COMICLINK AUCTIONS

THE AUCTION CHOICE FOR SMART SELLERS

ALL THESE SOLD FOR RECORD PRICES

- We get the HIGHEST REALIZED PRICES
- We charge HALF the commission
- We offer generous interest-free advances
- We don't charge fees for unmet reserves (you can only win)
- We have been in the comic business longest and have the most relevant bidders

ComicLink
AUCTIONS & EXCHANGE

www.comiclink.com
617-517-0062
buysell@comiclink.com

BUY AND BID ON COMICLINK.COM

CGC-GRADED COMICS
GOLDEN, SILVER AND BRONZE AGE COMICS
VINTAGE COMIC ART

SPECIALIZING IN VINTAGE COMICS

- Buy on the Exchange and at Auction
- Largest CGC Selection (10,000 +)
- Condition-Verified Gold, Silver & Bronze
- Impressive Original Comic Art
- New Listings throughout Every Day
- Want List Service that Really Works
- Expert Investment Advice
- Fraud Protection
- Satisfaction Guaranteed

ComicLink has the longest online presence of any vintage comic book & original art service. President Josh Nathanson is an Overstreet Advisor.

ComicLink
AUCTIONS & EXCHANGE
www.comiclink.com
617-517-0062
buysell@comiclink.com

METROPOLIS

COLLECTIBLES

www.metropoliscomics.com

VINTAGE COMIC BOOKS | ORIGINAL COMIC ART

Absolutely no other comic dealer buys or sells more Golden, Silver, & Bronze Age comics than Metropolis. We want to purchase your collection, large or small. We will treat you fairly and make your selling experience an enjoyable one.

BUYING

MILLIONS OF DOLLARS TO SPEND!

FREE APPRAISAL SERVICE!

WE PAY MORE BECAUSE

WE SELL MORE!

WE TRAVEL TO YOU!

IMMEDIATE PAYMENT!

OVER 100 YEARS COMBINED EXPERIENCE!

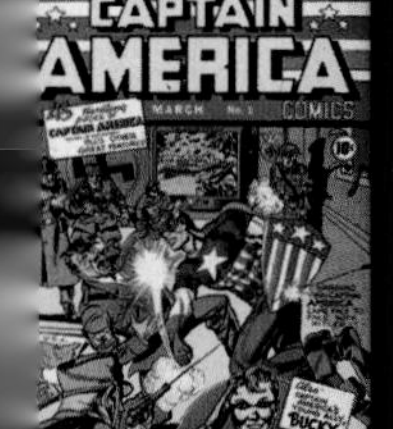

CALL TOLL-FREE

1-800-299-6387

Stephen Fishler, CEO 873 BROADWAY, SUITE 201, NEW YORK, NY 10003 Vincent Zurzolo, COO

Signed, Sealed & Guaranteed.

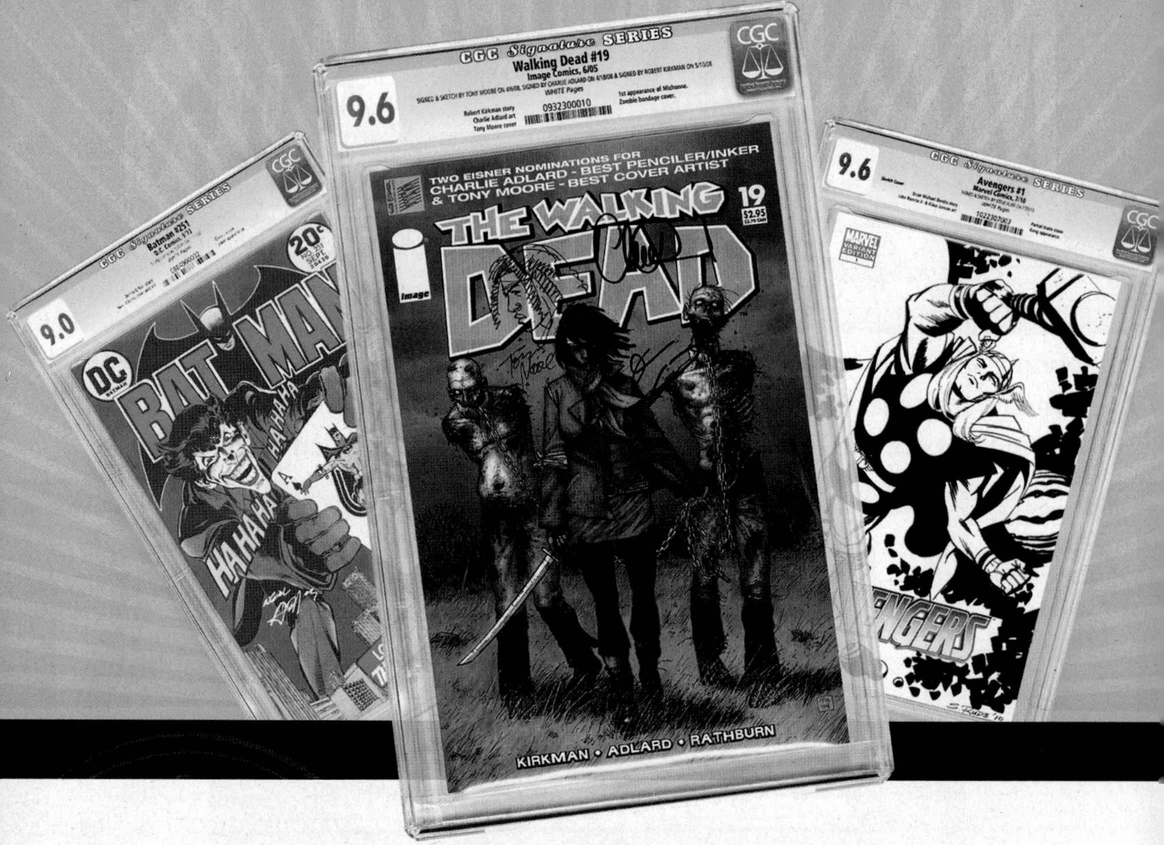

Authenticate your autographed comics to 100% certainty with the prestigious CGC *Signature* SERIES

At comic conventions throughout the year, CGC representatives are available to witness and verify the signing of your comics and then immediately submit them for grading and encapsulation for the CGC Signature Series designation. Your autographed comic book will be returned in a state-of-the-art, tamper-evident holder carrying the prestigious yellow label stating signature names, the date signed and (in some cases) the location – along with the general CGC grading information and integrity that our hobby has come to depend on.

The CGC Signature Series delivers the hobby's only 100% certified verification of an autograph's authenticity, making it preferred by collectors around the world.

Eliminate any question about the authenticity of your autographed comics!
Call 1-877-NM-COMIC or visit www.CGCcomics.com/signature to learn more.

P.O. Box 4738 | Sarasota, Florida 34230 | 1-877-NM-COMIC (662-6642) | www.CGCcomics.com

An Independent Member of the Certified Collectibles Group

COMIC CONNECT

WWW.COMICCONNECT.COM

WORLD'S PREMIER ONLINE COMIC MARKETPLACE & AUCTIONEER

SOLD! $1,500,000

SOLD! $1,100,000

SOLD! $1,000,000

SOLD! $575,000

SOLD! $465,000

SOLD! $436,000

SOLD! $2,161,000 WORLD RECORD

SOLD! $345,000

SOLD! $317,200

- In three years, we sold 20 copies of Action 1 - nobody else comes close!
- ComicConnect was the first to sell a comic book for $1 MILLION!
- ComicConnect holds the Guinness World Record at $2.161 MILLION!
- The three most expensive comics ever sold were all brokered by us!
- We have the best buyers and sellers. ComicConnect is where the action is!

IMMEDIATE CASH ADVANCES - SUPER FAST PAYMENT - FREE PRINT & ONLINE COLOR EVENT AUCTION CATALOG

INTEREST FREE TIME PAYMENTS - PHONE & ABSENTEE BIDDING - SMALL COMMISSION - NO BUYER'S PREMIUM

CONTACT US TODAY FOR A FREE CONSULTATION!

873 BROADWAY, SUITE 201, NEW YORK, NY 10003

P: 888.779.7377 | INT'L: 001.212.895.3999 | F: 212.260.4304

www.comicconnect.com | support@comicconnect.com

HERITAGE®

COMICS & COMIC ART AUCTIONS

HERITAGE AUCTIONS HAS SOLD $218 MILLION WORTH OF COMICS AND COMIC ART IN 12 YEARS, TRIPLE ALL OTHER COMIC AUCTIONEERS COMBINED!

BY FAR THE MOST WEB SITE VISITORS: No comics competitor comes remotely close — go to the independent tracking site compete.com and see for yourself!

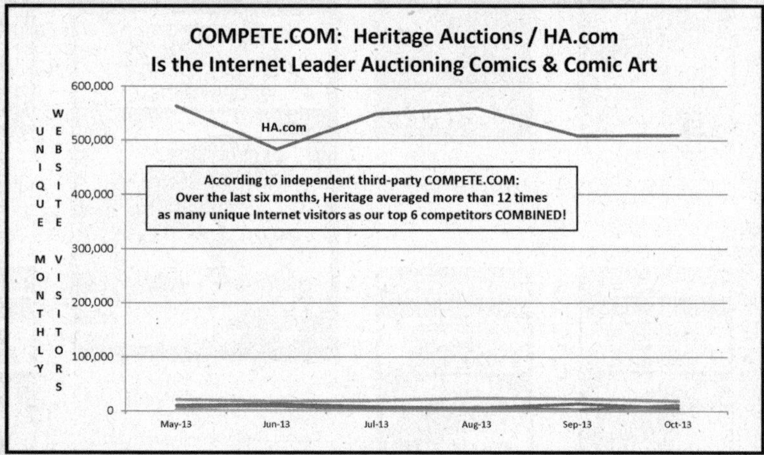

Competitor names and complete internet traffic details provided upon request.

Heritage has routinely advanced as much as $10 million on individual consignments, and currently has over $50 million available for cash advances.

HERITAGE HAS BEEN CHOSEN AS AUCTIONEER BY:

Stan Lee | Nicolas Cage | Joe Kubert | Steve Geppi
MAD Magazine | Random House | Playboy Magazine
The Joe Simon Estate | Gareb Shamus and Family

CALL OR EMAIL US TODAY!

WE LOOK FORWARD TO HEARING FROM YOU.

ED JASTER
877.HERITAGE (437.4824)
Ext. 1288
EdJ@HA.com

LON ALLEN
877.HERITAGE (437.4824)
Ext. 1261
LonA@HA.com

HERITAGE®

COMICS & COMIC ART AUCTIONS

HERITAGE SET THE RECORD AUCTION PRICE FOR A COMIC BOOK COLLECTION!

($3.9 Million for The Doug Schmell Collection in July 2012)

At HA.com, we publish ALL our auction results, not just a select few!

HERITAGE HAS UNPARALLELED MARKETING REACH

- Beautiful printed catalogs
- The most Web visits by far of any comics firm
- Aggressive advertising and cross-marketing

"Far as I'm concerned, the real superheroes are those great guys at Heritage. I really lucked out when I met 'em 'cause they got me prices that exceeded my wildest expectations, plus it was a real kick to work with them. I don't want this to sound like a TV commercial but, so help me Spidey, there's no one I'd rather entrust with my collection. Excelsior!"

– Stan Lee

Much more information in our ads on Pages 76–77, 78–79, 258–259, 267 and 1197!

3500 Maple Avenue | Dallas, Texas 75219 | 877.HERITAGE (437.4824) | Bid@HA.com

Annual Sales Exceed $900 Million | 850,000+ Online Bidder-Members

HERITAGE AUCTIONS HA.com

DALLAS | NEW YORK | BEVERLY HILLS | SAN FRANCISCO | HOUSTON | PARIS | GENEVA

TX Auctioneer licenses: Samuel Foose 11727; Robert Korver 13754; Andrea Voss 16406. • All comic auctions are subject to a 19.5% Buyer's Premium. HERITAGE Reg. U.S. Pat and TM off.

THE BEST BOOKS FOR BUYERS.
THE BEST PRICES FOR SELLERS.

Call us for a free consultation.

ComicLink
AUCTIONS & EXCHANGE

www.comiclink.com
617-517-0062
buysell@comiclink.com

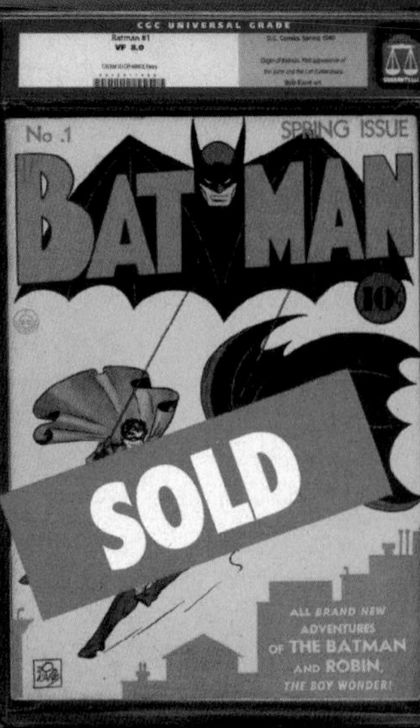

THE OVERSTREET® COMIC BOOK PRICE GUIDE

44TH EDITION

COMICS FROM THE 1500s-PRESENT INCLUDED
FULLY ILLUSTRATED CATALOGUE
& EVALUATION GUIDE

by ROBERT M. OVERSTREET

GEMSTONE PUBLISHING

Stephen A. Geppi, President & Chief Executive Officer
J.C. Vaughn, Vice-President of Publishing
Mark Huesman, Creative Director
Michael Solof, Advertising Sales Coordinator
Heather Winter, Office Manager • **Mike Wilbur**, Warehouse Operations
Tom Garey, Kathy Weaver, Brett Canby,
Angela Phillips-Mills, Jen Ruggles, Accounting Services

SPECIAL CONTRIBUTORS TO THIS EDITION

Robert Beerbohm • Dr. Arnold T. Blumberg • Scott Braden • Gene Gonzales • Mark Haynes • Ivan Kocmarek
Richard D. Olson, Ph.D. • S.C. Ringgenberg • Steve Saffel • Mark Squirek • J.C. Vaughn • Mark Wheatley

SPECIAL ADVISORS TO THIS EDITION

Grant Adey • David T. Alexander • Tyler Alexander • Lon Allen • Dave Anderson
David J. Anderson, DDS • Matt Ballesteros • Stephen Barrington • L.E. Becker • Robert L. Beerbohm
Jim Berry • Peter J. Bilelis • Steve Borock • Richard M. Brown • Shawn Caffrey • Paul Clairmont • Art Cloos
Gary Colabuono • Bill Cole • Jesse James Criscione • Frank Cwiklik • Zachary Davino • Brock Dickinson
Peter Dixon • Gary Dolgoff • John Dolmayan • Walter Durajlija • Ken Dyber • Bill Fidyk • Paul M. Figura
Stephen Fishler • Dan Fogel • Dan Gallo • Steven Gentner • Steve Geppi • Douglas Gillock
Tom Gordon III • Andy Greenham • Eric J. Groves • John Haines • Mark Haspel • Steven Houston • Nick Katradis
Ivan Kocmarek • Ben Lichtenstein • Stephen Lipson • Paul Litch • Doug Mabry • Brian Marcus • Jon McClure
Todd McDevitt • Mike McKenzie • Steve Mortensen • Marc Nathan • Josh Nathanson • Tom Nelson
Jamie Newbold • Terry O'Neill • Michael Pavlic • Bill Ponseti • Mick Rabin • Cathy Rader • Jeff Rader
Yolanda Ramirez • Rob Reynolds • Ben Samuels • Barry Sandoval • Alika Seki • Doug Simpson
Marc Sims • Mark Squirek • Tony Starks • West Stephan • Al Stoltz • Doug Sulipa • Chris Swartz
Brian Tatge • Maggie Thompson • Michael Tierney • Ted VanLiew • Frank Verzyl • John Verzyl
Rose Verzyl • Joseph Veteri • Todd Warren • Jeff Weaver • Mike Wilbur • Vincent Zurzolo, Jr.

See a full list of Overstreet Advisors on pages 1183-1187

NOTICE: Values for items pictured in this book are based on author's experience, consultations with a network of advisors including collectors specializing in various categories, and actual prices realized for specific items sold through private sales and auctions. The values offered in this book are approximations influenced by many factors including condition, rarity and demand, and they should serve as only guidelines, presenting an average range of what one might expect to pay for the items. In the marketplace, knowledge and opinions held by both sellers and buyers determine prices asked and prices paid. This is not a price list of items for sale or items wanted by the author or publisher. The author and the publisher shall not be held responsible for losses that may occur in the purchase, sale or other transaction of property because of information contained herein. Efforts have been made to present accurate information, but the possibility of error exists. Readers who believe that have discovered an error are invited to mail corrective information to the author, Robert M. Overstreet, at Gemstone Publishing, 1940 Greenspring Dr., Suite I, Timonium, MD 21093. Verified corrections will be incorporated into future editions of this book.

THE OVERSTREET COMIC BOOK PRICE GUIDE. Copyright © 1992, 1993, 1994, 1995, 1996, 1997, 1998, 1999, 2000, 2001, 2002, 2003, 2004, 2005, 2006, 2007, 2008, 2009, 2010, 2011, 2012, 2013, 2014 by Gemstone Publishing, Inc. All rights reserved. Printed in Canada. No part of this book may be used or reproduced in any manner whatsoever without written permission except in the case of brief quotations embodied in critical articles and reviews. For information, write to: Gemstone Publishing, 1940 Greenspring Dr., Suite I, Timonium, MD 21093 or email feedback@gemstonepub.com

All rights reserved. **THE OVERSTREET COMIC BOOK PRICE GUIDE (44th Edition)** is an original publication of Gemstone Publishing, Inc. This edition has never before appeared in book form.

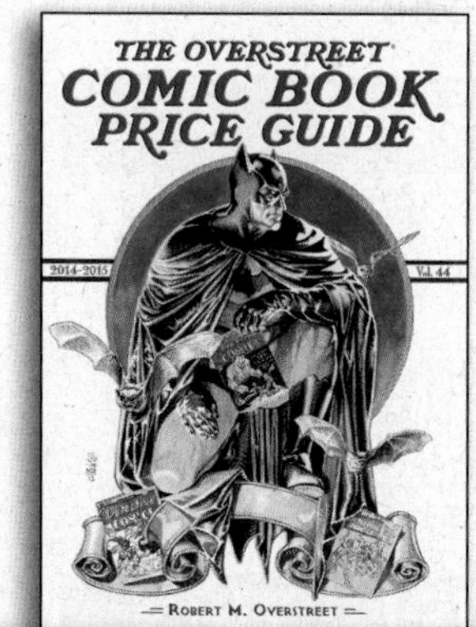

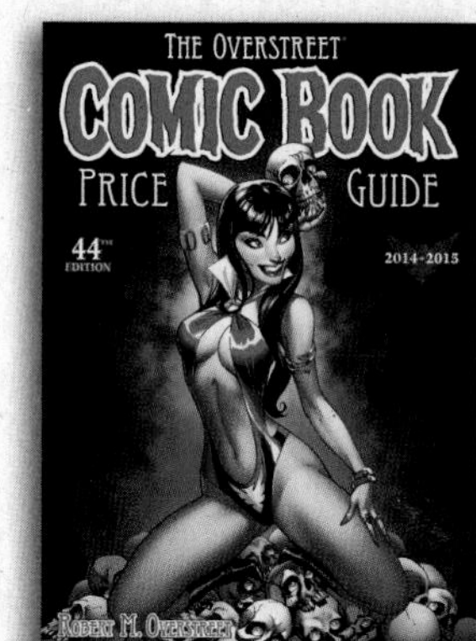

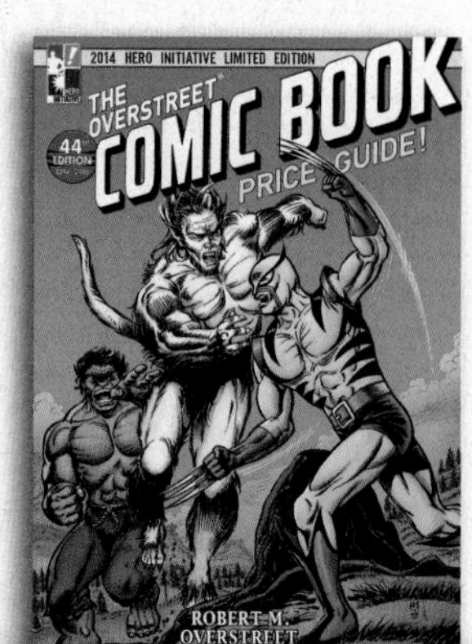

Batman: Art by J.G. Jones. Batman ©2014 DC Comics. Used by permission. All rights reserved.

Vampirella: Art by J. Scott Campbell and colors by Nei Ruffino. Vampirella ©2014 Dynamite Entertainment. Used by permission. All rights reserved.

Hero Initiative: Art by Herb Trimpe, inks by Tom Palmer and colors by Laura Martin. Wolverine, Hulk, and Wendigo ©2014 Marvel Characters, Inc. Used by permission. All rights reserved.

Overstreet® is a Registered Trademark of Gemstone Publishing, Inc.

Batman Hardcover Edition ISBN: 978-1-60360-157-3
Batman Soft Cover Edition ISBN: 978-1-60360-158-0

Vampirella Hardcover Edition ISBN: 978-1-60360-159-7
Vampirella Soft Cover Edition ISBN: 978-1-60360-160-3

Wolverine/Hero Initiative Hardcover Edition ISBN: 978-1-60360-161-0

Printed in Canada

10 9 8 7 6 5 4 3 2 1

Forty-Fourth Edition: July 2014

$1,000,000

$575,000

$465,000

$436,000

$345,000

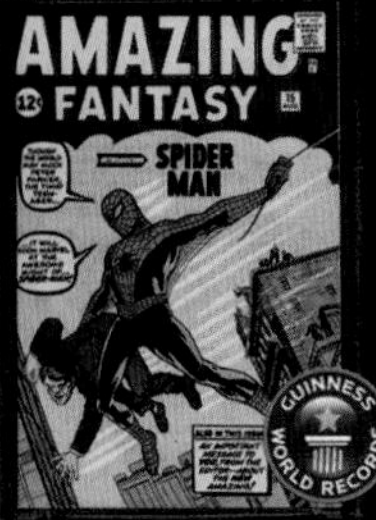

$1,100,000

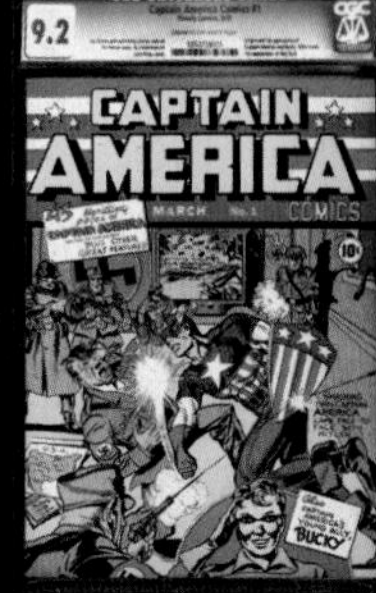

$343,057

$1,500,000

$325,000

THE COMICCONNECT DIFFERENCE

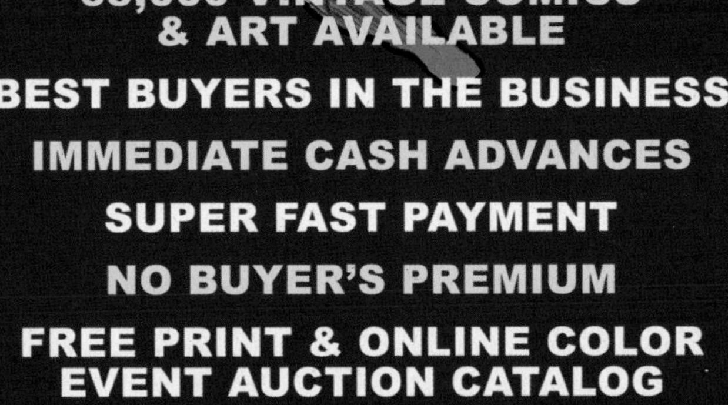

65,000 VINTAGE COMICS & ART AVAILABLE
BEST BUYERS IN THE BUSINESS
IMMEDIATE CASH ADVANCES
SUPER FAST PAYMENT
NO BUYER'S PREMIUM
FREE PRINT & ONLINE COLOR EVENT AUCTION CATALOG
INTEREST FREE TIME PAYMENTS*
PHONE & ABSENTEE BIDDING

$2,161,000

$323,000

*Time Payments are for certain lots only

WORLD'S PREMIER ONLINE COMIC MARKETPLACE & AUCTIONEER

LOW COMMISSIONS! MAXIMIZE YOUR PROFITS!
CALL TODAY TO CONSIGN FOR OUR NEXT EVENT AUCTION

Vincent Zurzolo
COO

COMICCONNECT

Rob Reynolds
Dir. of Consignments

Visit our website www.comicconnect.com or call us Toll Free at 888.779.7377
873 BROADWAY, SUITE 201, NEW YORK, NY 10003 | P: 212.895.3999 | F: 212.260.4304 | support@comicconnect.com

SELL ON COMICLINK.COM

WHERE YOU GET TOP DOLLAR
THE PREMIUM REAL-TIME EXCHANGE
THE PREFERRED AUCTION VENUE

MAXIMIZE YOUR RETURN

- Sell at Auction or on the Exchange
- Regularly Establishing Record Prices
- Longest Online Presence of any Comic Service
- Our Client Base & Experience are Unmatched
- Buyers are Waiting for Your High-Quality Items
- Pricing Experts can Maximize Value
- Grading Experts can Grade Your Comics
- Customer Service is Always Accessible
- Proven Track Record of Prompt Payment
- Cash Advance and Purchase Options Available

ComicLink makes the sales process easy!
Contact us to find out how to get the most money quickly for your vintage comics and art.

ComicLink
AUCTIONS & EXCHANGE
www.comiclink.com
617-517-0062
buysell@comiclink.com

TABLE OF CONTENTS

ACKNOWLEDGEMENTS

Since we began featuring original art on covers with *The Overstreet Comic Book Price Guide* #4, the *Guide* has been blessed to work with talent such as Joe Kubert, Will Eisner, Carl Barks, Wally Wood, Alex Schomburg, and so many other greats. Living up to that tradition is always our goal.

This year's additions to the cover artist honor roll include J.G. Jones and his incredible celebration of 75 years of Batman, and J. Scott Campbell's playful commemoration of Vampirella's 45th anniversary (with colorist Nei Ruffino), and we're so fortunate to have Herb Trimpe (along with the all-star team of inker Tom Palmer and colorist Laura Martin) return to Wolverine, a character he co-created 40 years ago, for our Hero Initiative edition.

This edition includes new articles by former staffer Scott Braden and former colleague Mark Squirek, as well as Ivan Kocmarek (thanks to Walter Durajlija), Steve Saffel, and S.C. Ringgenberg, contributions from illustrator Gene Gonzales, our friend Mark Wheatley, and former staffer Mark L. Haynes, as well as the usual Jack Bauer-style intense activities of our own Mark Huesman and J.C. Vaughn.

Special Thanks to the Overstreet Advisors who contributed to this edition, including Grant Adey, Austin Alexander, Bill Alexander, David Alexander, Tyler Alexander, Lon Allen, Dave Anderson, David J. Anderson, DDS, Matt Ballesteros, Stephen Barrington, L.E. Becker, Robert L. Beerbohm, Jim Berry, Peter Bilelis, Dr. Arnold T. Blumberg, Steve Borock, Richard M. Brown, Shawn Caffrey, Mike Carbonaro, Jon Chambers, Paul Clairmont, Art Cloos, Gary Colabuono, Bill Cole, Jesse James Criscione, Frank Cwiklik, Zachary Davino, Brock Dickinson, Peter Dixon, Gary Dolgoff, John Dolmayan, Walter Durajlija, Ken Dyber, Bill Fidyk, Paul M. Figura, Stephen Fishler, Dan Fogel, Dan Gallo, Steven Gentner, Steve Geppi, Douglas Gillock, Tom Gordon III, Andy Greenham, Eric J. Groves, John Haines, Jim Halperin, Mark Haspel, Steven Houston, Ivan Kocmarek, Ben Lichtenstein, Stephen Lipson, Paul Litch, Doug Mabry, Brian Marcus, Jon McClure, Todd McDevitt, Mike McKenzie, Steve Mortensen, Mark Nathan, Josh Nathanson, Tom Nelson, Jamie Newbold, Terry O'Neill, Michael Pavlic, Bill Ponseti, Mick Rabin, Jeff and Cathy Rader, Yolanda Ramirez, Rob Reynolds, Ben Samuels, Barry Sandoval, Alika Seki, Doug Simpson, Marc Sims, Mark Squirek, Tony Starks, West Stephan, Al Stoltz, Doug Sulipa, Chris Swartz, Brian Tatge, Maggie Thompson, Michael Tierney, Ted VanLiew, Frank Verzyl, John Verzyl, Rose Verzyl, Joseph Veteri, Todd Warren, Jeff Weaver, Eddie Wendt, Mike Wilbur, Mark Zaid, Vincent Zurzolo, Jr., as well as to our additional contributors, including Stephen Baer, Jack Borges, Alec Boyd, Mike Bromberg, Dr. Jonathan Calure, Tom Christopher, Bruce Fitch, Al Frieze, Tim Holl, Paul Howley, Robert Hundertmark, Mike Kacala, Ben Labonog, Jason Lohr, Boyd Magers, Rod Matlack, Bill Parker, Kevin Poling, Tom Saranello, and Tom Trombley. Without their active participation, this project would not have been possible.

Additionally, I would like to personally extend my thanks to all of those who encouraged and supported first the creation of and then subsequently the expansion of the *Guide* over the past four decades. While it's impossible in this brief space to individually acknowledge every individual, mention is certainly due to Lon Allen (Golden Age data); Mark Arnold (Harvey data); Larry Bigman (Frazetta-Williamson data); Bill Blackbeard (Platinum Age cover photos); Steve Borock and Mark Haspel (Grading); Glenn Bray (Kurtzman data); Gary Carter (DC data); J. B. Clifford Jr. (EC data); Gary Coddington (Superman data); Gary Colabuono (Golden Age ashcan data); Wilt Conine (Fawcett data); Chris Cormier (Miracleman data); Dr. S. M. Davidson (Cupples & Leon data); Al Dellinges (Kubert data); Stephen Fishler (10-Point Grading system); Chris Friesen (Glossary additions); David Gerstein (Walt Disney Comics data); Kevin Hancer (Tarzan data); Charles Heffelfinger and Jim Ivey (March of Comics listing); R. C. Holland and Ron Pussell (Seduction and Parade of Pleasure data); Grant Irwin (Quality data); Richard Kravitz (Kelly data); Phil Levine (giveaway data); Paul Litch (Copper & Modern Age data); Dan Malan & Charles Heffelfinger (Classic Comics data); Jon McClure (Whitman data); Fred Nardelli (Frazetta data); Michelle Nolan (Love comics); Mike Nolan (MLJ, Timely, Nedor data); George Olshevsky (Timely data); Dr. Richard Olson (Grading and Yellow Kid info); Chris Pedrin (DC War data); Scott Pell ('50s data); Greg Robertson (National data); Don Rosa (Late 1940s to 1950s data); Matt Schiffman (Bronze Age data); Frank Scigliano (Little Lulu data); Gene Seger (Buck Rogers data); Rick Sloane (Archie data); David R. Smith, Archivist, Walt Disney Productions (Disney data); Bill Spicer and Zetta DeVoe (Western Publishing Co. data); Tony Starks (Silver and Bronze Age data); Al Stoltz (Golden Age & Promo data); Doug Sulipa (Bronze Age data); Don and Maggie Thompson (Four Color listing); Mike Tiefenbacher & Jerry Sinkovec (Atlas and National data); Raymond True & Philip J. Gaudino (Classic Comics data); Jim Vadeboncoeur Jr. (Williamson and Atlas data); Richard Samuel West (Victorian Age and Platinum Age data); Kim Weston (Disney and Barks data); Cat Yronwode (Spirit data); Andrew Zerbe and Gary Behymer (M. E. data).

Finally, thanks, as always, to our advertisers, whose support makes this project possible, and to all of you who have purchased this edition.

MOST EXPERIENCE RECORD PRICES LOW COMMISSIONS

THE GREATEST RETURN ON YOUR COLLECTION

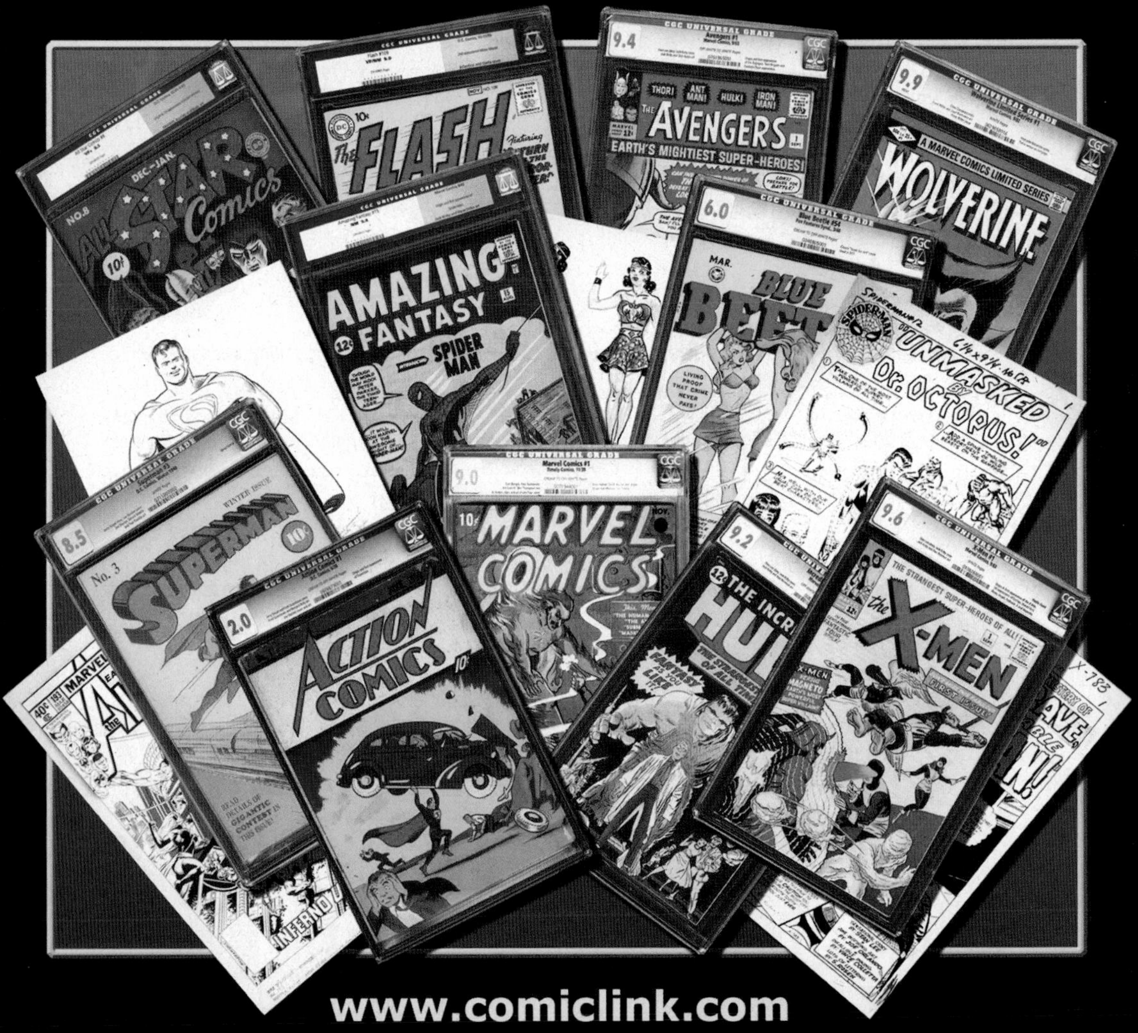

www.comiclink.com

buysell@comiclink.com 617-517-0062

CONSIGN TODAY!!

ONLY 10% TO SELL ON THE HOTTEST CGC CONSIGNMENT SITE!!!

PEDIGREECOMICS.COM Sells More CGC GRADED MARVEL COMICS Than Any Other Dealer in the World!... and Routinely Establishes New Record Sale Prices for its Superior Inventory of CGC Graded Silver and Bronze Age Marvels!

Ⓟedigree Comics deals exclusively in CGC Graded Comics and Magazines, so our customers can buy and sell books with ease, confidence and without any guesswork!

Ⓟedigree specializes in Ultra High Grade Marvels from the Silver, Bronze and Copper Ages. The site offers a HUGE SELECTION OF OVER 5,000 CGC BOOKS, bolstered with many "newly graded gems" from owner Doug Schmell's inventory of nationally recognized pedigrees!

Ⓟedigree offers the absolute LOWEST CONSIGNMENT FEE in the industry! ONLY 10% with no hidden costs. We do all the work, you take home 90%... Sweet!

Ⓟedigree WILL BUY YOUR COMICS! Doug Schmell has paid the highest recorded prices for countless individual comics and entire collections. (see our 2 page ad in this edition for details). Ask anyone in the hobby! You're assured professionalism and the best possible offer!

Ⓟedigree caters to an ever-growing clientele of high grade CGC collectors and aggressively promotes and markets it's services to attract new buyers and consignors!

Doug Schmell has been an avid collector for over 35 years. As a fan, he understands your passion for the hobby and returns every call and email.

In 2012, Doug's Personal Collection and #1 CGC Registry Sets Sold at Auction for over 3.94 MILLION DOLLARS!
(a record price for a comic book collection)

PedigreeComics.com®

Pedigree Comics, Inc. • 12541 Equine Lane • Wellington, FL 33414
PedigreeComics.com • email: DougSchmell@pedigreecomics.com
Office: (561) 422-1120 • Cell: (561) 596-9111 • Fax: (561) 422-1120

All Fantastic Four (the "Thing" and Human Torch) Character(s) © Copyright of Disney/Marvel Comics

Comic Investors LLC

Get the most from your collection

Collectors now have an advisor to help them make the right choice when selling or consigning their collection!

The 1st Call you should make:

(844)-MYCOMIC

joe@comicinvestors.com

ARE YOU SELLING YOUR LIFELONG COLLECTION OR HAVE YOU BEEN LEFT WITH A COLLECTION TO SELL?

Experience the Difference first hand by making us your first call when selling your collection!

Take these 3 easy steps to getting the most out of your collection!

Gather as much information about your collection. How many comics, what is the cover price and what comic titles you own. If possible, make a list on paper or your computer.

Set aside 5 to 10 minutes to talk with our experts.

Call (844) MYCOMIC or Email joe@comicinvestors.com

We are investment and comic professionals, not dealers, we can pay 60 to 90% of MARKET value for vintage comic books.

After turning thru pages of ads basically stating the same messages that they can pay the most or have millions in cash on hand or are the biggest comic buyer, collectors and comic sellers often make the wrong choice. Now there is a one-stop solution to help you sell your comic collection.....

We recommend a solution that will yield the highest dollar amount for YOU based on YOUR collection.

This may not always mean us making an offer for your collection. Sometimes a seller can realize more money by having us sell your collection or get you in contact with the right auction house.

Visit Our Website www.comicinvestors.com

COLLECTORS CHOOSE CGC

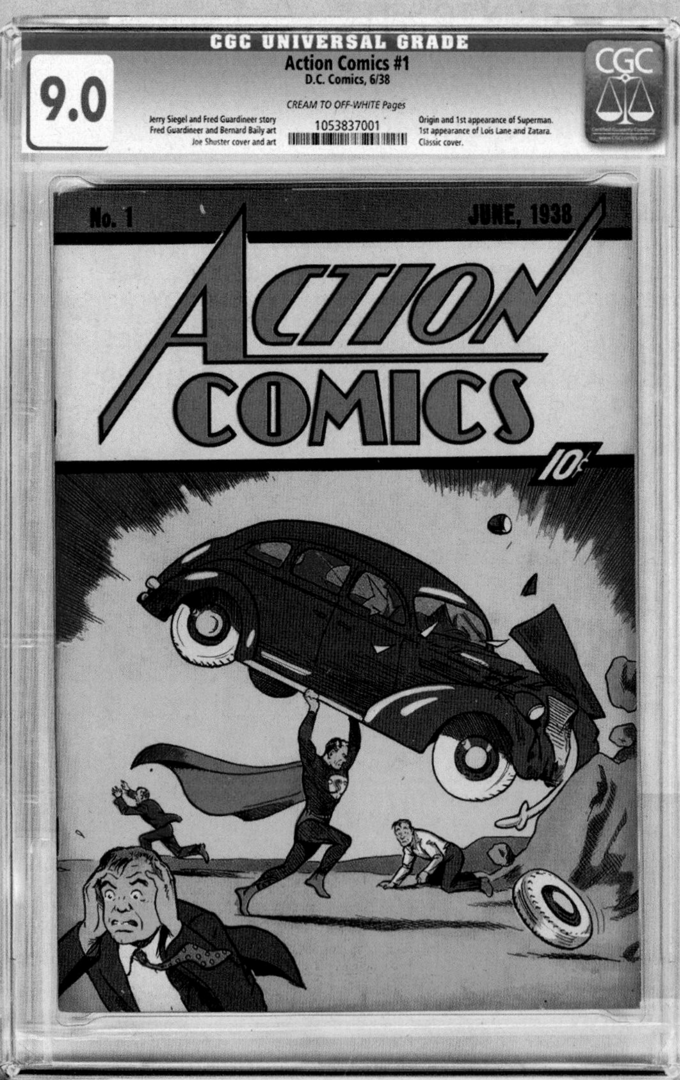

Collectors enjoy peace of mind when purchasing CGC-certified comics. Every CGC book has been reviewed by the hobby's most experienced team of professionals. It's the label smart collectors look for — online, at conventions, wherever the hobby takes them.

Our state-of-the-art, tamper-proof holder provides long-term protection for your comics.

CGC®
Certified Guaranty Company

An Independent Member of the Certified Collectibles Group

"The addition of CGC's independent, third-party certification to the marketplace has been one of the most important changes for collectors and dealers alike in the last decade."

— **Robert M. Overstreet**
The Overstreet Comic Book Price Guide

CGC Grading Services

CGC is the most preferred third-party comic book certification service, having graded more than two million comics in its 15 years. Our industry-leading grading team is prohibited from the commercial buying and selling of comics, to ensure accuracy and impartiality. Each book is evaluated by our team, and any detected restoration is noted.

Community Resources

With a membership in the CGC Collectors Society, collectors can interact on our Message Boards, receive monthly eNewsletters, access our Comics Population Report and more. Most notably, members can showcase their collections online in the CGC Registry, and compete in the annual CGC Registry Awards.

Learn more about CGC and submit your comics today! Visit www.CGCcomics.com

The trusted authority

for your favorite pursuit.

Founded in 1999, Certified Guaranty Company is the hobby's most preferred third-party grading service for collectible comics, magazines, photos and lobby cards. CGC offers professional condition analysis, including thorough restoration detection, before grading and encapsulating your collectibles in our state-of-the-art, archival-safe holders. CGC does not buy or sell collectibles—we're committed to providing an independent opinion you can always trust, so you can buy and sell with confidence.

To learn more, visit www.certifiedguaranty.com

P.O. Box 4738 | Sarasota, Florida 34230 | 1-877-NM-COMIC (662-6642) | www.CGCcomics.com

www.mycomicshop.com/sell

Visit our web site to find out why collectors and dealers just like you sell us over 120,000 comics a month. Our easy online selling system lets you turn your unwanted comics and graphic novels into cash.

"Thanks so much for being there. For personal reasons, I've needed to liquidate my prized comic collection of 40 years. I procrastinated, moved them around, sold a few on eBay, but really just let them sit for a very long time. Then, finding you, you purchased my bulk as a collection, but advised me to sell my older and key issues via your online want list system where I'd likely do better. I appreciated that you tried to help ME on what to do vs. just "sell it to us cheap". I think I'm about at $10,000 just from you. So, finally, I'm about to send my prizes, and I have confidence you will be fair. I'm also impressed that you upgrade many of my comics above the grades I gave them, even though it meant you'd owe me even more money! So, thanks for turning something that could have been very, very difficult into a process that was easy and painless."

- Dan D., Leawood, KS

Mycomicshop owner Buddy Saunders has been buying and selling comics since 1961. Start selling today:

www.mycomicshop.com/sell
817-860-7827 Mon-Fri 9AM to 6PM CST
buytrade@mycomicshop.com

Retailers: sell us your overstock

- We are always buying overstock comics and TPs published within the past 2 months.
- Visit www.mycomicshop.com/retailnetwork to start selling your overstock.

CONSIGN
Your Comic Books

www.mycomicshop.com/consign

Dozens of dealers advertise here. Why choose us?

- **We provide the largest comic-buying customer base available.** More buyers means your items sell more quickly and fetch higher prices. Mycomicshop.com has more visitors and buyers than any other comic retailer or comic-focused auction service.
- **Free eBay listings.** Your consignments are listed simultaneously on mycomicshop.com and eBay at no extra charge, giving your items unparalleled visibility in the market. We are the only major consignment service that offers this.
- **We make selling "raw" comics as easy as selling CGC-graded slabs.** All consignments are graded free of charge, and because our customers trust our grading, you'll get higher prices than if you listed the comics yourself on eBay. We can recommend CGC-grading when the cost/benefit warrants it, and handle the CGC submission for you at our full 20% dealer discount.

We are the fastest-growing consignment service. Why? Low 4-10% commission, strong prices, hassle-free sales, and an industry-leading sales platform. Call 682-232-4855 or visit www.mycomicshop.com/consign to learn more. Cash advances up to $1M available.

Este Bagato
Consignment Director
682-232-4855
consignment@mycomicshop.com

CCS The World's Leading COMIC BOOK PRESSING SERVICE

Over 10 years, CCS's professionals have developed an unparalleled pressing process that not only maximizes the potential of each comic book, but maintains its originality. Matt Nelson, president, has pressed more than 100,000 comic books of all types throughout his career—including the most valuable and sought-after issues.

before

after

Trust CCS for:

- Expert screening services
- Easy-to-use online submission form
- Fast turnaround and shipment savings costs for submissions transferred to CGC
- Quick Press (for lower-value comics)

For information on our pressing services and to submit, visit CCSpaper.com today.

About CCS

In November 2012, the Certified Collectibles Group (CCG) acquired Classics Incorporated, the world's leading comic book pressing service. Under its new name, CCS joins fellow CCG member Certified Guaranty Company (CGC) in its long-standing commitment to enhancing the comic book collecting experience for collectors across the world.

How to Submit

To submit your books for expert pressing by CCS, all you need is an Associate Membership in the CGC Collectors Society. You'll enjoy direct submission privileges to CCS and CGC—the world's leading comic book grading and encapsulation service—along with many other benefits. Join the Collectors Society today at **collectors-society.com/join**

1-855-CCS-1711 | CCSpaper.com

We Want Your

We Buy it All!

- Golden-Age 1933-1955
- Silver-Age 1956-1969
- Bronze-Age 1970-1985
- Original Comic Artwork

No hassles and no excuses!

Just Cash, Baby!

- No Collection too Large or too Small
- Travel the Globe to Buy Books we Need
- 30 Years Experience

Senior Advisor Overstreet Price Guide

LOOKING FOR A
COMIC SHOP NEAR YOU?
COMIC SHOP LOCATOR SERVICE
COMICS
comicshoplocator.com
888-COMIC-BOOK

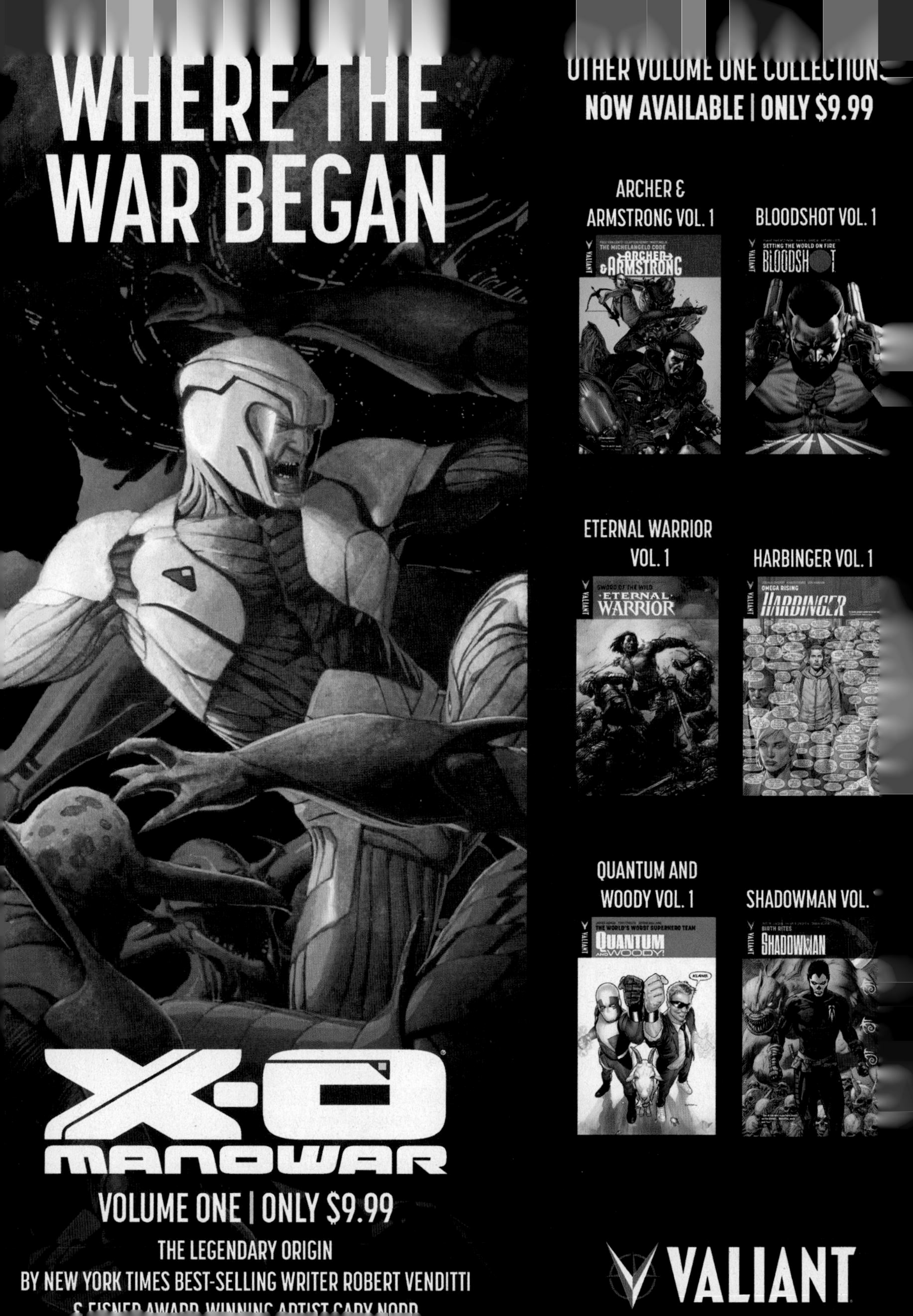

WHERE THE WAR BEGAN

X-O MANOWAR

VOLUME ONE | ONLY $9.99

THE LEGENDARY ORIGIN

BY NEW YORK TIMES BEST-SELLING WRITER ROBERT VENDITTI

& EISNER AWARD-WINNING ARTIST CARY NORD

OTHER VOLUME ONE COLLECTIONS

NOW AVAILABLE | ONLY $9.99

ARCHER & ARMSTRONG VOL. 1

BLOODSHOT VOL. 1

ETERNAL WARRIOR VOL. 1

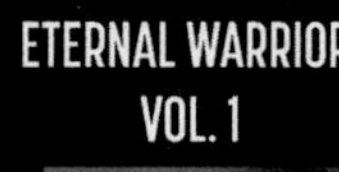

HARBINGER VOL. 1

QUANTUM AND WOODY VOL. 1

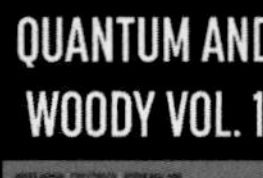

SHADOWMAN VOL. 1

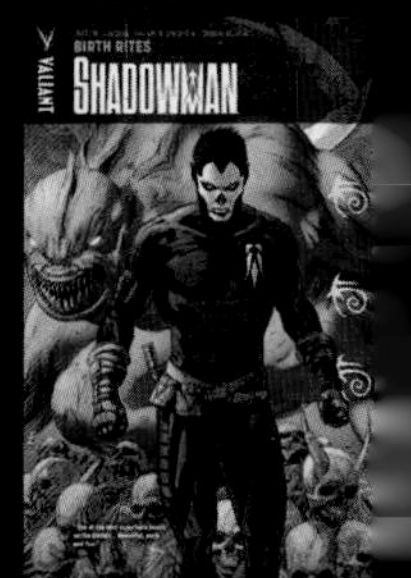

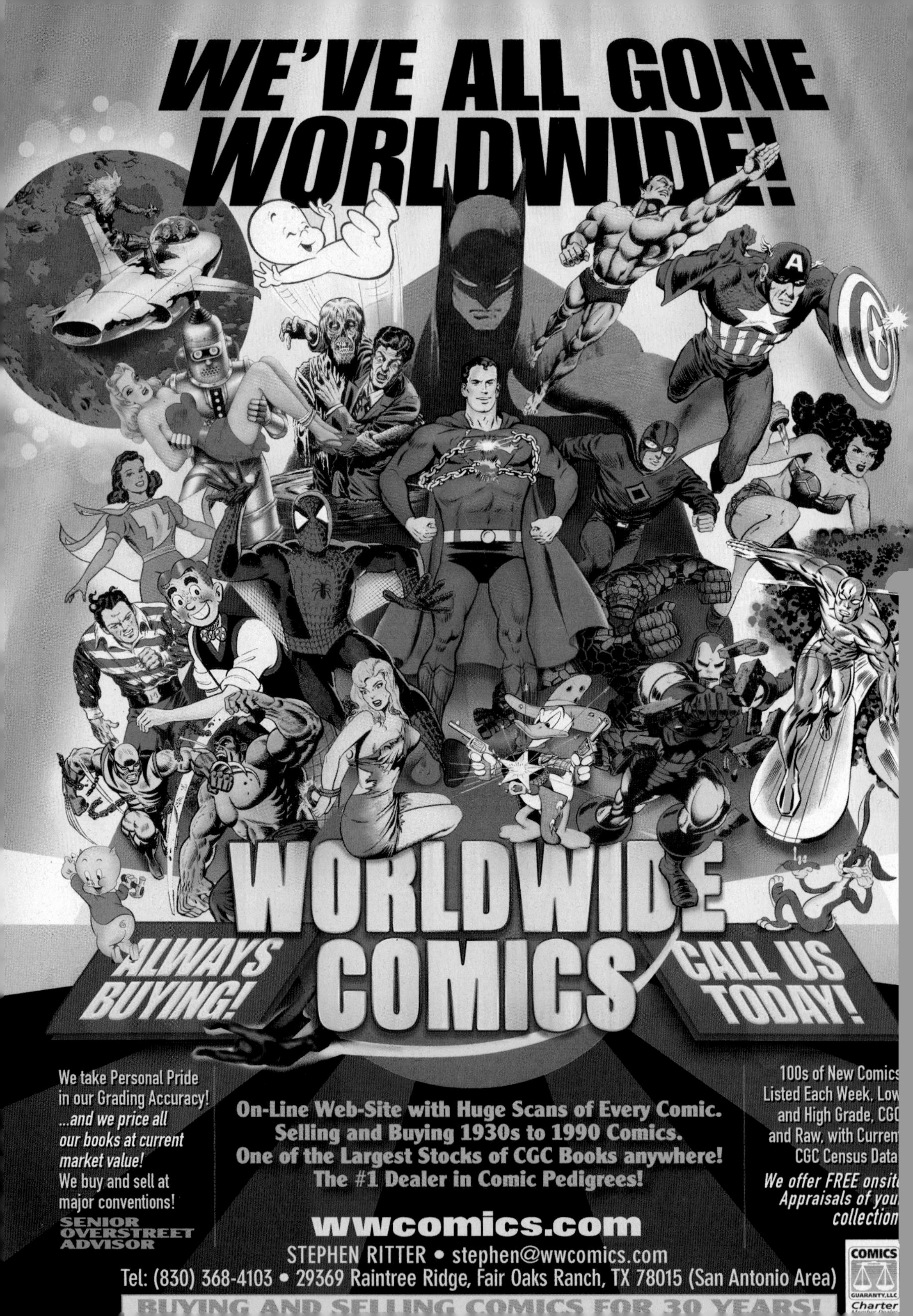

WE'VE ALL GONE WORLDWIDE!

WORLDWIDE COMICS

ALWAYS BUYING!

CALL US TODAY!

We take Personal Pride in our Grading Accuracy!
...and we price all our books at current market value!
We buy and sell at major conventions!
SENIOR OVERSTREET ADVISOR

On-Line Web-Site with Huge Scans of Every Comic.
Selling and Buying 1930s to 1990 Comics.
One of the Largest Stocks of CGC Books anywhere!
The #1 Dealer in Comic Pedigrees!

100s of New Comics Listed Each Week, Low and High Grade, CGC and Raw, with Current CGC Census Data
We offer FREE onsite Appraisals of your collection

wwcomics.com

STEPHEN RITTER • stephen@wwcomics.com
Tel: (830) 368-4103 • 29369 Raintree Ridge, Fair Oaks Ranch, TX 78015 (San Antonio Area)

BUYING AND SELLING COMICS FOR 30 YEARS!

HEROES Aren't Hard To Find

AMERICA'S COMIC SOURCE

HEROES AREN'T HARD TO FIND is one of the largest and most well-known comics retailers in the country. We carry a complete line of new comics, graphic novels, and manga; as well as back issues, Silver and Golden Age comics, statues, specialty items, and our own line of comics collecting supplies.

Located in the heart of the historic Elizabeth neighborhood near Uptown Charlotte, we work hard to foster a family-friendly atmosphere, while carrying an incredibly diverse line of comics from every genre. **Heroes is always buying comic collections, give us a call.**

We are also the proud organizers of

America's Favorite Comic Convention every summer since 1982, featuring the best creators and dealers in the business! You don't want to miss our **Annual Art Auction** where guests of the show create one-of-a-kind artwork while you watch!

1957 EAST 7th STREET, CHARLOTTE, NC 28204 10-9 MON-SAT, 1-6 SUN, 704.375.7462

MORE INFO ON THE WEB AT HEROESONLINE.COM

Captain America created by Joe Simon & Jack Kirby © & ™ 2012 Marvel Comics Art by Travis Charest

CREATING TOMORROW'S CLASSICS...TODAY.

WE ARE BOOM! STUDIOS COME INNOVATE WITH US

WWW.BOOM-STUDIOS.COM

Consign & Sell in Pedigree Comics'...

Pedigree's "Time-Based Auction" format runs for ten (10) days and features only **CGC certified comic books and magazines with a minimum value and opening bid of $100.00 or higher.** **Plus, there is No Buyers Premium!**

GRAND AUCTIONS are held Bi-Monthly (every 2 months) as a separate event on the Pedigree Comics website. Check the "Latest News" section of the site every day for all the news and updates on the upcoming Grand Auction!

Realize the absolute maximum profit on your CGC certified books by consigning to an upcoming Grand Auction and utilizing Pedigree Comics' Climbing Scale as follows:

90% Sellers commission for each consigned item with a winning bid up to $10,000 (Pedigree charges only 10%);

91% Sellers Commission for each consigned item with a winning bid over $10,000 and up to $25,000 (Pedigree charges only 9%);

92% Sellers Commission for each consigned item with a winning bid over $25,000 and up to $50,000 (Pedigree charges only 8%);

94% Sellers Commission for each consigned item with a winning bid over $50,000 and up to $100,000 (Pedigree charges only 6%);

95% Sellers Commission for each consigned item with a winning bid over $100,000. (Pedigree charges only 5%).

Midgard's Next GRAND AUCTION Fast Approaches Mortals!

Pedigree charges the "hands-down" Lowest Commission Rates of any auction site in the comics industry and consistently sets New Sales Records in every Grand Auction! There is always an Amazing Selection of High Grade and Ultra High Grade CGC Graded Comics and Magazines in Pedigree's Grand Auctions!

PedigreeComics.com®

...for more details!!

CGC Comics Guaranty, LLC Charter Member Dealer

Pedigree Comics, Inc. • 12541 Equine Lane • Wellington, FL 33414
PedigreeComics.com • email: DougSchmell@pedigreecomics.com
Office: (561) 422-1120 • Cell: (561) 596-9111 • Fax: (561) 422-1120

Auction Reporting Partner GPAnalysis

All Sales Listed Reported to GPAnalysis.com • Thor © Copyright of Disney / Marvel Comics

BASED ON THE SERIES OF NOVELS FEATURING
HONOR HARRINGTON

MATT HAWKINS | LINDA SEJIC

TALES OF HONOR™

ONGOING MONTHLY

TOP COW PRODUCTIONS, INC.

STUDIOS

neatstuff
COLLECTIBLES LLC

BUYING ENTIRE COLLECTIONS!

What I buy...

- G.I. JOE/ BARBIES
- BIG LITTLE BOOKS
- MOVIE POSTERS
- PULPS
- ORIGINAL ART
- MARX PLAYSETS
- MARVEL MANIA
- DISNEY
- NON SPORTS CARDS
- STATUES
- BISQUE FIGURES
- TOY ROBOTS
- BOARD GAMES
- MOVIE MEMORABILIA
- BASEBALL & SPORTS
- ALL PAPER COLLECTIBLES
- STAR WARS
- MARILYN MONROE
- FLASH GORDON
- SPIDER-MAN
- KING KONG
- PETER MAX, BEATLES
- '60s ROCK & ROLL
- ROY ROGERS
- JAMES BOND
- JAMES DEAN
- BUCK ROGERS
- MARVEL SUPER HEROES
- TARZAN
- ELVIS PRESLEY
- KISS TOYS & COMICS
- LITTLE NEMO

Golden Age Comics › Silver Age Comics › Original Comic Art › Toys

Why do ALL the other dealers in this book sell to me?

Because over the past ten years or so I have been buying comics from dealers throughout the country. In fact, over the years I have bought comics from just about every dealer who advertises in this book. I spend millions of dollars a year buying. If professional dealers sell me comics, why can't you? A dealer is extremely knowledgeable, has shown his comics to all kinds of buyers from retail customers to every other dealer in the country at shows. They choose to sell to me because of honesty, financial reliability, and of course the prices I pay.

I travel to YOU!
Unlimited funds available!
Payment in full on the spot!

We buy it all in one FREE call

1 (800) 224.9588

buyingeverything@yahoo.com

sellmyneatstuff.com

Be a *PREVIEWS* Insider

Are you looking for the **latest info** on **new releases, prevues** of **upcoming books, creator interviews, convention news** and **more?**

Be the **first to know** what's hitting comic book shops this week! **Special contests** and **prizes** for ***PREVIEWS*** Insiders!

Get the **FREE** weekly ***PREVIEWS***world**.com** E-newsletter!

SIGN-UP TODAY AT
www.***PREVIEWS***world**.com**/subscribe

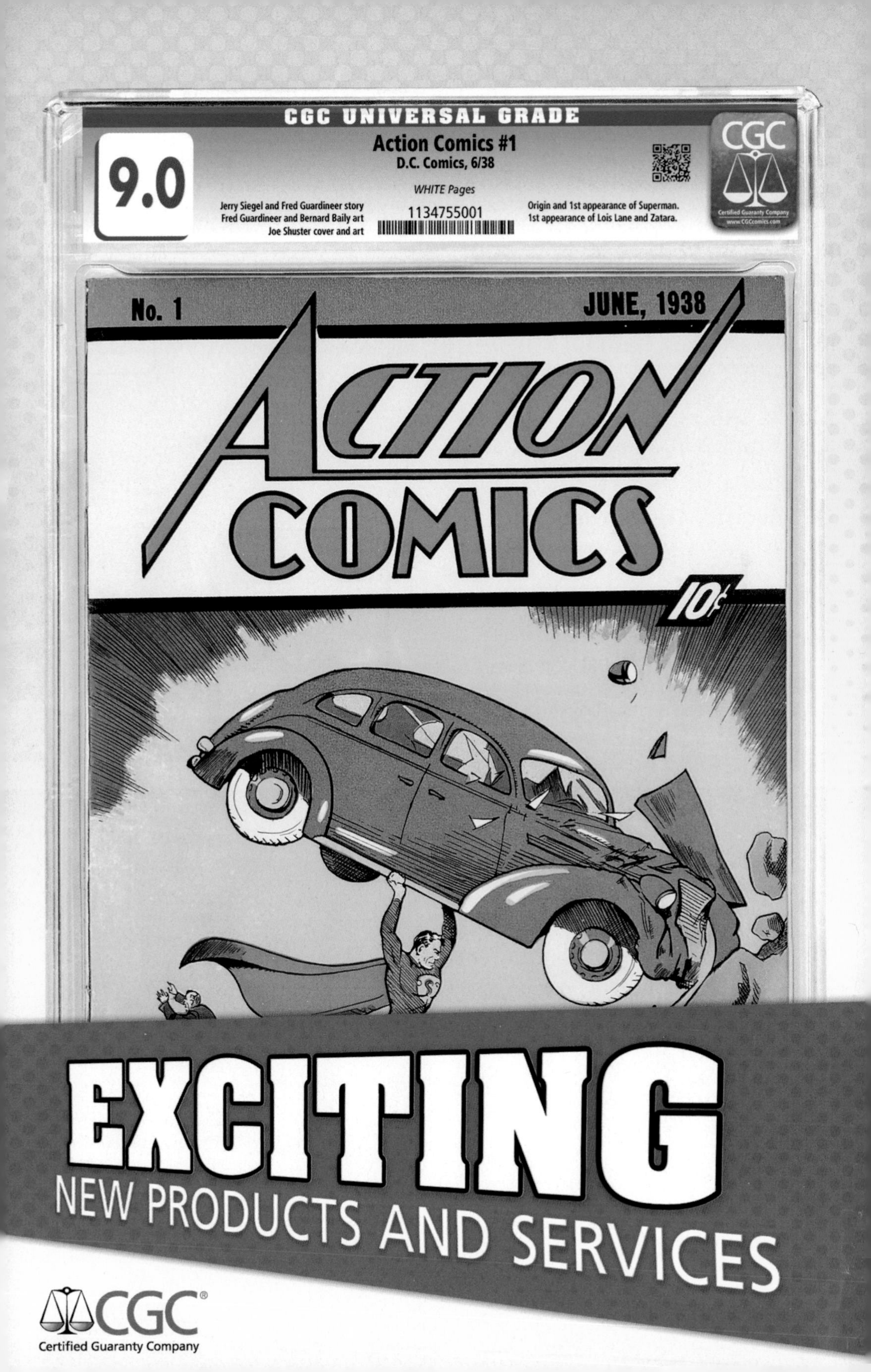

CGC UNIVERSAL GRADE

9.0

Action Comics #1
D.C. Comics, 6/38

WHITE Pages

Jerry Siegel and Fred Guardineer story
Fred Guardineer and Bernard Baily art
Joe Shuster cover and art

1134755001

Origin and 1st appearance of Superman.
1st appearance of Lois Lane and Zatara.

No. 1

JUNE, 1938

ACTION COMICS

10¢

EXCITING
NEW PRODUCTS AND SERVICES

New Offerings

Conservation Label

Specific repairs done to improve the structural integrity and long-term preservation of a comic book will now be classified as "conservation" and designated with a blue/purple label. These repairs include tear seals, support, staple replacement, piece reattachment and certain kinds of cleaning.

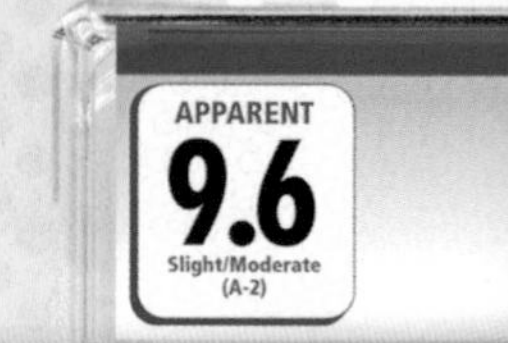

Restoration Scale

CGC has expanded its restoration grade designations. CGC now utilizes a five-point scale for quantity and the designation of "amateur" or "professional" will be expanded into three categories. Every type of restoration found on each book will be individually graded for quantity and quality, with a cumulative score determining the final restoration grade assigned.

APPARENT
9.6
Slight/Moderate
(A-2)

Mobile Site

Now you can verify a CGC collectible on the go with the new CGC mobile page: m.CGCcomics.com

CGC Registry Custom Sets

Showcase your collection, the way you collect it. The Custom Sets area of the Registry allows you to create your own set definitions, including the theme and slots.

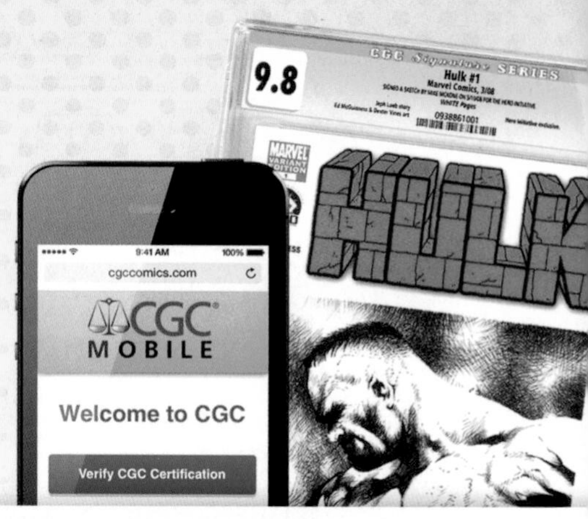

Coming Soon

CGC will be offering the option of a QR code that will allow the interior page images to be viewed online once the book as been encapsulated.

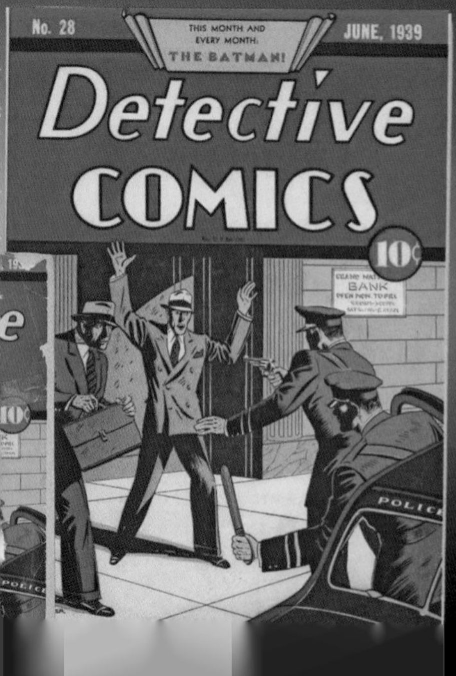

About CCS

In November 2012, the Certified Collectibles Group (CCG) acquired Classics Incorporated, the world's leading comic book pressing service. Under its new name, CCS joins fellow CCG member Certified Guaranty Company (CGC) in its long-standing commitment to enhancing the comic book collecting experience for collectors across the world.

How to Submit

To submit your books for expert pressing by CCS, all you need is an Associate Membership in the CGC Collectors Society. You'll enjoy direct submission privileges to CCS and CGC—the world's leading comic book grading and encapsulation service—along with many other benefits. Join the Collectors Society today at **collectors-society.com/join**

An Independent Member of the Certified Collectibles Group

Why send your comics to CGC for grading?

2.6 Million Comics Graded — Since opening for business 14 years ago, CGC has graded over 2.6 million books – and changed the comic collecting hobby for the better while doing it.

Longevity and Stability — The majority of our grading staff has been with us over 10 years! That's one reason our grading has remained consistent over the years. Any new graders are mentored and their grading closely scrutinized by the original grading team, to ensure their grading skills make our grade.

Increase Your Comic's Value — CGC certification consistently helps comics realize greater value at auction. Compare similar ungraded and graded books on sites such as eBay and Heritage Auctions to see for yourself.

The Trusted Authority — CGC has been the hobby's most preferred third-party grading service for collectible comics, magazines, photos and lobby cards since its founding. CGC offers professional condition analysis, including thorough restoration detection, before grading and encapsulating your collectibles in our state-of-the-art, archival-safe holders. Once a comic has been graded and encapsulated, it is guaranteed to be in the condition specified on the label—a source of reassuring confidence to many collectors.

"The addition of CGC's independent, third-party certification to the marketplace has been one of the most important changes for collectors and dealers alike in the last decade."

Robert M. Overstreet
The Overstreet Comic Book Price Guide

CCS

The World's Leading COMIC BOOK PRESSING SERVICE

Over 10 years, CCS's professionals have developed an unparalleled pressing process that not only maximizes the potential of each comic book, but maintains its originality. Matt Nelson, president, has pressed more than 100,000 comic books of all types throughout his career—including the most valuable and sought-after issues.

Trust CCS For:

- Expert screening services
- Easy-to-use online submission form
- Fast turnaround and shipment savings costs for submissions transferred to CGC
- Quick Press (for lower-value comics)

For information on our pressing services and to submit, visit CCSpaper.com today.

1-877-NM-COMIC • www.CGCcomics.com

CERTIFICATION NOTICE

CGC guarantees this comic book to be genuine and inspected by a minimum of one pre-grader and two graders. The assigned grade represents our opinion, as grading is subjective. Clerical error with respect to the description or grade of a comic book that would be readily noticed on inspection will be corrected at no charge. Certain books may receive a "pedigree" designation at CGC's discretion and based on supplied information believed to be accurate. The CGC holder is designed to be tamper-evident and has other security features to discourage fraudulent holder tampering. The CGC holder must be completely intact with unbroken corner posts in order to be considered an authentic certified CGC book.

Proper storage is essential to the preservation of your comic book. Extremes in light, temperature, moisture, vibration, temperature changes and other environmental hazards can contribute to the deterioration of a comic book sealed in a CGC holder. For maximum protection, keep your CGC certified comic books in an immobile, dark, temperature and humidity controlled area. A restoration check has been performed on this book. Detected restoration is noted on this label in general or specific terms. While the market determines the value of comics, many experts agree restored books have less value (in many cases substantially less) than an unrestored book of the same type and grade. A good faith effort is made to detect restoration, but CGC does not warrant this process or the results. If restoration is detected, most restored books will be assigned a marked and color-coded "restored" label. At the sole discretion of CGC, very minor color-touch or glue may be assigned a marked and color coded "Universal" label, however, a description of the detected restoration, in general or specific terms, will be disclosed. With this exception, the "Universal" marked and color-coded CGC certified books have been examined for restoration and none was found.

Certification by CGC does not assure liquidity, or assure universal acceptance of the CGC grading opinion, or eliminate the risks associated with a speculative and unregulated market.

The CGC holder is designed to open in the event that removal of the book is desired. Opening the holder voids the CGC certification. To avoid damage to the book, extreme care in following the correct procedure for removal must be exercised. CGC will not be financially responsible for damage that occurs to a book while not in our possession. If you are not familiar with the holder opening procedure contact an authorized CGC dealer or CGC Customer Service at 1.877.NM.COMIC, for assistance.

©2006 Certified Guaranty Company, LLC

"CGC is the visionary and leader in comic book grading. I cannot envision seeing the 'Mona Lisa of our industry' protected and preserved in any other holder!! Showcasing this specimen in a CGC holder along with the ability of viewing its interior while protected in their encapsulation is a dream come true!!"

Darren Adams | President
Pristinecomics.com/West Coast Sports Cards

P.O. Box 4738, Sarasota, Florida 34230 | 877-NM-COMIC (662-6642) | CGCcomics.com

• SOLID GRADING, SOLID REPUTATION, COMPETITIVE PRICING •

CGC AND NON-CGC GOLDEN AGE, SILVER AGE AND BRONZE AGE. ALL GENRES

CGC AND NON-CGC GOLDEN AGE, SILVER AGE AND BRONZE AGE. ALL GENRES

Have you been to large comic shows and only purchased 1 or 2 books?

Do you wish that all of a dealer's high grade selection could be in just one location?

Are you having difficulty in locating that hard-to-find issue?

Are you looking to upgrade from VF (8.0) to NM- (9.2) or NM (9.4)?

Large selection of CGC and non-CGC issues covering multiple genres.

All characters ©2009 respective copyright holders.

WELCOME TO THE WEB SITE DEDICATED TO THE BUYING AND SELLING OF CGC AND NON-CGC GOLDEN AGE, SILVER AGE AND BRONZE AGE COLLECTIBLES!

HighGradeComics.com

WILL BATTLE FOR YOUR BUSINESS!

I understand the emotional attachment involved when selling your collection.

I pay very fairly and the most important thing will happen: the check will clear.

ROBERT C. STORMS
17 Bethany Drive, Commack, NY 11725
Tel # 631-543-1917 Fax # 631-864-1921
Email: BobStorms@Highgradecomics.com

Want lists accepted and actually looked at.

• SOLID GRADING, SOLID REPUTATION, COMPETITIVE PRICING •

THE CLASSIC MAGAZINES, REMASTERED AND COLLECTED FOR THE FIRST TIME!

ORDER YOURS TODAY!

DYNAMITE® WWW.DYNAMITE.COM @DYNAMITECOMICS /DYNAMITECOMICS

Try Pedigree Comics' Awesome...

Raw to Riche$

CONSIGNMENT SERVICE!™

Pedigree Comics will transport your ungraded comics and/or magazines directly to CGC headquarters for submission. After a consultation regarding what you plan on sending us, all you'll have to do is carefully pack and ship the books to our offices... and your work is done!!!

Pedigree makes frequent trips to CGC's offices in Sarasota, Florida (usually once every 6 weeks). Your books will be safely and securely delivered for grading. Pedigree Comics, Inc. incurs all the risks involving the transport and delivery of your comics and magazines to and from CGC and is fully covered for any potential loss or damage to your books.

Pedigree will submit your books in person under the Pedigree Comics, Inc. account in the appropriate grading service (tier) and fill out all necessary submission forms. You do not lay out any of the grading costs in advance. We will deduct the grading costs (at our 20% discounted rate) from the sale of your CGC graded books on our website. There are no hidden fees or costs!!

Pedigree will pick up your graded books from CGC and safely transport them to our offices. This will save you from the potential hazards and expenses of having CGC ship the books back to you directly!

Pedigree will inventory, scan and upload your CGC graded books onto the PedigreeComics.com website where they will be listed in the New Arrivals Section or an upcoming Grand Auction. The books will be listed under your personal account and you will receive email notification of every bid and purchase made.

Pedigree does all the work while you can relax and watch your CGC graded books sell on our website. All of this for only 10% commission! You receive exactly 90% of the sale(s) price(s) of your book(s) after the deduction of the grading costs.

Pedigree Pays Extremely Fast! Your consignment check(s) will be mailed out within two weeks of the respective sales!

ALL THAT SERVICE FOR ONLY 10%!!
Take Advantage Now!... 'Dat Fee is Way Too Low to Last!
PedigreeComics.com®

Raw to Riche$ Consignment Service™ is a registered trademark of Pedigree Comics, Inc.

CGC
Comics Guaranty, LLC
Charter Member Dealer

Pedigree Comics, Inc. • 12541 Equine Lane • Wellington, FL 33414
PedigreeComics.com • email: DougSchmell@pedigreecomics.com
Office: (561) 422-1120 • Cell: (561) 596-9111 • Fax: (561) 422-1120

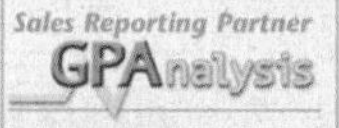
Sales Reporting Partner
GPAnalysis

All Fantastic Four (the "Thing") Character(s) © Copyright of Disney / Marvel Comics

THE INDUSTRY'S LEADING "TOP OF THE LINE" BAG!

With twice the thickness of 1 mil bags, Mylites 2 is the most economical Mylar sleeve on the market. Get maximum archival protection from a name you can trust.

Mylites 2 are available at your local comic shop! Ask for them by name!

Premium Archival Protection, For Your Entire Collection.

egerber.com

SEE OUR OTHER ADS IN THIS GUIDE FOR MORE INFORMATION

LOOK NO FURTHER

THAN RARE BOOKS & COMICS

WHEN THINKING OF SELLING YOUR COLLECTION!

WE BUY...

Golden, Silver and Bronze Age Comics, Big Little Books, Pulp Magazines and original art.

No collection is too large!

Immediate funds available for $500,000 or more...

WHAT WE DO FOR YOU

Pay exceptional prices for collections of interest.

We pay up to 110% of Guide for many desirable comics.

Travel to you to review your collection.

Provide a fair and honest value assessment.

Buy all grades and comic titles before 1975.

We will respect you and your collection. (No high pressure calls)

Offer generous finder fees that result in the purchase of a collection.

© character of DC Comics

CREDENTIALS

Special Advisor to the Overstreet Guide 1985–present (see our other ads in this book for further credential information)

JAMES PAYETTE
RARE BOOKS & COMICS
P.O. Box 750 • Bethlehem, NH 03574
Tel (603) 869-2097 • Fax (603) 869-3475
jimpayette@msn.com
jamespayettecomics.com

FIND THE BEST ON THE WEB!

D.I.G Auctions

WWW.DIAMONDGALLERIES.COM

GALLERYQUESTIONS@DIAMONDGALLERIES.COM

COMIC BOOK CERTIFICATION SERVICE

CBCS

Expert, Impartial, Third-Party Grading

www.CBCScomics.com Toll Free: 844-870-CBCS

Follow us on Facebook and Twitter!

neatstuff

COLLECTIBLES LLC

BUYING!!!!!

WHAT I BUY....

- ENTIRE INTACT COLLECTIONS AND DEALER STOCKS
- PLATINUM AGE, GOLDEN AGE, SILVER AGE, AND MODERN COMICS
- TOYS, PULPS, PREMIUMS, MAGAZINES, PAPER COLLECTIBLES
- SPORTS AND NON-SPORTS CARDS
- MUSIC COLLECTIBLES
- MOVIE POSTERS
- WE BUY EVERYTHING, ANYWHERE

DESPERATE FOR ORIGINAL COMIC ART!

I BUY EVERYTHING AND ANYTHING RELATED TO COMICS AND POPULAR CULTURE

Why do ALL the other dealers in this book sell to me ?

BECAUSE over the past ten years or so I have been buying comics from dealers throughout the country . In fact, over the years I have bought comics from just about every dealer who advertises in this book. I spend millions of dollars a year buying. If professional dealers sell me comics why can't you ? A dealer is extremely knowledgeable, has shown his comics to all kinds of buyers from retail customers to every other dealer in the country at shows. They choose to sell to me because of honesty, financial reliability, and of course the prices I pay.

I travel to YOU !
Unlimited funds available !
Payment in full on the spot !

buyingeverything@yahoo.com
sellmyneatstuff.com

We Buy It All in Just One Call!
Toll FREE
1 (800) 224.9588
Ask for Brian !

BUYING COLLECTIONS!

Large amount of ready cash available for immediate purchase of
Silver Age Comics
Golden Age Comics
Original Comic Book Art

JOE TED JOSE LISA

Ted VanLiew
27 years experience
Advisor to the
Overstreet Price Guide

SUPERWORLDCOMICS.COM
456 Main St., Holden, MA 01520
508-829-2259 OR 508-UBWACKY
ted@superworldcomics.com

REX

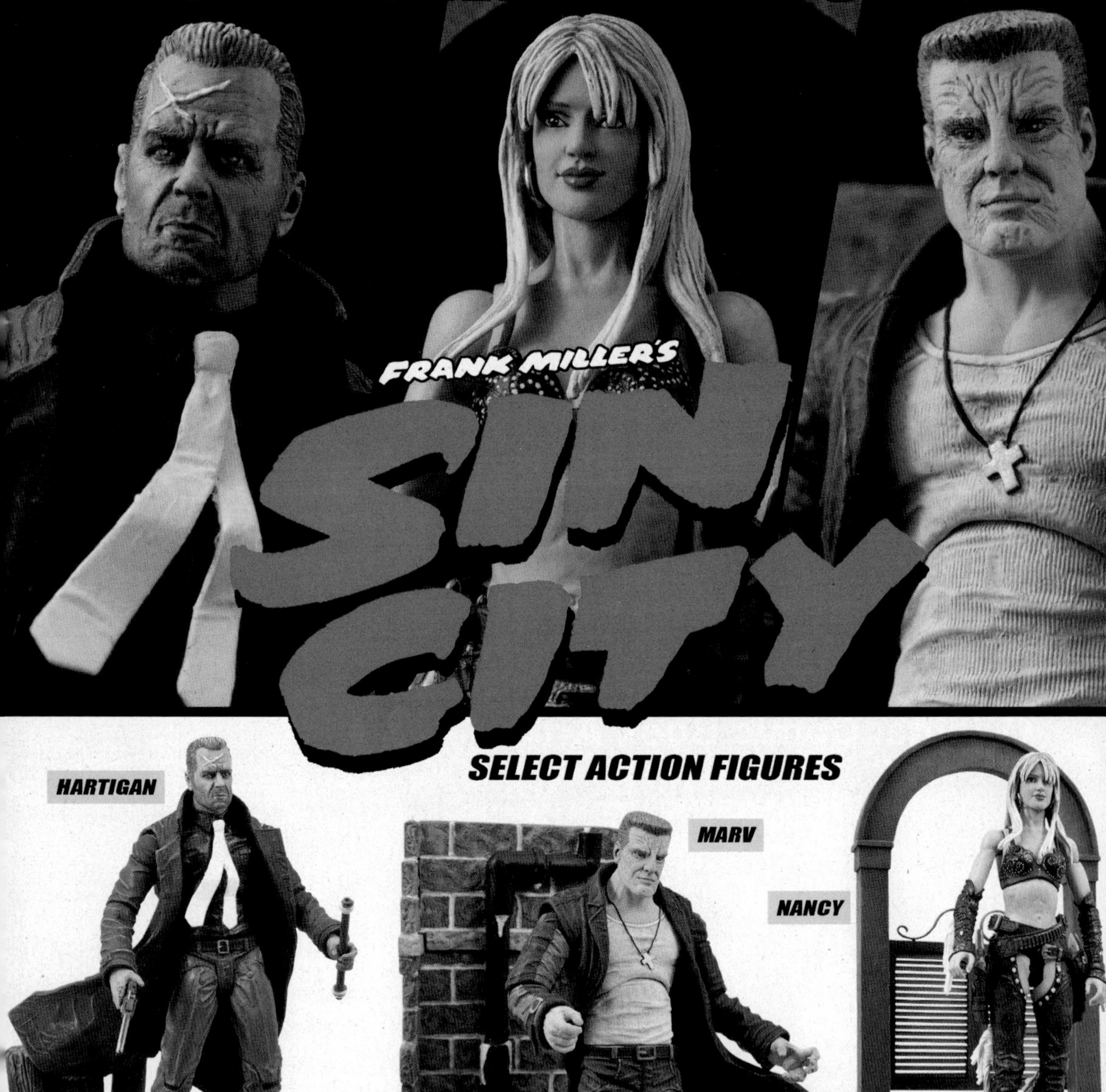

Are you ready to return to Sin City? The first series of 7", fully poseable Select figures from DST includes Marv, Hartigan and Nancy, all based on their appearances in the 2005 feature film. Each figure comes packaged with a base and accessories, in display packaging with spine reference artwork. Sculpted by Jean St. Jean!

DIAMOND SELECT TOYS™
diamondselecttoys.com

MIRAMAX™
TROUBLEMAKER STUDIOS

COMIC SHOP LOCATOR SERVICE
comicshoplocator.com
888-COMIC-BOOK

© 2014 Miramax, LLC. All Rights Reserved. DIAMOND SELECT TOYS, the DIAMOND SELECT TOYS logo are trademarks of Diamond Select Toys, LLC. © 2014 Diamond Select Toys and Collectibles, LLC. All Rights Reserved. Final product may vary.

The Best Comic Book Club Ever... Just Got Better!!!

CARDS ONE COMIC BOOK COLLECTOR CLUB

Over $150 Retail Value!

Over 200 Items in each CLUB MEMBERSHIP

Only $24.99 with Free Shipping!

CHOOSE YOUR CLUB

Standard Club

Comic Book Collector Club
JOIN TODAY!!!!

GET ALL THESE CLUB BENEFITS ***OVER $150 IN RETAIL VALUE***

- 35 Different Vintage Comic Books Guaranteed no Duplication of Books!!
- Comic Book Hero Collector Set
- 10 Super Hero and Super Villain Vintage Unopened Trading Card Packs
- Super Hero & Super Villain Stickers
- Super Hero Graphic Novel
- Random Selection of Super Hero & Super Villain Trading Cards
- Comic Book Promo Cards
- 100 Comic Book Protection Bags
- Comic Book and Trading Card Magazine Subscription
- Membership into the "Comic Book of the Month Club"
- Email Newsletters and Current Comic Book Specials

Join or Rejoin Today for a One Time Only Fee of only $24.99 with Free Shipping CBCC2

Mega-Size your Club!!!

STANDARD CLUB + 40 CLUB
Get 40 Additional Comic Books Added to Standard Club for only $15 More
$39.99 / 40 CLUB
CBCC5

STANDARD CLUB + 500 CLUB
Get 500 Additional Comic Books Added to Standard Club for only $100 More
$124.99/ 500 CLUB
CBCC7

STANDARD CLUB + 100 CLUB
Get 100 Additional Comic Books Added to Standard Club for only $30 More
$54.99/ 100 CLUB
CBCC6

STANDARD CLUB + 1000 CLUB
Get 1000 Additional Comic Books Added to Standard Club for only $175 More
$199.99/ 1000 CLUB
CBCC8

ALL MEGA DEALS COME WITH FREE SHIPPING & HANDLING!!!

Your ONE STOP SHOP FOR COMICS, SUPPLIES & MORE!

www.CARDSONE.com 1.888.472-3161

Earth Alliance #1 Review
08 June 2014 11:55 AM | No Comments

Big Trouble in Little China #1 Review
07 June 2014 1:54 PM | No Comments

Nailbiter #2 Review
04 June 2014 2:01 PM | No Comments

Maleficent Review
30 May 2014 8:08 AM | No Comments

X-Men No More Humans OGN
09 June 2014 8:35 AM | No Comments

COMIC NEWS

X-Men No More Humans OGN

The X-Men awaken to find [...]

The Riverdale Podcast Episode #118! – Afterlife With Archie Book One! w/ Special Guest Barbara Ann!

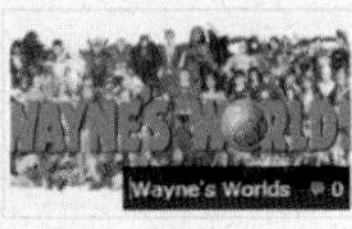

Wayne's Worlds: Angry Birds #1

Who ever gets too much [...]

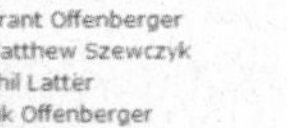

MURCIELAGA SHE-BAT #14

MURCIELAGA SHE-BAT #14 On Sale [...]

Tarot #86Dlx & #55 Glow Cover bundle FLASH SALE

Two Cool Goodies -Two Days [...]

VOTING OPENS IN INAUGURAL TRUE BELIEVERS COMIC AWARDS

LOG ON to http://www.truebelieverscomica to cast [...]

JUSTA LOTTA FUNKO: Toy Tokyo Red Batmobile POP! Exclusive?

If you have been following [...]

COSPLAY GIRL OF THE WEEK!

This week's cosplay girl of [...]

Action News from Captain Action

We thought we were going [...]

Dave Cockrum's personal X-Men comics collection

Dave Cockrum created and co-created [...]

PHOENIX COMICON 2014: The Dark Times Gallery Edition

Star Wars: Dark Times Gallery [...]

FIRST COMICS NEWS™ STAFF

REPORTERS

Francis Sky
Grant Offenberger
Matthew Szewczyk
Phil Latter
Rik Offenberger

COLUMNISTS

Alex Simmons
Anthony Kingsley Frizzera
Bob Almond
Dark Mark
Giovanni Aria
Holly Golightly
Josh Waldrop
Mark Heike
Matthew Szewczyk
Michael Dunne
Michael Netzer
Miguel Ortiz
Susan Lee

REVIEWERS

Christopher Kutz
Francis Sky
Giovanni Aria
Matthew Szewczyk
Jez
Michael Souza
Patrick McCrone
Tanya Tate
Wayne Hall

PODCASTERS

Jamie Coville
Jonathan Merrifield
Matthew Szewczyk
Patrick McCrone
Ric Croxton

PHOTOGRAPHERS

Amy Dunne
Denny Offenberger

EDITOR-IN-CHIEF

Rik Offenberger

BUREAU CHIEFS

Chris J. Thompson
Phil Latter

SENIOR EDITOR

Matthew Szewczyk

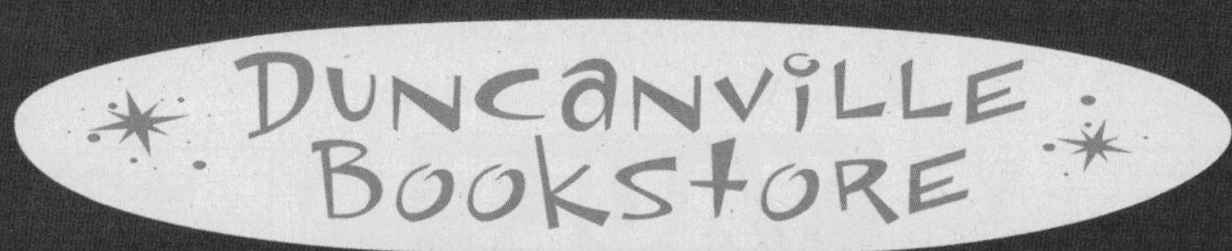

Comics ✶ Toys ✶ Games

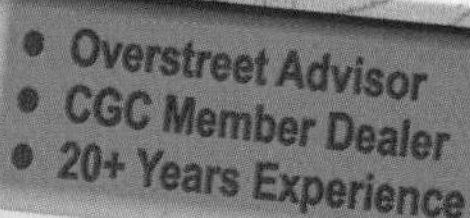

We Are <u>ALWAYS</u> Buying!!!

Golden Age to Modern Age Comics, Toys,
Action Figures, Movie Posters, Records,
Magazines, Pulps, & All Things Pop Culture

No Collection Too Large Or Too Small
Willing To Travel If Need Be

Paying Fair Market Value For All Ages Of Comics & Toys
We Buy It ALL! No Cherry Picking

We Will Pay Over Guide Prices For The Most Desirable Comics
We Are Willing To Pay A Finder's Fee For Assistance In Acquiring A Collection.

You Have Lots Of Options When Selling Your Collection. Give Us A Chance, You Will Not Be Disappointed!

3200 sq. ft. Retail Location
Located In The DFW Metroplex

Ebay Seller: AndyMac2570
We Ship Worldwide With Fast & Safe Shipping
With Over 10,000 Positive Feedbacks
Accurate & Consistent Grading

We Travel To 20+ Conventions A Year

All characters © their respective copyright holders.

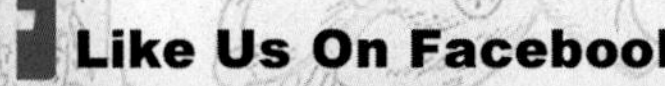

Follow Us On Twitter

www.duncanvillebookstore.com AndyMac2570@aol.com
101 W. Camp Wisdom Rd. Suite J, Duncanville, TX 75116
Open 7 Days A Week 10am—7pm
(972) 298-7546

A NEW ERA IN COMIC BOOK SERVICES

GET IT GRADED!®

GRADING | RE - GRADING | PRE - SCREENING | PRESSING

FEATURES

UNBIASED GRADING

SIMPLE ONLINE ORDERING

MUSEUM QUALITY CASES

INFORMATIVE TOP PANELS

NO SUBMISSION MINIMUMS

DIRECT SUBMISSIONS

PRIVATE PLACEMENTS

www.VaultGrading.com

PRE-ORDER NEW COMIC BOOKS SLABBED & GRADED

WHOLESALE ACCOUNTS AVAILABLE

www.VaultGradedComics.com

NEW YORK, NY • SAN DIEGO, CA

For more information contact us at sales@vaultgrading.com or toll free 855.222.5599

DO YOU OWN SIGNED COMIC BOOKS?...

PGX is offering a NEW SERVICE!

THE AUTHENTICATION EDITION!

Now you can have your signed comic books professionally authenticated, graded, and encapsulated! No one else in the comic book industry offers this service! For more info, visit us at www.pgxcomics.com

www.csacomics.com

COMICLINK AUCTIONS

THE AUCTION CHOICE FOR SMART SELLERS

ALL THESE SOLD FOR RECORD PRICES

- We get the HIGHEST REALIZED PRICES
- We charge HALF the commission
- We offer generous interest-free advances
- We don't charge fees for unmet reserves (you can only win)
- We have been in the comic business longest and have the most relevant bidders

ComicLink
AUCTIONS & EXCHANGE

www.comiclink.com
617-517-0062
buysell@comiclink.com

ALWAYS SEEKING THE FOLLOWING

DC COMICS 1936-1993

MARVEL COMICS 1958-1991

TIMELY COMICS 1939-1947

ATLAS COMICS 1948-1957

PULPS/FANTASY MAGAZINES 1928-1961

WARREN/MARVEL MAGAZINES 1958-1981

CALL NOW FOR IMMEDIATE PAYMENT!

DON'T WANT TO SELL WHOLESALE?

After 41 years in the hobby, I am extremely confident that I have the most consignor-friendly consignment program in the industry!

Along with the better comics that come in each collection, I also handle the cheaper comics that most auction companies won't take on consignment. Keep in mind that the only way to TRULY MAXIMIZE the value of your collection is to sell every comic individually. Don't let some other auction house bulk-lot your treasured comics!

CALL NOW FOR DETAILS
Office (972) 539-9190
Mobile (973) 432-4070

William Hughes' Vintage Collectables

MOVIE POSTERS • COMIC BOOKS • SPORTS MEMORABILIA

P.O. Box 270244 Flower Mound, TX 75027
Office: 972-539-9190
Mobile: 973-432-4070 Fax: 972-691-8837

www.VintageCollectables.net
Email: whughes199@yahoo.com
eBay User: NJPOWER2000

Dallas * New York * Los Angeles * Chicago

GREG REECE'S RARE COMICS

Overstreet Advisor
20 Years Experience
CGC Member Dealer

www.gregreececomics.com

Phone: 240-575-8600
E-mail: greg@gregreececomics.com
Frederick, MD

$2,000,000 CASH AVAILABLE FOR IMMEDIATE PAYMENT!
We travel anywhere!
Actual purchases from the last few years:
Toronto, CANADA $14,500
Chicago, IL $44,500
Cleveland, OH $6,500
Philadelphia, PA $50,000
New York, NY $74,000
Columbus, OH $6,800
Irving, TX $35,800
Baltimore, MD $42,500
San Antonio, TX $20,000
Knoxville, TN $22,000
Sterling, VA $85,000
New Orleans, LA $55,000
Raleigh, NC $15,000
Midlothian, VA $28,000
Fort Walton Beach, FL $5,000
St Petersburg, FL $8,700
Blacksburg, VA $13,000
• No waiting for YOUR $$. Full payment made on the spot!
• We buy it all, small to large collections.
• No nonsense. We treat you fairly.
• References available.

Your Silver and Golden Age Comics are...

WANTED

We're currently looking to buy your Silver Age and Golden Age comic books. Whether you're looking to sell either an entire run of books or a few single issues **Bill Cole Enterprises** is interested in buying it from you or selling it on consignment in our highly visible eBay store!

We know times are tough so if you need some extra income, then now is the time to part with those comics that may be taking up space in your basements and attics

Even if you don't want to part with your prized collection, then please visit our website for a full selection of preservation supplies to **"Protect what you collect"**SM. From Mylar® sleeves to acid-free boxes we offer you the highest quality products to keep your comics safe. Make sure that they're preserved well into the next era!

For more information please go to:

www.bcemylar.com

Sign up for our discount coupons and our monthly e-mail newsletter!

View our eBay auctions at www.ebay.com Seller ID: bcemylar

PO Box 60 • Randolph, MA 02368-0060 • Phone: 1-781-986-2653 • Fax 1-781-986-2656 • email: sales@bcemylar.com

All comics are copyrights of their respective owners. Mylar® is a registered trademark of DuPont Teijin films. Their brands of archival quality polyester films are Mylar® type D and Melinex® 456 and 455 of which they are exclusive manufacturers.

STOP!

If you have a comic collection to sell

BIG or **SMALL**

Read This:

I am a comic collector with *VERY* deep pockets and I love the thrill of buying new collections.

You meet the most fascinating people and hear their amazing stories about how they put their collections together.

Think of how much time and effort you have invested. Think of the fun and excitement you have had.

Last year I purchased over *$250,000.00* in collections.
Serious money for Serious collectors.

Each and every book gets an accurate grade and Realistic pricing

You had a great time collecting why shouldn't selling be the same?

>>>> NO LIES <<<<<< >>>>>> NO BS <<<<

<<<<<<<<<<< NO GAMES >>>>>>>>>>>

JIM 914.523.7491

great.wazu.comics@gmail.com

YOUR

Comic Book Social Network.

Sign up today for your **FREE** account.
Get news, read reviews, share photos, make friends,
post blogs, watch videos & more!

COMICWOW!

www.ComicWow.com

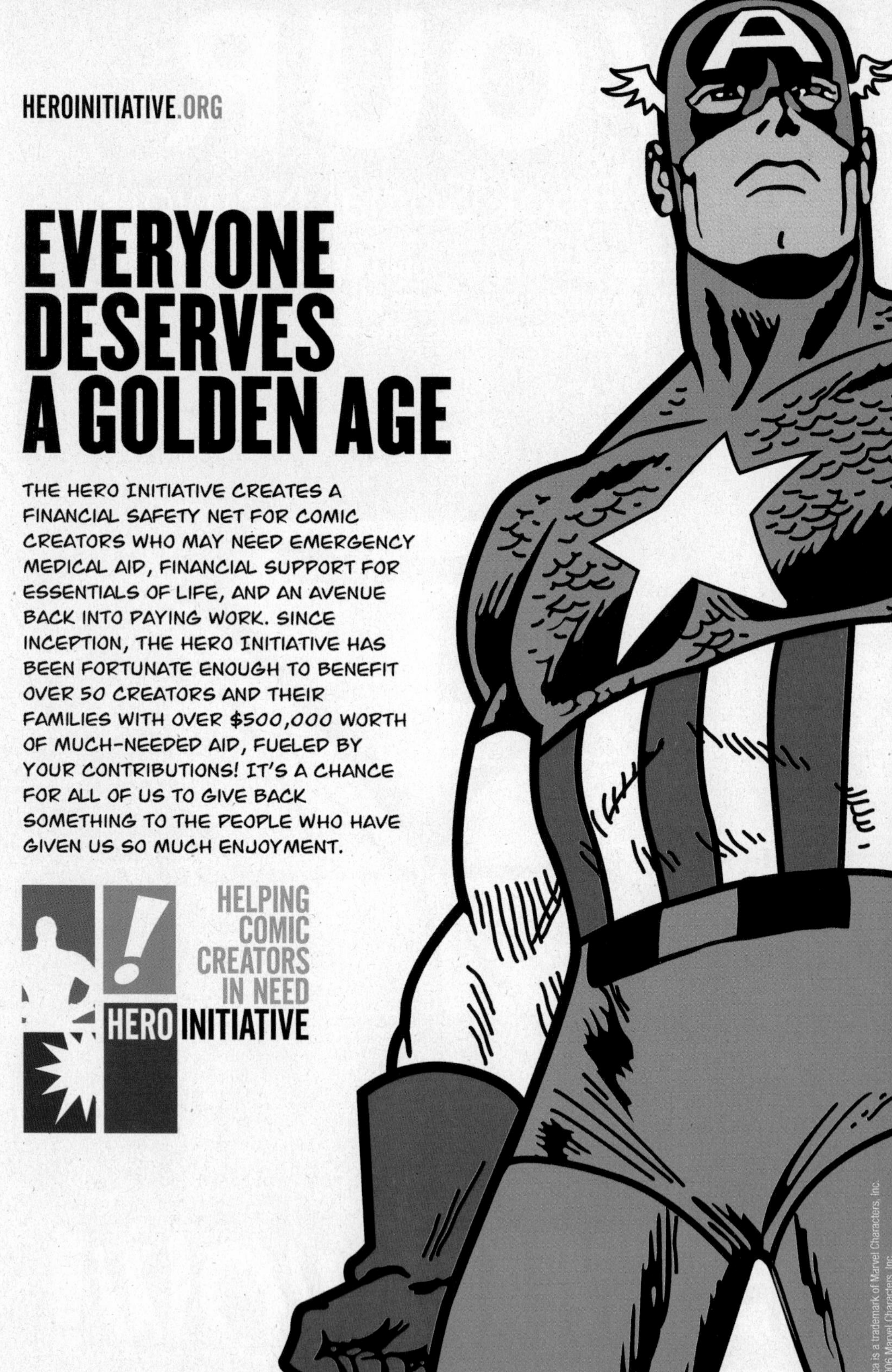
HEROINITIATIVE.ORG
EVERYONE DESERVES A GOLDEN AGE
THE HERO INITIATIVE CREATES A FINANCIAL SAFETY NET FOR COMIC CREATORS WHO MAY NEED EMERGENCY MEDICAL AID, FINANCIAL SUPPORT FOR ESSENTIALS OF LIFE, AND AN AVENUE BACK INTO PAYING WORK. SINCE INCEPTION, THE HERO INITIATIVE HAS BEEN FORTUNATE ENOUGH TO BENEFIT OVER 50 CREATORS AND THEIR FAMILIES WITH OVER $500,000 WORTH OF MUCH-NEEDED AID, FUELED BY YOUR CONTRIBUTIONS! IT'S A CHANCE FOR ALL OF US TO GIVE BACK SOMETHING TO THE PEOPLE WHO HAVE GIVEN US SO MUCH ENJOYMENT.
HELPING COMIC CREATORS IN NEED
HERO INITIATIVE
Captain America is a trademark of Marvel Characters, Inc.
Copyright ©2006 Marvel Characters, Inc.

6 Out of 10 Con-Goers Have Never Experienced a Comic Shop.

Come see what you're missing!

There's a lot to see and do at your local comic shop. From great comic books, graphic novels and toys, to cool events like Free Comic Book Day, creator signings, and more. It's 100% convention—100% of the time. So come see what you're missing. To find a comic shop near you, visit comicshoplocator.com.

*PREVIEWS*world.com • ToyChestNews.com • ComicShopLocator.com • FreeComicBookDay.com • Halloween ComicFest.com • KidsComics.com • GameTradeMagazine.com

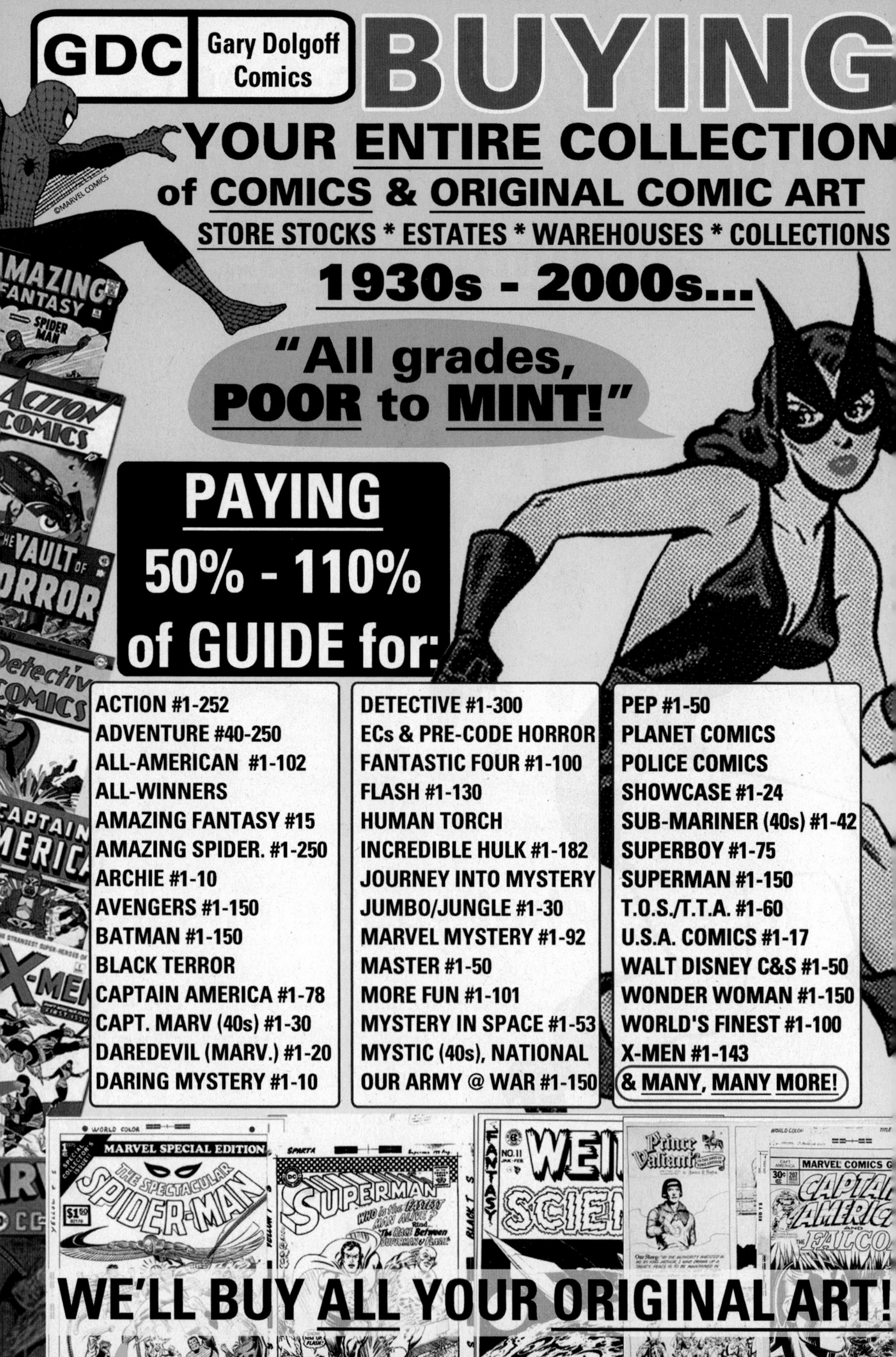
GDC
Gary Dolgoff Comics
BUYING
YOUR ENTIRE COLLECTION
of COMICS & ORIGINAL COMIC ART
STORE STOCKS * ESTATES * WAREHOUSES * COLLECTIONS
1930s - 2000s...
"All grades, POOR to MINT!"
PAYING
50% - 110%
of GUIDE for:
ACTION #1-252
ADVENTURE #40-250
ALL-AMERICAN #1-102
ALL-WINNERS
AMAZING FANTASY #15
AMAZING SPIDER. #1-250
ARCHIE #1-10
AVENGERS #1-150
BATMAN #1-150
BLACK TERROR
CAPTAIN AMERICA #1-78
CAPT. MARV (40s) #1-30
DAREDEVIL (MARV.) #1-20
DARING MYSTERY #1-10
DETECTIVE #1-300
ECs & PRE-CODE HORROR
FANTASTIC FOUR #1-100
FLASH #1-130
HUMAN TORCH
INCREDIBLE HULK #1-182
JOURNEY INTO MYSTERY
JUMBO/JUNGLE #1-30
MARVEL MYSTERY #1-92
MASTER #1-50
MORE FUN #1-101
MYSTERY IN SPACE #1-53
MYSTIC (40s), NATIONAL
OUR ARMY @ WAR #1-150
PEP #1-50
PLANET COMICS
POLICE COMICS
SHOWCASE #1-24
SUB-MARINER (40s) #1-42
SUPERBOY #1-75
SUPERMAN #1-150
T.O.S./T.T.A. #1-60
U.S.A. COMICS #1-17
WALT DISNEY C&S #1-50
WONDER WOMAN #1-150
WORLD'S FINEST #1-100
X-MEN #1-143
& MANY, MANY MORE!
WE'LL BUY ALL YOUR ORIGINAL ART!
©MARVEL COMICS

SELL YOUR COMICS & ORIGINAL ART

GDC Gary Dolgoff Comics

to GARY DOLGOFF!

"The Industry Professional, with a heart!..."

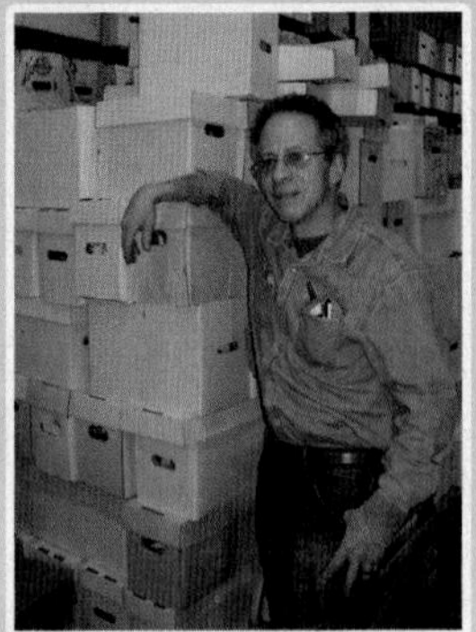

WHY SELL TO ME?

I'm able to pay more than most dealers in this book, because I take everything into account when I evaluate your collection. I also have a large staff & warehouse (800,000+ comics in stock), so I'm able to sell comics over time. Namely, I don't need to resell collections right-away for a 'quick-buck'...

- **30+ Years Experience (Buying Collections)**
- **I Buy ALL GRADES! (POOR to MINT)**
- **Great Reputation for being Fair and Honest**
- **I will happily buy your Whole Collection!**
- **Will Travel Worldwide (for certain collections)**
- **Immediate Payment ($500 to $500,000+)**

© DC Comics

Gary D Sez: "Live the good life... consider 'selling to Dolgoff'!"

Gary Dolgoff Comics
116 Pleasant St. STE #213
Easthampton, MA 01027

Call us anytime,
TOLL FREE: **1-866-830-4367**

gdcomics on ebay • email: gary@gdcomics.com • web: gdcomics.com

HOT FLIPS

comic book supplies

WWW.HOTFLIPS.COM

COMIC BOOK SUPPLIES, FOR COMIC BOOK COLLECTORS, BY COMIC BOOK COLLECTORS

COMIC BOOK BOXES

BAGS & BOARDS

CHARLES & JEFF CERRITO
CO-OWNERS

TOP LOADERS

LIKE US ON FACEBOOK | HOT FLIPS SUPPLIES

WWW.HOTFLIPS.COM

COMIC BOOK SUPPLIES, FOR COMIC BOOK COLLECTORS, BY COMIC BOOK COLLECTORS

WHOLESALE & RETAIL

CALL FOR WHOLESALE PRICING

WE BUY COMICS!!

BEST QUALITY & BEST CUSTOMER SERVICE

WE SHIP INTERNATIONALLY

CALL TOLL FREE: 1-800-922-FLIP (3547)

WE TRAVEL TO SHOWS ALL OVER THE USA, ALL YEAR LONG...

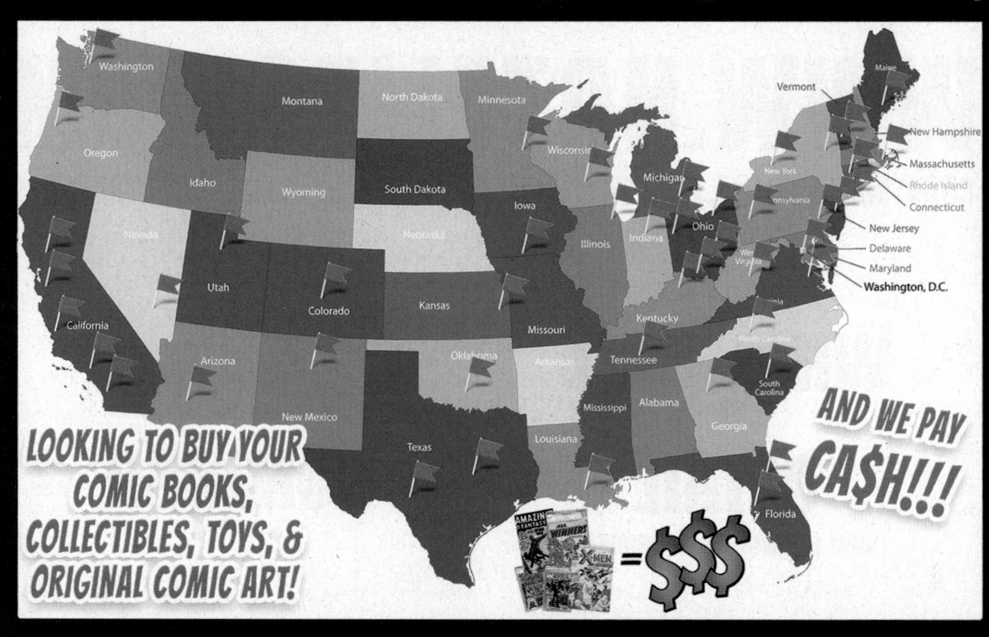

HERE ARE MOST OF THE CITIES WE WILL BE VISITING IN THE NEXT CALENDAR YEAR:

ALBUQUERQUE, NM
ANAHEIM, CA
ATLANTA, GA
ATLANTIC CITY, NJ
AUSTIN, TX
BALTIMORE, MD
BOSTON, MA
CHICAGO, IL
CLEVELAND, OH
COLUMBUS, OH
DENVER, CO
INDIANAPOLIS, IN
LOS ANGELES, CA
LOUISVILLE, KY
MINNEAPOLIS, MN
NASHVILLE, TN
NEW ORLEANS, LA
NEW YORK, NY
PHILADELPHIA, PA
PHOENIX, AZ
RENO, NV
RICHMOND, VA
SACRAMENTO, CA
SALT LAKE CITY, UT
SAN FRANCISCO, CA
SAN JOSE, CA
SEATTLE, WA
TAMPA BAY, FL
TORONTO (CANADA)
TULSA, OK

For a complete comic buying travel schedule, as well as what comics we are buying - Visit:
GETCASHFORCOMICS.COM

And follow us on Facebook:
FACEBOOK.COM/GETCASHFORCOMICS

WHY SELL TO US?

★ IN THE PAST YEAR WE'VE SPENT

$27,250,000 DOLLARS

ON BUYING COMIC BOOKS, COLLECTIBLES, TOYS, AND ORIGINAL COMIC ART!

★ WE MAKE FAST & FAIR OFFERS - TYPICALLY WITHIN 24 HOURS!

★ WILLING TO TRAVEL TO YOU AT A MOMENT'S NOTICE!

★ BEST OF ALL - WE PAY CA$H

TRY GETTING THAT FROM AN AUCTION HOUSE!

(IF CASH DOESN'T WORK FOR YOU, WE CAN ALSO PAY BY CHECK, WIRE, OR MONEY ORDER!)

WHEN YOU'RE READY TO SELL YOUR COMIC BOOKS & BE PAID TOP DOLLAR IN CASH THERE'S ONLY ONE COMPANY TO CALL:

GETCASHFORCOMICS.COM

CALL OR EMAIL US TODAY!

WHETHER YOU HAVE ONE BOOK TO SELL OR 10,000
CONTACT US TODAY TO DISCUSS IT.
THREE EASY WAYS TO GET IN CONTACT WITH US:

1. Call us toll free at 1-866-461-0640
2. Use our contact form at www.getcashforcomics.com
3. Email us at buying@GetCashForComics.com

Buy and Build Up Your CGC Collection

at PedigreeComics.com

Reach for Midgard's Best Selection of High-Grade Marvel and DC CGC CERTIFIED COMICS!

PEDIGREE COMICS IS THE ULTIMATE CGC COLLECTORS PARADISE!

The website's consignment section is routinely stocked with thousands of High-Grade CGC Certified Comics and Magazines, spanning all genres.

Check the "New Arrivals" section every day for the newly uploaded high-grade books!

PEDIGREE'S GRAND AUCTIONS ARE HELD BI-MONTHLY...

(every 2 months) as a separate event on the Pedigree Comics website. The auctions run for (10) days and feature hundreds of CGC Certified Comics and Magazines, many of which are the highest graded on the CGC Census.

Check the "Latest News" section every day for news and updates on the upcoming Grand Auction!

"The CGC Collectors Paradise"

Pedigree Comics, Inc. • 12541 Equine Lane • Wellington, FL 33414
PedigreeComics.com • email: DougSchmell@pedigreecomics.com
Office: (561) 422-1120 • Cell: (561) 596-9111 • Fax: (561) 422-1120

Auction Reporting Partner GPAnalysis

PASSION for COLLECTING...

When it comes to passion for collecting, dedication to the hobby, and amassing high-grade, award winning runs... few measure up to Pedigree Comics' CEO and President, Doug Schmell, who sold his personal collection of Silver Age Marvels in 2012 for over 3.94 Million Dollars (a record price for a comic book collection).

So, who is best qualified to help you build your collection and find you the books and upgrades you need?

Over the past 20 plus years, I have amassed over fifteen thousand Marvel comic books, most of which are in very high grade condition. When CGC was in the process of forming in March, 1999, I was one of a handful of collectors asked to attend their start-up meeting and provide input to the creation of this third party grading service. When the CGC commenced operations later that year and began encapsulating and grading comic books for the public, I began submitting my runs of Marvel titles. Now, known as "Captain Tripps" on the CGC Registry and chat boards, I have come to be recognized as one of the leading collectors of Marvel Silver and Bronze Age comics, with many of my books being the highest graded copies in existence. In fact, I received the coveted Achievement in Comics Collecting 2006, awarded by the CGC Comics Registry, in honor of the outstanding runs of Marvel comics I had registered since November, 2003, including the highest graded set of virtually every Marvel Silver Age and Bronze Age title.

Although I sold the majority of my Bronze Age titles when I moved to Florida in 2004, I kept and continued to add to my Silver Age sets, looking for upgrades on any individual issue whenever possible. The formation of this collection, which has been painstakingly pared down to around 700 books, took an incredible amount of effort, time, expense, and patience. The stories I could tell of meeting at diners, post offices in Northern New Jersey, law offices, street corners in New York City, dealers' tables, and comic stores around the country in order to obtain that missing issue or coveted upgrade, would blow your mind. My decision to sell the collection was based on my feeling that I had reached a sort of collector's Nirvana, that I had finally obtained every sought after pedigreed issue or top of the CGC census book I could possibly find. The long journey has taken me to this point in time and I couldn't be any happier.

Let me help you find the same fulfillment I have!
Email me at dougschmell@pedigreecomics.com
or call me today at 1-561-422-1120.

PedigreeComics.com

Visit the ToonSeum: Pittsburgh's Museum of Comic and Cartoon Art

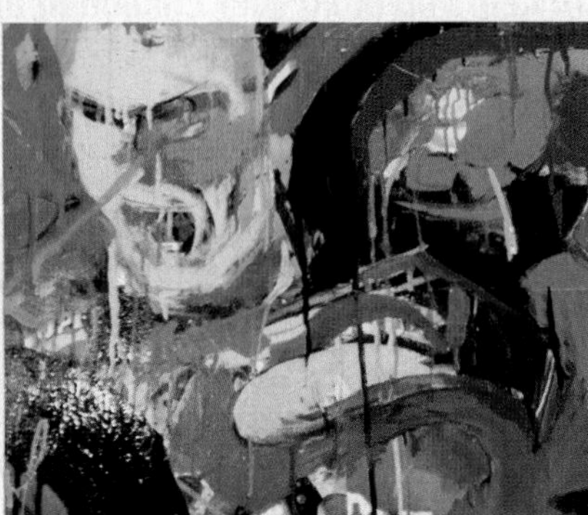

THE TOONSEUM IS A BOUTIQUE MUSEUM DEDICATED TO the comic and cartoon arts located in downtown Pittsburgh, PA.

The mission of the ToonSeum is to celebrate the art of cartooning in all its varied forms. From comic strips to comic books, to animation and illustration art.

Our goal is to promote a deeper appreciation of cartoonists and their work through hands-on workshops, community outreach, cartoon-oriented educational programming, and exhibitions of original cartoon art.

Our exhibits change every few months. Visit toonseum.org for all the latest exhibit and event information.

Collectors Wanted.
The ToonSeum is always interested in working with collectors willing to loan works to our exhibits or to donate artwork to the museums' holdings. For details, please contact our executive director Joe Wos at 412.760.1896.

945 Liberty Avenue, Pittsburgh, PA 15222 • 412.232.0199

Our exhibits have featured original artwork from:

Charles Schulz
Jack Kirby
Mary Blair
Dan Piraro
Winsor McCay
Gene Colan
Dale Messick
Chuck Jones
Joe Shuster
Stephan Pastis
Mike Peters
Bill Griffith
Trina Robbins
Bill Plympton
Ron Frenz
Ramona Fradon
Dik Brown
Mort Walker
John Romita
and many more!

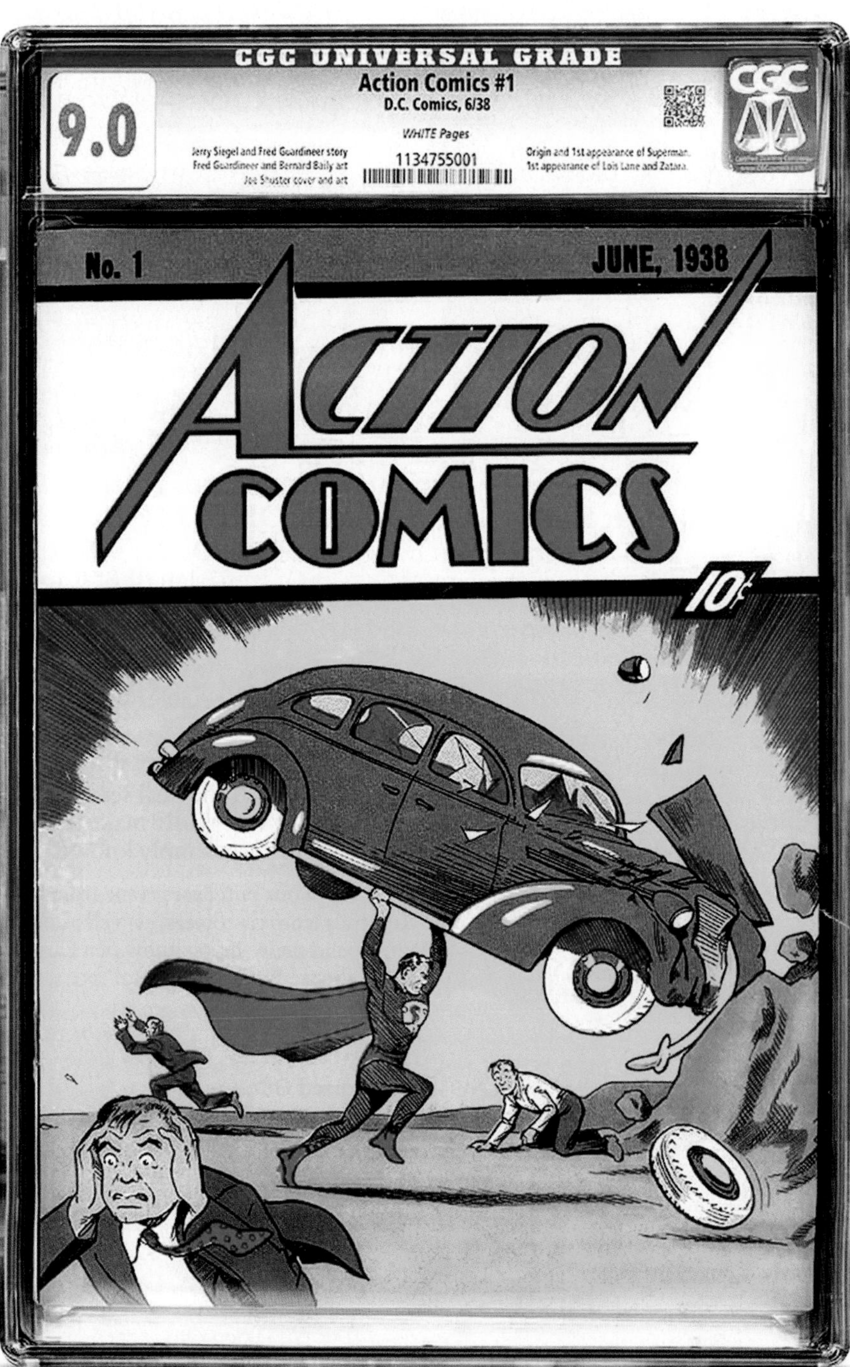
CGC UNIVERSAL GRADE
9.0
Action Comics #1
D.C. Comics, 6/38
WHITE Pages
Jerry Siegel and Fred Guardineer story
Fred Guardineer and Bernard Baily art
Joe Shuster cover and art
1134755001
Origin and 1st appearance of Superman.
1st appearance of Lois Lane and Zatara.
CGC
No. 1
JUNE, 1938
ACTION
COMICS
10¢

WE ARE BUYING!

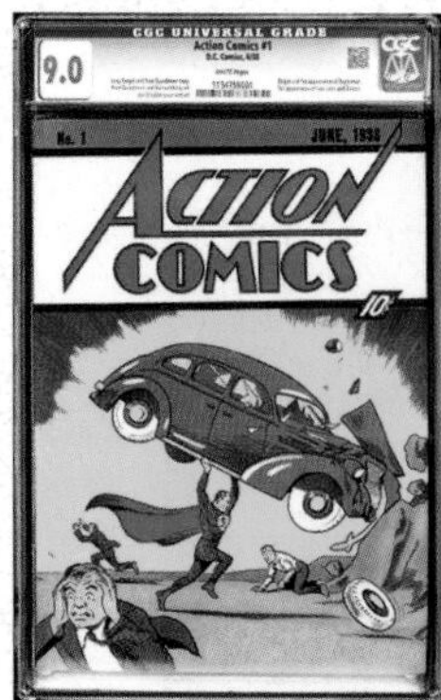

HIGHEST GRADED AC#1
1 OF 2 COPIES WE OWN!

Photo of Stan Lee & Darren (owner of Pristine Comics) taken at **STAN LEE'S WALK OF FAME INDUCTION.**

Stan Proudly Holding A Pair Of Our 9.9s
(Both *The Highest Graded* Copies Of Iron Man #1 & Cap #100)

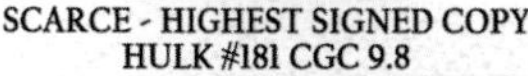

SCARCE - HIGHEST SIGNED COPY
HULK #181 CGC 9.8

GENEROUS Finder's Fees Paid!

Just Ask Andre. If the deal seems too large just **CALL ME**. I will gladly make it worth your while in the form simply known as **CA$H**.

Many of our purchases come from referrals - Referrals from customers, as well as other dealers. We depend on it. If you know of a Large Collection, Warehouse Find, Estate Deal ..etc ... **CALL ME.**

You Will NOT Be Squeezed Out...
and You Will Be Paid In CA$H. Referrals Mean Everything To Us.
Let Me Place Your Photo In Next Year's Overstreet Price Guide! CALL DARREN 253-941-1986

The #1 BUYER ON THE WEST COAST Is Actively Looking For:

- **Comic Books** (Pre 1989)
- **Magic the Gathering** (Boxes, Cases, Singles)
- **Comic Art**
- **Sports Cards** (Singles, boxes, Cases)

QUIT WASTING YOUR TIME !!!

If you're having to look through a "Price Guide" to decide if what you have is worth a lot of $$$

Do yourself a favor. Put the book down, pick up the phone and dial....

253-941-1986

1986/87 Fleer Basketball Factory Case
The Holy Grail Of Modern Day Basketball
Contains Michael Jordan's Rookie Card & Is
The Most Valuable Sports
Card Product Of the Last 40 Years.

BGS GRADED "10"
BETA BLACK LOTUS
The Highest & Only
BGS 10 Beta Black Lotus
The Holy Grail of Magic The Gathering

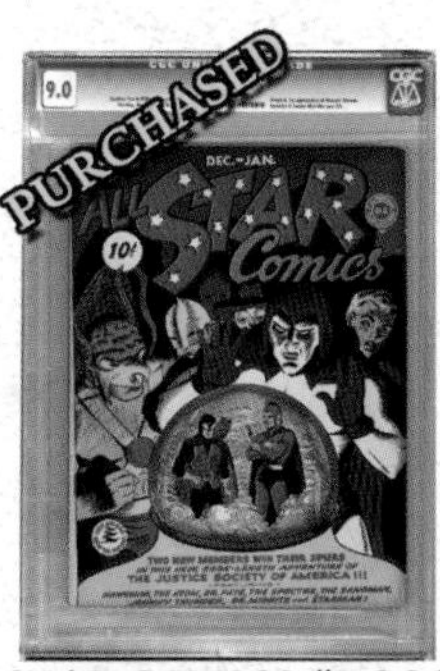

ALL STAR COMICS #8 CGC 9.0
Highest Graded Copy
1st Appearance Wonder Woman

STAN LEE SIGNATURE SERIES

Photo of Stan Lee Signing
Amazing Fantasy #15 for Pristinecomics.com

Avengers #57 CGC 9.8 Signature Series
Single Highest Signed Copy

WANTED!

MAGIC

MAGIC THE GATHERING
ALPHA & BETA BOOSTER BOXES
PAYING $25,000 PER BOX

OUR RETAIL SHOWROOM IS OPEN 7 DAYS A WEEK

conveniently located between Seattle & Tacoma and only minutes from Sea-Tac International Airport. Just off Interstate 5 in Federal Way.

WEST COAST SPORTSCARDS
2008 South 314th Street. Federal Way, WA 98003
Located just minutes from Seattle & Tacoma
CALL: 253-941-1986

Offic
Overst
Advis

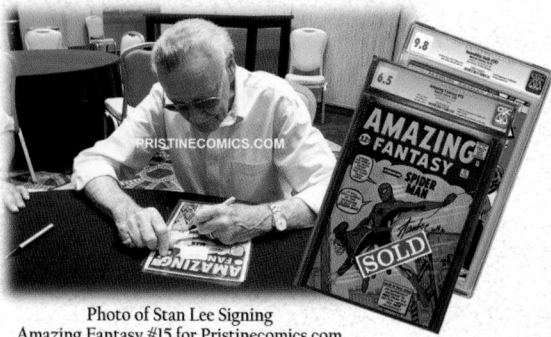

Coming to eBay August 2014

PRESENTED BY
PRISTINE COMICS

ACTION COMICS #1

9.0 grading by CGC
with white pages

WEST COAST SPORTS CARDS
PRISTINE COMICS
253-941-1986

pop culture with character

GEPPI'S
entertainment
MUSEUM

BOOK YOUR WEDDINGS, CORPORATE EVENTS, HOLIDAY PARTIES, BIRTHDAY PARTIES AND MEETINGS AT GEPPI'S ENTERTAINMENT MUSEUM!

LOCATED IN HISTORIC CAMDEN STATION AT BALTIMORE'S PREMIER DESTINATION OF CAMDEN YARDS.

Geppi's Entertainment Museum is a tribute to the characters, toys and collectibles of our past and present. Our main gallery can accommodate up to 400 for an amazing cocktail party. Our third floor is the perfect spot for an intimate sit down dinner.

To Make Your Party a Night to Remember: Contact Nadja Martens
Sales Manager - Events • Phone: 410-625-7063 • FAX: 410-625-7090
www.geppismuseum.com

CONSIGN NOW
WWW.HAKES.COM

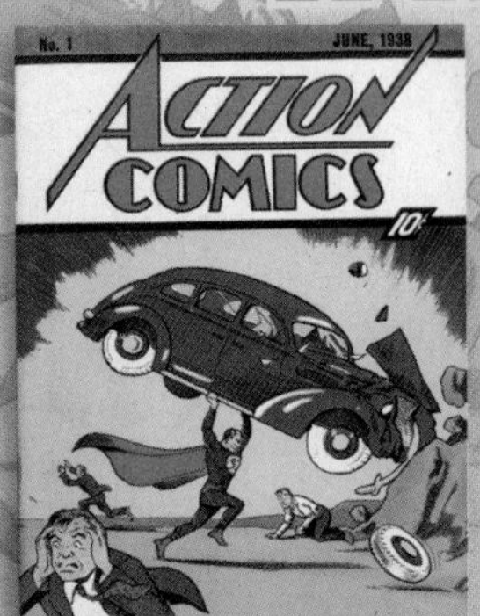

MICKEY
MECHANICAL
BANK
$28,750

KRESGE
ROBIN
MEGO
$12,197

MARILYN MONROE
OWNED DRESS
$15,180

THE BEATLES GIANT BOBBING
HEAD DISPLAY FIGURES SET
$33,674

MICKEY & MINNIE DISPLAY DOLLS
BY CHARLOTTE CLARK
$151,534

HAKE'S AMERICANA & COLLECTIBLES

SWAN COVER ORIGINAL ART $112,015

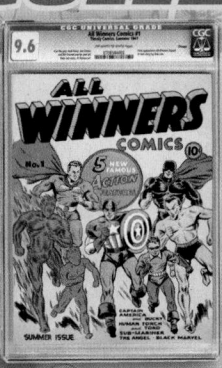

ALL-WINNERS #1 CGC 9.6 $95,200

KIRBY COVER ORIGINAL ART $95,156

1910 "POP" LLOYD BASEBALL CARD $94,875

PROVEN RESULTS FOR 5 DECADES

CONSIGN YOUR QUALITY COLLECTIBLES TODAY!

FOR CONSIGNMENT INFORMATION
VISIT: HAKES.COM
Hake's Americana & Collectibles
PO Box 12001 - York, PA 17402
866.404.9800

1907 $20 GOLD COIN $29,500

HENDRIX POSTER $7,974

HOUND OF THE BASKERVILLES POSTER $17,906

MAXX FX ALIEN PROTOTYPE $4,554

HARDING AND COOLIDGE BUTTON $29,601

PEANUTS SUNDAY ORIGINAL ART $41,264

BILLY BARRIX RECORD $13,210

WHEN YOU WANT TO SELL YOUR
COMIC BOOKS
AND WANT TO BE
PAID IN
CA$H
GET CA$H FOR COMICS
CALL THE BEST!
GET CA$H FOR COMICS
GET CA$H FOR COMICS
AMAZING FANTASY
SPIDER MAN
THE WALKING DEAD
GET CA$H FOR COMICS!
9.0
THE STRANGEST SUPER-HEROES OF ALL!
X-MEN
Fantastic Four
THE COMING OF GALACTUS!
$

WHY SELL TO US?

★ IN THE PAST YEAR WE'VE SPENT

$27,250,000 DOLLARS

ON BUYING COMIC BOOKS, COLLECTIBLES, TOYS, AND ORIGINAL COMIC ART!

★ WE MAKE FAST & FAIR OFFERS - TYPICALLY WITHIN 24 HOURS!

★ WILLING TO TRAVEL TO YOU AT A MOMENT'S NOTICE!

★ BEST OF ALL - WE PAY **CA$H**

TRY GETTING THAT FROM AN AUCTION HOUSE!

(IF CASH DOESN'T WORK FOR YOU, WE CAN ALSO PAY BY CHECK, WIRE, OR MONEY ORDER!)

WHEN YOU'RE READY TO SELL YOUR COMIC BOOKS & BE PAID TOP DOLLAR IN CASH THERE'S ONLY ONE COMPANY TO CALL:

GETCASHFORCOMICS.COM

CALL OR EMAIL US TODAY!

WHETHER YOU HAVE ONE BOOK TO SELL OR 10,000 CONTACT US TODAY TO DISCUSS IT.

THREE EASY WAYS TO GET IN CONTACT WITH US:

1. Call us toll free at 1-866-461-0640
2. Use our contact form at www.getcashforcomics.com
3. Email us at buying@GetCashForComics.com

THE COUNTDOWN FOR THE SPECIAL 45TH ANNIVERSARY EDITION BEGINS NOW!

WOULD YOU LIKE TO ADVERTISE
IN THE BOOK KNOWN AS

THE BIBLE OF COMIC BOOK COLLECTORS?

SINCE 1970, THE OVERSTREET COMIC BOOK PRICE GUIDE
HAS BEEN THE GO TO DESTINATION
FOR SERIOUS COMIC BOOK ENTHUSIASTS,
DEALERS AND HISTORIANS!

- Full Page Color ads start at $2,500!
- Full Page B&W ads start at $900!
- Save 10% when you take three or more ads of the same size & type!
- Save 10% with our Early Bird rates!
- Save 20% with both discounts!

For additional rates, specs or technical information, contact

Michael Solof

Advertising Sales Coordinator

(410) 625-7062

somike@geppismuseum.com

Early Bird Deadline
December 2, 2014

Standard Rate Deadline
March 4, 2015

WWW.GEMSTONEPUB.COM

Paul Gulacy • Captain Action

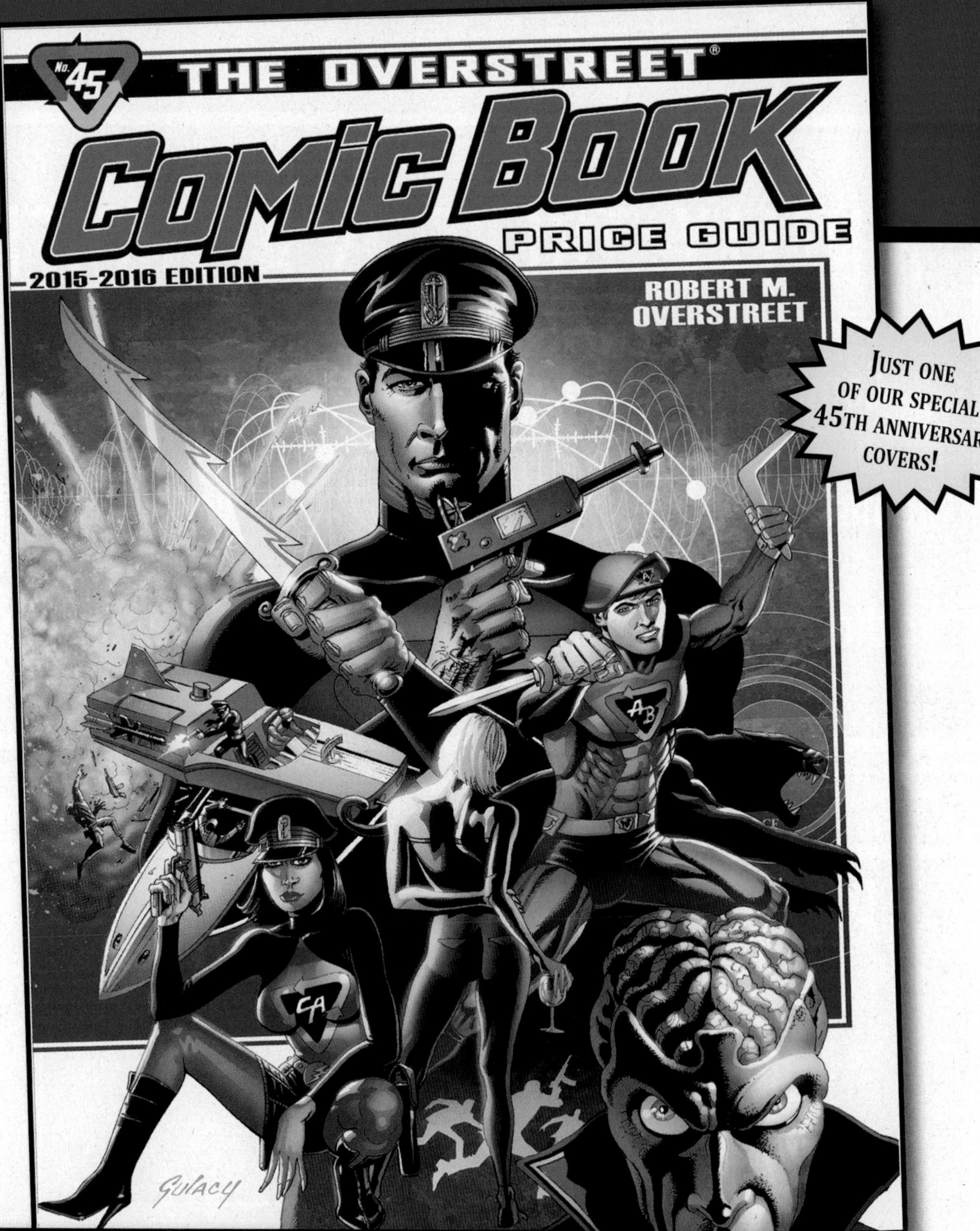

See Paul Gulacy's original art and so much more at Geppi's Entertainment Museum!

Captain Action and related characters ©2014 and TM Captain Action Enterprises, LLC. Used by Permission. Overstreet® is a Registered Trademark of Gemstone Publishing, Inc.

WWW.GEMSTONEPUB.COM

FINALLY, THERE IS A CHOICE.

Comic book grading leaps forward with CBCS.

Equipped with the experience, the integrity, and the technology to offer unmatched service and value.

Led by names you already KNOW and TRUST.

Steve Borock
The first name in comic book certification.

West Stephan
Golden Age and Pedigree Expert.

www.CBCScomics.com Toll Free: 844-870-CBCS

COMIC BOOK CERTIFICATION SERVICE

GUARANTEED TURNAROUND TIMES

--you receive CREDIT if we're late.

LOW prices combined with quick, guaranteed turnaround times, and FREE online grader's notes. Our newly designed, tamper evident "Shield" holder with a crystal clear inner sleeve made of archival PETG, uses cutting-edge technology to protect your comic.

CBCS
PO Box 33048
St. Petersburg,
FL 33733
(727) 803-6822

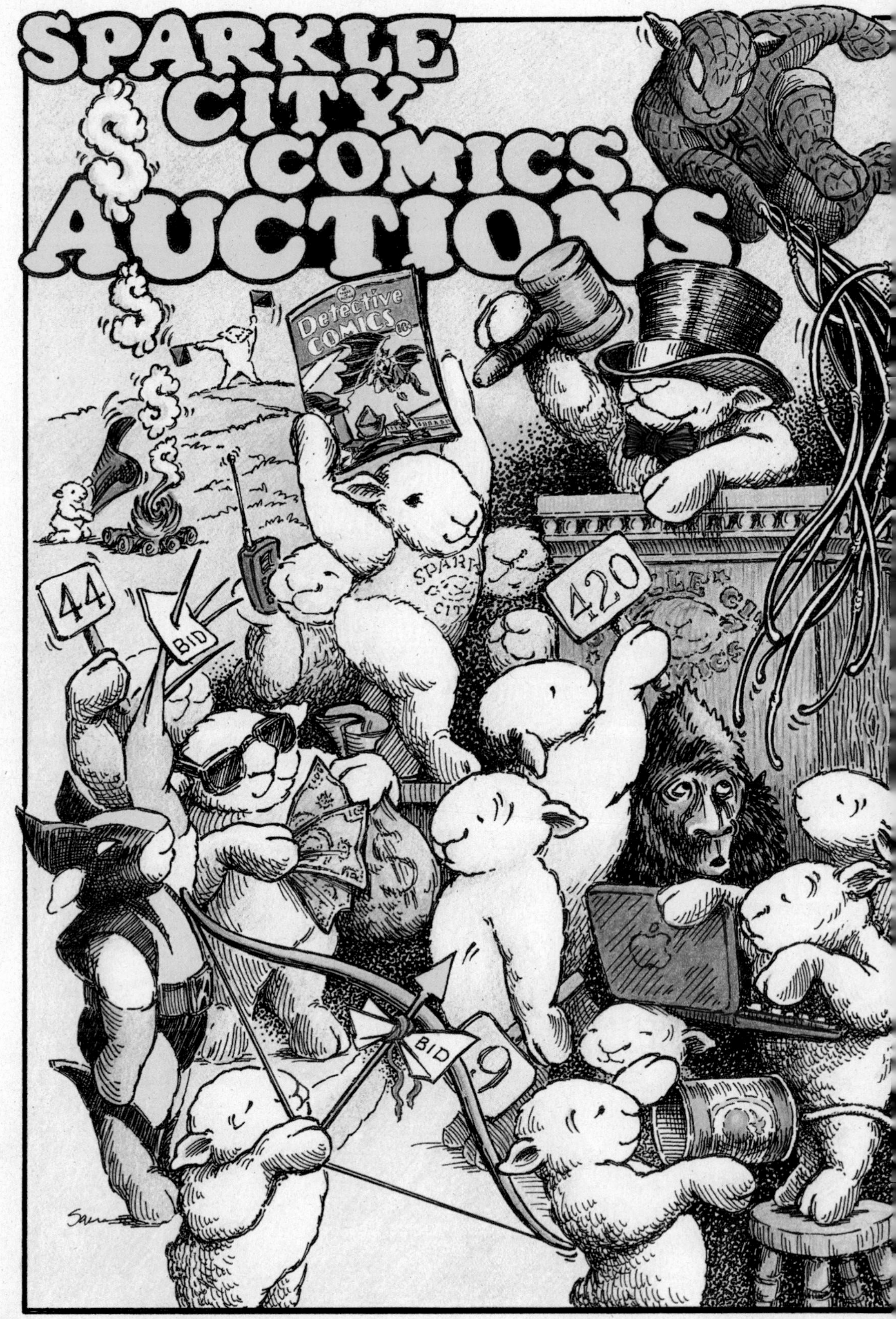
SPARKLE CITY COMICS AUCTIONS
Detective COMICS
44
BID
420
BID
9

SPARKLE CITY COMICS AUCTIONS

FOR THE FIRST TIME
CONSIGN YOUR ENTIRE COLLECTION INTACT!
Comics, Toys, Art – Raw and graded!

Do you want the ABSOLUTE MOST money for your lifetime collection?

Sparkle City Comics is proud to announce that for the first time, qualified collections are being considered for consignment INTACT!

DO NOT let other auctions houses or dealers come in and cherry pick your collection, leaving you with everything else. DO NOT let other auction houses or dealers come in and ONLY VALUE YOUR KEY COMICS, taking all the rest for free!

Do you have collectibles other than comics?

Whether it's magazines, Original Art, Toys, Cards, Statues, records, gold/silver or even Civil War relics; We can sell it all for you!

ONLY SPARKLE CITY COMICS can help you market and expose your entire collection to millions of collectors and get the most money possible, by a mile! We will handle your collection as though it was ours, maximizing the value on your key issues and selling the more common segments quickly en masse.

ONLY SPARKLE CITY COMICS can sell 10c books to $1,000,000 books, customize it to your needs and get it done FAST!

STOP calling in lowball offers and cherry pickers. Start maximizing your return from years of collecting by calling me NOW at:

1-800-215-4006

buyingeverything@yahoo.com

WWW.SPARKLECITYCOMICS.COM

eBay ID – sparklecitycomics
Positive Feedback – 49091+
Top Seller Plus
1 Seller of CGC Comics
on eBay

HERITAGE®

COMICS & COMIC ART AUCTIONS

QUESTIONS TO ASK YOUR *PROSPECTIVE AUCTIONEER*

- Do you make all of your previous price results available online so I can judge your performance, or do you cite only your most impressive results?
- Do you cross-market my items to bidders from other categories to drive my consignment prices higher?
- Do you have a world-class website that makes it easy for people to track and bid on my lots?
- Do you mail thousands of exquisite, printed catalogs to the top collectors throughout the world?
- Do you offer in-person viewing open to the public, so my premium quality books won't sell for generic prices?
- Do you offer live public auctions for your top items, with both proxy and real-time internet and telephone bidding?

At Heritage Auctions, the answer to all of the above questions is *YES*.

And there's more at Heritage that no one else in the comic hobby can come close to matching:

- An award-winning website that attracts an average of 30,000 daily visitors.
- 850,000+ bidder-members in 38 cross-marketed specialties.
- $900+ million in annual auction and private sales.
- Over $50 million in equity and owners' capital.
- Every consignor since our first auction in 1976 has been paid in full and right on schedule.

All of the above is why we have successfully auctioned more than 150,000 consignments, 75% of which have come from repeat consignors.

We invite your call or email us right now to discuss your comic treasures and how Heritage can serve you.

Call or e-mail us today! We look forward to hearing from you.

ED JASTER
877.HERITAGE (437.4824)
Ext. 1288
EdJ@HA.com

LON ALLEN
877.HERITAGE (437.4824)
Ext. 1261
LonA@HA.com

HERITAGE®

COMICS & COMIC ART AUCTIONS

As a result of our total marketing efforts (print marketing, web marketing, videos, coast-to-coast displays, a full-color catalog and more) this comic

SOLD FOR

$1,075,500

2/10

(in not nearly as strong a market as exists today), attracting bidders over the $500,000 level from six different countries.

3500 Maple Avenue | Dallas, Texas 75219 | 877.HERITAGE (437.4824) | Bid@HA.com

Annual Sales Exceed $900 Million | 850,000+ Online Bidder-Members

HERITAGE AUCTIONS HA.com

DALLAS | NEW YORK | BEVERLY HILLS | SAN FRANCISCO | HOUSTON | PARIS | GENEVA

TURN THE PAGE FOR MUCH MORE INFO ABOUT HERITAGE

TX Auctioneer licenses: Samuel Foose 11727; Robert Korver 13754; Andrea Voss 16406. • All comic auctions are subject to a 19.5% Buyer's Premium.

HERITAGE®

COMICS & COMIC ART AUCTIONS

START A BIDDING WAR FOR YOUR COMIC COLLECTION!

SOLD FOR $191,200 2/14

SOLD FOR $492,937 7/12

SOLD FOR $567,625 8/13

We don't make money until you make money! Our commission is a percentage of your sale price, so we can only maximize our fee by maximizing competitive bidding. We promote our auctions heavily because it's in your best interest and ours!

TO FIND OUT MORE ABOUT WHAT HERITAGE CAN DO FOR YOU, SEE OUR ADS ON PAGES 6–7, 76–77, 258–259, 267 AND 1197!

Heritage buys collections too! $3.1 million paid for a single collection in 2009

Contact us to find out more:

Ed Jaster
877.HERITAGE (437.4824)
ext. 1288
EdJ@HA.com

Lon Allen
877.HERITAGE (437.4824)
ext. 1261
LonA@HA.com

HERITAGE®

COMICS & COMIC ART AUCTIONS

MORE EXPOSURE FOR SELLERS AT HERITAGE!

Beautiful printed catalogs entice bidders to bid higher.

Our **heavily advertised** Signature® auctions are among the biggest events in the comic book hobby. The live sessions have bidders participating by phone, in person, and over the Internet.

Auction archive of Comics and Original Art — every item we've ever auctioned with full descriptions, images and actual prices realized. We don't hide our past results (and we don't intermix retail sales with our auction records)!

EXCLUSIVE AUCTIONEER OF THESE OUTSTANDING PERSONAL COLLECTIONS:

The Kerby Confer Collection
$3.9 million sold

The Doug Schmell Collection
$3.9 million sold

The Billy Wright Collection
$3.6 million sold

Heritage's experts will guide you through the consignment process and help you get the most money for your treasured items. Call or email us today!

3500 Maple Avenue | Dallas, Texas 75219 | 877.HERITAGE (437.4824) | Bid@HA.com

Annual Sales Exceed $900 Million | 850,000+ Online Bidder-Members

DALLAS | NEW YORK | BEVERLY HILLS | SAN FRANCISCO | HOUSTON | PARIS | GENEVA

TX Auctioneer licenses: Samuel Foose 11727; Robert Korver 13754; Andrea Voss 16406. - All comic auctions are subject to a 19.5% Buyer's Premium

SELL ON COMICLINK.COM

WHERE YOU GET TOP DOLLAR
THE PREMIUM REAL-TIME EXCHANGE
THE PREFERRED AUCTION VENUE

MAXIMIZE YOUR RETURN

- Sell at Auction or on the Exchange
- Regularly Establishing Record Prices
- Longest Online Presence of any Comic Service
- Our Client Base & Experience are Unmatched
- Buyers are Waiting for Your High-Quality Items
- Pricing Experts can Maximize Value
- Grading Experts can Grade Your Comics
- Customer Service is Always Accessible
- Proven Track Record of Prompt Payment
- Cash Advance and Purchase Options Available

ComicLink makes the sales process easy! Contact us to find out how to get the most money quickly for your vintage comics and art.

www.comiclink.com
617-517-0062
buysell@comiclink.com

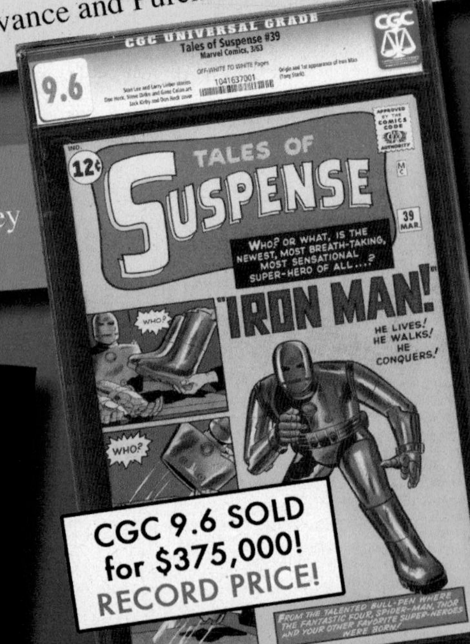

HAS THERE EVER BEEN A BETTER TIME TO BE A *COMIC BOOK FAN?*
WITH COMIC BOOK-INSPIRED MOVIES, TV SHOWS AND VIDEO GAMES, MORE PEOPLE THAN EVER ARE *DISCOVERING* THE CHARACTERS AND STORIES WE LOVE!

THAT'S *COOL* BECAUSE AS *GREAT* AS MANY OF THE OTHER INCARNATIONS HAVE BEEN, COMICS STILL DO IT *BEST*!

"BUT CHANCES ARE THAT IF YOU'RE READING *THIS* BOOK, YOU ALREADY *LOVE* COMICS OR KNOW SOMEONE WHO DOES."

"IN JUST A MOMENT, WE'LL GET DOWN TO *BASICS*..."

WE HOPE YOU'LL FIND THIS BOOK TO BE A SUPERB REFERENCE, NO MATTER WHAT TYPE OF COMICS YOU LIKE.

OUR *MARKET REPORTS* START ON PAGE 89, AND THEY OFFER THE INSIGHT OF THE *OVERSTREET ADVISORS* ABOUT BACK ISSUE SALES...
AND WE HAVE TONS OF PRICING DATA, TOP COMICS, GRADING TIPS, AND MORE!

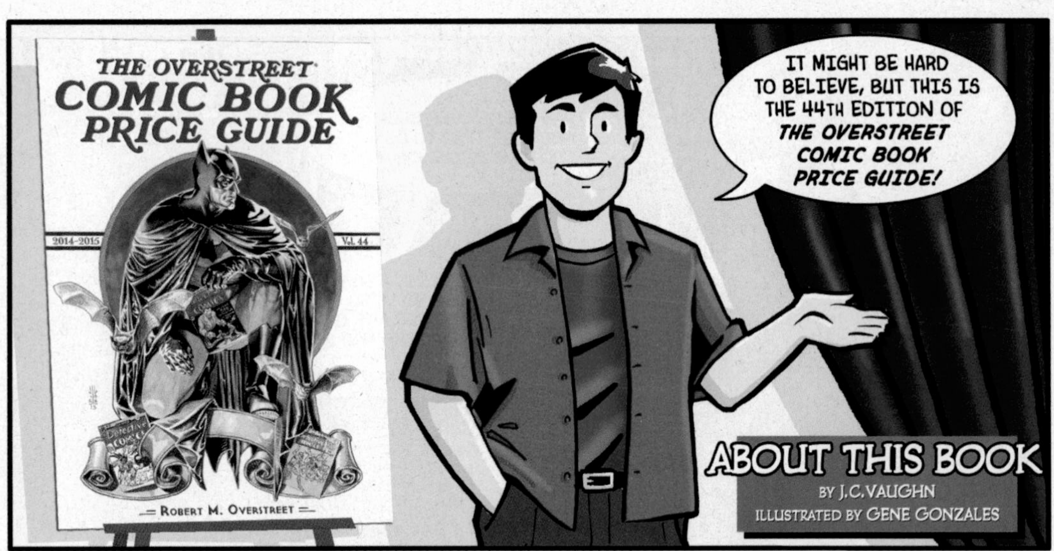
THE OVERSTREET COMIC BOOK PRICE GUIDE
2014-2015
Vol. 44
ROBERT M. OVERSTREET
IT MIGHT BE HARD TO BELIEVE, BUT THIS IS THE 44TH EDITION OF *THE OVERSTREET COMIC BOOK PRICE GUIDE!*

ABOUT THIS BOOK

BY J.C. VAUGHN

ILLUSTRATED BY GENE GONZALES

ACTION COMICS
GREEN LANTERN GREEN ARROW
9.4
DETECTIVE COMICS
AMAZING FANTASY
SPIDER MAN

"SINCE THE *GUIDE*'S DEBUT IN 1970, THERE HAVE BEEN A LOT OF CHANGES IN THE MARKETPLACE. FOR INSTANCE, THERE HAVE ALWAYS BEEN RECORD PRICES, BUT THESE DAYS THEY CAN MAKE *INTERNATIONAL NEWS...*"

"WHEN YOU KEEP UP WITH *RECORD PRICES*, WHAT'S *SELLING*, WHAT'S *NOT* SELLING, AND WHAT'S SUDDENLY *IN DEMAND*, IT HELPS YOU KNOW WHAT YOU SHOULD BE WILLING TO PAY OR WHEN TO SELL."

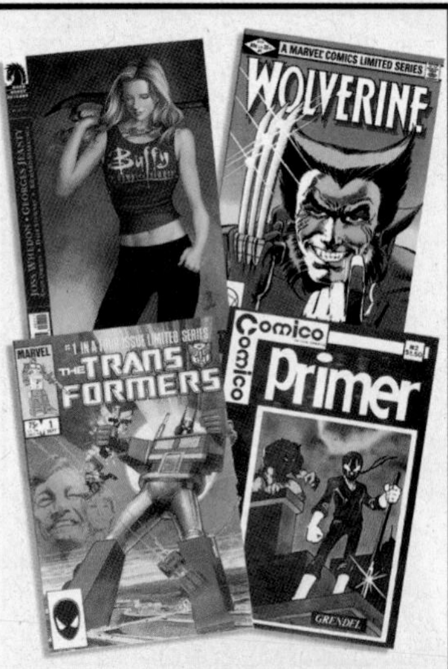
Buffy
A MARVEL COMICS LIMITED SERIES
WOLVERINE
THE TRANSFORMERS
Comico
Primer
GRENDEL

AND THERE HAVE BEEN LOTS OF OTHER CHANGES, TOO. WE'VE BEEN STUDYING THIS FOR *FOUR DECADES* NOW AND ONE THING IS REALLY CLEAR...

THE MORE YOU *KNOW* ABOUT COMICS, THE MORE YOU *WANT* TO KNOW. AND WE'VE BEEN HAPPY TO HELP PEOPLE LEARN FOR *44 YEARS*.

ONE OF THE COOL THINGS ABOUT COMIC BOOKS IS THAT THERE ARE LOTS OF NEW ONES TO DISCOVER...

AND THERE ARE LITERALLY HUNDREDS OF THOUSANDS OF DIFFERENT BACK ISSUES, TOO!

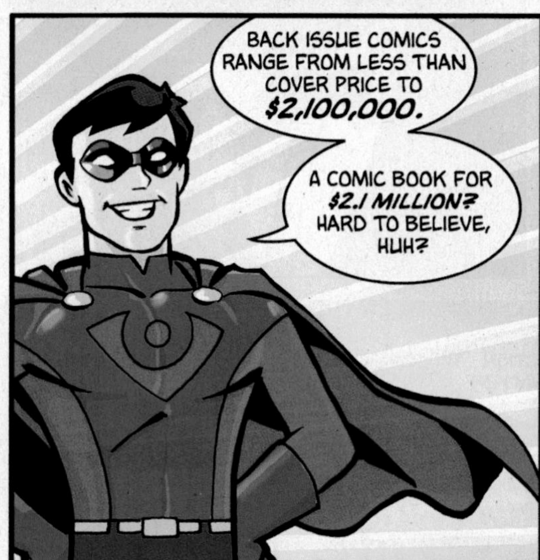
BACK ISSUE COMICS RANGE FROM LESS THAN COVER PRICE TO **$2,100,000.**
A COMIC BOOK FOR ***$2.1 MILLION?*** HARD TO BELIEVE, HUH?

THE FIRST COMIC TO HIT $1 MILLION WAS ***ACTION COMICS*** #1, THE FIRST APPEARANCE OF ***SUPERMAN***.
THE SECOND, JUST A FEW DAYS LATER, WAS ***DETECTIVE COMICS*** #27, THE FIRST APPEARANCE OF ***BATMAN***.
ANOTHER ACTION #1 SOLD FOR ***$1.5 MILLION*** JUST A SHORT WHILE AFTER THAT.

MANY OTHERS HAVE SOLD FOR RECORD PRICES IN THE LAST YEAR OR SO, EVEN WITH THE TOUGH ECONOMY NATIONALLY.

THE GRADE AND SCARCITY OF THE ISSUES HAVE A LOT TO DO WITH THAT. WE'LL GET INTO THAT IN JUST A BIT...

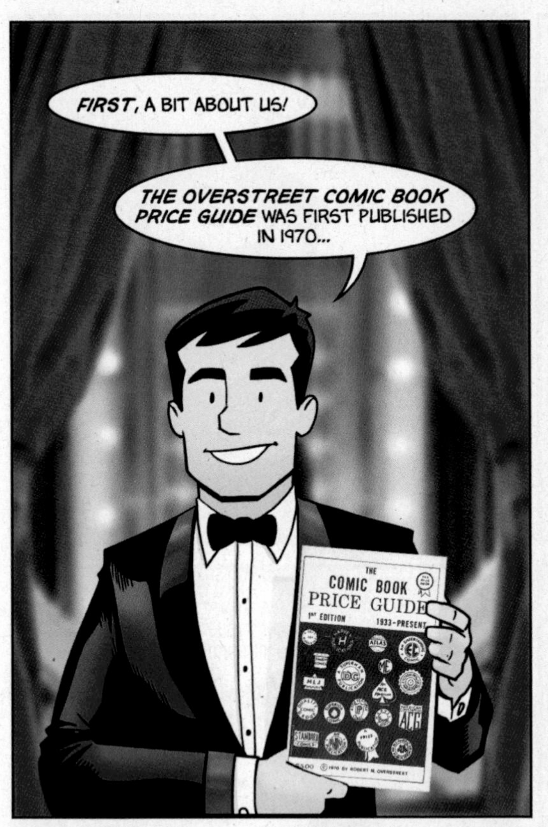

FIRST, A BIT ABOUT US!
THE OVERSTREET COMIC BOOK PRICE GUIDE WAS FIRST PUBLISHED IN 1970...
THE COMIC BOOK PRICE GUIDE
1ST EDITION 1933-PRESENT

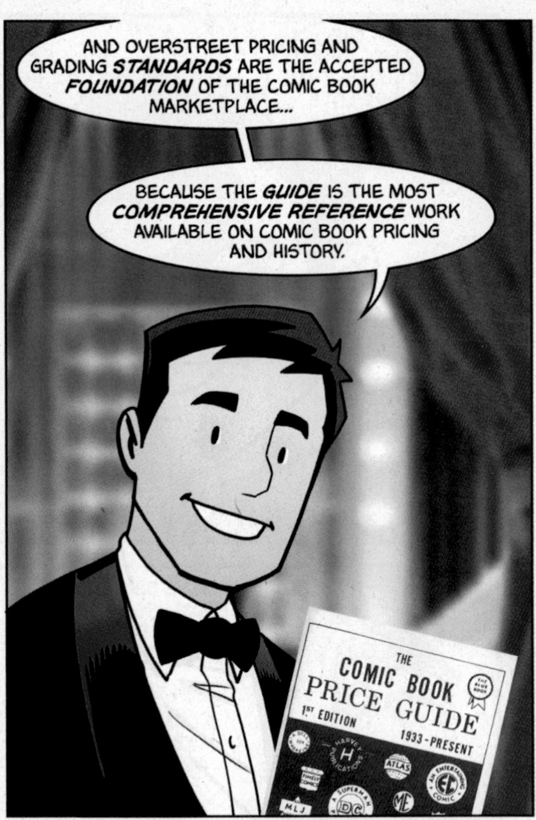

AND OVERSTREET PRICING AND GRADING STANDARDS ARE THE ACCEPTED FOUNDATION OF THE COMIC BOOK MARKETPLACE...
BECAUSE THE GUIDE IS THE MOST COMPREHENSIVE REFERENCE WORK AVAILABLE ON COMIC BOOK PRICING AND HISTORY.
THE COMIC BOOK PRICE GUIDE
1ST EDITION 1933-PRESENT

COMICS ARE LISTED *ALPHABETICALLY BY TITLE*, REGARDLESS OF PUBLISHER...

THE MAIN PRICING SECTION FEATURES COMICS FROM 1934 TO PRESENT.

THIS BOOK ALSO INCLUDES...

Big Little Books
Promotional Comics
Pioneer Age Comics
Victorian Age Comics
Platinum Age Comics

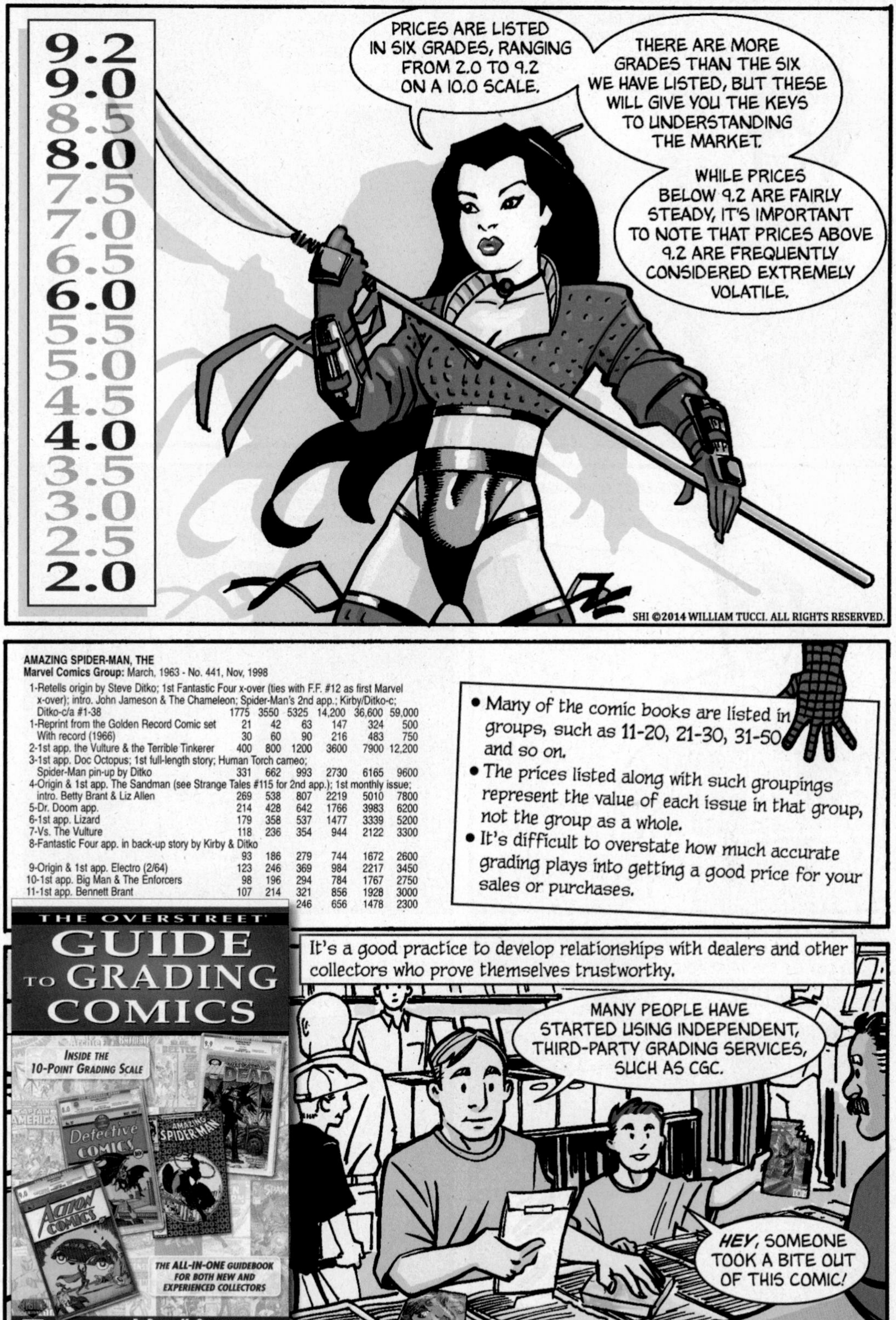

9.2
9.0
8.5
8.0
7.5
7.0
6.5
6.0
5.5
5.0
4.5
4.0
3.5
3.0
2.5
2.0

PRICES ARE LISTED IN SIX GRADES, RANGING FROM 2.0 TO 9.2 ON A 10.0 SCALE.

THERE ARE MORE GRADES THAN THE SIX WE HAVE LISTED, BUT THESE WILL GIVE YOU THE KEYS TO UNDERSTANDING THE MARKET.

WHILE PRICES BELOW 9.2 ARE FAIRLY STEADY, IT'S IMPORTANT TO NOTE THAT PRICES ABOVE 9.2 ARE FREQUENTLY CONSIDERED EXTREMELY VOLATILE.

SHI ©2014 WILLIAM TUCCI. ALL RIGHTS RESERVED.

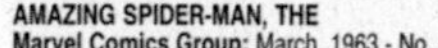

AMAZING SPIDER-MAN, THE
Marvel Comics Group: March, 1963 - No. 441, Nov, 1998

1-Retells origin by Steve Ditko; 1st Fantastic Four x-over (ties with F.F. #12 as first Marvel x-over); intro. John Jameson & The Chameleon; Spider-Man's 2nd app.; Kirby/Ditko-c; Ditko-c/a #1-38	1775	3550	5325	14,200	36,600	59,000
1-Reprint from the Golden Record Comic set	21	42	63	147	324	500
With record (1966)	30	60	90	216	483	750
2-1st app. the Vulture & the Terrible Tinkerer	400	800	1200	3600	7900	12,200
3-1st app. Doc Octopus; 1st full-length story; Human Torch cameo; Spider-Man pin-up by Ditko	331	662	993	2730	6165	9600
4-Origin & 1st app. The Sandman (see Strange Tales #115 for 2nd app.); 1st monthly issue; intro. Betty Brant & Liz Allen	269	538	807	2219	5010	7800
5-Dr. Doom app.	214	428	642	1766	3983	6200
6-1st app. Lizard	179	358	537	1477	3339	5200
7-Vs. The Vulture	118	236	354	944	2122	3300
8-Fantastic Four app. in back-up story by Kirby & Ditko	93	186	279	744	1672	2600
9-Origin & 1st app. Electro (2/64)	123	246	369	984	2217	3450
10-1st app. Big Man & The Enforcers	98	196	294	784	1767	2750
11-1st app. Bennett Brant	107	214	321	856	1928	3000
			246	656	1478	2300

- Many of the comic books are listed in groups, such as 11-20, 21-30, 31-50 and so on.
- The prices listed along with such groupings represent the value of each issue in that group, not the group as a whole.
- It's difficult to overstate how much accurate grading plays into getting a good price for your sales or purchases.

THE BEST PART IS THERE ARE MANY DIFFERENT WAYS TO COLLECT.

YOU CAN CHOOSE TO FOLLOW INDIVIDUAL PUBLISHERS, WRITERS, ARTISTS, CHARACTERS...

YOU CAN COLLECT SUPERHEROES, WAR COMICS, WESTERNS, ROMANCE OR WHATEVER YOU LIKE...

YOU CAN CHOOSE #1 ISSUES, FIRST APPEARANCES, CROSSOVERS, OR MANY OTHER VARIATIONS.

THE BEST THING TO COLLECT IS WHAT YOU LIKE, NOT WHAT SOMEONE ELSE LIKES.

WHETHER IT'S SPIDER-MAN OR EVERY COMIC THAT CAME OUT THE MONTH YOU WERE BORN, IT'S BEST TO DO IT WITH A PLAN.

THE BEST WAY TO HAVE A GOOD PLAN IS TO FIRST GET INFORMED.

CAPTAIN ACTION ©2014 CAPTAIN ACTION ENTERPRISES. ALL RIGHTS RESERVED.

THE BEST WAY TO GET INFORMED IS TO GO TO THE EXPERTS!
CAN'T I SAY "OR ELSE!" AFTER THAT?

DOCTOR EVIL ©2014 CAPTAIN ACTION ENTERPRISES. ALL RIGHTS RESERVED.

LEARN THE INS AND OUTS OF COLLECTING, INCLUDING HOW TO TAKE CARE OF YOUR COLLECTION!

SHI ©2014 WILLIAM TUCCI. ALL RIGHTS RESERVED.

Learn how to grade your comics and why the grades make a difference!

SHERLOCK DOME ©2014 J.C. VAUGHN & GENE GONZALES. ALL RIGHTS RESERVED.

LEARN WHAT TO EXPECT AT CONVENTIONS OR WHEN BUYING AND SELLING COMICS.
AND MAYBE HOW TO FIGHT ZOMBIES...

IT'S ALSO IMPORTANT TO REMEMBER THAT THIS BOOK IS A GUIDE, NOT A DEALER'S PRICE LIST. THE MARKET SETS THE PRICES.

BILLY BOB DRIWAHL ©2014 J.C. VAUGHN & VINCENT SPENCER. ALL RIGHTS RESERVED.

WITH INPUT FROM A NETWORK OF EXPERIENCED ADVISORS INCLUDING WELL ESTABLISHED COLLECTORS, DEALERS AND HISTORIANS OF POPULAR CULTURE, WE HAVE UNDERTAKEN SIGNIFICANT EFFORT TO ASSEMBLE THIS PRICING INFORMATION.

THE RESULTING LISTINGS COME THROUGH THE OBSERVATION AND DOCUMENTATION OF PRICES REALIZED THROUGH HOBBY AND TRADE SHOWS, CATALOG SALES, RETAIL SALES, AND INTERNET, LIVE AND MAIL-IN AUCTIONS. DOCUMENTED PERSONAL SALES MAY ALSO BE INCLUDED.

WE HAVE EARNED OUR REPUTATION FOR OUR CAUTIOUS, CONSERVATIVE APPROACH TO PRICING.

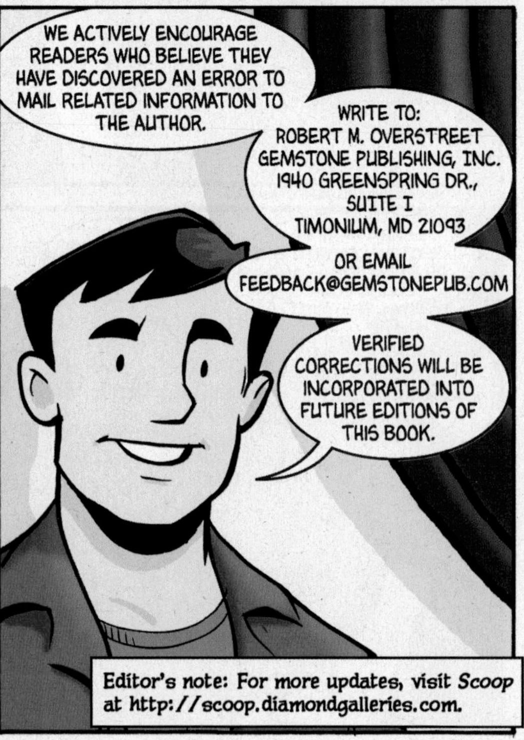
WE ACTIVELY ENCOURAGE READERS WHO BELIEVE THEY HAVE DISCOVERED AN ERROR TO MAIL RELATED INFORMATION TO THE AUTHOR.
WRITE TO: ROBERT M. OVERSTREET GEMSTONE PUBLISHING, INC. 1940 GREENSPRING DR., SUITE I TIMONIUM, MD 21093
OR EMAIL FEEDBACK@GEMSTONEPUB.COM
VERIFIED CORRECTIONS WILL BE INCORPORATED INTO FUTURE EDITIONS OF THIS BOOK.
Editor's note: For more updates, visit *Scoop* at http://scoop.diamondgalleries.com.

SILVER AGE BOOKS SET RECORDS
WHILE GOLDEN AGE PRICES REMAINED STEADY

by Robert M. Overstreet

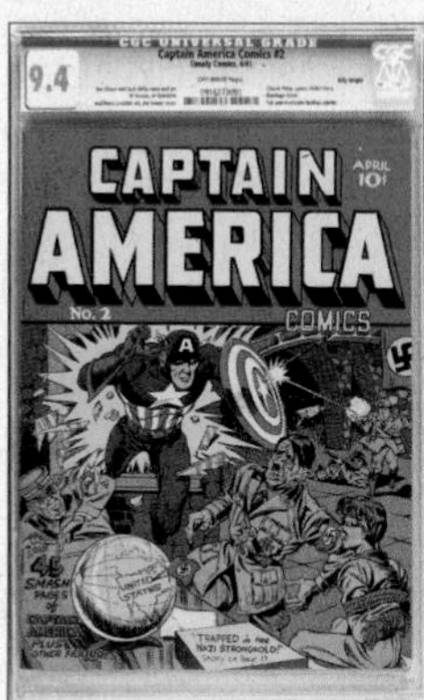

A few examples of noteworthy sales: ***Action Comics #1*** *in CGC 3.0 for $388,375,* ***All-American Comics #16*** *in CGC 8.0 for $203,150,* ***Batman #1*** *in CGC 9.2 for $567,625, and* ***Captain America Comics #2*** *in CGC 9.4 for $83,650.*

2013 was a banner year for the stock market reaching an historic high by year's end. Savings and investment accounts did well while unemployment remained high and the government stayed deadlocked. Gold rebounded in early 2014 while collectibles auctions received active bidding on a diversity of items. Reported by Forbes, Christie's sold a contemporary piece of art last year bringing a record breaking $142.4 million and also achieved $691.6 million, the highest amount ever raised in one auction. Last August a rare 1967 Ferrari Spider sold at auction for a world record price of $27.5 million and in September a '67 Corvette brought $3.2 million in a new auction record. In November probably the best known Clovis point sold for a record $276,000 at Morphy's Auctions. January 2014 saw a rare 1794 silver dollar go for a record price of $10,016,875. As you can see, investment dollars are chasing a diversity of rare items, including comic books.

West Stephan points out "Every so often the comics marketplace has a big event that changes the hobby in a positive way. In 1970, the *Overstreet Price Guide* changed the hobby forever. In 1990, the *Gerber Photo-Journals* changed how the collector was able to view books that were virtually unseen by most of us. Then in late 1990s eBay changed the way we bought and sold comics. In 2000, Certified books changed the way collectors and investors bought and sold again, giving us renewed confidence in buying comics that were not restored or overgraded. I am predicting 2014 will be another benchmark year for our hobby."

Eric Groves recalls "I can recall when early entrepreneurial comic book dealers for the first time made it possible to acquire elusive back issues, Phil Seuling, Claude Held, Ken Mitchell. Their sale lists were the precursors of Bob Overstreet's *Comic Book Price Guide*. How things have changed. High grade comics are now professionally graded and sealed, establishing them as investment vehicles."

Golden Age

Golden Age books had a strong year in 2013-2014 especially with the keys selling for record prices, such as *Action Comics* #1, *Detective Comics* #27, *Whiz Comics* #2(#1), *Batman* #1, *Captain America Comics* #1, *Pep Comics* #22, *Superman* #1, etc. These books enjoy high demand even for coverless copies and copies with missing pages. With so many books being locked up in plastic due to certification, collectors are turning more and more to collecting covers. With the *Gerber Photo-Journals* as reference, collectors are scanning the covers and singling out the best covers for their want lists. Barry Sandoval of Heritage Auctions agrees. "We are definitely seeing Golden Age collecting become more and more about the covers than any other consideration." World War II cover themes showing Nazi or Japanese continue to be popular. Especially when Hitler, Mussolini, Tojo and Hirohito appear.

West Stephan writes "Timely War-era books (1939-1945) still show incredible demand and upward movement." In the Pre-Code crime and Horror Genre, decapitation, gory, face melting covers continue to bring increased prices. Ben Samuels states "High-grade Golden Age comics of all sorts are eagerly sought out by legions of collectors. He continues "Pre-Code Horror comics from all publishers seem to be enjoying a strong market, in all grades. Especialy issues with shocking or gory cover art."

Paul Clairmont of PNJ Comics points out "We saw a substantial upward trend in the interest of comic books. It appears being a comic geek has become acceptable as the media has picked up on record-breaking internet auction results and hit shows such as *The Big Bang Theory* have made it socially acceptable to collect and invest in comics."

Dan Gallo writes: "The characters we love, like Spider-Man, Batman, and Wolverine, will always "be." Just like Mickey Mouse, they will be with us forever and there will always be people who want to have their first appearances..."

Terry O'Neill of Terry's Comics writes "Sales from 2012 to 2013 have been slightly down from last year, although sales in certain geographic regions reflected strong local economies. Most comic conventions had very good attendance but show sales had not increased and in some cases decreased due to more fans of pop culture and cosplay attending."

Dave Anderson points out "Although 2013 saw some stabilization of prices, activity and sales remained strong. There is certainly an awareness among collectors of previous sales and when they occurred, and there is some resistance to paying significantly more for a book with a reported recent sale when the same book goes up for sale again. Fresh books that have been unavailable for long periods of time tend to fare better. There is also resistance to paying more for books where the grade has been increased due to re-grading by CGC. Most higher profile sales are well documented these days, so it is easy to track the sales history of most books."

Art Cloos writes "By the end of 2013, my wife and I have attended over 40 comic, art and toy shows over the course of 2013. There is a healthy hobby out there with fans and collectors looking for deals and for both new collectors and dealers looking to learn about how the comic world works. The Golden Age Batman and Superman titles continue to be strong sellers with *Detective Comics* #27 to #40 being in very high demand. Lower grade copies of these books will sell well above *Guide* with little trouble when they are available."

Art Cloos continues "Single owner collections continue to appear. Not all make headlines though because many of these collections do not rise to the level of a pedigree collection with the kind of condition that a pedigree must contain. Jesse James Criscione states "Graded comics seemed to attract a whole new generation of investors. Record sales continue to exceed previous unbreakable records. This new generation of buyers seem to consider the highest bids establishing the true value of a CGC copy, regardless of census or basic standard pricing used in the comic book community."

Golden Age Sales

Action Comics #1, CGC 3.0 $388,375(8/13), #2 CGC 5.0 $26,290, #3 CGC 1.0 $4,182, #4 CGC 5.0 $6,871, #11 CGC 7.5 $7,767, #13 CGC 3.5 $34,200, #20 CGC 3.5 $2,868, #34 CGC 9.0 $3,346, #66 CGC 9.2 $3,884

Adventure Comics #36 CGC 5.5 $5,676

All-American Comics #16 CGC 8.0 $203,150, CGC 3.0 $128,174, #17 CGC 9.0 $20,315

All-American Men of War #2 VG $657, #28 FVF $538

Alley Oop Four Color #3VF $567

All Negro Comics #1 VF- $8,400

All Select Comics #1, CGC 9.0 $22,705, #11VF/NM $3,585

All Star Comics #3 CGC 3.0 $4,780, #8 CGC 5.0 $14,937, CGC 1.5 $3,585

All Winners #1 CGC 9.2 $35,850, #21 FN $2,868

Amazing Mystery Funnies V2#2, CGC 3.0 $1,374, V2#3

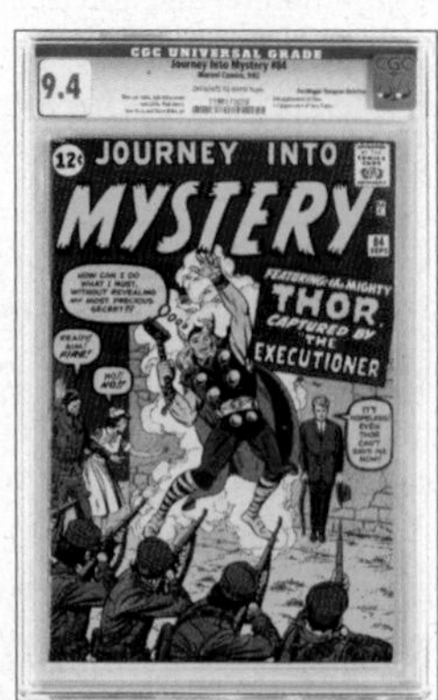

The diverse high grade collection of ***Don and Maggie Thompson*** *was auctioned off at Heritage Auctions with part 1 presented in the November 2013 auction bringing $835,382! Part 2 was featured in their February 2014 auction. Their* ***Avengers #1*** *in CGC 9.4 sold for $89,625, their* ***Incredible Hulk #1*** *in CGC 8.5 went for $58,256, their* ***Journey Into Mystery*** *#83 in CGC 9.2 sold for $77,675 and their* ***Journey Into Myste****ry #84 in CGC 9.4 brought $31,070.*

CGC 7.5 $2,151, V2#4 CGC 7.5 $5,377
Archie Comics #1, CGC 6.5 $62,778, VG- $20,315, CGC 1.0 $6,900, #4 VG $4,929, #7 VG/FN $1,494
Batman #1, CGC 9.2 $567,625, CGC 7.5(slight-r) $35,850, CGC NG, no cvr, 1st wrap missing $5,078, #2 CGC 8.5 $23,900, #3 CGC 9.2 $40,331, #5 CGC 9.2 $16,730, #7 CGC 9.0 $13,145, #8 CGC 9.0 $11,352, #9 CGC 9.4 $28,680, #11 CGC 9.0 $15,380, #17 CGC 9.2 $7,540
Black Cat #50 CGC 9.2 $6,274
Blue Beetle #4 CGC 9.0 $1,792, #54 CGC 7.0 $2,629,
Captain America Comics #1, CGC 7.0 $94,000, CGC 3.5 $32,265, #2 CGC 9.4 $83,650, CGC 8.5 $28,680, CGC 8.0 $22,705, #3 CGC 9.2 $43,319, CGC 3.5 $7,170
Captain Marvel Advs. #1 CGC 2.5 $2,270
Casper, The Friendly Ghost #1, CGC 8.5 $7,170, $4,887, CGC 7.5 $3,910, CGC 6.5 $2,629, CGC 5.0 $1,075, #10 CGC 9.0 $862
Catman #5 VF/NM(Mile High) $3,400
Crash Comics #4 FN #2,270, #5 CGC 8.5 $1900
Crime Does Not Pay #22 CGC 7.0 $4,481, CGC 5.5 $1,850, #24 CGC 7.5 $4,500, CGC 7.0 $3,585, CGC 3.5 $1,613, #27 CGC 9.0 $1,314
Crime Patrol #14 VF $657
Crime Reporter #2 VF- $777
Crime SuspenStories #22 CGC 9.2 $17,000
Crypt of Terror #17 CGC 7.0 $1,046
Daredevil Battles Hitler CGC 5.0 $4,200
Detective Comics #3 CGC 1.8 $3,884, #18 CGC 8.5 (Mile High) $26,290, #29 CGC 6.5(sli.r) $8,962, CGC 2.0 $10,755, #33, CGC 8.0 $68,712, #35, CGC 3.0 $16,730, CGC 1.5 $7,170, #38, CGC 0.5 $2,629, #45 CGC 9.2 $7,469
Donald Duck Four Color #178 CGC 8.5 $1,700
Fight Against Crime #20 VF/VF+ $6,122
Flash Comics #1 CGC 5.0 $18,522, CGC 1.5 $7,767
Flying Saucers 1952 CGC 9.2 $1,554
Forbidden Love #1 CGC 9.0 $2,390, CGC 8.5 $2,151, #2, CGC 9.4 $2,629, CGC 8.5 $538
Great Comics #3VG+ $3,585, FN $4,481
Green Hornet Comics #1 CGC 9.0 $8,365
Green Lantern #1 CGC 9.0 $44,812, CGC 5.0 $5,975
Hit Comics #25 CGC 7.0 $1,700
Jackpot Comics #4 CGC 3.5 $18,000, CGC 2.0 $8,350, no cvr, pg. missing $537
Keen Detective Funnies #9 CGC 8.5 $1,792
Little Dot #1 CGC 9.0 $10,157, CGC 8.0 $6,572, #2 CGC 9.0 $2,629, #4 CGC 9.2 $1,912
Little Lotta #1 CGC 8.5 $1,553
Looney Tunes #1 CGC 5.0 $2,629
Marvel Comics #1 CGC 8.0(ext. r) $23,900, CGC 0.5 $11,500
Marvel Mystery #8 CGC 5.5 $3,303
Mask #1 CGC 5.5 $1,673, #2 CGC 4.5 $956
Moon Girl #1 CGC 7.5 $717, #2 CGC 9.0 $1,792
More Fun #55 CGC 9.4 (Mile High) $47,800, #101 CGC 5.0 $1,650
Mystic Comics #4 CGC 4.5 $2,629
New York Worlds Fair 1939 CGC 7.0 $13,145
Peanuts #1 CGC 8.5 $13,145
Pep Comics #8 CGC 9.0 $2,987
Phantom Lady #17 CGC 4.5 $3,107, #18 CGC 6.5 $717, #23 CGC 8.0 $11,352
Reform School Girl CGC 5.5 $3107, CGC 6.5(slight r) $2,390
Science Comics #7 CGC 4.5 $334
Secret Diary of Eerie Adventures CGC 3.5 $1,912
Seven Seas Comics #5 CGC 9.0 $1,792
Silver Streak #8 CGC 7.0 $3,884, CGC 5.0 $2,161
Spirit #22 FN+ $1,434, VG $600
Sub-Mariner #1 CGC 3.5 $4,800, #2 CGC 2.5 $777, #14 CGC 6.5 $1,314, #23 CGC 8.0 $1,075
Superboy #1 CGC 9.0 $14,937, CGC 8.5 $11,352
Superman #1 CGC 6.0(Ext. R) $20,574, #2 CGC 1.0 $2031, #14 CGC 8.0 $8,365, CGC 7.5 $4,780, #17 CGC 8.0 $12,547, CGC 6.5 $3,585, #20 CGC 9.2 $5,079, #24 CGC 6.0 $1,314, #33 CGC 9.2 $2,270, #72 CGC 9.2 $1,434
Superman's Girlfriend Lois Lane #1 CGC 5.5 $1,553, #2 CGC 7.5 $568,
Superman's Pal Jimmy Olsen #1 CGC 4.0 $747
Tarzan Single Series #20 CGC 8.0 $956, CGC 7.0 $1,135
Terrific Comics #2 CGC 8.0 (Mile High) $1,434
Terry-Toons #1 CGC 9.0 $2,868
Thrilling Comics #12 CGC 8.0 $836, #29 CGC 9.0 $1,016, #46 CGC 8.5 $1,792
Top-Notch Comics #21 CGC 8.0 $717
Two-Gun Kid #1 CGC 9.2(Mile High) $3,226, CGC 7.5 $717
Uncle Scrooge 4-Color #386 CGC 7.0 $657, #495 CGC 9.4 $5,377, $2,629
United States Marines #3 CGC 7.5 $657
USA Comics #10 CGC 6.5 $3,286, CGC 3.0 $1,195
V-Comics #2 CGC 9.0 $2,031
Venus #10, CGC 9.2 $1,673, #15 CGC 4.0 $807, #16 CGC 6.0 $836, #18 CGC 6.0 $2,270, #19 CGC 6.0 $2,868
Walt Disney's Comics & Stories #1 CGC 9.0 $35,850, CGC 6.5 $7,767, #2 CGC 9.4 $26,290, #3 CGC 9.2 $14,340, #4 CGC 7.5 $3,884, CGC 6.5 $1,912, #7, CGC 9.0 $9,918, #10 CGC 8.5 $1,494, #11 CGC 7.5 $1,016, #12 CGC 9.0 $5,079
War Against Crime #1 CGC 7.5 $1,673
Weird Tales of the Future #2 CGC 6.5 $1,314, #3, CGC 4.0 $896, #5 CGC 6.0 $1,613,
Whiz Comics #1 CGC 4.5 (MP restoration) $7,500, #3(#2) CGC 2.5 $1,195, #4 CGC 7.0 $1,792, #8 CGC 9.0 $2,390
Wonder Woman #1, CGC 5.5 $9,261, #3 CGC 5.5 $986, #5 CGC 8.5 $1,733, #105 CGC 7.0 $896
Wonderworld #3 CGC 3.0 $1,613
Young Allies #9 CGC 8.0 $2,629

Silver Age: Most Silver Age keys continued to be in high demand throughout the year with record sales being reported. Art Cloos reports "Silver Age interest by collectors tends to favor Marvel without question. With an ever increasing presence in movies and now TV, Spider-Man, Thor, X-Men, The

© MAR

© MAR

© MAR

© MAR

*Key **Silver Age** books that sold last year are: **Amazing Fantasy #15**, CGC 8.5 $120,100, **Fantastic Four #1** CGC 9.2 went for $191,200, **Tales of Suspense #39** CGC 9.6 auctioned at $262,900, and an **X-Men #1** CGC 9.4 went for $83,650.*

Avengers, etc. find their titles in great demand. High grade rules, but in many of the local shows we go to, it is clear that lower grade Marvel and DC Silver Age books will sell and sell well if priced at *Guide* being more affordable in those grades. One trend we have noticed quite strongly at these smaller shows is the increasing number of many quite serious women and young buyers who attend, know what they want and look to buy them." Gary Dolgoff writes "Pre-Hero Marvels are great sellers in all grades, across the board (and have great stories and art by Kirby and Ditko!)."

Sales of Silver Age through Modern Age

Adventure Comics #210 CGC 7.0 $3,000, #247 CGC 5.0 $2,000

Amazing Fantasy #15 CGC 9.0 $120,000, CGC 8.5 $120,100, CGC 8.0 $71,700, CGC 7.0 $37,344, CGC 6.5 $26,290, CGC 5.0 $15,535, CGC 4.0 $9,002, CGC 3.0 $6,200

Amazing Spider-Man #1 CGC 8.0 $22,705, CGC 7.5 $15,000, CGC 6.5 $7,170, GD $1,700, #4, CGC 9.0 $5,377, #14 CGC 9.6 $15,535, Annual #1 CGC 9.2 $2,868

Avengers #1 CGC 9.4 $95,600, $89,625, CGC 8.5 $11,950, VF $8,962, CGC 8.0 $9,859, CGC 5.5 $4,000, CGC 4.0 $2,600, GD- $500, #2 VF/NM $1,800, #4 CGC 9.6 $23,900, CGC 9.2 $7,767, #5 CGC 9.2 $2,629

Brave & the Bold #28 CGC 7.0 $8,962, CGC 6.0 $4,780, CGC 5.5 $3,585, CGC 4.5 $3,000, #29 CGC 9.0 $8,365

Cerebus The Aardvark #1 CGC 9.4 $7,767, CGC 9.0 $1,853

Conan The Barbarian #1 CGC 9.6 $1,553, CGC 9.4 $836

Daredevil #1 CGC 9.6 $31,070, VF/NM $6,300, CGC 8.0 $2,868

Devil Kids Starring Hot Stuff #1 CGC 9.6 $3,107

Fantastic Four #1 CGC 9.2 $191,200, CGC 7.0 $21,510, CGC 6.5 $11,651, CGC 5.5 $15,535, CGC 4.5 $4,182, CGC 3.0 $3,500, #2 CGC 9.8 $65,725, CGC 8.5 $4,780, #4 CGC 8.5 $4,630, #5 CGC 9.4 $41,825

Flash #105 CGC 8.5 $11,352, CGC 7.0 $2,987, CGC 5.5 $1,500, CGC 3.0 $508, #110 CGC 9.0 $5,079, #123 CGC 9.2 $8,365, $6,572, CGC 8.0 $1,434

Friendly Ghost Casper #1 CGC 8.0 $657

Giant-Size X-Men #1 CGC 9.2 $1,500

G.I. Combat #87 CGC 7.5 $1,316

Green Lantern #1 CGC 9.0 $10,755, CGC 7.5 $2,031, #11, CGC 9.0 $10,755, #76 CC 9.4 $3,346

Harvey Hits #9 CGC 9.4 $4,780

Hero For Hire #1 CGC 9.8 $4,300, CGC 9.2 $500, CGC 9.0 $263, CGC 8.5 $263, $185, CGC 7.5 $227

Hot Stuff, the Little Devil #1 CGC 8.5 $5,979, CGC 7.5 $1,195, #2 CGC 8.5 $896

Incredible Hulk #1 CGC 8.5 $58,256, CGC 7.0 $17,327, CGC 6.5 $14,340, CGC 6.0 $8,962, CGC 5.5 $7,000, CGC 4.0 $6,572, CGC 3.5 $4,780, CGC 1.8 $3,600,#2 CGC 8.5 $5,079, #3 CGC 9.4 $23,900, #4 CGC 9.2 $7,767, #181 CGC 9.6 $4,182, CGC 8.0 $1,400

Iron Man #1 CGC 9.2 $1,255, CGC 9.0 $1,075

Journey Into Mystery #83 CGC 9.4 $171,000, CGC 9.2 $77,675, CGC 9.0 $35,850, CGC 8.5 $26,000, CGC 7.0 $8,300, CGC 6.5 $6,572, CGC 6.0 $5,228, #84 CGC 9.4 $31,070, #85 CGC 9.0 $4,481, CGC 8.0 $2,500, CGC 5.5 $4,300, #89 CGC 9.2 $3,107

Justice League of America #1 CGC 7.5 $4,481, CGC 7.0 $2,629

Little Lotta #3 CGC 9.4 $836,

Marvel Spotlight #5 CGC 9.8 $13,145

Richie Rich #5 CGC 9.2 $1,553, #11 CGC 9.2 $896, #12 CGC 9.2 $1,494

Richie Rich Millions #1 CGC 9.4 $3,585

Sgt. Fury #1 CGC 9.4 $28,680, CGC 9.0 $10,157, CGC 8.5 $7,170, CGC 7.0 $2,270

Showcase #4 CGC 9.0 $60,000, CGC 7.5 $26,290, CGC 5.0 $8,365, CGC 4.5 $5,377, CGC 2.0 $2150, #8 CGC 6.0 $2,629, #13 CGC 8.5 $3,884, #22 CGC 8.0 $17,925, CGC 7.5 $8,962, CGC 7.0 $4,780, CGC 6.5 $4,630, CGC 4.0 $1,400, #34 CGC 8.0 $956, #37 CGC 9.2 $3,884, #43 CGC 8.5 $358

Silver Surfer #1 CGC 9.4 $2,987, CGC 9.2 $1,450

Star Wars #1(35¢) CGC 9.4 $15,535, CGC 6.5 $1,105

Strange Tales #110 CGC 9.6 $44,812, CGC 9.4 $28,680, CGC

8.0 $6,572, CGC 7.5 $2,390, Annual #2 CGC 9.2 $3,107
Strange Worlds #3 CGC 9.0 $2,031
Tales of Suspense #39 CGC 9.6 $262,900, CGC 9.4 $83,650, CGC 9.2 $47,800, CGC 8.5 $15,535, CGC 8.0 $9,261, FN/FN+ $5,000, CGC 6.0 $4,481, CGC 4.5 $3,400, #40, CGC 9.2 $7,767, #41 VF+ $1,150, #45 CGC 9.2 $2,151, #49 CGC 94 $4,780, #50 CGC 9.4 $3,107, CGC 9.0 $1,195, #57 CGC 9.4 $5,975, CGC 9.0 $2,031, #58 CGC 9.4 4,182
Tales To Astonish #27 CGC 7.5 $10,456, VF- $7,500, VG+ $2,400, GD $1,000, GD+ $1,400, GD/VG $1,700, #35 CGC 9.0 $10,157, #49 CGC 9.2 $926, #60 CGC 9.4 $1,673,
Teenage Mutant Ninja Turtles #1 CGC 9.6 $8,962, CGC 8.5 $2,900, CGC 8.0 $3,400, CGC 7.5 $2,200, CGC 5.5 $1,000
Teen Titans #1 CGC 9.4 $2,151, CGC 9.2 $986
Thor #126 CGC 9.4 $2,151
Turok, Son of Stone #1('66) CGC 9.2 $335
Underdog #1 CGC 9.6 $508
Walking Dead #1 CGC 9.8 $1,792, #2, CGC 9.2 $269
X-Men #1 CGC 9.4 $83,650, CGC 9.0 $26,681, CGC 8.5 $14,937, CGC 7.5 $8,066, CGC 7.0 $6,000, CGC 5.0 $2,800, CGC 4.5 $2,200, CGC 2.0 $1,50

Bronze Age

Christopher Swartz points out "Oversaturation of the market with high grade copies from pressing has started to take its toll on the Bronze Age prices." Tom Nelson of Top Notch Comics agrees "The longtime established key of *Incredible Hulk* #181 is stronger than it has every been. I remember looking back at *Hulk* #181 about 5 years ago, a copy in Good 2.0 condition was selling for around $50 while a certified 9.8 was hitting record highs of $25,000. Now a low grade Good condition book would run you $300 on eBay while a certified 9.8 can be picked up for $8.000."

Gary Dolgoff reports "Generally, the more popular titles sell well throughout the Bronze Age, and I have trouble keeping the early 1970s mainline Marvels, *Batman* and *Detective Comics* in stock. Also early to mid-1970s Horror comics (*House of Mystery, House of Secrets*, etc.) sell well." Ken Dyber of Cloud 9 Comics agrees "DC Horror does seem to continue to sell well in all conditions as this is some of the best artwork not only from the Bronze Age, but arguably from all time periods. *Detective* and *Batman* continue to be some of the best-selling books in all grades, especially the *Batma*n issues. *Hero for Hire* #1 needs a dramatic price increase in Guide. A CGC 9.8 recently sold for $4300!" Terry O'Neill of Terry's Comics writes "This era has been on fire for the past few years. Most back issue dealers will agree that they are the most requested titles of the past year. With so many first appearances and number one issues of many key characters, it has finally come to dominate the back issue market."

Copper Age

Christopher Swartz reports "*Teenage Mutant Ninja Turtles* #1 is the king of the Copper Age with copies in all grades (CGC 9.6 $7,400, CGC 8.5 $2,900, CGC 8.0 $3,400, CGC 7.5 $2,200, CGC 5.5 $1,000) selling very easily. Ken Dyber of Cloud 9 Comics states." This could be the hottest time period in comics. I have to start off by saying Harley Quinn! All appearances are hot. *Batman Adventures* (1992) #12 (1st app.) should move up." Tom Nelson, Top Notch Comics reports "The 1980s Copper Age books have seen a huge speculator boom this year as Hollywood's continual announcement of a superhero or villain being piloted in a future TV show or feature film."

© DC

One of the hot books from the 1990s, **Batman Adventures #12** features the first comic appearance of Harley Quinn.

Modern Age

Paul Clairmont of PNJ Comics reports "This is easily the most volatile area of comic books. Print runs are at all-time lows compared to any other time in comic publishing history. People are continuing to try and find the next *Walking Dead* #1 and this is dangerous speculation" Doug Mabry of the Great Escape points out, "We continue to see increases in sales of new comics, with of course *The Walking Dead* leading the way." Steven Houston and John Dolmayan of Torpedo Comics report that "*The Walking Dead* series seems to be a perfect storm of collectability, a low print-run to start, almost being cancelled, followed by a slow increase in sales and then an explosion of attention after the cable television show hit the mainstream. Those who had been collecting from the start watched the market in amazement as their issues doubled, tripled and tripled again in value." Stephen Barrington also reports "Image has enjoyed great success with its *Walking Dead* series with back issues being impossible to keep in stock. Just when we think we have ordered plenty, we are proven wrong."

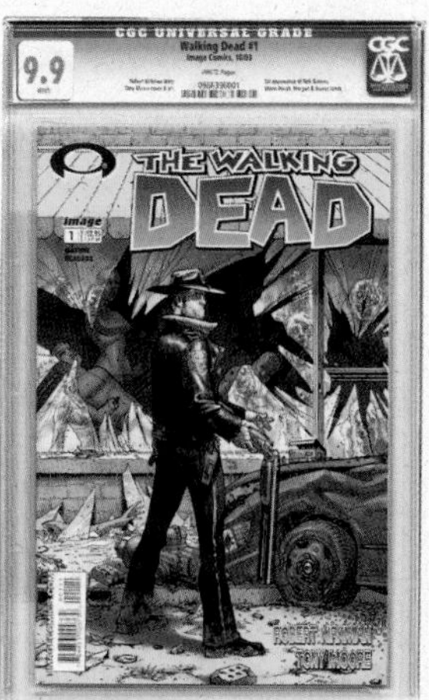

© Robert Kirkman

Comic buyers are looking for the next title to match the explosive price surges of **The Walking Dead**.

Original Comic Art

The upswing in demand for original comic art (both covers and interior pages) continued to set record prices throughout last year. More and more collectors are buying displayable original art to enhance their comic book collections.

A few EC covers, pages and complete stories sold at auction. The cover for *Haunt of Fear* #25 fetched $31,070 and the cover for *Tales From the Crypt* #43 sold at $41,825. The classic Feldstein covers for *Weird Fantasy* #11 sold for $65,725 and the cover to #17(1953) brought $44,812 and the recreated cover painting by Feldstein for *Weird Fantasy* #8 sold for $8,962. The cover to *Weird Science* #6 (1951) brought $20,315 and the cover to *Weird Science* #15 (1952) sold for $71,700. Wally Wood's *Two-Fisted Tales* #33 7-Page story art "Atom Bomb" sold for $31,070. Graham Ingels classic 7-page story "The Ventriloquists Dummy" from *Tales From the Crypt* sold for $17,327. An original story art from *National Comics* #13 by Will Eisner and Lou Fine (9 pgs.) sold for $53,775 while the splash page by Eisner for a *Spirit Section* dated 1/5/47 went for $5,079 and an enterior "Spirit" page by Eisner sold for $2,718. A Frank Frazetta oil painting, "*The Tempest*" sold for $65,725. His cover painting for *Vampirella* #5 (1970) brought $286,800 last August. A *Mickey Mouse* daily strip art dated 11/5/37 went for $5,676. A *Krazy Kat* Sunday Comic Strip page dated 5/2/20 went for $16,730. An original Gouache painted cover for *King of the Royal Mounted* #10 sold for $2,390. The original cover to *Justice League of America* #14 by Murphy Anderson (1962) sold for $55,812. The original cover art for *Conan The Barbarian* #4 (1971) by Barry Smith sold for $87,235.

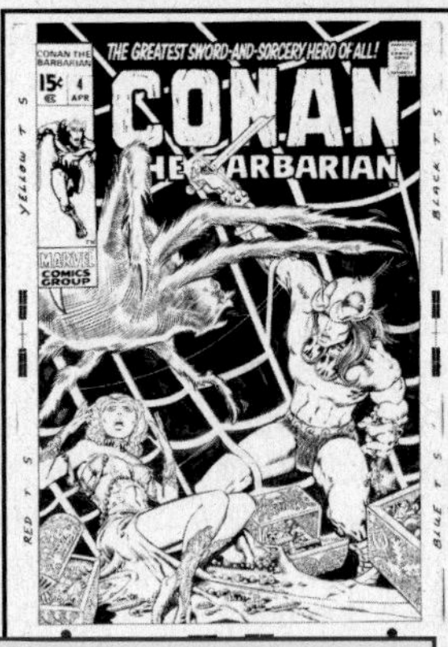

Among the notable sales of original art were Al Feldstein's classic cover to **Weird Fantasy #11** for $65,725 and Barry Smith's cover to **Conan the Barbarian #4** for $87,235.

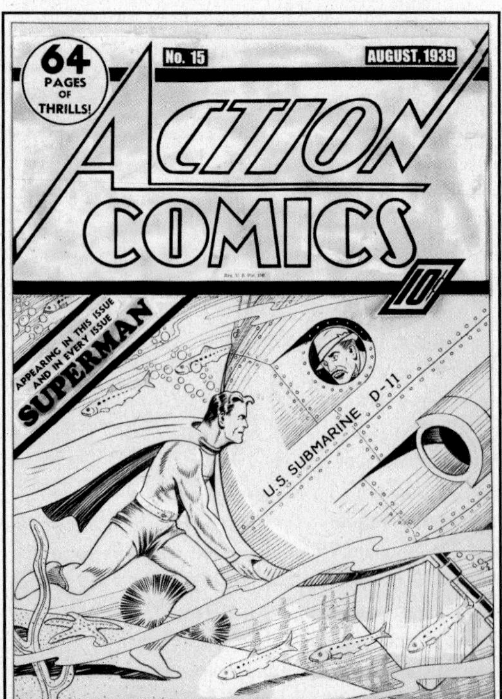

This original cover art for **Action Comics #15** by Fred Guardineer is the earliest known Superman cover art in existence. It sold for $286,800 in February 2014.

Pedigree collections 2013

The Don and Maggie Thompson large Silver Age collection was released through Heritage Auctions with part I in November, 2013 which realized $835,384! Part 2 of this collection was presented in the February, 2014 auction.

The Thomas Haas Golden Age collection and the Christopher Forbes Golden Age Collection were sold last year. Books from historic Pedigree collections appeared sporadically in all the top auctions held last year. Mile High (Edgar Church), Larson, Pennsylvania, White Mountain, Gaines file copies, Northford, and others were represented selling to eager buyers.

In Summary

2013 was another year in which hundreds of thousands of comic books were sold off web sites, from mailing lists, at conventions and at comic book stores. Prices realized were again mixed depending on rarity, character and grade.

The following market reports were submitted from some of our many advisors and are published here for your information. The opinions in these reports belong to each contributor and do not necessarily reflect the views of the publisher or the staff of *The Overstreet Comic Book Price Guide* or Gemstone Publishing.

They will provide important insights into the thinking of many key players in the marketplace.

See you next year!

Bob

Robert M. Overstreet
Publisher

OVERSTREET COVER SUBJECTS
FIRST APPEARANCES

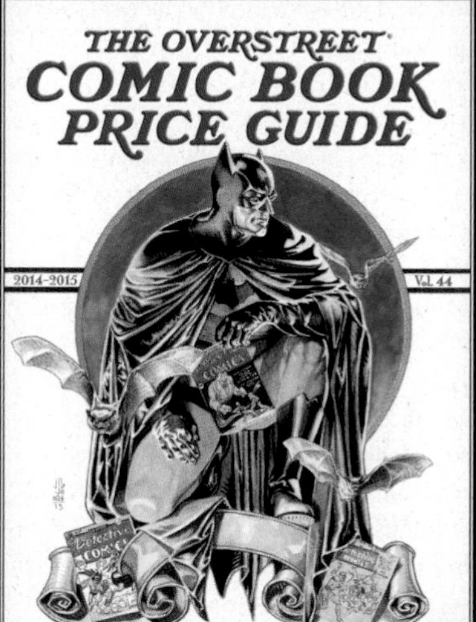

BATMAN
DETECTIVE COMICS #27
MAY 1939
2014 NM- PRICE: $1,650,000

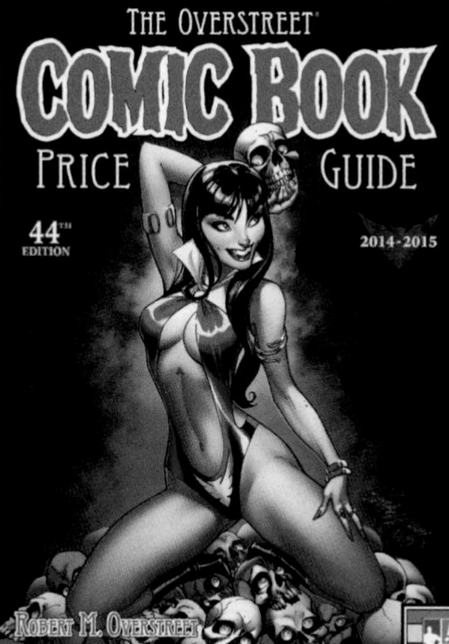

WOLVERINE
INCREDIBLE HULK #181
NOVEMBER 1974
2014 NM- PRICE: $2,000

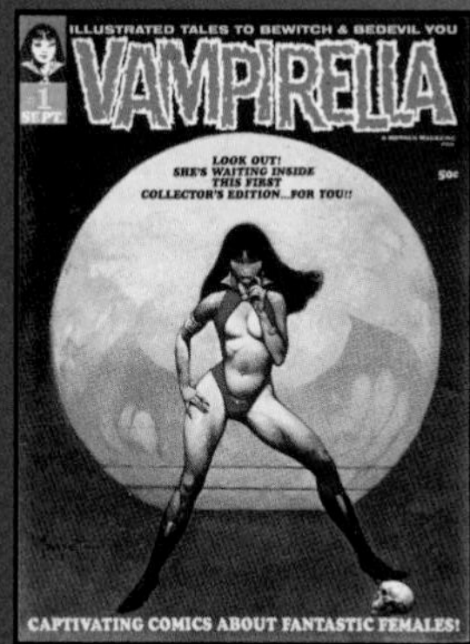

VAMPIRELLA
VAMPIRELLA #1
SEPTEMBER 1969
2014 NM- PRICE: $1,150

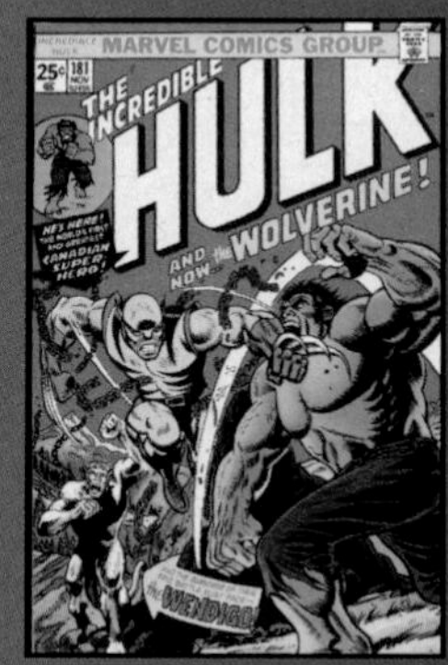

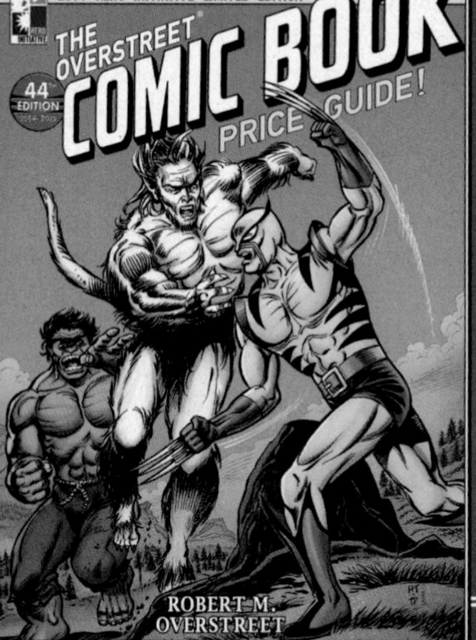

THE HULK
INCREDIBLE HULK #1
MAY 1962
2014 NM- PRICE: $120,000

Grant Adey
Halo Certification, Australia

First up, as out going proprietor of Fats Comics I'd like to thank everyone who supported my shop and wish new owners Justin & Talia Visona all the best. During my 12 years at the helm of Fats Comics the team past and present clocked a lot of firsts, mainly due to the excellent help and education from my American friends. Record price achieved for Frew *Phantom* #1 with Metropolis Comics. The Estate of Lee Falk With CGC and Comic Connect which set record prices I believe will stand forever. Being appointed a Overstreet advisor is without a doubt a great honor, a fact I am proud of and to be the first Australian advisor.

A new challenge. To build Australia's first collectibles certification company.

Certification to me is no stranger, racing motorcycles for a living in my youth it is common that your machine must meet specification standards for class, speed and time records. So applying the same principals to collectibles, a manual will be required and a group of unbiased knowledgeable scrutineers. Working in the comics, collectibles and antique industry for the last 12 years gave me access to the very best of industry and collecting minds, harnessing that wealth of knowledge and the answer to most questions is on the money. My team specializing in Australiana includes comics, toys, trading cards, art, coins, autographs, racing, sports. We work with private collectors and auctioneers suppling archival graded case sealed or day of sale only certification meaning a tamper evident seal fitting the item, autograph verification and working with artists to protect their intellectual rights.

Building a lab and workshop - The lab and procedures, cost effective technology thanks to China made the fit out fairly easy, digital microscopes, digital recorders, ultra sonic welders, photographic equipment etc. Procedures took a little more time getting things in the right sequence to make the job flow. Some graders prefer written notes while others prefer to record their findings by voice. Stored as an audio file. I tried the audio on a doll we were asked to certify, I found it clumsy at first but with practice it's very efficient coupled with photography of each section.

The workshop, 7 months of R & D, late nights. The decision was made to keep comic, magazine and trading card cases manufactured in house. Months of plastic type, manufacturing technics, properties of plastic, tooling costs, testing, the workshop in comparison to the lab was intense. Manufacturing in Australia is incredibly difficult, the "out source" of the '90s / 2000s has left us in a position with very few choices, we have a total national population similar to New York, large production runs are out of the question, and cost effective small production runs are pretty much impossible. By manufacturing in house we control the production runs, I guess it was worth all the hair pulling. The up side is no delays, no raw material freight costs, we start or stop case production as required. The end result is a compact workshop with speed and energy efficiency.

Supanova comic convention in November 2013 was the launch of Halo Certifications comics division. Fats Comics and Urban Fiction Comics, the small team went to bat with a 2 week old brand new product with absolutely zip advertising. Big ask of the guys, I sat and waited for the results of day 1 to roll in. The guys displayed Halo Cert. side by side with the other graded comics they have in stock. Halo Cert. represented about 1 in 4 on display. End of day 1 we have a pulse, day 2 people are talking and handing in submissions, senior grader JT is doing autograph verifications, modern grader Rus is at the Fats Comics booth talking grading with customers. End of day 3, one third of Halo Certs. available had been sold. A fairly stout outcome for a product never seen by the general public.

With that said Ace Comics & Games supported me in this endeavour from the start, actually retailing the first Halo cert. Ace is Brisbane's longest serving original owner retail chain of comic shops and warehouse. They have always supported local comic industry, like local artists, publishers, conventions, to serving smaller comic shops with inventory from their warehouse.

Ten days prior to the convention Urban Fiction comics received their first shipment of Halo certs. With brass kahunas they went straight to the meat grinder eBay with a brand new product auctioning 4 Halo certified comics - new DC lenticular covers, starting bid $1. Ye of little faith thought "oh boy, we're gunna get mashed." But 7 days later Joker's Daughter #1 (*Batman: The Dark Knight* #23.4) went for $126, and 3 others finished around $75 each.

New issue comics appear to be on the menu for certification, mmmm, mixed reaction, very early days, select customers of new issues are certifying some pretty good speculative issues of variants, sketch covers and low print run comics.

Most expensive comic in for grading so far (2 months from release of HC) Frew *Phantom* #2 in 4.0 . Value $10-$12k. The comic first came to light in 1999, Fats Comics sold it in 2000, my first year at Fats Comics, for $6500. Two owners later to see this gem cross my desk at Halo Cert. was very cool, a good 13 years later.

For submissions of restored comics, we return them as submitted free of charge. We also offer an archival case, no opinion given, whoch receives the "AO" (archival only) classification for customers.

Changing the way comic shops and collectors do business here, buyers are asking sellers if they have the comic graded, and if it's not as advertised, can they have a refund. On the other hand sellers are having comics graded to receive a fair market value. The variety of books we have seen in the last 2 months of operations are Golden Age in the 1.5 to 4.0, Silver Age keys in the 4.0 to 6.5, Bronze 8.5 average grade with some 9.2, Modern 9.2, comic shop and collectors new issue submissions improving quickly from 9.2 to 9.6 / 9.8.

With only 2 months of production as I write my 2013 report, the outlook for 2014 is strong. Special thanks to Jamie Newbold whose advice on technical matters is precise, and the guys who supported and shared in Australia's first certification company, Greg Rowe, Mike Clark, the Halo Cert. team of graders and workshop staff, and my old yankee buddy Jared Stern of Maryland.

This is Slim signing off from the furthermost outpost.

DAVID T. ALEXANDER
TYLER ALEXANDER, EDDIE WENDT & AUSTIN ALEXANDER
CULTUREANDTHRILLS.COM
CULTURE AND THRILLS COLLECTIBLES GALLERY

Action Comics #1 was the highlight book of the year for 2013. Every year we receive an abundance of calls from people who have just located a copy of *Action Comics* #1 and want to sell it to us. Almost all of these calls result in the owner of the book finding out he has a *Famous First Edition* reprint.

As we reported in last year's Market Report, one of the calls about *Action Comics* #1 that we received turned out to be the real deal and we obtained the book, got it graded and displayed it at several conventions before selling it at auction. The grade was 1.8 and the book sold for $175,000. This is the book that you are thrilled to get your hands on and heartbroken when you sell it. As you might recall from last year's Market Report, the book was found inside a wall of a house built in 1940 and was being used for insulation. The house was in the cold north near Canada and had been purchased by a contractor for $10,000 with the intention of doing some minor renovation and reselling it. A leak in the roof damaged the drywall and when he opened the wall to determine what repairs needed to be done, the *Action* #1 fell out. The book was in the hands of a person who never had a comic book in his life. There was a huge amount of publicity surrounding this book when it was offered for sale and almost every newspaper in the country picked up the story. There is much more information about this book and how it was found that I will not go into here, but if you see me at a comic show this year stop me, say hello, and I'll share a few more details. Selling it just makes us get out and look harder and deeper for the next copy.

Speaking of looking harder, we did acquire a massive amount of material in the past year. In an unusual circumstance we restricted our buying area to the East Coast and Midwest sections of the country. This was not propose driven, it was because the significant calls we received were all from west of the Mississippi. Our van died a noble death in the fall after hauling millions of valuable collectibles for hundreds of thousands of miles. Although we picked up lots of material while we were on the road we have been impressed by the quantity and quality of material that is being brought into our retail store.

© Nedor

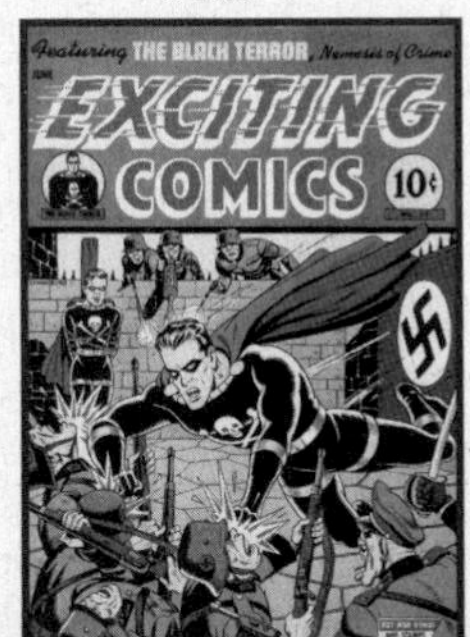

Schomburg WWII covers like **Exciting Comics #33** are in high demand.

One of our reasons for obtaining a retail location was to offer sellers a place to quickly dispose of their collections for a fair price. Local comic shops constantly contact us to offer any vintage material that comes their way. We have been opened for about a year and a half and have a steady flow of collectibles coming in the door. At this point I should note that our store carries almost no new material, unlike just about every comic book shop in the U.S., and we do not rely on new comic sales to keep the doors open. Our focus is on vintage material. Old-timers will remember the comic stores of the early 1970s when each store was different and had inventory that was not duplicated at the next store down the street. I might be trying to turn back the clock but I really like to offer our customers items that can be found nowhere else.

Interest in collecting has been strong in the last year. Everyone felt the pressure of the downturn in 2008-2009 and we are all seeing the upswing flourish this year. A number of fans lost their collections in the economic collapse and a few even lost their homes. Most of them are back in the collecting mode and rightly so. When you think about it, a lot of the fun of collecting is the treasure hunt.

Increased Popularity: Nedor Comics have had higher demand in the last few months. Their popularity reminds me of Timely Comics about 35 years ago. Many are selling for above *Guide* prices, and there is an increased demand recently. It doesn't hurt that Alex Schomburg, who did many Timely WWII covers, was one of the most prolific cover artists for Nedor. When Nedor dropped the WWII theme issues, Schomburg continued working and created an impressive amount of jungle and sci-fi covers. The issues with WWII covers can bring up to 3x-4x *Guide* particularly if a super-hero is fighting Nazi or Japanese soldiers. Many of the Nedor (Thrilling Pubs) pulp issues contain art by Schomburg. This is a field that most comic book collectors are not comfortable with. Those that do take the pulp plunge are generally very happy.

DC and Timely Golden Age super-hero issues are in constant demand. Superman, Batman and Captain America issues will forever lead the public conscience as they are as ingrained in Americana as baseball and apple pie. It really makes me feel good to see that my childhood hobby has become a field of national prominence. With the popularity of the big budget comic book movies it seems that comic collecting is something to by proud of these days, it is no longer "America's Secret Hobby."

Atlas Comics, the bridge between the patriotic Timely heroes and the Marvel Universe, have always been popular collectors items. Currently they are more than popular and have experienced some dramatic price increases. As an example *Strange Tales* #28, which is broken out as a key issue in the *Guide,* is selling at 4x-5x *Guide* values. Other Atlas issues going for multiples of *Guide* are *Strange Tales* #40, *Tales to Astonish* and *Tales of*

Suspense first issues, *Combat Kelly*, *Black Rider*, Korean War issues, horror and sci-fi titles, any Jack Kirby issues and issues with Joe Maneely covers. Maneely died in the late 1950s and was the top Atlas artist. How would our lives be different today if he had survived to help create the Marvel superheroes?

Tarzan comics are showing signs of making a comeback. For several years the Edgar Rice Burroughs titles have been fairly dormant. Recently we have seen renewed interest in both the Dell series and the reprint titles from United Features Syndicate, *Tip Top* and *Sparkler*. There are a lot of hard core Burroughs fans but the interest we have recently experienced has come strictly from comic book collectors. In addition Tarzan Big Little Books have had interest along with many other Big Little Book titles. The *Guide* began to list these several years ago and prices have not seen many changes. Could it be that collectors now see these as underpriced? Current interest has come from seasoned collectors. Have you ever noticed that almost every Antique Shop in America has a hand full of Big Little Books, all with spines missing that are offered at $50 each and up?

Pre-Code Horror has seen some incredible price gains during the past year. Many of the Atlas titles are selling for 2x-4x *Guide* values. Many of the short running titles featured grotesque violence, vampirism, dismemberment, hanging, injury to the eye and acid in the face, witchcraft, cannibalism, Atomic Bomb stories, murder, weird menace, flying saucers, occult themes, torture, zombies, criminal behavior and generally reprehensible acts. These books are now good for all the wrong reasons and, man, are they fun to read and collect.

Archie Comics had a big boost last year. Archies have always had a solid following but demand ramped up for *Archie's Madhouse*, *Josie*, *Sabrina*, *Betty & Veronica* and *Katy Keene*. We have also witnessed an unnatural demand for the original series. Issues prior to #50 seem hard to find in higher grades. When we consider who the original comics were meant to entertain it actually seems like a small miracle that any of these early issues exist in high grades. These early issues have a constant creep towards increased values. It does not seem like much after a year to year comparison, but check value increases during a five year period.

Recent Sales: *Amazing Fantasy* #15 CGC 4.5 $18,000, *Amazing Spider-Man* #1 CGC 5.5 $5,400, *Aquaman* #35 F/VF $275, *Avengers* #1 CGC 4.5 $,2500, *Batman Adventures* #12 NM $180, *Battle* #1 CGC 7.5 $617, *Bobby* #1 CGC 9.2 $425, *Black Panther* #1 CGC 9.8 $395, *Camera Comics* #1 CGC 8.5 $350, *Captain Britain* #1 CGC 9.8 $1,300, *Captain Britain* #8 NM $225, *Daredevil* #1 CGC 8.0 $3,375, *Daring Love* #1 CGC 4.5 $1,300, *Ghost Rider* #6 VF $350, *Giant-Size X-Men* #1 CGC 8.5 Stan Lee $1,200, *Ideal Comics* #1 CGC 9.0 $1,300, *Incredible Hulk* #181 CGC 9.0 $2,000, *Mask* #1 CGC 7.0 $2,300, *Mitzi* #1 CGC 8.5 $525, *Mopsy* #1 VF $335, *My Girl Pearl* #1 CGC 8.5 $594, *My Intimate Affair* #1 CGC 9.2 $450, *Nova* #1 CGC 9.8 $650, *Our Army at War* #1 VG $400, *Pep Comics* #1 F/G $950, *Sad Sack* #1 CGC 5.5 $600, *Sgt Fury and His Howling Commandos* #5 VF $325, *Superman* 6 CGC 6.0 $1,800, *Tales of Suspense* #57 CGC 8.0 $2,500, *Weird War* #1 VF $400, *Wilbur* #7 VF $250, and *World's Finest* #3 VG $1,400.

Conventions: Face-to-face activity is an important part of this hobby. There is nothing like interacting with other collectors, seeing the items that they treasure and swapping stories about deals lost and found. For a long time the internet put a halt to a lot of this type activity. Many smaller conventions disappeared as the internet became the new meeting place for collectors. Without a doubt the internet does have an important place in this field but it can be a cold, sterile and sometimes hostile environment.

After the initial infatuation with the internet began to subside fans started returning to the shows. Both large and small events began to thrive. In Central Florida we are fortunate to have some fantastic events take place several times each year. The Megacon in Orlando has experienced continued growth and draws many out of state dealers and collectors. It is a multimedia event and like the San Diego Comic-Con attracts lots of cosplay people who have no interest in buying or selling old funny books. People have distinctly different agendas at this show but it is still fun to attend and well worth the efforts of the dealers who set up here.

The Tampa Comic Con is the new blockbuster in Florida. It was a small regional event for about a decade but changed hands a few years ago and has morphed into a giant event that takes place at the Tampa Convention Center. Late last year, the first show at that facility had an attendance of just south of 30,000 people. Nobody expected that kind of turnout, particularly the Tampa Police Dept. as they had their hands full with traffic and crowd control. I thought the event was fantastic and sold a lot of Golden Age books. Our whole staff is looking forward to the second event scheduled for early August.

One of the coolest and most casual events is the Central Florida Comic Swap Meet. This get together is basically aimed at Golden Age collectors and for almost four years has taken place at the homes of various local fans. The event draws about 20-30 people and everybody brings books to display, talk about and maybe sell. It is a fun one day event with a "hang out with your pals" atmosphere. The organizers have produced a T-shirt for participants which was given out at each of the four events. I have attended the last two and had a great time, looked at magnificent collections and sold some super books and eaten some killer food. You guys who have opened your homes have gone way beyond the call of duty and everyone has been really happy with the menu. There have been a few out of state collectors show up at the last two swap meets. If you have an interest in becoming involved with this group check the CGC chat boards as info about the next event will appear there.

As a tribute to the 1970s comic cons we have promoted a Comic Book Swap Meet that takes place in the parking lot of our store every few months. Selling spaces are available for

$15. This allows collectors to take a space and sell off their extras and books they no longer collect. In the 1970s about a third of every dealers room was collectors selling their extras. In the early 1980s when convention table charges hit $150, the private collector/seller disappeared. This is our attempt to return to the past. I can still remember the summers in the mid 1970s when I would hit seven cons in seven weeks from Phoenix to New York City. The great thing was that I never paid more than $25 for a table at any of these shows. We are trying to regenerate the energy and excitement of those early 1970s shows.

Last year one of my long time clients pointed out that no one has advertised in more editions of the Guide than I have. My ads have appeared continuously since the Second Edition.

The hobby has shown growth in the last year and is strong because new fans are entering the field. Many have been drawn in because of the comic book films and become hard core collectors. I often get the question "Are there any original owner Golden Age and Silver Age collections that have not yet been discovered?"

Without hesitation, the answer is YES.

Dave Anderson, DDS
Collector

Although 2013 saw some stabilization of prices, activity and sales remained strong. There were not as many new finds, especially in Golden Age, so much of the activity consisted of recycling of already known books. There is certainly an awareness among collectors of previous sales and when they occerred thanks to GPAnalysis reporting and there is some resistance to paying significantly more for a book with a reported recent sale when the same book goes up for sale again. Fresh books that have been unavailable for long periods of time tend to fare better.

There is also resistance to paying more for books where the grade has been increased due to re-grading by CGC. Most higher profile sales are well documented these days so it is easy to track the sales history of most books. It is also becoming increasingly obvious that the preferred way to sell comic books is via acution whether by eBay or one of the many comic book auction companies. This is a trend that started in the mid to late 1990s and currently accounts for the majority of all comic book sales.

Stephen Barrington
with Jon Chambers
Flea Market Comics

The 2013 year started disasterously in January with the shop being burglarized to the tune of $15,000 in comics from the 1930s to the present. The local police didn't seem too interested in investigating and none of the comics were recovered. Diamond Comics sent out a bulletin to all the comic shops it services for which we were very appreciative.

The 2013 *Overstreet Price Guide* was a big hit with the collectors this year with sales topping last year's by a significant margin. The anticipation always builds in late May with the San Diego Comic-Con not coming fast enough for the new edition. The reference material packed into the *Guide* is nothing short of amazing.

New Comic Sales: Marvel's twice-a-month schedule for its titles has become very annoying to our customers. As a result, sales have fallen on many of the X-titles. *Superior Spider-Man* is the exception for Marvel's core titles. The *Infinity* series and crossovers proved to be more popular than expected. However, another bone of contention for the Marvel followers is the constant relaunches of its main characters. Starting over at number one has become a running joke in our shop.

The Marvel and DC new issue sales are about 50-50. Reordering from Diamond on DC is a lot easier than for Marvels. It seems they deliberately do not print a sufficient number of copies of its popular titles. Image has enjoyed great success with its *Walking Dead* series with back issues being impossible to keep in stock. Just when we think we have ordered plenty, we are proven wrong. Sigh! *The Walking Dead* trade paperbacks are extremely good sellers with Image and Diamond keeping them readily available.

DC's Villains Month was a nightmare when it came to ordering. The different ordering schedules confused everyone. And to top it off, the stories were not exactly a hit with our readers. The speculators on the 3-D covers flooded eBay with hundreds if not thousands of copies, depressing prices. The market for these in our area crashed shortly thereafter.

Of all the new comic sales, Batman titles rule supreme. There may be too many being offered in 2014; but time will tell. Marvel has too many titles out, diluting their sales.

Silver Age Marvels: *Amazing Spider-Man* is our top back issue seller while *Fantastic Four, Journey Into Mystery/Thor, Tales Of Suspense/Iron Man, Tales To Astonish/Hulk* are terrible sellers. Most *X-Men* and *Wolverine* and non-*Amazing* titles from the past 20 years are in our $1.00 or four for a $1.00 section. It seems every time someone brings a collection in, it's the same issues over and over again. We buy a lot because most people are just trying to get rid of them and these comics sell well in our bargain sections. The four-for-a dollar section is our most popular in the shop and as a result, we go through thousands a month.

We recently got in a nice selection of prime Silver Age Marvels (including key issues) in excellent condition, but most still sit on the wall displays or in the back-issue boxes. These have been discounted a number of times, but still no takers on most of them.

Silver Age DCs really don't do much better though there has been a small spike on Superman titles (*Action* and *Superman*). *Justice League of America, The Atom, Green Lantern, Hawkman* and even Batman titles have flatlined. The lesser known titles (*Challengers of the Unknown, Metal Men, Rip Hunter, Time Master* and *Sea Devils*) seem to be completely forgotten. We store these under the tables because of space limitations in our shop. If someone requests them, then we can pull them out. We sell these up to 60 and 70 percent off. One exception is DC War comics; they are requested often.

Some of the most requested numbers of *Amazing Spider-Man* continue to be #50 (1st Kingpin), the non-code 'drug' issues (#96-98), #101 (1st Morbius), the 'death' issues, #121 and #122, 1st Punisher (#129), #238 (1st Hobgoblin), #252 (black costume) and #300, 1st Venom.

The absolute hottest Bronze Age Marvels are *Incredible Hulk* #181 (and #180, #182), 1st *Wolverine*, *Giant-Size X-Men* #1, *X-Men* #94, and *Iron Man* #55 (1st Thanos). Unfortunately, some of the other places in town tend to put triple *Guide* prices on these issues, pricing them out of most of the collectors' range. We go by strict *Overstreet Guide* prices and discount those to make them more appealing.

Two Silver Age DC issues that go quickly are *Detective Comics* #359 (the 1st appearance of the Barbara Gordon Batgirl) and *Batman* #181 (1st Poison Ivy).

Which Prices Should Go Up: *Amazing Spider-Man* #129 (1st Punisher) is always a hot item as well as #s 121, 122 (death issues, Green Goblin, Gwen Stacy). The "drug" issues not approved by the Code (#96-98) sell in any condition. *Incredible Hulk* (#180-182)in lower grades sell well but the *Guide* prices don't reflect it since many collectors will pay slightly more for these in good and very good condition.

The first appearance of the Barbara Gordon Batgirl (*Detective* #359) sells in multiples of *Guide*. *X-Men* issues #141 and #142 (Days Of Future Past) has shown a lot of interest due to the new X-Men movie.

An encouraging trend is the steady influx of new readers with *My Little Pony* titles and childrens' comics leading the way. The main titles based on cartoons featuring the perennials (Superman, Batman, Spider-Man, Wonder Woman and the Hulk) do very well in our give-away program and are a big hit with parents. For many (ages 3 to 8) it is their first comic book.

Which Prices Should Go Down: All Silver Age *Fantastic Four* meet a lot of price resistance and seem to be too high in the *Guide*. ALL 1940s and 1950s Dells (including Disneys) seem to be a bit over the top. Overall, comics from the last 45 years seem to be very plentiful in grades up to Fine. A trend we noticed is the acceptance of lower grade issues, key or not. CGC has only moved up a little since last year and Golden Age sales are few.

After starting compiling information for the *Guide* in the early '70s, I've been at it for 40 years. Turning 61 this past spring is a little sobering. However, my passion for collecting is still strong.

Lauren Becker
Warp 9 Comics

Another year come and gone. Comics are still a strong focal point within the media and the "civilian" population. There is now a greater awareness of the comic shop, and more so, a larger awareness of the comic con. Conventions are now considered the new "destination points". A place where it's actually COOL to hang out, cos-play (dressing up in costume for all you old timers out there), and meet comic/media celebrities (hopefully). Conventions all over the country are experiencing HUGE spikes in attendance. Cons that were once topping 6000 people (still not bad), are now bringing in almost 20,000 or MORE!!! It's a great time to be a collectibles dealer!

DC Comics: The New 52 is becoming old hat. Numbers keep dropping off on the low tier titles. Some are even lower than BEFORE the New 52. Noticeably in the Superman family, the Green Lantern family (especially after Geoff Johns left), and even the JLA family (ie: *Flash*, *Aquaman*, etc.). The ONLY family of titles that HAVEN'T dropped is the BATMAN family of titles. *Batman* (by Snyder and Capullo) is still a consistent seller. As are *Nightwing*, *Batgirl*, and *Detective Comics*. Even *Batwing* gained a few new readers for us, as did *Catwoman*, ESPECIALLY when #23 was released with the first appearance of Joker's Daughter. This issue is a strong $10.00 back issue.

DC tried a massive 5th week event called "Villains Month", where all the Villain one shots would have a 3-D lenticular cover. The problem was when the books were already produced BEFORE the solicitations went out. The books were heavily allocated, and a speculator frenzy hit. The allocations were between 5-90% per title. The best sellers are the Harley Quinn and Joker's Daughter one shots, each getting $25.00 and $45.00 respectively.

Marvel Comics: Enough with the #1s already! Relaunching the titles at new #1s is getting tedious and trite! Another *Wolverine* series? Another NEW *Wolverine* series? More X-Men titles? Another Avengers title?

STOP THE INSANITY!

Although, to be fair, Marvel did have a great hit on its hands with the new *Superior Spider-Man* title. *Amazing Spider-Man* #700 (the last issue before *Superior* arrived) was really under-ordered at most shops. To be fair, the price point ($7.99!!), was enough to make most retailers stop and think, even with all of the extra variant cover incentives! The 1:200 variant with the unused Steve Ditko cover from *Amazing Fantasy* #15 was, without a doubt, THE hottest variant of the year with sales topping $800.00 raw (non CGC'ed) at one point! Regular copies of this issue went as high as $30.00!

Image Comics: The mighty *Walking Dead* is teetering a bit. The early issues have cooled a bit, BUT #1 is still exceptionally strong! The TV show is still giving it legs and still getting new fans into the shop. Issue #115 which was the 100th Charles Adlard issue was a special multi-cover issue which did exceptionally well. The NYCC variant was as high as $20.00 at one point, but has since cooled off to a respectable $5-10 comic.

Saga has been heating up, with our last NM/M copy of #1going for $125.00!!! Crazy for a book that hasn't received a movie/TV deal...yet.

Our Image sales for new #1s are huge, but after that first issue, they taper off big time. Good case in point was *East of West*. We ordered 200 copies and sold almost HALF in the first week. By issue #5, we ordered 20% and were NOT selling out. Not to say that this is a bad thing, but most people are speculating on the first issue, kind of a "done at one" and gone. Image is now back to being a speculator company, as many fans want to try and catch lightning in a bottle again (*Walking Dead*) and try to cash in on that TV/movie deal moolah. Image fans and Independent fans are trying this. Which leads me to...

Independents: *Rachel Rising* from Abstract Studios. A book that at times you could find in a $1 box. Uh-oh! Not so fast! A potential TV deal? Now $100.00 on line just like that! Time to scoop up ALL #1 independents you say? Not so fast...

Six Gun from Oni Press. A potential TV deal, and the comic shoots up to $100+ overnight! What's that? TV deal cancelled? Oh well...back down to $20.00 (still respectable).

Not to say that you should stay away from indies. There are some fine ones out right now that are great reads. Unfortunately, they are attached to movie/TV deals, so finding them at an affordable price is difficult.

Another indie that's been really hot right now is *Afterlife With Archie*! First print #1s have been closing at $10.00 minimum for us. Most retailers couldn't gauge this book, and many missed out! It's not all gags in this book, in fact, it has many adult like themes inside (nothing explicit though).

Back Issues: Certain back issues have just been going nuts! A few examples from the Silver Age include...

Amazing Spider-Man #1 (2.0)...$3000.00
Tales of Suspense #39 (2.0)...$1800.00
Tales to Astonish #13 (1st Groot 3.0)...$1000.00!!!
Fantastic Four #52 (8.0)...$600.00
Marvel Super Heroes #18 (1st Guardians of the Galaxy 8.5)...$300.00
Journey into Mystery #83 COVERLESS...$425.00
Avengers #1 COVERLESS...$300.00

These books are just getting older and more expensive. Notice I didn't say "difficult to find", because, truthfully, some of these books are still out there at almost every comic con, on line, or at least 5 stores per state. But, as auction prices become increasingly higher, collectors, especially newer ones, have to have that comic. Especially KEY books! Five years ago, no one would look at a coverless *Avengers* #1, and $100.00 would have been ridiculous. Now with a movie, AND 50 years of age, $300.00 seems like a bargain (well, to the buyer).

Bronze and Copper Age comics are starting to increase also. Sales include...

Incredible Hulk #181 (8.0)...1500.00
Iron Man #55 (8.0)...$400.00
Jimmy Olsen #135 (1st Darkseid 8.0)...$100.00
Batman #232 (8.0)...$200.00
Captain America #212 (35 cent edition without the "Marvel Comics Group" logo...4.0)...$1000.00 (yep...One Thousand Bucks...not a typo).

And lest I forget, Modern Age comics (all NM/MT/9.6-9.8)

New Mutants #98...$200.00
Amazing Spider-Man #300...$200.00
Superman #75...$20.00
Harley Quinn #1(1999)...$20.00
Batman Adventures #12...$125.00
Guardians of the Galaxy #1 (2006)...$60.00
Walking Dead #108 (1st Ezekiel)...CGC 9.8 $150.00

Again, this is just a SMALL sampling of what some sales are like. At cons, Modern Age books fly with large frequency, unlike Silver Age sales (which do better on line or within our store).

Jim Berry
Collector

Hello, everyone, and thank you for taking the time to read my report. This is my fourth report in as many years and I feel fortunate to contribute to this tome once again.

I'm a collector and part-time dealer based in Portland, Oregon and Seattle. I buy and sell on eBay as jb233 where I have a small store and never enough time to list all the books I'd like. I've been collecting and trading old comics since the late '70s and started working in a comic shop (Canyon Park Stamp, Coin and Comics) in the Seattle area in 1984 when I was still a sophmore in high-school. Currently, I make my living as a photographer, filmmaker and writer - but my first love, my true love, is old comics.

It's been another interesting year for comics in my region. I purchased a handful of great original owner collections in the earlier part of the year, and, in the latter part of the year, found virtually nothing. Clearly, this region of the country is, comparatively, comic poor when it comes to Golden Age material (or at least compared to the East). And, my sense is that original owner Silver Age is getting harder to find as well. Largely due to the web and eBay, sellers have a direct connection to a vast marketplace. In some regards, there is too much information, too many options, especially when an uneducated seller sees the potential for some huge, imagined profit based on unrealistic "Buy It Now" prices on eBay. The bottom line is that competition is fierce for old original owner

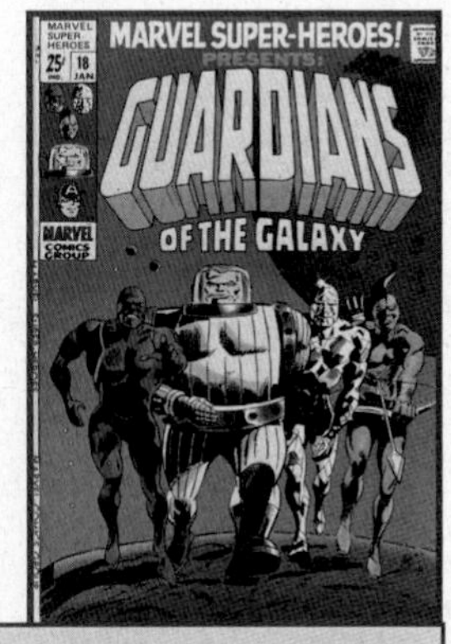

© MAR

***Marvel Super-Heroes* #18 is going nuts on the back market.**

comics as people have come to understand that old comics are actually money.

And then there's CGC and the continuing bifurcation that slabbing has created. Most dealers and collectors agree: CGC has become necessary in the hobby. But most also agree that the change has not always been for the better. The main issue is the level of inconsistency through the years, especially when it comes to the 9.2 – 9.8 grades. It becomes hard to stomach the amazing prices achieved for a 9.8 versus a 9.2 of the exact same book. I personally own a 9.8 *Batman* comic from 2000 that has two visible points of stress on the spine and a corner that shows some fraying. I also own a CGC 9.0 comic from the late '40s, a Crippen "D" book no less, that is, virtually, problem free. The spine is perfect. The corners are sharp. I went through the book with a fine-tooth comb before I slabbed it and, when compared to the 9.8 *Batman*, it clearly is the higher grade comic – and it's 50 years older! I've heard this same sort of story from virtually every dealer and collector I've talked with over the years. It seems as if no one is completely happy with CGC but no one is willing to put up much of a fuss either. There's no going back. There's no fighting the power. But still, it's a little sad to see how progress has changed the hobby - You can't smell the paper through a plastic slab.

Progress . . . One collection of note from earlier this year was an original owner set of books from the late '40s and '50s, around 300 comics in nice grades with a focus on TV and movie titles. There were quite a few Dell *Tarzan*, many Four Color movie titles, and then several little runs featuring old stars like Alan Ladd, Dale Evans, Jimmy Durante, and Jack Armstrong. It was a great stack of books with a lot of covers I'd never seen before. But when the owner and I started looking at the *Guide*, I told him that there was no way I'd be able to come close to Overstreet prices on his books due mainly to the fact that today's collector doesn't know who most of these people are. Despite what the *Guide* suggests, most of these books might sell for around five bucks each on eBay which means, sadly, that I can only offer pennies on the dollar for them.

I'll never forget the hurt look on that old man's face, but as anyone who watches eBay's general Golden Age section, or tries to sell these old titles can attest, the market for Golden Age has become quite specialized, focusing on key or unusual covers, World War II books, artists like Schomburg, L.B. Cole, Fine, Ditko, Baker, Wolverton, and Frazetta, as well as Timely, DC super-hero, pre-Code horror, and science fiction. There's a pulse for Disney and Archie as well, but beyond that, things start to slide down a steep and slippery slope.

In Portland, we welcomed Wizard World for the first time. The show wasn't great for sellers of old comics from the dealers I spoke with. But as we all know, old comics aren't really the focus of the big shows. Celebrities signing, promoting, and mugging, Cosplay, and Adam West's Batmobile – I'm not suggesting that there's anything wrong with that. It's just another piece of progress. Thankfully, there are still lots of old comics to be had at these shows.

For the first time in 34 years, The Second Genesis comic show didn't happen in Portland in 2013 – a real bummer as this is a real comic show in a real basement space with nothing but boxes of old comics and a few long tables of local artists and writers. From the information on their website, they cited several reasons for not putting the show together (personal conflicts and timing issues with the venue) but I wonder if they're feeling a little squeezed by the other big regional shows as well. I hope not and I'm crossing my fingers that they'll be back in 2014.

A shout out to John Hill, a square dealer and all-around good guy, who's starting a brick and mortar shop in Auburn, Washington. Hill's Of Comics will have lots of books, old and new. Tell him I sent you and he'll either give you a good deal or kick you out immediately. Also, thanks Josh for the great lunches and the comic talks throughout the year.

Finally, a sincere thanks to Mr. Overstreet and the crew at Gemstone for the incredible job they do producing this book. What would we do without our bible?

Here are a few notable books bought, sold, or bid-on – all eBay sales of no-reserve auctions:
America's Best #8 (FN-) $345
Startling Comics #53 (VG) $146
Action Comics #35 (VG) $276
Suspense #7 (VG) $163
Green Hornet #20 (VG) $200
Catman #14 (VG) $305
Catman #28 (VG) $676
Buster Crabbe #4 (FN+) $223
Moon Girl #1 (FN) $827
Superman's Pal Jimmy Olsen #1 (GD/VG) $680
Captain America #34 (GD) $550
Pocket Comics #2 (GD) $174
Strange Tales #89 (GD+) $256
Superman #14 (GD+) $565
Weird Mysteries #5 (GD+) $920
G.I. Combat #1 (VG) $266
Fight Against Crime #20 (VF) $6122 (!)
Tales To Astonish #13 (CGC 7.0) $2420
Brenda Starr #14 (CGC 7.0) $1900
The Witness #1 (CGC 5.5) $616
Iron Fist #14 (CGC 9.6) $650
Amazing Fantasy #15 (CGC 4.0) $8500
Amazing Fantasy #15 (CGC 6.5) $20,766

Thanks again and happy hunting in 2014.

Peter J. Bilelis, Esq.
Collector

Just finished reading the last of the 2012 *Guide* Market Reports. Wow, so many diverse opinions! From one collector's perspective, I can tell you that not everything is selling at or above *Guide*; and the sky isn't falling. Based on what I've seen, I think a more appropriate generalization would be – some books, whether because of title, character, cover, grade, or hype are currently aggressively escalating in demand (and realized sale prices), while the majority of books fall into one of two categories: (a) continue to appreciate at a slow/steady rate; or (b) are becoming less relevant due to forgotten heroes and other causes and, therefore, remaining flat or diminishing in value. Now, instead of penning a market report that simply focuses on personal purchase/sales data, I decided to do market research and analysis on the causal connection between some current market dynamics and sale/hammer prices, and then see how it reconciled with my (anecdotal) experiences. Given I collect (rather than deal) comic books, this type of data helps in my decision-making process, so I think it might be of value to other collectors too. I will focus on Golden Age (GA) examples, but much of this report really applies to most any hobby segment.

The general axiom is that sale/hammer prices are primarily driven by demand and perceived scarcity of the material. For 99% of the market, books sell at prices that can be reconciled with *Guide* estimated values. There is, however, a continuing trend of very high-grade key books, typically "blue chips" (generally, books with characters that transcend hobby interest, like Superman, Batman and Spider-Man) selling for prices that far exceed *Guide* estimated values. As one example, there is a copy of *Detective Comics* #35 being auctioned as I write this Market Report. It is currently listed as having been bid to $54k. Regardless of actual sale price (not always the best indicator of value), is this particular copy really worth so much more than the *Guide* estimated value? Well, it might be – right now. This type of book has several important criteria that push its value. It is a coveted pre-Robin *Detective* and features a Batman cover. Pre-Robin *Detective* Batman covers (except for *Detective* #36) typically draw a premium and seem to have constantly growing demand. And like *Detective* #31, this book is considered to: (a) have one of the all-time classic Batman covers (and splash pages); (b) be scarce in the marketplace; and (c) be very rare in grade. Granted, CGC 7.5 is not technically high grade, but then everything is relative. This is one of the nicest copies yet graded by CGC. And this is a rare "public" sale of a nicer graded *Detective* #35. So, it's easy to see why some people would be willing to pay a premium for this type of book. *Detective* #29 is another book that, due to the above qualities and similar scarcity "hype" (despite more than several copies entering the market over the past few years), constantly commands a premium that many consider to be justified while others deem it absurd.

Often, the fall-out from a record sale is that many dealers will: (a) assume the record sale affects the value of the same book in lower grades and will then price their lower grade copies more aggressively; and (b) bump up the prices on surrounding issues of the same title. One typical dealer justification for the price bump is that the record sale of a book is simply validation that the particular book in any grade and, further, the entire title is hot and undervalued by the *Guide*. The data I reviewed, however, rarely supported this theory.

Deciding how to approach the purchase of most any collectible book really depends on several basic factors including:
(A) **What Book is Under Consideration?** If it's a blue chip book, assume it will remain in-demand for the foreseeable future and relatively stable in value appreciation. This also explains why hobbyists feel comfortable in sometimes paying a small premium for even mid and lower grade copies of important blue chip books. But again, a spike in price to a particular high-grade copy of a blue chip book rarely means the book in every grade or the entire title is in need of a valuation overhaul. And, just because a book is "in demand" doesn't guarantee staying power or a good investment. If the book is a: (a) non-blue chip; or (b) "niche book" (e.g., obscure book with no distinguishing factors; book that contains the exploits of a forgotten character, etc.), historical data suggests these books, even if "hot" right now, appreciate more slowly over the long-haul and, in the case of "niche books," are more susceptible to plateauing and depreciation in value. Before paying a premium for a currently "hot" book, consider that the demand for it might be temporary rather than a true paradigm shift in value.
(B) **Scarcity in the Marketplace**. When an in-demand book rarely turns up for sale, assume there are several people that will pay a premium to secure it. While this helps explain why some books sell at prices well over *Guide* estimated values, scarcity alone isn't necessarily dispositive of a prudent purchasing decision. Historically, many books considered rare (e.g., books deemed rare by the *Guide*; books not pictured, or deemed rare, in *Gerber's Photo-Journal*, etc.) do well, even if not blue chip books. But value is often less stable on non-blue chips, and prices may vary considerably on this material. And, historically, when another similarly graded copy emerges, it often does not command the same premium. In other cases off-beat books have enjoyed growing "cult-followings" and many years have passed without another copy emerging for sale, making the book's proud owner smile as his/her book increases in demand and value.
(C) **At what Price have other Similar Items Recently Sold?** This is definitely good data for a purchasing decision. There are companies that provide a sort of "ticker-tape" like service, in that actual sales data (of certain CGC graded books) is collected and made available to customers. But this type of data (in a vacuum) doesn't necessarily provide a full picture of the market for a given book. As an example, a *Boy Comics* #11 in CGC 9.0 came up for sale a few years ago. A friend wanted it and reviewed the on-line actual sales data to determine how much to bid. At the time, the "ticker-tape" service reported the two best copies to be a CGC 9.0 (that sold for approx. 2.5X *Guide*) and a CGC 9.6 (Mile High copy). The friend concluded 2.5X *Guide* to be the right price for a CGC 9.0. Of course, this decision did not consider several other important factors. The data reported by the "ticker-tape" service, while accurate, didn't report on all sales of CGC books nor did it have any data for any/all raw copy sales. The friend's conclusion also didn't consider that the first CGC 9.0 sale

was the sale of the highest graded copy at the time. The MH copy was subsequently graded a CGC 9.6, knocking the CGC 9.0 off its "best" pedestal. So, the price paid for the first CGC 9.0 included a "best" premium. Was the second CGC 9.0 still worth approximately 2.5X then-current *Guide*? Well, it didn't sell at the same *Guide* multiple as did the first CGC 9.0. This illustrates one reason why the sale prices between two copies of the same book in the same grade can be quite different.

(D) **Do you Know what you are Buying?** Seems like a riddle, but if you are considering purchasing: (a) the highest graded copy (other than say a 9.9 or 10); or (b) one of the highest graded copies of a given book that is not in very high grade (e.g. CGC 7.5 *Detective* #35, again), conventional wisdom suggests that the purchaser doesn't really know what he/she is buying. As an example, if you buy an *Amazing Spider-Man* #1 in say CGC 9.0, you know what you are buying – a nice higher grade copy that has been bested by many other copies. There is an established market for this book in this grade, and its value is known and relatively stable. If, on the other hand (hypothetically) the CGC 9.0 *ASM* #1 was the single highest graded copy when you bought it and the general consensus was that a nicer copy would not come along, you thought you were buying the "best" copy. Over time, this perception may prove to be fact or not. A 9.0 has proven not to be a terribly high grade (for this era), allowing room for a nicer copy (or copies) to emerge and knock your copy from its "best" pedestal. This also makes a "highest graded copy" much more volatile and subject to price fluctuation, given there is no established market for it, and its value is somewhat based on a premium for its "uniqueness." This same logic applies to a book like the CGC 7.5 *Detective* #35. While considered scarce in the marketplace, the grade allows sufficient room for it to be bested, potentially relegating it to a position of less prominence.

How does this stack up with my personal buying/selling experience? Well, it certainly confirms much of what I've seen throughout the course of the year. While I wouldn't pay $54k for a CGC 7.5 *Detective* #35, I would pay over *Guide* value for this and several other books I am finding difficulty locating (like a higher grade copy of *Action* #39, *Detective* #187 and *Master* #27!).But it is also important to keep in mind that this is just an overview. Books sell at prices that don't necessarily correlate with *Guide* value (up and down) for many reasons not discussed here, such as: speculation, based on an upcoming Hollywood film about the book's character; an auction event in which the flood of choice material makes the sale of each piece at fair market value impossible due to a lack of available hobby dollars; a dealer who is willing to make a short sale for one reason or another; etc. And, if experience has taught me anything, it's that collecting comic books is not a science and logic doesn't necessarily factor in when there is an item you "must have."

Good luck hunting in 2014...

Steve Borock
President/Primary Grader
Comic Book Certification Service (CBCS)

As always, I would like to thank Bob Overstreet for all he has done for our hobby. We would not be where we are today without his dedication and professionalism over the last 45 years. Others in his position could have taken advantage of the power that the *Guide* wields, but not Bob. He has successfully held a steady course keeping the hobby safe for collectors and sellers alike. Thanks, Bob!

I would also like to thanks J.C. Vaughn and Mark Huesman, as these fellow hobbyists never get the credit they deserve for working year round to make sure they put out the finest price guide printed.

As you might have seen from my header above, I have stopped buying and selling comic books. By the time you read this, I will have opened a comic book certification (grading) company: CBCS. As many of you might know, I helped start the only successful certification service in our hobby, which opened in 2000. I, along with Mark Haspel, helped create the grading standards most of us use in the hobby today, helped create the first tamper-evident holder (slab), trained many professional graders, brought to light how much undisclosed restoration was really prevalent in our hobby, and more. You can read about CBCS in the ads placed as well as the article written about CBCS in this *Guide*. If you would like more information, please visit www.cbcscomics.com/

On to the real market report:

The market is still on fire and healthier than ever. Certain books have lost some of their value while certain other books have skyrocketed in prices. It seems that many high grade, non-key Silver Age Marvels, while still bringing a premium, have slowed down a bit as more come onto the market place. Most early 10¢ DCs in high grade sell for multiples of *Guide* due to their scarcity.

With Golden Age, on the other hand, most "mainstream" titles (*Action Comics*, *Detective Comics*, *Captain America*, etc), and hard-to-find Golden Age comics (Centaurs and "classic covers" as examples) have seen an upward swing in prices.

Bronze Age comics seem to be the flavor of the month, mostly due to movies and TV shows being announced. Once an announcement that a Bronze Age character even might be hitting the screen, first appearances seem to fly off dealers websites and convention booths. Marvel's TV show, *Agents of S.H.I.E.L.D.*, is a perfect example. The minute "Operation: Deathlok" was shown on the show, everybody was out looking for *Astonishing Tales* #25. It became the book everybody wanted and prices moved up.

Modern comics are a real "mine field" when it comes to investing. *The Walking Dead* is an anomaly. While the comic is a great read with a low print run, it is the TV show that has raised prices through the roof. That said, most of the "hot" Moderns, as witnessed over the years, don't always hold value. I always believe that most "hot" Moderns can be bought for much less money once hype dies down. Speculating in the Modern market is the most dangerous of games unless bought to "flip" right away. All that said, I love reading new comics, there is some great material being published these days, but I believe, as an investment, you are better off putting money into comics that are pre-1968.

I would like to give a shout out to the Hero Initiative (www.heroinitiative.org/). It's my favorite charity in our hobby. Please check them out. This year marks the fifth consecutive year that there is a Hero Initiative exclusive edition of the *Guide*, and all of the proceeds from it go to this great 501(C)(3) charity.

I will end this report the way I have done for years. This is for the newer people in our hobby, as I hope the more seasoned collectors already know this. Even though I believe in this market and have been in it since I was a kid, there is no such thing as a free lunch. If you are going to invest in comic books (or original comic art), you had better love what you buy. If the economy ever gets really bad, just like if you own stocks, precious metals, or anything else considered an investment, you will not be able to sell them for a really high price very quickly and you can certainly not use them to house or feed you and your family in times of need. The best advice I can give, and have been doing so for as long as I can remember, is: "Buy what you love and can afford." It's really that simple.

Just enjoy collecting and reading comic books, enjoy the friendships we make in this wonderful hobby, look around and enjoy all the cool stuff our hobby has to offer from original comic art to movies based on our favorite characters to comic memorabilia, and it will all seem worthwhile in the end.

I hope to see and talk with many of you reading this at the many upcoming conventions I attend!

Thank you for taking the time to read this and HAPPY COLLECTING!

Richard M. Brown
Collector

There is a saying, "Look to the Stars!" I always consider how Hollywood is treating us. With Iron Man being a household word, early *Tales of Suspense* issues are easy to recommend. Gwyneth Paltrow's strong portrayal of Pepper Potts makes *Tales of Suspense* #45 (1st Pepper Potts and Happy Hogan) an interesting investment. Collecting *Tales of Suspense* #52 (1st Black Widow) and #57 (1st Hawkeye) is also a fine idea. With Scarlet Witch and Quicksilver coming to the next Avengers movie, watch *Avengers* #16 and *X-Men* #4.

Comic Prices on the Rise: *Amazing Spider-Man* #9 and other early Electro appearances should benefit from Jamie Foxx's upcoming portrayal of the character in the next Spider-Man movie. Also, *Iron Man* #55 with the 1st Thanos.

Comic Prices on the Decline: Think Green. While Hulk and Green Arrow are getting excellent help from Hollywood, Green Lantern didn't work as a movie. Recent comic prices reflect that.

Pricing Adjustments?: *Avengers* #1 and *Avengers* #4 up! Early Spider-Man appearances and *Strange Tales Annual* #1 are scarce. Lots of *Strange Tales* and *Tales of Suspense* should go up.

Paul Clairmont
PNJ Comics

2013 was a blockbuster year for PNJ Comics! In our first full year of business we thought the biggest challenge would be finding enough back issue material to sustain everyday operations while raising enough capital for year over year growth and expansion. Through non-stop hard work and ambitious short, mid and long term goals we exceeded expectations in both areas. In a little over one year we expanded our inventory by 7,500% and continue to acquire new material on a weekly basis with a specific goal of carrying hard to find and high grade back issues. We grew so quickly that our biggest challenge is having the man power to process the collections we've acquired. Maybe this is a testament to the state of the economy or baby boomers spring cleaning. Being assertive and "beating the bushes" was vital for us to be "first to market" on some of the single highest CGC graded key and hot books.

We saw a substantial upward trend in the interest of comic books. It appears being a comic geek has become acceptable as the media has picked up on record breaking internet auction results and hit shows such as *The Big Bang Theory* have made it socially acceptable to collect and invest in comics. Not to mention the movies. All have acted as a spark to flame the growing demand. People are also buying into comic books to diversify their investment portfolios. Move over real estate and gold.... comic books are taking some of that pie. Add the regular "die hard" collectors who continue to fill in holes and upgrade to higher grade copies and the forecast for 2014 looks promising.

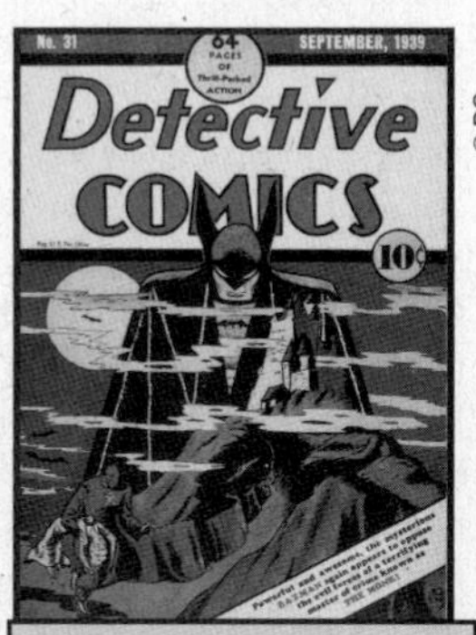

© DC

Mainstream Golden Age titles, like **Detective Comics** have seen an upward swing in prices.

When it comes to collectibles there seems to be two common themes to desirability: Rarity/Scarcity and Condition. We have witnessed firsthand that this is no different with comic books.

Although it is essential to stock as large of a variety as possible it is important to know your market demand and have the resources to sell. A business acquaintance once told me before we started PNJ Comics that his key to success was, "think globally - not locally" Being able to make new contacts and build clientele through our website and eBay is vital to back issue sales. Traveling to conventions is also effective but the time and effort in setting up boxes of inventory and travel expenses can be a higher risk to the bottom line. eBay is the undisputed king of internet sales venues. It doesn't represent the true picture of all sales. Patience is a virtue as well. Often auctions running for 7 days can miss potential clients. Setting up "Buy it Now" or "Best Offers" has provided the most consistently stronger sales results.

We saw some incredible results attributed to being the "first to market" with some strong sales. PNJ Comics was the first to have the only CGC 9.8 copy of *Alf* #48 with its infamous "rape cover". It sold for nearly $250 USD. In March of 2013, PNJ Comics also sold the first (and only) CGC 9.8 copy of *Marvel Preview* #7 featuring the 1st appearance of Rocket "Rocky" Raccoon for $2,000 USD. That sale was soon followed by the first (and only) copy of a CGC 9.8 *Marvel Preview* #11 featuring the 2nd appearance of Star Lord for $1,000 USD in July 2013. This same collection of *Marvel Preview* magazines yielded a CGC 9.6 of *Marvel Preview* #4 and CGC 9.8 copy of *Marvel Preview* #2.

In January 2013 we were selling CGC 9.8 copies of *Incredible Hulk* #271 for approximately $200 and as of this writing in November 2013 we have sold multiple copies for $500 USD. We also sold multiple copies of *X-Men* #141 in CGC 9.8 for $500 USD. No doubt the movie phenomenon helped spur these results as interest shifted the spotlight to these books.

We have seen growing interest throughout the year for established characters and franchises such as the Black Panther, Dr. Strange, Ant-Man and Star Wars. First appearances of any character in any title sell very well and very often above *Guide* prices. This interest grows as the movies draw closer and more attention is given through media outlets. Once San Diego Comic-Con releases more announcements we expect some of this to soar sky-high with our money on Star Wars as early buzz seems to be in favor with nostalgic fans of the franchise and comic collectors.

Canadian Price Variants: Another area of growing interest is niche books such as Canadian Price Variants. Marvel and DC are the most common so I'll only discuss them for the sake of example, but there are also Gold Key, Archie and many more. Marvel and DC both released separate pricing for Canada in October 1982 and continued well into the late '80s. These books are approximately 1/10th the original printing of the U.S counterpart and can be recognized with the single 75¢ or 95¢ cent price on the cover while less common books are $1.00, $1.60, $2.10, $3.50 etc. (All single Canadian prices).

With a low print run and distribution of these particular books circulated to the general public through venues such as grocery and convenience stores on spinner racks many were abused as they were enjoyed by their intended audience and not die hard collectors buying at specialty shops with direct editions. This has made it very difficult to find the books in high grade. Most copies are in lower condition than Very Fine. We sell high grade Canadian Editions at strong premiums over the regular print run. Non-keys sell for 25%-50% above *Guide* and keys can bring 100% to 1000% above *Guide* price. PNJ Comics is proud to have hundreds, even thousands of these books in high grade. Although mainstream titles naturally perform better, when it comes to Canadian Price Variants, all titles sell well. Make no mistake, it's a niche market but has created scarcity amongst an age in books that many people thought were mass produced. DC issues seem scarcer than Marvel but that is likely due to Winnipeg earning a reputation as a "Marvel City".

Just as difficult to find in high grade are newsstand editions. They are often in lower grade than their direct edition counterparts as mentioned above in the sources of distribution. Although not as scarce as Canadian newsstand editions they are scarce in Very Fine+ or better and once again bring consistent premium over the direct editions.

Scarcity of High Grade Copper Age: Another area that is picking up is issues near the end of a title's print run. As the title lost interest, fewer copies were ordered and therefore less produced. For instance, Marvel's line of Star Comics had many titles geared towards kids. *Masters of the Universe* #12 and #13 are more difficult to find in high grade than #1. PNJ Comics sold a CGC 9.8 copy of *Masters of the Universe* #12 in June 2013 for $500 USD.

This holds true for many titles such as *Ewoks, Droids* and pretty much any title from any publisher during the '80s and '90s. Long ignored in back issue dollar bins, people are finally realizing that these titles and issues are not easy to find in high grade. Other titles such as *Peter Porker, Spectacular Spider-Ham* and *Captain Carrot and His Amazing Zoo Crew* are fantastic parody books taking a page from Disney and incorporating animal characters as some of our favorite and most popular super-heroes. These do well as sets and again, are difficult in high grade as they spent most of their lives in quarter/dollar bins and were not ideally stored.

While a lot of attention was paid to books such as *Marvel Secret Wars* #8 and hoarded in high grade, everyone neglected books that weren't as popular and 25+ years later they are kicking themselves for not collecting these hard to find titles now. Add in the Canadian Price Variant element to the search and you have yourself a new resurgence of interest in Copper Age books.

Bronze Age: With the crop of new movies continuing to be green-lighted for production there are many books showing interest that were under collectors' radars. One of the best series that is still underappreciated and undervalued is *Jungle Action* beginning at issue #5. It features the Black Panther's first solo series but issue #5 is a reprint of a previously released *Avengers* book. Issue #6 is the first new material and is well written. It's certainly a sleeper title that few collectors, at the time of this writing are aware of. Another character that is showing a modest comeback is Fin Fang Foom.

Arguably the most popular pre-hero monster that first appeared in *Strange Tales* #89. It is a very little known fact that it took 13 years for his 2nd appearance to occur in the pages of *Astonishing Tales* #24, even though #23 also features the character. Issue #24 is noted as the 2nd appearance and boasts a great battle cover between Fin Fang Foom and Colussus (another favorite amongst pre-hero monster books). There are so few high grade copies available that collectors will find it frustrating getting their hands on these books in anything better then Very Fine/Near Mint (9.0). If a studio decides to include Fin Fang Foom in a movie this book has potential to be one of the best investment books even though it already brings prices 4 times above listed *Guide* price in any grade. All you have to do is look at the 1st appearance of Groot and what the *Guardians of the Galaxy* movie has done for him. Other books that are tough to find in high grade and rare in high grade are "Fast Willie Jackson". This Afro American style Archie humor book is a short lived series with the latter issues very difficult to find in anything better then Very Fine. Unfortunately, these niche books don't have history behind them and are therefore, very underappreciated for their social relevance.

Silver Age: *Fantastic Four* #52 is one book that is soaring. It's odd that *Fantastic Four* #53, which features the Black Panther's first origin and is a continuation of *Fantastic Four* #52, is not being scooped up by collectors as readily especially with its dark cover which makes it tough to find in high grade. This might be a good example of how the "1st appearance" mentality that speculators have, and not die hard collectors, is influencing demand. *Tales of Suspense* #57 saw steady growth and we sold more privately to die hard collectors. This is one issue that is hard to find in high grade. Although it seems to be off the radar momentarily as of this writing, we suspect it hasn't even begun to peak and will climb higher in 2014.

We are bewildered by the disparity between some of the Silver Age books and listed *Guide* prices. Although mainstream titles such as *Amazing Spider-Man* and *Fantastic Four* are readily available in large quantity few dealers, including ourselves, have a deep inventory of Pre-Hero books. These little gems always bring premiums of 50% to 400% of *Guide* in nearly any grade. They just aren't as common yet collectors are having a difficult time completing runs due to their scarcity. This is just one example we'll touch on to illustrate our opinion.

With Pre-Hero books, we took a moment to examine the "prototypes" phenomenon of many of the issues. Although the character images are often very loosely based on current mainstream characters the concepts have the same redeeming qualities. Given that scenario, we have found a few others for fun that we feel should be broken out in the *Overstreet Price Guide*. Here's a few for your consideration and to have fun.

Journey into Mystery #56 features a story with loosely based characteristics and concepts of "Fin Fang Foom".

Journey into Mystery #63 features a story penciled by the great Spider-Man artist, Steve Ditko and mentions a scientist named "Otto". Could this be a prototype of Dr. Octopus?

Journey into Mystery #66 features another Ditko penciled story of a character resembling "The Thing" from Fantastic Four.

Journey into Mystery #72 features a tiny "ant-like" civilization of people living on a baseball glove. Could this be more practice for the eventual Ant-Man character?

Journey into Mystery #74 has an alien race that has some attributes of "the Skrulls" one month before the release of *Fantastic Four* #2.

Journey into Mystery #78 is already recognized for having a prototype character of Doctor Strange but there is also a story that features an all-consuming being hell bent on destroying planets just like Galactus.

Journey into Mystery #81 has a possible prototype we thought was the most interesting. There is a story featuring a character that resembles Dr. Donald Blake, the character even goes on to become a knight during the medieval times and defeats a dragon before returning to the present day where he once again assumes the character very similar to Donald Blake. We may be reaching but thought it was too coincidental as it was only 2 issues before the true characters were featured in *Journey into Mystery* #83.

We'll let you be the judge but given some of the loosely resembled prototypes that are broken out in the *Overstreet Price Guide* we feel these unlisted prototypes should receive some recognition and possibly broken out as well. PNJ Comics sell these books on our website using the prototype features we have discussed.

Modern Age: This is easily the most volatile area of comic books. Print runs are at all-time lows compared to any other time in comic publishing history. There is the usual keen marketing by publishers to bury collectors with variant covers, blank sketch covers, 3D covers and many other gimmicks to earn collector's dollars. On any given week there are a handful of #1 issues for weekly new titles. It makes your head spin trying to dissect through what to buy. Our best advice is to collect what you like, keep it simple. People are continuing to try and find the next "*Walking Dead* #1" and this is dangerous speculation. Sure, there are some books that are released, tossed on eBay by the secondary market and some are lucky enough to make a short term profit, but spending hours going to different shops to find these books cuts into those profits quickly as "time is money". Many others are left holding more 3D or variant covers than the market is willing to pay for them. These books always come back to earthling prices. If you like roller coaster rides and spending hours of your precious time searching, we wish you the best of luck. Don't forget, most shop owners are 2 steps ahead of you.

As we mentioned earlier, print runs on Modern books are at all-time lows. We've seen the cycles over and over again throughout the years. "Hot now, Hot potato and then Hot many years later". A savvy buyer holding for the long term might find themselves doing well with these extremely low print runs. For example, a comic such as *SpongeBob SquarePants* has a print run of approximately 7,000 books per month and books like *Avengers, Superior Spider-Man* and *Batman* are around 100,000 books per month. What book will be tougher to find in high grade 15 years from now? If history has taught us anything we have a pretty good indication but we'll let you decide for yourself. One of the books that came out in the latter part of 2013 was *Afterlife With Archie*. This series has some excellent potential and is our pick as the best new book in 2013. It snuck past many collectors when it was released in October 2013 and has the usual variant covers but collectors soon realized there was a variant cover to the *Life With Archie* #23 magazine that was released in 2012. With a rumored print run of approximately 3,000 books in total, less when you count the "Afterlife With Archie" variant cover of this magazine, it just might be one of the most sought after magazines of the Modern Age.

Finally, PNJ Comics is a family-run business. We are honored and privileged to earn the designation of Overstreet Advisor in our first year of business. The success we have achieved is from relentless long hours, a lot of research, working very hard as a team and surrounding ourselves with positive and creative people. I also want to thank all the clients for giving us a chance during our first year. You meet some very good people in this business and learn the "Spirit of the 12 year Old" lives in many of us, fostering those collecting memories in adulthood. With that being said, I want to say a big "Thank you" to the most important people, my father for introducing me to this hobby which to this day still holds the fondest childhood memories of going to the comic shop every Saturday morning together. My wife, Nicole, you are the reason we started the business. Your love, support and hard work is what inspires me to get up each day and tackle the longest days I've ever worked. Without you, there is no business. Finally, my little super-hero, Jack, your imagination and creativity inspire me to follow my childhood dreams. This is the best team of super-heroes!!

ART CLOOS
COLLECTOR/HISTORIAN

It is an honor to be named a Price Guide Advisor and I greatly thank Bob Overstreet and Jeff Vaughn for allowing me to contribute here. I can vividly remember the excitement of going through the first *Guide* I ever bought, #4, way back in the day and each year since *The Guide* has found a place in my collection. My approach here will be as a collector who has been active in the hobby since the early 1970s and who has seen much change over that time and my focus on the books I collect.

First of all, by the end of December 2013, as I write this in late November, my wife and I will have attended over 40 comic, art and toy shows over the course of 2013. Based on that attendance alone it is not any kind of an exaggeration to say that there is a healthy hobby out there with fans and collectors looking for deals and for both new collectors and dealers looking to learn about how the comic world works. High end books of course continue to lead the pack in any of the ages that have been named in terms of prices realized. DC definitely has the edge in Golden Age sales. The Golden Age Batman and Superman titles continue to be strong sellers with *Detective Comics* #27 to #40 being in very high demand. Lower grade copies of these books will sell well above *Guide* with little trouble when they are available. Mid 1950s DCs continue to be very difficult to find in 5.0 or better and disappear quickly when they show for sale.

Traditionally people who collect comics do not always collect toys with the reverse being true for toy collectors. However, with a rapidly growing group of collectors who have an intense interest in collecting Wonder Woman toys and memorabilia (and who are driving the prices of those vintage items up in some cases quite significantly) these same collectors are increasingly going after Gold and Silver Age Wonder Woman comics and this is a trend that I have been observing for the last few years now and which I expect to continue in the future. These collectors want the first series *Wonder Woman* run and can be expected to (and in many cases are already) move on to her appearances in *Sensation Comics* and *Comic Cavalcade* as time goes by. The Holy Grail for them is a toss up between *Wonder Woman* #1 and *All Star Comics* #8. Many of them have not yet discovered 1944's *The Big All American Comic* which features Wonder Woman along with the Flash and Green Lantern but this is certainly a book Wonder Woman collectors will have on their radar in time. *World's Finest* continues to be a very difficult and under valued (though that is changing somewhat) title if you want to complete the first 100 issues. With 70 solo appearances of Batman and Superman before their first team up in issue #71 the early issues are the last frontier for collectors who want solo Golden Age Batman stories as well as Superman ones. Finding the early to late 1950 issues in anything resembling high grade is simply not easy. With both Superman and Batman appearing together on the silver screen in 2015, this is a title that bears watching.

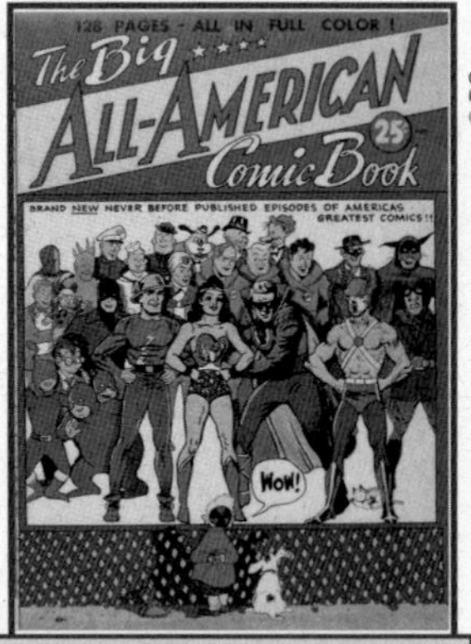

© DC

Wonder Woman collectors have **Big All-American Comic Book #1** on their radar.

Second of all, Silver Age interest by collectors tends to favor Marvel without question. *Showcase* #4 might have started the Silver Age but *Amazing Fantasy* #15 rules it. With an ever increasing presence in movies and now TV, Spider-Man,

Thor, X-Men, The Avengers, etc. find their titles in great demand. High grade rules, but in many of the local shows we go to, it is clear that lower grade Marvel and DC Silver Age books will sell and sell well if priced at *Guide* being more affordable in those grades. *Amazing Fantasy* #15 will sell at almost any grade. The result however is that those same books are inching up in value as demand increases. In terms of DCs, there are Silver and Bronze Age titles that are more and more sought out by collectors. Examples of these are *Detective Comics* #359 (the first Barbara Gordon Batgirl) and many of the Neal Adams covers from *Detective* and *Batman,* such as his homage to *Detective Comics* #31 on the cover of *Batman* #227. His Joker covers are of course also rising in demand and this is driving up the prices of those books in high grade. It will be interesting to see how the movies and TV productions that are in various states of planning by DC as I type this will be able to compete with Marvel's output and, as in the case of the before mentioned *World's Finest* title above, how they will affect sales of vintage DC books.

Third on my list for this year is to note that local shows have become the breeding ground for both newer collectors and dealers who are not ready to face the challenge of a "big time" show. What is really cool about them is that it is possible to find books that do not always appear on the display racks at bigger shows. Dells, Archies, Fox and the more obscure titles that seldom come up for sale can be found often at very reasonable prices. One trend we have noticed quite strongly at these smaller shows (as well as the big time cons) is the increasing number of many quite serious women and young buyers who attend, know what they want and look to buy at them. This has been verified by dealers we speak to and is a most welcome development which it is hoped will continue.

The fourth item for this report is my documented sales list for 2013 which includes *Showcase* #6 FN- at $900, *World's Finest* #66 FN at $350, *All-American* #33 PA copy (6.5) at $500, *Comic Cavalcade* # 3 VG at $350, *Sensation* #5 VG+ at $395, *Journey into Mystery* #95 FN- at $78, *All Star* #39 FN at $240, *All-American* #88 "D" book VF at $700, All-American #70 VG+ at $225, *All Star* #55 FN- at $200, *All Star* #52 FN at $250, *All Star* #47 VG at $200, *Teen Titans* 1st series #21 NM at $145, *Sensation* #53 GD at $170, *Sensation* #10 GD at $150, *Sensation* #50 VG at $125, *World's Finest* #6 VG at $285, *World's Finest* #57 (7.0) at $400, *World's Finest* # 56 GD+ at $60, *World's Finest* #64 VG at $300, *World's Finest* #67 VG at $300, *Amazing Spider-Man* #26 VG+ at $120, *Wonder Woman* # 1 (3.0) at $3,000 and *Detective* #97 VF at $475, (a Herbert Skogland book more on this below).

Finally as each New Year begins for the hobby it is not unusual to hear that the days of original owner collections surfacing and coming to the market are over, but the past few years of course show this is simply not true. Single owner collections continue to appear. Not all make headlines though because many of these collections do not rise to the level of a pedigree collection with the kind of condition that a pedigree must contain. These books when they come to light are broken up and sold with little or no fanfare and disappear into dealer's bins and buyer's collections and generally are lost to comic history. This brings me to one Mr. Herbert Skogland. In early 2013 the 90 year old Mr. Skogland walked into a small upstate NY comic store and asked the owner if he was interested in buying Mr. Skogland's comic collection. It consisted of approximately (according to the store owner) 800 books spanning over 50 years of collecting. A highlight of the collection was a run of *Batman* from #1 in 1940 running complete into the 1980s where the collection finally ended. There was a *Sensation* #1, runs of *Detective Comics, Green Lantern* and many others. As can be found in many books designated as pedigree collections, Mr. Skogland marked his books to keep track of them with many having his stamped name on both the cover and title page of the first story. A numbering system seemed to be used as well. This was not a pedigree find though because the one dominant feature of this collection was that the great majority of the books were very low grade, making the collection unfit for pedigree status. The *Batman* #1 was coverless, and the *Sensation* #1 was called a 3.0 by the store owner who bought the collection. The books had been loaned out to friends who in turn loaned out their books, and condition was the last thing any of them seemed to care about. Despite this there was a group of maybe 200 higher grade books that were in some cases very desirable to a collector. I bought one of them myself even though I had the book already as I wanted a piece of this collection's history. This collection represents a lifetime of effort by a collector who obviously had a great affection if not outright love for his books and it seemed wrong to me that his work of a lifetime would simply be lost to comic history except perhaps for a buyer of one of these books who might wonder who Herbert Skogland was and so I tell his story here to preserve its history. His collection has now been largely broken up, sold to both collectors and dealers. There are many like him out there with single owner collections that, because they are not pedigree worthy, and as a result not high ticket items in the market place, have been lost to documentation and a place in comic history. There will be more I am sure and it would be nice if some record of collections like this could be kept as a part of the history of comic collecting though I have no illusion that this either would or could happen in the future.

As 2014 is about to begin we look forward to a strong year for the hobby and can only imagine what new surprises the year in collecting will bring.

JESSE JAMES CRISCIONE
JESSE JAMES COMICS

This was a year when we saw Conventions peak, Cosplay become true mainstream, and the Comic Book industry explode not just in sales but also in vast increases in value in almost every genre across the board.

Comic book stores across the nation, either new or old, were scrambling all year. Almost every week, scrambling for the hot Variants coming out from both DC and Marvel. This boosted sales on regular covers to hit the levels required get these variants for their shelves. Though DC's attempt to revolutionize the comic variant scene with their lenticulars didn't go as planned, it opened up the flood gates to all companies that you will have to innovate to stay afloat in the coming years.

Characters like Deadpool, Harley Quinn, Joker, and yes even Joker's Daughter dominated the comic books scene not just in comics and toys but in the video game world as well. Thanos and the Guardians of the Galaxy gave truth to the fact that some dead back issues can all of a sudden become a treasure overnight. Image's *Walking Dead* seemed to own the market every month of the year between Comic and Trade sales.

Graded comics also seemed to attract a whole new generation of investors. Record sales continue to exceed previous unbreakable records. This new generation of buyers seem to consider the highest bids establishing the true value of a CGC copy, regardless of census or basic standard pricing used in the comic book community over the past few decades.

Movies continue to dominate our industry but in most cases have little effect on the overall comic book market. Other than Thanos, there really haven't been any key movies to move the value of our more mainstream titles. *Avengers*, *Thor*, *Captain America* or *Hulk* seem to be at a very slow pace of value growth but still a solid investment for the future.

The upcoming year looks to be promising. However, as fears starts to rise over the abundance of conventions there is a possibility of over-saturation of product, spreading out of creators, and the allure of what a convention is supposed to be. Fans want to be able to save up for two or three conventions a year to get that hard-to-get Gem they have always wanted. Now that choice lingers due to the fact that dealer might be doing 20 shows a year and by time they get to their town they may not have a vast variety like they normally do.

Overall, with that said, the industry continues to drive new issue sales and the opening of new stores is abundant. Really it's going to be up to the fans to decide if they are willing to pay $3.99 to $7.99 for a new issue. Are they willing to chase that variant? Finally are the temptations of digital still many years away for an industry that embraces the far future but relies on our past. Someone with a comic book in hand is a fan for our future.

Most requested comics in 2013:
Deadpool Vol. 3 #1
New Mutants #98
Iron Man #55
NYX #3
Howard the Duck #12
X-Force #6
New Teen Titans #44
Joker's Daughter 3d (*Batman: The Dark Knight* #23.4)
X-Men #282
X-Men #266
Coyote #11

BROCK DICKINSON
COLLECTOR

As in past years, I'll be focusing my report on the late Bronze through the Copper and Modern periods. While this area of collecting doesn't generate the headlines that books from the Golden and Silver Ages do, this is an important segment of the hobby for a number of reasons. First, this era of collecting is far larger than previous eras (covering some 30+ years), so the sheer range and volume of material is significant. Second, because it connects to the current new comics market, this era is actively collected by a far larger cohort of people than earlier eras. Finally, enough time has passed from the Golden and Silver Ages (and, to a lesser extent, the early Bronze Age) to ensure that most key books in those ages are well-known, with new keys emerging only slowly. The very "newness" of the post-1980 market means that new keys emerge very rapidly, often causing significant price spikes. The flip side of this, of course, is also true – that rapid price corrections or crashes can occur. All of this creates a segment of the market that is both broad and volatile, and it is impossible in the space of a few pages to cover all the hot spots and trends. As always, I merely do my best to hit a few of the key trends, and look at things that may have some longer lasting or wider impacts.

Perhaps the biggest story this year is the rapid rise of Copper Age books. Way back in 1993 I wrote a piece for *Overstreet Comic Book Monthly*, tracking the rise of Bronze Age collectors… these were a strange, young breed of collector driving books like *Marvel Spotlight* #5 (first Ghost Rider) to dizzying values of $100 or more. I suggested – to some skepticism at the time – that Bronze comics were a new frontier, and that a new generation of collectors was going to reshape the hobby. Flash forward 20 years, and we're on the cusp of the same phenomenon, but with the Copper Age as the new focus. Books once considered both plentiful and worthless are suddenly being traded for hundreds of dollars, and a "gold rush" mentality has started to take hold. The clear leader in this phenomenon is *New Mutants* #98 featuring the first appearance of Deadpool, with raw NM copies frequently selling in the $150-$200 range. Graded copies will sell for significantly more, and a "Gem Mint" CGC 10 copy sold for $15,449 this year. Other books, including *New Mutants* #87, *Batman* #386 and *Amazing Spider-Man* #300 are showing similar trends. In fact, the latter half of 2013 was characterized by a series of rapid price spikes on books as they were identified as "keys" by this new wave of Copper collectors.

Collectors have always had a challenge defining the exact time frame that falls within the Bronze Age, and the same holds true of the Copper Age. In a general sense, it probably runs from about 1982 to about 1992 – but books on either side of that barrier by a year or two are frequently described as "Copper Age" books. While it will likely be years before a true list of Copper keys is identified, here's my (humble!) first attempt to create a list of the "Top 40" Copper books over the past year. It is not meant to be comprehensive, but rather to capture a range of books (in only alphabetical order) from Marvel, DC and other publishers that have seen renewed interest and price hikes in the past year:

- *Albedo* #2
- *Amazing Spider-Man* #252, #298, #300, #361
- *Archie's Girls, Betty and Veronica* #320
- *Batman* #368, #386, #404, #426
- *Batman Adventures* #12
- *Bone* #1
- *Caliber Presents* #1
- *Comico Primer* #2
- *DC Comics Presents* #26, #47
- *Evil Ernie* #1
- *Incredible Hulk* #271, #340
- *Iron Man* #282
- *John Byrne's Next Men* #21
- *Marvel Super Heroes Secret Wars* #8
- *Miracleman* #15
- *New Mutants* #87, #98, *Annual* #2
- *Omega Men* #3
- *Sandman* #1
- *Superman* #423
- *Superman: The Man of Steel* #17, #18
- *Swamp Thing* #20, #37
- *Tales of the New Teen Titans* #44
- *Teenage Mutant Ninja Turtles* #1
- *Uncanny X-Men* #266, #282
- *Vampirella* #113
- *X-Factor* #6, #24

Any list of this type will, by nature, be somewhat arbitrary, but if this seems like something useful, I'd be happy to incorporate feedback into revised, expanded or updated lists for future updates.

The story this year is not all Copper, however – there also seemed to be a bit of a return to collecting specific characters. Certainly all Deadpool and Harley Quinn appearances were hot, but the excitement around these characters is, if anything, intensifying. The *Deadpool* series of 1997 was particularly strong on the back issue market, and issues above #50 routinely sold in the $20-$40 range. For Harley Quinn, her first appearance in *Batman Adventures* #12 ($150) and early appearances in *Batman: Mad Love* ($40) and *Batman: Harley Quinn* ($80) were all red hot, with demand far outstripping supply. Many of Harley's early appearances were in animated Batman titles aimed at children, and VF or better copies are scarce – and will often command $15-$20 or more. Even issues of her more common 2002 series generally draw about $8-$12 per copy. When it comes to Harley, low print runs and high demand mean that basically anything is a quick seller.

Perhaps of greater interest to traditional collectors, however, is the way in which *Batman* and *Amazing Spider-Man* heated up this year. *Batman* books between #300 and #400 were particularly hot, with many setting new records. Early Jason Todd appearances and first appearances of villains led the way, but many books in this era – traditionally seen as common – have spiked to $50 or more. *Batman* #386 ($100) is a particular breakout book, but all issues were moving. By the end of the year, the heat was extending back into the Batman run, with issues #250 and up starting to heat up again. *Amazing Spider-Man* is also increasingly hot, with key books, Venom and Carnage appearances, the McFarlane run and scarcer issues leading the way. Many issues between #200 and #500 are heating up, but especially keys like #252 (first black costume) #298 (first McFarlane), #300 (first Venom), #317 (early Venom), #361 (first Carnage), #410 (Carnage), #441 (last issue in original numbering), and Campbell covers (especially #s 601, 606 and 607). The renumbered issues #1-30 (from 1999 to 2002) are attracting a lot of interest, especially the scarcer #19-29. In fact, issues #28 and #29 are thought to be the lowest-printed issues of *Amazing Spider-Man* ever (at 48,559 and 48,804 copies respectively), and are attracting attention on that basis.

The New 52 from DC continues to be surprisingly strong. While the gimmicks and events (such as the lenticular 3D covers this past year) dominate discussion, some books continue to rise on the back market. *Batman* in particular continues to shock – who would have thought a couple of years ago that #1 would easily be a $65 book? The print run on some of these titles is large, but with most copies disappearing into collections, there are relatively few available on the back market. With demand rising as a result of Scott Snyder's strong run on the title, latecomers are paying significant premiums to get caught up. The first 6 or 8 issues of *Batman* are very strong sellers. Other titles, including *Nightwing*, continue to show similar strength, with the supposedly scarce #4 routinely selling for $30 or more.

The New 52 is not the only new universe launched in the past couple of years. Valiant has rolled out an outstanding set of tightly-connected books, with sales appearing to hold strong across the board. To date this has not been matched by back issue activity, though the possibility of future increases remains. Perhaps anticipating the impact of this line, 1990s Valiant prices rose across the board in last year's *Guide*, and while some of this may have been warranted, the rises were perhaps a little too aggressive. Having said that, the later issues of 1990s Valiant titles and the later Acclaim issues of Valiant characters are genuinely scarce, and routinely sell for multiples of *Guide*.

Marvel's response to the New 52 has been Marvel Now, and – more recently – All-New Marvel Now. While many of these books have been successful in the new issue market, back issue prices have been relatively stable... the constant renumbering and relaunching of Marvel titles has tended to mitigate against collectors seeking out back issues of hot titles (such as *Daredevil*) for any sustained period of time, though with a couple of exceptions (such as *Hawkeye*).

Announcements regarding movies and television programs were also a major factor this year. This was a huge driver for Marvel back issues, with anything connected to the Guardians of the Galaxy leading the way. *Incredible Hulk* #271 ($80), *Marvel Preview* #7 ($160) and *Incredible Hulk Annual* #5 ($40) were among the beneficiaries of this trend, but it soon spread more widely. Essentially, speculators have begun to seek out high grade copies of the first appearances of many of Marvel's "cosmic heroes", which has driven prices on formerly quiet books through the roof. *Nova* #1 from 1976 has become a $40 book, with CGC 9.8 copies reaching above $500, while *Ms. Marvel* #1 from 1977 commands similar prices. Both of these books were seen as dollar bin fodder not too long ago… but if those prices shock you, consider that *Darkhawk* #1 from 1991, while still in the $3-$4 range raw, is now commanding $100 in CGC 9.8. Nor are the "cosmic" characters the only spot of activity. Other hot issues linked to upcoming big and small screen adaptations include *Marvel Premiere* Ant-Man appearances in #47 ($60) and #48 ($20), while the earlier *Marvel Premiere* #15 with the first Iron Fist appearance is now a $200 book. While this has been a flashpoint for collectors this year, the movie-linked price rises often appear fickle or random. Last year's focus on Thanos appearances has given way to a new fixation this year on Ultron appearances. The appearance of Bishop in X-Men movie trailers has helped drive up values of *Uncanny X-Men* #282, but the first appearance of Blink – who pops up in those same trailers – in *Uncanny X-Men* #317 has not been as popular. And while some books in this area do appear to hold their value once a movie's cinematic run is done, many drop in value as popular attention moves elsewhere. This whole phenomenon is to be approached with caution.

The other major beneficiary of the movie/TV hype has been Image Comics. The transformation of Image over the past few years has been truly remarkable, and it has clearly become the most diverse publisher in the field, with many of its titles demonstrating extremely high levels of quality. The company's multimedia success with *The Walking Dead* has both cemented its books as strong potential investments in the minds of collectors, and as a sound launching pad for new properties in the minds of creators. Over the past year, this combination has spawned hit after hit, as collectors seek out high quality titles. Frequently, an announcement that a series has been optioned for movies or is in development for television has been enough to kick off a feeding frenzy, as collectors race to get ahead of "the next Walking Dead." This has produced some remarkable back market hits over the past 18 months, including *Saga* #1 ($100), *Thief of Thieves* #1 ($60), *Manhattan Projects* #1 ($30) and *Peter Panzerfaust* ($200). These books remain hot, but all good things must come to an end. This success has prompted rising print runs at Image, with the net effect that many more recent titles, while extremely popular, appear to be available in sufficient quantities to meet demand. This has had two effects. First, top Image titles now routinely outsell many Marvel and DC titles in the new comic market. Second, many speculators have moved on to books from smaller publishers, with mixed success. And in the midst of all of this, it goes without saying that *Walking Dead* remains a juggernaut. While early issues have not seen the massive run-up in values associated with the past couple of years, all pre-#100 issues are in demand, with later issues in this timeframe continuing to increase.

© Vaughan & Staples

Numerous Image titles have benefitted from rumors of TV/Movie deals.

This may not come as a complete surprise to many, but the increasing popularity of books graded by 3rd parties is continuing to reshape the hobby in significant ways. First, it's important to note that although there are a number of companies providing 3rd party grading services, the market is clear that CGC is the benchmark in this area, and CGC-graded books normally command a premium over their same-grade counterparts graded by other companies. From a market perspective, though, graded and encapsulated books also shift the focus of collecting. Most obviously, an encapsulated book cannot be read – thus the focus of the collecting shifts from the content of a comic to the appearance of a comic. The most immediate impact of this change is a focus on comic covers as a driver of collectability, which – by extension – leads us to comic artists. In the early days of comic collecting, the artist was king – attaching names like Schomburg, Baker, Frazetta or Kirby to books could dramatically increase their collectability. This trend continued into the early 1990s, when names like McFarlane, Lee and Liefeld drove values and created a comic brand in Image whose very name argued the artists' supremacy in the comic world. During the comic book crash of the 1990s, as a bubble based on rampant speculation burst, collectors chided themselves for having embraced "style" over "substance." This created a counter-movement that increasingly celebrated the cult of the writer over that of the artist, and figures like Alan Moore and Neil Gaiman came to dominate the field in the way that artists once had.

When those writers' stories can't be read anymore (because they're sealed in plastic cases), the artist returns to the fore – and once again, value begins to be driven by artists. In the past year or two, there's been a dramatic return to collecting key artists. Neal Adams has probably been the biggest beneficiary of this process, as covers showcasing his work have begun to spike. This is particularly true of his DC covers, but seems to be slowly spreading more widely. Though prices aren't yet rising, there are signs that even his 1990s Continuity Comics titles are seeing some interest. The same process appears to be taking hold with Bernie Wrightson covers, though this is not yet as advanced. Todd McFarlane covers are once again hot, and particularly on those titles or issues not traditionally associated with his work, like *Conan* #245 or *Batman* #423. Dave Stevens covers continue to be popular, and attract attention, with many of his covers now genuinely hard to find in high grade. And J. Scott Campbell covers can rise dramatically, as seen on books like *Elephantmen* #18, *Superior Spider-Man* #20, or *Amazing Spider-Man* #s 601, 607 and 608. In this latter case, Campbell's large and growing volume of work can mitigate against price increases, but perceived scarcity still makes some issues spike on the back market.

This cover-driven phenomenon produces some other interesting shifts in back market values. Brian Bolland's classic cover for *Wonder Woman* #72 – frequently copied for posters and statues – has become a much-sought book. The stark white cover is particularly prone to yellowing, and is hard to find in grades above VF. True NM copies will often command $50-$75 or more. The fascinating part of this example, though, is that the heat from #72 has carried across Bolland's run of covers, and while few have seen large price increases yet, these issues (#63-100) are increasingly difficult to find. A similar process is underway with the covers of Adam Hughes. His iconic cover for *Catwoman* (2002) #51 – a riff on the television show Lost – now commands $30-$40, but the broader impact is that his entire *Catwoman* cover run (#43-83) is heating up. Hughes covers in general are doing well, with the final few issues of *Tomb Raider* (#48-50) in particular demand, at about $15-$20 each.

Of course, the other major change spurred by 3rd party graded books is a shift to top condition books. In the Bronze era and later, only the absolute highest grades are truly desirable. Anything below a 9.8 is unlikely to command any premiums, a far cry from the day when certain unnamed other price guides were suggesting formulae such as "CGC 9.6 = 12 times raw value". But beyond the number grade, the increasingly popular mantra is "Buy the book, not the grade." Page colour is increasingly significant in this context, for example, with "white" pages commanding a significant premium over "white/off-white" pages. Similarly, collectors are increasingly looking for well-centred covers and other contributors to "eye appeal". Some are showing a preference for unpressed books, though CGC's inability – or unwillingness (pick your conspiracy theory) – to identify such books means this trend may be short-lived.

Another area of rising interest this year has been scarcer early issues of long-running independent titles. Antarctic Press' *Gold Digger* recently passed issue #200, while Radio Comix' anthropomorphic anthology *Furrlough* – though only published erratically now – is nearing the same issue. *Gold Digger* #1 is easily a $100 book, while *Furrlough* routinely fetches $50 or more. Other increasingly valued titles include early issues of *Femforce*, *Knights of the Dinner Table*, *Cavewoman* and *Heavy Metal*, among many others. Many of these titles are not presently included in the *Guide*, which can lead to widely varying prices. It will be interesting to see if this trend accelerates, and if it reaches into other long-running but more mainstream titles. Possible winners in this scenario might include titles like *Tarot: Witch of the Black Rose*, *Witchblade* or *Grimm Fairy Tales*. First issues of these titles command significant premiums already, and can be hard to find, but many early issues may be slated for further rises.

In last year's report, I suggested that Copper and Modern reprints were attracting some interest, particularly with DC's "Roman numeral" reprint identification system from the early 1990s. While interest remained steady in these books (especially the "Death of Superman" and "Batman: Knightfall" issues), it was Marvel reprints that began to attract more attention this year. Particularly popular were Marvel's gold and silver metallic ink second prints from the early-to-mid-1990s. Titles like *New Mutants* #87 and *Amazing Spider-Man* #361 were leading this trend, as collectors realized that these 2nd (and later) printings were much scarcer than the originals. Other reprints continued to be strong as well, with the increasingly sought after *Incredible Hulk* #377 (third print) commanding some significant prices, including a CGC 9.8 copy that sold for $661 in September.

As always, I hope my observation and insights are helpful to those who work so diligently to prepare the *Guide*, and to collectors who may be seeking new information. I genuinely value and enjoy the reports that my fellow advisors take the time to prepare, and I hope that my own contributions add to our hobby. As always, I appreciate feedback, discussion and ideas!

Gary Dolgoff
Gary Dolgoff Comics

2013 was a banner year for buying collections. I notice that a portion of the collections that I'm being offered (and most often purchasing) are from: (a) collectors who are retiring, and (b) (sadly enough) from spouses of collectors who have passed away. What I'm doing is what I've always been into doing: taking the time to evaluate each collection that I look at, so that the seller gets a fair-market assessment and offer for their collection…and treating the collections with respect. I know it's a 'tough call' to sell it, for those who do.

Some of the collections I bought this year:

The 'Bullet-Batch' Collection (the seller made his own bullets!) - over 400 boxes of comics, 1960s to present, including the '#1-ups' of most of the major 1960s & up titles (from *Fantastic Four* #1 up to *Green Lantern* #1 up, etc.).

The 'Nick Collection' (he told me and my assistants entertaining tales of his colorful past) - over 600 boxes of 1960s & up, including 'minor multiples' of nice-shape 1960s Marvels, and also a plethora of sets/runs of a title. This seller, who was very forthright and successful, entertainingly enough collected everything from *Winnie The Pooh* and *Woodsy Owl* (both sets sold right away) to *Justice League of America* #1-up, and runs of the Silver Age *Cap, Hulk* and *Iron Man.*

The Terry Golden-Age Collection - At first, he was only going to sell me a few 'marginal titles', but when I told him that for his lower-grade copies, I would pay him 80% of *Guide* for his *Captain America* issues and his large-logo *Action* issues and 100% of *Guide* for his *U.S.A. Comics*, and so forth, to my great delight, he mailed me his '*Collection entire*'...(and I must brag), that I paid him a few thousand more than he expected! He told me so after I gave him my offer. I kept some of those Timely issues (including the *USA* comic, of course) for my Collection.

Connecticut GA Collection - I paid the guy and his wife about 70% of *Guide* for his group. It included *Superman* #5 (awesome cover!) through #17, *Batman* #3 through #19 (most issues), and a box plus more of these grand 'moldy oldies' (they were in FR/GD to VG for the most part. And I must say, they're "great to git in all grades!"

Upper Midwest Collection (about 30 boxes of mostly oldies) - The nice lady had runs of *Wow Comics, Marvel Family*, plus a couple of boxes of pre-superhero Marvels, which are always "stellar sellers."

Tennessee Collection - This lady had a "small but potent collection" which included a CGC 3.5 *Action* #13 (4th Superman cover - I got over 5x *Guide* for that!), a VF *Showcase* #4;, *Marvel Comics* #1 in CGC 0.5 ('twas missing the back cover, and a chunk outta the last 4 pages, but still, it's a *Marvel* #1!) and much, much more...plus a nice li'l stack of valuable Original Comic Art (including a few Frazetta pen and ink pages), which I happily bought.

Yes, this was "indeedy" an "extra-happy"year for buying, and I got to keep a nice stack of stuff for myself, as well. What makes the buying "even happier" is that I finally "got hip" and enlarged my Warehouse staff, almost doubling it in size from 5 able assistants to 9 of 'em! I say that "It takes a village" to get my warehouse properly processed and get a decent amount of my stuff up for sale. Plus they're a good "jaunty batch of folks" to work with on a daily basis.

Golden Age (1930s - mid '50s): Timelys and early issues of *Action* and *Detective* - I've been finding that most of these go for well above *Guide* - so I've increased what I'm willing to pay on these, mostly to 80% of *Guide* and up, even on lower-grade issues (plus "I love 'em!")

Other DC Golden Age Superhero is solid-selling, for *Guide* or more, across-the-board, in all grades.

Fawcett, Quality, etc. sell generally for 80% of *Guide* or more for later '40s, *Guide* for early 1940s.

MLJ titles have been getting "more exotic-seeming" lately, with a number of them going for over *Guide*, especially *Hangman Comics*!

Pre-Code Horror sells great for *Guide*, sometimes more. I got 3x *Guide* for a later issue of a 'horror' *Venus* comic.

Crime Comics - many of them don't sell as briskly as one would think...at *Guide* or less.

Westerns, and especially Humor oldies, sell slowly for the most part...and often have to be moved for well under *Guide*.

Silver Age: Marvel's main titles (*Amazing Spider-Man, X-Men, Avengers, Fantastic Four, Incredible Hulk*, and *Iron Man*) as well as Marvels in general from 1964 and earlier, are such strong sellers, in all grades! (especially *Amazing Spidey* - the "strongest seller of all.")

The Sideline Titles (such as *Marvel Tales, Not Brand Ecch*, etc.) have been selling for 80% of *Guide* or so, but doing well enough by selling them in sets/runs.

Pre-Hero Marvels are great sellers in all grades, "across-the-board" (and have great stories and art by Kirby and Ditko!) They consistently sell, often for 20% over *Guide*. I've been getting over *Guide* - and often paying *Guide*, or close (sometimes more than *Guide*!)- for the #1 issues/1st appearances (*Amazing Fantasy* #15; *Amazing Spider-Man* #1; *Avengers* #1; *Daredevil* #1; *Fantastic Four* #1; *Incredible Hulk* #1; *Journey Into Mystery* #83 (1st app Thor), *Sgt. Fury* #1, *Strange Tales* #110 (1st Dr. Strange), *Tales Of Suspense* #39 (1st Iron Man), *Tales To Astonish* #27 (1st Ant-Man), and *X-Men* #1.

I've also been getting nice prices for premiere appearances for the 1st appearance of Flash (*Showcase* #4), *Brave & the Bold* #28 (1st Justice League), and Green Lantern (*Showcase* #22), and other DC 1st appearances. For most 12 cent & 15 cent cover DCs, I prefer selling in runs when possible, and for many of these titles - when they are in GD/VG or less - I find that I must discount somewhat, in order to keep sales of those "flowing" (except for the strongest titles, such as *Batman* and *Detective*). When Silver Age DCs are in strong VG or better, I often get *Guide* for those, as they usually appear in "read" condition.

Other non-DC/Marvel (1956-1971): 1960s Archie's sell on the slow side – although I don't advertise them much. Early 1950s and back Archie titles sell okay, especially in VG and better. Harvey comics also move 'so-so', except for *Richie Rich* #1 and a few other "early appearance" issues which can move okay, especially the #1s in nicer shape.

Bronze Age: *Amazing Spider-Man* #102-150 sell well, as do *X-Men* #94-142, and *Batman* #262 and earlier. *Detective Comics* #400 continues to be somewhat elusive and much sought-after.

Generally, the more popular titles sell well throughout the Bronze Age, and I have trouble keeping the early 1970s mainline Marvels, *Batman* and *Detective Comics* in stock.

Also, early to mid-1970s Horror comics (*House of Mystery, House of Secrets*, etc.) sell well enough (and one of the greatest reads of all-time in comics (in my opinion) is the 'immortal' Marvel – *Tomb of Dracula* #1-70 series). Me and my pal Joey still re-iterate with enthusiasm, 'For I am Dracula, Dracula, Dracula – lord of the undead'!!

I also find that for a lot of '70s titles, I sell well enough in sets/runs, especially the '70s Marvel titles ('most everything from Black Panther to Invaders).

Recent Comics (mid-1980s thru the 2000s): My enthusiasm for purchasing these babies has somewhat increased over the last year (especially with my increased staff who process them in droves.) I find that a growing number of my customers (both older, and newer) are enjoying buying these goodies, especially as runs-of-titles. I have bought and sold many thousands of these over the past year. As long as I can afford to "sell 'em cheap", especially in "quantity of an issue number", then it is worth buying! In all, I have around 10,000 *X-Men* issues between #s 145-200. I'm definitely a "long-term-fella".

Original Art: This year, I got lucky and got a small, but nice, Art Collection (including a few Frazetta pieces!) I hope to get more by paying "real good money" for Art when I run across it. Comic Art has jumped up in value over the last couple of decades in general, and why not, since "each piece is unique."

eBay and my Future Website: I've developed quite a following on eBay ('gdcomics'), and though their ever-changing rules are, shall we say, challenging, I do well with it. Sellers can (I must say, immodestly) trust my "gd-grading." I'm hoping to finally get my new website developed by the time you read this, or not too long after that.

Have a gr-reat comic book year!

Ken Dyber
Cloud 9 Comics

Greetings, time for another market report already. For those of your unfamiliar with Cloud 9, I am a dealer located in Portland, OR selling at conventions, and through my website *www.cloudninecomics.com*. (Cloud 9 is not a brick & mortar store). You can email me whenever at: ken@cloudninecomics.com or find my eBay listings under: Tasteecat, or on a VERY seldom occasion on the CGC chat boards under: Cloud9. The CGC boards are an increasingly valuable resource for people to find information or trade/sell comics, however it seems every time I say something, the responses are overly bitter or negative, so I try and stay away from dialogues and just read what's already posted. Hopefully this attitude/trend on the boards will change, as we're all in this together, and the more negative words you exhale onto others, the more word gets around (This after all, is a relatively small world we're involved in). So for pete's sake, stay positive!

The Year Overall: This year was a little down for me compared to last sales wise, but fairly close overall. Convention sales were down overall with a few exceptions being Portland & San Diego which were up & flat respectively. Portland though was up I think only because Wizard debuted a show, and Rose City expanded their size significantly (out two major weekend shows). San Diego was down considerably for the first 4 days from last year, but Sunday was quite strong, and I can only associate this with the fact that there were no panels, freebies, movie previews, contests, etc... when all that "stuff" is done at San Diego, people actually start spending money! Maybe San Diego could help their dealers by doing a few things like: A) Make it easier for attendees to attend & B) Only do these panels, celebrity guests, movie/video game previews, etc... all in the AM, and then in the PM let people filter out on the floor to shop. I have heard they are expanding the show floor next year, so we'll see how that affects things.

Regarding conventions, I've had several major dealers talk with me at shows stating that they are no longer setting up at shows at all, or maybe only their local show(s), as it's not worth it to them, as the show promoters are now asking on average around $800-$1300 for a 10x10 booth, with some shows like NY and San Diego around $2000 now! Then there are additional costs for all dealers of airfares, driving or shipping your inventory, the awful "drayage" costs by the local unions ($150 to fork lift my one pallet off a truck & bring it to my booth which takes all of 5 minutes to do... geez, I'm in the wrong biz, as that's about $1500 an hour!). These dealers now just come to shop, and then resell either at their store, or online on their websites or eBay. I ironically also am having more and more collectors/shoppers at conventions come up saying "Where are all the comic book dealers?" I think a majority of you non-dealers out that do not realize just how expensive it is for dealers to set up at shows between the costs of the booth, airfare, gas, freight, drayage, and sale tax, it is far from "easy money". I'm hoping some show promoters read this and consider freezing their continued annual increase of booth costs; as they are far outpacing inflation, and in reality, pricing out many dealers. I myself will be setting up at fewer shows in 2014 for this exact reason. Also, customers/collectors... please buy something at a show. I find it hard to believe you cannot find something you're excited about at a show. I certainly have never found a show without quite a few buying opportunities. If you do not support the dealers, they will stop showing up. Please, do not get me wrong, this is not a rant, but really quite an important point, as I feel that cons are reaching their peak either now, or in the near future, as all things go in cycles, as the costs will become too high, so less dealers will attend, and then collectors/shoppers will get frustrated, and then they'll stop coming, and then the con will begin to contract, and there will be no benefit to anyone.

Another trend at shows in the increase annually of the "Cosplay" crowd. Sure, I can see how it would be fun to dress up as your favorite character to walk around taking photos at a con. The thing that I find quite odd is that a very large majority of these people attending cons do not seem to be buying much. They are attending more for the social aspects (which there's nothing wrong with of course). But of the 7 shows I did this year, and the thousands of comics I sold at those shows, I think I can count the numbers of sales to people in costumes, and I sell all kinds of comics at shows, from $1 comics or high grade, keys & CGC books from the Golden Age to *Walking Dead*. This equates to high ticket sales for show promoters, but no real increase in sales to dealers. I love going to cons, as I grew up doing this, but I'm worried that there are some important underlying trends here that a majority of the general buying public isn't aware of, that could directly affect them, and over time, begin to diminish the enjoyment of attending cons, as there will be less of a variety of dealers setting up. This could lead to cons fractioning off, where say all the comic dealers stop setting up, and they begin a new much smaller size con of just comic book dealers, which has already happened in a few markets.

As for other things this past year… not much in the way of record prices compared with other years, and in fact, I've seen some very large percentage drops in blue-chip key issues, especially in the Silver Age high grade segment (bit more on this in the Silver Age section). If you're looking to purchase a book as an investment, flipping it in a few years or less could be a higher risk then initially thought. If you're purchasing an *Amazing Spider-Man* #1 to put away for your kids' college fund for 15 years, you should be alright, as almost all keys seems to flatten out for a few years or even drop some (just like the Gold, housing, stock market, etc…), but over the longer term, they have been showing quite consistent gains. GPAnalysis tracking system of CGC certified comics continues to be a valuable resource, and for serious collectors the $10 a month cost seems well worth it for the sale data available. However… I'm actually using this website less than I did a few years ago, as ComicLink, and quite a few dealers do not report their sales to this website, nor do they track all eBay sales, or raw books, or PGX books. So their data is far from complete. Quite a few sales are "luck of the draw" so to speak… presents for loved ones, where the buyer doesn't know the comic market at all, impulse buys, arbitrary location on a show floor at con (someone buys a *Hulk* #181 for $500, then an hour later "discovers" another dealers booth, who has a similar graded copy for $400). There is *Guide* pricing, GPAnalysis history, and then there is "other". On a piece chart these could arguably be split directly into thirds from a market share standpoint. So… what does this mean… to me, not only as a seller, but as a collector myself, if I see something I like, especially something uncommon, now is becoming more of a "gotta have" time period? Certain books, especially pre-Silver Age are setting their own rules when it comes to pricing. If, as a buyer, I see a dealer asking 5x *Guide* & 2x GPAnalysis for a Fine copy of a rare book, I may still look at it a good buy/investment with legs to grow in the immediate future. Some, but not all of this logic could be the page quality (which is becoming increasingly important), eye appeal, registry, staple condition, and sure it has defects, as we're talking about a Fine/6.0 copy, but what are the defects (piece missing, stain, small tear, creasing, etc…), also, are the defects mostly on the front or back or interior, etc… Many Golden Age Fine copies actually present better than a 7.0 or even 7.5 copy depending on what the defects are (ie: technical grade vs. eye appeal/presentation). That could be the reason why a CGC 6.0 copy sold for $1500 and a CGC 7.0 copy sold for $1400 (given both are in the relative same sale period/year). OK, here are some specifics on time periods…

Golden Age: Crime books… Not hot yet, but watch out, they are loaded with violent covers and stories, and have been ignored by collectors/dealers for some time now. Vastly undervalued and under the radar for years compared to their Superhero, Good Girl and Horror counterparts. Classic covers/key issues though… these are red hot! A *Crime SuspenStories* CGC 9.2 selling for $17,000 (not even the highest graded!). *Fight Against Crime* #20 is a much tougher book, and if a 9.2 copy was ever graded watch out for a jaw dropping sale (At the time of this writing 3x 7.5 copies are tied for the highest graded). A raw VF/VF+ copy sold on eBay for $6122 in November. I own a CGC 7.0 of this book, and that raw copy didn't look much, if any better than my graded 7.0 copy. Yet, 7.0 copies according to GPA are going for maybe around $4K at present. So... if that ones does hit the market again soon as a CGC 8.0 or 8.5… what do you think $8-10K? Also, this book should go up 200-300% in *Guide*, and be listed in the top 3 in the Top 10 Crime section in the front of *Guide*. *Crime Does Not Pay* #24 is also going through the roof, and has now surpassed #22 in value/demand, although #22 is a very tough book, brutal covers seem to be jumping leaps and bounds in demand at present. These are my "Big 3" of the Crime books, there are quite a few others, but if you're looking to invest, these are your blue-chips.

©WMG
Crime comics with classic covers, like **Crime SuspenStories #22, are red hot.**

Good girl books (GGA) are also still, which is quite shocking, undervalued, and many issues/titles need huge corrections in the *Guide*. *Fighting Yank* #21 is a classic cover (lingerie cover), and should be noted as such in the *Guide*. Mid-grade copies are going for around $1000 at present (*Guide* is currently at $195 for Fine/6.0). So that's around 6x *Guide* for mid-grade! Issue #23 is also a classic cover, and reminds one of *Suspense Comics* #3 with its woman sacrifice cover by those hooded villains. This one is selling around $600-$800 for mid-grade copies (*Guide* is $267 for Fine/6.0). That's 2.5-3x *Guide* for mid-grade copies of that one. Both are great covers, although I do think issue #21 has already surpassed #23 in demand, and is quickly becoming one of the most sought after GGA covers of all time. Fans of *Blue Beetle* #54 in particular may like this book for their collections. *Phantom Lady* #23 is also in need of a major price adjustment upwards in *Guide*. VF/8.0 copies are selling for around $11K! *Guide* is $1856. Ah… to say the *Guide* is off on this book would be a dramatic understatement. That's 5x *Guide* for VF copies. The CGC Census has only one 9.2 & two 8.0's copies graded. Doubling this book in *Guide* in all grades would be a good start, but still be considerably off.

A book to get now is *Thun'da* #1. This is the only comic drawn entirely by Frazetta, AND, it's a classic headlight cover! A CGC 9.6 sold in November 2013 for just under $14K, with a CGC 9.4 for $9K in 2010, however, mid-grade Fine to Very Fine copies currently can be bought for around $800. This is a huge spread between the scarce high grade copies, and these very nice mid-grade ones. Do not be surprised if these mid-grade copies you've been ignoring for years, all of a sudden begin selling for around $2K. *Junior Comics* are sought after across the board, and do not sell for quite as jaw-dropping prices, but are almost never available for sale at shows. The series across the board has killer covers and stories, but is lacking that one iconic cover to elevate the entire series, but as a series, it may be the strongest of all the GGA titles.

Looking to invest in the Golden Age but can't afford the obvious big ticket keys (ie: *Action* #1, *Detective* #27, etc.)? Classic covers are a great place to start. In addition to some of the titles listed above, you can go with Hitler/Nazi covers, Marvel Timelys (mostly *Cap* & *Marvel Mystery*), *Weird Tales of the Future* #2 & 5, *Captain Flight* #11, *Fight Comics* #31, *Pep* #22 and *Archie* #1 are just a few.

My one sleeper pick is *Batman* #139 (1st app. Bat-Girl) needs its own line listing, and should move upwards by about 20% in all grades. *Detective* #359 in the Silver Age (1st Barbara Gordon as Batgirl) is red hot in all grades, and I feel this book is flying a bit under the radar, however when I do get it in stock, it does sell quickly and almost always for my above *Guide* asking price.

Silver Age: DC Keys are starting to heat up again, especially female characters with *Action* #252 and *Detective* #359 jumping upwards on a monthly basis. *Adventure* #247 (1st Legion) has been slow for several years now, but still never seems to be on dealer walls at shows. Now is a GREAT time to buy this book if you can find a copy above VG, as lower grade copies are still on eBay fairly regularly. Imagine a Legion futuristic sci-fi movie staring someone like Jennifer Lawrence (*Hunger Games*)? Remember, the Legion is a teenager club, and Hollywood has been moving more towards teenage driven blockbusters (*Hunger Games* and *Ender's Game* are recent examples). This book for sure will never attain that status again, but is extremely scarce in high grade, and as we've seen in recent years, all it takes is one jaw dropping sale, or one internet announcement (or even rumor... hey, they're making a Legion movie!... oh no, I just started a rumor!) to get everyone excited about a book again. Mark my words... there will be a Legion movie, and the longer DC waits to do it, the better, as I do feel DC is starting to move in the right direction with their films. If... yes if... the Justice League movie kills it, which we're all hoping for (the DC equivalent of *The Avengers*), well then... books like *Wonder Woman* #1, *Showcase* #4, *Flash* #105, *Detective* #225, and *Action* #252 could all be moving not just upward, but way upwards.

On the Marvel side I already mentioned *Strange Tales* #110 is blazing hot, as is *Tales to Astonish* #27 (1st Ant Man). I think *Tales to Astonish* #44 (1st Wasp) is a great buy right now, and set to take off. This book pre-dates many of the other Marvel superheroes, and she's a very important player in the Marvel universe (even leading the Avengers for a period). Also, *Tales of Suspense* #52, which is still quite a hot book, has legs to increase in value significantly due to all the Black Widow's movie appearances (and having Scarlett Johanson play the character doesn't hurt either). As for the possibly most in-demand book from this time period, other dealers may disagree, but I think *Incredible Hulk* #1 is now more in demand than *Amazing Fantasy* #15. It's less common, and sells faster when I get them in stock, and I have more people asking for it than *AF*15s at shows, mostly due to them being harder to find. This past year a CGC 9.0 sold for $120,000 on ComicLink, who don't report their sales to GPA.

Batman #153 should have its own line listing, as this is a book length story with Bat-Girl & Batwoman starring throughout it. It is also the first time Robin & Bat-Girl kiss! I suggest a 10-20% mark up across all listings for this one as Bat-Girl & Batwoman issues sell faster than issues they do not appear in.

Lastly, as I mentioned before... the game of flipping big time keys/investment grade books has become a bit more risky. Let's start with *AF*15's... CGC 8.5's: 2008 sale: $118,977 sale, 2009 sale: $104,563, 2010 sale: $108,000 & $105,000, and 2011 sales of $110,000 & $107,000. No sales in 2012 or 2013... Think about that... 6 years with around a 9% loss on that book! *Amazing Spider-Man* #1 in CGC 9.4: 2009 sale: $104,200 then another sale 5 months later for $83,650, 2013 sale: $93,964. I'd say hardly consistent on gains there. *Journey Into Mystery* #83 in CGC 9.4 (highest graded): 2012 sale: $222,200, 2013 sales: $171,000 & then another at $185,500. For the record... the $222,200 & $185,500 sales are of the exact same comic (same CGC serial #). That's almost a $40K loss in one year. I could go on and on, and of course, these books all had comparable jumps in growth (dot com'ish), but there was a period where they seemed as an automatic sure-thing investment with immediate return, now one must pay quite a bit more attention before dropping that kind of money.

Bronze Age: I've seen interest in this period drop dramatically in the last few years for common books/non keys. Key issues are probably my best sellers, many of which I can't keep in stock, but most non-keys, unless 9.6/9.8 ish copies or Good/2.0 copies have to be sold in bulk or at 1/2 off to even get any interest. DC Horror though does seem to continue to sell well in all conditions as this is some of the best artwork not only from the Bronze Age, but arguably from all time periods.

Hero For Hire #1 needs a dramatic price increase in *Guide*, as this is one of my best selling comics from any time period. I constantly find myself sold out. I recommend a 100% increase in guide for Good – Fine and a 50% increase for VF – NM grades in *Guide*, with further upward adjustments needed next year. A CGC 9.8 recently sold for $4300! NM-/9.2s are going for around $500 at present (66% above *Guide*). VGs have been selling for $50 for me without a blink (*Guide* is $26).

Detective Comics and *Batman* continue to be some of the best-selling books from this time period in all grades, especially the Batman issues. *Detective* #411 (1st Talia) has been hot for years, and needs about a 50% increase in *Guide* in all grades. The book has cooled slightly, as more people have finally discovered this one, but still a strong seller. *Batman* #227 has finally slowed down a bit and stabilized. But issues #232 and 234 both fly off the shelves, especially #232. Keep an eye on this book (#232 – 1st Ra's al Ghul (Talia's father)), as in my humble opinion, this one just seems WAY undervalued given what great characters the Ghul family are. It's a classic Neal Adams cover, and another book I just can't keep in stock. CGC 9.8s seem a great buy right now hovering around $2000-$2500.

Amazing Spider-Man #121 & 122 both continue to sell quite fast in all grades, and need further upward adjustments, especially #121 (Death of Gwen Stacy), as the demand for this book is almost 2x, and should be reflected as a higher price point in *Guide* over #122 (maybe 10% higher in *Guide*). #129 (1st Punisher) continues to sell quickly, but has stalled at higher pricing tiers (should move up still 25-50% in Good-Fine grades) for the last few years, however #194 (1st Black Cat) is red hot, and needs a 25-50% increase in *Guide* in all grades. Bronze *Spideys* continue to sell well, and I'm seeing a great sign of things to come here: teenagers are buying these! Almost every show I did this year I had a boy or two (usually out with their mother, father, or sometimes with other friends), buying several copies of either late Silver Age or Bronze Age books in the $30-$60 range per book! I go out of my way to be nice to teenagers, as they are the future in the collectibles field, and they seem to have increased buying power these days (I was once in their shoes, having first set up as a dealer myself in CT at the ripe age of 13!).

Iron Man #94 is a Jack Kirby cover, and should have a separate line listing noting it as such. Also, issue 96 (1st new Guardsman) should have its own line listing with NM- pricing at $20.

Spire Christian Comics continue to be strong sellers in all grades with many people attracted to them for their strange stories/titles, with some people trying to collect them all, and others simply finding that one oddball title that works for them. All titles in all grades should go up with a suggested line listing for most titles of $3, $5, $7, $10, $12 $15. *Hansi* in particular is quite popular, and is the most requested and valuable by far.

Copper/Modern Age: Ah… the Copper Age… when does it begin & end?? Some say 1980s. eBay has it from 1984-1991, which to me seems like a strange and arbitrary time period to select. To me, maybe a better choice is Perez's reintroduction of the Teen Titans with *New Teen Titans* #1 (Nov. 1980), which is also the same year cover prices became $.50. As for when this time period ends, I've always associated it with the new publisher boom of Image and Valiant, among quite a few others of course. Image was founded in 1992 and Valiant's first set of original titles (*Harbinger*, *X-O Manowar*, *Rai* and *Shadowman*) were also launched this year. So this would put this time period from 1980-1992, and these seem to be logical markers for the beginning and end of this period. Another possible ending to the Copper/beginning to the Modern Age could be Todd McFarlane's launch of *Spider-Man* #1 in 1990. I do feel though that more people consider the smaller publisher boom as the beginning of the Modern Age, which would be 1992. I'm sure this will be open for debate for years, but the definitions of this period have always felt a little unclear to me, as per say when the Silver Age begins (the reintroduction of superheroes with *Showcase* #4). If anyone has better suggestions, I'm all ears, so give me a shout via email sometime or at a convention (just don't shout AT me!).

Now, with that said… this could now be the hottest time period in comics (I know, I can't believe I'm saying this either), but only for the "In-the-know" crowd at this point. So many stores and dealers have ignored these books for so long, there are tremendous buying opportunities here. I have to start off by saying HARLEY QUINN!! All appearances are hot. Line listings need to be made for all early appearances. Here are some of my suggested pricing and line listings: *The Batman Adventures* (1992 series) #12 (1st app.) should move up to $150 for NM- (and will probably grow next year). Other appearances in this series include *Annual* #1 (3rd appearance) $20 & #28 (4th appearance) $18. Additionally, *Batman Adventures Mad Love* TPB is the 2nd appearance and 1st origin of Harley Quinn with as far as I know, 3 printings, all of which are selling well. I suggest NM- listings for this: $50 (1st), $25 (2nd), $10 (3rd). *Batman & Robin Adventures* has 2 early appearances that I know of: #5 (Joker/Harley cover/story along with a Poison Ivy appearance ($10) and #8 ($8). *Batman Adventures* (2003 series) also has Harley Quinn appearance in #3 (cover with Joker) $10. Lastly, a series almost completely under the radar (except for Harley fans) is *Batman: Gotham Adventures* (1998 series) with appearances in issues #10, 14, 29, 43 & 45 (All $10). I am hardly by any means a Harley Quinn fan, or claim to be an expert, so I'm guessing I've missed some other early appearances, but in general, they all need line listings with at least $10 for NM- to bring the *Guide* up to market on this character.

A prime example, and one of my investment picks… *Avengers* #196, the first full Taskmaster, and in my humble opinion, a classic cover from this time period (also his first cover appearance). CGC 9.8s are going for around $300 at present with mid-grade raw copies going on eBay for around

$20. However... there are only around an average of 8 copies of CGC 9.8s selling a year at present. I'm sure this number will increase significantly as more copies are slabbed (no thanks to me!), but this is still a 34 year old comic, so don't expect that number to go into the hundreds. This character has loads of potential in the Marvel Universe and is still way under-used appearance wise. Issues #195 & #196 need to be separated in the *Guide*, with a suggested NM- line listing of $15 and $40 respectively, with probably an upward adjustment in next year's *Guide* by at least 50% from there.

Another series from the Copper/Modern period that is tremendously undervalued is the *Agent X* series with Deadpool and Taskmaster appearing in its 15 issues. Complete sets are only going for around $40-$50 at present, so keep an eye on these books. Deadpool... what can one say, *New Mutants* #98 is the *Hulk* #181 for the younger generation and is probably the 4th most popular superhero (if you can even call him that) behind Spider-Man, Batman & Wolverine. The original 1997 69 issue series needs some major price adjustments in the *Guide*. The entire series needs line listings as NM- copies of ANY issue sell around $7/$8. Key issues are now much more clearly defined so here are my suggestions on NM- prices (although I'm sure I've missed a few keys or am a bit off on some prices): #1 $40 #2 $20, #3&4 $15, #5-10 $12, #11 $35, #12-26 $7, #27 $15, #28-36 $7, #37 $15, #38-41 $7 #42 $30, #43 $7, #44 $22, #45-50 $7, #51&52 $12, #53 $6, #54 $55, #55 $40, #56&57 $10, #58-64 $7, #65 $30, #66-68 $15 #69 $25 & both Annuals $25. As for Deadpool's 2008 63 issue series, the key issues are not as clearly defined here, but #1 could have a lined listing of $15 as a good starting point. The two four issue mini-series should both come up by double in *Guide* at a minimum with sales for the entire sets going for $20-$40 on eBay any given day.

©DC

Batman Adventures: Mad Love starring Harley Quinn is getting LOTS of attention.

Also going through the roof is *New Mutants Annual* #2 with CGC 9.8s going for around $350 and raw NM- copies going for around $60. Same is true for *X-Factor* #6. These are books that went from being $5-$10 NM- raw comics that didn't have much demand, to going for $50 or more almost overnight. *Spawn* #9 (1st Angela) is another to keep your eye on. *Thor* #344 (1st Malekith) has jumped to a $125 CGC 9.8 book and has room to grow. *Tales of the Teen Titans* #44 (Dick Grayson becomes Nightwing) is selling quite well in all grades with CGC 9.8s going for around $225. *Superman: The Man of Steel* #18 (1st full Doomsday) has also really picked up, and needs to jump in *Guide* to around $35 for NM- copies, with CGC 9.8s going for around $150 with room to grow. This one I've always been a big fan of, and think it could easily become a $300 book in 9.8 sooner then we'd expect. Think about how many strong villains Superman has... yeah... not many. I'm really only hitting on books that are clearly established with sales history though. What about *Alpha Flight* #33, 1st Lady Deathstrike? This was a tremendously popular series during the heart of the Copper Age with 130 issues (more than *New Mutants*, *New Teen Titans*, *Transformers* which all have bonafied key issues). This book doesn't even have a line listing in the *Guide*? CGC 9.8s are actually selling for the exact same as *Thor* #344s, yet, this book isn't getting near the hype. Raw copies can still be found in $1 bins at shows. There must be other keys in this series (#51 for example is Jim Lee's first Marvel work, and first work on Wolverine). For the last year or two, I've been buying more comics from the 1980s and 1990s than I ever have before. Most are still worth next to nothing, but there are many going up 1000% in just a few months for one reason or another (ie: $3 to $30).

Simpsons Comics #1 should move up to $25 for NM-/9.2. Valiant's *Solar Man of the Atom* #1 should go up to $20 for NM-/9.2 and #10 should go up to $25 for NM-/9.2. This issue #10 commands big money for 9.8s, which presently are going for around $400! Dark Horse's *Predator* #1 from 1989 (1st appearance) should go up to $25 in NM-/9.2 with 9.8s trading for around $125.

As for X-Men, finally there seems to be a break-out book from their Modern age (vol. 2 1991) series. *New X-Men* #128 (becomes titled *New X-Men* with issue #114) is the first appearance of Fantomex. This book warrants a NM- line listing of $25, and may need to up moved upward in next year's *Guide* if it continues to perform well. This is just a brief appearance towards the end of the issue. Issue #129 also needs a separate line listing of $10 at NM-, as this is the first full appearance and first cover of Fantomex. Could this character become the next Deadpool? Remember what happened to *New Mutants* #98 about 6 years ago. These are books that can most likely still be found in dollar boxes. Also in the X family, *X-Factor* #6 (1st full Apocalypse) has exploded selling around $50 in NM-. Issue #5 sells well too, but for much less. This price break makes me think *New X-Men* #129 is way undervalued at present, and may one day surpass #128, especially with the character on the cover. *X-Factor* #24 (1st full Archangel) is also selling quite well, and should move upwards in *Guide* to maybe $35 in NM-, as should *X-Factor* #1, which should have a line listing of $15 in NM-.

Wolverine (1st series) #154 & 155 (Liefeld covers) both deserve line listings of $15 in NM-, as these are Deadpool cover/stories with CGC 9.8s of both going for around $60-$75. *Avengers* #257 (1st Nebula – Guardians of the Galaxy) needs its own line listing in the *Guide*, with a NM- price of $10.

Iron Man issues #271-275 are the Dragon Seed Saga where Iron Man (both Jim Rhodes and Tony Stark) battle

Fin Fang Foom and the Mandarin. Fin Fang Foom's first appearance in *Strange Tales* #89 is possibly one of the toughest Silver Age keys to find in any grade (let along high grade), and is always a quick seller, so keep an eye on the value/demand for this story line. Issues #271 and 274 are Fin Fang Foom covers, and the entire five issue story line is quite good. Also, issue #279 is a cover story vs. Ronan The Accuser, whose first appearance in *Fantastic Four* #65 has a lot of people speculating on a movie appearance soon. Look for demand to possibly increase for these issues.

All issues of *The Walking Dead* continue to sell quite well. Issue #1 seems to have finally cooled off and stabilized in price in almost all grades with 9.8s dropping under $2,000 for the time being. Issues #2 and #3 though both seem to be moving up substantially in value, especially in 9.8, with #2s going for around $1,000, and #3s going for around $600. A line listing needs to be added for issue #33, which I think will become remembered as a classic cover in the run, and story. This issue in which Michonne brutally tortures the Governor sells quite fast whenever we get them in. I suggest a NM- listing of $50. Also, issue #48 needs to be updated in the *Guide* to state that it is the "Death of the Governor" in addition to the deaths of Lori, Herschel & others. This is one of the most brutal/disturbing issues in the series, and should move up to $60 in NM-.

Teenage Mutant Ninja Turtles #1 has heated up again in a big way, with CGC 9.2/NM- copies going for around $3500-$4000 and mid-grade copies for $1200-$1800. I think I must ask this every year… Can we please put a line listing in this *Guide* for *TNMTs* #1?!! $3500 for NM-/9.2 would be dead on for a starting point. Prices DO NOT vary wildly on it, they are very consistent. Thank you very much.

Last year I suggested a new COPPER/MODERN AGE TOP 25 section in the front of the *Guide*, as this is our most traded section of the market. Here are my suggestions for the list (updated from last year although not published in the guide last year). These prices are based off raw & slabbed sales throughout the past several years of online & convention sales (I'm sure I forgot some, but this is a great starting point):

1. *Gobbledygook* #1: $6000
2. *Teenage Mutant Ninja Turtles* #1: $3500
3. *Gobbledygook* #2: $2500
4. *Miracleman* #1 Gold Edition: $1200
5. *Walking Dead* #1: $1000
6. *Albedo* #2: $950
7. *Bone* #1: $650
8. *Miracleman* #1 Blue Edition: $600
9. *Vampirella* #113: $500
10. *Batman* #608 Retailer Incentive Edition: $400
11. *Walking Dead* #2: $325
12. *Chew* #1: $300
13. *Walking Dead* #19: $275
14. *Walking Dead* #27: $225
15. *Walking Dead* #3: $200
16. *Amazing Spider-Man* #300: $180
17. *Knights of the Dinner Table* #1: $175
18. *Primer* #2: #$170
19. *Grendel* #1: #$160
20. *New Mutants* #98: 160
21. *Walking Dead* #4: $150
22. *Batman Adventures*: $150
23. *Y The Last Man* #1: $130
24. *Peter Panzerfaust* #1 $125
25. *The Goon* #1 $120
25. *Cry For Dawn* #1 #120

Magazines: As the trend continues with various magazine titles being CGC'd (*Playboy* & *Sports Illustrated* for example), I do think the *Guide* needs to include more magazines that have been associated with the comic book scene. *Famous Monsters of Filmland* is an obvious example that should be included in the *Guide*. If *Eerie*, *Creepy* and *Vampirella* are in this guide (all Warren Magazine publications), then why isn't *Famous Monsters* (also Warren Magazine)? I know the *Guide* has been focused on U.S. comics, but I think a very strong case can be made for including *Warrior Magazine* (UK), as the first appearances of V For Vendetta & Miracleman (Marvel Man) can be found here, among others. I've found most of these magazines are in demand, but not for terribly high prices (almost comparable to Archies in this regard from the same time period). Depending on grade, time period, $3, $5 & $10 for lower grade copies tends to get them moving quick, with $20-$25 for higher grade. High grade (NM-/9.2) copies seem very low in *Guide* due to how scarce they are, however I honestly am not sure if the demand is currently there. Since a majority of these magazines are horror related, one would think due to the popularity of *The Walking Dead*, that horror fans would start going back and seeking out these great magazines from 4 to 5 decades earlier. Heck, there are people willing to pay $50 for a CGC 9.8 of some random newer issue of *Walking Dead* (say issue 82), which they can't even read. One could buy 2 or 3 high grade copies from one of these horror magazines from 30-40 years ago for the same price and be able to read them. Humans sure do love reading about and watching monsters on TV/Film, so this is a market segment to really start looking at closer.

Thanks to everyone that's read my market report, visited the website, and said hello at one of the cons. I look forward to meeting more of you, and another year in the hobby!

BILL FIDYK
COLLECTOR

In the area of comic magazines—the raccoon is king! With the current *Guardians of the Galaxy* movie speculation running full throttle, *Marvel Preview* #4 and #7 are in very high demand. I sold a VF/NM copy of *Marvel Preview* #7 for $500 this year and thought it was an insane price to pay. However, I now see 9.0s selling for close to a thousand dollars. The price for *Marvel Preview* #4 has also skyrocketed. Not surprisingly, more copies of these two magazines have surfaced and have been brought to market in the past few months. In fact, I have seen more copies for sale now than I have in the past twenty years. I don't think these books are rare—I think they have been sitting in dealer warehouses and private collections for years. The movie hype has caused more people to notice them, dig them out and slab them. Speculators are shelling out big money to grab a copy before the movie comes out and the same people buying up these mags are turning around and flipping them for a quick profit. I also suspect that the prices on both of these mags will come back down to earth quickly after the movie is released. Honestly, how much more room do these magazines have to grow price wise? Will anyone really care about these characters in the long term? Do Rocket Racoon and Starlord have the same level of importance and significance to the Marvel Universe as Thanos does? I would proceed with caution and levelheadedness when purchasing these books. Nonetheless, I am very pleased that any comic in a magazine format is seeing this much attention.

Marvel/Curtis Magazines: The horror titles by Marvel seem to be in steady demand by Bronze horror collectors. *Monsters Unleashed*, *Vampire Tales*, *Tales of the Zombie* and *Dracula Lives* always seem to be at the top of collectors' lists due to the fact that many Bronze Age horror fans cross over into magazine territory looking for additional stories of favorite characters. However, one title that often gets overlooked is *Monsters of the Movies*. This title, which is Marvel's version of Warren's *Famous Monsters*, is a great read that primarily features articles on classic horror films and actors. What many people don't know is that issue one has a short six page comic in the first issue titled "The Demon that Devoured Hollywood" by Roy Thomas with Barry Windsor Smith art. Since it technically included comic art—it really should be listed in the *Guide*.

Warren Publishing: *Creepy*, *Vampirella* and *Eerie* are still the big three for Warren but are ironically only a small fraction of what the publisher put out. While *The Guide* lists a handful of issues of each title as being scarce due to low print runs—it seems that anything from issue #30-80 in *Creepy* is tough to find as well as issues #40-65 of *Eerie*. Mainly, many collectors go after certain artists featured in these titles. Anything with Wrightson and Corben art are always in demand as well as issues featuring a Frazetta cover. Most notably for me—*Creepy* #9,10,11 were amongst the hardest of the earlier issues to find for any of the Warren titles. Surprisingly, I finally managed to find all three this year but it took me years to find high grade copies. These magazines feature a ton of great stories and artwork and are always in steady demand.

Skywald: This is a publisher that only put out a small amount of magazines but also some of the most inventive. Issues continue to rise in price and these magazines are truly scarce. Truly Near Mint copies are almost impossible to find and fetch high prices. More and more, comic collectors are discovering these magazines and the great artists and writers that worked on them. Buckler, Byrne, Marcos and even Bill Everett just to name a few have been featured in these magazines. Very few slabbed copies are on the CGC census and very few come up for sale at all—even in low grade. I know many collectors that horde multiple copies of each title. If you see them, especially in high grade, grab them!

Paul M. Figura
Tenth Planet Comics and Games

When you own a comic shop, you have to make sure to have a few things in place first. Such as, a list of the people you can count on in times of need. First you should find a good lawyer, as an example, for when your loving wife isn't so understanding about why you do this. Next, a doctor, for those little stress relievers he prescribes for you, when you try to explain to your wife about how you spent the kid's college fund on a "can't miss" collection of gems. Last but not least, your psychiatrist for the reassurance of the *why* do you do this.

Speaking just about our little corner of the world and not retail nationwide, sales over the past few years, specifically in our market place has slowed to a snail's pace. The immediate surrounding area has 6 comic specialty stores, all within a 6 mile radius. That means every decision you make about products to carry monumental. The burden falls upon you to make the orders perfect. The store has to sell through everything ordered, to maximize your profit potential, getting the most out of every dollar spent. Do you take the chance of ordering enough to keep your shelf reasonably stocked in hopes that the casual consumer will eventually come back through, and keep spending in your store? All that aside, keeping your customers happy is key. Going that little bit above and beyond is what keeps them coming back. They have the ability to spend their hard earned money anywhere, so your goal is to keep them spending with you. Bring your personality with you, BE that person behind the bar that can converse with everyone. Business is business, and a little bit of personality goes a long way. I by NO means am claiming to be an expert on everything pertaining to comic retail. I am just another comic retailer, with some ideas on how to do things, and trying to keep my family stable. All while working a business that I have a passion for. If you don't have that fire burning, you might as well walk away now and keep your sanity. Or, as we like to say around the shop from time to time "We're just trying to be decent men in an indecent world!"

Loving what you do makes certain things easier. There was a time you could look at what a customer was buying and do some suggestive selling. Suggest a similar title, or storyline. If I felt strongly about the book I was recommending, I would just give the customer that particular issue to read and get them interested in the series. Such as, a belated wedding present, of *Walking Dead* Volume One to a friend and a customer, still has us laughing as he cursed me while buying volume nineteen. Right now with little to no walk-in traffic, that is getting harder and harder to do. Just know your customers. Something as simple as: greeting them by their first name as they walk in, knowing their likes and dislikes is what gives your store that personal touch. I look at all my customers and see friends, not just someone that comes in and shops with us. That makes the customers WANT to come back. Want to spend money in your store. It makes your store feel like home to them. A store that they look forward to visiting, as often as possible.

This brings us to the shaky economy. What does the retailer do? You need to create some excitement from the few people that still come in and shop. Most of them are on a limited budget. (Thank you one and all for still being the few remaining loyal customers!) You need to find those few desirable items that you can cross reference with the comics that customers still want and can afford!

Whether we like it or not, all comic specialty stores are in this together, from the big chain store, to the mom and pop neighborhood shops. Bitter feud driven rivals, and those friendly managed shops must work together to find a common solution. What fuels our passion and how we can relay those feelings to the general public may be the key. The answer is not in a movie; it is in that musty smelling paper that you hold in your hand marveling at the art of a past era. The future of the comic industry in general is depending upon us for the answer. We should be brothers helping brothers, find a way to unite shops, have open discussions on what problems we are facing and how best to cope with them. Can there be a doubt that the new shop in Hooterville is having a problem that any one of a hundred shops across the country, if not the world has already faced? Hopefully we haven't doomed ourselves yet. If something isn't said or done, and individual stores keep failing, and all that are left are the huge chain retailers, what does that mean to new or young collectors? There has to be more to this than just a dollar sign. Why did we get into this in the first place? All of us need to visit that part of ourselves again.

© Advance Mags.

*Dynamite has successfully brought back characters from the Pulp era. (**The Shadow** #22 shown)*

Will there be anyone left to fill that niche role? Common Man Comics! New and young readers welcome! As we review the trends and prices of comics, shouldn't we also be working to secure a healthier retail market, where individual specialty comic stores are the source of our information? Would that not promote a growth in the industry? Provided of course that the powers that be are also on the same page as the retailers, and listen to our voice.

To stay alive in the current state of economic affairs, our goal should be to make things fun and affordable once again for collectors. At the major conventions people are more than willing to drop money on all the current pop culture items, while the comic die-hards sit there with their huge displays of some really fantastic Gold and Silver back issues wondering if they are going to make their table costs. What prices are fair when someone has to pay $60 to $160 just to walk through the door? (Thanks Wizard).

DC Comics with the New 52 is trying hard to take back the spotlight that they held from the Golden through the Silver Eras. Some successes and a bunch of misses is what we are experiencing. The start of the New 52 had a ton of people jumping on board, although there were a lot of speculators just grabbing books in hopes of that rare gem. Now 2 years into this new universe, the line has been trimmed some, allowing the cream to rise to the top. Characters like Batman, have held strong sales, and the story lines have warranted it. The new creative team for *Aquaman* should be given high praises for the way they have re-invented that character, they have done such an amazing job taking a much maligned character and making him a force to be reckoned with, along with Mera! It is sad to say, even with a great story line with the H'el on Earth saga, that sales of Superman are not what they once were. How can you own such an iconic character and have it misfire time and time again? THAT needs to be looked at seriously.

Marvel on the other hand seems to be stuck in this endless loop of "BIG EVENTS" and are throwing them at us one after another (although, we here at the store are waiting for the big reveal next year in Marvel's Age Of Ultron that Walt Disney actually IS Ultron!). We are seeing more and more people getting tired of this and abandoning titles after the main story line is complete. Characters like Wolverine, while still popular, are on a decline due to a lot of overuse, and most people are still curious as to what this Marvel Now is all about.

There are some great independent comics now being distributed. Dynamite should be applauded for breathing new life into the characters of a bygone era of comics and pulps, The Shadow, Doc Savage, The Phantom, The Spider, Red Sonja; as well as Dark Horse with Conan, just to name a few. Conan has not had a great go of it since his hey day with Marvel. Now those books are a real latter day gem! But in the hands of the independent publisher, the casual comic people just see more titles instead of classic characters being brought about for a new generation. That shelf space is being taken up by the Image "let's throw as many titles at the wall and see what sticks" philosophy, and it is a horrible shame. It gets to be disheartening to see those titles get no recognition in an over-flooded independent market, for some other titles that won't even be remembered a year from now.

As far as pricing goes, Golden and Silver Age books should still hold that place of honor for collectors. Those decades were the creative foundation for our love of comics and the whole media circus that surrounds it. The pricing of comics from those years should reflect that. But what about the comics from the late '70s, '80s, and '90s? Also anything from 2000 on? Those books are so over-produced and were bought by collectors in multiple copies with the belief that comic prices will continue to soar. With the economy the way it is today, it's hard to get the casual shopper to come in, browse and have one of your sales staff be able to interest them on a certain title. We are doing no favors feeding them the belief that current comics are going to be of any extreme value. People are dumping collections with the hopes that there is a huge value and market for these books, and there definitely is not. With that being the case, how can we even pretend to hope of a future for our "hobby". We continue to take common comics and price them way out of the hands of anyone younger than 14 can afford to pay for them? With all the distractions available to teens and young adults, video games, computer gaming and social networking, Netflix, and even the new downloadable comics, what does that mean for the future of the old brick and mortar stores?

A neighboring store has had a *Spider-Man* #1 on display for a while, something like that you have to create some excitement about. Again the economy comes into play. Only those that can afford the luxury of prime back issues are looking for them, and not the low end issues you see everywhere. We get the usual run of '80s through the 2000s books come in pretty regular, but recently some medium grade *Detective Comics* found their way into the store. Those books are usually good movers, once again depending upon the pricing, with those *Detective Comics* came a huge run of '60s *Wonder Woman*. Early *Wonder Woman* is not a book you see walking through the doors with any regularity. This selection had some nice clean copies, and we have confidence that they will move well. I know I suggestively stated that books from the '80s-on are somewhat over-priced, there are a few exceptions as you might imagine. *Secret War* #8 is still selling well and getting a premium price, people love that black Spidey suit! The clamor over *Ultimate Spider-Man* #1 has seemed to die down, with those books sitting just a bit longer than they used to before getting snatched up by an excited collector. In the past few years, we have moved a large run of *Batman*, from Golden Age to present. Although they sold well, it was sad to see what they sold at, and kind of hard to let go. *Detective* #27 and #31 in somewhat low grade sold quicker and with much less stressing over. Low grade copies of *Lois Lane* #1 had a lot of interest, but no takers, and a low grade copy of *Lois Lane* #70, the first Silver Age appearance of Catwoman had no takers, even at a show that had Julie Newmar in attendance.

What about those "hidden" rare treasures? The Golden Age Fawcetts, *Captain Marvel*, *The Marvel Family*, *Captain Midnight*, *Bulletman*, and *Spy Smasher* just to name a few. I find it hard to believe that Golden Age treasures like that can be found relatively cheap. Those prices do not seem appropriate for such a long standing character from the classic era of comics. Captain Marvel ranks right up there in comic history right next to Superman. It is about time those books are paid the respect they are due. DC who owns those properties now have done another amazing job of making Black Adam one of their darkest villains with a rich background. Even before the New 52 Black Adam was not a total villain, until pushed into it, and now he is a villain you want to really see more of! Why not a Captain Marvel film? It seems that even Hollywood as well as the general public have forgotten those early Fawcett heroes. I really do hope that they will soon come back to notice!

Do the movies contribute any revenue to stores? Do they increase the value of books that were once hidden in our dank and musty basements? Only if you are lucky enough to have those books in stock that either have the first appearances of the characters, or the story the movie was based on. Does that mean that the prices of the comics that have movie characters in them should escalate? Hollywood has been given a free hand in writing the scripts using our beloved heroes; and stories. Ok, not all of them are horrible, although I do hear a lot of complaints in the store about the movies. My only reply is (and those of you who know me will already have repeated what I say) "Just enjoy the movies for what they are. Be thankful that that are using the media that we enjoy to make these films. Back when I was growing up, all we had was the black and white version of *The Adventures of Superman*, and then, they could only do so much with making you believe a man could fly. Not all of those stories and books should increase in value. A movie based on Deadpool will certainly drive the price of the first appearance up, but again, those are books from the "let's print more and more often '80s." Anyhow, the ripple effect from the movies to the stores has defiantly slowed.

Ok, movies and television do help promote comics, that is a given. But that does not necessarily translate to a rise in comic prices, or sales. The largest waste of space in the stores has been the back issue bins. Do we blame the weak economy? I know you might be tired of me placing the blame on the economy. I say this because a mentor of mine always said, I don't want to hear about the weather or that there is too much construction being the cause of poor sales. We have to be honest here, when sales dip, there is a reason for it. It may not be the reason we want to hear, but none the less it is a viable reason. Do we place blame on a disinterested fan base? Or perhaps we should point the finger at the mega stories that appear every spring like clockwork. Those stories that crossover into every title and place a drain on our time, our interest, and our cash flow. Pointing the finger is the easy part. Until we find a way to come together as an industry and work towards promoting our product, things are going to continue to be tough on the comic retailer, causing the comic consumer to pay the ultimate price.

Dan Gallo
Comic Art Con

I love this stuff. The whole all-encompassing genre, from movies to merchandise to the very books themselves, I feel very fortunate to be able to do this full time. All day every day my life revolves around the hobby, (and I wouldn't change a thing!).

My niche in our hobby is CGC graded key issues and original comic book art. I do this full time and every year is the same; there is an insatiable appetite for quality material. Will people ever not care about *Incredible Hulk* #181? Will there ever come a time when collectors don't want an *X-Men* #1? Will the market ever turn its back on a *Tales of Suspense* #39? If the answer is yes then the world would surely be at an end. The characters we love, like Spider-Man, Batman, and Wolverine, will always "be." Just like Mickey Mouse, they will be with us forever and there will always be people who want to have their first appearances. They may not want their second appearance but they will always want their first. Some collectors buy everything while others are more selective but the overlap is always the key issues. They are in the most demand, they see the most appreciation, and they are the most liquid. These are the books I deal in every day. No matter how hard I try I can't grow my inventory because the demand is just too great.

Collectors always ask me what's hot and sometimes that is not the right question to ask. What they should be asking is what is going to be hot? For the disclaimer, I don't have a crystal ball and you never know how things will shake out in the future but I do believe that the following books are either undervalued and or poised for a jump.

From the Silver Age, I absolutely love *Fantastic Four* #4, the first SA appearance of Namor. No one is paying attention right now and the book is totally undervalued. The census for CGC graded copies is in the neighborhood of *Strange Tales* #110 and *Brave and the Bold* #28, which are low compared to high census books like *Daredevil* #1 and *Avengers* #4. Early SA, low census, low price point…this book is poised to move although it probably will need some help from a movie tie in. If Ant-Man can be a hot property, then so can the Sub-Mariner!

From the Bronze Age, for the first time I see real potential for movement in middle grade keys. Traditionally, BA key books were affordable in higher grade so middle grade copies were often ignored. As higher graded copies have gotten more expensive the middle grade alternatives are now bargains by comparison and cost conscious collectors are snatching them up. I have already started to see overlapping of prices between 5.0 and 7.5 on key issues as the market tries to figure out this new found demand.

From the Modern Age, I love *Teenage Mutant Ninja Turtles* #2-4. Of course I love #1; it's a monster and the best book from the 1980s, but the #2, #3, & #4 have been available on the cheap for too long. With the property getting a reboot and a new generation of fans being exposed to them, the time is right to gobble up the early issues. Another favorite of mine is *New Mutants* #87, the first appearance of Cable. At one time it was much more popular book but today with all the people going gaga over *New Mutants* #98, the first Deadpool, the #87 has slipped. Isn't that when you are supposed to buy something though? I remember the #98 fetching $200 in 9.8 not to long ago and now it is double that. I see that as a real possibility of happening with the #87 as well and having a potential X-Force movie in the works with Cable being THE guy, well,… seems like a no brainer to me.

Another book that used to be more popular was *Punisher Limited Series* #1. After *Amazing Spider-Man* #129, I think it is the best Punisher book to own. The census is relatively low for a book from that era and if you search around you won't find too many available. I like it. Lastly, *Amazing Spider-Man* #361, the first Carnage, is on the move. For years this book was available in the $80-$100 range for 9.8s but over the last year it has inched up and now sells in the $150 range and it has plenty of room to grow. One can never underestimate the staying power of anything Spidey. I remember a few years ago thinking *ASM* #300 was topped out at $500 only to watch it keep going and going. We are in the middle of one of those runs with *ASM* #194, the first Black Cat right now. I would grab a #361 now while it's not that crazy. Actually, you might want to grab two!

I couldn't conclude my market overview without a few words about original comic book art. As co-promoter of Comic Art Con, I have seen firsthand how much fun the Original Art market is. Even if you have never thought about collecting OA, I recommend picking up at least one page to hang on your wall, (but be forewarned, buying just one page of art can be like eating just one potato chip…it's near impossible). You love the hobby, you love the characters, you love the books so why not have something unique, something that no one else has, an original page of comic book art!? Trust me, it's very cool! If you are already a collector or if you are curious about getting started you should pick up *The Overstreet Guide To Collecting Comic & Animation Art.* Sometimes breaking into a new market can be scary. This handbook makes it easier.

As in any hobby, buy what you like. After all, it is your collection and not mine. If there is an investment component to your focus then always buy the best because if and when the time comes for you to cash out there will be no shortage of buyers for the blue chip stuff.

Stephen H. Gentner
Collector

Greetings! I have attended a few larger comic cons this year, The Wizard Con and The Rose City Comic Con here in my hometown of Portland, Oregon. Just a quick word about cons now. In the dank and murky past, comic conventions were about buying comic books, and meeting writers and artists. Now they are infused with "Pop Culture" to the point of overwhelming the comic book function dramatically. Movie stars, old sci-fi TV stars, toys, fantasy swords, HUNDREDS of costumed people, clothing, statues, models, movies, music...

I could go on. Incredibly, in this sea of distracting sights and sounds, I actually found books I was looking for at BOTH shows! But here is the salient point to my kvetching...there were huge crowds and huge interest! A more dramatic display of the viability and financial success of these comic cons could NOT have been more evident. This goes hand in glove with my perspective on the market as a whole, which is good. The public's enjoyment of comic books both as investments and entertainment continues in a very healthy fashion. With the availability of *The Overstreet Price Guide*, the GPA Market Service and CGC Census data, collectors, investors, and market watchers can observe in real time how their books are doing, as well as plot their next moves in or out of the comic marketplace. As a collector, I tend to operate with heart as well as head in parking my dollars. Those two tools and sleuthing eBay along with the various auction and dealer sites affirms and illuminates potential purchases, while tracking previous acquisitions. Slabbed books are as much a commodity now as corn or orange juice!...(but lots more fun to read!).

© MAR

Prices are soaring for 1st appearances of upcoming Marvel movie villains like Ultron in **Avengers #55.**

Movie premieres of comic-related characters are incredibly strong and profitable now. The big movie companies are vying with one another putting out amazing sci-fi and super hero movies with special effects never dreamt of before. Compare the first *Superman* movie with the last two Superman movies. Batman, Iron Man, the Avengers, Thor, ... and more coming. These features shine a bright light on our hobby and the comics and characters we love. I myself have had to go after the first appearances of Thanos, Ultron, The Vision, and others before the speculation prices took me deeper into my pocket than I wanted to go! The larger point being more and more people are enjoying, identifying with, and pursuing comic books in our hobby for more reasons than ever before. One scenario I came across was a person with a family business investing large sums of money for long term investments in classic comic books!...WITH the blessing and encouragement of his investment counselors!! My Dad would always talk about how he loved double tax exempt bonds from Puerto Rico with a 5% yield. "Stephen, I wish I could get MORE of these...!" Compared to catching a wave with a great comic book in great condition and doubling, or trebling your investment makes that almost laughable. Old school and new school. Now if I could just learn how to SPEND appreciation, I'd have it made.

Some of the books I have secured this year are the aforementioned *Avengers* #55, first "Ultron", *Invincible Iron Man* #55, first "Thanos", *Avengers* #57, first "Vision", *X-Factor* #6, first "Apocalypse" in CGC 9.6, 9.6, 9.2, and 9.8 respectively. Some I bought slabbed, but most were bought raw and submitted for grade. I have generally bought raw books over the years, but recently, I have been submitting more acquisitions to confirm my grading eye with CGC standards. (But AFTER I had read them!). These movie tie-in purchases are fun in that you get to see how the comic books compare to how the movies portray them. Hit movies equate to hit pricing! Those notwithstanding, I also picked up a glorious *All Star Comics* #11 from 1942. It has the first full "Wonder Woman" segment in the series after her brief first appearance in *All Star Comics* #8. I continue to be drawn to World War Two comic books of the Golden Age. The history of our country in the crucible of that conflict is mirrored in the propaganda, flag waving, patriotic comics of that era. I have mentioned before in my reports how my favorite artist Alex Schomburg's covers in this period for Standard/Nedor, Continental, Harvey, and Timely only get better with age. For composition, proportion, frenetic action, and unflattering artistic stereotyping of the Nazis and Japanese, these propaganda covers by Schomburg are tops!

Other purchases were the new "lenticular" 3D covers that DC put out in their "Villains" series. Due to a shortage of the goop necessary to produce these brilliant covers, shortages on some titles led to hot spots...notably the "Harley Quinn" cover. I also picked up four sketch variants to the "New 52", *Batman*, *Flash*, *Action*, and *Green Lantern*.The *Batman* cover by Greg Capullo is really tasty! Last but not least I also found at the Rose City Con a Golden Age Collection discovered by Comic Safari. It is called the "Lake Golden Age" Collection. I purchased the *Batman* #4 in CGC 6.0 with brilliant colors and white pages! In the collection were an *All Star* #1, #3 ,#4, #5, *Batman* #1, #3, #4, #5, #6, *Detective* #29, #30, #31, #33, #35, *Superman* #1, #2, #3, #4, plus more. You don't often get a chance to see such a gaudy display of Golden Age keys in one place at one time! The idea this collection would be in attendance with all the mayhem of the Comic Con was a wonderful thing! Thanks for reading, and I'll see you next year!

Eric J. Groves
The Comic Art Foundation

The remembrance of things past: so it is with senior status in this hobby of ours. I'm old enough to recall the great comic book purge of the early 1950s and the institution of the repressive Comics Code Authority. Old enough to have grown up reading the great continuity comic strips of the '40s and '50s and the epics of the master comic artist Carl Barks. Old enough to have been present at the inception of organized fandom in the 1960s. I can recall when early entrepreneurial comic book dealers for the first time made it possible to acquire elusive back issues: Phil Sueling, Claude Held, Ken Mitchell. Their sale lists were the precursors of Bob Overstreet's *Comic Book Price Guide*. Then there were the first conventions, with rag tag armies of hucksters and seekers, carting cardboard boxes of comics into funky second rate hotels, the only ones that would have us.

How things have changed. High grade comics are now professionally graded and sealed, establishing them as investment vehicles for those who can afford to buy them, mostly at high end auctions. The once humble San Diego Comic-Con is now an international media phenomenon, dedicated to promoting the latest motion pictures related to comics. Many years of diligent and determined research has resulted in the encyclopedic volume which we advise, the *Price Guide*. It is invaluable, of course, as are the institutional memories of those who assisted it along the way. So, we take the long view. We seniors know from whence we came. Where do we go now? Herewith, some thoughts.

First, there is the never ending discussion about the relationship between comics and motion pictures. Who helps who the most? Are movie producers indebted to comic creators for their inspiration and success? Or are comics and their collectors the beneficiaries of the many films based on comics? In terms of sheer dollars, it seems film comes out ahead. But hugely successful movies like *The Dark Knight* and *The Avengers*, in our opinion, confer a benefit not only on comic makers but on the collecting community as a whole. It is, in a sense, about respectability. Movies legitimize comics as art, or literature, in the larger culture. The irony is that movies based on comics are really nothing new, see the *Flash Gordon* serials circa 1940. What is new is the spectacular production values of films mostly based on Marvel characters. From our perspective, the important thing at the end of the day is that comics be written and drawn for those who love them, not for the suits who run the movie studios, no offense.

Second, the market continues to teach us the same lesson every year: never underestimate the Golden Age. If we price the books fairly, we can sell *Action, Adventure, Batman, Detective, Flash, Green Lantern, Sensation, Superman* and *Wonder Woman* all day long, especially in the lower grades with a modest discount. We can't keep for very long Timelys like *All Winners, Captain America, Human Torch, Marvel Mystery* or *Young Allies*. Not only that, but put out a reasonably priced copy of *Catman* or *Black Terror* or *Hangman* and off they go. Why? Because they are American artifacts, icons. Put a modern comic in your right hand and a Golden Ager in your left, like a scale. Feel the heft of that old book which sold itself with the use of primary colors and pure fantasy. We sell many Golden Age comics to fans under forty simply because they want to experience possessing one. It's the difference between a Packard and a Smart car.

Third, as to the Silver Age. The holy grails are still the same: *Amazing Fantasy* #15, *Spidey* #1, *FF* #1, *Tales of Suspense* #39, etc. In historic perspective, these books look prettier as each year passes. They impart a certain innocence, suggesting it was all a merry experiment between Stan Lee, Steve Ditko and Jack Kirby. It was such fun back then. Who would have guessed that fifty years on, Marvel would so masterfully exploit these characters for billions in film revenue? It's great entertainment with comics writ large. The only problem with Silver Age back issues is this: at a certain point in time, many titles become quite common, especially second tier characters like Hawkman, Aquaman, Rip Hunter and others. But the DC titles carried over from the Golden Age, such as *Batman* and *Superman*, sell steadily.

Fourth, there is the Atomic Age. We sell a lot of books from this era, perhaps because collectors know we are always on the lookout for them. Fans are still in the hunt for the work of Frazetta, Wood, Baker, Wolverton, Toth and Reed Crandall. Good girl art books are reliable sellers. So is pre-Code horror, especially L.B. Cole covers, so long as such books are reasonably priced. Atlas titles are highly desirable. And, despite the many reprints, collectors want original ECs, except for *Mad* and *Panic*, which are a little slow.

Fifth, those who buy old comic books have settled into two communities. There are those who collect them, most often in runs, because they want the thrill of just looking at them and reading them. Then there is the investment community whose interest lies chiefly in obtaining the highest CGC graded copy of certain keys. This arrangement works well up to a point, but the inherent risk of a bubble is still there. Speculation is rarely healthy in any collecting community for the usual reason: if highly invested collectors decide to dump their collections simultaneously, values can be driven into the dirt.

Finally, we think the back issue comic book market is stable and encouraging. Recent price adjustments have been appropriate. There is simply no substitute for a good comic book. A life full of appreciation for comic art is not misspent. Sometimes I reflect back on the efforts to destroy comics when I was a child and how all the kids on my block hid their EC's from their parents. And then I realize: we won. *We won.*

John Haines
John Haines Rare Comics

2013 surprised us on two fronts: Sales for new comics experienced extremely strong growth while back issue and vintage comics slowed overall. We look at the market from three distinct views: 1) Brick and Mortar Store, 2) Convention Sales 3) Internet/Catalog Sales.

Brick and Mortar store: Comics and Friends is now into our fifth year and we continue to grow. At the store, new comics and trades lead the way for us, with back issue/vintage comics next, followed by Manga, then action figures, Heroclix, Magic the Gathering, statues, and t-shirts all contributing their fair share. Most of our Marvel titles continued to grow (although reader fatigue on X titles and Avengers titles is popping up due to over-saturation). Ditto DC although some momentum was lost during the confusion of "Villains Month." Dark Horse held steady for us, IDW and Boom increased, Dynamite dipped somewhat but was offset by growth in strong Image series. Top sellers of the year: *Walking Dead* #115, *Forever Evil* #1, *Harley Quinn* #1, *Dexter* #1, *Sons of Anarchy* #1, *Batman/ Superman* #1, *Regular Show* #1, *Superman Unchained* #1, *Superior Spider-Man* #1, *Justice League of America* #1, *Uncanny X-Men* #1, *Guardians of the Galaxy* #1, *X-Men* #1, *Infinity* #1, *Sandman: Overture* #1, and *Amazing X-Men* #1. Of course all issues of *Batman, Deadpool,* and *Superior Spider-Man* sold like crazy. Great new 2nd tier titles that sold well for us (and which you should check out if you haven't already): *God is Dead, East of West, Sex Criminals, Velvet, Lazarus,* and *True Lives of the Killjoys.*

Convention sales: The convention world has changed. Other than at a select few shows (which we'll get into later) the majority of people are no longer coming to search for vintage comics for their collections. Most are attending for Cosplay, Publisher Exclusives, and to meet and get things signed by their favorite creators. Wizard Ohio clinched it for us – this multiple day show was strongly attended with almost no dealer activity. This has been coming for a while and shouldn't surprise anyone. There are still a few true comic conventions out there – The Baltimore Comicon, The Pittsburgh Comicon, and Gem City tops among them on the East Coast. We now focus on those types of shows along with solid local one day conventions.

We host the Lake Effect Comic Book Convention which is a one day show that has built a reputation for having one of the strongest selections of vintage comics in Northeast Ohio over the past four years, so there is still a place for old-style Comic Book conventions. That all said, sales have shifted also – collectors are focusing on low cost, common issues where they can pick up large volume for low cost – price point pricing is king: box after box of $1 comics, $3 comics, $5 comics, etc. Wall books still go – they always do – but box stock has slowed tremendously over the year – and we constantly replenish our box stock. Overall, convention sales dipped for us during 2013 – we still love getting out there into the fray to buy, sell, trade, and talk comics with knowledgeable collectors.

What are collectors looking for: *Amazing Fantasy* #15 – the single most asked for comic at the shows we attend, followed closely by low number *Amazing Spider-Man, Avengers* #1 and #4 – we had and sold multiple copies of each this year. *Incredible Hulk* #181 – asked for constantly, *Amazing Spider-Man* #121 #122 and #129 – sell out as soon as they are put out for sale. *New Mutants* #98 with first appearance of Deadpool - hot as a pistol – cannot keep them. *Batman* #121 – still sells instantly. *Detective Comics* #359 1st Silver-Age Batgirl – sells over *Guide* levels. *Brave and the Bold* #28 – we went through multiple copies this year. *X-Men* issues have slowed a little bit as have *Showcase* – we do expect these to stay slow for long.

On the Golden Age side, things are still very strong – limited supply with constant demand will tend to do that. We buy all year long and were particularly pleased when we picked up a large 100+ Golden Age collection this summer all between 1940 and 1943 with plenty of Timely, MLJ, Quality, and DC – almost all were gone within the first month to long-time customers. We kept pushing and picked up a small quantity of high quality early EC horror comics (with a few pre-trend issues) from a discerning long-time collector and half of them went at the first show we attended. We recently acquired another small amount of early Golden Age between 1940 and 1944 and anticipate it will all sell when we attend the Gem City con in April. Again – Golden Age wall books sell quickly, box stock takes a bit longer but we still have collectors with want lists digging through them.

Internet/Catalog Sales: If you price it right, it all sells. Our internet sales continue to grow. While we sell current comics along with vintage comics online – the vintage comics have held steady and the current comics have exploded for us. Our customers like us to offer long runs of issues which allows them to save on shipping fees – so that's what we try to give them.

What is selling in the vintage arena: Westerns – can't believe it but we are in a growth period for vintage Westerns (the cheaper the better) – enjoy it while it lasts. Dells on the other hand, particularly the more pricy Barks issues are dormant – we sell more non-Barks right now – as an experiment, we offered all our *Walt Disney Comics and Stories, Uncle Scrooge,* and *Donald Duck* at 50% off (which we never do) – and were surprised to see not many takers. What else? Neal Adams continues to kill, The Archie Spire Christian series is red hot, *Amazing Spider-Man, Batman, Classics Illustrated,* Whitman DC variants, Marvel Price variants, Golden Age strip reprints – all are steady and in demand. Bronze Age horror is experiencing a mini-boomlet – again the prices on most of these are well within the range of anyone. And, there is still a strong contingent out there who only want CGC encapsulated comics regardless of condition.

What will happen next year is anyone's guess. As always we council collectors to buy what they like instead of chasing trends. If you do that, you'll never be disappointed with your collection.

Steven Houston & John Dolmayan
Torpedo Comics

To begin, I would like say that I'm honored to finally have the opportunity to contribute to the *Overstreet Guide,* it's something I've been dreaming of since the early 1990s.

A Brief Overview 2012-2013: Before getting into specifics, I would like to mention the four aspects of the comic industry that either had a direct effect on Torpedo Comics, or at the very least, came up in discussions regarding our business plan for the new Year. Beginning after Comic Con in 2012, the full effect of Marvel's *Avengers* movie on back-issues really began to impact our sales. This was compounded by the pending release of Marvel's next big budget project, the *Guardians of the Galaxy* movie, causing sales to spike on other cosmic theme titles. Not since the madness of 'Batmania' in 1989, had movies had such an effect on back-issues sales, making this easily the most important comic related aspect of 2013 for Torpedo.

Another important part of the 2012-2013 year for us was the phenomenal success of the *Walking Dead* cable television series, which kept our sales of all *Walking Dead* merchandise ticking along nicely, be it soft cover trade paperbacks, large format hardcovers, or massive compendiums.

Another cable television show that also had an effect on our business this year (indirectly via convention attendance) was the *Heroes of Cosplay* reality television show. This program showcased the flamboyant (and extremely competitive) world of super-hero/animation theme costuming at comic conventions, attracting an audience the comic industry has been courting for years – females.

A relatively new aspect of the industry, but still something that seemed to be shaking some corners of the industry to its core, was the continued growth of digital (or downloaded) comics. Still in its embryonic stages, digital comic media has had little effect on Torpedo Comics at this time, however if the major publishers decide to make vast amounts of their vintage inventories available for download – who knows what will happen? The final aspect of the year and perhaps the most perplexing for us was the exploding convention attendances across the entire United States. Perhaps the combination of the last few years of massively successful super-hero movies, combined with the exposure the *Heroes of Cosplay* show, brought a whole new audience to conventions, whatever the reasons, comic conventions seemed to be the place to be seen at in 2013, as people who have never read a comic in their lives swarmed various conventions.

Movies, Movies, Movies: The unprecedented success of recent super-hero movies has brought both old collectors back to the fold and newer collectors seeking to pick up their first key issues. We have experienced former collectors coming back, curious about comics again, as well as current collectors deciding to finally make that certain large purchase, usually an issue they may not had the financial ability to purchase in years past. A great example of this phenomenon for us this year, were the sale of three *Avengers* #1s – all to collectors who had the entire run except the first issue and all who had decided that with all the exposure the Avengers were getting via the movies, they had better bite the bullet and get the first issue now.

Something similar occurred with another set of collectors and speculators throughout 2012 and into 2013, and that was the mad rush to pick up copies of *Iron Man* #55 – the first appearance of Thanos (the villain who appeared at the end of *The Avengers* movie). In fact, when rumors began to spread concerning which characters were going to appear in the next *Avengers* and *Guardians of the Galaxy* movies, we had a second wave of collector/speculators fall upon our stock like a ravening horde of army ants! So in 2013, seeking to be ahead of the curve, we had many customers pouring over our back issue inventory pulling out almost everything movie related. Suddenly Captain Marvel was hot again, especially issues #25-33 (the Thanos war) as well as the 1970s Jim Starlin issues of *Warlock* (#9-15), in fact everything Thanos related suddenly disappeared from our stock. Also on collectors want-lists again (just like the glory days of 1992) were titles like *Logan's Run* #6 (Thanos back-up story), *Daredevil* #105 (Moondragon appearance) as well as *Avengers Annual* #7 and *Marvel Two-in-One Annual* #2 (the second Thanos war). Rumors concering the Avengers sequel and the new Captain America movie stimulated sales of *Avengers* #55 (first Ultron), *Avengers* #57 (1st Vision) and *Captain America* #117 (1st Falcon). When word began to spread about just how serious Marvel were regarding the *Guardians of the Galaxy* movie, customers feverishly began looking for *Marvel Super-Heroes* #18 (first Guardians), *Marvel Preview* magazine #7 (first Rocket Raccoon), *Incredible Hulk* #271 (first color Rocket Raccoon), *Rocket Raccoon* limited series #1-4 (are you kidding me!!!), *Strange Tales* #180 (first Gamora), *Tales to Astonish* #13 (first Groot) and finally, *Marvel Preview* magazine #4 (first Starlord). At every show we attended, we had sales of *Marvel Presents* #3-12 (Guardians) as well as *Defenders* #26-29 and *Giant-Size Defenders* #5 (all Guardians appearances), *Marvel Premiere* #1-2 (Warlock), *Thor Annual* #6 (Guardians) and *Marvel Team-Up* #55 (Warlock).

In terms of DC Comics, sales related to movies were weak, with negligible activity, apart from the few forward thinking individuals who were betting on Darkseid appearing in a possible Justice League movie. Thus we had sales of a few copies of *Superman's Pal Jimmy Olsen* #134-135 (1st Darkseid) as well as a nice $3000 sale of a CGC 4.5 *Brave and the Bold* #28 (1st Justice League). In conclusion, back-issue sales have been vibrant regarding anything the collecting public deems 'hot' or soon to be hot. However, I have noticed a cooling down of sales on titles currently devoid of any movie activity or rumored activity – more on this thorny subject in the Silver and Bronze Age reports.

Conventions: Torpedo Comics attended shows in Arizona, Anaheim, San Jose, San Diego and two shows in Las Vegas in 2013, most of which were well attended with Comic Con being the monster we all know it is. The Arizona show was a rather subdued affair, located in Phoenix, the show seemed to drag on with little passion from customers, except for having books signed. The only thing we could do was buy, buy, buy. We picked up some nice raw copies of *Incredible Hulk* #2-6, two copies of *Captain America* #100 as well as picking up about three hundred more common nice condition 'box books'.

Wondercon was a big show, with the book of the show apparently being *Tales to Astonish* #27 (first Ant-Man), we had three copies at the shows start, each being rather low grade, the first, a GD condition copy sold for $1000, the next was a GD+ which sold for $1400 and the final copy was a GD/VG which sold for $1700! Ironically, as soon as we were sold out, it was if every person who came to the booth needed a *Tales to Astonish* #27. So common were the requests that I asked one of the customers what was going on, and he mentioned the Ant-Man movie – suddenly it all became clear. It was at this show that I also began to get requests for *Avengers* #55 (1st Ultron), something was going on here again, especially after one customer bought the only two medium grade copies we had. We sold an *Incredible Hulk* #1 CGC 5.5 for $7000 at the show and then set off to find some *Tales to Astonish* #27s! Not a bad show, but a shadow of its former self compared to the San Francisco location.

Las Vegas was home to its first successful comic convention in memory this year. Held at the South Point Casino, the organizers went all out as they heavily advertised the special guests – Stan Lee and Jim Lee. Both days of the show were crowded, due to the intelligent show planning, which kept fans in line either for a signature and a photo from Stan, or a signature from Jim. Astonishingly, we sold a CGC 7.5 *Amazing Spider-Man* #1 for $15,000 at the show as well as a CGC 9.6 copy of *Silver Surfer* #1 for $5000. In fact the *Silver Surfer* book was the big seller for us at the show as we sold an additional three raw copies of issue #1, all in VF- condition for $600 each.

The biggest show of the year of course is Comic Con in San Diego, a massive event these last few years due to the Hollywood incursion. Upon arrival, I noticed the lack of hotel space as well as elevated customer requests for tickets that seemed impossible to purchase. Also rather annoying for some of our customers was the lack of parking at the event, unless you were there at 6 AM! I also noticed the huge lines of people heading towards to now legendary 'Hall H', with the escalators leading up to the second floor almost bending under the weight of thousands of attendees and unfortunately I also noticed that some of our loyal annual customers did not make it to the show.

The amount of people in costume was incredible, it seems the world of Cosplay has exploded these last few years as I witnessed groups of fans in various costumes roaming around, meeting other groups, which would lead to loud screams of approval from both groups as they were being photographed by hoards of MEN with massive cameras. What was the effect of all these new attendees on our sales at the show? Zilch I'm afraid, I don't know what the Cosplay fans collect, but what ever it is, we did not have it.

In terms of comic activity, the most requested book was *Avengers* #57 (1st Vision) with *Amazing Spider-Man* #121 (death of Gwen Stacy) coming in a close second. The lessons we have learned over the last five years were really brought into focus this year as we began to phase out lower grade (common) Silver and Bronze Age books, while increasing our inventory of higher grade product. One of the major reasons for this is due to the cost of booth space at Comic Con. Basically, we can fit approximately 24 long boxes of inventory in our booth space at the show and as such, if a book is going to be in the boxes, it had better be worth it. To that end, we upgraded our selection, pulling out $10 copies of VG grade Silver Age books, and replaced them with $60 VF copies. I spent months double-checking the grade of each book and utilized a new system to mark each book's grade with a fancy 'Torpedo Comics' sticker, which noted a given books grade. This created a sense of uniformity within the boxes, which seemed to go down very well with our customers -- especially one dealer who went through our entire selection pulling out nearly everything graded 9.0 or above.

Some of our regular customers who we had seen at Wondercon in Anaheim warned us they may not be able to come to Comic Con, a warning I took with a grain of salt as I though to myself, "Who can resist Comic Con"? Well it turns out that a third of our regular customers did not come to the show, either due to the fact they could not get tickets, or that they refused to battle the massive crowds in an effort to have a 'good time' purchasing comics. Troubling times indeed if this scenario keeps repeating itself.

Silver Age Report: While at the booth at Comic Con in 2012, John (Dolmayan) and myself discussed what Torpedo Comics needed in 2013 and among the many subjects we discussed, perhaps the most important was in regards to our Silver Age purchases. Instead of purchasing regular collections with large amounts of 'box books', we decided to concentrate of getting the major keys of the era. To that end we managed to accumulate most of the major keys, such as: *Amazing Fantasy* #15, *Amazing Spider-Man* #1, *Atom* #1, *Avengers* #1, #4, *Brave and the Bold* #28, *Daredevil* #1, *Fantastic Four* #1, #4, #5, #48, *Incredible Hulk* #1, *Journey into Mystery* #83, #85, *Showcase* #4, #22, *Strange Tales* #110, *Tales to Astonish* #27 and *X-Men* #1. The one book that we had no luck with was *Tales of Suspense* #39 (1st Iron Man) this year, which just gave us a little more idea on just how tough this issue is to find, in any condition. Luckily for us, our purchasing plan paid off this year, as it seemed as though collectors who go after 'runs' of comics were a little quiet this year, while those collectors searching for the right key issue to spend some money on were very active. Combined with the collectors swarming into the Silver Age market because of the *Avengers* and *Guardians of the Galaxy* movies, it seemed as though collectors were 'taking the leap' as we say and finally nailing down some major keys. Good examples of this is the sale of two *Showcase* #4s, one for $5000 and the other for $60,000 – that copy being an astonishing CGC 9.0 grade. We sold two *Amazing Fantasy* #15s, two *Amazing Spider-Man* #1s, three *Avengers* #1s, a *Brave and the Bold* #28, two *Fantastic Four* #1s, an *Incredible Hulk* #1 and FOUR *X-Men* #1s – a banner year for keys, if I do say so myself. One thing that is very interesting is the fact that all the aforementioned keys were CGC copies, with potential customers unwilling to purchase raw copies within the same price range.

In terms of raw sales, the secondary keys as I like to call

them, such as *Captain America* #100 were moving at an even faster pace, proving to be a more vibrant area for us in 2013. Always popular are the '1968 keys', such, *Captain Marvel* #1, *Doctor Strange* #169, *Incredible Hulk* #102, *Iron Man* #1, *Nick Fury Agent of SHIELD* #1, *Silver Surfer* #1, *Sub-Mariner* #1 and of course the aforementioned *Captain America* #100. Spending a few hundred dollars on one of these keys seemed very easy for collectors this year, especially if the grade was a VF. The hottest book from the 1968 keys was the *Silver Surfer*, with *Captain America* #100 next, followed by *Iron Man* #1. Another of the secondary keys that was asked for was *Thor* #126 (from 1966), a book that has shot up in price from FN to VF condition in recent years.

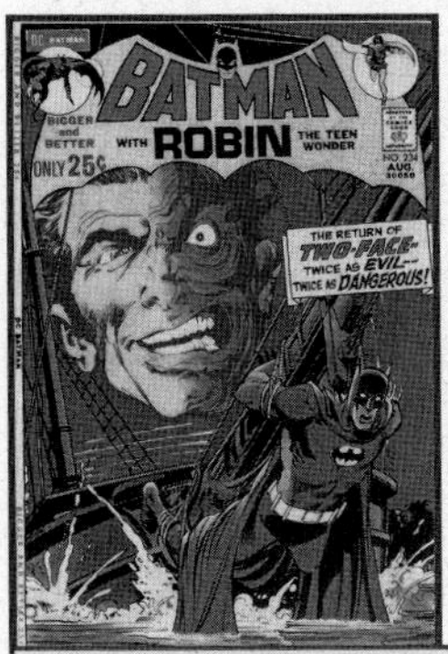

© DC

Neal Adams' early Batman issues have dominated sales. (**Batman** #234 shown)

Turning to DC Comics for a moment, although a little subdued compared to the frenzy of Marvel sales, we did move some nice DC keys. We sold a CGC 7.0 *Adventure Comics* #210 (1st Krypto) as well as CGC 5.0 *Adventure Comics* #247 (1st Legion). We sold low-grade raw copies of the *Atom* #1, *Green Lantern* #1 and *Justice League of America* #1, but to be honest I was a little disappointed in DC regular Silver Age titles, as interest in some of the titles like *Challengers of the Unknown*, *Doom Patrol* and *Hawkman* seems to waning as the original DC collectors move on, or pass on, with few new collectors to replace them. The reason for this? Well I have my theories, but rather than fill up page after page of theory, I will just say that with contemporary DC readers so far removed from the continuity of DC's Silver and Bronze Ages, is it any wonder that interest in the marginal DC 1960s books is low.

Significant Silver Age Sales 2012-2013:

Adventure Comics #210 CGC 7.0	$3000
Adventure Comics #247 CGC 5.0	$2000
Amazing Fantasy #15 CGC 1.8	$4500
Amazing Fantasy #15 CGC 3.0 (res)	$3500
Amazing Spider-Man #1 CGC 6.0 (res)	$3000
Amazing Spider-Man #1 CGC 7.5	$15,000
Avengers #1 CGC 4.0	$2600
Avengers #1 CGC 4.0 (off-white pgs.)	$2750
Avengers #1 CGC 5.5	$4000
Batman #121 CGC 6.5	$1200
Batman #189 CGC 9.6	$1300
Brave and the Bold #28 CGC 4.5	$3000
Fantastic Four #1 CGC 3.0	$3500
Incredible Hulk #1 CGC 5.5	$7000
Journey into Mystery #85 CGC 8.0	$2200
Journey into Mystery #85 CGC 8.0	$2500
Showcase #4 CGC 9.0	$60,000
Showcase #22 CGC 4.0	$1400
Showcase #34 CGC 8.0	$1400
Silver Surfer #1 CGC 9.6	$5000
X-Men #1 CGC 2.0	$1500
X-Men #1 CGC 5.0	$2700
X-Men #1 CGC 7.0	$6000
X-Men #1 CGC 7.5	$8000

Bronze Age Report: Once again to be brutally honest, Marvel Comics dominated our sales of 1970s era comics. The reason for this: movies, movies and more movies. For example, the re-booted Spider-Man franchise has brought in many collectors looking for *Amazing Spider-Man* #121 (death of Gwen Stacy), the *Avengers* movie has totally reinvigorated sales on all cosmic theme characters, such as Thanos and Captain Marvel, while the rumors swirling around the future *Guardians of the Galaxy* movie had collectors feverishly hunting for every character who is going to be featured in the movie.

Over at DC, Neal Adams, whose work on *Batman* and *Detective* seems to have undergone a major renaissance this year, dominated our sales. One funny aspect of our convention season this year was the fact that it seemed as though Neal attended every comic convention across the United States in 2012-2013 and ironically he was always close to our booth. This lead to a steady stream of Neal's fans, purchasing issues that featured his work to have signed. The consequences of this were that by the end of Comic Con this year, our *Batman* and *Detective* runs featuring Neal's work had been savaged, forcing us to push his fans onto *Green Lantern* and *X-Men* issues. Finally, as if providing further evidence of Mr. Adams' current collectability, we had two beautiful CGC 9.8 copies of Neal's *Batman* work sell this year, issue #232, which sold for $2550 and issue #234 which sold for $3000 – yes indeed, Mr. Adams was hot this year.

For us, one of the most requested books of 2013 was *House of Secrets* #92 (first Swamp Thing), unfortunately for us, we did not have a single issue to sell all year and I have loyal Torpedo customers, seemingly foaming at the mouth for that issue, especially in 9.2 or above. The usual Bronze keys, such as *Incredible Hulk* #181 and *Giant-Size X-Men* #1 have been joined by *Iron Fist* #14 (1st Sabretooth), *Marvel Premiere* #15 (1st Iron Fist), *Iron Man* #55 (1st Thanos), *Hero for Hire* #1 (1st Luke cage), *Marvel Spotlight* #5 (1st Ghost Rider) and *Werewolf by Night* #32 (1st Moon Knight) as most requested. Interestingly enough, *Ghost Rider* #1, *X-Men* #94, *Marvel Team-Up* #1, *Marvel Spotlight* #2 (1st Werewolf) and *Green Lantern* #76 have slowed for us a little in 2013.

Other issues of interest this year have been *Fantastic Four* #112 (vs. the Hulk) issues #120-123 (Silver Surfer appearances), *Incredible Hulk* #122 (vs. the Thing), issue #141 (1st Doc Samson), *Iron Man* #54 (1st Moondragon), issue #128 (Demon in a bottle classic), *Green Lantern* #78-89 (Neal Adams issues), *Avengers* #116-118, *Defenders* #9-11

(Avengers/Defenders war), *Sub-Mariner* #34-35 (Defenders prologue) and *Thor* #193 (Silver Surfer appearance).

Significant Bronze Age Sales:

Amazing Spider-Man #129 CGC 9.8	$5000
Batman #232 CGC 9.8	$3000
Batman #234 CGC 9.8	$2550
Giant-Size X-Men #1 CGC 9.2	$1500
Giant-Size X-Men #1 CGC 9.2	$1500
Giant-Size X-Men #1 CGC 9.4	$2500
Giant-Size X-Men #1 CGC 9.8	$7000
Incredible Hulk #181 CGC 8.0	$1400
Iron Fist #14 CGC 9.8	$1400

The Copper Age (Opinion): Those of you reading this report will notice that I have not used the 'Copper Age' designation. I must admit, I'm a little reticent to use this designation as in terms of actual years, as it supposedly relates to the years 1984 through 1992. To create this age of comics, the Bronze Age had to be stretched out from the original 1970-1979, to 1970 through 1984. This in turn, created the Modern Age, which currently covers the years 1984 through 1992. Although adopted by eBay, in my experience, these designations do not currently exists in dealer's back-issue selections across the United States. Maybe I missed it, but I did not ever see any major debate or discussion regarding this subject, for me, it just seemed to appear with the publication of the 34th edition of the *Overstreet Guide* in 2004. To date we have not stretched the Golden Age up to 1959, or pushed the Silver Age up to 1973, so why stretch out the Bronze Age to 1984? I would love to get some feedback on this subject, or even spark some lively debate.

1980s Comics: 1980s comics have become increasingly dependent on condition to make sales. Let's be honest here – nothing from the major publishers is really rare from the 1980s, so what does one do with this era of comics? Basically dealers have the option of selling FN/VF copies of most 1980s books at vast discounts at one of the smaller shows, 'smaller' being the operative word here, as with costs at major shows so high, only extremely inexperienced sellers (amateurs) would bring $1 books to a major show. Sales of the more common medium grade 1980s books are also under pressure from both Marvel's and DC's aggressive trade paperback publishing strategies. Fans that used to purchase huge runs of 'reading copies' now have the choice of purchasing reprints via trades or the new omnibus formats.

In regards to actual key books from this era, I have noticed a mediocre demand for the once highly sought after independent titles such as *Albedo* #2 (Usagi Yojimbo), *Love & Rockets* #1, *Mage* #6 (1st color Grendel) and *Primer* #2 (1st Grendel). *Teenage Mutant Ninja Turtles* seems to be still on many collectors want lists, especially issues #1-4. One odd observation I have witnessed, is high-end Silver Age collectors asking for the typical 1960s keys and then asking about high-grade copies of *TMNT*! Never under-estimate the power of a high-grade *Turtles* issue.

The best selling and most asked for 1980s back-issue is still *Amazing Spider-Man* #300. We sold a CGC 9.6 copy for $290 and a 9.8 copy for $850. Once again the impact of CGC cannot be underestimated as original 1980s collectors are sending in their high-grade keys and quite often end up being tempted to sell them, after witnessing some of the amazing prices being realized for these books. In regards to Marvel, the other hot 1980s keys are: *Amazing Spider-Man* #252 (1st black costume), *Avengers* #195 (1st brief Taskmaster appearance), *Avengers* #196 (1st full Taskmaster) – we sold a 9.8 copy of this issue for $290, *Captain America* #241 (Punisher appearance), *Daredevil* #168 (1st Elektra) and *Incredible Hulk* #340 (Wolverine appearance). The collecting hysteria concerning the *Guardians of the Galaxy* movie has proven not to be just a Silver and Bronze Age thing, with customer after customer requesting copies of *Incredible Hulk* #271 (1st Marvel Universe Rocket Raccoon) and more recently, *Avengers* #257 (1st Nebula). Amazingly, *Incredible Hulk* #271 was for many years a nothing issue, guiding at $4, not even having a listing by itself, now issues in CGC 9.8 sell for over $500! Other Marvel issues of the era include *Star Wars* #107 (last issue), *Ghost Rider* #81 (last issue), *Uncanny X-Men* #248 (1st Jim Lee) and finally getting some attention after years in the cold, *Thor* #337 (1st Walt Simonson). In regards to DC, high-grade Batmans still sell, including *Batman* #357 (1st Jason Todd), *Batman* #400, #404-407 (Year One), *Batman* #428 (death of Robin), *Batman The Dark Knight* #1 and *Batman: The Killing Joke* (we sold a CGC 9.9 copy for $500).

1990s Comics: Once thought of as a wasteland of comics, a true low-point in the history of the medium, some comics published in the 1990s seem to be getting a second look, most notably from former collectors (from the early 1990s) who have now matured and are ready to spend money recapturing 'their' youth. The 28 to 35 year-old age range seem particularly interested on either finishing sets they did not finish back in the day, or replace collections that they either sold, or lost. Obviously there is a massive amount of over-printed material from the 1990s, that may need another one hundred years to become collectible, but surprising to many is the fact that some 1990s comics did not have massive print-runs, especially after 1995.

Perhaps the poster boy of gimmick covers and slick marketing campaigns, Valiant Comics, has seen some new life in terms of sales for their pre-Unity issues. CGC has really benefited from this Valiant resurgence as collectors are sending in hundreds of these low print-run comics in the hope of getting 9.8 or above grades. Some of the Valiant issues have become almost mythical, whispered about on blogs, such as the *Bloodshot* #0 Gold edition – error version, rumored to have a print run as low as 15 or as high as 300! What is not a rumor, is the price a CGC 9.8 copy of the aforementioned issue went for in 2009, an astounding $2000. Another fascinating aspect of collecting Valiant Comics is managing to get complete runs, with some of the later issues of titles such as *X-O Manowar*, *Solar* and *Harbinger* not as easy to find as everyone thought.

In terms of the most popular and most asked for issues from the 1990s, *Next Men* #21 (1st Hellboy) is still much sought after, while Marvel and DC collectors are still looking for *Amazing Spider-Man* #363 (1st Carnage), *Iron Man* #282 (1st War Machine), *Uncanny X-Men* #266 (1st Gambit), *Uncanny X-Men* #282 (1st Bishop), *Batman* #497 (breaking of the bat), *Batman Adventures* #12 (1st Harley Quinn), *Batman Adventures: Mad Love* (origin Harley Quinn), *Batman: Vengeance of Bane* (1st Bane), and of course, the current 1990s king of the back-issues, *New Mutants* #98 (1st Deadpool), an issue that sold for over $15,000 in CGC 10.0 condition!

A personal observation regarding 1990s comics (not including Image Comics) is the fact that collectors are beginning to realize that the actual way in which comics were created back in the 1990s was the last time the industry had dense story telling, or to use modern comic vernacular – a lack of 'decompression' – the method of slowing a given issue's story pace, down to a crawl. Although not as fast paced as 1980s or Bronze Age stories, readers of 1990s comics will notice a stark difference between stories created in the 1990s and those of the Modern era (2000-present), that difference basically boils down to value for money. This is of course due to the fact that in the 1990s, monthly comic stories were not being designed for neat packaging within trade paperbacks and as such, if a given story was written (designed) for publication in four issues, that's what would occur, instead of today, where that four issue story is padded out, becoming a six issue story – perfect for the trade. If a collector/reader is looking for thousands of inexpensive comics that feature story-dense plotting which have not yet been published in trades – the 1990s is the place to look.

Modern Comics (2000-Present): Looking in on this era of comics from the outside (as Torpedo does not currently sell Modern comics), I have come to the conclusion that the sheer overwhelming abundance of trade paperbacks (in all their myriad formats) currently depresses the value of common back-issues, leaving only limited edition variant issues with much value. On a personal level, I happen to think that with today's embarrassingly low print-runs, the regular issues of today comics may one day end up being rather hard to find, but that is purely theoretical at this time. The one series that does not suffer from this syndrome is of course, *The Walking Dead*, with original issue prices breaking records for sales, as well as thousands of trade paperbacks being sold to readers (every week) just wanting to read the stories without going bankrupt. In regards to comic material published in the modern era, I have not seen anything to match the enthusiasm for *The Walking Dead*, from either Marvel or DC.

The Walking Dead series seems to be a perfect storm of collectability, a low print-run to start, almost being cancelled, followed by a slow increase in sales and then an explosion of attention after the cable television show hit the mainstream. Those who had been collecting from the start watched the market in amazement as their issues doubled, tripled and tripled again in value and this is the main reason I believe the industry has nothing to fear in regards to digital comics. If a collector purchased *The Walking Dead* from issue #1, off the rack, then that person has a highly sought after run of expensive comics that they can sell – it's the nature of comics, the collectors mentality that pervades the industry and what sometimes rewards said collector with valuable collectibles. Digital comics can't compete with this facet of the comics industry, as electronic computer files have no actual value. When the next hot book hits the market, what do you think collectors will want – the original issue that has real value, or the digital download that ends up on their hard drive? That is not to say digital comics have no place in the industry, far from it, as I personally feel that digital comics can be used to market comic stories to an audience that is unaware of comic shops, thus bringing this curious demographic into the stores and possibly creating future sales.

In Conclusion: I became an advisor to the *Overstreet Comic Book Price Guide* in 2012, a position I take very seriously. Thus, over the last few months, I have been sending in copious amounts of suggestions to the *Guide*, in the hope of expanding the *Guide*'s information, specifically concerning the comics of the 1980s and 1990s. I believe that the more information the *Guide* has, the better for all concerned. To this end, I have been passing on my 30 years of accumulated fan and retail knowledge to the staff at the *Guide*, with the hope that I can make the *Guide* even better (hey! I have all this stuff in my head, it has to go somewhere). The *Guide* has an amazing amount of information pertaining to the Gold, Silver and Bronze Age eras, so much so, that I have little to add to those eras, however I have made it my task to bring the same amount of scrutiny to the comics of the 1980s and 1990s. In regards to Torpedo Comics, we will be embarking on more shows than ever in 2014, and I look forward to sharing any new information with my fellow dealers (and the staff of the Guide) in the next *Overstreet Comic Book Price Guide*.

IVAN KOCMAREK
COLLECTOR

My first market report has to do more with looking ahead to 2014 rather than looking back on 2013 but I do want to mention a couple of things about last year.

2013 was about the beginning of the "Rise of the Canadian Whites" or, as I like to call them, the WECA books (see my article in this issue). Like Ditko's Gorgo rousing under 6,000 fathoms of ocean or Smaug's eye opening beneath a waterfall of gold coins, the WECA books began to shake off their slumber in 2013. Awareness of the scarcity of these books and their fundamental place in the history of comics in Canada and in the general Canadian psyche has begun to up the ante in acquiring them. Collectors of these books are not restricted to Canada, there also seem to be closeted "Whites" collectors in the U.S. and the U.K.

I had the good fortune of securing a 6.5 copy of *Wow*

Comics #1 for about $600. Most VG-FN non-key Bell Features issues seemed to command prices of between $250-500 with similar non-key Anglo-American and Educational Publications books going for $150-250 (the later colour Anglo-American books of 1945-46 going for $50-125 in the same condition). Non-key VG-FN Maple Leaf Publication books, on the other hand due to their scarcity and production quality, seem to garner the highest tier prices probably ranging from $300-600.

One of the most notable finds of last year was a run of the first seven issues of Canada's first real comic book title *Better Comics* published by Maple Leaf Publications in Vancouver. These represent the first seven monthly issues of *Better Comics* running from March 1941 to September. After this, with issue number 8, *Better Comics* became bi-monthly. This collection of higher grade *Betters* (7.0 to 9.0) was found in Alberta and the strange thing was that three copies of the second Maple Leaf Publications title *Union Jack – Lucky Comics* #1 and one copy of *Union Jack- Lucky Comics* #3 and a second copy of *Better Comics* #5 also surfaced from this same collection. These books should come out as a pedigree collection once they are certified by CGC.

2014 finds WECA books having a solid representation in the *Guide* with my article elsewhere in this issue. By the time you read this, our Canadian Whites Project Group (Walter Durajlija, Stephen Lipson, Jim Finlay, Tony Andrews, and myself) will have our GCD-style website/database up and running at www.canadianwhites.ca . Two Toronto comic super-heroines, Hope Nicholson and Rachel Richey should also have their reprint edition of all the Nelvana stories from the 31 issues of *Triumph Comics* on the stands. A documentary on the Canadian Whites by director Will Pascoe titled "Lost Heroes" is also scheduled to be aired in the early part of 2014 on Super Channel in Canada and the Canadian Whites are expected to have a small permanent display (right next to a Captain Canuck display) at Walter Durajlija's Big B Niagara comic book store in Niagara Falls, Canada.

Whether you call them Whites or WECA books, 2014 should be a breakout year for them.

Editor's note: Please be sure to check out our in-depth feature article on Canadian Whites on Page 1160.

Ben Lichtenstein
Zapp Comics

Greetings from New Jersey! Last year, we reported strong sales and things only got crazier in 2013. Basically, the buying public has a fever for any first appearances, in particular when it is connected to an upcoming movie. Prices on comics such as *Avengers* #55(Ultron), *Marvel Premiere* #47(Scott Lang Ant-Man) and many others have jumped to 4 to 6 times *Guide* upon announcement of a movie storyline.

New issues have shown steady growth and while digital comics sales continue to show growth, paper floppies are still selling well. Marvel books are hit and miss in sales. There is still a sense of disorder and confusion in their line-up titles, which has hurt sales. *Superior Spider-Man* is our best seller overall, with solid sales on *Deadpool* and some of the Avengers titles. Overall, DC has maintained a more streamlined universe. Sales on the Batman titles, in particular *Batman* by Snyder, continue to roar ahead. *Superman, Green Lantern, Flash* and *Wonder Woman* continue to sell steadily, at higher levels than the Pre-New 52 days. The Independent publishers have had some well-written gems emerge, along with lots of mediocre product. A few titles that are showing strength are *Black Science, Sex Criminals, Manifest Destiny, Deadly Class,* and a few others.

The recent back issue market has been quite volatile. Many of last year's hot Image have fizzled. A trend we're seeing now is the #1 issue of most Image books selling out and popping in price, but then dropping off dramatically by issue 3 or 4. *Saga, East of West* and *Walking Dead* are still very strong for us, with back issues flying and prices holding steady. Other titles, such as *Peter Panzerfaust, Morning Glories, Thief of Thieves,* etc. have slowed down quite a bit, with the exception of #1 1st prints on these titles, which sell easily every time we stock them. *Walking Dead* back issues are strong and prices held steady from last year. *Saga* continually sells, with #1 at $100, #2 at $20 and #3 at #15. *East of West* sells well at $9 for us.

DC New 52 back issues are very strong, with high prices seen on some of the early issues. *Batman* is king, with #1 1st Prints selling fast from $50 to $70, #2 at $10, #3 at $12, #4 at $30, #5 at $12, #6 at $30, #7 at $12, #8 at $10, #9 at $15, $13 at $12. Almost all of the Death of the Family tie-ins are selling briskly, with *Batgirl* #13 and *Catwoman* #13 at $20 each and the others are $5 to $8 apiece. Almost all of the titles from DC New 52 are seeing solid back issue sales. Marvel Now back issues are steady, but only a very few have seen price appreciation.

A most welcome trend we saw strengthen in 2013 is Copper Age and Modern back issues really attracting a lot of attention. Although print runs on many of these are obviously fairly high, there is high demand. We moved at least 50 raw copies of *X-Factor* #6 from $15 to $50 and many CGC 9.8 from $240 to $420 apiece. *New Mutants* #87 keep heating up, sold many raws at $25 to $60, and #98 is an instant sell at $100 to $150 raw and $225 in 9.6, $400 in 9.8.

Overall, an interesting development is the strong prices on fine to Very Fine copies of hot books, as buyers are happy to own a copy, without much emphasis given to condition. The usual spread between a 9.6 and an 8.0 is not in seen at all when it's a hot first appearance.

See ya at the shop and on the road!

Stephen Lipson
Collector

In 2013, it can be stated that it was a remarkable year for Canadian Golden Age comic books (AKA: Canadian Whites), in terms of bringing awareness to the marketplace.

These wartime era comics hosted a stable of superheroes that where both analogous and indigenous to Canada. Such iconic heroes as Nelvana of the Northern Lights and her brethren spoke to Canada's role on both the Home front and smashing the Axis abroad.

These comics were published primarily from 1941-1946, as a result of the implementation of the War Exchange Conservation Act. Essentially items that were deemed non-essential were prohibited for import into Canada, including but not limited to, pulp literature. As a result, Canada started its own fledgling comic book industry. One can refer to the extensive article appearing in the back of this edition of the *Overstreet Comic Book Price Guide* for more information pertaining to the Golden Age Canadian comic book publishing companies and featured heroes within their pages.

Several collections came to light in 2013, of which I was the recipient.

Notable 2013 Canadian Golden Age Comic Sales:
Freelance # 1 Good $1000.00
Canada Jack # NN VG+ One-Shot $1200.00
Triumph Comics # 12 G+ $600.00
Triumph Comics # 3 G/VG $750.00
Wow Comics # 1 G/VG $550.00
Better Comics Vol 2 # 1 F/VF $1500.00
Speed Savage # NN One-Shot VG+ $1200.00

The impetus for strong sales stem from a surge in demand for these very rare and sought after books, coupled with the imminent release of the Lost Heroes Movie, which is slated for release in Spring of 2014. In fact, the demand has increased exponentially over the last 8 years, with many new collectors entering the marketplace striving to acquire these vestiges of Canadian pop-culture.

When I entered this collecting arena back in 2004, there were roughly five known collectors of these books. I would suggest that figure has increased tenfold as of this writing, and I anticipate that we will see a continued increase in the number of collectors entering the arena moving forward.

Canadian Golden Age collections are coming to market.

Collectors in this milieu of collecting are both aggressive and passionate about acquiring these books, as it is estimated that there are between only 1-10 copies extant of each comic book. As a result, rarity and desirability drives the market, irrespective of condition. For example, as of this writing I can confirm that only 6 copies of the key issue of *Triumph-Adventure Comics* #1 (1st appearance of Nelvana of the Northern Lights) remain in existence. I also anticipate that many more books of this nature will be coming to market via both auction houses and private collections in 2014, which will provide more hard data on realized sales.

Editor's note: As mentioned previously in this section of the Guide, please be sure to check out our in-depth feature article on Canadian Whites on Page 1160.

Doug Mabry
The Great Escape

Greetings from Tennessee and Kentucky! 2013 was an historic year in the mid-South. In addition to extremely strong sales in back issues, our Nashville stores were able to participate in the two new big conventions in town. It was wonderful to see our part of the country finally see some of these big happenings, and I think the attendance at both conventions showed that we're definitely able to support bigger shows.

The comic market continues to be strong for all four of our stores. We continue to see increases in sales of new comics, with of course *The Walking Dead* leading the way. But it's in the Back Issue arena that we've seen some excitement. We've had some great original owner collections come into the stores in the last year. One collection had an *Amazing Spider-Man* #1 and an *X-Men* #1 that a man's mother had saved for him all these years. Neither one lasted more than a couple of days. We've also had several smaller original owner collections pop up. And of course, we've been able to travel all around the South buying collections. In the early Fall, we were able to get a collection from Arkansas that totaled over 20,000 books.

Comic sales break down for us in this way: Shows do well for us, but mostly with tons of cheap $1.00 comics. We can sell several thousand of them in a weekend at a good show. In store sales are steady across most genres and ages, although it goes without saying that high grade and keys always sell quickest. Silver Age DC seems to be slower for us than Marvels, though. And we can't seem to keep *Amazing Spider-Man* below #150 in stock. Also, all of the Carnage Spider-Man appearances go for well over *Guide*. Humor and funny animal books do well for us, but usually only at a substantial discount. eBay sales are a mixed bag. We do really well with complete runs. Golden Age also does well. Most of the Silver Age and newer books only bring about half *Guide* or less on eBay, though. But we do send most of the original comic art we get to eBay, and it always does great.

Sales of note this year:

Golden Age: *Plastic Man* #2 GD $181.99, *Fight Comics* #31 VG $284.99, *Planet Comics* #22 VG $310.99, *Detective Comics* #85 GD- $149.99, *Tally Ho* #1 VF (signed by Frazetta) $355.00, *Superman* #24, GD-, $324.99.

Silver Age: *Adventure Comics* #247 GD- $399.99, *Amazing Spider-Man* #1 GD $1,699.99, *X-Men* #1 GD $879.99, *Rip Hunter* #1 VG $99.99, *Hot Wheels* #1 NM- $99.99, *Incredible Hulk* #181 GD- $199.99, VG- $249.99, VG

$269.99, *Avengers* #4 GD+ $249.99.
Original Art: *Savage Sword of Conan* #15, page 18, by John Buscema/Alfredo Alcala $5,000.00.

Brian Marcus
Cavalier Comics

Greetings from Wise, VA! We celebrated our 20th anniversary this past year and it was a milestone. It's been a very busy year and I'm a bit rushed to get this done with all the collections we picked up toward the end of the year so let's get to it!

While attending the Tri-State Comic Con in Huntington, WV in March 2013, I was talking to Michael Browning and he told me about a collection that was up for sale. A gentlemen named Golden Butler Adkins passed away and willed his entire collection to the Masonic lodge to which he was a member. Mike gave us the contact info and it took us two months to get a chance to see this collection. When we finally did, it was worth it. Over 47,000 comics in 200 long boxes, what an amazing sight it was. The collection consisted of runs of Marvel, DC, Gold Key, and Charlton from the early 1960s up to just a few years ago. Even though the early stuff was low grade, all the key books were there. *Amazing Fantasy* #15, *Hulk* #1, *Fantastic Four* #1, *Justice League of America* #1 and much more. After a few months, we were able to come to an agreement and acquired the collection in early September. We are still going through it as of this writing but I can report that we've sold the *X-Men* #1 in Good condition for $1045 and the *Amazing Spider-Man* #1 in VG for $4000. Many books will be sent to CGC then off to Comiclink for auction. We are calling this the "Butler" collection.

We also had a chance to buy several comics off of a minor celebrity in Louisville, KY this past summer. Purchases included runs of high grade Marvel horror magazines, Marvel and DC horror titles, high grade Gold Key Walt Disney digests and several key books such as *Green Lantern* #76 and *Tales of Suspense* #57.

We only do around 5 or 6 conventions a year but with the collections we've acquired recently, that number will likely double.

New comic sales for DC have been consistent with *Batman* and *Superman Unchained* leading the pack. As for Marvel, sales have slipped but *Superior Spider-Man* has picked up. Event books from both companies are falling flat the past year. Come on guys, let's just get back to good storytelling in the individual books instead of some huge world changing event twice a year.

Sales of *Walking Dead*, *Saga* and *East of West* been very strong. Image keeps putting out some solid books. The only thing notable from Dark Horse this past year has been the *Star Wars* Lucas Draft.

My dollar bin sales have been burning it up the past year. I've always had a great selection of cheap books and my customers love it! Trade Paperback sales have been up which makes up for the slower new book sales.

Modern Age keys continue to sell well like *Amazing Spider-Man* #300, *X-Men* #266, *Next Men* #21 and especially *Batman Adventures* #12. Anything with Harley Quinn is difficult to keep in stock. *X-Factor* #6 is heating up with the announcement of Apocalypse for the next X-Men movie.

Notable in store sales include *Detective Comics* #400 CGC 8.0 $150, *Silver Surfer* #1 F+ $175, #4 Fine $135, Batman Death in the Family set $80, *Watchmen* #1-12 $100.

Jon McClure
Collector

Hello to friends and fellow collectors from Portland, Oregon! My best sales this year were Golden Age books of all types, at 150-200% *Guide*, sold in antique stores and mall spaces, largely as novelties and memory triggers. *Iron Man* #55 and *Scooby Doo* #1 are among the hottest books just as they were last year, and I am perpetually sold out of such books in any grade. Hard to find horror mags like Eerie Publications and Skywald are hot, and the latter is especially hard to find. Bronze Age horror remains a top mover for me across the board, with Marvel reprints surprisingly as popular, for the most part, as DC non-reprints from the same years (1972-1975), probably because of the era covers, by John Romita and other talents.

© MAR

Amazing Spider-Man #171 and other 35¢ variants are among the top issues of the Bronze Age.

Archie 15-cent cover price variants surface so rarely that it is hard to say what their current market values are, but their scarcity appears to be 200-500 to 1, based on Doug Sulipa's inventory as it has been lamely argued that such books are Canadian price variants and not U.S. test market variants. The majority of 15-cent Archie variants issues have been confirmed to exist since my variant article appeared in *Overstreet Guide* #40, pages 1010-1038, as have many other types of variants, including new types and subtypes of variants. I am compiling information for a variant update that should be completed and ready by the time *OPG* #47 arrives.

In my opinion, based on dollar sales realized, only three non-variant comics, namely *Green Lantern* #76, *Incredible Hulk* #181, and *Cerebus* #1, should be considered in the top 10 Bronze issues, with the other seven being a mix of Marvel 30 and 35-cent cover price variants; such examples include *Amazing Spider-Man* #169-173, *Kid Colt* #218-220, *Scooby Doo* #1, *Star Wars* #2-4. A number of Marvel 30-cent cover price variants among the ultra-scarce western and horror titles are routinely breaking the $1,000 barrier in mid-grade, that is, when they surface at all. Eight out of ten top ten Bronze Age comics listed are almost entirely common keys, because they are books with regularly reported sales and historical significance, as opposed to non-standard scarce books bringing much higher prices, of variant nature or not. Collectors and obsessives are primarily the backbone of such unusual but understandable acquisitions.

I ask you to consider for a moment the potential sale of a high grade *Action* #1, with or without provenance, and then consider how rarely a comic of such rarity and magnitude hits the market. Without reported sales related to such key items, how does one adjust upward annually, over a period of many years, other than speculatively, without an actual sale to refer to, an assigned or assumed value? Bob Overstreet has for decades been tasked to employ a careful logic to theorize an ultimate and relative value based on pop culture significance, based on similar iconic key book sale quite conservatively, a strategy that he has had no choice but to employ given circumstance. For the sake of argument, let's say a copy of *Detective Comics* #1 landed on the desk of any shaker and mover dealer, in any CGC certified grade higher than VF 8.0 tomorrow... regardless of the auction hammer, the book would automatically go to a higher incremental dollar value in the *Guide* (*Detective Comics* #1, theoretically the 21st most valuable comic ever published, is listed at $92,000 in VF 8.0 in *OPG* #43 because no better copy has been to date been viewed) without any reported sales based on educated assumptions and existing price spreads. Although convenient, such price formulas fail to accurately convey the sluggish FN/VF to VF market when compared to the marketability of lower grade reading copies.

The true financial value of any comic, beyond personal significance, ought to include a genuine dollar worth, as in "I'm cashing out today." Comics are not liquid commodities like gold, and silver, and other standard trade items. Comic books are, by nature, speculative. Collectors, quick-flip speculators, long-term investors, and dealers all know such considerations are true and fully valid, but again, the top 10 Bronze Age comic book list is based on historical significance and reported sales, which is a polar opposite to instant liquidity and therefore, a conceptually fluid relative value. Three notable Bronze Age variant sales from the past year that were sold on eBay include *DC Comics Presents* #22 Whitman variant, which sold on 09/13 for $402 in raw 4.5 VG+; *Kid Colt Outlaw* #208 which sold on 12/23/13 for $1628 in raw 7.0 F/VF; and *Weird Wonder Tales* #15 which sold on 12/19/13 for $255 in raw 2.0 condition.

Early Direct Marvel Comics Editions beginning 2/77 and running through 5/79 (1-3/78, 7/78, and 3-4/79 seem to have been skipped) are far scarcer than newsstand editions of the same era, selling in the $40-$125 range depending on desirability, grade, and scarcity. Such books were distributed by Whitman in Whitman bags, but are the same books; in the early direct market, this non-returnable higher discount tier was made possible and profitable by creating the "special market edition" option via distribution in Whitman bags, in grocery and department stores respectively. Such books were mistakenly referred to as "Marvel Whitmans" for many years.

Best regards to everyone everywhere until next year!

TODD MCDEVITT
NEW DIMENSION COMICS

Since I think it's valuable to know where the insight in these market reports is coming from, here is a little history on me. I started out with a small store in my hometown of Ellwood City, Pennsylvania in 1986. Since then, New Dimension Comics has grown to 5 stores surrounding the Pittsburgh area. When I started, I thought it would be just me in one store having fun selling comics. I never expected to grow to 5 stores and 50-some employees. All this time dedicating my life to comics seems to have earned me the chance to rant here once a year. I hope you can find some nugget of usefulness buried in here somewhere!

Buying Overview: I easily get offered 3-5 collections a day. I feel that it is my job to turn over every stone and dig into what is being offered to me. Of course, it's mostly schlock from the '80s and '90s. I will always buy it, but with a huge overstock on most of it, I use the phrase "pennies apiece" a lot when describing what I will pay. The joke is that I would make a great doctor since I deliver bad news so well. Folks usually aren't excited to hear that comics they paid $2-3 each for will now just return them a fraction of that. But, many are realistic, enjoyed their reading, and part with them comfortably. The other end of the spectrum is the vintage stuff. As I write this, I was offered a *Batman* #1 yesterday and another great batch of books from 1941-1942 just today. It's very comforting to know that these finds still happen. I have many hungry customers for them. Between 5 store locations, attending conventions, wholesale activity, and other venues, they go out the door quickly. My job most days is just to keep the NDC machine fed with cool comics!

Convention Scene: Many big cons are turning into autograph & sketch events. As such, I often have better success at small, regional, 1-day shows. They are more affordable, both for me to set up and for attendees to pay a small admission price. There are 2 distinct crowds here. Fans that want to pay a lot for an autograph/photo or sketch opportunity and collectors who want to expand their collection. These don't seem to overlap much. Maybe a few will go after a Stan Lee "experience" since he is such an icon to comic fans as well, but shows that focus on celebrities are not drawing much in the way of comic fans. So, at these small shows, I typically bring a giant array of cheap Silver Age, often $3 each, sometime $1 or $5 each (different stocks). This has made my life much easier. I buy a TON of collections and the only challenge is churning through them all quickly. In my early days, I would bag, board, look up, price, and sort them all. That takes forever! These days, I process a collection of oldies by dividing them into chunks of $1, $3, $5, $10 (often displayed on a rack as specials), and "real" books that are worth the time to showcase. Even with this shortcut, I am still overwhelmed with old comics to process. Just this year, having built my $3 selection to 45 long boxes, I had to create ANOTHER stock, currently at about 30 long boxes. Many of these comics may "book" for $10-15, but with so many rolling in, I have to keep them moving with attractive pricing.

Golden Age: Same story here. I can't get enough. What popular books do roll in, I sell right away. This past years sales include *Planet Comics, Young Allies, Superman, Rangers Comics*, tons of ECs, and many more I can't recall. Every year, I vow I will do a better job of tracking key sales to mention them here and I always forget. Sometimes these sales are pretty big piles too, often to other dealers who must see some room in my grading/pricing to make a buck elsewhere. We all have different needs, different customers. Same here. Heck, I have traded 2 comics for 30 long boxes just this year! Another note, it seems the low grade, even incomplete, books that are highly desirable sell way above *Guide*. Books that are in demand due to their classic covers make this happen the best. I have put crazy, "I'll keep looking at it if no one buys it" prices on a few this past year and they still sold.

Silver Age: Here's a rant I have been stewing on for a few years now. I use it often when buying collections and it seems to apply the most to Silver Age. Keys rule. I have made up a ratio of 30-to-1. Totally my gut, but I would love to survey and research to get a real sense of this statistic. The idea is that for every 1 person who collects say *Amazing Spider-Man*, there are 30 who are buying just the key issues. This makes the demand for a *Spidey* #1 FAR outweighing even the #2. Sure, the value is higher already, but to me I look at the #1 as a quick seller since the market for that key is hungry. But the #2, I'll have it for a while. It will sell, but likely to a guy collecting the run. And there are just fewer of those guys. So, another way to say this is that fans just buying keys are driving the price up on them far more than those seeking out the full runs. On another point here, I have to mention how the films, especially the Marvel movies, have driven demand. It's like they have provided justification for fans, some who might not have been too inclined to pull the trigger on pricey keys in the past, to spend a wad of cash on a funny book. Maybe they are justifying it to themselves, their wives, or their financial adviser. I have one fellow who has an amazing collection. Every year, he mentions to his financial consultant about selling it. And so far, every year he replies saying that "if you are seeing that kind of growth, I can't see any other place to put that money that makes sense". Wow. Talk about validation!

Modern Age: New comics are like fruit. Best fresh. Old fruit gets discounted. Really old fruit gets mashed up and made into pies. OK, maybe that last part doesn't make sense, but my point is that new comics, still the best seller in my 5 stores, rule. I compare it to opening weekend of a film. Fans who can't wait to see it flock to theaters to spend top dollar to see it first. Same with new comics. Monthly readers can't wait to read the next chapter. Some movie patrons will wait for the DVD release. Maybe they want to wait for the reviews and feedback to influence their decision to see it. In comics, this is graphic novels. Wait, see if it's well liked/reviewed, and read a whole story. Side note, I have tried to stop using the term "trade paperbacks". No one outside our industry knows what that means. I have watched my staff say it to soccer moms and them glaze over. I think "graphic novel" is more descriptive and socially consumable. Please join me in dropping one of these barriers discouraging new people from entering our fantastic hobby. Graphic novels!!

Back Issues: I love back issues. While many stores have not been able to justify dedicating the sales floor for them, I have always believed that it is an essential part of the identity of a comic book shop. That passion has translated into my 5 stores with a robust, constantly updated back issue selection. Additionally, I host many bargain priced sales events each year. Most legendarily, I open the basement of my biggest store twice per year and offer the comics at $1 each. Almost 500,000 comics, all sorted. It justifies my existence to see fans come from FAR away, many making a weekend out of it, to dive in. So, how do I make this work? Buying. Lots of buying. It's important to me to keep the flow of fresh stocks rolling in. So, I have been more aggressive than ever buying large, often hundreds of long boxes at a time, overstock bulk inventories. It has taken me 28 years to establish a solid clientele for these, but since I'm one of the few that has given this category focus, I just need to keep feeding the beast!

Steve Mortensen
Miracle Comics

Comics are no longer for nerds but an integral part of popular culture. Ten years ago the average person had no idea who Thor was, or the Avengers, Iron Man, or the X-Men. Now many have become fans and look forward to the movies. This has had a dramatic effect on the comic book industry, especially the back issue market. New collectors are entering the market and old collectors are getting back into the hobby. Another interesting change is the growing international market. At least 10% of my sales are going to international buyers. This is up from less than 5% ten years ago.

Most of my sales are in Bronze, Copper, and Modern Age comics. I love that niche, since I began collecting comics as a child in the 1980s. Some notable sales in 2013 include: *DC Comics Presents* #26 CGC 9.8 (1st New Teen Titans) for $301; *Amazing Spider-Man* #189 CGC 9.8 for $128, #199 CGC 9.8 for $95, #300 CGC 9.8 for $688, #316 CGC 9.8 (McFarlane Venom cover) for $125, #361 CGC 9.8 (1st Carnage) for $129; *Saga* #1 CGC 9.8 for $172; *Deadpool Kills the Marvel Universe* #1 CGC 9.9 MINT for $100; *Captain Britain* #1 CGC 9.0 (UK edition) for $198; *Haunt of Horror* #1 CGC 9.8 (Marvel Magazine) for $121; *Marvel Tales* #146 CGC 9.8 (*Amazing Spider-Man* #9 reprint) for $81; *Transformers* #1 CGC 9.8 (Marvel) for $182; *Daredevil* #232 CGC 9.8 (Miller story, 1st Nuke) for #128; *Swamp Thing* #3 CGC 9.8 (Wrightson art) for $298; *Punisher* #1

CGC 9.8 (1987, ongoing series) for $73; *Star Wars Annual* #2 CGC 9.8 for $411; *Secret Wars* #8 CGC 9.8 (Black Costume) for $128; *Web of Spider-Man* #1 CGC 9.8 for $70; *Marvel Super Heroes Contest of Champions* #1 CGC 9.8 (Marvel's first mini-series) for $108; *Star Wars* #1 CGC 9.8 (Bronze Age) for $535; *Think Tank* #1 CGC 9.8 for $63; *Tomb of Dracula* #58 CGC 9.8 (Blade cover) for $93; *Incredible Hulk* #340 CGC 9.8 for $212; *Thor* #337 CGC 9.8 (1st Beta Ray Bill) for $192; *Predator* #2 CGC 9.8 (Dark Horse) for $128; *Champions* #1 CGC 9.8 for $275; *Marvel Comics Super Special* #1 CGC 7.5 (Kiss) for $127; *Infinity Gauntlet* #1 CGC 9.8 for $111; *Walking Dead* #9 CGC 9.8 for $142, #27 CGC 9.8 (1st Governor) for $350; *Batman* #442 CGC 9.8 (1st Tim Drake as Robin) for $91; *New Mutants* #87 CGC 9.8 for $187; *Macross* #1 CGC 9.8 (Robotech) for $258; *Spider-Man and His Amazing Friends* #1 CGC 9.8 (NBC Cartoon) for $131; *Uncanny X-Men* #141 CGC 9.8 for $360; *Spawn* #10 CGC 9.8 (Cerebus cover) for $158; *Booster Gold* #1 CGC 9.8 (1st app) for $199; *Thing* #1 CGC 9.8 for $124; *Classic X-Men* #1 CGC 9.8 for $159; *Spider-Man* #13 CGC 9.8 (McFarlane black costume cover) for $81; *Spectacular Spider-Man* #64 CGC 9.8 (1st Cloak & Dagger) for $281.

The most surprising sale to me was the *Marvel Tales* #146 CGC 9.8 for $81. I think it was the most non-descript book in the lot, which suggests that collectors are not just flocking to key books but purchasing issues to fill runs in their collections. True, the book offers an affordable alternative to *Amazing Spider-Man* #9 in a similar grade, but what a premium in CGC 9.8!

For those of you looking to invest in Modern comics, I recommend checking out the titles from Image Comics. They continue to produce original stories with great art, and many collectors are buying them up in hope of finding the next *Walking Dead*. One example is *Peter Panzerfaust*, which was published in 2012. In the UK, the BBC plans a television series around the World War II Peter Pan take-off. Copies in CGC 9.8 are selling in the $300-400 range – as part of the hype surrounding the possibility of the series making it to TV. Another such comic, although not published by Image but by Abstract Studio, is *Rachel Rising*. It is a modern day horror comic combining elements of *The Exorcist* and *Lost*. It is selling between $400-500 in CGC 9.8 – a very tough grade on a book with most of the copies having spine damage. It had a very small print run and is expected to be made into a television series as well.

Looking ahead, I think we will see a nice spike in price for key *Star Wars* issues. There may even be some surprises in the 1990-2000s Dark Horse issues as characters may be pulled into the new movies and their first appearances may go up in value. Of course the holy grail of *Star Wars* collectors is issue #1 from 1977. The copies I've been able to find have been selling in the $500 range in CGC 9.8 with white pages. The 35-cent variant continues to rise in value with the sale of a CGC 9.4 copy in August for $15,535.

Marc Nathan
Cards, Comics and Collectibles
The Baltimore Comic-Con

Every year we do a very large Free Comic Book Day. Last year, we had Frank Cho, Adam Kubert, and Steve Conley, among others, just giving away comics, having cosplayers, and everything else we do. I imagine that we will have to do something even bigger – and that's based upon the fact that my anniversary is on May 1. So, it's a nice coincidence that Free Comic Book Day was established on the time that I opened – May 1, 1984. Also, it's nice that Marvel puts out movies just for us, too. Just for fun. [laughter]

Unchanged in 30 Years: *X-Men* still sells real well, and so does *Amazing Spider-Man.*

What Has Changed?: In 1984, *Batman* did not sell well. In fact, *Batman* did not sell well until *The Dark Knight* and *Batman* #400. Those two books together started the interest in *Batman*. And today, the book just percolates up and down to the point that it's sometimes the best-selling book and sometimes it is a Top 15 kind of book – but always an interesting book. But now, since 1989 on, it's been a super book.

I would say that seven or eight years ago, there was a definitive line between us – the comic book market – and mainstream pop culture. Even though *Star Wars*, and *Indiana Jones*, and *Aliens*, and anything like that were peripherally ours – it was *kind of* ours. Now, all of pop culture seems to be reflective of what we do, and there is no line between mainstream pop culture and us. And with things like *Walking Dead*, *Adventure Time*, and *The Big Bang Theory*, as well as all the Marvel movies, and even the DC movies, we are the absolute mainstream. We are what we sell and what we do.

In addition to that, the back part of the *Previews* catalog is much more reflective of pop culture than it was in the past. In your lifetime did you ever think that you would be able to buy a Moon Knight glass? There's much more things to buy and be merchandized. There's not just comics, there's toys and statues, banks, clocks and anything imaginable with our characters on it.

There are so many characters that are being merchandized to us now. Sure, a Spider-Man or Superman beach ball seemed to be an absolute, but did we ever imagine that a one-time secondary hero like Iron Man would be Marvel's best known character in the year of 2013? That would have been crazy talk 15 years ago. And, you know, there was a period of time coming out of "Heroes Reborn" that *Iron Man*, I think, would have been borderline being canceled. There was a period of time where they didn't know what to do with the character. Now, he seems to be – for some unknown reason – the center of the universe.

When Marvel Did Well, The Industry Did Well: Yes, Marvel kept the lights on. But DC has since had a lot of things going right for them, including their trade paperback and hardcover program which seems to succeed and exceed better than most anyone's – which, I'm sure, stupefies a lot of people. Although Marvel is quickly catching up, and has quickly caught up. It's funny, sitting here a couple of days before Christmas, can I keep a copy of *Infinity Gauntlet* on the shelf? There are things like that which seem obvious, but thankfully I have it to keep it on the shelf. Thankfully it is in print. It seems obvious, but there was a period of time when the most successful Marvel stories were not in collections. Now, thankfully, most of them are.

Marvel collections sell briskly and wonderfully. So, in terms of where DC is, I'd say Marvel has caught up. And there are certain things like the *Walking Dead* trade paperback program that are beating *Sandman, Preacher*, and all those collections. With that said, there are still DC collections that keep going and going and going. I feel like I have to reorder one or two every week.

© CN

The success of **Adventure Time** shows the mainstreaming of comics pop culture.

And then DC comes up with certain things like "The New 52" and the 3-D covers of this year that blows away everything else in the month (of their release). The current state of affairs at DC is still a "we'll see," but boy, I have to tell you that every week that goes by, because of the accessibility of 25+ issues, I feel like I'm gaining people *again* after the 3-D covers on DC monthlies. The readers may not know everything that's going on, but it seems easy for them to try to get caught up and into it. Then you have other things like TV's *Arrow*, which is creating interest in all of DC Comics' characters again.

Speculators: In the '90s when the speculator boom was happening, there really wasn't the ability for collectors to sell comics on eBay or through other auction houses. There were only local shows for the speculator to sell his books right away. What I'm seeing now is the regular customer, the guy who comes in and buys his *Batman* every month anyway, buying the 3-D covers or buying whatever trick there is – and buying three or four of them. He's buying the one for himself and stashing it, then selling the rest because he is his own auction house now. He can take one comic and see how it does. Yes, I notice people buying certain things that are reported hot, more than one copy, be it the latest Image hot, under-printed #1, or anything like that. And flipping it to supplement themselves.

Now, everybody's their own retail outlet for that. But as far as it crashing like it did in the '90s, I can't really foresee that. The crash was really generated by people who got burned. Today's speculators aren't really holding on to a *Harbinger* #0 or a *X-Men* #1 or an *X-Force* #1 or any million-printed book thinking they are going to be rich. They're not thinking about 10 years from now, or even three years from now, they are doing it now. They buy the book because they heard it sold out from the publisher, and they believe they can get $10 or $20 right now – which is what they're doing.

They are not waiting, holding, and hoping. They are buying. Because of the Internet news sites, they know exactly what to buy. They are not guessing themselves or considering it an afterthought, they are reading that a book sold out on a news site, buying it in their local stores, and selling it within weeks. They are an educated consumer.

I don't have anyone in this store buying 10 copies of a book speculating for something that will never happen. They are buying what they believe to be a genuine collectible because they read about it already – or they want three copies of them. Sometimes they do. If a new Image book comes out with a hot creator or creators, in some cases, they buy three of them because they like Ed Brubaker or Mark Millar or Grant Morrison or someone. They are buying it for that sake and not for the sake of a shiny cover.

Modern Comics: It seems that what's happening with Image back issues is not necessarily the result of under-printed issues, but perhaps a very informed consumer base. There's now a second wave in which customers who are already reading a title learn that there could be a TV show or movie based on a particular comic.

When my customers read that a book could be a larger property, they go ballistic. Anything like that blows up from being a $20 book to a $50 or $80 item, or wherever it goes. It will go how high it can go. There were rumors for things, and then the rumors escalate, and it may or may not happen. But in the rumor time, and that would be the rumor time of *Chew*, *Rachel Rising* or *Thief of Thieves*, when that happens, boy they escalate fast because my customers know; they are an educated buyers.

They read the news sites and think that a property has been optioned. Of course, back in the day, everything was optioned and nothing was made. People would walk up and down San Diego, and they would buy every property for a minimal fee, and held it against the other guy. And things never got developed. But now, with news sites, people know that this is happening. And when they are attached to a well-known creator, something is most likely to happen. And when it seems likely, again, it escalates faster – and there's a known. If Robert Kirkman is attached to *Thief of Thieves*, that seems likelier that it could be made into a TV or movie property. Obviously, Robert is going to make another series someday.

The Walking Dead's sales and success has creators looking at Image again. The money that *Walking Dead* is generating for Image has allowed them to do many things and to take better chances. And again attract super names and super creative people.

Silver Age: Silver Age Marvels across the board are selling as well as they ever have in 30 years. Now, there was a period of time in the late '80s and early '90s, during the market boom, where *Guide* to *Guide*, month to month, things were jumping. That may not be the case across the board. However, anything relating to a movie, which at Marvel could be anything. Every character is rumored, or is being done, or has done a movie. And there is interest in a great scope than we collect. If we collect Steve Ditko and Jack Kirby, they are collecting the first appearance of S.H.I.E.L.D. and Iron Man – and I hear Ant-Man is going to be a movie. Those movie-related titles are being sold as fast as any store can get them and any show can supply them. There is an insatiable market for the Marvel keys, first appearances, #1s, and epic) storylines. Those kind of things speculate and burst.

Silver DCs are percolating. Some things seem very quiet. You know, it's funny with DCs because you can say they are quiet, and then something happens and it wakes up. Do I believe that issues of *Atom* and *Metal Men* and *Hawkman* are quiet? Certainly. *Mystery In Space* and Adam Strange – they get quiet. Ten cent *Batman*, there are not enough of them in the world for the collectors – certainly not enough in grade. *Superman* always sells, *Action* and *Adventure* sell occasionally. *Green Lantern* – probably at this point – are overpriced. I'm talking about real Silver Age *Green Lanterns*, not Neal Adams. With the Neal Adams *Green Lantern*, there is no end in sight. Silver Age Neal Adams books there is no end to them, because Neal is doing so many shows now and he is everywhere. That's part of it, I think.

There's still a speculative market and whispers of a *Justice League* movie, so that makes *Justice League of America* #1 and *Brave and the Bold* #28 spike out. There's still *Showcase* #4, which is infinitely rare. There is still *Flash* #123, which is so cool that once you show it to someone they have to have it. There are certain books that will always be that way, but as a whole, you can still find a good bargain in the market place. I think that you can go to a convention and buy the right classic DCs at a bargain, and it would be the right thing to do. I don't think buying lesser DC keys at a bargain is a bad thing to do. I think you can buy *Flash* #105, and *Brave and the Bold* first appearances of any character is a good thing, because you never know. Looking for *Showcase* #30 or *Aquaman* #1 may sound like a foolish task, but just wait for the whispers of an *Aquaman* project, because its probably being discussed somewhere as the next big franchise. I think that if Warner wanted to make something as silly as *Metamorpho*, it might make a great movie. You could get the whole run of *Metamorpho* very cheaply at any point right now, but not for long if something like that were to come out. Something like that can happen, although it may not be *Metamorpho*, it might be *Angel and the Ape*. We don't know, but it may be something as silly as that.

This may sound stupid and silly, but ten years ago if I were to suggest an *Ant-Man* movie, a *Guardians of a Galaxy* movie, or a raccoon in a Marvel movie, you would have said "no way." And yet, you know that Warner Bros. is going to do something to counter this and there are plenty of things that seem foolish, yet they probably aren't if handled well. I would think a *Hawkman* movie would be great. When it comes to Silver Age, I think everything is wide open and I think everything is in play. I think that instead of being on the wave, that being ahead of the wave is buying any Silver Age first appearance. I think the smart collectors are and I think that's already been established. I think that when you look at *Showcase* #27 and, say, the first Sea Devils, why can't that make a good TV show. Why can't it be – or why can't it be anything. It certainly could be. Anything like that can happen because its owned, its out there, and it can be made. And, silly ones have already been done, you know – just not across the board.

Golden Age: Obviously, early Golden Age and World War II Gold sells quick and fast. Gold prices of standard, well-known super-hero books are holding strong and always sell. There are certain conventions in the country, and in this store, too, where they always sell. There are certain aspects of Gold that are esoteric that takes a longer time to sell, but that doesn't mean that they don't or won't. To break it down: Timelys always sell well, super-hero DCs always sell well, World War II covers always sell faster and quicker – mostly from dealer to dealer. Whereas Fiction House or Lev Gleason titles, or anything like that sell much slower. Dells still sell well, certain Dells sell great.

Real esoteric Golden Age titles sell wonderfully. And breaking into the '50s, pre-Code horror sells wonderfully well. Atlas sells probably above *Guide* in cases, especially if it's above VG. ECs sell great, in spite of being reprinted a thousand times. Especially if it has a specific cover, they sell above *Guide*. Sometimes well above *Guide* if it is the right cover. Most folks know that. The collector knows that – and the person who has it knows it generally.

Variants: Variants by the publisher, from what I see by online sales, ones that sell the best are ones drawn by the best people. It's like what I've always said: If its a chase cover, make it worth having. And you know who those guys are. If the best artists are doing your 1:50 or 1:100 cover, then that's what collectors want. They want that artist. If it's a 1:50 or 1:100 cover drawn by a guy who doesn't have that stature of collectability – he's just really good – that cover won't sell well. There's just a handful of people in the market who collectors chase down their variants. If there is a chase variant by a certain guy – I'm trying hard not to name names – his covers will always explode in the marketplace, because his fans have to have everything that that guy draws. Whereas a really nice cover drawn by a standard guy just sits. In addition, if it's just a black-and-white version of a cover they already bought, it's not necessarily that important either. You know, just like a sketch cover or a line-art cover of a book that they have already seen colored, it's just okay.

Now, all my store variants are not being bought by speculators. They are being bought by people who want everything of that book or that character. In addition to that, if I do have a specific person drawing the cover, he obviously has an audience also. In addition to that, whatever publisher that I do a variant with, there are people that collect everything by that publisher. There are people out there that own every comic by BOOM! or every comic by Dynamite, or every Marvel comic. And if you do one that's something that (collectors) have to seek out and find, when they find out it is out there, the collector has to have everything.

If (a collector) owns every comic book that Dynamite has made, and they want a complete collection, they have to find out how to track down the variant at Cards, Comics and Collectibles in Reisterstown, Maryland. That does happen.

Our Variants: There are a lot of reasons we decided to do our variants, both for our store and for The Baltimore Comic-Con. Some of the publishers that I am doing this with, I have great friendships. And I want to help them. Partially, also, because I am at most national level shows, I have an opportunity outside of Reisterstown to sell them, as well as on our website – I have lots of ways to sell them. They're also wonderful things for store signings or to create an event. Or even a show signing. If I do a specific variant for a convention, I can have that person sitting in my booth doing a signing. There are lots of aspects to it.

But why I am doing it in general, I guess the basic answer is that I just enjoy it. I really like to do it, and I see no end in the long term. If anyone thought they could do this for a short term gain, there's no way. That's living in a dream world. That's digging in the backyard for gold. This is selling a print run for a long time and believing in what you are buying. That can be a longtime thing. And no way do you go to a convention and think you'll sell 1,000 of something. You sell dozens, and you take them to the next show and sell dozens, and dozens, and dozens. And it's profitable over a long period of time. So, you better have storage, you better have a well-thought process – which, when I agreed to do this, I thought about it as a long-term project. This wasn't something that I was going to do in a short period of time and see how it works. There's no way that would have worked.

Digital Comics: Boy, a year and a half ago, weren't all brick-and-mortar stores worried about digital comics? And yet, I have to say that for a brief period of time, there was a concern. A lot of focus was put on it, and a lot of marketing money was spent on it. A lot of time was dealt with it.

Running the convention, though, gave me a different insight than some people who were really fearful. While running the convention I saw – because I had to manage it – the hundreds to thousands of people waiting in line to meet wonderful creators like David Finch and Jim Lee. And they weren't holding their iPad to get signed. They were holding physical things like comic books to get autographed.

The aspect that I would say was established at the San Diego Comic-Con in the '70s, that Jack Kirby and Carl Barks specifically put forward, was that they were infinitely accessible and kind and wonderful to their fans. And when they met a gratified fan, they were gratified back. It's something that you don't get from the movies or even folks that write books.

Almost every weekend, you can meet your favorite comic book celebrity or at least one of them. And 99% of creators are just as kind and wonderful as Jack Kirby and Carl Barks established dozens and dozens of years ago. And it has carried on, for the most part, to future generations of comic book creators – where they are absolutely gratified and kind to their fans.

As long as they are that way, why wouldn't fans want an autograph on something, and that something tends to be a comic book. That aspect of it – with conventions growing and lines getting longer and there is more accessibility all across the country – so every fan has their chance to meet their favorite creator at some point. There's always going to be comics because it's just how the fans want to have them.

Sure, the digital age is important, but I think the digital comic is just another format. I think that a digital comic is just another format like a hardcover or a slipcase or anything else – it's just another aspect. And I have the specific person in mind when I say he bought *Kingdom Come* four months in a row. Then he bought the skinny little hardcover. Then he bought the *Absolute*. And then he bought a digital comic. And he bought all of them. Why? Because he loves that book so much that he owns them all to this day in those different formats. Now, can you explain that? I can't. I think that's more of the norm.

I think that digital comics' effect on what we're doing is tiny. I don't think at this point that it's the earth-shattering thing we thought it could be. There was a great fear of it a few years ago. Now, I think we have jumped that track. There are specific sales charts that I have seen that suggest that print is far exceeding digital sales to the point that they have to take a second look at us. And I think part of it is that we are doing our job smarter and better, publishers are being more supportive of what we are doing, and the aspect of conventions certainly helps. And when I say that, and I can say this specifically, when I announce a specific guest at my show, my sales for the books of that guy increase. When I say Garth Ennis is coming back to Baltimore, and Garth Ennis launches a new book with Dynamite, Dynamite's sales increase because there's a "pamphlet" to get autographed. When I announce something like Garth Ennis, I know that throughout this general area, *Preacher* #1 is going to become a signature series comic book that goes from a normal back issue to a very expensive piece of collectible.

That happens. Then you go back to that everybody is their own auction house. The convention gives them that ability. Again, it all goes back to the person sitting at the table is all so kind and so genuine to the fan that they want this to succeed that way. Again, I don't think they are getting their iPad signed or even their phone. I don't think that happens.

Other Changes: This will really open up a can of worms in the collectible market of what we do, and I think its specific to the largest places where we sell things at – like the New York and San Diego shows. I think New York and San Diego – not yet Baltimore or Charlotte or MegaCon . . .not yet those shows – but at the largest of conventions, the 150,000 person convention, we are meeting some people who are wandering through our halls for the first time, whose only interest in what we do is what they like from different mediums. They want a *Tales of Suspense* #39, a *Journey Into*

Mystery #83, or even an *Iron Man* #1 – or those kind of things. They have zero interest in a *Journey Into Mystery* #84 or an *Iron Man* #2. They have zero interest in it. They want an *Iron Man* #1 or #55 – they don't want anything else, to the point that if this trend continues then more and more people will enter our arena only wanting those books, and, boy, its coming fast.

We believed that it only happened in auction houses where it was for the high-end. We know that major celebrities like Steven Spielberg or Nicolas Cage bought *Batman* #1, *Action* #1 and *Superman* #1, and maybe not *Superman* #8. We knew that. And they would only buy high-end through auction houses or specific retailers they were friends with. Now it's happening to people who are coming into the door for the first time, because they saw a movie or watched a TV show. They might buy a *Walking Dead* #1 but they have no interest in #6. I think if that trend continues, from a retailer perspective, it will make an *Iron Man* #2 almost worthless in the long run. Especially to shows like New York and San Diego where the cost of doing the show is so expensive, why take an *Iron Man* #2 when I might get only a portion of *Guide* because no one is interested in it in that audience? But everyone wants an *Iron Man* #1, where at that point, *Guide* doesn't even matter. It's going to be a fight to the finish where 100,000 people are going to want what there's only 15 of in the room. And if that's the case, the room is only going to have those books in it, if that continues.

And if that trend continues, it will be a trend in the marketplace that might only happen in those specific markets. But if it does, it has to be reflective to the *Guide* in that an *Iron Man* #1 to an *Iron Man* #2 could be as ludicrous as 1,000 to one. As crazy as that sounds, if you compare it to the numbers of the audience of the conventions, there are many national show retailers that buy at those events. And they put books away for those shows. But if I have 10 copies of *Amazing Spider-Man* #129, and I sell them all at New York for multiples of *Guide* because there's rumors of a *Punisher* movie or something, with the trend, what does that do to the next day? What does that do to the day after the New York show?

It means that I'm willing to pay *Guide* for one of these media-related books because I'm getting multiples of *Guide*. The *Guide* should show it, but it is a dangerous slope because everyday sales don't require that. It requires it four times out of the year, or three times out of the year. But it will be the marketplace on those days, Its very specific, but its absolutely happening. It affects my buying habits year around.

Overstreet Advisor Scott Braden assisted with the preparation of this market report.

JOSH NATHANSON
DOUGLAS GILLOCK
COMICLINK

2013 was another exciting year in the hobby with ComicLink buyers and sellers utilizing ComicLink Auctions as well as the Comic Book Exchange and Comic Art Exchange in order to buy and sell valuable comic books and comic art to add to their collections and maximize returns.

Demand is ever-present for comic books from the Silver Age genre. Major Marvel keys led the way in 2013 with exceptional results for several premiere and first appearance issues achieved. Just a few examples include *Avengers* #1 CGC 9.4 $132,500, *Amazing Fantasy* #15 CGC 8.5 for $120,100, $85,000 for an 8.0 and $44,555 for a CGC 7.0, *Amazing Spider-Man* #1 CGC 9.4 $110,000 and CGC 9.0 for $42,900, *Fantastic Four* #1 CGC 8.5 for $64,000, *Fantastic Four* #12 CGC 9.6 $65,000, *Tales to Astonish* #27 (first Ant-Man) CGC 8.5 $22,000, and *Incredible Hulk* #1 CGC 6.5 for $14,600.

Important early Silver Age DCs also heated up in 2013 with sales like *Brave and the Bold* #28 CGC 5.5 for $5,000, *Showcase* #4 CGC 5.5 for $9644, and *Showcase* #8 CGC 9.2 for $29,000. Other notable 2013 Silver Age sales included *Amazing Spider-Man* #25 CGC 9.8 for $10,739, *Amazing Spider-Man* #58 CGC 9.8 for $8,377, *Batman* #156 CGC 9.6 for $7,170, Batman #227 CGC 9.4 CVA for $1,899, *Captain America* #109 CGC 9.8 Signature Series for $3,300, *Detective Comics* #359 CGC 9.2 for $1,832, *Fantastic Four* #3 CGC 8.5 CVA for $6,655, *Journey Into Mystery* #55 CGC 7.5 White Mountain for $2,251, *Peanuts* #1 CGC 9.8 for $6,100, *Our Army at War* #151 CGC 9.4 for $3,433, and *Tales of Suspense* #48 CGC 9.8 for $14,050.

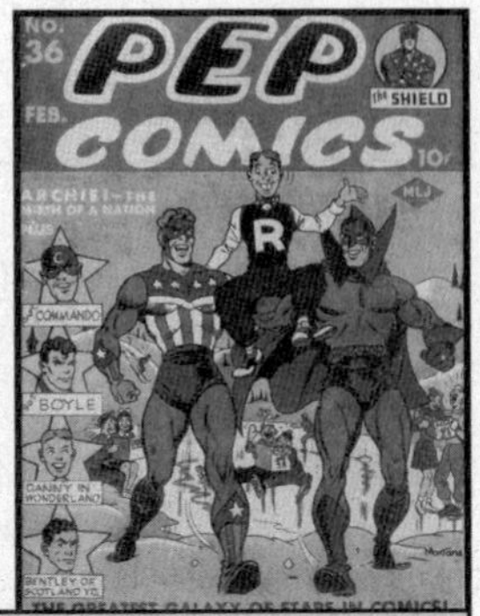

© AP

Pep Comics #36 was one of the record-setters from the Golden Age.

Major Golden Age keys were also a focus for many of these buyers in 2013. Just a handful of examples of these include sales such as *Detective Comics* #27 CGC 3.5 $215,000, *Detective Comics* #38 CGC 9.4 Allentown $135,000, *Superman* #1 CGC 1.8 for $64,000, *Captain America Comics* #1 CGC 6.0 $65,000, *Sensation Comics* #1 CGC 8.0 for $28,500, *Flash Comics* #1 CGC 3.5 for $15,461, *Archie Comics* #1 CGC 3.0 for $29,010, *Detective Comics* #38 CGC 2.5 for $7655, *All-American Comics* #16 CGC 3.0 (slightly brittle) for $21,363, and *Human Torch* #2 (#1) CGC 6.5 for $11,111.

Just a few examples of some other key, high grade, and "classic cover" Golden Age record sales included *Action Comics* #59 CGC 8.5 for $9,225, *Batman* #48 CGC 9.0 for $4,800, *Batman* #55 CGC 9.4 for $17,450, *Captain America Comics* #37 CGC 8.0 for $7,800, *Crime SuspenStories* #20 CGC 9.6 Gaines file copy for $8,988, *Crime SuspenStories* #22 CGC 9.2 for $17,000, *Giant Comics Edition* #12 CGC 7.0 for $9,300, *Jackpot Comics* #4 CGC 3.0 for $6,100, *Little Dot* #1 CGC 9.6 (first Richie Rich, single highest) for

$25,928, *Pep Comics* #36 CGC 2.5 for $5,600, *Startling Comics* #49 CGC 9.0 for $8,255, and *Whiz Comics* #4 CGC 9.4 for $20,551.

Scarcity and particularly scarcity in grade are key factors here with buyers extremely educated on the availability of these items and stepping up aggressively when they did come to market. The Golden Age market is also extremely cover driven right now and even at the lower end of the pricing spectrum a book with a stand-out cover can blow the doors off *Guide* prices when properly promoted.

Highlights of the Bronze and Modern eras were also found with the very top of the grading spectrum leading the way. The single highest CGC graded example of Deadpool's first appearance, *New Mutants* #98 CGC 10 hit $15,449, demonstrating the impressive appeal of this 1992 issue, while a CGC 9.9 example sold for $4400. High grade Spideys also over performed with a CGC 9.9 *Amazing Spider-Man* #125 selling for $4700 and *Amazing Spider-Man* #121 CGC 9.6 CVA for $2255.

Other impressive Bronze and Modern key and high grade sales included *Conan* #4 CGC 9.8 for $2,005, *Iron Man* #55 CGC 9.8 for $9,000 and a rare double cover CGC 9.8 for $13,025, *House of Secrets* #92 CGC 9.2 for $1,820, and *Star Wars* #1 CGC 9.8 Signature Series for $2.101.

Original comic art continues to draw the attention of more and more collectors and this segment of ComicLink's business has been incredibly dynamic in the past few years. Silver Age Marvel art lead the way with the record breaking $221,000 sale of Jack Kirby's complete 16-page *Thor* #134 story at the front of the pack. Other Kirby sales this year included his *Captain America* #212 cover art for $38,750, an unpublished 1979 Conan pin-up for $26,250, a *Silver Surfer* graphic povel page for $25,250, and a complete 13-page pre-hero story from *Tales of Suspense* #22 for $64,000.

Other impressive art sales in this growing market included a Steve Ditko *Amazing Spider-Man* #32 panel page for $56,555, an *Amazing Spider-Man* #37 panel page for $36,000, and a #30 panel page for $37,778, Gil Kane's *Avengers* #144 cover for $39,000, a Jim Lee *Batman* #614 Hush page for $15,001, a Paolo Rivera *Daredevil* cover for $16,500, a John Buscema *Silver Surfer: Judgement Day* splash for $9,600, Ernie Chan's *Batman* #282 cover for $9,100, a Marie Severin tribute pin-up to Bill Everett from *Sub-Mariner* #65 for $10,000, a Todd McFarlane *Amazing Spider-Man* #328 panel page for $8,100, a 1950 Burne Hogarth *Tarzan* Sunday for $10,500, a John Byrne *Fantastic Four* #246 panel page for $7,988, a Michael Turner *Superman/Batman* splash for $12,916, an Alex Schomburg *Marvel Mystery Comics* #43 cover recreation for $19,250, a Bernie Wrightson *House of Mystery* #225 splash for $12,260, and a Jim Steranko *X-Men* #51 panel page for $20,000.

The first months of 2014 have already shown exceptional results across all eras with auction and exchange sales such as the record $275,000 sale of *Journey into Mystery* #83 CGC 9.4 featuring the first appearance of Thor, *Sub-Mariner Comics* #1 CGC 9.2 $105,000, a *Batman* #1 CGC 4.0 for $52,000, *Amazing Fantasy* #15 CGC 7.5 for $59,800, *Tales to Astonish* #35 CGC 9.6 Western Penn (first Ant-Man in costume) for $66,000, a John Byrne *X-Men* #114 panel page for $26,250, a Jack Kirby *X-Men* #9 Marvel Girl pin-up for $25,250, and a rare "Canadian White" *Nelvana* #1 CGC 6.5 for $13,750.

With results like these leading off the year, 2014 seems poised to be another record-breaker not just for ComicLink, but for the industry as a whole. It does not seem like we can get enough material of quality to satiate our collector-investors! If you've got some, give us a call!

Tom Nelson
Top Notch Comics

Lots of buying and selling during the 2013 year, by far our biggest dollar increase. We primarily sell in our eBay store "topnotchcomics" which has around 2500 fixed price listings and weekly CGC auctions of 35-80 books.

Late Silver Age is a point where many new collectors enter the vintage comic market as Early Silver Age is just too expensive. *Iron Man* #1 leads the way followed by *Captain America* #100, *Silver Surfer* #1, *Sub-Mariner* #1 and *Conan* #1 from 1970. These books are benchmark books in the Marvel Universe, and a decade ago these were considered too common to have serious collector values. That has not proven to be the case as they are some of the hottest books that have skyrocketed in value in the past 15 years. I still see these books with room to move, especially in low to mid grade. Some sales: *Conan* #1 CGC 7.0 $170.00, CGC 9.4 $550.00, *Silver Surfer* #1 CGC 7.5 $500.00, 2.0 $100, *Iron Man* #1 CGC 4.5 $250.00, *Captain America* #100 GD $50.00, CGC 7.5 $300.00, CGC 9.6 $1500.00. *Sub-Mariner* #1 Fair $15.00, FN $75.00, CGC 9.0 $300.00.

The Bronze Age keys continue to be hot this year with many new books moving to key status. The longtime established key of *Incredible Hulk* #181 is stronger than it has ever been. I remember looking back at *Hulk* #181 about 5 years ago, a copy in Good 2.0 condition was selling for around $50.00 while a certified 9.8 was hitting record highs of $25,000.00. Now a low grade Good book would run you $300.00 on eBay while a certified 9.8 can be picked up for $8,000.00. Five years ago the spread between Good and NM- was 1-500. Now the spread is 1-25. That to me is a strong collecting demand. Increased demand has the minimum value going up while the über high grade has settled to an established reality. This is good for our hobby.

Giant-Size X-Men #1 has been strong with copies in all grades selling within a few weeks of us getting them into stock. Some other hot books have been *Iron Man* #55 (first Thanos) which has been selling on par with *Amazing Spider-Man* #129 (first Punisher). *Amazing Spider-Man* Bronze keys have been among our best selling books, especially issues #129, #121, and #194 followed by #122. The #121 has outpaced the #122 almost two to one now as the #122 remains flat with sales while the #121 is on fire. The #194 (first Black

Cat) still has a huge upside.

Batman books continue to be the biggest DC collectable run with the Neal Adams covers leading the way: *Batman* #221 (Beatles), #227 (classic cover), #232 (1st Ra's al Ghul), #234 (Two-Face), #251 (Joker cover), *Detective* #411 (1st Talia), #400 (Man-Bat). The *Green Lantern* Neal Adams run is very collectable with the #76 leading the way. The #87 (first John Stewart) is an undervalued book. Some sales: *Giant-Size X-Men* #1 GD 2.0 $200.00, CGC 9.4 $1500.00, CGC 9.6 $2600.00, *Amazing Spider-Man* #129 FN $250.00, CGC 9.0 $700.00, *Batman* #227 GD $50.00, VG/FN $100.00, CGC 8.0 $350.00, *Batman* #234 GD- 1.8 $20.00, VG/FN $60.00, CGC 9.0 $250.00, *Batman* #251 VG/FN 5.0 $80.00, CGC 8.0 200.00.

Some Bronze keys that really took off this year: *Superman's Pal Jimmy Olsen* #134 (Darkseid), *Nova* #1, *X-Men* #101 (Phoenix), *Ms. Marvel* #1, *Hero for Hire* #1 (Luke Cage), *Marvel Preview* magazine #4 (1st Starlord), #7 (1st Rocket Raccoon). Some sales include *Superman's Pal Jimmy Olsen* #134 6.0 $80.00, 6.5 $125.00, CGC 7.5 $200.00, CGC 8.0 $322.00. *Nova* #1 CGC 9.0 $100.00, CGC 9.4 $150.00, CGC 9.6 $250.00, CGC 9.8 $500.00, *X-Men* #101 GD 2.0 $28.00, 5.0 $70.00, 6.5 $75.00, 7.5 $80.00. *Marvel Preview* #4 CGC 9.6 $600.00, CGC 9.8 $1900.00. Future Bronze picks to watch: *Rom* #1, *Marvel Premiere* #15, *Iron Fist* #1, and *Ms. Marvel* #18.

The 1980s Copper Age books have seen a huge speculator boom this year as Hollywood's continual announcement of a superhero or villain being piloted in a future TV show or feature film. The collector scramble begins as books skyrocket within days of the announcement online, local comic shops and online retailers can't keep up with the current price swings as they are stripped of books at perceived bargains.

Some red hot books from the 1980s are *Uncanny X-Men* #141 (Days of Future Past), *X-Factor* #6 (Apocalypse), *Batman* #386 (Black Mask), *Incredible Hulk* #271 (Rocket Raccoon), *Teen Titans* #44 (Nightwing). Some of the perennial keys *Amazing Spider-Man* #300 sells instantly with the #298 and #299 seeing increased demand. Some other keys that have seen an increased in demand this year, many selling for double in the past 12 months. *Saga of the Swamp Thing* #37 (Constantine), *New Teen Titans* #2 (Deathstroke), *Dark Knight Returns* #1, *Sandman* #1, *Wolverine* Limited #1, *Wolverine* #1, *Punisher* Limited #1, *Amazing Spider-Man* #238 (Hobgoblin), *Secret Wars* #8, *DC Comics Presents* #26 (Teen Titans), #47 (Masters of Universe). Some collective runs like McFarlane *Spider-Man* run, Frank Miller *Daredevil* run, *Batman* #404-407, *Batman* #426-429. Some future picks to watch *Booster Gold* #1, *Thing* #1, *Green Arrow* #1, *Rocket Raccoon* #1, *Caliber Presents* #1 (The Crow), *She-Hulk* #1, *X-Factor* #23 (Archangel). Sales: *Secret Wars* #8 VF $35.00, CGC 9.8 $135, *Amazing Spider-Man* #300 CGC 9.8 $800.00, CGC 9.6 $275.00, VF+ $135.00, FN $79.95. *Incredible Hulk* #271 VF $75.00, CGC 9.6 $250.00, CGC 9.8 $500.00, *Saga of the Swamp Thing* #37 VF $70.00, CGC 9.6 $125.00, CGC 9.8 $300.00, *Amazing Spider-Man* #238 CGC 9.6 $200.00, VF $80.00. *Teen Titans* #44 CGC 9.8 $300.00, VF $25.00. *New Teen Titans* #2 GD $10.00, VG $20.00, CGC 9.6 $150.00, CGC 9.8 $400.00.

Marvel's Star Comics line has an interesting collectable demand, seems the #1s are the easiest to find while the final few issues can be quite scarce for an '80s book. There is crossover interest in the Star line with characters like Strawberry Shortcake, Star Wars Ewoks and Droids, Thundercats, Chuck Norris and Masters of the Universe. There may be some future winners in the Star line, pick them up now while they can still be had on the cheap.

For 1990s books, the mega Marvel Key is *New Mutants* #98 (1st Deadpool) which has blossomed to the most collectable Marvel book of the decade. The DC mega key now is Harley Quinn's first appearance in *Batman Adventures* #12 (1992). Her next collectable book is *Batman: Mad Love* (1994), followed by *Batman: Harley Quinn* from 1999. It's great to see a book escalate slowly over the years without a movie or TV announcement to stir up interest. Other keys from the decade which have seen an increased demand is *Superman: The Man of Steel* #18 (1st Doomsday), *Preacher* #1 and *Preacher* preview has elevated its status due to a movie announcement, *Amazing Spider-Man* #361 (1st Carnage). There are classic covers which are quickly becoming breakout books: *Amazing Spider-Man* #316 and *Amazing Spider-Man* #19 from Volume Two, as both of these covers feature Venom. *Batman Adventures* #12 started the year off with sales of $300.00 in 9.8 up to $875.00 for a 9.8 copy by the fall, we sold a copy in FN for $50.00 and by the end of the year a VF copy $175.00. *Man of Steel* #18 CGC 9.8 $150.00, but in VF $10.00. *New Mutants* #98 FN $100.00, VF 8.0 $125.00, VF/NM 9.0 $150.00, CGC 9.6 $235.00, CGC 9.8 $400.00. *Preacher* #1 early in the year CGC 9.8 $150.00 by the end of the year *Preacher* #1 CGC 9.8 $500.00. Future picks to watch: *Deadpool* #1, and *Man of Steel* #17.

For the decade of the 2000s, *The Walking Dead* is still the mega collectable of the decade. While the keys are still solid books, they have seemed to plateau out with price resistance. *Y the Last Man* #1 and the run of *Y the Last man* is very collectable, the *Spider-Man* run has collectable books in it with the 9/11 all Black cover issue #36 having been a hot book with CGC signature series. *Guardians of the Galaxy* Volume Two (2008-2010) #1-25 is a collectable run. Future picks from this decade is the *Harley Quinn* #1-38 run with issue #1 from 2000, *Y the Last Man* run #1-60.

For 2010s books, there have been some ups and downs in the past 3 years as collectors look for the next *Walking Dead* to buy into before the hype. Many of the Image titles have seen a substantial increase over cover price, but not *Walking Dead* status. Some collectable #1s are *Saga, Peter Panzerfaust,* and *Thief of Thieves.* The DC New 52 continues to build collector interest with *Batman* leading the way, with Near Mint copies the #1 at $75.00, #4 at $40.00, and #5 at $40.00. Amazing Spider-Man #700 was a sellout with multiple variant covers becoming collectable as well. The original cover to the #700 seems to be a winner along with the Ditko 1-200 Variant. There are going to be some future picks within the *Amazing Spider-Man* variants #650-700 book run, time will tell so get your collection filled in before some get priced out. *Amazing Spider-Man* is the #1 collectable run, so there will be future breakouts.

The convention scene is hopping as what used to be medium size shows of 2000-5000 attendees now have moved to large convention centers and are big established shows with over 10,000 attendees. The mega shows now have over 50,000 attendees. There is an increased amount of costumed "cosplayers" which includes many females who enjoy the con. Comics will continue to be part of the conventions but the artists and celebrities bring in the crowds. It's still good news as people are having fun and the convention circuit just keeps growing. Growing is good for our hobby, so let's see how big it can get.

Jamie Newbold
Southern California Comics

Since opening our store in 1997, we've acquired the inventories of six comic book stores that closed due to financial concerns (one additional store felt it was time to retire). The comic books we acquired numbered in the tens of thousands. The majority consisted of Modern Age books, as expected. Accounting for a mass amount of those Modern Age purchases were excess quantities the owners ordered in order to obtain variant issues. The sheer weight of the unsold bulk broke the banks of each of the stores. The variant craze of the 1990s matches up with the variant craze we're in now. The modifier that advances current sales for variants is eBay after the CGC process. Unfortunately, stores are ordering heavy for the variant cover reason with no financial outlet for the unsold bulk books. Storage fees or inefficient utilization of space for this glut just add to the overhead for all those comics. Is the 1990s collapse doomed to repeat?

Trying to decipher and deconstruct the comic book market is an extremely tedious task. This year we've seen dramatic spikes in the new comics market and back issue market based solely on speculation. Rumors spread like wildfire on the internet and literally within minutes of a story surfacing, we receive calls to see if we have that book in stock that's hot at the moment. The speculation drives sales of all ages of books – Gold, Silver, Modern – even children's books. Buzz that a new television show is being shopped around that's based on a comic book makes the first issue of that title like gold. Hearsay that a well-know actor will have an integral role in the new comic-based movie as a particular hero or villain makes that character's first appearance a desirable book. Books in which no one had any prior interest sell out fast and drive prices up quickly.

This year we've seen prices and demand for *Avengers* #55 skyrocket when the rumor hit that Ultron is to play a key role in the next *Avengers* flick. The *X-Men* books that feature the 'Days of Future Past' storyline currently fetch prices far beyond *Guide* once people caught wind that it would be the premise of the new *X-Men* film. Speculators try to beat each other out for the next hot ticket book. A consistent pattern we see in new comic sales is the same as last year – Image number ones. Everyone wants to score the next *Walking Dead* success story. Image first issues, no matter how much we inflate our orders, last on our shelves for mere hours. Speculators snatch these up in multiple quantities trying to cash in on the next big thing. There is no apparent limit to the prices people are willing to spend to get in on the ground floor. Titles with small print runs or those shopped-out to be multi-media events can carry hefty price tags. *East Of West*, *Saga* and *Peter Panzerfaust* drove speculation crazy with their introductory #1s. Some Image stuff isn't available at any store nationwide. Either because smaller stores may not order much or due to the breeding speculation based upon scarcity or availability.

© MAR

Comics like *Hawkeye* #11 grab new readers with their original ideas.

That being said, this year we experienced another comic event: DC's Villains Month with lenticular covers. We received multiple announcements of various difficulties: a shortage of the material used to create these covers, allocated distribution among stores, and a lousy chance of getting our complete orders we placed months earlier. We were barraged with questions and people trying to pre-order the books in order to secure a purchase. Once we received the actual books, we had people coming out of the woodworks clamoring and stepping over one another trying to snag the 3-D covers.

For four weeks, an influx of people who've never stepped inside a comic book store came in to participate in the spectacle of Villains Month.

It's always a good thing when you can grab a new audience and entice them into collecting or just reading comics by trying something new. This year we saw a newer title come out with an issue told from a dog's point of view. *Hawkeye* #11 gave the reader a chance to see the world through Lucky aka Arrow aka Pizza Dog's eyes. It's such an original – not to mention adorable – idea that definitely garnered many new readers!

The comic book market sometimes can be quite volatile. It's as strong as ever with the rumor mill operating non-stop and new or rehashed stories attracting new audiences, buyers, and the occasional reader.

This year we have seen an increased demand for '70s and '80s books. The best-selling titles from this time period are the *Amazing Spider-Man* and *Batman*. We normally throw books from this time period in our bargain $1 boxes, but recently the request for these comics has increased, elevating books once priced at a buck. Now they carry prices of $3-$5.

People who grew up in the '70s and '80s buy back the comics they read as children. This is the pattern of a 20-year cycle, meaning that the books that were new 20 years ago become desirable again. Now, that cycle is bringing more interest to our early '90s comics. As a result, old issues of *Spawn* #1 are selling through at our store! Once again, customers are picking up copies of the black poly-bagged Death of Superman. Prices are low compared to their heyday but certainly more profitable than five years before.

Deadpool and Harley Quinn stand out now as class 'A' 1990s collectors books. Traditional Marvel and DC titles from the '90s remain at the lowest point in their value. Movies and television may change that for some of them. Certainly the wealth of live-action programming and theatre releases give all titles potential. But the current spread of choices, at least by Marvel Entertainment, is goosing up the property values on a whole bunch of characters (Netflix 2015!).

Graphic novels and trade paperbacks (HCs and SCs) are strong sellers at our store. We increased our floor space almost two years ago and need to expand yet again to accommodate a growing inventory! The only reason we even consider this rent increase is because the sale of trades is so active that we believe they will offset the extra fees. We try to keep one or two of just about everything in stock. We only buffer volumes where history has shown the need: Batman and DC New 52, *Walking Dead*, Vertigo, and a little bit of just about everything Marvel. But really, trades went from being an aspect to being necessary to paying the rent, all in quick-step over the last couple of years. This year more so than last year, and so on. The power of a comic book store is its ability to relate to customers. We can talk trades – try finding that at Barnes and Noble!

We must be feeling the impact of digital comic book sales because generally, our weekly comics aren't flying off the shelves. We don't participate in a partnership with ComiXology. We know the market for them is growing and we assume we've lost customers that went over to digital. But we can't prove any of that because our customers never talk about it. We have no way of knowing where digital fits into our business. The only feedback we get is from customers that prefer paper over LCD.

Important Sales And Purchases: In March of 2013, we had the opportunity to purchase an incredible collection out of Los Angeles from the relatives of a woman who had recently passed away. This notable collection was so special due not only to the rarity of female collectors in our hobby, but that the stockpile spanned over half a century with nearly 30,000 books. She collected comics her entire life. The most remarkable book to come out of this collection was a *Showcase* #4. Due to the way this book was stored, it came to us at an estimated grade of about a 4.5 - 5.0. We pressed the book here at the store up to about an 8.5, but knew that structurally the book had the potential to be a 9.0. I was taught the pressing process by a professional paper conservationist. He runs his own paper restorative lab here in San Diego and showed me techniques for proper pressing. He assisted in my equipment purchase and trained me on usage. But despite pressing hundreds of books for clients and ourselves, we know there are some tasks requiring finery we can only achieve on occasion.

We sent the book off to Matt Nelson who was able to take the book and press it into a CGC graded 9.0. Being one of the highest graded copies known to exist, this *Showcase* #4 promptly attracted a buyer! We knew that this collection was something very spectacular, and wanted a way to pay homage to the owner and her passion as a collector. A CGC pedigree was considered, but with the input of several prominent collectors, it was decided that the collection overall did not meet the average quality necessary to warrant a pedigree. This significant collection that spanned from the '50s and up until 2012 deserved more than just a plain old bag and board. So, we decided that creating our own Certificate of Authenticity for the Southern California Comics Collection would be fitting. We personalized the certificate to the woman, celebrating her collection and life of dedication and enthusiasm for the comic book collecting hobby. Her collection was notable for the copies that were high-grade or had white paper, or both. She loved the DC ten-centers of her youth and took good care of those. Somehow many of those copies were not edge-tanned like later copies in the collection. Quite a bit of attention was paid to those books early in the collection's display at our store. They sold well and are really very addictive to some collectors (myself included).

Another large Silver Age collection surfaced out of Los Angeles just after the summer. The owner called around to several dealers on both coasts. He settled on our store partly due to the volume of positive Yelp.com comments we'd stacked. The majority of our local, potential sellers often 'Yelp' us to figure out if we shall be their destination. Good customer service goes a long way for us. Craigslist ads now run amuck here in town. Offers to buy comics fill the want listings daily and despite that we still see collections enter our doors with the same general frequency. Several large box counts filled with '70s to present have circulated through our store this past year. Mostly commons. In one case we absorbed about thirty short boxes of inherited material that included multiples of Modern Age keys. Lots of *ASM* #300s and *New Mutants* #98s. These are my store's bread-and-butter books. No self-respecting comic dealer can denigrate the quick cash these books continue to bring.

Unfortunately, eBay is awash in the same thing and continues to be a place where the unethical still beguile the uninformed. More guys are surfacing with eBay purchases that did not prove to be as advertised. We've helped the unsuspecting realize their *Hulk* #181s are off-grade, their 1960s *Batman* is missing a centerfold, or the creases on the spines of those '90s keys really do matter. In at least one instance we acted as a third-party intermediary to provide PayPal with documentation to support a purchase complaint. That purchase involved a customer of mine with an eBay purchase graded way off the mark. NM was clearly VG but the seller fought the refund. PayPal forced the refund after reviewing our appraisal and satisfied the buyer. Clearly, lessons about doing business online are still not reaching everyone.

We made a couple of cool sales outside of the larger collections:

Marvels

Amazing Spider-Man #5 CGC 7.5 $999
Amazing Spider-Man #129 CGC 9.4 $1,500
Amazing Spider-Man Annual #2 CGC 9.4 $1050
Avengers #1 CGC 6.0 $3325
Avengers #4 CGC 7.0 $1900
Incredible Hulk #181 CGC 9.6 $4,200
Journey Into Mystery Annual #1 CGC 9.4 $2400
Nick Fury, Agent of S.H.I.E.L.D. #6 CGC 9.8 $1,633
Strange Tales #110 CGC 8.0 $3800
Tales of Suspense #39 CGC 5.5 $3,500
X-Men #1 CGC 5.5 $3000
X-Men #2 CGC 7.0 $951

DCs

G.I. Combat #87 CGC 7.5 $1,316
Flash #105 CGC 5.5 $1,500
World's Finest #4 CGC 5.5 $438

Others

More Fun Comics #101 CGC 5.0 $1,650
Tip Top Comics #36 CGC 7.5 $317
Walking Dead #1 CGC 9.8 $1,650

Which Prices Should Go Up?: Might it be time for *Overstreet* to list NM 9.4 prices? With the overwhelming number of 9.4 key books alone, we need a place to judge their raw values. GPA, the major auction site archives, eBay's recorded sales, and our own sales experience can provide only so much information. We need one more source of information to provide balance to the question of potential values for raw 9.4s. I understand the data may be dated even as the annual *Guide* distributes, but so it's true of the 9.2s and such.

Which Prices Should Come Down?: The same stuff we all gripe about each year. Low grade books and Modern commons are strictly bargain box books. Additionally, there are too many copies of late '70s Bronze Age comics in the world. Ten to fifteen years ago, hustlers here in town were rampantly singing the praises of these books' return value. Finally they stopped and it's over. I'm sitting on a lot of copies of late '70s *X-Men* and *Amazing Spider-Man*. There's little demand for these comics at *Overstreet* prices.

Are There Any Specific Issues That Need A Substantial Price Adjustment?: We had a recent sale of a *Batman* #181 (intro. Poison Ivy) of which we marked up 20% of the *Guide*'s pricing. When we received an interested buyer within minutes of the book being listed on our online inventory, a quick check of the recent sales of this title proved that we had not priced it correctly. We increased the price another $100 and it sold within days.

All the Neal Adams Bat-books from the Silver-to-Bronze Age transition are all way under-priced from a Fine grade on. The demand for those books is greater than any other Silver Age DC title. In fact, Batman keys and first appearances could possibly tolerate price bumps on their own.

As always, my store operates on a 'team principal'. I disseminate the workload amongst the employees freeing me up to recover from surgery and travel. I give three of my employees credit for learning the ropes and carrying more of the task-load. Sam for her advanced skills with pressing and her assistance with this market report. I thank Matt for his knowledge of our business and his writing skills. I thank Kristin for running the whole shebang as my second-in-command.

Terry O'Neill
Terry's Comics/Nationwide Comics
CalComicCon

This report focuses on Convention and mail order aspects of comic collecting. Sales from 2012 to 2013 have been slightly down from last year, although sales in certain geographic regions reflected strong local economies. Most comic conventions had very good attendance but show sales had not increased and in some cases decreased due to more fans of pop culture and Cosplay attending conventions. These attendees are often young and get the passes to attend shows as soon as they are available. This can leave out old time collectors who are generally not so tech savvy. Three of the largest shows in 2013 were sold out before the shows opened: Emerald City ComicCon in Seattle, San Diego Comic-Con, and New York ComicCon. As a result, fewer serious collectors can attend these "Comic Conventions " every year. Fewer collectors, fewer sales. Fortunately, catalog sales were strong all year long and were supplemented by selling CGC or PGX graded comics on eBay. We will try to put more comics online and on auction sites in 2014.

Golden Age: Sales of this material has been steady, especially when we get comics in mid to high grade. Finding enough quality material from this era is always a challenge. We pay at least 50% of *Guide* for any comic from 1948 or older, no matter what the genre. It can be difficult to determine the value of some of this material, as some *OPG* prices are very high because of strong demand from decades ago. As collection were filled, demand dropped but prices are slow to correct. Other scarce titles sell so infrequently, that the *OPG* has not reflected their actual value because there are few recorded sales to determine this. Sales: *Walt Disney's Comics & Stories* #1 3.5 $3,600, *Zoot* #14 8.0 $550, *Captain America Comics* #66 3.0 $550, *Black Terror* #8 5.0 $500, *Batman* #49 5.0 $450, *X-Mas Comics* #7 4.5 $495.

Atom Age (1946-1955): I love Atom Age comics. The variety and relative scarcity of many titles is a collectors dream. If you have collected all the Silver, Bronze or Copper Age you ever wanted, then try collecting Atom Age comics. It is a challenge to find almost any title from this period in higher grade, as so many were poorly handled, read and re-read, and many were published on poor quality paper.

Especially scarce are comics that were primarily read by girls with Teen/Romance titles like *Archie*, *Pep*, *Millie*, *Patsy Walker* and *My Own Romances*, being examples that are often sought but rarely completed. Girls grew up to be women, and unlike most men, moved on to other interests, throwing their comics away. Some sales of note: *Young Men* #24 3.0 $450, *Lorna Jungle Girl* #9 7.5 $275, *Meet Corliss Archer* #1 5.0 $255, *Texan* #15 9.0 $250, *Strange Worlds* #1 (Avon) 3.5 $240.

Silver Age: Sales of Silver Age comics are always good. But due to large price increases in key books, some collectors are looking at Bronze Age as a better investment. That said, it is still the major source of annual income at Terry's Comics. Lately Movie/TV tie-in characters such as Ultron (*Avengers* #54 & #55), Guardians of the Galaxy (*Marvel Super Heroes* #18) & Groot (*Tales to Astonish* #13) have caused otherwise uncared for titles to sell briskly and above *Guide*. There is no way for the *OPG* to reflect these trends because they happen suddenly then fizzle out slowly. Some sales of note: *Strange Tales* #110 7.0 $1200, *Brave & the Bold* #28 1.0 $400 #34 5.0 $200, *Green Lantern* #1 2.0 $350, *Amazing Spider-Man* #3 3.0 $468, #38 9.0 $333, *Fantastic Four* #1 2.5 $2400, #48 5.0 $425, *Incredible Hulk* #2 3.5 $390, *G.I. Combat* #87 CGC 6.0 $750, *X-Men* #5 CGC 8.0 $500.

Bronze Age: This era has been on fire for the past few years. Most back issue dealers will agree that they are the most requested titles of the past year. With so many first appearances and number one issues of many key characters, it has finally come to dominate the back issue market.

Luke Cage Power Man #1 has been selling as fast as I can get it. As always, *Hulk* #181 sells fast. *Tomb of Dracula* titles, especially #1 and #10, sell well, and *Marvel Spotlight* #2 and *Werewolf by Night* titles are also selling. *Doctor Strange*, *Howard the Duck*, and *SHIELD* are being added to collections once more. *Star Wars* titles are finally selling again. Now that Disney owns Marvel and LucasFilms, we may one day see Mickey Mouse and Spider-Man teamed up against Darth Vader. The DC titles that are selling fast are: anything with Neal Adams especially *Batman* #232, *Superman* #317, and *Green Lantern* #85. Berni Wrightson, Swamp Thing, especially *House of Secrets* #92 sell well, as do some of the others great DC Mystery titles like *Witching Hour*, *House of Mystery*, and *Unexpected* with covers by Kaluta, Toth, Wood, Alcala, Redondo and Morrow. Here also Movie/TV tie-in characters such as Thanos (*Iron Man* #55), Darkseid (*Superman's Pal Jimmy Olsen* #134) and Rocket Raccoon (*Incredible Hulk* #271) are comics that were once slow sellers or in dollar boxes. Sales of note: *Conan* #1 8.5 $270 #3 9.0 $200, *Daredevil* #168 9.4 $200, *Marvel Spotlight* #2 9.0 $200, *House of Secrets* #92 6.0 $180, *Hulk* #180 9.2 $425, #181 8.5 $1200, *Batman* #232 5.0 $175, *Green Lantern* #76 5.0 $250, *Marvel Premiere* #15 9.0 $125.

Magazines: As was the case with Bronze Age, many of these are sleepers with first appearances and first issues in abundance. The number of fine artists and illustrators are substantial, especially in Warren and Marvel Magazines like *Creepy*, *Eerie*, *Vampirella*, *Savage Sword of Conan*, and *Vampire Tales*. With most of the EC pool of talent in early issues and a host of soon-to-be-famous artists like Richard Corben, Berni Wrightson, Jim Starlin, Frank Brunner, Michael Ploog, Jose Gonzalez, Alex Nino, Bruce Jones, Pablo Marcos and so many other greats, why are these titles not in greater demand? Not to mention covers by Frank Frazetta, Ken Kelly, Boris Vallejo, Vaughn Bodé and even Steve Ditko art. Sales of note: *Vampirella* #1 CGC 7.0 $247, *Deadly Hands of Kung Fu* #14 9.0 $150.

Modern Age & Independents: This era has been getting more and more requests. The amount of money spent on these comics has steadily increased over the years. DC has way more requested material in this era. Batman titles such as *Nightwing* and *Harley Quinn*, also Superman titles are selling well. For Indy titles, *Walking Dead* leads followed by *Teen Age Mutant Ninja Turtles* (all), *Grimm Fairy Tales*, *Fables* and some Valiant titles like *Rai* and *Harbinger*. Dark Horse, *Conan* and *Aliens* are often requested. Even *Simpsons Comics & Stories* #1 is getting around $50 in nice condition and other Bongo titles are in demand. Sales of note: *Teenage Mutant Ninja Turtles* #1 3rd $150, *Harbinger* #0 9.4 $120.

Graded Books: Because these do not sell as well at shows for us, we focus on internet, catalog and auction sales for them. While we still get record breaking prices on some material that is graded, few comics sell for the record prices of a few years ago. The CGC census shows how common many comics really are, even in high grade. If you buy a comic for over a thousand dollars, no matter what the grade, the safest way is to buy it slabbed, which should have had a good restoration check. Sales: *Fantastic Four* #27 CGC 9.2 $1400, *Incredible Hulk* #1 CGC 3.5 $4800, *Iron Man* #1 CGC 9.0 $1050.

Internet Sales: We currently list CGC graded comics on the internet. This translates into steady sales for prices at or above GPA. This is a great way for a person to sell a small collection and get top dollar, if done right. If you have a large collection of comics with only a few keys or high grade books, your best option is to sell to a dealer you trust. Keep in mind they have to make money and have a lot of overhead. You will get one lump sum and be done with it and they will do the work. Auction houses are a good way to sell certain comics of high value, but keep in mind that they will be only available for a small window of time and may not go for the actual market value. The auction house will get its percentage regardless of what your collectable sells for. Most of our entire inventory is at www.Terryscomics.com

In summary, collectors enter and leave this hobby all the time, which cause the dynamics to change yearly. Some collectors are following the latest trends, others are trying to build a long term portfolio. Still others like certain artists or storylines, and of course there are the hard core collectors that have to have everything Marvel or DC or all the DC War comics or Batmans. Regardless of why you collect, stick to what you like and you will never be disappointed if and when you decide to sell.

Michael Pavlic
Purple Gorilla Comics

"A Year Passes Like Nothing..." declares the cover copy to *The Fabulous Furry Freak Brothers* #3 and brother, don't I know it! Time already for another Market Report?

I'd like to acknowledge three people who continually have provided much needed support, counsel and stock this past year: Dave Hermary of Amazing Fantasy in Red Deer Alberta, Ben Falconer, head honcho at Phoenix Comics here in Calgary and Sgt. Erock, from parts unknown. Also, thanks once more go to Doug Sulipa who suggested I submit a report. This and all future reports are dedicated to Doyle Kathol, this is all HIS fault! Lastly, but never leastly (yeah, it's not a word, but whadaya gonna do?), I want to say a heartfelt thank you to my customers, I am nothing but a neurotic guy with way too many comics without you.

2013 was the best in Purple Gorilla Comics' short five year history. There. Done my report and...hah? Details? Fine, fine. I sell back issues and extremely few new comics (more on that later). While I wish I could play with the big boys and buy and sell *Amazing Spidey* #1s all day long, in reality the bulk of the 30,000 comics for sale at PGC are from the 1980s and 1990s. But that's OK, there are plenty of people in my part of the world that want exactly that!

I'm located in a Flea Market here in Calgary. Every weekend, thousands of people walk through the Market and hundreds into my store. I get the Hard Core Collector, who buys his *Overstreet* the day it comes out. The Casual or Lapsed Fan, who remembers buying that hologram issue of *Spidey* when he was 12 years old and wants it again. The Old School Reader, who sees the *Classics Illustrated* and Dells hanging on my wall and is compelled to stare and reminisce. There's the Archie Digest Reader, who wants to buy five digests for $5 because they like them. Most importantly, I see many Brand New Readers, folks that may like the movie, TV show, cartoon, t-shirt of whichever character and now want to start in on the comics. All these people and more are welcome at PGC, it's for people who LOVE comics! Anyway, on to the specifics.

Marvel Comics: Far and away the majority of my sales are from the House that Stan, Jack and Steve built. Top titles include *Amazing Spider-Man, Uncanny X-Men, Avengers, Hulk, Iron Man, Thor, Venom, Wolverine, Spider-Man* (1990), *X-Men* (1991). Basically if it was a big seller for Marvel in 1993, it's a big seller for PGC in 2013. Recent sales: *Spider-Man* #1 (1990) unbagged $20, bagged $25. *Amazing Spider-Man* #300 (9.2) $200, *New Mutants* #98 (9.2) $150, *Amazing Spider-Man* #361 $45, *Secret Wars* #8 $50. Generally, when some Silver Age Marvel comes in, it's gone within a couple of weeks. Any *Amazing Spidey* below issue #252 fetches at least 1.5 of *Guide*, more if it's key or 6.0 or better. Even lower grade Marvels, not featuring the above mentioned characters or titles move quickly at *Guide*.

The speculating going on with movie announcements; I've sold a *Hulk* #272 for $85 because it has Rocket Raccoon in it. That seemed crazy to me, what if the movie is bad? Like *Howard the Duck* bad? Yes, everyone is looking for the next *Walking Dead* #1, but that book had a print run of 7300. How many *Hulk* #272 are out there? 150,000-200,000? More? Be careful people! Buy what you like to read, if it happens to go up in value, great. If not, so what? You like to read it!

DC Comics: If it is not Batman or Batman related or if it is not written by either Alan Moore or Neil Gaiman, people don't care. OK, it's not quite like that, but close. Top titles: *Batman* (but not *Detective*, go figure), *Catwoman, Nightwing, Robin, Batgirl, Wonder Woman, Watchmen, Sandman.* I should mention that I get more request for Harley Quinn comics and/or appearances than almost any other character and find it next to impossible to get them. The *Batman Adventures Mad Love* special that I had lasted a day and sold for $40.

Dell/Gold Key Comics: Westerns rule the roost here, followed by TV or movie tie-ins. Lower grade, 3.0-6.0 are actually more desired by my buyers because they want to read them without paying top dollar. A typical Western from the mid 1950s priced no higher than $20 will move faster than the same comic in 9.2. A good portion of my buyers of Dell and Gold Key are nostalgia seekers, not collectors. Disney, Looney Toons and related titles are also steady sellers and again, high grades are not desired.

© TMP

Spawn collectors are still out there buying up early issues. (***Spawn* #19** shown).

Whitman: The pre-pack September-December 1980 Whitman comics go for well above *Guide* in any shape, same for the 60 cent pre-packs and the 75 cent Canadian cover price variants. I'm starting to notice more people asking for these books.

Independent Publishers: The only Image Comics that move with consistency are *Spawn, Maxx* and *Witchblade. Spawn* #1 is an easy $25 book, *Maxx* #1 $10. There are many Spawn collectors out there, my stock has dwindled by 40% in one year! Dark Horse's *Aliens, Predator, Star Wars* and *Hellboy* are all decent sellers. Not much of note sells from the other publishers. The thing that struck me the most was the complete drop off in interest in *TMNT* in the last six months of 2013. Before that, Mirage *TMNT* sold for 1.5 *Guide*. Now? Not so much...

Underground Comix: *Freak Bros.* have a huge following, I've lost count of how many Omnibus collections I've sold, it's well over 50 in the last couple of years. Anything Crumb moves quickly at well above *Fogel*'s prices. Most Undergrounds go for higher than the *Underground Price*

Guide and I look forward to the new version to see if my experience is the norm. P. Bagge, D. Clowes and Hernandez Bros. comics do well. *Black Kiss* also seems to have a bit of a resurgence in the last 12 months.

Sets: Depending on the weekend, sets can contribute between 20-40% of total sales. I'll either bundle a story arc or five consecutive issues of a title into a package. Comics that do not sell as single issues can do well as sets. The Marvel, DC, Image and Dark Horse titles I mentioned earlier do well as sets too, but I consistently sell sets of *Lobo*, *Star Trek* (DC), *Marshal Law*, *Flash*, *Superman*, *Legends of the Dark Knight* (1989), *Silver Surfer*, *Fantastic Four*, *Buffy*, *Camelot 3000*, *Swamp Thing* and *Captain America*. All at *Guide* prices. Heck, I've sold *Guy Gardner* sets for crying out loud! Sets are the perfect way to get the Brand New Reader started!

New Comics: As mentioned earlier, I do carry a few new titles and one line of TPBs as well as the aforementioned *Freak Bros.* Omnibus. I carry *PowerPuff Girls*, *Beware the Batman*, *Scooby-Doo Team Up*, *My Little Pony* and the *Spidey* comic based on the cartoon. I feel it is essential to have something for the young readers. Modern Batman or Spider-Man comics are NOT kid friendly and until very recently there has been very little for little girls to buy. I don't know about you, good reader, but I started my comic obsession when I was 10 years old. I'm 46 now. We, as a comics industry, need these whipper-snappers to take our place when we shuffle off this mortal coil. Otherwise, the comic industry will die. The *My Little Pony* comics sell well for me, even though I have a strict "No Bronies" policy. I order 20 copies a month (much more for #1 and #2) and only have copies of issues #9-13 left.

I also order in the TPBs and hardcover *Walking Dead* collections. I'd be dumb not to, it's a huge seller, attracts new readers every week and keeps them coming back for more. I also ordered in *Afterlife with Archie*. This has exploded here. Archie has more reach in the minds of the general public, has been read more by the general public, than any other comic character. Everyone has read at least one. Everyone knows who Jughead is. So when Archie releases its first "not for kids" comic, I was ready. Or so I thought. 80 copies sold of both printings of #1, 30 copies sold of #2 in a week. This could be huge, folks! During the summer months, I sell 75-100 Archie digests a week at $1 each. People have literally grown up reading Archie. Now there's an Archie for grown-ups!

Comic Pages: I've been fortune enough to have a supply of pages (thanks Blaine Tufts!) come through PGC and while they are not Ditko or Kirby pages, there is a demand for them. Several Millie the Model and Kathy pages from the early 1960s came and went, no doubt helped by the appearance of Stan Lee in town at the Expo this year. Many people wanted to get something unique for Stan to sign, what's more unique than a page. They sold for $200 each and that was probably a good deal too! Sold several Archie pages for anywhere between $40-$100 each.

That's how the comic book world looked like from my little corner. Thanks to the fine folks at *Overstreet* for giving me this platform to blather on with and I hope we can all do this again next year!

Bill Ponseti
Collector

Greetings comic lovers! Another interesting and exciting year has come to a close, and I've made several observations about trends that impact the comic market.

Trend #1: If it is even rumored that a character will be in an upcoming movie, their first appearances skyrocket in price. We saw this with *Avengers* #55 (Ultron), *Supergirl* (Action Comics #252), *Brave and the Bold* #28 (Justice League) and even Groot from *Tales to Astonish* #13. There were a number of others as well, but these speculative ventures can be risky as well. When the *Green Lantern* movie didn't perform very well, *Showcase* #22 crashed back down to earth from all time high selling prices. I don't see Groot sustaining himself as a long term investment option. Neither Rocket Raccoon. But, for those who got on the bandwagon early, there was quite a bit of money to be made.

Trend#2: Marvel Keys in all grades continue to astound collectors and dealers alike. In 2013 I had a hankering to dabble in the Silver Age key market again, as I've always enjoyed those books. Particularly the Marvel Keys from 1961 – 1964. They've become such a commodity that collectors and dealers now discuss "how much per point" (CGC grade point) they are worth more than anything else about these comics. I spent some time with Greg Reece at the Baltimore Comic Con this year and he mentioned to me that every time he thinks he has a handle on what the ceiling is for *Amazing Fantasy* #15 is, the market proves him wrong. I've been wrong about a ceiling for this book for 25 years, and counting. So I took the plunge and bought a copy for my collection this year, as I'm afraid if I wait any longer I wouldn't be able to afford one. *Amazing Fantasy* #15, *Hulk* #1, *Fantastic Four* #1, *Journey into Mystery* #83 and *Tales of Suspense* #39 sell almost immediately in all grades. *Tales to Astonish* #27, *Strange Tales* #110 and *Daredevil* #1 had good years too, but not to the degree of their elder statesmen.

Trend #3: Golden Age comics finished the year with a flourish and prices were strong across the board. During the last major auction of the year that I participated in, nearly every Golden Age book in the auction sold at or well above current *Guide* prices. I bid on about 40 lots, 10 of those I bid strongly on, I won 3 lots. Even mid-run DC Golden Age titles, like *Superman* and *Batman* in VF were selling above *Guide*. I haven't seen that happen in quite a while. We are used to seeing key issues, *Captain America*s, early *Batman*s, pre-Robin *Detective*s, and super high grade pedigree titles sell for multiples of *Guide*, but other segments enjoyed strong growth this year as well. *Archie* #1 and *Pep* #22 are very hot and sell for record breaking prices whenever they are offered for sale.

Trend #4: Page quality and level of restoration have a big impact on price. Collectors have demonstrated with their wallets that they will pay more for comics with OW/W or better pages than they will for like graded comics with lesser page quality. In some cases books with White pages sold for more in head to head competition for copies a grade point higher with OW/W pages. In terms of restoration, the stigma has decreased as unrestored key comics have become just too expensive for most collectors to afford. But, copies with Moderate or Slight restoration have grown at a much higher rate. The slight category seems to be speculative as I think folks are hedging that they can get them unrestored and make a profit. Collectors are "upgrading" their keys by buying copies with less restoration, even if the numeric grade goes down from their current copy.

Now let's look at some of the segments in more detail:
Platinum Age: As I reported last year, collector interest in this area continues to increase. This segment was stagnant for a very long time, but there is renewed interest in some of these titles. Again this year, I competed on nearly every copy of *Famous Funnies a Carnival of Comics* that came to market at auction. In November, a nice 6.0 OW copy with the mailing envelope was auctioned off. I bid, I lost. It sold for over double *Guide* at $3346! Fortunately I was able to locate a 5.0 copy shortly afterwards that also had the mailing envelope, but had to pay a strong price to obtain it from another collector. *Century of Comics* is probably priced too highly in the *Guide*, but when it comes to market, like it did again this year, it still sells. I competed on this one in November as well, and lost again. It was a 5.5 copy and sold for over $4300. That's a fair chunk of change for that book. I've tried, unsuccessfully, to locate a copy of *Funnies on Parade*, so the hunt continues. When *Famous Funnies* Series 1 or *Famous Funnies* #1 come to auction, or private sale, they command five figures. So, at least for this sub-segment of Platinum, the market is quite strong.
Golden Age: As mentioned above, it has been another strong year for Golden Age, and I've been quite active this year in this segment. Also as mentioned above the usual suspects continue to climb out of reach for the rank and file collector, which shifts focus to other areas of the Golden Age that can be had for more realistic prices. Realism can be relative though, as it is still a pricey area to collect if superheroes are your bag. And as last year, more Silver Age collectors continue to migrate into Golden Age, and I've seen a larger contingent of 30 something, and even 20 something year old collectors buying Golden Age comics. That speaks very well for our hobby as a whole. I collect pretty much across the segment and have competition for every book I go after. Even Western titles. Sure, they aren't as hard, or as expensive, as the superhero genre, but I still had to pay a good bit to get some of the ones I was chasing.

Batman #1 had another amazing year, and *Captain America* #1 has grown just as fast in 2013. Some notable sales or purchases of mine this year: *Batman* #1 8.0 OW EP – $24,000, *Batman* #1 7.0 OW/W MP - $20,000, *Detective Comics* #140 2.5 CR/OW - $1100, *Green Lantern* #1 3.0 OW/W SA - $2600, *Green Lantern* #1 2.5 OW/W SP - $3000, *Green Lantern* #1 5.5 CR/OW $6000, *All-Flash Comics* #1 6.0 OW/W - $3000, *New York World's Fair* 1939 6.5 OW SP - $2500, *All Star Comics* #3 6.0 OW EP - $3500, *Comic Cavalcade* #1 5.5 OW/W - $2200, *Silver Streak Comics* #6 5.5 OW MP - $3000, *Superman* #76 8.5 OW/W - $2600, *Superman* #14 5.0 OW/W - $2500, *Detective Comics* #33 4.0 OW SA $6000, *Captain America Comics* #27 5.0 OW/W - $3000.
Silver Age: Marvel ruled the roost as usual but DC has been coming on strong thanks, in part, to movie projects like *Justice League* and *Man of Steel*. *Showcase* #4 keeps climbing and climbing and is now a very expensive book in all grades. *Brave and the Bold* #28, *Justice League* #1, *Action* #252 and *Detective Comics* #359 sell as fast as they are listed. On the Marvel side, the momentum hasn't slowed for the last few years one bit. I attended Chicago Comic Con, Baltimore Comic Con, Wizard World Philadelphia, and the local Philly Comic Con this year and anytime I pulled Marvel keys out of my bag I had many suitors. I stopped showing off my *Amazing Fantasy* #15 as I tired of saying no to dealers that wanted it! Some notable sales or purchases of mine this year: *Hulk* #1 4.5 OW/W - $6500, *Fantastic Four* #1 5.0 OW - $7000, *Detective Comics* #225 7.0 CR/OW - $2000, *Amazing Spider-Man* #1 5.0 OW/W - $4200, *X-Men* #1 5.0 OW - $2800, *Daredevil* #1 7.0 OW/W - $1475, *Avengers* #1 7.0 OW - $5000, *Amazing Fantasy* #15 4.0 OW - $10,500, *Tales of Suspense* 3.5 White, $2100.
Outlook: More of the same in 2014. I fully expect the trends mentioned in the opening of my report to continue and see no signs of slowing for the comic market. It is a very fun time to be collecting and my passion, even after over 40 years of collecting and dealing in comics, has not waned one bit. It might be stronger now than it ever has been. There is so much variety out there, and in spite of all my years in the hobby, I continually find something new to get me excited and put me on a path to chasing something else. If you haven't attended a major comic show in a while, I recommend you do. There is nothing like being around like-minded people and sharing your passion for comics with them in a setting like a comic convention. If you can't make a show, then perhaps join an online comic collecting community like the CGC Chat Boards or one of the comic focused groups on Facebook.

Happy Collecting!

Jeff & Cathy Rader
Offbeat Archives

This year has taken a bit of a turn for us, though a great one. We have turned from eBay as our primary sales outlet to doing more direct sales, and more fixed prices. It has been a most welcome turn of events for us, and we have met many more collectors of the odd, rare, and often absurd, in the world of comics, and associated collectibles.

There are so many facets to our hobby that there is something for everyone, within any collector's budget. This year we have seen even more extreme records broken but there are ways to get what fills your collecting needs at the right price. Our specialty is in the out-of-the-norm, so we do not deal in many mainstream titles, but the oddball, and overlooked, and rare areas have been more than great for us for yet another year. New discoveries are constantly being made, and unmined treasure unearthed. Being comic collectors, researchers, and indexers, we all have the uncanny ability to make that next find before the masses, and set a trend, instead of following it.

One bandwagon that has taken off like a rocket is Archie, Archie, and Archie. With the few copies of early *Peps* and *Archie Comics* coming to market, it seems that each new hammer price overshadows the previous. This publicity, and perceived investment opportunity, is gaining followers like zombies. I think that, due to the Archie phenomenon, other publishers' attempts at teen-age humor have been getting caught up in the wake. Not to the same degree, but I get countless requests for ACG's *Cookie*, Marvel/Atlas *Millie the Model*, *Katy Keene* (well, still an Archie), *Barbie*, and the like. It looks like stratospheric prices are bringing collectors around to titles that are within possible grasp of completeing runs.

Westerns, especially Atlas Marvels have also attracted the Marvel Maniacs as a means to get some early output, great stories, and art, from their fave publisher, yet on a totally different price point. The thing is that finding these treasures in grade has always been a challenge. When you do see what Kirby could do with a western like *Rawhide Kid* it's hard not to let the hook get set. Take a look at the cover to *Rawhide Kid* #22, or #39, and try to tell me that it could not become an all-consuming desire. For some reason though, I have been experiencing resistance to the Golden Age DC Western titles, other than the somewhat near-genre, *Tomahawk*. No idea why, because they are quality books, but the demand just nowhere reaches the Marvels. In the way of rarity, you can always go in search of the *Tom Mix* Ralston-Purina give-aways. Other publishers of Westerns do not exactly fly off the shelves either unless it is something that a non-comic collector wants, such as a Roy Rogers photo-cover...then it's gone in a flash.

Science Fiction, fantasy, and pre-hero monsters do great for us, but they need to be reasonably priced to make the sale. eBay has brought so much out of the woodwork that many of the books that fall within these genres can be cherry-picked off of the Net at the right price, and it is hard to stay in competition with the bargains being found online.

Pre-Code Horror, Crime, and *Seduction of the Innocent* books are usually gone before I get a chance to unpack them, and condition be damned. This is, by far, one of the HOTTEST areas of collecting. With decapitations/hangings/face burning/extreme violence, it seems that nearly everybody wants some of the type of comics that led to the downfall of EC, and the uprising of the supposedly all-knowing Comics Code Authority. The difference in comics, in a matter of a few mere months, went from over-the-top bloodthirsty violence to tame, and often redrawn/censored pale comparisons to their forerunners. Things have gotten to the point that with some of the above items even coverless copies are swooped up just so that one can have a copy.

Barbie, Katy Keene, Westerns, movie, toy-related, etc. most often go to non-comic collectors from those areas. And they do not seem to care about how we as a collective value them. If there is a title that has an outside collecting arena watch out on trying to get those books, there are some rabid buyers that are looking for the same thing, and they are not restrained by condition, and often price.

Due to the current status of grade-chasing, and "hotness" of certain titles, some books may be out of the reach of the average collector. There are countless ways around that, and still be satisfied with your collection. Love Pre-Code Horror and spooky stuff? Seek out ACGs, and Charltons. They both put out some really wonderful tales in which some rival the more known but...they are usually available for a fraction of other publishers. If you are a Marvel completist, and/or love Harvey comics then go for a run of Marvel's Star Comics line. It is a do-able task, but good luck getting a set of these kiddie comics in high grade. How about a Spider-Man cover that the superhero collectors bypass? Try Marvel's *Dennis the Menace* #7.

Another overlooked scarcity is the comic book/magazine that Marvel put out for us video game geeks in *BLIP – The Video Games Magazine*. Most of the contents would bore a current collector to death, but issue #2 has a crazy Spider-man playing a video game photo-cover, and there is a 6-page Spidey vs. Green Goblin comic story by John Romita. And you thought your Spideys were complete! *Blip* #6 is also notable in that it has a 6-page Incredible Hulk comic story. Getting the set of 7, especially in grade, is like trying to get high score on Donkey Kong. Speaking of, if you're a gamer, *Everything's Archie* #106 has a hilarious Donkey Kong/Pac Man cover. That just proves that WHATEVER you decide to collect, there is a whole world of comics out there for you to flip through and work on your collecting passions.

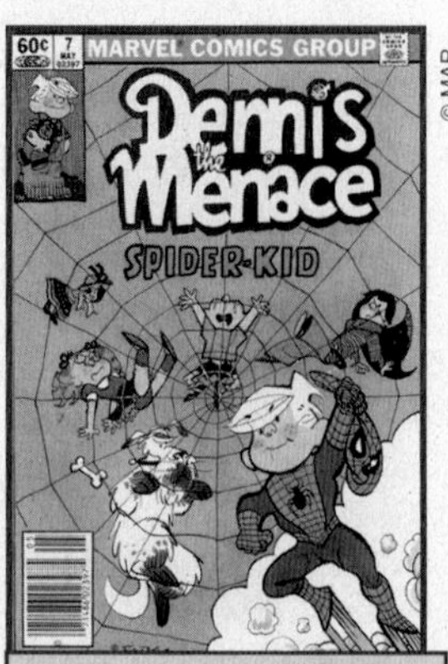

© MAR

Dennis the Menace #7 is a cover that many superhero collectors bypass.

Lesser titles and publishers have become sought after due to many runs shooting out of some collectors price range. Skywald, Atlas – with its array of brilliant artists, Tower (starting to come on strong), and so many others that are very fulfilling, yet can be had for a bargain compared to like books from the Big Two.

We always state to buy what you love but if you absolutely must look at comics as an investment then stick to the tried and true, stuff that has withstood the test of time such as *Incredible Hulk* #181, *Amazing Spider-Man* #129, *Iron Man* #55, and the like. At any given time there are "Hot" books that become a blip on the radar and fall back into obscurity solely due to the appearance of some fourth-rate character. Buying first issues is no guarantee either, despite a possible temporary jump. *Cerebus, Teenage Mutant Ninja Turtles, Bone*, and *The Walking Dead* are extreme exceptions to the rule. Anybody remember when *Trollords*, and *Samurai* were wall books? Check the bargain bins now.

As with coin collectors, stamp collectors, ANY collectors, rarity is key. Some comic collectors recognize that to a degree but if/when they ever take heed certain comics will spiral through the roof, while others are left behind. Rarity has already been recognized in certain publishers such as Centaur, and certain issues such as *Punch* and *Suspense* #3, but there are countless un-mined gems that are due for a huge jump once our outlook sees what most other collecting arenas recognize. That said, the CGC Census is a far from perfect gauge of rarity/scarcity. Countless collections will not see inside of a slab any time soon, and due to the "crack, press, & re-submit" trend the numbers will never be truly accurate. The only true way to know how Scarce, or Rare a comic is can be by either looking for it for ages, or learning from sources that have. Some comics that are perceived as hard to find are actually numerous, and others that are ignored can have but a handful of copies known. That's where we get our enjoyment in comics, digging up the impossible books for those in search. One of the downsides is that many rare books, including the Platinum books, get nowhere near enough true sales to get anywhere near an "average" price so report any sales. Many fail to get anywhere near *Guide* while others leave listed values in the dust. Try some of the more esoteric stuff that can bring immense personal pleasure in owning a rare, obscure item that every other kid on the block does not have.

One example of an affordable rarity is *Fiction Illustrated* #3 – Chandler, with a self portrait cover, and gorgeous interior artwork by Steranko. While the digest version of *Fiction Illustrated* #3 can be found here and there, finding the trade paperback format, referred to as "Chandler Deluxe Edition" in the ads, is a formidable task that took me a few years. This format truly is deserving of its "Scarce" designation, and the stunning Steranko artwork makes it a book to be on the lookout for.

Another area of interest that has taken on a new life is Comic magazines (Eerie Publications, Warren) and *Famous Monsters*. Now that they are slabbable, they have taken on a new life. Marvel's *Pussycat* has a fiendish fan following, and finding her individual stories in Goodman's (Marvel) men's mags has them scrambling to complete what is still being uncovered. Some magazine issues are particularly rare in high grade since they often sat in cheap bins. Same with Treasury Editions. These book were not amassed "in state" as many comics were, and those in grade are treasured.

If you want a fun collection, go with diversity. With so many books most can say, "I have one", "Me too", "Yeah but mine is
better than yours," By spreading your interests around in some of the less common areas you can easily have a unique collection that nobody else could duplicate.

The movie bump phenomenon is one of the riskiest ways for the collector to try to make a quick buck. Only the first in, and first out, make the $$$ and once the fad passes many are left holding overpriced hot potatoes that will stagnate. Comics is definitely not the path to fortune (unless you find the next pedigree collection) so if it is monetary reward you are looking for you are better off in stocks and bonds. In for pleasure, and the joy of discovery? Then comics it is.

The availability of reprints of all types has affected lower grade values. I have no reason anymore to seek out low grade books to read my old favorites. Ages ago I found what would certainly be considered a pedigree collection of all superhero Marvels, all easily 9.4-9.9. Once I let them go there is just no way in the world I would ever attempt a Marvel collection again, even if I had the finances. The Omnibuses, Essentials, Showcases, Masterworks, and the rest do the trick just fine, as they sure seem to be with countless others.

Another relatively affordable way to collect something different, and often rare, is non-U.S. comics. Many Stateside comics made their way into reprints all over the world, and often with different/newly drawn covers. Australian and U.K. Comics have much of what was popular here over the decades. There are also some indigenous comics that are fun to grab as well. Collecting Canadian comics has had a little overlap with U.S. Comics, but try to find some of their native titles such as the Canadian Whites, WWII-era comics that are cover-to-cover ingenuity that most missed out on by living a bit too far South. Mr. Monster is actually a Canuck, and was introduced in the *Canadian Super Duper Comics* #3, in 1947. There is a band of avid Canadian collectors currently working on a Canadian site and knowledge is going to jump in leaps and bounds. The interesting thing is that many have 1-2 surviving copies, and some issues are unknown, or currently extinct.

Some sales this year: *Funnyman* #1- Post-Superman Siegel & Shuster VG $41, *Super Funnies* #2 RARE Superior Mad-like Horror/crime satire VG- $135, *Jumbo Comics* #114 $35 FN+, *Peter Pat - Single Series* #8 racist content VG $37, *Tops Comics* #2004 (#4) not in *Gerber* Very rare GD $21, *King Solomon's Mines* #1 (NN) with bloody decapitation GD $17, *Guidebook to Comic Fandom* by Jerry Bails HG $76, *Cerebus* #2 sharp FN $152.50, *Magazineland* giveaway FN $26, *Best Cartoons Magazine* V3 #5, Marvel's *Pussycat* VG $20, *Cartoon Capers Magazine* V7 #5 Pussycat VG $17.50, U.K.'s *Triumph* #784 1939 UK One of the first ten Supermen cover of all $621, *Triumph* #813 with Superman story VG $111, *Jet-Man* #10 '46 Canadian White - Bell Overprint variant. Unique? FN $112, *Comic Crimes* #11 '46 Canadian White label variant FN $152, *Dell Giant Tales from the Tomb* L.B. Cole cover VG- $16, *The Gospel According to Superman* '73 Christian hardback with countless Superman reprints, and panel FN $25, *Archie* #50 with the Betty GGA cover that ALL Archie collectors are wanting VG $100 with countless others waiting in line for another.

Thank you all for yet another adventure-filled year in the fascinating world of comics! And a major "Thank You!" to Jean Bails for her initial edit. As we can not stress enough, buy what you love, and read what you buy.

Ben Samuels
Collector

It has been an interesting year for comic book collecting. There seem to be plenty of changes but as that old saying goes, "The more things change the more they stay the same."

Of course everyone knows that high-grade Silver Age key issues continue to set records. And high-grade Bronze Age key issues enjoy tremendous demand and command ever-higher prices. And I'm not breaking news to anyone when I mention that high-grade Golden Age comics of all sorts are eagerly sought out by legions of collectors. *X-Men* issues #94-143 CGC graded 9.6 and 9.8 are still bringing great prices. Vintage issues of *Amazing Spider-Man* in nice condition are like gold. This is all common knowledge. So what's new, you ask? Plenty!

Pre-Code horror comics from all publishers seem to be enjoying a strong market, in all grades. Especially issues with shocking or gory cover art. This year I sold *Horrific* #3 in VG (restored) for $370, *Out Of The Shadows* #8 in GD+ for $108, and *Bobby Benson's B-Bar-B Riders* #14 in VG/FN for $60. Ok, that last one wasn't too impressive; it has a cool bondage/decapitation cover but maybe the price wasn't stronger because of the weird horror/Western mash-up? I also saw a sale on eBay of a *Mister Mystery* #11 (CGC 4.0) for $524, *Weird Mysteries* #5 in GD to GD+ for $921, and *Chamber of Chills* (Harvey) #19 in VG+ for $438. *Crime SuspenStories* #22 seems to regularly sell for $500 or more in GD/VG to VG, which I find a little surprising because it is not a rare book by any means. But the Johnny Craig decapitation cover is certainly a classic and the *SOTI* and Senate investigation connections make it historically significant.

Obscure foreign comics, especially older ones, are gaining interest among more and more collectors. Vintage Canadian comics have a broad base of collectors and serious attempts are being made to catalog and research these rare books. Older Australian and British comics are attracting attention too. This year I sold several Australian comics from the 1950s for respectable prices but, as always, top condition is key to getting a good price. Sales of Australian comics include: *Batman* #29 in VF- for $56, *Love Illustrated* #4 in NM- for $71, *Superboy* #30 in VF for $61, *Super Adventure Comics* #28 in VF+ for $51, and *Super Adventure Comics* #73 in NM also for $51.

A few other nice sales I made this year include $104.37 for *Fantastic Four* #67 (CGC 8.5), $145.05 for *Uncanny X-Men* #121 (CGC 9.6), and getting $129.50 for Gladys Parker's *Mopsy* #1 in VG/FN was a very nice surprise.

Romance comics have a dedicated following of fans who love the often surprising tough and hard-hitting stories and great art from the pre-Code Golden Age, as well as the much more campy and sentimental material produced under the Comics Code during Silver Age. Golden Age issues from St. John, Harvey Comics, and of course Simon & Kirby's pioneering titles like *Young Romance Comics*, *Young Love*, and *Young Brides* which were published by Prize are consistent favorites among connoisseurs of the genre. In the Silver Age, DC's romance titles seem to be the most popular. Savvy collectors have discovered that some Harvey romance comics have fantastic artwork from Jack Kamen, Warren Kremer, John Prentice, and Matt Baker. Other stalwart artists of note that can be found in most Harvey romance comics include Bob Powell, Bill Draut, Manny Stallman and Lee Elias. The best Harvey romance books, by far, are the pre-Code issues. This is because after the Comics Code was introduced most issues consisted entirely of tame reprinted stories that had been radically censored.

Genuinely rare comics can still bring good prices too. This year I managed to locate a copy of *The Farmer's Daughter* (with cover and art by Howie Post) that looked about GD but was missing half a story page, so the grade was Poor. It sold for $62 -- not bad for an obscure incomplete humor comic! And a GD copy of *Captain Aero* #26 was on eBay recently. It is a *Gerber* "8" Photo-Journal "no-show" with a cool L.B. Cole outer-space cover and it sold for $225. Other books to watch for include many obscure promotional/giveaway comics, especially issues that deal with drugs & alcohol, race, religion, or politics. Some are very rare and can sell for surprising amounts of money when they are offered for sale.

But not all segments of the market are strong. Some eBay sales that I found disappointing this year were $22 for *Daredevil* #116 (CGC 9.2), $229 for *Four Color Comics* #386 (*Uncle Scrooge* #1) in VG+, $33 *Mystery In Space* #30 VG (President Eisenhower cover), $102 for *Captain Marvel, Jr.* #19 in FN, $76 for *Green Lama* #6 in VG (classic swastika cover), $36 for *Pictorial Romances* #4 (#1) VG+ (Matt Baker art), and a group of *Swamp Thing* #3 (VG/FN), #9 (VF/NM), and #10 (FN). All three issues had Bernie Wrightson art, and were signed by Bernie, but the lot sold for only $9.95!

Hollywood movies continue to keep popular comic book characters in the spotlight. Spider-Man seems to lead the pack these days but prices for nice vintage comics featuring the Avengers are particularly strong. *Avengers* #55 with the first appearance of Ultron-5 seems to be the "breakout" issue of the moment as people scramble to secure nice copies in anticipation of the upcoming film. I don't really keep up with modern comics anymore but I do know that back issues of *The Walking Dead* are selling like there's no tomorrow. I've seen CGC 9.8 issues of #1 often selling on eBay for over

$2,000 and even CGC 9.4 copies average around $1000. Those are what I call some killer prices! Other new areas of interest for many collectors are CGC certified Signature Series issues and blank sketch covers.

In the teen-age humor genre early issues of *Archie*, *Laugh*, copies of *Pep* featuring early appearances of that rascal from Riverdale, and *Jackpot* #4 through #9 are all in high demand with collectors eager to buy almost any issue they can locate, regardless of grade. Fox's *Sunny* and *Junior* with Al Feldstein art are still in high demand but collectors should beware that some later issues followed the "house style" Feldstein set for the titles but the covers and interior stories were drawn by other artists. Feldstein has denied drawing the cover of *Sunny* #13 and claims no involvement at all with issue #14. He also denied doing the cover and several interior stories in *Junior* #13. Additionally, while *Meet Corliss Archer* #1 is 100% Feldstein from cover to cover, Al says that he had nothing to do with either issue #2 or #3 of the series.

© HARV

Early issues of vintage Harvey characters never lack for interest. (**Richie Rich** #2 shown)

Vintage Harvey humor comics featuring their signature characters enjoy strong demand. Early issues of *Casper*, *Richie Rich*, *Little Dot*, plus *Hot Stuff* and *Devil Kids* never lack for interest from dedicated fans. Even *Little Lotta*, *Little Audrey*, and *Baby Huey* enjoy healthy popularity. However prices for *Stumbo Tinytown* seem to have peaked. Early issues of *Little Dot* seem especially difficult to find and there are some quirks to collecting the many varied Richie Rich titles. For example, *Richie Rich Zillions* #2 is considered scarcer than #1 and can bring higher prices.

Thanks to CGC and wider cultural appreciation of the American comic book, there seems to be some new influence by investors in the upper reaches of the hobby that helps drive the prices for the most expensive comics. And that introduces some interesting factors for this segment of the market. Namely, I believe that it magnifies the nostalgia factor and creates a focus on only the most iconic books. Someone who is spending six or seven figures on a single comic book will want something instantly recognizable, like Spidey, Batman, or Superman. And that lessens demand for older or second-tier characters like Captain Marvel, Plastic Man, Sub-Mariner, or the Spectre. For example, while *Journey Into Mystery* #83 (CGC 8.5) recently sold for $26,000, *More Fun Comics* #58 (CGC 9.4) featuring the Spectre sold for $9,462, and *Marvel Mystery Comics* #8 (CGC 5.5) featuring the Human Torch, Sub-Mariner, and The Angel went for $3,301. These books all sold in the same fairly high-profile comic auction.

Other new factors that may influence the market now and in the future include the plethora of information available on the internet. From the CGC census, to GPAnalysis, to the Heritage auction archive, the Grand Comics Database, and eBay completed auctions, there are more research tools available to collectors than ever before. There are also a myriad of downloadable vintage comics which have entered the public domain that are now available for free on several web sites. Another interesting resource is the top4comics.com web site which is attempting to catalog all known copies of *Action Comics* #1, *Detective Comics* #27, *Marvel Comics* #1, and *Superman* #1. The site has scans of all the books so far identified and certified issues are ranked by grade. The current counts (as I write this) show *Marvel Comics* #1 is the rarest with 36 copies listed while *Superman* #1 is the most common with 62 copies cataloged. *Detective Comics* #27 and *Action Comics* #1 weigh in with 38 and 41 copies, respectively.

The market for original art is another alternative competing for money from comic enthusiasts and it is a market that appears to be growing stronger all the time. Prices for prime material seem to go up monthly. It is a difficult market to quantify because every page is truly unique. Pulps are another option for collectors as these magazines have many connections to the world of comics and prices for desirable issues in nice condition reach new highs every year. Red Circle pulps were published by Martin Goodman who also founded Marvel/Timely Comics, and the *Marvel Stories* pulp from November 1940 (Vol 2, #2) has illustrations by Joe Simon and Jack Kirby as well as a one-page ad for Marvel Comics featuring a cameo by the Human Torch! Vintage under-the-counter girlie magazines, especially "spicy" titles with cover art by Enoch Bolles are another strong market with an enthusiastic following and rising prices.

Overall there are more options for collectors than ever before but there are also challenges, especially for the investor/collector. Whenever someone asks me what I think they should collect, what is "hot", or what is going to go up in value I always try to be honest and give them the best advice I can. I say, "You should collect stuff that you like." No one can see into the future and buying for profit is always a gamble. But if someone focuses on selecting material that they love there is always the simple pleasure of owning cool things. And really, isn't that what collecting comics is all about?

Barry Sandoval
Heritage Auctions

2013 was Heritage's second consecutive year of selling over $30 million worth of vintage comics and original comic art, so obviously we continue to be bullish on this category. **Don and Maggie Thompson Collection:** Although we receive auction consignments from many different sources, certainly the most fun from our point of view are the original-owner collections. We were excited to close out the year with the collection of two super-VIPs in our hobby, namely Maggie Thompson and the late Don Thompson. The Thompsons will be familiar to most any collector as the long-time editors of *Comics Buyer's Guide*. More importantly as far as their collection is concerned, they were already adults in the early 1960s when the Marvel superhero comics were published, so they handled their comics with care and respect. At the deadline for this report we had just offered the first installment of their collection, and those 80-odd books sold for more than three-quarters of a million dollars!

While CGC's census report is filling up for the Silver Age books, showing us there are more high-grade copies out there than some people thought, an original owner collection with the eye appeal of this one can still result in "auction fever," with prices to march.

Late 1970s/1980s Comics: Selling the staggering collection of Empire Comics of Rochester, NY has been an eye-opener for us. James and Anthony Furfferi, who ran the business, would routinely put away 20 or more copies of every new comic that came out from the late 1970s onward, and a high percentage have been grading out at CGC 9.8 today. We don't doubt that there were others putting away just as many copies as the Furfferi brothers did. This means it's a great time to be a buyer of this type of material. However, it's a bad time to be a seller of average, circulated copies of post-1975 comics, which no longer excite the serious collector very much. Why pay for them when you can get pristine copies relatively cheaply?

Classic Golden Age Covers: We are definitely seeing Golden Age collecting become more and more about the covers than any other consideration. *Phantom Lady* #17 *Guided* $5,920 in VF last year, but I think anyone with a copy for sale at that price would have seen a line around the block. *Star Spangled Comics* #7 with the first Newsboy Legion had roughly the same value, but you would be hard-pressed to find a taker at full *Guide*.

Ziff-Davis: We couldn't help notice the demand for this oddball publisher when anything in decent grade surfaces. Technically in the comics business for 10 years, they were really only active from 1950-1953. They have pulp-style painted covers, and some seem quite hard to find. The following have all sold for double *Guide* or more at Heritage recently: *Space Busters* #1 (Norm Saunders painted cover) and #2 (bondage cover), *Strange Confessions* #1, *Hot Rod King* #1 (Saunders cover and a book we've only offered three times in 12 years), and *Cloak and Dagger* #1 (another fantastic cover and seems to be hard to find).

Pre-Hero Marvel Monster Comics: A year ago we said that these issues were performing extremely well in high grade... well, in the meantime, they are selling well in any grade! We have seen certain sought-after issues sell over *Guide* even in VG or FN lately, and putting together a run takes more time and effort than a superhero run from a couple of years later. It would be exaggerating to call them rare, but some issues we might only offer once or twice a year, whereas any early *Spider-Man* issue we'll sell at one every couple of weeks.

DC Treasury Editions: When we auctioned some Near Mint copies of the DC treasuries recently we were pleased to see these fetch 1-5 times *Guide* at auction. Notice we said Near Mint – if you truly grade these by the same standards as a regular-size comic, NM copies are getting tough to come by. Marvel treasuries, however, seem to be plentiful even in high grade.

Original Comic Art: It is no longer news that five-and six-figure amounts are being paid for "prime" pages, but what continues to amaze is how well just about any 1960s through early 1980s art from a mainstream Marvel or DC title is selling. In every auction we'll have pieces that were purchased for $20 or $30 in the 1970s or 1980s and now fetch 100 times that amount, or more.

Among the highlights of our auctions this year were the original covers to *Watchmen* #1-12. These originally sold as one group lot for roughly $25,000 at a highly competitive Sotheby's auction in the early 1990s. In 2013 when we offered them as individual lots, they sold for almost half a million dollars! Our highest-dollar result of the year for a single lot was $478,000 for the Frank Miller cover art for *Batman: The Dark Knight Returns.*

© MAR

The first installment of the superb Don and Maggie Thompson pedigree was brought to market this past year.

Incidentally, while Marvel and DC superhero art has been the most lucrative category, there is a market for art from the most memorable "indies." Dan Clowes' cover for *Lloyd Llewellyn* #3 (1986) shocked most everyone by fetching $47,800, and we've sold key pages from Jaime Hernandez' *Love and Rockets* for thousands of dollars quite regularly.

If there's something we at Heritage can help you with, you'll find our contact information in our many ads in this book. We look forward to helping more collectors maximize the value of their four-color treasures in the coming year.

Alika Seki, P.E.
Maui Comics & Collectibles

This report is dedicated to the memory of Bruce Ellsworth, my mentor in comic appreciation and collecting. Bruce was the great nephew of Whitney Ellsworth, an editor and writer for DC Comics from the Golden Age. Through this relation, Bruce came into contact with some of the most incredible, iconic comics ever made. He also told me how he would haphazardly destroy those beautiful Golden Age comics as a kid reading the comics under the cover with a flashlight.

Bruce passed away at his residence in Waiehu, Maui in May of 2013 in his sleep with his loving wife, Melody, by his side. Bruce, as he told me very matter-of-factly, had come to Maui to die. He had just been deported from Australia for all of his multiple health woes, which I won't bother to list. If Bruce was one thing, it was brutally honest. If he was another, it was content. And even faced with his mortality, he couldn't help but enjoy his life – past, present and future simultaneously. We'd sit around and listen to records. He'd reminisce about his young days as a runaway from a blue-blooded, oil-rich family – playing blues and rock in the low and dirty clubs in New Orleans and all the trouble that went along. We would both dig feverishly through whatever new little collection we had found, somehow on this rock, where most people are ashamed to even admit they still collect comics. And he would confide in me how he had been preparing his affairs for his departure from this world.

I met Bruce in 2010, only 3 years before he passed, just about the time my first son was born. I had recently dug up the last dregs of my comic collection, which ended in the late 1990s – my college years. It was a wicker basket in the shape of a long box that my mom's Pomeranian had pissed on more than once, while I was away at college. About half was low grade Silver Age, semi-Key books that I had managed to get in middle school from a friend's dad's basement stash – the other half was "Death of Superman" and Fatal Attractions, and Image and Valiant and other typical '90s titles. When I met Bruce I was surprised at how nice he was, and how well he treated my comics, which were mostly beat up. I remember as a kid all the comic store guys of the world always seemed so rude and ready to cheat me out of my books, tell me how shitty they were and how little they were worth. Bruce was none of that. He would educate me about my books, about the artists and the writers, and how to grade them accurately. And he traded me books in better condition. He revived my love of comic collecting, which had died slowly over the years of becoming a young working professional.

We spent a couple years discovering little collections here and there and then one day Bruce told me that he had recommended I become an advisor in the 42nd edition of the *Guide*. I was stunned. Bruce had not only brought me back to collecting, but he had made one of my greatest nerd-dreams come true!

Unfortunately for Bruce he also trusted me to write our "store's" reports. And for those who don't know, there are no actual comic stores on Maui now. There used to be 5 actual stores at one point in the mid-'90s, but when the market crashed those stores all closed. The comic trade on this island has since degenerated into roving packs of comic-hungry collectors, who operate out of their homes and storage spaces - competing with each other for the few worthwhile collections that are surfacing. The last actual store to close was Compleat Comics. I remember going there as a kid. This past year Bruce bought out the remaining stock of Compleat Comics, which we are now selling at our "store". Our "store" used to be at Bruce's garage, and now it's been moved to my father-in-law's garage. If you're ever on Maui, feel free to contact me to come see the stash. See our B&W half page ad for information.

Recently Sold Collections (eBay seller: alikatime and in person): Low grade lot of Bronze Age Batman comics (*Batman* #227, 232 & 244, *Detective* #398-400-402 & 415), the Neal Adams covers. My personal favorite is the cover for *Detective* #244, where we see Batman sprawled out having just received a shirtless beatdown by Ra's al Ghul. Sold for $350 on eBay.

Low grade lot of Silver Age *Amazing Spider-Man* #16, 18, 19, 23. *Amazing Spider-Man* from the Silver Age in any grade and from the Bronze Age in higher grades are always consistent sellers. Sold for $250 on eBay.

Low grade lot of *TMNT* Role Playing Books 1985-1990 (about 5 books). The continued popularity of the Teenage Mutant Ninja Turtles as well as at least some pop-culture presence in some form or other since their emergence in 1984 has boosted demand and prices for early material. Even the role-playing books had a part in creating the TMNT mythos as it exists today. The RPG books served as a testing ground for personality traits and inter-personal stories that later made it into the accepted lore of the TMNT universe. Sold for $65 on eBay.

All Teenage Mutant Ninja Turtle-related comics, graphic novels, RPG books and other pre-1990 print material is always a good investment. You can usually find the original Mirage Studios run issues, even as low as #5 going for peanuts. Whereas the Turtles will always have staying power with the youth, and especially my generation which were the beneficiaries of late-'80s, early-'90s Turtlemania. I can't watch the new animated series on Nickelodeon with my son without smiling. And you better believe I bought him every single TMNT toy he asked for. I also am impatiently awaiting the August 2014 release of the TMNT movie. I reserve all judgments until I watch it, out of respect for Kevin Eastman – who has done and continues to do so much for new writers and artists, especially via his publication *Heavy Metal.*

Low to Mid-grade lot of *Iron Man* #1, 2, 3, 6, 7, 9. Sold for $350 on eBay. Low grade copies of these comics are abundant and that usually keeps the prices low, but due to the insanely popular movie franchise they remain a consistent seller. The main reason that Iron Man has risen so fast in popularity due mainly to Disney's treatment of the franchise. I am a fairly cynical guy, and have definitely used the term "Disney-fication" before to berate anything remotely kitchy or too-sweet. That being said, they are doing an incredible job with the portion of the Marvel Universe that they are controlling right now. They've got great actors, they've got great writers, they've got big budgets, but so does Fox with their X-Men movie franchise. So why has just about everything X-Men related that has come out to date (*Days of the Future Past* has not yet been released as of this report), been for the most part unfulfilling, leather-jacket clad, crap? Why am I left wondering whether I even give a care about the once mighty X-Men anymore? In one single word: Costumes.

Disney nailed it on all counts for the Avengers and their costumes. Thor had his 4 inexplicably placed circles on the front of his armor, Iron Man was yellow and Red, Black Widow was black and skin-tight, Cap was Cap, and even the Hulk had on his signature purple pants (the only notable miss was Hawkeye who wore black leather, and gave us a bad *Fox X-Men-esque* taste in my mouth). They may have made slight modifications to the costumes or appearances, but all-in-all they made every fanboys' dream come true and also managed to bring a whole new section of the population into the comic collecting fold. These movies are ultimately triumphs of the genre and show what these movies can achieve. Fox's treatments on the other hand…

From Fox's first installment of *X-Men* in 2000 I have been consistently let down and disappointed with only a few highlights to break my fall. Highlights for the Fox X-M*en* where Colossus goes metal for about 5 seconds to protect the children, *X-2* where we at last get an X-Man that resembles his comic counterpart with Nightcrawler, and of course Magneto's helmet. And for anyone who wants to raise the issue of Hugh Jackman's *Wolverine*; just because the guy looks like him don't mean a whole hell of a lot. Nobody gives a flip about Logan in street clothes unless Frank Miller is doing the art! Until he dons a skin-tight yellow and brown jumpsuit with a giant X on the belt and futuristic shoulder pads and goes into Berserker mode in a room full of henchman I will not be convinced!

To recover from that nerd-rant, I also sold a 50 long box collection of early 1990s full runs from all of the most popular Marvel, DC, Image, Valiant, Dark Horse and other publisher titles. The original owner had lived next to the Dark Horse office in the early and mid-1990s and also maintained multiple subscriptions through Mile High Comics. He brought the collection to the Big Island with him when he moved, where I purchased them and shipped them to Maui, and eventually sold them to a gentleman from Oahu. I kept the complete run (#1-189 including annuals and specials) of minty-fresh *Dark Horse Presents* for my own personal reading pleasure. Sold the *Daredevil* #1-380 complete run for $2,700 on eBay. The remainder of the collection was sold for $5,000 in person.

Garage Sale/Craigslist Finds: Last year I bought a low to mid-grade Bronze Age lot of *Uncanny X-Men* from a recent widow selling her husband's hobby stuff in the parking lot of Kihei Village Apartments. I had contacted her through a Craigslist ad. Despite my previous X-Men rant, they are still my favorite characters and I believe strongly in the value of these comics, especially the Bronze Age issues, which I have noticed are becoming more popular than the Silver age issues recently (aside from Neal Adams and Havok related issues). There was also a lot of other stuff in her collection, such as a complete run of *ROM* #1-31 and some scattered higher grade *Conan the Barbarian* in the upper 100s of the series, which I gave to Bruce. Bruce was also a big fan of Conan, in any incarnation. Conan is how Bruce introduced me to the work of Frank Frazetta, and officially blew my tiny little mind.

Also through Craigslist I found a garage sale that had comics, with a phone number in the ad. I called and they said that they would drop off the remaining comics after the garage sale (about 4 long boxes and a giant tub of baseball cards) for $15. I told them it was a deal. When I got the collection I found a list of comics that the original owner had made. Somebody had already gotten the *New Mutants* #98 and *Incredible Hulk* #340 that were in the collection. My heart was broken. And to show you what a small island and collecting community we have on Maui, the very next day I was talking with another collector I knew, and he had been the guy who got to the comics at the garage sale on the other side of the island. *New Mutants* #98 seems to be holding its value after the price spike it went through in recent years with rumors of a *Deadpool* movie. I wonder if all the delays and possible cancelation of the project will bring the price back down? Or are people just finally realizing how awesome *Deadpool* is, and will we see a sustained price in the triple digits for this issue? Only time will tell, but I'm holding all my copies for now.

It's easy to get caught up in all the recent mainstream attention to comics (I am certainly guilty of sporting a nerd-boner every time I see a preview for the new *Guardians of the Galaxy* movie), but in these turbulent political times it is also important to remember the counter-culture of America. Underground comics from the era when the American counter-culture emerged and made itself known (the 1960s and 70s) are historical blueprints on how to construct the mindset for social and political change.

I am by no means an expert on the genre, but I was fortunate enough to have Bruce to educate me with his incredible collection of Underground comics. As he put it, it is "the largest collection of Underground Comics" in the Pacific. His collection included a lot of file copies from Last Gasp and Kitchen Sink publishing, among others. Out of all the comics he had amassed over the years, he took the most pride in his collection of Undergrounds. Through Bruce I grew a great appreciation for R. Crumb (among others like Spain, Corben, Moebius, etc.) and his incredible representation of the under-represented anxieties that come as symptoms to the various societal pressures in modern America. I had always been a fan of the Beat writers of the same time period (like, Kerouac and Kesey and Burroughs and Bukowski), and had no idea what a great supplement to the literature the comics of that time made. And to put it all in context Bruce always had good stories about the trouble he would get into during that time in San Francisco. Trouble with the cops, smoking grass, chasing girls, playing music and having good, old-fashioned American fun. You know, the kind of fun that the NSA would snatch your ass in a van off the street for having.

Bruce had a good run. His love of comics was unparalleled. During his service one of his friends, Uncle Wayne, said something that really stuck with me. Uncle Wayne said, "When we die, our form is gone, but our energy continues on and travels freely. When we wish to visit with Bruce all we need is to ask that he come and see through our eyes, and feel through our hands. Through this experience he can live again. Think of this when you read an old comic that was a favorite of his, and feel the pages."

Thank you to all the *OPG* staff that has made this transition so easy for our little "store." Aloha, a hui hou! And remember to – NERD OUT WITH YOUR BIRD OUT!

Doug Simpson
Paradise Comics

Some say that the days and weeks just blend together, not in 2013! Every single day was a new challenge. What do we market heavily? What do we order conservatively? What collections do we buy first?

After some long days and nights we finally saw some increase in sales this year over last. Our total sales increased by 6% with graphic novels making the largest contribution at 10% growth. Generally our new issue sales continue to be on the decline.

The greatest area of growth in-store remains our sale of graphic novels. This is definitely the direction the hobby is going and the major companies have started producing more stories in only this format. The release of *Avengers: Endless Wartime, Hellboy And The Midnight Circus,* and *Fairest In All the Land* are just a few examples. Most of our new customers are coming to pick up graphic novels instead of regular monthly issues.

The impact of digital comics is being felt by many retailers, and it looks like they will be a major part of the hobby in the years to come. Hollywood continues to help our sales with the increasing visibility of its mainstream comic movies including *Thor 2: The Dark World, Iron Man 3,* and *The Man of Steel.* Let's hope the *Avengers 2* and *Captain America: Winter Soldier* releases continue the trend by bringing more buyers into the market.

Key issues from the Silver and Bronze Age are still selling incredibly well and don't seem to be slowing down at all. I simply can't keep up with the demand for high-grade Silver and Bronze Age books – from *Action* to *X-Men*, people want them in the highest grades and as fast as possible. I would need a full-time employee just to keep up with the want lists I am being handed daily. The usual suspects are always involved: *Amazing Fantasy* #15, *Incredible Hulk* #1, *Fantastic Four* #1, *Daredevil* #1, *Giant-Size X-Men* #1, *Incredible Hulk* #181, and *X-Men* #94, but I'm also seeing some new ones. *Marvel Spotlight* #5 and 12, *Hero for Hire* #1,*Marvel Premiere* #15 and *Marvel Super-Heroes* #18 are just a few examples.

Golden Age sales are slowly picking up, and with so many collectors pursuing high-grade Silver Age, buyers are finding some great deals. Don't get me wrong, there was always a market for Golden Age Hero comics, but never at *Guide*, and usually well below. I really can't see this trend changing in the near future.

Silver Age sales are in the stratosphere, and high-grade copies are selling faster than I can get them in. Everyone wants book from the 1960s regardless of condition and cost. For DC Silver Age, Hero and Horror comics have seen the greatest growth in sales, while Romance has slowed right down. It could just be the affordability but DC bin stock sells way more in volume than its Marvel counterpart. Batman is the key mover for DC along with *Justice League of America.* Marvel Silver Age is selling very well, with *Amazing Spider-Man* and *X-Men* leading the way, and demand for *Avengers, Thor,* and *Iron Man* increasing. The Marvel Silver Age market is always strong and doesn't look to be slowing down anytime soon.

Bronze Age comic sales are through the roof in high grade, and demand for mid-grade copies has increased as well. Marvel leads the way in this category because of Byrne *X-Men* (#108-143) and all *Amazing Spider-Man* issues between #100 and #200. These issues are on almost everyone's list and, if I had an entire box of each, they would be gone in days.

Modern books are selling again. A new market of younger readers is coming into the shop looking for titles that they can pick up and enjoy without knowing any of the history of the characters. The Marvel Now Avengers books, and the entire Ultimate line fill this niche. *All New X-Men* is consistently our best selling X-book, easily outselling *Uncanny X-Men.*

I can't continue my report without mentioning CGC and their fantastic service. Not only would our sales have been slower, but also, we wouldn't have grown as quickly if it hadn't been for them providing the only guaranteed way to corroborate condition and confirm restoration on high-quality books.

CGC continues to be the ultimate standard in independent third-party grading. I would like to mention that CGC is still the exclusive grading company for Paradise Comics.

Some recent CGC sales include:
Amazing Spider-Man #40 CGC 9.4 $2000.00
Amazing Spider-Man #41 CGC 9.2 $1050.00
Avengers #1 CGC 5.5 $2700.00
Incredible Hulk #1 CGC 1.8 $3600.00
Journey Into Mystery #83 CGC 5.5 4300.00
Showcase #22 CGC 7.5 $2200.00
Silver Surfer #1 CGC 9.2 $1450.00
Sub-Mariner Comics #1 CGC 3.5 $4800.00
Walking Dead #1 CGC 9.8 $2200.00
X-Men #1 CGC 4.5 $2200.00
CGC Signature Series *Giant-Size X-Men* #1 CGC 9.6 $3500.00
CGC Signature Series *Amazing Spider-Man* #129 9.4 $1400.00

Online sales on both our eBay Store and Website (WWW.PARADISECOMICS.COM) continued to grow all year and we are looking forward to even better sales in 2014.

For the first time in a couple of years we returned to conventions as a fully set up retailer and it was a great success. In 2014 we will be doing some more shows so look for the Paradise booth at a comic book convention near you!

Marc Sims and Walter Durajlija
Big B Comics

Right off the bat we want to thank the *Overstreet Comic Book Price Guide* team for another stellar edition of the *Guide*. With so many new people entering the hobby we think there is no better starting point than our *Guide*. All the tools are here for veteran and newbie alike. Grading, pricing, historical context, information on storage, and these market overviews written by the hobby's experts are all invaluable tools to help get the new collector started and to help get us veterans active in sharing what we've learned over the past year. All the advisors who took the time to post these reports are due a special thanks.

Big B Comics had a banner 2013. Our 3 retail stores all showed solid growth as did our convention sales. Big B Comics Hamilton, Barrie and Niagara Falls (all in Ontario, Canada) enjoyed strong new comic sales, comic book related pop culture sales, and back issue comic sales. We see no reason for this trend to stop so we're still optimistic about the future of our hobby and our industry!

The Big B Comics website www.bigbcomics.com is a friendly site that delivers information our customers look for in an organized and entertaining way. Please visit the site and help us with some feedback!

This past year showed just how much the comic community is clamouring for quality and innovative comic book releases. DC's Villains month in September 2013 was a huge hit. Image had a banner year offering a strong selection of new and exciting title launches like *East of West* and *Sex Criminals* mixed with old stalwarts like *Saga* and *The Walking Dead*. Now if we can only get Marvel to come out with a competent monthly comic strategy! Their editorial direction is shamefully short-sighted, chasing immediate dollars with constant relaunches. The relaunch leads to an immediate drop off in sales, which in turn leads to more relaunches. It's like watching a dog chase its tail, except the dog only has one eye and three legs so it trips and falls more often than not.

In looking at recent industry numbers we like seeing the growing chunk of the pie shared by the so-called secondary publishers of comics like Dark Horse, Image, IDW, Boom, and others. Marvel and DC combine for under two thirds of the market here in early 2014, leaving over a third of the market to the other guys. That's a far cry from even 5 years ago when one could routinely see combined market share of 80-90% for the big two. In addition, Marvel and DC are very close to each other which theoretically should lead to healthy competition and a stronger market for all.

The back issue comic book market was very active for us this past year. Big B Comics bought a nice $25,000 collection in June of 2013, just in time for summer at the stores and the Niagara and Toronto comic cons. This collection consisted of long runs of Marvel Silver and Bronze Age in mid-grade with most of the major keys present. Turnover was pretty solid, especially on anything key. Another substantial late '50s to early '60s DC collection was purchased late in 2013. This collection was of note because the books in it had exceptional grades. The average grade was VF on long runs of titles like *Flash*, *Batman*, *Detective*, *JLA*, and *Wonder Woman*. These are the sorts of runs that we just do not see all that often and the result has been VERY brisk sales. Intermixed throughout the year we also had several nice little pickups that when added up surely would equal a couple more significant sized collections. In fact there wasn't much we turned away this year. Keeping stock fresh is important; with old comics it really is about sourcing quality books on a consistent basis.

One dramatic shift in recent years has been our focus on actively picking up and pricing more aggressively certain back issues from the '90s. Five years ago this stuff was mostly junk but now demand is growing. Key comics from this period are hot and we think they'll get even hotter. Books like the black bagged Death of Superman, *Amazing Spider-Man* #361, and our personal favorite *X-Force* #2 (2nd Deadpool) languished for years but lately have shown strong demand. Remember that new collectors coming into the market are generally younger and books from this era resonate with them. The trick is to identify which books from this era will rise to the top of the collecting heap.

Highlights of back issue sales from 2013:

Action Comics #252 VG+ $700
Amazing Fantasy #15 CGC 1.8 $5000
Amazing Spider-Man #14 CGC 8.5 $2500
Amazing Spider-Man #15 CGC 9.2 $2500, CGC 8.5 $900
Amazing Spider-Man #129 CGC 9.6 $1900, CGC 9.2, 4 sales $1200-1300
Batman #121 GD $450 (heavy water damage – still sold in 1 day!)
Brave and the Bold #28 GD $1300
Detective Comics #39 CGC 8.0 (P) $1500
Detective Comics #411 CGC 9.6 $1800
Fantastic Four #1 CGC 1.8 (A) $1900
Green Lantern #1 FN+ $1500
Green Lantern #7 VF+ $900
Incredible Hulk #181, multiple mid grade copies $900-$1000
Journey into Mystery #83 FR/GD $1200
Strange Tales #115 CGC 8.0 $550
Walking Dead #1 CGC 9.6 $1250
Walking Dead #19 CGC 9.8 SS $900

© MAR

Thanks to Deadpool's 2nd appearance, a slow mover like ***X-Force* #2** has sprung back to life.

Run books continue to be the sector slowly losing ground in the market as demand shrinks compared to supply. There are three trends worth watching: 1) new collectors focusing their entire collections on key issues 2) established collectors switching over to key issues and/or finishing their runs, and 3) the rising costs of buying quality comics. All these factors point to a weakening trend in run books which will continue as time goes on.

The Bronze Age market stabilized a bit this year. Negative trends on books like *Hulk* #181, *ASM* #129, *X-Men* #94, *GL* #76 seemed to have "bottomed out" in 2013 and in some cases rebounded.

Low to Mid grade copies of all the Silver and Bronze Age keys were the big price gainers in 2013. Opting to pick up a nice respectable copy of say a *Hulk* #181 has caused the prices of 4.0 to 7.0 copies to shoot up while 9.2 to 9.6 copies just crept ahead. Ditto for the Silver Age; look at how well 2.0 copies of *Amazing Fantasy* #15 did against say 6.0 copies.

We're still high on the potential of the Golden Age era. Last year we picked up a *Skippy's Own Book of Comics* at CGC 8.0 and a *Famous Funnies* #1 CGC 6.0 because we see a strong growth potential for these very early comic books. Sure we'll have to hold books like this for a little while but at today's market prices we think there are some great deals out there with good future growth potential.

Canadian Golden Age comics known as "Canadian Whites" will be making a splash this year. Check out Ivan Kocmarek's excellent essay at the back of the *Guide* to find out more about these very cool Golden Age comics. This year Big B acquired a high grade run of Maple Leaf Publishing's *Better Comics* #1-7 and *Lucky Comics* #1 and #3, *Better* is the 1st "Canadian Whites" book while *Lucky* is the second title from Maple Leaf. These comics are extremely rare, especially in grade, making this an unprecedented find.

We have said this the last couple years but it is worth repeating. The grade driven back issue market in the Modern Age is problematic. Paying money for the number on a plastic holder (eg CGC 9.9s) is not sound investing. We've been proven wrong on this stand lately as people are cashing in big on these books but we are still advising people to stay away. The bubble will burst. Simply put the utility of the incremental increase in grade from 9.8 to 9.9 is almost nonexistent. The value lies in the assigned grade and that's a dangerous thing to bank on. Most of these modern books are plentiful in high grade and 9.9s may not turn out to be as rare as you might think. Throw your money at strong tight 9.4s or 9.6s. They usually look just as good and can be had for a fraction of the price!

Our comic book fan website www.comicbookdaily.com (CBD) had another great year. Walter's *Undervalued Spotlight* and *Auction Highlights* blogs are still going strong and enjoying increasing readership. The comments section of the site can often be a great place to learn insights into our hobby not easily found anywhere else. We invite anyone interested in the hardcore collecting aspect of comics to join us for a fun time. You just might learn something!

As we stated last year American pop culture continues to drive global pop culture. The reserves of our pop culture heritage are rich and deep. Our influence is wide and it will continue to get wider; we're in every corner of the world! We still encourage people to invest in the comics that are the foundation of this growing global pop culture phenomenon.

Finally, both of us would like to acknowledge and thank the Big B Comics team for the great work that they do. We are fortunate to work with such passionate and dedicated people every day.

Tony Starks
Comics Ina Flash!

After several years of being a regular Debbie Downer with my market reports, this one will be comparatively upbeat.

The past year has seen a market that – well – it's hard to find just one word. It's complex, but there is some zeal out there. Low and mid grade run type books appear to be stabilizing. There is even some passion again for these books as the prices are now appealing to many collectors. The market remains strong for key books and for high grade material. And the market is basically crazy for anything connected to or rumored to be connected to an upcoming movie or TV show.

As details leak out about upcoming characters in movies or TV shows, the rush is on. A few examples: *Avengers* #28 – 1st appearance of the Collector who will be starring in the *Guardians of the Galaxy* movie. *Avengers* #54 and #55 – Ultron, the villain of the next Avengers movie. *Tales of the Teen Titans* #44 – first Nightwing. *Superman's Pal Jimmy Olsen* #133 (1st app) and *Forever People* #1 (1st full app) of Darkseid – rumored to be the villain in the upcoming *JLA* movie.

In my last few market reports, I have been saying that run issues of Gold/Silver/Bronze in average condition were requiring deep discounts to sell. At least 50%, oftentimes more off *Guide* prices. To be sure, I still have to discount low and mid grade copies of run Silver/Bronze books. But the discounts aren't as steep and there are noticeably more buyers.

Here is what I believe is going on. 1) The economy has improved. 2) For a number of years now, a LOT of collectors been selling off their common books in the attempt to raise the money to purchase high grade key issues. This just further beat down the prices of common books. Most collectors have given up the high grade key quest. The big keys all command five and six figure prices in high grade. It's just not possible for average collector to raise the $60,000 that an *Avengers* #1 in 9.2 would command. Or if they could, it would require selling virtually every other book they own. A lot, - if not most collectors – have decided that a mid grade copy of *Avengers* #1 only costs $2000-$4000 and they don't have to sell everything comic they own it to buy it. 3) Tying in with #2, collectors by nature want to own more than a handful of books. The current prices on average grade run books are very appealing to a lot of collectors. 4) Any common book today can become a key issue when the character gets featured in a movie or TV. Collectors are seeing value again in collecting runs and titles. If you were working on a run of *Avengers* last year, you probably could have picked up a FN to VF copy of issue #55 for less than $50. Now it's worth $200 or more.

My last statement. That's the crazy part of the market right now. There are just so many "hot" books. Every month seems to bring new surprises, new key books. *Incredible Hulk* #272 and Rocket Raccoon anyone? *Nova* #1 has doubled in price (both Guardians of the Galaxy). Darkseid's early appearances (Justice League movie) in *Superman's Pal Jimmy Olsen* #134 and *Forever People* #1. *Captain America* #360 (1st Crossbones – next CA movie) *Thor* #344 (1st Malekith – *Thor 2*) *Tales of the Teen Titans* #44 (Dick Grayson becomes Nightwing – rumors fly for appearance in Superman/Batman or own movie). *Marvel Feature* #1 (1st Defenders) *Marvel Premiere* #15 (1st Iron Fist) *Hero for Hire* #1 (1st Luke Cage) and *Alias* #1 are all seeing increased demand due to the upcoming Netflix shows in 2014. It's hard to make a list because it's out of date in a couple of months.

So a few representative sales – high, low and average:
Sales of run type books – typically 35-40% off *OPG*: *Adventure Comics* #303 FN ($21), *Anthro* #1 GD ($3.00), *ASM* #52 VG/FN ($20), *Avengers* #70 VF+ ($23), *Captain Marvel* (1968) #2 VF ($30), *Fantastic Four* #28 VG/FN ($75), *Green Lantern* #81 NM- ($95), *Iron Man* #2 VF ($35), *Sub-Mariner* #6 VG/FN ($5), *Thor* #180 VF ($23), *X-Men* #57 VG/FN ($19), and *X-Men* #89 PGX 9.2 ($93).
Sales at or close to *OPG*: *Avengers* #16 VG/FN ($57), *Captain Marvel* #1 FN ($45), *Conan* #26 NM ($17), *Demon* #1 VF+ ($53), *New Gods* #1 FN/VF ($40), *Spectacular Spider-Man* #2 NM ($28), *Thor* #152 NM ($100), *The Virginian* #1 VG/FN ($8), *X-Men* #12 VG/FN ($100), and *X-Men* #65 NM ($210)
Sales above *OPG*: *Avengers* #28 VG/FN ($37), *Avengers* #54 CGC 5.5 ($95), *Avengers* #55 CGC 7.0 ($179), *Avengers* #112 NM- (1st Mantis) ($70), *Captain America* #100 VG ($75), *Fear* #1 PGX 9.0 ($75), *Forever People* #1 CGC 9.0 ($171), *Iron Man* #1 VG ($300), *Rima* #1 CGC 9.8 ($71), *Tales of the Teen Titans* #44 CGC 9.4 ($77), and *Thor* #344 PGX 9.8 ($135).
A few other notable sales of restored SA Key books: *Amazing Fantasy* #15 CGC 6.5 (Moderate Professional) ($7300). *Avengers* #1 CGC 9.2 (Slight Professional) Signature Series ($8500)

So what to take away from the above examples? Key books are selling for *OPG* or more. A few key issues in low to mid grade are way undervalued in the *OPG*: *Amazing Spider-Man* #129, *Incredible Hulk* #181, *Iron Man* #1 come immediately to mind. Introducing extremely popular characters – or in the case of *Iron Man* #1 the starting point for many collections – these books are bringing much more than the normal "spreads" would call for in low to mid grade. Also interesting is that in lower grades especially they sell for about the same amount of money raw as they do slabbed.

Better books – NM grades and minor keys are bringing around *OPG*. Maybe a little less, maybe a little more depending on the particular book

Run and common books still require significant discounts to sell. But it's 35-40% now instead of the 50% or more of a couple of years ago. And there are more buyers than before.

So there's my report. The market today is mixed – but it's a lot better mix than just a year ago.

West Stephan
Comic Book Certification Service (CBCS)

Timely comics and DC comics continue to be the stable rocks of the Golden Age. Timely War-era books (1939-1945) still show incredible demand and upward movement. Superman, Batman, and Wonder Woman will always have a stable collector and investor base. Flash and Green Lantern are holding their own while *Leading Comics* and *More Fun Comics* have lost some desirability. We need a Spectre/Dr. Fate movie DC! Come on already!

Hitler covers are still being bought at record prices. Robot covers are doing especially well too. Good Girl books sell very well but *Phanotm Lady*, *Jo-Jo*, *Rulah*, *Sunny*, and *Junior* seem to be the best sellers. Horror titles are doing very well. Titles like Atlas' *Mystery Tales* and *Astonishing* seem to have found a lot of new interest. Expect all Atlas horror to continue to rise in price and popularity.

Every so often the comics marketplace has a big event that changes the hobby in a positive way. In 1970, *The Overstreet Comic Book Price Guide* changed the hobby forever. In 1990, the Gerber *Photo-Journals* changed how the collector was able to view books that were virtually unseen by most of us. Then in the late 1990s, eBay changed the way we bought and sold comics. In 2000, certified books changed the way collectors and investors bought and sold again, giving us renewed confidence in buying comics that were not restored or overgraded. I am predicting 2014 will be another benchmark year for our hobby. It can only get better!

Al Stoltz
Basement comics

I cannot believe that Christmas is almost upon us and it is time to write yet another market report for *The Overstreet Price Guide* !! The year has flown by and I spent most of it chasing comics and weird items and watching what was trending at the shows I either attended or actually set up at for 2013. I have to say that the year seemed to get more predictable as it went along and helped me to come up with a business model for 2014 that I feel will work a lot better and make the bottom line a little stronger.

First step was to secure a new place to do business out of and that means space and more space to fill with comics we own and more we hope to buy. It took almost the whole year and we went through three different companies that were offering spaces to finally secure a 3,000 square foot warehouse with offices only twelve miles away from my house. While I almost came close to losing my mind dealing with these "worse than Used Car Salesmen" to get a large space to sort comics and to better organize our almost 13,000 eBay listings I believe in the end this will be a boon to future plans we have started to move forward with and when this contract is up may have to seek a bigger place to call home.

Our primary means of selling comics is still eBay and it was our 15th year selling comics and other stuff through this system, but as usual eBay tries to make it hard for you to make a decent buck. Rule changes and "improvements" on their end made us scramble to make changes to appease the Gods of eBay but we have stayed about the 15th largest seller of comics on the site and were amazed that they have seemed to purge over 10,000 sellers of comics off the site due to the new rules of selling. I still think it is a great place to sell comics and probably has been responsible for keeping the back issue market decent for even longer due to demand for old comics from out of the USA. That being said, I am glad Australia, our biggest buyer of comics outside USA, has a strong appetite for old comics and old Australian editions of comics that we keep posting. I am hoping that a move to a bigger place to work out of and hiring another set of hands or two to post items and pack will move the eBay operation along and be more profitable.

Comic Book Shows: Only set up at five shows for 2013 and visited another five or more as well and watched the crowds and where money was being traded for comics the most. There seems to be a ton of interest in comics but more from a Current issue interest to whatever movie-related comic that used to be in our overstock piles and now is a slabbed piece of Gold for the moment. The new DC lenticular covers seemed to be the rage at the last couple of shows I went to for the year and I have to admit they looked pretty cool. Will they have long term staying power in the market? Up to the fickle collectors but most could end up in deep discount bins by 2014 and beyond. The other big sellers of comics were the guys who worked hard to make comics affordable and by the bunch. Under $5.00 models of selling and especially $2.00 models of selling did tremendous business this year at shows and perhaps are responsible for creating new and maybe longer term buyers of older material in the end. Maybe that buyer will want to spend a little more to buy the key issues or look harder to find books to create a collection. I have also watched as discounts on regular box inventories at shows is now always at 30-50% off or more BUT it actually seems to drive sales and push items that were perhaps over-priced finally, or due to market shift and time do not really deserve to be at the level they are currently listed at for a value. The value is...what someone is going to pay...that is market value and it seems that answer is cheaper and well packaged at shows.

Better books at shows, and by that I mean Key Marvels and DCs...Golden Age Keys and Pedigree Copies or just rare and unusual stuff still does well and the circle of buyers for that material stays the same. I have grown fond of saying these days that you need at most 100 of the best selling books and 10 of each and that would be all you ever need to carry. *New Mutants* #98....yup right here next to *Amazing Spider-Man* #129 and *Incredible Hulk* #181...there you go happy buyers! At each four-day show we did this year we did notice that better books and items on the hunt by the hard core "get in the show early" crowd sold great on set up day and maybe another day but for the other days at the show vintage seemed to be a tough item to sell. I have been going to comic shows for 38 years now and have seen all kinds of trends and changes to the market and this may be yet another twist and turn to the hobby.

We did score lots of cool stuff this year and had little problem selling Keys and better books and even oddball stuff like Treasury Editions. Even pulps had moments of quick sales and happy buyers. Comic art, like a cool lot of very early art by Arthur Sudyam, sold at Mega Con to a great collector of the obscure like me and he seemed genuinely pleased to take it home. Sold a small collection of WWII Propaganda items that we may never see again. It was like last year I guess, a small mix of all kinds of material from Westerns to Archie to Art to Weird stuff made our bottom line happen and I am sure the same thing will be the answer to a successful 2014 by next December as well.

Doug Sulipa
Doug Sulipa's Comic World

The origins of comics can arguably be traced back to the Stone Age when cavemen told stories with pictures carved on walls. The Comic Book format that most us collect began circa 1933 and thus is 80 years old. Most print media is fast on the decline and headed for extinction. This worries comic collectors as print runs keep declining, as they fail to recognize the transformation of the Media as the total package involved. When you correctly view comics in the current Age, it includes (in multiple languages and countries around the World): Comics in Print Format (Books, Colloring Books, Comic Books as Periodicals, Digests, Graphic Novels, Hardcovers, Magazines, Newspapers, Paperbacks, Posters & more), Documentaries, Electronic Media (Internet & Mobile Phone), Films/Movies (8, 16 & 35 mm Film, VHS, DVD, Blu-Ray), Games (Board Games, Puzzles, Role-Playing, Video Game etc), Kindle Reader, Music (Cassette tape, CD, 8-Track, Vinyl Record), News, Radio, Television & More. Add to that an endless stream of memorabilia, collectibles and disposable items too, including: Action Figures, Bikes, Blankets, Bobble-Heads, Candy, Caps/Hats, Clothing, Coins, Costumes, Curtains, Drinks and their Containers, Food Containers, Fridge Magnets, Games, Keychains, Lithos, Lunch Boxes, Model Kits, Non-Sport Cards, Original Art, Patches, Radios, Rings, Stamps, Statues, Stickers, Toys, Wallets and much more. Given that colossal amount of items related to comics today and adding the current growing population of the world, comics today are unquestionably currently the most popular they have ever been in their entire history, and are still growing in all related Mass Media. Warner Brothers owns DC Comics. The Walt Disney company bought Marvel Comics in 2009 and Star Wars in 2012, so you can bet the explosion of related items has just begun. Comic books as print media still have very high value as low priced source material for all the aforementioned items above, if they make a bit of money that is a bonus, if they only break ever that is still great. Even as a loss leader, they have great potential, at very low cost. It was a small investment for Marvel to produce the *Alias* series from 2001, which will now reap the rewards of becoming a TV series for Netflix in the near future. Collectors are a stange breed, as they prefer to collect the ORIGINAL items, rather than reprints, if they can afford them.

Since tastes are ever changing and evolving, there will always also be overproduced comics out of favor and slow sellers. They might stay stagant in price for years, but given time they gain value, simply by inflation and cover prices of new items, so one needs only to be patient. If you want to be an investor in comics, do NOT buy just anything, do your homework, read market reports, ask advanced collectors and dealers, check out auctions, dealer sites, conventions, eBay and flea markets. If you are spending larger amounts of money and are not an expert at recognizing strictly graded condition, then beware, buy low price items, CGC graded items, and strict graded items from trusted experienced sellers, until you are confident about grading.

Collectors need to think about LIQUIDITY. Comics were produced as disposable entertainment objects, once you have read them you are to have used up their value, if you can salvage any value at all out of common comics after that, that should be considered found money. You will probably NOT be able to fund your children's education or your retirement with common comics. They are not cash or bonds, you cannot buy groceries with them. To educate yourself, when you make a purchase, immediately ask another seller what he would buy that same item for. Chances are that if 90% or more of your comics collection is 1981 and newer, you will have to become a Dealer and sell them yourself, to get any noteable money from your collection. Your options include: (1) eBay (2) Craigslist (3) kijiji (4) your local newspaper (5) local flea markets (6) sell or trade to your local second hand bookstores; "book" stores often have a low selection of comics, while comic shops might be overstocked; (7) have a garage sale listing comics as the main feature (many people will show up) and sell most common 1980s to the present comics in the 50 cents to $1.00 each price range; the ones that have a *Guide* value of $5.00 or more, you can ask $1.00 each or more (or 20-35% of *Guide*). Note: Comics sold in complete sets or runs (complete consecutive runs of 10, 20 or 30 comics in one lot are recommended) sold at 10% to 50% off *Guide* (based on popularity and scarcity), sell near equally as good as a decent selling key issue of same value.

In the 1980s fans and collectors both thought Bronze Age comics were common in high grade and would never be worth anything. They were all very wrong, as prices exploded and many comics are scarce to rare in high grade. In the last decade, fans and collectors both thought Copper Age comics were common in high grade and would never be worth anything; they are again very wrong, as many key issue prices are exploding as I write this and many of these comics are scarce to rare in high grade. Many think that Modern Age comics are common and worthless, but with the lowest print runs in the history of comics, any key issue that becomes hot has overnight explosive potential. Since all these characters started in the comic books that we know and love, they will always be collectible.

Once again the hottest comics of the year were those related to current and upcoming TV and movies, with many items experiencing skyrocketing prices. Even many veteran advanced collectors have been drawn into the frenzy. If there is one thing I have learned in 42+ years experience as a dealer, it is to sell the comics the customers want, when they want them. Often this involves buying hot comics at 100-200% or more of *Guide*, and marking the price up from there and selling immediately, even if at a modest profit. Many collectors get sucked into the "I have it and you don't" phenomena that makes them overpay for items that are on everybody's "must have" list. The mistake they make is buying at or over the peak price, when the next "must have" hot book comes along, the previous "must have" items can drop in value, or stay stagnant for up to 10 years, or longer. Most collectors are now in the habit of buying as prices are peaking, when it is actually the time to be selling these "must have" books (I have been making a good living for 42 years by selling at the right time. Rather than buying the current "must have" book at 600% *Guide*, you are usually better off buying 6 undervalued key issues with lots of future potential at current *Guide* levels.

This year there were so many collectors diverted from their regular collecting practices by hot TV and movies, that many non-Key Silver and Bronze Age titles saw slow downs in sales. The marketplace noted a lot of price corrections on CGC graded comics, often with items like uneventful 1966-1969 Marvel super-hero comics in CGC 9.4 selling at 9.0 *Guide* or lower prices. In fact many high grade non-Key issues now sell at below *Guide* prices, meanwhile the GD-FN copies on same comics are now undervalued in *Guide* and sell OK at current *Guide* levels. The newest phenomena is that many Marvel and DC Key issues that are priced at $100 or more in VF, sell much better in GD to FN grades at 125% to 200% current *Guide* prices. This is partly because smart sellers realize they are undervalued in GD-FN at current *Guide* levels, as the price spreads are now too wide, so the dealer pays full *Guide* and makes his markup from there. The hot TV and movies trend appears to be recurring for the forseeable next 2-5 years before the next reevaluation occurs.

Meanwhile, this is the time to buy up the bargain priced undervalued CGC comics, and the undervalued affordable key issues with future potential.

Alternative / Independent Comics: Since Copper Age comics have picked up in demand, so have alternative comics from that era and beyond. Those from popular media have always sold faster, including: (Adult, *Aliens*, Animated Cartoons, Anne Rice, *Avengers*(TV), *Bone*, *Buffy*, Classics, Comic Strip Reprints, *Crow*, Dave Stevens art (everything), *Dick Tracy*, Doc Savage, EC Reprints, *Elric*, *Green Hornet*,

Horror (most), H.P. Lovecraft, Indiana Jones, James Bond, *Man from UNCLE*, Movie adaptations, Phantom, *Planet of the Apes*, *Predator*, *Robotech*, Rock and Personality comics, Robert E. Howard, The Shadow, Sherlock Holmes, *Simpsons*, Spirit, *Star Wars*, any with top comic artists, Tarzan, TV Shows, Underground, Vampires, Vietnam War, Werewolf, Zombies, etc.

Collectors are highly interested in all 1980 and older Alternative Comics, including: Ground-Level comics, Underground comics, Ditto-Zines and Fanzines. Most of these have small print runs and are never seen by the average collector. When you add to that the challenge of locating these scarce and cool items, and at still reasonable price levels, it is easy to see why many fans get hooked. We have over 100,000 different independent comics from the 1975-2010+ era in stock, one of the biggest selection anywhere, with well over 1/3 not listed in the *Overstreet Guide*. Only about 10% of them were overprinted, giving the false impression that they are all common and worthless. Millions of these comics were dumped in bargain bins and many are no longer common in high grade, because of over-handling. Many had small print runs of only 1000-5000 copies, making them among the scarcest comics of the last 40 years, yet about 95% can bought for under $5.00, so now is the time to buy the scarcer issues, while they're still affordable.

I present a hit list of many of the hot issues, bestsellers and suggested issues to watch and buy up. Many bring 135-200% *Guide* if strictly graded: *Albedo* #0,1,2, *Aliens* #1(5/1988), all Alan Moore titles, *Amazing Heroes* 1984 Preview (1st Spider-Man's Black Costume Anywhere?), *Armour*, *Army of Darkness*, *Berni Wrightson Master of Macabre*, *Big Apple* #1(Wood-a), *Bizarre Sex* #9 (1st full Omaha the Cat Dancer), Blackthorne, *3-D Zone* and other 3-D comics (G.I. Joe, Star Wars, Transformers, Harvey, TV etc), *Blazing Combat* (Apple), *Blood of Dracula*(Wrightson issues), *Bone* #1-10, *Caliber Presents* #1(1st Crow), *Cerebus* #1-21, *Cody Starbuck*(1978), 1980's Continuity Comics (Neal Adams), *Cobalt Blue*(1977), *Critters* #1-5, 48-50(scarce), *Creatures of the ID* #1(1st Madman), *Crow* (1989) #1-4, *Cry for Dawn* #1-8, *Crusaders* #1(Southern Knights), *Dark Horse Presents* #1, #24 (1st Aliens), #36(1st Aliens vs. Predator), 51-62, 5th Anniversary Special (1st Sin City), *Deadworld* (graphic covers), *Death Rattle* #8(1st Xenozoic Tales), *Destroyer Duck* #1(1st Groo), *Dick Tracy* (Blackthorne) #71-99(low print), *Dick Tracy* Reuben Award series, *Echo of Futurepast*, *Eddie Campbell's Bacchus*, *Eightball*, *Elflord* (Nightwind; 1980-82; all rare) #1-14, V2#1, *Elfquest* #1, *Fantasy Quarterly* #1(1st Elfquest), *Femzine*(Paragon) #1,2, *Flaming Carrot* #1, *Faust* (Rebel) #1-5; *Faust* #11-13 (low print and scarce = $35-$50 each), *Femforce*, *Galaxia*, *Gasm*, *Gobbledygook* (1984) #1, 2, *Grendel* #40 (Last issue 2/1990), *Harbinger* #0(Pink), 1-6, *Hate*, *Hobbit*, *Hot Stuf* (Sal Q), *How to Draw* series (Transformers and GI Joe), *I Lusiphur* #1, 3, *Imagine*(Star Reach), *John Byrne's Next Men* #21(1st Hellboy), *Judge Dredd*, *Justice Machine* (Noble) #1-3 and Annual #1, *Justice Machine* Annual #1(1st Elementals), *Leather and Lace*, *Lone Wolf and Cub* # 1,41-45, *Love and Rockets* #1 (1981; 1st Series; Hernandez Bros pub Mag; B&W Covers; $1.00 cover Price; prototype for the 1982 regular series is quite rare, with only 800 copies printed: estimated value in VF/NM = $250-$400), *Love and Rockets* #1(Fall/1982), 2-10, *Macross* (Comico) #1 (12/1984; 1st Robotech), *Mage* (the Hero Discovered; Comico; 1984-86) #1,6,7, *Magnus Robot Fighter* #0, 1- 8, 12, Magazine #1-4, *Malibu Sun* #13(5/1992; 1st Spawn in print; VF= $50+), *Megaton* #3(1st Savage Dragon), 8, Explosion, *Miracleman* #10-24 especially #15 (Death of Kid Miracleman), *Mr. A* series (Ditko), *Mister X* #1(Vortex), *Nexus* #1(Capital 1981), 2,3, *Ninja High School* (1986/87), *Nucleus* #1(1979 Cerebus by Sim), *Oktoberfest* #1(1976 Dave Sim and Day-a), *Omaha Cat Dancer* #1, *Omega* #1(1987 Rebel; Tim Vigil), *Omen* (Vigil), *ORB* #1(Scarce), all Paragon Pub (pre-1982 titles, *Femzine*, etc), *Phantacea*(1977; Dave Sim), *Planet of the Apes*(all), *Power Comics*(1970s), *Predator* #1(1989), *Primer* (Comico) #2(1st Grendel), 5(1st Sam Kieth?), #6(1st Evangeline; 1st pro Chuck Dixon), *Quadrant*, *Quack* #1 (7/1976; First Printing; first published pro comics art by Dave Stevens), and 2-6, *Rai* (Valiant Pub; 1992) #0 (11/1992; first FULL appearance of Bloodshot; movie in the works), 1-5, *Realm* #4 (Arrow pub; 1st Deadworld), *Reid Fleming* #1(1980; 1st), *Rocketeer Special Edition* #1 and *Adventure Magazine* #1, *R.I.P.D.* (Dark Horse; 1999-2000) #1-4(Basis for 2013 movie), *Rock Comics* (Tavloid; Adams-a), *Rust* #12(Now; 1988; 1st Terminator), *Solar* #1,10, *Spawn* #9 (Neil Gaiman 1st Angela), *Star Reach*, *Starslayer* #2(1st Rocketeer), *Tales Too Terrible to Tell Terrology* (Low Print) #1-11, *Tank Girl*, *Teenage Mutant Ninja Turtles* (Mirage 1984-1993) #1(all printings), #2-4(1st Prints), #4 (5/1987; 2nd Print misprint variant, manfactured in error with the wraparound-c meant for *Tales of TMNT* #1, most copies destroyed, high grade copies bring $300-600), *Terminator* #12(Now Pub; 1st John Connor), *Terminator: The Burning Earth* #1 (1st pro Alex Ross work), *Tick* #1, *2000 AD* #2(1st Judge Dredd; VF with stickers = $1000+), *Transit*, *Twisted Tales*, *Uncensored Mouse*, *Untamed Love*, *Usagi Yojimbo* #1-5, Valiant comics (Pre-*Unity* issues and last issues), *Vanguard Illustrated* #7(1st modern Mr. Monster), *Vortex* #2(Vortex; 1st Mister X cover), *Wally Wood's Thunder Agents*, *Weird Romance*, *Windblade* #1(Nightwynd; 1982; Barry Blair; rare; VF=$100+), *World of Wood*, *Xenozoic Tales*, *Yummy Fur*, *Zen* (1987), *Zot* and more;

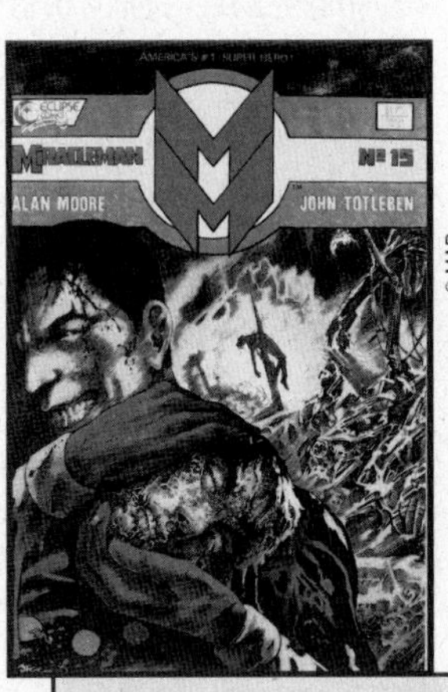

© MAR

***Miracleman* #15 is a hot issue.**

Archie Comics: This was our all-time best year for Archie back issue sales, with key issues and Cheryl Blossom leading the way. The first 28 appearances of Cheryl Blossom (10/1982 thru 6/1985) are all RED HOT, especially the first appearance in each title. My new minimum price on these key issues is: (VF/NM=$35; VF=$25; FN=$15; VG=$10; GD=$5; for first appearances in each title issues = add 50-100% or more). The issues include: *Archie Comics* #323-326, *Archie's Girls Betty And Veronica* #320 (1st app.), 321-322, 326-328, *Archie's Pals 'n' Gals* #161 (1st solo app.), *Archie At Riverdale High* #89,90,92,96-99,103 (1st Cheryl date with Archie), *Archie's TV Laugh-Out* #91, *Archie Giant Series* #526 (1 pg. cameo), #530, *Betty And Me* #136 (1 panel cameo), *Everything's Archie* #104,107, *Jughead* #325 (2nd app.), *Laugh* #380, and *Pep Comics* #396 (9/1984). Canadian Newsstand Cover Price Variants exist on all of these, and bring a premium price of 135-200% over the current value of USA editions.

Archie's Girls Betty And Veronica is especially hot. Recent CGC eBay sales: (#320; 9.0=$400; 7.5=$325; Canadian 7.0 = $480)(#321; 9.2=$200; 9.0=$150)(#322; 9.6=$300; 8.0=$175). Also hot is *Jughead* #325 (8.0=$149; Canadian 7.0 = $200).

The 1990-1991 *Explorers of the Unknown* series #1-3 and #6 (cameo) featured Agent Blaze Blossom of the CIA, a futuristic version of Cheryl Blossom. Otherwise from 7/1985 to 10/1994 there were very few appearances of Cheryl Blossom. The 4-part "Love Showdown" storyline in 11-12/1994 (*Archie* #429, *Betty* #19, *B&V* #82, and *Veronica* #39) made Cheryl Blossom a superstar at Archie Comics, with VF/NM copies still at only around the $10.00 range, sure to be a great long term investment. The 4 different *Cheryl Blossom* mini-series from 1995-1997 are all under-valued, as is the 1997-2001 main series #1-37. This is a surprisingly difficult lot of 50 different 1995-2001 Modern Comics to complete.

The 1961-1962 era Horror and Sci-Fi issues are Red Hot (*Archie* #123-125,127, *Archie Giant* #17, 19, *Betty & Veronica* #70,73,75,77,79,80, *Jokebook* #58,59,76, *Jughead* #77-82,85,86,88, *Laugh* #128,129, 130 (Creature), 132,133,136, 139, *Life with Archie* #9,11,35,39, *Little Archie* #18,20,22, *Madhouse* #6,8,11,13,15-26,29,35,36,38,42,48, 51,58,60, *Pals 'N' Gals* #18, *Pep* #151-154, 158-158 and others are hard to find, bringing 125-200% *Guide*.)

Demand for the Archie Teenage Mutant Ninja Turtles comics has been 3-5 times bigger than the Mirage Pub. ones for over 5 years, with no signs of slowing. The Archie editions had widespread newsstand distribution, thus those are the ones the general public bought when the movies, toys and cartoons all hit the market. The 1988-1990 titles are mostly still relatively common, but the 1991-up issues are Scarce. *TMNT Adventures* #50-72, *Specials* #6-10 and *Digests* all had low print runs and are now quite hard to find, still bringing 200-400% *Guide*, with virtually every dealer everywhere sold out (#72 in VF/NM brings $30-$50). The Mighty Mutant Animals in *TMNT Adventures* are still hot (1st app in #19, and #51-54). *The Mighty Mutant Animals* (4/1992-6/1993) is a hot title (current VF/NM values are: #1-5=$6; #6-8=$10; #9=$15); *TMNT Adventures Special* (1992-1994) is a hot title (current VF/NM values are: #1-6=$7; #7-9=$12; #10=$20). *TMNT Mutant Universe Sourcebook* is a hot title (current VF/NM values are = #1,2=$10; *Update*=$15).

Other best sellers and hot key issues include (with percentage of *Guide* #43 they sell at in brackets): *Afterlife With Archie* #1(6+ Variant covers), *Archie and Me* #1,49,67,160, 161, *Archie Comics* #1-100,133,158,185(1st "The Archies" band-s / TV Cartoon related) 189,200,283, 300,322,326, 336,356(Calgary Olympics), 400,429, 600-605,616,617 (125-150%), *Archie All-Star Special Series*; (Winter/1975; 164 pages, 4 different = 200%), *Archie as Pureheart*(120%), *Archie at Riverdale High* #1,47,113, *Archie Giant Series* (all B&V, Josie and Sabrina issues = 125-150%), #1-7,8(B&V as Devils-c), 9(Adams), 10-20,26,32,142,143, 195,196, 597, 603,620(Edmonton Mall), 632, *Archie All Canadian Digest* #1(Scarce; 300%), *Archie's Girls Betty & Veronica* #1-30(125-150%), 31-200(120-135%), #75(B&V sell souls to Devil; 200%), 105,118(1st Superteen), 119,123,127,199 (Spanking panel), 300,339,347, Annual #1-8, *Archie's Jokebook* #44-48 (Neal Adams = 125-135%), 100, 102, 124, 200, 288 (200%), *Archie's Madhouse* #22(150%), Sabrina issues(125-135%); #36 = 1st Salem the Cat and Annual #3 Origin Sabrina, *Archie's Mechanics* (135%), *Archie's Pal Jughead* #1-20, 58(Adams), 78,81,83,84,86(1st app of the Brain), 87,90(Jughead selling Tranquilizer drugs-c), 100,101 (125-135%), *Archie's Pals N Gals* #1-10, 12(Adams), 15 (Adams) (125%), 19 (Marilyn Monroe), 23 (1st Josie = 200-400%), #29 (Beatles 150%), 40(Superteen and Pureheart), 41-53, 54(Satan meets Veronica), 71-72(2-part drugs story); 100, 176,198,200,202(end of Archie's jalopy), 224, *Archie's Ten Issue Collectors Set* #1-10(Giveaway 125-150%), *Archie's TV Laughout* #1-23(125%), 91(200%), 92,93,96, 100-105(120-150%), *Betty and Me* #1-10(125%), 16(200%), 23(150%), 40(125%), 79-86(Betty Cooper Mysteries; 79-81 (Drago the Vampire; 125%), 139 (Katy Keene collecting-s), 160 (Wheel of Fortune parody-s), 200(150%), *Black Hood*(1983 = 150%), *Cartoon Network Ppresents Space Ghost* #1(200%), *Chilling Advs. in Sorcery*(150%), *Christmas with Archie* Treasury (200%), *Cosmo the Merry Martian*(125%), *Everything's Archie* #1,100,157, *Fast Willie Jackson* #1-7 (200%), *Flintstones* #1-10(150%), 11-22 (200%), *The Fly* (1983-84 = 150%), *Ginger* (120-135%), *Hanna-Barbera All Stars* (200%), *Hanna-Barbera Presents* (200%), *Jetsons* (200%), *Josie* #1(150%), 2-20(125%), 42(1st Alan M. Mayberry), 43 (Alexandra Cabot and Sebastian the Cat discover their witchcraft powers), 45 (200%), 46-74(125-150%), 100-106(Low Print; 150%), *JCP Presents Thunder Agents* (200%), *Jughead* #352(200%), *Jughead as Capt. Hero*(125%), *Jughead Fantasy* #1-3, *Jughead's Folly* #1(1st Elvis in comics 125%), *Katy Keene*(1983-1990) (#1-20 =150%; #21-32=200%; #33=300%), *Laugh Comics* #20-100,127-150,164,166,168, 200,300,400(120-150%); *Laugh* #106-109,111,113(Neal Adams; 150%); *Life with Archie*

(1958) #1-20, 45-58, 59(1st app Little Sabrina), 60-66,100, 113,172, 176,190, 200,238,279,286(125%), *Life With Archie* Magazine #1, 16 (Kevin Keller gay wedding), 23(11/2012; 1st app Afterlife With Archie on variant cover by Francavilla = $20-$30+); *Little Archie* #1-66(125%), *Madhouse* #95-97(Horror 150%), *Mighty Crusaders*(1983-85 = 150%), *Pep Comics* #22-127(120-135%), 138-140(Neal Adams 200%), 150-160(150%), 161(Josie Begins 200%), 162-170,200,224 (1st Hot Dog), 298,300,393,400,411 (150%); *Red Circle Sorcery*(150%), *Riverdale Rambling* (Archie Fanzine = $5-12 ea), *Sabrina* #1-17, 71-77 (135-150%), *Scooby Doo*(200%), *The Shield* (1983-84 = 150%); *Sonic the Hedgehog* #1-50 (120-150%), *Sonic the Hedgehog* #1/4 (1991-1992; SEGA Game Ashcan; 1st App Sonic in comics; scarce; VF/NM $50); scarcer Spire titles [*Archie and Big Ethyl*(150%), *Archie and Mr Weatherbee*(150%), *Circus*(200%), *Date Book*(150%), *Festival*(150%), *Roller Coaster*(200%), *Sports Scene* (200%), *Christmas with Archie* (Giant; 250%), *Jughead Soul Food*=150%] *Suzie*(120-135%), *Tales Calculated to Drive you Bats* (120%), *That Wilkin Boy*(150%), *Thunder Agents* (Archie; 150%), *Whiz Kids* (Archie and Radio Shack $5 ea), *Wilbur* (Katy Keene #5-56,58-69 and DeCarlo art in later issues = 120%);

Captain Canuck Comics: From 7/2013 to 1/2014 *Captain Canuck the Animated Cartoons* - Episode #1 thru Episode #4 were released online, with more to come. Old and new fans are very excited. Richard Comely is a popular guest at Canadian comic conventions, with long lines for his autograph. Minds Eye Entertainment is developing a feature film for the big screen. Over the years, there have been many licensed Captain Canuck products, including t-shirts, sweatshirts, doodle posters, etc.

By far our bestselling set (all publishers and titles) for the last 5 years has been *Captain Canuck* #1-14 with Special #1 (1975-1981) with over 150 sets sold in that period at $39 to $55 range. Captain Canuck is Canada's most famous title, all the main titles were distributed in the USA, but probably 90% of the print run was distributed to Canada, thus uncommon to scarcer in USA. The 1975-1981 issues are getting scarcer in strict VF/NM or better. I have again SOLD OUT of original Treasury sized #4 (2/1977; 1st Print; 150% *Guide*); #4 (2/1977; 2nd print, one of the rarest comics of the entire Bronze Age, lists at $30 in FN in *Overstreet*, but sells for around $500 in that grade if my some miracle you can find one). Canadian *Time Magazine* April 28/1997 (VG/FN $15). Comely confirmed small print runs for *Captain Canuck Re-Born* (1993/1994); #0 (English = 90,000 copies; VF $9), #0 (French = 6000; VF $30), #1 (47,000 Newsstand green-c; VF $8); #1 (40,000 bagged gold-c; VF $10); #1(French = 6000; VF $30); #2 (30,000; VF $12), #3 (8,000 copies, but most copies destroyed thus rare; VF = $100). 99% of all Capt Canuck 1975-81 original art was donated to Canada's National Archives, thus the few left command high prices. Comely's *Star Rider and the Peace Machine* #1-2 (1982; VF $6 ea) are getting scarcer too. All memorabilia and promo items are fast sellers. Captain Canuck #15 (8/2004; 150 copies) is virtually impossible to find. In 2013 raw copies in NM sold on eBay for $450 and $510.

Charlton Comics: We have about 35,000 Charlton comics in stock, with 95% of 1960-1986 issues in stock and a great selection of 50% of the 1940s-1959 issues too. The Horror titles as usual were the bestselling titles, especially in affordable GD-FN condition ranges. Strict VF or better are still uncommon, with VF/NM or better scarce to rare. Investors like VF/NM or better copies, but there are very few CGC graded copies. Key issues are 10-100 scarcer in High Grade than the same era Marvel and DC keys, yet only a few collectors ever notice this fact. The 1945-1950 issues are all very scarce, with most 1951-1957 issues also scarce, all being in high demand for a growing number of completionists who gladly buy them in any complete grades (at 120-150% *Guide*). The 1958-1969 Silver Age issues are uncommon to scarce, but with some legwork most sets are possible to complete in a reasonable amount of time. These are in moderate demand (at 115-125% *Guide*). The 1970-1986 Bronze Age issues are uncommon, with most of the 1984-1984 being "Lower Print" and scarcer issues. These are in above-average demand (at 120-135% *Guide*).

We sell far more Hanna-Barbera comics from all publishers (one of our specialties) than Walt Disney cartoon comics. This is because several generations grew up on H-B cartoons in their home daily on TV as kids, while Disney was more often exprienced as an occasional one-shot movie theatre film. Most of the 1950s and 1960s War and Western comics are above average sellers. All the other genres are solid steady sellers (at 115-125% *Guide*) including: Adult Cartoons, Cartoon, Crime, Funny Animals, History, Humor/Parody, Licensed Characters, Movie, Hot Rod, Jungle, Martial Arts, Mythology, Mystery, Newspaper Comic Strip, Pirates, Pop Music Stars, Radio, Romance, Science, SF, Soap Opera, Superhero, Teenage, and TV. The scarcer items include: Digests, Comic Magazines, Horror Mags and Non-Comic mags (Adult Cartoon, Crossword and Puzzle mags, Horror Film mags, Kung-Fu and Karate mags, *Sick* mag, True Romance mags, True Western mags. These fascinate many collectors and are above average sellers.

DC Comics: The DC Comics related movies, TV shows and Video Game comics are the most requested, (at 125-500% *Guide*). This includes (In Production and/or Confirmed); Black Mask (Batman Video Game), Booster Gold TV, Doomsday (rumored), Flash TV (Barry Allen), Green Arrow TV (Smallville and Arrow), Justice League Movie, Man of Steel movie (with Batman), Nightwing (rumored), Preacher TV, Sandman movie (Gaiman), Y the Last Man and more. Other HOT key issues include appearances by: Animal Man, Batgirl, Black Canary, Black Orchid, Brainiac, Deathstroke, Duela Dent (aka Joker's Daughter aka Harlequin), Freedom Fighters, Guy Gardner, Huntress, John Stewart, pre-1990 JSA comics, Kid Flash (Wally West the new Flash), Lobo, Lori Lemaris, Mon-El, Red Hood, early Sgt. Rock, Star Sapphire, Supergirl, Toyman, Ultra-Boy, Wonder Girl, Zatanna, etc.

First appearances of all the major villains for all the major Super-Heroes are way up in demand, and almost all are a good buy even at 125-150% *Guide* in strictly graded condition. I believe the *Guide* now undervalues almost all Hot and Key issues in GD through FN Grades (and often in VF too), so when almost anything gets hot, they can be considered wholesale prices, and retail prices can vary from 150-400% *Guide* for raw copies. Meanwhile high grade copies often bring lower premiums, unless CGC graded. A few of the HOT villains include: Bane, Bizarro, Black Mask, Catwoman, Clayface, Darkseid, Doomsday, Faora Hu-Ul, Gauntlet of Super-Villians (*Flash* #130 and all first appearances), General Zod, Grodd, Harley Quinn, Joker, Man-Bat, Mr. Freeze, Parasite, Phantom Zone villains, Poison Ivy, Penguin, Professor Zoom the Reverse Flash, Metallo, Ra's Al Ghul, Riddler, Scarecrow, Secret Society of Super Villians, Sinestro, Talia al Ghul, Titano, Two-Face, Vandal Savage, etc.

Ordinary non-Key issues of common and uncommon DC and Marvel Comics from 1960-1980 were slower sellers, thus many were sold at discounted prices on eBay this year. Since DCs of the period are scarcer than Marvels in general, they are expected to rebound, if buyers and sellers remain patient. I made up dozens of bargain lower grade copy sets at 25-50% off *Guide* on these and they actually sold quite well to happy buyers who just wanted affordable reading copies. Meanwhile I held back the better more presentable copies for the long haul, and if given time, they eventually sell themselves at *Guide* levels, as we get an endless stream of buyers filling out runs.

Superman The Movie from 1978 introduced General Zod to the general public. Terence Stamp played the Phantom Zone criminal who was also featured in the DC Treasury *All-New Collector's Edition* #C-62 and *DC Special Series* #25. In the eyes of the general public, General Zod rivals Lex Luthor as the top Superman villain in the TV and film media. The first and second 2-panel cameo appearances of General Zod were in *Adventure* #283 and #293, with #283 bringing 150-300% *Guide*. The first and second full appearances of General Zod were in *Action Comics* #297, 298. See also *Action Comics* #471-473 for General Zod's appearance along with the first 3 appearances of Faora Hu-Ul (after *Crisis* renamed as Zaora.) The villainess from the Phantom Zone appeared in 7 episodes of the *Smallville* TV series in 2009-2010, in the *Man of Steel* 2013 movie she appeared as Faora-Ul. Faora Hu-Ul and General Zod also appear in 1979 *World of Krypton* and 1982 *Phantom Zone* mini-series.

Movie and TV Related, Bestsellers and other Hot Key issues in 2013 included (with percentage of *Guide* #43 they sell at in brackets); *Action Comics* #297 (1st full General Zod; GD-N=300%; VF-NM=200%) #298(2nd full Zod; GD-FN=200%; VF-NM=150%) #309 (JFK GD-FN=200%; VF-NM=150%); #440 (1st Grell on Green Arrow 150%); #471-473 (Faora Hu-Ul; 150%); #484(w Rare 3-D Superman Doll = 400%); #521(Vixen-c/s; 300%); #583 (150%); *Adventure Comics* #229(10/1956; First SA app in title of GA version of Green Arrow = George Papp-a; First SA Aquaman = Ramona Fradon-a; GD-FN=140%; VF-NM = 120%); #250, 256 (#250 = 7/1958, 1st Kirby Green Arrow; #256 = 1/1959, first transformative new origin for Green Arrow, as he becomes the new SA Hero by Jack Kirby; GD-FN=200%; VF-NM = 150%); #251–255 (early new Green Arrow by Jack Kirby; GD-FN=125%; VF-NM = 110%); #257-266,268,269 (Green Arrow; 110%); #283 (1st Zod 2 panel cameo; GD-FN=200%; VF-NM=150%) #293(2nd Zod 2 panel cameo; 120%); #461,462 (Death GA Batman; 125%); *All-New Collector's Ed* #C-62 (Superman The Movie; Zod; 150%); *Animal Man* #1-10(150%); *DC Special Series* #25(Superman II with Zod 125%); *All-American Men Of War* #89 (art in comic re-imagined by top American pop artist Roy Lichtenstein for his famous paintings "Whaam!" and "As I opened Fire"; 250%).

Batman older Key issues (most GD-FN=135-160%; VF-NM=120-140%) #121(1st Mr. Freeze), 131, 139 (1st Original Batgirl), 155[1st SA Penguin), 171(1st SA Riddler), 181(1st Poison Ivy), 183, 189(1st Scarecrow 150%), 197, (all Neal Adams art or cover issues), 219, 222(150%), 227(200%), 232-235,237, 240, 243-245,251. Batman newer Key issues #357[1st Jason Todd, later Red Hood; 300%); #366,368 (120%); #386 (1st Black Mask; 1000%); #387 (Black Mask; 500%); #357-402 (Lowest Print Runs in the History of Title 75,303-97,741 per month = 150%); 497(135%), 426-429(125%); *Batman Family* #6 (1st Duela Dent, Two-Face's daughter in her guise as the Joker's Daughter, later becomes Harlequin, an inspiration / prototype character of Harley Quinn; 200%) #9[2nd Joker's Daughter, 1st Duela Dent as Penguin, Riddler and Scarecrow Daughters; 150%); #16 [Joker's Daughter 125%]; *Batman Adventures* #12(1st Harley Quinn; 300%); Batman Adventures: Mad Love (200%); *Batman: Sword of Azrael* #1-4(125%), *Batman Vengeance of Bane* #1(150%); *Batman Killing Joke* (150%), *Booster Gold* (1986) #1(200%); #2-25(150%) *Crisis of Infinite Earths* #7,8 (120%); DC Whitman Variants = see Whitman section; *DC Comics Presents* #26 (1st New Teen Titans 150%); #47(1st He-Man; 300%).

DC reprints (2nd, 3rd, 4th and more printings) = In almost all cases, these are much Scarcer with many that are Rare, as compared to the Common First Printings (Variant collectors have paid $25 to $100 each for some of the Rare issues). The best known ones are *Batman* #397(7/1986), 398.399,401-403,408-416,421-425,430-432 all had 2nd Printings in 1989, with some issues up to 8 printings. Some are NOT identified as Reprints, but have newer ads after the cover dates. All of these Reprints have different ads on the back covers than original 1st Printings. All the reprints have the same value as the 1st Prints. NOTE: Variant collectors will pay 50-200% Premiums for these scarcer reprints.

Detective Comics older Key issues (most GD-FN=135-160%; VF-NM=120-140%) #359 (1st Batgirl 150%), 363-365,369,(all Neal Adams Art or Cover issues), 370,371,384, 400(150%), 411 (200%), #482-569 (lowest Print Runs for title, 64,635-89,635 copies 150%); #521(Green Arrow series begins 200%); #524(175%), 553(2nd Black Mask; 400%), 569, 570, 572, 574-578; *Doom Patrol* #19,35,36,42-44,87 (150%); *Flash* #139(1st Prof Zoom Reverse Flash; GD-FN =300%; VF-NM=200%); #147,153,165,175,186 (2nd to 6th Reverse Flash 125-150%), #275-276 (Reverse Flash Kills Iris Allen wife of Flash; 200%), #323 (Flash vs. Reverse Flash; 400%), 324 (Flash kills Reverse Flash; 600%); #350 (return of Reverse Flash and Iris Allen 200%); *Flash* (1987) #1 (150%); *Firestorm* #61 Variant(150%), *Forever People* #1 (1st Full Darkseid; 150%); *Green Arrow* (1988) #1, 75, 97-100, 101,104,110,111,125,137(150%); #0 (1st Connor Hawke 200%); #96(300%); *Green Lantern* #7(1st Sinestro; GD-FN =200%; VF-NM=150%); #9,11,15,18 (2nd to 5th Sinestro = 125%) #16 (1st SA Star Sapphire; 120%); #59 (1st Guy Gardner 135%); #87 (2nd Guy Gardner; 1st John Stewart 125%); #116 (1st Guy Gardner as GL; 125%), 141(150%), #192(Re-intro Star 150%), 194-195(125%), *Hawkman* #4 (1st Zatanna; GD-FN=200%; VF-NM=150%); *Hellblazer* #1-10, 27(150%); *Justice League of America* #4 (Green Arrow joins JLA; GD-FN=125%; VF-NM = 110%); #137 (Superman meets Captain Marvel 150%), 183-185 (New Gods, Mr. Miracle, JSA vs Darkseid) = 150%; *Justice League* (1987) #1 and 3(Variant) = 150%; *Last Days of JSA* #1 = 150%; *Leading* #1(Winter 1941; 2nd Green Arrow? 110%); *Legends* #6(1st new JLA by Byrne; 150%); *Legion of Super-Heroes* #37,38 (Death of Superboy; 150%); *Masters Of The Universe* #1-3(150%); *More Fun Comics* #73 (11/1941; 1st Aquaman; 1st Oliver Queen the Green Arrow and 1st Speedy; GD-FN = 125%; VF or Better = ??); *New Gods* #1-2 (early Darkseid = 125%); *New Teen Titans* (1980) #1-2 (150%); *Omega Men* #3 (1st Lobo; 150%); *Preacher* #1 (500%), 2-20(200%); *Sandman* (1989) #1(250%), #2-7,9, 11-21,23-30(150%); #8,10,22(All 200%); *Shazam!* #1 (2/1973); a CGC 9.8 copy sold for $2500 in 2013; *Strange Adventures* #180,184,190,195,201(Animal Man; GD-FN =200%; VF-NM=150%); #205,206(GD-FN=150%; VF-NM=125%); *Superboy* #68(1st Bizarro; GD-FN=200%; VF-NM=150%); *Superman* Keys (most GD-FN=135-160%; VF-NM=120-140%) #123 (Supergirl tryout), 125 (Lois as Power Girl), 127(1st Titano), 129(1st Lori Lemaris Mermaid), 233(1st New Direction Superman; classic Adams-c), 423 (Last issue; Alan Moore); *Superman* #75 (Death of Superman 150%); *Superman: The Man of Steel* #17 (1st cameo Doomsday; 200%); #18 (1st full Doomsday 500%); #18 (has 5 Printings; 5th Print = Rare); *Superman's Pal Jimmy Olsen* #133 (1st app. Kirby's Fourth World; GD-FN=200%; VF-NM= 150%); #134(1st cameo Darkseid 150%); 135(2nd cameo Darkseid 150%); *Swamp Thing, Saga Of...*; Alan Moore) #20-30 (150%); #37(200%); #31-36,38-64 (135%), 171(400%); *Tales of Teen Titans* #44 (1st Nightwing), *Teen Titans* (1966) #1, 20-23(GD-FN=135%; VF-NM=120%); #46 (Joker's Daughter begins, third app overall = 150%); #47 (125%); #48(Joker's Daughter becomes Harlequin = 1st App = 150%); #49-52(Duela Dent as Harlequin appears 125%); *V for Vendetta* #1-12(150%); *Wonder Woman* (1942-1986) #61-120 (Low Print 125-150%); #159,177-204(125%); #267-268 (1st Copper Age Animal Man 150%); #281-283, 291-293,300,329(150%); *World's Finest* #84 (10/1956; First SA app in title of GA version of Green Arrow; GD-FN =135%; VF-NM = 120%); #96 (10/1958), 97-99 (new SA version of Green Arrow by Jack Kirby; GD-FN=135%; VF-NM=120%); #95, 100-140 (Green Arrow appears); #71,88, 90,94,113,125,129,144,148,154,156,169, 173-178,198-200 (GD-FN=120-135%; VF-NM=110-120%); #215,217,244-253, 300(125%); #323(200%); *Y: The Last Man* #1(150%); #2-60(200%).

Dell Comics: These have been strong and steady sellers for over 40+ years, if a seller is patient everything they produced sells, but only if the dealer has a good selection. We have about 20,000 Dell comics in stock, with 95% of 1955-1972 issues in stock. These have widespread international demand, many comics selling to non-collectors who are nostalgic about the characters and just want a few examples. Price seems to be the most important factor to most of the majority of buyers, with over 90% of what actually sells in the FR/GD to FN condition range. The price spreads in the *Guide* do not reflect the real market on these. Most FN/VF or better copies have major price resistance and are slow sellers (usually only selling if I do not have a more affordable copy in stock). We have about 35,000 Charlton comics in stock, with 95% of 1960-1986 issues in stock being First and Key issues, *Tarzan, Turok,* Carl Barks art comics, better Hanna-Barbera, better cartoon and popular TV and Movie comics. Dell comics in CGC graded VF/NM 9.0, NM- 9.2 and NM 9.4 often need to be priced at 25% to 50% off *Guide* to sell. Most Dell comics in GD-FN are under-valued in the *Guide*, while most VF-NM Dells are overvalued in *Guide*, this was caused by using the same Price to Condition spreads for Dell as wide as for Marvel and DC Superhero comics, while that is not the reality of the marketplace.

©Jay Ward

***Bullwinkle** is a best-selling Dell title (#1 shown).*

The Bestselling Titles (GD-FN = 120-140% *Guide*; FN/VF-VF/NM= 75-115% *Guide*) included: *Adventures of Mighty Mouse, Air War, Andy Panda* #35-56 (Chilly Willy backup-s issues), *Annie Oakley, Bat Masterson, Beetle Bailey, Beep Beep Road Runner, Ben Bowie, Beverly Hillbillies, Bewitched, Big Valley, Brave Eagle, Bugs Bunny, Bullwinkle, Cheyenne, Chilly Willy, Cisco Kid, Colt 45, Combat, Creature,* Dell Giants (Bugs Bunny, Lone Ranger, Little Lulu, Nancy, Tarzan, Western Roundup, Yogi Bear, etc), *Dracula, Dunc & Loo, Felix the Cat, Flintstones, Flying Nun, Flying Saucers, Four*

Color (over 100 Hot issues, over 300 issues in High Demand, about 700 are moderate sellers, with only about 200 being slower sellers), *Frankenstein, Fritzi Ritz* (with Peanuts), *F-Troop, Gene Autry* #101-121, *Get Smart, Ghost Stories, Gidget, Have Gun Will Travel, Hogans Heroes, Howdy Doody, Huckleberry Hound, I Dream of Jeannie, I Love Lucy, Indian Chief, Jetsons, John Carter of Mars, John Wayne* (all), *Jungle War, King of Royal Mounted, Kona, Laramie, Lawman, Leave it to Beaver, Little Lulu, Lone Ranger* #1-10, 112-145, *Looney Tunes* #1-50, 201-246, *March of Comics* (50% of this Promo giveaway series are above average sellers), *Maverick, McHale's Navy, Melvin Monster, Monkees, Movie Classics* (Western, SF and Horror), *Mummy, Nancy* (Peanuts-s, Oona-s, Stanley-a), *New Funnies* #65-120, 241-288, *Outer Limits, Peanuts, Pogo, Ponytail, Popeye, Quick Draw McGraw, Rawhide, Real McCoys, Red Ryder* #1-118, *Ricky Nelson, Rifleman, Rin Tin Tin* #18-38 (TV's Rusty and the Cavalry of Fort Apache issues), *Rocky and Friends, Roy Rogers* #119-145, *Sgt. Preston, Smokey Stover, Tales of Wells Fargo, Tarzan* #1-30, 80-131, *Thirteen, Tip Top* #211-225(with Nancy and Peanuts), *Tom and Jerry* #60-100, *Tonto, Top Cat, Turok, Twilight Zone, Voyage to Bottom of Sea, Wolfman, Woody Woodpecker, Wyatt Earp, Yak Yak, Yogi Bear* and *Zorro*.

Gold Key Comics: I have 35,000 Gold Key comics in stock, with about 95% of everthing in stock. We had above average sales on GD-FN copies this year. Strictly graded VF or better copies remain hard to find, but sell well on the right books. Non-Key issues on less popular titles are harder to sell in VF or better. The bestselling titles (GD-FN = 120-150% *Guide*; FN/VF-VF/NM= 110-125% *Guide*) included: *Addams Family, Amazing Chan, Atom Ant, Astro Boy, Auggie Doggie, Avengers* (TV) #1(Photo back-c), *Bamm Bamm, Banana Splits, Battle of the Planets, Beatles Yellow Submarine, Beneath Planet of Apes, Beep Beep* #1-10, *Beetle Bailey, Boris Karloff, Bugs Bunny* #86-100, *Bullwinkle, Cave Kids, Close Shaves of Pauline Peril, Daffy Duck* #31-50, *Dagar*, Dan Curtis (Giveaways) #1-9, *Daniel Boone, Dark Shadows, Doc Savage, Dr. Solar, Family Affair, Fat Albert, Flash Gordon, Flintstones, Frankenstein Jr, Fun-In, Funky Phantom, George of the Jungle, Gold Key Spotlight, Gomer Pyle, Grimm's Ghost, Hair Bear Bunch*, Hanna-Barbera (all #1 and Key issues), *Hanna-Barbera Super TV Heroes, Hanna-Barbera Bandwagon, Happy Days, Honey West, H.R. Pufnstuf, Huckleberry Hound, Inspector, Jetsons, John Carter, Jonny Quest, Kortak, Kroft Supershow, Lancelot Link, Land of Giants, Laredo, Lidsville, Little Lulu* #207 up, *Little Monsters, Lone Ranger, Looney Tunes* #1-10, Lucy Show, *Magilla Gorilla, Marge's Little Lulu* #165-206, *Magnus Robot Fighter, Mars Patrol, Mighty Samson, Mighty Hercules, Mighty Mouse, Milton Monster, Mr. Ed, Mr. & Mrs. J. Evil Scientist, Munsters, My Favorite Martian, Nancy & Sluggo, Occult Files of Dr. Spector, Peanuts, Peter Potomus, Phantom, Pink Panther, Popeye, Quick Draw McGraw, Ripley's Believe it or Not, Rifleman, Rocky & Fiendish Friends, Scooby-Doo* (Red Hot), *Secret Squirrel, Snagglepuss, Snooper & Blabber, Space Family Robinson, Space Ghost, Space Mouse, Spine Tingling Tales, Star Stream, Star Trek* #1-9, *Supercar, Tarzan, Tasmanian Devil* #1, *Three Stooges, Time Tunnel, Top Cat, Turok and Twilight Zone, UFO Flying Saucers, Underdog*, all Variants (see Variant Comics in this Report), *Wacky Races, Wacky Witch, Wagon Train, Wild Wild West, Woody Woodpecker* #75-100, and *Yakkey Doodle*. ** *Mod Love* #6201(#1; One-Shot; 1967) remains Rare and sells at 200-400% *Guide* #43 Prices;

Marvel Comics: The Movie and TV show-related Marvel Comics were the most requested, (at 125-500% *Guide* #43), plus a few added Hot Key issues, includes (in production and/or confirmed); *Agents of SHIELD* TV, *Ant-Man* (Henry Pym and Scott Lang), *Amazing Spider-Man* movie (Black Cat and Gwen Stacy), Beta Ray Bill, *Big Hero Six* - Disney Movie, Blink, *Black Panther* movie, Black Widow (Movie appearances), *Capt. America* movie (AIM, Bucky, Falcon, Red Skull), *Capt. Marvel* (Thanos related), Legend of Conan (King Conan movie with Arnold Schwarzenegger), *Daredevil* (Netflix TV), *Defenders* (Netflix TV Mini series), Doctor Strange movie, Fantomex, *Guardians of the Galaxy* movie (still Red Hot; Collector, Drax, Gambit, Gamora, Groot, *Iron Fist* (Netflix TV), *Iron Man* (Jim Rhodes War Machine), *Luke Cage Power Man* (Netflix TV), Marvel Man / *Quasar*, Rocket Raccoon, Starlord), Hawkeye (*TOS* #57), Inhumans movie (rumored; *FF* #36 38, 41-47; Medusa, Gorgon, Inhumans, Black Bolt and Maximus, with Origins in Thor), Jessica Jones (Netflix TV = *Alias* and *Pulse*), Ms. Marvel (Carol Danvers - *Avengers* film and new reboot series), Nick Fury in multiple movies, Mystique, Nova movie (Rumored), Psylocke (Elizabeth Betsy Braddock in 1976 *Capt. Britain* #8-10), Puck (*Alpha Flight* #1 in X-Men movie), Rogue, *Punisher, Star Wars* (3 more Disney Films - Boba Fett is Hot), *Thor* (Algim The Elf / Kurse, Malekith, Warriors 3), Vision (Avengers movie?), Warlock (Thanos related), Warpath, Wolverine (Mariko, Silver Samurai, Viper and Yashida), X-Force movie (Cable, Deadpool), X-Men movie (Days of Future Past movie from #141-142; followed by Apocalypse in next Film)

First appearances of all the major villains for all the major Super-Heroes are way up in demand, and almost all are a good buy even at 125-150% *Guide* in strictly graded condition. A few of the Hot Villains include; Apocalypse, Bullseye, Carnage, the Collector, Destroyer, Dormammu, Drax, Elektra, Enchantress and Executioner, Fin Fang Foom, Graviton (Agents of Shield), Korvac, Mandarin, Modok (*TOS* #93,94), Nebula (Guardians), Red Skull and Cosmic Cube (Capt. America film), Ronan (*FF* #65 re Guardians), Sabretooth, Silver Samurai, Taskmaster, Thanos, Ultron-5 (*Avengers 2* Movie), Venom (and early Symbiote black costume)

Movie and TV related, bestsellers and other Hot Key issues in 2013 included (with percentage of *Guide* #43 they sell at in brackets, or Grade/Price); *Alf* #48 (400%); *Alias* #1 (1st Jessica Jones 300%); *Alpha Flight* #1(1983; 1st Puck; 200%); #51(1st Jim Lee 200%); *Alpha Flight* V2 #17(1998; Chronological 1st Big Hero Six; VF/NM = $20); *Amazing Spider-Man* #119-122(GD-FN = 150%; VF-NM = 120%)

#194(1st Black Cat; GD-FN = 200%; VF-NM = 150%); #195,204,205,226,227,(2nd thru 5th Black Cat 125%); #229,230(Juggernaut; VF/NM = $16); #238, 252 (Canadian 75 Cent Variants = 200%); #233-279 (Canadian Newsstand Cover Price Variants, printed in USA = 200%); #300 (1st Venom 125%), #315-317 (Venom; 135%), #298,299,301-314,318-328(McFarlane 125%); #344-345(135%); #361 (Carnage, 200%); #430, 431 (Carnage and Silver Surfer; VF/NM- = $25); *Annihilation: Conquest* #6 (1st new Guardians VF/NM = $40); *Astonishing Tales* #21-22(First IT, the Living Colossus 120%) #23-24(Fin Fang Foom 150%); #25(120%); #29(Guardians 200%); *Avengers* #28 [1st Collector 150%); #46 (Re-intro Ant-Man 135%); #51(2nd Collector 125%);#54-55(250%); #57(1st Vision; GD-FN = 300%; VF-NM = 200%); #58 (2nd Vision 125%); #62 (classic Black Panther-c/s = Reprinted in *Jungle Action* #5; 125%); #119 (Collector 125%); #125 (Thanos 150%); #134-135 (Revised true origin of GA Human Torch becoming The Vision; 150%); #144 (1st Hellcat 150%); #158 (1st Graviton aka Dr. Franklin Hall = 250%); #167-177(classic Korvac Saga with Guardians, Capt. Marvel and Ms. Marvel; 200%); #181(1st Scott Lang who becomes the new Ant-Man 250%); #183(Ms. Marvel joins 200%); #195-196 (Taskmaster 200%) *Avengers Annual* #7(Thanos 120%), #224-270 (Canadian Newsstand Cover Price Variants, printed in USA = 200%); Annual #10(1st Rogue 120%); *Black Panther* #1(1977 130%); *Captain America* #117(1st Falcon; GD-FN = 250%; VF-NM = 175%); #153-155(150%), #180-181 (135%); #217 (1st Bronze Age Marvel Man; NM- = $50); *Captain Britain* (1976 UK); #1,2,24 (with Bonus inserts; VF/NM = $50 each); #8 [1st Betsy Braddock aka Psylocke; VF/NM = $250); #9-10 (2nd and 3rd Betsy Braddock; VF/NM = $25 each); *Captain Britain Monthly* (2nd series); #8 (1st app and Origin Meggan Braddock as a Super-Heroine-c/s, later Gloriana; VF/NM = $50); *Conan the Barbarian* #1(G-FN = 150%; VF-NM = 120%); #23-24 (135%); #58-59(150%); #139-185(Canadian Newsstand Cover Price Variants, printed in USA = 200%); #251-260 (VF/NM $6); #261-270(VF/NM $9); #271-274(VF/NM $12);#275(VF/NM $40); *Daredevil* #18,43,50-53,105,131, 132,141,146 (all 125%); #111(1st Silver Samurai 150%); *Darkhawk* #1 (CGC 9.8 = $100+); *Deadpool* (1997-2002); #1-53(200%); #54, 55(Punisher VF/NM = $30 ea); #55-60 (300%); #61-68(400%); #69(VF/NM $30); *Baby's First Deadpool Book* (VF/NM $40); *Defenders* #1(150%); #2-25 (125%); #26-29,36 (Guardians 200%); #94,96(200%); *Doctor Strange* #169(1968; GD-FN = 200%; VF-NM = 150%); #170-183(125%); *Droids* #1-8 (*Star Wars* 150%); *Ewoks* #1-14 (*Star Wars* 150%); *Fantastic Four* #36 (1st Medusa 150%); #38,41-43 (2nd-5th Medusa 120%); #44(1st Gorgon 150%); #45(1st Inhumans; GD-FN = 300%; VF-NM = 200%); #46 (1st full Black Bolt GD-FN = 150%; VF-NM = 135%); #47(1st Maximus 150%); #52-53(1st/2nd Black Panther GD-FN = 200%; VF-NM = 150%); #65(1st Ronan; G-FN = 200%; VF-NM = 150%); #66-67(Warlock 125%); #110(Error 150%); #247-293(Canadian Newsstand Cover Price Variants, printed in USA = 200%); *Ghost Rider* (1973) #1-5(125%); *G.I. Joe* #21(150%); #26, 27, 93-96,139-154 (all 125%); #155(GD-FN = 200%; VF-NM = 150%); Special #1(GD-FN = 200%; VF-NM = 150%); *Giant-Size Defenders* #5 (Guardians 150%); *Hero For Hire* #1(150%); #2-16(125%); *Human Fly* #1-19(150%); *Incredible Hulk* #102(135%); #121,122,126,140,141,161, 162 (all 125%); #234(1st Quasar VF/NM $30); #271 (Rocket Raccoon; GD-FN = 600%; VF-NM = 400%); #276-322 (Canadian Newsstand Cover Price Variants, printed in USA = 200%); #331-334,336-345 (McFarlane 135%); Annual #5 (2nd app Groot VF/NM $60); *Inhumans* (1975) #1(150%); #2-12(125%); *Iron Fist* #1(1975 150%); #2-15 (125%); *Iron Man* #1(GD-FN = 150%; VF-NM = 125%); #55 (150%); #88 (early Thanos 150%); #118(1st Jim Rhodes 150%); #169(150%); #163-209(Canadian Newsstand Cover Price Variants, printed in USA = 200%); #281(VF/NM = $8); #282(VF/NM = $12); #284(VF/NM = $9); *Journey Into Mystery* #83-86(120%); #103 (GD-FN = 200%; VF-NM = 150%); #112-115,118,119(all 125%); *Jungle Action* #1-4, 11-23(125%); #5,6,8,24(200%); #7,9,10(150%); *Logan's Run* #6 (Thanos 135%); *Longshot* #1-6(150%); *Marvel Age* #12 (3/1984 1st Spider-Man black costume; VF/NM $15); *Marvel Comics Super Special* #7 (Sgt. Pepper's Lonely Hearts Club Band; RARE; Not issued in USA; Pérez-a; French Softcover VF = $200; French Hardcover VF = $300; French Softcover combo with #4 Beatles VF = $250); *Marvel Feature* #1-3 (Defenders 135%); #4 (Antman; GD-FN = 300%; VF-NM = 200%); #5-10(150%); #11-12(125%); *Marvel Premiere* #1-14 (125%) #15(1st *Iron Fist*; GD-FN = 200%; VF-NM = 150%); #16-24(125%); #47(150%) 48(120%); *Marvel Presents* #3(Guardians 200%); #4-12(150%); *Marvel Preview* #4 (1st Star-Lord 2000%); #7 (1st Rocket Raccoon 2500%); #11,14,15,18(2nd-4th Star-Lord 600%); #3,8,10 (All 150%); *Marvel Spotlight* (1971) #28-29(125%); #30 (1st solo Warriors 3 = 200%) #32 (150%); *Marvel Spotlight* (1981-1981) #6-7 (origin of Star-Lord 250%); *Marvel Super-Heroes* #13(1st Carol Danvers later becomes Ms. Marvel; GD-FN = 600%; VF-NM = 400%); #15 (Medusa 150%); #18(1st Guardians Of The Galaxy; GD-FN = 600%; VF-NM = 400%); *Marvel Super-Heroes Secret Wars* #8(1st black costume; USA=120%; Canadian Variant=200%); *Marvel Team-Up* #57 (2nd Silver Samurai 200%); #83,84,85 (Silver Samurai 150%); #86(Guardians 200%); *Marvel Team-Up*

©MAR

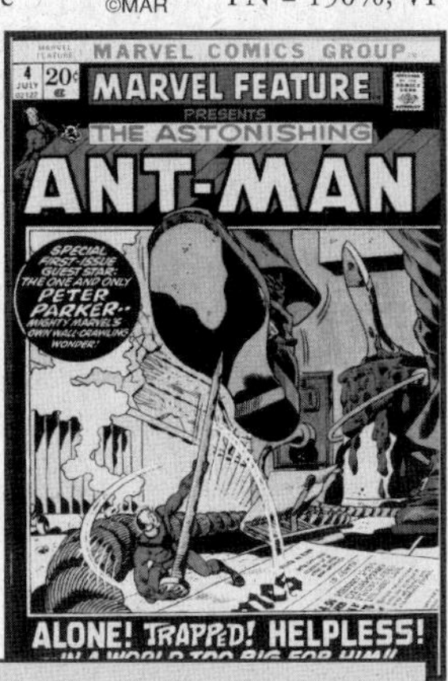

Even Ant-Man is a part of the Marvel Movie Madness sweeping the comics hobby.

#141 (scarcest 1st black costume in high grade; 200%); *Marvel Two-In-One* #5 (2nd Guardians of the Galaxy 200%); #61 (Starhawk and Guardians 200%); *Marvel Two-In-One Annual* #2 (Death of Thanos; GD-FN = 150%; VF-NM = 125%); #4 (3rd Graviton aka Dr. Franklin Hall 150%); Masters Of The Universe #12 (Death of He-Man 200%); #13 (Death of Skeletor 200%); *Ms. Marvel* #1,18(both 135%); *The 'Nam* #81-84 (low print and scarce 400%), *New Mutants* #5(Silver Samurai 150%); #16(1st Warpath 400%); #86-87 (1st Cable 150%); #98 (1st Deadpool; GD-FN = 250%; VF-NM = 175%); #100 (1st X-Force 300%), Annual #2(1st U.S. Psylocke 125%); *Nick Fury* (1968) #1(150%); #4 (Origin 150%); #2,3,5-7(125%); *Nova* #1(1976 150%); *Power Man* #17(1st issue with new title 150%); #48-50 (Iron Fist begins; Byrne-a; 200%); *Punisher* (1986) #1(150%); *Punisher* (1987) #1,10(150%), 100-104(250%); *Pulse* #1(Jessica Jones VF/NM = $10); *Rocket Raccoon* (1986) #1-4(150%) *Rom* #75(150%); *Secret Wars II* #4(1st app. and Origin of Kurse 150%); *Silver Surfer* (1968) #1,3,4 (GD-FN = 130%; VF-NM = 110%), (1987) #1, 34-38(150%), (1988-89 Moebius Mini) #1,2(200%); *Smurfs* (1982) #1-3(variants with Star Wars Jedi Arena game ad on back-c 150%), Treasury Edition #1(Scarce 200%); *Spectacular Spider-Man* #64(1st Cloak And Dagger 200%); #69,70,81-83(150%); #90(200%); #71-117(Canadian Newsstand Cover Price Variants, printed in USA = 200%); *Spider-Man* (1990) #1(Platinum 150%), #1(Gold UPC 150%); #1 (No Price on Comic 150%); *Spider-Man and His Amazing Friends* #1(250%); *Spidey Super Stories* #1-10(135%); #39 (early Thanos 200%); *Star Wars* (1977) #1(125%); #6 (1st first published Marvel art by Dave Stevens 150%); #42 (1st Boba Fett 300%); #68 (re-intro Boba Fett; USA=250%; Canadian Variant=500%); #100-106(120%); #107(135%); #64-106 (Canadian Newsstand Cover Price Variants, printed in USA = 200%); *Strange Tales* #89(1st Fin Fang Foom 250%); #97(1st Aunt May and Uncle Ben 200%); #110(1st Dr. Strange; GD-FN = 200%; VF-NM = 150%), 115(Origin Dr. Strange; GD-FN = 150%; VF-NM = 125%); #126 (1st Clea and Dormammu 200%) #135(1st SHIELD; 150%); #169 (150%); #180 (1st Gamora 200%); #179,181,182(135%); *Sub-Mariner* (1968) #34-35 (Defenders prelude; GD-FN = 200%; VF-NM = 150%); *Sunfire And Big Hero Six* #1 (600%), 2-3(300%); *Tales Of Suspense* #50(1st Mandarin; GD-FN = 200%; VF-NM = 150%); #57 (1st Hawkeye; GD-FN = 200%; VF-NM = 150%); #58-60,62,65,66 (125%) #93 (1st cameo Modok 150%); #94 (1st full Modok 200%); #97(1st app of Whiplash 125%); *Tales To Astonish* #27 (1st Ant-Man; GD-FN = 200%; VF-NM = 150%); *Thor* #126, 134,136,158,159(GD-FN = 125%; VF-NM = 110%); #146-151(Origin of Inhumans; GD-FN = 150%; VF-NM = 125%); #162,168,169 (Galactus; GD-FN = 150%; VF-NM = 125%); #163-166(Him/Warlock; GD-FN = 135%; VF-NM = 110%); #332-333 (Dracula; USA=200%; Canadian Variant = 500%); #337(1st Beta Ray Bill; US Edition = 200%; Canadian Variant = 400%); #344(1st Malekith 200%); #347(1st Algim The Elf, later Kurse; VF/NM $20) #411-412 (1st New Warriors 150%) *Thor Annual* #6(/1977; Korvac and Guardians 150%); *Transformers* #1, 61-80 (150%); *TV Stars* #3(Dave Stevens 3rd Marvel Art 150%); *Warlock* (1972) #10(Origin Thanos and Gamora later of Guardians 150%); *Web of Spider-Man* #18(1st Venom behind scenes 17 months before *ASM* #298 = 500%); *Weird Wonder Tales* #19(2nd *TTA* #13-r = 1st Groot-s 150%); *What If?* (1977) #11,16(2nd and 4th Marvel Art by Dave Stevens; 150%); *What If?* (1989 2nd) #105(1st Spider-Girl 175%); *Where Monsters Dwell* #6(11/1970; 1st *TTA* #13-r = 1st Groot-s 200%); *Wolverine* (1982; Miller mini) #2-4 (Canadian Newsstand Cover Price Variants, printed in USA = 200%); *Wolverine* (1988) #1(150%); #2-4 (Lord Shingen Yashida and Yukio / Earth 616 appear; 2-3=Silver Samurai); #2 (1st Silver Samurai battle; 150%); #10(1st Sabertooth battle; 120%); *X-Factor* #5(500%), 6(200%), 23-24(160%); *X-Men* (Uncanny) #118(Mariko 120%); #129(125%); #141-142 (Days of Future Past 125%); #158,162-164,171,184 (all 125%); #172-173 (Yukio and Wolverine 135%); 174(Silver Samurai 125%); #193(Warpath 150%); #201(1st Baby Nathan Cable 150%); #162-208(Canadian Newsstand Cover Price Variants, printed in USA = 200%); #244(1st Jubilee 150%), #248(1st Jim Lee 125%) #266 (1st Gambit 150%) #316 (1st Blink 150%), Annual #14 (1st Gambit = 5 Page appearance precedes X-Men #266 125%); *X-Men* (1991) #128 (1st Fantomex and Uncanny X-Force; VF/NM = $20).

©Warren

The list of high demand Warren magazines always includes **Vampirella**.

Warren, Skywald And Misc Horror And SF Magazines: Demand for Warren mags is still strong. The more afforable GD-FN copies are the most requested and thus the hardest to keep in stock. VF/NM or better high grade copies are still good sellers if unslabbed, with CGC slabbed copies being slower movers. Demand for *Famous Monsters* has been up all year, especially #1-30 in all grades. The high-demand Warren mags and scarcer issues include (percentages of *Guide* #43 are listed): *Blazing Combat* #1 and Anthology (GD-FN =400% *Guide*; VF-9.2=200%), *Comix International* #1 (200%), *Creepy* #9,11,19,29,76,79,146 (GD-FN=150% *Guide*; 8.0-9.2=125%), #32 (GD-FN=200% *Guide*; VF-9.2=150%), #10,14,17,18,34,39,46,47,50,53,63,70,71,78, 85, 91,113,132-145 (GD-FN=135% *Guide*; 8.0-9.2=110%), *Best of Creepy* paperback (VF $30), *Dracula* (TPB; GD-FN =200% *Guide*; 8.0-9.2=150%), *Dracula* (UK NEL / New English Library mag editions #1-12 VF set = $200); *Edgar*

Allan Poe's Fall of the House of Usher HC and SC (GD-FN =200% *Guide*; VF-9.2=150%), *Eerie* #1, 23(GD-FN=300% *Guide*; VF-9.2=200%), #8, 25, 48, 135(GD-FN=150% *Guide*; VF-9.2=125%), #17(GD-FN=500% *Guide*; VF-9.2=300%), *Eerie* #18, 24, 28, 38-41,45, 60, 81,125,128, 130-134,136-139 (GD-FN=135% *Guide*; 8.0-9.2=110%), *Famous Monsters* #1(VF=$1800; FN=$900; VG=$600), 2-10 (VF = $300-$900 ea; VG=$150-$400), 11-30(VF=$150-$300 ea; VG=$50=$125), 1962 Yearbook #1(VF $250; VG=$100), *Famous Monsters* (Dynacomm) #200(1993), 203, 205(VF = $25-35 ea); #201,206,211-214,216/217,219,221, 223,224(VF $20-$25 ea); others up to #250 ($10-$15 ea); *FM* Convention Books (1974, 1975; VF = $75+ ea), *FM* Paperbacks (VF = $75-100 ea; VG=$35), *Flintstones at New York World's Fair* 1964(1st print; 150%), *HELP* magazine (Kurtzman) (Note; Spines split easily, thus tough in VF or better) #1(VF $75+); #2-5, 9, 13,15, 16, 21-26(VF=$40-$60); others (VF = $25-$40); (*HELP* Paperbacks #1,2(VF $35); *Heidi Saha* (500 Printed? Very Rare; VF=$900; FN=$500; G=$250); *Monsters and Heroes* (Warren Related; Pub by Larry Ivie; 1967-1969; VF = $30-$50); *Monsterland / Forrest J. Ackerman's Monsterland* (1984-1987) #1-17(VF= $12-$20); *Monster World* (replaces *Famous Monsters* #70-79) #3(VF $60+); #4(VF $40+); #1,2,5-10(VF = $20-30); *Odd World of Richard Corben* (GD-FN=300% *Guide*; 8.0-9.2 =200%), *On the Scene / Freakout* #nn (#1; Fall 1967; GD-FN=150% *Guide*; 8.0-9.2=125%), *Screen Thrills* (1962-1965) #1,10(VF $75+); #2-4(VF $50); *Spacemen* (Note: spines split easily, thus tough in VF or better) #1,3(VF=$200+); #2,4-8 and Yearbook (VF=$50-$75); *Spirit Special* (Mail only, approx. 1500 printed; GD-FN=150% *Guide*; 8.0-9.2 =125%), *Outer Space Spirit* (TPB; VF $35); *Teen Love Stories* #1-3(GD-FN=125% *Guide*; 8.0-9.2=150%), *Tiny Tim* (125%); *Vampirella* #1,3,112,113 (125-135% *Guide*) #2,4-8,11,12,16,19,32-34,36,41,45,46,48,49,51,52,61,63,64, 77, 78,89,90,100-111(115-125% *Guide*); #32-34 (Note: spines split easily); Annual #1(125%), *Vampirella Special* #1(softcover=125%; rare hardcover=300%), *Vampirella* paperbacks #1-3(VF $30), 4-6(VF $50); *Vampirella* UK mags #1-4(VF $50 ea); *Warren Presents* #13, 14(150%); *Wildest Westerns/Favorite Westerns of Filmland* (Note: spines split easily, thus tough in VF or better) #1(VF=$200; GD=$50); #2(VF=$100; GD=$35); #3-6(VF=$60; GD=$20).

Skywald Magazines (*Nightmare*, *Psycho* and *Scream*) are always top sellers for us. They are very hard to restock once sold, with VF or better copies especially difficult. I usually buy them at 65-80% *Guide* and resell them at 140-160% *Guide*. Strict graded VF/NM or better copies are very hard to find. When I find them, I sell them instantly at: 9.0=150%; 9.2=150%; 9.4=200% or 9.2 Guide. *King* magazine #1 (rare 200%) and #2(Scarce 150%).

Eerie Pub, Modern Day, and Stanley Horror Comic mags (packed with pre-Code Horror and published with no Comic Code) are in very high demand in GD-FN, especially in lowest graded Reading copies. About 75% of the copies we get in stock in FR/GD thru VG sell within just a few weeks and usually most of what we have in stock is in about FN/VF to VF average. Most of the titles have scarcer issues and thus most of the sets are quite difficult to complete (the 1966-1970 issues and 1977 and newer issues are generally the hardest to find. The 1971-1976 issues represent most copies still found for sale in the marketplace. Examples in FN/VF, VF and VF+ are all slow sellers, as most collectors want either Reading copies, or Investment copies. Strictly graded VF/NM copies are more popular, with 9.2-9.4 copies in better demand. We sell them at these rates: GD-FN=140-160%; FN/VF, VF,VF+=100-115%; VF/NM=120-130%; 9.2=150%. *The Weird Indexes of Eerie Publications* by Mike Howlett is a MUST have book for fans (mind boggling list of cover, art and original pre-Code source listings, with checklist and cross references); *Weird Vampire Tales* and *Terrors of Dracula* list the publisher as Modern Day, which is a pseudonym for Eerie Pub and they are perhaps their scarcest titles and among our fastest sellers. The Stanley Pub mags have a lot of pre-Code Horror reprints and are about 50% scarcer than Eerie Pub mags, thus are also in higher demand.

Oddball scarce finds: *Mysticogryfil, the Journal of Wonder* (A&W Pub Coy; SF and Comic Fanzine) #1(VF = $60); #2 (5/1975; Neal Adams-a, Jack Kirby-a and interview; first published cover and art by Dave Stevens. Cover art is dated as 1974 by David Stevens. Dave Stevens illos on pages 2,8,27; VF = $125); #3(Winter 1976-77; Dave Stevens-s = page 21-22, Dave Stevens-a = page 3, 23; VF = $75); *Weird Mysteries* (Pastime Pub; B&W Comics and illustrated text-s mag) Volume 1 #1(3-5/1959; Tuska-ca; Reinman, Torres, Burgos, Orlando-a; VF = $200).

Whitman Comics: The Whitman Variants of DC Comics are up in demand, with diminishing supply. Since they were sold in Pre-Packs only, mainly in Big Box and chain stores, they sold mainly to readers from the General Public, with most being thrown out, and the remaining copies mostly well used in the FR/GD to VG/FN condition range. For these, higher grade starts at Fine or Better, with perhaps only about 10% of surviving copies in FN 6.0 or Higher grades.

This year it became evident that the eight June 1980 Variants are by far the scarest, typically with ZERO copies of any of them on eBay. They include: *Action* #508, *Batman* #324, *DC Comics Presents* #22, *Flash* #286, *JLA* #179, *Legion* #264, *New Advs. of Superboy* #6, and *Superman* #348 [VG/FN copies of these typically bring $50+ at eBay auctions. VF/NM copies are Rare to Non-Existant and would bring in the $100-$150 range]. The exception is: *DC Comics Presents* #22 = the #1 Rarest DC Whitman thought to NOT exist until about 3/2012. There are currently five known copies in exisitance. In 9/2013, I sold a raw VG+ copy for $402.00 at eBay auction.

The rare 8-12/1980 Whitman comics (of former Gold Key titles) had a temporary slowdown after the Random House File Copies find a few years back. A small amout of High Grade scarce 8-12/1980 issues surfaced in that collection, but all got quickly absorbed into permanent collections, and once again there are very few VF or better copies in the

Marketplace at any qiven time. Typically only about 10% of the copies in the Marketplace are in FN 6.0 or better. Demand for 8-12/1980 issues has TRIPLED in the last year, with Raw copies at record high asking and selling prices for Raw copies on eBay. My new minimum selling prices on these is: [VF/NM=$90; VF=$65; FN=$36; VG=$24; GD=$12]. I often see overgraded Raw copies at 50% to 100% higher than these prices on eBay.

Quantities of the Rare 8-12/1980 Whitman comics so far graded by CGC, according to CGC's December 14/2013 Census; *Battle of the Planets* #7(33), 8(27), 9(30), *Beep Beep* #91(3), 92(6), 93(7), *Black Hole* #4(15), *Buck Rogers* #8(3), 9(9); *Bugs Bunny* #221(17), 222(5 total for 40 and 50 cent Variants combined), *Chip 'N' Dale* #67(5), 68(8), 69(11), *Daffy Duck* #129(4), 130(9), 131(9), *Daisy and Donald* #45(6), #46(6), #47(19); *Donald Duck* #221(9), 222 (21), 223(23), 224(19); *Flash Gordon* #30(11), *Huey, Dewey and Louie* #65(4), #66(7), *Little Lulu* #260(x37), 261(26); *Looney Tunes* #33(8), 34(14), #35(11), *Mickey Mouse* #207(8), 208(20), 209(10); *Pink Panther* #75(9), 76(17), #77(16); *Popeye* #158(8), #159(5); *Porky Pig* #97(11), 98(18); *Super Goof* #60(10), 61(15), 62(5); *Tom and Jerry* #330(6), #331(8), #332(12); *Tweety and Sylvester* #105(10), #106(6), #107(6); *Uncle Scrooge* #179(54), #180(19), #181(21); *Walt Disney's Comics and Stories* #479(8), 480(27), 481(7), 482(13), 483(7); *Winnie the Pooh* #20(2), #21(4), 22(13); *Woody Woodpecker* #190(14), 191(8); *Yosemite Sam* #68(8), #69(21), #70(8).

Battle of the Planets #7-9 have more copies slabbed than other titles, as many dealers judge them as a "better" title and more worthwhile to slab. Take note that there are still only 50% of the 68 different (34 different issues) with 9 or fewer copies graded by CGC. The Big-4 (*Donald Duck* #222, *Little Lulu* #260, *Uncle Scrooge* #179, *WD Comics & Stories* #480) have been well known TOUGH issues for 30 years and were the first to bring record prices on eBay, now listing relatively high in the *Guide*, thus a disproportionate number of copies have been CGC graded, they are still scarce and in huge demand in spite of what the skewed CGC quantities would indicate. On 6/12/2013 *Black Hole* #4 in CGC NM/M: 9.8 sold for $2653.00 on ComicConnect.

The early Direct editions of Marvel Comics from 2/1977-12/1977, 1978 and 1979 (most with black diamond) are often mistaken to be Whitman Marvel. In reality, only the plastic bag is Whitman, so once the comics are removed they are identical to Marvel Direct editions, as they are one and the same. There are approx 200+ comics published thus in each of these years, with an estimated total of 600-700 existing in the period. The 1977 issues are usually scarcest, and typically command 50% over *Guide* premiums, while 1978-1979 issues on average sell at about a 25% over *Guide* premium. Since they are not broken out in the *Guide*, most collectors are unaware that they exist. A few issues were not published as early Direct editions in the period, probably a publiher error and seem likely to not exist. Knowledge and statistics are still hard to find on these, with no detailed research on scarcity. Some issues seem quite rare, with a few collectors having searched to fill in gaps in their collections for 5-10 years, with little or no luck. I would not be surprised to see some of these Rare evasive issues bring $50 to $100 in middle grades on eBay, if they ever surface.

Christopher Swartz Collector

2013 has been a great year for comics, at least reading wise concerning many of the current published monthly comic books. DC's new 52 Universe has a solid following and I especially like *Justice League Dark* and *Suicide Squad.* Marvel has continued to do well with titles like the *Superior Spider-Man* and the well written (Jason Aaron) *Incredible Hulk* series. There were a few comic book related big budget movies that were released this year, such as *The Man of Steel, The Wolverine, Thor The Dark World, Kick-Ass 2,* and *Iron Man 3* (which was complete crap). Surprisingly these movies did not significantly impact the comic book prices of their comic book counterparts, as in the past. The only issue that had a large price increase as direct result of an associated movie was *Adventure Comics* #277, featuring the 1st General Zod. For the most part there were not any major price increases in the market place besides early key Golden Age appearances of Batman, Superman, Wonder Woman, along with a few Silver Age keys (*Amazing Fantasy* #15, *Incredible Hulk* #1, *Sgt. Fury* #1, *Strange Tales* #110, and *Showcase* #4). I think collectors have finally started to realize that the bubble has burst for high grade non-key Golden and Silver Age issues. The same can be said for all high grade CGC 9.4 and above Bronze Age issues, including keys. Now let's bust open the comic book marketplace for 2013 like a high school kegger.

Golden Age – DC: Nothing changing much here with *Action Comics* (#1-13) and *Detective Comics* (#27-40) still being the most collected DC issues. These early Superman and Batman appearances all sell well above *Guide* value and will continue to spark more interest, especially with the Batman/Superman movie on the horizon. The most undervalued DC Golden Age keys continue to be *Action Comics* #2 and *Detective Comics* #28. When you consider their importance, factored in with their scarcity compared to the two issues that preceded them a month prior, they are bargain priced. My two picks for Batman and Superman issues that I think will take a big leap in collectability and value are *Detective Comics* #15 and *Action Comics* #12. *Detective* #15 features a full page ad of *Action Comics* #1 dated May 1938 and *Action* #12 features an ad page of *Detective Comics* #27, which was released at the same time as *Detective Comics* #27 itself.

All copies of *Flash Comics* #1 and *All Star Comics* #8 have all sold above *Guide* value when offered during 2013. Other DC keys have not fared as well, such as: *All-American Comics* #16, *Green Lantern* #1, *All Star Comics* #3, and *Adventure Comics* #40. While these issues are all definite keys, they all sell for way less than when offered in previous years. I think this is attributed to the fact that most Golden Age collectors are now hitting retirement age and selling their collections, or just not willing to spend outlandish prices for second tier characters. I personally appreciate the importance of these issues, however I do know that there are very few collectors from my generation who collect Golden Age comics. This is also a factor for the sudden decline in prices and a trend I do not see changing unless younger collectors start collecting Golden Age comics. As I stated last year *Batman* #1 continues to be the most collected issue of this era and deserves to be ranked as the fourth most valuable comic, right behind *Superman* #1. A *Batman* #1 CGC 9.2 copy sold for $567,625 earlier this year, making that a record selling price for a copy of *Batman* #1.

Golden Age – Timely/Marvel: *Captain America Comics* still continues to be the most collected Timely series with issues #1, 3, and 46 (Holocaust cover) being the biggest sellers. A *Captain America* #1 CGC 3.5 (SS Joe Simon) sold for $32,625 this year. All other Timelys have been in demand but all sell for under *Guide* value. *Marvel Comics* #1, *Human Torch* #1, and *Sub-Mariner* #1 have all sold for fractions of what they have in previous years.

All other Golden Age: *Pep Comics* #22 and *Archie Comics* #1 continue to be in demand. An *Archie Comics* #1 CGC 6.5 copy sold for $62,778 in December 2013. I am not an Archie fan, but apparently there are a few collectors with disposable income because I do not see these types of prices to continue to be realized for Archie issues. 2013 has been a good year for *Whiz Comics* #1 with multiple copies selling, with even restored copies being snatched up. A *Whiz* #1 CGC 4.5 (MP restoration) sold for $7,500. Disney titles have had a lot of buying/selling activity with anything containing Carl Barks art selling near *Guide* value in mid to high grade. Good girl issues *Phantom Lady* #17 and *Blue Beetle* #54 always sell above *Guide* value when offered. High grade EC Horror comics continue to be in demand but the collector base for ECs is starting to dwindle.

Silver Age – Marvel: *Amazing Fantasy* #15 is still the most collected book from this era, selling in all grades (CGC 7.0 $33,000, CGC 4.0 $8,300, CGC 3.0 $6,200). However, I feel that *AF* #15 has finally reached its price plateau, at least for the near future. *Incredible Hulk* #1 has been one of the best sellers this past year with copies selling for strong prices (CGC 8.5 $58,000, CGC 6.0 $8,900, CGC 3.5 $4,700). *Journey Into Mystery* #83 was very popular, mostly due to the Thor sequel being released in late 2013. A CGC 9.2 copy sold for $77,675 in November 2013. *Avengers* #1, *Fantastic Four* #1 and *Amazing Spider-Man* #1 still are always in demand, but collectors are not paying the premium prices for them as in previous years. *Sgt. Fury and His Howling Commandos* #1 and *Strange Tales* #110 are no longer undervalued books with copies selling at above *Guide* value in all grades. *Avengers* #55 has sold for multiple times *Guide* value in high grade after Ultron was announced to be the main villain in the upcoming Avengers sequel.

Silver Age – DC: 2013 was a very good year for DC keys, with multiple copies of *Showcase* #4 selling for significant prices. A CGC 9.0 copy sold for $50,000, while all grades of this issue sold for above *Guide* value (CGC 7.5 $26,000, CGC 5.0 $8,300, CGC 2.0 $2,150). There are many collectors who forget that *Showcase* #4 was the most valued Silver Age key for decades until the late '90s when *AF* #15 dethroned it. When you compare how many copies of *AF* #15 that have been graded (2,043 copies) to *Showcase* #4 (281), *Showcase* #4 is waiting to explode. Of course how DC and Warner Bros. handles The Flash on the big screen and in comics will also have a major impact on the demand for *Showcase* #4. Other DC keys that were major sellers were: *Adventure* #247, *Batman* #121, *Brave and the Bold* #28, *Flash* #105, and *Showcase* #22.

Bronze Age – Marvel: All Bronze Age books except the major keys (*Incredible Hulk* #181, *Amazing Spider-Man* #129, *Iron Man* #55, and *Marvel Spotlight* #5) deserve a price decrease. High grade copies of Bronze Age keys which sold for insane amounts have been steadily decreasing in selling price month after month. Oversaturation of the market with high grade copies from pressing has started to take its toll on the Bronze Age prices. A CGC 9.8 *Incredible Hulk* #181 sold for $8,066 in November 2013 and high grade copies continue to sell for less and less each year. I would not even contemplate buying a CGC 9.2 or higher book at the current prices unless you plan on actually holding onto the book for a significant amount of time. Even then you might not be able to resell the book for what you paid for it today. As I stated before, look to pick up Bronze Age keys in VF condition to save a considerable amount of money. A book that has shown a vast amount of interest this past year has been *Marvel Super-Heroes* #18, featuring the 1st Guardians of The Galaxy. However, if the upcoming movie bombs, look for interest to quickly disappear.

Bronze Age – DC: DC Bronze Age has taken a huge decrease in demand with the few exceptions being high grade copies of *Green Lantern* #76 and *Batman* #227 and #232.

Copper Age: There are a few issues in the Copper Age that are always consistent sellers. *Amazing Spider-Man* #300 always sells for $200 or more in CGC 9.4 or higher. 2013 has seen multiple copies of *Evil Ernie* #1 CGC 9.8 sell for over $600 each. *Teenage Mutant Ninja Turtles* #1 is the king of the Copper Age with copies in all grades (CGC 9.6 $7,400, CGC 8.5 $2,900, CGC 8.0 $3,400, CGC 7.5 $2,200, CGC 5.5 $1,000) selling very easily.

San Diego Comic-Con: The Con is always fun but if you are looking to find key issues for a decent price then do not even bother. Almost every dealer at the Con marks up their prices by 20% for any key issue. Now if you are looking for good deals on trades or Modern issues you will find some great deals to be had. I usually spend $400-500 on trades alone, because they are offered at 50% or more off of retail price. The big pick-up for me at Con was obtaining the original Javier Saltares cover art to *Ghost Rider* #1 and I am very appreciative to Albert Moy for helping me acquire this piece.

Important Sales or Purchases:
Batman #59 CGC 5.0 (Crippen pedigree) $500
Detective Comics #37 CGC 1.0 $1,700
Detective Comics #39 CGC 1.0 (SS Jerry Robinson) $850
Flash Comics #1 CGC 5.5 (restored MP) $5,750
Evil Ernie #1 CGC 9.4 $135
More Fun Comics #73 CGC 7.5 (restored MP) $3,250
Primer #2 CGC 9.4 $150
Showcase #4 CGC 2.0 $2,150
Whiz Comics #1(#2) CGC 7.5 (restored EP trimmed) $6,000

On an end note, please remember that collectibles, such as comic books are only worth (monetary wise) what someone else is willing to pay for them. The fair market value of comic books will always fluctuate, but as long as you are a fan of comics, buy what you like without your main concern being making a profit, you can continue to take satisfaction in this hobby. My best advice that I can offer to collectors is to never make a large purchase solely for potential resell profit and do not exceed your financial means. Going into debt to purchase a comic book is never a good idea, but neither is being addicted to strippers, so who am I to offer advice. Until next year and Hollywood making *Power Pack* into a movie, stay fan-boys my friends.

Brian Tatge
Motor City Comics

For those out there that don't know me, I love comics! All of them, new and old. So I have always tried to have my finger on the pulse of what's going on in the industry. The best way to tell the trends is by watching what was going on in the title at the current time. "Oh, Sinestro is going to have a big story line coming up!" (Reading *Previews* 3 months ahead of time) I could then speculate that *Green Lantern* #7 was going to have a spike in interest. And if the story was really awesome the interest was going to be even bigger.

Now you don't even have to read ANY comics to tell what's going to be hot. Just keep up with what's going on in *Variety* and *Entertainment Weekly* magazines. We are a very fickle lot, collectors, if it's not right in our face, we don't care. But you get national news of a movie being done that will feature such and such character, we gotta have it!

And with that being said, what is going to be hot? Well, there's the obvious *X-Men* #4 with the first Quicksilver and the Scarlet Witch. *Avengers* #16 where they join the Avengers. *Avengers* #54 and #55 with the first Ultron. And, for some reason, people are speculating that Agent Coulson might be The Vision. So there has been a spike in interest in that one again. Seems like it might be logical that we would see Vision as he was created by Ultron to destroy the Avengers. Then we have books that went crazy, *X-Men* #141 and 142. But don't forget the little ones that have great potential. Preacher has been announced as a movie, there was a tweet from Bryan Singer that had the words X-Men Apocalyspe and *X-Factor* #5 and 6 have gone up. X-Force also, so you see the interest in *New Mutants* #87 and #98 (with the Deadpool movie in limbo, it still has interest.) Then you have the backlash from sleepers that end up with a great television show like *Walking Dead* and *Arrow*. Causing books like *Walking Dead* #1 and #19 and *More Fun Comics* #73 to instantly have a large fan base of people wanting them. And just the hint of another character in a show (The Flash on Arrow) and *Showcase* #4 is back on everyone's radar. And *Captain America* #117 with the Falcon is one I almost forgot.

Now what to watch for (not in a good sense) is putting too much into a book. Meaning which ones MIGHT have reached their peak. Some people don't realize what the backlash from a bad movie can do. If you are doing this as an investment, you really should sell the books before the movie comes out. Because if it flops you will instantly see the prices stall and start to drop (or with big key books, not move in price.) And everyone has been on the *Iron Man* #55 bandwagon along with *Marvel Preview* #4 and #7 (Star Lord and Rocket Raccoon) and *Tales to Astonish* #13 with Groot. But these Guardians of the Galaxy characters are "unknown properties" to the mass public. And even comic people are leery about the movie. It's a gamble, but if it goes over big with the younger audience it could be bigger than any other Marvel movie so far. Similarly, when *The Walking Dead* TV series is on a mid-season break, you see the interest go down. And the moment it comes back, BAM! the interest returns. So be sure to keep up with what's going on in the current issues, the television show, and the movies. Because before you know it, it could be the same universe.

In closing, as I've always told people who ask me "What should I get?": always collect what you like. That way you always get what you want. And don't be afraid to pay a little more for that book that you've been looking for. You are paying for peace of mind. Because you know you're going to buy it. So the longer you "think" about it, the longer you give someone else to buy it right out from underneath you. And in that moment you realize you lost it, you would have instantly paid whatever price to get it.

And if you haven't noticed, Pop Culture has popped. Making any book, new or old, with a movie or TV tie-in gold. These books, and the industry, have reached a "Rock Star" status. And all of us, dealers, collectors and speculators are the keepers of all that rocks!

Michael Tierney
Collector's Edition
& The Comic Book Store

2013 was a lucky year when it came to finding and selling rare back issues. Started with a Fine copy of the 35 cent variant of *Star Wars* #1, which sold for $400 in less than an hour after being put under the display glass.

Just two days later, I picked up another rare book that I hadn't seen since the late Eighties: a one-owner Fine copy of the original *Teenage Mutant Ninja Turtles* #1 -- First Printing. It took only two weeks to sell this to a person who heard that we had a copy through fan buzz, and completed his 'Ultimate Collector's Quest.' As he said, "Some books you just have to see in front of you before buying."

But, by a wide margin, the biggest sale of the year was the first appearance of Spider-Man in *Amazing Fantasy* #15, with a VG+ (4.5) copy that sold for $7,600 within hours after being acquired.

Moving almost as fast was the first appearance of Iron Man in a GD- copy of *Tales of Suspense* #39 that sold for $600 after only one day. Soon after, a copy of *Tales to Astonish* #36 (with an early Ant-Man appearance) that had been sitting around sold in FN+ for $300.

And all that was before the end of March.

Back issue sales continued to multiply the steady growth we've seen over the last several years, so much so that we stopped running sales on them. The demand was just too strong to justify lowering the prices!

And the sales of new comics also jumped up substantially again this year.

The 2013 marketing push started with the Batman family crossover series, Death of the Family. While well received, it lacked the major event of the original Death in the Family, where Jason Todd's Robin was killed. This time, they sneaked the death of Robin Damian Wayne into *Batman Inc.* #8 after the event was over and with no advance warning. We turned away hundreds of disappointed customers when DC threw this curveball, but didn't back it up by printing extra. It was a huge missed opportunity, and it did not translate into digital sales for them. The resistance to digital is so great, that I rarely carry DC's digital combo comics. Almost no one buys them.

September was trouble. It has been a traditionally tricky month to order for. For some retailers, it's probably a good month with students returning to town for school. For me, it's bad because all of my customers are either paying for school or for their kid's school. In my 34 years of placing orders for this month, I've rarely turned a profit. Many Septembers have been my worst months ever. This was the month with the '90s Jim Lee *X-Men* #1 fiasco, for which I still have several hundred Mint copies of every cover. The exception was a couple of years ago, when DC relaunched their entire universe.

So, when DC came up with Villains Month where every DC Universe book sported a 3D lenticular cover, I played it safe and ordered normal numbers, which, with higher cover prices, was still a 25% increase in dollars gambled. Then came the allocations, and then the allocations were allocated. Didn't have enough of these 3D 'event books' to even cover regular reserves on some titles. And the 2D covers that I ordered on a one-to-one ratio to replace the allocation shortages just sat on the shelf. Exceptions were Harley Quinn and the Joker's Daughter, and Lobo to a lesser extent. While DC did allow returns of the 2Ds at a later date, it didn't help September. I didn't just lose money for the month, September hemorrhaged money.

Villains Month also brings up another point of contention that both DC and Marvel don't seem to have figured out. Their penchant for using fractal numbering is making life difficult for collectors. Used to be, if you could count, then you could maintain your comic collection. Add into the mix Marvel's habit of continually relaunching every series with a new round of #1 issues, and I'd guess they're ensuring the future of guide books. Collecting comics nowadays requires the use of a roadmap to navigate the numbering, which becomes a roadblock for novice collectors.

Other than the Thanos-themed *Infinity* mini-series, for Marvel the marketing plan was the same as it is every year, as Marvel Now restarted another bunch of titles with new #1 issues. Fortunately, their movie properties continued to help draw in huge crowds. These new customers unfortunately became confused when trying to find a good starting point, or worse, disillusioned when trying to find mainstream material for their children aged ten and under.

Marvel and DC seem to have lost the art of the All Ages comic. It's an abandoned niche market and possibly the most important market of sustainable future growth, that independent publishers are now starting to aggressively exploit.

My Little Pony first exploded out of the gate and quickly ran through several sold out printings. Since then, other media related titles like *Adventure Time*, *Regular Show*, *Bravest Warriors* and *Spongebob Comics* have become sensations at first, but quickly faded with time. All the while, *My Little Pony* never lost pace and kept running laps all around all the other All Ages competition all year long. *My Little Pony* put the "All" in All Ages, because they don't just appeal to young girls, as I often saw crowds as large as thirty to forty grown adult 'Bronies' arrive at the same time to buy Ponies.

©AP

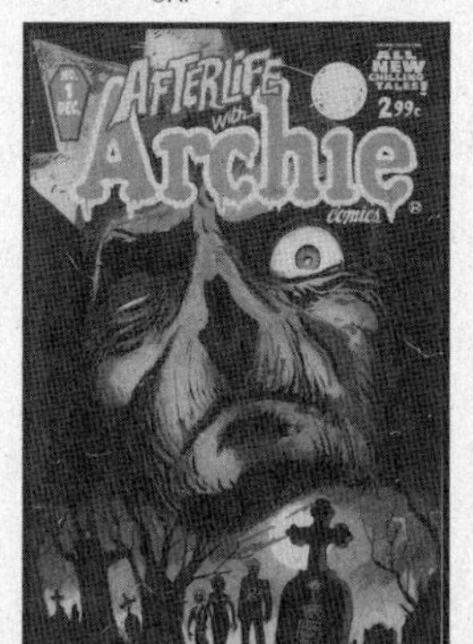

***Afterlife With Archie** is a monster hit. (#1 shown)*

Traditional Archie titles sold moderately at the start of the year, but their New Crusaders return to the Super Hero market just didn't fly. After that, even Archie stopped selling unless it was as a zombie comic. However, *Afterlife with Archie* was a big hit.

Despite last year's *Dredd* movie doing poorly at the box office, when it was released to the home market, sales of the back issue comics exploded -- for about three weeks. After that, Judge Dredd comic sales fell off the map. Just another example of the varied influence of movies on comics.

But back to the key subject of digital.

While it doesn't sell for us, digital does bring us new readers, who give it a try and then come looking to discover the real thing. Understanding the effect of digital comes down to understanding the importance of presentation. With books, a block of text is a block of text, whether it's on a sheet of paper or an electronic screen. With music, the sound is the product, not the delivery system. But with comics, the delivery system is as important as sound is to music, and the presentation of comics does not translate well from page to screen. True, publishers do continue to enhance the digital experience, but most readers today still prefer the tactile presentation of a printed two-page spread.

Instead of being a threat to sales, for us digital has been a great advertising tool. In that respect, digital is almost as strong a promotional tool as the super-hero movies. And like movies, as much as digital seems to have increased the sales of new comics, it also seems to have been a triggering factor in the steadily rising demand for old comics, which continued their hot pace throughout the year. The month of November saw the individual number of back issue units sold rise as high as 60% of the number of new comic units sold at one location. This all resulted in many more sales of note throughout the year.

For Marvel, the *Amazing Spider-Man* is always in high demand. Key sales include #17 $160 in VG+, and the first appearance of the Punisher in a FN- copy of #129 for $100. First appearances are always fast moving books, with an *Avengers* #1 selling in GD- for $500. A cameo appearance of Wolverine in the *Incredible Hulk* #182 went quickly for $36 in VG. And the first appearance of Deadpool in *New Mutants* #98 sold in FN+ for $80. The last issue of Marvel's *Star Wars* #107 sold in FN+ for $35.00

Building anticipation for the 2014 X-Men movie moved a lot of their comics. Sold *Giant-Size X-Men* #1 in VG- for $85.00. In the original series, sold #22 in FN- for $35, #23 in VG+ for $28, #25 in FN+ for $60, #31 in VG+ for $23, #35 in GD for $20. Even the reprints were moving, with #75 selling in FN- for $35, #80 in VF- for $45, #81 in VF for $50, #86 in VG+ for $19, #88 in FN- for $15, and #91 in VF+ for $24.75. Also sold a large number of modern era after the Seventies relaunch, with the hottest demand tied to the Days of Future Past, with two copies of #141 selling for $40 in VF+ and NM, and multiple copies of #142 selling in FN- for $13.25, VF- for $30, and VF+ for $40.

DC's Silver Age demand was just as hot as Marvel's. *Aquaman* #1 sold in VG+ for $168.75. *Justice League of America* #1 went for $450 in VG+, while #18 in VG- went for $45, and #34 in VG+ for $29. Sold 2 copies of *Green Lantern* #4, one in FN- for $95 and another in GD for $42. Other *Green Lantern* sales included #18 in GD+ for $21, #36 in VG+ for $20, and #59 in FN- for $45.

Horror and mystery books were also moving. One example was *House of Mystery* #143 in FN+ for $56.25. Sold a rare copy of *Phantom Stranger* Volume One #2 in VG- for $150. But super-heroes are the mainstay of DC. The introduction of Poison Ivy into *Batman* sold three different copies of #181, two GD- copies for $18 and $21, and a VG copy for $52. #203 sold in VG+ for $22, #223 in FN for $20, #227 in FN- for $39, #234 in VG+ for $40, and #244 in FN+ for #29. Even hotter was the #1 issue of the New 52 relaunch, which was selling in NM for $60, and the variant in NM for $75.

Superman continues to be popular, as #79 sold in FN- for $175. *Superboy* #52 went for $44 in GD+ and #67 for $41.25 in VG. DC's Bronze Age *Shazam!* #1 sold in NM for $35.00, and Fawcett's Golden Age *Whiz* #123 in VG+ sold for $30.

Had a lot of Romance comics that had been sitting around for years with old prices on them suddenly draw some strong activity. Key sales were *Campus Romance* #1 in GD for $30, *Girls' Romances* #24 in GD+ for $18.75 and #79 in VG+ for $12, *Glamorous Romances* #24 in GD+ for $18.25 and #77 in FN+ for $12, two copies of *Romantic Love* #11 -- one in FN- for $25 and another in GD- for $11.00, *Romantic Secrets* #31 in FN+ for $15, *Secret Romances* #5 in VG+ for $19.50, *Teenage Temptations* #1 in VG for $38.50 and #4 in VG for $13, *Tessie the Typist* #13 in VG- for $15.5-, *True Love Pictorial* #6 in VF+ for $37.50, *Untamed Love* #3 in GD+ for $23.50, and *Young Romance* #47 in GD+ for $29.50.

Sold a lot of other back issues from other publishers, like *Space Family Robinson* #1 in GD+ for $20, but nothing really compares to Marvel and DC when it comes to the demand for back issue comics across all the ages of comics manufacturing.

Ted VanLiew
Superworld Comics

This has been a very encouraging year! The economy is definitely picking up, at least in some sectors. We are seeing evidence of this in an increased willingness of buyers to spend more freely. It certainly helps that comic books have become one of the foremost collectibles in the world. The intrinsic coolness of the hobby is being discovered by an increasing number of collectors and investors. The smashing success of superhero movies hasn't hurt either! Many characters are becoming household words. With the various big time auction houses pumping out material on a regular basis, our profile has risen, as well.

While high grade Silver Age books are the core of what we sell, more unique Golden Age books are seeing a resurgence. Various Timely titles, especially WWII era books are always in great demand. Very difficult to locate in higher grades but they sell in all grades, especially since they're more affordable in lower grades. Nedors, or "poor man's Timelys" are going stronger than ever. Many have great covers, some by Schomburg, are cheaper than Timelys, but unfortunately are not easy to find.

Golden Age DCs remain a popular staple, especially the Batman and Superman titles. *Sensation* and *Wonder Woman* are good, as she's a DC mainstay, and the books are very inexpensive. *Flash, Green Lantern, All Star* and other titles that feature major characters are very steady sellers. The secondary titles such as *Leading* and *Comic Cavalcade* are less predictable but have their following.

The Golden Age is rife with books that are somewhat lesser known or obscure, but are popular. *Speed* or *Prize* comics are almost nonexistent in the market so when we get 'em, they fly. Strangely enough, titles like *Four Favorites* and *Four Most*, which have a lot of blah covers and aren't all that sought after, have some really weird frenetic covers on earlier issues. Those earlier ones are really tough to find, and fly when we get 'em.

Centaurs and Fox titles remain popular. There are so many others, but we'll leave it at that for Golden Age for now.

Atom Age is similar, as there are so many great books, some well known and some obscure. Atlas pre-code and post-code horror and mystery titles are on fire, as are almost any pre-Code horror, sci-fi, or mystery books in high grade. The more outrageous or tasteless a cover is, the more sought after the book. I don't know what that says about us!

In Silver Age almost anything halfway decent in high grade will find a buyer. The early Marvels are still supreme, although ten cent and early twelve cent DCs are very scarce in better grades. (I've yet to see a VF or better copy of *Action* #242 in ten years of looking!) Pre-Hero Marvels have become very popular. Many collectors are charmed by them; their look and content. The Kirby/Ditko axis is irresistible.

In the DC realm, I've come to realize that the Curt Swan/George Klein stuff is quite colorful and charming. Everybody loves the stuff by Infantino and Anderson which is the *Flash*, Sci-Fi, Mystery, *Hawkman* and Batman books, but there are others that are deserving of attention, such as anything by Ruben Moreira or Alex Toth, two criminally overlooked artists—they never drew superhero comics so they are not well remembered.

Collectors have become more particular with Bronze Age books. Due to the great supply of material, there is more of a pickiness and desire for only the highest grades on most issues. The exceptions are the key issues, such as *Marvel Spotlight* #5, *Iron Man* #55, and *Iron Fist* #14, to name just a few. Most Neal Adams issues are great, especially the ones in which he drew the interiors as well as his memorable covers.

Original Art is an interesting area that we have been involved in for a few years now. It's referred to as "The Wild West" since there's no uniformity in pricing, such as Bob Overstreet pioneered in the comics. The vintage, important pages have skyrocketed in price, but there are still so many great values to be had on others.

Important Sales And Purchases: Part of our success this past year has been our good fortune to be able to purchase some very special collections. One consisted of entirely pre-Code crime books of exceptional quality, and another large, lifetime collection of Golden and Silver Age comics containing many rarities. We dubbed this one the "Lynski Collection" in honor of Larry Lynski, who compiled the collection, but passed away this year. Here are some of the sales:

Action Comics #13 CGC 3.5 - $34,200; *Amazing Mystery Funnies* Vol 1, #4, VF - $4500, Vol. 2 #4 FN/VF - $2200, Vol 2, #5 VF - $9500; *Amazing Spider-Man* #1 VG - $3600, #4 VF+ - $2900, #6 VF/NM - $3900, #14 VF+ - $1950, #15 VF/NM - $1300, #16 NM- $1800, #40 CGC 9.4 $1450, #42 CGC 9.6 $1400; *Avengers* #1 VF $8500, #2 VF/NM $1800, #3 VF/NM $1450, #4 CGC 9.2 $7500, #4 CGC 8.5 Signature Series $3300, #5 NM- $1800, #8 CGC 9.4 $1500, #9 NM- $1500, #16 NM- $950; *Captain America Comics* #13 FN $2100, #36 VG- $1450, #66 VF+ $3000; *Crime Does Not Pay* #22 CGC 5.5 $1850, #24 CGC 7.5 $4500; *Daredevil* #1 VF/NM $6300; *Detective Comics* #11 CGC 7.5 $8500, #69 VG/F $1200; *Fantastic Four* #1 VG/F $5500, #2 FN/VF $2200, #6 NM- $6400, #7 VF/NM $2700, #12 VF- $2200, #15 CGC 9.4 $2750, #16 CGC 9.4 $2750, #20 CGC 9.6 $5400, #23 CGC 9.6 $3600, #48 CGC 9.6 $4200; *Fight Against Crime* #20 CGC 7.0 $3050; *Keen Detective Funnies* #18 VF $2500, #20 FN/VF $3400; *Journey Into Mystery* #83 CGC 7.0 $8300; *Marvel Comics* #1 CGC 0.5 $11,500; *Tales of Suspense* #39 FN/FN+ $5000, #39 CGC 4.5 $3400, #40 VF $1400, #41 VF+ $1150, #42 VF/NM $1170, #52 CGC 9.0 $1375, 59 NM- $1100; *Tales To Astonish* #27 VF- $7500.

Joseph Veteri, Esq. Comic Verification Authority/ Comic Art Con

Founded in 2011, Comic Verification Authority's mission is to enable collectors, dealers, and investors with a wide range of experience levels to quickly and easily identify examples with outstanding relative eye appeal in a given certified CGC grade. CVA verification allows these premium-quality examples to be easily identified and additionally, it allows for easy recognition of these examples in an online setting, where comic books cannot be inspected in person. We have reviewed literally tens of thousands of CGC graded comics in the past two years and have identified exceptional examples across all eras. Some of these comics have since sold and set record prices in grade, demonstrating the power of the CVA verification in the market.

Some of the many record prices that were achieved on CVA stickered comics in 2013 were as follows: *Amazing Fantasy* #15 CGC 7.0 $44,555, *Sub-Mariner Comics* #17 CGC 9.0 $3,020 (just shy of double the last recorded sale), *Flash Comics* #33 CGC 8.0 $2,600 (next highest sale was $975 for a non-CVA copy in July 2011), *Detective Comics* #128 CGC 9.2 $5,322 (*Guide* price in 9.2 is $2,400), *Detective Comics* #62 CGC 5.5 $2,200 (the best previously recorded recent non-CVA-sale for a CGC 6.0 was $1,483 in August 2013), *Fantastic Four* #1 CGC 7.0 $19,750 (compared to a 12 month average sale price of $14,658 for non-CVA examples), *Fantastic Four* #3 CGC 8.5 $6,655 (another non-CVA 8.5 sold before this one for $4,510 in 2013), *Marvel Mystery* #19 CGC 9.2 $7,069, *Incredible Hulk* #1 CGC 5.5 $8,250, *Tales to Astonish* #1 CGC 8.0 $5,750, *Amazing Spider-Man* #4 CGC 7.0 $1,505, *Amazing Spider-Man* #50 9.2 $2,422, *Batman* #24 CGC 7.0 $719, *Captain Marvel Advs.* #5 CGC 8.5 $2,222, *Fantastic Four* #49 CGC 9.4 $2,702, *Marvel Mystery Comics* #34 CGC 8.5 $6,238, *Marvel Mystery Comics* #68 CGC 9.0 $2,433 and *Uncanny X-Men* #129 CGC 9.8 $625. And this is just a small sample of the hundreds of CVA stickered comics that sold this year and achieved record results for the sellers.

In every field, collectors want exceptional value for their money - the certified comic book market is no exception. Now there is an easy way to identify comic books with higher visual appeal than others assigned the same numerical grade by CGC - simply look for the CVA Exceptional sticker. If the CVA sticker is on a book, that means CVA has reviewed the book in person and has rendered an opinion that it is one of the nicest examples that one can find in that particular grade. That increases the likelihood that when the buyer receives the book, he or she will be very happy with its eye appeal. CVA stickered books have strong structure and exceptional eye appeal for the assigned grade – they are the "keepers" in your collection!

CVA provides buyers with an additional layer of protection and the ability to make a more informed decision, fostering greater confidence in the quality of their purchases. Likewise, it enables sellers of CVA verified comic books assurance and confidence in identifying these examples as being premium-quality in grade and in advertising them accordingly.

CVA's proprietary, tamper-evident holographic sticker provides assurance that the comic book you own has met our strict standards for outstanding eye appeal and superior structure within the numerical grade assigned by CGC. CVA's distinctive sticker allows collectors, dealers and investors, with any level of experience, to easily identify these premium-quality examples in any grade. A CVA endorsement adds value for anyone interested in the CGC graded comic book market, buyers and sellers alike.

CVA is delivering strong results for sellers and putting premium copies in the hands of collectors. It has been an eventful two years and we are looking forward to expanding our services in 2014 and beyond! For more information go to www.cvacomics.com.

I also am the co-founder and co-promoter of Comic Art Con, "The First Exclusive Comic Art Convention". The convention has grown since its inception in 2009 (it is held every March and September). Thanks again to all of the dealers, comic artists and attendees that have made the show a success! For more information go to www.comicartshowcase.com.

Todd Warren
Collector

What's Hot? Key issues, classic covers and movie tie-ins! What's Not? Everything else. This is a generalization, of course, but it isn't far from the truth!

I see more and more comic collectors who aren't interested in completing runs of their favorite titles, but instead target specific key or classic issues from a particular genre or era. I'm guilty of it myself as I collect primarily Golden and Silver Age super-hero keys. But this collecting mentality has created the interesting dichotomy where a small number of vintage comic books are in high demand and sell easily at strong prices, while the rest, the average, everyday issues are a tough sell in anything but high grade condition.

This observation isn't news to many readers here. Keys have always been worth more and have sold more easily. The 'classic cover' market really began to take off with the publication of the *Gerber Photo Journals*, the advent of the Internet, and the introduction of CGC graded comics (which are sealed, preventing the comic from being read but accentuating the cover). And characters rumored to be appearing in an upcoming movie have long received a boost due to the hype.

Golden Age: Superman and Batman continued their dominance of the Golden Age market in 2013 with *Action Comics* #1-23, and the *Action* war covers, *Superman* #1, *Detective Comics* #27-37, and *Batman* #1 continuing to sell quickly at strong and sometimes record setting prices.

Wonder Woman for a long time has languished behind DC's bigger heroes, Superman and Batman, but that appears to be changing. Wonder Woman's big three Golden Age keys, *All Star Comics* #8, *Sensation Comics* #1, and *Wonder Woman* #1 all have begun selling at very strong prices. Whether the renewed interest in the character is due to movie speculation or just a realization that the key books of such a major character were a bargain is open to debate, but whatever the reason, Wonder Woman is back!

©MAR

Captain America Comics is one of the hottest Golden Age titles (#3 shown)

Flash and Green Lantern also showed a slight uptick in demand during the year. *Flash Comics* #1 is showing signs of life, with several copies appearing in auctions and bringing good prices this past year. The more common *All-Flash* #1, however, consistently sells at a significant discount to *Guide*. *All-American Comics* #16 is in high demand, but is very scarce and rarely comes up for sale. *Green Lantern* #1, with its excellent cover, has also shown renewed attention this past year. I myself sold a nice restored copy and then purchased another unrestored copy for my collection.

Captain America continues to be one of the hottest Golden Age titles. *Captain America Comics* #1 has been climbing the ladder of major Golden Age keys and is a book that seems to be on everyone's wishlist. And all of the War era issues of Captain America, with their amazing covers by Alex Schomburg, continue to be in high demand.

For Captain Marvel, the early issues of *Whiz Comics* and *Captain Marvel Adventures* are good sellers and still relatively cheap in the *Guide* when compared to a character like Superman. It appears DC is trying to put the spotlight back on the character by using him in the upcoming Justice

League animated film. If he does catch on again, look out. He was once the best-selling super-hero of all, and lightning may strike twice! *Captain Marvel Adventures* #1 is an especially difficult book to find in anything above VG. Low grade copies are available, but many of them have split spines due to the lower quality paper used for that particular issue. I'll keep looking!

Besides the blue-chip super-hero titles, other hot Golden Age books include any World War II themed cover, especially Hitler covers, classic Good Girl art covers, especially those by Matt Baker, and early Archie appearances.

Golden Age Comic Sales

• *Ace Comics* #11 (1st Phantom) CGC 7.5 $3,200
• *Blue Beetle* #1 (Rockford copy) CGC 4.5 $1,100
• *Daredevil Battles Hitler* #1 CGC 5.0 $4,200
• *Four Color* #178 (1st Uncle Scrooge) CGC 8.5 $1,700
• *Green Lantern* #1 F/VF restored $3,300
• *Hit Comics* #25 (1st Kid Eternity) CGC 7.0 $1,700
• *Single Series* #20 (Classic Tarzan cover) CGC 6.0 $750

Silver Age: Marvel Silver Age keys remains super hot and sell easily, and dealers sometimes have trouble keeping them in stock. One dealer happily told me after I made a purchase, "Well, now I have to go find another one of those!" Leading the way is *Amazing Fantasy* #15, which continues to be the biggest Silver Age book in existence. Every time I think I've got a handle on pricing for this book, it goes to the next level. *Fantastic Four* #1 and *Incredible Hulk* #1 are also incredibly hot. Even lower grade copies of these books sell for big money compared to just a few years ago. *Strange Tales* #110 jumped this year on the news of a Dr. Strange movie in the works.

DC Silver Age keys appear to be a bargain when compared to their Marvel counterparts. Some of them have been hot though. *Brave and the Bold* #28 and *Showcase* #4 are trending upward on news of a Justice League of America movie.

Silver Age Comic Sales

• *Tales of Suspense* #39 VG/F $3,250
• *Tales to Astonish* #27 VG+ $2,400
• *X-Men* #1 CGC 5.0 $2,800

Restored Key Comics: I think it's time the *Overstreet Guide* adds pricing data for restored copies of the major keys. With prices continuing to climb for the most important comics, many collectors turn to restored copies as their only way to affordably acquire their 'holy grails'. For some issues such as *Batman* #1 and *Superman* #1, more than half of the copies on the CGC census are restored, so a large percentage of copies in the marketplace are currently under-represented by the *Guide*.

Pulps: I keep meeting more and more Golden Age comic collectors who are also passionate Pulp collectors. It's good to see this offshoot of the comic collecting community continuing to thrive and develop.

Pulps got a boost this year with the publication of *The Alluring Art of Margaret Brundage: Queen of Pulp Pin-up Art*, which highlights her incredible work as cover artist for *Weird Tales, Magic Carpet* and others in the 1930s and 1940s. Brundage cover Pulps continue to be amongst the hottest Pulps out there and sell quickly in all grades.

Pulp Sales

• *Magic Carpet*, Jan 1933, VG+ $300 (Brundage cover)
• *Magic Carpet*, Apr 1933, VG $300
• *Magic Carpet*, Oct 1933, VG- $400 (classic Brundage-c)
• *Magic Carpet*, Jan 1934, VG $500 (Brundage-c, 1st Red Sonya)
• *Weird Tales*, Apr 1929, G/VG, $250 (Lovecraft's *The Dunwich Horror*)
• *Weird Tales*, Nov 1932, VG/F, $450 (1st Bran Mak Morn)
• *Weird Tales*, Dec 1932, VG $1000 (1st Conan the Cimmerian)
• *Weird Tales*, Jun 1933 VG, $600 (Brundage-c, Conan story)
• *Weird Tales*, Oct 1933, VG+ $1200 (classic Brundage Batwoman-c, Conan story)
• *Weird Tales*, Sep 1934, F $500 (Brundage-c, Conan story)

Jeff Weaver
Victory Comics

We at Victory Comics are happy to provide our inaugural Overstreet market report. As an active seller online, at conventions, and in a brick and mortar store, we hope to provide you with useful observations from each of these three related, but distinct comic book marketplaces.

In so many ways there has never been a better time to be into comics. The internet and comic shows have made almost every existing book available to collectors whether they are in a big city or a small town. It's a far cry from the days of my youth in a small Vermont town, thumbing through the Robert Crestohl mimeographed mail order catalog and hunting down new comics at a local bookstore and pharmacy. Not only are vintage books more accessible than ever (the same not being true of new comics, unfortunately), the prices for many non-key, vintage books have come down substantially.

The news is full of reports of all-time high prices for key vintage books. And our experience is that there continues to be considerable upward pressure on the prices of these books, especially in high grade. Marvel keys are on fire. But this represents only a small fraction of the overall material available in the back-issue marketplace. *Amazing Fantasy* #15 seems to be going nowhere but up. But what about *Amazing Spider-Man* #84 in VG+, *Captain America* #185 in Fine or *Thor* #145 in Good? These are the type of books that constitute the broader back-issue market. For this type of non-key, Silver and Bronze Age material there is no upward pressure at all due to plentiful supply.

Does that mean the market is in trouble? I know a lot of dealers who are holding large quantities of this material who think so. But these new lower prices (which seem to have stabilized so we are not in a free fall situation whatsoever) are resulting in far more sales of vintage material. Which market is healthier: one where the item is twice as expensive but no one buys it or the one where the item costs half as much but there is active buying and selling? I'd say the latter. So now is the time for collectors to discover - or rediscover - that great vintage material at a bargain.

Lower prices are just one of the changes happening in our hobby. Everywhere you turn, what was once our niche hobby (after having been a dominant pop culture influence in the 1940s) has taken over the mainstream. Comic shows across the country collectively bring out hundreds of thousands of people. Superhero and sci-fi/fantasy dominate the big screen and even the small screen (which is ironic given that TV almost killed the comic business) with shows like *The Walking Dead* and *The Big Bang Theory*.

Below we offer some observations about how these larger forces are impacting the various sectors of the comic market: the retail brick and mortar store, the comic show, and online selling.

The Comic Store Front: It's pretty clear that the number of individual new monthly comics sold in this county will never ever approach the astronomical numbers of the Golden Age. What comic store owner doesn't just sigh when he sees *Archie* #20 from 1946 boldly emblazoned with the subheading 1,306,000 million copies printed. (Of course, books then were returnable so some percentage was never sold, but even so it's an impressive number). Today if a book sells 100,000 a month it's considered an overwhelming success. That relationship is more stark if you consider that the US population today is estimated to be over 314 million and in 1946 it was less than 142 million.

All that being said about the macro picture, new monthly comics continue to have a robust and dedicated following, and the success of comic-based movies and television demonstrate the role of comics as an inexpensive proving ground for stories and characters that can be transitioned to the screen. Unfortunately, while comics have been a great feeder of storylines for movies, the film and television arms of the media companies seem to be doing very little in a deliberate way to drive those massive movie audiences into the stores that sell the source material for these blockbuster films. For a start, the film divisions could throw the Diamond Comic Shop Locator URL up on the screen in the theaters before these movies begin.

But I digress.

Victory Comics, in its fourth year as a retail store, continues to see growth both in the number of subscribers and the number of subscriptions per subscriber. Interest in the source material for popular movies and television shows has led many people to come looking for it or material like it. Added to the existing core of long-time comic devotees, the audience for comics is more diverse than ever. That's a huge positive for the long-term health of our hobby.

Unfortunately, the availability of new comics is limited largely to those areas where the population density will sustain a brick and mortar comic store. If the current direct market had existed when I was a child there is every likelihood that I would never have seen an actual comic book while growing up. Of course comics are available by mail order but nothing captures new readers like holding and reading a book in person.

Instead of figuring out how to expose new readers to printed books, the comic companies are investing in so-called digital comics. This may give current readers a more convenient medium on which to read their comics. But in terms of bringing it new readers in any numbers it will be a dead end.

Imagine if during the rise of television the comic companies had decided to sink money into Television Comics, that is, programs featuring a comic sitting on a table with its pages slowly being turned so you the viewer could read it on TV. Even people who like comics would switch the channel if they hadn't already fallen asleep.

As ludicrous as this example sounds, it is exactly the type of reasoning that propels the digital comic experiment. The truth is that what will save comics in the face of the digital age is that same thing that saved comics during the television age. Good stories that speak to readers and that are broadly disseminated throughout the population.

Imagine instead of spending money on digital comics, the comic companies disseminated inexpensive reprint material they already own outside the direct market so it didn't compete with current books. Perhaps it could be funded in part with regional advertising directing readers to area direct market stores, new comic mail order houses, or area comic conventions. Wouldn't that make more sense than trying to entice new readers to view static sequential art on a dynamic digital device? Comics are and have always been one of the most exciting things you can do with a piece of paper. But why would someone -- not already a comic reader -- go online to read Batman comics on a platform that with new video game technology essentially lets them BE Batman?

Not a sermon, just a thought. Ok, maybe a bit of a sermon.

On a more positive side, Free Comic Book Day continues to be -- hands down -- the most successful marketing effort in the modern history of our hobby. It has become an institution and it draws huge crowds. At Victory Comics we always have the storm troopers on-hand and we love to showcase local creators. Many stores feature big-name creators very successfully. We haven't brought in the big guns yet but maybe this year. Hey, Stan, what are doing on the first Saturday in May?

Two years into it, DC's new 52 reboot continues to show itself to have been a smart move. There have been some casualties along the way but overall it has been a real success for DC and comic stores. DC also hit a home run with its lenticular covers. Everyone had fearful flashbacks of the 1990s but the covers looked great and they sold extremely well. (A shout-out goes to Chuck Rozanski of Mile High Comics who on his own sent us free copies of lenticulars we were not going to get as a result of a tragic, fatal UPS truck accident. Our thanks to Chuck.)

Marvel has had a little difficulty figuring out how to respond. The constant renumbering and re-renumbering (or is it un-renumbering?) seems not to have any long-term impact. But as we write this, the numbering is about to change again. Marvel sales are nonetheless strong at our store but DC is running with them neck and neck, whereas before the DC reboot Marvel had a clear advantage, at least in our store.

Among the independent titles, break outs continue to challenge the big boys. *Walking Dead*, *Thief of Thieves*, *Saga*, and others demonstrate the vitality of the part of the new comic marketplace.

In terms of back issues, they sell well for us due in large part to the fact that we maintain the largest selection of vintage material in the DC metro area. We have a growing cadre of back-issue buyers who visit at regular intervals because they know we are always bringing new material back from conventions. While it is harder to reach them initially, we do find that once we do, back issue buyers will travel much further to find the material they need than will new book customers.

©MAR

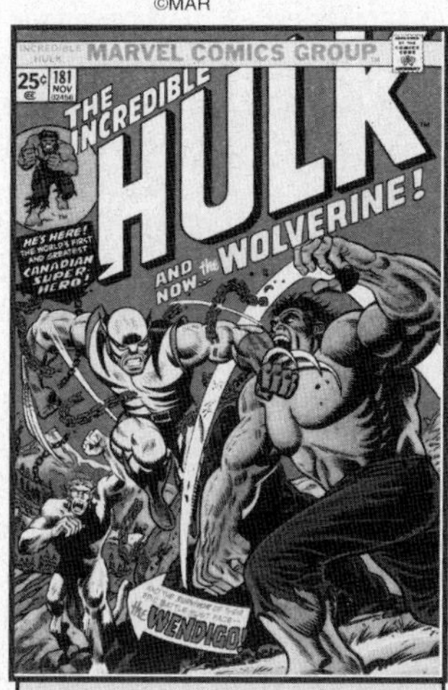

Bronze keys like **Incredible Hulk #181** sell well everywhere.

Items that consistently sell well in our retail store are modern semi-keys like *Incredible Hulk* #340, *Uncanny X-Men* #266, *Secret Wars* #8, the Miller limited *Wolverine* series and *New Mutants* #98. *Walking Dead* issues sell well. We've sold a #1 first print in our store this year, and many other early and key issues. Bronze keys are also move well: *X-Men* #94, *Giant-Size X-Men* #1, *Incredible Hulk* #181. Of course these books sell everywhere. Very recent back issues of current popular titles also do very well in the store.

Our retail store is not only an outlet for vintage books but also an incredibly important source of vintage books. This year we took in an original-owner Timely collection. It included a dozen *Captain America* and *Marvel Mystery* issues plus a smattering of non-Timely material. We also acquired a run of *Walt Disney Comics & Stories* from #1 up. We were offered a couple of very nice Silver Age collections, and an immeasurable amount of Bronze and Modern material – the vast majority of which we purchased.

The Shows: While our retail store is only 4 years old, Victory Comics has over a decade of comic show experience. Some of the most visible changes to our industry have occurred in the area of comic shows. Over the last decade the trend has been that many shows are not just about comics but instead focus on pop culture more generally,

San Diego Comic-Con, the NY Comic Con and its sister show C2E2 in Chicago, and the Wizard World shows all over the country have become mass market, pop culture extravaganzas that turn out massive crowds. It is quite incredible to be at one of these shows.

Comics are a part of these modern pop culture shows, but only a part. As a group, the attendees at these shows are far younger than the vintage comic collector community. Many are interested in comics but are not collectors in the traditional sense of the word. The overwhelming popularity of these events can result in tickets being sold out up to a year in advance.

But while the crowds are huge, the dynamic for vintage comics at these shows has changed. One phenomenon we have observed is the rise of the frequent online auctions and sites like eBay and their impact on the vintage comic show scene. At one time, the only place to see and buy vintage material was at shows. So collectors would save up for their next show and spend their entire collecting budget for six or eight months over the course of a weekend.

Now with weekly auctions being held by a number of online houses, the necessity of buying at a show has significantly declined. That means shows are often not just about making sales but about creating relationships with collectors who may buy less from you at a show than they once did but who may spend more later if you sell online. Many dealers also attend shows in order to buy material that they then can sell online or at their stores.

Here's a quick run-down on the shows I exhibited at or attended for the purpose of buying material this past year:

San Diego Comic-Con: Let's be clear. SDCC is an incredible experience. The exhibits from the big media companies, publishers and toy manufacturers are unbelievable. There are movie screenings. There are always new toys and other products being released. Many are exclusives and some are difficult to get even if you are there. (Note: Stay clear of the Hasbro booth at the opening of preview night unless you are prepared for an incredibly dangerous stampede of hundreds of fans created by the way they handle the sales of exclusives. It is completely avoidable but apparently no one in risk management has seen what goes on there.) While it is indeed impressive, it is perhaps the least comic-focused of all the comic cons.

New York Comic Con and Chicago's C2E2: Both of these shows are huge pop culture events. However, both are much more comic focused than SDCC. Vintage comic sales in New York are brisk. The crowds are intense. It's becoming, if it isn't already, the SDCC of the east. The dealer area is large and there is a wide selection of material from all eras and in all price categories despite the relatively high cost of exhibiting in the Big Apple.

C2E2 is the sister show in Chicago. While not as large as the NYCC, C2E2 is an impressive show. Parts of the show last year were very difficult to move through because of the throngs of fans. I count that as a positive. The scale of the show is more manageable than NY. C2E2 is held in the Spring at the McCormick Center. There are a lot of dealers there with material of all types, comic and non-comic.

Wizard World: Wizard World is not one show, or even two shows. It's a slew of shows across the country and the number appears to be ever increasing. The Wizard World show model is built on its long list of celebrity guests who are available for autographs and photo ops. (Shatner and I look great together by the way.) In addition to the dozens of celebrities, the Wizard shows include a busy dealer area.

The flagship show is Wizard World Chicago which is held every year near O'Hare Airport. Wizard Chicago predates C2E2 by many, many years and was the undisputed king of the Midwest shows for a long time. Recent years have shown that Chicago can successfully host two major shows and Wizard Chicago remains one of the must-attend national shows of the year.

The other show Wizard show which I attended last year was Philadelphia. It had a different feel than in past years in part due to the layout of the hall. While Wizard Philly has never been as big from a vintage comics sales standpoint as its Chicago brother, there is a strong presence by the East Coast dealer community so there is plenty of vintage material. This year we expect to increase substantially the number of Wizard shows on our schedule so next year's report will give you a broader view of the success of the Wizard expansion.

Baltimore Comic-Con: If vintage comics are your thing, you cannot miss this gem. Others may have found success moving in the Pop Culture direction but this show's success rests on its focus on comic books. In addition to an overflowing dealer room, Baltimore Comic-Con features a seemingly endless list of comic creator talent. If you want to buy vintage comics and interact with the creator community this show is worth the trip from anywhere in the country. Sales are always great here, and in part because we are only 45 miles away we traditionally have our largest display of the year at this show. This upcoming year the show is going from two days to three.

Megacon: We have exhibited at Orlando's annual spring show for the last few years. And even in that time it has gone through some changes. When I first exhibited there was a small core of vintage dealers in a sea of manga merchants. While manga, anime and the like still have a big presence at the show the number of vintage dealers has grown. Because this show is really the first of the year on the East Coast, dealers often have fresh material. Consequently, sales are generally strong here.

Other shows where one can find a wealth of vintage material include HeroesCon in North Carolina and Motor City Con outside of Detroit. I visited both this year as a buyer and had a lot of success. Both of these promoters do a great job bringing in top dealers with tons of vintage material. Finally, we attended a new Washington DC-based show called Awesome Con. If this show can grow its list of vintage dealers it may develop into a destination in future years. First year attendance was unexpectedly strong. This year the show is occupying considerably more space.

Online Selling: The impact of the internet on the vintage comic market cannot be overstated. In many ways this is the most diverse of the three comic marketplaces. It ranges from dealers selling on their own websites to those selling on eBay to the large online auction houses. The pricing adjustments we discussed above are driven substantially by the incredible quantities available 24 hours a day on the internet.

We continue to see increases in our sales overseas. Most are to English speaking countries (Canada, Australia, and the UK) but significant numbers of books are going all over Europe, Asia and Latin America.

While the internet offers opportunities for exposure, it also puts you in direct competition with sellers from around the world. So differentiating one's business and proper branding have become more and more important. EBay remains popular and has low barriers to entry. But the costs of selling on eBay and an ever- growing thicket of bureaucracy make it difficult to navigate. (I always know that I'm going to buy a collection when the owner turns down my initial offer so he can sell it himself on eBay. Two weeks is usually the length of that experiment.) We generally have 2500 to 3000 items on eBay at any given time.

What sells for us online? A little of everything. And in some cases, a lot of everything. That's its beauty. You are reaching such a large audience that there is potentially a buyer out there for anything. We have had success selling Silver and Bronze books, both keys and non-keys. We have sold Timelys, vintage Richie Rich and Archies, *Famous Monsters*, and esoteric Gold. At the end of 2013, we saw very strong worldwide sales of Silver Age runs when prices were discounted.

Because the online universe is populated with buyers who never go to a comic store or to a comic show, it makes sense that pricing patterns are different. That means it can be profitable to buy books at shows that one knows will do better online and vice versa.

Given our recent experience we expect over time that online sales will become an ever more important part of our vintage comic business.

Vincent Zurzolo, Frank Cwiklik & Rob Reynolds
Metropolis Collectibles
ComicConnect.com

Vincent Zurzolo - Metropolis Collectibles and ComicConnect.com

It is a very little known fact that in the Chinese calendar, 2013, while being the year of the snake was also the year of the vintage comic book. It's a fact, look it up. All joking aside, the comic market continues to be robust, strong and filled with aggressive activity.

Every year I espouse the strength of the comic market and it may sound like a sales pitch or propaganda but it has been the truth. The vintage comic market continues to grow and appreciate. Now, of course not every part of the market is constantly appreciating, but mainstream Golden Age, key covers, early and high grade Silver Age and a multitude of comics tied into upcoming movie projects have seen appreciation.

To give you an idea of how strong the market is, in November, a client who had never purchased a vintage comic book as an adult called my showroom, set up an appointment, came in, picked out a group of high grade Silver Age Marvels and spent over $100,000 on his first purchase. New buyers coming into the market, people who loved comics as children and young adults, have come back to the market.

Why? Their discretionary income increases, combine that with nostalgia and a realization that not only is this a fulfilling place to put one's money, it can also be very profitable.

Half of 2014 will be gone by the time you read this market report but my feeling is that it will be an excellent year for vintage comics. My prediction for this year is increased growth in the market. Specifically the Golden Age key, Silver Age Marvel and DC, almost anything tied to a movie appearance will potentially increase in value. As interest rates remain close to zero at banks and people continue to look for places to diversify, the comic market will continue to see growth from existing and new buyers will come into the market.

©Dave Sim

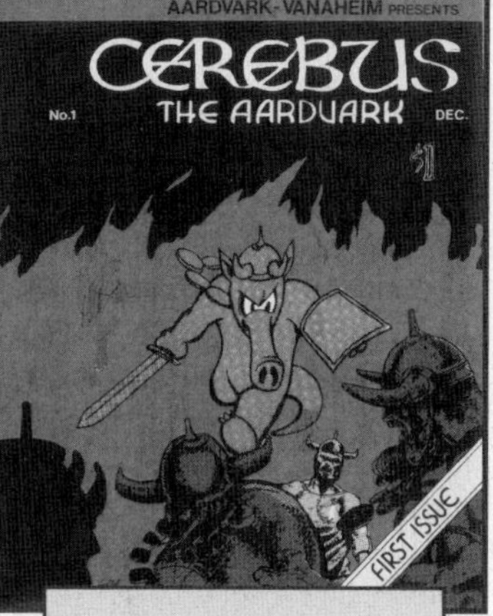

AARDVARK-VANAHEIM PRESENTS
CEREBUS
THE AARDVARK
No.1
DEC.
FIRST ISSUE

High grade Bronze is back after a recent slump (**Cerebus** #1 shown)

Through the expansion of Hollywood superhero movies the iconic American characters many of us have known all our lives will become part of the local lexicon of children, adolescents and adults in countries all over the world. As this happens it will increase the number of buyers and open people's eyes to the magnificent storytelling and artistry of vintage comics.

In the Golden Age market watch the evergreen titles like *Superman*, *Action*, *Batman*, *Detective*, *Captain America* and *Marvel Mystery*. Still under-priced, pick up as many Nedor and Better published comics as you can. Great art and fun stories. You'll love them. Golden Age *Wonder Woman*, *Sensation* and *All Star* #8 are all still under-valued and have been selling extremely well.

Silver Age Marvels continue to dominate the comic collectible/investment landscape. These characters connect to generations of collectors. Marvel's Silver Age counterparts at DC are tougher to find and when they come into the market in high grade, they get scooped up as well.

Incredible Hulk #181, *Amazing Spider-Man* #129, *House of Secrets* #92, *Green Lantern* #76, *Cerebus* #1, *X-Men* #94 and *Giant-Size X-Men* #1 are all still highly sought after. The Bronze Age market had fallen as there was a glut of high end copies hitting the market. Since then it has plateaued and is now back. As Hollywood continues to mine the mountain, watch as more Bronze Age characters hit the silver screen.

In the Copper/Modern market I think buying key issues like *Batman: The Dark Knight Returns*, *Wolverine* (mini-series), *Watchmen*, *Teenage Mutant Ninja Turtles*, *The Crow*, *The Walking Dead* and *New Mutants*, most of these close to reaching the 25-30 year old mark, will continue to grow in value.

Always present in my mind is how fortunate I am to be doing what I am doing. As a child with just a couple of quarters in my pocket drooling over the comics on the spinner rack at the local five and dime, I could never imagine my life's passion could become my career. I love comics, the art form, the stories the lessons to be taught and the fun and excitement they bring me. Thank you to all of our customers. Without you none of this would be possible.

So in closing, the more things change the more things stay the same. Isn't that how it works?

Frank Cwiklik - ComicConnect.com
A Year In The Life Of Metropolis

Every year, these reports seem to be due sooner, or at least it feels that way. And every year, time goes by faster, and as we grow our business at Metropolis and ComicConnect, expanding our client base worldwide, it gets tougher and tougher to distill a year's activity down to just a simple market report. So, instead, let's walk back through the year 2013 from our perspective and try to get a handle on the breakneck pace of change and the incredible gains made by our company specifically, and the vintage comics market in general. Overall, there is a lot to be excited about, and a lot to be proud of…

January 2013: The first month of the year always feels like a bit of a hangover. As with most retail companies, the holidays and the end of the year are a last-minute frenzy, keeping us on our toes and working around the clock. In our case, things are especially hectic with the end-of-year ComicConnect auctions, plus preparation for the coming year's convention schedule, and getting in last minute requests and sales for clientele looking to spend that year-end bonus or pick up a little holiday gift. In 2013, however, January was anything but a hangover, as we hit the ground running with great sales, ringing phones, and a buzzing web site. Just glancing one year back at the top sales for that month, the number of orders and invoices clearing over the $4000 mark is amazing, as a number of Mile High comics sold on the back of the previous year's record-breaking Church sales in our auctions.

As usual, the frenzy attending big sales records led to longterm and newer clients heating up our phone lines looking to get in on the action, while several old-school buyers we haven't heard from in some time got in touch to pick up some more esoteric material, including nearly complete runs of classic horror titles such as *Astonishing* and *Spellbound*. In fact, as in past years, diversity was the order of the day throughout the year, as collectors enticed by the rising values of the die-hard Marvel and DC Gold and Silver Keys diversified into more niche markets and "caviar" titles, from high-grade war to super-rare romance.

However, it was the pedigrees that ruled the roost as the year began. Top sales of the month included a 9.2 CGC Rockford *Detective Comics* #91; a lovely 8.0 CGC *Batman* #6; the White Mountain 9.2 CGC *House of Mystery* #2; and the River City 8.5 CGC issue 9 of the classic pre-Code horror *The Thing*. A number of Mile High copies of *Whiz Comics* also enjoyed brisk sales, and Golden Age DC mid-grades did unusually well. Mostly, though, the sales pattern became apparent in January and remained solid throughout the year: while big sales of big books were common, the majority of orders were small, reliable, unusual orders, with a surprising and revealing emphasis on late Bronze through Copper material.

Many of the new buyers entering our site were picking up small groups of 1980s *Batman*, late 1970s *Amazing Spider-Man*, late-'80s indie comics, and slabbed high-grade Marvels and DC in general under the $100 mark. In fact, the sub-$100 high-grade market was one of our best areas of growth, as new clients excited by the growing market but not yet ready or able to buy top-ticket books got their collections started with 9.8 comics from the mid '70s to late 1980s. It's an encouraging sign, as this is the next generation of comics collectors and investors, already on the prowl for good buys and smart plays, and already saving up for their first major key.

The year was off to a very auspicious start.

February 2013: And then off to London! We're delighted by the explosive growth in business to overseas clients, and I think it comes as a result of three things. Firstly, the media attention paid to our recent record sales of *Action Comics* #1, *Amazing Fantasy* #15, etc, has attracted world-wide attention, and has piqued the interest of serious, deep-pocketed buyers in other countries who are looking for unusual and stable alternative investment strategies other than the art market or antiques trade, which have grown increasingly closed-off and difficult for new buyers to penetrate.

©DIS

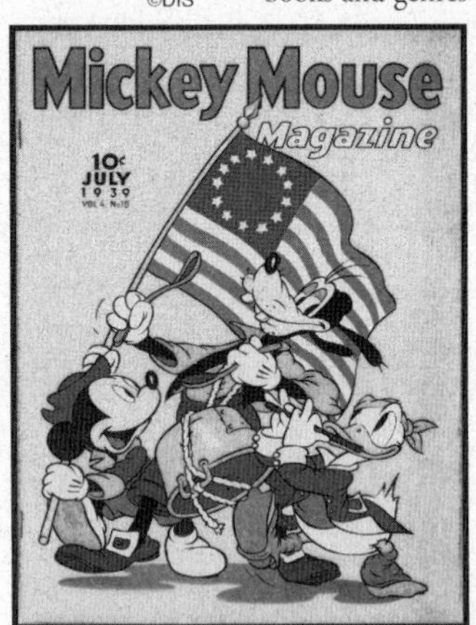

Overseas buyers snapped up copies of **Mickey Mouse Magazine** (Vol. 4 #10 shown)

Secondly, the runaway success of the Big Two publishers' movie and TV franchises has introduced European, Asian, and Middle Eastern audiences to these characters in a way the comics themselves never really could, and savvy fans hungry for ways to parlay that passion into a full-time hobby has led them to our site. Lastly, the success of the American convention model has inspired enterprenurial comics fans across the globe to copy the comic-con template in their home countries, with equal emphasis on video games and pop culture, and this has led to our visits overseas, which have been succeeding beyond expectations.

I personally was delighted to have my first chance to visit London, and as a lifelong anglophile instantly fell in love with the town, delighting in the culture, history, and most especially the instantly likeable people of the UK. The show itself, the London SuperCon, was a smash success for us, as we made sales numbers that rivaled the bigger NYC shows – a complete surprise and a very, very happy one. We were busy nonstop, and found that the buyers visiting our table were completely knowledgeable, ready to buy, eager to see our selection, and very easy to work with. Sales highlights included a GD+ *Amazing Spider-Man* #1 and an 8.0 CGC #4; a GD *Amazing Fantasy* #15; a 6.5 CGC *Captain America* #19; and a sparkling 9.0 CGC *World's Finest* #46.

Interestingly, another pattern was established with this show, where instead of the usual requests for the same keys or early Silver Age Marvels before the show, the books customers asked for were extremely wide-ranging in style and interest, and were often obscure or neglected treasures. I strongly feel that the days are over when we or other dealers can line up the same 100 or so obvious keys and chestnuts on a wall and be done with it – buyers, even new ones, are much savvier than in the past and tend to be focused on very specific, unusual, and personal collecting habits, making our job both harder (trying to guess what people will want ahead of time is way tougher) but also more fun (as long-dormant books and genres now have new life and give us chances to show off fun material that might have otherwise been forgotten!). I eagerly look forward to the 2014 London show – as of this writing (just after New Year's 2014), we already have three clients requesting material for the con!

March 2013: In like a lion, indeed – our banner sale of a splendid *Flash Comics* #1 7.0 CGC Library copy was easily the highlight of our March, as the harsh winter faded mercifully into a bright, successful Spring. A *Fantastic Four* #1 6.5 CGC also sold for $15,000 and Golden Age *Superman*, *Batman*, *Action*, and *Detective* proved suddenly very popular, as scores of low-to-higher-grade copies of WWII-era DC hero exploits did brisk business. As well, classic horror continued its stealth comeback, as high-grade issues of *Tales of the Mysterious Traveller* sold alongside some readers' grade ECs, classic Atlas pre-code horror issues, and some great L.B. Cole horror and weirdie covers, including *Terrors of the Jungle* #9 (a personal favorite). Meanwhile, Marvel keys continued their market dominance, as the brief first appearance of Wolverine, his one-panel cameo *in Incredible Hulk* #180, sold at 9.8 for the healthy sum of $3,200. The Mile High pedigree continued to attract buyers, as a wonderful

NM *Shadow Comics* V.7 #6 sold to a dedicated Church collector, and several overseas clients continued our international sales success, buying up a number of Disney Duck comics, including a 9.4 CGC *Four Color* #348. Disney comics, in fact, continue to be a silent success story for us, as we quietly rack up impressive sales numbers selling these classic Barks treasures to clients from Europe and Asia, where these stories are revered even more than in the United States.

April 2013: C2E2, the first of the big two Chicago conventions, was again a rousing success. Chicago has quickly become the preeminent convention town for us, as the Reed show, and the August Wizard con, have slowly grown over time to rival even the mighty NYC shows for attendance and sales numbers. We always look forward to visiting the Windy City, home of some of the finest restaurants in the country, and some of the nicest and most friendly people we encounter on the road. Due to illness, I was sadly unable to attend the 2013 C2E2, but our Executive Assistant, Brandon Peck, ably filled in and instantly befriended our regular clientele with his easy manner and terrific personal attention to detail.

Fantastic Four #48 9.8 CGC was easily the sales highlight of the show, which also saw sales of *Avengers* #1 7.5 CGC, *Amazing Spider-Man* #4 8.0 CGC, *Master Comics* #22 7.5 CGC, and the Gaines NM+ *Tales From the Crypt* #24. ECs in general, in fact, were very strong at this show, with several serious EC buyers adding some wonderful books to their collection, and, as with other cons, requests tended to be more varied and unusual, with more horror, romance, and second-tier Golden Age hero titles being brought in for enthusiastic clientele.

In fact, requests and pre-show sales have come to account for nearly 75% of our con sales, a complete flip from even five years ago. I have a feeling that as conventions become more focused on pop culture and what Red Letter Media call the "Celebrity Zoo" autograph alley, buyers become more selective about their time and buying habits, hitting the show early to avoid crowds and doing less browsing and more targeting buying. This creates an interesting challenge for us and other show dealers, one which may fundamentally transform the way comic sellers and buyers may do business at cons in future. We may be headed for a truly major shift in the market as a result, and while the vintage comics business on the whole is extremely healthy and growing rapidly, the long-time status of comic cons as the central buying venue may be phasing out in favor of online sales and the auction model, and what will replace it at cons is yet to be seen. Interesting times.

May 2013: I've been evangelizing for years about the relatively undervalued Golden Age *Wonder Woman* run, and *Wonder Woman* keys and high-grades in general. Out of any major hero series of the Golden Age, *WW* and *Sensation* are far and away the scarcest and toughest to complete, with some issues remaining in numbers of less than 200.

My predictions came to fruition in May of 2013, as a 9.0 *All Star Comics* #8 sold for the eye-watering price of $115,000, proving that the value of key issues starring the Amazon princess are rapidly on the up and up, as savvy investors swoop in on these issues in anticipation of DC's aggressive rebranding and remarketing of the character as they pump up their movie and TV franchises. ECs also continued their incredible comeback, as high-grade Gaines copies flew off the shelves by the score to dedicated collectors, and new buyers who completed their Silver and Golden key runs hungrily searched for new territory to conquer.

The NM Mile High *Whiz* #22 continued the pedigree streak, as well as Northford, White Mountain, and River City copies of classic horror titles such as *Astonishing*, *Marvel Tales*, *Suspense*, and the *Wings* Church-Mile High 9.6 #19.

June 2013: Wizard's forays into the NYC market continued with their 2013 Wizard NYC ComicCon, at which Marvel keys once again ruled the roost, as an *Amazing Fantasy* #15 3.5 sold for $8,700, an amazing sum for a book that sold in the same grade only two years prior for $5,500! *AF* #15 is one of the few bulletproof books on the market and it goes without saying that it continues to be the most popular comic we display at cons, without fail. The Wizard NYC con also saw the sales of an *Amazing Spider-Man* #1 VG, the 9.4 CGC Bethlehem copy of *Spook* #24, and a *Journey Into Mystery* #83 5.5 CGC.

Once again, the Church/Mile High pedigree ruled the roost in online sales, with the sale of a *Shadow Comics* Vol 1 #2 NM- selling for over $15,000. Disneys also remained strong, as overseas clients snapped up rare *Mickey Mouse Magazines* and high-grade Duck titles. Overall, we spent much of our time ramping up to…

July 2013: San Diego! This show has become the centerpiece of the year, as so much energy, time and resources are dedicated to preparing for easily the biggest, most expansive con on the planet. I personally look forward to getting to spend a week each year visiting friends and spending time in one of the prettiest cities on the West Coast, and marveling at the small army of volunteers required to corral the nearly quarter-of-a-million fans who descend on this town every year. I've come to know the city rather well, and have many friends there, so it's becoming almost a second home for me, making the time spent there not only memorable from a working perspective, but as a chance to recharge the batteries and get pumped for selling comics all over again!

This year's show proved the massive and rapid changes on the convention template caused by the success of comics throughout media – rather than a steady stream of comics buyers keeping the booth crowded, we experiences flurries of activity, as buyers hit the booth early to get their specific wants filled, leaving the rest of the day open for new faces and new fans for whom this may have been their first chance at seeing such rare keys and treasures up close and in person. As a result, while business was strong, it was less a parade of big key sales and more a flurry of requests and pre-sales, all esoteric, unusual, and wonderfully varied material, from under $100 apiece to five-figure rarities, all brought for an increasingly sophisticated and discerning clientele who knew exactly what they wanted and were ready to go.

That's not to say we didn't have some fantastic sales at the show. *Amazing Fantasy* #15 continued to amaze, as a 4.5 CGC sold for $10,000 (again, for comparison, a copy in the same grade sold at the 2009 SDCC for $5,900), as well as a raw GD/VG (the copy seen on TV's *Pawn Stars*, in fact, which is kind of cool). As usual, *Wonder Woman* was very popular with savvy buyers (we have sold at least one *WW* key or high grade at every SDCC I've attended), as the 9.4 CGC Mile High *Wonder Woman* #21 sold for $4,400, as did the 9.4 CGC *Sensation Comics* #7 and the NM San Francisco *Sensation* #60. Other key sales included an *X-Men* #1 in 7.5 CGC for $9250, a *Giant-Size X-Men* #1 9.8 CGC for $5,900, and an *Amazing Spider-Man* #121 9.8 CGC for $3,000. Disneys and ECs again proved their staying power, including the 9.6 CGC Gaines copy of *Weird Fantasy* #12.

August 2013: And then came Wizard World Chicago, which always used to seem like the afterparty to San Diego's big blowout, but is now a formidable juggernaut in its own right. Again, Chicago has become one of my favorite cities, and I'm always happy to have an excuse to visit. In addition, the tight-knit little village that Rosemont becomes when the con is in town makes for a wonderful clubhouse atmosphere that makes this one of the friendliest and most relaxing of shows, a real treat after the nonstop blitz of San Diego. The show this year was moved to the opposite end of the hall due to construction, and while the Wizard staff did their best to make the transition painless, it'll be nice to be back in the front hall next year.

As always, the Chicago summer show was a great place for buyers looking for awesome keys and rarities at reasonable grades and prices. As a result, we did well with *Avengers* #1 G/VG and 7.0 CGC, *Daredevil* #1 VG, *Fantastic Four* #48 9.4 CGC, and *Incredible Hulk* #181 9.4 CGC. Golden Age *Batman* were also strong, including a *Batman* #6 8.0 CGC selling for $3600, and a FN *Detective Comics* #48 was representative of the solid, mid-level sales of Golden Age in general that helped raise the numbers for this show and make for another banner year. Requests were once again the bulk of the show, and customers were on the prowl for everything from high-grade Silver Age *Superman* to romance comics to mid-grade pre-hero Atlas titles.

September 2013: Hello Baltimore! We've heard for years about the Baltimore ComicCon, and how it's quickly become one of the destination shows of the year, and we figured it was high time to check it out for ourselves – and boy are we glad we did! It's a terrific, old-school comic show, with eager buyers, full of comic dealers, great fun, and very well run. We had a very successful first year, anchored by sales of an *Amazing Fantasy* #15 VG- for $8250 (seriously, this book just doesn't stop), a *Strange Tales* #101 9.4 CGC for $10,500, and a beautiful restored *Flash Comics* #1 in VF for $12,800. Mile High *Police Comics* also proved popular in B-More, as did pedigrees in general, Timely Caps, and, a favorite of mine, several romance cheesecake covers, including the VF- file copy of *Personal Love* #21 and the ever-popular *Torchy* #1, which also sold in VF- condition. We will definitely be back for the next Baltimore show, considering the rock-solid results of this first outing!

October 2013: If the San Diego con is the Summer monster, then the great beast of the Autumn season must be New York Comic Con, easily the second-biggest comic convention of the year. As usual, tens of thousands descended on the west side of Manhattan for the pop culture event of the season, and, as usual, we were swamped with requests for material from clients. In past years, this show has been overwhelming and exhausting, but the good folks at Reed seem to have gotten the crowd control and floor layout down to an art form, making the 2013 outing one of the most enjoyable and memorable yet.

Unlike past shows, this year's NYCC was less about home-run keys and more a steady and healthy procession of requests, sales to folks filling in their want lists, and unusual sales of more esoteric material. A very strong show, it was full of one-of-a-kind sales like the 9.0 CGC *Amazing Mystery Funnies* V.2 #3 file copy, which sold for $3,000, the Mile High *Bill Barnes* #2 in NM, which sold for $3,000, the classic *Famous Funnies* #210, which sold in 9.0 CGC condition for $1,725, and, of course, a copy of the ubiquitous *Amazing Fantasy* #15 sold in GD- condition for $4,000.

The remainder of our Javits sales were of collectors' material, including Fiction House, pre-hero Atlas, Fawcetts, MLJs, etc. Again, it's interesting that even at the second-biggest show of the year, the sales are no longer about just the top 20 keys, but rarer, more obscure titles and classic Golden and Silver Age rarities, and especially at this show, we noticed that people stopping to buy had much deeper and more varied knowledge of comics history than in years past.

October also saw the sale of an *Amazing Fantasy* #15 7.5 CGC for $65,000 to a new client who, excited by the recent growth of big-ticket books, was actively moving out of other collectibles and into comics. We've had several such new clients join our customer base over the past year, serious investors who are burnt out on other alternative investments, scared off by the regulations and fluctuations of the stock market, and excited by the growth potential of the still-new comics investment field. All of these new clients give me boundless optimism for the future of our hobby, and I am pleased to report that all of these new buyers come armed with data, knowledge, and willingness to learn about the history of the medium, and an eagerness to dive deeper than the obvious top keys. Very healthy signs indeed.

November 2013: The sale of an *All-Star* #7 9.2 Mile High pedigree capped off the continuing resurgence of this esteemed pedigree. In fact, the two constants of the year are the return of the pedigree in importance to buyers, and the continuing growth of interest in non-DC and Marvel vintage comics and genre series. The sale of a *Teenage Mutant Ninja Turtles* #1 in 9.4 CGC for $5,250 was an indicator of how popular this series remained, and of the next frontier in vintage comics collecting, namely the Copper Age rarities such as the early *Turtles* issues, *Cerebus*, *Nexus*, and the like.

As readers who came of age during the indie explosion of the early 1980s enter the market with disposable income and an interest in investing, they are likely to be attracted to these comics, which are their equivalents of *Action* #1 or *Detective* #27. Also of note is the sudden influence of gaming on recent sales spikes, as the announcement of Black Mask in the recent Arkham Origins game led to a sudden and unexpected flurry of demand for his premiere appearances in *Batman* #386 and #387 and for prices of those issues in high grade to go as high as ten times *Guide* practically overnight. As gaming has become the most popular and profitable entertainment medium in the world, it will be interesting to see if there are any further influences from hero gaming on the key issue market. (And, if you haven't yet played any of the Arkham games, they may be the best portrayal of the Batman universe in any non-comics medium to date, play them immediately!)

Of course, movies continue to drive key issue prices. The announcement of *Guardians of the Galaxy* movie, and the *Age of Ultron* storyline in the next *Avengers* movie, have led to a feeding frenzy for key appearances of those characters and story arcs, and the confirmation of the Rhino and Electro as the next *Spider-Man* movie villains have led to those debuts flying out of inventory as fast as we can stock them. I expect this trend to continue, as Marvel and DC squeeze every property they can into their respective movie and TV projects, and more and more previously moribund keys may pop as a result. In short, keep an eye on the pages of Variety for the next comic buying trends…!

December 2013: Another visit from another client interested in moving into comics investment led to another fine sale of an *Amazing Fantasy* #15, this time a 5.0 CGC for $15,000. By year's end, it was apparent that there was no one who wasn't aware of how far Metro had helped take the market into the mainstream. Where once I would have to explain what I do all day when asked what I do for a living, now people immediately mention seeing a report on the news about an *Action* #1, or a segment on the morning news we shot at a convention, or a viral news story about record-breaking comic prices that showed up on their Facebook page. Where once we'd have to explain why and how people are buying and selling comics as an investment, now people come to us armed for bear and ready to buy and sell.

We closed out our year of pedigrees with more Mile High sales, including issues of *Top-Notch* and *Blue Beetle*, and a Crowley 8.5 CGC copy of *Suspense Comics* #1 at $5300. We also wrapped up a year of terrific sales by finding a home for Superman #4 8.5 CGC at $9250, and continued a trend of selling high-grade *Avengers* as fast as we can get them into stock – in fact, the *Avengers* may be the turn-around title of the year, as issues that lay dormant for years sprang back to life as Marvel's *Avengers* movies continue to gain popularity and break box office records.

I expect that, when next year rolls around, I will once again be surprised to see another market report is due and will think to myself, wait, didn't I just do one of these, like, three days ago? The good news is that time is flying because we are having fun – we get to bring this big, childlike, wondrous grin to faces every day matching up passionate collectors with their dream comics, and in doing so, make the collecting and buying of vintage comics legitimate and respected in the eyes of the greater public. Over the next year, we will be aggressively expanding our business worldwide, adding more shows overseas and targeting more non-US clientele. We'll also be expanding our want list capabilities, working harder on matching up buyers with their grails and sought-after rarities, and working on making our customer service even more personalized and direct than even before. It's a truly exciting time to be in the comic collecting hobby – we're glad you're with us.

©MAR

High grade **Avengers** sell as fast as they go into stock. (#3 shown)

Robert Reynolds - ComicConnect.com

As usual, Golden Age comics were the strongest of both our auctions and our marketplace. We saw dramatic increases in every key and strong pushes in the values of lesser titles as Silver Age buyers graduated to the Golden Age. DC titles stayed strong while Timelys saw huge increases across the board. Centaurs and Fiction House titles also enjoyed a strong following of collectors and corresponding prices.

Golden Age: Church was the first and last name of the 2013 ComicConnect auction season. The world's best pedigree collection found a new home in the ComicConnect Event Auctions. We sold over 300 Church copies in our four *Event Auctions* with nearly 200 of those for over $1,000 each. Collectors and investors flocked to runs of *Action Comics*, *Adventures into the Unknown*, *Blackhawk*, *Blue Bolt*, *Crack Comics*, *Magic Comics*, *Rangers Comics*, *Shadow Comics*, and the rarely offered *Young King Cole*. With the success of the Church copies in our auctions, we expect much more of the same in 2014 as smart consignors know, no other auction house comes close to the numbers we've achieved with the pedigree.

Top 2013 Edgar Church Copy Sales: *Action Comics* #81 CGC 9.8 $9,300, *Action Comics* #96 CGC 9.8 $11,801, *All Star Comics* #7 CGC 9.2 $16,000, *Amazing Mystery Funnies* V2 #2 CGC 9.4 $12,900, *Blue Beetle* #2 CGC 9.0 $8,900, *Blue Beetle* #3 CGC 9.2 $9,100, *Exciting Comics* #60 CGC 9.8 $11,785, *Flash Comics* #3 CGC 9.6 $17,500, *Flash Comics* #4 CGC 9.4 $11,100, *Funny Pages* V.3 #7 CGC 9.2 $12,066, *Green Hornet Comics* #24 CGC 9.4 $8,622, *National Comics* #2 CGC 9.6 $8,300, *Shadow Comics* # # CGC 9.6 $7,911, *Silver Streak Comics* #5 CGC 9.0 $9,300, *Sure-Fire Comics* #1 CGC 9.2 $7,400, *Thrilling Comics* #44 CGC 9.4 $14,700, and *Wonder Woman* #10 CGC 9.2 $7,001.

Our auctions set Golden Age records throughout the year. In June, we sold a copy of *Action Comics* #1 CGC 1.5 for $175,000 that caught the attention of the world's press. The world's most important comic was found in the wall of a home that was in the process of gut-renovation. The story appeared on NBC's *Today Show*, in *USA Today*, Yahoo, Reuters, the UK's *Daily Mail* and dozens of other news sites and blogs. In our December Event Auction, we set records with *Captain America Comics* #1 CGC 1.5 $26,499 and *Archie Comics* #1 CGC 1.0 surprised everyone with a $13,204 hammer price.

©DC

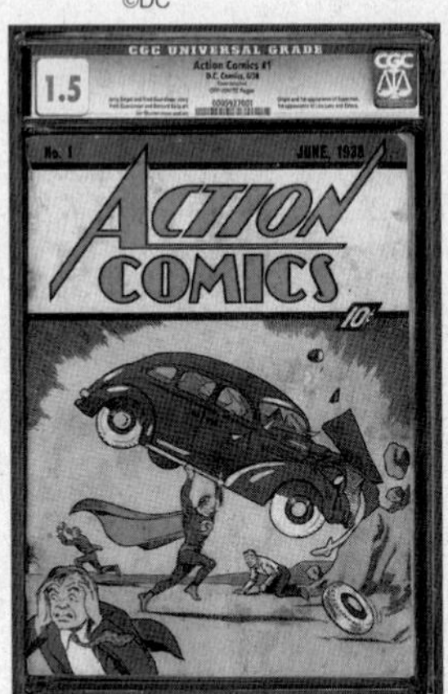

This CGC-graded 1.5 issue of **Action Comics #1** sold for a new record in that grade.

Top 2013 Golden Age Sales: *Action Comics* #1 CGC 1.5 $175,000 (record price), #1 CGC 2.0 R $77,333, #10 CGC 3.0 $30,500, *All Select Comics* #1 CGC 8.5 $14,000, *Archie Comics* #1 CGC 1.0 $13,204, *Batman* #1 CGC 7.0 $119,013 (record price), #1 CGC 1.8 $27,500, *Captain America Comics* #1 CGC 9.2 $306,050, #1 CGC 7.0 $94,000 (record price), #15 CGC 9.4 $13,000, *Detective Comics* #35 CGC 7.5 $63,100 (record price), *Flash Comics* #1 CGC 9.0 $147,000, *Sensation Comics* #1 CGC 4.5 $13,700, Superman #1 CGC 8.0 R $37,000, #2 CGC 9.2 $94,000 (record price), *Terrific Comics* #5 CGC 8.0 $13,533, and *USA Comics* #11 CGC 9.2 $12,777.

Silver Age and Bronze Age: Big growth came from the speculative nature of collectors and the impending release of movies based on comic books. First appearances from Dr. Strange, the Guardians of the Galaxy, Ant-Man, Electro, and many more garnered attention and high prices in the auction. We expect more of the same in 2014.

Top 2013 Silver, Bronze and Modern Sales: *Amazing Fantasy* #15 CGC 7.5 $57,500, *Amazing Spider-Man* #1 CGC 9.4 $93,964, #3 CGC 9.6 $39,500, #9 CGC 9.8 $58,000 (record price), *Brave and the Bold* #28 CGC 8.5 $45,504, #28 CGC 8.5 $40,500, *Fantastic Four* #1 CGC 8.5 $60,000, #5 CGC 9.2 $22,800, #50 CGC 9.8 $44,007 Northland (record price), *Journey into Mystery* #83 CGC 9.4 $171,000, *Showcase* #4 CGC 8.0 $29,300, *Tales of Suspense* #39 CGC 9.6 $260,000, #39 CGC 9.0 $24,944, *Tales to Astonish* #27 CGC 9.0 $40,000, #35 CGC 9.2 $29,000, *Teenage Mutant Ninja Turtles* #1 CGC 9.8 $13,088, and *X-Men* #1 CGC 9.0 $23,100.

Original Art: The original comic book art and memorabilia section has grown from 30 pieces just a couple of years ago to nearly 300 lots in every auction. The cover to *Avengers* #56 by John Buscema and Frank Giacoia sold for $53,000 in the June Auction while the splash page to Silver Surfer by Buscema and Dan Adkins hit $21,500. The cover to *Marvel Team-Up* #25 by Gil Kane, John Romita and Giacoia hammered for $13,200. Two Alex Ross paintings, the cover to the *History of the DC Universe* trade paperback sold for $19,200 and a *Marvels* splash featuring the Silver Surfer and Galactus went for a high bid of $8,600. The classic Neal Adams cover to Superman #213 hit $10,055 and the cover to *World's Finest* #182 by Adams and Swan sold at auction for $11,201.

Collectors and investors spent more money in the 2013 ComicConnect auctions than ever before. Our quarterly Event Auctions achieved sales in the eight figures, a first for our company, while our Comic Book Marketplace boasts nearly 70,000 listings that amass hundreds of offers daily. The Event Auctions come complete with 120 page full color catalogs, sent to all of our very best buyers, and we never charge a buyer's premium. Sales have tripled since I joined the ComicConnect team in 2009 and I'm proud to be a part of the greatest auction house on the planet. Our three current Guinness World Records speak for themselves.

Still, we have so much more to do for our clients. Day in and out, we match up the world's best comics with the world's best buyers. To do so, I send hundreds of thousands of e-mails and make thousands of phone calls every year. In 2013, I travelled all throughout the United States, logged thousands of airline miles and nearly 100 hours of driving time to bring amazing collections back to our New York City gallery to prepare for our auctions.

At ComicConnect, Event Auctions come every three months so we're always asking "What's next?" The new ComicConnect website was totally revamped and is running better than ever. Our expanded auction schedule met increased client demand and we are also adding several new cities to our convention schedule. 2014 is shaping up to be the best yet. I'd like to thank every buyer, bidder, and consignor I've had the pleasure of assisting with their collections. We try very hard to make every client truly pleased and I'm grateful for the opportunity to be of service.

THE WAR REPORT

by Matt Ballesteros & the War Correspondents
Andy Greenham and Mick Rabin

It is our pleasure to present the now sixth publication of the War Report, produced annually and included as a special excerpt within each year's *Overstreet Comic Book Price Guide*. If you are a returning reader, thanks for your interest and continued support! If you are new to this sector of the *Price Guide*, allow me to explain the intention behind this annual submission. The War Report was born out of the necessity to answer, for ourselves and myriad inquiring enthusiasts, age old inquiries about the War comic niche—especially as they related to key issues, important characters, storylines, artwork, and of course to the skilled creative talent behind War comics themselves. It goes without saying that we also sought clarity regarding any given War comic's importance in the market, its ranking amongst its peers, and of course its potential long and/or short term value. All-in-all the War Report is a compilation of our personal opinions on the War comic market and the individual comics that make up the genre. We hope you enjoy it.

This report would not be what it is without the selfless contributions of my returning colleagues in arms, whom I fondly refer to as the War Correspondents. This year I am supported by the veteran contributors and War comic aficionados and luminaries Andy Greenham and Mick Rabin. Not only are these men constantly invaluable to me year end and year out, but they offer anyone their well rounded comic book wisdom and prowess through their discussions on CGC forums' "War Comic" thread. If you think this report is helpful, you will find reams of War comic intelligence on the CGC War forum, along with countless regulars who would be more than happy to assist you with any genre specific query. If you are new to the segment, I urge you to visit the thread and get yourself a wealth of invaluable information.

As it usually does, the War Report not only discusses base market events, spotlights particular issues, and forecasts potential values, but it also includes special ops reports on lesser known or more cryptic War-book-related matters. If you are a burgeoning War collector, I urge you to get your hands on previous copies of the *Overstreet Price Guide*, as each year we take the time to zero in on specific one-of-a-kind issues that we strongly believe have made or will make an impact. Not to mention, each report includes expositions on potentially lesser known, but meaningfully important War comic topics that may affect what you might want to collect, sell, and especially read. Finally, be sure to make use of our now refined comic book rankings that we originally developed some seven years ago after carefully making inventory of every kind of War comic we could unearth (for a short summary of how we came to catalogue and then rank War comics, read ***Definition of a "War Comic" Briefly Revisited*** directly below).

In short, we hope you enjoy this year's dispatch and, as always, we welcome your feedback on any part of our findings or viewpoints. Enjoy!

Definition of a "War Book" Briefly Revisited

If you want an in-depth look at our comprehensive classification process, I encourage you to pick up a copy of the *Overstreet Price Guide*, issues #39 or #40, or you can visit www.warcomicreport.com for more details. However, to provide a base foundation to our model, the following is our classification of a "War comic": After cataloging hundreds of War comic titles that we cross referenced both against this Guide and other comic book publications…

• We characterized War comics as "Stories centered on the military, which is involved in major armed conflicts" (*i.e., no cold war, police actions, spy stories, etc.*).

• We eliminated war stories with super-heroes *(by employing the notion that "a war story with a superhero is by definition a 'fantasy' story")*.

• We defined classifications for specific war themes. We selected "War Battle Tales" (*i.e., stories that were predominantly centered on characters engulfed in battle)*. Therefore, at this time, we purged classifications such as War Adventure, War Propaganda, and Tragedy in Wartime, etc.

© DC

• We categorized two main comic book ages:
The Golden Age and The Atom/Silver/Bronze Age *(Although there were certainly countless titles launched during the Atom and Silver age respectively, the two ages in the War category are inextricably meshed. With many Silver Age mammoths getting their start in the Atom Age and blossoming into and throughout the lifespan of the Silver Age. Conversely, our categorization also lumps Bronze into our Atom and Silver classifications for roughly the same reasons. The Bronze Age, though containing highly notable titles, was primarily begat from Silver Age titles.*

Nevertheless, we may otherwise separate these age taxonomies in years to come if the need arises).

News from the Front - Attrition

Much like the trench warfare of World War I, the War comic market has dug in. Although there have been some notable transactions and the unearthing of semi-occasional high-grade War comics in the last 12 months, it has been a fairly desolate battlefield. It's not that anything has really lost ground; there are just few skirmishes to report on. Consequently, this begs the question, why has the momentum in this genre flagged? The correspondents discussed this issue at length. Is this a sign of a weakening market? Are there fewer War comic collectors? Are there too many books saturating the market? In short, we concluded that the answer to all of these questions is: none of the above.

First, the market remains strong. Watching sales throughout 2013 and 2014 we witnessed that nearly all, excepting a few War comics, are retaining their value. Further, if it's a key book, it continues to appreciate boldly in value. Second, while admittedly the number of actual War comic collectors is hard to precisely quantify, but upon our review of the known facts about the pool of existing enthusiasts, we don't believe that there has been much change in the total number of interested collectors. For those few who may have left to pursue other collecting ventures, they have been replaced by new recruits—essentially the fresh rank and file who may be interested in an enduring and healthy non-superhero genre. Lastly, it is also our opinion that it's not a matter of oversaturation either, at least not in the mid-to-high-grade realm. Yes, abundant low grade War comics inundate most online channels, but that is just not the case when it comes to the aforementioned mid-to-high-grade copies; particularly high-grade keys (see rankings below in this report) which, in most cases, continue to sell for greater dollar values than previously recorded. In sum, it appears that the matter of a "quiet front" stems from the overwhelming lack of high-grade War comics overall.

If you are a returning reader, I am sure you are aware that we have now said this a couple of times in recent reports (I apologize for the inadvertent repetition); however, the difference here is that we have not seen a shortage of this magnitude over the last decade, or since War comics came to their current limelight. Trolling retail outlets, online stores, and auction houses is producing scant copies, and of these, very, very few keys. Consequently, we believe that this is a direct result of collectors actually hanging on to their War comics with fervor. You see, unlike a good number of super-hero comics (which we also collect by the way), there are few high grade copies on census. So it only stands to reason that equally fewer raw copies exist tucked away somewhere in someone's collection. Thus, the notion of actually selling your high grade War comic with the hope of replacing it one day now transcends financial factors. The hard reality is that there just may be no other copy like it (period). It likely means the expenditure of great effort to retrieve the same issue again, or worse, facing the likelihood you might never own it again. A terrifying thought for any kind of comic book collector!

Understanding the current paradigm of a landscape devoid of high-grade War comics, we also contemplated the scenario of a collection suddenly hitting the market. Nothing like that has happened in the last few years, but it would be interesting to see how the current market might respond—particularly if scarce, high-grade keys became available, that even "non-War" collectors would be interested in snapping up. Being connected to the War comic collecting community, we have the advantage of knowing where most of the rather robust War comic collections reside. While few such collections exist (and none that we believe will be imminently unleashed into the world anytime soon, it is always an intriguing thought to consider what percentage of general comic collectors might be enticed to the genre should an event like this were to take place? While we continue to reflect on that, I assure you that most of us long term War comic collectors are appreciating the serenity.

With War comics potentially being out of sight and out of mind, hardcore War comic collectors may have less competition to contend with. Something that we don't mind and I assure you something that will be appreciated for as long or as short as the tranquility lasts.

Battlefield Ops - Can a soldier walk amongst supermen?

Here's a concept that needs to be considered. Can or should *Our Army at War* #83 (featuring the first true appearance of Sgt. Rock) make Overstreet's Top 20 Silver Age Comics list? Our personal bias aside, we truly believe it should. We understand and respect Robert Overstreet's careful deliberations when it comes to modifying his lineup. Clearly, he can make no abrupt moves when a particular comic book suddenly becomes hot. The test, I am sure—in his eyes is sustained durability, i.e., whether a comic's ranking and importance can stand the test of time. In this case however, we are now talking about a comic book that has been definitively in the high profile spotlight since the early '90s and recently searing its previous annual sales figures with each concurrent year for at least half a decade now.

In short, our unwavering belief is that this specific issue has attained more defined stature as it continues to garner larger general collector interest and, of course, higher dollar values. When looking at it for depth, you couldn't ask for more. It is "the" pinnacle War comic to own. *Our Army at War* #83 features the first true appearance of a very important iconic character to both the comic book industry and to pop culture, it (he) was originated by some of the most respected creators of the industry, AND it is highly sought after by both War and non-War comic collectors. In short, it is a pedigree comic book worthy of a status such as making the Top 20 list. If the above isn't satisfactory enough, look back at our previous reports for annual accounts of high dollar sales of the comic or consider the smattering of recent sales that substantiate our claim. For instance, among other

Our Army at War #83 copies sold in the last 12 months, here's an example of a few sales we witnessed since our last report:

A raw 2.0 went for nearly $700.
A CGC 3.0 went for about $1000.
A CGC 4.0 went for $1800.
A CGC 6.0 went for over $4,000.

Compare these sales figures to say *Fantastic Four* #2 and *Fantastic Four* #4 (which are ranked #19 and #20 respectively in the Overstreet Top 20 Silver Age Books). It can be conservatively said that both these comics are fetching merely $4000 apiece for copies in CGC 8.0, as compared to *OAAW* #83 which is reaping the same exact dollar figures for much lesser grades (such as CGC 6.0s). Certainly, *OAAW#* 83 can go toe-to-toe with these two super-hero team examples. Moreover, considering that the last sale of *OAAW* #83 in CGC 8.0 went for nearly $17,000 three years ago, you might even ponder if it could take on venerable Top 20 listers such as *Flash* #105 and *Showcase* #8.

Can Sgt. Rock finally take his place amongst the ranks of super-hero books? We certainly believe he deserves it. Who knows, maybe he makes it into the Top 20 in this very Guide… or perhaps in next year's publication. Time will tell. Nevertheless, we strongly believe that THE first non-superhero, a soldier, will be invading the Top 20 list very soon!

A Feat of Valor (A War Comic Collecting Account by Andy Greenham)

It amazes me every year how fast time flies. Another year has passed and I find myself putting a bit of my thoughts, opinions, and experience into another War Report. Again, I'd like to thank Matt Ballesteros for considering me and giving me this opportunity to share with our beloved Overstreet readers.

I think I was probably 8 years old when I started collecting comic books. It all began in the same way that many kids' comic collections begin, by simply falling in love with comics. My dad owned a coin shop and next door was a used book store. They used to sell old comic books and I would go there whenever I had some money and buy what I thought was neat. I loved DC Horror and Mystery, anything 10 cent or 12 cent covers, and DC War. The Flash and the Incredible Hulk were also some of my favorites, but what really captivated me were Sgt. Rock and the Unknown Soldier. I always felt that those two guys had the greatest stories and fabulous art, and they kept a kid like me just always wanting more.

In 1994-95, something monumental happened. Chris Pedrin released a book called *Chris Pedrin's Big Five Information Guide*. I picked up a copy and was hooked. This book was all about DC War and I just stumbled on a gold mine! I distinctly recall thinking to myself "Finally, I know what I want to focus on! DC War!!" I remember reading and re-reading this guide over and over again. In fact, I can still read it again and enjoy it just as much as I did the first time. I remember Chris mentioning that the early DC War books were tough in grade at VF or above, and I noted his price guide portion. He said that the books were truly undervalued, and I agreed with him. After all, it made a lot of sense. The war stories were, for the most part, extremely well-written, and extremely well-drawn. When a kid picked one up, he was drawn in, and hooked. War books are tough to find in high grade because people would read them and re-read them. Then they would trade them with their friends for other War books. You can tell when a book is well-done and enjoyed greatly, just by looking at the poor shape of them. This was typical for War books—always in rough shape, rarely in high grade.

Immediately after that book came out, I was going to the local shops and traveling to conventions looking for deals. I was fortunate because I had just received a small inheritance and even though it wasn't a lot of money, I was able to purchase quite a lot of books. I tried to buy whatever I could afford, and I stayed away from the dinosaur issues. They were very pricey back then, and all I was trying to do was go for quantity. I was picking up one of each issue, and not really being concerned about the grade.

Then, I decided to set my goal, to complete the whole Big Five. For those of you that don't know, the Big Five consists of the 5 major War titles that DC put out. They are:

• *All American Men Of War* (118 issues)
• *G.I. Combat* (245 issues)
• *Our Army At War* (422 issues)(#s 301 to 422 are titled *Sgt. Rock*)
• *Our Fighting Forces* (181 issues)
• *Star Spangled War Stories* (269 issues)(#s 205-268 are titled *Unknown Soldier*)

– *AAMOW, GIC, OAAW, OFF*, and *SSWS* for short.

Not only did I decide to try to get one copy of every one of these books, but I also decided that I wanted them in nice grade as well. It was extremely tough finding these books in grade and I realized that fairly early on. I was trying to get all books in VF or better, but early War books (10 centers) didn't seem to exist in that kind of high grade. I would go to a comic show and pick up just one or two comics, if I was lucky. How in the world was I going to accomplish my goal if I can only find one book here, one book there? Patience is a virtue, but that was just too slow to bear. I decided to not be so picky with grades. If I found a copy, and I could afford it, I would pick it up. As long as the cover was attached, and I didn't have it, it would be mine. This was much more fun! I was adding books to my collection left and right. When I got a new group of DC War books, I would immediately pull out my Pedrin book and highlight them, indicating that I've already bought them. This book, I took to every convention, and opened and closed it so often that I've had to tape it together numerous times.

In September of 2007, I did it! I picked up every issue of the Big Five. 1235 books, all highlighted and sitting in their appropriate long boxes and CGC boxes. It was an amazing feeling of accomplishment and one that I am still very proud of today. For those interested, the last book that made my collection complete was *Our Army at War* #11. The second-last book for me was *Our Army at War* #12. As an aside, I also had the full run of *Weird War Tales*.

You're probably going to think I was out of my mind, but pretty much immediately after I completed my first run of the Big Five, I started out to put together a second run! On January 2nd, 2009, I accomplished the unthinkable. I did it again. I assembled two complete runs of these 5 DC war titles, 1235 books per run. The final book to complete this second set was *Star Spangled War Stories* #5. And while I was still very proud to achieve this second goal, I did feel that the first set was harder to put together than the second. So, why did I do it? I don't know. Collectors are strange people. Sometimes there is no answer to the question 'why.' You collectors reading this should understand.

Along the way, I noticed that some of these early 10 cent DC war books were just not around. Forget about the grade, some of these issues were just downright scarce! I'd just like to mention some of the books that were tougher for me. Here's a condensed list of tough books:

- *All-American Men of War* #13 and #15
- *G. I. Combat* #59 and #73
- *Our Army at War* #2, #11, #12, early 20s and early 30s
- *Our Fighting Forces* - none stick out
- *Star Spangled War Stories* #3, #8, #30-32

My advice for the reader, if you have a goal, no matter what it is, stick to it. With determination, anything can be accomplished. Now let's see who can put 3 sets together!

Taking Cover (By Andy Greenham)

As I try to do every year, I run a contest to determine the best cover of either a certain artist, or title, or genre, or era. Last year, I ran a Joe Kubert cover contest. This year I decided to run a Russ Heath "Survivor Series." For those of you who aren't familiar with these contests, I'll explain it quickly. First, I asked the members of the CGC boards for their nominations for their favorite Russ Heath cover. This could be any genre, any title, any era. I received 116 nominations, and I can assure you that none of these covers were second-rate. This is Russ Heath, for goodness sake! After I have the nominations, then the contest begins. Similar to the TV show "Survivor," the forum members will "vote off" their least favorite covers. You can imagine that as the rounds progress, and fewer and fewer covers remain that it starts to become a very difficult task. The top two winners in this contest were both war books. To be honest, this didn't come as a big surprise to me, but it was a nice feeling of reassurance that it wasn't just me who appreciated Russ' contributions to the war comic field.

Top 5 best Russ Heath comic cover contest:

1) *G. I. Combat* #80
2) *All American Men Of War* #94
3) *Marvel Tales* #130
4) *Journey Into Unknown Worlds* #49
5) *Star Spangled War Stories* #81

The Spoils of War

Now that we have been producing this report for over half a decade, it is not unusual to have readers and colleagues approach us about the investment value of certain war comics, and in some cases as to whether to delve into the entire genre.

So this very short segment was created with the aim of spotlighting specific war comic issues with investment potential and, at times, calling out those issues showing sluggish returns. This year we are analyzing two or three war comics or titles worthy of a mention, providing our (albeit biased) opinion of their standing in the comic book market.

Colossal Disclaimer: THE INFORMATION PROVIDED IN THIS SEGMENT MAY BE WHOLLY INACCURATE. None of the writers, contributors, or publishers of this report can be responsible for the accuracy of this information or for how you use this information, none are financial or investment ADVISORS and none can predict how the marketplace will ultimately value these books. USE AT YOUR OWN RISK.

These are merely the opinions of seasoned war comic collectors. We urge you to use caution when taking heed to any of our investment opinions.

Long Term Return

Atlas War – That's right, we are not fixating on one issue or title here, we are calling out an entire comic line. Folks, Atlas War is hot! ...Especially if it's in high grade. What's exciting here is to see widespread interest for an entire comic book line outside of the staple that is DC War. Prices for these books are escalating at a moderate, yet steadfast manner. They are selling quickly and for somewhat strong prices if in an 8.0 or 8.5 grade. For your information, Atlas War comics are scarce in VF and are typically single highest at 8.5, generally commanding $500 or more for each issue, which is a decent showing for a long undervalued War comic legacy. That said; these prices are still palatable in comparison to some highly priced superhero books and/or key DC War comics. If you have been even mildly contemplating a leap into the genre, here is a somewhat attainable investment segment to jump into. To give you a leg up, we recommend that you initially focus on the titles ***Battle*** and ***Combat***, as those will most likely be the first to go up in price AND scarcity. But, don't forget to snap up any high grade copies of ***War Comics*** and ***War Action*** while you are out on the hunt. We expect all of these to get you fairly reasonable returns within 5 years or less.

Short Term Return

***Battle* #1-10 (ATLAS)** – OK, so we have already spotlighted *Battle* in our endorsement of Atlas War, but if you want to get truly specific about solid movers, then we are talking about the first ten issues of *Battle*...If you can find any of these issues in 8.0 or better – snap 'em up! To be frank, any high grade issue of *Battle* is a very worthy pick up, but for short term investments, we think the first 10 issues will be the easiest to flip. Look at getting a nice return on your purchase as soon as one to two years.

Losing Ground

As a consequence of both fluctuating markets and collector interest, there are comics that also lose momentum, sometimes momentarily, sometimes for longer. Although we like to advocate the War comic genre as a whole, we also believe it is our duty to point out titles that may be showing lackluster performance against its peers. Our hope with this impartial approach is to nurture the genre by educating enthusiasts and stewarding said collectors toward improved or more calculated purchases, whether choosing between issues or negotiating for a better price overall. In this year's report we focus not on a certain issue or a particular title, but on the overall pricing being bestowed on middle-high grades in the Bronze Age.

Although super key books still command great prices, in reality, Bronze age War comics were selling better a couple of years ago. We believe that this is strongly influenced by the fact that dealers are being too aggressive with Bronze Age War book prices for issues under a 9.4 grade. In short, comics middle-grounding at 9.2 or a little less are overpriced in our opinion. Certainly 9.4s, 9.6s and decidedly most 9.8s should be getting their due, but 9.2s are being priced a bit steep for their condition. The adverse effect of course is that it has slowed movement and interest overall in that corner of our genre because seasoned collectors know that these prices are not reflective of their current actual value and thus are not purchasing them. We certainly appreciate the notion that certain dealers believe these comics can command high prices, but at this point this pricing for Bronze Age War comics has slowed that niche segment of the market, at least for middle grade comics. Dealers, we hope you consider this point as you append a price to your next 9.2 *Unknown Soldier*. With a little correcting, this should right itself. Nevertheless, take note gang and shop wisely.

Gaining Ground

Keep a keen eye on *Our Army at War* #168, the Unknown Soldier's first appearance. This has been quiet for a little while and we anticipate a little forward momentum on this comic. It's hard to say how much ground it may gain, but it is worthy of closer inspection.

Intel from the War Correspondents

Uncovering the Washtones (by Mick Rabin)

In this forum last year, I outlined the genesis of the 12+ page stories that began with a sputter in *G.I. Combat* #56 and gathered steam within the DC War comics genre until the extended storylines catalyzed stronger and more complex character development, eventually giving rise to the enduring character-driven series of Gunner & Sarge (*Our Fighting Forces*), Sgt. Rock (*Our Army at War*), and Haunted Tank (*G.I. Combat*), among others. Those stories were interesting not only for the writing, but for the art where there's a lot of evidence that the artists were given more leeway to explore the boundaries of the medium.

However, as interesting as the stories were in the DC Big-5 titles, it's pretty hard to deny the impact of cover after cover after cover from that mid-'50s time period. While Kubert is the name most associated with DC War covers between 1963-1985, it was Jerry Grandenetti who was the true "cover-king"—as my friend, Steve Fears, likes to call him—during the mid-'50s to the early '60s. It's through this time frame that many collectors have discovered a compelling and rewarding sub-genre of war books: washtone covers.

Often referred to as greytones [or mistakenly as "painted covers"], washtone covers have become universally lauded as some of the most eye-catching covers ever made in any genre of any era of any publisher.

That's EVER.

When you mention washtones, people can often rattle off specifics with some of the more famous examples, like the beautiful run of *Sea Devils* covers or the staggering Kubert *Hawkman* cover to *Brave and the Bold* #44. There are a few people outside of the War comics collectors' circles who have a vague notion that the War titles contain some beautiful washtone covers, but few have taken the time to explore much beyond *GIC* #87, which is widely recognized as one of the best. Fewer still know that *GIC* #87 is in the middle of the longest string of uninterrupted washtone covers in the history of comics—the "Perty-Thirty." Those 30 issues start with *GIC* #75 and continue unabated until *GIC* #104. Even *Sea Devils* can't touch that.

Apparently, the fellow who was the driving force behind all of those washtones, Jack Adler, thought that War comics and washtones were a good mix. Many collectors tend to agree. Every year or so, the CGC Message Boards run a "Favorite War Comics" survey which starts with favorite cover nominations in all of the runs; the list is always top-heavy with washtone covers. They also typically comprise more than half of the top-ten and, with the exception of *AAMOW* #94 (which is often mistaken for a washtone. . .but that's just Russ Heath's eye candy at work), they've always dominated the top spot.

The "Perty-Thirty" from *G.I. Combat* isn't the only place to find washtones in the Big-5, though. In fact, there are washtones across many DC genres (although they are nearly nonexistent in the superhero titles—only *Detective Comics* #239 from Jan., 1957 comes to mind) including Mystery/Sci-fi, *B&B*, *Showcase*, Romance, Western, Teen humor, and even the Funny Animals. However, the war titles in general were loaded with washtones.

As an aside, I want to tip my hat to Chris Pedrin whose seminal handbook, *The Chris Pedrin Big-5 War Comics* is 20 years old this year. That book has become THE go-to whenever it comes to looking up important information about War comics. Before it was published, I recall being struck by a number of these covers in the early '90s and having no reference (internet was around, but there weren't comics sites like the Grand Comics Database until the mid-2000s), so I'd have to sift through boxes at comics shows and make lists for myself. It was a lot of fun, but a bit harrowing because I was never sure which issues of which titles I was missing until I cobbled through the collections of a couple of DC completists. "*The Pedrin Guide*" solved that problem and went a step further with an interesting article about Jack Adler and his washtone magic. To be clear, Adler turned covers drawn by

Grandenetti, Heath, and Kubert into washtone covers, but there is more information about that in the Pedrin Guide article.

Luckily, I got my hands on some of the toughest ones like *Star Spangled War Stories* #45, the first-ever washtone in ANY of the titles. It's a spectacular Kubert washtone with a paratrooper in mid-jump from the belly of an airplane threatened with flack. Two other genuinely popular (in any grade) ones are *AAMOW* #35 and *GIC* #80 which both feature predominantly black covers. Then there's the Grandenetti trifecta of *GIC* #69, *GIC* #83, and *OFF* #71 which all feature sweating soldiers peering through the jungle foliage at the viewer with rifles at the ready.

For the sake of this column, I decided to compile a list of the washtones in all of the Big-5 titles and sort them by date. There are more washtones after Feb./Mar. 1964, but I decided to cap the list with *GIC* #104 which is at the end of the "Perty-Thirty." After that issue, they only appeared sporadically, but the practice lasted well into the 1970s. All in all, they comprise some of the most compelling and collectable issues in all of the Big-5 runs. For the uninitiated, there are some incredible surprises awaiting you.

THE GREAT WASHTONE LIST (for DC War's BIG 5)

AAMOW – All American Men of War
GIC – G.I. Combat
OAAW – Our Army at War
OFF – Our Fighting Forces
SSWS – Star Spangled War Stories

YEAR	MO.	AAMOW	GIC	OAAW	OFF	SSWS
1952	Aug.	127		1		131
1952	Sept.			2		132
1952	Oct.	128		3		133
1952	Nov.			4		3
1952	Dec.	2		5		4
1953	Jan.			6		5
1953	Feb.	3		7		6
1953	Mar.			8		7
1953	Apr.	4		9		8
1953	May			10		9
1953	June	5		11		10
1953	July			12		11
1953	Aug.	6		13		12
1953	Sept.			14		13
1953	Oct.	7		15		14
1953	Nov.			16		15
1953	Dec.	8		17		16
1954	Jan.			18		17
1954	Feb.	9		19		18
1954	Mar.			20		19
1954	Apr.	10		21		20
1954	May			22		21
1954	June	11		23		22
1954	July			24		23
1954	Aug.	12		25		24

YEAR	MO.	AAMOW	GIC	OAAW	OFF	SSWS
1954	Sept.	13		26		25
1954	Oct.	14		27	1	26
1954	Nov.	15		28		27
1954	Dec.	16		29	2	28
1955	Jan.	17		30		29
1955	Feb.	18		31	3	30
1955	Mar.	19		32		31
1955	Apr.	20		33	4	32
1955	May	21		34		33
1955	June	22		35	5	34
1955	July	23		36		35
1955	Aug.	24		37	6	36
1955	Sept.	25		38		37
1955	Oct.	26		39	7	38
1955	Nov.	27		40		39
1955	Dec.	28		41	8	40
1956	Jan.	29		42		41
1956	Feb.	30		43	9	42
1956	Mar.	31		44		43
1956	Apr.	32		45	10	44
1956	May	33		46		45
1956	June	34		47	11	46
1956	July	35		48		47
1956	Aug.	36		49	12	48
1956	Sept.	37		50	13	49
1956	Oct.	38		51	14	50
1956	Nov.	39		52	15	51
1956	Dec.	40		53	16	52
1957	Jan.	41	44	54	17	53
1957	Feb.	42	45	55	18	54
1957	Mar.	43	46	56	19	55
1957	Apr.	44	47	57	20	56
1957	May	45	48	58	21	57
1957	June	46	49	59	22	58
1957	July	47	50	60	23	59
1957	Aug.	48	51	61	24	60
1957	Sept.	49	52	62	25	61
1957	Oct.	50	53	63	26	62
1957	Nov.	51	54	64	27	63
1957	Dec.	52	55	65	28	64
1958	Jan.	53	56	66	29	65
1958	Feb.	54	57	67	30	66
1958	Mar.	55	58	68	31	67
1958	Apr.	56	59	69	32	68
1958	May	57	60	70	33	69
1958	June	58	61	71	34	70
1958	July	59	62	72	35	71
1958	Aug.	60	63	73	36	72
1958	Sept.	61	64	74	37	73
1958	Oct.	62	65	75	38	74
1958	Nov.	63	66	76	39	75
1958	Dec.	64	67	77	40	76
1959	Jan.	65	68	78	41	77
1959	Feb.	66	69	79	42	78

YEAR	MO.	AAMOW	GIC	OAAW	OFF	SSWS
1959	Mar.	67	70	80	43	79
1959	Apr.	68	71	81	44	80
1959	May	69	72	82	45	81
1959	June	70	73	83	46	82
1959	July	71	74	84	47	83
1959	Aug.	72	75	85	48	84
1959	Sept.	73	76	86	49	85
1959	Oct.	74	77	87	50	86
1959	Nov.	75	78	88	51	87
1959	Dec.	76		89	52	
1960	Jan.		79	90		88
1960	Feb.	77		91	53	
1960	Mar.		80	92		89
1960	Apr.	78		93	54	
1960	May		81	94		90
1960	June	79		95	55	
1960	July		60	96		91
1960	Aug.	80		97	56	
1960	Sept.	81	83	98		92
1960	Oct.			99	57	
1960	Nov.		84	100		93
1960	Dec.	82		101	58	
1961	Jan.		85	102		94
1961	Feb.	83		103	59	
1961	Mar.		86	104		95
1961	Apr.	84		105	60	
1961	May		87	106		96
1961	June	85		107	61	
1961	July		88	108		97
1961	Aug.	86		109	62	
1961	Sept.		89	110		98
1961	Oct.	87		111	63	
1961	Nov.		90	112		99
1961	Dec.	88		113	64	
1962	Jan.		91	114	65	100
1962	Feb.	89		115	66	
1962	Mar.		92	116		101
1962	Apr.	90		117	67	
1962	May		93	118	68	102
1962	June	91		119		
1962	July		94	120	69	103
1962	Aug.	92		121	70	
1962	Sept.		95	122		104
1962	Oct.	93		123	71	
1962	Nov.		96	124	72	105
1962	Dec.	94		125		
1963	Jan.		97	126	73	106
1963	Feb.	95		127	74	
1963	Mar.		98	128		107
1963	Apr.	96		129	75	
1963	May		99	130	76	108
1963	June	97		131		
1963	July		100	132	77	109
1963	Aug.	98		133	78	
1963	Sept.		101	134		110
1963	Oct.	99		135	79	
1963	Nov.		102	136	80	111
1963	Dec.	100		137		
1964	Jan.		103	138	81	112
1964	Feb.	101		139	82	
1964	Mar.		104	140		113

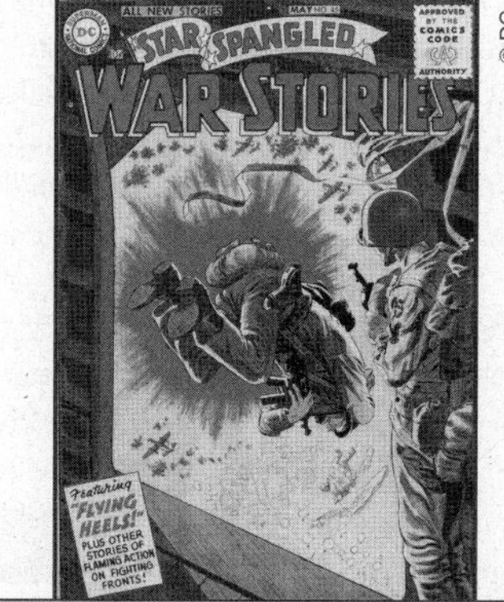

Star Spangled War Stories #45, the first washtone cover in the Big-5 titles

About Face, the Variants of War (By Andy Greenham)

As I collected every issue of the DC Big Five, I also bought any kind of variant that I could find. Even the slightest difference would be enough for me to add it to my collection.

Many of you are aware of direct edition comics vs. newsstand edition comics. Typically, the newsstand books would have a UPC code on the front cover. The direct edition books also had that box, but no UPC code, thus differentiating the two versions. Among other things, the non-UPC version would have the box filled with either Sgt. Rock's helmet, or an ad for DC comics, or sometimes even just left blank. I decided to try to get a copy of every newsstand book and a copy of every direct edition book. Below is a short list of the issues that I had found to have both variations. There may be earlier issues with two versions known, but my list will only include the books that I am aware of.

All-American Men of War
No variants

G. I. Combat
#223-228

Our Army At War
No variants

Our Fighting Forces
No variants

Sgt. Rock
#345-422

Star Spangled War Stories
No variants

Unknown Soldier
#250-268

...and for those interested:

Weird War Tales

#92-124

Please keep in mind that there are different variations that can be collected. I also picked up any Mark's Jeweller's inserts whenever I saw them.

Although I didn't specifically seek out the price variants, when I noticed that I had some with US prices and some with different Canadian prices, I kept one of each version.

Sgt. Rock #329 has a Whitman variant and that book is as tough as nails. If you see it, buy it, buy it, buy it!

Aside from these variants, I also wanted to collect every comic book that had any of my favorite DC War characters appearing in them. I think you'll be surprised at this little list that I've compiled. In alphabetical order (not importance):

Anarky #7 (Haunted Tank); *Brave and the Bold* #52 (Sgt. Rock/Haunted Tank/Johnny Cloud/Mlle. Marie); *Brave and the Bold* #84, #96, #108, #117, #124, #162 (Sgt. Rock); *Brave and the Bold* #146 (Unknown Soldier / DC and Whitman variants); *DC Comics Presents* #10 (Sgt. Rock), #42 (Unknown Soldier); *DC 100 Page Super Spectacular* #16 (Sgt. Rock); *DC Sampler* #1 (G.I. Combat, Sgt Rock); *DC Special* Vol 1 #5 (Sgt. Rock), Vol 2 #16 (?), Vol 2 #26 (Enemy Ace); *DC Special Blue Ribbon Digest* #7 (Sgt. Rock), #12 (Haunted Tank), #18 (Sgt. Rock), #21 (OAAW); *DC Special Series* #3 (Sgt. Rock), #8 (Sgt. Rock), #13 (Sgt. Rock), #18 (Sgt. Rock), #21 (Sgt. Rock), #22 (GIC); *DC Universe Holiday Bash* (1997) - #2 (Sgt. Rock/Easy Co.); *The Demon* #46-47 (Haunted Tank); *Detective Comics* #404 (Enemy Ace), #500(?), #501 (Mlle. Marie); *80 Page Giant* #7 (Sgt. Rock); *Fanboy* #4 (Sgt. Rock; *JLA* #159 (Enemy Ace), #160 (Enemy Ace); *Sgt. Rock's Prize Battle Tales*; *Showcase* #45 (Sgt. Rock), #57 (Enemy Ace), #58 (Enemy Ace); *Swamp Thing* #82 (Sgt. Rock), #83 (Enemy Ace); *World's Finest* #247 (Mlle. Marie), #248 (Sgt. Rock), #249 (Sgt. Rock).

I'm sure I'm missing some, but probably not too many. Good luck in the hunt, fellow war buffs!

GAINING RANK

Since our first report in *Overstreet* #39, we have been watchful of the market, paying keen attention to any fluctuations or changes. We carefully scrutinize interest and demand in all key issues of the genre which help manage the ranking of the top comics in the War category. It's important to know that after developing the initial rank listing (in 2008), we've been careful not to make any abrupt changes to the position of each of the comics. However, we are continuously making small tweaks as we either gather new intel on the books or see activity or changes in the market. This year however, in an effort to bring further clarity to the noteworthiness of each issue listed, we included a descriptor noting why a comic is meritorious of its ranking (see "merit" column below).

After careful deliberation we present the following war books rankings:

TOP 50 ATOM / SILVER / BRONZE AGE WAR COMICS OF 2014

ISSUE	2014 RANK	2013 RANK	MERIT
Our Army at War #83	1	1	1st true app of Sgt Rock (Kanigher/Kubert Master Sgt)
Sgt. Fury #1	2	2	1st app of Sgt Fury
G.I. Combat #87	3	3	1st app of Haunted Tank
Our Army at War #81	4	4	Sgt Rock prototype (Non Kanigher/Kubert "Sgt Rocky")
Our Army at War #82	5	5	Sgt Rock prototype (Non Kanigher/Kubert 4th grade rate Sgt)
G.I. Combat #68	6	6	Sgt Rock prototype (Kanigher/Kubert "The Rock" story
Two-Fisted Tales #18	7	7	1st issue to start EC War run
Frontline Combat #1	8	8	1st issue of EC all war title
Our Army at War #1	9	9	1st issue of Big Five war title
G.I. Combat #44	10	12	1st DC issue of Big Five war Title, early washtone
Our Army at War #90	11	10	How Sgt Rock got his stripes
Our Fighting Forces #1	12	11	1st issue of Big Five war title
Our Army at War #88	13	13	1st Sgt Rock cover (Kubert)
Star Spangled War Stories #131	14	14	1st issue of Big Five war title
Star Spangled War Stories #84	15	15	1st App of Mademoiselle Marie
All American Men of War #127	16	17	1st issue of Big Five war title
Our Fighting Forces #45	17	16	Gunner & Sarge run begins (Kanigher/ Grandenetti, predates OAAW #83)
Our Army at War #85	18	18	1st app of Ice Cream Soldier and 2nd Kubert Sgt. Rock
Our Army at War #84	19	20	2nd app of Sgt Rock
Our Army at War #91	20	19	1st all Sgt Rock issue
Our Army at War #151	21	21	1st app Of Enemy Ace

Our Army at War #112	22	22	Classic roster ("Brady Bunch") cover
G.I. Combat #1	23	23	1st issue of Quality Comics title
Star Spangled War Stories #90	24	24	1st Dinosaur "War That Time Forgot" ish
All American Men of War #28	25	25	1st Sgt Rock prototype (Kubert art)
All American Men of War #67	26	29	1st app of Gunner & Sarge (predates OAAW #83, not Grandenetti)
G.I. Combat #91	27	27	1st Haunted Tank Cover (washtone)
Our Army at War #86	28	26	Early Sgt Rock
Two-Fisted Tales Annual #1	29	28	Early 132 pg EC war annual
G.I. Combat #75	30	31	1st in "Perty Thirty" washtone run
Battle #1	31	35	1st issue of Atlas war title
Blazing Combat #1	32	30	1st issue of Warren war Magazine
Our Army at War #100	33	34	Scarce Kubert (black cover)
Star Spangled War Stories #151	34	33	1st solo app of Unknown Soldier
Combat #1	35	37	1st isssue of Atlas War title (black cover)
Fightin' Marines 15 (#1)	36	32	1st issue of St John war Title (Baker art)
G.I. Combat #69	37	36	1st in Grandenetti washtone trifecta (GIC #83 and OFF 71 are the others)
Foxhole #1	38	39	1st ish Mainline title (classic Kirby cover)
Our Army at War #128	39	40	Training & origin of Sgt Rock.
All American Men of War #82	40	38	1st app of Johnny Cloud
G.I. Combat #80	41	42	Classic washtone cover
Our Fighting Forces #49	42	41	1st app of Pooch
G.I. Combat #83	43	43	1st Big Al, Little Al & Charlie (2nd of Grandenetti washtone trifecta covers)
Our Army at War #168	44	46	1st app of the Unknown Soldier
Our Army at War #95	45	44	1st app of Bulldozer
Weird War Tales #1	46	45	1st issue in DC War & Fantasy title
Fightin' Marines #2	47	47	1st Canteen Kate (Matt Baker)
All American Men of War #18	48	48	1st Joe Kubert war cover
Combat Kelly #1	49	49	1st app of Combat Kelly (Heath art)
Sgt Rock's Prize Battle Tales #1	50	50	Kubert & Heath art

© WMG

Frontline Combat #1

© DC

G.I. Combat #44

© WARREN

Blazing Combat #1

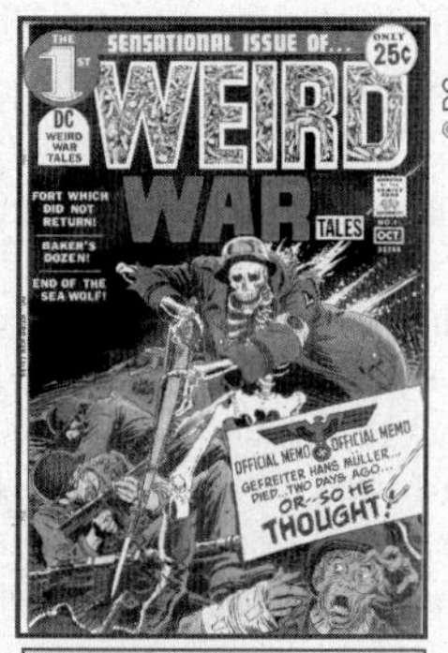

© DC

Weird War Tales#1

Here are some interesting facts about this year Top 50 Atom/Silver/Bronze Age War Comics rankings in 2014: *G.I. Combat* #44 (the 1st DC issue of the title), Atlas' *Combat* #1 and *Our Army at War* #168 (the 1st appearance of The Unknown Soldier) each moved up 2 slots since 2013. More importantly, *G.I. Combat* #44 crested its way into the top 10.

All American Men of War #67 (the first appearance of Gunner and Sarge) jumped 3 slots since last year.

Battle #1 was the biggest mover, leaping 4 slots to the 31st position and reflecting the recent flurry of action on all Atlas war comics.

Something significant to note, *G.I. Combat* #87, *Our Army at War* #81 and *Our Army at War* #82 all nearly tied in our voting process, scoring within fractions of a point from each other. Although they are all holding their positions from the previous year, it is possible we may see a change by next year; specifically, *Our Army at War* #82 gaining rank up from its current 5th position to a loftier spot. Keep an eye on those three books.

Our Army at War #83 (the 1st true Sgt Rock) and *Sgt. Fury* #1 (Sgt Fury's first appearance) continue to maintain their status as the #1 and #2 books of the genre respectively.

TOP 15 GOLDEN AGE WAR COMICS OF 2014

ISSUE	2014 RANK	2013 RANK	MERIT
Wings #1	1	1	1st issue in long running air war title
War Comics #1	2	2	1st comic completely devoted to war
Real Life #3	3	3	Hitler Cover (early 1942 WWII)
Contact Comics #1	4	4	1st issue of air battles title
Real Life Comics #1	5	5	1st issue of adventure title
Rangers Comics #8	6	6	US Rangers begin
Wings Comics #2	7	7	2nd issue of key air war title
Don Winslow #1 (1937)	8	9	Very early war adventure title
Bill Barnes Comics #1	9	8	1st issue of Air Ace title
Remember Pearl Harbor (nn)	10	10	1942 illustrated story of the battle
US Marines #2	11	11	Classic Cover (Bailey art)
American Library nn (#1)	12	12	"Thirty Seconds Over Tokyo" (movie)
Don Winslow #1 (1939)	13	13	Rare Four Color issue (#2)
American Library nn (#2)	14	14	Guadacanal Diary (painted cover)
Rangers Comics #26	15	15	Classic cover

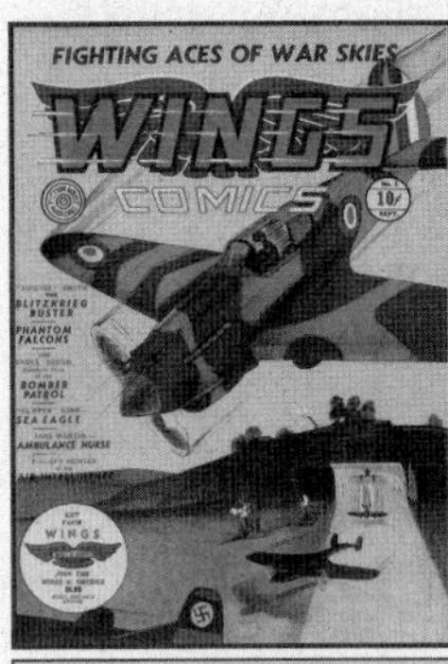

Wings Comics #1

TOP 5 ATLAS AND CHARLTON WAR COMICS of 2014

ISSUE	2014 RANK	2013 RANK	MERIT
Battle #1	1	1	1st issue of Atlas war title
Combat #1	2	2	1st issue of Atlas War title (black cover)
War Comics #1	3	3	1st issue of Atlas War title
War Action #1	4	4	1st issue of Atlas War title
War Comics #11	5	5	Classic flamethrower cover

TOP 5 CHARLTON WAR BOOKS OF 2014

ISSUE	2014 RANK	2013 RANK	MERIT
Fightin' Marines 15 (#1)	1	1	1st issue in St John war Title (Baker art)
Soldier & Marine #11	2	2	1st ish in short war title (Bob Powell art)
Attack #54	3	3	1st issue in short war title (100 pgs)
US Air Force #1	4	4	1st issue of Charlton war title
Fightin' Air Force #3	5	5	1st issue of Charlton war title

Attack #54

Closing Commendation (By Andy Greenham)

I just wanted to express my admiration to Joshua Dysart and Alberto Ponticelli. Together in 2008, they created a new series for the Unknown Soldier. This time, the war takes place in Uganda. Now, this is not the same Unknown Soldier that I grew up reading and loved so dearly, but it is still immensely enjoyable. The books are so well-written by Dysart, with gripping storytelling, you will feel that you're right there in Uganda. The gritty artwork by Ponticelli complements the writing perfectly that it truly seals the deal for me. Sadly, the series lasted only 25 issues, but I can't recommend it enough.

On that note, thanks for reading the War Report and see you next year!

Over and Out

Thanks for taking the time to read the War Report. We hope that you have found the information educational and informational and use it to broaden your collecting horizons. As always, I would like to thank everyone who contacted us throughout the year with their thoughts, comments, and support.

If you would like to discuss or challenge any of our deliberations, or would just like to share your own musings, please do not hesitate to contact the War Correspondents at **hq@warcomicreport.com**.

Again, we would like extend our humble thanks to the Overstreet team, particularly Bob Overstreet, J.C. Vaughn, and Mark Huesman. We appreciate your continued and enduring support.

Before we close on this edition, I would like to call out fans of other genres to produce your own reports. Whether, Western, Crime, Romance, Superhero or otherwise, it would be incredibly illuminating to get detailed insights about other categories. We've appreciated the singular limelight the war genre has been getting in the *Overstreet Comic Book Price Guide* all these years, but we assure you, there is room for others here.

As it has become customary, I want to express my deepest gratitude to the unflappable War Correspondents: Andy Greenham and Mick Rabin. Their unselfish contributions each year have made this report, and the valuable intel within, a meaningful chronicle for one of the most fascinating and interesting comic book genres ever published.

KEY SALES FROM 2013-2014

The following lists of sales were reported to Gemstone during the year and represent only a small portion of the total amount of important books that have sold.

GOLDEN AGE - ATOM AGE SALES

All Star Comics #39 FN $240
All Star Comics #52 FN $250
All Star Comics #55 FN- $200
All-American Comics #70 VG+ $225
All-American Comics #88 VF $700 "D" copy
Comic Cavalcade #3 VG $350
Detective Comics #85 GD- $149.99
Flash Comics #1 VF $12,800
Great Comics #3 VG+ $3,585
Human Torch #8 VG $1,150
Marvel Mystery Comics #36 GD/VG $550
Planet Comics #22 VG $310
Sensation Comics #5 VG+ $395
Sensation Comics #10 GD $150
Sensation Comics #40 VG $120
Sensation Comics #53 GD $170
Sensation Comics #75 GD- $74.99
Superman #24 GD- $324.99
USA Comics #13 FR $710
Weird Fantasy #13 #1 GD $157.50
World's Finest Comics #6 VG $285
World's Finest Comics #56 GD+ $60
World's Finest Comics #64 VG $300
World's Finest Comics #66 FN $350
World's Finest Comics #67 VG $300
Young Romance #1 FN- $188

SILVER AGE SALES

Adventure Comics #247 GD- $399.99
Amazing Fantasy #15 VG- $8,250
Amazing Fantasy #15 GD- $4,000
Amazing Spider-Man #1 GD $1,700
Amazing Spider-Man #2 GD+ $350
Amazing Spider-Man #3 GVG $400
Amazing Spider-Man #6 GVG $300
Amazing Spider-Man #13 GDVG $70
Amazing Spider-Man #13 GD+ $175
Amazing Spider-Man #26 VG+ $120
Amazing Spider-Man #26 VG $85
Amazing Spider-Man #39 FN $75
Avengers #4 GD+ $249.99
Green Lantern #54 FN $55
Hot Wheels #1 NM- $99.99
Incredible Hulk #3 GVG $300
Incredible Hulk #5 GD+ $215
Incredible Hulk #6 GD $140
Incredible Hulk #181 GD $180
Journey Into Mystery #83 FR/GD $780
Journey Into Mystery #95 FN- $78
Plastic Man #2 GD $181.99
Rip Hunter #1 VG $99.99
Sensation #60 NM $4,400 San Francisco
Showcase #6 FN- $900
Tales of Suspense #57 VF+ $1,500
Teen Titans #21 NM $145
X-Men #1 GD $880

BRONZE AGE TO MODERN AGE SALES

Annihilation: Conquest #6 NM- $49.99
Batman Adventures #12 NM $425
Batman Adventures #12 VF/NM $249.95
Guardians of the Galaxy (2008) #1 NM $121.49
Guardians of the Galaxy (2008) #24 NM $24.99
Incredible Hulk #181 VG $269.99
Incredible Hulk #181 GD- $199.99
Incredible Hulk #271 NM $129.99
Incredible Hulk #271 GD $30
Marvel Preview #7 FN $202.50
New Mutants #98 MT $245
New Mutants #98 NM $140
Rocket Raccoon #1 NM- $34.33
Saga #1 NM $37
Ultimate Spider-Man #1 NM $49.99
X-Men (Uncanny) #121 VF $79.99
X-Men (Uncanny) #137 VF/NM $94.99
Y: The Last Man #1 NM $99.99

Action Comics #1 CGC 2.0 $77,333 (restored)
Action Comics #1 CGC 1.5 $175,000
Action Comics #10 CGC 3.0 $30,500
Action Comics #19 CGC 7.5 $9,288
Action Comics #21 CGC 5.5 $2,375 white pages
Action Comics #31 CGC 8.0 $6,000 San Francisco
Action Comics #33 CGC 6.5 $1,050
Action Comics #36 CGC 6.5 $1,195
Action Comics #37 CGC 6.0 $800
Action Comics #59 CGC 8.5 $9,225
Action Comics #65 CGC 8.0 $700
Action Comics #81 CGC 9.8 $9,300
Action Comics #96 CGC 9.8 $11,801
All Select Comics #1 CGC 8.5 $14,000
All Star Comics #6 CGC 4.5 $362
All Star Comics #7 CGC 9.2 $16,000
All Winners Comics #3 CGC 7.0 $900 (restored)
All Winners Comics #4 CGC 8.0 $4,076
All-American Comics #16 CGC 3.0 $21,363
All-American Comics #35 CGC 6.5 $500 Penn
Amazing Mystery Funnies V2 #2 CGC 9.4 $12,900
Archie Comics #1 CGC 5.0 $13,204
Archie Comics #1 CGC 3.0 $29,010
Archie Comics #1 CGC 1.0 $13,204
Batman #1 CGC 9.2 $567,625
Batman #1 CGC 7.0 $119,013
Batman #1 CGC 4.0 $52,000
Batman #1 CGC 3.0 $35,501
Batman #1 CGC 1.8 $27,500
Batman #6 CGC 8.0 $3,600
Batman #9 CGC 7.0 $600
Batman #15 CGC 8.5 $3,255
Batman #23 CGC 7.0 $1,550
Batman #48 CGC 9.0 $4,800
Batman #55 CGC 9.4 $17,450
Big Shot Comics #46 CGC 9.6 $7,000 Mile High
Black Cat Mystery #50 CGC 9.0 $5,655
Blue Beetle #2 CGC 9.0 $8,900
Blue Beetle #3 CGC 9.2 $9,100,
Captain America Comics #1 CGC 9.2 $306,050
Captain America Comics #1 CGC 7.0 $94,000
Captain America Comics #1 CGC 7.0 $14,256 (restored)
Captain America Comics #1 CGC 6.5 $15,311 Stan Lee Sig.
Captain America Comics #1 CGC 6.0 $65,000
Captain America Comics #1 CGC 1.5 $26,499
Captain America Comics #1 CGC 1.5 $26,499
Captain America Comics #15 CGC 9.4 $13,000
Captain America Comics #34 CGC 7.5 $2,875
Captain America Comics #37 CGC 8.0 $7,800
Catman Comics #24 CGC 9.4 $16,000 Mile High
Catman Comics #28 CGC 4.0 $850
Crime SuspenStories #20 CGC 9.6 $8,988 Gaines file copy
Crime SuspenStories #22 CGC 9.2 $17,000
Detective Comics #1 CGC 0.5 $3,300
Detective Comics #27 CGC 3.5 $215,000
Detective Comics #33 CGC 8.0 $68,712
Detective Comics #35 CGC 7.5 $63,100
Detective Comics #38 CGC 9.4 $135,000 Allentown
Detective Comics #38 CGC 2.5 $7,655
Detective Comics #62 CGC 4.5 $1,100
Detective Comics #122 CGC 7.5 $1,777
Detective Comics #128 CGC 9.2 $5,322
Detective Comics #187 CGC 5.0 $1,000
Exciting Comics #60 CGC 9.8 $11,785
Famous Funnies #210 CGC 9.0 $1,725,
Fantastic Comics #6 CGC 9.0 $52 San Francisco
Feature Comics #61 CGC 9.6 $750 San Francisco
Flash Comics #1 CGC 9.0 $147,000
Flash Comics #1 CGC 3.5 $15,461
Flash Comics #3 CGC 9.6 $17,500
Flash Comics #4 CGC 9.4 $11,100
Flash Comics #88 CGC 9.0 $1,625
Funny Pages V.3 #7 CGC 9.2 $12,066
Giant Comics Edition #12 CGC 7.0 $9,300
Great Comics #3 CGC 3.5 $2,900
Green Hornet Comics #24 CGC 9.4 $8,622
Haunt of Fear #14 CGC 9.6 $2,888
Human Torch #8 CGC 7.5 $2,832
Human Torch #10 CGC 8.0 $4,700
Human Torch #18 CGC 8.0 $3,000
Human Torch #2 (#1) CGC 6.5 $11,111
Jackpot Comics #4 CGC 3.0 $6,100
Jackpot Comics #4 CGC 2.0 $6,265
Joe Palooka #2 CGC 8.5 $923
Keen Detective Funnies #24 CGC 3.5 $618
Kid Komics #7 CGC 9.0 $1,750
Marvel Mystery Comics #2 CGC 5.5 $10,088
Marvel Mystery Comics #15 CGC 7.5 $3,000
Marvel Mystery Comics #19 CGC 9.2 $7,069
Marvel Mystery Comics #28 CGC 8.0 $3,000
Marvel Mystery Comics #34 CGC 8.5 $4,488
Marvel Mystery Comics #45 CGC 8.0 $3,020
Marvel Mystery Comics #64 CGC 6.0 $935
Miss Fury #4 CGC 6.0 $650
More Fun Comics #101 CGC 5.5 $1,555
Mystery Tales #32 CGC 8.0 $2,100
Mystic Comics #9 CGC 6.0 $1,350
National Comics #2 CGC 9.6 $8,300
Nelvana #1 CGC 6.5 $13,750

Peanuts #1 CGC 9.8 $6,100
Pep Comics #36 CGC 2.5 $5,600
Reform School Girl # CGC 8.0 $9,900
Sensation Comics #1 CGC 8.0 $28,500
Sensation Comics #1 CGC 4.5 $13,700
Sensation Comics #7 CGC 9.4 $4,400
Shock SuspenStories #12 CGC 9.4 $1,414
Silver Streak Comics #5 CGC 9.0 $9,300
Speed Comics #24 CGC 9.6 $18,000 Mile High
Spirit #22 CGC 3.0 $605
Star Spangled Comics #44 CGC 9.0 $1,000
San Francisco
Startling Comics #49 CGC 9.0 $8,255
Startling Terror Tales #11 CGC 6.0 $1,300
Sub-Mariner Comics #1 CGC 9.2 $105,000
Sub-Mariner Comics #13 CGC 8.5 $5,800
Sub-Mariner Comics #15 CGC 6.5 $1,422
Sub-Mariner Comics #22 CGC 8.5 $1,257
Sub-Mariner Comics #6 CGC 7.5 $1,300
Superman #1 CGC 8.0 $37,000 (restored)
Superman #1 CGC 7.0 $26,000 (restored)
Superman #1 CGC 2.0 $62,111
Superman #1 CGC 1.8 $64,000
Superman #2 CGC 9.2 $94,000
Superman #2 CGC 5.0 $5,750
Superman #4 CGC 8.5 $9,250
Superman #31 CGC 6.5 $402
Superman #32 CGC 5.5 $395
Superman #53 CGC 9.0 $4,100
Superman #71 CGC 9.0 $1,751
Sure-Fire Comics #1 CGC 9.2 $7,400
Suspense Comics #1 CGC 8.5 $5,300 Crowley
Suspense Comics #3 CGC 3.0 $9,300
Suspense Comics #3 CGC 1.0 $6,000
Target Comics #7 CGC 6.0 $3,701
Terrific Comics #5 CGC 8.0 $13,533
Thrilling Comics #44 CGC 9.4 $14,700
USA Comics #11 CGC 9.2 $12,777
USA Comics #11 CGC 9.2 $12,777
Walt Disney's Comics & Stories #1 CGC 0.5 $640
Walt Disney's Comics & Stories #10 CGC 6.0 $638
Weird Tales of the Future #3 CGC 3.0 $480
Whiz Comics #4 CGC 9.4 $20,551
Wings Comics #112 CGC 8.0 $350 Mile High
Wonder Comics #3 CGC 8.5 $1,500
Wonder Comics #15 CGC 9.4 $4,522
Wonder Woman #1 CGC 3.0 $3,000
Wonder Woman #10 CGC 9.2 $7,001
Wonder Woman #21 CGC 9.4 $4,400 Mile High
Wonder Woman #79 CGC 8.5 $1,200
World's Best Comics #1 CGC 1.8 $800
World's Finest Comics #7 CGC 7.0 $850
World's Finest Comics #57 CGC 7.0 $400
Young Allies Comics #4 CGC 9.0 $6,200

SILVER AGE - SALES OF CGC-CERTIFIED COMICS

Action Comics #252 CGC 6.0 $1,611
Adventure Comics #210 CGC 7.0 $3,000
Adventure Comics #247 CGC 5.0 $2,000
Adventure Comics #283 CGC 8.5 $1,100
Amazing Adult Fantasy #12 CGC 9.4 $3,200
Amazing Fantasy #15 CGC 8.5 $120,100
Amazing Fantasy #15 CGC 8.0 $85,000
Amazing Fantasy #15 CGC 7.5 $65,000
Amazing Fantasy #15 CGC 7.5 $65,000
Amazing Fantasy #15 CGC 7.5 $59,800
Amazing Fantasy #15 CGC 7.5 $57,500
Amazing Fantasy #15 CGC 7.5 $55,500
Amazing Fantasy #15 CGC 7.0 $44,555
Amazing Fantasy #15 CGC 7.0 $44,555
Amazing Fantasy #15 CGC 7.0 $33,460
Amazing Fantasy #15 CGC 6.5 $27,000
Amazing Fantasy #15 CGC 6.0 $22,350
Amazing Fantasy #15 CGC 5.0 $13,400
Amazing Fantasy #15 CGC 4.5 $10,000
Amazing Fantasy #15 CGC 3.0 $3,500 (restored)
Amazing Fantasy #15 CGC 1.8 $4,500
Amazing Spider-Man #1 CGC 9.4 $110,000
Amazing Spider-Man #1 CGC 9.4 $93,964
Amazing Spider-Man #1 CGC 9.0 $42,900
Amazing Spider-Man #1 CGC 7.5 $15,000
Amazing Spider-Man #1 CGC 7.5 $12,400
Amazing Spider-Man #1 CGC 6.0 $3,000 (restored)
Amazing Spider-Man #1 CGC 2.5 $2,850
Amazing Spider-Man #1 CGC 2.0 $1,800
Amazing Spider-Man #2 CGC 8.5 $4,870
Amazing Spider-Man #3 CGC 9.6 $39,500
Amazing Spider-Man #3 CGC 9.2 $9,599
Amazing Spider-Man #4 CGC 5.0 $638
Amazing Spider-Man #6 CGC 9.8 $71,000
Amazing Spider-Man #9 CGC 9.8 $58,000
Amazing Spider-Man #9 CGC 4.0 $325
Amazing Spider-Man #10 CGC 9.8 $16,000
Amazing Spider-Man #13 CGC 9.2 $3,750
Amazing Spider-Man #25 CGC 9.8 $10,739
Amazing Spider-Man #58 CGC 9.8 $8,377
Amazing Spider-Man #63 CGC 9.8 $13,200
Avengers #1 CGC 9.4 $132,500
Avengers #1 CGC 9.4 $89,625
Avengers #1 CGC 9.2 $41,500
Avengers #1 CGC 6.5 $3,601
Avengers #1 CGC 5.5 $4,000

Avengers #1 CGC 5.0 $1,300
Avengers #1 CGC 4.0 $2,750 (off-white pgs.)
Avengers #1 CGC 4.0 $2,600
Avengers #4 CGC 9.6 $17,250
Avengers #4 CGC 8.5 $3,100
Avengers #8 CGC 9.8 $7,535
Avengers #58 CGC 9.6 $500
Batman #121 CGC 6.5 $1,200
Batman #156 CGC 9.6 $7,170
Batman #163 CGC 9.8 $8,080
Batman #189 CGC 9.6 $1,300
Brave and the Bold #28 CGC 9.2 $120,000
Brave and the Bold #28 CGC 8.5 $45,504
Brave and the Bold #28 CGC 8.5 $40,500
Brave and the Bold #28 CGC 5.5 $5,000
Brave and the Bold #28 CGC 4.5 $3,000
Captain America #109 CGC 9.8 $3,300 Sig. Series
Daredevil #1 CGC 6.5 $700
Daredevil #5 CGC 9.6 $2,051
Daredevil #7 CGC 9.4 $5,101
Daredevil #33 CGC 9.8 $1,322
Daredevil #37 CGC 9.6 $909
Daredevil #88 CGC 9.8 $605
Daredevil #92 CGC 9.8 $595
Detective Comics #359 CGC 9.2 $1,832
Doctor Strange #169 CGC 9.8 $2,300
Fantastic Four #1 CGC 8.5 $64,000
Fantastic Four #1 CGC 8.5 $60,000
Fantastic Four #1 CGC 7.5 $77,000
Fantastic Four #1 CGC 7.0 $19,750
Fantastic Four #1 CGC 3.0 $3,500
Fantastic Four #1 CGC 2.5 $2,400
Fantastic Four #1 CGC 2.5 $1,250
Fantastic Four #2 CGC 3.5 $630
Fantastic Four #3 CGC 8.5 $6,655
Fantastic Four #4 CGC 9.6 $37,499
Fantastic Four #4 CGC 9.4 $15,468 Thompson
Fantastic Four #5 CGC 9.4 $37,000
Fantastic Four #5 CGC 9.2 $22,800
Fantastic Four #5 CGC 9.2 $20,009
Fantastic Four #6 CGC 9.4 $10,268 Thompson
Fantastic Four #8 CGC 9.4 $9,800
Fantastic Four #9 CGC 9.6 $11,100
Fantastic Four #12 CGC 9.6 $65,000
Fantastic Four #12 CGC 9.6 $51,000
Fantastic Four #16 CGC 9.4 $3,972
Fantastic Four #19 CGC 9.6 $6,850
Fantastic Four #21 CGC 9.8 $7,090
Fantastic Four #23 CGC 9.4 $3,750 Twin Cities
Fantastic Four #36 CGC 9.6 $3,633
Fantastic Four #46 CGC 9.6 $2,759
Fantastic Four #48 CGC 9.6 $4,011
Fantastic Four #50 CGC 9.8 $44,007 Northland

Green Lantern #16 CGC 9.4 $3,200
Incredible Hulk #1 CGC 8.5 $58,256
Incredible Hulk #1 CGC 7.5 $26,055
Incredible Hulk #1 CGC 6.5 $14,600
Incredible Hulk #1 CGC 5.5 $8,800
Incredible Hulk #1 CGC 5.5 $7,000
Incredible Hulk #2 CGC 4.0 $650
Incredible Hulk #3 CGC 9.4 $18,250 Thompson
Incredible Hulk #4 CGC 9.4 $9,413 Thompson
Incredible Hulk #4 CGC 3.0 $225
Journey Into Mystery #52 CGC 9.2 $3,628
Journey Into Mystery #55 CGC 7.5 $2,251 White Mountain
Journey into Mystery #83 CGC 9.4 $275,000
Journey into Mystery #83 CGC 9.4 $171,000
Journey Into Mystery #83 CGC 9.2 $77,675 Thompson
Journey Into Mystery #83 CGC 4.0 $2,250
Journey Into Mystery #85 CGC 9.6 $35,000
Journey into Mystery #85 CGC 8.0 $2,500
Journey into Mystery #85 CGC 8.0 $2,200
Journey Into Mystery #87 CGC 9.4 $4,111
Journey Into Mystery #88 CGC 9.6 $7,600 Northland
Journey Into Mystery #103 CGC 9.8 $13,100
Masters of the Universe #12 CGC 9.8 $500
Nick Fury #1 CGC 9.4 $375
Our Army At War #83 CGC 4.0 $1,305
Our Army at War #151 CGC 9.4 $3,433
Phantom Stranger #1 CGC 6.0 $1,600
Showcase #4 CGC 9.0 $60,000
Showcase #4 CGC 8.0 $29,300
Showcase #4 CGC 5.5 $9,644
Showcase #8 CGC 9.2 $29,000
Showcase #22 CGC 4.0 $1,400
Showcase #34 CGC 8.0 $1,400
Silver Surfer #1 CGC 9.6 $5,000
Silver Surfer #4 CGC 9.8 $6,800
Strange Tales #101 CGC 9.6 $20,250
Strange Tales #101 CGC 9.4 $10,500
Strange Tales #110 CGC 9.6 $61,506
Strange Tales #110 CGC 9.6 $44,812
Strange Tales #110 CGC 8.0 $3,900
Strange Tales #110 CGC 5.0 $700
Strange Tales #115 CGC 9.4 $4,100 Thompson
Superman's Girlfriend, Lois Lane #2 CGC 8.0 $1,135
Tales of Suspense #39 CGC 9.6 $262,900
Tales of Suspense #39 CGC 9.6 $260,000
Tales of Suspense #39 CGC 9.4 $80,500
Tales Of Suspense #39 CGC 5.0 $3,800
Tales of Suspense #39 CGC 4.0 $3,100
Tales Of Suspense #39 CGC 3.0 $1,600
Tales of Suspense #40 CGC 9.4 $11,121 Pacific Coast
Tales of Suspense #48 CGC 9.8 $14,050

Tales of Suspense #57 CGC 9.6 $8,500
Tales of Suspense #57 CGC 9.2 $2,500
Tales of Suspense #57 CGC 9.0 $2,500
Tales of Suspense #59 CGC 9.8 $5,500
Tales to Astonish #27 CGC 9.2 $65,000
Tales to Astonish #27 CGC 9.0 $44,750
Tales to Astonish #27 CGC 9.0 $40,000
Tales to Astonish #27 CGC 8.5 $22,000
Tales to Astonish #27 CGC 3.5 $1,778
Tales to Astonish #35 CGC 9.6 $66,000 Western Penn
Tales to Astonish #35 CGC 9.2 $31,500
Tales to Astonish #35 CGC 9.2 $29,000
Tales to Astonish #39 CGC 9.0 $24,944
Tales to Astonish #44 CGC 9.8 $20,750 Northland
X-Men #1 CGC 9.6 $250,000
X-Men #1 CGC 9.0 $23,100
X-Men #1 CGC 8.5 $15,250
X-Men #1 CGC 7.5 $9,250
X-Men #1 CGC 7.5 $8,000
X-Men #1 CGC 7.0 $6,315
X-Men #1 CGC 7.0 $6,000
X-Men #1 CGC 5.0 $2,700
X-Men #1 CGC 5.0 $2,300
X-Men #1 CGC 2.0 $1,500
X-Men #4 CGC 9.4 $6,463 Thompson
X-Men #40 CGC 9.8 $2,800
X-Men #1 CGC 4.5 $2,500

BRONZE AGE - SALES OF CGC-CERTIFIED COMICS

All-Star Western #10 CGC 9.4 $1,045 Thompson
Amazing Spider-Man #121 CGC 9.8 $3,000
Amazing Spider-Man #121 CGC 9.6 $2,255
Amazing Spider-Man #129 CGC 9.8 $5,000
Amazing Spider-Man #200 CGC 9.9 $3,601
Archie's Pals 'N' Gals #161 CGC 9.4 $400
Avengers #55 CGC 9.8 $3,522
Batman #227 CGC 9.4 $1,899
Batman #232 CGC 9.8 $3,000
Batman #234 CGC 9.8 $2,550
Conan the Barbarian #4 CGC 9.8 $2,005
Conan the Barbarian #23 CGC 9.8 $1,000
Detective Comics #395 CGC 9.6 $3,346
Fantastic Four #123 CGC 9.2 $90
Giant-Size X-Men #1 CGC 9.8 $7,000
Giant-Size X-Men #1 CGC 9.8 $5,900
Giant-Size X-Men #1 CGC 9.4 $2,500
Giant-Size X-Men #1 CGC 9.2 $1,500
Green Lantern #76 CGC 9.4 $2,311
House of Secrets #92 CGC 9.2 $1,820
Incredible Hulk #180 CGC 9.6 $956
Incredible Hulk #181 CGC 8.5 $1,200
Incredible Hulk #181 CGC 8.0 $1,400
Incredible Hulk #181 CGC 7.0 $850
Incredible Hulk #181 CGC 5.0 $600
Incredible Hulk #271 CGC 9.8 $500
Iron Fist #14 CGC 9.8 $1,400
Iron Man #55 CGC 9.8 $13,025 (double cover)
Iron Man #55 CGC 9.8 $13,025
Iron Man #55 CGC 9.8 $9,000
Justice League of America #70 CGC 9.8 $955
Marvel Premiere #47 CGC 9.2 $150
Marvel Super-Heroes #18 CGC 9.8 $19,000
Spidey Super Stories #39 CGC 9.6 $300
Star Wars #1 CGC 9.8 $2,101 Sig. Series
Superman's Pal Jimmy Olsen #134 CGC 9.6 $1,553.50
Superman's Pal Jimmy Olsen #134 CGC 9.2 $375
Teenage Mutant Ninja Turtles #1 CGC 9.8 $13,088
Teenage Mutant Ninja Turtles #1 CGC 9.4 $5,250
X-Men #94 CGC 9.4 $1,434
X-Men #131 CGC 9.8 $1,237

COPPER - MODERN AGE - SALES OF CGC-CERTIFIED COMICS

Alf #48 CGC 9.8 $225
Amazing Spider-Man #252 CGC 9.8 $418.25
Amazing Spider-Man #252 CGC 9.8 $346.55
Amazing Spider-Man #300 CGC 9.9 $4,999
Batman #386 CGC 9.4 $165
Batman Adventures #12 CGC 9.8 $685
New Mutants #98 CGC 10.0 $15,449
New Mutants #98 CGC 9.9 $4,400
New Mutants #98 CGC 9.8 $418.25
Saga #1 CGC 9.8 $192.50
Teenage Mutant Ninja Turtles #1 CGC 9.4 $5,377.50
Teenage Mutant Ninja Turtles #1 CGC 8.5 $3,107.50
Teenage Mutant Ninja Turtles #1 CGC 8.0 $2,629
Teenage Mutant Ninja Turtles #3 CGC 9.4 $1,553.50
Walking Dead #1 CGC 9.8 $3,346
Walking Dead #1 CGC 9.8 $1,792.50
Walking Dead #1 CGC 9.6 $1,075.50
Walking Dead #7 CGC 9.8 $199.99
Walking Dead #19 CGC 9.8 $478
Walking Dead: Michonne Special #1 CGC 9.8 $53.99
Web of Spider-Man #1 CGC 9.9 $597.50
X-Men #141 CGC 9.8 $388.38

TOP COMICS

The following tables denote the rate of appreciation of the top Golden Age, Platinum Age, Silver Age and Bronze Age comics, as well as selected genres over the past year. The retail value for a Near Mint- copy of each comic (or VF where a Near Mint- copy is not known to exist) in 2014 is compared to its Near Mint- value in 2013. The rate of return for 2014 over 2013 is given. The place in rank is given for each comic by year, with its corresponding value in highest known grade. These tables can be very useful in forecasting trends in the market place. For instance, the investor might want to know which book is yielding the best dividend from one year to the next, or one might just be interested in seeing how the popularity of books changes from year to year. For instance, *Detective Comics* #31 was in 11th place in 2013 and has increased to 9th place in 2014. Premium books are also included in these tables and are denoted with an asterisk(*).

The following tables are meant as a guide to the investor. However, it should be pointed out that trends may change at anytime and that some books can meet market resistance with a slowdown in price increases, while others can develop into real comers from a presently dormant state. In the long run, if the investor sticks to the books that are appreciating steadily each year, he shouldn't go very far wrong.

TOP 100 GOLDEN AGE COMICS

TITLE/ISSUE#	2014 RANK	2014 NM- PRICE	2013 RANK	2013 NM- PRICE	$ INCR.	% INCR.
Action Comics #1	1	$2,100,000	1	$1,900,000	$200,000	11%
Detective Comics #27	2	$1,650,000	2	$1,500,000	$150,000	10%
Superman #1	3	$800,000	3	$720,000	$80,000	11%
All-American Comics #16	4	$600,000	4	$550,000	$50,000	9%
Marvel Comics #1	5	$500,000	5	$485,000	$15,000	3%
Batman #1	6	$460,000	6	$420,000	$40,000	10%
Captain America Comics #1	7	$315,000	7	$300,000	$15,000	5%
Action Comics #7	8	$230,000	8	$200,000	$30,000	15%
Detective Comics #31	9	$185,000	11	$150,000	$35,000	23%
Flash Comics #1	10	$180,000	9	$170,000	$10,000	6%
Pep Comics #22	11	$175,000	12	$140,000	$35,000	25%
More Fun Comics #52	12	$160,000	10	$155,000	$5,000	3%
Detective Comics #29	13	$155,000	14	$130,000	$25,000	19%
Action Comics #2	14	$150,000	13	$135,000	$15,000	11%
Action Comics #10	14	$150,000	17	$125,000	$25,000	20%
Whiz Comics #2 (#1)	14	$150,000	14	$130,000	$20,000	15%
Adventure Comics #40	17	$135,000	14	$130,000	$5,000	4%
Archie Comics #1	17	$135,000	19	$110,000	$25,000	23%
Detective Comics #33	17	$135,000	17	$125,000	$10,000	8%
All Star Comics #3	20	$105,000	20	$100,000	$5,000	5%
Action Comics #3	21	$100,000	25	$85,000	$15,000	18%
All Star Comics #8	21	$100,000	23	$90,000	$10,000	11%
Detective Comics #38	23	$95,000	21	$92,000	$3,000	3%
Detective Comics #1	24	VF $94,000	21	VF $92,000	$2,000	2%
Detective Comics #35	25	$90,000	27	$75,000	$15,000	20%
Marvel Mystery Comics #9	25	$90,000	24	$88,000	$2,000	2%
More Fun Comics #53	27	$82,000	26	$80,000	$2,000	3%
Detective Comics #28	28	$80,000	29	$72,000	$8,000	11%
Marvel Mystery Comics #2	28	$80,000	27	$75,000	$5,000	7%
Action Comics #13	30	$75,000	36	$60,000	$15,000	25%
Sub-Mariner Comics #1	31	$72,000	30	$70,000	$2,000	3%
Human Torch #2 (#1)	32	$68,000	31	$67,000	$1,000	1%
Green Lantern #1	33	$67,000	32	$66,000	$1,000	2%
Marvel Mystery Comics #5	34	$65,000	33	$62,000	$3,000	5%
Suspense Comics #3	34	$65,000	37	$58,000	$7,000	12%
Captain Marvel Adventures #1	36	$64,000	33	$62,000	$2,000	3%
Sensation Comics #1	36	$64,000	33	$62,000	$2,000	3%
Wonder Woman #1	38	$60,000	37	$58,000	$2,000	3%
Adventure Comics #48	39	$57,000	39	$56,000	$1,000	2%
New Fun Comics #1	40	VF $55,000	40	VF $54,000	$1,000	2%

TITLE/ISSUE#	2014 RANK	2014 NM- PRICE	2013 RANK	2013 NM- PRICE	$ INCR.	% INCR.
Superman #2	41	$54,000	41	$50,000	$4,000	8%
Action Comics #4	42	$50,000	42	$45,000	$5,000	11%
Action Comics #5	42	$50,000	42	$45,000	$5,000	11%
Action Comics #6	42	$50,000	42	$45,000	$5,000	11%
Captain America Comics #2	45	$48,000	42	$45,000	$3,000	7%
Walt Disney's Comics & Stories #1	46	$46,000	42	$45,000	$1,000	2%
Marvel Mystery Comics #3	47	$44,000	48	$42,000	$2,000	5%
Marvel Mystery Comics #4	47	$44,000	48	$42,000	$2,000	5%
*Marvel Mystery Comics 132 pg.	49	VF $43,500	47	VF $43,000	$500	1%
Batman #2	50	$42,000	50	$40,000	$2,000	5%
Daring Mystery Comics #1	50	$42,000	50	$40,000	$2,000	5%
All-American Comics #19	52	$41,000	50	$40,000	$1,000	3%
Captain America Comics #3	53	$39,000	55	$36,000	$3,000	8%
Detective Comics #36	54	$38,000	61	$32,000	$6,000	19%
More Fun Comics #54	54	$38,000	53	$37,000	$1,000	3%
*Captain America Comics 132 pg.	56	VF $37,000	53	VF $37,000	$0	0%
Action Comics #8	57	$36,000	61	$32,000	$4,000	13%
Action Comics #9	57	$36,000	61	$32,000	$4,000	13%
More Fun Comics #55	57	$36,000	56	$35,000	$1,000	3%
Wonder Comics #1	57	$36,000	61	$32,000	$4,000	13%
All Winners Comics #1	61	$35,000	56	$35,000	$0	0%
More Fun Comics #73	61	$35,000	59	$33,000	$2,000	6%
*Motion Picture Funnies Wkly #1	61	$35,000	56	$35,000	$0	0%
Amazing Man Comics #5	64	$34,000	59	$33,000	$1,000	3%
Famous Funnies-Series 1	64	VF $34,000	61	VF $32,000	$2,000	6%
Action Comics #15	66	$33,000	67	$30,000	$3,000	10%
Detective Comics #2	67	VF $32,000	67	VF $30,000	$2,000	7%
Detective Comics #37	67	$32,000	76	$27,000	$5,000	19%
Four Color Ser. 1 (Donald Duck) #4	67	$32,000	67	$30,000	$2,000	7%
Red Raven Comics #1	67	$32,000	67	$30,000	$2,000	7%
All-Select Comics #1	71	$31,500	66	$31,500	$0	0%
Mystic Comics #1	72	$31,000	67	$30,000	$1,000	3%
Marvel Mystery Comics #8	73	$30,000	73	$29,000	$1,000	3%
New Book of Comics #1	73	VF $30,000	67	VF $30,000	$0	0%
Silver Streak Comics #6	73	$30,000	73	$29,000	$1,000	3%
New York World's Fair 1939	76	VF/NM $29,000	73	VF/NM $29,000	$0	0%
Superman #3	76	$29,000	76	$27,000	$2,000	7%
Marvel Mystery Comics #10	78	$28,000	76	$27,000	$1,000	4%
All-American Comics #17	79	$27,000	80	$26,000	$1,000	4%
Wow Comics (FAW) #1	79	$27,000	76	$27,000	$0	0%
Action Comics #12	81	$26,000	103	$22,000	$4,000	18%
Action Comics #23	81	$26,000	96	$23,000	$3,000	13%
All-American Comics #18	81	$26,000	84	$25,000	$1,000	4%
Detective Comics #30	81	$26,000	84	$25,000	$1,000	4%
Green Giant Comics #1	81	$26,000	84	$25,000	$1,000	4%
New Fun Comics #6	81	VF $26,000	82	VF $25,500	$500	2%
Planet Comics #1	81	$26,000	82	$25,500	$500	2%
Young Allies Comics #1	81	$26,000	80	$26,000	$0	0%
Action Comics #17	89	$25,000	96	$23,000	$2,000	9%
Adventure Comics #73	89	$25,000	84	$25,000	$0	0%
All-American Comics #25	89	$25,000	89	$24,000	$1,000	4%
Captain America Comics #74	89	$25,000	96	$23,000	$2,000	9%
Detective Comics #3	89	VF $25,000	96	VF $23,000	$2,000	9%
Looney Tunes and Merrie Melodies #1	89	$25,000	89	$24,000	$1,000	4%
World's Best Comics #1	89	$25,000	84	$25,000	$0	0%
All Star Comics #1	96	$24,500	89	$24,000	$500	2%
Adventure Comics #61	97	$24,000	89	$24,000	$0	0%
Daredevil #1	97	$24,000	94	$23,500	$500	2%
Famous Funnies #1	97	VF $24,000	89	VF $24,000	$0	0%
Jumbo Comics #1	97	VF $24,000	101	VF $22,500	$1,500	7%
New Fun Comics #2	97	VF $24,000	94	VF $23,500	$500	2%

TOP 20 SILVER AGE COMICS

TITLE/ISSUE#	2014 RANK	2014 NM- PRICE	2013 RANK	2013 NM- PRICE	$ INCR.	% INCR.
Amazing Fantasy #15	1	$200,000	1	$175,000	$25,000	14%
Incredible Hulk #1	2	$120,000	2	$105,000	$15,000	14%
Fantastic Four #1	3	$110,000	2	$105,000	$5,000	5%
Showcase #4 (The Flash)	4	$70,000	4	$65,000	$5,000	8%
Amazing Spider-Man #1	5	$59,000	5	$58,000	$1,000	2%
Journey Into Mystery #83 (Thor)	6	$55,000	6	$50,000	$5,000	10%
X-Men #1	7	$42,000	7	$40,000	$2,000	5%
Tales of Suspense #39 (Iron Man)	8	$38,000	8	$36,000	$2,000	6%
Brave and the Bold #28	9	$36,000	11	$26,000	$10,000	38%
Avengers #1	10	$32,000	10	$28,000	$4,000	14%
Showcase #22 (Green Lantern)	10	$32,000	9	$30,000	$2,000	7%
Tales To Astonish #27 (Ant-Man)	10	$32,000	12	$25,000	$7,000	28%
The Flash #105	13	$22,000	13	$20,000	$2,000	10%
Justice League of America #1	14	$20,000	15	$17,000	$3,000	18%
Showcase #8 (The Flash)	15	$19,000	14	$18,500	$500	3%
Adventure Comics #247 (Legion)	16	$18,000	17	$16,500	$1,500	9%
Fantastic Four #5	16	$18,000	15	$17,000	$1,000	6%
Green Lantern #1	18	$15,500	18	$15,000	$500	3%
Showcase #9 (Lois Lane)	19	$14,000	19	$14,000	$0	0%
Fantastic Four #2	20	$12,800	20	$12,500	$300	2%

TOP 10 BRONZE AGE COMICS

TITLE/ISSUE#	2014 RANK	2014 NM- PRICE	2013 RANK	2013 NM- PRICE	$ INCR.	% INCR.
Star Wars #1 (35¢ price variant)	1	$5,500	1	$4,500	$1,000	22%
Green Lantern #76	2	$2,700	2	$2,700	$0	0%
Iron Fist #14 (35¢ price variant)	3	$2,200	3	$2,000	$200	10%
Cerebus #1	4	$2,100	5	$1,700	$400	24%
Incredible Hulk #181	5	$2,000	4	$1,800	$200	11%
Giant-Size X-Men #1	6	$1,350	6	$1,325	$25	2%
X-Men #94	7	$1,325	7	$1,300	$25	2%
House of Secrets #92	8	$1,225	8	$1,200	$25	2%
DC 100 Page Super Spectacular #5	9	$1,200	9	$1,175	$25	2%
Amazing Spider-Man #129	10	$1,000	10	$975	$25	3%

TOP 10 COPPER AGE COMICS

TITLE/ISSUE#	2014 RANK	2014 NM- PRICE	2013 RANK	2013 NM- PRICE	$ INCR.	% INCR.
Gobbledygook #1	1	$5,700	1	$5,600	$100	2%
Teenage Mutant Ninja Turtles #1	2	$3,500	-	-	-	-
Gobbledygook #2	3	$2,150	2	$2,100	$50	2%
Miracleman #1 Gold Edition	4	$1,500	3	$1,500	$0	0%
Albedo #2	5	$875	4	$850	$25	3%
Miracleman #1 Blue Edition	6	$850	4	$850	$0	0%
Vampirella #113	7	$550	6	$550	$0	0%
Grendel #1	8	$190	7	$190	$0	0%
Primer #2	9	$160	8	$160	$0	0%
Spider-Man #1 (2nd pr. w/Gold UPC)	10	$150	9	$150	$0	0%
Spider-Man #1 (Platinum)	10	$150	10	$130	$20	15%

TOP 20 BIG LITTLE BOOKS

BOOK #	TITLE	2014 RANK	2014 VF/NM PRICE	2013 RANK	2013 VF/NM PRICE	$ INCR.	% INCR.
731	Mickey Mouse the Mail Pilot (variant version of Mickey Mouse #717) (VG copy sold at auction for $7,170)						
nn	Mickey Mouse and Minnie Mouse at Macy's	2	$2,700	2	$2,700	$0	0%
nn	Mickey Mouse and Minnie March to Macy's	3	$2,200	3	$2,000	$200	10%
717	Mickey Mouse (skinny Mickey on-c)	3	$2,000	3	$2,000	$0	0%
W-707	Dick Tracy The Detective	5	$1,500	5	$1,500	$0	0%
725	Big Little Mother Goose HC	5	$1,300	5	$1,500	-$200	-13%
717	Mickey Mouse (reg. Mickey on-c)	7	$1,200	7	$1,200	$0	0%
nn	Mickey Mouse Silly Symphonies	8	$1,100	8	$1,100	$0	0%
721	Big Little Paint Book (336 pg.)	8	$1,000	8	$1,100	-$100	-9%
nn	Mickey Mouse the Mail Pilot (Great Big Midget Book)	11	$925	11	$925	$0	0%
725	Big Little Mother Goose SC	10	$900	10	$1,000	-$100	-10%
nn	Mickey Mouse (Great Big Midget Book)	12	$900	12	$900	$0	0%
nn	Mickey Mouse and the Magic Carpet	14	$900	14	$800	$100	13%
721	Big Little Paint Book (320 pg.)	12	$800	12	$900	-$100	-11%
nn	Mickey Mouse Sails For Treasure Island (Great Big Midget Book)	14	$800	14	$800	$0	0%
4063	Popeye Thimble Theater Starring... (2nd printing)	16	$700	16	$700	$0	0%
1126	Laughing Dragon of Oz	17	$650	-	$750	-$100	-13%
4063	Popeye Thimble Theater Starring...(1st pr.)	17	$600	17	$600	$0	0%
nn	Buck Rogers	17	$600	17	$600	$0	0%
nn	Buck Rogers in the City of Floating Globes	17	$600	17	$600	$0	0%

TOP 10 PLATINUM AGE COMICS

TITLE/ISSUE#	2014 RANK	2014 PRICE	2013 RANK	2013 PRICE	$ INCR.	% INCR.
Yellow Kid in McFadden Flats	1	FN $14,200	1	FN $14,000	$200	1%
Mickey Mouse Book (2nd printing)-variant	2	FN $8,000	2	FN $8,000	$0	0%
Little Sammy Sneeze	3	FN $6,000	3	FN $6,000	$0	0%
Mickey Mouse Book (1st printing)	4	VF $5,500	4	VF $5,500	$0	0%
Little Nemo 1906	5	FN $5,000	5	FN $5,000	$0	0%
Pore Li'l Mose	6	FN $4,200	6	FN $4,500	-$300	-7%
Little Nemo 1909	7	FN $4,000	7	FN $4,000	$0	0%
Yellow Kid #1	8	FN $3,600	9	FN $3,500	$100	3%
Buster Brown and His Resolutions 1903	9	FN $3,500	7	FN $4,000	-$500	-13%
Mickey Mouse Book (2nd printing)	9	VF $3,500	9	VF $3,500	$0	0%

TOP 10 CRIME COMICS

TITLE/ISSUE#	2014 RANK	2014 NM- PRICE	2013 RANK	2013 NM- PRICE	$ INCR.	% INCR.
Crime Does Not Pay #22	1	$10,500	1	$10,000	$500	5%
Crime Does Not Pay #24	2	$9,000	2	$8,500	$500	6%
Crime Does Not Pay #23	3	$4,800	3	$4,500	$300	7%
True Crime Comics #2	4	$3,200	4	$3,000	$200	7%
Crime Does Not Pay #33	5	$2,200	8	$1,900	$300	16%
True Crime Comics #3	5	$2,200	6	$2,000	$200	10%
The Killers #1	7	$2,150	5	$2,100	$50	2%
Crimes By Women #1	8	$2,000	6	$2,000	$0	0%
The Killers #2	9	$1,750	9	$1,700	$50	3%
Crime Does Not Pay, Best of ('44)	10	$1,700	10	$1,600	$100	6%

TOP 10 HORROR COMICS

TITLE/ISSUE#	2014 RANK	2014 NM- PRICE	2013 RANK	2013 NM- PRICE	$ INCR.	% INCR.
Eerie #1	1	$10,000	1	$9,500	$500	5%
Vault of Horror #12	2	$8,800	2	$8,700	$100	1%
Journey into Mystery #1	3	$8,000	4	$6,700	$1,300	19%
Tales of Terror Annual #1	3	VF $8,000	3	VF $7,600	$400	5%
Strange Tales #1	5	$7,200	5	$6,000	$1,200	20%
Tales to Astonish #1	6	$6,000	7	$5,200	$800	15%
Crypt of Terror #17	7	$5,500	6	$5,300	$200	4%
Haunt of Fear #15	8	$5,300	7	$5,200	$100	2%
Crime Patrol #15	9	$4,700	9	$4,700	$0	0%
House of Mystery #1	10	$4,000	10	$3,900	$100	3%

TOP 10 ROMANCE COMICS

TITLE/ISSUE#	2014 RANK	2014 NM- PRICE	2013 RANK	2013 NM- PRICE	$ INCR.	% INCR.
Giant Comics Edition #12	1	$8,000	1	$7,000	$1,000	14%
Negro Romance #1	2	$2,800	2	$2,700	$100	4%
Negro Romance #2	3	$2,300	3	$2,200	$100	5%
Negro Romance #3	3	$2,300	3	$2,200	$100	5%
Daring Love #1	5	$2,200	6	$1,800	$400	22%
Intimate Confessions #1	5	$2,200	5	$2,000	$200	10%
Giant Comics Edition #9	7	$1,800	7	$1,650	$150	9%
Giant Comics Edition #15	7	$1,800	8	$1,600	$200	13%
Forbidden Love #1	9	$1,500	-	$1,300	$200	15%
Modern Love #1	10	$1,450	9	$1,400	$50	4%

TOP 10 SCI-FI COMICS

TITLE/ISSUE#	2014 RANK	2014 NM- PRICE	2013 RANK	2013 NM- PRICE	$ INCR.	% INCR.
Mystery In Space #1	1	$6,700	1	$6,600	$100	2%
Showcase #17 (Adam Strange)	2	$6,400	2	$6,000	$400	7%
Journey Into Unknown Worlds #36	3	$4,600	7	$4,250	$350	8%
Strange Adventures #1	3	$4,600	3	$4,500	$100	2%
Showcase #15 (Space Ranger)	5	$4,500	4	$4,400	$100	2%
Mystery in Space #53	6	$4,400	5	$4,350	$50	1%
Weird Science-Fantasy Annual 1952	6	$4,400	5	$4,350	$50	1%
Fawcett Movie #15 (Man From Planet X)	8	$3,800	8	$3,800	$0	0%
Weird Fantasy #13 (#1)	8	$3,800	9	$3,700	$100	3%
Weird Science #12 (#1)	8	$3,800	9	$3,700	$100	3%

TOP 10 WESTERN COMICS

TITLE/ISSUE#	2014 RANK	2014 NM- PRICE	2013 RANK	2013 NM- PRICE	$ INCR.	% INCR.
Gene Autry Comics #1	1	$7,500	1	$7,500	$0	0%
*Lone Ranger Ice Cream 1939 2nd	2	VF $5,000	2	VF $6,000	-$1,000	-17%
Hopalong Cassidy #1	3	$4,500	3	$4,500	$0	0%
Roy Rogers Four Color #38	4	$4,250	4	$4,200	$50	1%
*Lone Ranger Ice Cream 1939	5	VF $4,000	4	VF $4,200	-$200	-5%
Red Ryder Comics #1	6	$3,800	6	$3,800	$0	0%
*Tom Mix Ralston #1	7	$3,600	7	$3,600	$0	0%
Western Picture Stories #1	8	$3,400	8	$3,300	$100	3%
John Wayne Adventure Comics #1	9	$3,300	9	$3,000	$300	10%
*Red Ryder Victory Patrol '42	10	$2,000	10	$2,000	$0	0%

GRADING DEFINITIONS

When grading a comic book, common sense must be employed. The overall eye appeal and beauty of the comic book must be taken into account along with its technical flaws to arrive at the appropriate grade.

10.0 GEM MINT (GM): This is an exceptional example of a given book - the best ever seen. The slightest bindery defects and/or printing flaws may be seen only upon very close inspection. The overall look is "as if it has never been handled or released for purchase." Only the slightest bindery or printing defects are allowed, and these would be imperceptible on first viewing. No bindery tears. Cover is flat with no surface wear. Inks are bright with high reflectivity. Well centered and firmly secured to interior pages. Corners are cut square and sharp. No creases. No dates or stamped markings allowed. No soiling, staining or other discoloration. Spine is tight and flat. No spine roll or split allowed. Staples must be original, centered and clean with no rust. No staple tears or stress lines. Paper is white, supple and fresh. No hint of acidity in the odor of the newsprint. No interior autographs or owner signatures. Centerfold is firmly secure. No interior tears.

9.9 MINT (MT): Near perfect in every way. Only subtle bindery or printing defects are allowed. No bindery tears. Cover is flat with no surface wear. Inks are bright with high reflectivity. Generally well centered and firmly secured to interior pages. Corners are cut square and sharp. No creases. Small, inconspicuous, lightly penciled, stamped or inked arrival dates are acceptable as long as they are in an unobtrusive location. No soiling, staining or other discoloration. Spine is tight and flat. No spine roll or split allowed. Staples must be original, generally centered and clean with no rust. No staple tears or stress lines. Paper is white, supple and fresh. No hint of acidity in the odor of the newsprint. Centerfold is firmly secure. No interior tears.

9.8 NEAR MINT/MINT (NM/MT): Nearly perfect in every way with only minor imperfections that keep it from the next higher grade. Only subtle bindery or printing defects are allowed. No bindery tears. Cover is flat with no surface wear. Inks are bright with high reflectivity. Generally well centered and firmly secured to interior pages. Corners are cut square and sharp. No creases. Small, inconspicuous, lightly penciled, stamped or inked arrival dates are acceptable as long as they are in an unobtrusive location. No soiling, staining or other discoloration. Spine is tight and flat. No spine roll or split allowed. Staples must be original, generally centered and clean with no rust. No staple tears or stress lines. Paper is off-white to white, supple and fresh. No hint of acidity in the odor of the newsprint. Centerfold is firmly secure. Only the slightest interior tears are allowed.

9.6 NEAR MINT+ (NM+): Nearly perfect with a minor additional virtue or virtues that raise it from Near Mint. The overall look is "as if it was just purchased and read once or twice." Only subtle bindery or printing defects are allowed. No bindery tears are allowed, although on Golden Age books bindery tears of up to 1/8" have been noted. Cover is flat with no surface wear. Inks are bright with high reflectivity. Well centered and firmly secured to interior pages. One corner may be almost imperceptibly blunted, but still almost sharp and cut square. Almost imperceptible indentations are permissible, but no creases, bends, or color break. Small, inconspicuous, lightly penciled, stamped or inked arrival dates are acceptable as long as they are in an unobtrusive location. No soiling, staining or other discoloration. Spine is tight and flat. No spine roll or split allowed. Staples must be original, generally centered, with only the slightest discoloration. No staple tears, stress lines, or rust migration. Paper is off-white, supple and fresh. No hint of acidity in the odor of the newsprint. Centerfold is firmly secure. Only the slightest interior tears are allowed.

9.4 NEAR MINT (NM): Nearly perfect with only minor imperfections that keep it from the next higher grade. Minor feathering that does not distract from the overall beauty of an otherwise higher grade copy is acceptable for this grade. The overall look is "as if it was just purchased and read once or twice." Subtle bindery defects are allowed. Bindery tears must be less than 1/16" on Silver Age and later books, although on Golden Age books bindery tears of up to 1/4" have been noted. Cover is flat with no surface wear. Inks are bright with high reflectivity. Generally well centered and secured to interior pages. Corners are cut square and sharp with ever-so-slight blunting permitted. A 1/16" bend is permitted with no color break. No creases. Small, inconspicuous, lightly penciled, stamped or inked arrival dates are acceptable as long as they are in an unobtrusive location. No soiling, staining or other discoloration apart from slight foxing. Spine is tight and flat. No spine roll or split allowed. Staples are generally centered; may have slight discoloration. No staple tears are allowed; almost no stress lines. No rust migration. In rare cases, a comic was not stapled at the bindery and therefore has a missing staple; this is not considered a defect. Any staple can be replaced on books up to Fine, but only vintage staples can be used on books from Very Fine to Near Mint. Mint books must have original staples. Paper is cream to off-white, supple and fresh. No hint of acidity in the odor of the newsprint. Centerfold is secure. Slight interior tears are allowed.

9.2 NEAR MINT- (NM-): Nearly perfect with only a minor additional defect or defects that keep it from Near Mint. A limited number of minor bindery defects are allowed. A light, barely noticeable water stain or minor foxing that does not distract from the beauty of the book is acceptable for this grade. Cover is flat with no surface wear. Inks are bright with only the slightest dimming of reflectivity. Generally well centered and secured to interior pages. Corners are cut square and sharp with ever-so-slight blunting permitted. A 1/16"-1/8" bend is permitted with no color break. No creases. Small, inconspicuous, lightly penciled, stamped or inked arrival dates are acceptable as long as they are in an unobtrusive location. No soiling, staining or other discoloration apart from slight foxing. Spine is tight and flat. No spine roll or split allowed. Staples may show some discoloration. No staple tears are allowed; almost no stress lines. No rust migration. In rare cases, a comic was not stapled at the bindery and therefore has a missing staple; this is not considered a defect. Any staple can be replaced on books up to Fine, but only vintage staples can be used on books from Very Fine to Near Mint. Mint books must have original staples. Paper is cream to off-white, supple and fresh. No hint of acidity in the odor of the newsprint. Centerfold is secure. Slight interior tears are allowed.

9.0 VERY FINE/NEAR MINT (VF/NM): Nearly perfect with outstanding eye appeal. A limited number of bindery defects are allowed. Almost flat cover with almost imperceptible wear. Inks are bright with slightly diminished reflectivity. An 1/8" bend is allowed if color is not broken. Corners are cut square and sharp with ever-so-slight blunting permitted but no creases. Several lightly penciled, stamped or inked arrival dates are acceptable. No obvious soiling, staining or other discoloration, except for very minor foxing. Spine is tight and flat. No spine roll or split allowed. Staples may show some discoloration. Only the slightest staple tears are allowed. A very minor accumulation of stress lines may be present if they are nearly imperceptible. No rust migration. In rare cases, a comic was not stapled at the bindery and therefore has a missing staple; this is not considered a defect. Any staple can be replaced on books up to Fine, but only vintage staples can be used on books from Very Fine to Near Mint. Mint books must have original staples. Paper is cream to off-white and supple. No hint of acidity in the odor of the newsprint. Centerfold is secure. Very minor interior tears may be present.

8.5 VERY FINE+ (VF+): Fits the criteria for Very Fine but with an additional virtue or small accumulation of virtues that improves the book's appearance by a perceptible amount.

8.0 VERY FINE (VF): An excellent copy with outstanding eye appeal. Sharp, bright and clean with supple pages. A comic book in this grade has the appearance of having been carefully handled. A limited accumulation of minor bindery defects is allowed. Cover is relatively flat with minimal surface wear beginning to show, possibly including some minute wear at corners. Inks are generally bright with moderate to high reflectivity. A 1/4" crease is acceptable if color is not broken. Stamped or inked arrival dates may be present. No obvious soiling, staining or other discoloration, except for minor foxing. Spine is almost flat with no roll. Possible minor color break allowed. Staples may show some discoloration. Very slight staple tears and a few almost very minor to minor stress lines may be present. No rust migration. In rare cases, a comic was not stapled at the bindery and therefore has a missing staple; this is not considered a defect. Any staple can be replaced on books up to Fine, but only vintage staples can be used on books from Very Fine to Near Mint. Mint books must have original staples. Paper is tan to cream and supple. No hint of acidity in the odor of the newsprint. Centerfold is mostly secure. Minor interior tears at the margin may be present.

7.5 VERY FINE– (VF–): Fits the criteria for Very Fine but with an additional defect or small accumulation of defects that detracts from the book's appearance by a perceptible amount.

7.0 FINE/VERY FINE (FN/VF): An above-average copy that shows minor wear but is still relatively flat and clean with outstanding eye appeal. A small accumulation of minor bindery defects is allowed. Minor cover wear beginning to show with interior yellowing or tanning allowed, possibly including minor creases. Corners may be blunted or abraded. Inks are generally bright with a moderate reduction in reflectivity. Stamped or inked arrival dates may be present. No obvious soiling, staining or other discoloration, except for minor foxing. The slightest spine roll may be present, as well as a possible moderate color break. Staples may show some discoloration. Slight staple tears and a slight accumulation of light stress lines may be present. Slight rust migration. In rare cases, a comic was not stapled at the bindery and therefore has a missing staple; this is not considered a defect. Any staple can be replaced on books up to Fine, but only vintage staples can be used on books from Very Fine to Near Mint. Mint books must have original staples. Paper is tan to cream, but not brown. No hint of acidity in the odor of the newsprint. Centerfold is mostly secure. Minor interior tears at the margin may be present.

6.5 FINE+ (FN+): Fits the criteria for Fine but with an additional virtue or small accumulation of virtues that improves the book's appearance by a perceptible amount.

6.0 FINE (FN): An above-average copy that shows minor wear but is still relatively flat and clean with no significant creasing or other serious defects. Eye appeal is somewhat reduced because of slight surface wear and the accumulation of small defects, especially on the spine and edges. A FINE condition comic book appears to have been read a few times and has been handled with moderate care. Some accumulation of minor bindery defects is allowed. Minor cover wear apparent, with minor to moderate creases. Inks show a major reduction in reflectivity. Blunted or abraded corners are more common, as is minor staining, soiling, discoloration, and/or foxing. Stamped or inked arrival dates may be present. A minor spine roll is allowed. There can also be a 1/4" spine split or severe color break. Staples show minor discoloration. Minor staple tears and an accumulation of stress lines may be present, as well as minor rust migration. In rare cases, a comic was not stapled at the bindery and therefore has a missing staple; this is not considered a defect. Any staple can be replaced on books up to Fine, but only vintage staples can be used on books from Very Fine to Near Mint. Mint books must have original staples. Paper is brown to tan and fairly supple with no signs of brittleness. No hint of acidity in the odor of the newsprint. Minor interior tears at the margin may be present. Centerfold may be loose but not detached.

5.5 FINE– (FN–): Fits the criteria for Fine but with an additional defect or small accumulation of defects that detracts from the book's appearance by a perceptible amount.

5.0 VERY GOOD/FINE (VG/FN): An above-average but well-used comic book. A comic in this grade shows some moderate wear; eye appeal is somewhat reduced because of the accumulation of defects. Still a desirable copy that has been handled with some care. An accumulation of bindery defects is allowed. Minor to moderate cover wear apparent, with minor to moderate creases and/or dimples. Inks have major to extreme reduction in reflectivity. Blunted or abraded corners are increasingly common, as is minor to moderate staining, discoloration, and/or foxing. Stamped or inked arrival dates may be present. A minor to moderate spine roll is allowed. A spine split of up to 1/2" may be present. Staples show minor discoloration. A slight accumulation of minor staple tears and an accumulation of minor stress lines may also be present, as well as minor rust migration. In rare cases, a comic was not stapled at the bindery and therefore has a missing staple; this is not considered a defect. Any staple can be replaced on books up to Fine, but only vintage staples can be used on books from Very Fine to Near Mint. Mint books must have original staples. Paper is brown to tan with no signs of brittleness. May have the faintest trace of an acidic odor. Centerfold may be loose but not detached. Minor tears may also be present.

4.5 VERY GOOD+ (VG+): Fits the criteria for Very Good but with an additional virtue or small accumulation of virtues that improves the book's appearance by a perceptible amount.

4.0 VERY GOOD (VG): The average used comic book. A comic in this grade shows some significant moderate wear, but still has not accumulated enough total defects to reduce eye appeal to the point that it is not a desirable copy. Cover shows moderate to significant wear, and may be loose but not completely detached. Moderate to extreme reduction in reflectivity. Can have an accumulation of creases or dimples. Corners may be blunted or abraded. Store stamps, name stamps, arrival dates, initials, etc. have no effect on this grade. Some discoloration, fading, foxing, and even minor soiling is allowed. As much as a 1/4" triangle can be missing out of the corner or edge; a missing 1/8" square is also acceptable. Only minor unobtrusive tape and other amateur repair allowed on otherwise high grade copies. Moderate spine roll may be present and/or a 1" spine split. Staples discolored. Minor to moderate staple tears and stress lines may be present, as well as some rust migration. Paper is brown but not brittle. A minor acidic odor can be detectable. Minor to moderate tears may be present. Centerfold may be loose or detached at one staple.

3.5 VERY GOOD– (VG–): Fits the criteria for Very Good but with an additional defect or small accumulation of defects that detracts from the book's appearance by a perceptible amount.

3.0 GOOD/VERY GOOD (GD/VG): A used comic book showing some substantial wear. Cover shows significant wear, and may be loose or even detached at one staple. Cover reflectivity is very low. Can have a book-length crease and/or dimples. Corners may be blunted or even rounded. Discoloration, fading, foxing, and even minor to moderate soiling is allowed. A triangle from 1/4" to 1/2" can be missing out of the corner or edge; a missing 1/8" to 1/4" square is also acceptable. Tape and other amateur repair may be present. Moderate spine roll likely. May have a spine split of anywhere from 1" to 1-1/2". Staples may be rusted or replaced. Minor to moderate staple tears and moderate stress lines may be present, as well as some rust migration. Paper is brown but not brittle. Centerfold may be loose or detached at one staple. Minor to moderate interior tears may be present.

2.5 GOOD+ (GD+): Fits the criteria for Good but with an additional virtue or small accumulation of virtues that improves the book's appearance by a perceptible amount.

2.0 GOOD (GD): Shows substantial wear; often considered a "reading copy." Cover shows significant wear and may even be detached. Cover reflectivity is low and in some cases completely absent. Book-length creases and dimples may be present. Rounded corners are more common. Moderate soiling, staining, discoloration and foxing may be present. The largest piece allowed missing from the front or back cover is usually a 1/2" triangle or a 1/4" square, although some Silver Age books such as 1960s Marvels have had the price corner box clipped from the top left front cover and may be considered Good if they would otherwise have graded higher. Tape and other forms of amateur repair are common in Silver Age and older books. Spine roll is likely. May have up to a 2" spine split. Staples may be degraded, replaced or missing. Moderate staple tears and stress lines may be present, as well as rust migration. Paper is brown but not brittle. Centerfold may be loose or detached. Moderate interior tears may be present.

1.8 GOOD- (GD-): Fits the criteria for Good but with an additional defect or small accumulation of defects that detracts from the book's appearance by a perceptible amount.

1.5 FAIR/GOOD (FR/GD): A comic showing substantial to heavy wear. A copy in this grade still has all pages and covers, although there may be pieces missing. Books in this grade are commonly creased, scuffed, abraded, soiled, and possibly unattractive, but still generally readable. Cover shows considerable wear and may be detached. Nearly no reflectivity to no reflectivity remaining. Store stamp, name stamp, arrival date and initials are permitted. Book-length creases, tears and folds may be present. Rounded corners are increasingly common. Soiling, staining, discoloration and foxing is generally present. Up to 1/10 of the back cover may be missing. Tape and other forms of amateur repair are increasingly common in Silver Age and older books. Spine roll is common. May have a spine split between 2" and 2/3 the length of the book. Staples may be degraded, replaced or missing. Staple tears and stress lines are common, as well as rust migration. Paper is brown and may show brittleness around the edges. Acidic odor may be present. Centerfold may be loose or detached. Interior tears are common.

1.0 FAIR (FR): A copy in this grade shows heavy wear. Some collectors consider this the lowest collectible grade because comic books in lesser condition are usually incomplete and/or brittle. Comics in this grade are usually soiled, faded, ragged and possibly unattractive. This is the last grade in which a comic remains generally readable. Cover may be detached, and inks have lost all reflectivity. Creases, tears and/or folds are prevalent. Corners are commonly rounded or absent. Soiling and staining is present. Books in this condition generally have all pages and most of the covers, although there may be up to 1/4 of the front cover missing or no back cover, but not both. Tape and other forms of amateur repair are more common. Spine roll is more common; spine split can extend up to 2/3 the length of the book. Staples may be missing or show rust and discoloration. An accumulation of staple tears and stress lines may be present, as well as rust migration. Paper is brown and may show brittleness around the edges but not in the central portion of the pages. Acidic odor may be present. Accumulation of interior tears. Chunks may be missing. The centerfold may be missing if readability is generally preserved (although there may be difficulty). Coupons may be cut.

0.5 POOR (PR): Most comic books in this grade have been sufficiently degraded to the point where there is little or no collector value; they are easily identified by a complete absence of eye appeal. Comics in this grade are brittle almost to the point of turning to dust with a touch, and are usually incomplete. Extreme cover fading may render the cover almost indiscernible. May have extremely severe stains, mildew or heavy cover abrasion to the point that some cover inks are indistinct/absent. Covers may be detached with large chunks missing. Can have extremely ragged edges and extensive creasing. Corners are rounded or virtually absent. Covers may have been defaced with paints, varnishes, glues, oil, indelible markers or dyes, and may have suffered heavy water damage. Can also have extensive amateur repairs such as laminated covers. Extreme spine roll present; can have extremely ragged spines or a complete, book-length split. Staples can be missing or show extreme rust and discoloration. Extensive staple tears and stress lines may be present, as well as extreme rust migration. Paper exhibits moderate to severe brittleness (where the comic book literally falls apart when examined). Extreme acidic odor may be present. Extensive interior tears. Multiple pages, including the centerfold, may be missing that affect readability. Coupons may be cut.

PUBLISHERS' CODES

The following abbreviations are used with cover reproductions throughout the book for copyright purposes:

ABC-**America's Best Comics**
AC-**AC Comics**
ACE-**Ace Periodicals**
ACG-**American Comics Group**
AJAX-**Ajax-Farrell**
AP-**Archie Publications**
BP-**Better Publications**
C & L-**Cupples & Leon**
CC-**Charlton Comics**
CEN-**Centaur Publications**
CCG-**Columbia Comics Group**
CG-**Catechetical Guild**
CHES-**Harry 'A' Chesler**
CLDS-**Classic Det. Stories**
CM-**Comics Magazine**
CN-**Cartoon Network**
CPI-**Conan Properties Inc.**
DC-**DC Comics, Inc.**
DELL-**Dell Publishing Co.**
DH-**Dark Horse**
DIS-**Disney Enterprises, Inc.**
DMP-**David McKay Publishing**
DS-**D. S. Publishing Co.**
EAS-**Eastern Color Printing Co.**
EC-**E. C. Comics**
ECL-**Eclipse Comics**
ENWIL-**Enwil Associates**
EP-**Elliott Publications**
ERB-**Edgar Rice Burroughs**
FAW-**Fawcett Publications**
FC-**First Comics**
FF-**Famous Funnies**
FH-**Fiction House Magazines**
FOX-**Fox Features Syndicate**
GIL-**Gilberton**
GK-**Gold Key**
GP-**Great Publications**
HARV-**Harvey Publications**
H-B-**Hanna-Barbera**
HILL-**Hillman Periodicals**
HOKE-**Holyoke Publishing Co.**
IM-**Image Comics**
KING-**King Features Syndicate**
LEV-**Lev Gleason Publications**
MAL-**Malibu Comics**
MAR-**Marvel Characters, Inc.**
ME-**Magazine Enterprises**
MLJ-**MLJ Magazines**
MS-**Mirage Studios**
NOVP-**Novelty Press**
NYNS-**New York News Syndicate**
PG-**Premier Group**
PINE-**Pines**
PMI-**Parents' Magazine Institute**
PRIZE-**Prize Publications**
QUA-**Quality Comics Group**
REAL-**Realistic Comics**
RH-**Rural Home**
S & S-**Street and Smith Publishers**
SKY-**Skywald Publications**
STAR-**Star Publications**
STD-**Standard Comics**
STJ-**St. John Publishing Co.**
SUPR-**Superior Comics**
TC-**Tower Comics**
TM-**Trojan Magazines**
TMP-**Todd McFarlane Prods.**
TOBY-**Toby Press**
TOPS-**Tops Comics**
UFS-**United Features Syndicate**
VAL-**Valiant**
VITL-**Vital Publications**
WB-**Warner Brothers.**
WEST-**Western Publishing Co.**
WHIT-**Whitman Publishing Co.**
WHW-**William H. Wise**
WMG-**William M. Gaines (E. C.)**
WP-**Warren Publishing Co.**
YM-**Youthful Magazines**
Z-D-**Ziff-Davis Publishing Co.**

OVERSTREET ADVISORS

Even before the first edition of *The Overstreet Comic Book Price Guide* was printed, author Robert M. Overstreet solicited pricing data, historical notations, and general information from a variety of sources. What was initially an informal group offering input quickly became an organized field of comic book collectors, dealers and historians whose opinions are actively solicited in advance of each edition of this book. Some of these Overstreet Advisors are specialists who deal in particular niches within the comic book world, while others are generalists who are interested in commenting on the broader marketplace. Each advisor provides information from their respective areas of interest and expertise, spanning the history of American comics.

While some choose to offer pricing and historical information in the form of annotated sales catalogs, auction catalogs, or documented private sales, assistance from others comes in the form of the market reports such as those beginning on page 96 in this book. In addition to those who have served as Overstreet Advisors almost since *The Guide*'s inception, each year new contributors are sought.

With that in mind, we are pleased to present our newest Overstreet Advisors:

THE CLASS OF 2014

DARREN ADAMS
Pristine Comics
Seattle, WA

SCOTT BRADEN
Comics Historian
Hanover, PA

CHARLES CERRITO
Hotflips
Farmingdale, NY

JEFF CERRITO
Hotflips
Farmingdale, NY

PAUL CLAIRMONT
PNJ Comics
Winnipeg, MB

PAUL FIGURA
Tenth Planet Comics and Games
Oak Lawn, IL

BRAD FOSTER
SharpComics.com
Plainfield, IL

IVAN KOCMAREK
Comics Historian
Hamilton, ON

STEPHEN LIPSON
Comics Historian
Mississauga, ON

DOUG MABRY
The Great Escape
Madison, TN

WILL MASON
GetCashForComics.com
New York

BRIAN MARCUS
Cavalier Comics
Wise, VA

ANDY McMAHON
Duncanville Bookstore
Duncanville, TX

VINCE OLIVA
Grader
CGC, LLC

BEN SAMUELS
Collector
St. Louis, MS

TODD SHEFFER
Hake's Americana
York, PA

BRIAN TATGE
Motor City Comics
Farmington Hills, MI

A complete listing of our Overstreet Advisors can be found on our title page and beginning on page 1183.

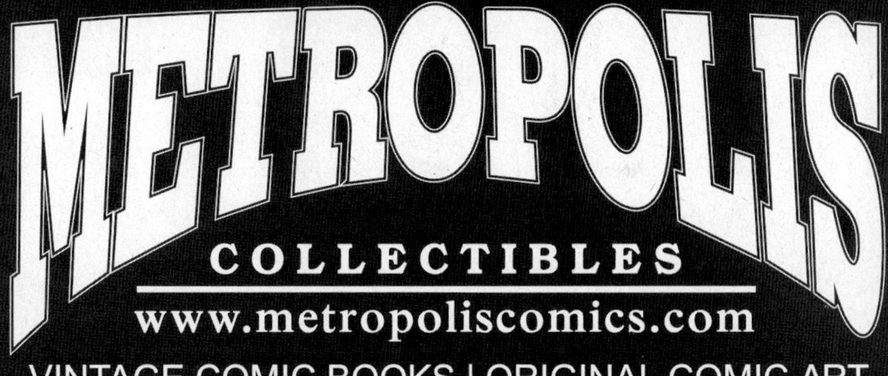

VINTAGE COMIC BOOKS | ORIGINAL COMIC ART

THE LARGEST DEALER OF VINTAGE COMIC BOOKS IN THE WORLD.

The Apex of Elegance and Class
Fine Vintage Collectibles
CGC
Comics Guaranty, LLC
CHARTER
MEMBER DEALER
Rob Hughes
Golden-Age
Silver-Age
Bronze-Age
Original Art
SENIOR ADVISOR OVERSTREET PRICE GUIDE
ALEX RAYMOND
Archangels
4629 Cass Street #9
Pacific Beach, CA 92109
RHughes@Archangels.com
Archangels.com
For the Connoisseur Collector

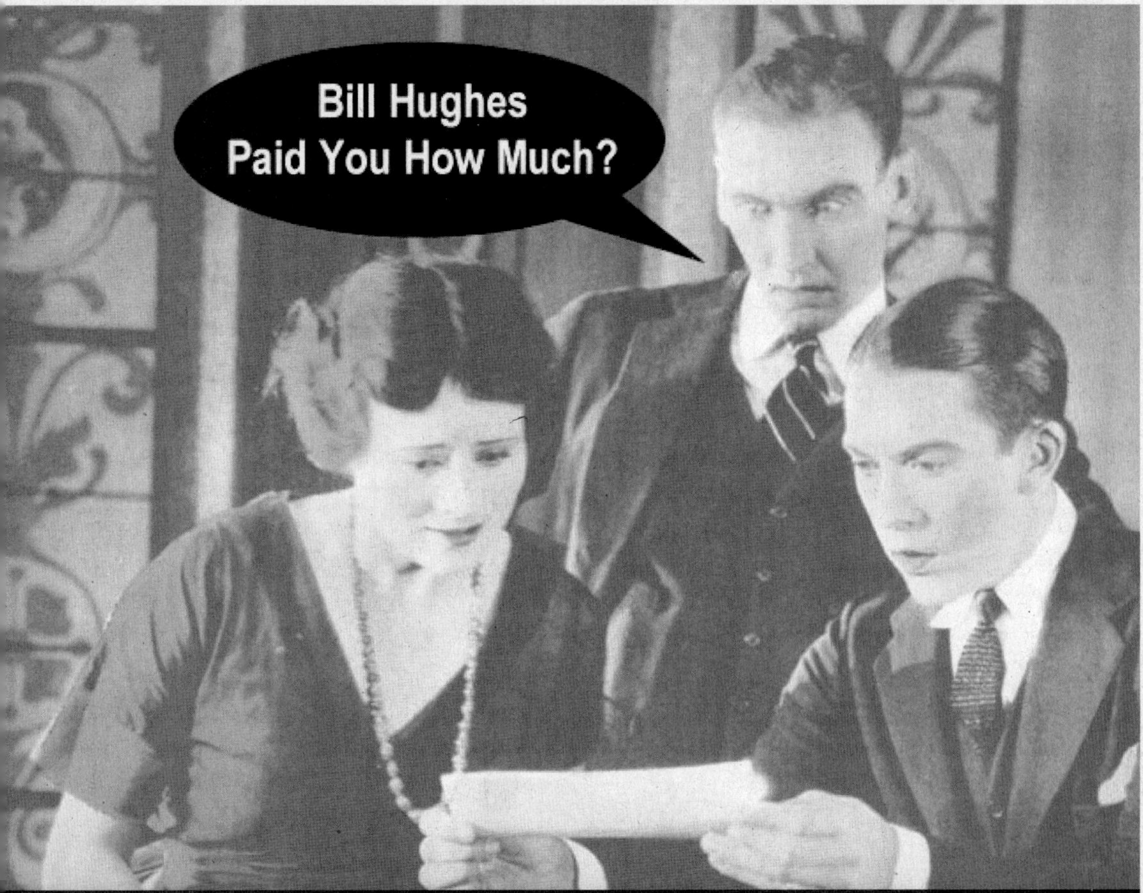

Bill Hughes
Paid You How Much?

CALL NOW FOR IMMEDIATE PAYMENT!!
ALWAYS SEEKING THE FOLLOWING:

Pre-1965 Disney Comics & Posters
Vintage Tarzan Books, Comics & Posters
Pre-1960 Western Comics & Posters
Early Popeye, Betty Boop & Krazy Kat
Vintage Our Gang, Marx Bros., 3-Stooges
Vintage Lone Ranger, Dick Tracy, Green Hornet
Charlie Chaplin, Buster Keaton, Harold Llyod
Horror & Sci-Fi Posters
Warren & Skywald Magazines
Pre-1961 Pulps and Fantasy Books

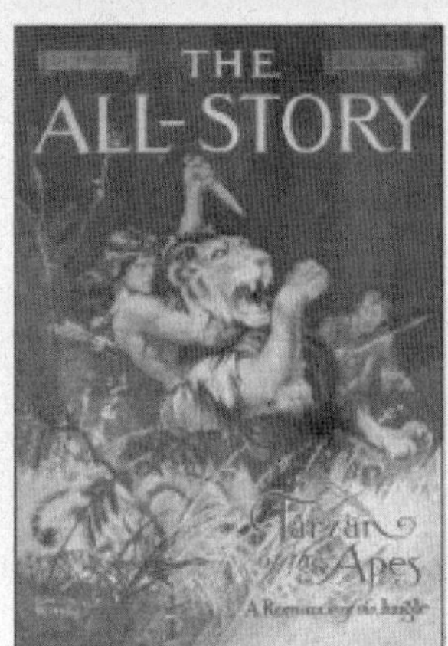

William Hughes' Vintage Collectables

P.O. Box 270244
Flower Mound, Texas 75027
Office: 972-539-9190
Mobile: 973-432-4070

eBay user: NJPOWER2000
www.VintageCollectables.net
Email: whughes199@yahoo.com

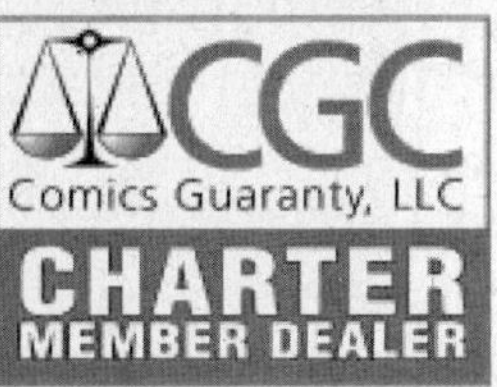

Senior Advisor
Overstreet
Price Guide

New York * Dallas * Los Angeles * Chicago

THE AMAZON.COM OF COMIC BOOKS

THE NATION'S LARGEST COMIC DEALER METROPOLIS

TRAVELING TO NYC?

WHETHER YOU ARE BUYING OR SELLING, CALL 1-800-229-6387 TO MAKE AN APPOINTMENT TO VISIT OUR AMAZING MANHATTAN SHOWROOM. OVER 125,000 COMICS AND ONE OF THE GREATEST COLLECTIONS OF ORIGINAL ART AND MOVIE POSTERS ON DISPLAY!

FAST & EASY SEARCH ENGINE! NEW COMICS ADDED DAILY!

BROWSE BY TITLE, PEDIGREE, NEW COLLECTIONS & MORE!

FEATURE GALLERY WITH THOUSANDS OF SCANS!

FREE APPRAISAL SERVICE! IMMEDIATE CASH OFFERS!

WORLD FAMOUS NEW YORK CITY SHOWROOM GALLERY!

FREE MAILING LIST FOR FIRST ALERTS & SPECIAL SALES!

AUTOMATED WANT LIST SERVICE—THE BEST IN THE BIZ!

HUGE DISCOUNT COMIC & GROUP LOT SELECTION!

SECURE ONLINE ORDERING! INTEREST FREE TIME PAYMENTS!

IN-DEPTH ARTICLES & INDUSTRY MARKET REPORTS!

NO INTERNET? ORDER TOLL-FREE OR SCHEDULE A VISIT!

METROPOLISCOMICS.COM, 873 BROADWAY SUITE 201, NEW YORK, NY 10003
PH: 212.260.4147 FX: 212.260.4304 TOLL-FREE 1.800.229.METRO (6387)
INTERNATIONAL: 001.212.260.4147 BUYING@METROPOLISCOMICS.COM

METROPOLIS THE NATION'S LARGEST COMIC DEALER

THE NATION'S LARGEST COMIC DEALER METROPOLIS

METROPOLIS

WE'RE CONFUSED!

We hope that someone who reads this will be able to explain why this kind of thing happens, because **we don't get it!**

The following is a true story...
At the biggest convention of the year, a dealer who traveled hundreds of miles to set up bought a high-grade **Fantastic Four #1** for roughly **1/2 the price** that we would have paid. After that comic passed through the hands of several dealers, Metropolis did in fact buy it. The fellow who initially sold it at the convention could easily have made ***seven thousand dollars more*** if he had sold it to us.

SHOULDN'T THESE GUYS KNOW BETTER? SHOULDN'T EVERYONE?

Is it still better to get more money for your comics than less? Does the Earth still revolve around the Sun? Are there still people out there who are not offering their books to Metropolis and losing money selling to the wrong guy?

If anyone out there can shed some light on why this still happens in this day and age, could you please let us know?

METROPOLISCOMICS.COM, 873 BROADWAY, SUITE 201, NEW YORK, NY 10003
PH: 212.260.4147 FX: 212.260.4304 TOLL-FREE: 1.800.229.METRO (6387)
INTERNATIONAL: 001.212.260.4147 BUYING@METROPOLISCOMICS.COM

METROPOLIS IS BUYING!

METROPOLIS

COLLECTIBLES

www.metropoliscomics.com

e following represents a sample of prices we will pay for your comic books. Other dealers say ey pay top dollar, but when it comes down to it, they simply do not. If you have comics to sell, invite you to contact every comic dealer in the country for offers. Then call us for your best er. We can afford to pay the highest price for your vintage comics because that is all we sell. you wish to sell us your comics, please ship us the books securely via FedEx with a tracking mber. If your collection is too large to ship, send us a detailed list and we'll travel to you. The ces below are for NM copies, but we are interested in all grades. Thank you.

on #1	$3,600,000
on #242	$18,000
enture #40	$100,000
enture #48	$70,000
enture #210	$22,000
American #16	$325,000
American #19	$40,000
Star #3	$145,000
azing Fantasy #15	$350,000
az. Spider-Man #1	$90,000
az. Spider-Man #129	$1,000
ngers #1	$65,000
ngers #4	$18,000
man #1	$400,000
ve & the Bold #28	$75,000
tain America #1	$335,000
ective #1	$120,000
ective #27	$2,500,000
ective #38	$80,000
Detective #168	$19,000
Detective #225	$25,000
Donald Duck #9	$28,000
Fantastic Comics #3	$50,000
Fantastic Four #1	$265,000
Fantastic Four #5	$44,000
Flash Comics #1	$375,000
Green Lantern #1 (GA)	$60,000
Green Lantern #1 (SA)	$22,000
Human Torch #2 (#1)	$100,000
Incredible Hulk #1	$250,000
Incredible Hulk #181	$2,000
Journey Into Mystery #83	$125,000
Justice League #1	$44,000
Marvel Comics #1	$340,000
More Fun #52	$175,000
More Fun #54	$38,000
More Fun #55	$38,000
New Fun #6	$40,000
Pep Comics #22	$250,000
Showcase #4	$250,000
Showcase #22	$100,000
Superboy #1	$25,000
Superman #1	$1,250,000
Superman #14	$45,000
Suspense Comics #3	$75,000
Tales of Suspense #39	$90,000
Tales to Astonish #27	$48,000
Target Comics V1 #7	$12,000
Walt Disney C&S #1	$55,000
Whiz #2 (#1)	$280,000
Wonder Woman #1	$50,000
Young Allies #1	$30,000
X-Men #1	$90,000

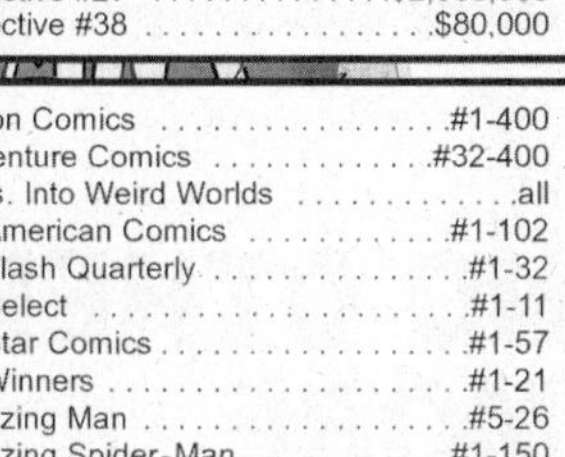

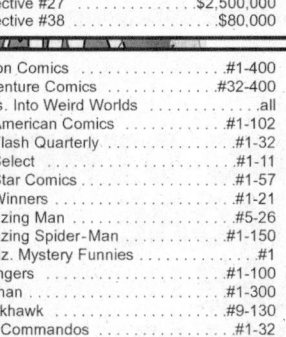

on Comics	#1-400
enture Comics	#32-400
s. Into Weird Worlds	all
American Comics	#1-102
Flash Quarterly	#1-32
Select	#1-11
Star Comics	#1-57
Winners	#1-21
azing Man	#5-26
azing Spider-Man	#1-150
az. Mystery Funnies	#1
ngers	#1-100
man	#1-300
ckhawk	#9-130
Commandos	#1-32
ve & the Bold	#1-100
tain America	#1-78
tain Marvel Advs.	#1-150
llengers	#1-25
ssic Comics	#1-169
nic Cavalcade	#1-63
edevil Comics	#1-60
ng Mystery	#1-8
ective Comics	#1-450
ald Duck 4-Colors	#4-up
tastic Four	#1-100
nt Comics	#1-86
Flash	#105-150
Flash Comics	#1-104
Funny Pages	#6-42
Green Lantern (GA)	#1-38
Green Lantern (SA)	#1-90
Hit Comics	#1-65
Human Torch	#2(#1)-38
Incredible Hulk	#1-6
Jimmy Olsen	#1-150
Journey Into Mystery	#1-125
Jumbo Comics	#1-167
Jungle Comics	#1-163
Justice League	#1-110
Mad	#1-50
Marvel Mystery	#1-92
Military Comics	#1-43
More Fun Comics	#7-127
Mystery in Space	#1-75
Mystic Comics	#1-up
National Comics	#1-75
New Adventure	#12-31
New Comics	#1-11
New Fun Comics	#1-6
Our Army at War	#1-200
Our Fighting Forces	#1-180
Planet Comics	#1-73
Rangers Comics	#1-69
Reform School Girl	all
Sensation Comics	#1-116
Showcase	#1-100
Star-Spangled Comics	#1-130
Strange Tales	#1-145
Sub-Mariner	#1-42
Superboy	#1-110
Superman	#1-250
Tales From The Crypt	#20-46
Tales of Suspense	#1-80
Tales to Astonish	#1-80
Terrific Comics	all
Thing	#1-17
USA Comics	#1-17
Weird Comics	#1-20
Weird Mysteries	#1-12
Weird Tales From The Future	all
Whiz Comics	#1-155
Wings Comics	#1-124
Wonder Woman	#1-200
Wonderworld	#3-33
World's Finest	#1-200
X-Men	#1-30

METROPOLISCOMICS.COM, 873 BROADWAY SUITE 201, NEW YORK, NY 10003
PH: 212.260.4147 FX: 212.260.4304 BUYING@METROPOLISCOMICS.COM

THE NATION'S LARGEST COMIC DEALER METROPOLIS

JUST THE FACTS

METROPOLIS

COLLECTIBLES

www.metropoliscomics.com

FACT 1: ABSOLUTELY NO OTHER COMIC DEALER BUYS MORE GOLDEN AND SILVER AGE COMICS THAN METROPOLIS.

Although the pages of the price guide are filled with other dealers offering to pay "top dollar," the simple truth is that Metropolis spends more money on more quality comic book collections year in and year out than any othe dealers in the country. We have the funds and the expertise to back up ou word. The fact is that we have spent nearly 8 million dollars on rare comic books and movie posters over the last year. If you have comic books to sell please call us at 1.800.229.6387. A generous finder's fee will be giver if you know of any comic book or movie poster collections that we purchas All calls will be strictly confidential.

FACT 2: ABSOLUTELY NO OTHER COMIC DEALER SELLS MORE GOLDEN AND SILVER AGE COMICS THAN METROPOLIS.

We simply have the best stock of Golden and Silver Age comic books in the country. The thousands of collectors familiar with our strict grading standards and excellent service can attest to this. Chances are, if you want it, we have it!

METROPOLISCOMICS.COM, 873 BROADWAY SUITE 201, NEW YORK, NY 10003
PH: 212.260.4147 FX: 212.260.4304 BUYING@METROPOLISCOMICS.COM
TOLL-FREE 1.800.229.M[illegible]RO (6387) INTERNA[illegible]NAL: 001.212.260.4147

ABSOLUTELY 100% FREE!

METROPOLIS

APPRAISAL SERVICE

If you'd like to know the value of your comics, why not ask the guys who *created* the universal 10 point grading scale? Metropolis offers the following absolutely free!

1. **VALUE APPRAISAL** to determine your comics' retail value based on all parameters including current desirability of the comic, relative scarcity and historical significance.

2. **COMPLETE EXAMINATION** of comics for all types of restoration.

3. **DOUBLE GRADING SYSTEM** to ensure greatest accuracy.

Our staff reflects over 75 years of comic evaluation and retail experience. There is not a more knowledgeable staff anywhere. For more info, call Toll-Free

1.800.229.METRO
(6 3 8 7)

Please limit the number of comics to 10.
Comics should be from 1930 -1975.
That is our field of expertise.

SELLER TIP :

Sometimes having your comics sealed by a 3rd party grader increases the value. Other times it won't and you only lose money on grading fees. Our consultation determines *when* and *when not* to have a comic "slabbed" saving you money.

METROPOLIS THE NATION'S LARGEST COMIC DEALER

METROPOLISCOMICS.COM, 873 BROADWAY SUITE 201, NEW YORK, NY 10003
PH: 212.260.4147 FX: 212.260.4304 BUYING@METROPOLISCOMICS.COM
TOLL-FREE 1.800.229.M RO (6387) INTERNATIONAL: 001.212.260.4147

ISN'T IT BETTER TO GET **MORE MONEY** FOR YOUR COMICS?

COMIC CONNECT

WWW.COMICCONNECT.COM

WORLD'S PREMIER ONLINE COMIC MARKETPLACE & AUCTIONEER

For over 30 years, the experts at ComicConnect have been recognized and renowned for selling the most sought after comic books and collections. Our services have been enlisted by individuals who are the most aggressive collectors in the market. ComicConnect will help you realize the best return when you are selling your comics.

In today's market, the decision of just how to sell your comics is critical. Making the right choice is like walking a tightrope without a net. Perhaps the most common pitfall novice sellers fall into is blindly consigning to the first auction house they come across. If you're considering parting with your collection, and think an auction house is the best way to go, we strongly advise you consider the following:

Do the Math. The commission rate an auction house charges you, the seller, is typically 15%. However, the auction house will also charge the bidder a "buyer's premium" of 19.5%. Make no mistake about it, a bidder in an auction simply deducts that additional 19.5% from the final price they are willing to pay. That's nearly a 35% cut from each and every transaction. By having their hand in the pocket of both the bidder and the seller, the auction house ensures the most profit for itself, while the consignor hemorrhages on their investment. With ComicConnect's small commission and No Buyer's Premiums, the rest of the proceeds go back into your pocket where it rightfully belongs.

When you consign to ComicConnect, you have at your disposal the services of the most experienced comic book sellers in the world. More importantly, you benefit from the thousands upon thousands of long-term customer relationships we've developed over the past 30 years. We're in it for the long haul, and will work with you to develop a strategy that will get you the highest return. We won't "square-peg" your collection into a formula that doesn't fit. We will pursue the avenue or avenues that work best for the comics you consign. Sometimes, that means selling your comics to the private individuals who pay the very best for being offered the very best. Oftentimes, we will arrange exclusive viewings at our showroom in Manhattan. We also maintain thousands of want lists of customers waiting in the wings for certain comic books to come to market - comic books that you may have in your collection.

If you're thinking of selling your comics, visit our online marketplace at ComicConnect.
For a free consultation, call us Toll Free at 888.779.7377 or email support@comicconnect.com.

873 BROADWAY, SUITE 201 NEW YORK, NY 10003 P: 212.895.3999 FX: 212.260.4304 COMICCONNECT.COM

Why should you sell on ComicConnect.com?

EXPERIENCE.

Over the last 25 years, the professionals at ComicConnect.com have sold more copies of...

Action Comics #1 than anyone on earth.

Detective Comics #27 than anyone on earth.

Amazing Fantasy #15 than anyone on earth.

Marvel Comics #1 than anyone on earth.

Superman #1 than anyone on earth.

Batman #1 than anyone on earth.

Showcase #4 than anyone on earth.

Fantastic Four #1 than anyone on earth.

Showcase #22 than anyone on earth.

Spider-Man #1 than anyone on earth.

All Star Comics #8 than anyone on earth.

All-American Comics #16 than anyone on earth.

Captain America #1 than anyone on earth.

Flash Comics #1 than anyone on earth.

More Fun Comics #52 than anyone on earth.

Adventure Comics #40 than anyone on earth.

Whiz Comics #2 (#1) than anyone on earth.

All Star Comics #3 than anyone on earth.

CONTACT US TODAY FOR A FREE CONSULTATION!

873 BROADWAY, SUITE 201, NEW YORK, NY 10003
P: 888.779.7377 | INT'L: 001.212.895.3999 | F: 212.260.4304
www.comicconnect.com | support@comicconnect.com

BIGGER AND BETTER

52 PAGES 25¢

COMICS INA FLASH!

52 PAGES 25¢

COMICS INA FLASH!

Giant-Size X-Men #1 © MCG

House of Secrets #92 © DC

We are the **KING** of **Bronze Age** books!

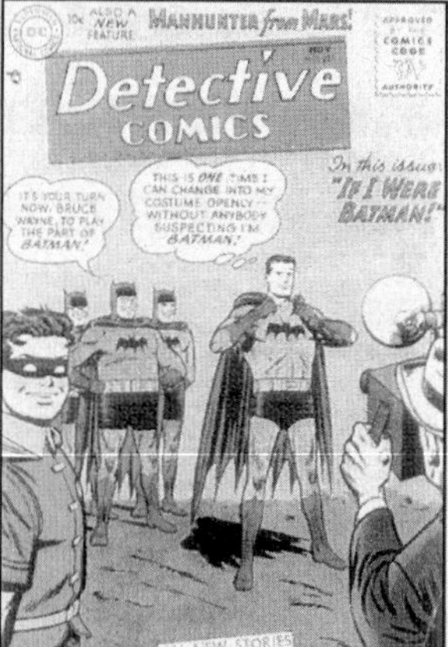

Detective Comics #225 © DC

Yes, we have plenty of **Silver Age** books too!

Showcase #4 © DC

BUY-SELL & TRADE COMICS 1956-1980

CONTACT US!! We'll send you our free photo packed catalogue which lists 1000's of comics with prices starting under $1.00!!

Tony Starks
COMICS INA FLASH®℠
PO Box 3611
Evansville, IN 47735-3611
Phone/FAX 812-401-6127
Outside USA 812-401-6127

NOW OFFERING:
Fast, Affordable & Professional comic book pressing service. Prices start at $8.00 a book. See our website for full details.

www.comicsinaflash.com
email: comicflash@aol.com

Comics Ina Flash! is a registered service mark of Tony Starks

JHV ASSOCIATES

is

BUYING COMICS

1935–1975

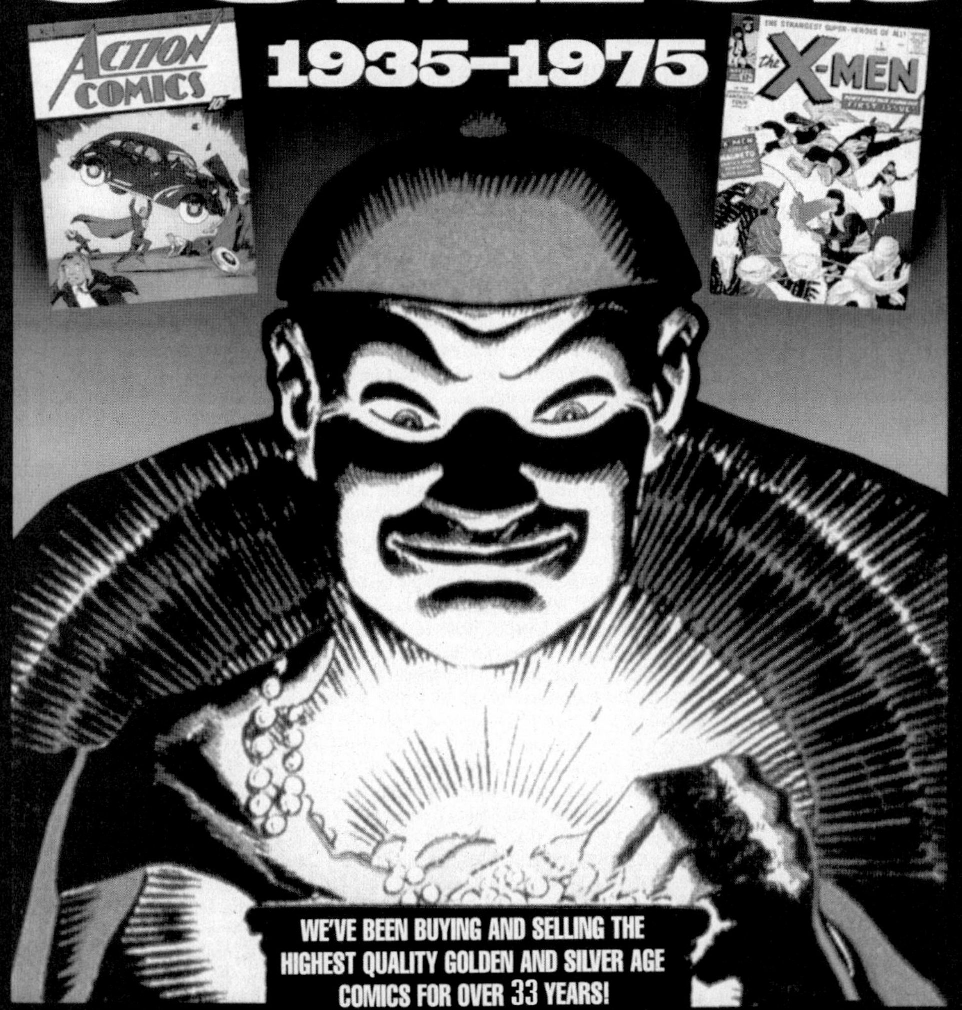

WE'VE BEEN BUYING AND SELLING THE HIGHEST QUALITY GOLDEN AND SILVER AGE COMICS FOR OVER 33 YEARS!

If you are thinking of selling your prized collection . . .call us! We'll fly anywhere to meet with you and we guarantee we'll treat you right!

Ask around (Even our competitors)...Our reputation Can't Be Beat!

P.O. BOX 317, WOODBURY HEIGHTS, NEW JERSEY 08097 TEL: 856-845-4010

E-MAIL: JHVASSOC@HOTMAIL.COM

WWW.JHVASSOCIATES.COM

VISIT MY EBAY STORE JHV ASSOC

www.dougcomicworld.com

DOUG SULIPA'S

COMIC WORLD

Box 21986
Steinbach, Manitoba
CANADA R5G 1B5
Ph: 1-204-346-3674 (8am-11pm)
Web site: www.dougcomicworld.com
Email: dsulipa@gmail.com Ebay Auctions: "dwscw"
Mail order since 1971! Overstreet Advisor!
Specialist in EVERYTHING!

1,300,000 COMICS & RELATED ITEMS: Specializing in 1960-2010 = 95% of ALL comics by ALL companies in Stock. Likely THE World's BIGGEST selection with Approx. 200,000 DIFFERENT Comics & Related items in stock. PLUS a Great Selection of 1940s-1950s & older too. (We especially like to carry everything valued at under $100). ** (200,000 Alternatives; 40,000 Archie; 35,000 Charlton; 3000 Classics; 6000 Comic/Cartoon Paperbacks; 15,000 Comic Digests; 70,000 Comic Magazines; 3000 Dennis the Menace; Fanzines & related; 350,000 DC; 20,000 DELL; 20,000 Disney; 3000 French & Foreign Language comics; 30,000 Gold Key; 5000 Hanna-Barbera; 8000 Harvey; 450,000 Marvel; 12,000 Richie Rich; 2000 Treasure Chest; 1500 Undergrounds; 13,000 UK British Marvel; 6000 Warren). ** **PLUS a big selection of:** ACG, Adult Cartoon, Atlas/Seaboard, Atlas/Marvel, Bananas mags, BLBs, Capt. Canuck, CARtoons, CGC graded, Coloring Books, Calendars, CBG, Christian/Religious, Comic Reader/Journal, Cracked, Dynamite, Eerie Pub., Fanzines, Fawcett Westerns, Giveaways, Gladstone, Heavy Metal, Help, Horror, Humor/Parody, MAD, Misc. Golden Age, National Lampoon, Platinum Age, Portfolios, RBCC, Romance, Sick, Skywald, Spire, Stanley, 3-D, Treasuries, Trib Comic, War, Tower, UK - British Annuals & Comics, Westerns & MORE. We have most of the hard to find Cartoon, Humor, Love, Teen, War & Western Comics & most main-stream Superhero & other popular titles too. Please ***SEND your*** SERIOUS ***WANT LIST*** of 50 or less "Most Wanted" items.
eBAY: See our many current auctions on eBay, for all the types of material we sell as "**dwscw**" (Our Feedback is at over +2400 = 100% Positive, at time of writing). **ABE Books**: See the BOOKS, Paperbacks, Pulps & other items we have listed on the internet at ABE books = "www.abebooks.com" & search sellers = "Comic World". **POSTERS**: We have 10,000 Movie & Video store Posters (1960-up & some older), PLUS about another 10,000 Chain Store type posters; 3000 Comic & Comic Promo posters. Send your want lists! **100,000 Vinyl RECORDS**: Most Standard issue records 1960-90 in stock & selection of '50s(most $5-25); 8000 Cassette tapes. **600,000 NON-SPORT TRADING CARDS**: Decent selection of 1950s-1980 singles; Huge Selection of 1981-1995 Singles, Sets & inserts; MAGIC the GATHERING; VIDEO GAMES; Collectible Atari 2600, Coleco, Intellivision, Nintendo, Sega, Vic-20 & some newer games. **BOARD GAMES**: Approx 1500 Vintage 1950s to 1980s Board Games; Character, TV, Comic & Misc. **16,000 VHS MOVIES**: Most Popular Theatre Movies in Stock; 1000's of Out-of-Print; Most are $5-$15 range; 3000 DVDs; Selection of old NEWSPAPERS, Sunday Comic Pages (1960s-early 1980s); 1000 AVON collectibles; 1000 old SOFT DRINK bottles. **250,000 MAGAZINES;** One of the World's biggest selection of ALL types of mags 1940s-2000+, some older: [70,000 Comic related; 10,000 Fantasy/SF/Horror; 10,000 Sports Illustrated; 5000 Misc. Sports; 10,000 Music; 10,000 Car, Hot Rod, Motorcycle; 10,000 Playboy & Penthouse; 8000 Misc. ADULT 1950s-2000+ (No XXX); 20,000 NEWS MAGS: Life, Time, Newsweek, McLeans, Look, Saturday Evening Post, Colliers,etc.; 5000 TV/Movie/Personality; 15,000 Comic Digests; 5000 Misc DIGESTS; Readers, Coronet, Mystery, SF, Childrens, etc.; 10,000 TV GUIDES 1950s-2000+; 3000 PULPS]. ** PLUS: Adventure, Aircraft, Argosy, Beckett, Bettie Page, Boxing, Childrens, Cosmopolitan, Crafts, Dime Novels (1885-1925), Ebony, Golf, High Times, Hobbies, Martial Arts, Model Airplane Cars Trains, Muscle mags, National Geographic, Omni, People Mag, Popular Mechanics, New Yorker, Price Guide mags, Punch, Railroad, RPG/Gaming, Rolling Stone, Scandal & Tabloid, Stephen King, Teen, Tennis, Traci Lords, True Detective, True Romance, UFO, US mag, Video Games, War/Military, Western, Women's Fashion, Wrestling; *** Please ***SEND your*** SERIOUS ***WANT LIST*** of 50 or less "Most Wanted" items.
MANITOBA Collection: (20,000+ Comics from this mainly 1971-1988 HIGH GRADE Pedigree Quality Collection from all Publishers).
250,000 Mass Market PAPERBACKS: ALL TYPES 1940-2000 from VINTAGE Rarities to Common Reading copies (40,000 F/SF/Horror; 60,000 Mystery; 10,000 Vintage Adult; 6000 Comic/Cartoon, 2000 Rare Canadian Collins White Circle; 3000 scarce Harlequin, #1-2000; 12,000 War/Military, 6000 TV; 4000 Biography; 15,000 Western; 10,000 Historical Fiction; Occult/UFO=4000; 10,000 NON-Fiction; 10,000 Romance; 50,000 Misc. General Fiction. PLUS: Children/ Juvenile, Sports, Music, Movie, Juvenile Delinquent, Drug, Estoteric, Good Girl Art, JFK, Star Trek, Character/Personality, Ace Doubles, ERB, REH, History, Literature, Religion & MORE. **60,000 HARDCOVERS**: A huge selection, of ALL types 1900-1990s+ including many lower cost Book Club & cheaper Reading copies. Most in the $5-$35 range, some cheaper, some better.

** **We have 600,000 Pounds of Inventory**: Our Website lists the equivalent of 6000 Typed Pages, in over 160 Categories (& still growing) of what INVENTORY is IN STOCK & ready to sell. They are NOT catalogued by price & conditon. (1) REQUEST Condition, Price & confirmation of availability; (2) State preferred Condition; (3) List up to a MAXIMUM of 50 items that interest you; (4) We will respond ASAP.

** **NO COMPUTER ??** Send your want list, or phone it in. We can make printouts & send by Mail = Phone for Cost of Printing Out & shipping. We will sell BULK Store & Dealer stock. **BUY US OUT** = Buy all our entire Comics & Related items Inventory (Approx; $6-$10 Million Retail - Instantly become one of the World's Leading dealers) for US $900,000. >> SATISFACTION ALWAYS GUARANTEED: 99.9% Satisfaction Rate!! **Strict Grading!** FULL TIME Mail Order ONLY, from our WAREHOUSE (NO Retail store). MAIL ORDER since 1971, with OVER 25,000 DIFFERENT Satisfied Customers, with over 250,000 completed orders. VISA, MC, Amex, MO, PAYPAL.

WEBSITE: (www.dougcomicworld.com) If we don't have what you want, maybe no one does.

GOLDEN AGE

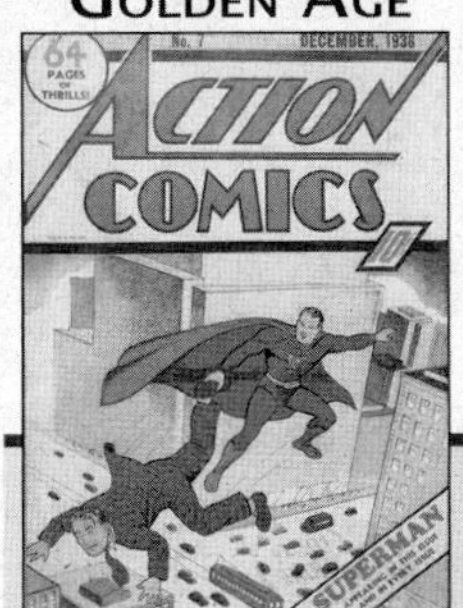

WANT LIST COMICS

SILVER AGE

WE FILL WANT LISTS

We have a simple question to ask . . . have you

E-MAILED

us your want list yet? Here is what it will cost you . . . 5 to 10 minutes of your time. Here is what you could stand to gain . . . SOME OR ALL OF THE COMIC BOOKS (CGC OR RAW) THAT YOU HAVE BEEN SEARCHING FOR THE LAST FEW YEARS!!!

WHAT ARE YOU WAITING FOR?

"The **Batman #1** you sold me was in the **nicest, unrestored condition** I've ever seen!", **Bob Overstreet, author "The Official Overstreet Comic Book Price Guide."**

"I'm glad that you have a **great selection** of **Golden Age** and **Silver Age** comics in stock. You have been able to constantly find books to fill some very tough missing holes in my collection. I also appreciate your **consistent, tight** grading and **fair** prices!"

Dan Hampton, Las Cruces, NM

These are just two of the **many** satisfied customers that have bought books from us in the past. Over the years, we have developed a **very strong return customer base** because we **ACCURATELY** price, grade, and describe books (in detail) over the phone and through the mail/email. If CGC books are desired, we can definitely fill those needs as well !!! In the past few years, we have acquired nearly **EVERY** major **Golden Age** and **Silver Age** book **more than once** for our many want list clients. These include books like **Action 1, Detective 1, Detective 27, Marvel 1, Superman 1** and more recent gems like **AF 15, FF 1, Hulk 1, Flash 105** and **Showcase 4, 8, 22. OUR SPECIALTY IS GOLD, SILVER, BRONZE, AND COPPER AGE BOOKS (1933 - 1993)**. Please check out our **great selection** of old books! (CGC or Raw).

We don't claim that we can fill every list all the time, but if any company can accomplish this, it **would certainly** be us! We can say this with **much confidence** because our representatives travel to the **majority** of the 50 states and Canada plus attend many of the major comic book conventions (San Diego, Chicago, Detroit, New York, etc.) to uncover books **you would not** have the opportunity to find. When we are not on the road, we spend **MANY** hours on the phone locating books from our **long** list of past and present comic sources we've developed over the **25 years** we have been dealing in comic books. When sending your want list either **E-MAIL** us, or mail us and include a self-addressed stamped envelope (if possible), **your phone number,** and a good time to reach you. We **DON'T** send out catalogs, so **please** ask for **specific** books and **conditions** desired. We will contact you **when** we find the items you've requested. **Phone calls are also welcomed. WE WILL GLADLY SUGGEST AND PERSONALLY PUT TOGETHER COMIC BOOK INVESTMENT PORTFOLIOS FOR BIG AND SMALL INVESTORS. OUR ADVICE IS ALWAYS FREE!**

SAVE YOURSELF ALL THE HASSLE AND LET US DO THE LOOKING FOR YOU!
CALL, FAX, MAIL, OR EMAIL US YOUR WANT LIST!

YOU HAVE NOTHING TO LOSE AND EVERYTHING ON YOUR WANT LIST TO GAIN!

Competitive pricing always. Accurate grading. **MANY CGC BOOKS AVAILABLE.** Friendly, courteous service. **Interest free time payments/layaways possible.** Checks, Money Orders, Visa, Mastercard, Discover and American Express accepted for total payment **OR** down payment on books. 7 day money back guarantee before a sale is considered final on all non-CGC books. No collect calls please.

PayPal payments accepted

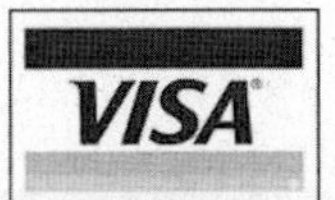

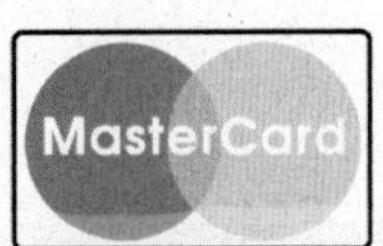

Our office/warehouse # is:
1-918-299-0440
Call us anytime between 1 pm and 8 pm, CST
Please ask for our private FAX #

WANT LIST COMICS
BOX 701932
TULSA, OK 74170-1932

Senior Advisor to the Overstreet Comic Price Guide
CBG Customer Service Award
References gladly provided!

Charter
Member Dealer

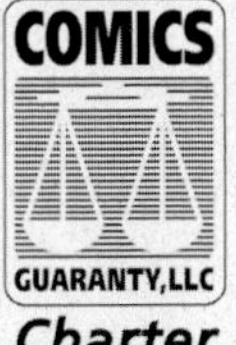

Charter
Member Dealer

Please e-mail your want list to wlc777@cox.net

PENDRAGON COMICS

Canada's Premier Store for quality Silver, Golden, and Bronze Age comics!

WE BUY ALL COMICS!
WE TRADE AND HELP UPGRADE!
WE BUY ENTIRE COLLECTIONS!
NO COLLECTION TOO BIG OR SMALL!
WE PAY CASH OR MONEY ORDER!
WE CAN EVEN PAY BY PAYPAL!

pendragoncomics@rogers.com

ALWAYS SELLING GREAT BOOKS...OUR TORONTO STORE HAS WALL TO WALL SHOWCASES OF GREAT COMICS. OUR SELECTION IS VAST, HAVING 60+ BINS OF VINTAGE HIGH GRADE QUALITY COMICS AND PLENTY OF LOWER PRICED READERS, INCLUDING MANY NON-SUPERHERO TITLES). LAST YEAR OUR HIGHLIGHTS WERE: DETECTIVE COMICS RUN #270-600, AVENGERS RUN #1-100, X-MEN RUN #1-29, FANTASTIC FOUR #12,25,26 AND CAPTAIN AMERICA COMICS #9.
COME ON IN, YOU WON'T BE DISAPPOINTED.

SEE US AT TORONTO'S BEST COMIC CONVENTION HOSTED BY HOBBYSTAR IN AUGUST!

THE SHOW BOASTS OVER 50,000 FANS FOR COMICS, TV/MOVIE, HORROR, SCI-FI AND ANIME. WE ARE THERE EVERY YEAR! (USUALLY LAST FRI, SAT & SUN IN AUGUST).

WE SPECIALIZE IN 1940-1970S COMICS
AN HONEST STORE FOR 20+ YEARS
AN OFFICIAL OVERSTREET ADVISOR
LAYAWAY POSSIBLE
*GREAT RESERVING SYSTEM
FOR NEW RELEASES!*

PENDRAGON COMICS

3759 LAKESHORE BLVD. WEST
TORONTO, ONTARIO, CANADA, M8W 1R1

416-253-6974 • OPEN WED – SUN

BUYING ALL COMICS

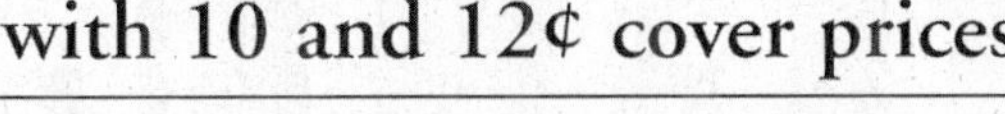

with 10 and 12¢ cover prices

TOP PRICES PAID!

IMMEDIATE CASH PAYMENT

Stop Throwing Away Those Old Comic Books!

I'm always paying top dollar
for any pre-1966 comic.
No matter what title or
condition, whether you have
one comic or a warehouse full.

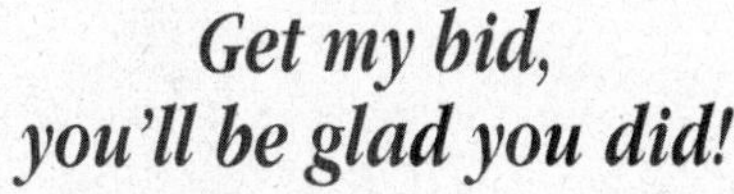

***Get my bid,
you'll be glad you did!***

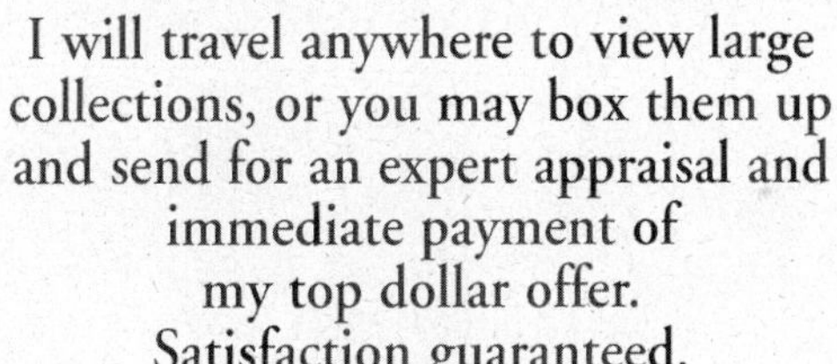

I will travel anywhere to view large
collections, or you may box them up
and send for an expert appraisal and
immediate payment of
my top dollar offer.
Satisfaction guaranteed.

For a quick reply
Send a List
of What You Have
or Call Toll Free

1-800-791-3037

or

1-608-345-8750

or write

Jef Hinds
P.O. Box 44803
Madison, WI 53744-4803

www.jhcomics.com

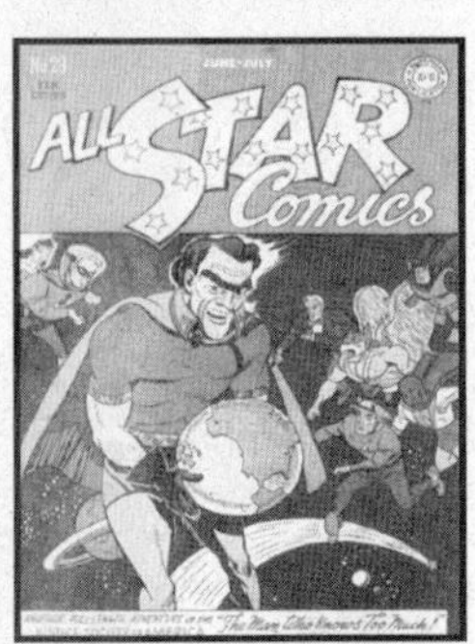

Human Torch, All Winners, Spider-Man, Captain America © Marvel, All Star, Batman, Superman © DC

FLORIDA

LONGEST RUNNING PRICE GUIDE ADVERTISER • FOUR DECADES AS PRICE GUIDE ADVISOR

DAVID T. ALEXANDER COLLECTIBLES

SHOP ONLINE AT DTACOLLECTIBLES.COM

FEATURING...
TYLER
EDDIE
LOCO
WE'RE ALWAYS BUYING!
Contact us to sell your comics.
Large quantities our specialty!
Call (813) 968-1805
VISIT OUR RETAIL STORE!
Culture and Thrills Collectibles Gallery
5205 N Florida Ave, Tampa, FL 33603
(813) 237-5400

- Paying Top Dollar for Your Collectibles (1900s-2000s)
- $500 TO $500,000+ Available for purchases
- 1 to 1,000,000+ Comics or other items, ‘No Problem’...
- BUYING: Comics, Original Art, Pulps, Mags, Toys, etc.
- 30+ Years Experience • We Pay You Immediately
- We’ll treat you & your items fairly & with respect...
- Best Reputation in the biz - We Never Under-pay!
- No knowledge of collectibles required, ‘it’s on us’
- We Travel, Expert Grading, Free Appraisals available...
- Every comic taken into account... so I can offer top $$$

We Travel...

(anywhere, anytime)

for ‘more valuable collections’...

Finders’ Fees Genuinely Paid

(For ‘info Leading to a Deal’...)

$100 to $10,000+, for a phone call!

TOLL FREE 1-866-830-4367

• **Gary Dolgoff Comics** • **email:** gary@gdcomics.com

116 Pleasant St. Suite #213, Easthampton, MA 01027 • **phone:** 413-529-0326

fax: 413-529-9824 • **ebay store:** http://stores.ebay.com/Gary-Dolgoff-Comics

GDC Gary Dolgoff Comics

GUY 'A': SOLD TO 'DEALER-X'

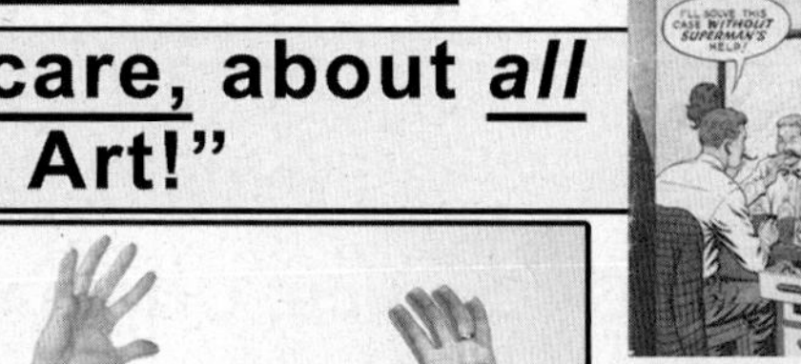

"He only took 10% of my collection 'into-account'! I 'UNDERSOLD MY COMICS'!"

DOLGOFF SEZ: "I do care, about *all* your Books & Art!"

GUY 'B': SOLD TO 'GARY-D'

"I sold to G.D.-COMICS... he paid 'top-dollar', because he ('took the time') to take all my comics & original art into account!"

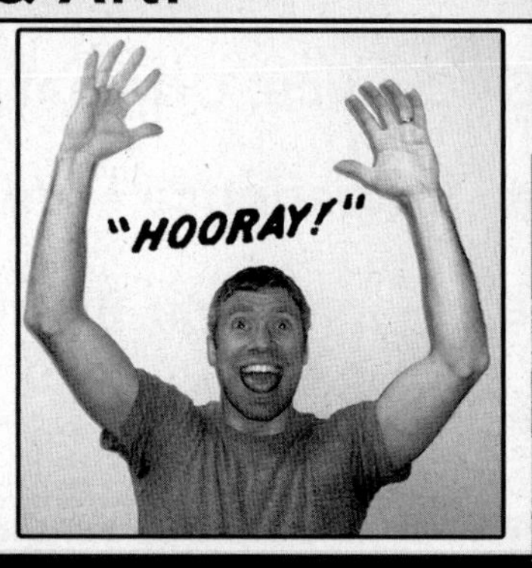

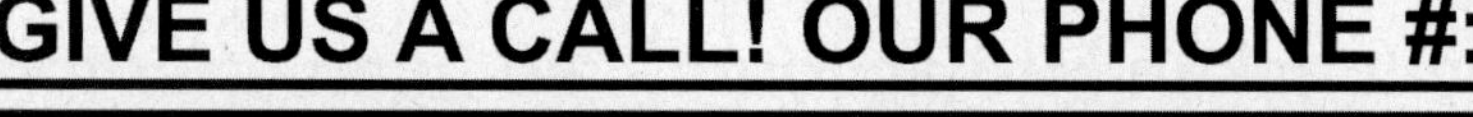

$1,000 to $500,000+... Immediately Available!

GIVE US A CALL! OUR PHONE #:

413-529-0326

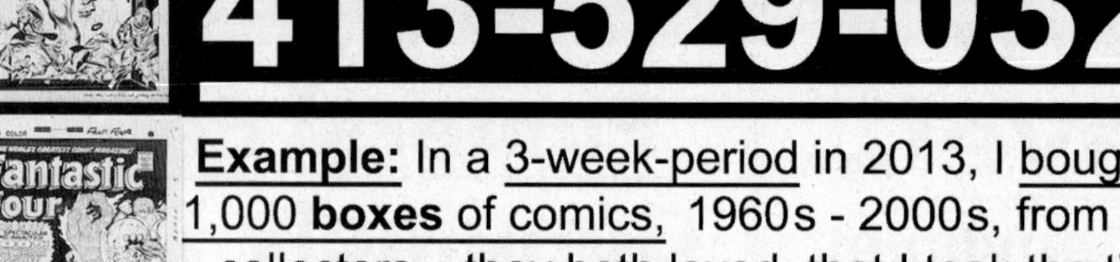

Example: In a 3-week-period in 2013, I bought over 1,000 **boxes** of comics, 1960s - 2000s, from various collectors... they both loved, that I took the time to professionally & efficiently EVALUATE THEIR 'COLLECTION-ENTIRE'! (instead of givng it the '30-minute-look', & making a 'cheesy-offer')...

I - G.D. - will 'roll up my sleeves', & give your collection/stock the attention that it deserves!

GDC Gary Dolgoff Comics

116 Pleasant St. Suite #213, Easthampton, MA 01027
PHONE: 413-529-0326 • **EMAIL:** gary@gdcomics.com
WEB: www.gdcomics.com • **eBay ID:** gdcomics

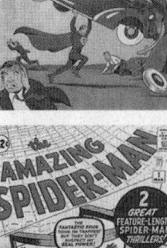

GDC Gary Dolgoff Comics

Thinking of Retiring?

(or just - 'Downsizing your Collection'?)

Don't Undersell your Collection (or Dealer's stock)...

Instead: Sell to the Dealer/Collector, who takes *all* of your Comics, Original Art, Magazines, etc... 'into account'...

A TRUE *'INDUSTRY-SECRET'!...*

Almost every dealer in this book may pay you 'good-money' for your 'top-books'... but will consider most of your collection as *incidental*, *free* (or, 'close-to-free') - for them...

On the 'other-hand'...

"WE WANT IT ALL!"...

AT G.D.COMICS -You will get - in addition to 'real good money' on your top books... you'll also get 'solid money', on... every-thing-else, in POOR to MINT condition! *('no-exaggeration')...*

GDC Gary Dolgoff Comics

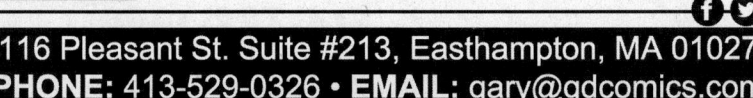

116 Pleasant St. Suite #213, Easthampton, MA 01027
PHONE: 413-529-0326 • **EMAIL:** gary@gdcomics.com
WEB: www.gdcomics.com • **eBay ID:** gdcomics

WE BUY OLD COMICS!
WE BUY OLD TOYS!
WE BUY ORIGINAL ART!
WE BUY STAR WARS/STAR TREK COLLECTIBLES!

BEST COMICS
INTERNATIONAL
EST. 1991

WE WILL BUY YOUR COLLECTION!
bestcomics.com
tommybest@aol.com
1300 Jericho Turnpike
New Hyde Park, NY 11040
516-328-1900
©2014 DC Comics.

Collect Comics?

Get our free catalog!

We Do Platinum, Golden, Silver & Bronze Back Issue Mail Order Right!

Here's what a few of our many satisfied customers say!

"I was very impressed with the packaging and speed of delivery." - Jack Eastwood, Murrieta, CA

"I have never dealt with a better mail order service." -Garth Ferris, Chico, CA

"I can count on you,...Precise Grading." -Carsten Pedersen, Hvidovre, Denmark

"RTS is my first source to find older comics for reasonable prices. Easy to use catalog & great service!" -Lance Leber, Monument, CO

"Thank you so much for your prompt service. Ordering from you is a really delightful experience. Your grading is unusually strict - most items were better than I expected." -Schultz Riggs, Jackson, MS

RTS Unlimited Inc, P.O. Box 150412, Dept OS44, Lakewood, CO 80215-0412
(303) 403-1840, Fax: (303) 403-1837, RTSUnlimited@earthlink.net, www.RTSUnlimited.com

Contact us today to get our huge illustrated free catalog! Platinum, Golden, Silver & Bronze comics, CGC graded comics, supplies, and more!! Over 30 years in business! We have the Rocky Mountain Region's most diverse selection of collectible back issue comics and supplies.

Photo-Journals!

This awesome resource to comic book collecting contains thousands of full color cover pictures in each volume! A must have for every comic collector!!

We can't recommend these books enough!

Thousands of full color pictures! Includes publication dates, artist information, articles and much more! Vol 1 & 2 focus on the Golden Age and also have scarcity data! The Golden Age volumes are only $65.95 each or $119.95 for both. Vol 3 & 4 are dedicated to Marvel Comics and are $27.95 each or $53.95 for both.

Special: Get all four volumes for only $164.95!

Shipping and handling: Continental US: please add $9.00 for the first Vol and $4.00 for each additional one. All others: please call for rates.

Note: Some volumes may have some minor cosmetic damage (The clear plastic coating is delaminating). ALL volumes are NEW and UNREAD.

To order: Call, fax, or e-mail a credit card order or Send check or money order to:

VISA

RTS Unlimited, Inc.
P.O. Box 150412
Lakewood, CO 80215
(303) 403-1840
Fax: (303) 403-1837
RTSUnlimited@earthlink.net
www.RTSUnlimited.com

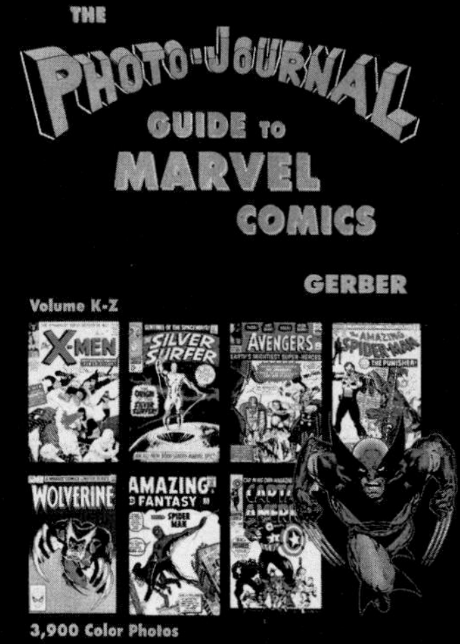

RTS Unlimited, Inc.

Dedicated to Customer Satisfaction!

DISCOVER...

Senior Advisor
Overstreet
Price Guide

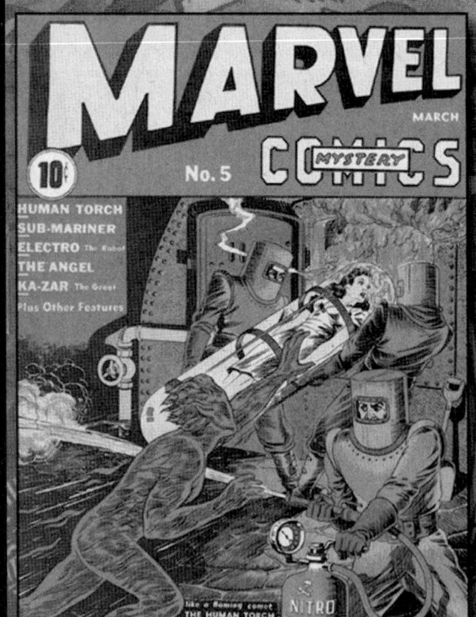

...HARLEY'S TROVE OF TIMELESS TREASURES

Golden Age • Silver Age • Bronze Age

For over 25 years, we have been supplying our clientele with the ***Finest Quality and Selection of Vintage Comic Books.*** By traveling to more than 30 comic book conventions in the USA, Canada, England, Australia and New Zealand each year and diligently searching for those rare and desirable comics our clients demand, it provides us with golden opportunities to purchase and offer one of the most ***Vast Selections of Golden Age, Silver Age and Bronze Age comics*** in the marketplace today.

Our material is Very Special and quite Diverse -- An ideal reflection of our client base. We cater to various wish-lists worldwide; from the very rare and unique items to super high-grade investment comics to the lower to mid-grade collector copies... ***We Have it All!***

And so, whatever type of comics you may be looking for, CGC certified or non-certified, be sure to give us a call. Our 25 years of Experience, Customer Service and Reputation is ***Second-to-None!***

• Accurate and Consistent Grading • Great Selection
• Competitive Pricing • Prompt & Professional Service
• Want-Lists Always Welcome • Complete Customer Satisfaction

No collection is too large or small. We will travel anywhere to view your comics and ***Pay the Highest Prices with Immediate Cash*** on hand. ***Make sure to Call Us First!***

Always Buying
Immediate Cash

Harley Yee

eBay ID
harleycomics

P.O. Box #51758
Livonia, MI 48151-5758 • USA
(800) 731-1029 • (734) 421-7921
(734) 421-7928 Fax
HarleyComx@aol.com HarleyYeeComics.com

YEEEEEEEE
Even the Mighty Subby knows that when it comes to Rare Comic Books, No One carries a Finer or more Vast Selection than Harley Yee.
Bill Guerre
Senior Advisor to Overstreet Price Guide
© Atlas/Marvel
When dealing with Yee, you will Soar with Glee! His Selection is Second-to-None.
HARLEY YEE
P.O. Box #51758 • Livonia, MI 48151-5758 USA
(800) 731-1029 or (734) 421-7921
(734) 421-7928 Fax
COMICS GUARANTY, LLC Charter Member Dealer
• Golden Age, Silver Age and Bronze Age Comics
• Hard-to-Find and Super High-Grade, Investment Books
• Lower to Mid-Grade, "Collector copy" Books
• Accurate Grading and Competitive Pricing
• Prompt and Professional Service
• Over 25 Years of "Hands On" Experience
• Want-List Service
• Setting Up at 30 or more Comic Conventions Every Year
HarleyYeeComics.com • HarleyComx@aol.com
eBay store: Harleycomics

COMIC COLLECTOR/DEALER

Paying up to **100% or more** of guide for many comics of interest

▼ POINTS TO CONSIDER ▼

TO SELL ON EBAY OR NOT TO SELL ON EBAY—THAT IS YOUR QUESTION?

- Consigning your comics to an eBay seller or an auction may not let you realize your collection's potential. EBay sellers and auctions charge 15% to 35% on every transaction regardless if they sell for less than guide. Many items sell for way below guide and you still pay all related charges. Many dealers buy these items well below market value. After you consider all charges and the final selling price you will generally net much less then we would pay. Selling to us there will be no charges, no waiting for payment. It's easy, and you will be treated with honesty and fairness.
- We have over 25 years experience in comic fandom. We have purchased many well-known collections while competing against other interested parties. Give us the chance to show you your top price.
- Being a collector/dealer gives us the ability to buy your entire collection and pay you the most for it. You will maximize your collection's value.

You have everything to gain by contacting us. WHY miss out on your BEST OFFER? Call 603-869-2097 today!

JAMES PAYETTE
Rare Books & Comics
P.O. Box 750 • Bethlehem, NH 03574
Tel (603) 869-2097 • Fax (603) 869-3475
www.jamespayettecomics.com
jimpayette@msn.com

CREDENTIALS

Special Advisor to Overstreet Guide	1985–present
Member AACBC	1990–present
Sotheby's Authenticating, Certification, and Grading committee	1991–2002
Experience as a Dealer/Collector	since 1975
CBG Customer Service Award Winner for many years	

PLEASE SEE OUR OTHER ADS FOR FURTHER REFERENCE

$ $ $ $ $ $ $ $ $ $ $ $ $ $ $

THE SELLER'S GUIDE

Yes, here are the pages you're looking for. These percentages will help you determine the sale value of your collection. If you do not find your title, call with any questions. We have purchased many of the major well-known collections. We are serious about buying your comics and paying you the most for them.

If you have comics or related items for sale call or send your list for a quote. No collection is too large or small. Immediate funds available of 500K and beyond.

These are some of the high prices we will pay. Percentages stated will be paid for any grade unless otherwise noted. All percentages based on this Overstreet Guide.

—JAMES PAYETTE

We are paying 100% of Guide for the following:

All Select	1-up	Marvel Mystery	11-up
All Winners	6-up	Pep	22-45
America's Best	1-up	Prize	2-50
Black Terror	1-25	Reform School Girl	1
Captain Aero	3-25	Speed	10-30
Captain America	11-up	Startling	2-up
Catman	1-up	Sub-Mariner	3-32
Dynamic	2-15	Thrilling	2-52
Exciting	3-50	U.S.A.	6-up
Human Torch	6-35	Wonder (Nedor)	1-up

We are paying 75% of Guide for the following:

Action 1-15
Adventure 247
All New 2-13
All Winners 1-5
Amazing Man all
Amazing Mystery Funnies all
Andy Devine
Arrow all
Captain America 1-10
Daredevil (2nd) 1
Detective 2-26
Detective Eye all
Detective Picture Stories all
Fantastic Four 1-2
Four Favorites 3-27
Funny Pages all
Funny Picture Stories all
Hangman all
Jumbo 1-10
Journey into Mystery 83
Keen Detective Funnies all
Marvel Mystery 1-10
Mystery Men all
Showcase 4
Spiderman 1-2
Superman 1
Superman's Pal 1
Tim McCoy all
Wonder (Fox)
Young Allies all

BUYING & SELLING GOLDEN & SILVER AGE COMICS SINCE 1975

$ $ $ $ $ $ $ $ $ $ $ $ $ $ $

We are paying 65% of Guide for the following:

Action 16-200
Adventure 32–100
All American
All Flash
All Top 8–18
Blonde Phantom
Blue Beetle 47–57
Brenda Starr 1–12
Crash
Daring Mystery
Fantastic
Flash (1st)
Hit 1–20
John Wayne
JO-JO 7–29
Kid Komics
Miss Fury
More Fun 52–107
Mysterious Adventure
Mystic (1st)
National 1–23
New Book of Comics
Pep 1–21
Phantom Lady
Phantom Stranger
Rangers 1-20
Rulah
Science (Fox)
Sensation
Silver Streak 1-17
Smash
Speed 1-20
Strange Tales 1–100
U.S.A. 1-5
Weird Comics
Zoot 7–16

We are paying 60% of Guide for the following:

Adventure 101–200
Adv. of Bob Hope 1–50
Adv. of Jerry Lewis 1-50
Adv. of Ozzie & Harriet
Air Fighters
All Star
Amazing Spiderman 3–10
America's Greatest
Batman 2-100
Blue Ribbon 2-20
Brave & the Bold 1–20
Bulletman
Captain Marvel
Captain Marvel Jr.
Captain Midnight
Challengers 1–10
Comic Cavalcade 1–29
Daredevil 1st 1–20
Detective 28-100
Dollman
Fantastic Four 3–10
Fight 1–30
Frontier Fighters
Green Hornet 1–20
Green Lantern (1st)
House of Mystery 1–50
House of Secrets 1–25
Ibis
Journey Into Mystery 1–115
Jumbo 11–50
Jungle 1–50
Lash Larue 1–46
Leading 1–14
Legend of D. Boone
Marvel Family
Mary Marvel
Master
Military
Modern
Movie Comics (D.C.)
My Greatest Adv. 1–50
Mystery in Space 1–50
Nickel
Planet
Police 1–20
Red Ryder 1-100
Saint
Shadow (1st)
Showcase 1–3, 5-20
Shield Wizard
Spy Smasher
Star Spangled
Superman 2–125
Superman's Pal 2–30
Strange Adventure 1–120
Superboy 1–50
Top-Notch
W.D. Comics & Stories 1–40
Whiz
World's Finest 1–110
Zip 1–39

We are also paying 50-100% of Guide for many other titles. Comics must be properly graded and complete. Please send your listing of comics for sale or a list of comics you wish to purchase. We are dealing in Marvels, D.C.'s, Timelys, Nedors, Western, Funny Material and much more! Please check our web site or send for our 100-page catalog. We will travel for large collections or, if you're passing through the area, call for an appointment.

JAMES PAYETTE
Rare Books & Comics
P.O. Box 750 • Bethlehem, NH 03574
Tel (603) 869-2097 • Fax (603) 869-3475
www.jamespayettecomics.com
jimpayette@msn.com

CREDENTIALS

Special Advisor to Overstreet Guide	1985–present
Member AACBC	1990–present
Sotheby's Authenticating, Certification, and Grading committee	1991–2002
Experience as a Dealer/Collector	since 1975
CBG Customer Service Award Winner for many years	

PLEASE SEE OUR OTHER ADS FOR FURTHER REFERENCE

THE COUNTDOWN FOR THE SPECIAL 45TH ANNIVERSARY EDITION BEGINS NOW!

WOULD YOU LIKE TO ADVERTISE
IN THE BOOK KNOWN AS

THE BIBLE OF COMIC BOOK COLLECTORS?

SINCE 1970, THE OVERSTREET COMIC BOOK PRICE GUIDE
HAS BEEN THE GO TO DESTINATION
FOR SERIOUS COMIC BOOK ENTHUSIASTS,
DEALERS AND HISTORIANS!

- **Full Page Color ads start at $2,500!**
- **Full Page B&W ads start at $900!**
- **Save 10% when you take three or more ads of the same size & type!**
- **Save 10% with our Early Bird rates!**
- **Save 20% with both discounts!**

For additional rates, specs or technical information, contact

Michael Solof
Advertising Sales Coordinator
(410) 625-7062
somike@geppismuseum.com

Early Bird Deadline
December 2, 2014

Standard Rate Deadline
March 4, 2015

WWW.GEMSTONEPUB.COM

PAUL GULACY • CAPTAIN ACTION

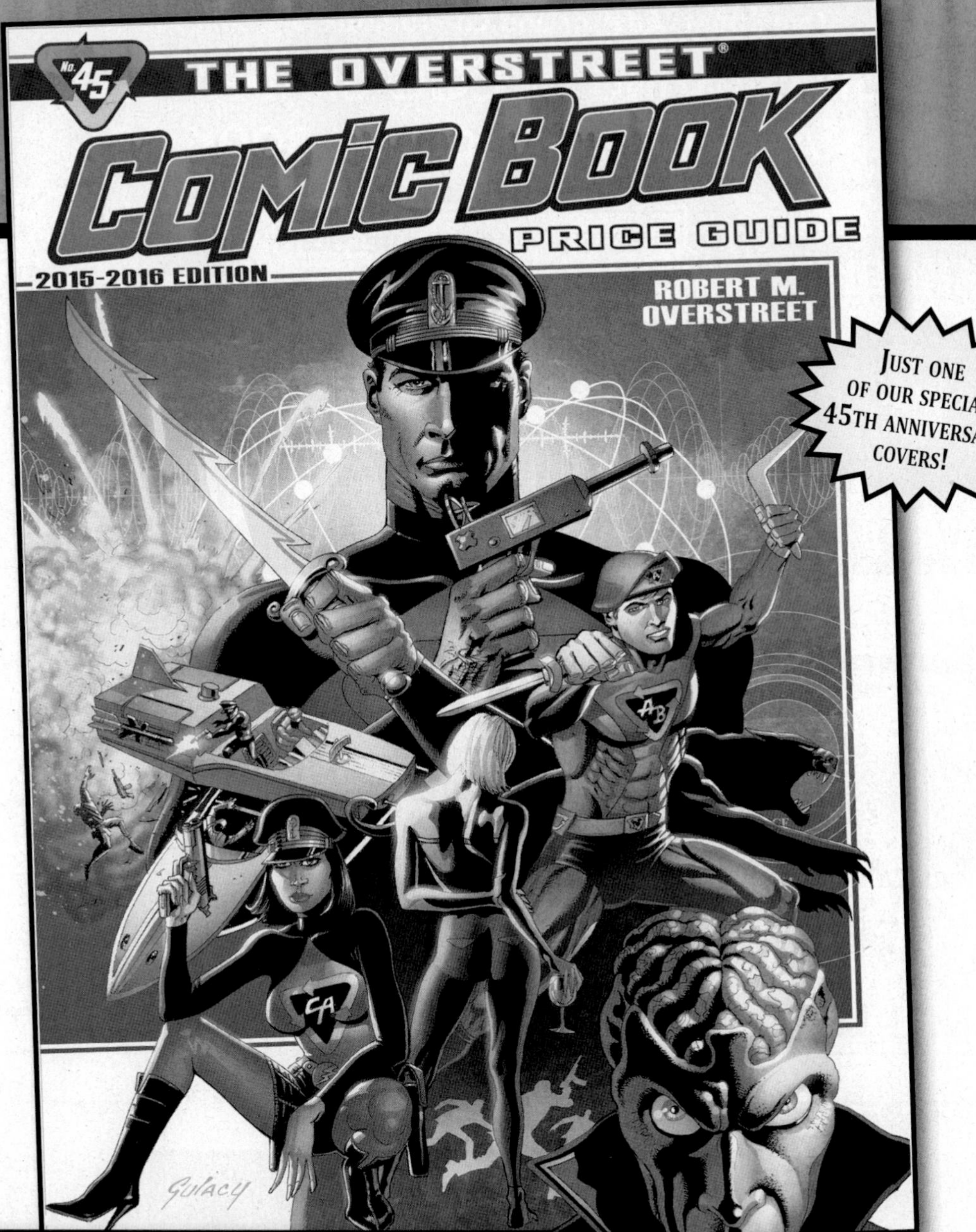

SEE PAUL GULACY'S ORIGINAL ART AND SO MUCH MORE AT GEPPI'S ENTERTAINMENT MUSEUM!

Captain Action and related characters ©2014 and TM Captain Action Enterprises, LLC. Used by Permission.
Overstreet® is a Registered Trademark of Gemstone Publishing, Inc.

WWW.GEMSTONEPUB.COM

DAN GALLO

Overstreet Advisor and Co-Promoter of Comic Art Con

SPECIALIZING IN CGC-GRADED BOOKS AND ORIGINAL COMIC BOOK ART

Buying entire collections,
(the bigger the better),
Individual Books,
CGC-Graded or Raw,
Gold, Silver, & Bronze Age,
Plus Original Art.
-- Will Travel --

Dan Gallo
Westchester County, NY

(954) 547-9063
dgallo1291@aol.com
eBay ID: dgallo1291

BIG B COMICS

ALWAYS BUYING COMICS
NO COLLECTION TOO BIG OR TOO SMALL

SHOP ONLINE FOR AWESOME GOLD, SILVER AND BRONZE AGE COMICS AT BIGBCOMICS.COM

EXCLUSIVE CAPTAIN CANUCK LICENSE HOLDER
EMAIL FOR A LIST OF CAPTAIN CANUCK PRODUCTS EXCLUSIVELY AT BIG B COMICS

BARRIE
241 Essa Road, Unit #1
Barrie, Ontario L4N 6B7
Phone: 705-739-1513
barrie@bigbcomics.com

NIAGARA FALLS
6689 Lundy's Lane
Niagara Falls, Ontario L2G 1V4
Phone: 289-296-2968
niagara@bigbcomics.com

HAMILTON
1045 Upper James Street
Hamilton, Ontario L9C 3A6
Phone: 905-318-9636
mailbox@bigbcomics.com

BIGBCOMICS.COM

AND DON'T FORGET TO VISIT
COMICBOOKDAILY.COM
DISCUSSING THE MINUTIAE OF THE COMIC BOOK WORLD

I BUY OLD COMICS 1930 to 1975

Any Title
Any Condition
Any Size Collection

Can Easily Travel to:
Atlanta
Chicago
Cincinnati
Dallas
Little Rock
Louisvillle
Memphis
St. Louis

I want your comics:
Superhero
Western
Horror
Humor
Romance

Leroy Harper
PO BOX 212
WEST PADUCAH, KY 42086

PHONE 270-748-9364
EMAIL LHCOMICS@hotmail.com

Over 20 years of experience

All characters © 2014 respective holders. All rights reserved

I BUY OLD COMICS 1930 to 1975

Any Title
Any Condition
Any Size Collection

Can Easily Travel to:
Atlanta
Chicago
Cincinnati
Dallas
Little Rock
Louisvillle
Memphis
St. Louis

I want your comics:
Superhero
Western
Horror
Humor
Romance

Leroy Harper
PO BOX 212
WEST PADUCAH, KY 42086

PHONE 270-748-9364
EMAIL LHCOMICS@hotmail.com

Over 20 years of experience

All characters © 2014 respective holders. All rights reserved

We Buy Comics

We are simply a professional, friendly and honest company
Feel free to call us anytime at 847.513.2666

Our Main Interests:

Comic Book Collections of any era consisting of 10,000 of more comics

High Grade Golden, Silver, or Bronze Age Collection

Comic Shop Overstock from the last three years

Uncirculated Comics from the 1960's to 1985

Revealed Treasures
165 N Archer Ave
Mundelein, IL 60060
Ebay Handle: Comics4Less
email oldcomics@yahoo.com

www.Comics4Less.com

We Sell Comics

Comics4Less Ebay Handle

Hundreds of no reserve Golden to Modern Age Comics every week

Comics4Less ComicCollectorlive.com Handle

Over 100,000 Comics listed from $1.00 to $5.00

Comics4Less Convention List

The Best $2.00 and $5.00 1970's-Current Comics
Wizard World Chicago/Ohio/Philadelphia
C2e2-Chicago
Planet Comic Con-Kansas City
Baltimore Comic Con
MCBA Springcon and Fallcon Minnesota

Revealed Treasures Comics4Less
165 N Archer Ave
Mundelein, IL 60060
Ebay Handle: Comics4Less
email oldcomics@yahoo.com

www.Comics4Less.com

MAIL ORDER CATALOGS

Good old-fashioned paper catalogs that you can hold in your hands.
Wide selection, reasonable prices, strict grading and great service.

Trusted mail order retailer since 1979.

OLD COMICS

40,000+ 1940s - 1970s

Gold-Silver-Bronze Comic Books

All publishers, All genres

Hero, Humor, Horror, Western, Teen, Romance, Movie/TV, Disney, Sci-Fi & more

MAGAZINES

15,000+ 1940s to now

Monsters, Sci-Fi, Horror, Humor, Movie/TV, Fanzines, Comic Format, Star Trek, Star Wars, Godzilla & more

Wide selection of rare, cult & interesting

Complete Comic Book Sets, Runs & Lots

All publishers & genres 1000s of sets, runs & lots at bargain prices

To have paper copies of these catalogs mailed to you, request "60-page Old Comics Catalog" with $4.00 (Outside US send $10.00), request "28-page Magazine Catalog" with $3.00 (Outside US send $7.00) or request 12-page "Complete Comic Book Sets Catalog" with $2.00 (Outside US send $5.00).
Send $6.00 to receive all three catalogs (Outside US send $15.00).
or view these individually priced back issues when you visit my website

MightyMags.com

PO Box 22916, St. Petersburg, FL 33742-2916

BUYING
BUYING
BUYING

I'm always buying the same types of things that I'm selling (old comics & magazines as mentioned above). Contact me through my website or by mail, especially if you live in the Tampa Bay area,if you are selling.

BUYING
BUYING
BUYING

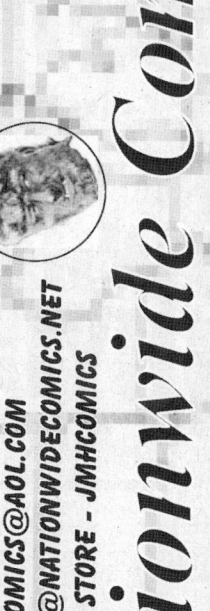

JOHN HAUSER
P.O. BOX 510673
NEW BERLIN, WI. 53151
262-789-1863
JMHCOMICS@AOL.COM
JOHN@NATIONWIDECOMICS.NET
E-BAY STORE - JMHCOMICS

TERRY O'NEILL
TERRY'S COMICS
P.O. BOX 2065
ORANGE, CA. 92859
PH: (714) 288-8993 OR
FAX: (714) 288-8992
INFO@TERRYSCOMICS.COM
TERRY@NATIONWIDECOMICS.NET

Nationwide Comics

SELLERS HOTLINE: 1 (800) 938-0325
WEB SITES: WWW.TERRYSCOMICS.COM
WWW.SOCALCOMICS.COM
WWW.JMHCOMICS.COM
WWW.PHILADELPHIACOMIC-CON.COM
WWW.CALCOMICCON.COM

DEREK WOYWOOD.
PHILADELPHIA COMIC-CON!
PO BOX 313
CLEMENTON, NJ 08021
PH: (856) 217-5737
DWOYWOOD@YAHOO.COM
DEREK@NATIONWIDECOMICS.NET

JAMIE NEWBOLD
SOUTHERN CALIFORNIA COMICS
CLAIREMONT MESA BL. #124
SAN DIEGO, CA. 92111
PH: (858) 715-8669 OR
SOCALCOM@AOL.COM
JAMIE@NATIONWIDECOMICS.NET

We buy and sell comics Nationwide.

WHO SAYS SIZE DOESN'T MATTER!!!!

ATTENTION

Dealers / Publishers / Collectors on Steroids

BUYING! BUYING! BUYING!

KEEP YOUR GOOD COMIC BOOKS and SELL US EVERYTHING YOU DON'T WANT!!

Cardsone is the Nation's Largest Mass Market Liquidators of comic books and we are always looking for more bulk comic book closeout deals to fill our orders. If you have large accumulations of Comic Books and want to clear out space give us a Call. We can handle any large size deal from a single pallet of comic books to an Entire Comic Book Warehouse Liquidation.

We are not interested in high grade or vintage comic books. Piece out your better comic books to the other guys to maximize the money you get for your overstock. We want the books that have been sitting around collecting dust and valuable storage space for years.

- ***Every deal... shipping is paid by us!!!***
- ***Get paid quick and easy!!!***
- ***We specialize in tractor trailer loads of comic books of 250k to 300k per load***
- ***On big deals... if you need us to come to you and load you up..... We will!!!***
- ***We don't care if you have 50,000 of the same issue. A mix is nice but not important***
- ***We only buy large accumations starting at 15,000 books or more***

For more information contact us:
rsales@cardsone.com • 423-472-3161 ext. 101

SELL CARDSONE YOUR BULK COMIC BOOK CLOSEOUTS & OVER RUNS... TODAY

Visit us at Cardsone.com or Like us on f /CardsoneTrading Cards

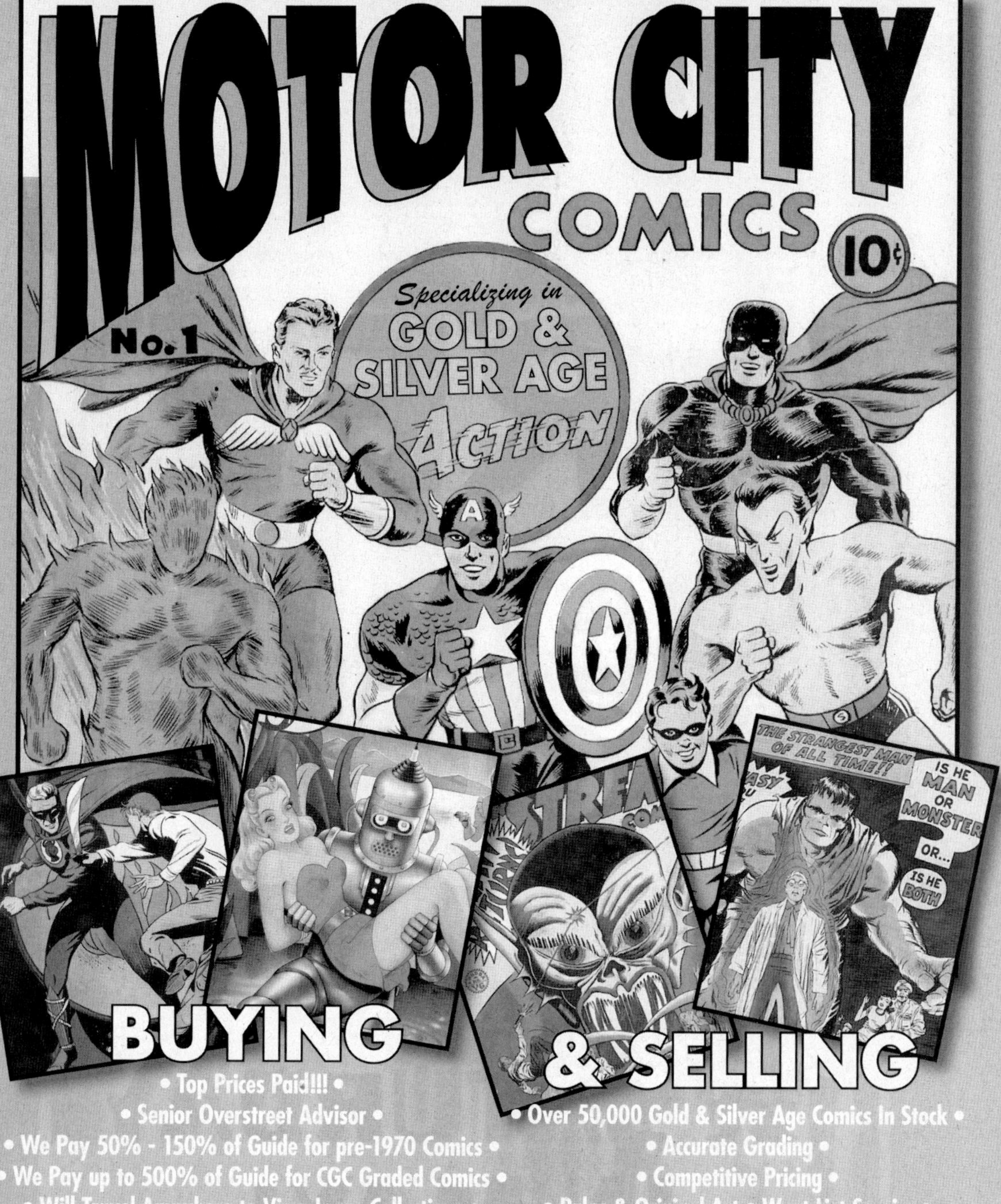
MOTOR CITY
COMICS
10¢
No. 1
Specializing in
GOLD & SILVER AGE
ACTION
THE STRANGEST MAN OF ALL TIME!!
IS HE MAN OR MONSTER OR... IS HE BOTH
BUYING
& SELLING
• Top Prices Paid!!! •
• Senior Overstreet Advisor •
• We Pay 50% - 150% of Guide for pre-1970 Comics •
• We Pay up to 500% of Guide for CGC Graded Comics •
• Will Travel Anywhere to View Large Collections •
• Consignment Sales •
• Over 50,000 Gold & Silver Age Comics In Stock •
• Accurate Grading •
• Competitive Pricing •
• Pulps & Original Art • Want List Service •
• Free Catalogs: call or write for your copy •
MOTOR CITY COMICS
33228 W. 12 MILE RD. • PMB 286 • FARMINGTON HILLS, MI 48334
(248) 426-8059 • FAX 426-8064 • www.motorcitycomics.com
Buying & Selling Premium Comics & Collectibles Since 1986

SAVE THE DATE!

FREE COMIC BOOK DAY

1st SATURDAY IN MAY!

www.freecomicbookday.com

COMICS TO ASTONISH
9400 SNOWDEN RIVER PKWY
COLUMBIA, MD 21045
MONDAY-SATURDAY 12-8PM
SUNDAY 12-6PM
We also buy Magic The Gathering
WE BUY!
- ALL COMICS 30'S TO 80'S!
- ENTIRE COLLECTIONS!
- BRONZE TO GOLDEN AGE!
- GRADED BOOKS!
CONTACT:
KEEGAN F. CONRAD
410-381-2732
COMICS2U@AOL.COM
WE HAVE OVER 80,000 BACK ISSUES!
NOVA ROCKS!
Check out our new website w/h tons of CGC books
CHECK OUT OUR WEB COMIC AT:
WWW.FATGUYBLACKGUYBALDGUY.COM
WWW.COMICSTOASTONISH.COM

HERITAGE®

COMICS & COMIC ART AUCTIONS

THE RESULTS SPEAK FOR THEMSELVES!

$6.7 Million
August 2013 Auction

$5.8 Million
Nov. 2013 Auction

$4 Million
May 2013 Auction

$4.3 Million
Feb. 2014 Auction

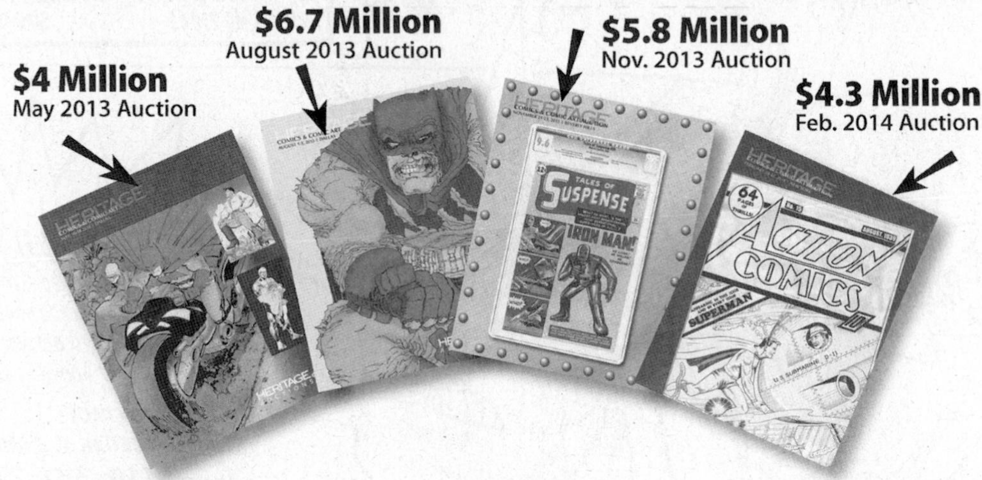

Sold for:
$388,375
8/13

Sold for:
$262,900
7/12

Sold for:
$203,150
7/12

TO FIND OUT MORE ABOUT WHAT HERITAGE CAN DO FOR YOU, SEE OUR ADS ON PAGES 6–7 AND 76–77, 78–79, 267 & 1197!

Call or email us today! We look forward to hearing from you.

Todd Hignite
877.HERITAGE (437.4824)
ext. 1790
ToddH@HA.com

Barry Sandoval
877.HERITAGE (437.4
ext. 1377
BarryS@HA.com

HERITAGE®

COMICS & COMIC ART AUCTIONS

HERE'S WHY ORIGINAL ART SELLERS CHOOSE HERITAGE:

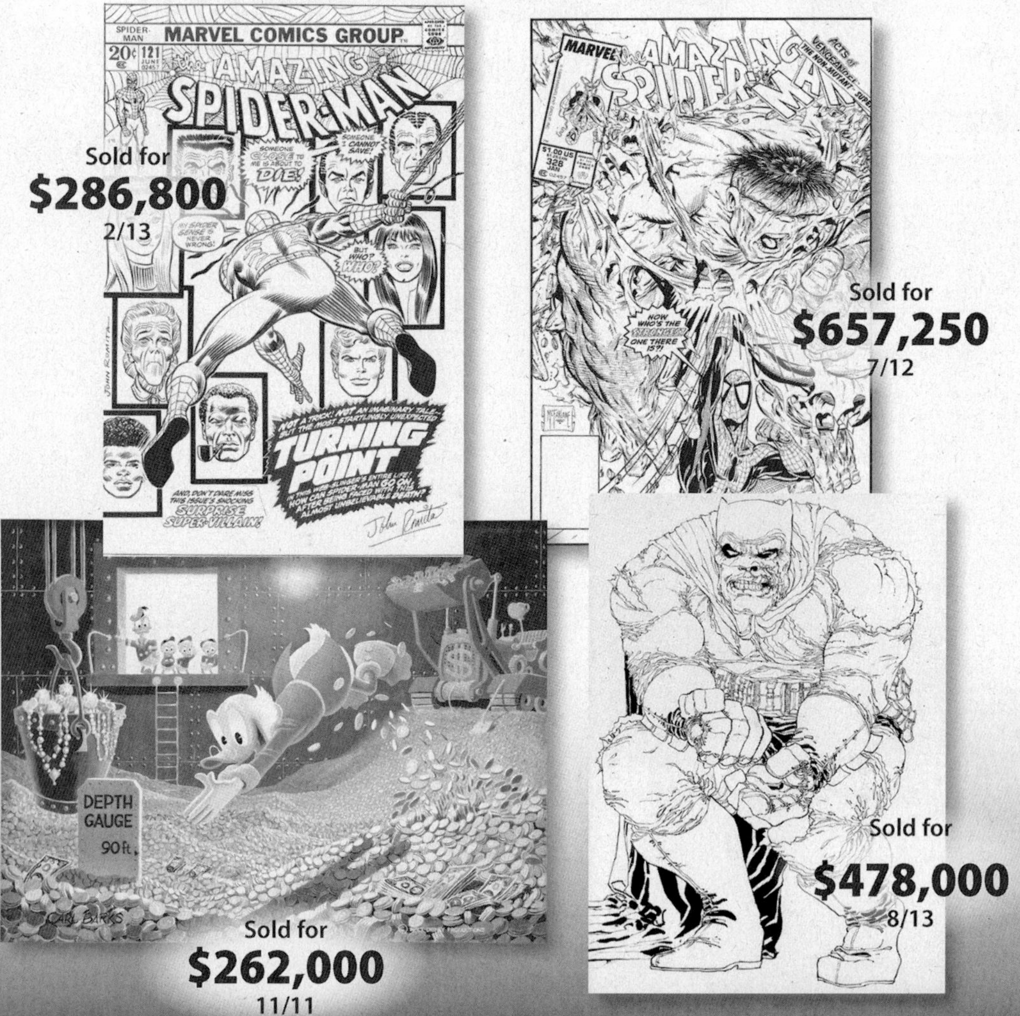

3500 Maple Avenue | Dallas, Texas 75219 | 877.HERITAGE (437.4824) | Bid@HA.com

Annual Sales Exceed $900 Million | 850,000+ Online Bidder-Members

HERITAGE HA.com AUCTIONS

DALLAS | NEW YORK | BEVERLY HILLS | SAN FRANCISCO | HOUSTON | PARIS | GENEVA

TX Auctioneer licenses: Samuel Foose 11727; Robert Korver 13754; Andrea Voss 16406. • All comic auctions are subject to a 19.5% Buyer's Premium. HERITAGE Reg. U.S. Pat and TM off.

UNBEATABLE!

RECORD SALES!

MILLIONS OF REASONS

to Consign with PEDIGREE and Sell in their GRAND AUCTIONS!...

PEDIGREE COMICS SALES:

Title	Grade	Pedigree	Price	Year
AVENGERS 4	CGC 9.8		$120,000	2013
BRAVE AND THE BOLD 28	CGC 9.2		$120,000	2013
JOURNEY INTO MYSTERY 83	CGC 9.4		$185,500	2013
TALES TO ASTONISH 27	CGC 9.4		$200,000	2013
TALES TO ASTONISH 27	CGC 9.2		$65,000	2013
TALES TO ASTONISH 35	CGC 9.6	WESTERN PENN	$125,000	2013
X-MEN 1	CGC 9.6		$250,000	2013
AVENGERS 1	CGC 9.4		$130,000	2013
AVENGERS 1	CGC 9.4	NORTHLAND	$185,000	2012
JOURNEY INTO MYSTERY 83	CGC 9.4		$222,200	2012
DETECTIVE COMICS 27	CGC 8.5 Apparent		$130,000	2012
AMAZING SPIDER-MAN 1	CGC 9.2	MASSACHUSETTS	$90,00	2011
JOURNEY INTO MYSTERY 83	CGC 9.2		$100,000	2011
X-MEN 1	CGC 9.4		$137,500	2011
TALES OF SUSPENSE 39	CGC 9.4		$147,500	2011
X-MEN 1	CGC 9.2		$60,000	2011
TALES TO ASTONISH 27	CGC 9.2		$45,000	2010
INCREDIBLE HULK 1	CGC 9.0		$100,000	2009
AVENGERS 2	CGC 9.8		$70,000	2009
FANTASTIC FOUR 1	CGC 9.6		$175,00 (PLUS TRADE)	2008
INCREDIBLE HULK 1	CGC 8.5		$32,500	2008
AMAZING SPIDER-MAN 1	CGC 9.0		$34,000	2007
FANTASTIC FOUR 1	CGC 8.5		$50,000	2007
STRANGE TALES ANNUAL 2	CGC 9.8	PACIFIC COAST	$25,000	2007
X-MEN 94	CGC 9.8		$25,000	2006
AMAZING SPIDER-MAN 1	CGC 9.6	WHITE MOUNTAIN	$110,000	2005
AMAZING FANTASY 15	CGC 9.4	WHITE MOUNTAIN	$150,000	2004
X-MEN 1	CGC 9.6	PACIFIC COAST	$100,000	2004

2009-2012 GRAND AUCTION RESULTS:

Title	Grade	Note	Price
TALES OF SUSPENSE 39	CGC 9.4		$102,500
FANTASTIC FOUR 2	CGC 9.6	WHITE MOUNTAIN	$87,000
JOURNEY INTO MYSTERY 83	CGC 9.0	TWIN CITIES	$52,000
FANTASTIC FOUR 1	CGC 9.4		$210,000
AMAZING FANTASY 15	CGC 9.2		$190,000
FANTASTIC FOUR 1	CGC 9.2		$143,000
TALES OF SUSPENSE 39	CGC 9.4		$114,990
FANTASTIC FOUR 1	CGC 8.5		$75,100
AVENGERS 4	CGC 9.6		$64,000
DAREDEVIL 1	CGC 9.6		$62,000
X-MEN 1	CGC 9.2		$55,000
FANTASTIC FOUR 1	CGC 8.0		$50,400
X-MEN 1	CGC 9.0		$33,333
INCREDIBLE HULK 181	CGC 9.8	CGC SIGNATURE SERIES	$32,001
X-MEN 94	CGC 9.8		$29,589
FANTASTIC FOUR 10	CGC 9.6		$27,999
AMAZING SPIDER-MAN 34	CGC 9.8		$25,250
FANTASTIC FOUR 26	CGC 9.6		$24,200
FANTASTIC FOUR 112	CGC 9.8		$24,017
AVENGERS 2	CGC 9.4		$13,500
NEW MUTANTS 98	CGC 9.9		$12,250

All Sales Listed Reported to GPAnalysis.com • All Fantastic Four Characters (the "Thing") © Copyright of Disney / Marvel Comics

Pedigree Comics, Inc. • 12541 Equine Lane • Wellington, FL 33414
PedigreeComics.com • email: DougSchmell@pedigreecomics.com
Office: (561) 422-1120 • Cell: (561) 596-9111 • Fax: (561) 422-1120

Sale Reporting Partner
GPAnalysis

PAYING TOP DOLLAR!...

COLLECTION PURCHASES:

$90,000 for runs of Winnipeg Collection in 1996
$98,000 for Slobodian Collection in 1998
$120,000 for runs of Bethlehem Collection in 1999
$150,000 for runs of River City Collection in 2000
$85,000 for runs of Northford Collection in 2001
$110,000 for "OO" Collection of Journey Into Mystery in 2002
$63,000 for Pacific Coast run of Tales to Astonish in 2004
$155,000 for Pacific Coast run of Tales of Suspense in 2005
$100,000 for Justice League of America CGC 1-3 Set in 2008
$103,000 for Mound City Collection in 2009
$208,000 for Twin Cities Collection Group in 2011
$287,000 for Saginaw Collection Runs in 2011
$600,000 for Cole Schave Silver Age Marvel Collection in 2013
$253,000 for Don/Maggie Thompson Collection Marvels in 2013

INDIVIDUAL COMIC PURCHASES:

Fantastic Four 1 (raw)... $32,000 1995
Amazing Spider-Man 1 (raw)... $25,000 1996
X-Men 1 CGC 9.6 Pacific Coast... $35,000 2000
Amazing Spider-Man 3 CGC 9.4 Massachusetts... $30,000 2001
Fantastic Four 2 CGC 9.4 White Mountain... $28,000 2001
Tales to Astonish 27 CGC 9.4... $25,000 2002
Amazing Spider-Man 2 CGC 9.6... $55,000 2002
Journey Into Mystery 83 CGC 9.4... $40,000 2002
Incredible Hulk 1 CGC 9.2 Northland... $47,500 2003
Tales of Suspense 39 CGC 9.4 White Mountain... $55,000 2004
Fantastic Four 3 CGC 9.4... $40,000 2005
Daredevil 1 CGC 9.4... $14,000 2006
Tales of Suspense 39 CGC 9.2... $24,000 2007
Fantastic Four 33 CGC 9.8... $22,500 2009
Amazing Spider-Man 55 CGC 9.8... $18,000 2009
Fantastic Four 1 CGC 9.2 White Mountain... $159,000 2010
Avengers 4 CGC 9.6... $40,000 2013
Brave and the Bold 28 CGC 9.2... $80,000 2013

Pedigree Comics, Inc. • 12541 Equine Lane • Wellington, FL 33414
PedigreeComics.com • email: DougSchmell@pedigreecomics.com
Office: (561) 422-1120 • Cell: (561) 596-9111 • Fax: (561) 422-1120

Sale Reporting Partner
GPAnalysis

JB²

PACIFIC NORTHWEST COMICS

OVERSTREET ADVISOR

WHAT WE BUY

- OLD COMIC BOOKS, ORIGINAL ART, TOYS AND CARDS ALSO BOARD GAMES AND RPGS (OLD AND MODERN).
- SPECIALIZING IN GOLD AND SILVER AGE COMICS.
- SINGLE ISSUES TO LIFELONG COLLECTIONS.
- WAREHOUSE, STORAGE, AND ESTATE FINDS.

WHY SELL TO US

- WE *LOVE* OLD COMICS AND WE ARE COLLECTORS FIRST WITH OVER 50 YEARS OF COMBINED EXPERIENCE IN THE HOBBY. BECAUSE THIS IS NOT OUR FULL-TIME BUSINESS, WE CAN AND WILL PAY MORE THAN YOUR AVERAGE DEALER.
- WE PRIDE OURSELVES ON BEING RESPECTFUL, HONEST, AND FRIENDLY.
- FREE IN-HOUSE APPRAISALS AND PHONE CONSULTATIONS.
- WE HAVE *CASH* ON HAND FOR LARGE COLLECTIONS.
- *FINDER'S FEES*: WE WILL PAY A HANDSOME FINDER'S FEE TO ANYONE WHO LEADS US TO A COLLECTION.

SEATTLE
JASON BESSONETTE
206.992.6424
TUNGLASHR@GMAIL.COM

PORTLAND
JIM BERRY
323.620.3329
JB233@NYU.EDU

COMIC BOOK CERTIFICATION SERVICE

CBCS

Expert, Impartial, Third-Party Grading

SHIELD YOUR COLLECTION!

www.CBCScomics.com Toll Free: 844-870-CBCS

Fogel's Underground Price & Grading Guide

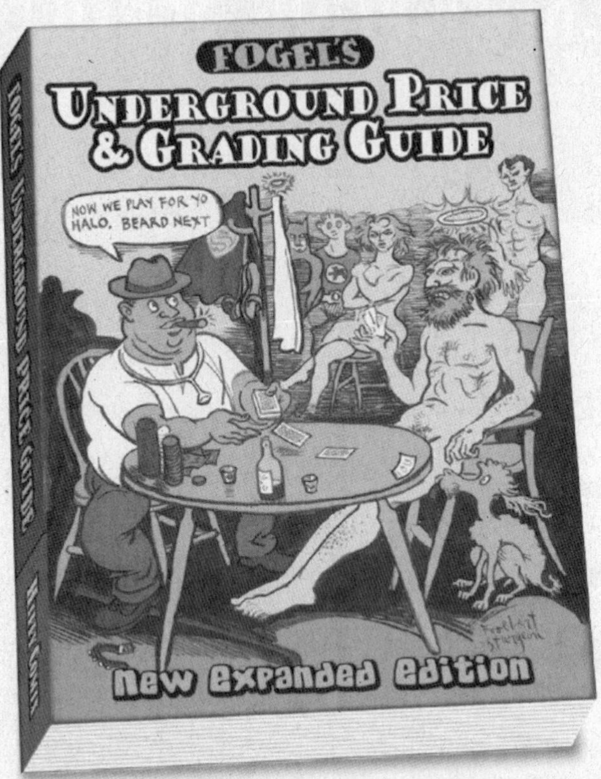

FRANK STACK LIMITED EDITION!

FINAL ARTWORK UNDER DEVELOPMENT

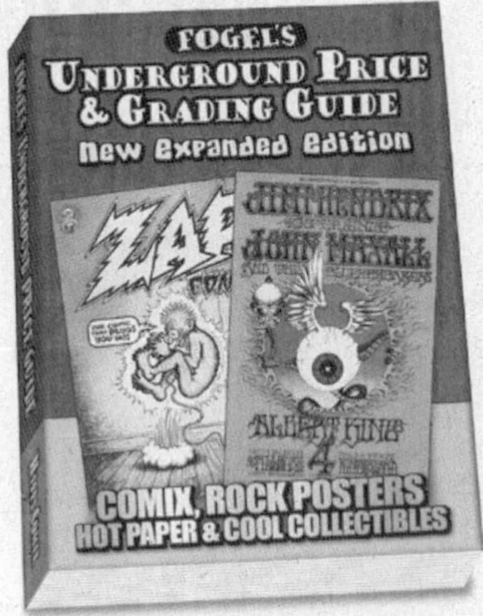

STANDARD EDITION

FINAL ARTWORK UNDER DEVELOPMENT

SPONSORED BY

THE BILL GRAHAM ARCHIVES

The "FUGG" is a mammoth, full-size trade paperback with updated prices and detailed listings on the hottest and newest (or newly discovered) underground and adult comic books, graphic novels, alternatives, independents, small press, and all titles not covered by *Overstreet's Comic Book Price Guide*.

Significantly expanded and updated special sections cover minicomics and international books. New sections also spotlight Tijuana Bibles, fanzines, tabloids, newspapers, and the first comprehensive Price and Grading Guide for rock posters of the psychedelic era! Plus a new, detailed, underground comix grading guide! Sponsored by the Bill Graham Archives at Wolfgang's Vault.

OVER 500 PAGES OF EXCLUSIVE CONTENT!

INTERVIEWS, ARTICLES, PHOTOS & FEATURES!

Available at HippyComix.com and finer comic book shops! Or call 510-220-6314!

COMIC ART APPRAISAL LLC

Appraisals for: Retail Value, Insurance, Donation, Estate, Equitable Distribution, Case Strategy, Deposition.

Comic Art Appraisal LLC

http://www.comicartappraisal.com

Comic Art Appraisal has been the foremost source for formal appraisals for comic books, original comic art, illustration art, original newspaper strip art and animation art for over 30 years. Collectors, dealers, financial institutions, museums, attorneys, galleries and the IRS have availed themselves of our services for establishing values for comic books, original comic art, original newspaper art and animation art. We have appraised over 1,000,000 individual items.

Free Evaluation Of Your Collectibles

See our site for a complete overview of our appraisal services.

Over 30 years Of Experience
Members Of American Appraisers Association
Members American Institute Of Conservation.

FANTASTIC FOUR #100
JACK KIRBY PENCILS
JOE SINNOTT INKS
1970 15 X10

Value Factors And Point Breakdown Comic Book Original Art

Potential Points	12	10	5	10	10	10	12	20	8	10	100
Factors	Condition	Configuration	Confirmation	Content	Context	Continuity	Creativity	Creator	Cross -over	Cyclical Interest	Total
FF #100 Cover	3	10	5	10	8	10	12	20	8	9	95

Never
sell a collectible without knowing the true value.
Price guides and auction records are rarely the entire picture.

Inquiries: Joe Mannarino or Nadia Mannarino
(201) 652 -1305
http://www.comicartappraisal.com

WANT TO BE SURPRISED
(IN A GOOD WAY)?
FROM COMICS TO COLORFORMS,
ROBOTS TO RECREATIONS,
ADD EBAY SELLER ID
DIGAUCTIONS
TO YOUR WATCH LIST!

D.G Auctions

FOR MORE INFORMATION CONTACT
DIAMOND INTERNATIONAL GALLERIES
CALL (443) 827-0441
EMAIL POKEVIN@DIAMONDGALLERIES.COM

HERITAGE®

COMICS & COMIC ART AUCTIONS

CONGRATULATIONS TO THE GARY DAHLBERG ESTATE
$2,000,000 SOLD IN HERITAGE AUCTIONS!

August 28, 2011

Mr. Barry Sandoval
Heritage Auctions
Dallas, Texas

Dear Barry,

I wanted to thank you and your colleagues for everything that Heritage has done marketing and auctioning the comic book collection of my late brother-in-law Gary Dahlberg.

When Gary passed away, the family knew very little about vintage comic collecting. We knew Gary's collection was valuable but had no idea how valuable. We discussed the collection with several of the leaders in the comic book collecting industry before selecting Heritage to represent us.

We were all thrilled to see Gary's collection featured in a special catalog with photographs and his personal biography, as well as in all of the printed mailers and brochures you put out before the Signature Auctions. With your cooperation and involvement, the collection was covered in many magazine and newspaper articles, making the front page of the Minneapolis Star Tribune. It was also shown on TV news. Heritage committed to using its considerable resourses in marketing this collection. You sure came through.

I was present at the first auction which featured extremely competitive bidding, and saw the first 400 comics sell for well over $1 million. Sales at this point are close to $2 million and still going strong.

I strongly feel that Heritage made sure that Gary's collection was prepared and presented in the most profitable way. In doing this, Gary's name and collection has become well known to every serious collector in the country. I don't think anyone could have done a better job.

I have talked to many people in your company over the last several months. Everyone I talked to was very patient with me and took the time to make sure all of my questions were completely answered. The entire family is impressed with your expertise and professionalism throughout the process. We all are extremely glad that we chose Heritage to represent us.

Sincerely,

Tom Madison

SOLD FOR $77,675

SOLD FOR $65,725

FOR MUCH MORE INFORMATION ON HERITAGE COMIC AND COMIC ART AUCTIONS, PLEASE SEE OUR OTHER ADS ON PAGES 6–7, 76–77, 78–79, 258–259, AND 1197!

To consign your comics or comic art to a Heritage auction, contact
LON ALLEN
877.HERITAGE (437.4824), ext. 1261
LonA@HA.com

GEOFFREY'S COMICS!

Just 10 minutes from LAX!

comicsonebay.com

(310) 538-3198

15900 Crenshaw Blvd

Torrance, CA 90249

California's LARGEST Golden, Silver and Bronze Age comic store!

WE BUY COMICS!

Brian Howard Art

Not many people can remember when they became passionate about a particular pastime- but I can. My love for comics started when I picked up my first comic book at age 6. This realm of colorful heroes and magical worlds transported me to foreign lands and mythical places.

But it was more than a passing phase—something I realized when I found myself unable to part with a single issue and only wanted to amass a bigger collection. Upon landing my first job at 12-years-old, all the money I earned went into my hobby as I dragged my parents to countless yard sales and flea markets in search of the kind of comics I wanted, but couldn't afford at enthusiast shows or stores. My love for the genre was cemented.

Neat Stuff Collectibles came to fruition shortly after I graduated from college. They say it's best when you love what you do so transitioning this pastime from recreation to vocation was an easy choice.

At the San Diego Comic Con, I was bitten by another bug: original comic art. The piece in question depicted a page from one of my favorite comic books ever. It was truly unique and one-of-a-kind, so I purchased it for sentimental reasons and never looked back.

So why should you place your comic art in my trust? Because even after all these years, I still get the same feeling when I look and touch this stuff as you do. I understand and respect the passion and thought that goes into amassing a comic compilation and most every dollar I earn gets reinvested back into my collection.

Let's chat comic art anytime.

Sincerely,

Brian Howard Schutzer

BUYING ORIGINAL ART

1-800-730-3954

buyingeverything@yahoo.com

www.comicartshop.com/neatstuff/

A Failure to Subscribe...

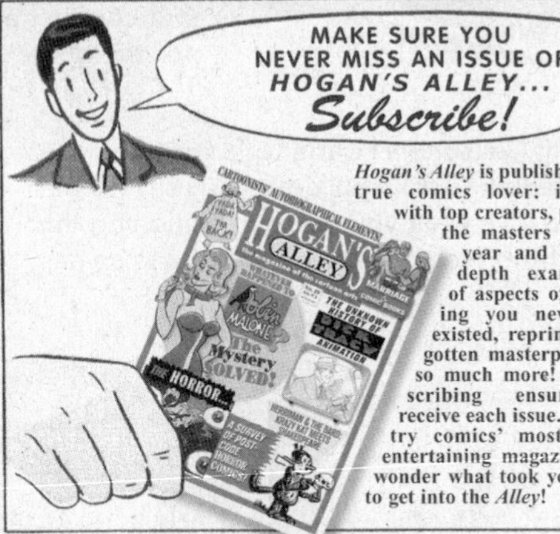

Hogan's Alley is published for the true comics lover: interviews with top creators, profiles of the masters of yesteryear and today, in-depth examinations of aspects of cartooning you never knew existed, reprints of forgotten masterpieces, and so much more! And subscribing ensures you receive each issue. Once you try comics' most literate, entertaining magazine, you'll wonder what took you so long to get into the *Alley*!

Limited back issues available.
Please check box and remit payment.
Price includes postage.

Issues 1–8 & 14
SOLD OUT

- ☐ Issue #9 ($10)
- ☐ Issue #10 ($10)
- ☐ Issue #11 ($10)
- ☐ Issue #12 ($8)
- ☐ Issue #13 ($8)
- ☐ Issue #15 ($8)
- ☐ Issue #16 ($8)
- ☐ Issue #17 ($8)
- ☐ Issue #18 ($8)
- ☐ Issue #19 ($8)

☐ Begin my subscription with Hogan's Alley #19!
I enclose $24 for four issues!

☐ Begin my subscription with Hogan's Alley #19, and also send me Hogan's Alley #18 immediately!
I enclose $30 for five issues!

☐ I don't rush into things. **Send me a sample issue for $3.**

Name ______

Address ______

City ______

State, Zip ______

Send your check or money order to:
HOGAN'S ALLEY, P.O. BOX 3872, DECATUR, GA 30031

OVERSTREET

Order back issues or subscriptions online at **hoganmag.com**
We accept Paypal! Send payment to **hoganmag@gmail.com**

$$ COLLECTORS ALWAYS PAY MORE FOR COMICS $$

If you want a vacation, or pay for life's thrills

A stack of old comics could pay all your bills.

Collectors pay more, comics give us chills!

Don't deal with dealers.
Collect $ from our collectors.™

CONTACT US TO BUY YOUR COMICS WITH **COURTESY & CASH**

(507) 400-0661 *Ask for Barry or Joe*

info@comicoop.com **www.comicoop.com**

THE BEST PLACE IN HOUSTON
(AND SURROUNDING AREAS)
TO SELL YOUR COMICS, TOYS, AND OTHER POP CULTURE COLLECTIBLES!

WE BUY: ORIGINAL ART!

GOLDEN AGE! SILVER AGE! BRONZE AGE! MODERN!
COMICS!
(WE'RE ONE OF THE FEW STORES IN TOWN THAT ACTUALLY STILL BUYS '90s COMIC BOOK COLLECTIONS)

WWW.THEPOPCULTURECOMPANY.COM
(281) 798 0777 - 11313 KATY FREEWAY - HOUSTON, TEXAS 77079
GET YOUR GEEK ON!

EVERYTHING COPYRIGHT © THEIR RESPECTIVE OWNERS.

Overstreet Advisors & CGC Authorized Dealer
"100% FAMILY OWNED & OPERATED"

- CANADIAN PRICE VARIANT & NEWSSTAND EDITION SPECIALISTS
- "HIGH GRADE" ~ "HARD TO FIND" ~ CGC BOOKS AVAILABLE
- LARGE INVENTORY OF SILVER, BRONZE AND COPPER COMICS
- STRICT AND ACCURATE GRADING ON RAW BOOKS
- CGC SUBMISSION SPECIALISTS SERVING CANADA 

LOOKING TO SELL YOUR COLLECTION
OR GET THE MOST FROM IT???
CONTACT US FIRST!!

WE OFFER: PRESCREEN & GRADING CONSULTATIONS
APPRAISAL SERVICES

WE BUY COLLECTIONS LARGE OR SMALL • WE TRAVEL TO YOU!!!

PAYING 100% OF PRICE GUIDE
FOR KEY & HIGH GRADE COMIC BOOKS

CONTACT: Paul, Nicole & Jack at (204) 416-8729 or (204) 509-8729
Email: info@pnjcomics.com ~ orders@pnjcomics.com
~ grading@pnjcomics.com

Visit us at www.pnjcomics.com

SERVING MANITOBA, SASKATCHEWAN, NORTHERN ONTARIO
& THE REST OF THE WORLD!!

"pnjcomics" ~ 100% positive feedback on ebay

BLASTOFF

Welcoming the future, treasuring the past

address: 5118 Lankershim Boulevard, North Hollywood, CA 91601

phone: (818) 980-BOOK | blastoffcomics.com | Open Every Day

BLASTOFF routinely offers a huge selection of vintage Golden, Silver and Bronze Age comics in the Southern California marketplace, and is quickly becoming one of the biggest consigners of comics, art and collectibles in Los Angeles. From our North Hollywood retail location, we offer rare comics from the collections of professional comics-industry heavyweights like **Mark Waid**, **Harlan Ellison**, **Karl Kesel** and many others.

BLASTOFF is always looking to acquire collections of any size, and is open to either purchase or consignment (with cash advance, naturally). While our store is based in Southern California, our Website has a global reach, and we've successfully sold our clients' collections to collectors around the world.

"What a delight to deal with someone who loves comics as much as I do. BLASTOFF's selection of high-grade vintage books for sale is astounding — and I'm not just saying that because some of them are mine!"

– **Mark Waid,** satisfied consigner

"For all the ages, there's only one place to buy the visual! It's Blastoff Comics, the standard all others salivate to meet."

– **Harlan Ellison,** satisfied consigner

Make sure to visit Blastoff Comics on Facebook!

Follow us on Twitter at @BlastoffComics

COMIC BOOK CERTIFICATION SERVICE

CBCS

Expert, Impartial, Third-Party Grading

SHIELD YOUR COMIC!

www.CBCScomics.com Toll Free: 844-870-CBCS

The #1 Auction Service
DEDICATED EXCLUSIVELY
to Comics, Original Art, Posters+More!

OUR 25 YEARS OF EXPERIENCE INCLUDE:

- Members of the prestigious Appraisers Association of America. Call for Estate, insurance and tax appraisals.
- We have represented ***FRANK FRAZETTA, MORT DRUCKER, CARMINE INFANTINO*** and others for original art sales.
- Exclusive Consultants to ***CHRISTIE'S AUCTION HOUSE.***

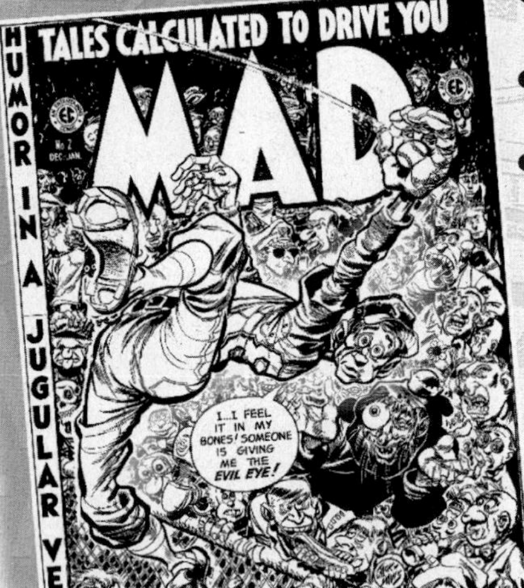

We are proud to be the #1 source of original comic art and related material dedicated exclusively to the field, including comic books and art, newspaper strip art, Disney, science fiction, fantasy, comic character toys, movie posters and animation. And we consistently attain **RECORD PRICES** for our consignors!.

ALL STAR AUCTIONS is also committed to offering collectors the absolute finest collectibles through a series of full-color catalogue auctions, interactive internet auctions and our exclusive **SIMUL-CONS**™.

We have been leaders in the field for over **25** years. We inaugurated and conducted 7 record-setting sales as exclusive consultants to ***CHRISTIE'S***, the renowned auction house. We are the official agents for ***FRANK FRAZETTA, MORT DRUCKER,*** and ***CARMINE INFANTINO*** (among others) for the sale of their original art; and we have served annually as official advisors to the ***OVERSTREET PRICE GUIDE***.

We enjoy an unparalleled record of honesty and integrity!

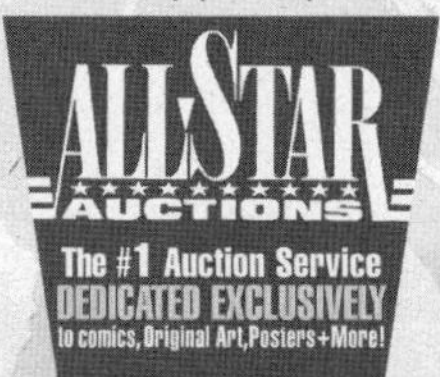

If you would like to participate,
either as a buyer or seller, please contact us in any of the following ways:
Office: (201) 652-1305 • Fax: (501) 325-6504 • e-mail: art@allstarauctions.net
www.allstarauctions.net

Over 25 Years of Experience!

ALLSTAR AUCTIONS

The most trusted name in comic collectibles auctions in the world!

Call us now to participate either buying, selling or for an insurance or Estate appraisal.

Let us help you realize the highest prices possible for all your prized possessions!

The #1 Auction Service DEDICATED EXCLUSIVELY to comics, Original Art, Posters + More!

www.allstarauctions.net

Office: (201) 652-1305

e-mail: art@allstarauctions.net

Fax #: (501) 325-6504

WWW.CYBERSPACECOMICS.COM

$$$ Cash For Comics $$$

Cyberspace Comics is currently buying comic collections and comic store overstock. We are also looking for Golden Age comics, Silver Age comics, Bronze Age comics, graphic novels, TPBs, hardcovers and any other type of comics out there! I'm paying good money for 10 cent comics and 12 cent comics. Especially Marvel Comics and DC Comics. Spider-Man, Avengers, X-Men, Fantastic Four, Thor, Batman!

I want them!

I'm also looking for Golden Age comics (1930s, 1940s, 1950s), Silver Age comics (1960s), Bronze Age comics (1970s) and even Indy comics - the weirder and more independent, the more interesting they become!

I know I am paying great prices! *How do I know that?* I've been buying comic books and collections from many of the other dealers advertising in this book who have bought collections from people just like you. If I buy your collection from another dealer, ask yourself: how much money did you leave on the table?

Cyberspace Comics offers an incredible selection of over <u>65,000 unique issues</u> ranging from the Golden Age to the present. Your order can even qualify for free shipping! See our selection here: www.cyberspacecomics.com/aa

Additionally, if you're after complete series or vintage comics, please visit our ebay store:

www.cyberspacecomics.com/ebay

steve@cyberspacecomics.com | 845-649-7957

Twitter: cyberspacecomix | Facebook: Cyberspace Comics

HEROTRADER

Buying and Selling Comic Books

And Collectibles

COMICS -COMIC SUPPLIES -TOYS -UNIQUE ITEMS

WE BUY COMICS!

what we buy

- -Golden, Silver, Bronze, & Modern age key issues
- -Original comic art
- -Vintage Monster Mags
- -Older toys and Sci-fi items
- -Comic related Collectibles

and Entire Collections

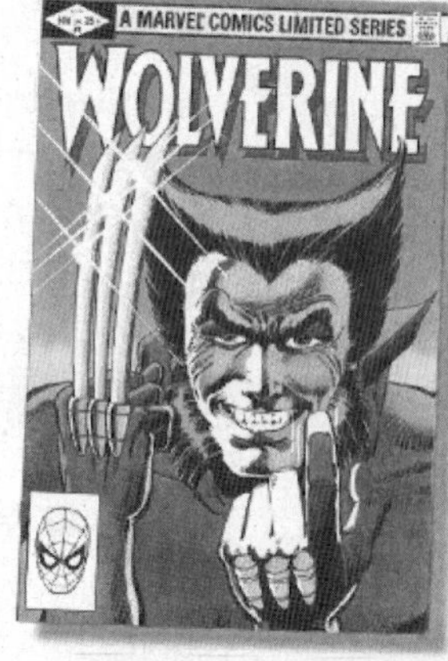

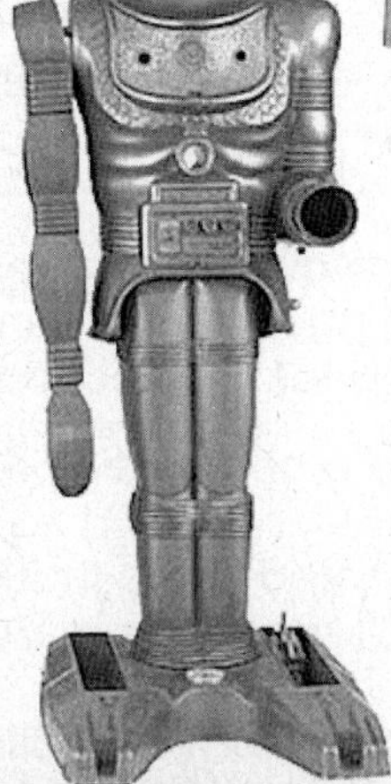
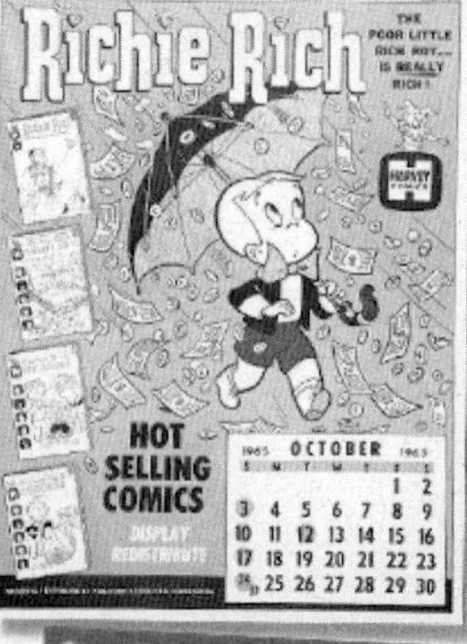

www.herotrader.com

email us: info@herotrader.com

Call us: (239) 910-4089

Mailing address:
2178 Andrea Lane #2
Fort Myers, FL 33912

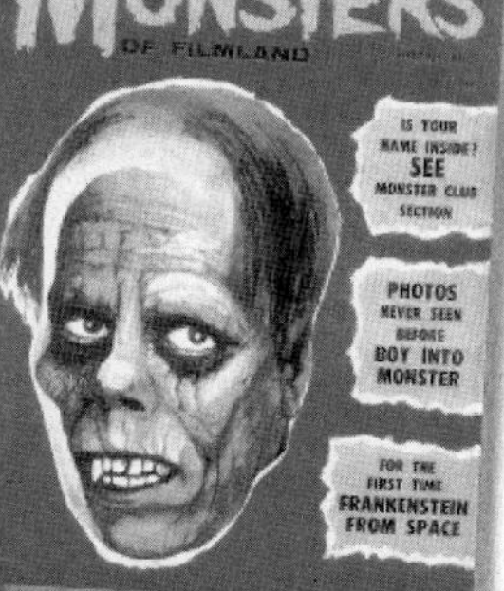

Look for our retail location in 2015

Comic Book Pressing Service:
Maximize your grades with our recognized pressing service! Contact us for details and pricing!

Sigs

We offer a wide range of CGC Signature Series books including many rare and hard to obtain celebrities and comic book artists. Past signings have included George Lucas, Arnold Schwarzenegger, Stan Lee, Chris Evans, Chris Hemsworth, Jessica Alba, Dan Aykroyd, and countless others.

We also offer our own limited edition comics known as "Sharp Variants" which are low print run issues.

Always Buying Gold, Silver, and Bronze Age Comics
We're interested in purchasing comic books from 1936-2000
Single books, collections, warehouse inventory, old store stock

We have a combined 54 years of market experience

Well respected in the Industry, with an easy to deal with no pressure business approach

We pay competitive rates for your collection and are able to travel anywhere in North America to view your comics with payment always available

References Available Upon Request

We offer both a Want List service and also a wide diverse selection of comic books in stock

Contact: Sales@SharpComics.com
410-848-0275
www.sharpcomics.com
www.facebook.com/sharpcomics

COMING IN OCTOBER 2014

THE

NEXT

COMIC HEAVEN AUCTION

OVER 8,000 GOLDEN AND SILVER AGE COMIC BOOKS WILL BE OFFERED

CALL OR E-MAIL US FOR A FREE CATALOG

Comic Heaven
John and Nanette Verzyl
P.O. Box 900
Big Sandy, TX 75755
1-903-636-5555
www.ComicHeaven.net

COMIC

B U Y

Sell us your Golden, Silver and Bronze Age comics.

No collection is too large or too small.

We will travel anywhere in the USA to buy collections we want.
Last year we traveled over 30,000 miles to buy comic books.

We are especially looking to buy:

- **Golden Age Timelys and DCs**
- **Fox/MLJ/ Nedor/ EC**
- **"Mile High" copies (Edgar Church Collection)**
- **"San Francisco", "Chicago" and other pedigree collections**
- **Silver Age Marvels and DCs**

HEAVEN

NOW CELEBRATING OUR 35th ANNIVERSARY!!

We Specialize In Purchasing Large Golden And Silver Age Collections

Comic Heaven
John and Nanette Verzyl
P.O. Box 900
Big Sandy, TX 75755
www.ComicHeaven.net
1-903-636-5555

www.comicheaven.net

- View large color scans of hundreds of rare comics up for bid

In our current Comic Heaven Auction

- See our entire auction catalog online
- Get info on upcoming auctions
- Some items available for immediate purchase

ORDER OUR FREE AUCTION CATALOG
By emailing us through our website
or by calling:

1-903-636-5555

Comic Heaven
John and Nanette Verzyl
P.O. Box 900
Big Sandy, TX 75755
www.ComicHeaven.net
1-903-636-5555

JOHN VERZYL AND DAUGHTER ROSE "HARD AT WORK"

John Verzyl started collecting comic books in 1965, and within ten years he had amassed thousands of Golden and Silver Age comic books. In 1979, with his wife Nanette, he opened "COMIC HEAVEN," a retail store devoted entirely to the buying and selling of comic books.

Over the years, John Verzyl has come to be recognized as an authority in the field of comic books. He has served as a special advisor to *The Overstreet Comic Book Price Guide* for the last 30 years. Thousands of his "mint" comics were photographed for Ernst Gerber's *Photo-Journal Guide to Comic Books*. His booths and displays at the annual San Diego Comic-Con, the August Chicago Comic Con, and the New York City Comic Con in October draw customers from all over the world.

The first COMIC HEAVEN AUCTION was held in 1987, and today his color-packed catalogs are mailed out to more than 12,000 interested collectors and dealers.

Comic Heaven
John and Nanette Verzyl
P.O. Box 900
Big Sandy, TX 75755
www.ComicHeaven.net
1-903-636-5555

THESE DIDN'T HAPPEN WITHOUT YOUR HELP.

The Overstreet Comic Book Price Guide doesn't happen by magic. A network of advisors – made up of experienced dealers, collectors and comics historians – gives us input for every edition we publish. If you spot an error or omission in this edition or any of our publications, let us know!

Write to us at
Gemstone Publishing Inc.,
1940 Greenspring Dr., Suite I,
Timonium, MD 21093.
Or e-mail **feedback@gemstonepub.com**.

We want your help!

BIG LITTLE BOOKS

INTRODUCTION

In 1932, at the depths of the Great Depression, comic books were not selling despite their successes in the previous two decades. Desperate publishers had already reduced prices to 25¢, but this was still too much for many people to spend on entertainment.

Comic books quickly evolved into two newer formats, the comics magazine and the Big Little Book. Both types retailed for 10¢.

Big Little Books began by reprinting the art (and adapting the stories) from newspaper comics. As their success grew and publishers began commissioning original material, movie adaptations and other entertainment-derived stories became commonplace.

GRADING

Before a Big Little Book's value can be assessed, its condition or state of preservation must be determined. A book in **Near Mint** condition will bring many times the price of the same book in **Poor** condition. Many variables influence the grading of a Big Little Book and all must be considered in the final evaluation. Due to the way they are constructed, damage occurs with very little use - usually to the spine, book edges and binding. More important defects that affect grading are: Split spines, pages missing, page browning or brittleness, writing, crayoning, loose pages, color fading, chunks missing, and rolling or out of square. The following grading guide is given to aid the novice:

9.4 Near Mint: The overall look is as if it was just purchased and maybe opened once; only subtle defects are allowed; paper is cream to off-white, supple and fresh; cover is flat with no surface wear or creases; inks and colors are bright; small penciled or inked arrival dates are acceptable; very slight blunting of corners at top and bottom of spine are common; outside corners are cut square and sharp. Books in this grade could bring prices of guide and a half or more.

9.0 Very Fine/Near Mint: Limited number of defects; full cover gloss with only very slight wear on book corners and edges; very minor foxing; very minor tears allowed, binding still square and tight with no pages missing; paper quality still fresh from cream to off-white. Dates, stamps or initials allowed on cover or inside.

8.0 Very Fine: Most of the cover gloss retained with minor wear appearing at corners and around edges; spine tight with no pages missing; cream/tan paper allowed if still supple; up to 1/4" bend allowed on covers with no color break; cover relatively flat; minor tears allowed.

6.0 Fine: Slight wear beginning to show; cover gloss reduced but still clean, pages tan/brown but still supple (not brittle); up to 1/4" split or color break allowed; minor discoloration and/or foxing allowed.

4.0 Very Good: Obviously a read copy with original printing luster almost gone; some fading and discoloration, but not soiled; some signs of wear such as corner splits and spine rolling; paper can be brown but not brittle; a few pages can be loose but not missing; no chunks missing; blunted corners acceptable.

2.0 Good: An average used copy complete with only minor pieces missing from the spine, which may be partially split; slightly soiled or marked with spine rolling; color flaking and wear around edges, but perfectly sound and legible; could have minor tape repairs but otherwise complete.

1.0 Fair: Very heavily read and soiled with small chunks missing from cover; most or all of spine could be missing; multiple splits in spine and loose pages, but still sound and legible, bringing 50 to 70 percent of good price.

0.5 Poor: Damaged, heavily weathered, soiled or otherwise unsuited for collecting purposes.

IMPORTANT

Most BLBs on the market today will fall in the **Good** to **Fine** grade category. When **Very Fine** to **Near Mint** BLBs are offered for sale, they usually bring premium prices.

A WORD ON PRICING

The prices are given for **Good**, **Fine** and **Very Fine/ Near Mint** condition. A book in **Fair** would be 50-70% of the **Good** price. **Very Good** would be halfway between the **Good** and **Fine** price, and **Very Fine** would be halfway between the **Fine** and **Very Fine/**

Near Mint price. The prices listed were averaged from convention sales, dealers' lists, adzines, auctions, and by special contact with dealers and collectors from coast to coast. The prices and the spreads were determined from sales of copies in available condition or the highest grade known. Since most available copies are in the **Good** to **Fine** range, neither dealers nor collectors should let the **Very Fine/Near Mint** column influence the prices they are willing to charge or pay for books in less than near perfect condition.

The prices listed reflect a six times spread from **Good** to **Very Fine/ Near Mint** (1 - 3 - 6). We feel this spread accurately reflects the current market, especially when you consider the scarcity of books in **Very Fine/Near Mint** condition. When one or both end sheets are missing, the book's value would drop about a half grade.

Books with movie scenes are of double importance due to the high crossover demand by movie collectors.

Abbreviations: a-art; c-cover; nn-no number; p-pages; r-reprint.

Publisher Codes: BRP-Blue Ribbon Press; **ERB**-Edgar Rice Burroughs; **EVW**-Engel van Wiseman; **FAW**-Fawcett Publishing Co.; **Gold**-Goldsmith Publishing Co.; **Lynn**-Lynn Publishing Co.; **McKay**-David McKay Co.; **Whit**-Whitman Publishing Co.; **World**-World Syndicate Publishing Co.

Terminology: *All Pictures Comics*-no text, all drawings; *Fast-Action*-A special series of Dell books highly collected; *Flip Pictures*-upper right corner of interior pages contain drawings that are put into motion when rifled; *Movie Scenes*-book illustrated with scenes from the movie. *Soft Cover*-A thin single sheet of cardboard used in binding most of the giveaway versions.

"Big Little Book" and "Better Little Book" are registered trademarks of Whitman Publishing Co. "Little Big Book" is a registered trademark of the Saalfield Publishing Co.

"Pop-Up" is a registered trademark of Blue Ribbon Press. "Little Big Book" is a registered trademark of the Saalfield Co.

Top 20 Big Little Books and related size books*

Issue#	Rank	Title	Price
731	1	Mickey Mouse the Mail Pilot (variant version of Mickey Mouse #717) (A VG copy sold at auction for $7,170)	
nn	2	Mickey Mouse and Minnie Mouse at Macy's	$2,700
nn	3	Mickey Mouse and Minnie March to Macy's	$2,200
717	4	Mickey Mouse (skinny Mickey on-c)	$2,000
W-707	5	Dick Tracy The Detective	$1,500
725	6	Big Little Mother Goose HC	$1,300
717	7	Mickey Mouse (reg. Mickey on-c)	$1,200
nn	8	Mickey Mouse Silly Symphonies	$1,100
721	9	Big Little Paint Book (336 pg.)	$1,000
nn	10	Mickey Mouse Mail Pilot (Great Big Midget Book)	$925
725	11	Big Little Mother Goose SC	$900
nn	11	Mickey Mouse (Great Big Midget Book)	$900
nn	11	Mickey Mouse and the Magic Carpet	$900
721	14	Big Little Paint Book (320 pg.)	$800
nn	14	Mickey Mouse Sails For Treasure Island (Great Big Midget Book)	$800
4063	16	Popeye Thimble Theater Starring... (2nd printing)	$700
1126	17	Laughing Dragon of Oz	$650
4063	18	Popeye Thimble Theater Starring... (1st printing)	$600
nn	18	Buck Rogers	$600
nn	18	Buck Rogers in the City of Floating Globes	$600

*Includes only the various sized BLBs; no premiums, giveaways or other divergent forms are included.

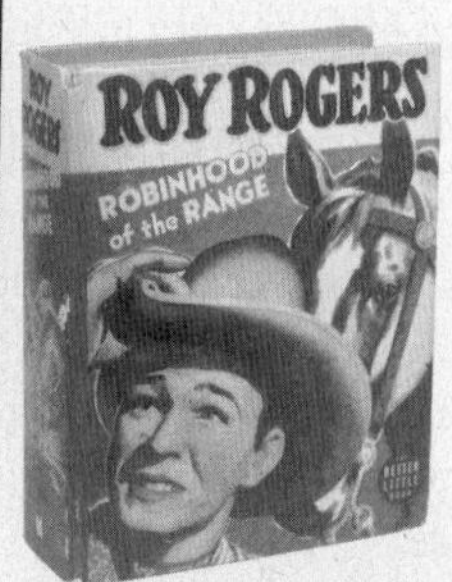

1425 - Andy Panda and Tiny Tom © WHIT

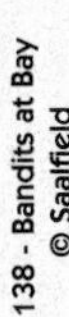

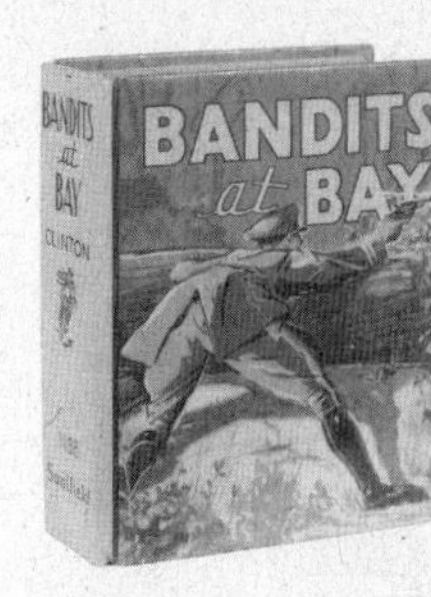

1138 - Bandits at Bay © Saalfield

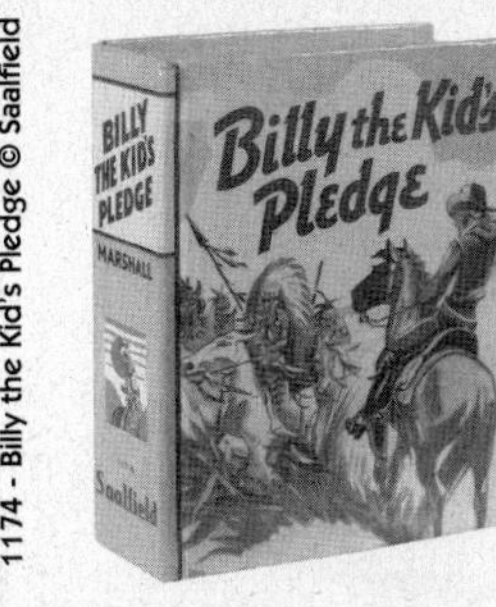

1174 - Billy the Kid's Pledge © Saalfield

GD FN VF/NM

1175-0- **Abbie an' Slats**, 1940, Saalfield, 400 pgs. 11.00 27.50 70.00

1182- **Abbie an' Slats-and Becky**, 1940, Saalfield, 400 pgs. 11.00 27.50 70.00

1177- **Ace Drummond**, 1935, Whitman, 432 pgs. 11.00 27.50 70.00

Admiral Byrd (See Paramount Newsreel ...)

nn- **Adventures of Charlie McCarthy and Edgar Bergen, The**, 1938, Dell, 194 pgs., Fast-Action Story, soft-c 20.00 50.00 140.00

1422- **Adventures of Huckleberry Finn, The**, 1939, Whitman, 432 pgs., Henry E. Vallely-a 10.00 25.00 65.00

1648- **Adventures of Jim Bowie** (TV Series), 1958, Whitman, 280 pgs. 4.00 10.00 26.00

1056- **Adventures of Krazy Kat and Ignatz Mouse in Koko Land**, 1934, Saalfield, 160 pgs., oblong size, hard-c, Herriman-c/a 57.00 143.00 400.00

1306- **Adventures of Krazy Kat and Ignatz Mouse in Koko Land**, 1934, Saalfield, 164 pgs., oblong size, soft-c, Herriman-c/a 64.00 160.00 450.00

1082- **Adventures of Pete the Tramp, The**, 1935, Saalfield, hard-c, by C. D. Russell 10.00 25.00 65.00

1312- **Adventures of Pete the Tramp, The**, 1935, Saalfield, soft-c, by C. D. Russell 10.00 25.00 65.00

1053- **Adventures of Tim Tyler**, 1934, Saalfield, hard-c, oblong size, by Lyman Young 20.00 50.00 140.00

1303- **Adventures of Tim Tyler**, 1934, Saalfield, soft-c, oblong size, by Lyman Young 20.00 50.00 140.00

1058- **Adventures of Tom Sawyer, The**, 1934, Saalfield, 160 pgs., hard-c, Park Sumner-a 10.00 25.00 65.00

1308- **Adventures of Tom Sawyer, The**, 1934, Saalfield, 160 pgs., soft-c, Park Sumner-a 10.00 25.00 65.00

1448- **Air Fighters of America**, 1941, Whitman, 432 pgs., flip picture 11.00 27.50 70.00

Alexander Smart, ESQ. (See Top Line Comics)

759- **Alice in Wonderland**, 1933, Whitman, 160 pgs., hard-c, photo-c, movie scenes 36.00 90.00 250.00

1481- **Allen Pike of the Parachute Squad U.S.A.**, 1941, Whitman, 432 pgs. 12.00 30.00 75.00

763- **Alley Oop and Dinny**, 1935, Whitman, 384 pgs., V. T. Hamlin-a 19.00 47.50 130.00

1473- **Alley Oop and Dinny in the Jungles of Moo**, 1938, Whitman, 432 pgs., V. T. Hamlin-a 19.00 47.50 130.00

nn- **Alley Oop and the Missing King of Moo**, 1938, Whitman, 36 pgs., 2 1/2" x 3 1/2", Penny Book 11.00 27.50 70.00

nn- **Alley Oop in the Kingdom of Foo**, 1938, Whitman, 68 pgs., 3 1/4" x 3 1/2", Pan-Am premium 26.00 65.00 180.00

nn- **Alley Oop Taming a Dinosaur**, 1938, Whitman, 68 pgs., 3 1/2" x 3 3/4", Pan-Am premium 26.00 65.00 180.00

nn- **"Alley Oop the Invasion of Moo,"** 1935, Whitman, 260 pgs., Cocomalt premium, soft-c; V. T. Hamlin-a 20.00 50.00 140.00

Andy Burnette (See Walt Disney's...)

Andy Panda (Also see Walter Lantz ...)

531- **Andy Panda**, 1943, Whitman, 3 3/4x8 3/4", Tall Comic Book, All Pictures Comics 14.00 35.00 100.00

1425- **Andy Panda and Tiny Tom**, 1944, Whitman, All Pictures Comics 10.00 25.00 65.00

1431- **Andy Panda and the Mad Dog Mystery**, 1947, Whitman, 288 pgs., by Walter Lantz 10.00 25.00 65.00

1441- **Andy Panda in the City of Ice**, 1948, Whitman, All Picture Comics, by Walter Lantz 10.00 25.00 65.00

1459- **Andy Panda and the Pirate Ghosts**, 1949, Whitman, 88 pgs., by Walter Lantz 10.00 25.00 65.00

1485- **Andy Panda's Vacation**, 1946, Whitman, All Pictures Comics, by Walter Lantz 10.00 25.00 65.00

15- **Andy Panda (The Adventures of)**, 1942, Dell, Fast-Action Story 14.00 35.00 100.00

707-10 - **Andy Panda and Presto the Pup**, 1949, Whitman 10.00 25.00 65.00

1130- **Apple Mary and Dennie Foil the Swindlers**, 1936, Whitman, 432 pgs. (Forerunner to Mary Worth) 10.00 25.00 65.00

1403- **Apple Mary and Dennie's Lucky Apples**, 1939, Whitman, 432 pgs. 10.00 25.00 65.00

GD FN VF/NM

2017- **(#17)-Aquaman-Scourge of the Sea**, 1968, Whitman, 260 pgs., 39 cents, hard-c, color illos 4.00 10.00 27.00

1192- **Arizona Kid on the Bandit Trail, The**, 1936, Whitman, 432 pgs. 10.00 25.00 60.00

1469- **Bambi** (Walt Disney's), 1942, Whitman, 432 pgs. 18.00 45.00 125.00

1497- **Bambi's Children** (Disney), 1943, Whitman, 432 pgs., Disney Studios-a 18.00 45.00 125.00

1138- **Bandits at Bay**, 1938, Saalfield, 400 pgs. 8.00 20.00 50.00

1459- **Barney Baxter in the Air with the Eagle Squadron**, 1938, Whitman, 432 pgs. 10.00 25.00 65.00

1083- **Barney Google**, 1935, Saalfield, hard-c 16.00 40.00 115.00

1313- **Barney Google**, 1935, Saalfield, soft-c 16.00 40.00 115.00

2031-(#31)- **Batman and Robin in the Cheetah Caper**, 1969, Whitman, 258 pgs. 4.00 10.00 27.00

5771- **Batman and Robin in the Cheetah Caper**, 1974, Whitman, 258 pgs., 49 cents 2.00 5.00 12.00

5771-1- **Batman and Robin in the Cheetah Caper**, 1974, Whitman, 258 pgs., 69 cents 2.00 5.00 12.00

5771-2- **Batman and Robin in the Cheetah Caper**, 1975?, Whitman, 258 pgs. 2.00 5.00 12.00

nn- **Beauty and the Beast**, nd (1930s), np (Whitman), 36 pgs., 3" x 3 1/2" Penny Book 4.00 10.00 22.00

Beep Beep The Road Runner (See Road Runner)

760- **Believe It or Not!**, 1933, Whitman, 160 pgs., by Ripley (c. 1931) 10.00 25.00 60.00

Betty Bear's Lesson (See Wee Little Books)

1119- **Betty Boop in Snow White**, 1934, Whitman, 240 pgs., hard-c; adapted from Max Fleischer Paramount Talkartoon 50.00 125.00 350.00

1119- **Betty Boop in Snow White**, 1934, Whitman, 240 pgs., soft-c; same contents as hard-c (Rare) 71.00 178.00 500.00

1158- **Betty Boop in "Miss Gullivers Travels,"** 1935, Whitman, 288 pgs., hard-c (Scarce) 57.00 143.00 400.00

2070- **Big Big Paint Book**, 1936, Whitman, 432 pgs., 8 1/2" x 11 3/8", B&W pages to color 21.00 52.50 150.00

1432- **Big Chief Wahoo and the Lost Pioneers**, 1942, Whitman, 432 pgs., Elmer Woggon-a 11.00 27.50 70.00

1443- **Big Chief Wahoo and the Great Gusto**, 1938, Whitman, 432 pgs., Elmer Woggon-a 11.00 27.50 70.00

1483- **Big Chief Wahoo and the Magic Lamp**, 1940, Whitman, 432 pgs., flip pictures, Woggon-c/a 11.00 27.50 70.00

725- **Big Little Mother Goose, The**, 1934, Whitman, 580 pgs. (Rare) Hardcover 163.00 408.00 1300.00

725- **Big Little Mother Goose, The**, 1934, Whitman, 580 pgs. (Rare) Softcover 123.00 308.00 900.00

1005- **Big Little Nickel Book**, 1935, Whitman, 144 pgs., Blackie Bear stories and Donna the Donkey 8.00 20.00 50.00

1006- **Big Little Nickel Book**, 1935, Whitman, 144 pgs., Blackie Bear stories, folk tales in primer style 8.00 20.00 50.00

1007- **Big Little Nickel Book**, 1935, Whitman, 144 pgs., Peter Rabbit, etc. 8.00 20.00 50.00

1008- **Big Little Nickel Book**, 1935, Whitman, 144 pgs., Wee Wee Woman, etc. 8.00 20.00 50.00

721- **Big Little Paint Book,** The, 1933, Whitman, 320 pgs., 3 3/4" x 8 1/2", for crayoning; first printing has green page ends; second printing has purple page ends (both are rare) 114.00 285.00 800.00

721- **Big Little Paint Book,** The, 1933, Whitman, 336 pgs., 3 3/4" x 8 1/2", for crayoning; first printing has green page ends; second printing has purple page ends (both are rare) 125.00 313.00 1000.00

1178- **Billy of Bar-Zero**, 1940, Saalfield, 400 pgs. 10.00 25.00 60.00

773- **Billy the Kid**, 1935, Whitman, 432 pgs., Hal Arbo-a 10.00 25.00 65.00

1159- **Billy the Kid on Tall Butte**, 1939, Saalfield, 400 pgs. 9.00 22.50 60.00

1174- **Billy the Kid's Pledge**, 1940, Saalfield, 400 pgs. 9.00 22.50 60.00

nn- **Billy the Kid, Western Outlaw**, 1935, Whitman, 260 pgs., Cocomalt premium, Hal Arbo-a, soft-c 12.00 30.00 85.00

1057- **Black Beauty**, 1934, Saalfield, hard-c 8.00 20.00 50.00

1307- **Black Beauty**, 1934, Saalfield, soft-c 8.00 20.00 50.00

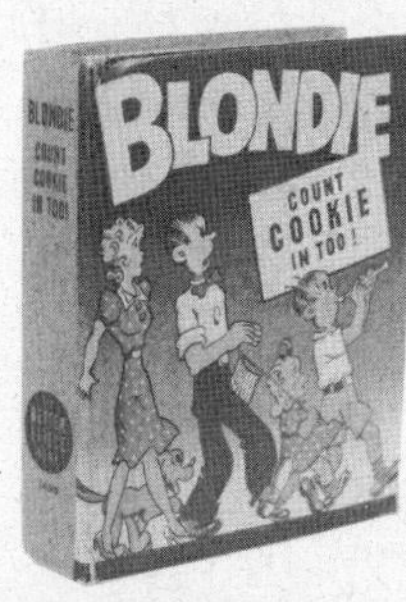
1430 - Blondie Count Cookie in Too! © WHIT

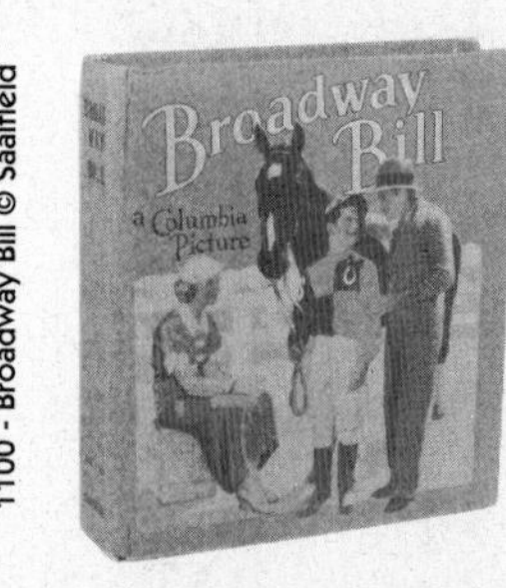
1100 - Broadway Bill © Saalfield

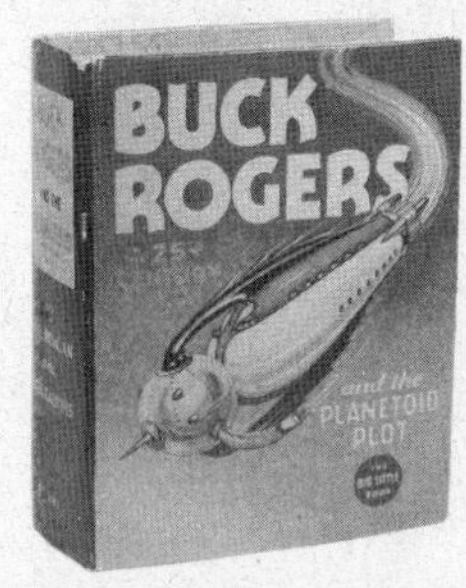
1197 - Buck Rogers and the Planetoid Plot © KING

GD FN VF/NM

1414- **Black Silver and His Pirate Crew**, 1937, Whitman, 300 pgs. 10.00 25.00 65.00

1447- **Blaze Brandon with the Foreign Legion**, 1938, Whitman, 432 pgs. 10.00 25.00 65.00

1410- **Blondie and Dagwood in Hot Water**, 1946, Whitman, 352 pgs., by Chic Young 10.00 25.00 60.00

1415- **Blondie and Baby Dumpling**, 1937, Whitman, 432 pgs., by Chic Young 10.00 25.00 65.00

1419- **Oh, Blondie the Bumsteads Carry On**, 1941, Whitman, 432 pgs., flip pictures, by Chic Young 10.00 25.00 65.00

1423- **Blondie Who's Boss?**, 1942, Whitman, 432 pgs., flip pictures, by Chic Young 10.00 25.00 65.00

1429- **Blondie with Baby Dumpling and Daisy**, 1939, Whitman, 432 pgs., by Chic Young 10.00 25.00 65.00

1430- **Blondie Count Cookie in Too!**, 1947, Whitman, 288 pgs., by Chic Young 10.00 25.00 60.00

1438- **Blondie and Dagwood Everybody's Happy**, 1948, Whitman, 288 pgs., by Chic Young 10.00 25.00 60.00

1450- **Blondie No Dull Moments**, 1948, Whitman, 288 pgs., by Chic Young 10.00 25.00 60.00

1463- **Blondie Fun For All**, 1949, Whitman, 288 pgs., by Chic Young 10.00 25.00 60.00

1466- **Blondie or Life Among the Bumsteads**, 1944, Whitman, 352 pgs., by Chic Young 10.00 25.00 65.00

1476- **Blondie and Bouncing Baby Dumpling**, 1940, Whitman, 432 pgs., by Chic Young 10.00 25.00 65.00

1487- **Blondie Baby Dumpling and All!**, 1941, Whitman, 432 pgs. flip pictures, by Chic Young 10.00 25.00 65.00

1490- **Blondie Papa Knows Best**, 1945, Whitman, 352 pgs., by Chic Young 10.00 25.00 60.00

1491- **Blondie-Cookie and Daisy's Pups**, 1943, Whitman, 1st printing, 432 pgs. 10.00 25.00 65.00

1491- **Blondie-Cookie and Daisy's Pups**, 1943, Whitman,. 2nd printing with different back-c & 352 pgs. 9.00 22.50 55.00

703-10- **Blondie and Dagwood Some Fun!**, 1949, Whitman, by Chic Young 8.00 20.00 48.00

21- **Blondie and Dagwood**, 1936, Lynn, by Chic Young 16.00 40.00 115.00

1108- **Bobby Benson on the H-Bar-O Ranch**, 1934, Whitman, 300 pgs., based on radio serial 12.00 30.00 75.00

Bobby Thatcher and the Samarang Emerald (See Top-Line Comics)

1432- **Bob Stone the Young Detective**, 1937, Whitman, 240 pgs., movie scenes 11.00 27.50 70.00

2002- **(#2)-Bonanza-The Bubble Gum Kid**, 1967, Whitman, 260 pgs., 39 cents, hard-c, color illos 4.00 10.00 27.00

1139- **Border Eagle, The**, 1938, Saalfield, 400 pgs. 8.00 20.00 50.00

1153- **Boss of the Chisholm Trail**, 1939, Saalfield, 400 pgs. 8.00 20.00 50.00

1425- **Brad Turner in Transatlantic Flight**, 1939, Whitman, 432 pgs. 10.00 25.00 60.00

1058- **Brave Little Tailor, The** (Disney), 1939, Whitman, 5" x 5 1/2", 68 pgs., hard-c (Mickey Mouse) 12.00 30.00 85.00

1427- **Brenda Starr and the Masked Impostor**, 1943, Whitman, 352 pgs., Dale Messick-a 12.00 30.00 80.00

1426- **Brer Rabbit** (Walt Disney's ...), 1947, Whitman, All Picture Comics, from "Song Of The South" movie 18.00 45.00 125.00

704-10- **Brer Rabbit**, 1949, Whitman 14.00 35.00 100.00

1059- **Brick Bradford in the City Beneath the Sea**, 1934, Saalfield, hard-c, by William Ritt & Clarence Gray 13.00 32.50 90.00

1309- **Brick Bradford in the City Beneath the Sea**, 1934, Saalfield, soft-c, by Ritt & Gray 13.00 32.50 90.00

1468- **Brick Bradford with Brocco the Modern Buccaneer**, 1938, Whitman, 432 pgs., by Wm. Ritt & Clarence Gray 10.00 25.00 60.00

1133- **Bringing Up Father**, 1936, Whitman, 432 pgs., by George McManus 12.00 30.00 85.00

1100- **Broadway Bill**, 1935, Saalfield, photo-c, 4 1/2" x 5 1/4", movie scenes (Columbia Pictures, horse racing) 11.00 27.50 70.00

1580- **Broadway Bill**, 1935, Saalfield, soft-c, photo-c, movie scenes 11.00 27.50 70.00

GD FN VF/NM

1181- **Broncho Bill**, 1940, Saalfield, 400 pgs. 10.00 25.00 60.00

nn- **Broncho Bill**, 1935, Whitman, 148 pgs., 3 1/2" x 4", Tarzan Ice Cream cup lid premium 25.00 62.50 175.00

nn- **Broncho Bill in Suicide Canyon** (See Top-Line Comics)

1417- **Bronc Peeler the Lone Cowboy**, 1937, Whitman, 432 pgs., by Fred Harman, forerunner of Red Ryder (also see Red Death on the Range) 10.00 25.00 60.00

nn- **Brownies' Merry Adventures, The**, 1993, Barefoot Books, 202 pgs., reprints from Palmer Cox's late 1800s books 3.00 7.50 18.00

1470- **Buccaneer, The**, 1938, Whitman, 240 pgs., photo-c, movie scenes 12.00 30.00 75.00

1646- **Buccaneers, The** (TV Series), 1958, Whitman, 4 1/2" x 5 1/4", 280 pgs., Russ Manning-a 4.00 10.00 25.00

1104- **Buck Jones in the Fighting Code**, 1934, Whitman, 160 pgs., hard-c, movie scenes 14.00 35.00 95.00

1116- **Buck Jones in Ride 'Em Cowboy** (Universal Presents), 1935, Whitman, 240 pgs., photo-c, movie scenes 14.00 35.00 95.00

1174- **Buck Jones in the Roaring West** (Universal Presents), 1935, Whitman, 240 pgs., movie scenes 14.00 35.00 95.00

1188- **Buck Jones in the Fighting Rangers** (Universal Presents), 1936, Whitman, 240 pgs., photo-c, movie scenes 14.00 35.00 95.00

1404- **Buck Jones and the Two-Gun Kid**, 1937, Whitman, 432 pgs. 10.00 25.00 65.00

1451- **Buck Jones and the Killers of Crooked Butte**, 1940, Whitman, 432 pgs. 10.00 25.00 65.00

1461- **Buck Jones and the Rock Creek Cattle War**, 1938, Whitman, 432 pgs. 10.00 25.00 65.00

1486- **Buck Jones and the Rough Riders in Forbidden Trails**, 1943, Whitman, flip pictures, based on movie; Tim McCoy app. 12.00 30.00 80.00

3- **Buck Jones in the Red Rider**, 1934, EVW, 160 pgs., movie scenes 21.00 52.50 150.00

8- **Buck Jones Cowboy Masquerade**, 1938, Whitman, 132 pgs., soft-c, 3 3/4" x 3 1/2", Buddy Book premium 24.00 60.00 170.00

15- **Buck Jones in Rocky Rhodes**, 1935, EVW, 160 pgs., photo-c, movie scenes 29.00 73.00 200.00

4069- **Buck Jones and the Night Riders**, 1937, Whitman, 7" x 9", 320 pgs., Big Big Book 39.00 98.00 275.00

nn- **Buck Jones on the Six-Gun Trail**, 1939, Whitman, 36 pgs., 2 1/2" x 3 1/2", Penny Book 10.00 25.00 60.00

nn- **Buck Jones Big Thrill Chewing Gum**, 1934, Whitman, 8 pgs., 2 1/2" x 3 1/2" (6 diff.) each... 14.00 35.00 100.00

742- **Buck Rogers in the 25th Century A.D.**, 1933, Whitman, 320 pgs., Dick Calkins-a 43.00 108.00 300.00

nn- **Buck Rogers in the 25th Century A.D.**, 1933, Whitman, 204 pgs.,Cocomalt premium, Calkins-a 29.00 73.00 200.00

765- **Buck Rogers in the City Below the Sea**, 1934, Whitman, 320 pgs., Dick Calkins-a 32.00 80.00 225.00

765- **Buck Rogers in the City Below the Sea**, 1934, Whitman, 324 pgs., soft-c, Dick Calkins-c/a (Rare) 57.00 143.00 400.00

1143- **Buck Rogers on the Moons of Saturn**, 1934, Whitman, 320 pgs., Dick Calkins-a 32.00 80.00 225.00

nn- **Buck Rogers on the Moons of Saturn**, 1934, Whitman, 324 pgs., premium w/no ads, soft 3-color-c, Dick Calkins-a 50.00 125.00 350.00

1169- **Buck Rogers and the Depth Men of Jupiter**, 1935, Whitman, 432 pgs., Calkins-a 34.00 85.00 240.00

1178- **Buck Rogers and the Doom Comet**, 1935, Whitman, 432 pgs., Calkins-a 31.00 78.00 220.00

1197- **Buck Rogers and the Planetoid Plot**, 1936, Whitman, 432 pgs., Calkins-a 31.00 78.00 220.00

1409- **Buck Rogers Vs. the Fiend of Space**, 1940, Whitman, 432 pgs., Calkins-a 40.00 100.00 280.00

1437- **Buck Rogers in the War with the Planet Venus**, 1938, Whitman, 432 pgs., Calkins-a 31.00 78.00 220.00

1474- **Buck Rogers and the Overturned World**, 1941, Whitman, 432 pgs., flip pictures, Calkins-a 33.00 83.00 230.00

1490- **Buck Rogers and the Super-Dwarf of Space**, 1943, Whitman, 11 Pictures Comics, Calkins-a 31.00 78.00 220.00

4057- **Buck Rogers, The Adventures of**, 1934, Whitman, 7" x 9 1/2",

Bulletman and the Return of Mr. Murder © FAW

L20 - Ceiling Zero © WB

1323 - Chandu the Magician © Saalfield

GD FN VF/NM

320 pgs., Big Big Book, "The Story of Buck Rogers on the Planet Eros," Calkins-c/a 71.00 178.00 500.00

nn- **Buck Rogers**, 1935, Whitman, 4" x 3 1/2", Tarzan Ice Cream cup premium (Rare) 86.00 215.00 600.00

nn- **Buck Rogers in the City of Floating Globes,** 1935, Whitman, 258 pgs., Cocomalt premium, soft-c, Dick Calkins-a 86.00 215.00 600.00

nn- **Buck Rogers Big Thrill Chewing Gum**, 1934, Whitman, 8 pgs., 2 1/2" x 3 " (6 diff.) each... 21.00 52.50 150.00

1135- **Buckskin and Bullets**, 1938, Saalfield, 400 pgs. 8.00 20.00 50.00

Buffalo Bill (See Wild West Adventures of ...)

nn- **Buffalo Bill**, 1934, World Syndicate, All pictures, by J. Carroll Mansfield 10.00 25.00 60.00

713- **Buffalo Bill and the Pony Express**, 1934, Whitman, hard-c, 384 pgs., Hal Arbo-a 11.00 27.50 70.00

nn- **Buffalo Bill and the Pony Express**, 1934, Whitman, soft-c, 384 pgs., Hal Arbo-a; three-color premium (Rare) 43.00 108.00 300.00

1194- **Buffalo Bill Plays a Lone Hand**, 1936, Whitman, 432 pgs., Hal Arbo-a 10.00 25.00 60.00

530- **Bugs Bunny**, 1943, Whitman, All Pictures Comics, Tall Comic Book, 3 1/4" x 8 1/4", reprints/Looney Tunes 1 & 5 17.00 42.50 120.00

1403- **Bugs Bunny and the Pirate Loot**, 1947, Whitman, All Pictures Comics 11.00 27.50 70.00

1435- **Bugs Bunny**, 1944, Whitman, All Pictures Comics 12.00 30.00 75.00

1440- **Bugs Bunny in Risky Business**, 1948, Whitman, All Pictures & Comics 11.00 27.50 70.00

1455- **Bugs Bunny and Klondike Gold**, 1948, Whitman, 288 pgs. 11.00 27.50 70.00

1465- **Bugs Bunny The Masked Marvel**, 1949, Whitman, 288 pgs. 11.00 27.50 70.00

1496- **Bugs Bunny and His Pals,** 1945, Whitman, All Pictures Comics; r/Four Color Comics #33 11.00 27.50 70.00

13- **Bugs Bunny and the Secret of Storm Island**, 1942, Dell,194 pgs., Fast-Action Story 27.00 68.00 190.00

706-10- **Bugs Bunny and the Giant Brothers**, 1949, Whitman 10.00 25.00 60.00

2007- **(#7)-Bugs Bunny-Double Trouble on Diamond Island**, 1967, Whitman, 260 pgs., 39 cents, hard-c, color illos 5.00 12.50 33.00

2029-**(#29)- Bugs Bunny, Accidental Adventure,** 1969, Whitman, 256 pgs., hard-c, color illos. 4.00 10.00 22.00

2952- **Bugs Bunny's Mistake**, 1949, Whitman, 3 1/4" x 4", 24 pgs., Tiny Tales, full color (5 cents) (1030-5 on back-c) 10.00 25.00 60.00

5757-2- **Bugs Bunny in Double Trouble on Diamond Island**,1967, (1980-reprints #2007), Whitman, 260 pgs., soft-c, 79 cents, B&W 2.00 5.00 14.00

5758- **Bugs Bunny, Accidental Adventure,** 1973, Whitman, 256 pgs., soft-c, B&W illos. 2.00 5.00 14.00

5758-1- **Bugs Bunny, Accidental Adventure,** 1973, Whitman, 256 pgs., soft-c, B&W illos. 2.00 5.00 14.00

5772- **Bugs Bunny the Last Crusader**, 1975, Whitman, 49 cents, flip-it book 2.00 5.00 14.00

5772-2- **Bugs Bunny the Last Crusader**, 1975, Whitman, $1.50, flip-it book 1.00 2.50 6.00

1169- **Bullet Benton**, 1939, Saalfield, 400 pgs. 10.00 25.00 60.00

nn- **Bulletman and the Return of Mr. Murder**, 1941, Fawcett, 196 pgs., Dime Action Book 39.00 98.00 275.00

1142- **Bullets Across the Border** (A Billy The Kid story), 1938, Saalfield, 400 pgs. 10.00 25.00 60.00

Bunky (See Top-Line Comics)

837- **Bunty** (Punch and Judy), 1935, Whitman, 28 pgs., Magic-Action with 3 pop-ups 12.00 30.00 80.00

1091- **Burn 'Em Up Barnes**, 1935, Saalfield, hard-c, movie scenes 10.00 25.00 60.00

1321- **Burn 'Em Up Barnes**, 1935, Saalfield, soft-c, movie scenes 10.00 25.00 60.00

1415- **Buz Sawyer and Bomber 13**,1946, Whitman, 352 pgs., Roy Crane-a 10.00 25.00 60.00

GD FN VF/NM

1412- **Calling W-1-X-Y-Z, Jimmy Kean and the Radio Spies**, 1939, Whitman, 300 pgs. 11.00 27.50 70.00

Call of the Wild (See Jack London's...)

1107- **Camels are Coming**, 1935, Saalfield, movie scenes 10.00 25.00 60.00

1587- **Camels are Coming**, 1935, Saalfield, movie scenes 10.00 25.00 60.00

nn- **Captain and the Kids, Boys Vill Be Boys, The**, 1938, 68 pgs., Pan-Am Oil premium, soft-c 12.00 30.00 85.00

1128- **Captain Easy Soldier of Fortune**, 1934, Whitman, 432 pgs., Roy Crane-a 11.00 27.50 70.00

nn- **Captain Easy Soldier of Fortune**, 1934, Whitman, 436 pgs., Premium, no ads, soft 3-color-c, Roy Crane-a 20.00 50.00 140.00

1474- **Captain Easy Behind Enemy Lines**, 1943, Whitman, 352 pgs., Roy Crane-a 11.00 27.50 70.00

nn- **Captain Easy and Wash Tubbs**, 1935, 260 pgs., Cocomalt premium, Roy Crane-a 11.00 27.50 70.00

1444- **Captain Frank Hawks Air Ace and the League of Twelve**, 1938, Whitman, 432 pgs. 11.00 27.50 70.00

nn- **Captain Marvel**, 1941, Fawcett, 196 pgs., Dime Action Book 50.00 125.00 350.00

1402- **Captain Midnight and Sheik Jomak Khan**, 1946, Whitman, 352 pgs. 16.00 40.00 115.00

1452- **Captain Midnight and the Moon Woman**, 1943, Whitman, 352 pgs. 18.00 45.00 125.00

1458- **Captain Midnight Vs. The Terror of the Orient**, 1942, Whitman, 432 pgs., flip pictures, Hess-a 18.00 45.00 125.00

1488- **Captain Midnight and the Secret Squadron**, 1941, Whitman, 432 pgs. 18.00 45.00 125.00

Captain Robb of.. (See Dirigible ZR90 ...)

nn- **Cauliflower Catnip Pearls of Peril**, 1981, Teacup Tales, 290 pgs., Joe Wehrle Jr.-s/a; deliberately printed on aged-looking paper to look like an old BLB 4.00 10.00 27.00

20- **Ceiling Zero,** 1936, Lynn, 128 pgs., 7 1/2" x 5", hard-c, James Cagney, Pat O'Brien photos on-c, movie scenes, Warner Bros. Pictures 11.00 27.50 70.00

1093- **Chandu the Magician**, 1935, Saalfield, 5" x 5 1/4", 160 pgs., hard-c, Bela Lugosi photo-c, movie scenes 13.00 32.50 90.00

1323- **Chandu the Magician**, 1935, Saalfield, 5" x 5 1/4", 160 pgs., soft-c, Bela Lugosi photo-c 14.00 35.00 100.00

Charlie Chan (See Inspector ...)

1459- **Charlie Chan Solves a New Mystery** (See Inspector..), 1940, Whitman, 432 pgs., Alfred Andriola-a 12.00 30.00 85.00

1478- **Charlie Chan of the Honolulu Police, Inspector**, 1939, Whitman, 432 pgs., Andriola-a 12.00 30.00 85.00

Charlie McCarthy (See Story Of ...)

734- **Chester Gump at Silver Creek Ranch**, 1933, Whitman, 320 pgs., Sidney Smith-a 13.00 32.50 90.00

nn- **Chester Gump at Silver Creek Ranch**, 1933, Whitman, 204 pgs., Cocomalt premium, soft-c, Sidney Smith-a 14.00 35.00 100.00

nn- **Chester Gump at Silver Creek Ranch**, 1933, Whitman, 52 pgs., 4" x 5 1/2", premium-no ads, soft-c, Sidney Smith-a 21.00 52.50 150.00

766- **Chester Gump Finds the Hidden Treasure**, 1934, Whitman, 320 pgs., Sidney Smith-a 12.00 30.00 85.00

nn- **Chester Gump Finds the Hidden Treasure**, 1934, Whitman, 52 pgs., 3 1/2" x 5 3/4", premium-no ads, soft-c, Sidney Smith-a 21.00 52.50 150.00

nn- **Chester Gump Finds the Hidden Treasure**, 1934, Whitman, 52 pgs., 4" x 5 1/2", premium-no ads, Sidney Smith-a 21.00 52.50 150.00

1146- **Chester Gump in the City Of Gold**, 1935, Whitman, 432 pgs., Sidney Smith-a 12.00 30.00 85.00

nn- **Chester Gump in the City Of Gold**, 1935, Whitman, 436 pgs., premium-no ads, 3-color, soft-c, Sidney Smith-a 24.00 60.00 165.00

1402- **Chester Gump in the Pole to Pole Flight**, 1937, Whitman, 432 pgs. 12.00 30.00 75.00

5- **Chester Gump and His Friends**, 1934, Whitman, 132 pgs., 3 1/2" x 3 1/2", soft-c, Tarzan Ice Cream cup lid premium

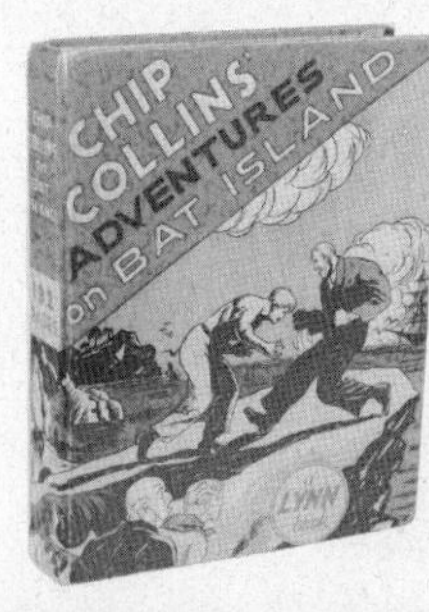

L14 - Chip Collins' Adventures on Bat Island © Lynn

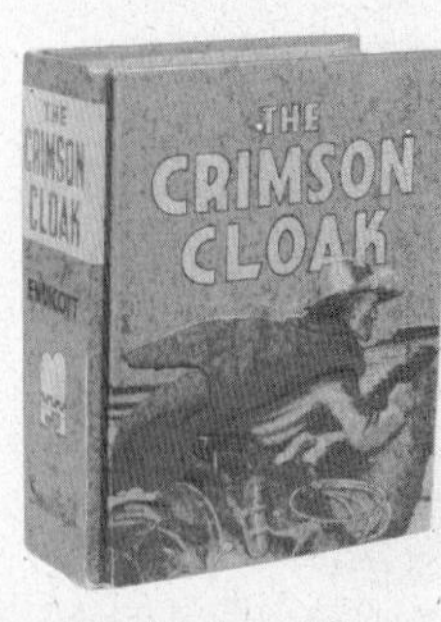

1161 - The Crimson Cloak © Saalfield

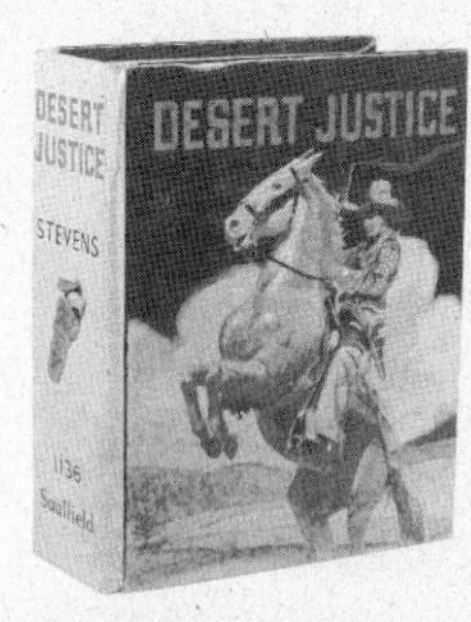

1136 - Desert Justice © Saalfield

GD FN VF/NM

23.00 57.50 160.00

nn- **Chester Gump at the North Pole**, 1938, Whitman, 68 pgs. soft-c, 3 3/4" x 3 1/2", Pan-Am giveaway 23.00 57.50 160.00

nn- **Chicken Greedy**, nd(1930s), np (Whitman), 36 pgs., 3" x 2 1/2", Penny Book 4.00 10.00 22.00

nn- **Chicken Licken**, nd (1930s), np (Whitman), 36 pgs., 3" x 2 1/2", Penny Book 4.00 10.00 22.00

1101- **Chief of the Rangers**, 1935, Saalfield, hard-c, Tom Mix photo-c, movie scenes from "The Miracle Rider" 13.00 32.50 90.00

1581- **Chief of the Rangers**, 1935, Saalfield, soft-c, Tom Mix photo-c, movie scenes 13.00 32.50 90.00

Child's Garden of Verses (See Wee Little Books)

L14- **Chip Collins' Adventures on Bat Island**, 1935, Lynn, 192 pgs. 11.00 27.50 70.00

2025- **Chitty Chitty Bang Bang**, 1968, Whitman, movie photos 4.00 10.00 27.00

Chubby Little Books, 1935, Whitman, 3" x 2 1/2", 200 pgs.

W803- **Golden Hours Story Book, The** 5.00 12.50 30.00

W803- **Story Hours Story Book, The** 5.00 12.50 30.00

W804- **Gay Book of Little Stories, The** 5.00 12.50 30.00

W804- **Glad Book of Little Stories, The** 5.00 12.50 30.00

W804- **Joy Book of Little Stories, The** 5.00 12.50 30.00

W804- **Sunny Book of Little Stories, The** 5.00 12.50 30.00

1453- **Chuck Malloy Railroad Detective on the Streamliner**,1938, Whitman, 300 pgs. 8.00 20.00 50.00

Cinderella (See Walt Disney's...)

Clyde Beatty (See The Steel Arena)

1410- **Clyde Beatty Daredevil Lion and Tiger Tamer**, 1939, Whitman, 300 pgs. 12.00 30.00 80.00

1480- **Coach Bernie Bierman's Brick Barton and the Winning Eleven**, 1938, 300 pgs. 10.00 25.00 60.00

1446- **Convoy Patrol** (A Thrilling U.S. Navy Story), 1942, Whitman, 432 pgs., flip pictures 10.00 25.00 60.00

1127- **Corley of the Wilderness Trail**, 1937, Saalfield, hard-c 10.00 25.00 60.00

1607- **Corley of the Wilderness Trail**, 1937, Saalfield, soft-c 10.00 25.00 60.00

1- **Count of Monte Cristo**, 1934, EVW, 160 pgs., (Five Star Library), movie scenes, hard-c (Rare) 20.00 50.00 140.00

1457- **Cowboy Lingo Boys' Book of Western Facts**, 1938, Whitman, 300 pgs., Fred Harman-a 8.00 20.00 50.00

1171- **Cowboy Malloy**, 1940, Saalfield, 400 pgs. 7.00 17.50 40.00

1106- **Cowboy Millionaire**, 1935, Saalfield, movie scenes with George O'Brien, photo-c, hard-c 12.00 30.00 80.00

1586- **Cowboy Millionaire**, 1935, Saalfield, movie scenes with George O'Brien, photo-c, soft-c 12.00 30.00 80.00

724- **Cowboy Stories**, 1933, Whitman, 300 pgs., Hal Arbo-a 10.00 25.00 65.00

nn- **Cowboy Stories**, 1933, Whitman, 52 pgs., soft-c, premium-no ads, 4" x 5 1/2" Hal Arbo-a 12.00 30.00 80.00

1161- **Crimson Cloak, The**, 1939, Saalfield, 400 pgs. 10.00 25.00 60.00

L19- **Curley Harper at Lakespur**, 1935, Lynn, 192 pgs. 10.00 25.00 60.00

5785-2- **Daffy Duck in Twice the Trouble**, 1980, Whitman, 260 pgs., 79 cents soft-c 1.00 2.50 6.00

2018-(#18)-**Daktari-Night of Terror**, 1968, Whitman, 260 pgs., 39 cents, hard-c, color illos 4.00 10.00 27.00

1010- **Dan Dunn And The Gangsters' Frame-Up**, 1937, Whitman, 7 1/4" x 5 1/2", 64 pgs., Nickel Book 29.00 73.00 200.00

1116- **Dan Dunn "Crime Never Pays,"** 1934, Whitman, 320 pgs., by Norman Marsh 8.00 20.00 50.00

1125- **Dan Dunn on the Trail of the Counterfeiters**, 1936, Whitman, 432 pgs., by Norman Marsh 8.00 20.00 50.00

1171- **Dan Dunn and the Crime Master**, 1937, Whitman, 432 pgs., by Norman Marsh 8.00 20.00 50.00

1417- **Dan Dunn and the Underworld Gorillas,** 1941, Whitman, All Pictures Comics, flip pictures, by Norman Marsh 8.00 20.00 50.00

1454- **Dan Dunn on the Trail of Wu Fang**, 1938, Whitman, 432 pgs., by Norman Marsh 10.00 25.00 65.00

1481- **Dan Dunn and the Border Smugglers**, 1938, Whitman, 432 pgs., by Norman Marsh 7.00 17.50 45.00

1492- **Dan Dunn and the Dope Ring**, 1940, Whitman, 432 pgs., by Norman Marsh 7.00 17.50 45.00

nn- **Dan Dunn and the Bank Hold-Up**, 1938, Whitman, 36 pgs., 2 1/2" x 3 1/2", Penny Book 8.00 20.00 50.00

nn- **Dan Dunn and the Zeppelin Of Doom**, 1938, Dell, 196 pgs., Fast-Action Story, soft-c 18.00 45.00 125.00

nn- **Dan Dunn Meets Chang Loo**, 1938, Whitman, 66 pgs., Pan-Am premium, by Norman Marsh 23.00 57.50 160.00

nn- **Dan Dunn Plays a Lone Hand**, 1938, Whitman, 36 pgs.,
2 1/2" x 3 1/2", Penny Book 8.00 20.00 50.00
3 3/4" x 3 1/2", Buddy book 24.00 60.00 170.00

6- **Dan Dunn Secret Operative 48 and the Counterfeiter Ring**, 1938, Whitman, 132 pgs., soft-c, 3 3/4" x 3 1/2", Buddy Book premium 24.00 60.00 170.00

9- **Dan Dunn's Mysterious Ruse**, 1936, Whitman, 132 pgs., soft-c, 3 1/2" x 3 1/2", Tarzan Ice Cream cup lid premium 24.00 60.00 170.00

1177- **Danger Trail North**, 1940, Saalfield, 400 pgs. 10.00 25.00 60.00

1151- **Danger Trails in Africa**, 1935, Whitman, 432 pgs. 12.00 30.00 80.00

nn- **Daniel Boone**, 1934, World Syndicate, High Lights of History Series, hard-c, All in Pictures 10.00 25.00 60.00

1160- **Dan of the Lazy L**, 1939, Saalfield, 400 pgs. 10.00 25.00 60.00

1148- **David Copperfield**, 1934, Whitman, hard-c, 160 pgs., photo-c, movie scenes (W. C. Fields) 12.00 30.00 80.00

nn- **David Copperfield**, 1934, Whitman, soft-c, 164 pgs., movie scenes 12.00 30.00 80.00

1151- **Death by Short Wave**, 1938, Saalfield 10.00 25.00 65.00

1156- **Denny the Ace Detective**, 1938, Saalfield, 400 pgs. 10.00 25.00 60.00

1431- **Desert Eagle and the Hidden Fortress, The**, 1941, Whitman, 432 pgs., flip pictures 10.00 25.00 65.00

1458- **Desert Eagle Rides Again, The**, 1939, Whitman, 300 pgs. 10.00 25.00 65.00

1136- **Desert Justice**, 1938, Saalfield, 400 pgs. 10.00 25.00 60.00

1484- **Detective Higgins of the Racket Squad**, 1938, Whitman, 432 pgs. 10.00 25.00 65.00

1124- **Dickie Moore in the Little Red School House**, 1936, Whitman, 240 pgs., photo-c, movie scenes (Chesterfield Motion Picts. Corp) 12.00 30.00 80.00

W-707- **Dick Tracy the Detective, The Adventures of**, 1933, Whitman, 320 pgs. (The 1st Big Little Book), by Chester Gould (Scarce) 188.00 470.00 1500.00

nn- **Dick Tracy Detective, The Adventures of**, 1933, Whitman, 52 pgs., 4" x 5 1/2", premium-no ads, soft-c, by Chester Gould 79.00 198.00 550.00

nn- **Dick Tracy Detective, The Adventures of**, 1933, Whitman, 52 pgs., 4" x 5 1/2", inside back-c & back-c ads for Sundial Shoes, soft-c, by Chester Gould 82.00 205.00 575.00

710- **Dick Tracy and Dick Tracy, Jr.** (The Advs. of ...), 1933, Whitman, 320 pgs., by Chester Gould 57.00 143.00 400.00

nn- **Dick Tracy and Dick Tracy, Jr.** (The Advs. of ...), 1933, Whitman, 52 pgs., premium-no ads, soft-c, 4" x 5 1/2", by Chester Gould 57.00 143.00 400.00

nn- **Dick Tracy the Detective and Dick Tracy, Jr.**, 1933, Whitman, 52 pgs., premium-no ads, 3 1/2"x 5 1/4", soft-c, by Chester Gould 57.00 143.00 400.00

723- **Dick Tracy Out West**, 1933, Whitman, 300 pgs., by Chester Gould 26.00 65.00 185.00

749- **Dick Tracy from Colorado to Nova Scotia**, 1933, Whitman, 320 pgs., by Chester Gould 24.00 60.00 170.00

nn- **Dick Tracy from Colorado to Nova Scotia**, 1933, Whitman, 204 pgs., premium-no ads, soft-c, by Chester Gould 26.00 65.00 185.00

1105- **Dick Tracy and the Stolen Bonds**, 1934, Whitman, 320 pgs., by Chester Gould 14.00 35.00 100.00

1112- **Dick Tracy and the Racketeer Gang**, 1936, Whitman, 432 pgs., by Chester Gould 14.00 35.00 95.00

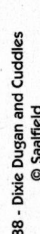

1420 - Dick Tracy and the Hotel Murders © UFS

1188 - Dixie Dugan and Cuddles © Saalfield

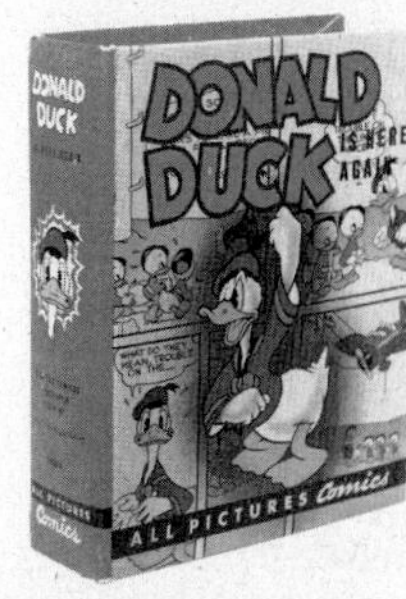
1484 - Donald Duck is Here Again! © DIS

GD FN VF/NM

1137- Dick Tracy Solves the Penfield Mystery, 1934, Whitman, 320 pgs., by Chester Gould 14.00 35.00 100.00
nn- Dick Tracy Solves the Penfield Mystery, 1934, Whitman, 324 pgs., premium-no ads, 3-color, soft-c, by Chester Gould 36.00 90.00 250.00
1163- Dick Tracy and the Boris Arson Gang, 1935, Whitman, 432 pgs., by Chester Gould 15.00 37.50 105.00
1170- Dick Tracy on the Trail of Larceny Lu, 1935, Whitman, 432 pgs., by Chester Gould 14.00 35.00 95.00
1185- Dick Tracy in Chains of Crime, 1936, Whitman, 432 pgs., by Chester Gould 15.00 37.50 105.00
1412- Dick Tracy and Yogee Yamma, 1946, Whitman, 352 pgs., by Chester Gould 14.00 35.00 95.00
1420- Dick Tracy and the Hotel Murders, 1937, Whitman, 432 pgs., by Chester Gould 15.00 37.50 105.00
1434- Dick Tracy and the Phantom Ship, 1940, Whitman, 432 pgs., by Chester Gould 15.00 37.50 105.00
1436- Dick Tracy and the Mad Killer, 1947, Whitman, 288 pgs., by Chester Gould 13.00 32.50 90.00
1439- Dick Tracy and His G-Men, 1941, Whitman, 432 pgs., flip pictures, by Chester Gould 15.00 37.50 105.00
1445- Dick Tracy and the Bicycle Gang, 1948, Whitman, 288 pgs., by Chester Gould 13.00 32.50 90.00
1446- Detective Dick Tracy and the Spider Gang, 1937, Whitman, 240 pgs., scenes from "Adventures of Dick Tracy" serial 19.00 47.50 130.00
1449- Dick Tracy Special F.B.I. Operative, 1943, Whitman, 432 pgs. by Chester Gould 15.00 37.50 105.00
1454- Dick Tracy on the High Seas, 1939, Whitman, 432 pgs., by Chester Gould 15.00 37.50 105.00
1460- Dick Tracy and the Tiger Lilly Gang, 1949, Whitman, 288 pgs., by Chester Gould 13.00 32.50 90.00
1478- Dick Tracy on Voodoo Island, 1944, Whitman, 352 pgs., by Chester Gould 13.00 32.50 90.00
1479- Detective Dick Tracy Vs. Crooks in Disguise, 1939, Whitman, 432 pgs., flip pictures, by Chester Gould 15.00 37.50 105.00
1482- Dick Tracy and the Wreath Kidnapping Case, 1945, Whitman, 352 pgs. 14.00 35.00 95.00
1488- Dick Tracy the Super-Detective, 1939, Whitman, 432 pgs., by Chester Gould 15.00 37.50 105.00
1491- Dick Tracy the Man with No Face, 1938, Whitman, 432 pgs. 15.00 37.50 105.00
1495- Dick Tracy Returns, 1939, Whitman, 432 pgs., based on Republic Motion Picture serial, Chester Gould-a 15.00 37.50 105.00
2001- (#1)-Dick Tracy-Encounters Facey, 1967, Whitman, 260 pgs., 39 cents, hard-c, color illos 4.00 10.00 27.00
3912- Dick Tracy Big Little Book Picture Puzzles, 1938, Whitman, 7 1/2" x 10 1/4" box with 2 jigsaw puzzles 50.00 125.00 350.00
Variant set, same cover w/2 puzzles showing Dick Tracy & Jr. in crime lab & Dick Tracy patting down a gangster 50.00 125.00 350.00
4055- Dick Tracy, The Adventures of, 1934, Whitman, 7" x 9 1/2", 320 pgs., Big Big Book, by Chester Gould 57.00 143.00 400.00
4071- Dick Tracy and the Mystery of the Purple Cross, 1938, 7" x 9 1/2", 320 pgs., Big Big Book, by Chester Gould (Scarce) 50.00 125.00 350.00
nn- Dick Tracy and the Invisible Man, 1939, Whitman, 3 1/4" x 3 3/4", 132 pgs., stapled, soft-c, Quaker Oats premium; NBC radio play script, Chester Gould-a 37.00 93.00 260.00
Vol. 2- Dick Tracy's Ghost Ship, 1939, Whitman, 3 1/2" x 3 1/2", 132 pgs., soft-c, stapled, Quaker Oats premium; NBC radio play script episode from actual radio show; Gould-a 37.00 93.00 260.00
3- Dick Tracy Meets a New Gang, 1934, Whitman, 3" x 3 1/2", 132 pgs., soft-c, Tarzan Ice Cream cup lid premium 36.00 90.00 250.00
11- Dick Tracy in Smashing the Famon Racket, 1938, Whitman, 3 3/4" x 3 1/2", Buddy Book-ice cream premium, by Chester Gould 36.00 90.00 250.00
nn- Dick Tracy Gets His Man, 1938, Whitman, 36 pgs., 2 1/2" x 3 1/2", Penny Book 8.00 20.00 50.00
nn- Dick Tracy the Detective, 1938, Whitman, 36 pgs., 2 1/2" x 3 1/2", Penny Book 8.00 20.00 50.00
9- Dick Tracy and the Frozen Bullet Murders, 1941, Dell, 196 pgs., Fast-Action Story, soft-c, by Gould 37.00 93.00 260.00
6833- Dick Tracy Detective and Federal Agent, 1936, Dell, 244 pgs., Cartoon Story Books, hard-c, by Gould 39.00 98.00 275.00
nn- Dick Tracy Detective and Federal Agent, 1936, Dell, 244 pgs., Fast-Action Story, soft-c, by Gould 34.00 85.00 240.00
nn- Dick Tracy and the Blackmailers, 1939, Dell, 196 pgs., Fast-Action Story, soft-c, by Gould 34.00 85.00 240.00
nn- Dick Tracy and the Chain of Evidence, Detective, 1938, Dell, 196 pgs., Fast-Action Story, soft-c, by Chester Gould 34.00 85.00 240.00
nn- Dick Tracy and the Crook Without a Face, 1938, Whitman, 68 pgs., 3 1/4" x 3 1/2", Pan-Am giveaway, Gould-c/a 29.00 73.00 200.00
nn- Dick Tracy and the Maroon Mask Gang, 1938, Dell, 196 pgs., Fast-Action Story, soft-c, by Gould 34.00 85.00 240.00
nn- Dick Tracy Cross-Country Race, 1934, Whitman, 8 pgs., 2 1/2" x 3", Big Thrill chewing gum premium (6 diff.) 12.00 30.00 85.00
nn- Dick Whittington and his Cat, nd(1930s), np(Whitman), 36 pgs., Penny Book 3.00 7.50 20.00
Dinglehoofer und His Dog Adolph (See Top-Line Comics)
Dinky (See Jackie Cooper in ...)
1464- Dirigible ZR90 and the Disappearing Zeppelin (Captain Robb of ...), 1941, Whitman, 300 pgs., Al Lewin-a 14.00 35.00 100.00
1167- Dixie Dugan Among the Cowboys, 1939, Saalfield, 400 pgs. 10.00 25.00 65.00
1188- Dixie Dugan and Cuddles, 1940, Saalfield, 400 pgs., by Striebel & McEvoy 10.00 25.00 65.00
Doctor Doom (See Foreign Spies... & International Spy...)
Dog of Flanders, A (See Frankie Thomas in ...)
1114- Dog Stars of Hollywood, 1936, Saalfield, photo-c, photo-illos 12.00 30.00 85.00
1594- Dog Stars of Hollywood, 1936, Saalfield, photo-c, soft-c, photo-illos 12.00 30.00 85.00
nn- Dolls and Dresses Big Little Set, 1930s, Whitman, box contains 20 dolls on paper, 128 sheets of clothing to color & cut out, includes crayons 36.00 90.00 250.00
Donald Duck (See Silly Symphony... & Walt Disney's ...)
800- Donald Duck in Bringing Up the Boys, 1948, Whitman, hard-c, Story Hour series 10.00 25.00 65.00
1404- Donald Duck (Says Such a Life) (Disney), 1939, Whitman, 432 pgs., Taliaferro-a 19.00 47.50 130.00
1411- Donald Duck and Ghost Morgan's Treasure (Disney), 1946, Whitman, All Pictures Comics, Barks-a; reprints FC #9 24.00 60.00 165.00
1422- Donald Duck Sees Stars (Disney), 1941, Whitman, 432 pgs., flip pictures, Taliaferro-a 18.00 45.00 125.00
1424- Donald Duck Says Such Luck (Disney), 1941, Whitman, 432 pgs., flip pictures, Taliaferro-a 18.00 45.00 125.00
1430- Donald Duck Headed For Trouble (Disney), 1942, Whitman, 432 pgs., flip pictures, Taliaferro-a 18.00 45.00 125.00
1432- Donald Duck and the Green Serpent (Disney), 1947, Whitman, All Pictures Comics, Barks-a; reprints FC #108 20.00 50.00 140.00
1434- Donald Duck Forgets To Duck (Disney), 1939, Whitman, 432 pgs., Taliaferro-a 18.00 45.00 125.00
1438- Donald Duck Off the Beam (Disney), 1943, Whitman, 352 pgs., flip pictures, Taliaferro-a 18.00 45.00 125.00
1438- Donald Duck Off the Beam (Disney), 1943, Whitman, 432 pgs., flip pictures, Taliaferro-a 18.00 45.00 125.00
1449- Donald Duck Lays Down the Law, 1948, Whitman, 288 pgs., Barks-a 18.00 45.00 125.00
1457- Donald Duck in Volcano Valley (Disney), 1949, Whitman, 288 pgs., Barks-a 18.00 45.00 125.00
1462- Donald Duck Gets Fed Up (Disney), 1940, Whitman, 432 pgs.,Taliaferro-a 18.00 45.00 125.00
1478- Donald Duck-Hunting For Trouble (Disney), 1938, Whitman, 432 pgs., Taliaferro-a 18.00 45.00 125.00
1484- Donald Duck is Here Again!, 1944, Whitman, All Pictures Comics, Taliaferro-a 18.00 45.00 125.00
1486- Donald Duck Up in the Air (Disney), 1945, Whitman, 352 pgs., Barks-a 20.00 50.00 140.00
705-10- Donald Duck and the Mystery of the Double X, (Disney), 1949, Whitman, Barks-a 12.00 30.00 80.00
2033-(#33)- Donald Duck, Luck of the Ducks, 1969, Whitman, 256 pgs.,

L13 - Donnie and the Pirates © Lynn

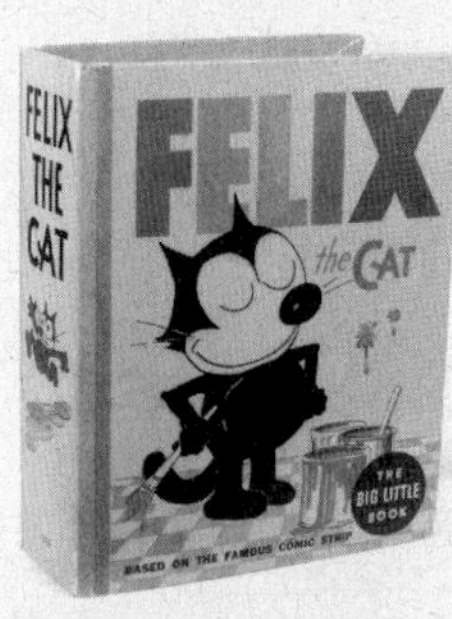

1129 - Felix the Cat © WHIT

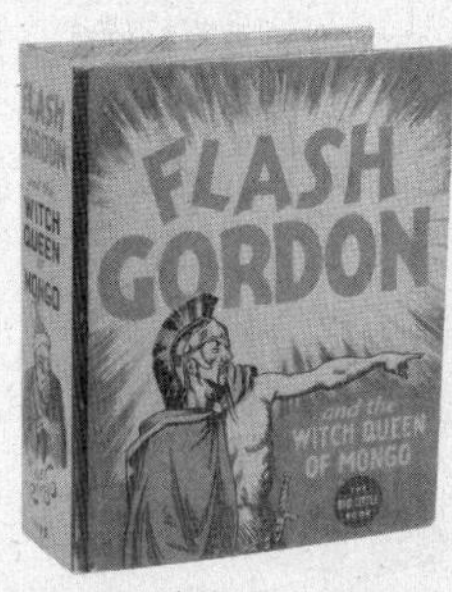

1190 - Flash Gordon and the Witch Queen of Mongo © KING

	GD	FN	VF/NM
hard-c, 39 cents, color illos.	4.00	10.00	22.00
2009-(#9)-Donald Duck-The Fabulous Diamond Fountain, (Walt Disney), 1967, Whitman, 260 pgs., 39 cents, hard-c, color illos	4.00	10.00	27.00
5756- Donald Duck-The Fabulous Diamond Fountain, (Walt Disney), 1973, Whitman, 260 pgs., 79 cents, soft-c, color illos	3.00	7.50	20.00
5756-1- Donald Duck-The Fabulous Diamond Fountain, (Walt Disney), 1973, Whitman, 260 pgs., 79 cents, soft-c, color illos	3.00	7.50	20.00
5756-2- Donald Duck-The Fabulous Diamond Fountain, (Walt Disney), 1973, Whitman, 260 pgs., 79 cents, soft-c, color illos	3.00	7.50	20.00
5760- Donald Duck in Volcano Valley (Disney), 1973, Whitman, 39 cents, flip-it book	3.00	7.50	20.00
5760-2- Donald Duck in Volcano Valley (Disney), 1973, Whitman, 79 cents, flip-it book	2.00	5.00	14.00
5764- Donald Duck, Luck of the Ducks, 1969, Whitman, 256 pgs., soft-c, 49 cents, color illos.	3.00	7.50	20.00
5773- Donald Duck - The Lost Jungle City, 1975, Whitman, 49 cents, flip-it book; 6 printings through 1980	2.00	5.00	14.00
nn- Donald Duck and the Ducklings, 1938, Dell, 194 pgs., Fast-Action Story, soft-c, Taliaferro-a	36.00	90.00	250.00
nn- Donald Duck Out of Luck (Disney), 1940, Dell, 196 pgs., Fast-Action Story, has Four Color #4 on back-c, Taliaferro-a	36.00	90.00	250.00
8- Donald Duck Takes It on the Chin (Disney), 1941, Dell, 196 pgs., Fast-Action Story, soft-c, Taliaferro-a	36.00	90.00	250.00
L13- Donnie and the Pirates, 1935, Lynn, 192 pgs.	10.00	25.00	60.00
1438- Don O'Dare Finds War, 1940, Whitman, 432 pgs.	10.00	25.00	60.00
1107- Don Winslow, U.S.N., 1935, Whitman, 432 pgs.	16.00	40.00	110.00
nn- Don Winslow, U.S.N., 1935, Whitman, 436 pgs., premium-no ads, 3-color, soft-c	19.00	47.50	130.00
1408- Don Winslow and the Giant Girl Spy, 1946, Whitman, 352 pgs.	12.00	30.00	75.00
1418- Don Winslow Navy Intelligence Ace, 1942, Whitman, 432 pgs., flip pictures	14.00	35.00	100.00
1419- Don Winslow of the Navy Vs. the Scorpion Gang, 1938, Whitman, 432 pgs.	14.00	35.00	100.00
1453- Don Winslow of the Navy and the Secret Enemy Base, 1943, Whitman, 352 pgs.	14.00	35.00	100.00
1489- Don Winslow of the Navy and the Great War Plot, 1940, Whitman, 432 pgs.	14.00	35.00	100.00
nn- Don Winslow U.S. Navy and the Missing Admiral, 1938, Whitman, 36 pgs., 2 1/2" x 3 1/2", Penny Book	7.00	17.50	40.00
1137- Doomed To Die, 1938, Saalfield, 400 pgs.	10.00	25.00	60.00
1140- Down Cartridge Creek, 1938, Saalfield, 400 pgs.	10.00	25.00	60.00
1416- Draftie of the U.S. Army, 1943, Whitman, All Pictures Comics	10.00	25.00	65.00
1100B- Dreams (Your dreams & what they mean), 1938, Whitman, 36 pgs., 2 1/2" x 3 1/2", Penny Book	3.00	7.50	20.00
24- Dumb Dora and Bing Brown, 1936, Lynn	11.00	27.50	70.00
1400- Dumbo, of the Circus - Only His Ears Grew! (Disney), 1941, Whitman, 432 pgs., based on Disney movie	18.00	45.00	125.00
10- Dumbo the Flying Elephant (Disney), 1944, Dell, 194 pgs., Fast-Action Story, soft-c	29.00	73.00	200.00
nn- East O' the Sun and West O' the Moon, nd (1930s), np (Whitman), 36 pgs., 3" x 2 1/2", Penny Book	3.00	7.50	20.00
774- Eddie Cantor in An Hour with You, 1934, Whitman, 154 pgs., 4 1/4" x 5 1/4", photo-c, movie scenes	12.00	30.00	85.00
nn- Eddie Cantor in Laughland, 1934, Goldsmith, 132 pgs., soft-c, photo-c, Vallely-a	12.00	30.00	85.00
1106- Ella Cinders and the Mysterious House, 1934, Whitman, 432 pgs.	12.00	30.00	75.00
nn- Ella Cinders and the Mysterious House, 1934, Whitman, 52 pgs., premium-no ads, soft-c, 3 1/2" x 5 3/4"	14.00	35.00	100.00

	GD	FN	VF/NM
nn- Ella Cinders, 1935, Whitman, 148 pgs., 3 1/4" x 4", Tarzan Ice Cream cup lid premium	24.00	60.00	165.00
nn- Ella Cinders Plays Duchess, 1938, Whitman, 68 pgs., 3 3/4" x 3 1/2", Pan-Am Oil premium	16.00	40.00	115.00
nn- Ella Cinders Solves a Mystery, 1938, Whitman, 68 pgs., Pan-Am Oil premium, soft-c	16.00	40.00	115.00
11- Ella Cinders' Exciting Experience, 1934, Whitman, 3 1/2" x 3 1/2", 132 pgs., Tarzan Ice Cream cup lid giveaway	24.00	60.00	165.00
1406- Ellery Queen the Adventure of the Last Man Club, 1940, Whitman, 432 pgs.	12.00	30.00	80.00
1472- Ellery Queen the Master Detective, 1942, Whitman, 432 pgs., flip pictures	12.00	30.00	80.00
1081- Elmer and his Dog Spot, 1935, Saalfield, hard-c	8.00	20.00	50.00
1311- Elmer and his Dog Spot, 1935, Saalfield, soft-c	8.00	20.00	50.00
722- Erik Noble and the Forty-Niners, 1934, Whitman, 384 pgs.	8.00	20.00	50.00
nn- Erik Noble and the Forty-Niners, 1934, Whitman, 386 pgs., 3-color, soft-c (Rare)	36.00	90.00	250.00
2019-(#19)- Fantastic Four in the House of Horrors, 1968, Whitman, 256 pgs., hard-c, color illos.	4.00	10.00	27.00
5775 - Fantastic Four in the House of Horrors, 1976, Whitman, 256 pgs., soft-c, color illos.	3.00	7.50	20.00
5775-1 - Fantastic Four in the House of Horrors, 1976, Whitman, 256 pgs., soft-c, color illos.	3.00	7.50	20.00
1058- Farmyard Symphony, The (Disney), 1939, 5" X 5 1/2", 68 pgs., hard-c	11.00	27.50	70.00
1129- Felix the Cat, 1936, Whitman, 432 pgs., Messmer-a	24.00	60.00	170.00
1439- Felix the Cat, 1943, Whitman, All Pictures Comics, Messmer-a	21.00	52.50	150.00
1465- Felix the Cat, 1945, Whitman, All Pictures Comics, Messmer-a	18.00	45.00	125.00
nn- Felix (Flip book), 1967, World Retrospective of Animation Cinema, 188 pgs., 2 1/2" x 4" by Otto Messmer	4.00	10.00	27.00
nn- Fighting Cowboy of Nugget Gulch, The, 1939, Whitman, 2 1/2" x 3 1/2", Penny Book	4.00	10.00	25.00
1401- Fighting Heroes Battle for Freedom, 1943, Whitman, All Pictures Comics, from "Heroes of Democracy" strip, by Stookie Allen	8.00	20.00	50.00
6- Fighting President, The, 1934, EVW (Five Star Library), 160 pgs., photo-c, photo ill., F. D. Roosevelt	10.00	25.00	60.00
nn- Fire Chief Ed Wynn and "His Old Fire Horse," 1934, Goldsmith, 132 pgs., H. Vallely-a, photo, soft-c	10.00	25.00	60.00
1464- Flame Boy and the Indians' Secret, 1938, Whitman, 300 pgs., Sekakuku-a (Hopi Indian)	8.00	20.00	50.00
22- Flaming Guns, 1935, EVW, with Tom Mix, movie scenes — Hardcover	43.00	108.00	300.00
(Scarce) — Softcover	50.00	125.00	350.00
1110- Flash Gordon on the Planet Mongo, 1934, Whitman, 320 pgs., by Alex Raymond	39.00	98.00	275.00
1166- Flash Gordon and the Monsters of Mongo, 1935, Whitman, 432 pgs., by Alex Raymond	37.00	93.00	260.00
nn- Flash Gordon and the Monsters of Mongo, 1935, Whitman, 436 pgs., premium-no ads, 3-color, soft-c, by Raymond	61.00	153.00	430.00
1171- Flash Gordon and the Tournaments of Mongo, 1935, Whitman, 432 pgs., by Alex Raymond	36.00	90.00	250.00
1190- Flash Gordon and the Witch Queen of Mongo, 1936, Whitman, 432 pgs., by Alex Raymond	36.00	90.00	250.00
1407- Flash Gordon in the Water World of Mongo, 1937, Whitman, 432 pgs., by Alex Raymond	31.00	78.00	215.00
1423- Flash Gordon and the Perils of Mongo, 1940, Whitman, 432 pgs., by Alex Raymond	29.00	73.00	200.00
1424- Flash Gordon in the Jungles of Mongo, 1947, Whitman, 352 pgs., by Alex Raymond	23.00	57.50	160.00
1443- Flash Gordon in the Ice World of Mongo, 1942, Whitman, 432 pgs., flip pictures, by Alex Raymond	30.00	75.00	210.00
1447- Flash Gordon and the Fiery Desert of Mongo, 1948, Whitman, 288 pgs., Raymond-a	23.00	57.50	160.00

Flintstones: A Friend From the Past © H-B

1461 - Gene Autry and the Red Bandit's Ghost © WHIT

The Ghost Gun Gang Meet Their Match © WHIT

GD FN VF/NM

1469- Flash Gordon and the Power Men of Mongo, 1943, Whitman, 352 pgs., by Alex Raymond 31.00 78.00 220.00

1479- Flash Gordon and the Red Sword Invaders, 1945, Whitman, 352 pgs., by Alex Raymond 29.00 73.00 200.00

1484- Flash Gordon and the Tyrant of Mongo, 1941, Whitman, 432 pgs., flip pictures, by Alex Raymond 31.00 78.00 220.00

1492- Flash Gordon in the Forest Kingdom of Mongo, 1938, Whitman, 432 pgs., by Alex Raymond 39.00 98.00 270.00

12- Flash Gordon and the Ape Men of Mor, 1942, Dell, 196 pgs., Fast-Action Story, by Alex Raymond 36.00 90.00 250.00

6833- Flash Gordon Vs. the Emperor of Mongo, 1936, Dell, 244 pgs., Cartoon Story Books, hard-c, Raymond-c/a 43.00 108.00 300.00

nn- Flash Gordon Vs. the Emperor of Mongo, 1936, Dell, 244 pgs., Fast-Action Story, soft-c, Alex Raymond-c/a 36.00 90.00 250.00

1467- Flint Roper and the Six-Gun Showdown, 1941, Whitman, 300 pgs. 10.00 25.00 60.00

2014-(#14)- Flintstones-The Case of the Many Missing Things, 1968, Whitman, 260 pgs., 39 cents, hard-c, color illos 4.00 10.00 27.00

nn- Flintstones: A Friend From the Past, 1977, Modern Promotions, 244 pgs., 49 cents, soft-c, flip pictures 2.00 5.00 11.00

nn- Flintstones: It's About Time, 1977, Modern Promotions, 244 pgs., 49 cents, soft-c, flip pictures 2.00 5.00 11.00

nn- Flintstones: Pebbles & Bamm-Bamm Meet Santa Claus, 1977, Modern Promotions, 244 pgs., 49 cents, soft-c, flip pictures 2.00 5.00 11.00

nn- Flintstones: The Great Balloon Race, 1977, Modern Promotions, 244 pgs., 49 cents, soft-c, flip pictures 2.00 5.00 11.00

nn- Flintstones: The Mystery of the Many Missing Things, 1977, Modern Promotions, 244 pgs., 49 cents, soft-c, flip pictures 2.00 5.00 11.00

2003-(#3)- Flipper-Killer Whale Trouble, 1967, Whitman, 260 pgs., hard-c, 39 cents, color illos 3.00 7.50 20.00

2032-(#32)- Flipper, Deep-Sea Photographer, 1969, Whitman, 256 pgs., hard-c, color illos. 3.00 7.50 20.00

1108- Flying the Sky Clipper with Winsie Atkins, 1936, Whitman, 432 pgs. 10.00 25.00 60.00

1460- Foreign Spies Doctor Doom and the Ghost Submarine, 1939, Whitman, 432 pgs., Al McWilliams-a 12.00 30.00 75.00

1100B- Fortune Teller, 1938, Whitman, 36 pgs., 2 1/2" x 3 1/2", Penny Book 3.00 7.50 20.00

1175- Frank Buck Presents Ted Towers Animal Master, 1935, Whitman, 432 pgs. 11.00 27.50 70.00

2015-(#15)-Frankenstein, Jr. - The Menace of the Heartless Monster, 1968, Whitman, 260 pgs., 39 cents, hard-c, color illos. 4.00 10.00 27.00

16- Frankie Thomas in A Dog of Flanders, 1935, EVW, movie scenes 12.00 30.00 75.00

1121- Frank Merriwell at Yale, 1935, 432 pgs. 10.00 25.00 60.00

Freckles and His Friends in the North Woods (See Top-Line Comics)

nn- Freckles and His Friends Stage a Play, 1938, Whitman, 36 pgs., 2 1/2" x 3 1/2", Penny Book 10.00 25.00 60.00

1164- Freckles and the Lost Diamond Mine, 1937, Whitman, 432 pgs., Merrill Blosser-a 11.00 27.50 70.00

nn- Freckles and the Mystery Ship, 1935, Whitman, 66 pgs., Pan-Am premium 12.00 30.00 75.00

1100B- Fun, Puzzles, Riddles, 1938, Whitman, 36 pgs., 2 1/2" x 3 1/2", Penny Book 3.00 7.50 20.00

1433- Gang Busters Step In, 1939, Whitman, 432 pgs., Henry E. Vallely-a 11.00 27.50 70.00

1437- Gang Busters Smash Through, 1942, Whitman, 432 pgs. 11.00 27.50 70.00

1451- Gang Busters in Action!, 1938, Whitman, 432 pgs. 11.00 27.50 70.00

nn- Gang Busters and Guns of the Law, 1940, Dell, 4" x 5", 194 pgs., Fast-Action Story, soft-c 27.00 68.00 190.00

nn- Gang Busters and the Radio Clues, 1938, Whitman, 36 pgs., 2 1/2" x 3 1/2", Penny Book 8.00 20.00 50.00

1409- Gene Autry and Raiders of the Range, 1946, Whitman, 352 pgs. 12.00 30.00 80.00

1425- Gene Autry and the Mystery of Paint Rock Canyon, 1947, Whitman, 288 pgs. 12.00 30.00 80.00

GD FN VF/NM

1428- Gene Autry Special Ranger, 1941, Whitman, 432 pgs., Erwin Hess-a 16.00 40.00 115.00

1433- Gene Autry in Public Cowboy No. 1, 1938, Whitman, 240 pgs., photo-c, movie scenes (1st Autry BLB) 29.00 73.00 200.00

1434- Gene Autry and the Gun-Smoke Reckoning, 1943, Whitman, 352 pgs. 16.00 40.00 110.00

1439- Gene Autry and the Land Grab Mystery, 1948, Whitman, 290 pgs. 12.00 30.00 75.00

1456- Gene Autry in Special Ranger Rule, 1945, Whitman, 352 pgs., Henry E. Vallely-a 16.00 40.00 110.00

1461- Gene Autry and the Red Bandit's Ghost, 1949, Whitman, 288 pgs. 11.00 27.50 70.00

1483- Gene Autry in Law of the Range, 1939, Whitman, 432 pgs. 16.00 40.00 110.00

1493- Gene Autry and the Hawk of the Hills, 1942, Whitman, 428 pgs., flip pictures, Vallely-a 16.00 40.00 110.00

1494- Gene Autry Cowboy Detective, 1940, Whitman, 432 pgs., Erwin Hess-a 16.00 40.00 110.00

700-10- Gene Autry and the Bandits of Silver Tip, 1949, Whitman 11.00 27.50 70.00

714-10- Gene Autry and the Range War, 1950, Whitman 11.00 27.50 70.00

nn- Gene Autry in Gun-Smoke, 1938, Dell, 196 pgs., Fast-Action story, soft-c 27.00 68.00 190.00

2035-(#35)- Gentle Ben, Mystery of the Everglades, 1969, Whitman, 256 pgs., hard-c, color illos. 3.00 7.50 20.00

1176- Gentleman Joe Palooka, 1940, Saalfield, 400 pgs. 10.00 25.00 60.00

George O'Brien (See The Cowboy Millionaire)

1101- George O'Brien and the Arizona Badman, 1936?, Whitman 10.00 25.00 60.00

1418- George O'Brien in Gun Law, 1938, Whitman, 240 pgs., photo-c, movie scenes, RKO Radio Pictures 10.00 25.00 60.00

1457- George O'Brien and the Hooded Riders, 1940, Whitman, 432 pgs., Erwin Hess-a 8.00 20.00 50.00

nn- George O'Brien and the Arizona Bad Man, 1939, Whitman, 36 pgs., 2 1/2" x 3 1/2", Penny Book 8.00 20.00 50.00

1462- Ghost Avenger, 1943, Whitman, 432 pgs., flip pictures, Henry Vallely-a 10.00 25.00 60.00

nn- Ghost Gun Gang Meet Their Match, The, 1939. Whitman, 2 1/2" x 3 1/2", Penny Book 8.00 20.00 50.00

nn- Gingerbread Boy, The, nd(1930s), np(Whitman), 36 pgs., Penny Book 2.00 5.00 15.00

1118- G-Man on the Crime Trail, 1936, Whitman, 432 pgs. 11.00 27.50 70.00

1147- G-Man Vs. the Red X, 1936, Whitman, 432 pgs. 12.00 30.00 80.00

1162- G-Man Allen, 1939, Saalfield, 400 pgs. 11.00 27.50 70.00

1173- G-Man in Action, A, 1940, Saalfield, 400 pgs., J.R. White-a 11.00 27.50 70.00

1434- G-Man and the Radio Bank Robberies, 1937, Whitman, 432 pgs. 12.00 30.00 80.00

1469- G-Man and the Gun Runners, The, 1940, Whitman, 432 pgs. 12.00 30.00 80.00

1470- G-Man vs. the Fifth Column, 1941, Whitman, 432 pgs., flip pictures 12.00 30.00 80.00

1493- G-Man Breaking the Gambling Ring, 1938, Whitman, 432 pgs., James Gary-a 12.00 30.00 80.00

nn- G-Man on Lightning Island, 1936, Dell, 244 pgs., Fast-Action Story, soft-c, Henry E. Vallely-a 24.00 60.00 170.00

nn- G-Man, Underworld Chief, 1938, Whitman, Buddy Book premium, 29.00 73.00 200.00

6833- G-Man on Lightning Island, 1936, Dell, 244 pgs., Cartoon Story Book, hard-c, Henry E. Vallely-a 18.00 45.00 125.00

4- G-Men Foil the Kidnappers, 1936, Whitman, 132 pgs., 3 1/2" x 3 1/2", soft-c, Tarzan Ice Cream cup lid premium 24.00 60.00 165.00

1157- G-Men on the Trail, 1938, Saalfield, 400 pgs. 10.00 25.00 60.00

1168- G Men on the Job, 1935, Whitman, 432 pgs. 12.00 30.00 75.00

nn- G-Men on the Job Again, 1938, Whitman, 36 pgs., 2 1/2" x 3 1/2", Penny Book 10.00 25.00 60.00

1159 - Hall of Fame of the Air © WHIT

1403 - Invisible Scarlet O'Neil © WHIT

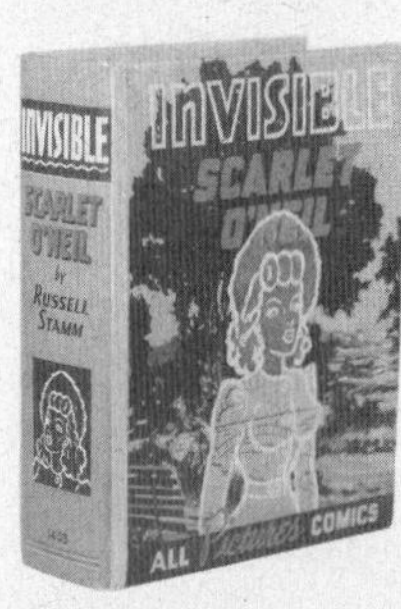

L11 - Jack London's Call of the Wild © Lynn

GD FN VF/NM

nn- G-Men and Kidnap Justice, 1938, Whitman, 68 pgs., Pan-Am premium, soft-c 12.00 30.00 75.00

nn- G-Men and the Missing Clues, 1938, Whitman, 36 pgs., 2 1/2"x 3 1/2", Penny Book 10.00 25.00 60.00

1097- Go Into Your Dance, 1935, Saalfield, 160 pgs.. photo-c, movie scenes with Al Jolson & Ruby Keeler 13.00 32.50 90.00

1577- Go Into Your Dance, 1935, Saalfield, 160 pgs., photo-c, movie scenes, soft-c 13.00 32.50 90.00

2021- Goofy in Giant Trouble (Walt Disney's ...), 1968, Whitman, hard-c, 260 pgs., 39 cents, color illos. 3.00 7.50 20.00

5751- Goofy in Giant Trouble (Walt Disney's ...), 1968, Whitman, soft-c, 260 pgs., 39 cents, color illos. 3.00 7.50 20.00

5751-2- Goofy in Giant Trouble, 1968 (1980-reprint of '67 version), Whitman, soft-c, 260 pgs., 79 cents, B&W 1.00 2.50 8.00

8- Great Expectations, 1934, EVW, (Five Star Library), 160 pgs., photo-c, movie scenes 14.00 35.00 100.00

1453- Green Hornet Strikes!, The, 1940, Whitman, 432 pgs., Robert Weisman-a 34.00 85.00 240.00

1480- Green Hornet Cracks Down, The, 1942, Whitman, 432 pgs., flip pictures, Henry Vallely-a 31.00 78.00 220.00

1496- Green Hornet Returns, The, 1941, Whitman, 432 pgs., flip pictures 34.00 85.00 240.00

5778- Grimm's Ghost Stories, 1976, Whitman, 256 pgs., Laura French-s adapted from fairy tales; blue spine & back-c 2.00 5.00 13.00

5778-1- Grimm's Ghost Stories, 1976, Whitman, 256 pgs., reprint of #5778; yellow spine & back-c 2.00 5.00 13.00

1172- Gullivers' Travels, 1939, Saalfield, 320 pgs., adapted from Paramount Pict. Cartoons (Rare) Hardcover 26.00 65.00 180.00
(Scarce) Softcover 29.00 73.00 205.00

nn- Gumps In Radio Land, The (Andy Gump and the Chest of Gold), 1937, Lehn & Fink Prod. Corp., 100 pgs., 3 1/4" x 5 1/2", Pebeco Tooth Paste giveaway, by Gus Edson 20.00 50.00 140.00

nn- Gunmen of Rustlers' Gulch, The, 1939, Whitman, 36 pgs., 2 1/2" x 3 1/2", Penny Book 7.00 17.50 40.00

1426- Guns in the Roaring West, 1937, Whitman, 300 pgs. 7.00 17.50 40.00

1647- Gunsmoke (TV Series), 1958, Whitman, 280 pgs., 4 1/2" x 5 3/4" 5.00 12.50 30.00

1101- Hairbreath Harry in Department QT, 1935, Whitman, 384 pgs., by J. M. Alexander 10.00 25.00 65.00

1413- Hal Hardy in the Lost Land of Giants, 1938, Whitman, 300 pgs., "The World 1,000,000 Years Ago" 10.00 25.00 65.00

1159- Hall of Fame of the Air, 1936, Whitman, 432 pgs., by Capt. Eddie Rickenbacker 8.00 20.00 50.00

nn- Hansel and Grethel, The Story of, nd (1930s), no publ., 36 pgs., Penny Book 2.00 5.00 15.00

1145- Hap Lee's Selection of Movie Gags, 1935, Whitman, 160 pgs., photos of stars 13.00 32.50 90.00

Happy Prince, The (See Wee Little Books)

1111- Hard Rock Harrigan-A Story of Boulder Dam, 1935, Saalfield, hard-c, photo-c, photo illos. 10.00 25.00 60.00

1591- Hard Rock Harrigan-A Story of Boulder Dam, 1935, Saalfield, soft-c, photo-c, photo illos. 10.00 25.00 60.00

1418- Harold Teen Swinging at the Sugar Bowl, 1939, Whitman, 432 pgs., by Carl Ed 10.00 25.00 60.00

nn- Hercules - The Legendary Journeys, 1998, Chronicle Books, 310 pgs., based on TV series, 1-color (brown) illos 1.00 2.50 9.00

1100B- Hobbies, 1938, Whitman, 36 pgs., 2 1/2" x 3 1/2", Penny Book 2.00 5.00 15.00

1125- Hockey Spare, The, 1937, Saalfield, sports book 7.00 17.50 40.00

1605- Hockey Spare, The, 1937, Saalfield, soft-c 7.00 17.50 40.00

728- Homeless Homer, 1934, Whitman, by Dee Dobbin, for young kids 4.00 10.00 25.00

17- Hoosier Schoolmaster, The, 1935, EVW, movie scenes 13.00 32.50 90.00

715- Houdini's Big Little Book of Magic, 1927 (1933), 300 pgs. 14.00 35.00 95.00

nn- Houdini's Big Little Book of Magic, 1927 (1933), 196 pgs., American Oil Co. premium, soft-c 14.00 35.00 95.00

GD FN VF/NM

nn- Houdini's Big Little Book of Magic, 1927 (1933), 204 pgs., Cocomalt premium, soft-c 14.00 35.00 95.00

Huckleberry Finn (See The Adventures of...)

nn- Huckleberry Hound Newspaper Reporter, 1977, Modern Promotions, 244 pgs., 49 cents, soft-c, flip pictures 2.00 5.00 13.00

1644- Hugh O'Brian TV's Wyatt Earp (TV Series), 1958, Whitman, 280 pgs. 5.00 12.50 30.00

5782-2- Incredible Hulk Lost in Time, 1980, 260 pgs., 79¢-c, soft-c, B&W 2.00 5.00 10.00

1424- Inspector Charlie Chan Villainy on the High Seas, 1942, Whitman, 432 pgs., flip pictures 14.00 35.00 95.00

1186- Inspector Wade of Scotland Yard, 1940, Saalfield, 400 pgs. 10.00 25.00 60.00

1194- Inspector Wade and The Feathered Serpent, 1939, Saalfield, 400 pgs. 10.00 25.00 60.00

1448- Inspector Wade Solves the Mystery of the Red Aces, 1937, Whitman, 432 pgs. 10.00 25.00 60.00

1148- International Spy Doctor Doom Faces Death at Dawn, 1937, Whitman, 432 pgs., Arbo-a 12.00 30.00 75.00

1155- In the Name of the Law, 1937, Whitman, 432 pgs., Henry E. Vallely-a 10.00 25.00 60.00

2012-(#12)-Invaders, The-Alien Missile Threat (TV Series), 1967, Whitman, 260 pgs., hard-c, 39 cents, color illos. 4.00 10.00 27.00

1403- Invisible Scarlet O'Neil, 1942, Whitman, All Pictures Comics, flip pictures 12.00 30.00 75.00

1406- Invisible Scarlet O'Neil Versus the King of the Slums, 1946, Whitman, 352 pgs. 10.00 25.00 60.00

1098- It Happened One Night, 1935, Saalfield, 160 pgs., Little Big Book, Clark Gable, Claudette Colbert photo-c, movie scenes from Academy Award winner 14.00 35.00 100.00

1578- It Happened One Night, 1935, Saalfield, 160 pgs., soft-c 14.00 35.00 100.00

Jack and Jill (See Wee Little Books)

1432- Jack Armstrong and the Mystery of the Iron Key, 1939, Whitman, 432 pgs., Henry E. Vallely-a 12.00 30.00 85.00

1435- Jack Armstrong and the Ivory Treasure, 1937, Whitman, 432 pgs., Henry Vallely-a 12.00 30.00 85.00

Jackie Cooper (See Story Of..)

1084- Jackie Cooper in Peck's Bad Boy, 1934, Saalfield, 160 pgs., hard, photo-c, movie scenes 15.00 37.50 105.00

1314- Jackie Cooper in Peck's Bad Boy, 1934, Saalfield, 160 pgs., soft, photo-c, movie scenes 15.00 37.50 105.00

1402- Jackie Cooper in "Gangster's Boy," 1939, Whitman, 240 pgs., photo-c, movie scenes 15.00 37.50 105.00

13- Jackie Cooper in Dinky, 1935, EVW, 160 pgs., movie scenes 15.00 37.50 105.00

nn- Jack King of the Secret Service and the Counterfeiters, 1939, Whitman, 36 pgs., 2 1/2" x 3 1/2", Penny Book, by John G. Gray 10.00 25.00 60.00

L11- Jack London's Call of the Wild, 1935, Lynn, 20th Cent. Pic., movie scenes with Clark Gable 12.00 30.00 80.00

nn- Jack Pearl as Detective Baron Munchausen, 1934, Goldsmith, 132 pgs., soft-c 12.00 30.00 85.00

1102- Jack Swift and His Rocket Ship, 1934, Whitman, 320 pgs. 16.00 40.00 110.00

1498- Jane Arden the Vanished Princess, Whitman, 300 pgs. 10.00 25.00 60.00

1179- Jane Withers in This is the Life (20th Century-Fox Presents...), 1935, Whitman, 240 pgs., photo-c, movie scenes 12.00 30.00 80.00

1463- Jane Withers in Keep Smiling, 1938, Whitman, 240 pgs., photo-c, movie scenes 12.00 30.00 80.00

Jaragu of the Jungle (See Rex Beach's ...)

1447- Jerry Parker Police Reporter and the Candid Camera Clue, 1941, Whitman, 300 pgs. 10.00 25.00 60.00

Jim Bowie (See Adventures of ...)

nn- Jim Brant of the Highway Patrol and the Mysterious Accident, 1939, Whitman, 36 pgs., 2 1/2" x 3 1/2", Penny Book 9.00 22.50 55.00

1466- Jim Craig State Trooper and the Kidnapped Governor, 1938, Whitman, 432 pgs. 10.00 25.00 60.00

1428 - Jim Starr of the Border Patrol © WHIT

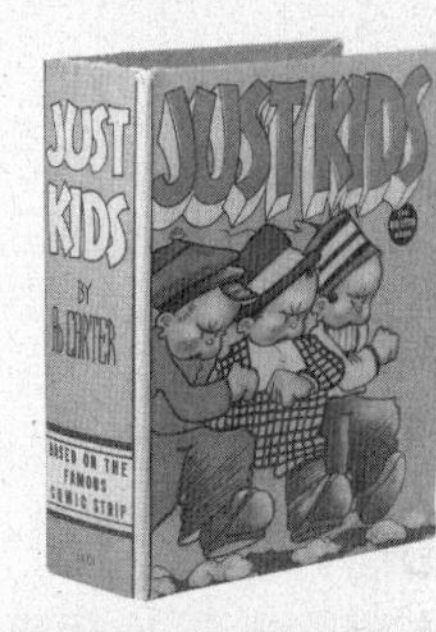

1401 - Just Kids © WHIT

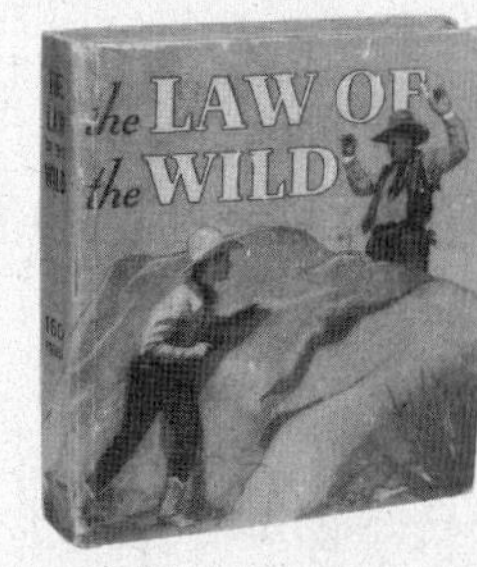

1322 - The Law of the Wild © Saalfield

	GD	FN	VF/NM
nn- Jim Doyle Private Detective and the Train Hold-Up, 1939, Whitman, 36 pgs., 2 1/2" x 3 1/2", Penny Book	10.00	25.00	65.00
1180- Jim Hardy Ace Reporter, 1940, Saalfield, 400 pgs., Dick Moores-a	10.00	25.00	65.00
1143- Jimmy Allen in the Air Mail Robbery, 1936, Whitman, 432 pgs.	10.00	25.00	65.00
27- Jimmy Allen in The Sky Parade, 1936, Lynn, 130 pgs., 5 x 7 1/2", Paramount Pictures, movie scenes	12.00	30.00	75.00
L15- Jimmy and the Tiger, 1935, Lynn, 192 pgs.	10.00	25.00	65.00
1428- Jim Starr of the Border Patrol, 1937, Whitman, 432 pgs.	10.00	25.00	65.00
Joan of Arc (See Wee Little Books)			
1105- Joe Louis the Brown Bomber, 1936, Whitman, 240 pgs., photo-c, photo-illos.	20.00	50.00	140.00
Joe Palooka (See Gentleman ...)			
1123- Joe Palooka the Heavyweight Boxing Champ, 1934, Whitman, 320 pgs., Ham Fisher-a	18.00	45.00	125.00
1168- Joe Palooka's Great Adventure, 1939, Saalfield	14.00	35.00	100.00
nn- Joe Penner's Duck Farm, 1935, Goldsmith, Henry Vallely-a	11.00	27.50	70.00
1402- John Carter of Mars, 1940, Whitman, 432 pgs., John Coleman Burroughs-a	50.00	125.00	350.00
nn- John Carter of Mars, 1940, Dell, 194 pgs., Fast-Action Story, soft-c	64.00	160.00	450.00
1164- Johnny Forty Five, 1938, Saalfield, 400 pgs.	10.00	25.00	60.00
John Wayne (See Westward Ho!)			
1100B- Jokes (A book of laughs galore), 1938, Whitman, 36 pgs., 2 1/2" x 3 1/2", Penny Book, laughing guy-c	2.00	5.00	15.00
1100B- Jokes (A book of side-splitting funny stories), 1938, Whitman, 36 pgs., 2 1/2" x 3 1/2", Penny Book, clowns on-c	2.00	5.00	15.00
2026-(#26)- Journey to the Center of the Earth, The Fiery Foe, 1968, Whitman	4.00	10.00	27.00
Jungle Jim (See Top-Line Comics)			
1138- Jungle Jim, 1936, Whitman, 432 pgs., Alex Raymond-a	20.00	50.00	140.00
1139- Jungle Jim and the Vampire Woman, 1937, Whitman, 432 pgs., Alex Raymond-a	20.00	50.00	140.00
1442- Junior G-Men, 1937, Whitman, 432 pgs., Henry E. Vallely-a	11.00	27.50	70.00
nn- Junior G-Men Solve a Crime, 1939, Whitman, 36 pgs., 2 1/2" x 3 1/2", Penny Book	11.00	27.50	70.00
1422- Junior Nebb on the Diamond Bar Ranch, 1938, Whitman, 300 pgs., by Sol Hess	11.00	27.50	70.00
1470- Junior Nebb Joins the Circus, 1939, Whitman, 300 pgs. by Sol Hess	11.00	27.50	70.00
nn- Junior Nebb Elephant Trainer, 1939, Whitman, 68 pgs., Pan-Am Oil premium, soft-c	13.00	32.50	90.00
1052- "Just Kids" (Adventures of ...), 1934, Saalfield, oblong size, by Ad Carter	18.00	45.00	125.00
1094- Just Kids and the Mysterious Stranger, 1935, Saalfield, 160 pgs., by Ad Carter	13.00	32.50	90.00
1184- Just Kids and Deep-Sea Dan, 1940, Saalfield, 400 pgs., by Ad Carter	12.00	30.00	75.00
1302- Just Kids, The Adventures of, 1934, Saalfield, oblong size, soft-c, by Ad Carter	20.00	50.00	140.00
1324- Just Kids and the Mysterious Stranger, 1935, Saalfield, 160 pgs., soft-c, by Ad Carter ,	13.00	32.50	90.00
1401- Just Kids, 1937, Whitman, 432 pgs., by Ad Carter	13.00	32.50	90.00
1055- Katzenjammer Kids in the Mountains, 1934, Saalfield, hard-c, oblong, H. H. Knerr-a	16.00	40.00	115.00
1305- Katzenjammer Kids in the Mountains, 1934, Saalfield, soft-c, oblong, H. H. Knerr-a	16.00	40.00	115.00
14- Katzenjammer Kids, The, 1942, Dell, 194 pgs., Fast-Action Story, H. H. Knerr-a	18.00	45.00	125.00
1411- Kay Darcy and the Mystery Hideout, 1937, Whitman, 300 pgs., Charles Mueller-a	12.00	30.00	80.00
1180- Kayo in the Land of Sunshine (With Moon Mullins), 1937, Whitman, 432 pgs., by Willard	13.00	32.50	90.00
1415- Kayo and Moon Mullins and the One Man Gang, 1939, Whitman, 432 pgs., by Frank Willard	11.00	27.50	70.00
7- Kayo and Moon Mullins 'Way Down South, 1938, Whitman, 132 pgs., 3 1/2" x 3 1/2", Buddy Book	21.00	52.50	150.00
1105- Kazan in Revenge of the North (James Oliver Curwood's...), 1937, Whitman, 432 pgs., Henry E. Vallely-a	11.00	25.00	60.00
1471- Kazan, King of the Pack (James Oliver Curwood's...), 1940, Whitman, 432 pgs.	9.00	22.50	55.00
1420- Keep 'Em Flying! U.S.A. for America's Defense, 1943, Whitman, 432 pgs., Henry E. Vallely-a, flip pictures	10.00	25.00	60.00
1133- Kelly King at Yale Hall, 1937, Saalfield	9.00	22.50	55.00
Ken Maynard (See Strawberry Roan & Western Frontier)			
5- Ken Maynard in "Wheels of Destiny," 1934, EVW, 160 pgs., movie scenes (scarce)	20.00	50.00	140.00
776- Ken Maynard in "Gun Justice," 1934, Whitman, 160 pgs., hard-c, movie scenes (Universal Pic.)	14.00	35.00	95.00
776- Ken Maynard in "Gun Justice," 1934, Whitman, 160 pgs., soft-c, movie scenes (Universal Pic.)	14.00	35.00	95.00
1430- Ken Maynard in Western Justice, 1938, Whitman, 432 pgs., Irwin Myers-a	11.00	27.50	70.00
1442- Ken Maynard and the Gun Wolves of the Gila, 1939, Whitman, 432 pgs.	11.00	27.50	70.00
nn- Ken Maynard in Six-Gun Law, 1938, Whitman, 36 pgs., 2 1/2" x 3 1/2", Penny Book	9.00	22.50	55.00
1134- King of Crime, 1938, Saalfield, 400 pgs.	10.00	25.00	60.00
King of the Royal Mounted (See Zane Grey)			
nn- Kit Carson, 1933, World Syndicate, by J. Carroll Mansfield, High Lights Of History Series, hard-c	10.00	25.00	60.00
nn- Kit Carson, 1933, World Syndicate, same as hard-c above but with a black cloth-c	10.00	25.00	60.00
1105- Kit Carson and the Mystery Riders, 1935, Saalfield, hard-c, Johnny Mack Brown photo-c, movie scenes	13.00	32.50	90.00
1585- Kit Carson and the Mystery Riders, 1935, Saalfield, soft-c, Johnny Mack Brown photo-c, movie scenes	13.00	32.50	90.00
Krazy Kat (See Adventures of...)			
2004- (#4)-Lassie-Adventure in Alaska (TV Series), 1967, Whitman, hard-c, 260 pgs., 39 cents, color illos	4.00	10.00	27.00
5754- Lassie-Adventure in Alaska (TV Series), 1973, Whitman, soft-c, 260 pgs., 49 cents, color illos	2.00	5.00	15.00
2027- Lassie and the Shabby Sheik (TV Series), 1968, Whitman, hard-c, 260 pgs., 39 cents	4.00	10.00	25.00
5762- Lassie and the Shabby Sheik (TV Series), 1972, Whitman, soft-c, 260 pgs., 39 cents	2.00	5.00	15.00
5769- Lassie, Old One-Eye (TV Series), 1975, Whitman, soft-c, 260 pgs., 49 cents, three printings	2.00	5.00	15.00
1132- Last Days of Pompeii, The, 1935, Whitman, 5 1/4" x 6 1/4", 260 pgs., photo-c, movie scenes	12.00	30.00	85.00
1128- Last Man Out (Baseball), 1937, Saalfield, hard-c	10.00	25.00	60.00
L30- Last of the Mohicans, The, 1936, Lynn, 192 pgs., movie scenes with Randolph Scott, United Artists Pictures	12.00	30.00	80.00
1126- Laughing Dragon of Oz, The, 1934, Whitman 432 pgs., by Frank Baum (scarce)	93.00	233.00	650.00
1086- Laurel and Hardy, 1934, Saalfield, 160 pgs., hard-c, photo-c, movie scenes	21.00	52.50	145.00
1316- Laurel and Hardy, 1934, Saalfield, 160 pgs. soft-c, photo-c, movie scenes	21.00	52.50	145.00
1092- Law of the Wild, The, 1935, Saalfield, 160 pgs., photo-c, movie scenes of Rex, The Wild Horse & Rin-Tin-Tin Jr.	11.00	27.50	70.00
1322- Law of the Wild, The, 1935, Saalfield, 160 pgs., photo-c, movie scenes, soft-c	11.00	27.50	70.00
1100B- Learn to be a Ventriloquist, 1938, Whitman, 36 pgs. 2 1/2" x 3 1/2", Penny Book	2.00	5.00	15.00
1149- Lee Brady Range Detective, 1938, Saalfield, 400 pgs.	9.00	22.50	55.00
L10- Les Miserables (Victor Hugo's ...), 1935, Lynn, 192 pgs., movie scenes	12.00	30.00	80.00
1441- Lightning Jim U.S. Marshal Brings Law to the West, 1940, Whitman, 432 pgs., based on radio program	10.00	25.00	65.00
nn- Lightning Jim Whipple U.S. Marshal in Indian Territory, 1939,			

1148 - The Little Green Door © Saalfield

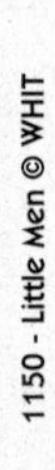

1150 - Little Men © WHIT

1416 - Little Orphan Annie in the Movies © WHIT

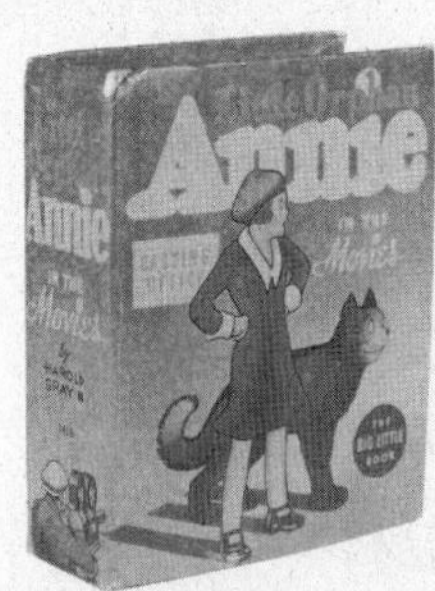

	GD	FN	VF/NM
Whitman, 36 pgs., 2 1/2" x 3 1/2", Penny Book	8.00	20.00	50.00
653- **Lions and Tigers** (With Clyde Beatty), 1934, Whitman, 160 pgs., photo-c movie scenes	12.00	30.00	85.00
1187- **Li'l Abner and the Ratfields**, 1940, Saalfield, 400 pgs., by Al Capp	14.00	35.00	95.00
1193- **Li'l Abner and Sadie Hawkins Day**, 1940, Saalfield, 400 pgs., by Al Capp	14.00	35.00	95.00
1198- **Li'l Abner in New York**, 1936, Whitman, 432 pgs., by Al Capp	15.00	37.50	105.00
1401- **Li'l Abner Among the Millionaires**, 1939, Whitman, 432 pgs., by Al Capp	15.00	37.50	105.00
1054- **Little Annie Rooney**, 1934, Saalfield, oblong - 4" x 8", All Pictures Comics, hard-c	14.00	35.00	100.00
1304- **Little Annie Rooney**, 1934, Saalfield, oblong - 4" x 8", All Pictures, soft-c	14.00	35.00	100.00
1117- **Little Annie Rooney and the Orphan House**, 1936, Whitman, 432 pgs.	11.00	27.50	70.00
1406- **Little Annie Rooney on the Highway to Adventure**, 1938, Whitman, 432 pgs.	11.00	27.50	70.00
1149- **Little Big Shot** (With Sybil Jason), 1935, Whitman, 240 pgs., photo-c, movie scenes	12.00	30.00	85.00
nn- **Little Black Sambo**, nd (1930s), np (Whitman), 36 pgs., 3" x 2 1/2", Penny Book	12.00	30.00	75.00
Little Bo-Peep (See Wee Little Books)			
Little Colonel, The (See Shirley Temple)			
1148- **Little Green Door, The**, 1938, Saalfield, 400 pgs.	10.00	25.00	60.00
1112- **Little Hollywood Stars**, 1935, Saalfield, movie scenes (Little Rascals, etc.), hard-c	12.00	30.00	85.00
1592- **Little Hollywood Stars**, 1935, Saalfield, movie scenes, soft-c	12.00	30.00	85.00
1087- **Little Jimmy's Gold Hunt**, 1935, Saalfield, 160 pgs., hard-c, Little Big Book, by Swinnerton	16.00	40.00	110.00
1317- **Little Jimmy's Gold Hunt**, 1935, Saalfield, 160 pgs., 4 1/4" x 5 3/4", soft-c, by Swinnerton	16.00	40.00	110.00
Little Joe and the City Gangsters (See Top-Line Comics)			
Little Joe Otter's Slide (See Wee Little Books)			
1118- **Little Lord Fauntleroy**, 1936, Saalfield, movie scenes, photo-c, 4 1/2" x 5 1/4", starring Mickey Rooney & Freddie Bartholomew, hard-c	10.00	25.00	60.00
1598- **Little Lord Fauntleroy**, 1936, Saalfield, photo-c, movie scenes, soft-c	10.00	25.00	60.00
1192- **Little Mary Mixup and the Grocery Robberies**, 1940, Saalfield	10.00	25.00	60.00
8- **Little Mary Mixup Wins A Prize**, 1936, Whitman, 132 pgs., 3 1/2" x 3 1/2", soft-c, Tarzan Ice Cream cup lid premium	24.00	60.00	165.00
1150- **Little Men**, 1934, Whitman, 4 3/4" x 5 1/4", movie scenes (Mascot Prod.), photo-c, hard-c	10.00	25.00	65.00
9- **Little Minister, The**,-Katharine Hepburn, 1935, 160 pgs., 4 1/4" x 5 1/2", EVW (Five Star Library), movie scenes (RKO)	14.00	35.00	100.00
1120- **Little Miss Muffet**, 1936, Whitman, 432 pgs., by Fanny Y. Cory	11.00	27.50	70.00
708- **Little Orphan Annie**, 1933, Whitman, 320 pgs., by Harold Gray, the 2nd Big Little Book	43.00	108.00	300.00
nn- **Little Orphan Annie**, 1928('33), Whitman, 52 pgs., 4" x 5 1/2", premium-no ads, soft-c, by Harold Gray	29.00	73.00	200.00
716- **Little Orphan Annie and Sandy**, 1933, Whitman, 320 pgs., by Harold Gray	24.00	60.00	170.00
716- **Little Orphan Annie and Sandy**, 1933, Whitman, 300 pgs., by Harold Gray	20.00	50.00	140.00
nn- **Little Orphan Annie and Sandy**, 1933, Whitman, 52 pgs., premium, no ads, 4" x 5 1/2", soft-c by Harold Gray	29.00	73.00	200.00
748- **Little Orphan Annie and Chizzler**, 1933, Whitman, 320 pgs., by Harold Gray	14.00	35.00	100.00
1010- **Little Orphan Annie and the Big Town Gunmen**, 1937, 7 1/4" x 5 1/2", 64 pgs., Nickel Book	12.00	30.00	85.00
nn- **Little Orphan Annie with the Circus**, 1934, Whitman, 320 pgs., same cover as L.O.A. 708 but with blue background, Ovaltine giveaway stamp inside front-c, by Harold Gray	36.00	90.00	250.00

	GD	FN	VF/NM
1103- **Little Orphan Annie with the Circus**, 1934, Whitman, 320 pgs.	14.00	35.00	100.00
1140- **Little Orphan Annie and the Big Train Robbery**, 1934, Whitman, 300 pgs., by Gray	14.00	35.00	100.00
1140- **Little Orphan Annie and the Big Train Robbery**, 1934, Whitman, 300 pgs., premium-no ads, soft-c, by Harold Gray	26.00	65.00	180.00
1154- **Little Orphan Annie and the Ghost Gang**, 1935, Whitman, 432 pgs. by Harold Gray	14.00	35.00	100.00
nn- **Little Orphan Annie and the Ghost Gang**, 1935, Whitman, 436 pgs., premium-no ads, 3-color, soft-c, by Harold Gray	26.00	65.00	180.00
1162- **Little Orphan Annie and Punjab the Wizard**, 1935, Whitman, 432 pgs., by Harold Gray	14.00	35.00	100.00
1186- **Little Orphan Annie and the $1,000,000 Formula**, 1936, Whitman, 432 pgs., by Gray	13.00	32.50	90.00
1414- **Little Orphan Annie and the Ancient Treasure of Am**, 1939, Whitman, 432 pgs., by Gray	12.00	30.00	80.00
1416- **Little Orphan Annie in the Movies**, 1937, Whitman, 432 pgs., by Harold Gray	12.00	30.00	80.00
1417- **Little Orphan Annie and the Secret of the Well**, 1947, Whitman, 352 pgs., by Gray	11.00	27.50	70.00
1435- **Little Orphan Annie and the Gooneyville Mystery**, 1947, Whitman, 288 pgs., by Gray	12.00	30.00	75.00
1446- **Little Orphan Annie in the Thieves' Den**, 1949, Whitman, 288 pgs., by Harold Gray	12.00	30.00	75.00
1449- **Little Orphan Annie and the Mysterious Shoemaker**, 1938, Whitman, 432 pgs., by Harold Gray	12.00	30.00	85.00
1457- **Little Orphan Annie and Her Junior Commandos**, 1943, Whitman, 352 pgs., by H. Gray	10.00	25.00	60.00
1461- **Little Orphan Annie and the Underground Hide-Out**, 1945, Whitman, 352 pgs., by Gray	10.00	25.00	60.00
1468- **Little Orphan Annie and the Ancient Treasure of Am**, 1949 (Misdated 1939), 288 pgs., by Gray	10.00	25.00	60.00
1482- **Little Orphan Annie and the Haunted Mansion**, 1941, Whitman, 432 pgs., flip pictures, by Harold Gray	12.00	30.00	80.00
3048- **Little Orphan Annie and Her Big Little Kit**, 1937, Whitman, 384 pgs., 4 1/2" x 6 1/2" box, includes miniature box of 4 crayons-red, yellow, blue and green	64.00	160.00	450.00
4054- **Little Orphan Annie, The Story of**, 1934, Whitman, 7" x 9 1/2", 320 pgs., Big Big Book, Harold Gray-c/a	30.00	75.00	210.00
nn- **Little Orphan Annie Gets into Trouble**, 1938, Whitman, 36 pgs., 2 1/2" x 3 1/2", Penny Book	9.00	22.50	55.00
nn- **Little Orphan Annie in Hollywood**, 1937, Whitman, 3 1/2" x 3 1/4", Pan-Am premium, soft-c	23.00	57.50	160.00
nn- **Little Orphan Annie in Rags to Riches**, 1939, Dell, 194 pgs., Fast-Action Story, soft-c	26.00	65.00	180.00
nn- **Little Orphan Annie Saves Sandy**, 1938, Whitman, 36 pgs., 2 1/2" x 3 1/2", Penny Book	10.00	25.00	60.00
nn- **Little Orphan Annie Under the Big Top**, 1938, Dell, 194 pgs., Fast-Action Story, soft-c	25.00	62.50	175.00
nn- **Little Orphan Annie Wee Little Books** (In open box) nn, 1934, Whitman, 44 pgs., by H. Gray			
L.O.A. And Daddy Warbucks	9.00	22.50	55.00
L.O.A. And Her Dog Sandy	9.00	22.50	55.00
L.O.A. And The Lucky Knife	9.00	22.50	55.00
L.O.A. And The Pinch-Pennys	9.00	22.50	55.00
L.O.A. At Happy Home	9.00	22.50	55.00
L.O.A. Finds Mickey	9.00	22.50	55.00
Complete set with box	57.00	143.00	400.00
nn- **Little Polly Flinders, The Story of**, nd (1930s), no publ., 36 pgs., 2 1/2" x 3", Penny Book	2.00	5.00	15.00
nn- **Little Red Hen, The**, nd(1930s), np(Whitman), 36 pgs., Penny Book	2.00	5.00	15.00
nn- **Little Red Riding Hood**, nd(1930s), np(Whitman), 36 pgs., 3" x 2 1/2", Penny Book	2.00	5.00	15.00
nn- **Little Red Riding Hood and the Big Bad Wolf** (Disney), 1934, McKay, 36 pgs., stiff-c, Disney Studio-a Sized (7 3/4" x 10")	24.00	60.00	170.00

1498 - Lone Ranger and the Silver Bullets © Lone Ranger Inc.

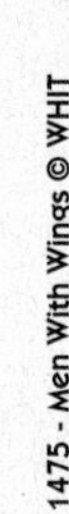

1475 - Men With Wings © WHIT

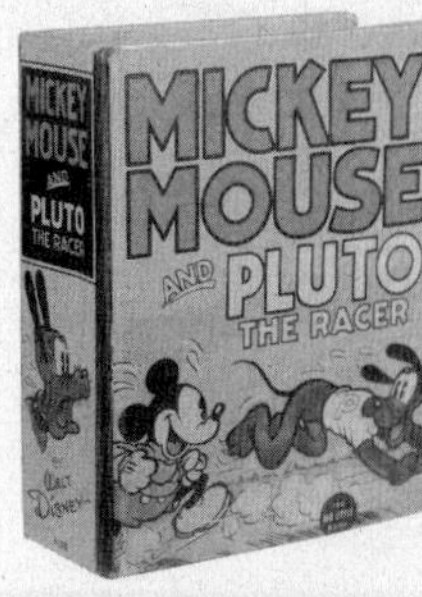

1128 - Mickey Mouse and Pluto the Racer © WDC

GD FN VF/NM

Different version (6 1/4" x 8 1/2") blue spine 16.00 40.00 115.00

757- **Little Women**, 1934, Whitman, 4 3/4" x 5 1/4", 160 pgs., photo-c, movie scenes, starring Katharine Hepburn 14.00 35.00 100.00

Littlest Rebel, The (See Shirley Temple)

1181- **Lone Ranger and his Horse Silver**, 1935, Whitman, 432 pgs., Hal Arbo-a 20.00 50.00 140.00

1196- **Lone Ranger and the Vanishing Herd**, 1936, Whitman, 432 pgs. 16.00 40.00 110.00

1407- **Lone Ranger and Dead Men's Mine, The**, 1939, Whitman, 432 pgs. 14.00 35.00 100.00

1421- **Lone Ranger on the Barbary Coast, The**, 1944, Whitman, 352 pgs., Henry Vallely-a 12.00 30.00 80.00

1428- **Lone Ranger and the Secret Weapon, The**, 1943, Whitman, 12.00 30.00 80.00

1431- **Lone Ranger and the Secret Killer, The**, 1937, Whitman 432 pgs., H. Anderson-a 16.00 40.00 110.00

1450- **Lone Ranger and the Black Shirt Highwayman, The**, 1939, Whitman, 432 pgs. 14.00 35.00 100.00

1465- **Lone Ranger and the Menace of Murder Valley, The**, 1938, Whitman, 432 pgs., Robert Wiseman-a 13.00 32.50 90.00

1468- **Lone Ranger Follows Through, The**, 1941, Whitman, 432 pgs., H.E. Vallely-a 13.00 32.50 90.00

1477- **Lone Ranger and the Great Western Span, The**, 1942, Whitman, 424 pgs., H. E. Vallely-a 12.00 30.00 80.00

1489- **Lone Ranger and the Red Renegades, The**, 1939, Whitman, 432 pgs. 16.00 40.00 110.00

1498- **Lone Ranger and the Silver Bullets**, 1946, Whitman, 352 pgs., Henry E. Vallely-a 12.00 30.00 80.00

712-10- **Lone Ranger and the Secret of Somber Cavern, The**, 1950, Whitman 10.00 25.00 65.00

2013- **(#13)-Lone Ranger Outwits Crazy Cougar, The**, 1968, Whitman, 260 pgs., 39 cents, hard-c, color illos 4.00 10.00 27.00

5774- **Lone Ranger Outwits Crazy Cougar, The**, 1976, Whitman, 260 pgs., 49 cents, soft-c, color illos 4.00 10.00 22.00

5774-1- **Lone Ranger Outwits Crazy Cougar, The**, 1979, Whitman, 260 pgs., 69 cents, soft-c, color illos 4.00 10.00 22.00

nn- **Lone Ranger and the Lost Valley, The**, 1938, Dell, 196 pgs., Fast-Action Story, soft-c 26.00 65.00 180.00

1405- **Lone Star Martin of the Texas Rangers**, 1939, Whitman, 432 pgs. 12.00 30.00 85.00

19- **Lost City, The**, 1935, EVW, movie scenes 12.00 30.00 80.00

1103- **Lost Jungle, The** (With Clyde Beatty), 1936, Saalfield, movie scenes, hard-c 12.00 30.00 80.00

1583- **Lost Jungle, The** (With Clyde Beatty), 1936, Saalfield, movie scenes, soft -c 11.00 27.50 70.00

753- **Lost Patrol, The**, 1934, Whitman, 160 pgs., photo-c, movie scenes with Boris Karloff 12.00 30.00 75.00

nn- **Lost World, The - Jurassic Park 2**, 1997, Chronicle Books, 312 pgs., adapts movie, 1-color (green) illos 3.00 7.50 20.00

1189- **Mac of the Marines in Africa**, 1936, Whitman, 432 pgs. 10.00 25.00 60.00

1400- **Mac of the Marines in China**, 1938, Whitman, 432 pgs. 10.00 25.00 60.00

1100B- **Magic Tricks** (With explanations), 1938, Whitman, 36 pgs., 2 1/2" x 3 1/2", Penny Book, rabbit in hat-c 2.00 5.00 15.00

1100B- **Magic Tricks** (How to do them), 1938, Whitman, 36 pgs., 2 1/2" x 3 1/2", Penny Book, genie-c 2.00 5.00 15.00

Major Hoople (See Our Boarding House)

2022-(#22)- **Major Matt Mason, Moon Mission**, 1968, Whitman, 256 pgs., hard-c, color illos. 4.00 10.00 27.00

1167- **Mandrake the Magician**, 1935, Whitman, 432 pgs., by Lee Falk & Phil Davis 16.00 40.00 110.00

1418- **Mandrake the Magician and the Flame Pearls**, 1946, Whitman, 352 pgs., by Lee Falk & Phil Davis 12.00 30.00 85.00

1431- **Mandrake the Magician and the Midnight Monster**, 1939, Whitman, 432 pgs., by Lee Falk & Phil Davis 14.00 35.00 95.00

1454- **Mandrake the Magician Mighty Solver of Mysteries**, 1941, Whitman, 432 pgs., by Lee Falk & Phil Davis, flip pictures 14.00 35.00 95.00

2011-(#11)-**Man From U.N.C.L.E., The**-The Calcutta Affair (TV Series), 1967, Whitman, 260 pgs., 39¢, hard-c, color illos 4.00 10.00 27.00

1429- **Marge's Little Lulu Alvin and Tubby**, 1947, Whitman, All Pictures Comics, Stanley-a 27.00 68.00 190.00

1438- **Mary Lee and the Mystery of the Indian Beads**, 1937, Whitman, 300 pgs. 10.00 25.00 60.00

1165- **Masked Man of the Mesa, The**, 1939, Saalfield, 400 pgs. 9.00 22.50 55.00

nn- **Mask of Zorro, The**, 1998, Chronicle Books, 312 pgs., adapts movie, 1-color (yellow-green) illos 1.00 2.50 9.00

1436- **Maximo the Amazing Superman**, 1940, Whitman, 432 pgs., Henry E. Vallely-a 12.00 30.00 80.00

1444- **Maximo the Amazing Superman and the Crystals of Doom**, 1941, Whitman,432 pgs., Henry E. Vallely-a 12.00 30.00 80.00

1445- **Maximo the Amazing Superman and the Supermachine**, 1941, Whitman, 432 pgs. 12.00 30.00 80.00

755- **Men of the Mounted**, 1934, Whitman, 320 pgs. 12.00 30.00 80.00

nn- **Men of the Mounted**, 1933, Whitman, 52 pgs., 3 1/2" x 5 3/4", premium-no ads; other versions with Poll Parrot & Perkins ad; soft-c 14.00 35.00 100.00

nn- **Men of the Mounted**, 1934, Whitman, Cocomalt premium, soft-c, by Ted McCall 10.00 25.00 60.00

1475- **Men With Wings**, 1938, Whitman, 240 pgs., photo-c, movie scenes (Paramount Pics.) 12.00 30.00 85.00

1170- **Mickey Finn**, 1940, Saalfield, 400 pgs., by Frank Leonard 10.00 25.00 865.00

717- **Mickey Mouse** (Disney), (1st printing) 1933, Whitman, 320 pgs., Gottfredson-a, skinny Mickey on cover 235.00 588.00 2000.00

717- **Mickey Mouse** (Disney), (2nd printing)1933, Whitman, 320 pgs., Gottfredson-a, regular Mickey on cover 150.00 375.00 1200.00

nn- **Mickey Mouse** (Disney), 1933, Dean & Son, Great Big Midget Book, 320 pgs. 123.00 308.00 900.00

731- **Mickey Mouse the Mail Pilot** (Disney), 1933, Whitman, (This is the same book as the 1st Mickey Mouse BLB #717(2nd printing) but with "The Mail Pilot" printed on the front. Lower left of back cover has a small box printed over the existing "No. 717." "No. 731" is printed next to it.) (Sold at auction in 2014 in VG+ condition for $7170, and in FR/GD condition for $2,500)

726- **Mickey Mouse in Blaggard Castle** (Disney), 1934, Whitman, 320 pgs., Gottfredson-a 30.00 75.00 210.00

731- **Mickey Mouse the Mail Pilot** (Disney), 1933, Whitman, 300 pgs., Gottfredson-a 30.00 75.00 210.00

731- **Mickey Mouse the Mail Pilot** (Disney), 1933, Whitman, 300 pgs., soft cover; Gottfredson-a (Rare) 64.00 160.00 450.00

nn- **Mickey Mouse the Mail Pilot** (Disney), 1933, Whitman, 292 pgs., American Oil Co. premium, soft-c, Gottfredson-a; another version 3 1/2" x 4 3/4" 30.00 75.00 210.00

nn- **Mickey Mouse the Mail Pilot** (Disney), 1933, Dean & Son, Great Big Midget Book (Rare) 124.00 310.00 925.00

750- **Mickey Mouse Sails for Treasure Island** (Disney), 1933, Whitman, 320 pgs., Gottfredson-a 30.00 75.00 210.00

nn- **Mickey Mouse Sails for Treasure Island** (Disney), 1935, Whitman, 196 pgs., premium-no ads, soft-c, Gottfredson-a (Scarce) 36.00 90.00 250.00

nn- **Mickey Mouse Sails for Treasure Island** (Disney), 1935, Whitman, 196 pgs., Kolynos Dental Cream premium (Scarce) 36.00 90.00 250.00

nn- **Mickey Mouse Sails for Treasure Island** (Disney), 1933, Dean & Son, Great Big Midget Book, 320 pgs. 114.00 285.00 800.00

756- **Mickey Mouse Presents a Walt Disney Silly Symphony** (Disney), 1934, Whitman, 240 pgs., Bucky Bug app. 29.00 73.00 200.00

801- **Mickey Mouse's Summer Vacation**, 1948, Whitman, hard-c, Story Hour series 12.00 30.00 85.00

1111- **Mickey Mouse Presents Walt Disney's Silly Symphonies Stories**, 1936, Whitman, 432 pgs., Donald Duck app. 29.00 73.00 200.00

1128- **Mickey Mouse and Pluto the Racer** (Disney), 1936, Whitman, 432 pgs., Gottfredson-a 24.00 60.00 170.00

1139- **Mickey Mouse the Detective** (Disney), 1934, Whitman, 300 pgs., Gottfredson-a 29.00 73.00 200.00

1139- **Mickey Mouse the Detective** (Disney), 1934, Whitman, 304 pgs.,

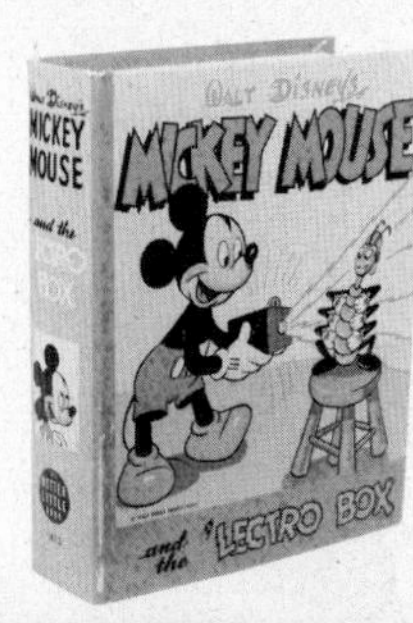

1413 - Mickey Mouse and the 'Lectro Box © DIS

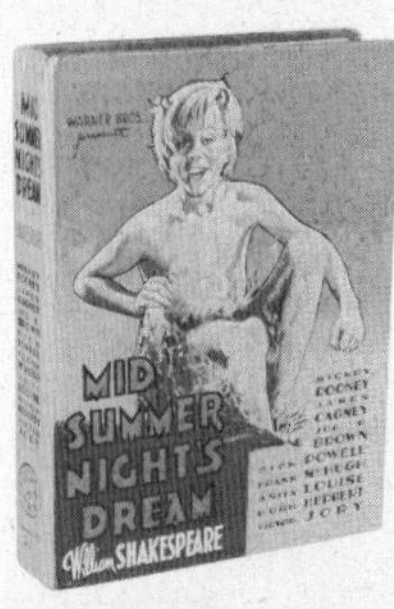

21 - Midsummer Night's Dream © EVW

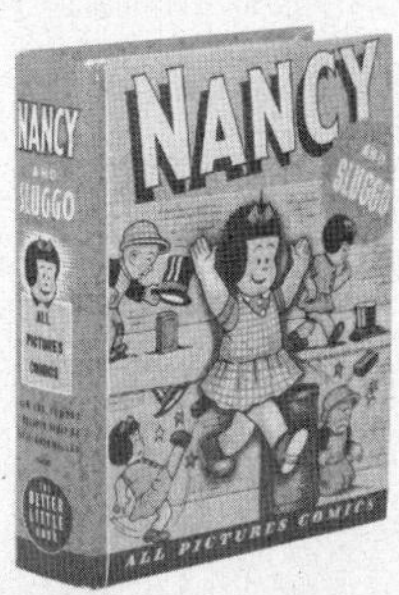

1400 - Nancy and Sluggo © WHIT

GD FN VF/NM

premium-no ads, soft-c, Gottfredson-a (Scarce) 43.00 108.00 300.00
1153- Mickey Mouse and the Bat Bandit (Disney), 1935, Whitman, 432 pgs., Gottfredson-a 26.00 65.00 180.00
nn- Mickey Mouse and the Bat Bandit (Disney), 1935, Whitman, 436 pgs., premium-no ads, 3-color, soft-c, Gottfredson-a (Scarce) 43.00 108.00 300.00
1160- Mickey Mouse and Bobo the Elephant (Disney), 1935, Whitman, 432 pgs., Gottfredson-a 26.00 65.00 180.00
1187- Mickey Mouse and the Sacred Jewel (Disney), 1936, Whitman, 432 pgs., Gottfredson-a 24.00 60.00 170.00
1401- Mickey Mouse in the Treasure Hunt (Disney), 1941, Whitman, 430 pgs., flip pictures of Pluto, Gottfredson-a 22.00 52.50 155.00
1409- Mickey Mouse Runs His Own Newspaper (Disney), 1937, Whitman, 432 pgs., Gottfredson-a 22.00 52.50 155.00
1413- Mickey Mouse and the 'Lectro Box (Disney), 1946, Whitman, 352 pgs., Gottfredson-a 16.00 40.00 115.00
1417- Mickey Mouse on Sky Island (Disney), 1941, Whitman, 432 pgs., flip pictures, Gottfredson-a; considered by Gottfredson to be his best Mickey story 22.00 52.50 155.00
1428- Mickey Mouse in the Foreign Legion (Disney), 1940, Whitman, 432 pgs., Gottfredson-a 22.00 52.50 155.00
1429- Mickey Mouse and the Magic Lamp (Disney), 1942, Whitman, 432 pgs., flip pictures 22.00 52.50 155.00
1433- Mickey Mouse and the Lazy Daisy Mystery (Disney), 1947, Whitman, 288 pgs. 16.00 40.00 115.00
1444- Mickey Mouse in the World of Tomorrow (Disney), 1948, Whitman, 288 pgs., Gottfredson-a 24.00 60.00 170.00
1451- Mickey Mouse and the Desert Palace (Disney), 1948, Whitman, 288 pgs. 16.00 40.00 115.00
1463- Mickey Mouse and the Pirate Submarine (Disney), 1939, Whitman, 432 pgs., Gottfredson-a 22.00 52.50 155.00
1464- Mickey Mouse and the Stolen Jewels (Disney), 1949, Whitman, 288 pgs. 21.00 52.50 145.00
1471- Mickey Mouse and the Dude Ranch Bandit (Disney), 1943, Whitman, 432 pgs., flip pictures 22.00 52.50 155.00
1475- Mickey Mouse and the 7 Ghosts (Disney), 1940, Whitman, 432 pgs., Gottfredson-a 22.00 52.50 155.00
1476- Mickey Mouse in the Race for Riches (Disney), 1938, Whitman, 432 pgs., Gottfredson-a 22.00 52.50 155.00
1483- Mickey Mouse Bell Boy Detective (Disney), 1945, Whitman, 352 pgs. 21.00 52.50 145.00
1499- Mickey Mouse on the Cave-Man Island (Disney), 1944, Whitman, 352 pgs. 21.00 52.50 145.00
2004- Mickey Mouse, Here Comes (Disney), 1936, Whitman, (Very Rare), 224 pgs., 12" x 8 1/4" box, with red, yellow and blue crayons, contains 224 loose pages to color, reprinted from early Mickey Mouse related movie and strip reprints 235.00 588.00 2000.00
2020-(#20)- Mickey Mouse, Adventure in Outer Space, 1968, Whitman, 256 pgs.,hard-c, color illos. 4.00 10.00 27.00
3059- Mickey Mouse Big Little Set (Disney), 1936, Whitman, 8 1/4" x 8 1/2", with crayons, box contains a 4" x 5 1/4" soft-c book with 160 pgs. of Mickey to color, reprinted from early Mickey Mouse BLBs, (Rare)
(a copy in NM sold for $1897 in Nov, 2011, a VF copy sold for $1147 in 2013)
5750- Mickey Mouse, Adventure in Outer Space, 1973, Whitman, 256 pgs.,soft-c, 39 cents, color illos. 2.00 5.00 15.00
3049- Mickey Mouse and His Big Little Kit (Disney), 1937, Whitman, 384 pgs., 4 1/2" x 6 1/2" box, includes miniature box of 4 crayons-red, yellow, blue and green 150.00 375.00 1210.00
3061- Mickey Mouse to Draw and Color (The Big Little Set), nd (early 1930s), Whitman, with crayons; box contains 320 loose pages to color, reprinted from early Mickey Mouse BLBs 123.00 308.00 880.00
4062- Mickey Mouse, The Story Of, 1935, Whitman, 7" x 9 1/2", 320 pgs., Big Big Book, Gottfredson-a 82.00 205.00 575.00
4062- Mickey Mouse and the Smugglers, The Story Of, 1935, Whitman, (Scarce), 7" x 9 1/2", 320 pgs., Big Big Book, same contents as above version; Gottfredson-a 82.00 205.00 575.00
708-10- Mickey Mouse on the Haunted Island (Disney), 1950, Whitman, Gottfredson-a 12.00 30.00 80.00
nn- Mickey Mouse and Minnie at Macy's, 1934 Whitman, 148 pgs., 3 1/4" x 3 1/2", soft-c, R. H. Macy & Co. Christmas giveaway (Rare, less than 20 known copies) 300.00 750.00 2700.00

GD FN VF/NM

nn- Mickey Mouse and Minnie March to Macy's, 1935, Whitman, 148 pgs., 3 1/2" x 3 1/2", soft-c, R. H. Macy & Co. Christmas giveaway (scarce) 259.00 648.00 2200.00
nn- Mickey Mouse and the Magic Carpet, 1935, Whitman, 148 pgs., 3 1/2"x 4", soft-c, giveaway, Gottfredson-a, Donald Duck app. 123.00 308.00 900.00
nn- Mickey Mouse Silly Symphonies, 1934, Dean & Son, Ltd (England), 48 pgs., with 4 pop-ups, Babes In The Woods, King Neptune
With dust jacket 138.00 345.00 1100.00
Without dust jacket 100.00 250.00 700.00
nn- Mickey Mouse the Sheriff of Nugget Gulch (Disney) 1938, Dell, 196 pgs., Fast-Action Story, soft-c, Gottfredson-a 36.00 90.00 250.00
nn- Mickey Mouse Waddle Book, 1934, BRP, 20 pgs., 7 1/2" x 10", forerunner of the Blue Ribbon Pop-Up books; with 4 removable articulated cardboard characters Book Only 100.00 200.00 500.00
(A complete copy in VG/FN w/VF dustjacket sold for $5676 in 2010)
(A copy in GD with dustjacket, no waddle sold for $190)
nn- Mickey Mouse with Goofy and Mickey's Nephews, 1938, Dell, Fast-Action Story, Gottfredson-a 36.00 90.00 250.00
16- Mickey Mouse and Pluto (Disney), 1942, Dell, 196 pgs., Fast-Action story 36.00 90.00 250.00
512- Mickey Mouse Wee Little Books (In open box), nn, 1934, Whitman, 44 pgs., small size, soft-c
Mickey Mouse and Tanglefoot 13.00 32.50 90.00
Mickey Mouse at the Carnival 13.00 32.50 90.00
Mickey Mouse Will Not Quit! 13.00 32.50 90.00
Mickey Mouse Wins the Race! 13.00 32.50 90.00
Mickey Mouse's Misfortune 13.00 32.50 90.00
Mickey Mouse's Uphill Fight 13.00 32.50 90.00
Complete set with box 96.00 240.00 675.00
1493- Mickey Rooney and Judy Garland and How They Got into the Movies, 1941, Whitman, 432 pgs., photo-c 12.00 30.00 75.00
1427- Mickey Rooney Himself, 1939, Whitman, 240 pgs., photo-c, movie scenes, life story 12.00 30.00 75.00
532- Mickey's Dog Pluto (Disney), 1943, Whitman, All Picture Comics, A Tall Comic Book , 3 3/4" x 8 3/4" 20.00 50.00 140.00
284- Midget Jumbo Coloring Book, 1935, Saalfield 43.00 108.00 300.00
2113- Midget Jumbo Coloring Book, 1935, Saalfield, 240 pgs. 43.00 108.00 300.00
21- Midsummer Night's Dream, 1935, EVW, movie scenes 12.00 30.00 85.00
nn- Minute-Man (Mystery of the Spy Ring), 1941, Fawcett, Dime Action Book 36.00 90.00 250.00
710- Moby Dick the Great White Whale, The Story of, 1934, Whitman, 160 pgs., photo-c, movie scenes from "The Sea Beast" 12.00 30.00 85.00
746- Moon Mullins and Kayo (Kayo and Moon Mullins-inside), 1933, Whitman, 320 pgs., Frank Willard-c/a 12.00 30.00 75.00
nn- Moon Mullins and Kayo, 1933, Whitman, Cocomalt premium, soft-c, by Willard 12.00 30.00 75.00
1134- Moon Mullins and the Plushbottom Twins, 1935, Whitman, 432 pgs., Willard-c/a 12.00 30.00 75.00
nn- Moon Mullins and the Plushbottom Twins, 1935, Whitman, 436 pgs., premium-no ads, 3-color, soft-c, by Willard 18.00 45.00 125.00
1058- Mother Pluto (Disney), 1939, Whitman, 68 pgs., hard-c 11.00 27.50 70.00
1100B- Movie Jokes (From the talkies), 1938, Whitman, 36 pgs., 2 1/2" x 3 1/2", Penny Book 2.00 5.00 15.00
1408- Mr. District Attorney on the Job, 1941, Whitman, 432 pgs., flip pictures 10.00 25.00 65.00
nn- Musicians of Bremen, The, nd (1930s), np (Whitman), 36 pgs., 3" x 2 1/2", Penny Book 2.00 5.00 15.00
1113- Mutt and Jeff, 1936, Whitman, 300 pgs., by Bud Fisher 26.00 65.00 180.00
1116- My Life and Times (By Shirley Temple), 1936, Saalfield, Little Big Book, hard-c, photo-c/illos 12.00 30.00 85.00
1596- My Life and Times (By Shirley Temple), 1936, Saalfield, Little Big Book, soft-c, photo-c/illos 12.00 30.00 85.00
1497- Myra North Special Nurse and Foreign Spies, 1938,

1109 - Oswald the Lucky Rabbit © DIS

1474 - The Phantom and the Sign of the Skull © KING

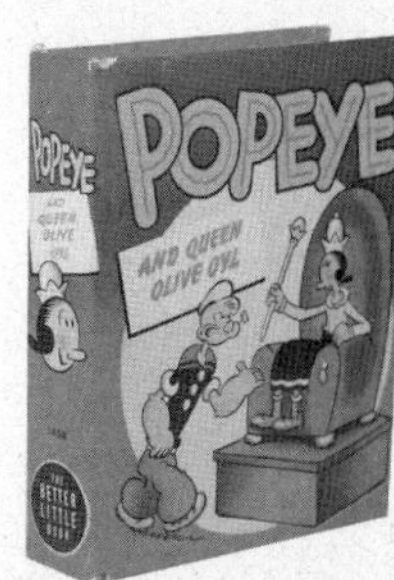

1458 - Popeye and Queen Olive Oyl © KING

GD FN VF/NM

Whitman, 432 pgs. 11.00 27.50 70.00

1400- Nancy and Sluggo, 1946, Whitman, All Pictures Comics, Ernie Bushmiller-a 12.00 30.00 75.00

1487- Nancy Has Fun, 1946, Whitman, All Pictures Comics 12.00 30.00 75.00

1150- Napoleon and Uncle Elby, 1938, Saalfield, 400 pgs., by Clifford McBride 11.00 27.50 70.00

1166- Napoleon Uncle Elby And Little Mary, 1939, Saalfield, 400 pgs., by Clifford McBride 11.00 27.50 70.00

1179- Ned Brant Adventure Bound, 1940, Saalfield, 400 pgs. 10.00 25.00 60.00

1146- Nevada Rides The Danger Trail, 1938, Saalfield, 400 pgs., J.R. White-a 10.00 25.00 60.00

1147- Nevada Whalen, Avenger, 1938, Saalfield, 400 pgs. 10.00 25.00 60.00

Nicodemus O'Malley (See Top-Line Comics)

1115- Og Son of Fire, 1936, Whitman, 432 pgs. 12.00 30.00 85.00

1419- Oh, Blondie the Bumsteads (See Blondie)

11- Oliver Twist, 1935, EVW (Five Star Library), movie scenes, starring Dickie Moore (Monogram Pictures) 12.00 30.00 80.00

718- Once Upon a Time, 1933, Whitman, 364 pgs., soft-c 12.00 30.00 80.00

712- 100 Fairy Tales for Children, The, 1933, Whitman, 288 pgs., Circle Library 10.00 25.00 60.00

1099- One Night of Love, 1935, Saalfield, 160 pgs., hard-c, photo-c, movie scenes, Columbia Pictures, starring Grace Moore 12.00 30.00 85.00

1579- One Night of Love, 1935, Sat, 160 pgs., soft-c, photo-c, movie scenes, Columbia Pictures, starring Grace Moore 12.00 30.00 85.00

1155- $1000 Reward, 1938, Saalfield, 400 pgs. 10.00 25.00 60.00

Orphan Annie (See Little Orphan ...)

L17- O'Shaughnessy's Boy, 1935, Lynn, 192 pgs., movie scenes, w/Wallace Beery & Jackie Cooper (Metro-Goldwyn-Mayer) 11.00 27.50 70.00

1109- Oswald the Lucky Rabbit, 1934, Whitman, 288 pgs. 16.00 40.00 115.00

1403- Oswald Rabbit Plays G-Man, 1937, Whitman, 240 pgs., movie scenes by Walter Lantz 18.00 45.00 125.00

1190- Our Boarding House, Major Hoople and his Horse, 1940, Saalfield, 400 pgs. 11.00 27.50 70.00

1085- Our Gang, 1934, Saalfield, 160 pgs., photo-c, movie scenes, hard-c 15.00 37.50 105.00

1315- Our Gang, 1934, Saalfield, 160 pgs., photo-c, movie scenes, soft-c 15.00 37.50 105.00

1451- "Our Gang" on the March, 1942, Whitman, 432 pgs., flip pictures, Vallely-a 15.00 37.50 105.00

1456- Our Gang Adventures, 1948, Whitman, 288 pgs. 12.00 30.00 85.00

nn- Paramount Newsreel Men with Admiral Byrd in Little America, 1934, Whitman, 96 pgs., 6 1/4" x 6 1/4", photo-c, photo ill. 14.00 35.00 100.00

nn- Patch, nd (1930s), np (Whitman), 36 pgs., 3" x 2 1/2", Penny Book 2.00 5.00 15.00

1445- Pat Nelson Ace of Test Pilots, 1937, Whitman, 432 pgs. 10.00 25.00 60.00

1411- Peggy Brown and the Mystery Basket, 1941, Whitman, 432 pgs., flip pictures, Henry E. Vallely-a 10.00 25.00 65.00

1423- Peggy Brown and the Secret Treasure, 1947, Whitman, 288 pgs., Henry E. Vallely-a 10.00 25.00 65.00

1427- Peggy Brown and the Runaway Auto Trailer, 1937, Whitman, 300 pgs., Henry E. Vallely-a 10.00 25.00 65.00

1463- Peggy Brown and the Jewel of Fire, 1943, Whitman, 352 pgs., Henry E. Vallely-a 10.00 25.00 65.00

1491- Peggy Brown in the Big Haunted House, 1940, Whitman, 432 pgs., Vallely-a 10.00 25.00 65.00

1143- Peril Afloat, 1938, Saalfield, 400 pgs. 10.00 25.00 60.00

1199- Perry Winkle and the Rinkeydinks, 1937, Whitman, 432 pgs., by Martin Branner 14.00 35.00 95.00

1487- Perry Winkle and the Rinkeydinks get a Horse, 1938, Whitman, 432 pgs., by Martin Branner 14.00 35.00 95.00

Peter Pan (See Wee Little Books)

nn- Peter Rabbit, nd(1930s), np(Whitman), 36 pgs., Penny Book, 3" x 2 1/2" 5.00 12.50 33.00

Peter Rabbit's Carrots (See Wee Little Books)

1100- Phantom, The, 1936, Whitman, 432 pgs., by Lee Falk & Ray Moore 27.00 68.00 190.00

1416- Phantom and the Girl of Mystery, The, 1947, Whitman, 352 pgs. by Falk & Moore 12.00 30.00 80.00

1421- Phantom and Desert Justice, The, 1941, Whitman, 432 pgs., flip pictures, by Falk & Moore 14.00 35.00 100.00

1468- Phantom and the Sky Pirates, The, 1945, Whitman, 352 pgs., by Falk & Moore 13.00 32.50 90.00

1474- Phantom and the Sign of the Skull, The, 1939, Whitman, 432 pgs., by Falk & Moore 16.00 40.00 110.00

1489- Phantom, Return of the..., 1942, Whitman, 432 pgs., flip pictures, by Falk & Moore 14.00 35.00 100.00

1130- Phil Burton, Sleuth (Scout Book), 1937, Saalfield, hard-c 7.00 17.50 40.00

Pied Piper of Hamlin (See Wee Little Books)

1466- Pilot Pete Dive Bomber, 1941, Whitman, 432 pgs., flip pictures 10.00 25.00 60.00

5776- Pink Panther Adventures in Z-Land, The, 1976, Whitman, 260 pgs., soft-c, 49 cents, B&W 1.00 2.50 8.00

5776-2- Pink Panther Adventures in Z-Land, The, 1980, Whitman, 260 pgs., soft-c, 79 cents, B&W 1.00 2.50 8.00

5783-2- Pink Panther at Castle Kreep, The, 1980, Whitman, 260 pgs., soft-c, 79 cents, B&W 1.00 2.50 8.00

Pinocchio and Jiminy Cricket (See Walt Disney's ...)

nn- Pioneers of the Wild West (Blue-c), 1933, World Syndicate, High Lights of History Series 7.00 17.50 40.00
With dustjacket 29.00 73.00 200.00

nn- Pioneers of the Wild West (Red-c), 1933, World Syndicate, High Lights of History Series 7.00 17.50 40.00

1123- Plainsman, The, 1936, Whitman, 240 pgs., photo-c, movie scenes with Gary Cooper (Paramount Pics.) 14.00 35.00 100.00

Pluto (See Mickey's Dog ... & Walt Disney's ...)

2114- Pocket Coloring Book, 1935, Saalfield 27.00 68.00 190.00

1060- Polly and Her Pals on the Farm, 1934, Saalfield, 164 pgs., hard-c, by Cliff Sterrett 12.00 30.00 80.00

1310- Polly and Her Pals on the Farm, 1934, Saalfield, soft-c 12.00 30.00 80.00

1051- Popeye, Adventures of..., 1934, Saalfield, oblong-size, E.C. Segar-a, hard-c 43.00 108.00 300.00

1088- Popeye in Puddleburg, 1934, Saalfield, 160 pgs., hard-c, E. C. Segar-a 18.00 45.00 125.00

1113- Popeye Starring in Choose Your Weppins, 1936, Saalfield, 160 pgs., hard-c, Segar-a 36.00 90.00 250.00

1117- Popeye's Ark, 1936, Saalfield, 4 1/2" x 5 1/2", hard-c, Segar-a 19.00 47.50 135.00

1163- Popeye Sees the Sea, 1936, Whitman, 432 pgs., Segar-a 20.00 50.00 140.00

1301- Popeye, Adventures of..., 1934, Saalfield, oblong-size, Segar-a 43.00 108.00 300.00

1318- Popeye in Puddleburg, 1934, Saalfield, 160 pgs., soft-c, Segar-a 19.00 47.50 135.00

1405- Popeye and the Jeep, 1937, Whitman, 432 pgs., Segar-a 20.00 50.00 140.00

1406- Popeye the Super-Fighter, 1939, Whitman, All Pictures Comics, flip pictures, Segar-a 19.00 47.50 135.00

1422- Popeye the Sailor Man, 1947, Whitman, All Pictures Comics 12.00 30.00 85.00

1450- Popeye in Quest of His Poopdeck Pappy, 1937, Whitman, 432 pgs., Segar-c/a 14.00 35.00 100.00

1458- Popeye and Queen Olive Oyl, 1949, Whitman, 288 pgs., Sagendorf-a 12.00 30.00 85.00

1459- Popeye and the Quest for the Rainbird, 1943, Whitman, Winner & Zaboly-a 14.00 35.00 95.00

1480- Popeye the Spinach Eater, 1945, Whitman, All Pictures Comics 12.00 30.00 85.00

1485- Popeye in a Sock for Susan's Sake, 1940, Whitman,

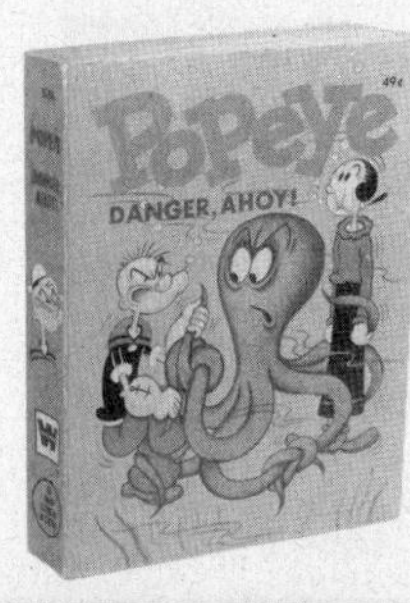
5768 - Popeye, Danger Ahoy! © KING

1176 - Powder Smoke Range © WHIT

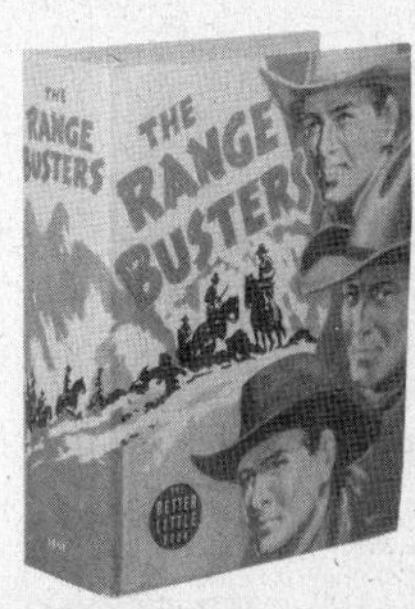

1441 - The Range Busters © WHIT

GD FN VF/NM

432 pgs., flip pictures 14.00 35.00 95.00

1497- Popeye and Caster Oyl the Detective, 1941, Whitman, 432 pgs. flip pictures, Segar-a 16.00 40.00 115.00

1499- Popeye and the Deep Sea Mystery, 1939, Whitman, 432 pgs., Segar-c/a 16.00 40.00 115.00

1593- Popeye Starring in Choose Your Weppins, 1936, Saalfield, 160 pgs., soft-c, Segar-a 16.00 40.00 115.00

1597- Popeye's Ark, 1936, Saalfield, 4 1/2" x 5 1/2", soft-c, Segar-a 16.00 40.00 115.00

2008-(#8)- Popeye-Ghost Ship to Treasure Island, 1967, Whitman, 260 pgs., 39 cents, hard-c, color illos 4.00 10.00 27.00

5755- Popeye-Ghost Ship to Treasure Island, 1973, Whitman, 260 pgs., soft-c, color illos 2.00 5.00 15.00

2034-(#34)- Popeye, Danger Ahoy!, 1969, Whitman, 256 pgs., hard-c, color illos. 4.00 10.00 25.00

5768- Popeye, Danger Ahoy!, 1975, Whitman, 256 pgs., soft-c, color illos. 2.00 5.00 15.00

4063- Popeye, Thimble Theatre Starring, 1935, Whitman, 7" x 9 1/2", 320 pgs., Big Big Book, Segar-c/a; (Cactus cover w/yellow logo) 86.00 215.00 600.00

4063- Popeye, Thimble Theatre Starring, 1935, Whitman, 7" x 9 1/2", 320 pgs., Big Big Book, Segar-c/a; (Big Balloon-c with red logo), (2nd printing w/same contents as above) 100.00 250.00 700.00

5761- Popeye and Queen Olive Oyl, 1973, 260 pgs., B&W, soft-c 4.00 10.00 27.00

5761-2- Popeye and Queen Olive Oyl, 1973 (1980-reprint of 1973 version), 260 pgs., 79 cents, B&W, soft-c 2.00 5.00 15.00

103- "Pop-Up" Buck Rogers in the Dangerous Mission (with Pop-Up picture), 1934, BRP, 62 pgs., The Midget Pop-Up Book w/Pop-Up in center of book, Calkins-a 121.00 303.00 850.00

206- "Pop-Up" Buck Rogers - Strange Adventures in the Spider Ship, The, 1935, BRP, 24 pgs., 8" x 9", 3 Pop-Ups, hard-c, by Dick Calkins 121.00 303.00 850.00

nn- "Pop-Up" Cinderella, 1933, BRP, 7 1/2" x 9 3/4", 4 Pop-Ups, hard-c
With dustjacket ($2.00) 68.00 170.00 475.00
Without dustjacket 57.00 143.00 400.00

207- "Pop-Up" Dick Tracy-Capture of Boris Arson, 1935, BRP, 24 pgs., 8" x 9", 3 Pop-Ups, hard-c, by Gould 68.00 170.00 475.00

210- "Pop-Up" Flash Gordon Tournament of Death, The, 1935, BRP, 24 pgs., 8" x 9", 3 Pop-Ups, hard-c, by Alex Raymond 114.00 285.00 800.00

202- "Pop-Up" Goldilocks and the Three Bears, The, 1934, BRP, 24 pgs., 8" x 9", 3 Pop-Ups, hard-c 36.00 90.00 250.00

nn- "Pop-Up" Jack and the Beanstalk, 1933, BRP, hard-c (50 cents), 1 Pop-Up 36.00 90.00 250.00

nn- "Pop-Up" Jack the Giant Killer, 1933, BRP, hard-c (50 cents), 1 Pop-Up 36.00 90.00 250.00

nn- "Pop-Up" Jack the Giant Killer, 1933, BRP, 4 Pop-Ups, hard-c
With dustjacket ($2.00) 68.00 170.00 475.00
Without dust jacket 57.00 143.00 400.00

nn- "Pop-Up" Little Black Sambo, (with Pop-Up picture), 1934, BRP, 62 pgs., The Midget Pop-Up Book, one Pop-Up in center of book 43.00 108.00 300.00

208- "Pop-Up" Little Orphan Annie and Jumbo the Circus Elephant, 1935, BRP, 24 pgs., 8" x 9 1/2", 3 Pop-Ups, hard-c, by H. Gray 68.00 170.00 475.00

nn- "Pop-Up" Little Red Ridinghood, 1933, BRP, hard-c (50 cents), 1 Pop-Up 43.00 108.00 300.00

nn- "Pop-Up" Mickey Mouse, The, 1933, BRP, 34 pgs., 6 1/2" x 9", 3 Pop-Ups, hard-c, Gottfredson-a (75 cents) 54.00 135.00 375.00

nn- "Pop-Up" Mickey Mouse in King Arthur's Court, The, 1933, BRP, 56 pgs., 7 1/2" x 9 1/4", 4 Pop-Ups, hard-c, Gottfredson-a
With dust jacket ($2.00) 123.00 308.00 900.00
Without dustjacket 93.00 233.00 650.00

101- "Pop-Up" Mickey Mouse in "Ye Olden Days" (with Pop-Up picture), 1934, 62 pgs., BRP, The Midget Pop-Up Book, one Pop-Up in center of book, Gottfredson-a 107.00 268.00 750.00

nn- "Pop-Up" Minnie Mouse, The, 1933, BRP, 36 pgs., 6 1/2" x 9", 3 Pop-Ups, hard-c (75 cents), Gottfredson-a 50.00 125.00 350.00

203- "Pop-Up" Mother Goose, The, 1934, BRP, 24 pgs., 8" x 9 1/4", 3 Pop-Ups, hard-c 43.00 108.00 300.00

nn- "Pop-Up" Mother Goose Rhymes, The, 1933, BRP, 96 pgs., 7 1/2" x 9 1/4", 4 Pop-Ups, hard-c
With dustjacket ($2.00) 46.00 115.00 325.00
Without dustjacket 43.00 108.00 300.00

209- "Pop-Up" New Adventures of Tarzan, 1935, BRP, 24 pgs., 8" x 9", 3 Pop-Ups, hard-c 107.00 268.00 750.00

104- "Pop-Up" Peter Rabbit, The (with Pop-Up picture), 1934, BRP, 62 pgs., The Midget Pop-Up Book, one Pop-Up in center of book 50.00 125.00 350.00

nn- "Pop-Up" Pinocchio, 1933, BRP, 7 1/2" x 9 3/4", 4 Pop-Ups, hard-c
With dustjacket ($2.00) 61.00 153.00 425.00
Without dust jacket 54.00 135.00 375.00

102- "Pop-Up" Popeye among the White Savages (with Pop-Up picture), 1934, BRP, 62 pgs., The Midget Pop-Up Book, one Pop-Up in center of book, E. C. Segar-a 61.00 153.00 425.00

205- "Pop-Up" Popeye with the Hag of the Seven Seas, The, 1935, BRP, 24 pgs., 8" x 9", 3 Pop-Ups, hard-c, Segar-a 68.00 170.00 475.00

201- "Pop-Up" Puss In Boots, The, 1934, BRP, 24 pgs., 3 Pop-Ups, hard-c 37.00 93.00 260.00

nn- "Pop-Up" Silly Symphonies, The (Mickey Mouse Presents His ...), 1933, BRP, 56 pgs., 9 3/4" x 7 1/2", 4 Pop-Ups, hard-c
With dust jacket ($2.00) 107.00 268.00 750.00
Without dust jacket 71.00 178.00 500.00

nn- "Pop-Up" Sleeping Beauty, 1933, BRP, hard-c, (50 cents), 1 Pop-up 41.00 103.00 290.00

212- "Pop-Up" Terry and the Pirates in Shipwrecked, The, 1935, BRP, 24 pgs., 8" x 9", 3 Pop-Ups, hard-c 71.00 178.00 500.00

211- "Pop-Up" Tim Tyler in the Jungle, The, 1935, BRP, 24 pgs., 8" x 9", 3 Pop-Ups, hard-c 46.00 115.00 325.00

1404- Porky Pig and His Gang, 1946, Whitman, All Pictures Comics, Barks-a, reprints Four Color #48 20.00 50.00 140.00

1408- Porky Pig and Petunia, 1942, Whitman, All Pictures Comics, flip pictures, reprints Four Color #16 & Famous Gang Book of Comics 12.00 30.00 85.00

1176- Powder Smoke Range, 1935, Whitman, 240 pgs., photo-c, movie scenes, Hoot Gibson, Harey Carey app. (RKO Radio Pict.) 11.00 27.50 70.00

1058- Practical Pig!, The (Disney), 1939, Whitman, 68 pgs., 5" x 5 1/2", hard-c 11.00 27.50 70.00

758- Prairie Bill and the Covered Wagon, 1934, Whitman, 384 pgs., Hal Arbo-a 10.00 25.00 60.00

nn- Prairie Bill and the Covered Wagon, 1934, Whitman, 390 pgs., premium-no ads, 3-color, soft-c, Hal Arbo-a 12.00 30.00 85.00

1440- Punch Davis of the U.S. Aircraft Carrier, 1945, Whitman, 352 pgs. 9.00 22.50 55.00

nn- Puss in Boots, nd(1930s), np(Whitman), 36 pgs., Penny Book 2.00 5.00 15.00

1100B- Puzzle Book, 1938, Whitman, 36 pgs., 2 1/2" x 3 1/2", Penny Book 3.00 7.50 20.00

1100B- Puzzles, 1938, Whitman, 36 pgs., 2 1/2" x 3 1/2", Penny Book 3.00 7.50 20.00

1100B- Quiz Book, The, 1938, Whitman, 36 pgs., 2 1/2" x 3 1/2", Penny Book 3.00 7.50 20.00

1142- Radio Patrol, 1935, Whitman, 432 pgs., by Eddie Sullivan & Charlie Schmidt (#1) 12.00 30.00 75.00

1173- Radio Patrol Trailing the Safeblowers, 1937, Whitman, 432 pgs. 10.00 25.00 60.00

1496- Radio Patrol Outwitting the Gang Chief, 1939, Whitman, 432 pgs. 10.00 25.00 60.00

1498- Radio Patrol and Big Dan's Mobsters, 1937, Whitman, 432 pgs. 10.00 25.00 60.00

nn- Raiders of the Lost Ark, 1998, Chronicle Books, 304 pgs., adapts movie, 1-color (green) illos 4.00 10.00 22.00

1441- Range Busters, The, 1942, Whitman, 432 pgs., Henry E. Vallely-a 10.00 25.00 60.00

1163- Ranger and the Cowboy, The, 1939, Saalfield, 400 pgs. 10.00 25.00 60.00

1154- Rangers on the Rio Grande, 1938, Saalfield, 400 pgs. 10.00 25.00 60.00

1443 - Red Ryder and the Rimrock Killer © WHIT

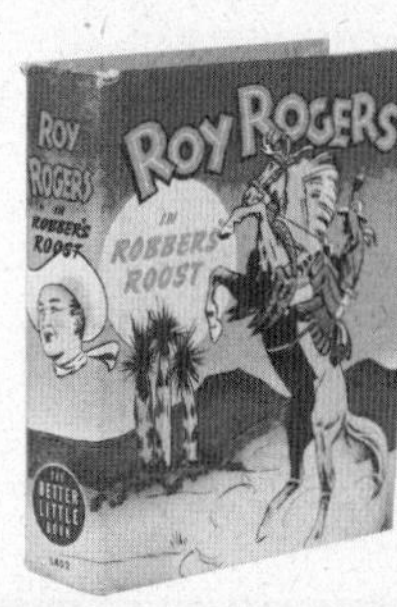

1452 - Roy Rogers in Robbers' Roost © WHIT

1495 - The Shadow and the Ghost Makers © WHIT

	GD	FN	VF/NM
1447- Ray Land of the Tank Corps, U.S.A., 1942, Whitman, 432 pgs., flip pictures, Hess-a	10.00	25.00	60.00
1157- Red Barry Ace-Detective, 1935, Whitman, 432 pgs., by Will Gould	12.00	30.00	85.00
1426- Red Barry Undercover Man, 1939, Whitman, 432 pgs., by Will Gould	12.00	30.00	75.00
20- Red Davis, 1935, EVW, 160 pgs.	11.00	27.50	70.00
1449- Red Death on the Range, The, 1940, Whitman, 432 pgs., Fred Harman-a (Bronc Peeler)	11.00	27.50	70.00
nn- Red Falcon Adventures, The, 1937, Seal Right Ice Cream, 8 pgs., set of 50 books, circular in shape			
Issue #1	64.00	160.00	450.00
Issue #2-5	43.00	108.00	300.00
Issue #6-10	36.00	90.00	250.00
Issue #11-50	21.00	52.50	150.00
nn- Red Hen and the Fox, The, nd(1930s), np(Whitman), 36 pgs., 3" x 2 1/2", Penny Book	3.00	7.50	18.00
1145- Red-Hot Holsters, 1938, Saalfield, 400 pgs.	10.00	25.00	60.00
1400- Red Ryder and Little Beaver on Hoofs of Thunder, 1939, Whitman, 432 pgs., Harman-c/a	13.00	32.50	90.00
1414- Red Ryder and the Squaw-Tooth Rustlers, 1946, Whitman, 352 pgs., Fred Harman-a	12.00	30.00	75.00
1427- Red Ryder and the Code of the West, 1941, Whitman, 432 pgs., flip pictures, by Harman	12.00	30.00	80.00
1440- Red Ryder the Fighting Westerner, 1940, Whitman, Harman-a	12.00	30.00	80.00
1443- Red Ryder and the Rimrock Killer, 1948, Whitman, 288 pgs., Harman-a	11.00	27.50	70.00
1450- Red Ryder and Western Border Guns, 1942, Whitman, 432 pgs., flip pictures, by Harman	12.00	30.00	80.00
1454- Red Ryder and the Secret Canyon, 1948, Whitman, 288 pgs., Harman-a	11.00	27.50	70.00
1466- Red Ryder and Circus Luck, 1947, Whitman, 288 pgs., by Fred Harman	11.00	27.50	70.00
1473- Red Ryder in War on the Range, 1945, Whitman, 352 pgs., by Fred Harman	12.00	30.00	75.00
1475- Red Ryder and the Outlaw of Painted Valley, 1943, Whitman, 352 pgs., by Harman	11.00	27.50	70.00
702-10- Red Ryder Acting Sheriff, 1949, Whitman, by Fred Hannan	10.00	25.00	65.00
nn- Red Ryder Brings Law to Devil's Hole, 1939, Dell, 196 pgs., Fast-Action Story, Harman-c/a	29.00	73.00	200.00
nn- Red Ryder and the Highway Robbers, 1938, Whitman, 36 pgs., 2 1/2" x 3 1/2", Penny Book	10.00	25.00	65.00
754- Reg'lar Fellers, 1933, Whitman, 320 pgs., by Gene Byrnes	11.00	27.50	70.00
nn- Reg'lar Fellers, 1933, Whitman, 202 pgs., Cocomalt premium, by Gene Byrnes	11.00	27.50	70.00
1424- Rex Beach's Jaragu of the Jungle, 1937, Whitman, 432 pgs.	9.00	22.50	55.00
12- Rex, King of Wild Horses in "Stampede," 1935, EVW, 160 pgs., movie scenes, Columbia Pictures	10.00	25.00	60.00
1100B- Riddles for Fun, 1938, Whitman, 36 pgs., 2 1/2" x 3 1/2", Penny Book	3.00	7.50	20.00
1100B- Riddles to Guess, 1938, Whitman, 36 pgs., 2 1/2" x 3 1/2", Penny Book	3.00	7.50	20.00
1425- Riders of Lone Trails, 1937, Whitman, 300 pgs.	10.00	25.00	65.00
1141- Rio Raiders (A Billy The Kid Story), 1938, Saalfield, 400 pgs.	10.00	25.00	65.00
2023-(#23)- The Road Runner, The Super Beep Catcher, 1968, Whitman, 256 pgs., hard-c, color illos.	1.00	2.50	9.00
5759- The Road Runner, The Super Beep Catcher, 1973, Whitman, 256 pgs., soft-c, 39 cents, B&W illos., and flip pictures	2.00	5.00	12.00
5767-2- Road Runner, The Lost Road Runner Mine, The, 1974 (1980), 260 pgs., 79 cents, B&W, soft-c	2.00	5.00	12.00
5784- The Road Runner and the Unidentified Coyote, 1974, Whitman, 260 pgs., soft-c, flip pictures	2.00	5.00	12.00
5784-2- The Road Runner and the Unidentified Coyote, 1980, Whitman, 260 pgs., soft-c, flip pictures	2.00	5.00	12.00
nn- Road To Perdition, 2002, Dreamworks, screenplay from movie, hard-c (Dreamworks and 20th Century Fox)	1.00	2.50	9.00
Robin Hood (See Wee Little Books)			
10- Robin Hood, 1935, EVW, 160 pgs., movie scenes w/Douglas Fairbanks (United Artists), hard-c	14.00	35.00	100.00
719- Robinson Crusoe (The Story of...), nd (1933), Whitman, 364 pgs., soft-c	12.00	30.00	75.00
1421- Roy Rogers and the Dwarf-Cattle Ranch, 1947, Whitman, 352 pgs., Henry E. Vallely-a	12.00	30.00	75.00
1437- Roy Rogers and the Deadly Treasure, 1947, Whitman, 288 pgs.	12.00	30.00	75.00
1448- Roy Rogers and the Mystery of the Howling Mesa, 1948, Whitman, 288 pgs.	12.00	30.00	75.00
1452- Roy Rogers in Robbers' Roost, 1948, Whitman, 288 pgs.	12.00	30.00	75.00
1460- Roy Rogers Robinhood of the Range, 1942, Whitman, 432 pgs., Hess-a (1st)	14.00	35.00	100.00
1462- Roy Rogers and the Mystery of the Lazy M, 1949, Whitman	10.00	25.00	65.00
1476- Roy Rogers King of the Cowboys, 1943, Whitman, 352 pgs., Irwin Myers-a, based on movie	16.00	40.00	110.00
1494- Roy Rogers at Crossed Feathers Ranch, 1945, Whitman, 320 pgs., Erwin Hess-a , 3 1/4" x 5 1/2"	12.00	30.00	75.00
701-10- Roy Rogers and the Snowbound Outlaws, 1949, 3 1/4" x 5 1/2"	10.00	25.00	60.00
715-10- Roy Rogers Range Detective, 1950, Whitman, 2 1/2" x 5"	10.00	25.00	60.00
nn- Sandy Gregg Federal Agent on Special Assignment, 1939, Whitman, 36 pgs., 2 1/2" x 3 1/2", Penny Book	9.00	22.50	55.00
Sappo (See Top-Line Comics)			
1122- Scrappy, 1934, Whitman, 288 pgs.	12.00	30.00	75.00
L12- Scrappy (The Adventures of...), 1935, Lynn, 192 pgs., movie scenes	12.00	30.00	75.00
1191- Secret Agent K-7,1940, Saalfield, 400 pgs., based on radio show	9.00	22.50	55.00
1144- Secret Agent X-9, 1936, Whitman, 432 pgs., Charles Flanders-a	15.00	37.50	105.00
1472- Secret Agent X-9 and the Mad Assassin, 1938, Whitman, 432 pgs., Charles Flanders-a	15.00	37.50	105.00
1161- Sequoia, 1935, Whitman, 160 pgs., photo-c, movie scenes	12.00	30.00	75.00
1430- Shadow and the Living Death, The, 1940, Whitman, 432 pgs., Erwin Hess-a	39.00	98.00	275.00
1443- Shadow and the Master of Evil, The, 1941, Whitman, 432 pgs., flip pictures, Hess-a	39.00	98.00	275.00
1495- Shadow and the Ghost Makers, The, 1942, Whitman, 432 pgs., John Coleman Burroughs-c	39.00	98.00	275.00
2024- Shazzan, The Glass Princess, 1968, Whitman, Hanna-Barbera	3.00	7.50	20.00
Shirley Temple (See My Life and Times & Story of..)			
1095- Shirley Temple and Lionel Barrymore Starring In "The Little Colonel," 1935, Saalfield, photo hard-c, movie scenes	18.00	45.00	125.00
1115- Shirley Temple in "The Littlest Rebel," 1935, Saalfield, photo-c, movie scenes, hard-c	18.00	45.00	125.00
1575- Shirley Temple and Lionel Barrymore Starring In "The Little Colonel," 1935, Saalfield, photo soft-c, movie scenes	18.00	45.00	125.00
1595- Shirley Temple in "The Littlest Rebel," 1935, Saalfield, photo-c, movie scenes, soft-c	18.00	45.00	125.00
1195- Shooting Sheriffs of the Wild West, 1936, Whitman, 432 pgs.	8.00	20.00	50.00
1169- Silly Symphony Featuring Donald Duck (Disney), 1937, Whitman, 432 pgs., Taliaferro-a	25.00	62.50	175.00
1441- Silly Symphony Featuring Donald Duck and His (MIS) Adventures (Disney), 1937, Whitman, 432 pgs., Taliaferro-a	25.00	62.50	175.00
1155- Silver Streak, The, 1935, Whitman, 160 pgs., photo-c, movie scenes (RKO Radio Pict.)	10.00	25.00	65.00
Simple Simon (See Wee Little Books)			
1649- Sir Lancelot (TV Series), 1958, Whitman, 280 pgs.	6.00	18.00	35.00

1419 - Skeezix on His Own in the Big City © WHIT

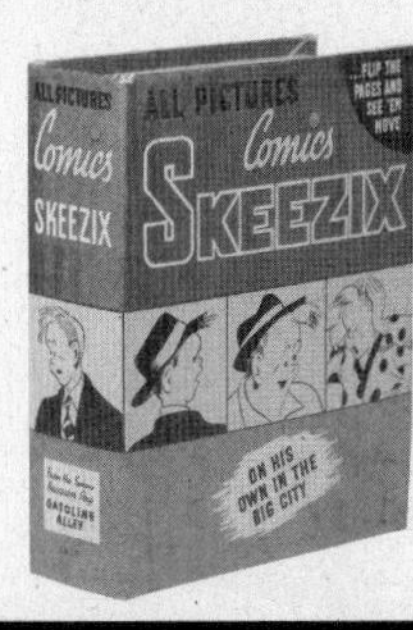

1152 - Son of Mystery © Saalfield

Star Wars - Episode 2 - Attack of the Clones © LucasFilm, Ltd.

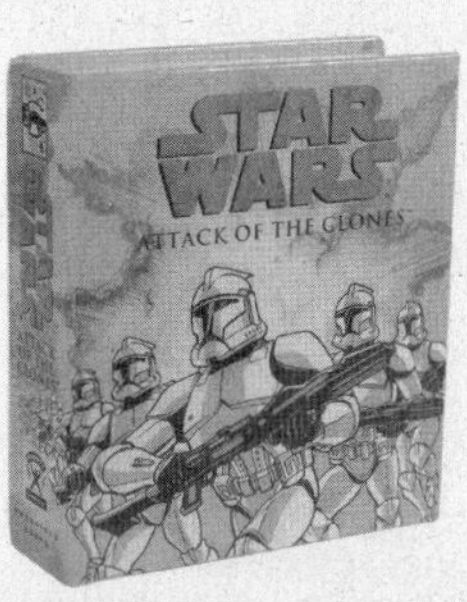

GD FN VF/NM

1112- Skeezix in Africa, 1934, Whitman, 300 pgs., Frank King-a 8.00 20.00 50.00

1408- Skeezix at the Military Academy, 1938, Whitman, 432 pgs., Frank King-a 8.00 20.00 50.00

1414- Skeezix Goes to War, 1944, Whitman, 352 pgs., Frank King-a 8.00 20.00 50.00

1419- Skeezix on His Own in the Big City, 1941, Whitman, All Pictures Comics, flip pictures, Frank King-a 8.00 20.00 50.00

761- Skippy, 1934, Whitman, 320 pgs., by Percy Crosby 8.00 20.00 50.00

4056- Skippy, The Story of, 1934, Whitman, 320 pgs., 7" x 9 1/2", Big Big Book, Percy Crosby-a 23.00 57.50 160.00

nn- Skippy, The Story of, 1934, Whitman, Phillips Dental Magnesia premium, soft-c, by Percy Crosby 8.00 20.00 50.00

1127- Skyroads (Hurricane Hawk's name not on cover), 1936, Whitman, 432 pgs., by Lt. Dick Calkins, Russell Keaton-a 11.00 27.50 70.00

1439- Skyroads with Clipper Williams of the Flying Legion, 1938, Whitman, 432 pgs., by Lt. Dick Calkins, Keaton-a 11.00 27.50 70.00

1127- Skyroads with Hurricane Hawk, 1936, Whitman, 432 pgs., by Lt. Dick Calkins, Russell Keaton-a 10.00 25.00 65.00

Smilin' Jack and his Flivver Plane (See Top-Line Comics)

1152- Smilin' Jack and the Stratosphere Ascent, 1937, Whitman, 432 pgs., Zack Mosley-a 12.00 30.00 85.00

1412- Smilin' Jack Flying High with "Downwind," 1942, Whitman, 432 pgs., Zack Mosley-a 12.00 30.00 80.00

1416- Smilin' Jack in Wings over the Pacific, 1939, Whitman, 432 pgs., Zack Mosley-a 12.00 30.00 80.00

1419- Smilin' Jack and the Jungle Pipe Line, 1947, Whitman, 352 pgs., Zack Mosley-a 12.00 30.00 75.00

1445- Smilin' Jack and the Escape from Death Rock, 1943, Whitman, 352 pgs., Mosley-a 12.00 30.00 75.00

1464- Smilin' Jack and the Coral Princess, 1945, Whitman, 352 pgs., Zack Mosley-a 12.00 30.00 75.00

1473- Smilin' Jack Speed Pilot, 1941, Whitman, 432 pgs., Zack Mosley-a 12.00 30.00 80.00

2- Smilin' Jack and his Stratosphere Plane, 1938, Whitman, 132 pgs., Buddy Book, soft-c, Zack Mosley-a 27.00 68.00 190.00

nn- Smilin' Jack Grounded on a Tropical Shore, 1938, Whitman, 36 pgs., 2 1/2" x 3 1/2", Penny Book 1000 25.00 60.00

11- Smilin' Jack and the Border Bandits, 1941, Dell, 196 pgs., Fast-Action Story, soft-c, Zack Mosley-a 24.00 60.00 170.00

745- Smitty Golden Gloves Tournament, 1934, Whitman, 320 pgs., Walter Berndt-a 12.00 30.00 75.00

nn- Smitty Golden Gloves Tournament, 1934, Whitman, 204 pgs., Cocomalt premium, soft-c, Walter Berndt-a 12.00 30.00 85.00

1404- Smitty and Herby Lost Among the Indians, 1941, Whitman, All Pictures Comics 10.00 25.00 60.00

1477- Smitty in Going Native, 1938, Whitman, 300 pgs., Walter Berndt-a 10.00 25.00 60.00

2- Smitty and Herby, 1936, Whitman, 132 pgs., 3 1/2" x 3 1/2", soft-c, Tarzan Ice Cream cup lid premium 24.00 60.00 170.00

9- Smitty's Brother Herby and the Police Horse, 1938, Whitman, 132 pgs., 3 1/4" x 3 1/2", Buddy Book-ice cream premium, by Walter Berndt 24.00 60.00 170.00

1010- Smokey Stover Firefighter of Foo, 1937, Whitman, 7 1/4" x 5 1/2", 64 pgs., Nickel Book, Bill Holman-a 12.00 30.00 85.00

1413- Smokey Stover, 1942, Whitman, All Pictures Comics, flip pictures, Bill Holman-a 12.00 30.00 85.00

1421- Smokey Stover the Foo Fighter, 1938, Whitman, 432 pgs., Bill Holman-a 12.00 30.00 85.00

1481- Smokey Stover the Foolish Foo Fighter, 1942, Whitman, All Pictures Comics 12.00 30.00 85.00

1- Smokey Stover the Fireman of Foo, 1938, Whitman, 3 3/4" x 3 1/2", 132 pgs., Buddy Book-ice cream premium, by Bill Holman 27.00 68.00 190.00

1100A- Smokey Stover, 1938, Whitman, 36 pgs., 2 1/2" x 3 1/2", Penny Book 10.00 25.00 65.00

nn- Smokey Stover and the Fire Chief of Foo, 1938, Whitman, 36 pgs., 2 1/2" x 3 1/2", Penny Book, yellow shirt on-c 10.00 25.00 65.00

nn- Smokey Stover and the Fire Chief of Foo, 1938, Whitman, 36 pgs., Penny Book, green shirt on-c 10.00 25.00 65.00

GD FN VF/NM

1460- Snow White and the Seven Dwarfs (The Story of Walt Disney's ...), 1938, Whitman, 288 pgs. 18.00 45.00 125.00

1136- Sombrero Pete, 1936, Whitman, 432 pgs. 10.00 25.00 60.00

1152- Son of Mystery, 1939, Saalfield, 400 pgs. 10.00 25.00 60.00

1191- SOS Coast Guard, 1936, Whitman, 432 pgs., Henry E. Vallely-a 10.00 25.00 65.00

2016-(#16)-Space Ghost-The Sorceress of Cyba-3 (TV Cartoon), 1968, Whitman, 260 pgs., 39¢-c, hard-c, color illos 10.00 25.00 60.00

1455- Speed Douglas and the Mole Gang-The Great Sabotage Plot, 1941, Whitman, 432 pgs., flip pictures 10.00 25.00 60.00

5779- Spider-Man Zaps Mr. Zodiac, 1976, 260 pgs., soft-c, B&W 1.00 2.50 9.00

5779-2- Spider-Man Zaps Mr. Zodiac, 1980, 260 pgs., 79¢-c, soft-c, B&W 1.00 2.50 6.00

1467- Spike Kelly of the Commandos, 1943, Whitman, 352 pgs. 10.00 25.00 60.00

1144- Spook Riders on the Overland, 1938, Saalfield, 400 pgs. 10.00 25.00 60.00

768- Spy, The, 1936, Whitman, 300 pgs. 12.00 30.00 75.00

nn- Spy Smasher and the Red Death, 1941, Fawcett, 4" x 5 1/2", Dime Action Book 43.00 108.00 300.00

1120- Stan Kent Freshman Fullback, 1936, Saalfield, 148 pgs., hard-c 8.00 20.00 50.00

1132- Stan Kent, Captain, 1937, Saalfield 8.00 20.00 50.00

1600- Stan Kent Freshman Fullback, 1936, Saalfield, 148 pgs., soft-c 8.00 20.00 50.00

1123- Stan Kent Varsity Man, 1936, Saalfield, 160 pgs., hard-c 8.00 20.00 50.00

1603- Stan Kent Varsity Man, 1936, Saalfield, 160 pgs., soft-c 8.00 20.00 50.00

nn- Star Wars - A New Hope, 1997, Chronicle Books, 320 pgs., adapts movie, 1-color (blue) illos 3.00 7.50 20.00

nn- Star Wars - Empire Strikes Back, The, 1997, Chronicle Books, 296 pgs., adapts movie, 1-color (blue) illos 3.00 7.50 20.00

nn- Star Wars - Episode 1 - The Phantom Menace, 1999, Chronicle Books, 344 pgs., adapts movie, 1-color (blue) illos 1.00 2.50 9.00

nn- Star Wars - Episode 2 - Attack of the Clones, 2002, Chronicle Books, 340 pgs., adapts movie, 1-color (blue) illos 1.00 2.50 9.00

nn- Star Wars - Return of the Jedi, 1997, Chronicle Books, 312 pgs., adapts movie, 1-color (blue) illos 3.00 7.50 20.00

1104- Steel Arena, The (With Clyde Beatty), 1936, Saalfield, hard-c, movie scenes adapted from "The Lost Jungle" 12.00 30.00 75.00

1584- Steel Arena, The (With Clyde Beatty), 1936, Saalfield, soft-c, movie scenes 12.00 30.00 75.00

1426- Steve Hunter of the U.S. Coast Guard Under Secret Orders, 1942, Whitman, 432 pgs. 10.00 25.00 60.00

1456- Story of Charlie McCarthy and Edgar Bergen, The, 1938, Whitman, 288 pgs. 10.00 25.00 60.00

Story of Daniel, The (See Wee Little Books)

Story of David, The (See Wee Little Books)

1110- Story of Freddie Bartholomew, The, 1935, Saalfield, 4 1/2" x 5 1/4", hard-c, movie scenes (MGM) 10.00 25.00 60.00

1590- Story of Freddie Bartholomew, The, 1935, Saalfield, 4 1/2" x 5 1/4", soft-c, movie scenes (MGM) 10.00 25.00 60.00

Story of Gideon, The (See Wee Little Books)

W714- Story of Jackie Cooper, The, 1933, Whitman, 240 pgs., photo-c, movie scenes, "Skippy" & "Sooky" movie 12.00 30.00 80.00

Story of Joseph, The (See Wee Little Books)

Story of Moses, The (See Wee Little Books)

Story of Ruth and Naomi (See Wee Little Books)

1089- Story of Shirley Temple, The, 1934, Saalfield, 160 pgs., hard-c, photo-c, movie scenes 11.00 27.50 70.00

1319- Story of Shirley Temple, The, 1934, Saalfield, 160 pgs., soft-c, photo-c, movie scenes 11.00 27.50 70.00

1090- Strawberry-Roan, 1934, Saalfield, 160 pgs., hard-c, Ken Maynard photo-c, movie scenes 11.00 27.50 70.00

1320- Strawberry-Roan, 1934, Saalfield, 160 pgs., soft-c, Ken Maynard photo-c, movie scenes 11.00 27.50 70.00

Streaky and the Football Signals (See Top-Line Comics)

5780-2- Superman in the Phantom Zone Connection, 1980, 260 pgs., 79¢-c, soft-c, B&W 1.00 2.50 9.00

1183 - Tailspin Tommy Air Racer © WHIT

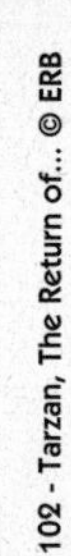

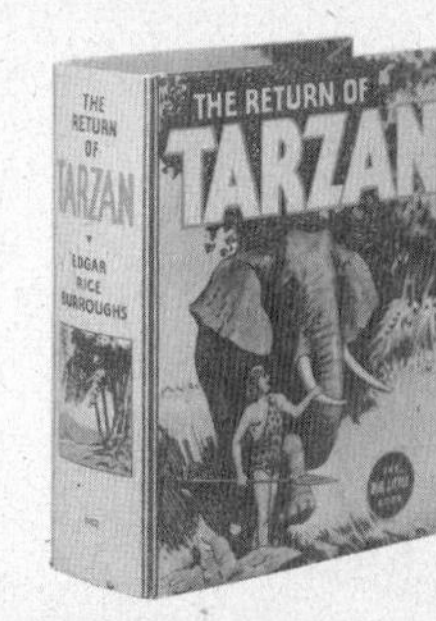

1102 - Tarzan, The Return of... © ERB

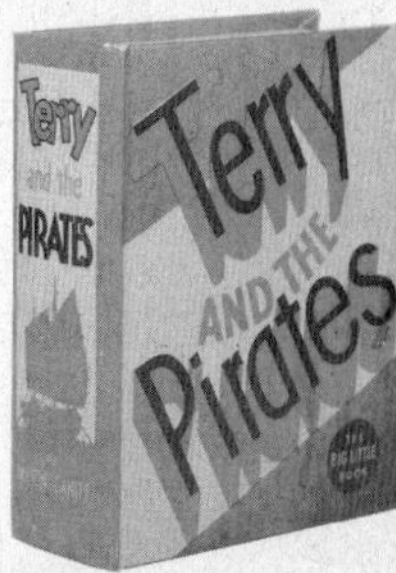

1156 - Terry and the Pirates © WHIT

	GD	FN	VF/NM
582- "Swap It" Book, The, 1949, Samuel Lowe Co., 260 pgs., 3 1/2" x 4 1/2"			
1. Little Tex in the Midst of Trouble	5.00	12.50	30.00
2. Little Tex's Escape	5.00	12.50	30.00
3. Little Tex Comes to the XY Ranch	5.00	12.50	30.00
4. Get Them Cowboy	5.00	12.50	30.00
5. The Mail Must Go Through! A Story of the Pony Express	5.00	12.50	30.00
6. Nevada Jones, Trouble Shooter	5.00	12.50	30.00
7. Danny Meets the Cowboys	5.00	12.50	30.00
8. Flint Adams and the Stage Coach	5.00	12.50	30.00
9. Bud Shinners and the Oregon Trail	5.00	12.50	30.00
10. The Outlaws' Last Ride	5.00	12.50	30.00
Sybil Jason (See Little Big Shot)			
747- Tailspin Tommy in the Famous Pay-Roll Mystery, 1933, Whitman, hard-c, 320 pgs., Hal Forrest-a (# 1)	12.00	30.00	85.00
747- Tailspin Tommy in the Famous Pay-Roll Mystery, 1933, Whitman, soft-c, 320 pgs., Hal Forrest-a (# 1)	12.00	30.00	85.00
nn- Tailspin Tommy the Pay-Roll Mystery, 1934, Whitman, 52 pgs., 3 1/2" x 5 1/4", premium-no ads, soft-c; another version with Perkins ad, Hal Forrest-a	18.00	45.00	125.00
1110- Tailspin Tommy and the Island in the Sky, 1936, Whitman, 432 pgs., Hal Forrest-a	11.00	27.50	70.00
1124- Tailspin Tommy the Dirigible Flight to the North Pole, 1934, Whitman, 432 pgs., H. Forrest-a	12.00	30.00	85.00
nn- Tailspin Tommy the Dirigible Flight to the North Pole, 1934, Whitman, 436 pgs., 3-color, soft-c, premium-no ads, Hal Forrest-a	29.00	73.00	200.00
1172- Tailspin Tommy Hunting for Pirate Gold, 1935, Whitman, 432 pgs., Hal Forrest-a	11.00	27.50	70.00
1183- Tailspin Tommy Air Racer, 1940, Saalfield, 400 pgs., hard-c	11.00	27.50	70.00
1184- Tailspin Tommy in the Great Air Mystery, 1936, Whitman, 240 pgs., photo-c, movie scenes	12.00	30.00	85.00
1410- Tailspin Tommy the Weasel and His "Skywaymen," 1941, Whitman, All Pictures Comics, flip pictures	10.00	25.00	65.00
1413- Tailspin Tommy and the Lost Transport, 1940, Whitman, 432 pgs., Hal Forrest-a	10.00	25.00	65.00
1423- Tailspin Tommy and the Hooded Flyer, 1937, Whitman, 432 pgs., Hal Forrest-a	11.00	27.50	70.00
1494- Tailspin Tommy and the Sky Bandits, 1938, Whitman 432 pgs., Hal Forrest-a	11.00	27.50	70.00
nn- Tailspin Tommy and the Airliner Mystery, 1938, Dell, 196 pgs., Fast-Action Story, soft-c, Hal Forrest-a	43.00	108.00	300.00
nn- Tailspin Tommy in Flying Aces, 1938, Dell, 196 pgs., Fast-Action Story, soft-c, Hal Forrest-a	43.00	108.00	300.00
nn- Tailspin Tommy in Wings Over the Arctic, 1934, Whitman, Cocomalt premium, Forrest-a	14.00	35.00	100.00
nn- Tailspin Tommy Big Thrill Chewing Gum, 1934, Whitman, 8 pgs., 2 1/2" x 3 " (6 diff.) each..	11.00	27.50	70.00
3- Tailspin Tommy on the Mountain of Human Sacrifice, 1938, Whitman, soft-c, Buddy Book	29.00	73.00	200.00
7- Tailspin Tommy's Perilous Adventure, 1934, Whitman, 132 pgs., 3 1/2" x 3 1/2" soft-c, Tarzan Ice Cream cup premium	29.00	73.00	200.00
nn- Tailspin Tommy, 1935, Whitman, 148 pgs., 3 1/2" x 4", Tarzan Ice Cream cup premium	32.00	80.00	225.00
L16- Tale of Two Cities, A, 1935, Lynn, movie scenes	12.00	30.00	85.00
744- Tarzan of the Apes, 1933, Whitman, 320 pgs., by Edgar Rice Burroughs (1st)	43.00	108.00	300.00
nn- Tarzan of the Apes, 1935, Whitman, 52 pgs., 3 1/2" x 5 1/4", soft-c, stapled, premium, no ad; another version with a Perkins ad	54.00	135.00	375.00
769- Tarzan the Fearless, 1934, Whitman, 240 pgs., Buster Crabbe photo-c, movie scenes, ERB	29.00	73.00	200.00
770- Tarzan Twins, The, 1934, Whitman, 432 pgs., ERB	82.00	205.00	575.00
770- Tarzan Twins, The, 1935, Whitman, 432 pgs., ERB	54.00	135.00	375.00
nn- Tarzan Twins, The, 1935, Whitman, 52 pgs., 3 1/2" x 5 3/4", premium-no ads, soft-c, ERB	68.00	170.00	475.00
nn- Tarzan Twins, The, 1935, Whitman, 436 pgs., 3-color, soft-c, premium-no ads, ERB	71.00	178.00	500.00
778- Tarzan of the Screen (The Story of Johnny Weissmuller), 1934, Whitman, 240 pgs., photo-c, movie scenes, ERB	29.00	73.00	200.00
1102- Tarzan, The Return of, 1936, Whitman, 432 pgs., Edgar Rice Burroughs	21.00	52.50	150.00
1180- Tarzan, The New Adventures of, 1935, Whitman, 160 pgs., Herman Brix photo-c, movie scenes, ERB	24.00	60.00	165.00
1182- Tarzan Escapes, 1936, Whitman, 240 pgs., Johnny Weissmuller photo-c, movie scenes, ERB	29.00	73.00	200.00
1407- Tarzan Lord of the Jungle, 1946, Whitman, 352 pgs., ERB	14.00	35.00	100.00
1410- Tarzan, The Beasts of, 1937, Whitman, 432 pgs., Edgar Rice Burroughs	21.00	52.50	145.00
1442- Tarzan and the Lost Empire, 1948, Whitman, 288 pgs., ERB	14.00	35.00	100.00
1444- Tarzan and the Ant Men, 1945, Whitman, 352 pgs., ERB	14.00	35.00	100.00
1448- Tarzan and the Golden Lion, 1943, Whitman, 432 pgs., ERB	20.00	50.00	140.00
1452- Tarzan the Untamed, 1941, Whitman, 432 pgs., flip pictures, ERB	20.00	50.00	140.00
1453- Tarzan the Terrible, 1942, Whitman, 432 pgs., flip pictures, ERB	20.00	50.00	140.00
1467- Tarzan in the Land of the Giant Apes, 1949, Whitman, ERB	14.00	35.00	100.00
1477- Tarzan, The Son of, 1939, Whitman, 432 pgs., ERB	20.00	50.00	140.00
1488- Tarzan's Revenge, 1938, Whitman, 432 pgs., ERB	20.00	50.00	140.00
1495- Tarzan and the Jewels of Opar, 1940, Whitman, 432 pgs.	20.00	50.00	140.00
4056- Tarzan and the Tarzan Twins with Jad-Bal-Ja the Golden Lion, 1936, Whitman, 7" x 9 1/2", 320 pgs., Big Big Book	60.00	150.00	470.00
709-10- Tarzan and the Journey of Terror, 1950, Whitman, 2 1/2" x 5", ERB, Marsh-a	10.00	25.00	65.00
2005- (#5)-Tarzan: The Mark of the Red Hyena, 1967, Whitman, 260 pgs., 39 cents, hard-c, color illos	4.00	10.00	27.00
nn- Tarzan, 1935, Whitman, 148 pgs., soft-c, 3 1/2" x 4", Tarzan Ice Cream cup premium, ERB (scarce)	86.00	215.00	600.00
nn- Tarzan and a Daring Rescue, 1938, Whitman, 68 pgs., Pan-Am premium, soft-c, ERB (blank back-c version also exists)	50.00	125.00	350.00
nn- Tarzan and his Jungle Friends, 1936, Whitman, 132 pgs., soft-c, 3 1/2" x 3 1/2", Tarzan Ice Cream cup premium, ERB (scarce)	86.00	215.00	600.00
nn- Tarzan in the Golden City, 1938, Whitman, 68 pgs., Pan-Am premium, soft-c, 3 1/2" x 3 3/4", ERB	50.00	125.00	350.00
nn- Tarzan The Avenger, 1939, Dell, 194 pgs., Fast-Action Story, ERB, soft-c	36.00	90.00	250.00
nn- Tarzan with the Tarzan Twins in the Jungle, 1938, Dell, 194 pgs., Fast-Action Story, ERB	36.00	90.00	250.00
1100B- Tell Your Fortune, 1938, Whitman, 36 pgs., 2 1/2" x 3 1/2", Penny Book	4.00	10.00	24.00
nn- Terminator 2: Judgment Day, 1998, Chronicle Books, 310 pgs., adapts movie, 1-color (blue-gray) illos	1.00	2.50	9.00
1156- Terry and the Pirates, 1935, Whitman, 432 pgs., Milton Caniff-a (#1)	14.00	35.00	100.00
nn- Terry and the Pirates, 1935, Whitman, 52 pgs., 3 1/2" x 5 1/4", soft-c, premium, Milton Caniff-a; 3 versions: No ad, Sears ad & Perkins ad	29.00	73.00	200.00
1412- Terry and the Pirates Shipwrecked on a Desert Island, 1938, Whitman, 432 pgs., Milton Caniff-a	12.00	30.00	85.00
1420- Terry and War in the Jungle, 1946, Whitman, 352 pgs., Milton Caniff-a	12.00	30.00	80.00
1436- Terry and the Pirates The Plantation Mystery, 1942, Whitman, 432 pgs., flip pictures, Milton Caniff-a	12.00	30.00	85.00
1446- Terry and the Pirates and the Giant's Vengeance, 1939, Whitman, 432 pgs., Caniff-a	12.00	30.00	85.00

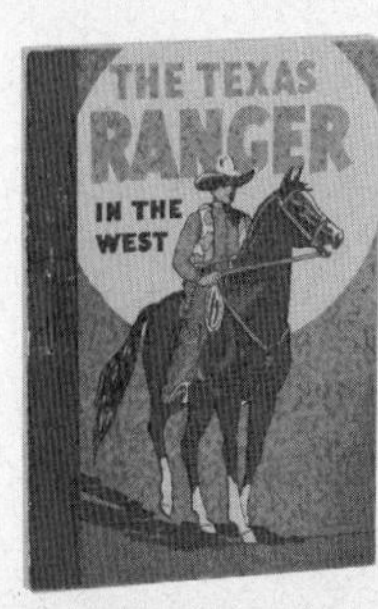

The Texas Ranger in the West © WHIT

1409 - Thumper and the Seven Dwarfs © DIS

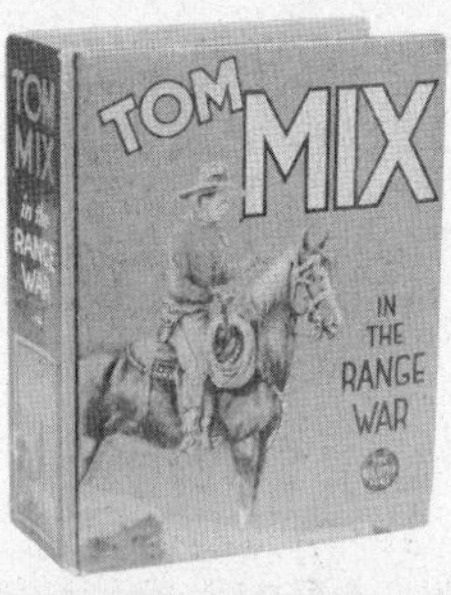

1166 - Tom Mix in the Range War © WHIT

		GD	FN	VF/NM
1499-	**Terry and the Pirates in the Mountain Stronghold**, 1941, Whitman, 432 pgs., Caniff-a	12.00	30.00	85.00
4073-	**Terry and the Pirates, The Adventures of**, 1938, Whitman, 7" x 9 1/2", 320 pgs., Big Big Book, Milton Caniff-a	39.00	98.00	275.00
4-	**Terry and the Pirates Ashore in Singapore**, 1938, Whitman, 132 pgs., 3 1/2" x 3 3/4", soft-c, Buddy Book premium	27.00	68.00	190.00
10-	**Terry and the Pirates Meet Again**, 1936, Whitman, 132 pgs., 3 1/2" x 3 1/2", soft-c, Tarzan Ice Cream cup lid premium	39.00	98.00	275.00
nn-	**Terry and the Pirates, Adventures of**, 1938, 36 pgs., 2 1/2" x 3 1/2", Penny Book, Caniff-a	10.00	25.00	60.00
nn-	**Terry and the Pirates and the Island Rescue**, 1938, Whitman, 68 pgs., 3 1/4" x 3 1/2", Pan-Am premium	21.00	52.50	150.00
nn-	**Terry and the Pirates on Their Travels**, 1938, 36 pgs., 2 1/2" x 3 1/2", Penny Book, Caniff-a	10.00	25.00	60.00
nn-	**Terry and the Pirates and the Mystery Ship**, 1938, Dell, 194 pgs., Fast-Action Story, soft-c	29.00	73.00	200.00
1492-	**Terry Lee Flight Officer U.S.A.**, 1944, Whitman, 352 pgs., Milton Caniff-a	12.00	30.00	75.00
7-	**Texas Bad Man, The** (Tom Mix), 1934, EVW, 160 pgs., (Five Star Library), movie scenes	18.00	45.00	125.00
1429-	**Texas Kid, The**, 1937, Whitman, 432 pgs.	8.00	20.00	50.00
1135-	**Texas Ranger, The**, 1936, Whitman, 432 pgs., Hal Arbo-a	8.00	20.00	50.00
nn-	**Texas Ranger, The**, 1935, Whitman, 260 pgs., Cocomalt premium, soft-c, Hal Arbo-a	12.00	30.00	75.00
nn-	**Texas Ranger and the Rustler Gang, The**, 1936, Whitman, Pan-Am giveaway	21.00	52.50	150.00
nn-	**Texas Ranger in the West, The**, 1938, Whitman, 36 pgs., 2 1/2" x 3 1/2", Penny Book	8.00	20.00	50.00
nn-	**Texas Ranger to the Rescue, The**, 1938, Whitman, 36 pgs., 2 1/2" x 3 1/2", Penny Book	8.00	20.00	50.00
12-	**Texas Ranger in Rustler Strategy, The**, 1936, Whitman, 132 pgs., 3 1/2" x 3 1/2", soft-c, Tarzan Ice Cream cup lid premium	26.00	65.00	180.00
	Tex Thorne (See Zane Grey)			
	Thimble Theatre (See Popeye)			
26-	**13 Hours By Air**, 1936, Lynn, 128 pgs., 5" x 7 1/2", photo-c, movie scenes (Paramount Pictures)	12.00	30.00	75.00
nn-	**Three Bears, The**, nd (1930s), np (Whitman), 36 pgs., 3" x 2 1/2", Penny Book	3.00	7.50	20.00
1129-	**Three Finger Joe** (Baseball), 1937, Saalfield, Robert A. Graef-a	8.00	20.00	50.00
nn-	**Three Little Pigs, The**, nd (1930s), np (Whitman), 36 pgs., 3" x 2 1/2", Penny Book	3.00	7.50	20.00
1131-	**Three Musketeers**, 1935, Whitman, 182 pgs., 5 1/4" x 6 1/4", photo-c, movie scenes	14.00	35.00	100.00
1409-	**Thumper and the Seven Dwarfs** (Disney), 1944, Whitman, All Pictures Comics	21.00	52.50	150.00
1108-	**Tiger Lady, The** (The life of Mabel Stark, animal trainer), 1935, Saalfield, photo-c, movie scenes, hard-c	10.00	25.00	60.00
1588-	**Tiger Lady, The**, 1935, Saalfield, photo-c, movie scenes, soft-c	10.00	25.00	60.00
1442-	**Tillie the Toiler and the Wild Man of Desert Island**, 1941, Whitman, 432 pgs., Russ Westover-a	11.00	27.50	70.00
1058-	**"Timid Elmer"** (Disney), 1939, Whitman, 5" x 5 1/2", 68 pgs., hard-c	11.00	27.50	70.00
1152-	**Tim McCoy in the Prescott Kid**, 1935, Whitman, 160 pgs., hard-c, photo-c, movie scenes	18.00	45.00	125.00
1193-	**Tim McCoy in the Westerner**, 1936, Whitman, 240 pgs., photo-c, movie scenes	1400	35.00	100.00
1436-	**Tim McCoy on the Tomahawk Trail**, 1937, Whitman, 432 pgs., Robert Weisman-a	12.00	30.00	75.00
1490-	**Tim McCoy and the Sandy Gulch Stampede**, 1939, Whitman, 424 pgs.	10.00	25.00	65.00
2-	**Tim McCoy in Beyond the Law**, 1934, EVW, Five Star Library, photo-c, movie scenes (Columbia Pict.) Hardcover	14.00	35.00	100.00
	(Rare) Softcover	36.00	90.00	250.00
10-	**Tim McCoy in Fighting the Redskins**, 1938, Whitman, 130 pgs., Buddy Book, soft-c	27.00	68.00	190.00
14-	**Tim McCoy in Speedwings**, 1935, EVW, Five Star Library, 160 pgs., photo-c, movie scenes (Columbia Pictures)	1900	47.50	135.00
nn-	**Tim the Builder**, nd (1930s), np (Whitman), 36 pgs., 3" x 2 1/2", Penny Book	3.00	7.50	20.00
	Tim Tyler (Also see Adventures of ...)			
1140-	**Tim Tyler's Luck Adventures in the Ivory Patrol**, 1937, Whitman, 432 pgs., by Lyman Young	10.00	25.00	65.00
1479-	**Tim Tyler's Luck and the Plot of the Exiled King**, 1939, Whitman, 432 pgs., by Lyman Young	10.00	25.00	60.00
767-	**Tiny Tim, The Adventures of**, 1935, Whitman, 384 pgs., by Stanley Link	12.00	30.00	85.00
1172-	**Tiny Tim and the Mechanical Men**, 1937, Whitman, 432 pgs., by Stanley Link	12.00	30.00	75.00
1472-	**Tiny Tim in the Big, Big World**, 1945, Whitman, 352 pgs., by Stanley Link	12.00	30.00	75.00
2006-	**(#6)-Tom and Jerry Meet Mr. Fingers**, 1967, Whitman, 39¢-c 260 pgs., hard-c, color illos.	4.00	10.00	27.00
5752-	**Tom and Jerry Meet Mr. Fingers**, 1973, Whitman, 39¢-c 260 pgs., soft-c, color illos., 5 printings	2.00	5.00	15.00
2030-	**(#30)- Tom and Jerry, The Astro-Nots**, 1969, Whitman, 256 pgs., hard-c, color illos.	3.00	7.50	20.00
5765-	**Tom and Jerry, The Astro-Nots**, 1974, Whitman, 256 pgs., soft-c, color illos.	2.00	5.00	15.00
5787-2-	**Tom and Jerry Under the Big Top**, 1980, Whitman, 79¢-c, 260 pgs., soft-c, B&W	2.00	5.00	15.00
723-	**Tom Beatty Ace of the Service**, 1934, Whitman, 256 pgs., George Taylor-a	12.00	30.00	75.00
nn-	**Tom Beatty Ace of the Service**, 1934, Whitman, 260 pgs., soft-c	12.00	30.00	75.00
1165-	**Tom Beatty Ace of the Service Scores Again**, 1937, Whitman, 432 pgs., Weisman-a	11.00	27.50	70.00
1420-	**Tom Beatty Ace of the Service and the Big Brain Gang**, 1939, Whitman, 432 pgs.	11.00	27.50	70.00
nn-	**Tom Beatty Ace Detective and the Gorgon Gang**, 1938?, Whitman, 36 pgs., 2 1/2" x 3 1/2", Penny Book	10.00	25.00	60.00
nn-	**Tom Beatty Ace of the Service and the Kidnapers**, 1938?, Whitman, 36 pgs., 2 1/2" x 3 1/2", Penny Book	10.00	25.00	60.00
1102-	**Tom Mason on Top**, 1935, Saalfield, 160 pgs., Tom Mix photo-c, from Mascot serial "The Miracle Rider," movie scenes, hard-c	18.00	45.00	125.00
1582-	**Tom Mason on Top**, 1935, Saalfield, 160 pgs., Tom Mix photo-c, movie scenes, soft-c	18.00	45.00	125.00
	Tom Mix (See Chief of the Rangers, Flaming Guns & Texas Bad Man)			
762-	**Tom Mix and Tony Jr. in "Terror Trail,"** 1934, Whitman, 160 pgs., movie scenes	18.00	45.00	125.00
1144-	**Tom Mix in the Fighting Cowboy**, 1935, Whitman, 432 pgs., Hal Arbo-a	12.00	30.00	85.00
nn-	**Tom Mix in the Fighting Cowboy**, 1935, Whitman, 436 pgs., premium-no ads, 3 color, soft-c, Hal Arbo-a	21.00	52.50	150.00
1166-	**Tom Mix in the Range War**, 1937, Whitman, 432 pgs., Hal Arbo-a	10.00	25.00	65.00
1173-	**Tom Mix Plays a Lone Hand**, 1935, Whitman, 288 pgs., hard-c, Hal Arbo-a	10.00	25.00	65.00
1183-	**Tom Mix and the Stranger from the South**, 1936, Whitman, 432 pgs.	10.00	25.00	65.00
1462-	**Tom Mix and the Hoard of Montezuma**, 1937, Whitman, H. E. Vallely-a	10.00	25.00	65.00
1482-	**Tom Mix and His Circus on the Barbary Coast**, 1940, Whitman, 432 pgs., James Gary-a	10.00	25.00	65.00
3047-	**Tom Mix and His Big Little Kit**, 1937, Whitman, 384 pgs., 4 1/2" x 6 1/2" box, includes miniature box of 4 crayons-red, yellow, blue and green	71.00	178.00	500.00
4068-	**Tom Mix and the Scourge of Paradise Valley**, 1937, Whitman, 7" x 9 1/2", 320 pgs., Big Big Book, Vallely-a	29.00	73.00	200.00
6833-	**Tom Mix in the Riding Avenger**, 1936, Dell, 244 pgs., Cartoon Story Book, hard-c	19.00	47.50	130.00
nn-	**Tom Mix Rides to the Rescue**, 1939, 36 pgs., 2 1/2" x 3", Penny Book	10.00	25.00	60.00
nn-	**Tom Mix Avenges the Dry Gulched Range King**, 1939, Dell, 196 pgs., Fast-Action Story, soft-c	20.00	50.00	140.00
nn-	**Tom Mix in the Riding Avenger**, 1936, Dell, 244 pgs., Fast-Action Story	20.00	50.00	140.00

1158 - Tracked by a G-Man
© Saalfield

1114 - Uncle Don's Strange Adventures
© WHIT

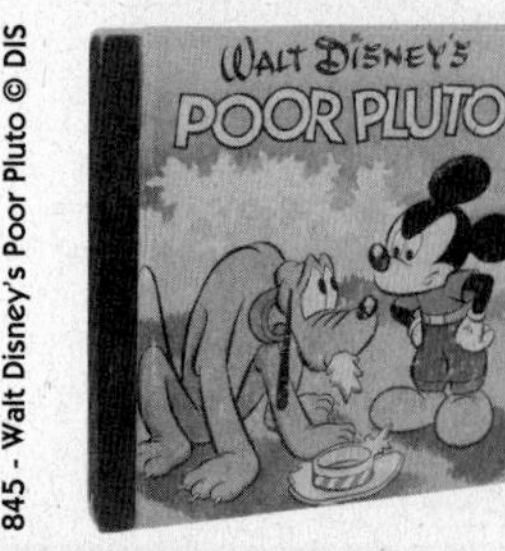

845 - Walt Disney's Poor Pluto © DIS

	GD	FN	VF/NM
nn- **Tom Mix the Trail of the Terrible 6**, 1935, Ralston Purina Co., 84 pgs., 3" x 3 1/2", premium	18.00	45.00	125.00
4- **Tom Mix and Tony in the Rider of Death Valley**, 1934, EVW, Five Star Library, 160 pgs., movie scenes (Universal Pictures), hard-c	17.00	42.50	120.00
4- **Tom Mix and Tony in the Rider of Death Valley**, 1934, EVW, Five Star Library, 160 pgs., movie scenes (Universal Pictures), soft-c (Rare)	36.00	90.00	250.00
7- **Tom Mix in the Texas Bad Man**, 1934, EVW, Five Star Library, 160 pgs., movie scenes, hard-c	18.00	45.00	125.00
7- **Tom Mix in the Texas Bad Man**, 1934, EVW, Five Star Library, 160 pgs., movie scenes; soft-c (Rare)	36.00	90.00	250.00
10- **Tom Mix in the Tepee Ranch Mystery**, 1938, Whitman, 132 pgs., Buddy Book, soft-c	21.00	52.50	150.00
1126- **Tommy of Troop Six** (Scout Book), 1937, Saalfield, hard-c	9.00	22.50	55.00
1606- **Tommy of Troop Six** (Scout Book), 1937, Saalfield, soft-c	9.00	22.50	55.00
Tom Sawyer (See Adventures of ...)			
1437- **Tom Swift and His Magnetic Silencer**, 1941, Whitman, 432 pgs., flip pictures	29.00	73.00	200.00
1485- **Tom Swift and His Giant Telescope**, 1939, Whitman, 432 pgs., James Gary-a	21.00	52.50	150.00
540- **Top-Line Comics** (In Open Box), 1935, Whitman, 164 pgs., 3 1/2" x 3 1/2", 3 books in set, all soft-c:			
Bobby Thatcher and the Samarang Emerald	16.00	40.00	110.00
Broncho Bill in Suicide Canyon	16.00	40.00	110.00
Freckles and His Friends in the North Woods	16.00	40.00	110.00
Complete set with box	50.00	125.00	350.00
541- **Top-Line Comics** (In Open Box), 1935, Whitman, 164 pgs., 3 1/2" x 3 1/2", 3 books in set; all soft-c:			
Little Joe and the City Gangsters	16.00	40.00	110.00
Smilin' Jack and His Flivver Plane	16.00	40.00	110.00
Streaky and the Football Signals	16.00	40.00	110.00
Complete set with box	50.00	125.00	350.00
542- **Top-Line Comics** (In Open Box), 1935, Whitman, 164 pgs., 3 1/2" x 3 1/2", 3 books in set; all soft-c:			
Dinglehoofer Und His Dog Adolph by Knerr	16.00	40.00	110.00
Jungle Jim by Alex Raymond	18.00	45.00	125.00
Sappo by Segar	18.00	45.00	125.00
Complete set with box	64.00	160.00	450.00
543- **Top-Line Comics** (In Open Box), 1935, Whitman, 164 pgs., 3 1/2" x 3 1/2", 3 books in set; all soft-c:			
Alexander Smart, ESQ by Winner	16.00	40.00	110.00
Bunky by Billy de Beck	16.00	40.00	110.00
Nicodemus O'Malley by Carter	16.00	40.00	110.00
Complete set with box	50.00	125.00	350.00
1158- **Tracked by a G-Man**, 1939, Saalfield, 400 pgs.	9.00	22.50	55.00
25- **Trail of the Lonesome Pine, The**, 1936, Lynn, movie scenes	12.00	30.00	85.00
nn- **Trail of the Terrible 6** (See Tom Mix ...)			
1185- **Trail to Squaw Gulch, The**, 1940, Saalfield, 400 pgs.	10.00	25.00	60.00
720- **Treasure Island**, 1933, Whitman, 362 pgs.	12.00	30.00	85.00
1141- **Treasure Island**, 1934, Whitman, 164 pgs., hard-c, 4 1/4" x 5 1/4", Jackie Cooper photo-c, movie scenes	12.00	30.00	85.00
1141- **Treasure Island**, 1934, Whitman, 164 pgs., soft-c, 4 1/4" x 5 1/4", Jackie Cooper photo-c, movie scenes	12.00	30.00	85.00
1018- **Trick and Puzzle Book**, 1939, Whitman, 100 pgs., soft-c	3.00	7.50	20.00
1100B- **Tricks Easy to Do** (Slight of hand & magic), 1938, Whitman, 36 pgs., 2 1/2" x 3 1/2", Penny Book	3.00	7.50	20.00
1100B- **Tricks You Can Do**, 1938, Whitman, 36 pgs., 2 1/2" x 3 1/2", Penny Book	3.00	7.50	20.00
5777- **Tweety and Sylvester, The Magic Voice**, 1976, Whitman, 260 pgs., soft-c, flip-it feature; 5 printings	2.00	5.00	11.00
1104- **Two-Gun Montana**, 1936, Whitman, 432 pgs., Henry E. Vallely-a	10.00	25.00	60.00
nn- **Two-Gun Montana Shoots it Out**, 1939, Whitman, 36 pgs., 2 1/2" x 3 1/2", Penny Book	10.00	25.00	60.00

	GD	FN	VF/NM
1058- **Ugly Duckling, The** (Disney), 1939, Whitman, 68 pgs., 5" x 5 1/2", hard-c	14.00	35.00	95.00
nn- **Ugly Duckling, The**, nd (1930s), np (Whitman), 36 pgs., 3" x 2 1/2", Penny Book	4.00	10.00	22.00
Unc' Billy Gets Even (See Wee Little Books)			
1114- **Uncle Don's Strange Adventures**, 1935, Whitman, 300 pgs., radio star-Uncle Don Carney	10.00	25.00	65.00
722- **Uncle Ray's Story of the United States**, 1934, Whitman, 300 pgs.	10.00	25.00	65.00
1461- **Uncle Sam's Sky Defenders**, 1941, Whitman, 432 pgs., flip pictures	10.00	25.00	60.00
1405- **Uncle Wiggily's Adventures**, 1946, Whitman, All Pictures Comics	12.00	30.00	85.00
1411- **Union Pacific**, 1939, Whitman, 240 pgs., photo-c, movie scenes	11.00	27.50	70.00
With Union Pacific letter	36.00	90.00	250.00
1189- **Up Dead Horse Canyon**, 1940, Saalfield, 400 pgs.	9.00	22.50	55.00
1455- **Vic Sands of the U.S. Flying Fortress Bomber Squadron**, 1944, Whitman, 352 pgs.	11.00	27.50	70.00
nn- **Visit to Santa Claus**, 1938?, Whitman, Pan Am premium by Snow Plane; soft-c (Rare)	29.00	73.00	200.00
1645- **Walt Disney's Andy Burnett on the Trail** (TV Series), 1958, Whitman, 280 pgs.	4.00	10.00	27.00
803- **Walt Disney's Bongo**, 1948, Whitman, hard-c, Story Hour Series	12.00	30.00	75.00
711-10-**Walt Disney's Cinderella and the Magic Wand**, 1950, Whitman, 2 1/2" x 5", based on Disney movie	10.00	25.00	65.00
845- **Walt Disney's Donald Duck and his Cat Troubles** (Disney), 1948, Whitman, 100 pgs., 5" x 5 1/2", hard-c	12.00	30.00	75.00
845- **Walt Disney's Donald Duck and the Boys**, 1948, Whitman, 100 pgs., 5" x 5 1/2", hard-c, Barks-a	21.00	52.50	150.00
2952- **Walt Disney's Donald Duck in the Great Kite Maker**, 1949, Whitman, 24 pgs., 3 1/4" x 4", Tiny Tales, full color (5 cents)	10.00	25.00	60.00
804- **Walt Disney's Mickey and the Beanstalk**, 1948, Whitman, hard-c, Story Hour Series	12.00	30.00	75.00
845- **Walt Disney's Mickey Mouse and the Boy Thursday**, 194 pgs., Whitman, 5" x 5 1/2", 100 pgs.	12.00	30.00	75.00
845- **Walt Disney's Mickey Mouse the Miracle Maker**, 1948, Whitman, 5" x 5 1/2", 100 pgs.	12.00	30.00	75.00
2952- **Walt Disney's Mickey Mouse and the Night Prowlers**, Whitman, 1949, 24 pgs., 3 1/4" x 4", Tiny Tales, full color (5 ¢)	10.00	25.00	60.00
5770- **Walt Disney's Mickey Mouse - Mystery at Disneyland**, Whitman, 1975, 260 pgs., four printings	2.00	5.00	13.00
5781-2- **Walt Disney's Mickey Mouse - Mystery at Dead Man's Cove**, Whitman, 1980, 260 pgs., two printings	2.00	5.00	11.00
845- **Walt Disney's Minnie Mouse and the Antique Chair**, 1948, Whitman, 5" x 5 1/2", 100 pgs.	12.00	30.00	75.00
1435- **Walt Disney's Pinocchio and Jiminy Cricket**, 1940, Whitman, 432 pgs.	25.00	62.50	175.00
nn- **Walt Disney's Pinocchio and Jiminy Cricket**, Fast Action Story, 1940, Dell, 432 pgs.	36.00	90.00	250.00
845- **Walt Disney's Poor Pluto**, 1948, Whitman, 5" x 5 1/2", 100 pgs., hard-c	12.00	30.00	75.00
1467- **Walt Disney's Pluto the Pup** (Disney), 1938, Whitman, 432 pgs., Gottfredson-a	16.00	40.00	110.00
1066- **Walt Disney's Story of Clarabelle Cow** (Disney), 1938, Whitman, 100 pgs.	12.00	30.00	75.00
66- **Walt Disney's Story of Dippy the Goof** (Disney), 1938, Whitman, 100 pgs.	12.00	30.00	75.00
1066- **Walt Disney's Story of Donald Duck** (Disney), 1938, Whitman, 100 pgs., hard-c, Taliaferro-a	12.00	30.00	75.00
1066- **Walt Disney's Story of Mickey Mouse** (Disney), 1938, Whitman, 100 pgs., hard-c, Gottfredson-a, Donald Duck app.	12.00	30.00	75.00
1066- **Walt Disney's Story of Minnie Mouse** (Disney), 1938, Whitman, 100 pgs., hard-c	12.00	30.00	75.00
1066- **Walt Disney's Story of Pluto the Pup**, (Disney), 1938, Whitman, 100 pgs., hard-c	12.00	30.00	75.00
2952- **Walter Lantz Presents Andy Panda's Rescue**, 1949, Whitman, Tiny Tales, full color (5 cents) (1030-5 on back-c)	10.00	25.00	60.00

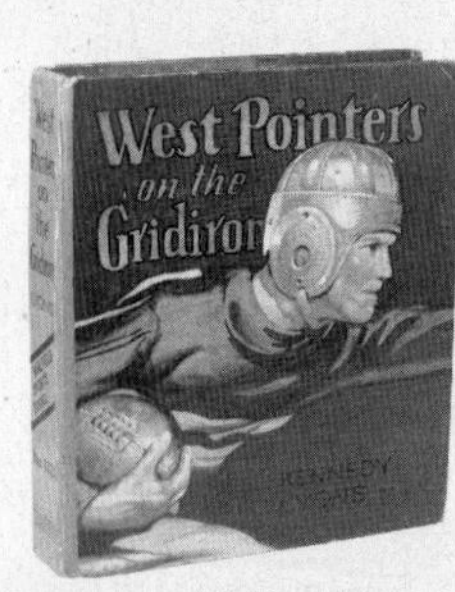

1121 - West Pointers on the Gridiron © Saalfield

2028 - Woody Woodpecker - The Sinister Signal © Walter Lantz

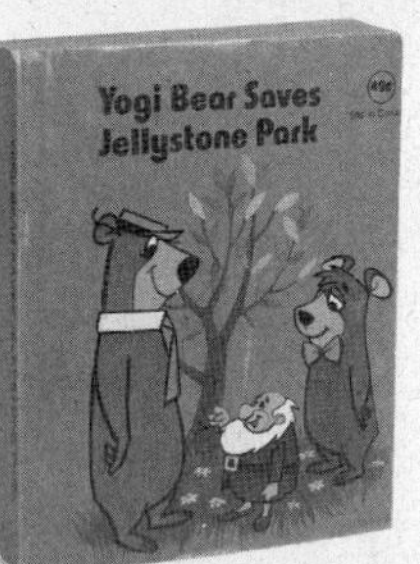

Yogi Bear Saves Jellystone Park © H-B

GD FN VF/NM

751- Wash Tubbs in Pandemonia, 1934, Whitman, 320 pgs., Roy Crane-a 12.00 30.00 75.00

nn- Wash Tubbs in Pandemonia, 1934, Whitman, 52 pgs., 4" x 5 1/2", premium-no ads, soft-c, Roy Crane-a 20.00 50.00 140.00

1455- Wash Tubbs and Captain Easy Hunting For Whales, 1938, Whitman, 432 pgs., Roy Crane-a 12.00 30.00 75.00

6- Wash Tubbs in Foreign Travel, 1934, Whitman, soft-c, 3 1/2" x 3 1/2", Tarzan Ice Cream cup premium 29.00 73.00 200.00

513- Wee Little Books (In Open Box), 1934, Whitman, 44 pgs., small size, 6 books in set (children's classics)
(Both Red box and Green box editions exist)
Child's Garden of Verses 5.00 12.50 30.00
The Happy Prince (The Story of) 5.00 12.50 30.00
Joan of Arc (The Story of) 5.00 12.50 30.00
Peter Pan (The Story of) 5.00 12.50 30.00
Pied Piper Of Hamlin 5.00 12.50 30.00
Robin Hood (A Story of...) 5.00 12.50 30.00
Complete set with box 31.00 78.00 220.00

514- Wee Little Books (In Open Box), 1934, Whitman, 44 pgs., small size, 6 books in set
Jack And Jill 5.00 12.50 30.00
Little Bo-Peep 5.00 12.50 30.00
Little Tommy Tucker 5.00 12.50 30.00
Mother Goose 5.00 12.50 30.00
Old King Cole 5.00 12.50 30.00
Simple Simon 5.00 12.50 30.00
Complete set with box 33.00 83.00 230.00

518- Wee Little Books (In Open Box), 1933, Whitman, 44 pgs., small size, 6 books in set, written by Thornton Burgess
Betty Bear's Lesson-1930 5.00 12.50 30.00
Jimmy Skunk's Justice-1933 5.00 12.50 30.00
Little Joe Otter's Slide-1929 5.00 12.50 30.00
Peter Rabbit's Carrots-1933 5.00 12.50 30.00
Unc' Billy Gets Even-1930 5.00 12.50 30.00
Whitefoot's Secret-1933 5.00 12.50 30.00
Complete set with box 33.00 83.00 230.00

519- Wee Little Books (In Open Box) (Bible Stories), 1934, Whitman, 44 pgs., small size, 6 books in set, Helen Janes-a
The Story of David 5.00 12.50 30.00
The Story of Gideon 5.00 12.50 30.00
The Story of Daniel 5.00 12.50 30.00
The Story of Joseph 5.00 12.50 30.00
The Story of Ruth and Naomi 5.00 12.50 30.00
The Story of Moses 5.00 12.50 30.00
Complete set with box 33.00 83.00 230.00

1471- Wells Fargo, 1938, Whitman, 240 pgs., photo-c, movie scenes 12.00 30.00 80.00

L18- Western Frontier, 1935, Lynn, 192 pgs., starring Ken Maynard, movie scenes 14.00 35.00 100.00

1121- West Pointers on the Gridiron, 1936, Saalfield, 148 pgs., hard-c, sports book 7.00 17.50 45.00

1601- West Pointers on the Gridiron, 1936, Saalfield, 148 pgs., soft-c, sports book 7.00 17.50 45.00

1124- West Point Five, The, 1937, Saalfield, 4 3/4" x 5 1/4", sports book, hard-c 7.00 17.50 45.00

1604- West Point Five, The, 1937, Saalfield, 4 1/4" x 5 1/4", sports book, soft-c 7.00 17.50 45.00

1164- West Point of the Air, 1935, Whitman, 160 pgs., photo-c, movie scenes 12.00 30.00 75.00

18- Westward Ho!, 1935, EVW, 160 pgs., movie scenes, starring John Wayne (Scarce) 57.00 143.00 400.00

1109- We Three, 1935, Saalfield, 160 pgs., photo-c, movie scenes, by John Barrymore, hard-c 10.00 25.00 60.00

1589- We Three, 1935, Saalfield, 160 pgs., photo-c, movie scenes, by John Barrymore, soft-c 10.00 25.00 60.00

Whitefoot's Secret (See Wee Little Books)

nn- Who's Afraid of the Big Bad Wolf, "Three Little Pigs" (Disney), 1933, McKay, 36 pgs., 6" x 8 1/2", stiff-c, Disney studio-a 27.00 68.00 190.00

nn- Wild West Adventures of Buffalo Bill, 1935, Whitman, 260 pgs., Cocomalt premium, soft-c, Hal Arbo-a 12.00 30.00 80.00

1096- Will Rogers, The Story of, 1935, Saalfield, photo-hard-c 8.00 20.00 50.00

1576- Will Rogers, The Story of, 1935, Saalfield, photo-soft-c 8.00 20.00 50.00

1458- Wimpy the Hamburger Eater, 1938, Whitman, 432 pgs., E.C. Segar-a 14.00 35.00 100.00

1433- Windy Wayne and His Flying Wing, 1942, Whitman, 432 pgs., flip pictures 10.00 25.00 60.00

1131- Winged Four, The, 1937, Saalfield, sports book, hard-c 10.00 25.00 60.00

1407- Wings of the U.S.A., 1940, Whitman, 432 pgs., Thomas Hickey-a 10.00 25.00 60.00

nn- Winning of the Old Northwest, The, 1934, World Syndicate, High Lights of History Series, full color-c 10.00 25.00 60.00

nn- Winning of the Old Northwest, The, 1934, World Syndicate, High Lights of History Series; red & silver-c 10.00 25.00 60.00

1122- Winning Point, The, 1936, Saalfield, (Football), hard-c 7.00 17.50 40.00

1602- Winning Point, The, 1936, Saalfield, soft-c 7.00 17.50 40.00

nn- Wizard of Oz Waddle Book, 1934, BRP, 20 pgs., 7 1/2" x 10", forerunner of the Blue Ribbon Pop-Up books; with 6 removable articulated cardboard characters. Book only 54.00 135.00 375.00
Dust jacket only 61.00 153.00 490.00
Near Mint Complete - $12,500

710-10-Woody Woodpecker Big Game Hunter, 1950, Whitman, by Walter Lantz 9.00 22.50 55.00

2010-(#10)-Woody Woodpecker-The Meteor Menace, 1967, Whitman, 260 pgs., 39¢-c, hard-c, color illos. 4.00 10.00 27.00

5753- Woody Woodpecker-The Meteor Menace, 1973, Whitman, 260 pgs., no price, soft-c, color illos. 1.00 2.50 6.00

2028- Woody Woodpecker-The Sinister Signal, 1969, Whitman 4.00 10.00 22.00

5763- Woody Woodpecker-The Sinister Signal, 1974, Whitman, 1st printing-no price; 2nd printing-39¢-c 1.00 2.50 6.00

23- World of Monsters, The, 1935, EVW, Five Star Library, movie scenes 12.00 30.00 85.00

779- World War in Photographs, The, 1934, Whitman, photo-c, photo illus. 9.00 22.50 55.00

Wyatt Earp (See Hugh O'Brian ...)

nn- Xena - Warrior Princess, 1998, Chronicle Books, 310 pgs., based on TV series, 1-color (purple) illos 1.00 2.50 9.00

nn- Yogi Bear Goes Country & Western, 1977, Modern Promotions, 244 pgs., 49 cents, soft-c, flip pictures 2.00 5.00 13.00

nn- Yogi Bear Saves Jellystone Park, 1977, Modern Promotions, 244 pgs., 49 cents, soft-c, flip pictures 2.00 5.00 13.00

nn- Zane Grey's Cowboys of the West, 1935, Whitman, 148 pgs., 3 3/4" x 4", Tarzan Ice Cream Cup premium, soft-c, Arbo-a 29.00 73.00 200.00

Zane Grey's King of the Royal Mounted (See Men of the Mounted)

1010- Zane Grey's King of the Royal Mounted in Arctic Law, 1937, Whitman, 7 1/4" x 5 1/2", 64 pgs., Nickel Book 12.00 30.00 75.00

1103- Zane Grey's King of the Royal Mounted, 1936, Whitman, 432 pgs. 10.00 25.00 65.00

nn- Zane Grey's King of the Royal Mounted, 1935, Whitman, 260 pgs., Cocomalt premium, soft-c 12.00 30.00 85.00

1179- Zane Grey's King of the Royal Mounted and the Northern Treasure, 1937, Whitman, 432 pgs. 10.00 25.00 60.00

1405- Zane Grey's King of the Royal Mounted the Long Arm of the Law, 1942, Whitman, All Pictures Comics 10.00 25.00 60.00

1452- Zane Grey's King of the Royal Mounted Gets His Man, 1938, Whitman, 432 pgs. 10.00 25.00 60.00

1486- Zane Grey's King of the Royal Mounted and the Great Jewel Mystery, 1939, Whitman, 432 pgs. 10.00 25.00 60.00

5- Zane Grey's King of the Royal Mounted in the Far North, 1938, Whitman, 132 pgs., Buddy Book, soft-c (Rare) 36.00 90.00 250.00

nn- Zane Grey's King of the Royal Mounted in Law of the North, 1939, Whitman, 36 pgs., 2 1/2" x 3 1/2", Penny Book 7.00 17.50 45.00

nn- Zane Grey's King of the Royal Mounted Policing the Frozen North, 1938, Dell, 196 pgs., Fast-Action Story, soft-c 18.00 45.00 125.00

1440- Zane Grey's Tex Thorne Comes Out of the West, 1937, Whitman, 432 pgs. 10.00 25.00 60.00

1465- Zip Saunders King of the Speedway, 1939, 432 pgs., Weisman-a 10.00 25.00 60.00

PROMOTIONAL COMICS

THE MARKETING OF A MEDIUM

by Dr. Arnold T. Blumberg, DCD

with new material and additional research by Sol M. Davidson, PhD, and Robert L. Beerbohm

Everyone wants something for free. It's in our nature to look for the quick fix, the good deal, the complimentary gift. We long to hit the lottery and quit our job, to win the trip around the world, or find that pot of gold at the end of the proverbial rainbow. Collectors in particular are certainly built to appreciate the notion of the "free gift," since it not only means a new item to collect and enjoy, but no risk or obligation in order to acquire it.

Ah, but there's the rub. Because things are not always what they seem, and "free gifts" usually come with a price. As the saying goes, "there's no such thing as a free lunch," so if it seems too good to be true, it probably is. This is the case even in the world of comics, where premiums and giveaways have a familiar agenda hidden behind the bright colors and fanciful stories. But where did it all begin?

Some of the earliest characters that were used as successful tools in promotional comics were Palmer Cox's creation "The Brownies." The illustration shown here showcases them drinking and endorsing Seal Brand Coffee.

EXTRA EXTRA

As we learn more about the early history of the comic book industry through continual investigation and the publishing of articles like those regularly featured in this book, we gain a much greater understanding of the financial and creative forces at work in shaping the medium, but perhaps one of the most intriguing and least recognized factors that influenced the dawn of comics is the concept of the premium or giveaway. (Note: Some of the historical information referenced in this article is derived from material also presented in Robert L. Beerbohm's introductory articles to the Platinum Age and Modern Age sections.)

The birth of the comic book as we know it today is intimately connected with the development of the comic strip in American newspapers and their use as an advertising and marketing tool for staple products such as bread, milk, and cereal. From the very beginning, comic characters have played several roles in pop culture, entertaining the youth of the country while also (sometimes none too subtly) acting as hucksters for whatever corporation foots the bill. From important staples to frivolous material produced simply to make a buck, these products have utilized the comics medium to sell, sell, sell. And what better way to hook a prospective customer than to give them "something for nothing?"

Starting in the 1850s, comics were being used in free almanacs such as **Elton's**, **Hostetter's** and **Wright's** to lure readers for the little booklets to sell patent medicine, farm products, tobacco, shoe polish, etc. Most of these are exceedingly rare today, hence it is difficult to compile an accurate history. More mention of these early precursors can be found in the Victorian Comics Era essay following this one. But although comic characters themselves were already being aggressively merchandised all around the world by the mid-1890s--as with, for example, Palmer Cox's **The Brownies**--the real starting point for the success of comics as a giveaway marketing mechanism can be traced to the introduction of **The Yellow Kid**, Richard Outcault's now legendary newspaper strip.

Newspaper publishers had already recognized that comic strips could boost circulation as well as please sponsors and advertisers by drawing more eyes to the page, so Sunday "supplements" were introduced to entice fans. Outcault's creation cemented the theory with proof of comic characters' marketing and merchandising power.

Soon after, Outcault (who had most likely been inspired by Cox's merchandising success with **The Brownies** in the first place) caught lightning in a bottle once more with **Buster Brown**, who has the distinction of being America's first nationally licensed comic strip character. Soon, comic strips proliferated throughout the nation's newspapers as tycoons like Hearst and Pulitzer recognized the drawing power of the new medium and fought circulation wars to capture the pennies of the nouveau readership. They paid exorbitant salaries to comic strip artists such as Rudolph Dirks (**Katzenjammer Kids**), and used the funnies as newspaper supplements and as premiums to attract readers. Corporations soon had the chance to license recognizable personas as their own personal pitchmen (or women or animals...). Comic character merchandise wasn't far behind, resulting in a boom of future collectibles now catalogued in volumes like **Hake's Price Guide to Character Toys**.

This unused cover was designed as the second cover for "Motion Picture Funnies Weekly." While the concept for this promotional comic title never caught on, the inaugural issue did feature the origin and first printed appearance of the Sub-Mariner.

TWO BIRTHS FOR THE PRICE OF ONE

Comic books themselves were at the heart of this movement, and giveaway and premium collections of comic strips not only appealed to children and adults alike, but provided the impetus for the birth of the modern comic book format itself. It could be said that without the concept of the giveaway comic or the marketing push behind it, there would be no comic book industry as we have it today. Well-known now is the story of how in spring 1933 Harry Wildenberg of Eastern Color Printing Company convinced Proctor & Gamble to sponsor the first modern comic book, **Funnies on Parade**, as a premium. Its success led to the first continuing comic book, **Famous Funnies**, and the rest, as they say, is history.

In 1935, while working on the printing presses of Eastern Color developing how modern comic books get printed, Juliun J. Proskauer came up with an idea for printing "Comic-Books-For-Industry." In July 1936 he made his first sale through his newly formed William C. Popper & Co. to David M. Davies, then advertising manager for Seagram's Distillers Corp. for three million copies of **Seagram's Merrymakers** in time for the 1936-37 Christmas season. "Thus was a new industry born," wrote **Printing News** in August 1945.

Even a casual perusal of the listings in this section of the Guide will dazzle the reader with the endless variety of purposes that this medium has served. Yes, promos have been used to hawk products from athletic equipment to zithers and zip codes, but comics are too versatile an art form to be confined to a few uses. They've swayed elections in cities (**The O'Dwyer Story**, 1949), in states (**Giant for a Day**: Jacob Javits, 1946) and nationwide (**The Story of Harry Truman**, 1948); solicited for charities (**Donald Duck and the Red Feather**, 1948); addressed health issues (**Blondie**, 1949, mental hygiene); discouraged kids from smoking (**Captain America Meets the Asthma Monster**, 1987); coached youngsters in sports skills (**Circling the Bases**, 1947, A.G. Spaulding); explained scientific complexities (**Adventures in Science**, 1946-61, GE); pleaded for social justice (**Consumer Comics**, 1975); espoused religious causes (**Oral Roberts' True Stories**, 1950s); protected the environment (**Our Spaceship Earth**, 1947); encouraged tourism (**Wyoming, The Cowboy State**, 1954); conveyed a sense of history (**Louisiana Purchase**, 1953); taught about computers (**Superman Radio Shack Giveaway**, 1980); trained employees (**Dial Finance Dialogues**, 1961-70) and executives (**Beneficial Finance System, Managing New Employees**, 1950s); cautioned safety (**Willy Wing Flap**, 1944(?)); announced corporate annual results (**Motorola Annual Report**, 1952); defended free enterprise (**Steve Merritt**, 1949); hammered communism (**How Stalin Hopes to Destroy America**, 1951); fought discrimination (**Mammy Yokum & the Great Dogpatch Mystery**, 1956, B'nai Brith); aided young workers in job-hunting (**The Job Scene**, 1969); battled the scourge of sickle cell anemia (**Where's Herbie**, 1972, U.S. H.E.W.); inspired the overcoming of adversity (**Al Capp by Li'l Abner**, 1946); fostered reading (**Linus Gets a Library Card**, 1960); recruited for the armed forces (**Li'l Abner Joins the Navy**, 1950); beguiled readers into learning languages (**Blondie**, 1949, Philadelphia pub-

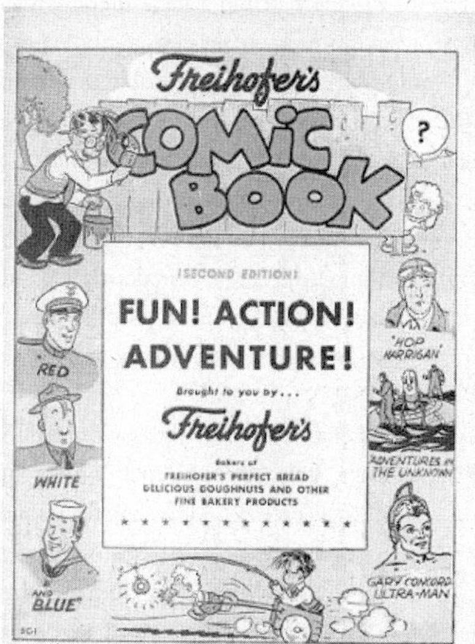

Every market and product has been on the promotional comic book bandwagon. Freihofer's Baking Company distributed a comic in the 1940s that featured reprinted pages from "All-American Comics."

lic schools); and even instructed in such delicate matters as birth control (**Escape from Fear**, 1950 (revised 1959, etc.), for Planned Parenthood).

READ ALL ABOUT IT

The impact of this new approach to advertising was not lost on the business world. Contrary to modern belief, comic books were hardly discounted by the adults of the time...at least not those who had the marketing savvy to recognize an opportunity - or a threat - when they saw one. In the April 1933 issue of **Fortune** magazine, an article titled "The Funny Papers" trumpeted the arrival of comics as a force to be reckoned with in the world of advertising and business, and what's more, a force to fear as well. At first providing a brief survey of the newspaper comic strip business (which for many of the magazine's readers must have seemed a foreign topic for serious discussion), the article goes on to examine the incredible financial draw of comics and their characters:

"Between 70 and 75 per cent {sic} of the readers of any newspaper follow its comic sections regularly...Even the advertiser has succumbed to the comic, and in 1932 spent well over $1,000,000 for comic-paper space."

"**Comic Weekly** is the comic section of seventeen Hearst Sunday papers...Advertisers who market their wares through balloon-speaking manikins {sic} may enjoy the proximity of Jiggs, Maggie, Barney Google, and other funny Hearst headliners."

Although the article continues to cast the notion of relying on comic strip material to sell product in a negative light, actually suggesting that advertisers who utilize comics are violating unspoken rules of "advertising decorum" and bringing themselves "down to the level" of comics (and since when have advertisers been stalwart preservers of good taste and high moral standards), there is no doubt that they are viewing comics in a new light. The comic characters have arrived by 1933...and they're ready to help sell your merchandise too.

Fortune wasn't the only one to take notice as World War II came and went. In 1948, Louis P. Birk, the head of Brevity, Inc., an important promotional comics publisher said, "Comics are serious business." In an article in **Printers' Ink** magazine, he estimated that more than 80 different "comic booklets" had been produced and more than 45,000,000 million copies distributed in the five years before 1948. But of course, comics were serious business long before businessman/historian Birk noted the fact for posterity.

THE MARCH OF WAR AND BEYOND

Through the relentless currents of time, comic strips, books, and the characters that starred in them became more and more an intrinsic part of American culture. During the turmoil of the Great Depression and World War II, comic characters in print and celluloid form entertained while informing and selling at the same time, and premium and giveaway comics came well and truly into their own, pushing everything from loaves of bread to war bonds.

In the 1950s and '60s, there was a shift in focus as the power of giveaway and premium comics was applied to more altruistic endeavors than simply selling something. Comic book format pamphlets, fully illustrated and often inventively written, taught children about banking, money, the dangers of poison and other household products, and even chronicled moments in American history. The comic book as giveaway was now not only a mar-

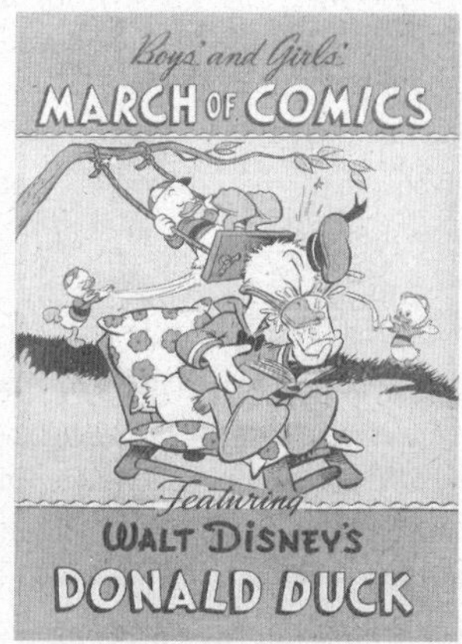

The promotional title "March of Comics" was a prolific comic that ran for 36 years and 488 issues featuring a variety of subjects and characters. (#20 shown)

keting gimmick--it was a tool for educating as well.

The 1970s and '80s saw another boom in premium and giveaway comics. Every product imaginable seemed to have a licensing deal with a comic book character, usually one of the prominent flag bearers of the Big Two, Marvel or DC. Spider-Man fought bravely against the Beetle for the benefit of All Detergent; Captain America allied himself with the Campbell Kids; and Superman helped a class of computer students beat a disaster-conjuring foe at his own game with the help of Radio Shack Tandy computers.

Newspapers rediscovered the power of comics, not just with enlarged strip supplements but with actual comic books. Spider-Man, the Hulk, and others turned up as giveaway comic extras in various American newspapers (including Chicago and Dallas publications), while a whole series of public information comics like those produced decades earlier used superheroes to caution children about the dangers of smoking, drugs, and child abuse.

Comics also turned up in a plethora of other toy products as the 1980s introduced kids to the joy of electronic games and action figures. Supplementary comics provided "free" with action figure and video game packages told the backstory about the product, adding depth to the play experience while providing an extra incentive to buy. Comics became an intrinsic part of the Atari line of video cartridges, for example, eventually spawning its own full-blown newsstand series as well.

As the twentieth century gave way to the twenty-first, giveaway comics were still being produced for inclusion in action figure and video game packages, as well as in conjunction with countless consumer items and corporations. It seems that the medium still has a lot to offer for all those companies desperate to make the most of their market share.

A COMIC BY ANY OTHER NAME

One of the earliest names for promotional comics was "special purpose comics." In their pursuit of superheroes, collectors have allowed promotional comics to lie fallow - under-appreciated and uncollected. Without a legitimate name, these products were given sundry other appellations - industrial comics, promos, giveaways, premiums, promics - each accurate but only for a small segment of the unorganized but lusty and lively medium. Perhaps no one name can cover all the variations and purposes of this branch of comic art, but for practical reasons if we accept the general premise that these comics were created to promote an idea, a product or a person, then "Promotional Comics" is probably as convenient a catch-all title as we can come up with.

We used the phrase "for practical reasons" because the word "practical" goes to the heart of promotional comics more than it does for any other comics product. What greater testimony is there to the medium's impact on American culture than to note their use by hard-headed, profit-minded business people and corporations? They invest their money and they expect results.

Today, premium comics continue to thrive and are still utilized as a valuable marketing and promotional tool. "Free" comics are still packaged with action figures and video games, and offered as mail-away premiums from a variety of product manufacturers. The comic industry itself has expanded its use of giveaway comics to self-promote as well, with "ashcan" and other giveaway editions turning up at conventions and comic shops to advertise upcoming series and special events. Many of these function as old-fashioned premiums, with a coupon or other response required from the reader to receive the comic.

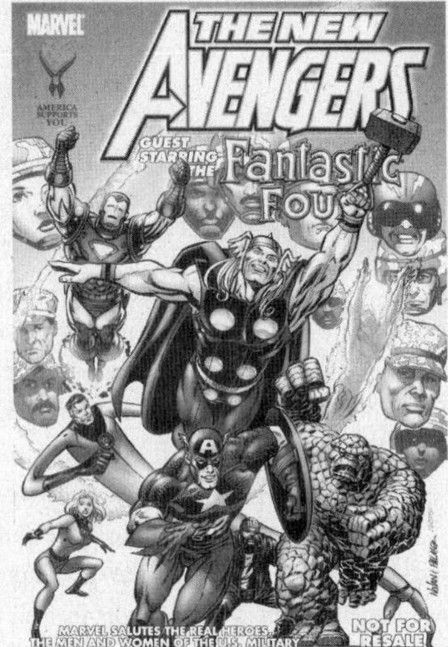

Today, promotional comics continue to be used as a marketing tool to reach both children and adults alike. This 2005 comic was produced by Marvel Comics as a salute to the men and women of the armed forces.

As for the supplements and giveaways printed all those years ago, they have spawned a collectible fervor all their own, thanks to their atypical distribution and frequent rarity. For that and the desire to delve deeper into comics history, we hope that by focusing more directly on this genre, we can enhance our understanding of this vital component in the development and history of the modern comic book.

Whether you're a collector or not, we're all motivated by that desire to get something for nothing. For as long as consumers are enticed by the notion of the "free gift," promotional comics will remain a vital marketing component in many business models, but they will also continue to fight the stigma that has long been associated with the industry as a whole. "Respectable" sources like **Fortune** may have taken notice of the power of comic-related advertising 71 years ago, but after all this time comics still fight an uphill battle to establish some measure of dignity for the medium. Perhaps the higher visibility of promotional comics will eventually prove to be a deciding factor in that intellectual war.

See ya in the funny papers.

Adventures @ eBay #1 © eBay

Adventures of the Big Boy #266 © Shoney's

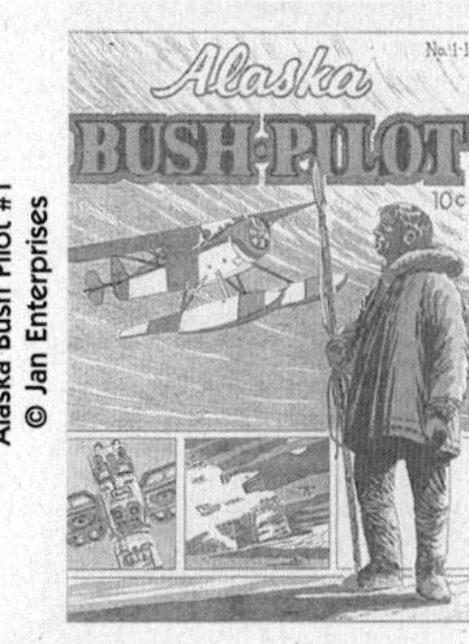

Alaska Bush Pilot #1 © Jan Enterprises

GD 2.0 | VG 4.0 | FN 6.0 | VF 8.0 | VF/NM 9.0 | NM- 9.2

ACTION COMICS
DC Comics: 1947 - 1998 (Giveaway)
1 (1976) paper cover w/10¢ price, 16 pgs. in color; reprints complete Superman story from #1 ('38) 3 6 9 20 32 42
1 (1976) Safeguard Giveaway; paper cover w/"free", 16 pgs. in color; reprints complete Superman story from #1 ('38) 3 6 9 20 32 42
1 (1983) paper cover w/10¢ price, 16 pgs. in color; reprints complete Superman story from #1 ('38) 3 6 9 14 20 25
1 (1987 Nestle Quik; 1988, 50¢) 1 2 3 5 7 9
1 (1992)-Came w/Reign of Superman packs 4.00
1 (1998 U.S. Postal Service, $7.95) Reprints entire issue; extra outer half-cover contains First Day Issuance of 32¢ Superman stamp with Sept. 10, 1998 Cleveland, OH postmark 1 2 3 5 6 8
Theater (1947, 32 pgs., 5" x 7", nn)-Vigilante story based on Columbia Vigilante serial; no Superman-c or story 65 130 195 416 708 1000

ACTION ZONE
CBS Television: 1994 (Promotes CBS Saturday morning cartoons)
1-WildC.A.T.s, T.M.N.Turtles, Skeleton Warriors stories; Jim Lee-c 4.00

ADVENTURE COMICS
IGA: No date (early 1940s) (Paper-c, 32 pgs.)
Two diff. issues; Super-Mystery-r from 1941 20 40 60 114 182 250

ADVENTURE IN DISNEYLAND
Walt Disney Productions (Dist. by Richfield Oil): May, 1955 (Giveaway, soft-c., 16 pgs)
nn 11 22 33 60 83 105

ADVENTURES @ EBAY
eBay: 2000 (6 3/4" x 4 1/2", 16 pgs.)
1-Judd Winick-a/Rucka & Van Meter-s; intro to eBay comic buying 2.50

ADVENTURES IN JET POWER
General Electric: 1950
nn 7 14 21 35 43 50

ADVENTURES OF BIG BOY (Also titled Adventures of the Big Boy)
Timely Comics/Webs Adv. Corp./Illus. Features: 1956 - Present (Giveaway) (East & West editions of early issues)
1-Everett-c/a 110 220 330 704 1202 1700
2-Everett-c/a 39 78 117 231 378 525
3-5: 4-Robot-c 20 40 60 114 182 250
6-10: 6-Sci/fic issue 9 18 27 52 126 190
11-20: 11,13-DeCarlo-a 7 14 21 44 72 100
21-30 4 8 12 25 40 55
31-50 3 6 9 16 24 32
51-100 2 4 6 9 13 16
101-150 2 4 6 8 10 12
151-240 1 2 3 5 7 9
241-265,267-269,271-300: 6.00
266-Superman x-over 3 6 9 17 26 35
270-TV's Buck Rogers-c/s 3 6 9 14 20 25
301-400 4.00
401-500 3.00
1-(2nd series - '76-'84,Paragon Prod.) (...Shoney's Big Boy) 1 3 4 6 8 10
2-20 5.00
21-50 3.00
Summer, 1959 issue, large size 6 12 18 42 79 115

ADVENTURES OF G. I. JOE
1969 (3-1/4x7") (20 & 16 pgs.)
First Series: 1-Danger of the Depths. 2-Perilous Rescue. 3-Secret Mission to Spy Island. 4-Mysterious Explosion. 5-Fantastic Free Fall. 6-Eight Ropes of Danger. 7-Mouth of Doom. 8-Hidden Missile Discovery. 9-Space Walk Mystery. 10-Fight for Survival. 11-The Shark's Surprise.
Second Series: 2-Flying Space Adventure. 4-White Tiger Hunt. 7-Capture of the Pygmy Gorilla. 12-Secret of the Mummy's Tomb.
Third Series: Reprinted surviving titles of First Series. Fourth Series: 13-Adventure Team Headquarters. 14-Search For the Stolen Idol.
each.... 3 6 9 17 26 35

ADVENTURES OF JELL-O MAN AND WOBBLY, THE
Welsh Publishing Group: 1991 ($1.25)
1 4.00

ADVENTURES OF KOOL-AID MAN
Marvel Comics: 1983 - No. 3, 1985 (Mail order giveaway)
Archie Comics: No. 4, 1987 - No. 8, 1989
1-8: 4-8-Dan DeCarlo-a/c 1 2 3 5 7 9

ADVENTURES OF MARGARET O'BRIEN, THE
Bambury Fashions (Clothes): 1947 (20 pgs. in color, slick-c, regular size) (Premium)
In "The Big City" movie adaptation (scarce) 20 40 60 120 195 270

ADVENTURES OF QUIK BUNNY
Nestle's Quik: 1984 (Giveaway, 32 pgs.)
nn-Spider-Man app. 2 4 6 9 13 16

ADVENTURES OF STUBBY, SANTA'S SMALLEST REINDEER, THE
W. T. Grant Co.: nd (early 1940s) (Giveaway, 12 pgs.)
nn 7 14 21 37 46 55

ADVENTURES OF VOTEMAN, THE
Foundation For Citizen Education Inc.: 1968
nn 4 8 12 27 44 60

ADVENTURES WITH SANTA CLAUS
Promotional Publ. Co. (Murphy's Store): No date (early 50's) (9-3/4x 6-3/4", 24 pgs., giveaway, paper-c)
nn-Contains 8 pgs. ads 6 12 18 29 36 42
16 pg. version 6 12 18 33 41 48

AIR POWER (CBS TV & the U.S. Air Force Presents)
Prudential Insurance Co.: 1956 (5-1/4x7-1/4", 32 pgs., giveaway, soft-c)
nn-Toth-a? Based on 'You Are There' TV program by Walter Cronkite 10 20 30 56 76 95

ALASKA BUSH PILOT
Jan Enterprises: 1959 (Paper cover)
1-Promotes Bush Pilot Club (Value will be based on sale)
NOTE: *A CGC certified 9.9 Mint sold for $632.50 in 2005.*

ALICE IN BLUNDERLAND
Industrial Services: 1952 (Paper cover, 16 pgs. in color)
nn-Facts about government waste and inefficiency 14 28 42 82 121 160

ALICE IN WONDERLAND
Western Printing Company/Whitman Publ. Co.: 1965; 1969; 1982
Meets Santa Claus(1950s), nd, 16 pgs. 6 12 18 28 34 40
Rexall Giveaway(1965, 16 pgs., 5x7-1/4) Western Printing (TV, Hanna-Barbera) 3 6 9 16 23 30
Wonder Bakery Giveaway(1969, 16 pgs, color, nn, nd) (Continental Baking Company) 3 6 9 15 22 28

ALICE IN WONDERLAND MEETS SANTA
No publisher: nd (6-5/8x9-11/16", 16 pgs., giveaway, paper-c)
nn 9 18 27 50 65 80

ALL ABOARD, MR. LINCOLN
Assoc. of American Railroads: Jan, 1959 (16 pgs.)
nn-Abraham Lincoln and the Railroads 6 12 18 28 34 40

ALL NEW COMICS
Harvey Comics: Oct, 1993 (Giveaway, no cover price, 16 pgs.)(Hanna-Barbera)
1-Flintstones, Scooby Doo, Jetsons, Yogi Bear & Wacky Races previews for upcoming Harvey's new Hanna-Barbera line-up 1 2 3 4 5 7
NOTE: *Material previewed in Harvey giveaway was eventually published by Archie.*

AMAZING SPIDER-MAN, THE
Marvel Comics Group
Acme & Dingo Children's Boots (1980)-Spider-Woman app. 2 4 6 11 16 20
Adventures in Reading Starring... (1990,1991) Bogdanove & Romita-c/a 5.00
Aim Toothpaste Giveaway (36 pgs., reg. size)-1 pg. origin recap; Green Goblin-c/story 2 4 6 9 13 16
Aim Toothpaste Giveaway (16 pgs., reg. size)-Dr. Octopus app. 2 4 6 9 13 16
All Detergent Giveaway (1979, 36 pgs.), nn-Origin-r 2 4 6 9 13 16
Amazing Fantasy #15 (8/02) reprint included in Spider-Man DVD Collector's Gift Set 5.00
Amazing Fantasy #15 (2006) News America Marketing newspaper giveaway 4.00
Amazing Spider-Man nn (1990, 6-1/8x9", 28 pgs.)-Shan-Lon giveaway; retells origin of Spider-Man; Bagley-a/Saviuk-c 2 4 6 8 10 12
Amazing Spider-Man nn (1990, 6-1/8x9", 28 pgs.)-Shan-Lon giveaway; reprints Amazing Spider-Man #303 w/McFarlane-c/a 2 4 6 8 10 12

Amazing Spider-Man: Riot at Robotworld © MAR

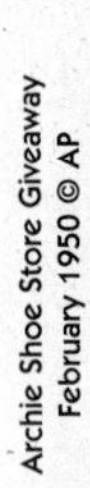
Archie Shoe Store Giveaway February 1950 © AP

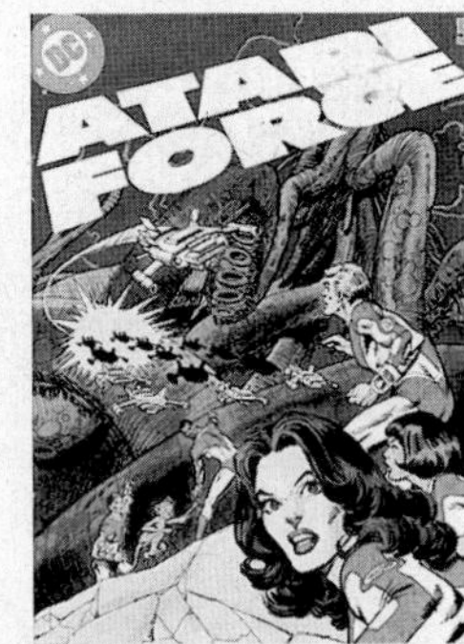

Atari Force #5 © Atari

GD 2.0 | VG 4.0 | FN 6.0 | VF 8.0 | VF/NM 9.0 | NM- 9.2

Amazing Spider-Man #1 Reprint (1990, 4-1/4x6-1/4", 28 pgs.)-Packaged with the book "Start Collecting Comic Books" from Running Press 4.00
Amazing Spider-Man #3 Reprint (2004)-Best Buy/Sony giveaway 2.50
Amazing Spider-Man #50 (Sony Pictures Edition) (8/04)-mini-comic included in Spider-Man 2 movie DVD Collector's Gift Set; r/#50 & various ASM covers with Dr. Octopus 2.50
Amazing Spider-Man #129 (Lion Gate Films) (6/04)-promotional comic given away at movie theaters on opening night for The Punisher 2.50
...& Power Pack (1984, nn)(Nat'l Committee for Prevention of Child Abuse) (two versions, mail offer & store giveaway)-Mooney-a; Byrne-c
Mail offer 2 4 6 9 11 14
Store giveaway 5.00
...& The Hulk (Special Edition)(6/8/80; 20 pgs.)-Supplement to Chicago Tribune
2 4 6 9 13 16
...& The Incredible Hulk (1981, 1982; 36 pgs.)-Sanger Harris or May D&F supplement to Dallas Times, Dallas Herald, Denver Post, Kansas City Star, Tulsa World; Foley's supplement to Houston Chronicle (1982, 16 pgs.)- "Great Rodeo Robbery"; The Jones Store-giveaway (1983, 16 pgs.) 2 4 6 11 16 20
...and the New Mutants Featuring Skids nn (National Committee for Prevention of Child Abuse/K-Mart giveaway)-Williams-c(i) 5.00
... Battles Ignorance (1992)(Sylvan Learning Systems) giveaway; Mad Thinker app. Kupperberg-a 1 2 3 5 7 9
...Captain America, The Incredible Hulk, & Spider-Woman (1981) (7-11 Stores giveaway; 36 pgs.) 2 4 6 10 14 18
...: Christmas in Dallas (1983) (Supplement to Dallas Times Herald) giveaway 2 4 6 10 14 18
...: Danger in Dallas (1983) (Supplement to Dallas Times Herald) giveaway 2 4 6 10 14 18
...: Danger in Denver (1983) (Supplement to Denver Post) giveaway for May D&F stores 2 4 6 10 14 18
..., Fire-Star, And Ice-Man at the Dallas Ballet Nutcracker (1983; supplement to Dallas Times Herald)-Mooney-p 2 4 6 10 14 18
Giveaway-Esquire Magazine (2/69)-Miniature-Still attached (scarce)
12 24 36 79 170 260
Giveaway-Eye Magazine (2/69)-Miniature-Still attached
9 18 27 58 114 170
...: Riot at Robotworld (1991; 16 pgs.)(National Action Council for Minorities in Engineering, Inc.) giveaway; Saviuk-c 1 2 3 5 6 8
..., Storm & Powerman (1982; 20 pgs.)(American Cancer Society) giveaway; also a 1991 2nd printing and a 1994 printing 1 2 3 5 6 8
...Vs. The Hulk (Special Edition; 1979, 20 pgs.)(Supplement to Columbus Dispatch)
2 4 6 13 18 22
...Vs. The Prodigy (Giveaway, 16 pgs. in color (1976, 5x6-1/2")-Sex education; (1 million printed; 35-50¢) 2 4 6 9 12 15
Spidey & The Mini-Marvels Halloween 2003 Ashcan (12/03, 8 1/2"x 5 1/2") Giarusso-s/a; Venom and Green Goblin app. 2.00

AMERICA MENACED!
Vital Publications: 1950 (Paper-c)
nn-Anti-communism 39 78 117 231 378 525

AMERICAN COMICS
Theatre Giveaways (Liberty Theatre, Grand Rapids, Mich. known): 1940's
Many possible combinations. "Golden Age" superhero comics with new cover added and given away at theaters. Following known: Superman #59, Capt. Marvel #20, 21, Capt. Marvel Jr. #5, Action #33, Classics Comics #8, Whiz #39. Value would vary with book and should be 70-80 percent of the original.

ANDY HARDY COMICS
Western Printing Co.:
...& the New Automatic Gas Clothes Dryer (1952, 5x7-1/4", 16 pgs.)
Bendix Giveaway (soft-c) 6 12 18 31 38 45

ANIMANIACS EMERGENCY WORLD
DC Comics: 1995
nn-American Red Cross 4.00

APACHE HUNTER
Creative Pictorials: 1954 (18 pgs. in color) (promo copy) (saddle stitched)
nn-Severin, Heath stories 15 30 45 85 130 175

AQUATEERS MEET THE SUPER FRIENDS
DC Comics: 1979
nn 2 4 6 10 14 18

ARCHIE AND HIS GANG (Zeta Beta Tau Presents...)
Archie Publications: Dec. 1950 (St. Louis National Convention giveaway)
nn-Contains new cover stapled over Archie Comics #47 (11-12/50) on inside; produced for Zeta Beta Tau 21 42 63 124 202 275

ARCHIE COMICS (Also see Sabrina)
Archie Publications
... And Friends and the Shield (10/02, 8 1/2"x 5 1/2") Diamond Comic Dist. 4.00
... And Friends - A Halloween Tale (10/98, 8 1/2"x 5 1/2") Diamond Comic Dist.; Sabrina and Sonic app.; Dan DeCarlo-a 4.00
... And Friends - A Timely Tale (10/01, 8 1/2"x 5 1/2") Diamond Comic Dist. 4.00
... And Friends Monster Bash 2003 (8 1/2"x 5 1/2") Diamond Comic Dist. Halloween 4.00
...And His Friends Help Raise Literacy Awareness In Mississippi nn (3/94)
1 2 3 5 6 8
...And His Friends Vs. The Household Toxic Wastes nn (1993, 16 pgs.) produced for the San Diego Regional Household Hazardous Materials Program
1 2 3 5 6 8
...And His Pals in the Peer Helping Program nn (2/91, 7"x4 1/2") produced by the FBI
1 2 3 5 6 8
...And the History of Electronics nn (5/90, 36 pgs.)-Radio Shack giveaway; Bender-c/a
1 2 3 5 6 8
Fairmont Potato Chips Giveaway-Mini comics 1970 (6 issues-nn's.,6 7/8" x 2 1/4", 8 pgs. each)
3 6 9 18 28 38
Fairmont Potato Chips Giveaway-Mini comics 1971 (4 issues-nn's.,6 7/8" x 5", 8 pgs. each)
3 6 9 18 28 38
Little Archie, The House That Wouldn't Move ('07, 8-1/2" x 5-3/8" Halloween mini-comic) 2.00
...'s Ham Radio Adventure (1997) Morse code instruction; Goldberg-a 6.00
...'s Weird Mysteries (9/99, 8 1/2"x 5 1/2") Diamond Comic Dist. Halloween giveaway 3.00
Tales From Riverdale (2006, 8 1/2"x 5 1/2") Diamond Comic Dist. Halloween giveaway 3.00
...: The Dawn of Time ('10, 8-1/2" x 5-3/8" Halloween mini-comic) 3.00
...: The Mystery of the Museum Sleep-In ('08, 8-1/2" x 5-3/8" Halloween mini-comic) 3.00
... Your Official Store Club Magazine nn (10/48, 9-1/2x6-1/2, 16 pgs.)- "Wolf Whistle" Archie on front-c; B. R. Baker Co. ad on back-c (a CGC 7.5 copy sold for $1912 in Feb. 2013)

ARCHIE SHOE-STORE GIVEAWAY
Archie Publications: 1944-50 (12-15 pgs. of games, puzzles, stories like Superman-Tim books, No nos. - came out monthly)
(1944-47)-issues 20 40 60 114 182 250
2/48-Peggy Lee photo-c 20 40 60 114 182 250
3/48-Marylee Robb photo-c 17 34 51 98 154 215
4/48-Gloria De Haven photo-c 20 40 60 114 182 250
5/48,6/48,7/48,10/48 17 34 51 98 154 215
8/48-Story on Shirley Temple 20 40 60 118 192 265
5/49-Kathleen Hughes photo-c 15 30 45 90 140 190
7/49 15 30 45 85 130 175
8/49-Archie photo-c from radio show 23 46 69 138 227 315
10/49-Gloria Mann photo-c from radio show 18 36 54 105 165 225
11/49,12/49, 2/50, 3/50 15 30 45 88 137 185

ARCHIE'S JOKE BOOK MAGAZINE (See Joke Book ...)
Archie Publications
Drug Store Giveaway (No. 39 w/new-c) 7 14 21 35 43 50

ARCHIE'S TEN ISSUE COLLECTOR'S SET (Title inside of cover only)
Archie Publications: June, 1997 - No. 10, June, 1997 ($1.50, 20 pgs.)
1-10: 1,7-Archie. 2,8-Betty & Veronica. 3,9-Veronica. 4-Betty. 5-World of Archie. 6-Jughead. 10-Archie and Friends each... 5.00

ASTRO COMICS
American Airlines (Harvey): 1968 - 1979 (Giveaway)(Reprints of Harvey comics)
1968-Richie Rich, Hot Stuff, Casper, Wendy on-c only; Spooky and Nightmare app. inside
4 8 12 23 37 50
1970-Casper, Spooky, Hot Stuff, Stumbo the Giant, Little Audrey, Little Lotta, & Richie Rich reprints. Five different versions 3 6 9 19 30 40
1973,1975,1976: 1973-Three different versions 2 4 6 13 18 22
1977-r/Richie Rich & Casper #20. 1978-r/Richie Rich & Casper #25. 1979-r/Richie Rich & Casper #30 (scarce) 2 4 6 11 16 20

ATARI FORCE
DC Comics: 1982 - No. 5, 1983
1-3 (1982, 5X7", 52 pgs.)-Given away with Atari games
1 2 3 5 6 8
4,5 (1982-1983, 52 pgs.)-Given away with Atari games (scarcer)
2 4 6 9 12 15

AURORA COMIC SCENES INSTRUCTION BOOKLET (Included with superhero model kits)
Aurora Plastics Co.: 1974 (6-1/4x9-3/4," 8 pgs., slick paper)
181-140-Tarzan; Neal Adams-a 3 6 9 18 27 36
182-140-Spider-Man. 4 8 12 23 37 50
183-140-Tonto(Gil Kane art). 184-140-Hulk. 185-140-Superman. 186-140-Superboy. 187-140-Batman. 188-140-The Lone Ranger(1974-by Gil Kane). 192-140-Captain

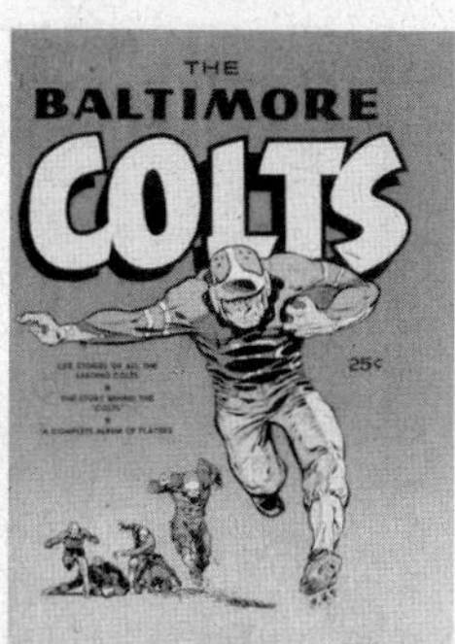

Baltimore Colts nn © AVC

Batman #121 Toys R Us Ed. © DC

Bionicle #9 © LEGO Toys

	GD 2.0	VG 4.0	FN 6.0	VF 8.0	VF/NM 9.0	NM- 9.2
America(1975). 193-140-Robin	3	6	9	16	23	30
BACK TO THE FUTURE						
Harvey Comics						
Special nn (1991, 20 pgs.)-Brunner-c; given away at Universal Studios in Florida						6.00
BALTIMORE COLTS						
American Visuals Corp.: 1950 (Giveaway)						
nn-Eisner-c	45	90	135	284	480	675
BAMBI (Disney)						
K. K. Publications (Giveaways): 1941, 1942						
1941-Horlick's Malted Milk & various toy stores; text & pictures; most copies mailed out with store stickers on-c	43	86	129	271	461	650
1942-Same as 4-Color #12, but no price (Same as '41 issue?) (Scarce)	97	194	291	621	1061	1500
BATMAN						
DC Comics: 1966 - Present						
Act II Popcorn mini-comic(1998)						4.00
Batman #121 Toys R Us edition (1997) r/1st Mr. Freeze						4.00
Batman #279 Mini-comic with Monogram Model kit (1995)						4.00
Batman #362 Mervyn's edition (1989)						5.00
Batman #608 New York Post edition (2002)						4.00
Batman Adventures #25 Best Western edition (1997)						4.00
Batman and Other DC Classics 1 (1989, giveaway)-DC Comics/Diamond Comic Distributors; Batman origin-r/Batman #47, Camelot 3000-r, Justice League-r('87), New Teen Titans-r						5.00
Batman and Robin movie preview (1997, 8 pgs.) Kellogg's Cereal promo						3.00
Batman Beyond Six Flags edition	1	2	3	5	6	8
Batman: Canadian Multiculturalism Custom (1992)						5.00
Batman Claritan edition (1999)						3.00
Kellogg's Poptarts comics (1966, Set of 6, 16 pgs.); All were folded and placed in Poptarts boxes. Infantino art on Catwoman and Joker issues. "The Man in the Iron Mask", "The Penguin's Fowl Play", "The Joker's Happy Victims", "The Catwoman's Catnapping Caper", "The Mad Hatter's Hat Crimes", "The Case of the Batman II" each....	4	8	12	28	47	65
Mask of the Phantasm (1993) Mini-comic released w/video	1	2	3	5	7	9
Onstar - Auto Show Special Edition (OnStar Corp., 2001, 8 pgs.) Riddler app.						3.00
Pizza Hut giveaway (12/77)-exact-r of #122,123; Joker-c/story	2	4	6	9	12	15
Prell Shampoo giveaway (1966, 16 pgs.)- "The Joker's Practical Jokes" (6-7/8x3-3/8")	8	16	24	54	102	150
Revell in pack (1995)						4.00
...: The 10-Cent Adventure (3/02, 10¢) intro. to the "Bruce Wayne: Murderer" x-over; Rucka-s/Burchett & Janson-a/Dave Johnson-c; these are alternate copies with special outer half-covers (at least 10 different) promoting comics, toys and games shops						3.00
BATMAN RECORD COMIC						
National Periodical Publications: 1966 (one-shot)						
1-With record (still sealed)	12	24	36	79	170	260
Comic only	7	14	21	49	92	135
BEETLE BAILEY						
Charlton Comics: 1969-1970 (Giveaways)						
Armed Forces ('69)-same as regular issue (#68)	2	4	6	10	14	18
Armed Forces ('70)	2	4	6	10	14	18
Bold Detergent ('69)-same as regular issue (#67)	2	4	6	10	14	18
Cerebral Palsy Assn. V2#71('69) - V2#73(#1,1/70)						2.00
Red Cross (1969, 5x7", 16 pgs., paper-c)	2	4	6	10	14	18
BELLAIRE BICYCLE CO.						
Bellaire Bicycle Co.: 1940 (promotional comic)						
nn-Contains Wonderworld #12 w/new-c. Contents can vary w/diff. 1940's books	30	60	90	177	289	400
BEST WESTERN GIVEAWAY						
DC Comics: 1999						
nn-Best Western hotels						2.50
BETTER LIFE FOR YOU, A						
Harvey Publications Inc.: (16 pgs., paper cover)						
nn-Better living through higher productivity	3	6	9	15	22	28
BEWARE THE BOOBY TRAP						
Malcolm Alter: 1970 (5" x 7")						
nn-Deals with drug abuse	4	8	12	23	37	50
B-FORCE (Milwaukee Brewers and Wisconsin Dental Asso.)						
Dark Horse Comics: 2001 (School and stadium giveaway)						
nn-Brewers players combat the evils of smokeless tobacco						3.00
BIG BOY (see Adventures of...)						
BIG JIM'S P.A.C.K.						
Mattel, Inc. (Marvel Comics): No date (1975) (16 pgs.)						
nn-Giveaway with Big Jim doll; Buscema/Sinnott-c/a	4	8	12	23	37	50
"BILL AND TED'S EXCELLENT ADVENTURE" MOVIE ADAPTATION						
DC Comics: 1989 (No cover price)						
nn-Torres-a						4.00
BIONICLE (LEGO robot toys)						
DC Comics: Jun, 2001 - No. 27, Nov, 2005 ($2.25/$3.25, 16 pages, available to LEGO club members)						
1	1	2	3	5	6	8
2-5						6.00
6-13						4.00
14-27						3.00
The Legend of Bionicle (McDonald's Mini-comic, 4-1/4 x 7")						4.00
Special Edition #0 (Six Heroes...One Destiny) '03 San Diego Comic Con; Ashley Wood-c						6.00
BLACK GOLD						
Esso Service Station (Giveaway): 1945? (8 pgs. in color)						
nn-Reprints from True Comics	6	12	18	27	33	38
BLADE SINS OF THE FATHER						
Marvel Comics: Aug, 1996 (24 pgs. with paper cover)						
1-Theatrical preview; possibly limited to 2000 copies (Value will be based on sale)						
BLAZING FOREST, THE (See Forest Fire and Smokey Bear)						
Western Printing: 1962 (20 pgs., 5x7", slick-c)						
nn-Smokey The Bear fire prevention	3	6	9	14	20	26
BLESSED PIUS X						
Catechetical Guild (Giveaway): No date (Text/comics, 32 pgs., paper-c)						
nn	6	12	18	33	41	48
BLIND JUSTICE (Also see Batman: Blind Justice)						
DC Comics/Diamond Comic Distributors: 1989 (Giveaway, squarebound)						
nn-Contains Detective #598-600 by Batman movie writer Sam Hamm, w/covers; published same time as originals?						6.00
BLONDIE COMICS						
Harvey Publications: 1950-1964						
1950 Giveaway	8	16	24	40	50	60
1962,1964 Giveaway	3	6	9	16	23	30
N. Y. State Dept. of Mental Hygiene Giveaway-(1950) Regular size; 16 pgs.; no #	4	8	12	23	37	50
N. Y. State Dept. of Mental Hygiene Giveaway-(1956) Regular size; 16 pgs.; no #	3	6	9	16	24	32
N. Y. State Dept. of Mental Hygiene Giveaway-(1961) Regular size; 16 pgs.; no #	3	6	9	15	22	28
BLOOD IS THE HARVEST						
Catechetical Guild: 1950 (32 pgs., paper-c)						
(Scarce)-Anti-communism (21 known copies)	239	478	717	1530	2615	3700
Black & white version (5 known copies), saddle stitched	103	206	309	659	1130	1600
Untrimmed version (only one known copy); estimated value - $1000						
NOTE: *In 1979 nine copies of the color version surfaced from the old Guild's files plus the five black & white copies.*						
BLUE BIRD CHILDREN'S MAGAZINE, THE						
Graphic Information Service: V1#2, 1957 - No. 10 1958 (16 pgs., soft-c, regular size)						
V1#2-10: Pat, Pete & Blue Bird app.	2	4	6	8	11	14
BLUE BIRD COMICS						
Various Shoe Stores: 1947 - 1950 (Giveaway, 36 pgs.)						
Charlton Comics: 1959 - 1964 (Giveaway)						
nn-(1947-50, not Charlton)(36 pgs.)-Several issues; Human Torch, Sub-Mariner app. in some	18	36	54	103	162	220
1959-(Charlton) Lil Genius, Wild Bill Hickok, Black Fury, Masked Raider, Timmy The Timid Ghost, Freddy (All #1)	3	6	9	14	20	26
1959-(Charlton, same 6 titles; all #2-5) except (#5) Masked Raider #21	3	6	9	14	20	25
1959-(#5) Masked Raider #21	3	6	9	15	22	28

Bozo the Clown © DELL

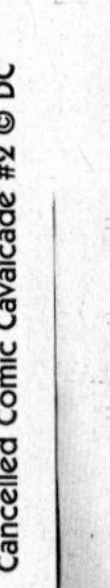

Cancelled Comic Cavalcade #2 © DC

Captain America and the Campbell Kids © MAR

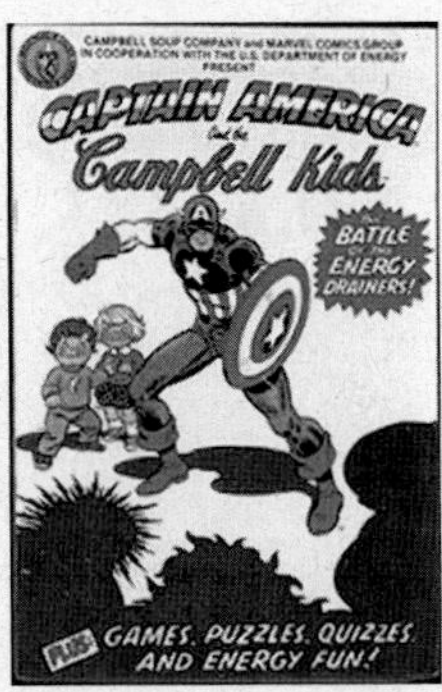

GD 2.0 | VG 4.0 | FN 6.0 | VF 8.0 | VF/NM 9.0 | NM- 9.2

1960-(6 titles, all #6-9) Black Fury, Masked Raider, Freddy, Timmy the Timid Ghost, Li'l Genius, Six Gun Heroes 3 6 9 14 19 24
1961-(All #10's) Black Fury, Masked Raider, Freddy, Timmy the Timid Ghost, Li'l Genius, Six Gun Heroes (Charlton) 2 4 6 13 18 22
1961-(All #11-13) Lil Genius, Wyatt Earp, Black Fury, Timmy the Timid Ghost, Atomic Mouse, Freddy 2 4 6 13 18 22
1962-(All #14) Lil Genius, Wyatt Earp, Black Fury, Timmy the Timid Ghost, Atomic Mouse, Freddy 2 4 6 13 18 22
1962-(6 titles, all #15) Lil Genius, Six Gun Heroes, Black Fury, Timmy the Timid Ghost, Texas Rangers, Freddy 2 4 6 13 18 22
1962-(7 titles, all #16) Lil Genius, Six Gun Heroes, Black Fury, Timmy the Timid Ghost, Texas Rangers, Wyatt Earp, Atomic Mouse 2 4 6 13 18 22
1963-(All #17) My Little Margie, Lil Genius, Timmy the Timid Ghost, Texas Rangers (Charlton) 2 4 6 9 13 16
1964-(All #18) Mysteries of Unexplored Worlds, Teenage Hotrodders, War Heroes, Wyatt Earp (Charlton) 2 4 6 9 13 16

NOTE: *Reprints comics of regular issue, with Blue Bird shoe promo on back cover, with upper front cover imprint of various shoe retailers. Printed from 1959 to 1962, with issues 1 thru 16. The 8 different front cover imprints for issues 1 thru 16 are, 1) Blue Bird Shoes, 2) Schiff's Shoes, 3) Big Shoe Store, 4) E.D. Edwards Shoe Store, 5) R & S Shoe store, 6) Federal Shoe Store, 7) Kirby's Shoes, 8) Gallenkamps.*

BOB & BETTY & SANTA'S WISHING WHISTLE (Also see A Christmas Carol, Merry Christmas From Sears Toyland, and Santa's Christmas Comic Variety Show)
Sears Roebuck & Co.: 1941 (Christmas giveaway, 12 pgs., oblong)
nn 20 40 60 114 182 250

BOBBY BENSON'S B-BAR-B RIDERS (Radio)
Magazine Enterprises/AC Comics
...in the Tunnel of Gold-(1936, 5-1/4x8"; 100 pgs.) Radio giveaway by Hecker-H.O. Company (H.O. Oats); contains 22 color pgs. of comics, rest in novel form 11 22 33 64 90 115
...And The Lost Herd-same as above 11 22 33 64 90 115

BOBBY SHELBY COMICS
Shelby Cycle Co./Harvey Publications: 1949
nn 5 10 14 20 24 28

BONE
Cartoon Books: Halloween, 2008 (8-1/2" x 5-3/8" mini-comic giveaway)
nn-Jeff Smith-s/a 2.00

BOY SCOUT ADVENTURE
Boy Scouts of America: 1954 (16 pgs., paper cover)
nn 5 10 14 20 24 28

BOYS' RANCH
Harvey Publications: 1951
Shoe Store Giveaway #5,6 (Identical to regular issues except Simon & Kirby centerfold replaced with ad) 14 28 42 76 108 140

BOZO THE CLOWN (TV)
Dell Publishing Co.: 1961
Giveaway-1961, 16 pgs., 3-1/2x7-1/4", Apsco Products 5 10 15 30 50 70

BRER RABBIT IN "ICE CREAM FOR THE PARTY"
American Dairy Association: 1955 (5x7-1/4", 16 pgs., soft-c) (Walt Disney) (Premium)
nn-(Scarce) 37 74 111 222 361 500

BUCK ROGERS (In the 25th Century)
Kelloggs Corn Flakes Giveaway: 1933 (6x8", 36 pgs)
370A-By Phil Nowlan & Dick Calkins; 1st Buck Rogers radio premium & 1st app. in comics (tells origin) (Reissued in 1995) 54 108 162 400 - -
with envelope 74 148 222 550 - -

BUGS BUNNY (Puffed Rice Giveaway)
Quaker Cereals: 1949 (32 pgs. each, 3-1/8x6-7/8")
A1-Traps the Counterfeiters, A2-Aboard Mystery Submarine, A3- Rocket to the Moon, A4-Lion Tamer, A5-Rescues the Beautiful Princess, B1-Buried Treasure, B2-Outwits the Smugglers, B3-Joins the Marines, B4-Meets the Dwarf Ghost, B5-Finds Aladdin's Lamp, C1-Lost in the Frozen North, C2-Secret Agent, C3-Captured by Cannibals, C4-Fights the Man from Mars, C5-And the Haunted Cave
each.... 8 16 24 40 50 60
Mailing Envelope (has illo of Bugs on front)(Each envelope designates what set it contains, A,B or C on front) 8 16 24 40 50 60

BUGS BUNNY (3-D)
Cheerios Giveaway: 1953 (Pocket size) (15 titles)
each.... 10 20 30 58 79 100
Mailing Envelope (has Bugs drawn on front) 10 20 30 58 79 100

BUGS BUNNY
DC Comics: May, 1997 ($4.95, 24 pgs., comic-sized)
1-Numbered ed. of 100,000; "1st Day of Issue" stamp cancellation on-c 6.00

BUGS BUNNY POSTAL COMIC
DC Comics: 1997 (64 pgs., 7.5" x 5")
nn -Mail Fan; Daffy Duck app. 4.50

BULLETMAN
Fawcett Publications
Well Known Comics (1942)-Paper-c, glued binding; printed in red (Bestmaid/Samuel Lowe giveaway) 15 30 45 85 130 175

BULLS-EYE (Cody of The Pony Express No. 8 on)
Charlton: 1955
Great Scott Shoe Store giveaway-Reprints #2 with new cover 18 36 54 103 162 220

BUSTER BROWN COMICS (Radio)(Also see My Dog Tige in Promotional sec.)
Brown Shoe Co.: 1945 - No. 43, 1959 (No. 5: paper-c)
nn, nd (#1,scarce)-Featuring Smilin' Ed McConnell & the Buster Brown gang "Midnight" the cat, "Squeaky" the mouse & "Froggy" the Gremlin; covers mention diff. shoe stores. Contains adventure stories 60 120 180 381 653 925
2 19 38 57 112 179 245
3,5-10 13 26 39 74 105 135
4 (Rare)-Low print run due to paper shortage 17 34 51 98 154 210
11-20 9 18 27 47 61 75
21-24,26-28 6 12 18 31 38 45
25,33-37,40,41-Crandall-a in all 10 20 30 56 76 95
29-32-"Interplanetary Police Vs. the Space Siren" by Crandall (pencils only #29) 10 20 30 58 79 100
38,39,42,43 6 12 18 31 38 45

BUSTER BROWN COMICS (Radio)
Brown Shoe Co: 1950s
...Goes to Mars (2/58-Western Printing), slick-c, 20 pgs., reg. size 14 28 42 76 108 140
...In "Buster Makes the Team!" (1959-Custom Comics) 8 16 24 44 57 70
...In The Jet Age ('50s), slick-c, 20 pgs., 5x7-1/4" 10 20 30 58 79 100
...Of the Safety Patrol ('60-Custom Comics) 3 6 9 17 26 35
...Out of This World ('59-Custom Comics) 7 14 21 35 43 50
...Safety Coloring Book ('58, 16 pgs.)-Slick paper 7 14 21 35 43 50

CALL FROM CHRIST
Catechetical Educational Society: 1952 (Giveaway, 36 pgs.)
nn 6 12 18 33 41 48

CANCELLED COMIC CAVALCADE
DC Comics, Inc.: Summer, 1978 - No. 2, Fall, 1978 (8-1/2x11", B&W)
(Xeroxed pgs. on one side only w/blue cover and taped spine)(Only 35 sets produced)
1-(412 pgs.) Contains xeroxed copies of art for: Black Lightning #12, cover to #13; Claw #13,14; The Deserter #1; Doorway to Nightmare #6; Firestorm #6; The Green Team #2,3.
2-(532 pgs.) Contains xeroxed copies of art for: Kamandi #60 (including Omac), #61; Prez #5; Shade #9 (including The Odd Man); Showcase #105 (Deadman), 106 (The Creeper); Secret Society of Super Villains #16 & 17; The Vixen #1; and covers to Army at War #2, Battle Classics #3, Demand Classics #1 & 2, Dynamic Classics #3, Mr. Miracle #26, Ragman #6, Weird Mystery #25 & 26, & Western Classics #1 & 2.
(A FN set of Number 1 & 2 was sold in 2005 for $3680; a VG set sold in 2007 for $2629)

NOTE: *In June, 1978, DC cancelled several of their titles. For copyright purposes, the unpublished original art for these titles was xeroxed, bound in the above books, published and distributed. Only 35 copies were made. Beware of bootleg copies.*

CAP'N CRUNCH COMICS (See Quaker Oats)
Quaker Oats Co.: 1963; 1965 (16 pgs.; miniature giveaways; 2-1/2x6-1/2")
(1963 titles)- "The Picture Pirates", "The Fountain of Youth", "I'm Dreaming of a Wide Isthmus". (1965 titles)- "Bewitched, Betwitched, & Betweaked", "Seadog Meets the Witch Doctor", "A Witch in Time" 5 10 15 31 53 75

CAPTAIN ACTION (Toy)
National Periodical Publications
...& Action Boy('67)-Ideal Toy Co. giveaway (1st app. Captain Action) 10 20 30 67 141 215

CAPTAIN AMERICA
Marvel Comics Group
...& The Campbell Kids (1980, 36pg. giveaway, Campbell's Soup/U.S. Dept. of Energy)

Captain Marvel and the Lts. of Safety #3 © FAW

Centipede #1 © Atari

Cheerios Premium W1
Donald Duck and the Pirates © DIS

	GD 2.0	VG 4.0	FN 6.0	VF 8.0	VF/NM 9.0	NM- 9.2
	2	4	6	9	13	16
...Goes To War Against Drugs(1990, no #, giveaway)-Distributed to direct sales shops; 2nd printing exists	1	2	3	5	6	8
...Meets The Asthma Monster (1987, no #, giveaway, Your Physician and Glaxo, Inc.)	1	2	3	5	6	8
Return of The Asthma Monster Vol. 1 #2 (1992, giveaway, Your Physician & Allen & Hanbury's)	1	2	3	5	6	8
...Vs. Asthma Monster (1990, no #, giveaway, Your Physician & Allen & Hanbury's)	1	2	3	5	6	8

CAPTAIN AMERICA COMICS
Timely/Marvel Comics: 1954

Shoestore Giveaway #77 — 100 200 300 635 1093 1550

CAPTAIN ATOM
Nationwide Publishers

...- Secret of the Columbian Jungle (16 pgs. in color, paper-c, 3-3/4x5-1/8")-Fireside Marshmallow giveaway — 6 12 18 28 34 40

CAPTAIN BEN DIX
Bendix Aviation Corporation: 1943 (Small size)

nn — 8 16 24 44 57 70

CAPTAIN BEN DIX IN ACTION WITH THE INVISIBLE CREW
Bendix Aviation Corp.: 1940s (nd), (20 pgs, 8-1/4"x11", heavy paper)

nn-WWII bomber-c; Japanese app. — 7 14 21 37 46 55

CAPTAIN BEN DIX IN SECRETS OF THE INVISIBLE CREW
Bendix Aviation Corp.: 1940s (nd), (32 pgs, soft-c)

nn — 7 14 21 35 43 50

CAPTAIN FORTUNE PRESENTS
Vital Publications: 1955 - 1959 (Giveaway, 3-1/4x6-7/8", 16 pgs.)

"Davy Crockett in Episodes of the Creek War", "Davy Crockett at the Alamo", "In Sherwood Forest Tells Strange Tales of Robin Hood" ('57), "Meets Bolivar the Liberator" ('59), "Tells How Buffalo Bill Fights the Dog Soldiers" ('57), "Young Davy Crockett" — 4 7 9 14 17 20

CAPTAIN GALLANT (...of the Foreign Legion) (TV)
Charlton Comics

Heinz Foods Premium (#1?)(1955; regular size)-U.S. Pictorial; contains Buster Crabbe photos; Don Heck-a — 1 3 4 6 8 10
Mailing Envelope — 20.00

CAPTAIN JOLLY ADVENTURES
Johnston and Cushing: 1950's, nd (Post Corn Fetti cereal giveaway) (5-1/4" x 4-1/2")

1-3: 1-Captain Jolly Advs. 2-Captain Jolly and His Pirate Crew in Off To Treasure Island. 3-C.J. & His Pirate Crew in The Terror Of The Deep — 2 4 5 7 8 10

CAPTAIN MARVEL ADVENTURES
Fawcett Publications

Bond Bread Giveaways-(24 pgs.; pocket size-7-1/4x3-1/2"; paper cover): "...& the Stolen City" ('48), "The Boy Who Never Heard of Capt. Marvel", "Meets the Weatherman" (1950) (reprint) each.... — 22 44 66 128 209 290
...Well Known Comics (1944; 12 pgs.; 8-1/2x10-1/2")-printed in red & in blue; soft-c; glued binding - (Bestmaid/Samuel Lowe Co. giveaway) — 15 30 45 94 147 200

CAPTAIN MARVEL ADVENTURES (Also see Flash and Funny Stuff)
Fawcett Publications (Wheaties Giveaway): 1945 (6x8", full color, paper-c)

nn- "Captain Marvel & the Threads of Life" plus 2 other stories (32 pgs.) — 70 140 350 700 - -

NOTE: *All copies were taped at each corner to a box of Wheaties and are never found in Fine or Mint condition. Prices listed for each grade include tape.*

CAPTAIN MARVEL AND THE LTS. OF SAFETY
Ebasco Services/Fawcett Publications: 1950 - 1951 (3 issues - no No.'s)

	GD	VG	FN	VF	VF/NM	NM-
nn (#1) "Danger Flies a Kite" ('50, scarce),	53	106	159	334	567	800
nn (#2)"Danger Takes to Climbing" ('50),	41	82	123	256	428	600
nn (#3)"Danger Smashes Street Lights" ('51)	41	82	123	256	428	600

CAPTAIN MARVEL, JR.
Fawcett Publications: (1944; 12 pgs.; 8-1/2x10-1/2")

...Well Known Comics (Printed in blue; paper-c, glued binding)-Bestmaid/Samuel Lowe Co. giveaway — 14 28 42 76 108 140

CARDINAL MINDSZENTY (The Truth Behind the Trial of...)
Catechetical Guild Education Society: 1949 (24 pgs., paper cover)

nn-Anti-communism — 11 22 33 64 90 115
Press Proof-(Very Rare)-(Full color, 7-1/2x11-3/4", untrimmed) Only two known copies — 300.00
Preview Copy (B&W, stapled), 18 pgs.; contains first 13 pgs. of Cardinal Mindszenty and was sent out as an advance promotion. Only one known copy — 300.00 - 400.00

NOTE: *Regular edition also printed in French. There was also a movie released in 1949 called "Guilty of Treason" which is a fact-based account of the trial and imprisonment of Cardinal Mindszenty by the Communist regime in Hungary.*

CARNIVAL OF COMICS
Fleet-Air Shoes: 1954 (Giveaway)

nn-Contains a comic bound with new cover; several combinations possible; Charlton's Eh! known — 5 10 15 24 30 35

CARTOON NETWORK
DC Comics: 1997 (Giveaway)

nn-reprints Cow and Chicken, Scooby-Doo, & Flintstones stories — 4.00

CARVEL COMICS (Amazing Advs. of Capt. Carvel)
Carvel Corp. (Ice Cream): 1975 - No. 5, 1976 (25¢; #3-5: 35¢) (#4,5: 3-1/4x5")

	GD	VG	FN	VF	VF/NM	NM-
1-3	1	2	3	5	6	8
4,5(1976)-Baseball theme	2	4	6	8	10	12

CASE OF THE WASTED WATER, THE
Rheem Water Heating: 1972? (Giveaway)

nn-Neal Adams-a — 4 8 12 27 44 60

CASPER SPECIAL
Target Stores (Harvey): nd (Dec, 1990) (Giveaway with $1.00 cover)

Three issues-Given away with Casper video — 6.00

CASPER, THE FRIENDLY GHOST (Paramount Picture Star...)(2nd Series)
Harvey Publications

	GD	VG	FN	VF	VF/NM	NM-
American Dental Association (Giveaways):						
...'s Dental Health Activity Book-1977	2	4	6	8	11	14
...Presents Space Age Dentistry-1972	2	4	6	9	13	16
..., His Den, & Their Dentist Fight the Tooth Demons-1974	2	4	6	9	13	16
Casper Rides the School Bus (1960, 7x3.5", 16 pgs.)	2	4	6	9	13	16

CELEBRATE THE CENTURY SUPERHEROES STAMP ALBUM
DC Comics: 1998 - No. 5, 2000 (32 pgs.)

1-5: Historical stories hosted by DC heroes — 4.00

CENTIPEDE
DC Comics: 1983

1-Based on Atari video game — 2 4 6 8 11 14

CENTURY OF COMICS
Eastern Color Printing Co.: 1933 (100 pgs.)
Bought by Wheatena, Malt-O-Milk, John Wanamaker, Kinney Shoe Stores, & others to be used as premiums and radio giveaways. No publisher listed.

nn-Mutt & Jeff, Joe Palooka, etc. reprints — 2230 4460 6690 17,000 - -

CHEERIOS PREMIUMS (Disney)
Walt Disney Productions: 1947 (16 titles, pocket size, 32 pgs.)

	GD	VG	FN	VF	VF/NM	NM-
Mailing Envelope for each set "W,X,Y & Z" (has Mickey illo on front)(each envelope designates the set it contains on the front)	11	22	33	60	83	105
Set "W"						
W1-Donald Duck & the Pirates	11	22	33	60	83	105
W2-Bucky Bug & the Cannibal King	7	14	21	37	46	55
W3-Pluto Joins the F.B.I.	7	14	21	37	46	55
W4-Mickey Mouse & the Haunted House	8	16	24	42	54	65
Set "X"						
X1-Donald Duck, Counter Spy	11	22	33	60	83	105
X2-Goofy Lost in the Desert	7	14	21	37	46	55
X3-Br'er Rabbit Outwits Br'er Fox	7	14	21	37	46	55
X4-Mickey Mouse at the Rodeo	8	16	24	42	54	65
Set "Y"						
Y1-Donald Duck's Atom Bomb by Carl Barks. Disney has banned reprinting this book	76	152	228	470	810	1175
Y2-Br'er Rabbit's Secret	7	14	21	37	46	55
Y3-Dumbo & the Circus Mystery	7	14	21	37	46	55
Y4-Mickey Mouse Meets the Wizard	8	16	24	42	54	65
Set "Z"						
Z1-Donald Duck Pilots a Jet Plane (not by Barks)	11	22	33	60	83	105
Z2-Pluto Turns Sleuth Hound	7	14	21	37	46	55
Z3-The Seven Dwarfs & the Enchanted Mtn.	8	16	24	42	54	65
Z4-Mickey Mouse's Secret Room	8	16	24	42	54	65

Cheerios 3-D Giveaways Set 2 #6 Mickey Mouse, Phantom Sheriff © DIS

Cinderella in "Fairest of the Fair" © DIS

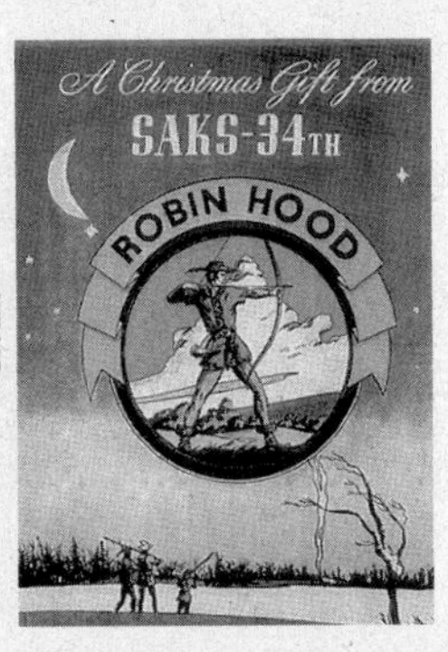

Classic Giveaways - Saks 34th St. © Saks

	GD 2.0	VG 4.0	FN 6.0	VF 8.0	VF/NM 9.0	NM- 9.2
CHEERIOS 3-D GIVEAWAYS (Disney)						
Walt Disney Productions: 1954 (24 titles, pocket size) (Glasses came in envelopes)						
Glasses only...	7	14	21	35	43	50
Mailing Envelope (no art on front)	8	16	24	42	54	65
(Set 1)						
1-Donald Duck & Uncle Scrooge, the Firefighters	9	18	27	47	61	75
2-Mickey Mouse & Goofy, Pirate Plunder	8	16	24	42	54	65
3-Donald Duck's Nephews, the Fabulous Inventors	9	18	27	47	61	75
4-Mickey Mouse, Secret of the Ming Vase	8	16	24	42	54	65
5-Donald Duck with Huey, Dewey, & Louie; ...the Seafarers (title on 2nd page)	9	18	27	47	61	75
6-Mickey Mouse, Moaning Mountain	8	16	24	42	54	65
7-Donald Duck, Apache Gold	9	18	27	47	61	75
8-Mickey Mouse, Flight to Nowhere	8	16	24	42	54	65
(Set 2)						
1-Donald Duck, Treasure of Timbuktu	9	18	27	47	61	75
2-Mickey Mouse & Pluto, Operation China	8	16	24	42	54	65
3-Donald Duck and the Magic Cows	9	18	27	47	61	75
4-Mickey Mouse & Goofy, Kid Kokonut	8	16	24	42	54	65
5-Donald Duck, Mystery Ship	9	18	27	47	61	75
6-Mickey Mouse, Phantom Sheriff	8	16	24	42	54	65
7-Donald Duck, Circus Adventures	9	18	27	47	61	75
8-Mickey Mouse, Arctic Explorers	8	16	24	42	54	65
(Set 3)						
1-Donald Duck & Witch Hazel	9	18	27	47	61	75
2-Mickey Mouse in Darkest Africa	8	16	24	42	54	65
3-Donald Duck & Uncle Scrooge, Timber Trouble	9	18	27	47	61	75
4-Mickey Mouse, Rajah's Rescue	8	16	24	42	54	65
5-Donald Duck in Robot Reporter	9	18	27	47	61	75
6-Mickey Mouse, Slumbering Sleuth	8	16	24	42	54	65
7-Donald Duck in the Foreign Legion	9	18	27	47	61	75
8-Mickey Mouse, Airwalking Wonder	8	16	24	42	54	65
CHESTY AND COPTIE (Disney)						
Los Angeles Community Chest: 1946 (Giveaway, 4pgs.)						
nn-(One known copy) by Floyd Gottfredson	77	154	231	493	847	1200
CHESTY AND HIS HELPERS (Disney)						
Los Angeles War Chest: 1943 (Giveaway, 12 pgs., 5-1/2x7-1/4")						
nn-Chesty & Coptie	50	100	150	315	533	750
CHOCOLATE THE FLAVOR OF FRIENDSHIP AROUND THE WORLD						
The Nestle Company: 1955						
nn	6	12	18	28	34	40
CHRISTMAS ADVENTURE, THE						
S. Rose (H. L. Green Giveaway): 1963 (16 pgs.)						
nn	2	4	6	9	13	16
CHRISTMAS ADVENTURES WITH ELMER THE ELF						
1949 (paper-c)						
nn	4	7	10	14	17	20
CHRISTMAS AT THE ROTUNDA (Titled Ford Rotunda Christmas Book 1957 on) (Regular size)						
Ford Motor Co. (Western Printing): 1954 - 1961 (Given away every Christmas at one location)						
1954-56 issues (nn's)	8	16	24	42	54	65
1957-61 issues (nn's)	7	14	21	37	46	55
CHRISTMAS CAROL, A						
Sears Roebuck & Co.: No date (1942-43) (Giveaway, 32 pgs., 8-1/4x10-3/4", paper cover)						
nn-Comics & coloring book	20	40	60	117	189	260
CHRISTMAS CAROL, A (Also see Bob & Santa's Wishing Whistle, Merry Christmas From Sears Toyland, and Santa's Christmas Comic Variety Show)						
Sears Roebuck & Co.: 1940s? (Christmas giveaway, 20 pgs.)						
nn-Comic book & animated coloring book	19	38	57	111	176	240
CHRISTMAS CAROLS						
Hot Shoppes Giveaway: 1959? (16 pgs.)						
nn	4	8	11	16	19	22
CHRISTMAS COLORING FUN						
H. Burnside: 1964 (20 pgs., slick-c, B&W)						
nn	2	4	6	11	16	20
CHRISTMAS DREAM, A						
Promotional Publishing Co.: 1950 (Kinney Shoe Store Giveaway, 16 pgs.)						

	GD 2.0	VG 4.0	FN 6.0	VF 8.0	VF/NM 9.0	NM- 9.2
nn	5	10	15	23	28	32
CHRISTMAS DREAM, A						
J. J. Newberry Co.: 1952? (Giveaway, paper cover, 16 pgs.)						
nn	4	8	12	18	22	25
CHRISTMAS DREAM, A						
Promotional Publ. Co.: 1952 (Giveaway, 16 pgs., paper cover)						
nn	4	8	12	18	22	25
CHRISTMAS FUN AROUND THE WORLD						
No publisher: No date (early 50's) (16 pgs., paper cover)						
nn	5	10	15	22	26	30
CHRISTMAS FUN BOOK						
G. C. Murphy Co.: 1950 (Giveaway, paper cover)						
nn-Contains paper dolls	6	12	18	28	34	40
CHRISTMAS IS COMING!						
No publisher: No date (early 50's?) (Store giveaway, 16 pgs.)						
nn-Santa cover	6	12	18	28	34	40
CHRISTMAS JOURNEY THROUGH SPACE						
Promotional Publishing Co.: 1960						
nn-Reprints 1954 issue Jolly Christmas Book with new slick cover	3	6	9	16	23	30
CHRISTMAS ON THE MOON						
W. T. Grant Co.: 1958 (Giveaway, 20 pgs., slick cover)						
nn	8	16	24	44	57	70
CHRISTMAS PLAY BOOK						
Gould-Stoner Co.: 1946 (Giveaway, 16 pgs., paper cover)						
nn	8	16	24	44	57	70
CHRISTMAS ROUNDUP						
Promotional Publishing Co.: 1960						
nn-Marv Levy-c/a	2	4	6	9	13	16
CHRISTMAS STORY CUT-OUT BOOK, THE						
Catechetical Guild: No. 393, 1951 (15¢, 36 pgs.)						
393-Half text & half comics	8	16	24	42	54	65
CHRISTMAS USA (Through 300 Years) (Also see Uncle Sam's...)						
Promotional Publ. Co.: 1956 (Giveaway)						
nn-Marv Levy-c/a	4	7	9	14	16	18
CHRISTMAS WITH SNOW WHITE AND THE SEVEN DWARFS						
Kobackers Giftstore of Buffalo, N.Y.: 1953 (16 pgs., paper-c)						
nn	8	16	24	42	54	65
CHRISTOPHERS, THE						
Catechetical Guild: 1951 (Giveaway, 36 pgs.) (Some copies have 15¢ sticker)						
nn-Stalin as Satan in Hell; Hitler & Lincoln app.	24	48	72	140	230	320
CHUCKY JACK'S A-COMIN'						
Great Smoky Mountains Historical Assn., Gatlinburg, TN: 1956 (Reg. size)						
nn-Life of John Sevier, founder of Tennessee	8	16	24	42	54	65
CINDERELLA IN "FAIREST OF THE FAIR" (Walt Disney)						
American Dairy Association (Premium): 1955 (5x7-1/4", 16 pgs., soft-c)						
nn	10	20	30	56	76	95
CINEMA COMICS HERALD						
Paramount Pictures/Universal/RKO/20th Century Fox/Republic:						
1941 - 1943 (4-pg. movie "trailers", paper-c, 7-1/2x10-1/2")(Giveaway)						
"Mr. Bug Goes to Town" (1941)	15	30	45	90	140	190
"Bedtime Story"	11	22	33	64	90	115
"Lady For A Night", John Wayne, Joan Blondell ('42)	18	36	54	107	169	230
"Reap The Wild Wind" (1942)	12	24	36	69	97	125
"Thunder Birds" (1942)	11	22	33	64	90	115
"They All Kissed the Bride"	11	22	33	64	90	115
"Arabian Nights" (nd)	12	24	36	69	97	125
"Bombardie" (1943)	11	22	33	64	90	115
"Crash Dive" (1943)-Tyrone Power	12	24	36	69	97	125
NOTE: *The 1941-42 issues contain line art with color photos. 1943 issues are line art.*						
CLASSICS GIVEAWAYS (Classic Comics reprints)						
12/41–Walter Theatre Enterprises (Huntington, WV) giveaway containing #2 (orig.) w/new generic-c (only 1 known copy)	84	168	252	538	919	1300

C-M-O Comics #1 © CEN

Comic Books #1 Talullah © Met. Printing Co.

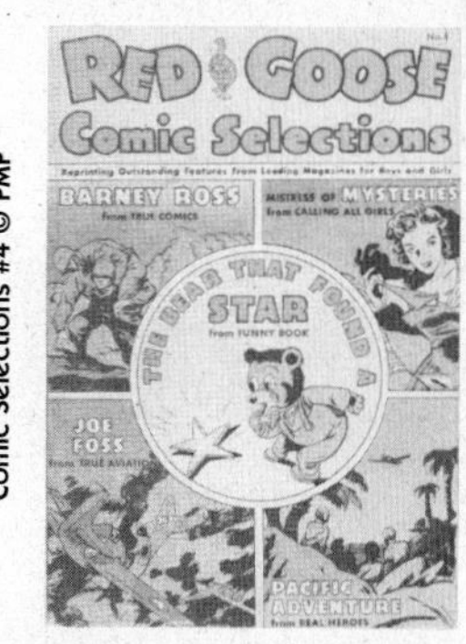

Comic Selections #4 © PMP

	GD 2.0	VG 4.0	FN 6.0	VF 8.0	VF/NM 9.0	NM- 9.2
1942–Double Comics containing CC#1 (orig.) (diff. cover) (not actually a giveaway) (very rare) (also see Double Comics) (only one known copy)	148	296	444	947	1624	2300
12/42–Saks 34th St. Giveaway containing CC#7 (orig.) (diff. cover) (very rare; only 6 known copies)	300	600	900	2010	3505	5000
2/43–American Comics containing CC#8 (orig.) (Liberty Theatre giveaway) (different cover) (only one known copy) (see American Comics)	97	194	291	621	1061	1500
12/44-Robin Hood Flour Co. Giveaway - #7-CC(R) (diff. cover) (rare) (edition probably 5 [22])	168	336	504	1075	1838	2600

NOTE: How are above editions determined without CC covers? 1942 is dated 1942, and CC#1-first reprint did not come out until 5/43. 12/42 and 2/43 are determined by blue note at bottom of first text page only in original edition. 12/44 is estimated from page width each reprint edition had progressively slightly smaller page width.

	GD	VG	FN	VF	VF/NM	NM-
1951–Shelter Thru the Ages (C.I. Educational Series) (actually Giveaway by the Ruberoid Co.) (16 pgs.) (contains original artwork by H. C. Kiefer) (there are 5 diff. back cover ad variations: "Ranch" house ad, "Igloo" ad, "Doll House" ad, "Tree House" ad & blank) (scarce)	55	110	165	352	601	850
1952–George Daynor Biography Giveaway (CC logo) (partly comic book/pictures/newspaper articles) (story of man who built Palace Depression out of junkyard swamp in NJ) (64 pgs.) (very rare; only 3 known copies, one missing back-c)	360	720	1080	2520	4410	6300
1953–Westinghouse/Dreams of a Man (C.I. Educational Series) (Westinghousebio./ Westinghouse Co. giveaway) (contains original artwork by H. C. Kiefer) (16 pgs.) (also French/Spanish/Italian versions) (scarce)	47	94	141	296	498	700
NOTE: Reproductions of 1951, 1952, and 1953 exist with color photocopy covers and black & white photocopy interior ("W.C.N. Reprint")	2	4	5	7	8	10
1951-53–Coward Shoe Giveaways (all editions very rare); 2 variations of back-c ad exist: With back-c photo ad: 5 (87), 12 (89), 22 (85), 32 (85), 49 (85), 69 (87), 72 (no HRN), 80 (0), 91 (0), 92 (0), 96 (0), 98 (0), 100 (0), 101 (0), 103-105 (all Os)	29	58	87	170	278	385
With back-c cartoon ad: 106-109 (all 0s), 110 (111), 112 (0)	31	62	93	186	303	420
1956–Ben Franklin 5-10 Store Giveaway (#65-PC with back cover ad) (scarce)	24	48	72	142	234	325
1956–Ben Franklin Insurance Co. Giveaway (#65-PC with diff. back cover ad) (very rare)	47	94	141	296	498	700
11/56–Sealtest Co. Edition - #4 (135) (identical to regular edition except for Sealtest logo printed, not stamped, on front cover) (only two copies known to exist)	28	56	84	165	270	375
1958–Get-Well Giveaway containing #15-CI (new cartoon-type cover) (Pressman Pharmacy) (only one copy known to exist)	27	54	81	162	266	370
1967-68–Twin Circle Giveaway Editions - all HRN 166, with back cover ad for National Catholic Press.						
2(R68), 4(R67), 10(R68), 13(R68)	3	6	9	21	32	42
48(R67), 128(R68), 535(576-R68)	4	8	12	22	34	45
16(R68), 68(R67)	5	10	15	30	48	65
12/69–Christmas Giveaway ("A Christmas Adventure") (reprints Picture Parade #4-1953, new cover) (4 ad variations)						
Stacey's Dept. Store	3	6	9	20	31	42
Anne & Hope Store	5	10	15	30	50	70
Gibson's Dept. Store (rare)	5	10	15	30	50	70
"Merry Christmas" & blank ad space	3	6	9	20	31	42

CLEAR THE TRACK!
Association of American Railroads: 1954 (paper-c, 16 pgs.)

	GD	VG	FN	VF	VF/NM	NM-
nn	5	10	15	24	30	35

CLIFF MERRITT SETS THE RECORD STRAIGHT
Brotherhood of Railroad Trainsmen: Giveaway (2 different issues)

	GD	VG	FN	VF	VF/NM	NM-
...and the Very Candid Candidate by Al Williamson	1	3	4	6	8	10
...Sets the Record Straight by Al Williamson (2 different-c: one by Williamson, the other by McWilliams)	1	3	4	6	8	10

CLYDE BEATTY COMICS (Also see Crackajack Funnies)
Commodore Productions & Artists, Inc.

	GD	VG	FN	VF	VF/NM	NM-
...African Jungle Book('56)-Richfield Oil Co. 16 pg. giveaway, soft-c	10	20	30	58	79	100

C-M-O COMICS
Chicago Mail Order Co.(Centaur): 1942 - No. 2, 1942 (68 pgs., full color)

	GD	VG	FN	VF	VF/NM	NM-
1-Invisible Terror, Super Ann, & Plymo the Rubber Man app. (all Centaur costume heroes)	94	188	282	597	1024	1450
2-Invisible Terror, Super Ann app.	57	114	171	362	619	875

COCOMALT BIG BOOK OF COMICS
Harry 'A' Chesler (Cocomalt Premium): 1938 (Reg. size, full color, 52 pgs.)

	GD	VG	FN	VF	VF/NM	NM-
1-(Scarce)-Biro-c/a; Little Nemo by Winsor McCay Jr., Dan Hastings; Jack Cole, Guardineer, Gustavson, Bob Wood-a	206	412	618	1318	2259	3200

COMIC BOOK (Also see Comics From Weatherbird)
American Juniors Shoe: 1954 (Giveaway)

Contains a comic rebound with new cover. Several combinations possible. Contents determine price.

COMIC BOOK CONFIDENTIAL
Sphinx Productions: 1988 (Giveaway, 16 pgs.)

1-Tie-in to a documentary about comic creators; creator biographies; Chester Brown-c 5.00

COMIC BOOK MAGAZINE
Chicago Tribune & other newspapers: 1940 - 1943 (Similar to Spirit sections) (7-3/4x10-3/4"; full color; 16-24 pgs. ea.)

	GD	VG	FN	VF	VF/NM	NM-
1940 issues	7	14	21	37	46	55
1941, 1942 issues	6	12	18	28	34	40
1943 issues	5	10	15	24	30	35

NOTE: *Published weekly. Texas Slim, Kit Carson, Spooky, Josie, Nuts & Jolts, Lew Loyal, Brenda Starr, Daniel Boone, Captain Storm, Rocky, Smokey Stover, Tiny Tim, Little Joe, Fu Manchu appear among others. Early issues had photo stories with pictures from the movies; later issues had comic art.*

COMIC BOOKS (Series 1)
Metropolitan Printing Co. (Giveaway): 1950 (16 pgs.; 5-1/4x8-1/2"; full color; bound at top; paper cover)

	GD	VG	FN	VF	VF/NM	NM-
1-Boots and Saddles; intro The Masked Marshal	6	12	18	28	34	40
1-The Green Jet; Green Lama by Raboy	20	40	60	114	182	250
1-My Pal Dizzy (Teen-age)	4	8	12	18	22	25
1-New World; origin Atomaster (costumed hero)	9	18	27	52	69	85
1-Talullah (Teen-age)	4	8	12	18	22	25

COMIC CAVALCADE
All-American/National Periodical Publications

	GD	VG	FN	VF	VF/NM	NM-
Giveaway (1944, 8 pgs., paper-c, in color)-One Hundred Years of Co-operation-r/Comic Cavalcade #9	47	94	141	296	498	700
Giveaway (1945, 16 pgs., paper-c, in color)-Movie "Tomorrow The World" (Nazi theme); r/Comic Cavalcade #10	61	122	183	390	670	950
Giveaway (c. 1944-45; 8 pgs, paper-c, in color)-The Twain Shall Meet-r/Comic Cavalcade #8	47	94	141	296	498	700

COMIC SELECTIONS (Shoe store giveaway)
Parents' Magazine Press: 1944-46 (Reprints from Calling All Girls, True Comics, True Aviation, & Real Heroes)

	GD	VG	FN	VF	VF/NM	NM-
1	5	10	15	22	26	30
2-6	4	8	11	16	19	22

COMICS FROM WEATHER BIRD (Also see Comic Book, Edward's Shoes, Free Comics to You & Weather Bird)
Weather Bird Shoes: 1954 - 1957 (Giveaway)

Contains a comic bound with new cover. Many combinations possible. Contents would determine price. Some issues do not contain complete comics, but only parts of comics. Value equals 40 to 60 percent of contents.

COMICS READING LIBRARIES (Educational Series)
King Features (Charlton Publ.): 1973, 1977, 1979 (36 pgs. in color) (Giveaways)

	GD	VG	FN	VF	VF/NM	NM-
R-01-Tiger, Quincy	2	4	6	8	11	14
R-02-Beetle Bailey, Blondie & Popeye	2	4	6	10	14	18
R-03-Blondie, Beetle Bailey	2	4	6	8	11	14
R-04-Tim Tyler's Luck, Felix the Cat	3	6	9	16	23	30
R-05-Quincy, Henry	2	4	6	8	11	14
R-06-The Phantom, Mandrake	3	6	9	16	23	30
1977 reprint(R-04)	2	4	6	9	13	16
R-07-Popeye, Little King	2	4	6	13	18	22
R-08-Prince Valiant (Foster), Flash Gordon	3	6	9	18	27	36
1977 reprint	2	4	6	11	16	20
R-09-Hagar the Horrible, Boner's Ark	2	4	6	10	14	18
R-10-Redeye, Tiger	2	4	6	8	11	14
R-11-Blondie, Hi & Lois	2	4	6	8	11	14
R-12-Popeye-Swee'pea, Brutus	2	4	6	13	18	22
R-13-Beetle Bailey, Little King	2	4	6	8	11	14
R-14-Quincy-Hamlet	2	4	6	8	11	14
R-15-The Phantom, The Genius	2	4	6	13	18	22
R-16-Flash Gordon, Mandrake	3	6	9	18	27	36
1977 reprint	2	4	6	10	14	18
Other 1977 editions....	2	4	6	8	10	12
1979 editions (68 pgs.)	2	4	6	8	10	12

NOTE: *Above giveaways available with purchase of $45.00 in merchandise. Used as a reading skills aid for small children.*

COMMANDMENTS OF GOD
Catechetical Guild: 1954, 1958

	GD	VG	FN	VF	VF/NM	NM-
300-Same contents in both editions; diff-c	5	10	15	24	29	34

Dan Curtis Giveaway #1
Dark Shadows © Dan Curtis

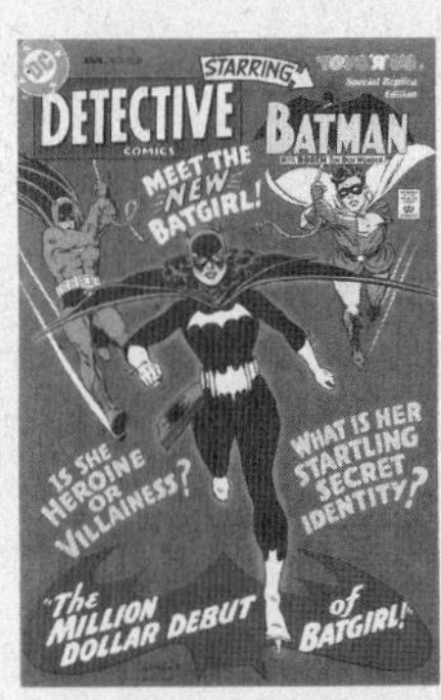

Detective Comics #359
Toys R Us Ed. © DC

Dick Tracy Sheds Light on the Mole
© NYNS

	GD 2.0	VG 4.0	FN 6.0	VF 8.0	VF/NM 9.0	NM- 9.2

COMPLIMENTARY COMICS
Sales Promotion Publ.: No date (1950's) (Giveaway)
1-Strongman by Powell, 3 stories 8 16 24 40 50 60

COPPER - THE OLDEST AND NEWEST METAL
Commercial Comics: 1959
nn 3 6 9 14 20 25

CRACKAJACK FUNNIES (Giveaway)
Malto-Meal: 1937 (Full size, soft-c, full color, 32 pgs.)(Before No. 1?)
nn-Features Dan Dunn, G-Man, Speed Bolton, Buck Jones, The Nebbs, Clyde Beatty, Freckles, Major Hoople, Wash Tubbs 97 194 291 621 1061 1500

CRAFTSMAN BOLT-ON SYSTEMS SAVE THE JUSTICE LEAGUE
DC Comics: 2012 (Giveaway promo for Craftsman Bolt-On Tool System)
1-Christian Duce-a/c; New-52 Justice League, The Key and Royal Flush Gang app. 3.00

CRISIS AT THE CARSONS
Pictorial Media: 1958 (Reg. size)
nn 5 10 15 24 30 35

CROSLEY'S HOUSE OF FUN (Also see Tee and Vee Crosley...)
Crosley Div. AVCO Mfg. Corp.: 1950 (Giveaway, paper cover, 32 pgs.)
nn-Strips revolve around Crosley appliances 5 10 15 22 26 30

DAGWOOD SPLITS THE ATOM (Also see Topix V8#4)
King Features Syndicate: 1949 (Science comic with King Features characters) (Giveaway)
nn-Half comic, half text; Popeye, Olive Oyl, Henry, Mandrake, Little King, Katzenjammer Kids app. 9 18 27 47 61 75

DAISY COMICS (Daisy Air Rifles)
Eastern Color Printing Co.: Dec, 1936 (5-1/4x7-1/2")
nn-Joe Palooka, Buck Rogers (2 pgs. from Famous Funnies No. 18, 1st full cover app.), Napoleon Flying to Fame, Butty & Fally 34 68 102 199 325 450

DAISY LOW OF THE GIRL SCOUTS
Girl Scouts of America: 1954, 1965 (16 pgs., paper-c)
1954-Story of Juliette Gordon Low 5 10 15 22 26 30
1965 2 4 6 9 12 15

DAN CURTIS GIVEAWAYS
Western Publishing Co.:1974 (3x6", 24 pgs., reprints)
1-Dark Shadows 2 4 6 11 16 20
2,6-Star Trek 2 4 6 11 16 20
3,4,7-9: 3-The Twilight Zone. 4-Ripley's Believe It or Not! 7-The Occult Files of Dr. Spektor. 8-Dagar the Invincible. 9-Grimm's Ghost Stories 2 4 6 9 12 15
5-Turok, Son of Stone (partial-r/Turok #78) 2 4 6 11 16 20

DANNY AND THE DEMOXICYCLE
Virginia Highway Safety Division: 1970s (Reg. size, slick-c)
nn 3 6 9 19 30 40

DANNY KAYE'S BAND FUN BOOK
H & A Selmer: 1959 (Giveaway)
nn 7 14 21 35 43 50

DAREDEVIL
Marvel Comics Group: 1993
...Vs. Vapora 1 (Engineering Show Giveaway, 16 pg.) - Intro Vapora 6.00

DAVY CROCKETT (TV)
Dell Publishing Co.
...Christmas Book (no date, 16 pgs., paper-c)-Sears giveaway
6 12 18 31 38 45
...Safety Trails (1955, 16pgs, 3-1/4x7")-Cities Service giveaway
8 16 24 40 50 60

DAVY CROCKETT
Charlton Comics
Hunting With... nn ('55, 16 pgs.)-Ben Franklin Store giveaway (Publ.-S. Rose)
5 10 15 24 30 35

DAVY CROCKETT
Walt Disney Prod.: (1955, 16 pgs., 5x7-1/4", slick, photo-c)
...In the Raid at Piney Creek-American Motors giveaway
8 16 24 40 50 60

DC SAMPLER
DC Comics: nn (#1) 1983 - No. 3, 1984 (36 pgs.; 6 1/2" x 10", giveaway)
nn(#1) -3: nn-Wraparound-c, previews upcoming issues. 3-Kirby-a
1 2 3 4 5 7

DC SPOTLIGHT
DC Comics: 1985 (50th anniversary special) (giveaway)
1-Includes profiles on Batman:The Dark Knight & Watchmen 6.00

DEATH JR. HALLOWEEN SPECIAL
Image Comics: Oct, 2006 (8-1/2"x 5-1/2", Halloween giveaway)
nn-Guy Davis-a/Joe Morrisey-s; wraparound-c 2.50

DENNIS THE MENACE
Hallden (Fawcett)
...& Dirt ('59)-Soil Conservation giveaway; r-# 36; Wiseman-c/a
3 6 9 14 20 26
...& Dirt ('68)-reprints '59 edition 2 4 6 8 11 14
...Away We Go('70)-Caladryl giveaway 2 4 6 8 10 12
...Coping with Family Stress-giveaway 2 4 6 8 10 12
...Takes a Poke at Poison('61)-Food & Drug Admin. giveaway; Wiseman-c/a
2 4 6 8 10 12
...Takes a Poke at Poison-Revised 1/66, 11/70 1 2 3 5 6 8
...Takes a Poke at Poison-Revised 1972, 1974, 1977, 1981
1 2 3 4 5 7

DESERT DAWN
E.C./American Museum of Natural History: 1935 (paper-c)
nn-Johnny Jackrabbit stars. Three known copies: A Fair copy (brittle) sold for $657 in 2007. A GD+ copy (brittle) sold for $2300 in 2005. Another Fair copy (brittle) sold for $690 in 2004

DETECTIVE COMICS (Also see other Batman titles)
National Periodical Publications/DC Comics
27 (1984)-Oreo Cookies giveaway (32 pgs., paper-c) r-/Det. #27,#38 & Batman #1 (1st Joker)
4 8 12 27 44 60
38 (1995) Blockbuster Video edition; reprints 1st Robin app. 3.00
38 (1997) Toys R Us edition 3.00
359 (1997) Toys R Us edition; reprints 1st Batgirl app. 3.00
373 (1997, 6 1/4" x 4") Warner Brothers Home Video 3.00

DICK TRACY GIVEAWAYS
1939 - 1958; 1990
Buster Brown Shoes Giveaway (1940s?, 36 pgs. in color); 1938-39-r by Gould
21 42 63 126 206 285
Gillmore Giveaway (See Superbook)
...Hatful of Fun (No date, 1950-52, 32pgs.; 8-1/2x10")-Dick Tracy hat promotion; Dick Tracy games, magic tricks. Miller Bros. premium 15 30 45 90 140 190
Motorola Giveaway (1953)-Reprints Harvey Comics Library #2; "The Case of the Sparkle Plenty TV Mystery" 7 14 21 37 46 55
Original Dick Tracy by Chester Gould, The (Aug, 1990, 16 pgs., 5-1/2x8-1/2")-Gladstone Publ.; Bread Giveaway 1 3 4 6 8 10
Popped Wheat Giveaway (1947, 16 pgs. in color)-1940-r; Sig Feuchtwanger Publ.; Gould-a
4 8 12 18 22 25
...Presents the Family Fun Book; Tip Top Bread Giveaway, no date or number (1940, Fawcett Publ., 16 pgs. in color)-Spy Smasher, Ibis, Lance O'Casey app.
39 78 117 240 395 550
Same as above but without app. of heroes & Dick Tracy on cover only
14 28 42 82 121 160
Service Station Giveaway (1958, 16 pgs. in color)(regular size, slick cover)-Harvey Info. Press 5 10 14 20 24 28
Shoe Store Giveaway (Weatherbird and Triangle Stores)(1939, 16 pgs.)-Gould-a
14 28 42 80 115 150

DICK TRACY SHEDS LIGHT ON THE MOLE
Western Printing Co.: 1949 (16 pgs.) (Ray-O-Vac Flashlights giveaway)
nn-Not by Gould 8 16 24 42 54 65

DICK WINGATE OF THE U.S. NAVY
Superior Publ./Toby Press: 1951; 1953 (no month)
nn-U.S. Navy giveaway 5 10 15 24 30 35
1(1953, Toby)-Reprints nn issue? (same-c) 5 10 14 20 24 28

DIG 'EM
Kellogg's Sugar Smacks Giveaway: 1973 (2-3/8x6", 16 pgs.)
nn-4 different issues 1 3 4 6 8 10

DOC CARTER VD COMICS
Health Publications Institute, Raleigh, N. C. (Giveaway): 1949 (16 pgs. in color) (Paper-c)
nn 20 40 60 114 182 250

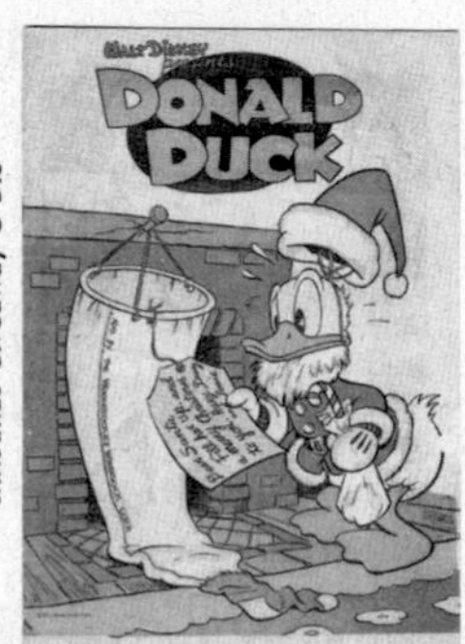

Donald Duck 1944 Christmas Giveaway © DIS

Famous Gang Book of Comics © WB

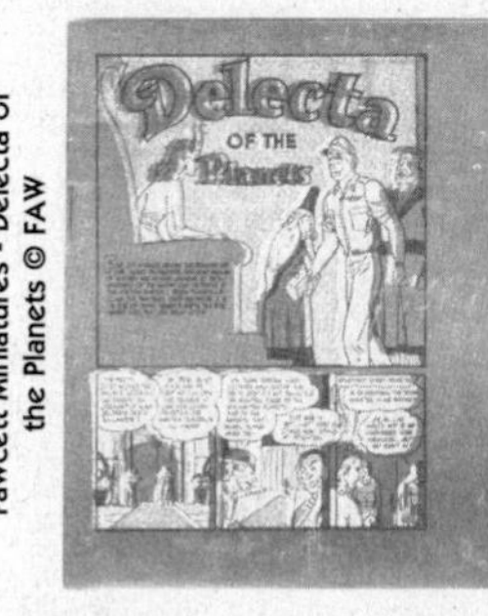

Fawcett Miniatures - Delecta of the Planets © FAW

	GD 2.0	VG 4.0	FN 6.0	VF 8.0	VF/NM 9.0	NM- 9.2

DONALD AND MICKEY MERRY CHRISTMAS (Formerly Famous Gang Book Of Comics)
K. K. Publ./Firestone Tire & Rubber Co.: 1943 - 1949 (Giveaway, 20 pgs.)
Put out each Christmas; 1943 issue titled "Firestone Presents Comics" (Disney)
1943-Donald Duck-r/WDC&S #32 by Carl Barks 77 154 231 493 847 1200
1944-Donald Duck-r/WDC&S #35 by Barks 74 148 222 470 810 1150
1945- "Donald Duck's Best Christmas", 8 pgs. Carl Barks; intro. & 1st app. Grandma Duck in comic books 107 214 321 680 1165 1650
1946-Donald Duck in "Santa's Stormy Visit", 8 pgs. Carl Barks 65 130 195 416 708 1000
1947-Donald Duck in "Three Good Little Ducks", 8 pgs. Carl Barks 65 130 195 416 708 1000
1948-Donald Duck in "Toyland", 8 pgs. Carl Barks 65 130 195 416 708 1000
1949-Donald Duck in "New Toys", 8 pgs. Barks 61 122 183 390 670 950

DONALD DUCK
K. K. Publications: 1944 (Christmas giveaway, paper-c, 16 pgs.)(2 versions)
nn-Kelly cover reprint 107 214 321 680 1165 1650

DONALD DUCK AND THE RED FEATHER
Red Feather Giveaway: 1948 (8-1/2x11", 4 pgs., B&W)
nn 20 40 60 117 189 260

DONALD DUCK IN "THE LITTERBUG"
Keep America Beautiful: 1963 (5x7-1/4", 16 pgs., soft-c) (Disney giveaway)
nn 5 10 15 31 53 75

DONALD DUCK "PLOTTING PICNICKERS" (See Frito-Lay Giveaway)

DONALD DUCK'S SURPRISE PARTY
Walt Disney Productions: 1948 (16 pgs.) (Giveaway for Icy Frost Twins Ice Cream Bars)
nn-(Rare)-Kelly-c/a 219 438 657 1402 2401 3400

DOT AND DASH AND THE LUCKY JINGLE PIGGIE
Sears Roebuck Co.: 1942 (Christmas giveaway, 12 pgs.)
nn-Contains a war stamp album and a punch out Jingle Piggie bank 12 24 36 67 94 120

DOUBLE TALK (Also see Two-Faces)
Feature Publications: No date (1962?) (32 pgs., full color, slick-c)
Christian Anti-Communism Crusade (Giveaway)
nn-Sickle with blood-c 16 32 48 94 147 200

DRUMMER BOY AT GETTYSBURG
Eastern National Park & Monument Association: 1976
nn-Fred Ray-a 3 6 9 14 20 25

DUMBO (Walt Disney's..., The Flying Elephant)
Weatherbird Shoes/Ernest Kern Co.(Detroit)/ Wieboldt's (Chicago): 1941
(K.K. Publ. Giveaway)
nn-16 pgs., 9x10" (Rare) 42 84 126 265 445 625
nn-52 pgs., 5-1/2x8-1/2", slick cover in color; B&W interior; half text, half reprints 4-Color No. 17 (Dept. store) 22 44 66 131 216 300

DUMBO WEEKLY
Walt Disney Prod.: 1942 (Premium supplied by Diamond D-X Gas Stations)(4 pgs. each)
1 41 82 123 256 428 600
2-16 14 28 42 82 121 160
Binder only (linen-like stock) 225
NOTE: *A cover and binder came separate at gas stations. Came with membership card.*

EAT RIGHT TO WORK AND WIN
Swift & Company: 1942 (16 pgs.) (Giveaway)
Blondie, Henry, Flash Gordon by Alex Raymond, Toots & Casper, Thimble Theatre(Popeye), Tillie the Toiler, The Phantom, The Little King, & Bringing up Father - original strips just for this book -(in daily strip form which shows what foods we should eat and why) 26 52 78 154 252 350

EDWARD'S SHOES GIVEAWAY
Edward's Shoe Store: 1954 (Has clown on cover)
Contains comic with new cover. Many combinations possible. Contents determines price, 50-60 percent of original. (Similar to Comics From Weatherbird & Free Comics to You)

ELSIE THE COW
D. S. Publishing Co.
Borden's cheese comic picture bk ("40, giveaway) 20 40 60 114 182 250
Borden Milk Giveaway-(16 pgs., nn) (3 ishs, "A Trip Through Space" and 2 others, 1957) 14 28 42 81 118 155
Elsie's Fun Book(1950; Borden Milk) 14 28 42 81 118 155
Everyday Birthday Fun With... (1957; 20 pgs.)(100th Anniversary); Kubert-a 14 28 42 81 118 155

	GD 2.0	VG 4.0	FN 6.0	VF 8.0	VF/NM 9.0	NM- 9.2

ESCAPE FROM FEAR
Planned Parenthood of America: 1956, 1962, 1969 (Giveaway, 8 pgs., color) (On birth control)
1956 edition 11 22 33 60 83 105
1962 edition 4 8 12 23 37 50
1969 edition 3 6 9 14 20 25

EVEL KNIEVEL
Marvel Comics Group (Ideal Toy Corp.): 1974 (Giveaway, 20 pgs.)
nn-Contains photo on inside back-c 4 8 12 27 44 60

FAMOUS COMICS (Also see Favorite Comics)
Zain-Eppy/United Features Syndicate: No date; Mid 1930's (24 pgs., paper-c)
nn-Reprinted from 1933 & 1934 newspaper strips in color; Joe Palooka, Hairbreadth Harry, Napoleon, The Nebbs, etc. (Many different versions known) 61 122 183 390 670 950

FAMOUS FAIRY TALES
K. K. Publ. Co.: 1942; 1943 (32 pgs.); 1944 (16 pgs.) (Giveaway, soft-c)
1942-Kelly-a 39 78 117 236 388 540
1943-r-/Fairy Tale Parade No. 2,3; Kelly-a 25 50 75 150 245 340
1944-Kelly-a 22 44 66 131 216 300

FAMOUS FUNNIES - A CARNIVAL OF COMICS
Eastern Color: 1933
36 pgs., no date given, no publisher, no number; contains strip reprints of The Bungle Family, Dixie Dugan, Hairbreadth Harry, Joe Palooka, Keeping Up With the Jones, Mutt & Jeff, Reg'lar Fellers, S'Matter Pop, Strange As It Seems, and others. This book was sold by M. C. Gaines to Wheatena, Malt-O-Milk, John Wanamaker, Kinney Shoe Stores, & others to be given away as premiums and radio giveaways (1933). Originally came with a mailing envelope. 486 972 1458 3550 6275 9000

FAMOUS GANG BOOK OF COMICS (Becomes Donald & Mickey Merry Christmas 1943 on)
Firestone Tire & Rubber Co.: Dec, 1942 (Christmas giveaway, 32 pgs., paper-c)
nn-(Rare)-Porky Pig, Bugs Bunny, Mary Jane & Sniffles, Elmer Fudd; r/Looney Tunes 68 136 204 435 743 1050

FANTASTIC FOUR
Marvel Comics
nn (1981, 32 pgs.) Young Model Builders Club 2 4 6 9 12 15
Vol. 3 #60 Baltimore Comic Book Show (10/02, newspaper supplement) 200,000 copies were distributed to Baltimore Sun home subscribers to promote Baltimore Comic Con 4.00

FATHER OF CHARITY
Catechetical Guild Giveaway: No date (32 pgs.; paper cover)
nn 5 10 15 24 29 34

FAVORITE COMICS (Also see Famous Comics)
Grocery Store Giveaway (Diff. Corp.) (detergent): 1934 (36 pgs.)
Book 1-The Nebbs, Strange As It Seems, Napoleon, Joe Palooka, Dixie Dugan, S'Matter Pop, Hairbreadth Harry, etc. reprints 100 200 300 635 1093 1550
Book 2,3 61 122 183 387 664 940

FAWCETT MINIATURES (See Mighty Midget)
Fawcett Publications: 1946 (3-3/4x5", 12-24 pgs.) (Wheaties giveaways)
Captain Marvel "And the Horn of Plenty"; Bulletman story 14 28 42 80 115 150
Captain Marvel "& the Raiders From Space"; Golden Arrow story 14 28 42 80 115 150
Captain Marvel Jr. "The Case of the Poison Press!" Bulletman story 14 28 42 80 115 150
Delecta of the Planets; C. C. Beck art; B&W inside; 12 pgs.; 3 printing variations (coloring) exist 20 40 60 114 182 250

FEARLESS FOSDICK
Capp Enterprises Inc.: 1951
...& The Case of The Red Feather 6 12 18 27 33 38

FIFTY WHO MADE DC GREAT
DC Comics: 1985 (Reg. size, slick-c)
nn 1 3 4 6 8 10

FIGHT FOR FREEDOM
National Assoc. of Mfgrs./General Comics: 1949, 1951 (Giveaway, 16 pgs.)
nn-Dan Barry-c/a; used in **POP**, pg. 102 6 12 18 31 38 45

FIRE AND BLAST
National Fire Protection Assoc.: 1952 (Giveaway, 16 pgs., paper-c)
nn-Mart Baily A-Bomb-c; about fire prevention 15 30 45 88 137 185

FIRE CHIEF AND THE SAFE OL' FIREFLY, THE

Flash Gordon Gordon Bread #2 ©KFS

Forest Fire © Commercial Comics

Frito-Lay Giveaways © DIS

	GD	VG	FN	VF	VF/NM	NM-
	2.0	4.0	6.0	8.0	9.0	9.2

GD VG FN VF VF/NM NM- 2.0 4.0 6.0 8.0 9.0 9.2

National Board of Fire Underwriters: 1952 (16 pgs.) (Safety brochure given away at schools) (produced by American Visuals Corp.)(Eisner)

nn-(Rare) Eisner-c/a 41 82 123 256 428 600

FLASH, THE
DC Comics

nn-(1990) Brochure for CBS TV series 4.00
The Flash Comes to a Standstill (1981, General Foods giveaway, 8 pages, 3-1/2 x 6-3/4", oblong) 2 4 6 10 14 18

FLASH COMICS (Also see Captain Marvel and Funny Stuff)
National Periodical Publications: 1946 (6-1/2x8-1/4", 32 pgs.)(Wheaties Giveaway)

nn-Johnny Thunder, Ghost Patrol, The Flash & Kubert Hawkman app.; Irwin Hasen-c/a 100 200 700 1000 - -

NOTE: *All known copies were taped to Wheaties boxes and are never found in mint condition. Copies with light tape residue bring the listed prices in all grades*

FLASH FORCE 2000
DC Comics: 1984

1-5 6.00

FLASH GORDON
Dell Publishing Co.: 1943 (20 pgs.)

Macy's Giveaway-(Rare); not by Raymond 58 116 174 371 636 900

FLASH GORDON
Harvey Comics: 1951 (16 pgs. in color, regular size, paper-c) (Gordon Bread giveaway)

1,2: 1-r/strips 10/24/37 - 2/6/38. 2-r/strips 7/14/40 - 10/6/40; Reprints by Raymond each.... 2 4 6 9 12 15

NOTE: *Most copies have brittle edges.*

FLINTSTONES FUN BOOK, THE
Denny's giveaway: 1990

1-20 1 2 3 5 6 8

FLOOD RELIEF
Malibu Comics (Ultraverse): Jan, 1994 (36 pgs.)(Ordered thru mail w/$5.00 to Red Cross)

1-Hardcase, Prime & Prototype app. 6.00

FOREST FIRE (Also see The Blazing Forest and Smokey Bear)
American Forestry Assn.(Commerical Comics): 1949 (dated-1950) (16 pgs., paper-c)

nn-Intro/1st app. Smokey The Forest Fire Preventing Bear; created by Rudy Wendelein; Wendelein/Sparling-a; 'Carter Oil Co.' on back-c of original 18 36 54 107 169 230

FOREST RANGER HANDBOOK
Wrather Corp.: 1967 (5x7", 20 pgs., slick-c)

nn-WIth Corey Stuart & Lassie photo-c 2 4 6 13 18 22

FORGOTTEN STORY BEHIND NORTH BEACH, THE
Catechetical Guild: No date (8 pgs., paper-c)

nn 5 10 15 23 28 32

FORK IN THE ROAD
U.S. Army Recruiting Service: 1961 (16 pgs., paper-c)

nn 2 4 6 11 16 20

48 FAMOUS AMERICANS
J. C. Penney Co. (Cpr. Edwin H. Stroh): 1947 (Giveaway) (Half-size in color)

nn - Simon & Kirby-a 11 22 33 62 86 110

FOXHOLE ON YOUR LAWN
No Publisher: No date

nn-Charles Biro art 4 7 10 14 17 20

FRANKIE LUER'S SPACE ADVENTURES
Luer Packing Co.: 1955 (5x7", 36 pgs., slick-c)

nn - With Davey Rocket 4 8 12 17 21 24

FREDDY
Charlton Comics

Schiff's Shoes Presents... #1 (1959)-Giveaway 4 8 11 16 19 22

FREE COMIC BOOK DAY EDITIONS (Now listed in the regular section)

FREE COMICS TO YOU FROM... (name of shoe store) (Has clown on cover & another with a rabbit) (Like comics from Weather Bird & Edward's Shoes)
Shoe Store Giveaway: Circa 1956, 1960-61

Contains a comic bound with new cover - several combinations possible; some Harvey titles known. Contents determine price.

FREEDOM TRAIN
Street & Smith Publications: 1948 (Giveaway)

nn-Powell-c w/mailer 16 32 48 94 147 200

FREIHOFER'S COMIC BOOK
All-American Comics: 1940s (7 1/2 x 10 1/4")

2nd edition-(Scarce) Cover features All-American Comics characters Ultra-Man, Hop Harrigan, Red, White and Blue and others 58 116 174 371 636 900

FRIENDLY GHOST, CASPER, THE
Harvey Publications: 1967 (16 pgs.)

American Dental Assoc. giveaway-Small size 3 6 9 17 25 32

FRITO-LAY GIVEAWAY
Frito-Lay: 1962 (3-1/4x7", soft-c, 16 pgs.) (Disney)

nn-Donald Duck "Plotting Picnickers" 5 10 15 30 50 70
nn-Ludwig Von Drake "Fish Stampede" 3 6 9 19 30 40
nn- Mickey Mouse & Goofy "Bicep Bungle" 3 6 9 21 33 45

FROM GOODWILL INDUSTRIES, A GOOD LIFE
Goodwill Industries: 1950s (regular size)

1 8 16 24 40 50 60

FRONTIER DAYS
Robin Hood Shoe Store (Brown Shoe): 1956 (Giveaway)

1 4 7 10 14 17 20

FRONTIERS OF FREEDOM
Institute of Life Insurance: 1950 (Giveaway, paper cover)

nn-Dan Barry-a 8 16 24 44 57 70

FUNNIES ON PARADE (Premium)(See Toy World Funnies)
Eastern Color Printing Co.: 1933 (36 pgs., slick cover)
No date or publisher listed

nn-Contains Sunday page reprints of Mutt & Jeff, Joe Palooka, Hairbreadth Harry, Reg'lar Fellers, Skippy, & others (10,000 print run). This book was printed for Proctor & Gamble to be given away & came out before Famous Funnies or Century of Comics. 1000 2000 3000 6000 11,000 16,000

FUNNY PICTURE STORIES
Comics Magazine Co./Centaur Publications: 1930s (Giveaway, 16-20 pgs., slick-c)

Promotes diff. laundries; has box on cover where "your Laundry Name" is printed 34 68 102 199 325 450

FUNNY STUFF (Also see Captain Marvel & Flash Comics)
National Periodical Publications (Wheaties Giveaway): 1946 (6-1/2x8-1/4")

nn-(Scarce)-Dodo & the Frog, Three Mouseketeers, etc.; came taped to Wheaties box; never found in better than fine 50 100 350 500 – –

FUTURE COP: L.A.P.D. (Electronic Arts video game)
DC Comics (WildStorm): 1998

nn-Ron Lim-a/Dave Johnson-c 2.50

GABBY HAYES WESTERN (Movie star)
Fawcett Publications

Quaker Oats Giveaway nn's(#1-5, 1951, 2-1/2x7") (Kagran Corp.)-...In Tracks of Guilt, ...In the Fence Post Mystery, ...In the Accidental Sherlock, ...In the Frame-Up, ...In the Double Cross Brand known 10 20 30 54 72 90
Mailing Envelope (has illo of Gabby on front) 10 20 30 54 72 90

GARY GIBSON COMICS (Donut club membership)
National Dunking Association: 1950 (Included in donut box with pin and card)

1-Western soft-c, 16 pgs.; folded into the box 5 10 14 20 24 28

GENE AUTRY COMICS
Dell Publishing Co.

...Adventure Comics And Play-Fun Book ('47)-32 pgs., 8x6-1/2"; games, comics, magic (Pillsbury premium) 22 44 66 132 216 300
Quaker Oats Giveaway(1950)-2-1/2x6-3/4"; 5 different versions; "Death Card Gang", "Phantoms of the Cave", "Riddle of Laughing Mtn.", "Secret of Lost Valley", "Bond of the Broken Arrow" (came in wrapper) each... 10 20 30 58 79 100
Mailing Envelope (has illo. of Gene on front) 10 20 30 58 79 100
3-D Giveaway(1953)-Pocket-size; 5 different 10 20 30 58 79 100
Mailing Envelope (no art on front) 8 16 24 44 57 70

GENE AUTRY TIM (Formerly Tim) (Becomes Tim in Space)
Tim Stores: 1950 (Half-size) (B&W Giveaway)

nn-Several issues (All Scarce) 19 38 57 109 172 235

GENERAL FOODS SUPER-HEROES

The Great People of Genesis © David C. Cook

Gulf Funny Weekly #356 © Gulf Oil Co.

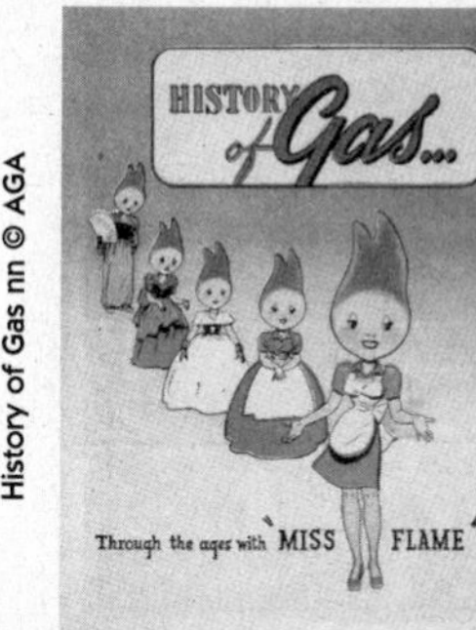

History of Gas nn © AGA

GD VG FN VF VF/NM NM-
2.0 4.0 6.0 8.0 9.0 9.2

DC Comics: 1979, 1980
1-4 (1979), 1-4 (1980) each... 12.00

G. I. COMICS (Also see Jeep & Overseas Comics)
Giveaways: 1945 - No. 73?, 1946 (Distributed to U. S. Armed Forces)
1-73-Contains Prince Valiant by Foster, Blondie, Smilin' Jack, Mickey Finn, Terry & the Pirates, Donald Duck, Alley Oop, Moon Mullins & Capt. Easy strip reprints (at least 73 issues known to exist) 8 16 24 42 54 65

GOLDEN ARROW
Fawcett Publications
...Well Known Comics (1944; 12 pgs.; 8-1/2x10-1/2"; paper-c; glued binding)- Bestmaid/ Samuel Lowe giveaway; printed in green 10 20 30 54 72 90

GOLDILOCKS & THE THREE BEARS
K. K. Publications: 1943 (Giveaway)
nn 13 26 39 74 105 135

GREAT PEOPLE OF GENESIS, THE
David C. Cook Publ. Co.: No date (Religious giveaway, 64 pgs.)
nn-Reprint/Sunday Pix Weekly 5 10 15 23 28 32

GREAT SACRAMENT, THE
Catechetical Guild: 1953 (Giveaway, 36 pgs.)
nn 5 10 15 22 26 30

GREEN JET COMICS, THE (See Comic Books, Series 1)

GRENADA
Commercial Comics Co.: 1983 (Giveaway produced by the CIA)
1-Air dropped over Grenada during the 1983 invasion 30.00

GRIT (YOU'VE GOT TO HAVE...)
GRIT Publishing Co.: 1959
nn-GRIT newspaper sales recruitment comic; Schaffenberger-a. Later version has altered artwork 5 10 15 22 26 30

GROWING UP WITH JUDY
1952
nn-General Electric giveaway 4 8 12 18 22 25

GULF FUNNY WEEKLY (Gulf Comic Weekly No. 1-4)(See Standard Oil Comics)
Gulf Oil Company (Giveaway): 1933 - No. 422, 5/23/41 (in full color; 4 pgs.; tabloid size to 2/3/39; 2/10/39 on, regular comic book size)(early issues undated)
1 66 132 198 419 722 1025
2-5 31 62 93 184 300 415
6-30 20 40 60 117 189 260
31-100 14 28 42 82 121 160
101-196 10 20 30 58 79 100
197-Wings Winfair begins(1/29/37); by Fred Meagher beginning in 1938 23 46 69 136 223 310
198-300 (Last tabloid size) 14 28 42 82 121 160
301-350 (Regular size) 9 18 27 52 69 85
351-422 8 16 24 42 54 65

GULLIVER'S TRAVELS
Macy's Department Store: 1939, small size
nn-Christmas giveaway 14 28 42 80 115 150

GUN THAT WON THE WEST, THE
Winchester-Western Division & Olin Mathieson Chemical Corp.: 1956 (Giveaway, 24 pgs.)
nn-Painted-c 5 10 15 24 30 35

HAPPINESS AND HEALING FOR YOU (Also see Oral Roberts'...)
Commercial Comics: 1955 (36 pgs., slick cover) (Oral Roberts Giveaway)
nn 9 18 27 52 69 85
NOTE: *The success of this book prompted Oral Roberts to go into the publishing business himself to produce his own material.*

HAPPI TIME FUN BOOK
Sears, Roebuck & Co.: 1940s - 1950s (32 pgs., soft-c)
nn-Comics, games, puzzles, & magic tricks cut -outs 4 7 10 14 17 20

HAPPY CHAMP, THE (The Story of Joker Osborn)
Western Publ.: 1965
nn-About water-skiing 3 6 9 19 30 40

HAPPY TOOTH
DC Comics: 1996
1 3.00

HARLEM YOUTH REPORT (Also see All-Negro Comics and Negro Romances)
Custom Comics, Inc.: 1964 (Giveaway)(No #1-4)
5-"Youth in the Ghetto" and "The Blueprint For Change"; distr. in Harlem only; has map of central Harlem on back-c (scarce) 57 114 171 456 1028 1600

HAWKMAN - THE SKY'S THE LIMIT
DC Comics: 1981 (General Foods giveaway, 8 pages, 3-1/2 x 6-3/4", oblong)
nn 2 4 6 10 14 18

HAWTHORN-MELODY FARMS DAIRY COMICS
Everybody's Publishing Co.: No date (1950's) (Giveaway)
nn-Cheerie Chick, Tuffy Turtle, Robin Koo Koo, Donald & Longhorn Legends 2 4 6 8 11 14

HENRY ALDRICH COMICS (TV)
Dell Publishing Co.
Giveaway (16 pgs., soft-c, 1951)-Capehart radio 3 6 9 17 26 35

HERE IS SANTA CLAUS
Goldsmith Publishing Co. (Kann's in Washington, D.C.): 1930s (16 pgs., 8 in color) (stiff paper covers)
nn 14 28 42 76 108 140

HERE'S HOW AMERICA'S CARTOONISTS HELP TO SELL U.S. SAVINGS BONDS
Harvey Comics: 1950? (16 pgs., giveaway, paper cover)
Contains: Joe Palooka, Donald Duck, Archie, Kerry Drake, Red Ryder, Blondie & Steve Canyon 20 40 60 114 182 250

HISTORY OF GAS
American Gas Assoc.: Mar, 1947 (Giveaway, 16 pgs., soft-c)
nn-Miss Flame narrates 8 16 24 40 50 60

HOME DEPOT, SAFETY HEROES
Marvel Comics.: Oct, 2005 (Giveaway)
nn-Spider-Man and the Fantastic Four on the cover; Olliffe-a/c; Roseman-s 2.50

HONEYBEE BIRDWHISTLE AND HER PET PEPI (Introducing...)
Newspaper Enterprise Assoc.: 1969 (Giveaway, 24 pgs., B&W, slick cover)
nn-Contains Freckles newspaper strips with a short biography of Henry Fornhals (artist) & Fred Fox (writer) of the strip 4 8 12 27 44 60

HOODS UP
Fram Corp.: 1953 (15¢, distributed to service station owners, 16 pgs.)
1-(Very Rare; only 2 known); Eisner-c/a in all (a CGC 9.0 copy sold for $1840 in 2006)
2-6-(Very Rare; only 1 known of #3, 2 known of #2,4) 48 96 144 302 514 725
NOTE: *Convertible Connie gives tips for service stations, selling Fram oil filters.*

HOOKED (Anti-drug comic distributed at NYC methadone clinics)
U.S. Dept. of Health: 1966 (giveaway, oblong)
nn-Distributed between May and July, 1966 3 6 9 19 30 40

HOPALONG CASSIDY
Fawcett Publications
Grape Nuts Flakes giveaway (1950,9x6") 14 28 42 78 112 145
...& the Mad Barber (1951 Bond Bread giveaway)-7x5"; used in **SOTI**, pgs. 308,309 18 36 54 103 162 220
...Meets the Brend Brothers Bandits (1951 Bond Bread giveaway, color, paper-c, 16 pgs., 3-1/2x7")- Fawcett Publ. 9 18 27 47 61 75
...Strange Legacy (1951 Bond Bread giveaway) 9 18 27 47 61 75
White Tower Giveaway (1946, 16pgs., paper-c) 9 18 27 52 69 85

HOPPY THE MARVEL BUNNY (WELL KNOWN COMICS)
Fawcett Publications: 1944 (8-1/2x10-1/2", paper-c)
Bestmaid/Samuel Lowe (printed in red or blue) 10 20 30 56 76 95

HOT STUFF, THE LITTLE DEVIL
Harvey Publications (Illustrated Humor):1963
Shoestore Giveaway 3 6 9 21 33 45

HOW KIDS ENJOY NEW YORK
American Airlines: 1966 (Giveaway, 40 pgs., 4x9")
nn-Includes 8 color pages by Bob Kane featuring a tour of New York and his studio (a VG copy sold for $180 and a FN+ sold for $250 in 2004)

HOW STALIN HOPES WE WILL DESTROY AMERICA
Joe Lowe Co. (Pictorial Media): 1951 (Giveaway, 16 pgs.)
nn 39 78 117 240 395 550

HURRICANE KIDS, THE (Also See Magic Morro, The Owl, Popular Comics #45)

If The Devil Would Talk © CG

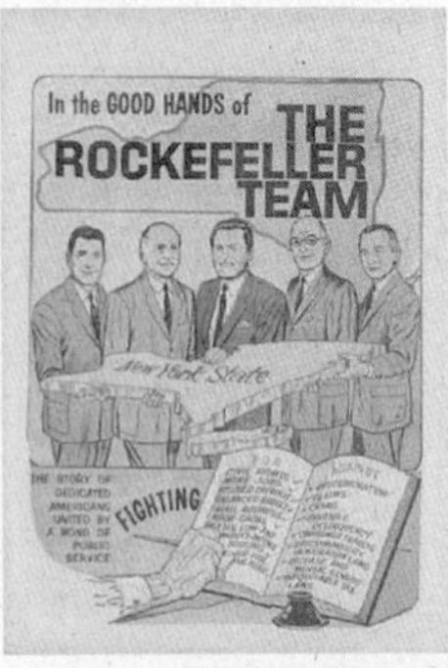

In The Good Hands of the Rockefeller Team © Country Art Studios

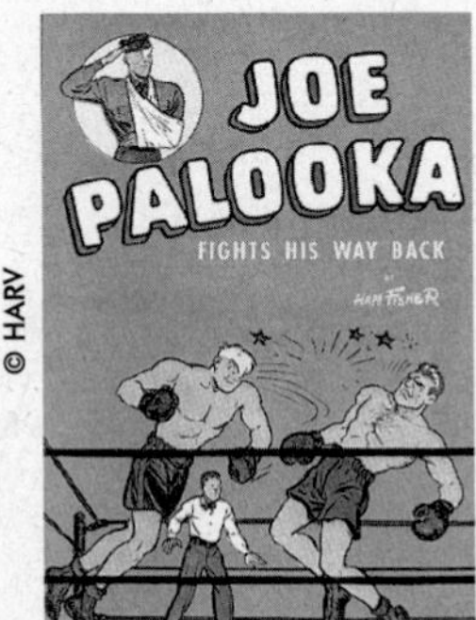

Joe Palooka Fights His Way Back © HARV

	GD 2.0	VG 4.0	FN 6.0	VF 8.0	VF/NM 9.0	NM- 9.2

R.S. Callender: 1941 (Giveaway, 7-1/2x5-1/4", soft-c)
nn-Will Ely-a. 8 16 24 44 57 70

IF THE DEVIL WOULD TALK
Roman Catholic Catechetical Guild/Impact Publ.: 1950; 1958 (32 pgs.; paper cover; in full color)
nn-(Scarce)-About secularism (20-30 copies known to exist); very low distribution
97 194 291 621 1061 1500
1958 Edition-(Impact Publ.); art & script changed to meet church criticism of earlier edition; 80 plus copies known to exist 33 66 99 194 317 440
Black & White version of nn edition; small size; only 4 known copies exist
36 72 108 211 343 475
NOTE: *The original edition of this book was printed and killed by the Guild's board of directors. It is believed that a very limited number of copies were distributed. The 1958 version was a complete bomb with very limited, if any, circulation. In 1979, 11 original, 4 1958 reprints, and 4 B&W's surfaced from the Guild's old files in St. Paul, Minnesota.*

IN LOVE WITH JESUS
Catechetical Educational Society: 1952 (Giveaway, 36 pgs.)
nn 7 14 21 37 46 55

INTERSTATE THEATRES' FUN CLUB COMICS
Interstate Theatres: Mid 1940's (10¢ on cover) (B&W cover) (Premium)
Cover features MLJ characters looking at a copy of Top-Notch Comics, but contains an early Detective Comic on inside; many combinations possible
11 22 33 64 90 115

IN THE GOOD HANDS OF THE ROCKEFELLER TEAM
Country Art Studios: No date (paper cover, 8 pgs.)
nn-Joe Simon-a 8 16 24 42 54 65

IRON GIANT
DC Comics: 1999 (4 pages, theater giveaway)
1-Previews movie 3.00

IRON HORSE GOES TO WAR, THE
Association of American Railroads: 1960 (Giveaway, 16 pgs.)
nn-Civil War & railroads 3 6 9 16 23 30

IRON MAN
Marvel Comics
Marvel Halloween Ashcan 2007 (8-1/2" x 5-3/8") updated origin; Michael Golden-c 2.00

IS THIS TOMORROW?
Catechetical Guild: 1947 (One Shot) (3 editions) (52 pgs.)
1-Theme of communists taking over the USA; (no price on cover) Used in **POP**, pg. 102 28 56 84 165 270 375
1-(10¢ on cover)(Red price on yellow circle) 28 56 84 165 270 375
1-(10¢ on cover)(Yellow price on black circle) 32 64 96 188 307 425
1-Has blank circle with no price on cover 32 64 96 188 307 425
Black & White advance copy titled "Confidential" (52 pgs.)-Contains script and art edited out of the color edition, including one page of extreme violence showing mob nailing a Cardinal to a door; (only two known copies). A VF+ sold in 2/08 for $3346. A NM 9.6 sold in 1/07 for $5975
NOTE: *The original color version first sold for 10 cents. Since sales were good, it was later printed as a giveaway. Approximately four million in total were printed. The two black and white copies listed plus two other versions as well as a full color untrimmed version surfaced in 1979 from the Guild's old files in St. Paul, Minnesota.*

IT'S FUN TO STAY ALIVE
National Automobile Dealers Association: 1948 (Giveaway, 16 pgs., heavy stock paper)
Featuring: Bugs Bunny, The Berrys, Dixie Dugan, Elmer, Henry, Tim Tyler, Bruce Gentry, Abbie & Slats, Joe Jinks, The Toodles, & Cokey; all art copyright 1946-48 drawn especially for this book 15 30 45 84 127 170

IT'S TIME FOR REASON - NOT TREASON
Liberty Lobby: 1967 (Reg. size, soft-c) (Anti-communist)
nn 6 12 18 38 69 100

JACK AND CHUCK LEARN THE HARD WAY
Commercia Comics/Wagner Electric Co.: 1950s (Reg. size, soft-c)
nn-Automotive giveaway 9 18 27 47 61 75

JACK & JILL VISIT TOYTOWN WITH ELMER THE ELF
Butler Brothers (Toytown Stores): 1949 (Giveaway, 16 pgs., paper cover)
nn 5 10 15 22 26 30

JACK ARMSTRONG (Radio)(See True Comics)
Parents' Institute: 1949
12-Premium version (distr. in Chicago only); Free printed on upper right-c; no price (Rare) 18 36 54 107 169 230

JACKIE JOYNER KERSEE IN HIGH HURDLES (Kellogg's Tony's Sports Comics)
DC Comics: 1992 (Sports Illustrated)
nn 5.00

JACKPOT OF FUN COMIC BOOK
DCA Food Ind.: 1957, giveaway (paper cover, regular size)
nn-Features Howdy Doody 11 22 33 64 90 115

JEDLICKA SHOES
DC Comics: 1961 (Funny animal-c)
nn-Contains Superman #142 8 16 24 56 108 160

JEEP COMICS
R. B. Leffingwell & Co.: 1945 - 1946
1-46 (Giveaways)-Strip reprints in all; Tarzan, Flash Gordon, Blondie, The Nebbs, Little Iodine, Red Ryder, Don Winslow, The Phantom, Johnny Hazard, Katzenjammer Kids; distr. to U.S. Armed Forces from 1945-1946 6 12 18 31 38 45

JINGLE BELLS CHRISTMAS BOOK
Montgomery Ward (Giveaway): 1971 (20 pgs., B&W inside, slick-c)
nn 6.00

JOAN OF ARC
Catechetical Guild (Topix) (Giveaway): No date (28 pgs., blank back-c)
nn-Ingrid Bergman photo-c; Addison Burbank-a 12 24 36 69 97 125
NOTE: *Unpublished version exists which came from the Guild's files.*

JOE PALOOKA (2nd Series)
Harvey Publications
...Body Building Instruction Book (1958 B&M Sports Toy giveaway, 16 pgs., 5-1/4x7")-Origin
9 18 27 47 61 75
...Fights His Way Back (1945 Giveaway, 24 pgs.) Family Comics
14 28 42 80 115 150
...in Hi There! (1949 Red Cross giveaway, 12 pgs., 4-3/4x6")
9 18 27 50 65 80
...in It's All in the Family (1945 Red Cross giveaway, 16 pgs., regular size)
9 18 27 52 69 85

JOE THE GENIE OF STEEL (Also see "Return of...")
U.S. Steel Corp., Pittsburgh, PA: 1950 (16 pgs, reg size)
nn-Joe Magarac, the Paul Bunyan of steel 9 18 27 50 65 80

JOHNNY JINGLE'S LUCKY DAY
American Dairy Assoc.: 1956 (16 pgs.; 7-1/4x5-1/8") (Giveaway) (Disney)
nn 5 10 15 24 30 35

JOHNSON MAKES THE TEAM
B.F. Goodrich: 1950 (Reg. size) (Football giveaway)
nn 6 12 18 31 38 45

JO-JOY (The Adventures of...)
W. T. Grant Dept. Stores: 1945 - 1953 (Christmas gift comic, 16 pgs., 7-1/16x10-1/4")
1945-53 issues 7 14 21 37 46 55

JOLLY CHRISTMAS BOOK (See Christmas Journey Through Space)
Promotional Publ. Co.: 1951; 1954; 1955 (36 pgs.; 24 pgs.)
1951-(Woolworth giveaway)-slightly oversized; no slick cover; Marv Levy-c/a
7 14 21 37 46 55
1954-(Hot Shoppes giveaway)-regular size-reprints 1951 issue; slick cover added; 24 pgs.; no ads 6 12 18 31 38 45
1955-(J. M. McDonald Co. giveaway)-reg. size 6 12 18 28 34 40

JOURNEY OF DISCOVERY WITH MARK STEEL (See Mark Steel)

JUMPING JACKS PRESENTS THE WHIZ KIDS
Jumping Jacks Stores giveaway: 1978 (In 3-D) with glasses (4 pgs.)
nn 6.00

JUNGLE BOOK FUN BOOK, THE (Disney)
Baskin Robbins: 1978
nn-Ice Cream giveaway 2 4 6 9 12 15

JUSTICE LEAGUE OF AMERICA
DC Comics: 1999 (included in Justice League of America Monopoly game)
nn - Reprints 1st app. in Brave and the Bold #28 2.50

KASCO KOMICS
Kasko Grainfeed (Giveaway): 1945; No. 2, 1949 (Regular size, paper-c)
1(1945)-Similar to Katy Keene; Bill Woggon-a; 28 pgs.; 6-7/8x9-7/8"
19 38 57 111 176 240

King James The King of Basketball © DC

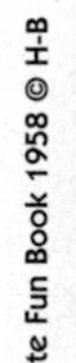

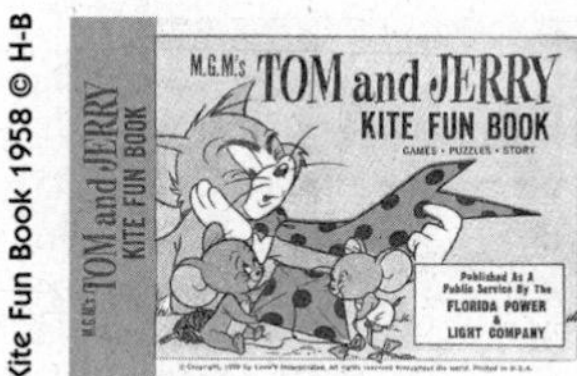

Kite Fun Book 1958 © H-B

Labor Is A Partner © CG

	GD 2.0	VG 4.0	FN 6.0	VF 8.0	VF/NM 9.0	NM- 9.2
2(1949)-Woggon-c/a	14	28	42	82	121	160

KATY AND KEN VISIT SANTA WITH MISTER WISH
S. S. Kresge Co. : 1948 (Giveaway, 16 pgs., paper-c)

nn	6	12	18	29	36	42

KELLOGG'S CINNAMON MINI-BUNS SUPER-HEROES
DC Comics: 1993 (4 1/4" x 2 3/4")

4 editions: Flash, Justice League America, Superman, Wonder Woman and the Star Riders
each..... 4.00

KERRY DRAKE DETECTIVE CASES
Publisher's Syndicate

...in the Case of the Sleeping City-(1951)-16 pg. giveaway for armed forces; paper cover
7 14 21 35 43 50

KEY COMICS
Key Clothing Co./Peterson Clothing: 1951 - 1956 (32 pgs.) (Giveaway)
Contains a comic from different publishers bound with new cover. Cover changed each year. Many combinations possible. Distributed in Nebraska, Iowa, & Kansas. Contents would determine price, 40-60 percent of original.

KING JAMES "THE KING OF BASKETBALL"
DC Comics: 2004 (Promo comic for LeBron James and Powerade Flava23 sports drink)

nn - Ten different covers by various artists; 4 covers for retail, 4 for mail-in, 1 for military commissaries, and 1 general market; Damion Scott-a/Gary Phillips-s 2.50

KIRBY'S SHOES COMICS
Kirby's Shoes: 1959 - 1961 (8 pgs., soft-c)

nn-Features Kirby the Golden Bear	3	5	7	10	12	14

KITE FUN BOOK
Pacific, Gas & Electric/Sou. California Edison/Florida Power & Light/ Missouri Public Service Co.: 1952 - 1998 (16 pgs, 5x7-1/4", soft-c)

1952-Having Fun With Kites (P.G.&E.)	12	24	36	69	97	125
1953-Pinocchio Learns About Kites (Disney)	41	82	123	256	428	600
1954-Donald Duck Tells About Kites-Fla. Power, S.C.E. & version with label issues -Barks pencils-8 pgs.; inks-7 pgs. (Rare)	258	516	774	1651	2826	4000
1954-Donald Duck Tells About Kites-P.G.&E. issue -7th page redrawn changing middle 3 panels to show P.G.&E. in story line; (All Barks-a) Scarce	206	412	618	1318	2259	3200
1955-Brer Rabbit in "A Kite Tail" (Disney)	27	54	81	158	259	360
1956-Woody Woodpecker (Lantz)	14	28	42	76	108	140
1957-Ruff and Reddy (exist?)						
1958-Tom And Jerry (M.G.M.)	9	18	27	52	69	85
1959-Bugs Bunny (Warner Bros.)	4	8	12	27	44	60
1960-Porky Pig (Warner Bros.)	4	8	12	28	47	65
1960-Bugs Bunny (Warner Bros.)	4	8	12	28	47	65
1961-Huckleberry Hound (Hanna-Barbera)	5	10	15	31	53	75
1962-Yogi Bear (Hanna-Barbera)	4	8	12	25	40	55
1963-Rocky and Bullwinkle (TV)(Jay Ward)	5	10	15	35	63	90
1963-Top Cat (TV)(Hanna-Barbera)	3	6	9	19	30	40
1964-Magilla Gorilla (TV)(Hanna-Barbera)	3	6	9	17	26	35
1965-Jinks, Pixie and Dixie (TV)(Hanna-Barbera)	3	6	9	15	22	28
1965-Tweety and Sylvester (Warner); S.C.E. version with Reddy Kilowatt app.	2	4	6	9	13	16
1966-Secret Squirrel (Hanna-Barbera); S.C.E. version with Reddy Kilowatt app.	5	10	15	30	50	70
1967-Beep! Beep! The Road Runner (TV)(Warner)	2	4	6	11	16	20
1968-Bugs Bunny (Warner Bros.)	2	4	6	13	18	22
1969-Dastardly and Muttley (TV)(Hanna-Barbera)	3	6	9	19	30	40
1970-Rocky and Bullwinkle (TV)(Jay Ward)	4	8	12	27	44	60
1971-Beep! Beep! The Road Runner (TV)(Warner)	2	4	6	11	16	20
1972-The Pink Panther (TV)	2	4	6	10	14	18
1973-Lassie (TV)	3	6	9	15	22	28
1974-Underdog (TV)	2	4	6	11	16	20
1975-Ben Franklin	2	4	6	8	10	12
1976-The Brady Bunch (TV)	3	6	9	16	23	30
1977-Ben Franklin (exist?)	2	4	6	8	10	12
1977-Popeye	2	4	6	9	13	16
1978-Happy Days (TV)	2	4	6	11	16	20
1979-Eight is Enough (TV)	2	4	6	9	13	16
1980-The Waltons (TV, released in 1981)	2	4	6	9	13	16
1982-Tweety and Sylvester	2	4	6	8	11	14
1984-Smokey Bear	1	3	4	6	8	10
1986-Road Runner	1	2	3	5	6	8
1997-Thomas Edison						4.00
1998-Edison Field (Anaheim Stadium)						3.00

KNOWING IS NOT ENOUGH
Commercial Comics: 1956 (Reg. size, paper-c) (Safety giveaway)

nn	7	14	21	35	43	50

KNOW YOUR MASS
Catechetical Guild: No. 303, 1958 (35¢, 100 Pg. Giant) (Square binding)

303-In color	7	14	21	35	43	50

KOLYNOS PRESENTS THE WHITE GUARD
Whitehall Pharmacal Co.: 1949 (paper cover, 8 pgs.)

nn	6	12	18	27	33	38

KOLYNOS PRESENTS THE WICKED WITCH
Whitehall Pharmacal Co.: 1951 (paper cover, 8 pgs.)

nn-Anti-tooth decay	4	7	10	14	17	20

K. O. PUNCH, THE (Also see Lucky Fights It Through & Sidewalk Romance)
E. C. Comics: 1948 (VD Educational giveaway)

nn-Feldstein-splash; Kamen-a	97	194	291	621	1061	1500

KOREA MY HOME (Also see Yalta to Korea)
Johnstone and Cushing: nd (1950s, slick-c, regular size)

nn-Anti-communist; Korean War	21	42	63	122	199	275

KRIM-KO KOMICS
Krim-ko Chocolate Drink: 5/18/35 - No. 6, 6/22/35; 1936 - 1939 (weekly)

1-(16 pgs., soft-c, Dairy giveaways)-Tom, Mary & Sparky Advs. by Russell Keaton, Jim Hawkins by Dick Moores, Mystery Island! by Rick Yager begin	14	28	42	76	108	140
2-6 (6/22/35)	10	20	30	56	76	95
Lola, Secret Agent; 184 issues, 4 pg. giveaways - all original stories each....	7	14	21	37	46	55

LABOR IS A PARTNER
Catechetical Guild Educational Society: 1949 (32 pgs., paper-c)

nn-Anti-communism	20	40	60	118	192	265
Confidential Preview-(8-1/2x11", B&W, saddle stitched)-only one known copy; text varies from color version, advertises next book on secularism (If the Devil Would Talk)	24	48	72	142	234	325

LADIES - WOULDN'T IT BE BETTER TO KNOW
American Cancer Society: 1969 (Reg. size)

nn	3	6	9	21	33	45

LADY AND THE TRAMP IN "BUTTER LATE THAN NEVER"
American Dairy Assoc. (Premium): 1955 (16 pgs., 5x7-1/4", soft-c) (Disney)

nn	8	16	24	44	57	70

LASSIE (TV)
Dell Publ. Co

The Adventures of... nn-(Red Heart Dog Food giveaway, 1949)-16 pgs, soft-c; 1st app. Lassie in comics	34	68	102	199	325	450

LIFE OF THE BLESSED VIRGIN
Catechetical Guild (Giveaway): 1950 (68pgs.) (square binding)

nn-Contains "The Woman of the Promise" & "Mother of Us All" rebound	7	14	21	35	43	50

LIGHTNING RACERS
DC Comics: 1989

1 4.50

LI'L ABNER (Al Capp's) (Also see Natural Disasters!)
Harvey Publ./Toby Press

...& the Creatures from Drop-Outer Space-nn (Job Corps giveaway; 36 pgs., in color) (entire book by Frank Frazetta)	21	42	63	124	202	280
...Joins the Navy (1950) (Toby Press Premium)	11	22	33	62	86	110
Al Capp by Li'l Abner (Circa 1946, nd, giveaway) Al Capp bio and his life as an amputee	11	22	33	62	86	110

LITTLE ALONZO
Macy's Dept. Store: 1938 (B&W, 5-1/2x8-1/2")(Christmas giveaway)

nn-By Ferdinand the Bull's Munro Leaf	9	18	27	50	65	80

LITTLE ARCHIE (See Archie Comics)

LITTLE DOT
Harvey Publications

Shoe store giveaway 2	4	8	12	27	44	60

Little Klinker © Little Klinker Ventures

Lone Ranger in "Milk For Big Mike" © L.R. Ents.

Magazineland USA nn © DC

	GD 2.0	VG 4.0	FN 6.0	VF 8.0	VF/NM 9.0	NM- 9.2

LITTLE FIR TREE, THE
W. T. Grant Co. : nd (1942) (8-1/2x11") (12 pgs. with cover, color & B&W, heavy paper) (Christmas giveaway)
nn-Story by Hans Christian Anderson; 8 pg. Kelly-r/Santa Claus Funnies (not signed); X-Mas-c 90 180 270 576 988 1400

LITTLE KLINKER
Little Klinker Ventures: Nov, 1960 (20 pgs.) (slick cover) (Montgomery Ward Giveaway)
nn - Christmas; Santa-c 2 4 6 11 16 20

LITTLE MISS SUNBEAM COMICS
Magazine Enterprises/Quality Bakers of America
Bread Giveaway 1-4(Quality Bakers, 1949-50)-14 pgs. each 6 12 18 31 38 45
Bread Giveaway (1957,61; 16pgs, reg. size) 5 10 15 24 30 35

LITTLE ORPHAN ANNIE
David McKay Publ./Dell Publishing Co.
Junior Commandos Giveaway (same-c as 4-Color #18, K.K. Publ.)(Big Shoe Store); same back cover as '47 Popped Wheat giveaway; 16 pgs; flag-c; r/strips 9/7/42-10/10/42 26 52 78 154 252 350
Popped Wheat Giveaway ('47)-16 pgs. full color; reprints strips from 5/3/40 to 6/20/40 4 8 12 18 22 25
Quaker Sparkies Giveaway (1940) 18 36 54 103 162 220
Quaker Sparkies Giveaway (1941, full color, 20 pgs.); "LOA and the Rescue"; r/strips 4/13/39-6/21/39 & 7/6/39-7/17/39. "LOA and the Kidnappers"; r/strips 11/28/38-1/28/39 15 30 45 94 147 200
Quaker Sparkies Giveaway (1942, full color, 20 pgs.); "LOA and Mr. Gudge"; r/strips 2/13/38-3/21/38 & 4/18/37-5/30/37. "LOA and the Great Am" 15 30 45 88 137 185

LITTLE TREE THAT WASN'T WANTED, THE
W. T. Grant Co. (Giveaway): 1960, (Color, 28 pgs.)
nn-Christmas story, puzzles and games 3 6 9 21 33 45

LOADED (Also see Re-Loaded)
DC Comics: 1995 (Interplay Productions)
1-Garth Ennis-s; promotes video game 4.00

LONE RANGER, THE
Dell Publishing Co.
Cheerios Giveaways (1954, 16 pgs., 2-1/2x7", soft-c) #1- "The Lone Ranger, His Mask & How He Met Tonto". #2- "The Lone Ranger & the Story of Silver" each.... 12 24 36 69 97 125
Doll Giveaways (Gabriel Ind.)(1973, 3-1/4x5")- "The Story of The Lone Ranger," "The Carson City Bank Robbery" & "The Apache Buffalo Hunt" 2 4 6 12 16 20
How the Lone Ranger Captured Silver Book(1936)-Silvercup Bread giveaway 55 110 165 352 601 850
...In Milk for Big Mike (1955, Dairy Association giveaway), soft-c; 5x7-1/4", 16 pgs. 10 20 30 58 79 100
Legend of The Lone Ranger (1969, 16 pgs., giveaway)-Origin The Lone Ranger 4 8 12 21 33 45
Merita Bread giveaway (1954, 16 pgs., 5x7-1/4")- "How to Be a Lone Ranger Health & Safety Scout" 14 28 42 80 115 150

LONE RANGER COMICS, THE
Lone Ranger, Inc. : Book 1, 1939(inside) (shows 1938 on-c) (52 pgs. in color; regular size) (Ice cream mail order)
Book 1-(Scarce)-The first western comic devoted to a single character; not by Vallely 600 1140 1710 4000 - -
2nd version w/large full color promo poster pasted over centerfold & a smaller poster pasted over back cover; includes new additional premiums not originally offered (Rare) 715 1430 2145 5000 - -

LOONEY TUNES
DC Comics: 1991, 1998
Claritin promotional issue (1998) 3.00
Colgate mini-comic (1998) 3.00
Tyson's 1-10 (1991) 4.00

LUCKY FIGHTS IT THROUGH (Also see The K. O. Punch & Sidewalk Romance)
Educational Comics: 1949 (Giveaway, 16 pgs. in color, paper-c)
nn-(Very Rare)-1st Kurtzman work for E. C.; V.D. prevention 142 284 426 909 1555 2200
nn-Reprint in color (1977) 7.00
NOTE: *Subtitled "The Story of That Ignorant, Ignorant Cowboy". Prepared for Communications Materials Center, Columbia University.*

LUDWIG VON DRAKE (See Frito-Lay Giveaway)

MACO TOYS COMIC
Maco Toys/Charlton Comics: 1959 (Giveaway, 36 pgs.)
1-All military stories featuring Maco Toys 3 6 9 14 19 24

MAD MAGAZINE
DC Comics: 1997, 1999, 2008
Special Edition (1997, Tang giveaway) 3.00
Stocking Stuffer (1999) 3.00
San Diego Comic-Con Edition (2008) Watchmen parody with Fabry-a; Aragonés cartoons 3.00

MAGAZINELAND USA
DC Comics: 1977
nn-Kubert-c/a 3 6 9 16 22 28

MAGIC MORRO (Also see Super Comics #21, The Owl, & The Hurricane Kids)
K. K. Publications: 1941 (7-1/2 x 5-1/4", giveaway, soft-c)
nn-Ken Ernst-a. 10 20 30 54 72 90

MAGIC OF CHRISTMAS AT NEWBERRYS, THE
E. S. London: 1967 (Giveaway) (B&W, slick-c, 20 pgs.)
nn 1 3 4 6 8 10

MAGIC SHOE ADVENTURE BOOK
Western Publications: 1962 - No. 3, 1963 (Shoe store giveaway, Reg. size)
nn-(1962) 5 10 15 34 60 85
1 (1963)-And the Flaming Threat 4 8 12 28 47 65
2 (1963)-And the Winning Run 4 8 12 28 47 65
3 (1963)-And the Missing Masterpiece Mystery 4 8 12 28 47 65

MAJOR INAPAK THE SPACE ACE
Magazine Enterprises (Inapac Foods): 1951 (20 pgs.) (Giveaway)
1-Bob Powell-c/a 6.00
NOTE: *Many warehouse copies surfaced in 1973.*

MAMMY YOKUM & THE GREAT DOGPATCH MYSTERY
Toby Press: 1951 (Giveaway)
nn-Li'l Abner 15 30 45 88 137 185
nn-Reprint (1956) 5 10 15 22 26 30

MAN NAMED STEVENSON, A
Democratic National Committee: 1952 (20 pgs., 5 1/4 x 7")
nn 9 18 27 47 61 75

MAN OF PEACE, POPE PIUS XII
Catechetical Guild: 1950 (See Pope Pius XII... & To V2#8)
nn-All Powell-a 7 14 21 35 43 50

MAN OF STEEL BEST WESTERN
DC Comics: 1997 (Best Western hotels promo)
3-Reprints Superman's first post-Crisis meeting with Batman 4.00

MAN WHO RUNS INTERFERENCE
General Comics, Inc./Institute of Life Insurance: 1946 (Paper-c)
nn-Football premium 5 10 15 22 26 30

MAN WHO WOULDN'T QUIT, THE
Harvey Publications Inc.: 1952 (16 pgs., paper cover)
nn-The value of voting 4 8 12 18 22 25

MARCH OF COMICS (Boys' and Girls'...#3-353)
K. K. Publications/Western Publishing Co.: 1946 - No. 488, April, 1982 (#1-4 are not numbered) (K.K. Giveaway) (Founded by Sig Feuchtwanger)
Early issues were full size, 32 pages, and were printed with and without an extra cover of slick stock, just for the advertiser. The binding was stapled if the slick cover was added; otherwise, the pages were glued together at the spine. Most 1948 - 1951 issues were full size,24 pages, pulp covers. Starting in 1952 they were half-size (with a few exceptions) and 32 pages with slick covers.1959 and later issues had only 16 pages plus covers. 1952 -1959 issues read oblong; 1960 and later issues read upright. All have new stories except where noted.
nn (#1, 1946)-Goldilocks; Kelly back-c (16 pgs., stapled) 47 94 141 296 498 700
nn (#2, 1946)-How Santa Got His Red Suit; Kelly-a (11 pgs., r/4-Color #61 from 1944) (16pgs., stapled) 30 60 90 177 289 400
nn (#3, 1947)-Our Gang (Walt Kelly) 36 72 108 211 343 475
nn (#4)-Donald Duck by Carl Barks, "Maharajah Donald", 28 pgs.; Kelly-c? (Disney) 757 1514 2271 5526 9763 14,000
5-Andy Panda (Walter Lantz) 19 38 57 111 176 240
6-Popular Fairy Tales; Kelly-c; Noonan-a(2) 20 40 60 120 195 270

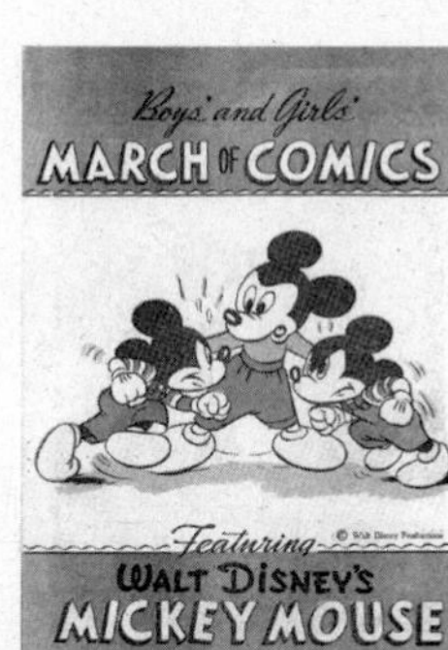

March of Comics #8 © DIS

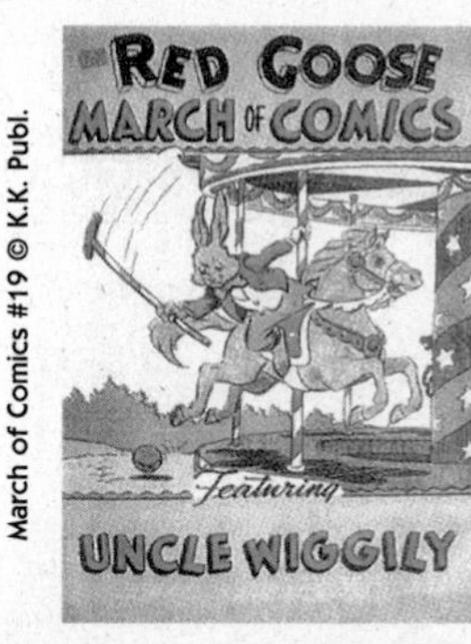

March of Comics #19 © K.K. Publ.

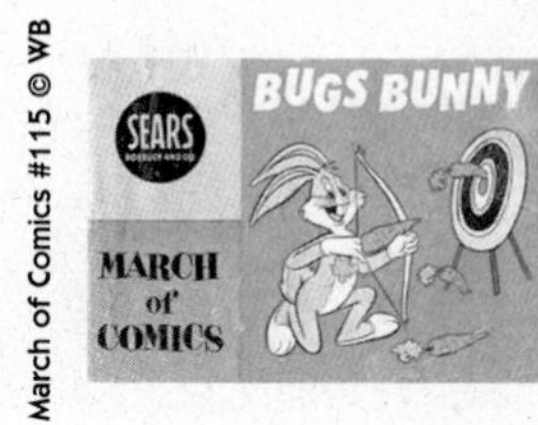

March of Comics #115 © WB

	GD 2.0	VG 4.0	FN 6.0	VF 8.0	VF/NM 9.0	NM- 9.2
7-Oswald the Rabbit	20	40	60	114	182	250
8-Mickey Mouse, 32 pgs. (Disney)	43	86	129	271	461	650
9(nn)-The Story of the Gloomy Bunny	13	26	39	74	105	135
10-Out of Santa's Bag	12	24	36	69	97	125
11-Fun With Santa Claus	11	22	33	60	83	105
12-Santa's Toys	11	22	33	60	83	105
13-Santa's Surprise	11	22	33	60	83	105
14-Santa's Candy Kitchen	11	22	33	60	83	105
15-Hip-It-Ty Hop & the Big Bass Viol	10	20	30	58	79	100
16-Woody Woodpecker (1947)(Walter Lantz)	14	28	42	81	118	155
17-Roy Rogers (1948)	21	42	63	124	202	280
18-Popular Fairy Tales	13	26	39	72	101	130
19-Uncle Wiggily	11	22	33	62	86	110
20-Donald Duck by Carl Barks, "Darkest Africa", 22 pgs.; Kelly-c (Disney)	271	542	813	1734	2967	4200
21-Tom and Jerry	12	24	36	67	94	120
22-Andy Panda (Lantz)	11	22	33	62	86	110
23-Raggedy Ann & Andy; Kerr-a	14	28	42	76	108	140
24-Felix the Cat, 1932 daily strip reprints by Otto Messmer	18	36	54	107	169	230
25-Gene Autry	18	36	54	105	165	225
26-Our Gang; Walt Kelly	17	34	51	100	158	215
27-Mickey Mouse; r/in M. M. #240 (Disney)	30	60	90	177	289	400
28-Gene Autry	18	36	54	103	162	220
29-Easter Bonnet Shop	9	18	27	47	61	75
30-Here Comes Santa	8	16	24	44	57	70
31-Santa's Busy Corner	8	16	24	44	57	70
32-No book produced						
33-A Christmas Carol (12/48)	9	18	27	47	61	75
34-Woody Woodpecker	11	22	33	64	90	115
35-Roy Rogers (1948)	20	40	60	115	185	255
36-Felix the Cat(1949); by Messmer; '34 strip-r	15	30	45	86	133	180
37-Popeye	14	28	42	81	118	155
38-Oswald the Rabbit	9	18	27	50	65	80
39-Gene Autry	17	34	51	98	154	210
40-Andy and Woody	9	18	27	50	65	80
41-Donald Duck by Carl Barks, "Race to the South Seas", 22 pgs.; Kelly-c	258	516	774	1651	2826	4000
42-Porky Pig	9	18	27	52	69	85
43-Henry	9	18	27	47	61	75
44-Bugs Bunny	10	20	30	56	76	95
45-Mickey Mouse (Disney)	21	42	63	124	202	280
46-Tom and Jerry	10	20	30	56	76	95
47-Roy Rogers	16	32	48	94	147	200
48-Greetings from Santa	6	12	18	31	38	45
49-Santa Is Here	6	12	18	31	38	45
50-Santa Claus' Workshop (1949)	6	12	18	31	38	45
51-Felix the Cat (1950) by Messmer	15	30	45	84	127	170
52-Popeye	12	24	36	67	94	120
53-Oswald the Rabbit	8	16	24	44	57	70
54-Gene Autry	15	30	45	86	133	180
55-Andy and Woody	8	16	24	42	54	65
56-Donald Duck; not by Barks; Barks art on back-c (Disney)	22	44	66	132	216	300
57-Porky Pig	8	16	24	44	57	70
58-Henry	7	14	21	35	43	50
59-Bugs Bunny	9	18	27	50	65	80
60-Mickey Mouse (Disney)	21	42	63	124	202	280
61-Tom and Jerry	8	16	24	44	57	70
62-Roy Rogers	16	32	48	94	147	200
63-Welcome Santa (1/2-size, oblong)	6	12	18	31	38	45
64(nn)-Santa's Helpers (1/2-size, oblong)	6	12	18	31	38	45
65(nn)-Jingle Bells (1950) (1/2-size, oblong)	6	12	18	31	38	45
66-Popeye (1951)	11	22	33	60	83	105
67-Oswald the Rabbit	8	16	24	42	54	65
68-Roy Rogers	15	30	45	90	140	190
69-Donald Duck; Barks-a on back-c (Disney)	20	40	60	117	189	260
70-Tom and Jerry	8	16	24	42	54	65
71-Porky Pig	8	16	24	44	57	70
72-Krazy Kat	9	18	27	50	65	80
73-Roy Rogers	15	30	45	84	127	170
74-Mickey Mouse (1951)(Disney)	19	38	57	111	176	246
75-Bugs Bunny	8	16	24	44	57	70
76-Andy and Woody	8	16	24	42	54	65

	GD 2.0	VG 4.0	FN 6.0	VF 8.0	VF/NM 9.0	NM- 9.2
77-Roy Rogers	15	30	45	84	127	170
78-Gene Autry (1951); last regular size issue	15	30	45	82	121	160

Note: All pre #79 issues came with or without a slick protective wrap-around cover over the regular cover which advertised Poll Parrot Shoes, Sears, etc. This outer cover protects the inside pages making them in nicer condition.
Issues with the outer cover are worth 15-25% more

	GD 2.0	VG 4.0	FN 6.0	VF 8.0	VF/NM 9.0	NM- 9.2
79-Andy Panda (1952, 5x7" size)	7	14	21	35	43	50
80-Popeye	9	18	27	50	65	80
81-Oswald the Rabbit	6	12	18	29	36	42
82-Tarzan; Lex Barker photo-c	15	30	45	84	127	170
83-Bugs Bunny	7	14	21	37	46	55
84-Henry	6	12	18	29	36	42
85-Woody Woodpecker	6	12	18	29	36	42
86-Roy Rogers	12	24	36	69	97	125
87-Krazy Kat	8	16	24	44	57	70
88-Tom and Jerry	6	12	18	31	38	45
89-Porky Pig	6	12	18	29	36	42
90-Gene Autry	12	24	36	67	94	120
91-Roy Rogers & Santa	12	24	36	67	94	120
92-Christmas with Santa	5	10	15	24	30	35
93-Woody Woodpecker (1953)	5	10	15	23	28	32
94-Indian Chief	10	20	30	54	72	90
95-Oswald the Rabbit	5	10	15	23	28	32
96-Popeye	10	20	30	54	72	90
97-Bugs Bunny	7	14	21	35	43	50
98-Tarzan; Lex Barker photo-c	14	28	42	82	121	160
99-Porky Pig	5	10	15	23	28	32
100-Roy Rogers	10	20	30	58	79	100
101-Henry	5	10	15	22	26	30
102-Tom Corbett (TV)('53, early app).; painted-c	12	24	36	67	94	120
103-Tom and Jerry	5	10	15	23	28	32
104-Gene Autry	10	20	30	56	76	95
105-Roy Rogers	10	20	30	56	76	95
106-Santa's Helpers	5	10	15	24	30	35
107-Santa's Christmas Book - not published						
108-Fun with Santa (1953)	5	10	15	24	30	35
109-Woody Woodpecker (1954)	5	10	15	24	30	35
110-Indian Chief	6	12	18	31	38	45
111-Oswald the Rabbit	5	10	15	22	26	30
112-Henry	4	9	13	18	22	26
113-Porky Pig	5	10	15	22	26	30
114-Tarzan; Russ Manning-a	14	28	42	82	121	160
115-Bugs Bunny	6	12	18	27	33	38
116-Roy Rogers	10	20	30	56	76	95
117-Popeye	10	20	30	54	72	90
118-Flash Gordon; painted-c	10	20	30	58	79	100
119-Tom and Jerry	5	10	15	22	26	30
120-Gene Autry	10	20	30	58	76	95
121-Roy Rogers	10	20	30	58	76	95
122-Santa's Surprise (1954)	5	10	15	22	26	30
123-Santa's Christmas Book	5	10	15	22	26	30
124-Woody Woodpecker (1955)	4	9	13	18	22	26
125-Tarzan; Lex Barker photo-c	14	28	42	78	112	145
126-Oswald the Rabbit	4	9	13	18	22	26
127-Indian Chief	7	14	21	35	43	50
128-Tom and Jerry	4	9	13	18	22	26
129-Henry	4	8	12	17	21	24
130-Porky Pig	4	9	13	18	22	26
131-Roy Rogers	10	20	30	56	76	95
132-Bugs Bunny	5	10	15	23	28	32
133-Flash Gordon; painted-c	10	20	30	58	76	95
134-Popeye	8	16	24	42	54	65
135-Gene Autry	10	20	30	56	76	95
136-Roy Rogers	10	20	30	56	76	95
137-Gifts from Santa	4	7	10	14	17	20
138-Fun at Christmas (1955)	4	7	10	14	17	20
139-Woody Woodpecker (1956)	4	9	13	18	22	26
140-Indian Chief	7	14	21	35	43	50
141-Oswald the Rabbit	4	9	13	18	22	26
142-Flash Gordon	10	20	30	56	76	95
143-Porky Pig	4	9	13	18	22	26
144-Tarzan; Russ Manning-a; painted-c	13	26	39	72	101	130
145-Tom and Jerry	4	9	13	18	22	26
146-Roy Rogers; photo-c	10	20	30	56	76	95

March of Comics #174 © L.R. Ents.

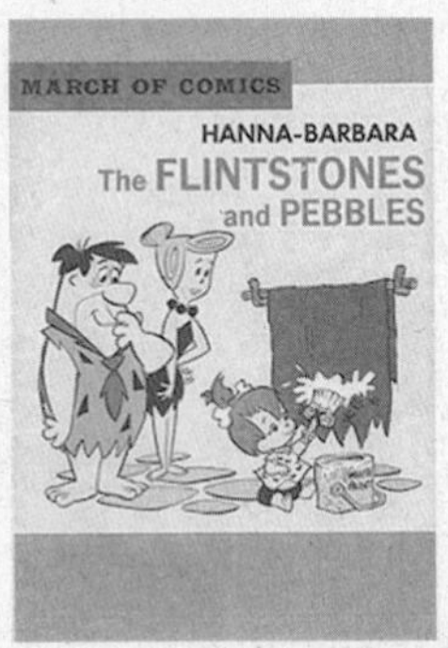

March of Comics #271 © H-B

March of Comics #285 © Osamu Tezuka

	GD 2.0	VG 4.0	FN 6.0	VF 8.0	VF/NM 9.0	NM- 9.2
147-Henry	4	8	11	16	19	22
148-Popeye	8	16	24	42	54	65
149-Bugs Bunny	5	10	15	22	26	30
150-Gene Autry	10	20	30	56	76	95
151-Roy Rogers	10	20	30	56	76	95
152-The Night Before Christmas	4	8	11	16	19	22
153-Merry Christmas (1956)	4	9	13	18	22	26
154-Tom and Jerry (1957)	4	9	13	18	22	26
155-Tarzan; photo-c	12	24	36	69	97	125
156-Oswald the Rabbit	4	9	13	18	22	26
157-Popeye	7	14	21	35	43	50
158-Woody Woodpecker	4	9	13	18	22	26
159-Indian Chief	7	14	21	35	43	50
160-Bugs Bunny	5	10	15	22	26	30
161-Roy Rogers	9	18	27	52	69	85
162-Henry	4	8	11	16	19	22
163-Rin Tin Tin (TV)	8	16	24	42	54	65
164-Porky Pig	4	9	13	18	22	26
165-The Lone Ranger	10	20	30	54	72	90
166-Santa and His Reindeer	4	7	10	14	17	20
167-Roy Rogers and Santa	9	18	27	52	69	85
168-Santa Claus' Workshop (1957, full size)	4	8	11	16	19	22
169-Popeye (1958)	7	14	21	35	43	50
170-Indian Chief	7	14	21	35	43	50
171-Oswald the Rabbit	4	8	12	17	21	24
172-Tarzan	11	22	33	60	83	105
173-Tom and Jerry	4	8	12	17	21	24
174-The Lone Ranger	10	20	30	54	72	90
175-Porky Pig	4	8	12	17	21	24
176-Roy Rogers	9	18	27	47	61	75
177-Woody Woodpecker	4	8	12	17	21	24
178-Henry	4	8	11	16	19	22
179-Bugs Bunny	4	8	12	17	21	24
180-Rin Tin Tin (TV)	7	14	21	37	46	55
181-Happy Holiday	4	7	9	14	16	18
182-Happi Tim	4	8	11	16	19	22
183-Welcome Santa (1958, full size)	4	7	9	14	16	18
184-Woody Woodpecker (1959)	4	8	11	16	19	22
185-Tarzan; photo-c	10	20	30	58	79	100
186-Oswald the Rabbit	4	8	11	16	19	22
187-Indian Chief	6	12	18	28	34	40
188-Bugs Bunny	4	8	11	16	19	22
189-Henry	4	7	10	14	17	20
190-Tom and Jerry	4	8	11	16	19	22
191-Roy Rogers	8	16	24	44	57	70
192-Porky Pig	4	8	11	16	19	22
193-The Lone Ranger	9	18	27	52	69	85
194-Popeye	6	12	18	31	38	45
195-Rin Tin Tin (TV)	7	14	21	35	43	50
196-Sears Special - not published						
197-Santa Is Coming	4	7	10	14	17	20
198-Santa's Helpers (1959)	4	7	10	14	17	20
199-Huckleberry Hound (TV)(1960, early app.)	8	16	24	42	54	65
200-Fury (TV)	6	12	18	28	34	40
201-Bugs Bunny	4	8	11	16	19	22
202-Space Explorer	8	16	24	42	54	65
203-Woody Woodpecker	4	7	10	14	17	20
204-Tarzan	9	18	27	52	69	85
205-Mighty Mouse	6	12	18	33	41	48
206-Roy Rogers; photo-c	8	16	24	42	54	65
207-Tom and Jerry	4	7	10	14	17	20
208-The Lone Ranger; Clayton Moore photo-c	10	20	30	58	79	100
209-Porky Pig	4	7	10	14	17	20
210-Lassie (TV)	6	12	18	33	41	48
211-Sears Special - not published						
212-Christmas Eve	4	7	10	14	17	20
213-Here Comes Santa (1960)	4	7	10	14	17	20
214-Huckleberry Hound (TV)(1961)	7	14	21	35	43	50
215-Hi Yo Silver	8	16	24	40	50	60
216-Rocky & His Friends (TV)(1961); predates Rocky and His Fiendish Friends #1 (see Four Color #1128)	9	18	27	52	69	85
217-Lassie (TV)	6	12	18	31	38	45
218-Porky Pig	4	7	10	14	17	20
219-Journey to the Sun	5	10	15	24	30	35

	GD 2.0	VG 4.0	FN 6.0	VF 8.0	VF/NM 9.0	NM- 9.2
220-Bugs Bunny	4	8	11	16	19	22
221-Roy and Dale; photo-c	8	16	24	42	54	65
222-Woody Woodpecker	4	7	10	14	17	20
223-Tarzan	9	18	27	50	65	80
224-Tom and Jerry	4	7	10	14	17	20
225-The Lone Ranger	8	16	24	40	50	60
226-Christmas Treasury (1961)	4	7	10	14	17	20
227-Letters to Santa (1961)	4	7	10	14	17	20
228-Sears Special - not published?						
229-The Flintstones (TV)(1962); early app.; predates 1st Flintstones Gold Key issue (#7)	10	20	30	54	72	90
230-Lassie (TV)	6	12	18	27	33	38
231-Bugs Bunny	4	8	11	16	19	22
232-The Three Stooges	9	18	27	52	69	85
233-Bullwinkle (TV) (1962, very early app.)	9	18	27	52	69	85
234-Smokey the Bear	5	10	15	23	28	32
235-Huckleberry Hound (TV)	7	14	21	35	43	50
236-Roy and Dale	7	14	21	35	43	50
237-Mighty Mouse	6	12	18	27	33	38
238-The Lone Ranger	8	16	24	40	50	60
239-Woody Woodpecker	4	7	10	14	17	20
240-Tarzan	8	16	24	44	57	70
241-Santa Claus Around the World	4	7	9	14	16	18
242-Santa's Toyland (1962)	4	7	9	14	16	18
243-The Flintstones (TV)(1963)	8	16	24	44	57	70
244-Mister Ed (TV); early app.; photo-c	7	14	21	35	43	50
245-Bugs Bunny	4	8	11	16	19	22
246-Popeye	6	12	18	27	33	38
247-Mighty Mouse	6	12	18	27	33	38
248-The Three Stooges	10	20	30	54	72	90
249-Woody Woodpecker	4	7	10	14	17	20
250-Roy and Dale	7	14	21	35	43	50
251-Little Lulu & Witch Hazel	11	22	33	60	83	105
252-Tarzan; painted-c	8	16	24	42	54	65
253-Yogi Bear (TV)	8	16	24	40	50	60
254-Lassie (TV)	6	12	18	27	33	38
255-Santa's Christmas List	4	7	10	14	17	20
256-Christmas Party (1963)	4	7	10	14	17	20
257-Mighty Mouse	6	12	18	27	33	38
258-The Sword in the Stone (Disney)	8	16	24	42	54	65
259-Bugs Bunny	4	8	11	16	19	22
260-Mister Ed (TV)	6	12	18	31	38	45
261-Woody Woodpecker	4	7	10	14	17	20
262-Tarzan	8	16	24	40	50	60
263-Donald Duck; not by Barks (Disney)	9	18	27	52	69	85
264-Popeye	6	12	18	27	33	38
265-Yogi Bear (TV)	6	12	18	31	38	45
266-Lassie (TV)	5	10	15	23	28	32
267-Little Lulu; Irving Tripp-a	10	20	30	56	76	95
268-The Three Stooges	9	18	27	47	61	75
269-A Jolly Christmas	3	6	8	12	14	16
270-Santa's Little Helpers	3	6	8	12	14	16
271-The Flintstones (TV)(1965)	8	16	24	44	57	70
272-Tarzan	8	16	24	40	50	60
273-Bugs Bunny	4	8	11	16	19	22
274-Popeye	6	12	18	27	33	38
275-Little Lulu; Irving Tripp-a	9	18	27	50	65	80
276-The Jetsons (TV)	12	24	36	67	94	120
277-Daffy Duck	4	8	11	16	19	22
278-Lassie (TV)	5	10	15	23	28	32
279-Yogi Bear (TV)	6	12	18	31	38	45
280-The Three Stooges; photo-c	9	18	27	47	61	75
281-Tom and Jerry	4	7	9	14	16	18
282-Mister Ed (TV)	6	12	18	31	38	45
283-Santa's Visit	4	7	9	14	16	18
284-Christmas Parade (1965)	4	7	9	14	16	18
285-Astro Boy (TV); 2nd app. Astro Boy	26	52	78	154	252	350
286-Tarzan	7	14	21	37	46	55
287-Bugs Bunny	4	8	11	16	19	22
288-Daffy Duck	4	7	10	14	17	20
289-The Flintstones (TV)	8	16	24	44	57	70
290-Mister Ed (TV); photo-c	5	10	15	24	30	35
291-Yogi Bear (TV)	6	12	18	27	33	38
292-The Three Stooges; photo-c	9	18	27	47	61	75

March of Comics #334 © CBS

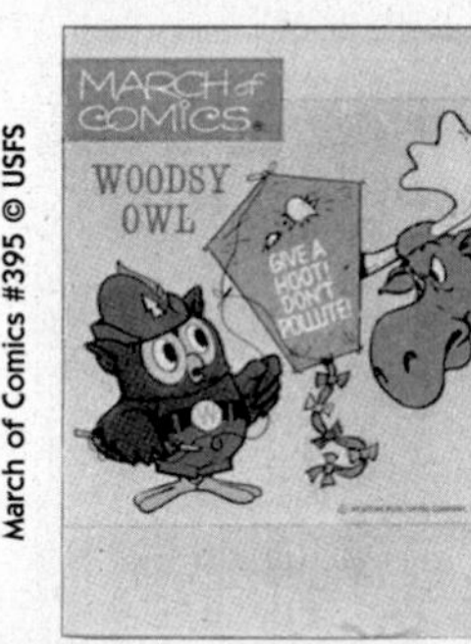

March of Comics #395 © USFS

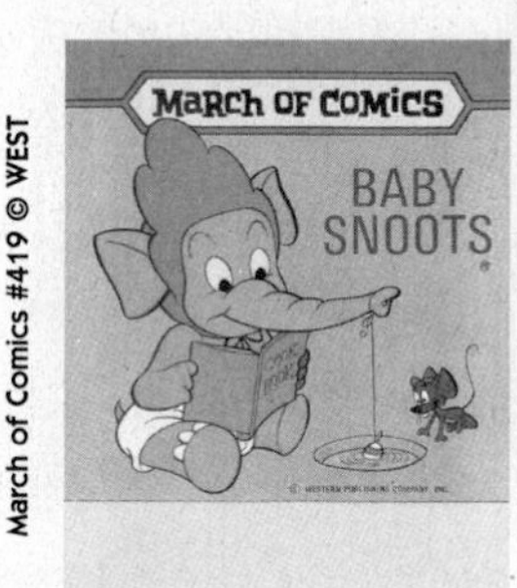

March of Comics #419 © WEST

	GD 2.0	VG 4.0	FN 6.0	VF 8.0	VF/NM 9.0	NM- 9.2
293-Little Lulu; Irving Tripp-a	8	16	24	42	54	65
294-Popeye	5	10	15	24	30	35
295-Tom and Jerry	4	7	9	14	16	18
296-Lassie (TV); photo-c	5	10	15	22	26	30
297-Christmas Bells	3	6	8	12	14	16
298-Santa's Sleigh (1966)	3	6	8	12	14	16
299-The Flintstones (TV)(1967)	8	16	24	44	57	70
300-Tarzan	7	14	21	37	46	55
301-Bugs Bunny	4	7	10	14	17	20
302-Laurel and Hardy (TV); photo-c	6	12	18	28	34	40
303-Daffy Duck	3	6	8	12	14	16
304-The Three Stooges; photo-c	8	16	24	44	57	70
305-Tom and Jerry	3	6	8	12	14	16
306-Daniel Boone (TV); Fess Parker photo-c	7	14	21	35	43	50
307-Little Lulu; Irving Tripp-a	7	14	21	37	46	55
308-Lassie (TV); photo-c	5	10	15	22	26	30
309-Yogi Bear (TV)	5	10	15	24	30	35
310-The Lone Ranger; Clayton Moore photo-c	10	20	30	58	79	100
311-Santa's Show	4	7	9	14	16	18
312-Christmas Album (1967)	4	7	9	14	16	18
313-Daffy Duck (1968)	3	6	8	12	14	16
314-Laurel and Hardy (TV)	6	12	18	27	33	38
315-Bugs Bunny	4	7	10	14	17	20
316-The Three Stooges	8	16	24	40	50	60
317-The Flintstones (TV)	8	16	24	42	54	65
318-Tarzan	7	14	21	35	43	50
319-Yogi Bear (TV)	5	10	15	24	30	35
320-Space Family Robinson (TV); Spiegle-a	11	22	33	62	86	110
321-Tom and Jerry	3	6	8	12	14	16
322-The Lone Ranger	7	14	21	37	46	55
323-Little Lulu; not by Stanley	5	10	15	24	30	35
324-Lassie (TV); photo-c	5	10	15	22	26	30
325-Fun with Santa	4	7	9	14	16	18
326-Christmas Story (1968)	4	7	9	14	16	18
327-The Flintstones (TV)(1969)	8	16	24	42	54	65
328-Space Family Robinson (TV); Spiegle-a	11	22	33	62	86	110
329-Bugs Bunny	4	7	10	14	17	20
330-The Jetsons (TV)	10	20	30	56	76	95
331-Daffy Duck	3	6	8	12	14	16
332-Tarzan	6	12	18	28	34	40
333-Tom and Jerry	3	6	8	12	14	16
334-Lassie (TV)	4	9	13	18	22	26
335-Little Lulu	5	10	15	24	30	35
336-The Three Stooges	8	16	24	40	50	60
337-Yogi Bear (TV)	5	10	15	24	30	35
338-The Lone Ranger	7	14	21	37	46	55
339-(Was not published)						
340-Here Comes Santa (1969)	3	6	8	12	14	16
341-The Flintstones (TV)	8	16	24	42	54	65
342-Tarzan	3	6	9	19	30	40
343-Bugs Bunny	2	4	6	10	14	18
344-Yogi Bear (TV)	3	6	9	16	23	30
345-Tom and Jerry	2	4	6	9	13	16
346-Lassie (TV)	3	6	9	15	21	26
347-Daffy Duck	2	4	6	9	13	16
348-The Jetsons (TV)	5	10	15	34	60	85
349-Little Lulu; not by Stanley	3	6	9	16	23	30
350-The Lone Ranger	3	6	9	17	26	35
351-Beep-Beep, the Road Runner (TV)	2	4	6	11	16	20
352-Space Family Robinson (TV); Spiegle-a	6	12	18	41	76	110
353-Beep-Beep, the Road Runner (1971) (TV)	2	4	6	11	16	20
354-Tarzan (1971)	3	6	9	17	26	35
355-Little Lulu; not by Stanley	3	6	9	16	23	30
356-Scooby Doo, Where Are You? (TV)	6	12	18	37	66	95
357-Daffy Duck & Porky Pig	2	4	6	8	11	14
358-Lassie (TV)	3	6	9	14	19	24
359-Baby Snoots	2	4	6	10	14	18
360-H. R. Pufnstuf (TV); photo-c	6	12	18	37	66	95
361-Tom and Jerry	2	4	6	8	11	14
362-Smokey Bear (TV)	2	4	6	8	11	14
363-Bugs Bunny & Yosemite Sam	2	4	6	9	13	16
364-The Banana Splits (TV); photo-c	5	10	15	33	57	80
365-Tom and Jerry (1972)	2	4	6	8	11	14
366-Tarzan	3	6	9	17	26	35

	GD 2.0	VG 4.0	FN 6.0	VF 8.0	VF/NM 9.0	NM- 9.2
367-Bugs Bunny & Porky Pig	2	4	6	9	13	16
368-Scooby Doo (TV)(4/72)	5	10	15	33	57	80
369-Little Lulu; not by Stanley	3	6	9	14	19	24
370-Lassie (TV); photo-c	3	6	9	14	19	24
371-Baby Snoots	2	4	6	9	13	16
372-Smokey the Bear (TV)	2	4	6	8	11	14
373-The Three Stooges	4	8	12	23	37	50
374-Wacky Witch	2	4	6	8	11	14
375-Beep-Beep & Daffy Duck (TV)	2	4	6	8	11	14
376-The Pink Panther (1972) (TV)	2	4	6	10	14	18
377-Baby Snoots (1973)	2	4	6	9	13	16
378-Turok, Son of Stone; new-a	6	12	18	42	79	115
379-Heckle & Jeckle New Terrytoons (TV)	2	4	6	8	11	14
380-Bugs Bunny & Yosemite Sam	2	4	6	8	11	14
381-Lassie (TV)	2	4	6	11	16	20
382-Scooby Doo, Where Are You? (TV)	5	10	15	30	50	70
383-Smokey the Bear (TV)	2	4	6	8	11	14
384-Pink Panther (TV)	2	4	6	8	11	14
385-Little Lulu	2	4	6	13	18	22
386-Wacky Witch	2	4	6	8	11	14
387-Beep-Beep & Daffy Duck (TV)	2	4	6	8	11	14
388-Tom and Jerry (1973)	2	4	6	8	11	14
389-Little Lulu; not by Stanley	2	4	6	13	18	22
390-Pink Panther (TV)	2	4	6	8	11	14
391-Scooby Doo (TV)	4	8	12	25	40	55
392-Bugs Bunny & Yosemite Sam	2	4	6	8	10	12
393-New Terrytoons (Heckle & Jeckle) (TV)	2	4	6	8	10	12
394-Lassie (TV)	2	4	6	9	13	16
395-Woodsy Owl	2	4	6	8	10	12
396-Baby Snoots	2	4	6	8	11	14
397-Beep-Beep & Daffy Duck (TV)	2	4	6	8	10	12
398-Wacky Witch	2	4	6	8	10	12
399-Turok, Son of Stone; new-a	6	12	18	40	73	105
400-Tom and Jerry	2	4	6	8	10	12
401-Baby Snoots (1975) (r/#371)	2	4	6	8	11	14
402-Daffy Duck (r/#313)	1	3	4	6	8	10
403-Bugs Bunny (r/#343)	2	4	6	8	10	12
404-Space Family Robinson (TV)(r/#328)	5	10	15	35	63	90
405-Cracky	1	3	4	6	8	10
406-Little Lulu (r/#355)	2	4	6	10	14	18
407-Smokey the Bear (TV)(r/#362)	2	4	6	8	10	12
408-Turok, Son of Stone; c-r/Turok #20 w/changes; new-a	5	10	15	34	60	85
409-Pink Panther (TV)	1	3	4	6	8	10
410-Wacky Witch	1	2	3	5	6	8
411-Lassie (TV)(r/#324)	2	4	6	9	13	16
412-New Terrytoons (1975) (TV)	1	2	3	5	6	8
413-Daffy Duck (1976)(r/#331)	1	2	3	5	6	8
414-Space Family Robinson (r/#328)	5	10	15	34	60	85
415-Bugs Bunny (r/#329)	1	2	3	5	6	8
416-Beep-Beep, the Road Runner (r/#353)(TV)	1	2	3	5	6	8
417-Little Lulu (r/#323)	2	4	6	10	14	18
418-Pink Panther (r/#384) (TV)	1	2	3	5	6	8
419-Baby Snoots (r/#377)	1	3	4	6	8	10
420-Woody Woodpecker	1	2	3	5	6	8
421-Tweety & Sylvester	1	2	3	5	6	8
422-Wacky Witch (r/#386)	1	2	3	5	6	8
423-Little Monsters	1	3	4	6	8	10
424-Cracky (12/76)	1	2	3	5	6	8
425-Daffy Duck	1	2	3	5	6	8
426-Underdog (TV)	3	6	9	21	33	45
427-Little Lulu (r/#335)	2	4	6	8	11	14
428-Bugs Bunny	1	2	3	4	5	7
429-The Pink Panther (TV)	1	2	3	4	5	7
430-Beep-Beep, the Road Runner (TV)	1	2	3	4	5	7
431-Baby Snoots	1	2	3	5	6	8
432-Lassie (TV)	2	4	6	8	10	12
433-437: 433-Tweety & Sylvester. 434-Wacky Witch. 435-New Terrytoons (TV). 436-Wacky Advs. of Cracky. 437-Daffy Duck	1	2	3	4	5	7
438-Underdog (TV)	3	6	9	19	30	40
439-Little Lulu (r/#349)	2	4	6	8	11	14
440-442,444-446: 440-Bugs Bunny. 441-The Pink Panther (TV). 442-Beep-Beep, the Road Runner (TV). 444-Tom and Jerry. 445-Tweety and Sylvester. 446-Wacky Witch	1	2	3	5	6	8

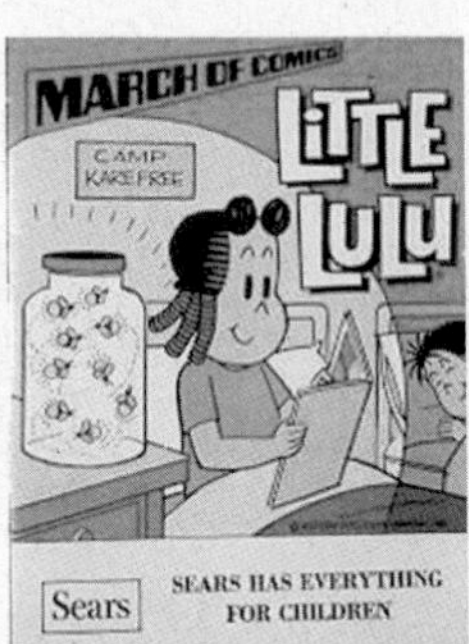

March of Comics #468 © Marjorie Buell

Marvel Guide to Collecting Comics © MAR

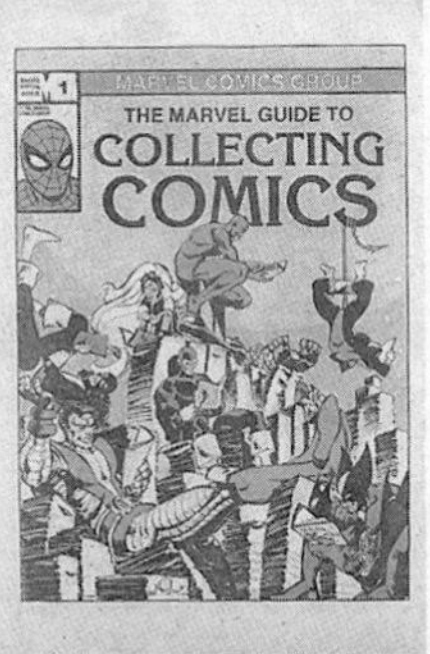

The Masked Pilot © R.S. Callender

	GD 2.0	VG 4.0	FN 6.0	VF 8.0	VF/NM 9.0	NM- 9.2
443-Baby Snoots	1	2	3	5	6	8
447-Mighty Mouse	2	4	6	8	10	12
448-455,457,458: 448-Cracky. 449-Pink Panther (TV). 450-Baby Snoots. 451-Tom and Jerry. 452-Bugs Bunny. 453-Popeye. 454-Woody Woodpecker. 455-Beep-Beep, the Road Runner (TV). 457-Tweety & Sylvester. 458-Wacky Witch	1	2	3	5	6	8
456-Little Lulu (r/#369)	2	4	6	8	10	12
459-Mighty Mouse	2	4	6	8	10	12
460-466: 460-Daffy Duck. 461-The Pink Panther (TV). 462-Baby Snoots. 463-Tom and Jerry. 464-Bugs Bunny. 465-Popeye. 466-Woody Woodpecker	1	2	3	5	6	8
467-Underdog (TV)	3	6	9	17	26	35
468-Little Lulu (r/#385)	1	2	3	5	6	8
469-Tweety & Sylvester	1	2	3	5	6	8
470-Wacky Witch	1	2	3	5	6	8
471-Mighty Mouse	1	3	4	6	8	10
472-474,476-478: 472-Heckle & Jeckle(12/80). 473-Pink Panther(1/81)(TV). 474-Baby Snoots. 476-Bugs Bunny. 477-Popeye. 478-Woody Woodpecker	1	2	3	5	6	8
475-Little Lulu (r/#323)	1	3	4	6	8	10
479-Underdog (TV)	3	6	9	16	23	30
480-482: 480-Tom and Jerry. 481-Tweety and Sylvester. 482-Wacky Witch	1	2	3	4	5	8
483-Mighty Mouse	1	3	4	6	8	10
484-487: 484-Heckle & Jeckle. 485-Baby Snoots. 486-The Pink Panther (TV). 487-Bugs Bunny	1	2	3	4	5	8
488-Little Lulu (4/82) (r/#335) (Last issue)	2	4	6	10	14	18

MARCH TO MARKET, THE
Swift & Co.: 1950 (Giveaway)

nn-The story of meat	3	6	8	11	13	15

MARGARET O'BRIEN (See The Adventures of...)

MARK STEEL
American Iron & Steel Institute: 1967, 1968, 1972 (Giveaway) (24 pgs.)

1967,1968- "Journey of Discovery with..."; Neal Adams art	4	8	12	27	44	60
1972- "...Fights Pollution"; N. Adams-a	2	4	6	11	16	20

MARTIN LUTHER KING AND THE MONTGOMERY STORY
Fellowship Reconciliation: 1957 (Giveaway, 16 pgs.) (A Spanish edition also exists)

nn-In color with paper-c (a CGC 9.2 copy sold for $350 and a FN+ sold for $200 in 2004)

MARTIN LUTHER KING AND THE MONTGOMERY STORY
Top Shelf/Fellowship Reconciliation: 2011, 2013 ($5.00, newsprint-c, 16 pgs.)

nn-(2011) Reprint of the 1957 giveaway published by Fellowship Reconciliation; stapled	5.00
nn-(2013) Reprint has glued binding unlike the stapled 2011 version	5.00

MARVEL COLLECTOR'S EDITION: X-MEN
Marvel Comics: 1993 (3-3/4x6-1/2")

1-4-Pizza Hut giveaways	5.00

MARVEL COMICS PRESENTS
Marvel Comics: 1987, 1988 (4 1/4 x 6 1/4, 20 pgs.)
...Mini Comic Giveaway

nn-(1988) Alf	1	2	3	5	6	8
nn-(1987) Captain America r/ #250	1	2	3	4	5	7
nn-(1987) Care Bears (Star Comics...)	1	2	3	4	5	7
nn-(1988) Flintstone Kids	1	2	3	5	6	8
nn-(1987) Heathcliffe (Star Comics...)	1	2	3	4	5	7
nn-(1987) Spider-Man-r/Spect. Spider-Man #21	1	2	3	4	5	7
nn-(1988) Spider-Man-r/Amazing Spider-Man #1	1	2	3	4	5	7
nn-(1988) X-Men-reprints X-Men #53; B. Smith-a	1	2	3	4	5	7

MARVEL GUIDE TO COLLECTING COMICS, THE
Marvel Comics: 1982 (16 pgs., newsprint pages and cover)

1-Simonson-c	1	2	3	4	5	7

MARVEL MINI-BOOKS
Marvel Comics Group: 1966 (50 pgs., B&W; 5/8x7/8") (6 different issues) (Smallest comics ever published) (Marvel Mania Giveaways)

Captain America, Millie the Model, Sgt. Fury, Hulk, Thor each...	2	4	6	11	16	20
Spider-Man	3	6	9	14	20	25

NOTE: *Each came from gum machines in six different color covers, usually one color: Pink, yellow, green, etc.*

MARVEL SUPER-HERO ISLAND ADVENTURES
Marvel Comics: 1999 (Sold at the park polybagged with Captain America V3 #19, one other comic, 5 trading cards and a cloisonn'e pin)

1-Promotes Universal Studios Islands of Adventures theme park	4.00

MARY'S GREATEST APOSTLE (St. Louis Grignion de Montfort)
Catechetical Guild (Topix) (Giveaway): No date (16 pgs.; paper cover)

nn	5	10	15	23	28	32

MASK
DC Comics: 1985

1-3	6.00

MASKED PILOT, THE (See Popular Comics #43)
R.S. Callender: 1939 (7-1/2x5-1/4", 16 pgs., premium, non-slick-c)

nn-Bob Jenney-a	8	16	24	44	57	70

MASTERS OF THE UNIVERSE (He-Man)
DC Comics: 1982 (giveaways with action figures, at least 35 different issues, unnumbered)

nn	2	4	6	8	10	12

MATRIX, THE (1999 movie)
Warner Brothers: 1999 (Recalled by Warner Bros. over questionable content)

nn-Paul Chadwick-s/a (16 pgs.); Geof Darrow-c	1	2	3	5	6	8

McCRORY'S CHRISTMAS BOOK
Western Printing Co: 1955 (36 pgs., slick-c) (McCrory Stores Corp. giveaway)

nn-Painted-c	5	10	15	22	26	30

McCRORY'S TOYLAND BRINGS YOU SANTA'S PRIVATE EYES
Promotional Publ. Co.: 1956 (16 pgs.) (Giveaway)

nn-Has 9 pg. story plus 7 pgs. toy ads	4	8	11	16	19	22

McCRORY'S WONDERFUL CHRISTMAS
Promotional Publ. Co.: 1954 (20 pgs., slick-c) (Giveaway)

nn	4	8	12	18	22	25

McDONALDS COMMANDRONS
DC Comics: 1985

nn-Four editions	5.00

MEDAL FOR BOWZER, A (Giveaway)
American Visuals Corp.: 1966 (8 pgs.)

nn-Eisner-c/script; Bowzer (a dog) survives untried pneumonia cure and earns his medal; (medical experimentation on animals)	15	30	45	103	227	350

MEET HIYA A FRIEND OF SANTA CLAUS
Julian J. Proskauer/Sundial Shoe Stores, etc.: 1949 (18 pgs.?, paper-c)(Giveaway)

nn	6	12	18	31	38	45

MEET THE NEW POST-GAZETTE SUNDAY FUNNIES
Pittsburgh Post Gazette: 3/12/49 (7-1/4x10-1/4", 16 pgs., paper-c)
Commercial Comics (insert in newspaper) (Rare)

Dick Tracy by Gould, Gasoline Alley, Terry & the Pirates, Brenda Starr, Buck Rogers by Yager, The Gumps, Peter Rabbit by Fago, Superman, Funnyman by Siegel & Shuster, The Saint, Archie, & others done especially for this book. A fine copy sold at auction in 1985 for $276.00.

	260	520	780	1700	-	-

MEN OF COURAGE
Catechetical Guild: 1949

Bound Topix comics-V7#2,4,6,8,10,16,18,20	6	12	18	31	38	45

MEN WHO MOVE THE NATION
Publisher unknown: (Giveaway) (B&W)

nn-Neal Adams-a	6	12	18	31	38	45

MERRY CHRISTMAS, A
K. K. Publications (Child Life Shoes): 1948 (Giveaway)

nn-Santa cover	8	16	24	44	57	70

MERRY CHRISTMAS
K. K. Publications (Blue Bird Shoes Giveaway): 1956 (7-1/4x5-1/4")

nn-Santa cover	4	8	12	18	22	25

MERRY CHRISTMAS FROM MICKEY MOUSE
K. K. Publications: 1939 (16 pgs.) (Color & B&W) (Shoe store giveaway)

nn-Donald Duck & Pluto app.; text with art (Rare); c-reprint/Mickey Mouse Mag. V3#3 (12/37)(Rare)	245	490	735	1568	2684	3800

MERRY CHRISTMAS FROM SEARS TOYLAND (See Santa's Christmas Comic, Bob & Betty & Santa's Wishing Whistle, and A Christmas Carol)
Sears Roebuck Giveaway: 1939 (16 pgs.) (Color)(Die-cut)

nn-Dick Tracy, Little Orphan Annie, The Gumps, Terry & the Pirates	103	206	309	659	1130	1600

Mickey Mouse Magazine V1 #10 © DIS

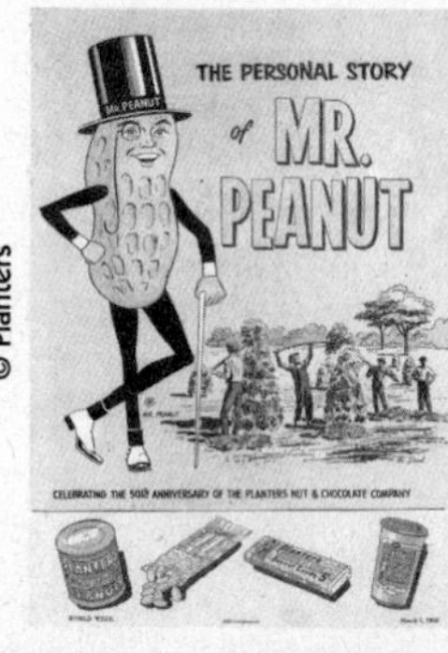

Mr. Peanut, The Personal Story of... © Planters

Natural Disasters! © GIS

GD 2.0 · VG 4.0 · FN 6.0 · VF 8.0 · VF/NM 9.0 · NM- 9.2

MICKEY MOUSE (Also see Frito-Lay Giveaway)
Dell Publ. Co
...& Goofy Explore Business(1978) 2 4 6 8 10 12
...& Goofy Explore Energy(1976-1978, 36 pgs.); Exxon giveaway in color; regular size 2 4 6 8 10 12
...& Goofy Explore Energy Conservation(1976-1978)-Exxon 2 4 6 8 10 12
...& Goofy Explore The Universe of Energy(1985, 20 pgs.); Exxon giveaway in color; regular size 1 2 3 5 7 9
The Perils of Mickey nn (1993, 5-1/4x7-1/4", 16 pgs.)-Nabisco giveaway w/ games, Nabisco coupons & 6 pgs. of stories; Phantom Blot app. 6.00

MICKEY MOUSE MAGAZINE
Walt Disney Productions: V1#1, Jan, 1933 - V1#9, Sept, 1933 (5-1/4x7-1/4")
No. 1-3 published by Kamen-Blair (Kay Kamen, Inc.)
(Scarce)-Distributed by dairies and leading stores through their local theatres.
First few issues had 5¢ listed on cover, later ones had no price.
V1#1 417 834 1668 5000 - -
2-4 150 300 600 1200 - -
5-9 100 200 400 800 - -

MICKEY MOUSE MAGAZINE
Walt Disney Productions: V1#1, 11/33 - V2#12, 10/35 (Mills giveaways issued by different dairies)
V1#1 129 258 387 826 1413 2000
2-12: 2-X-Mas issue 45 90 135 284 480 675
V2#1 (11/34) Donald Duck in sailor suit pg. 6 (cameo) 37 74 111 222 361 500
V2#2-4,6-12: 2-X-Mas issue. 4-St. Valentine-c 36 72 108 211 343 475
V2#5 (3/35) 1st app. Donald Duck in sailor outfit on-c 94 188 282 597 1024 1450

MICKEY MOUSE MAGAZINE
K.K. Publications: V4#1, Oct, 1938 (Giveaway)
V4#1 41 82 123 256 428 600

MIGHTY ATOM, THE
Whitman
Giveaway (1959, '63, Whitman)-Evans-a 3 6 9 16 23 30
Giveaway ('64r, '65r, '66r, '67r, '68r)-Evans-r? 2 4 6 10 14 18
Giveaway ('73r, '76r) 2 4 6 8 11 14

MILES THE MONSTER (Initially sold only at the Dover Speedway track)
Dover International Speedway, Inc.: 2006 ($3.00)
1,2-Allan Gross & Mark Wheatley-s/Wheatley-a 3.00

MILITARY COURTESY
Harvey Publications: (16 pgs.)
nn-Regulations and saluting instructions 5 10 14 20 24 28

MINUTE MAN
Sovereign Service Station giveaway: No date (16 pgs., B&W, paper-c blue & red)
nn-American history 3 6 8 12 14 16

MINUTE MAN ANSWERS THE CALL, THE
By M. C. Gaines: 1942,1943,1944,1945 (4 pgs.) (Giveaway inserted in Jr. JSA Membership Kit)
nn-Sheldon Moldoff-a 21 42 63 124 202 280

MIRACLE ON BROADWAY
Broadway Comics: Dec, 1995 (Giveaway)
1-Ernie Colon-c/a; Jim Shooter & Co. story; 1st known digitally printed comic book; 1st app. Spire & Knights on Broadway (1150 print run) 20.00
NOTE: *Miracle on Broadway was a limited edition comic given to 1100 VIPs in the entertainment industry for the 1995 Holiday Season.*

MISS SUNBEAM (See Little Miss Sunbeam Comics)

MR. BUG GOES TO TOWN (See Cinema Comics Herald)
K.K. Publications: 1941 (Giveaway, 52 pgs.)
nn-Cartoon movie (scarce) 68 136 204 435 743 1050

MR. PEANUT, THE PERSONAL STORY OF
Planters Nut & Chocolate Co.: 1956
nn 3 6 9 21 33 45

MOTHER OF US ALL
Catechetical Guild Giveaway: 1950? (32 pgs.)
nn 5 10 15 23 28 32

MOTION PICTURE FUNNIES WEEKLY (Amazing Man #5 on?)
First Funnies, Inc.: 1939 (Giveaway)(B&W, 36 pgs.) No month given; last panel in Sub-Mariner story dated 4/39 (Also see Colossus, Green Giant & Invaders No. 20)
1-Origin & 1st printed app. Sub-Mariner by Bill Everett (8 pgs.); Fred Schwab-c; reprinted in Marvel Mystery #1 with color added over the craft tint which was used to shade the black & white version; Spy Ring, American Ace (reprinted in Marvel Mystery #3) app.
(Rare)-only eight known copies, one near mint with white pages, the rest with brown pages. 5000 10,000 15,000 25,000 35,000 -
Covers only to #2-4 (set) 800
NOTE: Eight copies (plus one coverless) were discovered in 1974 in the estate of the deceased publisher. Covers only to issues No. 2-4 were also found which evidently were printed in advance along with #1. #1 was to be distributed only through motion picture movie houses. However, it is believed that only advanced copies were sent out and the motion picture houses not going for the idea. Possible distribution at local theaters in Boston suspected. The "pay" copy (graded at 9.0) was discovered after 1974, bringing the total known to nine. The last panel of Sub-Mariner contains a rectangular box with "Continued Next Week" printed in it. When reprinted in Marvel Mystery, the box was left in with lettering omitted.

MY DOG TIGE (Buster Brown's Dog)
Buster Brown Shoes: 1957 (Giveaway)
nn 5 10 15 24 30 35

MY GREATEST THRILLS IN BASEBALL
Mission of California: Date? (16 pg. Giveaway)
nn-By Mickey Mantle 54 108 162 343 574 825

MYSTERIOUS ADVENTURES WITH SANTA CLAUS
Lansburgh's: 1948 (paper cover)
nn 13 26 39 72 101 130

NAKED FORCE!
Commercial Comics: 1958 (Small size)
nn 3 6 8 11 13 15

NATURAL DISASTERS!
Graphic Information Service/ Civil Defense: 1956 (16 pgs., soft-c)
nn-Al Capp Li'l Abner-c; Li'l Abner cameo (1 panel); narrated by Mr. Civil Defense 10 20 30 54 72 90

NAVY: HISTORY & TRADITION
Stokes Walesby Co./Dept. of Navy: 1958 - 1961 (nn) (Giveaway)
1772-1778, 1778-1782, 1782-1817, 1817-1865, 1865-1936, 1940-1945:
1772-1778-16 pg. in color 5 10 15 22 26 30
1861: Naval Actions of the Civil War: 1865-36 pg. in color; flag-c 5 10 15 22 26 30

NEW ADVENTURE OF WALT DISNEY'S SNOW WHITE AND THE SEVEN DWARFS, A (See Snow White Bendix Giveaway)

NEW ADVENTURES OF PETER PAN (Disney)
Western Publishing Co.: 1953 (5x7-1/4", 36 pgs.) (Admiral giveaway)
nn 14 28 42 76 108 140

NEW AVENGERS... (Giveaway for U.S Military personnel)
Marvel Comics: 2005 - Present (Distributed by Army & Air Force Exchange Service)
... Guest Starring the Fantastic Four (4/05) Bendis-s/Jurgens-a/c 4.00
...: Pot of Gold (AAFES 110th Anniversary Issue) (10/05) Jenkins-s/Nolan-a/c 4.00
(#3) ...: Avengers & X-Men Time Trouble (4/06) Kirkman-s 4.00
(#4) ...: Letters Home (12/06) Capt. America, Punisher, Silver Surfer, Ghost Rider on-c 4.00
5-The Spirit of America (10/05) Captain America app. 4.00
6-Fireline (8/08) Spider-Man, Iron Man & Hulk app. Richards-a/Dave Ross-c 4.00
7-An Army of One (2009) Frank Cho pin-up on back-c 4.00
8-The Promise (12/09) Captain America (Bucky) app. 4.00

NEW FRONTIERS
Harvey Information Press (United States Steel Corp.) : 1958 (16 pgs., paper-c)
nn-History of barbed wire 3 6 9 14 19 24

NEW TEEN TITANS, THE
DC Comics: Nov. 1983
nn(11/83-Keebler Co. Giveaway)-In cooperation with "The President's Drug Awareness Campaign"; came in Presidential envelope w/letter from White House (Nancy Reagan) 1 2 3 4 5 7
nn-(re-issue of above on Mando paper for direct sales market); American Soft Drink Industry version; I.B.M. Corp. version 5.00

NEW USES FOR GOOD EARTH
Mined Land Conservation: 1960 (paper-c)
nn 3 6 9 19 30 40

NOLAN RYAN IN THE WINNING PITCH (Kellogg's Tony's Sports Comics)
DC Comics: 1992 (Sports Illustrated)
nn 5.00

OLD GLORY COMICS

The Owl © WEST

Peter Wheat, Advs. of ... #58 © Bakers Assocs.

Porky's Book of Tricks © WB

	GD	VG	FN	VF	VF/NM	NM-
	2.0	4.0	6.0	8.0	9.0	9.2

Chesapeake & Ohio Railway: 1944 (Giveaway)
nn-Capt. Fearless reprint 8 16 24 40 50 60

ON THE AIR
NBC Network Comic: 1947 (Giveaway, paper-c, regular size)
nn-(Rare) 18 36 54 105 165 225

OUT OF THE PAST A CLUE TO THE FUTURE
E. C. Comics (Public Affairs Comm.): 1946? (16 pgs.) (paper cover)
nn-Based on public affairs pamphlet "What Foreign Trade Means to You" 20 40 60 118 192 265

OUTSTANDING AMERICAN WAR HEROES
The Parents' Institute: 1944 (16 pgs., paper-c)
nn-Reprints from True Comics 5 10 15 22 26 30

OVERSEAS COMICS (Also see G.I. Comics & Jeep Comics)
Giveaway (Distributed to U.S. Armed Forces): 1944 - No. 105?, 1946 (7-1/4x10-1/4"; 16 pgs. in color)
23-105-Bringing Up Father (by McManus), Popeye, Joe Palooka, Dick Tracy, Superman, Gasoline Alley, Buz Sawyer, Li'l Abner, Blondie, Terry & the Pirates, Out Our Way 7 14 21 35 43 50

OWL, THE (See Crackajack Funnies #25 & Popular Comics #72)(Also see The Hurricane Kids & Magic Morro
Western Pub. Co./R.S. Callender: 1940 (Giveaway)(7-1/2x5-1/4")(Soft-c, color)
nn-Frank Thomas-a 15 30 45 86 133 180

OXYDOL-DREFT
Toby Press:1950 (Set of 6 pocket-size giveaways; distributed through the mail as a set) (Scarce)
1-3: 1-Li'l Abner. 2-Daisy Mae. 3-Shmoo 9 18 27 47 61 75
4-John Wayne; Williamson/Frazetta-c from John Wayne #3 12 24 36 67 94 120
5-Archie 11 22 33 62 86 110
6-Terrytoons Mighty Mouse 9 18 27 47 61 75
Mailing Envelope (has All Capp's Shmoo on front) 9 18 27 52 69 85

OZZIE SMITH IN THE KID WHO COULD (Kellogg's Tony's Sports Comics)
DC Comics: 1992 (Sports Illustrated)
nn-Ozzie Smith app. 5.00

PADRE OF THE POOR
Catechetical Guild: nd (Giveaway) (16 pgs., paper-c)
nn 5 10 15 24 30 35

PAUL TERRY'S HOW TO DRAW FUNNY CARTOONS
Terrytoons, Inc. (Giveaway): 1940's (14 pgs.) (Black & White)
nn-Heckle & Jeckle, Mighty Mouse, etc. 13 26 39 72 101 130

PEANUTS HALLOWEEN
Fantagraphics Books: Sept, 2008 (8-1/2" x 5-3/8" ashcan giveaway)
nn-Halloween themed reprints in color and B&W 2.00

PETER PAN (See New Adventures of Peter Pan)

PETER PENNY AND HIS MAGIC DOLLAR
American Bankers Association, N. Y. (Giveaway): 1947 (16 pgs.; paper-c; regular size)
nn-(Scarce)-Used in **SOTI**, pg. 310, 311 15 30 45 88 137 185
Diff. version (7-1/4x11")-redrawn, 16 pgs., paper-c 10 20 30 56 76 95

PETER WHEAT (The Adventures of...)
Bakers Associates Giveaway: 1948 - 1957? (16 pgs. in color) (paper covers)
nn(No.1)-States on last page, end of 1st Adventure of...; Kelly-a 26 52 78 154 252 350
nn(4 issues)-Kelly-a 14 28 42 82 121 160
6-10-All Kelly-a 10 20 30 54 72 90
11-20-All Kelly-a 9 18 27 50 65 80
21-35-All Kelly-a 8 16 24 40 50 60
36-66 6 12 18 28 34 40
...Artist's Workbook ('54, digest size) 6 12 18 28 34 40
...Four-In-One Fun Pack (Vol. 2, '54), oblong, comics w/puzzles 7 14 21 35 43 50
...Fun Book ('52, 32 pgs., paper-c, B&W & color, 8-1/2x10-3/4")-Contains cut-outs, puzzles, games, magic & pages to color 8 16 24 44 57 70
NOTE: *Al Hubbard art #36 on; written by Del Connell.*

PETER WHEAT NEWS
Bakers Associates: 1948 - No. 30, 1950 (4 pgs. in color)
Vol. 1-All have 2 pgs. Peter Wheat by Kelly 21 42 63 126 206 285
2-10 13 26 39 72 101 130
11-20 8 16 24 40 50 60
21-30 6 12 18 28 34 40
NOTE: *Early issues have no date & **Kelly** art.*

PINOCCHIO
Cocomalt/Montgomery Ward Co.: 1940 (10 pgs.; giveaway, linen-like paper)
nn-Cocomalt edition 43 86 129 271 456 640
nn-store edition 36 72 108 215 350 485

PIUS XII MAN OF PEACE
Catechetical Guild: No date (12 pgs.; 5-1/2x8-1/2") (B&W)
nn-Catechetical Guild Giveaway 6 12 18 31 38 45

PLOT TO STEAL THE WORLD, THE
Work & Unity Group: 1948, 16pgs., paper-c
nn-Anti commumism 18 36 54 103 162 220

POCAHONTAS
Pocahontas Fuel Company (Coal): 1941 - No. 2, 1942
nn(#1), 2-Feat. life story of Indian princess Pocahontas & facts about Pocahontas coal, Pocahontas, VA. 15 30 45 85 130 175

POLL PARROT
Poll Parrot Shoe Store/International Shoe
K. K. Publications (Giveaway): 1950 - No. 4, 1951; No. 2, 1959 - No. 16, 1962
1 ('50)-Howdy Doody; small size 18 36 54 107 169 230
2-4('51)-Howdy Doody 15 30 45 88 137 185
2('59)-16('62): 2-The Secret of Crumbley Castle. 5-Bandit Busters. 7-The Make-Believe Mummy. 8-Mixed Up Mission('60). 10-The Frightful Flight. 11-Showdown at Sunup. 12-Maniac at Mubu Island. 13-...and the Runaway Genie. 14-Bully for You. 15-Trapped In Tall Timber. 16-...& the Rajah's Ruby('62) 2 4 6 11 16 20

POPEYE
Whitman
Bold Detergent giveaway (Same as regular issue #94) 2 4 6 9 13 16
Quaker Cereal premium (1989, 16pp, small size,4 diff.)(Popeye & the Time Machine, --On Safari, --& Big Foot, --vs. Bluto) 2 4 6 8 10 12

POPEYE
Charlton (King Features) (Giveaway): 1972 - 1974 (36 pgs. in color)
E-1 to E-15 (Educational comics) 2 4 6 9 13 16
nn-Popeye Gettin' Better Grades-4 pgs. used as intro. to above giveaways (in color) 2 4 6 9 13 16

POPSICLE PETE FUN BOOK (See All-American Comics #6)
Joe Lowe Corp.: 1947, 1948
nn-36 pgs. in color; Sammy 'n' Claras, The King Who Couldn't Sleep & Popsicle Pete stories, games, cut-outs 10 20 30 58 79 100
Adventure Book ('48)-Has Classics ad with checklist to HRN #343 (Great Expectations #43) 9 18 27 52 69 85

PORKY'S BOOK OF TRICKS
K. K. Publications (Giveaway): 1942 (8-1/2x5-1/2", 48 pgs.)
nn-7 pg. comic story, text stories, plus games & puzzles 55 110 165 352 601 850

POST GAZETTE (See Meet the New...)

PUNISHER: COUNTDOWN (Movie)
Marvel Comics: 2004 (7 1/4" X 4 3/4" mini-comic packaged with Punisher DVD)
nn-Prequel to 2004 movie; Ennis-s/Dillon-a/Bradstreet-c 2.50

PURE OIL COMICS (Also see Salerno Carnival of Comics, 24 Pages of Comics, & Vicks Comics)
Pure Oil Giveaway: Late 1930's (24 pgs., regular size, paper-c)
nn-Contains 1-2 pg. strips; i.e., Hairbreadth Harry, Skyroads, Buck Rogers by Calkins & Yager, Olly of the Movies, Napoleon, S'Matter Pop, etc. Also a 16 pg. 1938 giveaway with Buck Rogers 34 68 102 204 332 460

QUAKER OATS (Also see Cap'n Crunch)
Quaker Oats Co.: 1965 (Giveaway) (2-1/2x5-1/2") (16 pgs.)
"Plenty of Glutton", starring Quake & Quisp; 3 6 9 14 19 24
"Lava Come-Back", "Kite Tale" 1 3 4 6 8 10

RAILROADS DELIVER THE GOODS!
Assoc. of American Railroads: Dec, 1954; Sept, 1957 (16 pgs., paper-c)
nn-The story of railway freight 6 12 18 28 34 40

RAILS ACROSS AMERICA!

Real Hit Comics #1 © FOX

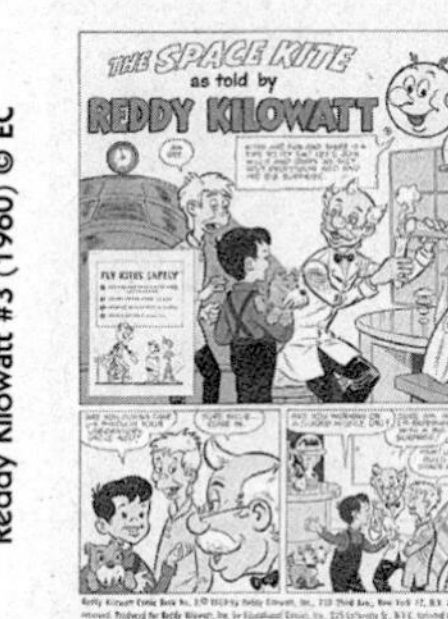

Reddy Kilowatt #3 (1960) © EC

Robin Hood - Ghosts of Waylea Castle © DIS

	GD 2.0	VG 4.0	FN 6.0	VF 8.0	VF/NM 9.0	NM- 9.2

Assoc. of American Railroads: nd (16 pgs.)

nn 6 12 18 28 34 40

READY THEN, READY NOW
Western Publications: 1966 (National Guard military giveaway, regular size)

nn 5 10 15 33 57 80

REAL FUN OF DRIVING!!, THE
Chrysler Corp.: 1965, 1966, 1967 (Regular size, 16 pgs.)

nn-Schaffenberger-a (12 pgs.) 1 2 3 5 6 8

REAL HIT
Fox Features Publications: 1944 (Savings Bond premium)

1-Blue Beetle-r; Blue Beetle on-c 15 30 45 90 140 190

NOTE: *Two versions exist, with and without covers. The coverless version has the title, No. 1 and price printed at top of splash page.*

RED BALL COMIC BOOK
Parents' Magazine Institute: 1947 (Red Ball Shoes giveaway)

nn-Reprints from True Comics 4 8 11 16 19 22

REDDY GOOSE
International Shoe Co. (Western Printing): No number, 1958?; No. 2, Jan, 1959 - No. 16, July, 1962 (Giveaway)

nn (#1) 4 8 12 23 37 50
2-16 3 6 9 14 20 25

REDDY KILOWATT (5¢) (Also see Story of Edison)
Educational Comics (E. C.): 1946 - No. 2, 1947; 1956 - 1965 (no month) (16 pgs., paper-c)

nn-A Visit With Reddy (1948-1954?) 9 18 27 50 65 80
nn-Reddy Made Magic (1946, 5¢) 13 26 39 72 101 130
nn-Reddy Made Magic (1958) 9 18 27 50 65 80
2-Edison, the Man Who Changed the World (3/4" smaller than #1) (1947, 5¢) 13 26 39 72 101 130
...Comic Book 2 (1954)- "Light's Diamond Jubilee" 9 18 27 54 72 90
...Comic Book 2 (1956, 16 pgs.)- "Wizard of Light" 9 18 27 52 69 85
...Comic Book 2 (1958, 16 pgs.)- "Wizard of Light" 9 18 27 50 65 78
...Comic Book 2 (1965, 16 pgs.)- "Wizard of Light" 4 8 12 28 44 60
...Comic Book 3 (1956, 8 pgs.)- "The Space Kite"; Orlando story; regular size 9 18 27 47 61 75
...Comic Book 3 (1960, 8 pgs.)- "The Space Kite"; Orlando story; regular size 4 8 12 28 44 60

NOTE: *Several copies surfaced in 1979.*

REDDY MADE MAGIC
Educational Comics (E. C.): 1956, 1958 (16 pgs., paper-c)

1-Reddy Kilowatt-r (splash panel changed) 11 22 33 60 83 105
1 (1958 edition) 6 12 18 31 38 45

RED ICEBERG, THE
Impact Publ. (Catechetical Guild): 1960 (10¢, 16 pgs., Communist propaganda)

nn-(Rare)- "We The People" back-c 27 54 81 194 435 675
2nd version- "Impact Press" back-c 23 46 69 161 351 540
3rd version- "Explains comic" back-c 23 46 69 161 351 540
4th version- "Impact Press w/World Wide Secret Heart Program ad" 23 46 69 161 351 540
5th version- "Chicago Inter-Student Catholic Action" back-c 23 46 69 161 351 540

NOTE: *This book was the Guild's last anti-communist propaganda book and had very limited circulation. 3 - 4 copies surfaced in 1979 from the defunct publisher's files. Other copies do turn up.*

RED RYDER COMICS
Dell Publ. Co.

Buster Brown Shoes Giveaway (1941, color, soft-c, 32 pgs.) 16 32 48 94 147 200
Red Ryder Super Book of Comics (1944, paper-c, 32 pgs.; blank back-c) Magic Morro app. 18 36 54 105 165 225
Red Ryder Victory Patrol-nn(1942, 32 pgs.)(Langendorf bread; includes cut-out membership card and certificate, order blank and "Slide-Up" decoder, and a Super Book of Comics in color (same content as Super Book #4 w/diff. cover (Pan-Am)) (Rare) 129 258 387 826 1413 2000
Red Ryder Victory Patrol-nn(1943, 32 pgs.)(Langendorf bread; includes cut-out "Rodeomatic" radio decoder, order coupon for "Magic V-Badge", cut-out membership card and certificate and a full color Super Book of comics comic book) (Rare) 97 194 291 621 1061 1500
Red Ryder Victory Patrol-nn(1944, 32 pgs.)-r-/#43,44; comic has a paper-c & is stapled inside a triple cardboard fold-out-c; contains membership card, decoder, map of R.R. home range, etc. Herky app. (Langendorf Bread giveaway; sub-titled 'Super Book of Comics') (Rare) 97 194 291 621 1061 1500
Wells Lamont Corp. giveaway (1950)-16 pgs. in color; regular size; paper-c; 1941-r 14 28 42 82 121 160

RETURN OF JOE THE GENIE OF STEEL (Also see Joe The Genie of Steel)
U. S. Steel Corp., Pittsburgh, PA/Commercial Comics: 1951 (U. S. Steel Corp. giveaway)

nn-Joe Magarac, the Paul Bunyan of steel 4 8 12 28 47 65

REX MORGAN M.D. TALKS ABOUT YOUR UNBORN CHILD
(No publisher) Fetal Alcohol, Tobacco & Firearms giveaway, 1980 (Reg. size, paper-c)

nn 3 6 9 19 30 40

RICHIE RICH, CASPER & WENDY NATIONAL LEAGUE
Harvey Publications: June, 1976 (52 pgs.) (newsstand edition also exists)

1 (Released-3/76 with 6/76 date) 3 6 9 15 22 28
1 (6/76)-2nd version w/San Francisco Giants & KTVU 2 logos; has "Compliments of Giants and Straw Hat Pizza" on-c 3 6 9 15 22 28
1-Variants for other 11 NL teams, similar to Giants version but with different ad on inside front-c 3 6 9 15 22 28

RIDE THE HIGH IRON!
Assoc. of American Railroads: Jan, 1957 (16 pgs.)

nn-The Story of modern passenger trains 5 10 15 24 30 35

RIPLEY'S BELIEVE IT OR NOT!
Harvey Publications

J. C. Penney giveaway (1948) 9 18 27 50 65 80

ROBIN HOOD (New Adventures of...)
Walt Disney Productions: 1952 (Flour giveaways, 5x7-1/4", 36 pgs.)

"New Adventures of Robin Hood", "Ghosts of Waylea Castle", & "The Miller's Ransom" each.... 4 7 10 14 17 20

ROBIN HOOD'S FRONTIER DAYS (...Western Tales, Adventures of... #1)
Shoe Store Giveaway (Robin Hood Stores): 1956 (20 pgs., slick-c)(7 issues?)

nn 6 12 18 31 38 45
nn-Issues with Crandall-a 8 16 24 42 54 65

ROCKETS AND RANGE RIDERS
Richfield Oil Corp.: May, 1957 (Giveaway, 16 pgs., soft-c)

nn-Toth-a 15 30 45 86 133 180

ROUND THE WORLD GIFT
National War Fund (Giveaway): No date (mid 1940's) (4 pgs.)

nn 11 22 33 64 90 115

ROY ROGERS COMICS
Dell Publishing Co.

...& the Man From Dodge City (Dodge giveaway, 16 pgs., 1954)-Frontier, Inc. (5x7-1/4") 12 24 36 69 97 125
Official Roy Rogers Riders Club Comics (1952; 16 pgs., reg. size, paper-c) 20 40 60 114 182 250

RUDOLPH, THE RED-NOSED REINDEER
Montgomery Ward: 1939 (2,400,000 copies printed); Dec, 1951 (Giveaway)

Paper cover-1st app. in print; written by Robert May; ill. by Denver Gillen 15 30 45 83 124 165
Hardcover version 19 38 57 109 172 235
1951 Edition (Has 1939 date)-36 pgs., slick-c printed in red & brown; pulp interior printed in four mixed-ink colors: red, green, blue & brown 11 22 33 62 86 110
1951 Edition with red-spiral promotional booklet printed on high quality stock, 8-1/2"x11", in red & brown, 25 pages composed of 4 fold outs, single sheets and the Rudolph comic book inserted (rare) 47 94 141 296 498 700

SABRINA THE TEENAGE WITCH
Archie Comic Publications: (8 1/2"x 5 1/2", Diamond Comic Dist. Halloween giveaway)

... And The Archies (2004)-Tania Del Rio-s/a; manga-style; Josie and the Pussycats app. 2.50

SAD CASE OF WAITING ROOM WILLIE, THE
American Visuals Corp. (For Baltimore Medical Society): (nd, 1950?) (14 pgs. in color; paper covers; regular size)

nn-By Will Eisner (Rare) 44 88 132 277 469 660

SAD SACK COMICS
Harvey Publications: 1957-1962

Armed Forces Complimentary copies, HD #1-40 (1957-1962) 3 6 9 15 22 28

SALERNO CARNIVAL OF COMICS (Also see Pure Oil Comics, 24 Pages of Comics, & Vicks

Salute to the Boy Scouts © AAR

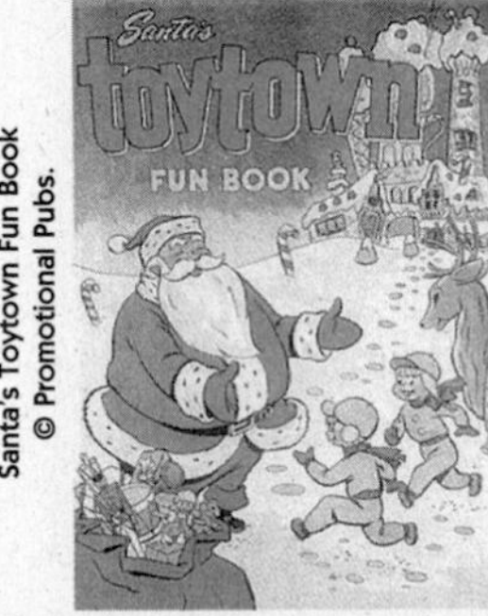

Santa's Toytown Fun Book © Promotional Pubs.

Sergeant Preston of the Yukon - How Yukon King... © Quaker

	GD 2.0	VG 4.0	FN 6.0	VF 8.0	VF/NM 9.0	NM- 9.2

Comics)
Salerno Cookie Co.: Late 1930s (Giveaway, 16 pgs, paper-c)
nn-Color reprints of Calkins' Buck Rogers & Skyroads, plus other strips from Famous Funnies 42 84 126 265 445 625

SALUTE TO THE BOY SCOUTS
Association of American Railroads: 1960 (16 pgs., paper-c, regular size)
nn-History of scouting and the railroad 3 6 9 16 23 30

SANTA AND POLLYANNA PLAY THE GLAD GAME
Western Publ.: Aug, 1960 (16 pgs.) (Disney giveaway)
nn 3 6 9 14 20 25

SANTA & THE BUCCANEERS
Promotional Publ. Co.: 1959 (Giveaway, paper-c)
nn-Reprints 1952 Santa & the Pirates 2 4 6 11 16 20

SANTA & THE CHRISTMAS CHICKADEE
Murphy's: 1974 (Giveaway, 20 pgs.)
nn 2 4 6 8 10 12

SANTA & THE PIRATES
Promotional Publ. Co.: 1952 (Giveaway)
nn-Marv Levy-c/a 4 8 12 17 21 24

SANTA CLAUS FUNNIES (Also see The Little Fir Tree)
W. T. Grant Co./Whitman Publishing: nd; 1940 (Giveaway, 8x10"; 12 pgs., color & B&W, heavy paper)
nn-(2 versions- no date and 1940) 14 28 42 80 115 150

SANTA IS HERE!
Western Publ. (Giveaway): 1949 (oblong, slick-c)
nn 6 12 18 33 38 45

SANTA ON THE JOLLY ROGER
Promotional Publ. Co. (Giveaway): 1965
nn-Marv Levy-c/a 2 4 6 8 10 12

SANTA! SANTA!
R. Jackson: 1974 (20 pgs.) (Montgomery Ward giveaway)
nn 1 3 4 6 8 10

SANTA'S BUNDLE OF FUN
Gimbels: 1969 (Giveaway, B&W, 20 pgs.)
nn-Coloring book & games 2 4 6 8 10 12

SANTA'S CHRISTMAS COMIC VARIETY SHOW (See Merry Christmas From Sears Toyland, Bob & Betty & Santa's Wishing Whistle, and A Christmas Carol)
Sears Roebuck & Co.: 1943 (24 pgs.)
Contains puzzles & new comics of Dick Tracy, Little Orphan Annie, Moon Mullins, Terry & the Pirates, etc. 53 106 159 334 567 800

SANTA'S CHRISTMAS TIME STORIES
Premium Sales, Inc.: nd (Late 1940s) (16 pgs., paper-c) (Giveaway)
nn 6 12 18 31 38 45

SANTA'S CIRCUS
Promotional Publ. Co.: 1964 (Giveaway, half-size)
nn-Marv Levy-c/a 2 4 6 8 11 14

SANTA'S FUN BOOK
Promotional Publ. Co.: 1951, 1952 (Regular size, 16 pgs., paper-c) (Murphy's giveaway)
nn 5 10 15 24 30 35

SANTA'S GIFT BOOK
No Publisher: No date (16 pgs.)
nn-Puzzles, games only 4 8 11 16 19 22

SANTA'S NEW STORY BOOK
Wallace Hamilton Campbell: 1949 (16 pgs., paper-c) (Giveaway)
nn 6 12 18 31 38 45

SANTA'S REAL STORY BOOK
Wallace Hamilton Campbell/W. W. Orris: 1948, 1952 (Giveaway, 16 pgs.)
nn 6 12 18 31 38 45

SANTA'S RIDE
W. T. Grant Co.: 1959 (Giveaway)
nn 3 6 9 14 19 24

SANTA'S RODEO
Promotional Publ. Co.: 1964 (Giveaway, half-size)
nn-Marv Levy-a 2 4 6 8 11 14

SANTA'S SECRET CAVE
W.T. Grant Co.: 1960 (Giveaway, half-size)
nn 2 4 6 11 16 20

SANTA'S SECRETS
Sam B. Anson Christmas giveaway: 1951, 1952? (16 pgs., paper-c)
nn-Has games, stories & pictures to color 4 8 12 17 21 24

SANTA'S STORIES
K. K. Publications (Klines Dept. Store): 1953 (Regular size, paper-c)
nn-Kelly-a 15 30 45 88 137 185
nn-Another version (1953, glossy-c, half-size, 7-1/4x5-1/4")-Kelly-a 11 22 33 62 86 110

SANTA'S SURPRISE
K. K. Publications: 1947 (Giveaway, 36 pgs., slick-c)
nn 8 16 24 40 50 60

SANTA'S TOYTOWN FUN BOOK
Promotional Publ. Co.: 1953 (Giveaway)
nn-Marv Levy-c 4 8 11 16 19 22

SANTA TAKES A TRIP TO MARS
Bradshaw-Diehl Co., Huntington, W.VA.: 1950s (nd) (Giveaway, 16 pgs.)
nn 4 8 11 16 19 22

SCHWINN BIKE THRILLS
Schwinn Bicycle Co.: 1959 (Reg. size)
nn 8 16 24 40 50 60

SCIENCE FAIR STORY OF ELECTRONICS
Radio Shack/Tandy Corp.: 1975 - 1987 (Giveaway)
11 different issues (approx. 1 per year) each.... 3.00

SCOOBY-DOO!
DC Comics.: 2002 (Burger King/Cartoon Network giveaway)
1 2.50

SEEING WASHINGTON
Commercial Comics: 1957 (also sold at 25¢)(Slick-c, reg. size)
nn 6 12 18 28 34 40

SERGEANT PRESTON OF THE YUKON
Quaker Cereals: 1956 (4 comic booklets) (Soft-c, 16 pgs., 7x2-1/2" & 5x2-1/2") Giveaways
"How He Found Yukon King", "The Case That Made Him A Sergeant", "How Yukon King Saved Him From The Wolves", "How He Became A Mountie"
each... 9 18 27 47 61 75

SHAZAM! (Visits Portland Oregon in 1943)
DC Comics: 1989 (69¢ cover)
nn-Promotes Super-Heroes exhibit at Oregon Museum of Science and Industry; reprints Golden Age Captain Marvel story 2 4 6 8 11 14

SHERIFF OF COCHISE, THE (TV)
Mobil: 1957 (16 pgs.) Giveaway
nn-Schaffenberger-a 4 9 13 18 22 26

SIDEWALK ROMANCE (Also see The K. O. Punch & Lucky Fights It Through)
Health Publications: 1950
nn-VD educational giveaway 39 78 117 240 395 550

SILLY PUTTY MAN
DC Comics: 1978
1 2 4 6 10 14 18

SKATING SKILLS
Custom Comics, Inc./Chicago Roller Skates: 1957 (36 & 12 pgs.; 5x7", two versions) (10¢)
nn-Resembles old ACG cover plus interior art 4 7 10 14 17 20

SKIPPY'S OWN BOOK OF COMICS (See Popular Comics)
No publisher listed: 1934 (Giveaway, 52 pgs., strip reprints)
nn-(Scarce)-By Percy Crosby 377 754 1131 2639 4620 6600
Published by Max C. Gaines for Phillip's Dental Magnesia to be advertised on the Skippy Radio Show and given away with the purchase of a tube of Phillip's Tooth Paste. This is the first four-color comic book of reprints about one character.

SKY KING "RUNAWAY TRAIN" (TV)

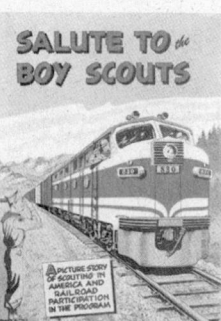

Snow White and the Seven Dwarfs (Bendix) © DIS

The Spirit (12/21/41) © Will Eisner

The Spirit (6/21/42) © Will Eisner

	GD 2.0	VG 4.0	FN 6.0	VF 8.0	VF/NM 9.0	NM- 9.2

National Biscuit Co.: 1964 (Regular size, 16 pgs.)

nn 5 10 15 35 63 90

SLAM BANG COMICS
Post Cereal Giveaway: No. 9, No date

9-Dynamic Man, Echo, Mr. E, Yankee Boy app. 9 18 27 50 65 80

SMILIN' JACK
Dell Publishing Co.

Popped Wheat Giveaway (1947)-1938 strip reprints; 16 pgs. in full color
2 4 6 8 11 14
Shoe Store Giveaway-1938 strip reprints; 16 pgs. 5 10 15 24 30 35
Sparked Wheat Giveaway (1942)-16 pgs. in full color 5 10 15 24 30 35

SMOKEY BEAR (See Forest Fire for 1st app.)
Dell Publ. Co.: 1959,1960

True Story of..., The -U.S. Forest Service giveaway-Publ. by Western Printing Co.; reprints 1st 16 pgs. of Four Color #932. Inside front-c differs slightly in 1959 & 1960 editions
6 12 18 28 34 40
1964,1969 reprints 3 6 9 14 19 24

SMOKEY STOVER
Dell Publishing Co.

General Motors giveaway (1953) 8 16 24 42 54 65
National Fire Protection giveaway(1953 & 1954)-16 pgs., paper-c
8 16 24 42 54 65

SNOW FOR CHRISTMAS
W. T. Grant Co.: 1957 (16 pgs.) (Giveaway)

nn 4 8 12 18 22 25

SNOW WHITE AND THE SEVEN DWARFS
Bendix Washing Machines: 1952 (32 pgs., 5x7-1/4", soft-c) (Disney)

nn 11 22 33 62 86 110

SNOW WHITE AND THE SEVEN DWARFS
Promotional Publ. Co.: 1957 (Small size)

nn 6 12 18 28 34 40

SNOW WHITE AND THE SEVEN DWARFS
Western Printing Co.: 1958 (16 pgs, 5x7-1/4", soft-c) (Disney premium)

nn- "Mystery of the Missing Magic" 6 12 18 31 38 45

SNOW WHITE AND THE 7 DWARFS IN "MILKY WAY"
American Dairy Assoc.: 1955 (16 pgs., soft-c, 5x7-1/4") (Disney premium)

nn 7 14 21 35 43 50

SOLDIER OF GOD
Conventual Franciscans of Marytown: 1982 ($1.00)

nn-Story of Father Maximilian Kobe, priest in WWII Poland; Ray Chatton-a 5.00

SPACE GHOST COAST TO COAST
Cartoon Network: Apr, 1994 (giveaway to Turner Broadcasting employees)

1-(8 pgs.); origin of Space Ghost 6.00

SPACE PATROL (TV)
Ziff-Davis Publishing Co. (Approved Comics)

...'s Special Mission (8 pgs., B&W, Giveaway) 45 90 135 284 480 675

SPARKY
Fire Protection Association: 1961 (Reg. size, paper-c)

nn 3 6 9 16 24 32

SPECIAL AGENT
Assoc. of American Railroads: Oct, 1959 (16 pgs.)

nn-The Story of the railroad police 6 12 18 28 34 40

SPECIAL DELIVERY
Post Hall Synd.: 1951 (32 pgs.; B&W) (Giveaway)

nn-Origin of Pogo, Swamp, etc.; 2 pg. biog. on Walt Kelly
(One copy sold in 1980 for $150.00)

SPECIAL EDITION (U. S. Navy Giveaways)
National Periodical Publications: 1944 - 1945 (Regular comic format with wording simplified, 52 pgs.)

1-Action (1944)-Reprints Action #80 57 114 171 362 619 875
2-Action (1944)-Reprints Action #81 57 114 171 362 619 875
3-Superman (1944)-Reprints Superman #33 57 114 171 362 619 875
4-Detective (1944)-Reprints Detective #97 57 114 171 362 619 875
5-Superman (1945)-Reprints Superman #34 57 114 171 362 619 875
6-Action (1945)-Reprints Action #84 57 114 171 362 619 875

NOTE: *Wayne Boring c-1, 2, 6. Dick Sprang c-4.*

SPIDER-MAN (See Amazing Spider-Man, The)

SPIRIT, THE (Weekly Comic Book)
Will Eisner: 6/2/40 - 10/5/52 (16 pgs.; 8 pgs.) (no cover) (in color)
(Distributed through various newspapers and other sources)

NOTE: **Eisner** script, pencils/inks for the most part from 6/2/40-4/26/42; a few stories assisted by Jack Cole, Fine, Powell and Kotsky.

6/2/40(#1)-Origin/1st app. The Spirit; reprinted in Police #11; Lady Luck (Brenda Banks) (1st app.) by Chuck Mazoujian & Mr. Mystic (1st. app.) by S. R. (Bob) Powell begin (rare) 245 490 735 1568 2684 3800
6/9/40(#2) 50 100 150 315 533 750
6/16/40(#3)-Black Queen app. in Spirit 34 68 102 199 325 450
6/23/40(#4)-Mr. Mystic receives magical necklace 26 52 78 154 252 350
6/30/40(#5) 26 52 78 154 252 350
7/7/40(#6)-1st app. Spirit carplane; Black Queen app. in Spirit
28 56 84 165 270 375
7/14/40(#7)-8/4/40(#10): 7/21/40-Spirit becomes fugitive wanted for murder
24 48 72 142 234 325
8/11/40-9/22/40: 9/15/40-Racist-c 22 44 66 132 216 300
9/29/40-Ellen drops engagement with Homer Creep 21 42 63 122 199 275
10/6/40-11/3/40 21 42 63 122 199 275
11/10/40-The Black Queen app. 21 42 63 122 199 275
11/17/40, 11/24/40 21 42 63 122 199 275
12/1/40-Ellen spanking by Spirit on cover & inside; Eisner-1st 3 pgs., J. Cole rest
24 48 72 142 234 325
12/8/40-3/9/41 16 32 48 94 147 200
3/16/41-Intro. & 1st app. Silk Satin 20 40 60 118 192 265
3/23/41-6/1/41: 5/11/41-Last Lady Luck by Mazoujian. 5/18/41-Lady Luck by Nick Viscardi begins, ends 2/22/42 15 30 45 90 140 190
6/8/41-2nd app. Satin; Spirit learns Satin is also a British agent
18 36 54 103 162 220
6/15/41-1st app. Twilight 17 34 51 98 154 210
6/22/41-Hitler app. in Spirit 16 32 48 94 147 200
6/29/41-1/25/42,2/8/42 14 28 42 81 118 155
2/1/42-1st app. Duchess 16 32 48 94 147 200
2/15/42-4/26/42-Lady Luck by Klaus Nordling begins 3/1/42
15 30 45 84 127 170
5/3/42-8/16/42-Eisner/Fine/Quality staff assists on Spirit
12 24 36 69 97 125
8/23/42-Satin cover splash; Spirit by Eisner/Fine although signed by Fine
17 34 51 98 154 210
8/30/42,9/27/42-10/11/42,10/25/42-11/8/42-Eisner/Fine/Quality staff assists on Spirit 12 24 36 67 94 120
9/6/42-9/20/42,10/18/42-Fine/Belfi art on Spirit; scripts by Manly Wade Wellman
9 18 27 50 65 80
11/15/42-12/6/42,12/20/42,12/27/42,1/17/43-4/18/43,5/9/43-8/8/43-Wellman/ Woolfolk scripts, Fine pencils, Quality staff inks 9 18 27 50 65 80
12/13/42,1/3/43,1/10/43,4/25/43,5/2/43-Eisner scripts/layouts; Fine pencils, Quality staff inks 10 20 30 54 72 90
8/15/43-Eisner script/layout; pencils/inks by Quality staff; Jack Cole-a
8 16 24 44 57 70
8/22/43-12/12/43-Wellman/Woolfolk scripts, Fine pencils, Quality staff inks; Mr. Mystic by Guardineer-10/10/43-10/24/43 8 16 24 44 57 70
12/19/43-8/13/44-Wellman/Woolfolk/Jack Cole scripts; Cole, Fine & Robin King-a; Last Mr. Mystic-5/14/44 8 16 24 42 54 65
8/20/44-12/16/45-Wellman/Woolfolk scripts; Fine art with unknown staff assists
8 16 24 42 54 65

NOTE: *Scripts/layouts by Eisner, or Eisner/Nordling, Eisner/Mercer or Spranger/Eisner; inks by Eisner or Eisner/Spranger in issues 12/23/45-2/2/47.*

12/23/45-1/6/46: 12/23/45-Christmas-c 9 18 27 52 69 85
1/13/46-Origin Spirit retold 13 26 39 72 101 130
1/20/46-1st postwar Satin app. 11 22 33 64 90 115
1/27/46-3/10/46: 3/3/46-Last Lady Luck by Nordling 9 18 27 52 69 85
3/17/46-Intro. & 1st app. Nylon 11 22 33 64 90 115
3/24/46,3/31/46,4/14/46 9 18 27 52 69 85
4/7/46-2nd app. Nylon 10 20 30 56 76 95
4/21/46-Intro. & 1st app. Mr. Carrion & His Pet Buzzard Julia
13 26 39 72 101 130
4/28/46-5/12/46,5/26/46-6/30/46: Lady Luck by Fred Schwab in issues 5/5/46-11/3/46 9 18 27 52 69 85
5/19/46-2nd app. Mr. Carrion 10 20 30 56 76 95
7/7/46-Intro. & 1st app. Dulcet Tone & Skinny 11 22 33 64 90 115

The Spirit (1/04/48) © Will Eisner

The Spirit (9/07/52) © Will Eisner

Steve Canyon's Secret Mission © HARV

	GD 2.0	VG 4.0	FN 6.0	VF 8.0	VF/NM 9.0	NM- 9.2
7/14/46-9/29/46	9	18	27	52	69	85
10/6/46-Intro. & 1st app. P'Gell	13	26	39	74	105	135
10/13/46-11/3/46,11/16/46-11/24/46	9	18	27	52	69	85
11/10/46-2nd app. P'Gell	11	22	33	62	86	110
12/1/46-3rd app. P'Gell	10	20	30	54	72	90
12/8/46-2/2/47	9	18	27	50	65	80

NOTE: *Scripts, pencils/inks by Eisner except where noted in issues 2/9/47-12/19/48.*

	GD 2.0	VG 4.0	FN 6.0	VF 8.0	VF/NM 9.0	NM- 9.2
2/9/47-7/6/47: 6/8/47-Eisner self satire	9	18	27	50	65	80
7/13/47- "Hansel & Gretel" fairy tales	11	22	33	64	90	115
7/20/47-Li'L Abner, Daddy Warbucks, Dick Tracy, Fearless Fosdick parody; A-Bomb blast-c	13	26	39	72	101	130
7/27/47-9/14/47	9	18	27	50	65	80
9/21/47-Pearl Harbor flashback	10	20	30	56	76	95
9/28/47-1st mention of Flying Saucers in comics-3 months after 1st sighting in Idaho on 6/25/47	17	34	51	98	154	210
10/5/47- "Cinderella" fairy tales	11	22	33	64	90	115
10/12/47-11/30/47	9	18	27	50	65	80
12/7/47-Intro. & 1st app. Powder Pouf	13	26	39	72	101	130
12/14/47-12/28/47	9	18	27	50	65	80
1/4/48-2nd app. Powder Pouf	10	20	30	54	72	90
1/11/48-1st app. Sparrow Fallon; Powder Pouf app.	10	20	30	54	72	90
1/18/48-He-Man ad cover; satire issue	10	20	30	54	72	90
1/25/48-Intro. & 1st app. Castanet	13	26	39	72	101	130
2/1/48-2nd app. Castanet	9	18	27	52	69	85
2/8/48-3/7/48	9	18	27	50	65	80
3/14/48-Only app. Kretchma	9	18	27	52	69	85
3/21/48,3/28/48,4/11/48-4/25/48	9	18	27	50	65	80
4/4/48-Only app. Wild Rice	9	18	27	52	69	85
5/2/48-2nd app. Sparrow	9	18	27	50	65	80
5/9/48-6/27/48,7/11/48,7/18/48: 6/13/48-TV issue	9	18	27	50	65	80
7/4/48-Spirit by Andre Le Blanc	8	16	24	42	54	65
7/25/48-Ambrose Bierce's "The Thing" adaptation classic by Eisner/Grandenetti	15	30	45	90	140	190
8/1/48-8/15/48,8/29/48-9/12/48	9	18	27	50	65	80
8/22/48-Poe's "Fall of the House of Usher" classic by Eisner/Grandenetti	15	30	45	90	140	190
9/19/48-Only app. Lorelei	10	20	30	54	72	90
9/26/48-10/31/48	9	18	27	50	65	80
11/7/48-Only app. Plaster of Paris	11	22	33	64	90	115
11/14/48-12/19/48	9	18	27	50	65	80

NOTE: *Scripts by Eisner or Feiffer or Eisner/Feiffer or Nordling. Art by Eisner with backgrounds by Eisner, Grandenetti, Le Blanc, Stallman, Nordling, Dixon and/or others in issues 12/26/48-4/1/51 except where noted.*

	GD 2.0	VG 4.0	FN 6.0	VF 8.0	VF/NM 9.0	NM- 9.2
12/26/48-Reprints some covers of 1948 with flashbacks	9	18	27	50	65	80
1/2/49-1/16/49	9	18	27	50	65	80
1/23/49,1/30/49-1st & 2nd app. Thorne	10	20	30	54	72	90
2/6/49-8/14/49	9	18	27	50	65	80
8/21/49,8/28/49-1st & 2nd app. Monica Veto	10	20	30	54	72	90
9/4/49,9/11/49	9	18	27	50	65	80
9/18/49-Love comic cover; has gag love comic ads on inside	10	20	30	54	72	90
9/25/49-Only app. Ice	9	18	27	52	69	85
10/2/49,10/9/49-Autumn News appears & dies in 10/9 issue	9	18	27	52	69	85
10/16/49-11/27/49,12/18/49,12/25/49	9	18	27	50	65	80
12/4/49,12/11/49-1st & 2nd app. Flaxen	9	18	27	52	69	85
1/1/50-Flashbacks to all of the Spirit girls-Thorne, Ellen, Satin, & Monica	4	28	42	76	108	140
1/8/50-Intro. & 1st app. Sand Saref	15	30	45	86	133	180
1/15/50-2nd app. Saref	13	26	39	72	101	130
1/22/50-2/5/50	9	18	27	50	65	80
2/12/50-Roller Derby issue	10	20	30	54	72	90
2/19/50-Half Dead Mr. Lox - Classic horror	11	22	33	64	90	115
2/26/50-4/23/50,5/14/50,5/28/50,7/23/50-9/3/50	9	18	27	50	65	80
4/30/50-Script/art by Le Blanc with Eisner framing	8	16	24	40	50	60
5/7/50,6/4/50-7/16/50-Abe Kanegson-a	8	16	24	40	50	60
5/21/50-Script by Feiffer/Eisner, art by Blaisdell, Eisner framing	8	16	24	40	50	60
9/10/50-P'Gell returns	10	20	30	54	72	90
9/17/50-1/7/51	9	18	27	50	65	80
1/14/51-Life Magazine cover; brief biography of Comm. Dolan, Sand Saref, Silk Satin, P'Gell, Sammy & Willum, Darling O'Shea, & Mr. Carrion & His Pet Buzzard Julia, with pin-ups by Eisner	11	22	33	64	90	115
1/21/51,2/4/51-4/1/51	9	18	27	50	65	80
1/28/51- "The Meanest Man in the World" by Eisner	11	22	33	64	90	115
4/8/51-7/29/51,8/12/51-Last Eisner issue	9	18	27	50	65	80
8/5/51,8/19/51-7/20/52-Not Eisner	8	16	24	40	50	60
7/27/52-(Rare)-Denny Colt in Outer Space by Wally Wood; 7 pg. S/F story of E.C. vintage	42	84	126	265	445	625
8/3/52-(Rare)- "Mission...The Moon" by Wood	42	84	126	265	445	625
8/10/52-(Rare)- "A DP On The Moon" by Wood	42	84	126	265	445	625
8/17/52-(Rare)- "Heart" by Wood/Eisner	39	78	117	240	395	550
8/24/52-(Rare)- "Rescue" by Wood	42	84	126	265	445	625
8/31/52-(Rare)- "The Last Man" by Wood	42	84	126	265	445	625
9/7/52-(Rare)- "The Man in The Moon" by Wood	42	84	126	265	445	625
9/14/52-(Rare)-Eisner/Wenzel-a	24	48	72	142	234	325
9/21/52-(Rare)- "Denny Colt, Alias The Spirit/Space Report" by Eisner/Wenzel	26	52	78	154	252	350
9/28/52-(Rare)- "Return From The Moon" by Wood	41	82	123	256	428	600
10/5/52-(Rare)- "The Last Story" by Eisner	22	44	66	132	216	300

Large Tabloid pages from 1946 on (Eisner) - Price 200 percent over listed prices.

NOTE: *Spirit sections came out in both large and small format. Some newspapers went to the 8-pg. format months before others. Some printed the pages so they cannot be folded into a small comic book section; these are worth less. (Also see Three Comics & Spiritman).*

SPY SMASHER
Fawcett Publications

	GD 2.0	VG 4.0	FN 6.0	VF 8.0	VF/NM 9.0	NM- 9.2
Well Known Comics (1944, 12 pgs., 8-1/2x10-1/2"), paper-c, glued binding, printed in green; Bestmaid/Samuel Lowe giveaway	15	30	45	83	124	165

STANDARD OIL COMICS (Also see Gulf Funny Weekly)
Standard Oil Co.: 1932-1934 (Giveaway, tabloid size, 4 pgs. in color)

	GD 2.0	VG 4.0	FN 6.0	VF 8.0	VF/NM 9.0	NM- 9.2
nn (Dec. 1932)	53	106	159	334	567	800
1-Series has original art	45	90	135	284	480	675
2-5	20	40	60	118	192	265
6-14: 14-Fred Opper strip, 1 pg.	14	28	42	76	108	140
1A (Jan 1933)	47	94	141	296	498	700
2A-14A (1933)	30	60	90	177	289	400
1B (1934)	37	74	111	222	361	500
2B-?B (1934)	30	60	90	177	289	400

NOTE: *Series A contains Frederick Opper's Si & Mirandi; Series B contains Goofus: He's From The Big City; McVittle by Walter O'Ehrle; interior strips include Pesty And His Pop & Smiling Slim by Sid Hicks.*

STAR TEAM
Marvel Comics Group: 1977 (6-1/2x5", 20 pgs.) (Ideal Toy Giveaway)

	GD 2.0	VG 4.0	FN 6.0	VF 8.0	VF/NM 9.0	NM- 9.2
nn	3	6	9	14	19	24

STEVE CANYON COMICS
Harvey Publications

	GD 2.0	VG 4.0	FN 6.0	VF 8.0	VF/NM 9.0	NM- 9.2
Dept. Store giveaway #3(6/48, 36pp)	10	20	30	54	72	90
...'s Secret Mission (1951, 16 pgs., Armed Forces giveaway); Caniff-a	9	18	27	47	61	75
Strictly for the Smart Birds (1951, 16 pgs.)-Information Comics Div. (Harvey) Premium	8	16	24	40	50	60

STORIES OF CHRISTMAS
K. K. Publications: 1942 (Giveaway, 32 pgs., paper cover)

	GD 2.0	VG 4.0	FN 6.0	VF 8.0	VF/NM 9.0	NM- 9.2
nn-Adaptation of "A Christmas Carol"; Kelly story "The Fir Tree"; Infinity-c	29	58	87	172	281	390

STORY HOUR SERIES (Disney)
Whitman Publ. Co.: 1948, 1949; 1951-1953 (36 pgs., paper-c) (4-3/4x6-1/2")
Given away with subscription to Walt Disney's Comics & Stories

	GD 2.0	VG 4.0	FN 6.0	VF 8.0	VF/NM 9.0	NM- 9.2
nn(1948)-Mickey Mouse and the Boy Thursday	12	24	36	67	94	120
nn(1948)-Mickey Mouse the Miracle Master	12	24	36	67	94	120
nn(1948)-Minnie Mouse and Antique Chair	12	24	36	67	94	120
nn(1949)-The Three Orphan Kittens(B&W & color)	9	18	27	47	61	75
nn(1949)-Danny-The Little Black Lamb	9	18	27	47	61	75
800(1948)-Donald Duck in "Bringing Up the Boys"	15	30	45	88	137	185
1953 edition	11	22	33	64	90	115
801(1948)-Mickey Mouse's Summer Vacation	10	20	30	56	76	95
1951, 1952 editions	7	14	21	35	43	50
802(1948)-Bugs Bunny's Adventures	9	18	27	50	65	80
803(1948)-Bongo	8	16	24	40	50	60
804(1948)-Mickey and the Beanstalk	9	18	27	47	61	75
805-15(1949)-Andy Panda and His Friends	8	16	24	40	50	60
806-15(1949)-Tom and Jerry	8	16	24	44	57	70
808-15(1949)-Johnny Appleseed	8	16	24	40	50	60

1948, 1949 Hard Cover Edition of each....30% - 40% more.

STOP AND GO, THE SAFETY TWINS
J.C. Penney: no date (giveaway)

	GD 2.0	VG 4.0	FN 6.0	VF 8.0	VF/NM 9.0	NM- 9.2
nn	5	10	15	24	30	35

STORY OF CHECKS THE
Federal Reserve Bank: 1979 (Reg. size)

	GD 2.0	VG 4.0	FN 6.0	VF 8.0	VF/NM 9.0	NM- 9.2
nn	1	3	4	6	8	10

STORY OF CHECKS AND ELECTRONIC PAYMENTS
Federal Reserve Bank: 1983 (Reg size)

Story of Harry S. Truman © DNC

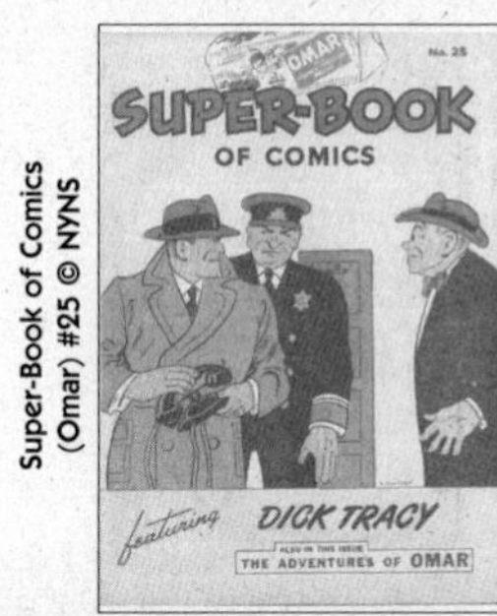

Super-Book of Comics (Omar) #25 © NYNS

Super Circus #1 © Cross Publ.

	GD 2.0	VG 4.0	FN 6.0	VF 8.0	VF/NM 9.0	NM- 9.2
nn	1	2	3	5	6	8

STORY OF CONSUMER CREDIT
Federal Reserve Bank: 1980 (Reg. size)

	GD	VG	FN	VF	VF/NM	NM-
nn	1	2	3	5	6	8

STORY OF EDISON, THE
Educational Comics: 1956 (16 pgs.) (Reddy Killowatt)

	GD	VG	FN	VF	VF/NM	NM-
nn-Reprint of Reddy Kilowatt #2(1947)	7	14	21	35	43	50

STORY OF FOREIGN TRADE AND EXCHANGE
Federal Reserve Bank: 1985 (Reg. size)

	GD	VG	FN	VF	VF/NM	NM-
nn	1	2	3	5	6	8

STORY OF HARRY S. TRUMAN, THE
Democratic National Committee: 1948 (Giveaway, regular size, soft-c, 16 pg.)

	GD	VG	FN	VF	VF/NM	NM-
nn-Gives biography on career of Truman; used in **SOTI**, pg. 311	14	28	42	76	108	140

STORY OF INFLATION, THE
Federal Reserve Bank: 1980s (Reg size)

	GD	VG	FN	VF	VF/NM	NM-
nn	1	3	4	6	8	10

STORY OF MONEY
Federral Reserve Bank: 1984 (Reg. size)

	GD	VG	FN	VF	VF/NM	NM-
nn	1	3	4	6	8	10

STORY OF THE BALLET, THE
Selva and Sons, Inc.: 1954 (16 pgs., paper cover)

	GD	VG	FN	VF	VF/NM	NM-
nn	4	8	11	16	19	22

STRANGE AS IT SEEMS
McNaught Syndicate: 1936 (B&W, 5" x 7", 24 pgs.)

	GD	VG	FN	VF	VF/NM	NM-
nn-Ex-Lax giveaway	8	16	24	44	57	70

STRAY
Dark Horse Comics: 2004 (8 1/2"x 5 1/2", Diamond Comic Dist. Halloween giveaway)

	GD	VG	FN	VF	VF/NM	NM-
nn-Reprint from The Dark Horse Book of Hauntings; Evan Dorkin-s/Jill Thompson-a						2.50

SUGAR BEAR
Post Cereal Giveaway: No date, circa 1975? (2 1/2" x 4 1/2", 16 pgs.)

	GD	VG	FN	VF	VF/NM	NM-
"The Almost Take Over of the Post Office", "The Race Across the Atlantic", "The Zoo Goes Wild" each...	1	2	3	5	6	8

SUNDAY WORLD'S EASTER EGG FULL OF EASTER MEAT FOR LITTLE PEOPLE
Supplement to the New York World: 3/27/1898 (soft-c, 16pg, 4"x8" approx., opens at top, color & B&W)(Giveaway)(shaped like an Easter egg)

	GD	VG	FN	VF	VF/NM	NM-
nn-By R.F. Outcault	18	36	54	107	169	230

SUPER BOOK OF COMICS
Western Publishing Co.: nd (1942-1943?) (Soft-c, 32 pgs.) (Pan-Am/Gilmore Oil/Kelloggs premiums)

	GD	VG	FN	VF	VF/NM	NM-
nn-Dick Tracy (Gilmore)-Magic Morro app. (2 versions: Dick Tracy Jr. on cover and a filing cabinet cover)	32	64	96	190	310	430
1-Dick Tracy & The Smuggling Ring; Stratosphere Jim app. (Rare) (Pan-Am)	32	64	96	190	310	430
1-Smilin' Jack, Magic Morro (Pan-Am)	14	28	42	76	108	140
2-Smilin' Jack, Stratosphere Jim (Pan-Am)	14	28	42	76	108	140
2-Smitty, Magic Morro (Pan-Am)	14	28	42	76	108	140
3-Captain Midnight, Magic Morro (Pan-Am)	22	44	66	131	216	300
3-Moon Mullins?	13	26	39	74	105	135
4-Red Ryder, Magic Morro (Pan-Am). Same content as Red Ryder Victory Patrol comic w/diff. cover	15	30	45	85	130	175
4-Smitty, Stratosphere Jim (Pan-Am)	13	26	39	74	105	135
5-Don Winslow, Magic Morro (Gilmore)	15	30	45	85	130	175
5-Don Winslow, Stratosphere Jim (Pan-Am)	15	30	45	85	130	175
5-Terry & the Pirates	17	34	51	98	154	210
6-Don Winslow, Stratosphere Jim (Pan-Am)-McWilliams-a	15	30	45	85	130	175
6-King of the Royal Mounted, Magic Morro (Pan-Am)	15	30	45	85	130	175
7-Dick Tracy, Magic Morro (Pan-Am)	19	38	57	112	179	245
7-Little Orphan Annie	11	22	33	64	90	115
8-Dick Tracy, Stratosphere Jim (Pan-Am)	17	34	51	98	154	210
8-Dan Dunn, Magic Morro (Pan-Am)	11	22	33	64	90	115
9-Terry & the Pirates, Magic Morro (Pan-Am)	17	34	51	98	154	210
10-Red Ryder, Magic Morro (Pan-Am)	15	30	45	85	130	175

SUPER-BOOK OF COMICS
Western Publishing Co.: (Omar Bread & Hancock Oil Co. giveaways) 1944 - No. 30, 1947 (Omar); 1947 - 1948 (Hancock) (16 pgs.)

NOTE: The Hancock issues are all exact reprints of the earlier Omar issues. The issue numbers were removed in some of the reprints.

	GD 2.0	VG 4.0	FN 6.0	VF 8.0	VF/NM 9.0	NM- 9.2
1-Dick Tracy (Omar, 1944)	15	30	45	94	147	200
1-Dick Tracy (Hancock, 1947)	14	28	42	78	112	145
2-Bugs Bunny (Omar, 1944)	8	16	24	40	50	60
2-Bugs Bunny (Hancock, 1947)	6	12	18	32	39	46
3-Terry & the Pirates (Omar, 1944)	11	22	33	60	83	105
3-Terry & the Pirates (Hancock, 1947)	10	20	30	54	72	90
4-Andy Panda (Omar, 1944)	8	16	24	40	50	60
4-Andy Panda (Hancock, 1947)	6	12	18	32	39	46
5-Smokey Stover (Omar, 1945)	6	12	18	32	39	46
5-Smokey Stover (Hancock, 1947)	5	10	15	24	30	35
6-Porky Pig (Omar, 1945)	8	16	24	40	50	60
6-Porky Pig (Hancock, 1947)	6	12	18	32	39	46
7-Smilin' Jack (Omar, 1945)	8	16	24	40	50	60
7-Smilin' Jack (Hancock, 1947)	6	12	18	32	39	46
8-Oswald the Rabbit (Omar, 1945)	6	12	18	32	39	46
8-Oswald the Rabbit (Hancock, 1947)	5	10	15	24	30	35
9-Alley Oop (Omar, 1945)	11	22	33	64	90	115
9-Alley Oop (Hancock, 1947)	11	22	33	60	83	105
10-Elmer Fudd (Omar, 1945)	6	12	18	32	39	46
10-Elmer Fudd (Hancock, 1947)	5	10	15	24	30	35
11-Little Orphan Annie (Omar, 1945)	8	16	24	42	53	64
11-Little Orphan Annie (Hancock, 1947)	7	14	21	36	45	54
12-Woody Woodpecker (Omar, 1945)	6	12	18	32	39	46
12-Woody Woodpecker (Hancock, 1947)	5	10	15	24	30	35
13-Dick Tracy (Omar, 1945)	11	22	33	64	90	115
13-Dick Tracy (Hancock, 1947)	11	22	33	60	83	105
14-Bugs Bunny (Omar, 1945)	6	12	18	32	39	46
14-Bugs Bunny (Hancock, 1947)	5	10	15	24	30	35
15-Andy Panda (Omar, 1945)	6	12	18	28	34	40
15-Andy Panda (Hancock, 1947)	5	10	15	24	30	35
16-Terry & the Pirates (Omar, 1945)	11	22	33	60	83	105
16-Terry & the Pirates (Hancock, 1947)	9	18	27	47	61	75
17-Smokey Stover (Omar, 1946)	6	12	18	32	39	46
17-Smokey Stover (Hancock, 1948?)	5	10	15	24	30	35
18-Porky Pig (Omar, 1946)	6	12	18	28	34	40
18-Porky Pig (Hancock, 1948?)	5	10	15	24	30	35
19-Smilin' Jack (Omar, 1946)	6	12	18	32	39	46
nn-Smilin' Jack (Hancock, 1948)	5	10	15	24	30	35
20-Oswald the Rabbit (Omar, 1946)	6	12	18	28	34	40
nn-Oswald the Rabbit (Hancock, 1948)	5	10	15	24	30	35
21-Gasoline Alley (Omar, 1946)	8	16	24	42	53	64
nn-Gasoline Alley (Hancock, 1948)	7	14	21	36	45	54
22-Elmer Fudd (Omar, 1946)	6	12	18	28	34	40
nn-Elmer Fudd (Hancock, 1948)	5	10	15	24	30	35
23-Little Orphan Annie (Omar, 1946)	8	16	24	40	50	60
nn-Little Orphan Annie (Hancock, 1948)	6	12	18	32	39	46
24-Woody Woodpecker (Omar, 1946)	6	12	18	28	34	40
nn-Woody Woodpecker (Hancock, 1948)	5	10	15	24	30	35
25-Dick Tracy (Omar, 1946)	11	22	33	60	83	105
nn-Dick Tracy (Hancock, 1948)	9	18	27	50	65	80
26-Bugs Bunny (Omar, 1946))	6	12	18	28	34	40
nn-Bugs Bunny (Hancock, 1948)	5	10	15	24	30	35
27-Andy Panda (Omar, 1946)	6	12	18	28	34	40
27-Andy Panda (Hancock, 1948)	5	10	15	24	30	35
28-Terry & the Pirates (Omar, 1946)	11	22	33	60	83	105
28-Terry & the Pirates (Hancock, 1948)	9	18	27	47	61	75
29-Smokey Stover (Omar, 1947)	6	12	18	28	34	40
29-Smokey Stover (Hancock, 1948)	5	10	15	24	30	35
30-Porky Pig (Omar, 1947)	6	12	18	28	34	40
30-Porky Pig (Hancock, 1948)	5	10	15	24	30	35
nn-Bugs Bunny (Hancock, 1948)-Does not match any Omar book	6	12	18	28	34	40

SUPER CIRCUS (TV)
Cross Publishing Co.

	GD	VG	FN	VF	VF/NM	NM-
1-(1951, Weather Bird Shoes giveaway)	8	16	24	40	50	60

SUPER FRIENDS
DC Comics: 1981 (Giveaway, no ads, no code or price)

	GD	VG	FN	VF	VF/NM	NM-
...Special 1 -r/Super Friends #19 & 36	2	4	6	9	12	15

SUPERGEAR COMICS
Jacobs Corp.: 1976 (Giveaway, 4 pgs. in color, slick paper)

	GD	VG	FN	VF	VF/NM	NM-
nn-(Rare)-Superman, Lois Lane; Steve Lombard app. (500 copies printed, over half destroyed?)	18	36	54	124	275	425

SUPERGIRL
DC Comics: 1984, 1986 (Giveaway, Baxter paper)

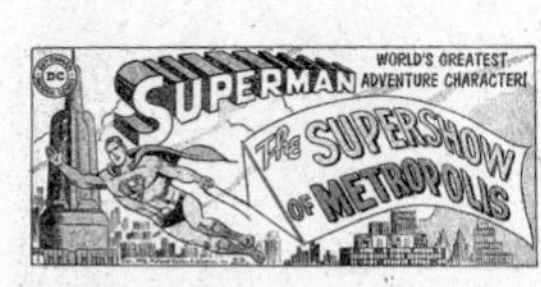

Superman (miniature) #1B © DC

Superman-Tim, May 1946 © DC

Tastee-Freez Comics #6 © Chicago Trib.

GD 2.0 | VG 4.0 | FN 6.0 | VF 8.0 | VF/NM 9.0 | NM- 9.2

GD 2.0 | VG 4.0 | FN 6.0 | VF 8.0 | VF/NM 9.0 | NM- 9.2

nn-(American Honda/U.S. Dept. Transportation) Torres-c/a
2 4 6 8 11 14

SUPER HEROES PUZZLES AND GAMES
General Mills Giveaway (Marvel Comics Group): 1979 (32 pgs., regular size)

nn-Four 2-pg. origin stories of Spider-Man, Captain America, The Hulk, & Spider-Woman
3 6 9 14 20 26

SUPERMAN
National Periodical Publ./DC Comics

72-Giveaway(9-10/51)-(Rare)-Price blackened out; came with banner wrapped around book; without banner 73 146 219 467 796 1125
72-Giveaway with banner 116 232 348 742 1271 1800
Bradman birthday custom (1988)(extremely limited distribution) - a CGC 9.6 copy sold for $2600, a NM copy sold for $1125, and a FN/VF copy sold for $800 in 2011-2012, plus a CGC 9.0 sold for $421 in 12/12
... For the Animals (2000, Doris Day Animal Foundation, 30 pgs.) polybagged with Gotham Adventures #22, Hourman #12, Impulse #58, Looney Tunes #62, Stars and S.T.R.I.P.E. #8 and Superman Adventures #41 2.50
Kelloggs Giveaway-(2/3 normal size, 1954)-r-two stories/Superman #55
28 56 84 165 270 375
Kenner: Man of Steel (Doomsday is Coming) (1995, 16 pgs.) packaged with set of Superman and Doomsday action figures 4.00
...Meets the Quik Bunny (1987, Nestles Quik premium, 36 pgs.)
1 2 3 5 6 8
Pizza Hut Premiums (12/77)-Exact reprints of 1950s comics except for paid ads (set of 6 exist?); Vol. 1-r#97 (#113-r also known) 1 3 4 6 8 10
Radio Shack Giveaway-36 pgs. (7/80) "The Computers That Saved Metropolis", Starlin/Giordano-a; advertising insert in Action #509, New Advs. of Superboy #7, Legion of Super-Heroes #265, & House of Mystery #282. (All comics were 68 pgs.) Cover of inserts printed on newsprint. Giveaway contains 4 extra pgs. of Radio Shack advertising that inserts do not have 1 2 3 5 6 8
Radio Shack Giveaway-(7/81) "Victory by Computer" 1 2 3 5 6 8
Radio Shack Giveaway-(7/82) "Computer Masters of Metropolis"
1 2 3 5 6 8

SUPERMAN ADVENTURES, THE (TV)
DC Comics: 1996 (Based on animated series)

1-(1996) Preview issue distributed at Warner Bros. stores 4.00
Titus Game Edition (1998) 2.50

SUPERMAN AND THE GREAT CLEVELAND FIRE
National Periodical Publ.: 1948 (Giveaway, 4 pgs., no cover) (Hospital Fund)

nn-In full color 65 130 195 416 708 1000

SUPERMAN AT THE GILBERT HALL OF SCIENCE
National Periodical Publ.: 1948 (Giveaway) (Gilbert Chemistry Sets / A.C. Gilbert Co.)

nn 37 74 111 222 361 500

SUPERMAN (Miniature)
National Periodical Publ.: 1942; 1955 - 1956 (3 issues, no #'s, 32 pgs.)
The pages are numbered in the 1st issue: 1-32; 2nd: 1A-32A, and 3rd: 1B-32B

No date-Py-Co-Pay Tooth Powder giveaway (8 pgs.; circa 1942)
41 82 123 256 428 600
1-The Superman Time Capsule (Kellogg's Sugar Smacks)(1955)
22 44 66 132 216 300
1A-Duel in Space (1955) 21 42 63 122 199 275
1B-The Super Show of Metropolis (also #1-32, no B)(1955)
21 42 63 122 199 275

NOTE: *Numbering variations exist. Each title could have any combination-#1, 1A, or 1B.*

SUPERMAN RECORD COMIC
National Periodical Publications: 1966 (Golden Records)

(With record)-Record reads origin of Superman from comic; came with iron-on patch, decoder, membership card & button; comic-r/Superman #125,146
10 20 30 69 147 225
Comic only 5 10 15 33 57 80

SUPERMAN'S BUDDY (Costume Comic)
National Periodical Publications: 1954 (4 pgs., slick paper-c; one-shot) (Came in box w/costume)

1-With box & costume 123 246 369 787 1344 1900
Comic only 55 110 165 352 601 850
1-(1958 edition)-Printed in 2 colors 17 34 51 98 154 210

SUPERMAN'S CHRISTMAS ADVENTURE
National Periodical Publications: 1940, 1944 (Giveaway, 16 pgs.)
Distributed by Nehi drinks, Bailey Store, Ivey-Keith Co., Kennedy's Boys Shop, Macy's Store, Boston Store

1(1940)-Burnley-a; F. Ray-c/r from Superman #6 (Scarce)-Superman saves Santa Claus. Santa makes real Superman Toys offered in 1940. 1st merchandising story; versions with Royal Crown Cola ad on front-c & Boston Store ad on front-c; cover art on each has the same layout but different art 360 720 1080 2520 4410 6300
nn(1944) w/Santa Claus & X-mas tree-c 97 194 291 621 1061 1500
nn(1944) w/Candy cane & Superman-c 97 194 291 621 1061 1500
nn(1944) w/1940-c (Santa over chimney); Superman image (from Superman #6) on back-c
97 194 291 621 1061 1500

SUPERMAN-TIM (Becomes Tim)
Superman-Tim Stores/National Periodical Publ.: Aug, 1942 - May, 1950 (Half size) (B&W Giveaway w/2 color covers) (Publ. monthly 2/43 on)

8/42 (#1)-All have Superman illos. 113 226 339 718 1234 1750
1/43 (#2) 39 78 117 231 378 525
2/43 (#3) 37 74 111 222 361 500
3/43 (#4) 37 74 111 222 361 500
4/43, 5/43, 6/43, 7/43, 8/43 34 68 102 199 325 450
9/43, 10/43, 11/43, 12/43 28 56 84 165 270 375
1/44-12/44 24 48 72 140 230 320
1/45-5/45, 10-12/45, 1/46-8/46 22 44 66 128 209 290
6/45-Classic Superman-c 23 46 69 138 227 315
7/45-Classic Superman flag-c 23 46 69 138 227 315
9/45-1st stamp album issue 48 96 114 302 509 715
9/46-2nd stamp album issue 41 82 123 256 428 600
10/46-1st Superman story 29 58 87 170 278 385
11/46, 12/46, 1/47-8/47 issues-Superman story in each; 2/47-Infinity-c.
All 36 pgs. 29 58 87 170 278 385
9/47-Stamp album issue & Superman story 40 80 120 246 411 575
10/47, 11/47, 12/47-Superman stories (24 pgs.) 29 58 87 170 278 385
1/48-7/48,10/48, 11/48, 2/49, 4/49-11/49 23 46 69 138 227 315
8/48-Contains full page ad for Superman-Tim watch giveaway
23 46 69 138 227 315
9/48-Stamp album issue 32 64 96 188 307 425
1/49-Full page Superman bank cut-out 23 46 69 138 227 315
3/49-Full page Superman boxing game cut-out 23 46 69 138 227 315
12/49-3/50, 5/50-Superman stories 25 50 75 150 245 340
4/50-Superman story, baseball stories; photo-c without Superman
29 58 87 170 278 385

NOTE: *All issues have Superman illustrations throughout. The page count varies depending on whether a Superman-Tim comic story is inserted. If it is, the page count is either 36 or 24 pages. Otherwise all issues are 16 pages. Each issue has a special place for inserting a full color Superman stamp. The stamp album issues had spaces for the stamps given away the past year. The books were mailed as a subscription premium. The stamps were given away free (or when you made a purchase) only when you physically came into the store.*

SUPER SEAMAN SLOPPY
Allied Pristine Union Council, Buffalo, NY: 1940s, 8pg., reg. size (Soft-c)

nn 4 8 12 17 21 24

SURVEY
Marvel Comics Group: 1948 (Readership survey for advertisers, reg. size)

nn-Harvey Kurtzman-c/a 65 130 195 416 708 1000

SWAMP FOX, THE
Walt Disney Productions: 1960 (14 pgs, small size) (Canada Dry Premiums)

Titles: (A)-Tory Masquerade, (B)-Turnabout Tactics, (C)-Rindau Rampage; each came in paper sleeve, books 1,2 & 3;
Set with sleeves 5 10 15 31 53 75
Comic only 2 4 6 13 18 22

SWORDQUEST
DC Comics/Atari Pub.: 1982, 52pg., 5"x7" (Giveaway with video games)

1,2-Roy Thomas & Gerry Conway-s; George Pérez & Dick Giordano-c/a in all
2 4 6 10 14 18
3-Low print 3 6 9 15 22 28

SYNDICATE FEATURES (Sci/fi)
Harry A. Chesler Syndicate: V1#3, 11/15/37 (Tabloid size, 3 colors, 4 pgs.) (Editors premium) (Came folded)

V1#3-Dan Hastings daily strips-Guardineer-a 155 310 465 992 1696 2400

TAKING A CHANCE
American Cancer Society: no date (giveaway)

nn-Anti-smoking 2 4 6 11 16 20

TASTEE-FREEZ COMICS (Also see Harvey Hits and Richie Rich)
Harvey Comics: 1957 (10¢, 36 pgs.)(6 different issues given away)

1-Little Dot on cover; Richie Rich "Ride 'Em Cowboy" story published one year prior to being printed in Harvey Hits #9. 10 20 30 64 132 200
2,4,5: 2-Rags Rabbit. 4-Sad Sack. 5-Mazie 2 4 6 16 23 30
3-Casper 3 6 9 21 32 40
6-Dick Tracy 3 6 9 21 32 40
nn-Brings You Space Facts and Fun Book 2 4 6 9 12 15

TAYLOR'S CHRISTMAS TABLOID

Terry and the Pirates Popped Wheat © DELL

Thumper HC © DIS

Triple-A Baseball Heroes (Omaha Royals) © MAR

GD 2.0 | VG 4.0 | FN 6.0 | VF 8.0 | VF/NM 9.0 | NM- 9.2

Dept. Store Giveaway: Mid 1930s, Cleveland, Ohio (Tabloid size; in color)
nn-(Very Rare)-Among the earliest pro work of Siegel & Shuster; one full color page called "The Battle in the Stratosphere", with a pre-Superman look; Shuster art thoughout. (Only 1 known copy) Estimated value... 4000.00

TAZ'S 40TH BIRTHDAY BLOWOUT
DC Comics: 1994 (K-Mart giveaway, 16 pgs.)
nn-Six pg. story, games and puzzles 4.00

TEE AND VEE CROSLEY IN TELEVISION LAND COMICS (Also see Crosley's House of Fun)
Crosley Division, Avco Mfg. Corp. : 1951 (52 pgs.; 8x11"; paper cover; in color) (Giveaway)
Many stories, puzzles, cut-outs, games, etc. 7 14 21 35 43 50

TEEN-AGE BOOBY TRAP
Commercial Comics: 1970 (Small size)
nn 4 7 10 14 17 20

TENNESSEE JED (Radio)
Fox Syndicate? (Wm. C. Popper & Co.): nd (1945) (16 pgs.; paper-c; reg. size; giveaway)
nn 20 40 60 117 189 260

TENNIS (...For Speed, Stamina, Strength, Skill)
Tennis Educational Foundation: 1956 (16 pgs.; soft cover; 10¢)
Book 1-Endorsed by Gene Tunney, Ralph Kiner, etc. showing how tennis has helped them 6 12 18 28 34 40

TERRY AND THE PIRATES
Dell Publishing Co.: 1939 - 1953 (By Milton Caniff)
Buster Brown Shoes giveaway(1938)-32 pgs.; in color 20 40 60 114 182 250
Canada Dry Premiums-Books #1-3(1953, 36 pgs.; 2x5")-Harvey; #1-Hot Shot Charlie Flies Again; 2-In Forced Landing; 3-Dragon Lady in Distress) 14 28 42 78 112 145
Gambles Giveaway (1938, 16 pgs.) 9 18 27 50 65 80
Gillmore Giveaway (1938, 24 pgs.) 9 18 27 52 69 85
Popped Wheat Giveaway(1938)-Strip reprints in full color; Caniff-a 2 4 6 8 10 12
Shoe Store giveaway (Weatherbird & Poll-Parrot)(1938, 16 pgs., soft-c)(2-diff.) 9 18 27 52 69 85
Sparked Wheat Giveaway(1942, 16 pgs.)-In color 9 18 27 52 69 85

TERRY AND THE PIRATES
Libby's Radio Premium: 1941 (16 pgs.; reg. size)(shipped folded in the mail)
"Adventure of the Ruby of Genghis Khan" - Each pg. is a puzzle that must be completed to read the story 400 800 1200 2600 - -

THAT THE WORLD MAY BELIEVE
Catechetical Guild Giveaway: No date (16 pgs.) (Graymoor Friars distr.)
nn 4 8 12 18 22 25

3-D COLOR CLASSICS (Wendy's Kid's Club)
Wendy's Int'l Inc.: 1995 (5 1/2" x 8", comes with 3-D glasses)
The Elephant's Child, Gulliver's Travels, Peter Pan, The Time Machine, 20,000 Leagues Under the Sea: Neal Adams-a in all each.... 3.50

350 YEARS OF AMERICAN DAIRY FOODS
American Dairy Assoc.: 1957 (5x7", 16 pgs.)
nn-History of milk 3 6 8 12 14 16

THUMPER (Disney)
Grosset & Dunlap: 1942 (50¢, 32pgs., hardcover book, 7"x8-1/2" w/dust jacket)
nn-Given away (along with a copy of Bambi) for a $2.00, 2-year subscription to WDC&S in 1942. (Xmas offer). Book only 15 30 45 90 140 190
Dust jacket only 10 20 30 56 76 95

TILLY AND TED-TINKERTOTLAND
W. T. Grant Co.: 1945 (Giveaway, 20 pgs.)
nn-Christmas comic 7 14 21 37 46 55

TIM (Formerly Superman-Tim; becomes Gene Autry-Tim)
Tim Stores: June, 1950 - Oct, 1950 (B&W, half-size)
4 issues; 6/50, 9/50, 10/50 known 17 34 51 98 154 210

TIM AND SALLY'S ADVENTURES AT MARINELAND
Marineland Restaurant & Bar, Marineland, CA: 1957 (5x7", 16 pgs., soft-c)
nn-copyright Oceanarium, Inc. 2 4 6 8 11 14

TIME MACHINE, THE
DC Comics: 2002 (10 pgs.)
nn-Promotes the 2002 DreamWorks movie 6.00

TIME OF DECISION
Harvey Publications Inc.: (16 pgs., paper cover)
nn-ROTC recruitment 4 7 10 14 17 20

GD 2.0 | VG 4.0 | FN 6.0 | VF 8.0 | VF/NM 9.0 | NM- 9.2

TIM IN SPACE (Formerly Gene Autry Tim; becomes Tim Tomorrow)
Tim Stores: 1950 (1/2 size giveaway) (B&W)
nn 14 28 42 78 112 145

TIM TOMORROW (Formerly Tim In Space)
Tim Stores: 8/51, 9/51, 10/51, Christmas, 1951 (5x7-3/4")
nn-Prof. Fumble & Captain Kit Comet in all 14 28 42 78 112 145

TIM TYLER'S LUCK
Standard Comics (King Feat. Syndicate): 1950s (Reg. size, slick-c)
nn-Felix the at app. 4 7 10 14 17 20

TITANS BEAT (Teen Titans)
DC Comics: Aug, 1996 (16 pgs., paper-c)
1-Intro./preview new Teen Titans members; Pérez-a 4.00

TOM MIX (...Commandos Comics #10-12)
Ralston-Purina Co.: Sept, 1940 - No. 12, Nov, 1942 (36 pgs.); 1983 (one-shot)
Given away for two Ralston box-tops; 1983 came in cereal box
1-Origin (life) Tom Mix; Fred Meagher-a 232 464 696 1485 2543 3600
2 53 106 159 334 567 800
3-9 41 82 123 256 428 600
10-12: 10-Origin Tom Mix Commando Unit; Speed O'Dare begins; Japanese sub-c. 12-Sci/fi-c 37 74 111 222 361 500
1983- "Taking of Grizzly Grebb", Toth-a; 16 pg. miniature 2 4 6 9 12 15

TOM SAWYER COMICS
Giveaway: 1951? (Paper cover)
nn-Contains a coverless Hopalong Cassidy from 1951; other combinations known 3 6 9 14 20 25

TOO MUCH, TOO LITTLE
Federal Reserve Bank: 1989 (Reg. size)
9-13 1 3 4 6 8 10

TOP-NOTCH COMICS
MLJ Magazines/Rex Theater: 1940s (theater giveaway, sepia-c)
1-Black Hood-c; content & covers can vary 43 86 129 271 461 650

TOPPS COMICS PRESENTS
Topps Comics: No. 0, 1993 (Giveaway, B&W, 36 pgs.)
0-Dracula vs. Zorro, Teenagents, Silver Star, & Bill the Galactic Hero 2.50

TOWN THAT FORGOT SANTA, THE
W. T. Grant Co.: 1961 (Giveaway, 24 pgs.)
nn 3 6 9 16 23 30

TOY LAND FUNNIES (See Funnies On Parade)
Eastern Color Printing Co.: 1934 (32 pgs., Hecht Co. store giveaway)
nn-Reprints Buck Rogers Sunday pages #199-201 from Famous Funnies #5. A rare variation of Funnies On Parade; same format, similar contents, same cover except for large Santa placed in center (value will be based on sale)

TOY WORLD FUNNIES (See Funnies On Parade)
Eastern Color Printing Co.: 1933 (36 pgs., slick cover, Golden Eagle and Wanamaker giveaway)
nn-Contains contents from Funnies On Parade/Century Of Comics. A rare variation of Funnies On Parade; same format, similar contents, same cover except for large Santa placed in center (value will be based on sale)

TRAPPED
Harvey Publications (Columbia Univ. Press): 1951 (Giveaway, soft-c, 16 pgs)
nn-Drug education comic (30,000 printed?) distributed to schools.; mentioned in **SOTI**, pgs. 256,350 2 4 6 8 10 12
NOTE: *Many copies surfaced in 1979 causing a setback in price; beware of trimmed edges, because many copies have a brittle edge.*

TRIPLE-A BASEBALL HEROES
Marvel Comics: 2007 (Minor league baseball stadium giveaway)
1-Special John Watson painted-c for Memphis, Durham and Buffalo; generic cover with team logos for each of the other 27 teams; Spider-Man, Iron Man, FF app. 3.00

TRIP TO OUTER SPACE WITH SANTA
Sales Promotions, Inc/Peoria Dry Goods: 1950s (paper-c)
nn-Comics, games & puzzles 5 10 15 22 26 30

TRIP WITH SANTA ON CHRISTMAS EVE, A
Rockford Dry Goods Co.: No date (Early 1950s) (Giveaway, 16 pgs., paper-c)
nn 5 10 15 22 26 30

TRUTH BEHIND THE TRIAL OF CARDINAL MINDSZENTY, THE (See Cardinal Mindszenty)

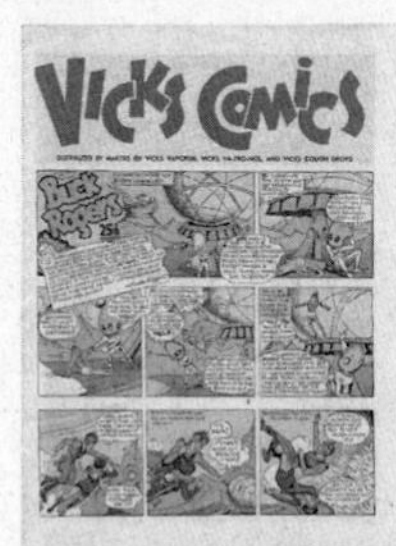

Vicks Comics (16-pg. giveaway) © EAS

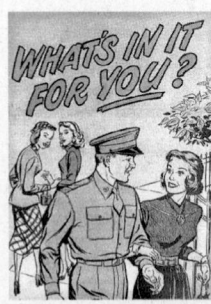

What's In It For You? © HARV

Wheaties A-3 © DIS

GD VG FN VF VF/NM NM-
2.0 4.0 6.0 8.0 9.0 9.2

24 PAGES OF COMICS (No title) (Also see Pure Oil Comics, Salerno Carnival of Comics, & Vicks Comics)
Giveaway by various outlets including Sears: Late 1930s
nn-Contains strip reprints-Buck Rogers, Napoleon, Sky Roads, War on Crime 31 62 93 186 303 420

TWO FACES OF COMMUNISM (Also see Double Talk)
Christian Anti-Communism Crusade, Houston, Texas: 1961 (Giveaway, paper-c, 36 pgs.)
nn 18 36 54 105 165 225

2001, A SPACE ODYSSEY (Movie)
Marvel Comics Group
Howard Johnson giveaway (1968, 8pp); 6 pg. movie adaptation, 2 pg. games, puzzles; McWilliams-a 2 4 6 9 12 15

UNCLE SAM'S CHRISTMAS STORY
Promotional Publ. Co.: 1958 (Giveaway)
nn-Reprints 1956 Christmas USA 2 4 6 10 13 16

UNCLE WIGGILY COMICS
Herberger's Clothing Store: 1942 (32 pgs., paper cover)
nn-Comic panels with 6 pages of puzzles 14 28 42 76 108 140

UNKEPT PROMISE
Legion of Truth: 1949 (Giveaway, 24 pgs.)
nn-Anti-alcohol 10 20 30 58 79 100

UNTOLD LEGEND OF THE BATMAN, THE
DC Comics: 1989 (28 pgs., 6X9", limited series of cereal premiums)
1-1st & 2nd printings known; Byrne-a 2 3 4 6 8 10
2,3: 1st & 2nd printings known 1 2 3 5 6 8

UNTOUCHABLES, THE (TV)
Leaf Brands, Inc.
Topps Bubblegum premiums produced by Leaf Brands, Inc.-2-1/2x4-1/2", 8 pgs. (3 diff. issues) "The Organization, Jamaica Ginger, The Otto Frick Story (drug), 3000 Suspects, The Antidote, Mexican Stakeout, Little Egypt, Purple Gang, Bugs Moran Story, & Lily Dallas Story" 3 6 9 16 23 30

VICKS COMICS (See Pure Oil Comics, Salerno Carnival of Comics & 24 Pages of Comics)
Eastern Color Printing Co. (Vicks Chemical Co.): nd (circa 1938) (Giveaway, 68 pgs. in color)
nn-Famous Funnies-r (before #40); contains 5 pgs. Buck Rogers (4 pgs. from F.F. #15, & 1 pg. from #16) Joe Palooka, Napoleon, etc. app. 54 108 162 343 592 840
nn-16 loose, untrimmed page giveaway; paper-c; r/Famous Funnies #14; Buck Rogers, Joe Palooka app. Has either "Vicks Comics" printed on cover or only a local store name as the logo. 22 44 66 131 216 300

WALT DISNEY'S COMICS & STORIES
K.K. Publications: 1942-1963 known (7-1/3"x10-1/4", 4 pgs. in color, slick paper) (folded horizontally once or twice as mailers) (Xmas subscription offer)
1942 mailer-r/Kelly cover to WDC&S 25; 2-year subscription + two Grosset & Dunlap hardcover books (32-pages each), of Bambi and of Thumper, offered for $2.00; came in an illustrated C&S envelope with an enclosed postage paid envelope
(Rare) Mailer only 21 42 63 126 206 285
with envelopes 27 54 81 158 259 360
1947,1948 mailer 17 34 51 98 154 210
1949 mailer-A rare Barks item: Same WDC&S cover as 1942 mailer, but with art changed so that nephew is handing teacher Donald a comic book rather than an apple, as originally drawn by Kelly. The tiny, 7/8"x1-1/4" cover shown was a rejected cover by Barks that was intended for C&S 110, but was redrawn by Kelly for C&S 111. The original art has been lost and this is its only app. (Rare) 39 78 117 233 377 520
1950 mailer-P.1 r/Kelly cover to Dell Xmas Parade 1 (without title); p.2 r/Kelly cover to C&S 101 (w/o title), but with the art altered to show Donald reading C&S 122 (by Kelly); hardcover book, "Donald Duck in Bringing Up the Boys" given with a $1.00 one-year subscription; P.4 r/full Kelly Xmas cover to C&S 99 (Rare) 17 34 51 98 154 210
1952 mailer-P1 r/cover WDC&S #88 14 28 42 80 115 150
1953 mailer-P.1 r/cover Dell Xmas Parade 4 (w/o title); insides offer "Donald Duck Full Speed Ahead," a 28-page, color, 5-5/8"x6-5/8" book, not of the Story Hour series; P.4 r/full Barks C&S 148 cover (Rare) 14 28 42 80 115 150
1963 mailer-Pgs. 1,2 & 4 r/GK Xmas art; P.3 r/a 1963 C&S cover (Scarce) 6 12 18 40 73 105
NOTE: *It is assumed a different mailer was printed each Xmas for at least twenty years.*

WALT DISNEY'S COMICS & STORIES
Walt Disney Productions: 1943 (36 pgs.) (Dept. store Xmas giveaway)
nn-X-Mas-c with Donald & the Boys; Donald Duck by Jack Hannah; Thumper by Ken Hultgren 43 86 129 271 461 650

WALT DISNEY'S DONALD DUCK
Gemstone Publishing: 2006
nn-(8-1/2"x 5-1/2", Halloween giveaway) r/"A Prank Above" -Barks-s/a; Rosa-s/a 2.50
nn-(2008, 8-1/2"x 5-1/2", Halloween giveaway) "The Halloween Huckster"; Rota-s/a 2.50

WALT DISNEY'S UNCLE SCROOGE
Gemstone Publishing
nn-(2007, 8-1/2"x 5-1/2", Halloween giveaway) Hound of the Whiskevilles; Barks-s/a 2.50

WARLORD
DC Comics: (Remco Toy giveaway, 2-3/4x4")
nn 5.00

WATCH OUT FOR BIG TALK
Giveaway: 1950
nn-Dan Barry-a; about crooked politicians 7 14 21 37 46 55

WEATHER-BIRD (See Comics From..., Dick Tracy, Free Comics to You..., Super Circus & Terry and the Pirates)
International Shoe Co./Western Printing Co.: 1958 - No. 16, July, 1962 (Shoe store giveaway)
1 4 8 12 24 38 52
2-16 3 6 9 14 19 24
NOTE: *The numbers are located in the lower bottom panel, pg. 1. All feature a character called Weather-Bird.*

WEATHER BIRD COMICS (See Comics From Weather Bird)
Weather Bird Shoes: 1955 (Giveaway)
nn-Contains a comic bound with new cover. Several combinations possible; contents determine price (40 - 60 percent of contents).

WEEKLY COMIC MAGAZINE
Fox Publications: May 12, 1940 (16 pgs.) (Others exist w/o super-heroes)
(1st Version)-8 pg. Blue Beetle story, 7 pg. Patty O'Day story; two copies known to exist. (a VF copy sold in 5/07 for $1553)
(2nd Version)-7 two-pg. adventures of Blue Beetle, Patty O'Day, Yarko, Dr. Fung, Green Mask, Spark Stevens, & Rex Dexter (two known copies, a FN sold in 2007 for $1912, other is GD)
(3rd version)-Captain Valor (only one known copy, in VG+; it sold in 2005 for $480) -
Discovered with business papers, letters and exploitation material promoting **Weekly Comic Magazine** for use by newspapers in the same manner of **The Spirit** weeklies. Interesting note: these are dated three weeks before the first Spirit comic. Letters indicate that samples may have been sent to a few newspapers. These sections were actually 15-1/2x22" pages which will fold down to an approximate 8x10" comic booklet. Other various comic sections were found with the above, but were more like the Sunday comic sections in format.

WE HIT THE JACKPOT
General Comics, Inc./American Affairs: 1947 (Promotional comic)
nn 6 12 18 31 38 45

WHAT DO YOU KNOW ABOUT THIS COMICS SEAL OF APPROVAL?
No publisher listed (DC Comics Giveaway): nd (1955) (4 pgs., slick paper-c)
nn-(Rare) 103 206 309 659 1130 1600

WHAT'S BEHIND THESE HEADLINES
William C. Popper Co.: 1948 (16 pgs.)
nn-Comic insert "The Plot to Steal the World" 6 12 18 31 38 45

WHAT'S IN IT FOR YOU?
Harvey Publications Inc.: (16 pgs., paper cover)
nn-National Guard recruitment 4 7 10 14 17 20

WHEATIES (Premiums)
Walt Disney Productions: 1950 & 1951 (32 titles, pocket-size, 32 pgs.)
Mailing Envelope (no art on front)(Designates sets A,B,C or D on front) 7 14 21 37 46 55

(Set A-1 to A-8, 1950)
A-1-Mickey Mouse & the Disappearing Island, A-5-Mickey Mouse, Roving Reporter each... 6 12 18 28 34 40
A-2-Grandma Duck, Homespun Detective, A-6-Li'l Bad Wolf, Forest Ranger, A-7-Goofy, Tightrope Acrobat, A-8-Pluto & the Bogus Money each... 5 10 15 24 30 35
A-3-Donald Duck & the Haunted Jewels, A-4-Donald Duck & the Giant Ape each... 8 16 24 42 54 65

(Set B-1 to B-8, 1950)
B-1-Mickey Mouse & the Pharoah's Curse, B-4-Mickey Mouse & the Mystery Sea Monster each... 6 12 18 31 38 45
B-2-Pluto, Canine Cowpoke, B-5-Li'l Bad Wolf in the Hollow Tree Hideout, B-7-Goofy & the Gangsters each... 5 10 15 24 30 35
B-3-Donald Duck & the Buccaneers, B-6-Donald Duck,Trail Blazer, B-8 Donald Duck, Klondike Kid each... 8 16 24 42 54 65

(Set C-1 to C-8, 1951)
C-1-Donald Duck & the Inca Idol, C-5-Donald Duck in the Lost Lakes, C-8-Donald Duck Deep-Sea Diver each... 8 16 24 42 54 65
C-2-Mickey Mouse & the Magic Mountain, C-6-Mickey Mouse & the Stagecoach Bandits each... 6 12 18 31 38 45
C-3-Li'l Bad Wolf, Fire Fighter, C-4-Gus & Jaq Save the Ship, C-7-Goofy, Big Game Hunter each... 5 10 15 24 30 35

The Wheel of Progress © AAR

Wisco/Klarer - Blaze Carson © FAW

X-Men The Movie © MAR

	GD 2.0	VG 4.0	FN 6.0	VF 8.0	VF/NM 9.0	NM- 9.2

(Set D-1 to D-8, 1951)
D-1-Donald Duck in Indian Country, D-5-Donald Duck, Mighty Mystic
each... 8 16 24 42 54 65
D-2-Mickey Mouse and the Abandoned Mine, D-6-Mickey Mouse & the Medicine Man
each... 6 12 18 31 38 45
D-3-Pluto & the Mysterious Package, D-4-Bre'r Rabbit's Sunken Treasure,
D-7-Li'l Bad Wolf and the Secret of the Woods, D-8-Minnie Mouse, Girl Explorer
each... 5 10 15 24 30 35
NOTE: *Some copies lack the Wheaties ad.*

WHEEL OF PROGRESS, THE
Assoc. of American Railroads: Oct, 1957 (16 pgs.)
nn-Bill Bunce 6 12 18 28 34 40

WHIZ COMICS (Formerly Flash Comics & Thrill Comics #1)
Fawcett Publications
Wheaties Giveaway(1946, Miniature, 6-1/2x8-1/4", 32 pgs.); all copies were taped at each corner to a box of Wheaties and are never found in very fine or mint condition; "Capt. Marvel & the Water Thieves", plus Golden Arrow, Ibis, Crime Smasher stories
80 160 400 - - -

WILD KINGDOM (TV) (Mutual of Omaha's...)
Western Printing Co.: 1965, 1966 (Giveaway, regular size, slick-c, 16 pgs.)
nn-Front & back-c are different on 1966 edition 2 4 6 9 12 15

WISCO/KLARER COMIC BOOK (Miniature)
Marvel Comics/Vital Publ./Fawcett Publ.: 1948 - 1964 (3-1/2x6-3/4", 24 pgs.)
Given away by Wisco "99" Service Stations, Carnation Malted Milk, Klarer Health Wieners, Fleers Dubble Bubble Gum, Rodeo All-Meat Wieners, Perfect Potato Chips, & others; see ad in Tom Mix #21
Blackstone & the Gold Medal Mystery (1948) 8 16 24 42 54 65
Blackstone "Solves the Sealed Vault Mystery" (1950) 8 16 24 42 54 65
Blaze Carson in "The Sheriff Shoots It Out" (1950) 8 16 24 42 54 65
Captain Marvel & Billy's Big Game (r/Capt. Marvel Adv. #76)
24 48 72 144 237 330
(Prices vary widely on this book)
China Boy in "A Trip to the Zoo" #10 (1948) 5 10 15 24 30 35
Indoors-Outdoors Game Book 4 7 10 14 17 20
Jim Solar Space Sheriff in "Battle for Mars", "Between Two Worlds", "Conquers Outer Space", "The Creatures on the Comet", "Defeats the Moon Missile Men", "Encounter Creatures on Comet", "Meet the Jupiter Jumpers", "Meets the Man From Mars", "On Traffic Duty", "Outlaws of the Spaceways", "Pirates of the Planet X", "Protects Space Lanes", "Raiders From the Sun", "Ring Around Saturn", "Robots of Rhea", "The Sky Ruby", "Spacetts of the Sky", "Spidermen of Venus", "Trouble on Mercury"
7 14 21 35 43 50
Johnny Starboard & the Underseas Pirates (1948) 5 10 15 22 26 30
Kid Colt in "He Lived by His Guns" (1950) 8 16 24 44 57 70
Little Aspirin as the "Crook Catcher" #2 (1950) 4 7 10 14 17 20
Little Aspirin in "Naughty But Nice" #6 (1950) 4 7 10 14 17 20
Return of the Black Phantom (not M.E. character)(Roy Dare)(1948)
6 12 18 28 34 40
Secrets of Magic 4 8 11 16 19 22
Slim Morgan "Brings Justice to Mesa City" #3 4 8 11 16 19 22
Super Rabbit(1950)-Cuts Red Tape, Stops Crime Wave!
9 18 27 50 65 80
Tex Farnum, Frontiersman (1948) 5 10 15 22 26 30
Tex Taylor in "Draw or Die, Cowpoke!" (1950) 7 14 21 35 43 50
Tex Taylor in "An Exciting Adventure at the Gold Mine" (1950)
6 12 18 31 38 45
Wacky Quacky in "All-Aboard" 3 6 8 12 14 16
When School Is Out 3 6 8 12 14 16
Willie in a "Comic-Comic Book Fall" #1 4 8 11 16 19 22
Wonder Duck "An Adventure at the Rodeo of the Fearless Quacker!" (1950)
9 18 27 47 61 75
Rare uncut version of three; includes Capt. Marvel, Tex Farnum, Black Phantom
Estimated value... 700.00
Rare uncut version of three; includes China Boy, Blackstone, Johnny Starboard & the Underseas Pirates Estimated value... 250.00
Rare uncut version of three; includes Willie in a "Comic-Comic Book Fall", Little Aspirin #2, Slim Morgan Brings Justice to Mesa City (a VF/FN copy sold for $54 in Nov. 2007)

WIZARD OF OZ
MGM: 1967 (small size)
"Dorothy and Friends Visit Oz", "Dorothy Meets the Wizard", "The Tin Woodsman Saves Dorothy" each... 2 4 6 8 10 12

WOLVERINE
Marvel Comics
145-(1999 Nabisco mail-in offer) Sienkiewicz-c 7 14 21 46 86 125
...Son of Canada (4/01, ed. of 65,000) Spider-Man & The Hulk app.; Lim-a 3.00

WOMAN OF THE PROMISE, THE
Catechetical Guild: 1950 (General Distr.) (Paper cover, 32 pgs.)
nn 6 12 18 28 34 40

WONDERFUL WORLD OF DUCKS (See Golden Picture Story Book)
Colgate Palmolive Co.: 1975
1-Mostly-r 1 3 4 6 8 10

WONDER WOMAN
DC Comics: 1977
Pizza Hut Giveaways (12/77)-Reprints #60,62 2 4 6 9 13 16
... - The Minotaur (1981, General Foods giveaway, 8 pages, 3-1/2 x 6-3/4", oblong) 2 4 6 13 18 22

WONDER WORKER OF PERU
Catechetical Guild: No date (5x7", 16 pgs., B&W, giveaway)
nn 5 10 15 27 33 38

WOODY WOODPECKER
Dell Publishing Co.
Clover Stamp-Newspaper Boy Contest('56)-9 pg. story-(Giveaway)
7 14 21 37 46 55
In Chevrolet Wonderland(1954-Giveaway)(Western Publ.)-20 pgs., full story line; Chilly Willy app. 18 36 54 103 162 220
...Meets Scotty MacTape(1953-Scotch Tape giveaway)-16 pgs., full size
18 36 54 103 162 220

WOOLWORTH'S CHRISTMAS STORY BOOK
Promotional Publ. Co.(Western Printing Co.): 1952 - 1954 (16 pgs., paper-c) (See Jolly Christmas Book)
nn: 1952 issue-Marv Levy c/a 6 12 18 33 41 48

WOOLWORTH'S HAPPY TIME CHRISTMAS BOOK
F. W. Woolworth Co. (Western Printing Co.): 1952 (Christmas giveaway)
nn-36 pgs. 6 12 18 31 38 45

WORLD'S FINEST COMICS
National Periodical Publ./DC Comics
Giveaway (c. 1944-45, 8 pgs., in color, paper-c)-Johnny Everyman-r/World's Finest
20 40 60 120 195 270
Giveaway (c. 1949, 8 pgs., in color, paper-c)- "Make Way For Youth" r/World's Finest; based on film of same name 18 36 54 107 169 230
#176, #179- Best Western reprint edition (1997) 3.00

WORLD'S GREATEST SUPER HEROES
DC Comics (Nutra Comics) (Child Vitamins, Inc.): 1977 (Giveaway, 3-3/4x3-3/4", 24 pgs.)
nn-Batman & Robin app.; health tips 2 4 6 9 13 16

WYOMING THE COWBOY STATE
1954 (Giveaway, slick-c)
nn 5 10 15 22 26 30

XMAS FUNNIES
Kinney Shoes: No date (Giveaway, paper cover, 36 pgs.?)
Contains 1933 color strip-r; Mutt & Jeff, etc. 29 58 87 172 281 390

X-MEN THE MOVIE
Marvel Comics/Toys R' Us: 2000
Special Movie Prequel Edition 5.00

X2 PRESENTS THE ULTIMATE X-MEN #2
Marvel Comics/New York Post: July, 2003
Reprint distributed inside issue of the New York Post 2.50

YALTA TO KOREA (Also see Korea My Home)
M. Phillip Corp. (Republican National Committee): 1952 (Giveaway, paper-c)
nn-(8 pgs.)-Anti-communist propaganda book 18 36 54 103 162 220

YOGI BEAR (TV)
Dell Publishing Co.
Giveaway ('84, '86)-City of Los Angeles, "Creative First Aid" & "Earthquake Preparedness for Children" 1 2 3 4 5 7

YOUR TRIP TO NEWSPAPERLAND
Philadelphia Evening Bulletin (Printed by Harvey Press): June, 1955 (14x11-1/2", 12 pgs.)
nn-Joe Palooka takes kids on newspaper tour 5 10 15 24 30 35

YOUR VOTE IS VITAL!
Harvey Publications Inc.: 1952 (5" x 7", 16 pgs., paper cover)
nn-The importance of voting 4 8 12 18 22 25

THE PIONEER AGE

The American Comic Book: 1500s–1828

For the last few years, we have featured a tremendous article by noted historian and collector Eric C. Caren on the foundations of what we now call "The Pioneer Age" of comics. We look forward to a new article on this significant topic in a future edition of *The Overstreet Comic Book Price Guide*. In the meantime, should you need it, Caren's article may be found in the 35th through 39th editions.

That said, even with the space constraints in this edition of the *Guide*, we could not possibly exclude reference to these incredible, formative works.

Why are these illustrations and sequences of illustrations important to the comic books of today?

German broadsheet, dated 1569.

The Murder of King Henry III (1589).

Quite frankly, because we can see in them the very building blocks of the comic art form.

The shooting of the Italian Concini (1617).

Over the course of just a few hundred years, we the evolution of narration, word balloons, panel-to-panel progression of story, and so much more. If these stories aren't developed first, how would be every have reached the point that that *The Adventures of Mr. Obadiah Oldbuck* could have come along in 1842?

As the investigation of comic book history has blown away the notion that comic books were a 20 century invention, it hasn't been easy to convince some, even with the clear, linear progression of the artful melding of illustration and words.

"Want to avoid an argument in social discourse? Steer clear of politics and religion. In the latter category, the most controversial subject is human evolution. Collectors can become just as squeamish when you start messing with the evolution of a particular collectible," Eric Caren wrote in his article. "In most cases, the origin of a particular comic character will be universally agreed upon, but try tackling the origin of printed comics and you are asking for trouble."

"The Bubblers Medley" (1720).

"Join, or Die" from the Pennsylvania Gazette, *May 9, 1754.*

"Amusement for John Bull..." from The European Magazine *(1783).*

But the evidence is there for any who choose to look. Before the original comics of the Golden Age, there were comic strip reprints collected in comic book form. The practice dated back decades earlier, of course, but coalesced into the current form when the realities of the Great Depression spawned the modern incarnation of the comic book and its immediate cousin, the Big Little Book.

Everything that came later, though, did so because the acceptance of the visual language had already been worked out. Before Spider-Man and the Hulk, before Superman and Batman, before the Yellow Kid, Little Nemo, and the Brownies, cartoonists and editorial illustrators were working out how to tell a story or simply convey their ideas in this new artform.

Without this sort of work, without these pioneers, we simply wouldn't be where we are today.

CONNECTICUT MIRROR.

Cartoons satirizing Napoleon on the front page of the Connecticut Mirror, dated January 7, 1811.

Another Napoleon cartoon, this time dubbing him "The Corsican Munchausen," from the London Strand, December 4, 1813.

"A Consultation at the Medical Board" from The Pasquin or General Satirist *(1821)*.

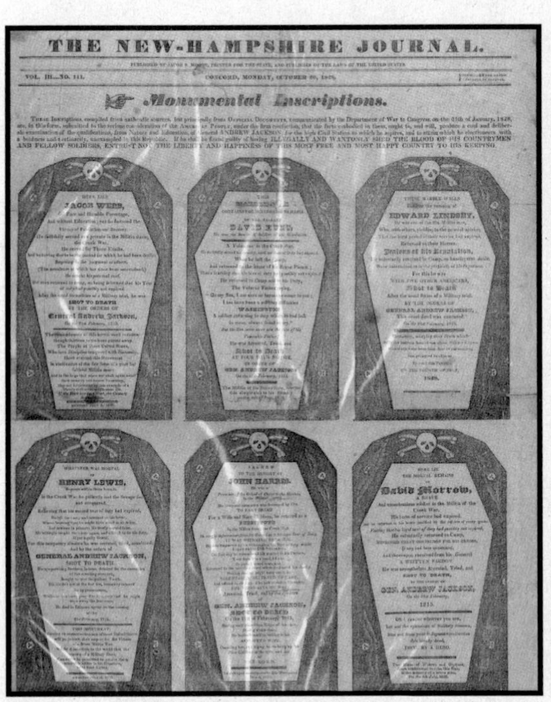

THE NEW-HAMPSHIRE JOURNAL.

CONCORD, MONDAY, OCTOBER 20, 1828.

Monumental Inscriptions.

JACOB WEBB,

EDWARD LINDSEY,

HENRY LEWIS,

JOHN HARRIS.

David Morrow,

GEN. ANDREW JACKSON.

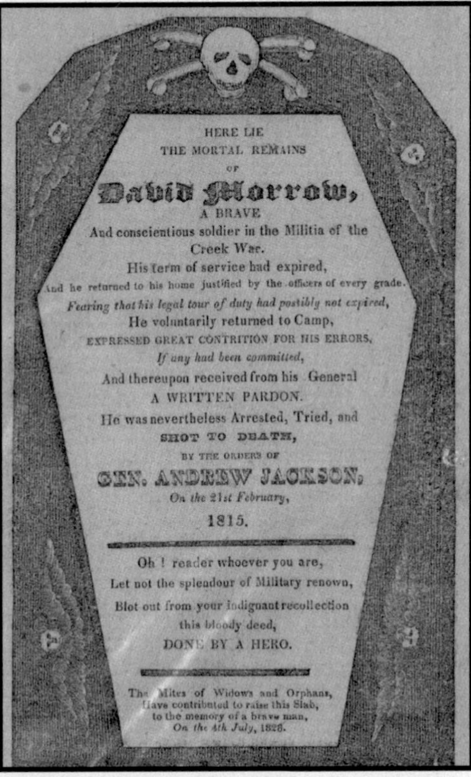

HERE LIE
THE MORTAL REMAINS
OF
David Morrow,
A BRAVE
And conscientious soldier in the Militia of the
Creek War.
His term of service had expired,
And he returned to his home justified by the officers of every grade.
Fearing that his legal tour of duty had possibly not expired,
He voluntarily returned to Camp,
EXPRESSED GREAT CONTRITION FOR HIS ERRORS,
If any had been committed,
And thereupon received from his General
A WRITTEN PARDON.
He was nevertheless Arrested, Tried, and
SHOT TO DEATH,
BY THE ORDERS OF
GEN. ANDREW JACKSON,
On the 21st February,
1815.

Oh! reader whoever you are,
Let not the splendour of Military renown,
Blot out from your indignant recollection
this bloody deed,
DONE BY A HERO.

The Mites of Widows and Orphans,
Have contributed to raise this Slab,
to the memory of a brave man,
On the 4th July, 1828.

Above left, the front page of The New Hampshire Journal, *dated October 20, 1828, with multiple tombstone "panels." To the right is a detail of the bottom right tombstone.*

THE VICTORIAN AGE

Comic Strips and Books: 1646-1900

A Concise History & Price Index Of The Field As Of 2014

ORIGINS OF EARLY AMERICAN COMIC STRIPS BEFORE THE YELLOW KID

by Robert Lee Beerbohm, Richard Samuel West & Richard D. Olson, PhD ©2014

(This article was originally created by Doug Wheeler, Robert Beerbohm and Richard D. Olson, PhD for CBPG #32 and continues to be revised annually by the current authors.) We welcome any and all corrections and additions. Special Thanks This Installment To Leonardo De Sa, Terrence Keegen, Gabriel Laderman and Joe Rainone.

Left: "The Burning of Mr. John Rogers," 1646 is the earliest-known North American cartoon printed on paper printed in the earliest children's primer in America.

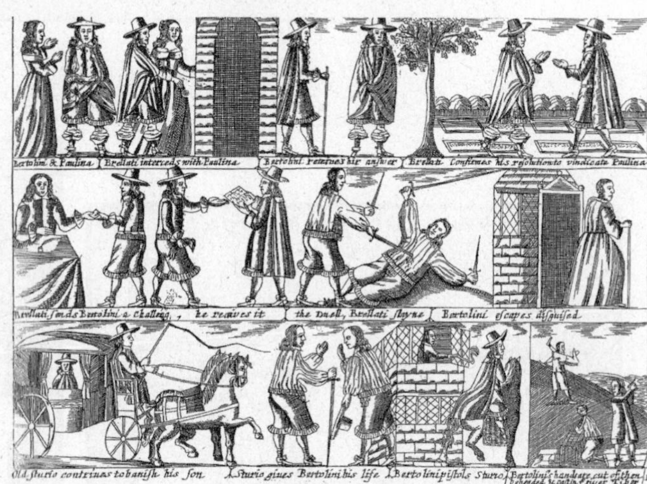

"God's Revenge For Murder" By John Reynolds, unknown artist, 1656. Earliest-known sequential comic "panel" strip created in the English language.

Left: From his pamphlet Plain Truth 1747 containing Ben Franklin's earliest-known cartoon titled "Heaven Helps Only Those Who Help Themselves" depicting ancient "super hero" Hercules in the upper right corner. Middle: "A Warm Place - Hell", one of two images definitely known to be drawn and engraved by Paul Revere, 1768. Word balloons had wide-spread usage in many cartoons in the 1700s. Right: The Tables Turned by James Gillray, 1797 commenting on an "invasion" of England by 1400 French convicts. The use of word balloons was wide spread in many parts of the world long before the Yellow Kid's parrot uttered a few words in 1896.

The Comic Almanac(k) debuted in America in 1831 with the earliest-known titles starting heavy with humor and sporting crude woodcut single panel cartoons. Ellm's American Comic Almanac was one of the first. By 1835 Davy Crockett, one of the nation's earliest national folk heroes, began issuing his own version. In the late 1840s the Comic Almanac(k)s began to offer tall-tale sequential comic strips which became somewhat commonplace in the 1850s, fueled by the advent of the California Gold Rush. They were instrumental in the development of the American comic strip and we will be reporting more new finds after further research into American folklore.

We have a lot of new discoveries to share with you again this year as amply evident in the price index which follows this year's history lesson. A quantum leap has finally been achieved in the area of introducing the comic book collecting world to *American Comic Almanac(k)s* as well as a huge multitude of American humor periodicals, many of which contained sequential comic strips.

This Victorian Era section is devoted to comic strips and books published during the years the United States expanded across the North American continent, fought a Civil War, shifted from an agrarian to an industrial society, "welcomed" waves of immigrants, and struggled over race, class, religion, temperance, and suffrage - and all of it depicted and satirized by generations of mostly now long-forgotten cartoonists. The social attitudes, beliefs, and conventions of 19th century America, the good as well as the bad, are to be found in abundance. Perhaps the first question to pop into most readers' minds will be, "What, beyond the happenstance of publication date, are Victorian Era comics?"

There has been a long slow-motion evolution of the comic strip which was not invented in America, contrary to many previous history books on the subject. One must examine many aspects of concurrent popular culture. The main aspect that we believe most distinguishes Victorian Era comic strips from those of later eras was the extremely rare use of word balloons within sequential (multi-picture) comic stories. When word balloons were used, it was nearly always within single-panel cartoons. On the occasions when they appeared inside a strip, with very few exceptions, the ballooned dialogue was inconsequential. Nineteenth-century comics tended to place both narration and dialogue beneath comic panels rather than within the panel's borders as they were thought by many to interfere with the art. Many of these comics are to the word balloon-strewn post-Yellow Kid comics of the 20th Century as silent movies are to the later "talkies." Just as sound changed how stories were structured on film, so too did comic strips change when the words were moved from beneath panels to inside them, and dialogue rather than narration drove the story in conjunction with the pictures.

The Victorian Era of actual comic strip books began on different dates in different nations, depending on when the first publication of a sequential comic book on their soil is known to have occurred. For the U.S. this happened when the American literary periodical *Brother Jonathan* printed the 40-page, 195-panel graphic novel *The Adventures of Mr. Obadiah Oldbuck* as a special extra dated September 14, 1842. Almost six decades later, America's Victorian comics came to their end, replaced by the onslaught of Platinum Age books reprinting newspaper strips from Bennett, Hearst, and Pulitzer Sunday comic sections, among many others.

There is considerable overlap between Victorian Era and Platinum Age comic books and strips. Those publications that continued from one century into the next, such as *Puck*, *Judge*, and *Life*, have their pre-1900 issues listed within the Victorian Age section, while their post-1899 issues can be found inside the Platinum Age. Some non-sequential (i.e., single-panel) American comic items existing prior to 1842 are also listed herein, going back to 1795. These belong to what could tentatively be called the Age of Caricature (1770s through 1830s). This was a fertile period for the art in England, when Gillray and Rowlandson, and, later, Cruikshank, Heath, and Seymour were that nation's top cartoonists. During the same period in the U.S., there were no artists who made their living as caricaturists, though William Charles, printer and engraver, did produce about two dozen spirited cartoon broadsides from 1805 to 1820, the most important ones concerning events of the War of 1812.

In addition, one can trace origins of American comic books to the humorous Comic Almanacs which began in earnest in the early 1830s.

The earliest known cartoon-like woodcut printed on paper in North America was in a Puritan children's book first published in 1646. Titled simply *The Burning of Mr. John Rogers*, it showed in flaming graphic detail what happens to those who stray from the flock and have to be burned at the stake. Dr. Wertham would have had a field day with that one!

Cartoon broadsides and other single panel images, often using word balloons, appeared from pre-Revolution days through the end of the 19th Century. The earliest known attributed cartoon, designed by the ubiquitous Benjamin Franklin, was "Heaven Helps Only Those Who Help Themselves," which first appeared in his pamphlet *Plain Truth* in 1747.

The most popularly remembered 18th-Century American cartoons are likely Franklin's "*Join or Die*" in 1754, representing the American Colonies as severed snake parts, and "*The Bloody Massacre Perpetrated in King Street*" -- Paul Revere's 1770 depiction of the Boston Massacre, which he pirated from the earlier Henry Pelham broadsheet cartoon "*The Fruits of Arbitrary Power.*"

In September 1826, John Warner Barber, New Haven, Ct. (1798-1885) designed and self-published the broadside *The Drunkard's Progress, Or The Direct Road to Poverty, Wretchedness and Ruin* showing in four stages sequentially "The Morning Dram" which is "The Beginning of Sorrow, " "The Grog Shop" with its "Bad Company," "The Confirmed Drunkard" in a state of "Beastly Intoxication," and the "Concluding Scene" with the family being driven off to the alms house. It is an interesting set of cuts, faintly reminiscent of Hogarth. Barber began his career in 1819, age 21, engraving on wood. He devoted most of his career to the multitude of art chores associated with book production. As late as 1870 he was issuing *Barber's Temperance Tracts,* which built upon his 1826 original plus four panels showing the positive effects of living without alcohol.

The first American whose fame was based primarily on his cartoons appears to be David Claypoole Johnston (1798-1865). Johnston provided illustrations for various almanacs, books, and periodicals, including the masthead for *Brother Jonathans*. Most notable of Johnston's comics work was his nine-issue series *Scraps*, which he self-published from 1828 to 1849. This series was highly influenced by George Cruikshank's series *Scraps and Sketches*, which first appeared in 1827. Because of the resemblance, Johnston became known in his day as "the American Cruikshank." Each issue of Johnston's *Scraps* consists of four large folio-sized pages, printed on one side, with nine to twelve single-panel cartoons per page, and each page often organized around a theme. Also popular was his comic album Outlines Illustrative of the Journal of F****** A*** K***** (1835), which parodied passages from the journal of recently published observations on America by British actress Fanny Kemble.

Johnston, himself a failed actor, had an interest in the theater his entire career. In addition to producing a number of prints depicting American actors in famous roles, he collaborated with actor Henry J. Finn to produce the 1831 *(American) Comic Annual*, with Finn as Editor and Johnston as artist, published by Richardson, Lord and Holbrook, Boston. It featured almost 30 full-page Johnston-designed copper engravings and woodcuts. Also that year, Finn solo produced *Finn's Comic Sketch Book*, a twelve-page album similar to Johnston's *Scraps* with upwards of half a dozen single-panel cartoons per page. It was published by Peabody and Co, of New York in business from 1831-1843. (Finn died tragically in a steamboat accident Jan. 13, 1840.)

Perhaps Johnston's most interesting contribution to the history of the comic strip in American came in 1837, when he produced the sequential comic broadside, *Illustrations of the Adventures & Achievements of the Renowned Don Quixote & his Doughty Squire Sancho Panza* (27.4 x 30.4 cm). This blank-reverse engraved print was an elaborate twelve-panel satire of the Andrew Jackson-Van Buren administration. It likely sold for 25 cents, seeing distribution in Boston, New York and Philadelphia. Much later, in 1863, Johnston drew another sequential comic broadside, *The House the Jeff Built* (27.5 x 36.7 cm), a bitter indictment of Jefferson Davis and the Southern slavocracy.

In July 1839, Wilson and Company, a newly formed New York printing firm, began publishing a mammoth newspaper by the name of *Brother Jonathan*. The publisher, J. Gregg Wilson had employed the newspaper format for *Brother Jonathan* to circumvent the higher postage rates imposed on magazines, but *Brother Jonathan* was a newspaper in format only -- it contained not a shred of news, instead specializing in serialized fiction, some of it written by Americans but most of it pirated from foreign sources. Despite the cost savings, the mammoth format had its limitations; when opened it measured a whopping three feet by four feet. So, once *Brother Jonathan* was an established success, Wilson and Day began in January 1841 the simultaneous publication of a magazine-sized quarto edition of *Brother Jonathan* that reprinted the contents of the mammoth edition.

Later that same year, to capitalize on the name recognition of their successful twin publications, Wilson and Company started issuing book-length *Brother Jonathan Extras* in the same format as the quarto magazine. These reprints are counted among the earliest paperback books in America. Most of the *Extra* numbers were pirated European novels. For example their eighth extra was the first American printing of a Charles Dickens novel. But for their ninth *Extra*, they did something no American publisher had ever done before -- they pirated a graphic novel, Rodolphe Töpffer's *The Adventures of Mr. Obadiah Oldbuck.* By reformatting *Oldbuck* from its original small oblong strip design to fit *Brother Jonathan's* standard quarto format Wilson and Company inadvertently made this edition (alone) of *Obadiah Oldbuck* resemble a modern comic book. *Oldbuck's* arrival on the shores of the New World would directly inspire a wave of American imitators. [*This first Wilson printing of Oldbuck from 1842 was reprinted in same-size limited edition facsimile by the Naples Comicon in 2003. An English translation by Leonardo De Sá of Töpffer's original draft is at leonardo desa.interdinamica. net/comics/lds/*]

Even though in 1904 (in its September 3 edition), *The New York Times* accurately identified the *Brother Jonathan Extra* as the first American comic book as well as Wilson & Co. utilizing Tilt & Bougue's original printing plates as well as still being in print for sale in New York at such a late date, Töpffer has already been largely forgotten in the New World. It is high time Töpffer received credit long overdue as the inventor of the modern comic strip, laying previously long-held myths to rest.

Töpffer (1799-1846) was a playwright, novelist, artist, and teacher from Geneva, Switzerland, who in 1827 had begun producing what he called "picture novels," sharing them with his friends and students. His earliest editions were self-published via lithography on transfer paper as they use the word "autographie" in their imprints. The earliest printers were J. Freydig, Frutiger (1830s) and Schmidt (1840s). These first sequential comic books, scripted in Töpffer's native French language, found their way to Paris and became an instant hit. According to Gombrich in *Art and Illusion* (1960), "Töpffer recognized that he could rely on the reader to supplement from their own lives what was omitted between the panels. This is crucial in the development of the sequential comic strip."

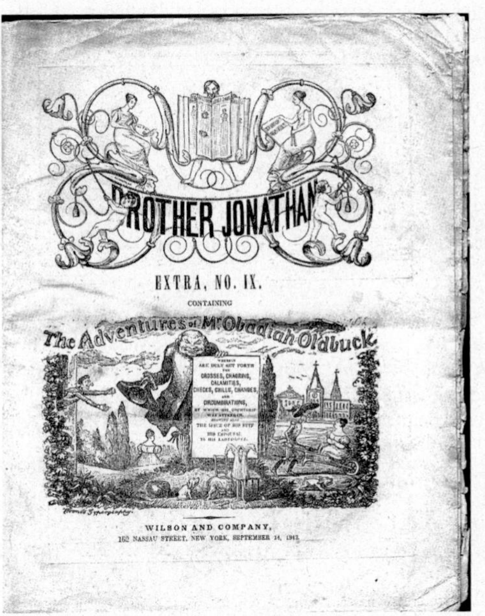

Cover to the subscriber version of the earliest-known sequential comic book published in America, The Adventures of Mr. Obadiah Oldbuck, Sept. 1842, Wilson & Co. New York, originally conceived in 1828 in Geneva Switzerland by creator Rodolphe Töpffer.

The demand for his comic books soon outstripped the supply, and pirated editions, redrawn by others, were created by Parisian publisher Aubert to capitalize on this. In a world where international copyright conventions did not exist, this was perfectly legal, if morally questionable. Thus, in 1841, London publisher Tilt and Bogue commissioned George Cruikshank to create an English version of Töpffer's *Les Amours de M. Vieux Bois* by pirating Aubert's pirated edition of the Geneva original.

This English translation, co-financed by George Cruikshank himself, sported a new cover page by George's brother Robert, based on a montage of Töpffer's scenes. Confirmation of this fact came when George Cruikshank's personal copy surfaced in auction recently with the inscription "Copied from a French book by my Brother Robert" above the title page with the same scene. This is the translation that was reprinted by America's Wilson and Company as *The Adventures of Mr. Obadiah Oldbuck* utilizing the original Tilt and Bogue printing plates.

Tilt and Bogue followed up their success by translating into English two additional stories of Töpffer's seven published graphic novels: *Beau Ogleby*, circa 1843 (originally Histoire de M. Jabot), and *Bachelor Butterfly* two years later (from *Histoire de M. Cryptogame)*. David Bogue also published picture-story strip books by John Leighton using the pseudonym Luke Limner. He wrote and drew beautiful comic books titled *London Out of Town or The Adventures of the Browns At The Seaside; Comic Art-Manufactures; and The Ancient Story of the Old Dame and Her Pig* starting in 1847, but none of these seem to have ever been republished in America. They follow a definite Töpffer influence. This growing body of comic book production was made easier by the spreading understanding of transfer paper lithography, otherwise the panels would have had to have been drawn and lettered mirror reverse. Gombrich referred to Töpffer's comic books as "the innocent ancestors of today's manufactured dreams... everywhere in these countless episodes of almost surrealist inconsequence we find a mastery of physiognomic characterization which sets the standard for such influential humorous draftsmen in the 19th century as Wilhelm Busch in Germany."

A Register of The New York City Book Trades 1821-1842 by Sidney F. & Elizabeth Stege12, Huttner (The Bibliographical Society of America, NYC, 1993) mentions Benjamin H. Day bought into *Brother Jonathan*'s publisher, Wilson and Company, in this year, becoming at some point an equal partner with owner J. Gregg Wilson. The Register lists them both as publishers of *Brother Jonathan* at the same address of 162 Nassau Street. Other historical artifacts state Day eventually became sole-owner and publisher. Exactly when has not yet been determined, though we have figured out with certainly before 1850 .

This is the same Benjamin H. Day who started the first successful penny newspaper in 1833, *The (New York) Sun*, transforming it in four short years into the largest circulation daily in the world at that time. He sold out his ownership of the Sun to his brother-in-law during the financial "panic" of 1837, a mistake he regretted the rest of his life. He re-emerged heavily involved in *Brother Jonathan* definitely by 1840 and as a partner by 1841. *Brother Jonathan's* offices were right next door to Tamany Hall. (See the first 20 minutes of the 2002 movie *Gangs of New York* to visualize the period atmosphere and their customer base.) According to *The Brothers Harper* by Eugene Exmen (Harper & Row, 1965), on page 125, "*Brother Jonathan...* offered in its weekly edition and also in special supplements very cheap reprints of English novels. In effect, it began a price-cutting war against the older established 'pirates' among the book publishers..." Day, it appears, had found the perfect project on which to build a new empire.

Desirous of repeating the success they had with *Obadiah Oldbuck*, Wilson and Company published the first American edition of *Bachelor Butterfly* in 1846. Three years later, they reformatted *Obadiah Oldbuck* back into its original British shape using lithography, dropping a handful of comic panels and altering the text to hide these deletions. Soon thereafter, they published other comic books for a steadily growing market that they had helped to stimulate. In recognition of their significant role in the dissemination of sequential comics, Wilson and Company deserve to be remembered as the first comic book publisher in America.

Back in Europe, perhaps inspired by his involvement with Töpffer's *Obadiah Oldbuck*, George Cruikshank soon created several sequential comic books of his own. These too found their way to America. *The Bachelor's Own Book*, published first in Britain in 1844, became the second known U.S. published sequential comic book when it was reprinted by Burgess, Stringer and Company the following year. Next was Cruikshank's masterpiece *The Bottle*, the Hogarthian-style tale of a man whose addiction to alcohol brings himself and his family to ruin. After debuting in London in 1847, it was reprinted the same year in a British-American co-publication between David Bogue and Americans Wiley and Putnam. Both printings were in huge folio form, available in either black and white or professionally hand-tinted versions. In 1848, the story saw American print again, this time in smaller form, placed at the front of the otherwise prose volume *Temperance Tales; Or, Six Nights with the Washing-tonians*. It continued to be reprinted by a variety of publishers into the early 20th Century. *The Bottle* was even reproduced onto painted glass slides and then projected by magic lantern onto a screen for the moral edification of temperance audiences. *The Drunkard's Children, Cruikshank's sequel to The Bottle*, was issued July 1, 1848 as a British-American-Australian co-publishing venture, but was less successful, and had not nearly as many reprints.

The Adventures of Obadiah Oldbuck, rare newly discovered 4th edition from mid 1850s. Says now "Published at Brother Jonathan Offices." Art & Story now accredited to the pseudonym "Timothy Crayon" - see Peter Piper ad previous page.

***The Strange and Wonderful Adventures of Bachelor Butterfly** by Rodolphe Töpffer (New York, 1846) was America's 3rd comic book; Wilson & Company's second comic book, this time out staying with the original European format.*

The most clearly sequential, as well as fun, of George Cruikshank's comic books was *The Tooth-Ache*, first issued in London in 1849. It was reprinted in America later that same year by Philadelphia map maker J.L. Smith. An additional concurrent version was also issued from Boston.

When closed, this booklet appears an unassuming 5-1/4 inches tall by 3-1/4 inches wide. Its striking feature is that the book folds open accordion style, stretching the entire 43-panel story along one single strip of paper, which when fully extended is seven feet, three inches long! *The Tooth-Ache* was issued in both black and white and professionally hand-colored editions. Abridged editions of the story, printed in black and white and with a "normal" page-turning rather than foldout presentation, appeared inside promotional giveaway comics issued by American companies in the 1880s.

Thanks to Töpffer, Cruikshank, and a handful of enterprising American publishers, the 1840s should be remembered as the decade when America first fell in love with the comics. It had seen the U.S. publication of six sequential comic books, as well as the importation of other comics with foreign imprints. America's growing interest in graphic humor was further stimulated by the growth of two other fields: the cartoon broadside and the humor magazine.

As mentioned before, the cartoon broadside had been a part of the American scene since pre-Revolution days, but it did not flourish until stone lithography (introduced in 1818 and in wide use by the 1830s) made the reproduction of images relatively fast and cheap. From the early 1830s into the mid 1840s, the leading producer of cartoon broadsides in America was New York printer H. R. Robinson, who either drew his own cartoons or employed others, especially E. W. Clay, to do it. Clay is notable for having produced the first sequential comic broadside in America. Published in 1834 and entitled, "This Is the House that Jack Built" (50 x 32 cm), the nine-panel parody of the classic nursery rhyme was an attack on the Jackson Administration. The dominant theme of American cartoon broadsides was political, as befitted a nation where politics was the leading spectator sport. As the American electorate grew increasingly educated and prosperous, the demand for cartoon broadside also increased. During the 1840s, lithographers in New York, Boston, and Philadelphia, entered the field to satisfy that demand. The best known of these, Nathaniel Currier, later Currier and Ives, joined the fray in 1848. The firm employed many artists, but its chief political cartoonist was Louis Maurer and its chief comic artist was Thomas Worth.

Except for the three previously cited sequential cartoon broadsides, nearly all of the cartoon broadsides published in America from 1832 to 1876, its dominant era, were single panels. From the 1860s onward, broadside series on a single comic theme became common, the most famous being Thomas Worth's *Darktown* series. These can be loosely categorized as sequential comics since they employed the same characters and formed a story of sorts when hung together on a wall, as was the publisher's expectation. Sequential art or not, the cartoon broadsides nearly always employed the speech balloons that later became one of the defining characteristic of the American comic strip.

During the same decade that sequential comics and cartoon broadsides were growing in popularity, the illustrated American humor magazine made its debut. The British comic weekly *Punch*, founded in 1841, was an immediate success, both in England and the United States. It was a handsomely printed quarto, initially twelve pages and later sixteen, with a repeating cover design, backed by a page of small advertisements, humorous text interspersed with comic spot art, and a single panel full-page cartoon. A significant subset of *Punch*'s subscriber base was located in the U.S., to which thousands of copies were exported on an ongoing trans-Atlantic basis. Inevitably, enterprising American publishers attempted to repulse this invader with a home-grown comic weekly. The first, *Yankee Doodle*, came to town (New York, that is) on October 10, 1846, for one year. *Judy* (November 28, 1846 to February 20, 1847), *The John-Donkey* (January 1 to October 21, 1848), and *The Elephant* (January 22 to February 19, 1848) soon followed. None of them was successful, but all of them continued to feed the growing American interest in comic art.

By the late 1840s, comic art was flourishing in America. The conditions were right for the production of the earliest known American-created sequential comic book. Brothers James and Donald Read, who had worked for a time as cartoonists on *Yankee Doodle*, were the creators of *Journey to the Gold Diggins by Jeremiah Saddlebags*. This spirited send-up of the California gold rush craze was published in June 1849 by Stringer and Townsend, the late publishers of *Judy*, and, soon after, by U. P. James of Cincinnati. This Töpffer-influenced comic book chronicles the adventures of its hero *Jeremiah Saddlebags* in his get-rich-quick quest for gold in California. It is highly sought by collectors of Western Americana. Interestingly, the back cover of the Stringer and Townsend edition carries an advertisement for *Rose and Gertrude* - a Genevese Story, one of Rodolphe Töpffer's non-comics prose novels.

Stringer and Townsend was making something of a name for itself as a publisher of comic art. It will be remembered that it was one of the 1845 participants in the American publication of *The Bachelor's Own Book*. And, then, in 1846-47, it published *Judy*. Its decision to issue *Jeremiah Saddlebags* was all in due course.

The Gold Rush proved to be a gold mine for American comic artists. Aside from being a featured topic in the 1849 edition of David Claypool Johnston's *Scraps*, in comic almanacs, and in Currier cartoon prints, it was the subject of several other significant sequential series. The first, *The Adventures of Mr. Tom Plump* (a fat man who nearly starves to death in his failed attempt at California Gold riches), saw print in 1850. The second, *The Adventures of Jeremiah Old-Pot* (a twelve-part burlesque narrative of a New York businessman who attempts to get rich selling tin in price-inflated California), ran throughout 1852 in *Yankee Notions*. Though the narrative was distinctly American in its humor, the artwork was probably German in origin. *Yankee Notions*' Publisher, T. W. Strong, built his business on recycling old woodcuts with new captions attached. It should be noted that the *Old-Pot* series, borrowed or otherwise, was the first sequential art to appear in an American humor magazine. *Yankee Notions*, published from 1852 to 1875, also has the distinction of being the first comic monthly published in America.

"Moses Keyser the Bowery Bully's Trip to the California Gold Mines," was a 13-page comic story that appeared in *Elton's Californian Comic All-My-Nack* for 1850. It was reprinted at least twice in the circa 1850-51 booklet *The Clown, Or The Banquet of Wit* and later again in *Sam Slick's Comic Almanac* in 1857. *The Clown* is also notable as the earliest known anthology of sequential comics, with the bonus that each multi-panel story is by a different artist. Many of the artists are as yet unidentified, and how much of it is original American material versus that reprinted from Europe is presently unknown. But verified are cartoons by George Cruikshank, Elton (American), the Read brothers, Grandville (French), and Richard Doyle (British). The Doyle contribution reprints the comics story "Brown, Jones and Robinson and How They Went to a Ball," which originally saw print in the August 24, 1850 issue of *Punch*. This is the first known American appearance of these Doyle characters, and was almost certainly pirated.

Richard Doyle's *The Foreign Tour of Messrs. Brown, Jones, and Robinson* is basically a travelogue in illustrated form, told via humorous episodes, part sequential cartoon sequences, and part snapshots of moments jumping forward in time. This halfway sequential format was ideal for most 19th Century cartoonists, who, with rare exception, had not quite grasped how to maintain a single sequential story for much longer than two dozen successive panels. Doyle had simplified Töpffer's formula in a manner most artists could attempt to emulate. Episodes of "*Brown, Jones, and Robinson*" originally appeared in *Punch* in 1850, until a dispute between the Roman Catholic Doyle and Punch's editors over an anti-Papal joke ended with Doyle's resignation. Doyle redrew and expanded the story into a single album, first seeing print in 1854 from British publisher Bradbury and Evans.

New York Publisher D. Appleton brought the album to America, reprinting it in 1860, 1871, and 1877. Next, Dick and Fitzgerald of New York pirated Doyle's story sometime in the early 1870s. Doyle's format from *Foreign Tour* was emulated again and again. Examples include: the 1857 *Mr. Hardy Lee, His Yacht*, by Charles Stedman; the 1860s- 1870s G. W. Carleton-published *Our Artist In...* series, set in various Latin American countries; the Augustus Hoppin 1870s sketch novels *On the Nile, Crossing the Atlantic*, and *Ups and Downs on Land and Water*; and *Life* founder John Ames Mitchell's 1881 (pre-Life) *The Summer School of Philosophy at Mt. Desert*. D. Appleton, the official, authorized American publisher of *Foreign Tour*, even commissioned an American artist - Toby - to create a sequel comic album involving Doyle's characters visiting the U.S. and Canada, published in 1872 as *The American Tour of Messrs Brown, Jones and Robinson*. In terms of influencing the development of mid-19th Century American comics, Doyle's *Foreign Tour* ranks with the works of Töpffer, Cruikshank, and Busch.

Doyle was also the author of an equally popular earlier cartoon series for Punch, titled, *In Manners and Customs of Ye Englyshe, Mr. Pips Hys Diary*, which was reprinted in 1849. In this work, Doyle told his story using a deliberately primitive almost stick-figure art style, combined with the Hogarthian structure of large single panel cartoons leaping forward in time with each picture.

Manners and Customs of Ye Harvard Studente, which ran in the first year of the *Harvard Lampoon* (1876-current), shows the clearest influence. The series by then student Francis Gilbert Attwood was collected in 1877 by Houghton Mifflin. Attwood followed it up with *Manners and Customs of Ye Bostonians*, again in the pages of the *Harvard Lampoon*, but it is unknown whether that series was ever reprinted in book form. Attwood later became one of the regular artists in *Life*.

The Extraordinary and Mirth-provoking Adventures by Sea and Land of Oscar Shanghai, inspired by Bachelor Butterfly, was issued May 1855 by Garrett and Company, Publishers, No. 18 Ann Street, New York. Oscar Shanghai has many misadventures including being swallowed by a whale, making a trip in a flying machine to Africa, where he is shot out of a huge bow by a "Black Prince" for refusing to marry a local princess of color. After more adventures, he makes it back home.

Oscar Shanghai's first publisher was confirmed in 2002 with the discovery of a very rare 36-page catalog from 1856 of books, pamphlets and prints handled by B.H. Day (successor to Wilson and Company) who was by this time publishing *Brother Jonathan* as a twice-a-year holiday pictorial only. The catalog has a few crossover advertisement pages from an associate publisher, Garrett and Company. This rediscovered treasure, which sold for $750 in 2002, contains within a sequential strip of one panel per page over 32 of those pages titled *"Peter Piper in Bengal,"* by John Tenniel, reprinted from four 1853 issues of *Punch*. In the narrative, Peter Piper tries his hand hunting all different kinds of wild game with many misadventures.

Amongst the many varied types of "Cheap Books" for sale in this rare catalog are the comic books *The Adventures of Obadiah Oldbuck, Bachelor Butterfly's Queer Love Adventures and Misfortunes*, and *The Fortunes of Ferdinand Flipper*, plus the aforementioned *Oscar Shanghai*. All were priced at "25¢ per copy, postage free, refunds paid out in stamps." There is also an advertisement for a comic book entitled *A Day's Sport - Or, Hunting Adventures of S. Winks Wattles, a Shopkeeper, Thomas Titt, a "legal gent," and Major Nicholas Noggin, a Jolly Good Fellow Generally* by Henry L. Stephens (1824-1882) of Philadelphia.

Stephens, later the political cartoonist for *Vanity Fair* (New York, 1859-1863) and a leading children's book illustrator, produced his first work, *Illustrations of the Poets: From Passages in the Life of Little Billy Vidkins*, a small wrappered album of 32 comic woodcuts, in 1849. It was first published by S. Robinson, of Philadelphia, and reprinted with variant titles several times in the 1850s including *Yankee Notions*. It is likely that Little *Billy Vidkins* was printed before *Jeremiah Saddlebags*, though more research is needed before making this claim.

Garrett and Company was also responsible for the 1856 publication of *The Sad Tale of the Courtship of Chevalier Slyfox-Wikof, Showing His Heart-Rending Astounding and Most Wonderful Love Adventures with Fanny Elssler and Miss Gambol*. This book parodied the very public relationship between the then-famous wealthy American aristocrat Henry Wikoff, and the even more famous European actress/ dancer Fanny Elssler. It is dated thusly because Wikoff's memoir is pictured in the comic book.

Apparently in late 1854 Garrett and Company formed a brief two-year partnership with Dick and Fitzgerald, officially becoming Garrett, Dick and Fitzgerald in November 1856, while continuing to operate out of the same 18 Ann Street address in New York. One month later they issued Richard Doyle's British published graphic novel *The Foreign Tour of Messrs. Brown, Jones, and Robinson,* reformatting it into the same oblong shape as Garrett's two prior comic books (which in turn were formatted in imitation of Töpffer's albums). This information came to light just this year. The interested scholar is encouraged to check out the new listings for Garrett's The Home Circle in the index.

In 1858, Garrett appears to have dropped out, leaving Dick and Fitzgerald alone with the former's book stock, his place of business, and most importantly, the printing plates for his comic books. For reasons unknown, Dick and Fitzgerald steered away from reprinting Garrett's comic books for more than a decade. But in the 1870s they resumed publication - not only of the three albums published by Garrett, but also of *Obadiah Oldbuck and Bachelor Butterfly* from Wilson and Company, and *Ferdinand Flipper* from *Brother Jonathan* - all of them also making use of the original printing plates. The inclusion of books from *Brother Jonathan*, Wilson and Company, and Garrett and Company all within the same promotional Peter Piper catalog from B.H. Day suggests that these early publishers of comic books had many over-lapping fields of interest,, and that Dick and Fitzgerald became the inheritor/acquirer of all of it. Dick and Fitzgerald also reprinted in the 1870s the earlier William T. Peter published *Ichabod Academicus* (how that title might have connected, if at all, with B.H. Day's business remains unclear). We can now say, though, that an evolving group of a handful of publishers was responsible, over a span of 46 years, beginning with the very first graphic novel published in America in 1842, for keeping in print in America a cluster of slightly over half a dozen graphic novels.

Tebbel's *History of Book Publishing* in the US (vol. 1, pages 351-2) states that Burgess and Stringer was dissolved in late 1840s and became two firms, Stringer and Townsend, and Burgess and Garrett. Burgess retired in 1850 and his nephew William Brisbane Dick stepped into the partnership, whereupon the new company was renamed Garrett, Dick and Fitzgerald. Garrett retired in 1851 and the firm became Dick and Fitzgerald. The firm persisted under that name until 1917.

Collections reprinting cartoons from Punch saw print in the U.S., such as *Merry Pictures by the Comic Hands*, imported for the 1859 Christmas Season, plus various John Leech, George Du Maurier, and Phil May books which appeared from the 1850s through 1910s. Finally, many American weekly newspapers and weekly and monthly magazines, humorous and non-humorous, reprinted cartoons from Punch. Such inclusions often became a prelude to switching to original material by American artists, if that publication find's cartoon section find American cartoonists of sufficient talent.

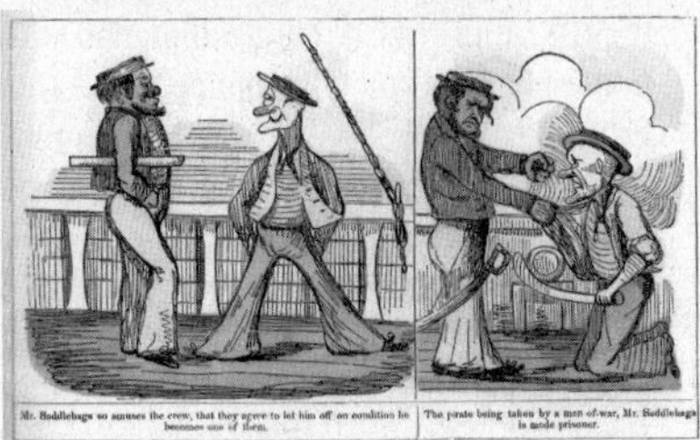

Journey to the Gold Diggins By Jeremiah Saddlebags, June 1849, so far the earliest known sequential comic book by American creators, J.A. and D.F. Read. Above: a couple sample pages. Note similarity to Töpffer's comics especially **Bachelor Butterfly**

Harper's Monthly, the leading American monthly, was a prime example. Soon after it commenced publication in November 1850, it began to carry a few pages of single panel cartoons reprinted from *Punch* at the rear of each issue. This evolved into reprinting sequential comic pages from the British periodical *Town Talk*, and then, starting December 1853, original sequential comics by the great Frank Bellew.

Bellew (1828-1888) should be regarded as the "Father of American Sequential Comics." Born in India, educated in France and England, he emigrated to America in 1850. His earliest work shows an influence from Doyle, but he rapidly developed his own unique art style. Bellew's comics, both sequential and single panel, graced nearly every American comic periodical published from the 1850s into the 1870s.

A month after the publication of the anonymous first installment of *Jeremiah Old-Pot* in *Yankee Notions*, Bellew began contributing his six-part, 18-panel comic series, *"Mr. Blobb in Search of a Physician"* to *The Lantern*, a New York comic weekly published from January 10, 1852 to July 2, 1853. The series ran in six of the nine issues published from January 31 through March 27, 1852. This was followed in April and May by the 16-panel, three-issue comic sequence *"Mr. Bulbear's Dream"*, which concluded with the main character awakened from his dream by falling out of bed, exactly like *Little Nemo* would do five decades later.

These two series were just the beginning for Bellew, who contributed a voluminous amount of work to the *New York Picayune* (1850-1860) (which he also edited for a time in 1857-58), *The Comic Monthly* (1859-1881), *Momus*, an 1860 comic daily, *The Phunniest of Awl* (1864-1867) (which he also edited), *Punchinello* (1870), and *Wild Oats* (1870-1881), to name the most prominent.

The Comic Monthly deserves special mention. Started in March 1859 and published by J. C. Haney and Company, of 119 Nassau Street, New York, *The Comic Monthly* was a profusely illustrated 16-page folio, the same size as *Harper's Weekly*. It focused its graphic satire on politics, the theater, and the comedy of everyday life. A preponderance of the purely comic satire took the form of sequential art. Here are random samplings of highlights from issues from 1860:

• February: "A Day of Humiliation, Fasting, Supplica-tion, and Prayer (four panels, unsigned), "New Year Calls under the Influence of Hard Times" (twelve panels, unsigned), "Young Trouble-some; or, Master Jacky's Holidays" (nineteen panels covering three and half pages, unsigned);

• April: "Four Years After Marriage" (sixteen panels, unsigned), "Our Masked Ball" (twelve panel centerspread, Bellew), "Trials of a Witness" (eight panels, Bellew);

• May: "Precocities of Young Springles" (seven panels, unsigned), "The Fight for the Championship" (twenty-four panel centerspread, Bellew), "Steam Applied to Music" (three panels, unsigned), "The Course of True Love" (four panels, Bellew);

• June: "Further Particulars of the Fight" (nine panel cover, Bellew), "The Man Who Went to See the Fight" (twelve panels, unsigned);

• July: "Explaining American Politics to an Intelligent Foreigner" (twelve panels, unsigned), "The Meerschaum Mania" (two panels, Bellew), "The Art of Stump Speaking" (ten panels, unsigned), "Our Little Friend, Tom Noddy" (three panels, unsigned); "The Japanese in New York" (twelve panel centerspread, Bellew), "The Observant Child" (three panels, unsigned), "Mr. Dibbs Goes to Pike's Peak and Comes Back Again" (fourteen panel back cover, unsigned);

• September: "The Zouave Fever" (four panel cover, unsigned), "Mr. Lupell" (two panels, Bellew), "The Prince of Wales in America" (twenty-four panel centerspread, J. H. Howard), "D'ye Think It's True?" (three panels, Bellew);

• October: "The Duties of the Wide Awake" (four panels, Bellew), "Our Charley (two panels, unsigned), "The Three Young Friends" (eighteen panel back cover, unsigned);

• November: "The Hanlon's (sic) At Home" (nine panel back cover, unsigned);

• December: "The Target Excursion" (seventeen panel centerspread, signed with an unidentifiable monogram); "The Sporting Critic" two panels, Bellew).

The Comic Monthly also published many multi-panel cartoons grouped under a single heading, which were not strictly sequential in nature. Bellew was the monthly's chief artist, assisted by Thomas Nast, A. R Waud, and others. Some of the unsigned art was certainly by Bellew, some by journeymen artists, and some of it pirated from European journals.

The Comic Monthly was not the first folio-sized humor magazine. Those laurels go to *The New York Picayune,* which began as a newspaper, switched to a folio in 1856, adopted *Punch's* format for thirty-five issues in 1857-58, and returned to a folio for the remainder of its run.

Frank Leslie's *Budget of Fun*, the greatest of the folio monthlies, began in January 1859 and was published until June 1878. Its star cartoonist during the sixties was William Newman (c. 1817-1870), one of the founding artists of Punch. As we have noted, *The Comic Monthly* began two months later.

Frank Leslie was born Henry Cart in Ipswich, England in 1821. He became a very skilled engraver before coming over to

Yankee Notions #1, January, 1852. This title began the first sequential comic strips in an American humor magazine, The Adventures of Jerimiah Old-Pot.

America in 1948. He first worked as manager for P.T. Barnum's *New York Illustrated News* for several years. in 1850 he legally had his name changed to Frank Leslie. He died in 1880 and his wife continued the numerous publications he was publishing. Many of Frank Leslie's periodicals had a lot of sequental comic art.

Quarto-sized monthlies to compete with the successful *Yankee Notions* were also proliferating. *Nick-Nax* was the first (May 1856 to December 1875), followed by *Phunny Phellow* (October 1859- 1876) and *Merryman's Comic Monthly* (January 1863 to December 1875), to name the most prominent.

Enterprising publishers continued to attempt an American comic weekly in the style of *Punch*. The most notable efforts, *Vanity Fair* (1859-1863), *Mrs. Grundy* (1865), and *Punchinello* (1870), were distinguished but unsuccessful.

Nearly all of them, weeklies and monthlies, to varying degrees, featured sequential comic art. By the time of the American Civil War, sequential comic art was a part of the American graphic landscape.

While Bellew stood out for his sequential comics, Thomas Nast (1840-1902) brought a new style to American political cartoons, of which he is regarded the father. Even though he created several sequential strips early in his career (especially for Nick-Nax in 1859), Nast made his name in the pages of the national news periodical, *Harper's Weekly*, for which he worked from 1862 until 1886. Nast was influenced more by the dark wood engravings of Franco-German illustrator Gustave Dore than by the cartoonists of *Punch*. His somber cartoons were a novelty in American cartooning. Nast in the pages of *Harper's Weekly* (and Newman in the pages of the *Budget of Fun*) popularized the extravagant double-page folio-sized cartoon, which had no precedent in European or American cartooning, save for the separately published cartoon broadsides. This format would come to full maturity after 1876 in the pages of *Puck* (1876-1918) and then *Judge* (1881-1947).

As Nast grew in prominence and success, American cartoonists increasingly emulated him. U.S. humor publications evolved towards an amalgamation of Nast and Punch, rather than sheer imitation of the latter. After the War, with Nast's style of cartoons more entrenched in American readers' minds, efforts to launch *Punch*-like American periodicals floundered quickly. *Mrs. Grundy*, ironically most famous for its cover design by Nast, died after a mere twelve issues (running July 8 to September 23, 1865). *Punchinello* (April 2 to December 24, 1870) struggled nine months before its backers gave up. *Punchinello* had been financed by Tammany Hall politicians Tweed and Sweeney, as counter-propaganda against Nast's ongoing assault upon their corruption. They attempted to buy and threaten Nast into silence, to no avail.

American comics continued their pull away from Anglo-Franco imitation with the infusion of a third major European influence – the German humor magazine. The German-American community swelled significantly after the failed revolution of 1848. These émigrés brought with them a culture of humor, expressed most flamboyantly in their native humor magazines, the most famous being *Kladderadatsch, Fliegende Blätter*, and *Münchener Bilderbogen*. As high in quality, as were the graphic artists who contributed to them, one German comic artist in particular excelled beyond the rest, his stories breaking out and crossing over into English language translations, the demand for which resulted in numerous printings. This artist, of course, was Heinrich Christian Wilhelm Busch (1832-1908).

Busch's work appeared in English in the 1860s in both British and American periodicals, often uncredited. For example, four of Busch's strips appeared in English in the pages of *Merryman's Monthly* in 1864, while in 1879 his graphic story "Fipps der Affe" was serialized across a 10-issue run of Puck as "Troddledums the Simian." The earliest known English language appearance of Busch in book form was *The Flying Dutchman, or The Wrath of Herr von Stoppelnoze*, in 1862, from New York publisher G. W. Carleton. Carleton not only pirated Busch's strip, but went so far as to credit the entire story to American poet John G. Saxe, with Busch's cartoons mere illustrations accompanying Saxe's prose!

The next known English language Busch book was **A** *Bushel of Merry Thoughts*, an 1868 London-published anthology collecting various Busch strips. Some of these same stories later appeared in the U.S.-published *The Mischief Book* (1880), newly translated and with a few more Busch tales added. One of these additions was "Hans Huckebein," a tale of a mischievous pet raven who in the end gets drunk and accidentally hangs himself. It became, at least in the States, Busch's second most popular sequential comic story. The unrepentant bird was promoted to title character in two later collections: the rare *Hookeybeak the Raven and Other Tales* in 1878 and *Jack Huckaback, the Scapegrace Raven*, circa 1888. There were also at least three trade card series in the 1870s and 1880s that reprinted the ending sequence, as *Fritz Spindle-Shanks, The Raven Black*.

The most popular Busch tale, though, was easily Max und Moritz, which in the U.S. saw print as *Max and Maurice - A Juvenile History in Seven Tricks*. Published in Boston in 1871, this English language version saw at minimum of 60 reprintings by the century's end, plus countless more printings thereafter. A separate British translation debuted in 1874, under the title *Max and Moritz*. It is well known that the later Rudolph Dirks comic strip series, Katzenjammer Kids, beginning in late

1897, was based on *Max und Moritz*.

According to documents found by comics historian Alfredo Castelli, *Katzenjammer Kids* may not have been pirated as has been assumed but was licensed by William Randolph Hearst instead. Hearst's *New York Journal* was published in different language editions for New York City's immigrant communities. In the German edition, the strip was published under its original name, *Max und Moritz*. Numerous other translations of Busch were published in America - too many to name in this article. Several can be found in the Victorian Age Price Index.

The most significant humor magazine of the 1870s, prior to the founding of the German-language *Puck* in 1876, was *Wild Oats* (1870-1881), which for part of its run also published a German-language edition, *Schnedereddeng*. In terms of the quality of its cartoons and comics, this New York City publication was in 1872 at an artistic level *Puck* would not achieve until 1880. Published by Winchell and Small (later Collin and Small) and distributed through the New York News Company, *Wild Oats* carried a cross-section of old and new generation comic artists, from the more established W. M. Avery, Frank Beard, Frank Bellew, E.S. Bisbee, Michael Angelo Woolf, and Thomas Worth, to up-and-comers such as Livingston Hopkins, Frederick Burr Opper, Palmer Cox, and James A. Wales.

Wild Oats began carrying sequential comic strips as early as #26, dated March 14, 1872, with the Livingston Hopkins strip pictured on the next page (we do not know anything yet about the first 25 issues). The very next issue has a Worth double-page spread titled "The Political Humpty Dumpty... Horace Greeley" told in eleven panels plus the sequential fictional "Graphic Account of the Assassination of Queen Victoria" and "Love As the Angels Love." "The Doings of the Japanese Embassy At Washington" related in twelve panels by W. M. Avery follows up in #28 April 11, 1872. An unknown hand drew "The Physiology of Moving" in six panels in #30. Hopkins returns with a beautiful intense 28-panel double-page spread in #31 May 23. Hopkins and Worth alternated for many issues with sequential comic strips on baseball, horse racing and other pertinent subjects of the day. In #45 December 5, 1872, E.S. Bisbee contributed his first sequential in seventeen panels and Worth showed up in "Humor and Pathos of a New England Thanksgiving" in eleven panels. Issue 47 expands the concept with a twelve-panel job by Bisbee, twenty-panel effort on one page by Hopkins and a three-panel effort by Worth. And on it goes through 1873 as well - comic strip after comic strip. Issue 58 June 5, 1873, includes a particularly humorous nineteen-panel double-pager drawn by someone still unknown titled "The Terrible Adventures of Messrs. Buster and Stumps, with the Indians" which begins with two white men heading out west in an effort to exterminate Indians - and their misadventures of not quite getting the job done. It reads across both pages in a unique evolution similar to Popeye #2052 (found in the Platinum listings). Issue 65 contains two nine-panel Thomas Worth strips "Only a Mad Dog Scare - Another Lesson For Nervous People" and "Only a Cholera Scare - Something For Nervous People to Read and Ponder Over." Issue 66 Sept 18, 1873, has the very funny Hopkins twelve-panel strip as well as two more ten-panel Worth strips on the delights of Hunting and Fishing plus one by Hopkins titled "The Adventures of Mr Old Party with Jersey Mosquitoes" in twelve-panels. All told, four comic strips in this issue. They obviously liked what they were doing, judging from the exuberance of the work.

The next issue has Worth's nine-panel report on "The Adventures of Young Muttonhead among the Free Lovers" which was all about the "free sex" convention recently held in Chicago. Issue 68 has a nine-panel "An Adventure with a New Jersey Mosquito" which smacks of Winsor McCay in subject and even art style. Maybe McCay was inspired by this for his later animated cartoon as well as earlier Rarebit Fiend. We'll never know for sure. On through 1875, *Wild Oats* presented sequential comic strips issue after issue. With #148, October 27, 1875, Frederick Opper contributes his very first Wild Oats cover, a political cartoon on inflation then rampant in the US. He does covers through at least #161 before a short break and then comes back with many more. In #158, January 5, 1876, Palmer Cox - some five years before inventing The Brownies - begins a wonderful series of 24-panel double page spread comic strips, with a couple sample titles being "The Adventures of Mr. and Mrs. Sprowl And Their Christmas Turkey-A Crashing Chasing Tearful Tragedy But Happily Ending Well" and "Bachelor Broke and Widow Snuggi: A Pictorial Account of Their Sleigh Ride and What Became of It."

Even though he had been contributing many covers and interior single panel jobs to *Wild Oats* for years, Frank Bellew does not show up with his first comic strip until #190, August 16, 1876, with a nine-panel effort he titled, "Rodger's Patent Mosquito Armour." By this time America's "Father of the sequential comic strip" had inspired many other cartoonists to try their hand telling stories with words and pictures.

Another highly desirable American graphic novel, sought especially by collectors of Western lore, is *Quiddities of an Alaskan Trip* by William H. Bell which debuted in 1873. Bell was Timothy O'Sullivan's assistant photographer on the 1871-74 expeditions of Lt. George Wheeler, surveying and mapping the western territories for the U.S. government. The story panels are laid out within ornate frames like those of stereograph cards, such as Bell was involved in creating on the expedition. It involves a parody of a trip from Washington, D.C., to survey the newly purchased territory of Alaska, which at the time was derisively referred to as "Seward's Folly." Bell published *Quiddities* in Portland, Oregon, in 1873, meaning that he drew it while he was on just such an expedition.

The seemingly disparate influences of Thomas Nast and German comics came together in the work of Austrian immigrant Joseph Keppler (1838-1894). Like many cartoonists in America, Keppler desired to rival Nast. Unlike most, he possessed the talent and drive to accomplish it. Keppler, trained as an artist but working as an actor, began contributing comic art to *Kikeriki* (1861-1923) in his native Vienna. He emigrated to St. Louis in 1868, where he took his first stab at starting a comic weekly, the German language *Die Vehme* (Aug 28, 1869 - Aug. 20, 1870). Seven months later, still in St. Louis, he tried again, launching another German language humor periodical, titled *Puck*. This German *Puck* began on March 18, 1871, joined by an English language version one year later, but both ended on Aug. 24, 1872.

Keppler moved to New York City and began working for Frank Leslie. His cartoons appeared in *Frank Leslie's Illustrated Newspaper*, Frank Leslie's *Budget of Fun*, and the Leslie-owned *Jolly Joker* and *Day's Doings*. (To capitalize on the 1876 Centennial Exposition in Philadelphia, Leslie published in that year a paperback collection of Centennial-related humor, *Centennial Fun*, most of which was Keppler's work.) Four years after the first *Puck* died, Keppler was ready to try again. He re-launched the German language edition of *Puck* in New York City on September 27, 1876.

This *Puck* was both familiar and exotic. Its format of an extravagant centerspread cartoon sandwiched between front and back cover cartoons had by this time become something of a comic periodical standard, certainly for the monthlies. But *Puck* was different from what had come before. The cartoons were lithographed, not engraved, which lent to them a softer, more pleasing quality, and they were in color, something virtually without precedent in American comic periodical literature.

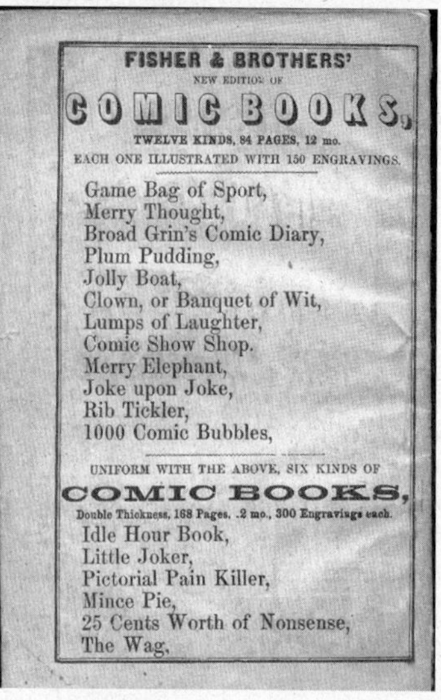

FISHER & BROTHERS'
NEW EDITION OF
COMIC BOOKS,
TWELVE KINDS, 84 PAGES, 12 mo.
EACH ONE ILLUSTRATED WITH 150 ENGRAVINGS.

Game Bag of Sport,
Merry Thought,
Broad Grin's Comic Diary,
Plum Pudding,
Jolly Boat,
Clown, or Banquet of Wit,
Lumps of Laughter,
Comic Show Shop.
Merry Elephant,
Joke upon Joke,
Rib Tickler,
1000 Comic Bubbles,

UNIFORM WITH THE ABOVE, SIX KINDS OF
COMIC BOOKS,
Double Thickness, 168 Pages, .2 mo., 300 Engravings each.
Idle Hour Book,
Little Joker,
Pictorial Pain Killer,
Mince Pie,
25 Cents Worth of Nonsense,
The Wag,

Earliest-known use of the description COMIC BOOKS dates from the early 1850s.

Initially, the magazine's cartoons were tinted in just one color, but *Puck* appeared, ambitiously, every week, and the coloring set it apart from anything else on American stands. The parallel English language edition of *Puck* was launched six months after the German version, on March 14, 1877. This English edition of *Puck* was a money-loser for several years, kept afloat by the German edition's profits and the determination of the English edition's literary editor, H.C. Bunner, not to give up. By 1880, *Puck* was a huge success. It became the new model for American humor publications. In time, Keppler hired other artists, most notably Frederick Burr Opper, Eugene Zimmerman ("Zim") and F. M. Howarth, and added black and white sequential comics to the magazine's interior and then, with increasing frequency in the early 1890s to the magazine's back cover. *Funny Folks* by F. M. Howarth, 1899, collected many early sequential comics from *Puck;* one of the titles many consider bridges the Victorian and Platinum Ages of comics. *Puck* was the model that inspired William Randolph Hearst to add a color comics section to his Sunday Journal in 1895.

With the first issue dated October 29, 1881, *Puck's* chief rival, *Judge*, was born. Founded by *Puck* artist James A. Wales, it also featured the work of Thomas Worth and Livingston Hopkins. *Judge* made several forays into *Puck*'s talent pool over the years. Its best capture was Eugene Zimmerman ("Zim"), who became for Judge the star artist that Frederick Burr Opper was for Puck.

Judge struggled financially for several years, and likely would have ceased publication had it not been for Puck's powerful performance during the 1884 election. *Puck*'s success galvanized Republican powerbrokers into recognizing the importance of the political cartoon weekly. They financed newspaperman W. J. Arkell's purchase of *Judge* in 1886 to turn it into a reliable Republican house organ.

Also worthy of mention is the New York City newspaper *The Daily Graphic* (March 4, 1873 to Sept 23, 1889), which claims the distinction of being the first regularly illustrated daily newspaper in the world, published every day except Sundays and holidays. The majority of its illustrations were portraits or depictions of news events, but nearly every issue contained some comic drawing, many of them gracing the front cover.

With so many pages to fill on a daily basis, *The Daily Graphic* became a rotating door for many young American cartoonists in the early stages of their careers (making one suspect that it was not the best paying gig in town). Within its pages, like needles to be found in the haystack of its more than 4800 issues, is early work by Livingston Hopkins (who mysteriously appears, vanishes, reappears, etc., for months to whole years at a time, right up to his 1884 departure to Australia), pre-*Life* work by Kemble, pre-*Harper*'s appearances by A.B. Frost and W.A. Rogers, pre-Puck and Judge Opper, C.J. Taylor, Hamilton, and Gillam. Old hats, too, appear at times, such as Michael Woolf and Frank Bellew, Sr.

Further, *The Daily Graphic* regularly plundered British periodicals for its back and sometimes center pages, not only perpetrating the usual swipes of single-panel *Punch* cartoons, but also stealing sequential strips from Punch's two main rival publications, *Judy* and *Fun*. This included occasionally reprinting (albeit at random) episodes of continuing British strips "The British Workman" by James Sullivan, and "McNab of that Ilk" by James Brown, though, strangely enough, not Marie Duval's *Ally Sloper*, despite the fact that *The Daily Graphic* did reprint some of Duval's non-"Sloper" strips. ("Ally Sloper" was a continuing sequential strip character who debuted in 1867, lasting into the 1920s, and had very successful solo British book collections of his strip appearances published as early as 1873, more than two decades prior to *Yellow Kid in McFadden*'s Flats).

Livingston Hopkins, whose art style changed like a chameleon from one year to the next, exhibited a definite Duval influence in his work within a year following the publication of the first *Ally Sloper* collection. Given that Hopkins worked for *The Daily Graphic* during the same period in which this newspaper was stealing cartoons from *Sloper*'s home publication, *Judy*, this can hardly be considered coincidental. Hopkins contributed a daily comic strip to *The Daily Graphic* in 1874-75, complete with word balloons. By the time Hopkins was preparing to emigrate to Australia to become lead cartoonist for the Sydney Bulletin, his art style was an imitation of Kemble's, who was also working at *The Daily Graphic.*

Life debuted on January 4, 1883, founded by J.A. Mitchell, and modeled after the Harvard Lampoon. It quickly rose to become the third main pillar of late 1800s American humor periodicals. Smaller in size, black and white, and priced the same as *Puck* and *Judge*, it nevertheless succeeded by appealing to a more genteel audience. Its earliest artists included Kemble and Palmer Cox, but its foremost artist was Charles Dana Gibson, becoming world renowned as the hand behind the graceful, aristocratic "Gibson Girls."

Unlike *Judge*, which had to become a low-brow imitation of *Life* to survive in the next century, and *Puck*, which attempted but failed to become an American version of the highbrow European humor magazines, Life transitioned into the 20th century virtually unaltered, and thrived. By the mid-1880s, with *Puck, Judge*, and *Life* all solidly in place, American comics and cartoon humor had come very much into their own, no longer looking first at Europe to take their cues.

Almanacs began to appear in America starting in 1639. Humor was introduced as early as 1647 by Samuel Danforth. A very important one was *Leed Almanac* beginning in 1687. John Tulley produced the first humorous almanac in 1688. James Franklin, brother of Ben, began the *Rhode Island Almanac* in 1728 using the name "Poor Robin" and his younger brother began *Poor Richard's Almanac* in 1732. Farmer's Almanac began in 1792 and used some humor.

The first comic almanac totally devoted to humor was published by Charles Ellm in Boston in 1831 and featured the artwork of D.C. Johnston. Perhaps the most famous comic almanacs (certainly the most valuable) are the *Davy Crockett* series (1835-1856) which began in Nashville, Tennessee. The comic periodicals all ended up issuing comic almanacs beginning with *Yankee Notions* in 1856 and continuing into the 1890s with a one-shot comic almanac published by *Judge* for the year 1894.

Beginning in the 1850s, a new breed of almanacs appeared. Usually created by medicine and farm product companies, they were distributed for free to promote the company's product. Competition amongst companies, whose goal was to get customers to read the almanacs and the advertisements contained therein again and again, meant that attention-getting humorous cartoons soon found their way back into these giveaway pamphlets. Initially their cartoons were done cheap, either poorly drawn or pirated from elsewhere, such as those found in the Hostetter's and Wright's almanac series. More elaborate promotional almanacs eventually did evolve, though, and amongst the best of these was *Barker's Illustrated Almanac*, first produced for the year 1878, and annually into the 1930s. Each *Barker's Almanac* contained ten to twelve full page cartoons, wonderful and bizarre in design, frequently racist, but also comically manic and crammed with details in a manner similar to Outcault's much later *Yellow Kid* pages. The cartoons in *Barker's Almanac* were so popular that in 1892, The Barker, Moore, and Mein Medicine Company published their first edition of *Barker's Komic Picture Souvenir*, reprinting nearly 150 pages of cartoons from their almanacs.

This first *Barker's Souvenir* features a wraparound color cover depicting people headed towards the Columbian World's Fair Exposition, which was to be held in Chicago the next year. It is the earliest confirmed "premium" comic book, sent to customers who mailed in a box label and outside wrapper from two different Barker's products. The *Souvenir* album was *Barker's* most in-demand premium. It was reprinted as a thick unnumbered booklet three more times in the 1890s, with the contents reorganized each time. Later, between 1901 and 1903, *Barker's* broke the album into three separate "Parts," each of which required still more box labels and wrappers to obtain. The 3-part series of reprint albums expanded to four parts circa 1906 or 1907. Both the 3 and 4-part album series had multiple printings.

Also very American in character were the country's promotional comics, which flourished throughout the latter half of the 19th century. They trace their beginnings to Comic Almanacs, which flourished in England and the United States since they first appeared in the 1830s. The first promotional comics which did not double as almanacs began to appear in the 1870s. They included the aforementioned reprints of Cruikshank and Busch strips, reprints of strips lifted from American sources (A.B. Frost's strip "The Bull Calf" was a particular favorite), and original material placing the product being promoted as the focus of the story. These original short cartoon dramas were in many ways similar in storyline to those found in modern television advertisements, except that the clothing is Victorian, and the claims, pre-F.D.A. and F.C.C., were unabashedly wild, over-the-top, and blunt. Chewing tobacco and snuff saved romances, calmed crying babies, and made the sick well. Stove polish that propelled you to wealth and power. Corsets that brought you a husband. The objective, of course, in an era before TV or radio, was to make each comic handout so entertaining that customers would want to keep and read the advertisement again and again.

The more wonderful graphics and outrageous claims tended to come from tobacco companies, who were using comic books and strips to sell their products more than a century before cries against "Joe Camel." The most elaborate of these were printed full color, and unfolded into a single long strip, just like Cruikshank's *The Tooth-Ache* from the 1840s, though usually limited to just the cover plus seven panels.

The earliest known anthology devoted to collecting the comic strips of a single American artist was A.B. Frost's *Stuff and Nonsense* in 1884. The next known American collection came in 1888, the very rare Frederick Burr Opper anthology, *Puck's Opper Book*. Both proved popular, so more Frost and Opper collections followed, to be joined within a few years by reprints collecting the cartoons and strips of Keppler, Kemble, Zim, Gibson, Mayer, Taylor, Frank Bellew's son "Chip," Howarth, Woolf, etc.

Puck, Judge, and *Texas Siftings* all began monthly Library series - 8-1/2" x 11" magazines, mostly black and white, which organized previously published material around one theme or one artist. For example, the first *Puck's Library* (July 1887) was titled "The National Game," and gathered beneath one cover *Puck* material poking fun at the game of baseball. The third (March 1888) and ninth (November 1889) issues of *Judge's Serial (later named Judge's Library)* were devoted entirely to the work of Zim.

Life tended more towards hardcover collections, such as its annual ten-issue series *The Good Things of Life* (1884-1893), which included cartoons and strips by Palmer Cox, T.S. Sullivant, Hy Mayer, and others. *The Good Things of Life* was published initially by the firm of White, Stokes, and Allen, but which by the fourth book, had become simply Frederick A. Stokes. Stokes published a number of other cartoon books in the 1880s and 1890s, the majority of them reprint collections. The experience he gained at this time with these reprint albums placed Stokes in the perfect position to pick up the wealth of material about to be created for the comics supplements of William R. Hearst's newspapers, making Stokes the first major publisher of the coming Platinum Age.

In 1892, Charles Scribner's Sons published A. B. Frost's *Bull Calf and Other Tales*. It contains sequential comic strip art on quite a few pages as well as single panel cartoons. By 1898, Charles Scribner's Sons also issued Kemble's *The Billy Goat and Other Comicalities* as a 112-page hardcover, which also has sequential comic strips.

In the early 1890s, the slum children cartoons of artist Michael Woolf (many of which were reprinted in the 1896 collection *99 Woolfs from Truth* and in the posthumous 1899 collection *Sketches of Lowly Life in a Great City*) were popular. *Truth* magazine, which followed Puck's format of color front cover, back cover and centerspread cartoons, but in style was more akin to the aristocratic Life, was initially unable to secure Woolf's services, creating an opportunity for the young cartoonist Richard F. Outcault, who desired to break into one of the weekly comic periodicals.

It was in his Woolf-inspired slum children cartoons for *Truth* that Outcault's prototype of the *Yellow Kid* first emerged. The bald, sack-clothed youngster made four appearances in *Truth*, starting with #372 on June 2, 1894, prior to his newspaper debut.

During the rise of Yellow Kid's popularity, he appeared in American comic magazines in parodies drawn by others, with politicians, even Hearst and Pulitzer, dressed up as the *Yellow Kid*. Such cartoons are known to have appeared in *Judge, Life, The Bee*, and *Vim* plus various newspapers across the country. More about the *Yellow Kid's* importance can be found in the Platinum Age section of this book.

While comics definitely have their roots in Europe, and the earliest American comic books either reprinted or emulated those of Europe, the direction of influence was by no means one way. By at least the 1870s, American cartoons were being published and seen in the Old World, as evidenced by the arrest in Spain of the on-the-lamb corrupt Tammany Hall politician Boss Tweed by Spanish police who recognized Tweed from a Nast cartoon.

European piracy of American cartoons was just as lucrative as the American piracy of Europeans. In the 1880s and '90s, the comics of Zim, Chip Bellew, and Charles Dana Gibson all saw reprint in Europe. In April 1899, *Pictorial Comedy*, a monthly magazine destined for a ten-year run, commenced publication in London. It was made up entirely of cartoons reprinted with permission from *Puck* and *Life*. F.M. Howarth's domestic comedies from *Puck* were favorites in France. American Hy Mayer was commissioned to create original comics work for *Black and White* (Britain), *Le Rire* (France), and *Fliegende Blätter*. Michael Woolf's slum children cartoons saw print in the British periodical *Pick-Me-Up*, during the same years that top British artist Phil May's first published work debuted in that publication. May later became famous for his Woolf-inspired street children cartoons as well as his influence on the development of comics in Australia.

As the 19th Century ended, American comics were coming to the fore worldwide, soon to explode into a position of dominance with the Platinum Age revolution brought about by the emergence of the color comic supplement in America's newspapers and the arrival of Richard F. Outcault's *Yellow Kid*.

END NOTE: Victorian Era comics were issued in many relatively obscure formats compared to what most of us are used to today. The Victorian Era section can only grow as there are many more heretofore undiscovered comics from the 1800s which have fallen off the radar of history. Some may wonder why some of the earlier items listed contain as of yet no prices. The reason is simple. These books are part of a relatively "new" market which is still establishing itself.

High-grade copies are almost unheard of in almost all instances. Some books may truly have only a handful left in existence. We are sure there are some known to have been published which no (as of yet) known copies have survived the ravages of time and neglect.

Each year expect another quantum leap in our ever-expanding knowledge of the fascinating earliest origins of the comic strip as it relates to North America. Your input in helping this section of the Guide grow and mature is most welcome!

Robert Lee Beerbohm first sold comics through the legendary RBCC beginning in 1966, set up at his first comicon in 1967, helped found the northern California Comics & Comix chain of stores in August 1972, co-hosted Berkeleycon 1973, the first UG creator-owned comix con and operated comic book stores from 1972-1994. He now owns Robert Beerbohm Comic Art that specializes in buying and selling scarce comics and related material from the 1840s-1980s. He has been compiling a detailed history book of the business of the American comic book for some time now and hopes to complete it soon.

Contact Robert directly at www.BLBComics.com

Richard Olson is an Research Professor Emeritus at the University of New Orleans. He published the Richard Outcault Collector for years. Reach Richard directly at: rolsonredoak@bellsouth.net

Richard Samuel West is the author of Satire on Stone: The Political Cartoons of Joseph Keppler (University of Illinois, 1988) and The San Francisco Wasp: An Illustrate History (Periodyssey Press, 2004) and editor of several cartoon collections. He is the owner of Periodyssey, a business that specializes in buying and selling significant and unusual American magazines. Richard can be reached at:

www.oldmagazines.com

All three are life-long collectors and students of all forms of the comics who welcome corrections and additions to this concise compilation of our earliest American comics heritage dating back almost two centuries. Happy Hunting!

The American Comic Almanac #5
1835 © Charles Ellms, NYC

The Strange and Wonderful Adventures
of Bachelor Butterfly by Rodolphe Töpffer
1870s © Dick & Fitzgerald, NYC

Barker's "Komic" Picture Souvenir, 3rd Edition
1894 © Barker, Moore & Klein Medicine Co.

COLLECTOR'S NOTE: Most of the books listed in this section were published well over a century before organized comics fandom began archiving and helping to preserve these fragile popular culture artifacts. With some of these comics now over 160 years old, they almost never surface in Fine+ or better shape. Be happy when you simply find a copy.

This year has seen price growth in quite a few comic books in this era. Since this section began growing almost a decade now, comic books from Wilson, Brother Jonathan, Huestis & Cozans, Garrett, Dick & Fitzgerald, Frank Leslie, Street & Smith and others continue to be recognized by the more savvy in this fine hobby as legitimate comic book collectors' items. We had been more concerned with simply establishing what is known to exist. For the most part, that work is now a *fait accompli* in this section compiled, revised, and expanded by Robert Beerbohm with special thanks this year to Terrance Keegan plus acknowledgment to Bill Blackbeard, Chris Brown, Alfredo Castelli, Darrell Coons, Leonardo De Sá, Scott Deschaine, Joe Evans, Ron Friggle, Tom Gordon III, Michel Kempeneers, Andy Konkykru, Don Kurtz, Richard Olson, Robert Quesinberry, Joseph Rainone, Steve Rowe, Randy Scott, John Snyder, Art Spiegelman, Steve Thompson, Richard Samuel West, Doug Wheeler and Richard Wright. Special kudos to long-time collector and scholar Gabriel Laderman.

The prices given for Fair, Good and Fine categories are for strictly graded editions. If you need help grading your item, we refer you to the grading section in this book or contact the authors of this essay. Items marked Scarce, Rare or Very Rare we are still trying to figure out how many copies might still be in existence. We welcome additions and corrections from any interested collectors and scholars at robert@BLBcomics.com

For ease ascertaining the contents of each item of this listing and the Platinum index list, we offer the following list of categories found immediately following most of the titles:
E - EUROPEAN ORIGINAL COMICS MATERIAL; Printed in Europe or reprinted in USA
G - GRAPHIC NOVEL (LONGER FORMAT COMIC TELLING A SINGLE STORY)
H - "HOW TO DRAW CARTOONS" BOOKS
I - ILLUSTRATED BOOKS NOTABLE FOR THE ARTIST, BUT NOT A COMIC.
M - MAGAZINE / PERIODICAL COMICS MATERIAL REPRINTS
N - NEWSPAPER COMICS MATERIAL REPRINTS
O - ORIGINAL COMIC MATERIAL NOT REPRINTED FROM ANOTHER SOURCE
P - PROMOTIONAL COMIC, EITHER GIVEN AWAY FOR FREE, OR A PREMIUM GIVEN IN CONJUNCTION WITH THE PURCHASE OF A PRODUCT.
S - SINGLE PANEL / NON-SEQUENTIAL CARTOONS

Measurements are in inches. The first dimension given is Height and the second is Width. Some original British editions are included in the section, so as to better explain and differentiate their American counterparts.

ACROBATIC ANIMALS
R.H. Russell: 1899 (9x11-7/8", 72 pgs, B&W, hard-c)
nn (Scarce) 150.00 300.00 600.00
NOTE: *Animal strips by Gustave Verbeck, presented 1 panel per page.*

ALMY'S SANTA CLAUS (P,E)
Edward C. Almy & Co., Providence, R.I.: nd (1880's) (5-3/4x4-5/8", 20 pgs, B&W, paper-c
nn - (Rare) 12.50 40.00 80.00
NOTE: *Department store Christmas giveaway containing an abbreviated 28-panel reprinting of George Cruikshank's **The Tooth-ache**. Santa Claus cover.*

AMERICAN COMIC ALMANAC, THE (OLD AMERICAN COMIC ALMANAC 1839-1846)
Charles Ellms: 1831-1846 (5x8, 52 pgs, B&W)
1 first American comic almanac ever prrinted 600.00 1200.00 2200.00
2-16 100.00 200.00 400.00
NOTE:#1 from 1831 is the First American Comic Almanac

AMERICAN PUNCH
American Punch Publishing Co: Jan 1879-March 1881, J.A. Cummings Engraving Co (last 3 ussues) (Quarto Monthly)
Most issues 25.00 50.00 150.00

THE AMERICAN WIT
Richardson & Collins, NY: 1867-68 (18-1/2x13. 8 pgs, B&W)
2/3 Frank Bellew single panels 50.00 100.00 200.00

AMERICAN WIT AND HUMOR
Harper & Bros, NY: 1859 (
nn - numerous McLenan sequential comic strips 100.00 200.00 450.00

ATTWOOD'S PICTURES - AN ARTIST'S HISTORY OF THE LAST TEN YEARS OF THE NINETEENTH CENTURY (M,S)
Life Publishing Company, New York: 1900 (11-1/4x9-1/8", 156 pgs, B&W, gilted blue hard-c)
nn - By Attwood 40.00 80.00 160.00
NOTE: *Reprints monthly calendar cartoons which appeared in **LIFE**, for 1887 through 1899.*

BACHELOR BUTTERFLY, THE VERITABLE HISTORY OF MR. (E,G)
D. Bogue, London: 1845 (5-1/2x10-1/4", 74 pgs, B&W, gilted hardcover)
nn - By Rodolphe Töpffer (Scarce) 500.00 1250.00 2800.00
nn - Hand colored edition (Very Rare) (no known sales)
NOTE: *This is the British Edition, translated from the re-engraved by Cham serialization found in **L'Illustration** - a periodical from Paris publisher Dubochet. Predates the first French collected edition. Third Töpffer comic book published in English. The first story page is numbered Page 3. Page 17 shows Bachelor Butterfly being swallowed by a whale.*

BACHELOR BUTTERFLY, THE STRANGE ADVENTURES OF (E,G)
Wilson & Co., New York: 1846 (5-3/8x10-1/8", 68 pgs, B&W, soft-c)

nn - By Rodolphe Töpffer (Very Rare) 600.00 1500.00 3000.00
nn - At least one hand colored copy exists (Very Rare) (no known sales)
NOTE: *2nd Töpffer comic book printed in the U.S., 3rd earliest known sequential comic book in the USA. Reprinted from the British D. Bogue 1845 edition, itself from the earlier French language **Histoire de Mr. Cryptogame**. Released the same year as the French Dubochet edition. Two variations known, the earlier printing with Page number 17 placed on the inside (left) bottom corner in error, with slightly later printings corrected to place page number 17 on the outside (right) bottom corner of that page. Another first printing indicator is pages 17 and 20 are printed on the wrong side of the page. For both printings: the first story page is numbered 2. Page 17 shows Bachelor Butterfly already in the whale. In most panels with 3 lines of text, the third line is indented further than the second, which is in turn indented further than the first.*

BACHELOR BUTTERFLY, THE STRANGE ADVENTURES
Brother Jonathan Press, NY: 1854 (5-1/2x10-5/8", 68 pgs, paper-c, B&W) (Very Rare)
nn - By Rodolphe Töpffer 250.00 500.00 1100.00

BACHELOR BUTTERFLY,THE STRANGE & WONDERFUL ADVENTURES OF
Dick & Fitzgerald, New York: 1870s-1888 (various printings 30 Cent cover price, 68 pgs, B&W, paper cover) (all versions Rare) (E,G)
nn - Black print on blue cover (5-1/2x10-1/2"); string bound 112.00 225.00 450.00
nn - Black print on green cover (5-1/2x10-1/2"); string bound 100.00 200.00 400.00
NOTE: *Reprints the earlier Wilson & Co. edition. Page 2 is the first story page. Page 17 shows Bachelor Butterfly already in the whale. In most panels with 3 lines of text, the second and third lines are equally indented in from the first. Unknown which cover (blue or green) is earlier.*

BACHELOR'S OWN BOOK. BEING THE PROGRESS OF MR. LAMBKIN, (GENT.) IN THE PURSUIT OF PLEASURE AND AMUSEMENT (E,O,G)
(See also PROGRESS OF MR. LAMBKIN)
D. Bogue, London: August 1, 1844 (5x8-1/4", 28 pgs printed one side only, cardboard cover & interior) (all versions Rare)
nn - First printing hand colored 200.00 400.00 750.00
nn - First printing black & white 200.00 400.00 750.00
NOTE: *First printing has misspellings in the title. "PURSUIT" is spelled "PERSUIT", and "AMUSEMENT" is spelled "AMUSEMEMT".*
nn - Second printing hand colored 200.00 400.00 750.00
nn - Second printing black & white 200.00 400.00 750.00
NOTE: Second printing. The misspelling of "PURSUIT" has been corrected, but "AMUSEMEMT" error is still present.
nn - Third printing hand colored No misspellings 200.00 400.00 750.00
nn - Third printing black & white 200.00 400.00 750.00
NOTE: *By George Cruikshank. This is the British Edition. Issued both in black & white, and professionally hand-colored editions. Hand-colored editions have survived in higher quantities than uncolored. Originally made with thin paper sheets covering the plates.*

BACHELOR'S OWN BOOK; OR, THE PROGRESS OF MR. LAMBKIN, (GENT.), IN THE PURSUIT OF PLEASURE AND AMUSEMENT, AND ALSO IN SEARCH OF HEALTH AND HAPPINESS, THE (E,O,G)
David Bryce & Son: Glasgow: 1884 (one shilling; 7-5/8 x5-7/8", 62 pgs printed one side only, illustrated hardcover, page edges guilt
nn - Reprints the 1844 edition with altered title 17.50 35.00 70.00
nn - soft cover edition exists 15.00 30.00 60.00

BACHELOR'S OWN BOOK. BEIN-G TWENTY-FOUR PASSAGES IN THE LIFE OF MR. LAMBKIN, GENT. (E,G)
Burgess, Stringer & Co., New York on cover; Carey & Hart, Philadelphia on title page: 1845 (31-1/4 cents, 7-1/2x4-5/8", 52 pgs, B&W, paper cover)
nn - By George Cruikshank (Very Rare) (no known sales)
NOTE: *This is the second known sequential comic book story published in America. Reprints the earlier British edition. Pages printed on one side only. New cover art by an unknown artist.*

BAD BOY'S FIRST READER (O,S)
G.W. Carleton & Co.: 1881 (5-3/4 x 4-1/8", 44 pgs, B&W, paper cover)
nn - By Frank Bellew (Senior) 50.00 100.00 200.00
NOTE: *Parody of a children's ABC primer, one cartoon illustration plus text per page. Includes one panel of Boss Tweed. Frank Bellew is considered the "Father of the American Sequential Comics."*

BALL OF YARN OR, QUEER, QUIANT & QUIZZICAL STORIES, UNRAVELED WITH NEARLY 200 COMIC ENGRAVINGS OF FREAKS, FOLLIES & FOIBLES OF QUEER FOLKS BY THAT PRINCE OF COMICS, ELTON, THE (M)
Philip. J. Cozans, 116 Nassau St, NY: early 1850s (7-1/4x3-1/2", 76 pgs, yellow-wraps)
nn - sequential comic strips plus singles (no known sales)
NOTE: Not known Mose Keyser-r, Jones, Smith & Robinson Goes To A Ball-r; The Adventures of Mr Goliah Starvemouse-r are all sequential comic strips printed in a number of sources

BARKER'S ILLUSTRATED ALMANAC (O,P,S)
Barker, Moore & Mein Medicine Co: 1878-1932+ (36 pgs, B&W, color paper-cr)
1878-1879 (Rare) 50.00 100.00 200.00
NOTE: *Not known yet what the cover art is.*
1880 Farmer Plowing Field-c 40.00 80.00 150.00
1881-1883 (Scarce,7-3/4x6-1/8") *4-mast ships & lighthouse-c* 40.00 80.00 150.00
1884-1889 (8x6-1/4") *Horse & Rider jumping picket fence-c* 40.00 80.00 150.00
1890-1897 (8-1/8x6-1/4") 40.00 80.00 150.00
1898-1899 (7-3/8x5-7/8") 40.00 80.00 150.00
1900+: see the Platinum Age Comics section (7x5-7/8")
NOTE: *Barker's Almanacs were actually issued in November of the year preceding the year which appears on the almanac. For example, the 1878 dated almanac was issued November 1877. They were given away to retailers of Barker's farm animal medicinal products, to in turn be given away to customers. Each Barker's Almanac contains 10 full page cartoons. These frequently included racist stereotypes of blacks. Each cartoon*

The Comical Adventures of Beau Ogleby
1843 © Tilt & Bogue, London

The Story of The Man of Humanity
and The Bull Calf by A. B. Frost
1890 © C.H. Fargo & Co.

Buzz A Buzz Or The Bees By Wilhelm Busch
1873 © Henry Holt And Company, New York

contained advertisements for Barker's products. It is unknown whether the cartoons appeared only in the almanacs, or if they also ran as newspaper ads or flyers. Originally issued with a metal hook attached in the upper left hand corner, which could be used to hang the almanac.

BARKER'S "KOMIC" PICTURE SOUVENIR (P,S)
Barker, Moore & Mein Medicine Co: nd (1892-94) (color cardboard cover, B&W interior) (all unnumbered editions Very Rare)

nn - (1892) (1st edition, 6-7/8x10-1/2, 150 pgs) wraparound cover showing people headed towards Chicago for the 1893 World's Fair 150.00 300.00 850.00
nn - (1893) (2nd edition, ??? pgs) same cover as 1st edition 150.00 300.00 850.00
nn - (1894) (3rd edition, 180 pgs, 6-3/4x10-3/8") 150.00 300.00 850.00
NOTE: *New cover art showing crowd of people laughing with a copy of Barker's Almanac.The crowd picture is flanked on both sides by picture of a tall thin person.*
nn - (1894) (4th edition, 124 pgs, 6-3/8x9-3/8") same-c as 3rd edition 150.00 300.00 800.00
NOTE: *Essentially same-c as 3rd edition, except flanking picture on left edge is now gone. The 2nd through 4th editions state their printing on the first interior page, in the paragraph beneath the picture of the Barker's Building. These have been confirmed as premium comic books, predating the Buster Brown premiums. They reprint advertising cartoons from Barker's Illustrated Almanac. For the 50 page booklets by this same name, numbered as "Part's, see the PLATINUM AGE SECTION. All "Editions in Parts", without exception, were published after 1900.*

BEAU OGLEBY, THE COMICAL ADVENTURES OF (E,G)
Tilt & Bogue: nd (c1843) (5-7/8x9-1/8", 72 pgs, printed one side only, green gilted hard-c, B&W)

nn - By Rodolphe Töpffer (Rare) 400.00 800.00 2100.00
nn - Hand coloured edition (Very Rare) (no known sales)
NOTE: *British Edition; no known American Edition. 2nd Töpffer comic book published in English. Translated from Paris publisher Aubert's unauthorized redrawn 1839 bootleg edition of Töpffer's* ***Histoire de Mr. Jabot****. The back most interior page is an advertisement for* ***Obadiah Oldbuck****, showing its comic book cover*

BEE, THE
Bee Publishing Co: May 16 1898-Aug 2 1898 (Chromolithographic Weekly)

most issues 50.00 100.00 200.00
8 June Yellow Kid Hearst cover issue 150.00 300.00 650.00

BEFORE AND AFTER. A LOCOFOCO CHRISTMAS PRESENT. (O, C)
D.C. Johnston, Boston: 1837 (4-3/4x3", 1 page, hand colored cardboard)

nn - (Very Rare) by David Claypoole Johnston (sold at auction for $400 in GD)
NOTE: *Pull-tab cartoon envelope, parodying the 1836 New York City mayoral election, picturing the candidate of the Locofoco Party smiling "Before the N.York election", then, when the tab is pulled, picturing him with an angry sneer "After the N.York election".*

BILLY GOAT AND OTHER COMICALITIES, THE (M)
Charles Scribner's Sons: 1898 (6-3/4x8-1/2", 116 pgs., B&W, Hardcover)

nn - By E. W. Kemble 125.00 250.00 600.00

BLACKBERRIES, THE (N.S) (see Coontown's 400)
R. H. Russell: 1897 (9"x12", 76 pgs, hard-c, every other page in color, every other page in one color sepia tone)

nn - By E. W. Kemble 162.00 325.00 1500.00
NOTE: *Tastefully done comics about Black Americana during the USA's Jim Crow days.*

BOOK OF BUBBLES, YE (S)
Endicott & Co., New York: March 1864 (6-1/4 x 9-7/8",160 pgs, guilt-illus. hard-c, B&W

nn - By unknown 150.00 300.00 600.00
NOTE: *Subtitle: A contribution to the New York Fair in aid of the Sanitary Commission; 68 single-sided pages of B&W cartoons, each with an accompanying limerick. A few are sequential.*

BOOK OF DRAWINGS BY FRED RICHARDSON (N,S)
Lakeside Press, Chicago: 1899 (13-5/8x10-1/2", 116 pgs, B&W, hard-c)

nn - 80.00 160.00 320.00
NOTE: *Reprinted from the* ***Chicago Daily News****. Mostly single panel. Includes one* ***Yellow Kid*** *parody, some Spanish-American War cartoons.*

BOTTLE, THE (E,O) (see also THE DRUNKARD'S CHILDREN, and TEA GARDEN TO TEA POT, and TEMPERANCE TALES; OR, SIX NIGHTS WITH THE WASHINGTONIANS)
D. Bogue, London, with others in later editions: nd (1846) (16-1/2x11-1/2", 16 pgs, printed one side only, paper cover)

D. Bogue, London (nd; 1846): first edition:
nn - Black & white (Scarce) 200.00 400.00 1000.00
nn - Hand colored (Rare) (no known sales)
D. Bogue, London, and Wiley and Putnam, New York (nd; 1847) : second edition, misspells American publisher "Putnam" as "Putman":
nn - Black & white (Scarce) 150.00 300.00 600.00
nn - Hand colored (Rare) (no known sales)
D. Bogue, London, and Wiley and Putnam, New York (nd; 1847) : third edition has "Putnam" spelled correctly.
nn - Black & white (Scarce) 150.00 300.00 600.00
nn - Hand colored (Rare) (no known sales)
D. Bogue, London, Wiley and Putnam, New York, and J. Sands, Sydney, New South Wales: (nd; 1847) : fourth edition with no misspellings
nn - Black & white (Scarce) 150.00 300.00 600.00
nn - Hand colored (Rare) (no known sales)
NOTE: *By George Cruikshank. Temperance/anti-alcohol story. All editions are in precisely identical format. The only difference is to be found on the cover, where it lists who published it. Cover is text only - no cover art.*

BOTTLE, THE HISTORY OF THE
J.C. Becket, 22 Grea St James St, Montreal, Canada: 1851 (9-1/8x6", B&W)

nn - From Engravings by Cruikshank 150.00 300.00 650.00
NOTE: *As published in The Canada Temperance Advocate.*

BOTTLE, THE (E)
W. Tweedie, London: nd (1862) (11-1/2x17-1/3", 16 pgs, printed one side only, paper cover)

nn - Black & white; By George Cruikshank (Scarce) 100.00 200.00 400.00
nn - Hand colored (Scarce) (no known sales)

BOTTLE, THE (E)
Geo. Gebbie, Philadelphia: nd (c.1871) (11-3/8x17-1/8", 42 pgs, tinted interior, hard-c)

nn - By George Cruikshank 100.00 200.00 400.00
NOTE: *New cover art (cover not by Cruikshank).*

BOTTLE, THE (E)
National Temperance, London: nd (1881) (11-1/2x16-1/2", 16 pgs, printed one side only, paper-c, color)

nn - By George Cruikshank 100.00 200.00 400.00
NOTE: *See Platinum Age section for 1900s printings.*

BOTTLE, THE (E)
Marques, Pittsburgh, PA: 1884/85 (6x8", 8 plates, full color, illustrated envelope)
nn - art not by Cruickshank; New Art 50.00 100.00 200.00
NOTE: Says Presented by J.M. Gusky, Dealer in Boots and Shoes

BROAD GRINS OF THE LAUGHING PHILOSOPHER
Dick & Fitzgerald,NY: 1870s
nn - (4) panel sequential strip 25.00 50.00 150.00

BROTHER JONATHAN
Wilson & Co/Benj H Day, 48 Beekman, NYC: 1839-???

July 4 1846 - ads for Obadiah & Butterfly 50.00 100.00 225.00
July 4 1856 catalog list - front cover comic strip 100.00 200.00 400.00
Xmas/New Years 1856 75.00 150.00 300.00
average large size issues 25.00 50.00 100.00
NOTE: has full page advert for Fredinand Flipper comic book116

BULL CALF, THE (P,M)
Various: nd (c1890's) (3-7/8x4-1/8", 16 pgs, B&W, paper-c)

nn - By A.B. Frost Creme Oatmeal Toilet Soap 25.00 50.00 150.00
nn - By A.B. Frost Thompson & Taylor Spice Co, Chicago 25.00 50.00 150.00
NOTE: *Reprints the popular strip story by Frost, with the art modified to place a sign for Creme Oatmeal Soap within each panel. The back cover advertises the specific merchant who gave this booklet away - multiple variations exist.*

BULL CALF AND OTHER TALES, THE (M)
Charles Scribner's Sons: 1892 (120 pgs., 6-3/4x8-7/8", B&W, illus. hard cover)

nn - By Arthur Burdett Frost 50.00 150.00 500.00
NOTE: *Blue, grey, tan hard covers known to exist.*

BULL CALF, THE STORY OF THE MAN OF HUMANITY AND THE (P,M)
C.H. Fargo & Co.: 1890 (5-1/4x6-1/4", 24 pgs, B&W, color paper-c)

nn - By A.B. Frost 50.00 100.00 200.00
NOTE: *Fargo shoe company giveaway; pages alternate between shoe advertisements and the strip story.*

BUSHEL OF MERRY THOUGHTS, A (see Mischief Book, The) (E)
Sampson Low Son & Marsten: 1868 (68 pgs, handcolored hardcover, B&W)

nn - (6-1/4 x 9-7/8", 138 pgs) red binding, publisher's name on title page only 200.00 400.00 800.00
nn - (6-1/2 x 10", 134 pgs) green binding, publisher's name on cover & title page 200.00 400.00 800.00
NOTE: *Cover plus story title pages designed by Leighton Brothers, based on Busch art. Translated by Harry Rogers (who is credited instead of Busch). This is a British publication, notable as the earliest known English language anthology collection of Wilhelm Busch comic strips. Page 13 of second story missing from all editions (panel dropped). Unknown which of the two editions was published first. A modern reprint, by Dover in 1971.*

BUTTON BURSTER, THE (M) (says on cover "ten cents hard cash")
M.J. Ivers & Co., 86 Nassau St., New York: 1873 (11x8-1/8", soft paper, B&W)

By various cartoonists (Very Rare) 125.00 250.00 500.00
NOTE: *Reprints from various 1873 issues of Wild Oats; has (5) different sequential comic strips: (3) by Livingston Hopkins, (1) by Thomas Worth, other one creator presently unknown; Bellew, Sr. single panel cartoons.*

BUZZ A BUZZ OR THE BEES (E)
Griffith & Farran, London: September 1872 (8-1/2x5-1/2", 168 pgs, printed one side only, orange, black & white hardcover, B&W interior)

nn - By Wilhelm Busch (Scarce) 112.00 225.00 450.00
NOTE: *Reprint published by Phillipson & Golder, Chester; text written by English to accompany Busch art.*

BUZZ A BUZZ OR THE BEES (E)
Henry Holt & Company, New York: 1873 (9x6", 96 pgs, gilted hardcover, hand colored)

nn - By Wilhelm Busch (Scarce) 100.00 200.00 450.00
NOTE: *Completely different translation than the Griffith & Farran version. Also, contains 28 additional illustrations by Park Benjamin. The lower page count is because the Henry Holt edition prints on both sides of each page, and the Griffith & Farran edition is printed one side only.*

CALENDAR FOR THE MONTH; YE PICTORIAL LYSTE OF YE MATTERS OF

The Carpet Bag #14
1851 © Snow & Wilder

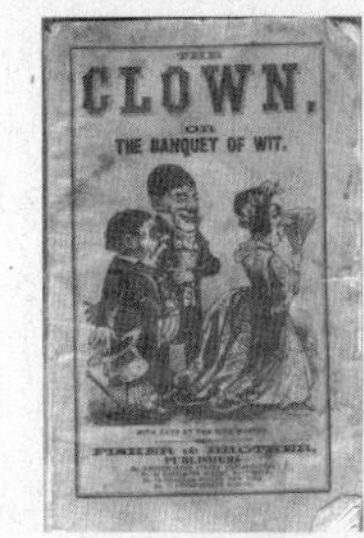

The Clown, or The Banquet of Wit
1851 © Fisher & Brother

Comic Monthly v6 #8
March 1865 © J.C.Haney, NY

INTEREST FOR SUMMER READING (P,M)
S.E. Bridgman & Company, Northampton, Mass: nd (c. late 1880's-1890's) (5-5/8x7-1/4", 64 pgs, paper-c, B&W)

nn - (Very Rare) T.S. Sullivant-c/a 100.00 200.00 400.00

NOTE: *Book seller's catalog, with every other page reprinting cartoons and strips (from Life??). Art by: Chips Bellew, Gibson, Howarth, Kemble, Sullivant, Townsend, Woolf.*

CARICATURE AND OTHER COMIC ART
Harper & Brothers, NY: 1877 (9-5/16x7-1/8", 360 pgs, B&W, green hard-c)

nn - By James Parton (over 200 illustrations) 30.00 60.00 200.00

NOTE: *This is the earliest known serious history of comics & related genre from around the world produced by an American. Parton was a cousin of Thomas Nast's wife Sarah. A large portion of this book was first serialized in **Harper's Monthly** in 1875.*

CARPET BAG, THE
Snow & Wilder, later Wilder & Pickard, Boston: March 21 1851-March 26 1853

Each average issue 25.00 50.00 100.00
Samuel "Mark Twain" Clemmons issues (first app in print) 600.00 1200.00 2500.00

NOTE: *Many issues contain cartoons by DC Johnston, Frank Bellew, others; literature includes Artemus Ward's Miss Partington who had a mischevious little Katzenjammer Kids-like brat. Carpet Bag was not considered derogatory pre-Civil War.*

CARROT-POMADE (O,G)
James G. Gregory, Publisher, New York: 1864 (9x6-7/8", 36 pgs, B&W)

nn - By Augustus Hoppin 70.00 140.00 280.00

NOTE: *The story of a quack remedy for baldness, sequentially told in the format parodying ABC primers. Has protective tissue pages (not part of page count).*

CARTOONS BY HOMER C. DAVENPORT (M,N,S)
De Witt Publishing House: 1898 (16-1/8x12", 102 pgs, hard-c, B&W)

nn 100.00 200.00 400.00

NOTE: *Reprinted from Harper's Weekly and the New York Journal. Includes cartoons about the Spanish-American War. Title page reads "Davenport's Cartoons".*

CARTOONS BY WILL E. CHAPIN (P,N,S)
The Times-Mirror Printing and Binding House, Los Angeles: 1899 (15-1/4x12", 98 pgs, hard-c, B&W)

nn - scarce 100.00 200.00 400.00

NOTE: *Premium item for subscribing to the Los-Angeles Times-Mirror newspaper, from which these cartoons were reprinted. Includes cartoons about the Spanish-American War.*

CARTOONS OF OUR WAR WITH SPAIN (N,S)
Frederick A. Stokes Company: 1898 (11-1/2x10", 72 pgs, hardcover, B&W)

nn - By Charles Nelan (r-New York Herald) 40.00 100.00 200.00
nn - 2nd printing noted on copy right page 30.00 60.00 120.00

CARTOONS OF THE WAR OF 1898 (E,M,N,S)
Belford, Middlebrook & Co., Chicago: 1898 (7x10-3/8",190 pgs, B&W, hard-c)

nn 50.00 100.00 200.00

NOTE: *Reprints single panel editorial cartoons on the Spanish-American War, from American, Spanish, Latino, and European newspapers and magazines, at rate of 2 to 6 cartoons per page. Art by Bart, Berryman, Bowman, Bradley, Chapin, Gillam, Nelan, Tenniel, others.*

CENTENNIAL FUN (O,S) (Rare)
Frank Leslie, Philadelphia: (July) 1876 (25¢, 11x8", 32 pgs, paper cover, B&W)

nn - By Joseph Keppler-c/a;Thomas Worth-a 150.00 300.00 600.00

NOTE: *Issued for the 1876 Centennial Exposition in Philadelphia. Exists with both black & white, and orange, black & white covers. One copy of the latter had an embossed newstand label from Partland, Maine, implying that the orange cover version, at least, was distributed and sold outside of Philadelphia.*

CHAMPAIGNE
Frank Leslie: June-Dec 1871

1-7 scarce 150.00 225.00 350.00

CHIC
Chic Publishing Co: 1880-81 (Chromolithographic Weekly)

1-38 Livingston Hopkins, Charles Kendrick, CW Weldon 75.00 150.00 300.00

CHILDREN'S CHRISTMAS BOOK, THE
The New York Sunday World: 1897 (10-1/4x8-3/4", 16 pgs, full color)

Dec 12, 1897 - By George Luks, G.H. Grant, Will Crawford, others) (Rare) 50.00 100.00 280.00

CHIP'S DOGS (M)
R.H. Russell and Son Publishers: 1895 hardcover, B&W)

nn - By Frank P. W. "Chip" Bellew 25.00 50.00 100.00
Early printing 80 pgs, 8-7/8x11-7/8"; dark green border of hardcover surrounds all four sides of pasted on cover image; pages arranged in error -- see NOTE below. (more scarce)
nn - By Frank P. W. "Chip" Bellew 12.50 25.00 50.00
Later printing 72 pgs, 8-7/8x11-3/4";green border only on the binding side (one side) of the cover image.

NOTE: *Both are strip reprints from **LIFE**. The difference in page count is due to more blank pages in the first printing -- all printings have the same comics contents, but with the pages in the first printing arranged differently. This is noticeable particularly in the 2-page strip "Getting a Pointer", which appears on the 2nd & 3rd to last pages of the later printings, but in the early printing the first half of this strip is near the middle of the book, while the last half appears on the 2nd to last story page.*

CHIP'S OLD WOOD CUTS (M,S)
R.H. Russell & Son: 1895 (8-7/8x11-3/4", 72 pgs, hardcover, B&W)

nn - By Frank P. W. ("Chip") Bellew 25.00 50.00 100.00
nn - 1897 reprint 15.00 30.00 60.00

CHIP'S UN-NATURAL HISTORY (O,S)
Frederick A. Stokes & Brother: 1888 (7x5-1/4", 64 pgs, hardcover, B&W)

nn - By Frank P. W. ("Chip") Bellew 12.50 25.00 50.00

NOTE: *Title page lists publisher as "Successors to White, Stokes & Allen."*

CLOWN, OR THE BANQUET OF WIT, THE (E,M,O)
Fisher & Brother, Philadelphia, Baltimore, New York, Boston: nd (c.1851) (7-3/8x4-1/2", 88 pgs, paper cover, B&W)

nn - (Very Rare; 3 known copies) 500.00 1000.00 2000.00

NOTE: *Earliest known multi-artist anthology of sequential comics; contains multiple sequential comics, plus numerous single panel cartoons. A mixture of reprinted and original material, involving both European and American artists. "Jones, Smith, and Robinson Goes to a Ball" by Richard Doyle (1st app. of Doyle's "Foreign Tour" in America, reprinted from PUNCH, August 24, 1850); "Moses Keyser The Bowery Bully's Trip to the Californian Gold Mines", by John H. Manning; "The Adventures of Mr. Gulp" (by the Read brothers?); more comics by artists unknown; cartoons by George Cruikshank, Grandville, Elton.*

COLD CUTS AND PICKLED EELS' FEET; DONE BROWN BY JOHN BROWN
P.J. Cozans, New York: nd (c1855-60) (B&W)

nn (Very Rare) 100.00 200.00 300.00

NOTE: *Mostly a children's book. But, pages 87 to 110, and 111 to 122, contain narrative sequential stories.*

COLLEGE SCENES (O,G)
N. Hayward, Boston: 1850 (5x6-3/4", 72 pgs, printed one side only, B&W lithography)

nn - (Rare) by Nathan Hayward 200.00 400.00 600.00

NOTE: *This is the 2nd such production for an American University; the first issued at Yale circa 1845, decent funny art of story about life of a Harvard student from his entrance thru graduation entirely in caricature. Has art on back cover as well.*

COLLEGE CUTS Chosen From The Columbia Spectator 1880-81-82 (S)
White & Stokes, NY: 1882 (8x9-5/8", 92 pgs, B&W)

By F. Benedict Herzog, H. McVickar, W. Bard McVickar, others 20.00 40.00 100.00
nn - 2nd edition reprint (1888) (8-1/4x10-3/8) 10.00 20.00 50.00

COMICAL COONS (M)
R.H. Russell: 1898 (8-7/8 x 11-7/8", 68 pgs, hardcover, B&W)

nn - By E. W. Kemble 300.00 600.00 1300.00

NOTE: *Black Americana collection of 2-panel stories.*

COMICAL ALMANAC
Anton Bicker, Cinncinati, OH: 1885 (9x6, 260 pgs, B&W, illustrated-c)

nn - two (12) page sequential Busch comic strips 50.00 100.00 200.00

COMIC ALMANAC, THE
John Berger. Baltimore: 1854-? (7-1/2x6-1/4, 36 pgs, B&W)

nn - 60.00 120.00 240.00

COMIC ANNUAL, AMERICAN (O,I)
Richardson, Lord, & Holbrook, Boston: 1831 (6-7/8x4-3/8", 268 pgs, B&W, hard-c)

nn - (Scarce) 150.00 300.00 600.00

NOTE: *Mostly text; front & back cover illustrations, 13 full page, and scattered smaller illustrations by David Claypoole Johnston; edited by Henry J. Finn.*

COMIC HISTORY OF THE UNITED STATES, (I)
Carleton & Co., NY: 1876 (6-7/8x5-1/8", 336 pgs, hardcover, B&W)

nn - By Livingston Hopkins. 12.50 25.00 50.00
2nd printing: Cassell, Petter, Galpin & Co.: 1880 (6-7/8x5-1/8", 336 pgs, hardcover, B&W)
nn - By Livingston Hopkins. 12.50 25.00 50.00

NOTE: *Text with many B&W illustrations; some are multi-panel comics. Not to beconfused with **Bill Nye's Comic History Of The U.S.** which contains Frederick Opper illustrations.*

COMIC MONTHLY, THE
J.C. Haney, N.Y.: March 1859-1880. (16 x 11-1/2", 30 pgs average, B&W)

Certain average issues with sequential comics 50.00 100.00 200.00
11 (Jan 1860) Bellew-c 25.00 50.00 100.00
v2#2 (Apr 1860) Bellew-c 25.00 50.00 100.00
v2#3 (May 1860) Bellew-c 25.00 50.00 100.00
v2#4 (June 1860) Comic Strip Cover 50.00 100.00 200.00
v2#5 (July 1860) Bellew-c; (12) panel Explaining American Politics To An Intelligent Foreigner; (10) panel The Art of Stump Speaking; (15) panel Mr. Dibbs Goes to Pike's Peak and Comes Back Again 100.00 200.00 400.00
v2#7 (Sept 1860) Comic Strip Cover; (24) panel double page spread The Prince of Wales In America 50.00 100.00 200.00
v2#8 (18) panel The Three Young Friends Sillouette Strip 25.00 50.00 100.00
v2#9 (Nov 1860) (9) panel sequential 25.00 50.00 100.00
v2#10 11 not indexed 25.00 50.00 100.00
v2#12 (Jan 1861) (12) panel double page spread 25.00 50.00 100.00

COMIC TOKEN FOR 1836, A COMPANION TO THE COMIC ALMANAC, THE
Charles Ellms, Boston: 1836 (8x5', 48 pgs, B&W)

nn - 50.00 100.00 200.00

COMIC WEEKLY, THE
???, NYC: 1881-???

issues with comic strips (Chips, etc) 60.00 125.00 250.00

Comics From Scribner's Magazine
1891 © Scribner's

The Comus Offering
1830-31 © B. Franklin Edmands

Elton's Californian Comic All-My-Nack #17
1850 © Elton's, NY

FR1.0 GD2.0 FN6.0

COMIC WORLD
???: 1876-1879 (Quarto Monthly)
issues with comic strips 37.50 75.00 150.00

COMICS FROM SCRIBNER'S MAGAZINE (M)
Scribner's: nd (1891) (10 cents, 9-1/2x6-5/8", 24 pgs, paper cover, side stapled, B&W)
nn - (Rare) F.M.Howarth C&A 125.00 250.00 500.00
NOTE: *Advertised in SCRIBNER'S MAGAZINE in the June 1891 issue, page 793, as available by mail order for 10 cents. Collects together comics material which ran in the back pages of Scribner's Magazine. Art by Attwood, "Chip" Bellew, Dões, Frost, Gibson, Zim.*

COMUS OFFERING CONTAINING HUMOROUS SCRAPS OF DIVERTING COMICALITIES, THE (O, S)
B. Franklin Edmands, 25 Court St, Boston: c1830-31 (8-7/8x10-3/4", 16 pgs, thin brown paper-c, blank on backs,
nn - (William F Straton, Engraver, 15 Water St, Boston) (no known sales)
NOTE: All hand-colored single panel cartoons format definitely inspired by D.C. Johnston's Scraps with every panel character using well-defined word balloons. Might become a seminal step in the evolution of the American comic book. More research is needed.

CONTRASTS AND CONCEITS FOR CONTEMPLATION BY LUKE LIMNER (O)
Ackerman & Co, 96 Strand, London: c1848 (9-3/4x6-1/4, 48 pgs, B&W)
nn - By John Leighton 50.00 100.00 200.00

COONTOWN'S 400 (M) (see **Blackberries**) (M)
The Life (Magazine) Co.: 1899 (10-15/16x8-7/8, 68 pgs, cloth light-brown hard-c, B&W
nn - By E.W. Kemble (scarce) 250.00 500.00 1500.00
NOTE: *Tastefully drawn depictions of Black Americana over one hundred years ago during Jim Crow days.*

CROSSING THE ATLANTIC (O,G)
James R. Osgood & Co., Boston: 1872 (10-7/8x16", 68 pgs, hardcover, B&W);
Houghton, Osgood & Co., Boston: 1880
1st printing - by Augustus Hoppin 50.00 100.00 200.00
2nd printing (1880; 66 pgs; 8-1/8x11-1/8") 32.50 65.00 150.00

C.R. PITT'S COMIC ALMANAC
C.R. Pitt: 1880 (7-1/2x4-5/8", 28 pgs)
nn - contains (8) panel sequential 50.00 100.00 200.00

CRUIKSHANK'S OMNIBUS: A VEHICLE FOR FUN AND FROLIC (E,S)
E. Ferrett & Co., Philadelphia: 1845 (25 cents, 7-1/2" x 4-5/8", 96 pgs, B&W, paper-c)
nn - By George Cruikshank c/a (Very Rare) 150.00 300.00 600.00
NOTE: *Mostly prose, with 10 plates of cartoons printed on one-side (about half the plates with multiple cartoons), plus illustrated cover, all by George Cruikshank. First (perhaps only) American printing of Cruikshank's Omnibus, which was published first in Britain. It is only a partial reprinting.*

CYCLISTS' DICTIONARY (S)
Morgan & Wright, Chicago: 1894 (5 x3-3/4, 80 pgs, soft-c, B&W
nn - By Unknown 37.50 75.00 150.00

THE DAILY GRAPHIC
The Graphic Company, 39 Park Place, NY: 1873-Sept 23, 1889 (14x20-1/2, 8 pgs, B&W)
Average issues with comic strips 15.00 20.00 40.00
Average issues without comic strips 10.00 15.00 30.00
NOTE:

DAVY CROCKETT'S COMIC ALMANACK
???, Nashville, TN, then elsewhere: 1835-end (32 pages plus wraps)
1 500.00 1000.00 2000.00
2-13 15 end 250.00 500.00 1000.00
14 contains (17) panel Crocket comic strip bio 1848 1000.00 1500.00 3000.00

DAY'S DOINGS (was The Last Sensation) (Becomes New York Illustrated Times)
James Watts, NYC: #1 June 6 1868-early 1876 (11x16, 16 pgs, B&W)
average issue with comic strips 10.00 15.00 25.00
Paul Pry & Alley Sloper character issues 25.00 50.00 100.00
Aug 19 1871 - First Alley Sloper in America?? 50.00 100.00 200.00
NOTE: *James Watts was a shadow company for Frank Leslie; outright sold to Frank Leslie in 1873. There are a lot of issues with comic strips from 1868 up.*

DAY'S SPORT - OR, HUNTING ADVENTURES OF S. WINKS WATTLES, A SHOPKEEPER, THOMAS TITT, A "LEGAL GENT," AND MAJOR NICHOLAS NOGGIN, A JOLLY GOOD FELLOW GENERALLY, A (O)
Brother Jonathan, NY: c1850s (5-7/8x8-1/4, 44 pgs)
nn - By Henry L. Stephens, Philadelphia (Very Rare) (no known sales)

DEVIL'S COMICAL OLDMANICK WITH COMIC ENGRAVINGS OF THE PRINCIPAL EVENTS OF TEXAS, THE
Turner & Fisher, NY & Philadelphia: 1837 (7-7/8x5", 24 pgs)
nn - many single panel cartoons 100.00 200.00 400.00

DIE VEHME, ILLUSTRIRTES WOCHENBLATT FUR SCHERZ UND ERNEST (M,O)
Heinrich Binder, St. Louis: No.1 Aug 28, 1869 - No.?? Aug 20, 1870 (10 cents, 8 pgs, B&W, paper-c) (see also PUCK)
1-?? (Very Rare) by Joseph Keppler 100.00 200.00 400.00
NOTE: *Joseph Keppler's first attempt at a weekly American humor periodical. Entirely in German. The title translates into: "**The Star Chamber: An Illustrated Weekly Paper in Fun and Ernest**".*

FR1.0 GD2.0 FN6.0

DOMESTIC MANNERS OF THE AMERICANS
The Imprint Society, Barre, Mass: 1969 (9-3/4 x 7-1/4", 390 pgs, hard-c in slipcase, B&W)
nn - 10.00 20.00 50.00
NOTE: *Reprints the 1832 edition of this book by Mrs. Trollope with an added insert. The 28-page insert is what is of primary interest to us -- it reproduces SCRAPS No. 4 (1833) by D.C. Johnston.*

DRUNKARD'S CHILDREN, THE (see also THE BOTTLE) (E,O)
David Bogue, London; John Wiley and G.P. Putnam, New York; J. Sands, Sydney, New South Wales: July 1, 1848 (16x11", 16 pgs, printed on one side only, paper-c)
nn - Black & white edition (Scarce) 300.00 600.00 950.00
nn - Hand colored edition (Rare) (no known sales)
NOTE: *Sequel story to THE BOTTLE, by George Cruikshank. Temperance/anti-alcohol story. British-American-Australian co-publication. Cover is text only - no cover art.*

DRUNKARD'S PROGRESS, OR THE DIRECT ROAD TO POVERTY, WRETCHEDNESS & RUIN, THE
J. W. Barber, New Haven, Conn.: Sept 1826 (single sheet)
nn - By John Warner Barber (Very Rare) (no known sales)
NOTE: *Broadside designed and printed by barber contains four large wood engravings showing "The Morning Dram" which is "The Beginning of Sorrow"; "The Grog Shop" with its "Bad Company"; "The Confirmed Drunkard" in a state of "Beastly Intoxication"; and the "Concluding Scene" with the family being drive off to the alms house. It is an interesting set of cuts, faintly reminiscent of Hogarth. Many modern reprints exist.*

DUEL FOR LOVE, A (O,P)
E.C. DeWitt & Co., Chicago: nd (c1880's) (3-3/8" x 2-5/8", 12 pgs, B&W, paper-c)
nn - Art by F.M. Howarth (Rare) 25.00 50.00 100.00
NOTE: *Advertising giveaway for DeWitt's Little Early Risers, featuring an 8-panel strip story, spread out 1 panel per page.*

DURHAM WHIFFS (O, P)
Blackwells Durham Tobacco Co: Jan 8 1878 (9x6.5", 8 pgs, color-c, B&W)
v1 #1 w/Trade Card Insert 37.50 75.00 150.00
NOTE: Sold in 2008 CGC 9.4 $1250

DYNALENE LAFLETS (P)
The Dynalene Company: nd (3 x 3-1/2", 16 pgs, B&W, paper cover)
nn - Dynalene Dyes promo (9) panel comic strip 25.00 50.00 75.00

ELEPHANT, THE
William H Graham, Tribune Building, NYC: Jan 22 1848-Feb 19 1848 (11x8.5", B&W)
1-5 Rare - single panel cartoons 150.00 300.00 600.00

ELTON'S COMIC ALL-MY-NACK (E,O.S)
Elton, Publisher, 18 Division & 98 Nassau St, NY: 1833-1852 (7-1/2x4-1/2", 36pgs, B&W
1-5 99% single panel cartoons 100.00 200.00 400.00
6 (1839) 100.00 200.00 400.00
NOTE: Two different covers & different interiors exist for this title and number
7-15 - 99% single panel cartoons 100.00 200.00 400.00
16 - contains 6 panel "A Tales of A Tayl-or" 1848-49 200.00 400.00 600.00
17 - contains "Moses Keyser, The Bowery Bully's Trip To the California Gold Mines" 1850 By John H. Manning, early comics creator, told in 15 panels 200.00 400.00 600.00
18-19 presently unknown contents 100.00 200.00 400.00
NOTE: *Contains both original American, and pirated European, cartoons. All single panel material, except where noted. Almanacs are published near the end of the year prior to that for which they are printed -- like calendars today. Thus, the 1833 No. 1 issue was really published in the last months of 1832. #17 has Elton's Californian Comic-All-My-Nack on the cover.*

ELTON'S COMIC ALMANAC (Publsiher change)
GW Cottrell & Co, Publishers & C Cornhill, Boston, Mass: 1853 (7-7/8x4-5/8,36pgs,B&W
20 - (2) sequential comic strips (9) panel "Jones, Smith and Robinson Goes To A Ball; (21) panel "The Adventures of Mr. Gulp" Rare 300.00 600.00 1200.00
NOTE: *Both strips appear in* The Clown, Or The Banquet of Wit

ELTON'S FUNNY ALMANACK (title change to Almanac)
Elton Publisher and Engraver, New York: 1846 (8x6-1/2", 36 pgs)
1 1846 50.00 100.00 200.00

ELTON'S FUNNY ALMANAC (#1 titled Almanack)
Elton & Co, New York: 1847-1853 (8x6-1/4, 36 pgs, B&W)
2 (1847) #3 (1848) 50.00 100.00 200.00
nn 1853 (8-1/8x4-7/8"; (5) panel comic strip "The Adventures of Mr. Goliah Starvemouse"

ELTON'S RIPSNORTER COMIC ALMANAC
Elton, 90 Nassau St, NY: 1850 (8x5, 24 pgs, B&W, paper-c)
nn - scarce 50.00 100.00 200.00

ENGLISH SOCIETY (S)
Harper & Brothers, Publishers, New York: 1897 (9-5/8x12-1/4", 206 pgs, B&W)
nn - by George Du Maurier 50.00 75.00 100.00

ENGLISH SOCIETY AT HOME (S)
James R. Osgood and Company: 1881 (10-7/8x8-5/8, 182 pgss, protective sheets on some pages - not included in pages count, hard-c, B&W 50.00 75.00 100.00
nn - by George Du Maurier

ENTER: THE COMICS (E,G)
University of Nebraska Press: 1965 (6-7/8x9-1/4", 120 pgs, hard-c)

The Evolution Of A Democrat
1888 © Paquet & Co, NY

Flying Leaves
1880s © E.R. Herrick & Company, New York

The Fools Paradise Mirth and Fun
For Old and Young
1883 © E.P. Dutton & Co, NYC

FR1.0 GD2.0 FN6.0

nn - By Ellen Weisse 25.00 50.00 100.00
NOTE: *Contains overview of Töpffer's life and career plus only published English translation of Töpffer's Monsieur Crepin (1837); appears to have been re-drawn by Weisse in the days before xerox machines.*

ESQUIRE BROWN AND HIS MULE, STORY OF
A.C. Meyer, Baltimore, Maryland: 1880s (5x3/7/8", 28 pgs, B&W)

Booklet (9 panel story plus cough remedies catalog) 25.00 50.00 100.00
Fold-Out of Booklet (9 panel version) 25.00 50.00 100.00

"EVENTS OF THE WEEK" REPRINTED FROM THE CHICAGO TRIBUNE
Henry O. Shepard Co, Chicago: 1894 (5-3/8x15-7/8", 110 pg, B&W, hard-c)

First Series, Second Series - By HR Heaton 37.50 75.00 150.00

EVERYBODY'S COMICK ALMANACK
Turner & Fisher, NY & Philadelphia: 1837 (7-7/8x5", 36 pgs, B&W)

nn 50.00 100.00 200.00

EVOLUTION OF A DEMOCRAT - A DARWINIAN TALE, THE (O,G)
Paquet & Co., New York: 1888 (25 cents, 7-7/8x5-1/2", 100 pgs, printed one side only, orange paper cover, B&W) (Very Rare)

nn - Written by Henry Liddell, art by G. Roberty 300.00 600.00 1200.00
NOTE: *Political parody about the rise of an Irishman through Tammany Hall. Grover Cleveland appears as linked with Tammany. Ireland becomes the next state in the USA.*

FABLES FOR THE TIMES (S, I)
R.H. Russell & Son, New York: 1896 (9-1/8x12-1/8", 52 pgs, yellow hard-c)

nn - By H.W. Phillips and T.S. Sullivant Scarce 75.00 150.00 300.00

FERDINAND FLIPPER, ESQ., THE FORTUNES OF (O,G)
Brother Jonathan, Publisher, NY: nd (1851) (5-3/4 x 9-3/8", 84 pgs, B&W, printed both sides)

nn - By Various (Very Rare) 700.00 1200.00 3000.00
NOTE: *Extended title: "...Commencing With A Period of Four Months And Anterior To His Birth Going Thru The Various Stages of His Infancy, Childhood, Verdant Years, Manhood, Middle Life, and Green and Ripe Old Age, And Ending A Short Time Subsequent to His Sudden Decease With His Final Exit, Funeral And Burial." Extremely unique comic book, put together by gathering 145 independent single illustrations and cartoons, by various artists, and stringing them together into a sequential story. The majority of panels are by Grandville. Also included are at least 19 signed Charles Martin, reprinted from 1847 issues of Yankee Doodle, 5 panels from D.C. Johnston, plus other panels by F.O.C. Darley, T.H. Matheson, and others. The story also contains several panels of Gold Rush content . Printed by E.A. Alverds. The 1851 date is derived from an advertisement found in the Oct-Dec 1851 issue of the Brother Jonathan newspaper. It ispossible, however, that it actually came out even earlier.*

FERDINAND FLIPPER, ESQ., THE FORTUNES OF (G)
Dick & Fitzgerald, New York: nd (1870's to 1888) (30 Cents, 84 pgs, B&W, paper cover)

nn - (Very Rare reprint - several editions possible) 375.00 750.00 1500.00

FINN'S COMIC ALMANAC
Marsh, Capen, & Lyon; Boston: 1835-??? (4.5x7.5, 36 pgs, B&W)

nn 100.00 200.00 400.00

FINN'S COMIC SKETCHBOOK (S)
Peabody & Co., 223 Broadway, NY: 1831 (10-1/2x16", 12 pgs, B&W)

nn - By Henry J. Finn (Very Rare) (no known sales)
NOTE: *Designs on copper plates; etched by J. Harris, NY; should have tissue paper in front of each plate.*

50 GREAT CARTOONS (M,P,S)
Ram's Horn Press: 1899 (14x10-3/4, 112 pgs, hard-c)

nn - By Frank Beard 30.00 60.00 120.00
NOTE: *Premium in return for a subscription to **The Ram's Horn** magazine.*

FISHER'S COMIC ALMANAC
Ames Fisher and Brother, No 12 North Sixth St, Philadelphia , Charles Small in NYC, Also in Boston: 1841-1868 (4-1/2 x 7-1/4, 36 pgs, B&W)

1-7 (1841-1847) 100.00 200.00 400.00
12 reprints mermaid-c with word balloon (1868) 100.00 200.00 400.00

F**** A*** K*****, OUTLINES ILLUSTRATIVE OF THE JOURNAL OF** (O,S)
D.C. Johnston, Boston: 1835 (9-5/16 x 6", 12 pgs, printed one side only, blue paper cover, B&W interior) (see also **SCRAPS**)

nn - by David Claypoole Johnston (Scarce) 600.00 1000.00 1500.00
NOTE: *This is a series of 8 plates parodying passages from the Journal of Fanny (Frances) A. Kemble, a British woman who wrote a highly negative book about American Culture after returning from the U.S. Though remembered now for her campaign against slavery, she was prejudiced against most everything American culture, thus inspiring Johnston's satire. Contains 4 protective sheets (not part of page count.)*

FLYING DUTCHMAN; OR, THE WRATH OF HERR VONSTOPPELNOZE, THE (E)
Carleton Publishing, New York: 1862 (7-5/8x5-1/4", 84 pgs, printed on one side only, gilted hardcover, B&W)

nn - By Wilhelm Busch (Scarce) 35.00 70.00 160.00
nn - 1975 Scarce 100 copy-r 74 pgs Visual Studies Workshop 5.00 10.00 20.00
NOTE: *This is the earliest known English language book publication of a Wilhelm Busch work. The story is plagiarized by American poet John G. Saxe, who is credited with the text, while the uncredited Busch cartoons are described merely as accompanying illustrations.*

FLYING LEAVES (E)
E.R. Herrick & Company, New York: nd (c1889/1890's) (8-1/4" x 11-1/2", 76 pgs, B&W interior, orange, b&w hard-c)

nn- (Scarce) 85.00 175.00 260.00

FR1.0 GD2.0 FN6.0

NOTE: *Reprints strips and single panel cartoons from 1888 Fliegende Blatter issues, translated into English. Various artists, including Bechstein, Adolf Hengeler, Lothar Meggendorfer, Emil Reinicke.*

FOOLS PARADISE WITH THE MANY ADVENTURES THERE AS SEEN IN THE STRANGE SURPRISING PEEP SHOW OF PROFESSOR WOLLEY COBBLE, THE (E)
(see also THE COMICAL PEEP SHOW)
John Camden Hotten, London: Nov 1871 (1 crown, 9-7/8x7-3/8", 172 pgs, printed one side only, gilted green hardcover, hand colored interior)

nn - By Wilhelm Busch (Rare) 400.00 800.00 1750.00
NOTE: *Title on cover is: **WALK IN! WALK IN!! JUST ABOUT TO BEGIN!!! the FOOLS PARADISE**; below the above title page. Anthology of Wilhelm Busch comics, translated into English.*

FOOLS PARADISE WITH THE MANY WONDERFUL SIGHTS AS SEEN IN THE STRANGE SURPRISING PEEP SHOW OF PROFESSOR WOLLEY COBBLE, FURTHER ADVENTURES IN (E)
Chatto & Windus, London: 1873 (10x7-3/8", 128 pgs, printed one side only, brown hardcover, hand colored interior)

nn - By Wilhelm Busch (Rare) 300.00 600.00 1320.00
NOTE: *Sequel to the 1871 **FOOLS PARADISE**, containing a completely different set of Busch stories, translated into English.*

FOOLS PARADISE MIRTH AND FUN FOR THE OLD & YOUNG (E)
Griffith & Farran, London: May 1883 (9-3/4x7-5/8", 78 pgs, color cover, color interior)

nn - By Wilhelm Busch (Rare) 100.00 200.00 420.00
NOTE: *Collection of selected stories reprinted from both the 1871 & 1873 **FOOLS PARADISE**.*

FOOLS PARADISE - MIRTH AND FUN FOR THE OLD & YOUNG (E)
E.P. Dutton and Co., NY: May 1883 (9-3/4x7-5/8", 78 pgs, color cover, color interior)

nn - By Wilhelm Busch (Rare) 100.00 200.00 420.00
NOTE: *Collection of selected stories reprinted from both the 1871 & 1873 **FOOLS PARADISE**.*

FOREIGN TOUR OFMESSRS. BROWN, JONES, AND ROBINSON, THE (see Messrs...)

FRANK LESLIE'S BOYS AND GIRLS
Frank Leslie, NYC: Oct 13 1866-#905 Feb 9 1884

average issue with comic strip 20.00 30.00 50.00

FRANK LESLIE'S BUDGET OF FUN
Frank Leslie, Ross & Tousey, 121 Nassau St, NYC: Jan 1859-1878 (newspaper size)

1-5 no comic strips 50.00 100.00 200.00
6 June 1859 (9) panel "The Wonderful Hunting Tour of Mr Borridge After the Deer" 75.00 150.00 300.00
7-9 no comic strips 25.00 50.00 100.00
10 Sept 1859 sequential comic strip 50.00 100.00 200.00
11 (8) panel sequential "Apropos of the Great Eastern" 50.00 100.00 200.00
12-14 25.00 50.00 100.00
15 Feb 1860 (12) panel "The Ballet Girl" strip 50.00 100.00 200.00
16-18 25.00 50.00 100.00
19 June 1860 comic strip front cover 100.00 200.00 300.00
NOTE: Cover is (11) panel "The Very Latest Fashionable Amusement..."; Back cover comic strip "Mr Jogg's Reasons For Preferring to Board to Keeping House" (7) panels using word balloons. Plus centerfold double page (18) panel spread "The New York May, Moving in General, and Mrs. Grundy's In Particular."
20 24 25 no comic strips 25.00 50.00 100.00
21 (7/15/60) (8) panel Mr Septimus Verdilater Visits the Baltimore Convention" 50.00 100.00 200.00
22 (8/1/60) (3) panel 25.00 50.00 100.00
23 (8/15/60) (12) panel "Superb Scheme For Perfecting of Dramatic Entertainment" 50.00 100.00 200.00
25 (9/15/60 (9) panel sequential 25.00 50.00 100.00
27 AbrahamLincoln Word Balloon cover 50.00 100.00 200.00
28 Wilhelm Busch sequential strip-r begin 50.00 100.00 200.00
29, 31-51 to be indexed next year 25.00 50.00 100.00
30 (12/15/60) (3) panel sequential strip 25.00 50.00 100.00
31 (Jan 1861) (12) panel The Boarding School Miss 25.00 50.00 100.00
32 (Feb 1861) (10) panel Telegraphic Horrors; Or, Mr Buchanan Undergoing A Series of Electric Shocks 50.00 100.00 200.00
35 (4/1/61) Abraham Lincoln Word Balloon cover 50.00 100.00 200.00
43 44 no sequential comic strips 25.00 50.00 100.00
45 (Nov 1861) (6) panel sequential; (11) panel The Budget Army and Infantry Tactics; First Bellew here? - Many Bellew full pagers begin 50.00 100.00 200.00
48 (Feb 1862) Bellew-c; (2) panel Bellew strip plus singles 50.00 100.00 200.00
49 (Mar 1862) Bellew-c; (16) panel Wilhelm Busch "The Fly Or The Disturbed Ducthman A Story without Words" 50.00 100.00 200.00
50 (April 1862) Bellew-c "Succession Bath" plus singles 25.00 50.00 100.00
51 (May 1862) Bellew-c; (25) panel Busch The Toothache (6) panel Definitions of the Day 50.00 100.00 200.00
52 (June 1862) Bellew-c; (9) panel A Cock & A Bull Expedition; (6) panel Bellew The First Campaign of the Home Guard 50.00 100.00 200.00
NOTE: Johnny Bull & Louis Napolean with Brother Jonathan
53-67 To Be Indexed in the Future 25.00 50.00 100.00
68 (11/18///63) (6) panel Bellew strip "Cuts On Cowards" 25.00 50.00 100.00
NOTE: contains (1) panel William Newman 1817-1870, mentor to Thomas Nast
71 (Feb 1864) Wiord Balloon Jefferson Davis-c 25.00 50.00 100.00
72 (Mar 1864) Word Balloon-c 25.00 50.00 100.00
73 (April 1864) Word Balloon-c in (6) panels 25.00 50.00 100.00

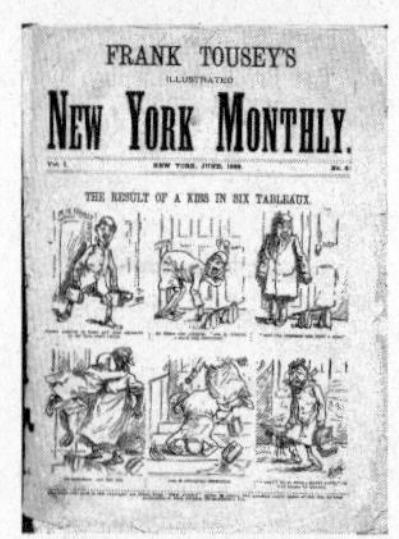

Frank Tousey's Illustrated New York Monthly #9
June 1882 © Frank Tousey

Funny Fellow's Own Book
1852 © Philip Cozans

Funny Folk by F.M. Howarth
1899© E.P. Dutton

FR1.0 GD2.0 FN6.0

74 (May 1864) Newman Word Balloon-c 25.00 50.00 100.00
75 77 78 no sequentials 25.00 50.00 100.00
76 (July 1864) Newman Word Balloon-c 25.00 50.00 100.00
79 (Oct 1864) Word Balloon-c 25.00 50.00 100.00
80 (Nov 1864) Robt E Lee & JeffDavis-c; no sequentials 25.00 50.00 100.00
81 (Dec 1864) Word Balloon "Abyss of War"-c 25.00 50.00 100.00
83 (2/18/65) Back-c (6) panel "Petroleum" 25.00 50.00 100.00
84 (Mar 1865) (6) panel sequential 25.00 50.00 100.00
85 (Apr 1865) Word Balloon-c 25.00 50.00 100.00
86 89 90 92 no sequentials 25.00 50.00 100.00
88 (7/6/65) (6) panel "Marriage" 25.00 50.00 100.00
91 (Oct 1865) (6) panel "Brief Confab At The Corner 25.00 50.00 100.00
93-98 yet to be indexed 25.00 50.00 100.00
99 (June 1866) (18) panel Mr Paul Peters Adventures While Trout-Fishing In The Adirondacks 50.00 100.00 200.00
100 (July 1866) (4) panel sequential comic strip 25.00 50.00 100.00
102 (Sept 1866) (6) panel sequential comic strip 25.00 50.00 100.00
103 (Oct 1866) (9) panel strip; (12) pane;l back cover Adventures of McTiffin At Long Branch 50.00 100.00 200.00
104 (Nov 1866) (4) panel; (23) panel "The Budget Rebuses; (2) panel Glut On Treason Market;back-c; (6) sequential strip 25.00 50.00 100.00
105 (12/18/66) Word Balloon-c; (20) panel sequential back-c 37.50 65.00 130.00
NOTE: Artists include William Newman (1863-1868), William Henry Shelton, Joseph Keppler (1873-1876), James A. Wales (1876-1878), Frederick Burr Opper (1878)

FRANK LESLIE'S LADY'S MAGAZINE
Frank Leslie, NYC: Feb 1863-Dec 1882 (8.5x12", typically 152 pgs)
issues with comic strips 20.00 40.00 50.00

FRANK LESLIE'S PICTORIAL WEEKLY
Frank Leslie, Ross & Tousey, 121 Nassau St, NYC:
average issue (Very Rare) 50.00 100.00 200.00

FRANK TOUSEY'S NEW YORK COMIC MONTHLY
Frank Tousey, NYC: (no known sales)

FREAKS
???, Philadelphia: Jan 8, 1881-April? 1881 (Chromolithographic Weekly)
(Very Rare) 50.00 100.00 300.00

FREELANCE, THE
A.M. Soteldo Jr, Edito, 292 Broadway, NYC: 1874-75 (Folio Weekly)
(Rare) 25.00 50.00 100.00

FREE MASONRY EXPOSED
Winchell & Small, 113 Fulton, NY: 1871 (7-5/8x10-1/2", 36pgs, blue paper-c, B&W)
nn- Thomas Worth Scarce 100.00 200.00 425.00
NOTE: Scathing satircal look at Free Masons thru many cartoons, their power waning by the 1870s

FREETHINKERS' PICTORIAL TEXT-BOOK, THE (S,O)
The Truth Seeker Company, New York: 1890, 1896, 1898 (9x12, hard-c, B&W)
1 (1890 edition) - Scarce 382 pgs By Watson Heston 200.00 400.00 800.00
1 (1896 edition) - Scarce 378 pgs By Watson Heston (1890-r)100.00 200.00 450.00
2 (1898 edition) - Scarce 408 pgs By Watson Heston 125.00 250.00 450.00
NOTE: *Sought after by collectors of Freethought/Atheism material. There is also 200 copy Modern Reprint.*

FRITZ SPINDLE-SHANKS, THE RAVEN BLACK
Cosack & C o, Buffalo, NY: 1870/80s (4-3/8x2-3/4", color)
(10) card comic strip set by Wilhelm Busch 25.00 50.00 100.00

FUN BY RALL
Unknown: circa 1865 (11x7-7/8", 68 pgs, soft-c, B&W)
nn - By presently unknown (Very Rare) 100.00 200.00 350.00
NOTE: *Wraparound soft cover like modern comic book; yellow paper cover with red & black ink.*

FUN FOR THE FAMILY IN PICTURES
D. Lothrop and Company: 1886 (4 x 7", 48 pgs, Silver & Red stiff-c; interior pages have various single color inks)
nn - By unknown hand 50.00 100.00 200.00
NOTE: *Single panel cartoons and sequential stories.*

FUN FROM LIFE
Frederick A Stokes & Brother, New York: 1889 (9 1/8 by 7 1/8, 72 pages, hard-c)
nn - Mostly by Frank "Chips" Bellew Jr 62.50 125.00 250.00
NOTE: *Contains both single panel and many sequential comics reprints from Life.*

FUNNYEST OF AWL AND THE FUNNIEST SORT OF PHUN, THE
AT Bellew Or W. Jennings Demorest, 121 Nassau St, NY : 1865-67 (30 issues, 16x11 tabloid 16 pgs B&W Monthly, 1-8 © American News; 9-on © A.T. Bellews)
1 (April 1864) Bellew-c 50.00 100.00 200.00
4 (1865) Bellew-c 50.00 100.00 200.00
5 (1865) Busch (20) panel comic srtip The Toothache 75.00 150.00 300.00
7 (1865) Bellew-c 50.00 100.00 200.00
8 (1865) Special Petroleum oil issue - much cartoon art 100.00 200.00 400.00
9 (July 1865) Bellew Bullfrog-c; centerfold double page spread hanging many Confederates; (6) panel strip hanging Jeff Davis 100.00 200.00 400.00
10 (Aug 1865) Bellew-c (13) panel Busch strip with two ducks, a frog and a butcher who gets the ducks in the end 100.00 200.00 400.00
11 (Sept 1865) Bellew Bull Frog Anti-French-c 50.00 100.00 200.00
13 14 15 (12/65-1/66) Bellew-c no sequential comic strips 50.00 100.00 200.00
16 (March 1866) address change to 39 Park Ave 50.00 100.00 200.00
22 (Sept 1866) 133 Nassau St 50.00 100.00 200.00
34 (Oct 1867) 133 Nassau St (7) panel Baseball comic strip; Last Known Issue - were there more? 100.00 200.00 400.00
NOTE: *Radical Republican politics distributed by Great American News Company; owned by Frank Bellew's wife as a front for her husband. When the Civil War ended, the brutal anti-Confederate comic strips and jokes switched to frogs and began attacking France. Funny thing, history says without France's help in the 1700s, there just might not have been a United States.*

FUNNY ALMANAC
Elton & Co., NY: 1853 (8-1/8x4-7/8, 36 pgs)
nn - sequential comic strip 50.00 100.00 200.00
NOTE: (5) panel strip "The Adventures of Mr. Goliah Starvemouse"

FUNNY FELLOWS OWN BOOK, A COMPANION FOR THE LOVERS OF FROLIC AND GLEE, THE (M,N)
Philip. J. Cozans, 116 Nassau ST, NY: 1852 (4-1/2x7-1/2", 196 pgs, burnt orange paper-c)
nn - contains many sequential comic strips (Very Rare) (no known sales)
NOTE: Collected from many different Comic Alamac(k)s including Mose Keyser (Calif Gold Rush); Jones, Smith and Robinson Goes To A Ball; Adventures of Mr. Gulp, Or the Effects of A Dinner Party; The Bowery Bully's Trip To The California Gold Mines plus lots more. This one is a sleeper so far.

FUNNY FOLK (M)
E. P. Dutton: 1899 (12x16-1/2", 90 pgs,14 strips in color-rest in b&w, hard-c)
nn - By Franklin Morris Howarth 162.50 325.00 1500.00
nn - London: J.M. Dent, 1899 embossed-c; same interior 200.00 450.00 900.00
NOTE: *Reprints many sequential strips & single panel cartoons from* ***Puck****. This is considered by many to be yet another "missing link" between Victorian & Platinum Age comic books. Most comic books 1900-1917 re-printing Sunday newspaper comic strips follow this size format, except using cardboard-c rather than hard-c.*

FUNNY SKETCHES...Also Embracing Comic Illustrations
Frank Harrison, New York: 1881 (6-5/8x5", 68 pgs, B&W, Color-c)
nn - contains (3) sequential comic strips; one strip is (6) pages long; plus one (3) pages; one more (2) pager 75.00 150.00 300.00

GIBSON BOOK, THE (M,S)
Charles Scribner's Sons & R.H. Russell, New York: 1906 (11-3/8x17-5/8", gilted red hard-c, B&W)
Book I 50.00 100.00 200.00
NOTE: *Reprints in whole the books: Drawings, Pictures of People, London,Sketches and Cartoons, Education of Mr. Pipp, Americans. 414 pgs. 1907 2nd editions exist same value.*
Book II 50.00 100.00 200.00
NOTE: *Reprints in whole the books: A Widow and Her Friends, The Weaker Sex, Everyday People, Our Neighbors. 314 pgs 1907 second edition for both also exists. Same value.*

GIBSON'S PUBLISHED DRAWINGS, MR. (M,S) (see Plat index for later issues post 1900)
R.H. Russell, New York: No.1 1894 - No. 9 1904 (11x17-3/4", hard-c, B&W)
nn (No.1; 1894) Drawings 96 pgs 30.00 60.00 120.00
nn (No.2; 1896) Pictures of People 92 pgs 30.00 60.00 120.00
nn (No.3; 1898) Sketches and Cartoons 94 pgs 30.00 60.00 120.00
nn (No.4; 1899) The Education of Mr. Pipp 88 pgs 30.00 60.00 120.00
nn (No.5; 1900) Americans 30.00 60.00 120.00
NOTE: *By Charles Dana Gibson cartoons, reprinted from magazines, primarily* ***LIFE****. The Education of Mr. Pipp tells a story. Series continues how long after 1904? Each of these books originally came in a boxx and are worth more with the box.*

GIRL WHO WOULDN'T MIND GETTING MARRIED, THE (O)
Frederick Warne & Co., London & New York: nd (c1870's) (9-1/2x11-1/2", 28 pgs, printed 1 side, paper-c, B&W)
nn - By Harry Parkes 62.50 125.00 250.00
NOTE: *Published simultaneously with its companion volume,* ***The Man Who Would Like to Marry****.*

GOBLIN SNOB, THE (O)
DeWitt & Davenport, New York: nd (c1853-56) (24 x 17 cm, 96 pgs, B&W, color hard-c)
nn - (Rare) by H.L. Stephens 250.00 500.00 1000.00

GOLDEN ARGOSY
Frank A. Munsey, 81 Warren St, NYC: 1880s (10-1/2x12, 16 pgs, B&W)
issues with full page comic strips by Chips and Bisbee 20.00 40.00 60.00

GOLDEN DAYS, THE
James Elverson, Publisher, NYC: March 6 1880-May 11 1907 weekly, 16 pgs
issues with comic strips 4.00 7.50 15.00
Horatio Alger issues 10.00 20.00 40.00
v10 #49-v11#1 1889 first Stratemeyer story 25.00 50.00 100.00

GOLDEN WEEKLY, THE
Frank Tousey, NYC: #1 Sept 25 1889-#145 Aug 18 1892 (10-3/4x14-1/2, 16 pgs, B&W)
average issue with comic striips 15.00 25.00 50.00

GREAT LOCOFOCO JUGGERNAUT, THE (S)
publisher unknown: Fall/Winter 1837 (7-5/8x3-1/4, handbill single page)
nn - By David Claypoole Johnston (a VG copy sold for $2000 in 2005)

The Story of Han's The Swapper Cover & First Two Panels
1865 © L. Pranc & Co, Boston

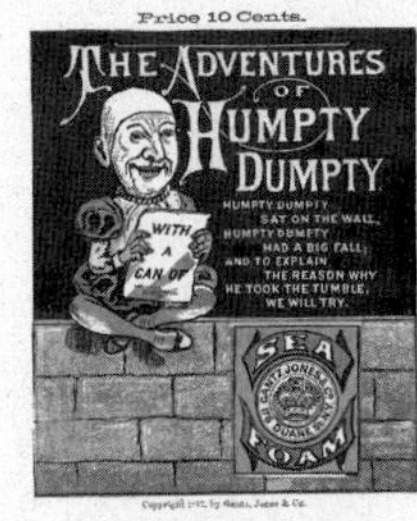

Humpty Dumpty, The Adventures of...
© Gantz, Jones and Co.

Imagerie d'Epinal
1888 © Mumoristic Publishing Co.

nn - **Imprint Society:** 1971 (reprint) 6.00 12.00 25.00

HALF A CENTURY OF ENGLISH HISTORY (S. M)
G.P. Putnam's Sons - The Knickerbocker Press, New York and London: 1884 (7-3/4 x 5-3/4", 316 pgs., illustrated hard-c)

nn - By Various 25.00 50.00 175.00
NOTE: *Subtitle: Pictorially Presented in a Series of Cartoons from the Collection of Mr. Punch. Comprising 150 plates by Doyle, Leech, Tenniel, and others, in which are portrayed the political careers of Peel, Palmerston, Russell, Cobden, Bright, Beaconsfield, Derby, Salisbury, Gladstone and other English statesmen.*

HAIL COLUMBIA! HISTORICAL, COMICAL, AND CENTENNIAL (O,S)
The Graphic Co., New York & Walter F. Brown, Providence, RI: 1876 (10x11-3/8", 60 pgs, red gilted hard-c, B&W)

nn - by Walter F. Brown (Scarce) 100.00 200.00 450.00

HANS HUCKEBEIN'S BATCH OF ODD STORIES ODDLY ILLUSTRATEDED
McLoughlin Bros., New York: 1880s (9-3/4x7-3/8, 36?? pg?

nn - By Wilhelm Busch (Rare) 75.00 150.00 300.00

HANS THE SWAPPER, THE STORY OF (O)
L. Pranc & Co., 159 Washington St, Boston: 1865 (33 inch long fold out in colors)

nn - unique fold out comic book on one long piece of paper 75.00 150.00 300.00

HARPER'S NEW MONTHLY MAGAZINE
Harper & Brothers, Franklin Square, NY: 1850-1870s (6-3/4x10, 140 pgs, paper-c, B&W)
1850s issues with comic strips in back advert section 20.00 30.00 50.00

HEALTH GUYED (I)
Frederick A. Stokes Company: 1890 (5-3/8 x 8-3/8, 56 pgs, hardcover, B&W)

nn - By Frank P.W. ("Chip") Bellew (Junior) 25.00 50.00 175.00
NOTE: *Text & cartoon illustration parody of a health guide.*

HEATHEN CHINEE, THE (O)
Western News Co.: 1870 (5-1/32x7-1/4, B&W, paper)
nn - 10 sheets printed on one side came in envelope 75.00 150.00 300.00

HITS AT POLITICS (M,S)
R.H. Russell, New York: 1899 (15" x 12", 156 pgs, B&W, hard-c)

nn - W.A. Rogers c/a 100.00 200.00 300.00
NOTE: *Collection of W.A. Rogers cartoons, all reprinted from Harper's Weekly. Includes Spanish-American War cartoons.*

THE HOME CIRCLE
Garrett & Co, NY: 1854-56 (26x19", 4 pgs, B&W)

	FR1.0	GD2.0	FN6.0
1 (1/54) beautiful ad of Garrett Building	100.00	200.00	400.00
2/4 (4/66) Cover ad for Yale College Scraps	100.00	200.00	400.00
2/5 (5/55) First ad for Oscas Shanghai	75.00	150.00	300.00
2/6 (6/55) another ad forOscas Snanghai	75.00	150.00	300.00
2/8 (#20) (8/55) Oscar Shanghai comic book cover repro	200.00	400.00	800.00
3/1 (#25) (1/56)	200.00	400.00	800.00
NOTE: Garrett's 2nd comic book Courtship of Chavalier Slyfox-Wikoff			
3/8 (#32) (8/56)	50.00	100.00	200.00
NOTE: First print ad for Foreign Tour of Messrs. Brown, Jones, and Robinson			
35 (11/56) first official Garrett, Dick & Fitzgerald issue	50.00	100.00	200.00
37 (1/57)	100.00	200.00	400.00

NOTE: Front page comic strip repro ad for Messrs. Brown, Jones, and Robinson's Foreign Tour; Back cover full of short sequentials, singles panel

HOME MADE HAPPY. A ROMANCE FOR MARRIED MEN IN SEVEN CHAPTERS (O,P)
Genuine Durham Smoking Tobacco & The Graphic Co.: nd (c1870's) (5-1/4 tall x 3-3/8" wide folded, 27" wide unfolded, color cardboard)

nn - With all 8 panels attached (Scarce) 30.00 60.00 200.00
nn - Individual panels/cards 5.00 10.00 25.00
NOTE: *Consists of 8 attached cards, printed on one side, which unfold into a strip story of title card & 7 panels. Scrapbook hobbyists in the 19th Century tended to pull the panels apart to paste into their scrapbooks, making copies with all panels still attached scarce.*

HOME PICTURE BOOK FOR LITTLE CHILDREN (E,P)
Home Insurance Company, New York: July 1887 (8 x 6-1/8", 36 pgs, b&w, color paper-c)

nn (Scarce) 40.00 80.00 160.00
NOTE: *Contains an abbreviated 32-panel reprinting of "The Toothache" by George Cruikshank. Remainder of booklet does not contain comics. Some copies known to exist do not contain The Toothache - buyer beware!*

HOOD'S COMICALITIES. COMICAL PICTURES FROM HIS WORKS (E,S)
Porter & Coates: 1880 (8-1/2x10-3/8", 104 pgs, printed one side, hard-c, B&W)

nn 30.00 50.00 100.00
NOTE: *Reprints 4 cartoon illustrations per page from the British Hood's Comic Annuals, which were poetry books by Thomas Hood.*

HOOKEYBEAK THE RAVEN, AND OTHER TALES (see also JACK HUCKABACK, THE SCAPEGRACE RAVEN) (E)
George Routledge and Sons, London & New York: nd (1878) (7-1/4x5-5/8", 104 pgs, hardcover, B&W)

nn - By Wilhelm Busch (Rare) 100.00 200.00 400.00

HOW ADOLPHUS SLIM-JIM USED JACKSON'S BEST, AND WAS HAPPY. A LENGTHY TALE IN 7 ACTS. (O,P)
Jackson's Best Chewing Tobacco & Donaldson Brothers: nd(c1870's) (5-1/8 tall x 3-3/8" wide folded, 27" wide unfolded, color cardboard)

nn - With all 8 panels attached (Scarce) 30.00 60.00 200.00
nn - Individual panels/cards 5.00 10.00 25.00
NOTE: *Consists of 8 attached cards, printed on one side, which unfold into a strip story of title card & 7 panels. Scrapbook hobbyists in the 19th Century tended to pull the panels apart topaste into their scrapbooks, making copies with all panels still attached scarce.*

HOW DAYS' DURHAM STANDARD OF THE WORLD SMOKING TOBACCO MADE TWO PAIRS OF TWINS HAPPY (O,P)
J.R. Day & Bro. Standard Durham Smoking Tobacco, Durham, NC: nd (c late 1870's/early 1880's) (3-5/8" x 5-1/2", folded, 21-3/4" tall unfolded, color cardboard)

nn- With all 6 panels attached (Scarce) 120.00 240.00 480.00
nn- Individual panels/cards 20.00 40.00 60.00
NOTE: *Highly sought by both Black Americana and Tobacciana collectors. Recurring mid-19th Century story about two African-American twin brothers who romance and marry a pair of African-American twin sisters. Although the text is racist at points, the art is not. Consists of 6 attached cards, printed on one side, which unfold downwards into a strip story of title card & 5 panels. Scrapbook hobbyists in the 19th Century tended to pull the panels apart and paste into their scrapbooks, making copies with all panels attached scarce. Note, there are numerous cartoon tellings of this same story, including several card series versions (with different art, and story variations, each time). But, the above is the only version which unfolds as a strip of attached cards. The cards from all the unattached versions are smaller sized, and thus distinguishable.*

HUGGINIANA; OR, HUGGINS' FANTASY, BEING A COLLECTION OF THE MOST ESTEEMED MODERN LITERARY PRODUCTIONS (I,S,P)
H.C. Southwick, New York: 1808 (296 pgs, printed one side, B&W, hard-c)

nn - (Very Rare)) (no known sales)
NOTE: *The earliest known surviving collected promotional cartoons in America. This is a booklet collecting 7 folded plus 1 full page flyer advertisements for barber John Richard Desborus Huggins, who hired American artists Elkanah Tisdale and William S. Leney to modify previously published illustrations into cartoons referring to his barber shop.*

HUMOROUS MASTERPIECES - PICTURES BY JOHN LEECH (E,M)
Frederick A. Stokes: nd (late 1900's - early 1910's) No.1-2 (5-5/8x3-7/8", 68 pgs, cardboard covers, B&W)

1- John Leech (single panel cartoon-r from **Punch**) 20.00 40.00 80.00
2- John Leech (single panel cartoon-r from **Punch**) 20.00 40.00 80.00

HUMOURIST, THE (E,I,S)
C.V. Nickerson and Lucas and Deaver, Baltimore: No.1 Jan 1829 - No.12 Dec 1829 (5-3/4x3-1/2", B&W text w/hand colored cartoon pg.)

Bound volume No.1-12 (Very Rare; copies in libraries 270 pgs) (no known sales)
NOTE: *Earliest known American published periodical to contain a cartoon every issue. Surviving individual issues currently unknown -- all information comes from 1 surviving bound volume. Each issue is mostly text, with one full page hand-colored cartoon. Bound volume contains an additional hand-colored cartoons at front of each six month set (total of 14 cartoons in volume). Cartoons appear to be of British origin, possibly by George Cruikshank.*

HUMPTY DUMPTY, ADVENTURES OF...(I,P)
1877 (Promotional 4x3-1/2", 12 page chapbook from Gantz, Jones & Co, 10¢-c.)

nn-Promotes Gantz Sea Foam Baking Powder; early app. of a costumed character, dressed as Humpty Dumpty 50.00 100.00 450.00

HUSBAND AND WIFE, OR THE STORY OF A HAIR. (O,P)
Garland Stoves and Ranges, Michigan Stove Co.: 1883 (4-3/16 tall x 2-11/16" wide folded, 16" wide unfolded, color cardboard)

nn - With all 6 panels attached (Scarce) 25.00 50.00 125.00
nn - Individual panels/cards 5.00 10.00 25.00
NOTE: *Consists of 6 attached cards, printed on one side, which unfold into a strip story of title card & 5 panels. Scrapbook hobbyists in the 19th Century tended to pull the panels apart topaste into their scrapbooks, making copies with all panels still attached scarce.*

ICHABOD ACADEMICUS, THE COLLEGE EXPERIENCES OF (O,G)
William T. Peters, New Haven, CT: 1850 (5-1/2x9-3/4",108 pgs, B&W)

nn - By William T. Peters (Rare) 1000.00 2000.00 4000.00
NOTE: *Pages are not uniform in size. Also, a copy showed up on eBay with misspelled Academicus. Has "n" instead of "m" - not known yet which printing is earliest version.*

ICHABOD ACADEMICUS, THE COLLEGE EXPERIENCES OF (O,G)
Dick & Fitzgerald, New York: nd (1870s-1888) (paper-c, B&W)

nn - By William T. Peters (Very Rare) 250.00 500.00 1000.00
NOTE: *Pages are uniform in size.*

ILLUSTRATED SCRAP-BOOK OF HUMOR AND INTELLIGENCE (M)
John J. Dyer & Co.: nd (c1859-1860)

nn - Very Rare 200.00 400.00 800.00
NOTE: *A "printed scrapbook" of images culled from some unidentified periodical. About half of it is illustrations that would have accompanied prose pieces. There are pages of single panel cartoons (multiple per page). And there are roughly 8 to 12 pages of sequential comics (all different stories, but appears to all be by the same presently unidentified artist).*

THE ILLUSTRATED WEEKLY
Chars C Lucas & Co, 11 Dey St, NY: 1876 (15x18", 8pgs, 8¢ per issue)

	FR1.0	GD2.0	FN6.0
2/8 (2/19/76) back-c all sequential comic strips	100.00	200.00	400.00
2/12 (3/18/76) full page of British-r sequentials	100.00	200.00	400.00
2/14 (4/1/76) April Fool Issue - (6) panel center; plus more	100.00	200.00	400.00
2/15 (4/8/76) (6) panel sequential	100.00	200.00	400.00
issues without comic strips	12.50	25.00	50.00

Jingo No. 3, Sept 24
1884 © Art Newspaper Co, Boston & NYC

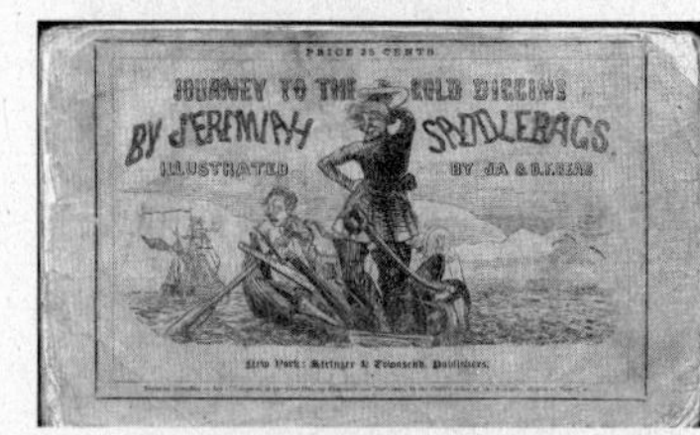

Journey To The Gold Diggings By Jeremiah Saddlebags
1849 © Various - First Original USA Comic Book

Judge, No. 1, October 29, 1881
1881 © Judge Publishing, NYC

FR1.0 GD2.0 FN6.0

ILLUSTRATIONS OF THE POETS: FROM PASSAGES IN THE LIFE OF LITTLE BILLY VIDKINS (See A Day's Sport...)
S. Robinson, Philadelphia: May 1849 (14.7 cm x 11.3 cm, 32 pgs, B&W)

nn - by Henry Stephens (very rare) (no known sales)
NOTE: *Predates Journey to the Gold Diggins By Jeremiah Saddlebags by a few months and is an original American proto-comic strip book. More research needs to be done. A later edition brought $800 in G/VG 2007*

IMAGERIE d'EPINAL (untrimmed individual sheets) (E)
Pellerin for Humoristic Publishing Co, Kansas City, Mo.: nd (1888) No.1-60 (15-7/8x11-3/4",single sheets, hand colored) (All are Rare)

1-14, 21, 22, 25-46, 49-60 - in the Album d'Images 17.50 35.00 70.00
15-20, 23,24, 47, 48 - not in the Album d'Images 30.00 60.00 120.00
NOTE: *Printed and hand colored in France expressly for the Humoristic Publishing Company . Printed on one side only. These are single sheets, sold separately. Reprints and translates the sheets from their original French.*

IMAGERIE d'EPINAL ALBUM d'IMAGES (E)
Pellerin for Humoristic Publishing Co., Kansas City. Mo: nd (1888) (15-1/2x11-1/2",108 pgs plus full color hard-c, hand colored interior)

nn - Various French artists (Rare) 400.00 800.00 2000.00
NOTE: *Printed and hand colored in France expressly for the Humoristic Publishing Company . Printed on one side only. This is supposedly a collection of sixty broadsheets, originally sold separately. All copies known only have fifty of the sixty known of these broadsheets (slightly bigger, before binding, trimming the margins in the process, down to 15-1/4x11-3/8".). Three slightly different covers known to exist, with or without the indication in French "Textes en Anglais" ("Texts in Englishi), with or without the general title "Contes de FEes" ("Fairy Tales"). All known copies were collected with sheets 15-20, 23,24, 47, and 48 missing.*

IN LAUGHLAND (M)
R.H. Russell, New York: 1899 (14-9/16x12", 72 pgs, hard-c)

nn - By Henry "Hy" Mayer (scarce) 150.00 300.00 600.00
NOTE: *Mostly strips plus single panel cartoon-r from various magazines. The majority are reprinted from Life, with the rest from: Truth, Dramatic Mirror, Black and White, Figaro Illustre, Le Rire, and Fliegende Blatter.*

IN THE "400" AND OUT (M,S) (see also **THE TAILOR-MADE GIRL**)
Keppler & Schwarzmann, New York: 1888 (8-1/4x12", 64 pgs, hardc, B&W)

nn - By C.J. Taylor 42.50 85.00 170.00
NOTE: *Cartoons reprinted from **Puck**. The "400" is a reference to New York City's aristocratic elite.*

IN VANITY FAIR (M,S)
R.H.Russell & Son, New York: 1896 (11-7/8x17-7/8", 80 pgs, hard-c, B&W)

nn - By A.B.Wenzell, r-LIFE and HARPER'S 45.00 90.00 180.00

JACK HUCKABACK, THE SCAPEGRACE RAVEN (see also HOOKEYBEAK THE RAVEN) (E)
Stroefer & Kirchner, New York: nd (c1877) (9-3/8x6-3/8", 56 pgs, printed one side only, hand colored hardcover, B&W interior)

nn - By Wilhelm Busch (Rare) 75.00 150.00 350.00
NOTE: *The 1877 date is derived from a gift signature on one known copy. The publication date might in truth be earlier.* There are also professionally hand colored copies known to exist which would be worth more.

JEFF PETTICOATS
American News Company, NY: July 1865 (23 inches folded out; 6-1/4x8 folded,, B&W)
nn - Very Rare Frank Bellew (6) panel sequential foldout (10¢) (no known sales)
NOTE: printed also in **FUNNYEST OF AWL AND THE FUNNIEST SORT OF PHUN** #9 (July 1865) (6) panel strip hanging Jeff Davis; This sold hundreds of thousand of copies in its day

JINGO (M,O)
Art Newspaper Co., Boston & New York: No.1 Sept 10, 1884 - No.11 Nov 19, 1884 (10 cents, 13-7/8" x 10-1/4",16 pgs, color front/back-c and center, remainder B&W, paper-c)

1-11(Rare) 50.00 100.00 200.00
NOTE: *Satirical Republican propaganda magazine, modeled after **Puck** and **Judge**, which was published during the last couple months of the 1884 Presidential Election campaign. The Republicans lost, **Jingo** ceased publication, and Republican backers soon after purchased **Judge** magazine.*

JOHN-DONKEY, THE (O, S)
George Dexter, Burgess, Stringer & Co., NYC: 1848 (10x7.5",16 pgs,B&W, 6¢

1 Jan 1 1848 75.00 150.00 300.00
2-end (last issue Aug 12 1848) 50.00 100.00 200.00

JOLLY JOKER
Frank Leslie, NY: 1862-1878 (B&W, 10¢)

20/6 (July 1877) (Bellew Opper cover & single panels 150.00 300.00 600.00

JOLLY JOKER, OR LAUGH ALL-ROUND
Dick & Fitzgerald, NY: 1870s? (8-1/4x4-7/8", 148, B&W, illustrated green cover)

nn - cartoons on every page 100.00 200.00 400.00

JONATHAN'S WHITTLINGS OF THE WAR (O, S)
T.W. Strong, 98 Nassau St, NYC: April 1854-July 8 1854 (11.5x8.5", 16 pgs, B&W)

1 April 1854 100.00 200.00 400.00
NOTE: *Begins Frank Bellew's sequential comic strip* "Mr. Hookemcumsnivey, A Russian Gentleman, Hears That His Country Is In A State of War"
2-12 (July 8 1854) Many Bellew & Hopkins 100.00 200.00 400.00

JOURNAL CARRIER'S GREETING
???, Minn, Minn: 1897-98? (giveaway promo, 10-1/8x8-1/4, 36, B&W, paper-c)
nn - rare 50.00 100.00 200.00

JOURNEY TO THE GOLD DIGGINS BY JEREMIAH SADDLEBAGS (O,G)
Various publishers: 1849 (25 cents, 5-5/8 x 8-3/4", 68 pgs, green & black paper cover, B&W interior)
nn -- New York edition, Stringer & Townsend, Publishers
(Very Rare) By J.A. and D.F. Read. 5000.00 8000.00 11,000.00
nn -- Cincinnati, Ohio edition, published by U.P. James
(Very Rare) By J.A. and D.F. Read. 5000.00 8000.00 11,000.00
nn -- 1950 reprint, with introduction, published by William P. Wreden, Burlingame, California: 1950 (5-7/8 x 9", 92 pgs, hardcover, color interior)
(390 copies printed) By J.A. and D.F. Read. 67.50 125.00 250.00
NOTE: *Earliest known original sequential comic book by an American creator; directly inspired by Töpffer's **Obadiah Oldbuck** and **Bachelor Butterfly** The New York and Cincinnati editions were both published in 1849, one soon after the other. Antiquarian Book sources have traditionally cited that the Cincinnati edition preceded the New York, but without referencing their evidence. Conflicting with this, the Cincinnati edition lists the New York publishers' 1849 copyright, while the New York edition makes no reference to the Cincinnati publishers. Such would indicate that the New York edition was first. Both are very rare, and until resolved both will be regarded as published simultaneously. A New York copy with missing back cover, detached front cover, and G/VG interior sold for $2000 in 2000. Two copies sold at auction in 2006 for $11,500 and 12,000. (Prices vary widely.)*

JUDGE (M,O)
Judge Publishing, New York: No.1 Oct 29, 1881 - No. 950, Dec ??, 1899 (10 cents, color front/back c and centerspread, remainder B&W, paper-c)

1 (Scarce) (no known sales)
2-26 (Volume 1; Scarce) 30.00 50.00 100.00
27-790,792-950 12.50 25.00 50.00
791 (12/12/1896; Vol.31) - classic satirical-c depicting Tammany Hall politicians as the Yellow Kid & Cox's Brownies 75.00 200.00 400.00
Bound Volumes (six month, 26 issue run each):
Vol. 1 (Scarce) (no known sales)
Vol. 2-30,32-37 140.00 280.00 600.00
Vol. 31 - includes issue 791 **YK/Brownies** parody 200.00 250.00 775.00
NOTE: *Rival publication to Puck. Purchased by Republican Party backers, following their loss in the 1884 Presidential Election, to become a Republican propaganda satire magazine.*

JUDGE, GOOD THINGS FROM
Judge Publishing Co., NY: 1887 (13-3/4x10.5", 68 pgs, color paper-c)

1 first printing 50.00 100.00 200.00
NOTE: Zimmerman, Hamilton, Victor, Woolf, Beard, Ehrhart, De Meza, Howarth, Smith, Alfred Mitchell

JUDGE'S LIBRARY (M)
Judge Publishing, New York: No.1, April 1890 - No. 141, Dec 1899 (10 cents, 11x8-1/8", 36 pgs, color paper-c, B&W)

1 10.00 20.00 40.00
2-141 10.00 20.00 40.00
151-??? (post-1900 issues; see Platinum Age section)
NOTE: ***Judge's Library** was a monthly magazine reprinting cartoons & prose from **Judge**, with each issue's material organized around the same subject. The cover art was often original. All issues were kept in print for the duration of the series, so later issues are more scarce than earlier ones.*

JUDGE'S QUARTERLY (M)
Judge Publishing Company/Arkell Publishing Company, New York: No.1 April 1892 - 31 Oct 1899 (25¢, 13-3/4x10-1/4", 64 pgs, color paper-c, B&W)

1-11 13-31 contents presently unknown to us 15.00 30.00 60.00
12 ZIM Sketches From Judge Jan 1895 100.00 200.00 400.00
NOTE: *Similar to **Judge's Library**, except larger in size, and issued quarterly. All reprint material, except for the cover art.*

JUDGE'S SERIALS (M,S)
Judge Publishing, New York: March 1888 (10x7.5", 36 pgs)

#3 - Eugene Zimmerman 100.00 200.00 400.00
NOTE: *A bit of sequential comic strips; mostly single panel cartoons. This series runs to at least #8.*

JUDY
Burgess, Stringer & Co., 17 Ann St, NYC: Nov 28 1846-Feb 20 47 (11x8.5",12 pgs,B&W)

1 Nov 28 1846 67.50 125.00 250.00
2-13 50.00 100.00 200.00

JUVENILE GEM, THE (see also THE ADVENTURES OF MR. TOM PLUMP, and OLD MOTHER MITTEN) (O,I)
Huestis & Cozans: nd (1850-1852) (6x3-7/8", 64 pgs, hand colored paper-c, B&W) (all versions Very Rare)

nn - First printing(s) publisher's address is 104 Nassau Street (1850-1851)
(1 copy sold for $800.00 in Fair)
nn - 2nd printing(s) publisher's address is 116 Nassau Street (1851-1852) (no known sales)
nn - 3rd printing(s) publisher's address is 107 Nassau Street (1852+) (no known sales)
NOTE: *The JUVENILE GEM is a gathering of multiple booklets under a single, hand colored cover (none of the interior booklets have the covers which they were given when sold separately). The publisher appears to have gathered whichever printings of each booklet were available when copies of THE JUVENILE GEM was assembled, so that the booklets within, and the conglomerate cover, may be from a mixture of printings. Contains two sequential comic booklets: THE ADVENTURES OF MR. TOM PLUMP, and OLD MOTHER MITTEN AND HER FUNNY KITTEN, plus five heavily illustrated children's booklets - **The Pretty Primer**, **The Funny Book**, **The Picture Book**, **The Two Sisters**, and **Story Of The Little Drummer**. Six of these -- including the two comic books -- were reprinted in the 1960's by Americana Review as a set of individual booklets, and included in a folder collectively titled "Six Children's Books of the 1850's".*

LANTERN, THE
Stringer & Townsend:1852-1853 (11x8-3/8", 12 pgs, soft paper, 6 ¢)

Leslie's Young America #1
1881 © Leslie & Company, NYC

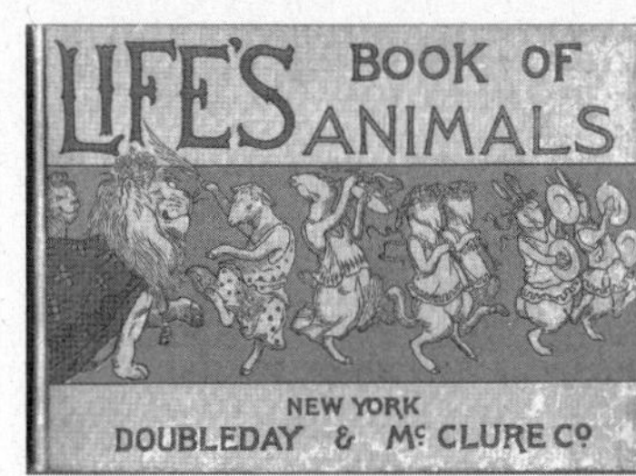

Life's Book of Animals
1888 © Doubleday & McClure Co.

Max and Maurice by Wilhelm Busch
1871 © Roberts Bros, Boston

FR1.0 GD2.0 FN6.0

1 Jan 10, 1852 37.50 75.00 150.00
2 25.00 50.00 100.00
3 First Frank Bellew cartoons onwards each issue 37.50 75.00 150.00
4 Bellew 's Mr Blobb begins 1/31/52 50.00 100.00 200.00
NOTE: *Bellew serial sequential comic strip "Mr Blobb In Search Of A Physician" becomes 2nd earliest known recurring character in American comic strips plus full page single panel Bellew cartoon "The Modern Frankenstein" take-off on Shelly's story.*
5 Hunsdale 2-panel "The Horrors of Slavery"; Mr Blobb 50.00 100.00 200.00
6 DF Read 15 panel "A Volley of Valentines"; Mr Blobb 50.00 100.00 200.00
7-8 10 Bellew's Mr Blobb continues 25.00 50.00 100.00
9 (4) panel "The Perils of Leap Year" MrBlobb 50.00 100.00 200.00
11 no Mr Blobb 20.00 40.00 80.00
12 Bellew's Mr Blobb continues 3/27/52 50.00 100.00 200.00
13 Bellew (10) panel sequential "Stump Speaking Studied" 50.00 100.00 200.00
14 no comic strips 20.00 40.00 80.00
15 Bellew's Mr Blobb ends (5) panel 4/17/52 50.00 100.00 200.00
16 Bellew begins new comic strip serial, "Mr. Bulbear, A Stockbroker, After having Supped at Delmonicos, Has A Dream", Part One, (6) panels 50.00 100.00 200.00
17 Bellew's Mr Bulbear continues 25.00 50.00 100.00
18 Bellew (8) panel "Trials of a Witness" 50.00 100.00 200.00
19 Bellew's Mr Bulbear's Dream continues 25.00 50.00 100.00
20-23 no comic strips 20.00 40.00 80.00
24 Bellew "Trials of a Publisher" (6) panel 50.00 100.00 200.00
25 comic strip "Travels of Jonathan Verdant"recurring character 25.00 50.00 100.00
26-49 contents to be indexed soon
50 (12/18/52) (2) panel Impertinent Smile 25.00 50.00 100.00
58 (2/12/53) (6) panel Trip to California 25.00 50.00 100.00
66 (4/9/53) (3) panel sequential strip 25.00 50.00 100.00

LAST SENSATION, THE (Becomes Day's Doings)
James Watts, NYC: Dec 27 1867-May 30 1868 (11x16 folio-size, 16 pgs, B&W)
issues with comic strips 50.00 100.00 200.00

LAUGH AND GROW FAT COMIC ALMANAC
Fisher & Brother, Philadelphia, New York & Boston: 1860-? (36 pgs)
nn 60.00 120.00 240.00

LEGEND OF SAM'L OF POSEN (O)
M.B. Curtis Company: 1884-85 (8x3-3/8", 44 pgs, Color-c, B&W interior)
nn - By M.B. Curtis 50.00 100.00 200.00
NOTE: Cover blurb says: From Early Days in Fatherland to affluence And Success in the Land of His Adoption, America

LESLIE'S YOUNG AMERICA (O. S)
Leslie & Co, 98 Chamber St, NY: 1881-82 (11-1/2x8", 5¢, B&W)
1 (7/9/81) back cover (6) panel strip 125.00 250.00 500.00
2 (7/16/81) back cover (9) panel strip 50.00 100.00 200.00
3 (7/23/81) back cover (16) panel Busch strip 67.50 125.00 250.00
9 (9/3/81) sequentials; Hopkins singles 50.00 100.00 200.00
15 (10/15/81) Zim or Frost? (6) panel strip 50.00 100.00 200.00
19 (11/12/81) (9) panel back-c strip 50.00 100.00 200.00
24 (4) panel strip 25 (2) panel back-c strip 50.00 100.00 200.00
26 27 (6) panel back-c strip 50.00 100.00 200.00
29 31 (12) panel strip 50.00 100.00 200.00
32 (2/11/82) (8) panel strip 50.00 100.00 200.00
issues without comic strips or Jules Verne 25.00 50.00 100.00
NOTE: Jules Verne stories begin with #1 and run thru at least #42

LIFE (M,O) (continues with Vol.35 No. 894+ in the Platinum Age section)
J.A.Mitchell: Vol.1 No.1 Jan. 4, 1883 - Vol.1 No.26 June 29, 1883 (10-1/4x8", 16 pgs, B&W, paper cover); J.A. Mitchell: Vol. 2 No. 27, July 5, 1883 - Vol. 6 No.148, Oct 29, 1885 (10-1/4x8-1/4", 16 pgs., B&W, paper cover); Mitchell & Miller: Vol.6 No.149, Nov. 5, 1885 - Vol. 31, No. 796, March 17, 1898 (10-3/8x8-3/8", 16 pgs., B&W, paper cover); Life Publishing Company: Vol. 31 No. 797, March 24, 1898 - Vol. 34 No. 893, Dec 28, 1899 (10-3/8 x 8-1/2", 20 pgs., B&W, paper cover)
1-26 (Scarce) (no known sales)
27-799 5.00 10.00 20.00
800 (4/7/1898) parody Yellow Kid / Spanish-American War cover (not by Outcault) 67.50 125.00 250.00
801-893 5.00 10.00 20.00
NOTE: *All covers for issues 1 - 26 are identical, apart from issue number & date.*
Hard bound collected volumes:
V. 1 (No.1-26) (Scarce) 67.50 125.00 250.00
V. 2-34 45.00 90.00 180.00
V. 31 YK #800 parody-c not by RFO 70.00 140.00 280.00
NOTE: *Because the covers of all issues in Volume 1 are identical, it was common practice to remove the covers before binding the issues together. This is not true of later volumes, though, in all volumes it was common to drop the advertising pages which appeared at the rear of each issue. Information on many more individual issues will expand next Guide.*

LIFE AND ADVENTURES OF JEFF DAVIS (I)
J.C. Haney & Co., NY: 1865 (10 cents, 7-1/2" x 4", 36 pgs, B&W, paper-c)
nn - By McArone (Scarce) 150.00 300.00 650.00
nn - 1974 Reprint (350) copies 6-3/4x4-3/8 50.00 10.00 20.00
nn - 1997 Reprint (7th Fla. Sutler, Clearwater, 6-3/4x4-1/4") – – 2.00
NOTE: *Humorous telling of the capture of Confederate President Jeff Davis in women's clothing, from the publisher of Merryman's Monthly. It contains an ad page for that publication; the material is perhaps reprinted from it. J.C. Haney licensed it to local printers, and so various publishers are found -- all printings currently regarded as simultaneous. (The Geo. H. Hees printing, Oswego, NY, contains an ad for the upcoming October 1865 issue of Merryman's Monthly, thus placing that printing in September 1865). Modern facsimile editions have been produced.*

LIFE IN PHILADELPHIA
W. Simpson, 66 Chestnut, Philadelphia; Siltart, No. 65 South Third St, Philadelphia: 1830 (7-3/4x6-7/8", 15 loose plates, hand colored copies exist, maybe B&W also)
nn - By Edward Williams Clay (1799-1857) (Very Rare) (no known sales)
NOTE: *First 13 plates etched, with many word balloons; scenes of exaggerated Black Americana in Philadelphia viewed one by one as broadsides. Had several publishers over the years. Was also eventually collected into a book of same name but only with the first 13 plates used; the last two not used in book. Collected book not yet viewed to share info.*

LIFE'S BOOK OF ANIMALS (M.S)
Doubleday & McClure Co.: 1898 (7-1/4x10-1/8", 88 pgs, color hardcover, B&W)
nn 25.00 50.00 100.00
NOTE: *Reprints funny animal single panel and strip cartoons reprinted from LIFE. Art by Blaisdell, Chip Bellew, Kemble, Hy Mayer, Sullivant, Woolf.*

LIFE'S COMEDY (M,S)
Charles Scribner's Sons: Series 1 1897 - Series 3 1898 (12x9-3/8", hardcover, B&W)
1 (142 pgs). 2, 3 (138 pgs) 60.00 120.00 240.00
NOTE: *Gibson a-1-3; c-3. Hy Mayer a-1-3. Rose O'Neill a-2-3. Stanlaws a-2-3. Sullivant a-1-2. Verbeek a-2. Wenzell a-1-3; c(painted)-2.*

LIFE, THE GOOD THINGS OF (M,S)
White, Stokes, & Allen, NY: 1884 - No.3 1886 ; Frederick A. Stokes, NY: No.4 1887; Frederick Stokes & Brother, NY: No.5 1888 - No.6 1889; Frederick A. Stokes Company, NY: No. 7 1890 - No.10 1893 (8-3/8x10-1/2", 74 pgs, gilted hardcover, B&W)
nn - 1884 (most common issue) 32.50 65.00 130.00
2 - 1885 32.50 65.00 130.00
3 - 1886 (76 pgs) 32.50 65.00 130.00
4 - 1887 (76 pgs) 32.50 65.00 130.00
5 - 1888 32.50 65.00 130.00
6 - 1889 32.50 65.00 130.00
7 - 1890 32.50 65.00 130.00
8 - 1891 (scarce) 50.00 100.00 200.00
9 - 1892 32.50 65.00 130.00
10 - 1893 32.50 65.00 130.00
NOTE: *Contains mostly single panel, and some sequential, comics reprinted from LIFE. Attwood a-1-4,10. Roswell Bacon a-5. Chip Bellew a-4-6. Frank Bellew a-4,6. Palmer Cox a-1. H. E. Dey a-5. C. D. Gibson a-4-10. F.M. Howarth a-5-6. Kemble a-1-3. Klapp a-5. Walt McDougall a-1-2. H. McVickar a-5; J. A. Mitchell a-5. Peter Newell a-2-3. Gray Parker a-4-5,7. J. Smith a-5. Albert E. Steiner a-5; T. S. Sullivant a-7-9. Wenzell a-8-10. Wilder a-3. Woolf a-3-6.*)

LIFE, THE SPICE OF (E,M,)
White and Allen: NY & London: 1888 (8-3/8x10-1/2",76 pgs, hard-c, B&W)
nn 50.00 100.00 200.00
NOTE: *Resembles **THE GOOD THINGS OF LIFE** in layout and format, and appears to be an attempt to compete with their former partner Frederick A. Stokes. However, the material is not from **LIFE**, but rather is reprinted and translated German sequential and single panel comics.*

LIFE'S PICTURE GALLERY (becomes LIFE'S PRINTS) (M,S,P)
Life Publishing Company, New York: nd (1898-1899) (paper cover, B&W) (all are scarce)
nn - (nd; 1898, 100 pgs, 5-1/4x8-1/2") Gibson-c of a woman with closed umbrella; 1st interior page announcing that after January 1, 1899 Gibson will draw exclusively for LIFE; the word "SPECIMEN" is printed in red, diagonally, across every print; a-Gibson, Rose O'Neill, Sullivant 37.50 75.00 150.00
nn - (nd; 1899, 128 pgs, 4-7/8x7-3/8") Gibson-c of a woman golfer; 1st interior page announcing that Gibson & Hanna, Jr. draw exclusively for LIFE; the word "SPECIMEN" is printed in red, horizontally, across every print. Includes prints from Gibson's **THE EDUCATION OF MR. PIPP**; a-Gibson, Sullivant 37.50 75.00 150.00
NOTE: *Catalog of prints reprinted from **LIFE** covers & centerspreads. The first catalog was given away free to anyone requesting it, but after many people got the catalog without ordering anything, subsequent catalogs were sold at 10 cents.*

LITTLE SICK BEAR, THE
Edwin W. Joy Co, San Francisco, CA: 1897 (6-1/4x5", 20 pgs, B&W, Scarce)
nn - By James Swinnerton one long sequential comic strip 200.00 400.00 800.00

LIGHT AND SHADE
William Drey Doppel Soap: 1892 (3-3/4x5-3/8", 20 pgs, B&W, color cover)
nn - By J.C. 50.00 100.00 200.00
NOTE: Contains (8) panel comic strip of black boy whose skin turns white using this soap.

LONDON OUT OF TOWN, OR THE ADVENTURES OF THE BROWNS AT THE SEA SIDE BY LUKE LIMNER, ESQ. (O)
David Bogue, 86 Fleet St, London: c1847 (5-1/2x4-1/4, 32 pgs, yellow paper hard-c, B&W
nn - By John Leighton 150.00 300.00 600.00
NOTE: one long sequential comic strip multiple-panel per page story; each page crammed with panels inspired by the Töpffer comic books Bogue began several years earlier.

LORGNETTE, THE (S)

Merryman's Monthly v3#5 with Bellew strip
May 1865 © J. C. Haney & Co., New York

Minneapolis Journal Cartoons Second Series
1895 © Minneapolis Journal

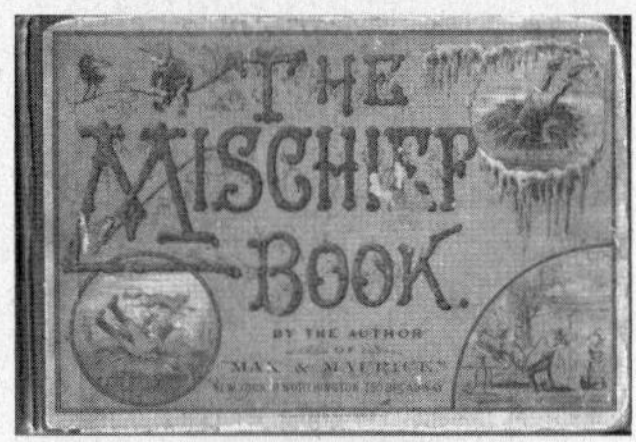

The Mischief Book by Wilhelm Busch
color cover art variation
1880 © R. Worthington, New York

FR1.0 GD2.0 FN6.0

George J Coombes, New York: 1886 (6-1/2x8-3/4, 38 pgs, hard-c, B&W)

nn - By J.K. Bangs 50.00 100.00 200.00

LOVING BALLAD OF LORD BATEMAN, THE (E,I)
G.W. Carleton & Co., Publishers, Madison Square, NY: 1871 (9x5-7/8",16 pgs, soft-c, 6¢)

nn - By George Cruikshank 50.00 100.00 200.00

MADISON'S EXPOSITION OF THE AWFUL & TERRIFYING CEREMONIES OF THE ODD FELLOWS
T.E. Peterson & Brothers, 306 Chestnut St, Phila: 1870s? (5-3/4x9-1/4, 68 pgs, B&W)
nn - single panel cartoons 50.00 100.00 200.00

MANNERS AND CUSTOMS OF YE HARVARD STUDENTE (M,S)
Houghton Mifflin & Co., Boston & Moses King, Cambridge: 1877 (7-7/8x11", 72 pgs, printed one side, hardc, B&W)

nn - by F.G. Attwood 75.00 150.00 300.00
NOTE: *Collection of cartoons originally serialized in the* ***Harvard Lampoon****. Attwood later became a major cartoonist for* ***Life****.*

MAN WHO WOULD LIKE TO MARRY, THE (O)
Frederick Warne & Co., London & New York: nd (c 1880's) (9-1/2x11-1/2", 28 pgs, printed 1 side, paper-c, B&W)

nn - By Harry Parkes 62.50 125.00 250.00
NOTE: *Published simultaneously with its companion volume,* ***The Girl Who Wouldn't Mind Getting Married****.*

MAX AND MAURICE: A JUVENILE HISTORY IN SEVEN TRICKS (E)
(see also Teasing Tom and Naughty Ned)
Roberts Brothers, Boston: 1871 first edition (8-1/8 x 5-1/2", 76 pgs, hard & soft-c B&W)

nn - By Wilhelm Busch (green or brown cloth hardbound) 275.00 550.00 1050.00
nn - exactly the same, but soft paper cover 162.00 325.00 650.00
NOTE: *Page count includes 56 pgs of art, two blank endpapers at the front (one colored), 8 pgs of ads at the back, two blank endpapers at the end (one colored), and the covers. Green or brown illustrated hardcover. The name of the author is given on the title page as "William Busch." We assume this to be the 1st edition. Back side of title page states: Entered according to Act of Congress, in the year 1870, by Roberts Brothers, In the office of the Librarian of Congress at Washington.*

nn - By Wilhelm Busch (1872 edition) 225.00 470.00 900.00
nn - 1875 reprint 100.00 200.00 450.00
nn - 1882 reprint (76 pgs, hand colored- c/a, 75¢) 100.00 200.00 400.00
nn- 1889 reprint with new art on cover printed in full color 100.00 200.00 400.00
NOTE: *Each of the above contains 56 pages of art and text in a transitional format between a regular children's book and a comic book (the page count difference is ad pages in back). Seminal inspiration for William Randolph Hearst to acquire as a "new comic" (following the wild success of Outcault's Yellow Kid) to license M&M from Busch and hire Rudolph Dirks in late 1897 to create a New York American newspaper incarnation. In Hearst's English language newspapers it was called The Katzenjammer Kids and in his German language NYC newspaper it was titled Max & Moritz, Busch's original title. At least 50 other reprints versions are reputed to exist printed thru 1900. Translated from the 1865 German original. We are still sorting out the edition confusion.*

MAX AND MAURICE: A JUVENILE HISTORY IN SEVEN TRICKS (E)
(see also Teasing Tom and Naughty Ned)
Little, Brown, and Company, Boston: 1898-1902 (8-1/8 x 5-3/4", 72 pgs, hardcover, black ink on orange paper) (various early reprints)

nn - 1898 , 1899 By Wilhelm Busch 50.00 100.00 200.00
nn - 1902 (64 pages, B&W) 10.00 30.00 90.00

MERRY MAPLE LEAVES Or A Summer In The Country (S)
E.P. Dutton And Company, New York: 1872 (9-3/8x7-3/8", 90 and 86 pgs pgs, hard-c)

nn - By Abner Perk 25.00 50.00 150.00
NOTE: *Each drawing contained in a maple leaf motif by Livingston Hopkins and others.*

MERRYMAN'S MONTHLY A COMIC MAGAZINE FOR THE FAMILY (M,O,E)
J.C. Haney & Co, NY: 1863-1875 (10-7/8x7-13/16", 30 pgs average, B&W)

Certain issues with sequential comics 100.00 200.00 400.00
NOTE: *Sequential strips by Frank Bellew Sr, Wilhelm Busch found so far; others?*

MERRYTHOUGHT, OR LAUGHTER FROM YEAR TO YEAR, THE
Fisher & Brother, Phila, Baltimore: early 1850s (4-1/2x7", B&W)
nn - many singles, some sequential (Very Rare) (no known sales)
NOTE: *See Vict article for back cover pic which is earliest known use of the term Comic Book*

MESSRS. BROWN, JONES, AND ROBINSON, THE FOREIGN TOUR OF
(see also **THE CLOWN, OR THE BANQUET OF WIT**) (E,M,O,G)
Bradbury & Evans, London: 1854 (11-5/8x9-1/2", 196 pgs, gilted hard-c, B&W)

nn - By Richard Doyle 35.00 70.00 200.00
nn - Bradbury & Evans 1900 reprint 20.00 40.00 80.00
NOTE: *Protective sheets between each page (not part of page count). Expanded and redrawn sequential comics story from the serialized episodes originally published in PUNCH. Also comes in a 174 pg 8-3/4x11" version.*

MESSRS. BROWN, JONES, AND ROBINSON, THE LAUGHABLE ADVENTURES OF (E,M,G)
Garrett, Dick & Fitzgerald, NY: nd (1856 or 1857) (5-3/4x9-1/4", 100 pgs, printed one side only, paper-c, B&W)

nn - (Very Rare) by Richard Doyle c/a 300.00 500.00 1100.00
NOTE: *1st American reprinting of the "Foreign Tour"; reformatted into a small oblong format. Links the earlier Garrett & Co. to the later Dick & Fitzgerald. Back cover reprints full size the Garrett & Co. version cover for Oscar Shanghai. Interior front cover reprints full size the Garrett & Co. version cover for Slyfox-Wikof. Issued without a title page.*

MESSRS. BROWN, JONES, AND ROBINSON, THE FOREIGN TOUR OF (E,M,G)
D. Appleton & Co., New York: 1860 & 1877 (11-5/8x9-1/2", 196 pgs, gilted hard-c, B&W)

nn - (1860 printing) by Richard Doyle 30.00 60.00 200.00
nn - (1871 printing) by Richard Doyle 30.00 60.00 150.00
nn - (1877 printing) by Richard Doyle 30.00 60.00 150.00
NOTE: *Protective sheets between each page (not part of page count). Reprints the Bradbury & Evans edition.*

MESSRS BROWN JONES AND ROBINSON, THE AMERICAN TOUR OF (O,G)
D. Appleton & Co., New York: 1872 (11-5/8x9-1/2", 158 pgs, printed one side only, B&W, green gilted hard-c)

nn - By Toby 70.00 140.00 400.00
NOTE: *Original American graphic novel sequel to Richard Doyle's Foreign Tour of Brown, Jones, and Robinson, with the same characters visiting New York, Canada, and Cuba. Protective sheets between each page (not part of page count).*

MESSRS. BROWN, JONES, AND ROBINSON, THE LAUGHABLE ADVEN. OF (E,M,G)
Dick & Fitzgerald, NY: nd (late 1870's - 1888) (5-3/4x9-1/4", 100 pgs, printed one side only, green paper-c, B&W)

nn - (Scarce) by Richard Doyle 100.00 200.00 450.00
NOTE: *Reprints the Garrett, Dick & Fitzgerald printing, with the following changes: Takes what had been page 12 in the Garrett, D&F printing (art by M.H. Henry), and makes it a title page, which is numbered page 1. The first story page, "Go to the Races", is numbered 2 (whereas it is numbered 1 in the Garrett, Dick & Fitzgerald version). Numbering stays ahead of the G,D&F edition by 1 page up through page 12, after which the page numbering becomes identical.*

MINNEAPOLIS JOURNAL CARTOONS (N,S)
Minneapolis Journal: nn 1894 - No.2 1895 (7-3/4" x 10-7/8", 76 pgs, B&W, paper-c)

nn (1894) (Rare) 50.00 100.00 200.00
Second Series (1895) (Rare) 50.00 100.00 200.00
nn- "War Cartoons" Jan 1899 (9x8", 160 pgs, paperback, punched & string bound) (Scarce) 24.00 96.00 170.00
NOTE: *Reprints single panel cartoons from the prior year, by Charles "Bart" L. Bartholomew.*

MISCHIEF BOOK, THE (E)
R. Worthington, New York: 1880 (7-1/8 x 10-3/4", 176 pgs, hard-c, B&W)

nn - Green cloth binding; green on brown cover; cover art by R. Lewis based on Busch art by Wilhelm Busch 175.00 350.00 735.00
nn - Blue cloth binding; hand colored cover; completely different cover art based on Busch by Wilhelm Busch 175.00 350.00 735.00
NOTE: *Translated by Abby Langdon Alger. American published anthology collection of Wilhelm Busch comic strips. Includes two of the strips found in the British "Bushel of Merry-Thoughts" collection, translated better, and with the dropped panel restored. Unknown which cover version was first.*

MISSES BROWN, JONES AND ROBINSON, THE FOREIGN TOUR OF THE (E,O,G)
Bickers & Sons, London: nd (c1850's) (12-1/4" x 9-7/8", 108 pgs, printed on one side, B&W, hard-c)

nn- "by Miss Brown" (Rare) 100.00 200.00 400.00
NOTE: *A female take on Doyle's Foreign Tour, by an unknown woman artist, using the pseudonym "Miss Brown."*

MISS MILLY MILLEFLEUR'S CAREER (S)
Sheldon & Co., NY: 1869 (10-3/4x9-7/8", 74 pgs, purple hard-c)

nn - Artist unknown (Rare) 75.00 150.00 300.00

MR PODGER AT COUP'S GREATEST SHOW ON EARTH HIS HAPS AND MISHAPS, THE ADVENTURES OF (O,S)
W.C. Coup, New York: 1884 (5-5/8x4-1/4", 20 pgs, color-c, B&W)

nn - Circus Themes; Similar to Barker's Comic Almanacs 25.00 50.00 100.00

MR. TOODLES' GREAT ELEPHANT HUNT (See Peter Piper in Bengal)
Brother Jonathan, NYC: 1850s (4-1/4x7-7/8", page count presently unknown)

nn - catalog contains comic strip (Very Rare) (no known sales)

MR. TOODLES' TERRIFIC ELEPHANT HUNT
Dick & Fitzgerald, NYC: 1860s (5-3/4x9-1/4", 32 pgs, paper-c, B&W) (Very Rare)

nn - catalog reprint contains 28 panel comic strip 150.00 300.00 600.00

MRS GRUNDY
Mrs Grundy Publishing Co, NYC: July 8 1865-Sept 30 1865 (weekly)

1-13 Thomas Nast, Hoppin, Stephens, 50.00 100.00 200.00

MUSEUM OF WONDERS, A (O,I)
Routledge & Sons: 1894 (13x10", 64 pgs, color-c, color thru out)

nn - By Frederick Opper 100.00 200.00 500.00

MY FRIEND WRIGGLES, A (Laughter) Moving Panorama, of His Fortunes And Misfortunes, Illustrated With Over 200 Engravings, of Most Comic Catastrophes And Side-Splitting Merriment) (O,G)
Stearn & Co, 202 Williams St, NY: 1850s (5-7/8x9-3/4", 100 pgs, B&W)

nn - By S. P. Avery (also the engraver) (Very Rare) 200.00 400.00 800.00

MY SKETCHBOOK (E,S)
Dana Estes & Charles E. Lauriat, Boston; J. Sabins & Sons, New York: circa 1880s (9-3/8x12", brown hard-c)

nn - By George Cruikshank 25.00 50.00 150.00
NOTE: *Reprints British editions 1834-36; extensive usage of word balloons.*

Nasby's Life Of Andy Jonson
1866 © Jesse Haney Company

99 "Woolf's" from Truth
1896 © Truth Company

The Adventures of Obadiah Oldbuck 4th printing
mid-1850s © Brother Jonathan Offices, NY

FR1.0 GD2.0 FN6.0

NASBY'S LIFE OF ANDY JONSON (O, M)
Jesse Haney Co., Publishers No. 119 Nassau St, NY: 1866 (4-1/2x7-1/2, 48 pgs, B&W)
nn - President Andrew Johnson satire 100.00 200.00 450.00
NOTE: Blurb further reads: With a True Pictorial History of His STumping Tour Out West By Petroleum V. Nasby, A Dimmicrat of Thirty Years Standing, And Who Allus Tuk His Licker Straight. Front of book has long sequential comic strip satire on President Andrew Johnson, misspelling his name on the cover on purpose.

NAST'S ILLUSTRATED ALMANAC
Harper & Brothers, Franklin Square, NYC: 1872-1874 (8x5.5", 80 pgs, B&W, 35¢)
nn 60.00 120.00 240.00

NAST'S WEEKLY (O,S)
???: 1892-93 (Quarto Weekly)
all issues scarce 50.00 100.00 200.00

NATIONAL COMIC ALMANAC
An Association of Gentlemen, Boston: 1838-?? (8.25x4.75", 34 pgs, B&W)
nn 60.00 120.00 240.00

NEW AMERICAN COMIC ALL-IMAKE (ELTON'S BASKET OF COMICAL SCRAPS), THE
Elton, Publisher, New York: 1839 (7-1/2x4-5/8, 24 pgs)
1 100.00 200.00 400.00

NEW BOOK OF NONSENSE, THE: A Contribution To The Great Central Fair In Aid of the Sanitary Commission (O,S)
Ashmead & Evans, No. 724 Chestnut St, Philadelphia: June 1864 (red hard-c)
nn - Artists unknown (Scarce) 50.00 150.00 300.00

NEW YORK ILLUSTRATED NEWS
Frank Leslie, NYC: 10/14/76-June 1884
average issues with comic strips 20.00 40.00 80.00

NEW YORK PICAYUNE (see PHUN FOTOCRAFT)
Woodward & Hutchings: 1850-1855 newspaper-size weekly; 1856-1857 Folio Monthly 16x10.5; 1857-1858 Quarto Weekly; 1858-1860 Quarto Weekly
Average Issue With Comic Strips 50.00 100.00 200.00
Issues with Full Front Page Comic Strip 100.00 200.00 400.00
NOTE: *Many issues contain Frank Bellew sequential comic strips & single panel cartoons. Later issues published by Woodward, Levison & Robert Gun (1853-1857) ; Levison & Thompson (1857-1860)*

NICK-NAX
Levison & Haney, NY: 1857-1858? (11x7-3/4", 32 pgs, B&W, paper-c)
v2 #10 Feb 1858 has many single panel cartoons 50.00 100.00 200.00

99 "WOOLFS" FROM TRUTH (see Sketches of Lowly Life in a Great City, Truth)
Truth Company, NY: 1896 (9x5-1/2", 72 pgs, varnished paper-like cloth hard-c, 25 cents)
nn - By Michael Angelo Woolf (Rare) 150.00 300.00 600.00
NOTE: *Woolf's cartoons are regarded as a primary influence on R.F. Outcault in the later development of The Yellow Kid newspaper strip. Copy sold in 2002 on eBay for $800.00.*

NONSENSE OR, THE TREASURE BOX OF UNCONSIDERED TRIFLES
Fisher & Brother, 12 North Sixth St, Phila, PA, 64 Baltimore St, Baltimore, MD: early 1850s (4-1/2x7", 128 pgs, B&W)
nn - much Davy Crocket sequential story-telling comic strips 250.00 500.00 1000.00

OBADIAH OLDBUCK, THE ADVENTURES OF MR. (E,G)
Tilt & Bogue, London: nd (1840-41) (5-15/16x9-3/16", 176 pgs,B&W, gilted hard-c)
nn - By Rodolphe Töpffer 800.00 1300.00 2900.00
nn - Hand coloured edition (Very Rare) (no known sales)
NOTE: *This is the British edition, translating the unauthorized redrawn 1839 edition from Parisian publisher Aubert, adapted from Töpffer's "Les Amours de Mr. Vieux Bois" (aka "Histoire de Mr. Vieux Bois"), originally published in French in Switzerland, in 1837 (2nd ed. 1839). Early 19th century books are often found rebound, with original cover and/or title page gone. To distinguish editions having no cover or title page: the British oblong editions (published by Tilt & Bogue) use Roman Numerals to number pages. American oblong shaped editions use Arabic Numerals. British are printed on one side only. This is the earliest known English language sequential comic book. Has a new title page with art by Robert Cruikshank.*

OBADIAH OLDBUCK, THE ADVENTURES OF MR. (E,G)
Wilson and Company, New York: September 14, 1842 (11-3/4x9", 44 pgs, B&W, yellow paper-c on bookstand editions, hemp paper interior)
Brother Jonathan Extra No. IX - Rare bookstand edition 2200.00 5000.00 10,000.00
Brother Jonathan Extra No. IX Very Rare subscriber/mailorder 2200.00 5000.00 10,000.00
NOTE: *By Rodolphe Töpffer. Earliest known sequential American comic book, reprinting the 1841 British edition. Pages are numbered with Roman numerals. States "BROTHER JONATHAN EXTRA - ADVENTURES OF MR. OBADIAH OLDBUCK." at the top of each page. Prints 2 to 3 tiers of panels on both sides of each page. Copies could be had for ten cents according to adverts in* ***Brother Jonathan****. By Rodolphe Töpffer with cover masthead design by David Claypool Johnston, and cover art beneath the masthead reprinting Robert Cruikshank's title page art from the Tilt & Bogue edition. A special, additional cover was added for copies sold on stands (it was not issued with mail order or subscriber copies). Only 1 known copy possesses (partially) this very thin outer yellow cover. A decent (subscriber) copy sold on eBay in later October 2002 for over $3500.00. In 2005, a G/VG for $20,000; and a VG for $20,000. An apparent GD copy sold in auction in 2007 for $9560. A FA/GD copy sold in 2008 for $4182.50. A bound edition sold in 2010 for $2270.50. (Prices vary widely.)*

OBADIAH OLDBUCK, THE ADVENTURES OF MR. (E,G)
Wilson & Co, New York: nd (1849) (5-11/16x8-3/8", 84 pgs, B&W,paper-c)
nn - by Rodolphe Töpffer; title page by Robert Cruikshank (Very Rare) 500.00 1200.00 4200.00
NOTE: *2nd Wilson & Co printing, reformatted into a small oblong format, with nine panels edited out, and text modified to smooth out this removal. Results in four less printed tiers/strips. Pages are numbered via Arabic numerals. Every panel on Pages 11, 14, 19, 21, 24, 34, 35 has one line of text. Reformatted to conform with British first edition.*

FR1.0 GD2.0 FN6.0

OBADIAH OLDBUCK, THE ADVENTURES OF MR. (E,G)
Wilson & Co, 162 Nassau, NY: nd (early-1850s) (5-11/16x8-3/8", 84 pgs, B&W, yellow-c
nn - 3rd USA Printing by Rodolphe Töpffer; title page by Robert Cruikshank (Very Rare) Says By Timothy Crayon, an obvious pseudonym 800.00 1600.00 4200.00
NOTE: Front cover banner the giant is holding says "Done With Drawings By Timothy Crayon, Gypsographer, 188 Comic Etchings On Antimony" Title page changes address to No. 15 Spruce-Street. (Late 162 Nassau Street.)

OBADIAH OLDBUCK, THE ADVENTURES OF MR..
Brother Jonathan Offices: ND (mid-1850s) (5-11/16x8-3/8", 84 pages, B&W, oblong)
nn - 4th printing; Originally by Rodolphe Töpffer (Very Rare) 500.00 1200.00 4200.00
NOTE: *Cover States: "New York: Published at the Brother Jonathan Office". Front cover banner the giant is holding says "Done With Drawings By Timothy Crayon, Gypsographer, 188 Comic Designs On Antimony."*

OBADIAH OLDBUCK, THE ADVENTURES OF MR. (E,G)
Dick & Fitzgerald, New York: nd (various printings; est. 1870s to 1888) (Thirty Cents, 84 pgs, B&W, paper-c) (all versions scarce)
nn - Black print on green cover(5-11/16x8-15/16"); string bound 200.00 400.00 1000.00
nn - Black print on blue cover; same format as green-c 200.00 400.00 1000.00
nn - Black print on white cover(5-13/16x9-3/16"); staple bound beneath cover); this is a later printing than the blue or green-c 200.00 400.00 1000.00
NOTE: *Reprints the abbreviated 1849 Wilson & Co. 2nd printing. Pages are numbered via Arabic numerals. Many of the panels on Pages 11, 14, 19, 21, 24, 34, 35 take two lines to print the same words found in the Wilson & Co version, which used only one text line for the same panels. Unknown whether the blue or green cover is earlier. White cover version has "thirty cents" line blackened out on the two copies known to exist. Robert Cruikshank's title page has been made the cover in the D&F editions.*

OLD FOGY'S COMIC ALMANAC
Philip J. Cozans, NY: 1858 (4-7/8x7-1/4, 48 pgs)
nn - sequential comic strip told one panel per page 50.00 100.00 200.00
NOTE: Contains (12) panel "Fourth of July in New York" sequential

OLD MOTHER MITTEN AND HER FUNNY KITTEN (see also **The Juvenile Gem**) (O)
Huestis & Cozans: nd(1850-1852) (6x3-7/8"12pgs, hand colored paper-c, B&W)
nn - first printing(s) publisher's address is 104 Nassau Street (1850-1851) (Very Rare) (no known sales)
NOTE: *A hand colored outer cover is highly rare, with only 1 recorded copy possessing it. Front cover image and text is repeated precisely on page 3 (albeit b&w), and only interior pages are numbered, together leading owners of coverless copies to believe they have the cover. The true back cover has ads for the publisher. Cover was issued only with copies which were sold separately - books which were bound together as part of THE JUVENILE GEM never had such covers.*

OLD MOTHER MITTEN AND HER FUNNY KITTEN (see JUVENILE GEM) (O)
Philip J. Cozans: nd (1850-1852) (6x3-7/8",12 pgs, hand colored paper-c, B&W)
nn - Second printing(s) publisher's address is 116 Nassau Street (1851-1852) (Very Rare) (no known sales)
nn - Third printing(s) publisher's address is 107 Nassau Street (1852+) (Very Rare) (no known sales)

OLD MOTHER MITTEN AND HER FUNNY KITTEN
Americana Review, Scotia, NY: nd (1960's) (6-1/4x4-1/8", 8 pgs, side-stapled, cardboard, B&W)
nn - Modern reprint 2.50 5.00 10.00
NOTE: *Issued within a folder titled SIX CHILDREN'S BOOKS OF THE 1850'S. States "Reprinted by American Review" at bottom of front cover. Reprints the 104 Nassau Street address.*

ON THE NILE (O,G)
James R. Osgood & Co., Boston: 1874 ; **Houghton, Osgood & Co., Boston:** 1880 (112 pgs, gilted green hardcover, B&W)
1st printing (1874; 10-3/4x16") - by Augustus Hoppin 45.00 90.00 180.00
2nd printing (1880; smaller sized) 32.50 65.00 130.00

OSCAR SHANGHAI, THE EXTRAORDINARY AND MIRTH-PROVKING ADVENTURES BY SEA & LAND OF (O, G)
Garrett & Co., Publishers, No. 18 Ann Street, New York: May 1855 (5-3/4x9-1/4", 100 pgs, printed one side only, paper-c, 25¢, B&W)
nn - Samuel Avery-c; interior by ALC Very Rare) 1000.00 2000.00 4000.00
NOTE: *Not much is known of this first edition as the data comes from a recently rediscovered* ***Brother Jonathan*** *catalog issued circa 1853-55. No original known yet to exist.*

OSCAR SHANGHAI, THE WONDERFUL AND AMUSING DOINGS BY SEA AND LAND OF (G)
Dick & Fitzgerald, 10 Ann St, NY: nd (1870s-1888) (25 ¢, 5-3/4x9-1/4", 100 pgs, printed one side only, green paper c, B&W)
nn - Cover by Samuel Avery; interior by ALC (Rare) 300.00 500.00 1000.00
NOTE: *Exact reprint of Garrett & Co original.*

OUR ARTIST IN CUBA (O)
Carleton, New York: 1865 (6-5/8x4-3/8", 120 pgs, printed one side only, gilted hard-c, B&W)
nn - By Geo. W. Carleton 37.50 75.00 150.00

OUR ARTIST IN CUBA, PERU, SPAIN, AND ALGIERS (O)
Carleton: 1877 (6-1/2x5-1/8", 156 pgs, hard-c, B&W)
nn - By Geo. W. Carleton 50.00 100.00 200.00
nn - By Geo. W. Carleton (wraps paper cover) (Rare) 45.00 90.00 180.00

The Wonderful and Amusing Doings by Sea & Land of Oscar Shanghai 1870s © Dick & Fitzgerald, New York

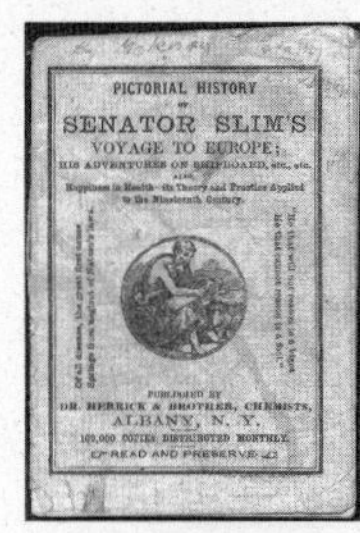

Pictorial History of Senator Slim's Voyage To Europe 1860 © Dr. Herrick & Brother, Albany, NY

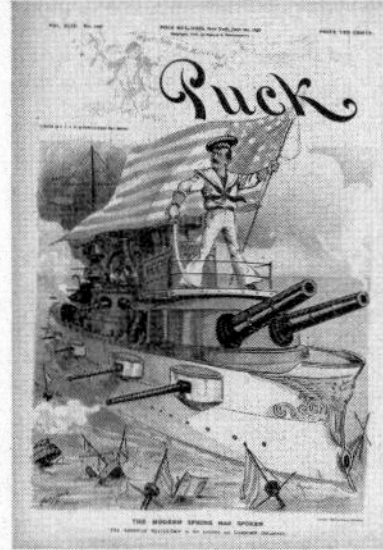

PUCK © Keppler & Schwarzman, NY

NOTE: *Reprints OUR ARTIST IN CUBA and OUR ARTIST IN PERU, then adds new section on Spain and Algiers.*

OUR ARTIST IN PERU (O)
Carleton, New York: 1866 (7-3/4x5-7/8", 68 pgs, gilted hardcover, B&W)
nn- By Geo. W. Carleton 37.50 75.00 150.00
NOTE: *Contains advertisement for the upcoming books **OUR ARTIST IN ITALY** and **OUR ARTIST IN FRANCE**, but no such publications have been found to date.*

PARSON SOURBALL'S EUROPEAN TOUR (O)
Duff and Ashmead: 1867 (6x7-1/2", 76 pgs, blue embossed title hard-c)
nn - By Horace Cope 100.00 200.00 400.00
NOTE: see **REV. MR. SOURBALL'S EUROPEAN TOUR, THE** for the soft paper cover version

PEN AND INK SKETCHES OF YALE NOTABLES (O,S)
Soule, Thomas and Winsor, St. Louis: 1872 (12-1/4x9-3/4", B&W)
By Squills 25.00 50.00 100.00
NOTE: *Printed by Steamlith Press, The R.P. Studley Company, St Louis.*

PETER PIPER IN BENGAL
Bengamin H Day.Publisher, Brother Jonathan Cheap Book Establishment, 48 Beekman, NY: 1953-55 (6-5/8x4-1/4, 36 pgs, yellow paper-c, B&W, 3 cents - two dollars per hundred) (Very Rare)
nn - By John Tenniel - 32 panel comic strip Punch-r 500.00 1000.00 2100.00
NOTE: *Actually also a catalog of inexpensive books, prints, maps and half a dozen comic books for sale on separate pages from publishers Day and Garrett - see full story of this brand new find in the Victorian Era essay. A complete copy with split spine sold in November 2002 for $750.00. Published date most likely 1855.*

THE PHILADELPHIA COMIC ALMANAC (S)
G. Strong, 44 Strawberry St, NYC: 1835 (8-1/2x5", 36 pgs)
nn - 100.00 200.00 600.00
NOTE: 77 engravings full of recurring cartoon characters but not sequential; early use of recurring characters.

PHIL MAY'S SKETCH BOOK (E,S,M)
R.H. Russell, New York: 1899 (14-5/8x10", 64 pgs, brown hard-c, B&W)
nn - By Phil May 32.50 65.00 130.00
NOTE: *American reprint of the British edition.*

PHUNNY PHELLOW, THE
Oakie, Dayton & Jones: Oct 1859-1876; **Street & Smith** 1876: (Folio Monthly)
average issue with Thomas Nast 50.00 100.00 200.00

PHUN FOTOCRAFT, KEWREUS KONSEETS KOMICALLY ILLUSTRATED BY A KWEER FELLER (N) (see **NEW YORK PICAYUNE)**
The New York Picayune, NY: 1850s (104 pgs)
nn - Mostly Frank Bellew, some John Leach 250.00 500.00 1000.00
NOTE: Many sequential comic strips as well as single cartoons all collected from The New York Picayune. Ross & Tousey, Agents, 121 Nassau St, NY. The Picayune ran many sequential comic strips in its decade.

PICTORIAL HISTORY OF SENATOR SLIM'S VOYAGE TO EUROPE
Dr. Herrick & Brother, Chemists, Albany, NY: 1860 (3-1/4x4-3/4", 32 pgs, B&W)
nn - By John McLenan Very Rare 150.00 300.00 600.00

PICTURES OF ENGLISH SOCIETY (Parchment-Paper Series, No.4) (M,S,E)
D. Appleton & Co., New York: 1884 (5-5/8x4-3/8", 108 pgs, paper-c, B&W)
4 - By George du Maurier; Punch-r 30.00 60.00 120.00
NOTE: *Every other page is a full page cartoon, with the opposite page containing the cartoon's caption.*

PICTURES OF LIFE AND CHARACTER (M,S,E)
Bradbury and Evans, London: No.1 1855 - No.5 c1864 (12-1/2x18", 100 pgs, illustrated hard-c, B&W)
nn (No.1) (1855) 32.50 65.00 130.00
2 (1858), 3 (1860) 32.50 65.00 130.00
4 (nd; c1862) 5 (nd; c1864) 32.50 65.00 130.00
nn (nd (late 1860's) 32.50 65.00 130.00
NOTE: 2-1/2x18-1/4", 494 pgs, green gilted-c) reprints 1-5 in one book
1-3 John Leech's... (nd; 12-3/8x10", ? pgs, red gilted-c). 25.00 50.00 100.00
NOTE: *Reprints John Leech cartoons from **Punch**. note that the Volume Number is mentioned only on the last page of these versions.*

PICTURES OF LIFE AND CHARACTER (E,M,S)
G.P. Putnam's Sons: 1880's (8-5/8x6-1/4", 218 pgs, hardcover, color-cr, B&W)
nn - John Leech (single panel **Punch** cartoon-r) 20.00 40.00 160.00
NOTE: *Leech reprints which extend back to the 1850s.*

PICTURES OF LIFE AND CHARACTER (Parchment-Paper Series) (E,M,S) (see also Humerous Masterpieces)
D. Appleton & Co., NY: 1884 (30¢, 5-3/4 x 4-1/2", 104 pgs, paper-c, B&W)
nn - John Leech (single panel **Punch** cartoon-r) 20.00 40.00 160.00
NOTE: *An advertisment in the back refers to a cloth-bound edition for 50 cents.*

PIPPIN AMONG THE WIDE-AWAKES (O,S)
Werill & Chapin, 113 Nassau St, NYC, NY): 1860 (6x4-1/2", 36 pgs, 6 cents)
nn - Artist unknown (Very Rare) 100.00 200.00 400.00

PLISH AND PLUM (E.G)
Roberts Brothers, Boston: 1883 (8-1/8x5-3/4", 80 pgs, hardcover, B&W)
nn - By Wilhelm Busch 40.00 80.00 200.00
nn - Reprint (Roberts Brothers, 1895) 40.00 80.00 200.00
nn - Reprint (Little, Brown & Co., 1899) 40.00 80.00 200.00
NOTE: *The adventures of two dogs.*

POUNDS OF FUN
Frank Tousey, 34 North Moore St, NY: 1881 (6-1/2x9-1/2", 68pgs, B&W)
nn - Bellew, Worth, Woolf, Chips 40.00 80.00 200.00

PRESIDENTS MESSAGE, THE
G.P. Putnam's Sons, NY: 1887 (5-3/4x7-5/8, 44 pgs)
nn - (19) Thomas Nast single panel full page cartoons 40.00 80.00 200.00

PROTECT THE U.S. FROM JOHN BULL - PROTECTION PICTURES FROM JUDGE
Judge Publishing, New York: 1888 ((10 cents, 6-7/8x10-3/8", 36 pgs, paper-c, B&W)
nn - (Scarce) 25.00 50.00 100.00
NOTE: *Reprints both cartoons and commentary from **Puck**, concerning the issue of tariffs which were then being debated in Congress. Art by Gillam, Hamilton, Victor.*

PUCK (German language edition, St. Louis) (M,O) (see also Die Vehme)
Publisher unknown, St. Louis: No.1, March 18, 1871 - No. ??, Aug. 24, 1872 (B&W, paper-c)
1-?? (Very Rare) by Joseph Keppler (no known sales)
NOTE: *Joseph Keppler's second attempt at a weekly humor periodical, following **Die Vehme** one year earlier. This was his first attempt to launch using the title **Puck**. This German language version ran for a full year before being joined by an English language version.*

PUCK (English language edition, St. Louis) (M,O)
Publisher unknown, St. Louis: No.1, March ?? 1872 - No. ??, Aug. 24, 1872 (B&W, paper c)
1-?? (Very Rare) by Joseph Keppler (no known sales)
NOTE: *Same material as in the German language edition, but in English.*

PUCK, ILLUSTRIRTES HUMORISTISCHES WOCHENBLATT (German language edition, NYC) (M,O)
Keppler & Schwarzmann, New York: No.1 Sept (27) 1876 - 1164 Dec ?? 1899 (10 cents, color front/back-c and centerspread, remainder B&W, paper-c)
1-26 (Volume 1; Rare) by Joseph Keppler - these issues precede the English language version, and contain cartoons not found in them. Includes cartoons on the controversial Tilden-Hayes 1876 Presidential Election debacle. (no known sales)
27-52 (Volume 2; Rare) by Joseph Keppler - contains some cartoon material not found in the English language editions. Particularly in the earlier issues. (no known sales)
53-1164 10.00 20.00 50.00
Bound Volumes (six month, 26 issue run each):
Vol. 1 (Rare) (no known sales)
Vol. 2-4 (Rare) (no known sales)
Vol. 5-47 62.50 125.00 250.00
NOTE: *Joseph Keppler's second, and successful, attempt to launch **Puck**. In German. The first six months precede the launch of the English language edition. Soon after (but not immediately after) the launch of the English edition, both editions began sharing the same cartoons, but, their prose material always remained different. The German language edition ceased publication at the end of 1899, while the English language edition continued into the early 20th Century. First American periodical to feature printed color every issue.*

PUCK (English language edition, NYC) (M,O)
Keppler & Schwarzmann, New York: No.1 March (14) 1877 - 1190 Dec ?? 1899 (10 cents, color front/back-c and centerspread, remainder B&W, paper-c)
1 (Rare) by Joseph Keppler (no known sales)
2-26 (Rare) by Joseph Keppler (no known sales)
27-1190 12.50 25.00 50.00
(see Platinum Age section for year 1900+ issues)
Bound volumes (six month, 26 issue run each):
Vol. 1 (Rare) (one set sold on eBay for $2300.00)
Vol. 2 (Scarce) (one set sold on eBay for $1500.00)
Vol. 3-6 (pre-1880 issues) 175.00 375.00 750.00
Vol. 7-46 140.00 300.00 600.00
NOTE: *The English language editions began six months after the German editions, and so the English edition numbering is always one volume number, and 26 issue numbers, behind its parallel German language edition. Pre-1880 & post-1900 issues are more scarce than 1880's & 1890's.*

PUCK (miniature) (M,P,I)
Keppler & Schwarzmann, New York: nd (c1895) (7x5-1/8", 12 pgs, color front & back paper-c, B&W interior)
nn - Scarce 25.00 50.00 110.00
NOTE: *C.J.Taylor-c; F.M.Howarth-a; F.Opper-a; giveaway item promoting **Puck's** various publications. Mostly text, with art reprinted from **Puck**.*

PUCK, CARTOONS FROM (M,S)
Keppler & Schwarzmann, New York: 1893 (14-1/4x11-1/2", 244 pgs, hard-c, mostly B&W)
nn - by Joseph Keppler (Signed and Numbered) 100.00 200.00 400.00
NOTE: *Reprints Keppler cartoons from 1877 to 1893, mostly in B&W, though a few in color, with a text opposite each cartoon explaining the situation then being satirized. Issued only in an edition of 300 numbered issues, signed by Keppler. Only 1/4 of the pages are cartoons.*

PUCK'S LIBRARY (M)
Keppler & Schwarzmann, New York: No.1, July, 1887 - No. 174, Dec, 1899 (10 cents, 11-1/2x8-1/4", 36 pgs, color paper-c, B&W)
1- "The National Game" (Baseball) 50.00 100.00 200.00
2-149 10.00 20.00 40.00
NOTE: ***Puck's Library** was a monthly magazine reprinting cartoons & prose from **Puck**, with each issue's*

Rays of Light
1886 © Morse Bros., Canton, Mass.

Scraps, New Series #1 by D.C. Johnston
1849 © D.C. Johnston, Boston

Shakespeare Would Ride The Bicycle If Alive Today
1896 © Cleveland Bicycles, Toledo, OH.

material organized around the same subject. The cover art was often original. All issues were kept in print for the duration of the series, so later issues are more scarce than earlier ones.

PUCK, PICKINGS FROM (M)
Keppler & Schwarzmann, New York: No.1, Sept, 1891 - No. 34, Dec, 1899 (25 cents, 13-1/4x10-1/4", 68 pgs, color paper-c, B&W)

1-34 Scarce 20.00 40.00 80.00
NOTE: *Similar to **Puck's Library**, except larger in size, and issued quarterly. All reprint material, except for the cover art. There also exist variations with "RAILROAD EDITION 30 CENTS" printed on the cover in place of the standard 25 cent price.*

PUCK'S OPPER BOOK (M)
Keppler & Schwarzmann, New York: 1888 (11-3/4x13-7/8", color paper-c, 68 pgs,interior B&W, 30¢)

nn - (Very Rare) by F. Opper 225.00 450.00 750.00
NOTE: *Puck's first book collecting work by a single artist.; mostly sequential comic strips.*

PUCK'S PRINTING BOOK FOR CHILDREN (S,O.I)
Keppler & Schwarzman, Pubs, NY: 1891 (10-3/8x7-7/8", 52 pgs, color-c, B&W and color)

nn - Frederick B Opper (Very Rare) (no known sales)
NOTE: *Left side printed in color; Right side B&W to be colored in.*

PUCK PROOFS (M,P,S)
Keppler & Schwarzmann, New York: nd (1906-1909) (74 pgs, paper cover; B&W) (all are Scarce)

nn - (c.1906, no price, 4-1/8x5-1/4") B&W painted -c of couple kissing over a chess board; 1905 & 1906-r 25.00 50.00 100.00
nn- (c.1909, 10 cents, 4-3/8x5-3/8") plain green paper-c; 76 pgs 1905-1909-r 25.00 50.00 100.00
NOTE: *Catalog of prints available from **Puck**, reprinting mostly cover & centerspread art from **Puck**. There likely exist more as yet unreported **Puck Proofs** catalogs. Art by Rose O'Neill.*

PUCK, THE TARIFF ?, CARTOONS AND COMMENTS FROM (M,S)
Keppler & Schwarzmann, New York: 1888 (10 cents, 6-7/8x10-3/8", 36 pgs, paper-c, B&W)

nn - (Scarce) 37.50 75.00 200.00
NOTE: *Reprints both cartoons and commentary from **Puck**, concerning the issue of tariffs which were then being debated in Congress. Art by Gillam, Keppler, Opper, Taylor.*

PUCK, WORLD'S FAIR
Keppler & Schwarzmann, PUCK BUILDING, World's Fair Grounds, Chicago: No.1 May 1, 1893 - No.26 Oct 30, 1893 (10 cents, 11-1/4x8-3/4, 14 pgs, paper-c, color front/back/center pages, rest B&W)(All issues Scarce to Rare)

1-26 30.00 60.00 130.00
1-26 bound volume: 500.00 1100.00 2200.00
NOTE: *Art by Joseph Keppler, F. Opper, F.M. Howarth, C.J. Taylor, W.A. Rogers. This was a separate, parallel run of **Puck**, published during the 1893 Chicago World's Fair from within the fairgrounds, and containing all new and different material than the regular weekly **Puck**. Smaller sized and priced the same, this originally sold poorly, and had not as wide distribution as **Puck**, and so consequently issues are much more rare than regular **Puck** issues from the same period. Not to be confused with the larger sized regular **Puck** issues from 1893 which sometimes also contained World's Fair related material, and sometimes had the words "World's Fair" appear on the cover. Can also be distinguished by the fact that **Puck's** issue numbering was in the 800's in 1893, while these issue number 1 through 26.*

PUNCHINELLO
Punchinello Publishing Co, NYC: April 2-Dec 24 1870 (weekly)

1-39 Henry L. Stephens, Frank Bellew, Bowlend 20.00 30.00 75.00
NOTE: *Funded by the Tweed Ring, mild politics attacking Grant Admin & other NYC newspapers. Bound copies exist.*

QUIDDITIES OF AN ALASKAN TRIP (O,G)
G.A. Steel & Co., Portland, OR: 1873 (6-3/4x10-1/2", 80 pgs, gilted hard-c, Red-c and Blue-c exist, B&W)

nn - By William H. Bell (Scarce) 350.00 750.00 1500.00
NOTE: *Highly sought Western Americana collectors. Parody of a trip from Washington DC to Alaska, by a member of the team which went to survey Alaska, purchase commonly known then as "Seward's Folly".*

"RAG TAGS" AND THEIR ADVENTURES, THE (N,S)
A. M. Robertson, San Francisco: 1899 (10-1/4x13-7/8, 84 pgs, color hard-c, B&W inside)

nn - By Arthur M. Lewis (SF Chronicle newspaper-r) (Scarce) 60.00 120.00 240.00

RAYS OF LIGHT (O,P)
Morse Bros., Canton, Mass.: No.1 1886 (7-1/8x5-1/8", 8 pgs, color paper-c, B&W)

1- (Rare) 50.00 100.00 200.00
NOTE: *Giveaway pamphlet in guise of an educational publication, consisting entirely of a sequential story in which a teacher instructs her classroom of young girls in the use of Rising Sun Stove Polish. Color front & back covers.*

RELIC OF THE ITALIAN REVOLUTION OF 1849, A
Gabici's Music Stores, New Orleans: 1849 (10-1/8x12-3/4", 144 pgs, hardcover)

nn - By G. Daelli (Scarce) 100.00 200.00 400.00
NOTE: *From the title page: "Album of fifty line engravings, executed on copper, by the most eminent artists at Rome in 1849; secreted from the papal police after the 'Restoration of Order,' And just imported into America."*

REMARKS ON THE JACOBINIAD (I,S)
E.W. Weld & W. Greenough, Boston: 1795-98 (8-1/4x5-1/8", 72 pgs, a number of B&W plates with text)

nn - Written by Rev. James Sylvester Gardner,artist unknown (Rare) (no known sales)
NOTE: *Early comics-type characters. Not sequential comics, but uses word balloons. Satire directed against "The Jacobin Club," supporters of the French Revolution and Radical Republicans. Gardner came to America from England in 1783, was minister of Trinity Church, Boston. There appears to be some reprints of this done as late as 1798.*

REV. MR. SOURBALL'S EUROPEAN TOUR, THE RECREATION OF A CITY, THE
Duffield Ashmead, Philadelphia: 1867 (7-5/8x6-1/4", 72 pgs, turquoise blue soft wrappers)

By Horace Cope (Rare) 50.00 100.00 200.00
NOTE: see **PARSON SOURBALL'S EUROPEAN TOUR** for the hard cover version.

RHYMES OF NONSENSE TRUTH & FICTION (S)
G.W. Carleton & Co, Publishers, NY: 1874 (10x7-3/4", 44 pgs, hard-c, B&W) (Very Rare)

nn - By Chaucer Jones and Michael Angelo Raphael Smith 100.00 200.00 400.00
NOTE: *Creator names obviously pseudonyms; looks like weak A.B. Frost.*

ROMANCE OF A HAMMOCK, THE - AS RECITED BY MR. GUS WILLIAMS IN "ONE OF THE FINEST" (O,P)
Unknown: 1880s (5-1/2x3-5/8" folded, 7 attached cardboard cards which fold out into a strip, color)

nn - By presently unknown Scarce 75.00 150.00 300.00
NOTE: *12-panel story, which one begins reading on one side of the folded-out strip, then flip to the other side to continue -- unlike the vast majority of folded strips, which are printed on only one side. This was a promotional handout, for a play titled "One of the Finest". The story pictured comes from a poem read in the play by then famous New York stage actor Gus Williams, who is pictured on the "cover"/title card."*

SAD TALE OF THE COURTSHIP OF CHEVALIER SLYFOX-WIKOF, SHOWING HIS HEART-RENDING ASTOUNDING & MOST WONDERFUL LOVE ADVENTURES WITH FANNY ELSSLER AND MISS GAMBOL, THE (O,G)
Garrett & Co., NY: Jan 1856 (25 ¢, 5-3/4x9-1/4", 100 pages, paper-c, B&W)

nn - By T.C. Bond ?? (Very Rare) 500.00 1000.00 2000.00
NOTE: *No surviving copies yet reported -- known via ads in Home Circle published by Garrett. Cover art by John McLenan and Samuel Avery. Graphic novel parodying the real-life romance between European actress/dancer Fanny Elssler and American aristocrat Henry Wikoff. The entire graphic novel is reprinted in the 1976 book "Fanny Elssler in America."*

SAD TALE OF THE COURTSHIP OF CHEVALIER SLYFOX-WIKOF, SHOWING HIS HEART-RENDING ASTOUNDING & MOST WONDERFUL LOVE ADVENTURES WITH FANNY ELSSLER AND MISS GUMBEL, THE (G) (25 cents printed on cover)
Dick And Fitzgerald, NY: 1870s-1888 (5-3/4x9-1/4", ??? pages, soft paper-c, B&W)

nn - By T.C. Bond ?? (Very Rare) 250.00 500.00 1000.00
NOTE: *Reprint of Garrett original printing before G,D&F partnership begins.*

SALT RIVER GUIDE FOR DISAPPOINTED POLITICIANS
Winchell, Small & Co., 113 Fulton St, NY: 1870s (16 pgs, 10¢)

nn - single panel cartoons from WIld Oats (Rare) 75.00 150.00 300.00

SAM SLICK'S COMIC ALMANAC
Philip J. Cozans, NYC: 1857 (7.5x4.5, 48 pgs, B&W) 100.00 200.00 400.00
NOTE: *Contains reprint of* "Moses Keyser the Bowery Bully's Trip to the California Gold Mines" *from* Elton's Comic Almanac #17 1850.

SCRAPS (O,S) (see also **F****** A*** K*******)
D.C. Johnston, Boston: 1828 - No.8 1840; New Series No.1 1849 (12 pgs, printed one side only, paper-c, B&W)

1 - 1828 (9-1/4 x 11-3/4") (Very Rare) (no known sales)
2 - 1830 (9-3/4 x 12-3/4") (Very Rare) (no known sales)
3 - 1832 (10-7/8 x 13-1/8") (Very Rare) (no known sales)
4 - 1833 (11 x 13-5/8") (Very Rare) (no known sales)
5- 1834 (10-3/8 x 13-3/8") (Very Rare) (no known sales)
6 - 1835 (10-3/8 x 13-1/4") red lettering in title SCRAPS (Very Rare) 250.00 500.00 1000.00
6 - 1835 (10-3/8 x 13-1/4") no red lettering in title (Rare) 200.00 400.00 880.00
7 - 1837 (10-3/4 x 13-7/8") 1st Edition (Very Rare) 200.00 400.00 880.00
7 - 1837 (10-3/4 x 13-3/4") 2nd Edition (so stated) 100.00 175.00 375.00
NOTE: *20 pgs. of text (double-sided), 4 pgs. of art (single-sided), plus the covers. There are no protective sheets between the art pages.*
8 - 1840 (10-1/2 x 13-7/8") (Rare) 200.00 400.00 880.00
New Series 1- 1849 (10-7/8 x 13-3/4") 125.00 250.00 475.00
NOTE: *By David Claypoole Johnston. All issues consist of four one-sided sheets with 9 to 12 single panel cartoons per sheet. The other pages are blank or text. With #1-5 the size of the pages can vary up to an inch. Contains 4 protective sheets (not part of page count) Only 1 3 4 and the 1849 New Series Number 1 has cover art along with 4 art pgs. (single sided) with 4 protective sheets and no text pages.New Series Number 1, as well as #6 with bo red lettering and the second printing of issue 7, have survived in higher numbers due to a 1940s warehouse discovery.*

THE SETTLEMENT OF RHODE ISLAND (O)
The Graphic Co. Photo-Lith 39 & 41, Park Place, New York: 1874 (11-3/8x10, 40 pgs, gilted blue hard-c

nn - Charles T. Miller & Walter F. Brown 50.00 100.00 250.00
NOTE: *This is also the Same Walter F. Brown that did "Hail Columbia".*

SHAKESPEARE WOULD RIDE THE BICYCLE IF ALIVE TODAY. "THE REASON WHY" (O,P,S)
Cleveland Bicycles H.A. Lozier & Co., Toledo, OH: 1896 (5-1/2x4",16 pgs, paper-c, color)

nn - By F. Opper (Rare) 70.00 140 .00 300.00
NOTE: *Original cartoons of Shakespearian characters riding bicycles; also popular amongst collectors of bicycle ephemera.*

Stuff and Nonsense by A.B. Frost
1884 © Charles Scribner's Sons

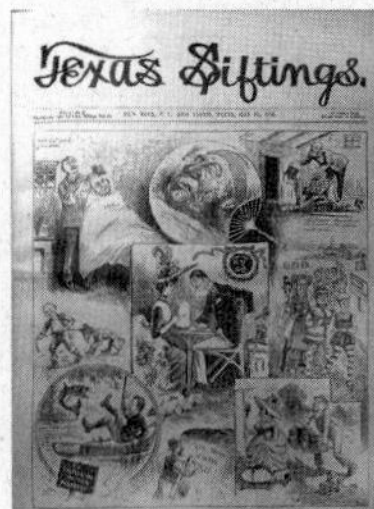

Texas Siftings v6 #2 May 15
1886 ©Texas Siftings Publishing Co.

The Adventures Of Mr. Tom Plump
1851 © Huestis & Cozans, NY

FR1.0 GD2.0 FN6.0

SHAKINGS - ETCHINGS FROM THE NAVAL ACADEMY BY A MEMBER OF THE CLASS OF '67 (O,S)
Lee & Shepard, Boston: 1867 (7-7/8x10", 132 pages, blue hard-c)
By: Park Benjamin 38.00 75.00 150.00
NOTE: *Park Benjamin later became editor of Harper's Bazaar magazine.*

SHOO FLY PICTORIAL (S)
John Stetson, Chestnut sT Theatre, Phila, PA: June 1870 (15-1/2x11-1/2", 8 pgs, B&W)
1 67.50 125.00 250.00

SHYS AT SHAKSPEARE
J.P. and T.C.P., Philadelphia: 1869 (9-1/4x6", 52 pgs)
nn - Artist unknown 75.00 150.00 300.00

SKETCHES OF LOWLY LIFE IN A GREAT CITY (M,S) (See 99 "Woolfs" From Truth)
G. P. Puntam's Sons: 1899 (8-5/8x11-1/4", 200 pgs, hard-c, B&W)
(reprints from Life and Judge of Woolf's cartoons of NYC slum children)
nn - By Michael Angelo Woolf 75.00 150.00 350.00
NOTE: *Woolf's cartoons are regarded as a primary influence on R.F. Outcault in the later development of The Yellow Kid newspaper strip.*

SNAP (O,S)
Valentine & Townsend, Tribune Bldg, NYC: March 13,1885 (17x11, 8 pgs, B&W)
1-Contains a sequential comic strip 50.00 100.00 175.00

SOCIETY PICTURES (M,S,E)
Charles H. Sergel Company, Chicago: 1895 (5-1/4x7-3/4", 168 pgs, printed 1 side, paper-c, B&W)
nn - By George du Maurier; reprints from **Punch**. 25.00 50.00 100.00

SOLDIERS AND SAILORS HALF DIME TALES OF THE LATE REBELLION
Soldiers & Sailors Publishing Co: 1868 (5-1/4x7-7/8", 32 pgs)
v1#1-#16 v2#1-#10 15.00 30.00 60.00
v2 #11 contains (5) page comic strip 25.00 50.00 100.00
NOTE: *Changes to Soldiers & Sailors Half Dime Magazine with v2 #1.*

SOUVENIR CONTAINING CARTOONS ISSUED BY THE PRESS BUREAU OF THE OHIO STATE REPUBLICAN EXECUTIVE COMMITTEE, A (S)
Ohio State Republican Executive Committee, Columbus, OH: 1899 (10-3/8x13-1/2, 248 pgs, Hard-c, B&W
nn - By William L. Bloomer (Scarce) 100.00 200.00 400.00

SOUVENIR OF SOHMER CARTOONS FROM PUCK, JUDGE, AND FRANK LESLIE'S (M,S,P)
Sohmer Piano Co.: nd(c.1893) (6x4-3/4", 16 pgs, paper-c, B&W)
nn 25.00 50.00 100.00
NOTE: *Reprints painted "cartoon" Sohmer Piano advertisements which appeared in the above publications. Artists include Keppler, Gillam, others.*

SPORTING NEW YORKER, THE
Ornum & Co, Beekman ST, NYC: 1870s
issues with sequential comic strips (Rare) 50.00 100.00 200.00

STORY OF THE MAN OF HUMANITY AND THE BULL CALF, THE
(see Bull Calf, The Story of The Man Of Humanity And The)
NOTE: *Reprints of two of A. B. Frost's mostfamous sequential comic strips.*

STREET & SMITH'S LITERARY ALBUM
Street & Smith, NY: #1 Dec 23 1865-#225 Apr 9 1870 (11-3/4x16-3/4", 16 pgs, B&W)
1 (23 Dec 1865) 10.00 30.00 50.00
2-129 131-225 (issues with short sequential strips) 7.50 15.00 30.00
130 (Steam Man satire parody) 100.00 200.00 300.00

STUFF AND NONSENSE (Harper's Monthly strip-r) (M)
Charles Scribner's Sons: 1884 (10-1/4x7-3/4", 100 pgs, hardcover, B&W)
nn - By Arthur Burdett Frost 100.00 185.00 375.00
nn - By A.B. Frost (1888 reprint, 104 pgs) 40.00 80.00 180.00
NOTE: *Earliest known anthology devoted to collecting the comic strips of a single American artist. 1888 2nd printing has a different cover and is layed out somewhat differently inside with a new title page, 3 added pages of cartoons, and a couple more illustrations. For more Frost, the 2nd is worth checki ng out also.*

STUMPING IT (LAUGHING SERIES BRICKTOP STORIES #8) (O,S)
Collin & Small, NY: 1876 (6-5/8x9-1/4, 68 pgs, perfect bound, B&W)
nn - Thomas Worth art abounds (some sequentials) 75.00 150.00 300.00
NOTE: Mainly single panel cartoons w/text; however, some sequential comic strips inside worth picking up

SUMMER SCHOOL OF PHILOSOPHY AT MT. DESERT, THE
Henry Holt & Co.: 1881 (10-3/8x8-5/8", 60 pgs, illus. gilt hard-c, B&W)
nn - By J. A. Mitchell 60.00 120.00 240.00
NOTE: *J.A.Mitchell went on to found **LIFE** two years later in 1883. Also, the long-running mascot for **LIFE** was Cupid - which you see multitudes of Cupids flying around in this story.*

SURE WATER CURE, THE
Carey Grey & Hart, Phila, PA: c1841-43 (8-/2x5, 32 pgs, B&W
nn - proto-comic-strip Very Rare 150.00 300.00 600.00

TAILOR-MADE GIRL, HER FRIENDS, HER FASHIONS, AND HER FOLLIES, THE
(see also IN THE "400" AND OUT) (M)
Charles Scribner's Sons, New York: 1888 (8-3/8x10-1/2", 68 pgs, hard-c, B&W)
nn - Art by C.J. Taylor 20.00 40.00 80.00
NOTE: *Format is a full page cartoon on every other page, with a script style vignette, written by Philip H. Welch, on every page opposite the art.*

TALL STUDENT, THE
Roberts Brothers, Boston: 1873 (7x5", 48 pgs, printed one side only, gilted hard-c, B&W)
nn - By Wilhelm Busch (Scarce) 37.50 75.00 150.00

TARIFF ?, CARTOONS AND COMMENTS FROM PUCK, THE (see Puck, The Tariff...)

TEASING TOM AND NAUGHTY NED WITH A SPOOL OF CLARK'S COTTON, THE ADVENTURES OF (O,P)
Clark's O.N.T. Spool Cotton: 1879 (4-1/4x3", 12 pgs, B&W, paper-c)
nn 17.50 35.00 70.00
NOTE: *Knock-off of the "First Trick" in Wilhelm Busch's **Max and Maurice**, modified to involve Clark's Spool Cotton in the story, with similar but new art by an artist identified as "HB". The back cover advertises the specific merchant who gave this booklet away -- multiple variations of back cover suspected.*

TEMPERANCE TALES; OR, SIX NIGHTS WITH THE WASHINGTONIANS, VOL I & II
W.A. Leary & Co., Philadelphia: 1848 (50¢, 6-1/8x4", 328 pgs, B&W, hard-c)
nn 100.00 200.00 425.00
NOTE: *Mostly text. This edition gathers Volume I & II together. The first 8 pages reprints George Cruikshank's **THE BOTTLE**, re-drawn & re-engraved by Phil A. Pilliner. Later editions of this book do not include **THE BOTTLE** reprint and are therefore of little interest to comics collectors.*

TEXAS SIFTINGS
Texas Siftings Publishing Co, Austin, Texas (1881-1887), **NYC** (1887-1897): 1881-1885 newspaper-size weekly; 1886-1897 folio weekly (15x10-3/4", 16 pgs, B&W 10¢
1881-1885 issues 25.00 50.00 100.00
v6#1 (5/8/86) (8) panel strip Afterwhich He Emigrated;
(16) panel The Tenor's Triumph Veni Vidi Vici 12.50 25.00 50.00
v6#2 (5/16/86) (5) panel sewuential 12.50 25.00 50.00
v6#3 no sequentials 12.50 25.00 50.00
v6#4 (5/29/86) Worth-c (4) panel Worth strip; (2) panel 12.50 25.00 50.00
v6#5 no sequentials 12.50 25.00 50.00
v6#6 (6/12/86) Comic Strip Cover (11) panels The Rise of a Great Artist
(5) panel sequential 50.00 100.00 200.00
v6#7 (6/19/86) Worth-c (2) panel Wiorth;
(10) panel Ha! Ha! The Honest Youth & the Lordly Villain 25.00 50.00 100.00
v6#8 (6/26/86) Worth-c; (15) panel The Kangaroo Hunter 25.00 50.00 100.00
v6#9 (7/3/86) Worth-c; Bellew (2) panel How Wives Get What They Want
12.50 25.00 50.00
v6#10 ((7/10/86) Baseball-c; (3) panel;
(5) panel A Story Without Words from Fliegende Blätter 12.50 25.00 50.00
v6 #11 12 13 Worth-c no sequentials 12.50 25.00 50.00
v6#14 (8/7/86) Wiorth-c; (7) panel Mrs Cleveland Presents
The President With A New Rocking Chair 12.50 25.00 50.00
v6#15 (8/14/86) Worth-c; (6) panel Worth strip 12.50 25.00 50.00
v6#16 (8/21/86) Worth-c Asleep At Post USA/Mexico Border
(6) panel sequential 12.50 25.00 50.00
v6#17 no sequrntials 12.50 25.00 50.00
v6#18 (9/4/86) Worth-c; (3) panel from Fliegende 12.50 25.00 50.00
v6#19 (9/11/86) Worth Anarchist & Uncle Sam-c;
(5) panel Duel of the Dudes 12.50 25.00 50.00
v6#20 (9/18/86) Worth-c (6) panel sequential 12.50 25.00 50.00
v6#21 (9/25/86) Worth-c; Verbeck single panel; (9) panel 12.50 25.00 50.00
v6#22 (10/2/86) Verbeck-c plus interiors 12.50 25.00 50.00
v6#23 (10/9/86) Worth-c Geronimo & Devil cover;
Verbeck and Chips singles 25.00 50.00 100.00
v6#24 (10/16/86) Worth-c Verbeck strip "Evolution" 12.50 25.00 50.00
v6#25 no sequential strips 12.50 25.00 50.00
v6#26 (10/30/86) Worth-c; (6) panel Verbeck "A Warning To Smokers"
12.50 25.00 50.00
NOTE: *Many Thomas Worth sequential comic strips. Frank Bellew and Dan McCarthy appear. Wilhelm Busch-r from German Fligende Blaetter. Later issues in 1890s comics become sporadic*

THAT COMIC PRIMER (S)
G.W. Carleton & Co., Publishers: 1877 (6-5/8x5", 52 pgs, paper soft-c, B&W)
nn - By Frank Bellew 75.00 150.00 300.00
NOTE: *Premium for the United States Life Insurance Company, New York.*

TIGER, THE LEFTENANT AND THE BOSUN, THE
Prudential Insurance Home Office, 878 & 880 Broad St, Newark, NJ: 1889 (4.5x3.25", 12 pgs) (Scarce)
nn - 8 panel sequential story in color 50.00 100.00 200.00

TOM PLUMP, THE ADVENTURES OF MR. (see also The Juvenile Gem) (O)
Huestis & Cozans, New York: nd (c1850-1851) (6x3-7/8", 12 pgs, hand colored paper-c, B&W)
nn- First printing(s) publisher's address is 104 Nassau Street (1850-1851)
(Very Rare) 750.00 1500.00 2900.00
NOTE: *California Gold Rush story. The hand colored outer cover is highly rare, with only 1 recorded copy possessing it. The front cover image and text is repeated precisely on page 3 (albeit b&w), and only interior pages are numbered, together leading owners of coverless copies to believe they have the cover. The true back*

Truth #372 (first app. The Yellow Kid) June 2 1894 © Truth Company, NY

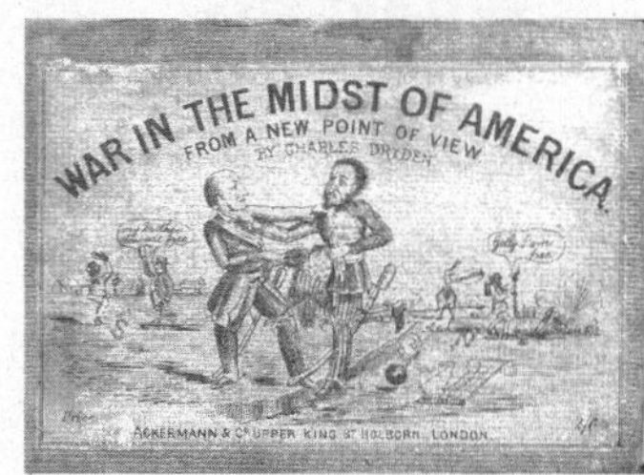

War in the Midst of America

Wild Oats #115 March 10 1875 © Winchell & Small, NYC

	FR1.0	GD2.0	FN6.0

cover contains ads for the publisher. The cover was issued only with copies which were sold separately - booklets which were bound together as part of ***THE JUVENILE GEM*** *never had such covers.*

TOM PLUMP, THE ADVENTURES OF MR. (see also The Juvenile Gem) (O)
Philip J. Cozans: nd (1851-1852) (6x3-7/8", 12 pgs,hand colored paper-c, B&W)

nn- Second printing(s) publisher's address is 116 Nassau Street (1851-1852) (Very Rare)	400.00	800.00	1600.00
nn- Third printing(s) publisher's address is 107 Nassau Street (1852+) (Very Rare)	400.00	800.00	1600.00

TOM PLUMP, THE ADVENTURES OF MR.
Americana Review, Scotia, NY: nd(1960's) (6-1/4x4-1/8", 8 pgs, side-stapled, cardboard-c, B&W)

nn - Modern reprint	-	12.00	24.00

NOTE: *Issued within a folder titled SIX CHILDREN'S BOOKS OF THE 1850'S. States "Reprinted by American Review" at bottom of front cover. Reprints the 104 Nassau Street address.)*

nn - Modern reprint (Scarce 1980s) (5-1/2x4-1/4", 8 pgs,side-stapled)	-	5.00	10.00

NOTE: *Photocopy reprint by a comix zine publisher, from an Americana Review cop; vailable by mail order*

TOOTH-ACHE, THE (E,O)
D. Bogue, London: 1849 (5-1/4x3-3/4)

nn - By Cruikshank, B&W (Very Rare)	250.00	500.00	1100.00
nn - By Cruikshank, hand colored (Rare)		(no known sales)	

NOTE: *Scripted by Horace Mayhew, art by George Cruikshank. This is the British edition. Price 1/6 b&w, 3 hand colored. In British editions, the panels are not numbered. Publisher's name appears on cover. Booklet's "pages" unfold into a single, long, strip.*

J.L. Smith, Philadelphia, PA: nd (1849) (5-1/8"x 3-3/4" folded, 86-7/8" wide unfolded, 26 pgs, cardboard-c, color, 15¢)

nn - By Cruikshank, hand colored (Very Rare)	400.00	800.00	1600.00

NOTE: *Reprints the D. Bogue edition. In American editions, the panels are numbered (43 panels, not counting front & back cover). Publisher's name stamped on inside front cover, plus printed along left-hand side of first interior page. Page 1 is pasted to inside back cover, and unfolds from there. Front cover not attached to back cover by design. Booklet's "pages" unfold into a single, long, strip (made from four individual strips pasted together on the blank back side). There is a fairly common1974 British Arts Council reprint.*

TRAMP, THE: His Tricks, Tallies, and Tell-Tales, with His Signs, Countersigns, Grips, Passwords and Villainies Exposed (O,S)
Dick & Fitzgerald, New York: 1878 (11-3/8x8, 36 pgs, paper-c, B&W, 25¢) (Rare)

1 Frank Bellew	150.00	300.00	650.00

NOTE: *Edited by Frank Bellew, A Bee And A Chip (Bellew's daughter and son Frank).*

TRUTH (See Platinum Age section for 1900-1906 issues)
Truth Company, NY: 1886-1906? (13-11/16x10-5/16", 16 pgs, process color-c & centerfolds, rest B&W)

1886-1887 issues	20.00	40.00	100.00
1888-1895 issues non Outcault issues	15.00	30.00	80.00
Mar 10 1894 - precursor Yellow Kid RFO	60.00	180.00	400.00
#372 June 2 1894 - first app Yellow Kid RFO	200.00	600.00	1200.00
June 23 1894 - precursor Yellow Kid R. F. Outcault	60.00	180.00	400.00
July 14 1894 -2nd app Yellow Kid RFO	110.00	330.00	700.00
Sept 15 1894 - (2) 3rd app YK RFO plus YK precursor	110.00	330.00	700.00
Feb 9 1895 - 4th app Yellow Kid RFO	110.00	330.00	700.00
1896-1899 issues	10.00	20.00	55.00

NOTE: *This magazine contains the earliest known appearances of* ***The Yellow Kid*** *by Richard Felton Outcault. Feb 9 1895 issue's YK cartoon was reprinted one week later in the* ***New York World*** *Feb 17 1895 edition. We are still sorting out further Outcault appearances. Truth also contained full color sequential strips by Hy Mayer on the back plus Woolf, Verbeek, etc.*

TRUTH, SELECTIONS FROM
Truth Company, NY: 1894-Spr 1897 (13-11/16x10-1/4, color-c, quarterly)

1-4	25.00	50.00	100.00
5-Outcault's early Yellow Kid	100.00	200.00	400.00
6-13	20.00	40.00	80.00

NOTE: *#5 reprints all early Outcault Yellow Kid appearances*

TURNER'S COMIC ALMANAC
Charles Strong, 298 Pearl St, NYC: ???-1843 (7.25x4.5", 36 pgs, B&W)

nn	60.00	120.00	240.00

TURNER'S COMICK ALMA-NACK
Turner & Fisher, NYC: 1844-?? (7.25x4.5", 36 pgs, B&W)

nn	60.00	120.00	240.00

TWO HUNDRED SKETCHES, HUMOROUS AND GROTESQUE, BY GUSTAVE DORE (E)
Frederick Warne & Co, London: 1867 (13-3/4x11-3/8, 94 pgs, hard-c, B&W)

nn - (1867) by Gustave Dore	100.00	200.00	500.00
nn - (Second Edition; 1871)- by Gustave Dore	50.00	100.00	240.00
nn - (Third Edition; 1870's)- by Gustave Dore	50.00	100.00	240.00
nn - (Fourth Edition; 1870's- by Gustave Dore	50.00	100.00	240.00

NOTE: *Contains sequential comics stories, single panel cartoons, and sketches. Reprints and translates material which originally appeared in the French publications "Le Journal pour Rire", circa 1848-49. Although dated 1867, it was likely published & available for the 1866 Christmas Season, as has been confirmed for the American edition. Printed by Dalziel. The American & first British editions were printed simultaneously, the American edition is not a reprint of the British.*

TWO HUNDRED SKETCHES, HUMOROUS AND GROTESQUE, BY GUSTAVE DORE (E)
Roberts Brothers, Boston: 1867 (13-3/4x11-3/8", 96 pgs, hard-c, B&W)

	FR1.0	GD2.0	FN6.0

nn - By Gustave Dore	100.00	200.00	500.00

NOTE: *Although dated 1867, it was published & available for the 1866 Christmas Season. Printed by Dalziel, in England, and imported to the USA expressly for a USA publisher.*

UNCLE JOSH'S TRUNK-FUL OF FUN
Dick & Fitzgerald, 18 Ann St, NY: 1870s (5-3/4x9", 68 pgs, B&W & Red-c, B&W inside)

nn - Rare	75.00	125.00	200.00

NOTE: Many single panel cartoons; (2) pages of early boxing sequential strip

UNCLE SAM'S COMIC ALMANAC
M.J. Meyers, NY: 1879 (11x8", 32 pgs)

nn -	50.00	100.00	200.00

UNDER THE GASLIGHT
Gaslight Publishing Co (Frank Tousey): Oct 13 1878-Apr 12 1879 (Folio, 16pgs)

1-27	75.00	125.00	200.00

UNITED STATES COMIC ALMANAC
King & Baird, Philadelphia: 1851-?? (7.5x4.5", 36 pgs, B&W)

nn	60.00	120.00	240.00

UPS AND DOWNS ON LAND AND WATER (O.G)
James R. Osgood & Co., Boston: 1871 ; **Houghton, Osgood & Co., Boston:** 1880 (108 pgs, gilted hard-c, B&W)

1st printing (1871; 10-3/4x16") - By Augustus Hoppin	45.00	90.00	180.00
2nd printing (1880; smaller sized)	32.50	65.00	130.00

NOTE: *Exists as blue or orange hard covers.*

VANITY FAIR
William A. Stephens (for Thompson & Camac): Dec 29 1859-July 4 1863 Quarto Weekly

average issues with comic strips	20.00	30.00	75.00

VERDICT, THE
Verdict Publishing Co: Dec 19 1898-Nov 12 1900 (Chromolithographic Weekly)

Average Issues	50.00	100.00	200.00

NOTE: Artists included George B. Luks, Horace Taylor, MIRS. Striking anti-Republican weekly full o fsome of the most savage political cartoons of the era. The last brilliant burst of energy for the political cartoon weekly

VERY VERY FUNNY (M,S)
Dick & Fitzgerald, New York: nd(c1880's) (10¢, 7-1/2x5", 68 pgs, paper-c, B&W)

nn - (Rare)	75.00	150.00	300.00

NOTE: *Unauthorized reprints of prose and cartoons extracted from Puck, Texas Siftings, and other publications. Includes art by Chips Bellew, Bisbee, Graetz, Opper, Wales, Zim.*

VIM
H. Wimmel, NYC: June 22-Aug 24 1898 (Chromolithographic Weekly)

average issue	50.00	100.00	200.00
Yellow Kid by Leon Barritt issues	75.00	150.00	300.00

WAR IN THE MIDST OF AMERICA. FROM A NEW POINT OF VIEW. (E,O,G)
Ackermann & Co., London: 1864 (4-3/8" x 5-7/8", folded, 36 feet wide unfolded, 80 pgs, hard-c, B&W)

nn- by Charles Dryden (rare)	400.00	800.00	1600.00

NOTE: *British graphic novel about the American Civil War, with a pro-Confederate bent. Adventures of a British artist who decides to visually summarize the American Civil War for his countrymen, from newspaper accounts. Reaching current events, he finds he can not finish the story until the War ends, and so he travels to America, to end it. Book unfolds into a single long strip (binding was issued split, to enable the unfolding).*

WASP, THE ILLUSTRATED SAN FRANCISCO
F. Korbel & Bros and Numerous Others: August 5 1876-April 25 1941 (Chromolithographic Weekly)

average 1800s issues with comic strips	50.00	100.00	200.00

WHAT I KNOW OF FARMING: Founded On The Experience of Horace Greeley (S)
The American News Company, New York: 1871 (7-1/4x4-1/2", paper-c, B&W)

nn - By Joseph Hull (Scarce)	35.00	70.00	140.00

NOTE: *Pay & Cox, Printers & Engravers, NY; political tract regarding Presidential elections.*

WILD FIRE
Wild Fire Co, NYC: Nov 30 1877-at least#16 Mar 1878 (Folio, 16 pgs)

1-16	25.00	50.00	100.00

WILD OATS, An Illustrated Weekly Journal of Fun, Satire, Burlesque, and Nits at Persons and Events of the Day (O)
Winchell & Small, 113 Fulton St /48 Ann St, NYC: Feb 1870-1881 (16-1/4x11", generally 16 pages, B&W, began as monthly, then bi-weekly, then weekly) All loose issues Very Rare (See *The Overstreet Price Guide* #35 2005 for a detailed index of single issue contents)

1-25 Very Rare - contents to be indexed next year	50.00	100.00	200.00
26-28 30 32 35 36 39 40 41 43-46 1872 (sequential strips)	50.00	100.00	200.00
29 33 37 42 no sequential strips	40.00	80.00	160.00
31 34 38 47 Hopkins sequential comic strips	50.00	100.00	200.00
48 (1/16/73) Worth 13 panel sequential; first Woolf-c	50.00	100.00	200.00
49 51 53 54 60 62 61 64 65 66 67 69 1873 sequential strips	50.00	100.00	200.00
50 52 56 59 63 71 no sequential strips	40.00	80.00	160.00
51 (Worth 18 panel double page spread, Woolf 9 panel	50.00	100.00	200.00
55 Hopkins 22 panel double page spread; Bellew-c	50.00	150.00	300.00

57 intense unknown 6 panel "Two Relics of Barbarism, or A Few Contrasted Pictures,

Wild Oats #139 August 25
1875 © Winchell & Small, NY

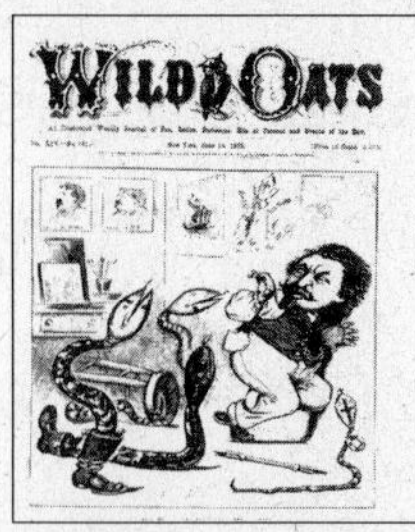

Wild Oats Vol. XIV #181374
June 14, 1876 © Winchell & Small

Yankee Notions #7 (v2#1)
July 1852 © T.W. Strong, NY

FR1.0 GD2.0 FN6.0

Showing the origin of the North American Indian 50.00 100.00 200.00
58 (6/5/73) unknown 19 panel double pager "The Terrible Adventures of Messrs Buster & Stumps, About Exterminating the Indians" reads across both pages like Popeye #2095 (1933); Woolf-c 100.00 200.00 400.00
68 (10/16/73) unknown 9 panel "Adv of New jersey Mosquito" looks like Winsor McCay type style: early inspiration for McCay's animated cartoon? 50.00 100.00 200.00
70 unknown 6 panel; Hopkins 6 panel "Hopkins novel: A Tale of True Love, with all the variations"; Bellew-c 50.00 100.00 200.00
72 (12/11/73) Worth 11 panel; Wales President Grant war-c 50.00 100.00 200.00
73 74 75 Hopkins sequential comic strip 75.00 150.00 300.00
76 77 sequential strips 50.00 100.00 200.00
78 Bellew 5 panel double pager 50.00 100.00 200.00
79-105 (March 1874-Dec 1874) contents presently unknown 50.00 100.00 200.00
106 107 111 no sequentials;Bellew-c #106 110;Wales-c #107 50.00 100.00 200.00
108 (1/20/75) Wales 12 panel double pg spread; Bellew-c 50.00 100.00 200.00
109 (1/27/75) unknown 6 panel; Wales-c 50.00 100.00 200.00
111 Busch 13 panel "The Conundrum of the Day - Is Lager Beer Intoxicating?"; Bellew-c 50.00 100.00 200.00
112 116 sequential comic strips 50.00 100.00 200.00
113 114 115 no sequentials Worth-c #114 40.00 80.00 160.00
117 intense Wales 6 panel "One of the Oppresions of the Civil Rights Laws"' Bellew-c 75.00 150.00 300.00
118-137 (3/31/75-8/4/75) no sequential comic strips 40.00 80.00 160.00
138 (8/18/75) Bellew Sr & Bellew "Chips" Jr singles appear 50.00 100.00 200.00
139-143 145-147 154-157 159 no sequentials 40.00 80.00 160.00
144 (9/29/75) Hopkins 8 panel sequential; Wales-c 50.00 100.00 200.00
148 (10/27/75) Opper's first cover; many Opper singles 75.00 150.00 300.00
149 150 151 152 153 all Opper-c and much interior work 50.00 100.00 200.00
158 (1/5/76) Palmer Cox 1rst comic strip 24 panel double page spread "The Adv of Mr & Mrs Sprowl And Their Christmas Turkey - A Crashing Chasing Tearful Tragedy But Happily Ending Well"; Opper-c 100.00 200.00 400.00
159 160 162 165 167 169-173 no sequentials 40.00 80.00 160.00
161 163 164 166 168 179 182 Palmer Cox sequential strips 100.00 200.00 400.00
174 (4/26/76) Cox 24 panel double pager "The Tramp's Progress; A Story of the West And the Union Pacific Railroad" 100.00 200.00 400.00
175-178 183-189 no sequentials 40.00 80.00 160.00
180 (6/7/76) Beard & Opper jam; Woolf, Bellew singles 50.00 100.00 200.00
181 more Mann two panel jobs; Opper-c 50.00 100.00 200.00
190 Bellew 9 panel "Rodger's Patent Mosquito Armour" 75.00 150.00 300.00
191-end contents to be indexed in the near future 40.00 80.00 160.00

NOTE: *There are very few lknown oose issues. All loose issues are Very Rare. Prices vary widely on this magazine. Issues with sequential comic strips would be in higher demand than issues with no comic strips. We present this index from the Library of Congress and New York Historical Society bound sets. We would love to hear from any one who turns up loose copies. This scarce humor bi-weekly contains easily a couple hundred original first-time published sequential comic strips found in most issues plus innumerable single panel cartoons in every issue*

WYMAN'S COMIC ALMANAC FOR THE TIMES
T.W.Strong, NY: 1854 (8x5", 24 pgs)
nn - 50.00 100.00 200.00

WOMAN IN SEARCH OF HER RIGHTS, THE ADVENTURES OF (G)
Lee & Shepard, Boston And New York: early 1870s (8-3/8x13", 40 pgs, hard-c)
By Florence Claxton (Very Rare) 450.00 900.00 1800.00
NOTE: *Earliest known original comic book sequential story by a woman; contains "nearly 100 original drawings by the author, which have been reproduced in fac-simile by the graphotype process of engraving." Tinted two color lithography; orange tint printed first, then printed 2nd time with black ink; early women's sufferage.*

WORLD OVER, THE (I)
G. W. Dillingham Company, New York: 1897 (192 pgs, hard-c)
nn - By Joe Kerr; 80 illustrations by R.F. Outcault (Rare) 300.00 600.00 1200.00
NOTE: soft cover editions also exist

WRECK-ELECTIONS OF BUSY LIFE (S)
Kellogg & Bulkeley: 1867 (9-1/4x11-3/4", ??? pages, soft-c)
nn - By J. Bowker (Rare) 100.00 200.00 400.00
NOTE: *Says "Sold by American News Company, New York" on cover.*

YANKEE DOODLE
W.H. Graham, Tribune Building, NYC: Oct 10 1846-Oct 2 1847 (Quarto weekly)
average issue 50.00 100.00 200.00

YANKEE NOTIONS, OR WHITTLINGS OF JONATHAN'S JACK-KNIFE
T.W. Strong, 98 Nassau St, NYC: Jan. 1852-1875 (11x8, 32 pgs, paper-c, 12.5¢, monthly)
1 Brother Jonathan character single panel cartoons 50.00 100.00 200.00
NOTE: *Begins continuing character sequential comic strip,* "The Adventures of Jeremiah Oldpot" *in* "A Bird in the Hand Is Worth Two in The Bush"
2-4 25.00 50.00 100.00
5 British X-Over 25.00 50.00 100.00
NOTE: *Single panel of John Bull & Brother Jonathan exchanging civilities (issues of* Punch & Yankee Notions)
6 end of Jeremiah Oldpot continued strip 25.00 50.00 100.00
v2#1 begin "Hoosier Bragg" sequential strip - six issue serial 25.00 50.00 100.00
v2#2 Feb 1853 two pg 12 panel sequential "Mr Vanity's Exploits, Arising Out Of A Valentine" 37.50 75.00 150.00
v2#3-v2#5 continues Hoosier Bragg 25.00 50.00 100.00
v2#6 Juen 1853 Lion Eats Hoosier Bragg, end of story 25.00 50.00 100.00
v3#1 begins referring to its cartoons as "Comic Art" 37.50 75.00 150.00

FR1.0 GD2.0 FN6.0

v4#1-V4#6 v5#1-v5#2 no sequential comic strips 20.00 40.00 80.00
v5#3 two sequential comic strips 37.50 75.00 150.00
NOTE: *Mr Take-A-Drop And The Maine Law (5) panels and The First Segar (7) panels (about smoking tobacco)*
v5#4 April 1856 begin Billy Vidkins 37.50 75.00 150.00
NOTE: *Begins reprinting "From Passages in the Life of Little Billy Vidkins, first issued as a stand alone proto-comic book in 1849 Illustrations of the Poets*
v5#5 The McBargem Guards (9) panel sequential; Vidkins 25.00 50.00 100.00
v5#6 v5 #9 no comics 20.00 40.00 80.00
v5#7 Billy Vidkins continues 25.00 50.00 100.00
v5#8 end of Vidkins By HL Stephens, Esq. 25.00 50.00 100.00
v5#10 (6) panel "How We Learn To Ride"; Timber is hero 25.00 50.00 100.00
v5#11 (7) panel "How Mr. Green Sparrowgrass Voted-A Warning For the Benefit of Quiet Citizens About To Excercize the Elective Franchise" plus Pt Two "How We Learn to Ride" 37.50 75.00 150.00
v5#12 (6) panel "How Mr Pipp Got Struck"; "The Eclipse" featuring Mr Phips; Pt 3 "How We Learn to Ride" 25.00 50.00 100.00
v6#1 (Jan 1857) (12) panel "A Tale of An Umbrella; (4) panel begins a serial "The Man Who Bought The Elephant; (8) panel How Our Young New Yorkers Celebrate New Years Day 25.00 50.00 100.00
v6#2 (Feb 1857) Pt 2 (4) panels The Man Who Bought the Elephant; (7) panel A Game of All Fours 25.00 50.00 100.00
v6#3 (Mar 1857) Pt 3 (4) panels The Man Who Bought the Elephant ending; (4) panel Ye Great Crinoline Monopoly 25.00 50.00 100.00
v6#4 no comic strips 25.00 50.00 100.00
v6#5 (May 1850) (3) panel A Short Trip to Mr Bumps, And How It Ended; (2) panel How mr Trembles Was Garrotted 25.00 50.00 100.00
v6#6 no comic strips 25.00 50.00 100.00
v6#7 (July 1857) (5) panel Alma Mater; (3) panel Three Tableaux In the Life of A Broadway Swell 25.00 50.00 100.00
v6 #8 9 no comic strips 25.00 50.00 100.00
v6#10 (Oct 1857) (3) panel Adv of Mr Near-Sight 25.00 50.00 100.00
v6#11 (Nov 1857) (11) panel Mrs Champignon's Dinner Party And the Way She Arranged Her Guests; (4) panel A Stroll in August 25.00 50.00 100.00
v6#12 (Dec 1857) (8) panel strip; (12) panel Young Fitz At A Blow Out in the Fifth Ave 25.00 50.00 100.00
v10#1 (Jan 1860) comic strip Bibbs at Central Park Skating Pond using word balloons 25.00 50.00 100.00

YE TRUE ACCOUNTE OF YE VISIT TO SPRINGFIELDE BY YE CONSTABEL HIS SPECIAL REPORTER
Frank Leslie: 1861 (5-1/8 x 5-1/4 or 93 inches when folded out, paper-c, B&W)
nn - Very Rare fold-out of 18 comic strip panels plus covers - -
NOTE: *8 panels contain word balloons (Very Rare - only one copy known to exist.) First printed in Frank Leslie's Budget of Fun Jan 1 1861 issue. Abraham Lincoln Biography.*

YE VERACIOUS CHRONICLE OF GRUFF & POMPEY IN 7 TABLEAUX. (O,P)
Jackson's Best Chewing Tobacco & Donaldson Brothers: nd (c1870's) (5-1/8 tall x 3-3/8" wide folded, 27" wide unfolded, color cardboard)
nn - With all 8 panels attached (Scarce) 40.00 80.00 160.00
nn - Individual panels/cards 6.00 12.00 24.00
NOTE: *Black Americana interest. Consists of 8 attached cards, printed on one side, which unfold into a strip story of title card & 7 panels. Scrapbook hobbyists in the 19th Century tended to pull the panels apart and paste into their scrapbooks, making copies with all panels attached scarce.*

YOUNG AMERICA (continues as Yankee Doodle)
T.W. Strong, NYC: 1856
1-30 John McLennon 50.00 100.00 200.00

YOUNG AMERICA'S COMIC ALMANAC
T.W. Strong, NY: 1857 (7-1/2x5", 24 pgs)
nn 50.00 100.00 200.00

THE YOUNG MEN OF AMERICA (becomes Golden Weekly) (S)
Frank Tousey, NYC: 1887-88 (14x10-1/4", 16 pgs, B&W)
527 (10/13/87) Bellew strip "Story of A Black Eye" 25.00 50.00 100.00
530 (11/3/87) Thomas Worth (6) panel strip 125
531 (11/10/87) Thomas Worth(3) panel strip
537 (12/22/87) H.E. Patterson (3) panel strip
544 (2/9/88) Caran s'Ache (6) panel strip-r 37.50 75.00 100.00
555 (4/26/88) Thomas Worth (3) panel strip
556 (5/3/88) Thomas Worth (6) panel strip; Kit Carson-c 75.00 150.00 300.00
569 (8/21/88) Frank Bellew (2) panel strip
570 (8/9/88) Kemble (2) panel strip
571 (8/16/88) Kemble (2) panel strip; first Davy Crockett 75.00 150.00 300.00
Issues with just single panel cartoons 10.00 20.00 40.00

ZIM'S QUARTERLY (M)
(13-13/16x10-1/4", 60 pgs, color-c; most;y B&W, some interior color)
1 - Eugene Zimmerman 112.50 225.00 450.00
NOTE: *Approx. half sequential comic strips, other half single panel cartoons.*

Any addititions or corrections to this section are always welcome, very much encouraged and can be sent to **feedback@gemstonepub.com** to be processed for next year's Guide.

THE PLATINUM AGE

The American Comic Book: 1883-1938

A Concise History & Price Index Of The Field As Of 2014

NEWSPAPERS HARNESS COMICS POWER MYRIAD FORMATS COMPETE

by Robert Lee Beerbohm and Richard D. Olson, PhD ©2014

(This article was originally created by Robert L. Beerbohm and Richard D. Olson beginning in CBPG #27 1997 and is revised annually as new information comes to light.)

The story of the success of the modern comic strip as we know it today is tied closely to the companies who sponsored and bought licenses from the copyright holder for the purpose of advertising products. Platinum Age comic books have come back into their own after languishing mostly forgotten for a few decades. With this series of comics history research updates now marking its first decade, these historically important books are seem by many now as very collectible. Online sources such as eBay and bookfinder.com have demonstrate that many of these Platinum books are actually not scarce at all as previously thought, though they are in any type of higher-grade condition. Even so, most Platinum Age books are much rarer than so-called Golden Age comic books, yet despite this scarcity, *Mutt & Jeff, Bringing Up Father, The Katzenjammer Kids*, and many more were more popular than say Superman and Batman when they were introduced. Recent research has come up with some more amazing rediscoveries. There is much that can be learned and applied to today's comics market by a simple historical examination of the medium's evolution over more than 160 years.

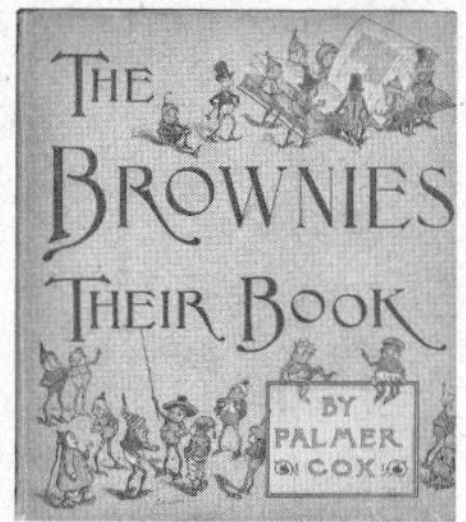

The Brownies' first book, 1887 by Palmer Cox, set a precedent for the Platinum Age, collecting and reprinting previously published material.

It should be noted that "ages" are applied to historical periods in the history of comics for convenience. In fact, ages typically overlap and there is no discrete beginning or ending for any given "age." This is the case with the Platinum Age, which clearly began with Palmer Cox's creation of *The Brownies* in 1883 even though it overlaps with the Victorian Age which ran through the end of the 19th Century. Cox introduced a qualitative change to the field, not an incremental quantitative change. Specifically, he produced art and verse for children in children's magazines and then merchandised those characters. He published work for children not only in books but in magazines and newspapers, and he merchandised his creations to an extent that had never been done previously.

Palmer Cox was born in 1840 near Granby, Quebec. He journeyed to Oakland, California in 1863, and began publishing cartoon, prose and poems in the local press and media outlets such as *The San Francisco Examiner* wherein by 1867 it has been reported he also began creating sequential comic strips, though none have yet surfaced.

His first book, ***Squibs of California***, was published in 1874. He subsequently moved to New York in 1875 and almost immediately began working for the magazine *Wild Oats*, of which more is written about in the preceding Victorian Age history introduction as well as a sample of his sequential work. He drew dozens of sequential comic strips for *Wild Oats*, a humor magazine so scarce only one issue has been offered on eBay in the past six years.

Soon thereafter he became a major contributor to the Scribner publications, including *The St. Nicholas*, an illustrated magazine for young folk. His first cartoon for them was "The Wasp And The Bee," published in the March 1879 cover-

The Brownies in the Philippines by Palmer Cox, Oct 1904 - scarce original art from the book. President Roosevelt is pictured within these multitudes of Brownie madness, a Cox "signature trademark." Cox's stories are comic strip-oriented in nature of time sequence as he boldly took his Brownies around the world.

date issue. While it is now clear that Cox used elves and brownie-like characters in his art for several different magazines as early as 1877 in *Harper's Young People* magazine as well as using Brownies-type characters beginning in the Feb 1881 issue of *Wide Awake*, the first true appearance of the Brownies in their own story using that title, a combination of art and verse was February, 1883, in *St. Nicholas*. Palmer Cox's *The Brownies* were the first North American comics-type characters to be internationally merchandised. Even though Cox was continuously doing sequential comic strips in magazines like *Wild Oats*, he left the popular medium of comics when he hit paydirt with *The Brownies*. For over a quarter of a century, Cox deftly combined the popular advertising motifs of animals and fairies into a wonderful, whimsical world of society at its best and worst.

The Brownies' first book was issued in 1887, titled *The Brownies: Their Book*; many more followed. Cox also added a run of his hugely popular characters in *Ladies Home Journal* from October 1891 through February 1895, as well as a special for December 1910. With the 1892-93 World's Fair, the merchandising exploded with a host of products, including pianos, paper dolls and other figurines, chairs, stoves, puzzles, cough drops, coffee, soap, boots, candy, and many more. *Brownies* material was being produced in Europe as well as the United States of America.

Cox tried out *The Brownies* as a newspaper strip in the *San Francisco Examiner* during 1898, where he had begun his newspaper career over 30 years before, and then in the *New York World* in 1900. It was then syndicated from 1903 through 1907. He seems to have retired from regularly drawing *The Brownies* with the January 1914 issue of *St. Nicholas* when he was 74. A wealthy man, he lived to the ripe old age of 84, spending his last decade in his home he affectionately called Brownie Castle, back in Granby, Quebec.

By the mid-1890s, while keeping careful track of steadily rising circulations of magazines with graphic humor such as *Harper's, Puck, St. Nicholas, Judge, Life* and *Truth*, New York based newspaper publishers began to recognize that illustrated humor would sell extra papers. This is what *The Yellow Kid* taught these publishers. Thus was born the Sunday "comic supplement." Most of the super star favorites were under contract with these magazines. However, there was an artist working for *Truth* who wasn't. Roy L McCardell, then a staffer at *Puck*, informed Morrill Goddard, Sunday Editor of *The New York World*, that he knew someone who could fit what was needed at the then-largest newspaper in America.

Richard F. Outcault (1863-1928) first introduced his street children strip in *Truth* #372, June 2, 1894, somewhat inspired by Michael Angelo Woolf's slum kids single panel cartoons in **Life** which had begun in the mid 1880s. The interested collector should seek out a copy of Woolf's *Sketches of Lowly Life In A Great City* (1899) listed in the *Guide* for comparison study. Edward Harrigan's play "O'Reilly and the Four Hundred," which had a song beginning with the words "Down in Hogan's Alley..." also likely provided direct inspiration.

It's also probable that Outcault's *Hogan's Alley* cast, including the *Yellow Kid*, was inspired by Charles W. Saalburg's *The Ting Lings*, which began in the *Chicago Inter Ocean Jr* supplement post-dated May 1, 1894 in the April 29, 1894 edition of Chicago Inter Ocean. That first episode is titled: "The Brownies Welcome The Ting-Lings."

There is also a definite similarity in Mickey Dugan's appearance and clothing style to Saalburg's creation which we will now examine in more detail thanks to welcome, on-going research by long time comics historian Allan Holtz supplemented by living comics history legend Bill Blackbeard.

Charles Saalzburg was an artist who was also the genius behind color printing in newspapers. He seems to have pioneered the concept from whom all others learned their craft.

On June 23, 1892 the *Chicago Inter Ocean* introduced a section with mostly editorial cartoons titled the *Illustrated Supplement*, commemorating the Democratic National Convention held in that city. Early regulars included Thomas Nast and Art Young. Starting June 26, the *Inter Ocean* began steadily issuing this weekly four page supplement, typically featuring full page editorial cartoons on its front and back covers. In May 1893 the supplement began coming out twice a week, and even greater frequency to daily during the *World Columbian Exposition* held in Chicago later that same year as it was used as a wrapper to attract sales from fair goers. Art Young did some of the color cover art and comic strips for the early Fair supplements, printing them right at the Fair to goggle-eyed fair tourists. Thomas Nast did some art as well during a visit he made to the Fair.

By September 10, 1893 the *Inter Ocean* introduced color, a multi-panel editorial comic strip by Charles Saalburg. The supplement used yellow ink, a further nail in the coffin of various Yellow Kid myths which had clouded serious comics scholarship in earlier decades before being proven wrong.

On October 1, Tom E. Powers introduced their first sequential non-political comic strip in color, a humorous pantomime.

As the Exposition ended in November, the contents were soon aimed more at children, enhanced with color added to the center as well by December 24, 1893, then changing its title to *Inter Ocean Jr* in January 1894. This was accomplished easily by folding the single four page sheet into eight pages.

In the January 1894 Saalburg began using Brownies-inspired characters in his color comic strips. The present theory is the *Ting-Ling* characters took over solo five months later in response to a presumed cease and desist letter which inevitably must have been issued from Palmer Cox to the *Inter Ocean*.

However, on July 8 1894, the *Inter Ocean Jr* stopped color and full page comics-type work in this supplement, devolving back to simple small spot art works. By mid-1894, color comics printing genius Saalburg had been lured to Pulitzer's New York World, becoming Art Director in charge of coloring for the new color printing press at the *New York World*. The color supplement was soon to be unleashed in the largest city in America.

By the November 18, 1894 issue of the *World*, Outcault was working for Goddard and Saalburg. Outcault produced a successful Sunday newspaper sequential comic strip in color with "The Origin of a New Species" on the back page in the World's first colored Sunday supplement. Long time pro Walt McDougall, a famous cartoonist reputed to have turned the 1884 Presidential race with a single cartoon that ran in the *World*, handled the cartoon art on the front page. Earlier, *The World* began running full page color single panels on May 21, 1893. McDougall did various other page panels during 1893, but it was Jan. 28, 1894 when the first sequence of comic pictures in a New York World newspaper appeared in panels in the same format as our comic strips today. It was a full page cut up into nine panels. This historic sequence was drawn entirely in pantomime, with no words, by Mark Fenderson.

The second page to appear in panels was an eight panel strip from February 4, 1894, also lacking words except for the title. This page was a collaboration between Walt McDougall and Mark Fenderson titled "The Unfortunate Fate of a Well-Intentioned Dog." From then on, many full page color strips by McDougall and Fenderson appeared; they were the first cartoonists to draw for the Sunday newspaper comic section. It was Outcault, however, who soon became the most famous cartoonist featured. After first appearing in black and white in Pulitzer's *The New York World* on February 17, 1895 and again on March 10, 1895, *The Yellow Kid* was introduced to the public in color on May 5, 1895.

Some have erroneously reported in scholarly journals that perhaps it was Frank Ladendorf's "Uncle Reuben," first introduced May 26, 1895, which became the first regularly recurring comics character in newspapers. This is wrong, as even Outcault's "Yellow Kid" began in Pulitzer's paper a good three months before *Uncle Reuben*. Until firm evidence to the contrary comes to light, that honor will forever be enshrined with Jimmy Swinnerton's *Little Bears* cartoon characters, found all over inside Hearst's *San Francisco Examiner* beginning October 14, 1893 with the first one called "Baby Monarch. Though never actually a comic strip, they nonetheless were the earliest presently-known recurring comics-type characters in American newspapers. In June 1895, a semi-regular "Little Bears" feature began. On January 26, 1896, children were introduced, the title eventually changed to "Little Bears and Tykes," forever confusing some scholars decades later. There never was a strip titled *Little Bears and Tigers,* as the *Tigers* were strictly for New York consumption when Hearst ordered Swinnerton to move to the Big Apple to compete better in the brewing comic strip wars.

The Yellow Kid's importance is widely recognized today as the first newspaper comic strip to demonstrate without a doubt that the general public was ready for full color comics. *The Yellow Kid* was the first in the USA to show that comics could increase newspaper sales, and that comic characters could be merchandised. *The Yellow Kid* was the headlining spark of what was soon dubbed by Hearst as "eight pages of polychromatic effulgence that makes the rainbow look like a lead pipe."

Ongoing research suggests that Palmer Cox's fabulous success with *The Brownies* was a direct inspiration for Richard Outcault's future merchandising work. The ultimate proof lies in the fourth Yellow Kid cartoon, which appeared in the February 9, 1895 issue of *Truth*. It was reprinted in the *New York World* eight days later on February 17, 1895, becoming the first Yellow Kid cartoon in the newspapers. The caption read "FOURTH WARD BROWNIES. MICKEY, THE ARTIST (adding a finishing touch) Dere, Chimmy! If Palmer Cox wuz t' see yer, he'd git yer copyrighted in a minute." The Yellow Kid was widely licensed in the greater New York area for all kinds of products, including gum and cigarette cards, toys, pinbacks, cookies, postcards, tobacco products, and appliances. There was also a short-lived humor magazine from Street & Smith named *The Yellow Kid*, featuring exquisite Outcault covers, plus a 196-page comic book from Dillingham & Co. known as *The Yellow Kid in McFadden's Flats,* dated to early 1897. Check out the covers in "The Platinum Age" three-page comic strip elsewhere in this Guide. In addition, there were several Yellow Kid plays produced, spawning other collectibles like show posters, programs and illustrated sheet music. (For those interested in more information regarding the Yellow Kid, it is available on the Internet at www.neponset.com/yellowkid.)

Mickey Dugan burned brightly for a few years as Outcault secured a copyright on the character with the United States Government by September 1896. By the time he completed the necessary paperwork, however, hundreds of business people

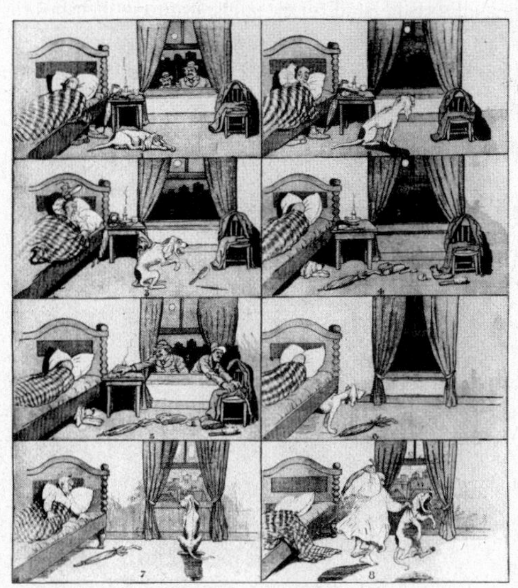

Walt McDougall & Mark Fenderson, the 2nd sequential comic strip in New York World, February 4, 1894, predates Yellow Kid in The World by over a year. Mark Fenderson drew the first NY World newspaper comic strip.

nationwide had pirated the image of The Yellow Kid and plastered it all over every product imaginable; mothers were even dressing their newborns to look like Dugan. Outcault, however, kept regularly utilizing images of *The Yellow Kid* in his comics style advertising work confirmed as late as 1915. Outcault soon found himself in a maelstrom not of his choosing, which probably pushed him to eventually drop the character. Outcault's creation went back and forth between newspaper giants Pulitzer and Hearst until Bennett's New York Herald mercifully snatched the cartoonist away in 1900 to do what amounted to a few relatively short-run strips. Later, he did one particular strip for a year–a satire of rural Black America titled *Pore Li'l Mose His Letters to his Mammy*, and then his newer creation, *Buster Brown*, debuted May 4, 1902. *Mose* had a very rare comic book collection published in 1902 by Cupples & Leon, now highly sought after by today's savvy collectors. Outcault continued drawing him in the background of occasional *Buster Brown* strips for many years to come.

William Randolph Hearst loved the comic strip medium ever since he was a little boy growing up on *Max & Moritz* by Wilhelm Busch in American collected book editions translated from the original German (these collections were first published in book form in 1871, serving as the influence for *The Katzenjammer Kids*). One of the ways Hearst responded to losing Outcault in 1900 was by purchasing the highly successful 23-year-old humor magazine *Puck* from the heirs of founder Joseph Keppler. With *Puck* and its exclusive cartoonist contracts, he commanded, among others, the very popular F. M. Howarth and Frederick Burr Opper's undivided attention. Opper first burst upon the comics scene in America back in 1880. Within a year Hearst had expanded this *National Lampoon* of its day into the colored Sunday comics section, *Puck-The Comic Weekly*. At first featuring Rudolph Dirk's *The Katzenjammer Kids* (1897), *Happy Hooligan* and other fine strips by the wildly popular Opper and a few others including Rudolph's brother Gus Dirks, the Hearst comic section steadily added more strips. For decades to come, there wasn't anything else that could compete with *Puck*. Hearst hired the best of the best and transformed *Puck* into the most popular comics section anywhere.

Outcault, meanwhile, followed in Palmer Cox's footprints a decade later by using the nexus of a World's Fair as a jumping off venue. *Buster Brown* was an instant sensation when he debuted as the new merchandising mascot of the Brown Shoe Company at the 1904 St. Louis World's Fair in a special Buster Brown Shoes pavilion. The character has the honor of being the first nationally licensed comic strip character in America with this time Outcault in almost full control. Many hundreds of different *Buster Brown* premiums have been issued. Comic books by Frederick A. Stokes Company featuring *Buster Brown & His Dog Tige* began as early as 1903 with *Buster Brown and His Resolutions*, simultaneously published in several different languages throughout the world.

After a few years, Buster and Outcault returned to Hearst in late 1905, joining what soon became the flagship of the comics world. Buster's popularity quickly spread all over the United States and then the world as he single-handedly spawned the first great comic strip licensing dynasty. For years, there were little people traveling from town to town performing as *Buster Brown* and selling shoes while accompanied by small dogs named Tige. Many other highly competitive licensed strips would soon follow. We suggest getting *Hake's Price Guide to Character Toys* for info on several hundred *Buster Brown* competitors, as well as several pages of the more fascinating *Buster Brown* material.

Soon there were many comic strip syndicates not only offering hundreds of various comic strips but also offering to license the characters for any company interested in paying the fee. The history of the comic strip with wide popularity since *The Yellow Kid* has been intertwined with giveaway premiums and character-based, store-bought merchandise of all kinds. Since its infancy as a profitable art form unto itself with *The Yellow Kid*, the comic strip world has profited from selling all sorts of "stuff" to the public featuring their favorite character or strip as its motif. American business gladly responded to the desire for comic character memorabilia with

Left: The Yellow Kid #1, March 20, 1897, Street & Smith as Howard Ainslee, NY.
Right: A rare full color "The Yellow Kid in McFadden's Flats" advertising sign promoting the first comic book featuring the Yellow Kid. The sign is from 1896 and measures 12x18".

The Adventures of Foxy Grandpa, late 1900, cover for the rare earliest known first edition of Carl "Bunny" Schultze's famous creation. He was one of the newspaper comics' first superstars.

Pore Li'l Mose by Richard Outcault, 1901. Bridges in between Yellow Kid and Buster Brown. Becoming scarce because many copies have been cut up.

thousands of fun items to enjoy and collect. Most of the early comics were not aimed specifically at kids, though children understandably enjoyed them as well.

Comic books have generally been associated with almost all of the licensed merchandise in this century. In the Platinum Age section beginning right after this essay, you will find a great many comic books in varied formats and sizes published before the advent of the first successful monthly newsstand comic magazine, *Famous Funnies*. What drove each of these evolutionary format changes was the need by their producers to make money so more books could be issued.

A very significant format was F. M. Howarth's *Funny Folks*, published in 1899 by E. P. Dutton and drawn from color as well as black and white pages of *Puck*. This rather large hardcover volume measured 16 1/2" wide by 12" tall. It contains numerous sequential comic strip pages as well as single gag illustrations. Howarth's art was a joy to behold and deserves wider recognition.

By Oct. 1900, Hearst had already caused Opper's *Folks In Funnyville* to be collected by publisher R. H. Russell, NY in a 12x9 hard cover format from his *New York Journal American Humorist* section. At the end of 1900, Carl Shultze had a first edition of *Vaudevilles and Other Things* published by Isaac H. Blanchard Co., NY. It measures 10 1/2" wide by 13" tall with 22 pages including covers. Each interior page is a 2 to 7 panel comic strip with lots of color.

There were also recently unearthed format variation second and third printings of *Vaudevilles* with the inscription "From the Originator of the 'Foxy Grandpa' Series" at the bottom of its front cover of the third printing. This note is lacking on the earlier first two editions, and it also switches format size to 11" tall by 13" wide. Discovered last year was a heretofore undocumented *The Adventures of Foxy Grandpa* - also issued in 1900 - new to the Platinum listings. The second number dated 1901 drops the words "The Adventures of..." from the title.

E. W. Kemble's *The Blackberries* had a color collection by 1901, also published by R. H. Russell, NY, as well as a few other comic-related volumes by Kemble still to be unearthed and properly identified. An earlier one was titled *Coontown's 400* (1899) newly listed this year. While the title is definitely not "PC" by today's standards, Kemble's drawings are excellent slices of African-American life in the USA with some humor injected. Kemble did a good job documenting aspects of life.

Confirmed is the exact format of Hearst's 1902 *The Katzenjammer Kids and Happy Hooligan And His Brother Gloomy Gus*. They both measure 15 5/16" wide by 10" tall and contain 88 pages including covers. Confirmed also is the fact that there are two separate editions with different covers for the pictured 1902 first edition and a 1903 Frederick Stokes edition of *Katzenjammer Kids* and *Happy Hooligan* with differing contents. They both are two different books entirely, and what confuses many collectors is that they have identical indicia title pages, but so does an entirely different *KK* from 1905.

Settling on a popular size of 17" wide by 11" tall, comic books were soon available that featured Charles "Bunny" Schultze's *Foxy Grandpa*, Rudolph Dirk's *The Katzenjammer Kids*, Winsor McCay's *Little Sammy Sneeze, Rarebit Fiend* and *Little Nemo*, and Fred Opper's *Happy Hooligan* and *Maud*, in addition to dozens of *Buster Brown* comic books. For well over a decade, these large-size, full-color volumes were the norm, retailing for 60¢. These collections offered full-size Sunday comics with the back side blank per page.

Though not the first daily newspaper strip, the very rare *Brainy Bowers and Drowsy Dugan* by R. W. Taylor is now crowned the first collection of strip reprints from a daily newspaper published in America. There are now four different collections of Brainy Bower known to exist.

The Outbursts of Everett True by A. D. Condo and J. W. Raper was first published by Saalfield in 1907 in an 88-page hardcover collection. It qualifies as the second daily comic strip collection as it predates the first *Mutt & Jeff* collection from Ball by three years. Condo & Raper's creation began its regular run several times a week in 1905 daily newspapers and lasted until 1927, when Condo became too sick to continue. This same *Everett True* collection was later truncated a bit by Saalfield in 1921 to 56 strips in just 32 pages measuring the standard 10"x10" Cupples & Leon size.

By 1908 Stokes had a large backlist of full color comic books for sale at 60¢ each. Some of these titles date back to 1903 and were reprinted over and over as demand warranted. Note the number of titles in the advertisement pulled from the back of *The Three Fun Makers* shown below.

With the ever-increasing popularity of Bud Fisher's new daily strip sensation, *Mutt & Jeff,* a new format was created for reprinting daily strips in black and white, a hardcover book about 15" wide by 5" tall, published by Ball starting in 1910 for five volumes. In 1912, Ball also branched out with at least the now-obscure *Doings of the Van Loons* by Fred I. Leipziger, a rare comic book in the same format as the *Mutt & Jeffs.*

Cartoons Magazine also began in 1912 and ran through 1921 before undergoing a radical format change. It is notable as a wonderful source for information on early comics and their creators. See also the Platinum index.

The next significant evolutionary change occurred in 1919, when Cupples & Leon began issuing their black and white daily strip reprint books in a new aforementioned format, about 10" wide by 10" tall, with four panels reprinted per page in a two by two matrix. These books were 52 pages for 25¢. The first ones featured *Bringing Up Father* and *Mutt & Jeff;* there were about 100 others.

By 1921, the last of the oblong (11"x15") color comic books were issued, with Cupples & Leon's *Jimmie Dugan* and *The Reg'lar Fellers* by Gene Byrne, and EmBee's *The Trouble Of Bringing Up Father* by self publisher George McManus. Of special historical interest, Embee issued the first 10¢ monthly comic book, *Comic Monthly,* with the first issue dated January 1922. A dozen 8-1/2"x9" issues were published, each featuring solo adventures of popular King Features strips. The monthly 10¢ comic book concept had finally arrived, though it would be more than a decade before it became truly successful.

Skippy by Percy Crosby debuted in the long-running humor magazine *Life* in the March 22, 1923 issue. By 1924 the first hard cover collection, *Life Presents Skippy*, was published. The newspaper comic strip debuted June 23, 1925 with the McClure syndicate. Hearst soon picked up a Sunday page a year later in mid-1926, then added a daily strip in 1929. By the 1930s it was red hot - think *Calvin & Hobbes or Peanuts* in popularity. In its day, it was one of the most popular comic strips ever created. Read the Modern era essay for more on *Skippy's* immense popularity.

In 1926, Cupples & Leon added a new 7" wide by 9" tall format with *Little Orphan Annie, Smitty,* and others. These were issued in both softcover and hardcover editions with dust jackets, and became extremely popular at 60¢ per copy.

Dell began publishing all original material in *The Funnies* in late 1929 in a larger tabloid format. At least three dozen issues were published before Delacorte threw in the towel. Even the extremely popular *Big Little Book*, introduced in 1932, can be viewed as a smaller version of the existing formats. The competition amongst publishers now included Dell, McKay, Sonnet, Saalfield and Whitman. The 1930s saw a definite shift in merchandising comic strip material from adults to children. This was the decade when Kellogg's placed *Buck Rogers* on the map, when Ovaltine issued tons of *Little Orphan Annie* material. Merchandising from such pioneers as Sam Gold and Kay Kamen spearheaded this next transformation of the comics biz beginning in the early 1930s.

Upwards of a thousand of these *Funnies On Parade* precursors, in all formats, were published through 1935 and were very popular. Towards the end of this era of once-popular comic book formats, beautiful collections of *Popeye, Mickey Mouse, Dick Tracy*, and many others were published which today command ever higher prices on the open market as they are rediscovered by the advanced collector who appreciates and enjoys truly great classic comics.

END NOTE: Each year we strive to add to the many 1930s variant formats. This Platinum Age section has grown as a result of advanced collectors who continue to report in with new finds. We encourage interested collectors and scholars to help with this section of the book, as each new data entry is very important for recovering our history. For corrections and additions to next year's next edition of *The Overstreet Guide* of some treasures you may have uncovered, please feel free to contact Gemstone Publishing at feedback@gemstonepub.com.

For further information on this era of American comic books, check out the previous evolving comics history essays in Guides #27,29-#40. Happy Hunting!

Banana Oil, a 1924 example of Cupples & Leon's then-revolutionary format from M.S. Publishers

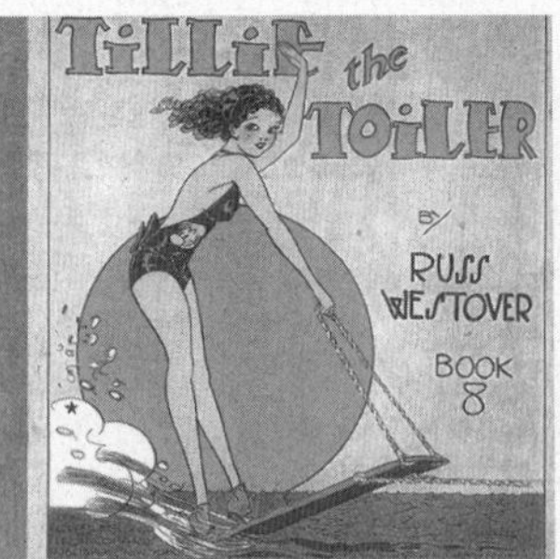

Tillie the Toiler #8 1933 from Cupples & Leon, another scarce number at the end of this once popular format.

David McKay published the last of the 10x10 comic books in 1935 as Famous Funnies grew in popularity.

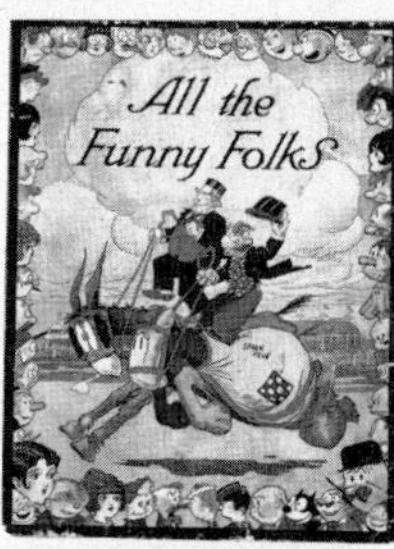

All the Funny Folks
© WPT

American-Journal-Examiner Joke Book
Special Supplement #12
1912 © New York American-Examiner

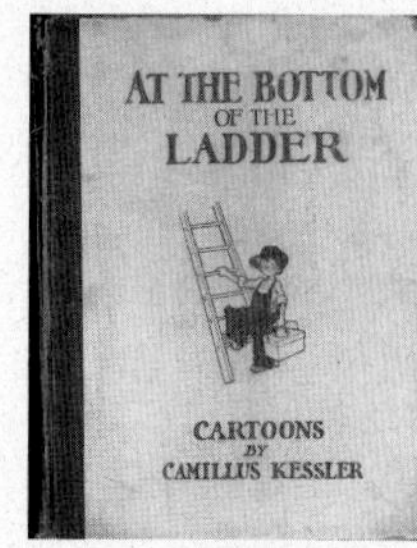

At The Bottom Of The Ladder
1926 © J.P. Lippincott Company

COLLECTOR'S NOTE: The books listed in this section were published many decades before organized comics fandom began archiving and helping to preserve these fragile popular culture artifacts. Consequently, copies of most all of these comics do not often surface in Fine+ or better shape. eBay has proven after more than a decade that many items once considered rare actually are not, though they almost always are in higher grades. For items marked scarce, we are trying to ascertain how many copies might still be in existence. Your input is always welcome.

Most Platinum Age comic books are in the Fair to VG range. If you want to collect these only in high grade, your collection will be extremely small. The prices given for Good, Fine and Very Fine categories are for strictly graded editions. If you need help grading your item, we refer you to the grading section in the front of this price guide or contact the authors of the Platinum essay. Most measurements are in inches. A few measurements are in centimeters. The first dimension given is Height and the second is Width.

For ease of ascertaining the contents of each item of this listing, there is a code letter or two following most titles we have been adding in over the years to aid you. A helpful list of categories pertaining to these codes can be found at the beginning of the Victorian Age pricing sections.This section created, revised, and expanded by Robert Beerbohm and Richard Olson with able assistance from Ray Agricola, Jon Berk, Bill Blackbeard, Roy Bonario, Ray Bottorff Jr., Chris Brown, Alfredo Castelli, Darrell Coons, Sol Davidson, Leonardo De Sá, Scott Deschaine, Mitchell Duval, Joe Evans, Tom Gordon III, Bruce Hamilton, Andy Konkykru, Don Kurtz, Gabriel Laderman, Bruce Mason, Donald Puff, Robert Quesinberry, Steve Rowe, Randy Scott, John Snyder, Art Spiegelman, Steve Thompson, Joan Crosby Tibbets, Richard Samuel West, Doug Wheeler, Richard Wright and Craig Yoe.

ADVENTURES OF EVA, PORA AND TED (M)
Evaporated Milk Association: 1932 (5x15", 16 pgs, B&W)

nn - By Steve 20.00 40.00 80.00
NOTE: *Appears to have had green, blue or white paper cover versions.*

ADVENTURES OF HAWKSHAW (N) (See Hawkshaw The Detective)
The Saalfield Publishing Co.: 1917 (9-3/4x13-1/2", 48 pgs., color & two-tone)

nn - By Gus Mager (only 24 pgs. of strips, reverse of each pg. is blank) 50.00 175.00 350.00
nn - 1927 Reprints 1917 issue 30.00 150.00 260.00
NOTE: *Started Feb 23, 1913-Sept 4, 1922, then begins again Dec 13, 1931-Feb 11, 1952.*

ADVENTURES OF SLIM AND SPUD, THE (M)
Prairie Farmer Publ. Co.: 1924 (3-3/4x 9-3/4", 104 pgs., B&W strip reprints)

nn 21.00 84.00 150.00
NOTE: *Illustrated mailing envelope exists postmarked out of Chicago, add 50%.*

ADVENTURES OF WILLIE WINTERS, THE (O,P)
Kelloggs Toasted Corn Flake Co.: 1912 (6-7/8x9-1/2", 20 pgs, full color)

nn - By Byron Williams & Dearborn Melvill 54.00 189.00 350.00

ADVENTURES OF WILLIE GREEN, THE (N) (see The Willie Green Comics)
Frank M. Acton Co.: 1915 (50¢, 52 pgs, 8-1/2X16", B&W, soft-c)

Book 1 - By Harris Brown; strip-r 54.00 189.00 350.00

A. E. F. IN CARTOONS BY WALLY, THE (N)
Don Sowers & Co.: 1933 (12x10-1/8", 88 pgs, hardcover B&W)

nn - By Wally Wallgren (WW One Stars & Stripes-r) 25.00 90.00 175.00

AFTER THE TOWN GOES DRY (I)
The Howell Publishing Co, Chicago: 1919 (48 pgs, 6-1/2x4", hardbound two color-c)

nn - By Henry C. Taylor; illus by Frank King 25.00 75.00 150.00

AIN'T IT A GRAND & GLORIOUS FEELING? (N) (Also see Mr. & Mrs.)
Whitman Publishing Co.: 1922 (9x9-3/4", 52 pgs., stiff cardboard-c)

nn - 1921 daily strip-r; B&W, color-c; Briggs-a 36.00 143.00 250.00
nn -(9x9-1/2", 28pgs., stiff cardboard-c)-Sunday strip-r in color (inside front-c says "More of the Married Life of Mr. & Mrs".) 36.00 143.00 250.00
NOTE: *Strip started in 1917; This is the 2nd Whitman comic book, after Brigg's MR. & MRS.*

ALL THE FUNNY FOLKS (I)
World Press Today, Inc.: 1926 (11-1/2x8-1/2", 112 pgs., color, hard-c)

nn-Barney Google, Spark Plug, Jiggs & Maggie, Tillie The Toiler, Happy Hooligan, Hans & Fritz, Toots & Casper, etc. 100.00 400.00 650.00
With Dust Jacket By Louis Biedermann 200.00 800.00 1400.00
NOTE: *Booklength race horse story masterfully enveloping all major King Features characters.*

ALPHONSE AND GASTON AND THEIR FRIEND LEON (N)
Hearst's New York American & Journal: 1902,1903 (10x15-1/4", Sunday strip reprints in color)

nn - (1902) - By Frederick Opper (scarce) 500.00 1800.00 -
nn - (1903) - By Frederick Opper (scarce) (72 pages) 500.00 1800.00 -
NOTE: *Strip ran Sept 22, 1901to at least July 17, 1904.*

ALWAYS BELITTLIN' (see Skippy; That Rookie From the 13th Squad; Between Shots)
Henry Holt & Co.: 1927 (6x8", hard-c with DJ,

nn -By Percy Crosby (text with cartoons) 43.00 172.00 300.00

ALWAYS BELITTLIN' (I) (see Skippy; That Rookie From the 13th Squad, Between Shots)
Percy Crosby, Publisher: 1933 (14 1/4 x 11", 72 pgs, hard-c, B&W)

nn - By Percy Crosby 43.00 172.00 300.00
NOTE: *Self-published; primarily political cartoons with text pages denouncing prohibition's gang warfare effects and cuts in the national defense budget as Crosby saw war looming in Europe and with Japan.*

AMERICAN-JOURNAL-EXAMINER JOKE BOOK SPECIAL SUPPLEMENT (O)
New York American: 1911-12 (12 x 9 3/4", 16 pgs) (known issues) (Very Rare)

1 Tom Powers Joke Book(12/10/11) 80.00 280.00 -
2 Mutt & Jeff Joke Book (Bud Fisher 12/17/11) 100.00 350.00 -
3 TAD's Joke Book (Thomas Dorgan 12/24/11) 80.00 300.00 -
4 F. Opper's Joke Book (Frederick Burr Opper 12/31/11) (contains Happy Hooligan) 100.00 350.00 -
5 not known to exist
6 Swinnerton's Joke Book (Jimmy Swinnerton 01/14/12) (contains Mr. Jack) 100.00 375.00 -
7 The Monkey's Joke Book (Gus Mager 01/21/12) (contains Sherlocko the Monk) 100.00 350.00 -
8 Joys And Glooms Joke Book (T. E. Powers 01/28/12) 80.00 280.00 -
9 The Dingbat Family's Joke Book (George Herriman 02/04/12) (contains early Krazy Kat & Ignatz) 200.00 700.00 -
10 Valentine Joke Book, A (Opper, Howarth, Mager, T. E. Powers 02/11/12) 80.00 280.00 -
11 Little Hatchet Joke Book (T. E. Powers 02/18/12) 80.00 280.00 -
12 Jungle Joke Book (Dirks, McCay 02/25/12) 100.00 400.00 -
13 The Hayseeds Joke Book (03/03/12) 80.00 280.00 -
14 Married Life Joke Book (T.E. Powers 03/10/12) 80.00 280.00 -
NOTE: *These were insert newspaper supplements similar to Eisner's later Spirit sections. A Valentine Joke Book recently surfaced from Hearst's Boston Sunday American proving that other cities besides New York City had these special supplements. Each issue also contains work by other cartoonists besides the cover featured creator and those already listed above such as Sidney Smith, Winsor McCay, Hy Mayer, Grace Weiderseim (later Drayton), others.*

AMERICA'S BLACK & WHITE BOOK 100 Pictured Reasons Why We Are At War (N,S)
Cupples & Leon: 1917 (10 3/4 x 8", 216 pgs)

nn - W. A. Rogers (New York Herald-r) 32.00 114.00 195.00

AMONG THE FOLKS IN HISTORY
Rand McNally Print Guild: 1935 (192 pgs, 8-1/2x9-1/2", hard-c, B&W)

nn - By Gaar Williams 21.00 84.00 150.00

AMONG THE FOLKS IN HISTORY
The Book and Print Guild: 1935 (200 pgs, 8-1/2x9-1/2:,

nn - By Gaar Williams 21.00 84.00 150.00
NOTE: *Both the above are evidently different editions and contain largely full-page, single panel cartoons similar to Briggs' work of that sort. 8 or 10 pages are broken into panels, usually with a this is how it was in the old days, this is how it is today theme.*

ANGELIC ANGELINA (N)
Cupples & Leon Company: 1909 (11-1/2x17", 56 pgs., 2 colors)

nn - By Munson Paddock 67.00 233.00 400.00
NOTE: *Strip ran March 22, 1908-Feb 7, 1909.*

ANDY GUMP, HIS LIFE STORY (I)
The Reilly & Lee Co, Chicago: 1924 (192 pgs, hardbound)

nn - By Sidney Smith (over 100 illustrations) 25.00 80.00 150.00

ANIMAL CIRCUS, THE (from Puggery Wee)
Rand McNally + Company: 1908 (48 pgs, 11x8-1/2", color-c, 3-color insides)

nn - By unknown 25.00 80.00 150.00
NOTE: *Illustrated verse, many pages with multiple illustrations.*

ANIMAL SERIALS
T. Y. Crowell: 1906 (9x6-7/8", 214 pgs, hard-c, B&W)

nn - By E Warde Blaisdell 20.00 80.00 150.00
NOTE: *Multi-page comic strip stories. Reprints of Sunday strip "Bunny Bright He's All-Right".*

A NOBODY'S SCRAP BOOK
Frederik A. Stokes Co., New York: 1900 (11" x 8-5/8", hard-c, color)

nn- (Scarce) 67.00 233.00 425.00
NOTE: *Designed in England, printed in Holland, on English paper -- which likely explains the mispelling of Frederick Stokes' name. Highly fragile paper. Strips and cartoons, all by the same unidentified artist, "A Nobody", almost certainly reprinted from somewhere, as they are very professional.*

AT THE BOTTOM OF THE LADDER (M)
J.P. Lippincott Company: 1926 (11x8-1/4", 296 pgs, hardcover, B&W)

nn - By Camillus Kessler 45.00 157.50 300.00
NOTE: *Hilarious single panel cartoons showing first jobs of then important "captains of industry."*

AUTO FUN, PICTURES AND COMMENTS FROM "LIFE"
Thomas Y. Crowell & Co.: 1905 (152 pgs, 9x7", hard-c, B&W)

nn -By various 45.00 157.00 300.00
NOTE: *The cover just has "Auto Fun" but the title page also has the subheading listed here. This is similar to other reprint books of Life cartoons printed in the guide. Largely single panel cartoons but also several sequential. One or more cartoons by Kemble, Levering, Dirks, Flagg, Sullivant. Sequential cartoons by Kemble, Levering, Sullivant, and the highpoint, a 2 pg 6 panel piece by Winsor McCay.*

BANANA OIL (N) (see also HE DONE HER WRONG)

Barney Google and Spark Plug #2
© C&L

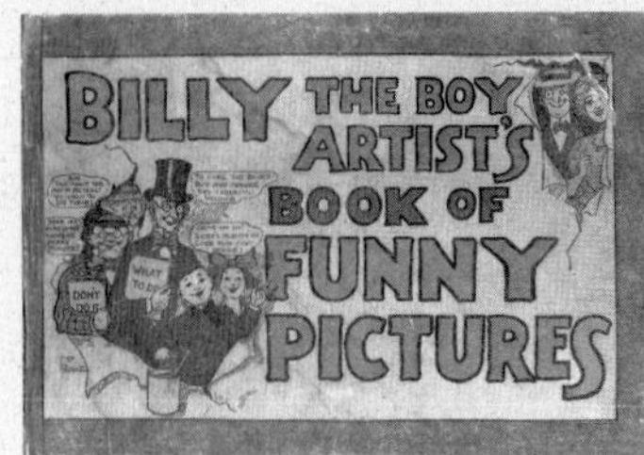

Bill the Boy Artist's Book by Ed Payne
1910 © C.M. Clark Publishing Co

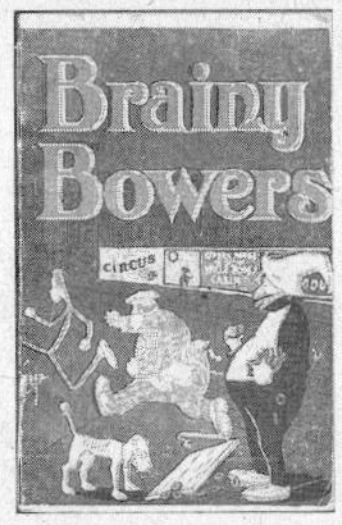

Brainy Bowers and Drowsy Duggan by R.W. Taylor
1905 © Star Publishing Co. - the first daily reprints

MS Publ. Co.: 1924 (9-7/8x10", 52 pgs., B&W)
nn - Milt Gross comic strips; not reprints 150.00 450.00 750.00

BARKER'S ILLUSTRATED ALMANAC (O,P,S) (See Barkers in Victorian Era section)
Barker, Moore & Mein Medicine Co: 1900-1932+ (36 pgs, B&W, color paper-c)
1900-1932+ (7x5-7/8") 20.00 70.00 150.00

BARKER'S "KOMIC" PICTURE SOUVENIR (P,S) (see Barker's in Victorian)
Barker, Moore & Mein Medicine Co: nd (Parts 1-3, 1901-1903; Parts 1-4, 1906+) (color cardboard-c, B&W interior, 50 pages)
Parts 1-3 (Rare, earliest printing, nd (1901)) 60.00 300.00 650.00
NOTE: *Same cover as 4th edition in Victorian Age Section, except has "Part 1", "Part 2", or "Part 3" printed in the blank space beneath the crate on which central figure is sitting. States "Edition in 3 Parts" on the first interior page, beneath the picture of the Barker's Building.*
Parts 1-3 (nd, c1901-1903) 50.00 200.00 425.00
NOTE: *New cover art on all Parts. States "Edition in 3 Parts" on the first interior page.*
Parts 1-4 (nd, c1906+) 50.00 100.00 325.00
NOTE: *States "Edition in 4 Parts" on the first interior page. Various printings known. These have been confirmed as premium comic books, predating the Buster Brown premiums. They reprint advertising cartoons from Barker's Illustrated Almanac. For the 50 page booklets by this same name, numbered as "Part"s, without exception, were published after 1900. Some editions are found to have 54 pages.*

BARNEY GOOGLE AND SPARK PLUG (N) (See **Comic Monthly**)
Cupples & Leon Co.: 1923 - No.6, 1928 (9-7/8x9-3/4"; 52 pgs., B&W, daily-r)
1 (nn)-By Billy DeBeck 60.00 240.00 450.00
2-4 (#5 & #6 do not exist) 46.00 186.00 350.00
NOTE: *Started June 17, 1919 as newspaper strip; Spark Plug introduced July 17, 1922; strip still running making it one of the oldest still in existence.*

BART'S CARTOONS FOR 1902 FROM THE MINNEAPOLIS JOURNAL (N,S)
Minneapolis Journal: 1903 (11x9", 102 pgs, paperback, B&W)
nn - By Charles L. Bartholomew 28.00 99.00 170.00

BELIEVE IT OR NOT! by Ripley (N,S)
Simon & Schuster: 1929 (8x 5-1/4", 68 pgs, red, B&W cover, B&W interior)
nn - By Robert Ripley (strip-r text & art) 60.00 125.00 250.00
NOTE: *1929 was the first printing of many reprintings . Strip began Dec 19, 1918 and is still running.*

BEN WEBSTER (N)
Standard Printing Company: 1928-1931 (13-3/4x4-7/16", 768 pgs, soft-c)
1 - "Bound to Win" 40.00 120.00 280.00
2 - "...in old Mexico 40.00 120.00 280.00
3 - "...At Wilderness Lake 40.00 120.00 280.00
4 - "...in the Oil Fields 40.00 120.00 280.00
NOTE: *Self Published by Edwin Alger, also contains fan's letter pages.*

BIG SMOKER
W.T. Blackwell & Co.: 1908 (16 pgs, 5-1/2x3-1/2", color-c & interior)
nn - By unknown 12.00 48.00 80.00
NOTE: *Stated reprint of 1878 version. no known copies yet of original printing.*

BILLY BOUNCE (I)
Donohue & Co.: 1906 (288 pgs, hardbound)
nn - By W.W. Denslow & Dudley Bragdon 150.00 525.00 925.00
NOTE: *Billy Bounce was created in 1901 as a comic strip by W. W. Denslow (strip ran from 1901 NOV 11 to 1905 DEC 3), but the series is best remembered in the C. W. Kahles version (from 1902 SEP 28). Denslow resumed his character in the above illustrated book.*

BILLY HON'S FAMOUS CARTOON BOOK (H)
Wasley Publishing Co.: 1927 (7-1/2x10", 68 pgs, softbound wraparound)
nn - By Billy Hon 12.00 48.00 80.00

BILLY THE BOY ARTIST'S BOOK OF FUNNY PICTURES (N)
C.M.Clark Publishing Co.: 1910 (9x12", hardcover-c, Boston Globe strip-r)
nn - By Ed Payne 125.00 400.00 750.00
NOTE: *This long lived strip ran in **The Boston Globe** from Nov 5 1899-Jan 7 1955; one of the longer run strips.*

BILLY THE BOY ARTIST'S PAINTING BOOK OF FUNNY PICTURES
(known to exist; more data required) - - -

BIRD CENTER CARTOONS: A Chronicle of Social Happenings (N,S)
A. C. McClurg & Co.: 1904 (12-3/8x9-1/2", 216 pgs, hardcover, B&W, single panels)
nn - By John McCutcheon 40.00 140.00 260.00
NOTE: *Strip began in **The Chicago Tribune** in 1903. Satirical cartoons and text concerning a mythical town.*

BLASTS FROM THE RAM'S HORN
The Rams Horn Company: 1902 (330 pgs, 7x9", B&W)
nn - By various 20.00 70.00 120.00
NOTE: *Cartoons reprinted from what was, apparently, a religious newspaper. Many cartoons by Frank Beard. Mostly single panel but occasionally sequential. Allegorical cartoons similar to the Christian Cartoons book. This book mixes cartoons and text sort of like the Caricature books. One or more cartoons on every page.*

BOBBY THATCHER & TREASURE CAVE (N)
Altemus Co.: 1932 (9x7", 86 pgs., B&W, hard-c)
nn - Reprints; Storm-a 54.00 189.00 400.00

BOBBY THATCHER'S ROMANCE (N)
The Bell Syndicate/Henry Altemus Co.: 1931 (8-3/4x7", color cover, B&W)
nn - By Storm 54.00 189.00 400.00

BOOK OF CARTOONS, A (M,S)
Edward T. Miller: 1903 (12-1/4x9-1/4", 120 pgs, hardcover, B&W)
nn - By Harry J. Westerman (Ohio State Journal-r) 20.00 70.00 120.00

BOOK OF DRAWINGS BY A.B. FROST, A (M,S)
P.F. Collier & Son: 1904 (15-3/8 x 11", 96 pgs, B&W)
nn - A.B. Frost 50.00 100.00 300.00
NOTE: *Pages alternate verses by Wallace Irwin and full-page plated by A.B.Frost. 39 plates.*

BOTTLE, THE (E) (see Victorian Age section for earlier printings)
Gowans & Gray, London & Glasgow: June 1905 (3-3/4x6", 72 pgs, printed one side only, paper cover, B&W)
nn - 1st printing (June 1905) 20.00 40.00 125.00
nn - 2nd printing (March 1906) 20.00 40.00 100.00
nn - 3rd printing (January 1911) 20.00 40.00 90.00
NOTE: *By George Cruikshank. Reprints both THE BOTTLE and THE DRUNKARD'S CHILDREN. Cover is text only - no cover art.*

BOTTLE, THE (E)
Frederick A. Stokes: nd (c1906) (3-3/4x6", 72 pgs, printed one side only, paper-c, B&W)
nn- by George Cruikshank 17.50 35.00 70.00
NOTE: *Reprint of the Gowans & Gray edition. Reprints both THE BOTTLE and THE DRUNKARD'S CHILDREN. Cover is text only - no cover art.*

BOYS AND FOLKS (N).
George H. Dornan Company: 1917 (10-1/4 x 8-1/4", 232 pgs. (single-sided), B&W strip-r.
nn - By Webster 21.00 64.00 150.00
NOTE: *Four sections: Life's Darkest Moments, Mostly About Folks, The Thrill That Comes Once in a Lifetime, and Our Boyhood Ambitions. Most are single-panel cartoons, but there are some sequential comic strips.*

BOY'S & GIRLS' BIG PAINTING BOOK OF INTERESTING COMIC PICTURES (N)
M. A. Donohue & Co.: 1914-16 (9x15, 70 pgs)
nn - By Carl "Bunny" Schultze (Foxy Grandpa-r) 81.00 284.00 -
#2 (1914) 81.00 284.00 -
#337 (1914) (sez "Big Painting & Drawing Book") 81.00 284.00 -
nn - (1916) (sez "Big Painting Book")(9-1/4x15") 81.00 284.00 -
NOTE: *These are all **Foxy Grandpa** items.*

BRAIN LEAKS: Dialogues of Mutt & Flea (N)
O. K. Printing Co. (Rochester Evening Times): 1911 (76 pgs, 6-5/8x4-5/8, hard-c, B&W)
nn - By Leo Edward O'Melia; newspaper strip-r 29.00 100.00 171.00

BRAINY BOWERS AND DROWSY DUGGAN (N)
Star Publishing: 1905 (7-1/4 x 4-9/16", 98 pgs., blue, brown & white color cover, B&W interior, 25¢) (daily strip-r 1902-04 Chicago Daily News)
#74 - By R. W. Taylor (Scarce) 600.00 1800.00 -
NOTE: *Part of a series of Atlantic Library Heart Series. Strip begins in 1901 and runs thru 1915. Taylor also created Yen the Janitor for the **New York World.***

BRAIN BOWERS AND DROWSY DUGAN (N)
Max Stein Pub. House, Chicago: 1905 (6-3/16x4-3/8", 64 pgs, B&W)
nn - By R.W. Taylor (Scarce) 600.00 1800.00 -
NOTE: *A coverless copy of this surfaced on eBay in 2002 selling for $700.00.;*

BRAINY BOWERS AND DROWSY DUGGAN GETTING ON IN THE WORLD WITH NO VISIBLE MEANS OF SUPPORT (STORIES TOLD IN PICTURES TO MAKE THEIR TELLING SHORT) (N)
Max Stein/Star Publishing: 1905 (7-3/8x5 1/8", 164 pgs, slick black, red & tan color cover, interior newsprint) (daily strip-r 1902-04 Chicago Daily News)
nn - By R. W. Taylor (Scarce) 500.00 1700.00 -
nn - Possible hard cover edition also? - - -
NOTE: *These Brainy Bowers editions are the earliest known daily newspaper strip reprint books.*

BRINGING UP FATHER (N)
Star Co. (King Features): 1917 (5-1/2x16-1/2", 100 pgs., B&W, cardboard-c)
nn - (Scarcer)-Daily strip- by George McManus 158.00 553.00 950.00

BRINGING UP FATHER (N)
Cupples & Leon Co.: 1919 - No. 26, 1934 (10x10", 52 pgs., B&W, stiff cardboard-c) (No. 22 is 9-1/4x9-1/2")
1-Daily strip-r by George McManus in all 25.00 100.00 325.00
2-10 25.00 100.00 250.00
11-20 40.00 200.00 375.00
21-26 (Scarcer) 60.00 300.00 550.00
The Big Book 1 (1926)-Thick book (hardcover, 142 pgs.) 127.00 508.00 900.00
w/dust jacket (rare) 183.00 732.00 1325.00
The Big Book 2 (1929) 96.00 384.00 700.00
w/dust jacket (rare) 183.00 732.00 1325.00
NOTE: *The Big Books contain 3 regular issues rebound. Strip began Jan 2 1913-May 28 2000.*

BRINGING UP FATHER, THE TROUBLE OF (N)
Embee Publ. Co.: 1921 (9-3/4x15-3/4", 46 pgs, Sunday-r in color)
nn - (Rare) 100.00 350.00 600.00
NOTE: *Ties with Mutt & Jeff (EmBee) and Jimmie Dugan And The Reg'lar Fellers (C&L) as the last of the*

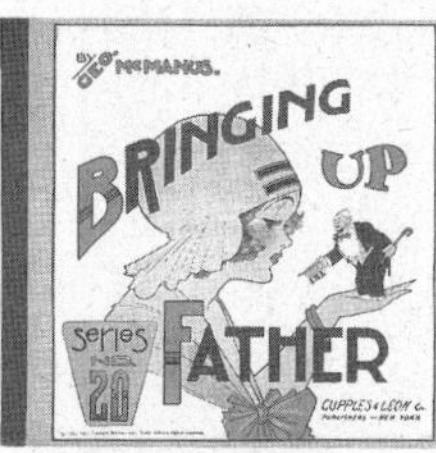

Bringing Up Father #20
1933 © Cupples & Leon

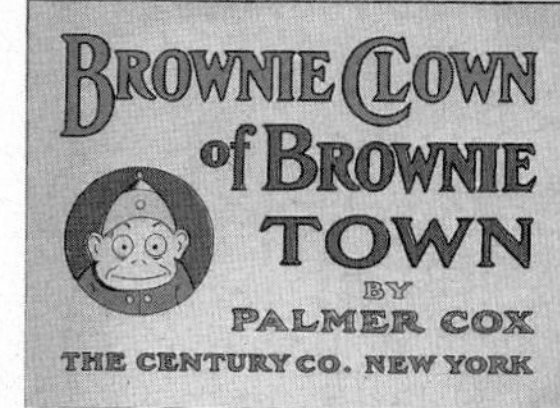

Brownie Clown of Brownie Town
© The Century Co.

Buster Brown His Dog Tige And Their Jolly Times
1906 © Cupples & Leon

GD2.0 FN6.0 VF8.0

oblong size era. This was self published by George McManus.

BRINGING UP FATHER (N) (see SAGARA'S ENGLISH CARTOONS
Publisher unknown (actually, unreadable), Tokyo: October 1924 (9-7/8" x 7-1/2", 90 pgs, color hard-c, B&W)

nn- (Scarce) by George McManus C&A (no known sales)
NOTE: *Published in Tokyo, Japan, with all strips in both English and Japanese, to facilitate learning English. Introduction by George McManus. Scarce in USA.*

BRONX BALLADS (I)
Simon & Schuster, NY: 1927 (9-1/2x7-1/4", hard-c, B&W)

nn - By Robert Simon and Harry Hershfield 36.00 143.00 250.00

BROWNIES, THE (not sequential comic strips)
The Century Co.: 1887 - 1914 (all came with dust jackets; add $100-150 to value if original dust jacket is included and intact)

Book 1 - The Brownies: Their Book (1887) 200.00 850.00 1200.00
Book 2 - Another Brownies Book (1890) 150.00 635.00 1000.00
Book 3 - The Brownies at Home (1893) 125.00 530.00 825.00
Book 4 - The Brownies Around the World (1894) 100.00 425.00 660.00
Book 5 - The Brownies Through the Union (1895) 100.00 425.00 660.00
Book 6 - The Brownies Abroad (1899) 100.00 425.00 660.00
Book 7 - The Brownies in the Philippines (1904) 100.00 425.00 660.00
Book 8 - The Brownies' Latest Adventures (1910) 100.00 425.00 660.00
Book 9 - The Brownies Many More Nights (1914) 100.00 425.00 660.00
...Raid on Kleinmaier Bros. (c. 1910, 16 pages) Kleinmaier Bros. Clothing, Marion, Ohio (no known sales)

BROWNIE CLOWN OF BROWNIE TOWN (N)
The Century Co.: 1908 (6-7/8 x 9-3/8", 112 pgs, color hardcover & interior)

nn - By Palmer Cox (rare; 1907 newspaper comic strip-r) 250.00 800.00 1000.00
NOTE: *The Brownies created 1883 in* ***St Nicholas Magazine.***

BUDDY TUCKER & HIS FRIENDS (N) (Also see **Buster Brown Nuggets**)
Cupples & Leon Co.: 1906 (11-5/8 x17", 58 pgs, color) (Scarce)

nn - 1905 Sunday strip-r by R. F. Outcault 500.00 1500.00 2500.00
NOTE: *Strip began Apr 30, 1905 thru at least Oct 1905.*

BUFFALO BILL'S PICTURE STORIES
Street & Smith Publications: 1909 (Soft cardboard cover)

nn - Very rare 67.00 233.00 400.00

BUGHOUSE FABLES (N) (see also **Comic Monthly**)
Embee Distributing Co. (King Features): 1921 (10¢, 4x4-1/2", 48 pgs.)

1-By Barney Google (Billy DeBeck) 46.00 186.00 350.00

BUG MOVIES (O) (Also see Clancy The Cop & Deadwood Gulch)
Dell Publishing Co.: 1931 (9-13/16x9-7/8", 52 pgs., B&W)

nn - Original material; Stookie Allen-a 150.00 300.00 500.00

BULL
Bull Publishing Company, New York: No.1, March, 1916 - No.12, Feb, 1917 (10 cents, 10-3/4x8-3/4", 24 pgs, color paper-c, B&W)

1-12 (Very Rare) – – –
NOTE: *Pro-German, Anti-British cartoon/humor monthly, whose goal was to keep the U.S. neutral and out of World War I. We know of no copies which have sold in the past few years.*

BUNNY'S BLUE BOOK (see also Foxy Grandpa) (N)
Frederick A. Stokes Co.: 1911 (10x15, 60¢)

nn - By Carl "Bunny" Schultze strip-r 100.00 350.00 –

BUNNY'S RED BOOK (see also Foxy Grandpa) (N)
Frederick A. Stokes Co.: 1912 (10-1/4x15-3/4", 64 pgs.)

nn - By Carl "Bunny" Schultze strip-r 100.00 350.00 –

BUNNY'S GREEN BOOK (see also Foxy Grandpa) (N)
Frederick A. Stokes Co.: 1913 (10x15")

nn - By Carl "Bunny" Schultze 100.00 350.00 –

BUSTER BROWN (C) (Also see Brown's Blue Ribbon Book of Jokes and Jingles & Buddy Tucker & His Friends)
Frederick A. Stokes Co.: 1903 - 1916 (Daily strip-r in color)

1903...& His Resolutions (11-1/4x16", 66 pgs.) by R. F. Outcault (Rare)-1st nationally distributed comic. Distr. through Sears & Roebuck 1600.00 3500.00 –
1904...His Dog Tige & Their Troubles (11-1/4x16-1/4", 66 pgs.)(Rare) 600.00 1800.00 –
1905...Pranks (11-1/4x16-3/8", 66 pgs.) 400.00 1450.00 –
1906...Antics (11x16-3/8", 66 pgs.) 400.00 1450.00 –
1906...And Company (11x16-1/2", 66 pgs.) 300.00 1050.00 –
1906...Mary Jane & Tige (11-1/4x16, 66 pgs.) 300.00 1050.00 –
NOTE: ***Yellow Kid*** *pictured on two pages.*
1908 Collection of Buster Brown Comics 250.00 835.00 –
1909 Outcault's Real Buster and The Only Mary Jane (11x16, 66 pgs, Stokes) 250.00 835.00 –
1910...Up to Date (10-1/8x15-3/4", 66 pgs.) 208.00 729.00 1200.00
1911...Fun And Nonsense (10-1/8x15-3/4", 66 pgs.) 183.00 642.00 1150.00
1912...The Fun Maker (10-1/8x15-3/4", 66 pgs.) -Yellow Kid (4 pgs.) 183.00 642.00 1150.00
1913...At Home (10-1/8x15-3/4", 56 pgs.) 167.00 583.00 1050.00
1914...And Tige Here Again (10x16, 62 pgs, Stokes) 153.00 535.00 1000.00
1915...And His Chum Tige (10x16, Stokes) 153.00 535.00 1000.00
1916...The Little Rogue (10-1/8x15-3/4", 62 pgs.) 162.00 567.00 1025.00
1917...And the Cat (5-1/2x 6-1/2, 26 pgs, Stokes) 115.00 402.00 750.00
1917...Disturbs the Family (5-1/2x 6 1/2, 26 pgs, Stokes
NOTE: *Story featuring statue of "the Chinese Yellow Kid"* 115.00 402.00 750.00
1917...The Real Buster Brown (5-1/2x 6 -/2, 26 pgs, Stokes 115.00 402.00 750.00

Frederick A. Stokes Co. Hard Cover Series (I)

...Abroad (1904, 10-1/4x8", 86 pgs., B&W, hard-c)-R. F. Outcault-a (Rare) 200.00 700.00 1100.00
...Abroad (1904, B&W, 67 pgs.)-R. F. Outcault-a 200.00 700.00 1100.00
NOTE: *Buster Brown Abroad is not an actual comic book, but prose with illustrations.*
..."Tige" His Story 1905 (10x8", 63 pgs., B&W) (63 illos.)
nn-By RF Outcault 143.00 500.00 –
...My Resolutions 1906 (10x8", B&W, 68 pgs.)-R.F. Outcault-a (Rare) 233.00 817.00 1400.00
...Autobiography 1907 (10x8", B&W, 71 pgs.) (16 color plates & 36 B&W illos) 67.00 233.00 440.00
...And Mary Jane's Painting Book 1907 (10x13-1/4", 60 pgs, both card & hardcover versions exist
nn-RFO (first printing blank on top of cover) 67.00 233.00 440.00
First Series- this is a reprint if it says First Series 67.00 233.00 440.00
Volume Two - By RFO 67.00 233.00 440.00
... My Resolutions by Buster Brown (1907, 68 pgs, small size, cardboard covers) scarce 43.00 150.00 285.00
NOTE: *Not actual comic book per se, but a compilation of the Resolutions panels found at the end of Outcault's Buster Brown newspaper strips.*

BUSTER BROWN (N)
Cupples & Leon Co./N. Y. Herald Co.: 1906 - 1917 (11x17", color, strip-r)
NOTE: *Early issues by R. F. Outcault; most C&L editions are not by Outcault.*

1906...His Dog Tige And Their Jolly Times (11-3/8x16-5/8", 68 pgs.) 300.00 1100.00 1800.00
1906...His Dog Tige & Their Jolly Times (11x16, 46 pgs.) 163.00 600.00 1025.00
1907...Latest Frolics (11-3/8x16-5/8", 66 pgs., r/'05-06 strips) 163.00 600.00 1025.00
1908...Amusing Capers (58 pgs.) 129.00 475.00 815.00
1909...The Busy Body (11-3/8x16-5/8", 62 pgs.) 129.00 475.00 815.00
1910...On His Travels (11x16", 58 pgs.) 115.00 402.00 750.00
1911...Happy Days (11-3/8x16-5/8", 58 pgs.) 115.00 402.00 750.00
1912...In Foreign Lands (10x16", 58 pgs) 115.00 402.00 750.00
1913...And His Pets (11x16", 58 pgs.) STOKES???? 115.00 402.00 750.00
1913...And His Pets (26 pg partial reprint) – – –
1914...Funny Tricks (11-3/8x16-5/8", 58 pgs.) 115.00 402.00 750.00
1916...At Play (10x16, 58 pgs) 115.00 402.00 750.00

BUSTER BROWN NUGGETS (N)
Cupples & Leon Co./N.Y.Herald Co.: 1907 (1905, 7-1/2x6-1/2", 36 pgs., color, strip-r, hard-c)(By R. F. Outcault) (NOTE: books are all unnumbered)

Buster Brown Goes Fishing, Goes Swimming, Plays Indian, Goes Shooting, Plays Cowboy, On Uncle Jack's Farm, Tige And the Bull, And Uncle Buster 40.00 150.00 300.00
Buddy Tucker Meets Alice in Wonderland 56.00 200.00 400.00
Buddy Tucker Visits The House That Jack Built 40.00 150.00 300.00

BUSTER BROWN MUSLIN SERIES (N)
Saalfield: 1907 (also contain copyright Cupples & Leon)

...Goes Fishing, Plays Indian, And the Donkey (1907, 6-7/8x6-1/8", 24 pgs., color)-r/1905 Sunday comics page by Outcault (Rare) 50.00 175.00 315.00
...Plays Cowboy (1907, 6-3/4x6", 10 pgs., color)-r/1905 Sunday comics page by Outcault (Rare) 50.00 175.00 315.00
NOTE: *These are muslin versions of the C&L BB Nugget series. Muslin books are all cloth books, made to be washable so as not easily stained/destroyed by very young children. The Muslin books contain one strip each (the title strip), to the more common NUGGET's three strips.*

BUSTER BROWN PREMIUMS (Advertising premium booklets)
Various Publishers: 1904 - 1912 (3x5" to 5x7"; sizes vary)

American Fruit Product Company, Rochester, NY

Buster Brown Duffy's 1842 Cider (1904, 7x5". 12 pgs, C.E. Sherin Co, NYC)
nn - By R. F. Outcault (scarce) 100.00 350.00 600.00

The Brown Shoe Company, St. Louis, USA

Set of five books (5x7", 16 pgs., color)
Brown's Blue Ribbon Book of Jokes and Jingles Book 1 (nn, 1904)-By R. F. Outcault; Buster Brown & Tige, Little Tommy Tucker, Jack & Jill, Little Boy Blue, Dainty Jane; The Yellow Kid app. on back-c (1st BB comic book premium) 300.00 1050.00 2000.00
Buster Brown's Blue Ribbon Book of Jokes and Jingles Book 2 (1905)-

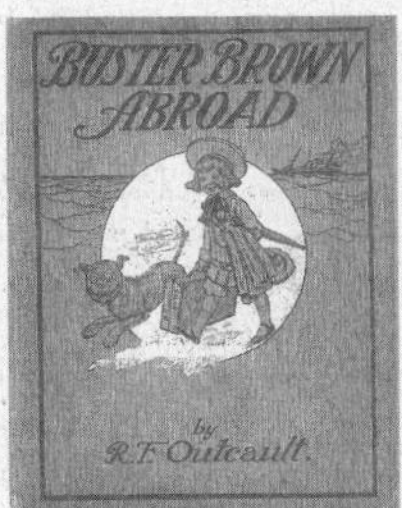

Buster Brown Abroad
1904 © Frederick A. Stokes Co.

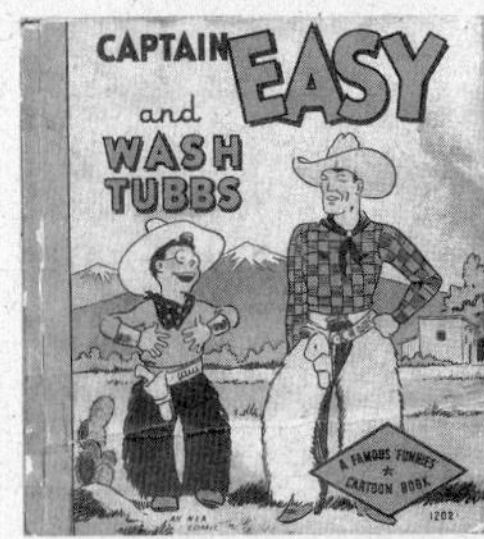

Captain Easy and Wash Tubbs by Roy Crane
1934 © Whitman Famous Comics Cartoon Book

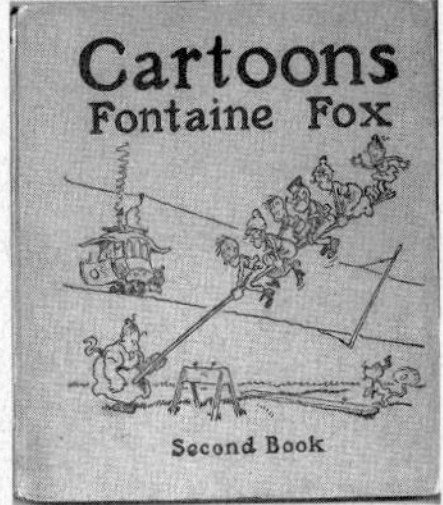

Cartoons Fontaine Fox Second Book
early 1920s © Harper & Bros, NY

Original color art by Outcault 200.00 600.00 1260.00
Buster's Book of Jokes & Jingles Book 3 (1909)
not by R.F. Outcault 150.00 400.00 840.00
NOTE: *Reprinted from the Blue Ribbon post cards with advert jingles added.*
Buster's Book of Instructive Jokes and Jingles Book 4 (1910)-Original color art
not by R.F. Outcault 150.00 585.00 1050.00
...Book of Travels nn (1912, 3x5")-Original color art not signed by Outcault
117.00 408.00 735.00
NOTE: *Estimated 5 or 6 known copies exist of books #1-4.*

The Buster Brown Bread Company

"Buster Brown" Bread Book of Rhymes, The (1904, 4x6", 12 pgs., half color, half B&W)- Original color art not signed by RFO 158.00 553.00 1000.00

Buster Brown's Hosiery Mills

"How Buster Brown Got The Pie" nn (nd, 7x5-1/4". 16 pgs, color paper cover and color interior By R.F. Outcault 83.00 292.00 525.00
"The Autobiography of Buster Brown" nn (nd,9x6-1/8", 36 pgs, text story & art by R.F. Outcault 83.00 292.00 525.00
NOTE: *Similar to, but a distinctly different item than "Buster Brown's Autobiography."*

The Buster Brown Stocking Company

Buster Brown Drawing Book, The nn (nd, 5x6", 20 pgs.)-B&W reproductions of 1903 R.F. Outcault art to trace 50.00 150.00 350.00
NOTE: *Reprints a comic strip from Burr McIntosh Magazine, which includes Buster, Yellow Kid, and Pore Li'l Mose (only known story involving all three.)*
Buster Brown Stocking Magazine nn (Jan. 1906, 7-3/4x5-3/8", 36 pgs.) R.F. Outcault
50.00 100.00 200.00
NOTE: *This was actually a store bought item selling for 5 cents per copy.*

Collins Baking Company

Buster Brown Drawing Book nn (1904, 5x3", 12 pgs.)-Original B&W art to trace, not signed by R.F. Outcault 50.00 150.00 315.00

C. H. Morton, St. Albans, VT

Merry Antics of Buster Brown, Buddy Tucker & Tige nn (nd, 3-1/2x5-1/2", 16 pgs.) -Original B&W art by R.F. Outcault 83.00 292.00 525.00

Ivan Frank & Company

Buster Brown nn (1904, 3x5", 12 pgs.)-B&W repros of R. F. Outcault Sunday pages (First premium to actually reproduce Sunday comic pages – may be first premium comic strip-r book?) 125.00 438.00 800.00
Buster Brown's Pranks (1904, 3-1/2x5-1/8", 12 pgs.)-reprints intro of Buddy Tucker into the BB newspaper strip before he was spun off into his own short lived newspaper strip
125.00 438.00 785.00

Kaufmann & Strauss

Buster Brown Drawing Book (1906, 28 pages, 5x3-1/2") Color Cover, B+W original story signed by Outcault, tracing paper inserted as alternate pages. Back cover imprinted for Nox' Em All Shoes 50.00 150.00 315.00

Pond's Extract

Buster Brown's Experiences With Pond's Extract nn (1904, 6-3/4x4-1/2", 28 pgs.) Original color art by R.F. Outcault (may be the first BB premium comic book with original art) 100.00 250.00 550.00

C. A. Cross & Co.

Red Cross Drawing Book nn (1906, 4-7/8x3-1/2", color paper -c, B&W interior, 12 pgs.)
50.00 150.00 315.00
NOTE: *This is for Red Cross coffee; not the health organization.*

Ringen Stove Company

Quick Meal Steel Ranges nn (nd, 5x3", 16 pgs.)-Original B&W art not signed by R.F. Outcault 50.00 150.00 315.00

Steinwender Stoffregen Coffee Co.

"Buster Brown Coffee" (1905, 4-7/8x3", color paper cover, B&W interior, 12 printed pages, plus 1 tracing paper page above each interior image (total of 8 sheets) (Very Rare)
83.00 292.00 525.00
NOTE: *Part of a BB drawing contest. If instructions had been followed, most copies would have ended up destroyed.*

U. S. Playing Card Company

Buster Brown - My Own Playing Cards (1906, 2-1/2x1-3/4", full color)
nn - By R. F. Outcault 42.00 147.00 250.00
NOTE: *Series of full color panels tell stories, average about 5 cards per story.*

Publisher Unknown

The Drawing Book nn (1906, 3-9/16x5", 8 pgs.)-Original B&W art to trace not by R.F. Outcault 50.00 150.00 300.00

BUTLER BOOK A Series of Clever Cartoons of Yale Undergraduate Life
Yale Record: June 16, 1913 (10-3/4 x 17", 34 pgs, paper cover B&W)
nn - By Alban Bernard Butler 21.00 73.00 130.00
NOTE: *Cartoons and strips reprinted from The Yale Record student newspaper.*

BUTTONS & FATTY IN THE FUNNIES
Whitman Publishing Co.: nd 1927 (10-1/4x15-1/2", 28pg., color)
W936 - Signed "M.E.B.", probably M.E. Brady; strips in color copyright The Brooklyn Daily Eagle; (very rare) 61.00 244.00 425.00

BY BRIGGS (M,N,P) (see also OLD GOLD THE SMOOTHER AND BETTER CIGARETTE)
Old Gold Cigarettes: nd (c1920's) (11" x 9-11/16", 44 pgs, cardboard-c, B&W)
nn- (Scarce) 20.00 70.00 130.00
NOTE: *Collection reprinting strip cartoons by Clare Briggs, advertising Old Gold Cigarettes. These strips originally appeared in various magazines, play program booklets, newspapers, etc. Some of the strips involve regular Briggs strip series. Contains all of the strips in the smaller, color "OLD GOLD" giveaways, plus more.*

CAMION CARTOONS
Marshall Jones Company: 1919 (7-1/2x5", 136 pgs, B&W)
nn - By Kirkland H. Day (W.W.One occupation) 20.00 70.00 120.00

CANYON COUNTRY KIDDIES (M)
Doubleday, Page & Co: 1923 (8x10-1/4", 88 pgs, hard-c, B&W)
nn - By James Swinnerton 39.00 137.00 260.00

CARLO (H)
Doubleday, Page & Co.: 1913 (8 x 9-5/8, 120 pgs, hardcover, B&W)
nn - By A.B. Frost 40.00 140.00 300.00
NOTE: *Original sequential strips about a dog. Became short lived newspaper comic strip in 1914. Originally published with a dust jacket which increases value 50%.*

CARTOON BOOK, THE
Bureau of Publicity, War Loan Organization, Treasury Department, Washington, D.C.: 1918 (6-1/2x4-7/8", 48 pgs, paper cover, B&W)
nn - By various artists 31.00 108.00 185.00
NOTE: *U.S. government issued booklet of WW I propaganda cartoons by 46 artists promoting the third sale of Liberty Loan bonds. The artists include: Berryman, Clare Briggs, Cesare, J. N. "Ding" Darling, Rube Goldberg, Kemble, McCutcheon, George McManus, F. Opper, T. E. Powers, Ripley, Satterfield, H. T. Webster, Gaar Williams.*

CARTOON CATALOGUE (S)
The Lockwood Art School, Kalamazoo, Mich.: 1919 (11-5/8x9, 52 pgs, B&W)
nn - Edited by Mr. Lockwood 20.00 60.00 140.00
NOTE: *Jammed with 100s of single panel cartoons and some sequential comics; Mr Lockwood began the very first cartoonist school back in 1892. Clare Briggs was one of his students.*

CARTOON COMICS
Lasco Publications, Detroit, Mich: #1, April 1930 - #2, May 1930 (8-3/6x5-1/5")
1, 2 - By Lu Harris 20.00 60.00 100.00
NOTE: *Contains recurring characters Hollywood Horace, Campus Charlie, Pair-A-Dice Alley and Jocko Monkey. Not much is presently known about the creator(s) or publisher.*

CARTOON HISTORY OF ROOSEVELT'S CAREER, A
The Review of Reviews Company: 1910 (276 pgs, 8-1/4x11",
nn - By various 43.00 129.00 325.00
NOTE: *Reprints editorial cartoons about Teddy Roosevelt from U.S. and international newspapers and cartoons from the humor magaines (Puck, Judge, etc.). A few cartoonists whose work is included are Dalrymple, Opper, McDougall, McCutcheon, Remington, Rogers, Kemble. Mostly single panel but 10 or so are sequential strips.*

CARTOON HUMOR
Collegian Press: 1938 (102 pgs, squarebound, B&W)
nn 20.00 70.00 120.00
NOTE: *Contains cartoons & strips by Otto Soglow, Syd Hoff, Peter Arno, Abner Dean, others.*

CARTOONIST'S PHILOSOPHY, A
Percy Crosby: 1931, HC, 252 pgs, 5-1/2x7-1/2", hard-c, celluloid dust wrapper
nn - By Percy Crosby (10 plates, 6 are of Skippy) 20.00 60.00 130.00
NOTE: *Crosby's partial autobiography regarding his return to France in 1929, and portrayals of Normandy, the "cliff dwellers" on Normandy cliffs (destroyed in WWII), his visit to London, comments on art, philosophy, several poems, and political dialogue. His description of his Cockney driver, "Harold" is amusing. Also describes his experience visiting Chicago to speak out against Capone, his concerns over the evils of Prohibition, and the economy prior to the 1929 crash. This book reveals he was aware of the dangers of his outspoken views, and is prophetic, re: his later years as political prisoner. Also reveals his religious beliefs.*

CARTOONS BY BRADLEY: CARTOONIST OF THE CHICAGO DAILY NEWS
Rand McNally & Company: 1917 (11-1/4x8-3/4", 112 pgs, hardcover, B&W)
nn - By Luther D. Bradley (editorial) 20.00 70.00 120.00

CARTOONS BY FONTAINE FOX (Toonerville Trolley) (S)
Harper & Brothers Publishers: nd early '20s (9x7-7/8", 102 pgs., hard-c, B&W)
Second Book- By Fontaine Fox (Toonerville-r) 150.00 300.00 500.00

CARTOONS BY HALLADAY (N,S)
Providence Journal Co., Rhode Island: Dec 1914 (116 pgs, 10-1/2x 7-3/4", hard-c, B&W)
nn- (Scarce) 50.00 125.00 250.00
NOTE: *Cartoons on Rhode Island politics, plus some Teddy Roosevelt & WW I cartoons.*

CARTOONS BY McCUTCHEON (S)
A. C. McClurg & Co.: 1903 (12-3/8x9-3/4", 212 pgs., hardcover, B&W)
nn - By John McCutcheon 20.00 70.00 120.00

CARTOONS BY W. A. IRELAND (S)
The Columbus-Evening Dispatch: 1907 (13-3/4 x 10-1/2", 66 pgs, hardcover)
nn - By W. A. Ireland (strip-r) 20.00 70.00 120.00

CARTOONS MAGAZINE (I,N,S)
H. H. Windsor, Publisher: Jan 1912-June 1921; July 1921-1923; 1923-1924; 1924-1927 (1912-July 1913 issues 12x9-1/4", 68-76 pgs; 1913-1921 issues 10x7", average 112 to 188 pgs, color covers)
1912-Jan-Dec 30.00 75.00 125.00
1913-1917 30.00 75.00 125.00

Cartoons Magazine Sept, 1917
by various creators © H. H. Windsor, Chicago

Charlie Chaplin in the Movies by Segar
1917 © Essaney

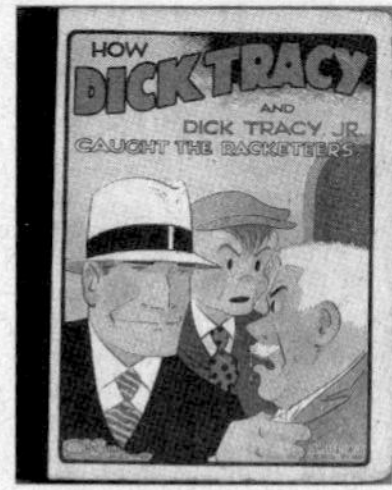

How Dick Tracy and Dick Tracy, Jr.
Caught the Racketeers by Chester Gould
1933 © Cupples & Leon

GD2.0 FN6.0 VF8.0

1917-(Apr) "How Comickers Regard Their Characters" 30.00 105.00 150.00
1917-(June) "A Genius of the Comic Page" - long article on George Herriman, Krazy Kat, etc with lots of Herriman art; "Cartoonists and Their Cars" 125.00 250.00 550.00
1918-1919 30.00 75.00 125.00
1920-June 1921 30.00 75.00 125.00
July 1921-1923 titled Wayside Tales & Cartoons Magazine 30.00 75.00 125.00
1923-1924 becomes Cartoons Magazine again 30.00 75.00 125.00
1924-1927 becomes Cartoons & Movie Magazine 30.00 75.00 125.00
NOTE: *Many issues contain a wealth of historical background on then current cartoonists of the day with an international slant; each issue profusely illustrated with many cartoons. We are unsure if this magazine continued after 1927.*

CARTOONS BY J. N. DARLING (S,N - some sequential strips)
The Register & Tribune Co., Des Moines, Iowa: 1909?-1920 (12x8-7/8",B&W)

Book 1 15.00 51.00 90.00
Book 2 Education of Alonzo Applegate (1910) 15.00 51.00 90.00
2nd printing 10.00 30.00 90.00
Book 3 Cartoons From The Files (1911) 15.00 51.00 90.00
Book 4 15.00 51.00 90.00
Book 5 In Peace And War (1916) 15.00 51.00 90.00
Book 6 Aces & Kings War Cartoons (Dec 1, 1918) 15.00 51.00 90.00
Book 7 The Jazz Era (Dec 1920) 15.00 51.00 90.00
Book 8 Our Own Outlines of History (1922) 15.00 51.00 90.00
NOTE: *Some of the most inspired hard hitting cartoons ever printed. Are there more?*

CARTOONS THAT MADE PRINCE HENRY FAMOUS, THE (N,S)
The Chicago Record-Herald: Feb/March 1902 (12-1/8" x 9", 32 pgs, paper-c, B&W)

nn- (Scarce) by McCutcheon 15.00 51.00 90.00
NOTE: *Cartoons about the visit of the British Prince Henry to the U.S.*

CAVALRY CARTOONS (O)
R. Montalboddi: nd (c1918) (14-1/4" x 11", 30 pgs, printed on one side, olive & black construction paper-c, B&W interior)

nn - By R.Montalboddi 20.00 55.00 100.00
NOTE: *Comics about life in the U.S.Cavalry during World War I, by a soldier who was in the 1st Cavalry.*

CHARLIE CHAPLIN (N)
Essanay/M. A. Donohue & Co.: 1917 (9x16", B&W, large size soft-c)

Series 1, #315-Comic Capers (9-3/4x15-3/4")-20 pgs. by Segar;
Series 1, #316-In the Movies 165.00 525.00 1200.00
#317-Up in the Air (20 pgs), #318-In the Army 165.00 525.00 1400.00
Funny Stunts-(12-1/2x16-3/8",16 color pgs) 165.00 525.00 1400.00
NOTE: *All contain pre-Thimble Theatre Segar art. The thin paper used makes high grade copies very scarce.*

CHASING THE BLUES
Doubleday Page: 1912 (7-1/2x10", 108 pgs., B&W, hard-c)

nn - By Rube Goldberg 150.00 525.00 900.00
NOTE: *Contains a dozen Foolish Questions, baseball, a few Goldberg poems and lots of sequential strips.*

CHRISTIAN CARTOONS (N,S)
The Sunday School Times Company: 1922 (7-1/4 x 6-1/8,104 pgs, brown hard-c, B&W)

nn - E.J. Pace 15.00 51.00 90.00
NOTE: *Religious cartoons reprinted from The Sunday School Times.*

CLANCY THE COP (O))
Dell Publishing Co.: 1930 - No. 2, 1931 (10x10", 52 pgs., B&W, cardboard-c)
(Also see Bug Movies & Deadwood Gulch)

1, 2-By VEP Victor Pazimino (original material; not reprints) 10000 250.00 500.00

CLIFFORD MCBRIDE'S IMMORTAL NAPOLEON & UNCLE ELBY (N)
The Castle Press: 1932 (12x17"; soft-c cartoon book)

nn - Intro. by Don Herod 36.00 144.00 250.00

COLLECTED DRAWINGS OF BRUCE BAIRNSFATHER, THE
W. Colston Leigh: 1931 (11-1/4x8-1/4 ", 168 pages, hardcover, B&W)

nn - By Bruce Bairnsfather 24.00 96.00 165.00

COMICAL PEEP SHOW
McLoughlin Bros: 1902 (36 pgs, B&W)

nn 24.00 96.00 165.00
NOTE: *Comic stories of Wilhelm Busch redrawn; two versions with green or gold front cover logos; back covers different.*

COMIC ANIMALS (I)
Charles E. Graham & Co.: 1903 (9-3/4x7-1/4", 90 pgs, color cover)

nn - By Walt McDougall (not comic strips) 43.00 150.00 260.00

COMIC CUTS (O)
H. L. Baker Co., Inc.: 5/19/34-7/28/34 (Tabloid size 10-1/2x15-1/2", 24 pgs., 5¢)
(full color, not reprints; published weekly; created for news stand sales)

V1#1 - V1#7(6/30/34), V1#8(7/14/34), V1#9(7/28/34)-Idle Jack strips 200.00 400.00 900.00
NOTE: *According to a 1958 Lloyd Jacquet interview, this short-lived comics mag was the direct inspiration for Major Malcolm Wheeler-Nicholson's* ***New Fun Comics****, not* ***Famous Funnies****.*

COMIC MONTHLY (N)
Embee Dist. Co.: Jan, 1922 - No. 12, Dec, 1922 (10¢, 8-1/2"x9", 28 pgs., 2-color covers)
(1st monthly newsstand comic publication) (Reprints 1921 B&W dailies)

1-Polly & Her Pals by Cliff Sterrett 375.00 1125.00 2300.00
2-Mike & Ike by Rube Goldberg 140.00 490.00 1000.00
3-S'Matter, Pop? 140.00 490.00 1000.00
4-Barney Google by Billy DeBeck 140.00 490.00 1000.00
5-Tillie the Toiler by Russ Westover 140.00 490.00 1000.00
6-Indoor Sports by Tad Dorgan 140.00 490.00 1000.00
NOTE: *#6 contains more Judge Rummy than Indoor Sports.*
7-Little Jimmy by James Swinnerton 140.00 490.00 1000.00
8-Toots and Casper b y Jimmy Murphy 140.00 490.00 1000.00
9-New Bughouse Fables by Barney Google 140.00 490.00 1000.00
10-Foolish Questions by Rube Goldberg 140.00 490.00 1000.00
11-Barney Google & Spark Plug by Billy DeBeck 140.00 490.00 1000.00
12-Polly & Her Pals by Cliff Sterrett 214.00 752.00 1500.00
NOTE: *This series was published by George McManus (Bringing Up Father) as Em & Rudolph Block, Jr., son of Hearst's cartoon editor for many years, as "Bee." One would have thought this series would have done very well considering the tremendous amount of talent assembled. All issues are extremely hard to find these days and rarely show up in any type of higher grade.*

COMIC PAINTING AND CRAYONING BOOK (H)
Saalfield Publ. Co.: 1917 (13-1/2x10", 32 pgs.) (No price on-c)

nn - Tidy Teddy by F. M. Follett, Clarence the Cop, Mr. & Mrs. Butt-In; regular comic stories to read or color 50.00 175.00 300.00

COMPLETE TRIBUNE PRIMER, THE (I)
Mutual Book Company: 1901 (7 1/4 x 5", 152 pgs, red hard-c)

nn - By Frederick Opper; has 75 Opper cartoons 25.00 75.00 125.00

COURTSHIP OF TAGS, THE (N)
McCormick Press: pre-1910 (9x4", 88 pgs, red & B&W-c, B&W interior)

nn - By O. E. Wertz (strip-r Wichita Daily Beacon) 25.00 75.00 125.00

DAFFYDILS (N)
Cupples & Leon Co.: 1911 (5-3/4x7-7/8", 52 pgs., B&W, hard-c)

nn - By "Tad" Dorgan 58.00 204.00 350.00
NOTE: *Also exists in self-published TAD edition: The T.A. Dorgan Company; unknown which is first printing.*

DAN DUNN SECRET OPERATIVE 48 (Also See Detective Dan) (N)
Whitman Publishing: 1937 ((5 1/2 x 7 1/4", 68pgs., color cardboard-c, B&W)

1010 And The Gangsters' Frame-Up 50.00 150.00 300.00
NOTE: *There are two versions of the book the later printing has a 5 cent cover price. Dick Tracy look-alike character by Norman Marsh.*

DANGERS OF DOLLY DIMPLE, THE (N)
Penn Tobacco Co.: nd (1930's) (9-3/8x7-7/8", 28 pgs, red cardboard-c, B&W)

nn - (Rare) by Walter Enright 25.00 88.00 150.00
NOTE: *Reprints newspaper comic strip advertisements, in which in every episode, Dolly Dimple's life is saved by Penn's Smoking Tobacco. - how very un-P.C. by today's standards.*

DEADWOOD GULCH (O) (See The Funnies 1929)(also see Bug Movies & Clancy The Cop)
Dell Publishing Co.: 1931 (10x10", 52 pgs., B&W, color covers, B&W interior)

nn - By Charles "Boody" Rogers (original material) 150.00 300.00 600.00

DESTINY A Novel In Pictures (O)
Farrar & Rinehart: 1930 (8x7", 424 pgs, B&W, hard-c, dust jacket?)

nn - By Otto Nuckel (original graphic novel) 25.00 100.00 175.00

DICK TRACY & DICK TRACY JR. CAUGHT THE RACKETEERS, HOW
Cupples & Leon Co.: 1933 (8-1/2x7", 88 pgs., hard-c) (See Treasure Box of Famous Comics) (N)

2-(Numbered on pg. 84)-Continuation of Stooge Viller book (daily strip reprints from 8/3/33 thru 11/8/33)(Rarer than #1) 100.00 400.00 800.00
With dust jacket... 175.00 500.00 1000.00

DICK TRACY & DICK TRACY JR. AND HOW THEY CAPTURED "STOOGE" VILLER (N)
Cupples & Leon Co.: 1933 (8-1/2x7", 100 pgs., hard-c, one-shot)
Reprints 1932 & 1933 Dick Tracy daily strips

nn(No.1)-1st app. of "Stooge" Viller 94.00 376.00 700.00
With dust jacket... 175.00 500.00 900.00

DIMPLES By Grace Drayton (N) (See Dolly Dimples)
Hearst's International Library Co.: 1915 (6 1/4 x 5 1/4, 12 pgs) (5 known)

nn-Puppy and Pussy; nn-She Goes For a Walk; nn-She Had A Sneeze; nn-She Has a Naughty Play Husband; nn-Wait Till Fido Comes Home 21.00 74.00 150.00

DOINGS OF THE DOO DADS, THE (N)
Detroit News (Universal Feat. & Specialty Co.): 1922 (50¢, 7-3/4x7-3/4", 34 pgs, B&W, red & white-c, square binding)

nn-Reprints 1921 newspaper strip "Text & Pictures" given away as prize in the Detroit News Doo Dads contest; by Arch Dale 43.00 173.00 360.00

DOING THE GRAND CANYON
Fred Harvey: 1922 (7 x 4-3/4", 24 pgs, B&W, paper cover)

nn - John McCutcheon 20.00 40.00 100.00

'Erbie And 'Is Playmates By F. Opper
1932 © Democratic National Committee

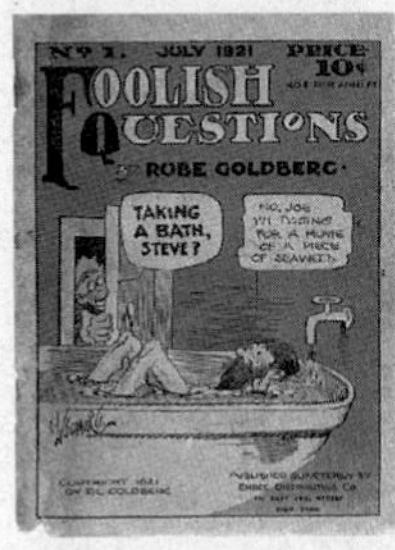

Foolish Questions by Rube Goldberg
1921 © EmBee Distributing Co., NY.

The Latest Adventures of Foxy Grandpa 1905
© Bunny Publ.

NOTE: *Text & 8 cartoons about visiting the Grand Canyon.*

DOINGS OF THE VAN-LOONS (N) (from same company as Mutt & Jeff #1-#5)
Ball Publications: 1912 (5-3/4X15-1/2", 68pg., B&W, hard-c)

nn - By Fred I. Leipziger (scarce) 72.00 252.00 600.00

DOLLY DIMPLES & BOBBY BOUNCE (See Dimples)
Cupples & Leon Co.: 1933 (8-3/4x7", color hardcover, B&W)

nn - Grace Drayton-a 24.00 96.00 165.00

DOO DADS, THE (Sleepy Sam and Tiny the Elephant)
Universal Feature * Specialty Co: 1922 (5-1/4x14", 36 pgs.,B&W, R&W-c,square binding)

nn - By Arch Dale 35.00 125.00 250.00

DRAWINGS BY HOWARD CHANDLER CHRISTIE (S, M)
Moffat, Yard & Company, NY: 1905 (11-7/8x16-1/2", 68 pgs, hard-c, B&W)

nn - Howard C. Christie 30.00 60.00 120.00
NOTE: *Reprints1898-1905 from Haprer & Bros, Ch. Scribners Sons, Leslie's, MacMillians, McLurg, Russell.*

DREAMS OF THE RAREBIT FIEND (N)
Frederick A. Stokes Co.:1905 (10-1/4x7-1/2", 68 pgs, thin paper cover all B&W) newspaper reprints from the New York Evening Telegram printed on yellow paper

nn-By Winsor "Silas" McCay (Very Rare) (Five copies known to exist)
Estimated value.... 900.00 2200.00 –
NOTE: *A G/VG copy sold for $2,045 in May 2004. This item usually turns up with fragile paper.*

DRISCOLL'S BOOK OF PIRATES (O)
David McKay Publ.: 1934 (9x7", 124 pgs, B&W, hardcover)

nn - By Montford Amory ("Pieces of Eight strip-r) 21.00 64.00 150.00

DUCKY DADDLES
Frederick A. Stokes Co: July 1911 (15x10")

nn - By Grace Weiderseim (later Drayton) strip-r 50.00 175.00 300.00

DUMBUNNIES AND THEIR FRIENDS IN RABBITBORO, THE (O)
Albertine Randall Wheelan: 1931 (8-3/4x7-1/8", 82 pgs, color hardcover, B&W)

nn - By Albertine Randall Wheelan (self-pub) 34.00 103.00 240.00

EDISON - INSPIRATION TO YOUTH (N)(Also see Life of Thomas---)
Thomas A. Edison, Incorporated: 1939 (9-1/2 x 6-1/2, paper cover, B&W)

nn - Photo-c 50.00 150.00 200.00
NOTE: *Reprints strip material found in the 1928 Life of Thomas A. Edison in Word and Picture.*

'ERBIE AND 'IS PLAYMATES
Democratic National Committee: 1932 (8x9-1/2, 16 pgs, B&W)

nn - By Frederick Opper (Rare) 100.00 200.00 425.00
NOTE: *Anti-Hoover/Pro-Roosevelt political comics.*

EXPANSION BEING BART'S BEST CARTOONS FOR 1899
Minneapolis Journal: 1900 (10-1/4x8-1/4", 124 pgs, paperback, B&W)

v2#1 - By Charles L. Bartholomew 24.00 84.00 145.00

FAMOUS COMICS (N)
King Features Synd. (Whitman Pub. Co.): 1934 (100 pgs., daily newspaper-r) (3-1/2x8-1/2"; paper cover)(came in an illustrated box)

684 (#1) - Little Jimmy, Katz Kids & Barney Google 40.00 103.00 240.00
684 (#2) - Polly, Little Jimmy, Katzenjammer Kids 40.00 103.00 240.00
684 (#3) - Little Annie Rooney, Polly and Her Pals, Katzenjammer Kids
40.00 103.00 240.00
Box price... 75.00 150.00 375.00

FAMOUS COMICS CARTOON BOOKS (N)
Whitman Publishing Co.: 1934 (8x7-1/4", 72 pgs, B&W hard-c, daily strip-r)

1200-The Captain & the Kids; Dirks reprints credited to Bernard Dibble 29.00 86.00 200.00
1202-Captain Easy & Wash Tubbs by Roy Crane; 2 slightly different versions of cover exist 34.00 103.00 240.00
1203-Ella Cinders By Conselman & Plumb 28.00 84.00 195.00
1204-Freckles & His Friends 25.00 75.00 175.00
NOTE: *Called Famous Funnies Cartoon Books inside back area sales advertisement.*

FANTASIES IN HA-HA (M)
Meyer Bros & Co.: 1900 (14 x 11-7/8", 64 pgs, color cover hardcover, B&W)

nn - By Hy Mayer 50.00 150.00 300.00

FELIX (N)
Henry Altemus Company: 1931 (6-1/2"x8-1/4", 52 pgs., color, hard-c w/dust jacket)

1-3-Sunday strip reprints of Felix the Cat by Otto Messmer. Book No. 2 r/1931 Sunday panels mostly two to a page in a continuity format oddly arranged so each tier of panels reads across two pages, then drops to the next tier. (Books 1 & 3 have not been documented.)(Rare)
Each 250.00 500.00 1000.00
With dust jacket 250.00 750.00 1200.00

FELIX THE CAT BOOK (N)
McLoughlin Bros.: 1927 (8"x15-3/4", 52 pgs, half in color-half in B&W)

nn - Reprints 23 Sunday strips by Otto Messmer from 1926 & 1927, every other one in color, two pages per strip. (Rare) 200.00 800.00 1600.00
260-Reissued (1931), reformatted to 9-1/2"x10-1/4" (same color plates, but one strip per every three pages), retitled ("Book" dropped from title) and abridged (only eight strips repeated from first issue, 28 pgs.).(Rare) 79.00 316.00 600.00

F. FOX'S FUNNY FOLK (see Toonerville Trolley; Cartoons by Fontaine Fox) (C)
George H. Doran Company: 1917 (10-1/4x8-1/4", 228 pgs, red, B&W cover, B&W interior, hardcover; dust jacket?)

nn - By Fontaine Fox (Toonerville Trolley strip-r) 150.00 450.00 750.00

52 CAREY CARTOONS (O,S)
Carey Cartoon Service, NY: 1915 (25 cents, 6-3/4" x 10-1/2", 118 pgs, printed on one side, color cardboard-c, B&W)

nn - (1915) War – – –
NOTE: *The Carey Cartoon Service supplied a weekly, hand-colored single panel cartoon broadsheet, on current news events, starting in 1906 or 1907, for window display in Carey Fountain Pen chain stores. These broadsheets were 22-1/2" x 33" in size. Starting circa 1915, Carey Fountain Pens began offering subscriptions for the broadsheets to other merchants, for window display in their stores as well. This collects, in B&W, the cartoons for 1915. An "Edition Deluxe" was also advertised, with all cartoons hand colored. It is currently unknown whether a reprint collection was only issued in 1915, or if other editions exist.*

52 LETTERS TO SALESMEN
Steven-Davis Company: 1927 (???)

nn - (Rare) 25.00 100.00 150.00
NOTE: *52 motivational letters to salesmen, with page of comics for each week, bound into embossed leather binder.*

FOLKS IN FUNNYVILLE (S)
R.H. Russell: 1900 (12"x9-1/4", 48 pgs.)(cardboard-c)

nn - By Frederick Opper 271.00 950.00 –
NOTE: *Reprinted from Hearst's NY Journal American Humorist supplements.*

FOOLISH QUESTIONS (S)
Small, Maynard & Co.: 1909 (6-7/8 x 5-1/2", 174 pgs, hardcover, B&W)

nn - By Rube Goldberg (first Goldberg item) 100.00 300.00 500.00
NOTE: *Comic strip began Oct 23, 1908 running thru 1941. Also drawn by George Frink in 1909.*

FOOLISH QUESTIONS THAT ARE ASKED BY ALL
Levi Strauss & Co./Small, Maynard & Co.: 1909 (5-1/2x5-3/4", 24 pgs, paper-c, B&W)

nn- (Rare) by Rube Goldberg 65.00 175.00 350.00

FOOLISH QUESTIONS (Boxed card set) (S)
Wallie Dorr Co., N.Y.: 1919 (5-1/4x3-3/4")(box & card backs are red)

nn - Boxed set w/52 B&W comics on cards; each a single panel gag complete set w/box
75.00 263.00 450.00
NOTE: *There are two diff sets put out simultaneously with the first set, by the same company. One set continues/picks up the numbering of the cards from the other set.*

FOOLISH QUESTIONS (S)
EmBee Distributing Co.: 1921 (10¢, 4x5 1/2; 52 pgs, 3 color covers; B&W)

1-By Rube Goldberg 46.00 160.00 300.00

FOXY GRANDPA
Foxy Grandpa Company, 33 Wall St, NY : 1900 (9x15", 84 pgs, full color, cardboard-c)

nn - By Carl Schultze (By Permission of New York Herald) 271.00 1200.00 –

NOTE: *This seminal comic strip began Jan 7, 1900 and was collected later that same year.*

FOXY GRANDPA (Also see The Funnies, 1st series) (N)
N. Y. Herald/Frederick A. Stokes Co./M. A. Donahue & Co./Bunny Publ. (L. R. Hammersly Co.): 1901 - 1916 (Strip-r in color, hard-c)

1901- 9x15" in color-N. Y. Herald 313.00 1000.00 –
1902- "Latest Larks of...", 32 pgs., 9-1/2x15-1/2" 164.00 575.00 –
1902- "The Many Advs. of...", 9x12", 148 pgs., Hammersly Co.
179.00 625.00 –
1903- "Latest Advs.", 9x15", 24 pgs., Hammersly Co. 164.00 575.00 –
1903- "...'s New Advs.", 11x15", 66 pgs., Stokes 164.00 575.00 –
1904- "Up to Date", 10x15", 66 pgs., Stokes 146.00 510.00 900.00
1904- "The Many Adventures of...", 9x15, 144pgs, Donohue 146.00 510.00 900.00
1905- "& Flip-Flaps", 9-1/2x15-1/2", 52 pgs. 146.00 510.00 900.00
1905- "The Latest Advs. of...", 9x15", 28, 52, & 68 pgs, M.A. Donohue Co.; re-issue of 1902 issue 104.00 365.00 700.00
1905- "Latest Larks of...", 9-1/2x15-1/2", 52 pgs., Donahue; re-issue of 1902 issue with more pages added 104.00 365.00 700.00
1905- "Latest Larks of...", 9-1/2x15-1/2", 24 pgs. edition, Donahue; re-issue of 1902 issue 104.00 365.00 700.00
1905- "Merry Pranks of...", 9-1/2x15-1/2", 28, 52 & 62 pgs., Donahue
104.00 365.00 700.00
1905-"...Surprises",10x15", color, 64 pg,Stokes, 60¢ 104.00 365.00 700.00
1906- "Frolics", 10x15", 30 pgs., Stokes 104.00 365.00 700.00
1907?-"...& His Boys",10x15", 64 color pgs, Stokes 104.00 365.00 700.00
1907- "Triumphs", 10x15", 62 pgs, Stokes 104.00 365.00 700.00
1908-"...Mother Goose", Stokes 104.00 365.00 700.00
1909- "...& Little Brother", 10x15, 58 pgs, Stokes 104.00 365.00 700.00

Giggles
© Pratt Food Co.

The Gumps #1 by Sidney Smith
1924 © Cupples & Leon

Hans and Fritz, Funny Larks of
1917 © Saalfield Publishing Co.

GD2.0 FN6.0 VF8.0

1911- "Latest Tricks", r-1910,1911 Sundays-Stokes Co. 104.00 365.00 700.00
1914-(9-1/2x15-1/2", 24 pgs.)-6 color cartoons/page, Bunny Publ. Co.
88.00 306.00 575.00
1915 - ...Always Jolly (10x16, Stokes) 88.00 306.00 575.00
1916- "Merry Book", (10x15", 64 pgs, Stokes) 88.00 306.00 575.00
1917-"...Adventures (5 1/2 x 6 1/2, 26 pgs, Stokes) 57.00 200.00 400.00
1917-"...Frolics (5 1/2 x 6 1/2, 26 pgs, Stokes) 57.00 200.00 400.00
1917-"...Triumphs (5 1/2 x 6 1/2, 26 pgs, Stokes) 57.00 200.00 400.00

FOXY GRANDPA, FUNNY TRICKS OF (The Stump Books)
M.A. Donahue Co, Chicago: approx 1903 (1-7/8x6-3/8", 44 pgs, blue hardcover)
nn - By Carl Schultze 54.00 189.00 325.00
NOTE: *One of a series of ten "stump" books; the only comics one.*

FOXY GRANDPA'S MOTHER GOOSE (I)
Stokes: October 1903 (10-11/16x8-1/2", 86 pgs, hard-c)
nn - By Carl Schultze (not comics - illustrated book) 54.00 189.00 325.00

FOXY GRANDPA SPARKLETS SERIES (N)
M. A. Donahue & Co.: 1908 (7-3/4x6-1/2"; 24 pgs., color)
"... Rides the Goat", "...& His Boys", "...Playing Ball", "...Fun on the Farm", "...Fancy Shooting", "...Show His Boys Up-To-Date Sports", "...Plays Santa Claus"
each.... 88.00 306.00 525.00
900- "Playing Ball"; Bunny illos; 8 pgs., linen like pgs., no date
73.00 254.00 435.00

FOXY GRANDPA VISITS RICHMOND (O,P)
Dietz Printing Co., Richmond, VA / Hotel Rueger: nd (c1920's) (5-7/8" x 4-1/2", 16 pgs, paper-c, B&W)
nn - (Scarce) By Bunny 25.00 88.00 175.00
NOTE: *Promotional comic given away to its guests by the Hotel Rueger, about Foxy Grandpa visiting and enjoying the Hotel. Originally came in an envelope, with the words "Foxy Grandpa Visits Richmond -- and Rueger's" printed on it.*

FOXY GRANDPA VISITS WASHINGTON, D.C. (P)
Dietz Printing Co., Richmond, VA / Hamilton Hotel: nd (c1920's) (5-7/8" x 4-1/2", 16 pgs, paper-c, B&W)
nn - (Scarce) By Bunny 25.00 88.00 150.00
NOTE: *Mostly reprints "... Visits Richmond", changing all references to Hotel Rueger, to Hamilton Hotel instead. Also, changes depictions of a waiter and a cook from black to white, plus incompletely erases the cover art on a book Foxy Grandpa falls asleep with (the latter is how we know that the Richmond version was first).*

FRAGMENTS FROM FRANCE (S)
G. P. Putnam & Sons: 1917 (9x6-1/4", 168 pgs, hardcover, $1.75)
nn - By Bruce Bairnsfather 25.00 88.00 150.00
NOTE: *WW1 trench warfare cartoons; color dust jacket.*

FUNNIES, THE (H) (See Clancy the Cop, Deadwood Gulch, Bug Movies)
Dell Publishing Co.: 1929 - No. 36, 10/18/30 (10¢; 5¢ No. 22 on) (16 pgs.)
Full tabloid size in color; not reprints; published every Saturday
1-My Big Brudder, Jonathan, Jazzbo & Jim, Foxy Grandpa, Sniffy, Jimmy Jams & other strips begin; first four-color comic newsstand publication; also contains magic, puzzles & stories 200.00 700.00 1400.00
2-21 (1930, 10¢) 150.00 300.00 600.00
22(nn-7/12/30-5¢) 150.00 300.00 600.00
23(nn-7/19/30-5¢), 24(nn-7/26/30-5¢), 25(nn-8/2/30), 26(nn-8/9/30), 27(nn-8/16/30), 28(nn-8/23/30), 29(nn-8/30/30), 30(nn-9/6/30), 31(nn-9/13/30), 32(nn-9/20/30), 33(nn-9/27/30), 34(nn-10/4/30), 35(nn-10/11/30), 36(nn, no date-10/18/30)
each.... 150.00 300.00 600.00

GASOLINE ALLEY (Also see Popular Comics & Super Comics) (N)
Reilly & Lee Publishers: 1929 (8-3/4x7", B&W daily strip-r, hard-c)
nn - By King (96 pgs.) 125.00 300.00 600.00
with scarce Dust Wrapper 250.00 500.00 1000.00
NOTE: *Of all the Frank King reprint books, this is the only one to reprint actual complete newspaper strips - all others are illustrated prose text stories.*

GIBSON'S PUBLISHED DRAWINGS, MR. (M,S) (see Victorian index for earlier issues)
R.H. Russell, New York: No.1 1894 - No. 9 1904 (11x17-3/4", hard-c, B&W)
nn (No.6; 1901) A Widow and her Friends (90 pgs.) 30.00 60.00 120.00
nn (No.7; 1902) The Social Ladder (88 pgs.) 30.00 60.00 120.00
8 - 1903 The Weaker Sex (88 pgs.) 30.00 60.00 120.00
9 - 1904 Everyday People (88 pgs.) 30.00 60.00 120.00
NOTE: *By Charles Dana Gibson cartoons, reprinted from magazines, primarily LIFE. The Education of Mr. Pipp tells a story. Series continues how long after 1904?*

GIGGLES
Pratt Food Co., Philadelphia, PA: 1908-09? (12x9", 8 pgs, color, 5 cents-c)
1-8: By Walt McDougall (#8 dated March 1909) 40.00 175.00 –
NOTE: *Appears to be monthly; almost tabloid size; yearly subscriptions was 25 cents.*

GOD'S MAN (H)
Jonathan Cape and Harrison Smith Inc.: 1929 (8-1/4x6", 298 pgs, B&W hardcover w/dust jacket) (original graphic novel in wood cuts)
nn - By Lynd Ward 43.00 171.00 300.00

GD2.0 FN6.0 VF8.0

GOLD DUST TWINS
N. K. Fairbank Co.: 1904 (4-5/8x6-3/4", 18 pgs, color and B&W)
nn - By E. W. Kemble (Rare) 40.00 80.00 160.00
NOTE: *Promo comic for Gold DustWashing Powder; includes page of watercolor paints.*

GOLF
Volland Co.: 1916 (9x12-3/4", 132 pgs, hard-c, B&W)
nn - By Clair Briggs 100.00 200.00 400.00

GUMPS, THE (N)
Landfield-Kupfer: No. 1, 1918 - No. 6, 1921; (B&W Daily strip-r)
Book No. 1(1918)(scarce)-cardboard-c, 5-1/4x13-1/3", 64 pgs., daily strip-r by Sidney Smith 75.00 250.00 500.00
Book No.2(1918)-(scarce); 5-1/4x13-1/3"; paper cover; 36 pgs. daily strip reprints by Sidney Smith 75.00 250.00 500.00
Book No. 3 100.00 350.00 700.00
Book No. 4 (1918) 5-3/8x13-7/8", 20 pgs. Color card-c 100.00 350.00 700.00
Book No. 5 10-1/4x13-1/2", 20 pgs. Color paper-c 100.00 350.00 700.00
Book No. 6 (Rare, 20 pgs, 8x13-3/8, strip-r 1920-21) 121.00 423.00 725.00

GUMPS, ANDY AND MIN, THE (N)
Landfield-Kupfer Printing Co., Chicago/Morrison Hotel: nd (1920s) (Giveaway, 5-1/2"x14", 20 pgs., B&W, soft-c)
nn - Strip-r by Sidney Smith; art & logo embossed on cover w/hotel restaurant menu on back-c or a hotel promo ad; 4 different contents of issues known
50.00 175.00 300.00

GUMPS, THE (N)
Cupples & Leon: 1924-1930 (10x10, 52 pgs, B&W)
1 - By Sidney Smith 61.00 244.00 450.00
2-7 39.00 154.00 300.00

THE GUMPS (P)
Cupples & Leon Company: 1924 (9 x 7-1/2", 28 pgs, paper cover)
nn (1924) 50.00 175.00 300.00
NOTE: *Promotional comic for Sunshine Andy Gump Biscuits. Daily strip-r from 1922-24.*

GUMP'S CARTOON BOOK, THE (N)
The National Arts Company: 1931 (13-7/8x10", 36 pgs, color covers, B&W)
nn - By Sidney Smith 57.00 228.00 450.00

GUMPS PAINTING BOOK, THE (N)
The National Arts Company: 1931 (11 x 15 1/4", 20 pgs, half in full color)
nn - By Sidney Smith 57.00 228.00 450.00

HALT FRIENDS! (see also **HELLO BUDDY**)
???: 1918? (4-3/8x5-3/4", 36 pgs, color-c, B&W, no cover price listed)
nn - Unknown 20.00 40.00 80.00
NOTE: *Says on front cover: "Comics of War Facts of Service Sold on its merits by Unemployed or Disabled Ex-Service Men. Credentials Shown On Request. Price - Pay What You Please." These are very common; contents vary widely.*

HAMBONE'S MEDITATIONS
Jahl & Co.: no date 1920 (6-1/8 x 7-1/2, 108 pgs, paper cover, B&W)
nn - By J. P. Alley 33.00 132.00 275.00
NOTE: *Reprint of racist single panel newspaper series, 2 cartoons per page.*

HAN OLA OG PER (N)
Anundsen Publishing Co, Decorah, Iowa: 1927 (10-3/8 x 15-3/4", 54 pgs, paper-c, B&W)
nn - American origin Norwegian language strips-r 33.00 131.00 230.00
NOTE: *1940s and modern reprints exist.*

HANS UND FRITZ (N)
The Saalfield Publishing Co.: 1917, 1927-29 (10x13-1/2", 28 pgs., B&W)
nn - By R. Dirks (1917, r-1916 strips) 96.00 335.00 600.00
nn - By R. Dirks (1923 edition- reprint of 1917 edition) 58.00 204.00 350.00
nn - By R. Dirks (1926 edition- reprint of 1917 edition) 58.00 204.00 350.00
The Funny Larks Of... By R. Dirks (©1917 outside cover; ©1916 inside indicia)
96.00 335.00 600.00
The Funny Larks Of... (1927) reprints 1917 edition of 1916 strips
Halloween-c 58.00 204.00 350.00
The Funny Larks Of... 2 (1929) 58.00 204.00 350.00
193 - By R. Dirks; contains 1916 Sunday strip reprints of Katzenjammer Kids & Hawkshaw the Detective - reprint of 1917 nn edition (1929) this edition is not rare
58.00 204.00 350.00

HAPPY DAYS (S)
Coward-McCann Inc.: 1929 (12-1/2x9-5/8", 110 pgs, hardcover B&W)
nn - By Alban Butler (WW 1 cartoons) 20.00 60.00 120.00

HAPPY HOOLIGAN (See Alphonse...) (N)
Hearst's New York American & Journal: 1902,1903
Book 1-(1902)-"And His Brother Gloomy Gus", By Fred Opper; has 1901-02-r; (yellow & black)(86 pgs.)(10x15-1/4") 600.00 1800.00 3000.00
New Edition, 1903 -10x15" 82 pgs. in color 350.00 1400.00 –

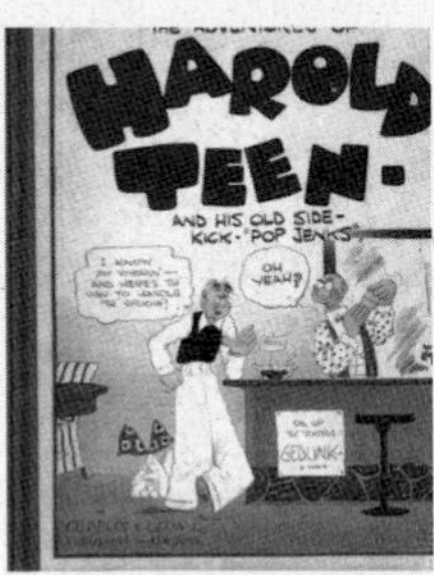

Harold Teen #2 by Carl Ed
1931 © Cupples & Leon

Jimmy By Jimmy Swinnerton
1905 © Frederick A. Stokes

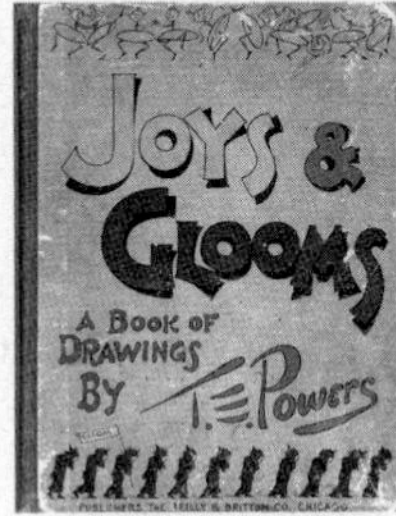

Joys & Glooms By T.E. Powers
1912 © Reilly & Britton Co.

GD2.0 FN6.0 VF8.0

NOTE: *Strip ran March 26, 1900-Aug 14, 1932 and is widely recognized as setting the format standard for all newspaper comic strips which came after it. Opper (1857-1937) was going blind towards the end.*

HAPPY HOOLIGAN (N) (By Fredrick Opper)
Frederick A. Stokes Co.: 1906-08 (10-1/4x15-3/4", cardboard color-c)
1906 - :Travels of...), 68 pgs,10-1/4x15-3/4", 1905-r 450.00 1000.00 –
1907 - "--Home Again", 68 pgs., 10x15-3/4", 60¢; full color-c 450.00 1000.00 –
1908 - "Handy--", 68 pgs, color 450.00 1000.00 –

HAPPY HOOLIGAN, THE STORY OF (G)
McLoughlin Bros.: No. 281, 1932 (12x9-1/2", 20 pgs., soft-c)
281-Three-color text, pictures on heavy paper 57.00 228.00 400.00
NOTE: *An homage to Opper's creation on its 30th Anniversary in 1932.*

HAROLD HARDHIKE'S REJUVENATION
O'Sullivan Rubber: 1917 (6-1/4x3-1/2, 16 pgs, B&W)
nn 25.00 100.00 175.00
NOTE: *Comic book to promote rubber shoe heels.*

HAROLD TEEN (N)
Cupples & Leon Co.: 1929 (9-7/8x9-7/8", 52 pgs, cardboard covers)
1 - By Carl Ed 50.00 200.00 500.00
nn - (1931, 8-11/16x6-7/8", 96 pgs, hardcover w/dj) 41.00 164.00 290.00
NOTE: *Title 2nd book:* ***HAROLD TEEN AND HIS OLD SIDE-KICK- POP JENKINS,*** *(Adv. of...). Precursor for Archie Andrews & crew; strip began May 4, 1919 running into 1959.*

HAROLD TEEN PAINT AND COLOR BOOK (N)
McLoughlin Bros Inc.: 1932 (13x9-3/4, 28 pgs, B&W and color)
#2054 25.00 100.00 175.00

HAWKSHAW THE DETECTIVE (See Advs. of..., Hans Und Fritz & Okay) (N)
The Saalfield Publishing Co.: 1917 (10-1/2x13-1/2", 24 pgs., B&W)
nn - By Gus Mager (Sunday strip-r) 54.00 190.00 325.00
nn - By Gus Mayer (1923 reprint of 1917 edition) 25.00 100.00 175.00
nn - By Gus Mager (1926 reprint of 1917 edition) 25.00 100.00 175.00
NOTE: *Runs Feb 23, 1913-Sept 4, 1922, starts again from Dec 13, 1931-Feb 11, 1952; Sherlock Holmes spoof.*

HEALTH IN PICTURES
American Public Health Association, NYC: 1930 (6-1/2" x 5-3/16", 76 pgs, green & black paper-c, B&W interior)
nn - By various 15.00 51.00 90.00
NOTE: *Collection of strips and cartoons put out by the Public Health Association, on topics ranging from boating and food safety, to small pox and typhoid prevention.*

HE DONE HER WRONG (O) (see also BANANA OIL)
Doubleday, Doran & Company: 1930 (8-1/4x 7-1/4", 276pgs, hard-c with dust jacket, B&W interiors)
nn - By Milt Gross 75.00 225.00 400.00
NOTE: *A seminal original-material wordless graphic novel, not reprints. Several modern reprints.*

HELLO BUDDY (see also **HALT FRIENDS**)
???: 1919? (4-3/8x5-3/4", 36 pgs, color-c, B&W, 15¢)
nn - Unknown 10.00 30.00 70.00
NOTE: *Says on front cover: "Comics of War Facts of Service Sold on its merits by Unemployed or Disabled Ex-Service Men." These are very common; contents vary widely.*

HENRY (N)
David McKay Co.: 1935 (25¢, soft-c)
Book 1 - By Carl Anderson 57.00 200.00 400.00
NOTE: *Strip began March 19 1932; this book ties with Popeye (David McKay) and Little Annie Rooney (David McKay) as the last of the 10x10" Platinum Age comic books.*

HENRY (M)
Greenberg Publishers Inc.: 1935 (11-1/4x 8-5/8", 72 pgs, red & blue color hard-c, dust jacket, B&W interiors) (strip-r from Saturday Evening Post)
nn - By Carl Anderson 57.00 200.00 400.00

HIGH KICKING KELLYS, THE (M)
Vaudeville News Corporation, NY: 1926 (5x11", B&W, two color soft-c)
nn - By Jack A. Ward (scarce) 40.00 160.00 280.00

HIGHLIGHTS OF HISTORY (N)
World Syndicate Publishing Co.: 1933-34 (4-1/2x4", 288 pgs)
nn - 5 different unnumbered issues; daily strip-r 10.00 40.00 70.00
NOTE: *Titles include Buffalo Bill, Daniel Boone, Kit Carson, Pioneers of the Old West, Winning of the Old Northwest. There are line drawing color covers and embossed hardcover versions. It is unknown which came out first.*

HOMER HOLCOMB AND MAY (N)
no publisher listed: 1920s (4 x 9-1/2", 40 pgs, paper cover, B&W)
nn - By Doc Bird Finch (strip-r) 10.00 40.00 70.00

HOME, SWEET HOME (N)
M.S. Publishing Co.: 1925 (10-1/4x10")
nn - By Tuthill 33.00 134.00 235.00

HOW THEY DRAW PROHIBITION (S)
Association Against Prohibition: 1930 (10x9", 100 pgs.)
nn - Single panel and multi-panel comics (rare) 71.00 285.00 500.00
NOTE: *Contains art by J.N. "Ding" Darling, James Flagg, Rollin Kirby, Winsor McCay, T.E. Powers, H.T. Webster, others. Also comes with a loose sheet listing all the newspapers where the cartoons originally appeared.*

HOW TO BE A CARTOONIST (H)
Saalfield Pub. Co: 1936 (10-3/8x12-1/2", 16 pgs, color-c, B&W)
nn - By Chas. H. Kuhn 10.00 40.00 70.00

HOW TO DRAW: A PRACTICAL BOOK OF INSTRUCTION (H)
Harper & Brothers: 1904 (9-1/4x12-3/8", 128 pgs, hardcover, B&W)
nn - Edited By Leon Barritt 57.00 228.00 400.00
NOTE: *Strips reprinted include: "Buster Brown" by Outcault, "Foxy Grandpa" by Bunny, "Happy Hooligan" by Opper, "Katzenjammer Kids" by Dirks, "Lady Bountiful" by Gene Carr, "Mr. Jack" by Swinnerton, "Panhandle Pete" by George McManus, "Mr E.Z. Mark" by F.M. Howarth others; non-character strips by Hy Mayer, Winsor McCay, T.E. Powers, others; single panel cartoons by Davenport, Frost, McDougall, Nast, W.A. Rogers, Sullivant, others.*

HOW TO DRAW CARTOONS (H)
Garden City Publishing Co.: 1926, 1937 (10 1/4 x 7 1/2, 150 pgs)
1926 first edition By Clare Briggs 25.00 75.00 150.00
1937 2nd edition By Clare Briggs 20.00 60.00 120.00
NOTE: *Seminal "how to" break into the comics syndicates with art by Briggs, Fisher, Goldberg, King, Webster, Opper, Tad, Hershfield, McCay, Ding, others. Came with Dust Jacket -add 50%.*

HOW TO DRAW FUNNY PICTURES: A Complete Course in Cartooning (H)
Frederick J. Drake & Co., Chicago: 1936 (10-3/8x6-7/8", 168 pgs, hardcover, B&W)
nn - By E.C. Matthews (200 illus by Eugene Zimmerman) 20.00 60.00 120.00

HY MAYER (M)
Puck Publishing: 1915 (13-1/2 x 20-3/4", 52 pgs, hardcover cover, color & B&W interiors)
nn - By Hy Mayer(strip reprints from Puck) 40.00 140.00 300.00

HYSTERICAL HISTORY OF THE CIVILIAN CONSERVATION CORPS
Peerless Engraving: 1934 (10-3/4x7-1/2", 104 pgs, soft-c, B&W)
nn - By various 20.00 60.00 120.00
NOTE: *Comics about CCC life, includes two color insert postcards in back.*

INDOOR SPORTS (N,S)
National Specials Co., New York: nd circa 1912 (25 cents, 6 x 9", 68 pgs, B&W)
nn - Tad 35.00 125.00 225.00
NOTE: *Cartoons reprinted from Hearst papers.*

IT HAPPENS IN THE BEST FAMILIES (N)
Powers Photo Engraving Co.: 1920 (52 pgs.)(9-1/2x10-3/4")
nn - By Briggs; B&W Sunday strips-r 29.00 114.00 200.00
Special Railroad Edition (30¢)-r/strips from 1914-1920 26.00 103.00 180.00

JIMMIE DUGAN AND THE REG'LAR FELLERS (N)
Cupples & Leon: 1921, 46 pgs. (11"x16")
nn - By Gene Byrne 71.00 284.00 500.00
NOTE: *Ties with EmBee's Mutt & Jeff and Trouble of Bringing Up Father as the last of this size.*

JIMMY (N) (see Little Jimmy Picture & Story Book)
N. Y. American & Journal: 1905 (10x15", 84 pgs., color)
nn - By Jimmy Swinnerton (scarce) 300.00 800.00 1500.00
NOTE: *James Swinnerton was one of the original first pioneers of the American newspaper comic strip.*

JIMMY AND HIS SCRAPES (N)
Frederick A. Stokes: 1906, (10-1/4x15-1/4", 66 pgs, cardboard-c, color)
nn - By Jimmy Swinnerton (scarce) 300.00 800.00 1500.00

JOE PALOOKA (N)
Cupples & Leon Co.: 1933 (9-13/16x10", 52 pgs., B&W daily strip-r)
nn - By Ham Fisher (scarce) 150.00 500.00 850.00

JOHN, JONATHAN AND MR. OPPER BY F. OPPER (S,I,N)
Grant, Richards, 48 Leicester Square, W.C.: 1903 (9-5/8x8-3/8", 108 pgs, hard-c B&W)
nn - Opper (Scarce) 50.00 200.00 380.00
NOTE: *British precursor-type companion to* WIllie And His Poppa *reprints from Hearst's NY American & Journal Opper cartoons interfacing* Uncle Sam *precursor* Brother Jonathan, John Bull. *Uses name* Happy Hooligan *in one cartoon, has* John Bull *smoking opium in another.*

JOLLY POLLY'S BOOK OF ENGLISH AND ETIQUETTE (S)
Jos. J. Frisch: 1931 (60 cents, 8 x 5-1/8, 88 pgs, paper-c, B&W)
nn - By Jos. J. Frisch 20.00 60.00 120.00
NOTE: *Reprint of single panel newspaper series, 4 per page, of English and etiquette lessons taught by a flapper.*

JOYS AND GLOOMS (N)
Reilly & Britton Co.: 1912 (11x8", 72 pgs, hard-c, B&W interior)
nn - By T. E. Powers (newspaper strip-r) 39.00 156.00 325.00

JUDGE - yet to be indexed

JUDGE'S LIBRARY - yet to be indexed

The Katzenjammer Kids
1921 © EmBee Publishing Co.

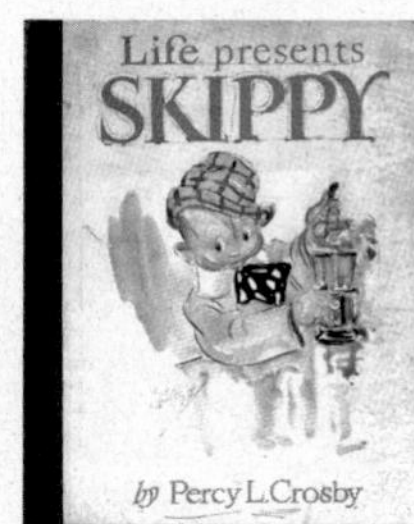

Life Presents Skippy by Percy L. Crosby
1924 © Life Publishing Company

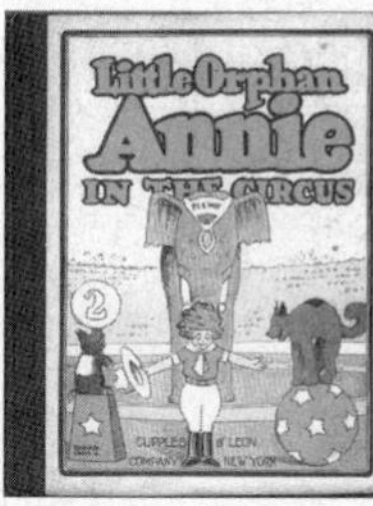

Little Orphan Annie by Harold Gray #2
1927© Cupples & Leon

GD2.0 **FN**6.0 **VF**8.0

JUST KIDS COMICS FOR CRAYON COLORING
King Features. NYC: 1928 (11x8-1/2, 16 pgs, soft-c)

nn - By Ad Carter 33.00 100.00 200.00
NOTE: *Porous better grade paper; top pics printed in color; lower in b&w to color.*

JUST KIDS, THE STORY OF (I)
McLoughlin Bros.: 1932 (12x9-1/2", 20 pgs., paper-c)

283-Three-color text, pictures on heavy paper 30.00 125.00 250.00

KAPTIN KIDDO AND PUPPO (N)
Frederick A. Stokes Co.: 1910-1913 (11x16-1/2", 62 pgs)

1910-By Grace Wiederseim (later Drayton) 40.00 140.00 240.00
1910-Turr-ble Tales of... By Grace Wiederseim (Edward Stern & Co., 11x16-1/2", 64 pgs.) 40.00 140.00 240.00
1913- ...'Speriences By Grace Drayton 40.00 140.00 240.00
NOTE: *Strip ran approx. 1909-1912.*

KATZENJAMMER KIDS, THE (Also see Hans Und Fritz) (N)
New York American & Journal: 1902,1903 (10x15-1/4", 86 pgs., color)
(By Rudolph Dirks; strip first appeared in 1897) © W.R. Hearst
NOTE: *All KK books 1902-1905 all have the same exact title page with a 1902 copyright by W.R. Hearst; almost always look instead on the front cover.*

1902 (Rare) (red & black); has 1901-02 strips 1000.00 2400.00 –
1903- **A New Edition** (Rare), 86 pgs 800.00 2100.00 –
1904- 10x15", 84 pgs 250.00 900.00 –
1905?-The Cruise of the, 10x15", 60¢, in color 250.00 900.00 –
1905-A Series of Comic Pictures, 10x15", 84 pgs. in color, possible reprint of 1904 edition 250.00 800.00 –
1905-Tricks of... (10x15", 66 pgs, Stokes) 250.00 800.00 –
1906-Stokes (10x16", 32 pgs. in color) 186.00 800.00 –
1907- The Cruise of the, 10x15", 62 pgs 1905-r? 186.00 800.00 –
1910-The Komical...(10x15) 150.00 450.00 800.00
1921-Embee Dist. Co., 10x16", 20 pgs. in color 150.00 450.00 800.00

KATZENJAMMER KIDS MAGIC DRAWING AND COLORING BOOK (N)
Sam L Gabriel Sons And Company: 1931 (8 1/2 x 12", 36 pages, stiff-c

838-By Knerr 50.00 200.00 350.00

KEEPING UP WITH THE JONESES (N)
Cupples & Leon Co.: 1920 - No. 2, 1921 (9-1/4x9-1/4",52 pgs.,B&W daily strip-r)

1,2-By Pop Momand 39.00 154.00 270.00

KID KARTOONS (N,S)
The Century Co.: 1922 (232 pgs, printed 1 side, 9-3/4 x 7-3/4", hard-c, B&W)

nn - By Gene Carr (Metropolitan Movies strip-r) 60.00 240.00 –

KING OF THE ROYAL MOUNTED (Also See Dan Dunn) (N)
Whitman Publishing: 1937 (5 1/2 x 7 1/4", 68 pgs., color cardboard-c, B&W)

1010 36.00 144.00 250.00

LADY BOUNTIFUL (N)
Saalfield Publ. Co./Press Publ. Co.: 1917 (13-3/8x10", 36 pgs, color cardboard-c, B&W interiors)

nn - By Gene Carr; 2 panels per page 50.00 150.00 275.00
193S - 2nd printing (13-1/8x10",28 pgs color-c, B&W) 33.00 117.00 200.00

LAUGHS YOU MIGHT HAVE HAD From The Comic Pages of Six Week Day Issues of the Post-Dispatch (N)
St. Louis Post-Dispatch: 1921 (9 x 10 1/2", 28 pgs, B&W, red ink cover)

nn - Various comic strips 39.00 154.00 270.00

LIFE, DOGS FROM (M)
Doubleday, Page & Company: nn 1920 - No.2 1926 (130 pgs, 11-1/4 x 9", color painted-c, hard-c, B&W)

nn (No.1) 120.00 360.00 –
Second Litter 80.00 320.00 –
NOTE: *Reprints strips & cartoons featuring dogs, from Life Magazine. Editted by Thomas L. Masson. Highly sought by collectors of dog ephemera. Art in both books is mostly by Robert L. Dickey. Other art: Carl Anderson-1,2; Barbes-1; Chip Bellew-1; Lang Campbell-1,2; Percy Crosby-1,2; Edwina-2; Frueh-2; R.B. Fuller-1; Gibson-1,2; Don Herold-2; Gus Mager-2; Orr-1; J.R. Shaver-1,2; T.S. Sullivant-2; Russ Westover-1,2; Crawford Young-1.*

LIFE OF DAVY CROCKETT IN PICTURE AND STORY, THE
Cupples & Leon: 1935 (8-3/4x7", 64 pgs, B&W hard-c, dust jacket)

nn - By C. Richard Schaare 29.00 116.00 200.00

LIFE OF THOMAS A. EDISON IN WORD AND PICTURE, THE (N)(Also see Edison...)
Thomas A. Edison Industries: 1928 (10x8", 56 pgs, paper cover, B&W)

nn - Photo-c 100.00 250.00 400.00
NOTE: *Reprints newspaper strip which ran August to November 1927.*

LIFE'S LITTLE JOKES (S)
M.S. Publ. Co.: No date (1924)(10-1/16x10", 52 pgs., B&W)

nn - By Rube Goldberg 64.00 257.00 525.00

LIFE, MINIATURE (see also LIFE (miniature reprint of of issue No. 1)) (M,P,S)

GD2.0 **FN**6.0 **VF**8.0

Life Publishing Co.: No. 1 - No. 4 1913, 1916, 1919 (5-3/4x4-5/8", 20 pgs, color paper-c

1- 3 (1913) 4 (1916) 5 (1919) (no known sales)
NOTE: *Giveaway item from Life, to promote subscriptions. All reprint material. No.2: James Montgomery Flagg-c; a-Chip Bellew, Gus Dirks, Gibson, F.M.Howarth, Art Young.*

LIFE'S PRINTS (was **LIFE'S PICTURE GALLERY -** See Victorian Age section) (M,S,P)
Life Publishing Company, New York: nd (c1907) (7x4-1/2", 132 pgs, paper cover, B&W)

nn - (nd; c1907) unillustrated black construction paper cover; reprints art from 1895-1907; art by J.M.Flagg, A.B.Frost, Gibson (Scarce) – – –
nn - (nd; c1908) b&w cardboard painted cover by Gibson, showing angel raising a champagne glass; reprints art from 1901-1908; art by J.M.Flagg, A.B.Frost, Gibson, Walt Kuhn, Art Young (Scarce) – – –
NOTE: *Catalog of prints reprinted from LIFE covers & centerspreads. There are likely more as yet unreported catalogs.*

LIFE, THE COMEDY OF LIFE
Life Publishing Company: 1907 (130 pgs, 11-3/4x9-1/4",embossed printed cloth covered board-c, B+W

nn - By various 20.00 80.00 120.00
NOTE: *Single cartoons and some sequential cartoons). Artists include Charles Dana Gibson, Harrison Cady, E.W. Kemble, James Montgomery Flagg.*

LILY OF THE ALLEY IN THE FUNNIES
Whitman Publishing Co.: No date (1927) (10-1/4x15-1/2"; 28 pgs., color)

W936 - By T. Burke (Rare) 57.00 228.00 400.00

LITTLE ANNIE ROONEY (N)
David McKay Co.: 1935 (25¢, soft-c)

Book 1 43.00 172.00 340.00
NOTE: *Ties with Henry & Popeye (David McKay) as the last of the 10x10" size Plat comic books.*

LITTLE ANNIE ROONEY WISHING BOOK (G) (See Happy Hooligan, Story of #281)
McLoughlin Bros.: 1932 (12x9-1/2", 16 pgs., soft-c, 3-color text, heavier paper)

282 - By Darrell McClure 41.00 144.00 250.00

LITTLE BIRD TOLD ME, A (E)
Life Publishing Co.: 1905? (96 pgs, hardbound)

nn - By Walt Kuhn (Life-r) 41.00 144.00 250.00

LITTLE FOLKS PAINTING BOOK (N)
The National Arts Company: 1931 (10-7/8 x 15-1/4", 20 pgs, half in full color)

nn - By "Tack" Knight (strip-r) 41.00 144.00 250.00

LITTLE JIMMY PICTURE AND STORY BOOK (I) (see Jimmy)
McLaughlin Bros., Inc.: 1932 (13-1/4 x 9-3/4", 20 pgs, cardstock color cover)

284 Text by Marion Kincaird; illus by Swinnerton 57.00 228.00 400.00

LITTLE JOHNNY & THE TEDDY BEARS (Judge-r) (M) (see Teddy Bear Books)
Reilly & Britton Co.: 1907 (10x14".; 68 pgs, green, red, black interior color)

nn - By J. R. Bray-a/Robert D. Towne-s 67.00 233.00 400.00

LITTLE JOURNEY TO THE HOME OF BRIGGS THE SKY-ROCKET, THE
Lockhart Art School: 1917 (10-3/4x7-7/8", 20 pgs, B&W) (I)

nn - About Clare Briggs (bio & lots of early art) 41.00 144.00 250.00

LITTLE KING, THE (see New Yorker Cartoon Albums for 1st appearance) (M)
Farrar & Reinhart, Inc: 1933 (10-1/4 x 8-3/4, 80 pgs, hardcover w/dust jacket

nn - By Otto Soglow (strip-r The New Yorker) 125.00 250.00 450.00
NOTE: *Copies with dust jacket are worth 50% more. Also exists in a 12x8-3/4 edition.*

LITTLE LULU BY MARGE (M)
Rand McNally & Company, Chicago: 1936 (6-9/16x6", 68 pgs, yellow hard-c, B&W)

nn - By Marjorie Henderson Buell 25.00 100.00 250.00
NOTE: *Begins reprinting single panel Little Lulu cartoons which began with Saturday Evening Post Feb. 23, 1935. This book was reprinted several times as late as 1940.*

LITTLE NAPOLEON
No publisher listed: 1924 , 50 pages, 10" by 10"; Color cardstock-c, B&W

nn - By Bud Counihan (Cupples &Leon format) 25.00 100.00 240.00

LITTLE NEMO (...in Slumberland) (N) (see also Little Sammy Sneeze, Dreams...Rarebit F)
Doffield & Co.(1906)/Cupples & Leon Co.(1909): 1906, 1909 (Sunday strip-r in color, cardboard covers)

1906-11x16-1/2" by Winsor McCay; 30 pgs. (scarce) 1500.00 5000.00 –
1909-10x14" by Winsor McCay (scarce) 1300.00 4000.00 –

LITTLE ORPHAN ANNIE (See Treasure Box of Famous Comics) (N)
Cupples & Leon Co.: 1926 - 1934 (8-3/4x7", 100 pgs., B&W daily strip-r, hard-c)

1 (1926)-Little Orphan Annie (softback see Treasure Box) 50.00 200.00 375.00
2 (1927)-In the Circus (softback see Wonder Box...) 36.00 144.00 275.00
3 (1928)-The Haunted House (softback see Wonder Box...) 36.00 144.00 275.00
4 (1929)-Bucking the World 36.00 144.00 275.00
5 (1930)-Never Say Die 30.00 120.00 225.00
6 (1931)-Shipwrecked 30.00 120.00 225.00
7 (1932)-A Willing Helper 25.00 100.00 200.00

The Trials of Lulu and Leander by Howarth
1906 © NY American & Journal

Maud the Mirthful Mule by Opper
1908 © Frederick A. Stokes

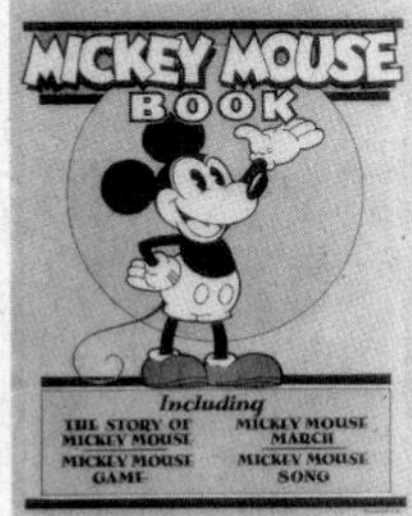

Mickey Mouse Book
1930 © Bibo & Lang

8 (1933)-In Cosmic City 25.00 100.00 200.00
9 (1934)-Uncle Dan (not rare) 25.00 100.00 200.00
NOTE: *Each book reprints dailies from the previous year. Each hardcover came with a dust jacket. Books with out dust jackets are worth 50% less. Many of copies of #9 Uncle Dan have been turning up on eBay recently.*

LITTLE ORPHAN ANNIE RUMMY CARDS (N)
Whitman Publishing Co., Racine: 1935 (box: 5 x 6 1/2" Cards: 3 1/2 x 2 1/4")

nn-Harold Gray 20.00 60.00 120.00
NOTE: *36 cards, including 1 instruction card, 5 character cards and 30 cards forming 5 sequential stories (6 cards each).*

LITTLE SAMMY SNEEZE (N) (see also Little Nemo, Dreams of A Rarebit Fiend)
New York Herald Co.: Dec 1905 (11x16-1/2", 72 pgs., color)

nn - By Winsor McCay (Very Rare) 3000.00 6000.00 –
NOTE: *Rarely found in fine to mint condition.*

LIVE AND LET LIVE
Travelers Insurance Co.: 1936 (5-3/4x7/3/4", 16 pgs. color and B&W)

nn - Bill Holman, Carl Anderson, etc 20.00 60.00 120.00

LULU AND LEANDER (N) (see also Funny Folk, 1899, in Victorian section)
New York American & Journal: 1904 (76 pgs); **William A Stokes & Co:** 1906

nn - By F.M. Howarth 300.00 750.00 1500.00
nn - The Trials of...(1906, 10x16", 68 pgs. in color) 300.00 750.00 1500.00
NOTE: *F. M. Howarth helped pioneer the American comic strip in the pages of PUCK magazine in the early 1890s before the Yellow Kid.*

MADMAN'S DRUM (O)
Jonathan Cape and Harrison Smith Inc.: 1930 (8-1/4x6", 274 pgs, B&W hardcover w/dust jacket) (original graphic novel in wood cuts)

nn - By Lynd Ward 50.00 175.00 300.00

MAMA'S ANGEL CHILD IN TOYLAND (I)
Rand McNally, Chicago: 1915 (128 pgs, hardbound)

nn - By M.T. "Penny" Ross & Marie C, Sadler 40.00 140.00 240.00
NOTE: *Mamma's Angel Child published as a comic strip by the "Chicago Tribune" 1908 Mar 1 to 1920 Oct 17.This novel dedicated to Esther Starring Richartz, "the original Mamma's Angel Kid."*

MAUD (N) (see also **Happy Hooligan**)
Frederick A. Stokes Co.: 1906 - 1908? (10x15-1/2", cardboard-c)

1906-By Fred Opper (Scarce), 66 pgs. color 400.00 1200.00 –
1907-The Matchless, 10x15" 70 pgs in color 300.00 900.00 –
1908-The Mirthful Mule, 10x15", 64 pgs in color 300.00 900.00 –
NOTE: *First run of strip began July 24, 1904 to at least Oct 6, 1907, spun out of* ***Happy Hooligan.***

MEMORIAL EDITION The Drawings of Clare Briggs (S)
Wm H. Wise & Company: 1930 (7-1/2x8-3/4", 284 pgs, pebbled false black leather, B&W) (posthumous boxed set of 7 books by Clare Briggs)

nn - The Days of Real Sport; nn-Golf; nn-Real Folks at Home; nn-Ain't it a Grand and Glorious Feeling?; nn-That Guiltiest Feeling; nn-Somebody's Always Taking the Joy Out of Life; nn-When a Feller Needs a Friend
Each book... 30.00 110.00 150.00
NOTE: *Also exists in a whitish cream colored paper back edition; first edition unknown presently.*

MENACE CARTOONS (M, S)
Menace Publishing Company, Aurora, Missouri: 1914 (10-3/8x8", 80 pgs, cardboard-c, B&W)

nn - (Rare) 50.00 150.00 450.00
NOTE: *Reprints anti-Catholic cartoons from K.K.K. related publication* ***The Menace.***

MEN OF DARING (N)
Cupples & Leon Co.: 1933 (8-3/4x7", 100 pgs)

nn - By Stookie Allen, intro by Lowell Thomas 30.00 90.00 200.00

MICKEY MOUSE BOOK
Bibo & Lang: 1930-1931 (12x9", stapled-c, 20 pgs., 4 printings)

nn - First Disney licensed publication (a magazine, not a book–see first book, Adventures of Mickey Mouse). Contains story of how Mickey met Walt and got his name; games, cartoons & song "Mickey Mouse (You Cute Little Feller)," written by Irving Bibo; Minnie, Clarabelle Cow, Horace Horsecollar & caricature of Walt shaking hands with Mickey. The changes made with the 2nd printing have been verified by billing affidavits in the Walt Disney Archives and include:Two Win Smith Mickey strips from 4/15/30 and 4/17/30 added to page 8 & back-c; "Printed in U.S.A." added to front cover; Bobette Bibo's age of 11 years added to title page; faulty type on the word "tail" corrected top of page 3; the word "start" added to bottom of page 7, removing the words "start 1 2 3 4" from the top of page 7; music and lyrics were rewritten on pages 12-14. A green ink border was added beginning with 2nd printing and some covers have inking variations. Art by Albert Barbelle, drawn in an Ub Iwerks style. Total circulation : 97,938 copies varying from 21,000 to 26,000 per printing.

1st printing. Contains the song lyrics **censored** in later printings, "When little Minnie's pursued by a big bad villain we feel so bad then we're glad when you up and kill him." Attached to the Nov. 15, 1930 issue of the Official Bulletin of the Mickey Mouse Club notes: "Attached to this Bulletin is a new Mickey Mouse Book that has just been published." This is thought to be the reason why a slightly disproportionate larger number of copies of the first printing still exist 700.00 1400.00 5500.00

GD2.0 FN6.0 VF8.0

2nd printing with a theater/advertising. Christmas greeting added to inside front cover (1 copy known with Dec. 27, 1930 date) – 8000.00 –
2nd-4th printings 600.00 1200.00 3500.00
NOTE: *Theater/advertising copies do not qualify as separate printings. Most copies are missing pages 9 & 10 which had a puzzle to be cut out. Puzzle (pages 9 and 10) cut out or missing, subtract 60% to 75%.*

MICKEY MOUSE COLORING BOOK (S)
Saalfield Publishing Company:1931 (15-1/4x10-3/4", 32 pgs, color soft cover, half printed in full color interior, rest B&W

871 - By Ub Iwerks & Floyd Gottfredson (rare) 450.00 1300.00 2600.00
NOTE: *Contains reprints of first MM daily strip ever, including the "missing" speck the chicken is after found only on the original daily strip art by Iwerks plus other very early MM art. There were several other Saalfield Mickey Mouse coloring books manufactured around the same time.*

MICKEY MOUSE, THE ADVENTURES OF (I)
David McKay Co., Inc.: Book I, 1931 - Book II, 1932 (5-1/2"x8-1/2", 32 pgs.)

Book I-First Disney book, by strict definition (1st printing-50,000 copies)(see Mickey Mouse Book by Bibo & Lang). Illustrated text refers to Clarabelle Cow as "Carolyn" and Horace Horsecollar as "Henry". The name "Donald Duck" appears with a non-costumed generic duck on back cover & inside, not in the context of the character that later debuted in the Wise Little Hen.
Hardback w/characters on back-c 75.00 300.00 725.00
Softcover w/characters on back-c 40.00 165.00 400.00
Version without characters on back-c 50.00 200.00 425.00
Book II-Less common than Book I. Character development brought into conformity with the Mickey Mouse cartoon shorts and syndicated strips. Captain Church Mouse, Tanglefoot, Peg-Leg Pete and Pluto appear with Mickey & Minnie 50.00 200.00 425.00

MICKEY MOUSE COMIC (N)
David McKay Co.: 1931 - No. 4, 1934 (10"x9-3/4", 52 pgs., card board-c) (Later reprints exist)

1 (1931)-Reprints Floyd Gottfredson daily strips in black & white from 1930 & 1931, including the famous two week sequence in which Mickey tries to commit suicide 300.00 1000.00 2000.00
2 (1932)-1st app. of Pluto reprinted from 7/8/31 daily. All pgs. from 1931 164.00 656.00 1200.00
3 (1933)-Reprints 1932 & 1933 Sunday pages in color, one strip per page, including the "Lair of Wolf Barker" continuity pencilled by Gottfredson and inked by Al Taliaferro & Ted Thwaites. First app. Mickey's nephews, Morty & Ferdie, one identified by name of Mortimer Fieldmouse, not to be confused with Uncle Mortimer Mouse who is introduced in the Wolf Barker story 214.00 856.00 1600.00
4 (1934)-1931 dailies, include the only known reprint of the infamous strip of 2/4/31 where the villainous Kat Nipp snips off the end of Mickey's tail with a pair of scissors 140.00 560.00 1050.00

MICKEY MOUSE (N)
Whitman Publishing Co.: 1933-34 (10x8-3/4", 34 pgs, cardboard-c)

948-1932 & 1933 Sunday strips in color, printed from the same plates as Mickey Mouse Book #3 by David McKay, but only pages 5-17 & 32-48 (including all of the "Wolf Barker" continuity) 157.00 629.00 1200.00
NOTE: *Some copies bound with back cover upside down. Variance doesn't affect value. Same art appears on front and back covers of all copies. Height of Whitman reissue trimmed 1/2 inch.*

MILITARY WILLIE
J. I. Austen Co.: 1907 (7x9-1/2", 12 pgs., every other page in color, stapled)

nn - By F. R. Morgan 70.00 245.00 400.00

MINNEAPOLIS TRIBUNE CARTOON BOOK (S)
Minneapolis Tribune: 1899-1903 (11-3/8x9-3/8", B&W, paper cover)

nn (#1) (1899) 28.00 99.00 170.00
nn (#2) (1900) 28.00 99.00 170.00
nn (#3) (1901) (published Jan 01, 1901) 28.00 99.00 170.00
nn (#4) (1902) (114 pgs) 28.00 99.00 170.00
nn (#5) (1903) (9x10-3/4",110 pgs, B&W; color-c) 28.00 99.00 170.00
NOTE: *All by Roland C. Bowman (editorial-r).*

MINUTE BIOGRAPHIES: INTIMATE GLIMPSES INTO THE LIVES OF 150 FAMOUS MEN AND WOMEN
Grossett & Dunlap: 1931, 1933 (10-1/4x7-3/4", 168 pgs, hardcover, B&W)

nn - By Nisenson (art) & Parker(text) 21.00 63.00 125.00
More.... (1933) 21.00 63.00 125.00

MISCHIEVOUS MONKS OF CROCODILE ISLE, THE (N)
J. I. Austen Co., Chicago: 1908 (8-1/2x11-1/2", 12 pgs., 4 pgs. in color)

nn - By F. R. Morgan; reads longwise 125.00 375.00 600.00

MR. & MRS. (Also see Ain't It A Grand and Glorious Feeling?) (N)
Whitman Publishing Co.: 1922 (9x9-1/2", 52 & 28 pgs., cardboard-c)

nn - By Briggs (B&W, 52 pgs.) 37.00 149.00 260.00
nn - 28 pgs.-(9x9-1/2")-Sunday strips-r in color 41.00 163.00 285.00
NOTE: *The earliest presently-known Whitman comic books*

MR. BLOCK (N)
Industrial Workers of the World (IWW): 1913, 1919

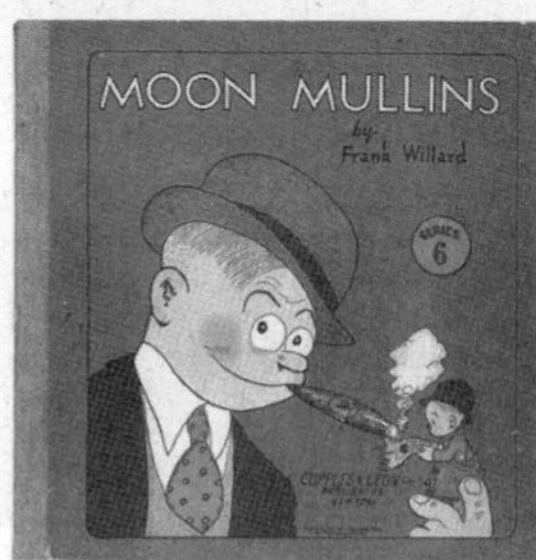

Moon Mullins #6 by Frank Willard
1932 © Cupples & Leon

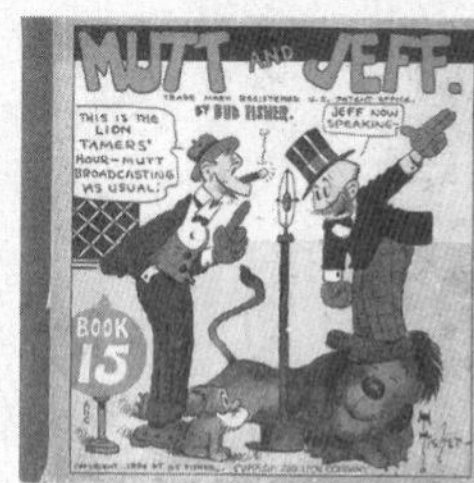

Mutt and Jeff #15 by Bud Fisher
1930 © Cupples & Leon

The Newlyweds by George McManus
1907 © Saalfield Publishing Co.

GD2.0 FN6.0 VF8.0

nn - By Ernest Riebe (C) 50.00 150.00 –
...And The Profiteers (original material) (H) 50.00 150.00 –
NOTE: *Mr Block was a daily strip published from 1912 NOV 7 to 1913 SEP ? by the socialist newspaper "Industrial Worker"; Mr Block was a "square" guy (his head was in fact a block) who enthusiastically supported the same system that exploited him. The noted Joe Hill wrote a song about him (Mr Block,1913, on the air of "It loooks me like a big time tonight") for the "Industrial Worker Songbook".*

MR. TWEE-DEEDLE (N)
Cupples & Leon: 1913, 1917 (11-3/8 x 16-3/4" color strips-r from NY Herald)
nn - By John B. Gruelle (later of Raggedy Ann fame) 350.00 900.00 1800.00
nn - "Further Adventures of..." By Gruelle 350.00 900.00 1800.00
NOTE: *Strip ran Feb 5, 1911-March 10, 1918.*

MONKEY SHINES OF MARSELEEN AND SOME OF HIS ADVENTURES (C)
McLaughlin Bros. New York: 1906 (10 x 12-3/8", 36 pgs, full color hardcover)
nn - By Norman E. Jennett strip-r NY Evening Telegram 100.00 250.00 450.00
NOTE: *Strip began in 1906 until at least March 13, 1910.*

MONKEY SHINES OF MARSELEEN (N)
Cupples & Leon Co.: 1909 (11-1/2 x 17", 58 pgs. in two colors)
nn - By Norman E. Jennett (strip-r New York Herald) 100.00 250.00 450.00

MOON MULLINS (N)
Cupples & Leon Co.: 1927 - 1933 (52 pgs., B&W daily strip-r)
Series 1 ('27)-By Willard 63.00 250.00 500.00
Series 2 ('28), Series 3 ('29), Series 4 ('30) 39.00 156.00 300.00
Series 5 ('31), 6 ('32), 7 ('33) 39.00 156.00 300.00
Big Book 1 ('30)-B&W (scarce) 100.00 400.00 750.00
w/dust jacket (rare) 183.00 732.00 1100.00

MOVING PICTURE FUNNIES
Saml Gabriel Sons & Company: 1918 (5-1/4 x 10-1/4", 52 pgs, B&W, illustrated hard-c)
nn 20.00 40.00 80.00
NOTE: *823 Comical illustrations that show a different scene when folded.*

MUTT & JEFF (...Cartoon, The) (N)
Ball Publications: 1911 - No. 5, 1916 (5-3/4 x 15-1/2", 72 pgs, B&W, hard-c)
1 (1910)(50¢) very common 71.00 286.00 550.00
2,3: 2 (1911)-Opium den panels; Jeff smokes opium (pipe dreams).
3 (1912) both very common 71.00 286.00 500.00
2-(1913) Reprint of 1911 edition with black ink cover 50.00 175.00 300.00
4 (1915) (50¢) (Scarce) 150.00 350.00 650.00
5 (1916) (Rare) -Photos of Fisher, 1st pg. (68 pages) 200.00 480.00 900.00
5-Scarce 84 page reprint edition 150.00 450.00 800.00
NOTE: *Mutt & Jeff first appeared in newspapers in 1907. Cover variations exist showing Mutt & Jeff reading various newspapers; i.e., The Oregon Journal, The American, and The Detroit News. Reprinting of each issue began soon after publication. No. 4 and 5 may not have been reprinted. Values listed include the reprints. Mutt & Jeff was the first successful American daily newspaper comic strip and as such remains one of the seminal strips of all time.*

MUTT & JEFF (N)
Cupples & Leon Co.: No. 6, 1919 - No. 22, 1934? (9-1/2x9-1/2", 52 pgs., B&W dailies, stiff-c)
6, 7 - By Bud Fisher (very common) 32.00 128.00 225.00
8-10 46.00 186.00 325.00
11-18 (Somewhat Scarcer) (#19-#22 do not exist) 60.00 å240.00 420.00
nn (1920) (Advs. of...) 11x16"; 44 pgs.; full color reprints of 1919 Sunday strips
93.00 372.00 650.00
Big Book nn (1926, 144 pgs., hardcovers) 114.00 456.00 800.00
w/dust jacket 193.00 772.00 1350.00
Big Book 1 (1928) - Thick book (hardcovers) 114.00 456.00 800.00
w/dust jacket (rare) 182.00 729.00 1275.00
Big Book 2 (1929) - Thick book (hardcovers) 114.00 456.00 800.00
w/dust jacket (rare) 182.00 729.00 1275.00
NOTE: *The Big Books contain three previous issues rebound.*

MUTT & JEFF (N)
Embee Publ. Co.: 1921 (9x15", color cardboard-c & interior)
nn - Sunday strips in color (Rare)- BY Bud Fisher 143.00 572.00 1100.00
NOTE: *Ties with The Trouble of Bringing Up Father (EmBee) and Jimmie Dugan & The Reg'lar Fellers (C&L) as the last of this size.*

MYSTERIOUS STRANGER AND OTHER CARTOONS, THE
McClure, Phillips & Co.: 1905 (12-3/8x9-3/4", 338 pgs, hardcover, B&W)
nn - By John McCutcheon 32.00 128.00 225.00

MY WAR - Szeged (Szuts)
Wm. Morrow Co.: 1932 (7x10-1/2", 210 pgs, hard-c, B&W)
nn - (All story panels, no words - powerful) 32.00 128.00 225.00

NAUGHTY ADVENTURES OF VIVACIOUS MR. JACK, THE
New York American & Journal: 1904 (15x10", color strips)
nn - By James Swinnerton; (Very Rare - 3 known copies) 900.00 1600.00 2200.00

NEBBS, THE (N)
Cupples & Leon Co.: 1928 (52 pgs., B&W daily strip-r)
nn - By Sol Hess; Carlson-a 40.00 160.00 280.00

GD2.0 FN6.0 VF8.0

NERVY NAT'S ADVENTURES (E)
Leslie-Judge Co.: 1911 (90 pgs, 85¢, 1903 strip reprints from **Judge**)
nn - By James Montgomery Flagg 75.00 263.00 450.00

THE NEWLYWEDS AND THEIR BABY (N)
Saalfield Publ. Co.: 1907 (13x10", 52 pgs., hardcover)
...& Their Baby' by McManus; daily strips 50% color 300.00 900.00 –
NOTE: *Strip ran Apr 10, 1904 thru Jan 14, 1906 and then May 19, 1907-Dec 5, 1916; was a huge success with Baby Snookums long before McManus invented Bringing Up Father; Snookums brought back as a topper strip over BUF Nov 19, 1944-Dec 30, 1956.*

THE NEWLYWEDS AND THEIR BABY'S COMIC PICTURES FOR PAINTING AND CRAYONING (N)
Saalfield Publishign Company: 1916 (10-1/4x14-3/4", 52 pgs. Cardboard-c)
nn - 44 B&W pages, covers, and one color wrap glued to B&W title page.
Color wrap: color title pg. & 3 pgs of color strips 83.00 290.00 500.00
nn - (1917, 10x14", 20 pgs, oblong, cardboard-c) partial reprint of 1916 edition
31.00 124.00 275.00

THE NEWLYWEDS AND THEIR BABY (N)
Saalfield Publishing Company: 1917 (10-1/8x13-9/16 ", 52 pgs, full color cardstock-c, some pages full color, others two color (orange, blue))
nn 83.00 290.00 450.00

NEW YORKER CARTOON ALBUM, THE (M)
Doubleday, Doran & Company Inc.: (1928-1931); **Harper & Brothers.:** (1931-1933); **Random House** (1935-1937), 12x9", various pg counts, hardcovers w/dust jackets)
1928: nn-114 pgs Arno, Held, Soglow, Williams, etc 20.00 60.00 120.00
1928: SECOND-114 pgs Arno, Bairnsfather, Gross, Held, Soglow, Williams
10.00 30.00 60.00
1930: THIRD-172 pgs Arno, Bairnsfather, Held, Soglow, Art Young
10.00 30.00 60.00
1931: FOURTH-154 pgs Arno, Held, Soglow, Steig, Thurber, Williams, Art Young, "Little King" by Soglow begins 10.00 30.00 60.00
1932: FIFTH-156 pgs Arno, Bairnsfather, Held, Hoff, Soglow, Steig, Thurber, Williams 10.00 30.00 60.00
1933: SIXTH-156 pgs same as above 10.00 30.00 60.00
1935: SEVENTH-164 pgs 10.00 30.00 60.00
1937: 168 pgs; Charles Addams plus same as above but no Little King, two page "Gone With The Wind" parody strip 10.00 30.00 60.00
NOTE: *Some sequential strips but mostly single panel cartoons.*

NIPPY'S POP (N)
The Saalfield Publishing Co.: 1917 (10-1/2x13-1/2", 36 pgs., B&W, Sunday strip-r)
nn - Charles M Payne (better known as S'Matter Pop) 43.00 152.00 260.00

OH, MAN (A Bully Collection of Those Inimitable Humor Cartoons) (S)
P.F. Volland & Co.: 1919 (8-1/2x13"; 136 pgs.)
nn - By Briggs 43.00 152.00 260.00
NOTE: *Originally came in illustrated box with Briggs art (box is Rare - worth 50% more with box).*

OH SKIN-NAY! (S)
P.F. Volland & Co.: 1913 (8-1/2x13", 136 pgs.)
nn - The Days Of Real Sport by Briggs 43.00 152.00 240.00
NOTE: *Originally came in illustrated box with Briggs art (box is Rare - worth 50% more with box).*

OLD GOLD THE SMOOTHER AND BETTER CIGARETTE...NOT A COUGH IN A CARLOAD (M,N,P) (see also BY BRIGGS)
Old Gold Cigarettes: nd (c1920's) (16 pgs, paper-c, color) (both Scarce)
nn- (4-1/4" x 3-7/8") cover strip is "Oh, Man!"; also contains: "Real Folks at Home", "Ain't It a Grand and Glorious Feelin?", "It Happens in the Best Regulated Families", and "Mr. and Mrs." (no known sales)
1440- (5-9/16" x 5-1/4") cover strip is "Frank and Ernest"; also contains: "That Guiltiest Feeling", "Real Folks at Home", "Oh, Man!", "When a Feller Needs a Friend". (no known sales)
NOTE: *Collection reprinting strip cartoons by Clare Briggs, advertising Old Gold Cigarettes. These strips originally appeared in various magazines, play program booklets, newspapers, etc. Some of the strips involve regular Briggs strip series. The two booklets contain a completely different set of comics.*

ON AND OFF MOUNT ARARAT (also see **Tigers**) (N)
Hearst's New York American & Journal: 1902, 86pgs. 10x15-1/4"
nn - Rare Noah's Ark satire by Jimmy Swinnerton (rare) 450.00 1500.00 –

ON THE LINKS (N)
Associated Feature Service: Dec, 1926 (9x10", 48 pgs.)
nn - Daily strip-r 25.00 100.00 175.00

ONE HUNDRED WAR CARTOONS (S)
Idaho Daily Statesman: 1918 (7-3/4x10", 102 pgs, paperback, B&W)
nn - By Villeneuve (WW I cartoons) 20.00 60.00 120.00

OUR ANTEDILUVIAN ANCESTORS (N,S)
New York Evening Journal, NY: 1903 (11-3/8x8-7/8", hardcover)
nn - By F Opper 75.00 200.00 400.00
NOTE: *There is a simultaneously published British edition, identical size and contents, from C. Arthur Pearson*

Percy and Ferdie
1921 © Cupples & Leon

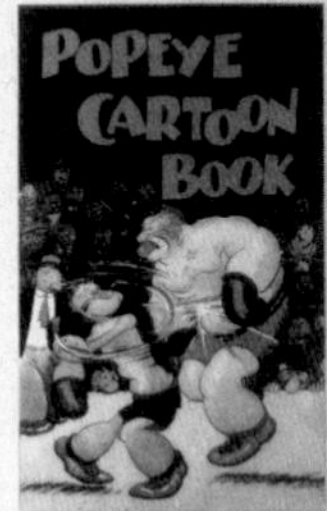

Popeye Cartoon Book
1934 © The Saalfield Co.

Roger Bean, R.G. #4
1917 © Indiana News Co., Distributors

 GD2.0 FN6.0 VF8.0

Ltd, London. A collection of single panel cartoons about cavemen. Similar to an earlier British cartoon book "Prehistoric Peeps from Punch", by E.T. Reed.

OUTBURSTS OF EVERETT TRUE, THE (N)
Saalfield Publ. Co.(Werner Co.): 1907 (92 pgs, 9-7/16x5-1/4")
1907 (2-4 panel strips-r)-By Condo & Raper 125.00 350.00 675.00
1921-Full color-c; reprints 56 of 88 cartoons from 1907 ed. (10x10", 32 pgs B&W) 125.00 225.00 350.00

OVER THERE COMEDY FROM FRANCE
Observer House Printing: nd (WW 1 era) (6x14", 60 pgs, paper cover)
nn - Artist(s) unknown 15.00 53.00 90.00

OWN YOUR OWN HOME (I)
Bobbs-Merrill Company, Indianapolis: 1919 (7-7/16x5-1/4")
nn - By Fontaine Fox – – –

PECKS BAD BOY (N)
Charles C. Thompson Co, Chicago (by Walt McDougal): 1906-1908 (strip-r)
The Adventures of... (1906) 11-1/2x16-1/4", 68 pgs 100.00 400.00 750.00
...& His Country Cousin Cynthia (1907) 12x16-1/2," 34 pgs In color 100.00 400.00 750.00
Advs. of...And His Country Cousins (1907) 5-1/2x10 1/2", 18 pgs In color 50.00 175.00 300.00
Advs. of...And His Country Cousins (1907) 11-1/2x16-1/4", 36 pgs 50.00 175.00 300.00
...& Their Advs With The Teddy Bear (1907) 5-1/2x10-1/2", 18 pgs in color 50.00 175.00 300.00
...& Their Balloon Trip To the Country (1907) 5-1/2x 10-1/2, 18 pgs in color 50.00 175.00 300.00
...With the Teddy Bear Show (1907) 5-1/2x 10-1/2 50.00 175.00 300.00
...With The Billy Whiskers Goats (1907) 5-1/2 x 10-1/2, 18 pgs in color 50.00 175.00 300.00
...& His Chums (1908) - 11x16-3/8", 36 pgs. Stanton & Van Vliet Co 100.00 400.00 750.00
...& His Chums (1908)-Hardcover; full color;16 pgs. 100.00 350.00 600.00
Advs. of...in Pictures (1908) (11x17, 36 pgs)-In color; Stanton & Van V. Liet Co. 100.00 400.00 700.00

PERCY & FERDIE (N)
Cupples & Leon Co.: 1921 (10x10", 52 pgs., B&W dailies, cardboard-c)
nn - By H. A. MacGill (Rare) 61.00 244.00 450.00

PETER RABBIT (N)
John H. Eggers Co. The House of Little Books Publishers: 1922 - 1923
B1-B4-(Rare)-(Set of 4 books which came in a cardboard box)-Each book reprints half of a Sunday page per page and contains 8 B&W and 2 color pages; by Harrison Cady (9-1/4x6-1/4", paper-c) each.... 43.00 172.00 300.00
Box only 57.00 228.00 400.00

PHILATELIC CARTOONS (M)
Essex Publishing Company, Lynn, Mass.: 1916 (8-11/16" x 5-7/8", 40 pgs, light blue construction paper-c, B&W interior)
nn - By Leroy S. Bartlett 25.00 75.00 175.00
NOTE: *Comics reprinted from The New England Philatelist.*

PICTORIAL HISTORY OF THE DEPARTMENT OF COMMERCE UNDER HERBERT HOOVER (see Picture Life of a Great American) (O)
Hoover-Curtis Campaign Committee of New York State: no date, 1928 (3-1/4 x 5-1/4, 32 pgs, paper cover, B&W)
nn - By Satterfield (scarce) 50.00 140.00 260.00
NOTE: *1928 Presidential Campaign giveaway. Original material, contents completely different from Picture Life of a Great American.*

PICTURE LIFE OF A GREAT AMERICAN (see Pictorial History of the Department of Commerce under Herbert Hoover) (O)
Hoover-Curtis Campaign Committee of New York State: no date, 1928 (paper cover, B&W)
nn - (8-3/4 x 7, 20 pgs) Text cover, 2 page text introduction, 18 pgs of comics (scarcer first print) 43.00 129.00 260.00
nn - (9 x 6-3/4,24 pgs) Illustrated cover,5 page text introduction, 18 pgs of comics (scarce) 43.00 129.00 260.00
NOTE: *1928 Presidential Campaign giveaway. Unknown which above version was published first. Both contain the same original comics material by Satterfield.*

PINK LAFFIN (I)
Whitman Publishing Co.: 1922 (9x12")(Strip-r; some of these actually text joke books)
...the Lighter Side of Life, ...He Tells 'Em, ...and His Family, ...Knockouts; Ray Gleason-a (All rare) each... 26.00 104.00 185.00

POLLY (AND HER PALS) - (N)
Newspaper Feature Service: 1916 (3x2-1/2", color)
Altogether: Three Rahs and a Tiger! by Cliff Sterrett 21.00 63.00 130.00
There Is A Limit To Pa's Patience by Cliff Sterrett 21.00 63.00 130.00
Pa's Lil Book Has Some Uncut Pages by Sterrett 21.00 63.00 130.00

NOTE: *Single newsprint sheet printed in full color on both sides, unfolds to show 12 panel story.*

POPEYE PAINT BOOK (N)
McLaughlin Bros, Inc., Springfield, Mass.: 1932 (9-7/8x13", 28 pgs, color-c)
2052 - By E. C. Segar 90.00 300.00 600.00
NOTE: *Contains a full color panel above and the exact same art in below panel n B&W which one was to color in; strip-r panels.*

POPEYE CARTOON BOOK (N)
The Saalfield Co.: 1934 (8-1/2x13", 40 pgs, cardboard-c)
2095-(scarce)-1933 strip reprints in color by Segar. Each page contains a vertical half of a Sunday strip, so the continuity reads row by row completely across each double page spread. If each page is read by itself, the continuity makes no sense. Each double page spread reprints one complete Sunday page from 1933 300.00 900.00 2500.00
12 Page Version 100.00 300.00 900.00

POPEYE (See **Thimble Theatre** for earlier Popeye-r from Sonnett) (N)
David McKay Publications: 1935 (25¢; 52 pgs, B&W) (By Segar)
1-Daily strip reprints- "The Gold Mine Thieves" 200.00 400.00 800.00
2-Daily strip-r (scarce) 200.00 400.00 900.00
NOTE: *Ties with Henry & Little Annie Rooney (David McKay) as the last of the 10x10" size books.*

PORE LI'L MOSE (N)
New York Herald Publ. by Grand Union Tea
Cupples & Leon Co.: 1902 (10-1/2x15", 78 pgs., color)
nn - By R. F. Outcault; Earliest known C&L comic book (scarce in high grade - very high demand) 1500.00 4200.00 –
NOTE: *Black Americana one page newspaper strips; falls in between Yellow Kid & Buster Brown. Complete copies have become scarce. Some have cut this book apart thinking that reselling individual pages will bring them more money.*

PRETTY PICTURES (M)
Farrar & Rinehart: 1931 (12 x 8-7/8", 104 pgs, color hardcover w/dust jacket, B&W; reprints from New Yorker, Judge, Life, Collier's Weekly)
nn - By Otto Soglow (contains "The Little King") 33.00 134.00 235.00

QUAINT OLD NEW ENGLAND (S)
Triton Syndicate: 1936 (5-1/4x6-1/4", 100 pgs, soft-c squarebound, B&W)
nn - By Jack Withycomb 36.00 144.00 250.00
NOTE: *Comics about weird doings in Old New England.*

RED CARTOONS (S)
Daily Worker Publishing Company: 1926 (12 x 9", 68 pgs,cardboard cover, B&W)
nn - By Various (scarce) 40.00 160.00 280.00
NOTE: *Reprint of American Communist Party editorial cartoons, from The Daily Worker, The Workers Monthly, and the Liberator. Art by Fred Ellis, William Gropper, Clive Weed, Art Young.*

REG'LAR FELLERS (See All-American Comics, Jimmie Dugan & The..., Popular Comics & Treasure Box of Famous Comics) (N)
Cupples & Leon Co./MS Publishing Co.: 1921-1929
1 (1921)-52 pgs. B&W dailies (Cupples & Leon, 10x10") 43.00 171.00 300.00
1925, 48 pgs. B&W dailies (MS Publ.) 39.00 157.00 275.00
Hardcover (1929, 8-3/4x7-1/2"; 96 pgs.)-B&W-r 54.00 214.00 375.00

REG'LAR FELLERS STORY PAINT BOOK
Whitman, Racine, Wisc.: 1932 (8-3/4x12-1/8", 132 pgs, red soft-c)
By Gene Byrnes 25.00 75.00 150.00

ROGER BEAN, R. G. (Regular Guy) (N)
The Indiana News Co, Distributers.: 1915 - No. 2, 1915 (5-3/8x17", 68 pgs., B&W, hardcovers); #3-#5 published by **Chas. B. Jackson:** 1916-1919
(No. 1 2 4 & 5 bound on side, No. 3 bound at top)
1-By Chas B. Jackson (68pgs.)(Scarce) 60.00 210.00 360.00
2- 5-5/8x17-1/8", 66 pgs (says 1913 inside - an obvious printing error) (red or green binding) 60.00 210.00 360.00
3-Along the Firing Line... (1916; 68 pgs, 6x17") 60.00 210.00 360.00
3-Along the Firing Line side-bound version 60.00 210.00 360.00
4-Into the Trenches and Out Again with... (1917, 68 pgs) 60.00 210.00 360.00
5 ...And The Reconstruction Period (1919, 5-3/8x15-1/2", 84 pgs) (Scarce) (has $1 printed on cover) 60.00 210.00 360.00
Baby Grand Editions 1-5 (10x10", cardboard-c) 60.00 210.00 360.00
NOTE: *No. 1 & 2 of the Twin Baby Grands (nd) 8-1/4x10-7/8", 52 pgs. #3 & #4 9x10-7/8" Cardboard cover. B&W strip reprints. Cover also says "Politics Pickles People Police."*
nn - 9x11, 68 pgs 60.00 210.00 360.00
NOTE: Has picture of Chic Jackson and a posthumous dedication from his three children. strip-r 1931-32

ROGER BEAN PHILOSOPHER
Schnull & Co: 1917 (5-1/2x17", 36 pgs., B&W, brown & black paper-c, square binding)
nn - By Chic Jackson (no known sales)

ROOKIE FROM THE 13TH SQUAD, THAT (N) (also Between Shots; Always Belittlin';Skippy)
Harper & Brothers Publishers: Feb. 1918 (8x9-1/4", 72 pgs, hardcover, B&W)
nn - By Lieut. P(ercy) L. Crosby 75.00 225.00 400.00
NOTE: *Strip began in 1917 at an Army base during basic training.*

ROUND THE WORLD WITH THE DOO-DADS (see Doings of the Doo-Dads, Doo Dads)
Universal Feature And Specialty Co, Chicago: 1922 (12x10-1/2", 52 pgs, B&W, red &

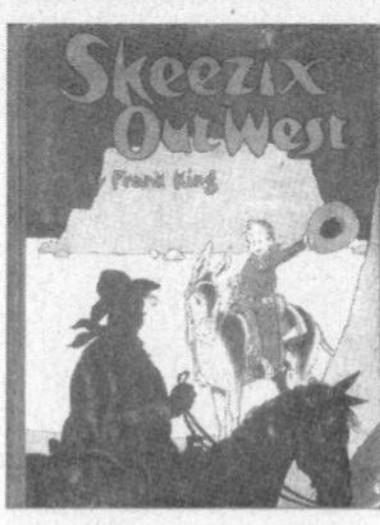
Skeezix Out West by Frank King
1928 © Reilly & Lee

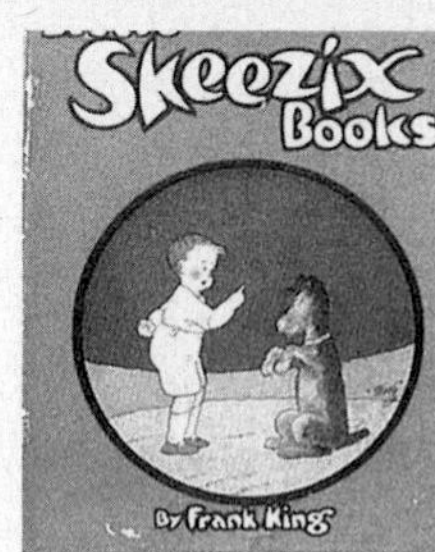

Little Skeezix Books by Frank King
1929 © Reilly & Lee

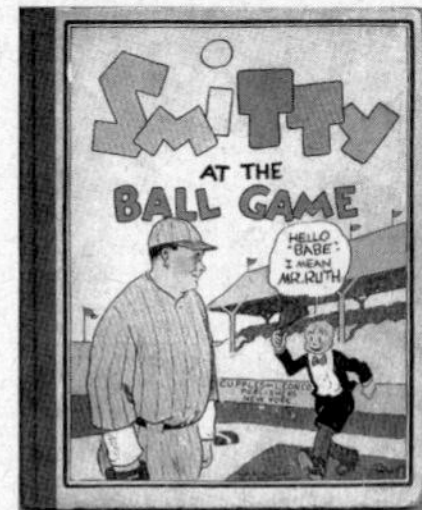

Smitty #2 By Walter Berndt
1929 © Cupples & Leon

light blue-c, square binding)

nn - By Arch Dale newspaper strip-r 43.00 173.00 300.00
NOTE: *Intermixed single panel and sequential comic strips with scenes from Scotland, Ireland, England, Holland, Italy, Spain, Egypt, Africa, and Lions & Elephants along the Nile River, China, Australia & back home.*

RUBAIYKT OF THE EGG
The John C Winston Co, Philadelphia: 1905 (7x5/12", 64 pgs, purple-c, B&W)

nn - By Clare Victor Dwiggins 20.00 60.00 125.00
NOTE: *Book is printed & cut into the shape of an egg.*

RULING CLAWSS, THE (N,S)
The Daily Worker: 1935 (192 pgs, 10-1/4 x 7-3/8", hard-c, B&W)

nn - By Redfield 60.00 240.00 –
NOTE: *Reprints cartoons from the American Communist Party newspaper The Daily Worker.*

SAGARA'S ENGLISH CARTOONS AND CARTOON STORIES (N)
Bunkosha, Tokyo: nd (c1925) (6-5/8" x 4-1/4", 272 pgs, hard-c, B&W)

nn- (Scarce) – – –
NOTE: *Published in Tokyo, Japan, with all strips in both English and Japanese, to facilitate learning English. Majority of book is Bringing Up Father by George McManus. Also contains Japanese strip Father Takes it Easy, by T. Sagara, reprinted from the Kokusai News Agency.*

SAM AND HIS LAUGH (N)
Frederick A. Stokes: 1906 (10x15", cardboard-c, Sunday strip-r in color)

nn - By Jimmy Swinnerton (Extremely Rare) 800.00 1400.00 2900.00
NOTE: *Strip ran July 24, 1904-Dec 26 1906; its ethnic humor might be considered racist by today's standards.*

SCHOOL DAYS (N)
Harper & Bros.: 1919 (9x8", 104 pgs.)

nn - By Clare Victor Dwiggins 75.00 150.00 300.00

SEAMAN SI - A Book of Cartoons About the Funniest "Gob" in the Navy (N)
Pierce Publishing Co.: 1916 (4x8-1/2, 200 pgs, hardcover, B&W); 1918 (4-1/8x8-1/4, 104 pgs, hardcover, B&W)

nn - By Perce Pearce (1916) 50.00 150.00 300.00
nn - 1918 - (Reilly & Britton Co.) 30.00 125.00 200.00
NOTE: *There exists two different covers for the 1918 reprints. The earlier edition was self published by the artist. The newspaper strip is sometimes also known as "The American Sailor."*

SECRET AGENT X-9 (N)
David McKay Pbll.: 1934 (Book 1: 84 pgs; Book 2: 124 pgs.) (8x7-1/2")

Book 1-Contains reprints of the first 13 weeks of the strip by Dashiell Hammett & Alex Raymond, complete except for 2 dailies 100.00 300.00 650.00
Book 2-Contains reprints immediately following contents of Book 1, for 20 weeks by Dashiell Hammett & Alex Raymond; complete except for two dailies. Last 5 strips misdated from 6/34, continuity correct 100.00 300.00 650.00

SILK HAT HARRY'S DIVORCE SUIT (N)
M. A. Donoghue & Co.: 1912 (5-3/4x15-1/2", oblong, B&W)

nn - Newspaper-r by Tad (Thomas A. Dorgan) 33.00 117.00 400.00

SINBAD A DOG'S LIFE (M)
Coward - McCann, Inc.: 1930 (11x 8-3/4", 104 pgs., single-sided, illustrated hard-c, B&W

nn - By Edwina 11.00 33.00 100.00
Sinbad...Again (1932, 10-15/16x 8-9/16", 104 pgs.) 11.00 33.00 100.00
NOTE: *Wordless comic strips from LIFE.*

SIS HOPKINS OWN BOOK AND MAGAZINE OF FUN
Leslie-Judge Co.: 1899-July 1911 (36 pgs, color-c, B&W) (merged into Judge's Library, later titled Film Fun)

any issue - By various 11.00 33.00 100.00
NOTE: *Zim, Flagg, Young, Newell, Adams, etc.*

SKEEZIX (Also see Gasoline Alley & Little Skeezix Books listed below) (I)
Reilly & Lee Co.: 1925 - 1928 (Strip-r, soft covers) (pictures & text)

...and Uncle Walt (1924)-Origin 26.00 104.00 180.00
...and Pal (1925), ...at the Circus (1926) 21.00 84.00 160.00
...& Uncle Walt (1927) (does this actually exist? reprint? never seen one yet)
...Out West (1928) 30.00 100.00 200.00
Hardback Editions... 34.00 136.00 235.00

SKEEZIX BOOKS, LITTLE (Also see Skeezix, Gasoline Alley) (G)
Reilly & Lee Co.: No date (1928, 1929) (Boxed set of three Skeezix books)

nn - Box with 3 issues of Skeezix. Skeezix & Pal, Skeezix at the Circus, Skeezix & Uncle Walt known. 1928 Set... 60.00 180.00 360.00
nn - Box with 4 issues of (3) above Skeezix plus "Out West" 80.00 330.00 550.00

SKEEZIX COLOR BOOK (N)
McLaughlin Bros. Inc, Springfield, Mass: 1929 (9-1/2x10-1/4", 28 pgs, one third in full color, rest in B&W)

2023 - By Frank King; strip-r to color 20.00 75.00 135.00

SKIPPY (see also Life Presents Skippy, Always Belittlin', That Rookie From 13th Squad)
No publisher listed: Circa 1920s (10x8", 16 pgs., color/B&W cartoons)

nn - By Percy Crosby 20.00 84.00 150.00

SKIPPY, LIFE PRESENTS (M)
Life Publishing Company & Henry Holt, NY: nd 1924 (134 pgs, 10-13/16x8-3/4", color hard-c, B&W

nn - By Percy L Crosby 100.00 300.00 500.00
NOTE: *Many sequential & single panel reprints from Skippy's earliest appearances in Life Magazine.*

SKIPPY
Greenberg, Publisher, Inc, NY: 1925. (11-14x8-5/8, 72 pgs, hard-c, B&W and color

nn - By Percy L. Crosby 50.00 150.00 300.00
NOTE: *Some but not all of these comics were also in Life Presents Skippy; issued with dust wrapper.*

SKIPPY AND OTHER HUMOR
Greenberg: Publisher, NY: 1929 (11-1/4x8-1/2",72 pgs,tan hard-c, B&W and color)

nn - By Percy L. Crosby 25.00 75.00 150.00
NOTE: *Came with a dust jacket.*

SKIPPY (I)
Grossett & Dunlap: 1929 (7-3/8x6, 370 pgs, hardcover text with some art)

nn - By Percy Crosby (issued with a dust jacket) 23.00 92.00 160.00
NOTE: *This is worth very little without the dust wrapper; very common without athe dust jacket.*

SKIPPY
Greenberg Press: 1930 (soft cover, ca. 16 pp.,

nn - By Percy Crosby (scarce) 50.00 175.00 300.00
NOTE: *Reprints from LIFE cartoons, color, b/w. Crosby told Greenberg to withdraw from the market as it cheapened the hard cover prior editions. Greenberg then stopped publishing per agreement, and sent Crosby all the copper & zinc bookplates, which were in Crosby estate until 1996.*

SKIPPY CRAYON AND COLORING BOOK (N)
McLoughlin Bros, Inc., Springfield, MA: 1931 (13x9-3/4", 28 pgs, color-c, color & B&W)

2050 - By Percy Crosby 28.00 84.00 195.00
NOTE: *This item says on the front cover: "Licensed by Percy Crosby" because he owned his creation. About half the pages have one panel pre-printed in full color with same one b&w below for person to copy the colors.*

SKIPPY RAMBLES (I)
G.P. Putnam's Sons: 1932 (7 1/8 x 5 1/8, 202 pgs)

nn - By Percy Crosby 21.00 84.00 150.00
NOTE: *Issued with a dustjacket. Has Skippy plates by Crosby every 4 or 5 pages.*

SKUDDABUD STARRY STORY SERIES - FOLK FROM THE FUTURE (O,G)
no publisher listed: 1936 (9" x 11-7/8", 48 pgs, cardboard-c, B&W)

Book One (Rare) "Parachuting" 21.00 84.00 150.00
NOTE: *By Columba Krebs. Top half of each page is a continuing strip story, while bottom half are different stories, in prose, about the same characters -- a race of aliens who have migrated to Earth, from their dying world.*

S'MATTER POP? (N)
Saalfield Publ. Co.: 1917 (10x14", 44 pgs., B&W, cardboard-c,)

nn - By Charlie Payne; in full color; pages printed on one side 48.00 169.00 290.00

S'MATTER POP? (N) (25 ¢ cover price)
E.I. Company, New York: 1927 (8-15/16x7-1/8", 52 pgs, yellow soft-c perfect bound

nn - By C.M. Payne (scarce) 24.00 84.00 145.00
NOTE: *First comic book published by Hugo Gernsback, noted for inventing Amazing Stories among other memorable science fiction pulps. The World Science Fiction Convention Award, The Hugo, is named for him.*

SMITTY (See Treasure Box of Famous Comics) (N)
Cupples & Leon Co.: 1928 - 1933 (9x7", 96 pgs., B&W strip-r, hardcover)

1928-(96 pgs. 7x8-3/4") By Walter Berndt 43.00 172.00 300.00
1929-At the Ball Game (Babe Ruth on cover) 57.00 229.00 450.00
1930-The Flying Office Boy, 1931-The Jockey, 1932-In the North Woods each... 31.00 126.00 250.00
1933-At Military School 31.00 126.00 250.00
NOTE: *Each hardbound was published with a dust jacket; worth 50% more with dust jacket. The 1929 edition is very popular with baseball collectors. Strip debuted Nov 27, 1922.*

SMOKEY STOVER (See Dan Dunn & King of the Royal Mounted) (N)
Whitman Publishing: 1937 (5 1/2 x 7 1/4", 68pgs., color cardboard-c, B&W)

1010 36.00 144.00 250.00

SOCIAL COMEDY (M)
Life Publishing Company: 1902 (11-3/4 x 9-1/2", 128 pgs, B&W, illustrated hardcover)

nn - Artists include C.D. Gibson & Kemble. 20.00 70.00 120.00
NOTE: *Reprints cartoons and a few sequential comics from LIFE. Came in unmarked slipcase.*

SOCIAL HELL, THE (O)
Rich Hill: 1902

nn - By Ryan Walker 21.00 74.00 130.00
NOTE: *"The conditions of workers and the corruption of a political system beholden to corporate interests have been a major focus of human rights concerns since the 19th century. This early graphic novel depicts the social evils of unreformed capitalism. Ryan Walker was a syndicate cartoonist for many mainstream newspapers as well as for the communist Daily Worker." This description comes from http://www.lib.uconn.edu/DoddCenter/ascexh3.html, where you can find also a reproduction of the cover. I add that Ryan Walker was the editor of "The Saint Louis Republic" comic section since its inception in 1897; the supplement published "Alma and Oliver", George McManus's first series.*

SPORT AND THE KID (see The Umbrella Man) (N)
Lowman & Hanford Co.: 1913 (6-1/4x6-5/8",114 pgs, hardcover, B&W&orange)

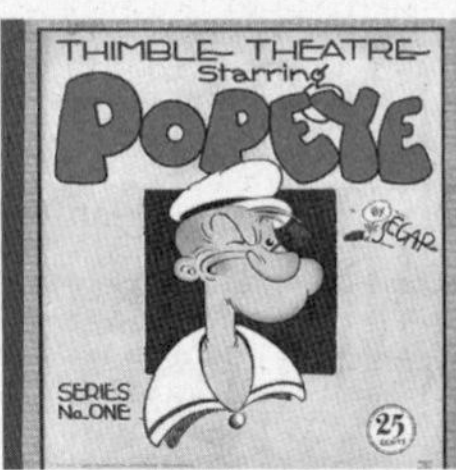

Thimble Theater #1 by E.C. Segar
1931 © Sonnet Publishing Co.

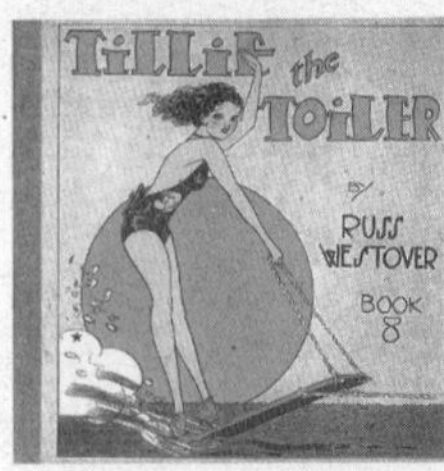

Tillie the Toiler #8 by Russ Westover
1933 © Cupples & Leon

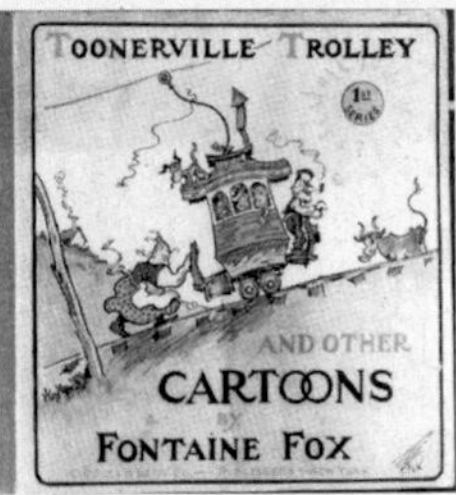

Toonerville Trolley And Other Cartoons
1921 © Cupples & Leon

GD2.0 FN6.0 VF8.0

nn - By J.R. "Dok" Hager 20.00 70.00 120.00

STORY OF CONNECTICUT (N)
The Hartford Times: Vol.1 1935 - Vol.3 1936 (10-1/2" x 7-3/8",304 pgs,color hard-c, B&W)

Vol.1 - 3 20.00 70.00 120.00
NOTE: *Collects a newspaper strip on Connecticut State history, which ran in the Hartford Times. Strip is in a similar format to "Texas History Movies". Also published in a plain, blue hardcover.*

STORY OF JAPAN IN CHINA, THE (N,S)
Trans-Pacific News Service, NYC: Vol. 3, No.1 March 10, 1938 (9" x 6", 36 pgs, construction paper-c, B&W)

Vol.3 No.1 21.00 64.00 150.00
NOTE: *Part of the "China Reference Series" of booklets, detailing the Japanese occupation and brutalization of China. Consists entirely of cartoons. The other booklets in the series have no cartoons. Art by: Ding, Fitzpatrick, Herblock, Herman, Rollin Kirby, Knox, Low, Manning, Orr, Shoemaker, Talburt.*

STRANGE AS IT SEEMS (S)
Blue-Star Publishing Co.: 1932 (64 pgs., B&W, square binding)

1-Newspaper-r (*Published with & without No. 1 and price on cover.*) 32.00 128.00 200.00
Ex-Lax giveaway (1936, B&W, 24 pgs., 5x7") - McNaught Synd. 13.00 52.00 90.00

SULLIVANT'S ABC ZOO (I)
The Old Wine Press: 1946 (11-3/4x9-3/8", hardcover)

nn - By T.S. Sullivant (Rare) – – –
NOTE: *Reprints Mitchell & Miller material 1895-1898 and Life Publishing 1898-1926.*

TAILSPIN TOMMY STORY & PICTURE BOOK (N)
McLoughlin Bros.: No. 266, 1931? (nd) (10x10-1/2", color strip-r)

266 - By Forrest 43.00 172.00 300.00

TAILSPIN TOMMY (Also see Famous Feature Stories & The Funnies)(N)
Cupples & Leon Co.: 1932 (100 pgs., hard-c) (B&W 1930 strip reprints)

nn - (Scarce)- by Hal Forrest & Glenn Chaffin 50.00 150.00 375.00

TALES OF DEMON DICK AND BUNKER BILL (O)
Whitman Publishing Co.: 1934 (5-1/4x10-1/2", 80 pgs, color hardcover, B&W)

793 - By Spencer 33.00 100.00 300.00

TARZAN BOOK (The Illustrated...) (N)
Grosset & Dunlap: 1929 (9x7", 80 pgs.)

1(Rare)-Contains 1st B&W Tarzan newspaper comics from 1929. By Hal Foster Cloth reinforced spine & dust jacket (50¢); Foster-c
With dust jacket... 86.00 344.00 600.00
Without dust jacket... 43.00 172.00 300.00
2nd Printing(1934, 25¢, 76 pgs.)-4 Foster pgs. dropped; paper spine, circle in lower right cover with 25¢ price. The 25¢ is barely visible on some copies 34.00 136.00 225.00
1967-House of Greystoke reprint-7x10", using the complete 300 illustrations/text from the 1929 edition minus the original indicia, foreword, etc. Initial version bound in gold paper & sold for $5.00. Officially titled **Burroughs Bibliophile #2**. A very few additional copies were bound in heavier blue paper. Gold binding... 2.25 6.75 20.00
Blue binding... 2.50 7.50 27.00

TARZAN OF THE APES TO COLOR (N)
Saalfield Publishing Co.: No. 988, 1933 (15-1/4x10-3/4", 24 pgs)
(Coloring book)

988-(Very Rare)-Contains 1929 daily reprints with some new art by Hal Foster. Two panels blown up large on each page with one at the top of opposing pages on every other double-page spread. Believed to be the only time these panels appeared in color. Most color panels are reproduced a second time in B&W to be colored 271.00 1084.00 2000.00

TARZAN OF THE APES The Big Little Cartoon Book (N)
Whitman Publishing Company: 1933 (4-1/2x3 5/8", 320 pgs, color-c, B&W)

744 - By Hal Foster (comic strips on every page) 60.00 175.00 325.00

TECK HASKINS AT OHIO STATE (S)
Lea-Mar Press: 1908 (7-1/4x5-3/8", 84 pgs, B&W hardcover)

nn - By W.A. Ireland; football cartoons-r from Columbus Ohio Evening Dispatch 28.00 99.00 170.00
NOTE: *Small blue & white patch of cover art pasted atop a color cloth quilt patter; pasted patch can easily peel off some copies.*

TECK 1909 (S)
Lea-Mar Press: 1909 (8-5/8 x 8-1/8", 124 pgs., B&W hardcover, 25¢)

nn - By W.A. Ireland; Ohio State University baseball cartoons-r from Columbus Evening Dispatch 28.00 99.00 170.00

TEDDY BEAR BOOKS, THE (M) (see also LITTLE JOHNNY AND THE TEDDY BEARS)
Reilly & Britton Co., Chicago: 1907 (7-1/16" x 5-3/8", 24 pgs, hard-c, color

The Teddy Bears Come to Life, The Teddy Bears at the Circus, The Teddy Bears in a Smashup, The Teddy Bears on a Lark, The Teddy Bears on a Toboggan, The Teddy Bears at School, The Teddy Bears Go Fishing, The Teddy Bears in Hot Water 21.00 63.00 150.00
NOTE: *Books are all unnumbered. C & A by J.R. Bray; s-Robert D. Towne. Reprints "Little Johnny & the Teddy Bears" strips, from Judge Magazine. Similar in format to the Buster Brown Nuggets series. All eight books debuted simultaneously.*

GD2.0 FN6.0 VF8.0

TEDDY BEARS IN FUN AND FROLIC (M) (see LITTLE JOHNNY & THE TEDDY BEARS)
Reilly & Britton Co., Chicago: 1908 (8-3/4" x 8-3/4", 50 pgs, cardboard-c, color)

nn - (Rare) by J.R. Bray-a; Robert D. Towne-s 100.00 400.00 700.00
NOTE: *Reprints "Little Johnny & the Teddy Bears" strips, from Judge Magazine. Unknown if there were any other "Teddy Bear" titles published in this format.*

THE TEENIE WEENIES
Reilly & Britton, Chicago: 1916 (16-3/8x10-1/2", 52 pgs, cardboard-c, full color)

nn - By Wm. Donahey (Chicago Tribune-r) 200.00 550.00 900.00

TERROR OF THE TINY TADS (see also UPSIDE DOWNS OF LITTLE LADY LOVEKINS AND OLD MAN MUFFAROO)
Cupples & Leon: 1909 (11x17, 26 Sunday strips in Black & Red, Stiff cardboard-c)

nn - By Gustave Verbeek (Very Rare) (no known sales)

TEXAS HISTORY MOVIES (N)
Various editions, 1928 to 1986 (B&W)

Book I -1928 Southwest Press (7-1/4 x 5-3/8, 56 pgs, cardboard cover) for the Magnolia Petroleum Company 50.00 125.00 250.00
nn - 1928 Southwest Press (12-3/8 x 9-1/4, 232 pgs, HC) 75.00 200.00 400.00
nn - 1935 Magnolia Petroleum Company (6 x 9, 132 pgs, paper cover) 21.00 63.00 130.00
NOTE: *Exists with either Wagon Train or Texas Flag & Lafitte/pirate covers.*
nn - 1943 Magnolia Petroleum Company (132 pgs, paper cover) 16.00 48.00 100.00
nn - 1963 Graphic Ideas Inc (11 x 8-1/2, softcover) 12.00 37.00 75.00
NOTE: *Reprints daily newspaper strips from the Dallas News, on Texas history. 1935 editions onward distributed within the Texas Public School System. Prior to that they appear to be giveaway comic books for the Magnolia Petroleum Company. There are many more editions than the ones pointed out above.*

THAT SON-IN-LAW OF PA'S! (N)
Newspaper Feature Service: 1914 (2-1/2 by 3", color)

nn - *Imprinted on back for THE LESTER SHOE STORE.* 15.00 25.00 50.00
NOTE: *Single sheet printed in full color on both sides, unfolds to show 12 panel story.*

THIMBLE THEATRE STARRING POPEYE (See also Popeye) (N)
Sonnet Publishing Co.: 1931 - No. 2, 1932 (25¢, B&W, 52 pgs.)(Rare)

1-Daily strip serial-r in both by Segar 157.00 650.00 1300.00
2 136.00 544.00 1100.00
NOTE: *The very first Popeye reprint book. The first Thimble Theatre Sunday page appeared Dec 19, 1919. Popeye first entered Thimble Theatre on Jan 17, 1929.*

THREE FUN MAKERS, THE (N)
Stokes and Company: 1908 (10x15", 64 pgs., color) (1904-06 Sunday strip-r)

nn - Maud, Katzenjammer Kids, Happy Hooligan 800.00 2000.00 –
NOTE: *This is the first comic book to compile more than one newspaper strip together.*

TIGERS (Also see On and Off Mount Ararat) (N)
Hearst's New York American & Journal: 1902, 86 pgs. 10x15-1/4"

nn - Funny animal strip-r by Jimmy Swinnerton 600.00 1600.00 –
NOTE: *The strip began as The Journal Tigers in The New York Journal Dec 12, 1897-Sept 28 1903*

TILLIE THE TOILER (N)
Cupples & Leon Co.: 1925 - No. 8, 1933 (52 pgs., B&W, daily strip-r)

nn (#1) By Russ Westover 54.00 216.00 400.00
2-8 50.00 175.00 360.00
NOTE: *First newspaper strip appearance was in January, 1921.*

TILLIE THE TOILER MAGIC DRAWING AND COLORING BOOK
Sam L Gabriel Sons And Company: 1931 (8-1/2 x 12", 36 pages, stiff-c)

838-By Russ Westover 39.00 156.00 275.00

TIMID SOUL, THE (N)
Simon & Schuster: 1931 (12-1/4x9", 136 pgs, B&W hardcover, dust jacket?)

nn - By H. T. Webster (newspaper strip-r) 40.00 120.00 260.00

TIM McCOY, POLICE CAR 17 (O)
Whitman Publishing Co.: 1934 (14-3/4x11", 32 pgs, stiff color covers)

674-1933 original material 100.00 350.00 550.00
NOTE: *Historically important as first movie adaptation in comic books.*

TOAST BOOK
John C. Winston Co: 1905 (7-1/4 x 6,104 pgs, skull-shaped book, feltcover, B&W)

nn - By Clare Dwiggins 50.00 175.00 300.00
NOTE: *Cartoon illustrations accompanying toasts/poems, most involving alcohol.*

TOM SAWYER & HUCK FINN (N)
Stoll & Edwards Co.:1925 (10x10-3/4", 52 pgs, stiff covers)

nn - By "Dwig" Dwiggins; 1923, 1924-r color Sunday strips 5000 200.00 350.00
NOTE: *By Permission of the Estate of Samuel L. Clemons and the Mark Twain Company.*

TOONERVILLE TROLLEY AND OTHER CARTOONS (N) (See Cartoons by Fontaine Fox)
Cupples & Leon Co.: 1921 (10 x10", 52 pgs., B&W, daily strip-r)

1 - By Fontaine Fox 100.00 350.00 550.00

TRAINING FOR THE TRENCHES (M)

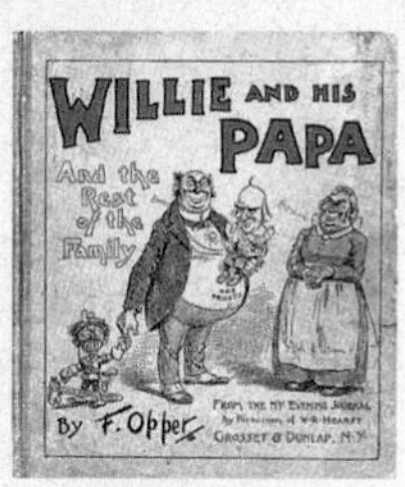

Willie and His Papa & the Rest of the Family by Opper
1901 © Grossett & Dunlap

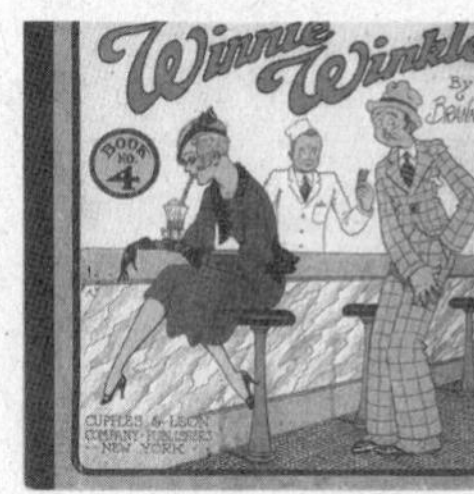

Winnie Winkle #4 by Branner
1933 © Cupples & Leon

The Yellow Kid #4 cover by Outcault
1897 © Howard Ainslee & Co.

	GD2.0	FN6.0	VF8.0

Palmer Publishing Company: 1917 (5-3/8 x 7", 20 pgs., paper-c, 10¢)

nn - By Lieut. Alban B. Butler, Jr.	21.00	84.00	150.00

NOTE: *Subtitle: "A book of humorous cartoons on a serious subject." Single-panels about military training.*

TREASURE BOX OF FAMOUS COMICS (N) (see Wonder Chest of Famous Comics)
Cupples & Leon Co.: 1934 8-1/2x(6-7/8", 36 pgs, soft covers) (Boxed set of 5 books)

Little Orphan Annie (1926)	21.00	84.00	165.00
Reg'lar Fellers (1928)	19.00	76.00	145.00
Smitty (1928)	19.00	76.00	145.00
Harold Teen (1931)	19.00	76.00	145.00
How Dick Tracy & Dick Tracy Jr. Caught The Racketeers (1933)	26.00	104.00	205.00
Softcover set of five books in box	160.00	640.00	1250.00
Box only	57.00	228.00	450.00

NOTE: *Dates shown are copyright dates; all books actually came out in 1934 or later. The softcovers are abbreviated versions of the hardcover editions listed under each character.*

T.R. IN CARTOONS (N)
A.C. McClurg & Co., Chicago: June 13, 1910 (10-5/8" x 8", 104? pgs, paper-c, B&W)

nn - By McCutcheon about Teddy Roosevelt	-	-	-

TRUTH (See Victorian section for earlier issues including the first Yellow Kid appearances)
Truth Company, NY: 1886-1906? (13-11/16x10-5/16", 16 pgs, process color-c & center-folds, rest B&W)

1900-1906 issues	20.00	40.00	75.00

TRUTH SAVE IT FROM ABUSE & OVERWORK BEING THE EPISODE OF THE HIRED HAND & MRS. STIX PLASTER, CONCERTIST (N)
Radio Truth Society of WBAP: no date, 1924 (6-3/8 x 4-7/8, 40 pgs, paper cover, B&W)

nn - By V.T. Hamlin (Very Rare)	100.00	400.00	700.00

NOTE: *Radio station WBAP giveaway reprints strips from the Ft. Worth Texas Star-Telegram set at local radio station. 1st collected work by V.T. Hamlin, pre-Alley Oop.*

TWENTY FIVE YEARS AGO (see At The Bottom Of The Ladder) (M,S)
Coward-McCann: 1931 (5-3/4x8-1/4, 328 pgs, hardcover, B&W)

nn - By Camillus Kessler	32.00	128.00	225.00

NOTE: *Multi-image panel cartoons showing historical events for dates during the year.*

UMBRELLA MAN, THE (N) (See Sport And The Kid)
Lowman & Hanford Co.: 1911 (8-7/8x5-7/8",112 pgs, hard-c, B&W & orange)

nn - By J.R. "Dok" Hager (Seattle Times-r)	20.00	70.00	120.00

UNCLE REMUS AND BRER RABBIT (N)
Frederick A. Stokes Co.: 1907 (64 pgs, hardbound, color)

nn - By Joel C Harris & J.M. Conde	50.00	175.00	300.00

UPSIDE DOWNS OF LITTLE LADY LOVEKINS AND OLD MAN MUFFAROO
(see also TERROR OF THE TINY TADS)
New York Herald: 1905 (?) (N)

nn - By Gustav Verbeck	150.00	450.00	750.00

VAUDEVILLES AND OTHER THINGS (N)
Isaac H. Blandiard Co.: 1900 (13x10-1/2", 22 pgs., color) plus two reprints

nn - By Bunny (Scarce)	400.00	1200.00	-
nn - 2nd print "By the Creator of Foxy Grandpa" on-c but only has copyright info of 1900 (10-1/2x15 1/2, 28 pgs, color)	450.00	900.00	-
nn - 3rd print. "By the creator of Foxy Grandpa" on-c; has both 1900 and 1901 copyright info (11x13")	350.00	700.00	-

WALLY - HIS CARTOONS OF THE A.E.F. (N)
Stars & Stripes: 1917 (96 and 108 pgs, B&W)

nn - By Abian A "Wally" Wallgren (7x18; 96 pgs)	25.00	75.00	150.00
nn - another edition (108 pgs, 7x17-1/2)	25.00	75.00	150.00

NOTE: *World War One cartoons reprints from Stars & Stripes; sold to U.S. servicemen with profits to go to French War Orphans Fund. various editions from 1917-1920; there might be more than what we list here.*

WAR CARTOONS (S)
Dallas News: 1918 (11x9", 112 pgs, hardcover, B&W)

nn - By John Knott (WWOne cartoons)	20.00	70.00	125.00

WAR CARTOONS FROM THE CHICAGO DAILY NEWS (N,S)
Chicago Daily News: 1914 (10 cents, 7-3/4x10-3/4", 68 pgs, paper-c, B&W)

nn - By L.D. Bradley	20.00	70.00	125.00

WEBER & FIELD'S FUNNYISMS (S,M,O)
Arkell Comoany, NY: 1904 (10-7/8x8", 112 pgs, color-c, B&W)

1 - By various (only issue?)	20.00	70.00	150.00

NOTE: *Contains some sequential & many single panel strips by Outcault, George Luks, CA David, Houston, L Smith, Hy Mayer, Verbeck, Woolf, Sydney Adams, Frank "Chip" Bellew, Eugene "ZIM" Zimmerman, Phil May, FT Richards, Billy Marriner, Grosvenor and many others.*

WE'RE NOT HEROES (O,S)
E.C. Wells and J.W. Moss: 1933 (8-11/16" x 5-7/8", 52 pgs, B&W interior)

nn - By Eddie Wells; red & black paper-c	10.00	30.00	60.00

NOTE: *Amateurish cartoons about World War I vets in the Walter Reed Veteran's Hospital.*

WHEN A FELLER NEEDS A FRIEND (S)
P. F. Volland & Co.: 1914 (11-11/16x8-7/8)

	GD2.0	FN6.0	VF8.0
nn - By Clare Briggs	37.00	131.00	225.00

NOTE: *Originally came in box with Briggs art (box is Rare); also numerous more modern reprints)*

WILD PILGRIMAGE (O)
Harrison Smith & Robert Haas: 1932 (9-7/8x7", 210 pgs, B&W hardcover w/dust jacket) (original wordless graphic novel in woodcuts)

nn - By Lynd Ward	50.00	175.00	300.00

WILLIE AND HIS PAPA AND THE REST OF THE FAMILY (I)
Grossett & Dunlap: 1901 (9-1/2x8", 200 pgs, hardcover from N.Y. Evening Journal by Permission of W. R. Hearst) (pictures & text)

nn - By Frederick Opper	100.00	260.00	450.00

NOTE: *Political satire series of single panel cartoons, involving whiny child Willie (President William McKinley), his rambunctious and uncontrollable cousin Teddy (Vice President Roosevelt), and Willie's Papa (trusts/monopolies) and their Maid (Senator) Hanna.*

WILLIE GREEN COMICS, THE (N) (see Adventures of Willie Green)
Frank M. Acton Co./Harris Brown: 1915 (8x15, 36 pgs); 1921 (6x10-1/8", 52 pgs, color paper cover, B&W interior, 25¢)

Book No. 1 By Harris Brown	45.00	158.00	270.00
Book 2 (#2 sold via mail order directly from the artist)(very rare)	45.00	172.00	300.00

NOTE: *Book No. 1 possible reprint of Adv. of Willie Green; definitely two different editions.*

WILLIE WESTINGHOUSE EDISON SMITH THE BOY INVENTOR (N)
William A. Stokes Co.: 1906 (10x16", 36 pgs. in color)

nn - By Frank Crane (Scarce)	350.00	850.00	1300.00

NOTE: *Comic strip began May 27, 1900 and ran thru 1914. Parody of inventors Westinghouse and Edison.*

WINNIE WINKLE (N) *Strip began as a daily Sept 20, 1920.*
Cupples & Leon Co.: 1930 - No. 4, 1933 (52 pgs., B&W daily strip-r)

1	43.00	172.00	375.00
2-4	29.00	116.00	300.00

WISDOM OF CHING CHOW, THE (see also The Gumps)
R. J. Jefferson Printing Co.: 1928 (4x3", 100 pgs, red & B&W cardboard cover) (newspaper strip-r The Chicago Tribune)

nn - By Sidney Smith (scarce)	30.00	90.00	150.00

WONDER CHEST OF FAMOUS COMICS (N) see Treasure Chest of Famous Comics)
Cupples & Leon Co.: 1935? 8-1/2x(6-7/8", 36 pgs, soft covers) (Boxed set of 5 books)

Little Orphan Annie #2 (1927) (Haunted House)	21.00	84.00	130.00
Little Orphan Annie #3 (1928) (in the Circus)	19.00	76.00	130.00
Smitty #2 (1929) (Babe Ruth app.)	19.00	76.00	130.00
Dolly Dimples and Bobby Bounce (1933) by Grace Drayton	19.00	76.00	130.00
How Dick Tracy & Dick Tracy Jr. Caught The Racketeers (1933)	26.00	104.00	185.00
Softcover set of five books in box	160.00	640.00	1125.00
Box only	57.00	228.00	400.00

NOTE: *Dates shown are original copyright dates of the first printings; all actually came out in 1934 or later. Extremely abbreviated versions of the hardcover editions listed under each character. It is suspected this came out the Christmas season following Teasure Chest of Famous Comics. which contains earlier editions.*

WORLD OF TROUBLE, A (S)
Minneapolis Journal: 1901 (10x8-3/4", 100 pgs, 40 pgs full color)

v3#1 - By Charles L. Bartholomew (editorial-r)	28.00	99.00	170.00

WRIGLEY'S "MOTHER GOOSE"
Wm. Wrigley Jr. Company, Chicago: 1915 (6" x 4", 28 pgs, full color)

nn - *Promotional comics for Wrigley's gum. Intro Wrigley's "Spearmen*	20.00	70.00	120.00
Book No. 2	20.00	70.00	120.00

YELLOW KID, THE (Magazine)(I) (becomes **The Yellow Book** #10 on)
Howard Ainslee & Co., N.Y.: Mar. 20, 1897 - #9, July 17, 1897
(5¢, B&W w/color covers, 52p., stapled) (not a comic book)

1-R.F. Outcault Yellow kid on-c only #1-6. The same Yellow Kid color ad app. on back-c #1-6 (advertising the New York Sunday Journal)	857.00	3600.00	-
2-6 (#2 4/3/97, #5 5/22/97, #6, 6/5/97)	743.00	2800.00	-
7-9 (Yellow Kid not on-c)	121.00	425.00	-

NOTE: *Richard Outcault's Yellow Kid from the Hearst New York American represents the very first successful newspaper comic strip in America. Listed here due to historical importance.*

YELLOW KID IN MCFADDEN'S FLATS, THE (N)
G. W. Dillingham Co., New York: 1897 (50¢, 7-1/2x5-1/2", 196 pgs., B&W, squarebound)

nn - The first "comic" book featuring The Yellow Kid; E. W. Townsend narrative w/R. F. Outcault Sunday comic page art-r & some original drawings (Prices vary widely. Rare.)	7000.00	14,200.00	-

NOTE: *A Fair condition copy sold for $2,901 in August 2004.; restored app VF sold for $10,500 in 2005. A copy in Fine+ (spine intact) and loose bacl cover sold for $17,000 in 2006.*

YESTERDAYS (S)
The Reilly & Lee Co.: 1930 (8-3/4 x 7-1/2", 128 pgs, illustrated hard-c with dust jacket

nn - Text and cartoons about Victorian times by Frank Wing	20.00	40.00	80.00

Any addititions or corrections to this section are always welcome, very much encouraged and can be sent to **feedback@gemstonepub.com** to be processed for next year's Guide.

1939

AT 75

By S.C. Ringgenberg

Batman was born in the shadows of the film noir era and dwelt there for the first year of his existence before being joined by Robin, the Boy Wonder, and then embarked on several decades of colorful, outlandish, and frequently silly sci-fi and fantasy-flavored adventures that totally changed the tone of the series. By the late 1960s, however, Batman had shucked the trappings of sci-fi, fantasy and camp and had returned to his roots as a shadowy, mysterious avenger, where he's lived ever since, abetted by a small army of talented creators that included Denny O'Neil, Neal Adams, Dick Giordano, Jim Aparo, Steve Englehart, Marshall Rogers, Frank Robbins, Frank Miller, Doug Moench, Kelley Jones, Archie Goodwin, and many others.

The Bat-Man, as he was initially known in *Detective Comics* #27 ("The Case of the Chemical Syndicate," the plot of which was heavily inspired by Theodore Tinsley's *Shadow* novel, *Partners of Peril*) had his origins in Bob Kane's desire to make more money doing comic books. It's really as simple as that. Kane had started out as a humor cartoonist and in 1939, was drawing strips like "Clip Carson" and others for DC.

As Kane recounted in his 1989 autobiography, *Batman & Me*, Batman grew out of a conversation with DC editor Vincent Sullivan: "'There's a character called Superman by Siegel and Shuster, and they are making $800 a week apiece. We're looking for another superhero. Do you think you could come up with one?' This was on Friday. I said, 'To make that kind of money, I'll have one for you on Monday!'" Kane said.

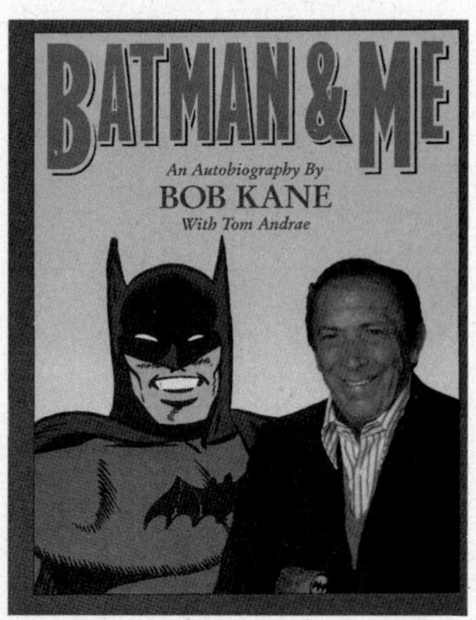

"So over the weekend I laid out a kind of naked superhero on the page. I placed a sheet of tracing paper over him so that I could create new costumes that might strike my fancy. Then, POW! It came to me in a flash...! I remembered Leonardo da Vinci's drawing of a bat-like flying machine," he said.

Writer Bill Finger, Kane's collaborator, recalled in *Steranko's History of Comics* that Kane had an idea for a character called Batman. "I went over to Kane's, and he had drawn a character, who looked very much like Superman with kind of reddish tights. Boots, no gloves, no gauntlets. With a small domino mask, swinging on a rope. It had two stiff wings sticking out, looking like bat wings..." Impressed, Finger also realized the idea needed refining. "I got *Webster's Dictionary* down off the shelf and was hoping they would have a drawing of a bat, and sure enough they did. I said, 'Notice the ears, why don't we duplicate the ears?' I suggested he draw what looked like a cowl. He experimented with various cowls. I suggested that he bring the cowl nosepiece down and make him mysterious and not show any eyes at all." For many years, Kane either denied or tried to minimize Finger's role as Batman's godfather and developer.

To further flesh out their initial conception, Kane and Finger looked at silent film star Douglas Fairbanks' athletic portrayal of Zorro, who played at being an indolent rich fop by day, but by night was a dark-cloaked avenger. This also made a strong impression on the young Kane. From the pulps, Kane and pulp writer Gardner Fox drew on Doc Savage's scientific detection and reliance on gadgetry. The Shadow's aura of dark mystery and ruthlessness also found their way into the embryonic Batman's personality.

Another pulp character that affected Batman's conception was "the Bat-Man," a villainous humanoid bat featured in *The Spider* pulp magazine that resembled the later Man-Bat character (created by Batman illustrator Neal Adams and veteran cartoonist Frank Robbins, who wrote Batman scripts for a short time in the '70s). The Black Bat, a pulp crime-fighter who debuted in 1939, and wore an all-black costume with a scalloped cape and finned gauntlets, was actually published several months after Batman's debut in *Detective* #27, but within a year, Batman's plain gloves (worn to avoid leaving fingerprints) had mutated into the familiar finned gauntlets that Batman wears to this day despite countless modifications to his costume. The Black Bat was a lawyer who was blinded, his face horribly burned, when a criminal threw acid in his face, a plot device later used for the venerable Batman villain, Two-Face, former district attorney Harvey Dent, who was added to the continuity in *Detective Comics* #66 (Aug. 1942)

In his autobiography, Kane also acknowledged the impression created by *The Bat Whispers* (1931), an early talkie (a remake of a silent film entitled simply *The Bat*, which was adapted from the 1920 stage play of the same name by Mary Roberts Rinehart and Avery Hopwood), whose villain wore a bat head mask that cast ominous bat-like shadows, and who signaled his next intended victim with a bat-signal thrown on walls. Lee Falk's jungle avenger, *The Phantom*, with white slits for eyes, and twin automatics on his hips, and Dick Tracy's hyper-stylized art and grotesque villains were two more of Batman's inspirations from the Sunday funnies of the 1930s. Radio's *Green Hornet*, a wealthy crime-fighter with an arsenal of gadgets and a high-powered auto, who debuted in 1936, clearly influenced Batman as well. It also bears repeating that Batman's utility belt was directly inspired by pulp hero Doc Savage's bulletproof utility vest, which had pockets packed with small explosives, smoke bombs, and gas grenades, lock picks, and a whole arsenal of miniaturized crime-fighting equipment.

The first issue of *Batman*, features in the second, untitled story, the Caped Crusader being captured by villainous mad scientist Dr. Hugo Strange, and stripped of his utility belt, but he escapes by combining explosive chemicals secreted in his hollow

CRIMINALS ARE A SUPERSTITIOUS COWARDLY LOT, SO MY DISGUISE MUST BE ABLE TO STRIKE TERROR INTO THEIR HEARTS. I MUST BE A CREATURE OF THE NIGHT, BLACK, TERRIBLE . . A . . A . .

- AS IF IN ANSWER, A HUGE BAT FLIES IN THE OPEN WINDOW!
A BAT! THAT'S IT! IT'S AN OMEN.. I SHALL BECOME A BAT!

AND THUS IS BORN THIS WEIRD FIGURE OF THE DARK.. THIS AVENGER OF EVIL. 'THE BATMAN'

boot heels, a plot device directly lifted from Doc Savage.

In addition to his early input on Batman's costume, Finger also created Commissioner Gordon, the only other character from the first Batman story who is still in the continuity, and later christened Gotham City in *Detective Comics* #48, Initially, Gordon's police hunted the Bat-Man as a dangerous vigilante, but soon (in *Batman* #7, October/November 1941) deputized Batman and Robin as honorary members of the Gotham City police.

One aspect of the character that has given added power to Batman's continuing appeal is that, unlike Superman, who gets his powers from being an extraterrestrial, any human could be Batman, given the willpower to train his body, and learn criminology, chemistry, and the myriad other disciplines Batman mastered after fifteen years of study.

Artist Jim Aparo, who began drawing Batman in *The Brave and The Bold* in 1968, and probably drew more Batman stories than other artist before his death in 2005, credited Batman's longevity to his very human vulnerability. "You relate to Batman because he's a human being like everybody else; but, he's far greater than we are because he's very athletic and he's very honed in on his senses..."

What spawned Wayne's obsessive quest to mold himself into a crime fighter is the stuff of comic book legend: his parents' brutal murder. Thomas and Martha Wayne were shot to death before their son's eyes by Joe Chill, whom Batman finally brought to justice in "The Origin of Batman" (*Batman* #47, June/July 1948). It was later revealed in 'The First Batman" (*Detective* #235, Sept. 1956) that Chill only pretended to be a stick-up man and murdered the Waynes on orders from Lew Moxon, a gangster Thomas Wayne had sent to prison years earlier. Batman's origin was further revised by having Martha Wayne's weak heart give out after seeing her husband shot. This same story also credited Thomas Wayne's crude Bat-Man masquerade costume worn at a party years before his death, which is shown on that issue's cover, with providing the subconscious inspiration for Bruce's choice of crime-fighting attire.

An interesting aspect of Frank Miller and David Mazzuchelli's later *Batman: Year One* mini-series in 1987 was the way Miller ignored the re-worked 1950s origin in which Martha Wayne had a heart attack after seeing her husband shot. Mazzuchelli's art, illustrating Miller's script, clearly shows both Wayne parents getting shot, thereby restoring the original brutal power to Batman's origin.

Having forged himself into a mental and physical marvel to fight crime, Bruce Wayne, in an origin first recounted in *Detective* #33, realized he needed some kind of disguise. Thinking out loud, Wayne's musings have now entered the annals of comic book legend: "Criminals are a superstitious and cowardly lot, so my disguise must be able to strike terror into their hearts. I must be a creature of the night, black, terrible…a…a… Fortunately, at that moment, a bat flew through Wayne's window, inspiring Wayne to utter: "A bat! That's it! It's an Omen! I shall become a bat!" Thus was Batman's distinctive gray and dark blue costume born.

Another likely factor in Batman's longevity is his reliance on technology to fight crime. Writer Gardner Fox was quick to have Batman use a batarang and gas pellets and silk rope from his utility belt in *Detective Comics* #31 and #32. The Batplane (or Bat-Gyro) had debuted in *Detective* #31, and Batman soon got his distinctively styled Batmobile (*Detective* #48) to replace the nondescript high-powered red roadster he used in the early stories. In February 1941, Batman was driving a red roadster with a bat-shaped hood ornament. This vehicle is the first car referred to as "the Batmobile." March 1941 is the last time Batman uses the red roadster, though in its final appearance it was drawn without the distinctive bat-shaped hood design.

The classic Batmobile (fashioned from "special reinforced glass and steel", and equipped with "special tires") with an enclosed cab, high, scalloped tail fin and bat-mask on the front grille, didn't appear until *Batman* #5 (Spring, 1941). In the April-May 1946 issue of *Batman*, the Dynamic Duo had installed "new rocket and jet-propulsion gadgets" to enable it to travel with comet-like speed. By *Detective* #149 (May, 1949), the Batmobile had also been modified so that it could travel through water. This Batmobile design lasted until *Detective* #152 (Feb. 1950) when it was introduced in a story entitled, the "Batmobile of 1950." The cover for that issue showed Batman welding part of the hood with a torch, while Robin applied an electric drill to a front fender. Behind them, a blackboard showed schematics of the new Batmobile that revealed its many crime-fighting features, including a knife-edge steel nose for cutting through barriers, a roof mounted searchlight capable of displaying the bat symbol, a radar antenna in the tail fin, rear-mounted rocket tubes, and a small laboratory set-up in the rear of the cab. That massive Batmobile was used until *Batman* #164 (June, 1954), when a smaller, sleeker Batmobile convertible with a stylized bat head emblazoned on the hood replaced it, which was then (in 1968) replaced with the futuristic Batmobile from the television show in *Detective* #371.

By the late '60s, after Robin had been packed off to college, TV's Batmobile had been replaced by a smaller, low-slung convertible with a bat emblem on the

Two of the movie Batmobiles on display at the 2012 Comic-Con International: San Diego

hood. In the movies made after the Batman feature film of 1967, which used the George Barris-styled Batmobile from the TV show, the Batmobile had become a high-tech, machine-gun equipped vehicle used in both *Batman* (1989) and its sequel *Batman Returns* (1992), while the third and fourth films, *Batman Forever* (1995) and *Batman and Robin*, used different Batmobile designs for each film.

By the time of *Batman Begins* (2005), *The Dark Knight* (2008), and *The Dark Knight Rises* (2012) films, the Batmobile has become a blocky, functional military-style vehicle called "the Tumbler" that is capable of racing over rooftops and zooming through the air. Batman was also given a powerful new Bat-cycle equipped with machine guns and capable of blinding speed.

Considering the level of pop culture recognition Batman currently enjoys, thanks to his presence on cable TV as an animated figure, and the popularity of the last three big-budget Batman films, it's interesting to remember that he started out his career playing second fiddle to Superman, and stayed in second place for the first three decades of his existence. Although Batman got his own syndicated newspaper strip around the same

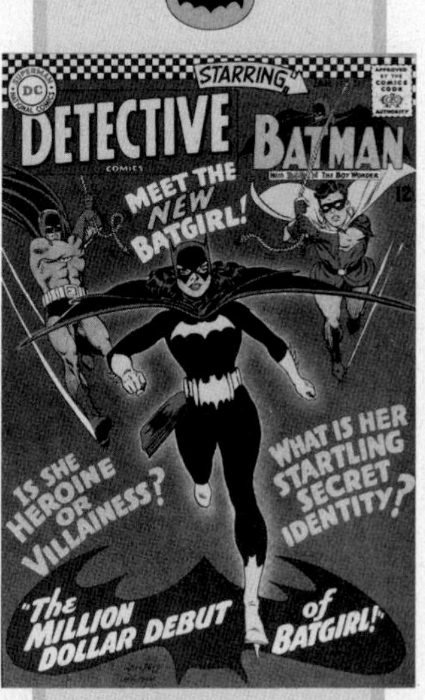

time Superman got his back in the early '40s, there was never a Batman radio program; he had to settle for guest starring on Superman's radio show. Up until the Bat-Mania craze of the mid-60s, spawned by his popular TV show, there were far more licensed Superman products throughout the '40s, '50s and early '60s.

By 1940, two years after he'd premiered, Superman already had a national fan club, the Supermen of America, and a small galaxy of licensed products, everything from t-shirts to paper dolls, wooden and plastic figurines, wind-up toys, puzzles, rings, and radio show premiums, followed in 1941 by series of 17 Technicolor theatrical cartoons, a pair of movie serials in 1948 and 1950, and then a long-running TV series beginning in 1951 that lasted until 1959 (it was one of the very first television shows filmed in color, an expensive proposition at the time).

Batman did beat Superman into the serial arena with the eponymous *Batman* serial in 1943, and then a follow-up entitled *Batman and Robin* in 1949. Unfortunately, both were cheap-looking affairs with none of the class of the higher-budgeted *Flash Gordon* serials.

The character had his first peak as a pop-culture figure in conjunction with the 1966 *Batman* television show, which in its first year was a ratings phenomenon that spawned a tidal wave of licensed Batman products. The offerings ran from sheets to wallpaper to toys, games, Halloween costumes, trading cards, and any other product you can think of, including All Star's Batman Slam Bang Vanilla Ice Cream from 1966, which featured Batman and Robin graphics on its packaging. However, when the Batman TV series was cancelled in 1968, it seemed that the era of the campy Batman was over. But what was there to replace it?

In retrospect, what Denny O'Neil, Neal Adams and Dick Giordano did seems an obvious choice: a return to Batman's roots as a dark, mysterious avenger. However, in 1968 and '69, it was a revelation for comics fans raised on the campy, sci-fi and fantasy-infused Batman stories of the previous decade to see Batman acting as a real detective and battling some genuinely scary menaces. As Neal Adams once noted, it was no secret that Batman was lousy in the '60s. The campy storylines and villains may have been fun, but they took the character far afield from his roots as a grim avenger who routinely brutalized or gunned down his enemies.

Since his creative resurgence in the late '60s, largely due to the talents of O'Neil,

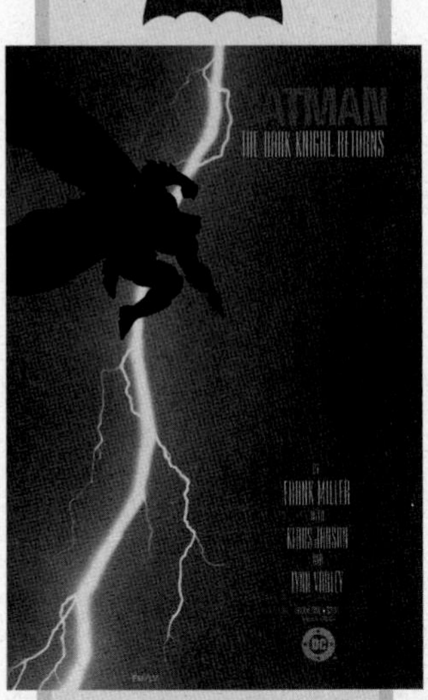

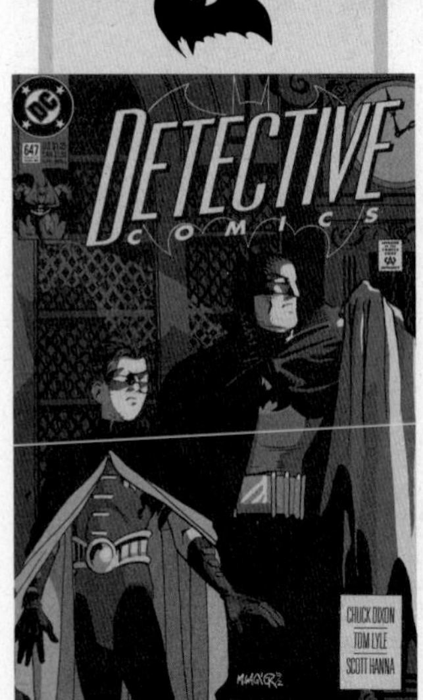

Adams, Giordano, and Frank Robbins, Batman has gone through a dizzying series of continuity, costume, and character changes, including having Dick Grayson replaced by several different Robins. The Bat-universe has gotten increasingly dark, as well. The Joker is no longer the clownish criminal he became in the '50s and '60s; he morphed back into the psychotic murderer he was in the first issue of *Batman*, poisoning people right and left with gleeful abandon. In Alan Moore and Brian Bolland's superb one-shot graphic novel, *The Killing Joke* (1988), the Joker cripples Barbara Gordon and then kidnaps and tortures Commissioner Gordon before Batman finally stops him. Also in 1988, The Joker also murdered then-current Robin, Jason Todd, based on the phoned-in votes of fans. But no matter how dark he gets, the Joker remains a white-faced green-haired super criminal who favors bad jokes and garish purple suits.

With the advent of the DC's *Crisis on Infinite Earths* miniseries (1985), Batman's continuity was retroactively revised in order to increase his appeal to modern readers, which included erasing the Earth-Two Batman, and revising Batman's origin so that Alfred Pennyworth raised him instead of his guardian, the corrupt Phillip Wayne. In addition, the revised continuity eliminated Batman as one of the founding members of the Justice League, though he did become the leader of the team in 1987, for a short while, any way.

Frank Miller's blockbuster four-issue miniseries, *Batman: The Dark Knight Returns* (1986), went a long way toward redefining Batman's persona in the popular imagination. It became one of the best-selling graphic novels ever, and the ripples of Miller's darker reimagining of the character are still being felt to this day. In it, an aging, retired Batman returns to fight crime, but is opposed by not only the Gotham City administration, but also by the U.S. government, and his old ally, Superman. The story ends with Batman ostensibly dead, but in reality he has dropped out of sight with Robin, Oliver Queen (the former Green Arrow), and some other followers to create an army that will return and establish order in the now-blighted United States.

Even his costume has gone through numerous changes. In the first year of his existence, Batman's costume went through numerous subtle changes to his gloves, belt and cowl, but by 1940, his costume had coalesced into the appearance it was to have until the "New Look" in 1964. After that, his costume stayed pretty much the same, though over the years, there were variations of it, including "The Rainbow Batman," (*Detective Comics* #241) "The Zebra Batman," (*Detective Comics* #275), even a kilt-clad Batman in *Detective* #198 ("The Lord of Batmanor").

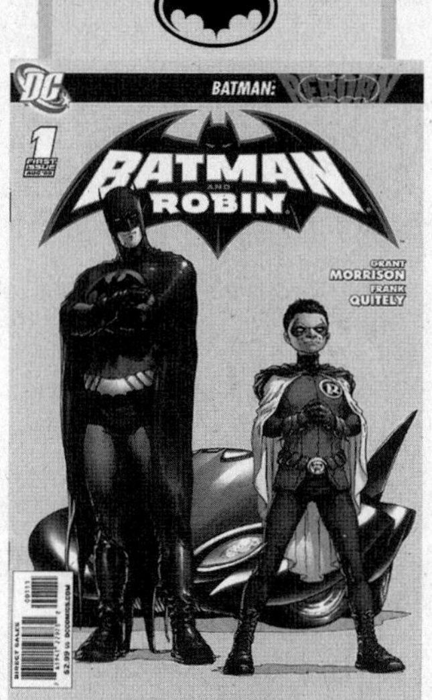

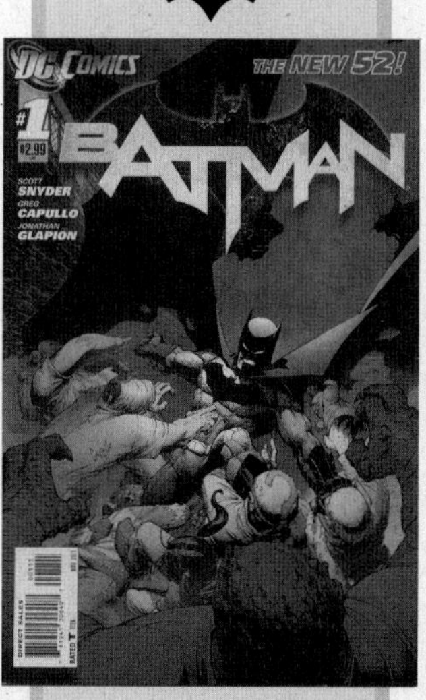

Starting with Tim Burton's 1989 film, Batman's costume has become an all-black, bulletproof bodysuit, which it has remained with subtle variations depending on who is writing and drawing the character. Kelley Jones, for instance, gave Batman perhaps the longest ears on his cowl of any artist. Following Frank Miller's *The Dark Knight Returns*, many artists have adopted the larger, military-style pouches on his utility belt, replacing the narrow cylinders of earlier decades.

Despite the dizzying series of retconned changes to his histories, and all the enemies he's defeated or killed, Batman's most notable accomplishment is his longevity and continued popularity. On his 75th anniversary, he deserves to be remembered as one of only three characters that have remained in continuous publication since their introductions (the others being Superman and Wonder Woman).

So, *Viva Batman*, long may his distinctive bat-shaped shadow loom over Gotham City!

COMICCONNECT HAS SOLD THE TOP THREE MOST EXPENSIVE COMICS OF ALL TIME

COMIC CONNECT

WWW.COMICCONNECT.COM

FOR 20 OF THE LAST 25 YEARS, THE EXPERTS AT COMICCONNECT HAVE HELD THE RECORD FOR SELLING THE MOST EXPENSIVE COMIC BOOK. THIS ACCOMPLISHMENT INCLUDES SELLING THE REIGNING GUINNESS WORLD RECORD OF $2.161 MILLION FOR THE HIGHEST GRADED COPY OF ACTION COMICS #1.

$2,161,000

YOU HAVE A CHOICE WHEN SELLING YOUR COMICS.
CHOOSE SMART. CHOOSE COMICCONNECT.

873 BROADWAY, SUITE 201, NEW YORK, NY 10003
P: 888.779.7377 | INT'L: 001.212.895.3999 | F: 212.260.4304
www.comicconnect.com | support@comicconnect.com

COMIC CONNECT

WWW.COMICCONNECT.COM

WORLD'S PREMIER ONLINE COMIC MARKETPLACE & AUCTIONEER

SOLD!
$1,500,000

SOLD!
$1,100,000

SOLD!
$1,000,000

SOLD!
$575,000

SOLD!
$465,000

SOLD!
$436,000

SOLD!
$2,161,000
WORLD RECORD

SOLD!
$345,000

SOLD!
$317,200

- In three years, we sold 20 copies of Action 1 - nobody else comes close!
- ComicConnect was the first to sell a comic book for $1 MILLION!
- ComicConnect holds the Guinness World Record at $2.161 MILLION!
- The three most expensive comics ever sold were all brokered by us!
- We have the best buyers and sellers. ComicConnect is where the action is!

IMMEDIATE CASH ADVANCES - SUPER FAST PAYMENT - FREE PRINT & ONLINE COLOR EVENT AUCTION CATALOG

INTEREST FREE TIME PAYMENTS - PHONE & ABSENTEE BIDDING - SMALL COMMISSION - NO BUYER'S PREMIUM

CONTACT US TODAY FOR A FREE CONSULTATION!

873 BROADWAY, SUITE 201, NEW YORK, NY 10003
P: 888.779.7377 | INT'L: 001.212.895.3999 | F: 212.260.4304
www.comicconnect.com | support@comicconnect.com

Abbott and Costello #2 © STJ

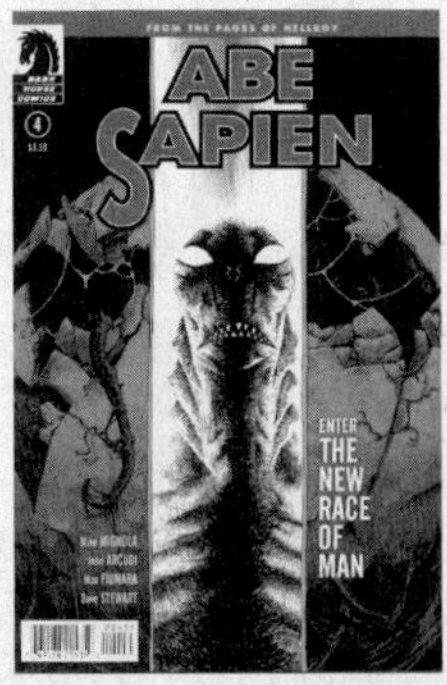

Abe Sapien #4 © Mike Mignola

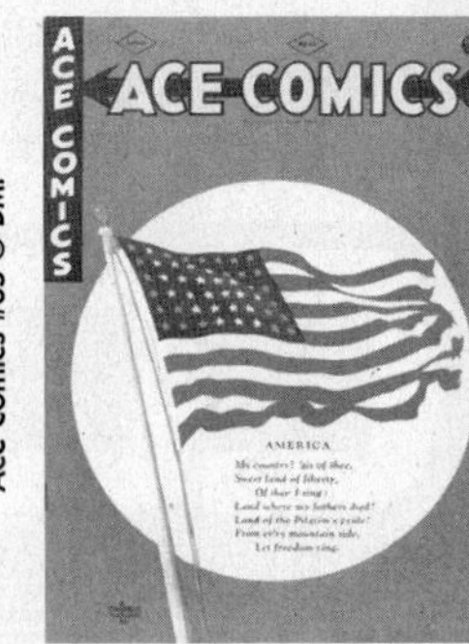

Ace Comics #65 © DMP

GD VG FN VF VF/NM NM-
2.0 4.0 6.0 8.0 9.0 9.2

The correct title listing for each comic book can be determined by consulting the indicia (publication data) on the beginning interior pages of the comic. The official title is determined by those words of the title in capital letters only, and not by what is on the cover. Titles are listed in this book as if they were one word, ignoring spaces, hyphens, and apostrophes, to make finding titles easier. Exceptions are made in rare cases. Comic books listed should be assumed to be in color unless noted "B&W".

Comic publishers are invited to send us sample copies for possible inclusion in future guides.

PRICING IN THIS GUIDE: Prices for **GD 2.0** (Good), **VG 4.0** (Very Good), **FN 6.0** (Fine), **VF 8.0** (Very Fine), **VF/NM 9.0** (Very Fine/Near Mint),and **NM– 9.2** (Near Mint–) are listed in whole U.S. dollars except for prices below $7 which show dollars and cents. **The minimum price listed is $3.00**, the cover price for current new comics. Many books listed at this price can be found in $1.00 boxes at conventions and dealers stores.

A-1 (See A-One)

ABADAZAD
CrossGen (Code 6): Mar, 2004 - No. 3, May, 2004 ($2.95)

1-3-Ploog-a/c; DeMatteis-s 3.00
1-2nd printing with new cover 3.00

ABATTOIR
Radical Comics: Oct, 2010 - No. 6, Aug, 2011 ($3.99/$3.50, limited series)

1-($3.99) Cansino-a/Levin & Peterí-s 4.00
2-6-($3.50) 3.50

ABBIE AN' SLATS (...With Becky No. 1-4) (See Comics On Parade, Fight for Love, Giant Comics Edition 2, Giant Comics Editions #1, Sparkler Comics, Tip Topper, Treasury of Comics, & United Comics)
United Features Syndicate: 1940; March, 1948 - No. 4, Aug, 1948 (Reprints)

	GD	VG	FN	VF	VF/NM	NM-
Single Series 25 ('40)	40	80	120	244	402	560
Single Series 28	33	66	99	194	317	440
1 (1948)	17	34	51	98	154	210
2-4: 3-r/Sparkler #68-72	10	20	30	58	79	100

ABBOTT AND COSTELLO (...Comics)(See Giant Comics Editions #1 & Treasury of Comics)
St. John Publishing Co.: Feb, 1948 - No. 40, Sept, 1956 (Mort Drucker-a in most issues)

	GD	VG	FN	VF	VF/NM	NM-
1	71	142	213	454	777	1100
2	38	76	114	228	369	510
3-9 (#8, 8/49; #9, 2/50)	27	54	81	158	259	360
10-Son of Sinbad story by Kubert (new)	32	64	96	188	307	425
11,13-20 (#11, 10/50; #13, 8/51; #15, 12/52)	19	38	57	109	172	235
12-Movie issue	20	40	60	115	185	255
21-30: 28-r/#8. 29,30-Painted-c	14	28	42	82	121	160
31-40: 33,38-Reprints	11	22	33	64	90	115
3-D #1 (11/53, 25¢)-Infinity-c	32	64	96	188	307	425

ABBOTT AND COSTELLO (TV)
Charlton Comics: Feb, 1968 - No. 22, Aug, 1971 (Hanna-Barbera)

	GD	VG	FN	VF	VF/NM	NM-
1	7	14	21	46	86	125
2	4	8	12	27	44	60
3-10	3	6	9	21	33	45
11-22	3	6	9	17	26	35

ABC (See America's Best TV Comics)

ABC: A-Z (one-shots)
America's Best Comics: Nov, 2005 - July, 2006 ($3.99, one-shots)

... Greyshirt and Cobweb (1/06) character bios; Veitch-s/a; Gebbie-a; Dodson-c 4.00
... Terra Obscura and Splash Brannigan (3/06) character bios; Barta-a; Dodson-c 4.00
... Tom Strong and Jack B. Quick (11/05) character bios; Sprouse-a; Nowlan-a; Dodson-c 4.00
... Top Ten and Teams (7/06) character bios; Ha & Cannon-a; Veitch-a; Dodson-c 4.00

ABE SAPIEN... (Hellboy character)
Dark Horse Comics: Apr, 2013 - Present ($3.50)

1-11: 1,2-Subtitled "Dark and Terrible"; Mignola & Allie-s/Fiumara-a/c. 8-Oeming-a 3.50
...: Drums of the Dead (3/98, $2.95) 1-Thompson-a. Hellboy back-up; Mignola-s/a/c 4.00
...: The Abyssal Plain (6/10 - No. 2, 7/10, $3.50) 1,2-Mignola & Arcudi-s/Snejbjerg-a 3.50
...: The Devil Does Not Jest (9/11 - No. 2, 10/11, $3.50) Mignola & Arcudi-s. 1-Two covers by Johnson & Francavilla 3.50
...: The Drowning (2/08 - No. 5, 6/08, $2.99) 1-5-Mignola-s/c; Alexander-a 3.50
...: The Haunted Boy (10/09, $3.50) 1-Mignola & Arcudi-s/Reynolds-a/Johnson-c 3.50

A. BIZARRO
DC Comics: Jul, 1999 - No. 4, Oct, 1999 (2.50, limited series)

1-4-Gerber-s/Bright-a 3.00

ABOMINATIONS (See Hulk)
Marvel Comics: Dec, 1996 - No. 3, Feb, 1997 ($1.50, limited series)

1-3-Future Hulk storyline 3.00

ABRAHAM LINCOLN LIFE STORY (See Dell Giants)

ABRAHAM STONE
Marvel Comics (Epic): July, 1995 - No. 2, Aug, 1995 ($6.95, limited series)

1,2-Joe Kubert-s/a 7.00

ABSENT-MINDED PROFESSOR, THE (See Shaggy Dog and the...)
Dell Publishing Co.: Apr, 1961 (Disney)

	GD	VG	FN	VF	VF/NM	NM-
Four Color #1199-Movie, photo-c; variant "Double Feature" edition; has a "Fabulous Formula" strip on back-c	7	14	21	48	89	130

ABSOLUTE VERTIGO
DC Comics (Vertigo): Winter, 1995 (99¢, mature)

	GD	VG	FN	VF	VF/NM	NM-
nn-1st app. Preacher. Previews upcoming titles including Jonah Hex: Riders of the Worm, The Invisibles (King Mob), The Eaters, Ghostdancing & Preacher	1	2	3	5	7	9

ABYSS, THE (Movie)
Dark Horse Comics: June, 1989 - No. 2, July, 1989 ($2.25, limited series)

1,2-Adaptation of film; Kaluta & Moebius-a 3.00

ACCELERATE
DC Comics (Vertigo): Aug, 2000 - No. 4, Nov, 2000 ($2.95, limited series)

1-4-Pander Bros.-a/Kadrey-s 3.00

ACCLAIM ADVENTURE ZONE
Acclaim Books: 1997 ($4.50, digest size)

1-Short stories of Turok, Troublemakers, Ninjak and others 4.50

ACE COMICS
David McKay Publications: Apr, 1937 - No. 151, Oct-Nov, 1949 (All contain some newspaper strip reprints)

	GD	VG	FN	VF	VF/NM	NM-
1-Jungle Jim by Alex Raymond, Blondie, Ripley's Believe It Or Not, Krazy Kat begin (1st app. of each)	320	640	960	2240	3920	5600
2	92	184	276	538	982	1425
3-5	63	126	189	403	689	975
6-10	47	94	141	296	498	700
11-The Phantom begins (1st app., 2/38) (in brown costume)	129	258	387	826	1413	2000
12-20	39	78	117	234	385	535
21-25,27-30	34	68	102	204	332	460
26-Origin & 1st app. Prince Valiant (5/39); begins series?	116	232	348	742	1271	1800
31-40: 37-Krazy Kat ends	22	44	66	132	216	300
41-60	15	30	45	88	137	185
61-64,66-76-(7/43; last 68 pgs.)	14	28	42	80	115	150
65-(8/42)-Flag-c	15	30	45	88	137	185
77-84 (3/44; all 60 pgs.)	12	24	36	67	94	120
85-99 (52 pgs.)	11	22	33	60	83	105
100 (7/45; last 52 pgs.)	12	24	36	67	94	120
101-134: 128-(11/47)-Brick Bradford begins. 134-Last Prince Valiant (all 36 pgs.)	10	20	30	56	76	95
135-151: 135-(6/48)-Lone Ranger begins	9	18	27	52	69	85

ACE KELLY (See Tops Comics & Tops In Humor)

ACE KING (See Adventures of Detective...)

ACES
Acme Press (Eclipse): Apr, 1988 - No. 5, Dec, 1988 ($2.95, B&W, magazine)

1-5 3.00

ACES HIGH
E.C. Comics: Mar-Apr, 1955 - No. 5, Nov-Dec, 1955

	GD	VG	FN	VF	VF/NM	NM-
1-Not approved by code	25	50	75	200	320	440
2	14	28	42	112	181	250
3-5	13	26	39	104	165	225

NOTE: *All have stories by* ***Davis, Evans, Krigstein,*** *and* ***Wood. Evans*** *c-1-5.*

ACES HIGH
Gemstone Publishing: Apr, 1999 - No. 5, Aug, 1999 ($2.50)

1-5-Reprints E.C. issues 4.00
Annual 1 ($13.50) r/#1-5 14.00

ACME NOVELTY LIBRARY, THE
Fantagraphics Books: Winter 1993-94 - Present (quarterly, various sizes)

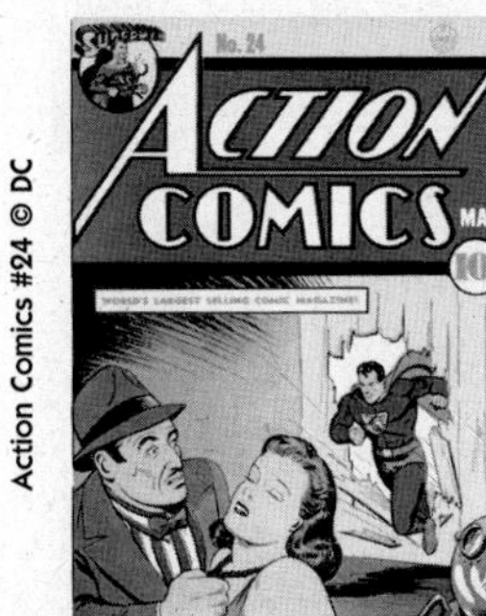

Action Comics #24 © DC

Action Comics #130 © DC

Action Comics #242 © DC

	GD 2.0	VG 4.0	FN 6.0	VF 8.0	VF/NM 9.0	NM- 9.2
1-Introduces Jimmy Corrigan; Chris Ware-s/a in all	1	3	4	6	8	10
1-2nd and later printings						4.00
2,3: 2-Quimby						6.00
4-Sparky's Best Comics & Stories	1	2	3	4	5	7
5-12: Jimmy Corrigan in all						5.00
13,15-($10.95-c)						11.00
14-($12.95-c) Concludes Jimmy Corrigan saga						13.00
16,19-($15.95, hardcover) Rusty Brown						16.00
17-($16.95, hardcover) Rusty Brown						17.00
18-($17.95, hardcover)						18.00
Jimmy Corrigan, The Smartest Kid on Earth (2000, Pantheon Books, Hardcover, $27.50, 380 pgs.) Collects Jimmy Corrigan stories; folded dust jacket						27.50
Jimmy Corrigan, The Smartest Kid on Earth (2003, Softcover, $17.95)						18.00

NOTE: *Multiple printings exist for most issues.*

ACROSS THE UNIVERSE: THE DC UNIVERSE STORIES OF ALAN MOORE (Also see DC Universe: The Stories of Alan Moore)
DC Comics: 2003 ($19.95, TPB)

	GD 2.0	VG 4.0	FN 6.0	VF 8.0	VF/NM 9.0	NM- 9.2
nn-Reprints selected Moore stories from '85-'87; Superman, Batman, Swamp Thing app.						20.00

ACTION ADVENTURE (War) (Formerly Real Adventure)
Gillmor Magazines: V1#2, June, 1955 - No. 4, Oct, 1955

	GD 2.0	VG 4.0	FN 6.0	VF 8.0	VF/NM 9.0	NM- 9.2
V1#2-4	6	12	18	31	38	45

ACTION COMICS (...Weekly #601-642) (Also see The Comics Magazine #1, More Fun #14-17 & Special Edition) (Also see Promotional Comics section)
National Periodical Publ./Detective Comics/DC Comics: 6/38 - No. 583, 9/86; No. 584, 1/87 - No. 904, Oct, 2011

	GD 2.0	VG 4.0	FN 6.0	VF 8.0	VF/NM 9.0	NM- 9.2
1-Origin & 1st app. Superman by Siegel & Shuster, Marco Polo, Tex Thompson, Pep Morgan, Chuck Dawson & Scoop Scanlon; 1st app. Zatara & Lois Lane; Superman story missing 4 pgs. which were included when reprinted in Superman #1; Clark Kent works for Daily Star; story continued in #2	130,000	260,000	390,000	900,000	1,500,000	2,100,000
1-Reprint, Oversize 13-1/2x10". **WARNING:** This comic is an exact reprint of the original except for its size. DC published it in 1974 with a second cover titling it as a Famous First Edition. There have been many reported cases of the outer cover being removed and the interior sold as the original edition. The reprint with the new outer cover removed is practically worthless. See Famous First Edition for value.						
2-O'Mealia non-Superman covers thru #6	8333	16,666	25,000	62,498	106,249	150,000
3 (Scarce)-Superman apps. in costume in only one panel	5556	11,112	16,668	41,670	70,835	100,000
4-6: 6-1st Jimmy Olsen (called office boy)	2778	5556	8334	20,835	35,418	50,000
7-2nd Superman cover	12,778	25,556	38,334	95,835	162,918	230,000
8,9	2000	4000	6000	15,000	25,500	36,000
10-3rd Superman cover by Shuster; splash panel used as cover art for Superman #1	8333	16,666	25,000	62,498	106,249	150,000
11,14: 1st X-Ray Vision? 14-Clip Carson begins, ends #41; Zatara-c	1000	2000	3000	7500	12,750	18,000
12-Has 1 panel Batman ad for Det. #27 (5/39); Zatara sci-fi cover	1444	2888	4332	10,830	18,415	26,000
13-Shuster Superman-c; last Scoop Scanlon; centerspread has a 2-page ad for Superman #1	5000	10,000	15,000	37,500	56,250	75,000
15-Guardineer Superman-c; has ad mentioning Detective Comics and Batman; full page ad for New York World's Fair 1939 with 25¢-c	1833	3666	5499	13,748	23,374	33,000
16-Has full page ad and 1 panel ad for New York World's Fair 1939 25¢ cover edition	583	1166	1749	4373	7437	10,500
17-Superman cover; last Marco Polo; full page ad for New York World's Fair 1939 with 15¢-c	1389	2778	4167	10,418	17,709	25,000
18-Origin 3 Aces; has a 1 panel ad for New York World's Fair 1939 at the end of the Superman story (ad also in #16,17,19)	583	1166	1749	4373	7437	10,500
19-Superman covers begin	1306	2612	3918	9795	16,648	23,500
20-The 'S' left off Superman's chest; Clark Kent works at 'Daily Star'	1278	2556	3834	9585	16,293	23,000
21-Has 2 ads for More Fun #52 (1st Spectre)	524	1048	1572	3825	6763	9700
22	514	1028	1542	3750	6625	9500
23-1st app. Luthor (w/red hair) & Black Pirate; Black Pirate by Moldoff; 1st mention of The Daily Planet (4/40)-Has 1 panel ad for Spectre in More Fun	1400	2800	4200	10,500	18,250	26,000
24,25: 24-Kent at Daily Planet. 25-Last app. Gargantua T. Potts, Tex Thompson's sidekick	459	918	1377	3350	5925	8500
26-28,30	423	846	1269	3000	5250	7500
29-1st Lois Lane-c (10/40)	449	898	1347	3278	5789	8300
31,32: 32-Intro/1st app. Krypto Ray Gun in Superman story by Burnley	300	600	900	1950	3375	4800
33-Origin Mr. America; Superman by Burnley; has half page ad for All Star Comics #3	300	600	900	2010	3505	5000
34,35,38,39	297	594	891	1901	3251	4600
36,40: 36-Classic robot-c. 40-(9/41)-Intro/1st app. Star Spangled Kid & Stripesy; Jerry Siegel photo	300	600	900	2070	3635	5200
37-Origin Congo Bill	300	600	900	1950	3375	4800
41	265	530	795	1694	2897	4100
42-1st app./origin Vigilante; Bob Daley becomes Fat Man; origin Mr. America's magic flying carpet; The Queen Bee & Luthor app; Black Pirate ends; not in #41	284	568	852	1818	3109	4400
43-46,48-50: 44-Fat Man's i.d. revealed to Mr. America. 45-1st app. Stuff (Vigilante's oriental sidekick)	258	516	774	1651	2826	4000
47-1st Luthor cover in comics (4/42)	343	686	1029	2400	4200	6000
51-1st app. The Prankster	245	490	735	1568	2684	3800
52-Fat Man & Mr. America become the Ameri-commandos; origin Vigilante retold; classic Superman and back-ups-c	300	600	900	2010	3505	5000
53-56,59,60: 56-Last Fat Man. 59-Kubert Vigilante begins?, ends #70. 60-First app. Lois Lane as Super-woman	213	426	639	1363	2332	3300
57-2nd Lois Lane-c in Action (3rd anywhere, 2/43)	219	438	657	1402	2401	3400
58-"Slap a Jap-c"	265	530	795	1694	2897	4100
61-Historic Atomic Radiation-c (6/43)	245	490	735	1568	2684	3800
62-Japan war-c	219	438	657	1402	2401	3400
63-Japan war-c; last 3 Aces	206	412	618	1318	2259	3200
64-Intro Toyman	187	374	561	1197	2049	2900
65-70	148	296	444	947	1624	2300
71-79: 74-Last Mr. America	116	232	348	742	1271	1800
80-2nd app. & 1st Mr. Mxyztplk-c (1/45)	145	290	435	921	1586	2250
81-88,90: 83-Intro Hocus & Pocus	107	214	321	680	1165	1650
89-Classic rainbow cover	116	232	348	742	1271	1800
91-99: 93-X-Mas-c. 99-1st small logo (8/46)	87	174	261	553	952	1350
100	129	258	387	826	1413	2000
101-Nuclear explosion-c (10/46)	194	388	582	1242	2121	3000
102-Mxyztplk-c	87	174	261	553	952	1350
103-107,109-120: 105,117-X-Mas-c	79	158	237	502	864	1225
108-Classic molten metal-c	92	184	276	584	1717	1425
121,122,124-126,128-140: 135,136,138-Zatara by Kubert	76	152	228	486	831	1175
123-(8/48) 1st time Superman flies, not leaps	81	162	243	518	884	1250
127-Vigilante by Kubert; Tommy Tomorrow begins (12/48, see Real Fact #6)	77	154	231	493	847	1200
141-150,152-157,159-161: 156-Lois as Super Woman. 161- Last 52 pgs.	74	148	222	470	810	1150
151-Luthor/Mr. Mxyztplk/Prankster team-up	90	180	270	576	988	1400
158-Origin Superman retold	139	278	417	883	1517	2150
162-180: 168,176-Used in **POP**, pg. 90. 173-Robot-c	71	142	213	454	777	1100
181-201: 191-Intro. Janu in Congo Bill. 198-Last Vigilante. 201-Last pre-code issue	68	136	204	435	743	1050
202-220,232: 212-(1/56)-Includes 1956 Superman calendar that is part of story. 232-1st Curt Swan-c in Action	58	116	174	371	636	900
221-231,233-240: 221-1st S.A. issue. 224-1st Golden Gorilla story. 228-(5/57)-Kongorilla in Congo Bill story (Congorilla try-out)	50	100	150	315	533	750
241,243-251: 241-Batman x-over. 248-Origin/1st app. Congorilla; Congo Bill renamed Congorilla. 251-Last Tommy Tomorrow	42	84	126	265	445	625
242-Origin & 1st app. Brainiac (7/58); 1st mention of Shrunken City of Kandor	250	500	875	2500	6000	9500
252-Origin & 1st app. Supergirl (5/59); 1st app. Metallo	270	540	945	2700	6850	11,000
253-2nd app. Supergirl	74	148	222	470	810	1150
254-1st meeting of Bizarro & Superman-c/story; 3rd app. Supergirl	51	102	153	318	539	760
255-1st Bizarro Lois Lane-c/story & both Bizarros leave Earth to make Bizarro World; 4th app. Supergirl	42	84	126	267	451	635
256-260: 259-Red Kryptonite used	32	64	96	188	307	425
261-1st X-Kryptonite which gave Streaky his powers; last Congorilla in Action; origin & 1st app. Streaky The Super Cat	36	72	108	216	351	485
262,264-266,268-270	28	56	84	165	270	375
263-Origin Bizarro World (continues in #264)	36	72	108	211	343	475
267(8/60)-3rd Legion app; 1st app. Chameleon Boy, Colossal Boy, & Invisible Kid, 1st app. of Supergirl as Superwoman.	60	120	180	381	653	925
271-275,277-282: 274-Lois Lane as Superwoman. 280-Brief origin of Superman & Supergirl retold; Brainiac-c. 282-Last 10¢ issue	24	48	72	142	234	325
276(5/61)-6th Legion app; 1st app. Brainiac 5, Phantom Girl, Triplicate Girl, Bouncing Boy, Sun Boy, & Shrinking Violet; Supergirl joins Legion	48	96	144	302	514	725
283(12/61)-Legion of Super-Villains app. 1st 12¢	13	26	39	89	195	300
284(1/62)-Mon-El app.	13	26	39	89	195	300
285(2/62)-12th Legion app; Brainiac 5 cameo; Supergirl's existence revealed to world; JFK & Jackie cameos	22	44	66	153	337	520

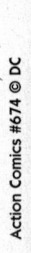

Action Comics #376 © DC

Action Comics #674 © DC

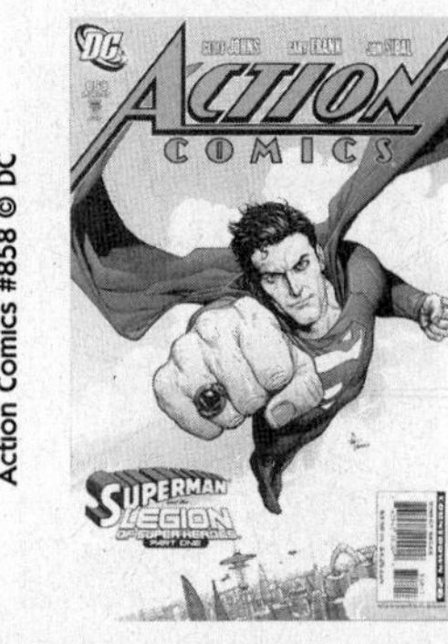

Action Comics #858 © DC

GD 2.0 | VG 4.0 | FN 6.0 | VF 8.0 | VF/NM 9.0 | NM- 9.2

286-287,289-292,294-299: 286(3/62)-Legion of Super Villains app. 287(4/62)-15th Legion app. (cameo). 289(6/62)-16th Legion app. (Adult); Lightning Man & Saturn Woman's marriage 1st revealed. 290(7/62)-Legion app. (cameo); Phantom Girl app. 1st Supergirl emergency squad. 291-1st meeting Supergirl & Mr. Mxyzptlk. 292-2nd app. Superhorse (see Adv.#293). 297-General Zod, Phantom Zone villains & Mon-El app. 298-General Zod app.; Legion cameo 11 22 33 76 163 250
288-Mon-El app.; r-origin Supergirl 12 24 36 79 170 260
293-Origin Comet (Superhorse) 13 26 39 89 195 300
300-(5/63) 13 26 39 86 188 290
301-303,305,307,308,310-312,315-320: 307-Saturn Girl app. 317-Death of Nor-Kan of Kandor. 319-Shrinking Violet app. 9 18 27 58 114 170
304,306,313: 304-Origin/1st app. Black Flame (9/63). 306-Brainiac 5, Mon-El app. 313-Batman app. 9 18 27 59 117 175
309-(2/64)-Legion app.; Batman & Robin-c & cameo; JFK app. (he died 11/22/63; on stands last week of Dec, 1963) 9 18 27 61 123 185
314-Retells origin Supergirl; J.L.A. x-over 9 18 27 59 117 175
321-333,335-339: 336-Origin Akvar (Flamebird) 7 14 21 48 89 130
334-Giant G-20; origin Supergirl, Streaky, Superhorse & Legion (all-r) 10 20 30 66 138 210
340-Origin, 1st app. of the Parasite; 2 pg. pin-up 11 22 33 76 163 250
341,344,350,358: 341-Batman app. in Supergirl back-up story. 344-Batman x-over. 350-Batman, Green Arrow & Green Lantern app. in Supergirl back-up story. 358-Superboy meets Supergirl 6 12 18 41 76 110
342,343,345,346,348,349,351-357,359: 342-UFO story. 345-Allen Funt/Candid Camera story. 6 12 18 40 73 105
347,360-Giant Supergirl G-33,G-45; 347-Origin Comet-r plus Bizarro story. 360-Legion app.-r; r/origin Supergirl 8 16 24 55 105 155
361-2nd app. Parasite 6 12 18 38 69 100
362-364,367-372,374-378: 362-366-Leper/Death story. 370-New facts about Superman's origin. 376-Last Supergirl in Action; last 12¢-c. 377-Legion begins (thru #392) 5 10 15 33 57 80
365,366: 365-JLA & Legion app. 366-JLA app. 5 10 15 34 60 85
373-Giant Supergirl G-57; Legion-r 8 16 24 51 96 140
379-399,401: 388-Sgt. Rock app. 392-Batman-c/app.; last Legion in Action; Saturn Girl gets new costume. 393-401-All Superman issues 3 6 9 19 30 40
400 4 8 12 23 37 50
402-Last 15¢ issue; Superman vs. Supergirl duel 3 6 9 20 31 42
403-413: All 52 pg. issues. 411-Origin Eclipso-(r). 413-Metamorpho begins, ends #418 3 6 9 19 30 40
414-424: 419-Intro. Human Target. 421-Intro Capt. Strong; Green Arrow begins. 422,423-Origin Human Target 2 4 6 9 13 16
425-Neal Adams-a(p); The Atom begins 3 6 9 15 22 28
426-431,433-436,438,439 2 4 6 8 10 12
432-1st Bronze Age Toyman app. (2/74) 2 4 6 13 18 22
437,443-(100 pg. Giants) 4 8 12 27 44 60
440-1st Grell-a on Green Arrow 2 4 6 10 14 18
441,442,444-448: 441-Grell-a on Green Arrow continues 2 4 6 8 10 12
449-(68 pgs.) 2 4 6 10 14 18
450-465,467-470,474-483,486,489-499: 454-Last Atom. 456-Grell Jaws-c. 458-Last Green Arrow 1 2 3 4 5 7
466,485,487,488: 466-Batman, Flash app. 485-Adams-c. 487,488-(44 pgs.). 487-Origin & 1st app. Microwave Man; origin Atom retold 1 2 3 5 7 9
471-(5/77) 1st app. Faora Hu-Ul 2 4 6 12 16 20
472,473-Faora app. 473-Faora, General Zod app. 2 4 6 9 13 16
481-483,485-492,495-499,501-505,507,508-Whitman variants (low print run; none show issue # on cover) 2 4 6 8 10 12
484-Earth II Superman & Lois Lane wed; 40th anniversary issue(6/78) 2 4 6 8 10 12
484-Variant includes 3-D Superman punchout doll in cello. pack; 4 different inserts; Canadian promo?) 3 6 9 17 26 35
500-($1.00, 68 pgs.)-Infinity-c; Superman life story retold; shows Legion statues in museum 2 4 6 8 10 12
501-543,545,547-551: 511-514-Airwave II solo stories. 513-The Atom begins. 517-Aquaman begins; ends #541. 521-1st app. The Vixen. 532,536-New Teen Titans cameo. 535,536-Omega Men app. 551-Starfire becomes Red-Star 5.00
504,505,507,508-Whitman variants (no cover price) 2 4 6 8 10 12
544-(6/83, Mando paper, 68 pgs.)-45th Anniversary issue; origins new Luthor & Brainiac; Omega Men cameo; Shuster-a (pin-up); article by Siegel 1 2 3 4 5 7
546-J.L.A., New Teen Titans app. 1 2 3 5 6 8
552,553-Animal Man-c & app. (2/84 & 3/84) 6.00
554-582 3.00
583-(9/86) Alan Moore scripts; last Earth 1 Superman story (cont'd from Superman #423)

GD 2.0 | VG 4.0 | FN 6.0 | VF 8.0 | VF/NM 9.0 | NM- 9.2

2 4 6 8 10 12
584-(1/87) Byrne-a begins; New Teen Titans app. 6.00
585-599: 586-Legends x-over. 596-Millennium x-over; Spectre app. 598-1st Checkmate 3.00
600-($2.50, 84 pgs., 5/88) 6.00
601-610,619-642: (#601-642 are weekly issues) ($1.50, 52 pgs.) 601-Re-intro The Secret Six; death of Katma Tui 4.00
611-618: 611-614-Catwoman stories (new costume in #611). 613-618-Nightwing stories 4.00
643-Superman & monthly issues begin again; Perez-c/a/scripts begin; swipes cover to Superman #1 6.00
644-649,651-661,663-666,668-673,675-683: 645-1st app. Maxima. 654-Part 3 of Batman storyline. 655-Free extra 8 pgs. 660-Death of Lex Luthor. 661-Begin $1.00-c. 675-Deathstroke cameo. 679-Last $1.00 issue. 683-Doomsday cameo 3.00
650,667: 650-($1.50, 52 pgs.)-Lobo cameo (last panel). 667-($1.75, 52 pgs.) 4.00
662-Clark Kent reveals i.d. to Lois Lane; story cont'd in Superman #53 4.00
674-Supergirl logo & c/story (reintro) 6.00
683-685-2nd & 3rd printings 3.00
684-Doomsday battle issue 4.00
685,686-Funeral for a Friend issues; Supergirl app. 4.00
687-($1.95)-Collector's Ed.w/die-cut-c 4.00
687-($1.50)-Newsstand Edition with mini-poster 3.00
688-699,701-703-($1.50): 688-Guy Gardner-c/story. 697-Bizarro-c/story. 703-(9/94)-Zero Hour 3.00
695-($2.50)-Collector's Edition w/embossed foil-c 4.00
700-($2.95, 68 pgs.)-Fall of Metropolis Pt 1, Guice-a; Pete Ross marries Lana Lang and Smallville flashbacks with Curt Swan art & Murphy Anderson inks 4.00
700-Platinum 15.00
700-Gold 18.00
0(10/94), 704(11/94)-719,721-731: 710-Begin $1.95-c. 714-Joker app. 719-Batman-c/app. 721-Mr. Mxyzptlk app. 723-Dave Johnson-c. 727-Final Night x-over. 3.00
720-Lois breaks off engagement w/Clark 4.00
720-2nd print. 3.00
732-749,751-767: 732-New powers. 733-New costume, Ray app. 738-Immonen-s/a(p) begins. 741-Legion app. 744-Millennium Giants x-over. 745-747-70's-style Superman vs. Prankster. 753-JLA-c/app. 757-Hawkman-c. 760-1st Encantadora. 761-Wonder Woman app. 765-Joker & Harley-c/app. 766-Batman-c/app. 3.00
750-($2.95) 4.00
768,769,771-774: 768-Begin $2.25-c; Marvel Family-c/app. 771-Nightwing-c/app. 772,773-Ra's al Ghul app. 774-Martian Manhunter-c/app. 3.00
770-($3.50) Conclusion of Emperor Joker x-over 4.00
775-($3.75) Bradstreet-c; intro. The Elite 4.00
776-799: 776-Farewell to Krypton; Rivoche-c. 780-782-Our Worlds at War x-over. 781-Hippolyta and Major Lane killed. 782-War ends. 784-Joker: Last Laugh; Batman & Green Lantern app. 793-Return to Krypton. 795-The Elite app. 798-Van Fleet-c 3.00
800-(4/03, $3.95) Struzan painted-c; guest artists include Ross, Jim Lee, Jurgens, Sale 4.00
801-811: 801-Raney-a. 809-The Creeper app. 811-Mr. Majestic app. 3.00
812-Godfall part 1; Turner-c; Caldwell-a(p) 4.00
812-2nd printing; B&W sketch-c by Turner 3.00
813-Godfall pt. 4; Turner-c; Caldwell-a(p) 4.00
814-824, 826-828,830-836: 814-Reis-a/Art Adams-c; Darkseid app.; begin $2.50-c. 815,816-Teen Titans-c/app. 820-Doomsday app. 826-Capt. Marvel app. 827-Byrne-c/a begin. 831-Villains United tie-in. 835-Livewire app. 836-Infinite Crisis; revised origin 3.00
825-($2.99, 40 pgs.) Doomsday app. 4.00
829-Omac Project x-over Sacrifice pt. 2 5.00
829-(2nd printing) red tone cover 4.00
837-843-One Year Later; powers return after Infinite Crisis; Johns & Busiek-s 3.00
844-Donner & Johns-s/Adam Kubert-a/c begin; brown-toned cover 4.00
844-Andy Kubert variant-c 5.00
844-2nd printing with red-toned Adam Kubert cover 3.00
845-849,851-857: 845-Bizarro-c/app.; re-intro. General Zod, Ursa & Non. 846-Jax-Ur app. 847-849-No Kubert-a. 851-Kubert-a/c. 855-857-Bizarro app.; Powell-a/c 3.00
850-($3.99) Supergirl and LSH app., origin re-told; Guedes-a/c 4.00
858-($3.50) Legion of Super-Heroes app.; 1st meeting re-told; Johns-s/Frank-a/c 4.00
858-Variant-c (Superman & giant Brainiac robot) by Frank 5.00
858-Second printing with regular cover with red background instead of yellow 3.00
858-Special Edition (7/10, $1.00) r/#858 with "What's Next?" cover logo 3.00
859-878: 859-863-Legion of Super-Heroes app.; var-c on each (859-Andy Kubert. 860-Lightle. 861-Grell. 862-Giffen. 863-Frank) 864-Batman and Lightning Lad app. 866-Brainiac returns 869-"Soda Pop" cover edition, 870-Pa Kent dies. 871-New Krypton; Ross-c 3.00
869-Initial printing recalled because of beer bottles on cover 4 8 12 23 37 50
879-896: 879-($3.99) Back-up Capt. Atom feature begins. 890-Luthor stories begin. 893-Comics debut of Chloe Sullivan (Smallville TV show) in regular DCU. 894-Death (Sandman) app. 896-Secret Six app. 4.00
897-899, 901-903-($2.99) 897-Joker app. 898-Larfleeze app. 899-Brainiac app. 3.00

Action Comics (2011 series) #23.1 © DC

Action Girl #18 © SLG

Adam Strange (2004 series) #1 © DC

	GD 2.0	VG 4.0	FN 6.0	VF 8.0	VF/NM 9.0	NM- 9.2

900 (6/11, $5.99, 96 pgs.) Conclusion of Luthor Black Ring saga; Doomsday app.; bonus short stories by various; Superman renounces U.S. citizenship 6.00
904-(10/11) Last issue of first volume; Doomsday app.; Rocafort-c 3.00
904-Variant-c by Ordway 5.00
#1,000,000 (11/98) Gene Ha-c; 853rd Century x-over 3.00
Annual 1 ('87, $2.95) Art Adams-c/a(p); Batman app. 5.00
Annual 2-6 ('89-'94, $2.95)-2-Pérez-c/a(i). 3-Armageddon 2001. 4-Eclipso vs. Shazam. 5-Bloodlines; 1st app. Loose Cannon. 6-Elseworlds story 4.00
Annual 7,9 ('95, '97, $3.95) 7-Year One story. 9-Pulp Heroes story 4.00
Annual 8 (1996, $2.95) Legends of the Dead Earth story 4.00
Annual 10 ('07, $3.99) Short stories by Johns & Donner and various incl. A. Adams, J. Kubert, Wight, Morales; origin of Phantom Zone, Mon-El; Metallo app.; Adam & Joe Kubert-c 4.00
Annual 11 (7/08, $4.99) Conclusion to General Zod story continued from #851; Kubert-a 5.00
Annual 12 (8/09, $4.99) Origin of Nightwing and Flamebird 5.00
Annual 13 (2/11, $4.99) 1st meeting of Luthor and Darkseid; Ra's al Ghul app. 5.00

NOTE: ***Supergirl's*** *origin in 262, 280, 285, 291, 305, 309.* ***N. Adams*** *c-356, 358, 359, 361-364, 366, 367, 370-374, 377-379i, 398-400, 402, 404,405, 419p, 466, 468, 469, 473i, 485.* ***Aparo*** *a-642.* ***Austin*** *c/a-682i.* ***Baily*** *a-24, 25.* ***Boring*** *a-164, 194, 211, 223, 233, 241, 250, 261, 266-268, 346, 348, 352, 356, 357.* ***Burnley*** *a-28-33; c-48?, 53-55, 58, 59?, 60-63, 65, 66p, 67p, 70p, 71p, 79p, 82p, 84-86p, 90-92p, 93p?, 94p, 107p, 108p.* ***Byrne*** *a-584-598p, 599i, 600p; c-584-591, 596-600.* ***Ditko*** *a-642.* ***Giffen*** *a-560, 563, 565, 577, 579; c-539, 560, 563, 565, 577, 579.* ***Grell*** *a-440-442, 444-446, 450-452, 456-458; c-456.* ***Guardineer*** *a-24, 25; c-8, 11, 12, 14-16, 18. 25.* ***Guice*** *a(p)-676-681, 683-698, 700; c-683, 685, 686, 687(direct), 688-693i, 694-696, 697i, 698-700.* ***Infantino*** *a-642.* ***Kaluta*** *c-613.* ***Bob Kane's*** *Clip Carson-14-41.* ***Gil Kane*** *a-443r, 493r, 539-541, 544-546, 551-554, 601-605, 642; c-535p, 540, 541, 544p, 545-549, 551-554, 580, 627.* ***Kirby*** *c-638.* ***Meskin*** *a-42-121(most).* ***Mignola*** *a-600, Annual 2; c-c-614.* ***Moldoff*** *a-23-25, 443r.* ***Mooney*** *a-667p.* ***Mortimer*** *c-153, 154, 159-172, 174, 178-181, 184, 186-189, 191-193, 196, 200, 206.* ***Orlando*** *a-617p; c-621.* ***Perez*** *a-600i, 643-652p, Annual 2p; c-529p, 602, 643-651, Annual 2p.* ***Quesada*** *c-Annual 4p.* ***Fred Ray*** *c-34, 36-46, 50-52.* ***Siegel & Shuster*** *a-1-27.* ***Paul Smith*** *c-608.* ***Starlin*** *a-509; c-631.* ***Leonard Starr*** *a-597i(part),* ***Staton*** *a-525p, 526p, 531p, 535p, 536p.* ***Swan/Moldoff*** *c-281, 286, 287, 293, 298, 334.* ***Thibert*** *c-676, 677p, 678-681, 684.* ***Toth*** *a-406, 407, 413, 431; c-616.* ***Tuska*** *a-486p, 550.* ***Williamson*** *a-568i.* ***Zeck*** *c-Annual 5*

ACTION COMICS (2nd series)(DC New 52)
DC Comics: Nov, 2011 - Present ($3.99)

1-Grant Morrison-s/Rags Morales-a/c; re-introduces Superman 1 3 4 6 8 10
1-Variant-c by Jim Lee of Superman in new armor costume 15.00
1-(2nd - 5th printings) 4.00
2-12: 2-Morales & Brent Anderson-a; behind the scenes sketch art and commentary. 3-Gene Ha & Morales-a. 4-Re-intro. Steel. 5-Flashback to Krypton; Andy Kubert-a. 6-Legion of Super-Heroes app.; Andy Kubert-a. 7-Gets the new costume; intro. Steel 4.00
2-12-Variant covers. 2-Van Sciver. 3-Ha. 4-Choi. 5,6-Morales. 8-Frank 5.00
13-17,19-23: 13-Re-intro of Krypto. 14-Neil deGrasse Tyson app. 15-Legion app. 4.00
18-($4.99) Last Morrison-s; Mxyzptlk, The Legion and the Wanderers app. 5.00
23.1, 23.2, 23.3, 23.4 (11/13, $2.99, regular covers) 3.00
23.1 (11/13, $3.99, 3-D cover) "Cyborg Superman #1" on cover; Zor-El & Brainiac app. 5.00
23.2 (11/13, $3.99, 3-D cover) "Zod #1" on cover; origin of Zod on Krypton; Faora app. 5.00
23.3 (11/13, $3.99, 3-D cover) "Lex Luthor #1" on cover; Kuder-c 5.00
23.4 (11/13, $3.99, 3-D cover) "Metallo #1" on cover; Fisch-s/Pugh-a 5.00
24-29: 25-Zero Year. 26-30-Kuder-a. 30-Doomsday app. 4.00
#0 (11/12, $3.99) Flashback to Lois' 1st Superman sighting; Oliver-a; 4.00
Annual 1 (12/12, $4.99) Superman vs. K-Man; Fisch-s/Hamner-a; Atomic Skull app. 5.00
Annual 2 (12/13, $4.99) Rocafort & Jurgens-a; H'El & Faora app.; back-up Mad sampler 5.00

ACTION COMICS
DC Comics: (no date)

1-Ashcan comic, not distributed to newsstands, only for in-house use. Cover art is the rejected art to Detective Comics #2 and interior from Detective Comics #1.
A CGC certified 9.0 copy sold for $17,825 in 2002 and for $29,000 in 2008.

ACTION FORCE (Also see G.I. Joe European Missions)
Marvel Comics Ltd. (British): Mar, 1987 - No. 50, 1988 ($1.00, weekly, magazine)

1,3: British G.I. Joe series. 3-w/poster insert 2 4 6 8 10 12
2,4 1 2 3 5 6 8
5-10 5.00
11-50 3.00
...Special 1 (7/87) Summer holiday special; Snake Eyes-c/app. 1 2 3 5 6 8
...Special 2 (10/87) Winter special; 5.00

ACTION FUNNIES
DC Comics: 1937/1938

nn - Ashcan comic, not distributed to newsstands, only for in house use. Cover art is Action Comics #3 and interior from Detective Comics #10. The Mallette/Brown copy in VG+ condition sold for $15,000 in 2005. A VF+ copy sold for $10,157.50 in 2012.

ACTION GIRL
Slave Labor Graphics: Oct, 1994 - No. 19 ($2.50/$2.75/$2.95, B&W)

1-19: 4-Begin $2.75-c. 19-Begin $2.95-c 3.00
1-6 ($2.75, 2nd printings): All read 2nd Print in indicia. 1-(2/96). 2-(10/95). 3-(2/96). 4-(7/96). 5-(2/97). 6-(9/97) 3.00
1-4 ($2.75, 3rd printings): All read 3rd Print in indicia. 3.00

ACTION PLANET COMICS
Action Planet: 1996 - No. 3, Sept, 1997 ($3.95, B&W, 44 pgs.)

1-3: 1-Intro Monster Man by Mike Manley & other stories 4.00
Giant Size Action Planet Halloween Special (1998, $5.95, oversized) 6.00

ACTUAL CONFESSIONS (Formerly Love Adventures)
Atlas Comics (MPI): No. 13, Oct, 1952 - No. 14, Dec, 1952

13,14 10 20 30 58 79 100

ACTUAL ROMANCES (Becomes True Secrets #3 on?)
Marvel Comics (IPS): Oct, 1949 - No. 2, Jan, 1950 (52 pgs.)

1 16 32 48 94 147 200
2-Photo-c 11 22 33 64 90 115

ADAM AND EVE
Spire Christian Comics (Fleming H. Revell Co.): 1975,1978 (35¢/39¢/49¢)

nn-By Al Hartley (1975 edition) 2 4 6 11 16 20
nn (1978 edition) 2 4 6 9 13 16

ADAM: LEGEND OF THE BLUE MARVEL
Marvel Comics: Jan, 2009 - No. 5, May, 2009 ($3.99, limited series)

1-5-Grevioux-s/Broome-a; Avengers app. 4.00

ADAM STRANGE (Also see Green Lantern #132, Mystery In Space #53 & Showcase #17)
DC Comics: 1990 - No. 3, 1990 ($3.95, 52 pgs, limited series, squarebound)

Book One - Three: Andy & Adam Kubert-c/a 4.00
...: The Man of Two Worlds (2003, $19.95, TPB) r/#1-3; sketch pages by Andy Kubert 20.00

ADAM STRANGE (Leads into the Rann/Thanagar War mini-series)
DC Comics: Nov, 2004 - No. 8, June, 2005 ($2.95, limited series)

1-8-Andy Diggle-s/Pascal Ferry-a/c. 1-Superman app. 3.00
...: Planet Heist TPB (2005, $19.99) r/series; sketch pages 20.00
... Special (11/08, $3.50) Takes place during Rann/Thanagar Holy War series; Starlin-s 4.00

ADAM-12 (TV)
Gold Key: Dec, 1973 - No. 10, Feb, 1976 (Photo-c)

1 6 12 18 37 66 95
2-10 3 6 9 21 33 45

ADDAMS FAMILY (TV cartoon)
Gold Key: Oct, 1974 - No. 3, Apr, 1975 (Hanna-Barbera)

1 7 14 21 46 86 125
2,3 5 10 15 33 57 80

ADLAI STEVENSON
Dell Publishing Co.: Dec, 1966

12-007-612-Life story; photo-c 3 6 9 21 33 45

ADOLESCENT RADIOACTIVE BLACK BELT HAMSTERS (See Clint)
Comic Castle/Eclipse Comics: 1986 - No. 9, Jan, 1988 ($1.50, B&W)

1-9: 1st & 2nd printings exist 3.00
1-Limited Edition 6.00
1-In 3-D (7/86), 2-4 ($2.50) 3.00
Massacre The Japanese Invasion #1 (8/89, $2.00) 3.00

ADOLESCENT RADIOACTIVE BLACK BELT HAMSTERS
Dynamite Entertainment: 2008 - No. 4, 2008 ($3.50, limited series)

1-4-Tom Nguyen-a/Keith Champagne-s; 2 covers by Nguyen and Oeming 3.50

ADRENALYNN (See The Tenth)
Image Comics: Aug, 1999 - No. 4, Feb, 2000 ($2.50)

1-4-Tony Daniel-s/Marty Egeland-a; origin of Adrenalynn 3.00

ADULT TALES OF TERROR ILLUSTRATED (See Terror Illustrated)

ADVANCED DUNGEONS & DRAGONS (Also see TSR Worlds)
DC Comics: Dec, 1988 - No. 36, Dec, 1991 (Newsstand #1 is Holiday, 1988-89) ($1.25-$1.75)

1-Based on TSR role playing game 4.00
2-36: 25-$1.75-c begins 3.00
Annual 1 (1990, $3.95, 68 pgs.) 4.00

ADVENTURE BOUND
Dell Publishing Co.: Aug, 1949

Four Color #239 5 10 15 34 60 85

ADVENTURE COMICS (Formerly New Adventure)(...Presents Dial H For Hero #479-490)
National Periodical Publications/DC Comics: No. 32, 11/38 - No. 490, 2/82; No. 491, 9/82 - No. 503, 9/83

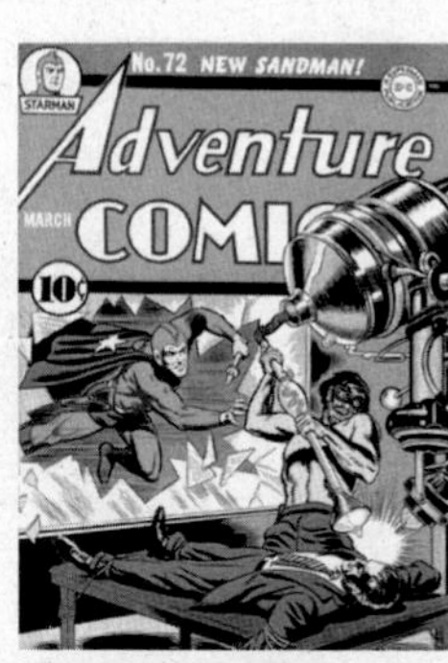

Adventure Comics #73 © DC

Adventure Comics #159 © DC

Adventure Comics #297 © DC

	GD 2.0	VG 4.0	FN 6.0	VF 8.0	VF/NM 9.0	NM- 9.2
32-Anchors Aweigh (ends #52), Barry O'Neil (ends #60, not in #33), Captain Desmo (ends #47), Dale Daring (ends #47), Federal Men (ends #70), The Golden Dragon (ends #36), Rusty & His Pals (ends #52) by Bob Kane, Todd Hunter (ends #38) and Tom Brent (ends #39) begin	440	880	1320	2500	3650	4800
33-35,37,38: 37-Cover used on Double Action #2	250	500	750	1400	2100	2800
36 (scarce)	226	452	678	1446	2473	3500
39(6/39)- Jack Wood begins, ends #42; early mention of Marijuana in comics	230	460	690	1300	1950	2600
40-(Rare, 7/39, on stands 6/10/39)-The Sandman begins by Bert Christman (who died in WWII); believed to be 1st conceived story (see N.Y. World's Fair for 1st published app.); Socko Strong begins, ends #54	6500	13,000	19,500	48,000	91,500	135,000
41-O'Mealia shark-c	622	1244	1866	4541	8021	11,500
42,44-Sandman-c by Flessel. 44-Opium story	838	1676	2514	6117	10,809	15,500
43,45: 45-Full page ad for Flash Comics #1	432	864	1296	3154	5577	8000
46,47-Sandman covers by Flessel. 47-Steve Conrad Adventurer begins, ends #76	622	1244	1866	4541	8021	11,500
48-1st app. The Hourman by Bernard Baily; Baily-c (Hourman c-48,50,52-59)	2750	5500	8250	20,500	38,750	57,000
49,50: 50-Cotton Carver by Jack Lehti begins, ends #64	300	600	900	1950	3375	4800
51,60-Sandman-c: 51-Sandman-c by Flessel.	377	754	1131	2639	4620	6600
52-59: 53-1st app. Jimmy "Minuteman" Martin & the Minutemen of America in Hourman; ends #78. 58-Paul Kirk Manhunter begins (1st app.), ends #72	258	516	774	1651	2826	4000
61-1st app. Starman by Jack Burnley (4/41); Starman c-61-72; Starman by Burnley in #61-80	1200	2400	3600	9000	16,500	24,000
62-65,67,68,70: 67-Origin & 1st app. The Mist; classic Burnley-c. 70-Last Federal Men	232	464	696	1485	2543	3600
66-Origin/1st app. Shining Knight (9/41)	284	568	852	1818	3109	4400
69-1st app. Sandy the Golden Boy (Sandman's sidekick) by Paul Norris (in a Bob Kane style); Sandman dons new costume	271	542	813	1734	2967	4200
71-Jimmy Martin becomes costumed aide to the Hourman; 1st app. Hourman's Miracle Ray machine	219	438	657	1402	2401	3400
72-1st Simon & Kirby Sandman (3/42, 1st DC work)	975	1950	2919	7100	12,550	18,000
73-Origin Manhunter by Simon & Kirby; begin new series; Manhunter-c (scarce)	1275	2550	3825	9550	17,275	25,000
74-78,80: 74-Thorndyke replaces Jimmy, Hourman's assistant; new Sandman-c begin by S&K. 75-Thor app. by Kirby; 1st Kirby Thor (see Tales of the Unexpected #16). 77-Origin Genius Jones; Mist story. 80-Last S&K Manhunter & Burnley Starman	194	388	582	1242	2121	3000
79-Classic Manhunter-c	290	580	870	1856	3178	4500
81-90: 83-Last Hourman. 84-Mike Gibbs begins, ends #102	123	246	369	787	1344	1900
91-Last Simon & Kirby Sandman	118	236	354	749	1287	1825
92-99,101,102: 92-Last Manhunter. 101-Shining Knight origin retold. 102-Last Starman, Sandman, & Genius Jones; most-S&K-c (Genius Jones cont'd in More Fun #108)	97	194	291	621	1061	1500
100-S&K-c	132	264	396	838	1444	2050
103-Aquaman, Green Arrow, Johnny Quick & Superboy all move over from More Fun Comics #107; 8th app. Superboy; Superboy-c begin; 1st small logo (4/46)	300	600	900	1950	3375	4800
104	110	220	330	704	1202	1700
105-110	77	154	231	493	847	1200
111-120: 113-X-Mas-c	70	140	210	445	765	1085
121,122-126,128-130: 128-1st meeting Superboy & Lois Lane	65	130	195	416	708	1000
127-Brief origin Shining Knight retold	66	132	198	419	722	1025
131-141,143-149: 132-Shining Knight 1st return to King Arthur time; origin aide Sir Butch	57	114	171	362	619	875
142-Origin Shining Knight & Johnny Quick retold	60	120	180	381	653	925
150,151,153,155,157,159,161,163-All have 6 pg. Shining Knight stories by Frank Frazetta. 159-Origin Johnny Quick. 161-1st Lana Lang app. in this title	70	140	210	445	765	1085
152,154,156,158,160,162,164-169: 166-Last Shining Knight. 168-Last 52 pg. issue	52	104	156	328	552	775
170-180	49	98	147	309	522	735
181-199: 189-B&W and color illo in **POP**	47	94	141	298	504	710
200 (5/54)	58	116	174	371	636	900
201-208: 207-Last Johnny Quick (not in 205)	43	86	129	271	461	650
209-Last pre-code issue; origin Speedy	44	88	132	276	468	670
210-1st app. Krypto (Superdog)-c/story (3/55)	360	720	1260	3300	6150	9000
211-213,215-219	41	82	123	256	428	600
214-2nd app. Krypto	74	148	222	470	810	1150
220-Krypto-c/sty	47	94	141	296	498	700
221-246: 229-1st S.A. issue; Green Arrow & Aquaman app. 237-1st Intergalactic Vigilante Squadron (6/57). 239-Krypto-c	37	74	111	222	361	500
247(4/58)-1st Legion of Super Heroes app.; 1st app. Cosmic Boy, Saturn Girl & Lightning Boy (later Lightning Lad in #267) (origin)	600	1200	1800	6000	12,000	18,000
248-252,254,255-Green Arrow in all: 255-Intro. Red Kryptonite in Superboy (used in #252 but with no effect)	31	62	93	186	303	420
253-1st meeting of Superboy & Robin; Green Arrow by Kirby in #250-255 (also see World's Finest #96-99)	36	72	108	216	351	485
256-Origin Green Arrow by Kirby	69	138	207	442	821	1200
257-259: 258-Green Arrow x-over in Superboy	25	50	75	147	241	335
260-1st Silver Age origin Aquaman (5/59)	76	152	228	486	831	1175
261-265,268,270: 262-Origin Speedy in Green Arrow. 270-Congorilla begins, ends #281,283	21	42	63	122	199	275
266-(11/59)-Origin & 1st app. Aquagirl (tryout, not same as later character)	21	42	63	126	206	285
267(12/59)-2nd Legion of Super Heroes; Lightning Boy now called Lightning Lad; new costumes for Legion	97	194	291	611	1406	2200
269-Intro. Aqualad (2/60); last Green Arrow (not in #206)	33	66	99	194	317	440
271-Origin Luthor retold	40	80	120	246	411	575
272-274,277-280: 279-Intro White Kryptonite in Superboy. 280-1st meeting Superboy & Lori Lemaris	20	40	60	114	182	250
275-Origin Superman-Batman team retold (see World's Finest #94)	25	50	75	150	245	340
276-(9/60) Robinson Crusoe-like story	20	40	60	117	189	260
281,284,287-289: 281-Last Congorilla. 284-Last Aquaman in Adv.; Mooney-a. 287,288-Intro Dev-Em, the Knave from Krypton. 287-1st Bizarro Perry White & Jimmy Olsen. 288-Bizarro-c. 289-Legion cameo (statues)	18	36	54	107	169	230
282(3/61)-5th Legion app; intro/origin Star Boy	39	78	117	240	395	550
283-Intro. The Phantom Zone; 1st app. of General Zod (cameo in 2 panels)	50	100	150	315	533	750
285-1st Tales of the Bizarro World-c/story (ends #299) in Adv. (see Action #255)	24	48	72	140	230	320
286-1st Bizarro Mxyzptlk; Bizarro-c	23	46	69	136	223	310
290(11/61)-9th Legion app; origin Sunboy in Legion (last 10¢ issue)	37	74	111	222	361	500
291,292,295-298: 291-1st 12¢ ish, (12/61). 292-1st Bizarro Lana Lang & Lucy Lane. 295-Bizarro-c; 1st Bizarro Titano	10	20	30	64	132	200
293(2/62)-13th Legion app; Mon-El app.; Legion of Super Pets 1st app./origin; 1st Superhorse; 2nd app. General Zod; 1st Bizarro Luthor & Kandor	37	74	111	222	361	500
294-1st Bizarro Marilyn Monroe, Pres. Kennedy.	12	24	36	79	170	260
299-1st Gold Kryptonite (8/62)	10	20	30	66	138	210
300-Tales of the Legion of Super-Heroes series begins (9/62); Mon-El leaves Phantom Zone (temporarily), joins Legion	50	100	150	390	870	1350
301-Origin Bouncing Boy	15	30	45	103	227	350
302-305: 303-1st app. Matter-Eater Lad. 304-Death of Lightning Lad in Legion	12	24	36	81	176	270
306-310: 306-Intro. Legion of Substitute Heroes. 307-1st app. Element Lad in Legion. 308-1st app. Lightning Lass in Legion. 309-1st app. Legion of Super-Monsters	11	22	33	73	157	240
311-320: 312-Lightning Lad back in Legion. 315-Last new Superboy story; Colossal Boy app. 316-Origins & powers of Legion given. 317-Intro. Dream Girl in Legion; Lightning Lass becomes Light Lass; Hall of Fame series begins. 320-Dev-Em 2nd app.	9	18	27	61	123	185
321-Intro. Time Trapper	8	16	24	56	108	160
322-330: 327-Intro/1st app. Lone Wolf in Legion. 329-Intro The Bizarro Legionnaires; intro. Legion flight rings	8	16	24	52	99	145
331-340: 337-Chlorophyll Kid & Night Girl app. 340-Intro Computo in Legion	7	14	21	48	89	130
341-Triplicate Girl becomes Duo Damsel	6	12	18	42	79	115
342-345,347-351: 345-Last Hall of Fame; returns in 356,371. 348-Origin Sunboy; intro Dr. Regulus in Legion. 349-Intro Universo & Rond Vidar. 351-1st app. White Witch	6	12	18	41	76	110
346-1st app. Karate Kid, Princess Projectra, Ferro Lad, & Nemesis Kid.	9	18	27	57	111	165
352,354-360: 354,355-Superman meets the Adult Legion. 355-Insect Queen joins Legion (4/67)	6	12	18	37	66	95
353-Death of Ferro Lad in Legion	7	14	21	44	82	120
361-364,366,368-370: 369-Intro Mordru in Legion	5	10	15	34	60	85
365,367: 365-Intro Shadow Lass (memorial to Shadow Woman app. in #354's Adult Legion-s); lists origins & powers of L.S.H. 367-New Legion headquarters	5	10	15	35	63	90

Adventure Comics #427 © DC

Adventure Comics #475 © DC

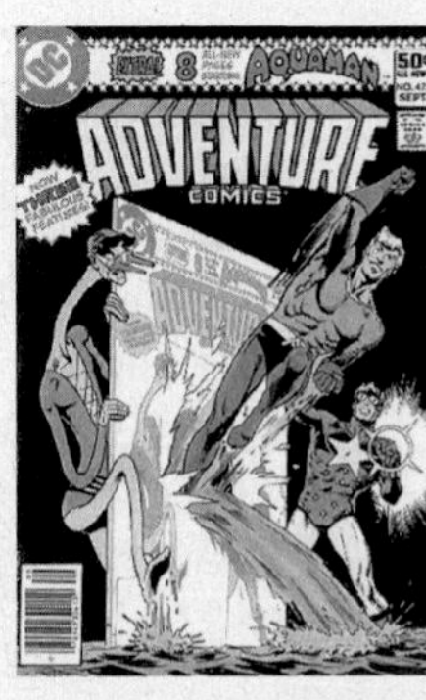

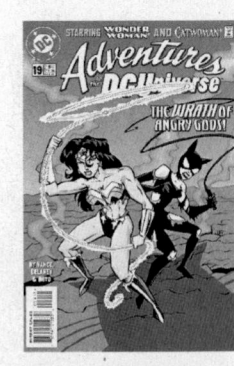

Adventures in the DCU #19 © DC

GD VG FN VF VF/NM NM-
2.0 4.0 6.0 8.0 9.0 9.2

371,372: 371-Intro. Chemical King (mentioned in #354's Adult Legion-s). 372-Timber Wolf & Chemical King join 5 10 15 35 63 90
373,374,376-380: 373-Intro. Tornado Twins (Barry Allen Flash descendants). 374-Article on comics fandom. 380-Last Legion in Adventure; last 12¢-c 5 10 15 33 57 80
375-Intro Quantum Queen & The Wanderers 5 10 15 34 60 85
381-Supergirl begins; 1st full length Supergirl story & her 1st solo book (6/69) 12 24 36 82 179 285
382-389 5 10 15 31 53 75
390-Giant Supergirl G-69 6 12 18 41 76 110
391-396,398 4 8 12 23 37 50
397-1st app. new Supergirl 5 10 15 31 53 75
399-Unpubbed G.A. Black Canary story 4 8 12 25 40 55
400-New costume for Supergirl (12/70) 5 10 15 31 53 75
401,402,404-408-(15¢-c) 3 6 9 17 26 35
403-68 pg. Giant G-81; Legion-r/#304,305,308,312 6 12 18 38 69 100
409-411,413-415,417-420-(52 pgs.): 413-Hawkman by Kubert r/B&B #44; G.A. Robotman-r/Det. #178; Zatanna by Morrow. 414-r-2nd Animal Man/Str. Advs. #184. 415-Animal Man-r/Str. Adv.#190 (origin recap). 417-Morrow Vigilante; Frazetta Shining Knight-r/Adv. #161; origin The Enchantress; no Zatanna. 418-Prev. unpub. Dr. Mid-Nite story from 1948; no Zatanna. 420-Animal Man-r/Str. Adv. #195 3 6 9 18 28 38
412-(52 pgs.) Reprints origin & 1st app. of Animal Man from Strange Adventures #180 3 6 9 18 28 38
416-Also listed as DC 100 Pg. Super Spectacular #10; Golden Age-r; r/1st app. Black Canary from Flash #86; no Zatanna 10 20 30 68 144 220
421-424: 424-Last Supergirl in Adventure 3 6 9 14 20 25
425-New look, content change to adventure; Kaluta-c; Toth-a, origin Capt. Fear 3 6 9 16 23 30
426,427: 426-1st Adventurers Club. 427-Last Vigilante 2 4 6 9 12 15
428-Origin/1st app. Black Orchid (c/story, 6-7/73) 5 10 15 33 57 80
429,430-Black Orchid-c/stories 3 6 9 20 31 42
431-Spectre by Aparo begins, ends #440. 5 10 15 35 63 90
432-439-Spectre app. 433-437-Cover title is Weird Adventure Comics. 436-Last 20¢ issue 3 6 9 21 33 45
440-New Spectre origin. 4 8 12 23 37 50
441-458: 441-452-Aquaman app. 443-Fisherman app. 445-447-The Creeper app. 446-Flag-c. 449-451-Martian Manhunter app. 450-Weather Wizard app. in Aquaman story. 453-458-Superboy app. 453-Intro. Mighty Girl. 457,458-Eclipso app. 1 3 4 6 8 10
459,460 (68 pgs.): 459-New Gods/Darkseid storyline concludes from New Gods #19 (#459 is dated 9-10/78) without missing a month. 459-Flash (ends #466), Deadman (ends #466), Wonder Woman (ends #464), Green Lantern (ends #460). 460-Aquaman (ends #478) 3 6 9 14 20 26
461-($1.00, 68 pgs.) Justice Society begins; ends 466 4 8 12 25 40 55
462-($1.00, 68 pgs.) Death Earth II Batman 5 10 15 31 53 75
463-466 ($1.00 size, 68 pgs.) 2 4 6 10 14 18
467-Starman by Ditko & Plastic Man begins; 1st app. Prince Gavyn (Starman). 2 4 6 8 11 14
468-490: 470-Origin Starman. 479-Dial 'H' For Hero begins, ends #490. 478-Last Starman & Plastic Man. 480-490: Dial 'H' For Hero 5.00
491-503: 491-100pg. Digest size begins; r/Legion of Super Heroes/Adv. #247, 267; Spectre, Aquaman, Superboy, S&K Sandman, Black Canary-r & new Shazam by Newton begin. 492,495,496,499-S&K Sandman-r/Adventure in all. 493-Challengers of the Unknown begins by Tuska w/brief origin. 493-495,497-499-G.A. Captain Marvel-r. 494-499-Spectre-r/Spectre 1-3, 5-7. 496-Capt. Marvel Jr. new-s, Cockrum-a. 498-Mary Marvel new-s; Plastic Man-r begin; origin Bouncing Boy-r/ #301. 500-Legion-r (Digest size, 148 pgs.).
501-503: G.A.-r 2 4 6 9 13 16
... 80 Page Giant (10/98, $4.95) Wonder Woman, Shazam, Superboy, Supergirl, Green Arrow, Legion, Bizarro World stories 5.00

NOTE: *Bizarro covers-285, 286, 288, 294, 295, 329. Vigilante app.-420, 426, 427.* ***N. Adams*** *a(r)-495i-498i; c-365-369, 371-373, 375-379, 381-383.* ***Aparo*** *a-431-433, 434i, 435, 436, 437i, 438i, 439-452, 503r; c-431-452.* ***Austin*** *a-449i 451i.* ***Bernard Baily*** *c-48, 50, 52-59.* ***Bolland*** *c-475.* ***Burnley*** *c-61-72, 116-120p.* ***Chaykin*** *a-438.* ***Ditko*** *a-467-478p; c-467p.* ***Creig Flessel*** *c-32, 33, 40, 42, 44, 46, 47, 51, 60.* ***Giffen*** *c-491p-494p, 500p.* ***Grell*** *a-435-437, 440.* ***Guardineer*** *c-34, 35, 45.* ***Infantino*** *a-416r.* ***Kaluta*** *c-425.* ***Bob Kane*** *a-38.* ***G. Kane*** *a-414r, 425; c-496-499, 537.* ***Kirby*** *a-250-256.* ***Kubert*** *a-413.* ***Meskin*** *a-81,125,127.* ***Moldoff*** *a-494i; c-49.* ***Morrow*** *a-413-415, 417, 422, 502r, 503r.* ***Netzer/Nasser*** *a-449-451.* ***Newton*** *a-459-461, 464-466, 491p, 492p.* ***Paul Norris*** *a-69.* ***Orlando*** *a-457p, 458p.* ***Perez*** *c-484-486, 490p.* ***Simon/Kirby*** *a-503r; c-73-97, 100-102.* ***Starlin*** *c-471.* ***Staton*** *a-445-447i, 456-458p, 459, 460, 461p-465p, 466,467p-478p, 502p(r); c-458, 461(back).* ***Toth*** *a-418, 419, 425, 431, 495p-497p.* ***Tuska*** *a-494p.*

ADVENTURE COMICS (Also see All Star Comics 1999 crossover titles)
DC Comics: May, 1999 ($1.99, one-shot)

1-Golden Age Starman and the Atom; Snejbjerg-a 3.00

ADVENTURE COMICS (See Final Crisis: Legion of Three Worlds)
DC Comics: No. 0, Apr, 2009 - No. 12, Aug, 2010; No. 516, Sept, 2010 - No. 529, Oct, 2011 ($1.00/$3.99)

0-($1.00) R/Adventure Comics #247; new Luthor & Brainiac back-up-s; Lopresti-c 3.00
1-7-($3.99) Superboy stories; Johns-s/Manapul-a; Legion back-up-s. 5-7-Blackest Night 4.00
1-12-Variant 7-panel covers by various numbered with original #504-#515 5.00
8-12: 8-11-New Krypton x-over. 11-Mon-El leaves 21st century. 12-Legion; Levitz-s 4.00
516-521: 516-(9/10, resumes original numbering) flashback to Legion formation; Atom back-ups. 521-Adult Legion resumes; Mon-El joins Green Lanterns 4.00
522-529-($2.99) Legion Academy. 523-527-Jimenez-a/c 3.00

ADVENTURE COMICS SPECIAL (See New Krypton issues in 2009 Superman titles)
DC Comics: Jan, 2009 ($2.99, one-shot)

... Featuring the Guardian - James Robinson-s/Pere Pérez-a; origin re-told; intro. Gwen 3.00

ADVENTURE INTO MYSTERY
Atlas Comics (BFP No. 1/OPI No. 2-8): May, 1956 - No. 8, July, 1957

1-Powell s/f-a; Forte-a; Everett-c 47 94 141 296 498 700
2-Flying Saucer story 26 52 78 154 252 350
3,6-Everett-c 23 46 69 136 223 310
4,5,7: 4-Williamson-a, 4 pgs; Powell-a. 5-Everett-c/a, Orlando-a. 7-Torres-a; Everett-c 24 48 72 144 237 330
8-Moreira, Sale, Torres, Woodbridge-a, Severin-c 23 46 69 136 223 310

ADVENTURE IS MY CAREER
U.S. Coast Guard Academy/Street & Smith: 1945 (44 pgs.)

nn-Simon, Milt Gross-a 22 44 66 128 209 290

ADVENTURERS, THE
Aircel Comics/Adventure Publ.: Aug, 1986 - No. 10, 1987? ($1.50, B&W)
V2#1, 1987 - V2#9, 1988; V3#1, Oct, 1989 - V3#6, 1990

1-Peter Hsu-a 1 2 3 5 6 8
1-Cover variant, limited ed. 2 4 6 9 12 15
1-2nd print (1986); 1st app. Elf Warrior 3.00
2,3, 0 (#4, 12/86)-Origin, 5-10, Book II, reg. & Limited Ed. #1 3.50
Book II, #2,3,0,4-9 3.00
Book III, #1 (10/89, $2.25)-Reg. & limited-c, Book III, #2-6 3.00

ADVENTURES (No. 2 Spectacular... on cover)
St. John Publishing Co.: Nov, 1949 - No. 2, Feb, 1950 (No. 1 ...in Romance on cover) (Slightly larger size)

1(Scarce); Bolle, Starr-a(2) 30 60 90 177 289 400
2(Scarce)-Slave Girl; China Bombshell app.; Bolle, L. Starr-a 41 82 123 256 428 600

ADVENTURES FOR BOYS
Bailey Enterprises: Dec, 1954

nn-Comics, text, & photos 8 16 24 40 50 60

ADVENTURES IN PARADISE (TV)
Dell Publishing Co.: Feb-Apr, 1962

Four Color #1301 5 10 15 34 60 85

ADVENTURES IN ROMANCE (See Adventures)

ADVENTURES IN SCIENCE (See Classics Illustrated Special Issue)

ADVENTURES IN THE DC UNIVERSE
DC Comics: Apr, 1997 - No. 19, Oct, 1998 ($1.75/$1.95/$1.99)

1-Animated style in all: JLA-c/app 5.00
2-11,13-17,19: 2-Flash app. 3-Wonder Woman. 4-Green Lantern. 6-Aquaman. 7-Shazam Family. 8-Blue Beetle & Booster Gold. 9-Flash. 10-Legion. 11-Green Lantern & Wonder Woman. 13-Impulse & Martian Manhunter. 14-Superboy/Flash race 3.50
12,18-JLA-c/app 3.50
Annual 1(1997, $3.95)-Dr. Fate, Impulse, Rose & Thorn, Superboy, Mister Miracle app. 4.50

ADVENTURES IN THE RIFLE BRIGADE
DC Comics (Vertigo): Oct, 2000 - No. 3, Dec, 2000 ($2.50, limited series)

1-3-Ennis-s/Ezquerra-a/Bolland-c 3.00
TPB (2004, $14.95) r/series and Operation Bollock series 15.00

ADVENTURES IN THE RIFLE BRIGADE: OPERATION BOLLOCK
DC Comics (Vertigo): Oct, 2001 - No. 3, Jan, 2002 ($2.50, limited series)

1-3-Ennis-s/Ezquerra-a/Fabry-c 3.00

ADVENTURES IN 3-D (With glasses)
Harvey Publications: Nov, 1953 - No. 2, Jan, 1954 (25¢)

1-Nostrand, Powell-a, 2-Powell-a 14 28 42 80 115 150

ADVENTURES INTO DARKNESS (See Seduction of the Innocent 3-D)
Better-Standard Publications/Visual Editions: No. 5, Aug, 1952- No. 14, 1954

5-Katz-c/a; Toth-a(p) 46 92 138 290 488 685
6-Tuska, Katz-a 36 72 108 211 343 475

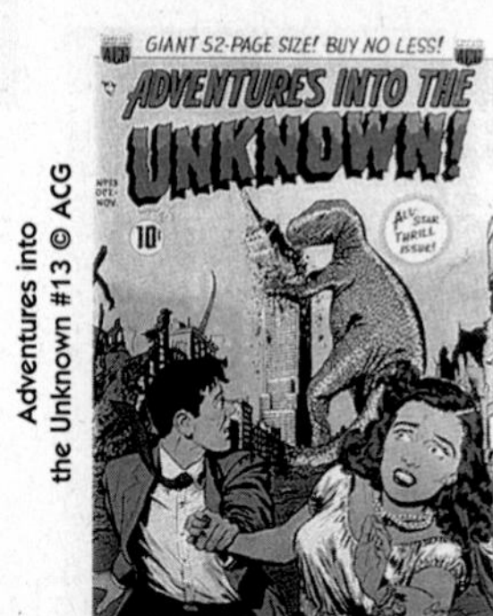

Adventures into the Unknown #13 © ACG

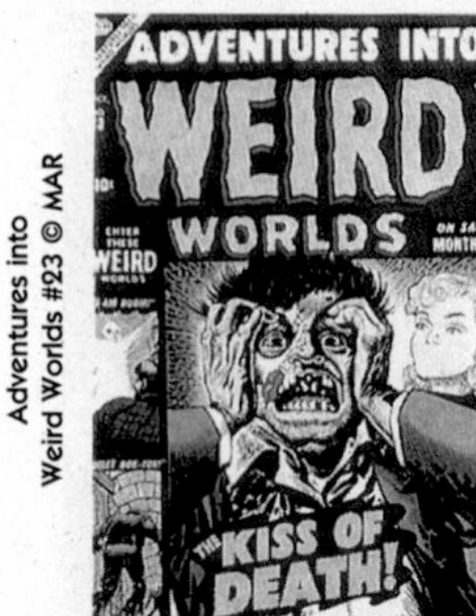

Adventures into Weird Worlds #23 © MAR

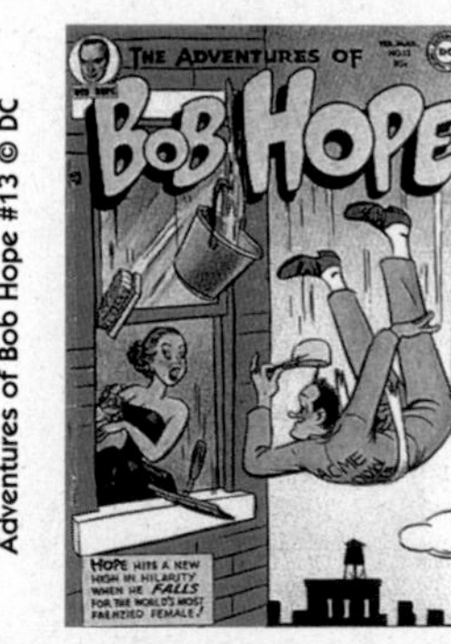

Adventures of Bob Hope #13 © DC

	GD 2.0	VG 4.0	FN 6.0	VF 8.0	VF/NM 9.0	NM- 9.2
7-9: 7-Katz-c/a. 8,9-Toth-a(p)	36	72	108	211	343	475
10-12: 10,11-Jack Katz-a. 12-Toth-a; lingerie panel	32	64	96	188	307	425
13-Toth-a(p); Cannibalism story cited by T. E. Murphy articles	40	80	120	244	402	560
14	26	52	78	154	252	350

NOTE: ***Fawcette** a-13. **Moreira** a-5. **Sekowsky** a-10, 11, 13(2).*

ADVENTURES INTO TERROR (Formerly Joker Comics)
Marvel/Atlas Comics (CDS): No. 43, Nov, 1950 - No. 31, May, 1954

	GD 2.0	VG 4.0	FN 6.0	VF 8.0	VF/NM 9.0	NM- 9.2
43(#1)	73	146	219	468	802	1135
44(#2, 2/51)-Sol Brodsky-c	43	86	129	271	456	640
3(4/51), 4	34	68	102	204	332	460
5-Wolverton-c panel/Mystic #6; Rico-c panel also; Atom Bomb story	37	74	111	222	361	500
6,8: 8-Wolverton text illo r-/Marvel Tales #104; prototype of Spider-Man villain The Lizard	32	64	96	192	314	435
7-Wolverton-a "Where Monsters Dwell", 6 pgs.; Tuska-c; Maneely-c panels	63	126	189	403	689	975
9,10,12-Krigstein-a. 9-Decapitation panels	31	62	93	182	296	410
11,13-20	25	50	75	150	245	340
21-24,26-31	24	48	72	140	230	320
25-Matt Fox-a	29	58	87	170	278	385

NOTE: ***Ayers** a-21. **Colan** a-3, 5, 14, 21, 24, 25, 28, 29; c-27. **Colletta** a-30. **Everett** c-13, 21, 25. **Fass** a-28, 29. **Forte** a-28. **Heath** a-43, 44, 4-6, 22, 24, 26; c-43, 9, 11. **Lazarus** a-7. **Maneely** a-7(3 pg.), 10, 11, 21., 22 c-15, 29. **Don Rico** a-4, 5(3 pg.). **Sekowsky** a-43, 3, 4. **Sinnott** a-8, 9, 11, 24, 28. **Tuska** a-14; c-7.*

ADVENTURES INTO THE UNKNOWN
American Comics Group: Fall, 1948 - No. 174, Aug, 1967 (No. 1-33: 52 pgs.)
(1st continuous series Supernatural comic; see Eerie #1)

	GD 2.0	VG 4.0	FN 6.0	VF 8.0	VF/NM 9.0	NM- 9.2
1-Guardineer-a; adapt. of 'Castle of Otranto' by Horace Walpole	245	490	735	1568	2684	3800
2,3: 3-Feldstein-a (9 pgs)	83	166	249	527	906	1285
4,5: 5- 'Spirit Of Frankenstein' series begins, ends #12 (except #11)	43	86	129	271	461	650
6-10	36	72	108	216	351	485
11-16,18-20: 13-Starr-a. 15-Hitler app.	30	60	90	177	289	400
17-Story similar to movie 'The Thing'	34	68	102	204	335	465
21-26,28-30	26	52	78	154	252	350
27-Williamson/Krenkel-a (8 pgs.)	32	64	96	188	307	425
31-50: 38-Atom bomb panels; Devil-c	20	40	60	118	192	265
51-(1/54)-(3-D effect-c/story)-Only white cover	41	82	123	256	428	600
52-58: (3-D effect-c/stories with black covers). 52-E.C. swipe/Haunt Of Fear #14	39	78	117	240	395	550
59-3-D effect story only; new logo	30	60	90	177	289	400
60-Wood*esque*-a by Landau	15	30	45	88	137	185
61-Last pre-code issue (1-2/55)	15	30	45	88	137	185
62-70	7	14	21	46	86	125
71-90: 80-Hydrogen bomb panel	6	12	18	37	66	95
91,96(#95 on inside),107,116-All have Williamson-a	6	12	18	40	73	105
92-95,97-99,101-106,108-115,117-128: 109-113,118-Whitney painted-c. 128-Williamson/Krenkel/Torres-a(r)/Forbidden Worlds #63; last 10¢ issue	5	10	15	31	53	75
100	5	10	15	34	60	85
129-153,157: 153,157-Magic Agent app.	4	8	12	23	37	50
154-Nemesis series begins (origin), ends #170	4	8	12	28	47	65
155,156,158-167,170-174: 174-Flying saucer-c	4	8	12	22	35	48
168-Ditko-a(p)	4	8	12	27	44	60
169-Nemesis battles Hitler	4	8	12	27	44	60
Nemesis Archives: Vol. One (Dark Horse Books, 9/08, $59.95) r/#154-170; creator bios						60.00

NOTE: *"Spirit of Frankenstein" series in 5, 6, 8-10, 12, 16. **Buscema** a-100, 106, 108-110, 158r, 165r. **Cameron** a-34. **Craig** a-152, 160. **Goode** a-45, 47, 60. **Landau** a-51, 59-63. **Lazarus** a-34, 48, 51, 52, 56, 58, 79, 87; c-31-56, 58. **Reinman** a-102, 111, 112, 115-118, 124, 130, 137, 141, 145, 164. **Whitney** c-12-30, 57, 59-on (most.) **Torres/Williamson** a-116.*

ADVENTURES INTO WEIRD WORLDS
Marvel/Atlas Comics (ACI): Jan, 1952 - No. 30, June, 1954

	GD 2.0	VG 4.0	FN 6.0	VF 8.0	VF/NM 9.0	NM- 9.2
1-Atom bomb panels	100	200	300	635	1093	1550
2-Sci/fic stories (2); one by Maneely	42	84	126	267	451	635
3-10: 7-Tongue ripped out. 10-Krigstein, Everett-a	34	68	102	199	325	450
11-20	28	56	84	165	270	375
21-Hitler in Hell story	36	72	108	211	343	475
22-26: 24-Man holds hypo & splits in two-c	25	50	75	150	245	340
27-Matt Fox end of world story-a; severed head-c	43	86	129	271	461	650
28-Atom bomb story; decapitation panels	28	56	84	165	270	375
29,30	21	42	63	126	206	285

NOTE: ***Ayers** a-8, 26. **Everett** a-4, 5; c-6, 8, 10-13, 18, 19, 22, 24, 25; a-4, 25. **Fass** a-7. **Forte** a-21, 24. **Al Hartley** a-2. **Heath** a-1, 4, 17, 22; c-7, 9, 20. **Maneely** a-2, 3, 11, 20, 22, 23, 25; c-1, 3, 22, 25-27, 29. **Reinman** a-24, 28. **Rico** a-13. **Robinson** a-13. **Sinnott** a-25, 30. **Tuska** a-1, 2, 12, 15. **Whitney** a-7. **Wildey** a-28. Bondage c-22.*

ADVENTURES IN WONDERLAND (Also see Uncle Charlies Fables)
Lev Gleason Publications: April, 1955 - No. 5, Feb, 1956 (Jr. Readers Guild)

	GD 2.0	VG 4.0	FN 6.0	VF 8.0	VF/NM 9.0	NM- 9.2
1-Maurer-a	11	22	33	62	86	110
2-4	7	14	21	37	46	55
5-Christmas issue	8	16	24	40	50	60

ADVENTURES OF ALAN LADD, THE
National Periodical Publ.: Oct-Nov, 1949 - No. 9, Feb-Mar, 1951 (All 52 pgs.)

	GD 2.0	VG 4.0	FN 6.0	VF 8.0	VF/NM 9.0	NM- 9.2
1-Photo-c	70	140	210	445	765	1085
2-Photo-c	39	78	117	231	378	525
3-6: Last photo-c	32	64	96	188	307	425
7-9	26	52	78	154	252	350

NOTE: ***Dan Barry** a-1. **Moreira** a-3-7.*

ADVENTURES OF ALICE (Also see Alice in Wonderland) (Becomes Alice at Monkey Island #3)
Civil Service Publ./Pentagon Publishing Co.: 1945

	GD 2.0	VG 4.0	FN 6.0	VF 8.0	VF/NM 9.0	NM- 9.2
1	15	30	45	83	124	165
2-Through the Magic Looking Glass	11	22	33	62	86	110

ADVENTURES OF BARON MUNCHAUSEN, THE
Now Comics: July, 1989 - No. 4, Oct, 1989 ($1.75, limited series)

	GD 2.0	VG 4.0	FN 6.0	VF 8.0	VF/NM 9.0	NM- 9.2
1-4: Movie adaptation						3.00

ADVENTURES OF BARRY WEEN, BOY GENIUS, THE
Image Comics: Mar, 1999 - No. 3, May, 1999 ($2.95, B&W, limited series)

	GD 2.0	VG 4.0	FN 6.0	VF 8.0	VF/NM 9.0	NM- 9.2
1-3-Judd Winick-s/a						3.00
...: Secret Crisis Origin Files (Oni, 7/04, Free Comic Book Day giveaway) - Winick-s/a						3.00
TPB (Oni Press, 11/99, $8.95) r/#1-3						9.00

ADVENTURES OF BARRY WEEN, BOY GENIUS 2.0, THE
Oni Press: Feb, 2000 - No. 3, Apr, 2000 ($2.95, B&W, limited series)

	GD 2.0	VG 4.0	FN 6.0	VF 8.0	VF/NM 9.0	NM- 9.2
1-3-Judd Winick-s/a						3.00
TPB (2000, $8.95)						9.00

ADVENTURES OF BARRY WEEN, BOY GENIUS 3, THE : MONKEY TALES
Oni Press: Feb, 2001 - No. 6, Feb, 2002 ($2.95, B&W, limited series)

	GD 2.0	VG 4.0	FN 6.0	VF 8.0	VF/NM 9.0	NM- 9.2
1-6-Judd Winick-s/a						3.00
TPB (2001, $8.95) r/#1-3; intro. by Peter David						9.00
...4 TPB (5/02, $8.95) r/#4-6						9.00

ADVENTURES OF BAYOU BILLY, THE (Based on video game)
Archie Comics: Sept, 1989 - No. 5, June, 1990 ($1.00)

	GD 2.0	VG 4.0	FN 6.0	VF 8.0	VF/NM 9.0	NM- 9.2
1-5: Esposito-c/a(i). 5-Kelley Jones-c						3.00

ADVENTURES OF BOB HOPE, THE (Also see True Comics #59)
National Per. Publ.: Feb-Mar, 1950 - No. 109, Feb-Mar, 1968 (#1-10: 52pgs.)

	GD 2.0	VG 4.0	FN 6.0	VF 8.0	VF/NM 9.0	NM- 9.2
1-Photo-c	213	426	639	1363	2332	3300
2-Photo-c	87	174	261	553	952	1350
3,4-Photo-c. 4-Horror-c	54	108	162	343	574	825
5-10	40	80	120	246	411	575
11-20	28	56	84	165	270	375
21-31 (2-3/55; last precode)	20	40	60	114	182	250
32-40	9	18	27	60	120	180
41-50	8	16	24	54	102	150
51-70	7	14	21	44	82	120
71-93	5	10	15	34	60	85
94-Aquaman cameo	5	10	15	34	60	85
95-1st app. Super-Hip & 1st monster issue (11/65)	7	14	21	44	82	120
96-105: Super-Hip and monster stories in all. 103-Batman, Robin, Ringo Starr cameos	5	10	15	33	57	80
106-109-All monster-c/stories by N. Adams-c/a	7	14	21	46	86	125

NOTE: *Buzzy in #34. Kitty Karr of Hollywood in #15, 17-20, 23, 28. Liz in #26, 109. Miss Beverly Hills of Hollywood in #7, 8, 10, 13, 14. Miss Melody Lane of Broadway in #15. Rusty in #23, 25. Tommy in #24. No 2nd feature in #2-4, 6, 8, 11, 12, 28-108.*

ADVENTURES OF CAPTAIN AMERICA
Marvel Comics: Sept, 1991 - No. 4, Jan, 1992 ($4.95, 52 pgs., squarebound, limited series)

	GD 2.0	VG 4.0	FN 6.0	VF 8.0	VF/NM 9.0	NM- 9.2
1-4: 1-Origin in WW2; embossed-c; Nicieza scripts; Maguire-c/a(p) begins, ends #3. 2-4-Austin-c/a(i). 3,4-Red Skull app.						5.00

ADVENTURES OF CYCLOPS AND PHOENIX (Also See Askani'son & The Further Adventures of Cyclops And Phoenix)
Marvel Comics: May, 1994 - No. 4, Aug, 1994 ($2.95, limited series)

	GD 2.0	VG 4.0	FN 6.0	VF 8.0	VF/NM 9.0	NM- 9.2
1-4-Characters from X-Men; origin of Cable						4.00
Trade paperback ($14.95)-reprints #1-4						15.00

ADVENTURES OF DEAN MARTIN AND JERRY LEWIS, THE

Adventures of Jerry Lewis #60 © DC

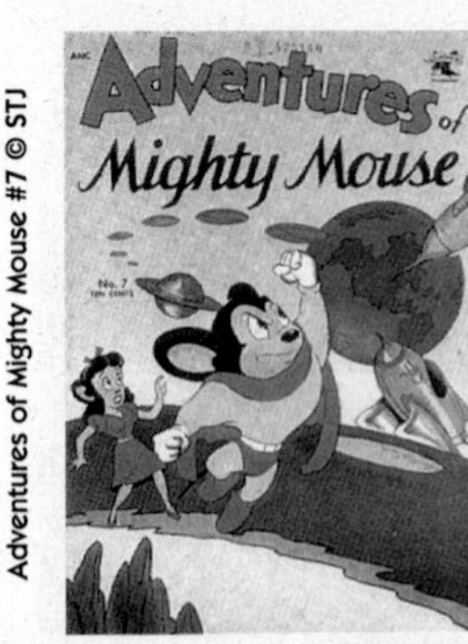

Adventures of Mighty Mouse #7 © STJ

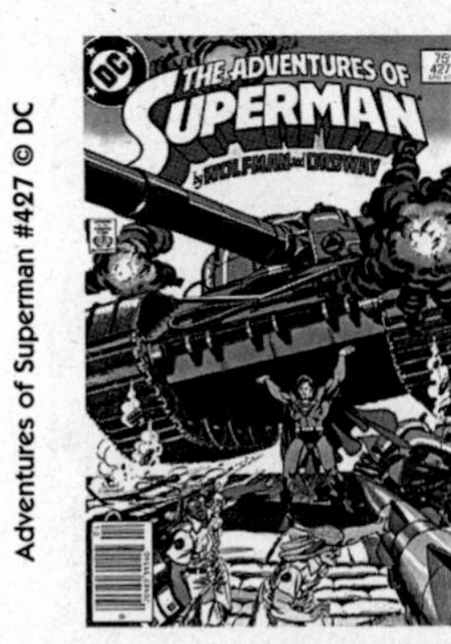

Adventures of Superman #427 © DC

(The Adventures of Jerry Lewis #41 on) (See Movie Love #12)
National Periodical Publications: July-Aug, 1952 - No. 40, Oct, 1957

	GD 2.0	VG 4.0	FN 6.0	VF 8.0	VF/NM 9.0	NM- 9.2
1	129	258	387	826	1413	2000
2-3 pg origin on how they became a team	55	110	165	352	601	850
3-10: 3- I Love Lucy text featurette	34	68	102	199	325	450
11-19: Last precode (2/55)	21	42	63	124	202	280
20-30	16	32	48	94	147	200
31-40	14	28	42	82	121	160

ADVENTURES OF DETECTIVE ACE KING, THE (Also see Bob Scully-- & Detective Dan)
Humor Publ. Corp.: No date (1933) (36 pgs., 9-1/2x12") (10¢, B&W, one-shot) (paper-c)

	GD 2.0	VG 4.0	FN 6.0	VF 8.0	VF/NM 9.0	NM- 9.2
Book 1-Along with Bob Scully & Detective Dan, the first comic w/original art & the first of a single theme.; Not reprints; Ace King by Martin Nadle (The American Sherlock Holmes). A Dick Tracy look-alike	475	950	1425	3800	-	-

ADVENTURES OF EVIL AND MALICE, THE
Image Comics: June, 1999 - No. 3, Nov, 1999 ($3.50/$3.95, limited series)

	GD 2.0	VG 4.0	FN 6.0	VF 8.0	VF/NM 9.0	NM- 9.2
1-3-Jimmie Robinson-s/a. 3-($3.95-c)						4.00

ADVENTURES OF FELIX THE CAT, THE
Harvey Comics: May, 1992 ($1.25)

	GD 2.0	VG 4.0	FN 6.0	VF 8.0	VF/NM 9.0	NM- 9.2
1-Messmer-r						5.00

ADVENTURES OF FORD FAIRLANE, THE
DC Comics: May, 1990 - No. 4, Aug, 1990 ($1.50, limited series, mature)

	GD 2.0	VG 4.0	FN 6.0	VF 8.0	VF/NM 9.0	NM- 9.2
1-4: Andrew Dice Clay movie tie-in; Don Heck inks						3.00

ADVENTURES OF HOMER COBB, THE
Say/Bart Prod. : Sept, 1947 (Oversized) (Published in the U.S., but printed in Canada)

	GD 2.0	VG 4.0	FN 6.0	VF 8.0	VF/NM 9.0	NM- 9.2
1-(Scarce)-Feldstein-c/a	39	78	117	240	395	550

ADVENTURES OF HOMER GHOST (See Homer The Happy Ghost)
Atlas Comics: June, 1957 - No. 2, Aug, 1957

	GD 2.0	VG 4.0	FN 6.0	VF 8.0	VF/NM 9.0	NM- 9.2
V1#1,2: 2-Robot-c	13	26	39	74	105	135

ADVENTURES OF JERRY LEWIS, THE (Adventures of Dean Martin & Jerry Lewis No. 1-40) (See Super DC Giant)
National Periodical Publ.: No. 41, Nov, 1957 - No. 124, May-June, 1971

	GD 2.0	VG 4.0	FN 6.0	VF 8.0	VF/NM 9.0	NM- 9.2
41	9	18	27	59	117	175
42-60	7	14	21	46	86	125
61-67,69-73,75-80	6	12	18	38	69	100
68,74-Photo-c (movie)	9	18	27	58	114	170
81,82,85-87,90,91,94,96,98,99	5	10	15	34	60	85
83,84,88: 83-1st Monsters-c/s. 84-Jerry as a Super-hero-c/s. 88-1st Witch, Miss Kraft	6	12	18	38	69	100
89-Bob Hope app.; Wizard of Oz & Alfred E. Neuman in MAD parody	6	12	18	41	76	110
92-Superman cameo	6	12	18	41	76	110
93-Beatles parody as babies	6	12	18	38	69	100
95-1st Uncle Hal Wack-A-Boy Camp-c/s	6	12	18	38	69	100
97-Batman/Robin/Joker-c/story; Riddler & Penguin app; Dick Sprang-c.	8	16	24	56	108	160
100	6	12	18	40	73	105
101,103,104-Neal Adams-c/a	7	14	21	46	86	125
102-Beatles app.; Neal Adams c/a	9	18	27	57	111	165
105-Superman x-over	6	12	18	41	76	110
106-111,113-116	4	8	12	28	47	65
112,117: 112-Flash x-over. 117-W. Woman x-over	6	12	18	40	73	105
118-124	4	8	12	27	44	60

NOTE: *Monster-c/s-90,93,96,98,101. Wack-A-Buy Camp-c/s-96,99,102,107,108.*

ADVENTURES OF JO-JOY, THE (See Jo-Joy)

ADVENTURES OF LASSIE, THE (See Lassie)

ADVENTURES OF LUTHER ARKWRIGHT, THE
Valkyrie Press/Dark Horse Comics: Oct, 1987 - No. 9, Jan, 1989 ($2.00, B&W) V2, #1, Mar, 1990 - V2#9, 1990 ($1.95, B&W)

	GD 2.0	VG 4.0	FN 6.0	VF 8.0	VF/NM 9.0	NM- 9.2
1-9: 1-Alan Moore intro., V2#1-9 (Dark Horse): r-1st series; new-c						4.00
TPB (1997, $14.95) r/#1-9 w/Michael Moorcock intro.						15.00

ADVENTURES OF MIGHTY MOUSE (Mighty Mouse Adventures No. 1)
St. John Publishing Co.: No. 2, Jan, 1952 - No. 18, May, 1955

	GD 2.0	VG 4.0	FN 6.0	VF 8.0	VF/NM 9.0	NM- 9.2
2	27	54	81	162	266	370
3-5	15	30	45	88	137	185
6-18	12	24	36	69	97	125

ADVENTURES OF MIGHTY MOUSE (2nd Series) (Becomes Mighty Mouse #161 on)
(Two No. 144's; formerly Paul Terry's Comics; No. 129-137 have nn's)
St. John/Pines/Dell/Gold Key: No. 126, Aug, 1955 - No. 160, Oct, 1963

	GD 2.0	VG 4.0	FN 6.0	VF 8.0	VF/NM 9.0	NM- 9.2
126(8/55), 127(10/55), 128(11/55)-St. John	10	20	30	56	76	95
nn(129, 4/56)-144(8/59)-Pines	5	10	15	30	50	70
144(10-12/59)-155(7-9/62) Dell	4	8	12	27	44	60
156(10/62)-160(10/63) Gold Key	4	8	12	27	44	60

NOTE: *Early issues titled "Paul Terry's Adventures of ...."*

ADVENTURES OF MIGHTY MOUSE (Formerly Mighty Mouse)
Gold Key: No. 166, Mar, 1979 - No. 172, Jan, 1980

	GD 2.0	VG 4.0	FN 6.0	VF 8.0	VF/NM 9.0	NM- 9.2
166-172	1	2	3	5	6	8

ADVS. OF MR. FROG & MISS MOUSE (See Dell Junior Treasury No. 4)

ADVENTURES OF OZZIE & HARRIET, THE (See Ozzie & Harriet)

ADVENTURES OF PATORUZU
Green Publishing Co.: Aug, 1946 - Winter, 1946

	GD 2.0	VG 4.0	FN 6.0	VF 8.0	VF/NM 9.0	NM- 9.2
nn's-Contains Animal Crackers reprints	6	12	18	28	34	40

ADVENTURES OF PINKY LEE, THE (TV)
Atlas Comics: July, 1955 - No. 5, Dec, 1955

	GD 2.0	VG 4.0	FN 6.0	VF 8.0	VF/NM 9.0	NM- 9.2
1	24	48	72	142	234	325
2-5	15	30	45	88	137	185

ADVENTURES OF PIPSQUEAK, THE (Formerly Pat the Brat)
Archie Publications (Radio Comics): No. 34, Sept, 1959 - No. 39, July, 1960

	GD 2.0	VG 4.0	FN 6.0	VF 8.0	VF/NM 9.0	NM- 9.2
34	3	6	9	21	33	45
35-39	3	6	9	17	26	35

ADVENTURES OF QUAKE & QUISP, THE (See Quaker Oats "Plenty of Glutton")

ADVENTURES OF REX THE WONDER DOG, THE (Rex...No. 1)
National Periodical Publ.: Jan-Feb, 1952 - No. 45, May-June, 1959; No. 46, Nov-Dec, 1959

	GD 2.0	VG 4.0	FN 6.0	VF 8.0	VF/NM 9.0	NM- 9.2
1-(Scarce)-Toth-c/a	168	336	504	1075	1838	2600
2-(Scarce)-Toth-c/a	71	142	213	454	777	1100
3-(Scarce)-Toth-a	55	110	165	347	594	840
4,5	43	86	129	268	454	640
6-10	37	74	111	222	361	500
11-Atom bomb-c/story; dinosaur-c/sty	40	80	120	246	411	575
12-19: 19-Last precode (1-2/55)	24	48	72	144	237	330
20-46	18	36	54	103	162	220

NOTE: ***Infantino, Gil Kane** art in 5-19 (most)*

ADVENTURES OF ROBIN HOOD, THE (Formerly Robin Hood)
Magazine Enterprises (Sussex Publ. Co.): No. 7, 9/57 - No. 8, 11/57
(Based on Richard Greene TV Show)

	GD 2.0	VG 4.0	FN 6.0	VF 8.0	VF/NM 9.0	NM- 9.2
7,8-Richard Greene photo-c. 7-Powell-a	15	30	45	83	124	165

ADVENTURES OF ROBIN HOOD, THE
Gold Key: Mar, 1974 - No. 7, Jan, 1975 (Disney cartoon) (36 pgs.)

	GD 2.0	VG 4.0	FN 6.0	VF 8.0	VF/NM 9.0	NM- 9.2
1(90291-403)-Part-r of $1.50 editions	2	4	6	13	18	22
2-7: 1-7 are part-r	2	4	6	8	11	14

ADVENTURES OF SNAKE PLISSKEN
Marvel Comics: Jan, 1997 ($2.50, one-shot)

	GD 2.0	VG 4.0	FN 6.0	VF 8.0	VF/NM 9.0	NM- 9.2
1-Based on Escape From L.A. movie; Brereton-c						4.00

ADVENTURES OF SPAWN, THE
Image Comics (Todd McFarlane Prods.): Jan, 2007; Nov, 2008 ($5.99)

	GD 2.0	VG 4.0	FN 6.0	VF 8.0	VF/NM 9.0	NM- 9.2
1,2-Printed adaptation of the Spawn.com web comic; Khary Randolph-a						6.00

ADVENTURES OF SPIDER-MAN, THE (Based on animated TV series)
Marvel Comics: Apr, 1996 - No. 12, Mar, 1997 (99¢)

	GD 2.0	VG 4.0	FN 6.0	VF 8.0	VF/NM 9.0	NM- 9.2
1-12: 1-Punisher app. 2-Venom cameo. 3-X-Men. 6-Fantastic Four						3.00

ADVENTURES OF SUPERBOY, THE (See Superboy, 2nd Series)

ADVENTURES OF SUPERMAN (Formerly Superman)
DC Comics: No. 424, Jan, 1987 - No. 499, Feb, 1993; No. 500, Early June, 1993 - No. 649, Apr, 2006 (This title's numbering continues with Superman #650, May, 2006)

	GD 2.0	VG 4.0	FN 6.0	VF 8.0	VF/NM 9.0	NM- 9.2
424-Ordway-c/a/Wolfman-s begin following Byrne's Superman revamp						4.00
425-435,437-462: 426-Legends x-over. 432-1st app. Jose Delgado who becomes Gangbuster in #434. 437-Millennium x-over. 438-New Brainiac app. 440-Batman app. 449-Invasion						3.00
436-Byrne scripts begin; Millennium x-over						3.50
463-Superman/Flash race; cover swipe/Superman #199						5.00
464-Lobo-c & app. (pre-dates Lobo #1)						5.00
465-479,481-495: 467-Part 2 of Batman story. 473-Hal Jordan, Guy Gardner x-over. 477-Legion app. 491-Last $1.00-c. 495-Forever People-c/story; Darkseid app.						3.00
480,496,497: 480-($1.75, 52 pgs.). 496-Doomsday cameo. 497-Doomsday battle issue						4.00
496,497-2nd printings						3.00

Adventures of Superman #636 © DC

Adventures of the Jaguar #5 © AP

Adventure Time #14 © Cartoon Network

	GD 2.0	VG 4.0	FN 6.0	VF 8.0	VF/NM 9.0	NM- 9.2

498,499-Funeral for a Friend; Supergirl app. 4.00
498-2nd & 3rd printings 3.00
500-($2.95, 68 pgs.)-Collector's edition w/card 5.00
500-($2.50, 68 pgs.)-Regular edition w/different-c 4.00
500-Platinum edition 30.00
501-($1.95)-Collector's edition with die-cut-c 3.50
501-($1.50)-Regular edition w/mini-poster & diff.-c 3.00
502-516: 502-Supergirl-c/story. 508-Challengers of the Unknown app. 510-Bizarro-c/story. 516-(9/94)-Zero Hour 3.00
505-($2.50)-Holo-grafx foil-c edition 3.50
0,517-523: 0-(10/94). 517-(11/94) 3.00
524-549,551-580: 524-Begin $1.95-c. 527-Return of Alpha Centurion (Zero Hour). 533-Impulse-c/app. 535-Luthor-c/app. 536-Brainiac app. 537-Parasite app. 540-Final Night x-over. 541-Superboy-c/app.; Lois & Clark honeymoon. 545-New powers. 546-New costume. 555-Red & Blue Supermen battle. 557-Millennium Giants x-over. 558-560: Superman Silver Age-style story; Krypto app. 561-Begin $1.99-c. 565-JLA app. 3.00
550-($3.50)-Double sized 4.00
581-588: 581-Begin $2.25-c. 583-Emperor Joker. 588-Casey-s 3.00
589-595: 589-Return to Krypton; Rivoche-c. 591-Wolfman-s. 593-595-Our Worlds at War x-over. 593-New Suicide Squad formed. 594-Doomsday-c/app. 3.00
596-Aftermath of "War" x-over has panel showing damaged World Trade Center buildings; issue went on sale the day after the Sept. 11 attack 6.00
597-599,601-624: 597-Joker: Last Laugh. 604,605-Ultraman, Owlman, Superwoman app. 606-Return to Krypton. 612-616,619-623-Nowlan-c. 624-Mr. Majestic app. 3.00
600-($3.95) Wieringo-a; painted-c by Adel; pin-ups by various 4.00
625,626-Godfall parts 2,5; Turner-c; Caldwell-a(p) 4.00
627-641,643-648: 627-Begin $2.50-c, Rucka-s/Clark-a/Ha-c begin. 628-Wagner-c. 631-Bagged with Sky Captain CD; Lois shot. 634-Mxyzptlk visits DC offices. 639-Capt. Marvel & Eclipso app. 641-OMAC app. 643-Sacrifice aftermath; Batman & Wonder Woman app. 3.00
642-OMAC Project x-over Sacrifice pt. 3; JLA app. 5.00
642-(2nd printing) red tone cover 3.00
649-Last issue; Infinite Crisis x-over, Superman vs. Earth-2 Superman 4.00
#1,000,000 (11/98) Gene Ha-c; 853rd Century x-over 3.00
Annual 1 (1987, $1.25, 52 pgs.)-Starlin-c & scripts 4.00
Annual 2,3 (1990, 1991, $2.00, 68 pgs.): 2-Byrne-c/a(i); Legion '90 (Lobo) app. 3-Armageddon 2001 x-over 4.00
Annual 4-6 ('92-'94, $2.50, 68 pgs.): 4-Guy Gardner/Lobo-c/story; Eclipso storyline; Quesada-c(p). 5-Bloodlines storyline. 6-Elseworlds sty. 4.00
Annual 7,9('95, '97, $3.95)-7-Year One story. 9-Pulp Heroes sty 4.00
Annual 8 (1996, $2.95)-Legends of the Dead Earth story 4.00
NOTE: ***Erik Larsen** a-431.*

ADVENTURES OF SUPERMAN
DC Comics: Jul, 2013 - Present ($3.99)

1-11-Short story anthology by various. 1-Lemire-s/a. 4-Timm-c. 6-Mongul app. 4.00

ADVENTURES OF THE DOVER BOYS
Archie Comics (Close-up): September, 1950 - No. 2, 1950 (No month given)

1,2 10 20 30 56 76 95

ADVENTURES OF THE FLY (The Fly #1-6; Fly Man No. 32-39; See The Double Life of Private Strong, The Fly, Laugh Comics & Mighty Crusaders)
Archie Publications/Radio Comics: Aug, 1959 - No. 30, Oct, 1964; No. 31, May, 1965

1-Shield app.; origin The Fly; S&K-c/a 50 100 150 390 870 1350
2-Williamson, S&K-a 26 52 78 182 404 625
3-Origin retold; Davis, Powell-a 21 42 63 147 324 500
4-Neal Adams-a(p)(1 panel); S&K-c; Powell-a; 2 pg. Shield story 14 28 42 97 214 330
5,6,9,10: 9-Shield app. 9-1st app. Cat Girl. 10-Black Hood app. 10 20 30 68 144 220
7,8: 7-1st S.A. app. Black Hood (7/60). 8-1st S.A. app. Shield (9/60) 11 22 33 76 163 250
11-13,15-20: 13-1st app. Fly Girl w/o costume. 16-Last 10¢ issue. 20-Origin Fly Girl retold 7 14 21 49 92 135
14-Origin & 1st app. Fly Girl in costume 8 16 24 55 105 155
21-30: 23-Jaguar cameo. 27-29-Black Hood 1 pg. strips. 30-Comet x-over (1st S.A. app.) in Fly Girl 6 12 18 38 69 100
31-Black Hood, Shield, Comet app. 6 12 18 40 73 105
Vol. 1 TPB ('04, $12.95) r/#1-4 & Double Life of Private Strong #1,2; foreward by Joe Simon 13.00
NOTE: ***Simon** c-2-4. **Tuska** a-1. Cover title to #31 is Flyman; Advs. of the Fly inside.*

ADVENTURES OF THE JAGUAR, THE (See Blue Ribbon Comics, Laugh Comics & Mighty Crusaders)
Archie Publications (Radio Comics): Sept, 1961 - No. 15, Nov, 1963

1-Origin Jaguar (1st app?) by J. Rosenberger 20 40 60 135 300 465
2,3: 3-Last 10¢ issue 10 20 30 68 144 220
4-6-Catgirl app. (#4's-c is same as splash pg.) 8 16 24 55 105 155
7-10: 10-Dinosaur-c 7 14 21 46 86 125
11-15:13,14-Catgirl, Black Hood app. in both 6 12 18 40 73 105

ADVENTURES OF THE MASK (TV cartoon)
Dark Horse Comics: Jan, 1996 - No. 12, Dec, 1996 ($2.50)

1-12: Based on animated series 3.00

ADVENTURES OF THE NEW MEN (Formerly Newmen #1-21)
Maximum Press: No. 22, Nov, 1996; No. 23, March, 1997 ($2.50)

22,23-Sprouse-c/a 3.00

ADVENTURES OF THE OUTSIDERS, THE (Formerly Batman & The Outsiders; also see The Outsiders)
DC Comics: No. 33, May, 1986 - No. 46, June, 1987

33-46: 39-45-r/Outsiders #1-7 by Aparo 3.00

ADVENTURES OF THE SUPER MARIO BROTHERS (See Super Mario Bros.)
Valiant: 1990 - No. 9, Oct, 1991 ($1.50)

V2#1 2 4 6 8 10 12
2-9 1 2 3 5 6 8

ADVENTURES OF THE THING, THE (Also see The Thing)
Marvel Comics: Apr, 1992 - No. 4, July, 1992, ($1.25, limited series)

1-4: 1-r/Marvel Two-In-One #50 by Byrne; Kieth-c. 2-4-r/Marvel Two-In-One #80,51 & 77; 2-Ghost Rider-c/story; Quesada-c. 3-Miller-r/Quesada-c; new Perez-a (4 pgs.) 3.00

ADVENTURES OF THE X-MEN, THE (Based on animated TV series)
Marvel Comics: Apr, 1996 - No. 12, Mar, 1997 (99¢)

1-12: 1-Wolverine/Hulk battle. 3-Spider-Man-c. 5,6-Magneto-c/app. 3.00

ADVENTURES OF TINKER BELL (See Tinker Bell, 4-Color No. 896 & 982)

ADVENTURES OF TOM SAWYER (See Dell Junior Treasury No. 10)

ADVENTURES OF YOUNG DR. MASTERS, THE
Archie Comics (Radio Comics): Aug, 1964 - No. 2, Nov, 1964

1 3 6 9 21 33 45
2 3 6 9 15 22 28

ADVENTURES ON OTHER WORLDS (See Showcase #17 & 18)

ADVENTURES ON THE PLANET OF THE APES (Also see Planet of the Apes)
Marvel Comics Group: Oct, 1975 - No. 11, Dec, 1976

1-Planet of the Apes magazine-r in color; Starlin-c; adapts movie thru #6 3 6 9 19 30 40
2-5: 5-(25¢-c edition) 2 4 6 11 16 20
5-7-(30¢-c variants, limited distribution) 4 8 12 27 44 60
6-10: 6,7-(25¢-c edition). 7-Adapts 2nd movie (thru #11) 2 4 6 11 16 20
11-Last issue; concludes 2nd movie adaptation 3 6 9 15 22 28
NOTE: ***Alcala** a-6-11r. **Buckler** c-2p. **Nasser** c-7. **Ploog** a-1-9. **Starlin** c-6. **Tuska** a-1-5r.*

ADVENTURES WITH THE DC SUPER HEROES (Interior also inserted into some DC issues)
DC Comics/Geppi's Entertainment Museum: 2007 Free Comic Book Day giveaway

"The Batman and Cal Ripken, Jr. Hall of Fame Edition "A Rare Catch" " in indicia 3.00

ADVENTURE TIME (With Finn & Jake) (Based on the Cartoon Network animated series)
Boom Entertainment (KaBOOM!): Feb, 2012 - Present ($3.99)

1-Cover A 20.00
1-Covers B & C; interlocking image 25.00
1-Cover D variant by Jeffrey Brown 30.00
1-Cover E wraparound 35.00
1-Second & third printings 5.00
2-Four covers 8.00
3-24,26-Multiple covers on all 4.00
25-($4.99) Art by Dustin Nguyen, Jess FInk, Jeffrey Brown & others; multiple covers 5.00
2013 Annual #1 (5/13, $4.99) Three covers; s/a by Langridge, Nguyen & others 5.00
2013 Spoooktacular (10/13, $4.99) Halloween-themed; s/a by Fraser Irving & others 5.00
2013 Summer Special (7/13, $4.99) Multiple covers 5.00
2014 Winter Special (1/14, $4.99) Multiple covers 5.00
... Cover Showcase (12/12, $3.99) Gallery of variant covers for #1-9; Paul Pope-c 4.00
... Free Comic Book Day Edition (5/12) Giveaway flip book with Peanuts 3.00

ADVENTURE TIME: CANDY CAPERS (Cartoon Network)
Boom Entertainment (KaBOOM!): Jul, 2013 - No. 6, Dec, 2013 ($3.99, limited series)

1-6-Multiple covers on all; McGinty-a 4.00

ADVENTURE TIME: MARCELINE AND THE SCREAM QUEENS (Cartoon Network)
Boom Entertainment (KaBOOM!): Jul, 2012 - No. 6, Dec, 2012 ($3.99, limited series)

1-6-Multiple covers on all 4.00

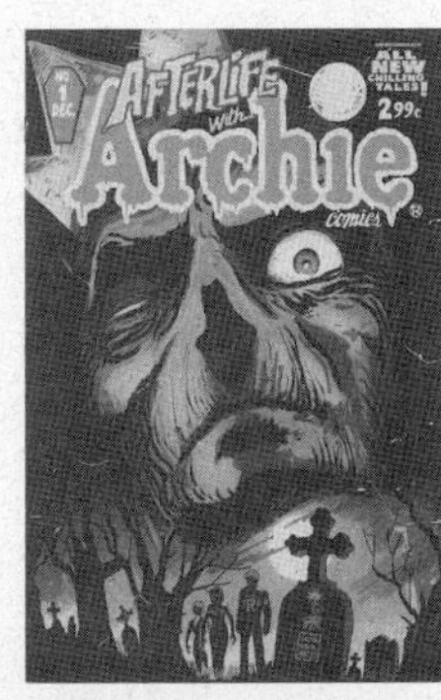

Afterlife with Archie #1 © AP

Age of Apocalypse #13 © MAR

Aggie Mack #8 © SUPR

	GD 2.0	VG 4.0	FN 6.0	VF 8.0	VF/NM 9.0	NM- 9.2

ADVENTURE TIME: THE FLIP SIDE (Cartoon Network)
Boom Entertainment (KaBOOM!): Jan, 2014 - No. 6, ($3.99, limited series)
1-4-Multiple covers on all; Tobin & Coover-s; Wook Jin Clark-a 4.00

ADVENTURE TIME WITH FIONNA & CAKE (Cartoon Network)
Boom Entertainment (KaBOOM!): Jan, 2013 - No. 6, Jun, 2013 ($3.99, limited series)
1-6-Multiple covers on all 4.00

AEON FLUX (Based on the 2005 movie which was based on the MTV animated series)
Dark Horse Comics: Oct, 2005 - No. 4, Jan, 2006 ($2.99, limited series)
1-4-Timothy Green II-a/Mike Kennedy-s 3.00
TPB (5/06, $12.95) r/series; cover gallery 13.00

AFRICA
Magazine Enterprises: 1955
1(A-1#137)-Cave Girl, Thun'da; Powell-c/a(4) 27 54 81 158 259 360

AFRICAN LION (Disney movie)
Dell Publishing Co.: Nov, 1955
Four Color #665 5 10 15 33 57 80

AFTER DARK
Sterling Comics: No. 6, May, 1955 - No. 8, Sept, 1955
6-8-Sekowsky-a in all 9 18 27 52 69 85

AFTER DARK (Co-created by Wesley Snipes)
Radical Comics: No. 0, Jun, 2010 - No. 3 ($1.00/$4.99, limited series)
0-($1.00) Milligan-s/Nentrup & Mattina-a 3.00
1-3-($4.99) Milligan-s/Manco-a 5.00

AFTERLIFE WITH ARCHIE
Archie Comic Publications: Sept, 2013 - Present ($2.99)
1-Aguirre-Sacasa-s/Francavilla-a; zombies in Riverdale; Sabrina app.; 4 covers 10.00
1-Second printing; new cover by Francavilla 3.00
2-Covers by Francavilla & Seeley; back-up short story r/Chilling Advs. in Sorcery 5.00
3,4-Covers by Francavilla & Seeley on each; back-up r/Chilling Advs. in Sorcery 3.00

AFTER THE CAPE
Image Comics (Shadowline): Mar, 2007 - No. 3, May, 2007 ($2.99, B&W, limited series)
1-3-Jim Valentino-s/Marco Rudy-a 3.00
... Volume One TPB (9/07, $12.99) r/series; scripts, sketch pages, character profiles 13.00
...II (11/07 - No. 3, 1/08, $2.99) 1-3-Jim Valentino-s/Sergio Carrera-a 3.00

AGAINST BLACKSHARD 3-D (Also see SoulQuest)
Sirius Comics: August, 1986 ($2.25)
1 3.00

AGENCY, THE
Image Comics (Top Cow): August, 2001 - No. 6, Mar, 2002 ($2.50/$2.95/$4.95)
1-5: 1-Jenkins-s/Hotz-a; three covers by Hotz, Turner, Silvestri. 3-5-($2.95) 3.00
6-($4.95) Flip-c preview of Jeremiah TV series 5.00
Preview (2001, 16 pgs.) B&W pages, cover previews, sketch pages 3.00

AGENT LIBERTY SPECIAL (See Superman, 2nd Series)
DC Comics: 1992 ($2.00, 52 pgs, one-shot)
1-1st solo adventure; Guice-c/a(i) 4.00

AGENTS, THE
Image Comics: Apr, 2003 - No. 6, Sept, 2003 ($2.95, B&W)
1-5-Ben Dunn-c/a in all 3.00
6-Five pg. preview of The Walking Dead #1 3 6 9 14 20 25

AGENTS OF ATLAS
Marvel Comics: Oct, 2006 - No. 6, Mar, 2007 ($2.99, limited series)
1-6: 1-Golden Age heroes Marvel Boy & Venus app.; Kirk-a 3.00
... MGC 1 (7/10, $1.00) r/#1 with "Marvel's Greatest Comics" logo on cover 3.00
HC (2007, $24.99, dustjacket) r/#1-6, What If? #9, agents' debuts in '40s-'50s Atlas comics, creator interviews, character design art 25.00

AGENTS OF ATLAS (Dark Reign)
Marvel Comics: Apr, 2009 - No. 11, Nov, 2009 ($3.99)
1-11: 1-Pagulayan-a; 2 covers by Art Adams and McGuinness; back-up with Wolverine app. 5-New Avengers app. 8-Hulk app. 4.00

AGENTS OF LAW (Also see Comic's Greatest World)
Dark Horse Comics: Mar, 1995 - No. 6, Sept, 1995 ($2.50)
1-6: 5-Predator app. 6-Predator app.; death of Law 3.00

AGENT X (Continued from Deadpool)
Marvel Comics: Sept. 2002 - No. 15, Dec, 2003 ($2.99/$2.25)
1-($2.99) Simone-s/Udon Studios-a; Taskmaster app. 3.50
2-9-($2.25) 2-Punisher app. 3.00
10-15-($2.99) 10,11-Evan Dorkin-s. 12-Hotz-a 3.00

AGE OF APOCALYPSE (See Uncanny X-Force)
Marvel Comics: May, 2012 - No. 14, Jun, 2013 ($2.99)
1-14: 1-Lapham-s/De La Torre-a/Ramos-c. 13-Leads into X-Termination x-over 3.00

AGE OF APOCALYPSE: THE CHOSEN
Marvel Comics: Apr, 1995 ($2.50, one-shot)
1-Wraparound-c 3.00

AGE OF BRONZE
Image Comics: Nov, 1998 - Present ($2.95/$3.50, B&W)
1-6-Eric Shanower-c/s/a 3.50
7-33-($3.50) 3.50
...Behind the Scenes (5/02, $3.50) background info and creative process 3.50
Image Firsts: Age of Bronze #1 (4/10, $1.00) r/#1 with "Image Firsts" cover logo 3.00
...Special (6/99, $2.95) Story of Agamemnon and Menelaus 3.50
A Thousand Ships (7/01, $19.95, TPB) r/#1-9 20.00
Sacrifice (9/04, $19.95, TPB) r/#10-19 20.00

AGE OF HEROES, THE
Halloween Comics/Image Comics #3 on: 1996 - No. 5, 1999 ($2.95, B&W)
1-5: James Hudnall scripts; John Ridgway-c/a 3.00
...Special ($4.95) r/#1,2 5.00
...Special 2 ($6.95) r/#3,4 7.00
...Wex 1 ('98, $2.95) Hudnall-s/Angel Fernandez-a 3.00

AGE OF HEROES (The Heroic Age)
Marvel Comics: Jul, 2010 - No. 4, Oct, 2010 ($3.99, limited series)
1-4-Short stories of Avengers members by various. 4-Jae Lee-c 4.00

AGE OF INNOCENCE: THE REBIRTH OF IRON MAN
Marvel Comics: Feb, 1996 ($2.50, one-shot)
1-New origin of Tony Stark 3.00

AGE OF REPTILES
Dark Horse Comics: Nov, 1993 - No. 4, Feb, 1994 ($2.50, limited series)
1-4: Delgado-c/a/scripts in all 3.00
... The Hunt 1-5 (5/96 - No. 5, 9/96, $2.95) Delgado-c/a/scripts in all; wraparound-c 3.00
... The Journey 1-4 (11/09 - No. 4, 7/10 $3.50) Delgado-c/a/scripts in all; wraparound-c 3.50

AGE OF THE SENTRY, THE
Marvel Comics: Nov, 2008 - No. 6, Mar, 2010 ($2.99, limited series)
1-6-Silver Age style stories. 1-Origin retold; Bullock-c. 3-Coover-a 3.00

AGE OF ULTRON
Marvel Comics: May, 2013 - No. 10, Aug, 2013 ($3.99, limited series)
1-10: 1-Wraparound cardstock foil-c. 1-5-Hitch-a/c. 6-Peterson & Pacheco-a, Hank Pym killed. 10-Polybagged; Angela joins the Marvel Universe 4.00
10AU (8/13, $3.99) Waid-s/Aralijo-a/Pichelli-c; Hank Pym's origin re-told 4.00

AGE OF X (X-Men titles crossover)
Marvel Comics: ($3.99, limited series)
... Alpha 1 (3/11, $3.99) Short stories by various; covers by Bachalo & Coipel 4.00
...: Universe 1,2 (5/11 - No. 2, 6/11, $3.99) Pham-a; Bianchi-c; Avengers & Spider-Man app. 4.00

AGGIE MACK
Four Star Comics Corp./Superior Comics Ltd.: Jan, 1948 - No. 8, Aug, 1949
1-Feldstein-a, "Johnny Prep" 41 82 123 256 428 600
2,3-Kamen-c 23 46 69 136 223 310
4-Feldstein "Johnny Prep"; Kamen-c 31 62 93 182 296 410
5-8-Kamen-c/a 25 50 75 150 245 340

AGGIE MACK
Dell Publishing Co.: Apr - Jun, 1962
Four Color #1335 4 8 12 28 47 65

AIR
DC Comics (Vertigo): Oct, 2008 - No. 24, Oct, 2010 ($2.99)
1-6,8-24-G. Willow Wilson-s/M.K. Perker-a 3.00
7-($1.00) Includes story re-cap 3.00
... A History of the Future TPB (2011, $14.99) r/#18-24 15.00
... Flying Machine TPB (2009, $12.99) r/#6-10; Wilson intro. 13.00
... Letters From Lost Countries TPB (2009, $9.99) r/#1-5; character sketch pages 10.00
... Pure Land TPB (2010, $14.99) r/#11-17 15.00

AIR ACE (Formerly Bill Barnes No. 1-12)

Air Ace V3 #3 © CN

Air Fighters Comics V2 #6 © HILL

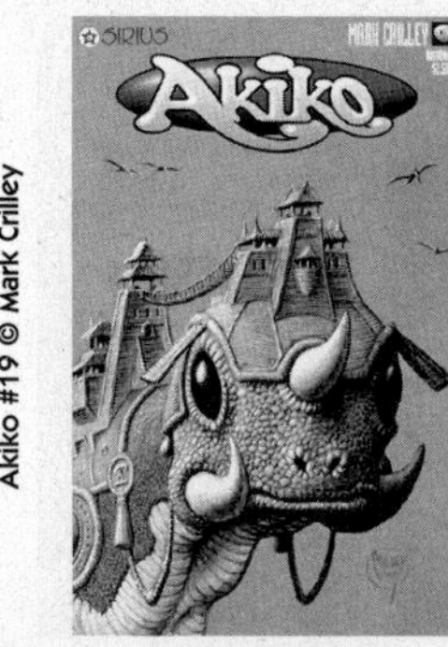

Akiko #19 © Mark Crilley

GD VG FN VF VF/NM NM-
2.0 4.0 6.0 8.0 9.0 9.2

Street & Smith Publications: V2#1, Jan, 1944 - V3#8(No. 20), Feb-Mar, 1947

V2#1-Nazi concentration camp-c 49 98 147 309 522 735
V2#2-Classic WWII-c 116 232 348 742 1271 1800
V2#3-12: 7-Powell-a 16 32 48 94 147 200
V3#1-6: 2-Atomic explosion on-c 14 28 42 80 115 150
V3#7-Powell bondage-c/a; all atomic issue 24 48 72 144 237 330
V3#8 (V5#8 on-c)-Powell-c/a 15 30 45 85 130 175

AIRBOY (Also see Airmaidens, Skywolf, Target: Airboy & Valkyrie)
Eclipse Comics: July, 1986 - No. 50, Oct, 1989 (#1-8, 50¢, 20 pgs., bi-weekly; #9-on, 36 pgs.; #34-on monthly)

1-4: 2-1st Marisa; Skywolf gets new costume. 3-The Heap begins 4.00
5-Valkyrie returns; Dave Stevens-c 1 3 4 6 8 10
6-49: 9-Begin $1.25-c; Skywolf begins. 11-Origin of G.A. Airboy & his plane Birdie. 28-Mr. Monster vs. The Heap. 33-Begin $1.75-c. 38-40-The Heap by Infantino. 41-r/1st app. Valkyrie from Air Fighters. 42-Begin $1.95-c. 46,47-part-r/Air Fighters. 48-Black Angel-r/A.F 3.00
50 ($4.95, 52 pgs.)-Kubert-c 5.00
NOTE: ***Evans*** c-21. ***Gulacy*** c-7, 20. ***Spiegle*** a-34, 35, 37. ***Ken Steacy*** painted c-17, 33.

AIRBOY COMICS (Air Fighters Comics No. 1-22)
Hillman Periodicals: V2#11, Dec, 1945 - V10#4, May, 1953 (No V3#3)

V2#11 61 122 183 390 670 950
12-Valkyrie-c/app. 53 106 159 334 567 800
V3#1,2(no #3) 40 80 120 246 411 575
4-The Heap app. in Skywolf 37 74 111 222 361 500
5,7,8,10,11 33 66 99 194 317 440
6-Valkyrie-c/app. 36 72 108 216 351 485
9-Origin The Heap 37 74 111 222 361 500
12-Skywolf & Airboy x-over; Valkyrie-c/app. 39 78 117 240 395 550
V4#1-Iron Lady app. 33 66 99 194 317 440
2,3,12: 2-Rackman begins 25 50 75 147 241 335
4-Simon & Kirby-c 30 60 90 177 289 400
5-9,11-All S&K-a 28 56 84 165 270 375
10-Valkyrie-c/app. 31 62 93 182 296 410
V5#1-4,6-11: 4-Infantino Heap. 10-Origin The Heap 19 38 57 112 179 245
5-Skull-c. 21 42 63 126 206 285
12-Krigstein-a(p) 20 40 60 115 185 255
V6#1-3,5-12: 6,8-Origin The Heap 18 36 54 107 169 230
4-Origin retold 21 42 63 126 206 285
V7#1-12: 7,8,10-Origin The Heap 18 36 54 105 165 225
V8#1-3,5-12 16 32 48 96 151 205
4-Krigstein-a 17 34 51 100 158 215
V9#1,3,4,6-12: 7-One pg. Frazetta ad 15 30 45 84 127 170
2-Valkyrie app. 15 30 45 88 137 185
5(#100) 15 30 45 88 137 185
V10#1-4 14 28 42 81 118 155
NOTE: ***Barry*** a-V2#3, 7. ***Bolle*** a-V4#12. ***McWilliams*** a-V3#7, 9. ***Powell*** a-V7#2, 3, V8#1, 6. ***Starr*** a-V5#1, 12. ***Dick Wood*** a-V4#12. Bondage-c V5#8.

AIRBOY MEETS THE PROWLER
Eclipse Comics: Aug, 1987 ($1.95, one-shot)

1-John Snyder, III-c/a 3.00

AIRBOY-MR. MONSTER SPECIAL
Eclipse Comics: Aug, 1987 ($1.75, one-shot)

1 3.00

AIRBOY VERSUS THE AIR MAIDENS
Eclipse Comics: July, 1988 ($1.95)

1 3.00

AIR FIGHTERS CLASSICS
Eclipse Comics: Nov, 1987 - No. 6, May, 1989 ($3.95, 68 pgs., B&W)

1-6: Reprints G.A. Air Fighters #2-7. 1-Origin Airboy 4.00

AIR FIGHTERS COMICS (Airboy Comics #23 (V2#11) on)
Hillman Periodicals: Nov, 1941; No. 2, Nov, 1942 - V2#10, Fall, 1945

V1#1-(Produced by Funnies, Inc.); No Airboy; Black Commander only app. 226 452 678 1446 2473 3500
2(11/42)-(Produced by Quality artists & Biro for Hillman); Origin & 1st app. Airboy & Iron Ace; Black Angel (1st app.), Flying Dutchman & Skywolf (1st app.) begin; Fuje-a; Biro-c/a 476 952 1428 3475 6138 8800
3-Origin/1st app. The Heap; origin Skywolf; 2nd Airboy app./c 206 412 618 1318 2259 3200
4-Japan war-c 174 348 522 1114 1907 2700
5-Japanese octopus War-c 161 322 483 1030 1765 2500
6-Japanese soldiers as rats-c 194 388 582 1242 2121 3000
7-Classic Nazi swastika-c 181 362 543 1158 1979 2800
8-12: 8,10,11-War covers 89 178 267 565 975 1385
V2#1-Classic Nazi War-c 96 192 288 610 1048 1485
2-Skywolf by Giunta; Flying Dutchman by Fuje; 1st meeting Valkyrie & Airboy (she worked for the Nazis in beginning); 1st app. Valkyrie (11/43); Valkyrie-c 142 284 426 909 1555 2200
3,4,6,8,9 60 120 180 381 658 935
5,7: 5-Flag-c; Fuje-a. 7-Valkyrie app. 64 128 192 406 696 985
10-Origin The Heap & Skywolf 69 138 207 442 759 1075
NOTE: ***Fuje*** *a-V1#2, 5, 7, V2#2, 3, 5, 7-9.* ***Giunta*** *a-V2#2, 3, 7, 9.*

AIRFIGHTERS MEET SGT. STRIKE SPECIAL, THE
Eclipse Comics: Jan, 1988 ($1.95, one-shot, stiff-c)

1-Airboy, Valkyrie, Skywolf app. 3.00

AIR FORCES (See American Air Forces)

AIRMAIDENS SPECIAL
Eclipse Comics: August, 1987 ($1.75, one-shot, Baxter paper)

1-Marisa becomes La Lupina (origin) 3.00

AIR RAIDERS
Marvel Comics (Star Comics)/Marvel #3 on: Nov, 1987- No. 5, Mar, 1988 ($1.00)

1,5: Kelley Jones-a in all 4.00
2-4: 2-Thunderhammer app. 3.00

AIRTIGHT GARAGE, THE (Also see Elsewhere Prince)
Marvel Comics (Epic Comics): July, 1993 - No. 4, Oct, 1993 ($2.50, lim. series, Baxter paper)

1-4: Moebius-c/a/scripts 5.00

AIR WAR STORIES
Dell Publishing Co.: Sept-Nov, 1964 - No. 8, Aug, 1966

1-Painted-c; Glanzman-c/a begins 4 8 12 27 44 60
2-8: 2,3-Painted-c 3 6 9 17 26 35

A.K.A. GOLDFISH
Caliber Comics: 1994 - 1995 (B&W, $3.50/$3.95)

...:Ace; ...:Jack; ...:Queen; ...:Joker; ...:King -Brian Michael Bendis-s/a 4.00
TPB (1996, $17.95) 20.00
Goldfish: The Definitive Collection (Image, 2001, $19.95) r/series plus promo art and new prose story; intro. by Matt Wagner 20.00
10th Anniversary HC (Image, 2002, $49.95) 50.00

AKIKO
Sirius: Mar, 1996 - No. 52, Feb, 2004 ($2.50/$2.95, B&W)

1-Crilley-c/a/scripts in all 5.00
2 4.00
3-39: 25-($2.95, 32 pgs.)-w/Asala back-up pages 3.00
40-49,51,52: 40-Begin $2.95-c 3.00
50-($3.50) 3.50
Flights of Fancy TPB (5/02, $12.95) r/various features, pin-ups and gags 13.00
TPB Volume 1,4 ('97, 2/00, $14.95) 1-r/#1-7. 4-r/#19-25 15.00
TPB Volume 2,3 ('98, '99, $11.95) 2-r/#8-13. 3- r/#14-18 12.00
TPB Volume 5 (12/01, $12.95) r/#26-31 13.00
TPB Volume 6,7 (6/03, 4/04, $14.95) 6-r/#32-38. 7-r/#40-47 15.00

AKIKO ON THE PLANET SMOO
Sirius: Dec, 1995 ($3.95, B&W)

V1#1-($3.95)-Crilley-c/a/scripts; gatefold-c 5.00
Ashcan ('95, mail offer) 3.00
Hardcover V1#1 (12/95, $19.95, B&W, 40 pgs.) 20.00
The Color Edition(2/00,$4.95) 5.00

AKIRA
Marvel Comics (Epic): Sept, 1988 - No. 38, Dec, 1995 ($3.50/$3.95/$6.95, deluxe, 68 pgs.)

1-Manga by Katsuhiro Otomo 3 6 9 16 23 30
1,2-2nd printings (1989, $3.95) 5.00
2 2 4 6 9 12 15
3-5 2 4 6 8 10 12
6-16 1 2 3 5 7 9
17-33: 17-$3.95-c begins 6.00
34-37: 34-(1994)-$6.95-c begins. 35-37: 35-(1995). 37-Texeira back-up, Gibbons, Williams pin-ups 2 4 6 8 10 12
38-Moebius, Allred, Pratt, Toth, Romita, Van Fleet, O'Neill, Madureira pin-ups 2 4 6 8 11 14

ALADDIN & HIS WONDERFUL LAMP (See Dell Jr Treasury #2)

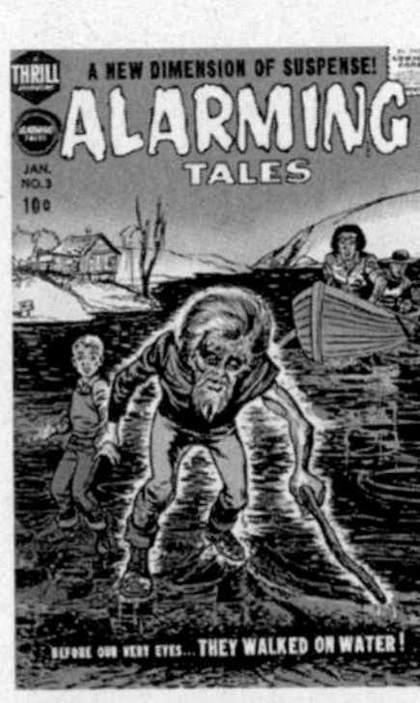

Alarming Tales #3 © HARV

Alex + Ada #1 © Luna & Vaughn

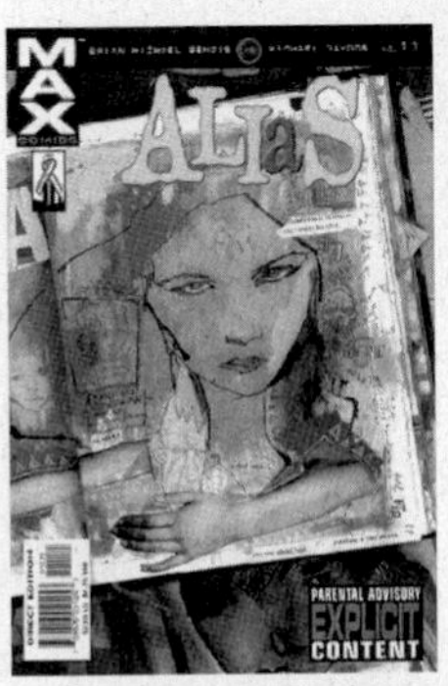

Alias #11 © MAR

ALAN LADD (See The Adventures of...)

ALAN MOORE'S AWESOME UNIVERSE HANDBOOK (Also see Across the Universe:...)
Awesome Entertainment: Apr, 1999 ($2.95, B&W)

	GD 2.0	VG 4.0	FN 6.0	VF 8.0	VF/NM 9.0	NM- 9.2
1-Alan Moore-text/ Alex Ross-sketch pages and 2 covers						5.00

ALAN MOORE...
DC Comics (WildStorm): TPB

	GD 2.0	VG 4.0	FN 6.0	VF 8.0	VF/NM 9.0	NM- 9.2
...'s Complete WildC.A.T.S. (2007, $29.99) r/#21-34,50; ...Homecoming & ...Gang War						30.00
...: Wild Worlds (2007, $24.99) r/various WildStorm one-shots and limited series						25.00

ALARMING ADVENTURES
Harvey Publications: Oct, 1962 - No. 3, Feb, 1963

	GD 2.0	VG 4.0	FN 6.0	VF 8.0	VF/NM 9.0	NM- 9.2
1-Crandall/Williamson-a	8	16	24	51	96	140
2-Williamson/Crandall-a	5	10	15	31	53	75
3-Torres-a	4	8	12	28	47	65

NOTE: ***Bailey** a-1, 3. **Crandall** a-1p, 2i. **Powell** a-2(2). **Severin** c-1-3. **Torres** a-2? **Tuska** a-1. **Williamson** a-1i, 2p.*

ALARMING TALES
Harvey Publications (Western Tales): Sept, 1957 - No. 6, Nov, 1958

	GD 2.0	VG 4.0	FN 6.0	VF 8.0	VF/NM 9.0	NM- 9.2
1-Kirby-c/a(4); Kamandi prototype story by Kirby	31	62	93	182	296	410
2-Kirby-a(4)	21	42	63	122	199	275
3,4-Kirby-a. 4-Powell, Wildey-a	17	34	51	98	154	210
5-Kirby/Williamson-a; Wildey-a; Severin-c	18	36	54	105	165	225
6-Williamson-a?; Severin-c	14	28	42	82	121	160

ALBEDO
Thoughts And Images: Summer, 1983 - No. 14, Spring, 1989 (B&W)
Antarctic Press: (Vol. 2) Jun, 1991 - No. 10 ($2.50)

	GD 2.0	VG 4.0	FN 6.0	VF 8.0	VF/NM 9.0	NM- 9.2
0-Yellow cover; 50 copies	14	28	42	97	214	330
0-White cover, 450 copies	8	16	24	51	96	140
0-Blue, 1st printing, 500 copies	7	14	21	46	86	125
0-Blue, 2nd printing, 1000 copies	4	8	12	25	40	55
0-3rd & 4th printing	3	6	9	14	19	24
1-Dark red - low print run	9	18	27	58	114	170
1-Bright red - low print run	6	12	18	37	66	95
2-(11/84) 1st app. Usagi Yojimbo by Stan Sakai; 2000 copies - no 2nd printing	35	70	105	252	564	875
3	3	6	9	19	30	40
4-Usagi Yojimbo-c	4	8	12	27	44	60
5-14	1	2	3	5	7	9
(Vol. 2) 1-10, Color Special						4.00

ALBEDO ANTHROPOMORPHICS
Antarctic Press: (Vol. 3) Spring, 1994 - No. 4, Jan, 1996 ($2.95, color);
(Vol. 4) Dec, 1999 - No. 2, Jan, 1999 ($2.95/$2.99, B&W)

	GD 2.0	VG 4.0	FN 6.0	VF 8.0	VF/NM 9.0	NM- 9.2
V3#1-4-Steve Gallacci-c/a. V4#1,2						3.00

ALBERTO (See The Crusaders)

ALBERT THE ALLIGATOR & POGO POSSUM (See Pogo Possum)

ALBION (Inspired by 1960s IPC British comics characters)
DC Comics (WildStorm): Aug, 2005 - No. 6, Nov, 2006 ($2.99, limited series)

	GD 2.0	VG 4.0	FN 6.0	VF 8.0	VF/NM 9.0	NM- 9.2
1-6-Alan Moore, Leah Moore & John Reppion-s/Shane Oakley-a; Dave Gibbons-c						3.00
TPB (2007, $19.99) r/series; intro by Neil Gaiman; reprints from 1960s British comics						20.00

ALBUM OF CRIME (See Fox Giants)

ALBUM OF LOVE (See Fox Giants)

AL CAPP'S DOGPATCH (Also see Mammy Yokum)
Toby Press: No. 71, June, 1949 - No. 4, Dec, 1949

	GD 2.0	VG 4.0	FN 6.0	VF 8.0	VF/NM 9.0	NM- 9.2
71(#1)-Reprints from Tip Top #112-114	15	30	45	84	127	170
2-4: 4-Reprints from Li'l Abner #73	11	22	33	64	90	115

AL CAPP'S SHMOO (Also see Oxydol-Dreft & Washable Jones & Shmoo)
Toby Press: July, 1949 - No. 5, Apr, 1950 (None by Al Capp)

	GD 2.0	VG 4.0	FN 6.0	VF 8.0	VF/NM 9.0	NM- 9.2
1-1st app. Super-Shmoo	29	58	87	170	278	385
2-5: 3-Sci-fi trip to moon. 4-X-Mas-c	20	40	60	115	185	255

AL CAPP'S WOLF GAL
Toby Press: 1951 - No. 2, 1952

	GD 2.0	VG 4.0	FN 6.0	VF 8.0	VF/NM 9.0	NM- 9.2
1-Edited-r from Li'l Abner #63	21	42	63	124	202	280
2-Edited-r from Li'l Abner #64	17	34	51	98	154	210

ALEISTER ARCANE
IDW Publishing: Apr, 2004 - No. 3, June, 2004 ($3.99, limited series)

	GD 2.0	VG 4.0	FN 6.0	VF 8.0	VF/NM 9.0	NM- 9.2
1-3-Steve Niles-s/Breehn Burns-a						4.00
TPB (10/04, $17.99) r/series; sketch pages						18.00

ALEXANDER THE GREAT (Movie)
Dell Publishing Co.: No. 688, May, 1956

	GD 2.0	VG 4.0	FN 6.0	VF 8.0	VF/NM 9.0	NM- 9.2
Four Color 688-Buscema-a; photo-c	6	12	18	41	76	110

ALEX + ADA
Image Comics: Nov, 2013 - Present ($2.99)

	GD 2.0	VG 4.0	FN 6.0	VF 8.0	VF/NM 9.0	NM- 9.2
1-5-Jonathan Luna-a/c; Sarah Vaughn & Luna-s						3.00

ALF (TV) (See Star Comics Digest)
Marvel Comics: Mar, 1988 - No. 50, Feb, 1992 ($1.00)

	GD 2.0	VG 4.0	FN 6.0	VF 8.0	VF/NM 9.0	NM- 9.2
1-Photo-c						5.00
1-2nd printing						3.00
2-19: 6-Photo-c						3.00
20-22: 20-Conan parody. 21-Marx Brothers. 22-X-Men parody						3.50
23-30: 24-Rhonda-c/app. 29-3-D cover						3.00
31-43,46,47,49						3.00
44,45: 44-X-Men parody. 45-Wolverine, Punisher, Capt. America-c						4.00
48-(12/91) Risqué Alf with seal cover	2	4	6	11	16	20
50-($1.75, 52 pgs.)-Final issue; photo-c						4.00
Annual 1-3: 1-Rocky & Bullwinkle app. 2-Sienkiewicz-c. 3-TMNT parody						4.00
...Comics Digest 1,2: 1-(1988)-Reprints Alf #1,2	1	3	4	6	8	10
Holiday Special 1,2 ('88, Wint. '89, 68 pgs.): 2-X-Men parody-c						4.00
Spring Special 1 (Spr/89, $1.75, 68 pgs.) Invisible Man parody						4.00
TPB (68 pgs.) r/#1-3; photo-c						5.00

ALFRED HARVEY'S BLACK CAT
Lorne-Harvey Productions: 1995 ($3.50, B&W/color)

	GD 2.0	VG 4.0	FN 6.0	VF 8.0	VF/NM 9.0	NM- 9.2
1-Origin by Mark Evanier & Murphy Anderson; contains history of Alfred Harvey & Harvey Publications; 5 pg. B&W Sad Sack story; Hildebrandts-c						6.00

ALGIE (LITTLE...)
Timor Publ. Co.: Dec, 1953 - No. 3, 1954

	GD 2.0	VG 4.0	FN 6.0	VF 8.0	VF/NM 9.0	NM- 9.2
1-Teenage	8	16	24	40	50	60
1-Algie #1 cover w/Secret Mysteries #19 inside	9	18	27	50	65	80
2,3	5	10	15	24	30	35
Accepted Reprint #2(nd)	3	6	8	12	14	16
Super Reprint #15	2	4	6	8	11	14

ALIAS:
Now Comics: July, 1990 - No. 5, Nov, 1990 ($1.75)

	GD 2.0	VG 4.0	FN 6.0	VF 8.0	VF/NM 9.0	NM- 9.2
1-5: 1-Sienkiewicz-c						3.00

ALIAS (Also see Jessica Jones apps. in New Avengers and The Pulse)
Marvel Comics (MAX Comics): Nov, 2001 - No. 28, Jan, 2004 ($2.99)

	GD 2.0	VG 4.0	FN 6.0	VF 8.0	VF/NM 9.0	NM- 9.2
1-Bendis-s/Gaydos-a/Mack-c; intro Jessica Jones; Luke Cage app.	1	2	3	5	6	8
2-4						5.00
5-28: 7,8-Sienkiewicz-a (2 pgs.) 16-21-Spider-Woman app. 22,23-Jessica's origin. 24-28-Purple; Avengers app.; flashback-a by Bagley						3.00
... MGC 1 (6/10, $1.00) r/#1 with "Marvel's Greatest Comics" logo on cover						3.00
HC (2002, $29.99) r/#1-9; intro. by Jeph Loeb						30.00
Omnibus (2006, $69.99, hardcover with dustjacket) r/#1-28 and What If Jessica Jones Had Joined the Avengers?; original pitch, script and sketch pages						70.00
Vol. 1: TPB (2003, $19.99) r/#1-9						20.00
Vol. 2: Come Home TPB (2003, $13.99) r/#11-15						14.00
Vol. 3: The Underneath TPB (2003, $16.99) r/#10,16-21						17.00

ALICE (New Adventures in Wonderland)
Ziff-Davis Publ. Co.: No. 10, 7-8/51 - No. 11(#2), 11-12/51

	GD 2.0	VG 4.0	FN 6.0	VF 8.0	VF/NM 9.0	NM- 9.2
10-Painted-c; Berg-a	27	54	81	160	263	365
11-(#2 on inside) Dave Berg-a	17	34	51	100	158	215

ALICE AT MONKEY ISLAND (Formerly The Adventures of Alice)
Pentagon Publ. Co. (Civil Service): No. 3, 1946

	GD 2.0	VG 4.0	FN 6.0	VF 8.0	VF/NM 9.0	NM- 9.2
3	10	20	30	56	76	95

ALICE IN WONDERLAND (Disney; see Advs. of Alice, Dell Jr. Treasury #1, The Dreamery, Movie Comics,Walt Disney Showcase #22, and World's Greatest Stories)
Dell Publishing Co.: No. 24, 1940; No. 331, 1951; No. 341, July, 1951

	GD 2.0	VG 4.0	FN 6.0	VF 8.0	VF/NM 9.0	NM- 9.2
Single Series 24 (#1)(1940)	51	102	153	321	541	760
Four Color 331, 341-"Unbirthday Party w/..."	13	26	39	86	188	290
1-(Whitman, 3/84, pre-pack only)-r/4-Color #331	2	4	6	11	16	20

ALIEN ENCOUNTERS (Replaces Alien Worlds)
Eclipse Comics: June, 1985 - No. 14, Aug, 1987 ($1.75, Baxter paper, mature)

	GD 2.0	VG 4.0	FN 6.0	VF 8.0	VF/NM 9.0	NM- 9.2
1-10: Nudity, strong language in all. 9-Snyder-a						4.00
11-14-Low print run						5.00

ALIEN LEGION (See Epic & Marvel Graphic Novel #25)

Aliens Alchemy #1 © 20th Cent. Fox

Aliens vs. Parker #4 © BOOM

Aliens vs. Predator: Eternal #4 © 20th Cent. Fox

GD VG FN VF VF/NM NM-
2.0 4.0 6.0 8.0 9.0 9.2

Marvel Comics (Epic Comics): Apr, 1984 - No. 20, Sept, 1987
nn-With bound-in trading card; Austin-i 4.00
2-20: 2-$1.50-c. 7,8-Portacio-i 3.00

ALIEN LEGION (2nd Series)
Marvel Comics (Epic): Aug, 1987(indicia)(10/87 on-c) - No. 18, Aug, 1990
V2#1-18-Stroman-a in all. 7-18-Farmer-i 3.00
...: Force Nomad TPB (Checker Book Pub. Group, 2001, $24.95) r/#1-11 25.00
...: Piecemaker TPB (Checker Book Pub. Group, 2002, $19.95) r/#12-18 20.00

ALIEN LEGION: (Series of titles; all Marvel/Epic Comics)
--BINARY DEEP, 1993 ($3.50, one-shot, 52 pgs.), nn-With bound-in trading card 4.00
--JUGGER GRIMROD, 8/92 ($5.95, one-shot, 52 pgs.) Book 1 6.00
--ONE PLANET AT A TIME, 5/93 - Book 3, 7/93 ($4.95, squarebound, 52 pgs.)
Book 1-3: Hoang Nguyen-a 5.00
--ON THE EDGE (The... #2 & 3), 11/90 - No. 3, 1/91 ($4.50, 52 pgs.)
1-3-Stroman & Farmer-a 4.50
--TENANTS OF HELL, '91 - No. 2, '91 ($4.50, squarebound, 52 pgs.)
Book 1,2-Stroman-c/a(p) 4.50

ALIEN NATION (Movie)
DC Comics: Dec, 1988 ($2.50; 68 pgs.)
1-Adaptation of film; painted-c 4.00

ALIEN PIG FARM 3000
Image Comics (RAW Studios): Apr, 2007 - No. 4, July, 2007 ($2.99, limited series)
1-4-Steve Niles, Thomas Jane & Todd Farmer-s/Don Marquez-a 3.00

ALIEN RESURRECTION (Movie)
Dark Horse Comics: Oct, 1997 - No. 2, Nov, 1997 ($2.50; limited series)
1,2-Adaptation of film; Dave McKean-c 3.00

ALIENS, THE (Captain Johner and...)(Also see Magnus Robot Fighter...)
Gold Key: Sept-Dec, 1967; No. 2, May, 1982
1-Reprints from Magnus #1,3,4,6-10; Russ Manning-a in all
3 6 9 19 30 40
2-(Whitman) Same contents as #1 1 2 3 5 6 8

ALIENS (Movie) (See Alien: The Illustrated..., Dark Horse Comics & Dark Horse Presents #24)
Dark Horse Comics: May, 1988 - No. 6, July, 1989 ($1.95, B&W, limited series)
1-Based on movie sequel; 1st app. Aliens in comics 3 6 9 14 20 26
1-2nd - 6th printings; 4th w/new inside front-c 3.00
2 2 4 6 8 10 12
2-2nd & 3rd printing, 3-6-2nd printings 3.00
3 1 2 3 5 7 9
4-6 5.00
Mini Comic #1 (2/89, 4x6")-Was included with Aliens Portfolio 4.00
Collection 1 ($10.95,)-r/#1-6 plus Dark Horse Presents #24 plus new-a 12.00
Collection 1-2nd printing (1991, $11.95)-On higher quality paper than 1st print;
Dorman painted-c 12.00
Hardcover ('90, $24.95, B&W)-r/1-6, DHP #24 30.00
... Omnibus Vol. 1 (7/07, $24.95, 9x6") r/1st & 2nd series and Aliens: Earth War 25.00
... Omnibus Vol. 2 (12/07, $24.95, 9x6") r/Genocide, Harvest and Colonial Marines series 25.00
... Omnibus Vol. 3 (3/08, $24.95, 9x6") r/Rogue, Salvation and Sacrifice, Labyrinth series 25.00
... Omnibus Vol. 4 (8/08, $24.95, 9x6") r/Music of the Spears, Stronghold, Berserker,
Mondo Pest and Mondo Heat series and one-shots 25.00
... Omnibus Vol. 5 (11/08, $24.95, 9x6") r/Alchemy, Survival, Havoc series and various 25.00
... Omnibus Vol. 6 (2/09, $24.95, 9x6") r/Apocalypse GN, Xenogenesis & one-shots 25.00
... Outbreak (3rd printing, 8/96, $17.95)-Bolton-c 18.00
Platinum Edition - (See Dark Horse Presents: Aliens Platinum Edition) -

ALIENS
Dark Horse Comics: V2#1, Aug, 1989 - No. 4, 1990 ($2.25, limited series)
V2#1-Painted art by Denis Beauvais 5.00
1-2nd printing (1990), 2-4 3.00
...: Nightmare Asylum TPB (12/96, $16.95) r/series; Bolton-c 17.00

ALIENS
Dark Horse Comics: May, 2009 - No. 4, Nov, 2009 ($3.50, limited series)
1-4-John Arcudi-s/Zach Howard-a. 1,2-Howard-c. 3,4-Swanland-c 3.50

ALIENS: (Series of titles, all Dark Horse)
--ALCHEMY, 10/97 - No. 3, 11/97 ($2.95),1-3-Corben-c/a, Arcudi-s 3.00
--APOCALYPSE - THE DESTROYING ANGELS, 1/99 - No. 4, 4/99 ($2.95)
1-4-Doug Wheatly-a/Schultz-s 3.00
--BERSERKERS, 1/95 - No. 4, 4/95 ($2.50) 1-4 3.00

GD VG FN VF VF/NM NM-
2.0 4.0 6.0 8.0 9.0 9.2

--COLONIAL MARINES, 1/93 - No. 10, 7/94 ($2.50) 1-10 3.00
--EARTH ANGEL. 8/94 ($2.95) 1-Byrne-a/story; wraparound-c 3.00
--EARTH WAR, 6/90 - No. 4, 10/90 ($2.50) 1-All have Sam Keith-a & Bolton painted-c 5.00
1-2nd printing, 3,4 3.00
2 4.00
--GENOCIDE, 11/91 - No. 4, 2/92 ($2.50) 1-4-Suydam painted-c. 4-Wraparound-c, poster 3.00
--GLASS CORRIDOR, 6/98 ($2.95) 1-David Lloyd-s/a 3.00
--HARVEST (See Aliens: Hive)
--HAVOC, 6/97 - No. 2, 7/97 ($2.95) 1,2: Schultz-s, Kent Williams-c, 40 artists including
Art Adams, Kelley Jones, Duncan Fegredo, Kevin Nowlan 3.00
--HIVE, 2/92 - No. 4,5/92 ($2.50) 1-4: Kelley Jones-c/a in all 3.00
...Harvest TPB ('98, $16.95) r/series; Bolton-c 17.00
--KIDNAPPED, 12/97 - No. 3, 2/98 ($2.50) 1-3 3.00
--LABYRINTH, 9/93 - No. 4, 1/94 ($2.50)1-4: 1-Painted-c 3.00
--LOVESICK, 12/96 ($2.95) 1 3.00
--MONDO HEAT, 2/96 ($2.50) nn-Sequel to Mondo Pest 3.00
--MONDO PEST, 4/95 ($2.95, 44 pgs.) nn-r/Dark Horse Comics #22-24 4.00
--MUSIC OF THE SPEARS, 1/94 - No. 4, 4/94 ($2.50) 1-4 3.00
--NEWT'S TALE, 6/92 - No. 2, 7/92 ($4.95) 1,2-Bolton-c 5.00
--PIG, 3/97 ($2.95)1 3.00
--PREDATOR: THE DEADLIEST OF THE SPECIES, 7/93 - No. 12,8/95 ($2.50)
1-Bolton painted-c; Guice-a(p) 5.00
1-Embossed foil platinum edition 10.00
2-12: Bolton painted-c. 2,3-Guice-a(p) 3.00
--PURGE, 8/97 ($2.95) nn-Hester-a 3.00
--ROGUE, 4/93 - No. 4, 7/93 ($2.50)1-4: Painted-c 3.00
--SACRIFICE, 5/93 ($4.95, 52 pgs.) nn-P. Milligan scripts; painted-c/a 5.00
--SALVATION, 11/93 ($4.95, 52 pgs.) nn-Mignola-c/a(p); Gibbons script 5.00
--SPECIAL, 6/97 ($2.50) 1 3.00
--STALKER, 6/98 ($2.50)1-David Wenzel-s/a 3.00
--STRONGHOLD, 5/94 - No. 4, 9/94 ($2.50) 1-4 3.00
--SURVIVAL, 2/98 - No. 3, 4/98 ($2.95) 1-3-Tony Harris-c 3.00
--TRIBES, 1992 ($24.95, hardcover graphic novel) Bissette text-s with Dorman painted-a 25.00
...softcover ($9.95) 10.00

ALIENS VS. PARKER (Not based on the Alien movie series)
BOOM! Studios: Mar, 2013 - No. 4, May, 2013 ($3.99, limited series)
1-4: 1-Paul Scheer & Nick Giovannetti-s; Bracchi-a/Noto-c 4.00

ALIENS VS. PREDATOR (See Dark Horse Presents #36)
Dark Horse Comics: June, 1990 - No. 4, Dec, 1990 ($2.50, limited series)
1-Painted-c 1 2 3 5 6 8
1-2nd printing 3.00
0-(7/90, $1.95, B&W)-r/Dark Horse Pres. #34-36 1 2 3 5 7 9
2,3 5.00
4-Dave Dorman painted-c 4.00
Annual (7/99, $4.95) Jae Lee-c 5.00
... : Booty (1/96, $2.50) painted-c 3.00
... Omnibus Vol. 1 (5/07, $24.95, 9x6") r/#1-4 & Annual; ...: War; ...: Eternal 25.00
... Omnibus Vol. 2 (10/07, $24.95, 9x6") r/...: Xenogenesis #1-4; ...: Deadliest of the Species;
...: Booty and stories from ... Annual 25.00
...: One For One (8/10, $1.00) r/#1 with red cover frame 3.00
... : Thrill of the Hunt (9/04, $6.95, digest-size TPB) Based on 2004 movie 7.00
... Wraith 1 (7/98, $2.95) Jay Stephens-s 3.00
--VS. PREDATOR: DUEL, 3/95 - No. 2, 4/95 ($2.50) 1,2 3.00
--VS. PREDATOR: ETERNAL, 6/98 - No. 4, 9/98 ($2.50)1-4: Edginton-s/Maleev-a; Fabry-c 3.00
--VS. PREDATOR: THREE WORLD WAR, 1/10 - No. 6, 9/10 ($3.50) 1-6-Leonardi-a 3.50
--VS. PREDATOR VS. THE TERMINATOR, 4/00 - No. 4, 7/00 ($2.95) 1-4: Ripley app. 3.00
--VS. PREDATOR: WAR, No. 0, 5/95 - No. 4, 8/95 ($2.50) 0-4: Corben painted-c 3.00
--VS. PREDATOR: XENOGENESIS, 12/99 - No. 4, 3/00 ($2.95) 1-4: Watson-s/Mel Rubi-a 3.00
--XENOGENESIS, 8/99 - No. 4, 11/99 ($2.95) 1-4: T&M Bierbaum-s 3.00

ALIEN TERROR (See 3-D Alien Terror)

ALIEN: THE ILLUSTRATED STORY (Also see Aliens)
Heavy Metal Books: 1980 ($3.95, soft-c, 8x11")

All-American Comics #4 © DC

All-American Comics #99 © DC

All-American Men of War #2 © DC

	GD 2.0	VG 4.0	FN 6.0	VF 8.0	VF/NM 9.0	NM- 9.2
nn-Movie adaptation; Simonson-a	3	6	9	14	19	24

ALIEN^{3} (Movie)
Dark Horse Comics: June, 1992 - No. 3, July, 1992 ($2.50, limited series)

	GD 2.0	VG 4.0	FN 6.0	VF 8.0	VF/NM 9.0	NM- 9.2
1-3: Adapts 3rd movie; Suydam painted-c						3.00

ALIEN WORLDS (Also see Eclipse Graphic Album #22)
Pacific Comics/Eclipse: Dec, 1982 - No. 9, Jan, 1985

	GD 2.0	VG 4.0	FN 6.0	VF 8.0	VF/NM 9.0	NM- 9.2
1,2,4: 2,4-Dave Stevens-c/a						6.00
3,5-7						4.00
8,9	1	2	3	4	5	7
3-D No. 1-Art Adams 1st published art	1	2	3	4	5	7

ALISON DARE, LITTLE MISS ADVENTURES (Also see Return of ...)
Oni Press: Sept, 2000 ($4.50, B&W, one-shot)

	GD 2.0	VG 4.0	FN 6.0	VF 8.0	VF/NM 9.0	NM- 9.2
1-J. Torres-s/J.Bone-c/a						4.50

ALISON DARE & THE HEART OF THE MAIDEN
Oni Press: Jan, 2002 - No. 2, Feb, 2002 ($2.95, B&W, limited series)

	GD 2.0	VG 4.0	FN 6.0	VF 8.0	VF/NM 9.0	NM- 9.2
1,2-J. Torres-s/J.Bone-c/a						3.00

ALISTER THE SLAYER
Midnight Press: Oct, 1995 ($2.50)

	GD 2.0	VG 4.0	FN 6.0	VF 8.0	VF/NM 9.0	NM- 9.2
1-Boris-c						3.00

ALL-AMERICAN COMICS (...Western #103-126, ...Men of War #127 on; also see The Big All-American Comic Book)
All-American/National Periodical Publ.: April, 1939 - No. 102, Oct, 1948

	GD 2.0	VG 4.0	FN 6.0	VF 8.0	VF/NM 9.0	NM- 9.2
1-Hop Harrigan (1st app.), Scribbly by Mayer (1st DC app.), Toonerville Folks, Ben Webster, Spot Savage, Mutt & Jeff, Red White & Blue (1st app.), Adventures in the Unknown, Tippie, Reg'lar Fellers, Skippy, Bobby Thatcher, Mystery Men of Mars, Daiseybelle, Wiley of West Point begin	580	1160	1740	4100	6900	9700
2-Ripley's Believe It or Not begins, ends #24	184	368	552	1168	2009	2850
3-5: 5-The American Way begins, ends #10	155	310	465	992	1696	2400
6,7: 6-Last Spot Savage; Popsicle Pete begins, ends #26, 28. 7-Last Bobby Thatcher	119	238	357	762	1306	1850
8-The Ultra Man begins & 1st-c app.	400	800	1200	2800	4900	7000
9,10: 10-X-Mas-c	113	226	339	718	1234	1750
11,15: 11-Ultra Man-c. 15-Last Tippie & Reg'lar Fellars; Ultra Man-c	155	310	465	992	1696	2400
12-14: 12-Last Toonerville Folks	110	220	330	704	1202	1700
16-(Rare)-Origin/1st app. Green Lantern by Sheldon Moldoff (c/a)(7/40) & begin series; appears in costume on-c & only one panel inside; created by Martin Nodell. Inspired in 1940 by a switchman's green lantern that would give trains the go ahead to proceed. G.L. cover pose swiped from last panel of a Jan, 1939 Flash Gordon Sunday page.	19,167	38,333	57,500	150,000	375,000	600,000
17-2nd Green Lantern	1200	2400	3600	9000	18,000	27,000
18-N.Y. World's Fair-c/story (scarce); The Atom app. in one panel announcing debut in next issue	1167	2334	3500	8800	17,400	26,000
19-Origin/1st app. The Atom (10/40); last Ultra Man	1950	3900	5850	14,600	27,800	41,000
20-Atom dons costume; Ma Hunkle becomes Red Tornado (1st app.)(1st DC costumed heroine, before Wonder Woman, 11/40); Rescue on Mars begins, ends #25; 1 pg. origin Green Lantern	584	1168	1752	4263	7532	10,800
21-Last Wiley of West Point & Skippy; classic Moldoff-c	497	994	1491	3628	6414	9200
22,23: 23-Last Daiseybelle; 3 Idiots begin, end #82	366	732	1098	2562	4481	6400
24-Sisty & Dinky become the Cyclone Kids; Ben Webster ends; origin Dr. Mid-Nite & Sargon, The Sorcerer in text with app.	383	766	1149	2681	4691	6700
25-Origin & 1st story app. Dr. Mid-Nite by Stan Asch; Hop Harrigan becomes Guardian Angel; last Adventure in the Unknown (scarce)	1150	2300	3450	8625	16,813	25,000
26-Origin/1st story app. Sargon, the Sorcerer	389	778	1167	2723	4762	6800
27: #27-32 are misnumbered in indicia with correct No. appearing on-c. Intro. Doiby Dickles, Green Lantern's sidekick	400	800	1200	2800	4900	7000
28-Hop Harrigan gives up costumed i.d.	213	426	639	1363	2332	3300
29,30	213	426	639	1363	2332	3300
31-40: 35-Doiby learns Green Lantern's i.d.	168	336	504	1075	1838	2600
41-50: 50-Sargon ends	134	268	402	851	1463	2075
51-60: 59-Scribbly & the Red Tornado ends	115	230	345	730	1258	1785
61-Origin/1st app. Solomon Grundy (11/44)	1000	2000	3000	7400	13,200	19,000
62-70: 70-Kubert Sargon; intro Sargon's helper, Maximillian O'Leary	96	192	288	610	1048	1485
71-88: 71-Last Red White & Blue. 72-Black Pirate begins (not in #74-82); last Atom. 73-Winky, Blinky & Noddy begins, ends #82. 79,83-Mutt & Jeff-c. 85-1st Crusher Crock (becomes Sportsmaster); Hasen "Derby" cover	77	154	231	489	837	1185
89-Origin & 1st app. Harlequin	145	290	435	921	1586	2250
90-99: 90-Origin/1st app. Icicle. 91,93,94,95-Harlequin-c. 99-Last Hop Harrigan	139	278	417	883	1517	2150
100-1st app. Johnny Thunder by Alex Toth (8/48); western theme begins (Scarce)	206	412	618	1318	2259	3200
101-Last Mutt & Jeff (Scarce)	142	284	426	909	1555	2200
102-Last Green Lantern, Black Pirate & Dr. Mid-Nite (Scarce)	271	542	813	1734	2967	4200

NOTE: *No Atom in 47, 62-69.* **Kinstler** *Black Pirate-89.* **Stan Aschmeier** *a (Dr. Mid-Nite) 25-84; c-7.* **Mayer** *c-1, 2(part), 6, 10.* **Moldoff** *c-16-23.* **Nodell** *c-31.* **Paul Reinman** *a (Green Lantern)-53-55p, 56-84, 87; (Black Pirate)-83-88, 90; c-52, 55-76, 78, 80, 81, 87.* **Toth** *a-88, 92, 96, 98-102; c(p)-92, 96-102. Scribbly by* **Mayer** *in #1-59. Ultra Man by* **Mayer** *in #8-19.*

ALL AMERICAN COMICS
DC Comics: April 1939

nn - Ashcan comic, not distributed to newsstands, only for in house use. Cover art is Advenure Comics #33 and interior from Detective Comics #23 (no known sales)

ALL-AMERICAN COMICS (Also see All Star Comics 1999 crossover titles)
DC Comics: May, 1999 ($1.99, one-shot)

	GD 2.0	VG 4.0	FN 6.0	VF 8.0	VF/NM 9.0	NM- 9.2
1-Golden Age Green Lantern and Johnny Thunder; Barreto-a						3.00

ALL-AMERICAN MEN OF WAR (Previously All-American Western)
National Periodical Publ.: No. 127, Aug-Sept, 1952 - No. 117, Sept-Oct, 1966

	GD 2.0	VG 4.0	FN 6.0	VF 8.0	VF/NM 9.0	NM- 9.2
127 (#1, 1952)	118	236	354	944	2122	3300
128 (1952)	54	108	162	432	966	1500
2(12-1/'52-53)-5	49	98	147	382	854	1325
6-Devil Dog story; Ghost Squadron story	38	76	114	281	633	985
7-10: 8-Sgt. Storm Cloud-s	38	76	114	281	633	985
11-16,18: 18-Last precode; 1st Kubert-c (2/55)	34	68	102	245	553	860
17-1st Frogman-s in this title	35	70	105	252	569	885
19,20,22-27	28	56	84	196	428	660
21-Easy Co. prototype	33	66	99	238	532	825
28 (12/55)-1st Sgt. Rock prototype; Kubert-a	49	98	147	382	854	1325
29,30,32-Wood-a	28	56	84	196	428	660
31,33,34,36-38,40: 34-Gunner prototype-s. 36-Little Sure Shot prototype-s. 38-1st S.A. issue	24	48	72	168	377	585
35-Greytone-c	28	56	84	202	451	700
39 (11/56)-2nd Sgt. Rock prototype; 1st Easy Co.?	36	72	108	266	596	925
41,43-47,49,50: 46-Tankbusters-c/s	21	42	63	147	324	500
42-Pre-Sgt. Rock Easy Co.-c/s	26	52	78	182	404	625
48-Easy Co.-c/s; Nick app.; Kubert-a	26	52	78	182	404	625
51-56,58-62,65,66: 61-Gunner-c/s	16	32	48	112	249	385
57(5/58),63,64 -Pre-Sgt. Rock Easy Co.-c/s	23	46	69	161	351	540
67-1st Gunner & Sarge by Andru & Esposito	46	92	138	340	770	1200
68,69: 68-2nd app. Gunner & Sarge. 69-1st Tank Killer-c/s	20	40	60	141	313	485
70	14	28	42	94	207	320
71-80: 71,72,76-Tank Killer-c/s. 74-Minute Commandos-c/s	12	24	36	81	176	270
81-Greytone-c	11	22	33	76	163	250
82-Johnny Cloud begins(1st app.), ends #117	23	46	69	161	356	550
83-2nd Johnny Cloud	13	26	39	91	201	310
84-88: 88-Last 10¢ issue	10	20	30	68	144	220
89-100: 89-Battle Aces of 3 Wars begins, ends #98	8	16	24	55	105	155
101-111,113-116: 111,114,115-Johnny Cloud	6	12	18	38	69	100
112-Balloon Buster series begins, ends #114,116	6	12	18	40	73	105
117-Johnny Cloud-c & 3-part story	6	12	18	40	73	105

NOTE: *Frogman stories in 17, 38, 44, 45, 50, 51, 53, 55-58, 63, 65, 66, 72, 76, 77.* **Colan** *a-112.* **Drucker** *a-47, 58, 61, 63, 65, 69, 71, 74, 77.* **Grandenetti** *c(p)-127, 128, 2-17(most).* **Heath** *a-14, 27, 32, 38, 41, 45, 47, 50, 51, 55-58, 62, 64, 71, 75, 76, 78, 95, 111-117; c-85, 91, 94-96, 100, 101, 110-112, others?* **Infantino** *a-8.* **Kirby** *a-29.* **Krigstein** *a-128('52), 2, 3, 5.* **Kubert** *a-22, 24, 28, 29, 33, 34, 36, 38, 39, 41-43, 47-50, 52, 53, 55, 56, 59, 60, 63-65, 69, 71-73, 76, 102, 103, 105, 106, 108, 114; c-41, 44, 52, 54, 55, 58, 64, 69, 76, 77, 79, 102-106, 108, 113-117, others? Tank Killer in 69, 71, 76 by* **Kubert**. **P. Reinman** *c-55, 57, 61, 62, 71, 72, 74-76, 80.* **J. Severin** *a-58.*

ALL AMERICAN MEN OF WAR
DC Comics: Aug/Sept. 1952

nn - Ashcan comic, not distributed to newsstands, only for in-house use. Cover art is All Star Western #58 and interior from Mr. District Attorney #21. A GD+ copy sold for $1195 in 2012.

ALL-AMERICAN SPORTS
Charlton Comics: Oct, 1967

	GD 2.0	VG 4.0	FN 6.0	VF 8.0	VF/NM 9.0	NM- 9.2
1	3	6	9	19	30	45

ALL-AMERICAN WESTERN (Formerly All-American Comics; Becomes All-American Men of War)
National Periodical Publ.: No. 103, Nov, 1948 - No. 126, June-July, 1952 (103-121: 52 pgs.)

103-Johnny Thunder & his horse Black Lightning continues by Toth, ends #126; Foley of The Fighting 5th, Minstrel Maverick, & Overland Coach begin; Captain Tootsie by Beck;

Alley Cat #6 © Alley Baggett

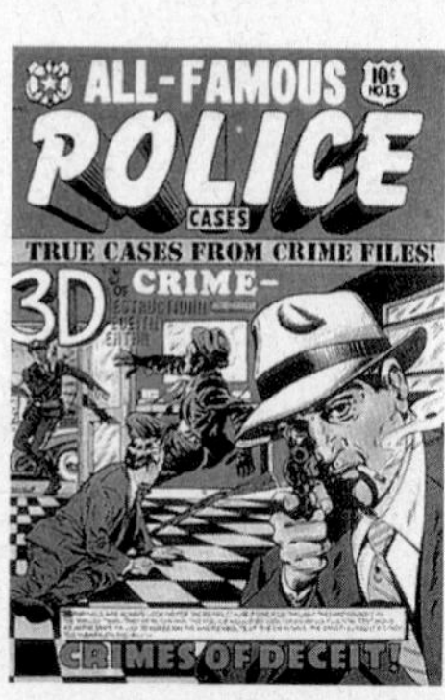

All-Famous Police Cases #13 © Star

All-Flash #7 © DC

	GD 2.0	VG 4.0	FN 6.0	VF 8.0	VF/NM 9.0	NM- 9.2
mentioned in Love and Death	52	104	156	328	552	775
104-Kubert-a	37	74	111	222	361	500
105,107-Kubert-a	31	62	93	186	303	420
106,108-110,112: 112-Kurtzman's "Pot-Shot Pete" (1 pg.)	26	52	78	154	252	350
111,114-116-Kubert-a	27	54	81	160	263	365
113-Intro. Swift Deer, J. Thunder's new sidekick (4-5/50); classic Toth-c; Kubert-a	29	58	87	170	278	385
117-126: 121-Kubert-a; bondage-c	20	40	60	114	182	250

NOTE: ***G. Kane** c(p)-112, 119, 120, 123. **Kubert** a-103-105, 107, 111, 112(1 pg.), 113-116, 121. **Toth** a 103-125; c(p)-103-111,113-116, 121, 122, 124-126. Some copies of #125 have #12 on-c.*

ALL COMICS
Chicago Nite Life News: 1945

	GD 2.0	VG 4.0	FN 6.0	VF 8.0	VF/NM 9.0	NM- 9.2
1	15	30	45	84	127	170

ALLEGRA
Image Comics (WildStorm): Aug, 1996 - No. 4, Dec, 1996 ($2.50)

	GD 2.0	VG 4.0	FN 6.0	VF 8.0	VF/NM 9.0	NM- 9.2
1-4						3.00

ALLEY CAT (Alley Baggett)
Image Comics: July, 1999 - No. 6, Mar, 2000 ($2.50/$2.95)

	GD 2.0	VG 4.0	FN 6.0	VF 8.0	VF/NM 9.0	NM- 9.2
Preview Edition						6.00
Prelude						5.00
Prelude w/variant-c						6.00
1-Photo-c						3.00
1-Painted-c by Dorian						4.00
1-Another Universe Edition, 1-Wizard World Edition						7.00
2-4: 4-Twin towers on-c						3.00
5,6-($2.95)						3.00
Lingerie Edition (10/99, $4.95) Photos, pin-ups, cover gallery						5.00
...Vs. Lady Pendragon ('99, $3.00) Stinsman-c						3.00

ALLEY OOP (See The Comics, The Funnies, Red Ryder and Super Book #9)
Dell Publishing Co.: No. 3, 1942

	GD 2.0	VG 4.0	FN 6.0	VF 8.0	VF/NM 9.0	NM- 9.2
Four Color 3 (#1)	44	88	132	326	738	1150

ALLEY OOP
Argo Publ.: Nov, 1955 - No. 3, Mar, 1956 (Newspaper reprints)

	GD 2.0	VG 4.0	FN 6.0	VF 8.0	VF/NM 9.0	NM- 9.2
1	16	32	48	92	144	195
2,3	12	24	36	67	94	120

ALLEY OOP
Dell Publishing Co.: 12-2/62-63 - No. 2, 9-11/63

	GD 2.0	VG 4.0	FN 6.0	VF 8.0	VF/NM 9.0	NM- 9.2
1	5	10	15	35	63	90
2	5	10	15	31	53	75

ALLEY OOP
Standard Comics: No. 10, Sept, 1947 - No. 18, Oct, 1949

	GD 2.0	VG 4.0	FN 6.0	VF 8.0	VF/NM 9.0	NM- 9.2
10	26	52	78	154	252	350
11-18: 17,18-Schomburg-c	20	40	60	120	195	270

ALLEY OOP ADVENTURES
Antarctic Press: Aug, 1998 - No. 3, Dec, 1998 ($2.95)

	GD 2.0	VG 4.0	FN 6.0	VF 8.0	VF/NM 9.0	NM- 9.2
1-3-Jack Bender-s/a						3.00

ALLEY OOP ADVENTURES (Alley Oop Quarterly in indicia)
Antarctic Press: Sept, 1999 - No. 3, Mar, 2000 ($2.50/$2.99, B&W)

	GD 2.0	VG 4.0	FN 6.0	VF 8.0	VF/NM 9.0	NM- 9.2
1-3-Jack Bender-s/a						3.00

ALL-FAMOUS CRIME (2nd series - Formerly Law Against Crime #1-3; becomes All-Famous Police Cases #6 on)
Star Publications: No. 8, 5/51 - No. 10, 11/51; No. 4, 2/52 - No. 5, 5/52;

	GD 2.0	VG 4.0	FN 6.0	VF 8.0	VF/NM 9.0	NM- 9.2
8 (#1-1st series)	22	44	66	132	216	300
9 (#2)-Used in **SOTI**, illo- "The wish to hurt or kill couples in lovers' lanes is a not uncommon perversion;" L.B. Cole-c/a(r)/Law-Crime #3	39	78	117	231	378	525
10 (#3)	20	40	60	117	189	260
4 (#4-2nd series)-Formerly Law-Crime	19	38	57	112	179	245
5 (#5) Becomes All-Famous Police Cases #6	19	38	57	112	179	245

NOTE: *All have **L.B. Cole** covers.*

ALL FAMOUS CRIME STORIES (See Fox Giants)

ALL-FAMOUS POLICE CASES (Formerly All Famous Crime #5)
Star Publications: No. 6, Feb, 1952 - No. 16, Sept, 1954

	GD 2.0	VG 4.0	FN 6.0	VF 8.0	VF/NM 9.0	NM- 9.2
6	20	40	60	114	182	250
7,8: 7-Baker story. 8-Marijuana story	19	38	57	109	172	235
9-16	17	34	51	98	154	210

NOTE: ***L. B. Cole** c-all; a-15, 1pg. **Hollingsworth** a-15.*

ALL-FLASH (...Quarterly No. 1-5)
National Per. Publ./All-American: Summer, 1941 - No. 32, Dec-Jan, 1947-48

	GD 2.0	VG 4.0	FN 6.0	VF 8.0	VF/NM 9.0	NM- 9.2
1-Origin The Flash retold by E. E. Hibbard; Hibbard c-1-10,12-14,16,31p.	1250	2500	3750	8750	14,875	21,000
2-Origin recap	271	542	813	1734	2967	4200
3,4	161	322	483	1030	1765	2500
5-Winky, Blinky & Noddy begins (1st app.), ends #32	116	232	348	742	1271	1800
6-10	106	212	318	673	1162	1650
11-13: 12-Origin/1st The Thinker. 13-The King app.	90	180	270	576	988	1400
14-Green Lantern cameo	106	212	318	673	1162	1650
15-20: 18-Mutt & Jeff begins, ends #22	82	164	246	528	902	1275
21-31	69	138	207	442	759	1075
32-Origin/1st app. The Fiddler; 1st Star Sapphire	139	278	417	883	1517	2150

All-Flash Quarterly ashcan (a recently discovered CGC 7.0 copy sold for $8150 in 2012)
NOTE: *Book length stories in 2-13, 16. Bondage c-31, 32. **Martin Nodell** c-15, 17-28.*

ALL FLASH (Leads into Flash [2nd series] #231)
DC Comics: Sept, 2007 ($2.99, one-shot)

	GD 2.0	VG 4.0	FN 6.0	VF 8.0	VF/NM 9.0	NM- 9.2
1-Wally West hunts down Bart's killers; Waid-s; two covers by Middleton & Sienkiewicz						3.00

ALL FOR LOVE (Young Love V3#5-on)
Prize Publications: Apr-May, 1957 - V3#4, Dec-Jan, 1959-60

	GD 2.0	VG 4.0	FN 6.0	VF 8.0	VF/NM 9.0	NM- 9.2
V1#1	8	16	24	54	102	150
2-6: 5-Orlando-c	5	10	15	31	53	75
V2#1-5(1/59), 5(3/59)	4	8	12	28	47	65
V3#1(5/59), 1(7/59)-4: 2-Powell-a	4	8	12	25	40	55

ALL FUNNY COMICS
Tilsam Publ./National Periodical Publications (Detective): Winter, 1943-44 - No. 23, May-June, 1948

	GD 2.0	VG 4.0	FN 6.0	VF 8.0	VF/NM 9.0	NM- 9.2
1-Genius Jones (see Adventure #77 for debut), Buzzy (1st app., ends #4), Dover & Clover (see More Fun #93) begin; Bailey-a	47	94	141	296	498	700
2	22	44	66	132	216	300
3-10	15	30	45	83	124	165
11-13,15,18,19-Genius Jones app.	14	28	42	80	115	150
14,17,20-23	10	20	30	56	76	95
16-DC Super Heroes app.	31	62	93	182	296	410

ALL GOOD
St. John Publishing Co.: Oct, 1949 (50¢, 260 pgs.)

	GD 2.0	VG 4.0	FN 6.0	VF 8.0	VF/NM 9.0	NM- 9.2
nn-(8 St. John comics bound together)	90	180	270	576	988	1400

NOTE: *Also see Li'l Audrey Yearbook & Treasury of Comics.*

ALL GOOD COMICS (See Fox Giants)
Fox Features Syndicate: No.1, Spring, 1946 (36 pgs.)

	GD 2.0	VG 4.0	FN 6.0	VF 8.0	VF/NM 9.0	NM- 9.2
1-Joy Family, Dick Transom, Rick Evans, One Round Hogan	27	54	81	158	259	360

ALL GREAT
William H. Wise & Co.: nd (1945?) (132 pgs.)

	GD 2.0	VG 4.0	FN 6.0	VF 8.0	VF/NM 9.0	NM- 9.2
nn-Capt. Jack Terry, Joan Mason, Girl Reporter, Baron Doomsday; Torture scenes	45	90	135	284	480	675

ALL GREAT COMICS (See Fox Giants)
Fox Feature Syndicate: 1946 (36 pgs.)

	GD 2.0	VG 4.0	FN 6.0	VF 8.0	VF/NM 9.0	NM- 9.2
1-Crazy House, Bertie Benson Boy Detective, Gussie the Gob	27	54	81	158	259	360

ALL GREAT COMICS (Formerly Phantom Lady #13? Dagar, Desert Hawk No. 14 on)
Fox Features Syndicate: No. 14, Oct, 1947 - No. 13, Dec, 1947 (Newspaper strip reprints)

	GD 2.0	VG 4.0	FN 6.0	VF 8.0	VF/NM 9.0	NM- 9.2
14(#12)-Brenda Starr & Texas Slim-r (Scarce)	57	114	171	362	621	880
13-Origin Dagar, Desert Hawk; Brenda Starr (all-r); Kamen-c; Dagar covers begin	65	130	195	416	708	1000

ALL-GREAT CONFESSION MAGAZINE (See Fox Giants)

ALL-GREAT CONFESSIONS (See Fox Giants)

ALL GREAT CRIME STORIES (See Fox Giants)

ALL GREAT JUNGLE ADVENTURES (See Fox Giants)

ALL HALLOW'S EVE
Innovation Publishing: 1991 ($4.95, 52 pgs.)

	GD 2.0	VG 4.0	FN 6.0	VF 8.0	VF/NM 9.0	NM- 9.2
1-Painted-c/a	1	2	3	4	5	7

ALL HERO COMICS
Fawcett Publications: Mar, 1943 (100 pgs., cardboard-c)

	GD 2.0	VG 4.0	FN 6.0	VF 8.0	VF/NM 9.0	NM- 9.2
1-Capt. Marvel Jr., Capt. Midnight, Golden Arrow, Ibis the Invincible, Spy Smasher, Lance O'Casey; 1st Banshee O'Brien; Raboy-c	181	362	543	1158	1979	2800

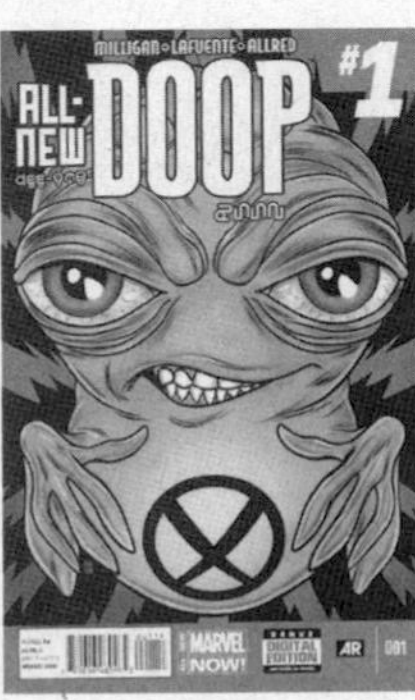

All-New Doop #1 © MAR

All-New X-Men #8 © MAR

All-Select Comics #1 © MAR

	GD 2.0	VG 4.0	FN 6.0	VF 8.0	VF/NM 9.0	NM- 9.2

ALL HUMOR COMICS
Quality Comics Group: Spring, 1946 - No. 17, December, 1949

	GD	VG	FN	VF	VF/NM	NM-
1	21	42	63	124	202	280
2-Atomic Tot story; Gustavson-a	14	28	42	76	108	140
3-9: 3-Intro Kelly Poole who is cover feature #3 on. 5-1st app. Hickory? 8-Gustavson-a	9	18	27	50	65	80
10-17	8	16	24	44	57	70

ALLIANCE, THE
Image Comics (Shadowline Ink): Aug, 1995 - No. 3, Nov, 1995 ($2.50)

1-3: 2-(9/95) 3.00

ALL LOVE (...Romances No. 26)(Formerly Ernie Comics)
Ace Periodicals (Current Books): No. 26, May, 1949 - No. 32, May, 1950

	GD	VG	FN	VF	VF/NM	NM-
26 (No. 1)-Ernie, Lily Belle app.	12	24	36	67	94	120
27-L. B. Cole-a	14	28	42	80	115	150
28-32	9	18	27	50	65	80

ALL-NEGRO COMICS
All-Negro Comics: June, 1947 (15¢)

	GD	VG	FN	VF	VF/NM	NM-
1 (Rare)	1833	3667	5500	9800	12,900	16,000

NOTE: *Seldom found in fine or mint condition; many copies have brown pages.*

ALL-NEW ATOM, THE (See The Atom and DCU Brave New World)
DC Comics: Sept, 2006 - No. 25, Sept, 2008 ($2.99)

1-25: 1-18-Simone-s. 1-Intro Ryan Choi; Byrne-a thru #3. 4-11-Barrows-a. 12,13-Chronos app. 14,15-Countdown x-over. 17,18-Wonder Woman app. 3.00
...: Future/Past TPB (2007, $14.99) r/#7-11 15.00
...: My Life in Miniature TPB (2007, $14.99) r/#1-6 and app. in DCU Brave New World #1 15.00
...: Small Wonder TPB (2008, $17.99) r/#17,18,21-25 18.00
...: The Hunt For Ray Palmer TPB (2008, $14.99) r/#12-16 15.00

ALL-NEW BATMAN: BRAVE & THE BOLD (See Batman: The Brave and the Bold)

ALL-NEW COLLECTORS' EDITION (Formerly Limited Collectors' Edition: see for C-57, C-59)
DC Comics, Inc.: Jan, 1978 - Vol. 8, No. C-62, 1979 (No. 54-58: 76 pgs.)

	GD	VG	FN	VF	VF/NM	NM-
C-53-Rudolph the Red-Nosed Reindeer	4	8	12	28	47	65
C-54-Superman Vs. Wonder Woman	4	8	12	25	40	55
C-55-Superboy & the Legion of Super-Heroes; Wedding of Lightning Lad & Saturn Girl; Grell-c/a	4	8	12	25	40	55
C-56-Superman Vs. Muhammad Ali: Wraparound Neal Adams-c/a; Adams & O'Neil-s (see "Superman Vs. Muhammad Ali" for reprint)	7	14	21	48	89	130
C-56-Superman Vs. Muhammad Ali (Whitman variant)-low print	9	18	27	58	114	170
C-57,C-59-(See Limited Collectors' Edition)						
C-58-Superman Vs. Shazam; Buckler-c/a	4	8	12	25	40	55
C-60-Rudolph's Summer Fun(8/78)	4	8	12	25	40	55
C-61-(See Famous First Edition-Superman #1)						
C-62-Superman the Movie (68 pgs.; 1979)-Photo-c from movie plus photos inside (also see DC Special Series #25)	3	6	9	15	22	28

ALL-NEW COMICS (...Short Story Comics No. 1-3)
Family Comics (Harvey Publications): Jan, 1943 - No. 14, Nov, 1946; No. 15, Mar-Apr, 1947 (10 x 13-1/2")

	GD	VG	FN	VF	VF/NM	NM-
1-Steve Case, Crime Rover, Johnny Rebel, Kayo Kane, The Echo, Night Hawk, Ray O'Light, Detective Shane begin (all 1st app.?); Red Blazer on cover only; Sultan-a; Nazi WWII-c	300	600	900	1980	3440	4900
2-Origin Scarlet Phantom by Kubert	123	246	369	787	1344	1900
3-Nazi war-c	97	194	291	621	1061	1500
4	84	168	252	538	919	1300
5-11: 5-Schomburg-c thru #11. 5,9-11-Japanese WWII-c. 6-8 Nazi WWII-c. 6-The Boy Heroes & Red Blazer (text story) begin, end #12; Black Cat app.; intro. Sparky in Red Blazer. 7-Kubert, Powell-a; Black Cat & Zebra app. 8,9: 8-Shock Gibson app.; Kubert, Powell-a; Schomburg-c. 9-Black Cat app.; Kubert-a. 10-The Zebra app. (from Green Hornet Comics); Kubert-a(3). 11-Girl Commandos, Man In Black app.	119	238	357	762	1306	1850
12-Kubert-a; Japanese WWII-c	58	116	174	371	636	900
13-Stuntman by Simon & Kirby; Green Hornet, Joe Palooka, Flying Fool app.; Green Hornet-c	50	100	150	315	533	750
14-The Green Hornet & The Man in Black Called Fate by Powell, Joe Flying Fool app.; Flying Fool app.; J. Palooka-c by Ham Fisher	41	82	123	256	428	600
15-(Rare)-Small size (5-1/2x8-1/2"; B&W; 32 pgs.). Distributed to mail subscribers only. Black Cat and Joe Palooka app.	155	310	465	992	1696	2400

NOTE: *Also see Boy Explorers No. 2, Flash Gordon No. 5, and Stuntman No. 3.* **Powell** *a-11.* **Schomburg** *c-5-11. Captain Red Blazer & Spark on c-5-11 (w/Boy Heroes #12).*

ALL-NEW DOOP (X-Men)
Marvel Comics: Jun, 2014 - Present ($3.99)

1-Milligan-s/Lafuente-a; Kitty Pryde and X-Men app. 4.00

ALL-NEW EXECUTIVE ASSISTANT: IRIS (Volume 4) (Also see Executive Assistant: Iris)
Aspen MLT: Sept, 2013 - Present ($1.00/$3.99)

1-($1.00) Buccellato-s/Qualano-a; multiple covers 3.00
2,3-($3.99) Multiple covers 4.00

ALL-NEW GHOST RIDER
Marvel Comics: May, 2014 - Present ($3.99)

1,2-Felipe Smith-s/Tradd Moore-a; origin of Robbie Reyes 4.00

ALL-NEW INVADERS
Marvel Comics: Mar, 2014 - Present ($3.99)

1-3: 1-Capt. America, Bucky, Namor & Jim Hammond team; Robinson-s/Pugh-a 4.00

ALL-NEW MARVEL NOW! POINT ONE
Marvel Comics: Mar, 2014 ($5.99, one-shot preview of upcoming series)

1-Previews of Loki, Silver Surfer, Black Widow, Ms. Marvel, Avengers, All-New Invaders 6.00

ALL-NEW OFFICIAL HANDBOOK OF THE MARVEL UNIVERSE A TO Z
Marvel Comics: 2006 - No. 12, 2006 ($3.99, limited series)

1-12-Profile pages of Marvel characters not covered in 2004-2005 Official Handbooks 4.00
...: Update 1-4 (2007, $3.99) Profile pages 4.00

ALL-NEW ULTIMATES
Marvel Comics: Jun, 2014 - Present ($3.99)

1-Miles Morales Spider-Man, Spider-Woman, Cloak and Dagger, and Bombshell team 4.00

ALL-NEW X-FACTOR
Marvel Comics: Mar, 2014 - Present ($3.99)

1-6-David-s/DiGiandomenico-a; Gambit, Polaris, Quicksilver, Danger app. 4.00

ALL-NEW X-MEN
Marvel Comics: Jan, 2013 - Present ($3.99)

1-Bendis-s; Immonen-a and wraparound-c; original X-Men time travel to present 4.00
2-24: 6-8-Marquez-a; Mystique app. 8-Avengers app. 16,17-Battle of the Atom tie-ins. 18-New uniforms. 22-24-Trial of Jean Grey; Guardians of the Galaxy app. 4.00
25-($4.99) Art by Marquez with pages by Timm, Mack, Young, Campbell & many others 5.00
Special #1 (12/13, $4.99) Superior Spider-Man and the Hulk app. 5.00

ALL NIGHTER
Image Comics: Jun, 2011 - No. 5, Oct, 2011 ($2.99, B&W, limited series)

1-5-David Haun-s/a/c 3.00

ALL-OUT WAR
DC Comics: Sept-Oct, 1979 - No. 6, Aug, 1980 ($1.00, 68 pgs.)

	GD	VG	FN	VF	VF/NM	NM-
1-The Viking Commando (origin), Force Three(origin), & Black Eagle Squadron begin	2	4	6	13	18	22
2-6	2	4	6	8	10	12

NOTE: **Ayers** *a(p)-1-6.* **Elias** *r-2.* **Evans** *a-1-6.* **Kubert** *c-16.*

ALL PICTURE ADVENTURE MAGAZINE
St. John Publishing Co.: Oct, 1952 - No. 2, Nov, 1952 (100 pg. Giants, 25¢, squarebound)

	GD	VG	FN	VF	VF/NM	NM-
1-War comics	37	74	111	222	361	500
2-Horror-crime comics	52	104	156	322	549	775

NOTE: *Above books contain three St. John comics rebound; variations possible.* **Baker** *art known in both.*

ALL PICTURE ALL TRUE LOVE STORY
St. John Publishing Co.: Oct., 1952 - No. 2, Nov., 1952 (100 pgs., 25¢)

	GD	VG	FN	VF	VF/NM	NM-
1-Canteen Kate by Matt Baker	57	114	171	362	619	875
2-Baker-c/a	41	82	123	256	428	600

ALL-PICTURE COMEDY CARNIVAL
St. John Publishing Co.: October, 1952 (100 pgs., 25¢)(Contains 4 rebound comics)

	GD	VG	FN	VF	VF/NM	NM-
1-Contents can vary; Baker-a	43	86	129	271	461	650

ALL REAL CONFESSION MAGAZINE (See Fox Giants)

ALL ROMANCES (Mr. Risk No. 7 on)
A. A. Wyn (Ace Periodicals): Aug, 1949 - No. 6, June, 1950

	GD	VG	FN	VF	VF/NM	NM-
1	15	30	45	85	130	175
2	10	20	30	54	72	90
3-6	9	18	27	50	65	80

ALL-SELECT COMICS (Blonde Phantom No. 12 on)
Timely Comics (Daring Comics): Fall, 1943 - No. 11, Fall, 1946

	GD	VG	FN	VF	VF/NM	NM-
1-Capt. America (by Rico #1), Human Torch, Sub-Mariner begin; Black Widow story (4 pgs.); Classic Schomburg-c	1650	3300	4950	11,000	21,500	32,000
2-Red Skull app.	568	1136	1704	4146	7323	10,500
3-The Whizzer begins	383	766	1149	2681	4691	6700

All Star Batman and Robin #4 © DC

All Star Comics #13 © DC

All-Star Squadron #47 © DC

GD 2.0 | VG 4.0 | FN 6.0 | VF 8.0 | VF/NM 9.0 | NM- 9.2

4,5-Last Sub-Mariner 300 600 900 2070 3635 5200
6-9: 6-The Destroyer app. 8-No Whizzer 258 516 774 1651 2826 4000
10-The Destroyer & Sub-Mariner app.; last Capt. America & Human Torch issue 258 516 774 1651 2826 4000
11-1st app. Blonde Phantom; Miss America app.; all Blonde Phantom-c by Shores 297 594 891 1901 3251 4600
NOTE: ***Schomburg** c-1-10. **Sekowsky** a-7. #7 & 8 show 1944 in indicia, but should be 1945.*

ALL SELECT COMICS 70th ANNIVERARY SPECIAL
Marvel Comics: Sept, 2009 ($3.99, one-shot)
1-New stories of Blonde Phantom and Marvex the Super Robot; r/Marvex G.A. app. 5.00

ALL SPORTS COMICS (Formerly Real Sports Comics; becomes All Time Sports Comics No. 4 on)
Hillman Periodicals: No. 2, Dec-Jan, 1948-49; No. 3, Feb-Mar, 1949
2-Krigstein-a(p), Powell, Starr-a 36 72 108 211 343 475
3-Mort Lawrence-a 22 44 66 132 216 300

ALL STAR BATMAN & ROBIN, THE BOY WONDER
DC Comics: Sept, 2005 - No. 10, Aug, 2008 ($2.99)
1-Two covers; retelling of Robin's origin; Frank Miller-s/Jim Lee-a/c 4.00
1-Diamond Retailer Summit Edition (9/05) sketch-c 60.00
2-10: 2-7-Two covers by Lee and Miller. 3-Black Canary app. 4-Six pg. Batcave gatefold.
10-Edition without profanity 3.00
8-10: 8,9-Variant cover by Neal Adams. 10-Variant-c by Quitely 5.00
10-Recalled edition with insufficiently covered profanity inside; Jim Lee-c 20.00
10-Recalled edition with variant Quitely-c 40.00
... Special Edition (2/06, $3.99) r/#1 with Lee pencil pages and Miller script; new Miller-c 4.00
Vol. 1 HC (2008, $24.99, dustjacket) r/#1-9; cover gallery, sketch pages; Schreck intro. 25.00
Vol. 1 SC (2009, $19.99) r/#1-9; cover gallery, sketch pages; Schreck intro. 20.00

ALL STAR COMICS
DC Comics: Spring 1940
1-Ashcan comic, not distributed to newsstands, only for in-house use. Cover art is Flash Comics #1 and interior from Detective Comics #37. A CGC certified 7.0 copy sold for $15,600 in 2002.

ALL STAR COMICS (All Star Western No. 58 on)
National Periodical Publ./All-American/DC Comics: Sum, 1940 - No. 57, Feb-Mar, 1951; No. 58, Jan-Feb, 1976 - No. 74, Sept-Oct, 1978
1-The Flash (#1 by E.E. Hibbard), Hawkman (by Shelly), Hourman (by Bernard Baily), The Sandman (by Creig Flessel), The Spectre (by Baily), Biff Bronson, Red White & Blue (ends #2) begin; Ultra Man's only app. (#1-3 are quarterly; #4 begins bi-monthly issues) 1200 2400 3600 9000 16,750 24,500
2-Green Lantern (by Martin Nodell), Johnny Thunder begin; Green Lantern figure swipe from the cover of All-American Comics #16; Flash figure swipe from cover of Flash Comics #8; Moldoff/Bailey-c (cut & paste-c.) 530 1060 1590 3869 6835 9800
3-Origin & 1st app. The Justice Society of America (Win/40); Dr. Fate & The Atom begin, Red Tornado cameo 4833 9667 14,500 36,500 70,750 105,000
3-Reprint, Oversize 13-1/2x10". **WARNING:** This comic is an exact reprint of the original except for its size. DC published it in 1974 with a second cover titling it as a Famous First Edition. There have been many reported cases of the outer cover being removed and the interior sold as the original edition. The reprint with the new outer cover removed is practically worthless. See Famous First Edition for value.
4-1st adventure for J.S.A. 530 1060 1590 3869 6835 9800
5-1st app. Shiera Sanders as Hawkgirl (1st costumed super-heroine, 6-7/41) 470 940 1410 3431 6066 8700
6-Johnny Thunder joins JSA 300 600 900 1950 3375 4800
7-Batman, Superman, Flash cameo; last Hourman; Doiby Dickles app. 343 686 1029 2400 4200 6000
8-Origin & 1st app. Wonder Woman (12-1/41-42)(added as 9 pgs. making book 76 pgs.; origin cont'd in Sensation #1; see W.W. #1 for more detailed origin); Dr. Fate dons new helmet; Hop Harrigan text stories & Starman begin; Shiera app.; Hop Harrigan JSA guest; Starman & Dr. Mid-Nite become members 4500 9000 13,500 33,750 66,875 100,000
9-11: 9-JSA's girlfriends cameo; Shiera app.; J. Edgar Hoover of FBI made associate member of JSA. 10-Flash, Green Lantern cameo; Sandman new costume. 11-Wonder Woman begins; Spectre cameo; Shiera app.; Moldoff Hawkman-c 300 600 900 1935 3343 4750
12-Wonder Woman becomes JSA Secretary 284 568 852 1803 3102 4400
13,15: Sandman w/Sandy in #14 & 15. 13-Hitler app. in book-length sci-fi story. 15-Origin & 1st app. Brain Wave; Shiera app. 252 504 756 1613 2757 3900
14-(12/42) Junior JSA Club begins; w/membership offer & premiums 258 516 774 1651 2826 4000
16-20: 19-Sandman w/Sandy. 20-Dr. Fate & Sandman cameo 219 438 657 1402 2401 3400
21-23: 21-Spectre & Atom cameo; Dr. Fate by Kubert; Dr. Fate, Sandman end. 22-Last Hop Harrigan; Flag-c. 23-Origin/1st app. Psycho Pirate; last Spectre & Starman 174 348 522 1114 1907 2700
24-Flash & Green Lantern cameo; Mr. Terrific only app.; Wildcat, JSA guest; Kubert Hawkman begins; Hitler-c 177 354 531 1124 1937 2750
25-27: 25-Flash & Green Lantern start again. 26-Robot-c. 27-Wildcat, JSA guest (#24-26: only All-American imprint) 152 304 456 965 1658 2350
28-32 135 270 405 864 1482 2100
33-Solomon Grundy & Doiby Dickles app; classic Solomon Grundy cover & last G.A. app. 360 720 1080 2520 4410 6300
34,35-Johnny Thunder cameo in both 129 258 387 826 1413 2000
36-Batman & Superman JSA guests 290 580 870 1856 3178 4500
37-Johnny Thunder cameo; origin & 1st app. Injustice Society; last Kubert Hawkman 174 348 522 1114 1907 2700
38-Black Canary begins; JSA Death issue 232 464 696 1485 2543 3600
39,40: 39-Last Johnny Thunder 123 246 369 787 1344 1900
41-Black Canary joins JSA; Injustice Society app. (2nd app.?) 123 246 369 787 1344 1900
42-Atom & the Hawkman don new costumes 123 246 369 787 1344 1900
43-49,51-56: 43-New logo; Robot-c. 55-Sci/Fi story. 56-Robot-c 123 246 369 787 1344 1900
50-Frazetta art, 3 pgs. 129 258 387 826 1413 2000
57-Kubert-a, 6 pgs. (Scarce); last app. G.A. Green Lantern, Flash & Dr. Mid-Nite 181 362 543 1158 1979 2800
V12 #58-(1976) JSA (Flash, Hawkman, Dr. Mid-Nite, Wildcat, Dr. Fate, Green Lantern, Robin & Star Spangled Kid) app.; intro. Power Girl 7 14 21 44 82 120
V12 #59,60: 59-Estrada & Wood-a 3 6 9 19 30 40
V12 #61-68: 62-65-Superman app. 64,65-Wood-c/a; Vandal Savage app. 66-Injustice Society app. 68-Psycho Pirate app. 3 6 9 19 30 40
V12 #69-1st Earth-2 Huntress (Helena Wayne) 5 10 15 31 53 75
V12 #70-73: 70-Full intro. of Huntress 3 6 9 19 30 40
V12 #74-(44 pgs.) Last issue, story continues in Adventure Comics #461 & 462 (death of Earth-2 Batman; Staton-c/a 4 8 12 28 47 65
(See Justice Society Vol. 1 TPB for reprints of V12 revival)
NOTE: *No Atom-27, 36; no Dr. Fate-13; no Flash-8, 9, 11-23; no Green Lantern-8, 9,11-23; Hawkman in 1-57 (only one to app. in all 57 issues); no Johnny Thunder-5, 36; no Wonder Woman-9, 10, 23. Book length stories in 4-9, 11-14, 18-22, 25, 26, 29, 30, 32-36, 40, 42, 43. Johnny Peril in #42-46, 48, 49, 51, 52,54-57. **Baily** a-1-10, 12, 13, 14i, 15-20. **Burnley** Starman-8-13; c-12, 13. **Grell** c-58. **E.E. Hibbard** c-3, 4, 6-10. **Infantino** c-40. **Kubert** Hawkman-24-30, 33-37. **Lampert/Baily/Flessel** c-1, 2. **Moldoff** Hawkman-3-23; c-11. **Mart Nodell** c-25i, 26i, 27-32. **Purcell** c-5. **Simon & Kirby** Sandman 14-17, 19. **Staton** a-66-74p. c-74p. **Toth** a-37(2), 38(2), 40, 41; c-38, 41. **Wood** a-58i-63i, 64, 65; c-63i, 64, 65. Issues 1-7, 9-16 are 68 pgs.; #8 is 76 pgs.; #17-19 are 60 pgs.; #20-57 are 52 pgs.*

ALL STAR COMICS (Also see crossover 1999 editions of Adventure, All-American, National, Sensation, Smash, Star Spangled and Thrilling Comics)
DC Comics: May, 1999 - No. 2, May, 1999 ($2.95, bookends for JSA x-over)
1,2-Justice Society in World War 2; Robinson-s/Johnson-c 3.00
1-RRP Edition 40.00
...80-Page Giant (9/99, $4.95) Phantom Lady app. 5.00

ALL STAR INDEX, THE
Independent Comics Group (Eclipse): Feb, 1987 ($2.00, Baxter paper)
1 1 2 3 5 6 8

ALL-STAR SQUADRON (See Justice League of America #193)
DC Comics: Sept, 1981 - No. 67, Mar, 1987
1-Original Atom, Hawkman, Dr. Mid-Nite, Robotman (origin), Plastic Man, Johnny Quick, Liberty Belle, Shining Knight begin 1 2 3 5 7 9
2-10: 3-Solomon Grundy app. 4,7-Spectre app. 8-Re-intro Steel, the Indestructable Man 5.00
11-46,48,49: 12-Origin G.A. Hawkman retold. 23-Origin/1st app. The Amazing Man. 24-Batman app. 25-1st app. Infinity, Inc. (9/83), 26-Origin Infinity, Inc.(2nd app.); Robin app. 27-Dr. Fate vs. The Spectre. 30-35-Spectre app. 33-Origin Freedom Fighters of Earth-X. 36,37-Superman vs. Capt. Marvel; Ordway-c. 41-Origin Starman 4.00
47-Origin Dr. Fate; McFarlane-a (1st full story)/part-c (7/85) 2 4 6 9 12 15
50-Double size; Crisis x-over 1 2 3 5 6 8
51-66: 51-56-Crisis x-over. 61-Origin Liberty Belle. 62-Origin The Shining Knight. 63-Origin Robotman. 65-Origin Johnny Quick. 66-Origin Tarantula 6.00
67-Last issue; retells first case of the Justice Society 1 2 3 5 6 8
Annual 1-3: 1(11/82)-Retells origin of G.A. Atom, Guardian & Wildcat; Jerry Ordway's 1st pencils for DC. (1st work was inking Carmine Infantino in Mystery in Space #117). 2(11/83)-Infinity, Inc. app. 3(9/84) 6.00
NOTE: ***Buckler** a-1-5; c-1, 3-5, 51. **Kubert** c-2, 7-18. JLA app. in 14, 15. JSA app. in 4, 14, 15, 19, 27, 28.*

ALL-STAR STORY OF THE DODGERS, THE
Stadium Communications: Apr, 1979 ($1.00)
1 2 4 6 9 13 16

ALL-STAR SUPERMAN (Also see FCBD edition in the Promotional Comics section)
DC Comics: Jan, 2006 - No. 12, Oct, 2008 ($2.99)
1-Grant Morrison-s/Frank Quitely-a/c 5.00

All Star Western (2011 series) #23 © DC

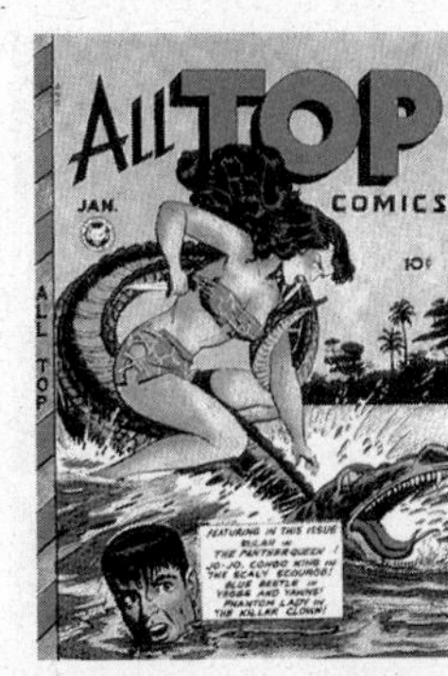

All Top Comics #9 © FOX

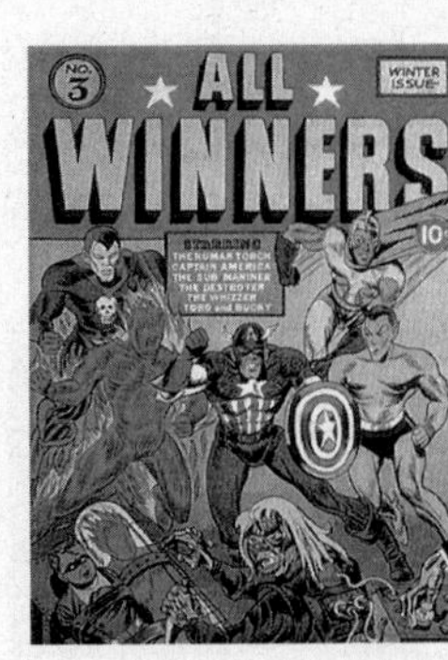

All Winners Comics #3 © MAR

GD VG FN VF VF/NM NM-
2.0 4.0 6.0 8.0 9.0 9.2

1-Variant-c by Neal Adams 20.00
1-Special Edition (2009, $1.00) r/#1 with "After Watchmen" cover logo frame 3.00
2-12: 3-Lois gets super powers. 7,8-Bizarro app. 3.00
Free Comic Book Day giveaway (6/08) reprints #1 3.00
Vol. 1 HC (2007, $19.99, dustjacket) r/#1-6; Bob Schreck intro. 20.00
Vol. 1 SC (2008, $12.99) r/#1-6; Schreck intro. 13.00
Vol. 2 HC (2009, $19.99, dustjacket) r/#7-12; Mark Waid intro. 20.00
Vol. 2 SC (2009, $12.99) r/#7-12; Mark Waid intro. 13.00

ALL STAR WESTERN (Formerly All Star Comics No. 1-57)
National Periodical Publ.: No. 58, Apr-May, 1951 - No. 119, June-July, 1961

58-Trigger Twins (ends #116), Strong Bow, The Roving Ranger & Don Caballero begin 47 94 141 296 498 700
59,60: Last 52 pgs. 28 56 84 165 270 375
61-66: 61-64-Toth-a 22 44 66 132 216 300
67-Johnny Thunder begins; Gil Kane-a 29 58 87 170 278 385
68-81: Last precode (2-3/55) 15 30 45 86 133 180
82-98: 97-1st S.A. issue 14 28 42 78 112 145
99-Frazetta-r/Jimmy Wakely #4 14 28 42 80 115 150
100 14 28 42 80 115 150
101-107,109-116,118,119 12 24 36 69 97 125
108-Origin J. Thunder; J. Thunder logo begins 22 44 66 132 216 300
117-Origin Super Chief 15 30 45 83 124 165
NOTE: ***Gil Kane** c(p)-58, 59, 61, 63, 64, 68, 69, 70-95(most), 97-199(most). **Infantino** art in most issues. Madame .44 app.- #117-119.*

ALL-STAR WESTERN (Weird Western Tales No. 12 on)
National Periodical Publications: Aug-Sept, 1970 - No. 11, Apr-May, 1972

1-Pow-Wow Smith-r; Infantino-a 5 10 15 34 60 85
2-Outlaw begins; El Diablo by Morrow begins; has cameos by Williamson, Torres, Kane, Giordano & Phil Seuling 5 10 15 31 53 75
3-Origin El Diablo 5 10 15 30 50 70
4-6: 5-Last Outlaw issue. 6-Billy the Kid begins, ends #8 3 6 9 21 33 45
7-9-(52 pgs.) 9-Frazetta-a, 3pgs.(r) 4 8 12 23 37 50
10-(52 pgs.) Jonah Hex begins (1st app., 2-3/72) 34 68 102 245 548 850
11-(52 pgs.) 2nd app. Jonah Hex; 1st cover 13 26 39 89 195 300
NOTE: ***Neal Adams** c-2-5; **Aparo** a-5. **G. Kane** a-3, 4, 6, 8. **Kubert** a-4r, 7-9r. **Morrow** a-2-4, 10, 11. No. 7-11 have 52 pgs.*

ALL STAR WESTERN (DC New 52)
DC Comics: Nov, 2011 - Present ($3.99)

1-29: 1-Jonah Hex in 1880s Gotham City; Gray & Palmiotti-s/Moritat-a. 2,3-El Diablo back-up. 9-11-Court of Owls. 10-Bat Lash back-up; Garcia-López-a. 13-16-Tomahawk back-up. 19-21-Booster Gold app. 21-28-Hex in present day. 22-Batman app. 27-Superman app. 4.00
#0 (11/12, $3.99) Jonah Hex's full origin; Gray & Palmiotti-s/Moritat-a 4.00

ALL SURPRISE (Becomes Jeanie #13 on) (Funny animal)
Timely/Marvel (CPC): Fall, 1943 - No. 12, Winter, 1946-47

1-Super Rabbit, Gandy & Sourpuss begin 43 86 129 271 461 650
2 21 42 63 124 202 280
3-10,12 17 34 51 98 154 210
11-Kurtzman "Pigtales" art 18 36 54 103 162 220

ALL TEEN (Formerly All Winners; All Winners & Teen Comics No. 21 on)
Marvel Comics (WFP): No. 20, January, 1947

20-Georgie, Mitzi, Patsy Walker, Willie app.; Syd Shores-c 22 44 66 132 216 300

ALL-TIME SPORTS COMICS (Formerly All Sports Comics)
Hillman Per.: V2, No. 4, Apr-May, 1949 - V2, No. 7, Oct-Nov, 1949 (All 52 pgs.)

V2#4 23 46 69 136 223 310
5-7: 5-(V1#5 inside)-Powell-a; Ty Cobb sty. 7-Krigstein-p; Walter Johnson & Knute Rockne sty 18 36 54 105 165 225

ALL TOP
William H. Wise Co.: 1944 (132 pgs.)

nn-Capt. V, Merciless the Sorceress, Red Robbins, One Round Hogan, Mike the M.P., Snooky, Pussy Katnip app. 37 74 111 222 361 500

ALL TOP COMICS (My Experience No. 19 on)
Fox Features Synd./Green Publ./Norlen Mag.: 1945; No. 2, Sum, 1946 - No. 18, Mar, 1949; 1957 - 1959

1-Cosmo Cat & Flash Rabbit begin (1st app.) 30 60 90 177 289 400
2 (#1-7 are funny animal) 15 30 45 86 133 180
3-7: Two diff. issues (7/47 & 9/47) 13 26 39 72 101 130
8-Blue Beetle, Phantom Lady, & Rulah, Jungle Goddess begin (11/47); Kamen-c 300 600 900 1920 3310 4700
9-Kamen-c 152 304 456 965 1658 2350
10-Kamen bondage-c 161 322 483 1030 1765 2500
11-13,15-17: 11,12-Rulah-c. 15-No Blue Beetle 124 248 372 787 1356 1925
14-No Blue Beetle; used in **SOTI**, illo- "Corpses of colored people strung up by their wrists" 187 374 561 1197 2049 2900
18-Dagar, Jo-Jo app; no Phantom Lady or Blue Beetle 82 164 246 528 902 1275
6(1957-Green Publ.)-Patoruzu the Indian; Cosmo Cat on cover only. 6(1958-Literary Ent.)-Muggy Doo; Cosmo Cat on cover only. 6(1959-Norlen)-Atomic Mouse; Cosmo Cat on-c only. 6(1959)-Little Eva. 6(Cornell)-Supermouse on-c 5 10 15 24 30 35
NOTE: *Jo-Jo by **Kamen**-12,18.*

ALL TRUE ALL PICTURE POLICE CASES
St. John Publishing Co.: Oct, 1952 - No. 2, Nov, 1952 (100 pgs.)

1-Three rebound St. John crime comics 46 92 138 290 488 685
2-Three comics rebound 34 68 102 204 332 460
NOTE: *Contents may vary.*

ALL-TRUE CRIME (...Cases No. 26-35; formerly Official True Crime Cases)
Marvel/Atlas Comics: No. 26, Feb, 1948 - No. 52, Sept, 1952
(OFI #26,27/CFI #28,29/LCC #30-46/LMC #47-52)

26(#1)-Syd Shores-c 36 72 108 211 343 475
27(4/48)-Electric chair-c 30 60 90 177 289 400
28-41,43-48,50-52: 35-37-Photo-c 14 28 42 82 121 160
42,49-Krigstein-a. 49-Used in **POP**, Pg 79 15 30 45 84 127 170
NOTE: ***Colan** a-46. **Keller** a-46. **Robinson** a-47, 50. **Sale** a-46. **Shores** c-26. **Tuska** a-48(3).*

ALL-TRUE DETECTIVE CASES (Kit Carson No. 5 on)
Avon Periodicals: #2, Apr-May, 1954 - No. 4, Aug-Sept, 1954

2(#1)-Wood-a 24 48 72 144 237 330
3-Kinstler-c 15 30 45 83 124 165
4-r/Gangsters And Gun Molls #2; Kamen-a 18 36 54 107 169 230
nn(100 pgs.)-7 pg. Kubert-a, Kinstler back-c 42 84 126 265 445 625

ALL TRUE ROMANCE (...Illustrated No. 3)
Artful Publ. #1-3/Harwell(Comic Media) #4-20?/Ajax-Farrell(Excellent Publ.) No. 22 on/Four Star Comic Corp.: 3/51 - No. 20, 12/54; No. 22, 3/55 - No. 30?, 7/57; No. 3(#31), 9/57;No. 4(#32), 11/57; No. 33, 2/58 - No. 34, 6/58

1 (3/51) 20 40 60 120 195 270
2 (10/51; 11/51 on-c) 13 26 39 74 105 135
3(12/51) - #5(5/52) 11 22 33 62 86 110
6-Wood-a, 9 pgs. (exceptional) 20 40 60 118 192 265
7-10 [two #7s: #7(11/52, 9/52 inside), #7(11/52, 11/52 inside)]. 10-Hollingsworth-c 10 20 30 58 79 100
11-13,16-19(9/54),20(12/54) (no #21): 11,13-Heck-a 9 18 27 50 65 80
14-Marijuana story 9 18 27 52 69 85
22: Last precode issue (1st Ajax, 3/55) 9 18 27 50 65 80
23-27,29,30(7/57): 29-Disbrow-a 8 16 24 44 57 70
28 (9/56)-L. B. Cole, Disbrow-a 12 24 36 67 94 120
3(#31, 9/57),4(#32, 11/57),33,34 (Farrell, '57- '58) 8 16 24 42 54 65

ALL WESTERN WINNERS (Formerly All Winners; becomes Western Winners with No. 5; see Two-Gun Kid No. 5)
Marvel Comics(CDS): No. 2, Winter, 1948-49 - No. 4, April, 1949

2-Black Rider (origin/1st app.) & his horse Satan, Kid Colt & his horse Steel, & Two-Gun Kid & his horse Cyclone begin; Shores c-2-4 74 148 222 470 810 1150
3-Anti-Wertham editorial 38 76 114 228 369 510
4-Black Rider i.d. revealed; Heath, Shores-a 38 76 114 228 369 510

ALL WINNERS COMICS (All Teen #20) (Also see Timely Presents: ...)
USA No. 1-7/WFP No. 10-19/YAI No. 21: Summer, 1941 - No. 19, Fall, 1946; No. 21, Winter, 1946-47; (No #20) (No. 21 continued from Young Allies No. 20)

1-The Angel & Black Marvel only app.; Capt. America by Simon & Kirby, Human Torch & Sub-Mariner begin (#1 was advertised as All Aces); 1st app. All-Winners Squad in text story by Stan Lee 1900 3800 5700 13,500 24,250 35,000
2-The Destroyer & The Whizzer begin; Simon & Kirby Captain America 530 1060 1590 3869 6835 9800
3 423 846 1269 3088 5444 7800
4-Classic War-c by Al Avison 470 940 1410 3431 6066 8700
5 326 652 978 2282 3991 5700
6-The Black Avenger only app.; no Whizzer story; Hitler, Hirohito & Mussolini-c 432 864 1296 3154 5577 8000
7-10 320 640 960 2240 3920 5600
11,13-15: 11-1st Atlas globe on-c (Winter, 1943-44; also see Human Torch #14). 14,15-No Human Torch 245 490 735 1568 2684 3800
12-Red Skull story; last Destroyer; no Whizzer story 300 600 900 2010 3505 5000

All-Winners Squad: Band of Brothers #1 © MAR

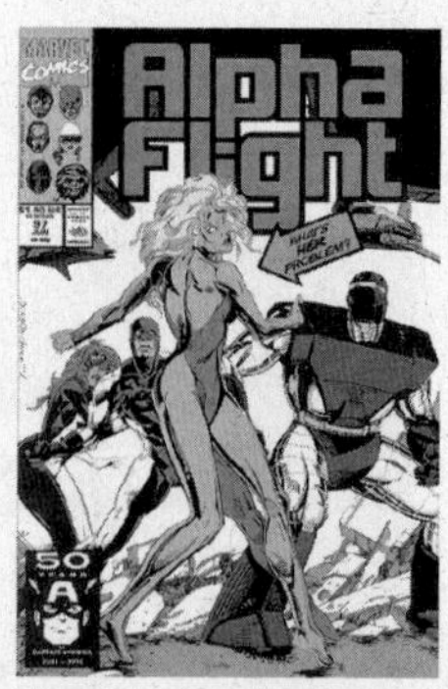

Alpha Flight #97 © MAR

Amazing Adult Fantasy #10 © MAR

GD VG FN VF VF/NM NM-
2.0 4.0 6.0 8.0 9.0 9.2

16-18: 16-No Human Torch 216 432 648 1372 2361 3350
19-(Scarce)-1st story app. & origin All Winners Squad (Capt. America & Bucky, Human Torch & Toro, Sub-Mariner, Whizzer, & Miss America; r-in Fantasy Masterpieces #10
892 1784 2676 6512 11,506 16,500
21-(Scarce)-All Winners Squad; bondage-c 687 1374 2061 5015 8858 12,700
NOTE: ***Everett*** *Sub-Mariner-1, 3, 4;* ***Burgos*** *Torch-1, 3, 4.* ***Schomburg*** *c-1, 7-18.* ***Shores*** *c-19p, 21.*
(2nd Series - August, 1948, Marvel Comics (CDS))
(Becomes All Western Winners with No. 2)
1-The Blonde Phantom, Capt. America, Human Torch, & Sub-Mariner app.
300 600 900 2010 3505 5000

ALL WINNERS COMICS 70th ANNIVERARY SPECIAL
Marvel Comics: Oct, 2009 ($3.99, one-shot)
1-New story of All Winners Squad; r/G.A. Capt America app. from All Winners #12 5.00

ALL-WINNERS SQUAD: BAND OF HEROES
Marvel Comics: Aug, 2011 - No. 5, Dec, 2011 ($2.99, unfinished limited series of 8 issues)
1-5-WWII story of the Young Avenger and Captain Flame; Jenkins-s/DiGiandomenico-a 3.00

ALL YOUR COMICS (See Fox Giants)
Fox Feature Syndicate (R. W. Voight): Spring, 1946 (36 pgs.)
1-Red Robbins, Merciless the Sorceress app. 22 44 66 128 209 290

ALMANAC OF CRIME (See Fox Giants)

AL OF FBI (See Little Al of the FBI)

ALONE IN THE DARK (Based on video game)
Image Comics: Feb, 2003 ($4.95)
1-Matt Haley-c/a; Jean-Marc & Randy Lofficier-s 5.00

ALPHA AND OMEGA
Spire Christian Comics (Fleming H. Revell): 1978 (49¢)
nn 2 4 6 9 13 16

ALPHA: BIG TIME (See Amazing Spider-Man #692-694)
Marvel Comics: Apr, 2013 - Present ($2.99)
1-5-Fialkov-s/Plati-a/Ramos-c. 1,3,5-Superior Peter Parker app. 4-Thor app. 3.00

ALPHA CENTURION (See Superman, 2nd Series & Zero Hour)
DC Comics: 1996 ($2.95, one-shot)
1 3.00

ALPHA FLIGHT (See X-Men #120,121 & X-Men/Alpha Flight)
Marvel Comics: Aug, 1983 - No. 130, Mar, 1994 (#52-on are direct sales only)
1-(52 pgs.) Byrne-a begins (thru #28) -Wolverine & Nightcrawler cameo 5.00
2-11,13-28: 2-Vindicator becomes Guardian; origin Marrina & Alpha Flight. 3-Concludes origin Alpha Flight. 6-Origin Shaman. 7-Origin Snowbird. 10,11-Origin Sasquatch. 13-Wolverine app. 16,17-Wolverine cameo. 17-X-Men x-over (mostly r-/X-Men #109). 20-New headquarters. 25-Return of Guardian. 28-Last Byrne issue 3.50
12-(52 pgs.)-Death of Guardian 4.00
29-32,35-49: 39-47,49-Portacio-a(i) 3.00
33-1st app. Lady Deathstrike; Wolverine app. 1 3 4 6 8 10
34-2nd app. Lady Deathstrike; origin Wolverine 6.00
50-Double size; Portacio-a(i) 4.00
51-Jim Lee's 1st work at Marvel (10/87); Wolverine cameo; 1st Lee Wolverine; Portacio-a(i)
1 2 3 5 6 8
52,53-Wolverine app.; Lee-a on Wolverine; Portacio-a(i); 53-Lee/Portacio-a 4.00
54-73,76-86,91-99,101-105: 54,63,64-No Jim Lee-a. 54-Portacio-a(i). 55-62-Jim Lee-a(p). 71-Intro The Sorcerer (villain). 91-Dr. Doom app. 94-F.F. x-over. 99-Galactus, Avengers app. 102-Intro Weapon Omega 3.00
74,75,87-90,100: 74-Wolverine, Spider-Man & The Avengers app. 75-Double size ($1.95, 52 pgs.). 87-90-Wolverine. 4 part story w/Jim Lee-c. 89-Original Guardian returns. 100-($2.00, 52 pgs.)-Avengers & Galactus app. 4.00
106-Northstar revealed to be gay 3.50
106-2nd printing (direct sale only) 3.00
107-109,112-119,121-129: 107-X-Factor x-over. 112-Infinity War x-overs 3.00
110,111: Infinity War x-overs, Wolverine app. (brief). 111-Thanos cameo 3.00
120-($2.25)-Polybagged w/Paranormal Registration Act poster 4.00
130-($2.25, 52 pgs.) 4.00
Annual 1,2 (9/86, 12/87) 4.00
...Classics Vol. 1 TPB (2007, $24.99) r/#1-8; character profile pages; Byrne interview 25.00
Special V2#1(6/92, $2.50, 52 pgs.)-Wolverine-c/story 4.00
NOTE: ***Austin*** *c-1i, 2i, 53i.* ***Byrne*** *c-81, 82.* ***Guice*** *c-85, 91-99.* ***Jim Lee*** *a(p)-51, 53, 55-62, 64; c-53, 87-90.* ***Mignola*** *a-29-31p.* ***Whilce Portacio*** *a(i)-39-47, 49-54.*

ALPHA FLIGHT (2nd Series)
Marvel Comics: Aug, 1997 - No. 20, Mar, 1999 ($2.99/$1.99)
1-($2.99)-Wraparound cover 6.00

GD VG FN VF VF/NM NM-
2.0 4.0 6.0 8.0 9.0 9.2

2,3: 2-Variant-c 4.00
4-11: 8,9-Wolverine-c/app. 3.00
12-($2.99) Death of Sasquatch; wraparound-c 4.00
13-20 3.00
.../Inhumans '98 Annual ($3.50) Raney-a 4.00

ALPHA FLIGHT (3rd Series)
Marvel Comics: May, 2004 - No. 12, April, 2005 ($2.99)
1-12: 1-6-Lobdell-s/Henry-c/a 3.00
... Vol. 1: You Gotta Be Kiddin' Me (2004, $14.99) r/#1-6 15.00

ALPHA FLIGHT (4th Series)
Marvel Comics: No. 0.1, Jul, 2011 - No. 8, Mar, 2012 ($2.99)
0.1-Pak & Van Lente-s/Oliver & Green-a; Kara Killgrave app. 3.00
1-(8/11, $3.99) Fear Itself tie-in; Eaglesham-a/Jimenez-c; bonus design sketch pages 4.00
2-8-($2.99) Fear Itself tie-ins. 2-Puck returns. 5-Taskmaster app. 7,8-Wolverine app. 3.00

ALPHA FLIGHT: IN THE BEGINNING
Marvel Comics: July, 1997 ($1.95, one-shot)
(-1)-Flashback w/Wolverine 3.00

ALPHA FLIGHT SPECIAL
Marvel Comics: July, 1991 - No. 4, Oct, 1991 ($1.50, limited series)
1-4: 1-3-r-A. Flight #97-99 w/covers. 4-r-A.Flight #100 3.00

ALPHA KORPS
Diversity Comics: Sept, 1996 ($2.50)
1-Origin/1st app. Alpha Korps 3.00

ALTERED IMAGE
Image Comics: Apr, 1998 - No. 3, Sept, 1998 ($2.50, limited series)
1-3-Spawn, Witchblade, Savage Dragon; Valentino-s/a 3.00

ALTER EGO
First Comics: May, 1986 - No. 4, Nov, 1986 (Mini-series)
1-4 3.00

ALTER NATION
Image Comics: Feb, 2004 - No. 4, Jun, 2004 ($2.95, limited series)
1-4: 1-Two covers by Art Adams and Barberi; Barberi-a 3.00

ALVIN (TV) (See Four Color Comics No. 1042 or Three Chipmunks #1)
Dell Publishing Co.: Oct-Dec, 1962 - No. 28, Oct, 1973
12-021-212 (#1) 8 16 24 51 96 140
2 5 10 15 31 53 75
3-10 4 8 12 28 47 65
11-"Chipmunks sing the Beatles' Hits" 5 10 15 31 53 75
12-28 4 8 12 23 37 50
Alvin For President (10/64) 4 8 12 28 47 65
...& His Pals in Merry Christmas with Clyde Crashcup & Leonardo 1 (25¢ Giant) (02-120-402)-(12-2/64) 6 12 18 42 79 115
Reprinted in 1966 (12-023-604) 4 8 12 23 37 50

ALVIN & THE CHIPMUNKS
Harvey Comics: July, 1992 - No. 5, May, 1994
1-5: 1-Richie Rich app. 5.00

AMALGAM AGE OF COMICS, THE: THE DC COMICS COLLECTION
DC Comics: 1996 ($12.95, trade paperback)
nn-r/Amazon, Assassins, Doctor Strangefate, JLX, Legends of the Dark Claw, & Super Soldier 13.00

AMANDA AND GUNN
Image Comics: Apr, 1997 - No. 4, Oct, 1997 ($2.95, B&W, limited series)
1-4 3.00

AMAZING ADULT FANTASY (Formerly Amazing Adventures #1-6; becomes Amazing Fantasy #15) (See Amazing Fantasy for Omnibus HC reprint of #1-15)
Marvel Comics Group (AMI): No. 7, Dec, 1961 - No. 14, July, 1962
7-Ditko-c/a begins, ends #14 46 92 138 368 834 1300
8-Last 10¢ issue 40 80 120 296 673 1050
9-13: 12-1st app. Mailbag. 13-Anti-communist story
39 78 117 289 657 1025
13-2nd printing (1994) 2 4 6 8 10 12
14-Prototype issue (Professor X) 43 86 129 318 722 1125

AMAZING ADVENTURE FUNNIES (Fantoman No. 2 on)
Centaur Publications: June, 1940 - No. 2, Sept. 1940
1-The Fantom of the Fair by Gustavson (r/Amaz. Mystery Funnies V2#7,V2#8),

Amazing Adventures #4 © MAR

Amazing Comics #1 © MAR

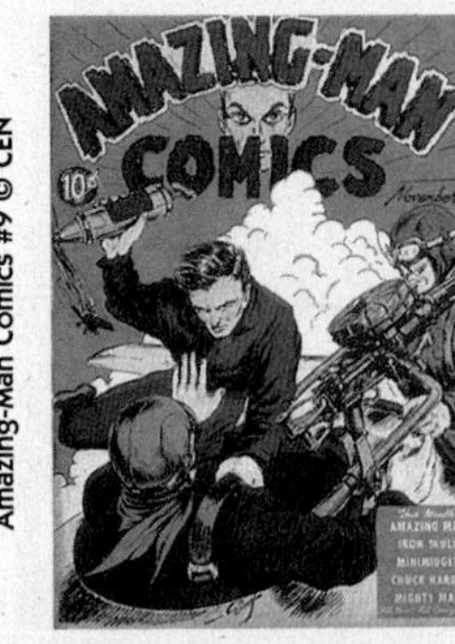

Amazing-Man Comics #9 © CEN

GD VG FN VF VF/NM NM-
2.0 4.0 6.0 8.0 9.0 9.2

The Arrow, Skyrocket Steele From the Year X by Everett (r/AMF #2);
Burgos-a 181 362 543 1158 1979 2800
2-Reprints; Published after Fantoman #2 116 232 348 742 1271 1800
NOTE: ***Burgos** a-1(2). **Everett** a-1(3). **Gustavson** a-1(5), 2(3). **Pinajian** a-2.*

AMAZING ADVENTURES (Also see Boy Cowboy & Science Comics)
Ziff-Davis Publ. Co.: 1950; No. 1, Nov, 1950 - No. 6, Fall, 1952 (Painted covers)

1950 (no month given) (8-1/2x11) (8 pgs.) Has the front & back cover plus Schomburg story used in Amazing Advs. #1 (Sent to subscribers of Z-D s/f magazines & ordered through mail for 10¢. Used to test market) 71 142 213 454 777 1100
1-Wood, Schomburg, Anderson, Whitney-a 89 178 267 565 975 1385
2-5: 2-Schomburg-a. 2,4,5-Anderson-a. 3,5-Starr-a 44 88 132 277 469 660
6-Krigstein-a 45 90 135 284 480 675

AMAZING ADVENTURES (Becomes Amazing Adult Fantasy #7 on) (See Amazing Fantasy for Omnibus HC reprint of #1-15)
Atlas Comics (AMI)/Marvel Comics No. 3 on: June, 1961 - No. 6, Nov, 1961

1-Origin Dr. Droom (1st Marvel-Age Superhero) by Kirby; Kirby/Ditko-a (5 pgs.) Ditko & Kirby-a in all; Kirby monster c-1-6 114 228 342 912 2056 3200
2 46 92 138 359 805 1250
3-6: 6-Last Dr. Droom 42 84 126 311 706 1100

AMAZING ADVENTURES
Marvel Comics Group: Aug, 1970 - No. 39, Nov, 1976

1-Inhumans by Kirby(p) & Black Widow (1st app. in Tales of Suspense #52) double feature begins 6 12 18 40 73 105
2-4: 2-F.F. brief app. 4-Last Inhumans by Kirby 3 6 9 21 33 45
5-8: Adams-a(p); 8-Last Black Widow; last 15¢-c 5 10 15 30 50 70
9,10: Magneto app. 10-Last Inhumans (origin-r by Kirby) 4 8 12 23 37 50
11-New Beast begins(1st app. in mutated form; origin in flashback); X-Men cameo in flashback (#11-17 are X-Men tie-ins) 17 34 51 117 259 400
12-17: 12-Beast battles Iron Man. 13-Brotherhood of Evil Mutants x-over from X-Men. 15-X-Men app. 16-Rutland Vermont - Bald Mountain Halloween x-over; Juggernaut app. 17-Last Beast (origin); X-Men app. 7 14 21 48 89 130
18-War of the Worlds begins (5/73); 1st app. Killraven; Neal Adams-a(p) 3 6 9 21 33 45
19-35,38,39: 19-Chaykin-a. 25-Buckler-a. 35-Giffen's first published story (art), along with Deadly Hands of Kung-Fu #22 (3/76) 1 3 4 6 8 10
36,37-(Regular 25¢ edition)(7-8/76) 1 3 4 6 8 10
36,37-(30¢-c variants, limited distribution) 4 8 12 23 37 50
NOTE: ***N. Adams** c-6-8. **Buscema** a-1p, 2p. **Colan** a-3-5p, 26p. **Ditko** a-24r. **Everett** a(i)3-5, 7-9. **Giffen** a-35i, 38p. **G. Kane** c-11, 25p, 29p. **Ploog** a-12i. **Russell** a-27-32, 34-37, 39; c-28, 30-32, 33i, 34, 35, 37, 39i. **Starlin** a-17. **Starlin** c-15p, 16, 17, 27. **Sutton** a-11-15p.*

AMAZING ADVENTURES
Marvel Comics Group: Dec, 1979 - No. 14, Jan, 1981

V2#1-Reprints story/X-Men #1 & 38 (origins) 2 4 6 11 13 20
2-14: 2-6-Early X-Men-r. 7,8-Origin Iceman 1 3 4 6 8 10
NOTE: ***Byrne** c-6p, 9p. **Kirby** a-1-14r; c-7, 9. **Steranko** a-12r. **Tuska** a-7-9.*

AMAZING ADVENTURES
Marvel Comics: July, 1988 ($4.95, squarebound, one-shot, 80 pgs.)

1-Anthology; Austin, Golden-a 5.00

AMAZING ADVENTURES OF CAPTAIN CARVEL AND HIS CARVEL CRUSADERS, THE
(See Carvel Comics in the Promotional Comics section)

AMAZING CHAN & THE CHAN CLAN, THE (TV)
Gold Key: May, 1973 - No. 4, Feb, 1974 (Hanna-Barbera)

1-Warren Tufts-a in all 3 6 9 21 33 45
2-4 3 6 9 16 23 30

AMAZING COMICS (Complete Comics No. 2)
Timely Comics (EPC): Fall, 1944

1-The Destroyer, The Whizzer, The Young Allies (by Sekowsky), Sergeant Dix; Schomburg-c 277 554 831 1759 3030 4300

AMAZING DETECTIVE CASES (Formerly Suspense No. 2?)
Marvel/Atlas Comics (CCC): No. 3, Nov, 1950 - No. 14, Sept, 1952

3 31 62 93 182 296 410
4-6: 6-Jerry Robinson-a 18 36 54 105 165 225
7-10 16 32 48 94 147 200
11,12: 11-(3/52)-Horror format begins. 12-Krigstein-a 42 84 126 265 445 625
13-(Scarce)-Everett-a; electrocution-c/story 45 90 135 284 480 675
14 39 78 117 240 395 550
NOTE: ***Colan** a-9. **Maneely** c-13. **Sekowsky** a-12. **Sinnott** a-13. **Tuska** a-10.*

AMAZING FANTASY (Formerly Amazing Adult Fantasy #7-14)
Atlas Magazines/Marvel: #15, Aug, 1962 (Sept, 1962 shown in indicia); #16, Dec, 1995 - #18, Feb, 1996

15-Origin/1st app. of Spider-Man by Steve Ditko (11 pgs.); 1st app. Aunt May & Uncle Ben; Kirby/Ditko-c 4000 8000 17,000 58,000 129,000 200,000
16-18 ('95-'96, $3.95): Kurt Busiek scripts; painted-c/a by Paul Lee 4.00
Amazing Fantasy #15: Spider-Man! (8/12, $3.99) recolored rep. of #15 and ASM #1 4.00
Amazing Fantasy Omnibus HC ("Amazing Adult Fantasy" on-c) (2007, $75.00, dustjacket) r/Amazing Adventures #1-6, Amazing Adult Fantasy #7-14 and Amazing Fantasy #15 with letter pages; foreword by Bissette; cover gallery from '70s reprint titles 75.00

AMAZING FANTASY (Continues from #6 in Araña: The Heart of the Spider)
Marvel Comics: Aug, 2004 - No. 20, June, 2006 ($2.99)

1-Intro. Anya Corazon; Fiona Avery-s/Mark Brooks-c/a 4.00
2-14,16-20: 3,4-Roger Cruz-a. 7-Intro. new Scorpion; Kirk-a. 10-Intro. Vampire By Night 13,14-Back-up Captain Universe stories. 16-20-Death's Head 3.00
15-($3.99) Spider-Man app.; intro 6 new characters incl. Mastermind Excello seen in World War Hulk series; s/a by various 4.00
Death's Head 3.0: Unnatural Selection TPB (2006, $13.99) r/#16-20 14.00
Scorpion: Poison Tomorrow (2005, $7.99, digest) r/#7-13 8.00

AMAZING GHOST STORIES (Formerly Nightmare)
St. John Publishing Co.: No. 14, Oct, 1954 - No. 16, Feb, 1955

14-Pit & the Pendulum story by Kinstler; Baker-c 38 76 114 228 369 510
15-r/Weird Thrillers #5; Baker-c, Powell-a 29 58 87 170 278 385
16-Kubert reprints of Weird Thrillers #4; Baker-c; Roussos, Tuska-a; Kinstler-a (1 pg.) 29 58 87 172 281 390

AMAZING HIGH ADVENTURE
Marvel Comics: 8/84; No. 2, 10/85; No. 3, 10/86 - No. 5, 1986 ($2.00)

1-5: Painted-c on all. 3,4-Baxter paper. 4-Bolton-c/a. 5-Bolton-a 4.00
NOTE: ***Bissette** a-4. **Severin** a-1, 3. **Sienkiewicz** a-1,2. **Paul Smith** a-2. **Williamson** a-2i.*

AMAZING JOY BUZZARDS
Image Comics: 2005 - No. 4, 2005 ($2.95, B&W with pink spot color in #1)

1-4-Mark Andrew Smith-s/Dan Hipp-a. 1-Mahfood back-c. 2-Morse back-c 3.00
Vol. 1 TPB (2005, $11.95) r/#1-4; bonus art and character design sketches 12.00
TPB (2008, $19.99) r/#1-4 and Vol. 2 #1-5 20.00

AMAZING JOY BUZZARDS (Volume 2)
Image Comics: Oct, 2005 - No. 5, Aug, 2006 ($2.99, B&W)

1-5: 1-Mark Andrew Smith-s/Dan Hipp-a. 4-Mahfood-a; Crosland-a. 5-Holgate-a 3.00
Vol. 2 TPB (2006, $12.99) r/#1-4; bonus art, pin-ups and character sketches 13.00

AMAZING-MAN COMICS (Formerly Motion Picture Funnies Weekly?)
(Also see Stars And Stripes Comics)
Centaur Publications: No. 5, Sept, 1939 - No. 26, Jan, 1942

5(#1)(Rare)-Origin/1st app. A-Man the Amazing Man by Bill Everett; The Cat-Man by Tarpe Mills (also #8), Mighty Man by Filchock, Minimidget & sidekick Ritty, & The Iron Skull by Burgos begins 1700 3400 5100 12,600 23,300 34,000
6-Origin The Amazing Man retold; The Shark begins; Ivy Menace by Tarpe Mills app. 371 742 1113 2600 4550 6500
7-Magician From Mars begins; ends #11 277 554 831 1759 3909 4300
8-Cat-Man dresses as woman 213 426 639 1363 2332 3300
9-Magician From Mars battles the 'Elemental Monster,' swiped into The Spectre in More Fun #54 & 55. Ties w/Marvel Mystery #4 for 1st Nazi War-c on a comic (2/40) 226 452 678 1446 2473 3500
10,11: 11-Zardi, the Eternal Man begins; ends #16; Amazing Man dons costume; last Everett issue 155 310 465 992 1696 2400
12,13 145 290 435 921 1586 2250
14-Reef Kinkaid, Rocke Wayburn (ends #20), & Dr. Hypno (ends #21) begin; no Zardi or Chuck Hardy 119 238 357 762 1306 1850
15,17-20: 15-Zardi returns; no Rocke Wayburn. 17-Dr. Hypno returns; no Zardi 107 214 321 680 1165 1650
16-Mighty Man's powers of super strength & ability to shrink & grow explained; Rocke Wayburn returns; no Dr. Hypno; Al Avison (a character) begins, ends #18 (a tribute to the famed artist) 113 226 339 718 1234 1750
21-Origin Dash Dartwell (drug-use story); origin & only app. T.N.T. 123 246 369 787 1344 1900
22-Dash Dartwell, the Human Meteor & The Voice app; last Iron Skull & The Shark; Silver Streak app. (classic-c) 300 600 900 2070 3635 5200
23-Two Amazing Man stories; intro/origin Tommy the Amazing Kid; The Marksman only app. 97 194 291 621 1061 1500
24-King of Darkness, Nightshade, & Blue Lady begin; end #26; 1st app. Super-Ann 97 194 291 621 1061 1500
25,26 (Scarce): Meteor Martin by Wolverton in both; 26-Electric Ray app. 300 600 900 1950 3375 4800
NOTE: ***Everett** a-5-11; c-5-11. **Gilman** a-14-20. **Giunta/Mirando** a-7-10. **Sam Glanzman** a-14-16, 18-21, 23. **Louis***

Amazing Mystery Funnies #19 © CEN

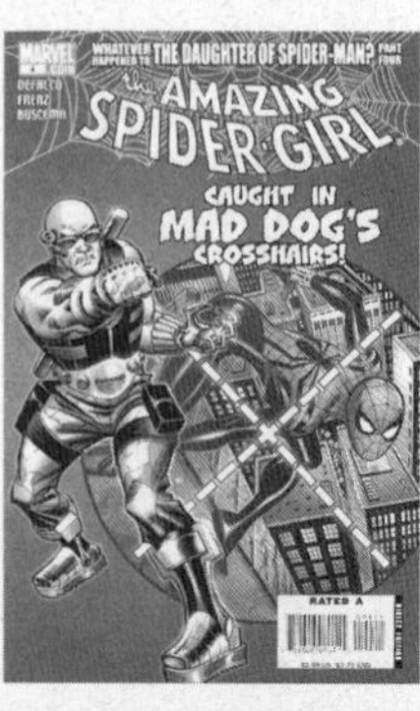

Amazing Spider-Girl #4 © MAR

Amazing Spider-Man #44 © MAR

GD VG FN VF VF/NM NM-
2.0 4.0 6.0 8.0 9.0 9.2

GD VG FN VF VF/NM NM-
2.0 4.0 6.0 8.0 9.0 9.2

*Glanzman a-6, 9-11, 14-21; c-13-19, 21. **Robert Golden** a-9. **Gustavson** a-6; c-22, 23. **Lubbers** a-14-21. **Simon** a-10. **Frank Thomas** a-6, 9-11, 14, 15, 17-21.*

AMAZING MYSTERIES (Formerly Sub-Mariner Comics No. 31)
Marvel Comics (CCC): No. 32, May, 1949 - No. 35, Jan, 1950 (1st Marvel Horror Comic)

32-The Witness app. 98 196 294 622 1074 1525
33-Horror format 45 90 135 284 480 675
34,35: Changes to Crime. 34,35-Photo-c 22 44 66 128 209 290

AMAZING MYSTERY FUNNIES
Centaur Publications: Aug, 1938 - No. 24, Sept, 1940 (All 52 pgs.)

V1#1-Everett-c(1st); Dick Kent Adv. story; Skyrocket Steele in the Year X on cover only
400 800 1200 2800 4900 7000
2-Everett 1st-a (Skyrocket Steele) 258 516 774 1651 2826 4000
3 142 284 426 909 1555 2200
3(#4, 12/38)-nn on cover, #3 on inside; bondage-c
148 296 444 947 1624 2300
V2#1-4,6: 2-Drug use story. 3-Air-Sub DX begins by Burgos. 4-Dan Hastings, Sand Hog begins (ends #5). 6-Last Skyrocket Steele 129 258 387 826 1413 2000
5-Classic Everett-c 290 580 870 1856 3178 4500
7 (Scarce)-Intro. The Fantom of the Fair & begins; Everett, Gustavson, Burgos-a
377 754 1131 2639 4620 6600
8-Origin & 1st app. Speed Centaur 165 330 495 1048 1799 2550
9-11: 11-Self portrait and biog. of Everett; Jon Linton begins; early Robot cover (11/39)
110 220 330 704 1202 1700
12 (Scarce)-1st Space Patrol; Wolverton-a (12/39); new costume Phantom of the Fair
216 432 648 1372 2361 3350
V3#1(#17, 1/40)-Intro. Bullet; Tippy Taylor serial begins, ends #24 (continued in The Arrow #2) 100 200 300 635 1868 1550
18,20: 18-Fantom of the Fair by Gustavson 97 194 291 621 1061 1500
19,21-24: Space Patrol by Wolverton in all 110 220 330 704 1202 1700

*NOTE: **Burgos** a-V2#3-9. **Eisner** a-V1#2, 3(2). **Everett** a-V1#2-4, V2#1, 3-6; c-V1#1-4, V2#3, 5, 18. **Filchock** a-V2#9. **Flessel** a-V2#6. **Guardineer** a-V1#4, V2#4-6; **Gustavson** a-V2#4, 5, 9-12, V3#1, 18, 19; c-V2#7, 9, 12, V3#1, 21, 22; **McWilliams** a-V2#9, 10. **TarpeMills** a-V2#2, 4-6, 9-12, V3#1. **Leo Morey**(Pulp artist) c-V2#10; text illo-V2#11. **FrankThomas** a-6-V2#11. **Webster** a-V2#4.*

AMAZING SAINTS
Logos International: 1974 (39¢)

nn-True story of Phil Saint 2 4 6 9 13 16

AMAZING SCARLET SPIDER
Marvel Comics: Nov, 1995 - No. 2, Dec, 1995 ($1.95, limited series)

1,2: Replaces "Amazing Spider-Man" for two issues. 1-Venom/Carnage cameos. 2-Green Goblin & Joystick-c/app. 3.00

AMAZING SCREW-ON HEAD, THE
Dark Horse Comics (Maverick): May, 2002 ($2.99, one-shot)

1-Mike Mignola-s/a/c 3.00

AMAZING SPIDER-GIRL (Also see Spider-Girl and What If...? (2nd series) #105)
Marvel Comics: No. 0, 2006; No. 1, Dec, 2006 - No. 30, May, 2009 ($2.99)

0-($1.99) Recap of the Spider-Girl series and character profiles; A.F. #15 cover swipe 3.00
1-14,16-24,26-($2.99) Frenz & Buscema-a. 9-Carnage returns. 19-Has #17 on cover 3.00
15,25,30-($3.99) 15-10th Anniversary issue. 25-Three covers 4.00
... Vol. 1: What Ever Happened to the Daughter of Spider-Man? TPB (2007, $14.99) r/#0-6 15.00
... Vol. 2: Comes the Carnage! TPB (2007, $13.99) r/#7-12 14.00
... Vol. 3: Mind Games TPB (2008, $13.99) r/#13-18 14.00

AMAZING SPIDER-MAN, THE (See All Detergent Comics, Amazing Fantasy, America's Best TV Comics, Aurora, Deadly Foes of..., Fireside Book Series, Friendly Neighborhood..., Giant-Size..., Giant Size Super-Heroes Featuring..., Marvel Age..., Marvel Collectors Item Classics, Marvel Fanfare, Marvel Graphic Novel, Marvel Knoghts..., Marvel Spec. Ed., Marvel Tales, Marvel Team-Up, Marvel Treasury Ed., New Avengers, Nothing Can Stop the Juggernaut, Official Marvel Index To..., Peter Parker..., Power Record Comics, Spectacular..., Spider-Man, Spider-Man Digest, Spider-Man Saga, Spider-Man 2099, Spider-Man Vs. Wolverine, Spidey Super Stories, Strange Tales Annual #2, Superior Spider-Man, Superman Vs. ..., Try-Out Winner Book, Ultimate Marvel Team-Up, Ultimate Spider-Man, Web of Spider- Man & Within Our Reach)

AMAZING SPIDER-MAN, THE
Marvel Comics Group: March, 1963 - No. 441, Nov, 1998

1-Retells origin by Steve Ditko; 1st Fantastic Four x-over (ties with F.F. #12 as first Marvel x-over); intro. John Jameson & The Chameleon; Spider-Man's 2nd app.; Kirby/Ditko-c; Ditko-c/a #1-38 1775 3550 5325 14,200 36,600 59,000
1-Reprint from the Golden Record Comic set 21 42 63 147 324 500
With record (1966) 30 60 90 216 483 750
2-1st app. the Vulture & the Terrible Tinkerer 400 800 1200 3600 7900 12,200
3-1st app. Doc Octopus; 1st full-length story; Human Torch cameo; Spider-Man pin-up by Ditko 331 662 993 2730 6165 9600
4-Origin & 1st app. The Sandman (see Strange Tales #115 for 2nd app.); 1st monthly issue; intro. Betty Brant & Liz Allen 269 538 807 2219 5010 7800
5-Dr. Doom app. 214 428 642 1766 3983 6200
6-1st app. Lizard 179 358 537 1477 3339 5200
7-Vs. The Vulture 118 236 354 944 2122 3300
8-Fantastic Four app. in back-up story by Kirby & Ditko
93 186 279 744 1672 2600
9-Origin & 1st app. Electro (2/64) 123 246 369 984 2217 3450
10-1st app. Big Man & The Enforcers 98 196 294 784 1767 2750
11-1st app. Bennett Brant 107 214 321 856 1928 3000
12-Doc Octopus unmasks Spider-Man-c/story 82 164 246 656 1478 2300
13-1st app. Mysterio 121 242 363 968 2184 3400
14-(7/64)-1st app. The Green Goblin (c/story)(Norman Osborn); Hulk x-over
176 352 528 1452 3276 5100
15-1st app. Kraven the Hunter; 1st mention of Mary Jane Watson (not shown)
86 172 258 688 1544 2400
16-Spider-Man battles Daredevil (1st x-over 9/64); still in old yellow costume
71 142 213 568 1284 2000
17-2nd app. Green Goblin (c/story); Human Torch x-over (also in #18 & #21)
77 154 231 616 1383 2150
18-1st app. Ned Leeds who later becomes Hobgoblin; Fantastic Four cameo; 3rd app. Sandman 46 92 138 368 834 1300
19-Sandman app. 36 72 108 266 596 925
20-Origin & 1st app. The Scorpion 63 126 189 504 1140 1775
21-2nd app. The Beetle (see Strange Tales #123) 38 76 114 285 641 1000
22-1st app. Princess Python 38 76 114 281 628 975
23-3rd app. The Green Goblin-c/story; Norman Osborn app.; Marvel Masterwork pin-up by Ditko; fan letter by Jim Shooter 46 92 138 350 788 1225
24 34 68 102 245 548 850
25-(6/65)-1st brief app. Mary Jane Watson (face not shown); 1st app. Spencer Smythe; Norman Osborn app. 38 76 114 285 641 1000
26-4th app. The Green Goblin-c/story; 1st app. Crime Master; dies in #27
39 78 117 289 657 1025
27-5th app. The Green Goblin-c/story; Norman Osborn app.
38 76 114 285 641 1000
28-Origin & 1st app. Molten Man (9/65, scarcer in high grade)
85 170 255 680 1525 2375
29,30 27 54 81 194 435 675
31-1st app. Harry Osborn who later becomes 2nd Green Goblin, Gwen Stacy & Prof. Warren. 34 68 102 245 548 850
32-38: 34-4th app. Kraven the Hunter. 36-1st app. Looter. 37-Intro. Norman Osborn. 38-(7/66)-2nd brief app. Mary Jane Watson (face not shown); last Ditko issue
21 42 63 147 324 500
39-The Green Goblin-c/story; Green Goblin's i.d. revealed as Norman Osborn; Romita-a begins (8/66; see Daredevil #16 for 1st Romita-a on Spider-Man)
36 72 108 259 580 900
40-1st told origin The Green Goblin-c/story 36 72 108 266 596 925
41-1st app. Rhino 36 72 108 259 580 900
42-(11/66)-3rd app. Mary Jane Watson (cameo in last 2 panels); 1st time face is shown 20 40 60 138 307 475
43-45,47-49: 44,45-2nd & 3rd app. The Lizard. 47-M.J. Watson & Peter Parker 1st date. 47-Green Goblin cameo; Harry & Norman Osborn app. 47,49-5th & 6th app. Kraven the Hunter 16 32 48 110 243 375
46-Intro. Shocker 17 34 51 117 259 400
50-1st app. Kingpin (7/67) 66 132 198 528 1189 1850
51-2nd app. Kingpin; Joe Robertson 1-panel cameo 20 40 60 140 310 485
52-58,60: 52-1st app. Joe Robertson & 3rd app. Kingpin. 56-1st app. Capt. George Stacy. 57,58-Ka-Zar app. 12 24 36 82 179 275
59-1st app. Brainwasher (alias Kingpin); 1st-c app. M. J. Watson
13 26 39 86 188 290
61-74: 61-1st Gwen Stacy cover app. 67-1st app. Randy Robertson. 69-Kingpin-c. 69,70-Kingpin app. 73-1st app. Silvermane. 74-Last 12¢ issue
10 20 30 64 132 200
75-83,87-89,91,92,95,99: 78,79-1st app. The Prowler. 83-1st app. Schemer & Vanessa (Kingpin's wife) 9 18 27 57 111 165
84-86,93: 84,85-Kingpin-c/story. 86-Re-intro & origin Black Widow in new costume. 93-1st app. Arthur Stacy 9 18 27 58 114 170
90-Death of Capt. Stacy 10 20 30 68 144 220
94-Origin retold 10 20 30 64 132 200
96-98-Green Goblin app. (97,98-Green Goblin-c); drug books not approved by CCA
10 20 30 66 138 210
100-Anniversary issue (9/71); Green Goblin cameo (2 pgs.)
13 26 39 91 201 310
101-1st app. Morbius the Living Vampire; Wizard cameo; Stan Lee co-plots with Roy Thomas; last 15¢ issue (10/71) 18 36 54 124 275 425
101-Silver ink 2nd printing (9/92, $1.75) 5.00
102-Origin & 2nd app. Morbius (25¢, 52 pgs.) 11 22 33 76 163 250

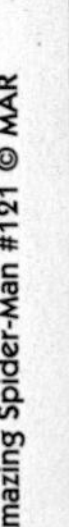

Amazing Spider-Man #246 © MAR

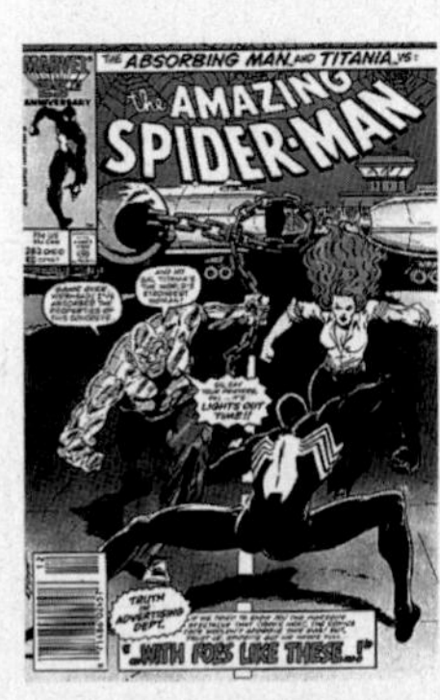

	GD 2.0	VG 4.0	FN 6.0	VF 8.0	VF/NM 9.0	NM- 9.2
103-118: 103,104-Roy Thomas-s. 104,111-Kraven the Hunter-c/stories. 105-109-Stan Lee-s. 108-1st app. Sha-Shan. 109-Dr. Strange-c/story. 110-1st app. Gibbon; Conway-s begin. 113-1st app. Hammerhead. 116-118-Reprints story from Spectacular Spider-Man Mag. in color with some changes	6	12	18	41	76	110
119,120-Spider-Man vs. Hulk (4 & 5/73)	9	18	27	57	111	165
121-Death of Gwen Stacy (6/73) (killed by Green Goblin) (reprinted in Marvel Tales #98 & 192)	23	46	69	161	356	550
122-Death of The Green Goblin-c/story (7/73) (reprinted in Marvel Tales #99 & 192)	21	42	63	147	324	500
123,126-128: 123-Cage app. 126-1st mention of Harry Osborn becoming Green Goblin	6	12	18	38	69	100
124-1st app. Man-Wolf (9/73)	7	14	21	46	86	125
125-Man-Wolf origin	6	12	18	40	73	105
129-1st app. The Punisher (2/74); 1st app. Jackal	80	160	240	480	740	1000
130-133: 131-Last 20¢ issue	5	10	15	34	60	85
134-(7/74); 1st app. Tarantula; Harry Osborn discovers Spider-Man's ID; Punisher cameo	6	12	18	38	69	100
135-2nd full Punisher app. (8/74)	9	18	27	58	114	170
136-1st app. Harry Osborn Green Goblin in costume	8	16	24	51	96	140
137-Green Goblin-c/story (2nd Harry Osborn Goblin)	6	12	18	37	66	95
138-141: 139-1st Grizzly. 140-1st app. Glory Grant	4	8	12	23	37	50
142,143-Gwen Stacy clone cameos: 143-1st app. Cyclone	4	8	12	23	37	50
144-147: 144-Full app. of Gwen Stacy clone. 145,146-Gwen Stacy clone storyline continues. 147-Spider-Man learns Gwen Stacy is clone	4	8	12	23	37	50
148-Jackal revealed	4	8	12	27	44	60
149-Spider-Man clone story begins, clone dies (?); origin of Jackal	7	14	21	46	86	125
150-Spider-Man decides he is not the clone	4	8	12	25	40	55
151-Spider-Man disposes of clone body; Len Wein-s begins; thru #180	4	8	12	25	40	55
152-160-(Regular 25¢ editions). 152-vs. the Shocker. 154-vs. Sandman. 156-1st Mirage. 157-159-Doc Octopus & Hammerhead app. 159-Last 25¢ issue(8/76). 160-Spider-Mobile destroyed	3	6	9	19	30	40
155-159-(30¢-c variants, limited distribution)	6	12	18	41	76	110
161-Nightcrawler app. from X-Men; Punisher cameo; Wolverine & Colossus app.	4	8	12	23	37	50
162-Punisher, Nightcrawler app.; 1st Jigsaw	4	8	12	23	37	50
163-168: 163-164-vs. the Kingpin. 165-vs. Stegron. 166-Stegron & the Lizard app. 167-1st app. Will O' The Wisp. 168-Will O' The Wisp app.	3	6	9	16	23	30
169-170,172-173: 169-Clone story recapped; Stan Lee Cameo. 170-Dr. Faustus app. 172-1st Rocket Racer. 173-vs Molten Man	3	6	9	16	23	30
171-Nova app. x-over w/Nova #12	3	6	9	17	26	35
169-173-(35¢-c variants, limited dist.)(6-10/77)	12	24	36	83	182	280
174,175-Punisher app.	3	6	9	19	30	40
176-180-Green Goblin app.	3	6	9	18	28	38
181-186: 181-Origin retold; gives life history of Spidey; Punisher cameo in flashback (1 panel). 182-(7/78)-Peter's first proposal to Mary Jane, but she declines (in #183). 183-Rocket Racer & the Big Wheel app. 184-vs. the second White Dragon. 185-Peter graduates college	3	6	9	14	20	25
187,188: 187-Captain America app. 188-vs. Jigsaw	3	6	9	16	23	30
189,190-Byrne-a; Man-Wolf app.	3	6	9	16	23	30
191-193,196-199: 191-vs. the Spider-Slayer. 192-Death of Spencer Smythe. 193-Peter & Mary Jane break up; the Fly app. 196-Faked death of Aunt May. 197-vs. the Kingpin. 198,199-Mysterio app.	2	4	6	11	16	20
NOTE: *Whitman 3-packs containing #192-194,196 exist.*						
194-1st app. Black Cat	7	14	21	46	86	125
195-2nd app. Black Cat & origin Black Cat	3	6	9	16	24	32
200-Giant origin issue (1/80); death of the burglar (from Amazing Fantasy #15)	3	6	9	21	33	45
201,202-Punisher app.	3	6	9	14	19	24
203-208,210-219: 203-3rd Dazzler (4/80). 204,205-Black Cat app. 204-last Wolfman-s. 206-Byrne-a. 207-vs Mesmero. 210-1st app. Madame Web. 211-Sub-Mariner app. 212-1st app. & origin Hydro-Man. 214,215-New Frightful Four app: Wizard, Trapster, Sandman & Llyra (Namor foe). 216-Madame Web app. 217-Sandman vs Hydro-Man. 219-Grey Gargoyle app. Frank Miller-c	2	4	6	9	12	15
209-Kraven the Hunter app; 1st app. origin Calypso	2	4	6	11	16	20
220-225,228: 220-Moon Knight app. 222-1st app. of the Whizzer as Speed Demon. 223-vs. The Red Ghost & the Super-Apes; Roger Stern-s begins. 224-Vulture app. 225-Foolkiller II-c/story.	1	3	4	6	8	10
226,227-Black Cat returns	2	4	6	9	12	15
229,230: Classic 'Nothing can stop the Juggernaut' story	2	4	6	11	16	20
231-237: 231,232-Cobra & Mr Hyde app. 233-Tarantula app. 234-Free 16 pg. insert "Marvel Guide to Collecting Comics", Tarantula & Will O' The Wisp app. 235-Origin Will 'O The Wisp. 236-Tarantula dies. 237-Stilt-Man app.	1	3	4	6	8	10
238-(3/83)-1st app. Hobgoblin (Ned Leeds); came with skin "Tattooz" decal. **NOTE:** The same decal appears in the more common Fantastic Four #252 which is being removed & placed in this issue as incentive to increase value. (No "Tattooz" were included in the Canadian edition) (Value listed is with or without tattooz)	7	14	21	49	92	135
239-2nd app. Hobgoblin & 1st battle w/Spidey	4	8	12	27	44	60
240-243,246-248: 240,241-Vulture app. (origin in #241). 242-Mary Jane Watson cameo (last panel). 243-Reintro Mary Jane after 4 year absence. 248-'The Kid Who Collects Spider-Man' story	1	3	4	6	8	10
244-3rd app. Hobgoblin (cameo)	2	4	6	9	12	15
245-(10/83)-4th app. Hobgoblin (cameo); Lefty Donovan gains powers of Hobgoblin & battles Spider-Man	2	4	6	9	12	15
249-251: 3 part Hobgoblin/Spider-Man battle. 249-Retells origin & death of 1st Green Goblin. 251-Last old costume	2	4	6	9	13	16
252-Spider-Man dons new black costume (5/84); ties with Marvel Team-Up #141 & Spectacular Spider-Man #90 for 1st new costume in regular title (See Marvel Super-Heroes Secret Wars #8 (12/84) for acquisition of costume); last Roger Stern-s	5	10	15	33	57	80
253-1st app. The Rose; Tom DeFalco-s begin	2	4	6	9	12	15
254,255,257,258: 254-Jack O' Lantern app. 255-1st app Black Fox. 257-Hobgoblin cameo; 2nd app. Puma; M.J. Watson reveals she knows Spidey's i.d. 258-Hobgoblin app.	1	3	4	6	8	10
256-1st app. Puma	2	4	6	9	12	15
259-Full Hobgoblin app.; Spidey back to old costume; origin Mary Jane Watson	2	4	6	9	12	15
260-Hobgoblin app.	2	4	6	8	10	12
261-Hobgoblin-c/story; painted-c by Vess	2	4	6	9	11	14
262-Spider-Man unmasked; photo-c	1	3	4	6	8	10
263,264,266-268: 266-Toad & Frogman app.; Peter David-s. 268-Secret Wars II x-over	1	2	3	5	6	8
265-1st app. Silver Sable (6/85)	2	4	6	9	13	16
265-Silver ink 2nd printing ($1.25)						4.00
269-270: 269-Spider-Man vs Firelord. 270 Avengers app.	1	3	4	6	8	10
271-274,277-280,282-283: 272-1st app. Slyde. 273-Secret Wars II x-over; Beyonder app. 274-Secret Wars II x-over; Zarathos app. (The Spirit of Vengeance). 277-Vess back-up art. 278-Scourge app; death of the Wraith. 279-Jack O' Lantern-c/s. 280-1st Sinister Syndicate: Beetle, Boomerang, Hydro-Man, Rhino, Speed Demon. 282-X-Factor app.	1	2	3	5	6	8
275-($1.25, 52 pgs.)-Hobgoblin-c/story; origin-r by Ditko	3	6	9	14	20	25
276-Hobgoblin app.	1	3	4	6	8	10
281-Hobgoblin battles Jack O'Lantern	1	3	4	6	8	10
284,285: 284-Punisher cameo; Gang War Pt. 1; Hobgoblin-c/story. 285-Punisher app.; minor Hobgoblin app.; last Tom DeFalco-s; Gang War Pt. 2	1	3	4	6	8	10
286-288: Gang War Parts 3-5. 286-Hobgoblin-c & app. (minor). 287-Hobgoblin app. (minor). 288-Full Hobgoblin app.; Gang War ends	1	3	4	6	8	10
289-(6/87, $1.25, 52 pgs.)-Hobgoblin's i.d. revealed as Ned Leeds; death of Ned Leeds; Macendale (Jack O'Lantern) becomes new Hobgoblin (1st app.)	3	6	9	14	20	25
290-292,295-297: 290-Peter proposes to Mary Jane; 1st David Michelinie-s. 291,292-Spider-Slayer app. 292-She accepts; leads into wedding in Amazing Spider-Man Annual #21. 295-'Mad Dog Ward' Pt.2; x-over w/Web of Spider-Man #33 & Spectacular Spider-Man #133. 296-297-Doc Octopus app.	1	2	3	5	6	8
293,294-Part 2 & 5 of Kraven story from Web of Spider-Man. 293-Continued from Web of Spider-Man #31; continues into Spectacular Spider-Man #131. 294-Death of Kraven; continued from Web of Spider-Man #32; continues in Spectacular Spider-Man #132	2	4	6	9	12	15
298-Todd McFarlane-c/a begins (3/88); 1st brief app. Eddie Brock who becomes Venom; (last pg.)	5	10	15	33	57	80
299-1st brief app. Venom with costume	4	8	12	25	40	55
300 ($1.50, 52 pgs.; 25th Anniversary)-1st full Venom app.; last black costume (5/88)	20	40	60	100	150	200
301-$1.00 issues begin. Classic McFarlane-c	3	6	9	14	20	25
302-305: 302-303-Silver Sable app. 304,305-Black Fox app. 304-1st bi-weekly issue	2	4	6	10	14	18
306-311,313,314: 306-Swipes-c from Action #1. 307-Chameleon app. 308-Taskmaster app. 309-1st app. Styx & Stone. 310-Killer Shrike app. 311-Inferno x-over; Mysterio app.	2	4	6	9	13	16
312-Hobgoblin battles Green Goblin; Inferno x-over	2	4	6	13	18	22
315,317-Venom app.	3	6	9	15	22	28
316-Classic Venom-c	3	6	9	16	23	30
318-323,325: 318-Scorpion app. 319-Bi-weekly begins again; Scorpion, Rhino, Backlash app.						

Amazing Spider-Man #355 © MAR

Amazing Spider-Man #375 © MAR

Amazing Spider-Man #411 © MAR

GD 2.0 | VG 4.0 | FN 6.0 | VF 8.0 | VF/NM 9.0 | NM- 9.2

320-'Assassination Nation Plot' Pt.1 (ends in issue #325); Paladin & Silver Sable app. 321-Paladin & Silver Sable app. 322-Silver Sable app. 323-Captain America app.
325-Captain America & Red Skull app. 1 3 4 6 8 10
324-Sabretooth app.; McFarlane cover only 2 4 6 8 10 12
326,327,329: 326-Acts of Vengeance x-over; vs Graviton. 327-Acts of Vengeance x-over; vs. Magneto; Cosmic storyline continues from Spectacular Spider-Man; Erik Larsen-a. 329-Acts of Vengeance x-over; vs. the Tri-Sentinel; Sebastian Shaw app.; Erik Larsen-a (continuous through issue #344) 6.00
328-Acts of Vengeance x-over; vs. the Hulk; last McFarlane issue
2 4 6 9 12 15
330,331-Punisher app. 331-Minor Venom app. 6.00
332,333-Venom-c/story 2 4 6 8 10 12
334-336,338-343: 334-339-Return of the Sinister Six. 341-Tarantula app; Spider-Man loses his cosmic powers. 342,343-Black Cat app. 4.00
337-Hobgoblin app. 5.00
344-(2/91) 1st app. Cletus Kasady (Carnage) 2 4 6 9 12 15
345-1st full app. Cletus Kasady; Venom cameo on last pg.; 1st Mark Bagley-a on Spider-Man
2 4 6 9 12 15
346,347-Venom app. 2 4 6 8 10 12
348,349,351-359: 348-Avengers x-over. 351-Bagley-a begins. 351,352-Nova of New Warriors app. 353-Darkhawk app.; brief Punisher app. 354-Punisher cameo & Nova, Night Thrasher (New Warriors), Darkhawk & Moon Knight app. 357,358-Punisher, Darkhawk, Moon Knight, Night Thrasher, Nova x-over. 358-3 part gatefold-c; last $1.00-c 3.00
350-($1.50, 52pgs.)-Origin retold; Spidey vs. Dr. Doom; last Erik Larsen-a pin-ups; Uncle Ben app. 4.00
360-Carnage cameo 4.00
361-(4/92) Intro. Carnage (the Spawn of Venom); begin 3 part story; recap of how Spidey's alien costume became Venom 3 6 9 16 23 30
361-($1.25)-2nd printing; silver-c 2 4 6 11 16 20
362,363-Carnage & Venom-c/story 2 4 6 8 10 12
362-2nd printing 1 3 4 6 8 10
364,366-373,376,377,381-387: 364-The Shocker app. (old villain). 366-Peter's parents-c/story; Red Skull, Viper & Taskmaster app. 367-Red Skull, Viper & Taskmaster app. 368-Invasion of the Spider-Slayers Pt.1 (through Pt.6 in #373). 369-Harry Osborn back-up (Gr. Goblin II). Electro app. 370-Black Cat & Scorpion app. 373-Venom back-up. 376,377-Cardiac app. 381,382-Hulk app. 383-The Jury app. 383-385-vs The Jury. 384-Venom/Carnage app. 386-Vulture app. 387-Vulture is de-aged & gets new costume 3.00
365-($3.95, 84 pgs.)-30th anniversary issue w/silver hologram on-c; Spidey/Venom/Carnage pull-out poster; contains 5 pg. preview of Spider-Man 2099 (1st app.); Spidey's origin retold; Lizard app.; reintro Peter's parents in Stan Lee 3 pg. text w/illo (story continues thru #370)
2 4 6 9 12 15
374-Venom-c/story 6.00
375-($3.95, 68 pgs.)-Holo-grafx foil-c; vs. Venom story; ties into Venom: Lethal Protector #1; Pat Olliffe-a. 1 2 3 5 6 8
378-380: Parts 3,7 and 11 of Maximum Carnage. 378-Continued from Web of Spider-Man #101; Venom vs Carnage; continues in Spider-Man #35. 379-Continued from Web of Spider-Man #102; Deathlok, Firestar, Black Cat & Morbius app.; continued in Spider-Man #36. 380-Continued from Web of Spider-Man #103; Captain America & Cloak and Dagger app.; continued in Spider-Man #37 5.00
388-($2.25, 68 pgs.)-Newsstand edition; Venom back-up & Cardiac & chance back-up; last David Michelinie-s (6-year run) 4.00
388-($2.95, 68 pgs.)-Collector's edition w/foil-c 5.00
389-1st JM DeMatteis-s; Trading Card insert (3 cards) attacked to the staples; harder to find in true high grade due to indents caused by the cards; Green Goblin app. 4.00
390-393,395,396: 390-393-vs. Shriek. 395-Puma app. 396-Daredevil & the Owl app. 3.00
390-($2.95)-Collector's edition polybagged w/16 pg. insert of new animated Spidey TV show plus animation cel 5.00
394-($2.95, 48 pgs.)-Deluxe edition; flip book w/Birth of a Spider-Man Pt. 2; silver foil both-c; Power & Responsibility Pt. 2; Judas Traveller, the Jackal and the Gwen Stacy Clone app. 1st app. Scrier 5.00
394-Newstand edition ($1.50-c) 7.00
397-($2.25)-Flip book w/Ultimate Spider-Man 4.00
398,399: 398-Web of Death Pt.3; continued from Spectacular Spider-Man #220; Doc Octopus & Kaine app.; continued in Spectacular Spider-Man #221. 399-Smoke and Mirrors Pt.2; continued from Web of Spider-Man #122; Jackal, Scarlet Spider, Gwen Stacy Clone app; continued in Spider-Man #56 5.00
400-($2.95)-Death of Aunt May; newsstand edition 3 6 9 16 23 30
400-($3.95)-Death of Aunt May; embossed grey overlay cover
2 4 6 10 14 18
400-Collector's Edition; white embossed-c; (10,000 print run)
4 8 12 27 44 60
401,402,405,406-409: 401-The Mark of Kaine Pt.2; continued from Web of Spider-Man #124; Scarlet Spider app; continues in Spider-Man #58. 402-Judas Traveller & Scrier app. 405-Exiled Pt.2; continued from Web of Spider-Man #128; Scarlet Spider app.; continues in Spider-Man #62. 406-1st full app. of the female Doc Octopus (Carolyn Trainer); continues in Spider-Man #63; Marvel Overpower card insert; harder to find in higher grades due to card indenting; last JM DeMatteis-s. 407-Human Torch, Sandman & Silver Sable app. Tom DeFalco-s (returns to Spider-Man; last-s in 1987). 408-Regular ed; Media Blizzard pt.2; Mysterio app; continued from Sensational Spider-Man #1; continues in Spider-Man #65. 409-The Return of Kaine Pt.3; continued from Spectacular Spider-Man #231; Kaine & Rhino app.; continues in Spider-Man #66 4.00
403-The Trial of Peter Parker Pt. 2; continued from Web of Spider-Man #126; Carnage app; continues in Spider-Man #60. 1 2 3 5 6 8
404-Maximum Clonage Pt.3; continued from Web of Spider-Man #127; Scarlet Spider, Jackal, Scrier & Kaine app; continued in Spider-Man #61 5.00
408-($2.95)-Polybagged version with TV theme song cassette; scarce in high grade due to damage caused by the cassette indenting the actual comic
7 14 21 46 86 125
408-Direct edition (without cassette & out of polybag) 5 10 15 31 53 75
408-Newstand edition; variant cover 5 10 15 33 57 80
410-Web of Carnage Pt.2; continued from Sensational Spider-Man #3; Carnage app; continues in Spider-Man #67 3 6 9 14 20 25
411,412,414,417-419,421-424: 411-Blood Brothers Pt.2; continued from Sensational Spider-Man #4; Gaunt app; continued in Spider-Man #68. 412-Blood Brothers Pt.6; continued from Sensational Spider-Man #5; vs Gaunt. 414-The Rose app. 417-Death of Scrier. 418-Revelations Pt.3; continued from Spectacular Spider-Man #240; Norman Osborn returns; 'death' of Peter and Mary Jane's baby (May Parker); continued in Spider-Man #75. 419-1st minor app. of The Black Tarantula. 422,423-Electro app. 424-Elektra app. 4.00
413-Contains a free packet of Island Twists Kool-Aid and Spider-Man For Kids magazine subscriber card; harder to find in true high grade 6.00
415-Onslaught Impact 2; Green Goblin (Phil Urich) app. vs. Mark IV Sentinels; last Mark Bagley-a (5 year run) 6.00
416-Epilogue to Onslaught; harder to find in high grade due to Marvel Overpower card insert
1 3 4 6 8 10
420-X-Man app. 6.00
425-($2.99)-48 pgs., wraparound-c; X-Man app 6.00
426,428,429,432,435-437,440: 426-Female Dr. Octopus app. 428-Dr. Octopus app. 429-Absorbing Man app. 432-Spider-Hunt Pt.2; continued from Sensational Spider-Man #25; Black Tarantula & Norman Osborn app. 433-Mr. Hyde app. 435-Identity Crisis; Black Tarantula & Kaine app. 436-Black Tarantula app. 437-Plantman app. 440-Gathering of Five Pt.2; continued from Sensational Spider-Man #32; John Byrne-s; Molten Man & Norman Osborn app; continued in Spider-Man #96 6.00
427-Return of Dr. Octopus; double-gatefold-c. 6.00
430-Carnage & Silver Surfer app. 2 4 6 11 16 20
431-Cosmic-Carnage vs Silver Surfer; Galactus cameo
3 6 9 19 30 40
432-Variant yellow-c 'Wanted Dead or Alive' 1 3 4 6 8 10
434-Identity Crisis; Black Tarantula app. 1 3 4 6 8 10
434-Variant 'Amazing Ricochet #1'-c 2 4 6 8 10 12
438-Daredevil app. 7.00
439-Alternate future story; Avengers app; last Tom DeFalco-s
1 2 3 5 6 8
441-The Final Chapter Pt.1; John Byrne-s; Norman Osborn app; last issue (Dec. 1998); story continues in Spider-Man #97 1 2 3 5 6 8
#500-up (See Amazing Spider-Man Vol. 2; series resumed original numbering after Vol. 2 #58)
#(-1) Flashback issue (7/97, $1.95-c) 3.00
Annual 1 (1964, 72 pgs.) Origin Spider-Man; 1st app. Sinister Six (Dr. Octopus, Electro, Kraven the Hunter, Mysterio, Sandman, Vulture) (new 41 pg. story); plus gallery of Spidey foes; early X-Men app. 91 182 273 728 1639 2550
Annual 2 (1965, 25¢, 72 pgs.) Reprints from #1,2,5 plus new Doctor Strange story
34 68 102 242 541 840
Special 3 (11/66, 25¢, 72 pgs.) New Avengers story & Hulk x-over; Doctor Octopus-r from #11,12; Romita-a 16 32 48 112 249 385
Special 4 (11/67, 25¢, 68 pgs.) Spidey battles Human Torch (new 41 pg. story)
13 26 39 89 195 300
Special 5 (11/68, 25¢, 68 pgs.) New 40 pg. Red Skull story; 1st app. Peter Parker's parents; last annual with new-a 11 22 33 73 157 240
Special 5-2nd printing (1994) 2 4 6 8 10 12
Special 6 (11/69, 25¢, 68 pgs.) Reprints 41 pg. Sinister Six story from annual #1 plus 2 Kirby/Ditko stories (r) 6 12 18 37 66 95
Special 7 (12/70, 25¢, 68 pgs.) All-r(#1,2) new Vulture-c
5 10 15 34 60 85
Special 8 (12/71) All-r 5 10 15 34 60 85
King Size 9 ('73) Reprints Spectacular Spider-Man (mag.) #2; 40 pg. Green Goblin-c/story (re-edited from 58 pgs.) 5 10 15 34 60 85
Annual 10 (1976) Origin Human Fly (vs. Spidey); new-a begins
3 6 9 15 22 28

Amazing Spider-Man V2 #5 © MAR

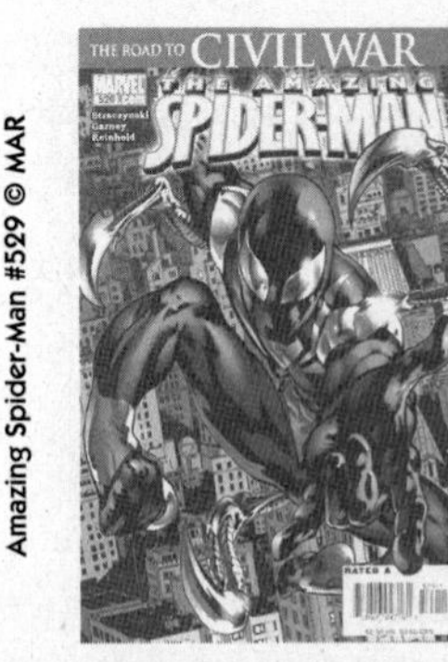

Amazing Spider-Man #529 © MAR

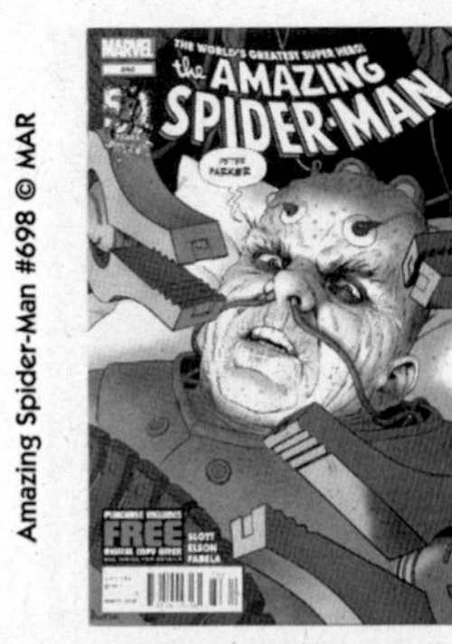

Amazing Spider-Man #698 © MAR

	GD	VG	FN	VF	VF/NM	NM-
	2.0	4.0	6.0	8.0	9.0	9.2

Annual 11-13 ('77-'79): 12-Spidey vs. Hulk-r/#119,120. 13-New Byrne/Austin-a; Dr. Octopus x-over w/Spectacular S-M Ann. #1 2 4 6 10 14 18
Annual 14 (1980) Miller-c/a(p); Dr. Strange app. 3 6 9 14 20 25
Annual 15 (1981) Miller-c/a(p); Punisher app. 3 6 9 17 26 35
Annual 16-20: 16 ('82)-Origin/1st app. new Capt. Marvel (female heroine). 17 ('83)-Kingpin app. 18 ('84)-Scorpion app.; JJJ weds. 19 ('85). 20 ('86)-Origin Iron Man of 2020 1 2 3 4 5 7
Annual 21 (1987) Special wedding issue; newsstand & direct sale versions exist & are worth same 2 4 6 9 12 15
Annual 22 (1988, $1.75, 68 pgs.) 1st app. Speedball; Evolutionary War x-over; Daredevil app. 6.00
Annual 23 (1989, $2.00, 68 pgs.) Atlantis Attacks; origin Spider-Man retold; She-Hulk app.; Byrne-c; Liefeld-a(p), 23 pgs. 5.00
Annual 24 (1990, $2.00, 68 pgs.) -Ant-Man app. 4.00
Annual 25 (1991, $2.00, 68 pgs.) 3 pg. origin recap; Iron Man app.; 1st Venom solo story; Ditko-a (6 pgs.) 5.00
Annual 26 (1992, $2.25, 68 pgs.) New Warriors-c/story; Venom solo story cont'd in Spectacular Spider-Man Annual #12 5.00
Annual 27 ('93, $2.95, 68 pgs.) Bagged w/card; 1st app. Annex 4.00
Annual 28 ('94, $2.95, 68 pgs.) Carnage-c/story 1 3 4 6 8 10
'96 Special-($2.95, 64 pgs.)-"Blast From The Past" 4.00
'97 Special-($2.99)-Wraparound-c,Sundown app. 4.00
Marvel Graphic Novel - Parallel Lives (3/89, $8.95) 2 4 6 8 10 12
...: Parallel Lives 1 (2012, $4.99) r/1989 GN 5.00
Marvel Graphic Novel - Spirits of the Earth (1990, $18.95, HC) 3 6 9 15 22 28
Super Special 1 (4/95, $3.95)-Flip Book 4.00
...: Skating on Thin Ice 1(1990, $1.25, Canadian)-McFarlane-c; anti-drug issue; Electro app. 1 2 3 5 7 9
...: Skating on Thin Ice 1 (2/93, $1.50, American) 4.00
...: Double Trouble 2 (1990, $1.25, Canadian) 6.00
...: Double Trouble 2 (2/93, $1.50, American) 3.00
...: Hit and Run 3 (1990, $1.25, Canadian)-Ghost Rider-c/story 1 2 3 5 7 9
...: Hit and Run 3 (2/93. $1.50, American) 3.00
... : Carnage (6/93, $6.95)-r/ASM #344,345,359-363 1 2 3 4 5 7
...: Chaos in Calgary 4 (Canadian; part of 5 part series)-Turbine,Night Rider, Frightful app. 2 4 6 8 11 14
...: Chaos in Calgary 4 (2/93, $1.50, American) 3.00
...: Deadball 5 (1993, $1.60, Canadian)-Green Goblin-c/story; features Montreal Expos 2 4 6 10 14 18

Note: Prices listed above are for English Canadian editions. French editions are worth double.

...: Soul of the Hunter nn (8/92, $5.95, 52 pgs.)-Zeck-c/a(p) 6.00
Wizard #1 Ace Edition ($13.99) r/#1 w/ new Ramos acetate-c 14.00
Wizard #129 Ace Edition ($13.99) r/#129 w/ new Ramos acetate-c 14.00

NOTE: ***Austin** a(i)-248, 335, 337, Annual 13; c(i)-188, 241, 242, 248, 331, 334, 343, Annual 25. **J. Buscema** a(p)-72, 73, 76-81, 84, 85. **Byrne** a-189p, 190p, 206p, Annual 3r, 6r, 7r, 13p; c-189p, 268, 296, Annual 12. **Ditko** a-1-38, Annual 1, Special 3(r), 2, 24(2); c-1i, 2-38. **Guice** c/a-Annual 18i. **Gil Kane** a(p)-89-105, 120-124, 150, Annual 10, 12i, 24p; c-90p, 96, 98, 99, 101-105p, 129p, 131p, 132p, 137-140p, 143p, 148p, 149p, 151p, 153p, 160p, 161p, Annual 10p, 24. **Kirby** a-8. **Erik Larsen** a-324, 327, 329-350; c-327, 329-350, 354i, Annual 25. **McFarlane** a-298p, 299p, 300-303, 304-323p, 325p, 328; c-298-325, 328. **Miller** c-218, 219. **Mooney** a-65i, 67-82i, 84-88i, 173i, 178i, 189i, 190i, 192i, 193i, 196-202i, 207i, 211-219i, 221i, 222i, 226i, 227i, 229-233i, Annual 11i, 17i. **Nasser** c-228p. **Nebres** a-Annual 24i. **Russell** c-357i. **Simonson** c-222, 337i. **Starlin** a-113i, 114i, 187p. **Williamson** a-365i.*

AMAZING SPIDER-MAN (Volume 2) (Some issues reprinted in "Spider-Man, Best Of" hardcovers)
Marvel Comics: Jan, 1999 - No. 700, Feb, 2013 ($2.99/$1.99/$2.25)

1-($2.99)-Byrne-a 6.00
1-Sunburst variant-c 1 2 3 5 6 8
1-($6.95) Dynamic Forces variant-c by the Romitas 1 3 4 6 8 10
1-Marvel Matrix sketch variant-c 1 3 4 6 8 10
2-($1.99) Two covers -by John Byrne and Andy Kubert 4.00
3-11: 4-Fantastic Four app. 5-Spider-Woman-c 3.00
12-($2.99) Sinister Six return (cont. in Peter Parker #12) 4.00
13-17: 13-Mary Jane's plane explodes 3.00
18,19,21-24,26-28: 18-Begin $2.25-c. 19-Venom-c. 24-Maximum Security 3.00
20-($2.99, 100 pgs.) Spider-Slayer issue; new story and reprints 4.00
25-($2.99) Regular cover; Peter Parker becomes the Green Goblin 4.00
25-($3.99) Holo-foil enhanced cover 5.00
29-Peter is reunited with Mary Jane 4.00
30-Straczynski-s/Campbell-c begin; intro. Ezekiel 6.00
31-35: Battles Morlun 4.00
36-Black cover; aftermath of the Sept. 11 tragedy in New York 3 6 9 16 23 30
37-49: 39-'Nuff Said issue 42-Dr. Strange app. 43-45-Doctor Octopus app. 46-48-Cho-c 3.00
50-Peter and MJ reunite; Captain America & Dr. Doom app.; Campbell-c 4.00
51-58: 51,52-Campbell-c. 55,56-Avery scripts. 57,58-Avengers, FF, Cyclops app. 3.00

	GD	VG	FN	VF	VF/NM	NM-
	2.0	4.0	6.0	8.0	9.0	9.2

(After #58 [Nov, 2003] numbering reverts back to original Vol. 1 with #500, Dec, 2003)

500-($3.50) J. Scott Campbell-c; Romita Jr. & Sr.-a; Uncle Ben app. 1 2 3 5 6 8
501-524: 501-Harris-c. 503-504-Loki app. 506-508-Ezekiel app. 509-514-Sins Past; intro. Gabriel and Sarah Osborn; Deodato-a. 519-Moves into Avengers HQ. 521-Begin $2.50-c 524-Harris-c 3.00
525,526-Evolve or Die x-over. 525-David-s. 526-Hudlin-s; Spider-Man loses eye 4.00
525-528-2nd printings with variant-c. 525-Ben Reilly costume. 526-Six-Armed Spidey. 527-Spider-Man 2099. 528-Spider-Ham 5.00
527,528: Evolve or Die pt.9, 12 3.00
529-Debut of red and gold costume; Garney-a 10.00
529-2nd printing 5.00
529-3rd printing with Wieringo-c 3.00
530,531-Titanium Man app.; Kirkham-a. 531-Begin $2.99-c 6.00
532-538-Civil War tie-in. 538-Aunt May shot 5.00
539-543-Back in Black. 539-Peter wears the black costume 3.00
544-($3.99) "One More Day" pt. 1; Quesada-a/Straczynski-s 4.00
545-(12/08, $3.99) "One More Day" pt. 4; Quesada-a/Straczynski-s, Peter & MJ's marriage un-done; r/wedding from ASM Annual #21; 2 covers by Quesada and Djurdjevic 4.00
546-($3.99) Brand New Day begins; McNiven-a; Deodato, Winslade, Land, Romita Jr.-a; 1st app. Mr. Negative 5.00
546-Variant-c by Bryan Hitch 8.00
546-Second printing with new McNiven-c of Peter Parker 4.00
546-MGC (7/10, $1.00) r/#546 with "Marvel's Greatest Comics" logo on cover 3.00
547-567: 547,548-McNiven-a. 549-551-Larroca-a. 550-Intro. Menace. 555-557-Bachalo-a. 559-Intro. Screwball. 560,561-MJ app. 565-New Kraven intro. 566,567-Spidey in Daredevil costume 3.00
568-($3.99) Romita Jr.-a begins; two covers by Romita Jr. and Alex Ross 6.00
568-Variant-c by John Romita Sr. 20.00
568-2nd printing with Romita Jr. Anti-Venom costume cover 4.00
569-Debut of Anti-Venom; Norman Osborn and Thunderbolts app.;Romita Jr.-c 4.00
569-Variant Venom-c by Granov 6.00
570-572-Two covers on each 3.00
573-($3.99) New Ways to Die conclusion; Spidey meets Stephen Colbert back-up; Ollife-a; two covers by Romita Jr. and Maguire 5.00
573-Variant cover with Stephen Colbert; cover swipe of AF #15 by Quesada 10.00
574-582: 577-Punisher app. 3.00
583-($3.99) Spidey meets Obama back-up story; regular Romita Sr. "Cougars" cover 10.00
583-($3.99) Obama variant-c with Spidey on left; Spidey meets Obama back-up story 30.00
583-($3.99) Second printing Obama variant-c with Spidey on right and yellow bkgrd 8.00
583-($3.99) 3rd-5th printings Obama variant-c: 3rd-Blue bkgrd w/flag. 4th-White bkgrd w/flag. 5th-Lincoln Memorial bkgrd 5.00
584-587, 589-599: 585-Menace ID revealed. 590,591-Fantastic Four app. 594-Aunt May engaged. 595-599-American Son; Osborn Avengers app. app. 3.00
588-($3.99) Conclusion to "Character Assassination"; Romita Jr.-a 4.00
600-(9/09, $4.99) Aunt May's wedding; Romita Jr.-a; Doc Octopus, FF app.; Mary Jane cameo; back-up story by Stan Lee; back-up with Doran-a; 2 covers by Romita Jr. & Ross 5.00
600-Variant covers by Romita Sr. and Quesada 10.00
601-604,606-611,613-616,618-621,623-627: 601-Back-up w/Quesada-a. 606,607-Black Cat app.; Campbell-c. 611-Deadpool-c/app. 612-The Gauntlet begins; Waid-s. 615,616-Sandman app. 621-Black Cat app. 624-Peter Parker fired. 626-Gaydos-a 3.00
605,612,617,622,628-($3.99): 605-Mayhew-c. 613-Rhino back-up story. 617-New Rhino. 622-Bianchi-c; Morbius app. 628-Captain Universe app. 4.00
629-633-($2.99)-Bachalo-a; Lizard app. 3.00
634-641-($3.99) 634-637-Grim Hunt; Kaine app. 635-Kraven returns. 638-641-"One Moment in Time" wedding flashback/ret-con; Quesada-s 4.00
638-641-Variant covers by Quesada 10.00
642-646-($2.99) Waid-s/Azaceta-a; interlocking covers by Djurdjevic 3.00
647-($4.99) Short stories by various; Djurdjevic-c; cover gallery of Brand New Day issues 5.00
648-691-($3.99) 648-Big Time begins; Ramos-a; Hobgoblin app. 654-Flash Thompson becomes Venom; Marla Jameson killed. 655-Martin-a. 657-660-Fantastic Four app. 666-673-Spider Island. 667-672-Ramos-a; Avengers app. 677-X-over w/Daredevil #8. 682-687-Avengers app. 4.00
654.1-(4/11, $2.99) Flash Thompson as Venom; Ramos-a 3.00
679.1-(4/12, $2.99) Morbius the Living Vampire app. 3.00
692-($5.99) Debut of Alpha; Ramos-a; back-up short stories 6.00
693-697: 694-Cover swipe of Superman vs. Spider-Man 4.00
698, 699, 699.1: 698-Doctor Octopus brain switch revealed. 699.1-Morbius origin 4.00
700-($7.99) Collage cover; Leads into Superior Spider-Man #1; back-up short stories 15.00
700-Variant skyline-c by Marcos 15.00
700-Second printing cover with Doctor Octopus on an ASM #300 swipe 8.00
700.1 - 700.5 (2/14, weekly limited series, $3.99) 700.1-Janson-a/Ferry-c 4.00
1999, 2000 Annual (6/99, '00, $3.50) 1999-Buscema-a 4.00
2001 Annual ($2.99) Follows Peter Parker: S-M #29; last Mackie-s 4.00

Amazing Spider-Man: The Movie #1 © MAR

Amazing World of DC Comics #9 © DC

Ame-Comi Girls #6 © DC

Annual 1 (2008, $3.99) McKone-a; secret of Jackpot revealed; death of Jackpot 4.00
Annual 36 (9/09, $3.99) Debut of Raptor; Olliffe-a 4.00
Annual 37 (7/10, $3.99) Untold 1st meeting with Captain America; back-up w/Olliffe-a 4.00
Annual 38 (6/11, $3.99) Deadpool & Hulk app.; Garbett-a/McNiven-c 4.00
Annual 39 (7/12, $3.99) Avengers app.; Garbett-a/c 4.00
...: Big Time 1 (8/11, $5.99) r/#648-650 6.00
Collected Edition #30-32 ($3.95) reprints #30-32 w/cover #30 4.00
... 500 Covers HC (2004, $49.99) reprints covers for #1-500 & Annuals; yearly re-caps 50.00
...: Ends of the Earth (7/12, $3.99) Silas-a/Fiumara-c; Big Hero Six app. 4.00
...: Family Business HC (2014, $24.99) Kingpin app.; Waid & Robinson-s/Dell'Otto-a 25.00
Free Comic Book Day 2011 (Spider-Man) 1-Ramos-c/a; Spider-Woman & Shang-Chi app. 3.00
.../Ghost Rider: Motorstorm 1 ('11, $2.99) r/#558-560 3.00
...: Hooky 1 (2012, $4.99) r/Marvel Graphic Novel #22 (1986) with Wrightson-a 5.00
...: Infested 1 (11/11, $3.99) Spider Island tie-in; short stories by various; Ramos-c 4.00
... Omnibus HC (2007, $99.99, dustjacket) r/Amazing Fantasy #15, Amazing Spider-Man #1-38, Annual #1,2, Strange Tales Annual #2 & Fantastic Four Annual #1; letter pages, bonus art, intro. by Stan Lee; bios, essays, Marvel Tales cover gallery 100.00
Spider-Man: Brand New Day - Extra!! #1 (9/08, $3.99) short stories; Bachalo,Olliffe-a 4.00
Spider-Man: Brand New Day Yearbook #1 (2008, $4.99) plot synopses; profile pages 5.00
... Spidey Sunday Spectacuar (7/11, $3.99) collects back-ups from ASM #634-645 4.00
...: Swing Shift (2007 FCBD Edition) Jimenez-c/a; Slott-s 4.00
...: Swing Shift Director's Cut (2008, $3.99) story from 2007 FCBD; Brand New Day info 4.00
The Many Loves of the Amazing Spider-Man (7/10, $3.99) short stories of Black Cat, Gwen & Carlie, and Mary Jane; s/a by various 4.00
...: The Short Halloween (7/09, $3.99) Bill Hader & Seth Meyers-s/Maguire-a 4.00
...: You're Hired 1 (5/11, $3.99) r/story from New York Daily News insert 4.00
...Vol. 1: Coming Home (2001, $15.95) r/#30-35; J. Scott Campbell-c 16.00
...Vol. 2: Revelations (2002, $8.99) r/#36-39; Kaare Andrews-c 9.00
...Vol. 3: Until the Stars Turn Cold (2002, $12.99) r/#40-45; Romita Jr.-c 13.00
...Vol. 4: The Life and Death of Spiders (2003, $11.99) r/#46-50; Campbell-c 12.00
...Vol. 5: Unintended Consequences (2003, $12.99) r/#51-56; Dodson-c 13.00
...Vol. 6: Happy Birthday (2003, $12.99) r/#57,58,500-502 13.00
...Vol. 7: The Book of Ezekiel (2004, $12.99) r/#503-508; Romita Jr.-c 13.00
...Vol. 8: Sins Past (2005, $12.99) r/#509-514; cover sketch gallery 13.00
...Vol. 9: Skin Deep (2005, $9.99) r/#515-518 10.00
...Vol. 10: New Avengers (2005, $14.99) r/#519-524 15.00
Brand New Day #1-3 (11/08-1/09, $3.99) reprints #546-551 4.00
Civil War: Amazing Spider-Man TPB (2007, $17.99) r/#532-538; variant covers 18.00

AMAZING SPIDER-MAN EXTRA! (Continued from Spider-Man: Brand New Day - Extra!! #1)
Marvel Comics: No. 2, Mar, 2009 - No. 3, May, 2009 ($3.99)

2,3: 2-Anti-Venom app.; Bachalo-a. 3-Ana Kraven app.; Jimenez-a 4.00

AMAZING SPIDER-MAN FAMILY (Also see Spider-Man Family)
Marvel Comics: Oct, 2008 - No. 8, Sept, 2009 ($4.99, anthology)

1-8-New tales and reprints. 1-Includes r/ASM #300; Granov-c. 2-Deodato-c. 5-Spider-Girl new story. 6-Origin of Jackpot 5.00

AMAZING SPIDER-MAN PRESENTS: AMERICAN SON
Marvel Comics: Jul, 2010 - No. 4, Oct, 2010 ($3.99, limited series)

1-4-Reed-s/Briones-a/Djurdjevic-c; Gabriel Stacy app. 4.00

AMAZING SPIDER-MAN PRESENTS: ANTI-VENOM - NEW WAYS TO LIVE
Marvel Comics: Nov, 2009 - No. 3, Feb, 2010 ($3.99, limited series)

1-3-Wells-s/Siqueira-a; Punisher app. 4.00

AMAZING SPIDER-MAN PRESENTS: JACKPOT
Marvel Comics: Mar, 2010 - No. 3, Jun, 2010 ($3.99, limited series)

1-3-Guggenheim-s/Melo-a; Boomerang and White Rabbit app. 4.00

AMAZING SPIDER-MAN: THE MOVIE
Marvel Comics: Aug, 2012 - No. 2, Aug, 2012 ($3.99, limited series)

1,2-Partial adaptation of the 2012 movie; Neil Edwards-a; photo covers 4.00

AMAZING SPIDER-MAN: THE MOVIE ADAPTATION
Marvel Comics: Mar, 2014 - No. 2, Apr, 2014 ($2.99, limited series)

1,2-Adaptation of the 2012 movie; Wellington Alves-a; photo covers 3.00

AMAZING WILLIE MAYS, THE
Famous Funnies Publ.: No date (Sept, 1954)

nn 83 166 249 530 908 1285

AMAZING WORLD OF DC COMICS
DC Comics: Jul, 1974 - No. 17, 1978 ($1.50, B&W, mail-order DC Pro-zine)

1-Kubert interview; unpublished Kirby-a; Infantino-c 6 12 18 42 79 115
2-4: 3-Julie Schwartz profile. 4-Batman; Robinson-c 5 10 15 31 53 75
5-Sheldon Mayer 4 8 12 28 47 65
6,8,13: 6-Joe Orlando; EC-r; Wrightson pin-up. 8-Infantino; Batman-r from Pop Tart giveaway. 13-Humor; Aragonés-c; Wood/Ditko-a; photos from serials of Superman, Batman, Captain Marvel 4 8 12 22 35 48
7,10-12: 7-Superman; r/1955 Pep comic giveaway. 10-Behind the scenes at DC; Showcase article. 11-Super-Villains; unpubl. Secret Society of S.V. story. 12-Legion; Grell-c/interview; 4 8 12 23 37 50
9-Legion of Super-Heroes; lengthy bios and history; Cockrum-c 6 12 18 42 79 115
14-Justice League 4 8 12 25 40 55
15-Wonder Woman; Nasser-c 5 10 15 30 50 70
16-Golden Age heroes 4 8 12 28 47 65
17-Shazam; G.A., 70s, TV and Fawcett heroes 4 8 12 25 40 55
Special 1 (Digest size) 3 6 9 20 31 42

AMAZING WORLD OF SUPERMAN (See Superman)

AMAZING X-MEN
Marvel Comics: Mar, 1995 - No. 4, July, 1995 ($1.95, limited series)

1-Age of Apocalypse; Andy Kubert-c/a 4.00
2-4 3.00

AMAZING X-MEN
Marvel Comics: Jan, 2014 - Present ($3.99)

1-5: 1-Nightcrawler returns; Aaron-s/McGuinness-a; wraparound-c 4.00

AMAZON
Comico: Mar, 1989 - No. 3, May, 1989 ($1.95, limited series)

1-3: Ecological theme; Steven Seagle-s/Tim Sale-a 3.00
1-3-(Dark Horse, 3/09 - No. 3, 5/09, $3.50) recolored reprint with creator interviews 3.50

AMAZON (Also see Marvel Versus DC #3 & DC Versus Marvel #4)
DC Comics (Amalgam): Apr, 1996 ($1.95, one-shot)

1-John Byrne-c/a/scripts 3.00

AMAZON ATTACK 3-D
The 3-D Zone: Sept, 1990 ($3.95, 28 pgs.)

1-Chaykin-a 6.00

AMAZONS ATTACK (See Wonder Woman #8 - 2006 series)
DC Comics: Jun, 2007 - No. 6, Late Oct, 2007 ($2.99, limited series)

1-6-Queen Hippolyta and Amazons attacks Wash., DC; Pfeifer-s/Woods-a 3.00

AMAZON WOMAN (1st Series)
FantaCo: Summer, 1994 - No. 2, Fall, 1994 ($2.95, B&W, limited series, mature)

1,2: Tom Simonton-c/a/scripts 3.00

AMAZON WOMAN (2nd Series)
FantaCo: Feb, 1996 - No. 4, May, 1996 ($2.95, B&W, limited series, mature)

1-4: Tom Simonton-a/scripts 3.00
...: Invaders of Terror ('96, $5.95) Simonton-a/s 6.00

AMBUSH (See Zane Grey, Four Color 314)

AMBUSH BUG (Also see Son of...)
DC Comics: June, 1985 - No. 4, Sept, 1985 (75¢, limited series)

1-4: Giffen-c/a in all 4.00
Nothing Special 1 (9/92, $2.50, 68pg.)-Giffen-c/a 4.00
Stocking Stuffer (2/86, $1.25)-Giffen-c/a 4.00

AMBUSH BUG: YEAR NONE
DC Comics: Sept, 2008 - No. 5, Jan, 2009; No. 7, Dec, 2009 ($2.99, limited series, no #6)

1-5,7-Giffen-s/a; Jonni DC app. 4-Conner-c. 7-Baltazar & Franco-a; Giffen-a 3.00

AME-COMI GIRLS (Based on the Anime-styled statue series)
DC Comics: Dec, 2012 - No. 5, Apr, 2013 ($3.99, printed version of digital-first series)

1-5: 1-Wonder Woman; Conner-c/a. 2-Batgirl. 3-Duela Dent; Naifeh-a 4.00

AME-COMI GIRLS (Based on the Anime-styled statue series)
DC Comics: May, 2013 - No. 8, Dec, 2013 ($3.99)

1-8: 1-Palmiotti & Gray-s/Francisco-a; story continues from earlier series 4.00

AMERICA AT WAR - THE BEST OF DC WAR COMICS (See Fireside Book Series)

AMERICA IN ACTION
Dell (Imp. Publ. Co.)/ Mayflower House Publ.: 1942; Winter, 1945 (36 pgs.)

1942-Dell-(68 pgs.) 17 34 51 98 154 210
1-(1945)-Has 3 adaptations from American history; Kiefer, Schrotter & Webb-a 14 28 42 76 108 140

AMERICAN, THE
Dark Horse Comics: July, 1987 - No. 8, 1989 ($1.50/$1.75, B&W)

American Vampire #30 © Snyder & DC

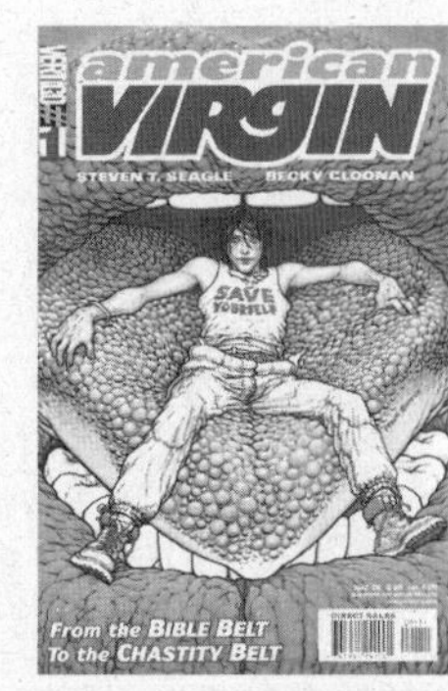

American Virgin #1 © Seagle & Cloonan

America's Best Comics #10 © STD

GD VG FN VF VF/NM NM-
2.0 4.0 6.0 8.0 9.0 9.2

1-8: ($1.50) 3.00
Collection ($5.95, B&W)-Reprints 6.00
Special 1 (1990, $2.25, B&W) 3.00

AMERICAN AIR FORCES, THE (See A-1 Comics)
William H. Wise(Flying Cadet Publ. Co./Hasan(No.1)/Life's Romances/ Magazine Ent. No. 5 on): Sept-Oct, 1944-No. 4, 1945; No. 5, 1951-No. 12, 1954

1-Article by Zack Mosley, creator of Smilin' Jack; German war-c 39 78 117 231 378 525
2-Classic-Japan war-c 68 136 204 432 741 1050
3,4-Japan war-c 20 40 60 114 182 250
NOTE: *All part comic, part magazine. Art by* ***Whitney, Chas. Quinlan, H. C. Kiefer,*** *and* ***Tony Dipreta.***
5(A-1 45)(Formerly Jet Powers), 6(A-1 54), 7(A-1 58), 8(A-1 65), 9(A-1 67), 10(A-1 74), 11(A-1 79), 12(A-1 91) 10 20 30 54 72 90
NOTE: ***Powell*** *c/a-5-12.*

AMERICAN CENTURY
DC Comics (Vertigo): May, 2001 - No. 27, Oct, 2003 ($2.50/$2.75)

1-Chaykin-s/painted-c; Tischman-a 4.00
2-27: 5-New story arc begins. 10-16,22-27-Orbik-c. 17-21-Silke-c. 18-$2.75-c begins 3.00
Hollywood Babylon (2002, $12.95, TPB) r/#5-9; w/sketch-to-art pages 13.00
Scars & Stripes (2001, $8.95, TPB) r/#1-4; Tischman intro. 9.00

AMERICAN DREAM (From the M2 Avengers)
Marvel Comics: Jul, 2008 - No. 5, Sept, 2008 ($2.99, limited series)

1-5-DeFalco-s/Nauck-a 3.00

AMERICAN FLAGG! (See First Comics Graphic Novel 3,9,12,21 & Howard Chaykin's..)
First Comics: Oct, 1983 - No. 50, Mar, 1988

1,21-27: 1-Chaykin-c/a begins. 21-27-Alan Moore scripts 4.00
2-20,28-49: 31-Origin Bob Violence 3.00
50-Last issue 4.00
Special 1 (11/86)-Introduces Chaykin's Time² 4.00
...: Hard Times TPB (6/85, $11.95) r/#1-7; intro. by Michael Moorcock; bonus materials 12.00
...: Definitive Collection Volume 1 HC (2008, $49.99) r/#1-14 and material from the...: Hard Times TPB; intro by Michael Chabon; afterword by Jim Lee 50.00

AMERICAN FREAK: A TALE OF THE UN-MEN
DC Comics (Vertigo): Feb, 1994 - No. 5, Jun, 1994 ($1.95, mini-series, mature)

1-5 3.00

AMERICAN GRAPHICS
Henry Stewart: No. 1, 1954; No. 2, 1957 (25¢)

1-The Maid of the Mist, The Last of the Eries (Indian Legends of Niagara) (sold at Niagara Falls) 11 22 33 60 83 105
2-Victory at Niagara & Laura Secord (Heroine of the War of 1812) 8 16 24 40 50 60

AMERICAN INDIAN, THE (See Picture Progress)

AMERICAN LIBRARY
David McKay Publ.: 1943 - No. 6, 1944 (15¢, 68 pgs., B&W, text & pictures)

nn (#1)-Thirty Seconds Over Tokyo (movie) 42 84 126 265 445 625
nn (#2)-Guadalcanal Diary; painted-c (only 10¢) 32 64 96 188 307 425
3-6: 3-Look to the Mountain. 4-Case of the Crooked Candle (Perry Mason). 5-Duel in the Sun. 6-Wingate's Raiders 16 32 48 94 147 200

AMERICAN: LOST IN AMERICA, THE
Dark Horse Comics: July, 1992 - No. 4, Oct, 1992 ($2.50, limited series)

1-4: 1-Dorman painted-c. 2-Phillips painted-c. 3-Mignola-c. 4-Jim Lee-c 3.00

AMERICAN SPLENDOR: (Series of titles)
Dark Horse Comics: Aug, 1996 - Apr, 2001 (B&W, all one-shots)

--**COMIC-CON COMICS** (8/96) 1-H. Pekar script. --**MUSIC COMICS** (11/97) nn-H. Pekar-s/ Sacco-a; r/Village Voice jazz strips. --**ODDS AND ENDS** (12/97) 1-Pekar-s. --**ON THE JOB** (5/97) 1-Pekar-s. --**A STEP OUT OF THE NEST** (8/94) 1-Pekar-s. --**TERMINAL** (9/99) 1-Pekar-s. --**TRANSATLANTIC** (7/98) 1-"American Splendour" on cover; Pekar-s 3.00
--**A PORTRAIT OF THE AUTHOR IN HIS DECLINING YEARS** (4/01, $3.99) 1-Photo-c. --**BEDTIME STORIES** (6/00, $3.95) 4.00

AMERICAN SPLENDOR
DC Comics: Nov, 2006 - No. 4, Feb, 2007 ($2.99, B&W)

1-4-Pekar-s/art by Haspiel and various. 1-Fabry-c 3.00
...: Another Day TPB (2007, $14.99) r/#1-4 15.00

AMERICAN SPLENDOR (Volume 2)
DC Comics (Vertigo): Jun, 2008 - No. 4, Sept, 2008 ($2.99, B&W)

1-4-Pekar-s/art by Haspiel and various. 1-Bond-c. 3-Cooke-c 3.00
...: Another Dollar TPB (2009, $14.99) r/#1-4 15.00

GD VG FN VF VF/NM NM-
2.0 4.0 6.0 8.0 9.0 9.2

AMERICAN SPLENDOR: UNSUNG HERO
Dark Horse Comics: Aug, 2002 - No. 3, Oct, 2002 ($3.99, B&W, limited series)

1-3-Pekar script/Collier-a; biography of Robert McNeill 4.00
TPB (8/03, $11.95) r/#1-3 12.00

AMERICAN SPLENDOR: WINDFALL
Dark Horse Comics: Sept, 1995 - No. 2, Oct,1995 ($3.95, B&W, limited series)

1,2-Pekar script 4.00

AMERICAN TAIL: FIEVEL GOES WEST, AN
Marvel Comics: Early Jan, 1992 - No. 3, Early Feb, 1992 ($1.00, limited series)

1-3-Adapts Universal animated movie; Wildman-a 3.00
1-($2.95-c, 69 pgs.) Deluxe squarebound edition 5.00

AMERICAN VAMPIRE
DC Comics (Vertigo): May, 2010 - Present ($3.99/$2.99)

1-10: 1-9-Snyder-s/Albuquerque-a. 1-5-Back-up story by Stephen King 4.00
1-5-Variant-c: 1-Jim Lee. 2-Berni Wrightson. 3-Andy Kubert. 5-Paul Pope 6.00
11-34-($2.99) 11-Santolouco-a. 12-Zezelj-a. 19-21-Bernet-a 3.00
... Anthology 1 (10/13, $7.99) Short stories by various; Albuquerque-c 8.00
...: The Long Road to Hell 1 (8/13, $6.99) Snyder-s/Albuquerque-a 7.00
HC (2010, $24.99, d.j.) r/#1-5; intro. by Stephen King; script pages and sketch art 25.00
...Volume Two HC (2011, $24.99, d.j.) r/#6-11; cover design art 25.00

AMERICAN VAMPIRE: LORD OF NIGHTMARES
DC Comics (Vertigo): Aug, 2012 - No. 5, Dec, 2012 ($2.99, limited series)

1-5-Set in 1954 England; Snyder-s/Nguyen-a/c. 2-Origin of Dracula 3.00

AMERICAN VAMPIRE: SECOND CYCLE
DC Comics (Vertigo): May, 2014 - Present ($3.99, limited series)

1-Snyder-s/Albuquerque-a/c 4.00

AMERICAN VAMPIRE: SURVIVAL OF THE FITTEST
DC Comics (Vertigo): Aug, 2011 - No. 5, Dec, 2011 ($2.99, limited series)

1-5-Set during WWII; Snyder-s/Murphy-a/c 3.00

AMERICAN VIRGIN
DC Comics (Vertigo): May, 2006 - No. 23, Mar, 2008 ($2.99)

1-23-Steven Seagle-s/Becky Cloonan-a in most. 1-3-Quitely-c. 4-14-Middleton-c 3.00
...: Head (2006, $9.99, TPB) r/#1-4; interviews with the creators and page development 10.00
...: Going Down (2007, $14.99, TPB) r/#5-9 15.00
...: Wet (2007, $12.99, TPB) r/#10-14 13.00
...: Around the World (Vol. 4) (2008, $17.99, TPB) r/#15-23 18.00

AMERICAN WAY, THE
DC Comics (WildStorm): Apr, 2006 - No. 8, Nov, 2006 ($2.99, limited series)

1-8-John Ridley-s/Georges Jeanty-a/c 3.00
TPB (2007, $19.99) r/series; covers; Jeanty sketch pages 20.00

AMERICA'S BEST COMICS
Nedor/Better/Standard Publications: Feb, 1942; No. 2, Sept, 1942 - No. 31, July, 1949 (New logo with #9)

1-The Woman in Red, Black Terror, Captain Future, Doc Strange, The Liberator, & Don Davis, Secret Ace begin 343 686 1029 2400 4200 6000
2-Origin The American Eagle; The Woman in Red ends 135 270 405 864 1482 2100
3-Pyroman begins (11/42, 1st app.; also see Startling Comics #18, 12/42) 119 238 357 762 1306 1850
4-6: 5-Last Capt. Future (not in #4); Lone Eagle app. 6-American Crusader app. 97 194 291 621 1061 1500
7-Hitler, Mussolini & Hirohito-c 258 516 774 1651 2826 4000
8-Last Liberator 94 188 282 597 1024 1450
9-The Fighting Yank begins; The Ghost app. 97 194 291 621 1061 1500
10-Flag-c 90 180 270 576 988 1400
11-Hirohito & Tojo-c. (10/44) 116 232 348 742 1271 1800
12 77 154 231 493 847 1200
13-Japanese WWII-c 97 194 291 621 1061 1500
14-17: 14-American Eagle ends; Doc Strange vs. Hitler story 66 132 198 419 722 1025
18-Classic-c 87 174 261 553 952 1350
19-21: 21-Infinity-c 60 120 180 381 653 925
22-Capt. Future app. 52 104 156 328 557 785
23-Miss Masque begins; last Doc Strange 62 124 186 409 697 985
24-Miss Masque bondage-c 61 122 183 390 670 950
25-Last Fighting Yank; Sea Eagle app. 47 94 141 296 498 700
26-31: 26-The Phantom Detective & The Silver Knight app.; Frazetta text illo & some panels in Miss Masque. 27,28-Commando Cubs. 27-Doc Strange. 28-Tuska Black Terror.

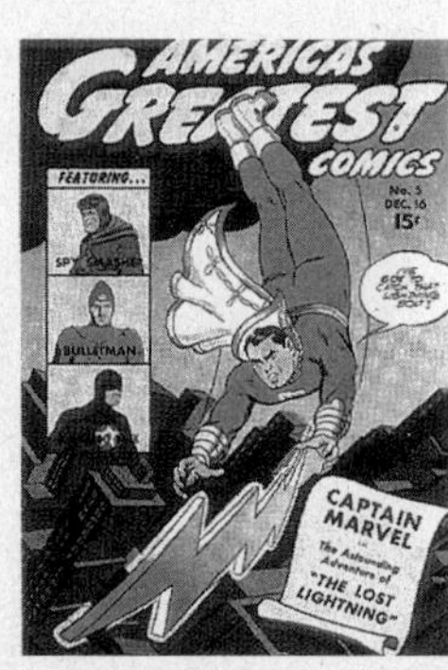

America's Greatest Comics #5 © FAW

Amethyst #1 © DC

Anarky #3 © DC

GD 2.0 | VG 4.0 | FN 6.0 | VF 8.0 | VF/NM 9.0 | NM- 9.2

29-Last Pyroman 45 90 135 284 480 675
NOTE: *American Eagle not in 3, 8, 9, 13. Fighting Yank not in 10, 12. Liberator not in 2, 6, 7. Pyroman not in 9, 11, 14-16, 23, 25-27.* ***Schomburg (Xela)*** *c-5, 7-31. Bondage c-18, 24.*

AMERICA'S BEST COMICS
America's Best Comics: 1999 - 2008
... Preview (1999, Wizard magazine supplement) - Previews Tom Strong, Top Ten, Promethea, Tomorrow Stories 3.00
... Primer (2008, $4.99, TPB) r/Tom Strong #1, Tom Strong's Terrific Tales, Top Ten #1, Promethea #1, Tomorrow Stories #1,6 5.00
... Sketchbook (2002, $5.95, square-bound)-Design sketches by Sprouse, Ross, Adams, Nowlan, Ha and others 6.00
Special 1 (2/01, $6.95)-Short stories of Alan Moore's characters; art by various; Ross-c 7.00
TPB (2004, $17.95) Reprints short stories and sketch pages from ABC titles 18.00

AMERICA'S BEST TV COMICS (TV)
American Broadcasting Co. (Prod. by Marvel Comics): 1967 (25¢, 68 pgs.)
1-Spider-Man, Fantastic Four (by Kirby/Ayers), Casper, King Kong, George of the Jungle, Journey to the Center of the Earth stories (promotes new TV cartoon show) 10 20 30 69 147 225

AMERICA'S BIGGEST COMICS BOOK
William H. Wise: 1944 (196 pgs., one-shot)
1-The Grim Reaper, The Silver Knight, Zudo, the Jungle Boy, Commando Cubs, Thunderhoof app. 43 86 129 271 461 650

AMERICA'S FUNNIEST COMICS
William H. Wise: 1944 - No. 2, 1944 (15¢, 80 pgs.)
nn(#1), 2-Funny Animal 24 48 72 142 234 325

AMERICA'S GOT POWERS
Image Comics: Apr, 2012 - No. 7, Oct, 2013 ($2.99, limited series)
1-7-Jonathan Ross-s/Bryan Hitch-a/c. 1-Wraparound-c 3.00

AMERICA'S GREATEST COMICS
Fawcett Publications: May?, 1941 - No. 8, Summer, 1943 (15¢, 100 pgs., soft cardboard-c)
1-Bulletman, Spy Smasher, Capt. Marvel, Minute Man & Mr. Scarlet begin; Classic Mac Raboy-c. 1st time that Fawcett's major super-heroes appear together as a group on a cover. Fawcett's 1st squarebound comic 343 686 1029 2400 4200 6000
2 145 290 435 921 1586 2250
3 113 226 339 718 1234 1750
4,5: 4-Commando Yank begins; Golden Arrow, Ibis the Invincible & Spy Smasher cameo in Captain Marvel 77 154 231 489 837 1185
6,7: 7-Balbo the Boy Magician app.; Captain Marvel, Bulletman cameo in Mr. Scarlet 68 136 204 435 743 1050
8-Capt. Marvel Jr. & Golden Arrow app.; Spy Smasher x-over in Capt. Midnight; no Minute Man or Commando Yank 68 136 204 435 743 1050

AMERICA'S SWEETHEART SUNNY (See Sunny, ...)

AMERICA VS. THE JUSTICE SOCIETY
DC Comics: Jan, 1985 - No. 4, Apr, 1985 ($1.00, limited series)
1-Double size; Alcala-a(i) in all 2 4 6 8 10 12
2-4: 3,4-Spectre cameo 1 2 3 5 7 9

AMERICOMICS
Americomics: April, 1983 - No. 6, Mar, 1984 ($2.00, Baxter paper/slick paper)
1-Intro/origin The Shade; Intro. The Slayer, Captain Freedom and The Liberty Corps; Perez-c 5.00
1,2-2nd printings ($2.00) 3.00
2-6: 2-Messenger app. & 1st app. Tara on Jungle Island. 3-New & old Blue Beetle battle. 4-Origin Dragonfly & Shade. 5-Origin Commando D. 6-Origin the Scarlet Scorpion 3.00
Special 1 (8/83, $2.00)-Sentinels of Justice (Blue Beetle, Captain Atom, Nightshade & The Question) 5.00

AMETHYST
DC Comics: Jan, 1985 - No. 16, Aug, 1986 (75¢)
1-16: 8-Fire Jade's i.d. revealed 3.00
Special 1 (10/86, $1.25) 4.00
1-4 (11/87 - 2/88)(Limited series) 3.00

AMETHYST, PRINCESS OF GEMWORLD (See Legion of Super-Heroes #298)
DC Comics: May, 1983 - No. 12, Apr, 1984 (Maxi-series)
1-(60¢) 5.00
1,2-(35¢): tested in Austin & Kansas City 3 6 9 19 30 40
2-12, Annual 1(9/84): 5-11-Pérez-c(p) 4.00
NOTE: *Issues #1 & 2 also have Canadian variants with a 75¢ cover price.*

AMORY WARS (Based on the Coheed and Cambria album The Second Stage Turbine Blade)
Image Comics: Jun, 2007 - No. 5, Jan, 2008 ($2.99, limited series)
1-5: 1-Claudio Sanchez-s/Gus Vasquez-a 3.00

AMORY WARS II
Image Comics: Jun, 2008 - No. 5, Oct, 2008 ($2.99, limited series)
1-5-Claudio Sanchez-s/Gabriel Guzman-a 3.00

AMORY WARS IN KEEPING SECRETS OF SILENT EARTH: 3
BOOM! Studios: May, 2010 - No. 12, Jun, 2011 ($3.99)
1-12: 1-Claudio Sanchez & Peter David-s/Chris Burnham-a. 1-Four covers 4.00

AMY RACECAR COLOR SPECIAL (See Stray Bullets)
El Capitán Books: July, 1997; Oct, 1999 ($2.95/$3.50)
1,2-David Lapham-a/scripts. 2-($3.50) 3.50

ANARCHO DICTATOR OF DEATH (See Comics Novel)

ANARKY (See Batman titles)
DC Comics: May, 1997 - No. 4, Aug, 1997 ($2.50, limited series)
1 3.50
2-4 3.00

ANARKY (See Batman titles)
DC Comics: May, 1999 - No. 8, Dec, 1999 ($2.50)
1-8: 1-JLA app.; Grant-s/Breyfogle-a. 3-Green Lantern app. 7-Day of Judgment; Haunted Tank app. 8-Joker-c/app. 3.00

ANCHORS ANDREWS (The Saltwater Daffy)
St. John Publishing Co.: Jan, 1953 - No. 4, July, 1953 (Anchors the Saltwater... No. 4)
1-Canteen Kate by Matt Baker (9 pgs.) 22 44 66 132 216 300
2-4 10 20 30 54 72 90

ANDY & WOODY (See March of Comics No. 40, 55, 76)

ANDY BURNETT (TV, Disney)
Dell Publishing Co.: Dec, 1957
Four Color 865-Photo-c 7 14 21 49 92 135

ANDY COMICS (Formerly Scream Comics; becomes Ernie Comics)
Current Publications (Ace Magazines): No. 20, June, 1948-No. 21, Aug, 1948
20,21: Archie-type comic 9 18 27 47 61 75

ANDY DEVINE WESTERN
Fawcett Publications: Dec, 1950 - No. 2, 1951
1-Photo-c 43 86 129 271 461 650
2-Photo-c 31 62 93 182 296 410

ANDY GRIFFITH SHOW, THE (TV)(1st show aired 10/3/60)
Dell Publishing Co.: #1252, Jan-Mar, 1962; #1341, Apr-Jun, 1962
Four Color 1252(#1) 33 66 99 238 532 825
Four Color 1341-Photo-c 30 60 90 216 483 750

ANDY HARDY COMICS (See Movie Comics #3 by Fiction House)
Dell Publishing Co.: April, 1952 - No. 6, Sept-Nov, 1954
Four Color 389(#1) 5 10 15 31 53 75
Four Color 447,480,515, #5,#6 4 8 12 25 40 55

ANDY PANDA (Also see Crackajack Funnies #39, The Funnies, New Funnies & Walter Lantz...)
Dell Publishing Co.: 1943 - No. 56, Nov-Jan, 1961-62 (Walter Lantz)
Four Color 25(#1, 1943) 46 92 138 354 797 1240
Four Color 54(1944) 25 50 75 175 388 600
Four Color 85(1945) 15 30 45 100 220 340
Four Color 130(1946),154,198 10 20 30 67 141 215
Four Color 216,240,258,280,297 8 16 24 51 96 140
Four Color 326,345,358 6 12 18 38 69 100
Four Color 383,409 5 10 15 33 57 80
16(11-1/52-53) - 30 4 8 12 28 47 65
31-56 4 8 12 23 37 50
(See March of Comics #5, 22, 79, & Super Book #4, 15, 27.)

A-NEXT (See Avengers)
Marvel Comics: Oct, 1998 - No. 12, Sept, 1999 ($1.99)
1-12: 1-Next generation of Avengers; Frenz-a. 2-Two covers. 3-Defenders app. 3.00
Spider-Girl Presents Avengers Next Vol. 1: Second Coming (2006, $7.99, digest) r/#1-6 8.00

ANGEL
Dell Publishing Co.: Aug, 1954 - No. 16, Nov-Jan, 1958-59
Four Color 576(#1, 8/54) 4 8 12 25 40 55
2(5-7/55) - 16 3 6 9 17 26 35

ANGEL (TV) (Also see Buffy the Vampire Slayer)
Dark Horse Comics: Nov, 1999 - No. 17, Apr, 2001 ($2.95/$2.99)

Angel and Faith #20 © 20th Cent. Fox

Angel and the Ape (2001 series) #2 © DC

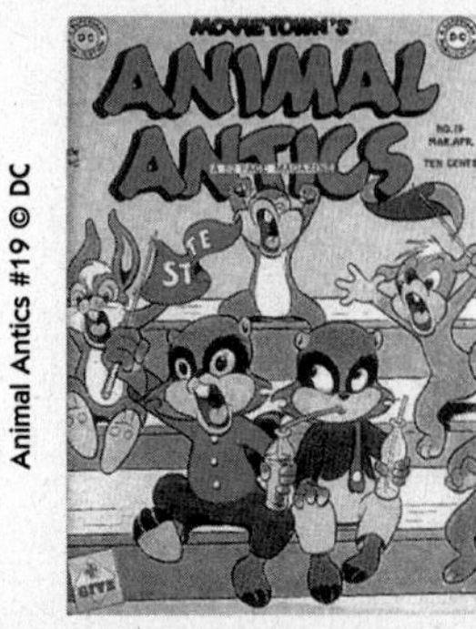

Animal Antics #19 © DC

	GD 2.0	VG 4.0	FN 6.0	VF 8.0	VF/NM 9.0	NM- 9.2
1-17: 1-3,5-7,10-14-Zanier-a. 1-4,7,10-Matsuda & photo-c. 16-Buffy-c/app.						3.00
...: Earthly Possessions TPB (4/01, $9.95) r/#5-7, photo-c						10.00
...: Surrogates TPB (12/00, $9.95) r/#1-3; photo-c						10.00

ANGEL (Buffy the Vampire Slayer)
Dark Horse Comics: Sept, 2001 - No. 4, May, 2002 ($2.99, limited series)

1-4-Joss Whedon & Matthews-s/Rubi-a; photo-c and Rubi-c on each 3.00

ANGEL (Buffy the Vampire Slayer) (Previously titled Angel: After the Fall)
IDW Publishing: No. 18, Feb, 2009 - No. 44, Apr, 2011 ($3.99)

18-44: Multiple covers on all. 25-Juliet Landau-s 4.00

ANGEL (one-shots) (Buffy the Vampire Slayer)
IDW Publishing: ($3.99/$7.49)

...: Connor (8/06, $3.99) Jay Faerber-s/Bob Gill-a; 4 covers + 1 retailer cover 4.00
...: Doyle (7/06, $3.99) Jeff Mariotte-s/David Messina-a; 4 covers + 1 retailer cover 4.00
...: Gunn (5/06, $3.99) Dan Jolley-s/Mark Pennington-a; 4 covers + 2 retailer covers 4.00
...: Illyria (4/06, $3.99) Peter David-s/Nicola Scott-a; 4 covers + 2 retailer covers 4.00
...: Masks (10/06, $7.49) short stories of Angel, Illyria, Cordilia & Lindsay; puppet Angel app. 8.00
... 100-Page Spectacular (4/11, $7.99) reprints of 4 issues; Runge-c 8.00
... Special • Lorne (3/10, $7.99) John Byrne-s/a; The Groosalugg app. 8.00
Team Angel 100-Page Spectacular (4/11, $7.99) reprints; Runge-c 8.00
...: Vs. Frankenstein (10/09, $3.99) John Byrne-s/a/c 4.00
...: Vs. Frankenstein II (10/10, $3.99) John Byrne-s/a/c 4.00
...: Wesley (6/06, $3.99) Scott Tipton-s/Mike Norton-a; 4 covers + 1 retailer cover 4.00
Spotlight TPB (12/06, $19.99) r/Connor, Doyle, Gunn, Illyria & Wesley one-shots 20.00
... Yearbook (5/11, $7.99) short stories by various; 3 covers 8.00

ANGELA
Image Comics (Todd McFarlane Prod.): Dec, 1994 - No. 3, Feb, 1995 ($2.95, lim. series)

	GD	VG	FN	VF	VF/NM	NM-
1-Gaiman scripts & Capullo-c/a in all; Spawn app.	1	2	3	5	6	8
2						6.00
3						5.00
Special Edition (1995)-Pirate Spawn-c	3	6	9	14	20	25
Special Edition (1995)-Angela-c	3	6	9	14	20	25
TPB ($9.95, 1995) reprints #1-3 & Special Ed. w/additional pin-ups						10.00

ANGEL: AFTER THE FALL (Buffy the Vampire Slayer) (Follows the last TV episode)
IDW Publishing: Nov, 2007 - No. 17, Feb, 2009 ($3.99)(Continues as Angel with #18)

1-Whedon & Lynch-s; multiple covers 5.00
2-17: Multiple covers on all 4.00

ANGELA/GLORY: RAGE OF ANGELS (See Glory/Angela: Rage of Angels)
Image Comics (Todd McFarlane Productions): Mar, 1996 ($2.50, one-shot)

1-Liefeld-c/Cruz-a(p); Darkchylde preview flip book 4.00
1-Variant-c 4.00

ANGEL: A HOLE IN THE WORLD (Adaptation of the 2-part TV episode)
IDW Publishing: Dec, 2009 - No. 5, Apr, 2010 ($3.99, limited series)

1-5-Fred becomes Illyria; Casagrande-a/c 4.00

ANGEL & FAITH (Follows Buffy the Vampire Slayer Season Eight)
Dark Horse Comics: Aug, 2011 - No. 25, Aug, 2013 ($2.99)

1-Gage-s/Isaacs-a; two covers by Morris & Chen 3.00
2-25-Two covers by Morris & Isaacs. 5-Harmony & Clem app.; Noto-a. 7-Drusilla app. 11-14-Willow & Connor app. 20-Spike app.; Archie style-c 3.00

ANGEL & FAITH SEASON 10
Dark Horse Comics: Apr, 2014 - Present ($3.50)

1-Gischler-s/Conrad-a; two covers by Fischer & Samnee 3.50

ANGEL AND THE APE (Meet Angel No. 7) (See Limited Collector's Edition C-34 & Showcase No. 77)
National Periodical Publications: Nov-Dec, 1968 - No. 6, Sept-Oct, 1969

	GD	VG	FN	VF	VF/NM	NM-
1-(11-12/68)-Not Wood-a	4	8	12	28	47	65
2-5-Wood inks in all. 4-Last 12¢ issue	3	6	9	19	30	40
6-Wood inks	3	6	9	21	33	45

ANGEL AND THE APE (2nd Series)
DC Comics: Mar, 1991 - No. 4, June, 1991 ($1.00, limited series)

1-4 3.00

ANGEL AND THE APE (3rd Series)
DC Comics (Vertigo): Oct, 2001 - No. 4, Jan 2002 ($2.95, limited series)

1-4-Chaykin & Tischman-s/Bond-a/Art Adams-c 3.00

ANGEL: AULD LANG SYNE (Buffy the Vampire Slayer)
IDW Publishing: Nov, 2006 - No. 5, Mar, 2007 ($3.99, limited series)

1-5: 1-Three covers plus photo-c; Tipton-s/Messina-a 4.00

ANGEL: BARBARY COAST (Buffy the Vampire Slayer)
IDW Publishing: Apr, 2010 - No. 3, Jun, 2010 ($3.99, limited series)

1-3-Angel in 1906 San Francisco; Tischman-s/Urru-a; 2 covers on each 4.00

ANGEL: BLOOD & TRENCHES (Buffy the Vampire Slayer)
IDW Publishing: Mar, 2009 - No. 4, June, 2009 ($3.99, B&W&Red, limited series)

1-4-Angel in World War II Europe; John Byrne-s/a/c 4.00

ANGEL: ILLYRIA: HAUNTED (Buffy the Vampire Slayer)
IDW Publishing: Nov, 2010 - No. 4, Feb, 2011 ($3.99, limited series)

1-4-Tipton & Huehner-s/Casagrande-a; 2 covers 4.00

ANGEL LOVE
DC Comics: Aug, 1986 - No. 8, Mar, 1987 (75¢, limited series)

1-8, Special 1 (1987, $1.25, 52 pgs.) 4.00

ANGEL: NOT FADE AWAY (Buffy the Vampire Slayer)
IDW Publishing: May, 2009 - No. 3, July, 2009 ($3.99, limited series)

1-3-Adaptation of TV show's final episodes; Mooney-a 4.00

ANGEL OF LIGHT, THE (See The Crusaders)

ANGEL: OLD FRIENDS (Buffy the Vampire Slayer)
IDW Publishing: Nov, 2005 - No. 5, Mar, 2006 ($3.99, limited series)

1-5: Four covers plus photo-c on each; Mariotte-s/Messina-a; Gunn, Spike and Illyria app. 4.00
... Cover Gallery (6/06, $3.99) gallery of variant covers for the series 4.00
... Cover Gallery (12/06, $3.99) gallery of variant covers; preview of Angel: Auld Lang Syne 4.00
TPB (2006, $19.99) r/series; gallery of Messina covers 20.00

ANGEL: ONLY HUMAN (Buffy the Vampire Slayer)
IDW Publishing: Aug, 2009 - No. 5, Dec, 2009 ($3.99, limited series)

1-5-Lobdell-s/Messina-a; covers by Messina and Dave Dorman 4.00

ANGEL: REVELATIONS (X-Men character)
Marvel Comics: July, 2008 - No. 5, Nov, 2008 ($3.99, limited series)

1-5-Origin from childhood re-told; Adam Pollina-a/Aquirre-Sacasa-s 4.00

ANGEL: SMILE TIME (Buffy the Vampire Slayer)
IDW Publishing: Dec, 2008 - No. 3, Apr, 2009 ($3.99, limited series)

1-3-Adaptation of TV episode; Messina-a; Messina and photo covers for each 4.00

ANGEL: THE CURSE (Buffy the Vampire Slayer)
IDW Publishing: June, 2005 - No. 5, Oct, 2005 ($3.99, limited series)

1-5-Four covers on each; Mariotte-s/Messina-a 4.00
TPB (1/06, $19.99) r/#1-5; cover gallery of Messina covers 20.00

ANGELTOWN
DC Comics (Vertigo): Jan, 2005 - No. 5, May, 2005 ($2.95, limited series)

1-5-Gary Phillips-s/Shawn Martinbrough-a 3.00

ANGELUS
Image Comics (Top Cow): Dec, 2007; Dec, 2009 - Nov, 2010 ($2.99)

... Pilot Season 1-(12/07) Sejic-a/c; Edington-s; origin re-told 3.00
1-6-Marz-s/Sejic-a; multiple covers on each 3.00

ANGRY CHRIST COMIX (See Cry For Dawn)

ANIMA
DC Comics: Mar, 1994 - No. 15, July, 1995 ($1.75/$1.95/$2.25)

1-7,0,8-15: 7-(9/94)-Begin $1.95-c; Zero Hour x-over 3.00

ANIMAL ADVENTURES
Timor Publications/Accepted Publ. (reprints): Dec, 1953 - No. 3, May?, 1954

	GD	VG	FN	VF	VF/NM	NM-
1-Funny animal	8	16	24	40	50	60
2,3: 2-Featuring Soopermutt (2/54)	6	12	18	28	34	40
1-3 (reprints, nd)	3	6	8	11	13	15

ANIMAL ANTICS
DC Comics: Feb, 1946

nn - Ashcan comic, not distributed to newsstands, only for in-house use. Cover art is Star Spangled Comics #49 and interior is Boy Commandos #12; a NM cover sold for $1000 in 2012, and FN/VF copy sold for $1553.50 in 2012.

ANIMAL ANTICS (Movietown... No. 24 on)
National Periodical Publ: Mar-Apr, 1946 - No. 23, Nov-Dec, 1949 (All 52 pgs.?)

	GD	VG	FN	VF	VF/NM	NM-
1-Raccoon Kids begins by Otto Feuer; many-c by Grossman; Seaman Sy Wheeler by Kelly in some issues; Grossman-a in most issues	45	90	135	284	480	675
2	25	50	75	147	241	335
3-10: 10-Post-c/a	16	32	48	94	147	200
11-23: 14,15,18,19-Post-a	12	24	36	69	97	125

Animal Man (2011 series) #1 © DC

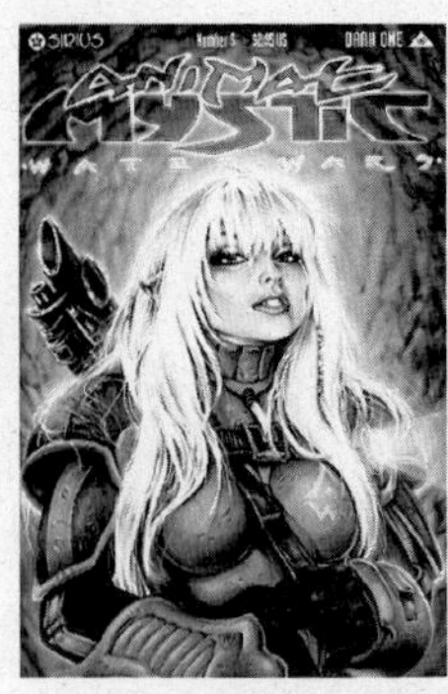

Animal Mystic Water Wars #5 © Greg Williams

Annex #2 © MAR

	GD	VG	FN	VF	VF/NM	NM-
	2.0	4.0	6.0	8.0	9.0	9.2

ANIMAL COMICS
Dell Publishing Co.: Dec-Jan, 1941-42 - No. 30, Dec-Jan, 1947-48

1-1st Pogo app. by Walt Kelly (Dan Noonan art in most issues)	109	218	327	692	1189	1685
2-Uncle Wiggily begins	53	106	159	334	567	800
3,5	25	50	75	175	388	600
4,6,7-No Pogo	14	28	42	96	211	325
8-10	17	34	51	117	257	400
11-15	11	22	33	73	157	240
16-20	8	16	24	54	102	150
21-30: 24-30- "Jigger" by John Stanley	7	14	21	44	82	120

NOTE: ***Dan Noonan** a-18-30. **Gollub** art in most later issues; c-29, 30. **Kelly** c-7-26, part #27-30.*

ANIMAL CRACKERS (Also see Adventures of Patoruzu)
Green Publ. Co./Norlen/Fox Feat.(Hero Books): 1946; No. 31, July, 1950; No. 9, 1959

1-Super Cat begins (1st app.)	20	40	60	114	182	250
2	11	22	33	60	83	105
31(Fox)-Formerly My Love Secret	8	16	24	44	57	70
9(1959-Norlen)-Infinity-c	5	10	15	22	26	30
nn, nd ('50s), no publ.; infinity-c	5	10	15	22	26	30

ANIMAL FABLES
E. C. Comics (Fables Publ. Co.): July-Aug, 1946 - No. 7, Nov-Dec, 1947

1-Freddy Firefly (clone of Human Torch), Korky Kangaroo, Petey Pig, Danny Demon begin	55	110	165	352	601	850
2-Aesop Fables begin	36	72	108	211	343	475
3-6	30	60	90	177	289	400
7-Origin Moon Girl	71	142	213	454	777	1100

ANIMAL FAIR (Fawcett's...)
Fawcett Publications: Mar, 1946 - No. 11, Feb, 1947

1-Hoppy the Marvel Bunny-c	28	56	84	165	270	375
2	14	28	42	82	121	160
3-6	12	24	36	67	94	120
7-11	10	20	30	54	72	90

ANIMAL FUN
Premier Magazines: 1953 (25¢, came w/glasses)

1-(3-D)-Ziggy Pig, Silly Seal, Billy & Buggy Bear	36	72	108	216	351	485

ANIMAL MAN (See Action Comics #552, 553, DC Comics Presents #77, 78, Last Days of Animal Man, Secret Origins #39, Strange Adventures #180 & Wonder Woman #267, 268)
DC Comics (Vertigo imprint #57 on): Sept, 1988 - No. 89, Nov, 1995 ($1.25/$1.50/$1.75/$1.95/$2.25, mature)

1-Grant Morrison scripts begin, ends #26	2	4	6	8	10	12
2-10: 2-Superman cameo. 6-Invasion tie-in. 9-Manhunter-c/story. 10-Psycho Pirate app.	1	2	3	4	5	7
11-49,51-55,57-89: 23,24-Psycho Pirate app. 24-Arkham Asylum story; Bizarro Superman app. 25-Inferior Five app. 26-Morrison apps. in story; part photo-c (of Morrison?)						3.00
50-($2.95, 52 pgs.)-Last issue w/Veitch scripts						5.00
56-($3.50, 68 pgs.)						5.00
Annual 1 (1993, $3.95, 68 pgs.)-Bolland-c; Children's Crusade Pt. 3						6.00
...: Deus Ex Machina TPB (2003, $19.95) r/#18-26; Morrison-s; new Bolland-c						20.00
...: Origin of the Species TPB (2002, $19.95) r/#10-17 & Secret Origins #39						20.00

NOTE: ***Bolland** c-1-63. 71-**Sutton**-a(i)*

ANIMAL MAN (DC New 52)
DC Comics: Nov, 2011 - No. 29, May, 2014 ($2.99)

1-Jeff Lemire-s/Travel Foreman-a/c; 1st printing with yellow cover background						8.00
1-Second printing (red cover background), Third printing (grey cover background)						3.00
2-29: 2-4 Foreman-a. 5-Huat-a. 10 Justice League Dark app. 13-17-Rotworld						3.00
#0 (11/12, $2.99) Lemire-s/Pugh-a/c; Buddy Baker's origin re-told						3.00
Annual 1 (7/12, $4.99) Swamp Thing app.; Lemire-s/Green-a						5.00
Annual 2 (9/13, $4.99) Lemire-s/Foreman-a						5.00

ANIMAL MYSTIC (See Dark One...)
Cry For Dawn/Sirius: 1993 - No. 4, 1995 ($2.95?/$3.50, B&W)

1	3	6	9	14	19	24
1-Alternate	4	8	12	22	34	45
1-2nd printing						5.00
2	2	4	6	10	14	18
2,3-2nd prints (Sirius)						3.50
3 ,4: 4-Color poster insert, Linsner-s	1	2	3	5	7	9
TPB ($14.95) r/series						18.00

ANIMAL MYSTIC WATER WARS
Sirius: 1996 - No. 6 ($2.95, limited series)

1-6-Dark One-c/a/scripts						5.00

ANIMAL WORLD, THE (Movie)
Dell Publishing Co.: No. 713, Aug, 1956

Four Color 713	4	8	12	25	40	55

ANIMANIACS (TV)
DC Comics: May, 1995 - No. 59, Apr, 2000 ($1.50/$1.75/$1.95/$1.99)

1	1	2	3	4	5	7
2-20: 13-Manga issue. 19-X-Files parody; Miran Kim-c; Adlard-a (4 pgs.)						4.00
21-59: 26-E.C. parody-c. 34-Xena parody. 43-Pinky & the Brain take over						3.00
A Christmas Special (12/94, $1.50, "1" on-c)						5.00

ANIMATED COMICS
E. C. Comics: No date given (Summer, 1947?)

1 (Rare) Funny Animal	89	178	267	570	978	1385

ANIMATED FUNNY COMIC TUNES (See Funny Tunes)

ANIMATED MOVIE-TUNES (Movie Tunes No. 3)
Margood Publishing Corp. (Timely): Fall, 1945 - No. 2, Sum, 1946

1,2-Super Rabbit, Ziggy Pig & Silly Seal	39	78	117	236	388	540

ANIMAX
Marvel Comics (Star Comics): Dec, 1986 - No. 4, June, 1987

1-4: Based on toys; Simonson-a						3.00

ANITA BLAKE (Circus of the Damned - The Charmer on cover)
Marvel Comics: July, 2010 - No. 5, Dec, 2010 ($3.99, limited series)

1-5-Laurell K. Hamilton & Jess Ruffner-s/Ron Lim-a/ Brett Booth-c						4.00
... - The Ingenue 1-5 (3/11 - No. 5, 10/11, $3.99) Hamilton & Ruffner-s/Lim-a/Booth-c						4.00
... - The Scoundrel 1-4 (11/11 - No. 5, 5/12, $3.99) Hamilton & Ruffner-s/Lim-a/Booth-c						4.00

ANITA BLAKE: VAMPIRE HUNTER GUILTY PLEASURES
Marvel Comics (Dabel Brothers): Dec, 2006 - No. 12, Aug, 2008 ($2.99)

1-Laurell K. Hamilton-s/Brett Booth-a; blue cover						6.00
1-Variant-c by Greg Horn						20.00
1-Sketch cover						25.00
1-2nd printing with red cover						3.00
2-Two covers						5.00
3-12						3.00
...: Handbook (2007, $3.99) profile pages of characters; glossary						4.00
... Volume One HC (6/07, $19.99, dust jacket) r/#1-6; cover gallery						20.00

ANITA BLAKE: VAMPIRE HUNTER THE FIRST DEATH, (LAURELL K. HAMILTON'S...)
Marvel Comics (Dabel Brothers): July, 2007 - No. 2, Dec, 2007 ($3.99)

1,2-Laurell K. Hamilton & Jonathon Green-s/Wellington Alves-a. 2-Marvel Zombie var-c						4.00
... HC (2008, $19.99, dust jacket) r/#1,2 & Guilty Pleasures Handbook						20.00

ANITA BLAKE, VAMPIRE HUNTER: THE LAUGHING CORPSE
Marvel Comics: Dec, 2008 - No. 5, Apr, 2009 ($3.99)

... - Book One (12/08 - No. 5, 4/09) 1-5-Laurell K. Hamilton-s/Ron Lim-a/c						4.00
... - Necromancer 1-5 (6/09 - No. 5, 11/09, $3.99) Lim-a/c						4.00
Anita Blake (Executioner on-c) #11-15 (12/09 - No. 15, 5/10) numbering continued; Lim-a						4.00

ANNE RICE'S INTERVIEW WITH THE VAMPIRE
Innovation Books: 1991 - No. 12, Jan, 1994 ($2.50, limited series)

1-12: Adapts novel; Moeller-a						3.00

ANNE RICE'S THE MASTER OF RAMPLING GATE
Innovation Books: 1991 ($6.95, one-shot)

1-Bolton painted-c; Colleen Doran painted-a						7.00

ANNE RICE'S THE MUMMY OR RAMSES THE DAMNED
Millennium Publications: Oct, 1990 - No. 12, Feb, 1992 ($2.50, limited series)

1-12: Adapts novel; Mooney-p in all						3.00

ANNE RICE'S THE WITCHING HOUR
Millennium Publ./Comico: 1992 - No. 13, Jan, 1993 ($2.50, limited series)

1-13						3.00

ANNETTE (Disney, TV)
Dell Publishing Co.: No. 905, May, 1958; No. 1100, May, 1960 (Mickey Mouse Club)

Four Color 905-Annette Funicello photo-c	21	42	63	147	324	500
Four Color 1100-...'s Life Story (Movie); A. Funicello photo-c	17	34	51	117	259	400

ANNEX (See Amazing Spider-Man Annual #27 for 1st app.)
Marvel Comics: Aug, 1994 - No. 4, Nov, 1994 ($1.75)

Annie Oakley #3 © MAR

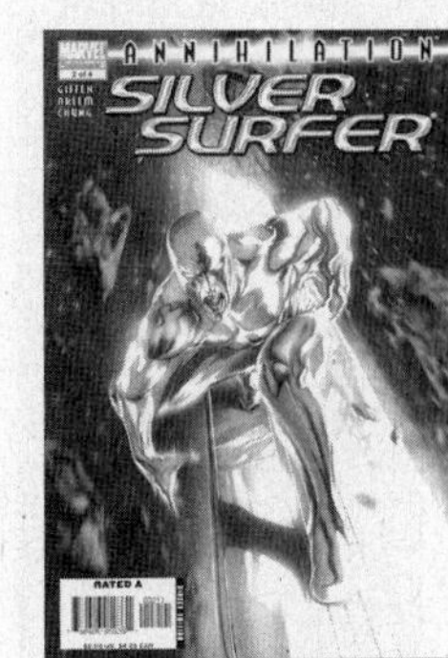

Annihilation: Silver Surfer #2 © MAR

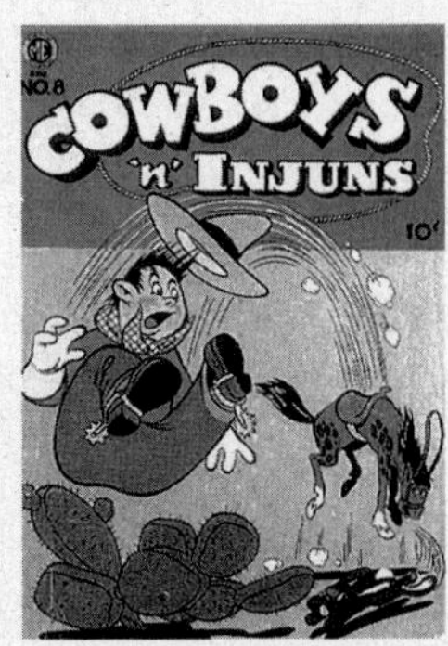

A-1 Comics #48 © ME

	GD 2.0	VG 4.0	FN 6.0	VF 8.0	VF/NM 9.0	NM- 9.2

GD VG FN VF VF/NM NM- 2.0 4.0 6.0 8.0 9.0 9.2

1-4: 1,4-Spider-Man app. 3.00

ANNIE
Marvel Comics Group: Oct, 1982 - No. 2, Nov, 1982 (60¢)

1,2-Movie adaptation 4.00
Treasury Edition ($2.00, tabloid size) 3 6 9 17 26 35

ANNIE OAKLEY (See Tessie The Typist #19, Two-Gun Kid & Wild Western)
Marvel/Atlas Comics(MPI No. 1-4/CDS No. 5 on): Spring, 1948 - No. 4, 11/48; No. 5, 6/55 - No. 11, 6/56

1 (1st Series, 1948)-Hedy Devine app. 52 104 156 328 552 775
2 (7/48, 52 pgs.)-Kurtzman-a, "Hey Look", 1 pg; Intro. Lana; Hedy Devine app; Captain Tootsie by Beck 30 60 90 177 289 400
3,4 24 48 72 144 237 330
5 (2nd Series, 1955)-Reinman-a ; Maneely-c 18 36 54 103 162 220
6-9: 6,8-Woodbridge-a. 9-Williamson-a (4 pgs.) 14 28 42 81 118 155
10,11: 11-Severin-c 14 28 42 76 108 140

ANNIE OAKLEY AND TAGG (TV)
Dell Publishing Co./Gold Key: 1953 - No. 18, Jan-Mar, 1959; July, 1965 (Gail Davis photo-c #3 on)

Four Color 438 (#1) 12 24 36 82 179 275
Four Color 481,575 (#2,3) 8 16 24 56 108 160
4(7-9/55)-10 7 14 21 46 86 125
11-18(1-3/59) 6 12 18 38 69 100
1(7/65-Gold Key)-Photo-c (c-r/#6) 4 8 12 27 44 60
NOTE: *Manning a-13. Photo back c-4, 9, 11.*

ANNIHILATION
Marvel Comics: May, 2006 - No. 6, Mar, 2007 ($3.99/$2.99, limited x-over series)

Prologue (5/06, $3.99, one-shot) Nova, Thanos and Silver Surfer app. 4.00
1-6: 1-(10/06) Giffen-s/DiVito-a; Annihilus app. 3.00
...: Heralds of Galactus 1,2 (4/07-5/07, $3.99) 2-Silver Surfer app. 4.00
...: Nova 1-4 (6/06-9/06, $2.99) Abnett & Lanning-s/Walker-a/Dell'Otto-c. 2,3-Quasar app. 3.00
...: Ronan 1-4 (6/06-9/06, $2.99) Furman-s/Lucas-a/Dell'Otto-c 3.00
... Saga (2007, $1.99) re-cap of the series; DiVito-c 3.00
...: Silver Surfer 1-4 (6/06-9/06, $2.99) Giffen-s/Arlem-a/Dell'Otto-c 3.00
...: Super-Skrull 1-4 (6/06-9/06, $2.99) Grillo-Marxuach-s/Titus-a/Dell'Otto-c 3.00
...: The Nova Corps Files (2006, $3.99) profile pages of characters and alien races 4.00
Annihilation Book 1 HC (2007, $29.99, dustjacket) r/Drax the Destroyer #1-4, Annihilation Prologue and Annihilation: Nova #1-4; sketch and layout pages 30.00
Annihilation Book 1 SC (2007, $24.99) same content as HC 25.00
Annihilation Book 2 HC (2007, $29.99, dustjacket) r/Annihilation: Silver Surfer #1-4, ...: Super Skrull #1-4 and ...: Ronan #1-4; sketch and layout pages 30.00
Annihilation Book 2 SC (2007, $24.99) same content as HC 25.00
Annihilation Book 3 HC (2007, $29.99, dustjacket) r/Annihilation #1-6, Annihilation: Heralds of Galactus #1,2 and Annihilation: Nova Corps Files; sketch pages 30.00
Annihilation Book 3 SC (2007, $24.99) same content as HC 25.00

ANNIHILATION: CONQUEST (Also see Nova 2007 series)
Marvel Comics: Jan, 2008 - No. 6, Jun, 2008 ($3.99/$2.99, limited x-over series)

Prologue (8/07, $3.99, one-shot) the new Quasar, Moondragon app.; Perkins-a 4.00
1-5-Raney-a; Ultron app. 3-Moondragon dies 5.00
6-($3.99) Guardians of the Galaxy team forms 1 3 4 6 8 10
... - Quasar 1-4 (9/07-No. 4, 12/07, $2.99) Gage-s/Lilly-a. 1-Super-Adaptoid app. 3.00
... - Starlord 1-4 (9/07-No. 4, 12/07, $2.99) Giffen-s/Green-a 6.00
... - Wraith 1-4 (9/07-No. 4, 12/07, $2.99) Hotz-a/Grillo-Marxuach-s 3.00
Annihilation: Conquest Book 1 HC (2008, $29.99, dustjacket) r/Prologue; ...Quasar #1-4, ...Star-Lord #1-4; Annihilation Saga; design pages 30.00

ANNIHILATORS
Marvel Comics: May, 2011 - No. 4, Aug, 2011 ($4.99, limited series)

1-4: Quasar, Silver Surfer, Beta-Ray Bill, Ronan, Gladiator app.; Huat-a 5.00

ANNIHILATORS: EARTHFALL
Marvel Comics: Nov, 2011 - No. 4, Feb, 2012 ($3.99, limited series)

1-4-Avengers app.; Abnett & Lanning-s/Huat-a/Christopher-c 4.00

ANOTHER WORLD (See Strange Stories From...)

ANSWER!, THE
Dark Horse Comics: Jan, 2013 - No. 4 ($3.99, limited series)

1-3-Dennis Hopeless-s/Mike Norton-a 4.00

ANT
Image Comics: Aug, 2005 - No. 11 ($2.99)

1-11: 1-Mario Gulley-s/a. 2-Savage Dragon & Spawn app. 3-Spawn-c/app. 3.00
Vol. 1: Reality Bites TPB (2006, $12.99) r/#1-4; sketch and concept art 13.00

ANTHRO (See Showcase #74)
National Periodical Publications: July-Aug, 1968 - No. 6, July-Aug, 1969

1-(7-8/68)-Howie Post-a in all 5 10 15 33 57 80
2-5: 5-Last 12¢ issue 3 6 9 21 33 45
6-Wood-c/a (inks) 4 8 12 23 37 50

ANTI-HITLER COMICS
New England Comics Press: Summer, 1992 ($2.75, B&W, one-shot)

1-Reprints Hitler as Devil stories from wartime comics 6.00

ANT-MAN (See Irredeemable Ant-Man, The)

ANT-MAN & WASP
Marvel Comics: Jan, 2011 - No. 3, Mar, 2011 ($3.99, limited series)

1-3-Tim Seeley-s/a; Espin-c; Tigra app. 4.00

ANT-MAN'S BIG CHRISTMAS
Marvel Comics: Feb, 2000 ($5.95, square-bound, one-shot)

1-Bob Gale-s/Phil Winslade-a; Avengers app. 6.00

ANT-MAN: SEASON ONE
Marvel Comics: 2012 ($24.99, hardcover graphic novel)

HC - Origin story; DeFalco-s/Domingues-a/Tedesco painted-c 25.00

ANTONY AND CLEOPATRA (See Ideal, a Classical Comic)

ANYTHING GOES
Fantagraphics Books: Oct, 1986 - No. 6, 1987 ($2.00, #1-5 color & B&W/#6 B&W, lim. series)

1-6: 1-Flaming Carrot app. (1st in color?); G. Kane-c. 2-6: 2-Miller-c(p); Alan Moore scripts; Kirby-a; early Sam Kieth-a (2 pgs.). 3-Capt. Jack, Cerebus app.; Cerebus-c by N. Adams. 4-Perez-c. 5-3rd color Teenage Mutant Ninja Turtles app. 3.50

A-1
Marvel Comics (Epic Comics): 1992 - No. 4, 1993 ($5.95, limited series, mature)

1-4: 1-Fabry-c/a, Russell-a, S. Hampton-a. 3-Bisley-c; Kent Williams-a. 4-McKean-a; Dorman-s/a 1 2 3 4 5 7

A-1
Titan Comics: Jul, 2013 - Present ($3.99)

1-5-Three serialized stories; three covers on each 4.00

A-1 COMICS (A-1 appears on covers No. 1-17 only)(See individual title listings for #11-139) (1st two issues not numbered.)
Life's Romances Publ.-No. 1/Compix/Magazine Ent.: 1944 - No. 139, Sept-Oct, 1955 (No #2)

nn-(1944) (See Kerry Drake Detective Cases)
1-Dotty Dripple (1 pg.), Mr. Ex, Bush Berry, Rocky, Lew Loyal (20 pgs.) 18 36 54 103 162 220
3-8,10: Texas Slim & Dirty Dalton, The Corsair, Teddy Rich, Dotty Dripple, Inca Dinca, Tommy Tinker, Little Mexico & Tugboat Tim, The Masquerader & others. 7-Corsair-c/s. 8-Intro Rodeo Ryan 11 22 33 62 86 110
9-All Texas Slim 11 22 33 64 90 115

(See Individual Alphabetical listings for prices)

11-Teena; Ogden Whitney-c
12,15-Teena
13-Guns of Fact & Fiction (1948). Used in **SOTI**, pg. 19; Ingels & Johnny Craig-a
14-Tim Holt Western Adventures #1
16-Vacation Comics; The Pixies, Tom Tom, Flying Fredd, & Koko & Kola
17-Tim Holt #2; photo-c; last issue to carry A-1 on cover (9-10/48)
18,20-Jimmy Durante; photo covers on both
19-Tim Holt #3; photo-c
21-Joan of Arc (1949)-Movie adaptation; Ingrid Bergman photo-covers & interior photos; Whitney-a
22-Dick Powell (1949)-Photo-c
23-Cowboys and Indians #6; Doc Holiday-c/story
24-Trail Colt #1-Frazetta-r in-Manhunt #13; Ingels-c; L. B. Cole-a
25-Fibber McGee & Molly (1949) (Radio)
26-Trail Colt #2-Ingels-c
27-Ghost Rider #1(1950)-Origin
28-Christmas-(Koko & Kola #6) ("50)
29-Ghost Rider #2-Frazetta-c (1950)
30-Jet Powers #1-Powell-a
31-Ghost Rider #3-Frazetta-c & origin ('51)
32-Jet Powers #2
33-Muggsy Mouse #1('51)
34-Ghost Rider #4-Frazetta-c (1951)
35-Jet Powers #3-Williamson/Evans-a
36-Muggsy Mouse #2; Racist-c
37-Ghost Rider #5-Frazetta-c (1951)
38-Jet Powers #4-Williamson/Wood-a
39-Muggsy Mouse #3
40-Dogface Dooley #1('51)
41-Cowboys 'N' Indians #7 (1951)
42-Best of the West #1-Powell-a
43-Dogface Dooley #2
44-Ghost Rider #6
45-American Air Forces #5-Powell-c/a
46-Best of the West #2
47-Thun'da, King of the Congo #1-Frazetta-c/a('52)
48-Cowboys 'N' Indians #8
49-Dogface Dooley #3
50-Danger Is Their Business #11 ('52)-Powell-a
51-Ghost Rider #7 ('52)
52-Best of the West #3

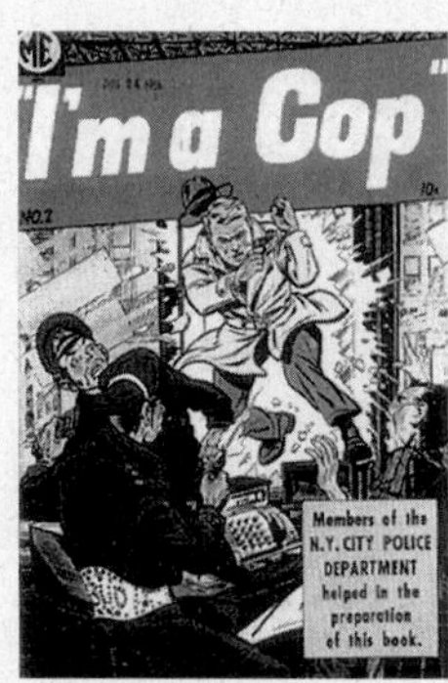

A-1 Comics #126 © ME

Aphrodite IX V2 #3 © TCOW

Approved Comics #3 © STJ

	GD 2.0	VG 4.0	FN 6.0	VF 8.0	VF/NM 9.0	NM- 9.2

53-Dogface Dooley #4
55-U.S. Marines #5-Powell-a
56-Thun'da #2-Powell-c/a
58-American Air Forces #7-Powell-a
60-The U.S. Marines #6-Powell-a
62-Starr Flagg, Undercover Girl #5 (#1) reprinted from A-1 #24
65-American Air Forces #8-Powell-a
67-American Air Forces #9-Powell-a
69-Ghost Rider #9(10/52)
71-Ghost Rider #10(12/52)- Vs. Frankenstein
74-American Air Forces #10-Powell-a
76-Best of the West #7
78-Thun'da #4-Powell-c/a
80-Ghost Rider #12(6/52)- One-eyed Devil-c
83-Thun'da #5-Powell-c/a
84-Ghost Rider #13(7-8/53)
86-Thun'da #6-Powell-c/a
88-Bobby Benson's B-Bar-B Riders #20
90-Red Hawk #11(1953)-Powell-c/a
91-American Air Forces #12-Powell-a
93-Great Western #8('54)-Origin The Ghost Rider; Powell-a
95-Muggsy Mouse #4
96-Cave Girl #12, with Thun'da; Powell-c/a
99-Muggsy Mouse #5
101-White Indian #12-Frazetta-a(r)
101-Dream Book of Romance #6 (4-6/54); Marlon Brando photo-c; Powell, Bolle, Guardineer-a
105-Great Western #9-Ghost Rider app.; Powell-a, 6 pgs.; Bolle-c
107-Hot Dog #1
108-Red Fox #15 (1954)-L.B. Cole-c/a; Powell-a
110-Dream Book of Romance #8 (10/54)-Movie photo-c
112-Ghost Rider #14 ('54)
114-Dream Book of Love #2- Guardineer, Bolle-a; Piper Laurie, Victor Mature photo-c
118-Undercover Girl #7-Powell-c
120-Badmen of the West #2
121-Mysteries of Scotland Yard #1; reprinted from Manhunt (5 stories)
124-Dream Book of Romance #8 (10-11/54)
126-I'm a Cop #2-Powell-a
128-I'm a Cop #3-Powell-a
130-Strongman #1-Powell-a (2-3/55)
132-Strongman #2
134-Strongman #3
136-Hot Dog #4
138-The Avenger #4-Powell-c/a

54-American Air Forces #6(8/52)- Powell-a
57-Ghost Rider #8
59-Best of the West #4
61-Space Ace #5('53)-Guardineer-a
63-Manhunt #13-Frazetta
64-Dogface Dooley #5
66-Best of the West #5
68-U.S. Marines #7-Powell-a
70-Best of the West #6
72-U.S. Marines #8-Powell-a(3)
73-Thun'da #3-Powell-c/a
75-Ghost Rider #11(3/52)
77-Manhunt #14
79-American Air Forces #11-Powell-a
81-Best of the West #8
82-Cave Girl #11(1953)-Powell-c/a; origin (#1)
85-Best of the West #9
87-Best of the West #10(9-10/53)
89-Home Run #3-Powell-a; Stan Musial photo-c
92-Dream Book of Romance #5- Photo-c; Guardineer-a
94-White Indian #11-Frazetta-a(r); Powell-c
97-Best of the West #11
98-Undercover Girl #6-Powell-c
100-Badmen of the West #1- Meskin-a(?)
103-Best of the West #12-Powell-a
104-White Indian #13-Frazetta-a(r) ('54)
106-Dream Book of Love #1 (6-7/54) -Powell, Bolle-a; Montgomery Clift, Donna Reed photo-c
109-Dream Book of Romance #7 (7-8/54). Powell-a; movie photo-c
111-I'm a Cop #1 ('54); drug mention story; Powell-a
113-Great Western #10; Powell-a
115-Hot Dog #3
116-Cave Girl #13-Powell-c/a
117-White Indian #14
119-Straight Arrow's Fury #1 (origin); Fred Meagher-c/a
122-Black Phantom #1 (11/54)
123-Dream Book of Love #3 (10-11/54)-Movie photo-c
125-Cave Girl #14-Powell-c/a
127-Great Western #11('54)-Powell-a
129-The Avenger #1('55)-Powell-c
131-The Avenger #2('55)-Powell-c/a
133-The Avenger #3-Powell-c/a
135-White Indian #15
137-Africa #1-Powell-c/a(4)
139-Strongman #4-Powell-a

NOTE: ***Bolle** a-110. Photo-c-17-22, 89, 92, 101, 106, 109, 110, 114, 123, 124.*

APACHE
Fiction House Magazines: 1951

	GD	VG	FN	VF	VF/NM	NM-
1	22	44	66	132	216	300
I.W. Reprint No. 1-r/#1 above	3	6	9	17	26	35

APACHE KID (Formerly Reno Browne; Western Gunfighters #20 on)
(Also see Two-Gun Western & Wild Western)
Marvel/Atlas Comics(MPC No. 53-10/CPS No. 11 on): No. 53, 12/50 - No. 10, 1/52; No. 11, 12/54 - No. 19, 4/56

	GD	VG	FN	VF	VF/NM	NM-
53(#1)-Apache Kid & his horse Nightwind (origin), Red Hawkins by Syd Shores begins	36	72	108	211	343	475
2(2/51)	18	36	54	105	165	225
3-5	14	28	42	76	108	140
6-10 (1951-52): 7-Russ Heath-a	11	22	33	64	90	115
11-19 (1954-56)	10	20	30	54	72	90

NOTE: ***Heath** a-7. c-11, 13. **Maneely** a-53; c-53(#1), 12, 14-16. **Powell** a-14. **Severin** c-17.*

APACHE MASSACRE (See Chief Victorio's...)

APACHE SKIES
Marvel Comics: Sept, 2002 - No. 4, Dec, 2002 ($2.99, limited series)

1-4-Apache Kid app.; Ostrander-s/Manco-c/a 3.00
TPB (2003, $12.99) r/#1-4 13.00

APACHE TRAIL
Steinway/America's Best: Sept, 1957 - No. 4, June, 1958

	GD	VG	FN	VF	VF/NM	NM-
1	11	22	33	62	86	110
2-4: 2-Tuska-a	8	16	24	40	50	60

APE (Magazine)
Dell Publishing Co.: 1961 (52 pgs., B&W)

	GD	VG	FN	VF	VF/NM	NM-
1-Comics and humor	4	8	12	27	44	60

APHRODITE IX
Image Comics (Top Cow): Sept, 2000 - No. 4, Mar, 2002 ($2.50)

1-3: 1-Four covers by Finch, Turner, Silvestri, Benitez 4.00
1-Tower Record Ed.; Finch-c 3.00
1-DF Chrome ($14.99) 15.00
4-($4.95) Double-sized issue; Finch-c 5.00
Convention Preview 10.00
...: Time Out of Mind TPB (6/04, $14.99) r/#1-4, & #0; cover gallery 15.00
Wizard #0 (4/00, bagged w/Tomb Raider magazine) Preview & sketchbook 5.00
#0-(6/01, $2.95) r/Wizard #0 with cover gallery 3.00

APHRODITE IX (Volume 2)
Image Comics (Top Cow): May, 2013 - Present ($2.99)

1-Free Comic Book Day giveaway; Hawkins-s/Sejic-a 3.00
2-9-($2.99) Hawkins-s/Sejic-a 3.00
... Hidden Files 1 (1/14, $2.99) Character profiles; Sejic-a 3.00

A+X (Avengers Plus X-Men)
Marvel Comics: Dec, 2012 - No. 18, May, 2014 ($3.99)

1-18: 1-Hulk & Wolverine team-up; Keown-c. 2-Black Widow/Rogue; Bachalo-c/a. 14-Superior Spider-Man app. 4.00
1-Variant baby-c by Skottie Young 5.00

APOCALYPSE AL
Image Comics: Feb, 2014 - No. 4 ($2.99, B&W)

1-3-Straczynski-s/Kotian-a; 2 covers on each 3.00

APOCALYPSE NERD
Dark Horse Comics: January, 2005 - No. 6, Oct, 2007 ($2.99, B&W)

1-6-Peter Bagge-s/a 3.00

APPARITION
Caliber Comics: 1995 ($3.95, 52 pgs., B&W)

1 ($3.95) 4.00
V2#1-6 ($2.95) 3.00
Visitations 4.00

APPLESEED
Eclipse Comics: Sept, 1988 - Book 4, Vol. 4, Aug, 1991 ($2.50/$2.75/$3.50, 52/68 pgs, B&W)

Book One, Vol. 1-5: 5-(1/89), Book Two, Vol. 1(2/89) -5(7/89): Art Adams-c, Book Three, Vol. 1(8/89) -4 ($2.75), Book Three, Vol. 5 ($3.50), Book Four, Vol. 1 (1/91) - 4 (8/91) ($3.50, 68 pgs.) 6.00

APPLESEED DATABOOK
Dark Horse Comics: Apr, 1994 - No. 2, May, 1994 ($3.50, B&W, limited series)

1,2: 1-Flip book format 4.00

APPROVED COMICS (Also see Blue Ribbon Comics)
St. John Publishing Co. (Most have no c-price): March, 1954 - No. 12, Aug, 1954 (Painted-c on #1-5,7,8,10)

	GD	VG	FN	VF	VF/NM	NM-
1-The Hawk #5-r	10	20	30	56	76	95
2-Invisible Boy (3/54)-Origin; Saunders-c	16	32	48	92	144	195
3-Wild Boy of the Congo #11-r (4/54)	10	20	30	56	76	95
4,5: 4-Kid Cowboy-r. 5-Fly Boy-r	10	20	30	56	76	95
6-Daring Adv.-r (5/54); Krigstein-a(2); Baker-c	14	28	42	76	108	140
7-The Hawk #6-r	10	20	30	56	76	95
8-Crime on the Run (6/54); Powell-a; Saunders-c	10	20	30	56	76	95
9-Western Bandit Trails #3-r, with new-c; Baker-c/a	14	28	42	76	108	140
10-Dinky Duck (Terrytoons)	6	12	18	31	38	45
11-Fightin' Marines #3-r (8/54); Canteen Kate app; Baker-c/a	14	28	42	76	108	140
12-Northwest Mounties #4-r(8/54); new Baker-c	14	28	42	76	108	140

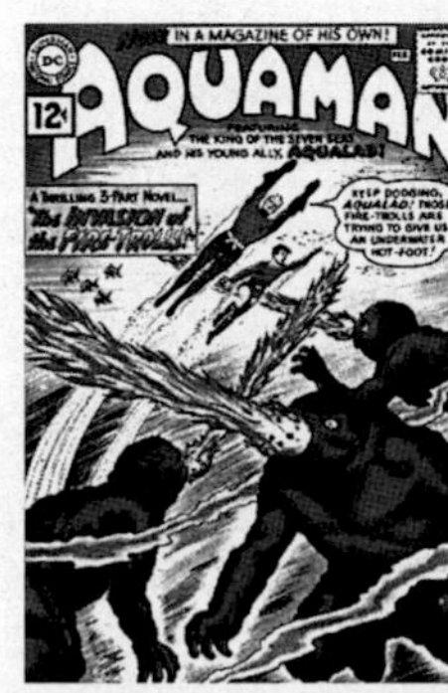

Aquaman #1 © DC

Aquaman (2011 series) #15 © DC

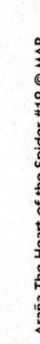

Araña The Heart of the Spider #12 © MAR

AQUAMAN (See Adventure Comics #260, Brave & the Bold, DC Comics Presents #5, DC Special #28, DC Special Series #1, DC Super Stars #7, Detective Comics, JLA, Justice League of America, More Fun #73, Showcase #30-33, Super DC Giant, Super Friends, and World's Finest Comics)

AQUAMAN (1st Series)
National Periodical Publications/DC Comics: Jan-Feb, 1962 - #56, Mar-Apr, 1971; #57, Aug-Sept,1977 - #63, Aug-Sept, 1978

	GD 2.0	VG 4.0	FN 6.0	VF 8.0	VF/NM 9.0	NM- 9.2
1-(1-2/62)-Intro. Quisp	93	186	279	744	1672	2600
2	31	62	93	223	499	775
3-5	18	36	54	128	284	440
6-10	12	24	36	83	182	280
11-1st app. Mera	11	22	33	76	163	250
12-17,19,20	10	20	30	64	132	200
18-Aquaman weds Mera; JLA cameo	10	20	30	69	147	225
21-28,30-32: 23-Birth of Aquababy. 26-Huntress app.(3-4/66). 30-Batman & Superman-c & cameo	6	12	18	42	79	115
29-1st app. Ocean Master, Aquaman's step-brother	8	16	24	51	96	140
33-1st app. Aqua-Girl (see Adventure #266)	7	14	21	46	86	125
34,36-40: 40-Jim Aparo's 1st DC work (8/68)	5	10	15	35	63	90
35-1st app. Black Manta	13	26	39	89	195	300
41-46,47,49: 45-Last 12¢-c	5	10	15	31	53	75
48-Origin reprinted	5	10	15	33	57	80
50-52-Deadman by Neal Adams	8	16	24	51	96	140
53-56('71): 56-1st app. Crusader; last 15¢-c	3	6	9	17	26	35
57('77)-63: 58-Origin retold	2	3	4	6	8	10
...: Death of a Prince TPB (2011, $29.99) r/#58-63 and Adventure #435-437,441-455						30.00

NOTE: ***Aparo** a-40-45, 46p, 47-59; c-58-63. **Nick Cardy** c-1-40. **Newton** a-60-63.*

AQUAMAN (1st limited series)
DC Comics: Feb, 1986 - No. 4, May, 1986 (75¢, limited series)

	GD 2.0	VG 4.0	FN 6.0	VF 8.0	VF/NM 9.0	NM- 9.2
1-New costume; 1st app. Nuada of Thierna Na Oge	1	2	3	4	5	7
2-4: 3-Retelling of Aquaman & Ocean Master's origins.						5.00
Special 1 (1988, $1.50, 52 pgs.)						4.00

NOTE: ***Craig Hamilton** c/a-1-4p. **Russell** c-2-4i.*

AQUAMAN (2nd limited series)
DC Comics: June, 1989 - No. 5, Oct, 1989 ($1.00, limited series)

	GD 2.0	VG 4.0	FN 6.0	VF 8.0	VF/NM 9.0	NM- 9.2
1-5: Giffen plots/breakdowns; Swan-a(p).						4.00
Special 1 (Legend of..., $2.00, 1989, 52 pgs.)-Giffen plots/breakdowns; Swan-a(p)						4.00

AQUAMAN (2nd Series)
DC Comics: Dec, 1991 - No. 13, Dec, 1992 ($1.00/$1.25)

	GD 2.0	VG 4.0	FN 6.0	VF 8.0	VF/NM 9.0	NM- 9.2
1-5						3.00
6-13: 6-Begin $1.25-c. 9-Sea Devils app.						3.00

AQUAMAN (3rd Series)(Also see Atlantis Chronicles)
DC Comics: Aug, 1994 - No. 75, Jan, 2001 ($1.50/$1.75/$1.95/$1.99/$2.50)

	GD 2.0	VG 4.0	FN 6.0	VF 8.0	VF/NM 9.0	NM- 9.2
1-(8/94)-Peter David scripts begin; reintro Dolphin						6.00
2-(9/94)-Aquaman loses hand						6.50
0-(10/94)-Aquaman replaces lost hand with hook.						6.50
3-8: 3-(11/94)-Superboy-c/app. 4-Lobo app. 6-Deep Six app.						3.50
9-69: 9-Begin $1.75-c. 10-Green Lantern app. 11-Reintro Mera. 15-Re-intro Kordax. 16-vs. JLA. 18-Reintro Ocean Master & Atlan (Aquaman's father). 19-Reintro Garth (Aqualad). 23-1st app. Deep Blue (Neptune Perkins & Tsunami's daughter). 23,24-Neptune Perkins, Nuada, Tsunami, Arion, Power Girl, & The Sea Devils app. 26-Final Night. 28-Martian Manhunter-c/app. 29-Black Manta-c/app. 32-Swamp Thing-c/app. 37-Genesis x-over. 41-Maxima-c/app. 43-Millennium Giants x-over; Superman-c/app. 44-G.A. Flash & Sentinel app. 50-Larsen-s begins. 53-Superman app. 60-Tempest marries Dolphin; Teen Titans app. 63-Kaluta covers begin. 66-JLA app.						3.00
70-75: 70-Begin $2.50-c. 71-73-Warlord-c/app. 75-Final issue						3.00
#1,000,000 (11/98) 853rd Century x-over						3.00
Annual 1 (1995, $3.50)-Year One story						4.00
Annual 2 (1996, $2.95)-Legends of the Dead Earth story						4.00
Annual 3 (1997, $3.95)-Pulp Heroes story						4.00
Annual 4,5 ('98, '99, $2.95)-4-Ghosts; Wrightson-c. 5-JLApe						4.00
...Secret Files 1 (12/98, $4.95) Origin-s and pin-ups						5.00

NOTE: ***Art Adams**-c, Annual 5. **Mignola** c-6. **Simonson** c-15.*

AQUAMAN (4th Series)(Titled Aquaman: Sword of Atlantis #40-on) (Also see JLA #69-75)
DC Comics: Feb, 2003 - No. 57, Dec, 2007 ($2.50/$2.99)

	GD 2.0	VG 4.0	FN 6.0	VF 8.0	VF/NM 9.0	NM- 9.2
1-Veitch-s/Guichet-a/Maleev-c						4.00
2-14: 2-Martian Manhunter app. 8-11-Black Manta app.						3.00
15-39: 15-San Diego flooded; Pfeifer-s/Davis-c begin. 23,24-Sea Devils app. 33-Mera returns. 39-Black Manta app.						3.00
40-Sword of Atlantis; One Year Later begins ($2.99-c) Guice-a ; two covers						4.00
41-49,51-57: 41-Two covers. 42-Sea Devils app. 44-Ocean Master app.						3.00
50-($3.99) Tempest app.; McManus-a						4.00
...Secret Files 2003 (5/03, $4.95) background on Aquaman's new powers; pin-ups						5.00
...: Once and Future TPB (2006, $12.99) r/#40-45						13.00
...: The Waterbearer TPB (2003, $12.95) r/#1-4, stories from Aquaman Secret Files and JLA/JSA Secret Files #1; JG Jones-c						13.00

AQUAMAN (DC New 52)
DC Comics: Nov, 2011 - Present ($2.99)

	GD 2.0	VG 4.0	FN 6.0	VF 8.0	VF/NM 9.0	NM- 9.2
1-23,24: 1-Geoff Johns-s/Ivan Reis-a/c. 7-13-Black Manta app. 14-17-Throne of Atlantis. 15,16-Justice League app. 24-Story of Atlan						3.00
23.1, 23.2 (11/13, $2.99, regular covers)						3.00
23.1 (11/13, $3.99, 3-D cover) "Black Manta #1" on cover; Crime Syndicate app.						5.00
23.2 (11/13, $3.99, 3-D cover) "Ocean Master #1" on cover; Crime Syndicate app.						5.00
25-($3.99) "Death of a King" finale; last Johns-s						4.00
26-29: 26-Parker-s/Pelletier-a begin					3.00	
#0 (11/12, $2.99) Aquaman & Vulko's return to Atlantis; Johns-s/Reis-a/c						3.00
Annual 1 (12/13, $4.99) The Others app.; Pelletier-c/Ostrander-s						5.00

AQUAMAN AND THE OTHERS (DC New 52)
DC Comics: Jun, 2014 - Present ($2.99)

	GD 2.0	VG 4.0	FN 6.0	VF 8.0	VF/NM 9.0	NM- 9.2
1-Jurgens-s/Medina-a						3.00

AQUAMAN: TIME & TIDE (3rd limited series) (Also see Atlantis Chronicles)
DC Comics: Dec, 1993 - No. 4, Mar, 1994 ($1.50, limited series)

	GD 2.0	VG 4.0	FN 6.0	VF 8.0	VF/NM 9.0	NM- 9.2
1-4: Peter David scripts; origin retold.						3.00
Trade paperback ($9.95)						10.00

AQUANAUTS (TV)
Dell Publishing Co.: May - July, 1961

	GD 2.0	VG 4.0	FN 6.0	VF 8.0	VF/NM 9.0	NM- 9.2
Four Color 1197-Photo-c	6	12	18	40	73	105

ARABIAN NIGHTS (See Cinema Comics Herald)

ARACHNOPHOBIA (Movie)
Hollywood Comics (Disney Comics): 1990 ($5.95, 68 pg. graphic novel)

	GD 2.0	VG 4.0	FN 6.0	VF 8.0	VF/NM 9.0	NM- 9.2
nn-Adaptation of film; Spiegle-a						6.00
Comic edition ($2.95, 68 pgs.)						4.00

ARAK/SON OF THUNDER (See Warlord #48)
DC Comics: Sept, 1981 - No. 50, Nov, 1985

	GD 2.0	VG 4.0	FN 6.0	VF 8.0	VF/NM 9.0	NM- 9.2
1,24,50: 1-1st app. Angelica, Princess of White Cathay. 24,50-(52 pgs.)						4.00
2-23,25-49: 3-Intro Valda. 12-Origin Valda. 20-Origin Angelica						3.00
Annual 1(10/84)						4.00

ARAÑA THE HEART OF THE SPIDER (See Amazing Fantasy (2004) #1-6)
Marvel Comics: March, 2005 - No. 12, Feb, 2006 ($2.99)

	GD 2.0	VG 4.0	FN 6.0	VF 8.0	VF/NM 9.0	NM- 9.2
1-12: 1-Avery-s/Cruz-a. 4-Spider-Man-c/app.						3.00
Vol. 1: Heart of the Spider (2005, $7.99, digest) r/Amazing Fantasy (2004) #1-6						8.00
Vol. 2: In the Beginning (2005, $7.99, digest) r/#1-6						8.00
Vol. 3: Night of the Hunter (2006, $7.99, digest) r/#7-12						8.00

ARCANA (Also see Books of Magic limited & ongoing series and Mister E)
DC Comics (Vertigo): 1994 ($3.95, 68 pgs., annual)

	GD 2.0	VG 4.0	FN 6.0	VF 8.0	VF/NM 9.0	NM- 9.2
1-Bolton painted-c; Children's Crusade/Tim Hunter story						4.00

ARCANUM
Image Comics (Top Cow Productions): Apr, 1997 - No. 8, Feb, 1998 ($2.50)

	GD 2.0	VG 4.0	FN 6.0	VF 8.0	VF/NM 9.0	NM- 9.2
1/2 Gold Edition						12.00
1-Brandon Peterson-s/a(p), 1-Variant-c, 4-American Ent. Ed.						3.50
2-8						3.00
3-Variant-c						4.00
...: Millennium's End TPB (2005, $16.99) r/#1-8 & #1/2; cover gallery and sketch pages						17.00

ARCHANGEL (See Uncanny X-Men, X-Factor & X-Men)
Marvel Comics: Feb, 1996 ($2.50, B&W, one-shot)

	GD 2.0	VG 4.0	FN 6.0	VF 8.0	VF/NM 9.0	NM- 9.2
1-Milligan story						3.00

ARCHARD'S AGENTS (See Ruse)
CrossGeneration Comics: Jan, 2003; Nov, 2003; Apr, 2004 ($2.95)

	GD 2.0	VG 4.0	FN 6.0	VF 8.0	VF/NM 9.0	NM- 9.2
1-Dixon-s/Perkins-a						3.00
...: The Case of the Puzzled Pugilist (11/03) Dixon-s/Perkins-a						3.00
Vol. 3 - Deadly Dare (4/04) Dixon-s/McNiven-a; preview of Lady Death: The Wild Hunt						3.00

ARCHENEMIES
Dark Horse Comics: Apr, 2006 - No. 4, July, 2006 ($2.99, limited series)

	GD 2.0	VG 4.0	FN 6.0	VF 8.0	VF/NM 9.0	NM- 9.2
1-4-Melbourne-s/Guichet-a						3.00

ARCHER & ARMSTRONG
Valiant: July (June inside), 1992 - No. 26, Oct, 1994 ($2.50)

	GD 2.0	VG 4.0	FN 6.0	VF 8.0	VF/NM 9.0	NM- 9.2
0-(7/92)-B. Smith-c/a; Reese-i assists						5.00

Archer & Armstrong #13 © VAL

Archie & Friends #47 © AP

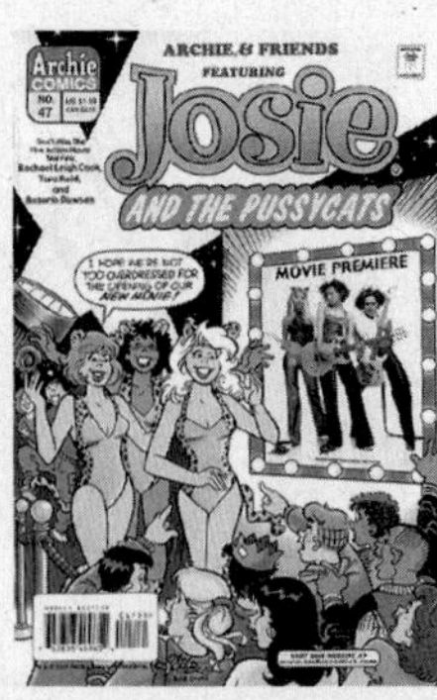

Archie Comics #4 © AP

	GD 2.0	VG 4.0	FN 6.0	VF 8.0	VF/NM 9.0	NM- 9.2
0-(with Gold Valiant Logo)	2	4	6	8	10	15
1,2: 1-(8/92)-Origin & 1st app. Archer; Miller-c; B. Smith/Layton-a. 2-2nd app. Turok (c/story); Smith/Layton-a; Simonson-c						5.00
3-7: 3,4-Smith-c&a(p) & scripts						4.00
8-($4.50, 52 pgs.)-Combined with Eternal Warrior #8; B. Smith-c/a & scripts; 1st app. Ivar the Time Walker						5.00
9-26: 10-2nd app. Ivar. 10,11-B. Smith-c. 21,22-Shadowman app. 22-w/bound-in trading card. 25-Eternal Warrior app. 26-Flip book w/Eternal Warrior #26						3.00
...: First Impressions HC (2008, $24.95) recolored reprints #0-6; new "Formation of the Sect" story by Jim Shooter and Sal Velutto; Shooter commentary; new cover by Golden						25.00

ARCHER & ARMSTRONG
Valiant Entertainment: Aug, 2012 - Present ($3.99)

	GD	VG	FN	VF	VF/NM	NM-
1-19: 1-Van Lente-s/Henry-a; two covers; origin. 5-8-Eternal Warrior app.						4.00
1,4-8-Pullbox variants: 1-Clayton Henry. 4-Juan Doe. 7,8-Emanuela Lupacchino						4.00
1-Variant-c by David Aja						10.00
1-Variant-c by Neal Adams						20.00
#0-(5/13, $3.99) Van Lente-s/Henry-a						4.00
...Archer #0-(2/14, $3.99) Van Lente-s/Pere Pérez-a; childhood origin						4.00

ARCHIE (See Archie Comics) (Also see Christmas & Archie, Everything's..., Explorers of the Unknown, Jackpot, Life With..., Little..., Oxydol-Dreft, Pep, Riverdale High, Teenage Mutant Ninja Turtles Adventures & To Riverdale and Back Again)

ARCHIE ALL CANADIAN DIGEST
Archie Publications: Aug, 1996 ($1.75, 96 pgs.)

	GD	VG	FN	VF	VF/NM	NM-
1	1	2	3	5	6	8

ARCHIE AMERICANA SERIES, BEST OF THE FORTIES
Archie Publications: 1991, 2002 ($10.95, trade paperback)

	GD	VG	FN	VF	VF/NM	NM-
Vol. 1,2-r/early strips from 1940s 1-Intro. by Steven King. 2-Intro. by Paul Castiglia						12.00

ARCHIE AMERICANA SERIES, BEST OF THE FIFTIES
Archie Publications: 1991 ($8.95, trade paperback)

	GD	VG	FN	VF	VF/NM	NM-
Vol. 2-r/strips from 1950's;						12.00
2nd printing (1998, $9.95)						12.00
Book 2 (2003, $10.95)						12.00

ARCHIE AMERICANA SERIES, BEST OF THE SIXTIES
Archie Publications: 1995 ($9.95, trade paperback)

	GD	VG	FN	VF	VF/NM	NM-
Vol. 3-r/strips from 1960s; intro. by Frankie Avalon.						12.00

ARCHIE AMERICANA SERIES, BEST OF THE SEVENTIES
Archie Publications: 1997, 2008 ($9.95/$10.95, trade paperback)

	GD	VG	FN	VF	VF/NM	NM-
Vol. 4 (1997, $9.95)-r/strips from 1970s						12.00
Vol. 8 Book 2 (2008, $10.95)-r/other strips from 1970s						12.00

ARCHIE AMERICANA SERIES, BEST OF THE EIGHTIES
Archie Publications: 2001 ($10.95, trade paperback)

	GD	VG	FN	VF	VF/NM	NM-
Vol. 5-r/strips from 1980s; foreward by Steve Geppi						12.00

ARCHIE AMERICANA SERIES, BEST OF THE '90S
Archie Publications: 2008 ($11.95, trade paperback)

	GD	VG	FN	VF	VF/NM	NM-
Vol. 9-r/strips from 1990s; new Lindsey cover						12.00

ARCHIE AND BIG ETHEL
Spire Christian Comics (Fleming H. Revell Co.): 1982 (69¢)

	GD	VG	FN	VF	VF/NM	NM-
nn-(Low print run)	2	4	6	13	18	22

ARCHIE & FRIENDS
Archie Comics: Dec, 1992 - No. 159, Feb, 2012 ($1.25-$2.99)

	GD	VG	FN	VF	VF/NM	NM-
1						5.00
2,4,10-14,17,18,20-Sabrina app. 20-Archie's Band-c						4.00
3,5-9,16						3.00
15-Babewatch-s with Sabrina app.						6.00
19-Josie and the Pussycats app.; E.T. parody-c/s						5.00
21-46						3.00
47-All Josie and the Pussycats issue; movie and actress profiles/photos						4.00
48-142: 48-56,58,60,96-Josie and the Pussycats-c/s. 79-Cheryl Blossom returns. 100-The Veronicas-c/app. 101-Katy Keene begins. 129-Begin $2.50. 130,131-Josie and the Pussycats. 137-Cosmo, Super Duck, Pat the Brat and other old characters app.						3.00
143-159: 143-Begin $2.99-c. 145-Jersey Shore spoof. 146,147-Twilite. 154-Little Archie						3.00

ARCHIE & FRIENDS DOUBLE DIGEST MAGAZINE
Archie Comics: Feb, 2011 - No. 33, Jan, 2014 ($3.99, digest-size)

	GD	VG	FN	VF	VF/NM	NM-
1-32: 1-Staton-a. 7-13-SuperTeens app.						4.00
33-($5.99, 320 pages) Double Double Digest						6.00

ARCHIE AND ME (See Archie Giant Series Mag. #578, 591, 603, 616, 626)
Archie Publications: Oct, 1964 - No. 161, Feb, 1987

GD VG FN VF VF/NM NM- 2.0 4.0 6.0 8.0 9.0 9.2

	GD	VG	FN	VF	VF/NM	NM-
1	14	28	42	96	211	325
2	8	16	24	56	108	160
3-5	6	12	18	40	73	105
6-10	5	10	15	30	50	70
11-20	3	6	9	21	33	45
21(6/68)-26,28-30: 21-UFO story. 26-X-Mas-c	3	6	9	16	24	32
27-Groovyman & Knowman superhero-s; UFO-sty	3	6	9	19	30	40
31-42: 37-Japan Expo '70-c/s	3	6	9	14	19	24
43-48,50-63-(All Giants): 43-(8/71) Mummy-s. 44-Mermaid-s. 62-Elvis cameo-c. 63-(2/74)	3	6	9	15	22	28
49-(Giant) Josie & the Pussycats-c/app.	3	6	9	20	31	42
64-66,68-99-(Regular size): 85-Bicentennial-s. 98-Collectors Comics	2	4	6	8	10	12
67-Sabrina app.(8/74)	2	4	6	10	14	18
100-(4/78)	2	4	6	8	11	14
101-120: 107-UFO-s	1	2	3	5	6	8
121(8/80)-159: 134-Riverdale 2001						6.00
160,161: 160-Origin Mr. Weatherbee; Caveman Archie gang story. 161-Last issue	1	2	3	5	6	8

ARCHIE AND MR. WEATHERBEE
Spire Christian Comics (Fleming H. Revell Co.): 1980 (59¢)

	GD	VG	FN	VF	VF/NM	NM-
nn - (Low print run)	2	4	6	13	18	22

ARCHIE...ARCHIE ANDREWS, WHERE ARE YOU? (...Comics Digest #9, 10; ...Comics Digest Mag. No. 11 on)
Archie Publications: Feb, 1977 - No. 114, May, 1998 (Digest size, 160-128 pgs., quarterly)

	GD	VG	FN	VF	VF/NM	NM-
1	3	6	9	17	26	35
2,3,5,7-9-N. Adams-a; 8-r-/origin The Fly by S&K. 9-Steel Sterling-r	2	4	6	10	14	18
4,6,10 ($1.00/$1.50)	2	4	6	8	11	14
11-20: 17-Katy Keene story	2	3	4	6	8	10
21-50,100	1	2	3	5	6	8
51-70						4.00
71-99,101-114: 113-Begin $1.95-c						3.00

ARCHIE AS PUREHEART THE POWERFUL (Also see Archie Giant Series #142, Jughead as Captain Hero, Life With Archie & Little Archie)
Archie Publications (Radio Comics): Sept, 1966 - No. 6, Nov, 1967

	GD	VG	FN	VF	VF/NM	NM-
1-Super hero parody	10	20	30	68	144	220
2	6	12	18	41	76	110
3-6	6	12	18	37	66	95

NOTE: *Evilheart cameos in all. Title: Archie As Pureheart the Powerful #1-3; ...As Capt. Pureheart-#4-6.*

ARCHIE AT RIVERDALE HIGH (See Archie Giant Series Magazine #573, 586, 604 & Riverdale High)
Archie Publications: Aug, 1972 - No. 113, Feb, 1987

	GD	VG	FN	VF	VF/NM	NM-
1	6	12	18	38	69	100
2	4	8	12	23	37	50
3-5	3	6	9	16	23	30
6-10	2	4	6	11	16	20
11-30	2	4	6	8	10	12
31(12/75)-46,48-50(12/77)	1	3	4	6	8	10
47-Archie in drag-s; Betty mud wrestling-s	2	4	6	10	14	18
51-80,100 (12/84)	1	2	3	5	6	8
81(8/81)-88, 91,93-95,98						6.00
89,90-Early Cheryl Blossom app. 90-Archies Band app.	3	6	9	14	20	26
92,96,97,99-Cheryl Blossom app. 96-Anti-smoking issue	2	4	6	11	16	20
101,102,104-109,111,112: 102-Ghost-c						6.00
103-Archie dates Cheryl Blossom-s	2	4	6	11	16	20
110,113: 110-Godzilla-s. 113-Last issue	1	2	3	5	6	8

ARCHIE COMICS (See Pep Comics #22 [12/41] for Archie's debut) (1st Teen-age comic; Radio show first aired 6/2/45 by NBC)
MLJ Magazines No. 1-19/Archie Publ. No. 20 on: Winter, 1942-43 - No. 19, 3-4/46; No. 20, 5-6/46 - Present

	GD	VG	FN	VF	VF/NM	NM-
1 (Scarce)-Jughead, Veronica app.; 1st app. Mrs. Andrews	8000	16,000	24,000	60,000	97,500	135,000
2 (Scarce)	1000	2000	3000	7600	13,800	20,000
3 (60 pgs.)(scarce)	622	1244	1866	4541	8021	11,500
4,5: 4-Article about Archie radio series. 5-Halloween-c	411	822	1233	2877	5039	7200
6,8-10: 6-X-Mas-c. 9-1st Miss Grundy cover	271	542	813	1734	2967	4200
7-1st definitive love triangle story	300	600	900	2010	3505	5000

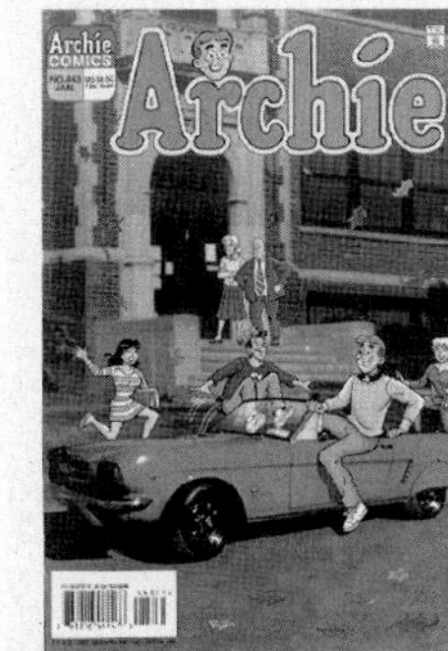

Archie Comics #443 © AP

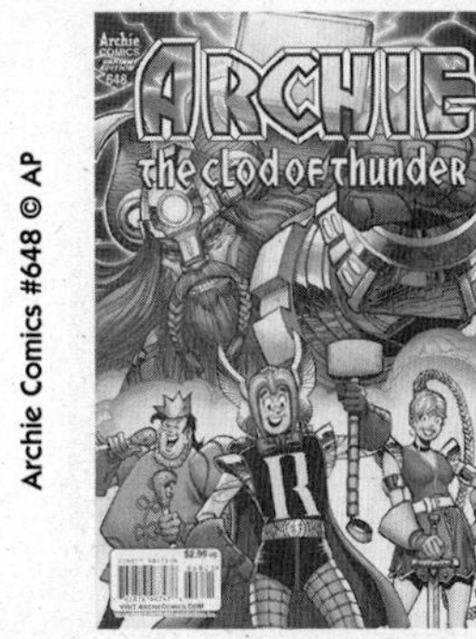

Archie Comics #648 © AP

Archie Comics Digest #160 © AP

GD 2.0 | VG 4.0 | FN 6.0 | VF 8.0 | VF/NM 9.0 | NM- 9.2

11-15: 15-Dotty & Ditto by Woggon 155 310 465 992 1696 2400
16-20: 15,17,18-Dotty & Ditto by Woggon. 16,19-Woggon-a. 18-Halloween pumpkin-c.
142 284 426 909 1555 2200
21-30: 23-Betty & Veronica by Woggon. 25-Woggon-a. 30-Coach Piffle app., a Coach Kleats prototype. 34-Pre-Dilton try-out (named Dilbert) 86 172 258 546 936 1325
31-40 52 104 156 328 552 775
41-49 40 80 120 246 411 575
50-Classic-c 65 130 195 416 708 1000
51-60 17 34 51 117 259 400
61-70 (1954): 65-70, Katy Keene app. 12 24 36 82 179 275
71-80: 72-74-Katy Keene app. 10 20 30 69 147 225
81-93,95-99 9 18 27 58 114 170
94-1st Coach Kleats in this title (see Pep #24) 9 18 27 62 126 190
100 10 20 30 64 132 200
101-122,126,128-130 (1962) 6 12 18 38 69 100
123-125,127-Horror/SF covers. 123-UFO-c/s 8 16 24 51 96 140
131,132,134-157,159,160: 137-1st Caveman Archie gang story
4 8 12 25 40 55
133 (12/62)-1st app. Cricket O'Dell 4 8 12 28 47 65
158-Archie in drag story 4 8 12 27 44 60
161(2/66)-184,186-188,190-195,197-199: 168-Superhero gag-c. 176,178-Twiggy-c
183-Caveman Archie gang story 3 6 9 17 26 35
185-1st "The Archies" Band story 4 8 12 25 40 55
189 (3/69)-Archie's band meets Don Kirshner who developed the Monkees
3 6 9 19 30 40
196 (12/69)-Early Cricket O'Dell app. 3 6 9 19 30 40
200 (6/70) 3 6 9 18 28 38
201-230(11/73): 213-Sabrina/Josie-c cameos. 229-Lost Child issue
2 4 6 11 16 20
231-260(3/77): 253-Tarzan parody 2 4 6 8 11 14
261-282, 284-299 1 3 4 6 8 10
283(8/79)-Cover/story plugs "International Children's Appeal" which was a fraudulent charity, according to TV's 20/20 news program broadcast July 20, 1979
2 4 6 8 10 12
300(1/81)-Anniversary issue 2 4 6 8 11 14
301-321,323-325,327-335,337-350: 323-Cheryl Blossom pin-up. 325-Cheryl Blossom app. 6.00
322-E.T. story 1 2 3 5 6 8
326-Early Cheryl Blossom story 2 4 6 11 16 20
336-Michael Jackson/Boy George parody 2 4 6 8 10 12
351-399: 356-Calgary Olympics Special. 393-Infinity-c; 1st comic book printed on recycled paper 5.00
400 (6/92)-Shows 1st meeting of Little Archie and Veronica 6.00
401-428 4.00
429-Love Showdown part 1 5.00
430-599: 467- "A Storm Over Uniforms" x-over parts 3,4. 538-Comic-Con issue 3.00
600-602: 600-(10/09) Archie proposes to Veronica. 601-Marries Veronica. 602-Twins born 4.00
603-605: 603-(1/10) Archie proposes to Betty. 604-Marries Betty. 605-Twins born 4.00
606-615,618-626: 609-Begin $2.99-c. 610-613-Man From RIVERDALE. 625-70th Anniversary. 626-Michael Strahan app. 3.00
616,617-Obama & Palin app.; two covers on each 4.00
627-630-Archie Meets KISS; 2 covers on each by Parent & Francavilla 4.00
631-654: 632-634-Archie marries Valerie from the Pussycats. 635-Jill Thompson var-c. 636-Gender swap. 641-644-Crossover with Glee; 2 covers. 648-Simonson var-c. 3.00
650-Variant "Battle of the Bands" cover by Fiona Staples 5.00
Annual 1 ('50)-116 pgs. (Scarce) 284 568 852 1818 3109 4400
Annual 2 ('51) 116 232 348 742 1271 1800
Annual 3 ('52) 66 132 198 419 722 1025
Annual 4,5 (1953-54) 46 92 138 290 488 685
Annual 6-10 (1955-59): 8,9-(100 pgs.). 10-(84 pgs.) Elvis record on-c
15 30 45 103 227 350
Annual 11-15 (1960-65): 12,13-(84 pgs.) 14,15-(68 pgs.)
9 18 27 60 120 180
Annual 16-20 (1966-70)(all 68 pgs.): 20-Archie's band-c
6 12 18 38 69 100
Annual 21,22,24-26 (1971-75): 21,22-(68 pgs.). 22-Archie's band-s.
24-26-(52 pgs.). 25-Cavemen-s 4 8 12 23 37 50
Annual 23-Archie's band-c/s; Josie/Sabrina-c 5 10 15 30 50 70
Annual Digest 27 ('75) 4 8 12 23 37 50
...28-30 3 6 9 14 20 25
...31-34 2 4 6 9 13 16
...35-40 (...Magazine #35 on) 1 3 4 6 8 10
...41-65 ('94) 5.00
...66-69 3.00
...All-Star Specials (Winter '75, $1.25)-6 remaindered Archie comics rebound in each; titles: "The World of Giant Comics", "Giant Grab Bag of Comics", "Triple Giant Comics" & "Giant Spec. Comics 5 10 15 30 50 70
NOTE: *Archies Band-s-185, 188-192, 197, 198, 201, 204, 205, 208, 209, 215, 329, 330; Band-c-191, 330. Cavemen Archie Gang-s-183, 192, 197, 208, 210, 220, 223, 282, 333, 335, 338, 340.* ***Al Fagly*** *c-17-35.* ***Bob Montana*** *c-38, 41-50, 58, Annual 1-4.* ***Bill Woggon*** *c-53, 54.*

ARCHIE COMICS DIGEST (...Magazine No. 37-95)
Archie Publications: Aug, 1973 - No. 267, Nov, 2010 (Digest-size, 160-128 pgs.)

1-1st Archie digest 9 18 27 57 111 165
2 5 10 15 30 50 70
3-5 4 8 12 23 37 50
6-10 3 6 9 16 23 30
11-33: 32,33-The Fly-r by S&K 2 4 6 10 14 18
34-60 1 3 4 6 8 10
61-80,100 1 2 3 5 6 8
81-99 5.00
101-140: 36-Katy Keene story 4.00
141-165 3.00
166-235,237-267: 194-Begin $2.39-c. 225-Begin $2.49-c 3.00
236-65th Anniversary issue, r/1st app. in Pep #22 and entire Archie Comics #1 (1942) 5.00
NOTE: ***Neal Adams*** *a-1, 2, 4, 5, 19-21, 24, 25, 27, 29, 31, 33. X-mas c-88, 94, 100, 106.*

ARCHIE COMICS (Free Comic Book Day editions) (Also see Pep Comics)
Archie Publications: 2003 - Present

... Free Comic Book Day Edition 1,2: 1-(7/03). 2-(9/04) 3.00
Little Archie "The Legend of the Lost Lagoon" FCBD Edition (5/07) Bolling-s/a 3.00
... Presents the Mighty Archie Art Players ('09) Free Comic Book Day giveaway 3.00
...'s 65th Anniversary Bash ('06) Free Comic Book Day giveaway 3.00
...'s Summer Splash FCBD Edition (5/10) Parent-a; Cheryl Blossom app. 3.00

ARCHIE COMICS PRESENTS: THE LOVE SHOWDOWN COLLECTION
Archie Publications: 1994 ($4.95, squarebound)

nn-r/Archie #429, Betty #19, Betty & Veronica #82, & Veronica #39
1 2 3 5 6 8

ARCHIE COMICS SUPER SPECIAL
Archie Publications: Dec, 2012 - Present ($9.99, squarebound magazine-sized, quarterly)

1-3: 1-Christmas themed. 2-Valentine's themed 10.00

ARCHIE DIGEST (Free Comic Book Day edition)
Archie Comic Publications: June/July 2014 (digest-size giveaway)

1-Reprints; Parent-c 3.00

ARCHIE DOUBLE DIGEST (See Archie's Double Digest Quarterly Magazine)

ARCHIE GETS A JOB
Spire Christian Comics (Fleming H. Revell Co.): 1977

nn 2 4 6 13 18 22

ARCHIE GIANT SERIES MAGAZINE
Archie Publications: 1954 - No. 632, July, 1992 (No #36-135, no #252-451)
(#1 not code approved) (#1-233 are Giants; #12-184 are 68 pgs.,#185-194,197-233 are 52 pgs.; #195,196 are 84 pgs.; #234-up are 36 pgs.)

1-Archie's Christmas Stocking 158 316 474 1003 1727 2450
2-Archie's Christmas Stocking('55) 77 154 231 493 847 1200
3-6-Archie's Christmas Stocking('56- '59) 53 106 159 334 567 800
7-10: 7-Katy Keene Holiday Fun(9/60); Bill Woggon-c. 8-Betty & Veronica Summer Fun (10/60); baseball story w/Babe Ruth & Lou Gehrig. 9-The World of Jughead (12/60); Neal Adams-a. 10-Archie's Christmas Stocking(1/61) 39 78 117 240 395 550
11,13,16,18: 11-Betty & Veronica Spectacular (6/61). 13-Betty & Veronica Summer Fun (10/61). 16-Betty & Veronica Spectacular (6/62). 18-Betty & Veronica Summer Fun (10/62)
25 50 75 150 245 340
12,14,15,17,19,20: 12-Katy Keene Holiday Fun (9/61). 14-The World of Jughead (12/61); Vampire-s. 15-Archie's Christmas Stocking (1/62). 17-Archie's Jokes (9/62); Katy Keene app. 19-The World of Jughead (12/62). 20-Archie's Christmas Stocking (1/63)
19 38 57 112 179 245
21,23,28: 21-Betty & Veronica Spectacular (6/63). 23-Betty & Veronica Summer Fun (10/63). 28-Betty & Veronica Summer Fun (9/64) 9 18 27 59 117 175
22,24,25,27,29,30: 22-Archie's Jokes (9/63). 24-The World of Jughead (12/63). 25-Archie's Christmas Stocking (1/64). 27-Archie's Jokes (8/64). 29-Around the World with Archie (10/64); Doris Day-s. 30-The World of Jughead (12/64) 8 16 24 54 102 150
26-Betty & Veronica Spectacular (6/64); all pin-ups; DeCarlo-c/a
9 18 27 60 120 180
31,33-35: 31-Archie's Christmas Stocking (1/65). 33-Archie's Jokes (8/65). 34-Betty & Veronica Summer Fun (9/65). 35-Around the World with Archie (10/65).
6 12 18 38 69 100
32-Betty & Veronica Spectacular (6/65); all pin-ups; DeCarlo-c/a
7 14 21 46 86 125

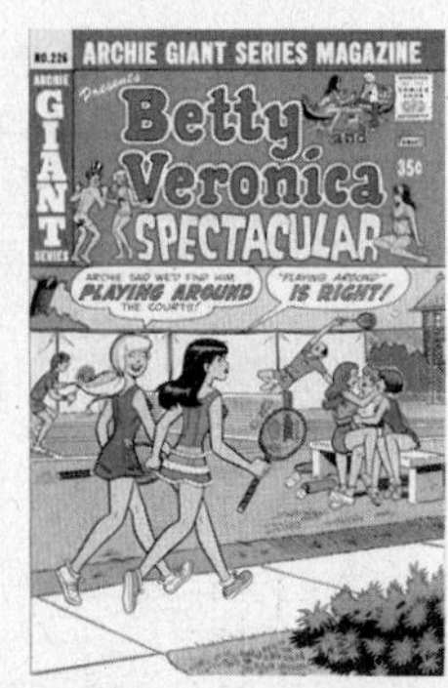

Archie Giant Series #226 © AP

Archie Giant Series #454 © AP

Archie Giant Series #610 © AP

GD 2.0 | VG 4.0 | FN 6.0 | VF 8.0 | VF/NM 9.0 | NM- 9.2

36-135-**Do not exist**

136-141: 136-The World of Jughead (12/65). 137-Archie's Christmas Stocking (1/66). 138-Betty & Veronica Spect. (6/66). 139-Archie's Jokes (6/66). 140-Betty & Veronica Summer Fun (8/66). 141-Around the World with Archie (9/66) 6 12 18 38 69 100

142-Archie's Super-Hero Special (10/66)-Origin Capt. Pureheart, Capt. Hero, and Evilheart 7 14 21 49 92 135

143-The World of Jughead (12/66); Capt. Hero-c/s; Man From R.I.V.E.R.D.A.L.E., Pureheart, Superteen app. 6 12 18 38 69 100

144-160: 144-Archie's Christmas Stocking (1/67). 145-Betty & Veronica Spectacular (6/67). 146-Archie's Jokes (6/67). 147-Betty & Veronica Summer Fun (8/67) 148-World of Archie (9/67). 149-World of Jughead (10/67). 150-Archie's Christmas Stocking (1/68). 151-World of Archie (2/68). 152-World of Jughead (2/68). 153-Betty & Veronica Spectacular (6/68). 154-Archie Jokes (6/68). 155-Betty & Veronica Summer Fun (8/68). 156-World of Archie (10/68). 157-World of Jughead (12/68). 158-Archie's Christmas Stocking (1/69). 159-Betty & Veronica Christmas Spectacular (1/69). 160-World of Archie (2/69); Frankenstein-s each... 4 8 12 23 37 50

161-World of Jughead (2/69); Super-Jughead-s; 11 pg. early Cricket O'Dell-s 4 8 12 25 40 55

162-183: 162-Betty & Veronica Spectacular (6/69). 163-Archie's Jokes(8/69). 164-Betty & Veronica Summer Fun (9/69). 165-World of Archie (9/69). 166-World of Jughead (9/69). 167-Archie's Christmas Stocking (1/70). 168-Betty & Veronica Christmas Spect. (1/70). 169-Archie's Christmas Love-In (1/70). 170-Jughead's Eat-Out Comic Book Mag. (12/69). 171-World of Archie (2/70). 172-World of Jughead (2/70). 173-Betty & Veronica Spectacular (6/70). 174-Archie's Jokes (8/70). 175-Betty & Veronica Summer Fun (9/70). 176-Li'l Jinx Giant Laugh-Out (8/70). 177-World of Archie (9/70). 178-World of Jughead (9/70). 179-Archie's Christmas Stocking(1/71). 180-Betty & Veronica Christmas Spect. (1/71). 181-Archie's Christmas Love-In (1/71). 182-World of Archie (2/71). 183-World of Jughead (2/71)-Last squarebound each... 3 6 9 17 26 35

184-189,193,194,197-199 (52 pgs.): 184-Betty & Veronica Spectacular (6/71). 185-Li'l Jinx Giant Laugh-Out (6/71). 186-Archie's Jokes (8/71). 187-Betty & Veronica Summer Fun (9/71). 188-World of Archie (9/71). 189-World of Jughead (9/71). 193-World of Archie (3/72).194-World of Jughead (4/72). 197-Betty & Veronica Spectacular (6/72). 198-Archie's Jokes (8/72). 199-Betty & Veronica Summer Fun (9/72) each... 3 6 9 15 22 28

190-Archie's Christmas Stocking (12/71); Sabrina-c 4 8 12 27 44 60

191-Betty & Veronica Christmas Spect.(2/72); Sabrina app. 4 8 12 23 37 50

192-Archie's Christmas Love-In (1/72); Archie Band-c/s 3 6 9 20 31 42

195-(84 pgs.)-Li'l Jinx Christmas Bag (1/72). 3 6 9 21 33 45

196-(84 pgs.)-Sabrina's Christmas Magic (1/72) 5 10 15 33 57 80

200-(52 pgs.)-World of Archie (10/72) 3 6 9 20 31 42

201-206,208-219,221-230,232,233 (All 52 pgs.): 201-Betty & Veronica Spectacular (10/72). 202-World of Jughead (11/72). 203-Archie's Christmas Stocking (12/72). 204-Betty & Veronica Christmas Spectacular (2/73). 205-Archie's Christmas Love-In (1/73). 206-Li'l Jinx Christmas Bag (12/72). 208-World of Archie (3/73). 209-World of Jughead (4/73). 210-Betty & Veronica Spectacular (6/73). 211-Archie's Jokes (8/73). 212-Betty & Veronica Summer Fun (9/73). 213-World of Archie (10/73). 214-Betty & Veronica Spectacular (10/73). 215-World of Jughead (11/73). 216-Archie's Christmas Stocking (12/73). 217-Betty & Veronica Christmas Spectacular (2/74). 218-Archie's Christmas Love-In (1/74). 219-Li'l Jinx Christmas Bag (12/73). 221-Betty & Veronica Spectacular (Advertised as World of Archie) (6/74). 222-Archie's Jokes (advertised as World of Jughead) (8/74). 223-Li'l Jinx (8/74). 224-Betty & Veronica Summer Fun (9/74). 225-World of Archie (9/74). 226-Betty & Veronica Spectacular (10/74). 227-World of Jughead (10/74). 228-Archie's Christmas Stocking (12/74). 229-Betty & Veronica Christmas Spectacular (12/74). 230-Archie's Christmas Love-In (1/75). 232-World of Archie (3/75). 233-World of Jughead (4/75) each... 2 4 6 11 16 20

207,220,231,243: Sabrina's Christmas Magic. 207-(12/72). 220-(12/73). 231-(1/75). 243-(1/76) each... 3 6 9 16 24 32

234-242,244-251 (36 pgs.): 234-Betty & Veronica Spectacular (6/75). 235-Archie's Jokes (8/75). 236-Betty & Veronica Summer Fun (9/75). 237-World of Archie (9/75) 238-Betty & Veronica Spectacular (10/75). 239-World of Jughead (10/75). 240-Archie's Christmas Stocking (12/75). 241-Betty & Veronica Christmas Spectacular (12/75). 242-Archie's Christmas Love-In (1/76). 244-World of Archie (3/76). 245-World of Jughead (4/76). 246-Betty & Veronica Spectacular (6/76). 247-Archie's Jokes (8/76). 248-Betty & Veronica Summer Fun (9/76). 249-World of Archie (9/76). 250-Betty & Veronica Spectacular (10/76). 251-World of Jughead each.... 2 4 6 9 12 15

252-451-**Do not exist**

452-454,456-466,468-478, 480-490,492-499: 452-Archie's Christmas Stocking (12/76). 453-Betty & Veronica Christmas Spectacular (12/76). 454-Archie's Christmas Love-In (1/77). 456-World of Archie (3/77). 457-World of Jughead (4/77). 458-Betty & Veronica Spectacular (6/77). 459-Archie's Jokes (8/77)-Shows 8/76 in error. 460-Betty & Veronica Summer Fun (9/77). 461-World of Archie (9/77). 462-Betty & Veronica Spectacular (10/77). 463-World of Jughead (10/77). 464-Archie's Christmas Stocking (12/77). 465-Betty & Veronica Christmas Spectacular (12/77). 466-Archie's Christmas Love-In (1/78). 468-World of Archie (2/78). 469-World of Jughead (2/78). 470-Betty & Veronica Spectacular(6/78). 471-Archie's Jokes (8/78). 472-Betty & Veronica Summer Fun (9/78). 473-World of Archie (9/78). 474-Betty & Veronica Spectacular (10/78). 475-World of Jughead (10/78). 476-Archie's Christmas Stocking (12/78). 477-Betty & Veronica Christmas Spectacular (12/78). 478-Archie's Christmas Love-In (1/79). 480-The World of Archie (3/79). 481-World of Jughead (4/79). 482-Betty & Veronica Spectacular (6/79). 483-Archie's Jokes (8/79). 484-Betty & Veronica Summer Fun(9/79). 485-The World of Archie (9/79). 486-Betty & Veronica Spectacular (10/79). 487-The World of Jughead (10/79). 488-Archie's Christmas Stocking (12/79). 489-Betty & Veronica Christmas Spectacular (1/80). 490-Archie's Christmas Love-in (1/80). 492-The World of Archie (2/80). 493-The World of Jughead (4/80). 494-Betty & Veronica Spectacular (6/80). 495-Archie's Jokes (8/80). 496-Betty & Veronica Summer Fun (9/80). 497-The World of Archie (9/80). 498-Betty & Veronica Spectacular (10/80). 499-The World of Jughead (10/80) each... 2 4 6 8 10 12

455,467,479,491,503-Sabrina's Christmas Magic: 455-(1/77). 467-(1/78). 479-(1/79) Dracula/Werewolf-s. 491-(1/80), 503(1/81) 2 4 6 11 16 20

500-Archie's Christmas Stocking (12/80) 2 4 6 8 11 14

501-514,516-527,529-532,534-539,541-543,545-550: 501-Betty & Veronica Christmas Spectacular (12/80). 502-Archie's Christmas Love-in (1/81). 504-The World of Archie (3/81). 505-The World of Jughead (4/81). 506-Betty & Veronica Spectacular (6/81). 507-Archie's Jokes (8/81). 508-Betty & Veronica Summer Fun (9/81). 509-The World of Archie (9/81). 510-Betty & Vernonica Spectacular (9/81). 511-The World of Jughead (10/81). 512-Archie's Christmas Stocking (12/81). 513-Betty & Veronica Christmas Spectacular (12/81). 514-Archie's Christmas Love-in (1/82). 516-The World of Archie(3/82). 517-The World of Jughead (4/82). 518-Betty & Veronica Spectacular (6/82). 519-Archie's Jokes (8/82). 520-Betty & Veronica Summer Fun (9/82). 521-The World of Archie (9/82). 522-Betty & Veronica Spectacular (10/82). 523-The World of Jughead (10/82).524-Archie's Christmas Stocking (1/83). 525-Betty and Veronica Christmas Spectacular (1/83). 526-Betty and Veronica Spectacular (5/83). 527-Little Archie (8/83). 529-Betty and Veronica Summer Fun (8/83). 530-Betty and Veronica Spectacular (9/83). 531-The World of Jughead (9/83). 532-The World of Archie (10/83). 534-Little Archie (1/84). 535-Archie's Christmas Stocking (1/84). 536-Betty and Veronica Christmas Spectacular (1/84). 537-Betty and Veronica Spectacular (6/84). 538-Little Archie (8/84). 539-Betty and Veronica Summer Fun (8/84). 541-Betty and Veronica Spectacular (9/84). 542-The World of Jughead (9/84). 543-The World of Archie (10/84). 545-Little Archie (12/84). 546-Archie's Christmas Stocking (12/84). 547-Betty and Veronica Christmas Spectacular (12/84). 548-?. 549-Little Archie. 550-Betty and Veronica Summer Fun each... 1 2 3 5 7 9

515,528,533,540,544: 515-Sabrina's Christmas Magic (1/82). 528-Josie and the Pussycats (8/83). 533-Sabrina; Space Pirates by Frank Bolling (10/83). 540-Josie and the Pussycats (8/84). 544-Sabrina the Teen-Age Witch (10/84). each... 2 4 6 10 14 18

551,562,571,584,597-Josie and the Pussycats 2 4 6 8 10 12

552-561,563-570,572-583,585-596,598-600: 552-Betty & Veronica Spectacular. 553-The World of Jughead. 554-The World of Archie. 555-Betty's Diary. 556-Little Archie (1/86). 557-Archie's Christmas Stocking (1/86). 558-Betty & Veronica Christmas Spectacular (1/86). 559-Betty & Veronica Spectacular. 560-Little Archie. 561-Betty & Veronica Summer Fun. 563-Betty & Veronica Spectacular. 564-World of Jughead. 565-World of Archie. 566-Little Archie. 567-Archie's Christmas Stocking. 568-Betty & Veronica Christmas Spectacular. 569-Betty & Veronica Spring Spectacular. 570-Little Archie. 571-Dracula-c/s. 572-Betty & Veronica Summer Fun. 573-Archie At Riverdale High. 574-World of Archie. 575-Betty & Veronica Spectacular. 576-Pep. 577-World of Jughead. 578-Archie And Me. 579-Archie's Christmas Stocking. 580-Betty and Veronica Christmas Spectacular. 581-Little Archie Christmas Special. 582-Betty & Veronica Spring Spectacular. 583-Little Archie. 585-Betty & Veronica Summer Fun. 586-Archie At Riverdale High. 587-The World of Archie (10/88); 1st app. Explorers of the Unknown. 588-Betty & Veronica Spectacular. 589-Pep (10/88). 590-The World of Jughead. 591-Archie & Me. 592-Archie's Christmas Stocking. 593-Betty & Veronica Christmas Spectacular. 594-Little Archie. 595-Betty & Veronica Spring Spectacular. 596-Little Archie. 598-Betty & Veronica Summer Fun. 599-The World of Archie (10/89); 2nd app. Explorers of the Unknown. 600-Betty and Veronica Spectacular each.... 6.00

601,602,604-609,611-629: 601-Pep. 602-The World of Jughead. 604-Archie at Riverdale High. 605-Archie's Christmas Stocking. 606-Betty and Veronica Christmas Spectacular. 607-Little Archie. 608-Betty and Veronica Spectacular. 609-Little Archie. 611-Betty and Veronica Summer Fun. 612-The World of Archie. 613-Betty and Veronica Spectacular. 614-Pep (10/90). 615-Veronica's Summer Special. 616-Archie and Me. 617-Archie's Christmas Stocking. 618-Betty & Veronica Christmas Spectacular. 619-Little Archie. 620-Betty and Veronica Spectacular. 621-Betty and Veronica Summer Fun. 622-Josie & the Pussycats; not published. 623-Betty and Veronica Spectacular. 624-Pep Comics. 625-Veronica's Summer Special. 626-Archie and Me. 627-World of Archie. 628-Archie's Pals 'n' Gals Holiday Special. 629-Betty & Veronica Christmas Spectacular. each.... 4.00

603-Archie and Me; Titanic app. 5.00

610-Josie and the Pussycats 1 2 3 4 5 7

630-631: 630-Archie's Christmas Stocking. 631-Archie's Pals 'n' Gals 4.00

Archie's Double Digest #66 © AP

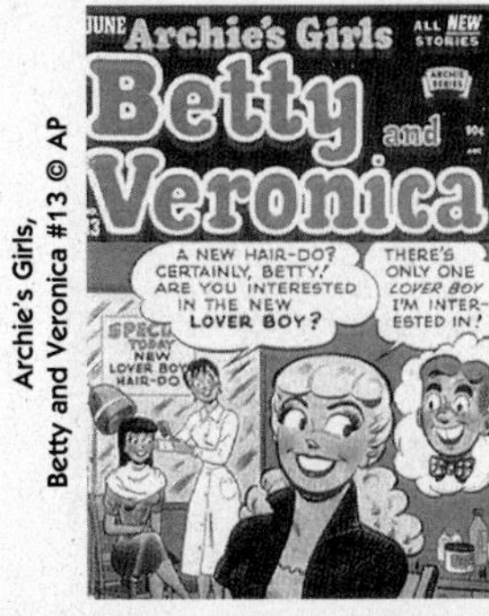

Archie's Girls, Betty and Veronica #13 © AP

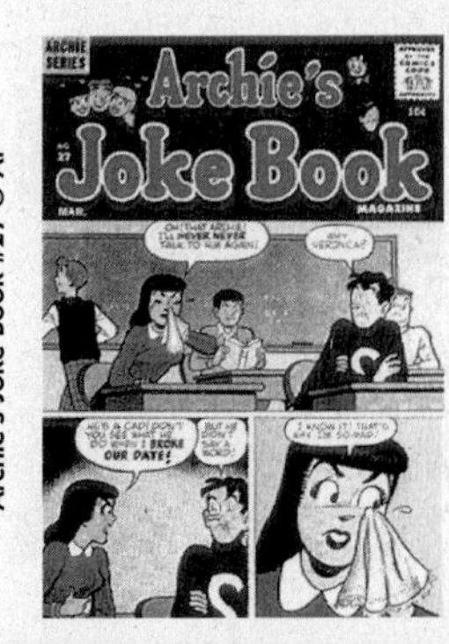

Archie's Joke Book #27 © AP

	GD 2.0	VG 4.0	FN 6.0	VF 8.0	VF/NM 9.0	NM- 9.2
632-Last issue; Betty & Veronica Spectacular	1	2	3	4	5	7

NOTE: *Archies Band-c-173,180,192; s-189,192. Archie Cavemen-165,225,232,244,249. Little Sabrina-527,534, 538,545,556,566. UFO-s-178,487,594.*

ARCHIE MEETS THE PUNISHER (Same contents as The Punisher Meets Archie)
Marvel Comics & Archie Comics Publ.: Aug, 1994 ($2.95, 52 pgs., one-shot)

	GD 2.0	VG 4.0	FN 6.0	VF 8.0	VF/NM 9.0	NM- 9.2
1-Batton Lash story, John Buscema-a on Punisher, Stan Goldberg-a on Archie	1	2	3	4	5	7

ARCHIE'S ACTIVITY COMICS DIGEST MAGAZINE
Archie Enterprises: 1985 - No. 4 (Annual, 128 pgs., digest size)

	GD 2.0	VG 4.0	FN 6.0	VF 8.0	VF/NM 9.0	NM- 9.2
1 (Most copies are marked)	2	4	6	9	13	16
2-4	1	2	3	5	7	9

ARCHIE'S CAR
Spire Christian Comics (Fleming H. Revell co.): 1979 (49¢)

	GD 2.0	VG 4.0	FN 6.0	VF 8.0	VF/NM 9.0	NM- 9.2
nn	2	4	6	13	18	22

ARCHIE'S CHRISTMAS LOVE-IN (See Archie Giant Series Mag. No. 169, 181,192, 205, 218, 230, 242, 454, 466, 478, 490, 502, 514)

ARCHIE'S CHRISTMAS STOCKING (See Archie Giant Series Mag. No. 1-6,10, 15, 20, 25, 31, 137, 144, 150, 158, 167, 179, 190, 203, 216, 228, 240, 452, 464, 476, 488, 500, 512, 524, 535, 546, 557, 567, 579, 592, 605, 617, 630)

ARCHIE'S CHRISTMAS STOCKING
Archie Comics: 1993 - No. 7, 1999 ($2.00-$2.29, 52 pgs.)(Bound-in calendar poster in all)

	GD 2.0	VG 4.0	FN 6.0	VF 8.0	VF/NM 9.0	NM- 9.2
1-Dan DeCarlo-c/a						5.00
2-5						4.00
6,7: 6-(1998, $2.25). 7-(1999, $2.29)						4.00

ARCHIE'S CIRCUS
Barbour Christian Comics: 1990 (69¢)

	GD 2.0	VG 4.0	FN 6.0	VF 8.0	VF/NM 9.0	NM- 9.2
nn	2	4	6	10	14	18

ARCHIE'S CLASSIC CHRISTMAS STORIES
Archie Comics: 2002 ($10.95, TPB)

	GD 2.0	VG 4.0	FN 6.0	VF 8.0	VF/NM 9.0	NM- 9.2
Volume 1 - Reprints stories from 1955-1964 Archie's Christmas Stocking issues						12.00

ARCHIE'S CLEAN SLATE
Spire Christian Comics (Fleming H. Revell Co.): 1973 (35/49¢)

	GD 2.0	VG 4.0	FN 6.0	VF 8.0	VF/NM 9.0	NM- 9.2
1-(35¢-c edition)(Some issues have nn)	3	6	9	14	19	24
1-(49¢-c edition)	2	4	6	10	14	18

ARCHIE'S DATE BOOK
Spire Christian comics (Fleming H. Revell Co.): 1981

	GD 2.0	VG 4.0	FN 6.0	VF 8.0	VF/NM 9.0	NM- 9.2
nn-(Low print)	2	4	6	13	18	22

ARCHIE'S DOUBLE DIGEST QUARTERLY MAGAZINE
Archie Comics: 1981 - Present ($1.95-$3.99, 256 pgs.) (Archie's Double Digest Magazine No. 10 on)

	GD 2.0	VG 4.0	FN 6.0	VF 8.0	VF/NM 9.0	NM- 9.2
1	3	6	9	16	23	30
2-10; 6-Katy Keene story.	2	4	6	10	14	18
11-30: 29-Pureheart story	2	4	6	8	10	12
31-50	1	2	3	4	5	7
51-70,100						5.00
71-99						4.00
101-237,239-250: 123-Begin $3.29-c. 170-Begin $3.69. 197-Begin $3.99-c.						4.00
238-Titled Archie Double Double Digest (4/13, $5.99, 320 pages)						6.00

ARCHIE'S FAMILY ALBUM
Spire Christian Comics (Fleming H. Revell Co.): 1978 (39¢/49¢, 36 pgs.)

	GD 2.0	VG 4.0	FN 6.0	VF 8.0	VF/NM 9.0	NM- 9.2
nn	2	4	6	13	18	22
nn (49¢-c edition)	2	4	6	9	13	16

ARCHIE'S FESTIVAL
Spire Christian Comics (Fleming H. Revell Co.): 1980 (49¢)

	GD 2.0	VG 4.0	FN 6.0	VF 8.0	VF/NM 9.0	NM- 9.2
nn	2	4	6	13	18	22

ARCHIE'S FUNHOUSE DOUBLE DIGEST
Archie Comics: Feb, 2014 - Present ($3.99, digest-size)

	GD 2.0	VG 4.0	FN 6.0	VF 8.0	VF/NM 9.0	NM- 9.2
1-4						4.00

ARCHIE'S GIRLS, BETTY AND VERONICA (Becomes Betty & Veronica)(Also see Veronica)
Archie Publications (Close-Up): 1950 - No. 347, Apr, 1987

	GD 2.0	VG 4.0	FN 6.0	VF 8.0	VF/NM 9.0	NM- 9.2
1	303	606	909	2121	3711	5300
2	124	248	372	787	1356	1925
3-5: 3-Betty's 1st ponytail. 4-Dan DeCarlo's 1st Archie work	73	146	219	467	796	1125
6-10: 10-Katy Keene app. (2 pgs.)	55	110	165	352	601	850
11-20: 11,13,14,17-19-Katy Keene app. 17-Last pre-code issue (3/55). 20-Debbie's Diary (2 pgs.)	41	82	123	256	428	600
21-30: 27,30-Katy Keene app. 29-Tarzan	32	64	96	188	307	425
31-43,45-50: 41-Marilyn Monroe and Brigitte Bardot mentioned. 45-Fabian 1 pg. photo & bio. 46-Bobby Darin 1 pg. photo & bio	21	42	63	126	206	285
44-Elvis Presley 1 pg. photo & bio	24	48	72	144	237	330
51-55,57-74: 67-Jackie Kennedy homage. 73-Sci-fi-c	9	18	27	57	111	165
56-Elvis and Bobby Darin records parody	10	20	30	66	138	210
75-Betty & Veronica sell souls to Devil	18	36	54	124	275	425
76-99: 82-Bobby Rydell 1 pg. illustrated bio; Elvis mentioned on-c. 83-Rick Nelson illo/text page. 84-Connie Francis 1 pg. illustrated bio	6	12	18	38	69	100
100	6	12	18	42	79	115
101-104, 106-117,120 (12/65): 113-Monsters-s	4	8	12	28	47	65
105-Beatles wig parody (5 pg. story)(9/64)	5	10	15	31	53	75
118-(10/65) 1st app./origin Superteen (also see Betty & Me #3)	6	12	18	41	76	110
119-2nd app./last Superteen story	5	10	15	31	53	75
121,122,124-126,128-140 (8/67): 135,140-Mod-c. 136-Slave Girl-s	3	6	9	19	30	40
123-"Jingo"-Ringo parody-c	4	8	12	23	37	50
127-Beatles Fan Club-s	5	10	15	31	53	75
141-156,158-163,165-180 (12/70)	3	6	9	15	22	28
157,164-Archies Band	3	6	9	18	28	38
181-193,195-199	2	4	6	11	16	20
194-Sabrina-c/s	3	6	9	18	28	38
200-(8/72)	3	6	9	14	19	24
201-205,207,209,211-215,217-240	2	4	6	8	10	12
206,208,210, 216: 206,208,216-Sabrina c/app. 206-Josie-c. 210-Sabrina app.	3	6	9	15	22	28
241 (1/76)-270 (6/78)	1	3	4	6	8	10
271-299: 281-UFO-s	1	2	3	5	7	9
300 (12/80)-Anniversary issue	2	4	6	8	10	12
301-309	1	2	3	4	5	7
310-John Travolta parody story	1	3	4	6	8	10
311-319						6.00
320 (10/82)-Intro. of Cheryl Blossom on cover and inside story (she also appears, but not on the cover, in Jughead #325 with same 10/82 publication date)	11	22	33	76	163	250
321-Cheryl Blossom app.	6	12	18	38	69	100
322-Cheryl Blossom app.; Cheryl meets Archie for the 1st time	7	14	21	46	86	125
323,326,329,330,331,333-338: 333-Monsters-s						6.00
324,325-Crickett O'Dell app.	2	4	6	9	12	15
327,328-Cheryl Blossom app.	3	6	9	19	30	40
332,339: 332-Superhero costume party. 339-(12/85) Betty dressed as Madonna.	2	4	6	9	12	15
340-346 Low print	1	3	4	6	8	10
347 (4/87) Last issue; low print	2	4	6	8	10	12
Annual 1 (1953)	129	258	387	826	1413	2000
Annual 2 (1954)	50	100	150	315	533	750
Annual 3-5 (1955-1957)	39	78	117	240	395	550
Annual 6-8 (1958-1960)	28	56	84	165	270	375

ARCHIE'S HOLIDAY FUN DIGEST
Archie Comics: 1997 - Present ($1.75/$1.95/$1.99/$2.19/$2.39/$2.49, annual)

	GD 2.0	VG 4.0	FN 6.0	VF 8.0	VF/NM 9.0	NM- 9.2
1-12-Christmas stories						3.00

ARCHIE'S JOKEBOOK COMICS DIGEST ANNUAL (See Jokebook...)

ARCHIE'S JOKE BOOK MAGAZINE (See Joke Book ...)
Archie Publ: 1953 - No. 3, Sum, 1954; No. 15, Fall, 1954 - No. 288, 11/82 (subtitled...Laugh-In #127-140; ...Laugh-Out #141-194)

	GD 2.0	VG 4.0	FN 6.0	VF 8.0	VF/NM 9.0	NM- 9.2
1953-One Shot (#1)	126	252	378	806	1378	1950
2	53	106	159	334	567	800
3 (no #4-14)	41	82	123	256	428	600
15-20: 15-Formerly Archie's Rival Reggie #14; last pre-code issue (Fall/54). 15-17-Katy Keene app.	27	54	81	158	259	360
21-30	16	32	48	94	147	200
31-43: 42-Bio of Ed "Kookie" Byrnes. 43-story about guitarist Duane Eddy	14	28	42	76	108	140
44-1st professional comic work by Neal Adams, 4 pgs.	32	64	96	192	314	435
45-47-N. Adams-a in all, 2-6 pgs.	19	38	57	111	176	240
48-Four pgs. N. Adams-a	19	38	57	111	176	240
49,50	6	12	18	41	66	90
51-56,60 (1962)	4	8	12	27	44	60
57-Elvis mentioned; Marilyn Monroe cameo	6	12	18	37	66	95

Archie's Mad House #4 © AP

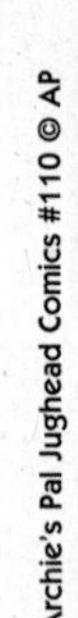
Archie's Pal Jughead Comics #110 © AP

Archie's Pals 'n' Gals #4 © AP

	GD 2.0	VG 4.0	FN 6.0	VF 8.0	VF/NM 9.0	NM- 9.2
58,59-Horror/Sci-Fi-c	6	12	18	40	73	105
61-80 (8/64): 66-(12¢ cover). 76-Robot-c	3	6	9	17	26	35
66-(15¢ cover variant)	3	6	9	21	33	45
81-89,91,92,94-99	3	6	9	14	20	25
90,93: 90-Beatles gag. 93-Beatles cameo	3	6	9	16	24	32
100 (5/66)	3	6	9	16	23	30
101,103-117,119-123,127,129,131-140 (9/69): 105-Superhero gag-c. 108-110-Archies Archers Band-s. 116-Beatles/Monkees/Bob Dylan cameos (posters)	2	4	6	11	16	20
102 (7/66) Archie Band prototype-c; Elvis parody panel, Rolling Stones mention	3	6	9	17	26	35
118,124,125,126,128,130: 118-Archie Band-c; Veronica & Groovers band-s. 124-Archies Band-c/app. 125-Beatles cameo (poster). 126,130-Monkees cameo. 128-Veronica/Archies Band app.	3	6	9	16	23	30
141-173,175-181,183-199	2	4	6	8	11	14
174-Sabrina-c. 182-Sabrina cameo	2	4	6	9	13	16
200 (9/74)	2	4	6	9	13	16
201-230 (3/77)	1	2	3	5	6	8
231-239,241-287						6.00
240-Elvis record-c	2	3	4	6	8	10
288-Last issue	1	2	3	4	5	7

NOTE: *Archies Band-c-118,124,147,172; 1 pg.-s-127,128,138,140,143,147,167; 2 pg.-s-124,131, 155. Sabrina app.-247,248,252-259,261,262,264,266-270,274,277,284-286.*

ARCHIE'S JOKES (See Archie Giant Series Mag. No. 17, 22, 27, 33, 139, 146, 154, 163, 174, 186, 198, 211, 222, 235, 247, 459, 471, 483, 495, 519)

ARCHIE'S LOVE SCENE
Spire Christian Comics (Fleming H. Revell Co.): 1973 (35¢/39¢/49¢/no price)

	GD 2.0	VG 4.0	FN 6.0	VF 8.0	VF/NM 9.0	NM- 9.2
1-(35¢ Edition)	3	6	9	14	19	24
1-(39¢/49¢ Edition/no price) (Some copies have nn)	2	4	6	10	14	18

ARCHIE'S LOVE SHOWDOWN SPECIAL
Archie Publications: 1994 ($2.00, one-shot)

	GD 2.0	VG 4.0	FN 6.0	VF 8.0	VF/NM 9.0	NM- 9.2
1-Concludes x-over from Archie #429, Betty #19, B&V #82, Veronica #39						4.00

ARCHIE'S MADHOUSE (Madhouse Ma-ad No. 67 on)
Archie Publications: Sept, 1959 - No. 66, Feb, 1969

	GD 2.0	VG 4.0	FN 6.0	VF 8.0	VF/NM 9.0	NM- 9.2
1-Archie begins	22	44	66	157	346	535
2	12	24	36	80	173	265
3-5	9	18	27	57	111	165
6-10	6	12	18	41	76	110
11-17 (Last w/regular characters)	5	10	15	35	63	90
18-21,23,29: 18-New format begins. 23-No Sabrina	5	10	15	31	53	75
22-1st app. Sabrina, the Teen-age Witch (10/62)	28	56	84	202	451	700
24-2nd app.Sabrina a	11	22	33	76	163	250
25,26,28-Sabrina app. 25-1st app. Captain Sprocket (4/63); 3rd app. Sabrina; sci-fi/horror-c	9	18	27	59	117	175
27-Sabrina-c; no story	7	14	21	49	92	135
30,34,38-40: No Sabrina. 34-Bordered-c begin.	4	8	12	25	40	55
31,33,37-Sabrina app.	7	14	21	46	86	125
32-Sabrina app.?	4	8	12	25	40	55
35-Beatles cameo. No Sabrina	4	8	12	28	47	65
36-1st Salem the Cat w/Sabrina story	9	18	27	62	126	190
41-48,51-57,60-62,64-66; No Sabrina 43-Mighty Crusaders cameo. 44-Swipes Mad #4 (Super-Duperman) in "Bird Monsters From Outer Space"	3	6	9	20	31	42
49,50,58,59,63-Sabrina stories	5	10	15	35	63	90
Annual 1 (1962-63) no Sabrina	7	14	21	48	89	130
Annual 2 (1964) no Sabrina	5	10	15	31	53	75
Annual 3 (1965)-r/1st app. Sabrina from #22	10	20	30	66	138	210
Annual 4,5('66-68)(Becomes Madhouse Ma-ad Annual #7 on); no Sabrina	4	8	12	25	40	55
Annual 6 (1969)-Sabrina the Teen-Age Witch-sty	6	12	18	37	66	95

NOTE: *Cover title to #61-65 is "Madhouse" and to #66 is "Madhouse Ma-ad Jokes". Sci-Fi/Horror covers 6, 8, 11, 13, 15-26, 29, 35, 36, 38, 42, 43, 48, 51, 58, 60.*

ARCHIE'S MECHANICS
Archie Publications: Sept, 1954 - No. 3, 1955

	GD 2.0	VG 4.0	FN 6.0	VF 8.0	VF/NM 9.0	NM- 9.2
1-(15¢; 52 pgs.)	98	196	294	622	1074	1525
2-(10¢)-Last pre-code issue	54	108	162	343	574	825
3-(10¢)	45	90	135	284	480	675

ARCHIE'S MYSTERIES (Continued from Archie's Weird Mysteries)
Archie Comics: No. 25, Feb, 2003 - No. 34, June, 2004 ($2.19)

	GD 2.0	VG 4.0	FN 6.0	VF 8.0	VF/NM 9.0	NM- 9.2
25-34- Archie and gang as "Teen Scene Investigators"						3.00

ARCHIE'S ONE WAY
Spire Christian Comics (Fleming H. Revell Co.): 1972 (35¢/39¢/49¢, 36 pgs.)

	GD 2.0	VG 4.0	FN 6.0	VF 8.0	VF/NM 9.0	NM- 9.2
nn-(35¢ Edition)	3	6	9	14	19	24
nn-(39¢, 49¢, no price editions)	2	4	6	10	14	18

ARCHIE'S PAL, JUGHEAD (Jughead No. 127 on)
Archie Publications: 1949 - No. 126, Nov, 1965

	GD 2.0	VG 4.0	FN 6.0	VF 8.0	VF/NM 9.0	NM- 9.2
1 (1949)-1st app. Moose (see Pep #33)	284	568	852	1818	3109	4400
2 (1950)	100	200	300	635	1093	1550
3-5	57	114	171	362	619	875
6-10: 7-Suzie app.	39	78	117	231	378	525
11-20: 20-Jughead as Sherlock Holmes parody	25	50	75	147	241	335
21-30: 23-25,28-30-Katy Keene app. 23-Early Dilton-s. 28-Debbie's Diary app.	18	36	54	103	162	220
31-50: 49-Archies Rock 'N' Rollers band-c	7	14	21	48	89	130
51-57,59-70: 59- Bio of Will Hutchins of TV's Sugarfoot. 68-Early Archie Gang Cavemen-s	5	10	15	34	60	85
58-Neal Adams-a	6	12	18	40	73	105
71-76,83,89-99: 72-Jughead dates Betty & Veronica. 83 (4/62) 1st mention of Secret Society of Jughead Hating Girls. 95-2nd app. Cricket O'Dell	4	8	12	27	44	60
77,78,80-82,85,86,88-Horror/Sci-Fi-c. 86(7/62) 1st app. The Brain	6	12	18	41	76	110
79-Creature From the Black Lagoon-c	7	14	21	48	89	130
84-1st app. Big Ethyl (5/62)	5	10	15	31	53	75
87-2nd app. of Big Ethyl; UGAJ (United Girls Against Jughead)-s	5	10	15	30	50	70
100	4	8	12	28	47	65
101-Return of Big Ethyl	4	8	12	27	44	60
102-126	3	6	9	19	30	40
Annual 1 (1953, 25¢)	86	172	258	546	936	1325
Annual 2 (1954, 25¢)-Last pre-code issue	41	82	123	260	440	620
Annual 3-5 (1955-57, 25¢)	32	64	96	188	307	425
Annual 6-8 (1958-60, 25¢)	21	42	63	122	199	275

ARCHIE'S PAL JUGHEAD COMICS (Formerly Jughead #1-45)
Archie Comic Publ.: No. 46, June, 1993 - No. 214, Sept, 2012 ($1.25-$2.99)

	GD 2.0	VG 4.0	FN 6.0	VF 8.0	VF/NM 9.0	NM- 9.2
46-214: 100-"A Storm Over Uniforms" x-over part 1,2. 166-Three Geeks cameo. 200-Tom Root-s; Sabrina cameo. 201-Begin $2.99-c						3.00

ARCHIE'S PALS 'N' GALS (Also see Archie Giant Series Magazine #628)
Archie Publ: 1952-53 - No. 6, 1957-58; No. 7, 1958 - No. 224, Sept, 1991
(...All News Stories on-c #49-59)

	GD 2.0	VG 4.0	FN 6.0	VF 8.0	VF/NM 9.0	NM- 9.2
1-(116 pgs., 25¢)	107	214	321	680	1165	1650
2(Annual)('54, 25¢)	49	98	147	309	522	735
3-5(Annual, '55-57, 25¢): 3-Last pre-code issue	36	72	108	216	351	485
6-10('58-'60)	22	44	66	128	209	290
11,13,14,16,17,20-(84 pgs.): 17-B&V paper dolls	14	28	42	78	112	145
12,15-(84 pgs.) Neal Adams-a. 12-Harry Belafonte 2 pg. photos & bio.	15	30	45	88	137	185
18-(84 pgs.) Horror/Sci-Fi-c	15	30	45	85	130	175
19-Marilyn Monroe app.	19	38	57	112	179	245
21,22,24-28,30 (68 pgs.)	6	12	18	40	73	105
23-(Wint./62) 6 pg. Josie-s with Pepper and Melody (1st app.) by DeCarlo; Betty in towel pin-up	27	54	81	189	420	650
29-Beatles satire (68 pgs.)	9	18	27	59	117	175
31(Wint. 64/65)-39 -(68 pgs.)	5	10	15	33	57	80
40-Early Superteen-s; with Pureheart	6	12	18	41	76	110
41(8/67)-43,45-50(2/69) (68 pgs.)	4	8	12	25	40	55
44-Archies Band-s; WEB cameo	4	8	12	28	47	65
51(4/69),52,55-64(6/71): 62-Last squarebound	3	6	9	18	28	38
53-Archies Band-c/s	3	6	9	21	33	45
54-Satan meets Veronica-s	5	10	15	34	60	85
65(8/70),67-70,73,74,76-81,83(6/74) (52 pgs.)	3	6	9	21	33	45
66,82-Sabrina-c	4	8	12	22	34	45
71,72-Two part drug story (8/72,9/72)	3	6	9	21	33	45
75-Archies Band-s	3	6	9	16	24	32
84-99	2	4	6	8	10	12
100 (12/75)	2	4	6	9	13	16
101-130(3/79): 125,126-Riverdale 2001-s	1	2	3	5	6	8
131-160,162-170 (7/84)						6.00
161 (11/82) 3rd app./1st solo Cheryl Blossom-s and pin-up; 2nd Jason Blossom	4	8	12	27	44	60
171-173,175,177-197,199: 197-G. Colan-a						5.00
174,176,198: 174-New Archies Band-s. 176-Cyndi Lauper-c. 198-Archie gang on strike at Archie Ent. offices						6.00

Archie's Rival Reggie #4 © AP

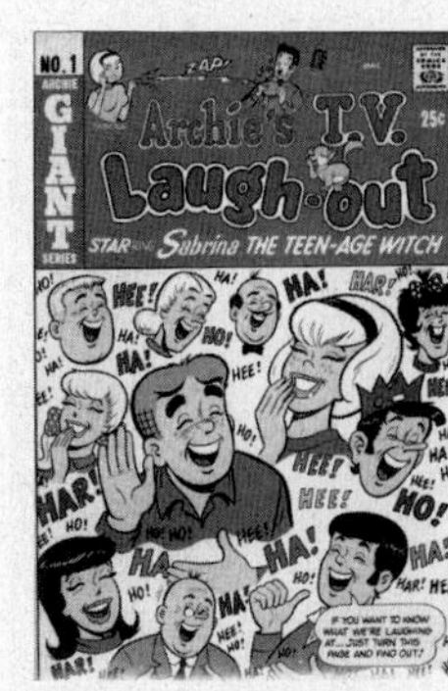

Archie's TV Laugh-Out #1 © AP

Aria #2 © Haberlin & Holguin

	GD 2.0	VG 4.0	FN 6.0	VF 8.0	VF/NM 9.0	NM- 9.2
200(9/88)-Illiteracy-s						6.00
201,203-223: Later issues $1.00 cover						4.00
202-Explains end of Archie's jalopy; Dezerland-c/s; James Dean cameo						6.00
224-Last issue						6.00

NOTE: *Archies Band-c-45,47,49,53,56; s-44,53,75,174. UFO-s-50,63,209,220.*

ARCHIE'S PALS 'N' GALS DOUBLE DIGEST MAGAZINE
Archie Comic Publications: Nov, 1992 - No. 146, Dec, 2010 ($2.50-$3.99)

	GD	VG	FN	VF	VF/NM	NM-
1-Capt. Hero story; Pureheart app.	2	4	6	8	10	12
2-10: 2-Superduck story; Little Jinx in all. 4-Begin $2.75-c	1	2	3	4	5	7
11-29						4.00
30-146: 40-Begin $2.99-c. 48-Begin $3.19-c. 56-Begin $3.29-c. 72-Begin $3.59-c. 100-Story uses screen captures from classic animated series. 102-Begin $3.69-c 125-128-"New Look" art; Moose and Midge break up. 130-Begin $3.99-c. 133-Reggie spotlight, also reprints early apps.						4.00

ARCHIE'S PARABLES
Spire Christian Comics (Fleming H. Revell Co.): 1973,1975 (39/49¢, 36 pgs.)

	GD	VG	FN	VF	VF/NM	NM-
nn-By Al Hartley; 39¢ Edition	3	6	9	14	19	24
49¢, no price editions	2	4	6	9	13	16

ARCHIE'S R/C RACERS (Radio controlled cars)
Archie Comics: Sept, 1989 - No. 10, Mar, 1991 (95¢/$1)

	GD	VG	FN	VF	VF/NM	NM-
1						6.00
2,5-7,10: 5-Elvis parody. 7-Supervillain-c/s. 10-UFO-c/s						4.00
3,4,8,9						3.00

ARCHIE'S RIVAL REGGIE (Reggie & Archie's Joke Book #15 on)
Archie Publications: 1949 - No. 14, Aug, 1954

	GD	VG	FN	VF	VF/NM	NM-
1-Reggie 1st app. in Jackpot Comics #5	95	190	285	603	1039	1475
2	43	86	129	271	461	650
3-5	34	68	102	204	332	460
6-10	24	48	72	140	230	320
11-14: Katy Keene in No. 10-14, 1-2 pgs.	19	38	57	109	172	235

ARCHIE'S RIVERDALE HIGH (See Riverdale High)

ARCHIE'S ROLLER COASTER
Spire Christian Comics (Fleming H. Revell Co.): 1981 (69¢)

	GD	VG	FN	VF	VF/NM	NM-
nn-(Low print)	2	4	6	13	18	22

ARCHIE'S SOMETHING ELSE
Spire Christian Comics (Fleming H. Revell Co.): 1975 (39/49¢, 36 pgs.)

	GD	VG	FN	VF	VF/NM	NM-
nn-(39¢-c) Hell's Angels Biker on motorcycle-c	3	6	9	14	19	24
nn-(49¢-c)	2	4	6	10	14	18
Barbour Christian Comics Edition ('86, no price listed)	2	3	4	6	8	10

ARCHIE'S SONSHINE
Spire Christian Comics (Fleming H. Revell Co.): 1973, 1974 (39/49¢, 36 pgs.)

	GD	VG	FN	VF	VF/NM	NM-
39¢ Edition	3	6	9	14	19	24
49¢, no price editions	2	4	6	9	13	16

ARCHIE'S SPORTS SCENE
Spire Christian Comics (Fleming H. Revell Co.): 1983 (no cover price)

	GD	VG	FN	VF	VF/NM	NM-
nn-(Low print)	2	4	6	13	18	22

ARCHIE'S SPRING BREAK
Archie Comics: 1996 - No. 5, 2000 ($2.00/$2.49, 48 pgs., annual)

	GD	VG	FN	VF	VF/NM	NM-
1-5: 1,2-Dan DeCarlo-c						4.00

ARCHIE'S STORY & GAME COMICS DIGEST MAGAZINE
Archie Enterprises: Nov, 1986 - No. 39, Jan, 1998 ($1.25-$1.95, 128 pgs., digest-size)

	GD	VG	FN	VF	VF/NM	NM-
1: Marked-up copies are common	2	4	6	11	16	20
2-10	2	4	6	8	10	12
11-20	1	2	3	4	5	7
21-39: 39-($1.95)						4.00

ARCHIE'S SUPER HERO SPECIAL (See Archie Giant Series Mag. No. 142)

ARCHIE'S SUPER HERO SPECIAL (...Comics Digest Mag. 2)
Archie Publications (Red Circle): Jan, 1979 - No. 2, Aug, 1979 (95¢, 148 pgs.)

	GD	VG	FN	VF	VF/NM	NM-
1-Simon & Kirby r-/Double Life of Pvt. Strong #1,2; Black Hood, The Fly, Jaguar, The Web app.	2	4	6	11	16	20
2-Contains contents to the never published Black Hood #1; origin Black Hood; N. Adams, Wood, McWilliams, Morrow, S&K-a(r); N. Adams-c. The Shield, The Fly, Jaguar, Hangman, Steel Sterling, The Web, The Fox-r	2	4	6	11	16	20

ARCHIE'S SUPER TEENS
Archie Comic Publications, Inc.: 1994 - No. 4, 1996 ($2.00, 52 pgs.)

	GD	VG	FN	VF	VF/NM	NM-
1-Staton/Esposito-c/a; pull-out poster						5.00
2-4: 2-Fred Hembeck script; Bret Blevins/Terry Austin-a						4.00

ARCHIE'S TV LAUGH-OUT ("...Starring Sabrina" on-c #1-50)
Archie Publications: Dec, 1969 - No. 105, Feb, 1986 (#1-7: 68 pgs.)

	GD	VG	FN	VF	VF/NM	NM-
1-Sabrina begins, thru #105	9	18	27	62	126	190
2 (68 pgs.)	5	10	15	35	63	90
3-6 (68 pgs.)	5	10	15	30	50	70
7-Josie begins, thru #105; Archie's & Josie's Bands cover logos begin	6	12	18	42	79	115
8-23 (52 pgs.): 10-1st Josie on-c. 12-1st Josie and Pussycats on-c. 14-Beatles cameo on poster	4	8	12	25	40	55
24-40: 37,39,40-Bicentennial-c	3	6	9	14	20	25
41,47,56: 41-Alexandra rejoins J&P band. 47-Fonz cameo; voodoo-s. 56-Fonz parody; B&V with Farrah hair-c	3	6	9	15	22	28
42-46,48-55,57-60	2	4	6	9	12	15
61-68,70-80: 63-UFO-s. 79-Mummy-s	1	3	4	6	8	10
69-Sherlock Holmes parody	1	3	4	6	8	10
81-90,94,95,97-99: 84 Voodoo-s	1	2	3	5	6	8
91-Early Cheryl Blossom-s; Sabrina/Archies Band-c	3	6	9	17	26	35
92-A-Team parody	1	3	4	6	8	10
93-(2/84) Archie in drag-s; Hill Street Blues-s; Groucho Marx parody; cameo parody app. of Batman, Spider-Man, Wonder Woman and others	2	4	6	9	12	15
96-MASH parody-s; Jughead in drag; Archies Band-c	1	3	4	6	8	10
100-(4/85) Michael Jackson parody-c/s; J&P band and Archie band on-c	2	4	6	10	14	18
101-104-Lower print run. 104-Miami Vice parody-c	1	2	3	5	7	9
105-Wrestling/Hulk Hogan parody-c; J&P band-s	2	4	6	9	12	15

NOTE: ***Dan DeCarlo-a** 78-up(most), **c**-89-up(most). **Archies Band-s** 2,7,9-11,15,20,25,37,64,65,67,68,70,73, 76,78,79,83,84,86,90,96,100,101; **Archies Band-c** 2,17,20,91,94,96,99-103. **Josie-s** 12,21,26,35,52,78,80,90. **Josie-c** 10,91,94. **Josie and the Pussycats (as a band in costume)-s** 7,9,10,37,38,41,42,66,84,99-101,105. **Josie w/Pussycats member Valerie &/or Melody-s** 17,20,22,25,27-29,31,33,36,39,40,43-51,53-65,67-77,79,81-83,85-89,92-94,102-104. **Josie w/Pussycats band-c** 12,14,17,18,22,24. **Sabrina-s** 1-9,11-86,88-106. **Sabrina-c** 1-18,21,23,27,49,91,94.*

ARCHIE'S VACATION SPECIAL
Archie Publications: Winter, 1994 - Present ($2.00/$2.25/$2.29/$2.49, annual)

	GD	VG	FN	VF	VF/NM	NM-
1						4.00
2-8: 8-(2000, $2.49)						3.00

ARCHIE'S WEIRD MYSTERIES (Continues as Archie's Mysteries)
Archie Comics: Feb, 2000 - No. 24, Dec, 2002 ($1.79/$1.99)

	GD	VG	FN	VF	VF/NM	NM-
1						3.50
2-24: 3-Mighty Crusaders app. 14-Super Teens-c/app.; Mighty Crusaders app.						3.00

ARCHIE'S WORLD
Spire Christian Comics (Fleming H. Revell Co.): 1973, 1976 (39/49¢)

	GD	VG	FN	VF	VF/NM	NM-
39¢ Edition	3	6	9	14	19	24
49¢ Edition, no price editions	2	4	6	9	13	16

ARCHIE 3000
Archie Comics: May, 1989 - No. 16, July, 1991 (75¢/95¢/$1.00)

	GD	VG	FN	VF	VF/NM	NM-
1,16: 16-Aliens-c/s						4.00
2-15: 6-Begin $1.00-c; X-Mas-c						3.00

ARCOMICS PREMIERE
Arcomics: July, 1993 ($2.95)

	GD	VG	FN	VF	VF/NM	NM-
1-1st lenticular-c on a comic (flicker-c)						4.00

AREA 52
Image Comics: Jan, 2001 - No. 4, June, 2001 ($2.95)

	GD	VG	FN	VF	VF/NM	NM-
1-4-Haberlin-s/Henry-a						3.00

ARES
Marvel Comics: Mar, 2006 - No. 5, July, 2006 ($2.99, limited series)

	GD	VG	FN	VF	VF/NM	NM-
1-5-Oeming-s/Foreman-a						3.00
...: God of War TPB (2006, $13.99) r/series						14.00

ARGUS (See Flash, 2nd Series) (Also see Showcase '95 #1,2)
DC Comics: Apr, 1995 - No. 6, Oct, 1995 ($1.50, limited series)

	GD	VG	FN	VF	VF/NM	NM-
1-6: 4-Begin $1.75-c						3.00

ARIA
Image Comics (Avalon Studios): Jan, 1999 - Present ($2.50)

	GD	VG	FN	VF	VF/NM	NM-
Preview (11/98, $2.95)						5.00
1-Anacleto-c/a	1	2	3	5	6	8
1-Variant-c by Michael Turner	1	2	3	5	6	8

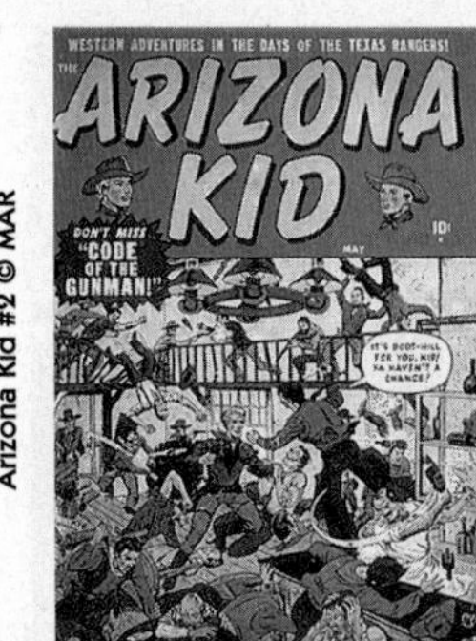

Arizona Kid #2 © MAR

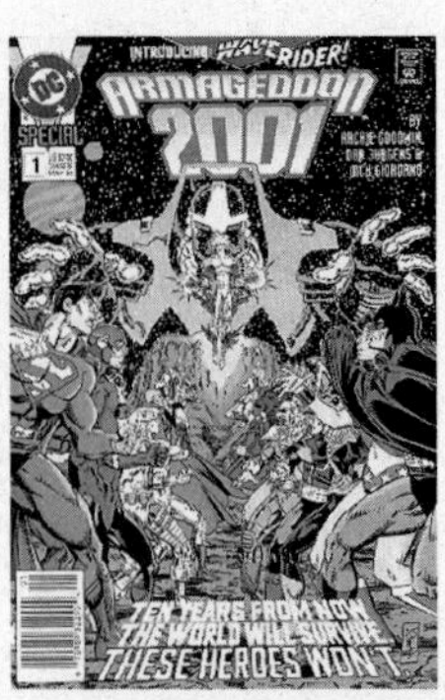

Armageddon 2001 #1 © DC

Army @ Love #2 © Rick Veitch

	GD 2.0	VG 4.0	FN 6.0	VF 8.0	VF/NM 9.0	NM- 9.2
1-($10.00) Alternate-c by Turner	1	3	4	6	8	10
1,2-(Blanc & Noir) Black and white printing of pencil art						3.00
1-(Blanc & Noir) DF Edition						5.00
2-4: 2,4-Anacleto-c/a. 3-Martinez-a						3.00
4-($6.95) Glow in the Dark-c	1	3	4	6	8	10
Aria Angela 1 (2/00, $2.95) Anacleto-a; 4 covers by Anacleto, JG Jones, Portacio and Quesada						3.00
Aria Angela Blanc & Noir 1 (4/00, $2.95) Anacleto-c						3.00
Aria Angela European Ashcan						10.00
Aria Angela 2 (10/00, $2.95) Anacleto-a/c						3.00
...: A Midwinter's Dream 1 (1/02, $4.95, 7"x7") text-s w/Anacleto panels						5.00
...: The Enchanted Collection (5/04, $16.95) r/Summer's Spell & The Uses of Enchantment						17.00

ARIA: SUMMER'S SPELL
Image Comics (Avalon Studios): Mar, 2002 - No. 2, Jun, 2002 ($2.95)

1,2-Anacleto-c/Holguin-s/Pajarillo & Medina-a 3.00

ARIA: THE SOUL MARKET
Image Comics (Avalon Studios): Mar, 2001 - No. 6, Dec, 2001 ($2.95)

1-6-Anacleto-c/Holguin-s 3.00
HC (2002, $26.95, 8.25" x 12.25") oversized r/#1-6 27.00
SC (2004, $16.95, 8.25" x 12.25") oversized r/#1-6 17.00

ARIA: THE USES OF ENCHANTMENT
Image Comics (Avalon Studios): Feb, 2003 - No. 4, Sept, 2003 ($2.95)

1-4-Anacleto-c/Holguin-s/Medina-a 3.00

ARIANE AND BLUEBEARD (See Night Music #8)

ARIEL & SEBASTIAN (See Cartoon Tales & The Little Mermaid)

ARION, LORD OF ATLANTIS (Also see Warlord #55)
DC Comics: Nov, 1982 - No. 35, Sept, 1985

1-Story cont'd from Warlord #62 4.00
2-35 3.00
... Special #1 (11/85) 4.00

ARION THE IMMORTAL (Also see Showcase '95 #7)
DC Comics: July, 1992 - No. 6, Dec, 1992 ($1.50, limited series)

1-6: 4-Gustovich-a(i) 3.00

ARISTOCATS (See Movie Comics & Walt Disney Showcase No. 16)

ARISTOKITTENS, THE (...Meet Jiminy Cricket No. 1)(Disney)
Gold Key: Oct, 1971 - No. 9, Oct, 1975

	GD	VG	FN	VF	VF/NM	NM-
1	3	6	9	19	30	40
2-5,7-9	3	6	9	14	19	24
6-(52 pgs.)	3	6	9	15	22	28

ARIZONA KID, THE (Also see The Comics & Wild Western)
Marvel/Atlas Comics(CSI): Mar, 1951 - No. 6, Jan, 1952

	GD	VG	FN	VF	VF/NM	NM-
1	22	44	66	132	216	300
2-4: 2-Heath-a(3)	13	26	39	72	101	130
5,6	10	20	30	58	79	100

NOTE: ***Heath** a-1-3; c-1-3. **Maneely** c-4-6. **Morisi** a-4-6. **Sinnott** a-6.*

ARK, THE (See The Crusaders)

ARKAGA
Image Comics: Sept, 1997 ($2.95, one-shot)

1-Jorgensen-s/a 3.00

ARKANIUM
Dreamwave Productions: Sept, 2002 - No. 5 ($2.95)

1-5: 1-Gatefold wraparound-c 3.00

ARKHAM ASYLUM: LIVING HELL
DC Comics: July, 2003 - No. 6, Dec, 2003 ($2.50, limited series)

1-6-Ryan Sook-a; Batman app. 3-Batgirl-c/app. 3.00

ARKHAM ASYLUM: MADNESS
DC Comics: 2010 ($19.99, HC graphic novel, dustjacket)

HC-Sam Kieth-s/a/c; Joker, Two-Face, Harley and Ivy app. 20.00
SC-(2011, $14.99) Sam Kieth-s/a/c; Joker, Two-Face, Harley and Ivy app. 15.00

ARKHAM REBORN
DC Comics: Dec, 2009 - No. 3, Feb, 2010 ($2.99, limited series)

1-3-David Hine-s/Jeremy Haun-a 3.00
Batman: Arkham Reborn TPB (2010, $12.99) r/#1-3, Detective Comics #864,865 and Batman: Battle For the Cowl: Arkham Asylum #1 13.00

ARMAGEDDON
Chaos! Comics: Oct, 1999 - No. 4, Jan, 2000 ($2.95, limited series)

Preview 5.00
1-4-Lady Death, Evil Ernie, Purgatori app. 3.00

ARMAGEDDON: ALIEN AGENDA
DC Comics: Nov, 1991 - No. 4, Feb, 1992 ($1.00, limited series)

1-4 3.00

ARMAGEDDON FACTOR, THE
AC Comics: 1987 - No. 2, 1987; No. 3, 1990 ($1.95)

1,2: Sentinels of Justice, Dragonfly, Femforce 3.00
3-($3.95, color)-Almost all AC characters app. 4.00

ARMAGEDDON: INFERNO
DC Comics: Apr, 1992 - No. 4, July, 1992 ($1.00, limited series)

1-4: Many DC heroes app. 3-A. Adams/Austin-a 3.00

ARMAGEDDON 2001
DC Comics: May, 1991 - No. 2, Oct, 1991 ($2.00, squarebound, 68 pgs.)

1-Features many DC heroes; intro Waverider 5.00
1-2nd & 3rd printings; 3rd has silver ink-c 4.00
2 4.00

ARMED & DANGEROUS
Acclaim Comics (Armada): Apr, 1996 - No.4, July, 1996 ($2.95, B&W)

1-4-Bob Hall-c/a & scripts 3.00
Special 1 (8/96, $2.95, B&W)-Hall-c/a & scripts. 3.00

ARMED & DANGEROUS HELL'S SLAUGHTERHOUSE
Acclaim Comics (Armada): Oct, 1996 - No. 4, Jan, 1997 ($2.95, B&W)

1-4: Hall-c/a/scripts. 3.00

ARMOR (AND THE SILVER STREAK) (Revengers Featuring... in indicia for #1-3)
Continuity Comics: Sept, 1985 - No.13, Apr, 1992 ($2.00)

1-13: 1-Intro/origin Armor & the Silver Streak; Neal Adams-c/a. 7-Origin Armor; Nebres-i 3.50

ARMOR (DEATHWATCH 2000)
Continuity Comics: Apr, 1993 - No. 6, Nov, 1993 ($2.50)

1-6: 1-3-Deathwatch 2000 x-over 3.00

ARMORINES (See X-O Manowar #25 for 16 pg. bound-in Armorines #0)
Valiant: June, 1994 - No. 12, June, 1995 ($2.25)

0-Stand-alone edition with cardstock-c 25.00
0-Gold 15.00
1 4.00
2-12: 7-Wraparound-c. 12-Byrne-c/swipe (X-Men, 1st Series #138) 3.00

ARMORINES (Volume 2)
Acclaim Comics: Oct, 1999 - No. 4 ($3.95/$2.50, limited series)

1-($3.95) Calafiore & P. Palmiotti-a 4.00
2,3-($2.50) 3.00

ARMOR X
Image Comics: March, 2005 - No. 4, June, 2005 ($2.95, limited series)

1-Keith Champagne-s/Andy Smith-a; flip covers on #2-4 3.00

ARMY AND NAVY COMICS (Supersnipe No. 6 on)
Street & Smith Publications: May, 1941 - No. 5, July, 1942

	GD	VG	FN	VF	VF/NM	NM-
1-Cap Fury & Nick Carter	52	104	156	328	557	785
2-Cap Fury & Nick Carter	31	62	93	182	296	410
3,4: 4-Jack Farr-c/a	23	46	69	136	223	310
5-Supersnipe app.; see Shadow V2#3 for 1st app.; Story of Douglas MacArthur; George Marcoux-c/a	53	106	159	334	567	800

ARMY @ LOVE
DC Comics (Vertigo): May, 2007 - No. 12, Apr, 2008;
V2 #1, Oct, 2008 - No. 6, Mar, 2009 ($2.99)

1-12-Rick Veitch-s/a(p); Gary Erskine-a(i) 3.00
(Vol. 2) 1-6-Veitch-s/a(p); Erskine-a(i) 3.00
...: Generation Pwned TPB (2008, $12.99) r/#6-12 13.00
...: The Hot Zone Club TPB (2007, $9.99) r/#1-5; intro. by Peter Kuper 10.00

ARMY ATTACK
Charlton Comics: July, 1964 - No. 4, Feb, 1965; V2#38, July, 1965 - No. 47, Feb, 1967

	GD	VG	FN	VF	VF/NM	NM-
V1#1	5	10	15	30	50	70
2-4(2/65)	3	6	9	19	30	40
V2#38(7/65)-47 (formerly U.S. Air Force #1-37)	3	6	9	16	23	30

NOTE: ***Glanzman** a-1-3. **Montes/Bache** a-44.*

ARMY AT WAR (Also see Our Army at War & Cancelled Comic Cavalcade)

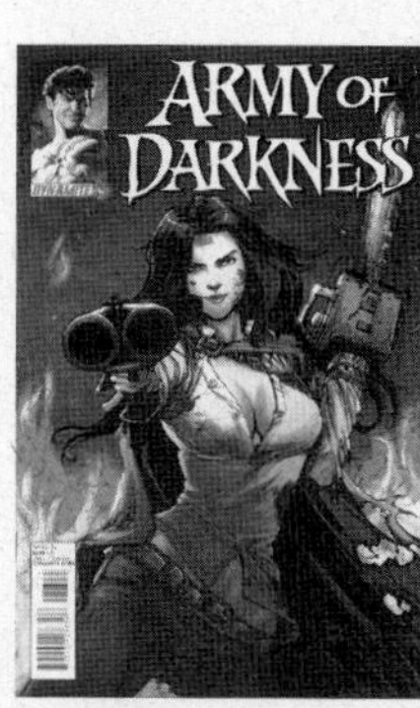
Army of Darkness V3 #13 © Orion

Arrow #5 © DC

Artifacts #28 © TCOW

GD VG FN VF VF/NM NM-
2.0 4.0 6.0 8.0 9.0 9.2

DC Comics: Oct-Nov, 1978
1-Kubert-c; all new story and art 2 4 6 11 16 20

ARMY OF DARKNESS (Movie)
Dark Horse Comics: Nov, 1992 - No. 2, Dec, 1992; No. 3, Oct, 1993 ($2.50, limited series)
1-3-Bolton painted-c/a 2 4 6 9 12 15
... Movie Adaptation TPB (2006, $14.99) r/#1-3; intro. by Busiek; Bruce Campbell interview 15.00

ARMY OF DARKNESS (Also see Marvel Zombies vs. Army of Darkness)
Dynamite Entertainment: 2005 - No. 13, 2007 ($2.99)
1-4 (Vs. Re-Animator):1,2-Four covers; Greene-a/Kuhoric-s. 3,4-Three covers 3.00
5-13: 5-7-Kuhoric-s/Sharpe-a; four covers. 8-11-Ash Vs. Dracula. 12,13-Death of Ash 3.00

ARMY OF DARKNESS: ...
Dynamite Entertainment: 2007 - No. 27, 2010 ($3.50/$3.99)
... From the Ashes 1-4-Kuhoric-s/Blanco-a; covers by Blanco & Suydam 3.50
5-8-(The Long Road Home); two covers on each 3.50
9-25: 9-12-(Home Sweet Hell), 13-King For a Day. 14-17-Hellbillies and Deadnecks 3.50
26,27-($3.99) Raicht-s/Cohn-a/c 4.00
...: Ash's Christmas Horror Special (2008, $4.99) Kuhoric-s/Simons-a; 2 covers 5.00
.../ Reanimator One Shot (2013, $4.99) Rahner-s/Valiente-a 5.00

ARMY OF DARKNESS VOLUME 3
Dynamite Entertainment: 2012 - No. 13, 2013 ($3.99)
1-13: 1-Female Ash; Michaels-a 4.00

ARMY OF DARKNESS: ASHES 2 ASHES (Movie)
Devil's Due Publ.: July, 2004 - No. 4, 2004 ($2.99, limited series)
1-4-Four covers for each; Nick Bradshaw-a 3.00
1-Director's Cut (12/04, $4.99) r/#1, cover gallery, script and sketch pages 5.00
TPB (2005, $14.99) r/series; cover gallery; Bradshaw interview and sketch pages 15.00

ARMY OF DARKNESS: ASH SAVES OBAMA
Dynamite Entertainment: 2009 - No. 4, 2009 ($3.50, limited series)
1-4-Serrano-s/Padilla-a; covers by Parrillo and Nauck. 4-Obama app. 3.50

ARMY OF DARKNESS: SHOP TILL YOU DROP DEAD (Movie)
Devil's Due Publ.: Jan, 2005 - No. 4, July, 2005 ($2.99, limited series)
1-4:1-Five covers; Bradshaw-a/Kuhoric-s. 2-4: Two covers. 3-Greene-a 3.00

ARMY OF DARKNESS VS. HACK/SLASH
Dynamite Entertainment: 2013 - No. 6, 2014 ($3.99, limited series)
1-6-Tim Seeley-s/Daniel Leister-a; multiple covers on each 4.00

ARMY OF DARKNESS / XENA
Dynamite Entertainment: 2008 - No. 4, 2008 ($3.50, limited series)
1-4-Layman-s/Montenegro-a; two covers on each 3.50

ARMY SURPLUS KOMIKZ FEATURING CUTEY BUNNY
Army Surplus Komikz/Eclipse Comics: 1982 - No. 5, 1985 ($1.50, B&W)
1-Cutey Bunny begins 2 4 6 8 10 12
2-5: 5-(Eclipse)-JLA/X-Men/Batman parody 4.50

ARMY WAR HEROES (Also see Iron Corporal)
Charlton Comics: Dec, 1963 - No. 38, June, 1970
1 5 10 15 34 60 85
2-10 3 6 9 20 31 42
11-21,23-30: 24-Intro. Archer & Corp. Jack series 3 6 9 16 23 30
22-Origin/1st app. Iron Corporal series by Glanzman 4 8 12 27 44 60
31-38 2 4 6 10 14 18
Modern Comics Reprint 36 ('78) 5.00
NOTE: *Montes/Bache a-1, 16, 17, 21, 23-25, 27-30.*

AROUND THE BLOCK WITH DUNC & LOO (See Dunc and Loo)

AROUND THE WORLD IN 80 DAYS (Movie) (See A Golden Picture Classic)
Dell Publishing Co.: Feb, 1957
Four Color 784-Photo-c 6 12 18 42 79 115

AROUND THE WORLD UNDER THE SEA (See Movie Classics)

AROUND THE WORLD WITH ARCHIE (See Archie Giant Series Mag. #29, 35, 141)

AROUND THE WORLD WITH HUCKLEBERRY & HIS FRIENDS (See Dell Giant No. 44)

ARRGH! (Satire)
Marvel Comics Group: Dec, 1974 - No. 5, Sept, 1975 (25¢)
1-Dracula story; Sekowsky-a(p) 3 6 9 18 28 38
2-5: 2-Frankenstein. 3-Mummy. 4-Nightstalker(TV); Dracula-c/app., Hunchback. 5-Invisible Man, Dracula 3 6 9 14 19 24
NOTE *Alcala a-2; c-3. Everett a-1r, 2r. Grandenetti a-4. Maneely a-4r. Sutton a-1-3.*

ARROW (See Protectors)
Malibu Comics: Oct, 1992 ($1.95, one-shot)
1-Moder-a(p) 3.00

ARROW (Based on the 2012 television series)
DC Comics: Jan, 2013 - Present ($3.99, printings of digital-first stories)
1-12: 1-Photo-c; origin retold; Grell-a. 8-12-Photo-c 4.00
1-Special Edition (2012, giveaway) Grell-c; back-up preview of Green Arrow #0 3.00

ARROW, THE (See Funny Pages)
Centaur Publications: Oct, 1940 - No. 2, Nov, 1940; No. 3, Oct, 1941
1-The Arrow begins(r/Funny Pages) 343 686 1029 2400 4200 6000
2,3: 2-Tippy Taylor serial continues from Amazing Mystery Funnies #24. 3-Origin Dash Dartwell, the Human Meteor; origin The Rainbow-r; bondage-c 161 322 483 1030 1765 2500
NOTE: *Gustavson a-1, 2; c-3.*

ARROWHEAD (See Black Rider and Wild Western)
Atlas Comics (CPS): April, 1954 - No. 4, Nov, 1954
1-Arrowhead & his horse Eagle begin 15 30 45 90 140 190
2-4: 4-Forte-a 10 20 30 56 76 95
NOTE: *Heath c-3. Jack Katz a-3. Maneely c-2. Pakula a-2. Sinnott a-1-4; c-1.*

ARROWSMITH (Also see Astro City/Arrowsmith flip book)
DC Comics (Cliffhanger): Sept, 2003 - No. 6, May, 2004 ($2.95)
1-6-Pacheco-a/Busiek-s 3.00
...: So Smart in Their Fine Uniforms TPB (2004, $14.95) r/#1-6 15.00

ARSENAL (Teen Titans' Speedy)
DC Comics: Oct, 1998 - No. 4, Jan, 1999 ($2.50, limited series)
1-4: Grayson-s. 1-Black Canary app. 2-Green Arrow app. 3.00

ARSENAL SPECIAL (See New Titans, Showcase '94 #7 & Showcase '95 #8)
DC Comics: 1996 ($2.95, one-shot)
1 3.00

ARTBABE
Fantagraphics Books: May, 1996 - Apr, 1999 ($2.50/$2.95/$3.50, B&W)
V1 #5, V2 #1-3 3.00
#4-($3.50) 3.50

ARTEMIS: REQUIEM (Also see Wonder Woman, 2nd Series #90)
DC Comics: June, 1996 - No. 6, Nov, 1996 ($1.75, limited series)
1-6: Messner-Loebs scripts & Benes-c/a in all. 1,2-Wonder Woman app. 3.00

ARTIFACTS
Image Comics (Top Cow): Jul, 2010 - Present ($3.99, intended as a limited series)
0-(5/10, free) Free Comic Book Day edition; Sejic-a 3.00
1-36: 1-6-Marz-s/Broussard-a. 1-Multiple covers; back-up origin of Witchblade. 7,8-Portacio-a. 9-12-Haun-a. 10-Wraparound-c by Sejic. 13-Keown-a. 14-25-Sejic-a 4.00
...Origins (1/12, $3.99) Two-page spread origins of the 13 artifacts; wraparound-c 4.00

ART OF HOMAGE STUDIOS, THE
Image Comics: Dec, 1993 ($4.95, one-shot)
1-Short stories and pin-ups by Jim Lee, Silvestri, Williams, Portacio & Chiodo 5.00

ART OF ZEN INTERGALACTIC NINJA, THE
Entity Comics: 1994 - No. 2, 1994 ($2.95)
1,2 3.00

ARZACH (See Moebius...)
Dark Horse Comics: 1996 ($6.95, one-shot)
nn-Moebius-c/a/scripts 1 2 3 4 5 7

ASCENSION
Image Comics (Top Cow Productions): Oct, 1997 - No. 22, Mar, 2000 ($2.50)
Preview 5.00
Preview Gold Edition 8.00
Preview San Diego Edition 2 4 6 8 10 12
0 4.00
1/2 6.00
1-David Finch-s/a(p)/Batt-s/a(i) 4.00
1-Variant-c w/Image logo at lower right 6.00
2-22 3.00
... Collected Edition 1,2 (1998 - No. 2, $4.95, squarebound) 1-r/#1,2. 2-r/#3,4 5.00
Fan Club Edition 5.00

ASH
Event Comics: Nov, 1994 - No. 6, Dec, 1995; No. 0, May, 1996 ($2.50/$3.00)

Ash: Cinder & Smoke #6 © Q&P

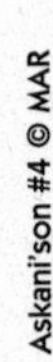

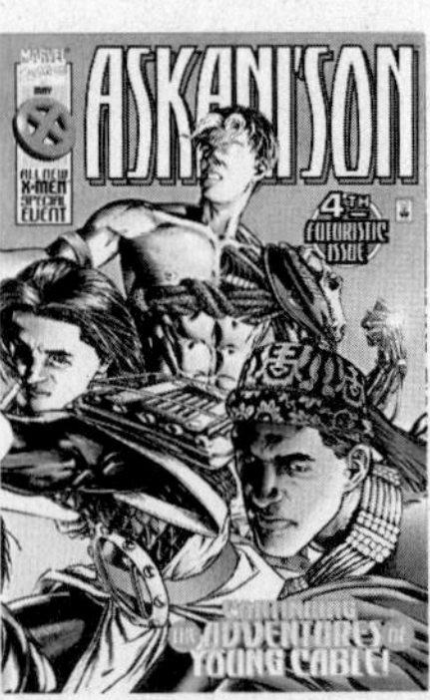

Askani'son #4 © MAR

Astonishing Tales #25 © MAR

	GD 2.0	VG 4.0	FN 6.0	VF 8.0	VF/NM 9.0	NM- 9.2

0-Present & Future (Both 5/96, $3.00, foil logo-c)-w/pin-ups 3.00
0-Blue Foil logo-c (Present and Future) (1000 each) 4.00
0-Silver Prism logo-c (Present and Future) (500 each) 10.00
0-Red Prism logo-c (Present and Future) (250 each) 20.00
0-Gold Hologram logo-c (Present and Future) (1000 each) 8.00
1-Quesada-p/story; Palmiotti-i/story: Barry Windsor-Smith pin-up
2 4 6 8 10 12
2-Mignola Hellboy pin-up 1 2 3 4 5 7
3,4: 3-Big Guy pin-up by Geoff Darrow. 4-Jim Lee pin-up 4.00
4-Fahrenheit Gold 7.00
4-6-Fahrenheit Red (5,6-1000) 8.00
4-6-Fahrenheit White 12.00
5, 6-Double-c w/Hildebrandt Bros.-a, Quesada & Palmiotti. 6-Texeira-c 3.00
5,6-Fahrenheit Gold (2000) 4.00
6-Fahrenheit White (500)-Texeira-c 12.00
Volume 1 (1996, $14.95, TPB)-r/#1-5, intro by James Robinson 15.00
Wizard Mini-Comic (1996, magazine supplement) 3.00
Wizard #1/2 (1997, mail order) 4.00

ASH AND THE ARMY OF DARKNESS
Dynamite Entertainment: 2013 - Present ($3.99)
1-5-Niles-s/Calero-a. 1-Three covers. 2-5-Two covers 4.00

ASH: CINDER & SMOKE
Event Comics: May, 1997 - No. 6, Oct, 1997 ($2.95, limited series)
1-6: Ramos-a/Waid, Augustyn-s in all. 2-6-variant covers by Ramos and Quesada 3.00

ASH: FILES
Event Comics: Mar, 1997 ($2.95, one-shot)
1-Comics w/text 3.00

ASH: FIRE AND CROSSFIRE
Event Comics: Jan, 1999 - No. 5 ($2.95, limited series)
1,2-Robinson-s/Quesada & Palmiotti-c/a 3.00

ASH: FIRE WITHIN, THE
Event Comics: Sept, 1996 - No. 2, Jan, 1997 ($2.95, unfinished limited series)
1,2: Quesada & Palmiotti-c/s/a 3.00

ASH/ 22 BRIDES
Event Comics: Dec, 1996 - No. 2, Apr, 1997 ($2.95, limited series)
1,2: Nicieza-s/Ramos-c/a 3.00

ASKANI'SON (See Adventures of Cyclops & Phoenix limited series)
Marvel Comics: Jan, 1996 - No. 4, May, 1996 ($2.95, limited series)
1-4: Story cont'd from Advs. of Cyclops & Phoenix; Lobdell/Loeb story; Gene Ha-c/a(p) 3.00
TPB (1997, $12.99) r/#1-4; Gene Ha painted-c 13.00

ASPEN (MICHAEL TURNER PRESENTS:...) (Also see Fathom)
Aspen MLT, Inc.: July, 2003 - No. 3, Aug, 2003 ($2.99)
1-Fathom story; Turner-a/Johns-s; interviews w/Turner & Johns; two covers by Turner 3.00
2,3:2-Fathom story; Turner-a/Johns-s; two covers by Turner; pin-ups and interviews 3.00
... Seasons: Fall 2005 (12/05, $2.99) short stories by various; Turner-c 3.00
... Seasons: Spring 2005 (4/05, $2.99) short stories by various; Turner-c 3.00
... Seasons: Summer 2006 (10/06, $2.99) short stories by various; Turner-c 3.00
... Seasons: Winter 2009 (3/09, $2.99) short stories by various; Benitez-c 3.00
... Showcase: Aspen Matthews 1 (7/08, $2.99) Caldwell-a 3.00
... Showcase: Kiani 1 (10/09, $2.99) Scott Clark-a; covers by Clark and Caldwell 3.00
... Sketchbook 1 (2003, $2.99) sketch pages by Michael Turner and Talent Caldwell 3.00
... Splash: 2006 Swimsuit Spectacular 1 (3/06, $2.99) pin-up pages by various; Turner-c 3.00
... Splash: 2007 Swimsuit Spectacular 1 (8/07, $2.99) pin-up pages by various; Turner-c 3.00
... Splash: 2008 Swimsuit Spectacular 1 (7/08, $2.99) pin-up pages by various; Turner-c 3.00
... Splash: 2010 Swimsuit Spectacular 1 (8/10, $2.99) pin-up pages by various; 2 covers 3.00

ASPEN SHOWCASE
Aspen MLT: Oct, 2008 ($2.99)
...: Benoist 1 (10/08) - Krul-s/Gunnell-a; two covers by Gunnell & Manapul 3.00
...: Ember 1 (2/09) - Randy Green-a; two covers by Gunnell & Green 3.00

ASSASSINS
DC Comics (Amalgam): Apr, 1996 ($1.95)
1 3.00

ASSASSIN'S CREED: THE FALL (Based on the Ubisoft Entertainment videogame)
DC Comics: Jan, 2011 - No. 3, Mar, 2011 ($3.99, limited series)
1-3-Cam Stewart & Karl Kerschl-s/a 4.00

ASSAULT ON NEW OLYMPUS PROLOGUE
Marvel Comics: Jan, 2010 ($3.99, one-shot)
1-Spider-Man, Hercules, Amadeus Cho app.; Granov-c; leads into Inc. Hercules #138 4.00

ASTONISHING (Formerly Marvel Boy No. 1, 2)
Marvel/Atlas Comics(20CC): No. 3, Apr, 1951 - No. 63, Aug, 1957
3-Marvel Boy continues; 3-5-Marvel Boy-c 107 214 321 680 1165 1650
4-6-Last Marvel Boy; 4-Stan Lee app. 74 148 222 470 810 1150
7-10: 7-Maneely s/f story. 10-Sinnott s/f story 40 80 120 246 411 575
11,12,15,17,20 37 74 111 222 361 500
13,14,16,18,19-Krigstein-a. 18-Jack The Ripper sty 38 76 114 228 369 510
21,22,24 30 60 90 177 289 400
23-E.C. swipe "The Hole In The Wall" from Vault Of Horror #16
32 64 96 188 307 425
25,29: 25-Crandall-a. 29-Decapitation-c 29 58 87 172 281 390
26-28 27 54 81 160 263 365
30-Tentacled eyeball-c/story; classic-c 54 108 162 343 574 825
31-37-Last pre-code issue 24 48 72 142 234 325
38-43,46,48-52,56,58,59,61 20 40 60 114 182 250
44,45,47,53-55,57,60: 44-Crandall swipe/Weird Fantasy #22. 45,47-Krigstein-a. 53-Ditko-a. 54-Torres-a, 55-Crandall, Torres-a. 57-Williamson/Krenkel-a (4 pgs.).
60-Williamson/Mayo-a (4 pgs.) 20 40 60 118 192 265
62,63: 62-Torres, Powell-a. 63-Woodbridge-a 20 40 60 117 189 260

NOTE: ***Ayers** a-16, 49. **Berg** a-36, 53, 56. **Cameron** a-50. **Gene Colan** a-12, 20, 29, 56. **Ditko** a-53. **Drucker** a-41, 62. **Everett** a-3-6(3), 6, 10, 12, 37, 47, 48, 58; c-3-5, 13,15, 16, 18, 29, 47, 49, 51, 53-55, 57, 59-63. **Fass** a-11, 34. **Forte** a-26, 48, 53, 58, 60. **Fuje** a-11. **Heath** a-8, 29; c-8, 9, 19, 22, 25, 26. **Kirby** a-56. **Lawrence** a-28, 37, 38, 42. **Maneely** a-7(2), 19; c-7, 31, 33, 34, 56. **Moldoff** a-33. **Morisi** a-10, 60. **Morrow** a-52, 61. **Orlando** a-47, 58, 61. **Pakula** a-10. **Powell** a-43, 44, 48. **Ravielli** a-26, 28. **Reinman** a-32, 34, 38. **Robinson** a-20. **J. Romita** a-7, 18, 24, 43, 57,61. **Roussos** a-55. **Sale** a-28, 38, 59; c-32. **Sekowsky** a-13. **Severin** c-46. **Shores** a-16, 60. **Sinnott** a-11, 30, 31. **Whitney** a-13. **Ed Win** a-20. Canadian reprints exist.*

ASTONISHING SPIDER-MAN AND WOLVERINE
Marvel Comics: Jul, 2010 - No. 6, Jul. 2011 ($3.99, limited series)
1-6-Adam Kubert-a/Jason Aaron-s. 1-Bonus pin-up gallery; wraparound-c 4.00
1-Director's Cut (10/10, $4.99) r/#1 with full script & B&W art 5.00
...: Another Fine Mess (6/11, $4.99) r/#1-3; wraparound-c 5.00

ASTONISHING TALES (See Ka-Zar)
Marvel Comics Group: Aug, 1970 - No. 36, July, 1976 (#1-7: 15¢; #8: 25¢)
1-Ka-Zar (by Kirby(p) #1,2; by B. Smith #3-6) & Dr. Doom (by Wood #1-4; by Tuska #5,6; by Colan #7,8; 1st Marvel villain solo series) double feature begins; Kraven the Hunter-c/story; Nixon cameo 6 12 18 38 69 100
2-Kraven the Hunter-c/story; Kirby, Wood-a 3 6 9 21 33 45
3-6: B. Smith-p; Wood-a-#3,4. 5,6-Red Skull 2-part story
4 8 12 23 37 50
7-Last 15¢ issue; Black Panther app. 3 6 9 16 23 30
8-(25¢, 52 pgs.)-Last Dr. Doom of series 3 6 9 21 33 45
9-All Ka-Zar issues begin; Lorna-r/Lorna #14 2 4 6 11 16 20
10-B. Smith/Sal Buscema-a. 3 6 9 14 20 25
11-Origin Ka-Zar & Zabu; death of Ka-Zar's father 2 4 6 13 18 22
12-2nd app.Man-Thing; by Neal Adams (see Savage Tales #1 for 1st app.)
4 8 12 28 47 65
13-3rd app.Man-Thing 3 6 9 20 31 42
14-20: 14-Jann of the Jungle-r (1950s); reprints censored Ka-Zar-s from Savage Tales #1. 17-S.H.I.E.L.D. begins. 19-Starlin-a(p). 20-Last Ka-Zar (continues into 1974 Ka-Zar series)
1 3 4 6 8 10
21-(12/73)-It! the Living Colossus begins, ends #24 (see Supernatural Thrillers #1)
4 8 12 23 37 50
22-24: 23,24-IT vs. Fin Fang Foom 3 6 9 17 26 35
25-1st app. Deathlok the Demolisher; full length stories begin, end #36; Perez's 1st work, 2 pgs. (8/74) 5 10 15 35 63 90
26-28,30 2 4 6 11 16 22
29-r/origin/1st app. Guardians of the Galaxy from Marvel Super-Heroes #18 plus-c w/4 pgs. omitted; no Deathlok story 2 4 6 9 12 15
31-34: 31-Watcher-r/Silver Surfer #3 2 4 6 10 13 16
35,36-(Regular 25¢ edition)(5,7/76) 2 4 6 10 13 16
35,36-(30¢-c, low distribution) 5 10 15 30 50 70

NOTE: ***Buckler** a-13i, 16p, 25, 26p, 27p, 28, 29p-36p; c-13, 25p, 26-30, 32-35p, 36. **John Buscema** a-9, 12p-14p, 16p; c-4-6p, 12p. **Colan** a-7p, 8p. **Ditko** a-21r. **Everett** a-6i. **G. Kane** a-11p, 15p; c-9, 10p, 11p, 14, 15p, 21p. **McWilliams** a-30i. **Starlin** a-19p; c-16p. **Sutton & Trimpe** a-8. **Tuska** a-5p, 6p, 8p. **Wood** a-1-4. **Wrightson** c-31i.*

ASTONISHING TALES (Anthology)
Marvel Comics: Apr, 2009 - No. 6, Sept, 2009 ($3.99, limited series)
1-6-Wolverine, Punisher, Iron Man and Iron Man 2020 app. 1-Wraparound-c 4.00

ASTONISHING THOR
Marvel Comics: Jan, 2011 - No. 5, Sept, 2011 ($3.99, limited series)
1-5: 1-Robert Rodi-s/Mike Choi-a/Esad Ribic-c 4.00

ASTONISHING X-MEN

Astonishing X-Men #2 © MAR

Astro City: Local Heroes #1 © Jukebox

Atari Force #13 © Atari

GD 2.0 | VG 4.0 | FN 6.0 | VF 8.0 | VF/NM 9.0 | NM- 9.2

Marvel Comics: Mar, 1995 - No. 4, July, 1995 ($1.95, limited series)
1-Age of Apocalypse; Magneto-c 4.00
2-4 3.00

ASTONISHING X-MEN
Marvel Comics: Sept, 1999 - No.3, Nov, 1999 ($2.50, limited series)
1-3-New team, Cable & X-Man app.; Peterson-a 3.00
TPB (11/00, $15.95) r/#1-3, X-Men #92 & #95, Uncanny X-Men #375 16.00

ASTONISHING X-MEN (See Giant-Size Astonishing X-Men for story folllowing #24)
Marvel Comics: July, 2004 - No. 68, Dec, 2013 ($2.99/$3.99)
1-Whedon-s/Cassaday-c/a; team of Cyclops, Beast, Wolverine, Emma Frost & Kitty Pryde 4.00
1-Director's Cut (2004, $3.99) different Cassaday partial sketch-c; cover gallery, sketch pages and script excerpt 5.00
1-Variant-c by Cassaday 10.00
1-Variant-c by Dell'Otto 5.00
2,3,5,6-X-Men battle Ord 3.00
4-Colossus returns 4.00
4-Variant Colossus cover by Cassaday 5.00
7-24: 7-Fantastic Four app. 9,10-X-Men vs. the Danger Room 3.00
7,9,10-12,19-24-Second printing variant covers 3.00
25-35: 25-Ellis-s/Bianchi-a begins; Bianchi wraparound-c. 31-Jimenez-a begins 3.00
36-68-($3.99): 36-Pearson wraparound-c; Way-s/Pearson-a. 44-47-McKone-a. 51-Northstar wedding; wraparound-c. 60-X-Termination tie-in 4.00
Annual 1 (1/13, $4.99) Gage-s/Baldeon-a; bonus r/Alpha Flight #106 5.00
.../Amazing Spider-Man: The Gauntlet Sketchbook ('09, giveaway) flip book preview 3.00
...: Ghost Boxes 1,2 (12/08-1/09, $3.99) Ellis-s/Davis & Granov-a; full Ellis script 4.00
... Saga (2006, $3.99) reprints highlights from #1-12; sketch pages and cover gallery 4.00
... Sketchbook Special ('08, $2.99) Costume sketches & blueprints by Bianchi & Larroca 3.00
...Vol. 1 HC (2006, $29.99, dust jacket) r/#1-12; interviews, sketch pages and covers 30.00
...Vol. 1: Gifted (2004, $14.99) r/#1-6; variant cover gallery 15.00
...Vol. 2: Dangerous (2005, $14.99) r/#7-12; variant cover gallery 15.00
...Vol. 3: Torn (2007, $14.99) r/#13-18; variant & sketch cover gallery 15.00

ASTONISHING X-MEN: XENOGENESIS
Marvel Comics: July, 2010 - No. 5, Apr, 2011 ($3.99, limited series)
1-5-Warren Ellis-s/Kaare Andrews-a/c. 1-Wraparound-c; script 4.00
1-Director's Cut (10/10, $4.99) r/#1 with full script & B&W art; cover sketches 5.00

ASTOUNDING SPACE THRILLS: THE COMIC BOOK
Image Comics: Apr, 2000 - No. 4, Dec, 2000 ($2.95, limited series)
1-4-Steve Conley-s/a. 2,3-Flip book w/Crater Kid 3.00
Galaxy-Sized Astounding Space Thrills 1 (10/01, $4.95) 5.00

ASTOUNDING WOLF-MAN
Image Comics: Jun, 2007 - No. 25, Nov, 2010 ($2.99)
1-Free Comic Boy Day issue; Kirkman-s/Howard-a; origin story 3.00
2-24: 11-Invincible x-over from Invincble #57 3.00
25-($4.99) Wraparound-c; Wolfcorps app. 5.00
Vol. 1 TPB (2008, $14.99) r/#1-7; sketch pages; Kirkman intro. 15.00

ASTRA
CPM Manga: 2001 - No. 8 ($2.95, B&W, limited series)
1-8: Created by Jerry Robinson; Tanaka-a. 1-Balent variant-c 3.00
TPB (2002, $15.95) r/#1-8; JH Williams III-c from #3 16.00

ASTRO BOY (TV) (See March of Comics #285 & The Original...)
Gold Key: August, 1965 (12¢)
1(10151-508) 1st app. Astro Boy in comics 24 48 72 168 372 575

ASTRO BOY THE MOVIE (Based on the 2009 CGI movie)
IDW Publishing: 2009 ($3.99, limited series)
...Official Movie Adaptation 1-4 (8/09 - No. 4, 9/09, $3.99) EJ Su-a 4.00
...Official Movie Prequel 1-4 (5/09 - No. 4, 8/09) Jourdan-a/c; Ashley Wood var-c on each 4.00

ASTRO CITY / ARROWSMITH (Flip book)
DC Comics (WildStorm Productions): Jun, 2004 ($2.95, one-shot flip book)
1-Intro. Black Badge; Ross-c; Arrowsmith a/c by Pacheco 3.00

ASTRO CITY (Also see Kurt Busiek's Astro City)
DC Comics (WildStorm Productions): Dec, 2004 - Dec, 2009 (one-shots)
...#1 Special Edition (8/10, $1.00) reprints first issue with "What's Next? cover logo 3.00
...: Astra Special 1,2 (11/09, 12/09, $3.99) Busiek-s/Anderson-a/Ross-c 4.00
... A Visitor's Guide (12/04, $5.95) short story, city guide and pin-ups by various; Ross-c 6.00
...: Beautie (4/08, $3.99) Busiek-s/Anderson-a/Ross-c; origin 4.00
...: Samaritan (9/06, $3.99) Busiek-s/Anderson-a/Ross-c; origin of Infidel 4.00
...: Shining Stars HC (2011, $24.99, d.j) r/...: Astra Special 1,2, ...: Beautie, ...: Samaritan, and ...: Silver Agent 1,2; bonus design art and Ross cover sketch art 25.00
...: Silver Agent 1,2 (8,9/10, $3.99) Busiek-s/Anderson-a/Ross-c 4.00

ASTRO CITY (Also see Kurt Busiek's Astro City)
DC Comics (Vertigo): Aug, 2013 - Present ($3.99)
1-10-Busiek-s/Anderson-a/Ross-c 4.00

ASTRO CITY: DARK AGE
DC Comics (WildStorm Productions): Aug, 2005 - No. 4, Dec, 2005 ($2.95, limited series)
Book One 1-4-Busiek-s/Anderson-a/Ross-c; Silver Agent and The Blue Knight app. 3.00
Book Two #1-4 (1/07-11/07, $2.99) Busiek-s/Anderson-a/Ross-c 3.00
Book Three #1-4 (7/09-10/09, $3.99) Busiek-s/Anderson-a/Ross-c 4.00
Book Four #1-4 (3/10-6/10, $3.99) Busiek-s/Anderson-a/Ross-c 4.00
... 1: Brothers and Other Strangers HC (2008, $29.99, d.j.) r/Book One #1-4, Book Two #1-4, and story from Astro City/Arrowsmith #1; Marc Guggenheim intro.; new Ross-c 30.00
... 1: Brothers and Other Strangers SC (2009, $19.99) same contents as HC 20.00
... 2: Brothers in Arms HC ('10, $29.99, d.j.) r/Book Three #1-4, Book Four #1-4, Ross-c 30.00

ASTRO CITY: LOCAL HEROES
DC Comics (WildStorm Productions): Apr, 2003 - No. 5, Feb, 2004 ($2.95, limited series)
1-5-Busiek-s/Anderson-a/Ross-c 3.00
HC (2005, $24.95) r/series; Kurt Busiek's Astro City V2 #21,22; stories from Astro City/Arrowsmith #1; and 9-11, The World's Finest... Vol. 2; Alex Ross sketch pages 25.00
SC (2005, $17.99) same contents as HC 18.00

ASYLUM
Millennium Publications: 1993 ($2.50)
1-3: 1-Bolton-c/a; Russell 2-pg. illos 3.00

ASYLUM
Maximum Press: Dec, 1995 - No. 11, Jan, 1997 ($2.95/$2.99, anthology) (#1-6 are flip books)
1-11: 1-Warchild by Art Adams, Beanworld, Avengelyne, Battlestar Galactica. 2-Intro Mike Deodato's Deathkiss. 4-1st app.Christian; painted Battlestar Galactica story begins. 6-Intro Bionix (Six Million Dollar Man & the Bionic Woman). 7-Begin $2.99-c. 8-B&W-a. 9- Foot Soldiers & Kid Supreme. 10-Lady Supreme by Terry Moore-c/app. 4.00

ATARI FORCE (Also see Promotional comics section)
DC Comics: Jan, 1984 - No. 20, Aug, 1985 (Mando paper)
1-(1/84)-Intro Tempest, Packrat, Babe, Morphea, & Dart 4.00
2-20 3.00
Special 1 (4/86) 4.00
NOTE: ***Byrne*** *c-Special 1i.* ***Giffen*** *a-12p, 13i.* ***Rogers*** *a-18p, Special 1p.*

A-TEAM, THE (TV) (Also see Marvel Graphic Novel)
Marvel Comics Group: Mar, 1984 - No. 3, May, 1984 (limited series)
1-3 6.00
1,2-(Whitman bagged set) w/75¢-c 2 4 6 8 10 12
3-(Whitman, no bag) w/75¢-c 1 2 3 5 6 8

A-TEAM: SHOTGUN WEDDING (Based on the 2010 movie)
IDW Publishing: Mar, 2010 - No. 4, Apr, 2010 ($3.99, limited series)
1-4-Co-plotted by Joe Carnahan; Stephen Mooney-a; Snyder III-c 4.00

A-TEAM: WAR STORIES (Based on the 2010 movie)
IDW Publishing: Mar, 2010 - Apr, 2010 ($3.99, series of one-shots)
...: B.A. (3/10) Dixon & Burnham-s/Maloney-a/Gaydos & photo-c 4.00
...: Face (4/10) Dixon & Burnham-s/Muriel-a/Gaydos & photo-c 4.00
...: Hannibal (3/10) Dixon & Burnham-s/Petrus-a/Gaydos & photo-c 4.00
...: Murdock (4/10) Dixon & Burnham-s/Vilanova-a/Gaydos & photo-c 4.00

ATHENA INC. THE MANHUNTER PROJECT
Image Comics: Dec, 2001; Apr, 2002 - No. 6 ($2.95/$4.95/$5.95)
...The Beginning (12/01, $5.95) Anacleto-c/a; Haberlin-s 6.00
1-5: 1-(4/02, $2.95) two covers by Anacleto 3.00
6-($4.95) 5.00
...: Agents Roster #1 (11/02, $5.95, 8 1/2 x 11") bios and sketch pages by Anacleto 6.00
Vol. 1 TPB (4/03, $19.95) r/#1-6 & Agents Roster; cover gallery 20.00

ATHENA
Dynamite Entertainment: 2009 - No. 4, 2010 ($3.50)
1-4-Murray-s/Neves-a; multiple covers on each. 1-Obama flip cover 3.50

ATLANTIS CHRONICLES, THE (Also see Aquaman, 3rd Series & Aquaman: Time & Tide)
DC Comics: Mar, 1990 - No. 7, Sept, 1990 ($2.95, limited series, 52 pgs.)
1-7: 1-Peter David scripts. 7-True origin of Aquaman; nudity panels 4.00

ATLANTIS, THE LOST CONTINENT
Dell Publishing Co.: May, 1961

Atlas #4 © MAR

The Atom #19 © DC

Atomic Comics #3 © Green Pub.

GD VG FN VF VF/NM NM-
2.0 4.0 6.0 8.0 9.0 9.2

GD VG FN VF VF/NM NM-
2.0 4.0 6.0 8.0 9.0 9.2

Four Color #1188-Movie, photo-c 9 18 27 58 114 170

ATLAS (See 1st Issue Special)

ATLAS
Dark Horse Comics: Feb, 1994 - No. 4, 1994 ($2.50, limited series)
1-4 3.00

ATLAS (Agents of Atlas)(The Heroic Age)
Marvel Comics: Jul, 2010 - No. 5, Nov, 2010 ($3.99/$2.99)
1-($3.99) Parker-s/Hardman-a/Dodson-c; 3-D Man app.; profile page 4.00
2-5-($2.99) 2,3,5-Pagulayan-c. 4-Jae Lee-c 3.00

ATLAS UNIFIED
Atlas Comics: No. 0, Oct, 2011 - No. 2, Feb, 2012 ($2.99, unfinished limited series)
0 Prelude: Midnight (10/11) Phoenix, Kromag, Sgt. Hawk app.; bonus sketch pages 3.00
1,2: 1-Three covers; Peyer-s/Salgado-a; x-over of Grim Ghost, Wulf, Phoenix & others 3.00

ATMOSPHERICS
Avatar Press: June, 2002 ($5.95, B&W, one-shot graphic novel)
1-Warren Ellis-s/Ken Meyer Jr.-painted-a/c 6.00

ATOM, THE (See Action #425, All-American #19, Brave & the Bold, D.C. Special Series #1, Detective Comics, Flash Comics #80, Hawkman, Identity Crisis, JLA, Power Of The Atom, Showcase #34 -36, Super Friends, Sword of The Atom, Teen Titans & World's Finest)

ATOM, THE (...& the Hawkman No. 39 on)
National Periodical Publ.: June-July, 1962 - No. 38, Aug-Sept, 1968
1-(6-7/62)-Intro Plant-Master; 1st app. Maya 93 186 279 744 1672 2600
2 31 62 93 223 499 775
3-1st Time Pool story; 1st app. Chronos (origin) 20 40 60 141 313 485
4,5: 4-Snapper Carr x-over 15 30 45 103 227 350
6,9,10 11 22 33 76 163 250
7-Hawkman x-over (6-7/63; 1st Atom & Hawkman team-up); 1st app. Hawkman since Brave & the Bold tryouts 23 46 69 161 356 550
8-Justice League, Dr. Light app. 12 24 36 79 170 260
11-15: 13-Chronos-c/story 9 18 27 60 120 180
16-20: 19-Zatanna x-over 7 14 21 46 86 125
21-28,30: 26-Two-page pin-up. 28-Chronos-c/story 6 12 18 41 76 110
29-1st solo Golden Age Atom x-over in S.A. 12 24 36 80 173 265
31-35,37,38: 31-Hawkman x-over. 37-Intro. Major Mynah; Hawkman cameo
5 10 15 35 63 90
36-G.A. Atom x-over 6 12 18 41 76 110
NOTE: ***Anderson*** *a-1-11i, 13i; c-inks-1-25, 31-35, 37.* ***Sid Greene*** *a-8i-37i.* ***Gil Kane*** *a-1p-37p; c-1p-28p, 29, 33p, 34; c-26i.* ***George Roussos*** *a-38i.* ***Mike Sekowsky*** *a-38p. Time Pool stories also in 6, 9,12, 17, 21, 27, 35.*

ATOM, THE (See All New Atom and Tangent Comics/ The Atom)

ATOM AGE (See Classics Illustrated Special Issue)

ATOM-AGE COMBAT
St. John Publishing Co.: June, 1952 - No. 5, Apr, 1953; Feb, 1958
1-Buck Vinson in all 53 106 159 334 567 800
2-Flying saucer story 32 64 96 192 314 435
3,5: 3-Mayo-a (6 pgs.). 5-Flying saucer-c/story 29 58 87 170 278 385
4 (Scarce) 32 64 96 192 314 435
1(2/58-St. John) 23 46 69 136 223 310

ATOM-AGE COMBAT
Fago Magazines: No. 2, Jan, 1959 - No. 3, Mar, 1959
2-A-Bomb explosion-c; 30 60 90 177 289 400
3 22 44 66 132 216 300

ATOMAN
Spark Publications: Feb, 1946 - No. 2, April, 1946
1-Origin & 1st app. Atoman; Robinson/Meskin-a; Kidcrusaders, Wild Bill Hickok, Marvin the Great app. 68 136 204 435 743 1050
2-Robinson/Meskin-a; Robinson c-1,2 42 84 126 265 445 625

ATOM & HAWKMAN, THE (Formerly The Atom)
National Periodical Publ: No. 39, Oct-Nov, 1968 - No. 45, Oct-Nov, 1969; No. 46, Mar, 2010
39-43: 40-41-Kubert/Anderson-a. 43-(7/69)-Last 12¢ issue; 1st S.A. app. Gentleman Ghost
5 10 15 34 60 85
44,45: 44-(9/69)-1st 15¢-c; origin Gentleman Ghost 5 10 15 34 60 85
46-(3/10, $2.99) Blackest Night crossover one-shot; Geoff Johns-s/Ryan Sook-a/c 3.00
NOTE: ***M. Anderson*** *a-39, 40i, 41i, 43, 44.* ***Sid Greene*** *a-40i-45i.* ***Kubert*** *a-40p, 41p; c-39-45.*

ATOM ANT (TV) (See Golden Comics Digest #2) (Hanna-Barbera)
Gold Key: January, 1966 (12¢)
1(10170-601)-1st app. Atom Ant, Precious Pup, and Hillbilly Bears
15 30 45 103 227 350

ATOM ANT & SECRET SQUIRREL (See Hanna-Barbera Presents)

ATOMIC AGE
Marvel Comics (Epic Comics): Nov, 1990 - No. 4, Feb, 1991 ($4.50, limited series, squarebound, 52 pgs.)
1-4: Williamson-a(i); sci-fi story set in 1957 4.50

ATOMIC ATTACK (True War Stories; formerly Attack, first series)
Youthful Magazines: No. 5, Jan, 1953 - No. 8, Oct, 1953 (1st story is sci/fi in all issues)
5-Atomic bomb-c; science fiction stories in all 41 82 123 256 428 600
6-8 28 56 84 165 270 375

ATOMIC BOMB
Jay Burtis Publications: 1945 (36 pgs.)
1-Superheroes Airmale & Stampy (scarce) 71 142 213 454 777 1100

ATOMIC BUNNY (Formerly Atomic Rabbit)
Charlton Comics: No. 12, Aug, 1958 - No. 19, Dec, 1959
12 12 24 36 69 97 125
13-19 8 16 24 42 54 65

ATOMIC COMICS
Daniels Publications (Canadian): Jan, 1946 (Reprints, one-shot)
1-Rocketman, Yankee Boy, Master Key app. 40 80 120 246 411 575

ATOMIC COMICS
Green Publishing Co.: Jan, 1946 - No. 4, July-Aug, 1946 (#1-4 were printed w/o cover gloss)
1-Radio Squad by Siegel & Shuster; Barry O'Neal app.; Fang Gow cover-r/ Detective Comics (Classic-c) 81 162 243 518 884 1250
2-Inspector Dayton; Kid Kane by Matt Baker; Lucky Wings, Congo King, Prop Powers (only app.) begin 55 110 165 352 601 850
3,4: 3-Zero Ghost Detective app.; Baker-a(2) each; 4-Baker-c
40 80 120 244 402 560

ATOMIC KNIGHTS (See Strange Adventures #117)
DC Comics: 2010 ($39.99, HC with dustjacket)
HC-Reprints the original 1960-64 run from debut in Strange Adventures #117 to S.A. #160; new intro. by Murphy Anderson 40.00

ATOMIC MOUSE (TV, Movies) (See Blue Bird, Funny Animals, Giant Comics Edition & Wotalife Comics)
Capitol Stories/Charlton Comics: 3/53 - No. 52, 2/63; No. 1, 12/84; V2#10, 9/85 - No. 12, 1/86
1-Origin & 1st app.; Al Fago-c/a in most 34 68 102 204 332 460
2 15 30 45 85 130 175
3-10: 5-Timmy The Timid Ghost app.; see Zoo Funnies
10 20 30 58 79 100
11-13,16-25 8 16 24 40 50 60
14,15-Hoppy The Marvel Bunny app. 9 18 27 50 65 80
26-(68 pgs.) 12 24 36 67 94 120
27-40: 36,37-Atom The Cat app. 6 12 18 29 36 42
41-52 5 10 15 22 26 30
1 (1984)-Low print run; rep/#7-c w/diff. stories 2 4 6 8 10 12
V2#10 (9/85) -12(1/86)-Low print run 1 3 4 6 8 10

ATOMIC RABBIT (Atomic Bunny #12 on; see Giant Comics #3 & Wotalife)
Charlton Comics: Aug, 1955 - No. 11, Mar, 1958
1-Origin & 1st app.; Al Fago-c/a in all? 30 60 90 177 289 400
2 14 28 42 80 115 150
3-10 10 20 30 56 76 95
11-(68 pgs.) 14 28 42 80 115 150

ATOMICS, THE
AAA Pop Comics: Jan, 2000 - No. 15, Nov, 2001 ($2.95)
1-11-Mike Allred-s/a; 1-Madman-c/app. 3.00
12-15-($3.50): 13-15-Savage Dragon-c/app. 15-Afterword by Alex Ross; colored reprint of 1st Frank Einstein story 3.50
...King-Size Giant Spectacular: Jigsaw (2000, $10.00) r/#1-4 10.00
...King-Size Giant Spectacular: Lessons in Light, Lava, & Lasers (2000, $8.95) r/#5-8 9.00
...King-Size Giant Spectacular: Running With the Dragon ('02, $8.95) r/#13-15 and r/1st Frank Einstein app. in color 9.00
...King-Size Giant Spectacular: Worlds Within Worlds ('01, $8.95) r/#9-12 9.00
Madman and the Atomics, Vol. 1 TPB (2007, $24.99) r/#1-15, cover gallery, pin-ups, afterword by Alex Ross 25.00
...: Spaced Out & Grounded in Snap City TPB (10/03, $12.95) r/one-shots - It Girl, Mr. Gum, Spaceman and Crash Metro & the Star Squad; sketch pages 13.00

ATOMIC SPY CASES
Avon Periodicals: Mar-Apr, 1950 (Painted-c)

Attack #1 © Youthful

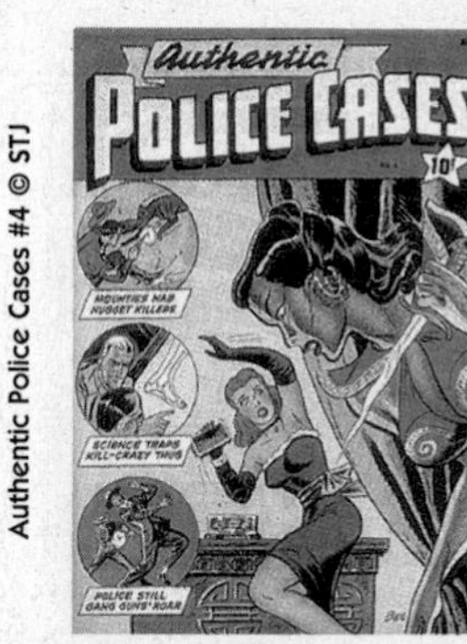

Authentic Police Cases #4 © STJ

The Authority #14 © WSP

GD 2.0 | VG 4.0 | FN 6.0 | VF 8.0 | VF/NM 9.0 | NM- 9.2

1-No Wood-a; A-bomb blast panels; Fass-a 39 78 117 230 375 520

ATOMIC THUNDERBOLT, THE
Regor Company: Feb, 1946 (one-shot) (scarce)
1-Intro. Atomic Thunderbolt & Mr. Murdo 64 128 192 406 696 985

ATOMIC TOYBOX
Image Comics: Dec, 1999 ($2.95)
1- Aaron Lopresti-c/s/a 3.00

ATOMIC WAR!
Ace Periodicals (Junior Books): Nov, 1952 - No. 4, Apr, 1953
1-Atomic bomb-c 152 304 456 965 1658 2350
2,3: 3-Atomic bomb-c 68 136 204 435 743 1050
4-Used in **POP**, pg. 96 & illo. 68 136 204 435 743 1050

ATOMIKA
Speakeasy Comics/Mercury Comics: Mar, 2005 - No. 6 ($2.99)
1-6: 1-Alex Ross-c/Sal Abbinanti-a/Dabb-s. 3-Fabry-c. 4-Four covers; Romita back-c 3.00
... God is Red TPB (5/06, $19.99) r/#1-6; cover gallery; Dabb foreword 20.00

ATOMIK ANGELS
Crusade Comics: May, 1996 - No. 4, Nov. 1996 ($2.50)
1-4: 1-Freefall from Gen 13 app. 3.00
1-Variant-c 4.00
Intrep-Edition (2/96, B&W, giveaway at launch party)-Previews Atomik Angels #1; includes Billy Tucci interview. 4.00

ATOM SPECIAL (See Atom & Justice League of America)
DC Comics: 1993/1995 ($2.50/$2.95)(68pgs.)
1,2: 1-Dillon-c/a. 2-McDonnell-a/Bolland-c/Peyer-s 4.00

ATOM THE CAT (Formerly Tom Cat; see Giant Comics #3)
Charlton Comics: No. 9, Oct, 1957 - No. 17, Aug, 1959
9 10 20 30 54 72 90
10,13-17 7 14 21 35 43 50
11,12: 11(64 pgs)-Atomic Mouse app. 12(100 pgs.) 11 22 33 62 86 110

ATTACK
Youthful Mag./Trojan No. 5 on: May, 1952 - No. 4, Nov, 1952; No. 5, Jan, 1953 - No. 5, Sept, 1953
1-(1st series)-Extreme violence 42 84 126 265 445 625
2,3-Both Harrison-c/a; bondage, whipping 24 48 72 142 234 325
4-Krenkel-a (7 pgs.); Harrison-a (becomes Atomic Attack #5 on) 24 48 72 142 234 325
5-(#1, Trojan, 2nd series) 17 34 51 98 154 210
6-8 (#2-4), 5 14 28 42 76 108 140

ATTACK
Charlton Comics: No. 54, 1958 - No. 60, Nov, 1959
54 (25¢, 100 pgs.) 12 24 36 69 97 125
55-60 7 14 21 35 43 50

ATTACK!
Charlton Comics: 1962 - No. 15, 3/75; No. 16, 8/79 - No. 48, 10/84
nn(#1)-('62) Special Edition 5 10 15 34 60 85
2('63), 3(Fall, '64) 4 8 12 22 35 48
V4#3(10/66), 4(10/67)-(Formerly Special War Series #2; becomes Attack At Sea V4#5): 3-Tokyo Rose story 3 6 9 18 28 38
1(9/71)-D-Day story 3 6 9 16 23 30
2-5: 2-Hitler app. 4-American Eagle app. 2 4 6 9 12 15
6-15(3/75): 8-Nixon app. 1 3 4 6 8 10
16(8/79) - 40 5.00
41-47 Low print run 7.00
48(10/84)-Wood-r; S&K-c (low print) 1 3 4 6 8 10
Modern Comics 13('78)-r 5.00
NOTE: *Sutton a-9, 10, 13.*

ATTACK!
Spire Christian Comics (Fleming H. Revell Co.): 1975 (39¢/49¢, 36 pgs.)
nn 2 4 6 10 14 18

ATTACK AT SEA (Formerly Attack!, 1967)
Charlton Comics: V4#5, Oct, 1968 (one-shot)
V4#5 3 6 9 18 28 38

ATTACK ON PLANET MARS (See Strange Worlds #18)
Avon Periodicals: 1951
nn-Infantino, Fawcette, Kubert & Wood-a; adaptation of Tarrano the Conqueror by Ray Cummings 90 180 270 576 988 1400

ATTITUDE LAD
Slave Labor Graphics: Apr, 1994 - No. 3, Nov, 1994 ($2.95, B&W)
1-3 3.00

AUDREY & MELVIN (Formerly Little...)(See Little Audrey & Melvin)
Harvey Publications: No. 62, Sept, 1974
62 2 4 6 9 13 16

AUGIE DOGGIE (TV) (See Hanna-Barbera Band Wagon, Quick-Draw McGraw, Spotlight #2, Top Cat & Whitman Comic Books)
Gold Key: October, 1963 (12¢)
1-Hanna-Barbera character 15 30 45 100 220 340

AUTHENTIC POLICE CASES
St. John Publishing Co.: 2/48 - No. 6, 11/48; No. 7, 5/50 - No. 38, 3/55
1-Hale the Magician by Tuska begins 51 102 153 318 539 760
2-Lady Satan, Johnny Rebel app. 32 64 96 188 307 425
3-Veiled Avenger app.; blood drainage story plus 2 Lucky Coyne stories; used in **SOTI**, illo. from Red Seal #16 54 108 162 343 574 825
4,5: 4-Masked Black Jack app. 5-Late 1930s Jack Cole-a(r); transvestism story 32 64 96 188 307 425
6-Matt Baker-c; used in **SOTI**, illo- "An invitation to learning", r-in Fugitives From Justice #3; Jack Cole-a; also used by the N.Y. Legis. Comm. 63 126 189 403 689 975
7,8,10-14: 7-Jack Cole-a; Matt Baker-a begins #8, ends #?; Vic Flint in #10-14. 10-12-Baker-a(2 each) 34 68 102 204 332 460
9-No Vic Flint 31 62 93 182 296 410
15-Drug-c/story; Vic Flint app.; Baker-c 36 72 108 211 343 475
16,17,19,22-Baker-c 29 58 87 170 278 385
18,20,21,23: Baker-a(i) 22 44 66 132 216 300
24-28 (All 100 pgs.): 26-Transvestism 41 82 123 250 418 585
29,31,32-Baker-c 22 44 66 130 213 295
30 18 36 54 103 162 220
33-38: 33-Baker-c. 34-Baker-c; r/#9. 35-Baker-c/a(2); r/#10. 36-r/#11; Vic Flint strip-r; Baker-c/a(2) unsigned. 37-Baker-c; r/#17. 38- Baker-c/a; r/#18 22 44 66 132 216 300
NOTE: ***Matt Baker** c-6-16, 17, 19, 22, 27, 29, 31-38; a-13, 16. Bondage c-1, 3.*

AUTHORITY, THE (See Stormwatch and Jenny Sparks: The Secret History of...)
DC Comics (WildStorm): May, 1999 - No. 29, Jul, 2002 ($2.50)
1-Wraparound-c; Warren Ellis-s/Bryan Hitch and Paul Neary-a 1 2 3 4 5 7
1-Special Edition (7/10, $1.00) r/#1 with "What's Next?" logo on cover 3.00
2-4 5.00
5-12: 12-Death of Jenny Sparks; last Ellis-s 4.00
13-Mark Millar-s/Frank Quitely-c/a begins 6.00
14-16-Authority vs. Marvel-esque villains 4.00
17-29: 17,18-Weston-a. 19,20,22-Quitely-a. 21-McCrea-a. 23-26-Peyer-s/Nguyen-a; new Authority. 25,26-Jenny Sparks app. 27,28-Millar-s/Art Adams-a/c 3.00
Annual 2000 ($3.50) Devil's Night x-over; Hamner-a/Bermejo-c 4.00
Absolute Authority Slipcased Hardcover (2002, $49.95) oversized r/#1-12 plus script pages by Ellis and sketch pages by Hitch 50.00
...: Earth Inferno and Other Stories TPB (2002, $14.95) r/#17-20, Annual 2000, and Wildstorm Summer Special; new Quitely-c 15.00
...: Human on the Inside HC (2004, $24.95, dust jacket) Ridley-s/Oliver-a/c 25.00
...: Human on the Inside SC (2004, $17.99) Ridley-s/Oliver-a/c 18.00
...: Kev (10/02, $4.95) Ennis-s/Fabry-c/a 5.00
...: Relentless TPB (2000, $17.95) r/#1-8 18.00
...: Scorched Earth (2/03, $4.95) Robbie Morrison-s/Frazer Irving-a/Ashley Wood-c 5.00
...: Transfer of Power TPB (2002, $17.95) r/#22-29 18.00
...: Under New Management TPB (2000, $17.95) r/#9-16; new Quitely-c 18.00

AUTHORITY, THE (See previews in Sleeper, Stormwatch: Team Achilles and Wildcats Version 3.0)
DC Comics (WildStorm): Jul, 2003 - No. 14, Oct, 2004 ($2.95)
1-14: 1-Robbie Morrison-s/Dwayne Turner-a. 5-Huat-a. 14-Portacio-a 3.00
#0 (10/03, $2.95) r/preview back-up-s listed above; Turner sketch pages 3.00
...: Fractured Worlds TPB (2005, $17.95) r/#6-14; cover gallery 18.00
...: Harsh Realities TPB (2004, $14.95) r/#0-5; cover gallery 15.00
.../Lobo: Jingle Hell (2/04, $4.95) Bisley-c/a; Giffen & Grant-s 5.00
.../Lobo: Spring Break Massacre (8/05, $4.99) Bisley-c/a; Giffen & Grant-s 5.00

AUTHORITY, THE (Volume 4) (The Lost Year)
DC Comics (WildStorm): Dec, 2006 - No. 2, May 2007; No. 3, Jan, 2010 - No. 12, Oct, 2010 ($2.99)
1,2-Grant Morrison-s/Gene Ha-a/c 3.00
1-Variant cover by Art Adams 5.00

Autumn Adventures #1 © DIS

Avengers #11 © MAR

	GD 2.0	VG 4.0	FN 6.0	VF 8.0	VF/NM 9.0	NM- 9.2

3-12: 3-(1/10) Morrison & Giffen-s/Robertson-a. 3-12-Ha-c. 12-Ordway-a 3.00
...Reader: The Lost Year (1/10, $2.99) r/#1,2 3.00
... Book One (2010, $17.99) r/#1-7; cover sketch art 18.00

AUTHORITY, THE (Volume 5) (World's End)
DC Comics (WildStorm): Oct, 2008 - No. 29, Jan, 2011 ($2.99)

1-29: 1-5-Simon Coleby-a/c; Lynch back-up story w/Hairsine-a/Gage-s. 21-Simonson-c 3.00
...: Rule Britannia TPB (2010, $19.99) r/#8-17 20.00
...: World's End TPB (2009, $17.99) r/#1-7 18.00

AUTHORITY, THE: MORE KEV
DC Comics (WildStorm): Jul, 2004 - No. 4, Dec, 2004 ($2.95, limited series)

1-4-Garth Ennis-s/Glenn Fabry-c/a 3.00
...: Kev TPB (2005, $14.99) r/Authority: Kev one-shot and Authority: More Kev series 15.00

AUTHORITY, THE: PRIME
DC Comics (WildStorm): Dec, 2007 - No. 6, May, 2008 ($2.99, limited series)

1-6-Gage-s/Robertson-c/a; Bendix app. 3.00
TPB (2008, $17.99) r/#1-6 18.00

AUTHORITY, THE: REVOLUTION
DC Comics (WildStorm): Dec, 2004 - No. 12, Dec, 2005 ($2.95/$2.99)

1-12-Brubaker-s/Nguyen-a. 5-Henry Bendix returns. 7-Jenny Sparks app. 3.00
...: Book One TPB (2005, $14.99) r/#1-6; cover gallery and Nguyen sketch pages 15.00
...: Book Two TPB (2006, $14.99) r/#7-12; cover gallery and Nguyen sketch pages 15.00

AUTHORITY, THE: THE MAGNIFICENT KEV
DC Comics (WildStorm): Nov, 2005 - No. 5, Feb, 2006 ($2.99, limited series)

1-5-Garth Ennis-s/Carlos Ezquerra-a/Glenn Fabry-c 3.00
TPB (2006, $14.99) r/#1-5 15.00

AUTOMATIC KAFKA
DC Comics (WildStorm): Sept, 2002 - No. 9, Jul, 2003 ($2.95)

1-9-Ashley Wood-c/a; Joe Casey-s 3.00

AUTOMATON
Image Comics (Flypaper Press): Sept, 1998 - No. 3, 1998 ($2.95, lim. series)

1-3-R.A. Jones-s/Peter Vale-a 3.00

AUTUMN
Caliber Comics: 1995 - No. 3, 1995 ($2.95, B&W)

1-3 3.00

AUTUMN ADVENTURES (Walt Disney's...)
Disney Comics: Autumn, 1990; No. 2, Autumn, 1991 ($2.95, 68 pgs.)

1-Donald Duck-r(2) by Barks, Pluto-r, & new-a 4.00
2-D. Duck-r by Barks; new Super Goof story 4.00

AVATAARS: COVENANT OF THE SHIELD
Marvel Comics: Sept, 2000 - No. 3, Nov, 2000 ($2.99, limited series)

1-3-Kaminski-s/Oscar Jimenez-a 3.00

AVATAR
DC Comics: Feb, 1991 - No. 3, Apr, 1991 ($5.95, limited series, 100 pgs.)

1-3: Based on TSR's Forgotten Realms 6.00

AVENGELYNE
Maximum Press: May, 1995 - No. 3, July, 1995 ($2.50/$3.50, limited series)

	GD	VG	FN	VF	VF/NM	NM-
1/2	2	4	6	8	10	12
1/2 Platinum						15.00
1-Newstand ($2.50)-Photo-c; poster insert						6.00
1-Direct Market ($3.50)-Chromium-c; poster	1	2	3	4	5	7
1-Glossy edition	2	4	6	12	16	20
1-Gold						12.00
2-3: 2-Polybagged w/card						3.00
3-Variant-c; Deodato pin-up						5.00
...Bible (10/96, $3.50)						4.00
.../Glory (9/95, $3.95) 2 covers						4.00
.../Glory Swimsuit Special (6/96, $2.95) photo and illos. covers						3.00
.../Glory: The Godyssey (9/96, $2.99) 2 covers (1 photo)						3.00
...Revelation One (Avatar, 1/01, $3.50) 3 covers by Haley, Rio, Shaw; Shaw-a						3.50
.../Shi (Avatar, 11/01, $3.50) Eight covers; Waller-a						3.50
...Swimsuit (8/95, $2.95)-Pin-ups/photos. 3-Variant-c exist (2 photo, 1 Liefeld-a)						4.00
...Swimsuit (1/96, $3.50, 2nd printing)-photo-c						4.00
Trade paperback (12/95, $9.95)						10.00
.../Warrior Nun Areala 1 (11/96, $2.99) also see Warrior Nun/Avengelyne						3.00

AVENGELYNE
Maximum Press: V2#1, Apr, 1996 - No. 14, Apr, 1997 ($2.95/$2.50)

V2#1-Four covers exist (2 photo-c). 4.00
V2#2-Three covers exist (1 photo-c); flip book w/Darkchylde 5.00
V2#0, 3-14: 0-(10/96).3-Flip book w/Priest preview. 5-Flip book w/Blindside 3.00

AVENGELYNE (Volume 3)
Awesome Comics: Mar, 1999 ($2.50)

1-Fraga & Liefeld-a 3.00

AVENGELYNE (4th series)
Image Comics: Jul, 2011 - No. 8, May, 2012 ($2.99)

1-8-Liefeld & Poulson-s/Gieni-a. 1-Three covers by Liefeld, Gieni, and Benitez 3.00

AVENGELYNE: ARMAGEDDON
Maximum Press: Dec, 1996 - No. 3, Feb, 1997 ($2.99, limited series)

1-3-Scott Clark-a(p) 3.00

AVENGELYNE: DEADLY SINS
Maximum Press: Feb, 1996 - No. 2, Mar, 1996 ($2.95, limited series)

1,2: 1-Two-c exist (1 photo, 1 Liefeld-a). 2-Liefeld-c; Pop Mhan-a(p) 3.00

AVENGELYNE/POWER
Maximum Press: Nov, 1995 - No.3, Jan, 1996 ($2.95, limited series)

1-3: 1,2-Liefeld-c. 3-Three variant-c. exist (1 photo-c) 3.00

AVENGELYNE · PROPHET
Maximum Press: May, 1996; No. 2, Feb. 1997 ($2.95, unfinished lim. series)

1,2-Liefeld-c/a(p) 3.00

AVENGER, THE (See A-1 Comics)
Magazine Enterprises: Feb-Mar, 1955 - No. 4, Aug-Sept, 1955

	GD	VG	FN	VF	VF/NM	NM-
1(A-1 #129)-Origin	40	80	120	244	402	560
2(A-1 #131), 3(A-1 #133) Robot-c, 4(A-1 #138)	27	54	81	160	263	365
IW Reprint #9('64)-Reprints #1 (new cover)	3	6	9	19	30	40

NOTE: *Powell a-2-4; c-1-4.*

AVENGERS, THE (TV)(Also see Steed and Mrs. Peel)
Gold Key: Nov, 1968 ("John Steed & Emma Peel" cover title) (15¢)

	GD	VG	FN	VF	VF/NM	NM-
1-Photo-c	13	26	39	89	195	300
1-(Variant with photo back-c)	17	34	51	117	259	400

AVENGERS, THE (See Essential..., Giant-Size..., JLA/..., Kree/Skrull War Starring..., Marvel Graphic Novel #27, Marvel Super Action, Marvel Super Heroes('66), Marvel Treasury Ed., Marvel Triple Action, New Avengers, Solo Avengers, Tales Of Suspense #49, West Coast Avengers & X-Men Vs....)

AVENGERS, THE (The Mighty Avengers on cover only #63-69)
Marvel Comics Group: Sept, 1963 - No. 402, Sept, 1996

	GD	VG	FN	VF	VF/NM	NM-
1-Origin & 1st app. The Avengers (Thor, Iron Man, Hulk, Ant-Man, Wasp); Loki app.	650	1300	2600	7500	19,750	32,000
2-Hulk leaves Avengers	107	214	321	856	1928	3000
3-2nd Sub-Mariner x-over outside the F.F. (see Strange Tales #107 for 1st); Sub-Mariner & Hulk team-up & battle Avengers; Spider-Man cameo (1/64)	79	158	237	632	1416	2200
4-Revival of Captain America who joins the Avengers; 1st Silver Age app. of Captain America & Bucky (3/64)	217	434	651	1790	4045	6300
4-Reprint from the Golden Record Comic set	13	26	39	91	201	310
With Record (1966)	20	40	60	135	300	465
5-Hulk app.	46	92	138	368	834	1300
6,8: 6-Intro/1st app. original Zemo & his Masters of Evil. 8-Intro Kang	36	72	108	259	580	900
7-Rick Jones app. in Bucky costume	38	76	114	281	628	975
9-Intro Wonder Man who dies in same story	50	100	150	400	900	1400
10-Intro/1st app. Immortus; early Hercules app. (11/64)	28	56	84	202	451	700
11-Spider-Man-c & x-over (12/64)	36	72	108	259	580	900
12-15: 15-Death of original Zemo	18	36	54	126	281	435
16-New Avengers line-up (Hawkeye, Quicksilver, Scarlet Witch join; Thor, Iron Man, Giant-Man, Wasp leave)	30	60	90	216	483	750
17,18: 17-Minor Hulk app.	12	24	36	84	185	285
19-1st app. Swordsman; origin Hawkeye (8/65)	14	28	42	96	211	325
20-22: Wood inks. 20-Intro. Power Man (Erik Josten)	10	20	30	66	138	210
23,24,26,27,29,30: 23-Romita Sr. inks (1st Silver Age Marvel work). 23,24-Avengers vs. Kang.	9	18	27	59	117	175
25-Dr. Doom-c/story	13	26	39	89	195	300
28-(5/66) First app. of The Collector; Giant-Man becomes Goliath	17	34	51	117	259	400
31-40: 32-1st Sons of the Serpent. 34-Last full Stan Lee plot/script. 35-1st Roy Thomas script w/Stan Lee plot. 38-40-Hercules app. 40-Sub-Mariner app.	7	14	21	49	92	135

41-46,50,52: 43-1st app. Red Guardian (dies in #44). 45-Hercules joins. 46-Ant-Man

Avengers #141 © MAR

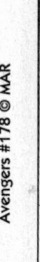

Avengers #178 © MAR

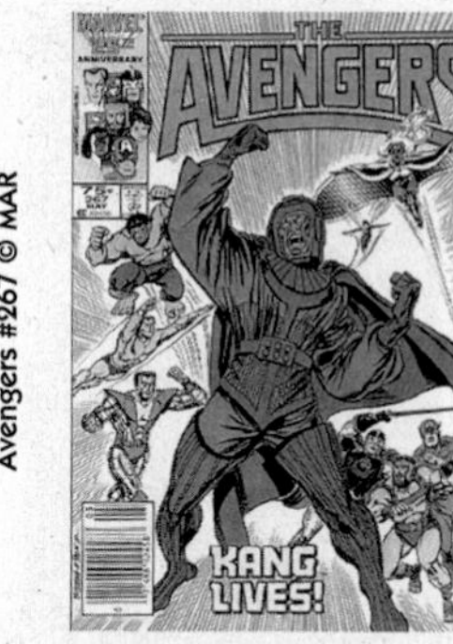

Avengers #267 © MAR

	GD 2.0	VG 4.0	FN 6.0	VF 8.0	VF/NM 9.0	NM- 9.2
returns (re-intro, 11/67). 52-Black Panther joins; 1st app. The Grim Reaper	7	14	21	44	82	120
47,49-Magneto-c/story	7	14	21	46	86	125
48-Origin/1st app. new Black Knight (1/68)	7	14	21	46	86	125
51-The Collector app.	7	14	21	48	89	130
53-X-Men app.	9	18	27	60	120	180
54-1st Ultron app. (1 panel); new Masters of Evil	10	20	30	64	132	200
55-1st full app. Ultron (8/68) (1 panel reveal in #54)	21	42	63	147	324	500
56-Zemo app; story explains how Capt. America became imprisoned in ice during WWII, only to be rescued in Avengers #4	8	16	24	51	96	140
57-1st app. S.A. Vision (10/68); death of Ultron-5	34	68	102	245	548	850
58-Origin The Vision	10	20	30	66	138	210
59-65: 59-Intro. Yellowjacket. 60-Wasp & Yellowjacket wed. 61-Dr. Strange app. 62-1st Man-Ape. 63-Goliath becomes Yellowjacket; Hawkeye becomes the new Goliath. 65-Last 12¢ issue	6	12	18	40	73	105
66-B. Smith-a; vs. Ultron-6	6	12	18	41	76	110
67-Ultron-6 cvr/sty; B. Smith-a	9	18	27	57	111	165
68-70: 69-1st brief app. Squadron Sinister (Dr. Spectrum, Hyperion, Nighthawk). 70-1st full app Nighthawk	6	12	18	37	66	95
71-1st app. The Invaders (12/69); Black Knight joins	8	16	24	54	102	150
72-79,81,82,84,86,90-91: 72-1st Zodiak; Captain Marvel & Nick Fury app. 73,74-Sons of the Serpent. 75-1st app. Arkon. 78-1st app. Lethal Legion (Man-Ape, Living Laser, Power Man, Grimm Reaper, Swordsman). 82-Daredevil app. 86-2nd Squadron Supreme app.	5	10	15	34	60	85
80-1st app. Red Wolf	6	12	18	37	66	95
83-Intro. The Liberators (Wasp, Valkyrie, Scarlet Witch, Medusa & the Black Widow)	6	12	18	38	69	100
85-1st app. Squadron Supreme (American Eagle, Dr. Spectrum, Hawkeye (Wyatt McDonald), Hyperion, Lady Lark, Nighthawk (Kyle Richmond), Tom Thumb, Whizzer)	6	12	18	37	66	95
87-Origin The Black Panther	6	12	18	38	69	100
88-Written by Harlan Ellison; Hulk app.	5	10	15	35	63	90
88-2nd printing (1994)	2	4	6	8	10	12
89-Classic Captain Marvel execution-c; beginning of Kree/Skrull War (runs through issue #97)	5	10	15	35	63	90
92-Last 15¢ issue; Neal Adams-c	6	12	18	40	73	105
93-(52 pgs.)-Neal Adams-c/a	13	26	39	89	195	300
94-96-Neal Adams-c/a	8	16	24	51	96	140
97-G.A. Capt. America, Sub-Mariner, Human Torch, Patriot, Vision, Blazing Skull, Fin, Angel, & new Capt. Marvel x-over	6	12	18	38	69	100
98,99: 98-Goliath becomes Hawkeye; Smith c/a(i). 99-Smith-c, Smith/Sutton-a	5	10	15	31	53	75
100-(6/72)-Smith-c/a; featuring everyone who was an Avenger	9	18	27	60	120	180
101-Harlan Ellison scripts	4	8	12	25	40	55
102-106,108,109	4	8	12	23	37	50
107-Starlin-a(p)	4	8	12	25	40	55
110,111-X-Men and Magneto app.	5	10	15	34	60	85
112-1st app. Mantis	5	10	15	34	53	75
113-115,119-124,126,128-130: 114-Swordsman returns; joins Avengers. 115-Prologue to Avengers/Defenders War. 119-Rutland, Vermont Halloween issue. 120-123-vs. Zodiac. 124-1st Star-Stalker. 126-Klaw & Solarr app. 129-Kang app; story continues in Giant-Size Avengers #2	3	6	9	19	30	40
116-118-Avengers/Defenders War; x-over w/Defenders #8-11. 116-Silver Surfer vs Vision. 117-Captain America vs. Sub-Mariner. 118-Avengers & Defenders vs. Loki & Dormammu	5	10	15	33	57	80
125-Thanos-c & brief app.; story continues in Captain Marvel #33	4	8	12	27	44	60
127-Ultron-7 app; story continues in Fantastic Four #150	3	6	9	21	33	45
131-133,136-140: 131,132-Vs. Kang. 131-1st Legion of the Unliving. 132-Continues in Giant-Size Avengers #3. 133-Origin of the Kree. 136-Ploog-r/Amazing Advs. #12. 137-Moondragon joins; Beast app; becomes provisional member; officially joins in #151; Wasp & Yellowjacket return	3	6	9	16	23	30
134,135-Origin of the Vision revised (also see Avengers Forever mini-series). 135-Continues in Giant-Size Avengers #4	4	8	12	23	37	50
141-143: 141-Squadron Supreme app; Pérez-a(p) begins. 142,143-Marvel Western heroes app. (Kid Colt, Rawhide Kid, Two-Gun Kid, Ringo Kid, Night Rider). 143-Vs. Kang (last 1970s app.)	2	4	6	12	15	20
144-Origin & 1st app. Hellcat (Patsy Walker)	3	6	9	17	26	35
145,146: Published out of sequence; Tony Isabella-s; originally intended to be in Giant-Size Avengers #5	2	4	6	9	12	15
146-149-(30¢-c variants, limited distribution)	4	8	12	27	44	60
147-149-(Reg. 25¢ editions)(5-7/76) Squadron Supreme app.	2	4	6	11	16	20
150-Kirby-a(r) pgs. 7-18 (from issue #16); pgs. 1-6 feature new-a by Pérez; new line-up: Capt. America, Iron Man, Scarlet Witch, Wasp, Yellowjacket, Vision & The Beast	2	4	6	11	16	20
150-(30¢-c variant, limited distribution)	4	8	12	27	44	60
151-Wonder Man returns w/new costume; Champions app.; The Collector app.	2	4	6	11	16	20
152-154,157,159,160,163: 152-1st app Black Talon. 154-vs. Attuma; continues in Super-Villain Team-up #9. 160-Grimm Reaper app. 163-Vs. The Champions	2	4	6	9	12	15
155,156-Dr. Doom app.	2	4	6	10	14	18
158-1st app. Graviton; Wonder Man vs. Vision; Jim Shooter plots begin	2	4	6	11	16	20
160-164-(35¢-c variants, limited dist.)(6-10/77)	7	14	21	44	82	120
161,162-Ultron-8 app; Henry Pym appears as Ant-Man. 162-1st app. Jocasta	2	4	6	11	16	20
164,165-Byrne-a; vs. Lethal Legion	2	4	6	10	14	18
166-Byrne-a; vs. Count Nefaria	2	4	6	12	15	20
167,168 – Guardians of the Galaxy app.	2	4	6	10	14	18
169,172,178-180: 172-Hawkeye rejoins	1	3	4	6	8	10
170,171-Ultron & Jocasta app. 170-Minor Guardians of the Galaxy app.	2	4	6	10	14	18
173-177-Korvac Saga issues; 173-175-The Collector app. 173,177-Guardians of the Galaxy app. 174-Thanos cameo. 176-Starhawk app.	2	4	6	8	10	12
181-(3/79) Byrne-a/Pérez-c; new line-up: Capt. America, Scarlet Witch, Iron Man, Wasp, Vision, Beast & The Falcon; debut of Scott Lang who becomes Ant-Man in Marvel Premiere #47 (4/79)	3	6	9	14	20	25
182-191-Byrne-a: 183-Ms. Marvel joins. 184-vs. Absorbing Man. 185-Origin Quicksilver & Scarlet Witch. 186-187-vs. Morded the Mystic. 188-Intro. The Elements of Doom. 189-Deathbird app. 190,191-vs. Grey Gargoyle	2	4	6	8	10	12
192-194,197-199: 197-199-vs Red Ronin	1	2	3	5	6	8
195-1st Taskmaster cameo	2	4	6	9	12	15
196-1st full Taskmaster app.	4	8	12	25	40	55
200-(10/80, 52 pgs.)-Ms. Marvel leaves; 1st actual app. of Marcus Immortus	2	4	6	8	10	12
201,203-210,212: 204,205-vs. Yellow Claw						5.00
202,214: 202-Ultron app. 214-Ghost Rider app.	1	2	3	4	5	7
211-New line-up: Capt. America, Iron Man, Tigra, Thor, Wasp & Yellowjacket; Angel, Beast, Dazzler app.	1	2	3	4	5	7
213,215,216,239,240,250: 213-Controversial Yellowjacket slapping Wasp issue; Yellowjacket leaves. 215,216-Silver Surfer app. 216-Tigra leaves. 239-(1/84) Avengers app. on David Letterman show. 240-Spider-Woman revived. 250-($1.00, 52 pgs; West Coast Avengers app. vs. Maelstrom						6.00
217-218,222,224-235,238: 217-Yellowjacket & Wasp return. 222-1st app. Egghead's Masters of Evil. 225,226-Black Knight app. 227-Roger Stern plots begin; Captain Marvel (Monica Rambeau) joins. 229-Death of Egghead. 230-Yellowjacket quits. 231-Iron Man leaves. 232-Starfox (Eros) joins. 233-Byrne-a. 234-Origin Quicksilver & Scarlet Witch. 238-Origin Blackout						5.00
219,220-Drax the Destroyer app. 220-Moondragon vs. Drax						6.00
221-Hawkeye & She-Hulk join; Spider-Man, Spider-Woman, Dazzler app.						6.00
223-Taskmaster app.	2	4	6	9	12	15
236,237-Spider-Man tries to join the Avengers						6.00
241-249,251-256,258-262: 242-Dr. Strange app. 243-Vision becomes chairman. 244,245-vs. Dire Wraiths. 246-248-Eternals app. 249-x-over with Thor #350. 252-vs. the Blood Brothers. 253-Vision vs. Quasimodo. 254-West Coast Avengers app. 255-John Buscema & Tom Palmer return as artists; 1st app Nebula's pirate crew. 256-Terminus app. 258-x-over with Amazing Spider-Man #269-270; Spider-Man & Firelord app. 258-260-Nebula app. 260-261-Secret Wars II X-over; Beyonder app. 262-Hercules vs. Sub-Mariner						4.00
257-1st app. Nebula (from the Guardians of the Galaxy movie)	3	6	9	14	20	25
263-(1/86) Return of Jean Grey, leading into X-Factor #1(story continues in FF #286)						6.00
264-265,267-269: 264-1st new Yellowjacket (Rita Demara) 266-Secret Wars II x-over; vs. The Beyonder. 267-269-Kang app.						3.00
266-Secret Wars II epilogue; Silver Surfer & Molecule Man app.						4.00
270-273-Baron Zemo and the new Masters of Evil app. 272-Alpha Flight app.						4.00
274-277-Baron Zemo and the new Masters of Evil app. in 'Siege of Avengers mansion'. 274-Hercules injured. 275-Jarvis severely beaten. 276-Thor returns. 277-Capt. America vs. Baron Zemo						5.00
278-283: 279-Capt. Marvel (Monica Rambeau) becomes Avengers leader; Dr. Druid joins. 280-Jarvis flashback issue. 281-283-Olympian Gods app. 282-Sub-Mariner rejoins						3.00
284,285-vs. the Olympian Gods. 285 Avengers vs. Zeus; Hercules recovers						4.00
286-299: 286-Fixer app. Awesome Android & Super Adaptoid app. 287-Mentallo app. 288-1st app. 'Heavy Metal' (TESS-One, Intergalactic Sentry #459, Machine Man,						

Avengers #402 © MAR

Avengers V2 #7 © MAR

Avengers V3 #6 © MAR

GD 2.0 | VG 4.0 | FN 6.0 | VF 8.0 | VF/NM 9.0 | NM- 9.2

Super-Adaptoid). 290-West Coast Avengers app. 291-$1.00 issues begin. 292-1st app. the Leviathan (Marrina). 293-Death of Marrina. 294-Capt. Marvel (Monica Rambeau) leaves. 295-vs. the Cross-Time Kangs. 297-Dr. Druid leaves; Thor, Black Knight & She-Hulk resign. 298-Inferno x-over. 299-Inferno x-over; New Mutants app. 3.00
300-(2/89, $1.75, 68 pgs., squarebound) New line-up; the Captain (Steve Rogers), Thor, Invisible Woman, Mr. Fantastic & Gilgamesh (formerly the Forgotten one) Inferno x-over; Simonson-a 4.00
301-304,306-313,319-325,327,330-343: 301-Firelord app; 1st app. Super-Nova. 302-Re-intro Quasar; Firelord app. 303-vs. Super-Nova. Quasar, Firelord & West Coast Avengers app.; Mr. Fantastic & Invisible Woman leave. 308-310-Eternals app. 311-313-Acts of Vengeance x-over. 312-Freedom Force app. 320-324-Alpha Flight app. 327-2nd app. Rage. 332,333-Dr. Doom app. 334-Intro. Thane Ector & the Brethren; Inhumans & Quicksilver app. 335-339-vs. the Brethren. 335-1st Steve Epting art. 341,342-New Warriors & Sons of the Serpent app. 343-Intro. the Gatherers; Bob Harras scripts begin (end #395); last $1.00-c 3.00
305,314-318: 305-Byrne scripts begin; most current & non-active Avengers app. 314-318-Spider-Man x-over. 4.00
326-1st app. Rage (11/90) 5.00
328,329: 328-Origin Rage. 329-New line-up (Capt. America, Quasar, Sersi, She-Hulk, Thor, Vision, Black Widow) Spider-Man becomes a reserve member; Rage & Sandman become probationary members 4.00
344,348-349,351-359: 344-1st app. Proctor, leader of the Gatherers. 349-Thor vs. Hercules. 351-Starjammers app. 352-354-Grimm Reaper app. 3.00
345,346-Operation Galactic Storm x-overs. 345-Pt.5-Deathbird app. 346-Pt.12-Intro. Starforce (super-powered Kree warriors) 4.00
347-Double-sized issue ($1.75, 39, pgs.) Operation Galactic Storm conclusion (Pt.19) end of the Kree/Shi'ar War; 'death' of the Supreme Intelligence 5.00
350-($2.50, 68 pgs.) Double gatefold-c showing-c to #1; r/#53 w/cover in flip book format; vs. The Starjammers 5.00
360-($2.95, 52 pgs.) Embossed all-foil-c; 30th ann. 5.00
361,362,364,365,367: 361-362-vs. the Gatherers. 364-365-vs. Galen-Kor of the Kree 4.00
363-($2.95, 52 pgs.)-All silver foil-c; vs. Proctor & the Gatherers; 1st cameo app. Deathcry (unnamed) 5.00
366-($3.95, 68 pgs.)-Embossed all gold foil-c; Deadpool app. in back-up story 5.00
368,376-378: 368-Bloodties pt.1; Avengers/X-Men x-over 3.00
369-($2.95)-Foil embossed-c; Bloodties pt.5; X-Men/Avengers vs. Exodus 5.00
370-373: 370-371-Ghaur the Deviant app. 372-373-vs. Proctor & the Gatherers 4.00
374-Bound-in trading card sheet; origin of Proctor as an alternate-Earth Black Knight revealed (scarcer in NM due to the card insert) 5.00
375-($2.00, 52 pgs.)-Regular ed.; Thunderstrike returns; leads into Malibu Comic's Black September; end of the Gatherers saga (since #343); death of Proctor; Black Knight & Sersi leave; last Epting-a 4.00
375-($2.50, 52 pgs.)-Collectors ed. 5.00
379-382-Regular editions: 379-Galen Kor & Kree Lunatic Legion app. 380-382-High Evolutionary app. 380-1st Mike Deodato-a. 381-Exodus app. 3.00
379-382-Marvel Double Feature editions ($2.50, 45 pgs.)-all have Giant-Man stories in a flip-book format 4.00
383-385: 383-Fantastic Force app. 384-Hercules stripped of immortality & banished from Olympus. 385-Red Skull app. 4.00
386-389, 398-399: 386-Red Skull app.; 'Taking of AIM' prelude; continues in Capt. America #440. 387-Taking of AIM Pt.2; Red Skull app.; re-intro Modok; continues in Capt. America #441. 388-Taking of AIM Pt.4; Red Skull & Modok app. 6.00
390-393: 390-'The Crossing' prelude; leads into Avengers: the Crossing #1. 391,392-The Crossing. 391-Overpower game card insert; scarcer in NM. 392-393-The Crossing 5.00
394,397: 394-The Crossing; 1st new Wasp; story cont. in Avengers Timeslide #1; 397-x-over w/Hulk #440-441 1 2 3 4 5 7
395-The Crossing/Timeslide; 'death' of Tony Stark; Bob Harras co-plot only, last work on Avengers 1 2 3 5 6 8
396-First Sign Pt.4; vs. the Zodiac 8.00
400-(Double-size, 32 pgs.)-Mark Waid scripts; Loki app. 7.00
401,402: 401-Onslaught Impact #1; Magneto app. 402-Onslaught Impact #2; vs. Onslaught & Holocaust; last issue; continues in X-Men #56 6.00
#500-503 (See Avengers Vol. 3; series resumed original numbering after Vol. 3 #84)
Special 1 (9/67, 25¢, 68 pgs.)-New-a; original & new Avengers team-up 11 22 33 76 163 250
Special 2 (9/68, 25¢, 68 pgs.)-New-a; original vs. new Avengers 8 16 24 51 96 140
Special 3 (9/69, 25¢, 68 pgs.)-r/Avengers #4 plus 3 Capt. America stories by Kirby (art); origin Red Skull 5 10 15 31 53 75
Special 4 (1/71, 25¢, 68 pgs.)-Kirby-r/Avengers #5,6 3 6 9 21 33 45
Special 5 (1/72, 52 pgs.)-All-reprint issue; Kirby-r Avengers #8/Heck-r w/Spider-Man from issue #11 3 6 9 20 31 42
Annual 6 (11/76) Pérez-a; Kirby-c; vs. Nuklo 2 4 6 11 16 20
Annual 7 (11/77)-Starlin-c/a; Warlock dies; Thanos app.; x-over w/Marvel Two-in-one Ann #2 5 10 15 34 60 85
Annual 8 (1978)-Dr. Strange, Ms. Marvel app. vs. Hyperion, Dr. Spectrum & Whizzer 2 4 6 8 11 14
Annual 9 (1979)-Newton-a(p); Intro. Arsenal 2 3 4 6 8 10
Annual 10 (1981)-Golden-a; X-Men cameo; 1st app. Rogue & Madelyne Pryor 5 10 15 33 57 80
Annual 11-13: 11 (1982)-Vs. The Defenders. 12 ('83)-Inhumans app. 13 ('84)-Ditko/Byrne-a 5.00
Annual 14-15,17-18: 14 ('85)-x-over w/Fantastic Four Ann. #19; vs. the Skrulls. 15 ('86)-vs. Freedom Force; x-over w/Avengers West Coast Ann. #1. 17('88)-Evolutionary War x-over. 18('89)-Atlantis Attacks 4.00
Annual 16 (1987)-x-over w/Avengers West Coast Ann. #2; Silver Surfer app. vs. the Grandmaster and Legion of the Unliving (including Drax, Captain Marvel & Green Goblin) 5.00
Annual 19-22: 19 ('90)-Terminus Factor Pt.5 (conclusion) continued from Avengers West Coast Ann. #5. 20 ('91)-Subterranean Saga Pt.1; cont. in Hulk Ann. #17. 21 ('92)-Citizen Kang pt.4; vs. Terminatrix. 22 ('93)-Bagged w/card; 1st app. Bloodwraith 4.00
Annual 23 (1994)-Buscema-a; Roy Thomas-s; vs. Loki & Pluto; x-over w/Thor Ann. #19 5.00
Avengers 1: The Coming of the Avengers! (2012, $3.99) recolored reprint/#1 5.00
...: Galactic Storm Vol. 1 ('06, $29.99, TPB) r/Kree-Shi'ar war from Avengers #345-346, Capt. America #398-399, Avengers West Coast #80-81, Quasar #32-33, Wonder Man #7-8, Iron Man #278 and Thor #445; new Epting-c 30.00
...: Galactic Storm Vol. 2 ('06, $29.99, TPB) r/Kree-Shi'ar war from Avengers #347, Capt. America #400-401, Avengers West Coast #82, Quasar #34-36, Wonder Man #9, Iron Man #279, Thor #446 and What If #55-56 30.00
...: Kang - Time and Time Again ('05, $19.99, TPB) r/Avengers #69-71 & 267-269, Thor #140 and Incredible Hulk #135 20.00
...Kree-Skrull War ('00, $24.95, TPB) new Neal Adams-c 25.00
...: Legends Vol. 3: George Perez ('03, $16.99)-r/#161,162,194-196,201, Ann. #6 & 8 17.00
Marvel Double Feature...Avengers/Giant-Man #379 ($2.50, 52 pgs.)-Same as Avengers #379 w/Giant-Man flip book 4.00
Marvel Graphic Novel - Deathtrap: The Vault (1991, $9.95) Venom-c/app. 2 4 6 8 10 12
The Korvac Saga TPB (2003, $19.95)-r/#167,168,170-177; Perez-c 20.00
The Serpent Crown TPB (2005, $15.99)-r/#141-144,147-149; Hellcat app. 16.00
The Yesterday Quest ($6.95)-r/#181,182,185-187 1 2 3 4 5 7
Under Siege ('98, $16.95, TPB) r/#270,271,273-277 17.00
...: Vision and the Scarlet Witch TPB (2005, $15.99) r/wedding from Giant-Size Avengers #4 and "Vision and the Scarlet Witch" mini-series #1-4 16.00
...: Visionaries ('99, $16.95)-r/early George Perez art 17.00

NOTE: ***Austin*** *c(i)-157, 167, 168, 170-177, 181, 183-188, 198-201, Annual 8.* ***John Buscema*** *a-41-44p, 46p, 47p, 49, 50, 51-62p, 74-77, 79-85, 87-91, 97, 105p, 121p, 124p,125p, 152, 153p, 255-279p, 281-302p; c-41-66, 68-71, 73-91, 97-99, 178, 256-259p, 261-279p, 281-302p.* ***Byrne*** *a-164-166p, 181-191p, 233p, Annual 13i, 14p; c-186-190p, 233p, 260, 305p; scripts-305-312.* ***Colan*** *a(p)-63-65, 111, 206-208, 210, 211; c(p)-65, 206-208, 210, 211.* ***Ditko*** *a-Annual 13.* ***Guice*** *a-Annual 12p.* ***Don Heck*** *a-9-15, 17-40, 157.* ***Kane*** *c-37p, 159p.* ***Kane/Everett*** *c-97.* ***Kirby*** *a-1-8p, Special 3r, 4r(p); c-1-30, 148, 151-158; layouts-14-16.* ***Ron Lim*** *c(p)-335-341.* ***Miller*** *c-193p.* ***Mooney*** *a-86i, 179p, 180p.* ***Nebres*** *a-178i; c-179i.* ***Newton*** *a-204p, Annual 9p.* ***Perez*** *a(p)-141, 143, 144, 148, 150, 154, 155, 160, 161, 162, 167,168, 170, 171, 194-196, 198-202, Annual 6, 8; c(p)-160-162, 164-166, 170-174, 181,183-185, 191, 192, 194-201, 379-382, Annual 8.* ***Starlin*** *c-121, 135.* ***Staton*** *a-127-134i.* ***Tuska*** *a-47i,48i, 51i, 53i, 54i, 106p, 107p, 135p, 137-140p, 163p. Guardians of the Galaxy app. in #167, 168, 170, 173, 175, 181.*

AVENGERS, THE (Volume Two)
Marvel Comics: V2#1, Nov, 1996 - No. 13, Nov, 1997 ($2.95/$1.95/$1.99) (Produced by Extreme Studios)

1-($2.95)-Heroes Reborn begins; intro new team (Captain America, Swordsman, Scarlet Witch, Vision, Thor, Hellcat & Hawkeye); 1st app. Avengers Island; Loki & Enchantress app.; Rob Liefeld-p & plot; Chap Yaep-p; Jim Valentino scripts; variant-c exists 5.00
1-($1.95)-Variant-c 6.00
2-13: 2,3-Jeph Loeb scripts begin, Kang app. 4-Hulk-c/app. 5-Thor/Hulk battle; 2 covers. 10,11,13-"World War 3"-pt. 2, x-over w/Image characters. 12-($2.99) "Heroes Reunited"-pt. 2 4.00
Heroes Reborn: Avengers (2006, $29.99, TPB) r/#1-12; pin-up and cover gallery 30.00

AVENGERS, THE (Volume Three)(See New Avengers for next series)
Marvel Comics: Feb, 1998 - No. 84, Aug, 2004; No. 500, Sept, 2004 - No. 503, Dec, 2004 ($2.99/$1.99/$2.25)

1-($2.99, 48 pgs.) Busiek-s/Pérez-a/wraparound-c; Avengers reassemble after Heroes Return 5.00
1-Variant Heroes Return cover 1 2 3 4 5 7
1-Rough Cut-Features original script and pencil pages 3.00
2-($1.99)Pérez-c, 2-Lago painted-c 4.00
3,4: 3-Wonder Man-c/app. 4-Final roster chosen; Perez poster 3.50
5-11: 5,6-Squadron Supreme-c/app. 8-Triathlon-c/app. 3.00
12-($2.99) Thunderbolts app. 4.00
12-Alternate-c of Avengers w/white background; no logo 15.00
13-24,26,28: 13-New Warriors app. 16-18-Ordway-s/a. 19-Ultron returns. 26-Immonen-a 3.00
16-Variant-c with purple background 5.00

Avengers #501 © MAR

Avengers (2013 series) #7 © MAR

Avengers Academy #18 © MAR

GD VG FN VF VF/NM NM-
2.0 4.0 6.0 8.0 9.0 9.2

25,27-($2.99) 25-vs. the Exemplars; Spider-Man app. 27-100 pgs. 4.00
29-33,35-47: 29-Begin $2.25-c. 35-Maximum Security x-over; Romita Jr.-a. 36-Epting-a; poster by Alan Davis. 38-Davis-a begins ($1.99-c) 3.00
34-($2.99) Last Pérez-a; Thunderbirds app. 4.00
48-($3.50, 100 pgs.) new story w/Dwyer-a & r/#98-100 4.00
49,51-59: 49-'Nuff Said story. 51-Anderson-a. 52-Reis-a. 57-Johns-s begin 3.00
50,60-($3.50): 50 Dwyer-a; Quasar app. 4.00
61-84: 61,62-Frank-a; new line-up. 63-Davis-a. 64-Reis-a. 65-70-Coipel-a. 75-Hulk app. 76-Jack of Hearts dies; Jae Lee-c. 77-(50¢-c) Coipel-a/Cassaday-c. 78,80,81-Coipel-a. 83,84-New Invaders app. 3.00

(After #84 [Aug, 2004], numbering reverted back to original Vol. 1 with #500, Sept, 2004)

500-($3.50) "Avengers Disassembled" begins; Bendis-s/Finch-a; Ant-Man (Scott Lang) killed, Vision destroyed 4.00
500-Director's Cut ($4.99) Cassaday foil variant-c plus interviews and galleries 5.00
501, 502-($2.25): 502-Hawkeye killed 3.00
503-($3.50) "Avengers Disassembled" ends; reprint pages from Avengers V1#16 4.00
#1 1/2 (12/99, $2.50) Timm-c/a; Stern-s; 1963-style issue 3.00
.../ Squadron Supreme '98 Annual ($2.99) 4.00
1999, 2000 Annual (7/99, '00, $3.50) 1999-Manco-a. 2000-Breyfogle-a 4.00
2001 Annual ($2.99) Reis-a; back-up-s art by Churchill 4.00
...: Above and Beyond TPB ('05, $24.99) r/#36-40,56, Annual 2001, & Avengers: The Ultron Imperative; Alan Davis-c 25.00
... Assemble HC ('04, $29.95, oversized) r/#1-11 & '98 Annual; Busiek intro.; Pérez pencil art and Busiek script from Avengers #1 30.00
... Assemble Vol. 2 HC ('05, $29.95, oversized) r/#12-22, #0 & Ann. 1999; Ordway intro. 30.00
... Assemble Vol. 3 HC ('06, $34.99, oversized) r/#23-34, #1 1/2 & Thunderbolts #42-44 35.00
... Assemble Vol. 4 HC ('07, $34.99, oversized) r/#35-40, Avengers 2000, Avengers 2001, Avengers: The Ultron Imperative, Maximum Security #1-3 & ...Dangerous Planet 35.00
... Assemble Vol. 5 HC ('07, $39.99, oversized) r/#41-56 and Avengers 2001 40.00
...: Clear and Present Dangers TPB ('01, $19.95) r/#8-15 20.00
...: Defenders War HC ('07, $19.99) r/#115-118 & Defenders #8-11; Englehart intro. 20.00
...: Disassembled HC ('06, $24.99) r/#500-503 & Avengers Finale; Director's Cut extras 25.00
...: Disassembled TPB ('05, $15.99) r/#500-503 & Avengers Finale; Director's Cut extras 16.00
...Finale 1 (1/05, $3.50) Epilogue to Avengers Disassembled; Neal Adams-c; art by various incl. Peréz, Maleev, Oeming, Powell, Mayhew, Mack, McNiven, Cheung, Frank 4.00
Free Comic Book Day (5/09, giveaway) New Avengers 1st battle vs. Dark Avengers 3.00
...: Living Legends TPB ('04, $19.99) r/#23-30; last Busiek/Pérez arc 20.00
...Supreme Justice TPB (4/01, $17.95) r/Squadron Supreme appearances in Avengers #5-7, '98 Annual, Iron Man #7, Capt. America #8, Quicksilver #10; Pérez-c 18.00
The Kang Dynasty TPB ('02, $29.99) r/#41-55 & 2001 Annual 30.00
The Morgan Conquest TPB ('00, $14.95) r/#1-4 15.00
.../Thunderbolts Vol. 1: The Nefaria Protocols (2004, $19.99) r/#31-34, 42-44 20.00
Ultron Unleashed TPB (8/99, $3.50) reprints early app. 4.00
Ultron Unlimited TPB (4/01, $14.95) r/#19-22 & #0 prelude 15.00
Wizard #0-Ultron Unlimited prelude 3.00
Vol. 1: World Trust TPB ('03, $14.99) r/#57-62 & Marvel Double-Shot #2 15.00
Vol. 2: Red Zone TPB ('04, $14.99) r/#64-70 15.00
Vol. 3: The Search For She-Hulk TPB ('04, $12.99) r/#71-76 13.00
Vol. 4: The Lionheart of Avalon TPB ('04, $11.99) r/#77-81 12.00
Vol. 5: Once an Invader TPB ('04, $14.99) r/#82-84, V1 #71; Invaders #0 & Ann #1 ('77) 15.00

AVENGERS (The Heroic Age)
Marvel Comics: July, 2010 - No. 34, Jan, 2013 ($3.99)

1-New team assembled; Bendis-s/Romita Jr.-a; Kang app.; back-up text Avengers history 6.00
1-Variant-c by Land 8.00
1-Variant covers by Djurdjevic and John Romita Sr. 12.00
1-3-Second printings 4.00
2,3: 2-Wonder Man app. 5.00
4-12: 4-6-Ultron app. 7-Red Hulk app. 12-Red Hulk joins 4.00
12.1 -(6/11, $2.99) Hitch & Neary-c/a; The Wizard & The Intelligencia app.; Ultron returns 3.00
13-24: 13-17-Fear Itself tie-ins. 13,15-Bachalo-a. 17-New Avengers app. 18-20-Acuña-a. 19-Vision returns, Storm joins 4.00
24.1 -(5/12, $2.99) Peterson-a; Magneto, She-Hulk app. 3.00
25-33: 25-30-Avengers vs. X-Men tie-in; Simonson-a. 31-34-Janet Van Dyne app. 4.00
34-($4.99) Art by Peterson, Mayhew & Dodson; Deodato, Simonson, Yu, Cheung, Coipel art pages; Bendis afterword 5.00
... Annual 1 (3/12, $4.99) Bendis-s/Dell'Otto-c/a; Wonder Man app. 5.00
... Assemble 1 (7/10, $3.99) Handbook-style profiles of Avengers, enemies, allies 4.00
...: Infinity Quest 1 (8/11, $4.99) r/#7-9 with variant covers 5.00
... Roll Call 1 (2012, $4.99) Updated handbook-style profiles of Avengers & enemies 5.00
... Spotlight (7/10, $3.99) Creator interviews, previews, history of the team; trivia 4.00

AVENGERS (Marvel NOW!)
Marvel Comics: Feb, 2013 - Present ($3.99)

1-13: 1-Hickman-s/Opeña-a/Weaver-c. 4-6-Adam Kubert-a 4.00
14-23: 14-17-Prelude to Infinity. 18-23-Infinity tie-ins 4.00
24-($4.99) Rogue Planet; Ribic-a; Iron Man 3030 app. 5.00
25-27-Hickman-s/Larroca-a. 27-Includes reprint of All-New Invaders #1 4.00
Annual (2/14, $4.99) Christmas-themed; Lafuente-a 5.00
...: Endless Wartime HC (2013, $24.99, OGN) Ellis-s/McKone-a; intro by Clark Gregg 25.00
...: The Enemy Within (7/13, $2.99) DeConnick-s/Hepburn-a; Captain Marvel tie-in 3.00

AVENGERS ACADEMY (The Heroic Age)(Also see Avengers Arena)
Marvel Comics: Aug, 2010 - No. 39, Jan, 2013 ($3.99/$2.99)

1-($3.99) Gage-s/McKone-a/c; Intro. team of Veil, Hazmat, Striker, Mettle, Finesse, Reptil 4.00
1-Variant-c by Djurdjevic 8.00
2-14,14.1 -($2.99) 3,4-Juggernaut app. 5-Molina-a. 7-Absorbing Man app.; Raney-a. 3.00
15-39: 15-20-Fear Itself tie-in. 22-Magneto app. 27,28-Runaways app. 29-33-Tie in to Avengers vs. X-Men event 3.00
... Giant Size 1 (7/11, $7.99) Young Allies and Arcade app.; Tobin-s/Baldeon-a 8.00

AVENGERS: AGE OF ULTRON POINT ONE (Free Comic Book Day)
Marvel Comics: 2012 (Free giveaway)

#0.1 - Reprints Avengers 12.1 (6/11); Bendis-s/Hitch & Neary-c/a 4.00

AVENGERS: A.I. (Follows Age of Ultron series)
Marvel Comics: Sept, 2013 - Present ($2.99)

1-11: 1-Humphries-s/Araújo-a; Hank Pym, Vision app. 7-Daredevil app. 3.00

AVENGERS AND POWER PACK ASSEMBLE!
Marvel Comics: June, 2006 - No. 4, Sept, 2006 ($2.99, limited series)

1-4-GuriHiru-a/Sumerak-s. 1-Capt. America app. 2-Iron Man. 3-Spider-Man, Kang app. 3.00
TPB (2006, $6.99, digest-size) r/#1-4 7.00

AVENGERS AND THE INFINITY GAUNTLET
Marvel Comics: Oct, 2010 - No. 4, Jan, 2011 ($2.99, limited series)

1-4: 1-Clevinger-s/Churilla-a; Dr. Doom and Thanos app. 1-Ramos-c. 2-Lim-c 3.00

AVENGERS ARENA
Marvel Comics: Feb, 2013 - No. 18, Jan, 2014 ($2.99)

1-18: 1-Avengers Academy members & Runaways in Arcade's Murder World; Walker-a 3.00

AVENGERS ASSEMBLE (Also see Marvel Universe Avengers Assemble)
Marvel Comics: May, 2012 - No. 25, May, 2014 ($3.99)

1-25: 1-Bendis-s/Bagley-a/c; movie roster in regular Marvel universe. 3-Thanos returns. 4-8-Guardians of the Galaxy app. 9-DeConnick-s begin. 13,14-Age of Ultron tie-in. 18-20-Infinity tie-in. 21-23-Inhumanity 4.00
Annual 1 (3/13, $4.99) Gage-s/Coker-a; spotlight on The Vision 5.00

AVENGERS: CELESTIAL QUEST
Marvel Comics: Nov, 2001 - No. 8, June, 2002 ($2.50/$3.50, limited series)

1-7-Englehart-s/Santamaría-a; Thanos app. 3.00
8-($3.50) 4.00

AVENGERS: CLASSIC
Marvel Comics: Aug, 2007 - No. 12, Juy, 2008 ($3.99/$2.99)

1,12-($3.99) 1-Reprints Avengers #1 ('63) with new stories about that era; Art Adams-c 4.00
2-11-($2.99) R/#2-11 with back-up w/art by Oeming and others 3.00

AVENGERS COLLECTOR'S EDITION, THE
Marvel Comics: 1993 (Ordered through mail w/candy wrapper, 20 pgs.)

1-Contains 4 bound-in trading cards 5.00

AVENGERS: EARTH'S MIGHTIEST HEROES
Marvel Comics: Jan, 2005 - No. 8, Apr, 2005 ($3.50, limited series)

1-8-Retells origin; Casey-s/Kolins-a 4.00
HC (2005, $24.99, 7 1/2" x 11" with dustjacket) r/#1-8 25.00

AVENGERS: EARTH'S MIGHTIEST HEROES (Based on the Disney animated series)
Marvel Comics: Jan, 2011 - No. 4, Apr, 2011 ($3.99)

1-4-Yost-s/Wegener-a. 1-Hero profile pages. 2-Villain profile pages 4.00

AVENGERS EARTH'S MIGHTIEST HEROES (Titled Marvel Universe... for #1)
Marvel Comics: Jun, 2012 - No. 17, Oct, 2013 ($2.99)

1-17-All ages title. 13-FF & Dr. Doom app. 17-Ant-Man, Luke Cage & Iron Fist app. 4.00

AVENGERS: EARTH'S MIGHTIEST HEROES II
Marvel Comics: Jan, 2007 - No. 8, May, 2007 ($3.99, limited series)

1-8-Retells time when the Vision joined; Casey-s/Rosado-a. 6-Hank & Janet's wedding 4.00
HC (2007, $24.99, 7 1/2" x 11" with dustjacket) r/#1-8; cover sketches 25.00

AVENGERS FAIRY TALES
Marvel Comics: May, 2008 - No. 4, Dec, 2008 ($2.99, limited series)

1-4: 1-Peter Pan-style tale; Cebulski-a/Lemos-a. 2-The Vision. 3-Miyazawa-a 3.00

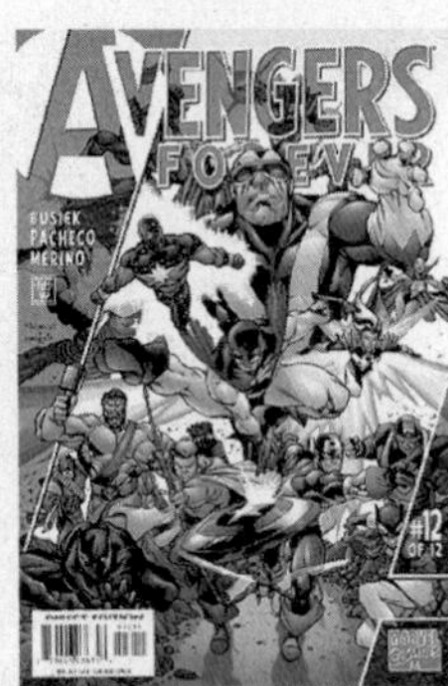

Avengers Forever #12 © MAR

Avengers Prime #3 © MAR

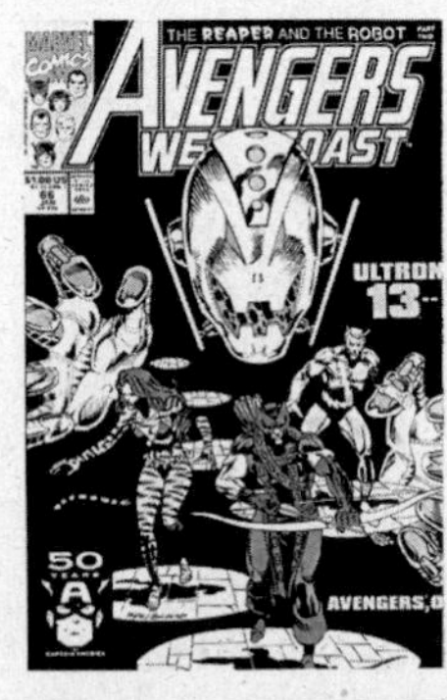

Avengers West Coast #66 © MAR

GD 2.0 | VG 4.0 | FN 6.0 | VF 8.0 | VF/NM 9.0 | NM- 9.2

AVENGERS FOREVER
Marvel Comics: Dec, 1998 - No. 12, Feb, 2000 ($2.99)
1-Busiek-s/Pacheco-a in all 4.00
2-12: 4-Four covers. 6-Two covers. 8-Vision origin revised. 12-Rick Jones becomes Capt. Marvel 3.00
TPB (1/01, $24.95) r/#1-12; Busiek intro.; new Pacheco-c 25.00

AVENGERS INFINITY
Marvel Comics: Sept, 2000 - No. 4, Dec, 2000 ($2.99, limited series)
1-4-Stern-s/Chen-a 3.00

AVENGERS/ INVADERS
Marvel Comics: Jul, 2008 - No. 12, Aug, 2009 ($2.99, limited series)
1-Invaders journey to the present; Alex Ross-c/Sadowski-a; Thunderbolts app. 3.00
2-12: 2-New Avengers app.; Perkins variant-c. 3-12-Variant-c on each 3.00
... Sketchbook (2008, giveaway) Ross and Sadowski sketch art; Krueger commentary 3.00

AVENGERS/ JLA (See JLA/Avengers for #1 & #3)
DC Comics: No, 2, 2003; No. 4, 2003 ($5.95, limited series)
2-Busiek-s/Pérez-a; wraparound-c; Krona, Galactus app. 6.00
4-Busiek-s/Pérez-a; wraparound-c 6.00

AVENGERS LOG, THE
Marvel Comics: Feb, 1994 ($1.95)
1-Gives history of all members; Pérez-c 3.00

AVENGERS NEXT (See A-Next and Spider-Girl)
Marvel Comics: Jan, 2007 - No. 5, Mar, 2007 ($2.99, limited series)
1-5-Lim-a/Wieringo-c; Spider-Girl app. 1-Avengers vs. zombies. 2-Thena app. 3.00
...: Rebirth TPB (2007, $13.99) r/#1-5 14.00

AVENGERS 1959
Marvel Comics: Dec, 2011 - No. 5, Mar, 2012 ($2.99, limited series)
1-5-Chaykin-s/a/c; Nick Fury, Kraven, Namora, Sabretooth, Dominic Fortune app. 3.00

AVENGERS ORIGINS (Series of one-shots)
Marvel Comics: Jan, 2012 ($3.99)
...: Ant-Man & The Wasp 1 (1/12) Aguirre-Sacasa-s/Hans-a/Djurdjevic-c; origin of both 4.00
...: Luke Cage 1 (1/12) Glass & Benson-s/Talajic-a/Djurdjevic-c; 4.00
...: Scarlet Witch & Quicksilver 1 (1/12) McKeever-s/Pierfederici-a/Djurdjevic-c 4.00
...: Thor 1 (1/12) K. Immonen-s/Barrionuevo-a/Djurdjevic-c 4.00
...: Vision 1 (1/12) Higgins & Siegel-s/Perger-a/Djurdjevic-c; Ultron-5 app. 4.00

AVENGERS PRIME (The Heroic Age)
Marvel Comics: Aug, 2010 - No. 5, Mar, 2011 ($3.99, limited series)
1-5-Thor, Iron Man & Steve Rogers; Bendis-s/Davis-a; Enchantress app. 4.00
1-Variant-c by Djurdjevic 8.00

AVENGERS: SEASON ONE
Marvel Comics: 2013 ($24.99, hardcover graphic novel)
HC - Origin story; Peter David-a/Tedesco painted-c; bonus script outline 25.00

AVENGERS: SOLO
Marvel Comics: Dec, 2011 - No. 5, Apr, 2012 ($3.99, limited series)
1-5-Hawkeye; back-up Avengers Academy 4.00

AVENGERS SPOTLIGHT (Formerly Solo Avengers #1-20)
Marvel Comics: No. 21, Aug, 1989 - No. 40, Jan, 1991 (75¢/$1.00)
21-Byrne-c/a 3.50
22-40: 26-Acts of Vengeance story. 31-34-U.S. Agent series. 36-Heck-i. 37-Mortimer-i. 40-The Black Knight app. 3.00

AVENGERS STRIKEFILE
Marvel Comics: Jan, 1994 ($1.75, one-shot)
1 3.00

AVENGERS: THE CHILDREN'S CRUSADE
Marvel Comics: Sept, 2010 - No. 9, May, 2012 ($3.99, limited series)
1-9-Young Avengers search for Scarlet Witch; Heinberg-s/Cheung-a. 6-9-X-Men app. 4.00
1-4-Variant-c. 1-Jelena Djurdjevic. 2-Travis Charest. 3,4-Art Adams 6.00
... - Young Avengers (5/11, $3.99) Takes place between #4&5; Alan Davis-a/c 4.00

AVENGERS: THE CROSSING
Marvel Comics: July, 1995 ($4.95, one-shot)
1-Deodato-c/a; 1st app. Thor's new costume 5.00

AVENGERS: THE INITIATIVE (See Civil War and related titles)
Marvel Comics: Jun, 2007 - No. 35, Jun, 2010 ($2.99)
1-Caselli-a/Slott-s/Cheung-c; War Machine app. 4.00

GD 2.0 | VG 4.0 | FN 6.0 | VF 8.0 | VF/NM 9.0 | NM- 9.2

2-35: 4,5-World War Hulk. 6-Uy-a. 14-19-Secret Invasion; 3-D Man app. 16-Skrull Kill Krew returns. 20-Tigra pregnancy revealed, 21-25-Ramos-a. 32-35-Siege 3.00
Annual 1 (1/08, $3.99) Secret Invasion tie-in; Cheung-c 4.00
... Featuring Reptil (5/09, $3.99) Gage-s/Uy-a 4.00
... Special 1 (1/09, $3.99) Slott & Gage-s/Uy-a 4.00
...: Vol. 1 - Basic Training HC (2007, $19.99, d.j.) r/#1-6 20.00
...: Vol. 1 - Basic Training SC (2008, $14.99) r/#1-6 15.00

AVENGERS: THE ORIGIN
Marvel Comics: Jun, 2010 - No. 5, Oct, 2010 ($3.99, limited series)
1-5-Casey-s/Noto-a/c; team origin (pre-Capt. America) re-told; Loki app. 4.00

AVENGERS: THE TERMINATRIX OBJECTIVE
Marvel Comics: Sept, 1993 - No. 4, Dec, 1993 ($1.25, limited series)
1 ($2.50)-Holo-grafx foil-c 4.00
2-4-Old vs. current Avengers 3.00

AVENGERS: THE ULTRON IMPERATIVE
Marvel Comics: Nov, 2001 ($5.99, one-shot)
1-Follow-up to the Ultron Unlimited ending in Avengers #42; BWS-c 6.00

AVENGERS, THOR & CAPTAIN AMERICA: OFFICIAL INDEX TO THE MARVEL UNIVERSE
Marvel Comics: Jun, 2010 - No. 15, 2001 ($3.99)
1-15-Each issue has chronological synopsies, creator credits, character lists for 30-40 issues of Avengers, Captain America and Journey Into Mystery starting with debuts 4.00

AVENGERS/THUNDERBOLTS
Marvel Comics: May, 2004 - No. 6, Sept, 2004 ($2.99, limited series)
1-6: Busiek & Nicieza-s/Kitson-c. 1,2-Kitson-a. 3-6-Grummett-a 3.00
Vol. 2: Best Intentions (2004, $14.99) r/#1-6 15.00

AVENGERS: TIMESLIDE
Marvel Comics: Feb, 1996 ($4.95, one-shot)
1-Foil-c 5.00

AVENGERS TWO: WONDER MAN & BEAST
Marvel Comics: May, 2000 - No. 3, July, 2000 ($2.99, limited series)
1-3: Stern-s/Bagley-c/a 3.00

AVENGERS/ULTRAFORCE (See Ultraforce/Avengers)
Marvel Comics: Oct, 1995 ($3.95, one-shot)
1-Wraparound foil-c by Pérez 4.00

AVENGERS UNDERCOVER (Follows Avengers Arena series)
Marvel Comics: May, 2014 - Present ($2.99)
1,2-Hopeless-s/Walker-a; Masters of Evil app. 3.00

AVENGERS UNITED THEY STAND
Marvel Comics: Nov, 1999 - No. 7, June, 2000 ($2.99/$1.99)
1-Based on the animated series 4.00
2-6-($1.99) 2-Avengers battle Hydra. 6-The Collector app. 3.00
7-($2.99) Devil Dinosaur-c/app.; The Collector app.; r/Avengers Action Figure Comic 4.00

AVENGERS UNIVERSE
Marvel Comics: Jun, 2000 - No. 3, Oct, 2000 ($3.99)
1-3-Reprints recent stories 4.00

AVENGERS UNPLUGGED
Marvel Comics: Oct, 1995 - No. 6, Aug, 1996 (99¢, bi-monthly)
1-6 3.00

AVENGERS VS. ATLAS (Leads into Atlas #1)
Marvel Comics: Mar, 2010 - No. 4, Jun, 2010 ($3.99, limited series)
1-4-Hardman-a; Ramos-c. 1-Back-up w/Miyazawa-a. 2-4-Original Avengers app. 4.00

AVENGERS VS. PET AVENGERS
Marvel Comics: Dec, 2010 - No. 4, Mar, 2011 ($2.99, limited series)
1-4-Eliopoulos-s/Guara-a; Fin Fang Foom app. 3.00

AVENGERS VS. X-MEN (Also see AVX: VS and AVX: Consequences)
Marvel Comics: No. 0, May, 2012 - No. 12, Dec, 2012 ($3.99/$4.99, bi-weekly limited series)
0-Bendis & Aaron-s; Frank Cho-a/c; Scarlet Witch and Hope featured 4.00
1-11: 1-5-Romita Jr. -a. 6,7,11-Coipel-a. 8-10-Adam Kubert-a. 11-Hulk app. 4.00
12-($4.99) Adam Kubert-a; Cyclops as Dark Phoenix 5.00

AVENGERS WEST COAST (Formerly West Coast Avengers)
Marvel Comics: No. 48, Sept, 1989 - No. 102, Jan, 1994 ($1.00/$1.25)
48,49: 48-Byrne-c/a & scripts continue thru #57 3.50
50-Re-intro original Human Torch 4.00
51-69,71-74,76-83,85,86,89-99: 54-Cover swipe/F.F. #1. 78-Last $1.00-c. 79-Dr. Strange

Avenging Spider-Man #21 © MAR

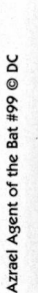

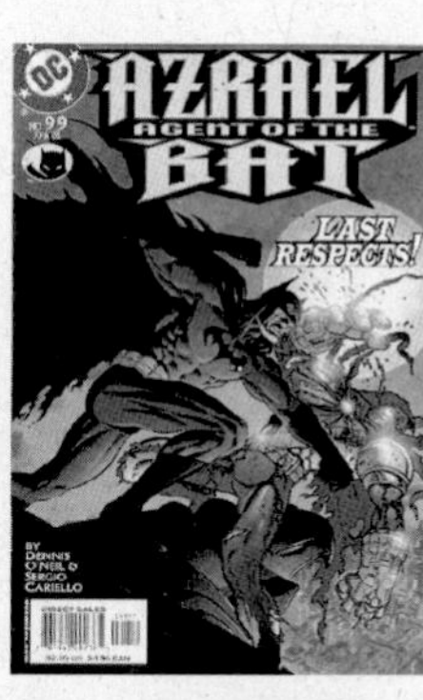

Azrael Agent of the Bat #99 © DC

Babe #6 © Prize

GD 2.0 | VG 4.0 | FN 6.0 | VF 8.0 | VF/NM 9.0 | NM- 9.2

x-over. 93-95-Darkhawk app. 3.00
70,75,84,87,88: 70-Spider-Woman app. 75 (52 pgs.)-Fantastic Four x-over. 84-Origin Spider-Woman retold; Spider-Man app. (also in #85,86). 87,88-Wolverine-c/story 4.00
100-($3.95, 68 pgs.)-Embossed all red foil-c 4.00
101,102: 101-X-Men x-over 5.00
Annual 5-8 ('90- '93, 68 pgs.)-5,6-West Coast Avengers in indicia. 7-Darkhawk app. 8-Polybagged w/card 4.00
...: Darker Than Scarlet TPB (2008, $24.99) r/#51-57,60-62; Byrne-s/a 25.00
...: Vision Quest TPB (2005, $24.99) r/#42-50; Byrne-s/a 25.00

AVENGERS WORLD
Marvel Comics: Mar, 2014 - Present ($3.99)
1-4: 1-Hickman & Spencer-s/Caselli-a 4.00

AVENGERS: X-SANCTION
Marvel Comics: Feb, 2012 - No. 4, May, 2012 ($3.99, limited series)
1-4-Loeb-s/McGuinness-a/c; Cable battles the Avengers. 3,4-Wolverine & Spidey app. 4.00

AVENGING SPIDER-MAN (Spider-Man and Avengers member team-ups)
Marvel Comics: Jan, 2012 - No. 22, Aug, 2013 ($3.99)
1-15: 1-3-Madureira-a/Wells-s; Madureira-c. 1-3-Red Hulk & Avengers app. 4-Hawkeye app. 5-Captain America app.; Yu-a. 11-Dillon-a. 12,13-Deadpool app. 14,15-Devil Dinosaur 4.00
1-Variant-c by Ramos 8.00
1-Variant-c by J. Scott Campbell 8.00
15.1 (2/13, $2.99) Follows Amazing Spider-Man #700; 1st Superior Spider-Man 5.00
16-22-Superior Spider-Man. 16-Wolverine & X-Men app. 18-Thor app. 22-Punisher app. 4.00
Annual 1 (12/12, $4.99) Spider-Man (Peter Parker) and The Thing; Zircher-c 5.00

AVIATION ADVENTURES AND MODEL BUILDING (True Aviation Advs. ...No. 15)
Parents' Magazine Institute: No. 16, Dec, 1946 - No. 17, Feb, 1947
16,17-Half comics and half pictures 8 16 24 42 54 65

AVIATION CADETS
Street & Smith Publications: 1943
nn 19 37 57 109 172 235

A-V IN 3-D
Aardvark-Vanaheim: Dec, 1984 ($2.00, 28 pgs. w/glasses)
1-Cerebus, Flaming Carrot, Normalman & Ms. Tree 4.00

AVX: CONSEQUENCES (Aftermath of Avengers Vs. X-Men series)
Marvel Comics: Dec, 2012 - No. 5, Jan, 2013 ($3.99, weekly limited series)
1-5-Cyclops in prison; Gillen-s/art by various 4.00

AVX: VS (Tie-in to Avengers Vs. X-Men series)
Marvel Comics: Jun, 2012 - No. 6, Nov, 2012 ($3.99, limited series)
1-6-Spotlight on the individual fights from Avengers Vs. X-Men #2; art by various 4.00

AWAKENING, THE
Image Comics: Oct, 1997 - No. 4, Apr, 1998 ($2.95, B&W, limited series)
1-4-Stephen Blue-s/c/a 3.00

AWESOME ADVENTURES
Awesome Entertainment: Aug, 1999 ($2.50)
1-Alan Moore-s/ Steve Skroce-a; Youngblood story 3.00

AWESOME HOLIDAY SPECIAL
Awesome Entertainment: Dec, 1997 ($2.50, one-shot)
1-Flip book w/covers of Fighting American & Coven. Holiday stories also featuring Kaboom and Shaft by regular creators. 3.00
1-Gold Edition 5.00

AWFUL OSCAR (Formerly & becomes Oscar Comics with No. 13)
Marvel Comics: No. 11, June, 1949 - No. 12, Aug, 1949
11,12 15 30 45 84 127 170

AWKWARD UNIVERSE
Slave Labor Graphics: 12/95 ($9.95, graphic novel)
nn 10.00

AXA
Eclipse Comics: Apr, 1987 - No. 2, Aug, 1987 ($1.75)
1,2 3.00

AXE COP: BAD GUY EARTH
Dark Horse Comics: Mar, 2011 - No. 3, May, 2011 ($3.50, limited series)
1-3-Malachai Nicolle-s/Ethan Nicolle-a 3.50

AXE COP: PRESIDENT OF THE WORLD
Dark Horse Comics: Jul, 2012 - No. 3, Sept, 2012 ($3.50, limited series)
1-3-Malachai Nicolle-s/Ethan Nicolle-a 3.50

AXEL PRESSBUTTON (Pressbutton No. 5; see Laser Eraser &...)
Eclipse Comics: Nov, 1984 - No. 6, July, 1985 ($1.50/$1.75, Baxter paper)
1-6: Reprints Warrior (British mag.). 1-Bolland-c; origin Laser Eraser & Pressbutton 3.00

AXIS ALPHA
Axis Comics: Feb, 1994 ($2.50, one-shot)
V1-Previews Axis titles including, Tribe, Dethgrip, B.E.A.S.T.I.E.S. & more; Pitt app. in Tribe story. 3.00

AZRAEL (...Agent of the Bat #47 on)(Also see Batman: Sword of Azrael)
DC Comics: Feb, 1995 - No. 100, May, 2003 ($1.95/$2.25/$2.50/$2.95)
1-Dennis O'Neil scripts begin 5.00
2,3 3.50
4-46,48-62: 5,6-Ras Al Ghul app. 13-Nightwing-c/app. 15-Contagion Pt. 5 (Pt. 4 on-c). 16-Contagion Pt. 10. 22-Batman-c/app. 23,27-Batman app. 27,28-Joker app. 35-Hitman app. 36-39-Batman, Bane app. 50-New costume. 53-Joker-c/app. 56,57,60-New Batgirl app. 3.00
47-($3.95) Flip book with Batman: Shadow of the Bat #80 4.00
63-74,76-92: 63-Huntress-c/app.; Azrael returns to old costume. 67-Begin $2.50-c. 70-79-Harris-c. 83-Joker x-over. 91-Bruce Wayne: Fugitive pt. 15 3.00
75-($3.95) New costume; Harris-c 4.00
93-100: 93-Begin $2.95-c. 95,96-Two-Face app. 100-Last issue; Zeck-c 3.00
#1,000,000 (11/98) Giarrano-a 3.00
Annual 1 (1995, $3.95)-Year One story 4.00
Annual 2 (1996, $2.95)-Legends of the Dead Earth story 4.00
Annual 3 (1997, $3.95)-Pulp Heroes story; Orbik-c 4.00
.../Ash (1997, $4.95) O'Neil-s/Quesada, Palmiotti-a 5.00
Plus (12/96, $2.95)-Question-c/app. 4.00

AZRAEL
DC Comics: Dec, 2009 - No. 18, May, 2011 ($2.99)
1-18: 1-9-Nicieza-s/Bachs-a. 1-Covers by Jock & Irving. 2,3-Jock-c. 5-Ragman app. 3.00
...: Angel in the Dark TPB (2010, $17.99) r/#1-6; cover gallery 18.00

AZRAEL: DEATH'S DARK KNIGHT
DC Comics: May, 2009 - No. 3, Jul, 2009 ($2.99, limited series)
1-Battle For the Cowl tie-in; Nicieza-s/Irving-a/March-c 3.00
TPB (2010, $14.99) r/#1-3, Batman Annual #27 and Detective Annual #11 15.00

AZTEC ACE
Eclipse Comics: Mar, 1984 - No. 15, Sept, 1985 ($2.25/$1.50/$1.75, Baxter paper)
1-$2.25-c (52 pgs.) 4.00
2-15: 2-Begin 36 pgs. 3.00
NOTE: *N. Redondo a-1i-8i, 10i. c-6-8i.*

AZTEK: THE ULTIMATE MAN
DC Comics: Aug, 1996 - No. 10, May 1997 ($1.75)
1-1st app. Aztek & Synth; Grant Morrison & Mark Millar scripts in all 6.00
2-9: 2-Green Lantern app. 3-1st app. Death-Doll. 4-Intro The Lizard King. 5-Origin. 6-Joker app.; Batman cameo. 7-Batman app. 8-Luthor app. 9-vs. Parasite-c/app. 4.00
10-JLA-c/app. 1 2 4 6 8 10
JLA Presents: Aztek the Ultimate Man TPB (2008, $19.99) r/#1-10 20.00
NOTE: ***Breyfogle** c-5p. **N. Steven Harris** a-1-5p. **Porter** c-1p. **Wieringo** c-2p.*

BABE (...Darling of the Hills, later issues)(See Big Shot and Sparky Watts)
Prize/Headline/Feature: June-July, 1948 - No. 11, Apr-May, 1950
1-Boody Rogers-a 31 62 93 182 296 410
2-Boody Rogers-a 18 36 54 107 169 230
3-11-All by Boody Rogers 16 32 48 94 147 200

BABE
Dark Horse Comics (Legend): July, 1994 - No. 4, Jan, 1994 ($2.50, lim. series)
1-4: John Byrne-c/a/scripts; ProtoTykes back-up story 3.00

BABE RUTH SPORTS COMICS (Becomes Rags Rabbit #11 on?)
Harvey Publications: April, 1949 - No. 11, Feb, 1951
1-Powell-a 40 80 120 246 411 575
2-Powell-a 27 54 81 158 259 360
3-11: Powell-a in most 22 44 66 130 213 295
NOTE: *Baseball c-2-4, 9. Basketball c-1, 6. Football c-5. Yogi Berra c/story-8. Joe DiMaggio c/story-3. Bob Feller c/story-4. Stan Musial c-9.*

BABES IN TOYLAND (Disney, Movie) (See Golden Pix Story Book ST-3)
Dell Publishing Co.: No. 1282, Feb-Apr, 1962
Four Color 1282-Annette Funicello photo-c 12 24 36 81 176 270

BABES OF BROADWAY

Baby Huey, The Baby Giant #2 © HARV

Babylon 5 #11 © WB

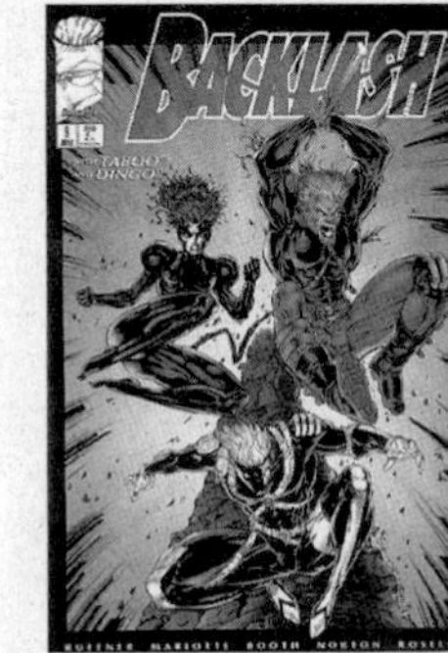

Backlash #9 © WSP

	GD 2.0	VG 4.0	FN 6.0	VF 8.0	VF/NM 9.0	NM- 9.2

Broadway Comics: May, 1996 ($2.95, one-shot)

1-Pin-ups of Broadway Comics' female characters; Alan Davis, Michael Kaluta, J. G. Jones, Alan Weiss, Guy Davis & others-a; Giordano-c. 3.00

BABE 2
Dark Horse Comics (Legend): Mar, 1995 - No. 2, May, 1995 ($2.50, lim. series)

1,2: John Byrne-c/a/scripts 3.00

BABY HUEY
Harvey Comics: No. 1, Oct, 1991 - No. 9, June, 1994 ($1.00/$1.25/$1.50, quarterly)

1 ($1.00): 1-Cover says "Big Baby Huey" 5.00
2-9 ($1.25-$1.50) 3.00

BABY HUEY AND PAPA (See Paramount Animated...)
Harvey Publications: May, 1962 - No. 33, Jan, 1968 (Also see Casper The Friendly Ghost)

	GD	VG	FN	VF	VF/NM	NM-
1	13	26	39	86	188	290
2	7	14	21	49	92	135
3-5	5	10	15	33	57	80
6-10	3	6	9	20	31	42
11-20	3	6	9	15	22	28
21-33	2	4	6	13	18	22

BABY HUEY DIGEST
Harvey Publications: June, 1992 (Digest-size, one-shot)

	GD	VG	FN	VF	VF/NM	NM-
1-Reprints	1	3	4	6	8	10

BABY HUEY DUCKLAND
Harvey Publications: Nov, 1962 - No. 15, Nov, 1966 (25¢ Giants, 68 pgs.)

	GD	VG	FN	VF	VF/NM	NM-
1	10	20	30	66	138	210
2-5	5	10	15	34	60	85
6-15	3	6	9	21	33	45

BABY HUEY, THE BABY GIANT (Also see Big Baby Huey, Casper, Harvey Hits #22, Harvey Comics Hits #60, & Paramount Animated Comics)
Harvey Publ: 9/56 - #97, 10/71; #98, 10/72; #99, 10/80; #100, 10/90; #101, 11/90

	GD	VG	FN	VF	VF/NM	NM-
1-Infinity-c	47	94	141	367	826	1285
2	21	42	63	147	324	500
3-Baby Huey takes anti-pep pills	13	26	39	89	195	300
4,5	9	18	27	61	123	185
6-10	6	12	18	40	73	105
11-20	5	10	15	31	53	75
21-40	4	8	12	23	37	50
41-60	3	6	9	16	23	30
61-79 (12/67)	2	4	6	13	18	22
80(12/68) - 95-All 68 pg. Giants	3	6	9	16	24	32
96,97-Both 52 pg. Giants	3	6	9	14	19	24
98-Regular size	2	4	6	9	12	15
99-Regular size	1	2	3	5	6	8
100,101 ($1.00)						4.00

BABYLON 5 (TV)
DC Comics: Jan, 1995 - No. 11, Dec, 1995 ($1.95/$2.50)

	GD	VG	FN	VF	VF/NM	NM-
1	2	4	6	8	11	14
2-5	1	2	3	5	7	9
6-11: 7-Begin $2.50-c	1	2	3	4	5	7
... The Price of Peace (1998, $9.95, TPB) r/#1-4,11						10.00

BABYLON 5: IN VALEN'S NAME
DC Comics: Mar, 1998 - No. 3, May, 1998 ($2.50, limited series)

1-3 4.00

BABY SNOOTS (Also see March of Comics #359,371,396,401,419,431,443,450,462,474,485)
Gold Key: Aug, 1970 - No. 22, Nov, 1975

	GD	VG	FN	VF	VF/NM	NM-
1	3	6	9	19	30	40
2-11	2	4	6	11	16	20
12-22: 22-Titled Snoots, the Forgetful Elefink	2	4	6	8	10	12

BACCHUS (Also see Eddie Campbell's ...)
Harrier Comics (New Wave): 1988 - No. 2, Aug, 1988 ($1.95, B&W)

1,2: Eddie Campbell-c/a/scripts. 3.00

BACHELOR FATHER (TV)
Dell Publishing Co.: No. 1332, 4-6/62 - No. 2, Sept.-Nov., 1962

	GD	VG	FN	VF	VF/NM	NM-
Four Color 1332 (#1), 2-Written by Stanley	6	12	18	42	79	115

BACHELOR'S DIARY
Avon Periodicals: 1949 (15¢)

	GD	VG	FN	VF	VF/NM	NM-
1(Scarce)-King Features panel cartoons & text-r; pin-up, girl wrestling photos; similar to Sideshow	110	220	330	704	1202	1700

BACK DOWN THE LINE
Eclipse Books: 1991 (Mature adults, 8-1/2 x 11", 52 pgs.)

nn (Soft-c, $8.95)-Bolton-c/a 9.00
nn (Limited Hard-c, $29.95) 30.00

BACKLASH (Also see The Kindred)
Image Comics (WildStorm Prod.): Nov,1994 - No. 32, May, 1997 ($1.95/$2.50)

1-Double-c; variant-double-c 4.00
2-7,9-32: 5-Intro Mindscape; 2 pinups. 19-Fire From Heaven Pt 2. 20-Fire From Heaven Pt 10. 31-WildC.A.T.S app. 3.00
8-($1.95, newsstand)-Wildstorm Rising Pt. 8 3.00
8-($2.50, direct market)-Wildstorm Rising Pt. 8 3.00
25-($3.95)-Double-size 4.00
...& Taboo's African Holiday (9/99, $5.95) Booth-s/a(p) 6.00

BACKLASH/SPIDER-MAN
Image Comics (WildStorm Productions): Aug, 1996 - No. 2, Sept, 1996 ($2.50, lim. series)

1,2: Pike (villain from WildC.A.T.S) & Venom app. 3.00

BACKPACK MARVELS (B&W backpack-sized reprint collections)
Marvel Comics: Nov, 2000 ($6.95, B&W, digest-size)

Avengers 1 -r/Avengers #181-189; profile pages 7.00
Spider-Man 1-r/ASM #234-240 7.00
X-Men 1-r/Uncanny X-Men #167-173 7.00
X-Men 2-r/Uncanny X-Men #174-179; new painted-c by Greg Horn 7.00

BACK TO THE FUTURE (Movie, TV cartoon)
Harvey Comics: Nov, 1991 - No. 4, June, 1992 ($1.25)

1-4: 1,2-Gil Kane-c; based on animated cartoon 3.00

BACK TO THE FUTURE: FORWARD TO THE FUTURE
Harvey Comics: Oct, 1992 - No. 3, Feb, 1993 ($1.50, limited series)

1-3 3.00

BAD ASS
Dynamite Entertainment: 2014 - Present ($3.99)

1-3-Hanna-s/Bessadi-a 4.00

BAD BLOOD
Dark Horse Comics: Jan, 2014 - No. 5, May, 2014 ($3.99, limited series)

1-5-Vampire story; Jonathan Maberry-s/Tyler Crook-a 4.00

BAD BOY
Oni Press: Dec, 1997 ($4.95, one-shot)

1-Frank Miller-s/Simon Bisley-a/painted-c 5.00

BAD COMPANY
Quality Comics/Fleetway Quality #15 on: Aug, 1988 - No. 19?, 1990 ($1.50/$1.75, high quality paper)

1-19: 5,6-Guice-c 3.00

BADGE OF JUSTICE (Formerly Crime And Justice #21)
Charlton Comics: No. 22, Jan, 1955; No. 2, Apr, 1955 - No. 4, Oct, 1955

	GD	VG	FN	VF	VF/NM	NM-
22(#1)-Giordano-c	10	20	30	58	79	100
2-4	7	14	21	35	43	50

BADGER, THE
Capital Comics(#1-4)/First Comics: Dec, 1983 - No. 70, Apr, 1991; V2#1, Spring, 1991

1 5.00
2-70: 52-54-Tim Vigil-c/a 3.00
50-($3.95, 52 pgs.) 4.00
V2#1 (Spring, 1991, $4.95) 5.00

BADGER, THE
Image Comics: V3#78, May, 1997 - V3#88 ($2.95, B&W)

78-Cover lists #1, Baron-s 3.00
79/#2, 80/#3, 81(indicia lists #80)/#4,82-88/#5-11 3.00

BADGER GOES BERSERK
First Comics: Sept, 1989 - No. 4, Dec, 1989 ($1.95, lim. series, Baxter paper)

1-4: 2-Paul Chadwick-c/a(2pgs.) 3.00

BADGER: SHATTERED MIRROR
Dark Horse Comics: July, 1994 - No. Oct, 1994 ($2.50, limited series)

1-4 3.00

BADGER: ZEN POP FUNNY-ANIMAL VERSION
Dark Horse Comics: July, 1994 - No. 2, Aug, 1994 ($2.50, limited series)

Badmen of Tombstone #1 © AVON

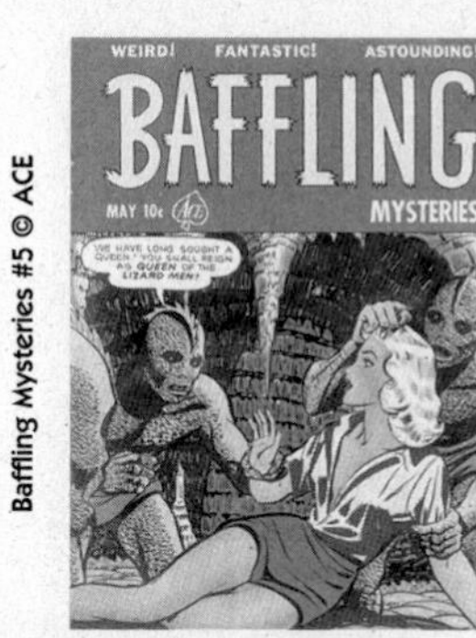

Baffling Mysteries #5 © ACE

Banana Splits #1 © H-B

GD 2.0 | VG 4.0 | FN 6.0 | VF 8.0 | VF/NM 9.0 | NM- 9.2

1,2 3.00

BAD GIRLS
DC Comics: Oct, 2003 - No. 5, Feb, 2004 ($2.50, limited series)
1-5-Steve Vance-s/Jennifer Graves-a/Darwyn Cooke-c 3.00
TPB (2009, $14.99) r/#1-5; Graves sketch pages 15.00

BAD IDEAS
Image Comics: Apr, 2004 - No. 2, July, 2004 ($5.95, B&W, limited series)
1,2-Chinsang-s/Mahfood & Crosland-a 6.00
..., Vol. 1: Collected! (2005, $12.99) r/#1,2 13.00

BADLANDS
Vortex Comics: May, 1990 ($3.00, glossy stock, mature)
1-Chaykin-c 3.00

BADLANDS
Dark Horse Comics: July, 1991 - No. 6, Dec, 1991 ($2.25, B&W, limited series)
1-6: 1-John F. Kennedy-c; reprints Vortex Comics issue 3.00

BADMEN OF THE WEST
Avon Periodicals: 1951 (Giant) (132 pgs., painted-c)
1-Contains rebound copies of Jesse James, King of the Bad Men of Deadwood, Badmen of Tombstone; other combinations possible.
Issues with Kubert-a... 41 82 123 250 418 585

BADMEN OF THE WEST! (See A-1 Comics)
Magazine Enterprises: 1953 - No. 3, 1954
1 (A-1 100)-Meskin-a? 22 44 66 132 216 300
2 (A-1 120), 3: 2-Larsen-a 15 30 45 85 130 175

BADMEN OF TOMBSTONE
Avon Periodicals: 1950
nn 18 36 54 103 162 220

BAD PLANET
Image Comics (Raw Studios): Dec, 2005 - No. 6, Nov, 2008 ($2.99)
1-6: 1-Thomas Jane & Steve Niles-s/Larosa & Bradstreet-a/c. 2-Wrightson-c. 3-3-D pages 3.00

BADROCK (Also see Youngblood)
Image Comics (Extreme Studios): Mar, 1995 - No. 2, Jan, 1996 ($1.75/$2.50)
1-Variant-c (3) 3.50
2-Liefeld-c/a & story; Savage Dragon app, flipbook w/Grifter/Badrock #2; variant-c exist 3.00
Annual 1(1995,$2.95)-Arthur Adams-c 4.00
Annual 1 Commemorative ($9.95)-3,000 printed 10.00
.../Wolverine (6/96, $4.95, squarebound)-Sauron app; pin-ups; variant-c exists 5.00
.../Wolverine (6/96)-Special Comicon Edition 5.00

BADROCK AND COMPANY (Also see Youngblood)
Image Comics (Extreme Studios): Sept, 1994 - No.6, Feb, 1995 ($2.50)
1-6 : 6-Indicia reads "October 1994"; story cont'd in Shadowhawk #17 3.00

BAFFLING MYSTERIES (Formerly Indian Braves No. 1-4; Heroes of the Wild Frontier No. 26-on)
Periodical House (Ace Magazines): No. 5, Nov, 1951 - No. 26, Oct, 1955
5 41 82 123 256 428 600
6-19,21-24: 8-Woodish-a by Cameron. 10-E.C. Crypt Keeper swipe on-c.
24-Last pre-code issue 28 56 84 165 270 375
20-Classic bondage-c 37 74 111 222 361 500
25-Reprints; surrealistic-c 20 40 60 114 182 250
26-Reprints 18 36 54 105 165 225
NOTE: ***Cameron** a-8, 10, 16-18, 20-22. **Colan** a-5, 11, 25r/5. **Sekowsky** a-5, 6, 22. Bondage c-20, 23. Reprints in 18(1), 19(1), 24(3).*

BALBO (See Master Comics #33 & Mighty Midget Comics)

BALDER THE BRAVE
Marvel Comics Group: Nov, 1985 - No. 4, 1986 (Limited series)
1-4: Simonson-c/a; character from Thor 4.00

BALLAD OF HALO JONES, THE
Quality Comics: Sept, 1987 - No. 12, Aug, 1988 ($1.25/$1.50)
1-12: Alan Moore scripts in all 3.00

BALL AND CHAIN
DC Comics (Homage): Nov, 1999 - No. 4, Feb, 2000 ($2.50, limited series)
1-4-Lobdell-s/Garza-a 3.00

BALLISTIC (Also See Cyberforce)
Image Comics (Top Cow Productions): Sept, 1995 - No. 3, Dec, 1995 ($2.50, limited series)
1-3: Wetworks app, Turner-c/a 3.00

GD 2.0 | VG 4.0 | FN 6.0 | VF 8.0 | VF/NM 9.0 | NM- 9.2

... Action (5/96, $2.95) Pin-ups of Top Cow characters participating in outdoor sports 3.00
... Imagery (1/96, $2.50, anthology) Cyberforce app. 3.00
.../ Wolverine (2/97, $2.95) Devil's Reign pt. 4; Witchblade cameo (1 page) 4.00

BALOO & LITTLE BRITCHES (Disney)
Gold Key: Apr, 1968
1-From the Jungle Book 4 8 12 23 37 50

BALTIMORE: ... (One-shots)
Dark Horse Comics: ($3.50)
... The Inquisitor (6/13) Mignola & Golden-s; Stenbeck-a/c 3.50
... The Play (11/12) Mignola & Golden-s; Stenbeck-a/c 3.50
... The Widow and the Tank (2/13) Mignola & Golden-s; Stenbeck-a/c 3.50

BALTIMORE: CHAPEL OF BONES
Dark Horse Comics: Jan, 2014 - No. 2, Feb, 2014 ($3.50, limited series)
1,2-Mignola & Golden-s; Stenbeck-a/c 3.50

BALTIMORE: DR. LESKOVAR'S REMEDY
Dark Horse Comics: Jun, 2012 - No. 2, Jul, 2012 ($3.50, limited series)
1,2-Mignola & Golden-s; Stenbeck-a/c 3.50

BALTIMORE: THE CURSE BELLS
Dark Horse Comics: Aug, 2011 - No. 5, Dec, 2011 ($3.50, limited series)
1-5-Mignola-s/c; Stenbeck-a. 1-Variant-c by Francavilla 3.50

BALTIMORE: THE INFERNAL TRAIN
Dark Horse Comics: Sept, 2013 - No. 3, Nov, 2013 ($3.50, limited series)
1-3-Mignola & Golden-s; Stenbeck-a/c 3.50

BALTIMORE: THE PLAGUE SHIPS
Dark Horse Comics: Aug, 2010 - No. 5, Dec, 2010 ($3.50, limited series)
1-5-Mignola-s/c; Stenbeck-a; Lord Baltimore hunting vampires in 1916 Europe 3.50

BAMBI (Disney) (See Movie Classics, Movie Comics, and Walt Disney Showcase No. 31)
Dell Publishing Co.: No. 12, 1942; No. 30, 1943; No. 186, Apr, 1948; 1984
Four Color 12-Walt Disney's... 46 92 138 340 770 1200
Four Color 30-Bambi's Children (1943) 40 80 120 296 673 1050
Four Color 186-Walt Disney's...; reprinted as Movie Classic Bambi #3 (1956)
14 28 42 96 211 325
1-(Whitman, 1984; 60¢)-r/Four Color #186 (3-pack) 2 4 6 10 14 18

BAMBI (Disney)
Grosset & Dunlap: 1942 (50¢, 7"x8-1/2", 32pg, hard-c w/dust jacket)
nn-Given away w/a copy of Thumper for a $2.00, 2-yr. subscription to WDC&S
in 1942 (Xmas offer). Book only 22 44 66 132 216 300
w/dust jacket 39 78 117 240 395 550

BAMM BAMM & PEBBLES FLINTSTONE (TV)
Gold Key: Oct, 1964 (Hanna-Barbera)
1 8 16 24 51 96 140

BANANA SPLITS, THE (TV) (See Golden Comics Digest & March of Comics No. 364)
Gold Key: June, 1969 - No. 8, Oct, 1971 (Hanna-Barbera)
1-Photo-c on all 8 16 24 56 108 160
2-8 5 10 15 34 60 85

BANANA SUNDAY
Oni Press: July, 2005 - No. 4, Oct, 2005 ($2.99, B&W, limited series)
1-4-Root Nibot-s/Colleen Coover-a 3.00
TPB (3/06, $11.95) r/#1-4; sketch gallery 12.00

BAND WAGON (See Hanna-Barbera Band Wagon)

BANG! TANGO
DC Comics (Vertigo): Apr, 2009 - No. 6, Sept, 2009 ($2.99, limited series)
1-6-Kelly-s/Sibar-a/Chaykin-c 3.00

BANG-UP COMICS
Progressive Publishers: Dec, 1941 - No. 3, June, 1942
1-Cosmo Mann & Lady Fairplay begin; Buzz Balmer by Rick Yager in all (origin #1)
98 196 294 622 1074 1525
2,3 50 100 150 315 533 750

BANISHED KNIGHTS (See Warlands)
Image Comics: Dec, 2001 - No. 4, June, 2002 ($2.95)
1-4-Two covers (Alvin Lee, Pat Lee) 3.00

BANNER COMICS (Becomes Captain Courageous No. 6)
Ace Magazines: No. 3, Sept, 1941 - No. 5, Jan, 1942
3-Captain Courageous (1st app.) & Lone Warrior & Sidekick Dicky begin;

Barbie #32 © Mattel

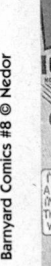

Barnyard Comics #8 © Nedor

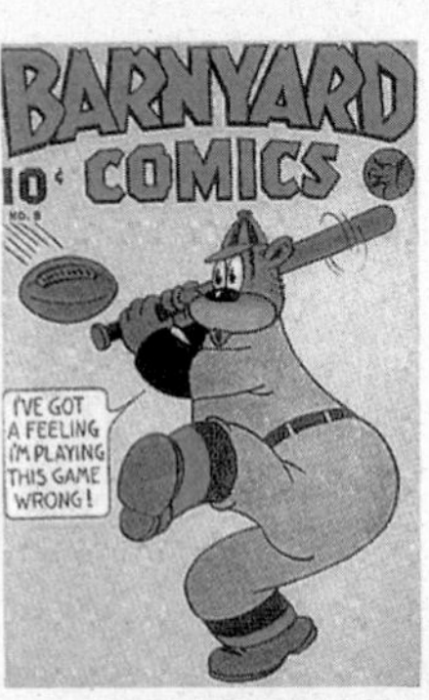

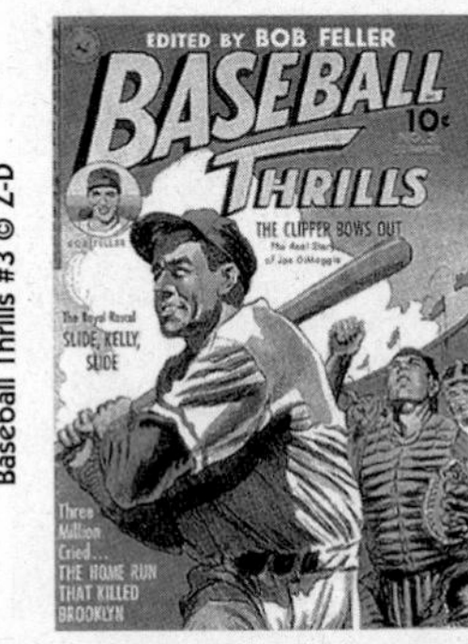

Baseball Thrills #3 © Z-D

	GD 2.0	VG 4.0	FN 6.0	VF 8.0	VF/NM 9.0	NM- 9.2
Jim Mooney-c	129	258	387	826	1413	2000
4,5: 4-Flag-c	77	154	231	493	847	1200

BARACK OBAMA (See Presidential Material: Barack Obama, Amazing Spider-Man #583, Savage Dragon #137)

BARACK THE BARBARIAN
Devil's Due Publishing: Jun, 2009 - No. 4, Oct, 2009 ($3.50/$3.99, limited series)

	GD 2.0	VG 4.0	FN 6.0	VF 8.0	VF/NM 9.0	NM- 9.2
...Quest For The Treasure of Stimuli 1-3-($3.50) Conan spoof with Barack Obama; Hama-s						3.50
...Quest For The Treasure of Stimuli 4-($3.99)						4.00
...: The Red of Red Sarah 1 ($5.99, B&W) Sarah Palin satire; Hama-s						6.00

BARBARIANS, THE
Atlas Comics/Seaboard Periodicals: June, 1975

	GD 2.0	VG 4.0	FN 6.0	VF 8.0	VF/NM 9.0	NM- 9.2
1-Origin, only app. Andrax; Iron Jaw app.; Marcos-a	2	4	6	13	18	22

BARBIE
Marvel Comics: Jan, 1991 - No. 63, Mar, 1996 ($1.00/$1.25/$1.50)

	GD 2.0	VG 4.0	FN 6.0	VF 8.0	VF/NM 9.0	NM- 9.2
1-Polybagged w/doorknob hanger; Romita-c	2	4	6	9	12	15
2-49,51-62	1	2	3	5	7	9
50,63: 50-(Giant). 63-Last issue	2	4	6	8	10	12
... And Baby Sister Kelly (1995, 99¢-c, part of a Marvel 4-pack) scarce	3	6	9	14	20	25

BARBIE & KEN
Dell Publishing Co.: May-July, 1962 - No. 5, Nov-Jan, 1963-64

	GD 2.0	VG 4.0	FN 6.0	VF 8.0	VF/NM 9.0	NM- 9.2
01-053-207(#1)-Based on Mattel toy dolls	36	72	108	259	580	900
2-4	26	52	78	182	404	625
5 (Last issue)	27	54	81	189	420	650

BARBIE FASHION
Marvel Comics: Jan, 1991 - No. 53, May, 1995 ($1.00/$1.25/$1.50)

	GD 2.0	VG 4.0	FN 6.0	VF 8.0	VF/NM 9.0	NM- 9.2
1-Polybagged w/Barbie Pink Card	2	4	6	9	12	15
2-49,51,52: 4-Contains preview to Sweet XVI	1	2	3	5	7	9
50,53: 50-(Giant). 53-Last issue	2	4	6	8	10	12

BARB WIRE (See Comics' Greatest World)
Dark Horse Comics: Apr, 1994 - No. 9, Feb, 1995 ($2.00/$2.50)

	GD 2.0	VG 4.0	FN 6.0	VF 8.0	VF/NM 9.0	NM- 9.2
1-9: 1-Foil logo						3.00
Trade paperback (1996, $8.95)-r/#2,3,5,6 w/Pamela Anderson bio						9.00

BARB WIRE: ACE OF SPADES
Dark Horse Comics: May, 1996 - No. 4, Sept, 1996 ($2.95, limited series)

	GD 2.0	VG 4.0	FN 6.0	VF 8.0	VF/NM 9.0	NM- 9.2
1-4: Chris Warner-c/a(p)/scripts; Tim Bradstreet-c/a(i) in all						3.00

BARB WIRE COMICS MAGAZINE SPECIAL
Dark Horse Comics: May, 1996 ($3.50, B&W, magazine, one-shot)

	GD 2.0	VG 4.0	FN 6.0	VF 8.0	VF/NM 9.0	NM- 9.2
nn-Adaptation of film; photo-c; poster insert.						3.50

BARB WIRE MOVIE SPECIAL
Dark Horse Comics: May, 1996 ($3.95, one-shot)

	GD 2.0	VG 4.0	FN 6.0	VF 8.0	VF/NM 9.0	NM- 9.2
nn-Adaptation of film; photo-c; 1st app. new look						4.00

BARKER, THE (Also see National Comics #42)
Quality Comics Group/Comic Magazine: Autumn, 1946 - No. 15, Dec, 1949

	GD 2.0	VG 4.0	FN 6.0	VF 8.0	VF/NM 9.0	NM- 9.2
1	24	48	72	144	237	330
2	15	30	45	83	124	165
3-10	12	24	36	69	97	125
11-14	10	20	30	54	72	90
15-Jack Cole-a(p)	10	20	30	56	76	95

NOTE: ***Jack Cole** art in some issues.*

BARNABY
Civil Service Publications Inc.: 1945 (25¢,102 pgs., digest size)

	GD 2.0	VG 4.0	FN 6.0	VF 8.0	VF/NM 9.0	NM- 9.2
V1#1-r/Crocket Johnson strips from 1942	5	10	14	20	24	28

BARNEY AND BETTY RUBBLE (TV) (Flintstones' Neighbors)
Charlton Comics: Jan, 1973 - No. 23, Dec, 1976 (Hanna-Barbera)

	GD 2.0	VG 4.0	FN 6.0	VF 8.0	VF/NM 9.0	NM- 9.2
1	4	8	12	23	37	50
2-11: 11(2/75)-1st Mike Zeck-a (illos)	3	6	9	14	20	25
12-23: 17-Columbo parody	2	4	6	10	14	18
Digest Annual (1972, B&W, 100 pgs.) (scarce)	4	8	12	25	40	55

BARNEY BAXTER (Also see Magic Comics)
David McKay/Dell Publishing Co./Argo: 1938 - No. 2, 1956

	GD 2.0	VG 4.0	FN 6.0	VF 8.0	VF/NM 9.0	NM- 9.2
Feature Books 15(McKay-1938)	41	82	123	256	428	600
Four Color 20(1942)	23	46	69	164	362	560
1,2 (1956-Argo)	9	18	27	50	65	80

BARNEY BEAR ...
Spire Christian Comics (Fleming H. Revell Co.): 1977-1982

	GD 2.0	VG 4.0	FN 6.0	VF 8.0	VF/NM 9.0	NM- 9.2
...Home Plate nn-(1979, 49¢), ...In Toyland nn-(1982, 49¢),...Lost and Found nn-(1979, 49¢), Out of The Woods nn-(1980, 49¢), Sunday School Picnic nn-(1981, 69¢), The Swamp Gang!-(1977, 39¢)	2	4	6	9	13	16

BARNEY GOOGLE & SNUFFY SMITH
Dell Publishing Co./Gold Key: 1942 - 1943; April, 1964

	GD 2.0	VG 4.0	FN 6.0	VF 8.0	VF/NM 9.0	NM- 9.2
Four Color 19(1942)	48	96	144	302	514	725
Four Color 40(1944)	18	36	54	126	281	435
Large Feature Comic 11(1943)	39	78	117	231	378	525
1(10113-404)-Gold Key (4/64)	4	8	12	25	40	55

BARNEY GOOGLE & SNUFFY SMITH
Toby Press: June, 1951 - No. 4, Feb, 1952 (Reprints)

	GD 2.0	VG 4.0	FN 6.0	VF 8.0	VF/NM 9.0	NM- 9.2
1	14	28	42	80	115	150
2,3	9	18	27	47	61	75
4-Kurtzman-a "Pot Shot Pete", 5 pgs.; reprints John Wayne #5	12	24	36	69	97	125

BARNEY GOOGLE AND SNUFFY SMITH
Charlton Comics: Mar, 1970 - No. 6, Jan, 1971

	GD 2.0	VG 4.0	FN 6.0	VF 8.0	VF/NM 9.0	NM- 9.2
1	3	6	9	16	24	32
2-6	2	4	6	11	16	20

BARNUM!
DC Comics (Vertigo): 2003; 2005 ($29.95, $19.95)

	GD 2.0	VG 4.0	FN 6.0	VF 8.0	VF/NM 9.0	NM- 9.2
Hardcover (2003, $29.95, with dust jacket)-Chaykin & Tischman-s/Henrichon-a						30.00
Softcover (2005, $19.95)-Chaykin & Tischman-s/Henrichon-a						20.00

BARNYARD COMICS (Dizzy Duck No. 32 on)
Nedor/Polo Mag./Standard(Animated Cartoons): June, 1944 - No. 31, Sept, 1950; No. 10, 1957

	GD 2.0	VG 4.0	FN 6.0	VF 8.0	VF/NM 9.0	NM- 9.2
1 (nn, 52 pgs.)-Funny animal	22	44	66	128	209	290
2 (52 pgs.)	14	28	42	78	112	145
3-5	10	20	30	58	79	100
6-12,16	9	18	27	52	69	85
13-15,17,21,23,26,27,29-All contain Frazetta text illos	10	20	30	58	79	100
18-20,22,24,25-All contain Frazetta-a & text illos	13	26	39	74	105	135
28,30,31	8	16	24	44	57	70
10 (1957)(Exist?)	4	7	10	14	17	20

BARRY M. GOLDWATER
Dell Publishing Co.: Mar, 1965 (Complete life story)

	GD 2.0	VG 4.0	FN 6.0	VF 8.0	VF/NM 9.0	NM- 9.2
12-055-503-Photo-c	4	8	12	23	37	50

BARRY WINDSOR-SMITH: STORYTELLER
Dark Horse Comics: Oct, 1996 - No. 9, July, 1997 ($4.95, oversize)

	GD 2.0	VG 4.0	FN 6.0	VF 8.0	VF/NM 9.0	NM- 9.2
1-9: 1-Intro Young Gods, Paradox Man & the Freebooters; Barry Smith-c/a/scripts						5.00
Preview						4.00

BAR SINISTER (Also see Shaman's Tears)
Acclaim Comics (Windjammer): Jun, 1995 - No. 4, Sept, 1995 ($2.50, lim. series)

	GD 2.0	VG 4.0	FN 6.0	VF 8.0	VF/NM 9.0	NM- 9.2
1-4: Mike Grell-c/a/scripts						3.00

BARTMAN (Also see Simpsons Comics & Radioactive Man)
Bongo Comics: 1993 - No. 6, 1994 ($1.95/$2.25)

	GD 2.0	VG 4.0	FN 6.0	VF 8.0	VF/NM 9.0	NM- 9.2
1-($2.95)-Foil-c; bound-in jumbo Bartman poster						6.00
2-6: 3-w/trading card						4.00

BART SIMPSON (See Simpsons Comics Presents Bart Simpson)

BASEBALL COMICS
Will Eisner Productions: Spring, 1949 (Reprinted later as a Spirit section)

	GD 2.0	VG 4.0	FN 6.0	VF 8.0	VF/NM 9.0	NM- 9.2
1-Will Eisner-c/a	70	140	210	445	765	1085

BASEBALL COMICS
Kitchen Sink Press: 1991 ($3.95, coated stock)

	GD 2.0	VG 4.0	FN 6.0	VF 8.0	VF/NM 9.0	NM- 9.2
1-r/1949 ish. by Eisner; contains trading cards						6.00

BASEBALL HEROES
Fawcett Publications: 1952 (one-shot)

	GD 2.0	VG 4.0	FN 6.0	VF 8.0	VF/NM 9.0	NM- 9.2
nn (Scarce)-Babe Ruth photo-c; baseball's Hall of Fame biographies	86	172	258	546	936	1325

BASEBALL'S GREATEST HEROES
Magnum Comics: Dec, 1991 - No. 2, May, 1992 ($1.75)

	GD 2.0	VG 4.0	FN 6.0	VF 8.0	VF/NM 9.0	NM- 9.2
1-Mickey Mantle #1; photo-c; Sinnott-a(p)						5.00
2-Brooks Robinson #1; photo-c; Sinnott-a(i)						4.00

BASEBALL THRILLS

Batgirl (2000 series) #14 © DC

Batgirl (2011 series) #11 © DC

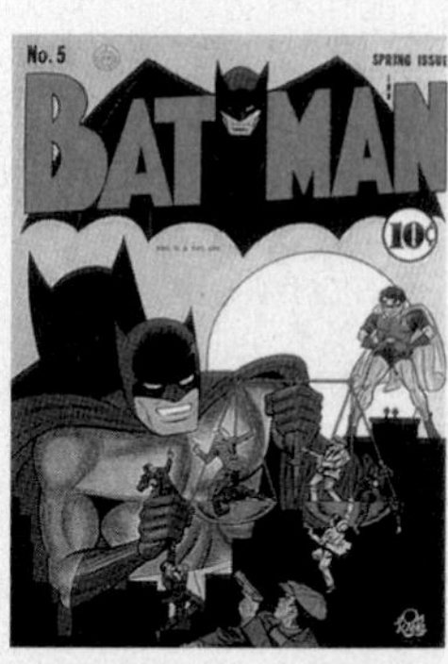

Batman #5 © DC

GD 2.0 | VG 4.0 | FN 6.0 | VF 8.0 | VF/NM 9.0 | NM- 9.2

Ziff-Davis Publ. Co.: No. 10, Sum, 1951 - No. 3, Sum, 1952 (Saunders painted-c No.1,2)

10(#1)-Bob Feller, Musial, Newcombe & Boudreau stories
44 88 132 277 469 660
2-Powell-a(2)(Late Sum, '51); Feller, Berra & Mathewson stories
32 64 96 188 307 425
3-Kinstler-c/a; Joe DiMaggio story 32 64 96 188 307 425

BASEBALL THRILLS 3-D
The 3-D Zone: May, 1990 ($2.95, w/glasses)

1-New L.B. Cole-c; life stories of Ty Cobb & Ted Williams 6.00

BASICALLY STRANGE (Magazine)
John C. Comics (Archie Comics Group): Dec, 1982 ($1.95, B&W)

1-(21,000 printed; all but 1,000 destroyed; pgs. out of sequence)
3 6 9 16 23 30
1-Wood, Toth-a; Corben-c; reprints & new art 2 4 6 13 18 22

BASIC HISTORY OF AMERICA ILLUSTRATED
Pendulum Press: 1976 (B&W) (Soft-c $1.50; Hard-c $4.50)

07-1999-America Becomes a World Power 1890-1920. 07-2251-The Industrial Era 1865-1915. 07-226x-Before the Civil War 1830-1860. 07-2278-Americans Move Westward 1800-1850. 07-2286-The Civil War 1850-1876; Redondo-a. 07-2294-The Fight for Freedom 1750-1783. 07-2308-The New World 1500-1750. 07-2316-Problems of the New Nation 1800-1830. 07-2324-Roaring Twenties and the Great Depression 1920-1940. 07-2332-The United States Emerges 1783-1800. 07-2340-America Today 1945-1976. 07-2359-World War II 1940-1945

Softcover editions each 1 2 3 4 5 7
Hardcover editions each 14.00

BASIL (...the Royal Cat)
St. John Publishing Co.: Jan, 1953 - No. 4, Sept, 1953

1-Funny animal 8 16 24 40 50 60
2-4 5 10 15 22 26 30
I.W. Reprint 1 2 4 6 9 12 15

BASIL WOLVERTON'S FANTASTIC FABLES
Dark Horse Comics: Oct, 1993 - No. 2, Dec, 1993 ($2.50, B&W, limited series)

1,2-Wolverton-c/a(r) 6.00

BASIL WOLVERTON'S GATEWAY TO HORROR
Dark Horse Comics: June, 1988 ($1.75, B&W, one-shot)

1-Wolverton-r 6.00

BASIL WOLVERTON'S PLANET OF TERROR
Dark Horse Comics: Oct, 1987 ($1.75, B&W, one-shot)

1-Wolverton-r; Alan Moore-c 6.00

BASTARD SAMURAI
Image Comics: Apr, 2002 - No. 3, Aug, 2002 ($2.95)

1-3-Oeming & Gunter-s; Shannon-a/Oeming-i 3.00
TPB (2003, $12.95) r/#1-3; plus sketch pages and pin-ups 13.00

BATGIRL (See Batman: No Man's Land stories)
DC Comics: Apr, 2000 - No. 73, Apr, 2006 ($2.50)

1-Scott & Campanella-a 6.00
1-(2nd printing) 3.00
2-10: 8-Lady Shiva app. 4.50
11-24: 12-"Officer Down" x-over. 15-Joker-c/app. 24-Bruce Wayne: Murderer pt. 2. 4.00
25-($3.25) Batgirl vs Lady Shiva 4.50
26-29: 27- Bruce Wayne: Fugitive pt. 5; Noto-a. 29-B.W.:F. pt. 13 3.50
30-49,51-73: 30-32-Connor Hawke app. 39-Intro. Black Wind. 41-Superboy-c/app. 53-Robin (Spoiler) app. 54-Bagged with Sky Captain CD. 55-57-War Games. 63,64-Deathstroke app. 67-Birds of Prey app. 73-Lady Shiva origin; Sale-c 3.00
50-($3.25) Batgirl vs Batman 4.00
Annual 1 ('00, $3.50) Planet DC; intro. Aruna 5.00
...: A Knight Alone (2001, $12.95, TPB) r/#7-11,13,14 13.00
...: Death Wish (2003, $14.95, TPB) r/#17-20,22,23,25 & Secret Files and Origins #1 15.00
...: Destruction's Daughter (2006, $19.99, TPB) r/#65-73 20.00
...: Fists of Fury (2004, $14.95, TPB) r/#15,16,21,26-28 15.00
...: Kicking Assassins (2005, $14.99, TPB) r/#60-64 15.00
... Secret Files and Origins (8/02, $4.95) origin-s Noto-a; profile pages and pin-ups 5.00
...: Silent Running (2001, $12.95, TPB) r/#1-6 13.00

BATGIRL (Cassandra Cain)
DC Comics: Sept, 2008 - No. 6, Feb, 2009 ($2.99)

1-6-Beechen-s/Calafiore-a 3.00

BATGIRL (Spoiler/Stephanie Brown)(Batman: Reborn)
DC Comics: Oct, 2009 - No. 24, Oct, 2011 ($2.99)

1-24: 1-7-Garbett-a/Noto-c. 3-New costume. 8-Caldwell-a. 9-14-Lau-c. 14-Supergirl app. 3.00
1-Variant-c by Hamner 5.00
...: Batgirl Rising TPB (2010, $17.99) r/#1-7 20.00
...: The Flood TPB (2011, $14.99) r/#9-14 15.00

BATGIRL (Barbara Gordon)(DC New 52)
DC Comics: Nov, 2011 - Present ($2.99)

1-Barbara Gordon back in costume; Simone-s/Syaf-a/Hughes-c 5.00
1-Second & Third printings 3.00
2-12: 2-6-Hughes-c. 3-Nightwing app. 7-12-Syaf-c. 9-Night of the Owls. 12-Batwoman app. 3.00
13-Die-cut cover; Death of the Family tie-in; Batwoman app. 10.00
13-24: 14-16-Death of the Family tie-in; Joker app. 20,21-Intro. The Ventriloquist 3.00
25-($3.99) Zero Year tie-in; Bennett-s/Pasarin-a 4.00
26-29: 27-Gothtopia tie-in. 28,29-Strix app. 3.00
#0 (11/12, $2.99) Batgirl origin updated; Simone-s/Benes-a 3.00
Annual 1 (12/12, $4.99) Catwoman and the Talons app.; Simone-s/Wijaya-a/Benes-c 5.00

BATGIRL ADVENTURES (See Batman Adventures, The)
DC Comics: Feb, 1998 ($2.95, one-shot) (Based on animated series)

1-Harley Quinn and Poison Ivy app.; Timm-c 1 3 4 6 8 10

BATGIRL SPECIAL
DC Comics: 1988 ($1.50, one-shot, 52 pgs)

1-Kitson-a/Mignola-c 1 2 3 5 7 9

BATGIRL: YEAR ONE
DC Comics: Feb, 2003 - No. 9, Oct, 2003 ($2.95, limited series)

1-9-Barbara Gordon becomes Batgirl; Killer Moth app.; Beatty & Dixon-s 3.00
TPB (2003, $17.95) r/#1-9 18.00

BAT LASH (See DC Special Series #16, Showcase #76, Weird Western Tales)
National Periodical Publications: Oct-Nov, 1968 - No. 7, Oct-Nov, 1969 (12¢/15¢)

1-(10-11/68, 12¢-c)-2nd app. Bat Lash; classic Nick Cardy-c/a in all
6 12 18 38 69 105
2-7: 6,7-(15¢-c) 4 8 12 27 44 60

BAT LASH
DC Comics: Feb, 2008 - No. 6, Jul, 2008 ($2.99, limited series)

1-6-Aragonés & Brandvold-s/John Severin-a. 1-Two covers by Severin and Simonson 3.00
...: Guns and Roses TPB (2008, $17.99) r/#1-6 18.00

BATMAN (See All Star Batman & Robin, Anarky, Aurora [in Promo. Comics section], Azrael, The Best of DC #2, Blind Justice, The Brave & the Bold, Cosmic Odyssey, DC 100-Page Super Spec. #14,20, DC Special, DC Special Series, Detective, Dynamic Classics, 80-Page Giants, Gotham By Gaslight, Gotham Nights, Greatest Batman Stories Ever Told, Greatest Joker Stories Ever Told, Heroes Against Hunger, JLA,The Joker, Justice League of America, Justice League Int., Legends of the Dark Knight, Limited Coll. Ed., Man-Bat, Nightwing, Power Record Comics, Real Fact #5, Robin, Saga of Ra's Al Ghul, Shadow of the..., Star Spangled, Super Friends, 3-D Batman, Untold Legend of..., Wanted... & World's Finest Comics)

BATMAN
National Per. Publ./Detective Comics/DC Comics: Spring, 1940 - No. 713, Oct, 2011 (#1-5 were quarterly)

1-Origin The Batman reprinted (2 pgs.) from Det. #33 w/splash from #34 by Bob Kane; see Detective #33 for 1st origin; 1st app. Joker (2 stories intended for 2 separate issues of Det. Comics which would have been 1st & 2nd app.); splash pg. to 2nd Joker story is similar to cover of Det. #40 (story intended for #40); 1st app. The Cat (Catwoman) (1st villainess in comics); has Batman story (w/Hugo Strange) without Robin originally planned for Det. #38; mentions location (Manhattan) where Batman lives (see Det. #31). This book was created entirely from the inventory of Det. Comics; 1st Batman/Robin pin-up on back-c; has text piece & photo of Bob Kane
22,000 44,000 66,000 155,000 307,500 460,000
1-Reprint, oversize 13-1/2x10". **WARNING**: This comic is an exact duplicate reprint of the original except for its size. DC published it in 1974 with a second cover titling it as a Famous First Edition. There have been many reported cases of the outer cover being removed and the interior sold as the original edition. The reprint with the new outer cover removed is practically worthless. See Famous First Edition for value.
2-2nd app. The Joker; 2nd app. Catwoman (out of costume) in Joker story; 1st time called Catwoman (NOTE: A 15¢-c for Canadian distr. exists.)
2000 4000 6000 15,000 28,500 42,000
3-3rd app Catwoman (1st in costume & 1st costumed villainess); 1st Puppet Master app.; classic Kane & Robinson-c 1075 2150 3225 8000 15,000 22,000
4-4th app. The Joker (see Det. #45 for 3rd); 1st mention of Gotham City in a Batman comic (on newspaper)(Win/40) 919 1838 2757 6709 11,855 17,000
5-1st app. the Batmobile with its bat-head front 703 1406 2109 5132 9066 13,000
6,7: 7-Bullseye-c; Joker app. 551 1102 1653 4022 7111 10,200
8-Infinity-c by Fred Ray; Joker app. 454 908 1362 3314 5857 8400
9-10:9-1st Batman x-mas story; Burnley-c. 10-Catwoman story (gets new costume)
432 864 1296 3154 5577 8000
11-Classic Joker-c by Ray/Robinson (3rd Joker-c, 6-7/42); Joker & Penguin app.

Batman #28 © DC

Batman #182 © DC

Batman #235 © DC

	GD 2.0	VG 4.0	FN 6.0	VF 8.0	VF/NM 9.0	NM- 9.2
	892	1784	2676	6512	11,506	16,500
12,15: 12-Joker app. 15-New costume Catwoman	343	686	1029	2400	4200	6000
13-Jerry Siegel (Superman's co-creator) appears in a Batman story; Batman parachuting on black-c	366	732	1098	2562	4481	6400
14-2nd Penguin-c; Penguin app. (12-1/42-43)	354	708	1062	2478	5578	6200
16-Intro/origin Alfred (4-5/43); cover is a reverse of #9 cover by Burnley; 1st small logo	632	1264	1896	4614	8157	11,700
17,20: 17-Classic war-c; Penguin app. 20-1st Batmobile-c (12-1/43-44); Joker app.	300	600	900	2010	3505	5000
18-Hitler, Hirohito, Mussolini-c.	389	778	1167	2723	4762	6800
19-Joker app.	226	452	678	1446	2473	3500
21,22,24,26,28-30: 21-1st skinny Alfred in Batman (2-3/44). 21,30-Penguin app. 22-1st Alfred solo-c/story (Alfred solo stories in 22-32,36); Catwoman & The Cavalier app. 28-Joker story	181	362	543	1158	1979	2800
23-Joker-c/story; classic black-c	303	606	909	2121	3711	5300
25-Only Joker/Penguin team-up; 1st team-up between two major villains	284	568	852	1818	3109	4400
27-Classic Burnley Christmas-c; Penguin app.	232	464	696	1485	2543	3600
31,32,34-36,39: 32-Origin Robin retold; Joker app. 35-Catwoman story (in new costume w/o cat head mask). 36-Penguin app.	129	258	387	826	1413	2000
33-Christmas-c	155	310	465	992	1696	2400
37,40,44-Joker-c/stories	219	438	657	1402	2401	3400
38-Penguin-c/story	161	322	483	1030	1765	2500
41-1st Sci-fi cover/story in Batman; Penguin app.(6-7/47)	116	232	348	742	1271	1800
42-2nd Catwoman-c (1st in Batman)(8-9/47); Catwoman story also.	206	412	618	1318	2259	3200
43-Penguin-c/story	135	270	405	864	1482	2100
45,46: 45-Christmas-c/story; Catwoman story. 46-Joker app.	103	206	309	659	1130	1600
47-1st detailed origin The Batman (6-7/48); 1st Bat-signal-c this title (see Detective #108); Batman tracks down his parent's killer and reveals i.d. to him	486	972	1458	3550	6275	9000
48-1000 Secrets of the Batcave; r-in #203; Penguin story	129	258	387	826	1413	2000
49-Joker-c/story; 1st app. Mad Hatter; 1st app. Vicki Vale	239	478	717	1530	2615	3700
50-Two-Face impostor app.	126	252	378	806	1378	1950
51,54,56,57,59,60: 57-Centerfold is a 1950 calendar; Joker app. 59-1st app. Deadshot; Batman in the future-c/story	100	200	300	635	1093	1550
52-Joker-c/story	174	348	522	1114	1907	2700
53-Joker story	103	206	309	659	1130	1600
55-Joker-c/stories	155	310	465	992	1696	2400
58,61: 58-Penguin-c. 61-Origin Batman Plane II	113	226	339	718	1234	1750
62-Origin Catwoman; Catwoman-c	194	388	582	1242	2121	3000
63-1st app. Killer Moth; Joker story; flying saucer story(2-3/51)	103	206	309	659	1130	1600
64,70-72,74-77,79: 70-Robot-c. 72-Last 52 pg. issue. 74-Used in **POP**, Pg. 90. 76-Penguin story. 79-Vicki Vale in "The Bride of Batman"	84	168	252	538	919	1300
65,69-Catwoman-c/stories	142	284	426	909	1555	2200
66,73-Joker-c/stories. 66-Pre-2nd Batman & Robin team try-out. 73-Vicki Vale story	148	296	444	947	1624	2300
67-Joker story	97	194	291	621	1061	1500
68,81-Two-Face-c/stories	107	214	321	680	1165	1650
78-(8-9/53)-Roh Kar, The Man Hunter from Mars story-the 1st lawman of Mars to come to Earth (green skinned)	100	200	300	635	1093	1550
80-Joker stories	97	194	291	621	1061	1500
82,83,87-89: 89-Last pre-code issue	81	162	243	518	884	1250
84-Catwoman-c/story; Two-Face app.	129	258	387	826	1413	2000
85,86-Joker story. 86-Intro Batmarine (Batman's submarine)	82	164	246	528	902	1275
90,91,93-96,98,99: 99-(4/56)-Last G.A. Penguin app.	71	142	213	454	777	1100
92-1st app. Bat-Hound-c/story	135	270	405	864	1482	2100
97-2nd app. Bat-Hound-c/story; Joker story	81	162	243	518	884	1250
100-(6/56)	300	600	900	1980	3440	4900
101-(8/56)-Clark Kent x-over who protects Batman's i.d. (3rd story)	73	146	219	467	796	1125
102-104,106-109: 103-1st S.A. issue; 3rd Bat-Hound-c/story	68	136	204	435	743	1050
105-1st Batwoman in Batman (2nd anywhere)	123	246	369	787	1344	1900
110-Joker story	69	138	207	442	759	1075
111-120: 112-1st app. Signalman (super villain). 113-1st app. Fatman; Batman meets his counterpart on Planet X w/a chest plate similar to S.A. Batman's design (yellow oval w/black design inside).	58	116	174	371	636	900
121- Origin/1st app. of Mr. Zero (Mr. Freeze).	181	362	543	1158	1979	2800
122,124-126,128,130: 122,126-Batwoman-c/story. 124-2nd app. Signal Man. 128-Batwoman cameo. 130-Lex Luthor app.	48	96	144	302	514	725
123,127: 123-Joker story; Bat-Hound app. 127-(10/59)-Batman vs. Thor the Thunder God c/story; Joker story; Superman cameo	50	100	150	315	533	750
129-Origin Robin retold; bondage-c; Batwoman-c/story (reprinted in Batman Family #8)	58	116	174	371	636	900
131-135,137-139,141-143: 131-Intro 2nd Batman & Robin series (see #66; also in #135,145, 154,159,163). 133-1st Bat-Mite in Batman (3rd app. anywhere). 134-Origin The Dummy (not Vigilante's villain). 139-Intro 1st original Bat-Girl; only app. Signalman as the Blue Bowman. 141-2nd app. original Bat-Girl. 143-(10/61)-Last 10¢ issue	42	84	126	265	445	625
136-Joker-c/story	48	96	144	302	514	725
140-Joker story, Batwoman-c/s; Superman cameo	43	86	129	271	461	650
144-(12/61)-1st 12¢ issue; Joker story	26	52	78	182	404	625
145,148-Joker-c/stories	27	54	81	194	435	675
146,147,149,150	20	40	60	140	310	485
151-154,156-158,160-162,164-168,170: 152-Joker story. 156-Ant-Man/Robin team-up(6/63). 164-New Batmobile(6/64) new look & Mystery Analysts series begins	16	32	48	112	249	385
155-1st S.A. app. The Penguin (5/63)	32	64	96	230	515	800
159,163-Joker-c/stories. 159-Bat-Girl app. 163-Last Bat-Girl app. until Teen Titans #50	21	42	63	147	324	500
169-2nd SA Penguin app.	18	36	54	126	281	435
171-1st Riddler app.(5/65) since Dec. 1948	46	92	138	368	834	1300
172-175,177,178,180,184	10	20	30	70	150	230
176-(80-Pg. Giant G-17); Joker-c/story; Penguin app. in strip-r; Catwoman reprint	12	24	36	83	182	280
179-2nd app. Silver Age Riddler	17	34	51	117	259	400
181-Batman & Robin poster insert; intro. Poison Ivy	38	76	114	285	641	1000
182,187-(80 Pg. Giants G-24, G-30); Joker-c/stories	11	22	33	75	160	245
183-2nd app. Poison Ivy	14	28	42	96	211	325
185-(80 Pg. Giant G-27)	11	22	33	73	157	240
186-Joker-c/story	11	22	33	75	160	245
188,191,192,194-196,199	9	18	27	58	114	170
189-1st S.A. app. Scarecrow; retells origin of G.A. Scarecrow from World's Finest #3(1st app.)	19	38	57	131	291	450
190-Penguin-c/app.	11	22	33	73	157	240
193-(80-Pg. Giant G-37)	10	20	30	68	144	220
197-4th S.A. Catwoman app. cont'd from Det. #369; 1st new Batgirl app. in Batman (5th anywhere)	15	30	45	100	220	340
198-(80-Pg. Giant G-43); Joker-c/story-r/World's Finest #61; Catwoman-r/Det. #211; Penguin-r; origin-r/#47	10	20	30	70	150	230
200-(3/68)-Joker cameo; retells origin of Batman & Robin; 1st Neal Adams work this title (cover only)	12	24	36	82	179	275
201-Joker story	7	14	21	46	86	125
202,204-207,209-212: 210-Catwoman-c/app. 212-Last 12¢ issue	6	12	18	42	79	115
203-(80 Pg. Giant G-49); r/#48, 61, & Det. 185; Batcave Blueprints	8	16	24	56	108	160
208-(80 Pg. Giant G-55); New origin Batman by Gil Kane plus 3 G.A. Batman reprints w/Catwoman, Vicki Vale & Batwoman	8	16	24	56	108	160
213-(80-Pg. Giant G-61); 30th anniversary issue (7-8/69); origin Alfred (r/Batman #16), Joker(r/Det. #168), Clayface; new origin Robin with new facts	9	18	27	61	123	185
214-217: 214-Alfred given a new last name- "Pennyworth" (see Detective #96)	6	12	18	37	66	95
218-(80-Pg. Giant G-67)	7	14	21	48	89	130
219-Neal Adams-a	8	16	24	51	96	140
220,221,224-226,229-231	5	10	15	34	60	85
222-Beatles take-off; art lesson by Joe Kubert	11	22	33	76	163	250
223,228,233: 223,228-(80-Pg. Giants G-73,G-79). 233-G-85-(68 pgs., "64 pgs." on-c)	7	14	21	46	86	125
227-Neal Adams cover swipe of Detective #31	25	50	75	175	388	600
232-(6/71) Adams-a. Intro/1st app. Ra's al Ghul; origin Batman & Robin retold; last 15¢ issue (see Detective #411 (5/71) for Talia's debut)	21	42	63	147	324	500
234-(9/71)-1st modern app. of Harvey Dent/Two-Face; (see World's Finest #173 for Batman as Two-Face; only S.A. mention of character); N. Adams-a; 52 pg. issues begin, end #242	20	40	60	135	300	465
235,236,239-242: 239-XMas-c. 241-Reprint/#5	6	12	18	40	73	105
237-N. Adams-a. 1st Rutland Vermont - Bald Mountain Halloween x-over. G.A. Batman-r/ Det. #37; 1st app. The Reaper; Wrightson/Ellison plots						

Batman #305 © DC

Batman #437 © DC

Batman #605 © DC

GD 2.0 | VG 4.0 | FN 6.0 | VF 8.0 | VF/NM 9.0 | NM- 9.2

13 26 39 91 201 310
238-Also listed as DC 100 Page Super Spectacular #8; Batman, Legion, Aquaman-r; G.A. Atom, Sargon (r/Sensation #57), Plastic Man (r/Police #14) stories; Doom Patrol origin-r; N. Adams wraparound-c 12 24 36 82 179 275
243-245-Neal Adams-a 8 16 24 56 108 160
246-250,252,253: 246-Scarecrow app. 253-Shadow-c & app. 5 10 15 34 60 85
251-(9/73)-N. Adams-c/a; Joker-c/story 11 22 33 76 163 250
254,256-259,261-All 100 pg. editions; part-r: 254-(2/74)-Man-Bat-c & app. 256-Catwoman app. 257-Joker & Penguin app. 258-First mention of Arkham (Hospital, renamed Arkham Asylum in #260). 259-Shadow-c/app. 7 14 21 44 82 120
255-(100 pgs.)-N. Adams-c/a; tells of Bruce Wayne's father who wore bat costume & fought crime (r/Det. #235); r/story Batman #22 8 16 24 51 96 140
260-(100 pgs.) Joker-c/story; 2nd Arkham Asylum (see #258 for 1st mention) 8 16 24 51 96 140
262 (68 pgs.) 5 10 15 33 57 80
263,264,266-285,287-290,292,293,295-299: 266-Catwoman back to old costume 3 6 9 14 20 25
265-Wrightson-a(i) 3 6 9 15 22 28
286,291,294: 294-Joker-c/stories 3 6 9 17 26 35
300-Double-size 3 6 9 19 30 40
301-(7/78)-310,312-315,317-320,325-331,333-352: 304-(44 pgs.). 306-3rd app. Black Spider. 307-1st app. Lucius Fox (1/79). 308-Mr. Freeze app. 310-1st modern app. The Gentleman Ghost in Batman; Kubert-c. 312,314,346-Two-Face-c/stories. 313-2nd app. Calendar Man. 318-Intro Firebug. 319-2nd modern age app. The Gentleman Ghost; Kubert-c. 344-Poison Ivy app. 345-1st app. new Dr. Death. 345,346,351-Catwoman back-ups 2 4 6 9 12 15
306-308,311-320,323,324,326-(Whitman variants; low print run; none show issue # on cover) 2 4 6 13 18 22
311,316,322-324: 311-Batgirl-c/story; Batgirl reteams w/Batman. 316-Robin returns. 322-324-Catwoman (Selina Kyle) app. 322,323-Cat-Man cameos (1st in Batman, 1 panel each). 323-1st meeting Catwoman & Cat-Man. 324-1st full app. Cat-Man this title 2 4 6 10 14 18
321,353,359-Joker-c/stories 3 6 9 14 20 25
332-Catwoman's 1st solo 2 4 6 11 16 20
354-356,358,360-365,369,370: 361-1st app Harvey Bullock 1 3 4 6 8 10
357-1st app. Jason Todd (3/83); see Det. #524; brief app. Croc (see Detective #523 (2/83) for earlier cameo 4 8 12 23 37 50
366-Jason Todd 1st in Robin costume; Joker-c/story 3 6 9 16 23 30
367-Jason in red & green costume (not as Robin) 2 4 6 8 11 14
368-1st new Robin in costume (Jason Todd) 2 4 6 13 18 22
371-385,388-399,401-403: 371-Cat-Man-c/story; brief origin Cat-Man (cont'd in Det. #538). 390-391-Catwoman app. 398-Catwoman & Two-Face app. 401-2nd app. Magpie (see Man of Steel #3 for 1st). 403-Joker cameo 1 2 3 5 6 8

NOTE: *Issues 397-399, 401-403, 408-416, 421-425, 430-432 all have 2nd printings in 1989; some with up to 8 printings. Some are not identified as reprints but have newer ads copyrighted after cover dates. All reprints have different back-c ads. All reprints are scarcer than 1st prints and have same value to variant collectors.*

386-Intro Black Mask (villain) 4 8 12 23 37 50
387-Intro Black Mask continues 2 4 6 9 12 15
400 ($1.50, 68pgs.)-Dark Knight special; intro by Stephen King; Art Adams/Austin-a 3 6 9 17 26 35
404-Miller scripts begin (end 407); Year 1; 1st modern app. Catwoman (2/87) 3 6 9 16 24 32
405-407: 407-Year 1 ends (See Detective Comics #575-578 for Year 2) 3 6 9 14 20 25
408-410: New Origin Jason Todd (Robin) 2 4 6 13 18 22
411-416,421,422,424,425: 411-Two-face app. 412-Origin/1st app. Mime. 414-Starlin scripts begin, end #429. 416-Nightwing-c/story 6.00
417-420: "Ten Nights of the Beast" storyline 2 4 6 8 10 12
423-McFarlane-c 2 4 6 9 12 15
426-($1.50, 52 pgs.)- "A Death In The Family" storyline begins, ends #429 3 6 9 14 20 25
427- "A Death In The Family" part 2. (Direct Sales version has inside back-c page for phone poll; newsstand version has an ad on inside back-c and UPC code on front-c) 2 4 6 11 16 20
428-Death of Robin (Jason Todd) 3 6 9 17 26 35
429-Joker-c/story; Superman app. 2 4 6 9 12 15
430-432 5.00
433-435-Many Deaths of the Batman story by John Byrne-c/scripts 5.00
436-Year 3 begins (ends #439); origin original Robin retold by Nightwing (Dick Grayson); 1st app. Timothy Drake (8/89) 2 4 6 9 12 15
436-441: 436-2nd printing. 437-Origin Robin cont. 440,441: "A Lonely Place of Dying" Parts 1 & 3 5.00
442-1st app. Timothy Drake in Robin costume 1 2 3 5 6 8
443-456,458,459,462-464: 445-447-Batman goes to Russia. 448,449-The Penguin Affair Pts 1 & 3. 450-Origin Joker. 450,451-Joker-c/stories. 452-454-Dark Knight Dark City storyline; Riddler app. 455-Alan Grant scripts begin, ends #466, 470. 464-Last solo Batman story; free 16 pg. preview of Impact Comics line 4.00
457-Timothy Drake officially becomes Robin & dons new costume 1 2 3 5 6 8
457-Direct sale edition (has #000 in indicia) 1 2 3 5 6 8
460,461,465-487: 460,461-Two part Catwoman story. 465-Robin returns to action with Batman. 470-War of the Gods x-over. 475-1st app. Renee Montoya. 475,476-Return of Scarface. 476-Last $1.00-c. 477,478-Photo-c 4.00
488-Cont'd from Batman: Sword of Azrael #4; Azrael-c & app. 1 2 3 5 6 8
489-Bane-c/story; 1st app. Azrael in Bat-costume 1 3 4 6 8 10
490-Riddler-c/story; Azrael & Bane app. 6.00
491,492: 491-Knightfall lead-in; Joker-c/story; Azrael & Bane app.; Kelley Jones-c begin. 492-Knightfall part 1; Bane app. 6.00
492-Platinum edition (promo copy) 2 4 6 9 12 15
493-496: 493-Knightfall Pt. 3. 494-Knightfall Pt. 5; Joker-c & app. 495-Knightfall Pt. 7; brief Bane & Joker apps. 496-Knightfall Pt. 9, Joker-c/story; Bane cameo 6.00
497-(Late 7/93)-Knightfall Pt. 11; Bane breaks Batman's back; B&W outer-c; Aparo-a(p); Giordano-a(i) 2 4 6 8 10 12
497-499: 497-2nd printing. 497-Newsstand edition w/o outer cover. 498-Knightfall part 15; Bane & Catwoman-c & app. (see Showcase 93 #7 & 8) 499-Knightfall Pt. 17; Bane app. 5.00
500-($2.50, 68 pgs.)-Knightfall Pt. 19; Azrael in new Bat-costume; Bane-c/story 5.00
500-($3.95, 68 pgs.)-Collector's Edition w/die-cut double-c w/foil by Joe Quesada & 2 bound-in post cards 1 2 3 5 6 8
501-508,510,511: 501-Begin $1.50-c. 501-508-Knightquest. 503,504-Catwoman app. 507-Ballistic app.; Jim Balent-a(p). 510-KnightsEnd Pt. 7. 511-(9/94)-Zero Hour; Batgirl-c/story 3.00
509-($2.50, 52 pgs.)-KnightsEnd Pt. 1 4.00
512-514,516-518: 512-(11/94)-Dick Grayson assumes Batman role 3.00
515-Special Ed.($2.50)-Kelley Jones-a begins; all black embossed-c; Troika Pt. 1 5.00
515-Regular Edition 3.00
519-534,536-549: 519-Begin $1.95-c. 521-Return of Alfred, 522-Swamp Thing app. 525-Mr. Freeze app. 527,528-Two Face app. 529-Contagion Pt. 6. 530-532-Deadman app. 533-Legacy prelude. 534-Legacy Pt. 5. 536-Final Night x-over; Man-Bat-c/app. 540,541-Spectre-c-app. 544-546-Joker & The Demon. 548,549-Penguin-c/app. 3.00
530-532 ($2.50)-Enhanced edition; glow-in-the-dark-c. 4.00
535-(10/96, $2.95)-1st app. The Ogre 4.00
535-(10/96, $3.95)-1st app. The Ogre; variant, cardboard, foldout-c 5.00
550-($3.50)-Collector's Ed., includes 4 collector cards; intro. Chase, return of Clayface; Kelley Jones-c 5.00
550-($2.95)-Standard Ed.; Williams & Gray-c 4.00
551,552,554-562: 551,552-Ragman c/app. 554-Cataclysm pt. 12. 3.00
553-Cataclysm pt.3 4.00
563-No Man's Land; Joker-c by Campbell; Bob Gale-s 5.00
564-574: 569-New Batgirl-c/app. 572-Joker and Harley app. 3.00
575-579: 575-New look Batman begins; McDaniel-a 3.00
580-598: 580-Begin $2.25-c. 587-Gordon shot. 591,592-Deadshot-c/app. 3.00
599-Bruce Wayne: Murderer pt. 7 3.50
600-($3.95) Bruce Wayne: Fugitive pt. 1; back-up homage stories in '50s, 60's, & 70s styles; by Aragonés, Gaudiano, Shanower and others 5.00
600-(2nd printing) 4.00
601-604, 606,607: 601,603-Bruce Wayne: Fugitive pt.3,13. 606,607-Deadshot-c/app. 3.00
605-($2.95) Conclusion to Bruce Wayne: Fugitive x-over; Noto-c 4.00
608-(12/02) Jim Lee-a/c & Jeph Loeb-s begin; Poison Ivy & Catwoman app. 10.00
608-2nd printing; has different cover with Batman standing on gargoyle 35.00
608-Special Edition; has different cover; 200 printed; used for promotional purposes (a CGC certified 9.2 copy sold for $700, and a CGC certified 9.8 copy sold for $2,100)
608-Special Edition (9/09, $1.00) printing has new "After Watchmen" logo cover frame 3.00
609-Huntress app. 9.00
610,611: 610-Killer Croc-c/app.; Batman & Catwoman kiss 8.00
612-Batman vs. Superman; 1st printing with full color cover 15.00
612-2nd printing with B&W sketch cover 20.00
613,614: 614-Joker-c/app. 7.00
615-617: 615-Reveals ID to Catwoman. 616-Ra's al Ghul app. 617-Scarecrow app. 5.00
618-Batman vs. "Jason Todd" 4.00
619-Newsstand cover; Hush story concludes; Riddler app. 5.00
619-Two variant tri-fold covers; one Heroes group, one Villains group 5.00
619-2nd printing with Riddler chess cover 5.00
620-Broken City pt. 1; Azzarello-s/Risso-a/c begin; Killer Croc app. 4.00
621-633: 621-625-Azzarello-s/Risso-a/c. 626-630-Winick-s/Nguyen-a/Wagner-c; Penguin & Scarecrow app. 631-633-War Games. 633-Conclusion to War Games x-over 3.00

Batman #671 © DC

Batman (2011 series) #5 © DC

Batman Chronicles Vol. 9 © DC

GD 2.0 | VG 4.0 | FN 6.0 | VF 8.0 | VF/NM 9.0 | NM- 9.2

634-638-Winick-s/Nguyen-a/Wagner-c; Red Hood app. 637-Amazo app. 638-Red Hood unmasked as Jason Todd 3.00
639-650: 640-Superman app. 641-Begin $2.50-c. 643,644-War Crimes; Joker app. 650-Infinite Crisis; Joker and Jason Todd app. 3.00
651-654-One Year Later; Bianchi-c 3.50
655-Begin Grant Morrison-s/Andy Kubert-a; Kubert-c w/red background 5.00
655-Variant cover by Adam Kubert, brown-toned image 20.00
656-Intro. Damian, son of Talia and Batman (see Batman: Son of the Demon) 8.00
657-Damian in Robin costume 5.00
658-665: 659-662-Mandrake-a. 663-Van Fleet-a. 664-Bane app. 3.00
666-675: 666-Future story of adult Damian; Andy Kubert-a. 667-669-Williams III-a. 670,671-Resurrection of Ra's al Ghul; Daniel-a. 671-2nd printing 3.00
676-Batman R.I.P. begins; Morrison-s/Daniel-a/Alex Ross-c 4.00
676-Variant-c by Tony Daniel 12.00
676-Second (red-tinted Daniel-c) & third (B&W Daniel-c) printings 3.00
677-680,682-685: Batman R.I.P.; Alex Ross-c. 678-Bat-Mite app. 682-685-Last Rites 3.00
677-Variant-c with Red Hood by Tony Daniel 10.00
677-Second printing with B&W&red-tinted Daniel-c 3.00
681-($3.99) Batman R.I.P. conclusion 4.00
686-($3.99) Gaiman-s/Andy Kubert-a; continues in Detective #853; Kubert sketch pgs.; covers by Kubert and Ross; 2nd & 3rd printings exist 4.00
687-($3.99) Batman: Reborn begins; Dick Grayson becomes Batman; Winick-s/Benes-a 4.00
688-699: 688-691-Bagley-a. 692-697,699-Tony Daniel-s/a. 692-Catwoman app. 3.00
700-(8/10, $4.99) Morrison-s; art by Daniel, Quitely, Finch & Andy Kubert; Finch-c 6.00
700-Variant-c by Mignola 10.00
701-712: 701,702-Morrison-s; R.I.P story. 704-Batman Inc. begins; Daniel-s/a 3.00
713-(10/11) Last issue of first volume; Nicieza-s; Robin flashbacks 3.00
#0 (10/94)-Zero Hour issue released between #511 & #512; Origin retold 3.00
#1,000,000 (11/98) 853rd Century x-over 3.00

	GD	VG	FN	VF	VF/NM	NM-
Annual 1 (8-10/61)-Swan-c	53	106	159	413	932	1450
Annual 2	24	48	72	168	372	575
Annual 3 (Summer, '62)-Joker-c/story	25	50	75	175	388	600
Annual 4,5	12	24	36	84	185	285
Annual 6,7 (7/64, 25¢, 80 pgs.)	10	20	30	69	147	225
Annual V5#8 (1982)-Painted-c	1	3	4	6	8	10
Annual 9,10,12: 9(7/85). 10(1986). 12(1988, $1.50)	1	2	3	4	5	7
Annual 11 (1987, $1.25)-Penguin-c/story; Moore-s	1	2	3	5	7	9

Annual 13 (1989, $1.75, 68 pgs.)-Gives history of Bruce Wayne, Dick Grayson, Jason Todd, Alfred, Comm. Gordon, Barbara Gordon (Batgirl) & Vicki Vale; Morrow-i 6.00
Annual 14-17 ('90-'93, 68 pgs.)-14-Origin Two-Face. 15-Armageddon 2001 x-over; Joker app. 15 (2nd printing). 16-Joker-c/s; Kieth-c. 17 (1993, $2.50, 68 pgs.)-Azrael in Bat-costume; intro Ballistic 4.00
Annual 18 (1994, $2.95) 4.00
Annual 19 (1995, $3.95)-Year One story; retells Scarecrow's origin 4.00
Annual 20 (1996, $2.95)-Legends of the Dead Earth story; Giarrano-a 4.00
Annual 21 (1997, $3.95)-Pulp Heroes story 4.00
Annual 22,23 ('98, '99, $2.95)-22-Ghosts; Wrightson-c. 23-JLApe; Art Adams-c 4.00
Annual 24 ('00, $3.50) Planet DC; intro. The Boggart; Aparo-a 4.00
Annual 25 ('06, $4.99) Infinite Crisis-revised story of Jason Todd; unused Aparo page 6.00
Annual 26 ('07, $3.99) Origin of Ra's al Ghul; Damian app. 4.00
Annual 27 ('09, $4.99) Azrael app.; Califiore-a; back-up story w/Kelley Jones-a 5.00
Annual 28 (2/11, $4.99) The Question, Nightrunner and Veil app.; Lau-c 5.00

NOTE: **Art Adams** *a-400p.* **Neal Adams** *c-200, 203, 210, 217, 219-222, 224-227, 229, 230, 232, 234, 236-241, 243-246, 251, 255, Annual 14.* **Aparo** *a-414-420, 426-435, 440-448, 450, 451, 480-483, 486-491, 494-500; c-414-416, 481, 482, 463i, 486, 487i.* **Bolland** *a-400; c-445-447.* **Burnley** *a-10, 12-18, 20, 22, 25, 27; c-9, 15, 16, 27, 28p, 40p, 42p.* **Byrne** *c-401, 433-435, 533-535, Annual 11.* **Travis Charest** *c-488-490p.* **Colan** *a-340p, 343-345p, 348-351p, 373p, 383p; c-343p, 345p, 350p.* **J. Cole** *a-238r.* **Cowan** *a-Annual 10p.* **Golden** *a-295p, 303p, 484, 485.* **Alan Grant** *scripts-455-466, 470, 474-476, 479, 480, Annual 16(part).* **Grell** *a-287, 288p, 289p, 290; c-287-290.* **Infantino/Anderson** *c-167, 173, 175, 181, 186, 191, 192, 194, 195, 198, 199.* **Infantino/Giella** *c-190.* **Kelley Jones** *a-513-519, 521-525, 527; c-491-499, 500(newsstand), 501-510, 513.* **Kaluta** *c-242, 248, 253, Annual 12.* **G. Kane/Anderson** *c-178-180.* **Bob Kane** *a-1, 2, 5; c-1-5, 7, 17.* **G. Kane** *a-(r)-254, 255, 259, 261, 353i.* **Kubert** *a-238r, 400; c-310, 319p, 327, 328, 344.* **McFarlane** *c-423.* **Mignola** *c-426-429, 452-454, Annual 18.* **Moldoff** *c-101-140.* **Moldoff/Giella** *a-164-175, 177-181, 183, 184, 186.* **Moldoff/Greene** *a-169, 172-174, 177-179, 181, 184.* **Mooney** *a-255r.* **Morrow** *a-Annual 13i.* **Newton** *a-305, 306, 328p, 331p, 332p, 337p, 338p, 346p, 352-357p, 360-372p, 374-378p; c-374p, 378p.* **Nino** *a-Annual 9.* **Irv Novick** *c-201, 202.* **Perez** *a-400; c-436-442.* **Fred Ray** *c-8, 10; w/Robinson-11.* **Robinson/Roussos** *a-12-17, 20, 22, 24, 25, 27, 28, 31, 33, 37.* **Robinson** *a-12, 14, 18, 22-32,34, 36, 37, 255r, 260r, 261r; c-6, 10, 12-14, 18, 21, 24, 26, 30, 37, 39.* **Simonson** *a-300p, 312p, 321p; c-300p, 312p, 366, 413i.* **P. Smith** *a-Annual 9.* **Dick Sprang** *c-19, 20, 22, 23, 25, 29, 31-36, 38, 51, 55, 66, 73, 76.* **Starlin** *c/a-402.* **Staton** *a-334.* **Sutton** *a-400.* **Wrightson** *a-265i, 400; c-320r. Bat-Hound app. in 92, 97, 103, 123, 125, 133, 156, 158. Bat-Mite app. in 133, 136, 144, 146, 158, 161. Batwoman app. in 105, 116, 122, 125, 128, 129, 131, 133, 139, 140, 141, 144, 145, 150, 151, 153, 154, 157, 159, 162, 163.* **Zeck** *c-417-420. Catwoman back-ups in 332, 345, 346, 348-351. Joker app. in 1, 2, 4, 5, 7-9, 11-13, 19, 20, 23, 25, 28, 32 & many more. Robin solo back-up stories in 337-339, 341-343.*

BATMAN (DC New 52)
DC Comics: Nov, 2011 - Present ($2.99/$3.99)

1-Snyder-s/Capullo-a/c 30.00
1-Variant-c by Van Sciver 50.00

GD 2.0 | VG 4.0 | FN 6.0 | VF 8.0 | VF/NM 9.0 | NM- 9.2

1-2nd-4th printings 3.00
2-4 3.00
2-5-Variant covers 2. Jim Lee. 3-Ivan Reis. 4-Mike Choi, 5-Burnham. 6-Frank 5.00
5-7-Court of Owls 3.00
5-7 Combo Pack ($3.99) polybagged with digital download code 4.00
8-11: 8-Begin $3.99-c. 8,9-Night of the Owls. 11-Court of the Owls finale 5.00
12-Story of Harper Row; Cloonan-a 4.00
13-Death of the Family; Joker and Harley Quinn app.; die-cut-c 8.00
14-20: 14-17-Death of the Family. 17-Death of the Family conclusion. 18-Andy Kubert-a 4.00
21-23: 21-Zero Year begins 4.00
23.1, 23.2, 23.3, 23.4 (11/13, $2.99, regular covers) 3.00
23.1 (11/13, $3.99, 3-D cover) "Joker #1" on cover; Andy Kubert-s/Andy Clarke-a 5.00
23.2 (11/13, $3.99, 3-D cover) "Riddler #1" on cover; Jeremy Haun-a 5.00
23.3 (11/13, $3.99, 3-D cover) "Penguin #1" on cover; Tieri-s/Duce-a/Fabok-c 5.00
23.4 (11/13, $3.99, 3-D cover) "Bane #1" on cover; Nolan-a/March-c 5.00
24-(12/13, $6.99) Batman vs. Red Hood at Ace Chemicals re-told; Dark City begins 7.00
24-New York Comic Con variant with Detective #27 cover swipe 10.00
25,29-($4.99) 25-All black cover; Doctor Death app. 5.00
26-28: 28-Nguyen-a; Harper Row as Bluebird; Stephanie Brown returns 4.00
#0 (11/12, $3.99) Flashbacks; Red Hood gang app. 4.00
Annual 1 (7/12, $4.99) Origin of Mr. Freeze; Snyder-s/Fabok-a 5.00
Annual 2 (9/13, $4.99) Origin of the Anchoress; Snyder-s; Jock-c 5.00
... Zero Year Director's Cut (9/13, $5.99) Reprints Batman #21 original pencil art pages with word balloons; Scott Snyder's script 6.00

BATMAN (Hardcover books and trade paperbacks)
...: ABSOLUTION (2002, $24.95)-Hard-c.; DeMatteis-s/Ashmore painted-a 25.00
...: ABSOLUTION (2003, $17.95)-Soft-c.; DeMatteis-s/Ashmore painted-a 18.00
...: A LONELY PLACE OF DYING (1990, $3.95, 132 pgs.)-r/Batman #440-442 & New Titans #60,61; Perez-c 6.00
...: ANARKY TPB (1999, $12.95) r/early appearances 13.00
...AND DRACULA: RED RAIN nn (1991, $24.95)-Hard-c.; Elseworlds storyline 32.00
...AND DRACULA: RED RAIN nn (1992, $9.95)-SC 12.00
...AND SON HC (2007, $24.99, dustjacket) r/Batman #655-658,663-666 25.00
...AND SON SC (2008, $14.99) r/Batman #655-658,663-666 15.00
...ANNUALS (See DC Comics Classics Library for reprints of early Annuals)
ARKHAM ASYLUM Hard-c; Morrison-s/McKean-a (1989, $24.95) 35.00
ARKHAM ASYLUM Soft-c ($14.95) 20.00
ARKHAM ASYLUM 15TH ANNIVERSARY EDITION Hard-c (2004, $29.95) reprint with Morrison's script and annotations, original page layouts; Karen Berger afterword 30.00
ARKHAM ASYLUM 15TH ANNIVERSARY EDITION Soft-c (2005, $17.99) 18.00
...: AS THE CROW FLIES-(2004, $12.95) r/#626-630; Nguyen sketch pages 13.00
BIRTH OF THE DEMON Hard-c (1992, $24.95)-Origin of Ra's al Ghul 30.00
BIRTH OF THE DEMON Soft-c (1993, $12.95) 15.00
BLIND JUSTICE nn (1992, $7.50)-r/Det. #598-600 7.50
BLOODSTORM (1994, $24.95,HC) Kelley Jones-c/a 28.00
BRIDE OF THE DEMON Hard-c (1990, $19.95) 25.00
BRIDE OF THE DEMON Soft-c ($12.95) 15.00
...: BROKEN CITY HC-(2004, $24.95) r/#620-625; new Johnson-c; intro by Schreck 25.00
...: BROKEN CITY SC-(2004, $14.99) r/#620-625; new Johnson-c; intro by Schreck 15.00
...: BRUCE WAYNE: FUGITIVE Vol. 1 ('02, $12.95)-r/ story arc 13.00
...: BRUCE WAYNE: FUGITIVE Vol. 2 ('03, $12.95)-r/ story arc 13.00
...: BRUCE WAYNE: FUGITIVE Vol. 3 ('03, $12.95)-r/ story arc 13.00
...: BRUCE WAYNE-MURDERER? ('02, $19.95)-r/ story arc 20.00
...: BRUCE WAYNE - THE ROAD HOME HC ('11, $24.99) r/Bruce Wayne: The Road Home one-shots 25.00
...: CASTLE OF THE BAT ($5.95)-Elseworlds story 6.00
...: CATACLYSM ('99, $17.95)-r/ story arc 18.00
...: CHILD OF DREAMS (2003, $24.95, B&W, HC) Reprint of Japanese manga with Kia Asamiya-s/a/c; English adaptation by Max Allan Collins; Asamiya interview 25.00
...: CHILD OF DREAMS (2003, $19.95, B&W, SC) 20.00
...CHRONICLES VOL. 1 (2005, $14.99)-r/apps. in Detective Comics #27-38; Batman #1 15.00
...CHRONICLES VOL. 2 (2006, $14.99)-r/apps. in Detective Comics #39-45 and NY World's Fair 1940; Batman #2,3 15.00
...CHRONICLES VOL. 3 (2007, $14.99)-r/apps. in Detective Comics #46-50 and World's Best Comics #1; Batman #4,5 15.00
...CHRONICLES VOL. 4 (2007, $14.99)-r/apps. in Detective Comics #51-56 and World's Finest Comics #2,3; Batman #6,7 15.00
...CHRONICLES VOL. 5 (2008, $14.99)-r/apps. in Detective Comics #57-61 and World's Finest Comics #4; Batman #8,9 15.00
...CHRONICLES VOL. 6 (2008, $14.99)-r/apps. in Detective Comics #62-65 and World's Finest Comics #5,6; Batman #10,11 15.00
...CHRONICLES VOL. 7 (2009, $14.99)-r/apps. in Detective Comics #66-70 and World's Finest Comics #7; Batman #12,13 15.00
...CHRONICLES VOL. 8 (2009, $14.99)-r/apps. in Detective Comics #71-74 and World's

Batman: Dark Joker - The Wild © DC

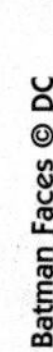

Batman Faces © DC

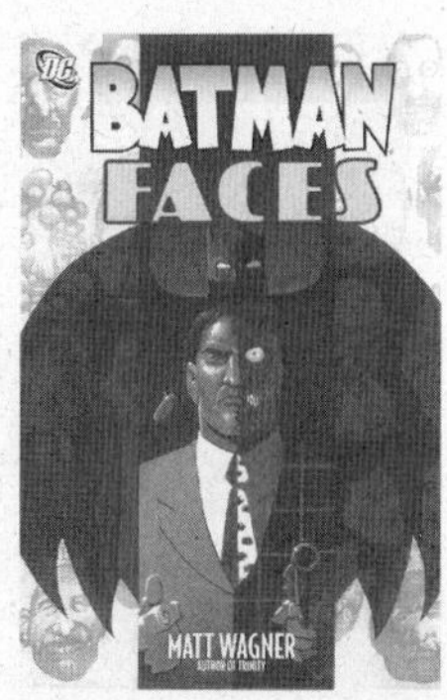

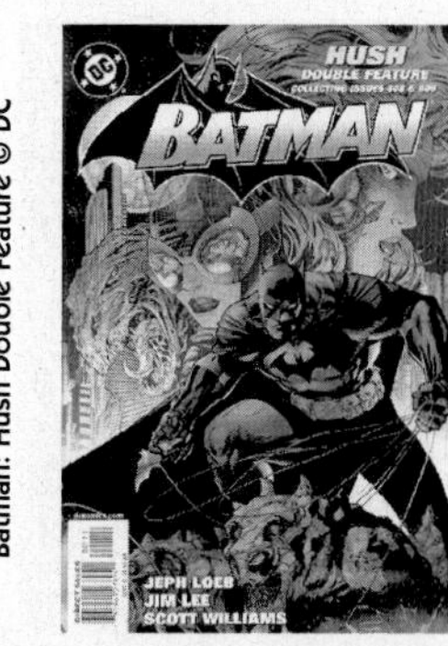

Batman: Hush Double Feature © DC

GD VG FN VF VF/NM NM-
2.0 4.0 6.0 8.0 9.0 9.2

Finest Comics #8,9; Batman #14,15 15.00

...CHRONICLES VOL. 9 (2010, $14.99)-r/apps. in Detective Comics #75-77 and World's Finest Comics #10; Batman #16,17 15.00

...CHRONICLES VOL. 10 (2010, $14.99)-r/apps. in Detective Comics #78-81 and World's Finest Comics #11; Batman #18,19 15.00

...: CITY OF CRIME (2006, $19.99) r/Detective Comics #800-808,811-814; Lapham-s 20.00

...: COLLECTED LEGENDS OF THE DARK KNIGHT nn (1994, $12.95)-r/Legends of the Dark Knight #32-34,38,42,43 13.00

...: CRIMSON MIST (1999, $24.95,HC)-Vampire Batman Elseworlds story Doug Moench-s/Kelley Jones-c/a 25.00

...: CRIMSON MIST (2001, $14.95,SC) 15.00

...: DARK JOKER-THE WILD (1993, $24.95,HC)-Elseworlds story; Moench-s/Jones-c/a 30.00

...: DARK JOKER-THE WILD (1993, $9.95,SC) 12.00

...DARK KNIGHT DYNASTY nn (1997, $24.95)-Hard-c.; 3 Elseworlds stories; Barr-s/ S. Hampton painted-a, Gary Frank, McDaniel-a(p) 28.00

...DARK KNIGHT DYNASTY Softcover (2000, $14.95) Hampton-c 15.00

...DEADMAN: DEATH AND GLORY nn (1996, $24.95)-Hard-c.; Robinson-s/ Estes-c/a 28.00

...DEADMAN: DEATH AND GLORY ($12.95)-SC 15.00

DEATH AND THE CITY (2007, $14.99, TPB)-r/Detective #827-834 15.00

DEATH BY DESIGN (2012, $24.99, HC)-Chip Kidd-s/Dave Taylor-s 25.00

DEATH IN THE FAMILY (1988, $3.95, trade paperback)-r/Batman #426-429 by Aparo 10.00

DEATH IN THE FAMILY: (2nd - 5th printings) 6.00

...: DETECTIVE (2007, $14.99, SC)-r/Detective Comics #821-826 15.00

...: DETECTIVE #27 HC (2003, $19.95)-Elseworlds; Uslan-s/Snejbjerg-a 20.00

...: DETECTIVE #27 SC (2004, $12.95)-Elseworlds; Uslan-s/Snejbjerg-a 13.00

DIGITAL JUSTICE nn (1990, $24.95, Hard-c.)-Computer generated art 30.00

... EARTH ONE HC (2012, $22.99)-Updated re-imagining of Batman's origin & debut; Geoff Johns-s/Gary Frank-a 23.00

... : EGO AND OTHER TALES HC (2007, $24.99)-r/Batman: Ego, Catwoman: Selina's Big Score, and stories from Batman Black and White and Solo; Darwyn Cooke-s/a 25.00

... : EGO AND OTHER TALES SC (2008, $17.99) same contents as HC 18.00

... :EVOLUTION (2001, $12.95, SC)-r/Detective Comics #743-750 13.00

... FACES (1995, $9.95, TPB) r/Legends of the Dark Knight #28-30 15.00

... FACES (2008, $12.99, TPB) Second printing 13.00

...: FACE THE FACE (2006, $14.99, TPB)-r/Batman #651-654, Detective #817-820 15.00

...: FALSE FACES HC (2008, $19.99)-r/Batman #588-590, Wonder Woman #160,161; Batman: Gotham City Secret Files #1 and Detective #787; Brian K. Vaughn intro. 20.00

...: FALSE FACES SC (2008, $14.99)-r/Batman #588-590, Wonder Woman #160,161; Batman: Gotham City Secret Files #1 and Detective #787; Brian K. Vaughn intro. 15.00

...: FORTUNATE SON HC (1999, $24.95) Gene Ha-a 25.00

...: FORTUNATE SON SC (2000, $14.95) Gene Ha-a 15.00

FOUR OF A KIND TPB (1998, $14.95)-r/1995 Year One Annuals featuring Poison Ivy, Riddler, Scarecrow, & Man-Bat 15.00

... GOING SANE (2008, $14.95, TPB) r/Legends of the Dark Knight #65-68,200 15.00

...: GOTHAM BY GASLIGHT (2006, $12.99, TPB) r/Gotham By Gaslight & Master of the Future one-shots; Elseworlds Batman vs. Jack the Ripper 13.00

...GOTHIC (1992, $12.95, TPB)-r/Legends of the Dark Knight #6-10 15.00

...GOTHIC (2007, $14.99, TPB)-r/Legends of the Dark Knight #6-10 15.00

...: HARVEST BREED-(2000, $24.95) George Pratt-s/painted-a 25.00

...: HARVEST BREED-(2003, $17.95) George Pratt-s/painted-a 18.00

...: HAUNTED KNIGHT-(1997, $12.95) r/ Halloween specials 15.00

...: HEART OF HUSH HC-(2009, $19.99) r/#Detective #846-850; pin-ups 20.00

...: HEART OF HUSH SC-(2010, $14.99) r/#Detective #846-850; pin-ups 15.00

...: HONG KONG HC (2003, $24.95, with dustjacket) Doug Moench-s/Tony Wong-a 25.00

...: HONG KONG SC (2004, $17.95) Doug Moench-s/Tony Wong-a 18.00

...: HUSH DOUBLE FEATURE-(2003, $3.95) r/#608,609(1st 2 Jim Lee-a issues) 6.00

...: HUSH SC-(2009, $24.99) r/#608-619; Wizard 0; variant cover gallery; Loeb intro 25.00

...: HUSH UNWRAPPED-(2011, $39.99, HC) r/#608-619's original Jin Lee pencil art 40.00

...: HUSH VOLUME 1 HC-(2003, $19.95) r/#608-612; & new 2 pg. origin w/Lee-a 20.00

...: HUSH VOLUME 1 SC-(2004, $12.95) r/#608-612; includes CD of DC GN art 13.00

...: HUSH VOLUME 2 HC-(2003, $19.95) r/#613-619; Lee intro & sketchpages 20.00

...: HUSH VOLUME 2 SC-(2004, $12.95) r/#613-619; Lee intro & sketchpages 13.00

...: ILLUSTRATED BY NEAL ADAMS VOLUME 1 HC-(2003, $49.95) r/Batman, Brave and the Bold, and Detective Comics stories and covers 50.00

...: ILLUSTRATED BY NEAL ADAMS VOLUME 2 HC-(2004, $49.95) r/Adams' Batman art from 1969-71; intro. by Dick Giordano 50.00

...: ILLUSTRATED BY NEAL ADAMS VOLUME 3 HC-(2006, $49.99) r/Adams' Batman art from 1971-74; covers, pin-ups and design art; intro. by Denny O'Neil 50.00

... IMPOSTERS TPB (2011, $14.99) r/Detective Comics #867-870 15.00

... INTERNATIONAL TPB (2010, $17.99) R/Batman: Scottish Connection, Batman in Barcelona: Dragon's Knight and Batman: Legends of the DK #52,53; Jim Lee-c 18.00

... IN THE FORTIES TPB ($19.95) Intro. by Bill Schelly 20.00

... IN THE FIFTIES TPB ($19.95) Intro. by Michael Uslan 20.00

... IN THE SIXTIES TPB ($19.95) Intro. by Adam West 20.00

GD VG FN VF VF/NM NM-
2.0 4.0 6.0 8.0 9.0 9.2

... IN THE SEVENTIES TPB ($19.95) Intro. by Dennis O'Neil 20.00

... IN THE EIGHTIES TPB ($19.95) Intro. by John Wells 20.00

.../ JUDGE DREDD FILES (2004, $14.95) reprints cross-overs 15.00

... :KING TUT'S TOMB TPB (2010, $14.99) r/Batman Confidential #26-28, Batman #353 and Brave and the Bold #164,171 15.00

... LEGACY-(1996, $17.95) reprints Legacy 18.00

...: LIFE AFTER DEATH HC-(2010, $19.99, dustjacket) r/#Batman #692-699 20.00

...: LONG SHADOWS HC-(2010, $19.99, dustjacket) r/#Batman #687-691 20.00

...: LONG SHADOWS SC-(2011, $14.99) r/#Batman #687-691 15.00

...: LOVERS & MADMEN-(See Batman Confidential)

...: MAD LOVE AND OTHER STORIES HC (2009, $19.99) r/Batman Adventures: Mad Love, Batman Advs. Holiday Special and other Dini/Timm collaborations; commentary 20.00

...: THE MANY DEATHS OF THE BATMAN (1992, $3.95, 84 pgs.)-r/Batman #433-435 w/new Byrne-c 6.00

...: MONSTERS (2009, $19.99, TPB)-r/Legends of the Dark Knight #71-73,83,84,89,90 20.00

...: THE MOVIES (1997, $19.95)-r/movie adaptations of Batman, Batman Returns, Batman Forever, Batman and Robin 20.00

...: NINE LIVES HC (2002, $24.95, sideways format) Motter-s/Lark-a 25.00

...: NINE LIVES SC (2003, $17.95, sideways format) Motter-s/Lark-a 18.00

...: OFFICER DOWN (2001, $12.95)-r/Commissioner shot x-over; Talon-c 13.00

.../ PLANETARY DELUXE HC (2011, $22.99)-r/Planetary/Batman: Night on Earth; script 23.00

...: PREY (1992, $12.95)-Gulacy/Austin-a 15.00

...: PRIVATE CASEBOOK HC (2008, $19.99)-r/Detective Comics #840-845 and story from DC Infinite Halloween Special #1 20.00

...: PRODIGAL (1997, $14.95)-Gulacy/Austin-a 15.00

...: R.I.P.: THE DELUXE EDITION HC (2009, $24.99)-r/Batman #676-683 and story from DC Universe #0 25.00

...: R.I.P.: SC (2010, $14.99)-r/Batman #676-683 and story from DC Universe #0 15.00

... SCARECROW TALES (2005, $19.99, TPB) r/Scarecrow stories & pin-ups from World's Finest #3 to present 20.00

...: SECRETS OF THE BATCAVE (2007, $17.99, TPB) r/Batcave stories 18.00

SHAMAN (1993, $12.95)-r/Legends/D.K. #1-5 15.00

...: SNOW (2007, $14.99, TPB)-r/Legends of the Dark Knight #192-196; Fisher-a 15.00

...: SON OF THE DEMON Hard-c (9/87, $14.95) (see Batman #655-658) 35.00

...: SON OF THE DEMON limited signed & numbered Hard-c (1,700) 60.00

...: SON OF THE DEMON Soft-c w/new-c ($8.95) 15.00

...: SON OF THE DEMON Soft-c (1989, $9.95, 2nd printing - 5th printing) 10.00

... : STRANGE APPARITIONS ($12.95) r/'77-'78 Englehart/Rogers stories from Detective #469-479; also Simonson-a 13.00

...: TALES OF THE DEMON (1991, $17.95, 212 pgs.)-Intro by Sam Hamm; reprints by Neal Adams(3) & Golden; contains Saga of Ra's al Ghul #1 20.00

TALES OF THE MULTIVERSE: BATMAN - VAMPIRE (2007, $19.99) r/Batman & Dracula: Red Rain, Batman: Bloodstorm and Batman: Crimson Mist; Van Lustbader foreword 20.00

...: TEN NIGHTS OF THE BEAST (1994, $5.95)-r/Batman #417-420 8.00

...: TERROR (2003, $12.95, TPB)-r/Legends of the Dark Knight #137-141; Gulacy-c 13.00

...: THE BLACK GLOVE (2009, $17.99, TPB) r/Batman #667-669,672-675 18.00

...: THE CHALICE (HC, '99, $24.95) Van Fleet painted-a 25.00

...: THE CHALICE (SC, '00, $14.95) Van Fleet painted-a 15.00

...: THE GREATEST STORIES EVER TOLD (2005, $19.99, TPB) Les Daniels intro. 20.00

...: THE GREATEST STORIES EVER TOLD VOLUME TWO (2007, $19.99, TPB) 20.00

...: THE JOKER'S LAST LAUGH ('08, $17.99) r/Joker's Last Laugh series #1-6 18.00

...: THE LAST ANGEL (1994, $12.95, TPB) Lustbader-s 15.00

...: THE RESURRECTION OF RA'S AL GHUL (2008, $29.99, HC w/DJ) r/x-over 30.00

...: THE RESURRECTION OF RA'S AL GHUL (2009, $19.99, SC) r/x-over 20.00

...: THE RING, THE ARROW AND THE BAT (2003, $19.95, TPB) r/Legends of the DCU #7-9 & Batman: Legends of the Dark Knight #127-131; Green Lantern & Green Arrow app. 20.00

...: THE STRANGE DEATHS OF BATMAN ('09, $19.99) r/Batman #291-294, Det. #347, World's Finest #184,269, Brave & the Bold #115, Nightwing #52; Aparo-c 20.00

...: THE WRATH ('09, $17.99) r/Batman Special #1 and Batman Confidential #13-16 18.00

...: THRILLKILLER (1998, $12.95, TPB)-r/series & Thrillkiller '62 15.00

...: TIME AND THE BATMAN HC ('11, $19.99) r/Batman #700-703; cover gallery 20.00

...: TWO-FACE AND SCARECROW YEAR ONE (2009, $19.99, TPB)-r/Year One: Batman Scarecrow #1,2 and Two Face: Year One #1,2 20.00

...: UNDER THE COWL (2010, $17.99, TPB)-r/app. Dick Grayson, Tim Drake, Damian Wayne, Jean Paul Valley and Terry McGinnis as Batman 18.00

...: UNDER THE HOOD (2005, $9.99, TPB)-r/Batman #635-641 10.00

...: UNDER THE HOOD Vol. 2 (2006, $9.99, TPB)-r/Batman #645-650 & Annual #25 10.00

...: UNDER THE RED HOOD (2011, $29.99, TPB)-r/Batman #635-641,645-650, Ann. #25 30.00

...: VENOM (1993, $9.95, TPB)-r/Legends of the Dark Knight #16-20; embossed-c 15.00

... VS. TWO-FACE (2008, $19.99, TPB) r/initial (Det. #80) & classic battles; Bianchi-c 20.00

...: WAR CRIMES (2006, $12.99, TPB) r/x-over; James Jean-c 13.00

... WAR DRUMS (2004, $17.95) r/Detective #790-796 & Robin #126-128 18.00

...: WAR GAMES ACT 1,2,3 (2005, $14.95/$14.99, TPB) r/x-over; James Jean-c; each.. 15.00

...: WHATEVER HAPPENED TO THE CAPED CRUSADER? HC-(2009, $24.99, d.j.) r/Batman

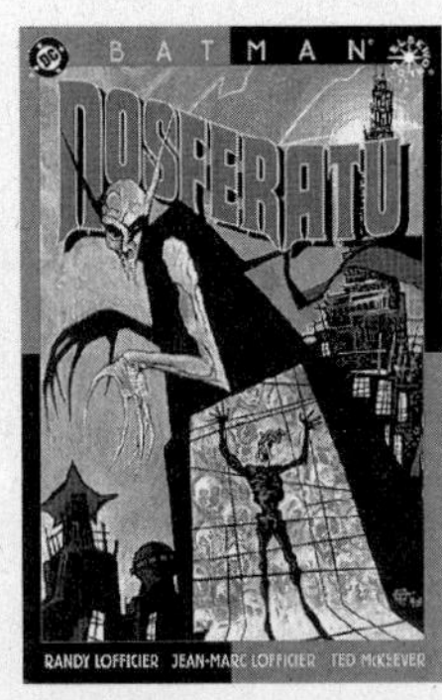

Batman: Nosferatu © DC

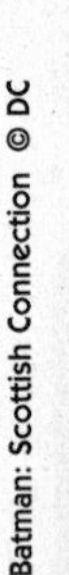

Batman: Scottish Connection © DC

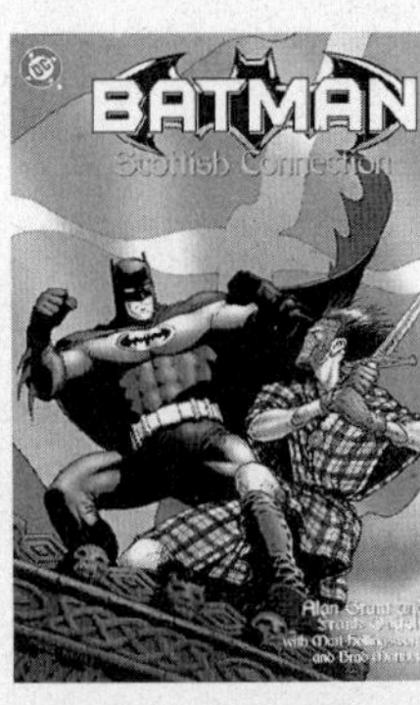

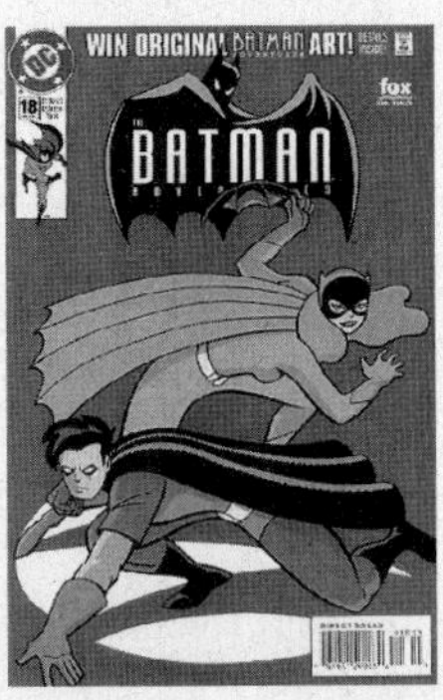

Batman Adventures #18 © DC

GD VG FN VF VF/NM NM-
2.0 4.0 6.0 8.0 9.0 9.2

#686, Detective #853 and other Gaiman Batman stories; Gaiman intro.; Andy Kubert sketch pages; new Kubert cover 25.00
...: WHATEVER HAPPENED TO THE CAPED CRUSADER? SC-(2010, $14.99) 15.00
YEAR ONE Hard-c (1988, $12.95) r/Batman #404-407 25.00
YEAR ONE (1988, $9.95, TPB)-r/Batman #404-407 by Miller; intro by Miller 15.00
YEAR ONE (TPB, 2nd & 3rd printings) 10.00
YEAR ONE Deluxe HC (2005, $19.99, die-cut d.j.) new intro. by Miller and developmental material from Mazzucchelli; script pages and sketches 20.00
YEAR ONE (Deluxe) SC (2007, $14.99) r/story plus bonus material from 2005 HC 15.00
YEAR TWO (1990, $9.95, TPB)-r/Det. 575-578 by McFarlane; wraparound-c 15.00

BATMAN (one-shots)
... ABDUCTION, THE (1998, $5.95) 6.00
... ALLIES SECRET FILES AND ORIGINS 2005 (8/05, $4.99) stories/pin-ups by various 5.00
... & ROBIN (1997, $5.95)-Movie adaptation 6.00
...: ARKHAM ASYLUM - TALES OF MADNESS (5/98, $2.95) Cataclysm x-over pt. 16 4.00
... : BANE (1997, $4.95)-Dixon-s/Burchett-a; Stelfreeze-c; cover art interlocks w/Batman:(Batgirl, Mr. Freeze, Poison Ivy) 6.00
... : BATGIRL (1997, $4.95)-Puckett-s/Haley,Kesel-a; Stelfreeze-c; cover art interlocks w/Batman:(Bane, Mr. Freeze, Poison Ivy) 6.00
... : BATGIRL (6/98, $1.95)-Girlfrenzy; Balent-a 4.00
... : BLACKGATE (1/97, $3.95) Dixon-s 5.00
... : BLACKGATE - ISLE OF MEN (4/98, $2.95) Cataclysm x-over pt. 8; Moench-s/Aparo-a 4.00
... BOOK OF SHADOWS, THE (1999, $5.95) 6.00
BROTHERHOOD OF THE BAT (1995, $5.95)-Elseworlds-s 6.00
... BULLOCK'S LAW (8/99, $4.95) Dixon-s 5.00
.../CAPTAIN AMERICA (1996, $5.95, DC/Marvel) Elseworlds story; Byrne-c/s/a 8.00
... : CATWOMAN DEFIANT nn (1992, $4.95, prestige format)-Milligan scripts; cover art interlocks w/Batman: Penguin Triumphant; special foil logo 6.00
.../CATWOMAN: FOLLOW THE MONEY (1/11, $4.99) Chaykin-c/s/a 5.00
... /DANGER GIRL (2/05, $4.95)-Leinil Yu-a/c; Joker, Harley Quinn & Catwoman app. 5.00
... /DAREDEVIL (2000, $5.95)-Barreto-a 6.00
...: DARK ALLEGIANCES (1996, $5.95)-Elseworlds story, Chaykin-c/a 7.00
...: DARK KNIGHT GALLERY (1/96, $3.50)-Pin-ups by Pratt, Balent, & others 4.00
...:DAY OF JUDGMENT (11/99, $3.95) 5.00
...:DEATH OF INNOCENTS (12/96, $3.95)-O'Neil-s/ Staton-a(p) 5.00
.../DEMON (1996, $4.95)-Alan Grant scripts 6.00
.../DEMON: A TRAGEDY (2000, $5.95)-Grant-s/Murray painted-a 6.00
...:D.O.A. (1999, $6.95)-Bob Hall-s/a 7.00
...:/DOC SAVAGE SPECIAL (2010, $4.99)-Azzarello-s/Noto-a/covers by JG Jones & Morales; preview of First Wave line (Batman, Doc Savage, The Spirit, Blackhawks) 5.00
...:DREAMLAND (2000, $5.95)-Grant-s/Breyfogle-a 6.00
... : EGO (2000, $6.95)-Darwyn Cooke-s/a 7.00
... 80-PAGE GIANT (8/98, $4.95) Stelfreeze-c 6.00
... 80-PAGE GIANT 1 (2/10, $5.99) Andy Kubert-c; Catwoman, Poison Ivy app. 6.00
... 80-PAGE GIANT 2 (10/99, $4.95) Luck of the Draw 6.00
... 80-PAGE GIANT 3 (7/00, $5.95) Calendar Man 6.00
... 80-PAGE GIANT 2011 (2/11, $5.95) Nguyen-c; short stories of villains by various 6.00
... 80-PAGE GIANT 2011 (10/11, $5.99) Nguyen-c; art by Naifeh & others 6.00
... FOREVER (1995, $5.95, direct market) 6.00
... FOREVER (1995, $3.95, newsstand) 4.00
FULL CIRCLE nn (1991, $5.95, 68 pgs.)-Sequel to Batman: Year Two 8.00
...GALLERY, The 1 (1992, $2.95)-Pin-ups by Miller, N. Adams & others 4.00
...GOLDEN STREETS OF GOTHAM (2003, $6.95) Elseworlds in early 1900s 7.00
...GOTHAM BY GASLIGHT (1989, $3.95) Elseworlds; Mignola-a/Augustyn-s 8.00
...GOTHAM CITY SECRET FILES 1 (4/00, $4.95) Batgirl app. 6.00
...: GOTHAM NOIR (2001, $6.95)-Elseworlds; Brubaker-s/Phillips-c/a 7.00
.../GREEN ARROW: THE POISON TOMORROW nn (1992, $5.95, square-bound, 68 pgs.) Netzer-c/a 8.00
...: HIDDEN TREASURES 1 (12/10, $4.99) unpubl. story Wrightson-a; r/Swamp Thing #7 5.00
HOLY TERROR nn (1991, $4.95, 52 pgs.)-Elseworlds story 6.00
.../HOUDINI: THE DEVIL'S WORKSHOP (1993, $5.95) 7.00
... :HUNTRESS/SPOILER - BLUNT TRAUMA (5/98, $2.95) Cataclysm pt. 13; Dixon-s/Barreto & Sienkiewicz-a 4.00
...: I, JOKER nn (1998, $4.95)-Elseworlds story; Bob Hall-s/a 6.00
...: IN BARCELONA: DRAGON'S KNIGHT 1 (7/09, $3.99) Waid-s/Olmos-a/Jim Lee-c 4.00
...: IN DARKEST KNIGHT nn (1994, $4.95, 52 pgs.)-Elseworlds story; Batman w/Green Lantern's ring. 6.00
...:JOKER'S APPRENTICE (5/99, $3.95) Von Eeden-a 5.00
...:JOKER'S DAUGHTER (4/14, $4.99) Bennett-s/Hetrick-a/Jeanty-c 5.00
.../ JOKER: SWITCH (2003, $6.95)-Bolton-a/Grayson-s 7.00
...:JUDGE DREDD: JUDGEMENT ON GOTHAM nn (1991, $5.95, 68 pgs.) Simon Bisley-c/a; Grant/Wagner scripts 8.00
...:JUDGE DREDD: JUDGEMENT ON GOTHAM nn (2nd printing) 6.00
...:JUDGE DREDD: THE ULTIMATE RIDDLE (1995, $4.95) 6.00
...:JUDGE DREDD: VENDETTA IN GOTHAM (1993, $5.95) 7.00
...: KNIGHTGALLERY (1995, $3.50)-Elseworlds sketchbook. 4.00
.../ LOBO (2000, $5.95)-Elseworlds; Joker app.; Bisley-a 6.00
...: MASK OF THE PHANTASM (1994, $2.95)-Movie adapt. 4.00
...: MASK OF THE PHANTASM (1994, $4.95)-Movie adapt. 6.00
...: MASQUE (1997, $6.95)-Elseworlds; Grell-c/s/a 7.00
...: MASTER OF THE FUTURE nn (1991, $5.95, 68 pgs.)-Elseworlds; sequel to Gotham By Gaslight; Barreto-a; embossed-c 6.00
...: MITEFALL (1995, $4.95)-Alan Grant script, Kevin O'Neill-a 6.00
... : MR. FREEZE (1997, $4.95)-Dini-s/Buckingham-a; Stelfreeze-c; cover art interlocks w/Batman:(Bane, Batgirl, Poison Ivy) 6.00
... /NIGHTWING: BLOODBORNE (2002, $5.95) Cypress-a; McKeever-c 6.00
...: NOEL (2011, $22.99, HC graphic novel with dustjacket) Lee Bermejo-s/a; Jim Lee intro.; Catwoman, Superman & The Joker app.; bonus sketch & layout art pages 23.00
...: NOSFERATU (1999, $5.95) McKeever-a 6.00
...: OF ARKHAM (2000, $5.95)-Elseworlds; Grant-s/Alcatena-a 6.00
...: OUR WORLDS AT WAR (8/01, $2.95)-Jae Lee-c 3.00
...: PENGUIN TRIUMPHANT nn (1992, $4.95)-Staton-a(p); foil logo 6.00
...•PHANTOM STRANGER nn (1997, $4.95) nn-Grant-s/Ransom-a 6.00
... : PLUS (2/97, $2.95) Arsenal-c/app. 4.00
... : POISON IVY (1997, $4.95)-J.F. Moore-s/Apthorp-a; Stelfreeze-c; cover art interlocks w/Batman:(Bane, Batgirl, Mr. Freeze) 6.00
.../POISON IVY: CAST SHADOWS (2004, $6.95) Van Fleet-c/a; Nocenti-s 7.00
.../PUNISHER: LAKE OF FIRE (1994, $4.95, DC/Marvel) 6.00
... :REIGN OF TERROR ('99, $4.95) Elseworlds 6.00
...RETURNS MOVIE SPECIAL (1992, $3.95) 4.00
...RETURNS MOVIE PRESTIGE (1992, $5.95, squarebound)-Dorman painted-c 6.00
...:RIDDLER-THE RIDDLE FACTORY (1995, $4.95)-Wagner script 6.00
...: ROOM FULL OF STRANGERS (2004, $5.95) Scott Morse-s/c/a 6.00
...: SCARECROW 3-D (12/98, $3.95) w/glasses 5.00
.../ SCARFACE: A PSYCHODRAMA (2001, $5.95)-Adlard-a/Sienkiewicz-c 6.00
...: SCAR OF THE BAT nn (1996, $4.95)-Elseworlds; Max Allan Collins script; Barreto-a 6.00
... :SCOTTISH CONNECTION (1998, $5.95) Quitely-a 6.00
... :SEDUCTION OF THE GUN nn (1992, $2.50, 68 pgs.) 5.00
.../SPAWN: WAR DEVIL nn (1994, $4.95, 52 pgs.) 6.00
... SPECIAL 1 (4/84)-Mike W. Barr story; Golden-c/a 1 2 3 5 6 8
.../SPIDER-MAN (1997, $4.95) Dematteis-s/Nolan & Kesel-a 6.00
... : THE ABDUCTION ('98, $5.95) 6.00
...: THE BLUE, THE GREY, & THE BAT (1992, $5.95)-Weiss/Lopez-a 7.00
... :THE HILL (5/00, $2.95)-Priest-s/Martinbrough-a 3.00
... :THE KILLING JOKE (1988, deluxe 52 pgs., mature readers)-Bolland-c/a; Alan Moore scripts; Joker cripples Barbara Gordon 3 6 9 17 26 35
...: THE KILLING JOKE (2nd thru 12th printings) 2 4 6 9 12 15
...: THE KILLING JOKE : THE DELUXE EDITION (2008, $17.99, HC) re-colored version along with Bolland-s/a from Batman Black and White #4; sketch pages; Tim Sale intro. 18.00
...: THE MAN WHO LAUGHS (2005, $6.95)-Retells 1st meeting with the Joker; Mahnke-a 7.00
...: THE OFFICIAL COMIC ADAPTATION OF THE WARNER BROS. MOTION PICTURE (1989, $2.50, regular format, 68 pgs.)-Ordway-c 4.00
...: THE OFFICIAL COMIC ADAPTATION OF THE WARNER BROS. MOTION PICTURE (1989, $4.95, prestige format, 68 pgs.)-same interiors but different-c 6.00
...: THE ORDER OF BEASTS (2004, $5.95)-Elseworlds; Eddie Campbell-a 6.00
...: THE SPIRIT (1/07, $4.99)-Loeb-s/Cooke-a; P'Gell & Commissioner Dolan app. 5.00
...: THE 10-CENT ADVENTURE (3/02, 10¢) intro. to the "Bruce Wayne: Murderer" x-over; Rucka-s/Burchett & Janson-a/Dave Johnson-c 3.00

NOTE: (Also see Promotional Comics section for alternate copies with special outer half-covers promoting local comic shops)

...: THE 12-CENT ADVENTURE (10/04, 12¢) intro. to the "War Games" x-over; Grayson-s/Bachs-a; Catwoman & Spoiler app. 3.00
...: TWO-FACE-CRIME AND PUNISHMENT-(1995, $4.95)-McDaniel-a 6.00
... : TWO FACES (11/98, $4.95) Elseworlds 6.00
...Vs. THE INCREDIBLE HULK (1995, $3.95)-r/DC Special Series #27 6.00
...: VILLAINS SECRET FILES (10/98, $4.95) Origin-s 6.00
... VILLAINS SECRET FILES AND ORIGINS 2005 (7/05, $4.99) Clayface origin w/ Mignola-a; Black Mask story, pin-up of villains by various; Barrionuevo-c 6.00

BATMAN ADVENTURES, THE (Based on animated series)
DC Comics: Oct, 1992 - No. 36, Oct, 1995 ($1.25/$1.50)

1-Penguin-c/story 6.00
1 ($1.95, Silver Edition)-2nd printing 3.00
2-6,8-11,13-19: 2,12-Catwoman-c/story. 3-Joker-c/story. 5-Scarecrow-c/story. 10-Riddler-c/story. 11-Man-Bat-c/story. 16-Joker-c/story; begin $1.50-c. 18-Batgirl-c/story. 19-Scarecrow-c/story. 4.00
7-Special edition polybagged with Man-Bat trading card 6.00
12-(9/93) 1st Harley Quinn app. in comics; 1st animated-version Batgirl app. in title 8 16 24 54 102 150

Batman and Robin (2011 series) #16 © DC

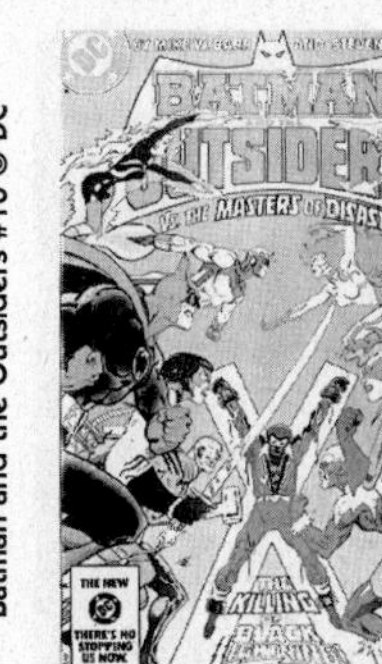

Batman and the Outsiders #10 © DC

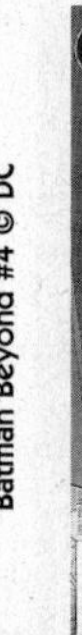
Batman Beyond #4 © DC

GD 2.0 | VG 4.0 | FN 6.0 | VF 8.0 | VF/NM 9.0 | NM- 9.2

20-24,26-32: 26-Batgirl app. 3.00
25-($2.50, 52 pgs.)-Superman app. 4.00
33-36: 33-Begin $1.75-c 3.00
Annual 1,2 ('94, '95): 2-Demon-c/story; Ra's al Ghul app. 4.00
...: Dangerous Dames & Demons (2003, $14.95, TPB) r/Annual 1,2, Mad Love & Adventures in the DC Universe #3; Bruce Timm painted-c 30.00
Holiday Special 1 (1995, $2.95) 5.00
The Collected Adventures Vol. 1,2 ('93, '95, $5.95) 10.00
TPB ('98, $7.95) r/#1-6; painted wraparound-c 10.00

BATMAN ADVENTURES (Based on animated series)
DC Comics: Jun, 2003 - No. 17, Oct, 2004 ($2.25)

1-Timm-c 4.00
1-Free Comic Book Day edition (6/03) Timm-c 4.00
2-17: 3,16-Joker-c/app. 4-Ra's al Ghul app. 6-8-Phantasm app. 14-Grey Ghost app. 3.00
Batman/Scooby-Doo Halloween Fest 1 (12/12, giveaway flipbook with Scooby-Doo) r/#1 3.00
Vol. 1: Rogues Gallery (2004, $6.95, digest size) r/#1-4 & Batman: Gotham Advs. #50 7.00
Vol. 2: Shadows & Masks (2004, $6.95, digest size) r/#5-9 7.00

BATMAN ADVENTURES, THE: MAD LOVE
DC Comics: Feb, 1994 ($3.95/$4.95)

1-Origin of Harley Quinn; Dini-s/Timm-c/a 4 8 12 23 37 50
1-($4.95, Prestige format) new Timm painted-c 2 4 6 11 16 20

BATMAN ADVENTURES, THE: THE LOST YEARS (TV)
DC Comics: Jan, 1998 - No. 5, May, 1998 ($1.95) (Based on animated series)

1-5-Leads into Fall '97's new animated episodes. 4-Tim Drake becomes Robin. 5-Dick becomes Nightwing 3.00
TPB-(1999, $9.95) r/series 12.00

BATMAN/ALIENS
DC Comics/Dark Horse: Mar, 1997 - No. 2, Apr, 1997 ($4.95, limited series)

1,2: Wrightson-c/a. 6.00
TPB-(1997, $14.95) w/prequel from DHP #101,102 15.00

BATMAN/ALIENS II
DC Comics/Dark Horse: 2003 - No. 3, 2003 ($5.95, limited series)

1-3-Edginton-s/Staz Johnson-a 6.00
TPB-(2003, $14.95) r/#1-3 15.00

BATMAN AND... (See Batman and Robin [2011 series] #19-on)

BATMAN AND ROBIN (See Batman R.I.P. and Batman: Battle For The Cowl series)
DC Comics: Aug, 2009 - No. 26, Oct, 2011 ($2.99)

1-Grant Morrison-s/Frank Quitely-a/c; Dick Grayson & Damian Wayne team 5.00
1-Variant cover by J.G. Jones 20.00
1-Second thru Fourth printings - recolored Quitely covers 3.00
2-16-Quitely-c. 2-Three printings. 4-6-Tan-a. 7-9-Stewart-a; Batwoman & Squire app. 13-15-Joker app.; Irving-a. 16-Bruce Wayne returns; Batman Inc. announced 3.00
2-Variant-c by Adam Kubert 10.00
17-26: 17-McDaniel-a/March-c. 21,22-Gleason-a. 23-25-Red Hood app. 3.00
... #1 Special Edition (6/10, $1.00) r/#1 with "What's Next?" cover logo 3.00
...: Batman and Robin Must Die - The Deluxe Edition HC (2011, $24.99) r/#13-16; cover and costume design sketch art 25.00
...: Batman Reborn - The Deluxe Edition HC (2010, $24.99) r/#1-6; design sketch art 25.00
...: Batman Reborn SC (2011, $14.99) r/#1-6; cover and character design sketch art 15.00
...: Batman vs. Robin - The Deluxe Edition HC (2010, $24.99) r/#7-12; cover sketch art 25.00

BATMAN AND ROBIN (DC New 52)(Cover title changes each issue starting with #19)
DC Comics: Nov, 2011 - Present ($2.99)

1-Bruce and Damian Wayne in costume; Tomasi-s/Gleason-a 3.00
2-14: 5,6-Ducard flashback. 9-Night of the Owls 3.00
15-Death of the Family tie-in; die-cut Joker cover 5.00
16-18: 16-Death of the Family tie-in. 18-Requiem 3.00
19-23: 19-Red Robin. 20-Red Hood. 21-Batgirl. 22-Catwoman. 23-Nightwing 3.00
23.1, 23.2, 23.3, 23.4 (11/13, $2.99, regular covers) 3.00
23.1 (11/13, $3.99, 3-D cover) "Two Face #1" on cover; March-a; Scarecrow app. 6.00
23.2 (11/13, $3.99, 3-D cover) "Court of Owls #1" on cover; history of the Owls 4.00
23.3 (11/13, $3.99, 3-D cover) "Ra's al Ghul #1" on cover; history of Ra's retold 4.00
23.4 (11/13, $3.99, 3-D cover) "Killer Croc #1" on cover; Croc's origin 4.00
24-29: 24-28-Two-Face. 25-Matches Malone app. 29-Aquaman 3.00
#0 (11/12, $2.99) Damian's childhood training with Talia; Tomasi-s/Gleason-a 3.00
Annual 1 (3/13, $4.99) Damian in the Batman #666 costume; Andy Kubert-c 5.00
Annual 2 (3/14, $4.99) Mahnke-a; flashback to Dick Grayson's first week as Robin 5.00

BATMAN AND ROBIN ADVENTURES (TV)
DC Comics: Nov, 1995 - No. 25, Dec, 1997 ($1.75) (Based on animated series)

1-Dini-s. 4.00
2-4,6-24: 2-4-Dini script. 4-Penguin-c/story. 9-Batgirl & Talia-c/story. 10-Ra's al Ghul-c/story. 11-Man-Bat app. 12-Bane-c/app. 13-Scarecrow-c/app. 15 Deadman-c/app. 16-Catwoman-c/app. 18-Joker-c/app. 24-Poison Ivy app. 3.00
5-Joker-c/story; Poison Ivy, Harley Quinn-c/app. 6.00
25-($2.95, 48 pgs.) 4.00
Annual 1,2 (11/96, 11/97): 1-Phantasm-c/app. 2-Zatara & Zatanna-c/app. 4.00
...: Sub-Zero(1998, $3.95) Adaptation of animated video 4.00

BATMAN AND SUPERMAN ADVENTURES: WORLD'S FINEST
DC Comics: 1997 ($6.95, square-bound, one-shot) (Based on animated series)

1-Adaptation of animated crossover episode; Dini-s/Timm-c. 8.00

BATMAN AND SUPERMAN: WORLD'S FINEST
DC Comics: Apr, 1999 - No. 10, Jan, 2000 ($4.95/$1.99, limited series)

1,10-($4.95, squarebound) Taylor-a 5.00
2-9-($1.99) 5-Batgirl app. 8-Catwoman-c/app. 3.00
TPB (2003, $19.95) r/#1-10 20.00

BATMAN AND THE OUTSIDERS (The Adventures of the Outsiders #33 on)
(Also see Brave & The Bold #200 & The Outsiders) (Replaces The Brave and the Bold)
DC Comics: Aug, 1983 - No. 32, Apr, 1986 (Mando paper #5 on)

1-Batman, Halo, Geo-Force, Katana, Metamorpho & Black Lightning begin 5.00
2-32: 5-New Teen Titans x-over. 9-Halo begins. 11,12-Origin Katana. 18-More info on Metamorpho's origin. 28-31-Lookers origin. 32-Team disbands 3.00
Annual 1,2 (9/84, 9/85): 2-Metamorpho & Sapphire Stagg wed 4.00
NOTE: ***Aparo** a-1-9, 11-13p, 16-20; c-1-4, 5i, 6-21, Annual 1, 2.* ***B. Kane** a-3r.* ***Layton** a-19i, 20i.* ***Lopez** a-3p.* ***Miller** c-Annual 1.* ***Perez** c-5p.* ***B. Willingham** a-14p.*

BATMAN AND THE OUTSIDERS (Continues as The Outsiders for #15-39)
DC Comics: Dec, 2007 - No. 14, Feb, 2009; No. 40, Jul, 2011 ($2.99)

1-14: 1-Batman, Catwoman, Martian Manhunter, Katana, Metamorpho, Thunder & Grace begin. 4-Batgirl joins. 11-13-Batman R.I.P. 3.00
40 (7/11) Final issue; Didio-s/Tan-a; history of the team 3.00
... Special (3/09, $3.99) Alfred assembles a new team; Andy Kubert-a; two covers 4.00
...: The Chrysalis TPB (2008, $14.99) r/#1-5 15.00
...: The Snare TPB (2008, $14.99) r/#6-10 15.00

BATMAN: ARKHAM CITY (Prequel to the video game)
DC Comics: Early Jul, 2011 - No. 5, Oct, 2011 ($2.99, limited series)

1-5-Dini-s/D'Anda-a; Joker app. 3.00
...: End Game (1/13, $6.99) Story bridges Arkham City and Arkham Unhinged series 7.00

BATMAN: ARKHAM UNHINGED (Based on the Batman: Arkham City video game)
DC Comics: Jun, 2012 - No. 20, Jan, 2014 ($2.99)

1-20: 1-Wilkins-c; Catwoman, Two-Face & Hugo Strange app. 3.00

BATMAN: BANE OF THE DEMON
DC Comics: Mar, 1998 - No. 4, June, 1998 ($1.95, limited series)

1-4-Dixon-s/Nolan-a; prelude to Legacy x-over 3.00

BATMAN: BATTLE FOR THE COWL (Follows Batman R.I.P. storyline)
DC Comics: May, 2009 - No. 3, Jul, 2009 ($3.99, limited series)

1-3-Tony Daniel-s/a/c; 2 covers on each 4.00
...: Arkham Asylum (6/09, $2.99) Hine-s/Haun-a/Ladronn-c 3.00
...: Commissioner Gordon (5/09, $2.99) Mandrake-a/Ladronn-c; Mr. Freeze app. 3.00
...: Man-Bat (6/09, $2.99) Harris-s/Calafiore-a/Ladronn-c; Dr. Phosphorus app. 3.00
...: The Network (7/09, $2.99) Nicieza-s/Calafiore & Kramer-a/Ladronn-c 3.00
...: The Underground (6/09, $2.99) Yost-s/Raimondi-a/Ladronn-c 3.00
Companion SC (2009, $14.99) r/ five one-shots 15.00
HC (2009, $19.99) r/#1-3 & Gotham Gazette: Batman Dead & Gotham Gazette: Batman Alive; gallery of variant covers and sketch art 20.00
SC (2010, $14.99) same contents as HC 15.00

BATMAN BEYOND (Based on animated series)
DC Comics: Mar, 1999 - No. 6, Aug, 1999 ($1.99, limited series)

1-6: 1,2-Adaptation of pilot episode, Timm-c 4.00
TPB (1999, $9.95) r/#1-6 15.00

BATMAN BEYOND (Based on animated series)(Continuing series)
DC Comics: Nov, 1999 - No. 24, Oct, 2001 ($1.99)

1-24: 1-Rousseau-a; Batman vs. Batman. 14-Demon-c/app. 21,22-Justice League Unlimited-c/app. 3.00
...: Return of the Joker (2/01, $2.95) adaptation of video release 4.00

BATMAN BEYOND (Animated series)(See Superman/Batman Annual #4)
DC Comics: Aug, 2010 - No. 6, Jan, 2011 ($2.99, limited series)

1-6: 1-Benjamin-a; Nguyen-c; return of Hush 3.00
1-Variant-c by J.H. Williams III 6.00

Batman Beyond Universe #5 © DC

Batman: Dark Victory #1 © DC

Batman Family #20 © DC

GD 2.0 VG 4.0 FN 6.0 VF 8.0 VF/NM 9.0 NM- 9.2

...: Hush Beyond TPB (2011, $14.99) r/#1-6 15.00

BATMAN BEYOND
DC Comics: Mar, 2011 - No. 8, Oct, 2011 ($2.99)
1-8: 1-3-Justice League app.; Beechen-s/Benjamin-a/Nguyen-c. 8-Inque app. 3.00
1-Variant-c by Darwyn Cooke 4.00

BATMAN BEYOND UNIVERSE
DC Comics: Oct, 2013 - Present ($3.99)
1-8: 1-Superman & the JLB app.; Sean Murphy-c. 8-Wonder Woman app. 4.00

BATMAN BEYOND UNLIMITED
DC Comics: Apr, 2012 - No. 18, Sept, 2013 ($3.99)
1-18: 1-Beechen-s/Breyfogle-a; Superman & Justice League back-ups; Nguyen-c. 17-Metal Men return; Marvel Family app. 18-New Batgirl 4.00

BATMAN: BLACK & WHITE
DC Comics: June, 1996 - No. 4, Sept, 1996 ($2.95, B&W, limited series)
1-Stories by McKeever, Timm, Kubert, Chaykin, Goodwin; Jim Lee-c; Allred inside front-c; Moebius inside back-c 4.00
2-4: 2-Stories by Simonson, Corben, Bisley & Gaiman; Miller-c. 3-Stories by M. Wagner, Janson, Sienkiewicz, O'Neil & Kristiansen; B. Smith-c; Russell inside front-c; Silvestri inside back-c. 4-Stories by Bolland, Goodwin & Gianni, Strnad & Nowlan, O'Neil & Stelfreeze; Toth-c; pin-ups by Neal Adams & Alex Ross 3.00
Hardcover ('97, $39.95) r/series w/new art & cover plate 40.00
Softcover ('00, $19.95) r/series 20.00
Volume 2 HC ('02, $39.95, 7 3/4"x12") r/B&W back-up-s from Batman: Gotham Knights #1-16; stories and art by various incl. Ross, Buscema, Byrne, Ellison, Sale; Mignola-c 40.00
Volume 2 SC ('03, $19.95, 7 3/4"x12") same contents as HC 20.00
Volume 2 SC ('08, $19.99, reg. size) same contents as HC 20.00
Volume 3 HC ('07, $24.99, reg. size) r/B&W back-up-s from Batman: Gotham Knights #17-49; stories and art by various incl. Davis, DeCarlo, Morse, Schwartz, Thompson; Miller-c 25.00

BATMAN: BLACK & WHITE
DC Comics: Nov, 2013 - No. 6, Apr, 2014 ($4.99, B&W, limited series)
1-6-Short story anthology by various. 1-Silvestri-c; Neal Adams-a. 2-Steranko-c; Nino-a. 3-Bermejo-s/a. 4-Conner-c; Allred-s/a. 6-Mahnke-c; Hughes, Cloonan, Chiang-a 4.00

BATMAN: BOOK OF THE DEAD
DC Comics: Jun, 1999 - No. 2, July, 1999 ($4.95, limited series, prestige format)
1,2-Elseworlds; Kitson-a 6.00

BATMAN CACOPHONY
DC Comics: Jan, 2009 - No. 3, Mar, 2009 ($3.99, limited series)
1-3-Kevin Smith-s/Walt Flanagan-a; Joker and Onomatoapoeia app.; Adam Kubert-c 4.00
1-3-Variant-c by Sienkiewicz 10.00
HC (2009, $19.99, d.j.) r/#1-3; Kevin Smith intro.; script for #3, cover gallery 20.00
SC (2010, $14.99) r/#1-3; Kevin Smith intro.; script for #3, cover gallery 15.00

BATMAN: CATWOMAN DEFIANT (See Batman one-shots)

BATMAN/ CATWOMAN: TRAIL OF THE GUN
DC Comics: 2004 - No. 2, 2004 ($5.95, limited series, prestige format)
1,2-Elseworlds; Van Sciver-a/Nocenti-s 6.00

BATMAN CHRONICLES, THE (See the Batman TPB listings for the Golden Age reprint series that shares this title)
DC Comics: Summer, 1995 - No. 23, Winter, 2001 ($2.95, quarterly)
1-3,5-19: 1-Dixon/Grant/Moench script. 3-Bolland-c. 5-Oracle Year One story, Richard Dragon app.,Chaykin-c. 6-Kaluta-c; Ra's al Ghul story. 7-Superman-c/app.11-Paul Pope-s/a. 12-Cataclysm pt. 10. 18-No Man's Land 4.00
4-Hitman story by Ennis, Contagion tie-in; Balent-c 2 4 6 8 10 12
20-23: 20-Catwoman and Relative Heroes-c/app. 21-Pander Bros.-a 4.00
...Gallery (3/97, $3.50) Pin-ups 4.00
...Gauntlet, The (1997, $4.95, one-shot) 6.00

BATMAN: CITY OF LIGHT
DC Comics: Dec, 2003 - No. 8, July, 2004 ($2.95, limited series)
1-8-Pander Brothers-a/s; Paniccia-s 3.00

BATMAN CONFIDENTIAL
DC Comics: Feb, 2007 - No. 54, May, 2011 ($2.99)
1-49,51-54: 1-6-Diggle-s/Portacio-a/c. 7-12-Cowan-a; Joker's origin. 13-16-Morales-a. 17-21-Batgirl vs. Catwoman; Maguire-a. 22-25-McDaniel-a; Joker app. 26-28-King Tut app.; Garcia-Lopez-a. 40-43-Kieth-s/a. 44-48-Mandrake-a/c 3.00
50-($4.99) Bingham-a; back-up Silver Age-style JLA story 5.00
...: Dead to Rights SC (2010, $14.99) r/#22-25,29,30 15.00
...: Lovers and Madmen HC (2008, $24.99, dustjacket) r/#7-12; Brad Meltzer intro. 25.00
...: Lovers and Madmen SC (2009, $14.99) r/#7-12; Brad Meltzer intro. 15.00
...: Rules of Engagement HC (2007, $24.99, dustjacket) r/#1-6 25.00
...: The Bat and the Beast SC (2010, $12.99) r/#31-35 13.00
...: The Cat and the Bat SC (2009, $12.99) r/#17-21 13.00
...: Vs. The Undead SC (2010, $14.99) r/#44-48 15.00

BATMAN: DARK DETECTIVE
DC Comics: Early July, 2005 - No. 6, Late September, 2005 ($2.99, limited series)
1-6-Englehart-s/Rogers & Austin-a; Silver St. Cloud and The Joker app. 3.00

BATMAN: DARK KNIGHT OF THE ROUND TABLE
DC Comics: 1999 - No. 2, 1999 ($4.95, limited series, prestige format)
1,2-Elseworlds; Giordano-a 6.00

BATMAN: DARK VICTORY
DC Comics: 1999 - No. 13, 2000 ($4.95/$2.95, limited series)
Wizard #0 Preview 3.00
1-($4.95) Loeb-s/Sale-c/a 5.00
2-12-($2.95) 3.00
13-($4.95) 5.00
Hardcover (2001, $29.95) with dust jacket; r/#0,1-13 30.00
Softcover (2002, $19.95) r/#0,1-13 20.00

BATMAN: DEATH AND THE MAIDENS
DC Comics: Oct, 2003 - No. 9, Aug, 2004 ($2.95, limited series)
1-Ra's al Ghul app.; Rucka-s/Janson-a 4.00
2-9: 9-Ra's al Ghul dies 3.00
TPB (2004, $19.95) r/#1-9 & Detective #783 20.00

BATMAN/ DEATHBLOW: AFTER THE FIRE
DC Comics/WildStorm: 2002 - No. 3, 2002 ($5.95, limited series)
1-3-Azzarello-s/Bermejo & Bradstreet-a 6.00
TPB (2003, $12.95) r/#1-3; plus concept art 13.00

BATMAN: DEATH MASK
DC Comics/CMX: Jun, 2008 - No. 4, Sept, 2008 ($2.99, B&W, limited series, right-to-left manga style)
1-4-Yoshinori Natsume-s/a 3.00
TPB (2008, $9.99, digest size) r/#1-4; interview with Yoshinori Natsume 10.00

BATMAN ETERNAL
DC Comics: Jun, 2014 - Present ($2.99, weekly series)
1-Snyder-s/Fabok-a; Professor Pyg & Jason Bard app. 3.00

BATMAN FAMILY, THE
National Periodical Pub./DC Comics: Sept-Oct, 1975 - No. 20, Oct-Nov, 1978 (#1-4, 17-on: 68 pgs.) (Combined with Detective Comics with No. 481)
1-Origin/2nd app. Batgirl-Robin team-up (The Dynamite Duo); reprints plus one new story begins; N. Adams-a(r); r/1st app. Man-Bat from Det. #400
4 8 12 28 47 65
2-5: 2-r/Det. #369. 3-Batgirl & Robin learn each's i.d.; r/Batwoman app. from Batman #105. 4-r/1st Fatman app. from Batman #113. 5-r/1st Bat-Hound app. from Batman #92
3 6 9 16 23 30
6-(7-8/76) Joker's daughter on cover (1st app.) 6 12 18 38 69 100
7,8,14-16: 8-r/Batwoman app.14-Batwoman app. 15-3rd app. Killer Moth. 16-Bat-Girl cameo (last app. in costume until New Teen Titans #47) 2 4 6 13 18 22
9-Joker's daughter-c/app. 4 8 12 23 37 50
10-1st revival Batwoman; Cavalier app.; Killer Moth app.
3 6 9 18 28 38
11-13,17-20: 11-13-Rogers-a(p): 11-New stories begin; Man-Bat begins. 13-Batwoman cameo. 17-($1.00 size)-Batman, Huntress begin; Batwoman & Catwoman 1st meet. 18-20: Huntress by Staton in all. 20-Origin Ragman retold
3 6 9 17 26 35

NOTE: ***Aparo*** *a-17; c-11-16.* ***Austin*** *a-12i.* ***Chaykin*** *a-14p.* ***Michael Golden*** *a-15-17,18-20p.* ***Grell*** *a-1; c-1.* ***Gil Kane*** *a-2r.* ***Kaluta*** *c-17, 19.* ***Newton*** *a-13.* ***Robinson*** *a-1r, 3i(r), 9r.* ***Russell*** *a-18i, 19i.* ***Starlin*** *a-17; c-18, 20.*

BATMAN: FAMILY
DC Comics: Dec, 2002 - No. 8, Feb, 2003 ($2.95/$2.25, weekly limited series)
1,8-($2.95): 1-John Francis Moore-s/Hoberg & Gaudiano-a 4.00
2-7-($2.25): 3-Orpheus & Black Canary app. 3.00

BATMAN: GATES OF GOTHAM
DC Comics: Jul, 2011 - No. 5, Late Oct, 2011 ($2.99, limited series)
1-5-Flashbacks to 1880s Gotham City; Snyder-s/Higgins-a 3.00

BATMAN: GCPD
DC Comics: Aug, 1996 - No. 4, Nov, 1996 ($2.25, limited series)
1-4: Features Jim Gordon; Aparo/Sienkiewicz-a 3.00

BATMAN: GORDON OF GOTHAM

Batman: Gotham Adventures #31 © DC

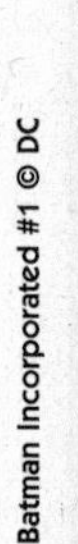
Batman Incorporated #1 © DC

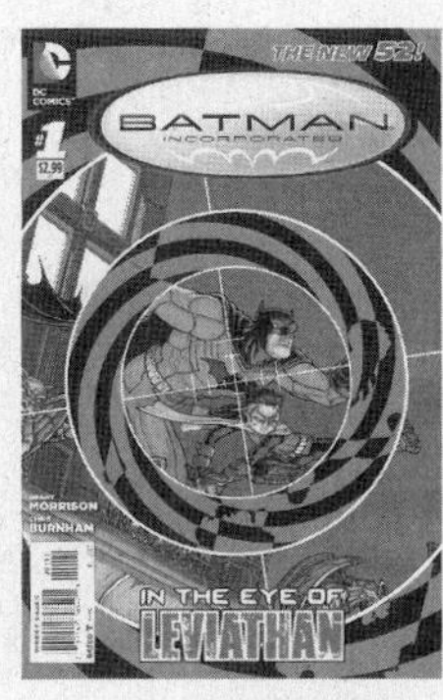

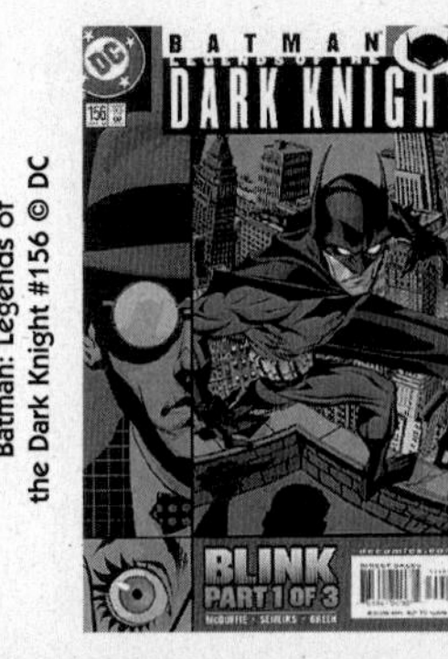

Batman: Legends of the Dark Knight #156 © DC

GD 2.0 | VG 4.0 | FN 6.0 | VF 8.0 | VF/NM 9.0 | NM- 9.2

DC Comics: June, 1998 - No. 4, Sept, 1998 ($1.95, limited series)
1-4: Gordon's early days in Chicago 3.00

BATMAN: GORDON'S LAW
DC Comics: Dec, 1996 - No. 4, Mar, 1997 ($1.95, limited series)
1-4: Dixon-s/Janson-c/a 3.00

BATMAN: GOTHAM ADVENTURES (TV)
DC Comics: June, 1998 - No. 60, May, 2003 ($2.95/$1.95/$1.99/$2.25)
1-($2.95) Based on Kids WB Batman animated series 4.00
2-3-($1.95): 2-Two-Face-c/app. 3.00
4-9,11-13,15-28: 4-Begin $1.99-c. 5-Deadman-c. 13-MAD #1 cover swipe 3.00
10,14,29,43,45-Harley Quinn app. 5.00
30-42,44,46-60: 31,60-Joker-c/app. 50-Catwoman-c/app. 58-Creeper-c/app. 3.00
TPB (2000, $9.95) r/#1-6 15.00

BATMAN: GOTHAM AFTER MIDNIGHT
DC Comics: July, 2008 - No. 12, Jun, 2009 ($2.99, limited series)
1-12-Steve Niles-s/Kelley Jones-a/c. 1-Scarecrow app. 2-Man-Bat app. 5,6-Joker app. 3.00
TPB (2009, $19.99) r/#1-12; John Carpenter intro.; Jones sketch pages 20.00

BATMAN: GOTHAM COUNTY LINE
DC Comics: 2005 - No. 3, 2005 ($5.99, square-bound, limited series)
1-3-Steve Niles-s/Scott Hampton-a. 2,3-Deadman app. 6.00
TPB (2006, $17.99) r/#1-3 18.00

BATMAN: GOTHAM KNIGHTS
DC Comics: Mar, 2000 - No. 74, Apr, 2006 ($2.50/$2.75)
1-Grayson-s; B&W back-up by Warren Ellis & Jim Lee 4.00
2-10-Grayson-s; B&W back-ups by various 3.00
11-($3.25) Bolland-c; Kyle Baker back-up story 4.00
12-24: 13-Officer Down x-over; Ellison back-up-s. 15-Colan back-up. 20-Superman-c/app. 3.00
25,26-Bruce Wayne: Murderer pt. 4,10 3.50
27-31: 28,30,31-Bruce Wayne: Fugitive pt. 7,14,17 3.00
32-49: 32-Begin $2.75-c; Kaluta-a back-up. 33,34-Bane-c/app. 35-Mahfood-a back-up. 38-Bolton-a back-up. 43-Jason Todd & Batgirl app. 44-Jason Todd flashback 3.00
50-54-Hush returns-Barrionuevo-a/Bermejo-c. 53,54-Green Arrow app. 4.00
55-($3.75) Batman vs. Hush; Joker & Riddler app. 5.00
56-74: 56-58-War Games; Jae Lee-c. 60-65-Hush app. 66-Villains United tie-in; Talia app. 3.00
Batman: Hush Returns TPB (2006, $12.99) r/#50-55,66; cover gallery 13.00

BATMAN: GOTHAM NIGHTS II (First series listed under Gotham Nights)
DC Comics: Mar, 1995 - No. 4, June, 1995 ($1.95, limited series)
1-4 3.00

BATMAN/GRENDEL (1st limited series)
DC Comics: 1993 - No. 2, 1993 ($4.95, limited series, squarebound; 52 pgs.)
1,2: Batman vs. Hunter Rose. 1-Devil's Riddle; Matt Wagner-c/a/scripts. 2-Devil's Masque; Matt Wagner-c/a/scripts 7.00

BATMAN/GRENDEL (2nd limited series)
DC Comics: June, 1996 - No. 2, July, 1996 ($4.95, limited series, squarebound)
1,2: Batman vs. Grendel Prime. 1-Devil's Bones. 2-Devil's Dance; Wagner-c/a/s 6.00

BATMAN: HARLEY & IVY
DC Comics: Jun, 2004 - No. 3, Aug, 2004 ($2.50, limited series)
1-3-Paul Dini-s/Bruce Timm-c/a 4.00
TPB (2007, $14.99) r/series; newly colored story from Batman: Gotham Knights #14 and Harley and Ivy: Love on the Lam series 15.00

BATMAN: HARLEY QUINN
DC Comics: 1999 ($5.95, prestige format)
1-Intro. of Harley Quinn into regular DC continuity; Dini-s/Alex Ross-c 4 8 12 23 37 50
1-(2nd printing) 1 3 4 6 8 10

BATMAN: HAUNTED GOTHAM
DC Comics: 2000 - No. 4, 2000 ($4.95, limited series, squarebound)
1-4-Doug Moench-s/Kelley Jones-c/a 6.00
TPB (2009, $19.99) r/#1-4 20.00

BATMAN/ HELLBOY/STARMAN
DC Comics/Dark Horse: Jan, 1999 - No. 2, Feb, 1999 ($2.50, limited series)
1,2: Robinson-s/Mignola-a. 2-Harris-c 5.00

BATMAN: HOLLYWOOD KNIGHT
DC Comics: Apr, 2001 - No. 3, Jun, 2001 ($2.50, limited series)
1-3-Elseworlds Batman as a 1940's movie star; Giordano-a/Layton-s 3.00

BATMAN/ HUNTRESS: CRY FOR BLOOD
DC Comics: Jun, 2000 - No. 6, Nov, 2000 ($2.50, limited series)
1-6: Rucka-s/Burchett-a; The Question app. 3.00
TPB (2002, $12.95) r/#1-6 13.00

BATMAN, INC.
DC Comics: Jan, 2011 - No. 8, Aug, 2011 ($3.99/$2.99)
1-3-Morrison-s/Paquette-a; covers by Paquette & Williams 4.00
4-8-($2.99) 4-Burnham-a, original Batwoman (Kathy Kane) app. 3.00
...: Leviathan Strikes (2/12, $6.99) Morrison-s/Burnham & Stewart-a; cover gallery 7.00

BATMAN INCORPORATED
DC Comics: Jul, 2012 - No. 13, Sept, 2013 ($2.99)
1-7-Morrison-s/Burnham-a/c. 2-Origin of Talia. 3-Matches Malone returns 3.00
1-Variant-c by Quitely 5.00
8-Death of Damian 5.00
9-13: 9,10,12,13-Morrison-s/Burnham-a/c 3.00
#0 (11/12, $2.99) Frazer Irving-a; the start of Batman Incorporated 3.00
... Special 1 (10/13, $4.99) Short stories about international Batmen; s/a by various 5.00

BATMAN: JEKYLL & HYDE
DC Comics: June, 2005 - No. 6, Nov, 2005 ($2.99, limited series)
1-6-Paul Jenkins-s; Two-Face app. 1-3-Jae Lee-a. 4-6-Sean Phillips-a 3.00
TPB (2008, $14.99) r/#1-6 15.00

BATMAN: JOKER TIME (...: It's Joker Time! on cover)
DC Comics: 2000 - No. 3 ($4.95, limited series, squarebound)
1-3-Bob Hall-s/a 6.00

BATMAN: JOURNEY INTO KNGHT
DC Comics: Oct, 2005 - No. 12, Nov, 2006 ($2.50/$2.99, limited series)
1-9-Andrew Helfer-s/Tan Eng Huat-a/Pat Lee-c 3.00
10-12-($2.99) Joker app. 3.00

BATMAN/ JUDGE DREDD "DIE LAUGHING"
DC Comics: 1998 - No. 2, 1999 ($4.95, limited series, squarebound)
1,2: 1-Fabry-c/a. 2-Jim Murray-c/a 6.00

BATMAN: KNIGHTGALLERY (See Batman one-shots)

BATMAN: LEAGUE OF BATMEN
DC Comics: 2001 - No. 2, 2001 ($5.95, limited series, squarebound)
1,2-Elseworlds; Moench-s/Bright & Tanghal-a/Van Fleet-c 6.00

BATMAN: LEGENDS OF THE DARK KNIGHT (Legends of the Dark...#1-36)
DC Comics: Nov, 1989 - No. 214, Mar, 2007 ($1.50/$1.75/$1.95/$1.99/$2.25/$2.50/$2.99)
1- "Shaman" begins, ends #5; outer cover has four different color variations, all worth same 5.00
2-10: 6-10- "Gothic" by Grant Morrison (scripts) 4.00
11-15: 11-15-Gulacy/Austin-a. 13-Catwoman app. 4.00
16-Intro drug Bane uses; begin Venom story 6.00
17-20 5.00
21-49,51-63: 38-Bat-Mite-c/story. 46-49-Catwoman app. w/Heath-c/a. 51-Ragman app.; Joe Kubert-c. 59,60,61-Knightquest x-over. 62,63-KnightsEnd Pt. 4 & 10 3.00
50-($3.95, 68 pgs.)-Bolland embossed gold foil-c; Joker-c/story; pin-ups by Chaykin, Simonson, Williamson, Kaluta, Russell, others 5.00
64-99: 64-(9/94)-Begin $1.95-c. 71-73-James Robinson-s,Watkiss-c/a. 74,75-McKeever-c/a/s. 76-78-Scott Hampton-c/a/s. 81-Card insert. 83,84-Ellis-s. 85-Robinson-s. 91-93-Ennis-s. 94-Michael T. Gilbert-s/a. 3.00
100-($3.95) Alex Ross painted-c; gallery by various 5.00
101-115: 101-Ezquerra-a. 102-104-Robinson-s 3.00
116-No Man's Land stories begin; Huntress-c 4.00
117-119,121-126: 122-Harris-c 3.00
120-ID of new Batgirl revealed 4.00
127-131: Return to Legends stories; Green Arrow app. 3.00
132-199, 201-204: 132-136 ($2.25-c) Archie Goodwin-s/Rogers-a. 137-141-Gulacy-a. 142-145-Joker and Ra's al Ghul app. 146-148-Kitson-a. 158-Begin $2.50-c 169-171-Tony Harris-c/a. 182-184-War Games. 182-Bagged with Sky Captain CD 3.00
200-($4.99) Joker-c/app. 5.00
205-214: 205-Begin $2.99-c. 207,208-Olivetti-a. 214-Deadshot app. 3.00
#0-(10/94)-Zero Hour; Quesada/Palmiotti-c; released between #64&65 3.00
Annual 1-7 ('91-'97, $3.50-$3.95, 68 pgs.): 1-Joker app. 2-Netzer-c/a. 3-New Batman (Azrael) app. 4-Elseworlds story. 5-Year One; Man-Bat app. 6-Legend of the Dead Earth story. 7-Pulp Heroes story 4.00
Halloween Special 1 (12/93, $6.95, 84 pgs.)-Embossed & foil stamped-c 1 2 3 5 6 8
Batman Madness-...Halloween Special (1994, $4.95) 6.00

Batman: Li'l Gotham #6 © DC

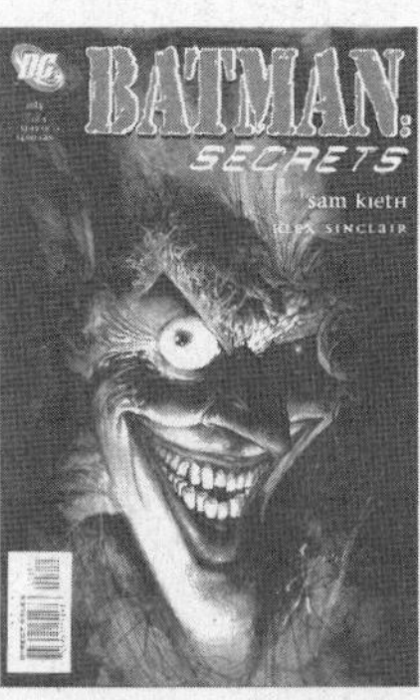

Batman: Secrets #3 © DC

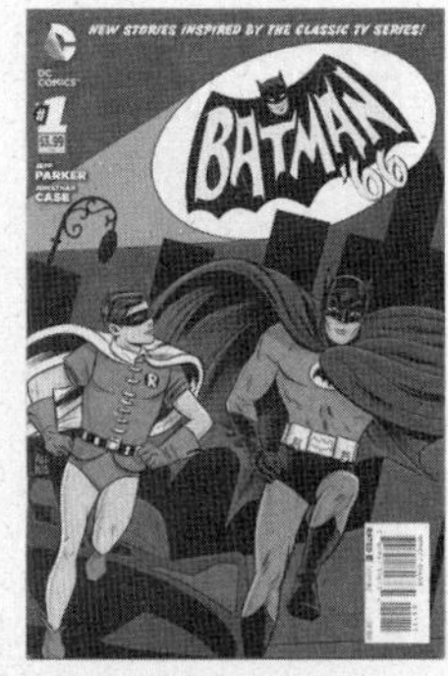

NEW STORIES INSPIRED BY THE CLASSIC TV SERIES!
BATMAN '66

Batman '66 #1 © DC

	GD	VG	FN	VF	VF/NM	NM-
	2.0	4.0	6.0	8.0	9.0	9.2

Batman Ghosts-...Halloween Special (1995, $4.95) 6.00

NOTE: ***Aparo** a-Annual 1. **Chaykin** scripts-24-26. **Giffen** a-Annual 1. **Golden** a-Annual 1. **Alan Grant** scripts-38, 52, 53. **Gil Kane** c/a-24-26. **Mignola** a-54; c-54, 62. **Morrow** a-Annual 3i. **Quesada** a-Annual 1. **James Robinson** scripts- 71-73. **Russell** c/a-42, 43. **Sears** a-21, 23; c-21, 23. **Zeck** a-69, 70; c-69, 70.*

BATMAN-LEGENDS OF THE DARK KNIGHT: JAZZ
DC Comics: Apr, 1995 - No. 3, June, 1995 ($2.50, limited series)
1-3 3.00

BATMAN: LI'L GOTHAM
DC Comics: Jun, 2013 - No. 12, May, 2014 ($2.99, printings of stories that 1st appeared online)
1-12-Dustin Nguyen-a/c; Nguyen & Fridolfs-s; holiday themed short stories 3.00
Halloween Comic Fest 2013 (12/13, no cover price) Halloween giveaway; r/#1 3.00

BATMAN/LOBO
DC Comics: Oct, 2007 - No. 2, Nov, 2007 ($5.99, squarebound, limited series)
1,2-Sam Kieth-s/a 6.00

BATMAN: MANBAT
DC Comics: Oct, 1995 - No. 3, Dec, 1995 ($4.95, limited series)
1-3-Elseworlds-Delano-script; Bolton-a 6.00
TPB-(1997, $14.95) r/#1-3 15.00

BATMAN: MITEFALL (See Batman one-shots)

BATMAN MINIATURE (See Batman Kellogg's)

BATMAN: NEVERMORE
DC Comics: June, 2003 - No. 5, Oct, 2003 ($2.50, limited series)
1-5-Elseworlds Batman & Edgar Allan Poe; Wrightson-c/Guy Davis-a/Len Wein-s 3.00

BATMAN: NO MAN'S LAND (Also see 1999 Batman titles)
DC Comics: (one shots)
nn (3/99, $2.95) Alex Ross-c; Bob Gale-s; begins year-long story arc 4.00
Collector's Ed. (3/99, $3.95) Ross lenticular-c 6.00
#0 (: Ground Zero on cover) (12/99, $4.95) Orbik-c 6.00
...: Gallery (7/99, $3.95) Jim Lee-c 4.00
...: Secret Files (12/99, $4.95) Maleev-c 6.00
TPB ('99, $12.95) r/early No Man's Land stories; new Batgirl early app. 13.00
No Law and a New Order TPB(1999, $5.95) Ross-c 8.00
Volume 2 ('00, $12.95) r/later No Man's Land stories; Batgirl(Huntress) app.; Deodato-c 13.00
Volume 3-5 ('00,'01 $12.95) 3-Intro. new Batgirl. 4-('00). 5-('01) Land-c 13.00

BATMAN: ODYSSEY
DC Comics: Sept, 2010 - No. 6, Feb, 2011 ($3.99, limited series)
1-6-Neal Adams-s/a/c. 1-Man-Bat app.; bonus sketch pages. 5,6-Joker app. 4.00
1-6-Variant B&W-version cover 5.00
Vol. 2 (12/11 - No. 7, 6/12) 1-7-Neal Adams-s/a/c 4.00

BATMAN: ORPHANS
DC Comics: Early Feb, 2011 - No. 2, Late Feb, 2011 ($3.99, limited series)
1,2-Berganza-s/Barberi-a/c 4.00

BATMAN: ORPHEUS RISING
DC Comics: Oct, 2001 - No. 5, Feb, 2002 ($2.50, limited series)
1-5-Intro. Orpheus; Simmons-s/Turner & Miki-a 3.00

BATMAN: OUTLAWS
DC Comics: 2000 - No. 3, 2000 ($4.95, limited series)
1-3-Moench-s/Gulacy-a 6.00

BATMAN: PENGUIN TRIUMPHANT (See Batman one-shots)

BATMAN/PREDATOR III: BLOOD TIES
DC Comics/Dark Horse Comics: Nov, 1997 - No. 4, Feb, 1998 ($1.95, lim. series)
1-4: Dixon-s/Damaggio-c/a 4.00
TPB-(1998, $7.95) r/#1-4 10.00

BATMAN/RA'S AL GHUL (See Year One:...)

BATMAN RETURNS MOVIE SPECIAL (See Batman one-shots)

BATMAN: RIDDLER-THE RIDDLE FACTORY (See Batman one-shots)

BATMAN: RUN, RIDDLER, RUN
DC Comics: 1992 - Book 3, 1992 ($4.95, limited series)
Book 1-3: Mark Badger-a & plot 6.00

BATMAN SCARECROW (See Year One:...)

BATMAN: SECRET FILES
DC Comics: Oct, 1997 ($4.95)
1-New origin-s and profiles 6.00

BATMAN: SECRETS
DC Comics: May, 2006 - No. 5, Sept, 2006 ($2.99, limited series)
1-5-Sam Kieth-s/a/c; Joker app. 3.00
TPB (2007, $12.99) r/series 13.00

BATMAN: SHADOW OF THE BAT
DC Comics: June, 1992 - No. 94, Feb, 2000 ($1.50/$1.75/$1.95/$1.99)
1-The Last Arkham-c/story begins; Alan Grant scripts in all 4.00
1-($2.50)-Deluxe edition polybagged w/poster, pop-up & book mark 5.00
2-7: 4-The Last Arkham ends. 7-Last $1.50-c 3.00
8-28: 14,15-Staton-a(p). 16-18-Knightfall tie-ins. 19-28-Knightquest tie-ins w/Azrael as Batman. 25-Silver ink-c; anniversary issue 3.00
29-($2.95, 52 pgs.)-KnightsEnd Pt. 2 4.00
30-72: 30-KnightsEnd Pt. 8. 31-(9/94)-Begin $1.95-c; Zero Hour. 32-(11/94). 33-Robin-c. 35-Troika-Pt.2. 43,44-Cat-Man & Catwoman-c. 48-Contagion Pt. 1; card insert. 49-Contagion Pt.7. 56,57,58-Poison Ivy-c/app. 62-Two-Face app. 69,70-Fate app. 3.00
35-($2.95)-Variant embossed-c 4.00
73,74,76-78: Cataclysm x-over pts. 1,9. 76-78-Orbik-c 3.00
75-($2.95) Mr. Freeze & Clayface app.; Orbik-c 4.00
79,81,82: 79-Begin $1.99-c; Orbik-c 3.00
80-($3.95) Flip book with Azrael #47 4.00
83-No Man's Land; intro. new Batgirl (Huntress) 15.00
84,85-No Man's Land 4.00
86-94: 87-Deodato-a. 90-Harris-c. 92-Superman app. 93-Joker and Harley app. 94-No Man's Land ends 3.00
#0 (10/94) Zero Hour; released between #31&32 3.00
#1,000,000 (11/98) 853rd Century x-over; Orbik-c 3.00
Annual 1-5 ('93-'97 $2.95-$3.95, 68 pgs.): 3-Year One story; Poison Ivy app. 4-Legends of the Dead Earth story; Starman cameo. 5-Pulp Heroes story; Poison Ivy app. 4.00

BATMAN '66 (Characters and likenesses based on the 1966 television series)
DC Comics: Sept, 2013 - Present ($3.99, printings of stories that first appeared online)
1-Jeff Parker-s/Jonathan Case-a/Mike Allred-c; Riddler & Catwoman app. 4.00
1-Variant-c by Jonathan Case 6.00
2-9: 2-Penguin & Mr. Freeze app.; Templeton-a. 3-Joker app. 5-Batgirl app. 4.00

BATMAN: SON OF THE DEMON (Also see Batman #655-658 and Batman Hardcovers)
DC Comics: 2006 ($5.99, reprints the 1987 HC in comic book format)
nn-Talia has Batman's son; Mike W. Barr-s/Jerry Bingham-a; new Andy Kubert-c 6.00

BATMAN-SPAWN: WAR DEVIL (See Batman one-shots)

BATMAN SPECTACULAR (See DC Special Series No. 15)

BATMAN: STREETS OF GOTHAM (Follows Batman: Battle For The Cowl series)
DC Comics: Aug, 2009 - No. 21, May, 2011 ($3.99$2.99)
1-18: 1-Dini-s/Nguyen-a; back-up Manhunter feature; Jeanty-a. 10,11-Zsasz app. 4.00
19-21-($2.99) 19-Joker app. 3.00
...- Hush Money HC (2010, $19.99) r/#1-4, Detective #852 and Batman #685 20.00
...- Hush Money SC (2011, $14.99) r/#1-4, Detective #852 and Batman #685 15.00
...- Leviathan HC (2010, $19.99) r/#5-11 20.00
...- The House of Hush HC (2011, $22.99) r/#12-14,16-21 23.00

BATMAN STRIKES!, THE (Based on the 2004 animated series)
DC Comics: Nov, 2004 - No. 50, Dec, 2008 ($2.25)
1,2,4-50: 1,11-Penguin app. 2-Man-Bat app. 4-Bane app. 9-Joker app. 18-Batgirl debut. 29-Robin debuts. 32,33-Cal Ripken 8-pg. insert. 44-Superman app. 3.00
1-Free Comic Book Day edition (6/05) Penguin app. 3.00
3-($2.95) Joker-c/app.; Catwoman & Wonder Woman-r from Advs. in the DCU 4.00
Jam Packed Action (2005, $7.99, digest) adaptations of two TV episodes 8.00
... Vol. 1: Crime Time (2005, $6.99, digest) r/#1-5 7.00
... Vol. 2: In Darkest Knight (2005, $6.99, digest) r/#6-10 7.00

BATMAN/ SUPERMAN
DC Comics: Aug, 2013 - Present ($3.99)
1-4-Greg Pak-s/Jae Lee-a/c; Catwoman & Wonder Woman app. 4.00
3.1 (11/13, $2.99, regular cover) 3.00
3.1 (11/13, $3.99, 3-D cover) "Doomsday #1" on cover; Booth-a; Zod app. 6.00
5-7-Booth-a; reads sideways; Mongul app. 4.00
8,9-First Contact x-over with Worlds' Finest #20,21; Power Girl & Huntress app.; Lee-a 4.00
Annual 1 (5/14, $5.99) Supergirl, Krypto, Cyborg, Batgirl, Red Hood app.; Jae Lee-c 6.00

BATMAN/ SUPERMAN/WONDER WOMAN: TRINITY
DC Comics: 2003 - No. 3, 2003 ($6.95, limited series, squarebound)
1-3-Matt Wagner-s/a/c. 1-Ra's al Ghul & Bizarro app. 7.00
HC (2004, $24.95, with dust-jacket) r/series; intro. by Brad Meltzer 30.00
SC (2004, $17.99) r/series; intro. by Brad Meltzer 18.00

BATMAN: SWORD OF AZRAEL (Also see Azrael & Batman #488,489)

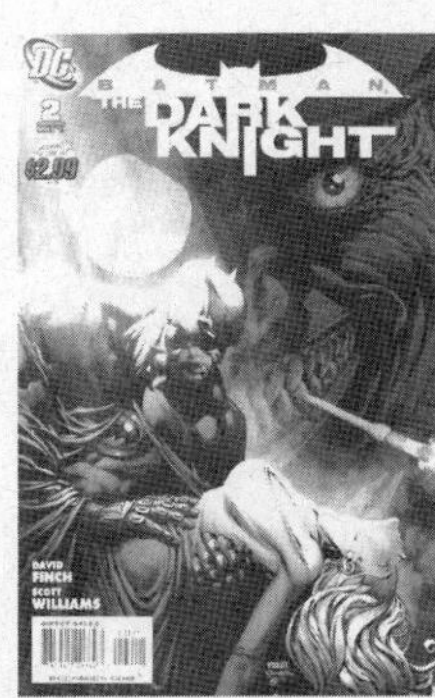

Batman: The Dark Knight #2 © DC

Batman: The Monster Men #1 © DC

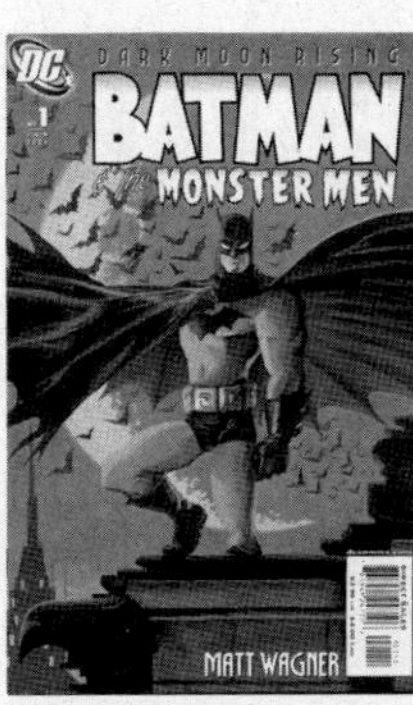

Batman: The Return #1 © DC

GD 2.0 | VG 4.0 | FN 6.0 | VF 8.0 | VF/NM 9.0 | NM- 9.2

GD 2.0 | VG 4.0 | FN 6.0 | VF 8.0 | VF/NM 9.0 | NM- 9.2

DC Comics: Oct, 1992 - No. 4, Jan, 1993 ($1.75, limited series)
1-Wraparound gatefold-c; Quesada-c/a(p) in all; 1st app. Azrael 2 4 6 9 12 15
2-4: 4-Cont'd in Batman #488 1 2 3 5 6 8
Silver Edition 1-4 (1993, $1.95)-Reprints #1-4 3.00
Trade Paperback (1993, $9.95)-Reprints #1-4 12.00
Trade Paperback Gold Edition 18.00

BATMAN/ TARZAN: CLAWS OF THE CAT-WOMAN
Dark Horse Comics/DC Comics: Sept, 1999 - No. 4, Dec, 1999 ($2.95, limited series)
1-4: Marz-s/Kordey-a 3.00

BATMAN: TENSES
DC Comics: 2003 - No. 2, 2003 ($6.95, limited series)
1,2-Joe Casey-s/Cully Hamner-a; Bruce Wayne's first year back in Gotham 7.00

BATMAN: THE ANKH
DC Comics: 2002 - No. 2, 2002 ($5.95, limited series)
1,2-Dixon-s/Van Fleet-a 6.00

BATMAN: THE BRAVE AND THE BOLD (Based on the 2008 animated series)
DC Comics: Mar, 2009 - No. 22, Dec, 2010 ($2.50/$2.99)
1-18: 1-Power Girl app. 4-Sugar & Spike cameo. 7-Doom Patrol app. 9-Catman app. 3.00
19-22-($2.99) Cyborg Superman and the Green Lantern Corps app. 22-Aquaman app. 3.00
TPB (2009, $12.99) r/#1-6 13.00
...: Emerald Knight TPB (2011, $12.99) r/#13,14,16,18,19,21 13.00
...: The Fearsome Fangs Strike Again TPB (2010, $12.99) r/#7-12 13.00

BATMAN: THE BRAVE AND THE BOLD (Titled "All New Batman: Brave & the Bold" for #1-13)
DC Comics: Jan, 2011 - No. 16, Apr, 2012 ($2.99)
1-16: 1-Superman. 4-Wonder Woman app. 8-Aquaman app. 9-Hawkman app. 3.00

BATMAN: THE CULT
DC Comics: 1988 - No. 4, Nov, 1988 ($3.50, deluxe limited series)
1-Wrightson-a/painted-c in all 1 2 3 5 6 8
2-4 6.00
Trade Paperback (1991, $14.95)-New Wrightson-c; Starlin intro. 25.00
Trade Paperback (2009, $19.99) 20.00

BATMAN: THE DARK KNIGHT
DC Comics: Jan, 2011 - No. 5, Oct, 2011 ($3.99/$2.99)
1-David Finch-s/a; Penguin & Killer Croc app.; covers by Finch and Clarke 4.00
2-5-($2.99) Demon app. 3.00

BATMAN: THE DARK KNIGHT (DC New 52)
DC Comics: Nov, 2011 - Present ($2.99)
1-29: 1-Jenkins & Finch-s/Finch-a/c; White Rabbit debut. 3-Flash app. 5,6-Superman app. 6,7-Bane app. 9-Night of the Owls. 22-25-Maleev-a. 28-Van Sciver-a/c 3.00
23.1, 23.2, 23.3, 23.4 (11/13, $2.99, regular covers) 3.00
23.1 (11/13, $3.99, 3-D cover) "Ventriloquist #1" on cover; Simone-s/Santacruz-a 6.00
23.2 (11/13, $3.99, 3-D cover) "Mr. Freeze #1" on cover; Gray & Palmiotti-s 5.00
23.3 (11/13, $3.99, 3-D cover) "Clayface#1" on cover; Richards-a 5.00
23.4 (11/13, $3.99, 3-D cover) "Joker's Daughter #1" on cover; origin story; Jeanty-a 12.00
#0 (11/12, $2.99) Hurwitz-s/Suayan & Ryp-a; flashback to aftermath of parents' murder 3.00
Annual 1 (7/13, $4.99) Hurwitz-s/Kudranski-a/Maleev-c; Scarecrow, Penguin Mad Hatter 5.00

BATMAN: THE DARK KNIGHT RETURNS (Also see Dark Knight Strikes Again)
DC Comics: Mar, 1986 - No. 4, 1986 ($2.95, squarebound, limited series)
1-Miller story & c/a(p); set in the future 5 10 15 35 63 90
1,2-2nd & 3rd printings, 3-2nd printing 1 3 4 6 8 10
2-Carrie Kelley becomes 1st female Robin 3 6 9 19 30 40
3-Death of Joker; Superman app. 3 6 9 14 20 25
4-Death of Alfred; Superman app. 3 6 9 14 20 25
Hardcover, signed & numbered edition ($40.00)(4000 copies) 275.00
Hardcover, trade edition 60.00
Softcover, trade edition (1st printing only) 2 4 6 11 16 20
Softcover, trade edition (2nd thru 8th printings) 2 4 6 8 10 12
10th Anniv. Slipcase set ('96, $100.00): Signed & numbered hard-c edition (10,000 copies), sketchbook, copy of script for #1, 2 color prints 135.00
10th Anniv. Hardcover ('96, $45.00) 50.00
10th Anniv. Softcover ('97, $14.95) 18.00
Hardcover 2nd printing ('02, $24.95) with 3 1/4" tall partial dustjacket 25.00
NOTE: *The #2 second printings can be identified by matching the grey background colors on the inside front cover and facing page. The inside front cover of the second printing has a dark grey background which does not match the lighter grey of the facing page. On the true 1st printings, the backgrounds are both light grey. All other issues are clearly marked.*

BATMAN: THE DOOM THAT CAME TO GOTHAM
DC Comics: 2000 - No. 3, 2001 ($4.95, limited series)
1-3-Elseworlds; Mignola-c/s; Nixey-a; Etrigan app. 6.00

BATMAN: THE KILLING JOKE (See Batman one-shots)

BATMAN: THE LONG HALLOWEEN
DC Comics: Oct, 1996 - No. 13, Oct, 1997 ($2.95/$4.95, limited series)
1-($4.95)-Loeb-s/Sale-c/a in all 1 2 3 5 6 8
2-5($2.95): 2-Solomon Grundy-c/app. 3-Joker-c/app., Catwoman, Poison Ivy app. 6.00
6-10: 6-Poison Ivy-c. 7-Riddler-c/app. 5.00
11,12 4.00
13-($4.95, 48 pgs.)-Killer revelations 6.00
Special Edition (Halloween Comic Fest 2013) (12/13, free giveaway) r/#1 3.00
Absolute Batman: The Long Halloween (2007, $75.00, oversized HC) r/series; interviews with the creators; Sale sketch pages; action figure line; unpubbed 4-page sequence 75.00
HC-($29.95) r/series 30.00
SC-($19.95) 20.00

BATMAN: THE MAD MONK ("Batman & the Mad Monk" on cover)
DC Comics: Oct, 2006 - No. 6, Mar, 2007 ($3.50, limited series)
1-6-Matt Wagner-s/a/c. 1-Catwoman app. 3.50
TPB (2007, $14.99) r/#1-6 15.00

BATMAN: THE MONSTER MEN ("Batman & the Monster Men" on cover)
DC Comics: Jan, 2006 - No. 6, June, 2006 ($2.99, limited series)
1-6-Matt Wagner-s/a/c 3.00
TPB (2006, $14.99) r/#1-6 15.00

BATMAN: THE OFFICIAL COMIC ADAPTATION OF THE WARNER BROS. MOTION PICTURE
(See Batman one-shots)

BATMAN: THE RETURN
DC Comics: Jan, 2011 ($4.99, one-shot)
1-Morrison-s/Finch-a; covers by Finch & Ha; costume design sketch art; script pages 5.00

BATMAN: THE RETURN OF BRUCE WAYNE (Follows Batman's "death" in Final Crisis #6)
DC Comics: Early Jul, 2010 - No. 6, Dec, 2010 ($3.99, limited series)
1-6-Bruce Wayne's time travels; Morrison-s/Andy Kubert-c. 1-Sprouse-a. 4-Jeanty-a 4.00
1-Second & third printings; 4.00
1-6-Variant covers: 1-Sprouse. 2-Irving. 3-Paquette. 4-Jeanty. 5-Sook. 6-Garbett 8.00
... - The Deluxe Edition HC (2011, $29.99) r/#1-6; sketch pages 30.00

BATMAN: THE ULTIMATE EVIL
DC Comics: 1995 ($5.95, limited series, prestige format)
1,2-Barrett, Jr. adaptation of Vachss novel. 6.00

BATMAN: THE WIDENING GYRE
DC Comics: Oct, 2009 - No. 6, Sept, 2010 ($3.99/$2.99/$4.99, limited series)
1-($3.99) Kevin Smith-s/Walt Flanagan-a; debut Baphomet; Demon app.; Sienkiewicz-c 4.00
1-5-Variant covers by Gene Ha 8.00
2-5-($2.99) 2-Silver St. Cloud returns. 5-Catwoman app. 3.00
6-($4.99) Joker, Deadshot & Catwoman app. 5.00
6-Variant cover by Gene Ha 10.00
HC (2010, $19.99, dj) r/#1-6; variant covers; afterword by Kevin Smith 20.00

BATMAN 3-D (Also see 3-D Batman)
DC Comics: 1990 ($9.95, w/glasses, 8-1/8x10-3/4")
nn-Byrne-a/scripts; Riddler, Joker, Penguin & Two-Face app. plus r/1953 3-D Batman; pin-ups by many artists 2 4 6 8 10 12

BATMAN: TOYMAN
DC Comics: Nov, 1998 - No. 4, Feb, 1999 ($2.25, limited series)
1-4-Hama-s 3.00

BATMAN: TURNING POINTS
DC Comics: Jan, 2001 - No. 5, Jan, 2001 ($2.50, weekly limited series)
1-5: 2-Giella-a. 3-Kubert-c/Giordano-a. 4-Chaykin-c/Brent Anderson-a. 5-Pope-c/a 3.00
TPB (2007, $14.99) r/#1-5 15.00

BATMAN: TWO-FACE-CRIME AND PUNISHMENT (See Batman one-shots)

BATMAN: TWO-FACE STRIKES TWICE
DC Comics: 1993 - No. 2, 1993 ($4.95, 52 pgs.)
1,2-Flip book format w/Staton-a (G.A. side) 6.00

BATMAN UNSEEN
DC Comics: Early Dec, 2009 - No. 5, Feb, 2010 ($2.99, limited series)
1-5-Doug Moench-s/Kelley Jones-a/c. Black Mask app. 3.00
SC (2010, $14.99) r/#1-5 15.00

Battle #9 © MAR

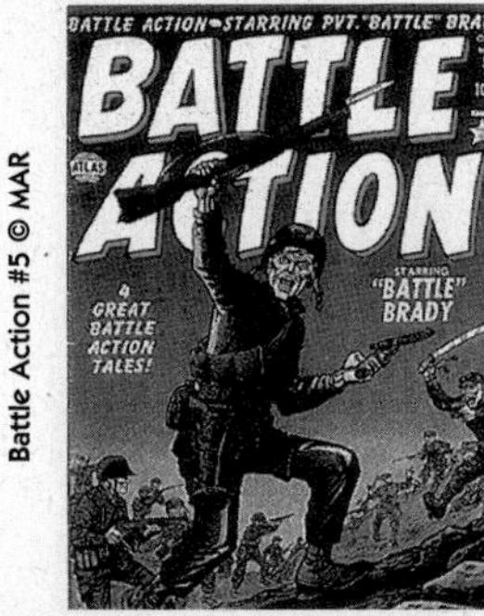

Battle Action #5 © MAR

Battle Cry #11 © Stanmor

GD VG FN VF VF/NM NM-
2.0 4.0 6.0 8.0 9.0 9.2

GD VG FN VF VF/NM NM-
2.0 4.0 6.0 8.0 9.0 9.2

BATMAN: VENGEANCE OF BANE (Also see Batman #491)
DC Comics: Jan, 1993; 1995 ($2.50, 68 pgs.)
... Special 1 - Origin & 1st app. Bane; Dixon-s/Nolan & Barreto-a/Fabry-c
4 8 12 27 44 60
... Special 1 (2nd printing) 1 3 4 6 8 10
.... II nn (1995, $3.95)-sequel; Dixon-s/Nolan & Barreto-a/Fabry-c
2 4 6 9 12 15

BATMAN VERSUS PREDATOR
DC Comics/Dark Horse Comics: 1991 - No. 3, 1992 ($4.95/$1.95, limited series) (1st DC/Dark Horse x-over)
1 (Prestige format, $4.95)-1 & 3 contain 8 Batman/Predator trading cards; Andy & Adam Kubert-a; Suydam painted-c 1 2 3 5 6 8
1-3 (Regular format, $1.95)-No trading cards 4.00
2,3-(Prestige)-2-Extra pin-ups inside; Suydam-c 6.00
TPB (1993, $5.95, 132 pgs.)-r/#1-3 w/new introductions & forward plus new wraparound-c by Dave Gibbons 1 3 4 6 8 10

BATMAN VERSUS PREDATOR II: BLOODMATCH
DC Comics: Late 1994 - No. 4, 1995 ($2.50, limited series)
1-4-Huntress app.; Moench scripts; Gulacy-a 4.00
TPB (1995, $6.95)-r/#1-4 1 3 4 6 8 10

BATMAN VS. THE INCREDIBLE HULK (See DC Special Series No. 27)

BATMAN: WAR ON CRIME
DC Comics: Nov, 1999 ($9.95, treasury size, one-shot)
nn-Painted art by Alex Ross; story by Alex Ross and Paul Dini 10.00

BATMAN/ WILDCAT
DC Comics: Apr, 1997 - No. 3, June, 1997 ($2.25, mini-series)
1-3: Dixon/Smith-s: 1-Killer Croc app. 3.00

BATMAN: YEAR 100
DC Comics: 2006 - No. 4, 2006 ($5.99, squarebound, limited series)
1-4-Paul Pope-s/a/c 6.00
TPB (2007, $19.99) r/series 20.00

BAT MASTERSON (TV) (Also see Tim Holt #28)
Dell Publishing Co.: Aug-Oct, 1959; Feb-Apr, 1960 - No. 9, Nov-Jan, 1961-62
Four Color 1013 (#1) (8-10/59) 10 20 30 66 138 210
2-9: Gene Barry photo-c on all. 2,3,6-Two different back-c exist; variants have a comic strip on the back-c 6 12 18 38 69 100

BATS (See Tales Calculated to Drive You Bats)

BATS, CATS & CADILLACS
Now Comics: Oct, 1990 - No. 2, Nov, 1990 ($1.75)
1,2: 1-Gustovich-a(i); Snyder-c 3.00

BAT-THING
DC Comics (Amalgam): June, 1997 ($1.95, one-shot)
1-Hama-s/Damaggio & Sienkiewicz-a 3.00

BATTLE
Marvel/Atlas Comics(FPI #1-62/ Male #63 on): Mar, 1951 - No. 70, Jun, 1960
1 42 84 126 265 445 625
2 22 44 66 132 216 300
3-10: 4-1st Buck Pvt. O'Toole. 10-Pakula-a 18 36 54 105 165 225
11-20: 11-Check-a. 17-Classic Hitler story 15 30 45 86 133 180
21,23-Krigstein-a 15 30 45 90 140 190
22,24-36: 32-Tuska-a. 36-Everett-a 14 28 42 82 121 160
37-Kubert-a (Last precode, 2/55) 15 30 45 84 127 170
38-40,42-48 14 28 42 76 108 140
41,49: 41-Kubert/Moskowitz-a. 49-Davis-a 14 28 42 80 115 150
50-54,56-58: 56-Colan-a; Ayers-a 13 26 39 74 105 135
55-Williamson-a (5 pgs.) 14 28 42 80 115 150
59-Torres-a 14 28 42 76 108 140
60-62: 60,62-Combat Kelly app. 61-Combat Casey app.
13 26 39 74 105 135
63-Ditko-a 18 36 54 105 165 225
64-66-Kirby-a. 66-Davis-a; has story of Fidel Castro in pre-Communism days (an admiring profile) 20 40 60 117 189 260
67,68: 67-Williamson/Crandall-a (4 pgs.); Kirby, Davis-a. 68-Kirby/Williamson-a (4 pgs.); Kirby/Ditko-a 20 40 60 118 192 265
69,70: 69-Kirby-a. 70-Kirby/Ditko-a 20 40 60 117 189 260
NOTE: ***Andru** a-37. **Berg** a-8, 38, 14, 60-62. **Colan** a-19, 33, 43, 55. **Everett** a-36, 50, 70; c-56, 57. **Heath** a-6, 9, 13, 31, 69; c-6, 9, 12, 26, 35, 37. **Kirby** c-64-69. **Maneely** a-4, 6, 7, 31, 61; c-4, 22, 27, 33, 43, 48, 59, 61. **Orlando** a-47. **Powell** a-53, 55. **Reinman** a-4, 8-10, 14, 26, 32, 48. **Robinson** a-9, 39. **Romita** a-14, 26. **Severin** a-28, 32-34, 66-69; c-36, 50, 55. **Sinnott** a-33, 37, 63, 66. **Whitney** s-10. **Woodbridge** a-52, 55.*

BATTLE ACTION
Atlas Comics (NPI): Feb, 1952 - No. 12, 5/53; No. 13, 10/54 - No. 30, 8/57
1-Pakula-a 33 66 99 194 317 440
2 18 36 54 103 162 220
3,4,6,7,9,10: 6-Robinson-c/a. 7-Partial nudity 14 28 42 78 112 145
5-Used in **POP**, pg. 93,94 14 28 42 78 112 145
8-Krigstein-a 14 28 42 80 115 150
11-15 (Last precode, 2/55) 13 26 39 74 105 135
16-30: 20-Romita-a. 22-Pakula-a. 27,30-Torres-a 12 24 36 67 94 120
NOTE: *Battle Brady app. 5-7, 10-12. **Berg** a-3. **Check** a-11. **Everett** a-7; c-13, 25. **Heath** a-3, 8, 18; c-3,15, 18, 21. **Maneely** a-1; c-5. **Reinman** a-1, 2, 20. **Robinson** a-6, 7; c-6. **Shores** a-7(2), 12, 20; c-11. **Sinnott** a-3, 27. **Woodbridge** a-28, 30.*

BATTLE ATTACK
Stanmor Publications: Oct, 1952 - No. 8, Dec, 1955
1 15 30 45 83 124 165
2 9 18 27 50 65 80
3-8: 3-Hollingsworth-a 8 16 24 44 57 70

BATTLEAXES
DC Comics (Vertigo): May, 2000 - No. 4, Aug, 2000 ($2.50, limited series)
1-4: Terry LaBan-s/Alex Horley-a 3.00

BATTLE BEASTS
Blackthorne Publishing: Feb, 1988 - No. 4, 1988 ($1.50/$1.75, B&W/color)
1-4: 1-3- (B&W)-Based on Hasbro toys. 4-Color 3.00

BATTLE BEASTS
IDW Publishing: Jul, 2012 - No. 4, Oct, 2012 ($3.99, limited series)
1-4-Curnow-s/Schiti-a; 2 covers on each 4.00

BATTLE BRADY (Formerly Men in Action No. 1-9; see 3-D Action)
Atlas Comics (IPC): No. 10, Jan, 1953 - No. 14, June, 1953
10: 10-12-Syd Shores-c 19 38 57 111 176 240
11-Used in **POP**, pg. 95 plus B&W & color illos 14 28 42 78 112 145
12-14 12 24 36 69 97 125

BATTLE CHASERS
Image Comics (Cliffhanger): Apr, 1998 - No. 4, Dec, 1998;
DC Comics (Cliffhanger): No. 5, May, 1999 - No. 8, May, 2001 ($2.50)
Image Comics: No. 9, Sept, 2001 ($3.50)
Prelude (2/98) 1 3 4 6 8 10
Prelude Gold Ed. 1 3 4 6 8 10
1-Madureira & Sharrieff-s/Madureira-a(p)/Charest-c 1 2 3 5 7 9
1-American Ent. Ed. w/"racy" cover 1 3 4 6 8 10
1-Gold Edition 9.00
1-Chromium cover 20.00
1-2nd printing 3.00
2 5.00
2-Dynamic Forces BattleChrome cover 2 4 6 8 10 12
3-Red Monika cover by Madureira 4.00
4-8: 4-Four covers. 6-Back-up by Adam Warren-s/a. 7-Three covers (Madureira, Ramos, Campbell) 3.00
9-($3.50, Image) Flip cover/story by Adam Warren 4.00
...: A Gathering of Heroes HC ('99, $24.95) r/#1-5, Prelude, Frank Frazetta Fantasy Ill.; cover gallery 25.00
...: A Gathering of Heroes SC ('99, $14.95) 15.00
...Collected Edition 1,2 (11/98, 5/99, $5.95) 1-r/#1,2. 2-r/#3,4 6.00

BATTLE CLASSICS (See Cancelled Comic Cavalcade)
DC Comics: Sept-Oct, 1978 (44 pgs.)
1-Kubert-r; new Kubert-c 2 4 6 8 10 12

BATTLE CRY
Stanmor Publications: 1952 (May) - No. 20, Sept, 1955
1 18 36 54 105 165 225
2-(7/52) 11 22 33 62 86 110
3,5-10: 8-Pvt. Ike begins, ends #13,17 9 18 27 52 69 85
4-Classic E.C. swipe 10 20 30 58 79 100
11-20 9 18 27 47 61 75
NOTE: ***Hollingsworth** a-9; c-20.*

BATTLEFIELD (War Adventures on the...)
Atlas Comics (ACI): April, 1952 - No. 11, May, 1953
1-Pakula, Reinman-a 27 54 81 158 259 360
2-5: 2-Heath, Maneely, Pakula, Reinman-a 15 30 45 86 133 180
6-11 13 26 39 74 105 135

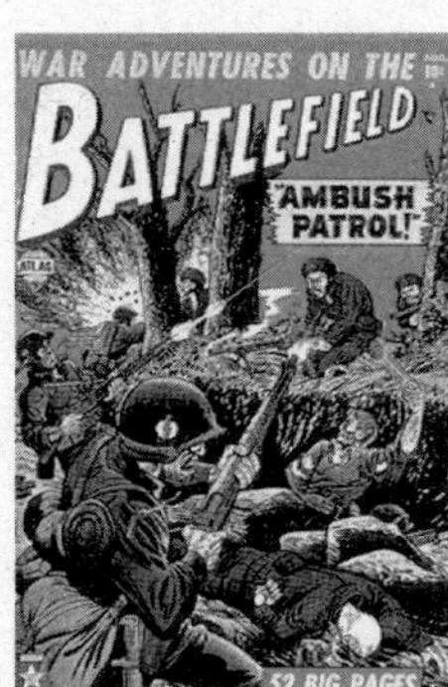

Battlefield #3 © MAR

Battlefields #7 © Spitfire Prods.

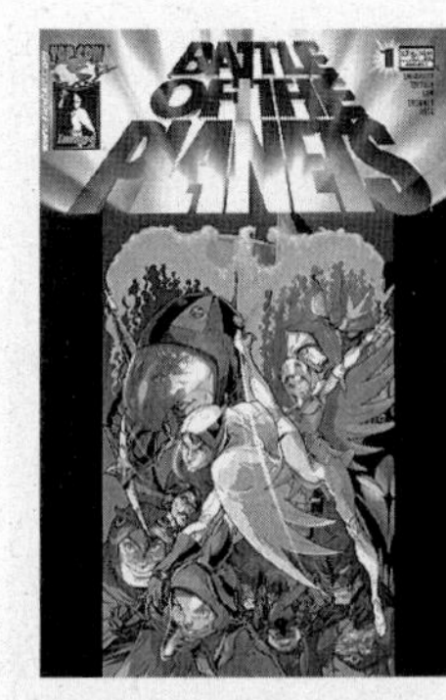
Battle of the Planets #1 © TCOW

NOTE: *Colan a-11. Everett a-8. Heath a-1, 2, 5p,7; c-2, 8, 9, 11. Ravielli a-11.*

BATTLEFIELD ACTION (Formerly Foreign Intrigues)
Charlton Comics: No. 16, Nov, 1957 - No. 62, 2-3/66; No. 63, 7/80 - No. 89, 11/84

	GD 2.0	VG 4.0	FN 6.0	VF 8.0	VF/NM 9.0	NM- 9.2
V2#16	9	18	27	47	61	75
17,20-30: 29-D-Day story	6	12	18	28	34	40
18,19-Check-a (2 stories in #18)	3	6	9	21	33	45
31-34,36-62(1966): 55,61-Hitler app.	3	6	9	16	23	30
35-Hitler-c	3	6	9	19	30	40
63-80(1983-84)						5.00
81-83,85-89 (Low print run)	1	2	3	4	5	7
84-Kirby reprints; 3 stories	1	3	4	6	8	10

NOTE: *Montes/Bache a-43, 55, 62. Glanzman a-87r.*

BATTLEFIELDS
Dynamite Entertainment: 2008 - No. 9, 2010 ($3.50, limited series then numbered issues)

	NM- 9.2
...: Dear Billy 1-3 ('09 - No. 3, '09, $3.50) Ennis-s/Snejbjerg-a/Cassaday-c.1-Leach var-c	3.50
...: Happy Valley 1-3 ('09 - No. 3, '09, $3.50) Ennis-s/Holden-a/Leach-c	3.50
...: The Night Witches 1-3 ('08 - No. 3, '09, $3.50) Ennis-s/Braun-a/Cassaday-c; Russian female pilots in WW2. 1-Leach var-c	3.50
...: The Tankies 1-3 ('09 - No. 3, '09, $3.50) Ennis-s/Ezquerra-a/Cassaday-c.1-Leach var-c	3.50
4-9: 4-6-Ezquerra-a/Leach-c. 7-9-Sequel to "The Night Witches"; Braun-a	3.50

BATTLEFIELDS (Volume 2)
Dynamite Entertainment: 2012 - No. 6, 2013 ($3.99, limited series)

	NM- 9.2
1-6: 1-3-Ennis-s/Ezquerra-a/Leach-c. 4-6-Braun-a	4.00

BATTLE FIRE
Aragon Magazine/Stanmor Publications: Apr, 1955 - No. 7, 1955

	GD 2.0	VG 4.0	FN 6.0	VF 8.0	VF/NM 9.0	NM- 9.2
1	14	28	42	80	115	150
2-(6/55)	9	18	27	47	61	75
3-7	8	16	24	42	54	65

BATTLE FOR A THREE DIMENSIONAL WORLD
3D Cosmic Publications: May, 1983 (20 pgs., slick paper w/stiff-c, $3.00)

	GD 2.0	VG 4.0	FN 6.0	VF 8.0	VF/NM 9.0	NM- 9.2
nn-Kirby c/a in 3-D; shows history of 3-D	2	4	6	8	11	14

BATTLEFORCE
Blackthorne Publishing: Nov, 1987 - No. 2, 1988 ($1.75, color/B&W)

	NM- 9.2
1,2: Based on game. 1-In color. 2-B&W	3.00

BATTLE FOR INDEPENDENTS, THE (Also See Cyblade/Shi & Shi/Cyblade: The Battle For Independents)
Image Comics (Top Cow Productions)/Crusade Comics: 1995 ($29.95)

	GD 2.0	VG 4.0	FN 6.0	VF 8.0	VF/NM 9.0	NM- 9.2
nn-Boxed set of all editions of Shi/Cyblade & Cyblade/Shi plus new variant	3	6	9	19	30	40

BATTLE FOR THE PLANET OF THE APES (See Power Record Comics)

BATTLEFRONT
Atlas Comics (PPI): June, 1952 - No. 48, Aug, 1957

	GD 2.0	VG 4.0	FN 6.0	VF 8.0	VF/NM 9.0	NM- 9.2
1-Heath-c	39	78	117	231	378	525
2-Robinson-a(4)	20	40	60	114	182	250
3-5-Robinson-a	15	30	45	90	140	190
6-10: Combat Kelly in No. 6-10. 6-Romita-a	14	28	42	82	121	160
11-22,24-28: 14,16-Battle Brady app. 22-Teddy Roosevelt & His Rough Riders story. 28-Last pre-code (2/55)	14	28	42	76	108	140
23,43-Check-a	14	28	42	72	112	145
29-39,41,44-47	12	24	36	69	97	125
40,42-Williamson-a	14	28	42	78	112	145
48-Crandall-a	13	26	39	74	105	135

NOTE: *Ayers a-18, 19, 32, 35. Berg a-44. Colan a-21, 22, 32, 33, 35, 38, 40, 42, 43, 45. Drucker a-28, 29. Everett a-44. Heath c-23, 26, 27, 29, 32. Maneely a-21-23, 26; c-2, 7, 13, 22, 34, 35, 41. Morisi a-42. Morrow a-41.Orlando a-47. Powell a-19, 21, 25, 29, 32, 40, 47. Robinson a-1-3, 4&5(4); c-4, 5. Robert Sale a-19. Severin a-32; c-40, 42, 45. Sinnott a-26, 45, 48. Woodbridge a-45, 46.*

BATTLEFRONT
Standard Comics: No. 5, June, 1952

	GD 2.0	VG 4.0	FN 6.0	VF 8.0	VF/NM 9.0	NM- 9.2
5-Toth-a	15	30	45	84	127	170

BATTLE GODS: WARRIORS OF THE CHAAK
Dark Horse Comics: Apr, 2000 - No. 4, July, 2000 ($2.95)

	NM- 9.2
1-4-Francisco Ruiz Velasco-s/a	3.00

BATTLE GROUND
Atlas Comics (OMC): Sept, 1954 - No. 20, Sept, 1957

	GD 2.0	VG 4.0	FN 6.0	VF 8.0	VF/NM 9.0	NM- 9.2
1	26	52	78	154	252	350
2-Jack Katz-a (11/54)	15	30	45	85	130	175
3,4: 3-Jack Katz-a. 4-Last precode (3/55)	14	28	42	76	108	140
5-8,10 (3/56)	12	24	36	69	97	125
9,11,13,18: 9-Krigstein-a. 11,13,18-Williamson-a in each	14	28	42	78	112	145
12,15-17,19,20	11	22	33	64	90	115
14-Kirby-a	15	30	45	84	127	170

NOTE: *Ayers a-4, 13, 16. Colan a-3, 11, 13. Drucker a-7, 12, 13, 20. Heath c-2, 3, 5, 7, 13. Maneely a-3, 14, 19; c-1, 18, 19. Orlando a-17. Pakula a-11. Reinman a-2. Severin a-4, 5, 12, 19. c-20. Sinnott a-7, 16. Tuska a-11.*

BATTLE HEROES
Stanley Publications: Sept, 1966 - No. 2, Nov, 1966 (25¢, squarebound giants)

	GD 2.0	VG 4.0	FN 6.0	VF 8.0	VF/NM 9.0	NM- 9.2
1	4	8	12	23	37	50
2	3	6	9	17	26	35

BATTLE HYMN
Image Comics: Jan, 2005 - No. 5, Oct, 2005 ($2.95/$2.99, limited series)

	NM- 9.2
1-5-WW2 super team; B. Clay Moore-s/Jeremy Haun-a; flip cover on #1-4	3.00

BATTLE OF THE BULGE (See Movie Classics)

BATTLE OF THE PLANETS (Based on syndicated cartoon by Sandy Frank)
Gold Key/Whitman No. 6 on: 6/79 - No. 10, 12/80

	GD 2.0	VG 4.0	FN 6.0	VF 8.0	VF/NM 9.0	NM- 9.2
1: Mortimer a-1-4,7-10	5	10	15	31	53	75
2-6,10	3	6	9	20	31	42
7-Low print run	5	10	15	34	60	85
8,9-Low print run: 8(11/80). 9-(3-pack only?)	5	10	15	31	53	75

BATTLE OF THE PLANETS (Also see Thundercats/...)
Image Comics (Top Cow): Aug, 2002 - No. 12, Sept, 2003 ($2.95/$2.99)

	NM- 9.2
1-($2.95) Alex Ross-c & art director; Tortosa-a(p); re-intro. G-Force	3.00
1-($5.95) Holofoil-c by Ross	6.00
2-11-($2.99) Ross-c on all	3.00
12-($4.99)	5.00
#1/2 (7/03, $2.99) Benitez-c; Alex Ross sketch pages	3.00
... Battle Book 1 (5/03, $4.99) background info on characters, equipment, stories	5.00
... : Jason 1 (7/03, $4.99) Ross-c; Erwin David-a; preview of Tomb Raider: Epiphany	5.00
... : Mark 1 (5/03, $4.99) Ross-c; Erwin David-a; preview of BotP: Jason	5.00
.../Thundercats 1 (Image/WildStorm, 5/03, $4.99) 2 covers by Ross & Campbell	5.00
.../Witchblade 1 (2/03, $5.95) Ross-c; Christina and Jo Chen-a	6.00
Vol. 1: Trial By Fire (2003, $7.99) r/#1-3	8.00
Vol. 2: Blood Red Sky (9/03, $16.95) r/#4-9	17.00
Vol. 3: Destroy All Monsters (11/03, $19.95) r/#10-12, ...: Jason, ...: Mark, .../Witchblade	20.00
Vol. 1: Digest (1/04, $9.99, 7-3/8x5", B&W) r/#1-9 & ...: Mark	10.00
Vol. 2: Digest (8/04, $9.99, B&W) r/#10-12, ...: Jason, ...: Manga #1-3, .../Witchblade	10.00

BATTLE OF THE PLANETS: MANGA
Image Comics (Top Cow): Nov, 2003 - No. 3, Jan, 2004 ($2.99, B&W)

	NM- 9.2
1-3-Edwin David-a/David Wohl-s; previews for Wanted & Tomb Raider #35	3.00

BATTLE OF THE PLANETS: PRINCESS
Image Comics (Top Cow): Nov, 2004 - No. 6, May, 2005 ($2.99, B&W, limited series)

	NM- 9.2
1-6-Tortosa-a/Wohl-s. 1-Ross-c. 2-Tortosa-c	3.00

BATTLE POPE
Image Comics: June, 2005 - No. 14, Apr, 2007 ($2.99/$3.50, reprints 2000 B&W series in color)

	NM- 9.2
1-5-Kirkman-s/Moore-a	3.50
6-10,12-14-($3.50) 14-Wedding	3.50
11-($4.99) Christmas issue	5.00
... Vol. 1: Genesis TPB (2006, $12.95) r/#1-4; sketch pages	13.00
... Vol. 2: Mayhem TPB (2006, $12.99) r/#5-8; sketch pages	13.00
... Vol. 3: Pillow Talk TPB (2007, $12.99) r/#9-11; sketch pages	13.00

BATTLER BRITTON (British comics character who debuted in 1956)
DC Comics (WildStorm): Sept, 2006 - No. 5, Jan, 2007 ($2.99, limited series)

	NM- 9.2
1-5-WWII fighter pilots; Garth Ennis-s/Colin Wilson-a	3.00
TPB (2007, $19.99) r/#1-5; background of the character's British origins in the 1950s	20.00

BATTLE REPORT
Ajax/Farrell Publications: Aug, 1952 - No. 6, June, 1953

	GD 2.0	VG 4.0	FN 6.0	VF 8.0	VF/NM 9.0	NM- 9.2
1	14	28	42	76	108	140
2-6	8	16	24	44	57	70

BATTLE SCARS
Marvel Comics: Jan, 2012 - No. 6, Jun, 2012 ($2.99, limited series)

	GD 2.0	VG 4.0	FN 6.0	VF 8.0	VF/NM 9.0	NM- 9.2
1-Intro. Marcus Johnson; Eaton-a/Pagulayan-c	1	3	4	6	8	10
2-5: 4-Deadpool app. 5-Nick Fury app.						4.00
6-Marcus Johnson becomes Nick Fury Jr.; resembles movie version; Agent Coulson app.	1	3	4	6	8	10

BATTLE SQUADRON
Stanmor Publications: April, 1955 - No. 5, Dec, 1955

Battlestar Galactica (2014) #9 © Universal

Battle Stories #1 © FAW

Batwoman #1 © DC

	GD 2.0	VG 4.0	FN 6.0	VF 8.0	VF/NM 9.0	NM- 9.2
1	12	24	36	67	94	120
2-5: 3-Iwo Jima & flag-c	8	16	24	40	50	60

BATTLESTAR GALACTICA (TV) (Also see Marvel Comics Super Special #8)
Marvel Comics Group: Mar, 1979 - No. 23, Jan, 1981

	GD	VG	FN	VF	VF/NM	NM-
1: 1-5 adapt TV episodes	2	4	6	9	12	15
2-23: 1-3-Partial-r	1	3	4	6	8	10

NOTE: *Austin c-9i, 10i. **Golden** c-18. **Simonson** a(p)-4, 5, 11-13, 15-20, 22, 23; c(p)-4, 5,11-17, 19, 20, 22, 23.*

BATTLESTAR GALACTICA (TV) (Also see Asylum)
Maximum Press: July, 1995 - No. 4, Nov, 1995 ($2.50, limited series)

1-4: Continuation of 1978 TV series 4.00
Trade paperback (12/95, $12.95)-reprints series 13.00

BATTLESTAR GALACTICA (1978 TV series)
Realm Press: Dec, 1997 - No. 5, July, 1998 ($2.99)

1-5-Chris Scalf-s/painted-a/c 3.00
...Search For Sanctuary (9/98, $2.99) Scalf & Kuhoric-s 3.00
...Search For Sanctuary Special (4/00, $3.99) Kuhoric-s/Scalf & Scott-a 4.00

BATTLESTAR GALACTICA (2003-2009 TV series)
Dynamite Entertainment: No. 0, 2006 - No. 12, 2007 (25¢/$2.99)

0-(25¢-c) Two covers; Pak-s/Raynor-a 3.00
1-($2.99) Covers by Turner, Tan, Raynor & photo-c; Pak-s/Raynor-a 3.00
2-12-Four covers on each 3.00
... Pegasus (2007, $4.99) story of Battlestar Pegasus & Admiral Cain; 2 covers 5.00
... Volume 1 HC (2007, $19.99) r/#0-4; cover gallery; Raynor sketch pages; commentary 20.00
... Volume 1 TPB (2007, $14.99) r/#0-4; cover gallery; Raynor sketch pages; commentary 15.00
... Volume 2 HC (2007, $19.99) r/#5-8; cover gallery; Raynor sketch pages 20.00
... Volume 2 TPB (2007, $14.99) r/#5-8; cover gallery; Raynor sketch pages 15.00

BATTLESTAR GALACTICA, (Classic...) (1978 TV series characters)
Dynamite Entertainment: 2006 - No. 5 ($2.99)

1-5: 1-Two covers by Dorman & Caldwell; Rafael-a. 2-Two covers 3.00

BATTLESTAR GALACTICA, (Classic...) (Volume 2) (1978 TV series characters)
Dynamite Entertainment: 2013 - Present ($3.99)

1-9: 1-5-Two covers by Alex Ross & Chris Eliopoulos on each; Abnett & Lanning-s 4.00

BATTLESTAR GALACTICA: APOLLO'S JOURNEY (1978 TV series)
Maximum Press: Apr, 1996 - No. 3, June, 1996 ($2.95, limited series)

1-3: Richard Hatch scripts 4.00

BATTLESTAR GALACTICA: CYLON APOCALYPSE (1978 TV series characters)
Dynamite Entertainment: 2007 - No. 4, 2007 ($2.99, limited series)

1-4-Carlos Rafael-a; 4 covers on each 3.00
TPB (2007, $14.99) r/series with cover gallery 15.00

BATTLESTAR GALACTICA: CYLON WAR (2003-2009 TV series)
Dynamite Entertainment: 2009 - No. 4, 2010 ($3.99, limited series)

1-3-First cylon war 40 years before the Caprica attack; Raynor-a; 2 covers 4.00

BATTLESTAR GALACTICA: GHOSTS (2003-2009 TV series)
Dynamite Entertainment: 2008 - No. 4, 2009 ($4.99, 40 pgs., limited series)

1-4-Intro. of the Ghost Squadron; Jerwa-s/Lau-a/Calero-c 5.00

BATTLESTAR GALACTICA: JOURNEY'S END (1978 TV series)
Maximum Press: Aug, 1996 - No. 4, Nov, 1996 ($2.99, limited series)

1-4-Continuation of the T.V. series 4.00

BATTLESTAR GALACTICA: ORIGINS (2003-2009 TV series)
Dynamite Entertainment: 2007 - No. 11, 2008 ($3.50)

1-11: 1-4-Baltar's origin; multiple covers. 5-8-Adama's origin. 9-11-Starbuck & Helo 3.50

BATTLESTAR GALACTICA: SEASON III
Realm Press: June/July, 1999 - No. 3, Sept, 1999 ($2.99)

1-3: 1-Kuhoric-s/Scalf & Scott-a; two covers by Scalf & Jae Lee. 2,3-Two covers 3.00
Gallery (4/00, $3.99) short story and pin-ups 4.00
1999 Tour Book (5/99, $2.99) 3.00
1999 Tour Book Convention Edition (6.99) 7.00
...Special: Centurion Prime (12/99, $3.99) Kuhoric-s 4.00

BATTLESTAR GALACTICA: SEASON ZERO (2003-2009 TV series)
Dynamite Entertainment: 2007 - No. 12, 2008 ($2.99)

1-12-Set 2 years before the Cylon attack; multiple covers 3.00
.../The Lone Ranger 2007 Free Comic Book Day Edition; flip book with Cassaday Lone Ranger-c 3.00

BATTLESTAR GALACTICA: SPECIAL EDITION (TV)
Maximum Press: Jan, 1997 ($2.99, one-shot)

1-Fully painted; Scalf-c/s/a; r/Asylum 3.00

BATTLESTAR GALACTICA: STARBUCK (TV)
Maximum Press: Dec, 1995 - No. 3, Mar, 1996 ($2.50, limited series)

1-3 4.00

BATTLESTAR GALACTICA: STARBUCK, (Classic...) (1978 TV series characters)
Dynamite Entertainment: 2013 - No. 4, 2014 ($3.99, limited series)

1-4-Tony Lee-s/Eman Casallos-a. 1-Childhood flashback 4.00

BATTLESTAR GALACTICA: THE COMPENDIUM (TV)
Maximum Press: Feb, 1997 ($2.99, one-shot)

1 3.00

BATTLESTAR GALACTICA: THE ENEMY WITHIN (TV)
Maximum Press: Nov, 1995 - No. 3, Feb, 1996 ($2.50, limited series)

1-3: 3-Indicia reads Feb, 1995 in error. 4.00

BATTLESTAR GALACTICA: THE FINAL FIVE (2003 series)
Dynamite Entertainment: 2009 - No. 4, 2009 ($3.99, limited series)

1-4-Raynor-a; 2 covers on each 4.00

BATTLESTAR GALACTICA ZAREK (2003 series)
Dynamite Entertainment: 2007 - No. 4, 2007 ($3.50, limited series)

1-4-Origin story of political activist Tom Zarek; 2 covers on each 3.50

BATTLE STORIES (See XMas Comics)
Fawcett Publications: Jan, 1952 - No. 11, Sept, 1953

	GD	VG	FN	VF	VF/NM	NM-
1-Evans-a	16	32	48	94	147	200
2	10	20	30	56	76	95
3-11	9	18	27	47	61	75

BATTLE STORIES
Super Comics: 1963 - 1964

	GD	VG	FN	VF	VF/NM	NM-
Reprints #10-13,15-18: 10-r/U.S Tank Commandos #? 11-r/? 11, 12,17-r/Monty Hall #?; 13-Kintsler-a (1pg).15-r/American Air Forces #7 by Powell; Bolle-r. 18-U.S. Fighting Air Force #?	2	4	6	9	13	16

BATTLETECH (See Blackthorne 3-D Series #41 for 3-D issue)
Blackthorne Publishing: Oct, 1987 - No. 6, 1988 ($1.75/$2.00)

1-6: Based on game. 1-Color. 2-Begin B&W 3.00
Annual 1 ($4.50, B&W) 5.00

BATTLETECH
Malibu Comics: Feb, 1995 ($2.95)

0 3.00

BATTLETECH FALLOUT
Malibu Comics: Dec, 1994 - No. 4, Mar, 1995 ($2.95)

1-4-Two edi. exist #1; normal logo 3.00
1-Gold version w/foil logo stamped "Gold Limited Edition 8.00
1-Full-c holographic limited edition 6.00

BATTLETIDE (Death's Head II & Killpower...)
Marvel Comics UK, Ltd.: Dec, 1992 - No. 4, Mar, 1993 ($1.75, mini-series)

1-4: Wolverine, Psylocke, Dark Angel app. 3.00

BATTLETIDE II (Death's Head II & Killpower...)
Marvel Comics UK, Ltd.: Aug, 1993 - No. 4, Nov, 1993 ($1.75, mini-series)

1-($2.95)-Foil embossed logo 4.00
2-4: 2-Hulk-c/story 3.00

BATWING (DC New 52)
DC Comics: Nov, 2011 - Present ($2.99)

1-24: 1-3,5-Judd Winick-s/Ben Oliver-a. 4-Origin; Chriscross-a. 9-Night of the Owls 3.00
25-($3.99) Zero Year tie-in; Luke Fox's first meeting with Batman; Conner-c 4.00
26-29: 26,27-Darwyn Cooke-c 3.00
#0 (11/12, $2.99) origin of David Zavimbe; Winick-s/To-a 3.00

BATWOMAN (See 52 #9 & 11 for debut and Detective Comics #854-860)
DC Comics: No. 0, Jan, 2011; No. 1, Nov, 2011 - Present ($2.99)

0-(1/11) Williams III-s; art by Williams III and Reeder; Williams III-c 3.00
0-(1/11)-Variant-c by Reeder 5.00
1-New DC 52; Williams III-a; Williams III & Blackman-s; Bette Kane app. 5.00
2-24: 2-Cameron Chase returns. 6-8-Reeder-a/c. 9-11,15,18-20,22,23-McCarthy-a. 12-17-Wonder Woman app. 21-Francavilla-a; Killer Croc app. 3.00
25-($3.99) Zero Year tie-in; Maggie Sawyer & Bruce Wayne app. 4.00
26-29: 26-29-Wolf Spider 3.00
#0 (11/12, $2.99) Flashback to Kate's training; Williams III-a 3.00

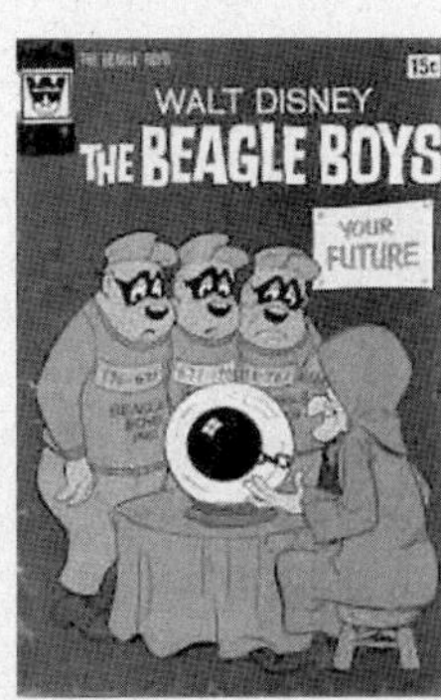

Beagle Boys #16 © DIS

Beast #2 © MAR

Beautiful Killer #1 © Black Bull

	GD 2.0	VG 4.0	FN 6.0	VF 8.0	VF/NM 9.0	NM- 9.2

... Elegy The Deluxe Edition HC (2010, $24.99, d.j.) r/Detective #854-860; gallery of variant covers, sketch art and script pages; intro. by Rachel Maddow 25.00
... Elegy SC (2011, $17.99) same contents as Deluxe HC 18.00

BAY CITY JIVE
DC Comics (WildStorm): Jul, 2001 - No. 3, Sept, 2001 ($2.95, limited series)

1-3: Intro Sugah Rollins in 1970s San Francisco; Layman-s/Johnson-a 3.00

BAYWATCH COMIC STORIES (TV) (Magazine)
Acclaim Comics (Armada): May, 1996 - No. 4, 1997 ($4.95) (Photo-c on all)

1-4: Photo comics based on TV show 5.00

BEACH BLANKET BINGO (See Movie Classics)

BEAGLE BOYS, THE (Walt Disney)(See The Phantom Blot)
Gold Key: 11/64; No. 2, 11/65; No. 3, 8/66 - No. 47, 2/79 (See WDC&S #134)

	GD	VG	FN	VF	VF/NM	NM-
1	5	10	15	30	50	70
2-5	3	6	9	17	26	35
6-10	3	6	9	15	22	28
11-20: 11,14,19-r	2	4	6	11	16	20
21-30: 27-r	2	4	6	8	11	14
31-47	1	3	4	6	8	10

BEAGLE BOYS VERSUS UNCLE SCROOGE
Gold Key: Mar, 1979 - No. 12, Feb, 1980

	GD	VG	FN	VF	VF/NM	NM-
1	2	4	6	9	13	16
2-12: 9-r	1	2	3	5	6	8

BEANBAGS
Ziff-Davis Publ. Co. (Approved Comics): Winter, 1951 - No. 2, Spring, 1952

	GD	VG	FN	VF	VF/NM	NM-
1,2	13	26	39	74	105	135

BEANIE THE MEANIE
Fago Publications: No. 3, May, 1959

	GD	VG	FN	VF	VF/NM	NM-
3	5	10	15	24	30	35

BEANY AND CECIL (TV) (Bob Clampett's...)
Dell Publishing Co.: Jan, 1952 - 1955; July-Sept, 1962 - No. 5, July-Sept, 1963

	GD	VG	FN	VF	VF/NM	NM-
Four Color 368	20	40	60	138	307	475
Four Color 414,448,477,530,570,635(1/55)	12	24	36	82	179	275
01-057-209 (#1)	11	22	33	77	166	255
2-5	9	18	27	58	114	170

BEAR COUNTRY (Disney)
Dell Publishing Co.: No. 758, Dec, 1956

	GD	VG	FN	VF	VF/NM	NM-
Four Color 758-Movie	5	10	15	31	53	75

BEAST (See X-Men)
Marvel Comics: May, 1997 - No. 3, 1997 ($2.50, mini-series)

1-3-Giffen-s/Nocon-a 3.00

BEAST BOY (See Titans)
DC Comics: Jan, 2000 - No. 4, Apr, 2000 ($2.95, mini-series)

1-4-Justiano-c/a; Raab & Johns-s 3.00

B.E.A.S.T.I.E.S. (Also see Axis Alpha)
Axis Comics: Apr, 1994 ($1.95)

1-Javier Saltares-c/a/scripts 3.00

BEASTS OF BURDEN (See Dark Horse Book of Hauntings, ...Monsters, ...The Dead, ...Witchcraft)
Dark Horse Comics: Sept, 2009 - No. 4, Dec, 2009 ($2.99, limited series)

1-4-Evan Dorkin-s/Jill Thompson-a/c 3.00
...: Hunters & Gatherers (3/14, $3.50) Evan Dorkin-s/Jill Thompson-a/c 3.50
...: Neighborhood Watch (8/12, $3.50) Evan Dorkin-s/Jill Thompson-a/c 3.50
Volume 1: Animal Rites HC (6/10, $19.99) r/#1-4 & short stories from Dark Horse Books 20.00

BEATLES, THE (See Girls' Romances #109, Go-Go, Heart Throbs #101, Herbie #5, Howard the Duck Mag. #4, Laugh #166, Marvel Comics Super Special #4, My Little Margie #54, Not Brand Echh, Strange Tales #130, Summer Love, Superman's Pal Jimmy Olsen #79, Teen Confessions #37, Tippy's Friends & Tippy Teen)

BEATLES, THE (Life Story)
Dell Publishing Co.: Sept-Nov, 1964 (35¢)

	GD	VG	FN	VF	VF/NM	NM-
1-(Scarce)-Stories with color photo pin-ups; Paul S. Newman-s (photo-c)	44	88	132	326	738	1150

BEATLES EXPERIENCE, THE
Revolutionary Comics: Mar, 1991 - No. 8, 1991 ($2.50, B&W, limited series)

1-8: 1-Gold logo 5.00

BEATLES YELLOW SUBMARINE (See Movie Comics under Yellow...)

BEAUTIFUL KILLER
Black Bull Comics: Sept., 2002 - No. 3, Jan, 2003 ($2.99, limited series)

...Limited Preview Edition (5/02, $5.00) preview pgs. & creator interviews 5.00
1-Noto-a/Palmiotti-s; Hughes-c; intro Brigit Cole 3.00
2,3: 2-Jusko-c. 3-Noto-c 3.00
TPB (5/03, $9.99) r/#1-3; cover gallery and Adam Hughes sketch pages 10.00

BEAUTIFUL PEOPLE
Slave Labor Graphics: Apr, 1994 ($4.95, 8-1/2x11", one-shot)

nn 5.00

BEAUTIFUL STORIES FOR UGLY CHILDREN
DC Comics (Piranha Press): 1989 - No. 30, 1991 ($2.00/$2.50, B&W, mature)

Vol. 1-20: 12-$2.50-c begins 4.00
21-25 5.00

	GD	VG	FN	VF	VF/NM	NM-
26-30-(Lower print run)	1	2	3	4	5	7

A Cotton Candy Autopsy ($12.95, B&W)-Reprints 1st two volumes 13.00

BEAUTY AND THE BEAST, THE
Marvel Comics Group: Jan, 1985 - No. 4, Apr, 1985 (limited series)

1-4: Dazzler & the Beast from X-Men; Sienkiewicz-c on all 4.00

BEAUTY AND THE BEAST (Graphic novel)(Also see Cartoon Tales & Disney's New Adventures of...)
Disney Comics: 1992

nn-($4.95, prestige edition)-Adapts animated film 7.00
nn-($2.50, newsstand edition) 4.00

BEAUTY AND THE BEAST
Disney Comics: Sept., 1992 - No. 2, 1992 ($1.50, limited series)

1,2 3.00

BEAUTY AND THE BEAST: PORTRAIT OF LOVE (TV)
First Comics: May, 1989 - No. 2, Mar, 1990 ($5.95, 60 pgs., squarebound)

1,2: 1-Based on TV show, Wendy Pini-a/scripts. 2-...: Night of Beauty; by Wendy Pini 6.00

BEAVER VALLEY (Movie)(Disney)
Dell Publishing Co.: No. 625, Apr, 1955

	GD	VG	FN	VF	VF/NM	NM-
Four Color 625	5	10	15	35	63	90

BEAVIS AND BUTTHEAD (MTV's...)(TV cartoon)
Marvel Comics: Mar, 1994 - No. 28, June, 1996 ($1.95)

	GD	VG	FN	VF	VF/NM	NM-
1-Silver ink-c. 1, 2-Punisher & Devil Dinosaur app.	1	3	4	6	8	10

1-2nd printing 4.00
2,3: 2-Wolverine app. 3-Man-Thing, Spider-Man, Venom, Carnage, Mary Jane & Stan Lee cameos; John Romita, Sr. art (2 pgs.) 5.00
4-28: 5-War Machine, Thor, Loki, Hulk, Captain America & Rhino cameos. 6-Psylocke, Polaris, Daredevil & Bullseye app. 7-Ghost Rider & Sub-Mariner app. 8-Quasar & Eon app. 9-Prowler & Nightwatch app. 11-Black Widow app. 12-Thunderstrike & Bloodaxe app. 13-Night Thrasher app. 14-Spider-Man 2099 app. 15-Warlock app. 16-X-Factor app. 25-Juggernaut app. 4.00

BECK & CAUL INVESTIGATIONS
Gauntlet Comics (Caliber): Jan, 1994 - No. 5, 1995? ($2.95, B&W)

1-5 3.00
Special 1 ($4.95) 5.00

BEDKNOBS AND BROOMSTICKS (See Walt Disney Showcase No. 6 & 50)

BEDLAM!
Eclipse Comics: Sept, 1985 - No. 2, Sept, 1985 (B&W-r in color)

1,2: Bissette-a 3.00

BEDTIME STORIES FOR IMPRESSIONABLE CHILDREN
Moonstone Books: Nov, 2010 ($3.99, B&W)

1-Short story anthology; Vaughn, Kuhoric & Tinnell-s; 3 covers 4.00

BEDTIME STORY (See Cinema Comics Herald)

BEELZELVIS
Slave Labor Graphics: Feb, 1994 ($2.95, B&W, one-shot)

1 3.00

BEEP BEEP, THE ROAD RUNNER (TV) (See Dell Giant Comics Bugs Bunny Vacation Funnies #8 for 1st app.) (Also see Daffy & Kite Fun Book)
Dell Publishing Co./Gold Key No. 1-88/Whitman No. 89 on: July, 1958 - No. 14, Aug-Oct, 1962; Oct, 1966 - No. 105, 1984

	GD	VG	FN	VF	VF/NM	NM-
Four Color 918 (#1, 7/58)	11	22	33	73	157	240
Four Color 1008,1046 (11-1/59-60)	7	14	21	44	82	120
4(2-4/60)-14(Dell)	6	12	18	37	66	95
1(10/66, Gold Key)	6	12	18	40	73	105

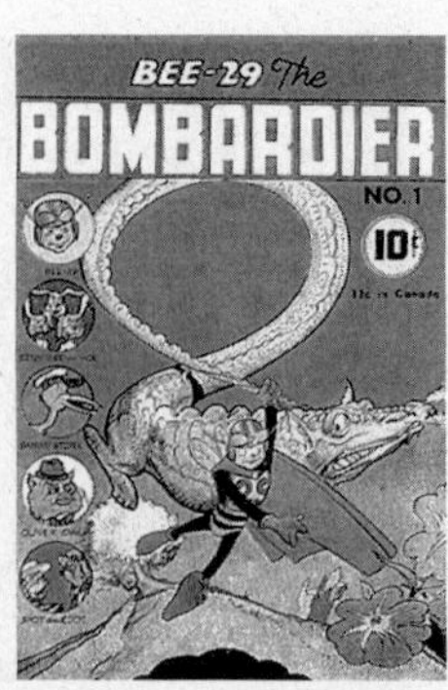

Bee 29, The Bombardier #1 © Neal Pub.

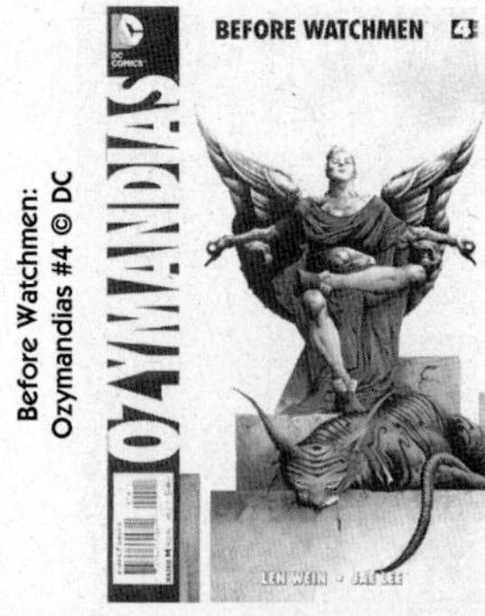

Before Watchmen: Ozymandias #4 © DC

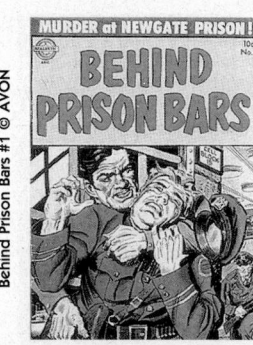

Behind Prison Bars #1 © AVON

	GD 2.0	VG 4.0	FN 6.0	VF 8.0	VF/NM 9.0	NM- 9.2
2-5	4	8	12	27	44	60
6-14	3	6	9	19	30	40
15-18,20-40	3	6	9	16	23	30
19-With pull-out poster	4	8	12	25	40	55
41-50	3	6	9	14	19	24
51-70	2	4	6	9	13	16
71-88	2	3	4	6	8	10
89,90,94-101: 100(3/82), 101(4/82)	2	4	6	8	10	12
91(8/80), 92(9/80), 93 (3-pack?) (low printing)	5	10	15	31	53	75
102-105 (All #90189 on-c; nd or date code; pre-pack) 102(6/83), 103(7/83), 104(5/84), 105(6/84)	3	6	9	16	24	32
#63-2970 (Now Age Books/Pendulum Pub. Comic Digest, 1971, 75¢, 100 pages, B&W) collection of one-page gags	4	8	12	27	44	60

NOTE: *See March of Comics #351, 353, 375, 387, 397, 416, 430, 442, 455. #5, 8-10, 35, 53, 59-62, 68-r; 96-102, 104 are 1/3-r.*

BEETLE BAILEY (See Giant Comic Album, Sarge Snorkel; also Comics Reading Libraries in the Promotional Comics section)
Dell Publishing Co./Gold Key #39-53/King #54-66/Charlton #67-119/Gold Key #120-131/Whitman #132: #459, 5/53 - #38, 5-7/62; #39, 11/62 - #53, 5/66; #54, 8/66 - #65, 12/67;#67, 2/69 - #119, 11/76; #120, 4/78 - #132, 4/80

	GD 2.0	VG 4.0	FN 6.0	VF 8.0	VF/NM 9.0	NM- 9.2
Four Color 469 (#1)-By Mort Walker	11	22	33	76	163	250
Four Color 521,552,622	7	14	21	44	82	120
5(2-4/56)-10(5-7/57)	5	10	15	35	63	90
11-20(4-5/59)	4	8	12	28	47	65
21-38(5-7/62)	3	6	9	20	31	42
39-53(5/66)	3	6	9	17	26	35
54-65 (No. 66 publ. overseas only?)	3	6	9	16	23	30
67-69: 69-Last 12¢ issue	3	6	9	14	20	25
70-99	2	4	6	9	13	16
100	2	4	6	11	16	20
101-111,114-119	1	3	4	6	8	10
112,113-Byrne illos. (4 each)	2	4	6	9	12	18
120-132	1	2	3	4	5	7

BEETLE BAILEY
Harvey Comics: V2#1, Sept, 1992 - V2#9, Aug, 1994 ($1.25/$1.50)

	GD 2.0	VG 4.0	FN 6.0	VF 8.0	VF/NM 9.0	NM- 9.2
V2#1						5.00
2-9-($1.50)						3.50
Big Book 1(11/92),2(5/93)(Both $1.95, 52 pgs.)						4.00
Giant Size V2#1(10/92),2(3/93)(Both $2.25,68 pgs.)						4.00

BEETLEJUICE (TV)
Harvey Comics: Oct, 1991 ($1.25)

	GD 2.0	VG 4.0	FN 6.0	VF 8.0	VF/NM 9.0	NM- 9.2
1						5.00

BEETLEJUICE CRIMEBUSTERS ON THE HAUNT
Harvey Comics: Sept, 1992 - No. 3, Jan, 1993 ($1.50, limited series)

	GD 2.0	VG 4.0	FN 6.0	VF 8.0	VF/NM 9.0	NM- 9.2
1-3						4.00

BEE 29, THE BOMBARDIER
Neal Publications: Feb, 1945

	GD 2.0	VG 4.0	FN 6.0	VF 8.0	VF/NM 9.0	NM- 9.2
1-(Funny animal)	36	72	108	211	343	475

BEFORE THE FANTASTIC FOUR: BEN GRIMM AND LOGAN
Marvel Comics: July, 2000 - No. 3, Sept, 2000 ($2.99, limited series)

	GD 2.0	VG 4.0	FN 6.0	VF 8.0	VF/NM 9.0	NM- 9.2
1-3-The Thing and Wolverine app.; Hama-s						3.00

BEFORE THE FANTASTIC FOUR: REED RICHARDS
Marvel Comics: Sept, 2000 - No. 3, Dec, 2000 ($2.99, limited series)

	GD 2.0	VG 4.0	FN 6.0	VF 8.0	VF/NM 9.0	NM- 9.2
1-3-Peter David-s/Duncan Fegredo-c/a						3.00

BEFORE THE FANTASTIC FOUR: THE STORMS
Marvel Comics: Dec, 2000 - No. 3, Feb, 2001 ($2.99, limited series)

	GD 2.0	VG 4.0	FN 6.0	VF 8.0	VF/NM 9.0	NM- 9.2
1-3-Adlard-a						3.00

BEFORE WATCHMEN: COMEDIAN (Prequel to 1986 Watchmen series)
DC Comics: Aug, 2012 - No. 6, Jun, 2013 ($3.99, limited series)

	GD 2.0	VG 4.0	FN 6.0	VF 8.0	VF/NM 9.0	NM- 9.2
1-6-Brian Azzarello-s/J.G. Jones-a/c; The Comedian during the Vietnam War; back-up Crimson Corsair serial in #1-4; Higgins-a						4.00
1-Variant-c by Jim Lee						30.00
1-6-Variant covers. 1-Risso. 2-Bradstreet. 3-Leon. 4-Stelfreeze. 5-Frank. 6-Albuquerque						8.00

BEFORE WATCHMEN: DOLLAR BILL (Prequel to 1986 Watchmen series)
DC Comics: Mar, 2013 ($3.99, one-shot)

	GD 2.0	VG 4.0	FN 6.0	VF 8.0	VF/NM 9.0	NM- 9.2
1-Len Wein-s/Steve Rude-a/c; origin and demise of Dollar Bill						4.00
1-Variant-c by Jim Lee						60.00
1-Variant-c by Darwyn Cooke						8.00

BEFORE WATCHMEN: DR. MANHATTAN (Prequel to 1986 Watchmen series)
DC Comics: Oct, 2012 - No. 4, Apr, 2013 ($3.99, limited series)

	GD 2.0	VG 4.0	FN 6.0	VF 8.0	VF/NM 9.0	NM- 9.2
1-4-Straczynski-s/Hughes-a/c; back-up Crimson Corsair serial in #1-3; Higgins-a						4.00
1-Variant-c by Jim Lee						30.00
1-4-Variant covers. 1-Pope. 2-Russell. 3-Neal Adams. 4-Sienkiewicz						8.00

BEFORE WATCHMEN: MINUTEMEN (Prequel to 1986 Watchmen series)
DC Comics: Aug, 2012 - No. 6, Mar, 2013 ($3.99, limited series)

	GD 2.0	VG 4.0	FN 6.0	VF 8.0	VF/NM 9.0	NM- 9.2
1-6-Darwyn Cooke-a/c; The team flashback to 1939; back-up Crimson Corsair serial in #1-5; Higgins-a						4.00
1-Variant-c by Jim Lee						20.00
1-6-Variant covers. 1-Golden. 2-Garcia-Lopez-c. 3-Chiang. 4-Rude. 6-Cloonan						8.00

BEFORE WATCHMEN: MOLOCH (Prequel to 1986 Watchmen series)
DC Comics: Jan, 2013 - No. 2, Feb, 2013 ($3.99, limited series)

	GD 2.0	VG 4.0	FN 6.0	VF 8.0	VF/NM 9.0	NM- 9.2
1,2-Straczynski-s/Risso-a/c; origin; back-up Crimson Corsair serial in both; Higgins-a						4.00
1-Variant-c by Jim Lee						30.00
1,2-Variant covers. 1-Matt Wagner. 2-Olly Moss						6.00

BEFORE WATCHMEN: NITE OWL (Prequel to 1986 Watchmen series)
DC Comics: Aug, 2012 - No. 4, Feb, 2013 ($3.99, limited series)

	GD 2.0	VG 4.0	FN 6.0	VF 8.0	VF/NM 9.0	NM- 9.2
1-4-Straczynski-s/Andy Kubert-a/c; Joe Kubert-a(i) in #1-3; back-up Crimson Corsair serial in #1-3; Higgins-a						4.00
1-Variant-c by Jim Lee						20.00
1-4-Variant covers. 1-Nowlan. 2-Finch. 3-Samnee. 4-Van Sciver						8.00

BEFORE WATCHMEN: OZYMANDIAS (Prequel to 1986 Watchmen series)
DC Comics: Sept, 2012 - No. 6, Apr, 2013 ($3.99, limited series)

	GD 2.0	VG 4.0	FN 6.0	VF 8.0	VF/NM 9.0	NM- 9.2
1-6-Len Wein-s/Jae Lee-a/c; origin of master plan; back-up Crimson Corsair serial in #1-4; Higgins-a						4.00
1-Variant-c by Jim Lee						20.00
1-6-Variant covers. 1-Jimenez. 2-Noto. 3-Carnevale. 4-Kaluta. 5-Thompson. 6-Sook						8.00

BEFORE WATCHMEN: RORSCHACH (Prequel to 1986 Watchmen series)
DC Comics: Oct, 2012 - No. 4, Apr, 2013 ($3.99, limited series)

	GD 2.0	VG 4.0	FN 6.0	VF 8.0	VF/NM 9.0	NM- 9.2
1-4-Azzarello-s/Bermejo-a/c; back-up Crimson Corsair serial in #1-3; Higgins-a						4.00
1-Variant-c by Jim Lee						40.00
1-4-Variant covers. 1-Steranko. 2-Jock. 3-Kidd. 4-Reis						8.00

BEFORE WATCHMEN: SILK SPECTRE (Prequel to 1986 Watchmen series)
DC Comics: Aug, 2012 - No. 4, Dec, 2013 ($3.99, limited series)

	GD 2.0	VG 4.0	FN 6.0	VF 8.0	VF/NM 9.0	NM- 9.2
1-4-Cooke & Conner-s/Conner-a/c; back-up Crimson Corsair serial in all; Higgins-a						4.00
1-Variant-c by Jim Lee						40.00
1-4-Variant covers. 1-Dave Johnson. 2-Middleton. 3-Allred. 4-Timm						8.00

BEHIND PRISON BARS
Realistic Comics (Avon): 1952

	GD 2.0	VG 4.0	FN 6.0	VF 8.0	VF/NM 9.0	NM- 9.2
1-Kinstler-c	34	68	102	204	332	460

BEHOLD THE HANDMAID
George Pflaum: 1954 (Religious) (25¢ with a 20¢ sticker price)

	GD 2.0	VG 4.0	FN 6.0	VF 8.0	VF/NM 9.0	NM- 9.2
nn	6	12	18	31	38	45

BELIEVE IT OR NOT (See Ripley's...)

BEN AND ME (Disney)
Dell Publishing Co.: No. 539, Mar, 1954

	GD 2.0	VG 4.0	FN 6.0	VF 8.0	VF/NM 9.0	NM- 9.2
Four Color 539	4	8	12	27	44	60

BEN BOWIE AND HIS MOUNTAIN MEN
Dell Publishing Co.: 1952 - No. 17, Nov-Jan, 1958-59

	GD 2.0	VG 4.0	FN 6.0	VF 8.0	VF/NM 9.0	NM- 9.2
Four Color 443 (#1)	8	16	24	54	102	150
Four Color 513,557,599,626,657	5	10	15	31	53	75
7(5-7/56)-11: 11-Intro/origin Yellow Hair	4	8	12	25	40	55
12-17	4	8	12	23	37	50

BEN CASEY (TV)
Dell Publishing Co.: June-July, 1962 - No. 10, June-Aug, 1965 (Photo-c)

	GD 2.0	VG 4.0	FN 6.0	VF 8.0	VF/NM 9.0	NM- 9.2
12-063-207 (#1)	5	10	15	35	63	90
2(10/62),3,5-10	4	8	12	23	37	50
4-Marijuana & heroin use story	4	8	12	27	44	60

BEN CASEY FILM STORIES (TV)
Gold Key: Nov, 1962 (25¢) (Photo-c)

	GD 2.0	VG 4.0	FN 6.0	VF 8.0	VF/NM 9.0	NM- 9.2
30009-211-All photos	6	12	18	38	69	100

BENEATH THE PLANET OF THE APES (See Movie Comics & Power Record Comics)

BEN FRANKLIN (See Kite Fun Book)

BEN HUR

Ben 10 #1 © Cartoon Network

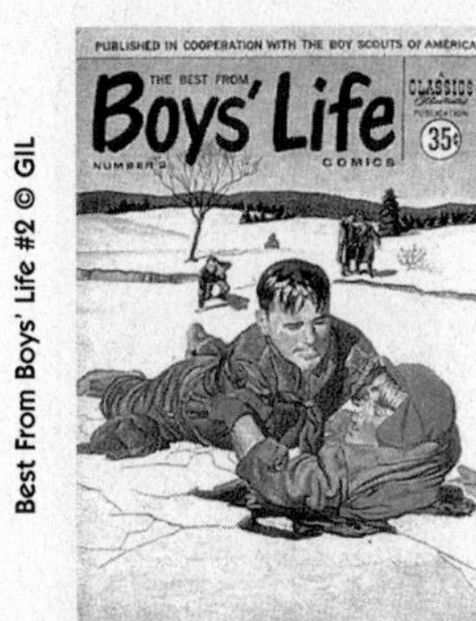

Best From Boys' Life #2 © GIL

Best of DC #45 © DC

GD VG FN VF VF/NM NM-
2.0 4.0 6.0 8.0 9.0 9.2

Dell Publishing Co.: No. 1052, Nov, 1959
Four Color 1052-Movie, Manning-a 9 18 27 58 114 170

BEN ISRAEL
Logos International: 1974 (39¢)
nn-Christian religious 2 4 6 10 14 18

BEN 10 (Cartoon Network)
IDW Publishing: Nov, 2013 - No. 4, Feb, 2014 ($3.99, limited series)
1-4: Henderson-s/Purcell-a; multiple covers on each 4.00

BEOWULF (Also see First Comics Graphic Novel #1)
National Periodical Publications: Apr-May, 1975 - No. 6, Feb-Mar, 1976
1 2 4 6 8 11 14
2,3,5,6: 5-Flying saucer-c/story 1 2 3 5 6 8
4-Dracula-c/s 1 2 3 5 7 9

BERNI WRIGHTSON, MASTER OF THE MACABRE
Pacific Comics/Eclipse Comics No. 5: July, 1983 - No. 5, Nov, 1984 ($1.50, Baxter paper)
1-5: Wrightson-c/a(r). 4-Jeff Jones-r (11 pgs.) 6.00

BERRYS, THE (Also see Funny World)
Argo Publ.: May, 1956
1-Reprints daily & Sunday strips & daily Animal Antics by Ed Nofziger
6 12 18 29 36 42

BERZERKER (Milo Ventimiglia Presents...)
Image Comics (Top Cow): No. 0, Feb, 2009 - No. 6, Jun, 2010 ($2.99/$3.99)
0-3-Jeremy Haun-a/Rick Loverd-s/Dale Keown-c. 0-Creator interviews 3.00
4-6-($3.99) Covers by Haun & Keown 4.00

BERZERKERS (See Youngblood V1#2)
Image Comics (Extreme Studios): Aug, 1995 - No. 3, Oct, 1995 ($2.50, limited series)
1-3: Beau Smith scripts, Fraga-a 3.00

BEST COMICS
Better Publications: Nov, 1939 - No. 4, Feb, 1940(10-11/16" wide x 8" tall, reads sideways)
1-(Scarce)-Red Mask begins(1st app.) & c/s-all 116 232 348 742 1271 1800
2-4: 4-Cannibalism story 61 122 183 390 670 950

BEST FROM BOY'S LIFE, THE
Gilberton Company: Oct, 1957 - No. 5, Oct, 1958 (35¢)
1-Space Conquerors & Kam of the Ancient Ones begin, end #5; Bob Cousy photo/story
13 26 39 72 101 130
2,3,5 8 16 24 42 54 65
4-L.B. Cole-a 8 16 24 44 57 70

BEST LOVE (Formerly Sub-Mariner Comics No. 32)
Marvel Comics (MPI): No. 33, Aug, 1949 - No. 36, April, 1950 (Photo-c 33-36)
33-Kubert-a 15 30 45 83 124 165
34 (10/49) 10 20 30 58 79 100
35,36-Everett-a 11 22 33 64 90 115

BEST OF ARCHIE, THE
Perigee Books: 1980 ($7.95, softcover TPB)
nn-Intro by Michael Uslan & Jeffrey Mendel 5 10 15 34 60 85

BEST OF BUGS BUNNY, THE
Gold Key: Oct, 1966 - No. 2, Oct, 1968
1,2-Giants 4 8 12 27 44 60

BEST OF DC, THE (Blue Ribbon Digest) (See Limited Coll. Ed. C-52)
DC Comics: Sept-Oct, 1979 - No. 71, Apr, 1986 (100-148 pgs; mostly reprints)
1-Superman, w/"Death of Superman"-r 2 4 6 11 16 20
2,5-9: 2-Batman 40th Ann. Special. 5-Best of 1979. 6,8-Superman. 7-Superboy. 9-Batman, Creeper app. 2 4 6 8 10 12
3-Superfriends 2 4 6 9 12 15
4-Rudolph the Red Nosed Reindeer 2 4 6 9 13 16
10-Secret Origins of Super Villains; 1st ever Penguin origin-s
3 6 9 15 22 28
11-16,18-20: 11-The Year's Best Stories. 12-Superman Time and Space Stories.13-Best of DC Comics Presents. 14-New origin stories of Batman villains. 15-Superboy. 16-Superman Anniv. 18-Teen Titans new-s., Adams, Kane-a; Perez-c. 19-Superman. 20-World's Finest
1 2 3 5 7 9
17-Supergirl 2 4 6 8 10 12
21,22: 21-Justice Society. 22-Christmas; unpublished Sandman story w/Kirby-a
2 4 6 10 14 18
23-27: 23-(148 pgs.)-Best of 1981. 24 Legion, new story and 16 pgs. new costumes. 25-Superman. 26-Brave & Bold. 27-Superman vs. Luthor
2 4 6 9 12 15
28,29: 28-Binky, Sugar & Spike app. 29-Sugar & Spike, 3 new stories; new Stanley & his Monster story 2 4 6 9 13 16
30,32-36,38,40: 30-Detective Comics. 32-Superman. 33-Secret origins of Legion Heroes and Villains. 34-Metal Men; has #497 on-c from Adv. Comics. 35-The Year's Best Comics Stories (148 pgs.). 36-Superman vs. Kryptonite. 38-Superman. 40-World of Krypton
2 4 6 9 12 15
31-JLA 2 4 6 10 14 18
34-Corrected version with "#34" on cover 2 4 6 10 14 18
37,39: 37-"Funny Stuff", Mayer-a. 39-Binky 2 4 6 10 14 18
41,43,45,47,49,53,55,58,60,63,65,68,70: 41-Sugar & Spike new stories with Mayer-a. 43,49,55-Funny Stuff. 45,53,70-Binky. 47,65,68-Sugar & Spike. 58-Super Jrs. Holiday Special; Sugar & Spike. 60-Plop!; Wood-c(r) & Aragonés-r (5/85). 63-Plop!; Wrightson-a(r)
3 6 9 14 19 24
42,44,46,48,50-52,54,56,57,59,61,62,64,66,67,69,71: 42,56-Superman vs. Aliens. 44,57,67-Superboy & LSH. 46-Jimmy Olsen. 48-Superman Team-ups. 50-Year's best Superman. 51-Batman Family. 52 Best of 1984. 54,56,59-Superman. 61-(148 pgs.)Year's best. 62-Best of Batman 1985. 69-Year's best Team stories. 71-Year's best
2 4 6 10 14 18

NOTE: ***N. Adams*** *a-2r, 14r, 18r, 26, 51.* ***Aparo*** *a-9, 14, 26, 30; c-9, 14, 26.* ***Austin*** *a-51i.* ***Buckler*** *a-40p; c-16, 22.* ***Giffen*** *a-50, 52; c-33p.* ***Grell*** *a-33p.* ***Grossman*** *a-37.* ***Heath*** *a-26.* ***Infantino*** *a-10r, 18.* ***Kaluta*** *a-40.* ***G. Kane*** *a-10r, 18r; c-40, 44.* ***Kubert*** *a-10r, 21, 26.* ***Layton*** *a-21.* ***S. Mayer*** *c-29, 37, 41, 43, 47; a-28, 29, 37, 41, 43, 47, 58, 65, 68.* ***Moldoff*** *c-64p.* ***Morrow*** *a-40; c-40.* ***W. Mortimer*** *a-39p.* ***Newton*** *a-5, 51.* ***Perez*** *a-24, 50p; c-18, 21, 23.* ***Rogers*** *a-14, 51p.* ***Simonson*** *a-11r.* ***Spiegle*** *a-52.* ***Starlin*** *a-51.* ***Staton*** *a-5, 21.* ***Tuska*** *a-24.* ***Wolverton*** *a-60.* ***Wood*** *a-60, 63; c-60, 63.* ***Wrightson*** *a-60. New art in #14, 18, 24.*

BEST OF DENNIS THE MENACE, THE
Hallden/Fawcett Publications: Summer, 1959 - No. 5, Spring, 1961 (100 pgs.)
1-All reprints; Wiseman-a 7 14 21 44 72 100
2-5 4 8 12 28 44 60

BEST OF DONALD DUCK, THE
Gold Key: Nov, 1965 (12¢, 36 pgs.)(Lists 2nd printing in indicia)
1-Reprints Four Color #223 by Barks 7 14 21 46 86 125

BEST OF DONALD DUCK & UNCLE SCROOGE, THE
Gold Key: Nov, 1964 - No. 2, Sept, 1967 (25¢ Giants)
1(30022-411)('64)-Reprints 4-Color #189 & 408 by Carl Barks; cover of F.C. #189 redrawn by Barks 8 16 24 54 102 150
2(30022-709)('67)-Reprints 4-Color #256 & "Seven Cities of Cibola" & U.S. #8 by Barks
7 14 21 44 82 120

BEST OF HORROR AND SCIENCE FICTION COMICS
Bruce Webster: 1987 ($2.00)
1-Wolverton, Frazetta, Powell, Ditko-r 1 2 3 5 6 8

BEST OF JOSIE AND THE PUSSYCATS
Archie Comics: 2001 ($10.95, TPB)
1-Reprints 1st app. and noteworthy stories 12.00

BEST OF MARMADUKE, THE
Charlton Comics: 1960
1-Brad Anderson's strip reprints 3 6 9 19 30 40

BEST OF MS. TREE, THE
Pyramid Comics: 1987 - No. 4, 1988 ($2.00, B&W, limited series)
1-4 3.00

BEST OF RAY BRADBURY, THE
ibooks: 2003 ($18.95, TPB)
The Graphic Novel - Reprints from Ray Bradbury Comics; adaptations by various 19.00

BEST OF THE BRAVE AND THE BOLD, THE (See Super DC Giant)
DC Comics: Oct, 1988 - No. 6, Jan, 1989 ($2.50, limited series)
1-6: Neal Adams-r, Kubert-r & Heath-r in all 4.00

BEST OF THE SPIRIT, THE
DC Comics: 2005 ($14.99, TPB)
nn-Reprints 1st app. and noteworthy stories; intro by Neil Gaiman; Eisner bio. 15.00

BEST OF THE WEST (See A-1 Comics)
Magazine Enterprises: 1951 - No. 12, April-June, 1954
1(A-1 42)-Ghost Rider, Durango Kid, Straight Arrow, Bobby Benson begin
41 82 123 256 428 600
2(A-1 46) 22 44 66 128 209 290
3(A-1 52), 4(A-1 59), 5(A-1 66) 18 36 54 105 165 225
6(A-1 70), 7(A-1 76), 8(A-1 81), 9(A-1 85), 10(A-1 87), 11(A-1 97), 12(A-1 103) 15 30 45 84 127 170

Best Romance #5 © STD

Betty #22 © AP

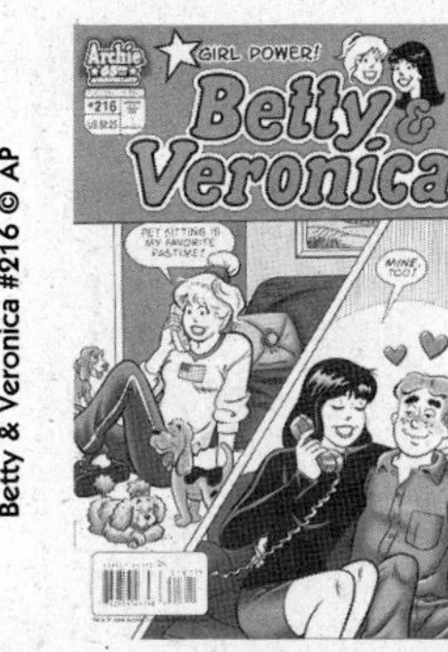

Betty & Veronica #216 © AP

	GD 2.0	VG 4.0	FN 6.0	VF 8.0	VF/NM 9.0	NM- 9.2

NOTE: *Bolle a-9. Borth a-12. Guardineer a-5, 12. Powell a-1, 12.*

BEST OF UNCLE SCROOGE & DONALD DUCK, THE
Gold Key: Nov, 1966 (25¢)

1(30030-611)-Reprints part 4-Color #159 & 456 & Uncle Scrooge #6,7 by Carl Barks 7 14 21 44 82 120

BEST OF WALT DISNEY COMICS, THE
Western Publishing Co.: 1974 ($1.50, 52 pgs.) (Walt Disney)
(8-1/2x11" cardboard covers; 32,000 printed of each)

96170-Reprints 1st two stories less 1 pg. each from 4-Color #62 6 12 18 37 66 95
96171-Reprints Mickey Mouse and the Bat Bandit of Inferno Gulch from 1934 (strips) by Gottfredson 6 12 18 37 66 95
96172-r/Uncle Scrooge #386 & two other stories 6 12 18 37 66 95
96173-Reprints "Ghost of the Grotto" (from 4-Color #159) & "Christmas on Bear Mountain" (from 4-Color #178) 6 12 18 37 66 95

BEST ROMANCE
Standard Comics (Visual Editions): No. 5, Feb-Mar, 1952 - No. 7, Aug, 1952

5-Toth-a; photo-c 15 30 45 85 120 175
6,7-Photo-c 10 20 30 56 76 95

BEST SELLER COMICS (See Tailspin Tommy)

BEST WESTERN (Formerly Terry Toons? or Miss America Magazine
Marvel Comics (IPC): V7#24(#57)?; Western Outlaws & Sheriffs No. 60 on)
No. 58, June, 1949 - No. 59, Aug, 1949

58,59-Black Rider, Kid Colt, Two-Gun Kid app.; both have Syd Shores-c 20 40 60 117 189 260

BETA RAY BILL: GODHUNTER
Marvel Comics: Aug, 2009 - No. 3, Oct, 2009 ($3.99, limited series)

1-3-Kano-a; Thor and Galactus app.; reprints form Thor #337-339. 2,3-Silver Surfer app. 4.00

BETRAYAL OF THE PLANET OF THE APES (Set 20 years before the first movie)
BOOM! Studios: Nov, 2011 - No. 4, Feb, 2012 ($3.99, limited series)

1-4-Dr. Zaius app.; Bechko-s/Hardman-a. 1-Three covers. 2-Two covers 4.00

BETTIE PAGE COMICS
Dark Horse Comics: Mar, 1996 ($3.95)

1-Dave Stevens-c; Blevins & Heath-a; Jaime Hernandez pin-up 2 4 6 10 14 18

BETTIE PAGE COMICS: QUEEN OF THE NILE
Dark Horse Comics: Dec, 1999 - No. 3, Apr, 2000 ($2.95, limited series)

1-3-Silke-s/a; Stevens-c 2 4 6 8 10 12

BETTIE PAGE COMICS: SPICY ADVENTURE
Dark Horse Comics: Jan, 1997 ($2.95, one-shot, mature)

nn-Silke-c/s/a 2 4 6 8 10 12

BETTY (See Pep Comics #22 for 1st app.)
Archie Comics: Sept, 1992 - No. 195, Jan, 2012 ($1.25-$2.99)

1 6.00
2-18,20-24: 20-1st Super Sleuther-s 4.00
19-Love Showdown part 2 5.00
25-Pin-up page of Betty as Marilyn Monroe, Madonna, Lady Di 5.00
26-50 3.00
51-195: 57- "A Storm Over Uniforms" x-over part 5,6. 186-Begin $2.99-c 3.00

BETTY AND HER STEADY (Going Steady with Betty No. 1)
Avon Periodicals: No. 2, Mar-Apr, 1950

2 11 22 33 60 83 105

BETTY AND ME
Archie Publications: Aug, 1965 - No. 200, Aug, 1992

1 10 20 30 66 138 210
2,3: 3-Origin Superteen 6 12 18 38 69 100
4-8: Superteen in new costume #4-7; dons new helmet in #5, ends #8. 5 10 15 31 53 75
9,10: Girl from R.I.V.E.R.D.A.L.E. 9-UFO-s 4 8 12 27 44 60
11-15,17-20(4/69) 3 6 9 21 33 45
16-Classic cover; w/risqué cover dialogue 5 10 15 35 63 90
21,24-35: 33-Paper doll page 3 6 9 16 23 30
22-Archies Band-s 3 6 9 16 24 32
23-I Dream of Jeannie parody 3 6 9 19 30 40
36(8/71),37,41-55 (52 pgs.): 42-Betty as vamp-s 3 6 9 16 23 30
38-Sabrina app. 4 8 12 23 37 50
39-Josie and Sabrina cover cameos 3 6 9 19 30 40
40-Archie & Betty share a cabin 3 6 9 17 26 35
56(4/71)-80(12/76): 79 Betty Cooper mysteries thru #86. 79-81-Drago the Vampire-s 2 4 6 9 13 16
81-99: 83-Harem-c. 84-Jekyll & Hyde-c/s 2 4 6 8 10 12
100(3/79) 2 4 6 9 12 15
101,118: 101-Elvis mentioned. 118-Tarzan mentioned 1 2 3 5 7 9
102-117,119-130(9/82): 103,104-Space-s. 124-DeCarlo-c begins 7.00
131-138,140,142-147,149-154,156-158: 135,136-Jason Blossom app. 136-Cheryl Blossom cameo. 137-Space-s. 138-Tarzan parody 5.00
139,141,148: 139-Katy Keene collecting-s; Archie in drag-s. 141-Tarzan parody-s. 148-Cyndi Lauper parody-s 6.00
155,159,160(8/87): 155-Archie in drag-s. 159-Superhero gag-c. 160-Wheel of Fortune parody 6.00
161-169,171-199 4.00
170,200: 170-New Archie Superhero-s 6.00

BETTY AND VERONICA (Also see Archie's Girls...)
Archie Enterprises: June, 1987 - Present (75¢-$2.99)

1 2 3 4 6 8 10
2-10 6.00
11-30 4.00
31-81 3.00
82-Love Showdown part 3 5.00
83-270: 242-Begin $2.50-c. 247-Begin $2.99-c. 264-270-Two covers 3.00
267-Mermaid variant-c by Fiona Staples 10.00
... Free Comic Book Day Edition #1 (6/05) Katy Keene-c/app.; Cheryl Blossom app. 3.00

BETTY & VERONICA ANNUAL DIGEST (...Digest Magazine #1-4, 44 on; ...Comics Digest Mag. #5-43)(Continues as Betty & Veronica Friends Double Digest #209-on)
Archie Publications: Nov, 1980 - No. 208, Nov, 2010 ($1.00/-$2.69, digest size)

1 3 6 9 15 22 28
2-10: 2(11/81-Katy Keene story), 3(8/82) 2 4 6 9 13 16
11-30 1 3 4 6 8 10
31-50 1 2 3 4 5 7
51-70 4.00
71-191: 110-Begin $2.19-c. 135-Begin $2.39-c. 165-Begin $2.49. 185-Includes reprint of Archie's Girls B&V #1 (1950) and new story where 1950 & 2008 B&V meet 3.00
192-208: 192-Begin $2.69-c 3.00

BETTY & VERONICA ANNUAL DIGEST MAGAZINE
Archie Comics: Sept, 1989 - No. 16, Aug, 1997 ($1.50/$1.75/$1.79, 128 pgs.)

1 1 2 3 5 7 9
2-10: 9-Neon ink logo 5.00
11-16: 16-Begin $1.79-c 3.00

BETTY & VERONICA CHRISTMAS SPECTACULAR (See Archie Giant Series Magazine #159, 168, 180, 191, 204, 217, 229, 241, 453, 465, 477, 489, 501, 513, 525, 536, 547, 558, 568, 580, 593, 606, 618)

BETTY & VERONICA DOUBLE DIGEST MAGAZINE
Archie Enterprises: 1987 - Present ($2.25-$3.99, digest size, 256 pgs.)(...Digest #12 on)

1 2 4 6 8 10 12
2-10 1 2 3 4 5 7
11-25: 5,17-Xmas-c. 16-Capt. Hero story 5.00
26-50 4.00
51-150: 87-Begin $3.19-c. 95-Begin $3.29-c. 114-Begin $3.59-c. 142-Begin $3.69-c 4.00
151-211,213-222: 151-(7/07)-Realistic style Betty & Veronica debuts (thru #154). 160-Cheryl Blossom spotlight. 170-173-Realistic style 4.00
212-Titled Betty & Veronica Double Double Digest (6/13, $5.99, 320 pages) 6.00
Betty & Veronica: in Bad Boy Trouble Vol.1 TPB (2007, $7.49) r/new style from #151-154 8.00

BETTY & VERONICA FRIENDS DOUBLE DIGEST (Continues from B&V Digest Mag. #208)
Archie Publications: No. 209, Jan, 2011 - Present ($3.99, digest size)

209-236: 209-Cheryl Blossom app. 4.00
237-Titled Betty & Veronica Friends Double Double Digest ($5.99, 320 pages) 6.00

BETTY & VERONICA SPECTACULAR (See Archie Giant Series Mag. #11, 16, 21, 26, 32, 138, 145, 153, 162, 173, 184, 197, 201, 210, 214, 221, 226, 234, 238, 246, 250, 458, 462, 470, 482, 486, 494, 498, 506, 510, 518, 522, 526, 530, 537, 552, 559, 563, 569, 575, 582, 588, 600, 608, 613, 620, 623, and Betty & Veronica)

BETTY AND VERONICA SPECTACULAR
Archie Comics: Oct, 1992 - No. 90, Sept, 2009 ($1.25/$1.50/$1.75/$1.99/$2.19/$2.25/$2.50)

1-Dan DeCarlo-c/a 5.00
2-90: 48-Cheryl Blossom leaves Riverdale. 64-Cheryl Blossom returns 3.00

BETTY & VERONICA SPRING SPECTACULAR (See Archie Giant Series Magazine #569, 582, 595)

BETTY & VERONICA SUMMER FUN (See Archie Giant Series Mag. #8, 13, 18, 23, 28, 34, 140, 147, 155, 164, 175, 187, 199, 212, 224, 236, 248, 460, 484, 496, 508, 520, 529, 539, 550, 561, 572, 585, 598, 611, 621)
Archie Comics: 1994 - Present ($2.00/$2.25/$2.29)

Beware #6 © TM

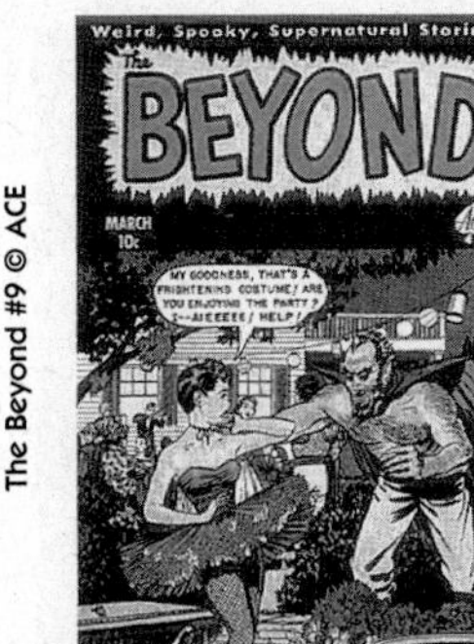

The Beyond #9 © ACE

Big All-American Comic Book #1 © DC

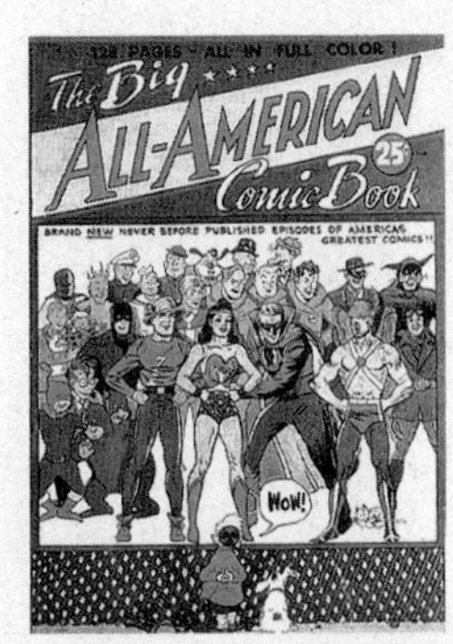

	GD	VG	FN	VF	VF/NM	NM-
	2.0	4.0	6.0	8.0	9.0	9.2

1-($2.00, 52 pgs. plus poster) 4.00
2-6: 5-($2.25-c). 6-($2.29-c) 3.00
Vol. 1 (2003, $10.95) reprints stories from Archie Giant Series editions 12.00

BETTY BOOP'S BIG BREAK
First Publishing: 1990 ($5.95, 52 pgs.)
nn-By Joshua Quagmire; 60th anniversary ish. 6.00

BETTY PAGE 3-D COMICS
The 3-D Zone: 1991 ($3.95, "7-1/2x10-1/4," 28 pgs., no glasses)
1-Photo inside covers; back-c nudity 2 4 6 8 11 14

BETTY'S DIARY (See Archie Giant Series Magazine No. 555)
Archie Enterprises: April, 1986 - No. 40, Apr, 1991 (#1:65¢; 75¢/95¢)
1 1 2 3 4 5 7
2-10 4.00
11-40 3.00

BETTY'S DIGEST
Archie Enterprises: Nov, 1996 - No. 2 ($1.75/$1.79)
1,2 3.00

BEVERLY HILLBILLIES (TV)
Dell Publishing Co.: 4-6/63 - No. 18, 8/67; No. 19, 10/69; No. 20, 10/70; No. 21, Oct, 1971
1-Photo-c 12 24 36 83 182 280
2-Photo-c 8 16 24 51 96 140
3-9: All have photo covers 6 12 18 40 73 105
10: No photo cover 5 10 15 30 50 70
11-21: All have photo covers. 18-Last 12¢ issue. 19-21-Reprint #1-3 (covers and insides)
5 10 15 33 57 80
NOTE: *#1-9, 11-21 are photo covers.*

BEWARE (Formerly Fantastic; Chilling Tales No. 13 on)
Youthful Magazines: No. 10, June, 1952 - No. 12, Oct, 1952
10-E.A. Poe's Pit & the Pendulum adaptation by Wildey; Harrison/Bache-a; atom bomb and shrunken head-c 64 128 192 406 696 985
11-Harrison-a; Ambrose Bierce adapt. 42 84 126 265 445 625
12-Used in **SOTI**, pg. 388; Harrison-a 42 84 126 265 445 625

BEWARE
Trojan Magazines/Merit Publ. No. ?: No. 13, 1/53 - No. 16, 7/53; No. 5, 9/53 - No. 15, 5/55
13(#1)-Harrison-a 63 126 189 403 689 975
14(#2, 3/53)-Krenkel/Harrison-c; dismemberment, severed head panels
42 84 126 265 445 625
15,16(#3, 5/53; #4, 7/53)-Harrison-a 40 80 120 244 402 560
5,9,12,13 39 78 117 240 395 550
6-Ill. in **SOTI**- "Children are first shocked and then desensitized by all this brutality." Corpse on cover swipe/V.O.H. #26; girl on cover swipe/Advs. Into Darkness #10
71 142 213 454 777 1100
7,8-Check-a 40 80 120 244 402 560
10-Frazetta/Check-c; Disbrow, Check-a 90 180 270 576 988 1400
11-Disbrow-a; heart torn out, blood drainage 42 84 126 265 445 625
14,15: 14-Myron Fass-c. 15-Harrison-a 36 72 108 211 343 475
NOTE: ***Fass** a-5, 6, 8; c-6, 11, 14. **Forte** a-8. **Hollingsworth** a-15(#3), 16(#4), 9; c-16(#4), 8, 9. **Kiefer** a-16(#4), 5, 6, 10.*

BEWARE (Becomes Tomb of Darkness No. 9 on)
Marvel Comics Group: Mar, 1973 - No. 8, May, 1974 (All reprints)
1-Everett-c; Kirby & Sinnott-r ('54) 3 6 9 21 33 45
2-8: 2-Forte, Colan-r. 6-Tuska-a. 7-Torres-r/Mystical Tales #7
3 6 9 14 20 25
NOTE: ***Infantino** a-4r. **Gil Kane** c-4. **Wildey** a-7r.*

BEWARE TERROR TALES
Fawcett Publications: May, 1952 - No. 8, July, 1953
1-E.C. art swipe/Haunt of Fear #5 & Vault of Horror #26
52 104 156 328 552 775
2 36 72 108 211 343 475
3-5,7 30 60 90 177 289 400
6-Classic skeleton-c 36 72 108 211 343 475
8-Tothish-a; people being cooked-c 39 78 117 231 378 525
NOTE: ***Andru** a-2. **Bernard Bailey** a-1; c-1-5. **Powell** a-1, 2, 8. **Sekowsky** a-2.*

BEWARE THE BATMAN (Based on the Cartoon Network series)
DC Comics: Dec, 2013 - Present ($2.99)
1-6: 1-Anarky app. 4-Man-Bat app. 6-Killer Croc app. 3.00

BEWARE THE CREEPER (See Adventure, Best of the Brave & the Bold, Brave & the Bold, 1st Issue Special, Flash #318-323, Showcase #73, World's Finest Comics #249)
National Periodical Publications: May-June, 1968 - No. 6, Mar-Apr, 1969 (All 12¢ issues)
1-(5-6/68)-Classic Ditko-c; Ditko-a in all 8 16 24 54 102 150
2-6: 2-5-Ditko-c. 2-Intro. Proteus. 6-Gil Kane-c 5 10 15 31 53 75

BEWARE THE CREEPER
DC Comics (Vertigo): June, 2003 - No. 5, Oct, 2003 ($2.95, limited series)
1-5-Female vigilante in 1920s Paris; Jason Hall-s/Cliff Chiang-a 3.00

BEWITCHED (TV)
Dell Publishing Co.: 4-6/65 - No. 11, 10/67; No. 12, 10/68 - No. 13, 1/69; No. 14, 10/69
1-Photo-c 12 24 36 84 185 285
2-No photo-c 7 14 21 46 86 125
3-13-All have photo-c. 12-Rep. #1. 13-Last 12¢-c 6 12 18 40 73 105
14-No photo-c; reprints #2 5 10 15 31 53 75

BEYOND!
Marvel Comics: Sept, 2006 - No. 6, Feb, 2007 ($2.99, limited series)
1-6-McDuffie-s/Kolins-a; Spider-Man, Venom, Gravity, Wasp app. 6-Gravity dies 3.00
HC (2007, $19.99, dustjacket) r/series; cover sketches and sketch design pages 20.00

BEYOND, THE
Ace Magazines: Nov, 1950 - No. 30, Jan, 1955
1-Bakerish-a(p) 47 94 141 296 498 700
2-Bakerish-a(p) 32 64 96 188 307 425
3-10: 10-Woodish-a by Cameron 22 44 66 132 216 300
11-20: 18-Used in **POP**, pgs. 81,82 19 38 57 111 176 240
21-26,28-30 18 36 54 107 169 230
27-Used in **SOTI**, pg. 111 19 38 57 111 176 240
NOTE: ***Cameron** a-10, 11p, 12p, 15, 16, 21-27, 30; c-20. **Colan** a-6, 13, 17. **Sekowsky** a-2, 3, 5, 7, 11, 14, 27r. No. 1 was to appear as Challenge of the Unknown No. 7.*

BEYOND THE FRINGE (Based on the TV series Fringe)
DC Comics: May, 2012 ($3.99, one-shot)
1-Joshua Jackson-s/Jorge Jimenez-a/Drew Johnson-c 4.00

BEYOND THE GRAVE
Charlton Comics: July, 1975 - No. 6, June, 1976; No. 7, Jan, 1983 - No. 17, Oct, 1984
1-Ditko-a (6 pgs.); Sutton painted-c 4 8 12 23 37 50
2-6: 2-5-Ditko-a; Ditko c-2,3,6 3 6 9 15 22 28
7-17: ('83-'84) Reprints. 8,11,16-Ditko-a. 11-Staton-a. 13-Aparo-c(r). 15-Sutton-c (low print run). 16-Palais-a 1 2 3 5 6 8
Modern Comics Reprint 2('78) 6.00
NOTE: ***Howard** a-4. **Kim** a-1. **Larson** a-4, 6.*

BIBLE, THE: EDEN
IDW Publishing: 2003 ($21.99, hardcover graphic novel)
HC-Scott Hampton painted-a; adaptation of Genesis by Dave Elliot and Keith Giffen 22.00

BIBLE TALES FOR YOUNG FOLK (...Young People No. 3-5)
Atlas Comics (OMC): Aug, 1953 - No. 5, Mar, 1954
1 27 54 81 158 259 360
2-Everett, Krigstein-a; Robinson-c 18 36 54 105 165 225
3-5: 4,5-Robinson-c 15 30 45 88 137 185

BIG (Movie)
Hit Comics (Dark Horse Comics): Mar, 1989 ($2.00)
1-Adaptation of film; Paul Chadwick-c 3.00

BIG ALL-AMERICAN COMIC BOOK, THE (See All-American Comics)
All-American/National Per. Publ.: 1944 (132 pgs., one-shot) (Early DC Annual)
1-Wonder Woman, Green Lantern, Flash, The Atom, Wildcat, Scribbly, The Whip, Ghost Patrol, Hawkman by Kubert (1st on Hawkman), Hop Harrigan, Johnny Thunder, Little Boy Blue, Mr. Terrific, Mutt & Jeff app.; Sargon on cover only; cover by Kubert/Hibbard/Mayer and others 649 1298 1947 4738 8369 12,000

BIG BABY HUEY (See Baby Huey)

BIG BANG COMICS (Becomes Big Bang #4)
Caliber Press: Spring, 1994 - No. 4, Feb, 1995; No. 0, May, 1995 ($1.95, lim. series)
1-4-($1.95-c) 3.00
0-(5/95, $2.95) Alex Ross-c; color and B&W pages 3.00
Your Big Book of Big Bang Comics TPB ('98, $11.00) r/#0-2 11.00

BIG BANG COMICS (Volume 2)
Image Comics (Highbrow Ent.): V2#1, May, 1996 - No. 35, Jan, 2001 ($1.95-$3.95)
1-23,26: 1-Mighty Man app. 2-4-S.A. Shadowhawk app. 5-Begin $2.95-c. 6-Curt Swan/Murphy Anderson-c. 7-Begin B&W. 12-Savage Dragon-c/app. 16,17,21-Shadow Lady 3.00
24,25,27-35-($3.95): 35-Big Bang vs. Alan Moore's "1963" characters 4.00
...Presents the Ultiman Family (2/05, $3.50) 3.50

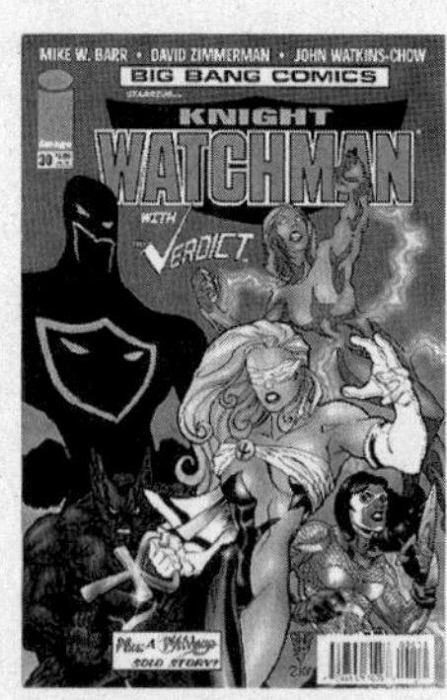

Big Bang Comics #30 © Carlson

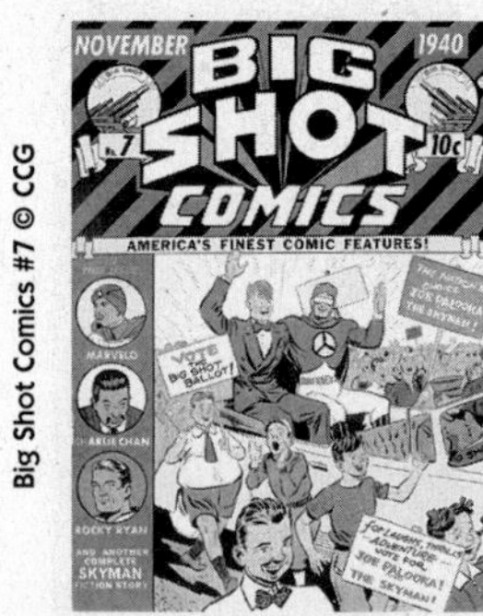

Big Shot Comics #7 © CCG

Big-3 #3 © FOX

GD 2.0 | VG 4.0 | FN 6.0 | VF 8.0 | VF/NM 9.0 | NM- 9.2

...Round Table of America (2/04, $3.95) Don Thomas-a 4.00
...Summer Special (8/03, $4.95) World's Nastiest Nazis app. 5.00

BIG BANG PRESENTS (Volume 3)
Big Bang Comics: July, 2006 - No. 5 ($2.95/$3.95, B&W)
1,2: 1-Protoplasman (Plastic Man homage) 3.00
3-5-($3.95) 3-Origin of Protoplasman. 4-Flip book 4.00

BIG BLACK KISS
Vortex Comics: Sep, 1989 - No, 3, Nov, 1989 ($3.75, B&W, lim. series, mature)
1-3-Chaykin-s/a 4.00

BIG BLOWN BABY (Also see Dark Horse Presents)
Dark Horse Comics: Aug, 1996 - No. 4, Nov, 1996 ($2.95, lim. series, mature)
1-4: Bill Wray-c/a/scripts 3.00

BIG BOOK OF ..., THE
DC Comics (Paradox Press): 1994 - 1999 (B&W)($12.95 - $14.95)
nn-...**BAD**,1998 ($14.95),...**CONSPIRACIES**, 1995 ($12.95), ...**DEATH**,1994 ($12.95), ...**FREAKS**, 1996 ($14.95), ...**GRIMM**, 1999 ($14.95), ...**HOAXES**, 1996 ($14.95), ...**LITTLE CRIMINALS**, 1996 ($14.95), ...**LOSERS**,1997 ($14.95), **MARTYRS**, 1997 ($14.95), ...**SCANDAL**,1997 ($14.95), ...**THE WEIRD WILD WEST**,1998 ($14.95), ...**THUGS**, 1997 ($14.95), ...**UNEXPLAINED**, 1997 ($14.95), ...**URBAN LEGENDS**, 1994 ($12.95), ...**VICE**, 1999 ($14.95), ...**WEIRDOS**, 1995 ($12.95) cover price

BIG BOOK OF FUN COMICS (See New Book of Comics)
National Periodical Publications: Spring, 1936 (Large size, 52 pgs.) (1st comic book annual & DC annual)
1 (Very rare)-r/New Fun #1-5 2300 4600 6900 15,000 - -

BIG BOOK ROMANCES
Fawcett Publications: Feb, 1950 (no date given) (148 pgs.)
1-Contains remaindered Fawcett romance comics - several combinations possible
50 100 150 315 533 750

BIG CHIEF WAHOO
Eastern Color Printing/George Dougherty (distr. by Fawcett): July, 1942 - No. 7, Wint., 1943/44?(no year given)(Quarterly)
1-Newspaper-r (on sale 6/15/42) 42 84 126 265 445 625
2-Steve Roper app. 23 46 69 136 223 310
3-5: 4-Chief is holding a Katy Keene comic 18 36 54 105 165 225
6-7 14 28 42 82 121 160
NOTE: *Kerry Drake in some issues.*

BIG CIRCUS, THE (Movie)
Dell Publishing Co.: No. 1036, Sept-Nov, 1959
Four Color 1036-Photo-c 6 12 18 37 66 95

BIG COUNTRY, THE (Movie)
Dell Publishing Co.: No. 946, Oct, 1958
Four Color 946-Photo-c 6 12 18 40 73 105

BIG DADDY DANGER
DC Comics: Oct, 2002 - No. 9, June, 2003 ($2.95, limited series)
1-9-Adam Pollina-s/a/c 3.00

BIG DADDY ROTH (Magazine)
Millar Publications: Oct-Nov, 1964 - No. 4, Apr-May, 1965 (35¢)
1-Toth-a; Batman & Robin parody 16 32 48 110 243 375
2-4-Toth-a 10 20 30 69 147 225

BIGFOOT
IDW Publishing: Feb, 2005 - No. 4, May, 2005 ($3.99, limited series)
1-4-Steve Niles & Rob Zombie-s/Richard Corben-a/c 4.00

BIGG TIME
DC Comics (Vertigo): 2002 ($14.95, B&W, graphic novel)
nn-Ty Templeton-s/c/a 15.00

BIG GUY AND RUSTY THE BOY ROBOT, THE (Also See Madman Comics #6,7 & Martha Washington Stranded In Space)
Dark Horse (Legend): July, 1995 - No. 2, Aug, 1995 ($4.95, oversize, limited series)
1,2-Frank Miller scripts & Geoff Darrow-c/a 1 2 3 4 5 7
Trade paperback (10/96, $14.95)-r/1,2 w/cover gallery 15.00

BIG HAIR PRODUCTIONS
Image Comics: Feb, 2000 - No. 2, Mar, 2000 ($3.50, B&W)
1,2 3.50

BIG HERO ADVENTURES (See Jigsaw)

BIG HERO 6 (Also see Sunfire & Big Hero Six)
Marvel Comics: Nov, 2008 - No. 5, Mar, 2009 ($3.99, limited series)
1-5-Claremont-s/Nakayama-a; 1-Character design pages & Handbook entries 4.00
...: Brave New Heroes 1 (11/12, $8.99) r/#1-5 9.00

BIG JON & SPARKIE (Radio)(Formerly Sparkie, Radio Pixie)
Ziff-Davis Publ. Co.: No. 4, Sept-Oct, 1952 (Painted-c)
4-Based on children's radio program 19 38 57 109 172 235

BIG LAND, THE (Movie)
Dell Publishing Co.: No. 812, July, 1957
Four Color 812-Alan Ladd photo-c 8 16 24 51 96 140

BIG LIE, THE
Image Comics: Sept, 2011 ($3.99, one-shot)
1-Revisits the 9-11 attacks; Rick Veitch-s/a(p); Thomas Yeates-c 4.00

BIG RED (See Movie Comics)

BIG SHOT COMICS
Columbia Comics Group: May, 1940 - No. 104, Aug, 1949
1-Intro. Skyman; The Face (1st app.; Tony Trent), The Cloak (Spy Master), Marvelo, Monarch of Magicians, Joe Palooka, Charlie Chan, Tom Kerry, Dixie Dugan, Rocky Ryan begin; Charlie Chan moves over from Feature Comics #31 (4/40)
277 554 831 1759 3030 4300
2 94 188 282 597 1024 1450
3-The Cloak called Spy Chief; Skyman-c 84 168 252 538 919 1300
4,5 60 120 180 381 653 925
6-10: 8-Christmas-c 48 96 144 302 514 725
11-13 45 90 135 284 480 675
14-Origin & 1st app. Sparky Watts (6/41) 48 96 144 302 514 725
15-Origin The Cloak 53 106 159 334 567 800
16-20 39 78 117 231 378 525
21-23,27,30: 30-X-Mas-c, WWII-c 32 64 96 192 314 435
24-Classic Tojo-c. 90 180 270 576 988 1400
25-Hitler-c 65 130 195 416 708 1000
26,29-Japanese WWII-c. 29-Intro. Capt. Yank; Bo (a dog) newspaper strip-r by Frank Beck begin, ends #104. 39 78 117 240 395 550
28-Hitler, Tojo & Mussolini-c 97 194 291 621 1061 1500
31,33-40 24 48 72 140 230 320
32-Vic Jordan newspaper strip reprints begin, ends #52; Hitler, Tojo & Mussolini-c
87 174 261 553 952 1350
41,42,44,45,47-50: 42-No Skyman. 50-Origin The Face retold
20 40 60 120 195 270
43-Hitler-c 77 154 231 493 847 1200
46-Hitler, Tojo-c (6/44) 76 152 228 486 831 1175
51-Tojo Japanese war-c 36 72 108 216 351 485
52-56,58-60: 18 36 54 103 162 220
57-Hitler, Tojo Halloween mask-c 40 80 120 244 402 560
61-70: 63 on-Tony Trent, the Face 14 28 42 82 121 160
71-80: 73-The Face cameo. 74-(2/47)-Mickey Finn begins. 74,80-The Face app. in Tony Trent. 78-Last Charlie Chan strip-r 14 28 42 76 108 140
81-90: 85-Tony Trent marries Babs Walsh. 86-Valentines-c
11 22 33 62 86 110
91-99,101-104: 69-94-Skyman in Outer Space. 96-Xmas-c
10 20 30 56 76 95
100 11 22 33 64 90 115
NOTE: ***Mart Bailey** art on "The Face" No. 1-104. **Guardineer** a-5. Sparky Watts by **Boody Rogers**-No. 14-42, 77-104, (by others No. 43-76). Others than Tony Trent wear "The Face" mask in No. 46-63, 93. Skyman by **Ogden Whitney**-No. 1, 2, 4, 12-37, 49, 70-101. Skyman covers-No. 1, 3, 7-12, 14, 16, 20, 27, 89, 95, 100.*

BIG SMASH BARGAIN COMICS
No publisher listed: Early 1950s (25¢, 160pgs., Canadian reprints)
1-4: Contains 4 comics from various companies bundled with new cover (scarce)
34 68 102 199 325 450

BIG TEX
Toby Press: June, 1953
1-Contains (3) John Wayne stories-r with name changed to Big Tex
11 22 33 62 86 110

BIG-3
Fox Features Syndicate: Fall, 1940 - No. 7, Jan, 1942
1-Blue Beetle, The Flame, & Samson begin 232 464 696 1485 2543 3600
2 86 172 258 546 936 1325
3-5 61 122 183 390 670 950
6,7: 6-Last Samson. 7-V-Man app. 47 94 141 296 498 700

Biker Mice From Mars #1 © MAR

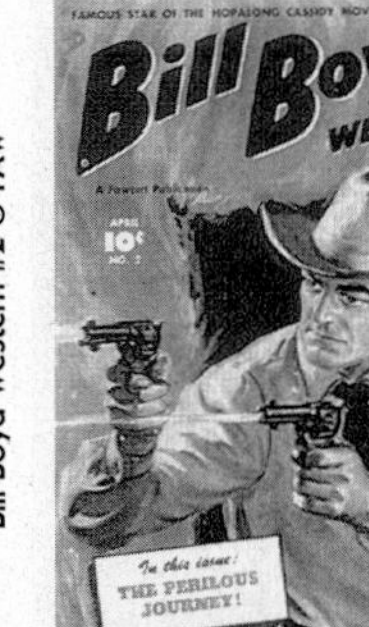

Bill Boyd Western #2 © FAW

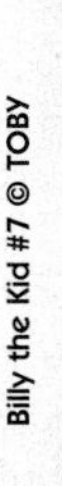
Billy the Kid #7 © TOBY

	GD 2.0	VG 4.0	FN 6.0	VF 8.0	VF/NM 9.0	NM- 9.2

BIG TOP COMICS, THE (TV's Great Circus Show)
Toby Press: 1951 - No. 2, 1951 (No month)

	GD	VG	FN	VF	VF/NM	NM-
1	11	22	33	60	83	105
2	9	18	27	47	61	75

BIG TOWN (Radio/TV) (Also see Movie Comics, 1946)
National Periodical Publ: Jan, 1951 - No. 50, Mar-Apr, 1958 (No. 1-9: 52pgs.)

	GD	VG	FN	VF	VF/NM	NM-
1-Dan Barry-a begins	68	136	204	438	749	1060
2	36	72	108	216	351	485
3-10	21	42	63	126	206	285
11-20	16	32	48	92	144	195
21-31: Last pre-code (1-2/55)	13	26	39	74	105	135
32-50: 46-Grey tone cover	10	20	30	56	76	95

BIG VALLEY, THE (TV)
Dell Publishing Co.: June, 1966 - No. 5, Oct, 1967; No. 6, Oct, 1969

	GD	VG	FN	VF	VF/NM	NM-
1: Photo-c #1-5	5	10	15	31	53	75
2-6: 6-Reprints #1	3	6	9	21	33	45

BIKER MICE FROM MARS (TV)
Marvel Comics: Nov, 1993 - No. 3, Jan, 1994 ($1.50, limited series)

	GD	VG	FN	VF	VF/NM	NM-
1-3: 1-Intro Vinnie, Modo & Throttle. 2-Origin						4.00

BILL & TED'S BOGUS JOURNEY
Marvel Comics: Sept, 1991 ($2.95, squarebound, 84 pgs.)

	GD	VG	FN	VF	VF/NM	NM-
1-Adapts movie sequel						4.00

BILL & TED'S EXCELLENT COMIC BOOK (Movie)
Marvel Comics: Dec, 1991 - No. 12, 1992 ($1.00/$1.25)

	GD	VG	FN	VF	VF/NM	NM-
1-12: 3-Begin $1.25-c						3.00

BILL BARNES COMICS (...America's Air Ace Comics No. 2 on) (Becomes Air Ace V2#1 on; also see Shadow Comics)
Street & Smith Publications: Oct, 1940(No. month given) - No. 12, Oct, 1943

	GD	VG	FN	VF	VF/NM	NM-
1-23 pgs.-comics; Rocket Rooney begins	95	190	285	603	1039	1475
2-Barnes as The Phantom Flyer app.; Tuska-a	48	96	144	302	514	725
3-5	41	82	123	256	428	600
6,8,10,12	37	74	111	222	361	500
7-(1942) Story about dropping atomic bomb on Japan	42	84	126	265	445	625
9-Classic WWII cover	47	94	141	296	498	700
11-Japanese WWII Gremlin cover	39	78	117	231	378	525

BILL BATTLE, THE ONE MAN ARMY (Also see Master Comics No. 133)
Fawcett Publications: Oct, 1952 - No. 4, Apr, 1953 (All photo-c)

	GD	VG	FN	VF	VF/NM	NM-
1	14	28	42	76	108	150
2	9	18	27	47	61	75
3,4	8	16	24	42	54	65

BILL BLACK'S FUN COMICS
Paragon #1-3/Americomics #4: Dec, 1982 - No. 4, Mar, 1983 ($1.75/$2.00, Baxter paper) (1st AC comic)

	GD	VG	FN	VF	VF/NM	NM-
1-(B&W fanzine; 7x8-1/2"; low print) Intro. Capt. Paragon, Phantom Lady & Commando D	2	4	6	13	18	22
2-4: 2,3-(B&W fanzines; 8-1/2x11"). 3-Kirby-c. 4-($2.00, color)-Origin Nightfall (formerly Phantom Lady); Nightveil app.; Kirby-a	1	3	4	6	8	10

BILL BOYD WESTERN (Movie star; see Hopalong Cassidy & Western Hero)
Fawcett Publ: Feb, 1950 - No. 23, June, 1952 (1-3,7,11,14-on: 36 pgs.)

	GD	VG	FN	VF	VF/NM	NM-
1-Bill Boyd & his horse Midnite begin; photo front/back-c	30	60	90	177	289	400
2-Painted-c	16	32	48	94	147	200
3-Photo-c begin, end #23; last photo back-c	14	28	42	80	115	150
4-6(52 pgs.)	12	24	36	69	97	125
7,11(36 pgs.)	10	20	30	56	76	95
8-10,12,13(52 pgs.)	10	20	30	58	79	100
14-22	9	18	27	52	69	85
23-Last issue	10	20	30	56	76	95

BILL BUMLIN (See Treasury of Comics No. 3)

BILL ELLIOTT (See Wild Bill Elliott)

BILLI 99
Dark Horse Comics: Sept, 1991 - No. 4, 1991 ($3.50, B&W, lim. series, 52 pgs.)

	GD	VG	FN	VF	VF/NM	NM-
1-4: Tim Sale-c/a						4.00

BILL STERN'S SPORTS BOOK
Ziff-Davis Publ. Co.(Approved Comics): Spring-Sum, 1951 - V2#2, Win, 1952

	GD	VG	FN	VF	VF/NM	NM-
V1#10-(1951) Whitney painted-c	21	42	63	122	199	275
2-(Sum/52; reg. size)	16	32	48	94	147	200
V2#2-(1952, 96 pgs.)-Krigstein, Kinstler-a	21	42	63	126	206	285

BILL THE BULL: ONE SHOT, ONE BOURBON, ONE BEER
Boneyard Press: Dec, 1994 ($2.95, B&W, mature)

	GD	VG	FN	VF	VF/NM	NM-
1						3.00

BILLY AND BUGGY BEAR (See Animal Fun)
I.W. Enterprises/Super: 1958; 1964

	GD	VG	FN	VF	VF/NM	NM-
I.W. Reprint #1, #7('58)-All Surprise Comics #?(Same issue-r for both)	2	4	6	10	14	18
Super Reprint #10(1964)	2	4	6	8	11	14

BILLY BATSON AND THE MAGIC OF SHAZAM! (Follows Shazam: The Monster Society of Evil mini-series)
DC Comics: Sept, 2008 - No. 21, Dec, 2010 ($2.25/$2.50, all ages title)

	GD	VG	FN	VF	VF/NM	NM-
1-17: 1-4-Mike Kunkel-s/a/c; Theo (Black) Adam app. 5-DeStefano-a. 13-16-Black Adam						3.00
1-Variant B&W sketch cover						3.50
18-21 ($2.99) 21-Justice League cameo						3.00
TPB (2010, $12.99) r/#1-6; cover and haracter sketches						13.00
...: Mr. Mind Over Matter TPB (2011, $12.99) r/#7-12						13.00

BILLY BUCKSKIN WESTERN (2-Gun Western No. 4)
Atlas Comics (IMC No. 1/MgPC No. 2,3): Nov, 1955 - No. 3, Mar, 1956

	GD	VG	FN	VF	VF/NM	NM-
1-Mort Drucker-a; Maneely-c/a	15	30	45	90	140	190
2-Mort Drucker-a	10	20	30	56	76	95
3-Williamson, Drucker-a	12	24	36	67	94	120

BILLY BUNNY (Black Cobra No. 6 on)
Excellent Publications: Feb-Mar, 1954 - No. 5, Oct-Nov, 1954

	GD	VG	FN	VF	VF/NM	NM-
1	9	18	27	52	69	85
2	6	12	18	29	36	42
3-5	5	10	15	24	30	35

BILLY BUNNY'S CHRISTMAS FROLICS
Farrell Publications: 1952 (25¢ Giant, 100 pgs.)

	GD	VG	FN	VF	VF/NM	NM-
1	21	42	63	124	202	280

BILLY MAKE BELIEVE
United Features Syndicate: No. 14, 1939

	GD	VG	FN	VF	VF/NM	NM-
Single Series 14	31	62	93	182	296	410

BILLY NGUYEN, PRIVATE EYE
Caliber Press: V2#1, 1990 ($2.50)

	GD	VG	FN	VF	VF/NM	NM-
V2#1						3.00

BILLY THE KID (Formerly The Masked Raider; also see Doc Savage Comics & Return of the Outlaw)
Charlton Publ. Co.: No. 9, Nov, 1957 - No. 121, Dec, 1976; No. 122, Sept, 1977 - No. 123, Oct, 1977; No. 124, Feb, 1978 - No. 153, Mar, 1983

	GD	VG	FN	VF	VF/NM	NM-
9	10	20	30	58	79	100
10,12,14,17-19: 12-2 pg Check-sty	8	16	24	40	50	60
11-(68 pgs.)-Origin & 1st app. The Ghost Train	9	18	27	50	65	80
13-Williamson/Torres-a	8	16	24	44	57	70
15-Origin; 2 pgs. Williamson-a	8	16	24	44	57	70
16-Williamson-a, 2 pgs.	8	16	24	42	54	65
20-26-Severin-a(3-4 each)	8	16	24	44	57	70
27-30: 30-Masked Rider app.	3	6	9	18	28	38
31-40	3	6	9	15	22	28
41-60	2	4	6	13	18	22
61-65	2	4	6	10	14	18
66-Bounty Hunter series begins.	3	6	9	14	20	25
67-80: Bounty Hunter series; not in #79,82,84-86	2	4	6	10	14	18
81-84,86-90: 87-Last Bounty Hunter. 88-1st app. Mr. Young of the Boothill Gazette	2	4	6	8	10	12
85-Early Kaluta-a (4 pgs.)	2	4	6	9	13	16
91-123: 110-Mr. Young of Boothill app. 111-Origin The Ghost Train. 117-Gunsmith & Co., The Cheyenne Kid app.	1	2	3	5	6	8
124(2/78)-153						6.00
Modern Comics 109 (1977 reprint)						5.00

NOTE: ***Boyette*** *a-88-110.* ***Kim*** *a-73.* ***Morsi*** *a-12,14.* ***Sattler*** *a-118-123.* ***Severin*** *a(r)-121-129, 134; c-23, 25.* ***Sutton*** *a-111.*

BILLY THE KID ADVENTURE MAGAZINE
Toby Press: Oct, 1950 - No. 29, 1955

	GD	VG	FN	VF	VF/NM	NM-
1-Williamson/Frazetta-a (2 pgs) r/from John Wayne Adventure Comics #2; photo-c	31	62	93	182	296	410

Billy West #3 © STD

Birds of Prey #35 © DC

Bishop the Last X-Man #4 © MAR

	GD 2.0	VG 4.0	FN 6.0	VF 8.0	VF/NM 9.0	NM- 9.2

2-Photo-c 12 24 36 69 97 125
3-Williamson/Frazetta "The Claws of Death", 4 pgs. plus Williamson art 34 68 102 199 325 450
4,5,7,8,10: 4,7-Photo-c 9 18 27 52 69 85
6-Frazetta assist on "Nightmare"; photo-c 15 30 45 83 124 165
9-Kurtzman Pot-Shot Pete; photo-c 11 22 33 64 90 115
11,12,15-20: 11-Photo-c 8 16 24 42 54 65
13-Kurtzman-r/John Wayne #12 (Genius) 9 18 27 47 61 75
14-Williamson/Frazetta; r-of #1 (2 pgs.) 10 20 30 56 76 95
21,23-29 7 14 21 37 46 55
22-Williamson/Frazetta-r(1pg.)/#1; photo-c 8 16 24 42 54 65

BILLY THE KID AND OSCAR (Also see Fawcett's Funny Animals)
Fawcett Publications: Winter, 1945 - No. 3, Fall, 1946 (Funny animal)

1 15 30 45 86 133 180
2,3 10 20 30 58 79 100

BILLY THE KID'S OLD TIMEY ODDITIES
Dark Horse Comics: Apr, 2005 - No. 4, July, 2005 ($2.99, limited series)

1-4-Eric Powell-s/c; Kyle Hotz-a 4.00
TPB (2005, $13.95) r/series 14.00
... and the Ghostly Fiend of London (9/10 - No. 4, 12/10, $3.99) 1-4-Powell-s/c; Kyle Hotz-a; Goon back-up; Powell-s/a 4.00
... and the Orm of Loch Ness (10/12 - No. 4, 1/13, $3.50) 1-4-Powell-s/Hotz-a/c 4.00

BILLY WEST (Bill West No. 9,10)
Standard Comics (Visual Editions): 1949-No. 9, Feb, 1951; No. 10, Feb, 1952

1 16 32 48 92 144 195
2 10 20 30 56 76 95
3-6,9,10 9 18 27 50 65 80
7,8-Schomburg-c 10 20 30 56 76 95

NOTE: ***Celardo** a-1-6, 9; c-1-3. **Moreira** a-3. **Roussos** a-2.*

BING CROSBY (See Feature Films)

BINGO (...Comics) (H. C. Blackerby)
Howard Publ.: 1945 (Reprints National material)

1-L. B. Cole opium-c; blank back-c 36 72 108 216 351 485

BINGO, THE MONKEY DOODLE BOY
St. John Publishing Co.: Aug, 1951; Oct, 1953

1(8/51)-By Eric Peters 8 16 24 44 57 70
1(10/53) 7 14 21 35 43 50

BINKY (Formerly Leave It to...)
National Periodical Publ./DC Comics: No. 72, 4-5/70 - No. 81, 10-11/71; No. 82, Summer/77

72-76 4 8 12 27 44 60
77-79: (68 pgs.). 77-Bobby Sherman 1pg. story w/photo. 78-1 pg. sty on Barry Williams of Brady Bunch. 79-Osmonds 1pg. story 5 10 15 35 63 90
80,81 (52 pgs.)-Sweat Pain story 5 10 15 31 53 75
82 (1977, one-shot) 4 8 12 27 44 60

BINKY'S BUDDIES
National Periodical Publications: Jan-Feb, 1969 - No. 12, Nov-Dec, 1970

1 7 14 21 46 86 125
2-12: 3-Last 12¢ issue 4 8 12 27 44 60

BIONIC MAN (TV)
Dynamite Entertainment: 2011 - No. 26, 2013 ($3.99)

1-26: 1-Kevin Smith & Phil Hester-s; Lau-a; multiple covers. 12-15-Bigfoot app. 4.00
Annual 1 (2013, $4.99) The Venus Probe; Beatty-s/Mayhew-c 5.00

BIONIC MAN VS. THE BIONIC WOMAN (TV)
Dynamite Entertainment: 2013 - No. 5, 2013 ($3.99, limited series)

1-5-Champagne-s/Luis-a; 3 covers on each 4.00

BIONIC WOMAN, THE (TV)
Charlton Publications: Oct, 1977 - No. 5, June, 1978

1 4 8 12 25 40 55
2-5 3 6 9 17 26 35

BIONIC WOMAN, THE (TV)
Dynamite Entertainment: 2013 - No. 10, 2013 ($3.99)

1-10: 1-Tobin-s/Renaud-c/Carvalho-a; origin re-told 4.00

BIRDS OF PREY (Also see Black Canary/Oracle: Birds of Prey)
DC Comics: Jan, 1999 - No. 127, Apr, 2009 ($1.99/$2.50/$2.99)

1-Dixon-s/Land-c/a 1 3 4 6 8 10
2-4 6.00
5-7,9-15: 15-Guice-a begins. 4.00
8-Nightwing-c/app.; Barbara & Dick's circus date 3 6 9 19 30 40
16-38: 23-Grodd-c/app. 26-Bane app. 32-Noto-c begin 3.00
39,40-Bruce Wayne: Murderer pt. 5,12 3.50
41-Bruce Wayne: Fugitive pt. 2 4.00
42-46: 42-Fabry-a. 45-Deathstroke-c/app. 3.00
47-74,76-91: 47-49-Terry Moore-s/Conner & Palmiotti-a; Noto-c. 50-Gilbert Hernandez-s begin. 52,54-Metamorpho app. 56-Simone-s/Benes-a begin. 65,67,68,70-Land-c. 76-Debut of Black Alice (from Day of Vengeance). 86-Timm-a (7 pgs.) 3.00
75-($2.95) Pearson-c; back-up story of Lady Blackhawk 4.00
92-99,101-127: 92-One Year Later. 94-Begin $2.99-c; Prometheus app. 96,97-Black Alice app. 98,99-New Batgirl app. 99-Black Canary leaves the team. 104-107-Secret Six app. 3.00
100-($3.99) new team recruited; Black Canary origin re-told 4.00
TPB (1999, $17.95) r/ previous series and one-shots 18.00
...: Batgirl 1 (2/98, $2.95) Dixon-s/Frank-c 5.00
...: Batgirl/Catwoman 1 ('03, $5.95) Robertson-a; cont'd in BOP: Catwoman/Oracle 1 6.00
...: Between Dark & Dawn TPB (2006, $14.99) r/#69-75 15.00
...: Blood and Circuits TPB (2007, $17.99) r/#96-103 18.00
...: Catwoman/Oracle 1 ('03, $5.95) Cont'd from BOP: Batgirl/Catwoman 1; David Ross-a 6.00
...: Club Kids TPB (2008, $17.99) r/#109-112,118 18.00
...: Dead of Winter TPB (2008, $17.99) r/#104-108 18.00
...: Metropolis or Dust TPB (2008, $17.99) r/#113-117 18.00
...: Of Like Minds TPB (2004, $14.95) r/#55-61 15.00
...: Old Friends, New Enemies TPB (2003, $17.95) r/#1-6, ...: Batgirl, ...: Wolves 18.00
...: Perfect Pitch TPB (2007, $17.99) r/#86-90,92-95 18.00
...: Platinum Flats TPB (2009, $17.99) r/#119-124 18.00
...: Revolution 1 (1997, $2.95) Frank-c/Dixon-s 5.00
... Secret Files 2003 (8/03, $4.95) Short stories, pin-ups and profile pages; Noto-c 5.00
...: Sensei and Student TPB (2005, $17.95) r/#62-68 18.00
...: The Battle Within TPB (2006, $17.99) r/#76-85 18.00
...: The Ravens 1 (6/98, $1.95)-Dixon-s; Girlfrenzy issue 4.00
...: Wolves 1 (10/97, $2.95) Dixon-s/Giordano & Faucher-a 5.00

BIRDS OF PREY (Brightest Day)
DC Comics: Jul, 2010 - No. 15, Oct, 2011 ($2.99)

1-Simone-s/Benes-a/c; Hawk and Dove join team, Penguin app. 3.00
1-Variant cover by Chiang 5.00
2-15: 2-4-Penguin app. 7-10-"Death of Oracle". 11-Catman app. 14,15-Tucci-a 3.00
... End Run HC (2011, $22.99, d.j.) r/#1-6 23.00

BIRDS OF PREY (DC New 52)
DC Comics: Nov, 2011 - Present ($2.99)

1-24: 1-Swierczynski-s/Saiz-a; intro. Starling. 2-Katana & Poison Ivy join. 4-Batgirl joins. 9-Night of the Owls. 16-Strix joins. 18-20-Mr. Freeze app. 3.00
25-($3.99) Zero Year tie-in; flashback to Dinah's childhood; John Lynch app. 4.00
26-29: 26-Birds vs. Basilisk. 28-Gothtopia tie-in; Ra's al Ghul app. 3.00
#0 (11/12, $2.99) Black Canary and Batgirl first meeting; Molenaar-a/Lau-c 3.00

BIRDS OF PREY: MANHUNT
DC Comics: Sept, 1996 - No. 4, Dec, 1996 ($1.95, limited series)

1-Features Black Canary, Oracle, Huntress, & Catwoman; Chuck Dixon scripts; Gary Frank-c on all. 1-Catwoman cameo only 1 2 3 5 6 8
2-4 6.00

NOTE: ***Gary Frank** c-1-4. **Matt Haley** a-1-4p. **Wade Von Grawbadger** a-1i.*

BIRTH CAUL, THE
Eddie Campbell Comics: 1999 ($5.95, B&W, one-shot)

1-Alan Moore-s/Eddie Campbell-a 6.00

BIRTH OF THE DEFIANT UNIVERSE, THE
Defiant Comics: May, 1993

nn-Contains promotional artwork & text; limited print run of 1000 copies. 2 4 6 8 11 14

BISHOP (See Uncanny X-Men & X-Men)
Marvel Comics: Dec, 1994 - No.4, Mar, 1995 ($2.95, limited series)

1-4: Foil-c; Shard & Mountjoy in all. 1-Storm app. 4.00

BISHOP THE LAST X-MAN
Marvel Comics: Oct, 1999 - No. 16, Jan, 2001 ($2.99/$1.99/$2.25)

1-($2.99)-Jeanty-a 4.00
2-8-($1.99): 2-Two covers 3.00
9-11,13-16: 9-Begin $2.25-c. 15-Maximum Security x-over; Xavier app. 3.00
12-($2.99) 4.00

BISHOP: XAVIER SECURITY ENFORCER
Marvel Comics: Jan, 1998 - No.3, Mar, 1998 ($2.50, limited series)

Bizarro World HC © DC

Black Beetle #4 © Francesco Francavilla

Black Cat Comics #11 © HARV

GD 2.0 VG 4.0 FN 6.0 VF 8.0 VF/NM 9.0 NM- 9.2

1-3: Ostrander-s 3.00

BITE CLUB
DC Comics (Vertigo): Jun, 2004 - No. 6, Nov, 2004 ($2.95, limited series)

1-6-Chaykin-s/Tischman-a/Quitely-c 3.00
TPB Digest (2005, $9.99) r/#1-6; cover gallery 10.00
The Complete Bite Club TPB (2007, $19.99) r/#1-6 and ...: Vampire Crime Unit #1-5 20.00

BITE CLUB: VAMPIRE CRIME UNIT
DC Comics (Vertigo): Jun, 2006 - No. 5 ($2.99, limited series)

1-5:1-Chaykin & Tischman-s/Hahn-a/Quitely-c. 4-Chaykin-c 3.00

BIZARRE ADVENTURES (Formerly Marvel Preview)
Marvel Comics Group: No. 25, 3/81 - No. 34, 2/83 (#25-33: Magazine-$1.50)

25,26: 25-Lethal Ladies. 26-King Kull; Bolton-c/a 2 4 6 8 10 12
27,28: 27-Phoenix, Iceman & Nightcrawler app. 28-The Unlikely Heroes; Elektra by Miller; Neal Adams-a 2 4 6 10 14 18
29,30,32,33: 29-Stephen King's Lawnmower Man. 30-Tomorrow; 1st app. Silhouette. 32-Gods; Thor-c/s. 33-Horror; Dracula app.; photo-c 2 3 4 6 8 10
31-After The Violence Stops; new Hangman story; Miller-a 2 4 6 8 10 12
34 ($2.00, Baxter paper, comic size)-Son of Santa; Christmas special; Howard the Duck by Paul Smith 1 2 3 5 7 9
NOTE: ***Alcala** a-27i. **Austin** a-25i, 28i. **Bolton** a-26, 32. **J. Buscema** a-27p, 29, 30p; c-26. **Byrne** a-31 (2 pg.). **Golden** a-25p, 28p. **Perez** a-27p. **Rogers** a-25p. **Simonson** a-29; c-29. **Paul Smith** a-34.*

BIZARRO COMICS!
DC Comics: 2001 ($29.95, hardcover, one-shot)

HC-Short stories of DC heroes by various alternative cartoonists including Dorkin, Pope, Haspiel, Kidd, Kochalka, Millionaire, Stephens, Wray; includes "Superman's Babysitter" by Kyle Baker from Elseworlds 80-Page Giant recalled by DC; Groening-c 30.00
Softcover (2003, $19.95) 20.00

BIZARRO WORLD
DC Comics: 2005 ($29.95, hardcover, one-shot)

HC-Short stories by various alternative cartoonists including Bagge, Baker, Dorkin, Dunn, Kupperman, Morse, Oswalt, Pekar, Simpson, Stewart; Jaime Hernandez-c 30.00
Softcover (2006, $19.99) 20.00

BLACK ADAM (See 52 and Countdown)
DC Comics: Oct, 2007 - No. 6, Mar, 2008 ($2.99, limited series)

1-6: 1-Mahnke-a/c; Isis returns; Felix Faust app. 3.00
...: The Dark Age TPB (2008, $17.99) r/#1-6; Alex Ross-c 18.00

BLACK AND WHITE (See Large Feature Comic, Series I)

BLACK & WHITE (Also see Codename: Black & White)
Image Comics (Extreme): Oct, 1994 - No. 3, Jan, 1995 ($1.95, limited series)

1-3: Thibert-c/story 3.00

BLACK & WHITE MAGIC
Innovation Publishing: 1991 ($2.95, 98 pgs., B&W w/30 pgs. color, squarebound)

1-Contains rebound comics w/covers removed; contents may vary 4.00

BLACK AXE
Marvel Comics (UK): Apr, 1993 - No. 7, Oct, 1993 ($1.75)

1-4: 1-Romita Jr.-c. 2-Sunfire-c/s 3.00
5-7: 5-Janson-c; Black Panther app. 6,7-Black Panther-c/s 3.00

BLACKBALL COMICS
Blackball Comics: Mar, 1994 ($3.00)

1-Trencher-c/story by Giffen; John Pain by O'Neill 3.00

BLACK BAT, THE
Dynamite Entertainment: 2013 - Present ($3.99)

1-9-Buccellato-s/Cliquet-a; multiple covers on each 4.00

BLACKBEARD'S GHOST (See Movie Comics)

BLACK BEAUTY (See Son of Black Beauty)
Dell Publishing Co.: No. 440, Dec, 1952

Four Color 440 5 10 15 30 50 70

BLACK BEETLE, THE
Dark Horse Comics: Jan, 2013 - No. 4, Jun, 2013 ($3.99, limited series)

1-4-Francavilla-s/a/c 4.00

BLACK BOLT: SOMETHING INHUMAN THIS WAY COMES
Marvel Comics: Sept, 2013 ($7.99, one-shot)

1-Reprints Black Bolt app. in Amazing Adventures #5-10 & Avengers #95 8.00

GD 2.0 VG 4.0 FN 6.0 VF 8.0 VF/NM 9.0 NM- 9.2

BLACKBURNE COVENANT, THE
Dark Horse Comics: Apr, 2003 - No. 4, July, 2003 ($2.99, limited series)

1-4-Nicieza-s/Raffaele-a 3.00
TPB (2003, $12.95) r/#1-4 13.00

BLACK CANARY (See All Star Comics #38, Flash Comics #86, Justice League of America #75 & World's Finest #244)
DC Comics: Nov, 1991 - No. 4, Feb, 1992 ($1.75, limited series)

1-4 3.00

BLACK CANARY
DC Comics: Jan, 1993 - No. 12, Dec, 1993 ($1.75)

1-7 3.00
8-12: 8-The Ray-c/story. 9,10-Huntress-c/story 3.00

BLACK CANARY (Follows Oliver Queen's marriage proposal in Green Arrow #75)
DC Comics: Early Sept, 2007 - No. 4, Late Oct, 2007 ($2.99, bi-weekly limited series)

1-4-Bedard-s/Siqueira-a 3.00
... Wedding Planner 1 (11/07, $2.99) Roux-c/Ferguson & Norrie-a 3.00

BLACK CANARY/ORACLE: BIRDS OF PREY (Also see Showcase '96 #3)
DC Comics: 1996 ($3.95, one-shot)

1-Chuck Dixon scripts & Gary Frank-c/a. 1 2 3 5 7 9

BLACK CAT (AMAZING SPIDER-MAN PRESENTS...)
Marvel Comics: Aug, 2010 - No. 4, Dec, 2010 ($3.99, limited series)

1-4-Van Meter-s/Pulido-a/Conner-c; Spider-Man & Ana Kraven app. 4.00

BLACK CAT COMICS (...Western #16-19; ...Mystery #30 on)
(See All-New #7,9, The Original Black Cat, Pocket & Speed Comics)
Harvey Publications (Home Comics): June-July, 1946 - No. 29, June, 1951

1-Kubert-a; Joe Simon c-1,2 81 162 243 518 884 1250
2-Kubert-a 41 82 123 250 418 585
3,4: 4-The Red Demons begin (The Demon #4 & 5) 34 68 102 204 332 460
5,6,7: 5,6-The Scarlet Arrow app. in ea. by Powell; S&K-a in both. 6-Origin Red Demon. 7-Vagabond Prince by S&K plus 1 more story 39 78 117 240 395 550
8-S&K-a; Kerry Drake begins, ends #13 36 72 108 214 347 480
9-Origin Stuntman (r/Stuntman #1) 39 78 117 230 375 520
10-20: 14,15,17-Mary Worth app. plus Invisible Scarlet O'Neil-#15,20,24 27 54 81 158 259 360
21-26 21 42 63 126 206 285
27,28: 27-Used in **SOTI**, pg. 193; X-Mas-c; 2 pg. John Wayne story. 28-Intro. Kit, Black Cat's new sidekick 23 46 69 136 223 310
29-Black Cat bondage-c; Black Cat stories 22 44 66 130 213 295

BLACK CAT MYSTERY (Formerly Black Cat; ...Western Mystery #54; ...Western #55,56; ...Mystery #57; ...Mystic #58-62; Black Cat #63-65)
Harvey Publications: No. 30, Aug, 1951 - No. 65, Apr, 1963

30-Black Cat on cover and first page only 36 72 108 211 343 475
31,32,34,37,38,40 29 58 87 170 278 385
33-Used in **POP**, pg. 89; electrocution-c 34 68 102 199 325 450
35-Atomic disaster cover/story 36 72 108 216 351 485
36,39-Used in **SOTI**: #36-Pgs. 270,271; #39-Pgs. 386-388 34 68 102 204 332 460
41-43 28 56 84 165 270 375
44-Eyes, ears, tongue cut out; Nostrand-a 32 64 96 188 307 425
45-Classic "Colorama" by Powell; Nostrand-a 60 120 180 381 653 925
46-49,51-Nostrand-a in all. 51-Story has blank panel covering censored art (post-Code) 30 60 90 177 289 400
50-Check-a; classic Warren Kremer-c showing a man's face & hands burning away 206 412 618 1318 2259 3200
52,53 (r/#34 & 35) 18 36 54 107 169 230
54-Two Black Cat stories (2/55, last pre-code) 20 40 60 115 185 255
55,56-Black Cat app. 18 36 54 107 169 230
57(7/56)-Kirby-c 20 40 60 115 185 255
58-60-Kirby-a(4). 58,59-Kirby-c. 60,61-Simon-c 23 46 69 136 223 310
61-Nostrand-a; "Colorama" r/#45 21 42 63 122 199 275
62 (3/58)-E.C. story swipe 18 36 54 107 169 230
63-65: Giants(10/62,1/63, 4/63); Reprints; Black Cat app. 63-origin Black Kitten. 65-1 pg. Powell-a 20 40 60 120 195 270
NOTE: ***Kremer** a-37, 39, 43; c-36, 37, 47. **Meskin** a-51. **Palais** a-30, 31(2), 32(2), 33-35, 37-40. **Powell** a-32-35, 36(2), 40, 41, 43-53, 57. **Simon** c-63-65. **Sparling** a-44. Bondage c-32, 34, 43.*

BLACK COBRA (Bride's Diary No. 4 on) (See Captain Flight #8)
Ajax/Farrell Publications(Excellent Publ.): No. 1, 10-11/54; No. 6(No. 2), 12-1/54-55; No. 3, 2-3/55

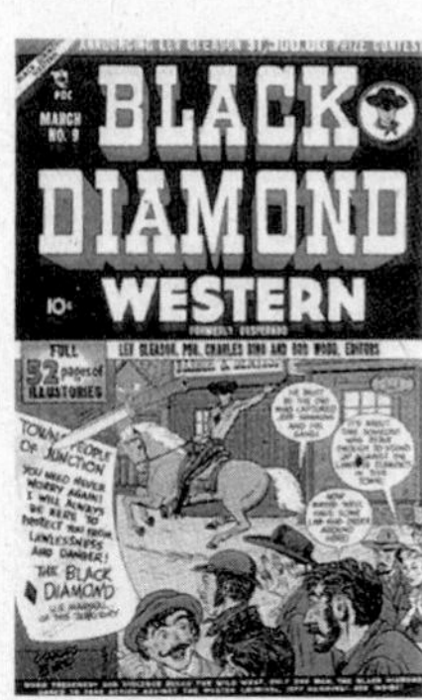

Black Diamond Western #9 © LEV

Blackest Night: Superman #3 © DC

Blackhawk #19 © QUA

	GD 2.0	VG 4.0	FN 6.0	VF 8.0	VF/NM 9.0	NM- 9.2
1-Re-intro Black Cobra & The Cobra Kid (costumed heroes)	37	74	111	222	361	500
6(#2)-Formerly Billy Bunny	20	40	60	114	182	250
3-(Pre-code)-Torpedoman app.	19	38	57	109	172	235

BLACK CONDOR (Also see Crack Comics, Freedom Fighters & Showcase '94 #10,11)
DC Comics: June, 1992 - No. 12, May, 1993 ($1.25)

1-8-Heath-c 3.00
9-12: 9,10,12-Heath-c. 9,10-The Ray app. 12-Batman-c/app. 3.00

BLACK CROSS SPECIAL (See Dark Horse Presents)
Dark Horse Comics: Jan, 1988 ($1.75, B&W, one-shot)(Reprints & new-a)

1-1st printing 4.00
1-(2nd printing) has 2 pgs. new-a 3.00

BLACK CROSS: DIRTY WORK (See Dark Horse Presents)
Dark Horse Comics: Apr, 1997 ($2.95, one-shot)

1-Chris Warner-c/s/a 3.00

BLACK DIAMOND
Americomics: May, 1983 - No. 5, 1984 (no month)($2.00-$1.75, Baxter paper)

1-3-Movie adapt.; 1-Colt back-up begins 4.00
4,5 3.00

NOTE: ***Bill Black** a-1i; c-1. **Gulacy** c-2-5. Sybil Danning photo back-c-1.*

BLACK DIAMOND WESTERN (Formerly Desperado No. 1-8)
Lev Gleason Publ: No. 9, Mar, 1949 - No. 60, Feb, 1956 (No. 9-28: 52 pgs.)

	GD 2.0	VG 4.0	FN 6.0	VF 8.0	VF/NM 9.0	NM- 9.2
9-Black Diamond & his horse Reliapon begin; origin & 1st app. Black Diamond	21	42	63	122	199	275
10	12	24	36	69	97	125
11-15	10	20	30	54	72	90
16-28(11/49-11/51)-Wolverton's Bingbang Buster	14	28	42	76	108	140
29-40: 31-One pg. Frazetta anti-drug ad	9	18	27	47	61	75
41-50,53-59	8	16	24	40	50	60
51-3-D effect-c/story	15	30	45	85	130	175
52-3-D effect story	14	28	42	81	118	155
60-Last issue	8	16	24	44	57	70

NOTE: ***Biro** c-9-35?. **Cooper** a-12. **Myron Foss** a-54-58, c-54-56, 58. **Guardineer** a-9, 12, 15, 18. **Jack Keller** a-12. **Kida** a-9. **Maurer** a-10. **Ed Moore** a-16. **Morisi** a-55. **William Overgard** a-9-23. **Tuska** a-10, 48. **Bill Walton** a-57.*

BLACK DRAGON, THE
Marvel Comics (Epic Comics): May, 1985 - No. 6, Oct, 1985 (Baxter paper, mature)

1-6: 1-Chris Claremont story & John Bolton painted-c/a in all 4.00
TPB (Dark Horse, 4/96, $17.95, B&W, trade paperback) r/#1-6; intro by Anne McCaffrey 18.00

BLACK DYNAMITE (Based on the Michael Jai White film)
IDW Publishing: Dec, 2013 - Present ($3.99)

1-Ash-s/Wimberly-a; multiple covers 4.00

BLACKEST NIGHT (2009 Green Lantern & DC crossover) (Leads into Brightest Day series)
DC Comics: No. 0, Jun, 2009 - No. 8, May, 2010 ($3.99, limited series)

0-Free Comic Book Day edition; Johns-s/Reis-a; profile pages of different corps 3.00
1-8: 1-($3.99) Black Lantern Corps arises; Johns-s/Reis-c/a; Hawkman & Hawkgirl killed. 4-Nekron rises. 8-Dead heroes return 5.00
1-Variant cover by Van Sciver 10.00
1-3,5: 2nd-4th printings 4.00
2-8: 2-Cascioli variant-c. 3-Van Sciver variant-c. 4-7-Migliari variant-c. 8-Mahnke var-c 8.00
... Director's Cut (6/10, $5.99) Commentary with story panels; cover gallery, script pgs. 6.00
HC (2010, $29.99, d.j.) r/#0-8 & Blackest Night Director's Cut; variant cover gallery 30.00
SC (2011, $19.99) r/#0-8 & Blackest Night Director's Cut; variant cover gallery 20.00
...: Black Lantern Corps Vol. 1 HC (2010, $24.99, d.j.) r/BN: Batman, BN: Superman, and BN: Titans series; cover gallery and character sketch designs 25.00
...: Black Lantern Corps Vol. 1 SC (2011, $19.99) same contents as HC edition 20.00
...: Black Lantern Corps Vol. 2 HC (2010, $24.99, d.j.) r/BN: The Flash, BN: JSA, and BN: Wonder Woman series; cover gallery and character sketch designs 25.00
...: Rise of the Black Lanterns HC (2010, $24.99) r/one-shots Atom and Hawkman #46, Catwoman #83, Phantom Stranger #42, Power of Shazam #48, The Question #37, Starman #81, Weird Western Tales #71, Green Arrow #30 & Adventure Comics #7; sketch art 25.00
...: Rise of the Black Lanterns SC (2011, $19.99) same contents as HC edition 20.00

BLACKEST NIGHT: BATMAN (2009 Green Lantern & DC crossover)
DC Comics: Oct, 2009 - No. 3, Dec, 2009 ($2.99, limited series)

1-3: 1-Bat-parents rise as Black Lanterns; Deadman app.; Syaf-a/Andy Kubert-c; 2 printings. 3-Flying Graysons return 3.00
1-3-Variant-c by Sienkiewicz 5.00

BLACKEST NIGHT: JSA (2009 Green Lantern & DC crossover)
DC Comics: Feb, 2010 - No. 3, Apr, 2010 ($2.99, limited series)

1-3-Original Sandman, Dr. Midnite and Mr. Terrific rise; Barrows-a/c 3.00
1-3-Variant-c by Gene Ha 5.00

BLACKEST NIGHT: SUPERMAN (2009 Green Lantern & DC crossover)
DC Comics: Oct, 2009 - No. 3, Dec, 2009 ($2.99, limited series)

1-3-Earth-2 Superman and Lois become Black Lanterns; Barrows-a/c; 2 printings 3.00
1-3-Variant-c by Shane Davis 5.00

BLACKEST NIGHT: TALES OF THE CORPS (2009 Green Lantern & DC crossover)
DC Comics: Sept, 2009 - No. 3, Sept, 2009 ($3.99, weekly limited series)

1-3-Short stories by various; interlocking cover images. 3-Commentary on B.N. #0 4.00
HC (2010, $24.99) r/#1-3 & Adventure Comics #4,5 & Green Lantern #49; sketch art 25.00
SC (2011, $19.99) r/#1-3 & Adventure Comics #4,5 & Green Lantern #49; sketch art 20.00

BLACKEST NIGHT: THE FLASH (2009 Green Lantern & DC crossover)
DC Comics: Feb, 2010 - No. 3, Apr, 2010 ($2.99, limited series)

1-3-Rogues vs. Dead Rogues; Johns-s/Kolins-a 3.00
1-3-Variant-c by Manapul 5.00

BLACKEST NIGHT: TITANS (2009 Green Lantern & DC crossover)
DC Comics: Oct, 2009 - No. 3, Dec, 2009 ($2.99, limited series)

1-3-Terra and the original Hawk return; Benes-a/c 3.00
1-3-Variant-c by Brian Haberlin 5.00

BLACKEST NIGHT: WONDER WOMAN (2009 Green Lantern & DC crossover)
DC Comics: Feb, 2010 - No. 3, Apr, 2010 ($2.99, limited series)

1-3-Maxwell Lord returns; Rucka-s/Scott-a/Horn-c. 2,3-Mera app.; Star Sapphire 3.00
1-3-Variant-c by Ryan Sook 5.00

BLACK FLAG (See Asylum #5)
Maximum Press: Jan, 1995 - No.4, 1995; No. 0, July, 1995 ($2.50, B&W) (No. 0 in color)

Preview Edition (6/94, $1.95, B&W)-Fraga/McFarlane-c. 3.00
0-4: 0-(7/95)-Liefeld/Fraga-c. 1-(1/95). 3.00
1-Variant cover 5.00
2,4-Variant covers 3.00

NOTE: ***Fraga** a-0-4, Preview Edition; c-1-4. **Liefeld/Fraga** c-0. **McFarlane/Fraga** c-Preview Edition.*

BLACK FURY (Becomes Wild West No. 58) (See Blue Bird)
Charlton Comics Group: May, 1955 - No. 57, Mar-Apr, 1966 (Horse stories)

	GD 2.0	VG 4.0	FN 6.0	VF 8.0	VF/NM 9.0	NM- 9.2
1	12	24	36	67	94	120
2	7	14	21	37	46	55
3-10	6	12	18	28	34	40
11-15,19,20	4	8	10	18	22	25
16-18-Ditko-a	12	24	36	67	94	120
21-30	4	7	10	14	17	20
31-57	3	6	8	12	14	16

BLACK GOLIATH (See Avengers #32-35,41,54 and Civil War #4)
Marvel Comics Group: Feb, 1976 - No. 5, Nov, 1976

	GD 2.0	VG 4.0	FN 6.0	VF 8.0	VF/NM 9.0	NM- 9.2
1-Tuska-a(p) thru #3	3	6	9	14	20	25
2-5: 2-4-(Regular 25¢ editions). 4-Kirby-c/Buckler-a	2	4	6	9	13	16
2-4-(30¢-c variants, limited distribution)(4,6,8/76)	4	8	12	23	37	50

BLACKHAWK (Formerly Uncle Sam #1-8; see Military Comics & Modern Comics)
Comic Magazines(Quality)No. 9-107(12/56); National Periodical Publications No. 108 (1/57) -250; DC Comics No. 251 on: No. 9, Winter, 1944 - No. 243, 10-11/68; No. 244, 1-2/76 - No. 250, 1-2/77; No. 251, 10/82 - No. 273, 11/84

	GD 2.0	VG 4.0	FN 6.0	VF 8.0	VF/NM 9.0	NM- 9.2
9 (1944)	258	516	774	1651	2826	4000
10 (1946)	107	214	321	680	1165	1650
11-15: 14-Ward-a; 13,14-Fear app.	74	148	222	470	810	1150
16-19	63	126	189	403	689	975
20-Classic Crandall bondage-c; Ward Blackhawk	97	194	291	621	1061	1500
21-30 (1950)	48	96	144	302	514	725
31-40: 31-Chop Chop by Jack Cole	39	78	117	240	395	550
41-49,51-60: 42-Robot-c	34	68	102	199	325	450
50-1st Killer Shark; origin in text	37	74	111	222	361	500
61,62: 61-Used in **POP**, pg. 91. 62-Used in **POP**, pg. 92 & color illo	30	60	90	177	289	400
63-70,72-80: 65-H-Bomb explosion panel. 66-B&W & color illos **POP**. 67-Hitler-s. 70-Return of Killer Shark; atomic explosion panel. 75-Intro. Blackie the Hawk	28	56	84	168	274	380
71-Origin retold; flying saucer-c; A-Bomb panels	32	64	96	192	314	435
81-86: Last precode (3/55)	25	50	75	150	245	340
87-92,94-99,101-107: 91-Robot-c. 105-1st S.A.	21	42	63	122	199	275
93-Origin in text	21	42	63	124	202	280
100	25	50	75	150	245	340
108-1st DC issue (1/57); re-intro. Blackie, the Hawk, their mascot; not in #115	36	72	108	266	596	925

Blackhawk #216 © DC

Black Knight #1 © MAR

Black Lightning #8 © DC

GD 2.0 | VG 4.0 | FN 6.0 | VF 8.0 | VF/NM 9.0 | NM- 9.2

109-117: 117-(10/57)-Mr. Freeze app. 13 26 39 91 201 310
118-(11/57)-Frazetta-r/Jimmy Wakely #4 (3 pgs.) 14 28 42 94 207 320
119-130 (11/58): 120-Robot-c 11 22 33 72 154 235
131-140 (9/59): 133-Intro. Lady Blackhawk 9 18 27 61 123 185
141-150,152-163,165,166: 141-Cat-Man returns-c/s. 143-Kurtzman-r/Jimmy Wakely #4. 150-(7/60)-King Condor returns. 166-Last 10¢ issue
8 16 24 51 96 140
151-Lady Blackhawk receives & loses super powers 8 16 24 54 102 150
164-Origin retold 8 16 24 54 102 150
167-180 6 12 18 37 66 95
181-190 5 10 15 31 53 75
191-196,199: 196-Combat Diary series begins 4 8 12 27 44 60
197,198,200: 197-New look for Blackhawks. 198-Origin retold
4 8 12 28 47 65
201,202,204-210 3 6 9 21 33 45
203-Origin Chop Chop (12/64) 4 8 12 25 40 55
211-227,229-243(1968): 230-Blackhawks become superheroes; JLA cameo 242-Return to old costumes 3 6 9 17 26 35
228-Batman, Green Lantern, Superman, The Flash cameos.
3 6 9 19 30 40
244 ('76) -250: 250-Chuck dies 1 2 3 5 6 8
251-273: 251-Origin retold; Black Knights return. 252-Intro Domino. 253-Part origin Hendrickson. 258-Blackhawk's Island destroyed. 259-Part origin Chop-Chop.
265-273 (75¢ cover price) 4.00

NOTE: ***Chaykin*** *a-260; c-257-260, 262.* ***Crandall*** *a-10, 11, 13, 16?, 18-20, 22-26, 30-33, 35p, 36(2), 37, 38?, 39-44, 46-50, 52-58, 60, 63, 64, 66, 67; c-14-20, 22-63(most except #28-33, 36, 37, 39).* ***Evans*** *a-244, 245,246i, 248-250i.* ***G. Kane*** *c-263, 264.* ***Kubert*** *c-244, 245.* ***Newton*** *a-266p.* ***Severin*** *a-257.* ***Spiegle*** *a-261-267, 269-273; c-265-272.* ***Toth*** *a-260p.* ***Ward*** *a-16-27(Chop Chop, 8pgs. ea.); pencilled stories-No. 17-63(approx.).* ***Wildey*** *a-268. Chop Chop solo stories in #10-95?*

BLACKHAWK
DC Comics: Mar, 1988 - No. 3, May, 1988 ($2.95, limited series, mature)

1-3: Chaykin painted-c/a/scripts 4.00

BLACKHAWK (Also see Action Comics #601)
DC Comics: Mar, 1989 - No. 16, Aug, 1990 ($1.50, mature)

1 4.00
2-6,8-16: 16-Crandall-c swipe 3.00
7-($2.50, 52 pgs.)-Story-r/Military #1 4.00
Annual 1 (1989, $2.95, 68 pgs.)-Recaps origin of Blackhawk, Lady Blackhawk, and others 4.00
Special 1 (1992, $3.50, 68 pgs.)-Mature readers 4.00

BLACKHAWK INDIAN TOMAHAWK WAR, THE
Avon Periodicals: 1951 (Also see Fighting Indians of the Wild West)

nn-Kinstler-c; Kit West story 20 40 60 115 185 255

BLACKHAWKS (DC New 52)
DC Comics: Nov, 2011 - No. 8, Jun, 2012 ($2.99)

1-8: 1-Costa-s/Nolan & Lashley-a 3.00

BLACK HEART ASSASSIN
Iguana Comics: Jan, 1994 ($2.95)

1 3.00

BLACK HOLE (See Walt Disney Showcase #54) (Disney, movie)
Whitman Publishing Co.: Mar, 1980 - No. 4, Sept, 1980

11295(#1) (1979, Golden, $1.50-c, 52 pgs., graphic novel; 8 1/2x11") Photo-c; Spiegle-a. 3 6 9 14 20 25
1-3: 1,2-Movie adaptation. 2,3-Spiegle-a. 3-McWilliams-a; photo-c.
3-New stories 2 4 6 9 12 15
4-Sold only in pre-packs; new story; Spiegle-a 10 20 30 64 132 200

BLACK HOOD, THE (See Blue Ribbon, Flyman & Mighty Comics)
Red Circle Comics (Archie): June, 1983 - No. 3, Oct, 1983 (Mandell paper)

1-Morrow, McWilliams, Wildey-a; Toth-c 6.00
2,3: The Fox by Toth-c/a; Boyette-a. 3-Morrow-a; Toth wraparound-c 4.00
NOTE: *Also see Archie's Super-Hero Special Digest #2*

BLACK HOOD
DC Comics (Impact Comics): Dec, 1991 - No. 12, Dec, 1992 ($1.00)

1 4.00
2-12: 11-Intro The Fox. 12-Origin Black Hood 3.00
Annual 1 (1992, $2.50, 68 pgs.)-w/Trading card 4.00

BLACK HOOD COMICS (Formerly Hangman #2-8; Laugh Comics #20 on; also see Black Swan, Jackpot, Roly Poly & Top-Notch #9)
MLJ Magazines: No. 9, Wint., 1943-44 - No. 19, Sum., 1946 (on radio in 1943)

9-The Hangman & The Boy Buddies cont'd 115 230 345 730 1253 1775
10-Hangman & Dusty, the Boy Detective app. 65 130 195 416 708 1000
11-Dusty app.; no Hangman 52 104 156 328 552 775
12-18: 14-Kinstler blood-c. 17-Hal Foster swipe from Prince Valiant; 1st issue with "An Archie Magazine" on-c 46 92 138 290 488 685
19-I.D. exposed; last issue 53 106 159 334 567 800
NOTE: *Hangman by* ***Fuje*** *in 9, 10.* ***Kinstler*** *a-15, c-14-16.*

BLACK JACK (Rocky Lane's...; formerly Jim Bowie)
Charlton Comics: No. 20, Nov, 1957 - No. 30, Nov, 1959

20 9 18 27 52 69 85
21,27,29,30 6 12 18 31 38 45
22,23: 22-(68 pgs.). 23-Williamson/Torres-a 8 16 24 42 54 65
24-26,28-Ditko-a 10 20 30 56 76 95

BLACK KNIGHT, THE
Toby Press: May, 1953; 1963

1-Bondage-c 32 64 96 188 307 425
Super Reprint No. 11 (1963)-Reprints 1953 issue 3 6 9 19 25 32

BLACK KNIGHT, THE
Atlas Comics (MgPC): May, 1955 - No. 5, April, 1956

1-Origin Crusader; Maneely-c/a 103 206 309 659 1130 1600
2-Maneely-c/a(4) 68 136 204 435 743 1050
3-5: 4-Maneely-c/a. 5-Maneely-c, Shores-a 53 106 159 334 567 800

BLACK KNIGHT (See The Avengers #48, Marvel Super Heroes & Tales To Astonish #52)
Marvel Comics: June, 1990 - No. 4, Sept, 1990 ($1.50, limited series)

1-4: 1-Original Black Knight returns. 3,4-Dr. Strange app. 3.00
... (MDCU) 1 (01/10, $3.99) Origin re-told; Frenz-a; originally from Marvel Digital Comics 4.00
NOTE: ***Buckler*** *c-1-4p*

BLACK KNIGHT: EXODUS
Marvel Comics: Dec, 1996 ($2.50, one-shot)

1-Raab-s; Apocalypse-c/app. 3.00

BLACK LAMB, THE
DC Comics (Helix): Nov, 1996 - No, 6, Apr, 1997 ($2.50, limited series)

1-6: Tim Truman-c/a/scripts 3.00

BLACKLIGHT (From ShadowHawk)
Image Comics: June, 2005 - No. 2, Jul, 2005 ($2.99)

1,2-Toledo & Deering-a/Wherle-s 3.00

BLACK LIGHTNING (See The Brave & The Bold, Cancelled Comic Cavalcade, DC Comics Presents #16, Detective #490 and World's Finest #257)
National Periodical Publ./DC Comics: Apr, 1977 - No. 11, Sept-Oct, 1978

1-Origin Black Lightning 2 4 6 9 13 16
2,3,6-10 1 2 3 5 6 8
4,5-Superman-c/s. 4-Intro Cyclotronic Man 1 3 4 6 8 10
11-The Ray new solo story 2 4 6 8 10 12
NOTE: ***Buckler*** *c-1-3p, 6-11p. #11 is 44 pgs.*

BLACK LIGHTNING (2nd Series)
DC Comics: Feb, 1995 - No. 13, Feb, 1996 ($1.95/$2.25)

1-5-Tony Isabella scripts begin, ends #8 3.00
6-13: 6-Begin $2.25-c. 13-Batman-c/app. 3.00

BLACK LIGHTNING: YEAR ONE
DC Comics: Mar, 2009 - No. 6, May, 2009 ($2.99, bi-weekly limited series)

1-6-Van Meter-s/Hamner-a. 1-Two printings (white and yellow cover title logos) 3.00
TPB (2009, $17.99) r/#1-6 18.00

BLACK MAGIC (...Magazine) (Becomes Cool Cat V8#6 on)
Crestwood Publ. V1#1-4,V6#1-V7#5/Headline V1#5-V5#3,V7#6-V8#5: 10-11/50 - V4#1, 6-7/53: V4#2, 9-10/53 - V5#3, 11-12/54; V6#1, 9-10/57 - V7#2, 11-12/58: V7#3, 7-8/60 - V8#5, 11-12/61 (V1#1-5, 52pgs.; V1#6-V3#3, 44pgs.)

V1#1-S&K-a, 10 pgs.; Meskin-a(2) 161 322 483 1030 1765 2500
2-S&K-a, 17 pgs.; Meskin-a 69 138 207 438 752 1065
3-6(8-9/51)-S&K, Roussos, Meskin-a 58 116 174 371 636 900
V2#1(10-11/51),4,5,7(#13),9(#15),12(#18)-S&K-a 40 80 120 244 402 560
2,3,6,8,10,11(#17) 32 64 96 190 310 430
V3#1(#19, 12/52). - 6(#24, 5/53)-S&K-a 33 66 99 194 317 440
V4#1(#25, 6-7/53), 2(#26, 9-10/53)-S&K-a(3-4) 34 68 102 204 332 460
3(#27, 11-12/53)-S&K-a; Ditko-a (2nd published-a); also see Captain 3-D, Daring Love #1, Strange Fantasy #9, & Fantastic Fears #5 (Fant. Fears was 1st drawn, but not 1st publ.)
63 126 189 403 689 975
4(#28)-Eyes ripped out/story-S&K, Ditko-a 45 90 135 284 480 675
5(#29, 3-4/54)-S&K, Ditko-a 36 72 108 216 351 485
6(#30, 5-6/54)-S&K, Powell?-a 29 58 87 170 278 385

Black Orchid #19 © DC

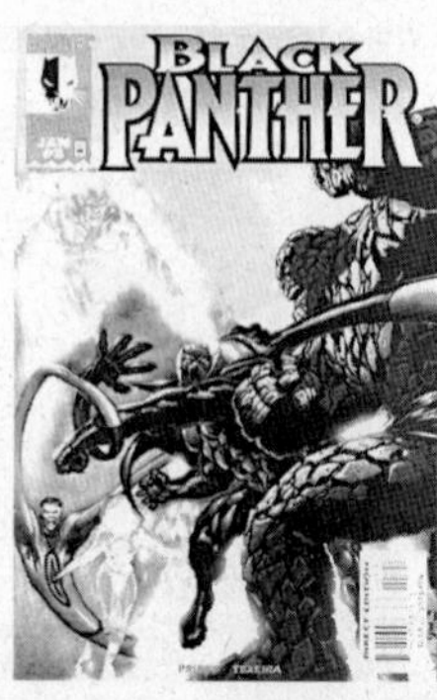

Black Panther V2 #3 © MAR

Black Panther (2005 series) #26 © MAR

GD 2.0 | VG 4.0 | FN 6.0 | VF 8.0 | VF/NM 9.0 | NM- 9.2

V5#1(#31, 7-8/54 - 3(#33, 11-12/54)-S&K-a 20 40 60 117 189 260
V6#1(#34, 9-10/57), 2(#35, 11-12/57) 12 24 36 69 97 125
3(1-2/58) - 6(7-8/58) 12 24 36 69 97 125
V7#1(9-10/58) - 3(7-8/60), 4(9-10/60) 10 20 30 56 76 95
5(11-12/60)-Hitler-c; Torres-a 18 36 54 103 162 220
6(1-2/61)-Powell-a(2) 10 20 30 56 76 95
V8#1(3-4/61)-Powell-c/a 10 20 30 56 76 95
2(5-6/61)-E.C. story swipe/W.F. #22; Ditko, Powell-a
11 22 33 60 83 105
3(7-8/61)-E.C. story swipe/W.F. #22; Powell-a(2) 11 22 33 60 83 105
4(9-10/61)-Powell-a(5) 10 20 30 56 76 95
5-E.C. story swipe/W.S.F. #28; Powell-a(3) 11 22 33 60 83 105

NOTE: ***Bernard Baily** a-V4#6?, V5#3(2). **Grandenetti** a-V2#3, 11. **Kirby** c-V1#1-6, V2#1-12, V3#1-6, V4#1, 2, 4-6, V5#1-3. **McWilliams** a-V3#2i. **Meskin** a-V1#1(2), 2, 3, 4(2), 5(2), 6, V2/1, 2, 3(2), 4(3), 5, 6(2), 7-9, 11, 12i, V3#1(2), 5, 6, V5#1(2), 2. **Orlando** a-V6#1, 4, V7#2; c-V6/1-6. **Powell** a-V5#1?. **Roussos** a-V1#3-5, 6(2), V2#3(2), 4, 5(2), 6, 8, 9, 10(2), 11, 12p, V3#1(2), 2i, 5, V5#2. **Simon** a-V2#12, V3#2, V7#5? c-V4#3?, V7#3?, 4, 5?, 6?, V8#1-5. **Simon & Kirby** a-V1#1, 2(2), 3-6, V2#1, 4, 5, 7, 9, 12, V3#1-6, V4#1(3), 2(4), 3(2), 4(2), 5, 6, V5#1-3; c-V2#1. **Leonard Starr** a-V1#1. **Tuska** a-V6#3, 4. **Woodbridge** a-V7#4.*

BLACK MAGIC
National Periodical Publications: Oct-Nov, 1973 - No. 9, Apr-May, 1975

1-S&K reprints 3 6 9 16 24 32
2-8-S&K reprints 2 4 6 10 14 18
9-S&K reprints 2 4 6 11 16 20

BLACKMAIL TERROR (See Harvey Comics Library)

BLACK MASK
DC Comics: 1993 - No. 3, 1994 ($4.95, limited series, 52 pgs.)

1-3 5.00

BLACK OPS
Image Comics (WildStorm): Jan, 1996 - No. 5, May, 1996 ($2.50, lim. series)

1-5 3.00

BLACK ORCHID (See Adventure Comics #428 & Phantom Stranger)
DC Comics: Holiday, 1988-89 - No. 3, 1989 ($3.50, lim. series, prestige format)

Book 1,3: Gaiman scripts & McKean painted-a in all 6.00
Book 2-Arkham Asylum story; Batman app. 1 2 3 5 6 8
TPB (1991, $19.95) r/#1-3; new McKean-c 20.00

BLACK ORCHID
DC Comics: Sept, 1993 - No. 22, June, 1995 ($1.95/$2.25)

1-22: Dave McKean-c all issues 3.00
1-Platinum Edition 12.00
Annual 1 (1993, $3.95, 68 pgs.)-Children's Crusade 4.00

BLACKOUT
Dark Horse Comics: Mar, 2014 - Present ($2.99)

1-Barbiere-s/Lorimer-a; King Tiger back-up by Stradley-s/Doug Wheatley-a 3.00

BLACKOUTS (See Broadway Hollywood...)

BLACK PANTHER, THE (Also see Avengers #52, Fantastic Four #52, Jungle Action & Marvel Premiere #51-53)
Marvel Comics Group: Jan, 1977 - No. 15, May, 1979

1-Jack Kirby-s/a thru #12 4 8 12 25 40 55
2-13: 4,5-(Regular 30¢ editions). 8-Origin 2 4 6 13 18 22
4,5-(35¢-c variants, limited dist.)(7,9/77) 6 12 18 38 69 100
14,15-Avengers x-over. 14-Origin 3 6 9 16 23 30
...By Jack Kirby Vol. 1 TPB (2005, $19.99) r/#1-7; unused covers and sketch pages 20.00
...By Jack Kirby Vol. 2 TPB (2006, $19.99) r/#8-12 by Kirby and #13 non-Kirby 20.00

NOTE: ***J. Buscema** c-15p. **Layton** c-13i.*

BLACK PANTHER
Marvel Comics Group: July, 1988 - No. 4, Oct, 1988 ($1.25)

1-4-Gillis-s/Cowan & Delarosa-a 4.00

BLACK PANTHER (Marvel Knights)
Marvel Comics: Nov, 1998 - No. 62, Sept, 2003 ($2.50)

1-Texeira-a/c; Priest-s 6.00
1-($6.95) DF edition w/Quesada & Palmiotti-c 1 2 3 5 6 8
2-4: 2-Two covers by Texeira and Timm. 3-Fantastic Four app. 4.00
5-35,37-40: 5-Evans-a. 6-8-Jusko-a. 8-Avengers-c/app. 15-Hulk app. 22-Moon Knight app. 23-Avengers app. 25-Maximum Security x-over. 26-Storm-c/app. 28-Magneto & Sub-Mariner-c/app. 29-WWII flashback meeting w/Captain America. 35-Defenders-c/app. 37-Luke Cage and Falcon-c/app. 3.00
36-($3.50, 100 pgs.) 35th Anniversary issue incl. r/1st app. in FF #52 4.00
41-56: 41-44-Wolverine app. 47-Thor app. 48,49-Magneto app. 3.00
57-62: 57-Begin $2.99-c. 59-Falcon app. 3.00
...: The Client (6/01, $14.95, TPB) r/#1-5 15.00
... 2099 #1 (11/04, $2.99) Kirkman-s/Hotz-a/Pat Lee-c 3.00

BLACK PANTHER (Marvel Knights)
Marvel Comics: Apr, 2005 - No. 41, Nov, 2008 ($2.99)

1-Reginald Hudlin-s/John Romita Jr. & Klaus Janson-a; covers by Romita & Ribic 5.00
1-2nd printing; variant-c by Ribic 3.00
2-7,9-15,17-20: 7-House of M; Hairsine-a. 10-14-Luke Cage app. 12,13-Blade app. 17-Linsner-c. 19-Doctor Doom app. 3.00
8-Cho-c; X-Men app. 4.00
8-2nd printing variant-c 3.00
16-($3.99) Wedding of T'Challa and Storm; wraparound Cho-c; Hudlin-s/Eaton-a 4.00
21-Civil War x-over; Namor app. 8.00
21-2nd printing with new cover and Civil War logo 3.00
22-25-Civil War: 23-25-Turner-c 4.00
26-41: 26-30-T'Challa and Storm join the Fantastic Four. 27-30-Marvel Zombies app. 28-30-Suydam-c. 39-41-Secret Invasion 3.00
Annual 1 (4/08, $3.99) Hudlin-s/Stroman & Lashley-a; alternate future; Uatu app. 4.00
...: Bad Mutha TPB (2006, $10.99) r/#10-13 11.00
...: Civil War TPB (2007, $17.99) r/#19-25 18.00
...: Four the Hard Way TPB (2007, $13.99) r/#26-30; page layouts and character designs 14.00
...: Little Green Men TPB (2008, $10.99) r/#31-34 11.00
...: The Bride TPB (2006, $14.99) r/#14-18; interview with the dress designer 15.00
...: Who Is The Black Panther HC (2005, $21.99) r/#1-6; Hudlin afterword; cover gallery 22.00
...: Who Is The Black Panther SC (2006, $14.99) r/#1-6; Hudlin afterword; cover gallery 15.00

BLACK PANTHER
Marvel Comics: Apr, 2009 - No. 12, Mar, 2010 ($3.99/$2.99)

1-($3.99) Hudlin-s/Lashley-a; covers by Campbell & Lashley; Dr. Doom app. 4.00
2-12-($2.99) 2-6-Campbell-c. 6-Shuri becomes female Black Panther 3.00

BLACK PANTHER/CAPTAIN AMERICA: FLAGS OF OUR FATHERS
Marvel Comics: Jun, 2010 - No. 4, Sept, 2010 ($3.99, limited series)

1-4-Hudlin-s/Cowan-a; WW2 story; Howling Commandos & Red Skull app. 4.00

BLACK PANTHER: PANTHER'S PREY
Marvel Comics: May, 1991 - No. 4, Oct, 1991 ($4.95, squarebound, lim. series, 52 pgs.)

1-4: McGregor-s/Turner-a 5.00

BLACK PANTHER: THE MAN WITHOUT FEAR (Continues from Daredevil #512)
Marvel Comics: No. 513, Feb, 2011 - No. 523, Nov, 2011 ($2.99)

513-523: 513-Shadowland aftermath; Liss-s/Francavilla-a/Bianchi-c. 521-523-Fear Itself 3.00
513-Variant-c by Francavilla 5.00

BLACK PANTHER: THE MOST DANGEROUS MAN ALIVE
Marvel Comics: No. 523.1, Nov, 2011 - No. 529, Apr, 2012 ($2.99)

523.1, 524-529: 523.1-Palo-a/Zircher-c. 524-Spider Island tie-in; Lady Bullseye app. 3.00

BLACK PEARL, THE
Dark Horse Comics: Sept, 1996 - No. 5, Jan, 1997 ($2.95, limited series)

1-5: Mark Hamill scripts 3.00

BLACK PHANTOM (See Tim Holt #25, 38)
Magazine Enterprises: Nov, 1954 (one-shot) (Female outlaw)

1 (A-1 #122)-The Ghost Rider story plus 3 Black Phantom stories; Headlight-c/a
37 74 111 222 361 500

BLACK PHANTOM
AC Comics: 1989 - No. 3, 1990 ($2.50, B&W; #2 color)(Reprints & new-a)

1-3: 1-Ayers-r, Bolle-r/B.P. #1-3-Redmask-r 3.00

BLACK PHANTOM, RETURN OF THE (See Wisco)

BLACK RIDER (Western Winners #1-7; Western Tales of Black Rider #28-31; Gunsmoke Western #32 on)(See All Western Winners, Best Western, Kid Colt, Outlaw Kid, Rex Hart, Two-Gun Kid, Two-Gun Western, Western Gunfighters, Western Winners, & Wild Western)
Marvel/Atlas Comics(CDS No. 8-17/CPS No. 19 on): No. 8, 3/50 - No. 18, 1/52; No. 19, 11/53 - No. 27, 3/55

8 (#1)-Black Rider & his horse Satan begin; 36 pgs; Stan Lee photo-c as Black Rider) 43 86 129 271 461 650
9-52 pgs. begin, end #14 23 46 69 136 223 310
10-Origin Black Rider 28 56 84 165 270 375
11-14: 14-Last 52pgs. 18 36 54 103 162 220
15-19: 19-Two-Gun Kid app. 15 30 45 86 133 180
20-Classic-c; Two-Gun Kid app. 16 32 48 94 147 200
21-27: 21-23-Two-Gun Kid app. 24,25-Arrowhead app. 26-Kid Colt app. 27-Last issue; last precode. Kid Colt app. The Spider (a villain) burns to death
14 28 42 82 121 160

NOTE: ***Ayers** c-22. **Jack Keller** a-15, 26, 27. **Maneely** a-14; c-16, 17, 25, 27. **Syd Shores** a-19, 21, 22, 23(3),*

Black Science #2 © Rick Remender

Black Terror #14 © BP

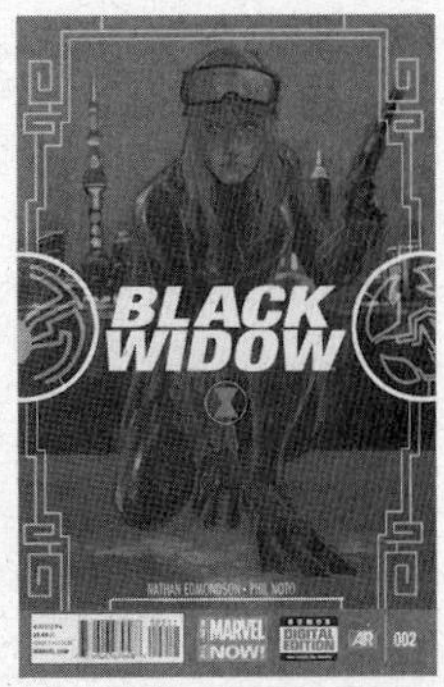

Black Widow (2014 series) #2 © MAR

	GD 2.0	VG 4.0	FN 6.0	VF 8.0	VF/NM 9.0	NM- 9.2

24(3), 25-27; c-19, 21, 23. ***Sinnott*** *a-24, 25.* ***Tuska*** *a-12, 19-21.*

BLACK RIDER RIDES AGAIN!, THE
Atlas Comics (CPS): Sept, 1957
1-Kirby-a(3); Powell-a; Severin-c 26 52 78 154 252 350

BLACK SEPTEMBER (Also see Avengers/Ultraforce, Ultraforce (1st series) #10 & Ultraforce/Avengers)
Malibu Comics (Ultraverse): 1995 ($1.50, one-shot)
Infinity-Intro to the new Ultraverse; variant-c exists. 3.00

BLACK SCIENCE
Image Comics: Nov, 2013 - Present ($3.50)
1-Remender-s/Scalera-a; multiple covers 10.00
2 6.00
3,4 4.00

BLACKSTONE (See Super Magician Comics & Wisco Giveaways)

BLACKSTONE, MASTER MAGICIAN COMICS
Vital Publ./Street & Smith Publ.: Mar-Apr, 1946 - No. 3, July-Aug, 1946
1 37 74 111 218 354 490
2,3 21 42 63 122 199 275

BLACKSTONE, THE MAGICIAN (...Detective on cover only #3 & 4)
Marvel Comics (CnPC): No. 2, May, 1948 - No. 4, Sept, 1948 (No #1) (Cont'd from E.C. #1?)
2-The Blonde Phantom begins, ends #4 82 164 246 528 902 1275
3,4: 3-Blonde Phantom by Sekowsky 47 94 141 298 504 710

BLACKSTONE, THE MAGICIAN DETECTIVE FIGHTS CRIME
E. C. Comics: Fall, 1947
1-1st app. Happy Houlihans 54 108 162 347 594 840

BLACK SUN (X-Men Black Sun on cover)
Marvel Comics: Nov, 2000 - No. 5, Nov, 2000 ($2.99, weekly limited series)
1-(...: X-Men), 2-(...: Storm), 3-(...: Banshee and Sunfire), 4-(...: Colossus and Nightcrawler), 5-(...: Wolverine and Thunderbird); Claremont-s in all; Evans interlocking painted covers; Magik returns 3.00

BLACK SUN
DC Comics (WildStorm): Nov, 2002 - No. 6, Jun, 2003 ($2.95, limited series)
1-6-Andreyko-s/Scott-a 3.00

BLACK SWAN COMICS
MLJ Magazines (Pershing Square Publ. Co.): 1945
1-The Black Hood reprints from Black Hood No. 14; Bill Woggon-a; Suzie app. Caribbean Pirates-c 21 42 63 124 202 280

BLACK TARANTULA (See Feature Presentations No. 5)

BLACK TERROR (See America's Best Comics & Exciting Comics)
Better Publications/Standard: Winter, 1942-43 - No. 27, June, 1949
1-Black Terror, Crime Crusader begin 360 720 1080 2520 4410 6300
2 148 296 444 947 1624 2300
3-Nazi WWII-c 116 232 348 742 1271 1800
4,5-Nazi & Japanese WWII-c 103 206 309 659 1130 1600
6-8: 6,8-Classic Nazi WWII-c. 7-Classic Japanese WWII-c; The Ghost app. 116 232 348 742 1271 1800
9,10-Nazi & Japanese WWII-c 90 180 270 576 988 1400
11,13-19 56 112 168 356 608 860
12-Japanese WWII-c 65 130 195 416 708 1000
20-Classic-c; The Scarab app. 66 132 198 419 722 1025
21-Miss Masque app. 60 120 180 381 653 925
22-Part Frazetta-a on one Black Terror story 57 114 171 362 619 875
23,25-27 51 102 153 321 541 760
24-Frazetta-a (1/4 pg.) 52 104 156 328 552 775
NOTE: ***Schomburg (Xela)*** *c-2-27; bondage c-2, 17, 24.* ***Meskin*** *a-27.* ***Moreira*** *a-27.* ***Robinson/Meskin*** *a-23, 24(3), 25, 26.* ***Roussos/Mayo*** *a-24.* ***Tuska*** *a-26, 27.*

BLACK TERROR, THE (Also see Total Eclipse)
Eclipse Comics: Oct, 1989 - No. 3, June, 1990 ($4.95, 52 pgs., squarebound, limited series)
1-3: Beau Smith & Chuck Dixon scripts; Dan Brereton painted-c/a 5.00

BLACK TERROR (Also see Project Superpowers)
Dynamite Entertainment: 2008 - No. 14, 2011 ($3.50/$3.99)
1-14-Golden Age hero. 1-Alex Ross-c/Mike Lilly-a; various variant-c exist 4.00

BLACKTHORNE 3-D SERIES
Blackthorne Publishing Co.: May, 1985 - No. 80, 1989 ($2.25/$2.50)
1-Sheena in 3-D #1. D. Stevens-c/retouched-a 1 2 3 5 6 8
2-10: 2-MerlinRealm in 3-D #1. 3-3-D Heroes #1. Goldyn in 3-D #1. 5-Bizarre 3-D Zone #1. 6-Salimba in 3-D #1. 7-Twisted Tales in 3-D #1. 8-Dick Tracy in 3-D #1. 9-Salimba in 3-D #2. 10-Gumby in 3-D #1 6.00
11-19: 11-Betty Boop in 3-D #1. 12-Hamster Vice in 3-D #1. 13-Little Nemo in 3-D #1. 14-Gumby in 3-D #2. 15-Hamster Vice #6 in 3-D. 16-Laffin' Gas #6 in 3-D. 17-Gumby in 3-D #3. 18-Bullwinkle and Rocky in 3-D #1. 19-The Flintstones in 3-D #1 6.00
20(#1),26(#2),35(#3),39(#4),52(#5),62,71(#6)-G.I. Joe in 3-D. 62-G.I. Joe Annual 2 4 6 8 11 14
21-24,27-28: 21-Gumby in 3-D #4. 22-The Flintstones in 3-D #2. 23-Laurel & Hardy in 3-D #1. 24-Bozo the Clown in 3-D #1. 27-Bravestarr in 3-D #1. 28- Gumby in 3-D #5 6.00
25,29,37-The Transformers in 3-D 2 4 6 10 14 18
30-Star Wars in 3-D #1 3 6 9 14 19 24
31-34,36,38,40: 31-The California Raisins in 3-D #1. 32-Richie Rich & Casper in 3-D #1. 33-Gumby in 3-D #6. 34-Laurel & Hardy in 3-D #2. 36-The Flintstones in 3-D #3. 38-Gumby in 3-D #7. 40-Bravestarr in 3-D #2 6.00
41-46,49,50: 41-Battletech in 3-D #1. 42-The Flintstones in 3-D #4. 43-Underdog in 3-D #1 44-The California Raisins in 3-D #2. 45-Red Heat in 3-D #1 (movie adapt.). 46-The California Raisins in 3-D #3. 49-Rambo in 3-D #1. 49-Sad Sack in 3-D #1. 50-Bullwinkle For President in 3-D #1 6.00
47,48-Star Wars in 3-D #2,3 2 4 6 9 13 16
51,53-60: 51-Kull in 3-D #1. 53-Red Sonja in 3-D #1. 54-Bozo in 3-D #2. 55-Waxwork in 3-D #1 (movie adapt.). 57-Casper in 3-D #1. 58-Baby Huey in 3-D #1. 59-Little Dot in 3-D #1. 60-Solomon Kane in 3-D #1 6.00
61,63-70,72-80: 61-Werewolf in 3-D #1. 63-The California Raisins in 3-D #4. 64-To Die For in 3-D #1. 65-Capt. Holo in 3-D #1. 66-Playful Little Audrey in 3-D #1. 67-Kull in 3-D #2. 69-The California Raisins in 3-D #5. 70-Wendy in 3-D #1. 72-Sports Hall of Shame #1. 74-The Noid in 3-D #1. 75-Moonwalker in 3-D #1 (Michael Jackson movie adapt.). 76-79. 80-The Noid in 3-D #2 1 2 3 4 5 7

BLACK WIDOW (Marvel Knights) (Also see Marvel Graphic Novel)
Marvel Comics: May, 1999 - No. 3, Aug, 1999 ($2.99, limited series)
1-(June on-c) Devin Grayson-s/J.G. Jones-c/a; Daredevil app. 5.00
1-Variant-c by J.G. Jones 6.00
2,3 4.00
...Web of Intrigue (6/99, $3.50) r/origin & early appearances 4.00
TPB (7/01, $15.95) r/Vol. 1 & 2; Jones-c 16.00

BLACK WIDOW (Marvel Knights) (Volume 2)
Marvel Comics: Jan, 2001 - No. 3, May, 2001 ($2.99, limited series)
1-3-Grayson & Rucka-s/Scott Hampton-c/a; Daredevil app. 3.00

BLACK WIDOW (Marvel Knights)
Marvel Comics: Nov, 2004 - No. 6, Apr, 2005 ($2.99, limited series)
1-6-Sienkiewicz-a/Land-c 3.00

BLACK WIDOW (Continues in Widowmaker #1)
Marvel Comics: Jun, 2010 - No. 8, Jan, 2011 ($3.99/$2.99)
1-($3.99) Liu-s/Acuña-a; Wolverine app.; back-up history text 4.00
1-Variant photo-c of Scarlett Johansson from Iron Man 2 movie 8.00
2-8-($2.99) 2-5-Acuña-a. 2,3-Elektra app. 3.00

BLACK WIDOW (All-New Marvel Now!)
Marvel Comics: Mar, 2014 - Present ($3.99)
1-5: 1-Edmonson-s/Noto-a/c. 3-5-Maria Hill app. 4.00

BLACK WIDOW & THE MARVEL GIRLS
Marvel Comics: Feb, 2010 - No. 4, Apr, 2010 ($2.99, limited series)
1-4-Tobin-s. 1-Enchantress app. 2-Avengers app. 4-Storm app.; Miyazawa-a 3.00

BLACK WIDOW: DEADLY ORIGIN
Marvel Comics: Jan, 2010 - No. 4, Apr, 2010 ($3.99, limited series)
1-4-Granov-c; origin retold. 1-Wolverine and Bucky app. 3-Daredevil app. 4.00

BLACK WIDOW: PALE LITTLE SPIDER (Marvel Knights) (Volume 3)
Marvel Comics: Jun, 2002 - No. 3, Aug, 2002 ($2.99, limited series)
1-3-Rucka-s/Kordey-a/Horn-c 3.00

BLACK WIDOW 2 (THE THINGS THEY SAY ABOUT HER) (Marvel Knights)
Marvel Comics: Nov, 2005 - No. 6, Apr, 2006 ($2.99, limited series)
1-6-Phillips & Sienkiewicz-a/Morgan-s; Daredevil app. 3.00
TPB (2006, $15.99) r/#1-6 16.00

BLACKWULF
Marvel Comics: June, 1994 - No. 10, Mar, 1995 ($1.50)
1-($2.50)-Embossed-c; Angel Medina-a 4.00
2-10 3.00

BLADE (The Vampire Hunter)
Marvel Comics

Blade (2006 series) #1 © MAR

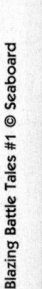

Blazing Battle Tales #1 © Seaboard

Blazing Comics #2 © Enwil

GD 2.0 | VG 4.0 | FN 6.0 | VF 8.0 | VF/NM 9.0 | NM- 9.2

1-(3/98, $3.50) Colan-a(p)/Christopher Golden-s 4.00
... Black & White TPB (2004, $15.99, B&W) reprints from magazines Vampire Tales #8,9; Marvel Preview #3,6; Crescent City Blues #1 and Marvel Shadow and Light #1 16.00
San Diego Con Promo (6/97) Wesley Snipes photo-c 3.00
...Sins of the Father (10/98, $5.99) Sears-a; movie adaption 6.00
Blade 2: Movie Adaptation (5/02, $5.95) Ponticelli-a/Bradstreet-c 6.00

BLADE (The Vampire Hunter)
Marvel Comics: Nov, 1998 - No. 3, Jan, 1999 ($3.50/$2.99)

1-($3.50) Contains Movie insider pages; McKean-a 4.00
2,3-($2.99): 2-Two covers 3.00

BLADE (Volume 2)
Marvel Comics (MAX): May, 2002 -No. 6, Oct, 2002 ($2.99)

1-6-Bradstreet-c/Hinz-s. 1-5-Pugh-a. 6-Homs-a 3.00

BLADE
Marvel Comics: Nov, 2006 - No. 12, Oct, 2007 ($2.99)

1-12: 1-Chaykin-a/Guggenheim-s; origin retold; Spider-Man app. 2-Dr. Doom-c/app. 5-Civil War tie-in; Wolverine app. 6-Blade loses a hand. 10-Spider-Man app. 3.00
...: Sins of the Father TPB (2007, $14.99) r/#7-12; afterword by Guggenheim 15.00
...: Undead Again TPB (2007, $14.99) r/#1-6; letters pages from #1&2 15.00

BLADE OF THE IMMORTAL (Manga)
Dark Horse Comics: June, 1996 - No. 131, Nov, 2007 ($2.95/$2.99/$3.95, B&W)

1-Hiroaki Samura-s/a in all 1 3 4 6 8 10
2-5: 2-#1 on cover in error 6.00
6-10 5.00
11,19,20,34-($3.95, 48 pgs.): 34-Food one-shot 4.00
12-18,21-33,35-41,43-105,107-131: 12-20-Dreamsong. 21-28-On Silent Wings. 29-33-Dark Shadow. 35-42-Heart of Darkness. 43-57-The Gathering 3.00
42-($3.50) Ends Heart of Darkness 3.50
106-($3.99) 4.00

BLADE RUNNER (Movie)
Marvel Comics Group: Oct, 1982 - No. 2, Nov, 1982

1,2-r/Marvel Super Special #22; 1-Williamson-c/a. 2-Williamson-a 4.00

BLADE: THE VAMPIRE-HUNTER
Marvel Comics: July, 1994 - No. 10, Apr, 1995 ($1.95)

1-($2.95)-Foil-c; Dracula returns; Wheatley-c/a 4.00
2-10: 2,3,10-Dracula-c/app. 8-Morbius app. 3.00

BLADE: VAMPIRE-HUNTER
Marvel Comics: Dec, 1999 - No. 6, May, 2000 ($3.50/$2.50)

1-($3.50)-Bart Sears-s; Sears and Smith-a 4.00
2-6-($2.50): 2-Regular & Wesley Snipes photo-c 3.00

BLAIR WITCH CHRONICLES, THE
Oni Press: Mar, 2000 - No. 4, July, 2000 ($2.95, B&W, limited series)

1-4-Van Meter-s.1-Guy Davis-a. 2-Mireault-a 3.00
1-DF Alternate-c by John Estes 4.00
TPB (9/00, $15.95) r/#1-4 & Blair Witch Project one-shot 16.00

BLAIR WITCH: DARK TESTAMENTS
Image Comics: Oct, 2000 ($2.95, one-shot)

1-Edington-s/Adlard-a; story of murderer Rustin Parr 3.00

BLAIR WITCH PROJECT, THE (Movie companion, not adaptation)
Oni Press: July, 1999 ($2.95, B&W, one-shot)

1-(1st printing) History of the Blair Witch, art by Edwards, Mireault, and Davis; Van Meter-s; only the stick figure is red on the cover 5.00
1-(2nd printing) Stick figure and title lettering are red on cover 4.00
1-(3rd printing) Stick figure, title, and creator credits are red on cover 3.00
DF Glow in the Dark variant-c ($10.00) 10.00

BLAST (Satire Magazine)
G & D Publications: Feb, 1971 - No. 2, May, 1971

1-Wrightson & Kaluta-a/Everette-c 7 14 21 48 89 130
2-Kaluta-c/a 5 10 15 35 63 90

BLAST CORPS
Dark Horse Comics: Oct, 1998 ($2.50, one-shot, based on Nintendo game)

1-Reprints from Nintendo Power magazine; Mahn-a 3.00

BLASTERS SPECIAL
DC Comics: 1989 ($2.00, one-shot)

1-Peter David scripts; Invasion spin-off 4.00

GD 2.0 | VG 4.0 | FN 6.0 | VF 8.0 | VF/NM 9.0 | NM- 9.2

BLAST-OFF (Three Rocketeers)
Harvey Publications (Fun Day Funnies): Oct, 1965 (12¢)

1-Kirby/Williamson-a(2); Williamson/Crandall-a; Williamson/Torres/Krenkel-a; Kirby/Simon-c 6 12 18 41 76 110

BLAZE
Marvel Comics: Aug, 1994 - No. 12, July, 1995 ($1.95)

1-($2.95)-Foil embossed-c 4.00
2-12: 2-Man-Thing-c/story. 11,12-Punisher app. 3.00

BLAZE CARSON (Rex Hart #6 on)(See Kid Colt, Tex Taylor, Wild Western, Wisco)
Marvel Comics (USA): Sept, 1948 - No. 5, June, 1949

1-Tex Taylor app.; Shores-c 28 56 84 165 270 375
2,4,5: 2-Tex Morgan app.; Shores-c. 4-Two-Gun Kid app. 5-Tex Taylor app. 19 38 57 109 172 235
3-Used by N.Y. State Legis. Comm. (injury to eye splash); Tex Morgan app. 20 40 60 114 182 250

BLAZE: LEGACY OF BLOOD (See Ghost Rider & Ghost Rider/Blaze)
Marvel Comics (Midnight Sons imprint): Dec, 1993 - No. 4, Mar, 1994 ($1.75, limited series)

1-4 3.00

BLAZE OF GLORY
Marvel Comics: Feb, 2000 - No. 4, Mar, 2000 ($2.99, limited series)

1-4-Ostrander-s/Manco-a; Two-Gun Kid, Rawhide Kid, Red Wolf and Ghost Rider app. 3.00
TPB (7/02, $9.99) r/#1-4 10.00

BLAZE THE WONDER COLLIE (Formerly Molly Manton's Romances #1?)
Marvel Comics(SePI): No. 2, Oct, 1949 - No. 3, Feb, 1950 (Both have photo-c)

2(#1), 3-(Scarce) 25 50 75 150 245 340

BLAZING BATTLE TALES
Seaboard Periodicals (Atlas): July, 1975

1-Intro. Sgt. Hawk & the Sky Demon; Severin, McWilliams, Sparling-a; Nazi-c by Thorne 3 6 9 14 19 24

BLAZING COMBAT (Magazine)
Warren Publishing Co.: Oct, 1965 - No. 4, July, 1966 (35¢, B&W)

1-Frazetta painted-c on all 25 50 75 175 388 600
2 8 16 24 51 96 140
3,4: 4-Frazetta half pg. ad 7 14 21 44 82 120
nn-Anthology (reprints from No. 1-4) (low print) 8 16 24 51 96 140

NOTE: ***Adkins** a-4. **Colan** a-3,4,nn. **Crandall** a-all. **Evans** a-1,4. **Heath** a-4,nn. **Morrow** a-1-3,nn. **Orlando** a-1-3,nn. **J. Severin** a-all. **Torres** a-1-4. **Toth** a-all. **Williamson** a-2. and **Wood** a-3,4,nn.*

BLAZING COMBAT: WORLD WAR I AND WORLD WAR II
Apple Press: Mar, 1994 ($3.75, B&W)

1,2: 1-r/Colan, Toth, Goodwin, Severin, Wood-a. 2-r/Crandall, Evans, Severin, Torres, Williamson-a 4.00

BLAZING COMICS (Also see Blue Circle Comics and Red Circle Comics)
Enwil Associates/Rural Home: 6/44 - #3, 9/44; #4, 2/45; #5, 3/45; #5(V2#2), 3/55 - #6(V2#3), 1955?

1-The Green Turtle, Red Hawk, Black Buccaneer begin; origin Jun-Gal; classic Japanese WWII splash 54 108 162 346 591 835
2-5: 3-Briefer-a. 5-(V2#2 inside) 37 74 111 222 361 500
5(3/55, V2#2-inside)-Black Buccaneer-c, 6(V2#3-inside, 1955)-Indian/Japanese-c; cover is from Apr. 1945 20 40 60 118 192 265

NOTE: *No. 5 & 6 contain remaindered comics rebound and the contents can vary. Cloak & Daggar, Will Rogers, Superman 64, Star Spangled 130, Kaanga known. Value would be half of contents.*

BLAZING SIXGUNS
Avon Periodicals: Dec, 1952

1-Kinstler-c/a; Larsen/Alascia-a(2), Tuska?-a; Jesse James, Kit Carson, Wild Bill Hickok app. 18 36 54 107 169 230

BLAZING SIXGUNS
I.W./Super Comics: 1964

I.W. Reprint #1,8,9: 1-r/Wild Bill Hickok #26, Western True Crime #? & Blazing Sixguns #1 by Avon; Kinstler-c. 8-r/Blazing Western #?; Kinstler-c. 9-r/Blazing Western #1; Ditko-r; Kintsler-c reprinted from Dalton Boys #1 2 4 6 10 14 18
Super Reprint #10,11,15-17: 10,11-r/The Rider #2,1. 15-r/Silver Kid Western #?. 16-r/Buffalo Bill #?; Wildey-r; Severin-c. 17(1964)-r/Western True Crime #? 2 4 6 10 14 18
12-Reprints Bullseye #3; S&K-a 3 6 9 18 28 38
18-r/Straight Arrow #? by Powell; Severin-c 2 4 6 10 14 18

BLAZING SIX-GUNS (Also see Sundance Kid)
Skywald Comics: Feb, 1971 - No. 2, Apr, 1971 (52 pgs.)

Blazing West #3 © ACG

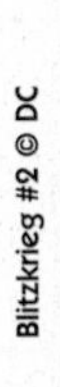
Blitzkrieg #2 © DC

Blonde Phantom #22 © MAR

	GD 2.0	VG 4.0	FN 6.0	VF 8.0	VF/NM 9.0	NM- 9.2
1-The Red Mask (3-D effect, not true 3-D), Sundance Kid begin (new-s), Avon's Geronimo reprint by Kinstler; Wyatt Earp app.	3	6	9	14	20	25
2-Wild Bill Hickok, Jesse James, Kit Carson-r plus M.E. Red Mask-r (3-D effect)	2	4	6	10	14	18

BLAZING WEST (The Hooded Horseman #21 on)
American Comics Group (B&I Publ./Michel Publ.): Fall, 1948 - No. 20, Nov-Dec, 1951

	GD 2.0	VG 4.0	FN 6.0	VF 8.0	VF/NM 9.0	NM- 9.2
1-Origin & 1st app. Injun Jones, Tenderfoot & Buffalo Belle; Texas Tim & Ranger begins, ends #13	20	40	60	117	189	260
2,3 (1-2/49)	11	22	33	64	90	115
4-Origin & 1st app. Little Lobo; Starr-a (3-4/49)	10	20	30	58	79	100
5-10: 5-Starr-a	9	18	27	52	69	85
11-13	8	16	24	44	57	70
14(11-12/50)-Origin/1st app. The Hooded Horseman	14	28	42	76	108	140
15-20: 15,16,18,19-Starr-a	9	18	27	52	69	85

BLAZING WESTERN
Timor Publications: Jan, 1954 - No. 5, Sept, 1954

	GD 2.0	VG 4.0	FN 6.0	VF 8.0	VF/NM 9.0	NM- 9.2
1-Ditko-a (1st Western-a?); text story by Bruce Hamilton	19	38	57	111	176	240
2-4	9	18	27	50	65	80
5-Disbrow-a; L.B. Cole-c	9	18	27	52	69	85

BLINDSIDE
Image Comics (Extreme Studios): Aug, 1996 ($2.50)

	GD 2.0	VG 4.0	FN 6.0	VF 8.0	VF/NM 9.0	NM- 9.2
1-Variant-c exists						3.00

BLINK (See X-Men Age of Apocalypse storyline)
Marvel Comics: March, 2001 - No. 4, June, 2001 ($2.99, limited series)

	GD 2.0	VG 4.0	FN 6.0	VF 8.0	VF/NM 9.0	NM- 9.2
1-4-Adam Kubert-c/Lobdell-s/Winick-script; leads into Exiles #1						3.00

BLIP
Marvel Comics Group: 2/1983 - 1983 (Video game mag. in comic format)

	GD 2.0	VG 4.0	FN 6.0	VF 8.0	VF/NM 9.0	NM- 9.2
1-1st app. Donkey Kong & Mario Bros. in comics, 6pgs. comics; photo-c	2	3	4	6	8	10
2-Spider-Man photo-c; 6pgs. Spider-Man comics w/Green Goblin	2	4	6	8	10	12
3,4,6						6.00
5-E.T., Indiana Jones; Rocky-c	1	2	3	4	5	7
7-6pgs. Hulk comics; Pac-Man & Donkey Kong Jr. Hints	1	2	3	5	6	8

BLISS ALLEY
Image Comics: July, 1997 - No. 2, Sept, 1997 ($2.95, B&W)

	GD 2.0	VG 4.0	FN 6.0	VF 8.0	VF/NM 9.0	NM- 9.2
1,2-Messner-Loebs-s/a						3.00

BLITZKRIEG
National Periodical Publications: Jan-Feb, 1976 - No. 5, Sept-Oct, 1976

	GD 2.0	VG 4.0	FN 6.0	VF 8.0	VF/NM 9.0	NM- 9.2
1-Kubert-c on all	4	8	12	25	40	55
2-5	3	6	9	16	24	32

BLOCKBUSTERS OF THE MARVEL UNIVERSE
Marvel Comics: March, 2011 ($4.99, one-shot)

	GD 2.0	VG 4.0	FN 6.0	VF 8.0	VF/NM 9.0	NM- 9.2
1-Handbook-style summaries of Marvel crossover events like Civil War & Heroes Reborn						5.00

BLONDE PHANTOM (Formerly All-Select #1-11; Lovers #23 on)(Also see Blackstone, Marvel Mystery, Millie The Model #2, Sub-Mariner Comics #25 & Sun Girl)
Marvel Comics (MPC): No. 12, Winter, 1946-47 - No. 22, Mar, 1949

	GD 2.0	VG 4.0	FN 6.0	VF 8.0	VF/NM 9.0	NM- 9.2
12-Miss America begins, ends #14	187	374	561	1197	2049	2900
13-Sub-Mariner begins (not in #16)	108	216	324	686	1181	1675
14,15: 15-Kurtzman's "Hey Look"	102	204	306	648	1112	1575
16-Captain America with Bucky story by Rico(p), 6 pgs.; Kurtzman's "Hey Look" (1 pg.)	129	258	387	826	1413	2000
17-22: 22-Anti Wertham editorial	87	174	261	553	952	1350

NOTE: *Shores c-12-18.*

BLONDIE (See Ace Comics, Comics Reading Libraries (Promotional Comics section), Dagwood, Daisy & Her Pups, Eat Right to Work..., King & Magic Comics)
David McKay Publications: 1942 - 1946

	GD 2.0	VG 4.0	FN 6.0	VF 8.0	VF/NM 9.0	NM- 9.2
Feature Books 12 (Rare)	84	168	252	538	919	1300
Feature Books 27-29,31,34(1940)	21	42	63	126	206	285
Feature Books 36,38,40,42,43,45,47	20	40	60	114	182	250
...1944 (Hard-c, 1938, B&W, 128 pgs.)-1944 daily strip-r	16	32	48	94	147	200

BLONDIE & DAGWOOD FAMILY
Harvey Publ. (King Features Synd.): Oct, 1963 - No. 4, Dec, 1965 (68 pgs.)

	GD 2.0	VG 4.0	FN 6.0	VF 8.0	VF/NM 9.0	NM- 9.2
1	5	10	15	30	50	70
2-4	3	6	9	19	30	40

BLONDIE COMICS (...Monthly No. 16-141)
David McKay #1-15/Harvey #16-163/King #164-175/Charlton #177 on:
Spring, 1947 - No. 163, Nov, 1965; No. 164, Aug, 1966 - No. 175, Dec, 1967; No. 177, Feb, 1969 - No. 222, Nov, 1976

	GD 2.0	VG 4.0	FN 6.0	VF 8.0	VF/NM 9.0	NM- 9.2
1	36	72	108	211	343	475
2	18	36	54	105	165	225
3-5	15	30	45	85	130	175
6-10	14	28	42	76	108	140
11-15	10	20	30	56	76	95
16-(3/50; 1st Harvey issue)	11	22	33	62	86	110
17-20: 20-(3/51)-Becomes Daisy & Her Pups #21 & Chamber of Chills #21	5	10	15	34	60	85
21-30	5	10	15	31	53	75
31-50	4	8	12	27	44	60
51-80	4	8	12	23	37	50
81-99	3	6	9	21	33	45
100	4	8	12	25	40	55
101-124,126-130	3	6	9	17	26	35
125 (80 pgs.)	4	8	12	27	44	60
131-136,138,139	3	6	9	16	24	32
137,140-(80 pgs.)	4	8	12	25	40	55
141-147,149-154,156,160,164-167	3	6	9	16	23	30
148,155,157-159,161-163 are 68 pgs.	3	6	9	21	33	45
168-175	2	4	6	11	16	20
177-199 (no #176)-Moon landing-c/s	2	4	6	9	13	16
200-Anniversary issue; highlights of the Bumsteads	2	4	6	10	14	18
201-210,213-222	2	4	6	8	10	12
211,212-1st & 2nd app. Super Dagwood	2	4	6	9	13	16
Blondie, Dagwood & Daisy by Chic Young #1(Harvey, 1953, 100 pg. squarebound giant) new stories; Popeye (1 pg.) and Felix (1pg.) app.	32	64	96	188	307	425

BLOOD
Marvel Comics (Epic Comics): Feb, 1988 - No. 4, Apr, 1988 ($3.25, mature)

	GD 2.0	VG 4.0	FN 6.0	VF 8.0	VF/NM 9.0	NM- 9.2
1-4: DeMatteis scripts & Kent Williams-c/a						5.00

BLOOD AND GLORY (Punisher & Captain America)
Marvel Comics: Oct, 1992 - No. 3, Dec, 1992 ($5.95, limited series)

	GD 2.0	VG 4.0	FN 6.0	VF 8.0	VF/NM 9.0	NM- 9.2
1-3: 1-Embossed wraparound-c by Janson; Chichester & Clarke-s						6.00

BLOOD & ROSES: FUTURE PAST TENSE (Bob Hickey's...)
Sky Comics: Dec, 1993 ($2.25)

	GD 2.0	VG 4.0	FN 6.0	VF 8.0	VF/NM 9.0	NM- 9.2
1-Silver ink logo						3.00

BLOOD & ROSES: SEARCH FOR THE TIME-STONE (Bob Hickey's...)
Sky Comics: Apr, 1994 ($2.50)

	GD 2.0	VG 4.0	FN 6.0	VF 8.0	VF/NM 9.0	NM- 9.2
1						3.00

BLOOD AND SHADOWS
DC Comics (Vertigo): 1996 - Book 4, 1996 ($5.95, squarebound, mature)

	GD 2.0	VG 4.0	FN 6.0	VF 8.0	VF/NM 9.0	NM- 9.2
Books 1-4: Joe R. Lansdale scripts; Mark A. Nelson-c/a.						6.00

BLOOD AND WATER
DC Comics (Vertigo): May, 2003 - No. 5, Sept, 2003 ($2.95, limited series)

	GD 2.0	VG 4.0	FN 6.0	VF 8.0	VF/NM 9.0	NM- 9.2
1-5-Judd Winick-s/Tomm Coker-a/Brian Bolland-c						3.00
TPB (2009, $14.99) r/#1-5						15.00

BLOOD: A TALE
DC Comics (Vertigo): Nov, 1996 - No. 4, Feb, 1997 ($2.95, limited series)

	GD 2.0	VG 4.0	FN 6.0	VF 8.0	VF/NM 9.0	NM- 9.2
1-4: Reprints Epic series w/new-c; DeMatteis scripts; Kent Williams-c/a						3.00
TPB (2004, $19.95) r/#1-4						20.00

BLOODBATH
DC Comics: Early Dec, 1993 - No. 2, Late Dec, 1993 ($3.50, 68 pgs.)

	GD 2.0	VG 4.0	FN 6.0	VF 8.0	VF/NM 9.0	NM- 9.2
1-Neon ink-c; Superman app.; new Batman-c /app.						4.00
2-Hitman 2nd app.	1	2	3	4	5	7

BLOODHOUND
DC Comics: Sept, 2004 - No. 10, June, 2005 ($2.95)

	GD 2.0	VG 4.0	FN 6.0	VF 8.0	VF/NM 9.0	NM- 9.2
1-10: 1-Jolley-s/Kirk-a/Johnson-c. 5-Firestorm app. (cont. from Firestorm #7)						3.00

BLOODHOUND: CROWBAR MEDICINE
Dark Horse Comics: Oct, 2013 - No. 5, Mar, 2014 ($3.99)

	GD 2.0	VG 4.0	FN 6.0	VF 8.0	VF/NM 9.0	NM- 9.2
1-5-Jolley-s/Kirk-a/c						4.00

BLOOD LEGACY
Image Comics (Top Cow): May, 2000 - No. 4, Nov, 2000; Apr, 2003 ($2.50/$4.99)

	GD 2.0	VG 4.0	FN 6.0	VF 8.0	VF/NM 9.0	NM- 9.2
...: The Story of Ryan 1-4-Kerri Hawkins-s. 1-Andy Park-a(p); 3 covers						3.00
...: The Young Ones 1 (4/03, $4.99, one-shot) Basaldua-c/a						5.00

Blood of Dracula #1 © Apple Comics

Bloodshot (2013 series) #1 © VAL

Blue Beetle #8 © FOX

GD	VG	FN	VF	VF/NM	NM-
2.0	4.0	6.0	8.0	9.0	9.2

Preview Special ('00, $4.95) B&W flip-book w/The Magdalena Preview 5.00

BLOODLINES: A TALE FROM THE HEART OF AFRICA (See Tales From the Heart of Africa)
Marvel Comics (Epic Comics): 1992 ($5.95, 52 pgs.)
1-Story cont'd from Tales From... 6.00

BLOOD OF DRACULA
Apple Comics: Nov, 1987 - No. 20?, 1990 ($1.75/$1.95, B&W)($2.25 #14,16 on)
1-3,5-14,20: 1-10-Chadwick-c 4.00
4,16-19-Lost Frankenstein pgs. by Wrightson 1 2 3 4 5 7
15-Contains stereo flexidisc ($3.75) 5.00

BLOOD OF THE DEMON (Etrigan the Demon)
DC Comics: May, 2005 - No. 17, Sept, 2006 ($2.50/$2.99)
1-14-Byrne-a(p) & plot/Pfeifer-script. 3,4-Batman app. 13-One Year Later 3.00
15-17-($2.99) 3.00

BLOOD OF THE INNOCENT (See Warp Graphics Annual)
WaRP Graphics: 1/7/86 - No. 4, 1/28/86 (Weekly mini-series, mature)
1-4 3.00

BLOODPACK
DC Comics: Mar, 1995 - No. 4, June,1995 ($1.50, limited series)
1-4 3.00

BLOODPOOL
Image Comics (Extreme): Aug, 1995 - No. 4, Nov, 1995 ($2.50, limited series)
1-4: Jo Duffy scripts in all 3.00
Special (3/96, $2.50)-Jo Duffy scripts 3.00
Trade Paperback (1996, $12.95)-r/#1-4 13.00

BLOOD RED DRAGON (Stan Lee and Yoshiki's...)
Image Comics: No. 0, Aug, 2011 - No. 3, Nov, 2011 ($3.99)
0-3-Goff-s/Soriano-a 4.00

BLOODSCENT
Comico: Oct, 1988 ($2.00, one-shot, Baxter paper)
1-Colan-p 3.00

BLOODSEED
Marvel Comics (Frontier Comics): Oct, 1993 - No. 2, Nov, 1993 ($1.95)
1,2: Sharp/Cam Smith-a 3.00

BLOODSHOT (See Eternal Warrior #4 & Rai #0)
Valiant/Acclaim Comics (Valiant): Feb, 1993 - No. 51, Aug, 1996 ($2.25/$2.50)
0-(3/94, $3.50)-Wraparound chromium-c by Quesada(p); origin 5.00
0-Gold variant; no cover price 10.00
Note: There is a "Platinum variant" ; press run error of Gold ed. (25 copies exist) (A CGC certified 9.8 copy sold for $2,067 in 2004)
1-($3.50)-Chromium embossed-c by B. Smith w/poster 5.00
2-5,8-14: 3-$2.25-c begins; cont'd in Hard Corps #5. 4-Eternal Warrior-c/story. 5-Rai & Eternal Warrior app. 14-(3/94)-Reese-c(i) 3.00
6,7: 6-1st app. Ninjak (out of costume). 7-In costume 4.00
15(4/94)-51: 16-w/bound-in trading card. 51-Bloodshot dies? 3.00
Yearbook 1 (1994, $3.95) 4.00
Special 1 (3/94, $5.95)-Zeck-c/a(p); Last Stand 6.00
...: Blood of the Machine HC (2012, $24.99) r/#1-8; new 8 pg. story; intro by VanHook 25.00

BLOODSHOT (Volume Two)
Acclaim Comics (Valiant): July, 1997 - No. 16, Oct, 1998 ($2.50)
1-16: 1-Two covers. 5-Copycat-c. X-O Manowar-c/app 3.00

BLOODSHOT (Re-titled Bloodshot and H.A.R.D.Corps with #14)
Valiant Entertainment: July, 2012 - Present ($3.99)
1-13: 1-Sweirczynski-s/Garcia & Lozzi-a. 10-13-Harbinger Wars tie-ins 4.00
1-9-Pullbox variants 4.00
1-Variant-c by David Aja 15.00
1-Variant-c by Esad Ribic 20.00
14-21-Bloodshot and H.A.R.D.Corps 4.00
#0 (8/13) Kindt-s/ChrisCross-a; covers by Lupacchino & Bullock 4.00
Bloodshot and H.A.R.D.Corps #0 (2/14, $3.99) History of Project Rising Spirit 4.00

BLOODSTONE
Marvel Comics: Dec, 2001 - No. 4, Mar, 2002 ($2.99)
1-4-Intro. Elsa Bloodstone; Abnett & Lanning-s/Lopez-a 3.00

BLOODSTREAM
Image Comics: Jan, 2004 - No. 4, Dec, 2004 ($2.95)
1-4-Adam Shaw painted-a 3.00

BLOODSTRIKE (See Supreme V2#3)
Image Comics (Extreme Studios): 1993 - No. 22, May, 1995; No. 25, May, 1994 ($1.95/$2.50)
1-22, 25: Liefeld layouts in early issues. 1-Blood Brothers prelude. 2-1st app. Lethal. 5-1st app. Noble. 9-Black and White part 6 by Art Thibert; Liefeld pin-up. 9,10-Have coupon #3 & 7 for Extreme Prejudice #0. 10-(4/94). 11-(7/94). 16:Platt-c; Prophet app. 17-19-polybagged w/card . 25-(5/94)-Liefeld/Fraga-c 3.00
NOTE: *Giffen* story/layouts-4-6. *Jae Lee* c-7, 8. *Rob Liefeld* layouts-1-3. *Art Thibert* c-6i.

BLOODSTRIKE
Image Comics: No. 26, Mar, 2012 - No. 33, Dec, 2012 ($2.99/$3.99)
26-29: 26-Two covers by Seeley & Liefeld; Seeley-s/Gaston-a 3.00
30-33-($3.99) 32,33-Suprema app. 4.00

BLOODSTRIKE ASSASSIN
Image Comics (Extreme Studios): June, 1995 - No. 3, Aug, 1995; No. 0, Oct, 1995 ($2.50, limited series)
0-3: 3-(8/95)-Quesada-c. 0-(10/95)-Battlestone app. 3.00

BLOOD SWORD, THE
Jademan Comics: Aug, 1988 - No. 53, Dec, 1992 ($1.50/$1.95, 68 pgs.)
1-53-Kung Fu stories in all 4.00

BLOOD SWORD DYNASTY
Jademan Comics: 1989 -No. 41, Jan, 1993 ($1.25, 36 pgs.)
1-Ties into Blood Sword 4.00
2-41: Ties into Blood Sword 3.00

BLOOD SYNDICATE
DC Comics (Milestone): Apr, 1993 - No. 35, Feb, 1996 ($1.50/-$3.50)
1-($2.95)-Collector's Edition; polybagged with poster, trading card, & acid-free backing board (direct sale only) 4.00
1-9,11-24,26,27,29,33-34: 8-Intro Kwai. 15-Byrne-c. 16-Worlds Collide Pt. 6; Superman-c/app. 17-Worlds Collide Pt. 13. 29-(99¢); Long Hot Summer x-over 3.00
10,28,30-32: 10-Simonson-c. 30-Long Hot Summer x-over 3.00
25-($2.95, 52 pgs.) 4.00
35-Kwai disappears; last issue 4.00

BLOODWULF
Image Comics (Extreme): Feb, 1995 - No. 4, May, 1995 ($2.50, limited series)
1-4: 1-Liefeld-c w/4 diferent captions & alternate-c. 3.00
Summer Special (8/95, $2.50)-Jeff Johnson-c/a; Supreme app; story takes place between Legend of Supreme #3 & Supreme #23. 3.00

BLOODY MARY
DC Comics (Helix): Oct, 1996 - No. 4, Jan, 1997 ($2.25, limited series)
1-4: Garth Ennis scripts; Ezquerra-c/a in all 3.50
TPB (2005, $19.99) r/#1-4 and Bloody Mary: Lady Liberty #1-4 20.00

BLOODY MARY: LADY LIBERTY
DC Comics (Helix): Sept, 1997 - No. 4, Dec, 1997 ($2.50, limited series)
1-4: Garth Ennis scripts; Ezquerra-c/a in all 3.00

BLUE
Image Comics (Action Toys): Aug, 1999 - No. 2, Apr, 2000 ($2.50)
1,2-Aronowitz-s/Struzan-c 3.00

BLUEBEARD
Slave Labor Graphics: Nov, 1993 - No. 3, Mar, 1994 ($2.95, B&W, lim. series)
1-3: James Robinson scripts. 2-(12/93) 3.00
Trade paperback (6/94, $9.95) 13.00
Trade paperback (2nd printing, 7/96, $12.95)-New-c 13.00

BLUE BEETLE, THE (Also see All Top, Big-3, Mystery Men & Weekly Comic Magazine)
Fox Publ. No. 1-11, 31-60; Holyoke No. 12-30: Winter, 1939-40 - No. 57, 7/48; No. 58, 4/50 - No. 60, 8/50
1-Reprints from Mystery Men #1-5; Blue Beetle origin; Yarko the Great-r/from Wonder Comics /Wonderworld #2-5 all by Eisner; Master Magician app.; (Blue Beetle in 4 different costumes) 470 940 1410 3431 6066 8700
2-K-51-r by Powell/Wonderworld #8,9 177 354 531 1124 1937 2750
3-Simon-c 132 264 396 838 1444 2050
4-Marijuana drug mention story 90 180 270 576 988 1400
5-Zanzibar The Magician by Tuska 77 154 231 493 847 1200
6-Dynamite Thor begins (1st); origin Blue Beetle 73 146 219 467 796 1125
7,8-Dynamo app. in both. 8-Last Thor 66 132 198 419 722 1025
9-12: 9,10-The Blackbird & The Gorilla app. in both. 10-Bondage/hypo-c. 11(2/42)-The Gladiator app. 12(6/42)-The Black Fury app. 58 116 174 371 636 900
13-V-Man begins (1st app.), ends #19; Kubert-a; centerfold spread 68 136 204 435 743 1050

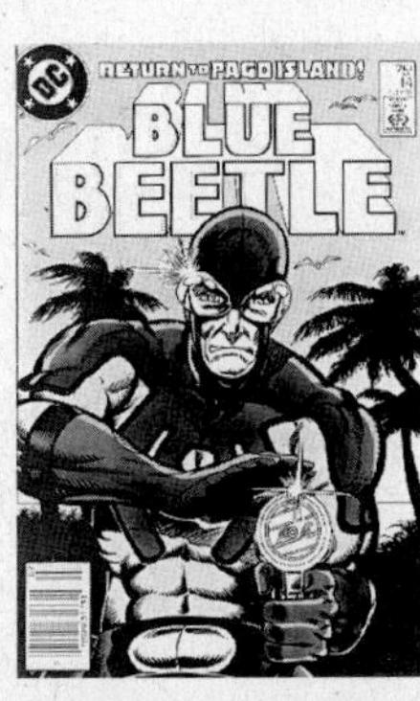

Blue Beetle (1986 series) #14 © DC

Blue Beetle (2011 series) #7 © DC

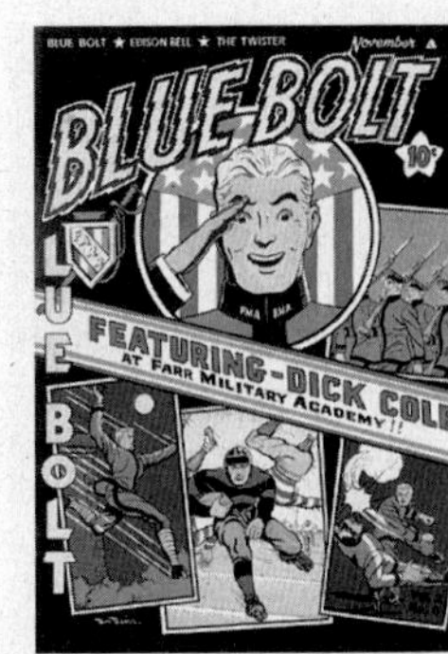

Blue Bolt V2 #6 © NOVP

	GD 2.0	VG 4.0	FN 6.0	VF 8.0	VF/NM 9.0	NM- 9.2
14,15-Kubert-a in both. 14-Intro. side-kick (c/text only), Sparky (called Spunky #17-19); BB vs. The Red Robe (Red Skull swipe)	58	116	174	371	636	900
16-18: 17-Brodsky-c	49	98	147	309	522	735
19-Kubert-a	51	102	153	318	539	760
20-Origin/1st app. Tiger Squadron; Arabian Nights begin	52	104	156	325	555	785
21-26: 24-Intro. & only app. The Halo. 26-General Patton story & photo	40	80	120	246	411	575
27-Tamaa, Jungle Prince app.	39	78	117	231	378	525
28-30(2/44)	36	72	108	211	343	475
31(6/44), 33,34,36-40: 34-38-"The Threat from Saturn" serial.	32	64	96	188	307	425
32-Hitler-c	81	162	243	518	884	1250
35-Extreme violence	39	78	117	231	378	525
41-45 (#43 exist?)	31	62	93	186	303	420
46-The Puppeteer app.	34	68	102	204	332	460
47-Kamen & Baker-a begin	165	330	495	1048	1799	2550
48-50	118	236	354	749	1287	1825
51,53	102	204	306	648	1112	1575
52-Kamen bondage-c; true crime stories begin	155	310	465	992	1696	2400
54-Used in **SOTI**. Illo, "Children call these 'headlights' comics"; classic-c	300	600	900	2010	3505	5000
55-57: 56-Used in **SOTI**, pg. 145. 57(7/48)-Last Kamen issue; becomes Western Killers?	98	196	294	622	1074	1525
58(4/50)-60-No Kamen-a	21	42	63	126	206	285

NOTE: *Kamen a-47-51, 53, 55-57; c-47, 49-52.* ***Powell*** *a-4(2). Bondage-c 9-12, 46, 52.*

BLUE BEETLE (Formerly The Thing; becomes Mr. Muscles No. 22 on)
(See Charlton Bullseye & Space Adventures)
Charlton Comics: No. 18, Feb, 1955 - No. 21, Aug, 1955

	GD 2.0	VG 4.0	FN 6.0	VF 8.0	VF/NM 9.0	NM- 9.2
18,19-(Pre-1944-r). 18-Last pre-code issue. 19-Bouncer, Rocket Kelly-r	21	42	63	122	199	275
20-Joan Mason by Kamen	26	52	78	154	252	350
21-New material	20	40	60	118	192	265

BLUE BEETLE (Unusual Tales #1-49; Ghostly Tales #55 on)(See Captain Atom #83 & Charlton Bullseye)
Charlton Comics: V2#1, June, 1964 - V2#5, Mar-Apr, 1965; V3#50, July, 1965 - V3#54, Feb-Mar, 1966; #1, June, 1967 - #5, Nov, 1968

	GD 2.0	VG 4.0	FN 6.0	VF 8.0	VF/NM 9.0	NM- 9.2
V2#1-Origin/1st S.A. app. Dan Garrett-Blue Beetle	8	16	24	52	99	145
2-5: 5-Weiss illo; 1st published-a?	5	10	15	33	57	80
V3#50-54-Formerly Unusual Tales	5	10	15	31	53	75
1(1967)-Question series begins by Ditko	9	18	27	60	120	180
2-Origin Ted Kord-Blue Beetle (see Capt. Atom #83 for 1st Ted Kord Blue Beetle); Dan Garrett x-over	5	10	15	35	63	90
3-5 (All Ditko-c/a in #1-5)	5	10	15	33	57	80
1,3(Modern Comics-1977)-Reprints	1	2	3	5	6	8

NOTE: *#6 only appeared in the fanzine 'The Charlton Portfolio.'*

BLUE BEETLE (Also see Americomics, Crisis On Infinite Earths, Justice League & Showcase '94 #2-4)
DC Comics: June, 1986 - No. 24, May, 1988

	NM- 9.2
1-Origin retold; intro. Firefist	4.00
2-10,15-19,21-24: 2-Origin Firefist. 5-7-The Question app. 21-Millennium tie-in	3.00
11-14-New Teen Titans x-over	3.50
20-Justice League app.; Millennium tie-in	3.50

BLUE BEETLE (See Infinite Crisis, Teen Titans, and Booster Gold #21)
DC Comics: May, 2006 - No. 36, Apr, 2009 ($2.99)

	NM- 9.2
1-Hamner-a/Giffen & Rogers-s; Guy Gardner app.	4.00
1-2nd & 3rd printings	3.00
2-36: 2-2nd printing exists. 2-4-Oracle app. 5-Phantom Stranger app. 16-Eclipso app. 18,33-Teen Titans app. 20-Sinestro Corps. 21-Spectre app. 26-Spanish issue	3.00
...: Black and Blue TPB (2010, $17.99) r/#27,28,35,36 & Booster Gold #21-25,28,29	18.00
...: Boundaries TPB (2009, $14.99) r/#29-34	15.00
...: End Game TPB (2008, $14.99) r/#20-26; English script for #26	15.00
...: Reach For the Stars TPB (2008, $14.99) r/#13-19	15.00
...: Road Trip TPB (2007, $12.99) r/#7-12	13.00
...: Shellshocked TPB (2006, $12.99) r/#1-6	13.00

BLUE BEETLE (DC New 52) (Also see Threshold)
DC Comics: Nov, 2011 - No. 16, Mar, 2013 ($2.99)

	NM- 9.2
1-16: 1-Bedard-s/Ig Guara-a; new origin. 9-Green Lantern (Kyle) app. 11-Booster Gold	3.00
#0 (11/12, $2.99) Origin of the scarab	3.00

BLUEBERRY (See Lt. Blueberry & Marshal Blueberry)
Marvel Comics (Epic Comics): 1989 - No. 5, 1990 ($12.95/$14.95, graphic novel)

	GD 2.0	VG 4.0	FN 6.0	VF 8.0	VF/NM 9.0	NM- 9.2
1,3,4,5-($12.95)-Moebius-a in all	3	6	9	14	19	24
2-($14.95)	3	6	9	14	20	26

BLUE BOLT
Funnies, Inc. No. 1/Novelty Press/Premium Group of Comics: June, 1940 - No. 101 (V10#2), Sept-Oct, 1949

	GD 2.0	VG 4.0	FN 6.0	VF 8.0	VF/NM 9.0	NM- 9.2
V1#1-Origin Blue Bolt by Joe Simon, Sub-Zero Man, White Rider & Super Horse, Dick Cole, Wonder Boy & Sgt. Spook (1st app. of each)	331	662	993	2317	4059	5800
2-Simon & Kirby's 1st art & 1st super-hero (Blue Bolt)	194	388	582	1242	2121	3000
3-1 pg. Space Hawk by Wolverton; 2nd S&K-a on Blue Bolt (same cover date as Red Raven #1); Simon-c	174	348	522	1114	1907	2700
4-S&K-a; classic Everett shark-c	161	322	483	1030	1765	2500
5-S&K-a; Everett-a begins on Sub-Zero; 1st time S&K names app. in a comic	142	284	426	909	1555	2200
6,8-10-S&K-a	126	252	378	806	1378	1950
7-S&K-c/a	152	304	456	965	1658	2350
11,12: 11-Robot-c	119	238	357	762	1306	1850
V2#1-Origin Dick Cole & The Twister; Twister x-over in Dick Cole, Sub-Zero, & Blue Bolt; origin Simba Karno who battles Dick Cole thru V2#5 & becomes main supporting character V2#6 on; battle-c	41	82	123	256	428	600
2-Origin The Twister retold in text	36	72	108	211	343	475
3-5: 5-Intro. Freezum	31	62	93	182	296	410
6-Origin Sgt. Spook retold	27	54	81	158	259	360
7-12: 7-Lois Blake becomes Blue Bolt's costume aide; last Twister. 12-Text-sty by Mickey Spillaine	22	44	66	132	216	300
V3#1-3	19	38	57	109	172	235
4-12: 4-Blue Bolt abandons costume	15	30	45	88	137	185
V4#1-Hitler, Tojo, Mussolini-c	68	136	204	435	743	1050
V4#2-12: 3-Shows V4#3 on-c, V4#4 inside (9-10/43). 5-Infinity-c. 8-Last Sub-Zero	13	26	39	74	105	135
V5#1-8, V6#1-3,5-10, V7#1-12	12	24	36	67	94	120
V6#4-Racist cover	24	48	72	140	230	320
V8#1-6,8-12, V9#1-4,7,8, V10#1(#100),V10#2(#101)-Last Dick Cole, Blue Bolt	10	20	30	56	76	95
V8#7,V9#6,9-L. B. Cole-c	22	44	66	128	209	290
V9#5-Classic fish in the face-c	22	44	66	128	209	290

NOTE: ***Everett*** *c-V1#4, 11, V2#1, 2.* ***Gustavson*** *a-V1#1-12, V2#1-7.* ***Kiefer*** *c-V3#1.* ***Rico*** *a-V6#10, V7#4. Blue Bolt not in V9#8.*

BLUE BOLT (Becomes Ghostly Weird Stories #120 on; continuation of Novelty Blue Bolt) (...Weird Tales of Terror #111,112,...Weird Tales #113-119)
Star Publications: No. 102, Nov-Dec, 1949 - No. 119, May-June, 1953

	GD 2.0	VG 4.0	FN 6.0	VF 8.0	VF/NM 9.0	NM- 9.2
102-The Chameleon, & Target app.	39	78	117	240	395	550
103,104-The Chameleon app. 104-Last Target	39	78	117	231	378	525
105-Origin Blue Bolt (from #1) retold by Simon; Chameleon & Target app.; opium den story	63	126	189	403	689	975
106-Blue Bolt by S&K begins; Spacehawk reprints from Target by Wolverton begin, ends #110; Sub-Zero begins; ends #109	61	122	183	390	670	950
107-110: 108-Last S&K Blue Bolt reprint. 109-Wolverton-c(r)/inside Spacehawk splash. 110-Target app.	60	120	180	381	653	925
111,112: 111-Red Rocket & The Mask-r; last Blue Bolt; 1pg. L. B. Cole-a. 112-Last Torpedo Man app.	55	110	165	352	601	850
113-Wolverton's Spacehawk-r/Target V3#7	57	114	171	362	619	875
114,116: 116-Jungle Jo-r	55	110	165	352	601	850
115-Sgt. Spook app.	57	114	171	362	619	875
117-Jo-Jo & Blue Bolt-r	56	112	168	356	608	860
118-"White Spirit" by Wood	57	114	171	362	619	875
119-Disbrow/Cole-c; Jungle Jo-r	56	112	168	356	608	860
Accepted Reprint #103(1957?, nd)	14	28	42	80	115	150

NOTE: ***L. B. Cole*** *c-102-108, 110 on.* ***Disbrow*** *a-112(2), 113(3), 114(2), 115(2), 116-118.* ***Hollingsworth*** *a-117.* ***Palais*** *a-112r. Sci/Fi c-105-110. Horror c-111.*

BLUE BULLETEER, THE (Also see Femforce Special)
AC Comics: 1989 ($2.25, B&W, one-shot)

	NM- 9.2
1-Origin by Bill Black; Bill Ward-a	4.00

BLUE BULLETEER (Also see Femforce Special)
AC Comics: 1996 ($5.95, B&W, one-shot)

	NM- 9.2
1-Photo-c	6.00

BLUE CIRCLE COMICS (Also see Red Circle Comics, Blazing Comics & Roly Poly Comic Book)
Enwil Associates/Rural Home: June, 1944 - No. 6, Apr, 1945

	GD 2.0	VG 4.0	FN 6.0	VF 8.0	VF/NM 9.0	NM- 9.2
1-The Blue Circle begins (1st app.); origin & 1st app. Steel Fist	36	72	108	216	351	485
2	21	42	63	122	199	275

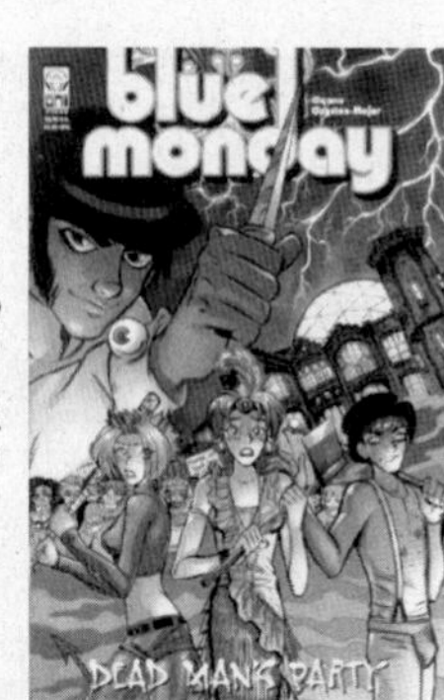

Blue Monday: Dead Man's Party © Chynna Clugston

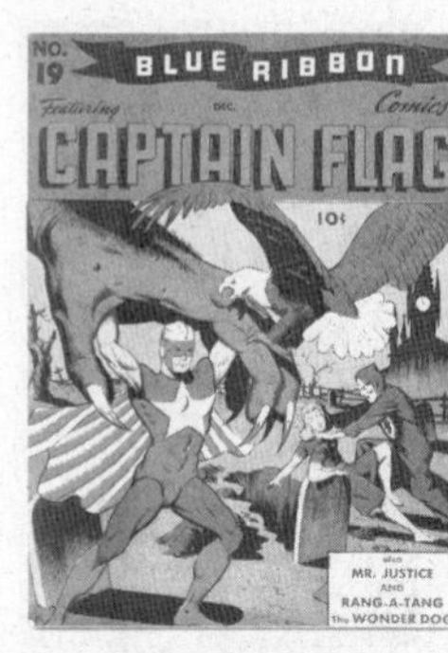

Blue Ribbon Comics #19 © MLJ

Bob Colt #4 © FAW

GD VG FN VF VF/NM NM-
2.0 4.0 6.0 8.0 9.0 9.2

3-Hitler parody-c 41 82 123 256 428 600
4-6: 5-Last Steel Fist. 20 40 60 114 182 250
6-(Dated 4/45, Vol. 2#3 inside)-Leftover covers to #6 were later restapled over early 1950's coverless comics; variations of the coverless comics exist.
Colossal Features known. 20 40 60 114 182 250

BLUE DEVIL (See Fury of Firestorm #24, Underworld Unleashed, Starman (2nd) #38, Infinite Crisis and Shadowpact)
DC Comics: June, 1984 - No. 31, Dec, 1986 (75¢/$1.25)

1 4.00
2-16,19-31: 4-Origin Nebiros. 7-Gil Kane-a. 8-Giffen-a 3.00
17,18-Crisis x-over 3.50
Annual 1 (11/85)-Team-ups w/Black Orchid, Creeper, Demon, Madame Xanadu, Man-Bat & Phantom Stranger 4.00

BLUE MONDAY: ... (one-shots)
Oni Press: Feb, 2002 - Present (B&W, Chynna Clugston-Major-s/a/c in all)

Dead Man's Party (10/02, $2.95) Dan Brereton painted back-c 3.00
Inbetween Days (9/03, $9.95, 8" x 5-1/2") r/Dead Man's Party, Lovecats, & Nobody's Fool 10.00
Lovecats (2/02, $2.95) Valentine's Day themed 3.00
Nobody's Fool (2/03, $2.95) April Fool's Day themed 3.00
Thieves Like Us (12/08, $3.50) Part 1 of an unfinished 5-part series 3.50

BLUE MONDAY: ABSOLUTE BEGINNERS
Oni Press: Feb, 2001 - No. 4, Sept, 2001 ($2.95, B&W, limited series)

1-4-Chynna Clugston-Major-s/a/c 3.00
TPB (12/01, $11.95, 8" x 6") r/series 12.00

BLUE MONDAY: PAINTED MOON
Oni Press: Feb, 2004 - No. 4, Mar, 2005 ($2.99, B&W, limited series)

1-4-Chynna Clugston-Major-s/a/c 3.00
TPB (4/05, $11.95, digest-sized) r/series; sketch pages 12.00

BLUE MONDAY: THE KIDS ARE ALRIGHT
Oni Press: Feb, 2000 - No. 3, May, 2000 ($2.95, B&W, limited series)

1-3-Chynna Clugston-Major-s/a/c. 1-Variant-c by Warren. 2-Dorkin-c 3.00
3-Variant cover by J. Scott Campbell 4.00
TPB (12/00, $10.95, digest-sized) r/#1-3 & earlier short stories 11.00

BLUE PHANTOM, THE
Dell Publishing Co.: June-Aug, 1962

1(01-066-208)-by Fred Fredericks 3 6 9 20 31 42

BLUE RIBBON COMICS (...Mystery Comics No. 9-18)
MLJ Magazines: Nov, 1939 - No. 22, Mar, 1942 (1st MLJ series)

1-Dan Hastings, Richy the Amazing Boy, Rang-A-Tang the Wonder Dog begin (1st app. of each); Little Nemo app. (not by W. McCay); Jack Cole-a(3)
(1st MLJ comic) 245 490 735 1568 2684 3800
2-Bob Phantom, Silver Fox (both in #3), Rang-A-Tang Club & Cpl. Collins begin
(1st app. of each); Jack Cole-a 119 238 357 762 1306 1850
3-J. Cole-a 79 158 237 502 864 1225
4-Doc Strong, The Green Falcon, & Hercules begin (1st app. each); origin & 1st app.
The Fox & Ty-Gor, Son of the Tiger 87 174 261 553 952 1350
5-8: 8-Last Hercules; 6,7-Biro, Meskin-a. 7-Fox app. on-c
65 130 195 416 708 1000
9-(Scarce)-Origin & 1st app. Mr. Justice (2/41) 303 606 909 2121 3711 5300
10-13: 12-Last Doc Strong. 13-Inferno, the Flame Breather begins, ends #19; Devil-c
111 222 333 705 1215 1725
14,15,17,18: 15-Last Green Falcon 95 190 285 603 1039 1475
16-Origin & 1st app. Captain Flag (9/41) 161 322 483 1030 1765 2500
19-22: 20-Last Ty-Gor. 22-Origin Mr. Justice retold 94 188 282 597 1024 1450
NOTE: ***Biro** c-3-5; a-2 (Cpl. Collins & Scoop Cody). **S. Cooper** c-9-17. 20-22 contain "Tales From the Witch's Cauldron" (same strip as "Stories of the Black Witch" in Zip Comics). Mr. Justice c-9-18. Captain Flag c-16-18 (w/Mr. Justice), 19-22.*

BLUE RIBBON COMICS (Becomes Teen-Age Diary Secrets #4)
(Also see Approved Comics, Blue Ribbon Comics and Heckle & Jeckle)
Blue Ribbon (St. John): Feb, 1949 - No. 6, Aug, 1949

1-Heckle & Jeckle (Terrytoons) 15 30 45 85 130 175
2(4/49)-Diary Secrets; Baker-c 43 86 129 271 461 650
3-Heckle & Jeckle (Terrytoons) 11 22 33 62 86 110
4(6/49)-Teen-Age Diary Secrets; Baker c/a(2) 45 90 135 284 480 675
5(8/49)-Teen-Age Diary Secrets; Oversize; photo-c; Baker-a(2)- Continues
as Teen-Age Diary Secrets 58 116 174 371 636 900
6-Dinky Duck(8/49)(Terrytoons) 8 16 24 42 54 65

BLUE RIBBON COMICS
Red Circle Prod./Archie Ent. No. 5 on: Nov, 1983 - No. 14, Dec, 1984

GD VG FN VF VF/NM NM-
2.0 4.0 6.0 8.0 9.0 9.2

1-S&K-r/Advs. of the Fly #1,2; Williamson/Torres-r/Fly #2; Ditko-c
1 2 3 5 6 8
2-7,9,10: 3-Origin Steel Sterling. 5-S&K Shield-r; new Kirby-c. 6,7-The Fox app. 6.00
8-Toth centerspread; Black Hood app.; Neal Adams-a(r)
1 2 3 4 5 7
11,13,14: 11-Black Hood. 13-Thunder Bunny. 14-Web & Jaguar 6.00
12-Thunder Agents; Noman new Ditko-a 1 2 3 5 6 8
NOTE: ***N. Adams** a(r)-8. **Buckler** a-4i. **Nino** a-2i. **McWilliams** a-8. **Morrow** a-8.*

BLUE STREAK (See Holyoke One-Shot No. 8)

BLUNTMAN AND CHRONIC TPB(Also see Jay and Silent Bob, Clerks, and Oni Double Feature)
Image Comics: Dec, 2001 ($14.95, TPB)

nn-Tie-in for "Jay & Silent Bob Strike Back" movie; new Kevin Smith-s/Michael Oeming-a; r/app. from Oni Double Feature #12 in color; Ben Affleck & Jason Lee afterwords 15.00

BLYTHE (Marge's)
Dell Publishing Co.: No. 1072, Jan-Mar, 1960

Four Color 1072 5 10 15 33 57 80

B-MAN (See Double-Dare Adventures)

BO (Tom Cat #4 on) (Also see Big Shot #29 & Dixie Dugan)
Charlton Comics Group: June, 1955 - No. 3, Oct, 1955 (A dog)

1-3: Newspaper reprints by Frank Beck; Noodnik the Eskimo app.
8 16 24 40 50 60

BOATNIKS, THE (See Walt Disney Showcase No. 1)

BOB BURDEN'S ORIGINAL MYSTERYMEN PRESENTS
Dark Horse Comics: 1999 - No. 4 ($2.95/$3.50)

1-3-Bob Burden-s/Sadowski-a(p) 3.50
4-($3.50) All Villain issue 3.50

BOBBY BENSON'S B-BAR-B RIDERS (Radio) (See Best of The West, The Lemonade Kid & Model Fun)
Magazine Enterprises/AC Comics: May-June, 1950 - No. 20, May-June, 1953

1-The Lemonade Kid begins; Powell-a (Scarce) 41 82 123 256 428 600
2 17 34 51 98 154 210
3-5: 4,5-Lemonade Kid-c (#4-Spider-c) 14 28 42 76 108 140
6-8,10 13 26 39 72 101 130
9,11,13-Frazetta-c; Ghost Rider in #13-15 by Ayers-a. 13-Ghost Rider-c
37 74 111 222 361 500
12,17-20: 20-(A-1 #88) 11 22 33 64 90 115
14-Decapitation/Bondage-c & story; classic horror-c 29 58 87 170 278 385
15-Ghost Rider-c 22 44 66 132 216 300
16-Photo-c 14 28 42 80 115 150
1 (1990, $2.75, B&W)-Reprints; photo-c & inside covers 3.00
NOTE: ***Ayers** a-13-15, 20. **Powell** a-1-12(4 ea.), 13(3), 14-16(Red Hawk only); c-1-8,1 0, 12. Lemonade Kid in most 1-13.*

BOBBY COMICS
Universal Phoenix Features: May, 1946

1-By S. M. Iger 10 20 30 58 79 100

BOBBY SHERMAN (TV)
Charlton Comics: Feb, 1972 - No. 7, Oct, 1972

1-Based on TV show "Getting Together" 5 10 15 33 57 80
2-7: Photo-c on all. 7-Bobby Sherman for President 4 8 12 23 37 50

BOB COLT (Movie star)(See XMas Comics)
Fawcett Publications: Nov, 1950 - No. 10, May, 1952

1-Bob Colt, his horse Buckskin & sidekick Pablo begin; photo front/back-c
begin 24 48 72 142 234 325
2 14 28 42 80 115 150
3-5 12 24 36 67 94 120
6-Flying Saucer story 10 20 30 58 79 100
7-10: 9-Last photo back-c 9 18 27 52 69 85

BOB HOPE (See Adventures of... & Calling All Boys #12)

BOB MARLEY, TALE OF THE TUFF GONG (Music star)
Marvel Comics: Aug, 1994 - No, 3, Nov, 1994 ($5.95, limited series)

1-3 6.00

BOB POWELL'S TIMELESS TALES
Eclipse Comics: March, 1989 ($2.00, B&W)

1-Powell-r/Black Cat #5 (Scarlet Arrow), 9 & Race for the Moon #1 3.00

BOB SCULLY, THE TWO-FISTED HICK DETECTIVE (Also see Advs. of Detective Ace King and Detective Dan)
Humor Publ. Co.: No date (1933) (36 pgs., 9-1/2x11", B&W, paper-c; 10¢-c)

Body Doubles #1 © DC

Bomb Queen III #2 © J. Robinson

Bone #55 © Jeff Smith

	GD 2.0	VG 4.0	FN 6.0	VF 8.0	VF/NM 9.0	NM- 9.2

nn-By Howard Dell; not reprints; along with Advs. of Det. Ace King and Detective Dan, the first comic w/original art & the first of a single theme; has a blue 2-tone cover 475 950 1425 3800 - -

BOB SON OF BATTLE
Dell Publishing Co.: No. 729, Nov, 1956

Four Color 729 4 8 12 23 37 50

BOB STEELE WESTERN (Movie star)
Fawcett Publications/AC Comics: Dec, 1950 - No. 10, June, 1952; 1990

1-Bob Steele & his horse Bullet begin; photo front/back-c begin 37 74 111 222 361 500
2 19 38 57 109 172 235
3-5: 4-Last photo back-c 14 28 42 82 121 160
6-10: 10-Last photo-c 13 26 39 72 101 130
1 (1990, $2.75, B&W)-Bob Steele & Rocky Lane reprints; photo-c & inside covers 3.00

BOB SWIFT (Boy Sportsman)
Fawcett Publications: May, 1951 - No. 5, Jan, 1952

1 10 20 30 58 79 100
2-5: Saunders painted-c #1-5 7 14 21 35 43 50

BOB, THE GALACTIC BUM
DC Comics: Feb, 1995 - No. 4, June, 1995 ($1.95, limited series)

1-4: 1-Lobo app. 3.00

BODY BAGS
Dark Horse Comics (Blanc Noir): Sept, 1996 - No. 4, Jan, 1997 ($2.95, mini-series, mature) (1st Blanc Noir series)

1,2-Jason Pearson-c/a/scripts in all. 1-Intro Clownface & Panda 5.00
3,4 4.00
Body Bags 1 (Image Comics, 7/05, $5.99) r/#1&2 6.00
Body Bags 2 (Image Comics, 8/05, $5.99) r/#3&4 6.00
...: 3 The Hard Way (Image, 2/06, $5.99) new story & r/Dark Horse Presents Annual 1997 and Dark Horse Maverick 2000; Pearson-c 6.00
...: One Shot (Image, 11/08, $5.99) wraparound-c; Pearson-c/a/s 6.00

BODYCOUNT (Also see Casey Jones & Raphael)
Image Comics (Highbrow Entertainment): Mar, 1996 - No. 4, July, 1996 ($2.50, lim. series)

1-4: Kevin Eastman-a(p)/scripts; Simon Bisley-c/a(i); Turtles app. 3.00

BODY DOUBLES (See Resurrection Man)
DC Comics: Oct, 1999 - No. 4, Jan, 2000 ($2.50, limited series)

1-4-Lanning & Abnett-s. 2-Black Canary app. 4-Wonder Woman app. 3.00
...(Villains) (2/98, $1.95, one-shot) 1-Pearson-c; Deadshot app. 3.00

BOFFO LAFFS
Paragraphics: 1986 - No. 5 ($2.50/$1.95)

1-($2.50) First comic cover with hologram 4.00
2-5 3.00

BOLD ADVENTURES
Pacific Comics: Oct, 1983 - No. 3, June, 1984 ($1.50)

1-Time Force, Anaconda, & The Weirdling begin 3.00
2,3: 2-Soldiers of Fortune begins. 3-Spitfire 3.00
NOTE: *Kaluta c-3. Nebres a-1-3. Nino a-2, 3. Severin a-3.*

BOLD STORIES (Also see Candid Tales & It Rhymes With Lust)
Kirby Publishing Co.: Mar, 1950 - July, 1950 (Digest size, 144 pgs.)

March issue (Very Rare) - Contains "The Ogre of Paris" by Wood 213 426 639 1363 2332 3300
May issue (Very Rare) - Contains "The Cobra's Kiss" by Graham Ingels (21 pgs.) 181 362 543 1158 1979 2800
July issue (Very Rare) - Contains "The Ogre of Paris" by Wood 161 322 483 1030 1765 2500

BOLT AND STAR FORCE SIX
Americomics: 1984 ($1.75)

1-Origin Bolt & Star Force Six 3.00
Special 1 (1984, $2.00, 52pgs., B&W) 4.00

BOMBARDIER (See Bee 29, the Bombardier & Cinema Comics Herald)

BOMBAST
Topps Comics: 1993 ($2.95, one-shot) (Created by Jack Kirby)

1-Polybagged w/Kirbychrome trading card; Savage Dragon app.; Kirby-c; has coupon for Amberchrome Secret City Saga #0 4.00

BOMBA THE JUNGLE BOY (TV)
National Periodical Publ.: Sept-Oct, 1967 - No. 7, Sept-Oct, 1968 (12¢)

1-Intro. Bomba; Infantino/Anderson-c 4 8 12 23 37 50
2-7 3 6 9 16 23 30

BOMBER COMICS
Elliot Publ. Co./Melverne Herald/Farrell/Sunrise Times: Mar, 1944 - No. 4, Winter, 1944-45

1-Wonder Boy, & Kismet, Man of Fate begin 87 174 261 553 952 1350
2-Hitler-c and 8 pg. story 118 236 354 749 1287 1825
3: 2-4-Have Classics Comics ad to HRN 20 48 96 144 302 514 725
4-Hitler, Tojo & Mussolini-c; Sensation Comics #13-c/swipe; has Classics Comics ad to HRN 20. 111 222 333 705 1215 1725

BOMB QUEEN
Image Comics (Shadowline): Feb, 2006 - No. 4, May, 2006 ($3.50, mature)

1-4-Jimmie Robinson-s/a 3.50
... Vs. Blacklight One Shot #1 (8/06, $3.50) Robinson-a; Shadowhawk app. 3.50
..., Vol. 1: WMD: Woman of Mass Destruction TPB (7/06, $12.99) r/#1-4; bonus art 13.00

BOMB QUEEN II
Image Comics (Shadowline): Oct, 2006 - No. 3, Dec, 2006 ($3.50, mature)

1-3-Jimmie Robinson-s/a; intro. The Four Queens 3.50
..., Vol. 2: Dirty Bomb - Queen of Hearts TPB (7/07, $14.99) r/#1-3 & Blacklight One Shot; bonus art; Robinson interview 15.00

BOMB QUEEN III THE GOOD, THE BAD & THE LOVELY
Image Comics (Shadowline): Mar, 2007 - No. 4, Jun, 2007 ($3.50, mature)

1-4-Jimmie Robinson-a/Jim Valentino-s; Blacklight & Rebound app. 1-Linsner-c 3.50

BOMB QUEEN IV SUICIDE BOMBER
Image Comics (Shadowline): Aug, 2007 - No. 4, Dec, 2007 ($3.50, mature)

1-4-Jim Robinson-s/a. 3-She-Spawn app. 3.50

BOMB QUEEN (Volume 5)
Image Comics (Shadowline): May, 2008 - No. 6, Mar, 2009 ($3.50, mature)

Vol. 5 #1-6-Jim Robinson-s/a 3.50
Vol. 6 #1-4: 1-(9/09 - No. 4, 1/11, $3.50) Obama satire 3.50
Vol. 7 #1-4 (12/11 - No. 4, 5/12) Bomb Queen returns in 2112 3.50
... Presents: All Girl Comics (5/09, $3.50) Dee Rail, Blacklight, Rebound, Tempest app. 3.50
... Presents: All Girl Special (7/11, $3.50) President Palin app. 3.50
... vs. Hack/Slash (2/11, $3.50) Cassie and Vlad app.; Robinson-s/a 3.50

BONANZA (TV)
Dell/Gold Key: June-Aug, 1960 - No. 37, Aug, 1970 (All Photo-c)

Four Color 1110 (6-8/60) 29 58 87 203 444 685
Four Color 1221,1283, & #01070-207, 01070-210 15 30 45 100 220 340
1(12/62-Gold Key) 16 32 48 107 236 365
2 9 18 27 58 114 170
3-10 7 14 21 44 82 120
11-20 5 10 15 34 60 85
21-37: 29-Reprints 5 10 15 30 50 70

BONE
Cartoon Books #1-20, 28 on/Image Comics #21-27: Jul, 1991 - No. 55, Jun, 2004 ($2.95, B&W)

1-Jeff Smith-c/a in all 50 100 150 325 475 625
1-2nd printing 2 4 6 9 12 15
1-3rd thru 5th printings 4.00
2-1st printing 6 12 18 42 79 115
2-2nd & 3rd printings 4.00
3-1st printing 5 10 15 35 63 90
3-2nd thru 4th printings 4.00
4,5 4 8 12 25 40 55
6-10 2 4 6 13 18 22
11-20 6.00
13 1/2 (1/95, Wizard) 2 4 6 8 10 12
13 1/2 (Gold) 2 4 6 9 12 15
21-37: 21-1st Image issue 5.00
38-($4.95) Three covers by Miller, Ross, Smith 1 2 3 4 5 7
39-55-($2.95) 4.00
1-27-($2.95): 1-Image reprints begin w/new-c. 2-Allred pin-up. 3.00
... Holiday Special (1993, giveaway) 2 3 4 6 8 10
... Reader -($9.95) Behind the scenes info 10.00
... Sourcebook-San Diego Edition 3.00
...10th Anniversary Edition (8/01, $5.95) r/#1 in color; came with figure 6.00
Complete Bone Adventures Vol 1,2 ('93, '94, $12.95, r/#1-6 & #7-12) 15.00
...: One Volume Edition (2004, $39.95, 1300 pgs.) r/#1-54; extra material 40.00
Volume 1-($19.95, hard-c)-"Out From Boneville" 20.00
Volume 1-($12.95, soft-c) 13.00

The Book of Fate #4 © DC

The Books of Faerie #3 © DC

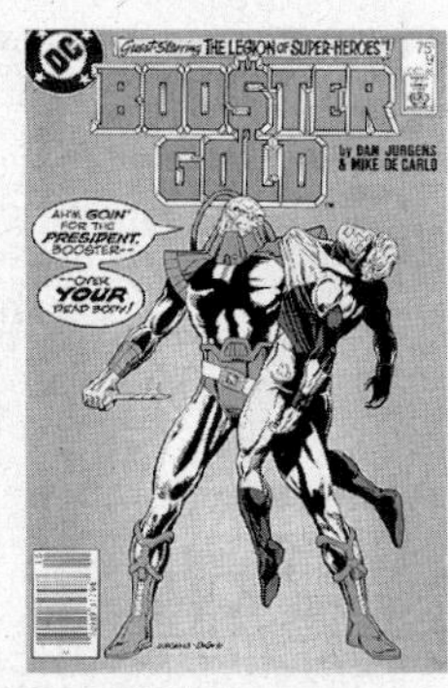

Booster Gold #9 © DC

	GD 2.0	VG 4.0	FN 6.0	VF 8.0	VF/NM 9.0	NM- 9.2

Volume 2,5-($22.95, hard-c)-"The Great Cow Race" & "Rock Jaw" 23.00
Volume 2,5-($14.95, soft-c) 15.00
Volume 3,4-($24.95, hard-c)-"Eyes of the Storm" & "The Dragonslayer" 25.00
Volume 3,4,7-($16.95, soft-c) 17.00
Volume 6-($15.95, soft-c)-"Old Man's Cave" 16.00
Volume 7-($24.95, hard-c)-"Ghost Circles" 25.00
Volume 8-($23.95, hard-c)-"Treasure Hunters" 24.00
NOTE: *Printings not listed sell for cover price.*

BONGO (See Story Hour Series)

BONGO & LUMPJAW (Disney, see Walt Disney Showcase #3)
Dell Publishing Co.: No. 706, June, 1956; No. 886, Mar, 1958

	GD	VG	FN	VF	VF/NM	NM-
Four Color 706 (#1)	5	10	15	33	57	80
Four Color 886	4	8	12	28	47	65

BONGO COMICS ...
Bongo Comics: 2005 - 2012 (Free Comic Book Day giveaways)

Gimme Gimme Giveaway! (2005) - Short stories from Simpsons Comics, Futurama Comics and Radioactive Man 3.00
Free-For-All! (2006, 2007, 2008, 2009, 2010, 2011,2013) - Short stories in each 3.00
Free-For-All! 2012 - Flip book withSpongeBob Comics 3.00

BONGO COMICS PRESENTS RADIOACTIVE MAN (See Radioactive Man)

BON VOYAGE (See Movie Classics)

BOOF
Image Comics (Todd McFarlane Prod.): July, 1994 - No. 6, Dec, 1994 ($1.95)

1-6 3.00

BOOF AND THE BRUISE CREW
Image Comics (Todd McFarlane Prod.): July, 1994 - No. 6, Dec, 1994 ($1.95)

1-6 3.00

BOOK AND RECORD SET (See Power Record Comics)

BOOK OF ALL COMICS
William H. Wise: 1945 (196 pgs.)(Inside f/c has Green Publ. blacked out)

	GD	VG	FN	VF	VF/NM	NM-
nn-Green Mask, Puppeteer & The Bouncer	53	106	159	334	567	800

BOOK OF ANTS, THE
Artisan Entertainment: 1998 ($2.95, B&W)

1-Based on the movie Pi; Aronofsky-s 3.00

BOOK OF BALLADS AND SAGAS, THE
Green Man Press: Oct, 1995 - No. 4 ($2.95/$3.50/$3.25, B&W)

1-4: 1-Vess-c/a; Gaiman story. 3.50

BOOK OF COMICS, THE
William H. Wise: No date (1944) (25¢, 132 pgs.)

	GD	VG	FN	VF	VF/NM	NM-
nn-Captain V app.	44	88	132	277	469	660

BOOK OF FATE, THE (See Fate)
DC Comics: Feb, 1997 - No. 12, Jan, 1998 ($2.25/$2.50)

1-12: 4-Two-Face-c/app. 6-Convergence. 11-Sentinel app. 3.00

BOOK OF LOST SOULS, THE
Marvel Comics (Icon): Dec, 2005 - No. 6, June, 2006 ($2.99)

1-6-Colleen Doran-a/c; J. Michael Straczynski-s 3.00
... Vol. 1: Introductions All Around (2006, $16.99, TPB) r/series 17.00

BOOK OF LOVE (See Fox Giants)

BOOK OF NIGHT, THE
Dark Horse Comics: July, 1987 - No. 3, 1987 ($1.75, B&W)

1-3: Reprints from Epic Illustrated; Vess-a 3.00
TPB-r/#1-3 15.00
Hardcover-Black-c with red crest 100.00
Hardcover w/slipcase (1991) signed and numbered 50.00

BOOK OF THE DEAD
Marvel Comics: Dec, 1993 - No. 4, Mar, 1994 ($1.75, limited series, 52 pgs.)

	GD	VG	FN	VF	VF/NM	NM-
1-4: 1-Ploog Frankenstein & Morrow Man-Thing-r begin; Wrightson-r/Chamber of Darkness #7. 2-Morrow new painted-c; Chaykin/Morrow Man-Thing; Krigstein-r/Uncanny Tales #54; r/Fear #10. 3-r/Astonishing Tales #10 & Starlin Man-Thing. 3,4-Painted-c	1	2	3	5	6	8

BOOKS OF DOOM (Dr. Doom from Fantastic Four)
Marvel Comics: Jan, 2006 - No. 6, June, 2006 ($2.99, limited series)

1-6-Life story/origin of Dr. Doom; Brubaker-s/Raimondi-a/Rivera-c 3.00
Fantastic Four: Books of Doom HC (2006, $19.99) r/#1-6 20.00
Fantastic Four: Books of Doom SC (2007, $14.99) r/#1-6 15.00

BOOKS OF FAERIE, THE
DC Comics (Vertigo): Mar, 1997 - No. 3, May, 1997 ($2.50, limited series)

1-3-Gross-a 3.00
TPB (1998, $14.95) r/#1-3 & Arcana Annual #1 15.00

BOOKS OF FAERIE, THE : AUBERON'S TALE
DC Comics (Vertigo): Aug, 1998 - No. 3, Oct, 1998 ($2.50, limited series)

1-3-Gross-a 3.00

BOOKS OF FAERIE, THE : MOLLY'S STORY
DC Comics (Vertigo): Sept, 1999 - No. 4, Dec, 1999 ($2.50, limited series)

1-4-Ney Rieber-s/Mejia-a 3.00

BOOKS OF MAGIC
DC Comics: 1990 - No. 4, 1991 ($3.95, 52 pgs., limited series, mature)

	GD	VG	FN	VF	VF/NM	NM-
1-Bolton painted-c/a; Phantom Stranger app.; Gaiman scripts in all	1	3	4	6	8	10
2,3: 2-John Constantine, Dr. Fate, Spectre, Deadman app. 3-Dr. Occult app.; minor Sandman app.	1	2	3	4	5	7
4-Early Death-c/app. (early 1991)	1	2	3	5	6	8

Trade paperback-($19.95)-Reprints limited series 20.00

BOOKS OF MAGIC (Also see Hunter: The Age of Magic and Names of Magic)
DC Comics (Vertigo): May, 1994 - No. 75, Aug, 2000 ($1.95/$2.50, mature)

	GD	VG	FN	VF	VF/NM	NM-
1-Charles Vess-c	2	4	6	8	10	12
1-Platinum	2	4	6	13	18	22
2-4: 4-Death app.	1	2	3	4	5	7

5-14: Charles Vess-c 4.00
15-75: 15-$2.50-c begins. 22-Kaluta-c. 25-Death-c/app; Bachalo-c. 51-Peter Gross-s/a begins. 55-Medley-a 3.00
Annual 1-3 (2/97, 2/98, '99, $3.95) 4.00
Bindings (1995, $12.95, TPB)-r/#1-4 13.00
Death After Death (2001, $19.95, TPB)-r/#42-50 20.00
Girl in the Box (1999, $14.95, TPB)-r/#26-32 15.00
Reckonings (1997, $12.95, TPB)-r/#14-20 13.00
Summonings (1996, $17.50, TPB)-r/#5-13, Vertigo Rave #1 17.50
The Burning Girl (2000, $17.95, TPB)-r/#33-41 18.00
Transformations (1998, $12.95, TPB)-r/#21-25 13.00

BOOKS OF MAGICK, THE : LIFE DURING WARTIME (See Books of Magic)
DC Comics (Vertigo): Sept, 2004 - No. 15, Dec, 2005 ($2.50/$2.75)

1-15: 1-Spencer-s/Ormston-a/Quitely-c; Constantine app. 2-Bagged with Sky Captain CD 6-Fegredo-a. 7-Constantine & Zatanna-c 3.00
... Book One TPB (2005, $9.95) r/#1-5 10.00

BOONDOCK SAINTS (Based on the movie)
12-Gauge Comics: May, 2010 - No. 2, Jun, 2010 ($3.99, limited series)

...: In Nomine Patris 1,2-Troy Duffy-s/Guus Floor-a 4.00
...: In Nomine Patris Vol. 2 (10/10 - No. 2, 11/10): 1,2-Duffy-s/Floor-a 4.00
...: In Nomine Patris Vol. 3 (3/11 - No. 2, 4/11): 1,2-Duffy-s/Floor-a 4.00

BOOSTER GOLD (See Justice League #4)
DC Comics: Feb, 1986 - No. 25, Feb, 1988 (75¢)

1-Dan Jurgens-s/a(p) 5.00
2-25: 4-Rose & Thorn app. 6-Origin. 6,7,23-Superman app. 8,9-LSH app. 22-JLI app. 24,25-Millennium tie-ins 4.00
NOTE: ***Austin** c-22i. **Byrne** c-23i.*

BOOSTER GOLD (See DC's weekly series 52)
DC Comics: Oct, 2007 - No. 47, Oct, 2011 ($3.50/$2.99/$3.99)

1-Geoff Johns-s/Dan Jurgens-a(p); covers by Jurgens and Art Adams; Rip Hunter app. 5.00
2-20: 3-Jonah Hex app. 4-Barry Allen app. 5-Joker and Batgirl app. 8-Superman app. 3.00
21-29-($3.99) 21-Blue Beetle back-ups begin. 22-New Teen Titans app. 23-Photo-c. 26,27-Blackest Night; Ted Kord rises. 29-Cyborg Superman app. 4.00
30-47-($2.99): 32-34-Giffen & DeMatteis-s. 32-Emerald Empress app. 40-Origin retold. 43-Legion of S.H. app. 44-47-Flashpoint tie-in; Doomsday app. 3.00
#0-(4/08) Blue Beetle (Ted Cord) returns; takes place between #6&7 3.00
#1,000,000-(9/08) Michelle Carter returns; takes place between #10&11 3.00
...: Blue and Gold (2008, $24.99, HC w/d.j.) r/#0,7-10,#1,000,000; cover sketches 25.00
...: Day of Death (2010, $14.99, SC) r/#20-25 and Brave and the Bold #23 15.00
...: 52 Pick-Up (2008, $24.99, HC w/d.j.) r/#1-6, original design sketches from Jurgens 25.00
...: Past Imperfect (2011, $17.99, SC) r/#32-38 18.00
...: Reality Lost (2009, $14.99, SC) r/#11,12,15-19 15.00
...: The Tomorrow Memory (2010, $17.99, SC) r/#26-31 18.00

BOOTS AND HER BUDDIES

Borderland: Origins #2 © Gearbox

The Bouncer #11 © FOX

Boy Comics #11 © LEV

Standard Comics/Visual Editions/Argo (NEA Service): No. 5, 9/48 - No. 9, 9/49; 12/55 - No. 3, 1956

	GD 2.0	VG 4.0	FN 6.0	VF 8.0	VF/NM 9.0	NM- 9.2
5-Strip-r	17	34	51	98	154	210
6,8	12	24	36	67	94	120
7-(Scarce)	14	28	42	82	121	160
9-(Scarce)-Frazetta-a (2 pgs.)	27	54	81	158	259	360
1-3(Argo-1955-56)-Reprints	6	12	18	31	38	45

BOOTS & SADDLES (TV)
Dell Publ. Co.: No. 919, July, 1958; No. 1029, Sept, 1959; No. 1116, Aug, 1960

	GD 2.0	VG 4.0	FN 6.0	VF 8.0	VF/NM 9.0	NM- 9.2
Four Color 919 (#1)-Photo-c	6	12	18	42	79	115
Four Color 1029, 1116-Photo-c	5	10	15	31	53	75

BORDERLANDS: ORIGINS (Based on the video game)
IDW Publishing: Nov, 2012 - No. 4, Feb, 2013 ($3.99, limited series)

	GD 2.0	VG 4.0	FN 6.0	VF 8.0	VF/NM 9.0	NM- 9.2
1-4: 1-Spotlight on Roland. 2-Lilith. 3-Mordecai. 4-Brick						4.00

BORDER PATROL
P. L. Publishing Co.: May-June, 1951 - No. 3, Sept-Oct, 1951

	GD 2.0	VG 4.0	FN 6.0	VF 8.0	VF/NM 9.0	NM- 9.2
1	14	28	42	82	121	160
2,3	10	20	30	56	76	95

BORDER WORLDS (Also see Megaton Man)
Kitchen Sink Press: 7/86 - No. 7, 1987; V2#1, 1990 - No. 4, 1990 ($1.95-$2.00, B&W, mature)

	GD 2.0	VG 4.0	FN 6.0	VF 8.0	VF/NM 9.0	NM- 9.2
1-7, V2#1-4: Donald Simpson-c/a/scripts						3.00

BORIS KARLOFF TALES OF MYSTERY (TV) (...Thriller No. 1,2)
Gold Key: No. 3, April, 1963 - No. 97, Feb, 1980

	GD 2.0	VG 4.0	FN 6.0	VF 8.0	VF/NM 9.0	NM- 9.2
3-5-(Two #5's, 10/63,11/63): 5-(10/63)-11 pgs. Toth-a.	5	10	15	31	53	75
6-8,10: 10-Orlando-a	4	8	12	25	40	55
9-Wood-a	4	8	12	27	44	60
11-Williamson-a, 8 pgs.; Orlando-a, 5 pgs.	4	8	12	27	44	60
12-Torres, McWilliams-a; Orlando-a(2)	4	8	12	21	33	45
13,14,16-20	3	6	9	18	28	38
15-Crandall	3	6	9	19	30	40
21-Jeff Jones-a(3 pgs.) "The Screaming Skull"	3	6	9	19	30	40
22-Last 12¢ issue	3	6	9	16	23	30
23-30: 23-Reprint; photo-c	3	6	9	15	22	28
31-50: 36-Weiss-a	3	6	9	14	19	24
51-74: 74-Origin & 1st app. Taurus	2	4	6	10	14	18
75-79,87-97: 90-r/Torres, McWilliams-a/#12; Morrow-c	2	4	6	9	12	15
80-86-(52 pgs.)	2	4	6	10	14	18
Story Digest 1(7/70-Gold Key)-All text/illos.; 148 pp.	5	10	15	31	53	75

(See Mystery Comics Digest No. 2, 5, 8, 11, 14, 17, 20, 23, 26)
NOTE: ***Bolle** a-51-54, 56, 58, 59. **McWilliams** a-12, 14, 18, 19, 72, 80, 81, 93. **Orlando** a-11-15, 21. Reprints: 78, 81-86, 88, 90, 92, 95, 97.*

BORIS KARLOFF THRILLER (TV) (Becomes Boris Karloff Tales...)
Gold Key: Oct, 1962 - No. 2, Jan, 1963 (84 pgs.)

	GD 2.0	VG 4.0	FN 6.0	VF 8.0	VF/NM 9.0	NM- 9.2
1-Photo-c	10	20	30	64	132	200
2	6	12	18	40	73	105

BORIS THE BEAR
Dark Horse Comics/Nicotat Comics #13 on: Aug, 1986 - No. 34, 1990 ($1.50/$1.75/$1.95, B&W)

	GD 2.0	VG 4.0	FN 6.0	VF 8.0	VF/NM 9.0	NM- 9.2
1, 8, Annual 1 (1988, $2.50): 8-(44 pgs.)						4.00
1 (2nd printing),2,3,4A,4B,5-12, 14-34						3.00
13-1st Nicotat Comics issue						3.00

BORIS THE BEAR INSTANT COLOR CLASSICS
Dark Horse Comics: July, 1987 - No. 3, 1987 ($1.75/$1.95)

	GD 2.0	VG 4.0	FN 6.0	VF 8.0	VF/NM 9.0	NM- 9.2
1-3						3.00

BORN
Marvel Comics: 2003 - No. 4, 2003 ($3.50, limited series)

	GD 2.0	VG 4.0	FN 6.0	VF 8.0	VF/NM 9.0	NM- 9.2
1-4-Frank Castle (the Punisher) in 1971 Vietnam; Ennis-s/Robertson-a						3.50
HC (2004, $17.99) oversized reprint of series; proposal, layout pages						18.00
Punisher: Born SC (2004, $13.99) r/series; proposal, layout pages						14.00

BORN AGAIN
Spire Christian Comics (Fleming H. Revell Co.): 1978 (39¢)

	GD 2.0	VG 4.0	FN 6.0	VF 8.0	VF/NM 9.0	NM- 9.2
nn-Watergate, Nixon, etc.	3	6	9	19	30	40

BOUNCE, THE
Image Comics: May, 2013 - Present ($2.99)

	GD 2.0	VG 4.0	FN 6.0	VF 8.0	VF/NM 9.0	NM- 9.2
1-11-Casey-s/Messina-a						3.00

BOUNCER, THE (Formerly Green Mask #9)
Fox Features Syndicate: 1944 - No. 14, Jan, 1945

	GD 2.0	VG 4.0	FN 6.0	VF 8.0	VF/NM 9.0	NM- 9.2
nn(1944, #10?)	31	62	93	186	303	420
11 (9/44)-Origin; Rocket Kelly, One Round Hogan app.	23	46	69	136	223	310
12-14: 14-Reprints no # issue	19	38	57	111	176	240

BOUNTY GUNS (See Luke Short's..., Four Color 739)

BOX OFFICE POISON
Antarctic Press: 1996 - No. 21, Sept, 2000 ($2.95, B&W)

	GD 2.0	VG 4.0	FN 6.0	VF 8.0	VF/NM 9.0	NM- 9.2
1-Alex Robinson-s/a in all	1	2	3	4	5	7
2-5						4.00
6-21, ...Kolor Karnival 1 (5/99, $2.99)						3.00
...Super Special 0 (5/97, $4.95)						5.00
Sherman's March: Collected BOP Vol. 1 (9/98, $14.95) r/#0-4						15.00
TPB (2002, $29.95, 608 pgs.) r/entire series						30.00

BOY AND HIS 'BOT, A
Now Comics: Jan, 1987 ($1.95)

	GD 2.0	VG 4.0	FN 6.0	VF 8.0	VF/NM 9.0	NM- 9.2
1-A Holiday Special						3.00

BOY AND THE PIRATES, THE (Movie)
Dell Publishing Co.: No. 1117, Aug, 1960

	GD 2.0	VG 4.0	FN 6.0	VF 8.0	VF/NM 9.0	NM- 9.2
Four Color 1117-Photo-c	6	12	18	37	66	95

BOY COMICS (Captain Battle No. 1 & 2; Boy Illustories No. 43-108) (Stories by Charles Biro) (Also see Squeeks)
Lev Gleason Publ. (Comic House): No. 3, Apr, 1942 - No. 119, Mar, 1956

	GD 2.0	VG 4.0	FN 6.0	VF 8.0	VF/NM 9.0	NM- 9.2
3 (No.1)-1st app. & origin Crimebuster (ends #110), Bombshell (ends #8) Young Robin Hood (ends # 32), Yankee Longago (ends #28), Hero of the Month (ends #31), Case 1001-1005, 1006-1009 (ends #10); Swoop Storm begins (ends #32); Pepper Casey only app.; 1st app. Iron Jaw; Crimebuster's pet monkey Squeeks begins	320	640	960	2240	3920	5600
4-Hitler, Tojo Mussolini-c; Iron Jaw app. Little Wise Guys (prototype of later version) begins, ends #5	171	342	513	1086	1868	2650
5-Japanese war-c	113	226	339	718	1234	1750
6-Origin Iron Jaw; origin & death of Iron Jaw's son killed by his father; Hitler app.; Little Dynamite begins, ends #39; 1st Iron Jaw-c	320	640	960	2240	3920	5600
7-Flag & Hitler, Tojo, Mussolini-c; Dickey Dean app.	148	296	444	947	1624	2300
8-Death of Iron Jaw; Iron Jaw-c & spash pg.	103	206	309	659	1130	1600
9-Iron Jaw sty/classic-c	148	296	444	947	1624	2300
10-Return of Iron Jaw; classic Biro Iron Jaw/Nazi-c	174	348	522	1114	1907	2700
11-Iron Jaw sty/classic-c	110	220	330	704	1202	1700
12-Classic Japanese WWII bondage torture interrogation-c	90	180	270	576	988	1400
13-Nazi firing squad-c	77	154	231	493	847	1200
14-Iron Jaw-c	81	162	243	518	884	1250
15-Death of Iron Jaw, killed by The Rodent	90	180	270	576	988	1400
16,18,20 (2/45)	47	94	141	296	498	700
17-(8/44)-Flag-c; The Moth app.	48	96	144	302	514	725
19-One of the greatest all-time stories	53	106	159	334	567	800
21-24: 24-Concentration camp story	32	64	96	192	314	435
25-Devil-c; hanging story (52 pgs.)	39	78	117	240	395	550
26-Bondage, torture-c/story (68 pgs.)	42	84	126	268	452	635
27-29,31,32-(All 68 pgs.). 28-Yankee Longago ends. 32-Swoop Storm & Young Robin Hood end	34	68	102	204	332	460
30-(10/46, 68 pgs.)-Origin Crimebuster retold from #3 w/Iron Jaw; Nazi work camp story	39	78	117	235	385	535
33-40: 34-Crimebuster story (2); suicide-c/story	22	44	66	132	216	300
41-50-41-Daredevil illus. text story	19	38	57	111	176	240
51-59: 57(9/50)-Dilly Duncan begins, ends #71	16	32	48	94	147	200
60-(12/50)-Iron Jaw returns c/sty	18	36	54	105	165	225
61-Origin Crimebuster & Iron Jaw retold c/sty	20	40	60	114	182	250
62-(2/51)-Death of Iron Jaw explained w/Iron Jaw-c	19	38	57	111	176	240
63-67,69-72: 63-McWilliams-a	14	28	42	76	108	140
68,73-Iron Jaw c/sty; 73-Frazetta 1 pg. ad	14	28	42	80	115	150
74,78,81-Iron Jaw c/sty (2-3)	12	24	36	67	94	120
75-77,84	11	22	33	62	86	110
79,80-Iron Jaw sty: 80(8/52)-1st app. Rocky X of the Rocketeers; becomes "Rocky X" #101; Iron Jaw, Sniffer & the Deadly Dozen in #80-118	11	22	33	64	90	115
82-Iron Jaw-c (apps. in one panel)	11	22	33	62	86	110
83,85-88-Iron Jaw c/sty. 87-The Deadly Dozen begins; becomes Iron Jaw #88 (4/53)	11	22	33	64	90	115

89(5/53)-92-The Claw serial app. in Rocky X (also see Silver Streak & Daredevil); on-c. 89-"Iron Jaw" becomes "Sniffrer & Iron Jaw" (ends #118); Iron Jaw c/story in all

Boy Commandos #8 © DC

The Boys #10 © Spitfire

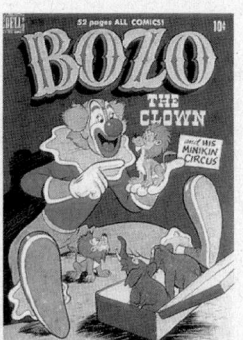

Bozo the Clown FC #285 © Capitol

GD 2.0 | VG 4.0 | FN 6.0 | VF 8.0 | VF/NM 9.0 | NM- 9.2

12 24 36 67 94 120
93-Claw cameo & last app.; Woodesque-a on Rocky X by Sid Check; Iron Jaw-c/sty
11 22 33 64 90 115
94-97-Iron Jaw-c/sty in all 11 22 33 60 83 105
98,100:(4/54): 98-Rocky X by Sid Check 11 22 33 62 86 110
99,101-107,109,111,119: 101-Rocky X becomes spy strip. 106-Robin Hood app. 111-Crimebuster becomes Chuck Chandler, ends #119
10 20 30 54 72 90
108-(2/55)-Kubert & Ditko-a (Crimebuster, 8 pgs.) 11 22 33 62 86 110
110,112-118-Kubert-a 10 20 30 58 79 100
(See Giant Boy Book of Comics)
NOTE: *Boy Movies in 3-5,40,41. Iron Jaw app. 3,4,6,8,10,11,13-15; returns-60,62, 68, 69, 72-79, 81-118; c-60-62, 73, 74, 78, 81-83, 85-97.* ***Biro*** *c-all.* ***Jack Alderman*** *a-26.* ***Dan Barry*** *a-31,32, 35-38.* ***Al Borth*** *a- 51.* ***Dick Briefer*** *a-3-28, 124.* ***Sid Check*** *a-93, 98.* ***Ditko*** *a-108.* ***Bob Fujitani (Fuje)*** *a-55, 18pgs.* ***Jerry Gandenetti*** *a-52.* ***R. W. Hall*** *a-19-22.* ***Hubbell*** *a-30, 106, 108, 110, 111.* ***Joe Kubert*** *a-108, 110, 112-118.* ***Kenneth Landau*** *a-92.* ***George Mandel*** *a-3-30.* ***Norman Maurer*** *a-4-9, 12, 13, 31, 32, 35, 41, 43, 46, 51, 57, 61, 73, 74, 78-83.* ***Bob Montana*** *a-4, 16, 19.* ***Pete Morisi*** *a-111.* ***William Overgard*** *a-68, 71, 74, 86, 88.* ***Palais*** *a-14, 16, 17, 19, 20, 25, 26. among others.* ***Tuska*** *a-30.* ***Bob Wood*** *a-8-13.*

BOY COMMANDOS (See Detective #64 & World's Finest Comics #8)
National Periodical Publications: Winter, 1942-43 - No. 36, Nov-Dec, 1949

1-Origin Liberty Belle; The Sandman & The Newsboy Legion x-over in Boy Commandos; S&K-a, 48 pgs.; S&K cameo? (classic WWII-c) 400 800 1200 2800 4900 7000
2-Last Liberty Belle; Hitler-c; S&K-a, 46 pgs.; WWII-c
239 478 717 1530 2615 3700
3-S&K-a, 45 pgs.; WWII-c 135 270 405 864 1482 2100
4-6: All WWII-c. 6-S&K-a 84 168 252 538 919 1300
7-10: All WWII-c 53 106 159 334 567 800
11-13: All WWII-c. 11-Infinity-c 39 78 117 240 395 550
14,16,18-19-All have S&K-a. 18-2nd Crazy Quilt-c 32 64 96 192 314 435
15-1st app. Crazy Quilt, their arch nemesis 41 82 123 250 418 585
17,20-Sci/fi-c/stories 39 78 117 235 385 535
21,22,25: 22-3rd Crazy Quilt-c; Judy Canova x-over 26 52 78 154 252 350
23-S&K-c/a(all) 35 70 105 208 339 470
24-1st costumed superhero satire-c (11-12/47). 31 62 93 182 296 410
26-Flying Saucer story (3-4/48)-4th of this theme; see The Spirit 9/28/47(1st), Shadow Comics V7#10 (2nd, 1/48) & Captain Midnight #60 (3rd, 2/48)
31 62 93 186 303 420
27,28,30: 30-Cleveland Indians story 25 50 75 150 245 340
29-S&K story (1) 27 54 81 158 259 360
31-35: 32-Dale Evans app. on-c & in story. 33-Last Crazy Quilt-c. 34-Intro. Wolf, their mascot 22 44 66 132 216 300
36-Intro The Atomobile c/sci-fi story (Scarce) 41 82 123 250 418 585
The Boy Commandos by Joe Simon & Jack Kirby Volume One HC (2010, $49.99) reprints apps. in Detective #64-72, World's Finest #8,9 & Boy Commandos #1,2; Buhle intro. 50.00
NOTE: *Most issues signed by* ***Simon & Kirby*** *are not by them.* ***S&K*** *c-1-9, 13, 14, 17, 21, 23, 24, 30-32.* ***Feller*** *c-30.*

BOY COMMANDOS
National Per. Publ.: Sept-Oct, 1973 - No. 2, Nov-Dec, 1973 (G.A. S&K reprints)

1,2: 1-Reprints story from Boy Commandos #1 plus-c & Detective #66 by S&K. 2-Infantino/Orlando-c 2 4 6 10 14 18

BOY COMMANDOS COMICS
DC Comics: Sept/Oct. 1942

1-Ashcan comic, not distributed to newsstands, only for in-house use. Cover art is the splash page from the Boy Commandos story in Detective Comics #68 interior is from an unidentified issue of Detective Comics (A FN- copy sold for $1912 in 2012)
nn - (9-10/42) Ashcan comic, not distributed to newsstands, only for in-house use. Cover art is the splash page from the Boy Commandos story in Detective Comics #68 interior is from Detective Comics #68 (no known sales)

BOY COWBOY (Also see Amazing Adventures & Science Comics)
Ziff-Davis Publ. Co.: 1950 (8 pgs. in color)

nn-Sent to subscribers of Ziff-Davis mags. & ordered through mail for 10¢; used to test market for Kid Cowboy 33 66 99 194 317 440

BOY DETECTIVE
Avon Periodicals: May-June, 1951 - No. 4, May, 1952

1 20 40 60 117 189 260
2-4: 3,4-Kinstler-c 14 28 42 81 118 155

BOY EXPLORERS COMICS (Terry and The Pirates No. 3 on)
Family Comics (Harvey Publ.): May-June, 1946 - No. 2, Sept-Oct, 1946

1-Intro The Explorers, Duke of Broadway, Calamity Jane & Danny Dixon…Cadet; S&K-c/a, 24 pgs. 76 152 228 486 831 1175
2-(Rare)-Small size (5-1/2x8-1/2"; B&W; 32 pgs.) Distributed to mail subscribers only; S&K-a 135 270 405 864 1482 2100
(Also see All New No. 15, Flash Gordon No. 5, and Stuntman No. 3)

GD 2.0 | VG 4.0 | FN 6.0 | VF 8.0 | VF/NM 9.0 | NM- 9.2

BOY ILLUSTORIES (See Boy Comics)

BOY LOVES GIRL (Boy Meets Girl No. 1-24)
Lev Gleason Publications: No. 25, July, 1952 - No. 57, June, 1956

25(#1) 13 26 39 74 105 135
26,27,29-33: 30-33-Serial, 'Loves of My Life 9 18 27 50 65 80
34-42: 39-Lingerie panels 9 18 27 47 61 75
28-Drug propaganda story 9 18 27 50 65 80
43-Toth-a 9 18 27 52 69 85
44-50: 47-Toth-a? 49-Roller Derby-c. 50-Last pre-code (2/55)
8 16 24 44 57 70
51-57: 57-Ann Brewster-a 8 16 24 40 50 60

BOY MEETS GIRL (Boy Loves Girl No. 25 on)
Lev Gleason Publications: Feb, 1950 - No. 24, June, 1952 (No. 1-17: 52 pgs.)

1-Guardineer-a 19 38 57 109 172 235
2 11 22 33 64 90 115
3-10 11 22 33 60 83 105
11-24 10 20 30 56 76 95
NOTE: ***Briefer*** *a-24.* ***Fuje*** *c-3,7. Painted-c 1-17. Photo-c 19-21, 23.*

BOYS, THE
DC Comics (WildStorm)/Dynamite Ent. #7 on: Oct, 2006 - No. 72, 2012 ($2.99/$3.99)

1-Garth Ennis-s/Darick Robertson-a 6.00
2-6 4.00
7-42-(Dynamite Ent.,). 19-Origin of the Homelander. 23-Variant-c by Cassaday 3.00
43-64,66-71-($3.99) Russ Braun-a in most. 54,55-McCrea-a 4.00
65,72-($4.99): 65-End of the Homelander. 72-Last issue; bonus pin-ups; cover gallery 5.00
#1: Dynamite Edition (2009, $1.00) r/#1; flip book with Battlefields Night Witches 3.00
...: Herogasm 1-6 (2009 - No. 6, 2009, $2.99) Ennis-s/McCrea-a 3.00
... Volume 1: The Name of the Game TPB (2007, $14.99) r/#1-6; intro. by Simon Pegg 15.00
... Volume 2: Get Some TPB (2008, $19.99) r/#7-14 20.00
... Volume 3: Good For The Soul TPB (2008, $19.99) r/#15-22 20.00
... Volume 4: We Gotta Go Now TPB (2009, $19.99) r/#23-30; cover gallery 20.00
... Volume 5: Herogasm TPB (2009, $19.99) r/#Herogasm #1-6 20.00

BOYS, THE: BUTCHER, BAKER, CANDLESTICKMAKER
Dynamite Entertainment: 2011 - No. 6, 2011 ($3.99, mature)

1-6-Garth Ennis-s/Darick Robertson-a; Billy Butcher's early years 4.00

BOYS, THE: HIGHLAND LADDIE
Dynamite Entertainment: 2010 - No. 6, 2011 ($3.99, mature)

1-6-Garth Ennis-s/John McCrea-a 4.00

BOYS' AND GIRLS' MARCH OF COMICS (See March of Comics)

BOYS' RANCH (Also see Western Tales & Witches' Western Tales)
Harvey Publ.: Oct, 1950 - No. 6, Aug, 1951 (No.1-3, 52 pgs.; No. 4-6, 36 pgs.)

1-S&K-c/a(3) 58 116 174 371 636 900
2-S&K-c/a(3) 40 80 120 246 411 575
3-S&K-c/a(2); Meskin-a 39 78 117 231 378 525
4-S&K-c/a, 5 pgs. 34 68 102 199 325 450
5,6-S&K-c, splashes & centerspread only; Meskin-a
20 40 60 114 182 250

BOZO (Larry Harmon's Bozo, the World's Most Famous Clown)
Innovation Publishing: 1992 ($6.95, 68 pgs.)

1-Reprints Four Color #285(#1) 1 2 3 4 5 7

BOZO THE CLOWN (TV) (Bozo No. 7 on)
Dell Publishing Co.: July, 1950 - No. 4, Oct-Dec, 1963

Four Color 285(#1) 17 34 51 114 252 390
2(7-9/51)-7(10-12/52) 9 18 27 63 129 195
Four Color 464,508,551,594(10/54) 9 18 27 57 111 165
1(nn, 5-7/62) 7 14 21 44 82 120
2 - 4(1963) 5 10 15 35 63 90

BOZZ CHRONICLES, THE
Marvel Comics (Epic Comics): Dec, 1985 - No. 6, 1986 (Lim. series, mature)

1-6-Logan/Wolverine look alike in 19th century. 1,3,5-Blevins-a 3.00

B.P.R.D. (Bureau of Paranormal Research and Defense) (Also see Hellboy titles)
Dark Horse Comics: (one-shots)

... Dark Waters (7/03, $2.99) Guy Davis-c/a; Augustyn-s 3.00
... Night Train (9/03, $2.99) Johns & Kolins-s; Kolins & Stewart-a 3.00
... The Ectoplasmic Man (6/08, $2.99) Stenbeck-a/Mignola-c; origin of Johann Kraus 3.00
... There's Something Under My Bed (11/03, $2.99) Pollina-a/c 3.00
... The Soul of Venice (5/03, $2.99) Oeming-a/c; Gunter & Oeming-s 3.00
... The Soul of Venice and Other Stories TPB (8/04, $17.95) r/one-shots & new story

B.P.R.D. 1948 #1 © Mike Mignola

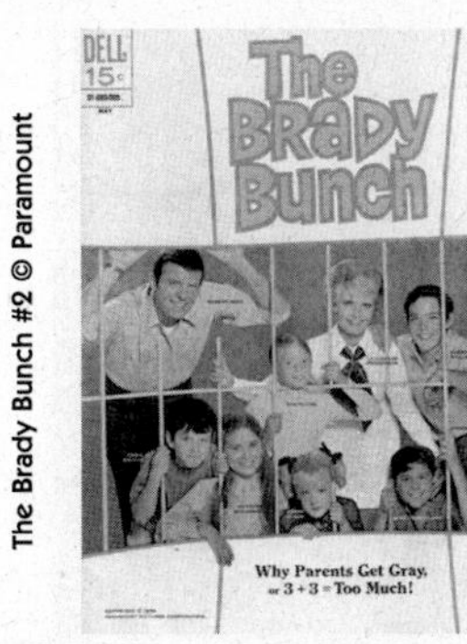

The Brady Bunch #2 © Paramount

Brain Boy #1 © DH

GD 2.0 VG 4.0 FN 6.0 VF 8.0 VF/NM 9.0 NM- 9.2

by Mignola and Cam Stewart; sketch pages by various 18.00
... War on Frogs (6/08,12/08, 6/09, 12/09, $2.99) 1-Trimpe-a/Mignola-c; Abe Sapien app. 2-Severin-a. 3-Moline-a. 4-Snejbjerg 3.00

B.P.R.D.: GARDEN OF SOULS
Dark Horse Comics: Mar, 2007 - No. 5, July, 2007 ($2.99, limited series)
1-5-Mignola & Arcudi-s/Guy Davis-a/Mignola-c 3.00

B.P.R.D.: HELL ON EARTH
Dark Horse Comics: ($3.50, limited series)
... Exorcism (6/12 - No. 2, 7/12) 1,2-Mignola-s/Stewart-a/Kalvachev -c 3.50
... Gods (1/11 - No. 3, 3/11) 1-Mignola & Arcudi-s/Guy Davis-a; Ryan Sook-c 3.50
... Monsters (7/11 - No. 2, 8/11) 1,2-Mignola & Arcudi-s. 1-Sook & Francavilla covers 3.50
... New World (8/10 - No. 5, 12/10) 1-5-Mignola & Arcudi-s/Guy Davis-a/c 3.50
... Russia (9/11 - No. 5, 1/12) 1-5-Mignola & Arcudi-s/Crook-a 3.50
... The Devil's Engine (5/12 - No. 3, 7/12) 1-3-Mignola & Arcudi-s/Crook-a/Fegredo-c 3.50
... The Long Death (2/12 - No. 3, 4/12) 1-3-Mignola & Arcudi-s/Harren-a/Fegredo-c 3.50
... The Pickens County Horror (3/12 - No. 2, 4/12) 1,2-Mignola & Allie-s/Latour-a 3.50
... The Transformation of J.H. O'Donnell (5/12) 1-Mignola & Allie-s/Fiumara-a 3.50
... The Return of the Master (8/12 - No. 5, 12/12) 1-5-Mignola & Arcudi-s/Crook-a; 3-5-Also numbered as #100-102 on cover and indicia 3.50
103-117: 103-(1/13). 103,104-The Abyss of Time. 105,106-A Cold Day in Hell 3.50

B.P.R.D.: HOLLOW EARTH (Mike Mignola's...)
Dark Horse Comics: Jan, 2002 - No. 3, June, 2002 ($2.99, limited series)
1-3-Mignola, Golden & Sniegoski-s/Sook-a/Mignola-c; Hellboy and Abe Sapien app. 3.00
... and Other Stories TPB (1/03; 7/04, $17.95) r/#1-3, Hellboy: Box Full of Evil, Abe Sapien: Drums of the Dead, and Dark Horse Extra; plus sketch pages 18.00

B.P.R.D.: KILLING GROUND
Dark Horse Comics: Aug, 2007 - No. 5, Dec, 2007 ($2.99, limited series)
1-5-Mignola & Arcudi-s/Guy Davis-a/c 3.00

B.P.R.D.: KING OF FEAR
Dark Horse Comics: Jan, 2010 - No. 5, May, 2010 ($2.99, limited series)
1,2-Mignola & Arcudi-s/Guy Davis-a; Mignola-c 3.00

B.P.R.D.: 1946
Dark Horse Comics: Jan, 2008 - No. 5, May, 2008 ($2.99, limited series)
1-5-Mignola & Dysart-s/Azaceta-a; Mignola-c 3.00

B.P.R.D.: 1947
Dark Horse Comics: Jul, 2009 - No. 5, Nov, 2009 ($2.99, limited series)
1-5-Mignola & Dysart-s/Bá & Moon-a; Mignola-c 3.00

B.P.R.D.: 1948
Dark Horse Comics: Oct, 2012 - No. 5, Feb, 2013 ($3.50, limited series)
1-5-Mignola & Arcudi-s/Fiumara-a; Johnson-c 3.50

B.P.R.D.: PLAGUE OF FROGS
Dark Horse Comics: Mar, 2004 - No. 5, July, 2004 ($2.99, limited series)
1-5-Mignola-s/Guy Davis-c/a 3.00
TPB (1/05, $17.95) r/series; sketchbook pages & afterword by Davis & Mignola 18.00

B.P.R.D.: THE BLACK FLAME
Dark Horse Comics: Sept, 2005 - No. 6, Jan, 2006 ($2.99, limited series)
1-6-Mignola & Arcudi-s/Guy Davis-a/ Mignola-c 3.00
TPB (7/06, $17.95) r/series; sketchbook pages & afterword by Davis & Mignola 18.00

B.P.R.D.: THE BLACK GODDESS
Dark Horse Comics: Jan, 2009 - No. 5, May, 2009 ($2.99, limited series)
1-5-Mignola & Arcudi-s/Guy Davis-a/Nowlan-c 3.00

B.P.R.D.: THE DEAD
Dark Horse Comics: Nov, 2004 - No. 5, Mar, 2005 ($2.99, limited series)
1-5-Mignola-s/Guy Davis-c/a 3.00

B.P.R.D.: THE DEAD REMEMBERED
Dark Horse Comics: Apr, 2011 - No. 3, Jun, 2011 ($3.50, limited series)
1-3-Mignola-s; Moline-a; Jo Chen-c. 1-Variant-c by Moline 3.50

B.P.R.D.: THE UNIVERSAL MACHINE
Dark Horse Comics: Apr, 2006 - No. 5, Aug, 2006 ($2.99, limited series)
1-5-Mignola & Arcudi-s/Guy Davis-a/Mignola-c. 5-Mignola-a (5 pgs.) 3.00
TPB (1/07, $17.95) r/series; sketchbook pages by Davis; Mignola afterword 18.00

B.P.R.D.: THE WARNING
Dark Horse Comics: July, 2008 - No. 5, Nov, 2008 ($2.99, limited series)
1-5-Mignola & Arcudi-s/Guy Davis-c/a 3.00

B.P.R.D.: VAMPIRE
Dark Horse Comics: Mar, 2013 - No. 5, Jul, 2013 ($3.50, limited series)
1-5-Mignola-s/Bá & Moon-a; Moon-c 3.50

BRADLEYS, THE (Also see Hate)
Fantagraphics Books: Apr, 1999 - No. 6, Jan, 2000 ($2.95, B&W, limited series)
1-6-Reprints Peter Bagge's-s/a 3.00

BRADY BUNCH, THE (TV)(See Kite Fun Book and Binky #78)
Dell Publishing Co.: Feb, 1970 - No. 2, May, 1970 (photo-c)
1 10 20 30 68 114 220
2 8 16 24 54 102 150

BRAIN, THE
Sussex Publ. Co./Magazine Enterprises: Sept, 1956 - No. 7, 1958
1-Dan DeCarlo-a in all including reprints 13 26 39 74 105 135
2,3 9 18 27 47 61 75
4-7 4 8 12 27 44 60
I.W. Reprints #1-4,8-10('63),14: 2-Reprints Sussex #2 with new cover added 2 4 6 9 13 16
Super Reprint #17,18(nd) 2 4 6 9 13 16

BRAINBANX
DC Comics (Helix): Mar, 1997 - No. 6, Aug, 1997 ($2.50, limited series)
1-6: Elaine Lee-s/Temujin-a 3.00

BRAIN BOY
Dell Publishing Co.: Apr-June, 1962 - No. 6, Sept-Nov, 1963 (Painted c-#1-6)
Four Color 1330(#1)-Gil Kane-a; origin 10 20 30 64 132 200
2(7-9/62),3-6: 4-Origin retold 6 12 18 41 76 110

BRAIN BOY
Dark Horse Comics: Sept, 2013 - Present ($2.99)
1-3-Van Lente-s/Silva-a/Olivetti-c 3.00
#0-(12/13, $2.99) Reprints stories from Dark Horse Presents #23-25; Olivetti-c 3.00

BRAM STOKER'S BURIAL OF THE RATS (Movie)
Roger Corman's Cosmic Comics: Apr, 1995 - No.3, June, 1995 ($2.50)
1-3: Adaptation of film; Jerry Prosser scripts 3.00

BRAM STOKER'S DRACULA (Movie)(Also see Dracula: Vlad the Impaler)
Topps Comics: Oct, 1992 - No. 4, Jan, 1993 ($2.95, limited series, polybagged)
1-(1st & 2nd printing)-Adaptation of film begins; Mignola-c/a in all; 4 trading cards & poster; photo scenes of movie 4.00
1-Crimson foil edition (limited to 500) 8.00
2-4: 2-Bound-in poster & cards. 4 trading cards in both. 3-Contains coupon to win 1 of 500 crimson foil-c edition of #1. 4-Contains coupon to win 1 of 500 uncut sheets of all 16 trading cards 4.00

BRAND ECHH (See Not Brand Echh)

BRAND OF EMPIRE (See Luke Short's...Four Color 771)

BRASS
Image Comics (WildStorm Productions): Aug, 1996 - No. 3, May, 1997 ($2.50, lim. series)
1-($4.50) Folio Ed.; oversized 4.50
1-3: Wiesenfeld-s/Bennett-a. 3-Grunge & Roxy(Gen 13) cameo 3.00

BRASS
DC Comics (WildStorm): Aug, 2000 - No. 6, Jan, 2001 ($2.50, limited series)
1-6-Arcudi-s 3.00

BRATH
CrossGeneration Comics: Feb, 2003 - No. 14, June, 2004 ($2.95)
Prequel-Dixon-s/Di Vito-a 3.00
1-14: 1-(3/03)-Dixon-s/Di Vito-a 3.00
Vol. 1: Hammer of Vengeance (2003, $9.95) Digest-sized reprint of Prequel & #1-6 10.00

BRATPACK/MAXIMORTAL SUPER SPECIAL
King Hell Press: 1996 ($2.95, B&W, limited series)
1,2: Veitch-s/a 3.00

BRATS BIZARRE
Marvel Comics (Epic/Heavy Hitters): 1994 - No. 4, 1994 ($2.50, limited series)
1-4: All w/bound-in trading cards 3.00

BRAVADOS, THE (See Wild Western Action)
Skywald Publ. Corp.: Aug, 1971 (52 pgs., one-shot)
1-Red Mask, The Durango Kid, Billy Nevada-r; Bolle-a; 3-D effect story 3 6 9 14 19 24

Brave and the Bold #2 © DC

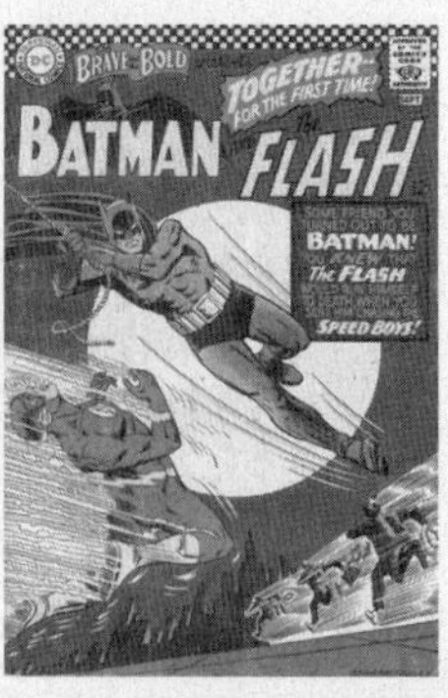

Brave and the Bold #67 © DC

Brave and the Bold #141 © DC

BRAVE AND THE BOLD, THE (See Best Of... & Super DC Giant) (Replaced by Batman & The Outsiders)
National Periodical Publ./DC Comics: Aug-Sept, 1955 - No. 200, July, 1983

	GD 2.0	VG 4.0	FN 6.0	VF 8.0	VF/NM 9.0	NM- 9.2
1-Viking Prince by Kubert, Silent Knight, Golden Gladiator begin; part Kubert-c	303	606	909	2500	5650	8800
2	121	242	363	968	2184	3400
3,4	64	128	192	512	1156	1800
5-Robin Hood begins (4-5/56, 1st DC app.), ends #15; see Robin Hood Tales #7	66	132	198	528	1189	1850
6-10: 6-Robin Hood by Kubert; last Golden Gladiator app.; Silent Knight; no Viking Prince. 8-1st S.A. issue	45	90	135	333	754	1175
11-22,24: 12,14-Robin Hood-c. 18,21-23-Grey tone-c. 22-Last Silent Knight. 24-Last Viking Prince by Kubert (2nd solo book)	36	72	108	259	580	900
23-Viking Prince origin by Kubert; 1st B&B single theme issue & 1st Viking Prince solo book	44	88	132	326	738	1150
25-1st app. Suicide Squad (8-9/59)	86	172	258	688	1544	2400
26,27-Suicide Squad	29	58	87	209	467	725
28-(2-3/60)-Justice League intro./1st app.; origin/1st app. Snapper Carr	750	1500	3000	10,000	23,000	36,000
29-Justice League (4-5/60)-2nd app. battle the Weapons Master; robot-c	214	428	642	1766	3983	6200
30-Justice League (6-7/60)-3rd app.; vs. Amazo	172	344	516	1419	3210	5000
31-1st app. Cave Carson (8-9/60); scarce in high grade; 1st try-out series	39	78	117	289	657	1025
32,33-Cave Carson	22	44	66	156	346	535
34-Origin/1st app. Silver-Age Hawkman, Hawkgirl & Byth (2-3/61); Gardner Fox story, Kubert-c/a ; 1st S.A. Hawkman tryout series; 2nd in #42-44; both series predate Hawkman #1 (4-5/64)	145	290	435	1196	2698	4200
35-Hawkman by Kubert (4-5/61)-2nd app.	37	74	111	274	612	950
36-Hawkman by Kubert; origin & 1st app. Shadow Thief (6-7/61)-3rd app.	34	68	102	245	548	850
37-Suicide Squad (2nd tryout series)	18	36	54	126	281	435
38,39-Suicide Squad. 38-Last 10¢ issue	16	32	48	110	243	375
40,41-Cave Carson Inside Earth (2nd try-out series). 40-Kubert-a. 41-Meskin-a	12	24	36	84	185	285
42-Hawkman by Kubert (2nd tryout series); Hawkman earns helmet wings; Byth app.	19	38	57	131	291	450
43-Hawkman by Kubert; more detailed origin	23	46	69	161	356	550
44-Hawkman by Kubert; grey-tone-c	19	38	57	131	291	450
45-49-Strange Sports Stories by Infantino	8	16	24	56	108	160
50-The Green Arrow & Manhunter From Mars (10-11/63); 1st Manhunter x-over outside of Detective Comics (pre-dates House of Mystery #143); team-ups begin	16	32	48	112	249	385
51-Aquaman & Hawkman (12-1/63-64); pre-dates Hawkman #1	18	36	54	124	275	425
52-(2-3/64)-3 Battle Stars; Sgt. Rock, Haunted Tank, Johnny Cloud, & Mlle. Marie team-up for 1st time by Kubert (c/a)	21	42	63	147	324	500
53-Atom & The Flash by Toth	9	18	27	59	117	175
54-Kid Flash, Robin & Aqualad; 1st app./origin Teen Titans (6-7/64)	37	74	111	274	612	950
55-Metal Men & The Atom	8	16	24	54	102	150
56-The Flash & Manhunter From Mars	8	16	24	54	102	150
57-Origin & 1st app. Metamorpho (12-1/64-65)	16	32	48	110	243	375
58-2nd app. Metamorpho by Fradon	9	18	27	61	123	185
59-Batman & Green Lantern; 1st Batman team-up in Brave and the Bold	11	22	33	73	157	240
60-Teen Titans (2nd app.)-1st app. new Wonder Girl (Donna Troy), who joins Titans (6-7/65)	18	36	54	124	275	425
61-Origin Starman & Black Canary by Anderson	11	22	33	76	163	250
62-Origin Starman & Black Canary cont'd. 62-1st S.A. app. Wildcat (10-11/65); 1st S.A. app. of G.A. Huntress (W.W. villain)	10	20	30	68	144	220
63-Supergirl & Wonder Woman	8	16	24	52	99	145
64-Batman Versus Eclipso (see H.O.S. #61)	8	16	24	51	96	140
65-Flash & Doom Patrol (4-5/66)	6	12	18	37	66	95
66-Metamorpho & Metal Men (6-7/66)	6	12	18	37	66	95
67-Batman & The Flash by Infantino; Batman team-ups begin, end #200 (8-9/66)	6	12	18	42	79	115
68-Batman/Metamorpho/Joker/Riddler/Penguin-c/story; Batman as Bat-Hulk (Hulk parody)	8	16	24	51	96	140
69-Batman & Green Lantern	6	12	18	38	69	100
70-Batman & Hawkman; Craig-a(p)	6	12	18	38	69	100
71-Batman & Green Arrow	6	12	18	38	69	100
72-Spectre & Flash (6-7/67); 4th app. The Spectre; predates Spectre #1	6	12	18	40	73	105
73-Aquaman & The Atom	6	12	18	37	66	95
74-Batman & Metal Men	6	12	18	37	66	95
75-Batman & The Spectre (12-1/67-68); 6th app. Spectre; came out between Spectre #1 & #2	6	12	18	38	69	100
76-Batman & Plastic Man (2-3/68); came out between Plastic Man #8 & #9	6	12	18	37	66	95
77-Batman & The Atom	6	12	18	37	66	95
78-Batman, Wonder Woman & Batgirl	6	12	18	38	69	100
79-Batman & Deadman by Neal Adams (8-9/68); early Deadman app.	9	18	27	61	123	185
80-Batman & Creeper (10-11/68); N. Adams-a; early app. The Creeper; came out between Creeper #3 & #4	8	16	24	52	99	145
81-Batman & Flash; N. Adams-a	8	16	24	52	99	145
82-Batman & Aquaman; N. Adams-a; origin Ocean Master retold (2-3/69)	8	16	24	52	99	145
83-Batman & Teen Titans; N. Adams-a (4-5/69)	8	16	24	52	99	145
84-Batman (G.A., 1st S.A. app.) & Sgt. Rock; N. Adams-a; last 12¢ issue (6-7/69)	8	16	24	52	99	145
85-Batman & Green Arrow; 1st new costume for Green Arrow by Neal Adams (8-9/69)	10	20	30	66	138	210
86-Batman & Deadman (10-11/69); N. Adams-a; story concludes from Strange Adventures #216 (1-2/69)	8	16	24	52	99	145
87-Batman & Wonder Woman	4	8	12	27	44	60
88-Batman & Wildcat	4	8	12	27	44	60
89-Batman & Phantom Stranger (4-5/70); early Phantom Stranger app. (came out between Phantom Stranger #6 & 7	4	8	12	25	40	55
90-Batman & Adam Strange	4	8	12	25	40	55
91-Batman & Black Canary (8-9/70)	4	8	12	25	40	55
92-Batman; intro the Bat Squad	4	8	12	25	40	55
93-Batman-House of Mystery; N. Adams-a	7	14	21	44	82	120
94-Batman-Teen Titans	4	8	12	25	40	55
95-Batman & Plastic Man	3	6	9	20	31	42
96-Batman & Sgt. Rock; last 15¢ issue	3	6	9	21	33	45
97-Batman & Wildcat; 52 pg. issues begin, end #102; reprints origin & 1st app. Deadman from Strange Advs. #205	3	6	9	21	33	45
98-Batman & Phantom Stranger; 1st Jim Aparo Batman-a?	3	6	9	21	33	45
99-Batman & Flash	3	6	9	21	33	45
100-(2-3/72, 25¢, 52 pgs.)-Batman-Green Lantern-Green Arrow-Black Canary-Robin; Deadman-r by Adams/Str. Advs. #210	5	10	15	35	63	90
101-Batman & Metamorpho; Kubert Viking Prince	3	6	9	20	31	42
102-Batman-Teen Titans; N. Adams-a(p)	5	10	15	30	50	70
103-107,109,110: Batman team-ups: 103-Metal Men. 104-Deadman. 105-Wonder Woman. 106-Green Arrow. 107-Black Canary. 109-Demon. 110-Wildcat	3	6	9	14	20	26
108-Sgt. Rock	3	6	9	15	22	28
111-Batman/Joker-c/story	3	6	9	18	28	38
112-117: All 100 pgs.; Batman team-ups: 112-Mr. Miracle. 113-Metal Men; reprints origin/1st Hawkman from Brave and the Bold #34; r/origin Multi-Man/Challengers #14. 114-Aquaman. 115-Atom; r/origin Viking Prince from #23; r/Dr. Fate/Hourman/Solomon Grundy/Green Lantern from Showcase #55. 116-Spectre. 117-Sgt. Rock; last 100 pg. issue	5	10	15	30	50	70
118-Batman/Wildcat/Joker-c/story	3	6	9	16	24	32
119,121-123,125-128,132-140: Batman team-ups: 119-Man-Bat. 121-Metal Men. 122-Swamp Thing. 123-Plastic Man/Metamorpho. 125-Flash. 126-Aquaman. 127-Wildcat. 128-Mr. Miracle. 132-Kung-Fu Fighter. 133-Deadman. 134-Green Lantern. 135-Metal Men. 136-Metal Men/Green Arrow. 137-Demon. 138-Mr. Miracle. 139-Hawkman. 140-Wonder Woman	2	4	6	8	10	12
120-Kamandi (68 pgs.)	3	6	9	14	19	24
124-Sgt. Rock; Jim Aparo app. on cover & in story	2	4	6	9	12	15
129,130-Batman/Green Arrow/Atom parts 1 & 2; Joker & Two Face-c/stories	3	6	9	14	20	25
131-Batman & Wonder Woman vs. Catwoman-c/sty	2	4	6	10	14	18
141-Batman/Black Canary vs. Joker-c/story	2	4	6	13	18	22
142-160: Batman team-ups: 142-Aquaman. 143-Creeper; origin Human Target (44 pgs.). 144-Green Arrow; origin Human Target part 2 (44 pgs.). 145-Phantom Stranger. 146-G.A. Batman/Unknown Soldier. 147-Supergirl. 148-Plastic Man; X-Mas-c. 149-Teen Titans. 150-Anniversary issue; Superman. 151-Flash. 152-Atom. 153-Red Tornado. 154-Metamorpho. 155-Green Lantern. 156-Dr. Fate. 157-Batman vs. Kamandi (ties into Kamandi #59). 158-Wonder Woman. 159-Ra's Al Ghul. 160-Supergirl.	1	3	4	6	8	10
145(11/79)-147,150-159,165(8/80)-(Whitman variants; low print run; none show issue # on cover)	2	4	6	10	14	18
161-181,183-190,192-195,198,199: Batman team-ups: 161-Adam Strange. 162-G.A. Batman/						

Brave and the Bold (2007 series) #5 © DC

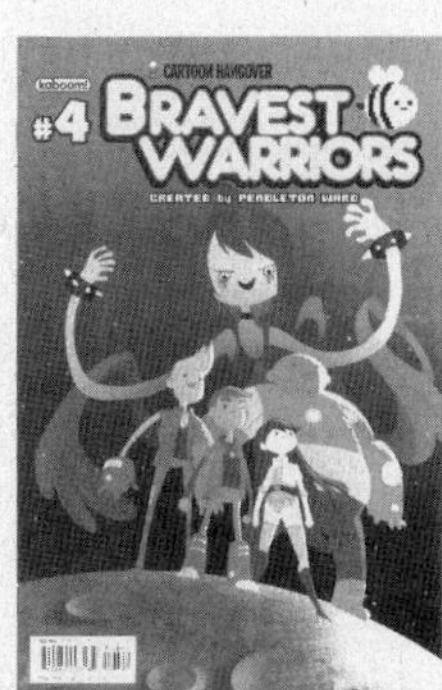

Bravest Warriors #4 © Frederator

Brenda Starr #14 © SUPR

Sgt. Rock. 163-Black Lightning. 164-Hawkman. 165-Man-Bat. 166-Black Canary; Nemesis (intro) back-up story begins, ends #192; Penguin-c/story. 167-G.A. Batman/Blackhawk; origin Nemesis. 168-Green Arrow. 169-Zatanna. 170-Nemesis. 171-Scalphunter. 172-Firestorm. 173-Guardians of the Universe. 174-Green Lantern. 175-Lois Lane. 176-Swamp Thing. 177-Elongated Man. 178-Creeper. 179-Legion. 180-Spectre. 181-Hawk & Dove. 183-Riddler. 184-Huntress & Earth II Batman. 185-Green Arrow. 186-Hawkman. 187-Metal Men. 188,189-Rose & the Thorn. 190-Adam Strange. 192-Superboy vs. Mr. I.Q. 194-Flash. 195-I...Vampire. 198-Karate Kid. 199-Batman vs. The Spectre 6.00

182-G.A. Robin; G.A. Starman app.; 1st modern app. G.A. Batwoman 2 4 6 8 10 12

191-Batman/Joker-c/story; Nemesis app. 2 4 6 8 11 14

196-Ragman; origin Ragman retold. 1 2 3 5 6 8

197-Catwoman; Earth II Batman & Catwoman marry; 2nd modern app. of G.A. Batwoman; Scarecrow story in Golden Age style 2 4 6 11 16 20

200-Double-sized (64 pgs.); printed on Mando paper; Earth One & Earth Two Batman app. in separate stories; intro/1st app. Batman & The Outsiders 2 4 6 8 10 12

NOTE: ***Neal Adams*** *a-79-86, 93, 100r, 102; c-75, 76, 79-86, 88-90, 93, 95, 99, 100r.* ***M. Anderson*** *a-115r; c-72i, 96i.* ***Andru/Esposito*** *c-25-27.* ***Aparo*** *a-98, 100-102, 104-125, 126i, 127-136, 138-145, 147, 148i, 149-152, 154, 155, 157-162, 168-170, 173-178, 180-182, 184, 186i-189i, 191i-193i, 195, 196, 200; c-105-109, 111-136, 137i, 138-175, 177, 180-184, 186-200.* ***Austin*** *a-166i.* ***Bernard Baily*** *c-32, 33, 58.* ***Buckler*** *a-185, 186p; c-137, 178p, 185p, 186p.* ***Giordano*** *a-143, 144.* ***Infantino*** *a-67p, 72p, 97r, 98r, 115r, 172p, 183p, 190p, 194p; c-45-49, 67p, 69p, 70p, 72p, 96p, 98r.* ***Kaluta*** *c-176.* ***Kane*** *a-115r; c-59, 64.* ***Kubert*** *&/or* ***Heath*** *a-1-24; reprints-101, 113, 115, 117.* ***Kubert*** *a-99r; c-22-24, 34-36, 40, 42-44, 52.* ***Mooney*** *a-114r.* ***Mortimer*** *a-64, 69.* ***Newton*** *a-153p, 156p, 165p.* ***Irv Novick*** *c-1(part), 2-21.* ***Fred Ray*** *a-78r.* ***Roussos*** *a-50, 76i, 114r.* ***Staton*** *148p. 52 pgs.-97, 100; 68 pgs.-120; 100 pgs.-112-117.*

BRAVE AND THE BOLD, THE
DC Comics: Dec, 1991 - No. 6, June, 1992 ($1.75, limited series)

1-6: Green Arrow, The Butcher, The Question in all; Grell scripts in all 4.00

NOTE: ***Grell*** *c-3, 4-6.*

BRAVE AND THE BOLD, THE
DC Comics: Apr, 2007 - No. 35, Aug, 2010 ($2.99)

1-Batman & Green Lantern team-up; Roulette app.; Waid-s/Peréz-c/a; 2 covers 4.00

2-32,34,35: 2-GL & Supergirl. 3-Batman & Blue Beetle vs. Fatal Five; Lobo app. 4-6-LSH app. 12-Megistus conclusion; Ordway-a. 14-Kolins-a. 16-Superman & Catwoman. 28-Blackhawks app. 29-Batman/Brother Power the Geek. 31-Atom/Joker 3.00

33-Batgirl, Zatanna & W.W.; prelude to Killing Joke 2 4 6 11 16 20

...: Demons and Dragons HC (2009, $24.99, dustjacket) r/#13-16; Brave & the Bold V1 #181, Flash V3 #107 and Impulse #17; Mark Waid commentary 25.00

...: Demons and Dragons SC (2010, $17.99) same contents as HC 18.00

...: Milestone SC (2010, $17.99) r/#24-26 and Static #12, Hardware #16, Xombi #6 18.00

Team-ups of the Brave and the Bold HC (2010, $24.99) r/#27-33 25.00

...: The Book of Destiny HC (2008, $24.99, dustjacket) r/#7-12; Ordway sketch pages 25.00

...: The Book of Destiny SC (2009, $17.99) r/#7-12; Ordway sketch pages 18.00

...: The Lords of Luck HC (2007, $24.99, dustjacket) r/#1-6 with Waid intro & annotations 25.00

...: The Lords of Luck SC (2008, $17.99) r/#1-6 with Waid intro & annotations 18.00

...: Without Sin SC (2009, $17.99) r/#17-22 18.00

BRAVE AND THE BOLD ANNUAL NO. 1 1969 ISSUE, THE
DC Comics: 2001 ($5.95, one-shot)

1-Reprints Silver Age team-ups in 1960s-style 80 pg. Giant format 6.00

BRAVE AND THE BOLD SPECIAL, THE (See DC Special Series No. 8)

BRAVE EAGLE (TV)
Dell Publishing Co.: No. 705, June, 1956 - No. 929, July, 1958

Four Color 705 (#1)-Photo-c 6 12 18 38 69 100

Four Color 770, 816, 879 (2/58), 929-All photo-c 4 8 12 27 44 60

BRAVE NEW WORLD (See DCU Brave New World)

BRAVE OLD WORLD (V2K)
DC Comics (Vertigo): Feb, 2000 - No. 4, May, 2000 ($2.50, mini-series)

1-4-Messner-Loeb-s/Guy Davis & Phil Hester-a 3.00

BRAVE ONE, THE (Movie)
Dell Publishing Co.: No. 773, Mar, 1957

Four Color 773-Photo-c 5 10 15 31 53 75

BRAVEST WARRIORS (Based on the animated web series)
BOOM! Entertainment (KaBOOM): Oct, 2012 - Present ($3.99)

1-18-Multiple covers on each 4.00

2014 Annual (1/14, $4.99) Short stories featuring Catbug; multiple covers 5.00

BRAVURA
Malibu Comics (Bravura): 1995 (mail-in offer)

0-wraparound holographic-c; short stories and promo pin-ups of Chaykin's Power & Glory, Gil Kane's & Steven Grant's Edge, Starlin's Breed, & Simonson's Star Slammers 5.00

1 1/2 7.00

BREACH
DC Comics: Mar, 2005 - No. 11, Jan, 2006 ($2.95/$2.50)

1-11: 1-Marcos Martin-a/Bob Harras-s; origin. 4-JLA-c/app. 3.00

BREAKDOWN
Devil's Due Publ.: Oct, 2004 - No. 6, Apr, 2005 ($2.95)

1-6: 1-Two covers by Dave Ross and Leinil Yu; Dixon-s/Ross-a 3.00

BREAKFAST AFTER NOON
Oni Press: May, 2000 - No. 6, Jan, 2001 ($2.95, B&W, limited series)

1-6-Andi Watson-s/a 3.00

TPB (2001, $19.95) r/series 20.00

BREAKING INTO COMICS THE MARVEL WAY
Marvel Comics: May, 2010 - No. 2, May, 2010 ($3.99, limited series)

1,2-Short stories by various newcomer artists; artist profiles 4.00

BREAKNECK BLVD.
MotioN Comics/Slave Labor Graphics Vol. 2: No. 0, Feb, 1994 - No. 2, Nov, 1994; Vol. 2#1, Jul, 1995 - #6, Dec., 1996 ($2.50/$2.95, B&W)

0-2, V2#1-6: 0-Perez/Giordano-c 3.00

BREAK-THRU (Also see Exiles V1#4)
Malibu Comics (Ultraverse): Dec, 1993 - No. 2, Jan, 1994 ($2.50, 44 pgs.)

1,2-Perez-c/a(p); has x-overs in Ultraverse titles 4.00

BREATH OF BONES: A TALE OF THE GOLEM
Dark Horse Comics: Jun, 2013 - No. 3, Aug, 2013 ($3.99, B&W, limited series)

1-3-Niles-s/Wachter-a 4.00

BREATHTAKER
DC Comics: 1990 - No. 4, 1990 ($4.95, 52 pgs., prestige format, mature)

Book 1-4: Mark Wheatley-painted-c/a & scripts; Marc Hempel-a 5.00

TPB (1994, $14.95) r/#1-4; intro by Neil Gaiman 15.00

'BREED
Malibu Comics (Bravura): Jan, 1994 - No. 6, 1994 ($2.50, limited series)

1-(48 pgs.)-Origin/1st app. of 'Breed by Starlin; contains Bravura stamps; spot varnish-c 4.00

2-6: 2-5-contains Bravura stamps. 6-Death of Rachel 3.00

...:Book of Genesis (1994, $12.95)-reprints #1-6 13.00

'BREED II
Malibu Comics (Bravura): Nov, 1994 - No. 6, Apr, 1995 ($2.95, limited series)

1-6: Starlin-c/a/scripts in all. 1-Gold edition 3.00

'BREED III
Image Comics: May, 2011 - No. 7, Dec, 2011 ($2.99)

1-7: Starlin-c/a/scripts in all 3.00

BREEZE LAWSON, SKY SHERIFF (See Sky Sheriff)

BRENDA LEE'S LIFE STORY
Dell Publishing Co.: July-Sept., 1962

01-078-209 8 16 24 51 86 120

BRENDA STARR (Also see All Great)
Four Star Comics Corp./Superior Comics Ltd.: No. 13, 9/47; No. 14, 3/48; V2#3, 6/48 - V2#12, 12/49

V1#13-By Dale Messick 95 190 285 603 1039 1475

14-Classic Kamen bondage-c 245 490 735 1568 2684 3800

V2#3-Baker-a? 73 146 219 467 796 1125

4-Used in **SOTI**, pg. 21; Kamen-c 87 174 261 553 952 1350

5-10 68 136 204 435 743 1050

11,12 (Scarce) 71 142 213 454 777 1100

NOTE: *Newspaper reprints plus original material through #6. All original #7 on.*

BRENDA STARR (...Reporter)(Young Lovers No. 16 on?)
Charlton Comics: No. 13, June, 1955 - No. 15, Oct, 1955

13-15-Newspaper-r 32 64 96 188 307 425

BRENDA STARR REPORTER
Dell Publishing Co.: Oct, 1963

1 10 20 30 68 144 220

BRER RABBIT (See Kite Fun Book, Walt Disney Showcase #28 and Wheaties)
Dell Publishing Co.: No. 129, 1946; No. 208, Jan, 1949; No. 693, 1956 (Disney)

Four Color 129 (#1)-Adapted from Disney movie "Song of the South" 22 44 66 156 346 535

Four Color 208 (1/49) 10 20 30 66 138 210

Brick Bradford #6 © STD

Brigade #6 © Rob Liefeld

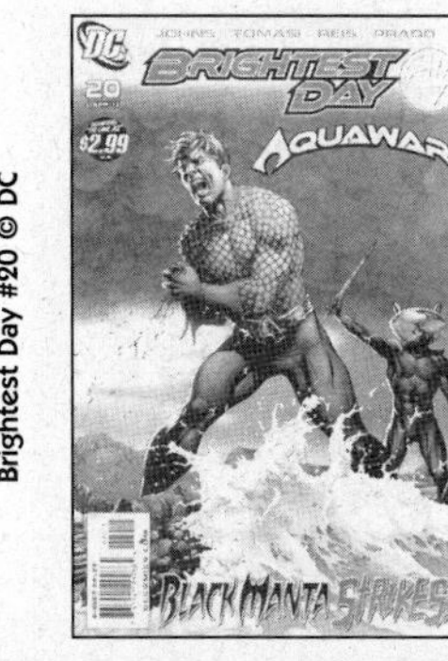

Brightest Day #20 © DC

	GD 2.0	VG 4.0	FN 6.0	VF 8.0	VF/NM 9.0	NM- 9.2
Four Color 693-Part-r #129	7	14	21	49	92	135

BRIAN BOLLAND'S BLACK BOOK
Eclipse Comics: July, 1985 (one-shot)

1-British B&W-r in color 4.00

BRIAN PULIDO'S LADY DEATH... (See Lady Death)

BRICK BRADFORD (Also see Ace Comics & King Comics)
King Features Syndicate/Standard: No. 5, July, 1948 - No. 8, July, 1949 (Ritt & Grey reprints)

	GD 2.0	VG 4.0	FN 6.0	VF 8.0	VF/NM 9.0	NM- 9.2
5	19	38	57	112	176	240
6-Robot-c (by Schomburg?).	39	78	117	240	395	550
7-Schomburg-c. 8-Says #7 inside, #8 on-c	15	30	45	94	147	200

BRIDE'S DIARY (Formerly Black Cobra No. 3)
Ajax/Farrell Publ.: No. 4, May, 1955 - No. 10, Aug, 1956

	GD 2.0	VG 4.0	FN 6.0	VF 8.0	VF/NM 9.0	NM- 9.2
4 (#1)	10	20	30	56	76	95
5-8	8	16	24	40	50	60
9,10-Disbrow-a	9	18	27	50	65	80

BRIDES IN LOVE (Hollywood Romances & Summer Love No. 46 on)
Charlton Comics: Aug, 1956 - No. 45, Feb, 1965

	GD 2.0	VG 4.0	FN 6.0	VF 8.0	VF/NM 9.0	NM- 9.2
1	12	24	36	69	97	125
2	8	16	24	40	50	60
3-6,8-10	3	6	9	21	33	45
7-(68 pgs.)	4	8	12	27	44	60
11-20	3	6	9	16	23	30
21-45	2	4	6	11	16	20

BRIDES ROMANCES
Quality Comics Group: Nov, 1953 - No. 23, Dec, 1956

	GD 2.0	VG 4.0	FN 6.0	VF 8.0	VF/NM 9.0	NM- 9.2
1	18	36	54	103	162	220
2	11	22	33	60	83	105
3-10: Last precode (3/55)	10	20	30	56	76	95
11-17,19-22: 15-Baker-a(p)?; Colan-a	9	18	27	50	65	80
18-Baker-a	11	22	33	64	90	115
23-Baker-c/a	15	30	45	85	130	175

BRIDE'S SECRETS
Ajax/Farrell(Excellent Publ.)/Four-Star: Apr-May, 1954 - No. 19, May, 1958

	GD 2.0	VG 4.0	FN 6.0	VF 8.0	VF/NM 9.0	NM- 9.2
1	15	30	45	84	127	170
2	9	18	27	52	69	85
3-6: Last precode (3/55)	8	16	24	44	57	70
7-11,13-19: 18-Hollingsworth-a	8	16	24	40	50	60
12-Disbrow-a	9	18	27	47	61	75

BRIDE-TO-BE ROMANCES (See True...)

BRIGADE
Image Comics (Extreme Studios): Aug, 1992 - No. 4, 1993 ($1.95, lim. series)

1-Liefeld part plots/scripts in all, Liefeld-c(p); contains 2 Brigade trading cards 4.00
1-Gold foil stamped logo edition 8.00
2-Contains coupon for Image Comics #0 & 2 trading cards 3.00
2-With coupon missing 2.00
3,4: 3-Contains 2 trading cards; 1st Birds of Prey. 4-Flip book featuring Youngblood #5 3.00

BRIGADE
Image Comics (Extreme): V2#1, May, 1993 - V2#22, July, 1995, V2#25, May, 1996 ($1.95/$2.50)

V2#1-22,25: 1-Gatefold-c; Liefeld co-plots; Blood Brothers part 1; Bloodstrike app. 2-(6/93, V2#1 on inside)-Foil merricote-c (newsstand ed. w/out foil-c exists). 3-Perez-c(i); Liefeld scripts. 8,9-Coupons #2 & 6 for Extreme Prejudice #0 bound-in. 11-(8/94, $2.50) WildC.A.T.S app. 16-Polybagged w/ trading card. 22-"Supreme Apocalypse" Pt. 4; w/ trading card 3.00
0-(9/93)-Liefeld scripts; 1st app. Warcry; Youngblood & Wildcats app.; 3.00
20-Variant-c. by Quesada & Palmiotti 3.00
Sourcebook 1 (8/94, $2.95) 3.00
1-(Awesome Ent., 7/00, $2.99) Flip book w/Century preview 4.00
1-(6/10, $3.99) Liefeld-s/Mychaels-a; covers by Liefeld & Mychaels 4.00

BRIGAND, THE (See Fawcett Movie Comics No. 18)

BRIGHTEST DAY (Also see Blackest Night and Green Lantern)
DC Comics: No. 0, Jun, 2010 - No. 24, Late Jun, 2011 ($3.99/$2.99)

0-($3.99) Johns & Tomasi-s/Pasarin-a/Finch-c 4.00
0-Variant-c by Reis 8.00
1-23-($2.99) 1-Black Manta returns. 4-Intro. Jackson (new Aqualad) 16-Aqualad origin. 18-Hawkman & Hawkgirl killed. 20-Aquaman killed 3.00
1-23: Variant covers. 1-6,9-18,20-23-by Reis, 7,8 White Lantern by Sook. 19-by Frank 6.00
24-($4.99) Swamp Thing and John Constantine return to DC universe 5.00
24-($4.99) Variant cover by Reis 8.00
...: The Atom Special (9/10, $2.99) Lemire-s/Asrar-a/Frank-c 3.00
... Volume 1 HC (2010, $29.99) r/#0-7; cover gallery 30.00
... Volume 2 HC (2011, $29.99) r/#8-16; cover gallery 30.00

BRIGHTEST DAY AFTERMATH: THE SEARCH FOR SWAMP THING
DC Comics: Aug, 2011 - No. 3, Oct, 2011 ($2.99, limited series)

1-3-Vankin-s/Castiello-a; covers by Syaf & Jones; John Constantine & Zatanna app. 3.00

BRILLIANT
Marvel Comics (Icon): Jul, 2011 - Present ($3.95, limited series)

1-5-Bendis-s/Bagley-a/c 4.00

BRING BACK THE BAD GUYS (Also see Fireside Book Series)
Marvel Comics: 1998 ($24.95, TPB)

1-Reprints stories of Marvel villains' secrets 25.00

BRINGING UP FATHER
Dell Publishing Co.: No. 9, 1942 - No. 37, 1944

	GD 2.0	VG 4.0	FN 6.0	VF 8.0	VF/NM 9.0	NM- 9.2
Large Feature Comic 9	31	62	93	186	303	420
Four Color 37	17	34	51	117	259	400

BRING ON THE BAD GUYS (See Fireside Book Series)

BRING THE THUNDER
Dynamite Entertainment: 2010 - No. 4, 2011 ($3.99)

1-4-Alex Ross-c/Ross & Nitz-s/Tortosa-a 4.00

BROADWAY HOLLYWOOD BLACKOUTS
Stanhall: Mar-Apr, 1954 - No. 3, July-Aug, 1954

	GD 2.0	VG 4.0	FN 6.0	VF 8.0	VF/NM 9.0	NM- 9.2
1	16	32	48	94	147	200
2,3	12	24	36	69	97	125

BROADWAY ROMANCES
Quality Comics Group: January, 1950 - No. 5, Sept, 1950

	GD 2.0	VG 4.0	FN 6.0	VF 8.0	VF/NM 9.0	NM- 9.2
1-Ward-c/a (9 pgs.); Gustavson-a	39	78	117	240	395	550
2-Ward-a (9 pgs.); photo-c	27	54	81	158	259	360
3-5: All-Photo-c	15	30	45	86	133	180

BROKEN ARROW (TV)
Dell Publishing Co.: No. 855, Oct, 1957 - No. 947, Nov, 1958

	GD 2.0	VG 4.0	FN 6.0	VF 8.0	VF/NM 9.0	NM- 9.2
Four Color 855 (#1)-Photo-c	5	10	15	33	57	80
Four Color 947-Photo-c	5	10	15	30	50	70

BROKEN CROSS, THE (See The Crusaders)

BROKEN PIECES
Aspen MLT: No. 0, Sept, 2011; Oct, 2011 - No. 5, Dec, 2012 ($2.50/$3.50, limited series)

0-($2.50)-Roslan-s/Kaneshiro-a; three covers 3.00
1-5: 1-($3.50)-Roslan-s/Kaneshiro-a; three covers 3.50

BROKEN TRINITY
Image Comics (Top Cow): July, 2008 - No. 3, Nov, 2008 ($2.99, limited series)

1-3-Witchblade, Darkness & Angelus app.; Marz-s/Sejic & Hester-a; two covers 3.00
...: Aftermath 1 (4/09, $2.99) Marz & Hill-s/Lucas & Kirkham-a 3.00
...: Angelus 1 (12/08, $2.99) Marz-s/Stelfreeze-a; two covers 3.00
...: Pandora's Box 1-6 (2/10 - No. 6, 4/11 $3.99) Tommy Lee Edwards-c 4.00
...: The Darkness 1 (8/08, $2.99) Hester-s/Lucas-a; two covers 3.00
...: Witchblade 1 (12/08, $2.99) Marz-s/Blake-a; two covers 3.00

BRONCHO BILL (See Comics On Parade, Sparkler & Tip Top Comics)
United Features Syndicate/Standard(Visual Editions) No. 5-on: 1939 - 1940; No. 5, 1?/48 - No. 16, 8?/50

	GD 2.0	VG 4.0	FN 6.0	VF 8.0	VF/NM 9.0	NM- 9.2
Single Series 2 ('39)	52	104	156	328	557	785
Single Series 19 ('40)(#2 on cvr)	42	84	126	265	445	625
5	15	30	45	85	130	175
6(4/48)-10(4/49)	10	20	30	56	76	95
11(6/49)-16	9	18	27	50	65	80

NOTE: ***Schomburg** c-6, 7, 9-13, 15, 16.*

BROOKS ROBINSON (See Baseball's Greatest Heroes #2)

BROTHER BILLY THE PAIN FROM PLAINS
Marvel Comics Group: 1979 (68pgs.)

	GD 2.0	VG 4.0	FN 6.0	VF 8.0	VF/NM 9.0	NM- 9.2
1-B&W comics, satire, Jimmy Carter-c & x-over w/Brother Billy peanut jokes. Joey Adams-a (scarce)	4	8	12	27	44	60

BROTHERHOOD, THE (Also see X-Men titles)
Marvel Comics: July, 2001 - No. 9, Mar, 2002 ($2.25)

1-Intro. Orwell & the Brotherhood; Ribic-a/X-s/Sienkiewicz-c 3.00
2-9: 2-Two covers (JG Jones & Sienkiewicz). 4-6-Fabry-c. 7-9-Phillips-c/a 3.00

Brute Force #1 © MAR

Buccaneers #24 © QUA

Buck Jones #2 © DELL

BROTHER POWER, THE GEEK (See Saga of Swamp Thing Annual & Vertigo Visions)
National Periodical Publications: Sept-Oct, 1968 - No. 2, Nov-Dec, 1968

	GD 2.0	VG 4.0	FN 6.0	VF 8.0	VF/NM 9.0	NM- 9.2
1-Origin; Simon-c(i?)	5	10	15	31	53	75
2	3	6	9	19	30	40

BROTHERS, HANG IN THERE, THE
Spire Christian Comics (Fleming H. Revell Co.): 1979 (49¢)

	GD 2.0	VG 4.0	FN 6.0	VF 8.0	VF/NM 9.0	NM- 9.2
nn	2	4	6	13	18	22

BROTHERS IN ARMS (Based on the World War II military video game)
Dynamite Entertainment: 2008 - No. 4, 2008 ($3.99/$3.50)

	GD 2.0	VG 4.0	FN 6.0	VF 8.0	VF/NM 9.0	NM- 9.2
1-($3.99) Fabbri-a; two covers by Fabbri & Sejic						4.00
2-4-($3.50) Two covers by Fabbri & Sejic on each						3.50

BROTHERS OF THE SPEAR (Also see Tarzan)
Gold Key/Whitman No. 18: June, 1972 - No. 17, Feb, 1976; No. 18, May, 1982

	GD 2.0	VG 4.0	FN 6.0	VF 8.0	VF/NM 9.0	NM- 9.2
1	5	10	15	31	53	75
2-Painted-c begin, end #17	3	6	9	18	28	38
3-10	3	6	9	15	22	28
11-18: 12-Line drawn-c. 13-17-Spiegle-a. 18(5/82)-r/#2; Leopard Girl-r	2	4	6	11	16	20

BROTHERS, THE CULT ESCAPE, THE
Spire Christian Comics (Fleming H. Revell Co.): 1980 (49¢)

	GD 2.0	VG 4.0	FN 6.0	VF 8.0	VF/NM 9.0	NM- 9.2
nn	3	6	9	14	19	24

BROWNIES (See New Funnies)
Dell Publishing Co.: No. 192, July, 1948 - No. 605, Dec, 1954

	GD 2.0	VG 4.0	FN 6.0	VF 8.0	VF/NM 9.0	NM- 9.2
Four Color 192(#1)-Kelly-a	12	24	36	82	179	275
Four Color 244(9/49), 293 (9/50)-Last Kelly c/a	9	18	27	60	120	180
Four Color 337(7-8/51), 365(12-1/51-52), 398(5/52)	5	10	15	34	60	85
Four Color 436(11/52), 482(7/53), 522(12/53), 605	5	10	15	33	57	80

BRUCE GENTRY
Better/Standard/Four Star Publ./Superior No. 3: Jan, 1948 - No. 8, Jul, 1949

	GD 2.0	VG 4.0	FN 6.0	VF 8.0	VF/NM 9.0	NM- 9.2
1-Ray Bailey strip reprints begin, end #3; E. C. emblem appears as a monogram on stationery in story; negligee panels	61	122	183	390	670	950
2,3	39	78	117	231	378	525
4-8	26	52	78	154	252	350

NOTE: *Kamenish a-2-7; c-1-8.*

BRUCE JONES' OUTER EDGE
Innovation: 1993 ($2.50, B&W, one-shot)

	GD 2.0	VG 4.0	FN 6.0	VF 8.0	VF/NM 9.0	NM- 9.2
1-Bruce Jones-c/a/script						3.00

BRUCE LEE (Also see Deadly Hands of Kung Fu)
Malibu Comics: July, 1994 - No. 6, Dec, 1994 ($2.95, 36 pgs.)

	GD 2.0	VG 4.0	FN 6.0	VF 8.0	VF/NM 9.0	NM- 9.2
1-6: 1-(44 pgs.)-Mortal Kombat prev., 1st app. in comics. 2,6-(36 pgs.)						5.00

BRUCE WAYNE: AGENT OF S.H.I.E.L.D. (Also see Marvel Vs. DC #3 & DC Vs. Marvel #4)
Marvel Comics (Amalgam): Apr, 1996 ($1.95, one-shot)

	GD 2.0	VG 4.0	FN 6.0	VF 8.0	VF/NM 9.0	NM- 9.2
1-Chuck Dixon scripts & Cary Nord-c/a.						3.00

BRUCE WAYNE: THE ROAD HOME (See Batman: The Return of Bruce Wayne)
(See Batman: Bruce Wayne - The Road Home HC for reprints)
DC Comics: Dec, 2010 ($2.99, series of one-shots with interlocking covers)

	GD 2.0	VG 4.0	FN 6.0	VF 8.0	VF/NM 9.0	NM- 9.2
...: Batgirl 1 - Bryan Miller-s/Pere Pérez-a						3.00
...: Batman and Robin 1 - Nicieza-s/Richards-a; Vicki Vale app.						3.00
...: Catwoman 1 - Fridolfs-s/Nguyen-a; Harley & Ivy app.						3.00
...: Commissioner Gordon 1 - Beechen-s/Kudranski-a; Penguin app.						3.00
...: Oracle 1 - Andreyko-s/Padilla-a; Man-Bat & Manhunter app.						3.00
...: Outsiders 1 - Barr-s/Saltares-a						3.00
...: Ra's al Ghul 1 - Nicieza-s/McDaniel-a						3.00
...: Red Robin 1 - Nicieza-s/Bachs-a; Ra's al Ghul app.						3.00

BRUISER
Anthem Publications: Feb, 1994 ($2.45)

	GD 2.0	VG 4.0	FN 6.0	VF 8.0	VF/NM 9.0	NM- 9.2
1						3.00

BRUTE, THE
Seaboard Publ. (Atlas): Feb, 1975 - No. 3, July, 1975

	GD 2.0	VG 4.0	FN 6.0	VF 8.0	VF/NM 9.0	NM- 9.2
1-Origin & 1st app; Sekowsky-a(p)	3	6	9	15	22	28
2-Sekowsky-a(p); Fleisher-s	2	4	6	10	14	18
3-Brunner/Starlin/Weiss-a(p)	2	4	6	13	18	22

BRUTE & BABE
Ominous Press: July, 1994 - No. 2, Aug, 1994

	GD 2.0	VG 4.0	FN 6.0	VF 8.0	VF/NM 9.0	NM- 9.2
1-($3.95, 8 tablets plus-c)-"...It Begins..."; tablet format						4.00
2-($2.50, 36 pgs.)-"Mael's Rage", 2-(40 pgs.)-Stiff additional variant-c						3.00

BRUTE FORCE
Marvel Comics: Aug, 1990 - No. 4, Nov, 1990 ($1.00, limited series)

	GD 2.0	VG 4.0	FN 6.0	VF 8.0	VF/NM 9.0	NM- 9.2
1-4: Animal super-heroes; Delbo & DeCarlo-a						3.00

B-SIDES (The Craptacular...)
Marvel Comics: Nov, 2002 - No. 3, Jan, 2003 ($2.99, limited series)

	GD 2.0	VG 4.0	FN 6.0	VF 8.0	VF/NM 9.0	NM- 9.2
1-3-Kieth-c/Weldele-a. 2-Dorkin-a (1 pg.) 2-FF cameo. 3-FF app.						3.00

BUBBLEGUM CRISIS: GRAND MAL
Dark Horse Comics: Mar, 1994 - No. 4, June, 1994 ($2.50, limited series)

	GD 2.0	VG 4.0	FN 6.0	VF 8.0	VF/NM 9.0	NM- 9.2
1-4-Japanese manga						3.00

BUBBLEGUN
Aspen MLT: Jun, 2013 - No. 5, Mar, 2014 ($1.00/$3.99)

	GD 2.0	VG 4.0	FN 6.0	VF 8.0	VF/NM 9.0	NM- 9.2
1-($1.00) Roslan-s/Bowden-a; multiple covers						3.00
2-5-($3.99) Multiple covers on each						4.00

BUCCANEER
I. W. Enterprises: No date (1963)

	GD 2.0	VG 4.0	FN 6.0	VF 8.0	VF/NM 9.0	NM- 9.2
I.W. Reprint #1(r-/Quality #20), #8(r-/#23): Crandall-a in each	3	6	9	16	23	30

BUCCANEERS (Formerly Kid Eternity)
Quality Comics: No. 19, Jan, 1950 - No. 27, May, 1951 (No. 24-27: 52 pgs.)

	GD 2.0	VG 4.0	FN 6.0	VF 8.0	VF/NM 9.0	NM- 9.2
19-Captain Daring, Black Roger, Eric Falcon & Spanish Main begin; Crandall-a	48	96	144	302	514	725
20,23-Crandall-a	36	72	108	215	350	485
21-Crandall-c/a	39	78	117	236	388	540
22-Bondage-c	28	56	84	165	270	375
24-26: 24-Adam Peril, U.S.N. begins. 25-Origin & 1st app. Corsair Queen. 26-last Spanish Main	24	48	72	142	234	325
27-Crandall-c/a	34	68	102	205	335	465
Super Reprint #12 (1964)-Crandall-r/#21	3	6	9	16	23	30

BUCCANEERS, THE (TV)
Dell Publishing Co.: No. 800, 1957

	GD 2.0	VG 4.0	FN 6.0	VF 8.0	VF/NM 9.0	NM- 9.2
Four Color 800-Photo-c	6	12	18	40	73	105

BUCKAROO BANZAI (Movie)
Marvel Comics Group: Dec, 1984 - No. 2, Feb, 1985

	GD 2.0	VG 4.0	FN 6.0	VF 8.0	VF/NM 9.0	NM- 9.2
1,2-Movie adaptation; r/Marvel Super Special #33; Texiera-c/a						4.00

BUCKAROO BANZAI: RETURN OF THE SCREW
Moonstone: 2006 - No. 3, 2006 ($3.50, limited series)

	GD 2.0	VG 4.0	FN 6.0	VF 8.0	VF/NM 9.0	NM- 9.2
1-3: 1-Three covers by Haley, Stribling, Beck; Thompson-a						3.50
Preview (2006, 50¢) B&W preview; history of movie and spin-off projects						3.00

BUCK DUCK
Atlas Comics (ANC): June, 1953 - No. 4, Dec, 1953

	GD 2.0	VG 4.0	FN 6.0	VF 8.0	VF/NM 9.0	NM- 9.2
1-Funny animal stories in all	18	36	54	103	162	220
2-4: 2-Ed Win-a(5)	11	22	33	62	86	110

BUCK JONES (Also see Crackajack Funnies, Famous Feature Stories, Master Comics #7 & Wow Comics #1, 1936)
Dell Publishing Co.: No. 299, Oct, 1950 - No. 850, Oct, 1957 (All Painted-c)

	GD 2.0	VG 4.0	FN 6.0	VF 8.0	VF/NM 9.0	NM- 9.2
Four Color 299(#1)-Buck Jones & his horse Silver-B begin; painted back-c begins, ends #5	11	22	33	76	163	250
2(4-6/51)	7	14	21	44	82	120
3-8(10-12/52)	6	12	18	37	66	95
Four Color 460,500,546,589	6	12	18	38	69	100
Four Color 652,733,850	5	10	15	31	53	75

BUCK ROGERS (Also see Famous Funnies, Pure Oil Comics, Salerno Carnival of Comics, 24 Pages of Comics, & Vicks Comics)
Famous Funnies: Winter, 1940-41 - No. 6, Sept, 1943
NOTE: Buck Rogers first appeared in the pulp magazine Amazing Stories Vol. 3 #5 in Aug, 1928.

	GD 2.0	VG 4.0	FN 6.0	VF 8.0	VF/NM 9.0	NM- 9.2
1-Sunday strip reprints by Rick Yager; begins with strip #190; Calkins-c	331	662	993	2317	4059	5800
2 (7/41)-Calkins-c	139	278	417	883	1517	2150
3 (12/41), 4 (7/42)	118	236	354	749	1287	1825
5,6: 5-Story continues with Famous Funnies No. 80; Buck Rogers, Sky Roads. 6-Reprints of 1939 dailies; contains B.R. story "Crater of Doom" (2 pgs.) by Calkins not-r from Famous Funnies	98	194	294	622	1074	1525

BUCK ROGERS
Toby Press: No. 100, Jan, 1951 - No. 9, May-June, 1951

	GD 2.0	VG 4.0	FN 6.0	VF 8.0	VF/NM 9.0	NM- 9.2
100(#7)-All strip-r begin; Anderson, Chatton-a	31	62	93	182	296	410
101(#8), 9-All Anderson-a(1947-49-r/dailies)	23	46	69	136	223	310

Buck Rogers (2013 series) #1 © Dille Family

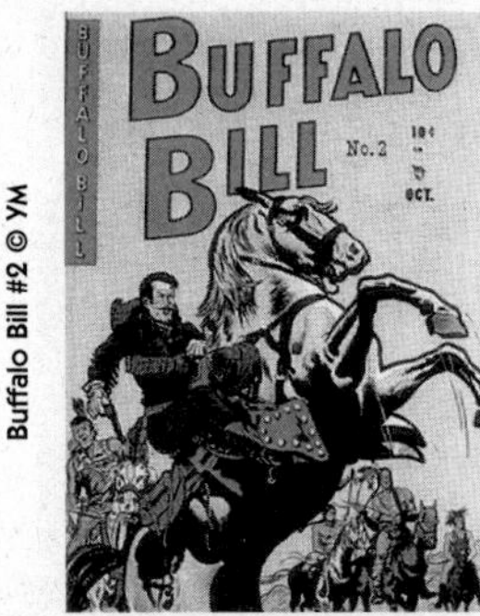

Buffalo Bill #2 © YM

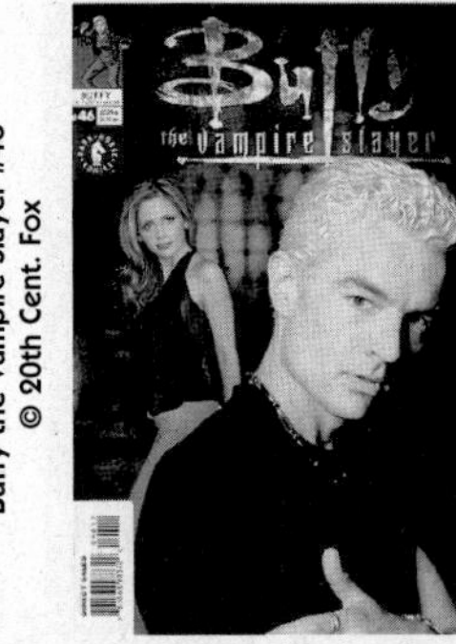

Buffy the Vampire Slayer #46 © 20th Cent. Fox

	GD 2.0	VG 4.0	FN 6.0	VF 8.0	VF/NM 9.0	NM- 9.2

BUCK ROGERS (...in the 25th Century No. 5 on) (TV)
Gold Key/Whitman No. 7 on: Oct, 1964; No. 2, July, 1979 - No. 16, May, 1982 (No #10; story was written but never released. #17 exists only as a press proof without covers and was never published)

	GD	VG	FN	VF	VF/NM	NM-
1(10128-410, 12¢)-1st S.A. app. Buck Rogers & 1st new B. R. in comics since 1933 giveaway; painted-c; back-c pin-up	10	20	30	64	132	200
2(7/79)-6: 3,4,6-Movie adaptation; painted-c	2	4	6	9	12	15
7,11 (Whitman)	2	4	6	11	16	20
8,9 (prepack)(scarce)	4	8	12	25	40	55
12-16: 14(2/82), 15(3/82), 16(5/82)	2	4	6	8	10	12
Giant Movie Edition 11296(64pp, Whitman, $1.50), reprints GK #2-4 minus cover; tabloid size; photo-c (See Marvel Treasury)	3	6	9	17	26	35
Giant Movie Edition 02489(Western/Marvel, $1.50), reprints GK #2-4 minus cover	3	6	9	16	24	32

NOTE: ***Bolle** a-2p,3p, Movie Ed.(p). **McWilliams** a-2i,3i, 5-11, Movie Ed.(i). Painted c-1-9,11-13.*

BUCK ROGERS (Comics Module)
TSR, Inc.: 1990 - No. 10, 1991 ($2.95, 44 pgs.)

1-10 (1990): 1-Begin origin in 3 parts. 2-Indicia says #1. 2,3-Black Barney back-up story. 4-All Black Barney issue; B. B.-c. 5-Indicia says #6; Black Barney-c & lead story; Buck Rogers back-up story. 10-Flip book (72pgs.) 4.00

BUCK ROGERS
Dynamite Entertainment: No. 0, 2009 - No. 12, 2010 (25¢/$3.50)

0-(25¢) Beatty-s/Rafael-a/Cassaday-c 3.00
1-12: 1-($3.50) Three covers by Cassaday, Ross and Wagner; origin re-told 3.50
Annual 1 (2011, $4.99) Rafael-a; covers by Rafael & Sadowski 5.00

BUCK ROGERS
Hermes Press: 2013 - No. 4, 2013 ($3.99)

1-4-Howard Chaykin-s/a/c 4.00

BUCKSKIN (TV)
Dell Publishing Co.: No. 1011, July, 1959 - No. 1107, June-Aug, 1960

	GD	VG	FN	VF	VF/NM	NM-
Four Color 1011 (#1)-Photo-c	6	12	18	41	76	110
Four Color 1107-Photo-c	6	12	18	38	69	100

BUCKY O'HARE (Funny Animal)
Continuity Comics: 1988 ($5.95, graphic novel)

	GD	VG	FN	VF	VF/NM	NM-
1-Golden-c/a(r); r/serial-Echo of Futurepast #1-6	1	2	3	4	5	7
Deluxe Hardcover ($40.00, 52 pg., 8 x 11")						40.00

BUCKY O'HARE
Continuity Comics: Jan, 1991 - No. 5, 1991 ($2.00)

1-6: 1-Michael Golden-c/a 3.00

BUDDIES IN THE U.S. ARMY
Avon Periodicals: Nov, 1952 - No. 2, 1953

	GD	VG	FN	VF	VF/NM	NM-
1-Lawrence-c	14	28	42	81	118	155
2-Mort Lawrence-c/a	10	20	30	56	76	95

BUFFALO BEE (TV)
Dell Publishing Co.: No. 957, Nov, 1958 - No. 1061, Dec-Feb, 1959-60

	GD	VG	FN	VF	VF/NM	NM-
Four Color 957 (#1)	8	16	24	51	96	140
Four Color 1002 (8-10/59), 1061	6	12	18	40	73	105

BUFFALO BILL (See Frontier Fighters, Super Western Comics & Western Action Thrillers)
Youthful Magazines: No. 2, Oct, 1950 - No. 9, Dec, 1951

	GD	VG	FN	VF	VF/NM	NM-
2-Annie Oakley story	14	28	42	81	118	155
3-9: 2-4-Walter Johnson-c/a. 9-Wildey-a	10	20	30	56	76	95

BUFFALO BILL CODY (See Cody of the Pony Express)

BUFFALO BILL, JR. (TV) (See Western Roundup)
Dell/Gold Key: Jan, 1956 - No. 13, Aug-Oct, 1959; 1965 (All photo-c)

	GD	VG	FN	VF	VF/NM	NM-
Four Color 673 (#1)	8	16	24	52	99	145
Four Color 742,766,798,828,856(11/57)	5	10	15	35	63	90
7(2-4/58)-13	5	10	15	31	53	75
1(6/65, Gold Key)-Photo-c(r/F.C. #798); photo-b/c	4	8	12	23	37	50

BUFFALO BILL PICTURE STORIES
Street & Smith Publications: June-July, 1949 - No. 2, Aug-Sept, 1949

	GD	VG	FN	VF	VF/NM	NM-
1,2-Wildey, Powell-a in each	14	28	42	80	115	150

BUFFY THE VAMPIRE SLAYER (Based on the TV series)(Also see Angel and Faith, Spike, Tales of the Vampires and Willow)
Dark Horse Comics: 1998 - No. 63, Nov, 2003 ($2.95/$2.99)

	GD	VG	FN	VF	VF/NM	NM-
1-Bennett-a/Watson-s; Art Adams-c	1	2	3	6	8	10
1-Variant photo-c	1	2	3	6	8	10
1-Gold foil logo Art Adams-c						15.00
1-Gold foil logo photo-c						20.00
2-4-Photo-c	1	3	4	6	8	10
5-15-Regular and photo-c. 4-7-Gomez-a. 5,8-Green-c						5.00
16-48: 29,30-Angel x-over. 43-45-Death of Buffy. 47-Lobdell-s begin. 48-Pike returns						3.00
50-($3.50) Scooby gang battles Adam; back-up story by Watson						4.00
51-63: 51-54-Viva Las Buffy; pre-Sunnydale Buffy & Pike in Vegas						3.00
Annual '99 ($4.95)-Two stories and pin-ups	1	2	3	4	5	7
...: A Stake to the Heart TPB (3/04, $12.95) r/#60-63						13.00
...: Chaos Bleeds (6/03, $2.99) Based on the video game; photo & Campbell-c						3.00
...: Creatures of Habit (3/02, $17.95) text with Horton & Paul Lee-a						18.00
...: Jonathan 1 (1/01, $2.99) two covers; Richards-a						3.00
...: Lost and Found 1 (3/02, $2.99) aftermath of Buffy's death; Richards-a						3.00
... Lovers Walk (2/01, $2.99) short stories by various; Richards & photo-c						3.00
...: Note From the Underground (3/03, $12.95) r/#47-50						13.00
...: Omnibus Vol. 1 (7/07, $24.95, 9x6") r/Spike & Dru #3, Origin #1-3 and Buffy #51-59						25.00
...: Omnibus Vol. 2 (9/07, $24.95, 9x6") r/Buffy #60-63 and various one-shots & specials						25.00
...: Omnibus Vol. 3 (1/08, $24.95, 9x6") r/Buffy #1-8,12,16, Annual '99						25.00
...: Omnibus Vol. 4 (5/08, $24.95, 9x6") r/Buffy #9-11,13-15,17-20,50 and various						25.00
...: Omnibus Vol. 5 (9/08, $24.95, 9x6") r/Buffy #21-28 and various one-shots & specials						25.00
...: Omnibus Vol. 6 (2/09, $24.95, 9x6") r/Buffy #29-38 and various one-shots & specials						25.00
...: One For One (9/10, $1.00) r/#1 with red cover frame						3.00
...: Reunion (6/02, $3.50) Buffy & Angel's; Espenson-s; art by various						3.50
...: Slayer Interrupted TPB (2003, $14.95) r/#56-59						15.00
...: Tales of the Slayers (10/02, $3.50) art by Matsuda and Colan; art & photo-c						3.50
...: The Death of Buffy TPB (8/02, $15.95) r/#43-46						16.00
...: Viva Las Buffy TPB (7/03, $12.95) r/#51-54						13.00
Wizard #1/2	1	2	3	6	8	9

BUFFY THE VAMPIRE SLAYER ("Season Eight" of the TV series)
Dark Horse Comics: Mar, 2007 - No. 40, Jan, 2011 ($2.99)

1-Joss Whedon-s/Georges Jeanty-a/Jo Chen-c 6.00
1-Variant cover by Jeanty 6.00
1-RRP with B&W Jeanty cover (edition of 1000) 85.00
1-4: 1-2nd thru 5th printings. 2-2nd-4th printings. 3,4-2nd & 3rd printings 3.00
2-5-Jeanty-a; covers by Chen & Jeanty 4.00
6-13,16-19-Two covers by Chen & Jeanty. 6-9-Faith app.; Vaughan-s. 10,11-Whedon-s. 12-15-Goddard-s; Dracula app. 16-19-Fray app.; Whedon-s/Moline-a 3.00
20-40: 20-28,31-40-Two covers by Chen and Jeanty. 20-Animation style flashback. 21,26-30-Espenson-s. 30-Hughes-c. 31-Whedon-s. 32-35-Meltzer-s. 36-40-Whedon-s 3.00
...: Riley (8/10, $3.50) Espensen-s/Moline-a; Riley Finn and Sam; Angel app. 3.50
... Tales of the Vampires (6/09, $2.99) Cloonan-s/Lolos-a; covers by Chen & Bá/Moon 3.00
...: Willow (12/09, $3.50) Whedon-s/Moline-a; Willow meets the Snake Guide 3.50
...: Volume One: The Long Way Home TPB (11/07, $15.95) r/#1-5 and variant covers 16.00
...: Volume Two: No Future for You TPB (6/08, $15.95) r/#6-10 and variant covers 16.00
...: Volume Three: Wolves at the Gate TPB (11/08, $15.95) r/#11-15 and variant covers 16.00
...: Volume Four: Time of Your Life TPB (5/09, $15.95) r/#16-20 and variant covers 16.00
...: Volume Five: Predators and Prey TPB (9/09, $15.95) r/#21-25 and variant covers 16.00
...: Volume Six: Retreat TPB (3/10, $15.99) r/#26-30 and stories from MySpace DHP 16.00
...: Volume Seven: Twilight TPB (10/10, $16.99) r/#31-35 and Willow one-shot 17.00
...: Volume Eight: Last Gleaming TPB (6/11, $16.99) r/#36-40 and Riley one-shot 17.00

NOTE: *Later printings have Jo Chen cover art with different credit graphics.*

BUFFY THE VAMPIRE SLAYER ("Season Nine" of the TV series)
Dark Horse Comics: Sept, 2011 - No. 25, Sept, 2013 ($2.99)

1-25: 1-Whedon-s/Jeanty-a; covers by Morris & Chen. 2-5-Chambliss-s; two covers by Morris & Jeanty. 5-Moline-a; Nikki flashback. 6,7-Two covers by Jeanty & Noto. 8-10-Richards-a. 14-Espenson-s; intro. Billy. 16-19-Illyria app. 3.00
....: Buffyverse Sampler (1/13, $4.99) r/#1, Angel & Faith #1, Spike #1, Willow #1 5.00
FCBD (5/12, giveaway) Buffy vs. Alien; Jeanty-a; flip book with The Guild 3.00

BUFFY THE VAMPIRE SLAYER (SEASON TEN)
Dark Horse Comics: Mar, 2014 - Present ($3.50)

1-Gage-s/Isaacs-a; covers by Morris & Isaacs 3.50

BUFFY THE VAMPIRE SLAYER: ANGEL
Dark Horse Comics: May, 1999 - No. 3, July, 1999 ($2.95, limited series)

1-3-Gomez-a; Matsuda-c & photo-c for each 3.00

BUFFY THE VAMPIRE SLAYER: GILES
Dark Horse Comics: Oct, 2000 ($2.95, one-shot)

1-Eric Powell-a; Powell & photo-c 3.00

BUFFY THE VAMPIRE SLAYER: HAUNTED
Dark Horse Comics: Dec, 2001 - No. 4, Mar, 2002 ($2.99, limited series)

1-4-Faith and the Mayor app.; Espenson-s/Richards-a 3.00
TPB (9/02, $12.95) r/series; photo-c 13.00

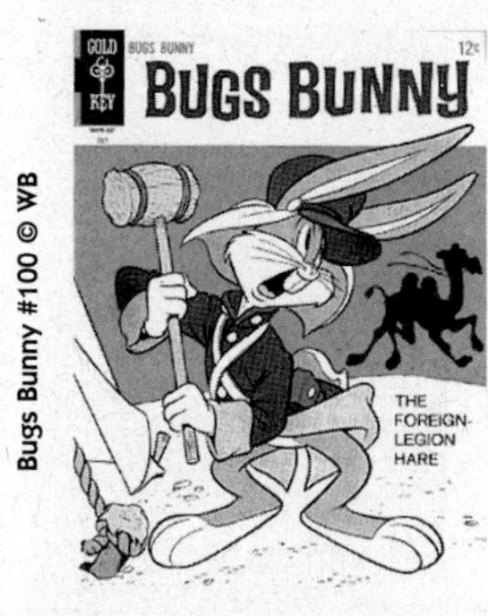

Bugs Bunny #100 © WB

Bulletman #7 © FAW

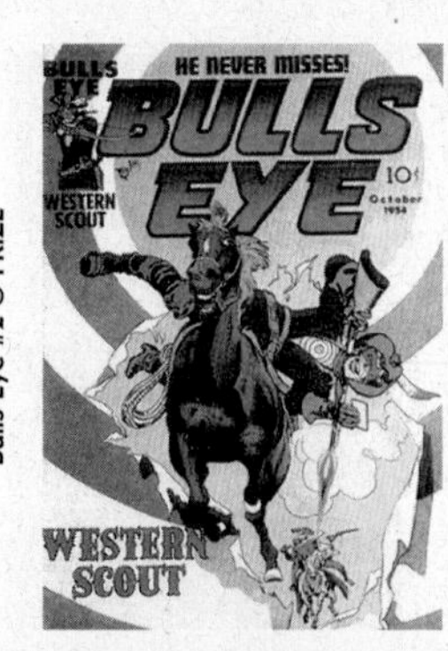

Bulls-Eye #2 © PRIZE

GD VG FN VF VF/NM NM-
2.0 4.0 6.0 8.0 9.0 9.2

GD VG FN VF VF/NM NM-
2.0 4.0 6.0 8.0 9.0 9.2

BUFFY THE VAMPIRE SLAYER: OZ
Dark Horse Comics: July, 2001 - No. 3, Sept, 2001 ($2.99, limited series)
1-3-Totleben & photo-c; Golden-s 3.00

BUFFY THE VAMPIRE SLAYER: SPIKE AND DRU
Dark Horse Comics: Apr, 1999; No. 2, Oct, 1999; No. 3, Dec, 2000 ($2.95)
1-3: 1,2-Photo-c. 3-Two covers (photo & Sook) 3.00

BUFFY THE VAMPIRE SLAYER: THE ORIGIN (Adapts movie screenplay)
Dark Horse Comics: Jan, 1999 - No. 3, Mar, 1999 ($2.95, limited series)
1-3-Brereton-s/Bennett-a; reg & photo-c for each 3.00

BUFFY THE VAMPIRE SLAYER: WILLOW & TARA
Dark Horse Comics: Apr, 2001 ($2.99, one-shot)
1-Terry Moore-a/Chris Golden & Amber Benson-s; Moore-c & photo-c 3.00
TPB (4/03, $9.95) r/#1 & W&T - Wilderness; photo-c 10.00

BUFFY THE VAMPIRE SLAYER: WILLOW & TARA - WILDERNESS
Dark Horse Comics: Jul, 2002 - No. 2, Sept, 2002 ($2.99, limited series)
1,2-Chris Golden & Amber Benson-s; Jothikaumar-c & photo-c 3.00

BUG
Marvel Comics: Mar, 1997 ($2.99, one-shot)
1-Micronauts character 3.00

BUGALOOS (Sid & Marty Krofft TV show)
Charlton Comics: Sept, 1971 - No. 4, Feb, 1972
1 5 10 15 30 50 70
2-4 3 6 9 19 30 40
NOTE: *No. 3(1/72) went on sale late in 1972 (after No. 4) with the 1/73 issues.*

BUGHOUSE (Satire)
Ajax/Farrell (Excellent Publ.): Mar-Apr, 1954 - No. 4, Sept-Oct, 1954
V1#1 22 44 66 132 216 300
2-4 14 28 42 80 115 150

BUGS BUNNY (See The Best of..., Camp Comics, Comic Album #2, 6, 10, 14, Dell Giant #28, 32, 46, Dynabrite, Golden Comics Digest #1, 3, 5, 6, 8, 10, 14, 15, 17, 21, 26, 30, 34, 39, 42, 47, Kite Fun Book, Large Feature Comic #8, Looney Tunes and Merry Melodies, March of Comics #44, 59, 75, 83, 97, 115, 132, 149, 160, 179, 188, 201, 220, 231, 245, 259, 273, 287, 301, 315, 329, 343, 363, 367, 380, 392, 403, 415, 428, 440, 452, 464, 476, 487, Porky Pig, Puffed Wheat, Story Hour Series #802, Super Book #14, 26 and Whitman Comic Books)

BUGS BUNNY (See Dell Giants for annuals)
Dell Publishing Co./Gold Key No. 86-218/Whitman No. 219 on: 1942 - No. 245, April, 1984
Large Feature Comic 8(1942)-(Rarely found in fine-mint condition)
245 490 735 1568 2684 3800
Four Color 33 ('43) 96 192 288 768 1734 2700
Four Color 51 32 64 96 230 515 800
Four Color 88 21 42 63 147 324 500
Four Color 123('46),142,164 15 30 45 100 220 340
Four Color 187,200,217,233 11 22 33 73 157 240
Four Color 250-Used in **SOTI**, pg. 309 11 22 33 76 163 250
Four Color 266,274,281,289,298('50) 9 18 27 60 120 180
Four Color 307,317(#1),327(#2),338,347,355,366,376,393
8 16 24 54 102 150
Four Color 407,420,432(10/52) 7 14 21 46 86 125
Four Color 498(9/53),585(9/54), 647(9/55) 6 12 18 37 66 95
Four Color 724(9/56),838(9/57),1064(12/59) 5 10 15 33 57 80
28(12-1/52-53)-30 5 10 15 34 60 85
31-50 4 8 12 28 47 65
51-85(7-9/62) 4 8 12 23 37 50
86(10/62)-88-Bugs Bunny's Showtime-(25¢, 80pgs.) 5 10 15 35 63 90
89-99 3 6 9 16 24 32
100 3 6 9 17 26 35
101-118: 108-1st Honey Bunny. 118-Last 12¢ issue 3 6 9 14 19 24
119-140 2 4 6 11 16 20
141-170 2 4 6 9 12 15
171-218: 218-Publ. by Whitman only? 2 4 6 8 10 12
219,220,225-237(5/82): 229-Swipe of Barks story/WDC&S #223. 233(2/82)
2 4 6 8 10 12
221(9/80),222(11/80)-Pre-pack? (Scarce) 4 8 12 25 40 55
223 (1/81, 50¢-c), 224 (3/81)-Low distr. 2 4 6 13 18 22
223 (1/81, 40¢-c) Cover price error variant 3 6 9 16 23 30
238-245 (#90070 on-c, nd, nd code; pre-pack): 238(5/83), 239(6/83), 240(7/83), 241(7/83), 242(8/83), 243(8/83), 244(3/84), 245(4/84) 3 6 9 14 19 24
NOTE: *Reprints-100,102-104,110,115,123,143,144,147,167,173,175-177,179-185,187,190.*
nn (Xerox Pub. Comic Digest, 1971, 100 pages, B&W)
collection of one-page gags 4 8 12 23 37 50
...Comic-Go-Round 11196-(224 pgs.)($1.95)(Golden Press, 1979)
4 8 12 25 40 55
...Winter Fun 1(12/67-Gold Key)-Giant 5 10 15 30 50 70

BUGS BUNNY
DC Comics: June, 1990 - No. 3, Aug, 1990 ($1.00, limited series)
1-3: Daffy Duck, Elmer Fudd, others app. 4.00

BUGS BUNNY (...Monthly on-c)
DC Comics: 1993 - No. 3, 1994? ($1.95)
1-3-Bugs, Porky Pig, Daffy, Road Runner 3.50

BUGS BUNNY (Digest-size reprints from Looney Tunes)
DC Comics: 2005 - Present ($6.99, digest)
Vol. 1: What's Up Doc? - Reprints from Looney Tunes #37,41,43-45,48,52,55,57-59,63 7.00

BUGS BUNNY & PORKY PIG
Gold Key: Sept, 1965 (Paper-c, giant, 100 pgs.)
1(30025-509) 6 12 18 38 69 100

BUGS BUNNY'S ALBUM (See Bugs Bunny, Four Color No. 498,585,647,724)

BUGS BUNNY LIFE STORY ALBUM (See Bugs Bunny, Four Color No. 838)

BUGS BUNNY MERRY CHRISTMAS (See Bugs Bunny, Four Color No. 1064)

BUILDING, THE
Kitchen Sink Press: 1987; 2000 (8 1/2" x 11" sepia toned graphic novel)
nn-Will Eisner-s/c/a 15.00
nn-(DC Comics, 9/00, $9.95) reprints 1987 edition 10.00

BULLET CROW, FOWL OF FORTUNE
Eclipse Comics: Mar, 1987 - No. 2, Apr, 1987 ($2.00, B&W, limited series)
1,2-The Comic Reader-r & new-a 3.00

BULLETMAN (See Fawcett Miniatures, Master Comics, Mighty Midget Comics, Nickel Comics & XMas Comics)
Fawcett Publications: Sum, 1941 - #12, 2/12/43; #14, Spr, 1946 - #16, Fall, 1946 (No #13)
1-Silver metallic-c 400 800 1200 2800 4900 7000
2-Raboy-c 177 354 531 1124 1937 2750
3,5-Raboy-c each 142 284 426 909 1555 2200
4 98 196 294 622 1074 1525
6,8-10: 10-Intro. Bulletdog 84 168 252 538 919 1300
7-Ghost Stories told by night watchman of cemetery begins; Eisnerish-a; hidden message "Chic Stone is a jerk". 94 188 282 597 1024 1450
11,12,14-16 (nn 13): 12-Robot-c 61 122 183 390 670 950
NOTE: ***Mac Raboy** c-1-3, 5, 6, 10. "Bulletman the Flying Detective" on cover #8 on.*

BULLET POINTS
Marvel Comics: Jan, 2007 - No. 5, May, 2007 ($2.99, limited series)
1-5: 1-Steve Rogers becomes Iron Man; Straczynski-s/Edwards-a. 4,5-Galactus app. 3.00
TPB (2007, $13.99) r/#1-5; layout pages by Edwards 14.00

BULLETPROOF MONK (Inspired the 2003 film)
Image Comics (Flypaper Press): 1998 - No. 3, 1999 ($2.95, limited series)
1-3-Oeming-a 3.00
...: Tales of the BPM (3/03, $2.95) Flip book; 2 covers by Sale; art by Sale, Oeming, Dave Johnson; Seann William Scott afterword 3.00
TPB (2002, $9.95) r/#1-3; foreword by John Woo 10.00

BULLETS AND BRACELETS (Also see Marvel Versus DC #3 & DC Versus Marvel #4)
Marvel Comics (Amalgam): Apr, 1996 ($1.95)
1-John Ostrander script & Gary Frank-c/a 3.00

BULLS-EYE (Cody of The Pony Express No. 8 on)
Mainline No. 1-5/Charlton No. 6,7: 7-8/54-No. 5, 3-4/55; No. 6, 6/55; No. 7, 8/55
1-S&K-c, 2 pgs.-a 68 136 204 435 743 1050
2-S&K-c/a 53 106 159 334 567 800
3-5-S&K-c/a(2 each). 4-Last pre-code issue (1-2/55). 5-Censored issue with tomahawks removed in battle scene 43 86 129 271 461 650
6-S&K-c/a 39 78 117 240 395 550
7-S&K-c/a(3) 43 86 129 271 461 650

BULLS-EYE COMICS (Formerly Komik Pages #10; becomes Kayo #12)
Harry 'A' Chesler: No. 11, 1944
11-Origin K-9, Green Knight's sidekick, Lance; The Green Knight, Lady Satan, Yankee Doodle Jones app. 50 100 150 315 533 750

BULLSEYE: GREATEST HITS (Daredevil villain)
Marvel Comics: Nov, 2004 - No. 5, Mar, 2005 ($2.99, limted series)

Buster Crabbe #12 © FF

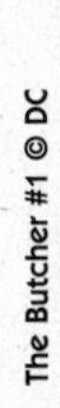

The Butcher #1 © DC

Buzzy #2 © DC

	GD 2.0	VG 4.0	FN 6.0	VF 8.0	VF/NM 9.0	NM- 9.2
1-5-Origin of Bullseye; Steve Dillon-a/Deodato-c. 3-Punisher app.						3.00
TPB (2005, $13.99) r/#1-5						14.00

BULLSEYE: PERFECT GAME (Daredevil villain)
Marvel Comics: Jan, 2011 - No. 2, Feb, 2011 ($3.99, limited series)

1,2-Huston-s/Martinbrough-a; Bullseye as baseball pitcher						4.00

BULLWHIP GRIFFIN (See Movie Comics)

BULLWINKLE (...and Rocky No. 22 on; See March of Comics #233 and Rocky & Bullwinkle) (TV) (Jay Ward)
Dell/Gold Key: 3-5/62 - #11, 4/74; #12, 6/76 - #19, 3/78; #20, 4/79 - #25, 2/80

Four Color 1270 (3-5/62)	16	32	48	110	243	375
01-090-209 (Dell, 7-9/62)	13	26	39	86	188	290
1(11/62, Gold Key)	12	24	36	80	173	265
2(2/63)	8	16	24	54	102	150
3(4/72)-11(4/74-Gold Key)	5	10	15	31	53	75
12-14: 12(6/76)-Reprints. 13(9/76), 14-New stories	3	6	9	17	26	35
15-25	2	4	6	11	16	20
Mother Moose Nursery Pomes 01-530-207 (5-7/62, Dell)	15	30	45	100	220	340

NOTE: *Reprints: 6, 7, 20-24.*

BULLWINKLE AND ROCKY (TV)
Charlton Comics: July, 1970 - No. 7, July, 1971

1-Has 1 pg. pin-up	6	12	18	40	73	105
2-7: 3-Snidely Whiplash app.	5	10	15	30	50	70

BULLWINKLE AND ROCKY
Star Comics/Marvel Comics No. 3 on: Nov, 1987 - No. 9, Mar, 1989

1-9: Boris & Natasha in all. 3,5,8-Dudley Do-Right app. 4-Reagan-c						5.00
Marvel Moosterworks (1/92, $4.95)	2	4	6	8	10	12

BUMMER
Fantagraphics Books: June, 1995 ($3.50, B&W, mature)

1						3.50

BUNNY (Also see Harvey Pop Comics and Fruitman Special)
Harvey Publications: Dec, 1966 - No. 20, Dec, 1971; No. 21, Nov, 1976

1-68 pg. Giants begin	7	14	21	49	92	135
2-10: 3-1st app. Fruitman. 6,8-10-Fruitman	4	8	12	28	47	65
11-18: 18-Last 68 pg. Giant	4	8	12	27	44	60
19-21-52 pg. Giants: 21-Fruitman app.	4	8	12	25	40	55

BURKE'S LAW (TV)
Dell Publ.: 1-3/64; No. 2, 5-7/64; No. 3, 3-5/65 (All have Gene Barry photo-c)

1-Photo-c	5	10	15	31	53	75
2,3-Photo-c	4	8	12	23	37	50

BURNING ROMANCES (See Fox Giants)

BUSTER BEAR
Quality Comics Group (Arnold Publ.): Dec, 1953 - No. 10, June, 1955

1-Funny animal	11	22	33	62	86	110
2	7	14	21	35	43	50
3-10	6	12	18	28	34	40
I.W. Reprint #9,10 (Super on inside)	2	4	6	9	13	16

BUSTER BROWN COMICS (See Promotional Comics section)

BUSTER BUNNY
Standard Comics(Animated Cartoons)/Pines: Nov, 1949 - No. 16, Oct, 1953

1-Frazetta 1 pg. text illo.	11	22	33	62	86	110
2	7	14	21	35	43	50
3-14,16	6	12	18	28	34	40
15-Racist-c	10	20	30	56	76	95

BUSTER CRABBE (TV)
Famous Funnies Publ.: Nov, 1951 - No. 12, 1953

1-1st app.(?) Frazetta anti-drug ad; text story about Buster Crabbe & Billy the Kid	39	78	117	236	388	540
2-Williamson/Evans-c; text story about Wild Bill Hickok & Pecos Bill	37	74	111	218	354	490
3-Williamson/Evans-c/a	39	78	117	231	378	525
4-Frazetta-c/a, 1pg.; bondage-c	47	94	141	296	498	700
5-Frazetta-c; Williamson/Krenkel/Orlando-a, 11pgs. (per Mr. Williamson)	127	254	381	807	1391	1975
6,8	19	38	57	109	172	235
7-Frazetta one pg. ad	19	38	57	111	176	240
9-One pg. Frazetta Boy Scouts ad (1st?)	15	30	45	94	147	200
10-12	12	24	36	69	97	125

NOTE: Eastern Color sold 3 dozen each NM file copies of #s 9-12 a few years ago.

BUSTER CRABBE (The Amazing Adventures of...)(Movie star)
Lev Gleason Publications: Dec, 1953 - No. 4, June, 1954

1,4: 1-Photo-c. 4-Flash Gordon-c	21	42	63	122	199	275
2,3-Toth-a	19	38	57	111	176	240

BUTCH CASSIDY
Skywald Comics: June, 1971 - No. 3, Oct, 1971 (52 pgs.)

1-Pre-code reprints and new material; Red Mask reprint, retitled Maverick; Bolle-a; Sutton-a	3	6	9	15	22	28
2,3: 2-Whip Wilson-r. 3-Dead Canyon Days reprint/Crack Western No. 63; Sundance Kid app.; Crandall-a	2	4	6	10	14	18

BUTCH CASSIDY (...& the Wild Bunch)
Avon Periodicals: 1951

1-Kinstler-c/a	20	40	60	114	182	250

NOTE: ***Reinman** story; Issue number on inside spine.*

BUTCH CASSIDY (See Fun-In No. 11 & Western Adventure Comics)

BUTCHER, THE (Also see Brave and the Bold, 2nd Series)
DC Comics: May, 1990 - No. 5, Sept, 1990 ($1.50, mature)

1-5: 1-No indicia inside						3.00

BUTCHER KNIGHT
Image Comics (Top Cow): Jan, 2001 - No. 4, June, 2001 ($2.95, limited series)

Preview (B&W, 16 pgs.) Dwayne Turner-c/a						3.00
1-4-Dwayne Turner-c/a						3.00

BUZ SAWYER (Sweeney No. 4 on)
Standard Comics: June, 1948 - No. 3, 1949

1-Roy Crane-a	28	56	84	165	270	375
2-Intro his pal Sweeney	15	30	45	88	137	185
3	12	24	36	69	97	125

BUZ SAWYER'S PAL, ROSCOE SWEENEY (See Sweeney)

BUZZ, THE (Also see Spider-Girl)
Marvel Comics: July, 2000 - No. 3, Sept, 2000 ($2.99, limited series)

1-3-Buscema-a/DeFalco & Frenz-s						3.00

BUZZARD (See The Goon)
Dark Horse Comics: Jun, 2010 - No. 3, Aug, 2010 ($3.50, limited series)

1-3-Eric Powell-c; Buzzard story w/Powell-s/a; Billy The Kid back-up; Powell-s/Hotz-a						3.50

BUZZ BUZZ COMICS MAGAZINE
Horse Press: May, 1996 ($4.95, B&W, over-sized magazine)

1-Paul Pope-c/a/scripts; Moebius-a						5.00

BUZZY (See All Funny Comics)
National Periodical Publications/Detective Comics: Winter, 1944-45 - No. 75, 1-2/57; No. 76, 10/57; No. 77, 10/58

1 (52 pgs. begin); "America's favorite teenster"	36	72	108	214	347	480
2 (Spr, 1945)	18	36	54	107	169	230
3-5	14	28	42	82	121	160
6-10	12	24	36	67	94	120
11-20	11	22	33	60	83	105
21-30	10	20	30	54	72	90
31,35-38	9	18	27	50	65	80
32-34,39-Last 52 pgs. Scribbly story by Mayer in each (these four stories were done for Scribbly #14 which was delayed for a year)	10	20	30	54	72	90
40-77: 62-Last precode (2/55)	9	18	27	47	61	75

BUZZY THE CROW (See Harvey Comics Hits #60 & 62, Harvey Hits #18 & Paramount Animated Comics #1)

BY BIZARRE HANDS
Dark Horse Comics: Apr, 1994 - No. 3, June, 1994 ($2.50, B&W, mature)

1-3: Lansdale stories						3.00

CABBOT: BLOODHUNTER (Also see Bloodstrike & Bloodstrike: Assassin)
Maximum Press: Jan, 1997 ($2.50, one-shot)

1-Rick Veitch-a/script; Platt-c; Thor, Chapel & Prophet cameos						3.00

CABLE (See Ghost Rider &..., & New Mutants #87) (Title becomes Soldier X)
Marvel Comics: May, 1993 - No. 107, Sept, 2002 ($3.50/$1.95/$1.50-$2.25)

1-($3.50, 52 pgs.)-Gold foil & embossed-c; Thibert a-1-4p; c-1-3						5.00
2-15: 3-Extra 16 pg. X-Men/Avengers ann. preview. 4-Liefeld-a assist; last Thibert-a(p). 6-8-Reveals that Baby Nathan is Cable; gives background on Stryfe. 9-Omega Red-c/story. 11-Bound-in trading card sheet						4.00

Cable #68 © MAR

The Call #1 © MAR

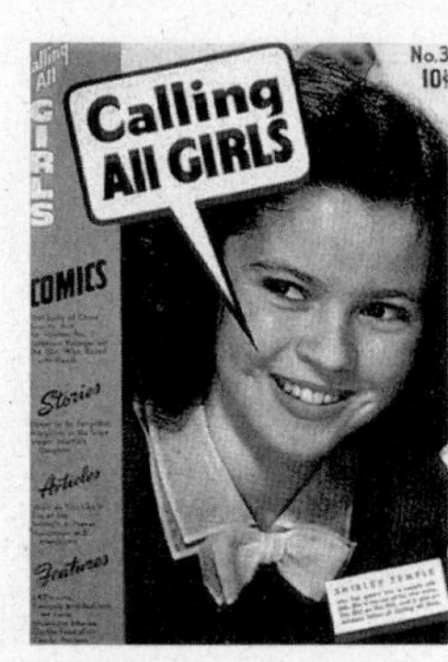

Calling All Girls #3 © PMI

GD VG FN VF VF/NM NM-
2.0 4.0 6.0 8.0 9.0 9.2

16-Newsstand edition 3.00
16-Enhanced edition 5.00
17-20-($1.95)-Deluxe edition, 20-w/bound in '95 Fleer Ultra cards 4.00
17-20-($1.50)-Standard edition 3.00
21-24, 26-44, -1(7/97): 21-Begin $1.95-c; return from Age of Apocalyse. 24-Grizzly dies. 28-vs. Sugarman; Mr. Sinister app. 30-X-Man-c/app.; Exodus app. 31-vs. X-Man. 32-Post app. 33-Post-c/app; Mandarin app (flashback); includes "Onslaught Update". 34-Onslaught x-over; Hulk-c/app; Apocalypse app. (cont'd in Hulk #444). 35-Onslaught x-over; Apocalypse vs. Cable. 36-w/card insert. 38-Weapon X-c/app; Psycho Man & Micronauts app. 40-Scott Clark-a(p). 41-Bishop-c/app. 3.00
25 ($3.95)-Foil gatefold-c 5.00
45-49,51-74: 45-Operation Zero Tolerance. 51-1st Casey-s. 54-Black Panther. 55-Domino-c/app. 62-Nick Fury-c/app.63-Stryfe-c/app. 67,68-Avengers-c/app. 71,73-Liefeld-a 3.00
50-($2.99) Double sized w/wraparound-c 4.00
75 -($2.99) Liefeld-c/a; Apocalypse: The Twelve x-over 4.00
76-79: 76-Apocalypse: The Twelve x-over 3.00
80-96: 80-Begin $2.25-c. 87-Mystique-c/app. 3.00
97-99,101-107: 97-Tischman-s/Kordey-a/c begin 3.00
100-($3.99) Dialogue-free 'Nuff Said back-up story 4.00
... Classic Vol. 1 TPB (2008, $29.99) r/#1-4, New Mutants #87, Cable: Blood & Metal #1,2 30.00
.../Machine Man '98 Annual ($2.99) Wraparound-c 4.00
.../X-Force '96 Annual ($2.95) Wraparound-c 4.00
...'99 Annual ($3.50) vs. Sinister; computer photo-c 4.00
...Second Genesis 1 (9/99, $3.99) r/New Mutants #99, 100 and X-Force #1; Liefeld-c 4.00
...: The End (2002, $14.99, TPB) r/#101-107 15.00

CABLE
Marvel Comics: May, 2008 - No. 25, Jun, 2010 ($2.99/$3.99)

1-23: 1-10-Olivetti-c/a. 1-Liefeld var-c. 2-Finch var-c. 3-Romita Jr. var-c. 4-Bishop app.; Djurdjevic var-c. 5-Silvestri var-c. 6-Liefeld var-c. 13-15-Messiah War x-over; Deadpool app. 16,17-Gulacy-a 3.00
24,25-($3.99) 24-Bishop app. 25-Deadpool app.; Medina-a 4.00

CABLE AND X-FORCE (Marvel NOW!)
Marvel Comics: Feb, 2013 - Present ($3.99)

1-19: 1-Hopeless-s/Larroca-a; Cable, Colossus, Domino, Forge & Dr. Nemesis team 4.00

CABLE - BLOOD AND METAL (Also see New Mutants #87 & X-Force #8)
Marvel Comics: Oct, 1992 - No. 2, Nov, 1992 ($2.50, limited series, 52 pgs.)

1-Fabian Nicieza scripts; John Romita, Jr.-c/a in both; Cable vs. Stryfe; 2nd app. of The Wild Pack (becomes The Six Pack); wraparound-c 5.00
2-Prelude to X-Cutioner's Song 5.00

CABLE/DEADPOOL ("Cable & Deadpool" on cover)
Marvel Comics: May, 2004 - No. 50, Apr, 2008 ($2.99)

1-49: 1-Nicieza-s/Liefeld-c. 7-9-X-Men app. 17-House of M. 21-Heroes For Hire app. 30,31-Civil War. 30-Great Lakes Avengers app. 33-Liefeld-c. 43,44-Wolverine app. 3.00
50-($3.99) Final issue; Spider-Man and the Avengers app. 4.00
Cable & Deadpool MCG 1 (7/11, $1.00) r/#1 with "Marvel's Greatest Comics" cover logo 3.00
... Vol. 1: If Looks Could Kill TPB (2004, $14.99) r/#1-6 15.00
... Vol. 2: The Burnt Offering TPB (2005, $14.99) r/#7-12 15.00
... Vol. 3: The Human Race TPB (2005, $14.99) r/#13-18 15.00
... Vol. 4: Bosom Buddies TPB (2006, $14.99) r/#19-24 15.00
... Vol. 5: Living Legends TPB (2006, $13.99) r/#25-29 14.00
... Vol. 6: Paved With Good Intentions TPB (2007, $14.99) r/#30-35 15.00
... Vol. 7: Separation Anxiety TPB (2007, $17.99) r/#36-42; sketch pages 18.00
Deadpool Vs. The Marvel Universe TPB (2008, $24.99) r/#43-50 25.00

CADET GRAY OF WEST POINT (See Dell Giants)

CADILLACS & DINOSAURS (TV)
Marvel Comics (Epic Comics): Nov, 1990 - No. 6, Apr, 1991 ($2.50, limited series)

1-6: r/Xenozoic Tales in color w/new-c 3.00
...In 3-D #1 (7/92, $3.95, Kitchen Sink)-With glasses 6.00

CADILLACS AND DINOSAURS (TV)
Topps Comics: V2#1, Feb, 1994 - V2#9, 1995 ($2.50, limited series)

V2#1-($2.95)-Collector's edition w/Stout-c & bound-in poster; Buckler-a; foil stamped logo; Giordano-a in all 6.00
V2#1-9: 1-Newsstand edition w/Giordano-c. 2,3-Collector's editions w/Stout-c & posters. 2,3-Newsstand ed. w/Giordano-c; w/o posters. 4-6-Collectors & Newsstand editions; Kieth-c. 7-9-Linsner-c 3.00

CAGE (Also see Hero for Hire, Power Man & Punisher)
Marvel Comics: Apr, 1992 - No. 20, Nov, 1993 ($1.25)

1,3,10,12: 3-Punisher-c & minor app. 10-Rhino & Hulk-c/app. 12-(52 pgs.)-Iron Fist app. 4.00
2,4-9,11,13-20: 9-Rhino-c/story; Hulk cameo 3.00

GD VG FN VF VF/NM NM-
2.0 4.0 6.0 8.0 9.0 9.2

CAGE (Volume 3)
Marvel Comics (MAX): Mar, 2002 - No. 5, Sept, 2002 ($2.99, mature)

1-5-Corben-c/a; Azzarello-s 3.00
HC (2002, $19.99, with dustjacket) r/#1-5; intro. by Darius James; sketch pages 20.00
SC (2003, $13.99) r/#1-5; intro. by Darius James 14.00

CAGED HEAT 3000 (Movie)
Roger Corman's Cosmic Comics: Nov, 1995 - No. 3, Jan, 1996 ($2.50)

1-3: Adaptation of film 3.00

CAGES
Tundra Publ.: 1991 - No. 10, May, 1996 ($3.50/$3.95/$4.95, limited series)

1-Dave McKean-c/a in all 2 4 6 8 10 12
2-Misprint exists 1 2 3 5 6 8
3-9: 5-$3.95-c begins 4.00
10-($4.95) 5.00

CAIN'S HUNDRED (TV)
Dell Publishing Co.: May-July, 1962 - No. 2, Sept-Nov, 1962

nn(01-094-207) 3 6 9 19 30 40
2 3 6 9 15 22 28

CAIN/VAMPIRELLA FLIP BOOK
Harris Comics: Oct, 1994 ($6.95, one-shot, squarebound)

nn-contains Cain #3 & #4; flip book is r/Vampirella story from 1993 Creepy Fearbook 1 2 3 5 7 9

CALIBAN
Avatar Press: Mar, 2014 - Present ($3.99)

1-Garth Ennis-s/Facundo Percio-a 4.00

CALIBER PRESENTS
Caliber Press: Jan, 1989 - No. 24, 1991 ($1.95/$2.50, B&W, 52 pgs.)

1-Anthology; 1st app. The Crow; Tim Vigil-c/a 6 12 18 37 66 95
2-Deadworld story; Tim Vigil-a 2 4 6 10 14 18
3-24: 15-24 ($3.50, 68 pgs.) 4.00

CALIBER PRESENTS: CINDERELLA ON FIRE
Caliber Press: 1994 ($2.95, B&W, mature)

1 3.00

CALIBER SPOTLIGHT
Caliber Press: May, 1995 ($2.95, B&W)

1-Kabuki app 3.50

CALIFORNIA GIRLS
Eclipse Comics: June, 1987 - No. 8, May, 1988 ($2.00, 40 pgs, B&W)

1-8: All contain color paper dolls 4.00

CALL, THE
Marvel Comics: June, 2003 - No. 4, Sept, 2003 ($2.25)

1-4-Austen-s/Olliffe-a 3.00

CALLING ALL BOYS (Tex Granger No. 18 on)
Parents' Magazine Institute: Jan, 1946 - No. 17, May, 1948 (Photo c-1-5,7,8)

1 15 30 45 90 140 190
2-Contains Roy Rogers article 10 20 30 56 76 95
3-7,9,11,14-17: 6-Painted-c. 11-Rin Tin Tin photo on-c; Tex Granger begins. 14-J. Edgar Hoover photo on-c. 15-Tex Granger-c begin 8 16 24 44 57 70
8-Milton Caniff story 10 20 30 56 76 95
10-Gary Cooper photo on-c 10 20 30 56 76 95
12-Bob Hope photo on-c 15 30 45 83 124 165
13-Bing Crosby photo on-c 14 28 42 76 108 140

CALLING ALL GIRLS
Parents' Magazine Institute: Sept, 1941 - No. 89, Sept, 1949 (Part magazine, part comic)

1 23 46 69 136 223 310
2-Photo-c 13 26 39 74 105 135
3-Shirley Temple photo-c 17 34 51 98 154 210
4-10: 4,5,7,9-Photo-c. 9-Flag-c 11 22 33 64 90 115
11-Tina Thayer photo-c; Mickey Rooney photo-b/c; B&W photo inside of Gary Cooper as Lou Gehrig in "Pride of Yankees" 14 28 42 76 108 140
12-20 10 20 30 54 72 90
21-39,41-43(10-11/45)-Last issue with comics 9 18 27 50 65 80
40-Liz Taylor photo-c 26 52 78 154 252 350
44-51(7/46)-Last comic book size issue 8 16 24 42 54 65
52-89 7 14 21 37 46 55

NOTE: ***Jack Sparling** art in many issues; becomes a girls' magazine "Senior Prom" with #90.*

The Call of Duty: The Wagon #1 © MAR

Camp Comics #2 © WHIT

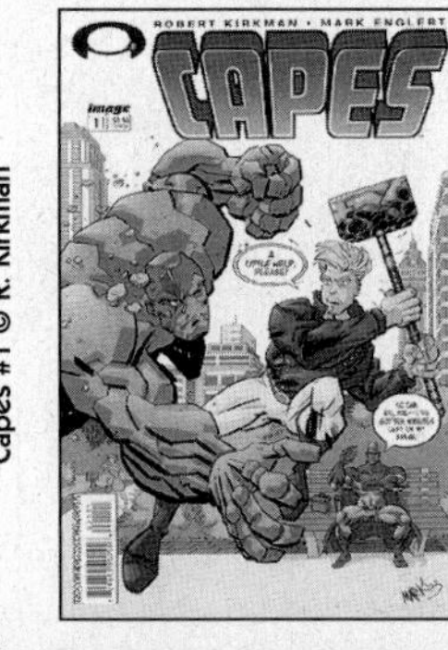

Capes #1 © R. Kirkman

CALLING ALL KIDS (Also see True Comics)
Parents' Magazine Institute: Dec-Jan, 1945-46 - No. 26, Aug, 1949

	GD 2.0	VG 4.0	FN 6.0	VF 8.0	VF/NM 9.0	NM- 9.2
1-Funny animal	15	30	45	90	140	190
2	10	20	30	54	72	90
3-10	8	16	24	44	57	70
11-26	8	16	24	40	50	60

CALL OF DUTY, THE : THE BROTHERHOOD
Marvel Comics: Aug, 2002 - No. 6, Jan, 2003 ($2.25)

	GD 2.0	VG 4.0	FN 6.0	VF 8.0	VF/NM 9.0	NM- 9.2
1-Exploits of NYC Fire Dept.; Finch-c/a; Austen & Bruce Jones-s						4.00
2-6-Austen-s						3.00
...Vol 1: The Brotherhood & The Wagon TPB (2002, $14.99) r/#1-6 & ...The Wagon #1-4						15.00

CALL OF DUTY, THE : THE PRECINCT
Marvel Comics: Sept, 2002 - No. 5, Jan, 2003 ($2.25, limited series)

	GD 2.0	VG 4.0	FN 6.0	VF 8.0	VF/NM 9.0	NM- 9.2
1-Exploits of NYC Police Dept.; Finch-c; Bruce Jones-s/Mandrake-a						3.00
2-4						3.00
...Vol 2: The Precinct TPB (2003, $9.99) r/#1-4						10.00

CALL OF DUTY, THE : THE WAGON
Marvel Comics: Oct, 2002 - No. 4, Jan, 2003 ($2.25, limited series)

	GD 2.0	VG 4.0	FN 6.0	VF 8.0	VF/NM 9.0	NM- 9.2
1-4-Exploits of NYC EMS Dept.; Finch-c; Austen-s/Zelzej-a						3.00

CALVIN (See Li'l Kids)

CALVIN & THE COLONEL (TV)
Dell Publishing Co.: No. 1354, Apr-June, 1962 - No. 2, July-Sept, 1962

	GD 2.0	VG 4.0	FN 6.0	VF 8.0	VF/NM 9.0	NM- 9.2
Four Color 1354(#1) (The last Four Color issue)	8	16	24	51	96	140
2	5	10	15	35	63	90

CAMELOT 3000
DC Comics: Dec, 1982 - No. 11, July, 1984; No. 12, Apr, 1985 (Direct sales, maxi series, Mando paper)

	GD 2.0	VG 4.0	FN 6.0	VF 8.0	VF/NM 9.0	NM- 9.2
1-12: 1-Mike Barr scripts & Brian Bolland-c/a begin. 5-Intro Knights of New Camelot						5.00
TPB (1988, $12.95) r/#1-12						15.00
...: The Deluxe Edition (2008, $34.99, HC) r/#1-12; oversized & recolored; Barr intro.; design and promotional art; original proposal page						40.00

NOTE: ***Austin** a-7i-12i. **Bolland** a-1-12p; c-1-12.*

CAMERA COMICS
U.S. Camera Publishing Corp./ME: July, 1944 - No. 9, Summer, 1946

	GD 2.0	VG 4.0	FN 6.0	VF 8.0	VF/NM 9.0	NM- 9.2
nn (7/44)	27	54	81	162	266	370
nn (9/44)	20	40	60	118	192	265
1(10/44)-The Grey Comet (slightly smaller page size than subsequent issues)	21	42	63	124	202	280
2-16 pgs. of photos with 32 pgs. of comics	15	30	45	85	130	175
3-Nazi WW II-c; photos	17	34	51	100	158	215
4-9: All 1/3 photos	14	28	42	78	112	145

CAMP CANDY (TV)
Marvel Comics: May, 1990 - No. 6, Oct, 1990 ($1.00, limited series)

	GD 2.0	VG 4.0	FN 6.0	VF 8.0	VF/NM 9.0	NM- 9.2
1-6: Post-c/a(p); featuring John Candy						5.00

CAMP COMICS
Dell Publishing Co.: Feb, 1942 - No. 3, April, 1942 (All have photo-c)(All issues are scarce)

	GD 2.0	VG 4.0	FN 6.0	VF 8.0	VF/NM 9.0	NM- 9.2
1- "Seaman Sy Wheeler" by Kelly, 7 pgs.; Bugs Bunny app.; Mark Twain adaptation	81	162	243	518	884	1250
2-Kelly-a, 12 pgs.; Bugs Bunny app.; classic-c	81	162	243	518	884	1250
3-(Scarce)-Dave Berg & Walt Kelly-a	61	122	183	390	670	950

CAMP RUNAMUCK (TV)
Dell Publishing Co.: Apr, 1966

	GD 2.0	VG 4.0	FN 6.0	VF 8.0	VF/NM 9.0	NM- 9.2
1-Photo-c	3	6	9	21	33	45

CAMPUS LOVES
Quality Comics Group (Comic Magazines): Dec, 1949 - No. 5, Aug, 1950

	GD 2.0	VG 4.0	FN 6.0	VF 8.0	VF/NM 9.0	NM- 9.2
1-Ward-c/a (9 pgs.)	36	72	108	216	351	485
2-Ward-c/a	27	54	81	158	259	360
3-5	15	30	45	84	127	170

NOTE: ***Gustavson** a-1-5. Photo c-3-5.*

CAMPUS ROMANCE (...Romances on cover)
Avon Periodicals/Realistic: Sept-Oct, 1949 - No. 3, Feb-Mar, 1950

	GD 2.0	VG 4.0	FN 6.0	VF 8.0	VF/NM 9.0	NM- 9.2
1-Walter Johnson-a; c-/Avon paperback #348	36	72	108	211	343	475
2-Grandenetti-a; c-/Avon paperback #151	25	50	75	147	241	335
3-c-/Avon paperback #201	25	50	75	147	241	335
Realistic reprint	15	30	45	86	133	180

CANADA DRY PREMIUMS (See Swamp Fox, The & Terry & The Pirates in the Promotional Comics section)

CANCELLED COMIC CAVALCADE (See the Promotional Comics section)

CANDID TALES (Also see Bold Stories & It Rhymes With Lust)
Kirby Publ. Co.: April, 1950; June, 1950 (Digest size) (144 pgs.) (Full color)

	GD 2.0	VG 4.0	FN 6.0	VF 8.0	VF/NM 9.0	NM- 9.2
nn-(Scarce) Contains Wood female pirate story, 15 pgs., and 14 pgs. in June issue; Powell-a	155	310	465	992	1696	2400

NOTE: *Another version exists with Dr. Kilmore by Wood; no female pirate story.*

CANDY (Teen-age)(Also see Police Comics #37)
Quality Comics Group (Comic Magazines): Autumn, 1947 - No. 64, Jul, 1956

	GD 2.0	VG 4.0	FN 6.0	VF 8.0	VF/NM 9.0	NM- 9.2
1-Gustavson-a	25	50	75	150	245	340
2-Gustavson-a	15	30	45	84	127	170
3-10	11	22	33	60	83	105
11-30	9	18	27	47	61	75
31-64: 64-Ward-c(p)?	8	16	24	40	50	60
Super Reprint No. 2,10,12,16,17,18('63- '64):17-Candy #12	2	4	6	10	14	18

NOTE: ***Jack Cole** 1-2 pg. art in many issues.*

CANDY COMICS
William H. Wise & Co.: Fall, 1944 - No. 3, Spring, 1945

	GD 2.0	VG 4.0	FN 6.0	VF 8.0	VF/NM 9.0	NM- 9.2
1-Two Scoop Scuttle stories by Wolverton	39	78	117	240	395	550
2,3-Scoop Scuttle by Wolverton, 2-4 pgs.	26	52	78	154	252	350

CANNON (See Heroes, Inc. Presents Cannon)

CANNON: DAWN OF WAR (Michael Turner's...)
Aspen MLT, Inc.: Nov, 2004 ($2.99)

	GD 2.0	VG 4.0	FN 6.0	VF 8.0	VF/NM 9.0	NM- 9.2
1-Turnbull-a; two covers by Turnbull and Turner						3.00

CANNONBALL COMICS
Rural Home Publishing Co.: Feb, 1945 - No. 2, Mar, 1945

	GD 2.0	VG 4.0	FN 6.0	VF 8.0	VF/NM 9.0	NM- 9.2
1-The Crash Kid, Thunderbrand, The Captive Prince & Crime Crusader begin; skull-c	116	232	348	742	1271	1800
2-Devil-c	87	174	261	553	952	1350

CANTEEN KATE (See All Picture All True Love Story & Fightin' Marines)
St. John Publishing Co.: June, 1952 - No. 3, Nov, 1952

	GD 2.0	VG 4.0	FN 6.0	VF 8.0	VF/NM 9.0	NM- 9.2
1-Matt Baker-c/a	77	154	231	493	847	1200
2-Matt Baker-c/a	49	98	147	309	522	735
3-(Rare)-Used in **POP**, pg. 75; Baker-c/a	57	114	171	362	619	875

CAPE, THE
IDW Publishing: Dec, 2010; Jul, 2011 - No. 4, Jan, 2012 ($3.99)

	GD 2.0	VG 4.0	FN 6.0	VF 8.0	VF/NM 9.0	NM- 9.2
1-(12/10) Zach Howard-c/a; Jason Ciaramella-s						4.00
1-4: 1-(7/11) Story continues from 12/10 issue						4.00
...: Legacy Edition (6/11, $5.99) r/#1 (12/10) with Joe Hill's original short story						6.00
...: 1969 (7/12 - No. 4, 10/12, $3.99) 1-4-Ciaramella-s; origin in Vietnam						4.00

CAPER
DC Comics: Dec, 2003 - No. 12, Nov, 2004 ($2.95, limited series)

	GD 2.0	VG 4.0	FN 6.0	VF 8.0	VF/NM 9.0	NM- 9.2
1-12: 1-4-Judd Winick-s/Farel Dalrymple-a. 5-8-John Severin-a. 9-12-Fowler-a						3.00

CAPES
Image Comics: Sept, 2003 - No. 3, Nov, 2003 ($3.50)

	GD 2.0	VG 4.0	FN 6.0	VF 8.0	VF/NM 9.0	NM- 9.2
1-3-Robert Kirkman-s/Mark Englert-a/c						3.50

CAP'N QUICK & A FOOZLE (Also see Eclipse Mag. & Monthly)
Eclipse Comics: July, 1984 - No. 3, Nov, 1985 ($1.50, color, Baxter paper)

	GD 2.0	VG 4.0	FN 6.0	VF 8.0	VF/NM 9.0	NM- 9.2
1-3-Rogers-c/a						3.00

CAPTAIN ACTION (Toy)
National Periodical Publications: Oct-Nov, 1968 - No. 5, June-July, 1969 (Based on Ideal toy)

	GD 2.0	VG 4.0	FN 6.0	VF 8.0	VF/NM 9.0	NM- 9.2
1-Origin; Wally Wood-a; Superman-c app.	6	12	18	38	69	100
2,3,5-Gil Kane/Wally Wood-a	5	10	15	31	53	75
4- Gil Kane-c	4	8	12	27	44	60

CAPTAIN ACTION COMICS (Toy)
Moonstone: No. 0, 2008 - Present (Based on the Ideal toy)

	GD 2.0	VG 4.0	FN 6.0	VF 8.0	VF/NM 9.0	NM- 9.2
0-($1.99) Origin re-told; Sparacio-a; three covers; character history by Michael Eury						3.00
1-5: 1-($3.99) Sparacio-a; intro. by Jim Shooter						4.00
... Comics Special 1 (2010, $5.99) 3 covers by Barreto, Ordway & Spiegle						6.00
... Exclusive Special 1 (2011, no price) Gulacy-c; Barreto-a						4.00
...: First Mission, Last Day (2008, $3.99) origin story re-told; Nicieza-s/Procopio-a						4.00
... King Size Special 1 (2011, $6.99) 1-Covers by Byrne, Wheatley & M. Benes						7.00
... Season 2 (2010, $3.99) 1-3: 1-Covers by Allred & Texiera; Obama app.						4.00
... Winter Special (2011, $4.99) Green Hornet & Kato on-c & text story						5.00

CAPTAIN AERO COMICS (Samson No. 1-6; also see Veri Best Sure Fire & Veri Best Sure Shot Comics)

Captain Aero Comics V2 #2 © HOKE

Captain America #115 © MAR

Captain America #234 © MAR

GD VG FN VF VF/NM NM-
2.0 4.0 6.0 8.0 9.0 9.2

Holyoke Publishing Co.: V1#7(#1), Dec, 1941 - V2#4(#10), Jan, 1943; V3#9(#11), Sept, 1943 -V4#3(#17), Oct, 1944; #21, Dec, 1944 - #26, Aug, 1946 (No #18-20)

V1#7(#1)-Flag-Man & Solar, Master of Magic, Captain Aero, Cap Stone, Adventurer begin; Nazi WWII-c 187 374 561 1197 2049 2900
8,10: 8(#2)-Pals of Freedom app. 10(#4)-Origin The Gargoyle; Kubert-a 94 188 282 597 1024 1450
9(#3)-Hitler-sty; Catman back-c; Alias X begins; Pals of Freedom app.; Nazi WWII-c 106 212 318 673 1162 1650
11,12(#5,6)-Kubert-a; Miss Victory in #6 74 148 222 470 810 1150
V2#1,2(#7,8): 8-Origin The Red Cross; Miss Victory app.; Brodsky-c(i) 52 104 156 328 557 785
3(#9)-Miss Victory app. 65 130 195 416 708 1000
4(#10)-Miss Victory app.; Japanese WWII-c 53 106 159 334 567 800
V3#9 - V3#12(#11-14): All Quinlan Japanese WWII-c. 9-Miss Victory app. 50 100 150 315 533 750
V3#13(#15),V4#2(#16): Schomburg Japanese WWII-c. 13-Miss Victory app. 58 116 174 371 636 900
V4#3(#17), 21-24-L. B. Cole Japanese WWII covers. 22-Intro/origin Mighty Mite. 54 108 162 343 574 825
25-L. B. Cole SciFi-c 61 122 183 390 670 950
26-L. B. Cole SciFi-c; Palais-a(2) (scarce) 181 362 543 1158 1979 2800
NOTE: *L.B. Cole c-17, 21-26. Hollingsworth a-23. Infantino a-23, 26. Schomburg c-15, 16.*

CAPTAIN AMERICA (See Adventures of..., All-Select, All Winners, Aurora, Avengers #4, Blood and Glory, Captain Britain 16-20, Giant-Size..., The Invaders, Marvel Double Feature, Marvel Fanfare, Marvel Mystery, Marvel Super-Action, Marvel Super Heroes V2#3, Marvel Team-Up, Marvel Treasury Special, Power Record Comics, Ultimates, USA Comics, Young Allies & Young Men)

CAPTAIN AMERICA (Formerly Tales of Suspense #1-99) (Captain America and the Falcon #134-223 & Steve Rogers: Captain America #444-454 appears on cover only)
Marvel Comics Group: No. 100, Apr, 1968 - No. 454, Aug, 1996

100-Flashback on Cap's revival with Avengers & Sub-Mariner; story continued from Tales of Suspense #99; Kirby-c/a begins 29 58 87 209 467 725
101-The Sleeper-c/story; Red Skull app. 9 18 27 57 111 165
102-104: 102-Sleeper-c/s. 103,104-Red Skull-c/sty 7 14 21 48 89 130
105-108: 107-Red Skull & Hitler-c 6 12 18 37 66 95
109-Origin Capt. America retold in detail 8 16 24 54 102 150
109-2nd printing (1994) 2 4 6 8 10 12
110-Rick Jones dons Bucky's costume & becomes Cap's partner; Hulk x-over; Steranko-a Classic Steranko-c 9 18 27 62 126 190
111,113-Classic Steranko-c/a: 111-Death of Steve Rogers. 113-Cap's funeral; Avengers app. 9 18 27 57 111 165
112-S.A. recovery retold; last Kirby-c/a 6 12 18 37 66 95
114-116,119,120: 114-Red Skull Cosmic Cube story. 115,116-Red Skull app; last 12c issue. 119-Cap vs. Red Skull; Cosmic Cube "destroyed"; Falcon app. 4 8 12 28 47 65
117-1st app. The Falcon (9/69) 15 30 45 103 227 350
118-2nd app. The Falcon 7 14 21 44 82 120
121-136,139,140: 121-Retells origin; Avengers app. 122-Cap vs. Scorpion. 124-Modok app. 125-Mandarin app. 129-Red Skull app. 133-The Falcon becomes Cap's partner; origin Modok. 139,140-Grey Gargoyle app; origin in #140 3 6 9 21 33 45
137,138-Spider-Man x-over 4 8 12 25 40 55
141,142-Grey Gargoyle app. 141-Last Stan Lee issue. 142-Last 15¢ issue 3 6 9 17 26 35
143-(52 pgs) Cap vs. Red Skull 3 6 9 21 33 45
144-New costume Falcon 3 6 9 17 26 35
145-152: 145-147-Cap vs. the Supreme Hydra. 148-Red Skull app. 151,152- Cap vs. Mr. Hyde 3 6 9 14 20 25
153-155: 153-1st brief app. Jack Monroe; return of 1950s Captain America. 154-1st full app. Jack Monroe (Nomad); 1950s Captain America and Avengers app. 155-Origin retold; origin Jack Monroe and the 1950s Captain America 3 6 9 19 30 40
156-Cap vs. the 1950s Captain America; Jack Monroe app; classic Cap vs Cap cover 3 6 9 16 23 30
157-170,177-179: 160-1st app. Solarr. 163-1st Serpent Squad: Viper, Eel and Cobra. 164-1st Nightshade. 165-167-Cap vs. Yellow Claw. 168-1st Helmut Zemo (as the Phoenix). 169,170-Vs. original Moonstone 2 4 6 9 12 15
171-Black Panther app. 2 4 6 12 16 20
172,173: X-Men x-over 3 6 9 16 23 30
174,175: X-Men x-over 2 4 6 18 22 25
176-End of Cap. Avengers app. 2 4 6 13 18 22
180-Intro/origin of Nomad (Steve Rogers) 3 6 9 15 22 28
181-Intro/origin new Cap. 2 4 6 11 16 20
182,184,185,187-192: 182,184,185-Red Skull app. 189,190-Cap vs. Nightshade. 191-Iron Man app. 192-Intro Dr. Karla Sofen (later becomes Moonstone) 2 4 6 8 10 12
183-Death of new Cap; Steve Rogers drops Nomad I.D; returns to being Capt. America 2 4 6 9 12 15
186-True origin The Falcon; Red Skull app. 2 4 6 9 12 15
193-Kirby-c/a begins 2 4 6 13 18 22
194-199-(Regular 25¢ edition)(4-7/76) 2 4 6 10 14 18
196-199-(30¢-c variants, limited distribution) 5 10 15 30 50 70
200-(Regular 25¢ edition)(8/76) 2 4 6 11 16 20
200-(30¢-c variant, limited distribution) 5 10 15 33 57 80
201-214-Kirby-c/a. 208-1st Arnim Zola. 209,210- Arnim Zola app. 210-212 –vs Red Skull 2 4 6 8 11 14
210-214-(35¢-c variants, limited dist.)(6-10/77) 6 12 18 38 69 100
215,216,218-229: 215-Origin retold. 216-r/Strange Tales #114. 226,227-Red Skull app. 228-Cap vs. Constrictor. 229-Marvel Man app. 1 2 4 5 6 9
217-Intro. Marvel Boy (Wendell Vaughan); becomes Marvel Man in #218; later becomes Quasar (2/78) 2 4 6 9 12 15
230,235: 230-Battles Hulk-c/story cont'd in Inc. Hulk #232. 235-(7/79) Daredevil x-over; Miller-a(p) 1 2 4 5 7 10
231-233,236-240,242-246: 233-"Death" of Sharon Carter. 244,245-Miller-c 1 2 3 4 5 7
234-Daredevil app. 1 2 3 4 6 8
241-Punisher app.; Miller-c 3 6 9 21 33 45
241-2nd print 4.00
247-252-Byrne-a 1 3 4 6 8 10
253,255: 253-Byrne-a; Baron Blood app. 255-Origin retold; Miller-c 2 4 6 8 11 14
254-Byrne-a; death of Baron Blood; intro new Union Jack 2 4 6 9 12 16
256-262: 257-Hulk app. 258-Zeck-a begins. 259-Cap vs. Dr. Octopus. 261,262-Red Skull app. 5.00
263-266: 263-Red Skull-c/story. 264-Original X-Men app. 265,266-Spider-Man app. 6.00
267-280: 267-1st app. Everyman. 268-Defenders app. 269-1st Team America. 272-1st Vermin. 273,274-Baron Strucker. 275-1st Baron Zemo (formally the Phoenix). 276-278-Cap vs. Baron Zemo. 279-(3/83)-Contains Tattooz skin decals. 280-Scarecrow app. 5.00
281-1950's Bucky returns. Spider-Woman and Viper app. 1 2 3 4 6 8
282-Bucky becomes new Nomad (Jack Monroe) **1** **3** **4** **6** 8 10
282-Silver ink 2nd print ($1.75) w/original date (6/83) 3.00
283-Cap vs. Viper 5.00
284,285,289,291-300: 284-Patriot (Jack Mace) app. 285-Death of Patriot. 293,294-Nomad app. 293-299-Red Skull and Baron Zemo app. 298-Origin Red Skull. 300- "Death" of Red Skull. 4.00
286-288-Deathlok app. 5.00
290-1st Mother Superior (Red Skull's daughter, later becomes Sin) 1 2 3 4 6 8
301-304,307-318,322,324-326,328-331: 301-Avengers app. 307-1st Madcap; 1st Mark Gruenwald-s (begins 8-year run). 308-Secret Wars II x-over. 310-1st Serpent Society. 312-1st Flag Smasher. 313-Death of Modok. 314-Squadron Supreme x-over. 317-Hawkeye & Mockingbird app. 318-Scourge app; death of Blue Streak and Adder. 322-Cap vs. Flag Smasher. 325-Nomad app. 328,330-Demolition Man (D-Man) app. 3.00
305,306-Captain Britain app. 4.00
319-321,327: 319-Scourge kills numerous villians 320-"Death"of Scourge. 321-Cap vs. Flag Smasher; classic Zeck cover Cap with machine gun. 327-Cap vs Super-Patriot 4.00
323-1st app. new Super-Patriot (see Nick Fury) 5.00
332-Old Captain America resigns 1 3 4 6 8 10
333-340; 333- Super Patriot becomes new Cap. 334-Intro new Bucky; Freedom Force app. 337-Serpent Society app; Avengers #4 homage-c; Steve Rogers becomes 'the Captain'; becomes Captain America again in issue #350. 339-Fall of the Mutants tie-in 4.00
341-343,345-349: 341-Cap vs Iron Man; x-over with Iron Man #228. 342-Cap vs. Viper and the Serpent Squad 3.00
344-($1.50, 52 pgs.)-Ronald Reagan cameo as a snake man 4.00
350-($1.75, 68 pgs.)-Return of Steve Rogers (original Cap) to original costume 6.00
351-382,384-396: 351-Nick Fury app. 357-Bloodstone hunt Pt. 1 (of 6). 358-359 Baron Zemo app. 365,366-Acts of Vengeance x-overs. 367-Magneto vs Red Skull. 372-378-Streets of Poison. 374-Bullseye app. 375-Daredevil app. 376-Black Widow app. 377-Bullseye vs. Crossbones; Red Skull app. 379-Quasar app. 380-382-Serpent Society app. 386-U.S. Agent app. 387-392-Superia Stratagem. 387-389-Red Skull back-up stories. 394-Red Skull app. 395-Thor app. (Eric Masterson; also in 396-397); Red Skull app. 396-Red Skull and new (1st) Jack O Lantern app; last $1.00-c 3.00
360-1st app. Crossbones; Baron Zemo app. 2 4 6 11 16 20
383-($2.00, 68 pgs., squarebound)-50th anniversary issue; Red Skull story; Jim Lee-c(i) 5.00
397-399,401-424,425: 397-New Jack O Lantern app. 398,399-Operation Galactic Storm x-overs. 401-Operation Galactic storm epilogue. 402-Begin 6 part Man-Wolf story w/Wolverine in #403-407. 405-410-New Jack O Lantern app. in back-up story. 406-Cable

Captain America #431 © MAR

Captain America V3 #5 © MAR

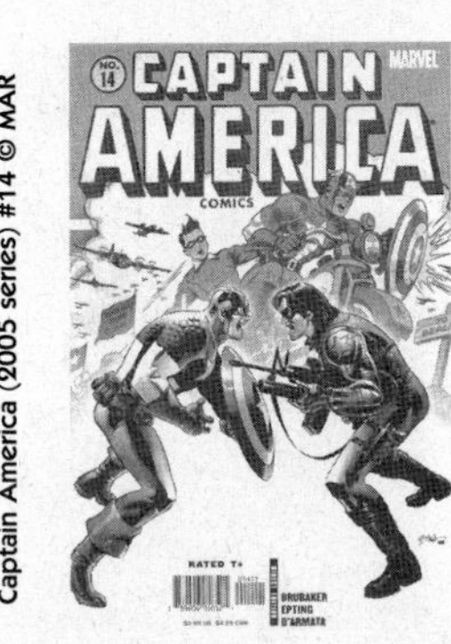

Captain America (2005 series) #14 © MAR

GD 2.0 | VG 4.0 | FN 6.0 | VF 8.0 | VF/NM 9.0 | NM- 9.2

& Shatterstar cameo. 407-Capwolf vs. Cable-c/story. 408-Infinity War x-over; Falcon back-up story. 409-Red Skull & Crossbones app. 410-Crossbones app. 414-Black Panther app. 419-Red Skull app; x-over with Silver Sable #15. 423- Cap vs. Namor-c/story 3.00
400-($2.25, 84 pgs.) Flip book format w/double gatefold-c; Operation Galactic Storm x-over; r/Avengers #4 plus-c contains cover pin-ups 1 2 3 5 6 8
425-($2.95, 52 pgs.)-Embossed Foil-c edition; Fighting Chance Pt. 1 4.00
425-($1.75, 52 pgs.)-non-embossed-c edition; Fighting Chance Pt. 1 5.00
426-439,442,443: 426-437-Fighting Chance Pt. 2-12. 427-Begins $1.50-c; bound-in trading card sheet. 428-1st Americop. 431-1st Free Spirit. 434-1st Jack Flag. 438-Fighting Chance epilogue. 443-Last Gruenwald issue 4.00
440,441-Avengers x-overs; 'Taking A.I.M" story 5.00
444-Mark Waid scripts & Ron Garney-c/a(p) begins, ends #454; Avengers app. 5.00
445-Operation rebirth Pt.1; vs Red Skull; Sharon Carter returns 5.00
446,447 – Operation Rebirth; Red Skull app. 446-Hitler app. 6.00
448-($2.95, double-sized issue) Waid script & Garney-c/a; Red Skull "dies" 5.00
449-Thor app; story x-overs with Thor, Iron Man and Avengers titles 5.00
450- "Man Without a Country" begins; Steve Rogers-c 4.00
450-Captain America-c with white background 6.00
451-453: 451-1st app. Cap's new costume. 453-Cap gets old costume back; Bill Clinton app. 4.00
454-Last issue of the regular series (8/96) 5.00
#600-up (See Captain America 2005 series, resumed original numbering after #50)
Special 1(1/71)-All reprint issue from Tales Of Suspense #63,69,70,71,75 5 10 15 34 60 85
Special 2(1/72, 52 pgs.)-All reprint issue from Tales Of Suspense #72-74 and Not Brand Echh #5 4 8 12 23 37 50
Annual 3('76, 52 pgs.)-Kirby-c/a(new) 3 6 9 16 23 30
Annual 4('77, 34 pgs.)-Magneto-c/story 3 6 9 16 23 30
Annual 5-7: (52 pgs.)('81-'83) 5.00
Annual 8(9/86)-Wolverine-c/story 3 6 9 19 30 40
Annual 9-13('90-'94, 68 pgs.)-9-Nomad back-up. 10-Origin retold (2 pgs.). 11-Falcon solo story. 12-Bagged w/card. 13-Red Skull-c/story 4.00
...Ashcan Edition ('95, 75¢) 3.00
... and the Falcon: Madbomb TPB (2004, $16.99) r/#193-200; Kirby-s/a 17.00
... and the Falcon: Nomad TPB (2006, $24.99) r/#177-186; Cap becomes Nomad 25.00
... and the Falcon: Secret Empire TPB (2005, $19.99) r/#169-176 20.00
... and the Falcon: The Swine TPB (2006, $29.99) r/#206-214 & Annual #3,4 30.00
... By Jack Kirby: Bicentennial Battles TPB (2005, $19.99) r/#201-205 & Marvel Treasury Special Featuring Captain America's Bicentennial Battles; Kirby-s/a 20.00
...: Deathlok Lives! nn(10/93, $4.95)-r/#286-288 6.00
...Drug War 1-(1994, $2.00, 52 pgs.)-New Warriors app. 4.00
...Man Without a Country(1998, $12.99, TPB)-r/#450-453 13.00
...Medusa Effect 1 (1994, $2.95, 68 pgs.)-Origin Baron Zemo 4.00
...Operation Rebirth (1996, $9.95)-r/#445-448 10.00
... 65th Anniversary Special (5/06, $3.99) WWII flashback with Bucky; Brubaker-s 5.00
...Streets of Poison ($15.95)-r/#372-378 16.00
...: The Movie Special nn (5/92, $3.50, 52 pgs.)-Adapts movie; printed on coated stock; The Red Skull app. 4.00

NOTE: ***Austin** c-225i, 239i, 246i. **Buscema** a-115p, 217p; c-136p, 217, 297. **Byrne** c-223(part), 238, 239, 247p-254p, 290, 291, 313p; a-247-254p, 255, 313p, 350. **Colan** a(p)-116-137, 256, Annual 5; c(p)-116-123, 126, 129. **Everett** a-136i, 137i; c-126i. **Garney** a(p)-444-454. **Gil Kane** a-145p; c-147p, 149p, 150p, 170p, 172-174, 180, 181p, 183-190p, 215, 216, 220, 221. **Kirby** a(p)-100-109, 112, 193-214, 216, Special 1, 2(layouts), Annual 3, 4; c-100-109, 112, 126p, 193-214. **Ron Lim** a(p)-366, 368-378, 380-386; c-366p, 368-378p, 379, 380-393p. **Miller** c-241p, 244p, 245p, 255p, Annual 5. **Mooney** a-149i. **Morrow** a-144. **Perez** c-243p, 246p. **Robbins** c(p)-183-187, 189-192, 225. **Roussos** a-140i, 168i. **Shores** a-102i, 107i, 109i. **Starlin/Sinnott** c-162. **Sutton** a-244i. **Tuska** a-112i, 215p, Special 2. **Waid** scripts-444-454. **Williamson** a-313i. **Wood** a-127i. **Zeck** a-263-289; c-300.*

CAPTAIN AMERICA (Volume Two)
Marvel Comics: V2#1, Nov, 1996 - No. 13, Nov, 1997($2.95/$1.95/$1.99)
(Produced by Extreme Studios)

1-($2.95)-Heroes Reborn begins; Liefeld-c/a; Loeb scripts; reintro Nick Fury 6.00
1-($2.95)-(Variant-c)-Liefeld-c/a 6.00
1-(7/96, $2.95)-(Exclusive Comicon Ed.)-Liefeld-c/a. 1 2 3 5 6 8
2-11,13: 5-Two-c. 6-Cable-c/app. 13-"World War 3"-pt. 4, x-over w/Image 3.00
12-($2.99) "Heroes Reunited"-pt. 4 4.00
Heroes Reborn: Captain America (2006, $29.99, TPB) r/#1-12 & Heroes Reborn #1/2 30.00

CAPTAIN AMERICA (Vol. Three) (Also see Capt. America: Sentinel of Liberty)
Marvel Comics: Jan, 1998 - No. 50, Feb, 2002 ($2.99/$1.99/$2.25)

1-($2.99) Mark Waid-s/Ron Garney-a 4.00
1-Variant cover 6.00
2-($1.99): 2-Two covers 3.00
3-11: 3-Returns to old shield. 4-Hawkeye app. 5-Thor-c/app. 7-Andy Kubert-c/a begin. 9-New shield 3.00
12-($2.99) Battles Nightmare; Red Skull back-up story 4.00
13-17,19-Red Skull returns 3.00
18-($2.99) Cap vs. Korvac in the Future 4.00
20-24,26-29: 20,21-Sgt. Fury back-up story painted by Evans 3.00
25-($2.99) Cap & Falcon vs. Hatemonger 4.00
30-49: 30-Begin $2.25-c. 32-Ordway-a. 33-Jurgens-s/a begins; U.S. Agent app. 36-Maximum Security x-over. 41,46-Red Skull app. 3.00
50-($5.95) Stories by various incl. Jurgens, Quitely, Immonen; Ha-c 6.00
.../Citizen V '98 Annual ($3.50) Busiek & Kesel-s 4.00
1999 Annual ($3.50) Flag Smasher app. 4.00
2000 Annual ($3.50) Continued from #35 vs. Protocide; Jurgens-s 4.00
2001 Annual ($2.99) Golden Age flashback; Invaders app. 4.00
...: To Serve and Protect TPB (2/02, $17.95) r/Vol. 3 #1-7 18.00

CAPTAIN AMERICA (Volume 4)
Marvel Comics: Jun, 2002 - No. 32, Dec, 2004 ($3.99/$2.99)

1-Ney Rieber-s/Cassaday-c/a 4.00
2-9-($2.99) 3-Cap reveals Steve Rogers ID. 7-9-Hairsine-a 3.00
10-32: 10-16-Jae Lee-a. 17-20-Gibbons-s/Weeks-a. 21-26-Bachalo-a. 26-Bucky flashback. 27,28-Eddie Campbell-a. 29-32-Red Skull app. 3.00
...Vol. 1: The New Deal HC (2003, $22.99) r/#1-6; foreward by Max Allan Collins 23.00
...Vol. 2: The Extremists TPB (2003, $13.99) r/#7-11; Cassaday-c 14.00
...Vol. 3: Ice TPB (2003, $12.99) r/#12-16; Jae Lee-a; Cassaday-c 13.00
...Vol. 4: Cap Lives TPB (2004, $12.99) r/#17-22 & Tales of Suspense #66 13.00
Avengers Disassembled: Captain America TPB (2004, $17.99) r/#29-32 and Captain America and the Falcon #5-7 18.00

CAPTAIN AMERICA
Marvel Comics: Jan, 2005 - No. 619, Aug, 2011 ($2.99/$3.99)

1-Brubaker-s/Epting-c/a; Red Skull app. 5.00
2-24: 10-House of M. 11-Origin of the Winter Soldier. 13-Iron Man app. 24-Civil War 3.00
6,8-Retailer variant covers 6.00
25-($3.99) Captain America shot dead; handcuffed red glove cover by Epting 10.00
25-($3.99) Variant edition with running Cap cover by McGuinness 8.00
25-($3.99) 2nd printing with "The Death of The Dream" cover by Epting 4.00
25-Director's Cut-($4.99) w/script with Brubaker commentary; pencil pages, variant and un-used covers gallery; article on media hype 6.00
26-33-Falcon & Winter Soldier app. 3.00
34-(3/08) Bucky becomes the new Captain America; Alex Ross-c 5.00
34-Variant-c by Steve Epting 5.00
34-($3.99) Director's Cut; includes script; pencil art, costume designs, cover gallery 5.00
34-DF Edition with Alex Ross portrait cover; signed by Ross 25.00
35-49-Bucky as Captain America. 43-45-Batroc app. 46,47-Sub-Mariner app. 3.00
50-(7/09, $3.99) Bucky's birthday flashbacks; Captain America's life synopsis; Martin-a 4.00
(After #50, numbering reverts to original with #600, Aug, 2009)
600-(8/09, $4.99) Covers by Ross and Epting; leads into Captain America: Reborn series; art by Guice, Chaykin, Ross, Eaglesham; commentary by Joe Simon; cover gallery 5.00
601-615,617-619-($3.99) 601-Gene Colan-a; 3 covers. 602-Nomad back-up feature begins. 606-Baron Zemo returns. 611-615-Trial of Captain America 4.00
615.1 (5/11, $2.99) Brubaker-s/Breitweiser-a/Acuña-c 3.00
616-(5/11, $4.99) 70th Anniversary Issue; short stories by Brubaker, Chaykin, Deodato, McGuinness, Grist and others, Charest-c 5.00
616-Variant-c by Epting 8.00
...: America's Avenger (8/11, $4.99) Handbook format profiles of friends and foes 5.00
... and Batroc (5/11, $3.99) Gillen-s/Arlem-a; Bucky vs. Batroc in Paris 4.00
... and Crossbones (5/11, $3.99) Harms-s/Shalvey-a/Tocchini-c 4.00
... and Falcon (5/11, $3.99) Williams-s/Isaacs-a/Tocchini-c 4.00
... and the First Thirteen (5/11, $3.99) Peggy Carter in WWII France 1943 4.00
... and the Secret Avengers (5/11, $3.99) DeConnick-s/Tocchini-a/c; Black Widow app. 4.00
... and Thor: Avengers 1 (9/11, $4.99) Movie version Cap; prequel to Thor movie; Lim-c 5.00
... By Ed Brubaker Omnibus Vol. 1 HC (2007, $74.99, dustjacket) r/#1-25; Capt. America 65th Anniv. Spec. and Winter Soldier: Winter Kills; Brubaker intro.; bonus material 75.00
Civil War: Captain America TPB (2007, $11.99) r/#22-24 & Winter Soldier: Winter Kills 12.00
...: Fighting Avenger (6/11, $4.99) 1st WWII mission; Gurihiru-a/c; Kitson var-c 5.00
...MGC #1 (5/10, $1.00) r/#1 with "Marvel's Greatest Comics" cover logo 3.00
...: Rebirth 1 (8/11, $4.99) r/origin & Red Skull apps. from Tales of Suspense #63,65-68 5.00
...: Red Menace Vol. 1 SC (2006, $11.99) r/#15-17 and 65th Anniversary Special 12.00
...: Red Menace Vol. 2 SC (2006, $10.99) r/#18-21; Brubaker interview 11.00
... Spotlight (7/11, $3.99) creator interviews; features on the movie and The Invaders 4.00
... Theater of War: America First! (2/09, $4.99) 1950s era tale; Chaykin-s/a; reprints 5.00
... Theater of War: America the Beautiful (3/09, $4.99) WW2 tale; Jenkins-s/Erskine-a 5.00
... Theater of War: Operation Zero-Point (12/08, $3.99) WW2 tale; Breitweiser-a 4.00
...: The Death of Captan America Vol. 1 HC (2007, $19.99) r/#25-30; variant covers 20.00
...: The Death of Captan America Vol. 2 HC (2008, $19.99) r/#31-36; variant covers 20.00
...Vol. 1: Winter Soldier HC (2005, $21.99) r/#1-7; concept sketches 22.00
...Vol. 1: Winter Soldier SC (2006, $16.99) r/#1-7; concept sketches 17.00
...: Who Won't Wield the Shield (6/10, $3.99) Deadpool & Forbush Man app. 4.00

Captain America (2013 series) #14 © MAR

Captain America Comics #21 © MAR

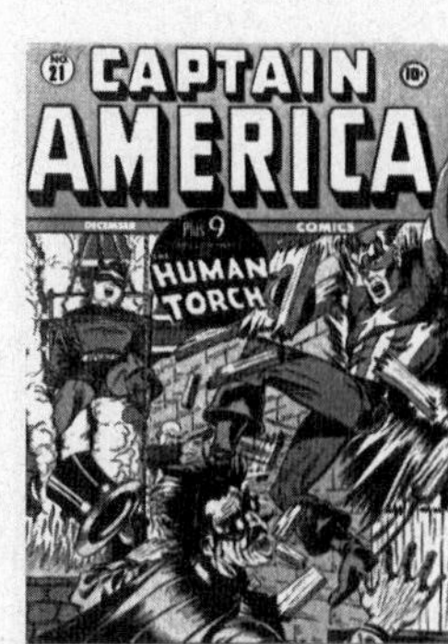

Captain America: Living Legend #1 © MAR

GD 2.0 VG 4.0 FN 6.0 VF 8.0 VF/NM 9.0 NM- 9.2

...: Winter Soldier Vol. 2 HC (2006, $19.99) r/#8,9,11-14 20.00
...: Winter Soldier Vol. 2 SC (2006, $14.99) r/#8,9,11-14 15.00

CAPTAIN AMERICA
Marvel Comics: Sept, 2011 - No. 19, Dec, 2012 ($3.99)

1-19: 1-5-Brubaker-s/McNiven-c/a. 1-Nick Fury & Baron Zemo app. 6-10-Davis-a/c 4.00
1-Variant-c by John Romita Sr. 8.00
1-Movie photo variant-c of Chris Evans in costume 5.00

CAPTAIN AMERICA (Marvel NOW!)
Marvel Comics: Jan, 2013 - Present ($3.99)

1-10-Remender-s/Romita Jr.-a/c; Cap in Dimension Z; Arnim Zola app.; 1st app. Jet Black. 10-Sharon Carter killed 4.00
11-19: 11,12,14,15-Pacheco-a; Nuke returns. 16-Red Skull app.; Alixe-a 4.00
...: Homecoming 1 (5/14, $3.99) Van Lente-s/Grummett-a; bonus rep of Capt. Am. #117 4.00

CAPTAIN AMERICA AND ... (Numbering continues from Captain America #619)
Marvel Comics: No. 620, Sept, 2011 - No. 640, Feb, 2013 ($2.99)

... Bucky 620-628: 620-624-Brubaker & Andreyko-s/Samnee-a/McGuinness-c. 620-Bucky's early WWII days. 625-628-Francavilla-c/a 3.00
... Hawkeye 629-632: 629-(6/12) Bunn-s/Vitti-aDell'Otto-c 3.00
... Iron Man 633-635: 635-(8/12) Bunn-s/Kitson-a/Andrasofszky-c; Batroc app. 3.00
... Namor 635.1 (10/12) World War II flashback; Will Conrad-a/Immonen-c 3.00
... Black Widow 636-640: 636-(11/12) Bunn-s/Francavilla-a/c 3.00

CAPTAIN AMERICA AND THE FALCON
Marvel Comics: May, 2004 - No. 14, June, 2005 ($2.99, limited series)

1-4-Priest-s/Sears-a 3.00
5-14: 5-8-Avengers Disassembled x-over. 6,7-Scarlet Witch app. 8-12-Modok app. 3.00
... Vol. 1: Two Americas (2005, $9.99) r/#1-4 10.00
... Vol. 2: Brothers and Keepers (2005, $17.99) r/#8-14 18.00

CAPTAIN AMERICA & THE KORVAC SAGA
Marvel Comics: Feb, 2011 - No. 4, May, 2011 ($2.99, limited series)

1-4-McCool-s/Rousseau-a/c. 4-Galactus app. 3.00

CAPTAIN AMERICA/BLACK PANTHER (See Black Panther/Captain America: Flags of Our Fathers)

CAPTAIN AMERICA COMICS
Timely/Marvel Comics (TCI 1-20/CmPS 21-68/MjMC 69-75/Atlas Comics (PrPI 76-78): Mar, 1941 - No. 75, Feb, 1950; No. 76, 5/54 - No. 78, 9/54
(No. 74 & 75 titled Capt. America's Weird Tales)

1-Origin & 1st app. Captain America & Bucky by S&K; Hurricane, Tuk the Caveboy begin by S&K; 1st app. Red Skull; Hitler-c (by Simon?); intro of the "Capt. America Sentinels of Liberty Club" (advertised on inside front-c.); indicia reads Vol. 2, Number 1
13,000 26,000 39,000 90,000 170,000 315,000
2-S&K Hurricane; Tuk by Avison (Kirby splash); classic Hitler-c
2050 4100 6150 15,400 31,700 48,000
3-Classic Red Skull-c & app; Stan Lee's 1st text (1st work for Marvel)
1750 3500 5250 13,000 26,000 39,000
4-Early use of full pg. panel in comic; back-c pin-up of Captain America and Bucky
1050 2100 3150 7980 14,490 21,000
5 1000 2000 3000 7300 12,900 18,500
6-Origin Father Time; Tuk the Caveboy ends 892 1784 2676 6512 11,506 16,500
7-Red Skull app.; classic-c 975 1950 2919 7100 12,550 18,000
8-10-Last S&K issue, (S&K centerfold #6-10) 757 1514 2271 5526 9763 14,000
11-Last Hurricane, Headline Hunter; Al Avison Captain America begins, ends #20; Avison-c(p) 524 1048 1572 3825 6763 9700
12-The Imp begins, ends #16; last Father Time 514 1028 1542 3750 6625 9500
13-Origin The Secret Stamp; classic-c 703 1406 2109 5132 9066 13,000
14,15 514 1028 1542 3450 6625 9500
16-Red Skull unmasks Cap; Red Skull-c 730 1460 2190 5329 9415 13,500
17-The Fighting Fool only app. 449 898 1347 3278 5789 8300
18-Classic-c 476 952 1428 3475 6138 8800
19-Human Torch begins #19 423 846 1269 3046 5323 7600
20-Sub-Mariner app.; no Human Torch 423 846 1269 3000 5250 7500
21-25: 25-Cap drinks liquid opium 415 830 1245 2905 5103 7300
26-30: 27-Last Secret Stamp; last 68 pg. issue. 28-60 pg. issues begin.
400 800 1200 2800 4900 7000
31-35,38-40: 34-Centerfold poster of Cap 360 720 1080 2520 4410 6300
36-Classic Hitler-c 514 1028 1542 3450 6625 9500
37-Red Skull app. 459 918 1377 3350 5925 8500
41-Last Japan War-c 303 606 909 2121 3711 5300
42-45 277 554 831 1759 3030 4300
46-German Holocaust-c; classic 649 1298 1947 4738 8369 12,000
47-Last German War-c 300 600 900 2010 3505 5000
48-58,60 197 388 582 1242 2121 3000
59-Origin retold 343 686 1029 2400 4200 6000
61-Red Skull-c/story 383 766 1149 2681 4691 6700
62,64,65: 65-Kurtzman's "Hey Look" 239 478 717 1530 2615 3700
63-Intro/origin Asbestos Lady 245 490 735 1568 2684 3800
66-Bucky is shot; Golden Girl teams up with Captain America & learns his i.d; origin Golden Girl 309 618 927 2163 3782 5400
67-69: 67-Captain America/Golden Girl team-up; Mxyztplk swipe; last Toro in Human Torch. 68-Sub-Mariner/Namora, and Captain America/Golden Girl team-up. 69-Human Torch/Sun Girl team-up. 300 600 900 2070 3635 5200
70-73: 70-Sub-Mariner/Namora, and Captain America/Golden Girl team-up. 70-SciFi-c/story. 71-Anti Wertham editorial; The Witness, Bucky app.
331 662 993 2317 4059 5800
74-(Scarce)(10/49)-Titled "Captain America's Weird Tales"; Red Skull-c & app.; classic-c 1250 2500 3750 9300 17,150 25,000
75(2/50)-Titled "C.A.'s Weird Tales"; no C.A. app.; horror cover/stories
331 662 993 2317 4059 5800
76-78(1954): Human Torch/Toro stories; all have communist-c/stories
206 412 618 1318 2259 3200
132-Pg. Issue (B&W-1942)(Canadian)-Very rare. Has blank inside-c and back-c; contains Marvel Mystery #33 & Captain America #18 w/cover from Captain America #22; same contents as one version of the Marvel Mystery annuals
6167 12,334 18,500 37,000 - -

NOTE: *Crandall a-2i, 3i, 9i, 10i.* ***Kirby*** *c-1, 2, 5-8p.* ***Rico*** *c-69-71.* ***Romita*** *c-77, 78.* ***Schomburg*** *c-3, 4, 26-29, 31, 33, 37-39, 41, 42, 45-54, 58.* ***Sekowsky*** *c-55, 56.* ***Shores*** *c-1i, 2i, 5-7i, 11i, 20-25, 30, 32, 34, 35, 40, 57, 59-67.* ***S&K*** *c-9, 10. Bondage c-3, 7, 15, 16, 34, 38.*

CAPTAIN AMERICA COMICS #1 70TH ANNIVERSARY EDITION
Marvel Comics: May, 2011 ($4.99, one-shot)

1-Recolored reprint of entire 1941 issue including Hurricane & Tuk stories; Ching-c 5.00

CAPTAIN AMERICA COMICS 70TH ANNIVERSARY SPECIAL
Marvel Comics: June, 2009 ($3.99, one-shot)

1-WWII flashback; Marcos Martin-a; Marcos-2 covers; r/Capt. America Comics #7 5.00

CAPTAIN AMERICA CORPS
Marvel Comics: Aug, 2011 - No. 5, Dec, 2011 ($2.99, limited series)

1-5-Stern-s/Briones-a/Jimenez-a; various versions of Captain America team-up 3.00

CAPTAIN AMERICA: DEAD MEN RUNNING
Marvel Comics: Mar, 2002 - No. 3, May, 2002 ($2.99, limited series)

1-3-Macan-s/Zezelj-a 3.00

CAPTAIN AMERICA: FIRST VENGEANCE (Based on the 2011 movie version)
Marvel Comics: Jul, 2011 - No. 4, Aug, 2011 ($2.99, limited series)

1-4-Van Lente-s; art by Luke Ross & others. 2-Movie photo-c 3.00

CAPTAIN AMERICA: FOREVER ALLIES
Marvel Comics: Oct, 2010 - No. 4, Jan, 2011 ($3.99, limited series)

1-4-Stern-s/Dragotta-a; Bucky in present & WW2 flashbacks; Young Allies app. 4.00

CAPTAIN AMERICA: HAIL HYDRA
Marvel Comics: Mar, 2011 - No. 5, Jul, 2011 ($2.99, limited series)

1-5-Cap vs. Hydra; Granov-c. 1-WWII flashback. 2-Kirby-style art by Scioli. 4-Hotz-a 3.00

CAPTAIN AMERICA: LIVING LEGEND
Marvel Comics: Dec, 2013 - No. 4, Feb, 2014 ($3.99, limited series)

1-4: 1-Diggle-s/Granov-a/c. 2-4-Alessio-a 4.00

CAPTAIN AMERICA: MAN OUT OF TIME
Marvel Comics: Jan, 2011 - No. 5, May, 2011 ($3.99, limited series)

1-5-Waid-s/Molina-a/Hitch-c; Cap's unfreezing in modern times re-told 4.00

CAPTAIN AMERICA/NICK FURY: BLOOD TRUCE
Marvel Comics: Feb, 1995 ($5.95, one-shot, squarebound)

nn-Chaykin story 6.00

CAPTAIN AMERICA/NICK FURY: THE OTHERWORLD WAR
Marvel Comics: Oct, 2001 ($6.95, one-shot, squarebound)

nn-Manco-a; Bucky and Red Skull app. 7.00

CAPTAIN AMERICA: PATRIOT
Marvel Comics: Nov, 2010 - No. 4, Feb, 2011 ($3.99, limited series)

1-4-Kesel-s/Breitweiser-a; 1-WW2 story; Patriot & the Liberty Legion app. 4.00

CAPTAIN AMERICA: REBORN (Titled Reborn in #1-3)
Marvel Comics: Sept, 2009 - No. 6, Mar, 2010 ($3.99, limited series)

1-6-Steve Rogers returns from the dead; Brubaker-s/Hitch & Guice-a. 1-Covers by Hitch, Ross & Quesada. 2-Origin re-told. 4-Joe Kubert var-c. 5-Cassaday var-c 4.00
1-4-Variant-c by Cassaday. 2-Variant-c by Sale. 5-Finch var-c 10.00

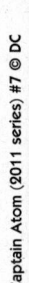

Captain America: Sentinel of Liberty #2 © MAR

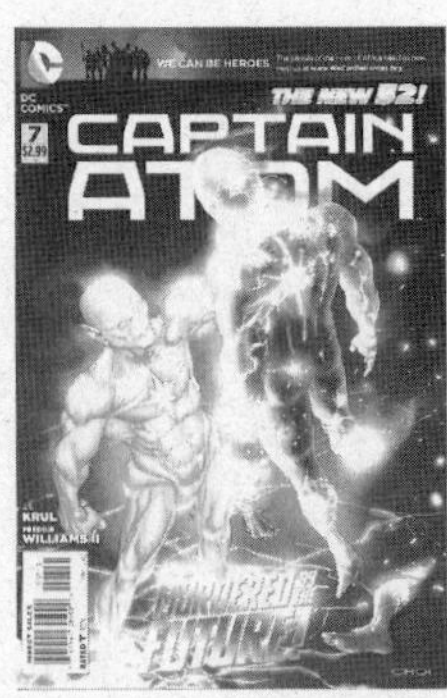

Captain Atom (2011 series) #7 © DC

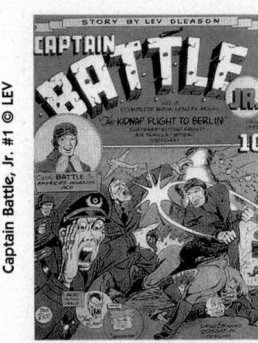

Captain Battle, Jr. #1 © LEV

GD 2.0 VG 4.0 FN 6.0 VF 8.0 VF/NM 9.0 NM- 9.2

GD 2.0 VG 4.0 FN 6.0 VF 8.0 VF/NM 9.0 NM- 9.2

... MGC #1 (5/11, $1.00) r/#1 with "Marvel's Greatest Comics" logo on cover 3.00
...: Who Will Wield the Shield? (2/10, $3.99) Aftermath of series; Guice & Luke Ross-a 4.00

CAPTAIN AMERICA: RED, WHITE & BLUE
Marvel Comics: Sept, 2002 ($29.99, one-shot, hardcover with dustjacket)

nn-Reprints from Lee & Kirby, Steranko, Miller and others; and new short stories and pin-ups by various incl. Ross, Dini, Timm, Waid, Dorkin, Sienkiewicz, Miller, Bruce Jones, Collins, Piers-Rayner, Pope, Deodato, Quitely, Nino; Stelfreeze-c 30.00
TPB (2007, $19.99) 20.00

CAPTAIN AMERICA, SENTINEL OF LIBERTY (See Fireside Book Series)

CAPTAIN AMERICA: SENTINEL OF LIBERTY
Marvel Comics: Sept, 1998 - No. 12, Aug, 1999 ($1.99)

1-Waid-s/Garney-a 3.00
1-Rough Cut ($2.99) Features original script and pencil pages 3.00
2-5: 2-Two-c; Invaders WW2 story 3.00
6-($2.99) Iron Man-c/app. 4.00
7-11: 8-Falcon-c/app. 9-Falcon poses as Cap 3.00
12-($2.99) Final issue; Bucky-c/app. 4.00

CAPTAIN AMERICA SPECIAL EDITION
Marvel Comics Group: Feb, 1984 - No. 2, Mar, 1984 ($2.00, Baxter paper)

1-Steranko-c/a(r) in both; r/ Captain America #110,111 6.00
2-Reprints the scarce Our Love Story #5, and C.A. #113
1 2 3 5 6 8

CAPTAIN AMERICA THEATER OF WAR
Marvel Comics: 2009 - 2010 ($3.99, series of one-shots)

...: A Brother in Arms (6/09) Jenkins-s/McCrea-a; WWII story 4.00
...: Ghosts of My Country (12/09) Jenkins-s/Bonetti-a/Guice-c 4.00
...: Prisoners of Duty (2/10) Higgins & Siegel-s/Padilla-a; WWII story 4.00
...: To Soldier On (10/09) Jenkins-s/Blanco-a/Noto-c; Captain America in Iraq 4.00

CAPTAIN AMERICA: THE CHOSEN
Marvel Comics: Nov, 2007 - No. 6, Mar, 2008 ($3.99, limited series)

1-6-Breitweiser-a/Morrell-s 4.00

CAPTAIN AMERICA: THE CLASSIC YEARS
Marvel Comics: Jun, 1998 -No. 2 (trade paperbacks)

1-($19.95) Reprints Captain America Comics #1-5 25.00
2-($24.95) Reprints Captain America Comics #6-10 25.00

CAPTAIN AMERICA: THE FIRST AVENGER ADAPTATION (MARVEL'S...)
Marvel Comics: Jan, 2014 - No. 2, Feb, 2014 ($2.99, limited series)

1,2-Adaptation of the 2011 movie; Peter David-s/Wellinton Alves-a/photo-c 3.00

CAPTAIN AMERICA: THE LEGEND
Marvel Comics: Sept, 1996 ($3.95, one-shot)

1-Tribute issue; wraparound-c 5.00

CAPTAIN AMERICA: THE 1940S NEWSPAPER STRIP
Marvel Comics: Aug, 2010 - No. 3, Oct, 2010 ($3.99, limited series)

1-3-Karl Kesel-s/a; new stories set in WW2, formatted like 1940s newspaper comics 4.00

CAPTAIN AMERICA: WHAT PRICE GLORY
Marvel Comics: May, 2003 - No. 4, May, 2003 ($2.99, weekly limited series)

1-4-Bruce Jones-s/Steve Rude & Mike Royer-a 3.00

CAPTAIN AMERICA: WHITE
Marvel Comics: No. 0, Sept, 2008 ($2.99, unfinished limited series)

0-Bucky's origin retold; Loeb-s/Sale-a; interviews with creators; Sale sketch art 3.00

CAPTAIN AMERICA: WINTER SOLDIER DIRECTOR'S CUT
Marvel Comics: Jun, 2014 ($4.99, one-shot)

1-Reprints Captain America (2005) #1; bonus Brubaker script & series proposal 5.00

CAPTAIN AND THE KIDS, THE (See Famous Comics Cartoon Books)

CAPTAIN AND THE KIDS, THE (See Comics on Parade, Katzenjammer Kids, Okay Comics & Sparkler Comics)
United Features Syndicate/Dell Publ. Co.: 1938 -12/39; Sum, 1947 - No. 32, 1955; Four Color No. 881, Feb, 1958

Single Series 1(1938) 110 220 330 704 1202 1700
Single Series 1(Reprint)(12/39- "Reprint" on-c) 48 96 144 302 514 725
1(Summer, 1947-UFS)-Katzenjammer Kids 18 36 54 103 162 220
2 11 22 33 62 86 110
3-10 10 20 30 54 72 90
11-20 8 16 24 44 57 70
21-32 (1955) 8 16 24 40 50 60
50th Anniversary issue-(1948)-Contains a 2 pg. history of the strip, including an account of the famous Supreme Court decision allowing both Pulitzer & Hearst to run the same strip under different names 17 34 51 98 154 210
Special Summer issue, Fall issue (1948) 11 22 33 62 86 110
Four Color 881 (Dell) 4 8 12 28 44 60

CAPTAIN ATOM
Nationwide Publishers: 1950 - No. 7, 1951 (5¢, 5x7-1/4", 52 pgs.)

1-Science fiction 42 84 126 265 445 625
2-7 24 48 72 142 234 325

CAPTAIN ATOM (Formerly Strange Suspense Stories #77)(Also see Space Adventures and Thunderbolt)
Charlton Comics: V2#78, Dec, 1965 - V2#89, Dec, 1967

V2#78-Origin retold; Bache-a (3 pgs.) 7 14 21 48 89 130
79-82: 79-1st app. Dr. Spectro; 3 pg. Ditko cut & paste /Space Adventures #24. 82-Intro. Nightshade (9/66) 5 10 15 33 57 80
83-86: Ted Kord Blue Beetle in all. 83-(11/66)-1st app. Ted Kord. 84-1st app. new Captain Atom 5 10 15 30 50 70
87-89: Nightshade by Aparo in all 5 10 15 30 50 70
83-85(Modern Comics-1977)-reprints 1 2 3 4 5 7
NOTE: *Aparo a-87-89. Ditko c/a(p) 78-89. #90 only published in fanzine 'The Charlton Bullseye' #1, 2.*

CAPTAIN ATOM (Also see Americomics & Crisis On Infinite Earths)
DC Comics: Mar, 1987 - No. 57, Sept, 1991 (Direct sales only #35 on)

1-(44 pgs.)-Origin/1st app. with new costume 4.00
2-49: 5-Firestorm x-over. 6-Intro. new Dr. Spectro. 11-Millennium tie-in. 14-Nightshade app. 16-Justice League app. 17-$1.00-c begins; Swamp Thing app. 20-Blue Beetle x-over. 24,25-Invasion tie-in 3.00
50-($2.00, 52 pgs.) 4.00
51-57: 57-War of the Gods x-over 3.00
Annual 1,2 ('88, '89)-1-Intro Major Force 4.00

CAPTAIN ATOM (DC New 52)
DC Comics: Nov, 2011 - No. 12, Oct, 2012; No. 0, Nov, 2012 ($2.99)

1-12-J.T. Krul-s/Freddie Williams II-a. 3-Flash app. 3.00
#0 (11/12, $2.99) origin of Captain Atom re-told 3.00

CAPTAIN ATOM: ARMAGEDDON (Restarts the WildStorm Universe)
DC Comics (WildStorm): Dec, 2005 - No. 9, Aug, 2006 ($2.99, limited series)

1-9-Captain Atom appears in WildStorm Universe; Pfeifer-s/Camuncoli-a. 1-Lee-c 3.00
TPB (2007, $19.99) r/series 20.00

CAPTAIN BATTLE (Boy Comics #3 on) (See Silver Streak Comics)
New Friday Publ./Comic House: Summer, 1941 - No. 2, Fall, 1941

1-Origin Blackout by Rico; Captain Battle begins (1st appeared in Silver Streak #10, 5/41) classic hooded villain bondage/torture-c 155 310 465 992 1696 2400
2-Doctor Horror only app. 82 164 246 528 902 1275

CAPTAIN BATTLE (2nd Series)
Magazine Press/Picture Scoop No. 5: No. 3, Wint, 1942-43; No. 5, Sum, 1943 (No #4)

3-Origin Silver Streak-r/SS#3; origin Lance Hale-r/Silver Streak; Simon-a(r) (52 pgs., nd) 73 146 219 467 796 1125
5-Origin Blackout retold (68 pgs.); Japanese WWII-c 65 130 195 416 708 1000

CAPTAIN BATTLE, JR.
Comic House (Lev Gleason): Fall, 1943 - No. 2, Winter, 1943-44

1-Nazi WWII-c by Rico. Hitler/Claw sty; The Claw vs. The Ghost 135 270 405 864 1482 2100
2-Wolverton's Scoop Scuttle; Don Rico-c/a; The Green Claw story is reprinted from Silver Streak #6; Japanese WWII bondage/torture-c by Rico 81 162 243 518 884 1250

CAPTAIN BEN DIX (See Promotional Comics section)

CAPTAIN BRITAIN (Also see Marvel Team-Up No. 65, 66)
Marvel Comics International: Oct. 13, 1976 - No. 39, July 6, 1977 (Weekly)

1-Origin; with Capt. Britain's face mask inside 4 8 12 23 37 50
2-Origin, part II; Capt. Britain's Boomerang inside 3 6 9 17 26 35
3-7,9-11: 3-Vs. Bank Robbers. 4-7-Vs. Hurricane. 9-11- Battles Dr. Synne 1 3 4 6 8 10
8-(12/76) 1st app. Betsy Braddock, the sister of Capt. Britain (Brian Braddock) who later becomes Psylocke (X-Men); 1st app. Dr. Synne 8 16 24 54 102 150
12-23,25-27: (scarce)-12,13-Vs. Dr. Synne. 14,15-Vs. Mastermind. 16-23,25,26-With Captain America. 17-Misprinted & color section reprinted in #18. 27-Origin retold 2 4 6 13 18 22
24-With C.B.'s Jet Plane inside 3 6 9 17 26 35

Captain Canuck #2 © R. Comely

Captain Easy #16 © NEA

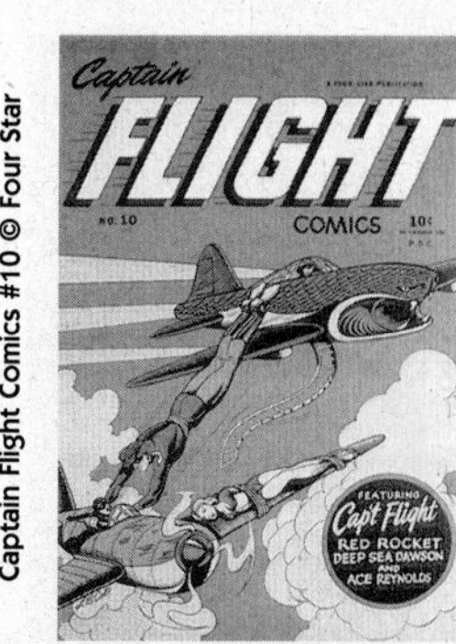

Captain Flight Comics #10 © Four Star

28-32,36-39: 28-32-Vs. Lord Hawk. 37-39-Vs. Highwayman & Munipulator 6.00
33-35-More on origin 1 2 3 4 5 7
Annual (1978, Hardback, 64 pgs.)-Reprints #1-7 with pin-ups of Marvel characters
3 6 9 15 22 28
Summer Special (1980, 52 pgs.)-Reprints 1 2 3 5 6 8

*NOTE: No. 1, 2, & 24 are rarer in mint due to inserts. Distributed in Great Britain only. Nick Fury-r by **Steranko** in 1-20, 24-31, 35-37. Fantastic Four-r by **J. Buscema** in all. New **Buscema**-a in 24-30. Story from No. 39 continues in Super Spider-Man (British weekly) No. 231-247. Following cancellation of his series, new Captain Britain stories appeared in "Super Spider-Man" (British weekly) No. 231-247. Captain Britain stories which appear in Super-Spider-Man No 248-253 are reprints of Marvel Team-Up No. 65&66. Capt. Britain strips also appeared in Hulk Comic (weekly) 1, 3-30, 42-55, 57-60, in Marvel Superheroes (monthly) 377-388, in Daredevils (monthly) 1-11, Mighty World of Marvel (monthly) 7-16 & Captain Britain (monthly) 1-14. Issues 1-23 have B&W & color, paper-c, & are 32 pgs. Issues 24 on are all B&W w/glossy-c & are 36 pgs.*

CAPTAIN BRITAIN AND MI: 13 (Also see Secret Invasion x-over titles)
Marvel Comics: Jul, 2008 - No. 15, Sept, 2009 ($2.99)

1-Skrull invasion; Black Knight app.; Kirk-a 4.00
1-2nd printing with Kirk variant-c; 3rd printing with B&W cover 3.00
2-15: 5-Blade app. 9,10-Dracula app. 3.00
... Annual 1 (8/09, $3.99) Land-c; Meggan in Hell; Dr. Doom cameo; Collins-a 4.00

CAPTAIN CANUCK
Comely Comix (Canada)(All distr. in U. S.): 7/75 - No. 4, 7/77; No. 4, 7-8/79 - No. 14, 3-4/81

1-1st app. Bluefox 1 3 4 6 8 10
2,3(5-7/76)-2-1st app. Dr. Walker, Redcoat & Kebec. 3-1st app. Heather 6.00
4(1st printing-2/77)-10x14-1/2"; (5.00); B&W; 300 copies serially numbered and signed with one certificate of authenticity 7 14 21 49 92 135
4(2nd printing-7/77)-11x17", B&W; only 15 copies printed; signed by creator Richard Comely, serially #'d and two certificates of authenticity inserted; orange cardboard covers (Very Rare) 10 20 30 69 147 225
4-14: 4(7-8/79)-1st app. Tom Evans & Mr. Gold; origin The Catman. 5-Origin Capt. Canuck's powers; 1st app. Earth Patrol & Chaos Corps. 8-Jonn 'The Final Chapter'. 9-1st World Beyond. 11-1st 'Chariots of Fire' story 6.00
15-(8/04, $15.00) Limited edition of unpublished issue from 1981; serially #'d edition of 150; signed by creator Richard Comely 5 10 15 34 60 85
... Legacy 1 (9-10/06) Comely-s/a 4.00
... Legacy Special Edition ($7.95, 52 pgs., limited ed. of 1000) Comely-s/a
1 3 4 6 8 10
Special Collectors Pack (polybagged) 2 4 6 8 10 12
Summer Special 1(7-9/80, 95¢, 64 pgs.) 6.00

NOTE: 30,000 copies of No. 2 were destroyed in Winnipeg.

CAPTAIN CANUCK: UNHOLY WAR
Comely Comix: Oct, 2004 - No. 3, Jan, 2005 ($2.50, limited series)

1-3-Riel Langlois-s/Drue Langlois-a 3.00

CAPTAIN CARROT AND HIS AMAZING ZOO CREW (Also see New Teen Titans & Oz-Wonderland War)
DC Comics: Mar, 1982 - No. 20, Nov, 1983

1-Superman app. 6.00
2-20: 3-Re-intro Dodo & The Frog. 9-Re-intro Three Mouseketeers, the Terrific Whatzit. 10,11-Pig Iron reverts back to Peter Porkchops. 20-Changeling app. 4.00

CAPTAIN CARROT AND THE FINAL ARK (DC Countdown tie-in)
DC Comics: Dec, 2007 - No. 3, Feb, 2008 ($2.99, limited series)

1-3-Bill Morrison-s/Scott Shaw!-a. 3-Batman, Red Arrow, Hawkgirl & Zatanna app. 3.00
TPB (2008, $19.99) r/#1-3; Captain Carrot and His Amazing Zoo Crew #1,14,15; New Teen Titans #16 and stories from Teen Titans (2003 series) #30,31; cover gallery 20.00

CAPTAIN CARVEL AND HIS CARVEL CRUSADERS (See Carvel Comics)

CAPTAIN CONFEDERACY
Marvel Comics (Epic Comics): Nov, 1991 - No. 4, Feb, 1992 ($1.95)

1-4: All new stories 3.00

CAPTAIN COURAGEOUS COMICS (Banner #3-5; see Four Favorites #5)
Periodical House (Ace Magazines): No. 6, March, 1942

6-Origin & 1st app. The Sword; Lone Warrior, Capt. Courageous app.; Capt. moves to Four Favorites #5 in May 84 168 252 538 919 1300

CAPT'N CRUNCH COMICS (See Cap'n...)

CAPTAIN DAVY JONES
Dell Publishing Co.: No. 598, Nov, 1954

Four Color 598 5 10 15 30 50 70

CAPTAIN EASY (See The Funnies & Red Ryder #3-32)
Hawley/Dell Publ./Standard(Visual Editions)/Argo: 1939 - No. 17, Sept, 1949; April, 1956

nn-Hawley(1939)-Contains reprints from The Funnies & 1938 Sunday strips by Roy Crane
89 178 267 565 975 1385
Four Color 24 (1943) 52 104 156 328 552 775
Four Color 111(6/46) 11 22 33 76 163 250
10(Standard-10/47) 13 26 39 74 105 135
11,12,14,15,17: 11-17 all contain 1930s & '40s strip-r 10 20 30 56 76 95
13,16: Schomburg-c 11 22 33 64 90 115
Argo 1(4/56)-Reprints 7 14 21 37 46 55

CAPTAIN EASY & WASH TUBBS (See Famous Comics Cartoon Books)

CAPTAIN ELECTRON
Brick Computer Science Institute: Aug, 1986 ($2.25)

1-Disbrow-a 3.00

CAPTAIN EO 3-D (Michael Jackson Disney theme parks movie)
Eclipse Comics: July, 1987 (Eclipse 3-D Special #18, $3.50, Baxter)

1-Adapts 3-D movie; Michael Jackson-c/app. 6.00
1-2-D limited edition 2 4 6 9 12 15
1-Large size (11x17", 8/87)-Sold only at Disney Theme parks ($6.95)
3 6 9 14 20 25

CAPTAIN FEARLESS COMICS (Also see Holyoke One-Shot #6, Old Glory Comics & Silver Streak #1)
Helnit Publishing Co. (Holyoke Publ. Co.): Aug, 1941 - No. 2, Sept, 1941

1-Origin Mr. Miracle, Alias X, Captain Fearless, Citizen Smith Son of the Unknown Soldier; Miss Victory (1st app.) begins (1st patriotic heroine? before Wonder Woman)
87 174 261 553 952 1350
2-Grit Grady, Captain Stone app. 51 102 153 321 541 760

CAPTAIN FLAG (See Blue Ribbon Comics #16)

CAPTAIN FLASH
Sterling Comics: Nov, 1954 - No. 4, July, 1955

1-Origin; Sekowsky-a; Tomboy (female super hero) begins; only pre-code issue; atomic rocket-c 41 82 123 256 428 600
2-4: 4-Flying saucer invasion-c 24 48 72 140 230 320

CAPTAIN FLEET (Action Packed Tales of the Sea)
Ziff-Davis Publishing Co.: Fall, 1952

1-Painted-c 16 32 48 94 147 200

CAPTAIN FLIGHT COMICS
Four Star Publications: May, 1944 - No. 10, Dec, 1945; No. 11, Feb-Mar, 1947

nn-Captain Flight begins 53 106 159 334 567 800
2-4: 4-Rock Raymond begins, ends #7 32 64 96 188 307 425
5-Bondage, classic torture-c; Red Rocket begins; the Grenade app. (scarce)
142 284 426 909 1555 2200
6-L. B. Cole-a, 8 pgs. 30 60 90 177 289 400
7-10: 7-L. B. Cole covers begin, end #11. 7-9-Japanese WWII-c. 8-Yankee Girl begins; intro. Black Cobra & Cobra Kid & begins. 9-Torpedoman app.; last Yankee Girl; Kinstler-a. 10-Deep Sea Dawson, Zoom of the Jungle, Rock Raymond, Red Rocket, & Black Cobra app; bondage-c 53 106 159 334 567 800
11-Torpedoman, Blue Flame (Human Torch clone) app.; last Black Cobra, Red Rocket; classic L. B. Cole sci-fi robot-c (scarce) 206 412 618 1318 2259 3200

CAPTAIN GALLANT (...of the Foreign Legion) (TV) (Texas Rangers in Action No. 5 on?)
Charlton Comics: 1955; No. 2, Jan, 1956 - No. 4, Sept, 1956

Non-Heinz version (#1)-Buster Crabbe photo on-c; full page Buster Crabbe photo inside front-c 8 16 24 44 57 70
(Heinz version is listed in the Promotional Comics section)
2-4: Buster Crabbe in all. 2-Crabbe photo back-c 6 12 18 31 38 45

CAPTAIN GLORY
Topps Comics: Apr, 1993 ($2.95) (Created by Jack Kirby)

1-Polybagged w/Kirbychrome trading card; Ditko-a & Kirby-c; has coupon for Amberchrome Secret City Saga #0 4.00

CAPTAIN HERO (See Jughead as...)

CAPTAIN HERO COMICS DIGEST MAGAZINE
Archie Publications: Sept, 1981

1-Reprints of Jughead as Super-Guy 2 4 6 10 14 18

CAPTAIN HOBBY COMICS
Export Publication Ent. Ltd. (Dist. in U.S. by Kable News Co.): Feb, 1948 (Canadian)

1 9 18 27 47 61 75

CAPT. HOLO IN 3-D (See Blackthorne 3-D Series #65)

CAPTAIN HOOK & PETER PAN (Movie)(Disney)
Dell Publishing Co.: No. 446, Jan, 1953

Four Color 446 8 16 24 54 102 150

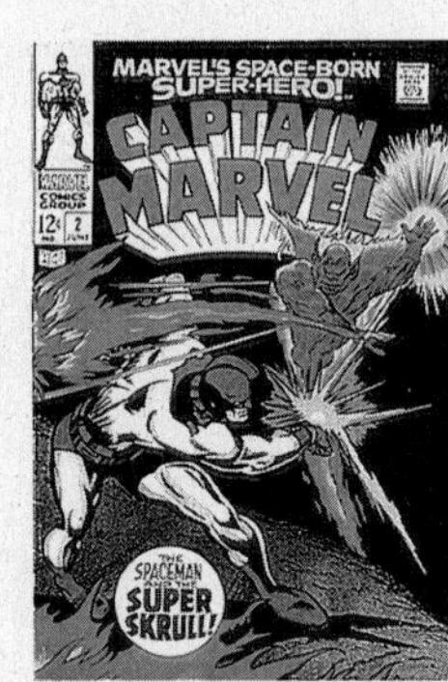

Captain Marvel #2 © MAR

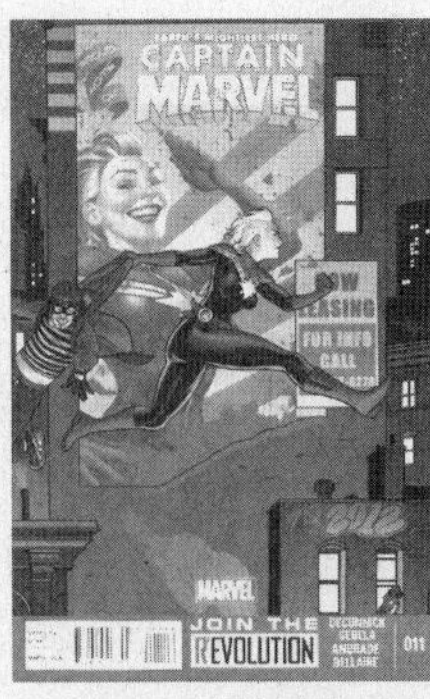

Captain Marvel (2012 series) #11 © MAR

Captain Marvel Adventures #19 © FAW

GD VG FN VF VF/NM NM-
2.0 4.0 6.0 8.0 9.0 9.2

CAPTAIN JET (Fantastic Fears No. 7 on)
Four Star Publ./Farrell/Comic Media: May, 1952 - No. 5, Jan, 1953
1-Bakerish-a 25 50 75 147 241 335
2 15 30 45 86 133 180
3-5,6(?) 12 24 36 69 97 125

CAPTAIN JOHNER & THE ALIENS
Valiant: May, 1995 - No. 2, May, 1995 ($2.95, shipped in same month)
1,2: Reprints Magnus Robot Fighter 4000 A.D. back-up stories; new Paul Smith-c 3.00

CAPTAIN JUSTICE (TV)
Marvel Comics: Mar, 1988 - No. 2, Apr, 1988 (limited series)
1,2-Based on the 1987 "Once a Hero" television series 3.00

CAPTAIN KANGAROO (TV)
Dell Publishing Co.: No. 721, Aug, 1956 - No. 872, Jan, 1958
Four Color 721 (#1)-Photo-c 13 26 39 86 188 290
Four Color 780, 872-Photo-c 11 22 33 73 157 240

CAPTAIN KIDD (Formerly Dagar; My Secret Story #26 on)(Also see Comic Comics & Fantastic Comics)
Fox Feature Syndicate: No. 24, June, 1949 - No. 25, Aug, 1949
24,25: 24-Features Blackbeard the Pirate 15 30 45 84 127 170

CAPTAIN MARVEL (See All Hero, All-New Collectors' Ed., America's Greatest, Fawcett Miniature, Gift, JSA, Kingdom Come, Legends, Limited Collectors' Ed., Marvel Family, Master No. 21, Mighty Midget Comics, Power of Shazam!, Shazam, Special Edition Comics, Whiz, Wisco (in Promotional Comics section), World's Finest #253 and XMas Comics)

CAPTAIN MARVEL (Becomes ...Presents the Terrible 5 No. 5)
M. F. Enterprises: April, 1966 - No. 4, Nov, 1966 (25¢ Giants)
nn-(#1 on pg. 5)-Origin; created by Carl Burgos 5 10 15 31 53 75
2-4: 3-(#3 on pg. 4)-Fights the Bat 3 6 9 21 33 45

CAPTAIN MARVEL (Marvel's Space-Born Super-Hero! Captain Marvel #1-6; see Giant-Size..., Life Of..., Marvel Graphic Novel #1, Marvel Spotlight V2#1 & Marvel Super-Heroes #12)
Marvel Comics Group: May, 1968 - No. 19, Dec, 1969; No. 20, June, 1970 - No. 21, Aug, 1970; No. 22, Sept, 1972 - No. 62, May, 1979
1 15 30 45 103 227 350
2-Super Skrull-c/story 8 16 24 51 96 140
3-5: 4-Captain Marvel battles Sub-Mariner 6 12 18 38 69 100
6-11: 11-Capt. Marvel given great power by Zo the Ruler; Smith/Trimpe-c; Death of Una 4 8 12 25 40 55
12,13,15,18-20 3 6 9 17 26 35
14-Capt. Marvel vs. Iron Man; last 12¢ issue. 4 8 12 25 40 55
16,17-New costume 4 8 12 23 37 50
21-Capt. Marvel battles Hulk; last 15¢ issue 4 8 12 28 47 65
22-24 3 6 9 16 23 30
25,26: 25-Starlin-c/a begins; Starlin's 1st Thanos saga begins (3/73), ends #34; Thanos cameo (5 panels). 26-Minor Thanos app. (see Iron Man #55); 1st Thanos-c 6 12 18 41 76 110
27,28-2nd & 3rd app. Thanos. 28-Thanos-c/s 6 12 18 38 69 100
29,30-Thanos cameos. 29-C.M. gains more powers 4 8 12 23 37 50
31-Thanos app.; last 20¢ issue. 4 8 12 25 40 55
32-Thanos-c & app. 5 10 15 30 50 70
33-Thanos-c & app.; Capt. Marvel battles Thanos; Thanos origin re-told 6 12 18 38 69 100
34-1st app. Nitro; C.M. contracts cancer which eventually kills him; last Starlin-c/a 4 8 12 23 37 50
35,37-40,42,46-48,50,53-56,59-62: 39-Origin Watcher 2 4 6 8 10 12
36,41,43,49: 36-R-origin/1st app. Capt. Marvel from Marvel Super-Heroes #12. 41,43-Wrightson part inks; #43-c(i). 49-Starlin & Weiss-p assists 2 4 6 8 11 14
44,45-(Regular 25¢ editions)(5,7/76) 2 4 6 8 10 12
44,45-(30¢-c variants, limited distribution) 4 8 12 27 44 60
51,52-(Regular 30¢ editions)(7,9/77) 2 4 6 8 10 12
51,52-(35¢-c variants, limited distribution) 5 10 15 30 50 70
57-Thanos appears in flashback 2 4 6 13 18 22
58-Thanos cameo 2 4 6 10 14 18
NOTE: ***Alcala*** *a-35.* ***Austin*** *a-46i, 49-53i; c-52i.* ***Buscema*** *a-18p-21p.* ***Colan*** *a(p)-1-4; c(p)-1-4, 8, 9.* ***Heck*** *a-5-10p, 16p.* ***Gil Kane*** *a-17-21p; c-17-24p, 37p, 53.* ***Starlin*** *a-36.* ***McWilliams*** *a-40i. #25-34 were reprinted in The Life of Captain Marvel.*

CAPTAIN MARVEL
Marvel Comics: Nov, 1989 ($1.50, one-shot, 52 pgs.)
1-Super-hero from Avengers; new powers 4.00

CAPTAIN MARVEL
GD VG FN VF VF/NM NM-
2.0 4.0 6.0 8.0 9.0 9.2
Marvel Comics: Feb, 1994 ($1.75, 52 pgs.)
1-(Indicia reads Vol 2 #2)-Minor Captain America app. 4.00

CAPTAIN MARVEL
Marvel Comics: Dec, 1995 - No. 6, May, 1996 ($2.95/$1.95)
1 ($2.95)-Advs. of Mar-Vell's son begins; Fabian Nicieza scripts; foil-c 4.00
2-6: 2-Begin $1.95-c 3.00

CAPTAIN MARVEL (Vol. 3) (See Avengers Forever)
Marvel Comics: Jan, 2000 - No. 35, Oct, 2002 ($2.50)
1-Peter David-s in all; two covers 4.00
2-10: 2-Two covers; Hulk app. 9-Silver Surfer app. 3.00
11-35: 12-Maximum Security x-over. 17,18-Starlin-a. 27-30-Spider-Man 2099 app. 3.00
Wizard #0-Preview and history of Rick Jones 4.00
...: First Contact (8/01, $16.95, TPB) r/#0,1-6 17.00

CAPTAIN MARVEL (Vol. 4) (See Avengers Forever)
Marvel Comics: Nov, 2002 - No. 25, Sept, 2004 ($2.25/$2.99)
1-Peter David-s/Chriscross-a ; 3 covers by Ross, Jusko & Chriscross 4.00
2-7: 2,3-Punisher app. 3-Alex Ross-c; new costume debuts. 4-Noto-c. 7-Thor app. 3.00
3-Sketchbook Edition-($3.50) includes Ross' concept design pages for new costume 4.00
8-25: 8-Begin $2.99-c; Thor app.; Manco-c. 10-Spider-Man-c/app. 15-Neal Adams-c 3.00
Vol. 1: Nothing To Lose (2003, $14.99, TPB) r/#1-6 15.00
Vol. 2: Coven (2003, $14.99, TPB) r/#7-12 15.00
Vol. 3: Crazy Like a Fox (2004, $14.99, TPB) r/#13-18 15.00
Vol. 4: Odyssey (2004, $16.99, TPB) r/#19-25 17.00

CAPTAIN MARVEL (Vol. 5) (See Secret Invasion x-over titles)
Marvel Comics: Jan, 2008 - No. 5, Jun, 2008 ($2.99)
1-5-Mar-Vell "from the past in the present"; McGuinness-c/Weeks-a 3.00
3,4-Skrull variant-c 4.00

CAPTAIN MARVEL
Marvel Comics: Sept, 2012 - No. 17, Jan, 2014 ($2.99)
1-16: 1-Carol Danvers as Captain Marvel; DeConnick-s/Soy-a. 13,14-The Enemy Within. 15,16-Infinity tie-in. 3.00
17-($3.99) Cameo of new Ms. Marvel (Kamala Khan); Andrade-a 4.00

CAPTAIN MARVEL
Marvel Comics: May, 2014 - Present ($3.99)
1,2: 1-Carol Danvers; DeConnick-s/Lopez-a. 2-Guardians of the Galaxy app. 4.00

CAPTAIN MARVEL ADVENTURES (See Special Edition Comics for pre #1)
Fawcett Publications: 1941 (March) - No. 150, Nov, 1953 (#1 on stands 1/16/41)
nn(#1)-Captain Marvel & Sivana by Jack Kirby. The cover was printed on unstable paper stock and is rarely found in Fine or Mint condition; blank back inside-c 3000 6000 9000 22,500 43,250 64,000
2-(Advertised as #3, which was counting Special Edition Comics as the real #1); Tuska-a 432 864 1296 3154 5577 8000
3-Metallic silver-c 320 640 960 2240 3920 5600
4-Three Lt. Marvels app. 216 432 648 1372 2361 3350
5 171 342 513 1086 1868 2650
6-10: 9-1st Otto Binder scripts on Capt. Marvel 126 252 378 806 1378 1950
11-15: 12-Capt. Marvel joins the Army. 13-Two pg. Capt. Marvel pin-up. 15-Comix Cards on back-c begin, end #26 103 206 309 659 1130 1600
16,17: 17-Painted-c 94 188 282 597 1024 1450
18-Origin & 1st app. Mary Marvel & Marvel Family (12/11/42); classic painted-c; Mary Marvel by Marcus Swayze 277 554 831 1759 3030 4300
19-Mary Marvel x-over; Christmas-c 81 162 243 518 884 1250
20,21,23-Attached to the cover, each has a miniature comic just like the Mighty Midget Comics #11, except that each has a full color promo ad on the back cover. Most copies were circulated without the miniature comic. These issues with miniatures attached are very rare, and should not be mistaken for copies with the similar Mighty Midget glued in its place. The Mighty Midgets had blank back covers except for a small victory stamp seal. Only the Capt. Marvel, Captain Marvel Jr. and Golden Arrow No. 11 miniatures have been positively documented as having been affixed to these covers. Each miniature was only partially glued by its back cover to the Captain Marvel comic making it easy to see if it's the genuine miniature rather than a Mighty Midget.
with comic attached.... 411 822 1233 2877 5039 7200
20,23-Without miniature 71 142 213 454 777 1100
21-Without miniature; Hitler-c 126 252 378 806 1378 1950
22-Mr. Mind serial begins; Mr. Mind first heard 97 194 291 621 1061 1500
24,25 68 136 204 432 746 1060
26-28,30: 26-Flag-c; subtle Mr. Mind 2-panel cameo. 27-1st full Mr. Mind app. (his voice was only heard over the radio before now) (9/43) 57 114 171 362 619 875
29-1st Mr. Mind-c (11/43) 63 126 189 403 689 975
31-35: 35-Origin Radar (5/44, see Master #50) 51 102 153 318 539 760
36-40: 37-Mary Marvel x-over 47 94 141 296 498 700
41-46: 42-Christmas-c. 43-Capt. Marvel 1st meets Uncle Marvel; Mary Batson cameo.

Captain Marvel, Jr. #6 © FAW

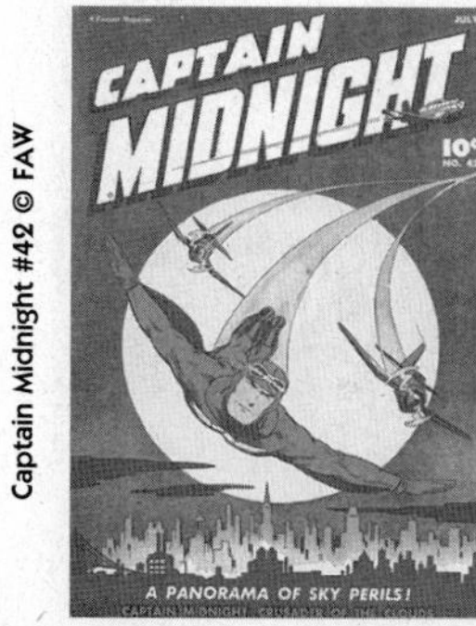

Captain Midnight #42 © FAW

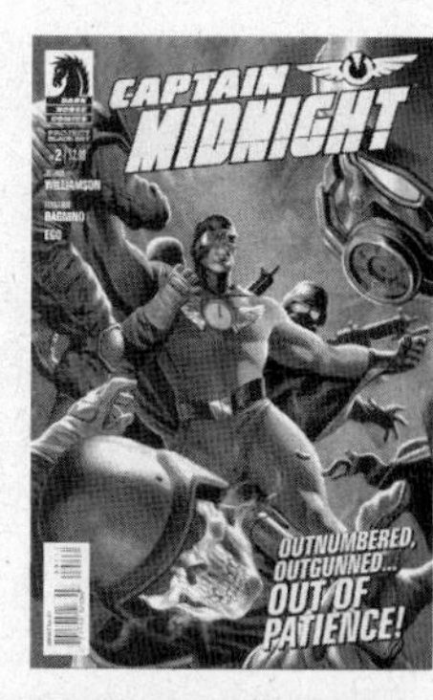

Captain Midnight #2 © DH

	GD 2.0	VG 4.0	FN 6.0	VF 8.0	VF/NM 9.0	NM- 9.2
46-Mr. Mind serial ends	39	78	117	240	395	550
47-50	37	74	111	222	361	500
51-53,55-60: 51-63-Bi-weekly issues. 52-Origin & 1st app. Sivana Jr.; Capt. Marvel Jr. x-over	33	66	99	194	317	440
54-Special oversize 68 pg. issue	34	68	102	199	325	450
61-The Cult of the Curse serial begins	36	72	108	211	343	475
62-65-Serial cont.; Mary Marvel x-over in #65	33	66	99	194	317	440
66-Serial ends; Atomic War-c	39	78	117	231	378	525
67-77,79: 69-Billy Batson's Christmas; Uncle Marvel, Mary Marvel, Capt. Marvel Jr. x-over. 71-Three Lt. Marvels app. 79-Origin Mr. Tawny	30	60	90	177	289	400
78-Origin Mr. Atom	34	68	102	199	325	450
80-Origin Capt. Marvel retold; origin scene-c	81	162	243	518	884	1250
81-84,86-90: 81,90-Mr. Atom app. 82-Infinity-c. 82,86,88,90-Mr. Tawny app.	30	60	90	177	289	400
85-Freedom Train issue	33	66	99	194	317	440
91-99: 92-Mr. Tawny app. 96-Gets 1st name "Tawky"	29	58	87	170	278	385
100-Origin retold; silver metallic-c	48	96	144	302	514	725
101-115,117-120	28	56	84	168	274	380
116-Flying Saucer issue (1/51)	33	66	99	194	317	440
121-Origin retold	37	74	111	218	354	490
122-137,139,140	28	56	84	168	274	380
138-Flying Saucer issue (11/52)	33	66	99	194	317	440
141-Pre-code horror story "The Hideous Head-Hunter"	31	62	93	186	303	420
142-149: 142-used in **POP**, pgs. 92,96	31	62	93	182	296	410
150-(Low distribution)	54	108	162	343	574	825

NOTE: *Swayze a-12, 14, 15, 18, 19, 40; c-12, 15, 19.*

CAPTAIN MARVEL AND THE GOOD HUMOR MAN (Movie)
Fawcett Publications: 1950

	GD 2.0	VG 4.0	FN 6.0	VF 8.0	VF/NM 9.0	NM- 9.2
nn-Partial photo-c w/Jack Carson & the Captain Marvel Club Boys	47	94	141	296	498	700

CAPTAIN MARVEL COMIC STORY PAINT BOOK (See Comic Story...)

CAPTAIN MARVEL, JR. (See Fawcett Miniatures, Marvel Family, Master Comics, Mighty Midget Comics, Shazam & Whiz Comics)

CAPTAIN MARVEL, JR.
Fawcett Publications: Nov, 1942 - No. 119, June, 1953 (No #34)

	GD 2.0	VG 4.0	FN 6.0	VF 8.0	VF/NM 9.0	NM- 9.2
1-Origin Capt. Marvel Jr. retold (Whiz #25); Capt. Nazi app. Classic Raboy-c	568	1136	1704	4146	7323	10,500
2-Vs. Capt. Nazi; origin Capt. Nippon	203	406	609	1289	2220	3150
3	115	230	345	730	1253	1775
4-Classic Raboy-c	121	242	363	768	1322	1875
5-Vs. Capt. Nazi	97	194	291	621	1061	1500
6-8: 8-Vs. Capt. Nazi	81	162	243	518	884	1250
9-Classic flag-c	94	188	282	597	1024	1450
10-Hitler-c	155	310	465	992	1696	2400
11,12,15-Capt. Nazi app.	68	136	204	435	743	1050
13-Classic Hitler, Tojo and Mussolini football-c	155	310	465	992	1696	2400
14,16-20: 14-Christmas-c. 16-Capt. Marvel & Sivana x-over. 17-Futuristic city-c. 19-Capt. Nazi & Capt. Nippon app.	57	114	171	362	619	875
21-30: 25-Flag-c	45	90	135	284	480	675
31-33,36-40: 37-Infinity-c	33	66	99	194	317	440
35-#34 on inside; cover shows origin of Sivana Jr. which is not on inside. Evidently the cover to #35 was printed out of sequence and bound with contents to #34	33	66	99	194	317	440
41-70: 42-Robot-c. 53-Atomic Bomb-c/story	27	54	81	160	263	365
71-99,101-104: 87,93-Robot-c. 104-Used in **POP**, pg. 89	24	48	72	140	230	320
100	27	54	81	162	266	370
105-114,116-118: 116-Vampira, Queen of Terror app.	26	52	78	154	252	350
115-Classic injury to eye-c; Eyeball story w/injury-to-eye panels	116	232	348	742	1271	1800
119-Electric chair-c (scarce)	76	152	228	486	831	1175

NOTE: *Mac Raboy c-1-28, 30-32, 57, 59 among others.*

CAPTAIN MARVEL PRESENTS THE TERRIBLE FIVE
M. F. Enterprises: Aug, 1966; V2#5, Sept, 1967 (No #2-4) (25¢)

	GD 2.0	VG 4.0	FN 6.0	VF 8.0	VF/NM 9.0	NM- 9.2
1	5	10	15	30	50	70
V2#5-(Formerly Captain Marvel)	3	6	9	21	33	45

CAPTAIN MARVEL'S FUN BOOK
Samuel Lowe Co.: 1944 (1/2" thick) (cardboard covers)(25¢)

	GD 2.0	VG 4.0	FN 6.0	VF 8.0	VF/NM 9.0	NM- 9.2
nn-Puzzles, games, magic, etc.; infinity-c	40	80	120	246	411	575

CAPTAIN MARVEL SPECIAL EDITION (See Special Edition)

CAPTAIN MARVEL STORY BOOK
Fawcett Publications: Summer, 1946 - No. 4, Summer?, 1948

	GD 2.0	VG 4.0	FN 6.0	VF 8.0	VF/NM 9.0	NM- 9.2
1-Half text	57	114	171	362	619	875
2-4	41	82	123	250	418	585

CAPTAIN MARVEL THRILL BOOK (Large-Size)
Fawcett Publications: 1941 (B&W w/color-c)

	GD 2.0	VG 4.0	FN 6.0	VF 8.0	VF/NM 9.0	NM- 9.2
1-Reprints from Whiz #8,10, & Special Edition #1 (Rare)	310	620	930	3100	-	-

NOTE: *Rarely found in Fine or Mint condition.*

CAPTAIN MIDNIGHT (TV, radio, films) (See The Funnies, Popular Comics & Super Book of Comics)(Becomes Sweethearts No. 68 on)
Fawcett Publications: Sept, 1942 - No. 67, Fall, 1948 (#1-14: 68 pgs.)

	GD 2.0	VG 4.0	FN 6.0	VF 8.0	VF/NM 9.0	NM- 9.2
1-Origin Captain Midnight, star of radio and movies; Captain Marvel cameo on cover	314	628	942	2198	3849	5500
2-Smashes the Jap Juggarnaut	155	310	465	992	1696	2400
3-Classic Nazi war-c	142	284	426	909	1555	2200
4,5: 4-Grapples the Gremlins	113	226	339	718	1234	1750
6-8	68	136	204	435	743	1050
9-Raboy-c	69	138	207	442	759	1075
10-Raboy Flag-c	71	142	213	454	777	1100
11-20: 11,17,18-Raboy-c. 16 (1/44)	48	96	144	302	514	725
21-Classic WWII-c	56	112	168	356	608	860
22,25-30: 22-War savings stamp-c	40	80	120	246	411	575
23-WWII Concentration Camp-c	53	106	159	334	567	800
24-Japan flag sunburst-c	58	116	174	371	636	900
31-40	31	62	93	182	296	410
41-59,61-67: 50-Sci/fi theme begins?	24	48	72	142	234	325
60-Flying Saucer issue (2/48)-3rd of this theme; see The Spirit 9/28/47(1st), Shadow Comics V7#10 (2nd, 1/48) & Boy Commandos #26 (4th, 3-4/48)	37	74	111	222	361	500

CAPTAIN MIDNIGHT
Dark Horse Comics: No. 0, Jun, 2013 - Present ($2.99)

	NM- 9.2
0-9: 0-Williamson-s/Ibáñez-a; WWII hero appears in modern times. 4,5-Skyman app.	3.00
One For One: Captain Midnight #1 (1/14, $1.00) r/#1	3.00

CAPTAIN NICE (TV)
Gold Key: Nov, 1967 (one-shot)

	GD 2.0	VG 4.0	FN 6.0	VF 8.0	VF/NM 9.0	NM- 9.2
1(10211-711)-Photo-c	6	12	18	37	66	95

CAPTAIN N: THE GAME MASTER (TV)
Valiant Comics: 1990 - No. 6? ($1.95, thick stock, coated-c)

	NM- 9.2
1-6: 4-6-Layton-c	5.00

CAPTAIN PARAGON (See Bill Black's Fun Comics)
Americomics: Dec, 1983 - No. 4, 1985

	NM- 9.2
1-Intro/1st app. Ms. Victory	4.00
2-4	3.00

CAPTAIN PARAGON AND THE SENTINELS OF JUSTICE
AC Comics: April, 1985 - No. 6, 1986 ($1.75)

	NM- 9.2
1-6: 1-Capt. Paragon, Commando D., Nightveil, Scarlet Scorpion, Stardust & Atoman	3.00

CAPTAIN PLANET AND THE PLANETEERS (TV cartoon)
Marvel Comics: Oct, 1991 - No. 12, Oct, 1992 ($1.00/$1.25)

	NM- 9.2
1-N. Adams painted-c	4.00
2-12: 3-Romita-c	3.00

CAPTAIN POWER AND THE SOLDIERS OF THE FUTURE (TV)
Continuity Comics: Aug, 1988 - No. 2, 1988 ($2.00)

	NM- 9.2
1,2: 1-Neal Adams-c/layouts/inks; variant-c exists.	3.00

CAPTAIN PUREHEART (See Archie as...)

CAPTAIN ROCKET
P. L. Publ. (Canada): Nov, 1951

	GD 2.0	VG 4.0	FN 6.0	VF 8.0	VF/NM 9.0	NM- 9.2
1	47	94	141	296	498	700

CAPT. SAVAGE AND HIS LEATHERNECK RAIDERS (...And His Battlefield Raiders #9 on)
Marvel Comics Group (Animated Timely Features): Jan, 1968 - No. 19, Mar, 1970 (See Sgt. Fury No. 10)

	GD 2.0	VG 4.0	FN 6.0	VF 8.0	VF/NM 9.0	NM- 9.2
1-Sgt. Fury & Howlers cameo	5	10	15	34	60	85
2,7,11: 2,4-Origin Hydra. 7-Pre-"Thing" Ben Grimm story. 11-Sgt. Fury app.	3	6	9	17	26	35
3-6,8-10,12-14: 14-Last 12¢ issue	3	6	9	16	23	30

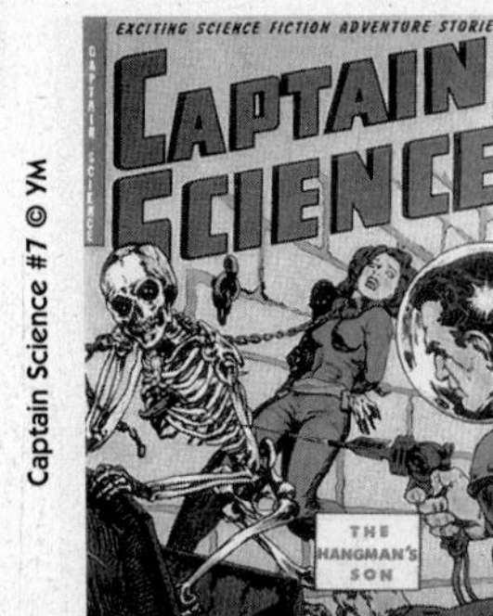

Captain Science #7 © YM

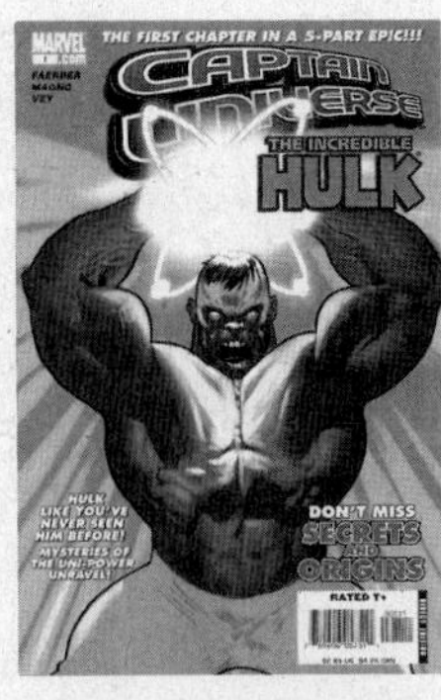

Captain Universe/Hulk #1 © MAR

Captain Wonder #1 © Haberlin Studios

GD VG FN VF VF/NM NM-
2.0 4.0 6.0 8.0 9.0 9.2

15-19 3 6 9 14 19 24
*NOTE: **Ayres/Shores** a-1-8,11. **Ayres/Severin** a-9,10,17-19. **Heck/Shores** a-12-15.*

CAPTAIN SCIENCE (Fantastic No. 8 on)
Youthful Magazines: Nov, 1950; No. 2, Feb, 1951 - No. 7, Dec, 1951
1-Wood-a; origin; 2 pg. text w/ photos of George Pal's "Destination Moon."
94 188 282 597 1024 1450
2-Flying saucer-c swiped Weird Science #13(#2)-c 53 106 159 334 567 800
3,6,7; 3,6-Bondage c-swipes/Wings #94,91 45 90 135 284 480 675
4,5-Wood/Orlando-c/a(2) each 86 172 258 546 936 1325
NOTE: *Fass a-4. Bondage c-3, 6, 7.*

CAPTAIN SILVER'S LOG OF SEA HOUND (See Sea Hound)

CAPTAIN SINBAD (Movie Adaptation) (See Fantastic Voyages of... & Movie Comics)

CAPTAIN STERNN: RUNNING OUT OF TIME
Kitchen Sink Press: Sept, 1993 - No. 5, 1994 ($4.95, limited series, coated stock, 52 pgs.)
1-5: Berni Wrightson-c/a/scripts 6.00
1-Gold ink variant 10.00

CAPTAIN STEVE SAVAGE (...& His Jet Fighters, No. 2-13)
Avon Periodicals: 1950 - No. 8, 1/53; No. 5, 9-10/54 - No. 13, 5-6/56
nn(1st series)-Harrison/Wood art, 22 pgs. (titled "...Over Korea")
41 82 123 256 428 600
1(4/51)-Reprints nn issue (Canadian) 20 40 60 114 182 250
2-Kamen-a 15 30 45 88 137 185
3-11 (#6, 11-12/54, last precode) 13 26 39 74 105 135
12-Wood-a (6 pgs.) 15 30 45 90 140 190
13-Check, Lawrence-a 14 28 42 76 108 140
NOTE: ***Kinstler** c-2-5, 7-9, 11. **Lawrence** a-8. **Ravielli** a-5, 9.*
5(9-10/54-2nd series)(Formerly Sensational Police Cases)
11 22 33 60 83 105
6-Reprints nn issue; Harrison/Wood-a 11 22 33 62 86 110
7-13: 9,10-Kinstler-c. 10-r/cover #2 (1st series). 13-r/cover #8 (1st series)
9 18 27 50 65 80

CAPTAIN STONE (See Holyoke One-Shot No. 10)

CAPT. STORM (Also see G. I. Combat #138)
National Periodical Publications: May-June, 1964 - No. 18, Mar-Apr, 1967
1-Origin 10 20 30 64 132 200
2-7,9-18: 3,6,13-Kubert-a. 4-Colan-a. 12-Kubert-c 6 12 18 42 79 115
8-Grey-tone-c 8 16 24 52 99 145

CAPTAIN 3-D (Super hero)
Harvey Publications: December, 1953 (25¢, came with 2 pairs of glasses)
1-Kirby/Ditko-a (Ditko's 3rd published work tied with Strange Fantasy #9, see also Daring Love #1 & Black Magic V4 #3); shows cover in 3-D on inside; Kirby/Meskin-c 12 24 36 69 97 125
NOTE: *Half price without glasses*

CAPTAIN THUNDER AND BLUE BOLT
Hero Comics: Sept, 1987 - No. 10, 1988 ($1.95)
1-10: 1-Origin Blue Bolt. 3-Origin Capt. Thunder. 6-1st app. Wicket. 8-Champions x-over 3.00

CAPTAIN TOOTSIE & THE SECRET LEGION (Advs. of...)(Also see Monte Hale #30,39 & Real Western Hero)
Toby Press: Oct, 1950 - No. 2, Dec, 1950
1-Not Beck-a; both have sci/fi covers 32 64 96 188 307 425
2-The Rocketeer Patrol app.; not Beck-a 20 40 60 114 182 250

CAPTAIN TRIUMPH (See Crack Comics #27)

CAPTAIN UNIVERSE... (5-part x-over)
Marvel Comics: 2005; Jan, 2006
.../ Daredevil 1 (1/06, $2.99) Part 2; Faerber-s/Santacruz-a 3.00
.../ Hulk 1 (1/06, $2.99) Part 1; Faerber-s/Magno-a 3.00
.../ Invisible Woman 1 (1/06, $2.99) Part 4; Faerber-s/Raiz-a; Gladiator app. 3.00
.../ Silver Surfer 1 (1/06, $2.99) Part 5; Faerber-s/Magno-a 3.00
.../ X-23 1 (1/06, $2.99) Part 3; Faerber-s/Portella-a; Scorpion app. 3.00
...: Power Unimaginable TPB (2005, $19.99)-Reprints from Marvel Spotlight #9-11, Incredible Hulk Ann. #10, Marvel Fanfare #25, Web of Spider-Man Ann. #5&6, Marvel Comics Presents #148, Cosmic Power Unlimited #5 20.00
...: The Hero Who Could Be You 1 (7/13, $7.99) r/Marvel Spotlight #9-11 & early apps. 8.00
...: Universal Heroes TPB (2005, $13.99) reprints .../Hulk, .../Daredevil, ...X-23 and back-up stories from Amazing Fantasy (2005) #13,14 14.00

CAPTAIN VENTURE & THE LAND BENEATH THE SEA (See Space Family Robinson)
Gold Key: Oct, 1968 - No. 2, Oct, 1969
1-r/Space Family Robinson serial; Spiegle-a 4 8 12 27 44 60

GD VG FN VF VF/NM NM-
2.0 4.0 6.0 8.0 9.0 9.2

2-Spiegle-a 4 8 12 23 37 50

CAPTAIN VICTORY AND THE GALACTIC RANGERS (Also see Kirby: Genesis)
Pacific Comics: Nov, 1981 - No. 13, Jan, 1984 ($1.00, direct sales, 36-48 pgs.) (Created by Jack Kirby)
1-1st app. Mr. Mind 4.00
2-13: 3-N. Adams-a 3.00
Special 1-(10/83)-Kirby c/a(p) 4.00
*NOTE: **Conrad** a-10, 11. **Ditko** a-6. **Kirby** a-1-3p; c-1-13.*

CAPTAIN VICTORY AND THE GALACTIC RANGERS
Jack Kirby Comics: July, 2000 - No. 2, Sept, 2000 ($2.95, B&W)
1,2-New Jeremy Kirby-s with reprinted Jack Kirby-a; Liefeld pin-up art 3.00

CAPTAIN VIDEO (TV) (See XMas Comics)
Fawcett Publications: Feb, 1951 - No. 6, Dec, 1951 (No. 1,5,6-36 pgs.; 2-4, 52 pgs.)
1-George Evans-a(2); 1st TV hero comic 103 206 309 659 1130 1600
2-Used in **SOTI**, pg. 382 66 132 198 419 722 1025
3-6-All Evans-a except #5 mostly Evans 55 110 165 352 601 850
NOTE: *Minor **Williamson** assists on most issues. Photo c-1, 5, 6; painted c-2-4.*

CAPTAIN WILLIE SCHULTZ (Also see Fightin' Army)
Charlton Comics: No. 76, Oct, 1985 - No. 77, Jan, 1986
76,77-Low print run 1 2 3 5 6 8

CAPTAIN WIZARD COMICS (See Meteor, Red Band & Three Ring Comics)
Rural Home: 1946
1-Capt. Wizard dons new costume; Impossible Man, Race Wilkins app.
36 72 108 216 351 485

CAPTAIN WONDER
Image Comics: Feb, 2011 ($4.99, 3-D comic with glasses)
1-Haberlin-s/Tan-a; sketch pages, crossword puzzle, paper dolls 5.00

CARBON GREY
Image Comics: Mar, 2011 - No. 3, May, 2011 ($2.99, limited series)
1-3-Khari Evans, Kinsun Loh & Hoang Nguyen-a; Nguyen-c 3.00
... Origins 1,2 (11/11 - No. 2, 3/12, $3.99) 1-Pop Mhan-a 4.00
Vol. 2 (7/12 - No. 3, 2/13, $3.99) 1-3-Gardner-s/Evans & Nguyen-a 4.00
Vol. 3 (12/13 - Present) 1,2-Gardner-s/Evans & Nguyen-a 4.00

CARE BEARS (TV, Movie)(See Star Comics Magazine)
Star Comics/Marvel Comics No. 15 on: Nov, 1985 - No. 20, Jan, 1989
1-20: Post-a begins. 11-$1.00-c begins. 13-Madballs app.
1 2 3 5 6 8

CAREER GIRL ROMANCES (Formerly Three Nurses)
Charlton Comics: June, 1964 - No. 78, Dec, 1973
V4#24-31 3 6 9 14 20 25
32-Elvis Presley, Herman's Hermits, Johnny Rivers line drawn-c
9 18 27 60 120 180
33-37,39-50: 39-Tiffany Sinn app. 2 4 6 13 18 22
38-(2/67) 1st app. Tiffany Sinn, C.I.A. Sweetheart, Undercover Agent (also see Secret Agent #10; Dominguel-a 3 6 9 16 24 32
51-78: 54-Jonnie Love anti-drup PSA. 67-Susan Dey pin-up. 70-David Cassidy pin-up
2 4 6 10 14 18

CAR 54, WHERE ARE YOU? (TV)
Dell Publishing Co.: Mar-May, 1962 - No. 7, Sept-Nov, 1963; 1964 - 1965 (All photo-c)
Four Color 1257(#1, 3-5/62) 7 14 21 49 92 135
2(6-8/62)-7 5 10 15 30 50 70
2,3(10-12/64), 4(1-3/65)-Reprints #2,3,&4 of 1st series
3 6 9 19 30 40

CARL BARKS LIBRARY OF WALT DISNEY'S GYRO GEARLOOSE COMICS AND FILLERS IN COLOR, THE
Gladstone: 1993 ($7.95, 8-1/2x11", limited series, 52 pgs.)
1-6: Carl Barks reprints 1 3 4 6 8 10

CARL BARKS LIBRARY OF WALT DISNEY'S COMICS AND STORIES IN COLOR, THE
Gladstone: Jan, 1992 - No. 51, Mar, 1996 ($8.95, 8-1/2x11", 60 pgs.)
1,2,6,8-51: 1-Barks Donald Duck-r/WDC&S #31-35; 2-r/#36,38-41; 6-r/#57-61; 8-r/#67-71; 9-r/#72-76; 10-r/#77-81; 11-r/#82-86; 12-r/#87-91; 13-r/#92-96; 14-r/#97-101; 15-r/#102-106; 16-r/#107-111; 17-r/#112,114,117,124,125; 18-r/#126-130; 19-r/#131,132(2),133,134; 20-r/#135-139; 21-r/#140-144; 22-r/#145-149; 23-r/#150-154; 24-r/#155-159; 25-r/#160-164; 26-r/#165-169; 27-r/#170-174;28-r/#175-179; 29-r/#180-184; 30-r/#185-189; 31-r/#190-194; 32-r/#195-199;33-r/#200-204; 34-r/#205-209; 35-r/#210-214; 36-r/#215-219; 37-r/#220-224; 38-r/#225-229; 39-r/#230-234; 40-r/#235-239; 41-r/#240-244; 42r/#245-249; 43-r/#250-254; 44-50; All contain one Heroes & Villains trading card each

Carnage: Mind Bomb #1 © MAR

Cartoon Cartoons #13 © Cartoon Net

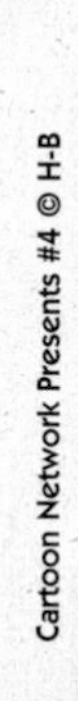
Cartoon Network Presents #4 © H-B

	GD 2.0	VG 4.0	FN 6.0	VF 8.0	VF/NM 9.0	NM- 9.2

	2	4	6	9	12	15
3,4,7: 3-r/#42-46. 4-r/#47-51. 7-r/#62-66.	2	4	6	11	16	20
5-r/#52-56	3	6	9	16	23	30

CARL BARKS LIBRARY OF WALT DISNEY'S DONALD DUCK ADVENTURES IN COLOR, THE
Gladstone: Jan, 1994 - No. 25, Jan, 1996 ($7.95-$9.95, 44-68 pgs., 8-1/2"x11")
(all contain one Donald Duck trading card each)

1-5,7-25-Carl Barks-r: 1-r/FC #9; 2-r/FC #29; 3-r/FC #62; 4-r/FC #108; 5-r/FC #147 & #79(Mickey Mouse); 7-r/FC #159. 8-r/FC #178 & 189. 9-r/FC #199 & 203; 10-r/FC 223 & 238; 11-r/Christmas Parade #1 & 2; 12-r/FC #296; 13-r/FC #263; 14-r/MOC #20 & 41; 15-r/FC 275 & 282; 16-r/FC #291&300; 17-r/FC #308 & 318; 18-r/Vac. Parade #1 & Summer Fun #2; 19-r/FC #328 & 367 — 2 4 6 9 12 15
6-r/MOC #4, Cheerios "Atom Bomb," D.D. Tells About Kites — 3 6 9 14 20 25

CARL BARKS LIBRARY OF WALT DISNEY'S DONALD DUCK CHRISTMAS STORIES IN COLOR, THE
Gladstone: 1992 ($7.95, 44pgs., one-shot)

nn-Reprints Firestone giveaways 1945-1949 — 2 4 6 10 14 18

CARL BARKS LIBRARY OF WALT DISNEY'S UNCLE SCROOGE COMICS ONE PAGERS IN COLOR, THE
Gladstone: 1992 - No. 2, 1993 ($8.95, limited series, 60 pgs., 8-1/2x11")

1-Carl Barks one pg. reprints — 3 6 9 16 23 30
2-Carl Barks one pg. reprints — 2 4 6 10 14 18

CARNAGE
Marvel Comics: Dec, 2010 - No. 5, Aug, 2011 ($3.99, limited series)

1-5-Spider-Man & Iron Man app.; Clayton Crain-a/c; Wells-s — 4.00
...: It's a Wonderful Life (10/96, $1.95) David Quinn scripts — 3.00
...: Mind Bomb (2/96, $2.95) Warren Ellis script; Kyle Hotz-a — 4.00

CARNAGE, U.S.A.
Marvel Comics: Feb, 2012 - No. 5 ($3.99, limited series)

1-4-Clayton Crain-a/c; Wells-s; Spider-Man & Avengers app. 3,4-Venom app. — 4.00

CARNATION MALTED MILK GIVEAWAYS (See Wisco)

CARNEYS, THE
Archie Comics: Summer, 1994 ($2.00, 52 pgs)

1-Bound-in pull-out poster — 4.00

CARNIVAL COMICS (Formerly Kayo #12; becomes Red Seal Comics #14)
Harry 'A' Chesler/Pershing Square Publ. Co.: 1945

nn (#13)-Guardineer-a — 19 38 57 109 172 235

CAROLINE KENNEDY
Charlton Comics: 1961 (one-shot)

nn-Interior photo covers of Kennedy family — 8 16 24 52 99 145

CAROUSEL COMICS
F. E. Howard, Toronto: V1#8, April, 1948

V1#8 — 8 16 24 44 57 70

CARS (Based on the 2006 Pixar movie)
Boom Entertainment: No. 0, Nov, 2009 - No. 7, Jun, 2010 ($2.99)

0-7: 0,1-Three covers on each. 2-7-Two covers on each — 3.00
...: Adventures of Tow Mater 1-4 (7/10 - No. 4, 10/10, $2.99) 1-Two covers — 3.00
...: Radiator Springs 1-4 (7/09 - No. 4, 10/09, $2.99) Two covers on each — 3.00
...: The Rookie 1-4 (3/09 - No. 4, 6/09, $2.99) Origin of Lightning McQueen — 3.00

CARS 2 (Based on the 2011 Pixar movie)
Marvel Worldwide (Disney Comics): Aug, 2011 - No. 2, Aug, 2011 ($3.99)

1,2-Movie adaptation; car profile pages — 4.00

CARS, WORLD OF (Free Comic Book Day giveaway)
BOOM Kids!: May, 2009

1-Based on the Disney/Pixar movie — 3.00

CARTOON CARTOONS (Anthology)
DC Comics: Mar, 2001 - No. 33, Oct, 2004 ($1.99/$2.25)

1-33-Short stories of Cartoon Network characters. 3,6,10,13,15-Space Ghost. 13-Begin $2.25-c. 17-Dexter's Laboratory begins — 3.00

CARTOON KIDS
Atlas Comics (CPS): 1957 (no month)

1-Maneely-c/a; Dexter The Demon, Willie The Wise-Guy, Little Zelda app. — 13 26 39 72 101 130

CARTOON NETWORK ACTION PACK (Anthology)
DC Comics: July, 2006 - No. 67, May, 2012 ($2.25/$2.50/$2.99)

1-31-Short stories of Cartoon Network characters. 1,4,6-Rowdyruff Boys app. — 3.00
32-67: 32-Begin $2.50-c. 50-Ben 10/Generator Rex team-up — 3.00

CARTOON NETWORK BLOCK PARTY (Anthology)
DC Comics: Nov, 2004 - No. 59, Sept, 2009 ($2.25/$2.50)

1,2,4-51-Short stories of Cartoon Network characters — 3.00
3-($2.95) Bonus pages — 4.00
52-59: 52-Begin $2.50-c. 59-Last issue; Powerpuff Girls app. — 3.00
Cartoon Network 2-in-1: Ben 10 Alien Force/The Secret Saturdays TPB (2010, $12.99) reprints stories from #26-42 — 13.00
Cartoon Network 2-in-1: Foster's Home For Imaginary Friends/Powerpuff Girls TPB (2010, $12.99) reprints stories from #19-21,23,25,26,28,30-32,34-38,41 — 13.00
... Vol. 1: Get Down! (2005, $6.99, digest) reprints from Dexter's Lab and Cartoon Cartoons — 7.00
... Vol. 2: Read All About It! (2005, $6.99, digest) reprints — 7.00
... Vol. 3: Can You Dig It?; ... Vol. 4: Blast Off! (2006, $6.99, digest) reprints — 7.00

CARTOON NETWORK PRESENTS
DC Comics: Aug, 1997 - No. 24, Aug, 1999 ($1.75-$1.99, anthology)

1-Dexter's Lab — 5.00
1-Platinum Edition — 1 2 3 5 7 9
2-10: 2-Space Ghost — 3.50
11-24: 12-Bizarro World — 3.00

CARTOON NETWORK PRESENTS SPACE GHOST
Archie Comics: Mar, 1997 ($1.50)

1-Scott Rosema-p — 6.00

CARTOON NETWORK STARRING... (Anthology)
DC Comics: Sept, 1999 - No. 18, Feb, 2001 ($1.99)

1-Powerpuff Girls — 5.00
2-18: 2,8,11,14,17-Johnny Bravo. 12,15,18-Space Ghost — 3.00

CARTOON TALES (Disney's...)
W.D. Publications (Disney): nd, nn (1992) ($2.95, 6-5/8x9-1/2", 52 pgs.)

nn-Ariel & Sebastian-Serpent Teen; Beauty and the Beast; A Tale of Enchantment; Darkwing Duck - Just Us Justice Ducks; 101 Dalmatians - Canine Classics; Tale Spin - Surprise in the Skies; Uncle Scrooge - Blast to the Past — 4.00

CARVERS
Image Comics (Flypaper Press): 1998 - No. 3, 1999 ($2.95)

1-3-Pander Bros.-a/Fleming-s — 3.00

CAR WARRIORS
Marvel Comics (Epic): June, 1991 - No. 4, Sept, 1991 ($2.25, lim. series)

1-4: 1-Says April in indicia — 3.00

CASANOVA
Image Comics: June, 2006 - No. 14, May, 2008 ($1.99, B&W & olive green or blue)

1-14: 1-7-Matt Fraction-s/Gabriel Bá-a/c. 8-14-Fabio Moon-a — 3.00
...: Luxuria TPB (2008, $12.99) r/#1-7; sketch pages and cover gallery — 13.00
1-4 (Marvel Comics, 10/10 - No. 4, 12/10, $3.99) Recolored reprints Image series #1-7 — 4.00
...: Gula (Marvel, 1/11 - No. 4, 4/11) r/Image series #8-14. 4-New story pages — 4.00
...: Avaritia (III) 1-4 (Marvel, 11/11 - No. 4, 8/12, $4.99) new story; Fraction-s/Bá-a — 5.00

CASE FILES: SAM & TWITCH (Also see the Spawn titles)
Image Comics: May, 2003 - No. 25, July, 2006 ($2.50/$2.95, color #1-6/B&W #7-on)

1-25: 1-5-Scott Morse-a/Marc Andreyko-s. 7-13-Paul Lee-a. 13-Niles-s — 3.00

CASE OF THE SHOPLIFTER'S SHOE (See Perry Mason, Feature Book No.50)

CASE OF THE WINKING BUDDHA, THE
St. John Publ. Co.: 1950 (132 pgs.; 25¢; B&W; 5-1/2x7-5-1/2x8")

nn-Charles Raab-a; reprinted in Authentic Police Cases No. 25 — 36 72 108 211 343 475

CASEY BLUE
DC Comics (WildStorm): Jul, 2008 - No. 6, Dec, 2008 ($2.99, limited series)

1-6-B. Clay Moore-s/Carlos Barberi-a — 3.00
...: Beyond Tomorrow TPB (2009, $19.99) r/#1-6; Barberi sketch pages — 20.00

CASEY-CRIME PHOTOGRAPHER (Two-Gun Western No. 5 on)(Radio)
Marvel Comics (BFP): Aug, 1949 - No. 4, Feb, 1950

1-Photo-c; 52 pgs. — 27 54 81 158 259 360
2-4: Photo-c — 19 38 57 111 176 240

CASEY JONES (TV)
Dell Publishing Co.: No. 915, July, 1958

Four Color 915-Alan Hale photo-c — 5 10 15 33 57 80

Casper and Friends #1 © HARV

Casper Giant Size #1 © HARV

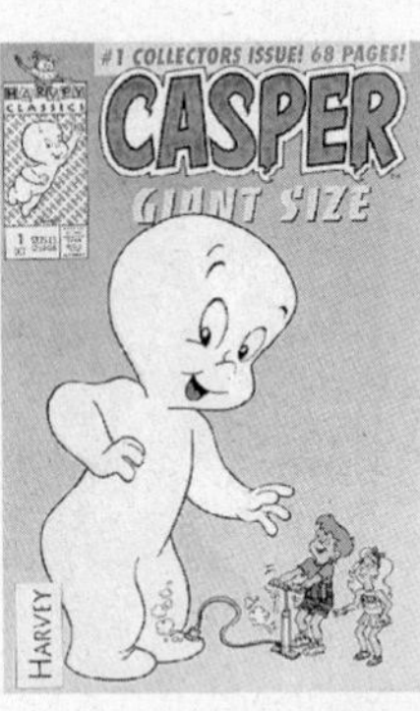

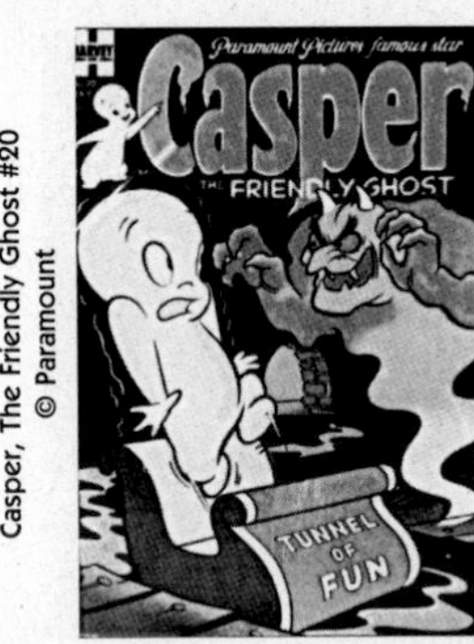

Casper, The Friendly Ghost #20 © Paramount

CASEY JONES & RAPHAEL (See Bodycount)
Mirage Studios: Oct, 1994 ($2.75, unfinished limited series)

	GD 2.0	VG 4.0	FN 6.0	VF 8.0	VF/NM 9.0	NM- 9.2
1-Bisley-c; Eastman story & pencils						3.00

CASEY JONES: NORTH BY DOWNEAST
Mirage Studios: May, 1994 - No. 2, July, 1994 ($2.75, limited series)

	GD 2.0	VG 4.0	FN 6.0	VF 8.0	VF/NM 9.0	NM- 9.2
1,2-Rick Veitch script & pencils; Kevin Eastman story & inks						3.00

CASPER ADVENTURE DIGEST
Harvey Comics: V2#1, Oct, 1992 - V2#8, Apr, 1994 ($1.75/$1.95, digest-size)

	GD 2.0	VG 4.0	FN 6.0	VF 8.0	VF/NM 9.0	NM- 9.2
V2#1: Casper, Richie Rich, Spooky, Wendy						5.00
2-8						3.50

CASPER AND...
Harvey Comics: Nov, 1987 - No. 12, June, 1990 (.75/$1.00, all reprints)

	GD 2.0	VG 4.0	FN 6.0	VF 8.0	VF/NM 9.0	NM- 9.2
1-Ghostly Trio						5.00
2-12: 2-Spooky; begin $1.00-c. 3-Wendy. 4-Nightmare. 5-Ghostly Trio. 6-Spooky. 7-Wendy. 8-Hot Stuff. 9-Baby Huey. 10-Wendy.11-Ghostly Trio. 12-Spooky						3.00

CASPER AND FRIENDS
Harvey Comics: Oct, 1991 - No. 5, July, 1992 ($1.00/$1.25)

	GD 2.0	VG 4.0	FN 6.0	VF 8.0	VF/NM 9.0	NM- 9.2
1-Nightmare, Ghostly Trio, Wendy, Spooky						4.00
2-5						3.00

CASPER AND FRIENDS MAGAZINE: Mar, 1997 - No. 3, July, 1997 ($3.99)

	GD 2.0	VG 4.0	FN 6.0	VF 8.0	VF/NM 9.0	NM- 9.2
1-3						4.00

CASPER AND NIGHTMARE (See Harvey Hits# 37, 45, 52, 56, 59, 62, 65, 68,71, 75)

CASPER AND NIGHTMARE (Nightmare & Casper No. 1-5)
Harvey Publications: No. 6, 11/64 - No. 44, 10/73; No. 45, 6/74 - No. 46, 8/74 (25¢)

	GD 2.0	VG 4.0	FN 6.0	VF 8.0	VF/NM 9.0	NM- 9.2
6: 68 pg. Giants begin, ends #32	5	10	15	31	53	75
7-10	3	6	9	21	33	45
11-20	3	6	9	17	26	35
21-37: 33-37-(52 pg. Giants)	3	6	9	14	20	26
38-46	2	4	6	10	14	18

NOTE: *Many issues contain reprints.*

CASPER AND SPOOKY (See Harvey Hits No. 20)
Harvey Publications: Oct, 1972 - No. 7, Oct, 1973

	GD 2.0	VG 4.0	FN 6.0	VF 8.0	VF/NM 9.0	NM- 9.2
1	3	6	9	17	26	35
2-7	2	4	6	10	14	18

CASPER AND THE GHOSTLY TRIO
Harvey Pub.: Nov, 1972 - No. 7, Nov, 1973; No. 8, Aug, 1990 - No. 10, Dec, 1990

	GD 2.0	VG 4.0	FN 6.0	VF 8.0	VF/NM 9.0	NM- 9.2
1	3	6	9	17	26	35
2-7	2	4	6	10	14	18
8-10						6.00

CASPER AND WENDY
Harvey Publications: Sept, 1972 - No. 8, Nov, 1973

	GD 2.0	VG 4.0	FN 6.0	VF 8.0	VF/NM 9.0	NM- 9.2
1: 52 pg. Giant	3	6	9	17	26	35
2-8	2	4	6	10	14	18

CASPER BIG BOOK
Harvey Comics: V2#1, Aug, 1992 - No. 3, May, 1993 ($1.95, 52 pgs.)

	GD 2.0	VG 4.0	FN 6.0	VF 8.0	VF/NM 9.0	NM- 9.2
V2#1-Spooky app.						4.00
2,3						4.00

CASPER CAT (See Dopey Duck)
I. W. Enterprises/Super: 1958; 1963

	GD 2.0	VG 4.0	FN 6.0	VF 8.0	VF/NM 9.0	NM- 9.2
1,7: 1-Wacky Duck #?.7-Reprint, Super No. 14('63)	2	4	6	9	13	16

CASPER DIGEST (...Magazine #?; ...Halloween Digest #8, 10)
Harvey Publications: Oct, 1986 - No. 18, Jan, 1991 ($1.25/$1.75, digest-size)

	GD 2.0	VG 4.0	FN 6.0	VF 8.0	VF/NM 9.0	NM- 9.2
1	1	3	4	6	8	10
2-18: 11-Valentine-c. 18-Halloween-c						6.00

CASPER DIGEST (...Magazine #? on)
Harvey Comics: V2#1, Sept, 1991 - V2#14, Nov, 1994 ($1.75/$1.95, digest-size)

	GD 2.0	VG 4.0	FN 6.0	VF 8.0	VF/NM 9.0	NM- 9.2
V2#1						5.00
2-14						3.50

CASPER DIGEST STORIES
Harvey Publications: Feb, 1980 - No. 4, Nov, 1980 (95¢, 132 pgs., digest size)

	GD 2.0	VG 4.0	FN 6.0	VF 8.0	VF/NM 9.0	NM- 9.2
1	2	4	6	9	13	16
2-4	1	2	3	5	7	9

CASPER DIGEST WINNERS
Harvey Publications: Apr, 1980 - No. 3, Sept, 1980 (95¢, 132 pgs., digest size)

	GD 2.0	VG 4.0	FN 6.0	VF 8.0	VF/NM 9.0	NM- 9.2
1	2	4	6	9	13	16
2,3	1	2	3	5	7	9

CASPER ENCHANTED TALES DIGEST
Harvey Comics: May, 1992 - No. 10, Oct, 1994 ($1.75, digest-size, 98 pgs.)

	GD 2.0	VG 4.0	FN 6.0	VF 8.0	VF/NM 9.0	NM- 9.2
1-Casper, Spooky, Wendy stories						5.00
2-10						4.00

CASPER GHOSTLAND
Harvey Comics: May, 1992 ($1.25)

	GD 2.0	VG 4.0	FN 6.0	VF 8.0	VF/NM 9.0	NM- 9.2
1						3.00

CASPER GIANT SIZE
Harvey Comics: Oct, 1992 - No. 4, Nov, 1993 ($2.25, 68 pgs.)

	GD 2.0	VG 4.0	FN 6.0	VF 8.0	VF/NM 9.0	NM- 9.2
V2#1-Casper, Wendy, Spooky stories						5.00
2-4						4.00

CASPER HALLOWEEN TRICK OR TREAT
Harvey Publications: Jan, 1976 (52 pgs.)

	GD 2.0	VG 4.0	FN 6.0	VF 8.0	VF/NM 9.0	NM- 9.2
1	3	6	9	17	26	35

CASPER IN SPACE (Formerly Casper Spaceship)
Harvey Publications: No. 6, June, 1973 - No. 8, Oct, 1973

	GD 2.0	VG 4.0	FN 6.0	VF 8.0	VF/NM 9.0	NM- 9.2
6-8	2	4	6	10	14	18

CASPER'S GHOSTLAND
Harvey Publications: Winter, 1958-59 - No. 97, 12/77; No. 98, 12/79 (25¢)

	GD 2.0	VG 4.0	FN 6.0	VF 8.0	VF/NM 9.0	NM- 9.2
1-84 pgs. begin, ends #10	16	32	48	112	249	385
2	9	18	27	59	117	175
3-10	7	14	21	44	82	120
11-20: 11-68 pgs. begin, ends #61. 13-X-Mas-c	5	10	15	35	63	90
21-40	4	8	12	28	47	65
41-61	3	6	9	16	24	32
62-77: 62-52 pgs. begin	2	4	6	9	13	16
78-98: 94-X-Mas-c	2	4	6	8	10	12

NOTE: *Most issues contain reprints w/new stories.*

CASPER SPACESHIP (Casper in Space No. 6 on)
Harvey Publications: Aug, 1972 - No. 5, April, 1973

	GD 2.0	VG 4.0	FN 6.0	VF 8.0	VF/NM 9.0	NM- 9.2
1: 52 pg. Giant	3	6	9	18	28	38
2-5	2	4	6	11	16	20

CASPER'S SCARE SCHOOL
Ape Entertainment: 2011 - No. 4 ($3.99, limited series)

	GD 2.0	VG 4.0	FN 6.0	VF 8.0	VF/NM 9.0	NM- 9.2
1,2-New short stories and classic reprints						4.00

CASPER STRANGE GHOST STORIES
Harvey Publications: October, 1974 - No. 14, Jan, 1977 (All 52 pgs.)

	GD 2.0	VG 4.0	FN 6.0	VF 8.0	VF/NM 9.0	NM- 9.2
1	3	6	9	18	28	38
2-14	2	4	6	11	16	20

CASPER, THE FRIENDLY GHOST (See America's Best TV Comics, Famous TV Funday Funnies, The Friendly Ghost..., Nightmare &..., Richie Rich and..., Tastee-Freez, Treasury of Comics, Wendy the Good Little Witch & Wendy Witch World)

CASPER, THE FRIENDLY GHOST (Becomes Harvey Comics Hits No. 61 (No. 6), and then continued with Harvey issue No. 7)(1st Series)
St. John Publishing Co.: Sept, 1949 - No. 5, Aug, 1951

	GD 2.0	VG 4.0	FN 6.0	VF 8.0	VF/NM 9.0	NM- 9.2
1(1949)-Origin & 1st app. Baby Huey & Herman the Mouse (1st comic app. of Casper and the 1st time the name Casper app. in any media, even films)	320	640	960	2240	3920	5600
2,3 (2/50 & 8/50)	110	220	330	704	1202	1700
4,5 (3/51 & 8/51)	77	154	231	493	847	1200

CASPER, THE FRIENDLY GHOST (Paramount Picture Star...)(2nd Series)
Harvey Publications (Family Comics): No. 7, Dec, 1952 - No. 70, July, 1958
Note: No. 6 is Harvey Comics Hits No. 61 (10/52)

	GD 2.0	VG 4.0	FN 6.0	VF 8.0	VF/NM 9.0	NM- 9.2
7-Baby Huey begins, ends #9	30	60	90	219	490	760
8,9	18	36	54	128	284	440
10-Spooky begins (1st app., 6/53), ends #70?	27	54	81	189	420	650
11,12: 2nd & 3rd app. Spooky	13	26	39	89	195	300
13-18: Alfred Harvey app. in story	11	22	33	76	163	250
19-1st app. Nightmare (4/54)	20	40	60	140	310	485
20-Wendy the Witch begins (1st app., 5/54)	27	54	81	194	435	675
21-30: 24-Infinity-c	9	18	27	59	117	175
31-40: 38-Early Wendy app. 39-1st app. Samson Honeybun. 40-1st app. Dr. Brainstorm	7	14	21	46	86	125
41-1st Wendy app. on-c	8	16	24	55	105	155
42-50: 43-2nd Wendy-c. 46-1st app. Spooky's girl Pearl.						

Castle: A Calm Before Storm #5 © ABC

The Cat #1 © MAR

Cat-Man Comics #10 © HOKE

	GD	VG	FN	VF	VF/NM	NM-
	2.0	4.0	6.0	8.0	9.0	9.2

GD VG FN VF VF/NM NM-
2.0 4.0 6.0 8.0 9.0 9.2

6 12 18 37 66 95

51-70 (Continues as Friendly Ghost... 8/58) 58-Early app. Bat Balfrey. 63-2nd app. Something the Baby Ghost. 66-1st app. Wildcat Witch 5 10 15 31 53 75

Harvey Comics Classics Vol. 1 TPB (Dark Horse Books, 6/07, $19.95) Reprints Casper's earliest appearances in this title, Little Audrey, and The Friendly Ghost Casper, mostly B&W with some color stories; history, early concept drawings and animation art 20.00

NOTE: *Baby Huey app. 7-9, 11, 121, 14, 16, 20. Buzzy app. 14, 16, 20. Nightmare app. 19, 27, 36, 37, 42, 46, 51, 53, 56, 70. Spooky app. 10-70. Wendy app. 20, 29-31, 35, 37, 38, 41-49, 51, 52, 54-58, 61, 64, 68.*

CASPER THE FRIENDLY GHOST (Formerly The Friendly Ghost...)(3rd Series)
Harvey Comics: No. 254, July, 1990 - No. 260, Jan, 1991 ($1.00)

254-260 3.00

CASPER THE FRIENDLY GHOST (4th Series)
Harvey Comics: Mar, 1991 - No. 28, Nov, 1994 ($1.00/$1.25/$1.50)

1-Casper becomes Mighty Ghost; Spooky & Wendy app. 5.00
2-28: 7,8-Post-a. 11-28-($1.50) 3.00

CASPER T.V. SHOWTIME
Harvey Comics: Jan, 1980 - No. 5, Oct, 1980

1 2 4 6 9 13 16
2-5 1 2 3 5 7 9

CASSETTE BOOKS (Classics Illustrated)
Cassette Book Co./I.P.S. Publ.: 1984 (48 pgs, b&w comic with cassette tape)

NOTE: *This series was illegal. The artwork was illegally obtained, and the Classics Illustrated copyright owner, Twin Circle Publ. sued to get an injunction to prevent the continued sale of this series. Many C.I. collectors obtained copies before the 1987 injunction, but now they are already scarce. Here again the market is just developing, but sealed mint copies of com ic and tape should be worth at least $25.*

1001 (CI#1-A2)New-PC 1002(CI#3-A2)CI-PC 1003(CI#13-A2)CI-PC
1004(CI#25)CI-LDC 1005(CI#10-A2)New-PC 1006(CI#64)CI-LDC

CASTILIAN (See Movie Classics)

CASTLE: A CALM BEFORE STORM (Based on the ABC TV series Castle)
Marvel Comics: Feb, 2013 - No. 5, Jul, 2013 ($3.99, limited series)

1-5-Peter David-s/Robert Atkins-a/Mico Suayan-c 4.00

CASTLE: RICHARD CASTLE'S ... (Based on the ABC TV series Castle)
Marvel Comics: 2011, 2012 ($19.99, hardcover graphic novels with dustjacket)

Deadly Storm HC (2011) - An "adaptation" of the show's fictional Derrick Storm novel; Bendis & DeConnick-s 20.00
Storm Season HC (2012) - Bendis & DeConnick-s/Lupacchino-a 20.00

CASTLEVANIA: THE BELMONT LEGACY
IDW Publishing: March 2005 - No. 5, July, 2005 ($3.99, limited series)

1-5-Marc Andreyko-s/E.J. Su-a 4.00

CASTLE WAITING
Olio: 1997 - No. 7, 1999 ($2.95, B&W)
Cartoon Books: Vol. 2, Aug, 2000 - No. 16 ($2.95/$3.95, B&W)
Fantagraphics Books: Vol. 3, 2006 - Present ($5.95/$3.95, B&W)

1-Linda Medley-s/a in all 1 2 3 5 6 8
2 4.00
3-7 3.00
The Lucky Road TPB r/#1-7 17.00
Hiatus Issue (1999) Crilley-c; short stories and previews 3.00
Vol. 2 #1-6,14-16 (#5&6 also have #12&13 on cover, for series numbering) 3.00
Vol. 3 #1 ($5.95) r/#15,16 and new story 6.00
Vol. 3 #2-15 ($3.95) 4.00

CASUAL HEROES
Image Comics (Motown Machineworks): Apr, 1996 ($2.25, unfinished lim. series)

1-Steve Rude-c 3.00

CAT, T.H.E. (TV) (See T.H.E. Cat)

CAT, THE (See Movie Classics)

CAT, THE (Female hero)
Marvel Comics Group: Nov, 1972 - No. 4, June, 1973

1-Origin & 1st app. The Cat (who later becomes Tigra); Mooney-a(i); Wood-c(i)/a(i) 4 8 12 23 37 50
2,3: 2-Marie Severin/Mooney-a. 3-Everett inks 3 6 9 14 20 25
4-Starlin/Weiss-a(p) 3 6 9 15 22 28

CATACLYSM
Marvel Comics: No. 0.1, Dec, 2013 ($3.99)

0.1-Fialkov-s; Galactus threatens the Ultimate Universe 4.00

CATACLYSM: THE ULTIMATES LAST STAND (Leads into Survive #1)
Marvel Comics: Jan, 2014 - No. 5, Apr, 2014 ($3.99, limited series)

1-5-Galactus in the Ultimate Universe; Ultimates & Spider-Man app.; Bendis-s/Bagley-a 4.00

CATACLYSM: ULTIMATES
Marvel Comics: Jan, 2014 - No. 3, Mar, 2014 ($3.99, limited series)

1-3-Ultimates vs. Galactus; Fialkov-s/Giandomenico-a 4.00

CATACLYSM: ULTIMATE SPIDER-MAN
Marvel Comics: Jan, 2014 - No. 3, Mar, 2014 ($3.99, limited series)

1-3-Spider-Man vs. Galactus; Bendis-s/Marquez-a 4.00

CATACLYSM: ULTIMATE X-MEN
Marvel Comics: Jan, 2014 - No. 3, Mar, 2014 ($3.99, limited series)

1-3-Fialkov-s/Martinez-a; Captain Marvel app. 4.00

CATALYST: AGENTS OF CHANGE (Also see Comics' Greatest World)
Dark Horse Comics: Feb, 1994 - No.7, Nov, 1994 ($2.00, limited series)

1-7: 1-Foil stamped logo 3.00

CATALYST COMIX (From Comics' Greatest World)
Dark Horse Comics: Jul, 2013 - Present ($2.99)

1-9: Amazing Grace, Frank Wells, and Agents of Change app.; Casey-s/Grampá-c 3.00

CATECHISM IN PICTURES
Catechetical Guild: Jan, 1958

311-Addison Burbank-a 8 16 24 40 50 60

CAT FROM OUTER SPACE (See Walt Disney Showcase #46)

CATHOLIC COMICS (See Heroes All Catholic...)
Catholic Publications: June, 1946 - V3#10, July, 1949

1 30 60 90 177 289 400
2 16 32 48 94 147 200
3-13(7/47): 11-Hollingsworth-a 14 28 42 82 121 160
V2#1-10 11 22 33 62 86 110
V3#1-10: Reprints 10-part Treasure Island serial from Target V2#2-11 (see Key Comics #5) 11 22 33 64 90 115

NOTE: ***Orlando** c-V2#10, V3#5, 6, 8.*

CATHOLIC PICTORIAL
Catholic Guild: 1947

1-Toth-a(2) (Rare) 39 78 117 240 395 550

CAT-MAN COMICS (Formerly Crash Comics No. 1-5)
Holyoke Publishing Co./Continental Magazines V2#12, 7/44 on:
5/41 - No. 17, 1/43; No. 18, 7/43 - No. 22, 12/43; No. 23, 3/44 - No. 26, 11/44; No. 27, 4/45 - No. 30, 12/45; No. 31, 6/46 - No. 32, 8/46

1(V1#6)-The Cat-Man new costume (see Crash Comics for 1st app.) by Charles Quinlan; Origin The Deacon & Sidekick Mickey, Dr. Diamond & Rag-Man; The Black Widow app. Blaze Baylor begins 432 864 1296 3154 5577 8000
2(V1#7) 226 452 678 1446 2473 3500
3(V1#8)-The Pied Piper begins; classic Hitler, Stalin & Mussolini-c 239 478 717 1530 2615 3700
4(V1#9) 155 310 465 992 1696 2400
5(V2#10, 12/41)-Origin/1st app. The Kitten, Cat-Man's sidekick; The Hood begins. (cover re-dated w/cat image printed over Nov. date). Most of The Kitten's cover image blocked with sidebar 168 336 504 1075 1838 2600
6(V2#11), 7(V2#12) 148 296 444 947 1624 2300
8(V2#13,3/42)-Origin Little Leaders; Volton by Kubert begins (his 1st comic book work) 181 362 543 1158 1979 2800
9 (V2#14, 4/42)-Japanese WWII-c 161 322 483 1030 1765 2500
10 (V2#15, 5/42)-Origin Blackout; Phantom Falcon begins 142 284 426 909 1555 2200
11 (V3#1, 6/42)-Kubert-a 142 284 426 909 1555 2200
12 (V3#2),15,17(1/43): 12-Volton by Brodsky, not Kubert 129 258 387 826 1413 2000
13-(9/42)(scarce) Weed of Doom (marijuana) 300 600 900 1950 3375 4800
14-(10/42) World War II-c; Brodsky-a 148 296 444 947 1624 2300
16 (V3#5, 12/42)-Hitler, Tojo, Mussolini, Goehring-c 300 600 900 1950 3375 4800
18 (V3#8, 7/43)-(scarce) 155 310 465 992 1696 2400
19 (V2#6, 9/43)-Hitler, Tojo, Mussolini-c 290 580 870 1856 3178 4500
20 (V2#7, 10/43)-Classic Hitler-c 331 662 993 2317 4059 5800
21,22 (V2#8, V2#9) 116 232 348 742 1271 1800
23 (V2#10, 3/44) World War II-c 129 258 387 826 1413 2000
nn(V3#13, 5/44) Rico-a; Schomburg Japanese WWII bondage-c (Rare) 226 452 678 1446 2473 3500
nn(V2#12, 7/44) L.B. Cole-a (4 pgs) 110 220 330 704 1202 1700
nn(V3#1, 9/44)-Origin The Golden Archer; Leatherface app.

Catwoman #94 © DC

Catwoman (2002 series) #66 © DC

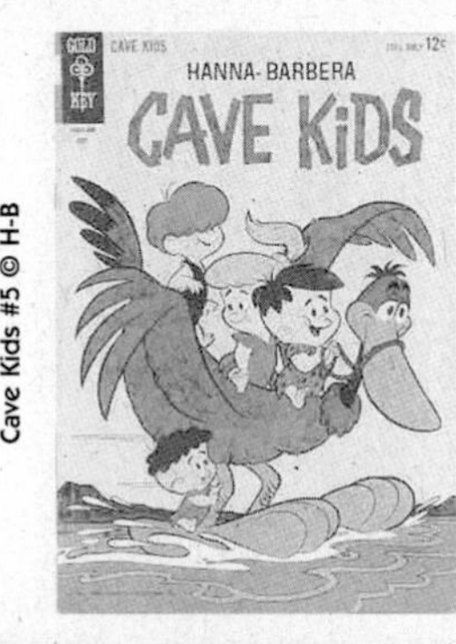

Cave Kids #5 © H-B

GD VG FN VF VF/NM NM-
2.0 4.0 6.0 8.0 9.0 9.2

110 220 330 704 1202 1700
nn(V3#2, 11/44)-L. B. Cole-c 129 258 387 826 1413 2000
27-Origins Catman & Kitten retold; L. B. Cole Flag-c; Infantino-a
161 322 483 1030 1765 2500
28-Dr. Macabre app.; L. B. Cole-c/a 213 426 639 1363 2332 3300
29-32-L. B. Cole-c; bondage-#30 155 310 465 992 1696 2400
NOTE: *Fuje a-11, 27, 28(2), 29(3), 30. Palais a-11, 16, 27, 28, 29(2), 30(2), 32; c-25(7/44). Rico a-11(2), 23, 27, 28.*

CAT TALES (3-D)
Eternity Comics: Apr, 1989 ($2.95)

1-Felix the Cat-r in 3-D 5.00

CATWOMAN (Also see Action Comics Weekly #611, Batman #404-407, Detective Comics, & Superman's Girlfriend Lois Lane #70, 71)
DC Comics: Feb, 1989 - No. 4, May, 1989 ($1.50, limited series, mature)

1 1 3 4 6 8 10
2-4: 3-Batman cameo. 4-Batman app. 1 2 3 5 7 9
Her Sister's Keeper (1991, $9.95, trade paperback)-r/#1-4 12.00

CATWOMAN (Also see Showcase '93, Showcase '95 #4, & Batman #404-407)
DC Comics: Aug, 1993 - No. 94, Jul, 2001 ($1.50-$2.25)

0-(10/94)-Zero Hour; origin retold. Released between #14&15 4.00
1-($1.95)-Embossed-c; Bane app.; Balent c-1-10; a-1-10p 6.00
2-20: 3-Bane flashback cameo. 4-Brief Bane app. 6,7-Knightquest tie-ins; Batman (Azrael) app. 8-1st app. Zephyr. 12-KnightsEnd pt. 6. 13-new Knights End Aftermath. 14-(9/94)-Zero Hour 4.00
21-24, 26-30, 33-49: 21-$1.95-c begins. 28,29-Penguin cameo app. 36-Legacy pt. 2. 38-40-Year Two; Batman, Joker, Penguin & Two-Face app. 46-Two-Face app. 3.00
25,31,32: 25-($2.95)-Robin app. 31,32-Contagion pt. 4 (Reads pt. 5 on-c) & pt. 9. 4.00
50-($2.95, 48 pgs.)-New armored costume 4.00
50-($2.95, 48 pgs.)-Collector's Ed.w/metallic ink-c 5.00
51-77: 51-Huntress-c/app. 54-Grayson-s begins. 56-Cataclysm pt.6. 57-Poison Ivy-c/app. 63-65-Joker-c/app. 72-No Man's Land; Ostrander-s begins 3.00
78-82: 80-Catwoman goes to jail 3.00
83,84,89-Harley Quinn-c/app. 83-Begin $2.25-c 5.00
85-88,90-94 3.00
#1,000,000 (11/98) 853rd Century x-over 3.00
Annual 1 (1994, $2.95, 68 pgs.)-Elseworlds story; Batman app.; no Balent-a 4.00
Annual 2,4 ('95, '97, $3.95) 2-Year One story. 4-Pulp Heroes 4.00
Annual 3 (1996, $2.95)-Legends of the Dead Earth story 4.00
...Plus 1 (11/97, $2.95) Screamqueen (Scare Tactics) app. 4.00
TPB ($9.95) r/#15-19, Balent-c 12.00

CATWOMAN (Also see Detective Comics #759-762)
DC Comics: Jan, 2002 - No. 82, Oct, 2008; No. 83, Mar, 2010 ($2.50/$2.99)

1-Darwyn Cooke & Mike Allred-a; Ed Brubaker-s 6.00
2-4 4.00
5-54: 5-9-Rader-a/Paul Pope-c. 10-Morse-c. 16-JG Jones-c. 22-Batman-c/app. 34-36-War Games. 43-Killer Croc app. 44-Hughes-c begin. 50-Zatanna app. 52-Catwoman kills Black Mask. 53-One Year Later; Helena born 3.00
55-82: 55-Begin $2.99-c. 56-58-Wildcat app. 74-Zatanna app. 75-78-Salvation Run 3.00
83-(3/10, $2.99) Blackest Night one-shot; Black Mask app.; Hughes-c 3.00
...: Catwoman Dies TPB (2008, $14.99) r/#66-72; Hughes cover gallery 15.00
...: Crime Pays TPB (2008, $14.99) r/#73-77 15.00
...: Crooked Little Town TPB (2003, $14.95) r/#5-10 & Secret Files; Oeming-c 15.00
...: It's Only a Movie TPB (2007, $19.99) r/#59-65 20.00
...: Relentless TPB (2005, $19.95) r/#12-19 & Secret Files 20.00
... Secret Files and Origins (10/02, $4.95) origin-s Oeming-a; profiles and pin-ups 5.00
...Selina's Big Score HC (2002, $24.95) Cooke-s/a; pin-ups by various 25.00
...Selina's Big Score SC (2003, $17.95) Cooke-s/a; pin-ups by various 18.00
...: The Dark End of the Street TPB (2002, $12.95) r/#1-4 & Slam Bradley back-up stories from Detective Comics #759-762 13.00
...: The Long Road Home TPB (2009, $17.99) r/#78-82 18.00
...: The Replacements TPB (2007, $14.99) r/#53-58 15.00
...: Wild Ride TPB (2005, $14.99) r/#20-24 & Secret Files #1 15.00

CATWOMAN (DC New 52)
DC Comics: Nov, 2011 - Present ($2.99)

1-Winick-s/March-a; Batman app. 5.00
2-12: 2-6-March-a. 7,8-Melo-a. 9-Night of the Owls 3.00
13-(12/12) Death of the Family tie-in; die-cut Joker mask-c 10.00
13-Second printing with chessboard-c 3.00
14-22: 14-Death of the Family tie-in; Joker app 3.00
23,24: 23-(10/13) Debut of Joker's Daughter in final panel. 24-Joker's Daughter app. 5.00
25,26,28,29: 25-Zero Year. 26-Joker's Daughter app. 28-Gothtopia 3.00
27-($3.99) Gothtopia x-over with Detective Comics #27; Olliffe & Richards-a 4.00
#0 (11/12, $2.99) Origin re-told; Nocenti-s/Melo-a/March-c 3.00
Annual 1 (7/13, $4.99) Nocenti-s/Duce-a; Penguin app. 5.00

CATWOMAN/ GUARDIAN OF GOTHAM
DC Comics: 1999 - No. 2, 1999 ($5.95, limited series)

1,2-Elseworlds; Moench-s/Balent-a 6.00

CATWOMAN: NINE LIVES OF A FELINE FATALE
DC Comics: 2004 ($14.95, TPB)

nn-Reprints notable stories from Batman #1 to the present; pin-ups by various; Bolland-c 15.00

CATWOMAN: THE MOVIE (2004 Halle Berry movie)
DC Comics: 2004 ($4.95/$9.95)

1-($4.95) Movie adaptation; Jim Lee-c and sketch pages; Derenick-a 5.00
... & Other Cat Tales TPB (2004, $9.95)-r/Movie adaptation; Jim Lee sketch pages, r/Catwoman #0, Catwoman (2nd series) #11 & 25; photo-c 10.00

CATWOMAN/VAMPIRELLA: THE FURIES
DC Comics/Harris Publ.: Feb, 1997 ($4.95, squarebound, 46 pgs.) (1st DC/Harris x-over)

nn-Reintro Pantha; Chuck Dixon scripts; Jim Balent-c/a 6.00

CATWOMAN: WHEN IN ROME
DC Comics: Nov, 2004 - No. 6, Aug, 2005 ($3.50, limited series)

1-6-Jeph Loeb-s/Tim Sale-a/c; Riddler app. 3.50
HC (2005, $19.99, dustjacket) r/series; intro by Mark Chiarello; sketch pages 20.00
SC (2007, $12.99) r/series; intro by Mark Chiarello; sketch pages 13.00

CATWOMAN/WILDCAT
DC Comics: Aug, 1998 - No. 4, Nov, 1998 ($2.50, limited series)

1-4-Chuck Dixon & Beau Smith-s; Stelfreeze-c 3.00

CAUGHT
Atlas Comics (VPI): Aug, 1956 - No. 5, Apr, 1957

1 23 46 69 136 223 310
2-4: 3-Maneely, Pakula, Torres-a. 4-Maneely-a 14 28 42 78 112 145
5-Crandall, Krigstein-a 14 28 42 81 118 155
NOTE: *Drucker a-2. Heck a-4. Severin c-1, 2, 4, 5. Shores a-4.*

CAVALIER COMICS
A. W. Nugent Publ. Co.: 1945; 1952 (Early DC reprints)

2(1945)-Speed Saunders, Fang Gow 20 40 60 117 189 260
2(1952) 12 24 36 67 94 120

CAVE GIRL (Also see Africa)
Magazine Enterprises: No. 11, 1953 - No. 14, 1954

11(A-1 82)-Origin; all Cave Girl stories 48 96 144 302 514 725
12(A-1 96), 13(A-1 116), 14(A-1 125)-Thunda by Powell in each
38 76 114 226 368 510
NOTE: *Powell c/a in all.*

CAVE GIRL
AC Comics: 1988 ($2.95, 44 pgs.) (16 pgs. of color, rest B&W)

1-Powell-r/Cave Girl #11; Nyoka photo back-c from movie; Powell/Bill Black-c; Special Limited Edition on-c 4.00

CAVE KIDS (TV) (See Comic Album #16)
Gold Key: Feb, 1963 - No. 16, Mar, 1967 (Hanna-Barbera)

1 6 12 18 38 69 100
2-5 4 8 12 23 37 50
6-16: 7,12-Pebbles & Bamm Bamm app. 16-1st Space Kidettes
3 6 9 19 30 40

CAVEWOMAN
Basement Comics: Jan, 1994 - No. 6, 1995 ($2.95)

1 5 10 15 31 53 75
2 3 6 9 16 23 30
3-6 2 4 6 9 12 15
...: Meets Explorers ('97, $2.95) 5.00
...: One-Shot Special (7/00, $2.95) Massey-s/a 5.00

CBLDF (Comic Book Legal Defense Fund) (See Liberty Comics)

CELESTINE (See Violator Vs. Badrock #1)
Image Comics (Extreme): May, 1996 - No. 2, June, 1996 ($2.50, limited series)

1,2: Warren Ellis scripts 3.00

CENTURION OF ANCIENT ROME, THE
Zondervan Publishing House: 1958 (no month listed) (B&W, 36 pgs.)

(Rare) All by Jay Disbrow 90 180 270 576 988 1400

Century West GN © H. Chaykin

Cerebus The Aardvark #179 © Dave Sim

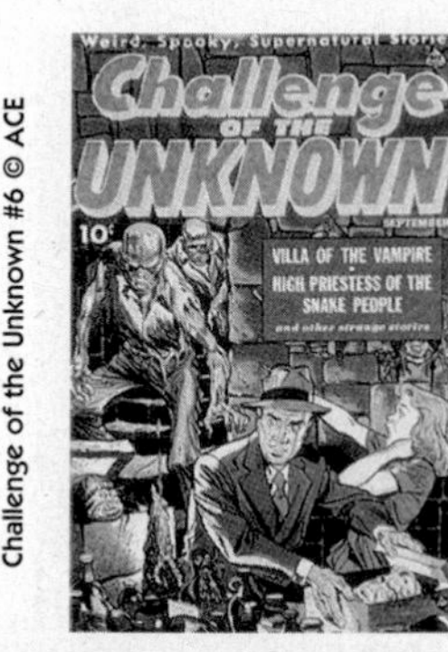

Challenge of the Unknown #6 © ACE

GD 2.0 | VG 4.0 | FN 6.0 | VF 8.0 | VF/NM 9.0 | NM- 9.2

CENTURIONS (TV)
DC Comics: June, 1987 - No. 4, Sept, 1987 (75¢, limited series)
1-4 4.00

CENTURY: DISTANT SONS
Marvel Comics: Feb, 1996 ($2.95, one-shot)
1-Wraparound-c 4.00

CENTURY OF COMICS (See Promotional Comics section)

CENTURY WEST
Image Comics: Sept, 2013 ($7.99, squarebound, graphic novel)
nn-Haward Chaykin-s/a/c 8.00

CEREBUS BI-WEEKLY
Aardvark-Vanaheim: Dec. 2, 1988 - No. 27, Nov. 24, 1989 ($1.25, B&W)
Reprints Cerebus The Aardvark #1-27
1-16, 18, 19, 21-27: 3.00
17-Hepcats app. 2 4 6 8 10 12
20-Milk & Cheese app. 2 4 6 10 12 15

CEREBUS: CHURCH & STATE
Aardvark-Vanaheim: Feb, 1991 - No. 30, Apr, 1992 ($2.00, B&W, bi-weekly)
1-30: r/Cerebus #51-80 3.00

CEREBUS: HIGH SOCIETY
Aardvark-Vanaheim: Feb, 1990 - No. 25, 1991 ($1.70, B&W)
1-25: r/Cerebus #26-50 3.00

CEREBUS JAM
Aardvark-Vanaheim: Apr, 1985
1-Eisner, Austin, Dave Sim-a (Cerebus vs. Spirit) 6.00

CEREBUS THE AARDVARK (See A-V in 3-D, Nucleus, Power Comics)
Aardvark-Vanaheim: Dec, 1977 - No. 300, March, 2004 ($1.70/$2.00/$2.25, B&W)
0 3.00
0-Gold 20.00
1-1st app. Cerebus; 2000 print run; most copies poorly printed
75 150 225 600 1350 2100
Note: *There is a counterfeit version known to exist. It can be distinguished from the original in the following ways: inside cover is glossy instead of flat, black background on the front cover is blotted or spotty. Reports show that a counterfeit #2 also exists.*
2-Dave Sim art in all 13 26 39 91 201 310
3-Origin Red Sophia 11 22 33 73 157 240
4-Origin Elrod the Albino 9 18 27 60 120 180
5,6 7 14 21 49 92 135
7-10 6 12 18 37 66 95
11,12: 11-Origin The Cockroach 5 10 15 31 53 75
13-15: 14-Origin Lord Julius 3 6 9 21 33 45
21-B. Smith letter in letter column 5 10 15 35 63 90
22-Low distribution; no cover price 4 8 12 25 40 55
23-30: 23-Preview of Wandering Star by Teri S. Wood. 26-High Society begins, ends #50
3 6 9 16 23 30
31-Origin Moonroach 3 6 9 16 24 32
32-40, 53-Intro. Wolveroach (brief app.) 2 4 6 8 10 12
41-50,52: 52-Church & State begins, ends #111; Cutey Bunny app.
1 2 3 5 7 9
51,54: 51-Cutey Bunny app. 54-1st full Wolveroach story
2 4 6 8 11 14
55,56-Wolveroach app.; Normalman back-ups by Valentino
1 3 4 6 8 10
57-100: 61,62: Flaming Carrot app. 65-Gerhard begins 4.00
101-160: 104-Flaming Carrot app. 112/113-Double issue. 114-Jaka's Story begins, ends #136. 139-Melmoth begins, ends #150. 151-Mothers & Daughters begins, ends #200 3.00
161-Bone app. 1 3 4 6 8 10
162-231: 175-($2.25, 44 pgs). 186-Strangers in Paradise cameo. 201-Guys storyline begins; Eddie Campbell's Bacchus app. 220-231-Rick's Story 3.00
232-265-Going Home 3.00
266-288,291-299-Latter Days: 267-Five-Bar Gate. 276-Spore (Spawn spoof) 3.00
289&290 ($4.50) Two issues combined 5.00
300-Final issue 3.00
Free Cerebus (Giveaway, 1991-92?, 36 pgs.)-All-r 4.00

CHAIN GANG WAR
DC Comics: July, 1993 - No. 12, June, 1994 ($1.75)
1-($2.50)-Embossed silver foil-c, Dave Johnson-c/a 4.00
2-4,6-12: 3-Deathstroke app. 4-Brief Deathstroke app. 6-New Batman (Azrael) cameo. 11-New Batman-c/story. 12-New Batman app. 3.00
5-($2.50)-Foil-c; Deathstroke app; new Batman cameo (1 panel) 4.00

CHAINS OF CHAOS
Harris Comics: Nov, 1994 - No. 3, Jan, 1995 ($2.95, limited series)
1-3-Re-Intro of The Rook w/ Vampirella 5.00

CHALLENGE OF THE UNKNOWN (Formerly Love Experiences)
Ace Magazines: No. 6, Sept, 1950 (See Web Of Mystery No. 19)
6- "Villa of the Vampire" used in N.Y. Joint Legislative Comm. Publ; Sekowsky-a
41 82 123 256 428 600

CHALLENGER, THE
Interfaith Publications/T.C. Comics: 1945 - No. 4, Oct-Dec, 1946
nn; nd; 32 pgs.; Origin the Challenger Club; Anti-Fascist with funny animal filler
71 142 213 454 777 1100
2-Classic Pandora's Box demons-c; Kubert-a 58 116 174 371 636 900
3,4: Kubert-a; 4-Fuje-a 48 96 144 302 514 725

CHALLENGERS OF THE FANTASTIC
Marvel Comics (Amalgam): June 1997 ($1.95, one-shot)
1-Karl Kesel-s/Tom Grummett-a 3.00

CHALLENGERS OF THE UNKNOWN (See Showcase #6, 7, 11, 12, Super DC Giant, and Super Team Family) (See Showcase Presents for B&W reprints)
National Per. Publ./DC Comics: 4-5/58 - No. 77, 12-1/70-71; No. 78, 2/73 - No. 80, 6-7/73; No. 81, 6-7/77 - No. 87, 6-7/78
1-(4-5/58)-Kirby/Stein-a(2); Kirby-c 221 442 663 1823 4112 6400
2-Kirby/Stein-a(2) 64 128 192 512 1156 1800
3-Kirby/Stein-a(2); Rocky returns from space with powers similar to the Fantastic Four (9/58)
54 108 162 432 966 1500
4-8-Kirby/Wood-a plus cover to #8 42 84 126 311 706 1100
9,10 25 50 75 175 388 600
11-Grey tone-c 27 54 81 189 420 650
12-15: 14-Origin/1st app. Multi-Man (villain) 17 34 51 119 265 410
16-22: 18-Intro. Cosmo, the Challengers Spacepet. 22-Last 10¢ issue
12 24 36 81 176 270
23-30 8 16 24 56 108 160
31-Retells origin of the Challengers 9 18 27 57 111 165
32-40 6 12 18 41 76 110
41-47,49,50,52-60: 43-New look begins. 47-1st Sponge-Man. 49-Intro. Challenger Corps. 55-Death of Red Ryan. 60-Red Ryan returns 5 10 15 31 53 75
48,51: 48-Doom Patrol app. 51-Sea Devils app. 5 10 15 33 57 80
61-68: 64,65-Kirby origin-r, parts 1 & 2. 66-New logo. 68-Last 12¢ issue.
4 8 12 23 37 50
69-73,75-80: 69-1st app. Corinna. 77-Last 15¢ issue 3 6 9 16 23 30
74-Deadman by Tuska/Adams; 1 pg. Wrightson-a 5 10 15 35 63 90
81,83-87: 81-(6-7/77). 83-87-Swamp Thing app. 84-87-Deadman app.
2 4 6 8 10 12
82-Swamp Thing begins (thru #87, c/s 2 4 6 9 12 15
NOTE: ***N. Adams** c-67, 68, 70, 72, 74i, 81i. **Buckler** c-83-86p. **Giffen** a-83-87p. **Kirby** a-75-80r; c-75, 77, 78. **Kubert** c-64, 66, 69, 76, 79. **Nasser** c/a-81p, 82p. **Tuska** a-73. **Wood** r-76.*

CHALLENGERS OF THE UNKNOWN
DC Comics: Mar, 1991 - No. 8, Oct, 1991 ($1.75, limited series)
1-Jeph Loeb scripts & Tim Sale-a in all (1st work together); Bolland-c 4.00
2-8: 2-Superman app. 3-Dr. Fate app. 6-G. Kane-c(p). 7-Steranko-c/swipe by Art Adams 3.00
... Must Die! (2004, $19.95, TPB) r/series; intro by Bendis; Sale sketch pages 20.00
NOTE: ***Art Adams** c-7. **Hempel** c-5. **Gil Kane** c-6p. **Sale** a-1-8; c-3, 8. **Wagner** c-4.*

CHALLENGERS OF THE UNKNOWN
DC Comics: Feb, 1997 - No. 18, July, 1998 ($2.25)
1-18: 1-Intro new team; Leon-c/a(p) begins. 4-Origin of new team. 11,12-Batman app. 15-Millennium Giants x-over; Superman-c/app. 3.00

CHALLENGERS OF THE UNKNOWN
DC Comics: Aug, 2004 - No. 6, Jan, 2005 ($2.95, limited series)
1-6-Intro. new team; Howard Chaykin-s/a 3.00

CHALLENGE TO THE WORLD
Catechetical Guild: 1951 (10¢, 36 pgs.)
nn 6 12 18 31 38 45

CHAMBER (See Generation X and Uncanny X-Men)
Marvel Comics: Oct, 2002 - No. 4, Jan, 2003 ($2.99, limited series)
1-4-Bachalo-c/Vaughan-s/Ferguson-a. 1-Cyclops app. 3.00

CHAMBER OF CHILLS (Formerly Blondie Comics #20; ...of Clues No. 27 on)
Harvey Publications/Witches Tales: No. 21, June, 1951 - No. 26, Dec, 1954
21 (#1) 52 104 156 328 552 775

Chamber of Chills #23 © HARV

The Champions #10 © MAR

Chaos! Quarterly #3 © B. Pulido

	GD 2.0	VG 4.0	FN 6.0	VF 8.0	VF/NM 9.0	NM- 9.2
22,24 (#2,4)	39	78	117	231	378	525
23 (#3)-Excessive violence; eyes torn out	39	78	117	240	395	550
5(2/52)-Decapitation, acid in face scene	39	78	117	240	395	550
6-Woman melted alive	39	78	117	231	378	525
7-Used in **SOTI**, pg. 389; decapitation/severed head panels	37	74	111	222	361	500
8-10: 8-Decapitation panels	31	62	93	186	303	420
11,12,14: 14-Spider-Man precursor (11/52)	25	50	75	150	245	340
13,15-24-Nostrand-a in all. 13,21-Decapitation panels. 18-Atom bomb panels. 20-Nostrand-c	30	60	90	177	289	400
25,26	20	40	60	117	189	260

NOTE: *About half the issues contain bondage, torture, sadism, perversion, gore, cannabalism, eyes ripped out, acid in face, etc.* ***Elias*** *c-4-11, 14-19, 21-26.* ***Kremer*** *a-12, 17.* ***Palais*** *a-21(1), 23.* ***Nostrand/Powell*** *a-13, 15, 16.* ***Powell*** *a-21, 23, 24('51), 5-8, 11, 13, 18-21, 23-25. Bondage-c-21, 24('51), 7. 25-r/#5; 26-r/#9.*

CHAMBER OF CHILLS
Marvel Comics Group: Nov, 1972 - No. 25, Nov, 1976

	GD	VG	FN	VF	VF/NM	NM-
1-Harlan Ellison adaptation	4	8	12	28	47	65
2-5: 2-1st app. John Jakes' Brak the Barbarian	3	6	9	16	24	32
6-25: 22,23-(Regular 25¢ editions)	3	6	9	14	20	26
22,23-(30¢-c variants, limited distribution)(5,7/76)	4	8	12	28	47	65

NOTE: ***Adkins*** *a-1i, 2i.* ***Brunner*** *a-2-4; c-4.* ***Chaykin*** *a-4.* ***Ditko*** *r-14, 16, 19, 23, 24.* ***Everett*** *a-3i, 11r,21r.* ***Heath*** *a-1r.* ***Gil Kane*** *c-2p.* ***Kirby*** *r-11, 18, 19, 22.* ***Powell*** *a-13r.* ***Russell*** *a-1p, 2p.* ***Shores*** *a-5 .* ***Williamson/Mayo*** *a-13r.* ***Robert E. Howard*** *horror story adaptation-2, 3.*

CHAMBER OF CLUES (Formerly Chamber of Chills)
Harvey Publications: No. 27, Feb, 1955 - No. 28, April, 1955

	GD	VG	FN	VF	VF/NM	NM-
27-Kerry Drake-r/#19; Powell-a; last pre-code	7	14	21	35	43	50
28-Kerry Drake	6	12	18	28	34	40

CHAMBER OF DARKNESS (Monsters on the Prowl #9 on)
Marvel Comics Group: Oct, 1969 - No. 8, Dec, 1970

	GD	VG	FN	VF	VF/NM	NM-
1-Buscema-a(p)	7	14	21	48	89	130
2,3: 2-Neal Adams scripts. 3-Smith, Buscema-a	4	8	12	28	47	65
4-A Conan-esque tryout by Smith (4/70); reprinted in Conan #16; Marie Severin/Everett-c	8	16	24	56	108	160
5,8: 5-H.P. Lovecraft adaptation. 8-Wrightson-c	4	8	12	25	40	55
6	3	6	9	21	33	45
7-Wrightson-c/a, 7pgs. (his 1st work at Marvel); Wrightson draws himself in 1st & last panels; Kirby/Ditko-r; last 15¢-c	5	10	15	35	63	90
1-(1/72; 25¢ Special, 52 pgs.)	4	8	12	25	40	55

NOTE: ***Adkins/Everett*** *a-8.* ***Buscema*** *a-Special 1r.* ***Craig*** *a-5.* ***Ditko*** *a-6-8r.* ***Heck*** *a-1, 2, 8, Special 1r.* ***Kirby*** *a(p)-4, 5, 7r.* ***Kirby/Everett*** *c-5.* ***Severin/Everett*** *c-6.* ***Shores*** *a-2, 3i, Special 1r.* ***Sutton*** *a-1, 2i, 4, 7, Special 1r.* ***Wrightson*** *c-7, 8.*

CHAMP COMICS (Formerly Champion No. 1-10)
Worth Publ. Co./Champ Publ./Family Comics(Harvey Publ.): No. 11, Oct, 1940 - No. 24, Dec, 1942; No. 25, April, 1943

	GD	VG	FN	VF	VF/NM	NM-
11-Human Meteor cont'd. from Champion	103	206	309	659	1130	1600
12-17,20: 14,15-Crandall-c. 20-The Green Ghost app.	81	162	243	518	884	1250
18,19-Simon-c. 19-The Wasp app.	103	206	309	659	1130	1600
21-23,25: 22-The White Mask app. 23-Flag-c	60	120	180	381	653	925
24-Hitler, Tojo & Mussolini-c	97	194	291	621	1061	1500

CHAMPION (See Gene Autry's...)

CHAMPION COMICS
Worth Publ. Co.: Oct, 1939 (ashcan)

nn-Ashcan comic, not distributed to newsstands, only for in house use. A FN/VF copy sold for $2,261.76 in 2010.

CHAMPION COMICS (Formerly Speed Comics #1?; Champ Comics No. 11 on)
Worth Publ. Co.(Harvey Publications): No. 2, Dec, 1939 - No. 10, Aug, 1940 (no No.1)

	GD	VG	FN	VF	VF/NM	NM-
2-The Champ, The Blazing Scarab, Neptina, Liberty Lads, Jungleman, Bill Handy, Swingtime Sweetie begin	129	258	387	826	1413	2000
3-7: 7-The Human Meteor begins?	79	158	237	502	864	1225
8-10: 8-Simon-c. 9-1st S&K-c (1st collaboration together). 10-Bondage-c by Kirby	200	400	600	1280	2190	3100

CHAMPIONS, THE
Marvel Comics Group: Oct, 1975 - No. 17, Jan, 1978

	GD	VG	FN	VF	VF/NM	NM-
1-Origin & 1st app. The Champions (The Angel, Black Widow, Ghost Rider, Hercules, Iceman); Venus x-over	4	8	12	23	37	50
2-4,8-10,16: 2,3-Venus x-over	2	4	6	11	16	20
5-7-(Regular 25¢ edition)(4-8/76) 6-Kirby-c	2	4	6	11	16	20
5-7-(30¢-c variants, limited distribution)	4	8	12	28	47	65
11-14,17-Byrne-a. 14-(Regular 30¢ edition)	2	4	6	13	18	22
14,15-(35¢-c variant, limited distribution)	5	10	15	33	57	80
15-(Regular 30¢ edition)(9/77)-Byrne-a	2	4	6	13	18	22
... Classic Vol. 1 TPB (2006, $19.99) r/#1-11; unused cover to #7						20.00
... Classic Vol. 2 TPB (2007, $19.99) r/#12-17, Iron Man Ann. #4, Avengers #163, Super-Villain Team-Up #14 and Peter Parker, The Spectacular Spider-Man #17-18						20.00

NOTE: ***Buckler/Adkins*** *c-3.* ***Byrne*** *a-11-15, 17.* ***Kane/Adkins*** *c-1.* ***Kane/Layton*** *c-11.* ***Tuska*** *a-3p, 4p, 6p, 7p. Ghost Rider c-1-4, 7, 8, 10, 14, 16, 17 (4, 10, 14 are more prominent).*

CHAMPIONS (Game)
Eclipse Comics: June, 1986 - No. 6, Feb, 1987 (limited series)

1-6: 1-Intro Flare; based on game. 5-Origin Flare — 3.00

CHAMPIONS (Also see The League of Champions)
Hero Comics: Sept, 1987 - No. 12, 1989 ($1.95)

1-12: 1-Intro The Marksman & The Rose. 14-Origin Malice — 3.00
Annual 1(1988, $2.75, 52 pgs.)-Origin of Giant — 4.00

CHAMPION SPORTS
National Periodical Publications: Oct-Nov, 1973 - No. 3, Feb-Mar, 1974

	GD	VG	FN	VF	VF/NM	NM-
1	3	6	9	16	23	30
2,3	2	4	6	9	12	15

CHANNEL ZERO
Image Comics: Feb, 1998 - No. 5 ($2.95, B&W, limited series)

1-5, ...Dupe (1/99) -Brian Wood-s/a — 3.00

CHAOS (See The Crusaders)

CHAOS! BIBLE
Chaos! Comics: Nov, 1995 ($3.30, one-shot)

1-Profiles of characters & creators — 3.50

CHAOS! CHRONICLES
Chaos! Comics: Feb, 2000 ($3.50, one-shot)

1-Profiles of characters, checklist of Chaos! comics and products — 3.50

CHAOS EFFECT, THE
Valiant: 1994

Alpha (Giveaway w/trading card checklist) — 3.00
Alpha-Gold variant, Alpha-Red variant, Omega-Gold variant — 5.00
Omega (11/94, $2.25); Epilogue Pt. 1, 2 (12/94, 1/95; $2.95) — 3.00

CHAOS! GALLERY
Chaos! Comics: Aug, 1997 ($2.95, one-shot)

1-Pin-ups of characters — 3.00

CHAOS! QUARTERLY
Chaos! Comics: Oct, 1995 -No. 3, May, 1996 ($4.95, quarterly)

1-3: 1-anthology; Lady Death-c by Julie Bell. 2-Boris "Lady Demon"-c — 5.00
1-Premium Edition (7,500) — 25.00

CHAOS WAR
Marvel Comics: Dec, 2010 - No. 4, Mr, 2011 ($3.99, limited series)

1-5-Hercules, Thor and others vs. Chaos King; Pham-a. 3-5-Galactus app. — 4.00
...: Alpha Flight 1 (1/11, $3.99) McCann-s/Brown-a — 4.00
...: Ares 1 (2/11, $3.99) Oeming-s/Segovia-a — 4.00
...: Chaos King 1 (1/11, $3.99) Kaluta-a/c; Monclair-s — 4.00
...: Dead Avengers 1-3 (1/11 - No. 3, 3/11, $3.99) Grummett-a; Capt. Marvel app. — 4.00
...: God Squad 1 (2/11, $3.99) Sumerak-s/Panosian-a — 4.00
...: Thor 1,2 (1/11 - No. 2, 2/11, $3.99) DeMatteis-s/Ching-a — 4.00
...: X-Men 1,2 (2/11 - No. 2, 3/11, $3.99) Braithwaite-a; Thunderbird, Banshee app. — 4.00

CHAPEL (Also see Youngblood & Youngblood Strikefile #1-3)
Image Comics (Extreme Studios): No. 1 Feb, 1995 - No. 2, Mar, 1995 ($2.50, limited series)

1,2 — 3.00

CHAPEL (Also see Youngblood & Youngblood Strikefile #1-3)
Image Comics (Extreme Studios): V2 #1, Aug, 1995 - No. 7, Apr, 1996 ($2.50)

V2#1-7: 4-Babewatch x-over. 5-vs. Spawn. 7-Shadowhawk-c/app; Shadowhunt x-over — 3.00
#1-Quesada & Palmiotti variant-c — 3.00

CHAPEL (Also see Youngblood & Youngblood Strikefile #1-3)
Awesome Entertainment: Sept, 1997 ($2.99, one-shot)

1 (Reg. & alternate covers) — 3.00

CHARISMAGIC
Aspen MLT: No. 0, Mar, 2011 - No. 6, Jul, 2012 ($1.99/$2.99/$3.50)

0-($1.99) Khary Randolph-a/ Vince Hernandez-s; 3 covers — 3.00
1-4-($2.99) 1-4-Four covers on each — 3.00
5,6-($3.50) Multiple covers on each — 3.50
...: The Death Princess 1-3 (11/12 - No. 3, 7/13, $3.99) Hernandez-s/Emilio Lopez-a — 4.00

Charismagic V2 #3 © Aspen MLT

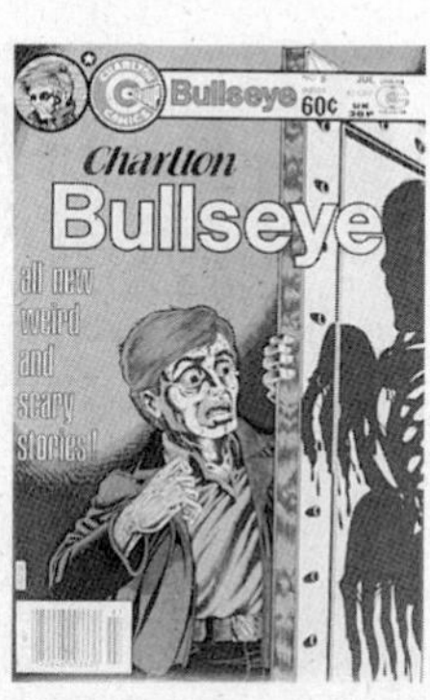

Charlton Bullseye #8 © CC

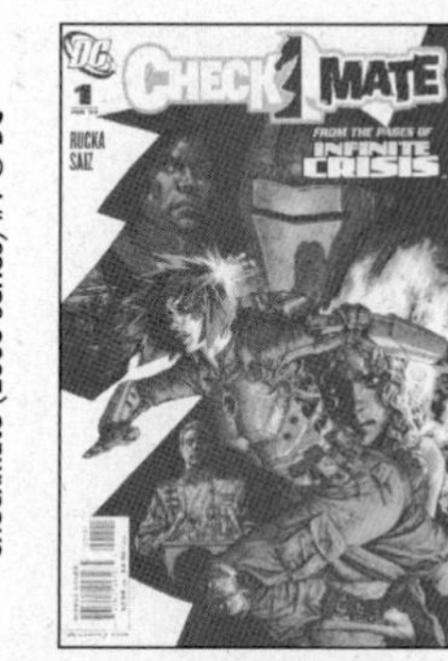

Checkmate (2006 series) #1 © DC

	GD 2.0	VG 4.0	FN 6.0	VF 8.0	VF/NM 9.0	NM- 9.2

CHARISMAGIC (Volume 2)
Aspen MLT: May, 2013 - No. 6, Nov, 2013 ($1.00/$3.99)

	GD	VG	FN	VF	VF/NM	NM-
1-($1.00) Vincenzo Cucca-a/ Vince Hernandez-s; multiple covers						3.00
2-6-($3.99) Multiple covers on each						4.00

CHARLEMAGNE (Also see War Dancer)
Defiant Comics: Mar, 1994 - No. 5, July, 1994 ($2.50)

	GD	VG	FN	VF	VF/NM	NM-
1/2 (Hero Illustrated giveaway)-Adam Pollina-c/a						3.00
1-(3/94, $3.50, 52 pgs.)-Adam Pollina-c/a.						4.00
2,3,5: Adam Pollina-c/a. 2-War Dancer app. 5-Pre-Schism issue.						3.00
4-($3.25, 52 pgs.)						4.00

CHARLIE CHAN (See Big Shot Comics, Columbia Comics, Feature Comics & The New Advs. of...)

CHARLIE CHAN (The Adventures of...) (Zaza The Mystic No. 10 on) (TV)
Crestwood(Prize) No. 1-5; Charlton No. 6(6/55) on: 6-7/48 - No. 5, 2-3/49; No.6, 6/55 - No. 9, 3/56

	GD	VG	FN	VF	VF/NM	NM-
1-S&K-c, 2 pgs.; Infantino-a	87	174	261	553	952	1350
2-5-S&K-c: 3-S&K-c/a	50	100	150	315	533	750
6 (6/55-Charlton)-S&K-c	37	74	111	222	361	500
7-9	20	40	60	118	192	265

CHARLIE CHAN
Dell Publishing Co.: Oct-Dec, 1965 - No. 2, Mar, 1966

	GD	VG	FN	VF	VF/NM	NM-
1-Springer-a/c	5	10	15	31	53	75
2-Springer-a/c	3	6	9	21	33	45

CHARLIE McCARTHY (See Edgar Bergen Presents...)
Dell Publishing Co.: No. 171, Nov, 1947 - No. 571, July, 1954 (See True Comics #14)

	GD	VG	FN	VF	VF/NM	NM-
Four Color 171	22	44	66	154	340	525
Four Color 196-Part photo-c; photo back-c	14	28	42	94	207	320
1(3-5/49)-Part photo-c; photo back-c	12	24	36	81	176	270
2-9(7/52; #5,6-52 pgs.)	7	14	21	48	89	130
Four Color 445,478,527,571	6	12	18	37	66	95

CHARLTON ACTION: FEATURING "STATIC" (Also see Eclipse Monthly)
Charlton Comics: No, 11, Oct, 1985 - No. 12, Dec, 1985

	GD	VG	FN	VF	VF/NM	NM-
11,12-Ditko-c/a; low print run	1	2	3	5	6	8

CHARLTON BULLSEYE
CPL/Gang Publications: 1975 - No. 5, 1976 ($1.50, B&W, bi-monthly, magazine format)

	GD	VG	FN	VF	VF/NM	NM-
1: 1 & 2 are last Capt. Atom by Ditko/Byrne intended for the never published Capt. Atom #90; Nightshade app.; Jeff Jones-a	4	8	12	28	47	65
2-Part 2 Capt. Atom story by Ditko/Byrne	3	6	9	20	31	42
3-Wrong Country by Sanho Kim	2	4	6	13	18	22
4-Doomsday + 1 by John Byrne	3	6	9	16	24	32
5-Doomsday + 1 by Byrne, The Question by Toth; Neal Adams back-c; Toth-c	4	8	12	23	37	50

CHARLTON BULLSEYE
Charlton Publications: June, 1981 - No. 10, Dec, 1982; Nov, 1986

	GD	VG	FN	VF	VF/NM	NM-
1-1st Blue Beetle app. since '74, 1st app. The Question since '75; 1st app. Rocket Rabbit; Neil The Horse shown on preview page	2	4	6	8	10	12
2-5: 2-Charlton debut of Neil The Horse; Rocket Rabbit app. 4-Vanguards						6.00
6-10: Low print run. 6-Origin & 1st app. Thunderbunny. 7-1st apps. of Captain Atom & Nightshade since '75. 9-1st app. Bludd.	1	2	3	5	7	9

NOTE: *Material intended for issue #11-up was published in **Scary Tales** #37-up.*

CHARLTON CLASSICS
Charlton Comics: Apr, 1980 - No. 9, Aug, 1981

	GD	VG	FN	VF	VF/NM	NM-
1-Hercules-r by Glanzman in all						6.00
2-9						5.00

CHARLTON CLASSICS LIBRARY (1776)
Charlton Comics: V10 No.1, Mar, 1973 (one-shot)

	GD	VG	FN	VF	VF/NM	NM-
1776 (title) - Adaptation of the film musical "1776"; given away at movie theatres; also a newsstand version	3	6	9	14	19	24

CHARLTON PREMIERE (Formerly Marine War Heroes)
Charlton Comics: V1#19, July, 1967; V2#1, Sept, 1967 - No. 4, May, 1968

	GD	VG	FN	VF	VF/NM	NM-
V1#19, V2#1,2,4: V1#19-Marine War Heroes. V2#1-Trio; intro. Shape, Tyro Team & Spookman. 2-Children of Doom; Boyette classic-a. 4-Unlikely Tales; Aparo, Ditko-a	3	6	9	15	22	28
V2#3-Sinistro Boy Fiend; Blue Beetle & Peacemaker x-over	3	6	9	17	26	35

CHARLTON SPORT LIBRARY - PROFESSIONAL FOOTBALL
Charlton Comics: Winter, 1969-70 (Jan. on cover) (68 pgs.)

	GD	VG	FN	VF	VF/NM	NM-
1	3	6	9	19	30	40

CHARMED (TV)
Zenescope Entertainment: No. 0, Jun, 2010 - Present ($3.50)

	GD	VG	FN	VF	VF/NM	NM-
0-19-Multiple covers on most						3.50

CHASE (See Batman #550 for 1st app.)(Also see Batwoman)
DC Comics: Feb, 1998 - No. 9, Oct, 1998; #1,000,000 Nov, 1998 ($2.50)

	GD	VG	FN	VF	VF/NM	NM-
1-9: Williams III & Gray-a. 1-Includes 4 Chase cards. 4-Teen Titans app. 7,8-Batman app. 9-GL Hal Jordan-c/app.						3.00
#1,000,000 (11/98) Final issue; 853rd Century x-over						3.00

CHASING DOGMA (See Jay and Silent Bob)

CHASSIS
Millenium Publications: 1996 - No. 3 ($2.95)

	GD	VG	FN	VF	VF/NM	NM-
1-3: 1-Adam Hughes-c. 2-Conner var-c.						3.00

CHASSIS
Hurricane Entertainment: 1998 - No. 3 ($2.95)

	GD	VG	FN	VF	VF/NM	NM-
0,1-3: 1-Adam Hughes-c. 0-Green var-c.						3.00

CHASSIS (Vol. 3)
Image Comics: Nov, 1999 - No. 4 ($2.95, limited series)

	GD	VG	FN	VF	VF/NM	NM-
1-4: 1-Two covers by O'Neil and Green. 2-Busch var-c.						3.00
1-($6.95) DF Edition alternate-c by Wieringo						7.00

CHASTITY
Chaos! Comics: (one-shots)

	GD	VG	FN	VF	VF/NM	NM-
#1/2 (1/01, $2.95) Batista-a						3.00
Heartbreaker (3/02, $2.99) Adrian-a/Molenaar-c						3.00
Love Bites (3/01, $2.99) Vale-a/Romano-c						3.00
Reign of Terror 1 (10/00, $2.95) Grant-s/Ross-a/Rio-c						3.00
Re-Imagined 1 (7/02, $2.99) Conner-c; Toledo-a						3.00

CHASTITY: CRAZYTOWN
Chaos! Comics: Apr, 2002 - No. 3, June, 2002 ($2.99, limited series)

	GD	VG	FN	VF	VF/NM	NM-
1-3-Nicieza-s/Batista-c/a						3.00

CHASTITY: LUST FOR LIFE
Chaos! Comics: May, 1999 - No. 3, July, 1999 ($2.95, limited series)

	GD	VG	FN	VF	VF/NM	NM-
1-3-Nutman-s/Benes-c/a						3.00

CHASTITY: ROCKED
Chaos! Comics: Nov, 1998 - No. 4, Feb, 1999 ($2.95, limited series)

	GD	VG	FN	VF	VF/NM	NM-
1-4-Nutman-s/Justiniano-c/a						3.00

CHASTITY: SHATTERED
Chaos! Comics: Jun, 2001 - No. 3, Sept, 2001 ($2.99, limited series)

	GD	VG	FN	VF	VF/NM	NM-
1-3-Kaminski & Pulido-s/Batista-c/a						3.00

CHASTITY: THEATER OF PAIN
Chaos! Comics: Feb, 1997 - No. 3, June, 1997 ($2.95, limited series)

	GD	VG	FN	VF	VF/NM	NM-
1-3-Pulido-s/Justiniano-c/a						3.00
TPB (1997, $9.95) r/#1-3						10.00

CHECKMATE (TV)
Gold Key: Oct, 1962 - No. 2, Dec, 1962

	GD	VG	FN	VF	VF/NM	NM-
1-Photo-c on both	5	10	15	33	57	80
2	5	10	15	30	50	70

CHECKMATE! (See Action Comics #598 and The OMAC Project)
DC Comics: Apr, 1988 - No. 33, Jan, 1991 ($1.25)

	GD	VG	FN	VF	VF/NM	NM-
1-33: 13: New format begins						3.00

NOTE: ***Gil Kane** c-2, 4, 7, 8, 10, 11, 15-19.*

CHECKMATE (See Infinite Crisis and The OMAC Project)
DC Comics: Jun, 2006 - No. 31, Dec, 2008 ($2.99)

	GD	VG	FN	VF	VF/NM	NM-
1-Rucka-s/Saiz-a/Bermejo-c; Alan Scott, Mr. Terrific, Sasha Bordeaux app.						4.00
1-2nd printing with B&W cover						3.00
2-31: 2,3-Kobra, King Faraday, Amanda Waller, Fire app. 13-15-Outsiders app. 26-Chimera origin						3.00
...: A King's GameTPB (2007, $14.99) r/#1-7						15.00
...: Chimera TPB (2009, $17.99) r/#26-31						18.00
...: Fall of the Wall TPB (2008, $14.99) r/#16-22						15.00
...: Pawn Breaks TPB (2007, $14.99) r/#8-12						15.00

CHERYL BLOSSOM (See Archie's Girls, Betty and Veronica #320 for 1st app.)
Archie Publications: Sept, 1995 - No. 3, Nov, 1995 ($1.50, limited series)

	GD	VG	FN	VF	VF/NM	NM-
1	2	4	6	9	12	15
2,3	1	2	3	5	7	9
Special 1-4 ('95, '96, $2.00)	1	2	3	5	7	9

Cheryl Blossom Special #3 © AP

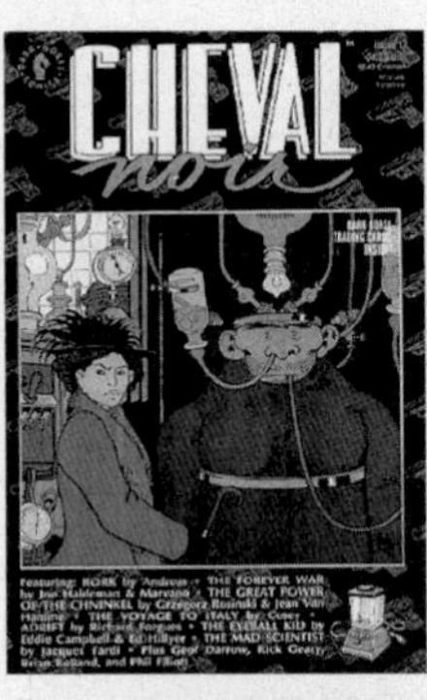

Cheval Noir #17 © DH

Children's Big Book #1 © Dorene

	GD	VG	FN	VF	VF/NM	NM-
	2.0	4.0	6.0	8.0	9.0	9.2

GD VG FN VF VF/NM NM- 2.0 4.0 6.0 8.0 9.0 9.2

CHERYL BLOSSOM (Cheryl's Summer Job)
Archie Publications: July, 1996 - No. 3, Sept, 1996 ($1.50, limited series)

1-3 1 2 3 4 5 7

CHERYL BLOSSOM (...Goes Hollywood)
Archie Publications: Dec, 1996 - No. 3, Feb, 1997 ($1.50, limited series)

1-3 1 2 3 4 5 7

CHERYL BLOSSOM
Archie Publications: Apr, 1997 - No. 37, Mar, 2001 ($1.50/$1.75/$1.79/$1.99)

1-Dan DeCarlo-c/a 2 4 6 8 10 12
2-10: 2-7-Dan DeCarlo-c/a 6.00
11-37: 32-Begin $1.99-c. 34-Sabrina app. 4.00

CHESTY SANCHEZ
Antarctic Press: Nov, 1995 - No. 2, Mar, 1996 ($2.95, B&W)

1,2 3.00
...Super Special (2/99, $5.99) 6.00

CHEVAL NOIR
Dark Horse Comics: 1989 - No. 48, Nov, 1993 ($3.50, B&W, 68 pgs.)

1 ($3.50) Dave Stevens-c 2 4 6 9 12 15
2-6,8,10 ($3.50): 6-Moebius poster insert 5.00
7-Dave Stevens-c 1 2 3 5 6 8
9,11,13,15,17,20,22 ($4.50, 84 pgs.) 6.00
12,18,19,21,23 ($3.95): 12-Geary-a; Mignola-c 5.00
14 ($4.95, 76 pgs.)(7 pgs. color) 6.00
16,24 ($3.75): 16-19-Contain trading cards 5.00
25,26 ($3.95): 26-Moebius-a begins 5.00
27-48 ($2.95): 33-Snyder III-c 4.00

NOTE: ***Bolland** a-2, 6, 7, 13, 14. **Bolton** a-2, 4, 45; c-4, 20. **Chadwick** c-13. **Dorman** painted c-16. **Geary** a-13, 14. **Kelley Jones** c-27. **Kaluta** a-6; c-6, 18. **Moebius** c-5, 9, 26. **Dave Stevens** c-1, 7. **Sutton** painted c-36.*

CHEW (See Walking Dead #61 for preview)
Image Comics: Jun, 2009 - Present ($2.99)

1-Layman-s/Guillory-a 10 20 30 66 138 210
1-(2nd-4th printings) 1 2 3 5 6 8
2-1st printing 3 6 9 19 30 40
2-5-(2nd & 3rd printings) 6.00
3-1st printing 2 4 6 11 16 20
4,5-1st printings 2 4 6 8 10 12
6-10 1 3 4 6 8 10
11-15: 15-Gatefold wraparound-c 1 2 3 5 6 8
16-24: 19-Neon green cover ink 5.00
25-40: 27-(6/12) Second Helping Edition 4.00
27-(5/11) Future issue released between #18 & #19 5.00
Image Firsts: Chew #1 (4/10, $1.00) r/#1 with "Image Firsts" cover logo 5.00

CHEYENNE (TV)
Dell Publishing Co.: No. 734, Oct, 1956 - No. 25, Dec-Jan, 1961-62

Four Color 734(#1)-Clint Walker photo-c 12 24 36 84 185 285
Four Color 772,803: Clint Walker photo-c 8 16 24 51 96 140
4(8-10/57) - 20: 4-9,13-20-Clint Walker photo-c. 10-12-Ty Hardin photo-c
6 12 18 37 66 95
21-25-Clint Walker photo-c on all 6 12 18 38 69 100

CHEYENNE AUTUMN (See Movie Classics)

CHEYENNE KID (Formerly Wild Frontier No. 1-7)
Charlton Comics: No. 8, July, 1957 - No. 99, Nov, 1973

8 (#1) 8 16 24 42 54 65
9,15-19 6 12 18 29 36 42
10-Williamson/Torres-a(3); Ditko-c 11 22 33 60 83 105
11-(68 pgs.)-Cheyenne Kid meets Geronimo 10 20 30 58 79 100
12-Williamson/Torres-a(2) 10 20 30 58 79 100
13-Williamson/Torres-a (5 pgs.) 8 16 24 44 57 70
14-Williamson-a (5 pgs.?) 8 16 24 42 54 65
20-22,24,25-Severin c/a(3) each 4 8 12 21 33 45
23,27-29 3 6 9 15 22 28
26,30-Severin-a 3 6 9 17 26 35
31-59 2 4 6 10 14 18
60-65 2 4 6 8 11 14
66-Wander by Aparo begins, ends #87 2 4 6 10 14 18
67-80 2 4 6 8 11 14
81-99: Apache Red begins #88, origin in #89 2 4 6 8 11 14
Modern Comics Reprint 87,89(1978) 5.00

CHIAROSCURO (THE PRIVATE LIVES OF LEONARDO DA VINCI)
DC Comics (Vertigo): July, 1995 - No. 10, Apr, 1996 ($2.50/$2.95, limited series, mature)

1-9: McGreal and Rawson-s/Truog & Kayanan-a 3.00
10-($2.95) 3.00
TPB (2005, $24.99) r/series; intro. by Alisa Kwitney, afterword by Pat McGreal 25.00

CHICAGO MAIL ORDER (See C-M-O Comics)

CHIEF, THE (Indian Chief No. 3 on)
Dell Publishing Co.: No. 290, Aug, 1950 - No. 2, Apr-June, 1951

Four Color 290(#1) 7 14 21 44 82 120
2 5 10 15 35 63 90

CHIEF CRAZY HORSE (See Wild Bill Hickok #21)
Avon Periodicals: 1950 (Also see Fighting Indians of the Wild West!)

nn-Fawcette-c 22 44 66 132 216 300

CHIEF VICTORIO'S APACHE MASSACRE (See Fight Indians of/Wild West!)
Avon Periodicals: 1951

nn-Williamson/Frazetta-a (7 pgs.); Larsen-a; Kinstler-c
50 100 150 315 533 750

CHILD IS BORN, A
Apostle Arts: Nov, 2011 ($5.99, one-shot)

nn-Story of the birth of Jesus; Billy Tucci-s/a; cover by Tucci & Sparacio 6.00
HC (7/12, $15.99) Includes bonus interview with Billy Tucci and sketch art 16.00

CHILDREN OF FIRE
Fantagor Press: Nov, 1987 - No. 3, 1988 ($2.00, limited series)

1-3: by Richard Corben 4.00

CHILDREN OF THE VOYAGER (See Marvel Frontier Comics Unlimited)
Marvel Frontier Comics: Sept, 1993 - No. 4, Dec, 1993 ($1.95, limited series)

1-($2.95)-Embossed glow-in-the-dark-c; Paul Johnson-c/a 4.00
2-4 3.00

CHILDREN'S BIG BOOK
Dorene Publ. Co.: 1945 (25¢, stiff-c, 68 pgs.)

nn-Comics & fairy tales; David Icove-a 15 30 45 85 130 175

CHILDREN'S CRUSADE, THE
DC Comics (Vertigo): Dec, 1993 - No. 2, Jan, 1994 ($3.95, limited series)

1,2-Gaiman scripts & Bachalo-a; framing issues for Children's Crusade x-over 4.00

CHILD'S PLAY: THE SERIES (Movie)
Innovation Publishing: May, 1991 - #3, 1991 ($2.50, 28pgs.)

1-3 3.00

CHILD'S PLAY 2 THE OFFICIAL MOVIE ADAPTATION (Movie)
Innovation Publishing: 1990 - No. 3, 1990 ($2.50, bi-weekly limited series)

1-3: Adapts movie sequel 3.00

CHILI (Millie's Rival)
Marvel Comics Group: 5/69 - No. 17, 9/70; No. 18, 8/72 - No. 26, 12/73

1 9 18 27 58 114 170
2,4,5 5 10 15 34 60 85
3-Millie & Chili visit Marvel and meet Stan Lee & Stan Goldberg (6 pgs.)
6 12 18 37 66 95
6-17 5 10 15 30 50 70
18-26 4 8 12 27 44 60
Special 1(12/71, 52 pgs.) 5 10 15 35 63 90

CHILLER
Marvel Comics (Epic): Nov, 1993 - No. 2, Dec, 1993 ($7.95, lim. series)

1,2-(68 pgs.) 1 2 3 5 6 8

CHILLING ADVENTURES IN SORCERY (...as Told by Sabrina #1, 2)
(Red Circle Sorcery No. 6 on)
Archie Publications (Red Circle Prods.): 9/72 - No. 2, 10/72; No. 3, 10/73 - No. 5, 2/74

1-Sabrina cameo as narrator 5 10 15 30 50 70
2-Sabrina cameo as narrator 3 6 9 17 26 35
3-5: Morrow-c/a, all. 4,5-Alcazar-a 2 4 6 11 16 20

CHILLING TALES (Formerly Beware)
Youthful Magazines: No. 13, Dec, 1952 - No. 17, Oct, 1953

13(No.1)-Harrison-a; Matt Fox-c/a 77 154 231 493 847 1200
14-Harrison-a 53 106 159 334 567 800
15-Matt Fox-c; Harrison-a 60 120 180 381 653 925
16-Poe adapt.-'Metzengerstein'; Rudyard Kipling adapt.- 'Mark of the Beast,'
by Kiefer; bondage-c 47 94 141 296 498 700

Chilling Tales of Horror V1 #6 © Stanley

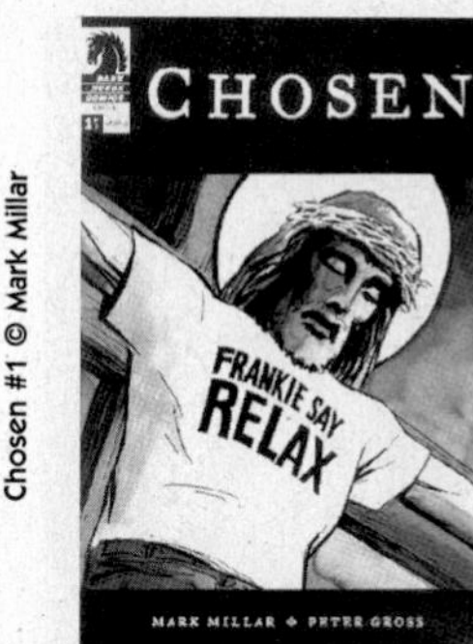

Chosen #1 © Mark Millar

Christmas with Mother Goose FC #126 © DELL

GD 2.0 | VG 4.0 | FN 6.0 | VF 8.0 | VF/NM 9.0 | NM- 9.2

17-Matt Fox-c; Sir Walter Scott & Poe adapt. 53 106 159 334 567 800

CHILLING TALES OF HORROR (Magazine)
Stanley Publications: V1#1, 6/69 - V1#7, 12/70; V2#2, 2/71 - V2#6, 10/71(50¢, B&W, 52 pgs.)
V1#1 8 16 24 56 108 160
2-4,(no #5),6,7: 7-Cameron-a 6 12 18 38 69 100
V2#2-6: 2-Two different #2 issues exist (2/71 & 4/71). 2-(2/71) Spirit of Frankenstein -r/Adventures into the Unknown #16. 4-(8/71) different from other V2#4(6/71) 5 10 15 35 63 90
V2#4-(6/71) r/9 pg. Feldstein-a from Adventures into the Unknown #3 6 12 18 37 66 95
NOTE: *Two issues of V2#2 exist, Feb, 1971 and April, 1971. Two issues of V2#4 exist, Jun, 1971 and Aug, 1971.*

CHILLY WILLY (Also see New Funnies #211)
Dell Publ. Co.: No. 740, Oct, 1956 - No. 1281, Apr-June, 1962 (Walter Lantz)
Four Color 740 (#1) 7 14 21 44 82 120
Four Color 852 (2/58),967 (2/59),1017 (9/59),1074 (2-4/60),1122 (8/60), 1177 (4-6/61), 1212 (7-9/61), 1281 5 10 15 30 50 70

CHIMERA
CrossGeneration Comics: Mar, 2003 - No. 4, July, 2003 ($2.95, limited series)
1-4-Marz-s/Peterson-c/a 3.00
Vol. 1 TPB (2003, $15.95) r/#1-4 plus sketch pages, 3-D models, how-to guides 16.00

CHIMICHANGA
Albatross Exploding Funny Books: 2010 ($3.00, B&W)
1-3-Eric Powell-s/a/c 3.00

CHINA BOY (See Wisco in the Promotional Comics section)

CHIN MUSIC
Image Comics: May, 2013 - Present ($2.99)
1,2-Steve Niles-s/Tony Harris-a/c 3.00

CHIP 'N' DALE (Walt Disney)(See Walt Disney's C&S #204)
Dell Publishing Co./Gold Key/Whitman No. 65 on: Nov, 1953 - No. 30, June-Aug, 1962; Sept, 1967 - No. 83, July, 1984
Four Color 517(#1) 10 20 30 66 138 210
Four Color 581,636 6 12 18 38 69 100
4(12/55-2/56)-10 5 10 15 33 57 80
11-30 4 8 12 28 47 65
1(Gold Key, 1967)-Reprints 3 6 9 19 30 40
2-10 2 4 6 13 18 22
11-20 2 4 6 9 12 15
21-40 2 4 6 8 10 12
41-64,70-77: 75(2/82), 76(2-3/82), 77(3/82) 1 2 3 5 7 9
65,66 (Whitman) 2 4 6 8 11 14
67-69 (3-pack? 1980): 67(8/80), 68(10/80) (scarce) 4 8 12 27 44 60
78-83 (All #90214; 3-pack, nd, nd code): 78(4/83), 79(5/83), 80(7/83), 81(8/83), 82(5/84), 83(7/84) 3 6 9 15 22 28
NOTE: *All Gold Key/Whitman issues have reprints except No. 32-35, 38-41, 45-47. No. 23-28, 30-42, 45-47, 49 have new covers.*

CHIP 'N DALE RESCUE RANGERS
Disney Comics: June, 1990 - No. 19, Dec, 1991 ($1.50)
1-New stories; origin begins 4.00
2-19: 2-Origin continued 3.00

CHIP 'N DALE RESCUE RANGERS
BOOM! Studios: Dec, 2010 - No. 8, Jul, 2011 ($3.99)
1-8: 1-Brill-s/Castellani-a; 3 covers 4.00
... Free Comic Book Day Edition (5/11) Flip book with Darkwing Duck 3.00

CHITTY CHITTY BANG BANG (See Movie Comics)

C.H.I.X.
Image Comics (Studiosaurus): Jan, 1998 ($2.50)
1-Dodson, Haley, Lopresti, Randall, and Warren-s/c/a 3.00
1-($5.00) "X-Ray Variant" cover 5.00
C.H.I.X. That Time Forgot 1 (8/98, $2.95) 3.00

CHOICE COMICS
Great Publications: Dec, 1941 - No. 3, Feb, 1942
1-Origin Secret Circle; Atlas the Mighty app.; Zomba, Jungle Fight, Kangaroo Man, & Fire Eater begin 155 310 465 992 1696 2400
2 77 154 231 493 847 1200
3-Double feature; Features movie "The Lost City" (classic cover); continued from Great Comics #3 174 348 522 1114 1907 2700

CHOLLY AND FLYTRAP (Arthur Suydam's...)(Also see New Adventures of...)
Image Comics: Nov, 2004 - No. 4, June, 2005 ($4.95/$5.95, limited series)
1-($4.95) Arthur Suydam-s/a/c 6.00
2-4-($5.95) 6.00

CHOO CHOO CHARLIE
Gold Key: Dec, 1969
1-John Stanley-a 5 10 15 35 63 90

CHOSEN
Dark Horse Comics: Jan, 2004 - No. 3, Aug, 2004 ($2.99, limited series)
1-Story of the second coming; Mark Millar-s/Peter Gross-a 4.00
2,3 3.00

CHRISTIAN (See Asylum)
Maximum Press: Jan, 1996 ($2.99, one-shot)
1-Pop Mhan-a 3.00

CHRISTIAN HEROES OF TODAY
David C. Cook: 1964 (36 pgs.)
nn 3 6 9 17 26 35

CHRISTMAS (Also see A-1 Comics)
Magazine Enterprises: No. 28, 1950
A-1 28 9 18 27 50 65 80

CHRISTMAS ADVENTURE, A (See Classics Comics Giveaways, 12/69)

CHRISTMAS ALBUM (See March of Comics No. 312)

CHRISTMAS ANNUAL
Golden Special: 1975 ($1.95, 100 pgs., stiff-c)
nn-Reprints Mother Goose stories with Walt Kelly-a 3 6 9 21 33 45

CHRISTMAS & ARCHIE
Archie Comics: Jan, 1975 ($1.00, 68 pgs., 10-1/4x13-1/4" treasury-sized)
1-(scarce) 5 10 15 34 60 85

CHRISTMAS BELLS (See March of Comics No. 297)

CHRISTMAS CARNIVAL
Ziff-Davis Publ. Co./St. John Publ. Co. No. 2: 1952 (25¢, one-shot, 100 pgs.)
nn 37 74 111 222 361 500
2-Reprints Ziff-Davis issue plus-c 18 36 54 103 162 220

CHRISTMAS CAROL, A (See March of Comics No. 33)

CHRISTMAS EVE, A (See March of Comics No. 212)

CHRISTMAS IN DISNEYLAND (See Dell Giants)

CHRISTMAS PARADE (See Dell Giant No. 26, Dell Giants, March of Comics No. 284, Walt Disney Christmas Parade & Walt Disney's...)

CHRISTMAS PARADE (Walt Disney's)
Gold Key: 1962 (no month listed) - No. 9, Jan, 1972 (#1,5: 80 pgs.; #2-4,7-9: 36 pgs.)
1 (30018-301)-Giant 8 16 24 51 96 140
2-6: 2-r/F.C. #367 by Barks. 3-r/F.C. #178 by Barks. 4-r/F.C. #203 by Barks. 5-r/Christmas Parade #1 (Dell) by Barks; giant. 6-r/Christmas Parade #2 (Dell) by Barks (64 pgs.); giant 5 10 15 35 63 90
7-Pull-out poster (half price w/o poster) 5 10 15 30 50 70
8-r/F.C. #367 by Barks; pull-out poster 5 10 15 35 63 90
9 4 8 12 25 40 55

CHRISTMAS PARTY (See March of Comics No. 256)

CHRISTMAS STORIES (See Little People No. 959, 1062)

CHRISTMAS STORY (See March of Comics No. 326 in the Promotional Comics section)

CHRISTMAS STORY, THE
Catechetical Guild: 1955 (15¢)
393-Addison Burbank-a 8 16 24 40 50 60

CHRISTMAS STORY BOOK (See Woolworth's Christmas Story Book)

CHRISTMAS TREASURY, A (See Dell Giants & March of Comics No. 227)

CHRISTMAS WITH ARCHIE
Spire Christian Comics (Fleming H. Revell Co.): 1973, 1974 (49¢, 52 pgs.)
nn-Low print run 3 6 9 15 22 28

CHRISTMAS WITH MOTHER GOOSE
Dell Publishing Co.: No. 90, Nov, 1945 - No. 253, Nov, 1949
Four Color 90 (#1)-Kelly-a 15 30 45 103 227 350
Four Color 126 ('46), 172 (11/47)-By Walt Kelly 11 22 33 76 163 250
Four Color 201 (10/48), 253-By Walt Kelly 10 20 30 64 132 200

Christmas with the Super-Heroes #1 © DC

Chyna #1 © Chaos!

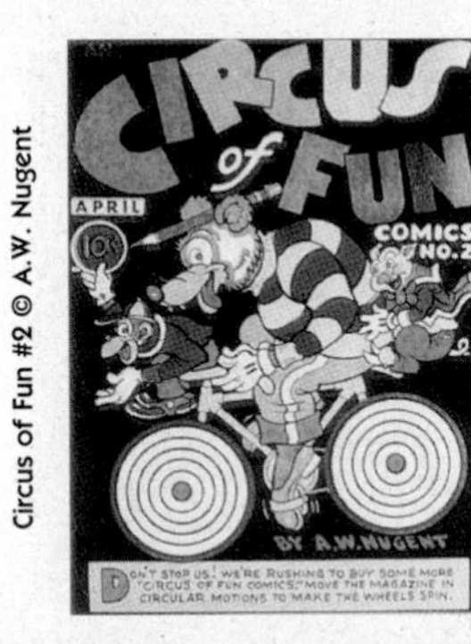

Circus of Fun #2 © A.W. Nugent

	GD 2.0	VG 4.0	FN 6.0	VF 8.0	VF/NM 9.0	NM- 9.2

GD VG FN VF VF/NM NM- 2.0 4.0 6.0 8.0 9.0 9.2

CHRISTMAS WITH SANTA (See March of Comics No. 92)

CHRISTMAS WITH THE SUPER-HEROES (See Limited Collectors' Edition)
DC Comics: 1988; No. 2, 1989 ($2.95)

1,2: 1-(100 pgs.)-All reprints; N. Adams-r, Byrne-c; Batman, Superman, JLA, LSH Christmas stories; r-Miller's 1st Batman/DC Special Series #21. 2-(68 pgs.)-Superman by Chadwick; Batman, Wonder Woman, Deadman, Green Lantern, Flash app.; Morrow-a; Enemy Ace by Byrne; all new-a 6.00

CHROMA-TICK, THE (...Special Edition, #1,2) (Also see The Tick)
New England Comics Press: Feb, 1992 - No. 8, Nov, 1993 ($3.95/$3.50, 44 pgs.)

1,2-Includes serially numbered trading card set 5.00
3-8 ($3.50, 36 pgs.): 6-Bound-in card 4.00

CHROME
Hot Comics: 1986 - No. 3, 1986 ($1.50, limited series)

1-3 3.00

CHROMIUM MAN, THE
Triumphant Comics: Aug, 1993 - No.10, May, 1994 ($2.50)

1-1st app. Mr. Death; all serially numbered 3.00
2-10: 2-1st app. Prince Vandal. 3-1st app. Candi, Breaker & Coil. 4,5-Triumphant Unleashed x-over. 8,9-(3/94). 10-(5/94) 3.00
0-(4/94)-Four color-c, 0-All pink-c & all blue-c; no cover price 3.00

CHROMIUM MAN: VIOLENT PAST, THE
Triumphant Comics: Jan, 1994 - No. 2, Jan, 1994 ($2.50, limited series)

1,2-Serially numbered to 22,000 each 3.00

CHRONICLES OF CONAN, THE (See Conan the Barbarian)

CHRONICLES OF CORUM, THE (Also see Corum...)
First Comics: Jan, 1987 - No. 12, Nov, 1988 ($1.75/$1.95, deluxe series)

1-12: Adapts Michael Moorcock's novel 3.00

CHRONOS
DC Comics: Mar, 1998 - No. 11, Feb. 1999 ($2.50)

1-11-J.F. Moore-s/Guinan-a 3.00
#1,000,000 (11/98) 853rd Century x-over 3.00

CHUCK (Based on the NBC TV series)
DC Comics (WildStorm): Aug, 2008 - No. 6, Jan, 2009 ($2.99, limited series)

1-6-Jeremy Haun-a/Kristian Donaldson-c; Noto back-up-a 3.00
TPB (2009, $19.99) r/#1-6; photo-c 20.00

CHUCKLE, THE GIGGLY BOOK OF COMIC ANIMALS
R. B. Leffingwell Co.: 1945 (132 pgs., one-shot)

1-Funny animal 23 46 69 136 223 310

CHUCK NORRIS (TV)
Marvel Comics (Star Comics): Jan, 1987 - No. 4, July, 1987

1-Ditko-a 2 4 6 8 10 12
2,3: Ditko-a 6.00
4-No Ditko-a (low print run) 1 2 3 4 5 8

CHUCK WAGON (See Sheriff Bob Dixon's...)

CHUCKY (Based on the 1988 killer doll movie Child's Play)
Devil's Due Publishing: Apr, 2007 - No. 4, Nov, 2007 ($3.50/$5.50)

1-3-Pulido-s/Medors-a; art & photo covers 5.00
4-($5.50) 1 2 3 4 5 7
TPB (2007, $18.99) r/series; gallery of variant covers; 4 pages of script and sketch art 19.00

CHYNA (WWF Wrestling)
Chaos! Comics: Sept, 2000; July, 2001 ($2.95/$2.99, one-shots)

1-Grant-s/Barrows-a; photo-c 3.00
1-($9.95) Premium Edition; Cleavenger-c 10.00
II -(7/01, $2.99) Deodato-a; photo-c 3.00

CICERO'S CAT
Dell Publishing Co.: July-Aug, 1959 - No. 2, Sept-Oct, 1959

1-Cat from Mutt & Jeff 4 8 12 28 47 65
2 4 8 12 25 40 55

CIMARRON STRIP (TV)
Dell Publishing Co.: Jan, 1968

1-Stuart Whitman photo-c 4 8 12 23 37 50

CINDER AND ASHE
DC Comics: May, 1988 - No. 4, Aug, 1988 ($1.75, limited series)

1-4: Mature readers 3.00

CINDERELLA (Disney) (See Movie Comics)
Dell Publishing Co.: No. 272, Apr, 1950 - No. 786, Apr, 1957

Four Color 272 11 22 33 76 163 250
Four Color 786-Partial-r #272 6 12 18 41 76 110

CINDERELLA
Whitman Publishing Co.: Apr, 1982

nn-Reprints 4-Color #272 1 2 3 4 5 7

CINDERELLA: FABLES ARE FOREVER (See Fables)
DC Comics (Vertigo): Apr, 2011 - No. 6, Sept, 2011 ($2.99, limited series)

1-6-Roberson-s/McManus-a/Zullo-c; Dorothy Gale app. 3.00

CINDERELLA: FROM FABLETOWN WITH LOVE (See Fables)
DC Comics (Vertigo): Jan, 2010 - No. 6, Jun, 2010 ($2.99, limited series)

1-6: Roberson-s/McManus-a/Zullo-c 3.00
TPB (2010, $14.99) r/#1-6 15.00

CINDERELLA LOVE
Ziff-Davis/St. John Publ. Co. No. 12 on: No. 10, 1950; No. 11, 4-5/51; No. 12, 9/51; No. 4, 10-11/51 - No. 11, Fall, 1952; No. 12, 10/53 - No. 15, 8/54; No. 25, 12/54 - No. 29, 10/55 (No #16-24)

10(#1)(1st Series, 1950)-Painted-c 20 40 60 117 189 260
11(#2, 4-5/51)-Crandall-a; Saunders painted-c 14 28 42 82 121 160
12(#3, 9/51)-Photo-c 14 28 42 76 108 140
4-8: 4,6,7-Photo-c 13 26 39 72 101 130
9-Kinstler-a; photo-c 14 28 42 78 112 145
10,11(Fall/'52): 10,11-Photo-c 13 26 39 72 101 130
12(St. John-10/53)-#13:13-Painted-c. 12 24 36 69 97 125
14-Matt Baker-a 16 32 48 94 147 200
15(8/54)-Matt Baker-c 30 60 90 177 289 400
25(2nd Series)(Formerly Romantic Marriage) Classic Matt Baker-c
50 100 150 315 533 750
26-Matt Baker-c; last precode (2/55) 30 60 90 177 289 400
27,29: Both Matt Baker-c 28 56 84 165 270 375
28 12 24 36 69 97 125

CINDY COMICS (...Smith No. 39, 40; Crime Can't Win No. 41 on)(Formerly Krazy Komics) (See Junior Miss & Teen Comics)
Timely Comics: No. 27, Fall, 1947 - No. 40, July, 1950

27-Kurtzman-a, 3 pgs: Margie, Oscar begin 25 50 75 150 245 340
28-31-Kurtzman-a 15 30 45 90 140 190
32-40: 33-Georgie story; anti-Wertham editorial 14 28 42 76 108 140
NOTE: *Kurtzman's "Hey Look"-#27(3), 29(2), 30(2), 31; "Giggles 'n' Grins"-28.*

CINNAMON: EL CICLO
DC Comics: Oct, 2003 - No. 5, Feb, 2004 ($2.50, limited series)

1-5-Van Meter-s/Chaykin-c/Paronzini-a 3.00

CIRCUS (...the Comic Riot)
Globe Syndicate: June, 1938 - No. 3, Aug, 1938

1-(Scarce)-Spacehawks (2 pgs.), & Disk Eyes by Wolverton (2 pgs.), Pewee Throttle by Cole (2nd comic book work; see Star Comics V1#11), Beau Gus, Ken Craig & The Lords of Crillon, Jack Hinton by Eisner, Van Bragger by Kane
486 972 1458 3550 6275 9000
2,3-(Scarce)-Eisner, Cole, Wolverton, Bob Kane-a in each
271 542 813 1734 2967 4200

CIRCUS BOY (TV) (See Movie Classics)
Dell Publishing Co.: No. 759, Dec, 1956 - No. 813, July, 1957

Four Color 759 (#1)-The Monkees' Mickey Dolenz photo-c
10 20 30 69 147 225
Four Color 785 (4/57), 813-Mickey Dolenz photo-c 9 18 27 59 117 175

CIRCUS COMICS
Farm Women's Pub. Co./D. S. Publ.: Apr, 1945 - No. 2, Jun, 1945; Wint., 1948-49

1-Funny animal 14 28 42 81 118 155
2 9 18 27 52 69 85
1(1948)-D.S. Publ.; 2 pgs. Frazetta 24 48 72 142 234 325

CIRCUS OF FUN COMICS
A. W. Nugent Publ. Co.: 1945 - No. 3, Dec, 1947 (A book of games & puzzles)

1 15 30 45 85 130 175
2,3 10 20 30 54 72 90

CISCO KID, THE (TV)
Dell Publishing Co.: July, 1950 - No. 41, Oct-Dec, 1958

Four Color 292(#1)-Cisco Kid, his horse Diablo, & sidekick Pancho & his horse Loco begin; line drawn cover 19 38 57 133 297 460

Cisco Kid #3 © DELL

Civil War #1 © MAR

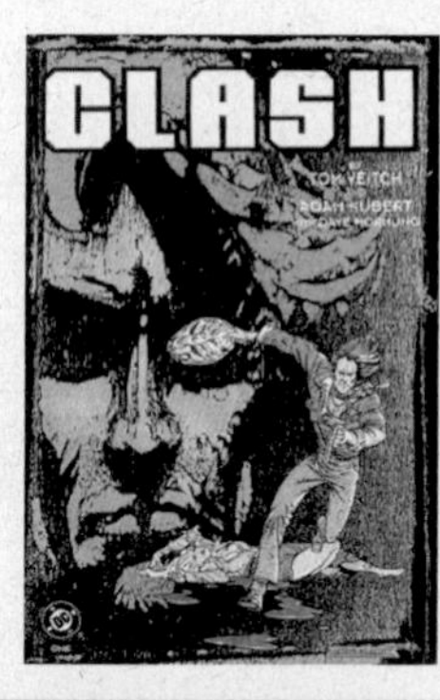

Clash #1 © Veitch & Kubert

	GD 2.0	VG 4.0	FN 6.0	VF 8.0	VF/NM 9.0	NM- 9.2
2(1/51) Painted-c begin	10	20	30	64	132	200
3-5	9	18	27	59	117	175
6-10	8	16	24	51	96	140
11-20	7	14	21	44	82	120
21-36-Last painted-c	6	12	18	37	66	95
37-41: All photo-c	7	14	21	46	86	125

NOTE: ***Buscema** a-40. **Ernest Nordli** painted c-5-16, 20, 35.*

CISCO KID COMICS
Bernard Bailey/Swappers Quarterly: Winter, 1944 (one-shot)

1-Illustrated Stories of the Operas: Faust; Funnyman by Giunta; Cisco Kid (1st app.) & Superbaby begin; Giunta-c 45 90 135 284 480 675

CITIZEN SMITH (See Holyoke One-Shot No. 9)

CITIZEN V AND THE V-BATTALION (See Thunderbolts)
Marvel Comics: June, 2001 - No. 3, Aug, 2001 ($2.99, limited series)

1-3-Nicieza-a; Michael Ryan-c/a 3.00
...: The Everlasting 1-4 (3/02 - No. 4, 7/02) Nicieza-s/LaRosa-a(p) 3.00

CITY OF HEROES (Online game)
Dark Horse Comics/Blue King Studios: Sept, 2002; May, 2004 - No. 7 ($2.95)

1-(no cover price) Dakan-s/Zombo-a 3.00
1-7-($2.95) 3.00

CITY OF HEROES (Online game)
Image Comics: June, 2005 - No. 20, Aug, 2007 ($2.99)

1-20: 1-Waid-s; Pérez-c. 6-Flip-c with City of Villains. 7-9-Jurgens-s 3.00

CITY OF OTHERS
Dark Horse Comics: Apr, 2007 - No. 4, Aug, 2007 ($2.99, limited series)

1-4-Bernie Wrightson-a/c; Steve Niles & Wrightson-s 3.00
TPB (2/08, $14.95) r/#1-4; Wrightson sketch pages 15.00

CITY OF SILENCE
Image Comics: May, 2000 - No. 3, July, 2000 ($2.50)

1-3-Ellis-s/Erskine-a 3.00
TPB (6/04, $9.95) r/#1-3; pin-up gallery 10.00

CITY OF THE LIVING DEAD (See Fantastic Tales No. 1)
Avon Periodicals: 1952

nn-Hollingsworth-c/a 54 108 162 343 574 825

CITY OF TOMORROW
DC Comics (WildStorm): June, 2005 - No. 6, Nov, 2005 ($2.99, limited series)

1-6-Howard Chaykin-s/a 3.00
TPB (2006, $19.99) r/#1-6 20.00

CITY PEOPLE NOTEBOOK
Kitchen Sink Press: 1989 ($9.95, B&W, magazine sized)

nn-Will Eisner-s/a 15.00
nn-(DC Comics, 2000) Reprint 10.00

CITY SURGEON (Blake Harper...)
Gold Key: August, 1963

1(10075-308)-Painted-c 4 8 12 23 37 50

CIVIL WAR (Also see Amazing Spider-Man for TPB)
Marvel Comics: July, 2006 - No. 7, Jan, 2007 ($3.99/$2.99, limited series)

1-($3.99) Millar-s/McNiven-a & wraparound-c 1 2 3 5 6 8
1-Variant cover by Michael Turner 2 4 6 9 12 15
1-Aspen Comics Variant cover by Turner 2 4 6 9 12 15
1-Director's Cut (2006, $4.99) r/#1 plus promo art, variant covers, sketches and script 5.00
2-($2.99) Spider-Man unmasks 1 2 3 4 5 7
2-Turner variant cover 5.00
2-B&W sketch variant cover 20.00
2-2nd printing 4.00
3-7: 3-Thor returns. 4-Goliath killed 5.00
3-7-Turner variant covers 6.00
3-7-B&W sketch variant covers 15.00
TPB (2007, $24.99) r/#1-7; gallery of variant covers 25.00
...: Battle Damage Report (2007, $3.99) Post-Civil War character profiles; McGuinness-c 4.00
...: Choosing Sides (2/07, $3.99) Colan-c; Howard the Duck app.; 2 covers by Yu & Colan 4.00
... Companion TPB (2007, $13.99) r/Civil War Files, ...:Battle Damage Report, Marvel Spotlight: Millar/McNiven, Marvel Spotlight: Civil War Aftermath and Daily Bugle CW 14.00
Daily Bugle Civil War Newspaper Special #1 (9/06, 50¢, newsprint) Daily Bugle "newspaper" overview of the crossover; Mayhew-a 3.00
...Files (2006, $3.99) profile pages of major Civil War characters; McNiven-c 4.00
...: Marvel Universe TPB (2007, $11.99) r/Civil War: Choosing Sides, CW: The Return, She-Hulk #8, CW: The Initiative; She-Hulk sketch page; variant cover gallery 12.00
...: MGC #1 (6/10, $1.00) r/#1 with "Marvel's Greatest Comics" cover logo 3.00
...: The Confession (5/07, $2.99) Maleev-c/a; Bendis-s 3.00
...: The Initiative (4/07, $4.99) Silvestri-c/a; previews of post-Civil War series 5.00
...: The Return (3/07, $2.99) Captain Marvel returns; The Sentry app.; Raney-a 3.00
...: The Road to Civil War TPB (2007, $14.99) r/New Avengers: Illuminati, Fantastic Four #536 & 537, Amazing Spider-Man #529-531; Spider-Man costume sketches by Bachalo 15.00
... War Crimes (2/07, $3.99) Kingpin in prison; Tieri-s/Staz Johnson-a 4.00
... War Crimes TPB (2007, $17.99) r/Civil War: War Crimes one-shot and Underworld #1-5 18.00
... X-Men Universe TPB (2007, $13.99) r/Cable & Deadpool #30-32; X-Factor #8,9 14.00

CIVIL WAR CHRONICLES (Reprints of Civil War and related Marvel issues)
Marvel Comics: Oct, 2007 - No. 12, Sept, 2008 ($4.99, limited series)

1-12: Reprints Civil War, Civil War: Frontline and x-over issues 5.00

CIVIL WAR: FRONTLINE (Tie-in to Civil War and related Marvel issues)
Marvel Comics: Aug, 2006 - No. 11, Apr, 2007 ($2.99, limited series)

1-Jenkins-s/Bachs-a/Watson-c; back-up stories by various 4.00
2-11: 3-Green Goblin app. 11-Aftermath of Civil War #7 3.00
... Book 1 TPB (2007, $14.99) r/#1-6 15.00
... Book 2 TPB (2007, $14.99) r/#7-11 15.00

CIVIL WAR: HOUSE OF M
Marvel Comics: Nov, 2008 - No. 5, Mar, 2009 ($2.99, limited series)

1-5-Gage-s/DiVito-a 3.00

CIVIL WAR MUSKET, THE (Kadets of America Handbook)
Custom Comics, Inc.: 1960 (25¢, half-size, 36 pgs.)

nn 3 6 9 15 22 28

CIVIL WAR: X-MEN (Tie-in to Civil War)
Marvel Comics: Sept, 2006 - No. 4, Dec, 2006 ($2.99, limited series)

1-4-Paquette-a/Hine-s; Bishop app. 3.00
1-Variant cover by Michael Turner 10.00
TPB (2007, $11.99) r/#1-4, profile pages of minor characters 12.00

CIVIL WAR: YOUNG AVENGERS & RUNAWAYS (Tie-in to Civil War)
Marvel Comics: Sept, 2006 - No. 4, Dec, 2006 ($2.99, limited series)

1-4-Caselli-a/Wells-s/Cheung-c 3.00
TPB (2007, $11.99) r/#1-4, profile pages of characters 12.00

CLAIRE VOYANT (Also see Keen Teens)
Leader Publ./Standard/Pentagon Publ.: 1946 - No. 4, 1947 (Sparling strip reprints)

nn 73 146 219 467 796 1125
2-Kamen-c 53 106 159 334 567 800
3-Kamen bridal-c; contents mentioned in Love and Death, a book by Gershom Legman(1949) referenced by Dr. Wertham in **SOTI** 69 138 207 442 759 1075
4-Kamen bondage-c 58 116 174 371 636900

CLANDESTINE (Also see Marvel Comics Presents & X-Men: ClanDestine)
Marvel Comics: Oct, 1994 - No.12, Sept, 1995 ($2.95/$2.50)

1-($2.95)-Alan Davis-c/a(p)/scripts & Mark Farmer-c/a(i) begin, ends #8; Modok app.; Silver Surfer cameo; gold foil-c 4.00
2-12: 2-Wraparound-c. 2,3-Silver Surfer app. 5-Origin of ClanDestine. 6-Capt. America, Hulk, Spider-Man, Thing & Thor-c; Spider-Man cameo. 7-Spider-Man-c/app; Punisher cameo. 8-Invaders & Dr. Strange app. 10-Captain Britain-c/app. 11-Sub-Mariner app. 3.00
Preview (10/94, $1.50) 3.00
... Classic HC (2008, $29.99, DJ) r/#1-8, Marvel Comics Presents #158, X-Men and Clandestine #1&2, sketch pages and cover gallery; Alan Davis afterword 30.00

CLANDESTINE
Marvel Comics: Apr, 2008 - No. 5, Aug, 2008 ($2.99, limited series)

1-5: 1-Alan Davis-c/a(p)/scripts & Mark Farmer-c/a(i). 2-5-Excalibur app. 3.00

CLASH
DC Comics: 1991 - No. 3, 1991 ($4.95, limited series, 52 pgs.)

Book One - Three: Adam Kubert-c/a 5.00

CLASSIC BATTLESTAR GALACTICA (See Battlestar Galactica, Classic...)

CLASSIC COMICS/ILLUSTRATED - INTRODUCTION
by Dan Malan

Since the first publication of this special introduction to the **Classics** section, a number of revisions have been made to further clarify the listings. **Classics** reprint editions prior to 1963 had either incorrect dates or no dates listed. Those reprint editions should be identified only by the highest number on the reorder list (HRN). Past *Guide*s listed what were calculated to be approximately correct dates, but many people found it confusing for the *Guide* to list a date not

Classic Comics #1 © GIL

Classic Comics #2 © GIL

Classic Comics #3 © GIL

GD	VG	FN	VF	VF/NM	NM-
2.0	4.0	6.0	8.0	9.0	9.2

listed in the comic itself.

We have also attempted to clear up confusion about edition variations, such as color, printer, etc. Such variations are identified by letters. Editions are determined by three categories. Original edition variations are designated as Edition 1A, 1B, etc. All reprint editions prior to 1963 are identified by HRN only. All reprint editions from 9/63 on are identified by the correct date listed in the comic.

Information is also included on four reprintings of **Classics**. From 1968-1976, Twin Circle, the Catholic newspaper, serialized over 100 **Classics** titles. That list can be found under non-series items at the end of this section. In 1972, twelve **Classics** were reissued as **Now Age Books Illustrated**. They are listed under **Pendulum Illustrated Classics**. In 1982, 20 **Classics** were reissued, adapted for teaching English as a second language. They are listed under **Regents Illustrated Classics**. Then in 1984, six **Classics** were reissued with cassette tapes. See the listing under **Cassette Books**.

UNDERSTANDING CLASSICS ILLUSTRATED
by Dan Malan

Since **Classics Illustrated** is the most complicated comic book series, with all its reprint editions and variations, changes in covers and artwork, a variety of means of identifying editions, and the most extensive worldwide distribution of any comic-book series, this introductory section is provided to assist you in gaining expertise about this series.

THE HISTORY OF CLASSICS

The **Classics** series was the brain child of Albert L. Kanter, who saw in the new comic-book medium a means of introducing children to the great classics of literature. In October of 1941 his Gilberton Co. began the **Classic Comics** series with **The Three Musketeers**, with 64 pages of storyline. In those early years, the struggling series saw irregular schedules and numerous printers, not to mention variable art quality and liberal story adaptations. With No.13 the page total was reduced to 56 (except for No. 33, originally scheduled to be No. 9), and with No. 15 the coming-next ad on the outside back cover moved inside. In 1945 the Jerry Iger Shop began producing all new CC titles, beginning with No. 23. In 1947 the search for a classier logo resulted in **Classics Illustrated**, beginning with No. 35, **Last Days of Pompeii**. With No. 45 the page total dropped again to 48, which was to become the standard.

Two new developments in 1951 had a profound effect upon the success of the series. One was the introduction of painted covers, instead of the old line drawn covers, beginning with No. 81, **The Odyssey**. The second was the switch to the major national distributor Curtis. They raised the cover price from 10 to 15 cents, making it the highest priced comic-book, but it did not slow the growth of the series, because they were marketed as books, not comics. Because of this higher quality image, **Classics** flourished during the fifties while other comic series were reeling from outside attacks. They diversified with their new **Juniors**, **Specials**, and **World Around Us** series.

Classics artwork can be divided into three distinct periods. The pre-Iger era (1941-44) was mentioned above for its variable art quality. The Iger era (1945-53) was a major improvement in art quality and adaptations. It came to be dominated by artists Henry Kiefer and Alex Blum, together accounting for some 50 titles. Their styles gave the first real personality to the series. The EC era (1954-62) resulted from the demise of the EC horror series, when many of their artists made the major switch to classical art.

But several factors brought the production of new CI titles to a complete halt in 1962. Gilberton lost its 2nd class mailing permit. External factors like television, cheap paperback books, and Cliff Notes were all eating away at their market. Production halted with No.167, **Faust**, even though many more titles were already in the works. Many of those found their way into foreign series, and are very desirable to collectors. In 1967, **Classics Illustrated** was sold to Patrick Frawley and his Catholic publication, Twin Circle. They issued two new titles in 1969 as part of an attempted revival, but succumbed to major distribution problems in 1971. In 1988, First Publishing acquired the rights to use the old CI series art, logo, and name from the Frawley Group, and released a short-lived series featuring contributions of modern creators. Acclaim Books and Twin Circles issued a series of **Classics** reprints from 1997-1998.

One of the unique aspects of the **Classics Illustrated** (CI) series was the proliferation of reprint variations. Some titles had as many as 25 editions. Reprinting began in 1943. Some **Classic Comics** (CC) reprints (r) had the logo format revised to a banner logo, and added a motto under the banner. In 1947 CC titles changed to the CI logo, but kept their line drawn covers (LDC). In 1948, Nos. 13, 18, 29 and 41 received second covers (LDC2), replacing covers considered too violent, and reprints of Nos. 13-44 had pages reduced to 48, except for No. 26, which had 48 pages to begin with.

Starting in the mid-1950s, 70 of the 80 LDC titles were reissued with new painted covers (PC). Thirty of them also received new interior artwork (A2). The new artwork was generally higher quality with larger art panels and more faithful but abbreviated storylines. Later on, there were 29 second painted covers (PC2), mostly by Twin Circle. Altogether there were 199 interior art variations (169 (O)s and 30 A2 editions) and 272 different covers (169 (O)s, four LDC2s, 70 new PCs of LDC (O)s, and 29 PC2s). It is mildly astounding to realize that there are nearly 1400 different editions in the U.S. CI series.

FOREIGN CLASSICS ILLUSTRATED

If U.S. Classics variations are mildly astounding, the veritable plethora of foreign CI variations will boggle your imagination. While we still anticipate additional discoveries, we presently know about series in 25 languages and 27 countries. There were 250 new CI titles in foreign series, and nearly 400 new foreign covers of U.S. titles. The 1400 U.S. CI editions pale in comparison to the 4000 plus foreign editions. The very nature of CI lent itself to flourishing as an international series. Worldwide, they published over one billion copies! The first foreign CI series consisted of six Canadian Classic Comic reprints in 1946.

The following chart shows when CI series first began in each country:
1946: Canada. 1947: Australia. 1948: Brazil/The Netherlands. 1950: Italy. 1951: Greece/Japan/Hong Kong(?)/England/Argentina/Mexico. 1952: West Germany. 1954: Norway. 1955: New Zealand/South Africa. 1956: Denmark/Sweden/Iceland. 1957: Finland/France. 1962: Singapore(?). 1964: India (8 languages). 1971: Ireland (Gaelic). 1973: Belgium(?) /Philippines(?) & Malaysia(?).

Significant among the early series were Brazil and Greece. In 1950, Brazil was the first country to begin doing its own new titles. They issued nearly 80 new CI titles by Brazilian authors. In Greece in 1951 they actually had debates in parliament about the effects of Classics Illustrated on Greek culture, leading to the inclusion of 88 new Greek History & Mythology titles in the CI series.

But by far the most important foreign CI development was the joint European series which began in 1956 in 10 countries simultaneously. By 1960, CI had the largest European distribution of any American publication, not just comics! So when all the problems came up with U.S. distribution, they literally moved the CI operation to Europe in 1962, and continued producing new titles in all four CI series. Many of them were adapted and drawn in the U.S., the most famous of which was the British CI #158A. Dr. No, drawn by Norman Nodel. Unfortunately, the British CI series ended in late 1963, which limited the European CI titles available in English to 15. Altogether there were 82 new CI art titles in the joint European series, which ran until 1976.

IDENTIFYING CLASSICS EDITIONS

HRN: This is the highest number on the reorder list. It should be listed in ( ) after the title number. It is crucial to understanding various CI editions.

ORIGINALS (O): This is the all-important First Edition. To determine (O)s,there is one primary rule and two secondary rules (with exceptions):

Rule No. 1: All (O)s and only (O)s have coming-next ads for the next number. **Exceptions**: No. 14(15) (reprint) has an ad on the last inside text page only. No. 14(0) also has a full-page outside back cover ad (also rule 2). Nos.55(75) and 57(75) have coming-next ads. (Rules 2 and 3 apply here). Nos. 168(0) and 169(0) do not have coming-next ads. No.168 was never reprinted; No. 169(0) has HRN (166). No. 169(169) is the only reprint.

Rule No. 2: On nos.1-80, all (O)s and only (O)s list 10c on the front cover. **Exceptions**: Reprint variations of Nos. 37(62), 39(71), and 46(62) list 10c on the front cover. (Rules 1 and 3 apply here.)

Rule No. 3: All (O)s have HRN close to that title No. **Exceptions**: Some reprints also have HRNs close to that title number: a few CC(r)s, 58(62), 60(62), 149(149), 152(149) 153(149), and title nos. in the 160's. (Rules 1 and 2 apply here.)

DATES: Many reprint editions list either an incorrect date or no date. Since Gilberton apparently kept track of CI editions by HRN, they often left the (O) date on reprints. Often, someone with a CI collection for sale will swear that all their copies are originals. That is why we are so detailed in pointing out how to identify original editions. Except for original editions, which should have a coming-next ad, etc., all CI dates prior to 1963 are incorrect! So you want to go by HRN only if it is (165) or below, and go by listed date if it is 1963 or later. There are a few (167) editions with incorrect dates. They could be listed either as (167) or (62/3), which is meant to indicate that they were issued sometime between late 1962 and early 1963.

COVERS: A change from CC to LDC indicates a logo change, not a cover change; while a change from LDC to LDC2, LDC to PC, or from PC to PC2 does indicate a new cover. New PCs can be identified by HRN, and PC2s can be identified by HRN and date. Several covers had color changes, particularly from purple to blue.

Notes: If you see 15 cents in Canada on a front cover, it does not necessarily indicate a Canadian edition. Editions with an HRN between 44 and 75, with 15 cents on the cover are Canadian. Check the publisher's address. An HRN listing two numbers with a / between them indicates that there are two different reorder lists in the front and back covers. Official Twin Circle editions have a full-page back cover ad for their TC magazine, with no CI reorder list. Any CI with just a Twin Circle sticker on the front is not an official TC edition.

TIPS ON LISTING CLASSICS FOR SALE

It may be easy to just list Edition 17, but Classics collectors keep track of CI editions in terms of HRN and/or date, (O) or (r), CC or LDC, PC or PC2, A1 or A2, soft or stiff cover, etc. Try to help them out. For originals, just list (0), unless there are variations such as color (Nos. 10 and 61), printer (Nos. 18-22), HRN (Nos. 95, 108, 160), etc. For reprints, just list HRN if it's (165) or below. Above that, list HRN and date. Also, please list type of logo/cover/art for the convenience of buyers. They will appreciate it.

CLASSIC COMICS (Also see Best from Boys Life, Cassette Books, Famous Stories, Fast Fiction, Golden Picture Classics, King Classics, Marvel Classics Comics, Pendulum Illustrated Classics, Picture Parade, Picture Progress, Regents Ill. Classics, Spitfire, Stories by Famous Authors, Superior Stories, and World Around Us.)

CLASSIC COMICS (Classics Illustrated No. 35 on)
Elliot Publishing #1-3 (1941-1942)/Gilberton Publications #4-167 (1942-1967) /Twin Circle Pub. (Frawley) #168-169 (1968-1971):

Classic Comics #4 © GIL

Classic Comics #6 © GIL

Classic Comics #7 © GIL

10/41 - No. 34, 2/47; No. 35, 3/47 - No. 169, Spring 1969
(Reprint Editions of almost all titles 5/43 - Spring 1971)
(Painted Covers (0)s No. 81 on, and (r)s of most Nos. 1-80)

Abbreviations:
A–Art; C or c–Cover; CC–Classic Comics; CI–Classics Ill.; Ed–Edition; LDC–Line Drawn Cover; PC–Painted Cover; r–Reprint

1. The Three Musketeers

Ed	HRN	Date	Details	A	C	GD 2.0	VG 4.0	FN 6.0	VF 8.0	VF/NM 9.0	NM- 9.2
1	–	10/41	Date listed-1941; Elliot Pub; 68 pgs.	1	1	470	940	1410	3431	6066	8700
2	10	–	10¢ price removed on all (r)s; Elliot Pub; CC-r	1	1	36	72	108	211	343	475
3	15	–	Long Isl. Ind. Ed.; CC-r	1	1	26	52	78	154	252	350
4	18/20	–	Sunrise Times Ed.; CC-r	1	1	19	38	57	109	172	235
5	21	–	Richmond Courier Ed.; CC-r	1	1	17	34	51	98	154	210
6	28	1946	CC-r	1	1	14	28	42	80	115	150
7	36	–	LDC-r	1	1	8	16	24	42	54	65
8	60	–	LDC-r	1	1	6	12	18	27	33	38
9	64	–	LDC-r	1	1	5	10	15	22	26	30
10	78	–	C-price 15¢;LDC-r	1	1	4	9	13	18	22	26
11	93	–	LDC-r	1	1	4	9	13	18	22	26
12	114	–	Last LDC-r	1	1	4	8	11	16	19	22
13	134	–	New-c; old-a; 64 pg. PC-r	1	2	3	6	9	18	28	38
14	143	–	Old-a; PC-r; 64 pg.	1	2	2	4	6	11	16	20
15	150	–	New-a; PC-r; Evans/Crandall-a	2	2	3	6	9	16	24	32
16	149	–	PC-r	2	2	2	4	6	8	11	14
17	167	–	PC-r	2	2	2	4	6	8	11	14
18	167	4/64	PC-r	2	2	2	4	6	8	11	14
19	167	1/65	PC-r	2	2	2	4	6	8	11	14
20	167	3/66	PC-r	2	2	2	4	6	8	11	14
21	166	11/67	PC-r	2	2	2	4	6	8	11	14
22	166	Spr/69	C-price 25¢ ; stiff-c; PC-r	2	2	2	4	6	8	11	14
23	169	Spr/71	PC-r; stiff-c	2	2	2	4	6	8	11	14

2. Ivanhoe

Ed	HRN	Date	Details	A	C	GD 2.0	VG 4.0	FN 6.0	VF 8.0	VF/NM 9.0	NM- 9.2
1	(O)	12/41?	Date listed-1941; Elliot Pub; 68 pgs.	1	1	239	478	717	1530	2615	3700
2	10	–	Price & 'Presents' removed; Elliot Pub; CC-r	1	1	32	64	96	188	307	425
3	15	–	Long Isl. Ind. ed.; CC-r	1	1	21	42	63	124	202	280
4	18/20	–	Sunrise Times ed.; CC-r	1	1	18	36	54	103	162	225
5	21	–	Richmond Courier ed.; CC-r	1	1	16	32	48	94	147	200
6	28	1946	Last 'Comics'-r	1	1	14	28	42	80	115	150
7	36	–	1st LDC-r	1	1	9	18	27	47	61	75
8	60	–	LDC-r	1	1	6	12	18	27	33	38
9	64	–	LDC-r	1	1	5	10	15	22	26	30
10	78	–	C-price 15¢; LDC-r	1	1	4	9	13	18	22	26
11	89	–	LDC-r	1	1	4	8	12	17	21	24
12	106	–	LDC-r	1	1	4	7	10	14	17	20
13	121	–	Last LDC-r	1	1	4	7	10	14	17	20
14	136	–	New-c&a; PC-r	2	2	5	10	15	25	31	36
15	142	–	PC-r	2	2	2	4	6	9	13	16
16	153	–	PC-r	2	2	2	4	6	9	13	16
17	149	–	PC-r	2	2	2	4	6	9	13	16
18	167	–	PC-r	2	2	2	4	6	8	11	14
19	167	5/64	PC-r	2	2	2	4	6	8	11	14
20	167	1/65	PC-r	2	2	2	4	6	8	11	14
21	167	3/66	PC-r	2	2	2	4	6	8	11	14
22A	166	9/67	PC-r	2	2	2	4	6	8	11	14
22B	166	–	Center ad for Children's Digest & Young Miss; rare; PC-r	2	2	6	12	18	40	73	105
23	166	R/68	C-Price 25¢; PC-r	2	2	2	4	6	8	11	14
24	169	Win/69	Stiff-c	2	2	2	4	6	8	11	14
25	169	Win/71	PC-r; stiff-c	2	2	2	4	6	8	11	14

3. The Count of Monte Cristo

Ed	HRN	Date	Details	A	C	GD 2.0	VG 4.0	FN 6.0	VF 8.0	VF/NM 9.0	NM- 9.2
1	(O)	3/42	Elliot Pub; 68 pgs.	1	1	155	310	465	992	1696	2400
2	10	–	Conray Prods; CC-r	1	1	27	54	81	158	259	360
3	15	–	Long Isl. Ind. ed.; CC-r	1	1	20	40	60	120	195	270
4	18/20	–	Sunrise Times ed.; CC-r	1	1	18	36	54	107	169	230
5	20	–	Sunrise Times ed.; CC-r	1	1	17	34	51	98	154	210
6	21	–	Richmond Courier ed.; CC-r	1	1	16	32	48	94	147	200
7	28	1946	CC-r; new Banner logo	1	1	14	28	42	80	115	150
8	36	–	1st LDC-r	1	1	9	18	27	47	61	75
9	60	–	LDC-r	1	1	6	12	18	27	33	38
10	62	–	LDC-r	1	1	6	12	18	29	36	42
11	71	–	LDC-r	1	1	5	10	14	20	24	28
12	87	–	C-price 15¢; LDC-r	1	1	4	9	13	18	22	26
13	113	–	LDC-r	1	1	4	7	10	14	17	20
14	135	–	New-c&a; PC-r; Cameron-a	2	2	3	6	9	17	26	35
15	143	–	PC-r	2	2	2	4	6	8	13	16
16	153	–	PC-r	2	2	2	4	6	8	13	16
17	161	–	PC-r	2	2	2	4	6	8	13	16
18	167	–	PC-r	2	2	2	4	6	8	11	14
19	167	7/64	PC-r	2	2	2	4	6	8	11	14
20	167	7/65	PC-r	2	2	2	4	6	8	11	14
21	167	7/66	PC-r	2	2	2	4	6	8	11	14
22	166	R/68	C-price 25¢; PC-r	2	2	2	4	6	8	11	14
23	169	–	Win/69 Stiff-c; PC-r	2	2	2	4	6	8	11	14

4. The Last of the Mohicans

Ed	HRN	Date	Details	A	C	GD 2.0	VG 4.0	FN 6.0	VF 8.0	VF/NM 9.0	NM- 9.2
1	(O)	8/42	Date listed-1942; Gilberton #4(0) on; 68 pgs.	1	1	132	264	396	838	1444	2050
2	12	–	Elliot Pub; CC-r	1	1	27	54	81	158	259	360
3	15	–	Long Isl. Ind. ed.; CC-r	1	1	20	40	60	120	195	270
4	20	–	Long Isl. Ind. ed.; CC-r; banner logo	1	1	18	36	54	105	165	225
5	21	–	Queens Home News ed.; CC-r	1	1	16	32	48	94	147	200
6	28	1946	Last CC-r; new	1	1	14	28	42	80	115	150
7	36	–	1st LDC-r	1	1	9	18	27	47	61	75
8	60	–	LDC-r	1	1	6	12	18	27	33	38
9	64	–	LDC-r	1	1	5	10	14	20	24	28
10	78	–	C-price 15¢; LDC-r	1	1	4	9	13	18	22	26
11	89	–	LDC-r	1	1	4	8	12	17	21	24
12	117	–	Last LDC-r	1	1	4	7	10	14	17	20
13	135	–	New-c; PC-r	1	2	5	10	15	24	30	35
14	141	–	PC-r	1	2	4	7	9	14	16	18
15	150	–	New-a; PC-r; Severin, L.B. Cole-a	2	2	6	12	18	27	33	38
16	161	–	PC-r	2	2	2	4	6	8	11	14
17	167	–	PC-r	2	2	2	4	6	8	11	14
18	167	6/64	PC-r	2	2	2	4	6	8	11	14
19	167	8/65	PC-r	2	2	2	4	6	8	11	14
20	167	8/66	PC-r	2	2	2	4	6	8	11	14
21	166	R/67	C-price 25¢; PC-r	2	2	2	4	6	8	11	14
22	169	Spr/69	Stiff-c; PC-r	2	2	2	4	6	8	11	14

5. Moby Dick

Ed	HRN	Date	Details	A	C	GD 2.0	VG 4.0	FN 6.0	VF 8.0	VF/NM 9.0	NM- 9.2
1A	(O)	9/42	Date listed-1942; Gilberton; 68 pgs.	1	1	155	310	465	992	1696	2400
1B			inside-c, rare free promo			239	478	717	1530	2615	3700

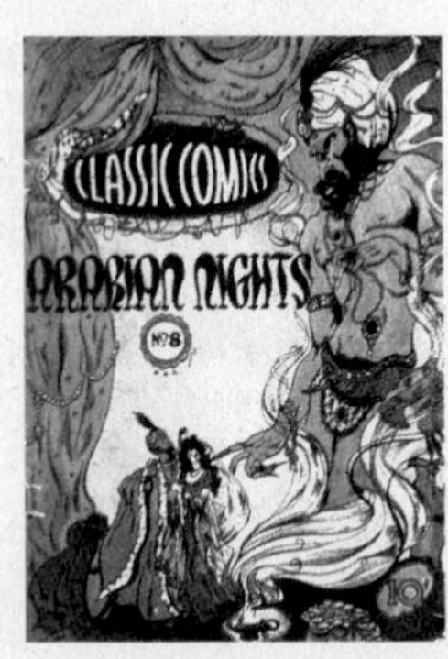

Classic Comics #8 © GIL

Classic Comics #10 © GIL

Classic Comics #12 © GIL

Ed	HRN	Date	Details	A	C	GD 2.0	VG 4.0	FN 6.0	VF 8.0	VF/NM 9.0	NM- 9.2
2	10	–	Conray Prods; Pg. 64 changed from 105 title list to letter from Editor; CC-r	1	1	28	56	84	165	270	375
3	15	–	Long Isl. Ind. ed.; Pg. 64 changed from Letter to the Editor to Ill. poem-Concord Hymn; CC-r	1	1	23	46	69	136	223	310
4	18/20	–	Sunrise Times ed.; CC-r	1	1	19	38	57	109	172	235
5	20	–	Sunrise Times ed.; CC-r	1	1	18	36	54	105	165	225
6	21	–	Sunrise Times ed.; CC-r	1	1	16	32	48	94	147	200
7	28	1946	CC-r; new banner logo	1	1	14	28	42	81	118	155
8	36	–	1st LDC-r	1	1	9	18	27	47	61	75
9	60	–	LDC-r	1	1	6	12	18	27	33	38
10	62	–	LDC-r	1	1	6	12	18	29	36	42
11	71	–	LDC-r	1	1	5	10	15	22	26	30
12	87	–	C-price 15¢; LDC-r	1	1	5	10	14	20	24	28
13	118	–	LDC-r	1	1	4	8	12	17	21	24
14	131	–	New c&a; PC-r	2	2	5	10	15	25	31	36
15	138	–	PC-r	2	2	2	4	6	9	12	16
16	148	–	PC-r	2	2	2	4	6	9	12	16
17	158	–	PC-r	2	2	2	4	6	9	12	16
18	167	–	PC-r	2	2	2	4	6	8	11	14
19	167	6/64	PC-r	2	2	2	4	6	8	11	14
20	167	7/65	PC-r	2	2	2	4	6	8	11	14
21	167	3/66	PC-r	2	2	2	4	6	8	11	14
22	166	9/67	PC-r	2	2	2	4	6	8	11	14
23	166	Win/69	New-c & c-price 25¢; Stiff-c; PC-r	2	3	3	6	9	16	23	30
24	169	Win/71	PC-r	2	3	3	6	9	14	19	24

6. A Tale of Two Cities

Ed	HRN	Date	Details	A	C	GD 2.0	VG 4.0	FN 6.0	VF 8.0	VF/NM 9.0	NM- 9.2
1	(O)	10/42	Date listed-1942; 68 pgs. Zeckerberg c/a	1	1	129	258	387	826	1413	2000
2	14	–	Elliot Pub; CC-r	1	1	24	48	72	142	234	325
3	18	–	Long Isl. Ind. ed.; CC-r	1	1	20	40	60	114	182	250
4	20	–	Sunrise Times ed.; CC-r	1	1	18	36	54	105	165	225
5	28	1946	Last CC-r; new banner logo	1	1	14	28	42	80	115	150
6	51	–	1st LDC-r	1	1	8	16	24	42	54	65
7	64	–	LDC-r	1	1	5	10	15	23	28	32
8	78	–	C-price 15¢; LDC-r	1	1	5	10	14	20	24	28
9	89	–	LDC-r	1	1	4	7	10	14	17	20
10	117	–	LDC-r	1	1	4	7	10	14	17	20
11	132	–	New-c&a; PC-r; Joe Orlando-a	2	2	5	10	15	25	31	36
12	140	–	PC-r	2	2	2	4	6	8	11	14
13	147	–	PC-r	2	2	2	4	6	8	11	14
14	152	–	PC-r; very rare	2	2	17	34	51	98	154	210
15	153	–	PC-r	2	2	2	4	6	9	13	16
16	149	–	PC-r	2	2	2	4	6	9	13	16
17	167	–	PC-r	2	2	2	4	6	8	11	14
18	167	6/64	PC-r	2	2	2	4	6	8	11	14
19	167	8/65	PC-r	2	2	2	4	6	8	11	14
20	166	5/67	PC-r	2	2	2	4	6	8	11	14
21	166	Fall/68	New-c & 25¢; PC-r	2	3	3	6	9	16	24	32
22	169	Sum/70	Stiff-c; PC-r	2	3	2	4	6	13	18	22

7. Robin Hood

Ed	HRN	Date	Details	A	C	GD 2.0	VG 4.0	FN 6.0	VF 8.0	VF/NM 9.0	NM- 9.2
1	(O)	12/42	Date listed-1942; first Gift Box ad-bc; 68 pgs.	1	1	100	200	300	635	1093	1550
2	12	–	Elliot Pub; CC-r	1	1	24	48	72	140	230	320
3	18	–	Long Isl. Ind. ed.; CC-r	1	1	19	38	57	111	176	240
4	20	–	Nassau Bulletin ed.; CC-r	1	1	18	36	54	103	162	220
5	22	–	Queens Cty. Times ed.; CC-r	1	1	16	32	48	94	147	200
6	28	–	CC-r	1	1	14	28	42	81	118	155
7	51	–	LDC-r	1	1	8	16	24	42	54	65
8	64	–	LDC-r	1	1	5	10	15	24	30	35
9	78	–	LDC-r	1	1	4	9	13	18	22	26
10	97	–	LDC-r	1	1	4	8	12	17	21	24
11	106	–	LDC-r	1	1	4	7	10	14	17	20
12	121	–	LDC-r	1	1	4	7	10	14	17	20
13	129	–	New-c; PC-r	1	2	5	10	15	25	31	36
14	136	–	New-a; PC-r	2	2	5	10	15	24	29	34
15	143	–	PC-r	2	2	2	4	6	9	13	16
16	153	–	PC-r	2	2	2	4	6	9	13	16
17	164	–	PC-r	2	2	2	4	6	8	11	14
18	167	–	PC-r	2	2	2	4	6	8	11	14
19	167	6/64	PC-r	2	2	2	4	6	8	11	14
20	167	5/65	PC-r	2	2	2	4	6	8	11	14
21	167	7/66	PC-r	2	2	2	4	6	8	11	14
22	166	12/67	PC-r	2	2	2	4	6	8	11	14
23	169	Sum/69	Stiff-c; c-price 25¢; PC-r	2	2	2	4	6	8	11	14

8. Arabian Nights

Ed	HRN	Date	Details	A	C	GD 2.0	VG 4.0	FN 6.0	VF 8.0	VF/NM 9.0	NM- 9.2
1	(O)	2/43	Original; 68 pgs. Lilian Chestney-c/a	1	1	152	304	456	965	1658	2350
2	17	–	Long Isl. ed.; pg. 64 changed from Gift Box ad to Letter from British Medical Worker; CC-r	1	1	52	104	156	323	549	775
3	20	–	Nassau Bulletin; Pg. 64 changed from letter to article-Three Men Named Smith; CC-r	1	1	42	84	126	265	445	625
4A	28	1946	CC-r; new banner logo, slick-c	1	1	31	62	93	182	296	410
4B	28	1946	Same, but w/stiff-c	1	1	31	62	93	182	296	410
5	51	–	LDC-r	1	1	22	44	66	128	209	290
6	64	–	LDC-r	1	1	19	38	57	111	176	240
7	78	–	LDC-r	1	1	18	36	54	105	165	225
8	164	–	New-c&a; PC-r	2	2	15	30	45	90	140	190

9. Les Miserables

Ed	HRN	Date	Details	A	C	GD 2.0	VG 4.0	FN 6.0	VF 8.0	VF/NM 9.0	NM- 9.2
1A	(O)	3/43	Original; slick paper cover; 68 pgs.	1	1	95	190	285	603	1039	1475
1B	(O)	3/43	Original; rough, pulp type-c; 68 pgs.	1	1	113	226	339	718	1234	1750
2	14	–	Elliot Pub; CC-r	1	1	26	52	78	154	252	350
3	18	3/44	Nassau Bul. Pg. 64 changed from Gift Box ad to Bill of Rights article; CC-r	1	1	22	44	66	128	209	290
4	20	–	Richmond Courier ed.; CC-r	1	1	19	38	57	111	176	240
5	28	1946	Gilberton; pgs. 60-64 rearranged/ illos added; CC-r	1	1	14	28	42	81	118	155
6	51	–	LDC-r	1	1	9	18	27	47	61	75
7	71	–	LDC-r	1	1	6	12	18	29	36	42
8	87	–	C-price 15¢; LDC-r	1	1	6	12	18	27	33	38
9	161	–	New-c&a; PC-r	2	2	7	14	21	37	46	55
10	167	9/63	PC-r	2	2	2	4	6	11	16	20
11	167	12/65	PC-r	2	2	2	4	6	11	16	20
12	166	R/1968	New-c & price 25¢; PC-r	2	3	3	6	9	17	26	35

10. Robinson Crusoe (Used in **SOTI**, pg. 142)

Ed	HRN	Date	Details	A	C	GD 2.0	VG 4.0	FN 6.0	VF 8.0	VF/NM 9.0	NM- 9.2
1A	(O)	4/43	Original; Violet-c; 68 pgs; Zuckerberg c/a	1	1	86	172	258	546	936	1325
1B	(O)	4/43	Original; blue-grey-c, 68 pgs.	1	1	94	188	282	597	1024	1450

Classic Comics #13 © GIL

Classic Comics #15 © GIL

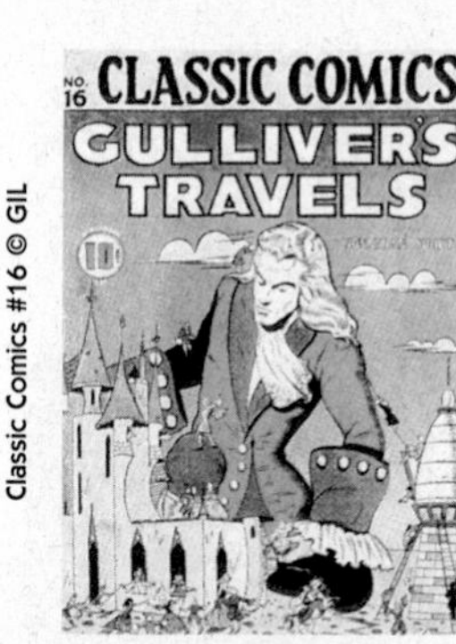

Classic Comics #16 © GIL

Ed	HRN	Date	Details	A	C	GD 2.0	VG 4.0	FN 6.0	VF 8.0	VF/NM 9.0	NM- 9.2
2A	14	–	Elliot Pub; violet-c; 68 pgs; CC-r	1	1	29	58	87	170	278	385
2B	14	–	Elliot Pub; blue-grey-c; CC-r	1	1	25	50	75	147	241	335
3	18	–	Nassau Bul. Pg. 64 changed from Gift Box ad to Bill of Rights article; CC-r	1	1	19	38	57	111	176	240
4	20	–	Queens Home News ed.; CC-r	1	1	16	32	48	94	147	200
5	28	1946	Gilberton; pg. 64 changes from Bill of Rights to WWII article-One Leg Shot Away; last CC-r	1	1	14	28	42	80	115	150
6	51	–	LDC-r	1	1	8	16	24	42	54	65
7	64	–	LDC-r	1	1	6	12	18	27	33	38
8	78	–	C-price 15¢; LDC-r	1	1	5	10	14	20	24	28
9	97	–	LDC-r	1	1	4	9	13	18	22	26
10	114	–	LDC-r	1	1	4	7	10	14	17	20
11	130	–	New-c; PC-r	1	2	5	10	15	25	31	36
12	140	–	New-a; PC-r	2	2	5	10	15	24	29	34
13	153	–	PC-r	2	2	2	4	6	8	11	14
14	164	–	PC-r	2	2	2	4	6	8	11	14
15	167	–	PC-r	2	2	2	4	6	8	11	14
16	167	7/64	PC-r	2	2	2	4	6	10	14	18
17	167	5/65	PC-r	2	2	2	4	6	10	14	18
18	167	6/66	PC-r	2	2	2	4	6	8	11	14
19	166	Fall/68	C-price 25¢; PC-r	2	2	2	4	6	8	11	14
20	166	R/68	(No Twin Circle ad)	2	2	2	4	6	9	13	16
21	169	Sm/70	Stiff-c; PC-r	2	2	2	4	6	9	13	16

11. Don Quixote

Ed	HRN	Date	Details	A	C	GD 2.0	VG 4.0	FN 6.0	VF 8.0	VF/NM 9.0	NM- 9.2
1	10	5/43	First (O) with HRN list; 68 pgs.	1	1	89	178	267	565	970	1375
2	18	–	Nassau Bulletin ed.; CC-r	1	1	23	46	69	136	223	310
3	21	–	Queens Home News ed.; CC-r	1	1	19	38	57	111	176	240
4	28	–	CC-r	1	1	14	28	42	81	118	155
5	110	–	New-PC; PC-r	1	2	7	14	21	35	43	50
6	156	–	Pgs. reduced 68 to 52; PC-r	1	2	4	7	10	14	17	20
7	165	–	PC-r	1	2	2	4	6	9	13	16
8	167	1/64	PC-r	1	2	2	4	6	9	13	16
9	167	11/65	PC-r	1	2	2	4	6	9	13	16
10	166	R/1968	New-c & price 25¢; PC-r	1	3	3	6	9	18	27	36

12. Rip Van Winkle and the Headless Horseman

Ed	HRN	Date	Details	A	C	GD 2.0	VG 4.0	FN 6.0	VF 8.0	VF/NM 9.0	NM- 9.2
1	11	6/43	Original; 68 pgs.	1	1	92	184	276	584	1005	1425
2	15	–	Long Isl. Ind. ed.; CC-r	1	1	24	48	72	142	234	325
3	20	–	Long Isl. Ind. ed.;	1	1	20	40	60	114	182	250
4	22	–	Queens Cty. Times ed.; CC-r	1	1	16	32	48	94	147	200
5	28	–	CC-r	1	1	14	28	42	80	115	150
6	60	–	1st LDC-r	1	1	8	16	24	40	50	60
7	62	–	LDC-r	1	1	5	10	15	23	28	32
8	71	–	LDC-r	1	1	4	9	13	18	22	26
9	89	–	C-price 15¢; LDC-r	1	1	4	8	12	17	21	24
10	118	–	LDC-r	1	1	4	7	10	14	17	20
11	132	–	New-c; PC-r	1	2	5	10	15	25	31	36
12	150	–	New-a; PC-r	2	2	5	10	15	24	29	34
13	158	–	PC-r	2	2	2	4	6	9	13	16
14	167	–	PC-r	2	2	2	4	6	9	13	16
15	167	12/63	PC-r	2	2	2	4	6	8	11	14
16	167	4/65	PC-r	2	2	2	4	6	8	11	14
17	167	4/66	PC-r	2	2	2	4	6	8	11	14
18	166	R/1968	New-c&price 25¢; PC-r; stiff-c	2	3	3	6	9	14	20	26
19	169	Sm/70	PC-r; stiff-c	2	3	2	4	6	10	14	18

13. Dr. Jekyll and Mr. Hyde (Used in **SOTI**, pg. 143)(1st horror comic?)

Ed	HRN	Date	Details	A	C	GD 2.0	VG 4.0	FN 6.0	VF 8.0	VF/NM 9.0	NM- 9.2
1	12	8/43	Original 60 pgs.	1	1	137	274	411	870	1498	2125
2	15	–	Long Isl. Ind. ed.; CC-r	1	1	36	72	108	211	343	475
3	20	–	Long Isl. Ind. ed.; CC-r	1	1	24	48	72	142	234	325
4	28	–	No c-price; CC-r	1	1	18	36	54	105	165	225
5	60	–	New-c; Pgs. reduced from 60 to 52; H.C. Kiefer-c; LDC-r	1	2	9	18	27	47	61	75
6	62	–	LDC-r	1	2	6	12	18	28	34	40
7	71	–	LDC-r	1	2	5	10	15	23	28	32
8	87	–	Date returns (erroneous); LDC-r	1	2	5	10	15	22	26	30
9	112	–	New-c&a; PC-r; Cameron-a	2	3	7	14	21	35	43	50
10	153	–	PC-r	2	3	2	4	6	9	13	16
11	161	–	PC-r	2	3	2	4	6	9	13	16
12	167	–	PC-r	2	3	2	4	6	8	11	14
13	167	8/64	PC-r	2	3	2	4	6	8	11	14
14	167	11/65	PC-r	2	3	2	4	6	8	11	14
15	166	R/68	C-price 25¢; PC-r	2	3	2	4	6	8	11	14
16	169	Wn/69	PC-r; stiff-c	2	3	2	4	6	8	11	14

14. Westward Ho!

Ed	HRN	Date	Details	A	C	GD 2.0	VG 4.0	FN 6.0	VF 8.0	VF/NM 9.0	NM- 9.2
1	13	9/43	Original; last outside bc coming-next ad; 60 pgs.	1	1	194	388	582	1242	2121	3000
2	15	–	Long Isl. Ind. ed.; CC-r	1	1	58	116	174	371	636	900
3	21	–	Queens Home News; Pg. 56 changed from coming-next ad to Three Men Named Smith; CC-r	1	1	46	92	138	290	488	685
4	28	1946	Gilberton; Pg. 56 changed again to WWII article-Speaking for America; last CC-r	1	1	39	78	117	242	401	560
5	53	–	Pgs. reduced from 60 to 52; LDC-r	1	1	36	72	108	216	351	485

15. Uncle Tom's Cabin (Used in **SOTI**, pgs. 102, 103)

Ed	HRN	Date	Details	A	C	GD 2.0	VG 4.0	FN 6.0	VF 8.0	VF/NM 9.0	NM- 9.2
1	14	11/43	Original; Outside-bc ad: 2 Gift Boxes; 60 pgs.; color var. on-c; green trunk,root on left & brown trunk, root on left	1	1	82	164	246	528	902	1275
2	15	–	Long Isl. Ind. listed- bottom inside-fc; also Gilberton listed bottom-pg. 1; CC-r; green root vs. brown root var. occurs again	1	1	26	52	78	154	252	350
3	21	–	Nassau Bulletin ed.; CC-r	1	1	20	40	60	117	189	260
4	28	–	No c-price; CC-r	1	1	14	28	42	82	121	160
5	53	–	Pgs. reduced 60 to 52; LDC-r	1	1	8	16	24	42	54	65
6	71	–	LDC-r	1	1	6	12	18	27	33	38
7	89	–	C-price 15¢; LDC-r	1	1	5	10	15	24	30	35
8	117	–	New-c/lettering changes; PC-r	1	2	5	10	15	25	31	36
9	128	–	'Picture Progress' promo; PC-r	1	2	2	4	6	10	14	18
10	137	–	PC-r	1	2	2	4	6	9	13	16
11	146	–	PC-r	1	2	2	4	6	9	13	16
12	154	–	PC-r	1	2	2	4	6	9	13	16
13	161	–	PC-r	1	2	2	4	6	8	11	14
14	167	–	PC-r	1	2	2	4	6	8	11	14
15	167	6/64	PC-r	1	2	2	4	6	8	11	14
16	167	5/65	PC-r	1	2	2	4	6	8	11	14

Classic Comics #17 © GIL

Classic Comics #20 © GIL

Classic Comics #21 © GIL

Ed	HRN	Date	Details	A	C	GD 2.0	VG 4.0	FN 6.0	VF 8.0	VF/NM 9.0	NM- 9.2
17	166	5/67	PC-r	1	2	2	4	6	8	11	14
18	166	Wn/69	New-stiff-c; PC-r	1	3	3	6	9	15	22	28
19	169	Sm/70	PC-r; stiff-c	1	3	2	4	6	10	14	18

16. Gulliver's Travels

Ed	HRN	Date	Details	A	C	GD 2.0	VG 4.0	FN 6.0	VF 8.0	VF/NM 9.0	NM- 9.2
1	15	12/43	Original-Lilian Chestney c/a; 60 pgs.	1	1	77	154	231	493	847	1200
2	18/20	–	Price deleted; Queens Home News ed; CC-r	1	1	22	44	66	128	209	290
3	22	–	Queens Cty. Times ed.; CC-r	1	1	18	36	54	105	165	225
4	28	–	CC-r	1	1	14	28	42	80	115	150
5	60	–	Pgs. reduced to 48; LDC-r	1	1	6	12	18	31	38	45
6	62	–	LDC-r	1	1	5	10	15	23	28	32
7	78	–	C-price 15¢; LDC-r	1	1	5	10	14	20	24	28
8	89	–	LDC-r	1	1	4	8	12	17	21	24
9	155	–	New-c; PC-r	1	2	5	10	15	25	31	36
10	165	–	PC-r	1	2	2	4	6	8	11	14
11	167	5/64	PC-r	1	2	2	4	6	8	11	14
12	167	11/65	PC-r	1	2	2	4	6	8	11	14
13	166	R/1968	C-price 25¢; PC-r	1	2	2	4	6	8	11	14
14	169	Wn/69	PC-r; stiff-c	1	2	2	4	6	8	11	14

17. The Deerslayer

Ed	HRN	Date	Details	A	C	GD 2.0	VG 4.0	FN 6.0	VF 8.0	VF/NM 9.0	NM- 9.2
1	16	1/44	Original; Outside-bc ad: 3 Gift Boxes; 60 pgs.	1	1	66	132	198	419	872	1025
2A	18	–	Queens Cty Times (inside-fc); CC-r	1	1	23	46	69	136	223	310
2B	18	–	Gilberton (bottom-pg. 1); CC-r; Scarce	1	1	33	66	99	194	317	440
3	22	–	Queens Cty. Times ed.; CC-r	1	1	19	38	57	109	172	235
4	28	–	CC-r	1	1	14	28	42	81	118	155
5	60	–	Pgs.reduced to 52; LDC-r	1	1	7	14	21	37	46	55
6	64	–	LDC-r	1	1	5	10	15	22	26	30
7	85	–	C-price 15¢; LDC-r	1	1	4	8	12	17	21	24
8	118	–	LDC-r	1	1	4	7	10	14	17	20
9	132	–	LDC-r	1	1	4	7	10	14	17	20
10	167	11/66	Last LDC-r	1	1	2	4	6	11	16	20
11	166	R/1968	New-c & price 25¢; PC-r	1	2	3	6	9	17	26	35
12	169	Spr/71	Stiff-c; letters from parents & educa-tors; PC-r	1	2	2	4	6	10	14	18

18. The Hunchback of Notre Dame

Ed	HRN	Date	Details	A	C	GD 2.0	VG 4.0	FN 6.0	VF 8.0	VF/NM 9.0	NM- 9.2
1A	17	3/44	Orig.; Gilberton ed; 60 pgs.	1	1	90	180	270	576	988	1400
1B	17	3/44	Orig.; Island Pub. Ed.; 60 pgs.	1	1	81	162	243	518	884	1250
2	18/20	–	Queens Home News ed.; CC-r	1	1	25	50	75	150	245	340
3	22	–	Queens Cty. Times ed.; CC-r	1	1	20	40	60	114	182	250
4	28	–	CC-r	1	1	18	36	54	105	165	225
5	60	–	New-c; 8pgs. de-leted; Kiefer-c; LDC-r	1	2	9	18	27	47	61	75
6	62	–	LDC-r	1	2	5	10	15	22	26	30
7	78	–	C-price 15¢; LDC-r	1	2	5	10	14	20	24	28
8A	89	–	H.C.Kiefer on bot-tom right-fc; LDC-r	1	2	4	9	13	18	22	26
8B	89	–	Name omitted; LDC-r	1	2	5	10	15	24	30	35
9	118	–	LDC-r	1	2	4	8	12	17	21	24
10	140	–	New-c; PC-r	1	3	7	14	21	35	43	50
11	146	–	PC-r	1	3	4	9	13	18	22	26
12	158	–	New-c&a; PC-r; Evans/Crandall-a	2	4	5	10	15	25	31	36
13	165	–	PC-r	2	4	2	4	6	9	13	16
14	167	9/63	PC-r	2	4	2	4	6	9	13	16
15	167	10/64	PC-r	2	4	2	4	6	9	13	16
16	167	4/66	PC-r	2	4	2	4	6	8	11	14
17	166	R/1968	New price 25¢; PC-r	2	4	2	4	6	8	11	14
18	169	Sp/70	Stiff-c; PC-r	2	4	2	4	6	8	11	14

19. Huckleberry Finn

Ed	HRN	Date	Details	A	C	GD 2.0	VG 4.0	FN 6.0	VF 8.0	VF/NM 9.0	NM- 9.2
1A	18	4/44	Orig.; Gilberton ed.; 60 pgs.	1	1	54	108	162	343	574	825
1B	18	4/44	Orig.; Island Pub.; 60 pgs.	1	1	57	114	171	362	619	875
2	18	–	Nassau Bulletin ed.; fc-price 15¢-Canada; no coming-next ad; CC-r	1	1	23	46	69	136	223	310
3	22	–	Queens City Times ed.; CC-r	1	1	19	38	57	111	176	240
4	28	–	CC-r	1	1	14	28	42	80	115	150
5	60	–	Pgs. reduced to 48; LDC-r	1	1	6	12	18	31	38	45
6	62	–	LDC-r	1	1	5	10	15	23	28	32
7	78	–	LDC-r	1	1	4	9	13	18	22	26
8	89	–	LDC-r	1	1	4	8	12	17	21	24
9	117	–	LDC-r	1	1	4	7	10	14	17	20
10	131	–	New-c&a; PC-r	2	2	5	10	15	24	30	35
11	140	–	PC-r	2	2	2	4	6	9	13	16
12	150	–	PC-r	2	2	2	4	6	9	13	16
13	158	–	PC-r	2	2	2	4	6	9	13	16
14	165	–	PC-r (scarce)	2	2	3	6	9	14	19	24
15	167	–	PC-r	2	2	2	4	6	8	11	14
16	167	6/64	PC-r	2	2	2	4	6	8	11	14
17	167	6/65	PC-r	2	2	2	4	6	8	11	14
18	167	10/65	PC-r	2	2	2	4	6	8	11	14
19	166	9/67	PC-r	2	2	2	4	6	8	11	14
20	166	Win/69	C-price 25¢; PC-r; stiff-c	2	2	2	4	6	8	11	14
21	169	Sm/70	PC-r; stiff-c	2	2	2	4	6	8	11	14

20. The Corsican Brothers

Ed	HRN	Date	Details	A	C	GD 2.0	VG 4.0	FN 6.0	VF 8.0	VF/NM 9.0	NM- 9.2
1A	20	6/44	Orig.; Gilberton ed.; bc-ad: 4 Gift Boxes; 60 pgs.	1	1	48	96	114	302	514	725
1B	20	6/44	Orig.; Courier ed.; 60 pgs.	1	1	41	82	123	256	428	600
1C	20	6/44	Orig.; Long Island Ind. ed.; 60 pgs.	1	1	41	82	123	256	428	600
2	22	–	Queens Cty. Times ed.; white logo banner; CC-r	1	1	20	40	60	114	182	250
3	28	–	CC-r	1	1	19	38	57	109	172	235
4	60	–	CI logo; no price; 48 pgs.; LDC-r	1	1	15	30	45	90	140	190
5A	62	–	LDC-r; Classics Ill. logo at top of pgs.	1	1	15	30	45	83	124	165
5B	62	–	w/o logo at top of pg. (scarcer)	1	1	15	30	45	86	133	180
6	78	–	C-price 15¢; LDC-r	1	1	14	28	42	81	118	155
7	97	–	LDC-r	1	1	14	28	42	78	112	145

21. 3 Famous Mysteries ("The Sign of the 4", "The Murders in the Rue Morgue", "The Flayed Hand")

Ed	HRN	Date	Details	A	C	GD 2.0	VG 4.0	FN 6.0	VF 8.0	VF/NM 9.0	NM- 9.2
1A	21	7/44	Orig.; Gilberton ed.; 60 pgs.	1	1	98	196	294	630	1078	1525
1B	21	7/44	Orig. Island Pub. Co.; 60 pgs.	1	1	102	204	306	650	1113	1575
1C	21	7/44	Original; Courier Ed.; 60 pgs.	1	1	89	178	267	565	970	1375
2	22	–	Nassau Bulletin ed.; CC-r	1	1	40	80	120	244	402	560
3	30	–	CC-r	1	1	28	56	84	165	270	375
4	62	–	LDC-r; 8 pgs. de-leted; LDC-r	1	1	22	44	66	128	209	290

Classic Comics #24 © GIL

Classic Comics #26 © GIL

Classic Comics #28 © GIL

Ed	HRN	Date	Details	A	C	GD 2.0	VG 4.0	FN 6.0	VF 8.0	VF/NM 9.0	NM- 9.2
5	70	–	LDC-r	1	1	20	40	60	117	189	260
6	85	–	C-price 15¢; LDC-r	1	1	18	36	54	107	169	230
7	114	–	New-c; PC-r	1	2	18	36	54	107	169	230

22. The Pathfinder

Ed	HRN	Date	Details	A	C	GD	VG	FN	VF	VF/NM	NM-
1A	22	10/44	Orig.; No printer listed; ownership statement inside fc lists Gilberton & date; 60 pgs.	1	1	47	94	141	296	498	700
1B	22	10/44	Orig.; Island Pub. ed.; 60 pgs.	1	1	41	82	123	256	428	600
1C	22	10/44	Orig.; Queens Cty Times ed. 60 pgs.	1	1	41	82	123	256	428	600
2	30	–	C-price removed; CC-r	1	1	15	30	45	85	130	175
3	60	–	Pgs. reduced to 52; LDC-r	1	1	6	12	18	27	33	38
4	70	–	LDC-r	1	1	5	10	15	22	26	30
5	85	–	C-price 15¢; LDC-r	1	1	4	9	13	18	22	26
6	118	–	LDC-r	1	1	4	8	12	17	21	24
7	132	–	LDC-r	1	1	4	7	10	14	17	20
8	146	–	LDC-r	1	1	4	7	10	14	17	20
9	167	11/63	New-c; PC-r	1	2	4	8	12	23	37	50
10	167	12/65	PC-r	1	2	2	4	6	11	16	20
11	166	8/67	PC-r	1	2	2	4	6	11	16	20

23. Oliver Twist (1st Classic produced by the Iger Shop)

Ed	HRN	Date	Details	A	C	GD	VG	FN	VF	VF/NM	NM-
1	23	7/45	Original; 60 pgs.	1	1	47	94	141	296	498	700
2A	30	–	Printers Union logo on bottom left-fc same as 23(Orig.) (very rare); CC-r	1	1	30	60	90	177	289	400
2B	30	–	Union logo omitted; CC-r	1	1	15	30	45	84	127	170
3	60	–	Pgs. reduced to 48; LDC-r	1	1	6	12	18	29	36	42
4	62	–	LDC-r	1	1	5	10	15	23	28	32
5	71	–	LDC-r	1	1	5	10	14	20	24	28
6	85	–	C-price 15¢; LDC-r	1	1	4	9	13	18	22	26
7	94	–	LDC-r	1	1	4	7	10	14	17	20
8	118	–	LDC-r	1	1	4	7	10	14	17	20
9	136	–	New-PC, old-a; PC-r	1	2	5	10	15	24	30	35
10	150	–	Old-a; PC-r	1	2	4	7	10	14	17	20
11	164	–	Old-a; PC-r	1	2	4	8	11	16	19	22
12	164	–	New-a; PC-r; Evans/Crandall-a	2	2	4	8	12	23	37	50
13	167	–	PC-r	2	2	2	4	6	11	16	20
14	167	8/64	PC-r	2	2	2	4	6	8	11	14
15	167	12/65	PC-r	2	2	2	4	6	8	11	14
16	166	R/1968	New 25¢; PC-r	2	2	2	4	6	8	11	14
17	169	Win/69	Stiff-c; PC-r	2	2	2	4	6	8	11	14

24. A Connecticut Yankee in King Arthur's Court

Ed	HRN	Date	Details	A	C	GD	VG	FN	VF	VF/NM	NM-
1	–	9/45	Original	1	1	41	82	123	256	428	600
2	30	–	No price circle; CC-r	1	1	15	30	45	84	127	170
3	60	–	8 pgs. deleted; LDC-r	1	1	6	12	18	27	33	38
4	62	–	LDC-r	1	1	5	10	15	23	28	32
5	71	–	LDC-r	1	1	5	10	15	22	26	30
6	87	–	C-price 15¢; LDC-r	1	1	4	9	13	18	22	26
7	121	–	LDC-r	1	1	4	8	12	17	21	24
8	140	–	New-c&a; PC-r	2	2	5	10	15	25	31	36
9	153	–	PC-r	2	2	2	4	6	9	13	16
10	164	–	PC-r	2	2	2	4	6	8	11	14
11	167	–	PC-r	2	2	2	4	6	8	11	14
12	167	7/64	PC-r	2	2	2	4	6	8	11	14
13	167	6/66	PC-r	2	2	2	4	6	8	11	14
14	166	R/1968	C-price 25¢; PC-r	2	2	2	4	6	8	11	14
15	169	Spr/71	PC-r; stiff-c	2	2	2	4	6	8	11	14

25. Two Years Before the Mast

Ed	HRN	Date	Details	A	C	GD	VG	FN	VF	VF/NM	NM-
1	–	10/45	Original; Webb/Heames-a&c	1	1	41	82	123	256	428	600
2	30	–	Price circle blank; CC-r	1	1	15	30	45	84	127	170
3	60	–	8 pgs. deleted; LDC-r	1	1	6	12	18	27	33	38
4	62	–	LDC-r	1	1	5	10	15	23	28	32
5	71	–	LDC-r	1	1	4	9	13	18	22	26
6	85	–	C-price 15¢; LDC-r	1	1	4	8	12	17	21	24
7	114	–	LDC-r	1	1	4	7	10	14	17	20
8	156	–	3 pgs. replaced by fillers; new-c; PC-r	1	2	5	10	15	25	31	36
9	167	12/63	PC-r	1	2	2	4	6	8	11	14
10	167	12/65	PC-r	1	2	2	4	6	8	11	14
11	166	9/67	PC-r	1	2	2	4	6	8	11	14
12	169	Win/69	C-price 25¢; stiff-c PC-r	1	2	2	4	6	8	11	14

26. Frankenstein (2nd horror comic?)

Ed	HRN	Date	Details	A	C	GD	VG	FN	VF	VF/NM	NM-
1	26	12/45	Orig.; Webb/Brewster a&c; 52 pgs.	1	1	111	222	333	713	1219	1725
2A	30	–	Price circle blank; no indicia; CC-r	1	1	32	64	96	188	307	425
2B	30	–	With indicia; scarce; CC-r	1	1	36	72	108	216	351	485
3	60	–	LDC-r	1	1	17	34	51	98	154	210
4	62	–	LDC-r	1	1	15	30	45	88	137	185
5	71	–	LDC-r	1	1	8	16	24	42	54	65
6A	82	–	C-price 15¢; soft-c LDC-r	1	1	7	14	21	37	46	55
6B	82	–	Stiff-c; LDC-r	1	1	8	16	24	42	54	65
7	117	–	LDC-r	1	1	5	10	15	22	26	30
8	146	–	New Saunders-c; PC-r	1	2	6	12	18	31	38	45
9	152	–	Scarce; PC-r	1	2	8	16	24	42	54	65
10	153	–	PC-r	1	2	2	4	6	10	14	18
11	160	–	PC-r	1	2	2	4	6	10	14	18
12	165	–	PC-r	1	2	2	4	6	9	13	16
13	167	–	PC-r	1	2	2	4	6	9	13	16
14	167	6/64	PC-r	1	2	2	4	6	9	13	16
15	167	6/65	PC-r	1	2	2	4	6	9	13	16
16	167	10/65	PC-r	1	2	2	4	6	9	13	16
17	166	9/67	PC-r	1	2	2	4	6	9	13	16
18	169	Fall/69	C-price 25¢; stiff-c PC-r	1	2	2	4	6	9	13	16
19	169	Spr/71	PC-r; stiff-c	1	2	2	4	6	9	13	16

27. The Adventures of Marco Polo

Ed	HRN	Date	Details	A	C	GD	VG	FN	VF	VF/NM	NM-
1	–	4/46	Original	1	1	41	82	123	256	428	600
2	30	–	Last 'Comics' reprint; CC-r	1	1	15	30	45	84	127	170
3	70	–	8 pgs. deleted; no c-price; LDC-r	1	1	5	10	15	24	30	35
4	87	–	C-price 15¢; LDC-r	1	1	4	9	13	18	22	26
5	117	–	LDC-r	1	1	4	7	10	14	17	20
6	154	–	New-c; PC-r	1	2	5	10	15	24	30	35
7	165	–	PC-r	1	2	2	4	6	8	11	14
8	167	4/64	PC-r	1	2	2	4	6	8	11	14
9	167	6/66	PC-r	1	2	2	4	6	8	11	14
10	169	Spr/69	New price 25¢; stiff-c; PC-r	1	2	2	4	6	8	11	14

28. Michael Strogoff

Ed	HRN	Date	Details	A	C	GD	VG	FN	VF	VF/NM	NM-
1	–	6/46	Original	1	1	41	82	123	256	428	600
2	51	–	8 pgs. cut; LDC-r	1	1	15	30	45	84	127	170
3	115	–	New-c; PC-r	1	2	6	12	18	31	38	45
4	155	–	PC-r	1	2	4	7	10	14	17	20
5	167	11/63	PC-r	1	2	2	4	6	9	13	16
6	167	7/66	PC-r	1	2	2	4	6	9	13	16
7	169	Sm/69	C-price 25¢; stiff-c PC-r	1	3	3	6	9	15	21	26

29. The Prince and the Pauper

Classic Comics #30 © GIL

Classic Comics #32 © GIL

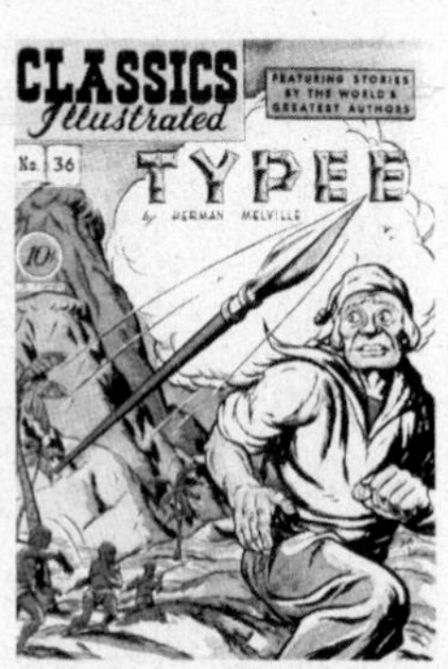

Classics Illustrated #36 © GIL

Ed	HRN	Date	Details	A	C	GD 2.0	VG 4.0	FN 6.0	VF 8.0	VF/NM 9.0	NM- 9.2
1	–	7/46	Orig.; "Horror"-c	1	1	60	120	180	381	653	925
2	60	–	8 pgs. cut; new-c by Kiefer; LDC-r	1	2	9	18	27	52	69	85
3	62	–	LDC-r	1	2	5	10	15	24	30	35
4	71	–	LDC-r	1	2	4	9	13	18	22	26
5	93	–	LDC-r	1	2	4	8	12	17	21	24
6	114	–	LDC-r	1	2	4	7	10	14	17	20
7	128	–	New-c; PC-r	1	3	5	10	15	24	30	35
8	138	–	PC-r	1	3	2	4	6	9	13	16
9	150	–	PC-r	1	3	2	4	6	9	13	16
10	164	–	PC-r	1	3	2	4	6	8	11	14
11	167	–	PC-r	1	3	2	4	6	8	11	14
12	167	7/64	PC-r	1	3	2	4	6	8	11	14
13	167	11/65	PC-r	1	3	2	4	6	8	11	14
14	166	R/68	C-price 25¢; PC-r	1	3	2	4	6	8	11	14
15	169	Sm/70	PC-r; stiff-c	1	3	2	4	6	8	11	14

30. The Moonstone

Ed	HRN	Date	Details	A	C	GD 2.0	VG 4.0	FN 6.0	VF 8.0	VF/NM 9.0	NM- 9.2
1	–	9/46	Original; Rico-c/a	1	1	41	82	123	256	428	600
2	60	–	LDC-r; 8pgs. cut	1	1	9	18	27	50	65	80
3	70	–	LDC-r	1	1	8	16	24	42	54	65
4	155	–	New L.B. Cole-c; PC-r	1	2	4	8	12	28	44	60
5	165	–	PC-r; L.B. Cole-c	1	2	3	6	9	16	23	30
6	167	1/64	PC-r; L.B. Cole-c	1	2	2	4	6	11	16	20
7	167	9/65	PC-r; L.B. Cole-c	1	2	2	4	6	10	14	18
8	166	R/1968	C-price 25¢; PC-r	1	2	2	4	6	9	13	16

31. The Black Arrow

Ed	HRN	Date	Details	A	C	GD 2.0	VG 4.0	FN 6.0	VF 8.0	VF/NM 9.0	NM- 9.2
1	30	10/46	Original	1	1	39	78	117	235	385	535
2	51	–	CI logo; LDC-r 8pgs. deleted	1	1	6	12	18	33	41	48
3	64	–	LDC-r	1	1	4	9	13	18	22	26
4	87	–	C-price 15¢; LDC-r	1	1	4	8	12	17	21	24
5	108	–	LDC-r	1	1	4	7	10	14	17	20
6	125	–	LDC-r	1	1	4	7	10	14	17	20
7	131	–	New-c; PC-r	1	2	5	10	15	24	30	35
8	140	–	PC-r	1	2	2	4	6	9	13	16
9	148	–	PC-r	1	2	2	4	6	9	13	16
10	161	–	PC-r	1	2	2	4	6	8	11	14
11	167	–	PC-r	1	2	2	4	6	8	11	14
12	167	7/64	PC-r	1	2	2	4	6	8	11	14
13	167	11/65	PC-r	1	2	2	4	6	8	11	14
14	166	R/1968	C-price 25¢; PC-r	1	2	2	4	6	8	11	14

32. Lorna Doone

Ed	HRN	Date	Details	A	C	GD 2.0	VG 4.0	FN 6.0	VF 8.0	VF/NM 9.0	NM- 9.2
1	–	12/46	Original; Matt Baker c&a	1	1	41	82	123	250	418	585
2	53/64	–	8 pgs. deleted; LDC-r	1	1	9	18	27	47	61	75
3	85	1951	C-price 15¢; LDC-r; Baker c&a	1	1	7	14	21	37	46	55
4	118	–	LDC-r	1	1	4	9	13	18	22	26
5	138	–	New-c; old-c becomes new title pg.; PC-r	1	2	6	12	18	28	34	40
6	150	–	PC-r	1	2	2	4	6	8	11	14
7	165	–	PC-r	1	2	2	4	6	8	11	14
8	167	1/64	PC-r	1	2	2	4	6	9	13	16
9	167	11/65	PC-r	1	2	2	4	6	9	13	16
10	166	R/1968	New-c; PC-r	1	3	3	6	9	16	24	32

33. The Adventures of Sherlock Holmes

Ed	HRN	Date	Details	A	C	GD 2.0	VG 4.0	FN 6.0	VF 8.0	VF/NM 9.0	NM- 9.2
1	33	1/47	Original; Kiefer-c; contains Study in Scarlet & Hound of the Baskervilles; 68 pgs.	1	1	129	258	387	826	1413	2000
2	53	–	"A Study in Scarlet" (17 pgs.) deleted; LDC-r	1	1	47	94	141	296	498	700
3	71	–	LDC-r	1	1	38	76	114	228	369	510
4A	89	–	C-price 15¢; LDC-r	1	1	30	60	90	117	289	400
4B	89	–	Kiefer's name omitted from-c	1	1	31	62	93	186	303	420

34. Mysterious Island (Last "Classic Comic")

Ed	HRN	Date	Details	A	C	GD 2.0	VG 4.0	FN 6.0	VF 8.0	VF/NM 9.0	NM- 9.2
1	35	2/47	Original; Webb/Heames-c/a	1	1	41	82	123	250	418	585
2	60	–	8 pgs. deleted; LDC-r	1	1	7	14	21	37	46	55
3	62	–	LDC-r	1	1	5	10	15	23	28	32
4	71	–	LDC-r	1	1	6	12	18	31	38	45
5	78	–	C-price 15¢ in circle; LDC-r	1	1	5	10	14	20	24	28
6	92	–	LDC-r	1	1	4	9	13	18	22	26
7	117	–	LDC-r	1	1	4	7	10	14	17	20
8	140	–	New-c; PC-r	1	2	5	10	15	24	30	35
9	156	–	PC-r	1	2	2	4	6	9	13	16
10	167	10/63	PC-r	1	2	2	4	6	8	11	14
11	167	5/64	PC-r	1	2	2	4	6	8	11	14
12	167	6/66	PC-r	1	2	2	4	6	8	11	14
13	166	R/1968	C-price 25¢; PC-r	1	2	2	4	6	8	11	14

35. Last Days of Pompeii (First "Classics Illustrated")

Ed	HRN	Date	Details	A	C	GD 2.0	VG 4.0	FN 6.0	VF 8.0	VF/NM 9.0	NM- 9.2
1	35	3/47	Original; LDC; Kiefer-c/a	1	1	41	82	123	250	418	585
2	161	–	New c&a; 15¢; PC-r; Kirby/Ayers-a	2	2	5	10	15	32	51	70
3	167	1/64	PC-r	2	2	3	6	9	16	22	28
4	167	7/66	PC-r	2	2	3	6	9	16	22	28
5	169	Spr/70	New price 25¢; stiff-c; PC-r	2	2	3	6	9	16	22	28

36. Typee

Ed	HRN	Date	Details	A	C	GD 2.0	VG 4.0	FN 6.0	VF 8.0	VF/NM 9.0	NM- 9.2
1	36	4/47	Original	1	1	29	58	87	170	278	385
2	64	–	No c-price; 8 pg. ed.; LDC-r	1	1	7	14	21	37	46	55
3	155	–	New-c; PC-r	1	2	5	10	15	24	30	35
4	167	9/63	PC-r	1	2	2	4	6	9	13	16
5	167	7/65	PC-r	1	2	2	4	6	9	13	16
6	169	Sm/69	C-price 25¢; stiff-c PC-r	1	2	2	4	6	9	13	16

37. The Pioneers

Ed	HRN	Date	Details	A	C	GD 2.0	VG 4.0	FN 6.0	VF 8.0	VF/NM 9.0	NM- 9.2
1	37	5/47	Original; Palais-c/a	1	1	27	54	81	158	259	360
2A	62	–	8 pgs. cut; LDC-r; price circle blank	1	1	6	12	18	28	34	40
2B	62	–	10¢; LDC-r;	1	1	29	58	87	170	278	385
3	70	–	LDC-r	1	1	4	8	12	17	21	24
4	92	–	15¢; LDC-r	1	1	4	8	11	16	19	22
5	118	–	LDC-r	1	1	4	7	10	14	17	20
6	131	–	LDC-r	1	1	4	7	10	14	17	20
7	132	–	LDC-r	1	1	4	7	10	14	17	20
8	153	–	LDC-r	1	1	4	7	10	14	17	20
9	167	5/64	LDC-r	1	1	2	4	6	9	13	16
10	167	6/66	LDC-r	1	1	2	4	6	9	13	16
11	166	R/1968	New-c; 25¢; PC-r	1	2	3	6	9	18	27	36

38. Adventures of Cellini

Ed	HRN	Date	Details	A	C	GD 2.0	VG 4.0	FN 6.0	VF 8.0	VF/NM 9.0	NM- 9.2
1	–	6/47	Original; Froehlich c/a	1	1	32	64	96	192	314	435
2	164	–	New-c&a; PC-r	2	2	3	6	9	18	27	36
3	167	12/63	PC-r	2	2	2	4	6	10	14	18
4	167	7/66	PC-r	2	2	2	4	6	10	14	18
5	169	Spr/70	Stiff-c; new price 25¢; PC-r	2	2	2	4	6	11	16	20

39. Jane Eyre

Ed	HRN	Date	Details	A	C	GD 2.0	VG 4.0	FN 6.0	VF 8.0	VF/NM 9.0	NM- 9.2
1	–	7/47	Original	1	1	31	62	93	186	303	420
2	60	–	No c-price; 8 pgs. cut; LDC-r	1	1	6	12	18	31	38	45
3	62	–	LDC-r	1	1	5	10	15	24	30	35
4	71	–	LDC-r; c-price 10¢	1	1	5	10	15	22	26	30

Classics Illustrated #42 © GIL

Classics Illustrated #44 © GIL

Classics Illustrated #48 © GIL

Ed	HRN	Date	Details	A	C	GD 2.0	VG 4.0	FN 6.0	VF 8.0	VF/NM 9.0	NM- 9.2
5	92	–	C-price 15¢; LDC-r	1	1	4	9	13	18	22	26
6	118	–	LDC-r	1	1	4	8	12	17	21	24
7	142	–	New-c; old-a; PC-r	1	2	6	12	18	28	34	40
8	154	–	Old-a; PC-r	1	2	4	8	12	17	21	24
9	165	–	New-a; PC-r	2	2	3	6	9	17	26	35
10	167	12/63	PC-r	2	2	3	6	9	14	19	24
11	167	4/65	PC-r	2	2	2	4	6	13	18	22
12	167	8/66	PC-r	2	2	2	4	6	13	18	22
13	166	R/1968	New-c; PC-r	2	3	5	10	15	31	53	75

40. Mysteries ("The Pit and the Pendulum", "The Advs. of Hans Pfall" & "The Fall of the House of Usher")

Ed	HRN	Date	Details	A	C	GD 2.0	VG 4.0	FN 6.0	VF 8.0	VF/NM 9.0	NM- 9.2
1	40	8/47	Original; Kiefer-c/a, Froehlich, Griffiths-a	1	1	58	116	174	371	636	900
2	62	–	LDC-r; 8pgs. cut	1	1	24	48	72	142	234	325
3	75	–	LDC-r	1	1	19	38	57	111	176	240
4	92	–	C-price 15¢; LDC-r	1	1	15	30	45	94	147	200

41. Twenty Years After

Ed	HRN	Date	Details	A	C	GD 2.0	VG 4.0	FN 6.0	VF 8.0	VF/NM 9.0	NM- 9.2
1	–	9/47	Original; 'horror'-c	1	1	39	78	117	235	385	535
2	62	–	New-c; no c-price 8 pgs. cut; LDC-r; Kiefer-c	1	2	7	14	21	37	46	55
3	78	–	C-price 15¢; LDC-r	1	2	5	10	15	23	28	32
4	156	–	New-c; PC-r	1	3	5	10	15	24	30	35
5	167	12/63	PC-r	1	3	2	4	6	8	11	14
6	167	11/66	PC-r	1	3	2	4	6	8	11	14
7	169	Spr/70	New price 25¢; stiff-c; PC-r	1	3	2	4	6	8	11	14

42. Swiss Family Robinson

Ed	HRN	Date	Details	A	C	GD 2.0	VG 4.0	FN 6.0	VF 8.0	VF/NM 9.0	NM- 9.2
1	42	10/47	Orig.; Kiefer-c&a;	1	1	24	48	72	140	230	320
2A	62	–	8 pgs. cut; outside bc: Gift Box ad; LDC-r	1	1	6	12	18	31	38	45
2B	62	–	8 pgs. cut; outside-bc: Reorder list; scarce; LDC-r	1	1	10	20	30	58	79	100
3	75	–	LDC-r	1	1	5	10	14	20	24	28
4	93	–	LDC-r	1	1	5	10	14	20	24	28
5	117	–	LDC-r	1	1	3	6	9	14	19	24
6	131	–	New-c; old-a; PC-r	1	2	3	6	9	15	21	26
7	137	–	Old-a; PC-r	1	2	2	4	6	10	14	18
8	141	–	Old-a; PC-r	1	2	2	4	6	10	14	18
9	152	–	New-a; PC-r	2	2	3	6	9	16	23	30
10	158	–	PC-r	2	2	2	4	6	8	11	14
11	165	–	PC-r	2	2	3	6	9	16	24	32
12	167	12/63	PC-r	2	2	2	4	6	8	11	14
13	167	4/65	PC-r	2	2	2	4	6	8	11	14
14	167	5/66	PC-r	2	2	2	4	6	8	11	14
15	166	11/67	PC-r	2	2	2	4	6	8	11	14
16	169	Spr/69	PC-r; stiff-c	2	2	2	4	6	8	11	14

43. Great Expectations (Used in **SOTI**, pg. 311)

Ed	HRN	Date	Details	A	C	GD 2.0	VG 4.0	FN 6.0	VF 8.0	VF/NM 9.0	NM- 9.2
1	43	11/47	Original; Kiefer-a/c	1	1	90	180	270	576	988	1400
2	62	–	No c-price; 8 pgs. cut; LDC-r	1	1	57	114	171	362	624	885

44. Mysteries of Paris (Used in **SOTI**, pg. 323)

Ed	HRN	Date	Details	A	C	GD 2.0	VG 4.0	FN 6.0	VF 8.0	VF/NM 9.0	NM- 9.2
1A	44	12/47	Original; 56 pgs.; Kiefer-c/a	1	1	65	130	195	416	708	1000
1B	44	12/47	Orig.; printed on white/heavier paper; (rare)	1	1	76	152	228	486	831	1175
2A	62	–	8 pgs. cut; outside-bc: Gift Box ad; LDC-r	1	1	30	60	90	177	289	400
2B	62	–	8 pgs. cut; outside-bc: reorder list; LDC-r	1	1	30	60	90	177	289	400
3	78	–	C-price 15¢; LDC-r	1	1	25	50	75	147	241	335

45. Tom Brown's School Days

Ed	HRN	Date	Details	A	C	GD 2.0	VG 4.0	FN 6.0	VF 8.0	VF/NM 9.0	NM- 9.2
1	44	1/48	Original; 1st 48pg. issue	1	1	20	40	60	114	182	250
2	64	–	No c-price; LDC-r	1	1	7	14	21	35	43	50
3	161	–	New-c&a; PC-r	2	2	3	6	9	16	24	32
4	167	2/64	PC-r	2	2	2	4	6	9	13	16
5	167	8/66	PC-r	2	2	2	4	6	9	13	16
6	166	R/1968	C-price 25¢; PC-r	2	2	2	4	6	9	13	16

46. Kidnapped

Ed	HRN	Date	Details	A	C	GD 2.0	VG 4.0	FN 6.0	VF 8.0	VF/NM 9.0	NM- 9.2
1	47	4/48	Original; Webb-c/a	1	1	20	40	60	114	182	250
2A	62	–	Price circle blank; LDC-r	1	1	7	14	21	35	43	50
2B	62	–	C-price 10¢; rare; LDC-r	1	1	31	62	93	182	296	410
3	78	–	C-price 15¢; LDC-r	1	1	5	10	14	20	24	28
4	87	–	LDC-r	1	1	4	9	13	18	22	26
5	118	–	LDC-r	1	1	4	7	10	14	17	20
6	131	–	New-c; PC-r	1	2	5	10	15	23	28	32
7	140	–	PC-r	1	2	2	4	6	9	13	16
8	150	–	PC-r	1	2	2	4	6	9	13	16
9	164	–	Reduced pg.width; PC-r	1	2	2	4	6	8	11	14
10	167	–	PC-r	1	2	2	4	6	8	11	14
11	167	3/64	PC-r	1	2	2	4	6	8	11	14
12	167	6/65	PC-r	1	2	2	4	6	8	11	14
13	167	12/65	PC-r	1	2	2	4	6	8	11	14
14	166	9/67	PC-r	1	2	2	4	6	8	11	14
15	166	Win/69	New price 25¢; PC-r; stiff-c	1	2	2	4	6	8	11	14
16	169	Sm/70	PC-r; stiff-c	1	2	2	4	6	8	11	14

47. Twenty Thousand Leagues Under the Sea

Ed	HRN	Date	Details	A	C	GD 2.0	VG 4.0	FN 6.0	VF 8.0	VF/NM 9.0	NM- 9.2
1	47	5/48	Orig.; Kiefer-a&c;	1	1	20	40	60	120	195	270
2	64	–	No c-price; LDC-r	1	1	6	12	18	28	34	40
3	78	–	C-price 15¢; LDC-r	1	1	4	9	13	18	22	26
4	94	–	LDC-r	1	1	4	8	12	17	21	24
5	118	–	LDC-r	1	1	4	7	10	14	17	20
6	128	–	New-c; PC-r	1	2	5	10	15	24	30	35
7	133	–	PC-r	1	2	2	4	6	10	14	18
8	140	–	PC-r	1	2	2	4	6	9	13	16
9	148	–	PC-r	1	2	2	4	6	9	13	16
10	156	–	PC-r	1	2	2	4	6	9	13	16
11	165	–	PC-r	1	2	2	4	6	9	13	16
12	167	–	PC-r	1	2	2	4	6	9	13	16
13	167	3/64	PC-r	1	2	2	4	6	9	13	16
14	167	8/65	PC-r	1	2	2	4	6	9	13	16
15	167	10/66	PC-r	1	2	2	4	6	9	13	16
16	166	R/1968	C-price 25¢; new-c PC-r	1	3	3	6	9	15	22	28
17	169	Spr/70	Stiff-c; PC-r	1	3	2	4	6	13	18	22

48. David Copperfield

Ed	HRN	Date	Details	A	C	GD 2.0	VG 4.0	FN 6.0	VF 8.0	VF/NM 9.0	NM- 9.2
1	47	6/48	Original; Kiefer-c/a	1	1	20	40	60	114	182	250
2	64	–	Price circle replaced by motif of boy reading; LDC-r	1	1	6	12	18	28	34	40
3	87	–	C-price 15¢; LDC-r	1	1	4	8	12	17	21	24
4	121	–	New-c; PC-r	1	2	5	10	15	22	26	30
5	130	–	PC-r	1	2	2	4	6	9	13	16
6	140	–	PC-r	1	2	2	4	6	9	13	16
7	148	–	PC-r	1	2	2	4	6	9	13	16
8	156	–	PC-r	1	2	2	4	6	9	13	16
9	167	–	PC-r	1	2	2	4	6	8	11	14
10	167	4/64	PC-r	1	2	2	4	6	8	11	14
11	167	6/65	PC-r	1	2	2	4	6	8	11	14
12	166	5/67	PC-r	1	2	2	4	6	8	11	14
13	166	R/67	PC-r; C-price 25¢	1	2	2	4	6	10	14	18
14	166	Spr/69	C-price 25¢; stiff-c PC-r	1	2	2	4	6	8	11	14
15	169	Win/69	Stiff-c; PC-r	1	2	2	4	6	8	11	14

49. Alice in Wonderland

Classics Illustrated #55 © GIL

Classics Illustrated #56 © GIL

Classics Illustrated #58 © GIL

Ed	HRN	Date	Details	A	C	GD 2.0	VG 4.0	FN 6.0	VF 8.0	VF/NM 9.0	NM- 9.2
1	47	7/48	Original; 1st Blum a & c	1	1	22	44	66	132	216	300
2	64	–	No c-price; LDC-r	1	1	8	16	24	42	54	65
3A	85	–	C-price 15¢; soft-c LDC-r	1	1	7	14	21	37	46	55
3B	85	–	Stiff-c; LDC-r	1	1	8	16	24	40	50	60
4	155	–	New PC, similar to orig.; PC-r	1	2	4	8	12	25	40	55
5	165	–	PC-r	1	2	3	6	9	17	26	35
6	167	3/64	PC-r	1	2	3	6	9	16	23	30
7	167	6/66	PC-r	1	2	4	8	12	27	44	60
8A	166	Fall/68	New-c; soft-c; 25¢ c-price; PC-r	1	3	4	8	12	25	40	55
8B	166	Fall/68	New-c; stiff-c; 25¢ c-price; PC-r	1	3	6	12	18	38	69	100

50. Adventures of Tom Sawyer (Used in **SOTI**, pg. 37)

Ed	HRN	Date	Details	A	C	GD 2.0	VG 4.0	FN 6.0	VF 8.0	VF/NM 9.0	NM- 9.2
1A	51	8/48	Orig.; Aldo Rubano a&c	1	1	20	40	60	114	182	250
1B	51	9/48	Orig.; Rubano c&a	1	1	20	40	60	114	182	250
1C	51	9/48	Orig.; outside-bc: blue & yellow only; rare	1	1	25	50	75	147	241	335
2	64	–	No c-price; LDC-r	1	1	5	10	15	23	28	32
3	78	–	C-price 15¢; LDC-r	1	1	4	8	12	17	21	24
4	94	–	LDC-r	1	1	4	7	10	14	17	20
5	117	–	LDC-r	1	1	2	4	6	10	14	18
6	132	–	LDC-r	1	1	2	4	6	10	14	18
7	140	–	New-c; PC-r	1	2	3	6	9	17	26	35
8	150	–	PC-r	1	2	2	4	6	9	13	16
9	164	–	New-a; PC-r	2	2	3	6	9	17	26	35
10	167	–	PC-r	2	2	2	4	6	9	13	16
11	167	1/65	PC-r	2	2	2	4	6	8	11	14
12	167	5/66	PC-r	2	2	2	4	6	8	11	14
13	166	12/67	PC-r	2	2	2	4	6	8	11	14
14	169	Fall/69	C-price 25¢; stiff-c; PC-r	2	2	2	4	6	8	11	14
15	169	Win/71	PC-r	2	2	2	4	6	8	11	14

51. The Spy

Ed	HRN	Date	Details	A	C	GD 2.0	VG 4.0	FN 6.0	VF 8.0	VF/NM 9.0	NM- 9.2
1A	51	9/48	Original; inside-bc illo: Christmas Carol	1	1	19	38	57	109	172	235
1B	51	9/48	Original; inside-bc illo: Man in Iron Mask	1	1	19	38	57	109	172	235
1C	51	8/48	Original; outside-bc: full color	1	1	19	38	57	109	172	235
1D	51	8/48	Original; outside-bc: blue & yellow only; scarce	1	1	20	40	60	115	185	255
2	89	–	C-price 15¢; LDC-r	1	1	5	10	14	20	24	28
3	121	–	LDC-r	1	1	4	8	12	17	21	24
4	139	–	New-c; PC-r	1	2	3	6	9	18	27	35
5	156	–	PC-r	1	2	2	4	6	9	13	16
6	167	11/63	PC-r	1	2	2	4	6	8	11	14
7	167	7/66	PC-r	1	2	2	4	6	8	11	14
8A	166	Win/69	C-price 25¢; soft-c; scarce; PC-r	1	2	3	6	9	15	21	26
8B	166	Win/69	C-price 25¢; stiff-c; PC-r	1	2	2	4	6	8	11	14

52. The House of the Seven Gables

Ed	HRN	Date	Details	A	C	GD 2.0	VG 4.0	FN 6.0	VF 8.0	VF/NM 9.0	NM- 9.2
1	53	10/48	Orig.; Griffiths a&c	1	1	19	38	57	109	172	235
2	89	–	C-price 15¢; LDC-r	1	1	5	10	14	20	24	28
3	121	–	LDC-r	1	1	4	8	12	17	21	24
4	142	–	New-c&a; PC-r; Woodbridge-a	2	2	5	10	15	25	31	36
5	156	–	PC-r	2	2	2	4	6	9	13	16
6	165	–	PC-r	2	2	2	4	6	8	11	14
7	167	5/64	PC-r	2	2	2	4	6	9	13	16
8	167	3/66	PC-r	2	2	2	4	6	8	11	14
9	166	R/1968	C-price 25¢; PC-r	2	2	2	4	6	8	11	14
10	169	Spr/70	Stiff-c; PC-r	2	2	2	4	6	8	11	14

53. A Christmas Carol

Ed	HRN	Date	Details	A	C	GD 2.0	VG 4.0	FN 6.0	VF 8.0	VF/NM 9.0	NM- 9.2
1	53	11/48	Original & only ed; Kiefer-c/a	1	1	24	48	72	142	234	325

54. Man in the Iron Mask

Ed	HRN	Date	Details	A	C	GD 2.0	VG 4.0	FN 6.0	VF 8.0	VF/NM 9.0	NM- 9.2
1	55	12/48	Original; Froehlich-a, Kiefer-c	1	1	19	38	57	109	172	235
2	93	–	C-price 15¢; LDC-r	1	1	5	10	15	23	28	32
3A	111	–	(O) logo lettering; scarce; LDC-r	1	1	6	12	18	31	38	45
3B	111	–	New logo as PC; LDC-r	1	1	5	10	15	23	28	32
4	142	–	New-c&a; PC-r	2	2	5	10	15	24	30	35
5	154	–	PC-r	2	2	2	4	6	9	13	16
6	165	–	PC-r	2	2	2	4	6	8	11	14
7	167	5/64	PC-r	2	2	2	4	6	8	11	14
8	167	4/66	PC-r	2	2	2	4	6	8	11	14
9A	166	Win/69	C-price 25¢; soft-c PC-r	2	2	3	6	9	15	21	26
9B	166	Win/69	Stiff-c	2	2	2	4	6	8	11	14

55. Silas Marner (Used in **SOTI**, pgs. 311, 312)

Ed	HRN	Date	Details	A	C	GD 2.0	VG 4.0	FN 6.0	VF 8.0	VF/NM 9.0	NM- 9.2
1	55	1/49	Original-Kiefer-c	1	1	19	38	57	109	172	235
2	75	–	Price circle blank; 'Coming Next' ad; LDC-r	1	1	5	10	15	24	30	35
3	97	–	LDC-r	1	1	3	6	9	14	19	24
4	121	–	New-c; PC-r	1	2	3	6	9	18	27	35
5	130	–	PC-r	1	2	2	4	6	9	13	16
6	140	–	PC-r	1	2	2	4	6	9	13	16
7	154	–	PC-r	1	2	2	4	6	9	13	16
8	165	–	PC-r	1	2	2	4	6	8	11	14
9	167	2/64	PC-r	1	2	2	4	6	8	11	14
10	167	6/65	PC-r	1	2	2	4	6	8	11	14
11	166	5/67	PC-r	1	2	2	4	6	8	11	14
12A	166	Win/69	C-price 25¢; soft-c PC-r	1	2	3	6	9	15	21	26
12B	166	Win/69	C-price 25¢; stiff-c PC-r	1	2	2	4	6	8	11	14

56. The Toilers of the Sea

Ed	HRN	Date	Details	A	C	GD 2.0	VG 4.0	FN 6.0	VF 8.0	VF/NM 9.0	NM- 9.2
1	55	2/49	Original; A.M. Froehlich-c/a	1	1	24	48	72	142	234	325
2	165	–	New-c&a; PC-r; Angelo Torres-a	2	2	8	16	24	40	50	60
3	167	3/64	PC-r	2	2	3	6	9	16	23	30
4	167	10/66	PC-r	2	2	3	6	9	16	23	30

57. The Song of Hiawatha

Ed	HRN	Date	Details	A	C	GD 2.0	VG 4.0	FN 6.0	VF 8.0	VF/NM 9.0	NM- 9.2
1	55	3/49	Original; Alex Blum-c/a	1	1	18	36	54	103	162	220
2	75	–	No c-price w/15¢ sticker; 'Coming Next' ad; LDC-r	1	1	5	10	15	24	30	35
3	94	–	C-price 15¢; LDC-r	1	1	5	10	14	20	24	28
4	118	–	LDC-r	1	1	3	6	9	14	19	24
5	134	–	New-c; PC-r	1	2	3	6	9	17	26	35
6	139	–	PC-r	1	2	2	4	6	9	13	16
7	154	–	PC-r	1	2	2	4	6	9	13	16
8	167	–	Has orig.date; PC-r	1	2	2	4	6	8	11	14
9	167	9/64	PC-r	1	2	2	4	6	8	11	14
10	167	10/65	PC-r	1	2	2	4	6	8	11	14
11	166	F/1968	C-price 25¢; PC-r	1	2	2	4	6	8	11	14

58. The Prairie

Ed	HRN	Date	Details	A	C	GD 2.0	VG 4.0	FN 6.0	VF 8.0	VF/NM 9.0	NM- 9.2
1	60	4/49	Original; Palais c/a	1	1	18	36	54	103	162	220
2A	62	–	No c-price; no coming-next ad; LDC-r	1	1	9	18	27	47	61	75
2B	62		10¢ (rare)	1	1	19	38	57	112	179	245

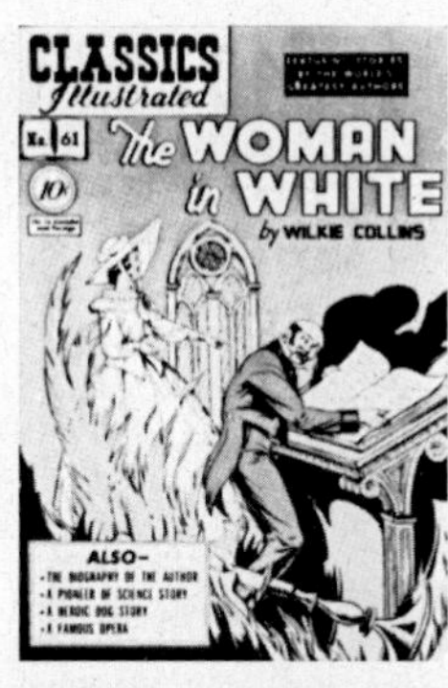

Classics Illustrated #61 © GIL

Classics Illustrated #65 © GIL

Classics Illustrated #69 © GIL

Ed	HRN	Date	Details	A	C	GD 2.0	VG 4.0	FN 6.0	VF 8.0	VF/NM 9.0	NM- 9.2
3	78	–	C-price 15¢ in dbl. circle; LDC-r	1	1	5	10	15	22	26	30
4	114	–	LDC-r	1	1	4	8	12	17	21	24
5	131	–	LDC-r	1	1	4	7	10	14	17	20
6	132	–	LDC-r	1	1	4	7	10	14	17	20
7	146	–	New-c; PC-r	1	2	5	10	15	23	28	32
8	155	–	PC-r	1	2	2	4	6	9	13	16
9	167	5/64	PC-r	1	2	2	4	6	8	11	14
10	167	4/66	PC-r	1	2	2	4	6	8	11	14
11	169	Sm/69	New price 25¢; stiff-c; PC-r	1	2	2	4	6	8	11	14

59. Wuthering Heights

Ed	HRN	Date	Details	A	C	GD 2.0	VG 4.0	FN 6.0	VF 8.0	VF/NM 9.0	NM- 9.2
1	60	5/49	Original; Kiefer-c/a	1	1	19	38	57	109	172	235
2	85	–	C-price 15¢; LDC-r	1	1	6	12	18	28	34	40
3	156	–	New-c; PC-r	1	2	5	10	15	25	31	36
4	167	1/64	PC-r	1	2	2	4	6	9	13	16
5	167	10/66	PC-r	1	2	2	4	6	9	13	16
6	169	Sm/69	C-price 25¢; stiff-c; PC-r	1	2	2	4	6	9	13	16

60. Black Beauty

Ed	HRN	Date	Details	A	C	GD 2.0	VG 4.0	FN 6.0	VF 8.0	VF/NM 9.0	NM- 9.2
1	62	6/49	Original; Froehlich-c/a	1	1	18	36	54	103	162	220
2	62	–	No c-price; no coming-next ad; LDC-r (rare)	1	1	20	40	60	114	182	250
3	85	–	C-price 15¢; LDC-r	1	1	5	10	15	23	28	32
4	158	–	New L.B. Cole-c/a; PC-r	2	2	7	14	21	35	43	50
5	167	2/64	PC-r	2	2	2	4	6	11	16	20
6	167	3/66	PC-r	2	2	2	4	6	11	16	20
7	166	R/1968	New-c&price, 25¢; PC-r	2	3	5	10	15	30	50	70

61. The Woman in White

Ed	HRN	Date	Details	A	C	GD 2.0	VG 4.0	FN 6.0	VF 8.0	VF/NM 9.0	NM- 9.2
1A	62	7/49	Original; Blum-c/a fc-purple; bc: top illos light blue	1	1	19	38	57	109	172	235
1B	62	7/49	Original; Blum-c/a fc-pink; bc: top illos light violet	1	1	19	38	57	109	172	235
2	156	–	New-c; PC-r	1	2	6	12	18	28	34	40
3	167	1/64	PC-r	1	2	2	4	6	11	16	20
4	166	R/1968	C-price 25¢; PC-r	1	2	2	4	6	11	16	20

62. Western Stories ("The Luck of Roaring Camp" and "The Outcasts of Poker Flat")

Ed	HRN	Date	Details	A	C	GD 2.0	VG 4.0	FN 6.0	VF 8.0	VF/NM 9.0	NM- 9.2
1	62	8/49	Original; Kiefer-c/a	1	1	17	34	51	98	154	210
2	89	–	C-price 15¢; LDC-r	1	1	5	10	15	23	28	32
3	121	–	LDC-r	1	1	3	6	9	15	21	26
4	137	–	New-c; PC-r	1	2	3	6	9	17	26	35
5	152	–	PC-r	1	2	2	4	6	8	11	14
6	167	10/63	PC-r	1	2	2	4	6	8	11	14
7	167	6/64	PC-r	1	2	2	4	6	8	11	14
8	167	11/66	PC-r	1	2	2	4	6	8	11	14
9	166	R/1968	New-c&price 25¢; PC-r	1	3	3	6	9	16	24	32

63. The Man Without a Country

Ed	HRN	Date	Details	A	C	GD 2.0	VG 4.0	FN 6.0	VF 8.0	VF/NM 9.0	NM- 9.2
1	62	9/49	Original; Kiefer-c/a	1	1	18	36	54	103	162	220
2	78	–	C-price 15¢ in double circle; LDC-r	1	1	5	10	15	23	28	32
3	156	–	New-c, old-a; PC-r	1	2	6	12	18	28	34	40
4	165	–	New-a & text pgs.; PC-r; A. Torres-a	2	2	5	10	15	23	28	32
5	167	3/64	PC-r	2	2	2	4	6	8	11	14
6	167	8/66	PC-r	2	2	2	4	6	8	11	14
7	169	Sm/69	New price 25¢; stiff-c; PC-r	2	2	2	4	6	8	11	14

64. Treasure Island

Ed	HRN	Date	Details	A	C	GD 2.0	VG 4.0	FN 6.0	VF 8.0	VF/NM 9.0	NM- 9.2
1	62	10/49	Original; Blum-c/a	1	1	19	38	57	109	172	235
2A	82	–	C-price 15¢; soft-c LDC-r	1	1	5	10	15	22	26	30
2B	82	–	Stiff-c; LDC-r	1	1	5	10	15	23	28	32
3	117	–	LDC-r	1	1	3	6	9	15	21	26
4	131	–	New-c; PC-r	1	2	3	6	9	17	26	35
5	138	–	PC-r	1	2	2	4	6	9	13	16
6	146	–	PC-r	1	2	2	4	6	9	13	16
7	158	–	PC-r	1	2	2	4	6	9	13	16
8	165	–	PC-r	1	2	2	4	6	8	11	14
9	167	–	PC-r	1	2	2	4	6	8	11	14
10	167	6/64	PC-r	1	2	2	4	6	8	11	14
11	167	12/65	PC-r	1	2	2	4	6	8	11	14
12A	166	10/67	PC-r	1	2	2	4	6	8	11	14
12B	166	10/67	w/Grit ad stapled in book	1	2	10	20	30	66	138	210
13	169	Spr/69	New price 25¢; stiff-c; PC-r	1	2	2	4	6	9	13	16
14	–	1989	Long John Silver's Seafood Shoppes; $1.95, First/Berkley Publ.; Blum-r	1	2						5.00

65. Benjamin Franklin

Ed	HRN	Date	Details	A	C	GD 2.0	VG 4.0	FN 6.0	VF 8.0	VF/NM 9.0	NM- 9.2
1	64	11/49	Original; Kiefer-c; Iger Shop-a	1	1	10	20	30	68	144	220
2	131	–	New-c; PC-r	1	2	5	10	15	24	30	35
3	154	–	PC-r	1	2	2	4	6	9	13	16
4	167	2/64	PC-r	1	2	2	4	6	9	13	16
5	167	4/66	PC-r	1	2	2	4	6	9	13	16
6	169	Fall/69	New price 25¢; stiff-c; PC-r	1	2	2	4	6	9	13	16

66. The Cloister and the Hearth

Ed	HRN	Date	Details	A	C	GD 2.0	VG 4.0	FN 6.0	VF 8.0	VF/NM 9.0	NM- 9.2
1	67	12/49	Original & only ed; Kiefer-a & c	1	1	32	64	96	192	314	435

67. The Scottish Chiefs

Ed	HRN	Date	Details	A	C	GD 2.0	VG 4.0	FN 6.0	VF 8.0	VF/NM 9.0	NM- 9.2
1	67	1/50	Original; Blum-a&c	1	1	15	30	45	90	140	190
2	85	–	C-price 15¢; LDC-r	1	1	5	10	15	23	28	32
3	118	–	LDC-r	1	1	3	6	9	15	21	26
4	136	–	New-c; PC-r	1	2	3	6	9	18	27	36
5	154	–	PC-r	1	2	2	4	6	9	13	16
6	167	11/63	PC-r	1	2	2	4	6	10	14	18
7	167	8/65	PC-r	1	2	2	4	6	9	13	16

68. Julius Caesar (Used in **SOTI**, pgs. 36, 37)

Ed	HRN	Date	Details	A	C	GD 2.0	VG 4.0	FN 6.0	VF 8.0	VF/NM 9.0	NM- 9.2
1	70	2/50	Original; Kiefer-c/a	1	1	15	30	45	90	140	190
2	85	–	C-price 15¢; LDC-r	1	1	5	10	15	22	26	30
3	108	–	LDC-r	1	1	4	9	13	18	22	26
4	156	–	New L.B. Cole-c; PC-r	1	2	6	12	18	28	34	40
5	165	–	New-a by Evans, Crandall; PC-r	2	2	5	10	15	24	30	35
6	167	2/64	PC-r	2	2	2	4	6	8	11	14
7	167	10/65	Tarzan books inside cover; PC-r	2	2	2	4	6	8	11	14
8	166	R/1967	PC-r	2	2	2	4	6	8	11	14
9	169	Win/69	PC-r; stiff-c	2	2	2	4	6	8	11	14

69. Around the World in 80 Days

Ed	HRN	Date	Details	A	C	GD 2.0	VG 4.0	FN 6.0	VF 8.0	VF/NM 9.0	NM- 9.2
1	70	3/50	Original; Kiefer-c/a	1	1	15	30	45	90	140	190
2	87	–	C-price 15¢; LDC-r	1	1	5	10	15	22	26	30
3	125	–	LDC-r	1	1	4	9	13	18	22	26
4	136	–	New-c; PC-r	1	2	5	10	15	25	31	36
5	146	–	PC-r	1	2	2	4	6	9	13	16
6	152	–	PC-r	1	2	2	4	6	9	13	16
7	164	–	PC-r	1	2	2	4	6	8	11	14
8	167	–	PC-r	1	2	2	4	6	8	11	14
9	167	7/64	PC-r	1	2	2	4	6	8	11	14
10	167	11/65	PC-r	1	2	2	4	6	8	11	14
11	166	7/67	PC-r	1	2	2	4	6	8	11	14
12	169	Spr/69	C-price 25¢; stiff-c;	1	2	2	4	6	8	11	14

Classics Illustrated #71 © GIL

Classics Illustrated #83 © GIL

						GD 2.0	VG 4.0	FN 6.0	VF 8.0	VF/NM 9.0	NM- 9.2

PC-r

70. The Pilot

Ed	HRN	Date	Details	A	C	GD 2.0	VG 4.0	FN 6.0	VF 8.0	VF/NM 9.0	NM- 9.2
1	71	4/50	Original; Blum-c/a	1	1	14	28	42	81	118	155
2	92	–	C-price 15¢; LDC-r	1	1	5	10	15	23	28	32
3	125	–	LDC-r	1	1	4	9	13	18	22	26
4	156	–	New-c; PC-r	1	2	6	12	18	28	34	40
5	167	2/64	PC-r	1	2	2	4	6	11	16	20
6	167	5/66	PC-r	1	2	2	4	6	9	13	16

71. The Man Who Laughs

Ed	HRN	Date	Details	A	C	GD 2.0	VG 4.0	FN 6.0	VF 8.0	VF/NM 9.0	NM- 9.2
1	71	5/50	Original; Blum-c/a	1	1	20	40	60	114	182	250
2	165	–	New-c&a; PC-r	2	2	14	28	42	80	115	155
3	167	4/64	PC-r	2	2	11	22	33	62	86	115

72. The Oregon Trail

Ed	HRN	Date	Details	A	C	GD 2.0	VG 4.0	FN 6.0	VF 8.0	VF/NM 9.0	NM- 9.2
1	73	6/50	Original; Kiefer-c/a	1	1	14	28	42	81	118	155
2	89	–	C-price 15¢; LDC-r	1	1	5	10	15	23	28	32
3	121	–	LDC-r	1	1	4	9	13	18	22	26
4	131	–	New-c; PC-r	1	2	5	10	15	25	31	36
5	140	–	PC-r	1	2	2	4	6	9	13	16
6	150	–	PC-r	1	2	2	4	6	9	13	16
7	164	–	PC-r	1	2	2	4	6	8	11	14
8	167	–	PC-r	1	2	2	4	6	8	11	14
9	167	8/64	PC-r	1	2	2	4	6	8	11	14
10	167	10/65	PC-r	1	2	2	4	6	8	11	14
11	166	R/1968	C-price 25¢; PC-r	1	2	2	4	6	8	11	14

73. The Black Tulip

Ed	HRN	Date	Details	A	C	GD 2.0	VG 4.0	FN 6.0	VF 8.0	VF/NM 9.0	NM- 9.2
1	75	7/50	1st & only ed.; Alex Blum-c/a	1	1	38	76	114	228	369	510

74. Mr. Midshipman Easy

Ed	HRN	Date	Details	A	C	GD 2.0	VG 4.0	FN 6.0	VF 8.0	VF/NM 9.0	NM- 9.2
1	75	8/50	1st & only edition	1	1	38	76	114	228	369	510

75. The Lady of the Lake

Ed	HRN	Date	Details	A	C	GD 2.0	VG 4.0	FN 6.0	VF 8.0	VF/NM 9.0	NM- 9.2
1	75	9/50	Original; Kiefer-c/a	1	1	14	28	42	81	118	155
2	85	–	C-price 15¢; LDC-r	1	1	5	10	15	24	30	35
3	118	–	LDC-r	1	1	5	10	14	20	24	28
4	139	–	New-c; PC-r	1	2	5	10	15	25	31	36
5	154	–	PC-r	1	2	2	4	6	9	13	16
6	165	–	PC-r	1	2	2	4	6	8	11	14
7	167	4/64	PC-r	1	2	2	4	6	8	11	14
8	167	5/66	PC-r	1	2	2	4	6	8	11	14
9	169	Spr/69	New price 25¢; stiff-c; PC-r	1	2	2	4	6	8	11	14

76. The Prisoner of Zenda

Ed	HRN	Date	Details	A	C	GD 2.0	VG 4.0	FN 6.0	VF 8.0	VF/NM 9.0	NM- 9.2
1	75	10/50	Original; Kiefer-c/a	1	1	14	28	42	81	118	155
2	85	–	C-price 15¢; LDC-r	1	1	5	10	15	23	28	32
3	111	–	LDC-r	1	1	3	6	9	16	21	26
4	128	–	New-c; PC-r	1	2	3	6	9	17	26	35
5	152	–	PC-r	1	2	2	4	6	9	13	16
6	165	–	PC-r	1	2	2	4	6	8	11	14
7	167	4/64	PC-r	1	2	2	4	6	8	11	14
8	167	9/66	PC-r	1	2	2	4	6	8	11	14
9	169	Fall/69	New price 25¢; stiff-c; PC-r	1	2	2	4	6	8	11	14

77. The Iliad

Ed	HRN	Date	Details	A	C	GD 2.0	VG 4.0	FN 6.0	VF 8.0	VF/NM 9.0	NM- 9.2
1	78	11/50	Original; Blum-c/a	1	1	14	28	42	81	118	155
2	87	–	C-price 15¢; LDC-r	1	1	5	10	15	24	30	35
3	121	–	LDC-r	1	1	3	6	9	15	21	26
4	139	–	New-c; PC-r	1	2	3	6	9	16	24	32
5	150	–	PC-r	1	2	2	4	6	9	13	16
6	165	–	PC-r	1	2	2	4	6	8	11	14
7	167	10/63	PC-r	1	2	2	4	6	8	11	14
8	167	7/64	PC-r	1	2	2	4	6	8	11	14
9	167	5/66	PC-r	1	2	2	4	6	8	11	14
10	166	R/1968	C-price 25¢; PC-r	1	2	2	4	6	8	11	14

78. Joan of Arc

Ed	HRN	Date	Details	A	C	GD 2.0	VG 4.0	FN 6.0	VF 8.0	VF/NM 9.0	NM- 9.2
1	78	12/50	Original; Kiefer-c/a	1	1	14	28	42	81	118	155
2	87	–	C-price 15¢; LDC-r	1	1	5	10	15	23	28	32
3	113	–	LDC-r	1	1	3	6	9	15	21	26
4	128	–	New-c; PC-r	1	2	3	6	9	17	26	35
5	140	–	PC-r	1	2	2	4	6	9	13	16
6	150	–	PC-r	1	2	2	4	6	9	13	16
7	159	–	PC-r	1	2	2	4	6	9	13	16
8	167	–	PC-r	1	2	2	4	6	8	11	14
9	167	12/63	PC-r	1	2	2	4	6	8	11	14
10	167	6/65	PC-r	1	2	2	4	6	8	11	14
11	166	6/67	PC-r	1	2	2	4	6	8	11	14
12	166	Win/69	New-c&price, 25¢; PC-r; stiff-c	1	3	3	6	9	16	24	32

79. Cyrano de Bergerac

Ed	HRN	Date	Details	A	C	GD 2.0	VG 4.0	FN 6.0	VF 8.0	VF/NM 9.0	NM- 9.2
1	78	1/51	Orig.; movie promo inside front-c; Blum-c/a	1	1	14	28	42	81	118	155
2	85	–	C-price 15¢; LDC-r	1	1	5	10	15	23	28	32
3	118	–	LDC-r	1	1	3	6	9	17	23	28
4	133	–	New-c; PC-r	1	2	3	6	9	16	24	32
5	156	–	PC-r	1	2	2	4	6	11	16	20
6	167	8/64	PC-r	1	2	2	4	6	11	16	20

80. White Fang (Last line drawn cover)

Ed	HRN	Date	Details	A	C	GD 2.0	VG 4.0	FN 6.0	VF 8.0	VF/NM 9.0	NM- 9.2
1	79	2/51	Orig.; Blum-c/a	1	1	14	28	42	81	118	155
2	87	–	C-price 15¢; LDC-r	1	1	5	10	15	24	30	35
3	125	–	LDC-r	1	1	3	6	9	15	21	26
4	132	–	New-c; PC-r	1	2	3	6	9	16	24	32
5	140	–	PC-r	1	2	2	4	6	9	13	16
6	153	–	PC-r	1	2	2	4	6	9	13	16
7	167	–	PC-r	1	2	2	4	6	8	11	14
8	167	9/64	PC-r	1	2	2	4	6	8	11	14
9	167	7/65	PC-r	1	2	2	4	6	8	11	14
10	166	6/67	PC-r	1	2	2	4	6	8	11	14
11	169	Fall/69	New price 25¢; PC-r; stiff-c	1	2	2	4	6	8	11	14

81. The Odyssey (1st painted cover)

Ed	HRN	Date	Details	A	C	GD 2.0	VG 4.0	FN 6.0	VF 8.0	VF/NM 9.0	NM- 9.2
1	82	3/51	First 15¢ Original; Blum-c	1	1	14	28	42	81	118	155
2	167	8/64	PC-r	1	1	2	4	6	11	16	20
3	167	10/66	PC-r	1	1	2	4	6	11	16	20
4	169	Spr/69	New, stiff-c; PC-r	1	2	3	6	9	18	27	36

82. The Master of Ballantrae

Ed	HRN	Date	Details	A	C	GD 2.0	VG 4.0	FN 6.0	VF 8.0	VF/NM 9.0	NM- 9.2
1	82	4/51	Original; Blum-c	1	1	13	26	39	72	101	130
2	167	8/64	PC-r	1	1	3	6	9	14	19	24
3	166	Fall/68	New, stiff-c; PC-r	1	2	3	6	9	18	27	36

83. The Jungle Book

Ed	HRN	Date	Details	A	C	GD 2.0	VG 4.0	FN 6.0	VF 8.0	VF/NM 9.0	NM- 9.2
1	85	5/51	Original; Blum-c Bossert/Blum-a	1	1	13	26	39	72	101	130
2	110	–	PC-r	1	1	2	4	6	10	14	18
3	125	–	PC-r	1	1	2	4	6	9	13	16
4	134	–	PC-r	1	1	2	4	6	9	13	16
5	142	–	PC-r	1	1	2	4	6	9	13	16
6	150	–	PC-r	1	1	2	4	6	9	13	16
7	159	–	PC-r	1	1	2	4	6	9	13	16
8	167	–	PC-r	1	1	2	4	6	8	11	14
9	167	3/65	PC-r	1	1	2	4	6	8	11	14
10	167	11/65	PC-r	1	1	2	4	6	8	11	14
11	167	5/66	PC-r	1	1	2	4	6	8	11	14
12	166	R/1968	New c&a; stiff-c; PC-r	2	2	3	6	9	18	28	38

84. The Gold Bug and Other Stories ("The Gold Bug", "The Tell-Tale Heart", "The Cask of Amontillado")

Ed	HRN	Date	Details	A	C	GD 2.0	VG 4.0	FN 6.0	VF 8.0	VF/NM 9.0	NM- 9.2
1	85	6/51	Original; Blum-c/a; Palais, Laverly-a	1	1	15	30	45	84	127	170
2	167	7/64	PC-r	1	1	11	22	33	62	86	110

Classics Illustrated #87 © GIL

Classics Illustrated #89 © GIL

Classics Illustrated #95 © GIL

85. The Sea Wolf

Ed	HRN	Date	Details	A	C	GD 2.0	VG 4.0	FN 6.0	VF 8.0	VF/NM 9.0	NM- 9.2
1	85	7/51	Original; Blum-c/a	1	1	11	22	33	64	90	115
2	121	–	PC-r	1	1	2	4	6	9	13	16
3	132	–	PC-r	1	1	2	4	6	9	13	16
4	141	–	PC-r	1	1	2	4	6	9	13	16
5	161	–	PC-r	1	1	2	4	6	8	11	14
6	167	2/64	PC-r	1	1	2	4	6	8	11	14
7	167	11/65	PC-r	1	1	2	4	6	8	11	14
8	169	Fall/69	New price 25¢; stiff-c; PC-r	1	1	2	4	6	8	11	14

86. Under Two Flags

Ed	HRN	Date	Details	A	C	GD 2.0	VG 4.0	FN 6.0	VF 8.0	VF/NM 9.0	NM- 9.2
1	87	8/51	Original; first delBourgo-a	1	1	11	22	33	64	90	115
2	117	–	PC-r	1	1	2	4	6	10	14	18
3	139	–	PC-r	1	1	2	4	6	9	13	16
4	158	–	PC-r	1	1	2	4	6	9	13	16
5	167	2/64	PC-r	1	1	2	4	6	8	11	14
6	167	8/66	PC-r	1	1	2	4	6	8	11	14
7	169	Sm/69	New price 25¢; stiff-c; PC-r	1	1	2	4	6	8	11	14

87. A Midsummer Nights Dream

Ed	HRN	Date	Details	A	C	GD 2.0	VG 4.0	FN 6.0	VF 8.0	VF/NM 9.0	NM- 9.2
1	87	9/51	Original; Blum c/a	1	1	11	22	33	64	90	115
2	161	–	PC-r	1	1	2	4	6	9	13	16
3	167	4/64	PC-r	1	1	2	4	6	8	11	14
4	167	5/66	PC-r	1	1	2	4	6	8	11	14
5	169	Sm/69	New price 25¢; stiff-c; PC-r	1	1	2	4	6	8	11	14

88. Men of Iron

Ed	HRN	Date	Details	A	C	GD 2.0	VG 4.0	FN 6.0	VF 8.0	VF/NM 9.0	NM- 9.2
1	89	10/51	Original	1	1	11	22	33	64	90	115
2	154	–	PC-r	1	1	2	4	6	9	13	16
3	167	1/64	PC-r	1	1	2	4	6	8	11	14
4	166	R/1968	C-price 25¢; PC-r	1	1	2	4	6	8	11	14

89. Crime and Punishment (Cover illo. in **POP**)

Ed	HRN	Date	Details	A	C	GD 2.0	VG 4.0	FN 6.0	VF 8.0	VF/NM 9.0	NM- 9.2
1	89	11/51	Original; Palais-a	1	1	13	26	39	72	101	130
2	152	–	PC-r	1	1	2	4	6	9	13	16
3	167	4/64	PC-r	1	1	2	4	6	8	11	14
4	167	5/66	PC-r	1	1	2	4	6	8	11	14
5	169	Fall/69	New price 25¢ stiff-c; PC-r	1	1	2	4	6	8	11	14

90. Green Mansions

Ed	HRN	Date	Details	A	C	GD 2.0	VG 4.0	FN 6.0	VF 8.0	VF/NM 9.0	NM- 9.2
1	89	12/51	Original; Blum-c/a	1	1	11	22	33	64	90	115
2	148	–	New L.B. Cole-c; PC-r	1	2	5	10	15	22	26	30
3	165	–	PC-r	1	2	2	4	6	8	11	14
4	167	4/64	PC-r	1	2	2	4	6	8	11	14
5	167	9/66	PC-r	1	2	2	4	6	8	11	14
6	169	Sm/69	New price 25¢; stiff-c; PC-r	1	2	2	4	6	8	11	14

91. The Call of the Wild

Ed	HRN	Date	Details	A	C	GD 2.0	VG 4.0	FN 6.0	VF 8.0	VF/NM 9.0	NM- 9.2
1	92	1/52	Orig.; delBourgo-a	1	1	11	22	33	64	90	115
2	112	–	PC-r	1	1	2	4	6	9	13	16
3	125	–	'Picture Progress' on back-c; PC-r	1	1	2	4	6	9	13	16
4	134	–	PC-r	1	1	2	4	6	9	13	16
5	143	–	PC-r	1	1	2	4	6	9	13	16
6	165	–	PC-r	1	1	2	4	6	9	13	16
7	167	–	PC-r	1	1	2	4	6	8	11	14
8	167	4/65	PC-r	1	1	2	4	6	8	11	14
9	167	3/66	PC-r	1	1	2	4	6	8	11	14
10	166	11/67	PC-r	1	1	2	4	6	8	11	14
11	169	Spr/70	New price 25¢; stiff-c; PC-r	1	1	2	4	6	8	11	14

92. The Courtship of Miles Standish

Ed	HRN	Date	Details	A	C	GD 2.0	VG 4.0	FN 6.0	VF 8.0	VF/NM 9.0	NM- 9.2
1	92	2/52	Original; Blum-c/a	1	1	11	22	33	64	90	115
2	165	–	PC-r	1	1	2	4	6	9	13	16
3	167	3/64	PC-r	1	1	2	4	6	9	13	16
4	166	5/67	PC-r	1	1	2	4	6	9	13	16
5	169	Win/69	New price 25¢ stiff-c; PC-r	1	1	2	4	6	9	13	16

93. Pudd'nhead Wilson

Ed	HRN	Date	Details	A	C	GD 2.0	VG 4.0	FN 6.0	VF 8.0	VF/NM 9.0	NM- 9.2
1	94	3/52	Orig.; Kiefer-c/a;	1	1	11	22	33	64	90	115
2	165	–	New-c; PC-r	1	2	2	4	6	11	16	25
3	167	3/64	PC-r	1	2	2	4	6	9	13	16
4	166	R/1968	New price 25¢; soft-c; PC-r	1	2	2	4	6	9	13	16

94. David Balfour

Ed	HRN	Date	Details	A	C	GD 2.0	VG 4.0	FN 6.0	VF 8.0	VF/NM 9.0	NM- 9.2
1	94	4/52	Original; Palais-a	1	1	11	22	33	64	90	115
2	167	5/64	PC-r	1	1	2	4	6	11	16	20
3	166	R/1968	C-price 25¢; PC-r	1	1	2	4	6	13	18	22

95. All Quiet on the Western Front

Ed	HRN	Date	Details	A	C	GD 2.0	VG 4.0	FN 6.0	VF 8.0	VF/NM 9.0	NM- 9.2
1A	96	5/52	Orig.; del Bourgo-a	1	1	14	28	42	81	118	155
1B	99	5/52	Orig.; del Bourgo-a	1	1	13	26	39	72	101	130
2	167	10/64	PC-r	1	1	3	6	9	15	22	28
3	167	11/66	PC-r	1	1	3	6	9	15	22	28

96. Daniel Boone

Ed	HRN	Date	Details	A	C	GD 2.0	VG 4.0	FN 6.0	VF 8.0	VF/NM 9.0	NM- 9.2
1	97	6/52	Original; Blum-a	1	1	11	22	33	62	86	110
2	117	–	PC-r	1	1	2	4	6	9	13	16
3	128	–	PC-r	1	1	2	4	6	9	13	16
4	132	–	PC-r	1	1	2	4	6	9	13	16
5	134	–	"Story of Jesus" on back-c; PC-r	1	1	2	4	6	9	13	16
6	158	–	PC-r	1	1	2	4	6	9	13	16
7	167	1/64	PC-r	1	1	2	4	6	8	11	14
8	167	5/65	PC-r	1	1	2	4	6	8	11	14
9	167	11/66	PC-r	1	1	2	4	6	8	11	14
10	166	Win/69	New-c; price 25¢; PC-r; stiff-c	1	2	3	6	9	15	22	28

97. King Solomon's Mines

Ed	HRN	Date	Details	A	C	GD 2.0	VG 4.0	FN 6.0	VF 8.0	VF/NM 9.0	NM- 9.2
1	96	7/52	Orig.; Kiefer-a	1	1	11	22	33	62	86	110
2	118	–	PC-r	1	1	2	4	6	9	13	16
3	131	–	PC-r	1	1	2	4	6	9	13	16
4	141	–	PC-r	1	1	2	4	6	9	13	16
5	158	–	PC-r	1	1	2	4	6	9	13	16
6	167	2/64	PC-r	1	1	2	4	6	8	11	14
7	167	9/65	PC-r	1	1	2	4	6	8	11	14
8	169	Sm/69	New price 25¢; stiff-c; PC-r	1	1	2	4	6	8	11	14

98. The Red Badge of Courage

Ed	HRN	Date	Details	A	C	GD 2.0	VG 4.0	FN 6.0	VF 8.0	VF/NM 9.0	NM- 9.2
1	98	8/52	Original	1	1	11	22	33	62	86	110
2	118	–	PC-r	1	1	2	4	6	9	13	16
3	132	–	PC-r	1	1	2	4	6	9	13	16
4	142	–	PC-r	1	1	2	4	6	9	13	16
5	152	–	PC-r	1	1	2	4	6	9	13	16
6	161	–	PC-r	1	1	2	4	6	9	13	16
7	167	–	Has orig.date; PC-r	1	1	2	4	6	9	13	16
8	167	9/64	PC-r	1	1	2	4	6	9	13	16
9	167	10/65	PC-r	1	1	2	4	6	9	13	16
10	166	R/1968	New-c&price 25¢; PC-r; stiff-c	1	2	3	6	9	16	23	30

99. Hamlet (Used in **POP**, pg. 102)

Ed	HRN	Date	Details	A	C	GD 2.0	VG 4.0	FN 6.0	VF 8.0	VF/NM 9.0	NM- 9.2
1	98	9/52	Original; Blum-a	1	1	11	22	33	64	90	115
2	121	–	PC-r	1	1	2	4	6	9	13	16
3	141	–	PC-r	1	1	2	4	6	9	13	16
4	158	–	PC-r	1	1	2	4	6	9	13	16
5	167	–	Has orig.date; PC-r	1	1	2	4	6	8	11	14
6	167	7/65	PC-r	1	1	2	4	6	8	11	14
7	166	4/67	PC-r	1	1	2	4	6	8	11	14
8	169	Spr/69	New-c&price 25¢; PC-r; stiff-c	1	2	3	6	9	16	23	30

Classics Illustrated #102 © GIL

Classics Illustrated #107 © GIL

Classics Illustrated #115 © GIL

100. Mutiny on the Bounty

Ed	HRN	Date	Details	A	C	GD 2.0	VG 4.0	FN 6.0	VF 8.0	VF/NM 9.0	NM- 9.2
1	100	10/52	Original	1	1	11	22	33	62	86	110
2	117	–	PC-r	1	1	2	4	6	9	13	16
3	132	–	PC-r	1	1	2	4	6	9	13	16
4	142	–	PC-r	1	1	2	4	6	9	13	16
5	155	–	PC-r	1	1	2	4	6	9	13	16
6	167	–	Has orig. date;PC-r	1	1	2	4	6	8	11	14
7	167	5/64	PC-r	1	1	2	4	6	8	11	14
8	167	3/66	PC-r	1	1	2	4	6	8	11	14
9	169	Spr/70	PC-r; stiff-c	1	1	2	4	6	8	11	14

101. William Tell

Ed	HRN	Date	Details	A	C	GD 2.0	VG 4.0	FN 6.0	VF 8.0	VF/NM 9.0	NM- 9.2
1	101	11/52	Original; Kiefer-c delBourgo-a	1	1	11	22	33	62	86	110
2	118	–	PC-r	1	1	2	4	6	9	13	16
3	141	–	PC-r	1	1	2	4	6	9	13	16
4	158	–	PC-r	1	1	2	4	6	9	13	16
5	167	–	Has orig.date; PC-r	1	1	2	4	6	8	11	14
6	167	11/64	PC-r	1	1	2	4	6	8	11	14
7	166	4/67	PC-r	1	1	2	4	6	8	11	14
8	169	Win/69	New price 25¢; stiff-c; PC-r	1	1	2	4	6	8	11	14

102. The White Company

Ed	HRN	Date	Details	A	C	GD 2.0	VG 4.0	FN 6.0	VF 8.0	VF/NM 9.0	NM- 9.2
1	101	12/52	Original; Blum-a	1	1	14	28	42	76	108	140
2	165	–	PC-r	1	1	3	6	9	16	23	30
3	167	4/64	PC-r	1	1	3	6	9	16	23	30

103. Men Against the Sea

Ed	HRN	Date	Details	A	C	GD 2.0	VG 4.0	FN 6.0	VF 8.0	VF/NM 9.0	NM- 9.2
1	104	1/53	Original; Kiefer-c; Palais-a	1	1	11	22	33	64	90	115
2	114	–	PC-r	1	1	4	8	11	16	19	22
3	131	–	New-c; PC-r	1	2	5	10	15	24	30	35
4	158	–	PC-r	1	2	4	7	10	14	17	20
5	149	–	White reorder list; came after HRN-158; PC-r	1	2	5	10	15	22	26	30
6	167	3/64	PC-r	1	2	2	4	6	9	13	16

104. Bring 'Em Back Alive

Ed	HRN	Date	Details	A	C	GD 2.0	VG 4.0	FN 6.0	VF 8.0	VF/NM 9.0	NM- 9.2
1	105	2/53	Original; Kiefer-c/a	1	1	11	22	33	62	86	110
2	118	–	PC-r	1	1	2	4	6	9	13	16
3	133	–	PC-r	1	1	2	4	6	9	13	16
4	150	–	PC-r	1	1	2	4	6	9	13	16
5	158	–	PC-r	1	1	2	4	6	9	13	16
6	167	10/63	PC-r	1	1	2	4	6	8	11	14
7	167	9/65	PC-r	1	1	2	4	6	8	11	14
8	169	Win/69	New price 25¢; stiff-c; PC-r	1	1	2	4	6	8	11	14

105. From the Earth to the Moon

Ed	HRN	Date	Details	A	C	GD 2.0	VG 4.0	FN 6.0	VF 8.0	VF/NM 9.0	NM- 9.2
1	106	3/53	Original; Blum-a	1	1	11	22	33	62	86	110
2	118	–	PC-r	1	1	2	4	6	9	13	16
3	132	–	PC-r	1	1	2	4	6	9	13	16
4	141	–	PC-r	1	1	2	4	6	9	13	16
5	146	–	PC-r	1	1	2	4	6	9	13	16
6	156	–	PC-r	1	1	2	4	6	9	13	16
7	167	–	Has orig. date; PC-r	1	1	2	4	6	8	11	14
8	167	5/64	PC-r	1	1	2	4	6	8	11	14
9	167	5/65	PC-r	1	1	2	4	6	8	11	14
10A	166	10/67	PC-r	1	1	2	4	6	8	11	14
10B	166	10/67	w/Grit ad stapled in book	1	1	9	18	27	59	117	175
11	169	Sm/69	New price 25¢; stiff-c; PC-r	1	1	2	4	6	8	11	14
12	169	Spr/71	PC-r	1	1	2	4	6	8	11	14

106. Buffalo Bill

Ed	HRN	Date	Details	A	C	GD 2.0	VG 4.0	FN 6.0	VF 8.0	VF/NM 9.0	NM- 9.2
1	107	4/53	Orig.; delBourgo-a	1	1	11	22	33	60	83	105
2	118	–	PC-r	1	1	2	4	6	9	13	16
3	132	–	PC-r	1	1	2	4	6	9	13	16
4	142	–	PC-r	1	1	2	4	6	9	13	16
5	161	–	PC-r	1	1	2	4	6	8	11	14
6	167	3/64	PC-r	1	1	2	4	6	8	11	14
7	166	7/67	PC-r	1	1	2	4	6	8	11	14
8	169	Fall/69	PC-r; stiff-c	1	1	2	4	6	8	11	14

107. King of the Khyber Rifles

Ed	HRN	Date	Details	A	C	GD 2.0	VG 4.0	FN 6.0	VF 8.0	VF/NM 9.0	NM- 9.2
1	108	5/53	Original	1	1	11	22	33	60	83	105
2	118	–	PC-r	1	1	2	4	6	9	13	16
3	146	–	PC-r	1	1	2	4	6	9	13	16
4	158	–	PC-r	1	1	2	4	6	9	13	16
5	167	–	Has orig.date; PC-r	1	1	2	4	6	8	11	14
6	167	10/66	PC-r	1	1	2	4	6	8	11	14

108. Knights of the Round Table

Ed	HRN	Date	Details	A	C	GD 2.0	VG 4.0	FN 6.0	VF 8.0	VF/NM 9.0	NM- 9.2
1A	108	6/53	Original; Blum-a	1	1	11	22	33	64	90	115
1B	109	6/53	Original; scarce	1	1	12	24	36	67	94	120
2	117	–	PC-r	1	1	2	4	6	9	13	16
3	165	–	PC-r	1	1	2	4	6	8	11	14
4	167	4/64	PC-r	1	1	2	4	6	8	11	14
5	166	4/67	PC-r	1	1	2	4	6	8	11	14
6	169	Sm/69	New price 25¢; stiff-c; PC-r	1	1	2	4	6	8	11	14

109. Pitcairn's Island

Ed	HRN	Date	Details	A	C	GD 2.0	VG 4.0	FN 6.0	VF 8.0	VF/NM 9.0	NM- 9.2
1	110	7/53	Original; Palais-a	1	1	11	22	33	64	90	115
2	165	–	PC-r	1	1	2	4	6	9	13	16
3	167	3/64	PC-r	1	1	2	4	6	9	13	16
4	166	6/67	PC-r	1	1	2	4	6	9	13	16

110. A Study in Scarlet

Ed	HRN	Date	Details	A	C	GD 2.0	VG 4.0	FN 6.0	VF 8.0	VF/NM 9.0	NM- 9.2
1	111	8/53	Original	1	1	15	30	45	84	127	170
2	165	–	PC-r	1	1	11	22	33	62	86	110

111. The Talisman

Ed	HRN	Date	Details	A	C	GD 2.0	VG 4.0	FN 6.0	VF 8.0	VF/NM 9.0	NM- 9.2
1	112	9/53	Original; last H.C. Kiefer-a	1	1	11	22	33	64	90	115
2	165	–	PC-r	1	1	2	4	6	9	13	16
3	167	5/64	PC-r	1	1	2	4	6	9	13	16
4	166	Fall/68	C-price 25¢; PC-r	1	1	2	4	6	9	13	16

112. Adventures of Kit Carson

Ed	HRN	Date	Details	A	C	GD 2.0	VG 4.0	FN 6.0	VF 8.0	VF/NM 9.0	NM- 9.2
1	113	10/53	Original; Palais-a	1	1	11	22	33	62	86	110
2	129	–	PC-r	1	1	2	4	6	9	13	16
3	141	–	PC-r	1	1	2	4	6	9	13	16
4	152	–	PC-r	1	1	2	4	6	9	13	16
5	161	–	PC-r	1	1	2	4	6	8	11	14
6	167	–	PC-r	1	1	2	4	6	8	11	14
7	167	2/65	PC-r	1	1	2	4	6	8	11	14
8	167	5/66	PC-r	1	1	2	4	6	8	11	14
9	166	Win/69	New-c&price 25¢; PC-r; stiff-c	1	2	3	6	9	14	20	25

113. The Forty-Five Guardsmen

Ed	HRN	Date	Details	A	C	GD 2.0	VG 4.0	FN 6.0	VF 8.0	VF/NM 9.0	NM- 9.2
1	114	11/53	Orig.; delBourgo-a	1	1	14	28	42	76	108	140
2	166	7/67	PC-r	1	1	4	8	12	23	37	50

114. The Red Rover

Ed	HRN	Date	Details	A	C	GD 2.0	VG 4.0	FN 6.0	VF 8.0	VF/NM 9.0	NM- 9.2
1	115	12/53	Original	1	1	14	28	42	76	108	140
2	166	7/67	PC-r	1	1	4	8	12	23	37	50

115. How I Found Livingstone

Ed	HRN	Date	Details	A	C	GD 2.0	VG 4.0	FN 6.0	VF 8.0	VF/NM 9.0	NM- 9.2
1	116	1/54	Original	1	1	14	28	42	80	115	150
2	167	1/67	PC-r	1	1	4	8	12	27	44	60

116. The Bottle Imp

Ed	HRN	Date	Details	A	C	GD 2.0	VG 4.0	FN 6.0	VF 8.0	VF/NM 9.0	NM- 9.2
1	117	2/54	Orig.; Cameron-a	1	1	14	28	42	80	115	150
2	167	1/67	PC-r	1	1	4	8	12	27	44	60

117. Captains Courageous

Classics Illustrated #122 © GIL

Classics Illustrated #127 © GIL

Classics Illustrated #132 © GIL

Ed	HRN	Date	Details	A	C	GD 2.0	VG 4.0	FN 6.0	VF 8.0	VF/NM 9.0	NM- 9.2
1	118	3/54	Orig.; Costanza-a	1	1	13	26	39	74	105	135
2	167	2/67	PC-r	1	1	3	6	9	14	20	26
3	169	Fall/69	New price 25¢; stiff-c; PC-r	1	1	3	6	9	14	20	26

118. Rob Roy

Ed	HRN	Date	Details	A	C	GD 2.0	VG 4.0	FN 6.0	VF 8.0	VF/NM 9.0	NM- 9.2
1	119	4/54	Original; Rudy & Walter Palais-a	1	1	14	28	42	80	115	150
2	167	2/67	PC-r	1	1	4	8	12	27	44	60

119. Soldiers of Fortune

Ed	HRN	Date	Details	A	C	GD 2.0	VG 4.0	FN 6.0	VF 8.0	VF/NM 9.0	NM- 9.2
1	120	5/54	Schaffenberger-a	1	1	13	26	39	72	101	130
2	166	3/67	PC-r	1	1	3	6	9	14	20	26
3	169	Spr/70	New price 25¢; stiff-c; PC-r	1	1	3	6	9	14	20	26

120. The Hurricane

Ed	HRN	Date	Details	A	C	GD 2.0	VG 4.0	FN 6.0	VF 8.0	VF/NM 9.0	NM- 9.2
1	121	6/54	Orig.; Cameron-a	1	1	13	26	39	72	101	130
2	166	3/67	PC-r	1	1	4	8	12	22	34	50

121. Wild Bill Hickok

Ed	HRN	Date	Details	A	C	GD 2.0	VG 4.0	FN 6.0	VF 8.0	VF/NM 9.0	NM- 9.2
1	122	7/54	Original	1	1	11	22	33	60	83	105
2	132	–	PC-r	1	1	2	4	6	9	13	16
3	141	–	PC-r	1	1	2	4	6	9	13	16
4	154	–	PC-r	1	1	2	4	6	9	13	16
5	167	–	PC-r	1	1	2	4	6	8	11	14
6	167	8/64	PC-r	1	1	2	4	6	8	11	14
7	166	4/67	PC-r	1	1	2	4	6	8	11	14
8	169	Win/69	PC-r; stiff-c	1	1	2	4	6	8	11	14

122. The Mutineers

Ed	HRN	Date	Details	A	C	GD 2.0	VG 4.0	FN 6.0	VF 8.0	VF/NM 9.0	NM- 9.2
1	123	9/54	Original	1	1	11	22	33	64	90	115
2	136	–	PC-r	1	1	2	4	6	9	13	16
3	146	–	PC-r	1	1	2	4	6	9	13	16
4	158	–	PC-r	1	1	2	4	6	9	13	16
5	167	11/63	PC-r	1	1	2	4	6	8	11	14
6	167	3/65	PC-r	1	1	2	4	6	8	11	14
7	166	8/67	PC-r	1	1	2	4	6	8	11	14

123. Fang and Claw

Ed	HRN	Date	Details	A	C	GD 2.0	VG 4.0	FN 6.0	VF 8.0	VF/NM 9.0	NM- 9.2
1	124	11/54	Original	1	1	11	22	33	64	90	115
2	133	–	PC-r	1	1	2	4	6	9	13	16
3	143	–	PC-r	1	1	2	4	6	9	13	16
4	154	–	PC-r	1	1	2	4	6	9	13	16
5	167	–	Has orig.date; PC-r	1	1	2	4	6	8	11	14
6	167	9/65	PC-r	1	1	2	4	6	8	11	14

124. The War of the Worlds

Ed	HRN	Date	Details	A	C	GD 2.0	VG 4.0	FN 6.0	VF 8.0	VF/NM 9.0	NM- 9.2
1	125	1/55	Original; Cameron-c/a	1	1	14	28	42	80	115	150
2	131	–	PC-r	1	1	2	4	6	10	14	18
3	141	–	PC-r	1	1	2	4	6	10	14	18
4	148	–	PC-r	1	1	2	4	6	10	14	18
5	156	–	PC-r	1	1	2	4	6	10	14	18
6	165	–	PC-r	1	1	2	4	6	13	18	22
7	167	–	PC-r	1	1	2	4	6	9	13	16
8	167	11/64	PC-r	1	1	2	4	6	10	14	18
9	167	11/65	PC-r	1	1	2	4	6	9	13	16
10	166	R/1968	C-price 25¢; PC-r	1	1	2	4	6	9	13	16
11	169	Sm/70	PC-r; stiff-c	1	1	2	4	6	9	13	16

125. The Ox Bow Incident

Ed	HRN	Date	Details	A	C	GD 2.0	VG 4.0	FN 6.0	VF 8.0	VF/NM 9.0	NM- 9.2
1	–	3/55	Original; Picture Progress replaces reorder list	1	1	11	22	33	60	83	105
2	143	–	PC-r	1	1	2	4	6	9	13	16
3	152	–	PC-r	1	1	2	4	6	9	13	16
4	149	–	PC-r	1	1	2	4	6	9	13	16
5	167	–	PC-r	1	1	2	4	6	8	11	14
6	167	11/64	PC-r	1	1	2	4	6	8	11	14
7	166	4/67	PC-r	1	1	2	4	6	8	11	14
8	169	Win/69	New price 25¢; stiff-c; PC-r	1	1	2	4	6	8	11	14

126. The Downfall

Ed	HRN	Date	Details	A	C	GD 2.0	VG 4.0	FN 6.0	VF 8.0	VF/NM 9.0	NM- 9.2
1	5/55	–	Orig.; 'Picture Progress' replaces reorder list; Cameron-c/a	1	1	11	22	33	64	90	115
2	167	8/64	PC-r	1	1	2	4	6	13	18	22
3	166	R/1968	C-price 25¢; PC-r	1	1	2	4	6	13	18	22

127. The King of the Mountains

Ed	HRN	Date	Details	A	C	GD 2.0	VG 4.0	FN 6.0	VF 8.0	VF/NM 9.0	NM- 9.2
1	128	7/55	Original	1	1	11	22	33	64	90	115
2	167	6/64	PC-r	1	1	2	4	6	11	16	20
3	166	F/1968	C-price 25¢; PC-r	1	1	2	4	6	11	16	20

128. Macbeth (Used in **POP**, pg. 102)

Ed	HRN	Date	Details	A	C	GD 2.0	VG 4.0	FN 6.0	VF 8.0	VF/NM 9.0	NM- 9.2
1	128	9/55	Orig.; last Blum-a	1	1	11	22	33	64	90	115
2	143	–	PC-r	1	1	2	4	6	9	13	16
3	158	–	PC-r	1	1	2	4	6	9	13	16
4	167	–	PC-r	1	1	2	4	6	8	11	14
5	167	6/64	PC-r	1	1	2	4	6	8	11	14
6	166	4/67	PC-r	1	1	2	4	6	8	11	14
7	166	R/1968	C-Price 25¢; PC-r	1	1	2	4	6	8	11	14
8	169	Spr/70	Stiff-c; PC-r	1	1	2	4	6	8	11	14

129. Davy Crockett

Ed	HRN	Date	Details	A	C	GD 2.0	VG 4.0	FN 6.0	VF 8.0	VF/NM 9.0	NM- 9.2
1	129	11/55	Orig.; Cameron-a	1	1	14	28	42	82	121	160
2	167	9/66	PC-r	1	1	11	22	33	62	86	110

130. Caesar's Conquests

Ed	HRN	Date	Details	A	C	GD 2.0	VG 4.0	FN 6.0	VF 8.0	VF/NM 9.0	NM- 9.2
1	130	1/56	Original; Orlando-a	1	1	11	22	33	64	90	115
2	142	–	PC-r	1	1	2	4	6	9	13	16
3	152	–	PC-r	1	1	2	4	6	9	13	16
4	149	–	PC-r	1	1	2	4	6	9	13	16
5	167	–	PC-r	1	1	2	4	6	8	11	14
6	167	10/64	PC-r	1	1	2	4	6	8	11	14
7	167	4/66	PC-r	1	1	2	4	6	8	11	14

131. The Covered Wagon

Ed	HRN	Date	Details	A	C	GD 2.0	VG 4.0	FN 6.0	VF 8.0	VF/NM 9.0	NM- 9.2
1	131	3/56	Original	1	1	6	12	18	40	73	105
2	143	–	PC-r	1	1	2	4	6	9	13	16
3	152	–	PC-r	1	1	2	4	6	9	13	16
4	158	–	PC-r	1	1	2	4	6	9	13	16
5	167	–	PC-r	1	1	2	4	6	8	11	14
6	167	11/64	PC-r	1	1	2	4	6	8	11	14
7	167	4/66	PC-r	1	1	2	4	6	8	11	14
8	169	Win/69	New price 25¢; stiff-c; PC-r	1	1	2	4	6	8	11	14

132. The Dark Frigate

Ed	HRN	Date	Details	A	C	GD 2.0	VG 4.0	FN 6.0	VF 8.0	VF/NM 9.0	NM- 9.2
1	132	5/56	Original	1	1	11	22	33	64	90	115
2	150	–	PC-r	1	1	2	4	6	9	13	16
3	167	1/64	PC-r	1	1	2	4	6	9	13	16
4	166	5/67	PC-r	1	1	2	4	6	9	13	16

133. The Time Machine

Ed	HRN	Date	Details	A	C	GD 2.0	VG 4.0	FN 6.0	VF 8.0	VF/NM 9.0	NM- 9.2
1	132	7/56	Orig.; Cameron-a	1	1	7	14	21	46	86	125
2	142	–	PC-r	1	1	2	4	6	10	14	18
3	152	–	PC-r	1	1	2	4	6	10	14	18
4	158	–	PC-r	1	1	2	4	6	9	13	16
5	167	–	PC-r	1	1	2	4	6	9	13	16
6	167	6/64	PC-r	1	1	2	4	6	10	14	18
7	167	3/66	PC-r	1	1	2	4	6	9	13	16
8	166	12/67	PC-r	1	1	2	4	6	9	13	16
9	169	Win/71	New price 25¢; stiff-c; PC-r	1	1	2	4	6	9	13	16

134. Romeo and Juliet

Ed	HRN	Date	Details	A	C	GD 2.0	VG 4.0	FN 6.0	VF 8.0	VF/NM 9.0	NM- 9.2
1	134	9/56	Original; Evans-a	1	1	6	12	18	42	79	115
2	161	–	PC-r	1	1	2	4	6	9	13	16

Classics Illustrated #140 © GIL

Classics Illustrated #146 © GIL

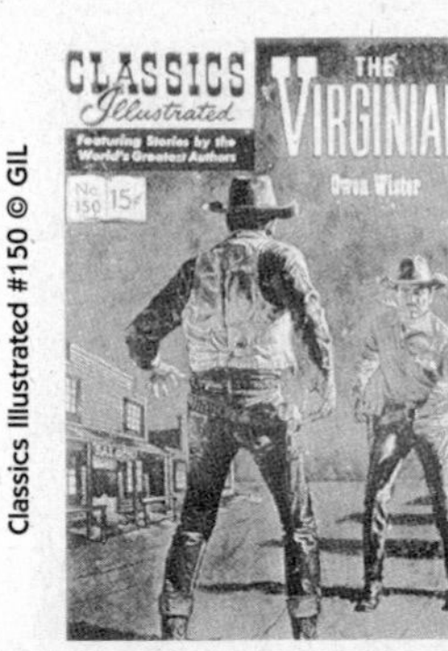

Classics Illustrated #150 © GIL

Ed	HRN	Date	Details	A	C	GD 2.0	VG 4.0	FN 6.0	VF 8.0	VF/NM 9.0	NM- 9.2
3	167	9/63	PC-r	1	1	2	4	6	8	11	14
4	167	5/65	PC-r	1	1	2	4	6	8	11	14
5	166	6/67	PC-r	1	1	2	4	6	8	11	14
6	166	Win/69	New c&price 25¢; stiff-c; PC-r	1	2	3	6	9	17	25	32

135. Waterloo

Ed	HRN	Date	Details	A	C	GD 2.0	VG 4.0	FN 6.0	VF 8.0	VF/NM 9.0	NM- 9.2
1	135	11/56	Orig.; G. Ingels-a	1	1	6	12	18	42	79	115
2	153	–	PC-r	1	1	2	4	6	9	13	16
3	167	–	PC-r	1	1	2	4	6	8	11	14
4	167	9/64	PC-r	1	1	2	4	6	8	11	14
5	166	R/1968	C-price 25¢; PC-r	1	1	2	4	6	8	11	14

136. Lord Jim

Ed	HRN	Date	Details	A	C	GD 2.0	VG 4.0	FN 6.0	VF 8.0	VF/NM 9.0	NM- 9.2
1	136	1/57	Original; Evans-a	1	1	6	12	18	42	79	115
2	165	–	PC-r	1	1	2	4	6	8	11	14
3	167	3/64	PC-r	1	1	2	4	6	8	11	14
4	167	9/66	PC-r	1	1	2	4	6	8	11	14
5	169	Sm/69	New price 25 ¢; stiff-c; PC-r	1	1	2	4	6	8	11	14

137. The Little Savage

Ed	HRN	Date	Details	A	C	GD 2.0	VG 4.0	FN 6.0	VF 8.0	VF/NM 9.0	NM- 9.2
1	136	3/57	Original; Evans-a	1	1	6	12	18	42	79	115
2	148	–	PC-r	1	1	2	4	6	9	13	16
3	156	–	PC-r	1	1	2	4	6	9	13	16
4	167	–	PC-r	1	1	2	4	6	8	11	14
5	167	10/64	PC-r	1	1	2	4	6	8	11	14
6	166	8/67	PC-r	1	1	2	4	6	8	11	14
7	169	Spr/70	New price 25¢; stiff-c; PC-r	1	1	2	4	6	8	11	14

138. A Journey to the Center of the Earth

Ed	HRN	Date	Details	A	C	GD 2.0	VG 4.0	FN 6.0	VF 8.0	VF/NM 9.0	NM- 9.2
1	136	5/57	Original	1	1	8	16	24	51	96	140
2	146	–	PC-r	1	1	2	4	6	11	16	20
3	156	–	PC-r	1	1	2	4	6	11	16	20
4	158	–	PC-r	1	1	2	4	6	9	13	16
5	167	–	PC-r	1	1	2	4	6	8	11	14
6	167	6/64	PC-r	1	1	2	4	6	13	18	22
7	167	4/66	PC-r	1	1	2	4	6	13	18	22
8	166	R/68	C-price 25¢; PC-r	1	1	2	4	6	10	14	18

139. In the Reign of Terror

Ed	HRN	Date	Details	A	C	GD 2.0	VG 4.0	FN 6.0	VF 8.0	VF/NM 9.0	NM- 9.2
1	139	7/57	Original; Evans-a	1	1	6	12	18	40	73	105
2	154	–	PC-r	1	1	2	4	6	9	13	16
3	167	–	Has orig.date; PC-r	1	1	2	4	6	8	11	14
4	167	7/64	PC-r	1	1	2	4	6	8	11	14
5	166	R/1968	C-price 25¢; PC-r	1	1	2	4	6	8	11	14

140. On Jungle Trails

Ed	HRN	Date	Details	A	C	GD 2.0	VG 4.0	FN 6.0	VF 8.0	VF/NM 9.0	NM- 9.2
1	140	9/57	Original	1	1	6	12	18	40	73	105
2	150	–	PC-r	1	1	2	4	6	9	13	16
3	160	–	PC-r	1	1	2	4	6	9	13	16
4	167	9/63	PC-r	1	1	2	4	6	8	11	14
5	167	9/65	PC-r	1	1	2	4	6	8	11	14

141. Castle Dangerous

Ed	HRN	Date	Details	A	C	GD 2.0	VG 4.0	FN 6.0	VF 8.0	VF/NM 9.0	NM- 9.2
1	141	11/57	Original	1	1	7	14	21	44	82	120
2	152	–	PC-r	1	1	2	4	6	9	13	16
3	167	–	PC-r	1	1	2	4	6	9	13	16
4	166	7/67	PC-r	1	1	2	4	6	9	13	16

142. Abraham Lincoln

Ed	HRN	Date	Details	A	C	GD 2.0	VG 4.0	FN 6.0	VF 8.0	VF/NM 9.0	NM- 9.2
1	142	1/58	Original	1	1	6	12	18	42	79	115
2	154	–	PC-r	1	1	2	4	6	9	13	16
3	158	–	PC-r	1	1	2	4	6	9	13	16
4	167	10/63	PC-r	1	1	2	4	6	8	11	14
5	167	7/65	PC-r	1	1	2	4	6	8	11	14
6	166	11/67	PC-r	1	1	2	4	6	8	11	14
7	169	Fall/69	New price 25¢; stiff-c; PC-r	1	1	2	4	6	8	11	14

143. Kim

Ed	HRN	Date	Details	A	C	GD 2.0	VG 4.0	FN 6.0	VF 8.0	VF/NM 9.0	NM- 9.2
1	143	3/58	Original; Orlando-a	1	1	6	12	18	40	73	105
2	165	–	PC-r	1	1	2	4	6	8	11	14
3	167	11/63	PC-r	1	1	2	4	6	8	11	14
4	167	8/65	PC-r	1	1	2	4	6	8	11	14
5	169	Win/69	New price 25¢; stiff-c; PC-r	1	1	2	4	6	8	11	14

144. The First Men in the Moon

Ed	HRN	Date	Details	A	C	GD 2.0	VG 4.0	FN 6.0	VF 8.0	VF/NM 9.0	NM- 9.2
1	143	5/58	Original; Woodbridge/Williamson/Torres-a	1	1	7	14	21	46	86	125
2	152	–	(Rare)-PC-r	1	1	8	16	24	51	96	140
3	153	–	PC-r	1	1	2	4	6	9	13	16
4	161	–	PC-r	1	1	2	4	6	8	11	14
5	167	–	PC-r	1	1	2	4	6	8	11	14
6	167	12/65	PC-r	1	1	2	4	6	8	11	14
7	166	Fall/68	New-c&price 25¢; PC-r; stiff-c	1	2	3	6	9	16	23	30
8	169	Win/69	Stiff-c; PC-r	1	2	2	4	6	10	16	20

145. The Crisis

Ed	HRN	Date	Details	A	C	GD 2.0	VG 4.0	FN 6.0	VF 8.0	VF/NM 9.0	NM- 9.2
1	143	7/58	Original; Evans-a	1	1	6	12	18	42	79	115
2	156	–	PC-r	1	1	2	4	6	9	13	16
3	167	10/63	PC-r	1	1	2	4	6	8	11	14
4	167	3/65	PC-r	1	1	2	4	6	8	11	14
5	166	R/68	C-price 25¢; PC-r	1	1	2	4	6	8	11	14

146. With Fire and Sword

Ed	HRN	Date	Details	A	C	GD 2.0	VG 4.0	FN 6.0	VF 8.0	VF/NM 9.0	NM- 9.2
1	143	9/58	Original; Woodbridge-a	1	1	6	12	18	42	79	115
2	156	–	PC-r	1	1	2	4	6	10	14	18
3	167	11/63	PC-r	1	1	2	4	6	9	13	16
4	167	3/65	PC-r	1	1	2	4	6	9	13	16

147. Ben-Hur

Ed	HRN	Date	Details	A	C	GD 2.0	VG 4.0	FN 6.0	VF 8.0	VF/NM 9.0	NM- 9.2
1	147	11/58	Original; Orlando-a	1	1	6	12	18	41	76	110
2	152	–	Scarce; PC-r	1	1	6	12	18	42	79	115
3	153	–	PC-r	1	1	2	4	6	9	13	16
4	158	–	PC-r	1	1	2	4	6	9	13	16
5	167	–	Orig.date; but PC-r	1	1	2	4	6	8	11	14
6	167	2/65	PC-r	1	1	2	4	6	8	11	14
7	167	9/66	PC-r	1	1	2	4	6	8	11	14
8A	166	Fall/68	New-c&price 25¢; PC-r; soft-c	1	2	3	6	9	16	24	32
8B	166	Fall/68	New-c&price 25¢; PC-r; stiff-c; scarce	1	2	3	6	9	21	33	45

148. The Buccaneer

Ed	HRN	Date	Details	A	C	GD 2.0	VG 4.0	FN 6.0	VF 8.0	VF/NM 9.0	NM- 9.2
1	148	1/59	Orig.; Evans/Jenny-a; Saunders-c	1	1	6	12	18	40	73	105
2	568	–	Juniors list only PC-r	1	1	2	4	6	9	13	16
3	167	–	PC-r	1	1	2	4	6	8	11	14
4	167	9/65	PC-r	1	1	2	4	6	8	11	14
5	169	Sm/69	New price 25¢; PC-r; stiff-c	1	1	2	4	6	8	11	14

149. Off on a Comet

Ed	HRN	Date	Details	A	C	GD 2.0	VG 4.0	FN 6.0	VF 8.0	VF/NM 9.0	NM- 9.2
1	149	3/59	Orig.;G.McCann-a; blue reorder list	1	1	6	12	18	42	79	115
2	155	–	PC-r	1	1	2	4	6	9	13	16
3	149	–	PC-r; white reorder list; no coming-next ad	1	1	2	4	6	9	13	16
4	167	12/63	PC-r	1	1	2	4	6	8	11	14
5	167	2/65	PC-r	1	1	2	4	6	8	11	14
6	167	10/66	PC-r	1	1	2	4	6	8	11	14
7	166	Fall/68	New-c & price 25¢; PC-r	1	2	3	6	9	16	23	30

150. The Virginian

Ed	HRN	Date	Details	A	C

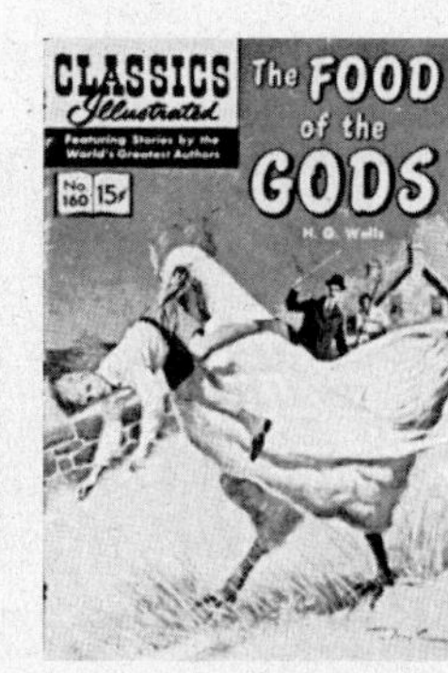

Classics Illustrated #160 © GIL

Classics Illustrated #162 © GIL

Classics Illustrated #167 © GIL

Ed	HRN	Date	Details	A	C	GD 2.0	VG 4.0	FN 6.0	VF 8.0	VF/NM 9.0	NM- 9.2
1	150	5/59	Original	1	1	7	14	21	44	82	120
2	164	–	PC-r	1	1	2	4	6	11	16	20
3	167	10/63	PC-r	1	1	3	6	9	15	21	26
4	167	12/65	PC-r	1	1	2	4	6	11	16	20

151. Won By the Sword

Ed	HRN	Date	Details	A	C	GD 2.0	VG 4.0	FN 6.0	VF 8.0	VF/NM 9.0	NM- 9.2
1	150	7/59	Original	1	1	6	12	18	42	79	115
2	164	–	PC-r	1	1	2	4	6	10	14	18
3	167	10/63	PC-r	1	1	2	4	6	10	14	18
4	166	7/67	PC-r	1	1	2	4	6	10	14	18

152. Wild Animals I Have Known

Ed	HRN	Date	Details	A	C	GD 2.0	VG 4.0	FN 6.0	VF 8.0	VF/NM 9.0	NM- 9.2
1	152	9/59	Orig.; L.B. Cole c/a	1	1	7	14	21	46	86	125
2A	149	–	PC-r; white reorder list; no coming-next ad; IBC: Jr. list #572	1	1	2	4	6	9	13	16
2B	149	–	PC-r; inside-bc: Jr. list to #555	1	1	2	4	6	9	13	16
2C	149	–	PC-r; inside-bc: has World Around Us ad; scarce	1	1	3	6	9	15	21	26
3	167	9/63	PC-r	1	1	2	4	6	8	11	14
4	167	8/65	PC-r	1	1	2	4	6	8	11	14
5	169	Fall/69	New price 25¢; stiff-c; PC-r	1	1	2	4	6	8	11	14

153. The Invisible Man

Ed	HRN	Date	Details	A	C	GD 2.0	VG 4.0	FN 6.0	VF 8.0	VF/NM 9.0	NM- 9.2
1	153	11/59	Original	1	1	7	14	21	49	92	135
2A	149	–	PC-r; white reorder list; no coming-next ad; inside-bc: Jr. list to #572	1	1	2	4	6	11	16	20
2B	149	–	PC-r; inside-bc: Jr. list to #555	1	1	2	4	6	13	18	22
3	167	–	PC-r	1	1	2	4	6	9	13	16
4	167	2/65	PC-r	1	1	2	4	6	9	13	16
5	167	9/66	PC-r	1	1	2	4	6	9	13	16
6	166	Win/69	New price 25¢; PC-r; stiff-c	1	1	2	4	6	9	13	16
7	169	Spr/71	Stiff-c; letters spelling 'Invisible Man' are 'solid' not 'invisible;' PC-r	1	1	2	4	6	9	13	16

154. The Conspiracy of Pontiac

Ed	HRN	Date	Details	A	C	GD 2.0	VG 4.0	FN 6.0	VF 8.0	VF/NM 9.0	NM- 9.2
1	154	1/60	Original	1	1	7	14	21	41	82	120
2	167	11/63	PC-r	1	1	2	4	6	13	18	22
3	167	7/64	PC-r	1	1	2	4	6	13	18	22
4	166	12/67	PC-r	1	1	2	4	6	13	18	22

155. The Lion of the North

Ed	HRN	Date	Details	A	C	GD 2.0	VG 4.0	FN 6.0	VF 8.0	VF/NM 9.0	NM- 9.2
1	154	3/60	Original	1	1	6	12	18	42	79	115
2	167	1/64	PC-r	1	1	2	4	6	11	16	20
3	166	R/1967	C-price 25¢; PC-r	1	1	2	4	6	10	14	18

156. The Conquest of Mexico

Ed	HRN	Date	Details	A	C	GD 2.0	VG 4.0	FN 6.0	VF 8.0	VF/NM 9.0	NM- 9.2
1	156	5/60	Orig.; Bruno Premiani-c/a	1	1	6	12	18	42	79	115
2	167	1/64	PC-r	1	1	2	4	6	10	14	18
3	166	8/67	PC-r	1	1	2	4	6	10	14	18
4	169	Spr/70	New price 25¢; stiff-c; PC-r	1	1	2	4	6	9	13	16

157. Lives of the Hunted

Ed	HRN	Date	Details	A	C	GD 2.0	VG 4.0	FN 6.0	VF 8.0	VF/NM 9.0	NM- 9.2
1	156	7/60	Orig.; L.B. Cole-c	1	1	7	14	21	44	82	120
2	167	2/64	PC-r	1	1	2	4	6	13	18	22
3	166	10/67	PC-r	1	1	2	4	6	13	18	22

158. The Conspirators

Ed	HRN	Date	Details	A	C	GD 2.0	VG 4.0	FN 6.0	VF 8.0	VF/NM 9.0	NM- 9.2
1	156	9/60	Original	1	1	7	14	21	44	82	120
2	167	7/64	PC-r	1	1	2	4	6	13	18	22
3	166	10/67	PC-r	1	1	2	4	6	13	18	22

159. The Octopus

Ed	HRN	Date	Details	A	C	GD 2.0	VG 4.0	FN 6.0	VF 8.0	VF/NM 9.0	NM- 9.2
1	159	11/60	Orig.; Gray Morrow-a; L.B. Cole-c	1	1	7	14	21	44	82	120
2	167	2/64	PC-r	1	1	2	4	6	13	18	22
3	166	R/1967	C-price 25¢; PC-r	1	1	2	4	6	13	18	22

160. The Food of the Gods

Ed	HRN	Date	Details	A	C	GD 2.0	VG 4.0	FN 6.0	VF 8.0	VF/NM 9.0	NM- 9.2
1A	159	1/61	Original	1	1	7	14	21	46	86	125
1B	160	1/61	Original; same, except for HRN	1	1	7	14	21	44	82	120
2	167	1/64	PC-r	1	1	2	4	6	13	18	22
3	166	6/67	PC-r	1	1	2	4	6	13	18	22

161. Cleopatra

Ed	HRN	Date	Details	A	C	GD 2.0	VG 4.0	FN 6.0	VF 8.0	VF/NM 9.0	NM- 9.2
1	161	3/61	Original	1	1	7	14	21	44	82	120
2	167	1/64	PC-r	1	1	3	6	9	14	19	24
3	166	8/67	PC-r	1	1	3	6	9	14	19	24

162. Robur the Conqueror

Ed	HRN	Date	Details	A	C	GD 2.0	VG 4.0	FN 6.0	VF 8.0	VF/NM 9.0	NM- 9.2
1	162	5/61	Original	1	1	7	14	21	44	82	120
2	167	7/64	PC-r	1	1	3	6	9	14	19	24
3	166	8/67	PC-r	1	1	3	6	9	14	19	24

163. Master of the World

Ed	HRN	Date	Details	A	C	GD 2.0	VG 4.0	FN 6.0	VF 8.0	VF/NM 9.0	NM- 9.2
1	163	7/61	Original; Gray Morrow-a	1	1	7	14	21	44	82	120
2	167	1/65	PC-r	1	1	2	4	6	13	18	22
3	166	R/1968	C-price 25¢; PC-r	1	1	2	4	6	13	18	22

164. The Cossack Chief

Ed	HRN	Date	Details	A	C	GD 2.0	VG 4.0	FN 6.0	VF 8.0	VF/NM 9.0	NM- 9.2
1	164	(1961)	Orig.; nd(10/61?)	1	1	6	12	18	41	76	110
2	167	4/65	PC-r	1	1	2	4	6	13	18	22
3	166	Fall/68	C-price 25¢; PC-r	1	1	2	4	6	13	18	22

165. The Queen's Necklace

Ed	HRN	Date	Details	A	C	GD 2.0	VG 4.0	FN 6.0	VF 8.0	VF/NM 9.0	NM- 9.2
1	164	1/62	Original; Morrow-a	1	1	7	14	21	44	82	120
2	167	4/65	PC-r	1	1	2	4	6	13	18	22
3	166	Fall/68	C-price 25¢; PC-r	1	1	2	4	6	13	18	22

166. Tigers and Traitors

Ed	HRN	Date	Details	A	C	GD 2.0	VG 4.0	FN 6.0	VF 8.0	VF/NM 9.0	NM- 9.2
1	165	5/62	Original	1	1	8	16	24	55	105	155
2	167	2/64	PC-r	1	1	3	6	9	21	33	45
3	167	11/66	PC-r	1	1	3	6	9	21	33	45

167. Faust

Ed	HRN	Date	Details	A	C	GD 2.0	VG 4.0	FN 6.0	VF 8.0	VF/NM 9.0	NM- 9.2
1	165	8/62	Original	1	1	11	22	33	75	160	245
2	167	2/64	PC-r	1	1	5	10	15	34	60	85
3	166	6/67	PC-r	1	1	5	10	15	34	60	85

168. In Freedom's Cause

Ed	HRN	Date	Details	A	C	GD 2.0	VG 4.0	FN 6.0	VF 8.0	VF/NM 9.0	NM- 9.2
1	169	Win/69	Original; Evans/Crandall-a; stiff-c; 25¢; no coming-next ad;	1	1	13	26	39	86	188	290

169. Negro Americans The Early Years

Ed	HRN	Date	Details	A	C	GD 2.0	VG 4.0	FN 6.0	VF 8.0	VF/NM 9.0	NM- 9.2
1	166	Spr/69	Orig. & last issue; 25¢; Stiff-c; no coming-next ad; other sources indicate publication date of 5/69	1	1	12	24	36	80	173	265
2	169	Spr/69	Stiff-c	1	1	7	14	21	44	82	120

NOTE: *Many other titles were prepared or planned but were only issued in British/European series.*

CLASSIC POPEYE (See Popeye, Classic)

CLASSIC PUNISHER (Also see Punisher)
Marvel Comics: Dec, 1989 ($4.95, B&W, deluxe format, 68 pgs.)

1-Reprints Marvel Super Action #1 & Marvel Preview #2 plus new story 5.00

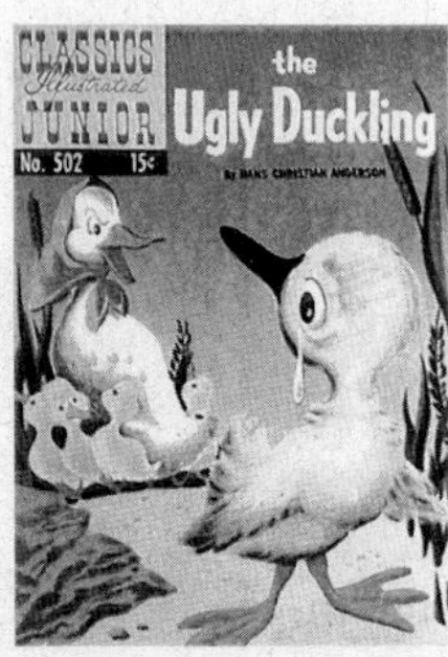

Classics Illustrated Junior #502 © GIL

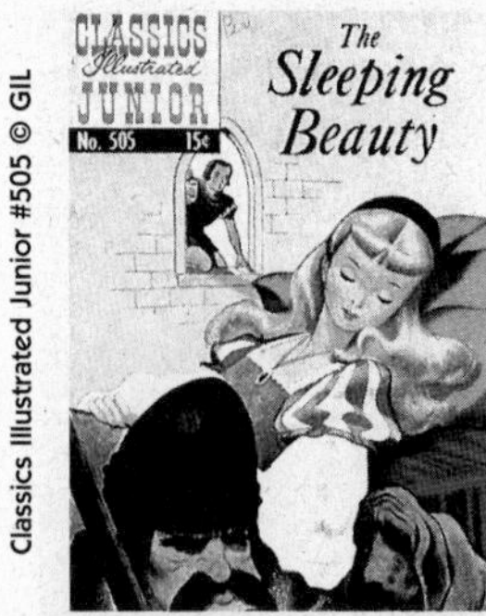

Classics Illustrated Junior #505 © GIL

Classics Illustrated Special Issue #159 © GIL

	GD 2.0	VG 4.0	FN 6.0	VF 8.0	VF/NM 9.0	NM- 9.2

CLASSIC RED SONJA
Dynamite Entertainment: 2010 - No. 4, 2010 ($3.99)

1-4-Newly colored reprints of stories from Savage Sword of Conan magazine 4.00

CLASSICS ILLUSTRATED
First Publishing/Berkley Publishing: Feb, 1990 - No. 27, July, 1991 ($3.75/$3.95, 52 pgs.)

1-27: 1-Gahan Wilson-c/a. 4-Sienkiewicz painted-c/a. 6-Russell scripts/layouts. 7-Spiegle-a. 9-Ploog-c/a. 16-Staton-a. 18-Gahan Wilson-c/a; 20-Geary-a. 26-Aesop's Fables (6/91). 26,27-Direct sale only 5.00

CLASSICS ILLUSTRATED
Acclaim Books/Twin Circle PublishingCo.: Feb, 1997 - Jan, 1998 ($4.99, digest-size) (Each book contains study notes)

A Christmas Carol-(12/97), A Connecticut Yankee in King Arthur's Court-(5/97), All Quiet on the Western Front-(1/98), A Midsummer's Night Dream-(4/97) Around the World in 80 Days-(1/98), A Tale of Two Cities-(2/97)Joe Orlando-r, Captains Courageous-(11/97), Crime and Punishment-(3/97), Dr. Jekyll and Mr. Hyde-(10/97), Don Quixote-(12/97), Frankenstein-(10/97), Great Expectations-(4/97), Hamlet-(3/97), Huckleberry Finn-(3/97), Jane Eyre-(2/97), Kidnapped-(1/98), Les Miserables-(5/97), Lord Jim-(9/97), Macbeth-(5/97), Moby Dick-(4/97), Oliver Twist-(5/97), Robinson Crusoe-(9/97), Romeo & Juliet-(2/97), Silas Marner-(11/97), The Call of the Wild-(9/97), The Count of Monte Cristo-(1/98), The House of the Seven Gables-(9/97), The Iliad-(12/97), The Invisible Man-(10/97), The Last of the Mohicans-(12/97), The Master of Ballantrae-(11/97), The Odyssey-(3/97), The Prince and the Pauper-(4/97), The Red Badge Of Courage-(9/97), Tom Sawyer-(2/97) Wuthering Heights-(11/97) 5.00

NOTE: *Stories reprinted from the original Gilberton Classic Comics and Classics Illustrated.*

CLASSICS ILLUSTRATED GIANTS
Gilberton Publications: Oct, 1949 (One-Shots - "OS")

These Giant Editions, all with new front and back covers, were advertised from 10/49 to 2/52. They were 50¢ on the newsstand and 60¢ by mail. They are actually four Classics in one volume. All the stories are reprints of the Classics Illustrated Series.

NOTE: There were also British hardback Adventure & Indian Giants in 1952, with the same covers but different contents: Adventure - 2, 7, 10; Indian - 17, 22, 37, 58. They are also rare.

	GD	VG	FN	VF	VF/NM	NM-
"An Illustrated Library of Great Adventure Stories" - reprints of No. 6,7,8,10 (Rare); Kiefer-c	152	304	456	965	1658	2350
"An Illustrated Library of Exciting Mystery Stories" - reprints of No. 30,21,40, 13 (Rare); Blum-c	161	322	483	1030	1765	2500
"An Illustrated Library of Great Indian Stories" - reprints of No. 4,17,22,37 (Rare); Blum-c	152	304	456	965	1658	2350

INTRODUCTION TO CLASSICS ILLUSTRATED JUNIOR

Collectors of Juniors can be put into one of two categories: those who want any copy of each title, and those who want all the originals. Those seeking every original and reprint edition are a limited group, primarily because Juniors have no changes in art or covers to spark interest, and because reprints are so low in value it is difficult to get dealers to look for specific reprint editions.

In recent years it has become apparent that most serious Classics collectors seek Junior originals. Those seeking reprints seek them for low cost. This has made the previous note about the comparative market value of reprints inadequate. Three particular reprint editions are worth even more. For the 535-Twin Circle edition, see Giveaways. There are also reprint editions of 501 and 503 which have a full-page bc ad for the very rare Junior record. Those may sell as high as $10-$15 in mint. Original editions of 557 and 558 also have that ad.

There are no reprint editions of 577. The only edition, from 1969, is a 25 cent stiff-cover edition with no ad for the next issue. All other original editions have coming-next ad. But 577, like C.I. #168, was prepared in 1962 but not issued. Copies of 577 can be found in 1963 British/European series, which then continued with dozens of additional new Junior titles.

PRICES LISTED BELOW ARE FOR ORIGINAL EDITIONS, WHICH HAVE AN AD FOR THE NEXT ISSUE.

NOTE: *Non HRN 576 copies- many are written on or colored . Reprints with 576 HRN are worth about 1/3 original prices. All other HRN #'s are 1/2 original price*

CLASSICS ILLUSTRATED JUNIOR
Famous Authors Ltd. (Gilberton Publications): Oct, 1953 - Spring, 1971

	GD	VG	FN	VF	VF/NM	NM-
501-Snow White & the Seven Dwarfs; Alex Blum-a	12	24	36	69	97	125
502-The Ugly Duckling	9	18	27	47	61	75
503-Cinderella	8	16	24	40	50	60
504-512: 504-The Pied Piper. 505-The Sleeping Beauty. 506-The Three Little Pigs. 507-Jack & the Beanstalk. 508-Goldilocks & the Three Bears. 509-Beauty and the Beast. 510-Little Red Riding Hood. 511-Puss-N Boots. 512-Rumpelstiltskin	6	12	18	27	33	38
513-Pinocchio	7	14	21	37	46	55
514-The Steadfast Tin Soldier	8	16	24	44	57	70
515-Johnny Appleseed	6	12	18	27	33	38
516-Aladdin and His Lamp	6	12	18	29	36	42
517-519: 517-The Emperor's New Clothes. 518-The Golden Goose. 519-Paul Bunyan	6	12	18	27	33	38
520-Thumbelina	6	12	18	29	36	42
521-King of the Golden River	6	12	18	27	33	38
522,523,530: 522-The Nightingale. 523-The Gallant Tailor. 530-The Golden Bird	5	10	15	24	30	35
524-The Wild Swans	6	12	18	29	36	42
525,526: 525-The Little Mermaid. 526-The Frog Prince	6	12	18	29	36	42
527-The Golden-Haired Giant	6	12	18	27	33	38
528-The Penny Prince	6	12	18	27	33	38
529-The Magic Servants	6	12	18	27	33	38
531-Rapunzel	6	12	18	27	33	38
532-534: 532-The Dancing Princesses. 533-The Magic Fountain. 534-The Golden Touch	5	10	15	23	28	32
535-The Wizard of Oz	8	16	24	44	57	70
536-The Chimney Sweep	6	12	18	27	33	38
537-The Three Fairies	6	12	18	28	34	40
538-Silly Hans	5	10	15	23	28	32
539-The Enchanted Fish	6	12	18	31	38	45
540-The Tinder-Box	6	12	18	31	38	45
541-Snow White & Rose Red	5	10	15	24	30	35
542-The Donkey's Tale	5	10	15	24	30	35
543-The House in the Woods	6	12	18	27	33	38
544-The Golden Fleece	6	12	18	31	38	45
545-The Glass Mountain	5	10	15	24	30	35
546-The Elves & the Shoemaker	5	10	15	24	30	35
547-The Wishing Table	6	12	18	27	33	38
548-551: 548-The Magic Pitcher. 549-Simple Kate. 550-The Singing Donkey. 551-The Queen Bee	5	10	15	23	28	32
552-The Three Little Dwarfs	6	12	18	27	33	38
553,556: 553-King Thrushbeard. 556-The Elf Mound	5	10	15	23	28	32
554-The Enchanted Deer	6	12	18	29	36	42
555-The Three Golden Apples	5	10	15	24	30	35
557-Silly Willy	6	12	18	28	34	40
558-The Magic Dish; L.B. Cole-c; soft and stiff-c exist on original	7	14	21	35	43	50
559-The Japanese Lantern; 1 pg. Ingels-a; L.B. Cole-c	7	14	21	35	43	50
560-The Doll Princess; L.B. Cole-c	7	14	21	35	43	50
561-Hans Humdrum; L.B. Cole-c	6	12	18	29	36	42
562-The Enchanted Pony; L.B. Cole-c	7	14	21	35	43	50
563,565-568,570: 563-The Wishing Well; L.B. Cole-c. 565-The Silly Princess; L.B. Cole-c. 566-Clumsy Hans; L.B. Cole-c. 567-The Bearskin Soldier; L.B. Cole-c. 570-The Pearl Princess	6	12	18	27	33	38
564-The Salt Mountain; L.B.Cole-c. 568-The Happy Hedgehog; L.B. Cole-c.	6	12	18	28	34	40
569,573: 569-The Three Giants.573-The Crystal Ball	5	10	15	23	28	32
571,572: 571-How Fire Came to the Indians. 572-The Drummer Boy	6	12	18	29	36	42
574-Brightboots	5	10	15	24	30	35
575-The Fearless Prince	6	12	18	28	34	40
576-The Princess Who Saw Everything	7	14	21	35	43	50
577-The Runaway Dumpling	8	16	24	44	57	70

NOTE: *Prices are for original editions. Last reprint - Spring, 1971.* ***Costanza*** *&* ***Schaffenberger*** *art in many issues.*

CLASSICS ILLUSTRATED SPECIAL ISSUE
Gilberton Co.: (Came out semi-annually) Dec, 1955 - Jul, 1962 (35¢, 100 pgs.)

	GD	VG	FN	VF	VF/NM	NM-
129-The Story of Jesus (titled ...Special Edition) "Jesus on Mountain" cover	18	36	54	105	165	225
"Three Camels" cover (12/58)	19	38	57	109	172	235
"Mountain" cover (no date)-Has checklist on inside b/c to HRN #161 & different testimonial on back-c	14	28	42	76	108	140
"Mountain" cover (1968 re-issue; has white 50¢ circle)	10	20	30	56	76	95
132A-The Story of America (6/56); Cameron-a	12	24	36	67	94	120
135A-The Ten Commandments(12/56)	11	22	33	64	90	115
138A-Adventures in Science(6/57); HRN to 137	11	22	33	60	83	105
138A-(6/57)-2nd version w/HRN to 149	7	14	21	35	43	50
138A-(12/61)-3rd version w/HRN to 149	7	14	21	35	43	50
141A-The Rough Rider (Teddy Roosevelt)(12/57); Evans-a	11	22	33	62	86	110
144A-Blazing the Trails West(6/58)- 73 pgs. of Crandall/Evans plus Severin-a	11	22	33	64	90	115
147A-Crossing the Rockies(12/58)-Crandall/Evans-a	11	22	33	62	86	110
150A-Royal Canadian Police(6/59)-Ingels, Sid Check-a	11	22	33	62	86	110
153A-Men, Guns & Cattle(12/59)-Evans-a (26 pgs.); Kinstler-a	11	22	33	62	86	110

Classic Star Wars #4 © Lucasfilm

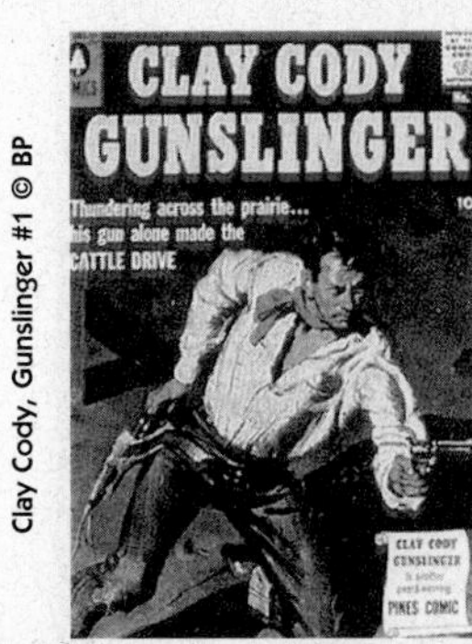

Clay Cody, Gunslinger #1 © BP

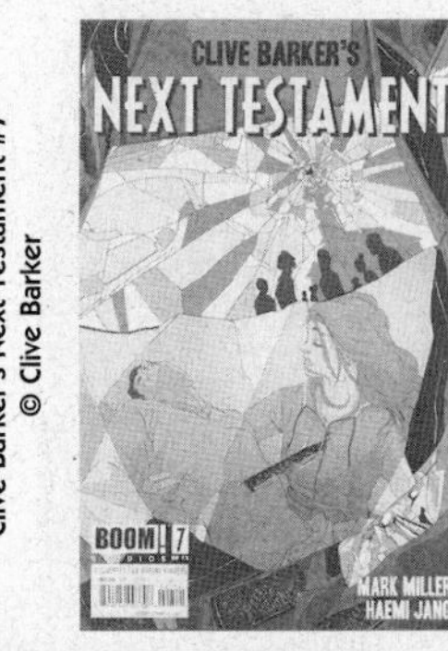

Clive Barker's Next Testament #7 © Clive Barker

GD 2.0 VG 4.0 FN 6.0 VF 8.0 VF/NM 9.0 NM- 9.2

156A-The Atomic Age(6/60)-Crandall/Evans, Torres-a
11 22 33 62 86 110
159A-Rockets, Jets and Missiles(12/60)-Evans, Morrow-a
11 22 33 62 86 110
162A-War Between the States(6/61)-Kirby & Crandall/Evans-a; Ingels-a
17 34 51 100 158 215
165A-To the Stars(12/61)-Torres, Crandall/Evans, Kirby-a
14 28 42 76 108 140
166A-World War II('62)-Torres, Crandall/Evans, Kirby-a
15 30 45 83 124 165
167A-Prehistoric World(7/62)-Torres & Crandall/Evans-a; two versions exist
(HRN to 165 & HRN to 167) 14 28 42 81 118 155
nn Special Issue-The United Nations (1964; 50¢; scarce); this is actually part of the European Special Series, which cont'd on after the U.S. series stopped issuing new titles in 1962. This English edition was prepared specifically for sale at the U.N. It was printed in Norway
50 100 150 315 533 750

NOTE: *There was another U.S. Special Issue prepared in 1962 with artwork by* ***Torres*** *entitled World War I. Unfortunately, it was never issued in any English-language edition. It was issued in 1964 in West Germany, The Netherlands, and some Scandanavian countries, with another edition in 1974 with a new cover.*

CLASSICS LIBRARY (See King Classics)

CLASSIC STAR WARS (Also see Star Wars)
Dark Horse Comics: Aug, 1992 - No. 20, June, 1994 ($2.50)

1-Begin Star Wars strip-r by Williamson; Williamson redrew portions of the panels to fit comic book format 6.00
2-10: 8-Polybagged w/Star Wars Galaxy trading card. 8-M. Schultz-c 4.00
11-19: 13-Yeates-c. 17-M. Schultz-c. 19-Evans-c 3.00
20-($3.50, 52 pgs.)-Polybagged w/trading card 4.00
Escape To Hoth TPB ($16.95) r/#15-20 17.00
The Rebel Storm TPB - r/#8-14 17.00
Trade paperback ($29.95, slip-cased)-Reprints all movie adaptations 30.00
NOTE: *Williamson c-1-5,7,9,10,14,15,20.*

CLASSIC STAR WARS: (Title series). **Dark Horse Comics**

--A NEW HOPE, 6/94 - No. 2, 7/94 ($3.95)
1,2: 1-r/Star Wars #1-3, 7-9 publ; 2-r/Star Wars #4-6, 10-12 publ. by Marvel Comics 4.00

--DEVILWORLDS, 8/96 - No.2, 9/96 ($2.50s)1,2: r/Alan Moore-s 3.00

--HAN SOLO AT STARS' END, 3/97 - No. 3, 5/97 ($2.95)
1-3: r/strips by Alfredo Alcala 3.00

--RETURN OF THE JEDI, 10/94 - No.2, 11/94 ($3.50)
1,2: 1-r/1983-84 Marvel series; polybagged with w/trading card 3.50

--THE EARLY ADVENTURES, 8/94 - No. 9, 4/95 ($2.50)1-9 3.00

--THE EMPIRE STRIKES BACK, 8/94 - No. 2, 9/94 ($3.95)
1-r/Star Wars #39-44 published by Marvel Comics 4.00

CLASSIC X-MEN (Becomes X-Men Classic #46 on)
Marvel Comics Group: Sept, 1986 - No. 45, Mar, 1990

1-Begins-r of New X-Men 6.00
2-10: 10-Sabretooth app. 4.00
11-42,44,45: 11-1st origin of Magneto in back-up story. 17-Wolverine-c. 27-r/X-Men #121. 26-r/X-Men #120; Wolverine-c/app. 35-r/X-Men #129. 39-New Jim Lee back-up story (2nd-a on X-Men) 1 2 3 5 6 8
43-Byrne-c/a(r); ($1.75, double-size) 4.00
NOTE: ***Art Adams*** *c(p)-1-10, 12-16, 18-23.* ***Austin*** *c-10,15-21,24-28i.* ***Bolton*** *back up stories in 1-28,30-35.* ***Williamson*** *c-12-14i.*

CLAW (See Capt. Battle, Jr., Daredevil Comics & Silver Streak Comics)

CLAWS (See Wolverine & Black Cat: Claws 2 for sequel)
Marvel Comics: Oct, 2006 - No. 3, Dec, 2006 ($3.99, limited series)

1-3-Wolverine and Black Cat team-up; Linsner-a/c 4.00
Wolverine & Black Cat: Claws HC (2007, $17.99, dustjacket) r/#1-3 & bonus Linsner art 18.00

CLAW THE UNCONQUERED (See Cancelled Comic Cavalcade)
National Periodical Publications/DC Comics: 5-6/75 - No. 9, 9-10/76; No. 10, 4-5/78 - No. 12, 8-9/78

1-1st app. Claw 2 4 6 8 10 12
2-12: 3-Nudity panel. 9-Origin 1 2 3 4 5 7
NOTE: ***Giffen*** *a-8-12p.* ***Kubert*** *c-10-12.* ***Layton*** *a-9i, 12i.*

CLAW THE UNCONQUERED (See Red Sonja/Claw: The Devil's Hands)
DC Comics: Aug, 2006 - No. 6, Jan, 2007 ($2.99)

1-6: 1,2-Chuck Dixon-s/Andy Smith; two covers by Smith & Van Sciver 3.00
TPB (2007, $17.99) r/#1-6; cover gallery 18.00

CLAY CODY, GUNSLINGER
Pines Comics: Fall, 1957

1-Painted-c 6 12 18 31 38 45

CLEAN FUN, STARRING "SHOOGAFOOTS JONES"
Specialty Book Co.: 1944 (10¢, B&W, oversized covers, 24 pgs.)

nn-Humorous situations involving Negroes in the Deep South
White cover issue... 21 42 63 122 199 275
Dark grey cover issue... 21 42 63 126 206 285

CLEMENTINA THE FLYING PIG (See Dell Jr. Treasury)

CLEOPATRA (See Ideal, a Classical Comic No. 1)

CLERKS: THE COMIC BOOK (Also see Tales From the Clerks and Oni Double Feature #1)
Oni Press: Feb, 1998 ($2.95, B&W, one-shot)

1-Kevin Smith-s 2 4 6 11 16 20
1-Second printing 4.00
...Holiday Special (12/98, $2.95) Smith-s 5.00
...The Lost Scene (12/99, $2.95) Smith-s/Hester-a 5.00

CLIFFHANGER (See Battle Chasers, Crimson, and Danger Girl)
WildStorm Prod./Wizard Press: 1997 (Wizard supplement)

0-Sketchbook preview of Cliffhanger titles 6.00

CLIMAX! (Mystery)
Gillmor Magazines: July, 1955 - No. 2, Sept, 1955

1 17 34 51 98 154 210
2 14 28 42 76 108 140

CLINT (Also see Adolescent Radioactive Black Belt Hamsters)
Eclipse Comics: Sept, 1986 - No. 2, Jan, 1987 ($1.50, B&W)

1,2 3.00

CLINT & MAC (TV, Disney)
Dell Publishing Co.: No. 889, Mar, 1958

Four Color 889-Alex Toth-a, photo-c 10 20 30 64 132 200

CLIVE BARKER'S BOOK OF THE DAMNED: A HELLRAISER COMPANION
Marvel Comics (Epic): Oct, 1991 - No. 3, Nov, 1992 ($4.95, semi-annual)

Volume 1-3-(52 pgs.): 1-Simon Bisley-c. 2-(4/92). 3-(11/92)-McKean-a (1 pg.) 5.00

CLIVE BARKER'S HELLRAISER (Also see Epic, Hellraiser Nightbreed –Jihad, Revelations, Son of Celluloid, Tapping the Vein & Weaveworld)
Marvel Comics (Epic Comics): 1989 - No. 20, 1993 ($4.50-6.95, mature, quarterly, 68 pgs.)

Book 1-4,10-16,18,19: Based on Hellraiser & Hellbound movies; Bolton-c/a; Spiegle & Wrightson-a (graphic album). 10-Foil-c. 12-Sam Kieth-a 6.00
Book 5-9 ($5.95): 7-Bolton-a. 8-Morrow-a 6.00
Book 17-Alex Ross-a, 34 pgs. 2 4 6 8 10 12
Book 20-By Gaiman/McKean 1 2 3 5 6 8
...Collected Best (Checker Books, '02, $21.95)-r/by various incl. Ross, Gaiman, Mignola 22.00
...Collected Best II ('03, $19.95)-r/by various incl. Bolton, L. Wachowski, Dorman 20.00
...Collected Best III ('04, $26.95)-r/by various incl. Bolton, L. Wachowski, Wrightson 27.00
...Dark Holiday Special ('92, $4.95)-Conrad-a 6.00
...Spring Slaughter 1 ('94, $6.95, 52 pgs.)-Painted-c 7.00
...Summer Special 1 ('92, $5.95, 68 pgs.) 6.00

CLIVE BARKER'S HELLRAISER
BOOM! Studios: Mar, 2011 - No. 20, Nov, 2012 ($3.99)

1-20: 1-Barker & Monfette-s/Manco-a; preview of Hellraiser Masterpieces; 3 covers 4.00
Annual 1 (3/12, $4.99) Hervás-a; three covers 5.00
2013 Annual (10/13, $4.99) Seifert-s/Hervás-a; Barker & Meares-s/Ordon-a 5.00
... Masterpieces 1-12 (11/11 - No. 12, 4/12, $3.99) reps from Marvel series. 1-Wrightson-a 4.00
...: The Dark Watch 1-12 (2/13 - No. 12, 1/14, $3.99) Tom Garcia-a; multiple covers 4.00
...: The Road Below 1-4 (10/12 - No. 4, 1/13, $3.99) Haemi Jang-a; multiple covers 4.00

CLIVE BARKER'S NEXT TESTAMENT
BOOM! Studios: May, 2013 - No. 12 ($3.99)

1-8: 1-Clive Barker & Mark Miller-s/Haemi Jang-a. 1-Four covers 4.00

CLIVE BARKER'S NIGHTBREED (Also see Epic)
Marvel Comics (Epic Comics): Apr, 1990 - No. 25, Mar, 1993 ($1.95/$2.25/$2.50, mature)

1-25: 1-4-Adapt horror movie. 5-New stories; Guice-a(p) 3.00

CLIVE BARKER'S THE HARROWERS
Marvel Comics (Epic Comics): Dec, 1993 - No. 6, May, 1994 ($2.50)

1-($2.95)-Glow-in-the-dark-c; Colan-c/a in all 4.00
2-6 3.00
NOTE: ***Colan*** *a(p)-1-6; c-1-3, 4p, 5p.* ***Williamson*** *a(i)-2, 4, 5(part).*

CLOAK AND DAGGER
Ziff-Davis Publishing Co.: Fall, 1952

Cloak and Dagger #4 © MAR

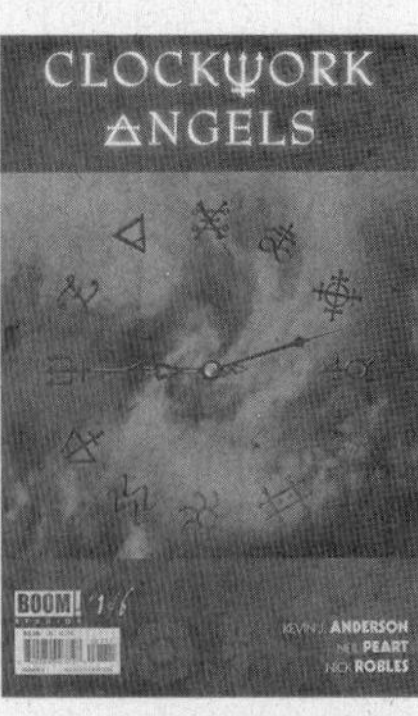
Clockwork Angels #1 © Core Music

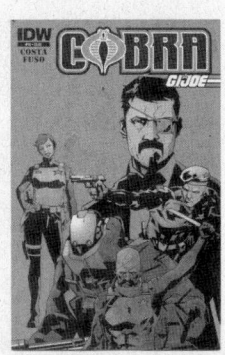

Cobra #18 © Hasbro

GD 2.0 VG 4.0 FN 6.0 VF 8.0 VF/NM 9.0 NM- 9.2

1-Saunders painted-c 32 64 96 192 314 435

CLOAK AND DAGGER (Also see Marvel Fanfare and Spectacular Spider-Man #64)
Marvel Comics Group: Oct, 1983 - No. 4, Jan, 1984 (Mini-series)

1-4-Austin-c/a(i) in all. 4-Origin 4.00

CLOAK AND DAGGER (2nd Series)(Also see Marvel Graphic Novel #34 & Strange Tales)
Marvel Comics Group: July, 1985 - No. 11, Jan, 1987

1-11: 9-Art Adams-p 3.00
...And Power Pack (1990, $7.95, 68 pgs.) 8.00
NOTE: *Mignola c-7, 8.*

CLOAK AND DAGGER (3rd Series listed as Mutant Misadventures Of...)

CLOAK AND DAGGER
Marvel Comics: May, 2010 ($3.99, one-shot)

1-Stuart Moore-s/Mark Brooks-a; X-Men app. 4.00

CLOBBERIN' TIME
Marvel Comics: Sept, 1995 ($1.95) (Based on card game)

nn-Overpower game guide; Ben Grimm story 3.00

CLOCK MAKER, THE
Image Comics: Jan, 2003 - No. 4, May, 2003 ($2.50, comic unfolds to 10"x13" pages)

1-4-Krueger-s 3.00
... Act Two (4/04, $4.95, standard format) Krueger-s/Matt Smith-c 5.00

CLOCKWORK ANGELS (Based on Neil Peart's story and lyrics from Rush's album)
BOOM! Studios: Mar, 2014 - No. 6 ($3.99, limited series)

1-Kevin J. Anderson-s/Nick Robles-a; two covers 4.00

CLONEZONE SPECIAL
Dark Horse Comics/First Comics: 1989 ($2.00, B&W)

1-Back-up series from Badger & Nexus 3.00

CLOSE ENCOUNTERS (See Marvel Comics Super Special & Marvel Special Edition)

CLOSE SHAVES OF PAULINE PERIL, THE (TV cartoon)
Gold Key: June, 1970 - No. 4, March, 1971

1 4 8 12 23 37 50
2-4 3 6 9 16 23 30

CLOWN COMICS (No. 1 titled Clown Comic Book)
Clown Comics/Home Comics/Harvey Publ.: 1945 - No. 3, Win, 1946

nn (#1) 14 28 42 76 108 140
2,3 9 18 27 47 61 75

CLOUDBURST
Image Comics: June, 2004 ($7.95, squarebound)

1-Gray & Palmiotti-s/Shy & Gouveia-a 8.00

CLOUDFALL
Image Comics: Nov, 2003 ($4.95, B&W, squarebound)

1-Kirkman-s/Su-a/c 5.00

CLOWNS, THE (I Pagliacci)
Dark Horse Comics: 1998 ($2.95, B&W, one-shot)

1-Adaption of the opera; P. Craig Russell-script 3.00

CLUBHOUSE RASCALS (#1 titled ...Presents?) (Also see Three Rascals)
Sussex Publ. Co. (Magazine Enterprises): June, 1956 - No. 2, Oct, 1956

1-The Brain app. in both; DeCarlo-a 8 16 24 44 57 70
2 7 14 21 35 43 50

CLUB "16"
Famous Funnies: June, 1948 - No. 4, Dec, 1948

1-Teen-age humor 14 28 42 76 108 140
2-4 8 16 24 44 57 70

CLUE COMICS (Real Clue Crime V2#4 on)
Hillman Periodicals: Jan, 1943 - No. 15(V2#3), May, 1947

1-Origin The Boy King, Nightmare, Micro-Face, Twilight, & Zippo
181 362 543 1158 1979 2800
2 (scarce) 84 168 252 538 919 1300
3-5 (9/43) 45 90 135 284 480 675
6,8,9: 8-Palais-c/a(2) 34 68 102 206 336 465
7-Classic concentration camp torture-c (3/44) 71 142 213 454 777 1100
10-Origin/1st app. The Gun Master & begin series; content changes to crime
(10/46) 36 72 108 216 351 485
11 (12/46) 25 50 75 150 245 340
12-Origin Rackman; McWilliams-a, Guardineer-a(2) 31 62 93 182 296 410
V2#1-Nightmare new origin; Iron Lady app.; Simon & Kirby-a (3/47)
54 108 162 343 574 825
V2#2-S&K-a(2)-Bondage/torture-c; man attacks & kills people with electric iron.
Infantino-a 70 140 210 445 765 1085
V2#3-S&K-a(3) 55 110 165 352 601 850

CLUELESS SPRING SPECIAL (TV)
Marvel Comics: May, 1997 ($3.99, magazine sized, one-shot)

1-Photo-c from TV show 4.00

CLUTCHING HAND, THE
American Comics Group: July-Aug, 1954

1-Gustavson, Moldoff-a 41 82 123 256 428 600

CLYDE BEATTY COMICS (Also see Crackajack Funnies)
Commodore Productions & Artists, Inc.: October, 1953 (84 pgs.)

1-Photo front/back-c; movie scenes and comics 22 44 66 132 216 300

CLYDE CRASHCUP (TV)
Dell Publishing Co.: Aug-Oct, 1963 - No. 5, Sept-Nov, 1964

1-All written by John Stanley 6 12 18 41 76 110
2-5 4 8 12 27 44 60

COBB
IDW Publishing: May, 2006 - No. 3, July, 2007 ($3.99, B&W)

1-3-Beau Smith-s/Eduardo Barreto-a/c; regular and retailer incentive covers 4.00

COBRA (G.I. Joe)
IDW Publishing: No. 10, Feb, 2012 - No. 21, Jan, 2013 ($3.99)

10-21 4.00
... Annual 2012: The Origin of Cobra Commander (1/12, $7.99) Dixon-s 8.00

CODENAME: ACTION
Dynamite Entertainment: 2013 - No. 5, 2014 ($3.99, limited series)

1-5-Captain Action; Chris Roberson-s/Jonathan Lau-a; multiple covers on each 4.00

CODE NAME: ASSASSIN (See 1st Issue Special)

CODENAME: DANGER
Lodestone Publishing: Aug, 1985 - No. 4, May, 1986 ($1.50)

1-4 3.00

CODENAME: FIREARM (Also see Firearm)
Malibu Comics (Ultraverse): June, 1995 - No. 5, Sept, 1995 ($2.95, bimonthly limited series)

0-5: 0-2-Alec Swan back-up story by James Robinson 3.00
NOTE: *Perez c-0.*

CODENAME: GENETIX
Marvel Comics UK: Jan, 1993 - No. 4, May, 1993 ($1.75, limited series)

1-4: Wolverine in all 3.00

CODENAME: KNOCKOUT
DC Comics (Vertigo): No. 0, Jun, 2001 - No. 23, June, 2003 ($2.50/$2.75)

0-15: Rodi-s in all. 0-5-Small Jr. -a. 1-Two covers by Chiodo & Cho. 7,8,10,11,12-Paquette-a.
6,9,13,14-Conner-a 3.00
16-23: 16-Begin $2.75-c. 23-Last issue; JG Jones-c 3.00

CODENAME SPITFIRE (Formerly Spitfire And The Troubleshooters)
Marvel Comics Group: No. 10, July, 1987 - No. 13, Oct, 1987

10-13: 10-Rogers-c/a (low printing) 3.50

CODENAME: STRYKE FORCE (Also See Cyberforce V1#4 & Cyberforce/Stryke Force: Opposing Forces
Image Comics (Top Cow Productions): Jan, 1994 - No. 14, Sept, 1995 ($1.95-$2.25)

0,1-14: 1-12-Silvestri stories, Peterson-a. 4-Stormwatch app. 14-Story continues in
Cyberforce/Stryke Force: Opposing Forces; Turner-a 3.00
1-Gold, 1-Blue 4.00

CODE OF HONOR
Marvel Comics: Feb, 1997 - No. 4, May, 1997 ($5.95, limited series)

1-4-Fully painted by various; Dixon-s 6.00

CODY OF THE PONY EXPRESS (See Colossal Features Magazine)
Fox Features Syndicate: Sept, 1950 (See Women Outlaws)(One shot)

1-Painted-c 14 28 42 82 121 160

CODY OF THE PONY EXPRESS (Buffalo Bill...) (Outlaws of the West #11 on;
Formerly Bullseye)
Charlton Comics: No. 8, Oct, 1955; No. 9, Jan, 1956; No. 10, June, 1956

8-Bullseye on splash pg; not S&K-a 8 16 24 44 57 70

Coffin Hill #1 © Kittridge & Paniagua

The Colonized #1 © Ryall & IDW

Combat Kelly #1 © MAR

	GD 2.0	VG 4.0	FN 6.0	VF 8.0	VF/NM 9.0	NM- 9.2
9,10: Buffalo Bill app. in all	6	12	18	29	36	42

CODY STARBUCK (1st app. in Star Reach #1)
Star Reach Productions: July, 1978

	GD	VG	FN	VF	VF/NM	NM-
nn-Howard Chaykin-c/a	3	6	9	14	20	25
2nd printing	2	4	6	8	10	12

NOTE: *Both printings say First Printing. True first printing is on lower-grade paper, somewhat off-register, and snow in snow sequence has green tint.*

CO-ED ROMANCES
P. L. Publishing Co.: November, 1951

	GD	VG	FN	VF	VF/NM	NM-
1	10	20	30	56	76	95

COFFEE WORLD
World Comics: Oct, 1995 ($1.50, B&W, anthology)

1-Shannon Wheeler's Too Much Coffee Man story 3.00

COFFIN, THE
Oni Press: Sept, 2000 - No. 4, May, 2001 ($2.95, B&W, limited series)

1-4-Hester-s/Huddleston-a 3.00
TPB (8/01, $11.95, TPB) r/#1-4 12.00

COFFIN HILL
DC Comics (Vertigo): Dec, 2013 - Present ($2.99)

1-6: 1-Caitlin Kittredge-s/Inaki Miranda-a; covers by Dave Johnson & Gene Ha 3.00

COLDER
Dark Horse Comics: Nov, 2012 - No. 5, Mar, 2013 ($3.99, limited series)

1-5-Tobin-s/Ferreyra-a/c 4.00

COLD WAR
IDW Publishing: Oct, 2011 - No. 4, Jan, 2012 ($3.99, limited series)

1-4-John Byrne-s/a/c; two covers on each 4.00

COLLIDER (See FBP: Federal Bureau Of Physics; title changed after issue #1)

COLLECTORS DRACULA, THE
Millennium Publications: 1994 - No. 2, 1994 ($3.95, color/B&W, 52 pgs., limited series)

1,2-Bolton-a (7 pgs.) 4.00

COLLECTORS ITEM CLASSICS (See Marvel Collectors Item Classics)

COLONIZED, THE
IDW Publishing: Apr, 2013 - No. 4, Jul, 2013 ($3.99, limited series)

1-4-Aliens vs. Zombies; Dave Sim-c/Chris Ryall-s/Drew Moss-a 4.00

COLORS IN BLACK
Dark Horse Comics: Mar, 1995 - No. 4, June, 1995 ($2.95, limited series)

1-4 3.00

COLOSSAL FEATURES MAGAZINE (Formerly I Loved) (See Cody of the Pony Express)
Fox Features Syndicate: No. 33, 5/50 - No. 34, 7/50; No. 3, 9/50 (Based on Columbia serial)

	GD	VG	FN	VF	VF/NM	NM-
33,34: Cody of the Pony Express begins. 33-Painted-c. 34-Photo-c	14	28	42	81	118	155
3-Authentic criminal cases	14	28	42	81	118	155

COLOSSAL SHOW, THE (TV cartoon)
Gold Key: Oct, 1969

	GD	VG	FN	VF	VF/NM	NM-
1	5	10	15	30	50	70

COLOSSUS (See X-Men)
Marvel Comics: Oct, 1997 ($2.99, 48 pgs., one-shot)

1-Raab-s/Hitch & Neary-a, wraparound-c 4.00

COLOSSUS COMICS (See Green Giant & Motion Picture Funnies Weekly)
Sun Publications (Funnies, Inc.?): March, 1940

	GD	VG	FN	VF	VF/NM	NM-
1-(Scarce)-Tulpa of Tsang(hero); Colossus app.	919	1838	2757	6709	11,855	17,000

NOTE: *Cover by artist that drew Colossus in Green Giant Comics.*

COLOUR OF MAGIC, THE (Terry Pratchett's...)
Innovation Publishing: 1991 - No. 4, 1991 ($2.50, limited series)

1-4: Adapts 1st novel of the Discworld series 3.00

COLT .45 (TV)
Dell Publishing Co.: No. 924, 8/58 - No. 1058, 11-1/59-60; No. 4, 2-4/60 - No. 9, 5-7/61

	GD	VG	FN	VF	VF/NM	NM-
Four Color 924(#1)-Wayde Preston photo-c on all	9	18	27	60	120	180
Four Color 1004,1058: 1004-Photo-b/c	7	14	21	48	89	130
4,5,7-9	7	14	21	48	89	130
6-Toth-a	8	16	24	51	96	140

COLUMBIA COMICS
William H. Wise Co.: 1943

	GD	VG	FN	VF	VF/NM	NM-
1-Joe Palooka, Charlie Chan, Capt. Yank, Sparky Watts, Dixie Dugan app.	29	58	87	170	278	385

COMANCHE
Dell Publishing Co.: No. 1350, Apr-Jun, 1962

	GD	VG	FN	VF	VF/NM	NM-
Four Color 1350-Disney movie; reprints FC #966 with title change from "Tonka" to "Comanche"; Sal Mineo photo-c	5	10	15	31	53	75

COMANCHEROS, THE
Dell Publishing Co.: No. 1300, Mar-May, 1962

	GD	VG	FN	VF	VF/NM	NM-
Four Color 1300-Movie, John Wayne photo-c	13	26	39	86	188	290

COMBAT
Atlas Comics (ANC): June, 1952 - No. 11, April, 1953

	GD	VG	FN	VF	VF/NM	NM-
1	36	72	108	211	343	475
2-Heath-c/a	18	36	54	105	165	225
3,5-9,11: 3-Romita-a. 6-Robinson-c; Romita-a	14	28	42	82	121	160
4-Krigstein-a	15	30	45	83	124	165
10-B&W and color illos. in **POP**; Sale-a, Forte-a	15	30	45	84	127	170

NOTE: *Combat Casey in 7-11.* **Heath** *a-2, 3; c-1, 2, 5, 9.* **Maneely** *a-1; c-3, 10.* **Pakula** *a-1.* **Reinman** *a-1.*

COMBAT
Dell Publishing Co.: Oct-Nov, 1961 - No. 40, Oct, 1973 (No #9)

	GD	VG	FN	VF	VF/NM	NM-
1	6	12	18	38	69	100
2,3,5	4	8	12	25	40	55
4-John F. Kennedy c/story (P.T. 109)	5	10	15	31	53	75
6,7,8(4-6/63), 8(7-9/63)	4	8	12	23	37	50
10-26: 26-Last 12¢ issue	3	6	9	19	30	40
27-40(reprints #1-14). 30-r/#4	3	6	9	14	19	24

COMBAT CASEY (Formerly War Combat)
Atlas Comics (SAI): No. 6, Jan, 1953 - No. 34, July, 1957

	GD	VG	FN	VF	VF/NM	NM-
6 (Indicia shows 1/52 in error)	21	42	63	124	202	280
7-R.Q. Sale-a	14	28	42	76	108	140
8-Used in **POP**, pg. 94	13	26	39	72	101	130
9,10,13-19-Violent art by R.Q. Sale; Battle Brady x-over #10	15	30	45	85	130	175
11,12,20-Last Precode (2/55)	11	22	33	64	90	115
21-34: 22,25-R.Q. Sale-a	11	22	33	60	83	105

NOTE: **Everett** *a-6.* **Heath** *c-10, 17, 19, 23, 30.* **Maneely** *c-6, 8, 15.* **Powell** *a-29(5), 30(5), 34.* **Severin** *c-26, 33, 34.*

COMBAT KELLY
Atlas Comics (SPI): Nov, 1951 - No. 44, Aug, 1957

	GD	VG	FN	VF	VF/NM	NM-
1-1st app. Combat Kelly; Heath-a	37	74	111	222	361	500
2	19	38	57	111	176	240
3-10	15	30	45	84	127	170
11-Used in **POP**, pgs. 94,95 plus color illo.	15	30	45	83	124	165
12-Color illo. in **POP**	14	28	42	81	118	155
13-16	13	26	39	72	101	130
17-Violent art by R. Q. Sale; Combat Casey app.	15	30	45	88	137	185
18-20,22-44: 18-Battle Brady app. 28-Last precode (1/55). 38-Green Berets story (8/56)	11	22	33	64	90	115
21-Transvestism-c	12	24	36	67	94	120

NOTE: **Berg** *a-8, 12-14, 15-17, 19-23, 25, 26, 28, 31-37, 39, 41-44; c-2.* **Colan** *a-42.* **Heath** *a-4, 18; c-31.* **Lawrence** *a-23.* **Maneely** *a-4(2), 6, 7(3), 8; c-4, 5, 7, 8, 10, 25, 29, 39.* **R.Q. Sale** *a-17, 25.* **Severin** *c-41, 42.* **Whitney** *a-5.*

COMBAT KELLY (...and the Deadly Dozen)
Marvel Comics Group: June, 1972 - No. 9, Oct, 1973

	GD	VG	FN	VF	VF/NM	NM-
1-Intro & origin new Combat Kelly; Ayers/Mooney-a; Severin-c (20¢)	3	6	9	19	30	40
2,5-8	2	4	6	11	16	20
3,4: 3-Origin. 4-Sgt. Fury-c/s	3	6	9	14	19	24
9-Death of the Deadly Dozen	3	6	9	16	23	30

COMBAT ZONE: TRUE TALES OF GIS IN IRAQ
Marvel Comics: 2005 ($19.99, squarebound)

Vol. 1-Karl Zinsmeister scripts adapted from his non-fiction books; Dan Jurgens-a 20.00

COMBINED OPERATIONS (See The Story of the Commandos)

COMEBACK (See Zane Grey 4-Color 357)

COMEDY CARNIVAL
St. John Publishing Co.: no date (1950's) (100 pgs.)

	GD	VG	FN	VF	VF/NM	NM-
nn-Contains rebound St. John comics	36	72	108	211	343	475

COMEDY COMICS (1st Series) (Daring Mystery #1-8) (Becomes Margie Comics #35 on)
Timely Comics (TCI 9,10): No. 9, April, 1942 - No. 34, Fall, 1946

9-(Scarce)-The Fin by Everett, Capt. Dash, Citizen V, & The Silver Scorpion app.; Wolverton-a; 1st app. Comedy Kid; satire on Hitler & Stalin; The Fin, Citizen V & Silver

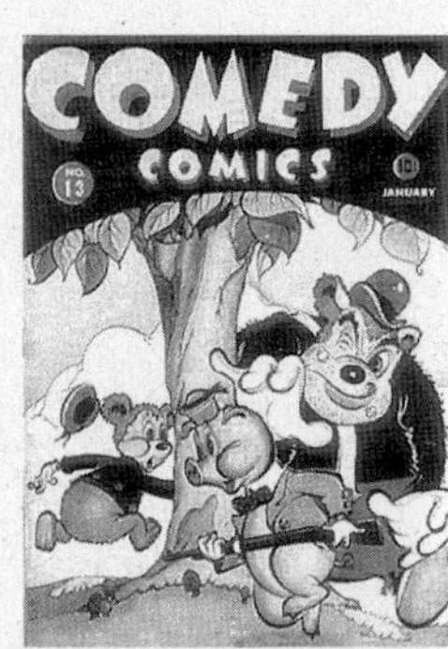

Comedy Comics #13 © MAR

The Comet #15 © AP

Comic Cavalcade #3 © DC

GD 2.0 | VG 4.0 | FN 6.0 | VF 8.0 | VF/NM 9.0 | NM- 9.2

Scorpion cont. from Daring Mystery 300 600 900 1980 3440 4900
10-(Scarce)-Origin The Fourth Musketeer, Victory Boys; Monstro, the Mighty app.
223 446 669 1416 2433 3450
11-Vagabond, Stuporman app. 58 116 174 371 636 900
12,13 21 42 63 122 199 275
14-Origin/1st app. Super Rabbit (3/43) plus-c 63 126 189 403 689 975
15-19 20 40 60 117 189 260
20-Hitler parody-c 39 78 117 231 378 525
21-Tojo-c 28 56 84 165 270 375
22-Hitler parody-c 39 78 117 231 378 525
23-32 15 30 45 85 138 175
33-Kurtzman-a (5 pgs.) 16 32 48 94 147 200
34-Intro Margie; Wolverton-a (5 pgs.) 28 56 84 165 270 375

COMEDY COMICS (2nd Series)
Marvel Comics (ACI): May, 1948 - No. 10, Jan, 1950
1-Hedy, Tessie, Millie begin; Kurtzman's "Hey Look" (he draws himself)
42 84 126 265 445 625
2 20 40 60 117 189 260
3,4-Kurtzman's "Hey Look" (?&3) 20 40 60 120 195 270
5-10 14 28 42 82 121 160

COMET, THE (See The Mighty Crusaders & Pep Comics #1)
Red Circle Comics (Archie): Oct, 1983 - No. 2, Dec, 1983
1-Re-intro & origin The Comet; The American Shield begins. Nino & Infantino art in both. Hangman in both 6.00
2-Origin continues. 5.00

COMET, THE
DC Comics (Impact Comics): July, 1991 - No. 18, Dec, 1992 ($1.00/$1.25)
1 4.00
2-18: 4-Black Hood app. 6-Re-intro Hangman. 8-Web x-over. 10-Contains Crusaders trading card. 4-Origin. Netzer(Nasser) c(p)-11,14-17 3.00
Annual 1 (1992, $2.50, 68 pgs.)-Contains Impact trading card; Shield back-up story 4.00

COMET MAN, THE (Movie)
Marvel Comics Group: Feb, 1987 - No. 6, July, 1987 (limited series)
1-6: 3-Hulk app. 4-She-Hulk shower scene-c/s. Fantastic 4 app. 5-Fantastic 4 app. 3.00
NOTE: ***Kelley Jones** a-1-6p.*

COMIC ALBUM (Also see Disney Comic Album)
Dell Publishing Co.: Mar-May, 1958 - No. 18, June-Aug, 1962
1-Donald Duck 8 16 24 51 96 140
2-Bugs Bunny 5 10 15 30 50 70
3-Donald Duck 6 12 18 40 73 105
4-6,8-10: 4-Tom & Jerry. 5-Woody Woodpecker. 6,10-Bugs Bunny. 8-Tom & Jerry. 9-Woody Woodpecker 4 8 12 27 44 60
7,11,15: Popeye. 11-(9-11/60) 4 8 12 28 47 65
12-14: 12-Tom & Jerry. 13-Woody Woodpecker. 14-Bugs Bunny
4 8 12 27 44 60
16-Flintstones (12-2/61-62)-3rd app. Early Cave Kids app.
7 14 21 46 86 125
17-Space Mouse (3rd app.) 5 10 15 30 50 70
18-Three Stooges; photo-c 7 14 21 46 86 125

COMIC BOOK
Marvel Comics-#1/Dark Horse Comics-#2: 1995 ($5.95, oversize)
1-Spumco characters by John K. 1 2 3 4 5 7
2-(Dark Horse) 6.00

COMIC BOOK GUY: THE COMIC BOOK (BONGO COMICS PRESENTS...) (Simpsons)
Bongo Comics: 2010 - No. 5, 2010 ($3.99/$2.99, limited series)
1-($3.99) Four-layer cover w/classic swipes incl. FF#1; intro Graphic Novel Kid 4.00
2-($2.99) 2-Stan Lee cameo. 3-Includes Little Lulu spoof. 4-CBG origin 3.00

COMIC CAPERS
Red Circle Mag./Marvel Comics: Fall, 1944 - No. 6, Fall, 1946
1-Super Rabbit, The Creeper, Silly Seal, Ziggy Pig, Sharpy Fox begin
36 72 108 211 343 475
2 19 38 57 111 176 240
3-6: 4-(Summer 1945) 16 32 48 94 147 200

COMIC CAVALCADE
All-American/National Periodical Publications: Winter, 1942-43 - No. 63, June-July, 1954
(Contents change with No. 30, Dec-Jan, 1948-49 on)
1-The Flash, Green Lantern, Wonder Woman, Wildcat, The Black Pirate by Moldoff (also #2), Ghost Patrol, and Red White & Blue begin; Scribbly app.; Minute Movie
865 1730 2595 6315 11,158 16,000
2-Mutt & Jeff begin; last Ghost Patrol & Black Pirate; Minute Movies
245 490 735 1568 2684 3800
3-Hop Harrigan & Sargon, the Sorcerer begin; The King app.
161 322 483 1030 1765 2500
4,5: 4-The Gay Ghost, The King, Scribbly, & Red Tornado app. 5-Christmas-c. 5-Prints ad for Jr. JSA membership kit that includes "The Minute Man Answers The Call"
155 310 465 992 1696 2400
6-10: 7-Red Tornado & Black Pirate app.; last Scribbly. 9-Fat & Slat app.; X-Mas-c
123 246 369 787 1344 1900
11,12,14: 12-Last Red White & Blue 97 194 291 621 1061 1500
13-Solomon Grundy app.; X-Mas-c 187 374 561 1197 2049 2900
15-Just a Story begins 98 196 294 622 1074 1525
16-20: 19-Christmas-c 90 180 270 576 988 1400
21-23: 22-Johnny Peril begins. 23-Harry Lampert-c (Toth swipes)
86 172 258 546 936 1325
24-Solomon Grundy x-over in Green Lantern 116 232 348 742 1271 1800
25-28: 25-Black Canary app.; X-Mas-c. 26-28-Johnny Peril app. 28-Last Mutt & Jeff
77 154 231 493 847 1200
29-(10-11/48)-Last Flash, Wonder Woman, Green Lantern & Johnny Peril; Wonder Woman invents "Thinking Machine"; 2nd computer in comics (after Flash Comics #52); Leave It to Binky story (early app.) 90 180 270 576 988 1400
30-(12-1/48-49)-The Fox & the Crow, Dodo & the Frog & Nutsy Squirrel begin
41 82 123 256 428 600
31-35 23 46 69 136 223 310
36-49: 41-Last squarebound issue 17 34 51 100 158 215
50-62(Scarce) 21 42 63 122 199 275
63(Rare) 34 68 102 204 332 460
NOTE: ***Grossman** a-30-63. **E.E. Hibbard** c-(Flash only)-1-4, 7-14, 16-19, 21. **Sheldon Mayer** a(2-3)-40-63. **Moulson** c(G.L.)-7, 15. **Nodell** c(G.L.)-9. **H.G. Peter** c(W. Woman only)-1, 3-21, 24. **Post** a-31, 36. **Purcell** c(G.L.)-2-5, 10. **Reinman** a(Green Lantern)-4-6, 8, 9, 13, 15-21; c(Gr. Lantern)-6, 8, 19. **Toth** a(Green Lantern)-26-28; c-27. Atom app.-22, 23.*

COMIC COMICS
Fawcett Publications: Apr, 1946 - No. 10, Feb, 1947
1-Captain Kid; Nutty Comics #1 in indicia 15 30 45 85 130 175
2-10-Wolverton-a, 4 pgs. each. 5-Captain Kidd app. Mystic Moot by Wolverton in #2-10? 15 30 45 84 127 170

COMIC LAND
Fact and Fiction Publ.: March, 1946
1-Sandusky & the Senator, Sam Stupor, Sleuth, Marvin the Great, Sir Passer, Phineas Gruff app.; Irv Tirman & Perry Williams art 15 30 45 85 130 175

COMICO CHRISTMAS SPECIAL
Comico: Dec, 1988 ($2.50, 44 pgs.)
1-Rude/Williamson-a; Dave Stevens-c 5.00

COMICO COLLECTION (Also see Grendel)
Comico: 1987 ($9.95, slipcased collection)
nn-Contains exclusive Grendel: Devil's Vagary, 9 random Comico comics, a poster and newsletter in black slipcase w/silver ink 25.00

COMICO PRIMER (See Primer)

COMIC PAGES (Formerly Funny Picture Stories)
Centaur Publications: V3#4, July, 1939 - V3#6, Dec, 1939
V3#4-Bob Wood-a 63 126 189 403 689 975
5,6: 6-Schwab-c 55 110 165 352 601 850

COMICS (See All Good)

COMICS, THE
Dell Publ. Co.: Mar, 1937 - No. 11, Nov, 1938 (Newspaper strip-r; bi-monthly)
1-1st app. Tom Mix in comics; Wash Tubbs, Tom Beatty, Myra North, Arizona Kid, Erik Noble & International Spy w/Doctor Doom begin
187 374 561 1197 2049 2900
2 82 164 246 528 902 1275
3-11: 3-Alley Oop begins 66 132 198 419 722 1025

COMICS AND STORIES (See Walt Disney's Comics and Stories)

COMICS & STORIES (Also see Wolf & Red)
Dark Horse Comics: Apr, 1996 - No. 4, July, 1996 ($2.95, lim. series) (Created by Tex Avery)
1-4: Wolf & Red app; reads Comics and Stories on-c. 1-Terry Moore-a. 2-Reed Waller-a 3.00

COMICS CALENDAR, THE (The 1946...)
True Comics Press (ordered through the mail): 1946 (25¢, 116 pgs.) (Stapled at top)
nn-(Rare) Has a "strip" story for every day of the year in color
40 80 120 242 401 560

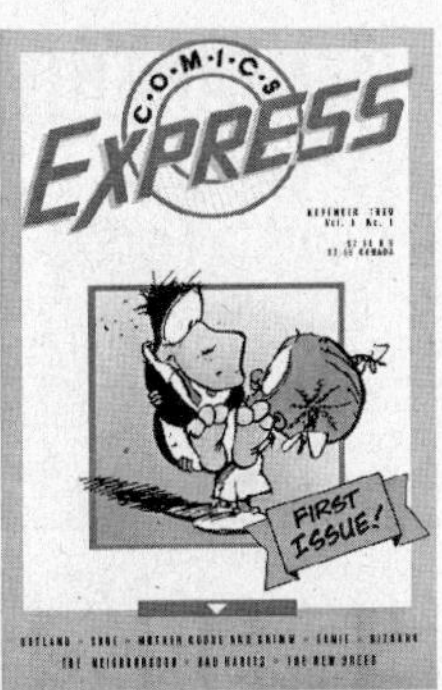

Comics Express #1 © ECL

Comics on Parade #12 © UFS

Commando Adventures #1 © MAR

GD 2.0 | VG 4.0 | FN 6.0 | VF 8.0 | VF/NM 9.0 | NM- 9.2

COMICS DIGEST (Pocket size)
Parents' Magazine Institute: Winter, 1942-43 (B&W, 100 pgs)
1-Reprints from True Comics (non-fiction World War II stories)
10 20 30 54 72 90

COMICS EXPRESS
Eclipse Comics: Nov, 1989 - No. 2, Jan, 1990 ($2.95, B&W, 68pgs.)
1,2: Collection of strip-r; 2(12/89-c, 1/90 inside) 4.00

COMICS FOR KIDS
London Publ. Co./Timely: 1945 (no month); No. 2, Sum, 1945 (Funny animal)
1-Puffy Pig, Sharpy Fox 26 52 78 154 252 350
2-Puffy Pig, Sharpy Fox 21 42 63 122 199 275

COMICS' GREATEST WORLD
Dark Horse Comics: Jun, 1993 - V4#4, Sept, 1993 ($1.00, weekly, lim. series)
Arcadia (Wk 1): V1#1,2,4: 1-X: Frank Miller-c. 2-Pit Bulls. 4-Monster. 3.00
1-B&W Press Proof Edition (1500 copies) 1 3 4 6 8 10
1-Silver-c; distr. retailer bonus w/print & cards 1 2 3 5 6 8
3-Ghost, Dorman-c; Hughes-a 4.00
Retailer's Prem. Emb. Silver Foil Logo-r/V1#1-4 1 3 4 6 8 10
Golden City (Wk 2: V2#1-4: 1-Rebel; Ordway-c. 2-Mecha; Dave Johnson-c.
3-Titan; Walt Simonson-c. 4-Catalyst; Perez-c. 3.00
1-Gold-c; distr. retailer bonus w/print & cards. 6.00
Retailer's Prem. Embos. Gold Foil Logo-r/V2#1-4 1 2 3 5 6 8
Steel Harbor (Week 3): V3#1-Barb Wire; Dorman-c; Gulacy-a(p) 4.00
2-4: 2-The Machine. 3-Wolfgang. 4-Motorhead 3.00
1-Silver-c; distr. retailer bonus w/print & cards 1 2 3 5 6 8
Retailer's Prem. Emb. Red Foil Logo-r/V3#1-4. 1 3 4 6 8 10
Vortex (Week 4): V4#1-4: 1-Division 13; Dorman-c. 2-Hero Zero; Art Adams-c.
3-King Tiger; Chadwick-a(p); Darrow-c. 4-Vortex; Miller-c. 3.00
1-Gold-c; distr. retailer bonus w/print & cards. 6.00
Retailer's Prem. Emb. Blue Foil Logo-r/V4#1-4. 1 2 3 5 6 8

COMICS' GREATEST WORLD: OUT OF THE VORTEX (See Out of The Vortex)

COMICS HITS (See Harvey Comics Hits)

COMICS MAGAZINE, THE (...Funny Pages #3)(Funny Pages #6 on)
Comics Magazine Co. (1st Comics Mag./Centaur Publ.): May, 1936 - No. 5, Sept, 1936 (Paper covers)
1-1st app. Dr. Mystic (a.k.a. Dr. Occult) by Siegel & Shuster (the 1st app. of a Superman prototype in comics). Dr. Mystic is not in costume but later appears in costume as a more pronounced prototype in More Fun #14-17. (1st episode of "The Koth and the Seven"; continues in More Fun #14; originally scheduled for publication at DC). 1 pg. Kelly-a; Sheldon Mayer-a 3600 7200 10,800 21,000 - -
2-Federal Agent (a.k.a. Federal Men) by Siegel & Shuster; 1 pg. Kelly-a
370 740 1110 2220 2960 3700
3-5 320 640 960 1920 2560 3200

COMICS NOVEL (Anarcho, Dictator of Death)
Fawcett Publications: 1947
1-All Radar; 51 pg anti-fascism story 34 68 102 204 332 460

COMICS ON PARADE (No. 30 on are a continuation of Single Series)
United Features Syndicate: Apr, 1938 - No. 104, Feb, 1955
1-Tarzan by Foster; Captain & the Kids, Little Mary Mixup, Abbie & Slats, Ella Cinders, Broncho Bill, Li'l Abner begin 383 766 1149 2681 4691 6700
2 (Tarzan & others app. on-c of #1-3,17) 135 270 405 864 1482 2100
3 103 206 309 659 1130 1600
4,5 81 162 243 518 884 1250
6-10 55 110 165 352 601 850
11-16,18-20 42 84 126 267 451 635
17-Tarzan-c 53 106 159 334 567 800
21-29: 22-Son of Tarzan begins. 22,24,28-Tailspin Tommy-c. 29-Last Tarzan issue
36 72 108 216 351 485
30-Li'l Abner 20 40 60 114 182 250
31-The Captain & the Kids 15 30 45 85 130 175
32-Nancy & Fritzi Ritz 14 28 42 78 112 145
33,36,39,42-Li'l Abner 16 32 48 94 147 200
34,37,40-The Captain & the Kids (10/41,6/42,3/43) 15 30 45 83 124 165
35,38-Nancy & Fritzi Ritz. 38-Infinity-c 14 28 42 76 108 140
41-Nancy & Fritzi Ritz 11 22 33 60 83 105
43-The Captain & the Kids 15 30 45 83 124 165
44 (3/44),47,50: Nancy & Fritzi Ritz 11 22 33 60 83 105
45-Li'l Abner 15 30 45 84 127 170
46,49-The Captain & the Kids 13 26 39 74 105 135
48-Li'l Abner (3/45) 15 30 45 84 127 170
51,54-Li'l Abner 14 28 42 76 108 140
52-The Captain & the Kids (3/46) 10 20 30 56 76 95
53,55,57-Nancy & Fritzi Ritz 10 20 30 56 76 95
56-The Captain & the Kids (r/Sparkler) 10 20 30 56 76 95
58-Li'l Abner; continues as Li'l Abner #61? 14 28 42 76 108 140
59-The Captain & the Kids 9 18 27 47 61 75
60-70-Nancy & Fritzi Ritz 8 16 24 44 57 70
71-99,101-104-Nancy & Sluggo: 71-76-Nancy only 8 16 24 42 54 65
100-Nancy & Sluggo 14 28 42 76 108 140
Special Issue, 7/46; Summer, 1948 - The Captain & the Kids app.
14 28 42 76 108 140
NOTE: Bound Volume (Very Rare) includes No. 1-12; bound by publisher in pictorial comic boards & distributed at the 1939 World's Fair and through mail order from ads in comic books (also see Tip Top)
300 600 900 1950 3375 4800
NOTE: *Li'l Abner reprinted from Tip Top.*

COMICS READING LIBRARIES (See the Promotional Comics section)

COMICS REVUE
St. John Publ. Co. (United Features Synd.): June, 1947 - No. 5, Jan, 1948
1-Ella Cinders & Blackie 12 24 36 69 97 125
2,4: 2-Hap Hopper (7/47). 4-Ella Cinders (9/47) 9 18 27 47 61 75
3,5: 3-Iron Vic (8/47). 5-Gordo No. 1 (1/48) 8 16 24 44 57 70

COMIC STORY PAINT BOOK
Samuel Lowe Co.: 1943 (Large size, 68 pgs.)
1055-Captain Marvel & a Captain Marvel Jr. story to read & color; 3 panels in color per pg. (reprints) 77 154 231 493 847 1200

COMIX BOOK
Marvel Comics Group/Krupp Comics Works No. 4,5: 1974 - No. 5, 1976 ($1.00, B&W, magazine) (#1-3 newsstand; #4,5 were direct distribution only)
1-Underground comic artists; 2 pgs. Wolverton-a 3 6 9 15 22 28
2,3: 2-Wolverton-a (1 pg.) 3 6 9 14 19 24
4(2/76), 4(5/76), 5 (Low distribution) 3 6 9 16 23 30
NOTE: *Print run No. 1-3: 200,000-250,000; No. 4&5: 10,000 each.*

COMIX INTERNATIONAL
Warren Magazines: Jul, 1974 - No. 5, Spring, 1977 (Full color, stiff-c, mail only)
1-Low distribution; all Corben story remainders from Warren; Corben-c on all
9 18 27 62 126 190
2,4: 2-Two Dracula stories; Wood, Wrightson-r; Crandall-a; Maroto-a.
4-Printing w/ 3 Corben sty 6 12 18 37 66 95
3-5: 3-Dax story. 4-(printing without Corben story). 4-Crandall-a. 4,5-Vampirella stories.
5-Spirit story; Eisner-a 5 10 15 33 57 80
NOTE: *No. 4 had two printings with extra **Corben** story in one. No. 3 may also have a variation. No. 3 has two Jeff Jones reprints from Vampirella.*

COMMANDER BATTLE AND THE ATOMIC SUB
Amer. Comics Group (Titan Publ. Co.): Jul-Aug, 1954 - No. 7, Aug-Sep, 1955
1 (3-D effect)-Moldoff flying saucer-c 53 106 159 334 567 800
2,4-7: 2-Moldoff-c. 4-(1-2/55)-Last pre-code; Landau-a. 5-3-D effect story (2 pgs.). 6,7-Landau-a. 7-Flying saucer-c 34 68 102 204 332 460
3-H-Bomb-c; Atomic Sub becomes Atomic Spaceship
36 72 108 211 343 475

COMMANDO ADVENTURES
Atlas Comics (MMC): June, 1957 - No. 2, Aug, 1957
1-Severin-c 14 28 42 82 121 160
2-Severin-c; Reinman & Romita-a; Drucker-a? 10 20 30 56 76 95

COMMANDOS
DC Comics: Oct. 1942
1-Ashcan comic, not distributed to newsstands, only for in-house use. Cover art is Boy Commandos #1 with interior being a Boy Commandos story from an unidentified issue of Detective Comics (a VF copy sold for $1254.75 in 2012)

COMMANDO YANK (See The Mighty Midget Comics & Wow Comics)

COMMON GROUNDS
Image Comics (Top Cow): Feb, 2004 - No. 6, July, 2004 ($2.99)
1-6: 1-Two covers; art by Jurgens and Oeming. 3-Bachalo, Jurgens-a. 4-Peréz-a 3.00
...: Baker's Dozen TPB (12/04, $14.99) r/#1-6; cover gallery; Holey Crullers pages 15.00

COMPLETE ALICE IN WONDERLAND (Adaptation of Carroll's original story)
Dynamite Entertainment: 2009 - Present ($4.99, limited series)
1-4-Leah Moore & John Reppion-s/Erica Awano-a/John Cassaday-c 5.00

COMPLETE BOOK OF COMICS AND FUNNIES

Complete Love Magazine V26 #3 © ACE

Conan #34 © Conan Properties

Conan the Adventurer #4 © Conan Properties

GD VG FN VF VF/NM NM-
2.0 4.0 6.0 8.0 9.0 9.2

William H. Wise & Co.: 1944 (25¢, one-shot, 196 pgs.)
1-Origin Brad Spencer, Wonderman; The Magnet, The Silver Knight by Kinstler, & Zudo the Jungle Boy app. 48 96 144 302 514 725

COMPLETE BOOK OF TRUE CRIME COMICS
William H. Wise & Co.: No date (Mid 1940's) (25¢, 132 pgs.)
nn-Contains Crime Does Not Pay rebound (includes #22) 161 322 483 1030 1765 2500

COMPLETE COMICS (Formerly Amazing Comics No. 1)
Timely Comics (EPC): No. 2, Winter, 1944-45
2-The Destroyer, The Whizzer, The Young Allies & Sergeant Dix; Schomburg-c 174 348 522 1114 1907 2700

COMPLETE DRACULA (Adaptation of Stoker's original story)
Dynamite Entertainment: 2009 - No. 5, 2009 ($4.99, limited series)
1-5-Leah Moore & John Reppion-s/Colton Worley-a/John Cassaday-c 5.00

COMPLETE FRANK MILLER BATMAN, THE
Longmeadow Press: 1989 ($29.95, hardcover, silver gilded pages)
HC-Reprints Batman: Year One, Wanted: Santa Claus--Dead or Alive, and The Dark Knight Returns 45.00

COMPLETE GUIDE TO THE DEADLY ARTS OF KUNG FU AND KARATE
Marvel Comics: 1974 (68 pgs., B&W magazine)
V1#1-Bruce Lee-c and 5 pg. story (scarce) 6 12 18 41 76 110

COMPLETE LOVE MAGAZINE (Formerly a pulp with same title)
Ace Periodicals (Periodical House): V26#2, May-June, 1951 - V32#4(#191), Sept, 1956
V26#2-Painted-c (52 pgs.) 14 28 42 76 108 140
V26#3-6(2/52), V27#1(4/52)-6(1/53) 10 20 30 56 76 95
V28#1(3/53), V28#2(5/53), V29#3(7/53)-6(12/53) 10 20 30 54 72 90
V30#1(2/54), V30#1(#176, 4/54),2,4-6(#181, 1/55) 10 20 30 54 72 90
V30#3(#178)-Rock Hudson photo-c 10 20 30 56 76 95
V31#1(#182, 3/55)-Last precode 9 18 27 52 69 85
V31#2(5/55)-6(#187, 1/56) 9 18 27 50 65 80
V32#1(#188, 3/56)-4(#191, 9/56) 9 18 27 50 65 80
NOTE: *(34 total issues). Photo-c V27#5-on. Painted-c V26#3.*

COMPLETE MYSTERY (True Complete Mystery No. 5 on)
Marvel Comics (PrPI): Aug, 1948 - No. 4, Feb, 1949 (Full length stories)
1-Seven Dead Men 50 100 150 315 533 750
2-4: 2-Jigsaw of Doom!; Shores-a. 3-Fear in the Night; Burgos-c/a (28 pgs.). 4-A Squealer Dies Fast 39 78 117 240 395 550

COMPLETE ROMANCE
Avon Periodicals: 1949
1-(Scarce)-Reprinted as Women to Love 47 94 141 296 498 700

CONAN (See Chamber of Darkness #4, Giant-Size..., Handbook of..., King Conan, Marvel Graphic Novel #19, 28, Marvel Treasury Ed., Power Record Comics, Robert E. Howard's.., Savage Sword of Conan, and Savage Tales)

CONAN
Dark Horse Comics: Feb, 2004 - No. 50, May, 2008 ($2.99)
0-(11/03, 25¢-c) Busiek-s/Nord-a 3.00
1-($2.99) Linsner-c/Busiek-s/Nord-a 5.00
1-(2nd printing) J. Scott Campell-c 3.00
1-(3rd printing) Nord-c 3.00
2-49: 18-Severin & Timm-a. 22-Kaluta-a (6 pgs.) 24-Harris-c. 29-31-Mignola-s 3.00
24-Variant-c with nude woman (also see Conan and the Demons of Khitai #3 for ad) 30.00
50-($4.99) Harris-c; new story and reprint from Conan the Barbarian #30 5.00
... and the Daughters of Midora (10/04, $4.99) Texiera-a/c 5.00
...: Born on the Battlefield TPB (6/08, $17.95) r/#0,8,15,23,32,45,46; Ruth sketch pages 18.00
...: FCBD 2006 Special (5/06) Paul Lee-a; flip book with Star Wars FCBD 2006 Special 3.00
...: One For One (8/10, $1.00) r/#1 with red cover frame 3.00
...: The Blood-Stained Crown and Other Stories TPB (1/08, $14.95) r/#18,26-28,39 15.00
...: The Weight of the Crown (1/10, $3.50) Darick Robertson-s/a; 2 covers by Robertson 3.50
HC Vol. 1: The Frost Giant's Daughter and Other Stories (2005, $24.95) r/#1-6, partial #7; signed by Busiek; Nord sketch pages 25.00
Vol. 1: The Frost Giant's Daughter and Other Stories (2005, $15.95) r/#1-6, partial #7 16.00
Vol. 2: The God in the Bowl and Other Stories HC (2005, $24.95) r/#9-14 25.00
Vol. 2: The God in the Bowl and Other Stories SC (2006, $15.95) r/#9-14 16.00
Vol. 3: The Tower of the Elephant and Other Stories HC (5/06, $24.95) r/#0,16,17,19-22 25.00
Vol. 3: The Tower of the Elephant and Other Stories SC (6/06, $15.95) r/#0,16,17,19-22 16.00
Vol. 4: The Hall of the Dead and Other Stories HC (5/07, $24.95) r/#0,24,25,29-31,33,34 25.00
Vol. 4: The Hall of the Dead and Other Stories SC (6/07, $17.95) r/#0,24,25,29-31,33,34 18.00
Vol. 5: Rogues in the House and Other Stories SC (3/08, $17.95) r/#0,37,38,41-44 18.00

GD VG FN VF VF/NM NM-
2.0 4.0 6.0 8.0 9.0 9.2

Vol. 6: The Hand of Nergal HC (10/08, $24.95) r/#0,47-50; sketch pages 25.00

CONAN AND THE DEMONS OF KHITAI
Dark Horse Comics: Oct, 2005 - No. 4, Jan, 2006 ($2.99, limited series)
1,2,4-Paul Lee-a/Akira Yoshida-s/Pat Lee-c 3.00
3-1st printing with red cover logo; letters page has image of Conan #24 nude variant-c 5.00
3-2nd printing with black cover logo; letters page has image of Conan #24 regular-c 3.00
TPB (7/06, $12.95) r/series 13.00

CONAN AND THE JEWELS OF GWAHLUR
Dark Horse Comics: Apr, 2005 - No. 3, June, 2005 ($2.99, limited series)
1-3-P. Craig Russell-s/a/c 3.00
HC (12/05, $13.95) r/series; P. Craig Russell interview and sketch pages 14.00

CONAN AND THE MIDNIGHT GOD
Dark Horse Comics: Dec, 2006 - No. 5, May, 2007 ($2.99, limited series)
1-5-Dysart-s/Conrad-a/Alexander-c 3.00
TPB (10/07, $14.95) r/#1-5 and Age of Conan: Hyborian Adventures one-shot 15.00

CONAN AND THE PEOPLE OF THE BLACK CIRCLE
Dark Horse Comics: Oct, 2013 - No. 4, Jan, 2014 ($3.50, limited series)
1-4-Van Lente-s/Olivetti-a/c 3.50

CONAN AND THE SONGS OF THE DEAD
Dark Horse Comics: July, 2006 - No. 5, Nov, 2006 ($2.99, limited series)
1-5-Timothy Truman-a/c; Joe Lansdale-s 3.00
TPB (4/07, $14.95) r/series; Truman sketch pages 15.00

CONAN: (Title Series): Marvel Comics
CONAN, 8/95 - No. 11, 6/96 ($2.95), 1-11: 4-Malibu Comic's Rune app. 3.00
...CLASSIC, 6/94 - No. 11, 4/95 ($1.50), 1-11: 1-r/Conan #1 by B. Smith, r/covers w/changes. 2-11-r/Conan #2-11 by Smith. 2-Bound w/cover to Conan The Adventurer #2 by mistake 3.00
...DEATH COVERED IN GOLD, 9/99 - No. 3, 11/99 ($2.99), 1-3-Roy Thomas-s/ John Buscema-a 3.00
...FLAME AND THE FIEND, 8/00 - No. 3, 10/00 ($2.99), 1-3-Thomas-s 3.00
...RETURN OF STYRM, 9/98 - No. 3, 11/98 ($2.99), 1-3-Parente & Soresina-a; painted-c 3.00
...RIVER OF BLOOD, 6/98 - No. 3, 8/98 ($2.50), 1-3 3.00
...SCARLET SWORD, 12/98 - No. 3, 2/99 ($2.99), 1-3-Thomas-s/Raffaele-a 3.00

CONAN: ISLAND OF NO RETURN
Dark Horse Comics: Jun, 2011 - No. 2, Jul, 2011 ($3.50, limited series)
1,2-Marz-s/Sears-a 3.50

CONAN: ROAD OF KINGS
Dark Horse Comics: Dec, 2010 - No. 12, Jan, 2012 ($3.50)
1-12: 1-Roy Thomas-s/Mike Hawthorne-a; covers by Wheatley & Keown 3.50

CONAN SAGA, THE
Marvel Comics: June, 1987 - No. 97, Apr, 1995 ($2.00/$2.25, B&W, magazine)
1-Barry Smith-r; new Smith-c 1 2 3 5 6 8
2-27: 2-9,11-new Barry Smith-c. 13,15-Boris-c. 17-Adams-r.18,25-Chaykin-r. 22-r/Giant-Size Conan 1,2 4.00
28-90: 28-Begin $2.25-c. 31-Red Sonja-r by N. Adams/SSOC #1; 1 pg. Jeff Jones-r. 32-Newspaper strip-r begin by Buscema. 33-Smith/Conrad-a. 39-r/Kull #1('71) by Andru & Wood. 44-Swipes-c/Savage Tales #1. 57-Brunner-r/SSOC #30. 66-r/Conan Annual #2 by Buscema. 79-r/Conan #43-45 w/Red Sonja. 85-Based on Conan #57-63 3.00
91-96 4.50
97-Last issue 1 2 3 4 5 7
NOTE: ***J. Buscema** r-32-on; c-86. **Chaykin** r-34. **Chiodo** painted c-63, 65, 66, 82. **G. Colan** a-47p. **Jusko** painted c-64, 83. **Kaluta** c-84. **Nino** a-37. **Ploog** a-50. **N. Redondo** painted c-48, 50, 51, 53, 57, 62. **Simonson** r-50-54, 56. **B. Smith** r-51. **Starlin** c-34. **Williamson** r-50i.*

CONAN THE ADVENTURER
Marvel Comics: June, 1994 - No. 14, July, 1995 ($1.50)
1-($2.50)-Embossed foil-c; Kayaran-a 4.00
2-14 3.00
2-Contents are Conan Classics #2 by mistake 3.00

CONAN THE BARBARIAN
Marvel Comics: Oct, 1970 - No. 275, Dec, 1993
1-Origin/1st app. Conan (in comics) by Barry Smith; 1st brief app. Kull; #1-9 are 15¢ issues 22 44 66 154 340 525
2 9 18 27 58 114 170
3-(Low distribution in some areas) 12 24 36 84 185 285
4,5 7 14 21 49 92 135
6-9: 8-Hidden panel message, pg. 14. 9-Last 15¢-c 6 12 18 37 66 95

Conan the Barbarian #150 © Conan Properties

Conan the Barbarian (2012) #18 © Conan Properties

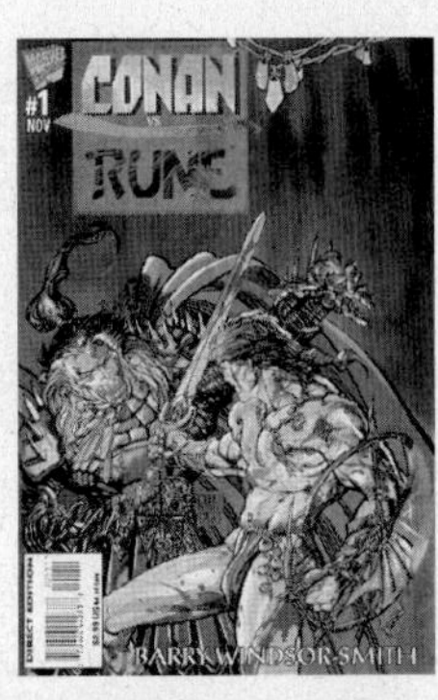

Conan vs. Rune #1 © MAR

GD 2.0 VG 4.0 FN 6.0 VF 8.0 VF/NM 9.0 NM- 9.2

10,11 (25¢ 52 pg. giants): 10-Black Knight-r; Kull story by Severin 6 12 18 42 79 115
12,13: 12-Wrightson-c(i) 5 10 15 34 60 85
14,15-Elric app. 6 12 18 38 69 100
16,19,20: 16-Conan-r/Savage Tales #1 5 10 15 33 57 80
17,18-No Barry Smith-a 4 8 12 27 44 60
21,22: 22-Has reprint from #1 4 8 12 28 47 65
23-1st app. Red Sonja (2/73) 6 12 18 41 76 110
24-1st full Red Sonja story; last Smith-a 6 12 18 40 73 105
25-John Buscema-c/a begins 3 6 9 16 23 30
26-30: 28-Centerfold ad by Mark Jewelers 2 4 6 13 18 22
31-36,38-40 2 4 6 9 12 15
37-Neal Adams-c/a; last 20¢ issue; contains pull-out subscription form 3 6 9 16 24 32
41-43,46-50: 48-Origin retold 2 4 6 8 10 12
44,45-N. Adams-i(Crusty Bunkers). 45-Adams-c 2 4 6 9 12 15
51-57,59,60: 59-Origin Belit 1 2 3 5 6 8
58-2nd Belit app. (see Giant-Size Conan #1) 2 4 6 8 11 14
61-65-(Regular 25¢ editions)(4-8/76) 1 2 3 4 5 7
61-65-(30¢-c variants, limited distribution) 5 10 15 30 50 70
66-99: 68-Red Sonja story cont'd from Marvel Feature #7. 75-79-(Reg. 30¢-c). 84-Intro. Zula. 85-Origin Zula. 87-r/Savage Sword of Conan #3 in color 6.00
75-79-(35¢-c variants, limited distribution) 5 10 15 33 57 80
100-(52 pg. Giant)-Death of Belit 1 3 4 6 8 10
101-114 4.00
115-Double size 5.00
116-199,201-231,233-249: 116-r/Power Record Comic PR31. 244-Zula returns 4.00
200,232: 200-(52 pgs.). 232-Young Conan storyline begins; Conan is born 5.00
250-(60 pgs.) 6.00
251-270: 262-Adapted from R.E. Howard story 5.00
271-274 1 2 3 5 6 8
275-($2.50, 68 pgs.)-Final issue; painted-c (low print) 3 6 9 16 23 30
King Size 1(1973, 35¢)-Smith-r/#2,4; Smith-c 3 6 9 19 30 40
Annual 2(1976, 50¢)-New full length story 2 4 6 10 14 18
Annual 3,4: 3('78)-Chaykin/N. Adams-r/SSOC #2. 4('78)-New full length story 2 4 6 8 10 12
Annual 5,6: 5(1979)-New full length Buscema story & part-c, 6(1981)-Kane-c/a 6.00
Annual 7-12: 7('82)-Based on novel "Conan of the Isles" (new-a). 8(1984). 9(1984). 10(1986). 11(1986). 12(1987) 4.00
Special Edition 1 (Red Nails) 4.00
The Chronicles of Conan Vol. 1: Tower of the Elephant and Other Stories (Dark Horse, 2003, $15.95) r/#1-8; afterword by Roy Thomas 16.00
The Chronicles of Conan Vol. 2: Rogues in the House and Other Stories (Dark Horse, 2003, $15.95) r/#9-13,16; afterword by Roy Thomas 16.00
The Chronicles of Conan Vol. 3: The Monster of the Monoliths and Other Stories (Dark Horse, 2003, $15.95) r/#14,15,17-21; afterword by Roy Thomas 16.00
The Chronicles of Conan Vol. 4: The Song of Red Sonja and Other Stories (Dark Horse, 2004, $15.95) r/#23-26 & "Red Nails" from Savage Tales; afterword by Roy Thomas 16.00
The Chronicles of Conan Vol. 5: The Shadow in the Tomb and Other Stories (Dark Horse, 2004, $15.95) r/#27-34; afterword by Roy Thomas 16.00
The Chronicles of Conan Vol. 6: The Curse of the Skull and Other Stories (Dark Horse, 2004, $15.95) r/#35-42; afterword by Roy Thomas 16.00
The Chronicles of Conan Vol. 7: The Dweller in the Pool and Other Stories (Dark Horse, 2005, $15.95) r/#43-51; afterword by Roy Thomas 16.00
The Chronicles of Conan Vol. 8: Brothers of the Blade and Other Stories (Dark Horse, 2005, $16.95) r/#52-59; afterword by Roy Thomas 17.00
The Chronicles of Conan Vol. 9: Riders of the River-Dragons and Other Stories (Dark Horse, 11/05, $16.95) r/#60-63,65,69-71; afterword by Roy Thomas 17.00
The Chronicles of Conan Vol. 10: When Giants Walk the Earth and Other Stories (Dark Horse, 3/06, $16.95) r/#72-77,79-82; afterword by Roy Thomas 17.00
The Chronicles of Conan Vol. 11: The Dance of the Skull and Other Stories (Dark Horse, 2/07, $16.95) r/#82-86,88-90; afterword by Roy Thomas 17.00
The Chronicles of Conan Vol. 12: The King Beast of Abombi and Other Stories (Dark Horse, 7/07, $16.95) r/#91,93-100; afterword by Roy Thomas 17.00
The Chronicles of Conan Vol. 13: Whispering Shadows and Other Stories (Dark Horse, 12/07, $16.95) r/#92,100-107; afterword by Roy Thomas 17.00
The Chronicles of Conan Vol. 14: Shadow of the Beast and Other Stories (Dark Horse, 3/08, $16.95) r/#92,108-115; afterword by Roy Thomas 17.00
The Chronicles of Conan Vol. 15: The Corridor of Mullah-Kajar and Other Stories (Dark Horse, 7/08, $16.95) r/#116-121 & Annual #2; afterword by Roy Thomas 17.00

NOTE: ***Arthur Adams*** *c-248, 249.* ***Neal Adams*** *a-116r(i); c-49i.* ***Austin*** *a-125, 126; c-125i, 126i.* ***Brunner*** *c-17i. c-40.* ***Buscema*** *a-25-36p, 38, 39, 41-56p, 58-63p, 65-67p, 68, 70-78p, 84-86p, 88-91p, 93-126p, 136p, 140, 141-144p, 146-158p, 159, 161, 162, 163p, 165-185p, 187-190p, Annual 2(3pgs.). 3-5p, 7p; c(p)-26, 36, 44, 46, 52, 56, 58, 59, 64, 65, 72, 78-80, 83-91, 93-103, 105-126, 136-151, 155-159, 161, 162, 168, 169, 171, 172, 174, 175, 178-185, 188, 189, Annual 4, 5, 7.* ***Chaykin*** *a-79-83.* ***Golden*** *c-152.* ***Kaluta*** *c-167.* ***Gil Kane*** *a-12p, 17p, 18p, 127-130, 131-134p; c-12p, 17p, 18p, 23, 25, 27-32, 34, 35, 38, 39, 41-43, 45-51, 53-55, 57, 60-63, 65-71, 73p, 76p, 127-134.* ***Jim Lee*** *c-242.* ***McFarlane*** *c-241p.* ***Ploog*** *a-57.* ***Russell*** *a-21; c-251i.* ***Simonson*** *c-135.* ***B. Smith*** *a-1-11p, 12, 13-15p, 16, 19-21, 23, 24; c-1-11, 13-16, 19-24p.* ***Starlin*** *a-64.* ***Wood*** *a-47r. Issue Nos. 3-5, 7-9, 11, 16-18, 21, 23, 25, 27-30, 35, 37, 38, 42, 45, 52, 57, 58, 65, 69-71, 73, 79-83, 99, 100, 104, 114, Annual 2 have original Robert E. Howard stories adapted. Issues #32-34 adapted from Norvell Page's novel* ***Flame Winds****.*

CONAN THE BARBARIAN (Volume 2)
Marvel Comics: July, 1997 - No. 3, Oct, 1997 ($2.50, limited series)

1-3-Castellini-a 3.00

CONAN THE BARBARIAN
Dark Horse Comics: Feb, 2012 - Present ($3.50)

1-25: 1-3-Brian Wood-s/Becky Cloonan-a. 1-Two covers by Carnevale & Cloonan 3.50
One for One: Conan the Barbarian #1 (1/14, $1.00) r/#1 3.00

CONAN THE BARBARIAN MOVIE SPECIAL (Movie)
Marvel Comics Group: Oct, 1982 - No. 2, Nov, 1982

1,2-Movie adaptation; Buscema-a 4.00

CONAN THE BARBARIAN
Dark Horse Comics: Feb, 2012 - Present ($3.50)

1-14: 1-3-Brian Wood-s/Becky Cloonan-a. 1-Two covers by Carnevale & Cloonan 3.50

CONAN THE BARBARIAN: THE MASK OF ACHERON (Based on the 2011 movie)
Dark Horse Comics: Jul, 2011 ($6.99, one-shot)

1-Stuart Moore-s/Gabriel Guzman-a/c 7.00

CONAN THE BARBARIAN: THE USURPER
Marvel Comics: Dec, 1997 - No. 3, Feb, 1998 ($2.50, limited series)

1-3-Dixon-s 3.00

CONAN: THE BOOK OF THOTH
Dark Horse Comics: Mar, 2006 - No. 4, June, 2006 ($4.99, limited series)

1-4-Origin of Thoth-amon; Len Wein & Kurt Busiek-s/Kelley Jones-a/c 5.00
TPB (12/06, $17.95) r/#1-4 18.00

CONAN THE CIMMERIAN
Dark Horse Comics: No. 0, Jun, 2008 - No. 25, Nov, 2010 (99¢/$2.99)

0-Follows Conan #50; Truman-s/Giorello-a/c 3.00
1-(7/08, $2.99) Two covers by Joe Kubert and Cho; Giorello & Corben-a 3.00
2-25: 2-7-Cho-c; Giorello & Corben-a. 8-18-Linsner-c. 14-Joe Kubert-a (7 pgs.) 3.00

CONAN THE DESTROYER (Movie)
Marvel Comics Group: Jan, 1985 - No. 2, Mar, 1985

1,2-r/Marvel Super Special 4.00

CONAN THE FRAZETTA COVER SERIES
Dark Horse Comics: Dec, 2007 - No. 8 ($3.50/$5.99/$6.99)

1-($3.50) Reprints from Dark Horse series with Frazetta covers 6.00
2,3-($5.99) 6.00
4-8-($6.99) 7.00

CONAN THE KING (Formerly King Conan)
Marvel Comics Group: No. 20, Jan, 1984 - No. 55, Nov, 1989

20-49 4.00
50-54 5.00
55-Last issue 1 2 3 5 6 8

NOTE: ***Kaluta*** *c-20-23, 24i, 26, 27, 30, 50, 52.* ***Williamson*** *a-37i; c-37i, 38i.*

CONAN: THE LEGEND (See Conan 2004 series)

CONAN: THE LORD OF THE SPIDERS
Marvel Comics: Mar, 1998 - No. 3, May, 1998 ($2.50, limited series)

1-3-Roy Thomas-s/Raffaele-a 3.00

CONAN THE SAVAGE
Marvel Comics: Aug, 1995 - No. 10, May, 1996 ($2.95, B&W, Magazine)

1-10: 1-Bisley-c. 4-vs. Malibu Comics' Rune. 5,10-Brereton-c 4.00

CONAN VS. RUNE (Also See Conan #4)
Marvel Comics: Nov, 1995 ($2.95, one-shot)

1-Barry Smith-c/a/scripts 4.00

CONCRETE (Also see Dark Horse Presents & Within Our Reach)
Dark Horse Comics: March, 1987 - No. 10, Nov, 1988 ($1.50, B&W)

1-Paul Chadwick-c/a in all 1 3 4 6 8 10
1-2nd print 3.00
2 6.00
3-Origin 5.00
4-10 4.00
A New Life 1 (1989, $2.95, B&W)-r/#3,4 plus new-a (11 pgs.) 4.00
Celebrates Earth Day 1990 ($3.50, 52 pgs.) 6.00

Concrete Eclectica #1 © P. Chadwick

Confessions of Romance #8 © STAR

Constantine #5 © DC

GD VG FN VF VF/NM NM-
2.0 4.0 6.0 8.0 9.0 9.2

Color Special 1 (2/89, $2.95, 44 pgs.)-r/1st two Concrete apps. from Dark Horse Presents #1,2 plus new-a 6.00
Depths TPB (7/05, $12.95)-r/#1-5, stories from DHP #1,8,10,150; other short stories 13.00
Land And Sea 1 (2/89, $2.95, B&W)-r/#1,2 6.00
Odd Jobs 1 (7/90, $3.50)-r/5,6 plus new-a 4.00
...Vol. 1: Depths ('05, $12.95, 9"x6") r/#1-5 & short stories 13.00
...Vol. 2: Heights ('05, $12.95, 9"x6") r/#6-10 & short stories 13.00
...Vol. 3: Fragile Creatures (1/06, $12.95, 9"x6") r/mini-series & short stories from DHP 13.00
...Vol. 4: Killer Smile (3/06, $12.95, 9"x6") r/mini-series & short stories from various 13.00
...Vol. 5: Think Like a Mountain (5/06, $12.95, 9"x6") r/mini-series & short stories 13.00
...Vol. 6: Strange Armor (7/06, $12.95, 9"x6") r/mini-series & short stories 13.00
...Vol. 7: The Human Dilemma (4/06, $12.95, 9"x6") r/mini-series 13.00

CONCRETE: (Title series), **Dark Horse Comics**

--ECLECTICA, 4/93 - No. 2, 5/93 ($2.95) 1,2 4.00

--FRAGILE CREATURE, 6/91 - No. 4, 2/92 ($2.50) 1-4 4.00

--KILLER SMILE, (Legend), 7/94 - No. 4, 10/94 ($2.95) 1-4 4.00

--STRANGE ARMOR, 12/97 - No. 5, 5/98 ($2.95, color) 1-5-Chadwick-s/c/a; retells origin 4.00

--THE HUMAN DILEMMA, 12/04 - No. 6, 5/05 ($3.50)
1-6: Chadwick-a/c & scripts; Concrete has a child 3.50

--THINK LIKE A MOUNTAIN, (Legend), 3/96 - No. 6, 8/96 ($2.95)
1-6: Chadwick-a/scripts & Darrow-c in all 4.00

CONDORMAN (Walt Disney)
Whitman Publishing: Oct, 1981 - No. 3, Jan, 1982
1-3: 1,2-Movie adaptation; photo-c 1 3 4 6 8 10

CONEHEADS
Marvel Comics: June, 1994 - No. 4, 1994 ($1.75, limited series)
1-4 3.00

CONFESSIONS ILLUSTRATED (Magazine)
E. C. Comics: Jan-Feb, 1956 - No. 2, Spring, 1956
1-Craig, Kamen, Wood, Orlando-a 30 60 90 177 289 400
2-Craig, Crandall, Kamen, Orlando-a 22 44 66 132 216 300

CONFESSIONS OF LOVE
Artful Publ.: Apr, 1950 - No. 2, July, 1950 (25¢, 7-1/4x5-1/4", 132 pgs.)
1-Bakerish-a 53 106 159 334 567 800
2-Art & text; Bakerish-a 34 68 102 199 325 450

CONFESSIONS OF LOVE (Formerly Startling Terror Tales #10; becomes Confessions of Romance No. 7 on)
Star Publications: No. 11, 7/52 - No. 14, 1/53; No. 4, 3/53- No. 6, 8/53
11-13: 12,13-Disbrow-a 17 34 51 98 154 210
14,5,6 14 28 42 81 118 155
4-Disbrow-a 15 30 45 83 124 165
NOTE: *All have* **L. B. Cole** *covers.*

CONFESSIONS OF ROMANCE (Formerly Confessions of Love)
Star Publications: No. 7, Nov, 1953 - No. 11, Nov, 1954
7 17 34 51 98 154 210
8 14 28 42 81 118 155
9-Wood-a 15 30 45 86 133 180
10,11-Disbrow-a 15 30 45 83 124 165
NOTE: *All have* **L. B. Cole** *covers.*

CONFESSIONS OF THE LOVELORN (Formerly Lovelorn)
American Comics Group (Regis Publ./Best Synd. Features): No. 52, Aug, 1954 - No. 114, June-July, 1960
52 (3-D effect) 32 64 96 188 307 425
53,55 12 24 36 69 97 125
54 (3-D effect) 31 62 93 182 296 410
56-Anti-communist propaganda story, 10 pgs; last pre-code (2/55) 15 30 45 86 133 180
57-90,100 9 18 27 52 69 85
91-Williamson-a 10 20 30 58 79 100
92-99,101-114 8 16 24 42 54 65
NOTE: **Whitney** *a-most issues; c-52, 53. Painted c-106, 107.*

CONFIDENTIAL DIARY (Formerly High School Confidential Diary; Three Nurses #18 on)
Charlton Comics: No. 12, May, 1962 - No. 17, Mar, 1963
12-17 3 6 9 15 21 26

CONGO BILL (See Action Comics & More Fun Comics #56)
National Periodical Publication: Aug-Sept, 1954 - No. 7, Aug-Sept, 1955
1 (Scarce) 200 400 600 1600 - -
2,7 (Scarce) 125 250 375 1000 - -
3-6 (Scarce). 4-Last pre-code issue 100 200 300 800 - -
NOTE: *(Rarely found in fine to mint condition.)* **Nick Cardy** *c-1-7.*

CONGO BILL
DC Comics (Vertigo): Oct, 1999 - No. 4, Jan, 2000 ($2.95, limited series)
1-4-Corben-c 3.00

CONGORILLA (Also see Actions Comics #224)
DC Comics: Nov, 1992 - No. 4, Feb, 1993 ($1.75, limited series)
1-4: 1,2-Brian Bolland-c 3.00

CONJURORS
DC Comics: Apr, 1999 - No. 3, Jun, 1999 ($2.95, limited series)
1-3-Elseworlds; Phantom Stranger app.; Barreto-c/a 3.00

CONNECTICUT YANKEE, A (See King Classics)

CONNOR HAWKE: DRAGON'S BLOOD (Also see Green Arrow titles)
DC Comics: Jan, 2007 - No. 6, Jun, 2007 ($2.99, limited series)
1-6-Chuck Dixon-s/Derec Donovan-a/c 3.00
SC (2008, $19.99) r/#1-6 20.00

CONQUEROR, THE
Dell Publishing Co.: No., 690, Mar, 1956
Four Color 690-Movie, John Wayne photo-c 14 28 42 94 207 320

CONQUEROR COMICS
Albrecht Publishing Co.: Winter, 1945
nn 22 44 66 132 216 300

CONQUEROR OF THE BARREN EARTH (See The Warlord #63)
DC Comics: Feb, 1985 - No. 4, May, 1985 (Limited series)
1-4: Back-up series from Warlord 3.00

CONQUEST
Store Comics: 1953 (6¢)
1-Richard the Lion Hearted, Beowulf, Swamp Fox 7 14 21 35 43 50

CONQUEST
Famous Funnies: Spring, 1955
1-Crandall-a, 1 pg.; contains contents of 1953 ish. 5 10 15 22 26 30

CONSPIRACY
Marvel Comics: Feb, 1998 - No. 2, Mar, 1998 ($2.99, limited series)
1,2-Painted art by Korday/Abnett-s 3.00

CONSTANTINE (Also see Hellblazer)
DC Comics (Vertigo): 2005 (Based on the 2005 Keanu Reeves movie)
...: The Hellblazer Collection (2005, $14.95) Movie adaptation and r/#1, 27, 41; photo-c 15.00
...: The Official Movie Adaptation (2005, $6.95) Seagle-s/Randall-a/photo-c 7.00

CONSTANTINE (Also see Justice League Dark)
DC Comics: May, 2013 - Present ($2.99)
1-Lemire & Fawkes-s/Guedes-a; two covers by Reis & Guedes 3.00
2-12: 2-The Spectre app. 5-Trinity War tie-in; Shazam app. 9-Forever Evil tie-in 3.00

CONSTRUCT
Caliber (New Worlds): 1996 - No. 6, 1997 ($2.95, B&W, limited series)
1-6: Paul Jenkins scripts 3.00

CONSUMED
Platinum Studios: July, 2007 - No. 4, Oct, 2007 ($2.99, limited series)
1-4-Linsner-c/Budd-a/Shumskas-Tait-s 3.00

CONTACT COMICS
Aviation Press: July, 1944 - No. 12, May, 1946
nn-Black Venus, Flamingo, Golden Eagle, Tommy Tomahawk begin 63 126 189 403 689 975
2-5: 3-Last Flamingo. 3,4-Black Venus by L. B. Cole. 5-The Phantom Flyer app. 43 86 129 271 461 650
6,11-Kurtzman's Black Venus; 11-Last Golden Eagle, last Tommy Tomahawk; Feldstein-a 48 96 144 302 514 725
7-10 39 78 117 240 395 550
12-Sky Rangers, Air Kids, Ace Diamond app.; L.B. Cole sci-fi cover 155 310 465 992 1696 2400
NOTE: **L. B. Cole** *a-3, 9; c-1-12.* **Giunta** *a-3.* **Hollingsworth** *a-5, 7, 10.* **Palais** *a-11, 12.*

CONTEMPORARY MOTIVATORS
Pendelum Press: 1977 - 1978 ($1.45, 5-3/8x8", 31 pgs., B&W)
14-3002 The Caine Mutiny; 14-3010 Banner in the Sky; 14-3029 God Is My Co-Pilot; 14-3037

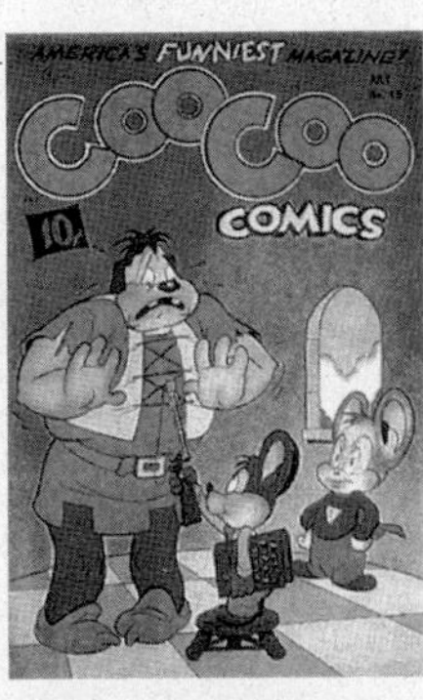

Coo Coo Comics #40 © STD

Cool World #2 © Paramount

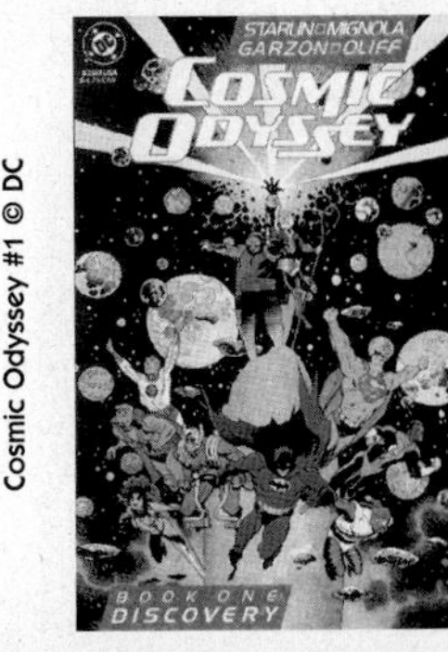

Cosmic Odyssey #1 © DC

GD 2.0 | VG 4.0 | FN 6.0 | VF 8.0 | VF/NM 9.0 | NM- 9.2

Guadalcanal Diary; 14-3045 Hiroshima; 14-3053 Hot Rod; 14-3061 Just Dial a Number; 14-3088 The Diary of Anne Frank; 14-3096 Lost Horizon
2 4 6 8 10 12

NOTE: *Also see Pendulum Illustrated Classics. Above may have been distributed the same.*

CONTEST OF CHAMPIONS (See Marvel Super-Hero...)

CONTEST OF CHAMPIONS II
Marvel Comics: Sept, 1999 - No. 5 ($2.50, limited series)
1-5-Claremont-s/Jimenez-a 3.00

CONTRACTORS
Eclipse Comics: June, 1987 ($2.00, B&W, one-shot)
1-Funny animal 3.00

CONTRACT WITH GOD, A
Baronet Publishing Co./Kitchen Sink Press: 1978 ($4.95/$7.95, B&W, graphic novel)
nn-Will Eisner-s/a 3 6 9 14 20 25
Reprint (DC Comics, 2000, $12.95) 13.00

CONVOCATIONS: A MAGIC THE GATHERING GALLERY
Acclaim Comics (Armada): Jan, 1996 ($2.50, one-shot)
1-pin-ups by various artists including Kaluta, Vess, and Dringenberg 3.00

COO COO COMICS (...the Bird Brain No. 57 on)
Nedor Publ. Co./Standard (Animated Cartoons): Oct, 1942 - No. 62, Apr, 1952
1-Origin/1st app. Super Mouse & begin series (cloned from Superman); the first funny animal super hero series (see Looney Tunes #5 for 1st funny animal super hero)
36 72 108 211 343 475
2 17 34 51 98 154 210
3-10: 10-(3/44) 13 26 39 74 105 135
11-33: 33-1 pg. Ingels-a 10 20 30 58 79 100
34-40,43-46,48-Text illos by Frazetta in all. 36-Super Mouse covers begin
13 26 39 72 101 130
41-Frazetta-a (6-pg. story & 3 text illos) 22 44 66 132 216 300
42,47-Frazetta-a & text illos. 16 32 48 94 147 200
49-(1/50)-3-D effect story; Frazetta text illo 15 30 45 83 124 165
50,51-3-D effect-c only. 50-Frazetta text illo 14 28 42 80 115 150
52-62: 56-58,61-Super Mouse app. 9 18 27 52 69 85

"COOKIE" (Also see Topsy-Turvy)
Michel Publ./American Comics Group(Regis Publ.): Apr, 1946 - No. 55, Aug-Sept, 1955
1-Teen-age humor 26 52 78 154 252 350
2-1st app. Tee-Pee Tim who takes over Ha Ha Comics later
15 30 45 84 127 170
3-10: 8-Bing Crosby app. 12 24 36 69 97 125
11-20: 12-Hedy Lamarr app. 13-Jackie Robinson mentioned. 15-Gregory Peck app. 16-Ub Iwerks (a creator of Mickey Mouse) name used. 18-Jane Russell-type Jane Bustle. 19-Cookie takes a dog to see Lassie movie 11 22 33 60 83 105
21-23,26,28-30: 26-Milt Gross & Starlett O'Hara stories. 28,30-Starlett O'Hara stories
9 18 27 50 65 80
24,25,27-Starlett O'Hara stories 9 18 27 52 69 85
31-34,37-48,50,52-55 8 16 24 42 54 65
35,36-Starlett O'Hara stories 9 18 27 47 61 75
49,51: 49-(6-7/54)-3-D effect-c/s. 51-(10-11/54) 8pg. TrueVision 3-D effect story
13 26 39 74 105 135

COOL CAT (What's Cookin' With...) (Formerly Black Magic)
Prize Publications: V8#6, Mar-Apr, 1962 - V9#2, July-Aug, 1962
V8#6, nn(V9#1, 5-6/62), V9#2 3 6 9 17 26 35

COOL WORLD (Movie by Ralph Bakshi)
DC Comics: Apr, 1992 - No. 4, Sept, 1992 ($1.75, limited series)
1-4: Prequel to animated/live action movie. 1-Bakshi-c. Bill Wray inks in all 3.00
Movie Adaptation nn ('92, $3.50, 68pg.)-Bakshi-c 4.00

COPPER CANYON (See Fawcett Movie Comics)

COPS (TV)
DC Comics: Aug, 1988 - No. 15, Aug, 1989 ($1.00)
1 ($1.50, 52 pgs.)-Based on Hasbro Toys 4.00
2-15: 14-Orlando-c(p) 3.00

COPS: THE JOB
Marvel Comics: June, 1992 - No. 4, Sept, 1992 ($1.25, limited series)
1-4: All have Jusko scripts & Golden-c 3.00

CORBEN SPECIAL, A
Pacific Comics: May, 1984 (one-shot)
1-Corben-c/a; E.A. Poe adaptation 6.00

GD 2.0 | VG 4.0 | FN 6.0 | VF 8.0 | VF/NM 9.0 | NM- 9.2

CORE, THE
Image Comics: July, 2008 ($3.99)
Pilot Season - Hickman-s/Rocafort-a 4.00

CORKY & WHITE SHADOW (Disney, TV)
Dell Publishing Co.: No. 707, May, 1956 (Mickey Mouse Club)
Four Color 707-Photo-c 6 12 18 40 73 105

CORLISS ARCHER (See Meet Corliss Archer)

CORMAC MAC ART (Robert E. Howard's...)
Dark Horse Comics: 1990 - No. 4, 1990 ($1.95, B&W, mini-series)
1-4: All have Bolton painted-c; Howard adapts. 3.00

CORNY'S FETISH
Dark Horse Comics: Apr, 1998 ($4.95, B&W, one-shot)
1-Renée French-s/a; Bolland-c 5.00

CORPORAL RUSTY DUGAN (See Holyoke One-Shot #2)

CORPSES OF DR. SACOTTI, THE (See Ideal a Classical Comic)

CORSAIR, THE (See A-1 Comics No. 5, 7, 10 under Texas Slim)

CORTEZ AND THE FALL OF THE AZTECS
Tome Press: 1993 ($2.95, B&W, limited series)
1,2 3.00

CORUM: THE BULL AND THE SPEAR (See Chronicles Of Corum)
First Comics: Jan, 1989 - No. 4, July, 1989 ($1.95)
1-4: Adapts Michael Moorcock's novel 3.00

COSMIC BOOK, THE
Ace Comics: Dec, 1986 - No. 1, 1987 ($1.95)
1,2: 1-(44pgs.)-Wood, Toth-a. 2-(B&W) 4.00

COSMIC BOY (Also see The Legion of Super-Heroes)
DC Comics: Dec, 1986 - No. 4, Mar, 1987 (limited series)
1-4: Legends tie-ins all issues 4.00

COSMIC GUARD
Devil's Due Publ.: Aug, 2004 - No. 6, Dec, 2005 ($2.99)
1-6-Jim Starlin-s/a 3.00

COSMIC HEROES
Eternity/Malibu Graphics: Oct, 1988 - No. 11, Dec, 1989 ($1.95, B&W)
1-11: Reprints 1934-1936's Buck Rogers newspaper strips #1-728 3.00

COSMIC ODYSSEY
DC Comics: 1988 - No. 4, 1988 ($3.50, limited series, squarebound)
1-4: Reintro. New Gods into DC continuity; Superman, Batman, Green Lantern (John Stewart) app; Starlin scripts, Mignola-c/a in all. 2-Darkseid merges Demon & Jason Blood (separated in Demon limited series #4) 5.00
TPB (1992,2009, $19.99) r/#1-4; Robert Greenberger intro. 20.00

COSMIC POWERS
Marvel Comics: Mar, 1994 - No. 6, Aug, 1994 ($2.50, limited series)
1,2-Thanos app. 1-Ron Lim-c/a(p). 2-Terrax 5.00
3-6: 3-Ganymede & Jack of Hearts app. 4.00

COSMIC POWERS UNLIMITED
Marvel Comics: May, 1995 - No. 5, May, 1996 ($3.95, quarterly)
1-5 4.00

COSMIC RAY
Image Comics: June, 1999 - No. 2 ($2.95, B&W)
1,2-Steven Blue-s/a 3.00

COSMIC SLAM
Ultimate Sports Entertainment: 1999 ($3.95, one-shot)
1-McGwire, Sosa, Bagwell, Justice battle aliens; Sienkiewicz-c 4.00

COSMO CAT (Becomes Sunny #11 on; also see All Top & Wotalife Comics)
Fox Publications/Green Publ. Co./Norlen Mag.: July-Aug, 1946 - No. 10, Oct, 1947; 1957; 1959
1 27 54 81 158 259 360
2 15 30 45 85 130 175
3-Origin (11-12/46) 19 38 57 109 172 235
4-Robot-c 14 28 42 78 112 145
5-10 11 22 33 60 83 105
2-4(1957-Green Publ. Co.) 6 12 18 27 33 38
2-4(1959-Norlen Mag.) 5 10 15 23 28 32

Countdown #39 © DC

Coup D'Etat: Sleeper #1 © WSP

Coven #6 © Awesome

	GD	VG	FN	VF	VF/NM	NM-
	2.0	4.0	6.0	8.0	9.0	9.2

GD VG FN VF VF/NM NM-
2.0 4.0 6.0 8.0 9.0 9.2

I.W. Reprint #1 2 4 6 11 16 20

COSMO THE MERRY MARTIAN
Archie Publications (Radio Comics): Sept, 1958 - No. 6, Oct, 1959

1-Bob White-a in all 15 30 45 90 140 190
2-6 11 22 33 60 83 105

COTTON WOODS
Dell Publishing Co.: No. 837, Sept, 1957

Four Color 837 4 8 12 25 40 55

COUGAR, THE (Cougar No. 2)
Seaboard Periodicals (Atlas): April, 1975 - No. 2, July, 1975

1,2: 1-Vampire; Adkins-a(p). 2-Cougar origin; werewolf-s; Buckler-c(p) 2 4 6 11 16 20

COUNTDOWN (See Movie Classics)

COUNTDOWN
DC Comics (WildStorm): June, 2000 - No. 8, Jan, 2001 ($2.95)

1-8-Mariotte-s/Lopresti-a 3.00

COUNTDOWN (Continued from 52 weekly series)
DC Comics: No. 51, July, 2007 - No. 1, June, 2008 ($2.99, weekly, limited series) (issue #s go in reverse)

51-Gatefold wraparound-c by Andy Kubert; Duela Dent killed; the Monitors app. 3.00
50-1: 50-Joker-c. 48-Lightray dies. 47-Mary Marvel gains Black Adam's powers. 46-Intro. Forerunner. 43-Funeral for Bart Allen. 39-Karate Kid-c 3.00
Countdown to Final Crisis Vol. 1 TPB (2008, $19.99) r/#51-39 20.00
Countdown to Final Crisis Vol. 2 TPB (2008, $19.99) r/#38-26 20.00
Countdown to Final Crisis Vol. 3 TPB (2008, $19.99) r/#25-13 20.00
Countdown to Final Crisis Vol. 4 TPB (2008, $19.99) r/#12-1 20.00

COUNTDOWN: ARENA (Takes place during Countdown #21-18)
DC Comics: Feb, 2008 - No. 4, Feb, 2008 ($3.99, weekly, limited series)

1-4-Battles between alternate Earth heroes; McDaniel-a; Andy Kubert variant-c on each 4.00
TPB (2008, $17.99) r/#1-4; variant covers 18.00

COUNTDOWN PRESENTS: LORD HAVOK & THE EXTREMISTS
DC Comics: Dec, 2007 - No. 8 ($2.99, limited series)

1-6: 1-Tieri-s/Sharp-a/c; Challengers From Beyond app. 3.00
TPB (2008, $17.99) r/#1-6 18.00

COUNTDOWN PRESENTS THE SEARCH FOR RAY PALMER (Leads into Countdown #18)
DC Comics: Nov, 2007 - Feb, 2008 ($2.99, series of one-shots)

...: Wildstorm (11/07) Part 1; The Authority app.; Art Adams-c/Unzueta-a 3.00
...: Crime Society (12/07) Earth-3 Owlman & Jokester app.; Igle-a 3.00
...: Red Rain (1/08) Vampire Batman app.; Kelley Jones-c; Jones, Battle & Unzueta-a 3.00
...: Gotham By Gaslight (1/08) Victorian Batman app.; Tocchini-a/Nguyen-c 3.00
...: Red Son (2/08) Soviet Superman app.; Foreman-a 3.00
...: Superwoman/Batwoman (2/08) Conclusion; gender-reversed heroes; Sook-c 3.00
TPB (2008, $17.99) r/one-shots 18.00

COUNTDOWN SPECIAL
DC Comics: Dec, 2007 - Jun, 2008 ($4.99, collection of reprints related to Countdown)

...: Eclipso (5/08) r/Eclipso #10 & Spectre #17,18 (1994); Sook-c 5.00
...: Jimmy Olsen (1/08) r/Superman's Pal, Jimmy Olsen #136,147,148; Kirby-s/a; Sook-c 5.00
...: Kamandi (6/08) r/Kamandi: The Last Boy on Earth #1,10,29; Kirby-s/a; Sook-c 5.00
...: New Gods (3/08) r/Forever People #1, Mr. Miracle #1, New Gods #7; Kirby-s/a; Sook-c 5.00
...: Omac (4/08) r/Omac (1974) #1, Warlord #37-39, DC Comics Presents #61; Sook-c 5.00
...: The Atom 1,2 (2/08) r/stories from Super-Team Family #11-14; Sook-c on both 5.00
...: The Flash (12/07) r/Rogues Gallery in Flash (1st series) #106,113,155,174; Sook-c 5.00

COUNTDOWN TO ADVENTURE
DC Comics: Oct, 2007 - No. 8, May, 2008 ($3.99, limited series)

1-8: 1-Adam Strange, Animal Man and Starfire app.; origin of Forerunner 4.00
TPB (2008, $17.99) r/#1-8 18.00

COUNTDOWN TO INFINITE CRISIS (See DC Countdown)

COUNTDOWN TO MYSTERY (See Eclipso: The Music of the Spheres TPB for reprint)
DC Comics: Nov, 2007 - No. 8, Jun, 2008 ($3.99, limited series)

1-8: 1-Doctor Fate, Eclipso, The Spectre and Plastic Man app. 4.00
TPB (2008, $17.99) r/#1-8 18.00

COUNT DUCKULA (TV)
Marvel Comics: Nov, 1988 - No. 15, Jan, 1991 ($1.00)

1,8: 1-Dangermouse back-up. 8-Geraldo Rivera photo-c/& app.; Sienkiewicz-a(i) 5.00
2-7,9-15: Dangermouse back-ups in all 4.00

COUNT OF MONTE CRISTO, THE
Dell Publishing Co.: No. 794, May, 1957

Four Color 794-Movie, Buscema-a 7 14 21 48 89 130

COUP D'ETAT (Oneshots)
DC Comics (WildStorm): April, 2004 ($2.95, weekly limited series)

...: Sleeper 1 (part 1 of 4) Jim Lee-a; 2 covers by Lee and Bermejo 3.00
...: Stormwatch 1 (part 2 of 4) D'Anda-a; 2 covers by D'Anda and Bermejo 3.00
...: Wildcats Version 3.0 1 (part 3 of 4) Garza-a; 2 covers by Garza and Bermejo 3.00
...: The Authority 1 (part 4 of 4) Portacio-a; 2 covers by Portacio and Bermejo 3.00
...: Afterword 1 (5/04) Profile pages and prelude stories for Sleeper & Wetworks 3.00
TPB (2004, $12.95) r/series and profile pages from Afterword 13.00

COURAGE COMICS
J. Edward Slavin: 1945

1,2,77 15 30 45 83 124 165

COURTNEY CRUMRIN
Oni Press: Apr, 2012 - No. 10, Feb, 2013 ($3.99)

1-10-Ted Naifeh-s/a 4.00

COURTNEY CRUMRIN...
Oni Press: July, 2005; July 2007; Dec, 2008 ($5.95, B&W, series of one-shots)

... And The Fire Thief's Tale (7/07) Naifeh-s/a 6.00
... And The Prince of Nowhere (12/08) Naifeh-s/a 6.00
... Tales (5/11) sequel to Tales Portrait of the Warlock...; Naifeh-s/a 6.00
... Tales Portrait of the Warlock as a Young Man (7/05) origin Uncle Aloysius; Naifeh-s/a 6.00

COURTNEY CRUMRIN & THE COVEN OF MYSTICS
Oni Press: Dec, 2002 - No. 4, March, 2003 ($2.95, B&W, limited series)

1-4-Ted Naifeh-s/a 3.00
TPB (9/03, $11.95, 8" x 5-1/2") r/#1-4 12.00

COURTNEY CRUMRIN & THE NIGHT THINGS
Oni Press: Mar, 2002 - No. 4, June, 2002 ($2.95, B&W, limited series)

1-4-Ted Naifeh-s/a 3.00
Free Comic Book Day Edition (5/03) Naifeh-s/a 3.00
TPB (12/02, $11.95) r/#1-4 12.00

COURTNEY CRUMRIN IN THE TWILIGHT KINGDOM
Oni Press: Dec, 2003 - No. 4, May, 2004 ($2.99, B&W, limited series)

1-4-Ted Naifeh-s/a 3.00
TPB (9/04, $11.95, digest-size) r/#1-4 12.00

COURTSHIP OF EDDIE'S FATHER (TV)
Dell Publishing Co.: Jan, 1970 - No. 2, May, 1970

1-Bill Bixby photo-c on both 5 10 15 33 57 80
2 4 8 12 23 37 50

COVEN
Awesome Entertainment: Aug, 1997 - No. 5, Mar, 1998 ($2.50)

Preview 1 2 3 5 6 8
1-Loeb-s/Churchill-a; three covers by Churchill, Liefeld, Pollina 1 2 3 5 6 8
1-Fan Appreciation Ed.(3/98); new Churchill-c 3.00
1+ :Includes B&W art from Kaboom 1 3 4 6 8 10
2-Regular-c w/leaping Fantom 6.00
2-Variant-c w/circle of candles 1 2 3 5 6 8
3-6-Contains flip book preview of ReGex 3.00
3-White variant-c 1 2 3 4 5 7
3,4: 3-Halloween wraparound-c. 4-Purple variant-c 3.00
...Black & White (9/98) Short stories 3.00
...Fantom Special (2/98) w/sketch pages 5.00

COVEN
Awesome Entertainment: Jan, 1999 - No. 3, June, 1999 ($2.50)

1-3: 1-Loeb-s/Churchill-a; 6 covers by various. 2-Supreme-c/app. 3-Flip book w/Kaboom preview 3.00
... Dark Origins (7/99, 2.50) w/Lionheart gallery 3.00

COVENANT, THE
Image Comics (Top Cow): 2005 ($9.99, squarebound, one-shot)

nn-Tone Rodriguez-a/Aron Coleite-s 10.00

COVERED WAGONS, HO (Disney, TV)
Dell Publishing Co.: No. 814, June, 1957 (Donald Duck)

Four Color 814-Mickey Mouse app. 5 10 15 31 53 75

COWBOY ACTION (Formerly Western Thrillers No. 1-4; Becomes Quick-Trigger Western

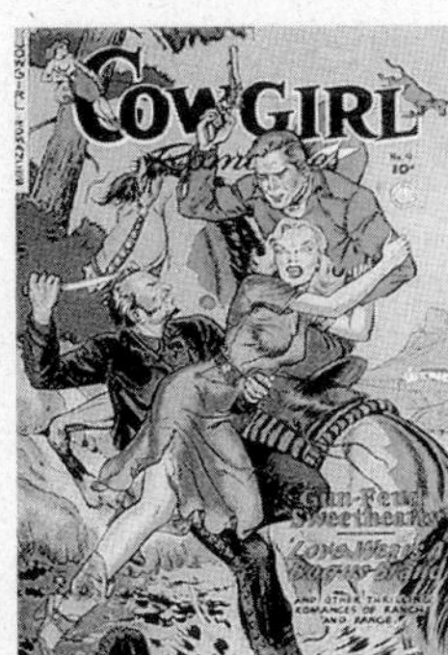

Cowgirl Romances #9 © FH

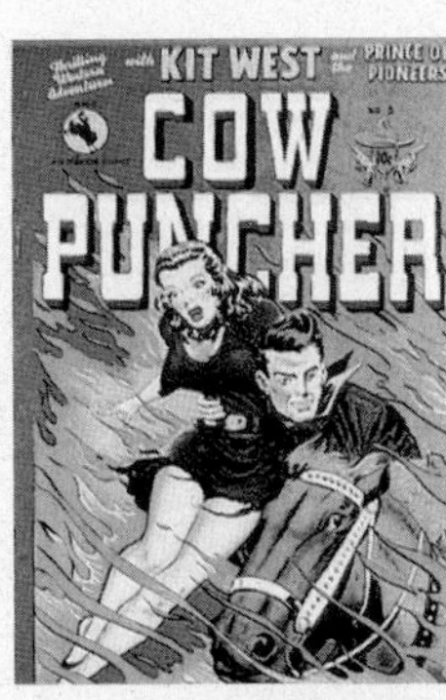

Cow Puncher #5 © AVON

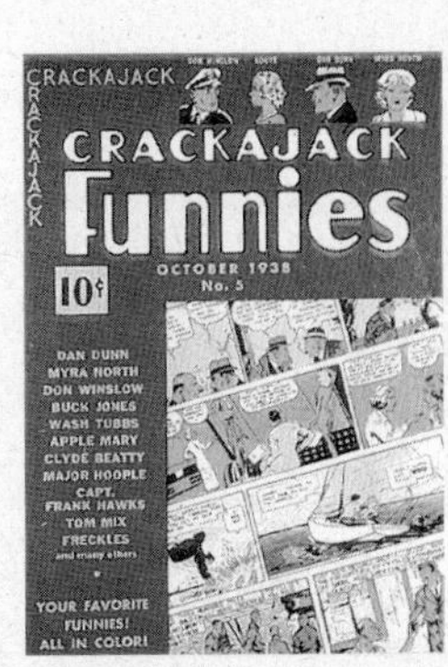

Crackajack Funnies #5 © DELL

	GD 2.0	VG 4.0	FN 6.0	VF 8.0	VF/NM 9.0	NM- 9.2

No. 12 on)
Atlas Comics (ACI): No. 5, March, 1955 - No. 11, March, 1956

5	14	28	42	80	115	150
6-10: 6-8-Heath-c	10	20	30	56	76	95
11-Williamson-a (4 pgs.); Baker-a	11	22	33	64	90	115

NOTE: *Ayers a-8. Drucker a-6. Maneely c/a-5, 6. Severin c-10. Shores a-7.*

COWBOY COMICS (Star Ranger #12, Stories #14)(Star Ranger Funnies #15)
Centaur Publishing Co.: No. 13, July, 1938 - No. 14, Aug, 1938

13-(Rare)-Ace and Deuce, Lyin Lou, Air Patrol, Aces High, Lee Trent, Trouble Hunters begin	168	336	504	1075	1838	2600
14-Filchock-c	103	206	309	659	1130	1600

NOTE: *Guardineer a-13, 14. Gustavson a-13, 14.*

COWBOY IN AFRICA (TV)
Gold Key: Mar, 1968

1(10219-803)-Chuck Connors photo-c	4	8	12	25	40	55

COWBOY LOVE (Becomes Range Busters?)
Fawcett Publications/Charlton Comics No. 28 on: 7/49 - V2#10, 6/50; No. 11, 1951; No. 28, 2/55 - No. 31, 8/55

V1#1-Rocky Lane photo back-c	15	30	45	88	137	185
2	8	16	24	44	57	70
V1#3,4,6 (12/49)	8	16	24	40	50	60
5-Bill Boyd photo back-c (11/49)	9	18	27	47	61	75
V2#7-Williamson/Evans-a	10	20	30	54	72	90
V2#8-11	7	14	21	35	43	50
V1#28 (Charlton)-Last precode (2/55) (Formerly Romantic Story?)	6	12	18	31	38	45
V1#29-31 (Charlton; becomes Sweetheart Diary #32 on)	6	12	18	28	34	40

NOTE: *Powell a-10. Marcus Swayze a-2, 3. Photo c-1-11. No. 1-3, 5-7, 9, 10 are 52 pgs.*

COWBOY ROMANCES (Young Men No. 4 on)
Marvel Comics (IPC): Oct, 1949 - No. 3, Mar, 1950 (All photo-c & 52 pgs.)

1-Photo-c	24	48	72	140	230	320
2-William Holden, Mona Freeman "Streets of Laredo" photo-c	17	34	51	98	154	210
3-Photo-c	15	30	45	85	130	175

COWBOYS 'N' INJUNS (...and Indians No. 6 on)
Compix No. 1-5/Magazine Enterprises No. 6 on: 1946 - No. 5, 1947; No. 6, 1949 - No. 8, 1952

1-Funny animal western	15	30	45	83	124	165
2-5-All funny animal western	10	20	30	54	72	90
6(A-1 23)-Half violent, half funny; Ayers-a	14	28	42	78	112	145
7(A-1 41, 1950), 8(A-1 48)-All funny	9	18	27	47	61	75
I.W. Reprint No. 1,7,10 (Reprinted in Canada by Superior, No. 7), 10('63)	2	4	6	11	16	20

COWBOY WESTERN COMICS (TV)(Formerly Jack In The Box; Becomes Space Western No. 40-45 & Wild Bill Hickok & Jingles No. 68 on; title:Cowboy Western Heroes No. 47 & 48; Cowboy Western No. 49 on)
Charlton (Capitol Stories): No. 17, 7/48 - No. 39, 8/52; No. 46, 10/53; No. 47, 12/53; No. 48, Spr, '54; No. 49, 5-6/54 - No. 67, 3/58 (nn 40-45)

17-Jesse James, Annie Oakley, Wild Bill Hickok begin; Texas Rangers app.	16	32	48	94	147	200
18,19-Orlando-c/a. 18-Paul Bunyan begins. 19-Wyatt Earp story	10	20	30	58	79	100
20-25: 21-Buffalo Bill story. 22-Texas Rangers-c/story. 24-Joel McCrea photo-c & adaptation from movie "Three Faces West". 25-James Craig photo-c & adaptation from movie "Northwest Stampede"	9	18	27	52	69	85
26-George Montgomery photo-c and adaptation from movie "Indian Scout"; 1 pg. bio on Will Rogers	10	20	30	58	79	100
27-Sunset Carson photo-c & adapts movie "Sunset Carson Rides Again" plus 1 other Sunset Carson story	39	78	117	240	395	550
28-Sunset Carson line drawn-c; adapts movies "Battling Marshal" & "Fighting Mustangs" starring Sunset Carson	20	40	60	114	182	250
29-Sunset Carson line drawn-c; adapts movies "Rio Grande" with Sunset Carson & "Winchester '73" w/James Stewart plus 5 pg. life history of Sunset Carson featuring Tom Mix	20	40	60	114	182	250
30-Sunset Carson photo-c; adapts movie "Deadline" starring Sunset Carson plus 1 other Sunset Carson story	39	78	117	240	395	550
31-34,38,39,47-50 (no #40-45): 50-Golden Arrow, Rocky Lane & Blackjack (r?) stories	9	18	27	47	61	75
35,36-Sunset Carson-c/stories (2 in each). 35-Inside front-c photo of Sunset Carson plus photo on-c	20	40	60	120	195	270
37-Sunset Carson stories (2)	15	30	45	94	147	200
46-(Formerly Space Western)-Space western story	15	30	45	94	147	200
51-57,59-66: 51-Golden Arrow(r?) & Monte Hale-r renamed Rusty Hall. 53,54-Tom Mix-r. 55-Monte Hale story(r?). 66-Young Eagle story. 67-Wild Bill Hickok and Jingles-c/story	7	14	21	35	43	50
58-(1/56, 15¢, 68 pgs.)-Wild Bill Hickok, Annie Oakley & Jesse James stories; Forgione-a	8	16	24	44	57	70
67-(15¢, 68 pgs.)-Williamson/Torres-a, 5 pgs.	9	18	27	50	65	80

NOTE: *Many issues trimmed 1" shorter. Maneely a-67(5). Inside front/back photo c-29.*

COWGIRL ROMANCES
Marvel Comics (CCC): No. 28, Jan, 1950 (52 pgs.)

28(#1)-Photo-c	22	44	66	128	209	290

COWGIRL ROMANCES
Fiction House Magazines: 1950 - No. 12, Winter, 1952-53 (No. 1-3: 52 pgs.)

1-Kamen-a	45	90	135	284	480	675
2	24	48	72	140	230	320
3-5: 5-12-Whitman-c (most)	21	42	63	122	199	275
6-9,11,12	20	40	60	118	192	265
10-Frazetta?/Williamson?-a; Kamen?/Baker-a; r/Mitzi story from Movie Comics #4 w/all new dialogue	36	72	108	211	343	475

COW PUNCHER (...Comics)
Avon Periodicals: Jan, 1947; No. 2, Sept, 1947 - No. 7, 1949

1-Clint Cortland, Texas Ranger, Kit West, Pioneer Queen begin; Kubert-a; Alabam stories begin	48	96	144	302	514	725
2-Kubert, Kamen/Feldstein-a; Kamen-c	40	80	120	244	402	560
3-5,7: 3-Kiefer story	30	60	90	177	289	400
6-Opium drug mention story; bondage, headlight-c; Reinman-a	39	78	117	233	384	535

COWPUNCHER
Realistic Publications: 1953 (nn) (Reprints Avon's No. 2)

nn-Kubert-a	14	28	42	76	108	140

COWSILLS, THE (See Harvey Pop Comics)

COW SPECIAL, THE
Image Comics (Top Cow): Spring-Summer 2000; 2001 ($2.95)

1-Previews upcoming Top Cow projects; Yancy Butler photo-c						3.00
Vol. 2 #1-Witchblade-c; previews and interviews						3.00

COYOTE
Marvel Comics (Epic Comics): June, 1983 - No. 16, Mar, 1986

1-10,15: 7-10-Ditko-a						4.00
11-1st McFarlane-a.	1	3	4	6	8	10
12-14,16: 12-14-McFarlane-a. 14-Badger x-over. 16-Reagan c/app.						6.00
Coyote Collection Vol. 1 (2005, $14.99) reprints from Coyote #1-7 & Scorpio Rose #1,2 plus Rogers layout pages for unpublished #3; Englehart intro.						15.00
Coyote Collection Vol. 2 (2005, $12.99) reprints from Coyote #1-4						13.00
Coyote Collection Vol. 3 (2006, $12.99) reprints from Coyote #5-8						13.00
Coyote Collection Vol. 4 (2007, $14.99) reprints from Coyote #9-12						15.00
Coyote Collection Vol. 5 (2007, $12.99) reprints from Coyote #13-16						13.00

CRACKAJACK FUNNIES (Also see The Owl)
Dell Publishing Co.: June, 1938 - No. 43, Jan, 1942

1-Dan Dunn, Freckles, Myra North, Wash Tubbs, Apple Mary, The Nebbs, Don Winslow, Tom Mix, Buck Jones, Major Hoople, Clyde Beatty, Boots begin	184	368	552	1168	2009	2850
2	73	146	219	467	796	1125
3	54	108	162	343	574	825
4	43	86	129	271	461	650
5-Nude woman on cover (10/38)	50	100	150	315	533	750
6-8,10: 8-Speed Bolton begins (1st app.)	39	78	117	240	395	550
9-(3/39)-Red Ryder strip-r begin by Harman; 1st app. in comics & 1st cover app.	171	342	513	1086	1868	2650
11-14	34	68	102	204	332	460
15-Tarzan text feature begins by Burroughs (9/39); not in #26,35	37	74	111	222	361	500
16-24: 18-Stratosphere Jim begins (1st app., 12/39). 23-Ellery Queen begins plus-c (1st comic book app., 5/40)	28	56	84	165	270	375
25-The Owl begins (1st app., 7/40); in new costume #26 by Frank Thomas (also see Popular Comics #72)	74	148	222	470	810	1150
26-30: 28-Part Owl-c	48	96	144	302	514	725
31-Owl covers begin, end #42	50	100	150	315	533	750
32-Origin Owl Girl	54	108	162	343	574	825

33-38: 36-Last Tarzan issue. 37-Cyclone & Midge begin (1st app.)

Crack Comics #13 © QUA

Cracked #8 © Major Mags.

Cracked #233 © GCC

GD VG FN VF VF/NM NM-
2.0 4.0 6.0 8.0 9.0 9.2

48 96 144 302 514 725
39-Andy Panda begins (intro/1st app., 9/41) 58 116 174 371 636 900
40-42: 42-Last Owl-c. 37 74 111 222 361 500
43-Terry & the Pirates-r 22 44 66 132 216 300
NOTE: ***McWilliams** art in most issues.*

CRACK COMICS (Crack Western No. 63 on)
Quality Comics Group: May, 1940 - No. 62, Sept, 1949

1-Origin & 1st app. The Black Condor by Lou Fine, Madame Fatal, Red Torpedo, Rock Bradden & The Space Legion; The Clock, Alias the Spider (by Gustavson), Wizard Wells, & Ned Brant begin; Powell-a; Note: Madame Fatal is a man dressed as a woman
465 930 1395 3395 5998 8600
2 219 438 657 1402 2401 3400
3 152 304 456 965 1658 2350
4 123 246 369 787 1344 1900
5-10: 5-Molly The Model begins. 10-Tor, the Magic Master begins
92 184 276 584 1005 1425
11-20: 13-1 pg. J. Cole-a. 15-1st app. Spitfire 82 164 246 528 902 1275
21-24: 23-Pen Miller begins; continued from National Comics #22. 24-Last Fine Black Condor
65 130 195 416 708 1000
25 50 100 150 315 533 750
26-Flag-c 58 116 174 371 636 900
27-(1/43)-Intro & origin Captain Triumph by Alfred Andriola (Kerry Drake artist) & begin series 97 194 291 621 1061 1500
28-30 41 82 123 256 428 600
31-39: 31-Last Black Condor 24 48 72 142 234 325
40-46 17 34 51 100 158 215
47-57,59,60-Capt. Triumph by Crandall 18 36 54 107 169 230
58,61,62-Last Captain Triumph 15 30 45 85 130 175
NOTE: *Black Condor by **Fine**: No. 1, 2, 5, 6, 8, 10-24; by **Sultan**: No. 3, 7; by **Fugitani**: No. 9. **Cole** a-34. **Crandall** a-61(unsigned); c-48, 49, 51-61. **Guardineer** a-17. **Gustavson** a-1, 2, 4, 7, 13, 17, 23. **McWilliams** a-15-27. Black Condor c-2, 4, 6, 8, 10, 12, 14, 16, 18, 20-26. Capt. Triumph c-27-62. The Clock c-1, 3, 5, 7, 9, 11, 13, 15, 17, 19.*

CRACK COMICS (Next Issue Project)
Image Comics: No. 63, Oct, 2011 ($4.99, one-shot)

63-Mimics style & format of a 1949 issue; Weiss-c; s/a by various; Capt Triumph app. 5.00

CRACK COMICS
Quality Comics: May 1940

1-Ashcan comic, not distributed to newsstands, only for in-house use. Cover art is the same as published version of Crack Comics #1with exception of text panel on bottom left of cover. A CGC certified 4.0 copy sold for $1,495 in 2005.

CRACKED (Magazine) (Satire) (Also see The 3-D Zone #19)
Major Magazines(#1-212)/Globe Communications(#213-346/American Media #347 on):
Feb-Mar, 1958 - No. 365, Nov, 2004

1-One pg. Williamson-a; Everett-c; Gunsmoke-s 23 46 69 161 356 550
2-1st Shut-Ups & Bonus Cut-Outs; Superman parody-c by Severin (his 1st cover on the title) Frankenstein-s 11 22 33 76 163 250
3-5 9 18 27 59 117 175
6-10: 7-Reprints 1st 6 covers on-c. 8-Frankenstein-c. 10-Wolverton-a
7 14 21 49 92 135
11-12, 13(nn,3/60), 6 12 18 38 69 100
14-Kirby-a 7 14 21 44 82 120
15-17, 18(nn,2/61), 19,20 5 10 15 35 63 90
21-27(11/62), 27(No.28, 2/63; mis-#d), 29(5/63) 5 10 15 31 53 75
30-40(11/64): 37-Beatles and Superman cameos 4 8 12 25 40 55
41-45,47-56,59,60: 47,49,52-Munsters. 51-Beatles inside-c. 59-Laurel and Hardy photos
3 6 9 21 33 45
46,57,58: 46,58-Man From U.N.C.L.E. 46-Beatles. 57-Rolling Stones
4 8 12 23 37 50
61-80: 62-Beatles cameo. 69-Batman, Superman app. 70-(8/68) Elvis cameo. 71-Garrison's Gorillas; W.C. Fields photos 3 6 9 16 23 30
81-99: 99-Alfred E. Neuman on-c 3 6 9 14 20 25
100 3 6 9 17 26 35
101-119: 104-Godfather-c/s. 108-Archie Bunker-s. 112,119-Kung Fu (TV). 113-Tarzan-s. 115-MASH. 117-Cannon. 118-The Sting-c/s 2 4 6 10 14 18
120(12/74) Six Million Dollar Man-c/s; Ward-a 2 4 6 13 18 22
121,122,124-126,128-133,136-140: 121-American Graffiti. 122-Korak-c/s. 124,131-Godfather-c/s. 128-Capone-c. 129,131-Jaws. 132-Baretta-c/s. 133-Space 1999. 136-Laverne and Shirley/Fonz-c. 137-Travolta/Kotter-c/s. 138-Travolta/Laverne and Shirley/ Fonz-c. 139-Barney Miller-c/s. 140-King Kong-c/s; Fonz-s
2 4 6 10 14 18
123-Planet of the Apes-c/s; Six Million Dollar Man 2 4 6 13 18 22
127,134,135: 127-Star Trek-c/s; Ward-a. 134-Fonz-c/s; Starsky and Hutch. 135-Bionic Woman-c/s; Ward-a 2 4 6 11 16 20

GD VG FN VF VF/NM NM-
2.0 4.0 6.0 8.0 9.0 9.2

141,151-Charlie's Angels-c/s. 151-Frankenstein 2 4 6 11 16 20
142,143,150,152-155,157: 142-MASH-c/s. 143-Rocky-c/s; King Kong-s. 150-(5/78) Close Encounters-c/s. 152-Close Enc./Star Wars-c/s. 153-Close Enc./Fonz-c/s. 154-Jaws II-c/s; Star Wars-s. 155-Star Wars/Fonz-c 2 4 6 9 13 16
144,149,156,158-160: 144-Fonz/Happy Days-c. 149-Star Wars/Six Mil.$ Man-c/s. 156-Grease/Travolta-c. 158-Mork & Mindy. 159-Battlestar Galactica-c/s; MASH-s. 160-Superman-c/s 2 4 6 11 16 20
145,147-Both have insert postcards: 145-Fonz/Rocky/L&S-c/s. 147-Star Wars-s; Farrah photo page (missing postcards-1/2 price) 3 6 9 14 20 26
146,148: 46-Star Wars-c/s with stickers insert (missing stickers-1/2 price). 148-Star Wars-c/s with inside-c color poster 3 6 9 16 23 30
161,170-Ward-a: 161-Mork & Mindy-c/s. 170-Dukes of Hazzard-c/s
2 4 6 8 11 14
162,165-168,171,172,175-178,180-Ward-a: 162-Sherlock Holmes-s. 165-Dracula-c/s. 167-Mork-c/s. 168,175-MASH-c/s. 168-Mork-s. 172-Dukes of Hazzard/CHiPs-c/s. 176-Barney Miller-c/s 2 4 6 8 10 12
163,179:163-Postcard insert; Mork & Mindy-c/s. 179-Insult cards insert; Popeye, Dukes of Hazzard-c/s 3 6 9 14 19 24
164,169,173,174: 164-Alien movie-c/s; Mork & Mindy-s. 169-Star Trek. 173,174-Star Wars-Empire Strikes Back. 173-SW poster 2 4 6 9 13 16
181,182,185-191,193,194,196-198-most Ward-a: 182-MASH-c/s. 185-Dukes of Hazzard-c/s; Jefferson-s. 187-Love Boat. 188-Fall Guy-s. 189-Fonz/Happy Days-c. 190,194-MASH-c/s. 191-Magnum P.I./Rocky-c; Magnum-s. 193-Knight Rider-s. 196-Dukes of Hazzard/Knight Rider-c/s. 198-Jaws III-c/s; Fall Guy-s 1 2 3 5 7 9
183,184,192,195,199,200-Ward-a in all: 183-Superman-c/s. 184-Star Trek-c/s. 192-E.T.-c/s; Rocky-s. 195-E.T.-c/s. 199-Jabba-c; Star Wars-s. 200-(12/83)
1 3 4 6 8 10
201,203,210-A-Team-c/s 6.00
202,204-206,211-224,226,227,230-233: 202-Knight Rider-s. 204-Magnum P.I.; A-Team-s. 206-Michael Jackson/Mr. T-c/s. 212-Prince-s; Cosby-s. 213-Monsters issue-c/s. 215-Hulk Hogan/Mr. T-c/s. 216-Miami Vice-s; James Bond-s. 217-Rambo-s; Cosby-s; A-Team-s. 218-Rocky-c/s. 219-Arnold/Commando-c/s; Rocky-s; Godzilla. 220-Rocky-c/s. 221-Stephen King app. 223-Miami Vice-s. 224-Cosby-s. 226-29th Anniv.; Tarzan-s; Aliens-s; Family Ties-s. 227-Cosby, Family Ties, Miami Vice-s. 230-Monkees-c/s; Elvis on-c; 232-Alf, Cheers, StarTrek-s. 233-Superman/James Bond-c/s; Robocop, Predator-s 5.00
207-209,225,234: 207-Michael Jackson-c/s. 208-Indiana Jones-c/s. 209-MichaelJackson/ Gremlins-c/s; Star Trek III-s. 225-Schwarzenegger/Stallone/G.I. Joe-c/s. 234-Don Martin-a begins; Batman/Robocop/Clint Eastwood-c/s 6.00
228,229: 228-Star Trek-c/s; Alf, Pee Wee Herman-s. 229-Monsters issue-c/s; centerfold with many superheroes 6.00
235,239,243,249: 235-1st Martin-c; Star Trek:TNG-s; Alf-s. 239-Beetlejuice-c/s; Mike Tyson-s. 243-X-Men and other heroes app. 249-Batman/Indiana Jones/Ghostbusters-c/s 6.00
236,244,245,248: 236-Madonna/Stallone-c/s; Twilight Zone-s. 244-Elvis-c/s; Martin-c. 245-Roger Rabbit-c/s. 248-Batman issue 6.00
237,238,240-242,246,247,250: 237-Robocop-s. 238-Rambo-c/s; Star Trek-s. 242-Dirty Harry-s, Ward-a. 246-Alf-s; Star Trek-s., Ward-a. 247-Star Trek-s. 250-Batman/Ghostbusters-s 4.00
251-253,255,256,259,261-265,275-278,281,284,286-297,299: 252-Star Trek-s. 253-Back to the Future-s. 255-TMNT-c/s. 256-TMNT-c/s; Batman, Bart Simpson on-c. 259-Die Hard II, Robocop-s. 261-TMNT, Twin Peaks-s. 262-Rocky-c/s; Rocky Horror-s. 265-TMNT-s. 276-Aliens III, Batman-s. 277-Clinton-c. 284-Bart Simpson-c; 90210-s. 297-Van Damme-s/photo-c. 299-Dumb & Dumber-c/s 4.00
254,257,266,267,272,280,282,285,298,300: 254-Back to the Future, Punisher-s; Wolverton-a, Batman-s, Ward-a. 257-Batman, Simpsons-s; Spider-Man and other heroes app. 266-Terminator-c/s. 267-Toons-c/s. 272-Star Trek VI-s. 280-Swimsuit issue. 282-Cheers-c/s. 285-Jurassic Park-c/s. 298-Swimsuit issue; Martin-c. 300-(8/95) Brady Bunch-c/s 5.00
258,260,274,279,283: 258-Simpsons-c/s; Back to the Future-s. 260-Spider-Man-c/s; Simpsons-s. 274-Batman-c/s. 279-Madonna-c/s. 283-Jurassic Park-c/s; Wolverine app. inside back-c 5.00
301-305,307-365: 365-Freas-c 3.00
306-Toy Story-c/s 4.00
Biggest... (Winter, 1977) 2 4 6 13 18 22
Biggest, Greatest... nn('65) 4 8 12 28 47 65
Biggest, Greatest... 2('66/67) - #5('69/70) 3 6 9 19 30 40
Biggest, Greatest... 6('70) - #12(Wint. '77) 3 6 9 14 19 24
Biggest, Greatest...13(Fall '78) - #21(Fall/Wint. '86) 2 4 6 8 11 14
...Blockbuster 1(Sum '87), 2('88), 3(Sum. '89) 1 3 4 6 8 10
...Blockbuster 4 - 6(Sum. '92) 6.00
...Collectors' Edition 4 ('73; formerly ...Special) 2 4 6 13 18 22
5-9,10(10/75) 2 4 6 11 16 20
11-19,20(11/17) 2 4 6 8 11 14
21,22,23(5/78): 23-Ward-a 2 4 6 8 11 14
(#24-62,64 not numbered)
1978 (nn; July, Sept, Nov, Dec) (#24-27) 2 4 6 8 11 14
1979 (nn; May, July, Sept, Nov, Dec) (#28-33) 2 4 6 8 11 14

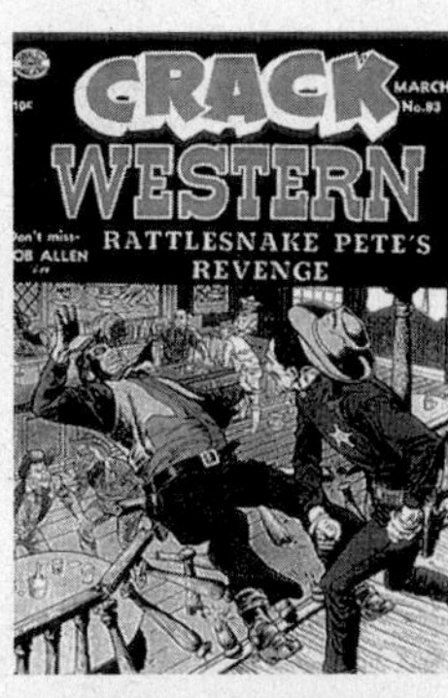

Crack Western #83 © QUA

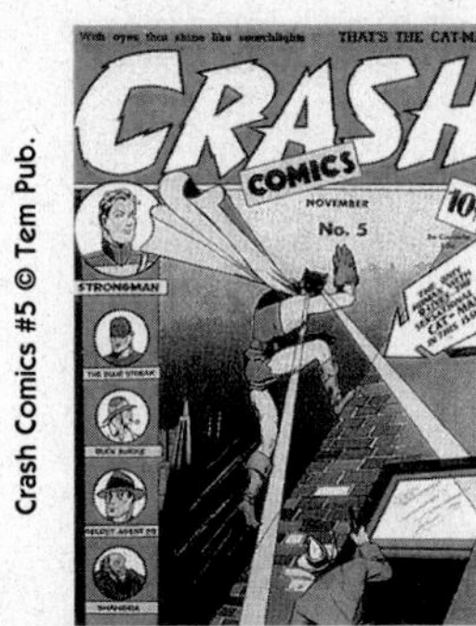

Crash Comics #5 © Tem Pub.

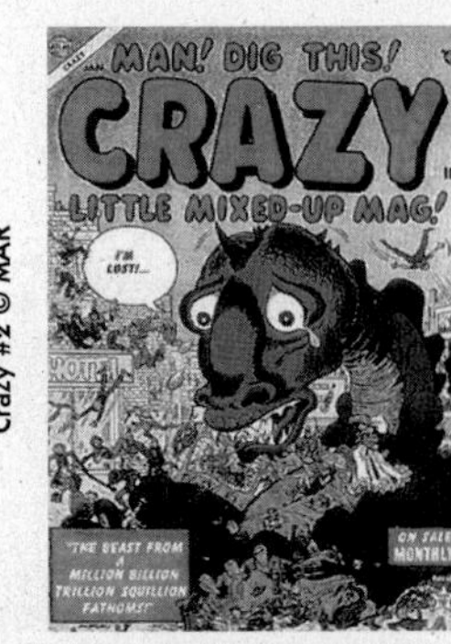

Crazy #2 © MAR

GD 2.0 | VG 4.0 | FN 6.0 | VF 8.0 | VF/NM 9.0 | NM- 9.2

1980 (nn; Feb, May, July, Sept, Nov, Dec) (#34-39) 1 3 4 6 8 10
1981 (nn; Feb, May, July, Sept, Nov, Dec) (#40-45) 1 3 4 6 8 10
1982 (nn; Feb, May, July, Sept, Nov, Dec) (#46-51) 1 3 4 6 8 10
1983 (nn; Feb, May, Sept, Nov, Dec) (#52-56) 1 3 4 6 8 10
1984 (nn; Feb, May, July, Nov) (#57-60) 1 2 3 4 5 7
1985 (nn; Feb) (#61) 1 2 3 4 5 7
62(9/85), nn(#63,11/85), 64(12/85), 65-69, 70(4/87) 1 2 3 4 5 7
71,72,73(100 pgs., 1/88), 74-79, 80(9/89) 5.00
81-96, 97(two diff. issues), 98-115: 83-Elvis, Batman parodies 5.00
116('98)-Last issue? 6.00
...Digest 1(Fall, '86, 148 pgs.), 2(1/87) 1 2 3 6 8 10
...Digest 3-5 1 2 3 4 5 7
...Party Pack 1,2('88) - 4('90) 4.00
...Shut-Ups 1(2/72) 3 6 9 17 26 35
...Shut-Ups 2('72) becomes Cracked Spec. #3 3 6 9 14 19 24
...Special 3('73; formerly Cracked Shut-Ups; ...Collectors' Edition#4 on)
2 4 6 13 18 22
... Summer Special 1(Sum. '91), 2(Sum. '92)-Don Martin-a 4.00
... Summer Special 3(Sum. '93) - 8(Sum. '98) 3.00
... Super (Vol. 2, formerly Super Cracked) 5(Wint. '91/92) - 14(Wint.'97/98) 3.00
Extra Special... 1(Spr. '76) 2 4 6 11 16 20
Extra Special... 2(Spr./Sum. '77) 2 4 6 10 14 18
Extra Special... 3(Wint. '79) - 9(Wint. '86) 1 2 3 4 5 7
Giant... nn('65) 5 10 15 33 57 80
Giant... 2('66) - 5('69) 3 6 9 21 33 45
Giant...6('70) - 12('76) 3 6 9 16 24 32
Giant...nn(9/77, #13), nn(1/78, #14), nn(3/78, #15), nn(5/78, #16), nn(7/78, #17), nn(11/78, #18), nn(3/79, #19), nn(7/79, #20), nn(10/79, #21), nn(12/79, #22), nn(3/80, #23), nn(7/80, #24) 2 4 6 11 16 20
Giant...nn(10/80, #25), nn(12/80, #26), nn(3/81, #27), nn(7/81, #28), nn(10/81, #29), nn(12/81, #30), nn(7/82, #31), nn(10/82, #32), nn(12/82, #33), nn(7/83, #34),
2 4 6 8 11 14
Giant...nn(10/83, #35), nn(12/83, #36), nn(3/84, #37), nn(7/84, #38), nn(10/84, #39), nn(3/85, #40), nn(7/85, #41), nn(10/85, #42) 1 2 3 5 7 9
Giant...43(3/86) - 46(1/87), 47(Wint. '88), 48(Wint. '89) 1 2 3 4 5 7
King Sized... 1('67) 4 8 12 25 40 55
King Sized... 2('68) - 5('71) 3 6 9 17 26 35
King Sized... 6('72) - 11('77) 3 6 9 14 20 26
King Sized... 12(Fall '78) - 17(Sum. '83) 2 4 6 8 11 14
King Sized... 18-20 (Sum/'86) (#21,22 exist?) 1 3 4 6 8 10
Spaced Out... 1-4 ('93 - '94) 5.00
Super... 1('68) 4 8 12 25 40 55
Super... 2('69) - 6('73) 3 6 9 19 30 40
Super... 7('74), 8(Spr. '75) - 10(Spr. '77) 3 6 9 15 22 28
Super... 11(Sum. '78) - 16(Fall '81) 2 4 6 11 16 20
Super... 17(Spr. '82) - 22(Fall '83) 2 4 6 8 11 14
Super... 23(Sum. '84, mis-numbered as #24) 2 4 6 8 11 14
Super... 24(Fall '84, correctly numbered) 2 4 6 8 11 14
Super... 25(Wint. '85) - 32(Fall '86) 2 4 6 8 10 12
Super... (Vol. 2) 1('87, 100 pgs.)-Severin & Elder-a 1 3 4 6 8 10
Super... (Vol. 2) 2(Sum. '88), 3(Wint. '89), 4(exist?)(Becomes Cracked Super) 6.00

NOTE: ***Burgos** a-1-10. **Colan** a-257. **Davis** a-5, 11-17, 24, 40, 80; c-12-14, 16. **Elder** a-5, 6, 10-13; c-10. **Everett** a-1-10, 23-25, 61; c-1. **Heath** a-1-3, 6, 13, 14, 17, 110; c-6. **Jaffee** a-5, 6. **Don Martin** c-235, 244, 247, 259, 261, 264. **Morrow** a-8-10. **Reinman** a-1-4. **Severin** c/a-in most all issues. **Shores** a-3-7. **Torres** a-7-10. **Ward** a-22-24, 27, 35, 40, 120-193, 195, 197-205, 242, 244, 246, 247, 250, 252-257. **Williamson** a-1 (1 pg.). **Wolverton** a-10 (2 pgs.), Giant nn('65). **Wood** a-27, 35, 40. Alfred E. Neuman c-177, 200, 202. Batman c-234, 248, 249, 256, 274. Captain America c-256. Christmas c-234, 243. Spider-Man c-260. Star Trek c-127, 169, 207, 228. Star Wars c-145, 146, 148, 149, 152, 155, 173, 174, 199. Superman c-183, 233. #144, 146 have free full-color pre-glued stickers. #145, 147, 155, 163 have free full-color postcards. #123, 137, 154, 157 have free iron-ons.*

CRACKED MONSTER PARTY
Globe Communications: July, 1988 - No. 27, Wint. 1999/2000

1 2 4 6 10 14 18
2-10 2 4 6 8 10 12
11-26 1 2 3 4 5 7
27-Interview with a Vampire-c/s 2 4 6 8 10 12

CRACKED'S FOR MONSTERS ONLY
Major Magazines: Sept, 1969 - No. 9, Sept, 1969; June, 1972

1 4 8 12 28 47 65
2-9, nn(6/72) 3 6 9 19 30 40

CRACK WESTERN (Formerly Crack Comics; Jonesy No. 85 on)
Quality Comics Group: No. 63, Nov, 1949 - No. 84, May, 1953 (36 pgs., 63-68,74-on)

63(#1)-Ward-c; Two-Gun Lil (origin & 1st app.)(ends #84), Arizona Ames, his horse Thunder (with sidekick Spurs & his horse Calico), Frontier Marshal (ends #70), & Dead Canyon Days (ends #69) begin; Crandall-a 18 36 54 107 169 230
64,65: 64-Ward-c. Crandall-a in both. 15 30 45 83 124 165
66,68-Photo-c. 66-Arizona Ames becomes A. Raines (ends #84)
13 26 39 72 101 130
67-Randolph Scott photo-c; Crandall-a 14 28 42 80 115 150
69(52pgs.)-Crandall-a 13 26 39 72 101 130
70(52pgs.)-The Whip (origin & 1st app.) & his horse Diablo begin (ends #84); Crandall-a 13 26 39 72 101 130
71(52pgs.)-Frontier Marshal becomes Bob Allen F. Marshal (ends #84); Crandall-c/a 14 28 42 80 115 150
72(52pgs.)-Tim Holt photo-c 12 24 36 67 94 120
73(52pgs.)-Photo-c 10 20 30 58 79 100
74-76,78,79,81,83-Crandall-c. 83-Crandall-a(p) 11 22 33 62 86 110
77,80,82 8 16 24 44 57 70
84-Crandall-c/a 12 24 36 67 94 120

NOTE: ***Crandall** c-71p, 74-81, 83p(w/**Cuidera**-i).*

CRASH COMICS (Cat-Man Comics No. 6 on)
Tem Publishing Co.: May, 1940 - No. 5, Nov, 1940

1-The Blue Streak, Strongman (origin), The Perfect Human, Shangra begin (1st app. of each); Kirby-a 343 686 1029 2400 4200 6000
2-Simon & Kirby-a 181 362 543 1158 1979 2800
3-Simon & Kirby-a 155 310 465 992 1696 2400
4-Origin & 1st app. The Cat-Man; S&K-a 383 766 1149 2681 4691 6700
5-1st Cat-Man-c & 2nd app.; Simon & Kirby-a 206 412 618 1318 2259 3200

NOTE: *Solar Legion by **Kirby** No. 1-5 (5 pgs. each). Strongman c-1-4. Catman c-5.*

CRASH DIVE (See Cinema Comics Herald)

CRASH METRO AND THE STAR SQUAD
Oni Press: May, 1999 ($2.95, B&W, one-shot)

1-Allred-s/Ontiveros-a 3.00

CRASH RYAN (Also see Dark Horse Presents #44)
Marvel Comics (Epic): Oct, 1984 - No. 4, Jan, 1985 (Baxter paper, lim. series)

1-4 3.00

CRAZY (Also see This Magazine is Crazy)
Atlas Comics (CSI): Dec, 1953 - No. 7, July, 1954

1-Everett-c/a 36 72 108 211 343 475
2 22 44 66 132 216 300
3-7: 4-I Love Lucy satire. 5-Satire on censorship 20 40 60 114 182 250

NOTE: ***Ayers** a-5. **Berg** a-1, 2. **Burgos** c-5, 6. **Drucker** a-6. **Everett** a-1-4. **Al Hartley** a-4. **Heath** a-3, 7; c-7. **Maneely** a-1-7, c-3, 4. **Post** a-3-6. Funny monster c-1-4.*

CRAZY (Satire)
Marvel Comics Group: Feb, 1973 - No. 3, June, 1973

1-Not Brand Echh-r; Beatles cameo (r) 3 6 9 16 23 30
2,3-Not Brand Echh-r; Kirby-a 2 4 6 10 16 20

CRAZY MAGAZINE (Satire)
Oct, 1973 - No. 94, Apr, 1983 (40-90¢, B&W magazine)
Marvel Comics: (#1, 44 pgs; #2-90, reg. issues, 52 pgs; #92-95, 68 pgs)'

1-Wolverton(1 pg.), Bode-a; 3 pg. photo story of Neal Adams & Dick Giordano; Harlan Ellison story; TV Kung Fu sty. 4 8 12 28 47 65
2-"Live & Let Die" c/s; 8pgs; Adams/Buscema-a; McCloud w5 pgs. Adams-a; Kurtzman's "Hey Look" 2 pg.-r 3 6 9 19 30 40
3-5: 3-"High Plains Drifter" w/Clint Eastwood c/s; Waltons app; Drucker, Reese-a. 4-Shaft-c/s; Ploog-a; Nixon 3 pg. app; Freas-a. 5-Michael Crichton's "Westworld" c/s; Nixon app.
3 6 9 16 24 32
6,7,18: 6-Exorcist c/s; Nixon app. 7-TV's Kung Fu c/s; Nixon app.; Ploog & Freas-a. 18-Six Million Dollar Man/Bionic Woman c/s; Welcome Back Kotter story
3 6 9 15 22 28
8-10: 8-Serpico c/s; Casper parody; TV's Police Story. 9-Joker cameo; Chinatown story; Eisner s/a begins; Has 1st 8 covers on-c. 10-Playboy Bunny-c; M. Severin-a; Lee Marrs-a begins; "Deathwish" story 3 6 9 14 20 26
11-17,19: 11-Towering Inferno. 12-Rhoda. 13-"Tommy" the Who Rock Opera. 14-Mandingo. 15-Jaws story. 16-Santa/Xmas-c; "Good Times" TV story; Jaws. 17-Bicentennial issue; Baretta; Woody Allen. 19-King Kong c/s; Reagan, J. Carter, Howard the Duck cameos, "Laverne & Shirley" 2 4 6 11 16 20
20,24,27: 20-Bicentennial-c; Space 1999 sty; Superheroes song sheet, 4pgs. 24-Charlie's Angels. 27-Charlie's Angels/Travolta/Fonz-c; Bionic Woman sty
3 6 9 14 19 24
21-23,25,26,28-30: 21-Starsky & Hutch. 22-Mount Rushmore/J. Carter-c; TV's Barney Miller; Superheroes spoof. 23-Santa/Xmas-c; "Happy Days" sty; "Omen" sty. 25-J. Carter-c/s; Grandenetti-a begins; TV's Alice; Logan's Run. 26-TV Stars-c; Mary Hartman, King Kong. 28-Donny & Marie Osmond-c/s; Marathon Man. 29-Travolta/Kotter-c; "One Day at a Time", Gong Show. 30-1977, 84 pgs. w/bonus; Jaws, Baretta, King Kong, Happy Days
2 4 6 9 12 15

Crazy #53 © MAR

Creator-Owned Heroes #8 © Paperfilms

Creatures on the Loose #23 © MAR

GD 2.0 | VG 4.0 | FN 6.0 | VF 8.0 | VF/NM 9.0 | NM- 9.2

31,33-35,38,40: 31-"Rocky"-c/s; TV game shows. 33-Peter Benchley's "Deep". 34-J. Carter-c; TV's "Fish". 35-Xmas-c with Fonz/Six Million Dollar Man/Wonder Woman/Darth Vader/ Travolta, TV's "Mash" & "Family Matters". 38-Close Encounters of the Third Kind-c/s. 40-"Three's Company-c/s 1 3 4 6 8 11

32-Star Wars/Darth Vader-c/s; "Black Sunday" 3 6 9 14 19 24

36,42,47,49: 36-Farrah Fawcett/Six Million Dollar Man-c; TV's Nancy Drew & Hardy Boys; 1st app. Howard The Duck in Crazy, 2 pgs. 42-84 pgs. w/bonus; TV Hulk/Spider-Man-c; Mash, Gong Show, One Day at a Time, Disco, Alice. 47-Battlestar Galactica xmas-c; movie "Foul Play". 49-1979, 84 pgs. w/bonus; Mork & Mindy-c; Jaws, Saturday Night Fever, Three's Company 2 4 6 9 12 15

37-1978, 84 pgs. w/bonus. Darth Vader-c; Barney Miller, Laverne & Shirley, Good Times, Rocky, Donny & Marie Osmond, Bionic Woman 2 4 6 13 18 22

39,44: 39-Saturday Night Fever-c/s. 44-"Grease"-c w/Travolta/O. Newton-John 2 4 6 11 16 20

41-Kiss-c & 1pg. photos; Disaster movies, TV's "Family", Annie Hall 4 8 12 27 44 60

43,45,46,48,51: 43-Jaws-c; Saturday Night Fever. 43-E.C. swipe from Mad #131. 45-Travolta/O. Newton-John/J. Carter-c; Eight is Enough. 46-TV Hulk-c/s; Punk Rock. 48-"Wiz"-c, Battlestar Galactica-s. 51-Grease/Mork & Mindy/D&M Osmond-c, Mork & Mindy-sty. "Boys from Brazil" 1 3 4 6 8 11

50,58: 50-Superman movie-c/sty, Playboy Mag., TV Hulk, Fonz; Howard the Duck, 1 pg. 58-1980, 84 pgs. w/32 pg. color comic bonus insert-Full reprint of Crazy Comic #1, Battlestar Galactica, Charlie's Angels, Starsky & Hutch 2 4 6 11 16 20

52,59,60,64: 52-1979, 84 pgs. w/bonus. Marlon Brando-c; TV Hulk, Grease. Kiss, 1 pg. photos. 59-Santa Ptd-c by Larkin; "Alien", "Moonraker", Rocky-2, Howard the Duck, 1 pg. 60-Star Trek w/Muppets-c; Star Trek sty; 1st app/origin Teen Hulk; Severin-a. 64-84 pgs. w/bonus Monopoly game satire. "Empire Strikes Back", 8 pgs., One Day at a Time 2 4 6 11 16 20

53,54,65,67-70: 53-"Animal House"-c/sty; TV's "Vegas", Howard the Duck, 1 pg. 54-Love at First Bite-c/sty, Fantasy Island sty, Howard the Duck 1 pg. 65-(Has #66 on-c, Aug/'80). "Black Hole" w/Janson-a; Kirby,Wood/Severin-a(r), 5 pgs. Howard the Duck, 3 pgs.; Broderick-a; Buck Rogers, Mr. Rogers. 67-84 pgs. w/bonus; TV's Kung Fu, Exorcist; Ploog-a(r). 68-American Gigolo, Dukes of Hazzard, Teen Hulk; Howard the Duck, 3 pgs. Broderick-a; Monster sty/5 pg. Ditko-a(r). 69-Obnoxio the Clown-c/sty; Stephen King's "Shining", Teen Hulk, Richie Rich, Howard the Duck, 3pgs; Broderick-a. 70-84 pgs. Towering Inferno, Daytime TV; Trina Robbins-a 1 3 4 6 8 10

55-57,61,63: 55-84 pgs. w/bonus; Love Boat, Mork & Mindy, Fonz, TV Hulk. 56-Mork/Rocky/ J. Carter-c; China Syndrome. 57-TV Hulk with Miss Piggy-c, Dracula, Taxi, Muppets. 61-1980, 84 pgs. Adams-a(r), McCloud, Pro wrestling, Casper, TV's Police Story. 63-Apocalypse Now-Coppola's cult movie; 3rd app. Teen Hulk, Howard the Duck, 3 pgs. 2 4 6 8 11 14

62-Kiss-c & 2 pg. app; Quincy, 2nd app. Teen Hulk 4 8 12 23 37 50

66-Sept/'80, Empire Strikes Back-c/sty; Teen Hulk by Severin, Howard the Duck, 3pgs. by Broderick 2 4 6 10 14 18

71,72,75-77,79: 71-Blues Brothers parody, Teen Hulk, Superheroes parody, WKRP in Cincinnati, Howard the Duck, 3pgs. by Broderick. 72-Jackie Gleason/Smokey & the Bandit II-c/sty, Shogun, Teen Hulk. Howard the Duck, 3pgs. by Broderick. 75-Flash Gordon movie c/sty; Teen Hulk, Cat in the Hat, Howard the Duck 3pgs. by Broderick. 76-84 pgs. w/bonus; Monster-sty w/ Crandall-a(r), Monster-stys(2) w/Kirby-a(r), 5pgs. ea; Mash, TV Hulk, Chinatown. 77-Popeye movie/R. Williams-c/sty; Teen Hulk, Love Boat, Howard the Duck 3 pgs. 79-84 pgs. w/bonus color stickers; has new material; "9 to 5" w/Dolly Parton, Teen Hulk, Magnum P.I., Monster-sty w/5pgs, Ditko-a(r), "Rat" w/Sutton-a(r), Everett-a, 4 pgs.(r) 1 3 4 6 8 10

73,74,78,80: 73-84 pgs. w/bonus Hulk/Spiderman Finger Puppets-c & bonus; "Live & Let Die, Jaws, Fantasy Island. 74-Dallas/"Who Shot J.R."-c/sty; Elephant Man, Howard the Duck 3pgs. by Broderick. 78-Clint Eastwood-c/sty; Teen Hulk, Superheroes parody, Lou Grant. 80-Star Wars, 2 pg. app; "Howling", TV's "Greatest American Hero" 2 4 6 8 11 14

81,84,86,87,89: 81-.Superman Movie II-c/sty; Wolverine cameo, Mash, Teen Hulk. 84-American Werewolf in London, Johnny Carson app; Teen Hulk. 86-Time Bandits-c/sty; Private Benjamin. 87-Rubix Cube-c; Hill Street Blues, "Ragtime", Origin Obnoxio the Clown; Teen Hulk. 89-Burt Reynolds "Sharkey's Machine", Teen Hulk 1 3 4 6 8 10

82-X-Men-c w/new Byrne-a, 84 pgs. w/new material; Fantasy Island, Teen Hulk, "For Your Eyes Only", Spiderman/Human Torch-r by Kirby/Ditko; Sutton-a(r); Rogers-a; Hunchback of Notre Dame, 5 pgs. 2 4 6 11 16 20

83-Raiders of the Lost Ark-c/sty; Hart to Hart; Reese-a; Teen Hulk 2 4 6 9 13 20

85,88: 85-84 pgs; Escape from New York, Teen Hulk; Kirby-a(r), 5 pgs, Poseidon Adventure, Flintstones, Sesame Street. 88-84 pgs. w/bonus Dr. Strange Game; some new material; Jeffersons, X-Men/Wolverine, 10 pgs.; Byrne-a; Apocalypse Now, Teen Hulk 1 3 4 6 8 11

90-94: 90-Conan-c/sty; M. Severin-a; Teen Hulk. 91-84 pgs, some new material; Bladerunner-c/sty, "Deathwish-II, Teen Hulk, Black Knight, 10 pgs.-'50s-r w/Maneely-a. 92-Wrath of Khan Star Trek-c/sty; Joanie & Chachi, Teen Hulk. 93-"E.T."-c/sty, Teen Hulk, Archie Bunkers Place, Dr. Doom Game. 94-Poltergeist, Smurfs, Teen Hulk, Casper, Avengers parody-8pgs. Adams-a 2 4 6 10 14 18

Crazy Summer Special #1 (Sum, '75, 100 pgs.)-Nixon, TV Kung Fu, Babe Ruth, Joe Namath, Waltons, McCloud, Chariots of the Gods 3 6 9 14 19 24

NOTE: ***N. Adams** a-2, 61r, 94p. **Austin** a-82i. **Buscema** a-2, 82. **Byrne** c-82p. **Nick Cardy** c-7, 8, 10, 12-16, Super Special 1. **Crandall** a-76r. **Ditko** a-68r, 79r, 82r. **Drucker** a-3. **Eisner** a-9-16. **Kelly Freas** c-1-6, 9, 11; a-7. **Kirby/Wood** a-66r. **Ploog** a-1, 4, 7, 67r, 73r. **Rogers** a-82. **Sparling** a-92. **Wood** a-65r. Howard the Duck in 36, 50, 51, 53, 54, 59, 63, 65, 66, 68, 69, 71, 72, 74, 75, 77. Hulk in 46, c-42, 46, 57, 73. Star Wars in 32, 66; c-37.*

CRAZYMAN
Continuity Comics: Apr, 1992 - No. 3, 1992 ($2.50, high quality paper)

1-($3.95, 52 pgs.)-Embossed-c; N. Adams part-i 4.00
2,3 ($2.50): 2-N. Adams/Bolland-c 3.00

CRAZYMAN
Continuity Comics: V2#1, 5/93 - No. 4, 1/94 ($2.50, high quality paper)

V2#1-4: 1-Entire book is die-cut. 2-(12/93)-Adams-c(p) & part scripts. 3-(12/93). 4-Indicia says #3, Jan. 1993 3.00

CRAZY, MAN, CRAZY (Magazine) (Becomes This Magazine is...?)
(Formerly From Here to Insanity)
Humor Magazines (Charlton): V2#1, Dec, 1955 - V2#2, June, 1956

V2#1,V2#2-Satire; Wolverton-a, 3 pgs. 16 32 48 94 147 200

CREATOR-OWNED HEROES
Image Comics: Jun, 2012 - No. 8, Jan, 2013 ($3.99)

1-8-Anthology of short stories by various and creator interviews 4.00

CREATURE, THE (See Movie Classics)

CREATURE COMMANDOS (See Weird War Tales #93 for 1st app.)
DC Comics: May, 2000 - No. 8, Dec, 2000 ($2.50, limited series)

1-8: Truman-s/Eaton-a 3.00

CREATURES OF THE ID
Caliber Press: 1990 ($2.95, B&W)

1-Frank Einstein (Madman) app.; Allred-a 3 6 9 21 33 45

CREATURES OF THE NIGHT
Dark Horse Books: Nov, 2004 ($12.95, hardcover graphic novel)

HC-Neil Gaiman-s/Michael Zulli-a/c 13.00

CREATURES ON THE LOOSE (Formerly Tower of Shadows No. 1-9)(See Kull)
Marvel Comics: No. 10, March, 1971 - No. 37, Sept, 1975 (New-a & reprints)

10-(15¢)-1st full app. King Kull; see Kull the Conqueror; Wrightson-a 7 14 21 48 89 130

	GD	VG	FN	VF	VF/NM	NM-
11-15: 13-Last 15¢ issue	3	6	9	19	30	40
16-Origin Warrior of Mars (begins, ends #21)	3	6	9	15	22	28
17-20	2	4	6	9	13	16
21-Steranko-c	3	6	9	16	24	32
22-Steranko-c; Thongor stories begin	3	6	9	17	26	35
23-29-Thongor-c/stories	1	3	4	6	8	10
30-Manwolf begins	3	6	9	19	30	40
31-33	2	4	6	9	13	16
34-37	2	4	6	8	10	12

NOTE: ***Crandall** a-13. **Ditko** r-15, 17, 18, 20, 22, 24, 27, 28. **Everett** a-16i(new). **Matt Fox** r-21i. **Howard** a-26i. **Gil Kane** a-16p, 17p, 19i; c-16, 17, 19, 20, 25, 29, 33p, 35p, 36p. **Kirby** a-10-15r, 16(2)r, 17r, 19r. **Morrow** a-20, 21. **Perez** a-33-37; c-34p. **Shores a-11. innott** r-21. **Sutton** c-10. **Tuska** a-30-32p.*

CREECH, THE
Image Comics: Oct, 1997 - No. 3, Dec, 1997 ($1.95/$2.50, limited series)

1-3: 1-Capullo-s/c/a(p) 3.00
TPB (1999, $9.95) r/#1-3, McFarlane intro. 10.00
Out for Blood 1-3 (7/01 - No. 3, 11/01; $4.95) Capullo-s/c/a 5.00

CREED
Hall of Heroes Comics: Dec, 1994 - No. 2, Jan, 1995 ($2.50, B&W)

	GD	VG	FN	VF	VF/NM	NM-
1	2	4	6	9	12	15
2	2	4	6	8	10	12

CREED
Lightning Comics: June, 1995 - No. 3 ($2.75/$3.00, B&W/color)

1-($2.75) 4.00
1-($3.00, color) 5.00
1-($9.95)-Commemorative Edition 10.00
1-TwinVariant Edition (1250? print run) 10.00
1-Special Edition; polybagged w/certificate 4.00
1 Gold Collectors Edition; polybagged w/certificate 3.00

The Creeper (2006 series) #1 © DC

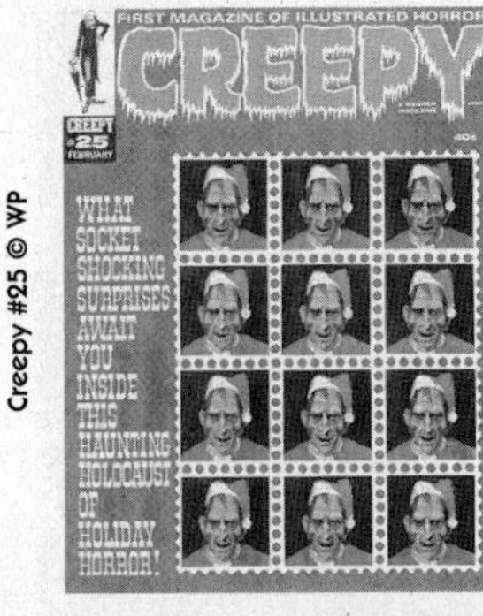

Creepy #25 © WP

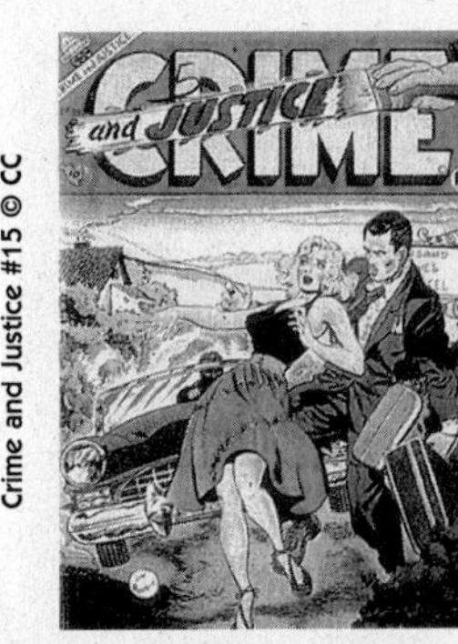

Crime and Justice #15 © CC

GD 2.0 | VG 4.0 | FN 6.0 | VF 8.0 | VF/NM 9.0 | NM- 9.2

2,3-($3.00, color)-Butt Naked Edition & regular-c 3.00
3-($9.95)-Commemorative Edition; polybagged w/certificate & card 10.00

CREED: CRANIAL DISORDER
Lightning Comics: Oct, 1996 ($3.00, limited series)

1-3-Two covers 3.00
1-($5.95)-Platinum Edition 6.00
2,3-($9.95)Ltd. Edition 10.00

CREED/TEENAGE MUTANT NINJA TURTLES
Lightning Comics: May, 1996 ($3.00, one-shot)

1-Kaniuga-a(p)/scripts; Laird-c; variant-c exists 3.00
1-($9.95)-Platinum Edition 10.00
1-Special Edition; polybagged w/certificate 5.00

CREEP, THE
Dark Horse Books: No. 0, Aug, 2012 - No. 4, Dec, 2012 ($2.99/$3.50)

0-Frank Miller-c; Arcudi-s/Case-a 3.50
1-4-($3.50): 1-Mignola-c. 2-Sook-c 3.50

CREEPER BY STEVE DITKO, THE
DC Comics: 2010 ($39.99, hardcover with dustjacket)

HC-Reprints Showcase #73, Beware the Creeper #1-6, First Issue Special #7 and apps. in World's Finest #249-255 and Cancelled Comic Cavalcade #2; intro. by Steve Niles 40.00

CREEPER, THE (See Beware..., Showcase #73 & 1st Issue Special #7)
DC Comics: Dec, 1997 - No. 11; #1,000,000 Nov, 1998 ($2.50)

1-11-Kaminski-s/Martinbrough-a(p). 7,8-Joker-c/app. 3.00
#1,000,000 (11/98) 853rd Century x-over 3.00

CREEPER, THE (See DCU Brave New World)
DC Comics: Oct, 2006 - No. 6, Mar, 2007 ($2.99, limited series)

1-6-Niles-s/Justiniano-a/c; Jack Ryder becomes the Creeper. 2-6-Batman app. 3.00
... - Welcome to Creepsville TPB ('07, $19.99) r/#1-6 & story from DCU Brave New World 20.00

CREEPS
Image Comics: Oct, 2001 - No. 4, May, 2002 ($2.95)

1-4-Mandrake-a/Mishkin-s 3.00

CREEPSHOW
Plume/New American Library Pub.: July, 1982 (softcover graphic novel)

1st edition-nn-(68 pgs.) Kamen-c/Wrightson-a; screenplay by Stephen King for the George Romero movie 4 8 12 27 44 60
2nd-7th printings 3 6 9 17 26 35

CREEPSVILLE
Laughing Reindeer Press: V2#1, Winter, 1995 ($4.95)

V2#1-Comics w/text 5.00

CREEPY (See Warren Presents)
Warren Publishing Co./Harris Publ. #146: 1964 - No. 145, Feb, 1983; No. 146, 1985 (B&W, magazine)

1-Frazetta-a (his last story in comics?); Jack Davis-c; 1st Warren all comics magazine; 1st app. Uncle Creepy 12 24 36 79 170 260
2-Frazetta-c & 1 pg. strip 8 16 24 52 99 145
3-8,11-13,15-17: 3-7,9-11,15-17-Frazetta-c. 7-Frazetta 1 pg. strip. 15,16-Adams-a. 16-Jeff Jones-a 6 12 18 37 66 95
9-Creepy fan club sketch by Wrightson (1st published-a); has 1/2 pg. anti-smoking strip by Frazetta; Frazetta-c; 1st Wood and Ditko art on this title; Toth-a (low print) 7 14 21 49 92 135
10-Brunner fan club sketch (1st published work) 6 12 18 38 69 100
14-Neal Adams 1st Warren work 6 12 18 38 69 100
18-28,30,31: 27-Frazetta-c 4 8 12 28 47 65
29,34: 29-Jones-a 5 10 15 30 50 70
32-(scarce) Frazetta-c; Harlan Ellison sty 8 16 24 51 96 140
33,35,37,39,40,42-47,49: 35-Hitler/Nazi-s. 39-1st Uncle Creepy solo-s, Cousin Eerie app.; early Brunner-a. 42-1st San Julian-c. 44-1st Ploog-a. 46-Corben-a 4 8 12 23 37 50
36-(11/70)1st Corben art at Warren 5 10 15 30 50 70
38,41-(scarce): 38-1st Kelly-c. 41-Corben-a 5 10 15 33 57 80
48,55,65-(1972, 1973, 1974 Annuals) #55 & 65 contain an 8 pg. slick comic insert. 48-(84 pgs.). 55-Color poster bonus (1/2 price if missing). 65-(100 pgs.) Summer Giant 5 10 15 30 50 70
50-Vampirella/Eerie/Creepy-c 5 10 15 33 57 80
51,54,56-61,64: All contain an 8 pg. slick comic insert in middle. 59-Xmas horror. 54,64-Chaykin-a 4 8 12 27 44 60
52,53,66,71,72,75,76,78-80: 71-All Bermejo-a; Space & Time issue. 72-Gual-a. 78-Fantasy issue. 79,80-Monsters issue 3 6 9 19 30 40
62,63-1st & 2nd full Wrightson story art; Corben-a; 8 pg. color comic insert 4 8 12 27 44 60
67,68,73 3 6 9 21 33 45
69,70-Edgar Allan Poe issues; Corben-a 4 8 12 23 37 50
74,77: 74-All Crandell-a. 77-Xmas Horror issue; Corben-a,Wrightson-a 4 8 12 23 37 50
81,84,85,88-90,92-94,96-99,102,104-112,114-118,120,122-130: 84,93-Sports issue. 85,97,102-Monster issue. 89-All war issue; Nino-a. 94-Weird Children issue. 96,109-Aliens issue. 99-Disasters. 103-Corben-a. 104-Robots issue. 106-Sword & Sorcery.107-Sci-fi. 116-End of Man. 125-Xmas Horror 2 4 6 10 14 18
82,100,101: 82-All Maroto issue. 100-(8/78) Anniversary. 101-Corben-a 3 6 9 14 20 26
83,95-Wrightson-a. 83-Corben-a. 95-Gorilla/Apes. 2 4 6 13 18 22
86,87,91,103-Wrightson-a. 86-Xmas Horror 2 4 6 13 18 22
113-All Wrightson-r issue 3 6 9 19 29 38
119,121: 119-All Nino issue.121-All Severin-r issue 2 4 6 13 18 22
131,133-136,138,140: 135-Xmas issue 2 4 6 13 18 22
132,137,139: 132-Corben. 137-All Williamson-r issue. 139-All Toth-r issue 3 6 9 14 20 26
141,143,144 (low dist.): 144-Giant, $2.25; Frazetta-c 3 6 9 17 26 35
142,145 (low dist.): 142-(10/82, 100 pgs.) All Torres issue. 145-(2/83) last Warren issue 3 6 9 19 30 40
146 ($2.95)-1st from Harris; resurrection issue 6 12 18 41 76 110
Year Book '68-'70: '70-Neal Adams, Ditko-a(r) 5 10 15 33 57 80
Annual 1971,1972 5 10 15 31 53 75
1993 Fearbook ($3.95)-Harris Publ.; Brereton-c; Vampirella by Busiek-s/Art Adams-a; David-s; Paquette-a 3 6 9 17 26 35
...:The Classic Years TPB (Harris/Dark Horse, '91, $12.95) Kaluta-c; art by Frazetta,Torres, Crandall, Ditko, Morrow, Williamson, Wrightson 25.00

NOTE: *All issues contain many good artists works:* ***Neal Adams, Brunner, Corben, Craig (Taycee), Crandall, Ditko, Evans, Frazetta, Heath, Jeff Jones, Krenkel, McWilliams, Morrow, Nino, Orlando, Ploog, Severin, Torres, Toth, Williamson, Wood, & Wrightson****; covers by* ***Crandall, Davis, Frazetta, Morrow, San Julian, Todd/Bode****; Otto Binder's "Adam Link" stories in No. 2, 4, 6, 8, 9, 12, 13, 15 with* ***Orlando*** *art.* ***Frazetta*** *c-2-7, 9-11, 15-17, 27, 32, 83r, 89r, 91r.* ***E.A. Poe*** *adaptations in 66, 69, 70.*

CREEPY (Mini-series)
Harris Comics/Dark Horse: 1992 - Book 4, 1992 (48 pgs, B&W, squarebound)

Book 1-4: Brereton painted-c on all. Stories and art by various incl. David (all), Busiek(2), Infantino(2), Guice(3), Colan(1) 2 4 6 8 10 12

CREEPY
Dark Horse Comics: July, 2009 - Present ($4.99, 48 pgs, B&W, quarterly)

1-16: 1-Powell-c; art by Wrightson, Toth, Alexander. 8,12-Corben-c 5.00

CREEPY THINGS
Charlton Comics: July, 1975 - No. 6, June, 1976

1-Sutton-c/a 3 6 9 14 19 24
2-6: Ditko-a in 3,5. Sutton c-3,4. 6-Zeck-c 2 4 6 8 10 12
Modern Comics Reprint 2-6(1977) 5.00

NOTE: ***Larson*** *a-2,6.* ***Sutton*** *a-1,2,4,6.* ***Zeck*** *a-2.*

CREW, THE
Marvel Comics: July, 2003 - No. 7, Jan, 2004 ($2.50)

1-7-Priest-s/Bennett-a; James Rhodes (War Machine) app. 3.00

CRIME AND JUSTICE (Badge Of Justice #22 on; Rookie Cop? No. 27 on)
Capitol Stories/Charlton Comics: March, 1951 - No. 21, Nov, 1954; No. 23, Mar, 1955 - No. 26, Sept, 1955 (No #22)

1 39 78 117 231 378 525
2 18 36 54 105 165 225
3-8,10-13: 6-Negligee panels 15 30 45 90 140 190
9-Classic story "Comics Vs. Crime" 30 60 90 177 289 400
14-Color illos in **POP**; story of murderer who beheads women 27 54 81 158 259 360
15-17,19-21,23,24: 15-Negligee panels. 23-Rookie Cop (1st app.) 12 24 36 69 97 125
18-Ditko-a 28 56 84 165 270 375
25,26: (scarce) 17 34 51 98 154 210

NOTE: ***Alascia*** *c-20.* ***Ayers*** *a-17.* ***Shuster*** *a-19-21; c-19. Bondage c-11, 12.*

CRIME AND PUNISHMENT (Title inspired by 1935 film)
Lev Gleason Publications: April, 1948 - No. 74, Aug, 1955

1-Mr. Crime app. on-c 40 80 120 244 402 560
2-Narrator, Officer Common Sense (a ghost) begins, ends #27? (see Crime Does Not Pay #41) 20 40 60 120 195 270
3-(6/48)-Used in **SOTI**, pg. 112; contains Biro & Gleason self censorship code of 12 listed restrictions 22 44 66 132 216 300
4,5 15 30 45 90 140 190

Crime Cases #9 © MAR

Crime Clinic #1 © Z-D

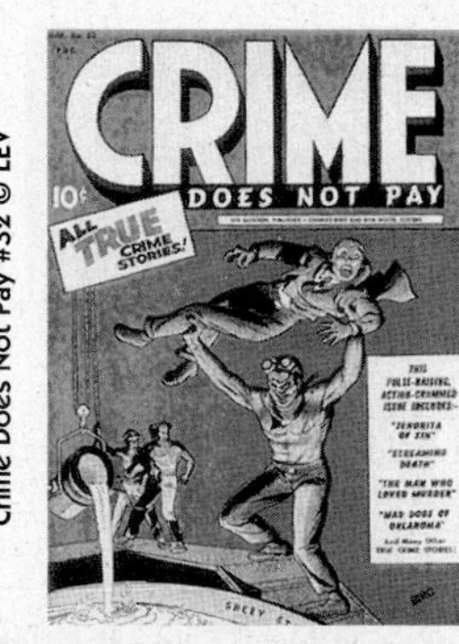

Crime Does Not Pay #32 © LEV

	GD 2.0	VG 4.0	FN 6.0	VF 8.0	VF/NM 9.0	NM- 9.2
6-10	14	28	42	80	115	150
11-20	12	24	36	69	97	125
21-30	11	22	33	60	83	105
31-38,40-44,46: 46-One pg. Frazetta-a	10	20	30	54	72	90
39-Drug mention story "The Five Dopes"	15	30	45	86	133	180
45- "Hophead Killer" drug story	15	30	45	86	133	180
47-53,55,57,60-65,70-74:	9	18	27	52	69	85
54-Electric Chair-c	10	20	30	56	76	95
56-Classic dagger/torture-c	11	22	33	64	90	115
58-Used in **POP**, pg. 79	11	22	33	62	86	110
59-Used in **SOTI**, illo "What comic-book America stands for"	34	68	102	204	332	460
66-Toth-c/a(4); 3-D effect issue (3/54); 1st "Deep Dimension" process	41	82	123	250	418	585
67- "Monkey on His Back" heroin story; 3-D effect issue	39	78	117	231	378	525
68-3-D effect issue; Toth-c (7/54)	32	64	96	188	307	425
69- "The Hot Rod Gang" dope crazy kids	15	30	45	85	130	175

NOTE: ***Belfi** a- 2, 3, 5. **Biro** c-most. **Al Borth** a-9, 35. **Cooper** a-9. **Joe Certa** a-8. **Tony Dipreta** a-3, 5, 15, 34. **Everett** a-31. **Bob Fujitani (Fuje)** a-2-20, 26, 27. **Joseph Gaguardi** a-15, 18, 20. **Fred Guardineer** a-2-5, 10-12, 14, 15, 17, 18, 20, 26-28, 32, 34, 35, 38-44, 51, 54. **Jack Keller** a-18. **Kinstler** c-69. **Martinott** a-13. **Al McWilliams** a-36, 41, 48, 49. **William Overgard** a-36. **Dick Rockwell** a-35, 51. **Robert Q. Sale** a-43. **George Tuska** a-28, 30, 51, 64, 70. Painted-c-31.*

CRIME AND PUNISHMENT: MARSHALL LAW TAKES MANHATTAN
Marvel Comics (Epic Comics): 1989 ($4.95, 52 pgs., direct sales only, mature)

	NM- 9.2
nn-Graphic album featuring Marshall Law	5.00

CRIME BIBLE: THE FIVE LESSONS (Aftermath of DC's 52 series)
DC Comics: Dec, 2007 - No. 5, Apr, 2008 ($2.99, limited series)

	NM- 9.2
1-5-Rucka-s; The Question (Renee Montoya) app. 3-Batwoman app.	3.00
The Question: The Five Books of Blood HC (2008, $19.99) r/#1-5	20.00
The Question: The Five Books of Blood SC (2009, $14.99) r/#1-5	15.00

CRIME CAN'T WIN (Formerly Cindy Smith)
Marvel/Atlas Comics (TCI 41/CCC 42,43,4-12): No. 41, 9/50 - No. 43, 2/51; No. 4, 4/51 - No. 12, 9/53

	GD 2.0	VG 4.0	FN 6.0	VF 8.0	VF/NM 9.0	NM- 9.2
41(#1)-"The Girl Who Planned Her Own Murder"	27	54	81	162	266	370
42(#2)	15	30	45	90	140	190
43(#3)-Horror story	20	40	60	114	182	250
4(4/51),5-12: 10-Possible use in **SOTI**, pg. 161	14	28	42	81	118	155

NOTE: ***Robinson** a-9-11. **Tuska** a-43.*

CRIME CASES COMICS (Formerly Willie Comics)
Marvel/Atlas Comics(CnPC No.24-8/MJMC No.9-12): No. 24, 8/50 - No. 27, 3/51; No. 5, 5/51 - No. 12, 7/52

	GD 2.0	VG 4.0	FN 6.0	VF 8.0	VF/NM 9.0	NM- 9.2
24 (#1, 52 pgs.)-True police cases	20	40	60	120	195	270
25-27(#2-4): 27-Morisi-a	15	30	45	85	130	175
5-12: 11-Robinson-a. 12-Tuska-a	14	28	42	80	115	150

CRIME CLINIC
Ziff-Davis Publishing Co.: No. 10, July-Aug, 1951 - No. 5, Summer, 1952

	GD 2.0	VG 4.0	FN 6.0	VF 8.0	VF/NM 9.0	NM- 9.2
10(#1)-Painted-c; origin Dr. Tom Rogers	29	58	87	170	278	385
11(#2),4,5: 4,5-Painted-c	20	40	60	114	182	250
3-Used in **SOTI**, pg. 18	20	40	60	117	189	260

NOTE: *All have painted covers by **Saunders**. **Starr** a-10.*

CRIME CLINIC
Slave Labor Graphics: May, 1995 - No. 2, Oct, 1995 ($2.95, B&W, limited series)

	NM- 9.2
1,2	3.00

CRIME DETECTIVE COMICS
Hillman Periodicals: Mar-Apr, 1948 - V3#8, May-June, 1953

	GD 2.0	VG 4.0	FN 6.0	VF 8.0	VF/NM 9.0	NM- 9.2
V1#1-The Invisible 6, costumed villains app; Fuje-c/a, 15 pgs.	34	68	102	199	325	450
2,5: 5-Krigstein-a	16	32	48	94	147	200
3,4,6,7,10-12: 6-McWilliams-a	14	28	42	82	121	160
8-Kirbyish-a by McCann	14	28	42	82	121	160
9-Used in **SOTI**, pg. 16 & "Caricature of the author in a position comic book publishers wish he were in permanently" illo.	40	80	120	244	402	560
V2#1,4,7-Krigstein-a: 1-Tuska-a	14	28	42	76	108	140
2,3,5,6,8-12 (1-2/52)	12	24	36	67	94	120
V3#1-Drug use-c	13	26	39	72	101	130
2-8	10	20	30	56	76	95

NOTE: ***Briefer** a-11, V3#1. **Kinstlerish**-a by **McCann**-V2#7, V3#2. **Powell** a-10, 11. **Starr** a-10.*

CRIME DETECTOR
Timor Publications: Jan, 1954 - No. 5, Sept, 1954

	GD 2.0	VG 4.0	FN 6.0	VF 8.0	VF/NM 9.0	NM- 9.2
1	23	46	69	136	223	310
2	14	28	42	81	118	155
3,4	13	26	39	72	101	130
5-Disbrow-a (classic)	24	48	72	140	230	320

CRIME DOES NOT PAY (Formerly Silver Streak Comics No. 1-21)
Comic House/Lev Gleason/Golfing: No. 22, June, 1942 - No. 147, July, 1955 (1st crime comic)(Title inspired by film)

	GD 2.0	VG 4.0	FN 6.0	VF 8.0	VF/NM 9.0	NM- 9.2
22 (23 on cover, 22 on indicia)-Origin The War Eagle & only app.; Chip Gardner begins; #22 was rebound in Complete Book of True Crime (Scarce)	568	1136	1704	4146	7323	10,500
23-(7/42) (Scarce)	300	600	900	1950	3375	4800
24-(11/42) Intro. & 1st app. Mr. Crime; classic Biro-c showing woman's head on fire being pushed onto hot stovetop burner	771	1542	2313	3855	6428	9000
25-(1/43) 2nd app. Mr. Crime; classic '40s crime-c	123	246	369	787	1344	1900
26-(3/43) 3rd app. Mr. Crime	103	206	309	659	1130	1600
27-Classic Biro-c pushing man into hot oven	123	246	369	787	1344	1900
28-30: 30-Wood and Biro app.	77	154	231	493	847	1200
31,32,34-40	43	86	129	271	461	650
33-(5/44) Classic Biro hanging & hatchet-c	142	284	426	909	1555	2200
41-(9/45) Origin & 1st app. Officer Common Sense	39	78	117	231	378	525
42-(11/45) Classic electrocution-c	53	106	159	334	567	800
43-46,48-50: 44-50 are 68 pg. issues. 44-"Legs" Diamond story. 50-(3/47)-1st issue to advertise 5 million readers on front-c. 58-(12/47)-shows 6 million readers (these ads believed to have influenced the crime comic wave of 1948)	27	54	81	158	259	360
47-(9/46)-Electric chair-c	41	82	123	256	428	600
51-70: 58(12/47)-Thomas Dun, killer of thousands (1565) story. 63,64-Possible use in **SOTI**, pg. 306. 63-Contains Biro & Gleason self censorship code of 12 listed restrictions (5/48)	20	40	60	117	189	260
71-99: 87-Chip Gardner begins, ends #100. 87-99-Painted-c	16	32	48	94	147	200
100-Painted-c	18	36	54	105	165	225
101-104,107-110: 101,102-Painted-c. 102-Chip Gardner app.	14	28	42	80	115	150
105-Used in **POP**, pg. 84	15	30	45	84	127	170
106,114-Frazetta-a, 1 pg.	14	28	42	81	118	155
111-Used in **POP**, pgs. 80 & 81; injury-to-eye sty illo	15	30	45	90	140	190
112,113,115-130	11	22	33	64	90	115
131-140	10	20	30	58	79	100
141,142-Last pre-code issue; Kubert-a(1)	12	24	36	67	94	120
143-Kubert-a in one story	12	24	36	67	94	120
144-146	10	20	30	58	79	100
147-Last issue (scarce); Kubert-a	16	32	48	94	147	200
1(Golfing-1945)	10	20	30	54	72	90
The Best of...(1944, 128 pgs.)-Series contains 4 rebound issues	110	220	330	704	1202	1700
...1945 issue	71	142	213	454	777	1100
...1946-48 issues	53	106	159	334	567	800
...1949-50 issues	45	90	135	284	480	675
...1951-53 issues (25¢)	39	78	117	240	395	550

NOTE: *Many issues contain violent covers and stories. Who Dunit by **Guardineer**-39-42, 44-105, 108-110; Chip Gardner by **Bob Jujitani (Fuge)**-88-103. **Alderman** a-29, 41-44, 49. **Dan Barry** a-67, 75. **Charles Biro** c-1-76, 122, 142. **Dick Briefer** a-29(2), 30, 31, 33, 37, 39. **G. Colan** a-105. **Tony Dipreta** a-79, 90, 92. **Fuje** c-88, 89, 91-94, 96, 98, 99, 102, 103. **Fred Guardineer** a-51, 57, 58(2), 66-68, 71, 74, 79, 81, 90, 92. **Joe Kubert** c-143. **Landau** a-118. **Al Mandell** a-37. **Norman Maurer** a-29, 39, 41, 42. **McWilliams** a-91, 93, 95, 100-103. **Rudy Palais** a-30, 33, **Bob Powell** a-146, 147. **George Tuska** a-48-50(2ea.), 51, 52 56, 57(2), 58, 60-64, 66-68, 71, 74, 81. Painted c-87-103. Bondage c-43, 62, 98.*

CRIME EXPOSED
Marvel Comics (PPI)/Marvel Atlas Comics (PrPI): June, 1948; Dec, 1950 - No. 14, June, 1952

	GD 2.0	VG 4.0	FN 6.0	VF 8.0	VF/NM 9.0	NM- 9.2
1(6/48)	36	72	108	216	351	485
1(12/50)	22	44	66	132	216	300
2	15	30	45	86	133	180
3-9,11,14	14	28	42	80	115	150
10-Used in **POP**, pg. 81	14	28	42	82	121	160
12-Krigstein & Robinson-a	14	28	42	82	121	160
13-Used in **POP**, pg. 81; Krigstein-a	15	30	45	83	124	165

NOTE: ***Keller** a-8, 10. **Maneely** c-8. **Robinson** a-11, 12. **Sale** a-4. **Tuska** a-3, 4.*

CRIMEFIGHTERS
Marvel Comics (CmPS 1-3/CCC 4-10): Apr, 1948 - No. 10, Nov, 1949

	GD 2.0	VG 4.0	FN 6.0	VF 8.0	VF/NM 9.0	NM- 9.2
1-Some copies are undated & could be reprints	27	54	81	162	266	370
2,3: 3-Morphine addict story	15	30	45	88	137	185
4-10: 4-Early John Buscema-a. 6-Anti-Wertham editorial. 9,10-Photo-c	14	28	42	81	118	155

Crime Incorporated #3 © FOX

Crime Mysteries #8 © Ribage

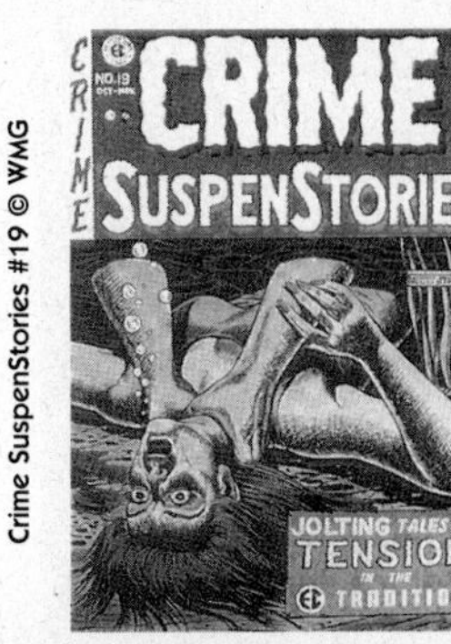

Crime SuspenStories #19 © WMG

GD VG FN VF VF/NM NM-
2.0 4.0 6.0 8.0 9.0 9.2

CRIME FIGHTERS (...Always Win)
Atlas Comics (CnPC): No. 11, Sept, 1954 - No. 13, Jan, 1955
11-13: 11-Maneely-a,13-Pakula, Reinman, Severin-a
13 26 39 72 101 130

CRIME-FIGHTING DETECTIVE (Shock Detective Cases No. 20 on; formerly Criminals on the Run)
Star Publications: No. 11, Apr-May, 1950 - No. 19, June, 1952 (Based on true crime cases)
11-L. B. Cole-c/a (2 pgs.); L. B. Cole-c on all 19 38 57 111 176 240
12,13,15-19: 17-Young King Cole & Dr. Doom app. 15 30 45 85 130 175
14-L. B. Cole-c/a, r/Law-Crime #2 16 32 48 94 147 200

CRIME FILES
Standard Comics: No. 5, Sept, 1952 - No. 6, Nov, 1952
5-1pg. Alex Toth-a; used in **SOTI**, pg. 4 (text) 24 48 72 140 230 320
6-Sekowsky-a 14 28 42 81 118 155

CRIME ILLUSTRATED (Magazine)
E. C. Comics: Nov-Dec, 1955 - No. 2, Spring, 1956 (25¢, Adult Suspense Stories on-c)
1-Ingels & Crandall-a 20 40 60 114 182 250
2-Ingels & Crandall-a 15 30 45 85 130 175
NOTE: ***Craig** a-2. **Crandall** a-1, 2; c-2. **Evans** a-1. **Davis** a-2. **Ingels** a-1, 2. **Krigstein/Crandall** a-1. **Orlando** a-1, 2; c-1.*

CRIME INCORPORATED (Formerly Crimes Incorporated)
Fox Features Syndicate: No. 2, Aug, 1950; No. 3, Aug, 1951
2 27 54 81 158 259 360
3(1951)-Hollingsworth-a 18 36 54 107 169 230

CRIME MACHINE (Magazine reprints pre-code crime and gangster comics)
Skywald Publications: Feb, 1971 - No. 2, May, 1971 (B&W, 68 pgs., roundbound)
1-Kubert-a(2)(r)(Avon); bikini girl in cake-c 5 10 15 35 63 90
2-Torres, Wildey-a; violent-c/a 4 8 12 27 44 60

CRIME MUST LOSE! (Formerly Sports Action?)
Sports Action (Atlas Comics): No. 4, Oct, 1950 - No. 12, April, 1952
4-Ann Brewster-a in all; c-used in N.Y. Legis. Comm. documents
20 40 60 117 189 260
5-10,12: 9-Robinson-a 14 28 42 82 121 160
11-Used in **POP**, pg. 89 15 30 45 84 127 170

CRIME MUST PAY THE PENALTY (Formerly Four Favorites; Penalty #47, 48)
Ace Magazines (Current Books): No. 33, Feb, 1948; No. 2, Jun, 1948 - No. 48, Jan, 1956
33(#1, 2/48)-Becomes Four Teeners #34? 40 80 120 246 411 575
2(6/48)-Extreme violence; Palais-a? 26 52 78 154 252 350
3,4,8: 3- "Frisco Mary" story used in Senate Investigation report, pg. 7. 4,8-Transvestism stories 20 40 60 117 189 260
5-7,9,10 15 30 45 85 130 175
11-19 14 28 42 82 121 160
20-Drug story "Dealers in White Death" 21 42 63 126 206 285
21-32,34-40,42-48: 44-Last pre-code 12 24 36 67 94 120
33(7/53)- "Dell Fabry-Junk King" drug story; mentioned in Love and Death
18 36 54 105 165 225
41-reprints "Dealers in White Death" 13 26 39 72 101 130
NOTE: ***Cameron** a-29-31, 34, 35, 39-41. **Colan** a-20, 31. **Kremer** a-3, 37r. **Larsen** a-32. **Palais** a-5?,37.*

CRIME MUST STOP
Hillman Periodicals: October, 1952 (52 pgs.)
V1#1(Scarce)-Similar to Monster Crime; Mort Lawrence, Krigstein-a
110 220 330 704 1202 1700

CRIME MYSTERIES (Secret Mysteries #16 on; combined with Crime Smashers #7 on)
Ribage Publ. Corp. (Trojan Magazines): May, 1952 - No. 15, Sept, 1954
1-Transvestism story; crime & terror stories begin 77 154 231 489 845 1200
2-Marijuana story (7/52) 47 94 141 296 498 700
3-One pg. Frazetta-a 42 84 126 265 445 625
4-Cover shows girl in bondage having her blood drained; 1 pg. Frazetta-a
90 180 270 576 988 1400
5-10 39 78 117 231 378 525
11,12,14 34 68 102 204 332 460
13-(5/54)-Angelo Torres 1st comic work (inks over Check's pencils); Check-a
39 78 117 234 385 535
15-Acid in face-c 50 100 150 315 533 750
NOTE: ***Fass** a-13; c-4, 6, 10. **Hollingsworth** a-10-13, 15; c-2, 12, 13, 15. **Kiefer** a-4. **Woodbridge** a-13? Bondage-c-1, 8, 12.*

CRIME ON THE RUN (See Approved Comics #8)

CRIME ON THE WATERFRONT (Formerly Famous Gangsters)
Realistic Publications: No. 4, May, 1952 (Painted cover)
4 29 58 87 170 278 385

CRIME PATROL (Formerly International #1-5; International Crime Patrol #6; becomes Crypt of Terror #17 on)
E. C. Comics: No. 7, Summer, 1948 - No. 16, Feb-Mar, 1950
7-Intro. Captain Crime 81 162 243 518 884 1250
8-14: 12-Ingels-a 71 142 213 454 777 1100
15-Intro. of Crypt Keeper (inspired by Witches Tales radio show) & Crypt of Terror (see Tales From the Crypt #33 for origin); used by N.Y. Legis. Comm.; last pg. Feldstein-a
269 538 807 2152 3426 4700
16-2nd Crypt Keeper app.; Roussos-a 171 342 513 1368 2184 3000
NOTE: ***Craig** c/a in most issues. **Feldstein** a-9-16. **Kiefer** a-8, 10, 11. **Moldoff** a-7.*

CRIME PATROL
Gemstone Publishing: Apr, 2000 - No. 10, Jan, 2001 ($2.50)
1-10: E.C. reprints 4.00
Volume 1,2 (2000, $13.50) 1-r/#1-5. 2-r/#6-10 14.00

CRIME PHOTOGRAPHER (See Casey...)

CRIME REPORTER
St. John Publ. Co.: Aug, 1948 - No. 3, Dec, 1948 (Indicia shows Oct.)
1-Drug club story 68 136 204 435 743 1050
2-Used in **SOTI**: illo- "Children told me what the man was going to do with the red-hot poker;" r/Dynamic #17 with editing; Baker-c; Tuska-a 103 206 309 659 1130 1600
3-Baker-c; Tuska-a 53 106 159 334 567 800

CRIMES BY WOMEN
Fox Features Syndicate: June, 1948 - No. 15, Aug, 1951; 1954 (True crime cases)
1-True story of Bonnie Parker 129 258 387 826 1413 2000
2,3: 3-Used in **SOTI**, pg. 234 71 142 213 454 777 1100
4,5,7-9,11-15: 8-Used in **POP**. 14-Bondage-c 65 130 195 416 708 1000
6-Classic girl fight-c; acid-in-face panel 77 154 231 493 847 1200
10-Used in **SOTI**, pg. 72; girl fight-c 68 136 204 435 743 1050
54(M.S. Publ.-'54)-Reprint; (formerly My Love Secret)
26 52 78 154 252 350

CRIMES INCORPORATED (Formerly My Past)
Fox Features Syndicate: No. 12, June, 1950 (Crime Incorporated No. 2 on)
12 27 54 81 160 263 365

CRIMES INCORPORATED (See Fox Giants)

CRIME SMASHER (See Whiz #76)
Fawcett Publications: Summer, 1948 (one-shot)
1-Formerly Spy Smasher 41 82 123 256 428 600

CRIME SMASHERS (Becomes Secret Mysteries No. 16 on)
Ribage Publishing Corp.(Trojan Magazines): Oct, 1950 - No. 15, Mar, 1953
1-Used in **SOTI**, pg. 19,20, & illo "A girl raped and murdered;" Sally the Sleuth begins
90 180 270 576 988 1400
2-Kubert-c 48 96 144 302 514 725
3,4 39 78 117 240 395 550
5-Wood-a 47 94 141 296 498 700
6,8-11: 8-Lingerie panel 32 64 96 188 307 425
7-Female heroin junkie story 36 72 108 211 343 475
12-Injury to eye panel; 1 pg. Frazetta-a 34 68 102 204 332 460
13-Used in **POP**, pgs. 79,80; 1 pg. Frazetta-a 34 68 102 204 332 460
14,15 26 52 78 154 252 350
NOTE: ***Hollingsworth** a-14. **Kiefer** a-15. Bondage c-7, 9.*

CRIME SUSPENSTORIES (Formerly Vault of Horror No. 12-14)
E. C. Comics: No. 15, Oct-Nov, 1950 - No. 27, Feb-Mar, 1955
15-Identical to #1 in content; #1 printed on outside front cover. #15 (formerly "The Vault of Horror") printed and blackened out on inside front cover with Vol. 1, No. 1 printed over it. Evidently, several of No. 15 were printed before a decision was made not to drop the Vault of Horror and Haunt of Fear series. The print run was stopped on No. 15 and continued on No. 1. All of the No. 15 issues were changed as described above.
171 342 513 1368 2184 3000
1 137 274 411 1096 1748 2400
2 69 138 207 552 876 1200
3-5: 3-Poe adaptation. 3-Old Witch stories begin 47 94 141 376 601 825
6-10: 9-Craig bio. 41 82 123 328 527 725
11,12,14,15: 15-The Old Witch guest stars 33 66 99 264 420 575
13,16-Williamson-a 34 68 102 272 436 600
17-Williamson/Frazetta-a (6 pgs.) Williamson bio. 49 98 147 392 621 850
18,19: 19-Used in **SOTI**, pg. 235 29 58 87 232 366 500
20-Classic hanging cover used in **SOTI**, illo "Cover of a children's comic book"
49 98 147 392 621 850

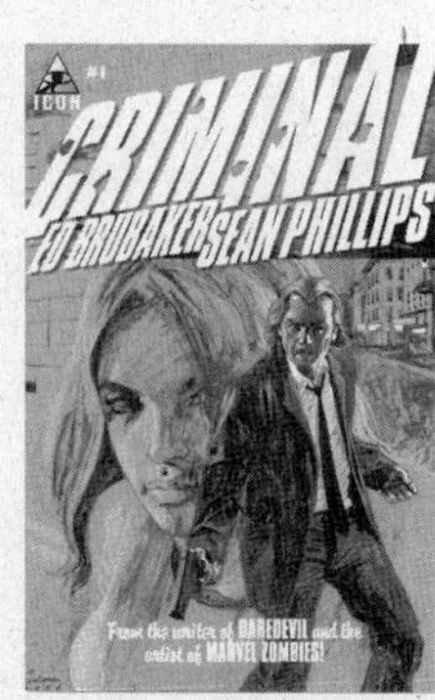

Criminal #1 © Brubaker & Phillips

Crimson #24 © Humberto Ramos

Crisis on Multiple Earths TPB © DC

	GD 2.0	VG 4.0	FN 6.0	VF 8.0	VF/NM 9.0	NM- 9.2
21,24-26: 24- "Food For Thought" similar to "Cave In" in Amazing Detective Cases #13 (1952)	21	42	63	168	272	375
22-Used in Senate investigation on juvenile delinquency; Ax decapitation-c	229	458	687	1832	2916	4000
23-Used in Senate investigation on juvenile delinquency	29	58	87	232	366	500
27-Last issue (Low distribution)	27	54	81	216	341	465

NOTE: ***Craig** a-1-21; c-1-18, 20-22. **Crandall** a-18-26. **Davis** a-4, 5, 7, 9-12, 20. **Elder** a-17,18. **Evans** a-15, 19, 21, 23, 25, 27; c-23, 24. **Feldstein** c-19. **Ingels** a-1-12, 14, 15, 27. **Kamen** a-2, 4-18, 20-27; c-25-27. **Krigstein** a-22, 24, 25, 27. **Kurtzman** a-1, 3. **Orlando** a-16, 22, 24, 26. **Wood** a-1, 3. Issues No. 1-3 were printed in Canada as "Weird Suspenstories." Issues No. 11-15 have E. C. "quickie" stories. No. 25 contains the famous "Are You a Red Dupe?" editorial. Ray Bradbury adaptations-15, 17.*

CRIME SUSPENSTORIES
Russ Cochran/Gemstone Publ.: Nov, 1992 - No. 27, May, 1999 ($1.50/$2.00/$2.50)

1-27: Reprints Crime SuspenStories series 4.00

CRIMINAL (Also see Criminal: The Sinners)
Marvel Comics (Icon): Oct, 2006 - No. 10, Oct, 2007 ($2.99)
Volume 2: Feb, 2008 - No. 7, Nov, 2008 ($3.50)

1-10-Ed Brubaker-s/Sean Phillips-a/c 3.00
Volume 2: 1-7-Brubaker-s/Phillips-a 3.50
... Vol. 1: Coward TPB (2007, $14.99) r/#1-5; intro. by Tom Fontana 15.00
... Vol. 2: Lawless TPB (2007, $14.99) r/#6-10; intro. by Frank Miller 15.00
... Vol. 3: The Dead and the Dying TPB (2008, $11.99) r/V2#1-4; intro. by John Singleton 12.00

CRIMINAL MACABRE: (limited series and one-shots)
Dark Horse Comics: ($2.99)

...: Cellblock 666 (9/08 - No. 4, 5/09)(#25-28 in series) 1-4-Niles-s/Stakal-a/Bradstreet-c 3.00
...: Die, Die, My Darling (4/12, $3.50) reprints serial from DHP #4-6; Staples-c 3.50
...: Feat of Clay (6/06, $2.99) Niles-s/Hotz-a/c 3.00
Free Comic Book Day: Criminal Macabre - Call Me Monster (5/11) flip book w/Baltimore 3.00
...: My Demon Baby (9/07 - No. 4, 4/08)(#21-24 in the series) 1-4-Niles-s/Stakal-a 3.00
...: No Peace For Dead Men (9/11, $3.99) Niles-s/Mitten-a/Staples-c 4.00
...: The Eyes of Frankenstein (9/13 - No. 4, 12/13 $3.99) 1-4-Niles-s/Mitten-a 4.00
...: The Goon (7/11, $3.99) Niles-s/Mitten-a; covers by Powell & Staples 4.00
...: They Fight By Night (11/12, $3.99) reprints serial from DHP #10-13; Staples-c 4.00
...: Two Red Eyes (12/06 - No. 4, 3/07) 1-4-Niles-s/Hotz-a/Bradstreet-c 3.00

CRIMINAL MACABRE: A CAL MCDONALD MYSTERY (Also see Last Train to Deadsville)
Dark Horse Comics: May, 2003 - No. 5, Sept, 2003 ($2.99)

1-5-Niles-s/Templesmith-a 3.00

CRIMINAL MACABRE: FINAL NIGHT - THE 30 DAYS OF NIGHT CROSSOVER
Dark Horse Comics: Dec, 2012 - No. 4, Mar, 2013 ($3.99, limited series)

1-4-Niles-s/Mitten-a/Erickson-c 4.00

CRIMINALS ON THE RUN (Formerly Young King Cole) (Crime Fighting Detective No. 11 on)
Premium Group (Novelty Press): V4#1, Aug-Sep, 1948-#10, Dec-Jan, 1949-50

	GD	VG	FN	VF	VF/NM	NM-
V4#1-Young King Cole continues	27	54	81	158	259	360
2-6: 6-Dr. Doom app.	23	46	69	136	223	310
7-Classic "Fish in the Face" c by L. B. Cole	54	108	162	343	574	825
V5#1,2 (#8,9),10: 9,10-L. B. Cole-c	21	42	63	122	199	275

NOTE: *Most issues have **L. B. Cole** covers. **McWilliams** a-V4#6, 7, V5#2; c-V4#5.*

CRIMINAL: THE LAST OF THE INNOCENT
Marvel Comics (Icon): Jun, 2011 - No. 4, Sept, 2011 ($3.50)

1-4-Ed Brubaker-s/Sean Phillips-a/c 3.50

CRIMINAL: THE SINNERS
Marvel Comics (Icon): Sept, 2009 - No. 5, Mar, 2010 ($3.50)

1-5-Ed Brubaker-s/Sean Phillips-a/c 3.50

CRIMSON (Also see Cliffhanger #0)
Image Comics (Cliffhanger Productions): May, 1998 - No. 7, Dec, 1998;
DC Comics (Cliffhanger Prod.): No. 8, Mar, 1999 - No. 24, Apr, 2001 ($2.50)

1-Humberto Ramos-a/Augustyn-s 5.00
1-Variant-c by Warren 8.00
1-Chromium-c 15.00
2-Ramos-c with street crowd, 2-Variant-c by Art Adams 4.00
2-Dynamic Forces CrimsonChrome cover 15.00
3-7: 3-Ramos Moon background-c. 7-Three covers by Ramos, Madureira, & Campbell 3.50
8-23: 8-First DC issue 3.00
24-($3.50) Final issue; wraparound-c 4.00
DF Premiere Ed. 1998 ($6.95) covers by Ramos and Jae Lee 7.00
Crimson: Scarlet X Blood on the Moon (10/99, $3.95) 4.00
Crimson Sourcebook (11/99, $2.95) Pin-ups and info 3.00
Earth Angel TPB (2001, $14.95) r/#13-18 15.00
Heaven and Earth TPB (1/00, $14.95) r/#7-12 15.00
Loyalty and Loss TPB ('99, $12.95) r/#1-6 15.00
Redemption TPB ('01, $14.95) r/#19-24 15.00

CRIMSON AVENGER, THE (See Detective Comics #20 for 1st app.)(Also see Leading Comics #1 & World's Best/Finest Comics)
DC Comics: June, 1988 - No. 4, Sept, 1988 ($1.00, limited series)

1-4 4.00

CRIMSON DYNAMO
Marvel Comics (Epic): Oct, 2003 - No. 6, Apr, 2004 ($2.50/$2.99)

1-4,6: 1-John Jackson Miller-s/Steve Ellis-a/c 3.00
5-($2.99) Iron Man-c/app. 4.00

CRIMSON PLAGUE
Event Comics: June, 1997 ($2.95, unfinished mini-series)

1-George Perez-a 3.00

CRIMSON PLAGUE (George Pérez's...)
Image Comics (Gorilla): June, 2000 - No. 2, Aug, 2000 ($2.95, mini-series)

1-George Pérez-a; reprints 6/97 issue with 16 new pages 3.00
2-($2.50) 3.00

CRISIS AFTERMATH: THE BATTLE FOR BLUDHAVEN (Also see Infinite Crisis)
DC Comics: Jun, 2006 - No. 6, Sept, 2006 ($2.99, limited series)

1-Atomic Knights return; Teen Titans app.; Jurgens-a/Acuna-c 4.00
1-2nd printing with pencil cover 3.00
2-6: 2-Intro S.H.A.D.E. (new Freedom Fighters) 3.00
TPB (2007, $12.99) r/#1-6 13.00

CRISIS AFTERMATH: THE SPECTRE (Also see Infinite Crisis, Gotham Central and Tales of the Unexpected)
DC Comics: Jul, 2006 - No. 3, Sept, 2006 ($2.99, limited series)

1-3-Crispus Allen becomes the Spectre; Pfeifer-s/Chiang-a/c 3.00
TPB (2007, $12.99) r/#1-3 and Tales of the Unexpected #1-3 13.00

CRISIS ON INFINITE EARTHS (Also see Official... Index and Legends of the DC Universe)
DC Comics: Apr, 1985 - No. 12, Mar, 1986 (maxi-series)

	GD	VG	FN	VF	VF/NM	NM-
1-1st DC app. Blue Beetle & Detective Karp from Charlton; Pérez-c on all	2	4	6	10	14	18
2-6: 6-Intro Charlton's Capt. Atom, Nightshade, Question, Judomaster, Peacemaker & Thunderbolt into DC Universe	2	4	6	8	10	12
7-Double size; death of Supergirl	3	6	9	14	19	24
8-Death of the Flash (Barry Allen)	2	4	6	13	18	22
9-11: 9-Intro. Charlton's Ghost into DC Universe. 10-Intro. Charlton's Banshee, Dr. Spectro, Image, Punch & Jewellee into DC Universe; Starman (Prince Gavyn) dies	2	4	6	8	10	12
12-(52 pgs.)-Deaths of Dove, Kole, Lori Lemaris, Sunburst, G.A. Robin & Huntress; Kid Flash becomes new Flash; 3rd & final DC app. of the 3 Lt. Marvels; Green Fury gets new look (becomes Green Flame in Infinity, Inc. #32)	2	4	6	9	13	16

Slipcased Hardcover (1998, $99.95) Wraparound dust-jacket cover by Pérez and Alex Ross; sketch pages by Pérez; intro by Wolfman 125.00
TPB (2000, $29.95) Wraparound-c by Pérez and Ross 30.00

NOTE: *Crossover issues: All Star Squadron 50-56,60; Amethyst 13; Blue Devil 17,18; DC Comics Presents 78,86-88,95; Detective Comics 558; Fury of Firestorm 41,42; G.I. Combat 274; Green Lantern 194-196,198; Infinity, Inc. 18-25 & Annual 1, Justice League of America 244,245 & Annual 3; Legion of Super-Heroes 16,18; Losers Special 1; New Teen Titans 13,14; Omega Men 31,33; Superman 413-415; Swamp Thing 44,46; Wonder Woman 327-329.*

CRISIS ON MULTIPLE EARTHS
DC Comics: 2002 - 2010 ($14.95, trade paperbacks)

TPB-(2003) Reprints 1st 4 Silver Age JLA/JSA crossovers from J.L.ofA. #21,22; 29,30; 37,38; 46,47; new painted-c by Alex Ross; intro. by Mark Waid 15.00
Volume 2 (2003, $14.95) r/J.L.ofA. #55,56; 64,65; 73,74; 82,83; new Ordway-c 15.00
Volume 3 (2004, $14.95) r/J.L.ofA. #91,92; 100-102; 107,108; 113; Wein intro., Ross-c 15.00
Volume 4 (2006, $14.99) r/J.L.ofA. #123-124 (Earth-Prime),135-137 (Fawcett's Shazam characters), 147-148 (Legion of Super-Heroes); Ross-c 15.00
Volume 5 (2010, $19.99) r/J.L.ofA. #159-160 (Jonah Hex, Enemy Ace), #171-172 (Murder of Mr. Terrific), 1#83-185 (New Gods & Darkseid); Pérez-c 20.00
... The Team-Ups Volume 1 (2005, $14.99) r/Flash #123,129,137,151; Showcase #55,56; Green Lantern #40, Brave and the Bold #61 and Spectre #7; new Ordway-c 15.00

CRITICAL MASS (See A Shadowline Saga: Critical Mass)

CRITTER
Big Dog Press: Jul, 2011 - No. 4, 2011; Jun, 2012 - Present ($3.50)

1-4-Multiple covers on all 3.50
Vol. 2 1-17-Multiple covers on all 3.50

CRITTERS (Also see Usagi Yojimbo Summer Special)

CrossGen Chronicles #2 © CRO

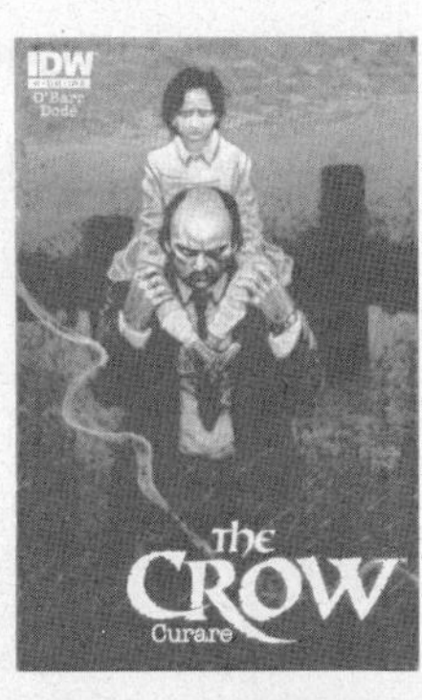

The Crow: Curare #1 © James O'Barr

Crown Comics #15 © G/M

Fantagraphics Books: 1986 - No. 50, 1990 ($1.70/$2.00, B&W)

	GD 2.0	VG 4.0	FN 6.0	VF 8.0	VF/NM 9.0	NM- 9.2
1-Cutey Bunny, Usagi Yojimbo app.	2	4	6	8	10	12
2,4,5,8,9						6.00
3,6,7,10-Usagi Yojimbo app.	1	2	3	5	6	8
11,14-Usagi Yojimbo app. 11-Christmas Special (68 pgs.)						5.00
12,13,15-22,24-37,39,40: 22-Watchmen parody; two diff. covers exist						3.00
23-With Alan Moore Flexi-disc ($3.95)						5.00
38-($2.75-c) Usagi Yojimbo app.						5.00
41-49						4.00
50 ($4.95, 84 pgs.)-Neil the Horse, Capt. Jack, Sam & Max & Usagi Yojimbo app.; Quagmire, Shaw-a	1	2	3	4	5	7
Special 1 (1/88, $2.00)						4.00

CROSS
Dark Horse Comics: No. 0, Oct, 1995 - No. 6, Apr, 1995 ($2.95, limited series, mature)

	GD 2.0	VG 4.0	FN 6.0	VF 8.0	VF/NM 9.0	NM- 9.2
0-6: Darrow-c & Vachss scripts in all						3.00

CROSS AND THE SWITCHBLADE, THE
Spire Christian Comics (Fleming H. Revell Co.): 1972 (35-49¢)

	GD 2.0	VG 4.0	FN 6.0	VF 8.0	VF/NM 9.0	NM- 9.2
1-Some issues have nn	3	6	9	15	22	28

CROSS BRONX, THE
Image Comics: Sept, 2006 - No. 4, Dec, 2006 ($2.99, limited series)

	GD 2.0	VG 4.0	FN 6.0	VF 8.0	VF/NM 9.0	NM- 9.2
1-4: 1-Oeming-a/c; Oeming & Brandon-s; Ribic var-c. 2-Johnson var-c. 4-Mack var-c						3.00

CROSSFIRE
Spire Christian Comics (Fleming H. Revell Co.): 1973 (39/49¢)

	GD 2.0	VG 4.0	FN 6.0	VF 8.0	VF/NM 9.0	NM- 9.2
nn	2	4	6	13	18	22

CROSSFIRE (Also see DNAgents)
Eclipse Comics: 5/84 - No. 17, 3/86; No. 18, 1/87 - No. 26, 2/88 ($1.50, Baxter paper) (#18-26 are B&W)

	GD 2.0	VG 4.0	FN 6.0	VF 8.0	VF/NM 9.0	NM- 9.2
1-11,14-26: 1-DNAgents x-over; Spiegle-c/a begins						3.00
12-Death of Marilyn Monroe; Dave Stevens-c	2	4	6	8	10	12
13-Death of Marilyn Monroe						6.00

CROSSFIRE AND RAINBOW (Also see DNAgents)
Eclipse Comics: June, 1986 - No. 4, Sept, 1986 ($1.25, deluxe format)

	GD 2.0	VG 4.0	FN 6.0	VF 8.0	VF/NM 9.0	NM- 9.2
1-3: Spiegle-a						3.00
4-Dave Stevens-c						6.00

CROSSGEN...
CrossGeneration Comics

	GD 2.0	VG 4.0	FN 6.0	VF 8.0	VF/NM 9.0	NM- 9.2
CrossGenesis (1/00) Previews CrossGen universe; cover gallery						3.00
...Primer (1/00) Wizard supplement; intro. to the CrossGen universe						3.00
...Sampler (2/00) Retailer preview book						3.00

CROSSGEN CHRONICLES
CrossGeneration Comics: June, 2000 - No. 8 ($3.95)

	GD 2.0	VG 4.0	FN 6.0	VF 8.0	VF/NM 9.0	NM- 9.2
1-Intro. to CrossGen characters & company						4.00
1-(no cover price) same contents, customer preview						4.00
2-8: 2-(3/01) George Pérez-c/a. 3-5-Pérez-a/Waid-s. 6,7-Nebres-c/a						4.00

CROSSING MIDNIGHT
DC Comics (Vertigo): Jan, 2007 - No. 19, Jul, 2008 ($2.99)

	GD 2.0	VG 4.0	FN 6.0	VF 8.0	VF/NM 9.0	NM- 9.2
1-19: 1-Carey-s/Fern-a/Williams III-c. 10-12-Nguyen-a						3.00
...: Cut Here TPB (2007, $9.99) r/#1-5						10.00
...: A Map of Midnight TPB (2008, $14.99) r/#6-12; afterword by Carey						15.00
...: The Sword in the Soul TPB (2008, $14.99) r/#13-19						15.00

CROSSING THE ROCKIES (See Classics Illustrated Special Issue)

CROSSOVERS, THE
CrossGeneration Comics: Feb, 2003 - No. 12 ($2.95)

	GD 2.0	VG 4.0	FN 6.0	VF 8.0	VF/NM 9.0	NM- 9.2
1-12-Robert Rodi-s. 1-6-Mauricet & Ernie Colon-a. 7-Staton-a begins						3.00
Vol. 1: Cross Currents (2003, $9.95) digest-sized reprints #1-6						10.00

CROW, THE (Also see Caliber Presents)
Caliber Press: Feb, 1989 - No. 4, 1989 ($1.95, B&W, limited series)

	GD 2.0	VG 4.0	FN 6.0	VF 8.0	VF/NM 9.0	NM- 9.2
1-James O'Barr-c/a/scripts	7	14	21	46	86	125
1-3-2nd printing						6.00
2-4	4	8	12	23	37	50
2-3rd printing						4.00

CROW, THE
Tundra Publishing, Ltd.: Jan, 1992 - No. 3, 1992 ($4.95, B&W, 68 pgs.)

	GD 2.0	VG 4.0	FN 6.0	VF 8.0	VF/NM 9.0	NM- 9.2
1-3: 1-r/#1,2 of Caliber series. 2-r/#3 of Caliber series w/new material. 3-All new material	1	2	3	5	6	8

CROW, THE
Kitchen Sink Press: 1/96 - No. 3, 3/96 ($2.95, B&W)

	GD 2.0	VG 4.0	FN 6.0	VF 8.0	VF/NM 9.0	NM- 9.2
1-3: James O'Barr-c/scripts						5.00
#0-A Cycle of Shattered Lives (12/98, $3.50) new story by O'Barr						4.00

CROW, THE
Image Comics (Todd McFarlane Prod.): Feb, 1999 - No. 10, Nov, 1999 ($2.50)

	GD 2.0	VG 4.0	FN 6.0	VF 8.0	VF/NM 9.0	NM- 9.2
1-10: 1-Two covers by McFarlane and Kent Williams; Muth-s in all. 2-6,10-Paul Lee-a						3.00
Book 1 - Vengeance (2000, $10.95, TPB) r/#1-3,5,6						11.00
Book 2 - Evil Beyond Reach (2000, $10.95, TPB) r/#4,7-10						11.00
Todd McFarlane Presents The Crow Magazine 1 (3/00, $4.95)						5.00

CROW, THE: CITY OF ANGELS (Movie)
Kitchen Sink Press: July, 1996 - No. 3, Sept, 1996 ($2.95, limited series)

	GD 2.0	VG 4.0	FN 6.0	VF 8.0	VF/NM 9.0	NM- 9.2
1-3: Adaptation of film; two-c (photo & illos.). 1-Vincent Perez interview						3.00

CROW, THE: CURARE
IDW Publishing: Jun, 2013 - No. 3, Aug, 2013 ($3.99, limited series)

	GD 2.0	VG 4.0	FN 6.0	VF 8.0	VF/NM 9.0	NM- 9.2
1-3-James O'Barr-s/Antoine Dodé-a; multiple covers on each						4.00

CROW, THE: DEATH AND REBIRTH
IDW Publishing: Jul, 2012 - No. 5, Nov, 2012 ($3.99, limited series)

	GD 2.0	VG 4.0	FN 6.0	VF 8.0	VF/NM 9.0	NM- 9.2
1-5-Shirley-s/Colden-a; multiple covers on each						4.00

CROW, THE: FLESH AND BLOOD
Kitchen Sink Press: May, 1996 - No. 3, July, 1996 ($2.95, limited series)

	GD 2.0	VG 4.0	FN 6.0	VF 8.0	VF/NM 9.0	NM- 9.2
1-3: O'Barr-c						3.00

CROW, THE: RAZOR - KILL THE PAIN
London Night Studios: Apr, 1998 - No. 3, July, 1998 ($2.95, B&W, lim. series)

	GD 2.0	VG 4.0	FN 6.0	VF 8.0	VF/NM 9.0	NM- 9.2
1-3-Hartsoe-s/O'Barr-painted-c						3.00
0(10/98) Dorien painted-c, Finale (2/99)						3.00
The Lost Chapter (2/99, $4.95), Tour Book-(12/97) pin-ups; 4 diff.-c						5.00

CROW, THE: PESTILENCE
IDW Publishing: Mar, 2014 - Present ($3.99, limited series)

	GD 2.0	VG 4.0	FN 6.0	VF 8.0	VF/NM 9.0	NM- 9.2
1-Frank Bill-s/Drew Moss-a; two covers						4.00

CROW, THE: SKINNING THE WOLVES
IDW Publishing: Dec, 2012 - No. 3, Feb, 2013 ($3.99, limited series)

	GD 2.0	VG 4.0	FN 6.0	VF 8.0	VF/NM 9.0	NM- 9.2
1-3-James O'Barr-s/Jim Terry-s/a; multiple covers on each						4.00

CROW, THE: WAKING NIGHTMARES
Kitchen Sink Press: Jan, 1997 - No. 4, 1998 ($2.95, B&W, limited series)

	GD 2.0	VG 4.0	FN 6.0	VF 8.0	VF/NM 9.0	NM- 9.2
1-4-Miran Kim-c						5.00

CROW, THE: WILD JUSTICE
Kitchen Sink Press: Oct, 1996 - No. 3, Dec, 1996 ($2.95, B&W, limited series)

	GD 2.0	VG 4.0	FN 6.0	VF 8.0	VF/NM 9.0	NM- 9.2
1-3-Prosser-s/Adlard-a						3.00

CROWN COMICS (Also see Vooda)
Golfing/McCombs Publ.: Wint, 1944-45; No. 2, Sum, 1945 - No. 19, July, 1949

	GD 2.0	VG 4.0	FN 6.0	VF 8.0	VF/NM 9.0	NM- 9.2
1- "The Oblong Box" E.A. Poe adaptation	45	90	135	284	480	675
2-Baker-a	34	68	102	199	325	450
3-Baker-a; Voodah by Baker	39	78	117	240	395	550
4-6-Baker-c/a; Voodah app. #4,5	36	72	108	211	343	475
7-Feldstein, Baker, Kamen-a; Baker-c	37	74	111	222	361	500
8-Baker-a; Voodah app.	28	56	84	165	270	375
9-11,13-19: Voodah in #10-19. 13-New logo	19	38	57	111	176	240
12-Master Marvin by Feldstein, Starr-a; Voodah-c	20	40	60	114	182	250

NOTE: ***Bolle** a-11, 13-16, 18, 19; c-11p, 15. **Powell** a-19. **Starr** a-11-13; c-11i.*

CRUCIBLE
DC Comics (Impact): Feb, 1993 - No. 6, July, 1993 ($1.25, limited series)

	GD 2.0	VG 4.0	FN 6.0	VF 8.0	VF/NM 9.0	NM- 9.2
1-6: 1-(99¢)-Neon ink-c. 1,2-Quesada-c(p). 1-4-Quesada layouts						3.00

CRUEL AND UNUSUAL
DC Comics (Vertigo): June, 1999 - No. 4, Sept, 1999 ($2.95, limited series)

	GD 2.0	VG 4.0	FN 6.0	VF 8.0	VF/NM 9.0	NM- 9.2
1-4-Delano & Peyer-s/McCrea-c/a						3.00

CRUSADER FROM MARS (See Tops in Adventure)
Ziff-Davis Publ. Co.: Jan-Mar, 1952 - No. 2, Fall, 1952 (Painted-c)

	GD 2.0	VG 4.0	FN 6.0	VF 8.0	VF/NM 9.0	NM- 9.2
1-Cover is dated Spring	79	158	237	502	864	1225
2-Bondage-c	54	108	162	343	574	825

CRUSADER RABBIT (TV)
Dell Publishing Co.: No. 735, Oct, 1956 - No. 805, May, 1957

	GD 2.0	VG 4.0	FN 6.0	VF 8.0	VF/NM 9.0	NM- 9.2
Four Color 735 (#1)	21	42	63	147	324	500
Four Color 805	16	32	48	111	246	380

The Crusades #12 © Seagle & Jones

Cryptozoic Man #1 © Flanagan & Johnson

CSI: NY - Bloody Murder #1 © CBS

	GD 2.0	VG 4.0	FN 6.0	VF 8.0	VF/NM 9.0	NM- 9.2

CRUSADERS, THE (Religious)
Chick Publications: 1974 - Vol. 17, 1988 (39/69¢, 36 pgs.)

Vol.1-Operation Bucharest ('74). Vol.2-The Broken Cross ('74). Vol.3-Scarface ('74). Vol.4-Exorcists ('75). Vol.5-Chaos ('75)	3	6	9	16	23	30
Vol.6-Primal Man? ('76)-(Disputes evolution theory). Vol.7-The Ark-(claims proof of existence, destroyed by Bolsheviks). Vol.8-The Gift-(Life story of Christ). Vol.9-Angel of Light-(Story of the Devil). Vol.10-Spellbound?-(Tells how rock music is Satanic & produced by witches). 11-Sabotage?. 12-Alberto. 13-Double Cross. 14-The Godfathers. (No. 6-14 low in distribution; loaded with religious propaganda.). 15-The Force. 16-The Four Horsemen	3	6	9	16	23	30
Vol. 17-The Prophet (low print run)	3	6	9	17	26	35

CRUSADERS (Southern Knights No. 2 on)
Guild Publications: 1982 (B&W, magazine size)

1-1st app. Southern Knights	2	4	6	9	12	16

CRUSADERS, THE (Also see Black Hood, The Jaguar, The Comet, The Fly, Legend of the Shield, The Mighty... & The Web)
DC Comics (Impact): May, 1992 - No. 8, Dec, 1992 ($1.00/$1.25)

1-8-Contains 3 Impact trading cards 4.00

CRUSADES, THE
DC Comics (Vertigo): 2001 - No. 20, Dec, 2002 ($3.95/$2.50)

...: Urban Decree ('01, $3.95) Intro. the Knight; Seagle-s/Kelley Jones-c/a 4.00
1-(5/01, $2.50) Sienkiewicz-c 3.00
2-20: 2-Moeller-c. 18-Begin $2.95-c 3.00

CRUSH
Dark Horse Comics: Oct, 2003 - No. 4, Jan, 2004 ($2.99, limited series)

1-4-Jason Hall-s/Sean Murphy-a 3.00

CRUSH, THE
Image Comics (Motown Machineworks): Jan, 1996 - No. 5, July, 1996 ($2.25, limited series)

1-5: Baron scripts 3.00

CRUX
CrossGeneration Comics: May, 2001 - No. 33, Feb, 2004 ($2.95)

1-33: 1-Waid-s/Epting & Magyar-a/c. 6-Pelletier-a. 13-Dixon-s begin. 25-Cover has fake creases and other aging 3.00
Atlantis Rising Vol. 1 TPB (2002, $15.95) r/#1-6 16.00
Test of Time Vol. 2 TPB (12/02, $15.95) r/#7-12 16.00
Vol. 3: Strangers in Atlantis (2003, $15.95) r/#13-18 16.00
Vol. 4: Chaos Reborn (2003, $15.95) r/#19-24 16.00

CRY FOR DAWN
Cry For Dawn Pub.: 1989 - No. 9 ($2.25, B&W, mature)

1	7	14	21	44	82	120
1-2nd printing	3	6	9	17	26	35
1-3rd printing	3	6	9	14	20	25
2	4	8	12	23	37	50
2-2nd printing	2	4	6	11	16	20
3	3	6	9	16	23	30
3a-HorrorCon Edition (1990, less than 400 printed, signed inside-c)						200.00
4-6	2	4	6	11	16	20
5-2nd printing	1	2	3	5	6	8
7-9	2	4	6	9	12	15
4-9-Signed & numbered editions	3	6	9	14	20	25

Angry Christ Comix HC (4/03, $29.99) reprints various stories; and 30 pgs. new material 30.00
...Calendar (1993) 35.00

CRYIN' LION COMICS
William H. Wise Co.: Fall, 1944 - No. 3, Spring, 1945

1-Funny animal	17	34	51	98	154	210
2-Hitler and Tojo app.	14	28	42	82	121	160
3	10	20	30	58	79	100

CRYPT
Image Comics (Extreme): Aug, 1995 - No.2, Oct. 1995 ($2.50, limited series)

1,2-Prophet app. 3.00

CRYPTIC WRITINGS OF MEGADETH
Chaos! Comics: Sept, 1997 - No. 4, Jun, 1998 ($2.95, quarterly)

1-4-Stories based on song lyrics by Dave Mustaine 3.00

CRYPT OF DAWN (see Dawn)
Sirius: 1996 ($2.95, B&W, limited series)

1-Linsner-c/s; anthology. 5.00
2, 3 (2/98) 4.00
4,5: 4- (6/98), 5-(11/98) 3.00
Ltd. Edition 20.00

CRYPT OF SHADOWS
Marvel Comics Group: Jan, 1973 - No. 21, Nov, 1975 (#1-9 are 20¢)

1-Wolverton-r/Advs. Into Terror #7	4	8	12	25	40	55
2-10: 2-Starlin/Everett-c	3	6	9	16	23	30
11-21: 18,20-Kirby-a	3	6	9	14	20	25

NOTE: ***Briefer*** *a-2r.* ***Ditko*** *a-13r, 18-20r.* ***Everett*** *a-6, 14r; c-2i.* ***Heath*** *a-1r.* ***Gil Kane*** *c-1, 6.* ***Mort Lawrence*** *a-1r, 8r.* ***Maneely*** *a-2r.* ***Moldoff*** *a-8.* ***Powell*** *a-12r, 14r.* ***Tuska*** *a-2r.*

CRYPT OF TERROR (Formerly Crime Patrol; Tales From the Crypt No. 20 on)
(Also see EC Archives • Tales From the Crypt)
E. C. Comics: No. 17, Apr-May, 1950 - No. 19, Aug-Sept, 1950

17-1st New Trend to hit stands	314	628	942	2512	4006	5500
18,19	166	332	498	1328	2114	2900

NOTE: ***Craig*** *c/a-17-19.* ***Feldstein*** *a-17-19.* ***Ingels*** *a-19.* ***Kurtzman*** *a-18.* ***Wood*** *a-18. Canadian reprints known; see Table of Contents.*

CRYPTOZOIC MAN (Comic Book Men)
Dynamite Entertainment: 2013 - No. 4, 2014 ($3.99, limited series)

1-Bryan Johnson-s/Walt Flanagan-a/c	2	4	6	9	12	15
2-4	1	3	4	6	8	10

CRYSIS (Based on the EA videogame)
IDW Publishing: Jun, 2011 - No. 6, Oct, 2011 ($3.99, limited series)

1-6: 1-Richard K. Moran-s/Peter Bergting-a; two covers 4.00

CSI: CRIME SCENE INVESTIGATION (Based on TV series)
IDW Publishing: Jan, 2003 - No. 5, May, 2003 ($3.99, limited series)

1-Two covers (photo & Ashley Wood); Max Allan Collins-s 4.00
2-5 4.00
Free Comic Book Day edition (7/04) Previews CSI: Bad Rap; The Shield: Spotlight; 24: One Shot; and 30 Days of Night 3.00
...: Case Files Vol. 1 TPB (8/06, $19.99) B&W rep/Serial TPB, CSI - Bad Rap and CSI - Demon House limited series 20.00
...: Serial TPB (2003, $19.99) r/#1-5; bonus short story by Collins/Wood 20.00
...: Thicker Than Blood (7/03, $6.99) Mariotte-s/Rodriguez-a 7.00

CSI: CRIME SCENE INVESTIGATION - BAD RAP
IDW Publishing: Aug, 2003 - No. 5, Dec, 2003 ($3.99, limited series)

1-5-Two photo covers; Max Allan Collins-s/Rodriguez-a 4.00
TPB (3/04, $19.99) r/#1-5 20.00

CSI: CRIME SCENE INVESTIGATION - DEMON HOUSE
IDW Publishing: Feb, 2004 - No. 5, Jun, 2004 ($3.99, limited series)

1-5-Photo covers on all; Max Allan Collins-s/Rodriguez-a 4.00
TPB (10/04, $19.99) r/#1-5 20.00

CSI: CRIME SCENE INVESTIGATION - DOMINOS
IDW Publishing: Aug, 2004 - No. 5, Dec, 2004 ($3.99, limited series)

1-5-Photo covers on all; Oprisko-s/Rodriguez-a 4.00

CSI: CRIME SCENE INVESTIGATION - DYING IN THE GUTTERS
IDW Publishing: Aug, 2006 - No. 5, Dec, 2006 ($3.99, limited series)

1-5-"Rich Johnston" murdered; comic creators (Quesada, Rucka, David, Brubaker, Silvestri and others) appear as suspects; Stephen Mooney-a; photo-c 4.00

CSI: CRIME SCENE INVESTIGATION - SECRET IDENTITY
IDW Publishing: Feb, 2005 - No. 5, Jun, 2005 ($3.99, limited series)

1-5-Photo covers on all; Steven Grant-s/Gabriel Rodriguez-a 4.00

CSI: MIAMI
IDW Publishing: Oct, 2003; Apr, 2004 ($6.99, one-shots)

... - Blood Money (9/04)-Oprisko-s/Guedes & Perkins-a 7.00
... - Smoking Gun (10/03)-Mariotte-s/Avilés & Wood-a 7.00
... - Thou Shalt Not... (4/04)-Oprisko-s/Guedes & Wood-a 7.00
TPB (2/05, $19.99) reprints one-shots 20.00

CSI: NY - BLOODY MURDER
IDW Publishing: July, 2005 - No. 5, Nov, 2005 ($3.99, limited series)

1-5-Photo covers on all; Collins-s/Woodward-a 4.00

C•23 (Jim Lee's...) (Based on Wizards of the Coast card game)
Image Comics: Apr, 1998 - No. 8, Nov, 1998 ($2.50)

1-8: 1,2-Choi & Mariotte-s/ Charest-c. 2-Variant-c by Jim Lee. 4-Ryan Benjamin-c. 5,8-Corben var-c. 6-Flip book with Planetary preview; Corben-c 3.00

CUD
Fantagraphics Books: 8/92 - No. 8, 12/94 ($2.25-$2.75, B&W, mature)

Curse of the Spawn #23 © TMP

Cyberella #2 © Chaykin & Cameron

Cyberforce V4 #1 © TCOW

GD 2.0 VG 4.0 FN 6.0 VF 8.0 VF/NM 9.0 NM- 9.2

1-8: Terry LaBan scripts & art in all. 6-1st Eno & Plum 3.00

CUD COMICS
Dark Horse Comics: Jan, 1995 - No. 8, Sept, 1997 ($2.95, B&W)

1-8: Terry LaBan-c/a/scripts. 5-Nudity; marijuana story 3.00
Eno and Plum TPB (1997, $12.95) r/#1-4, DHP #93-95 13.00

CUPID
Marvel Comics (U.S.A.): Dec, 1949 - No. 2, Mar, 1950

1-Photo-c 21 42 63 122 199 275
2-Bettie Page ('50s pin-up queen) photo-c; Powell-a (see My Love #4) 65 130 195 416 708 1000

CURIO
Harry 'A' Chesler: 1930's(?) (Tabloid size, 16-20 pgs.)

nn 20 40 60 114 182 250

CURLY KAYOE COMICS (Boxing)
United Features Syndicate/Dell Publ. Co.: 1946 - No. 8, 1950; Jan, 1958

1 (1946)-Strip-r (Fritzi Ritz); biography of Sam Leff, Kayoe's artist 20 40 60 114 182 250
2 14 28 42 76 108 140
3-8 11 22 33 62 86 110
United Presents...(Fall, 1948) 11 22 33 62 86 110
Four Color 871 (Dell, 1/58) 4 8 12 25 40 55

CURSED
Image Comics (Top Cow): Oct, 2003 - No. 4, Feb, 2004 ($2.99)

1-4-Avery & Blevins-s/Molenaar-a 3.00

CURSE OF DRACULA, THE
Dark Horse Comics: July, 1998 - No. 3, Sept, 1998 ($2.95, limited series)

1-3-Marv Wolfman-s/Gene Colan-a 3.00
TPB (2005, $9.95) r/series; intro. by Marv Wolfman 10.00

CURSE OF DREADWOLF
Lightning Comics: Sept, 1994 ($2.75, B&W)

1 3.00

CURSE OF RUNE (Becomes Rune, 2nd Series)
Malibu Comics (Ultraverse): May, 1995 - No. 4, Aug, 1995 ($2.50, lim. series)

1-4: 1-Two covers form one image 3.00

CURSE OF THE SPAWN
Image Comics (Todd McFarlane Prod.): Sept, 1996 - No. 29, Mar, 1999 ($1.95)

1-Dwayne Turner-a(p) 1 2 3 5 6 8
1-B&W Edition 2 4 6 9 13 16
2-3 5.00
4-29: 12-Movie photo-c of Melinda Clarke (Priest) 4.00
Blood and Sutures ('99, $9.95, TPB) r/#5-8 10.00
Lost Values ('00, $10.95, TPB) r/#12-14,22; Ashley Wood-c 11.00
Sacrifice of the Soul ('99, $9.95, TPB) r/#1-4 10.00
Shades of Gray ('00, $9.95, TPB) r/#9-11,29 10.00
The Best of the Curse of the Spawn (6/06, $16.99, TPB) B&W r/#1-8,12-16,20-29 17.00

CURSE OF THE WEIRD
Marvel Comics: Dec, 1993 - No. 4, Mar, 1994 ($1.25, limited series)
(Pre-code horror-r)

1-4: 1,3,4-Wolverton-r(1-Eye of Doom; 3-Where Monsters Dwell; 4-The End of the World). 2-Orlando-r. 4-Zombie-r by Everett; painted-c 1 2 3 5 6 8
NOTE: ***Briefer** r-2. **Davis** a-4r. **Ditko** a-1r, 2r, 4r; c-1r. **Everett** r-1. **Heath** r-1-3. **Kubert** r-3. **Wolverton** a-1r, 3r, 4r.*

CUSTER'S LAST FIGHT
Avon Periodicals: 1950

nn-Partial reprint of Cowpuncher #1 15 30 45 90 140 190

CUTEY BUNNY (See Army Surplus Komikz Featuring...)

CUTIE PIE
Junior Reader's Guild (Lev Gleason): May, 1955 - No. 3, Dec, 1955; No. 4, Feb, 1956; No. 5, Aug, 1956

1 9 18 27 47 61 75
2-5: 4-Misdated 2/55 6 12 18 31 38 45

CUTTING EDGE
Marvel Comics: Dec, 1995 ($2.95)

1-Hulk-c/story; Messner-Loebs scripts 3.00

CVO: COVERT VAMPIRIC OPERATIONS
IDW Publishing: June, 2003 ($5.99, one-shot)

1-Alex Garner-s/Mindy Lee-a(p) 6.00
... - Human Touch 1 (8/04, $3.99, one-shot) Hernandez & Garner-a 4.00
... - 100-Page Spectacular (4/11, $7.99) r/#1, African Blood #2 Rogue State #5 8.00
TPB (9/04, $19.99) r/#1 and ... - Artifact #1-3; intro. by Garner 20.00

CVO: COVERT VAMPIRIC OPERATIONS - AFRICAN BLOOD
IDW Publishing: Sept, 2006 - No. 4, May, 2007 ($3.99, limited series)

1-4-El Torres-s/Luis Czerniawski-a 4.00

CVO: COVERT VAMPIRIC OPERATIONS - ARTIFACT
IDW Publishing: Oct, 2003 - No. 3, Dec, 2003 ($3.99, limited series)

1-3-Jeff Mariotte-s/Gabriel Hernandez-a/Alex Garner-c 4.00

CVO: COVERT VAMPIRIC OPERATIONS - ROGUE STATE
IDW Publishing: Nov, 2004 - No. 5, Mar, 2005 ($3.99, limited series)

1-5-Jeff Mariotte-s/Vazquez-a 4.00
TPB (7/05, $19.99) r/#1-5; cover gallery 20.00

CYBERELLA
DC Comics (Helix): Sept, 1996 - No. 12, Aug, 1997 ($2.25/$2.50)(1st Helix series)

1-12: 1-5-Chaykin & Cameron-a. 1,2-Chaykin-c. 3-5-Cameron-c 3.00

CYBERFORCE
Image Comics (Top Cow Productions): Oct, 1992 - No. 4, 1993; No. 0, Sept, 1993 ($1.95, limited series)

1-Silvestri-c/a in all; coupon for Image Comics #0; 1st Top Cow Productions title 6.00
1-With coupon missing 2.00
2-4,0: 2-(3/93). 3-Pitt-c/story. 4-Codename: Stryke Force back-up (1st app.); foil-c. 0-(9/93)-Walt Simonson-c/a/scripts 3.00

CYBERFORCE
Image Comics (Top Cow Productions)/Top Cow Comics No. 28 on:
V2#1, Nov, 1993 - No. 35, Sept. 1997 ($1.95)

V2#1-24: 1-7-Marc Silvestri/Keith Williams-c/a. 8-McFarlane-c/a. 10-Painted variant-c exists. 18-Variant-c exists. 23-Velocity-c. 3.00
1-3: 1-Gold Logo-c. 2-Silver embossed-c. 3-Gold embossed-c 10.00
1-(99¢, 3/96, 2nd printing) 3.00
25-($3.95)-Wraparound, foil-c 4.00
26-35: 28-(11/96)-1st Top Cow Comics iss. Quesada & Palmiotti's Gabriel app. 27-Quesada & Palmiotti's Ash app. 3.00
Annual 1,2 (3/95, 8/96, $2.50, $2.95) 4.00
NOTE: *Annuals read Volume One in the indica.*

CYBERFORCE (Volume 3)
Image Comics (Top Cow): Apr, 2006 - No. 6, Nov, 2006 ($2.99)

1-6: 1-Pat Lee-a/Ron Marz-s; three covers by Pat Lee, Marc Silvestri and Dave Finch 3.00
#0-(6/06, $2.99) reprints origin story from Image Comics Hardcover Vol. 1 3.00
.../X-Men 1 (1/07, $3.99) Pat Lee-a/Ron Marz-s; 2 covers by Lee and Silvestri 4.00
Vol. 1 TPB (12/06, $14.99) r/#1-6, #0 & story from The Cow Quarterly; cover gallery 15.00

CYBER FORCE (Volume 4)
Image Comics (Top Cow): Dec, 2012 - Present (no cover price/$2.99)

1-8: 1-Silvestri & Hawkins-s/Pham-a; multiple covers on each 3.00

CYBERFORCE/HUNTER-KILLER
Image Comics (Top Cow Productions): July, 2009 - No. 5, Mar, 2010 ($2.99)

1-5-Waid-s/Rocafort-a; multiple covers on each 3.00

CYBERFORCE ORIGINS
Image Comics (Top Cow Productions): Jan, 1995 - No. 3, Nov, 1995 ($2.50)

1-Cyblade (1/95) 5.00
1-Cyblade (3/96, 99¢, 2nd printing) 3.00
1A-Exclusive Ed.; Tucci-c 4.00
2,3: 2-Stryker (2/95)-1st Mike Turner-a. 3-Impact 3.00
(#4) Misery (12/95, $2.95) 3.00

CYBERFORCE/STRYKEFORCE: OPPOSING FORCES (See Codename: Stryke Force #15)
Image Comics (Top Cow Productions): Sept, 1995 - No. 2, Oct, 1995 ($2.50, limited series)

1,2: 2-Stryker disbands Strykeforce. 3.00

CYBERFORCE UNIVERSE SOURCEBOOK
Image Comics (Top Cow Productions): Aug, 1994/Feb, 1995 ($2.50)

1,2-Silvestri-c 3.00

CYBERFROG
Hall of Heroes: June, 1994 - No. 2, Dec, 1994 ($2.50, B&W, limited series)

1-Ethan Van Sciver-c/a/scripts 3 6 9 14 20 25
2 1 3 4 6 8 10

CYBERFROG

Cyclone Comics #1 © Bilbara

Cyclops #1 © MAR

Dagar, Desert Hawk #22 © FOX

	GD 2.0	VG 4.0	FN 6.0	VF 8.0	VF/NM 9.0	NM- 9.2

Harris Comics: Feb, 1996 - No. 3, Apr, 1996 ($2.95)

0-3: Van Sciver-c/a/scripts. 2-Variant-c exists 6.00

CYBERFROG: (Title series), **Harris Comics**

--RESERVOIR FROG, 9/96 - No. 2, 10/96 ($2.95) 1,2: Van Sciver-c/a/scripts; wraparound-c 4.00

--3RD ANNIVERSARY SPECIAL, 1/97 - #2, ($2.50, B&W) 1,2 4.00

--VS. CREED, 7/97 ($2.95, B&W)1 4.00

CYBERNARY (See Deathblow #1)
Image Comics (WildStorm Productions): Nov, 1995 - No.5, Mar, 1996 ($2.50)

1-5 3.00

CYBERNARY 2.0
DC Comics (WildStorm): Sept, 2001 - No. 6, Apr, 2002 ($2.95, limited series)

1-6: Joe Harris-s/Eric Canete-a. 6-The Authority app. 3.00

CYBERPUNK
Innovation Publishing: Sept, 1989 - No. 2, Oct, 1989 ($1.95, 28 pgs.) Book 2, #1, May, 1990 - No. 2, 1990 ($2.25, 28 pgs.)

1,2, Book 2 #1,2:1,2-Ken Steacy painted-covers (Adults) 3.00

CYBERPUNK: THE SERAPHIM FILES
Innovation Publishing: Nov, 1990 - No. 2, Dec, 1990 ($2.50, 28 pgs., mature)

1,2: 1-Painted-c; story cont'd from Seraphim 3.00

CYBERPUNX
Image Comics (Extreme Studios): Mar, 1996 ($2.50)

1 3.00

CYBERRAD
Continuity Comics: 1991 - No. 7, 1992 ($2.00)(Direct sale & newsstand-c variations) V2#1, 1993 ($2.50)

1-7: 5-Glow-in-the-dark-c by N. Adams (direct sale only). 6-Contains 4 pg. fold-out poster; N. Adams layouts 3.00
V2#1-($2.95, direct sale ed.)-Die-cut-c w/B&W hologram on-c; Neal Adams sketches 4.00
V2#1-($2.50, newsstand ed.)-Without sketches 3.00

CYBERRAD DEATHWATCH 2000 (Becomes CyberRad w/#2, 7/93)
Continuity Comics: Apr, 1993 - No. 2, 1993 ($2.50)

1,2: 1-Bagged w/2 cards; Adams-c & layouts & plots. 2-Bagged w/card; Adams scripts 3.00

CYBER 7
Eclipse Comics: Mar, 1989 - #7, Sept, 1989; V2#1, Oct, 1989 - #10, 1990 ($2.00, B&W)

1-7, Book 2 #1-10: Stories translated from Japanese 3.00

CYBLADE
Image Comics (Top Cow Productions): Oct, 2008 - No. 4, Mar, 2009 ($2.99)

1-4: 1,2-Mays-a/Fialkov-s. 1-Two covers. 3,4-Ferguson-a 3.00
.../ Ghost Rider 1 (Marvel/Top Cow, 1/97, $2.95) Devil's Reign pt. 2 4.00
...: Pilot Season 1 (9/07, $2.99) Rick Mays-a 3.00

CYBLADE/SHI (Also see Battle For The Independents & Shi/Cyblade: The Battle For The Independents)
Image Comics (Top Cow Productions): 1995 ($2.95, one-shot)

	GD	VG	FN	VF	VF/NM	NM-
San Diego Preview	2	4	6	9	12	15
1-($2.95)-1st app. Witchblade	1	3	4	6	8	10
1-($2.95)-variant-c; Tucci-a						5.00

CYBRID
Maximum Press: July, 1995; No. 0, Jan, 1997 ($2.95/$3.50)

1-(7/95) 3.50
0-(1/97)-Liefeld-a/script; story cont'd in Avengelyne #4 3.50

CYCLONE COMICS (Also see Whirlwind Comics)
Bilbara Publishing Co.: June, 1940 - No. 5, Nov, 1940

	GD	VG	FN	VF	VF/NM	NM-
1-Origin Tornado Tom; Volton (the human generator), Tornado Tom, Kingdom of the Moon, Mister Q begin (1st app. of each)	71	142	213	454	777	1100
2	48	96	144	302	514	725
3-Classic-c (scarce)	107	214	321	680	1165	1650
4-(9/40)	48	96	144	302	514	725
5-(Scarce)	71	142	213	454	777	1100

Ashcan - (5/40) Not distributed to newsstands, only for in house use. Cover produced on green stock paper. A CGC certified FN (6.0) copy sold for $2,000 in 2006.

CYCLOPS (X-Men)
Marvel Comics: Oct, 2001 - No. 4, Jan, 2002 ($2.50, limited series)

1-4-Texeira-c/a. 1,2-Black Tom and Juggernaut app. 3.00

1-(5/11, $2.99, one-shot) Haspiel-a; Batroc and the Circus of Crime app. 3.00

CYCLOPS: RETRIBUTION
Marvel Comics: 1994 ($5.95, trade paperback)

	GD	VG	FN	VF	VF/NM	NM-
nn-r/Marvel Comics Presents #17-24	1	2	3	5	6	8

CY-GOR (See Spawn #38 for 1st app.)
Image Comics (Todd McFarlane Prod.): July, 1999 - No. 6, Dec, 1999 ($2.50)

1-6-Veitch-s 3.00

CYNTHIA DOYLE, NURSE IN LOVE (Formerly Sweetheart Diary)
Charlton Publications: No. 66, Oct, 1962 - No. 74, Feb, 1964

	GD	VG	FN	VF	VF/NM	NM-
66-74	3	6	9	14	19	24

DAFFODIL
Marvel Comics (Soleil): 2010 - No. 3, 2010 ($5.99, limited series)

1-3-English version of French comic; Brrémaud-s/Rigano-a 6.00

DAFFY (Daffy Duck No. 18 on)(See Looney Tunes)
Dell Publishing Co./Gold Key No. 31-127/Whitman No. 128 on: #457, 3/53 - #30, 7-9/62; #31, 10-12/62 - #145, 6/84 (No #132,133)

	GD	VG	FN	VF	VF/NM	NM-
Four Color 457(#1)-Elmer Fudd x-overs begin	10	20	30	70	150	230
Four Color 536,615('55)	6	12	18	42	79	115
4(1-3/56)-11('57)	5	10	15	33	57	80
12-19(1958-59)	4	8	12	28	47	65
20-40(1960-64)	3	6	9	20	31	42
41-60(1964-68)	3	6	9	16	23	30
61-90(1969-74)-Road Runner in most. 76-82-"Daffy Duck and the Road Runner" on-c	2	4	6	11	16	20
91-110	2	4	6	8	11	14
111-127	1	3	4	6	8	10
128,134-141: 139(2/82), 140(2-3/82), 141(4/82)	2	4	6	8	10	12
129(8/80),130,131 (pre-pack?) (scarce). 129-Sherlock Holmes parody-s	4	8	12	23	37	50
142-145(#90029 on-c; nd, nd code, pre-pack): 142(6/83), 143(8/83), 144(3/84), 145(6/84)	3	6	9	17	26	35
Mini-Comic 1 (1976; 3-1/4x6-1/2")	1	3	4	6	8	10

NOTE: *Reprint issues-No.41-46, 48, 50, 53-55, 58, 59, 65, 67, 69, 73, 81, 96, 103-108; 136-142, 144, 145(1/3-2/3-r). (See March of Comics No. 277, 288, 303, 313, 331, 347, 357,375, 387, 397, 402, 413, 425, 437, 460).*

DAFFY DUCK (Digest-size reprints from Looney Tunes)
DC Comics: 2005 ($6.99, digest)

Vol. 1: You're Despicable! - Reprints from Looney Tunes #38,43,45,47,51,53,54,58,61,62,66,70 7.00

DAFFY TUNES COMICS
Four-Star Publications: June, 1947; No. 12, Aug, 1947

	GD	VG	FN	VF	VF/NM	NM-
nn	10	20	30	56	76	95
12-Al Fago-c/a; funny animal	9	18	27	52	69	85

DAGAR, DESERT HAWK (Captain Kidd No. 24 on; formerly All Great)
Fox Features Syndicate: No. 14, Feb, 1948 - No. 23, Apr, 1949 (No #17,18)

	GD	VG	FN	VF	VF/NM	NM-
14-Tangi & Safari Cary begin; Good bondage-c/a	97	194	291	621	1061	1500
15,16-E. Good-a; 15-Bondage-c	54	108	162	343	574	825
19,20,22: 19-Used in **SOTI**, pg. 180 (Tangi)	50	100	150	315	533	750
21,23: 21-Bondage-c; "Bombs & Bums Away" panel in "Flood of Death" story used in **SOTI.** 23-Bondage-c	53	106	159	334	567	800

NOTE: *Tangi by **Kamen**-14-16, 19, 20; c-20, 21.*

DAGAR THE INVINCIBLE (Tales of Sword & Sorcery...) (Also see Dan Curtis Giveaways & Gold Key Spotlight)
Gold Key: Oct, 1972 - No. 18, Dec, 1976; No. 19, Apr, 1982

	GD	VG	FN	VF	VF/NM	NM-
1-Origin; intro. Villains Olstellon & Scor	4	8	12	23	37	50
2-5: 3-Intro. Graylin, Dagar's woman; Jarn x-over	3	6	9	14	19	24
6-1st Dark Gods story	2	4	6	9	13	16
7-10: 9-Intro. Torgus. 10-1st Three Witches story	2	4	6	9	13	16
11-18: 13-Durak & Torgus x-over; story continues in Dr. Spektor #15. 14-Dagar's origin retold. 18-Origin retold	2	4	6	8	10	12
19(4/82)-Origin-r/#18						6.00

NOTE: *Durak app. in 7, 12, 13. Tragg app. in 5, 11.*

DAGWOOD (Chic Young's) (Also see Blondie Comics)
Harvey Publications: Sept, 1950 - No. 140, Nov, 1965

	GD	VG	FN	VF	VF/NM	NM-
1	14	28	42	94	207	320
2	8	16	24	55	105	155
3-10	7	14	21	44	82	120
11-20	5	10	15	35	63	90
21-30	5	10	15	31	53	75
31-50: 33-Sci-Fi-c	4	8	12	28	47	65

Daily Bugle #1 © MAR

Dale Evans Comics #3 © DC

Damian, Son of Batman #1 © DC

GD 2.0 VG 4.0 FN 6.0 VF 8.0 VF/NM 9.0 NM- 9.2

51-70 3 6 9 21 33 45
71-100 3 6 9 17 26 35
101-121,123-128,130,135 3 6 9 16 23 30
122,129,131-134,136-140-All are 68-pg. issues 3 6 9 21 33 45
NOTE: *Popeye and other one page strips appeared in early issues.*

DAI KAMIKAZE!
Now Comics: June, 1987 - No. 12, Aug, 1988 ($1.75)
1-1st app. Speed Racer 5.00
1-Second printing 3.00
2-12 3.00

DAILY BUGLE (See Spider-Man)
Marvel Comics: Dec, 1996 - No. 3, Feb, 1997 ($2.50, B&W, limited series)
1-3-Paul Grist-s 3.00

DAISY AND DONALD (See Walt Disney Showcase No. 8)
Gold Key/Whitman No. 42 on: May, 1973 - No. 59, July, 1984 (no No. 48)
1-Barks-r/WDC&S #280,308 3 6 9 19 30 40
2-5: 4-Barks-r/WDC&S #224 2 4 6 11 16 20
6-10 2 4 6 9 12 15
11-20 1 3 4 6 8 10
21-41: 32-r/WDC&S #308 1 2 3 5 6 8
42-44 (Whitman) 2 4 6 8 11 14
45 (8/80),46-(pre-pack?)(scarce) 4 8 12 23 37 50
47-(12/80)-Only distr. in Whitman 3-pack (scarce) 5 10 15 33 57 80
48(3/81)-50(8/81): 50-r/#3 2 4 6 10 14 18
51-54: 51-Barks-r/4-Color #1150. 52-r/#2. 53(2/82), 54(4/82)
2 4 6 9 13 16
55-59-(all #90284 on-c, nd, nd code, pre-pack): 55(5/83), 56(7/83), 57(8/83), 58(8/83), 59(7/84) 3 6 9 16 23 30

DAISY & HER PUPS (Dagwood & Blondie's Dogs)(Formerly Blondie Comics #20)
Harvey Publications: No. 21, 7/51 - No. 27, 7/52; No. 8, 9/52 - No. 18, 5/54
21 (#1)-Blondie's dog Daisy and her 5 pups led by Elmer begin. Rags Rabbit app.
5 10 15 35 63 90
22-27 (#2-7): 26 has No. 6 on cover but No. 26 on inside. 23,25-The Little King app. 24-Bringing Up Father by McManus app. 25-27-Rags Rabbit app.
4 8 12 27 44 60
8-18: 8,9-Rags Rabbit app. 8,17-The Little King app. 11-The Flop Family Swan begins. 22-Cookie app. 11-Felix The Cat app. by 17,18-Popeye app.
4 8 12 25 40 55

DAISY DUCK & UNCLE SCROOGE PICNIC TIME (See Dell Giant #33)

DAISY DUCK & UNCLE SCROOGE SHOW BOAT (See Dell Giant #55)

DAISY DUCK'S DIARY (See Dynabrite Comics, & Walt Disney's C&S #298)
Dell Publishing Co.: No. 600, Nov, 1954 - No. 1247, Dec-Fef, 1961-62 (Disney)
Four Color 600 (#1) 7 14 21 44 82 120
Four Color 659, 743 (11/56) 5 10 15 35 63 90
Four Color 858 (11/57), 948 (11/58), 1247 (12-2/61-62)
5 10 15 31 53 75
Four Color 1055 (11-1/59-60), 1150 (12-1/60-61)-By Carl Barks)
8 16 24 54 102 150

DAISY HANDBOOK
Daisy Manufacturing Co.: 1946; No. 2, 1948 (10¢, pocket-size, 132 pgs.)
1-Buck Rogers, Red Ryder; Wolverton-a (2 pgs.) 21 42 63 122 199 275
2-Captain Marvel & Ibis the Invincible, Red Ryder, Boy Commandos & Robotman; Wolverton-a (2 pgs.); contains 8 pg. color catalog 21 42 63 122 199 275

DAISY MAE (See Oxydol-Dreft)

DAISY'S RED RYDER GUN BOOK
Daisy Manufacturing Co.: 1955 (25¢, pocket-size, 132 pgs.)
nn-Boy Commandos, Red Ryder; 1pg. Wolverton-a 15 30 45 85 130 175

DAKEN: DARK WOLVERINE
Marvel Comics: Nov, 2010 - No. 23, May, 2012 ($3.99/$2.99)
1-Camuncoli-a/c; Way & Liu-s; back-up history of the character 4.00
2-9, 9.1, 10-23-($2.99) 3,4-Fantastic Four app. 7-9-Crossover with X-23 #8,9; Gambit app. 9.1-Avengers app. 13-16-Moon Knight app. 17-19-Runaways app. 3.00

DAKKON BLACKBLADE ON THE WORLD OF MAGIC: THE GATHERING
Acclaim Comics (Armada): June, 1996 ($5.95, one-shot)
1-Jerry Prosser scripts; Rags Morales-c/a. 6.00

DAKOTA LIL (See Fawcett Movie Comics)

DAKTARI (Ivan Tors) (TV)
Dell Publishing Co.: July, 1967 - No. 3, Oct, 1968; No. 4, Oct, 1969
1-Marshall Thompson photo-c on all 4 8 12 23 37 50
2-4 3 6 9 17 26 35

DALE EVANS COMICS (Also see Queen of the West...)(See Boy Commandos #32)
National Periodical Publications: Sept-Oct, 1948 - No. 24, Jul-Aug, 1952 (No. 1-19: 52 pgs.)
1-Dale Evans & her horse Buttermilk begin; Sierra Smith begins by Alex Toth
58 116 174 371 636 900
2-Alex Toth-a 30 60 90 177 289 400
3-11-Alex Toth-a 20 40 60 114 182 250
12-20: 12-Target-c 14 28 42 80 115 150
21-24 14 28 42 82 121 160
NOTE: *Photo-c-1, 2, 4-14.*

DALGODA
Fantagraphics Books: Aug, 1984 - No. 8, Feb, 1986 (High quality paper)
1,8: 1- Fujitake-c/a in all. 8-Alan Moore story 4.00
2-7: 2,3-Debut Grimwood's Daughter. 3.00

DALTON BOYS, THE
Avon Periodicals: 1951
1-(Number on spine)-Kinstler-c 18 36 54 105 165 225

DAMAGE
DC Comics: Apr, 1994 - No. 20, Jan, 1996 ($1.75/$1.95/$2.25)
1-20: 6-(9/94)-Zero Hour. 0-(10/94). 7-(11/94). 14-Ray app. 3.00

DAMAGE CONTROL (See Marvel Comics Presents #19)
Marvel Comics: 5/89 - No. 4, 8/89; V2#1, 12/89 - No. 4, 2/90 ($1.00)
V3#1, 6/91 - No. 4, 9/91 ($1.25, all are limited series)
V1#1-4,V2#1-4,V3#1-4: V1#4-Wolverine app. V2#2,4-Punisher app. 1-Spider-Man app. 2-New Warriors app. 3,4-Silver Surfer app. 4-Infinity Gauntlet parody 3.00

DAMAGED
Radical Comics: Jul, 2011 - No. 6 ($3.99/$3.50, limited series)
1-($3.99) Lapham-s/Manco-a; covers by Maleev & Manco 4.00
2-4-($3.50) Maleev-c 3.50

DAMIAN: SON OF BATMAN
DC Comics: Dec, 2013 - No. 4, Mar, 2014 ($3.99, limited series)
1-4-Andy Kubert-s/c/a; near-future Damian; Ra's al Ghul & Talia app. 4.00
1-Variant-c by Tony Daniel 8.00

DAMNED
Image Comics (Homage Comics): June, 1997 - No. 4, Sept, 1997 ($2.50, limited series)
1-4-Steven Grant-s/Mike Zeck-c/a in all 3.00

DAMN NATION
Dark Horse Comics: Feb, 2005 - No. 3, Apr, 2005 ($2.99, limited series)
1-3-J. Alexander-a/Andrew Cosby-s 3.00

DAMSELS
Dynamite Entertainment: 2012 - No. 13, 2014 ($3.99)
1-13: 1-Leah Moore & John Reppion-s/Aneke-a. 1-Campbell-c. 2-8-Linsner-c 4.00
... Giant Killer One Shot (2013, $4.99) Leah Moore & John Reppion-s/Dietrich Smith-a 5.00

DAMSELS: MERMAIDS
Dynamite Entertainment: No. 0, 2013 - No. 5, 2013 ($3.99)
0-Free Comic Book Day giveaway; Sturges-s/Deshong-a/Hans-c 3.00
1-5-($3.99) Sturges-s/Deshong-a. 1-Two covers by Anacleto & Renaud. 2-5-Renaud-c 4.00

DANCES WITH DEMONS (See Marvel Frontier Comics Unlimited)
Marvel Frontier Comics: Sept, 1993 - No. 4, Dec, 1993 ($1.95, limited series)
1-($2.95)-Foil embossed-c; Charlie Adlard & Rod Ramos-a 4.00
2-4 3.00

DAN DARE
Virgin Comics: Nov, 2007 - No. 7, July, 2008 ($2.99/$5.99)
1-6-Ennis-s/Erskine-a. 1-Two covers by Talbot and Horn. 2-6-Two covers on each 3.00
7-($5.99) Double sized finale with wraparound Erskine-c; Gibbons variant-c 6.00

DANDEE: Four Star Publications: 1947 (Advertised, not published)

DAN DUNN (See Crackajack Funnies, Detective Dan, Famous Feature Stories & Red Ryder)

DANDY COMICS (Also see Happy Jack Howard)
E. C. Comics: Spring, 1947 - No. 7, Spring, 1948
1-Funny animal; Vince Fago-a in all; Dandy in all 42 84 126 265 445 625
2 31 62 93 182 296 410
3-7: 3-Intro Handy Andy who is c-feature #3 on 24 48 72 144 237 330

Danger Girl #2 © J. Scott Campbell

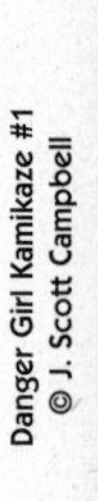

Danger Girl Kamikaze #1 © J. Scott Campbell

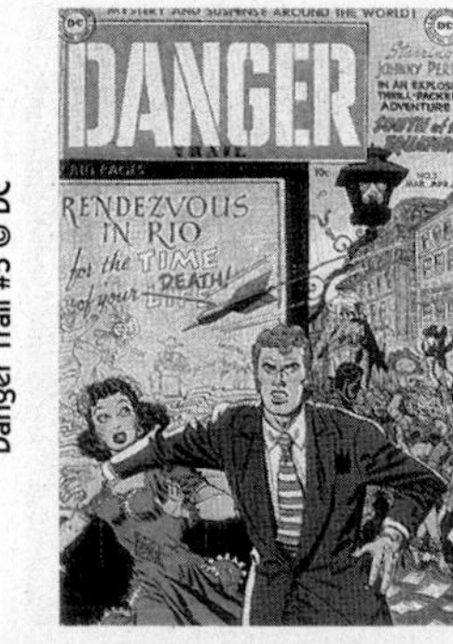

Danger Trail #5 © DC

	GD 2.0	VG 4.0	FN 6.0	VF 8.0	VF/NM 9.0	NM- 9.2

DANGER
Comic Media/Allen Hardy Assoc.: Jan, 1953 - No. 11, Aug, 1954

1-Heck-c/a	34	68	102	199	325	450
2,3,5,7,9-11:	18	36	54	105	165	225
4-Marijuana cover/story	21	42	63	122	199	275
6- "Narcotics" story; begin spy theme	20	40	60	114	182	250
8-Bondage/torture/headlights panels	22	44	66	128	209	290

NOTE: *Morisi a-2, 5, 6(3), 10; c-2. Contains some reprints from Danger & Dynamite.*

DANGER (Formerly Comic Media title)
Charlton Comics Group: No. 12, June, 1955 - No. 14, Oct, 1955

12(#1)	14	28	42	80	115	150
13,14: 14-r/#12	11	22	33	62	86	110

DANGER
Super Comics: 1964

Super Reprint #10-12 (Black Dwarf; #10-r/Great Comics #1 by Novack. #11-r/Johnny Danger #1. #12-r/Red Seal #14), #15-r/Spy Cases #26. #16-Unpublished Chesler material (Yankee Girl), #17-r/Scoop #8 (Capt. Courage & Enchanted Dagger), #18(nd)-r/Guns Against Gangsters #5 (Gun-Master, Annie Oakley, The Chameleon; L.B. Cole-r)	2	4	6	11	16	20

DANGER AND ADVENTURE (Formerly This Magazine Is Haunted; Robin Hood and His Merry Men No. 28 on)
Charlton Comics: No. 22, Feb, 1955 - No. 27, Feb, 1956

22-Ibis the Invincible-c/story (last G.A. app.); Nyoka app.; last pre-code issue	11	22	33	62	86	110
23-Lance O'Casey-c/sty; Nyoka app.; Ditko-a thru #27	13	26	39	72	101	130
24-27: 24-Mike Danger & Johnny Adventure begin	9	18	27	50	65	80

DANGER GIRL (Also see Cliffhanger #0)
Image Comics (Cliffhanger Productions): Mar, 1998 - No. 4, Dec, 1998;
DC Comics (Cliffhanger Prod.): No. 5, July, 1999 - No. 7, Feb, 2001

Preview-Bagged in DV8 #14 Voyager Pack						4.00
Preview Gold Edition						10.00
1-($2.95) Hartnell & Campbell-s/Campbell/Garner-a	1	2	3	5	6	8
1-($4.95) Chromium cover						48.00
1-American Entertainment Ed.						8.00
1-American Entertainment Gold Ed., 1-Tourbook edition						10.00
1-"Danger-sized" ed.; over-sized format	3	6	9	16	23	30
2-($2.50)						4.00
2-Smoking Gun variant cover	4	8	12	23	37	50
2-Platinum Ed.	5	10	15	31	53	75
2-Dynamic Forces Omnichrome variant-c	2	4	6	9	13	16
2-Gold foil cover						9.00
2-Ruby red foil cover	10	20	30	69	147	225
3,4: 3-c by Campbell, Charest and Adam Hughes. 4-Big knife variant-c						3.00
3,5: 3-Gold foil cover. 5-DF Bikini variant-c						5.00
4-6						3.00
7-($5.95) Wraparound gatefold-c; Last issue						6.00
...: Danger-Sized Treasury Edition #1 (IDW, 1/12, $9.99, 13" x 8-1/2") r/#1,2 & Preview						10.00
...: Hawaiian Punch (5/03, $4.95) Campbell-c; Phil Noto-a						5.00
...: Odd Jobs TPB (2004, $14.95) r/one-shots Hawaiian Punch, Viva Las Danger & Special; Campbell-c						15.00
San Diego Preview (8/98, B&W) flip book w/Wildcats preview						5.00
Sketchbook (2001, $6.95) Campbell-a; sketches for comics, toys, games						7.00
...Special (2/00, $3.50) art by Campbell, Chiodo, and Art Adams						3.50
... 3-D #1 (4/03, $4.95, bagged with 3-D glasses) r/ Preview & #1 in 3-D						5.00
...: Viva Las Danger (1/04, $4.95) Noto-a/Campbell-c						5.00
... :The Dangerous Collection nn (8/98; r-#1)						6.00
... :The Dangerous Collection 2,3: 2-(11/98, $5.95) r/#2,3. 3-('99) r/#4,5						6.00
... :The Dangerous Collection nn, 2-($10.00) Gold foil logo						10.00
... :The Ultimate Collection HC ($29.95) r/#1-7; intro by Bruce Campbell						30.00
... :The Ultimate Collection SC ($19.95) r/#1-7; intro by Bruce Campbell						20.00

DANGER GIRL AND THE ARMY OF DARKNESS
Dynamite Entertainment/ IDW Publ.: 2011 - No. 6, 2012 ($3.99, limited series)

1-6-Hartnell-s/Bolson-a. 1,2 Covers by Campbell, Bradshaw & Renaud						4.00

DANGER GIRL: BACK IN BLACK
DC Comics (Cliffhanger): Jan, 2006 - No. 4, Apr, 2006 ($2.99, limited series)

1-4-Hartnell-s/Bradshaw-a. 1-Campbell-c						3.00
TPB (2007, $12.99) r/series & covers						13.00

DANGER GIRL: BODY SHOTS
DC Comics (WildStorm): Jun, 2007 - No. 4, Sept, 2007 ($2.99, limited series)

1-4-Hartnell-s/Bradshaw-a						3.00
TPB (2007, $12.99) r/series & covers						13.00

DANGER GIRL/ G.I. JOE
IDW Publishing: Jul, 2012 - No. 5, Nov, 2012 ($3.99, limited series)

1-Hartnell-s/Royle-a; 2 covers by Campbell on each						4.00

DANGER GIRL KAMIKAZE
DC Comics (Cliffhanger): Nov, 2001 - No. 2, Dec., 2001 ($2.95, lim. series)

1,2-Tommy Yune-s/a						3.00

DANGER GIRL: REVOLVER
IDW Publishing: Jan, 2012 - No. 4, Apr, 2012 ($3.99, limited series)

1-4-Hartnell-s/Madden-a; covers by Campbell & Madden						4.00

DANGER GIRL: THE CHASE
IDW Publishing: Sept, 2013 - No. 4, Dec, 2013 ($3.99, limited series)

1-4-Hartnell-s/Tolibao-a. 1-Three covers (Panosian, Wallace & photo)						4.00

DANGER GIRL: TRINITY
IDW Publishing: Apr, 2013 - No. 4, Jul, 2013 ($3.99, limited series)

1-4-Hartnell-s/Campbell-c; art by Royle, Tolibao, & Molnar. 1-Variant-c by Garner						4.00

DANGER IS OUR BUSINESS!
Toby Press: 1953(Dec.) - No. 10, June, 1955

1-Captain Comet by Williamson/Frazetta-a, 6 pgs. (science fiction)	46	92	138	290	488	685
2	14	28	42	81	118	155
3-10	12	24	36	69	97	125
I.W. Reprint #9('64)-Williamson/Frazetta-r/#1; Kinstler-c	7	14	21	46	86	125

DANGER IS THEIR BUSINESS (Also see A-1 Comic)
Magazine Enterprises: No. 50, 1952

A-1 50-Powell-a	14	28	42	80	115	150

DANGER MAN (TV)
Dell Publishing Co.: No. 1231, Sept-Nov, 1961

Four Color 1231-Patrick McGoohan photo-c	9	18	27	61	123	185

DANGER TRAIL (Also see Showcase #50, 51)
National Periodical Publ.: July-Aug, 1950 - No. 5, Mar-Apr, 1951 (52 pgs.)

1-King Faraday begins, ends #4; Toth-a in all	129	258	387	826	1413	2000
2	92	184	276	584	1005	1425
3-(Rare) one of the rarest early '50s DCs	145	290	435	921	1586	2250
4,5: 5-Johnny Peril-c/story (moves to Sensation Comics #107); new logo (also see Comic Cavalcade #15-29)	68	136	204	432	746	1060

DANGER TRAIL
DC Comics: Apr, 1993 - No. 4, July, 1993 ($1.50, limited series)

1-4: Gulacy-c on all						3.00

DANGER UNLIMITED (See San Diego Comic Con Comics #2 & Torch of Liberty Special)
Dark Horse (Legend): Feb, 1994 - No. 4, May, 1994 ($2.00, limited series)

1-4: Byrne-c/a/scripts in all; origin stories of both original team (Doc Danger, Thermal, Miss Mirage, & Hunk) & future team (Thermal, Belebet, & Caucus). 1-Intro Torch of Liberty & Golgotha (cameo) in back-up story. 4-Hellboy & Torch of Liberty cameo in lead story						3.00
TPB (1995, $14.95)-r/#1-4; includes last pg. originally cut from #4						15.00

DAN HASTINGS (See Syndicate Features)

DANIEL BOONE (See The Exploits of..., Fighting... Frontier Scout...,The Legends of... & March of Comics No. 306)
Dell Publishing Co.: No. 1163, Mar-May, 1961

Four Color 1163-Marsh-a	5	10	15	31	53	75

DANIEL BOONE (TV) (See March of Comics No. 306)
Gold Key: Jan, 1965 - No. 15, Apr, 1969 (All have Fess Parker photo-c)

1-Back-c and last eight pages fold in half to form "Official Handbook Fess Parker as Daniel Boone Trail Blazers Club"	7	14	21	48	89	130
2-Back-c pin-up	5	10	15	30	50	70
3-5-Back-c pin-ups	4	8	12	25	40	55
6-15: 7,8-Back-c pin-up	3	6	9	19	30	40

DAN'L BOONE
Sussex Publ. Co.: Sept, 1955 - No. 8, Sept, 1957

1	14	28	42	80	115	150
2	10	20	30	54	72	90
3-8	8	16	24	40	50	60

Danny Blaze #1 © CC

Daredevil #19 © LEV

Daredevil #2 © MAR

	GD 2.0	VG 4.0	FN 6.0	VF 8.0	VF/NM 9.0	NM- 9.2

DANNY BLAZE (...Firefighter) (Nature Boy No. 3 on)
Charlton Comics: Aug, 1955 - No. 2, Oct, 1955

1-Authentic stories of fire fighting 13 26 39 74 105 135
2 9 18 27 50 65 80

DANNY DINGLE (See Sparkler Comics)
United Features Syndicate: No. 17, 1940

Single Series 17 27 54 81 158 259 360

DANNY THOMAS SHOW, THE (TV)
Dell Publishing Co.: No. 1180, Apr-June, 1961 - No. 1249, Dec-Feb, 1961-62

Four Color 1180-Toth-a, photo-c 13 26 39 89 195 300
Four Color 1249-Manning-a, photo-c 12 24 36 80 173 265

DANTE'S INFERNO (Based on the video game)
DC Comics (WildStorm): Feb, 2010 - No. 6, Jul, 2010 ($3.99, limited series)

1-6-Christos Gage-s/Diego Latorre-a 4.00
TPB (2010, $19.99) r/#1-6 20.00

DAOMU (Based on a novel series from China)
Image Comics: Feb, 2011 - Present ($2.99)

1-8-Kennedy Xu-s/Ken Chou-a 3.00

DARBY O'GILL & THE LITTLE PEOPLE (Movie)(See Movie Comics)
Dell Publishing Co.: 1959 (Disney)

Four Color 1024-Toth-a; photo-c. 9 18 27 57 111 165

DAREDEVIL ("Daredevil Comics" on cover of #2) (See Silver Streak Comics)
Lev Gleason Publications (Funnies, Inc. No. 1): July, 1941 - No. 134, Sept, 1956
(52 pgs. #52-80; 64 pgs. #35-41)(Charles Biro stories)

1-No. 1 titled "Dardedevil Battles Hitler," Classic battle issue as Daredevil teams up in each strip - The Silver Streak, Lance Hale, Cloud Curtis, Dickey Dean & Pirate Prince to battle Hitler; The Claw unites with Hitler and Japanese and battles Daredevil; Origin of Hitler feature story "The Man of Hate." Classic Hitler photo app. on-c
1275 2550 3825 9500 16,750 24,000
2-London (by Jerry Robinson), Pat Patriot (by Reed Crandall), Nightro, Real American No. 1 (by Briefer #2-11), Dash Dillon, Whirlwind begin; Dickie Dean, Pirate Prince end; intro. & only app. Pioneer, Champion of America & Times Square. The Claw continues #2-4 366 732 1098 2562 4481 6400
3-Intro./origin of 13. Newspaper editor has name "Roussos." Daredevil battles the Claw ill. text story 258 516 774 1651 2826 4000
4-The Claw captured and taken to New York Central Park Zoo. Whirlwind, the Blond Bomber begins, ends #6 206 412 618 1318 2259 3200
5-Ghost vs. Claw begins by Bob Wood, ends #20; 13 & Jinx begin; origin 13 retold in text; intro./origin Jinx, 13's sidekick; intro. Sniffer in Daredevil
155 310 465 992 1696 2400
6-(12/41)-Daredevil battles wolf with human brain. Dash Dillon ends
135 270 405 864 1482 2100
7,9: 7-(2/42), shows #6 on cover; delayed one month due to Pearl Harbor attack. 9-Daredevil vs. Daredevil-c; Sniffer strip begins, ends #69
110 220 330 704 1202 1700
8-Nazi WWII war-c. Nightro ends. Sniffer/Daredevil fight Nazi insurgents;
116 232 348 742 1271 1800
10-(5-42), "Remember Pearl Harbor" Japanese WWII-c; classic splash page w/American flag. Daredevil joins Air Corps. to fight Japanese. Ghost Battles Claw & Japanese. Last Whirlwind 135 270 405 864 1482 2100
11-Classic Quasimodo (hunchback of Notre Dame) bondage/torture-c/sty. London, Pat Patriot, Real America #1 end 402 804 1206 2573 4037 5500
12-Origin of The Claw; Scoop Scuttle by Wolverton begins (2-4 pgs.), ends #22, not in #21. Charles Biro biography. Dickey Dean, Pirate Prince return (both end #32)
139 278 417 883 1517 2150
13-Intro of Little Wise Guys (10/42)(also see Boy #4); Daredevil fights Nazi hooded cult; Ghost battles Claw, Hitler & Nazis in Britain; Bob Wood biography
107 214 321 680 1165 1650
14-Classic Daredevil facial portrait-c; Hitler app.; "Slap the Jap" game included
81 162 243 518 884 1250
15-Death of Meatball 103 206 309 659 1130 1600
16,17: 16-WWII-c w/freighter hit by German torpedo. Meatball is buried & Curly joins Little Wise Guys team. 17-Japanese WWII-c 73 146 219 467 796 1125
18-New origin of Daredevil (not same as Silver Streak #6). Hitler, Mussolini Tojo and Mickey Mouse app. on-c at carnival 123 246 369 787 1344 1900
19,20: Last Ghost vs. Claw 63 126 189 403 689 975
21-Reprints cover of Silver Streak #6 (on inside) plus intro. of The Claw from Silver Streak #1. The Claw strip begins by Bob Q. Siege, ends #31 84 168 252 538 919 1300
22,23: 22-Daredevil fights the Tramp. 23-Dickie Dean by Bob Montana
46 92 138 290 488 685
24-Bloody puppet show-c 53 106 159 334 567 800
25-1st Little Wise Guys-c without Daredevil 37 74 111 222 361 500
26,28-30 41 82 123 256 428 600
27-Bondage/torture-c 71 142 213 454 777 1100
31-Death of The Claw 83 166 249 530 908 1285
32-34: 32,33-Egbert app. 33-Roger Wilco begins, ends #35
34 68 102 206 336 465
35-37,39-41: 35-Two Daredevil stories begin, end #68; Chauncey app. 37-39-Go Along Gallagher app. (#35-41 are 64 pgs.); 41-Dickie Dean ends
36 72 108 216 351 485
38-Origin Daredevil retold from #18 47 94 141 296 498 700
42-Intro. Kilroy in Daredevil who unveils Daredevil's I.D.-c/sty
31 62 93 182 296 410
43-45,47,48-All Daredevil-c. 43-Daredevil in costume on-c & 1 panel only inside; 44-DD back in costume; i.d. revealed on-c. 29 58 87 170 278 385
46,50: DD not on-c 24 48 72 140 230 320
49-Wise Guys fight secret hooded group c/sty. DD not on-c
29 58 87 170 278 385
51,52,56-60,63-66,68,69-Last Daredevil & Sniffer (12/50). 56-Wise Guys start their own circus. DD not on-c 20 40 60 114 182 250
53-Daredevil/Wise Guys find lost palace of Zanzarah, an underground Egyptian tomb w/mummy & treasure; classic c/story. DD-c 21 42 63 126 206 285
54,55-Daredevil-c 21 42 63 122 199 275
61-Daredevil & Wise Guys in haunted house classic c/story. Daredevil/Wise Guys fly rocket into stratosphere. DD not on-c 21 42 63 126 206 285
62-Wise Guys in medieval times, a dream by Peewee locked in a medieval museum; classic c/story. DD not on-c 21 42 63 126 206 285
67-Last Daredevil-c 21 42 63 122 199 275
70-Little Wise Guys take over book without Daredevil. Daredevil removed from-c & logo; Air Devils w/Hot Rock Flanagan begins, ends #80 14 28 42 78 112 145
71-78,81: 81-Dilly Duncan begins, ends #134 10 20 30 58 79 100
79,80: 79-(10/51)-Daredevil returns; Wise Guys go to Africa. 80-Daredevil & Wise Guys blast into space & land on Mars; last Daredevil app. in title
12 24 36 67 94 120
82,90: One pg. Frazetta ad in both 10 20 30 58 79 100
83-89,91-99,101-134 10 20 30 54 72 90
100-(7/53) 12 24 36 67 94 120

NOTE: **Biro** *a-1-22, 38; c-1-134; script-1-134.* **Dan Barry** *a(Daredevil) 40-48;* **Roy Belft**-*a (Daredevil) 49-55.* **Bolle** *a-125.* **Al Borth**-*a(Daredevil) #57-59.* **Briefer** *a-1-11 (Real American #1); Pirate Prince-#1, 2, 12-31.* **Tony Dipreta**-*a(Wise Guys) #108-110, 112-134.* **R.W. Hall** *a-22.* **Carl Hubbell** *a-9-21, 23-26, 27(Daredevil), 28-32.* **Al Mandel** *a-13.* **Hy Mankin**-*a(Wise Guys)-#80, 81.* **Maurer**-*a(Daredevil)-23, 31, 37, 38, 41, 43-51, 53-67, 69; (Little Wise Guys)-70-89.* **McWilliams** *a-70, 73-80.* **Bob Montana** *a-12, 23, 27, 28, 31-33.* **Wm. Overgard**-*a(Daredevil) #67, (Wise Guys) 74-79, 83-85, 87.* **Jerry Robinson** *a(London) #2-8.* **Roussos** *a(Nightro)-2-8.* **Bob Q. Siege**-*a(Claw) 27-31; (Daredevil)-#35.* **Wolverton** *a-12-22.* **Bob Wood**-*a(The Claw)-1-20; (The Ghost)-5-20.* **Dick Wood** *sty-2-10, 13-22, 27-32.* **Daredevil** *not on-c #46,49-52,56-66,68-134.*

DAREDEVIL (...& the Black Widow #92-107 on-c only; see Giant-Size...,Marvel Advs., Marvel Graphic Novel #24, Marvel Super Heroes, '66 & Spider-Man &...)
Marvel Comics Group: Apr, 1964 - No. 380, Oct, 1998

1-Origin/1st app. Daredevil; intro Foggy Nelson & Karen Page; death of Battling Murdock; Bill Everett-c/a; reprinted in Marvel Super Heroes #1 (1966)
321 642 963 2648 5974 9300
2-Fantastic Four cameo; 2nd app. Electro (Spidey villain); Thing guest star
68 136 204 544 1222 1900
3-Origin & 1st app. The Owl (villain) 38 76 114 285 641 1000
4-Origin & 1st app. The Purple Man 34 68 102 245 548 850
5-Minor costume change; Wood-a begins 27 54 81 189 420 650
6-Mr. Fear app. 18 36 54 126 281 435
7-Daredevil battles Sub-Mariner & dons red costume for 1st time (4/65); Marvel Masterwork pin-up by Wood 71 142 213 568 1284 2000
8-10: 8-Origin/1st app. Stilt-Man 14 28 42 94 207 320
11-15: 12-1st app. Plunderer; Ka-Zar app. 13-Facts about Ka-Zar's origin; Kirby-a
10 20 30 66 138 210
16,17-Spider-Man x-over. 16-1st Romita-a on Spider-Man (5/66)
17 34 51 117 259 400
18-Origin & 1st app. Gladiator 10 20 30 64 132 200
19,20 8 16 24 55 105 155
21-26,28-30: 24-Ka-Zar app. 30-Thor app. 6 12 18 41 76 110
27-Spider-Man x-over 7 14 21 48 89 130
31-36,39,40: 36-Dr. Doom app. on last page. 39-1st Exterminator (later becomes Death-Stalker) 6 12 18 37 66 95
37,38: Daredevil vs. Dr. Doom. 38-Fantastic Four x-over; cont'd in F.F. #73
6 12 18 41 76 110
41,42,44-49: 41-Death Mike Murdock. 42-1st app. Jester. 45-Statue of Liberty photo-c 5 10 15 34 60 85
43-Daredevil battles Captain America; origin partially retold

Daredevil #100 © MAR

Daredevil #230 © MAR

Daredevil V2 #9 © MAR

GD 2.0 VG 4.0 FN 6.0 VF 8.0 VF/NM 9.0 NM- 9.2

7 14 21 44 82 120
50-53: 50-52-B. Smith-a. 53-Origin retold; last 12¢ issue
5 10 15 35 63 90
54-56,58-60: 54-Spider-Man cameo. 56-1st app. Death's Head (9/69); story cont'd in #57 (not same as new Death's Head) 4 8 12 27 44 60
57-Reveals i.d. to Karen Page; Death's Head app. 5 10 15 30 50 70
61-76,78-80: 79-Stan Lee cameo. 80-Last 15¢ issue 4 8 12 23 37 50
77-Spider-Man x-over 4 8 12 28 47 65
81-(52 pgs.) Black Widow begins (11/71). 5 10 15 34 60 85
82,84-99: 87-Electro-c/story 3 6 9 19 30 40
83-B. Smith layouts/Weiss-p 3 6 9 21 33 45
100-Origin retold 4 8 12 27 44 60
101-104,106,108-110,112-120: 113-1st brief app. Deathstalker. 114-1st full app. Deathstalker
3 6 9 16 23 30
105-Origin Moondragon by Starlin (12/73); Thanos cameo in flashback (early app.)
3 6 9 21 33 45
107-Starlin-c; Thanos cameo 3 6 9 17 26 35
111-1st app. Silver Samurai (4/74) 5 10 15 31 53 75
121-123,125-130,137: 126-1st new Torpedo 3 6 9 14 20 25
124-1st app. Copperhead; Black Widow leaves 3 6 9 16 23 30
131-Origin/1st app. new Bullseye (see Nick Fury #15) 9 18 27 60 120 180
132-2nd app. new Bullseye (Regular 25¢ edition) 5 10 15 34 60 85
132-(30¢-c variant, limited distribution)(4/76) 9 18 27 60 120 180
133-136-(Regular 25¢ editions). 133-Uri Geller app. 3 6 9 14 20 25
133-136-(30¢-c variants, limited distribution)(5-8/76) 4 8 12 23 37 50
138-Ghost Rider-c/story; Death's Head is reincarnated; Byrne-a
3 6 9 19 30 40
139,140,142-145,147-157: 142-Nova cameo. 147,148-(Reg. 30¢-c). 150-1st app. Paladin. 151-Reveals i.d. to Heather Glenn. 155-Black Widow returns. 156-The '60s Daredevil app.
2 4 6 13 18 22
141,146-Bullseye app. 3 6 9 21 33 45
146-(35¢-c variant, limited distribution) 6 12 18 38 69 100
147,148-(35¢-c variants, limited distribution) 5 10 15 30 50 70
158-Frank Miller art begins (5/79); origin/death of Deathstalker (see Captain America #235 & Spectacular Spider-Man #27 8 16 24 56 108 160
159 5 10 15 30 50 70
160,161-Bullseye app. 4 8 12 25 40 55
162-Ditko-a; no Miller-a 3 6 9 14 20 25
163,164: 163-Hulk cameo. 164-Origin retold 3 6 9 18 28 38
165-167,170 3 6 9 16 24 32
168-Origin/1st app. Elektra; 1st Miller scripts 10 20 30 66 138 210
169-2nd Elektra app. 5 10 15 31 53 75
171-173 3 6 9 16 23 30
174,175-Elektra app. 3 6 9 17 26 35
176-180-Elektra app. 178-Cage app. 179-Anti-smoking issue mentioned in the Congressional Record 3 6 9 16 24 32
181-(52 pgs.)-Death of Elektra; Punisher cameo out of costume
4 8 12 25 40 55
182-184-Punisher app. by Miller (drug issues) 3 6 9 14 20 26
185-191: 187-New Black Widow. 189-Death of Stick. 190-($1.00, 52 pgs.)-Elektra returns, part origin; 2 pin-ups. 191-Last Miller Daredevil 2 4 6 8 10 12
192-195,198,199,201-207,209-218,220-226,234-237: 226-Frank Miller plots begin 4.00
196-Wolverine-c/app. 2 4 6 9 13 16
197-Bullseye-c/app.; 1st app. Yuriko Oyama (who becomes Lady Deathstrike)
1 2 3 5 6 8
200,238: 200-Bullseye app. 238-Mutant Massacre; Sabretooth app. 6.00
208,219,228-233: 208-Harlan Ellison scripts borrowed from Avengers TV episode "House that Jack Built". 219-Miller-c/script. 228-233-Last Miller scripts 5.00
227-Miller scripts begin 6.00
239,240,242-247 3.00
241-Todd McFarlane-a(p) 5.00
248,249-Wolverine app. 6.00
250,251,253,258: 250-1st app. Bullet. 258-Intro The Bengal (a villain) 3.00
252,260 (52 pgs.): 252-Fall of the Mutants. 260-Typhoid Mary app. 5.00
254-Origin & 1st app. Typhoid Mary (5/88) 1 2 3 4 5 8
255,256,258: 255,256-2nd/3rd app. Typhoid Mary. 259-Typhoid Mary app. 5.00
257-Punisher app. (x-over w/Punisher #10) 1 3 4 6 8 10
261-281,283-294,296-299,301-304,307-318: 270-1st app. Black Heart. 272-Intro Shotgun (villain). 281-Silver Surfer cameo. 283-Capt. America app. 297-Typhoid Mary app.; Kingpin storyline begins. 292-D.G. Chichester scripts begin. 293-Punisher app. 303-Re-intro the Owl. 304-Garney-c/a. 309-Punisher-c.; Terror app. 310-Calypso-c 3.00
282,295,300,305,306: 282-Silver Surfer app. 295-Ghost Rider app. 300-($2.00, 52 pgs.) Kingpin story ends. 305,306-Spider-Man-c 4.00
319-Prologue to Fall From Grace; Elektra returns 6.00
319-2nd printing w/black-c 3.00
320-Fall From Grace Pt 1 5.00
321-Fall From Grace regular ed.; Pt 2; new costume; Venom app. 3.00
321-($2.00)-Wraparound Glow-in-the-dark-c ed. 5.00
322-Fall From Grace Pt 3; Eddie Brock app. 4.00
323,324-Fall From Grace Pt. 4 & 5: 323-Vs. Venom-c/story. 324-Morbius-c/story 4.00
325-($2.50, 52 pgs.)-Fall From Grace ends; contains bound-in poster 4.00
326-349,351-353: 326-New logo. 328-Bound-in trading card sheet. 330-Gambit app. 348-1st Cary Nord art in DD (1/96);"Dec" on-c. 353-Karl Kesel scripts; Nord-c/a begins; Mr. Hyde-c/app. 3.00
350-($2.95)-Double-sized 4.00
350-($3.50)-Double-sized; gold ink-c 5.00
354-374,376-379: Kesel scripts, Nord-c/a in all. 354-$1.50-c begins. 355-Larry Hama layouts; Pyro app. 358-Mysterio-c/app. 359-Absorbing Man cameo. 360-Absorbing Man-c/app. 361-Black Widow-c/app. 363,366-370-Gene Colan-a(p). 368-Omega Red-c/app. 372-Ghost Rider-c/app. 376-379-"Flying Blind", DD goes undercover for S.H.I.E.L.D. 3.00
375-($2.99) Wraparound-c; Mr. Fear-c/app. 4.00
380-($2.99) Final issue; flashback story 5.00
#(-1) Flashback issue (7/97, $1.95) Gene Colan-a/c 4.00
Special 1(9/67, 25¢, 68 pgs.)-New art/story 7 14 21 46 86 125
Special 2,3: 2(2/71, 25¢, 52 pgs.)-Entire book has Powell/Wood-r; Wood-c.
3(1/72, 52 pgs.)-Reprints 3 6 9 21 33 45
Annual 4(10/76) 2 4 6 11 16 20
Annual 4(#5)-10: ('89-94 68 pgs.)-5-Atlantis Attacks. 6-Sutton-a. 7-Guice-a (7 pgs.). 8-Deathlok-c/story. 9-Polybagged w/card 4.00
...: Born Again TPB ($17.95)-r/#227-233; Miller-s/Mazzucchelli-a & new-c 20.00
... By Frank Miller and Klaus Janson Omnibus HC (2007, $99.99, dustjacket) r/#158-161, 163-191 and What If...? #28; intros by Miller and Janson; interviews, bonus art 100.00
... By Frank Miller and Klaus Janson Omnibus Companion HC (2007, $59.99, die-cut d.j.) r/#219,226-233, Daredevil: The Man Without Fear #1-5, Daredevil: Love and War, and Peter Parker, the Spect. Spider-Man #27-28; bonus materials 60.00
.../Deadpool- (Annual '97, $2.99)-Wraparound-c 5.00
...: Fall From Grace TPB ($19.95)-r/#319-325 20.00
...: Gang War TPB ($15.95)-r/#169-172,180; Miller-s/a(p) 16.00
...Legends: (Vol. 4) Typhoid Mary TPB (2003, $19.95) r/#254-257,259-263 20.00
... :Love's Labors Lost TPB ($19.99)-r/#215-217,219-222,225,226; Mazzucchelli-c 20.00
.../Punisher TPB (1988, $4.95)-r/D.D. #182-184 (all printings) 6.00
...Visionaries: Frank Miller Vol. 1 TPB ($17.95) r/#158-161,163-167 18.00
...Visionaries: Frank Miller Vol. 2 TPB ($24.95) r/#168-182; new Miller-c 25.00
...Visionaries: Frank Miller Vol. 3 TPB ($24.95) r/#183-191, What If? #28,35 & Bizarre Adventures #28; new Miller-c 25.00
... Vs. Bullseye Vol. 1 TPB (2004, $15.99) r/#131-132,146,169,181,191 16.00
Wizard Ace Edition: Daredevil (Vol. 1) #1 (4/03, $13.99) Acetate Campbell-c 14.00

NOTE: ***Art Adams*** *c-238p, 239.* ***Austin*** *a-191i; c-151i, 200i.* ***John Buscema*** *a-136, 137p, 234p, 235p; c-86p, 136i, 137p, 142, 219.* ***Byrne*** *c-200p, 201, 203, 223.* ***Capullo*** *a-286p.* ***Colan*** *a(p)-20-49, 53-82, 84-98, 100, 110, 112, 124, 153, 154, 156, 157, 363, 366-370, Spec. 1p; c(p)-20-42, 44-49, 53-60, 71, 92, 98, 138, 153, 154, 156, 157, Annual 1.* ***Craig*** *a-50i, 52i.* ***Ditko*** *a-162, 234p, 235p, 264p; c-162.* ***Everett*** *c/a-1; inks-21, 83.* ***Garney*** *c/a-304.* ***Gil Kane*** *a-141p, 146-148p, 151p; c(p)-85, 90, 91, 93, 94, 115, 116, 119, 120, 125-128, 133, 139, 147, 152.* ***Kirby*** *c-2-4, 5p, 12p, 13p, 43.* ***Layton*** *c-202.* ***Miller*** *scripts-168-182, 183(part), 184-191, 219, 227-233; a-158-161p, 163-184p, 191p; c-158-161p, 163-184p, 185-189, 190p, 191.* ***Orlando*** *a-2-4p.* ***Powell*** *a-9p, 11p, Special 1r, 2r.* ***Simonson*** *c-199, 236p.* ***B. Smith*** *a-236p; c-51p, 52p, 217.* ***Starlin*** *a-105p.* ***Steranko*** *c-44i.* ***Tuska*** *a-39i, 145p.* ***Williamson*** *a(i)-237, 239, 240, 243, 248-257, 259-282, 283(part), 284, 285, 287, 288(part), 289(part), 293-300; c(i)-237, 243, 244, 248-257, 259-263, 265-278, 280-289, Annual 8.* ***Wood*** *a-5-8, 9i, 10, 11i, Spec. 2i; c-5i, 6-11, 164i.*

DAREDEVIL (Volume 2)(Marvel Knights)(Becomes Black Panther: The Man Without Fear #513)
Marvel Comics: Nov, 1998 - No. 512, Feb, 2011 ($2.50/$2.99)

1-Kevin Smith-s/Quesada & Palmiotti-a 12.00
1-($6.95) DF Edition w/Quesada & Palmiotti var.-c 15.00
1-($6.00) DF Sketch Ed. w/B&W-c 10.00
2-Two covers by Campbell and Quesada/Palmiotti 9.00
3-8: 4,5-Bullseye app. 5-Variant-c exists. 8-Spider-Man-c/app.; last Smith-s 6.00
9-15: 9-11-David Mack-s; intro Echo. 12-Begin $2.99-c; Haynes-a. 13,14-Quesada-a 4.00
16-19-Direct editions; Bendis-s/Mack-c/painted-a 4.00
18,19,21,22-Newsstand editions with variant cover logo "Marvel Unlimited Featuring... 4.00
20-($3.50) Gale-s/Winslade-a; back-up by Stan Lee-s/Colan-a; Mack-c 5.00
21-40: 21-25-Gale-s. 26-38-Bendis-s/Maleev-a. 32-Daredevil's ID revealed. 35-Spider-Man-c/app. 38-Iron Fist & Luke Cage app. 40-Dodson-a 3.50
41-(25¢-c) Begins "Lowlife" arc; Maleev-a; intro Milla Donovan 3.00
41-(Newsstand edition with 2.99¢-c) 3.00
42-45-"Lowlife" arc; Maleev-a 3.00
46-50-($2.99). 46-Typhoid Mary returns. 49-Bullseye app. 50-Art panels by various incl. Romita, Colan, Mack, Janson, Oeming, Quesada 3.00
51-64,66-74,76-81: 51-55-Mack-s/a; Echo app. 54-Wolverine-c/app. 61-64-Black Widow app. 71-Decalogue begins. 76-81-The Murdock Papers. 81-Last Bendis-s/Maleev-a 3.00
65-($3.99) 40th Anniversary issue; Land-c; art by Maleev, Horn, Bachalo and others 4.00
75-($3.99) Decalogue ends; Jester app. 4.00

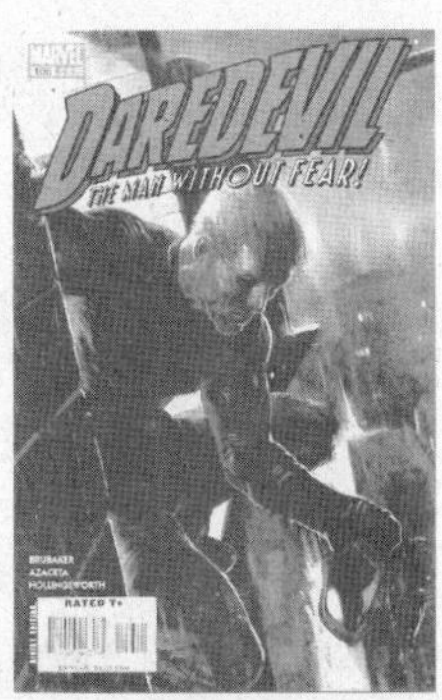

Daredevil V2 #106 © MAR

Daredevil (2014 series) #1 © MAR

Daredevil: Yellow #1 © MAR

GD 2.0 | VG 4.0 | FN 6.0 | VF 8.0 | VF/NM 9.0 | NM- 9.2

82-99,101-119: 82-Brubaker-s/Lark-a begin; Foggy "killed". 84-86-Punisher app. 87-Other Daredevil ID revealed. 94-Romita-c. 111-Lady Bullseye debut 3.00
82-Variant-c by McNiven 4.00
100-($3.99) Three covers (Djurdjevic, Bermejo and Turner); art by Romita Sr., Colan, Lark, Sienkiewicz, Maleev, Bermejo & Djurdjevic; sketch art gallery; r/Daredevil #90 (1972) 4.00
(After Vol. 2 #119, Aug, 2009, numbering reverts to original Vol. 1 with #500)
500-(10/09, $4.99) Kingpin, Lady Bullseye app.; back-up stories, pin-up & cover galleries; r/#191; five covers by Djurdjevic, Darrow, Dell'Otto, Ross and Zircher 5.00
501-512: 501-Daredevil takes over The Hand; Diggle-s begins; Ribic-c. 508-Shadowland begins. 512-Black Panther app. 3.00
Annual #1 (12/07, $3.99) Brubaker-s/Fernandez-a/Djurdjevic-c; Black Tarantula app. 4.00
... & Captain America: Dead on Arrival (2008, $4.99) English version of Italian story 5.00
... Black & White 1 (10/10, $3.99) B&W short stories by various; Aja-c 4.00
... Blood of the Tarantula (6/08, $3.99) Parks & Brubaker-s/Samnee-a/Djurdjevic-c 4.00
... By Brian Michael Bendis Omnibus Vol. 1 HC (2008, $99.99) oversized r/#16-19,26-50, and 56-60 100.00
... By Ed Brubaker Saga (2008, giveaway) synopsis of issues #82-110, preview of #111 3.00
... Cage Match 1 (7/10, $2.99) flashback early Luke Cage team-up; Chen-a 3.00
... MGC #26 (8/10, $1.00) r/#26 with "Marvel's Greatest Comics" logo on cover 3.00
...2099 #1 (11/04, $2.99) Kirkman-s/Moline-a 3.00
TPB ($9.95) r/#1-3 10.00
...Vol. 1 HC (2001, $29.99, with dustjacket) r/#1-11,13-15 30.00
...Vol. 1 HC (2003, $29.99, with dustjacket) r/#1-11,13-15; larger page size 30.00
...Vol. 2 HC (2002, $29.99, with dustjacket) r/#26-37; afterword by Bendis 30.00
...Vol. 3 HC (2004, $29.99, with dustjacket) r/#38-50; Maleev sketch pages 30.00
...Vol. 4 HC (2005, $29.99, with dustjacket) r/#56-65; Vol. 1 #81 (1971) Black Widow 30.00
...Vol. 5 HC (2006, $29.99, with dustjacket) r/#66-75 30.00
...Vol. 6 HC (2006, $34.99, with dustjacket) r/#76-81 & What If Karen Page Had Lived? 35.00
(Vol. 1) Visionaries TPB ($19.95) r/#1-8; Ben Affleck intro. 20.00
(Vol. 2) Parts of a Hole TPB (1/02, $17.95) r/#9-15; David Mack intro. 18.00
(Vol. 3) Wake Up TPB (7/02, $9.99) r/#16-19 10.00
...Vol. 4: Underboss TPB (8/02, $14.99) r/#26-31 15.00
...Vol. 5: Out TPB (2003, $19.99) r/#32-40 20.00
...Vol. 6: Lowlife TPB (2003, $13.99) r/#41-45 14.00
...Vol. 7: Hardcore TPB (2003, $13.99) r/#46-50 14.00
...Vol. 8: Echo - Vision Quest TPB (2004, $13.99) r/#51-55; David Mack-s/a 14.00
...Vol. 9: King of Hell's Kitchen TPB (2004, $13.99) r/#56-60 14.00
...Vol. 10: The Widow TPB (2004, $16.99) r/#61-65 & Vol. 1 #81 17.00
...Vol. 11: Golden Age TPB (2005, $13.99) r/#66-70 14.00
...Vol. 12: Decalogue TPB (2005, $14.99) r/#71-75 15.00
...Vol. 13: The Murdock Papers TPB (2006, $14.99) r/#76-81 15.00
...: The Devil Inside and Out Vol. 1 (2006, $14.99) r/#82-87; Brubaker & Lark interview 15.00
...: The Devil Inside and Out Vol. 2 (2007, $14.99) r/#88-93; Bermejo cover sketches 15.00
...: Hell To Pay Vol. 1 TPB (2007, $14.99) r/#94-99; Djurdjevic cover sketches 15.00
...: Hell To Pay Vol. 2 TPB (2008, $15.99) r/#100-105 16.00

DAREDEVIL (Volume 3)
Marvel Comics: Sept, 2011 - No. 36, Apr, 2014 ($3.99/$2.99)

1-($3.99) Mark Waid-s/Paolo Rivera-a; back-up tale with Marcos Martin-a 4.00
1-Variant-c by Marcos Martin 8.00
1-Variant-c by Neal Adams 10.00
2-10,10.1,11-20,23,24,25,27-36-($2.99) 2-Capt. America app. 3-Klaw returns. 4-6-Marcos Martin-a. 8-X-over w/Amazing Spider-Man #677; Spider-Man and Black Cat app. 11-Spider-Man app. 17-Allred-a. 30-Silver Surfer app. 32,33-Satana & monsters app. 3.00
21,22: 21-1st Superior Spider-Man app. (cameo). 22-Superior Spider-Man app. 5.00
26-($3.99) Bullseye and Lady Bullseye app.; back-up "Fighting Cancer" story 4.00
Annual 1 (10/12, $4.99) Alan Davis-s/a/c; Dr. Strange & ClanDestine app. 5.00

DAREDEVIL (Volume 4)
Marvel Comics: May, 2014 - Present ($3.99)

1,2-($3.99) Mark Waid-s/Chris Samnee-a; Murdock moves to San Francisco 4.00
#1.50-($4.99) 50th Anniversary issue; Murdock at 50; back-up Bendis-s/Maleev-a 5.00

DAREDEVIL/ BATMAN (Also see Batman/Daredevil)
Marvel Comics/ DC Comics: 1997 ($5.99, one-shot)

nn-McDaniel-c/a 6.00

DAREDEVIL BATTLES HITLER (See Daredevil #1 [1941 series])

DAREDEVIL: BATTLIN' JACK MURDOCK
Marvel Comics: Aug, 2007 - No. 4, Nov, 2007 ($3.99, limited series)

1-4-Wells-s/DiGiandomenico-a; flashback to the fixed fight 4.00
TPB (2007, $12.99) r/#1-4; page layouts and cover inks 13.00

DAREDEVIL COMICS (Golden Age title) (See Daredevil)

DAREDEVIL: DARK NIGHTS
Marvel Comics: Aug, 2013 - No. 8, Mar, 2014 ($3.99, limited series)

1-8: 1-3-Lee Weeks-s/a. 4,5-David Lapham-s/a; The Shocker app. 6-8-Conner-c 4.00

DAREDEVIL/ ELEKTRA: LOVE AND WAR
Marvel Comics: 2003 ($29.99, hardcover with dust jacket)

HC-Larger-size reprints of Daredevil: Love and War (Marvel Graphic Novel #24) & Elektra: Assassin; Frank Miller-s; Bill Sienkiewicz-a 30.00

DAREDEVIL: END OF DAYS
Marvel Comics: Dec, 2012 - No. 8, Aug, 2013 ($3.99, limited series)

1-8-Bendis & Mack-s/Janson & Sienkiewicz-a; death of Daredevil in the future 4.00

DAREDEVIL: FATHER
Marvel Comics: June, 2004 - No. 6, Feb, 2007 ($3.50/$2.99, limited series)

1-Quesada-s/a; Isanove-painted color 3.50
1-Director's Cut ($2.99) cover and page development art; partial sketch-c 3.00
2-6: 2-($2.99,10/05). 3-Santerians app. 3.00
HC (2006, $24.99) r/series; Lindelof intro.; sketch pages, cover pencils and bonus art 25.00

DAREDEVIL: NINJA
Marvel Comics: Dec, 2000 - No. 3, Feb, 2001 ($2.99, limited series)

1-3: Bendis-s/Haynes-a 3.00
1-Dynamic Forces foil-c 10.00
TPB (7/01, $12.95) r/#1-3 with cover and sketch gallery 13.00

DAREDEVIL NOIR
Marvel Comics: June, 2009 - No. 4, Sept, 2009 ($3.99, limited series)

1-4-Irvine-s/Coker-a; covers by Coker and Calero 4.00

DAREDEVIL: REBORN (Follows Shadowland x-over)
Marvel Comics: Mar, 2011 - No. 4, Jul, 2011 ($3.99, limited series)

1-4-Diggle-s/Gianfelice-a 4.00

DAREDEVIL: REDEMPTION
Marvel Comics: Apr, 2005 - No. 6, Aug, 2005 ($2.99, limited series)

1-6-Hine-s/Gaydos-a/Sienkiewicz-c 3.00
TPB (2005, $14.99) r/#1-6 15.00

DAREDEVIL: SEASON ONE
Marvel Comics: 2012 ($24.99, hardcover graphic novel)

HC - Story of early career, yellow costume; Johnston-s/Alves-a/Tedesco painted-c 25.00

DAREDEVIL/ SHI (See Shi/ Daredevil)
Marvel Comics/ Crusade Comics: Feb,1997 ($2.95, one-shot)

1 3.00

DAREDEVIL/ SPIDER-MAN
Marvel Comics: Jan, 2001 - No. 4, Apr, 2001 ($2.99, limited series)

1-4-Jenkins-s/Winslade-a/Alex Ross-c; Stilt Man app. 3.00
TPB (8/01, $12.95) r/#1-4; Ross-c 13.00

DAREDEVIL THE MAN WITHOUT FEAR
Marvel Comics: Oct, 1993 - No. 5, Feb, 1994 ($2.95, limited series) (foil embossed covers)

1-Miller scripts; Romita, Jr./Williamson-c/a 6.00
2-5 5.00
Hardcover 100.00
Trade paperback 20.00

DAREDEVIL: THE MOVIE (2003 movie adaptation)
Marvel Comics: March, 2003 ($3.50/$12.95, one-shot)

1-Photo-c of Ben Affleck; Bruce Jones-s/Manuel Garcia-a 3.50
TPB ($12.95) r/movie adaptation; Daredevil #32; Ultimate Daredevil & Elektra #1 and Spider-Man's Tangled Web #4; photo-c of Ben Affleck 13.00

DAREDEVIL: THE TARGET (Daredevil Bullseye on cover)
Marvel Comics: Jan, 2003 ($3.50, unfinished limited series)

1-Kevin Smith-s/Glenn Fabry-c/a 3.50

DAREDEVIL VS. PUNISHER
Marvel Comics: Sept, 2005 - No. 6, Jan, 2006 ($2.99, limited series)

1-5-David Lapham-s/a 3.00
TPB (2005, $15.99) r/#1-6 16.00

DAREDEVIL: YELLOW
Marvel Comics: Aug, 2001 - No. 6, Jan, 2002 ($3.50, limited series)

1-6-Jeph Loeb-s/Tim Sale-a/c; origin & yellow costume days retold 3.50
HC (5/02, $29.95) r/#1-6 with dustjacket; intro by Stan Lee; sketch pages 30.00
Daredevil Legends Vol. 1: Daredevil Yellow (2002, $14.99, TPB) r/#1-6 15.00

DARING ADVENTURES (Also see Approved Comics)
St. John Publishing Co.: Nov, 1953 (25¢, 3-D, came w/glasses)

Daring Love #1 © Gilmore

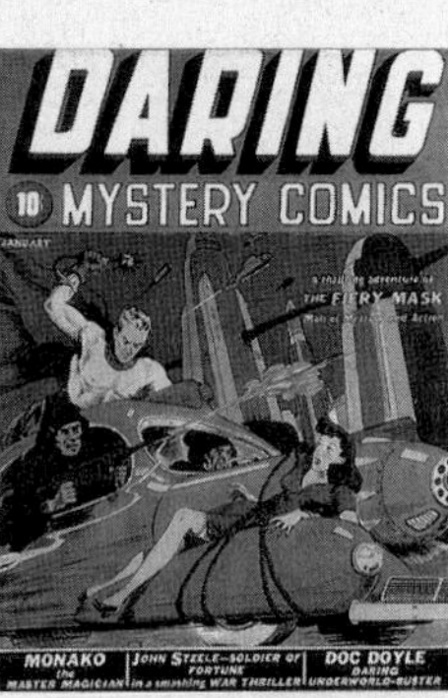

Daring Mystery Comics #1 © MAR

Dark Angel #6 © MAR

GD 2.0 | VG 4.0 | FN 6.0 | VF 8.0 | VF/NM 9.0 | NM- 9.2

GD 2.0 | VG 4.0 | FN 6.0 | VF 8.0 | VF/NM 9.0 | NM- 9.2

1 (3-D)-Reprints lead story from Son of Sinbad #1 by Kubert 26 52 78 154 252 350

DARING ADVENTURES
I.W. Enterprises/Super Comics: 1963 - 1964

I. W. Reprint #8-r/Fight Comics #53; Matt Baker-a 4 8 12 28 47 65
I.W. Reprint #9-r/Blue Bolt #115; Disbrow-a(3) 5 10 15 30 50 70
Super Reprint #10,11('63)-r/Dynamic #24,16; 11-Marijuana story; Yankee Boy app.; Mac Raboy-a 4 8 12 21 33 45
Super Reprint #12('64)-Phantom Lady from Fox (r/#14 only? w/splash pg. omitted); Matt Baker-a 9 18 27 57 111 165
Super Reprint #15('64)-r/Hooded Menace #1 6 12 18 37 66 95
Super Reprint #16('64)-r/Dynamic #12 3 6 9 19 30 40
Super Reprint #17('64)-r/Green Lama #3 by Raboy 4 8 12 25 40 55
Super Reprint #18-Origin Atlas from unpublished Atlas Comics #1 4 8 12 23 37 50

DARING COMICS (Formerly Daring Mystery) (Jeanie Comics No. 13 on)
Timely Comics (HPC): No. 9, Fall, 1944 - No. 12, Fall, 1945

9-Human Torch, Toro & Sub-Mariner begin 161 322 483 1030 1765 2500
10-12: 10-The Angel only app. 11,12-The Destroyer app. 135 270 405 864 1482 2100
NOTE: ***Schomburg** c-9-11. **Sekowsky** c-12? Human Torch, Toro & Sub-Mariner c-9-12.*

DARING CONFESSIONS (Formerly Youthful Hearts)
Youthful Magazines: No. 4, 11/52 - No. 7, 5/53; No. 8, 10/53

4-Doug Wildey-a; Tony Curtis story 19 38 57 111 176 240
5-8: 5-Ray Anthony photo on-c. 6,8-Wildey-a 14 28 42 82 121 160

DARING ESCAPES
Image Comics: Sept, 1998 - No. 4, Mar, 1999 ($2.95/$2.50, mini-series)

1-Houdini; following app. in Spawn #19,20 3.00
2-4-($2.50) 3.00

DARING LOVE (Radiant Love No. 2 on)
Gilmor Magazines: Sept-Oct, 1953

1–Steve Ditko's 1st published work (1st drawn was Fantastic Fears #5)(Also see Black Magic #27)(scarce) 142 284 426 909 1555 2200

DARING LOVE (Formerly Youthful Romances)
Ribage/Pix: No. 15, 12/52; No. 16, 2/53-c, 4/53-Indicia; No. 17-4/53-c & indicia

15 14 28 42 80 115 150
16,17: 17-Photo-c 13 26 39 72 101 130
NOTE: ***Colletta** a-15. **Wildey** a-17.*

DARING LOVE STORIES (See Fox Giants)

DARING MYSTERY COMICS (Comedy Comics No. 9 on; title changed to Daring Comics with No. 9)
Timely Comics (TPI 1-6/TCI 7,8): 1/40 - No. 5, 6/40; No. 6, 9/40; No. 7, 4/41 - No. 8, 1/42

1-Origin The Fiery Mask (1st app.) by Joe Simon; Monako, Prince of Magic (1st app.), John Steele, Soldier of Fortune (1st app.), Doc Denton (1st app.) begin; Flash Foster & Barney Mullen, Sea Rover only app; bondage-c 2000 4000 6000 15,000 28,500 42,000
2-(Rare)-Origin The Phantom Bullet (1st & only app.); The Laughing Mask & Mr. E only app.; Trojak the Tiger Man begins, ends #6; Zephyr Jones & K-4 & His Sky Devils app., also #4 1150 2300 3450 8700 15,850 23,000
3-The Phantom Reporter, Dale of FBI, Captain Strong only app.; Breeze Barton, Marvex the Super-Robot, The Purple Mask begin 578 1156 1734 4219 7460 10,700
4,5: 4-Last Purple Mask; Whirlwind Carter begins; Dan Gorman, G-Man app. 5-The Falcon begins (1st app.); The Fiery Mask, Little Hercules app. by Sagendorf in the Segar style; bondage-c 423 846 1269 3067 5384 7700
6-Origin & only app. Marvel Boy by S&K; Flying Flame, Dynaman, & Stuporman only app.; The Fiery Mask by S&K; S&K-c 486 972 1458 3550 6275 9000
7-Origin and 1st app. The Blue Diamond, Captain Daring by S&K, The Fin by Everett, The Challenger, The Silver Scorpion & The Thunderer by Burgos; Mr. Millions app. 411 822 1233 2877 5039 7200
8-Origin Citizen V; Last Fin, Silver Scorpion, Capt. Daring by Borth, Blue Diamond & The Thunderer; Kirby & part solo Simon-c; Rudy the Robot only app.; Citizen V, Fin & Silver Scorpion continue in Comedy #9 331 662 993 2317 5217 5800
NOTE: ***Schomburg** c-1-4, 7. **Simon** a-2, 3, 5. Cover features: 1-Fiery Mask; 2-Phantom Bullet; 3-Purple Mask; 4-G-Man; 5-The Falcon; 6-Marvel Boy; 7, 8-Multiple characters.*

DARING MYSTERY COMICS 70th ANNIVERARY SPECIAL
Marvel Comics: Nov, 2009 ($3.99, one-shot)

1-New story of The Phantom Reporter; r/app. in Daring Mystery #3 (1940); 2 covers 5.00

DARING NEW ADVENTURES OF SUPERGIRL, THE
DC Comics: Nov, 1982 - No. 13, Nov, 1983 (Supergirl No. 14 on)

1-Origin retold; Lois Lane back-ups in #2-12 1 2 3 5 6 8
2-13: 8,9-Doom Patrol app. 13-New costume; flag-c 4.00
NOTE: ***Buckler** c-1p, 2p. **Giffen** c-3p, 4p. **Gil Kane** c-6,8, 9, 11-13.*

DARK, THE
Continum Comics: Nov, 1990 - No. 4, Feb, 1993; V2#1, May, 1993 - V2#7, Apr?, 1994 ($1.95)

1-4: 1-Bright-p; Panosian, Hanna-i; Stroman-c. 2-(1/92)-Stroman-c/a(p). 4-Perez-c & part-i 3.00
V2#1,V2#2-6: V2#1-Red foil Bart Sears-c. V2#1-Red non-foil variant-c. V2#1-2nd printing w/blue foil Bart Sears-c. V2#2-Stroman/Bryant-a. 3-Perez-c(i). 3-6-Foil-c. 4-Perez-c & part-i; bound-in trading cards. 5,6-(2,3/94)-Perez-c(i). 7-(B&W)-Perez-c(i) 3.00
Convention Book 1 ,2(Fall/94, 10/94)-Perez-c 3.00

DARK ANGEL (Formerly Hell's Angel)
Marvel Comics UK, Ltd.: No. 6, Dec, 1992 - No. 16, Dec, 1993 ($1.75)

6-8,13-16: 6-Excalibur-c/story. 8-Psylocke app. 3.00
9-12-Wolverine/X-Men app. 3.50

DARK ANGEL: PHOENIX RESURRECTION (Kia Asamiya's...)
Image Comics: May, 2000 - No. 4, Oct, 2001 ($2.95)

1-4-Kia Asamiya-s/a. 3-Van Fleet variant-c 3.00

DARK AVENGERS (See Secret Invasion and Dark Reign titles)
Marvel Comics: Mar, 2009 - No. 16, Jul, 2010 ($3.99)

1-Norman Osborn assembles his Avengers; Bendis-s/Deodato-a/c 4.00
1-Variant Iron Patriot armor cover by Djurdjevic 8.00
2-16: 2-6-Bendis-s/Deodato-a/c. 2-4 Dr. Doom app. 7,8-Utopia x-over; X-Men app. 9-Nick Fury app. 11,12-Deodato & Horn-a. 13-16-Siege. 13-Sentry origin 4.00
Annual 1 (2/10, $4.99) Bendis-s/Bachalo-a; Marvel Boy new costume; Siege preview 5.00
,,,/ Uncanny X-Men: Exodus (11/09, $3.99) Conclusion of x-over; Deodato & Dodson-a 4.00
,,,/ Uncanny X-Men: Utopia (8/09, $3.99) Part 1 of x-over w/Uncanny X-Men #513,514 4.00

DARK AVENGERS (Title continues from Thunderbolts #174)
Marvel Comics: No. 175, Aug, 2012 - No. 190, Jul, 2013 ($2.99)

175-190: 175-New team assembles; Parker-s/Shalvey-a/Deodato-c 3.00

DARK AVENGERS: ARES
Marvel Comics: Dec, 2009 - No. 3, Feb, 2010 ($3.99, limited series)

1-3-Garcia-a/Gillen-s. 1-Nord-c. 2-Tan-c. 3-McGuinness-c 4.00

DARKCHYLDE (Also see Dreams of the Darkchylde)
Maximum Press #1-3/ Image Comics #4 on: June, 1996 - No. 5, Sept, 1997 ($2.95/ $2.50)

1-Randy Queen-c/a/scripts; "Roses" cover 6.00
1-American Entertainment Edition-wraparound-c 6.00
1-"Fashion magazine-style" variant-c 1 2 3 4 5 7
1-Special Comicon Edition (contents of #1) Winged devil variant-c 5.00
1-($2.50)-Remastered Ed.-wraparound-c 4.00
2(Reg-c),2-Spiderweb and Moon variant-c 6.00
3(Reg-c),3-"Kalvin Clein" variant-c by Drew 4.00
4,5(Reg-c), 4-Variant-c 4.00
5-B&W Edition, 5-Dynamic Forces Gold Ed. 8.00
0-(3/98, $2.50) 3.00
0-Remastered (1/01, $2.95) includes Darkchylde: Redemption preview 3.00
1/2-WIzard offer 4.00
1/2 Variant-c 6.00
... The Descent TPB ('98, $19.95) r/#1-5; bagged with Darkchylde The Legacy Preview Special 1998; listed price is for TPB only 20.00

DARKCHYLDE LAST ISSUE SPECIAL
Darkchylde Entertainment: June, 2002 ($3.95)

1-Wraparound-c; cover gallery 4.00

DARKCHYLDE REDEMPTION
Darkchylde Entertainment: Feb, 2001 - No. 2, Dec, 2001 ($2.95)

1,2: 1-Wraparound-c 3.00
1-Dynamic Forces alternate-c 6.00
1-Dynamic Forces chrome-c 16.00

DARKCHYLDE SKETCH BOOK
Image Comics (Dynamic Forces): 1998

1-Regular-c 8.00
1-DarkChrome cover 16.00

DARKCHYLDE SUMMER SWIMSUIT SPECTACULAR
DC Comics (WildStorm): Aug, 1999 ($3.95, one-shot)

1-Pin-up art by various 4.00

DARKCHYLDE SWIMSUIT ILLUSTRATED
Image Comics: 1998 ($2.50, one-shot)

Darkdevil #2 © MAR

Darkhawk #43 © MAR

Dark Horse Comics #6 © DH

	GD 2.0	VG 4.0	FN 6.0	VF 8.0	VF/NM 9.0	NM- 9.2

1-Pin-up art by various 3.00
1-(6.95) Variant cover 7.00
1-Chromium cover 15.00

DARKCHYLDE THE DIARY
Image Comics: June, 1997 ($2.50, one-shot)
1-Queen-c/s/ art by various 3.00
1-Variant-c 5.00
1-Holochrome variant-c 8.00

DARKCHYLDE THE LEGACY
Image Comics/DC (WildStorm) #3 on: Aug, 1998 - No. 3, June, 1999 ($2.50)
1-3: 1-Queen-c. 2-Two covers by Queen and Art Adams 3.00

DARK CLAW ADVENTURES
DC Comics (Amalgam): June, 1997 ($1.95, one-shot)
1-Templeton-c/s/a & Burchett-a 3.00

DARK CROSSINGS: DARK CLOUDS RISING
Image Comics (Top Cow): June, 2000; Oct, 2000 ($5.95, limited series)
1-Witchblade, Darkness, Tomb Raider crossover; Dwayne Turner-a 6.00
1-(Dark Clouds Overhead) 6.00

DARK CRYSTAL, THE (Movie)
Marvel Comics Group: April, 1983 - No. 2, May, 1983
1,2-Adaptation of film 4.00

DARK DAYS (See 30 Days of Night)
IDW Publishing: June, 2003 - No. 6, Dec, 2003 ($3.99, limited series)
1-6-Sequel to 30 Days of Night; Niles-s/Templesmith-a 4.00
1-Retailer variant (Diamond/Alliance Fort Wayne 5/03 summit) 15.00
TPB (2004, $19.99) r/#1-6; cover gallery; intro. by Eric Red 20.00

DARKDEVIL (See Spider-Girl)
Marvel Comics: Nov, 2000 - No. 3, Jan, 2001 ($2.99, limited series)
1-3: 1-Origin of Darkdevil; Kingpin-c/app. 3.00

DARK DOMINION
Defiant: Oct, 1993 - No. 10, July, 1994 ($2.50)
1-10-Len Wein scripts begin. 4-Free extra 16 pgs. 7-9-J.G. Jones-c/a. 10-Pre-Schism issue; Shooter/Wein script; John Ridgway-a 3.00

DARKER IMAGE (Also see Deathblow, The Maxx, & Bloodwulf)
Image Comics: Mar, 1993 ($1.95, one-shot)
1-The Maxx by Sam Kieth begins; Bloodwulf by Rob Liefeld & Deathblow by Jim Lee begin (both 1st app.); polybagged w/1 of 3 cards by Kieth, Lee or Liefeld 3.00
1-B&W interior pgs. w/silver foil logo 6.00

DARKEWOOD
Aircel Publishing: 1987 - No. 5, 1988 ($2.00, 28pgs, limited series)
1-5 3.00

DARK FANTASIES
Dark Fantasy: 1994 - No. 8, 1995 ($2.95)
1-Test print Run (3,000)-Linsner-c 1 2 3 5 6 8
1-Linsner-c 5.00
2-8: 2-4 (Deluxe), 2-4 (Regular), 5-8 (Deluxe; $3.95) 4.00
5-8 (Regular; $3.50) 3.50

DARK GUARD
Marvel Comics UK: Oct, 1993 - No. 4, Jan, 1994 ($1.75)
1-($2.95)-Foil stamped-c 4.00
2-4 3.00

DARKHAWK (Also see War of Kings)
Marvel Comics: Mar, 1991 - No. 50, Apr, 1995 ($1.00/$1.25/$1.50)
1-Origin/1st app. Darkhawk; Hobgoblin cameo 5.00
2,3,13,14: 2-Spider-Man & Hobgoblin app. 3-Spider-Man & Hobgoblin app. 13,14-Venom-c/story 4.00
4-12,15-24,26-49: 6-Capt. America & Daredevil x-over. 9-Punisher app. 11,12-Tombstone app. 19-Spider-Man & Brotherhood of Evil Mutants-c/story. 20-Spider-Man app. 22-Ghost Rider-c/story. 23-Origin begins, ends #25. 27-New Warriors-c/story. 35-Begin 3 part Venom story. 39-Bound-in trading card sheet 3.00
25,50: (52 pgs.)-Red holo-grafx foil-c w/double gatefold poster; origin of Darkhawk armor 4.00
Annual 1-3 ('92-'94,68 pgs.)-1-Vs. Iron Man. 2 -Polybagged w/card 4.00

DARKHOLD: PAGES FROM THE BOOK OF SINS (See Midnight Sons Unlimited)
Marvel Comics (Midnight Sons imprint #15 on): Oct, 1992 - No. 16, Jan, 1994
1-($2.75, 52 pgs.)-Polybagged w/poster by Andy & Adam Kubert; part 4 of Rise of the Midnight Sons storyline 4.00
2-10,12-16: 3-Reintro Modred the Mystic (see Marvel Chillers #1). 4-Sabertooth-c/sty. 5-Punisher & Ghost Rider app. 15-Spot varnish-c. 15,16-Siege of Darkness pt. 4&12 3.00
11-($2.25)-Outer-c is a Darkhold envelope made of black parchment w/gold ink 4.00

DARK HORSE BOOK OF..., THE
Dark Horse Comics: Aug, 2003 - Nov, 2006 ($14.95/$15.95, HC, 9 1/4" x 6 1/4")
... Hauntings (8/03, $14.95)-Short stories by various incl. Mignola (Hellboy), Thompson, Dorkin, Russell; Gianni-c 15.00
... Monsters (11/06, $15.95)-Short-s by Mignola, Thompson, Dorkin, Giffen, Busiek; Gianni-c 16.00
... The Dead (6/05, $14.95)-Short-s by Mignola, Thompson, Dorkin, Powell; Gianni-c 15.00
... Witchcraft (6/04, $14.95)-Short-s by Mignola, Thompson, Dorkin, Millionaire; Gianni-c 15.00

DARK HORSE CLASSICS (Title series), **Dark Horse Comics**
1992 ($3.95, B&W, 52 pgs. nn's): The Last of the Mohicans. 20,000 Leagues Under the Sea 4.00

DARK HORSE CLASSICS, 5/96 ($2.95) 1-r/Predator: Jungle Tales 3.00
--ALIENS VERSUS PREDATOR, 2/97 - No. 6, 7/97 ($2.95,) 1-6: r/Aliens Versus Predator 3.00
--GODZILLA: KING OF THE MONSTERS, 4/98 ($2.95) 1-6: 1-r/Godzilla: Color Special; Art Adams-a 3.00
--STAR WARS: DARK EMPIRE, 3/97 - No. 6, 8/97 ($2.95) 1-6: r/Star Wars: Dark Empire 3.00
--TERROR OF GODZILLA, 8/98 - No. 6, 1/99 ($2.95) 1-6-r/manga Godzilla in color; Art Adams-c 3.00

DARK HORSE COMICS
Dark Horse Comics: Aug, 1992 - No. 25, Sept, 1994 ($2.50)
1-Dorman double gategold painted-c; Predator, Robocop, Timecop (3-part) & Renegade stories begin 4.00
2-6,11-25: 2-Mignola-c. 3-Begin 3-part Aliens story; Aliens-c. 4-Predator-c. 6-Begin 4 part Robocop story. 12-Begin 2-part Aliens & 3-part Predator stories. 13-Thing From Another World begins w/Nino-a(i). 15-Begin 2-part Aliens: Cargo story. 16-Begin 3-part Predator story. 17-Begin 3-part Star Wars: Droids story & 3-part Aliens: Alien story; Droids-c. 19-Begin 2-part X story; X cover 3.00
7-Begin Star Wars: Tales of the Jedi 3-part story 1 2 3 4 5 7
8-1st app. X and begins; begin 4-part James Bond 6.00
9,10: 9-Star Wars ends. 10-X ends; Begin 3-part Predator & Godzilla stories 4.00
NOTE: *Art Adams c-11.*

DARK HORSE DOWN UNDER
Dark Horse Comics: June, 1994 - No. 3, Oct, 1994 ($2.50, B&W, limited series)
1-3 3.00

DARK HORSE MAVERICK
Dark Horse Comics: July, 2000; July, 2001; Sept, 2002 (B&W, annual)
2000-($3.95) Short stories by Miller, Chadwick, Sakai, Pearson 4.00
2001-($4.99) Short stories by Sakai, Wagner and others; Miller-c 5.00
...: Happy Endings (9/02, $9.95) Short stories by Bendis, Oeming, Mahfood, Mignola, Miller, Kieth and others; Miller-c 10.00

DARK HORSE MONSTERS
Dark Horse Comics: Feb, 1997 ($2.95, one-shot)
1-Reprints 3.00

DARK HORSE PRESENTS
Dark Horse Comics: July, 1986 - No. 157, Sept, 2000 ($1.50-$2.95, B&W)
1-1st app. Concrete by Paul Chadwick 2 4 6 9 13 16
1-2nd printing (1988, $1.50) 3.00
1-Silver ink 3rd printing (1992, $2.25)-Says 2nd printing inside 3.00
2-9: 2-6,9-Concrete app. 6.00
10-1st app. The Mask; Concrete app. 2 4 6 9 12 15
11-19,21-23: 11-19,21-Mask stories. 12,14,16,18,22-Concrete app. 15(2/88). 17-All Roachmill issue 6.00
20-(68 pgs.)-Concrete, Flaming Carrot, Mask 1 3 4 6 8 10
24-Origin Aliens-c/story (11/88); Mr. Monster app. 2 4 6 11 16 20
25-27,29-31,37-39,41,44,45,47-49: 38-Concrete. 44-Crash Ryan. 48,49-Contain 2 trading cards 3.00
28,33,40: 28-(52 pgs.)-Concrete app.; Mr. Monster story (homage to Graham Ingels). 33-(44 pgs.). 40-(52 pgs.)-1st Argosy story 4.00
32,34,35: 32-(68 pgs.)-Annual; Concrete, American. 34-Aliens-c/story. 35-Predator-c/app. 4.00
36-1st Aliens Vs. Predator story; painted-c, 36-Variant line drawn-c 1 2 3 5 6 8
42,43,46: 42,43-Aliens-c/stories. 46-Prequel to new Predator II mini-series 3.00
50-S/F story by Perez; contains 2 trading cards 4.00
51-53-Sin City by Frank Miller, parts 2-4; 51,53-Miller-c (see D.H.P. Fifth Anniversary Special for pt. 1) 1 2 3 4 6 8
54-61: 54-(9/91) The Next Men begins (1st app.) by Byrne; Miller-a/Morrow-c. Homocide by

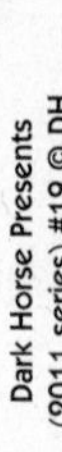
Dark Horse Presents (2011 series) #19 © DH

Dark Minds #1 © Dreamwave

Dark Mysteries #1 © Merit

Morrow (also in #55). 55-2nd app. The Next Men; parts 5 & 6 of Sin City by Miller; Miller-c. 56-(68 pg. annual)-part 7 of Sin City by Miller; part prologue to Aliens: Genocide; Next Men by Byrne. 57-(52 pgs.)-Part 8 of Sin City by Miller; Next Men by Byrne; Byrne & Miller-c; Alien Fire story; swipes cover to Daredevil #1. 58,59-Alien Fire stories. 58-61- Part 9-12 Sin City by Miller 5.00
62-Last Sin City (entire book by Miller, c/a; 52 pgs.) 1 3 4 6 8 10
63-66,68-79,81-84-($2.25): 64-Dr. Giggles begins (1st app.), ends #66; Boris the Bear story. 66-New Concrete-c/story by Chadwick. 71-Begin 3 part Dominque story by Jim Balent; Balent-c. 72-(3/93)-Begin 3-part Eudaemon (1st app.) story by Nelson 3.00
67-($3.95, 68 pgs.)-Begin 3-part prelude to Predator: Race War mini-series; Oscar Wilde adapt. by Russell 4.00
80-Art Adams-c/a (Monkeyman & O'Brien) 4.00
85-87,92-99: 85-Begin $2.50-c. 92, 93, 95-Too Much Coffee Man 3.00
88-91-Hellboy by Mignola. 1 2 3 5 6 8
NOTE: *There are 5 different Dark Horse Presents #100 issues*
100-1-Intro Lance Blastoff by Miller; Milk & Cheese by Evan Dorkin 4.00
100-2-Hellboy-c by Wrightson; Hellboy story by Mignola; includes Roberta Gregory & Paul Pope stories 6.00
100-3-100-5: 100-3-Darrow-c, Concrete by Chadwick; Pekar story. 100-4-Gibbons-c: Miller story, Geary story/a. 100-5-Allred-c, Adams, Dorkin, Pope 3.00
101-125: 101-Aliens c/a by Wrightson, story by Pope. 103-Kirby gatefold-c. 106-Big Blown Baby by Bill Wray. 107-Mignola-c/a. 109-Begin $2.95-c; Paul Pope-c. 110-Ed Brubaker-a/s. 114-Flip books begin; Lance Blastoff by Miller; Star Slammers by Simonson. 115-Miller-c. 117-Aliens-c/app. 118-Evan Dorkin-c/a. 119-Monkeyman & O'Brien. 124-Predator. 125-Nocturnals 3.00
126-($3.95, 48 pgs.)-Flip book: Nocturnals, Starship Troopers 4.00
127-134,136-140: 127-Nocturnals. 129-The Hammer. 132-134-Warren-a 3.00
135-($3.50) The Mark 3.50
141-All Buffy the Vampire Slayer issue 4.00
142-149: 142-Mignola-c. 143-Tarzan. 146,147-Aliens vs. Predator. 148-Xena 3.00
150-($4.50) Buffy-c by Green; Buffy, Concrete, Fish Police app. 4.50
151-157: 151-Hellboy-c/app. 153-155-Angel flip-c. 156,157-Witch's Son 3.00
Annual 1997 ($4.95, 64 pgs.)-Flip book; Body Bags, Aliens. Pearson-c; stories by Allred & Stephens, Pope, Smith & Morrow 1 2 3 5 6 8
Annual 1998 ($4.95, 64 pgs.) 1st Buffy the Vampire Slayer comic app.; Hellboy story and cover by Mignola 1 2 3 5 6 8
Annual 1999 (7/99, $4.95) Stories of Xena, Hellboy, Ghost, Luke Skywalker, Groo, Concrete, the Mask and Usagi Yojimbo in their youth. 5.00
Annual 2000 ($4.95) Girl sidekicks; Chiodo-c and flip photo Buffy-c 5.00
...Aliens Platinum Edition (1992)-r/DHP #24,43,43,56 & Special 11.00
...Fifth Anniversary Special nn (4/91, $9.95)-Part 1 of Sin City by Frank Miller (c/a); Aliens, Aliens vs. Predator, Concrete, Roachmill, Give Me Liberty & The American stories 25.00
The One Trick Rip-off (1997, $12.95, TPB)-r/stories from #101-112 13.00
NOTE: ***Geary** a-59, 60. **Miller** a-Special, 51-53, 55-62; c-59-62, 100-1; c-51, 53, 55, 59-62, 100-1. **Moebius** a-63; c-63, 70. **Vess** a-78; c-75, 78.*

DARK HORSE PRESENTS
Dark Horse Comics: Apr, 2011 - Present ($7.99, anthology)

1-34: 1-Frank Miller-c & Xerxes preview; Neal Adams-s/a. 1-3-Concrete by Chadwick. 1-8-Chaykin-s/a. 2,3,9-Corben-a. 3-Steranko interview. 7-Hellboy app. 10-Milk & Cheese. 12-17-Aliens; Kieth-a. 14-Flipbook. 18-Capt. Midnight. 23-26,29-34-Nexus. 25,26-Buffy. 28,29-Neal Adams-s/a. 31,32-Hellboy; McMahon-a 8.00

DARK HORSE TWENTY YEARS
Dark Horse Comics: 2006 (25¢, one-shot)

nn-Pin-ups by Dark Horse artists of other artists' Dark Horse characters; Mignola-c 3.00

DARK IVORY
Image Comics: Mar, 2008 - No. 4, Jan, 2009 ($2.99, limited series)

1-4-Eva Hopkins & Joseph Michael Linsner-s/Linsner-a/c 3.00

DARK KNIGHT (See Batman: The Dark Knight Returns & Legends of the...)

DARK KNIGHT STRIKES AGAIN, THE (Also see Batman: The Dark Knight Returns)
DC Comics: 2001 - No. 3, 2002 ($7.95, prestige format, limited series)

1-Frank Miller-s/a/c; sequel set 3 years after Dark Knight Returns; 2 covers 8.00
2,3 8.00
HC (2002, $29.95) intro. by Miller; sketch pages and exclusive artwork; cover has 3 1/4" tall partial dustjacket 30.00
SC (2002, $19.95) intro. by Miller; sketch pages 20.00

DARKLON THE MYSTIC (Also see Eerie Magazine #79,80)
Pacific Comics: Oct, 1983 (one-shot)

1-Starlin-c/a(r) 4.00

DARKMAN (Movie)
Marvel Comics: Sept, 1990; Oct, 1990 - No. 3, Dec, 1990 ($1.50)

1 (9/90, $2.25, B&W mag., 68 pgs.)-Adaptation of film 4.00
1-3: Reprints B&W magazine 3.00

DARKMAN
Marvel Comics: V2#1, Apr, 1993 -No. 6, Sept, 1993 ($2.95, limited series)

V2#1 ($3.95, 52 pgs.) 4.00
2-6 3.00

DARK MANSION OF FORBIDDEN LOVE, THE (Becomes Forbidden Tales of Dark Mansion No. 5 on)
National Periodical Publ.: Sept-Oct, 1971 - No. 4, Mar-Apr, 1972 (52 pgs.)

1 17 34 51 119 265 410
2-4: 2-Adams-c. 3-Jeff Jones-c 9 18 27 60 120 180

DARKMAN VS. THE ARMY OF DARKNESS (Movie crossover)
Dynamite Entertanment: 2006 - No. 4, 2007 ($3.50)

1-4: 1-Busiek & Stern-s/Fry-a; photo-c and Perez and Bradshaw covers 3.50

DARKMINDS
Image Comics (Dreamwave Prod.): July, 1998 - No. 8, Apr, 1999 ($2.50)

1-Manga; Pat Lee-s/a; 2 covers 1 3 4 6 8 10
1-2nd printing 3.00
2, 0-(1/99, $5.00) Story and sketch pages 5.00
3-8, 1/2-(5/99, $2.50) Story and sketch pages 3.00
... Collected 1,2 (1/99,3/99; $7.95) 1-r/#1-3. 2-r/#4-6 8.00
... Collected 3 (5/99; $5.95) r/#7,8 6.00

DARKMINDS (Volume 2)
Image Comics (Dreamwave Prod.): Feb, 2000 - No. 10, Apr, 2001 ($2.50)

1-10-Pat Lee-c 3.00
0-(7/00) Origin of Mai Murasaki; sketchbook 3.00

DARKMINDS: MACROPOLIS
Image Comics (Dreamwave Prod.): Jan, 2002 - No. 4, Dec, 2002 ($2.95)

Preview (8/01) Flip book w/Banished Knights preview 3.00
1-4-Jo Chen-a 3.00

DARKMINDS: MACROPOLIS (Volume 2)
Dreamwave Prod.: Sept, 2003 - No. 4, Jul, 2004 ($2.95)

1-4-Chris Sarracini-s/Kwang Mook Lim-a 3.00

DARKMINDS / WITCHBLADE (Also see Witchblade/Dark Minds)
Image Comics (Top Cow/Dreamwave Prod.): Aug, 2000 ($5.95, one-shot)

1-Wohl-s/Pat Lee-a; two covers by Silvestri and Lee 6.00

DARK MYSTERIES (Thrilling Tales of Horror & Suspense)
"Master" - "Merit" Publications: June-July, 1951 - No. 24, July, 1955

1-Wood-c/a (8 pgs.) 142 284 426 909 1555 2200
2-Classic skull-c; Wood/Harrison-c/a (8 pgs.) 116 232 348 742 1271 1800
3-9: 7-Dismemberment, hypo blood drainage stys 54 108 162 343 574 825
10-Cannibalism story; witch burning-c 68 136 204 435 743 1050
11-13,15-18: 11-Severed head panels. 13-Dismemberment-c/story. 17-The Old Gravedigger host 48 96 144 302 514 725
14-Several E.C. Craig swipes 49 98 147 309 522 735
19-Injury-to-eye panel; E.C. swipe; torture-c 97 194 291 621 1061 1500
20-Female bondage, blood drainage story 55 110 165 352 601 850
21,22: 21-Devil-c. 22-Last pre-code issue, misdated 3/54 instead of 3/55 39 78 117 240 395 550
23,24 26 52 78 154 252 350
NOTE: ***Cameron** a-1, 2. **Myron Fass** c/a-21. **Harrison** a-3, 7; c-3. **Hollingsworth** a-7-17, 20, 21, 23. **Wildey** a-5. Woodish art by **Fleishman**-9; c-10, 14-17. Bondage c-10, 18, 19.*

DARK NEMESIS (VILLAINS) (See Teen Titans)
DC Comics: Feb, 1998 ($1.95, one-shot)

1-Jurgens-s/Pearson-c 3.00

DARKNESS, THE (See Witchblade #10)
Image Comics (Top Cow Productions): Dec, 1996 - No. 40, Aug, 2001 ($2.50)

Special Preview Edition-(7/96, B&W)-Ennis script; Silvestri-a(p) 2 4 6 9 13 16
0 2 4 6 8 10 12
0-Gold Edition 16.00
1/2 1 3 4 6 8 10
1/2-Christmas-c 3 6 9 14 19 24
1/2-(3/01, $2.95) r/#1/2 w/new 6 pg. story & Silvestri-c 3.00
1-Ennis-s/Silvestri-a, 1-Black variant-c 2 4 6 9 12 15
1-Platinum variant-c 20.00
1-DF Green variant-c 12.00

The Darkness #100 © TCOW

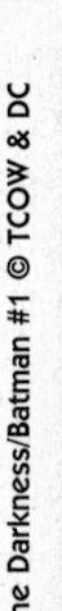
The Darkness/Batman #1 © TCOW & DC

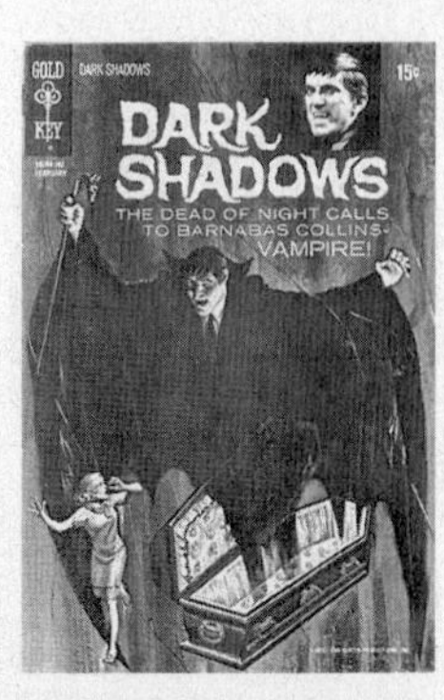
Dark Shadows #8 © Dan Curtis Prods.

	GD 2.0	VG 4.0	FN 6.0	VF 8.0	VF/NM 9.0	NM- 9.2
1,2: 1-Fan Club Ed.	1	3	4	6	8	10
3-5						6.00
6-10: 9,10-Witchblade "Family Ties" x-over pt. 2,3						4.00
7-Variant-c w/concubine	1	2	3	5	7	9
8-American Entertainment						6.00
8-10-American Entertainment Gold Ed.						7.00
11-Regular Ed.; Ennis-s/Silverstri & D-Tron-c						3.00
11-Nine (non-chromium) variant-c (Benitez, Cabrera, the Hildebrandts, Finch, Keown, Peterson, Portacio, Tan, Turner						4.50
11-Chromium-c by Silvestri & Batt						20.00
12-19: 13-Begin Benitez-a(p)						3.00
20-24,26-40: 34-Ripclaw app.						3.00
25-($3.99) Two covers (Benitez, Silvestri)						4.00
25-Chromium-c variant by Silvestri						8.00
.../ Batman (8/99, $5.95) Silvestri, Finch, Lansing-a(p)						6.00
...Collected Editions #1-4 ($4.95,TPB) 1-r/#1,2. 2-r/#3,4. 3- r/#5,6. 4- r/#7,8						6.00
...Collected Editions #5,6 ($5.95, TPB)5- r/#11,12. 6-r/#13,14						6.00
Deluxe Collected Editions #1 (12/98, $14.95, TPB) r/#1-6 & Preview						15.00
...: Heart of Darkness (2001, $14.95, TPB) r/ #7,8, 11-14						15.00
Holiday Pin-up-American Entertainment						5.00
Holiday Pin-up Gold Ed.-American Entertainment						7.00
Image Firsts: Darkness #1 (9/10, $1.00) r/#1 with "Image Firsts" logo on cover						3.00
Infinity #1 (8/99, $3.50) Lobdell-s						3.50
Prelude-American Entertainment						4.00
Prelude Gold Ed.-American Entertainment						9.00
Volume 1 Compendium (2006, $59.99) r/#1-40, V2 #1, Tales of the Darkness #1-4; #1/2, Darkness/Witchblade #1/2, Darkness: Wanted Dead; cover and sketch gallery						60.00
...: Wanted Dead 1 (8/03, $2.99) Texiera-a/Tieri-s						3.00
Wizard ACE Ed.- Reprints #1	2	4	6	8	10	12

DARKNESS (Volume 2)
Image Comics (Top Cow Productions): Dec, 2002 - No. 24, Oct, 2004 ($2.99)

	GD	VG	FN	VF	VF/NM	NM-
1-24: 1-6-Jenkins-s/Keown-a. 17-20-Lapham-s. 23,24-Magdalena app.						3.00
... Black Sails (3/05, $2.99) Marz-s/Cha-a; Hunter-Killer preview						3.00
... and Tomb Raider (4/05, $2.99) r/Darkness Prelude & Tomb Raider/Darkness Special						3.00
...: Resurrection TPB (2/04, $16.99) r/#1-6 & Vol. 1 #40						17.00
.../ The Incredible Hulk (7/04, $2.99) Keown-a/Jenkins-s						3.00
.../ Vampirella (7/05, $2.99) Terry Moore-s; two covers by Basaldua and Moore						3.00
... Vol. 5 TPB (2006, $19.99) r/#7-16 & The Darkness: Wanted Dead #1; cover gallery						20.00
... vs. Mr Hyde Monster War 2005 (9/05, $2.99) x-over w/Witchblade, Tomb Raider and Magdalena; two covers						3.00
.../ Wolverine (2006, $2.99) Kirkham-a/Tieri-s						3.00

DARKNESS (Volume 3) (Numbering jumps from #10 to #75)
Image Comics (Top Cow Productions): Dec, 2007 - Present ($2.99)

	GD	VG	FN	VF	VF/NM	NM-
1-10: 1-Hester-s/Broussard-a. 1-Three covers. 7-9-Lucas-a. 8-Aphrodite IV app.						3.00
75 (2/09, $4.99) Four covers; Hester-s/art by various						5.00
76-99,101-113,115-($2.99) 76-99,101-Multiple covers on each						3.00
100 (2/12, $4.99) Four covers; Hester-s/art by various; cover gallery; series timeline						5.00
114-($4.99) The Age of Reason Part 1; Hine-s/Haun-a; bonus Darkness timeline						5.00
116-($3.99) The Age of Reason Part 3; Hine-s/Haun-a						4.00
....: Butcher (4/08, $3.99) Story of Butcher Joyce; Levin-s/Broussard-a/c						4.00
...: Confession (5/11) Free Comic Boy Day giveaway; Broussard & Molnar-a						3.00
... / Darkchylde: Kingdom Pain 1 (5/10, $4.99) Randy Queen-s/a						5.00
... First Look (11/07, 99¢) Previews series; sketch pages						3.00
...: Lodbrok's Hand (12/08, $2.99) Hester-s/Oeming-a/c; variant-c by Carnevale						3.00
...: Shadows and Flame 1 (1/10, $2.99) Lucas-c/a						3.00
...: Vicious Traditions 1 (3/14, $3.99) Ales Kot-s/Dean Ormston-a/Dale Keown-c						4.00

DARKNESS: FOUR HORSEMEN
Image Comics (Top Cow): Aug, 2010 - No. 4, May, 2011 ($3.99, limited series)

1-4-Hine-s/Wamester-a — 4.00

DARKNESS: LEVEL...
Image Comics (Top Cow): No. 0, Dec, 2006 - No. 5, Aug, 2007 ($2.99, limited series)

0-5: 0-Origin of The Darkness in WW1; Jenkins-s. 1-Jackie's origin retold; Sejic-a — 3.00

DARKNESS/ PITT
Image Comics (Top Cow): Dec, 2006; Aug, 2009 - No. 3, Nov, 2009 ($2.99)

...: First Look (12/06) Jenkins script pages with Keown B&W and color art — 3.00
1-3: 1-(8/09) Jenkins-s/Keown-a; covers by Keown and Sejic. 2,3-Two covers — 3.00

DARKNESS/ SUPERMAN
Image Comics (Top Cow Productions): Jan, 2005 - No. 2, Feb, 2005 ($2.99, limited series)

1,2-Marz-s/Kirkham & Banning-a/Silvestri-c — 3.00

DARKNESS VS. EVA: DAUGHTER OF DRACULA
Dynamite Entertainment: 2008 - No. 4, 2008 ($3.50, limited series)

1-4-Leah Moore & John Reppion-s/Salazar-a; three covers on each — 3.50

DARK REIGN (Follows Secret Invasion crossover)
Marvel Comics: 2009 ($3.99/$4.99, one-shots)

	NM-
...: Files 1 (2009, $4.99) profile pages of villains tied in to Dark Reign x-over	5.00
...: Made Men 1 (11/09, $3.99) short stories by various incl. Pham, Leon, Oliver	4.00
...: New Nation 1 (2/09, $3.99) previews of various series tied in to Dark Reign x-over	4.00
...: The Cabal 1 (6/09, $3.99) Cabal members stories by various incl. Granov, Acuña	4.00
...: The Goblin Legacy 1 (2009, $3.99) r/ASM #39,40; Osborn history; Mayhew-a	4.00

DARK REIGN: ELEKTRA
Marvel Comics: May, 2009 - No. 5, Oct, 2009 ($3.99, limited series)

1-5-Mann-a/Bermejo-c; Elektra after the Skrull replacement. 2,3-Bullseye app. — 4.00

DARK REIGN: FANTASTIC FOUR
Marvel Comics: May, 2009 - No. 5, Sept, 2009 ($2.99, limited series)

1-5-Chen-a — 3.00

DARK REIGN: HAWKEYE
Marvel Comics: June, 2009 - No. 5, Mar, 2010 ($3.99, limited series)

1-5-Bullseye in the Dark Avengers; Raney-a/Langley-c. 5-Guinaldo-a — 4.00

DARK REIGN: LETHAL LEGION
Marvel Comics: Aug, 2009 - No. 3, Nov, 2009 ($3.99, limited series)

1-3-Santolouco-a/Edwards-c; Grim Reaper and Wonder Man app. — 4.00

DARK REIGN: MR. NEGATIVE (Also see Amazing Spider-Man #546)
Marvel Comics: Aug, 2009 - No. 3, Oct, 2009 ($3.99, limited series)

1-3-Jae Lee-c/Gugliotta-a; Spider-Man app. — 4.00

DARK REIGN: SINISTER SPIDER-MAN
Marvel Comics: Aug, 2009 - No. 4, Nov, 2009 ($3.99, limited series)

1-4-Bachalo-c/a; Venom/Scorpion as Dark Avenger Spider-Man — 4.00

DARK REIGN: THE HOOD
Marvel Comics: Jul, 2009 - No. 5, Nov, 2009 ($3.99, limited series)

1-5-Hotz-a/Djurdjevic-c — 4.00

DARK REIGN: THE LIST
Marvel Comics: 2009 - 2010 ($3.99, one-shots)

	NM-
... - Amazing Spider-Man (1/10, $3.99) Adam Kubert-c/a; back-up r/Pulse #5	4.00
... - Avengers (11/09, $3.99) Bendis-s/Djurdjevic-c/a; Ronin (Hawkeye) app.	4.00
... - Daredevil (11/09, $3.99) Diggle-s/Tan-c/a; Bullseye app.; leads into Daredevil #501	4.00
... - Hulk (12/09, $3.99) Pak-s/Oliver-a; Skaar app.; back-up r/Amaz. Spider-Man #14	4.00
... - Punisher (12/09, $3.99) Romita Jr.-a/c; Castle killed by Daken; preview of Franken-Castle in Punisher #11	6.00
... - Secret Warriors (12/09, $3.99) McGuinness-a/c; Nick Fury; back-up r/Steranko-a	4.00
... - Wolverine (12/09, $3.99) Ribic-a/c; Marvel Boy and Fantomex app.	4.00
... - X-Men (11/09, $3.99) Alan Davis-a/c; Namor app.; back-up r/Kieth-a	4.00

DARK REIGN: YOUNG AVENGERS
Marvel Comics: Jul, 2009 - No. 5, Dec, 2009 ($3.99, limited series)

1-5-Brooks-a; Osborn's Young Avengers vs. original Young Avengers — 4.00

DARK REIGN: ZODIAC
Marvel Comics: Aug, 2009 - No. 3, Nov, 2009 ($3.99, limited series)

1-3-Casey-s/Fox-a. 1-Human Torch app. — 4.00

DARKSEID (VILLAINS) (See Jack Kirby's New Gods and New Gods)
DC Comics: Feb, 1998 ($1.95, one-shot)

1-Byrne-s/Pearson-c — 3.00

DARKSEID VS. GALACTUS: THE HUNGER
DC Comics: 1995 ($4.95, one-shot) (1st DC/Marvel x-over by John Byrne)

nn-John Byrne-c/a/script — 6.00

DARK SHADOWS
Steinway Comic Publ. (Ajax)(America's Best): Oct, 1957 - No. 3, May, 1958

	GD 2.0	VG 4.0	FN 6.0	VF 8.0	VF/NM 9.0	NM- 9.2
1	30	60	90	177	289	400
2,3	20	40	60	117	189	260

DARK SHADOWS (TV) (See Dan Curtis Giveaways)
Gold Key: Mar, 1969 - No. 35, Feb, 1976 (Photo-c: 1-7)

	GD 2.0	VG 4.0	FN 6.0	VF 8.0	VF/NM 9.0	NM- 9.2
1(30039-903)-With pull-out poster (25¢)	20	40	60	135	300	465
1-With poster missing	7	14	21	48	89	130
2	8	16	24	54	102	150
3-With pull-out poster	9	18	27	60	120	180
3-With poster missing	5	10	15	35	63	90

Dark Tower: The Gunslinger Born #1 © Stephen King

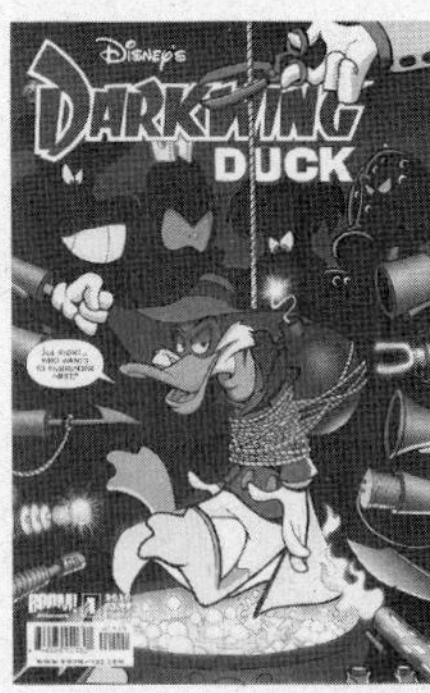

Darkwing Duck (2010 series) #1 © DIS

Darling Love #2 © AP

	GD 2.0	VG 4.0	FN 6.0	VF 8.0	VF/NM 9.0	NM- 9.2
4-7: 7-Last photo-c	6	12	18	38	69	100
8-10	5	10	15	30	50	70
11-20	4	8	12	27	44	60
21-35: 30-Last painted-c	4	8	12	23	37	50
Story Digest 1 (6/70, 148pp.)-Photo-c (low print)	7	14	21	46	86	125

DARK SHADOWS (TV) (See Nightmare on Elm Street)
Innovation Publishing: June, 1992 - No. 4, Spring, 1993 ($2.50, limited series, coated stock)

1-Based on 1991 NBC TV mini-series; painted-c 5.00
2-4 4.00

DARK SHADOWS: BOOK TWO
Innovation Publishing: 1993 - No. 4, July, 1993 ($2.50, limited series)

1-4-Painted-c. 4-Maggie Thompson scripts 4.00

DARK SHADOWS: BOOK THREE
Innovation Publishing: Nov, 1993 ($2.50)

1-(Whole #9) 4.00

DARK SHADOWS/VAMPIRELLA
Dynamite Entertainment: 2012 - No. 5, 2012 ($3.99, limited series)

1-5-Andreyko-s/Berkenkotter-a/Neves-c 4.00

DARK SHADOWS, VOLUME 1
Dynamite Entertainment: 2011 - No. 23, 2013 ($3.99)

1-23-Set in 1971. 1-Aaron Campbell-a; covers by Campbell & Francavilla 4.00

DARK SHADOWS: YEAR ONE
Dynamite Entertainment: 2013 - No. 6, 2013 ($3.99, limited series)

1-6-Origin of Barnabas Collins; Andreyko-s/Vilanova-a 4.00

DARKSTAR AND THE WINTER GUARD
Marvel Comics: Aug, 2010 - No. 3, Oct, 2010 ($3.99, limited series)

1-3-Gallaher-s/Ellis-a/Henry-c; back-up reprint from X-Men Unlimited #28 4.00

DARKSTARS, THE
DC Comics: Oct, 1992 - No. 38, Jan, 1996 ($1.75/$1.95)

1-1st app. The Darkstars 4.00
2-24,0,25-38: 5-Hawkman & Hawkwoman app. 18-20-Flash app. 24-(9/94)-Zero Hour. 0-(10/94). 25-(11/94). 30-Green Lantern app. 31-...vs. Darkseid. 32-Green Lantern app. 3.00

NOTE: *Travis Charest a(p)-4-7; c(p)-2-5; c-6-11. Stroman a-1-3; c-1.*

DARK TOWER: THE BATTLE OF JERICHO HILL (Based on Stephen King's Dark Tower)
Marvel Comics: Feb, 2010 - No. 5, Jun, 2010 ($3.99, limited series)

1-5-Peter David & Robin Furth-s/Jae Lee & Richard Isanove-a/c; variant-c for each 4.00

DARK TOWER: THE FALL OF GILEAD (Based on Stephen King's Dark Tower)
Marvel Comics: July, 2009 - No. 6, Jan, 2010 ($3.99, limited series)

1-6-Peter David & Robin Furth-s/Richard Isanove-a/Jae Lee-c; variant-c for each 4.00
Dark Tower: Guide to Gilead (2009, $3.99) profile pages of people and places 4.00

DARK TOWER: THE GUNSLINGER BORN (Based on Stephen King's Dark Tower series)
Marvel Comics: Apr, 2007 - No. 7, Oct, 2007 ($3.99, limited series)

1-Peter David & Robin Furth-s/Jae Lee & Richard Isanove-a; boyhood of Roland Deschain; afterword by Ralph Macchio; map of New Canaan 6.00
1-Variant cover by Quesada 8.00
1-Second printing with variant-c by Quesada 5.00
1-Sketch cover variant by Jae Lee 40.00
2-6-Jae Lee-c 4.00
2-Second printing with variant-c by Immonen 4.00
2-7-Variant covers. 2-Finch-c. 3-Yu-c. 4-McNiven-c. 5-Land-c. 6-Campbell. 7-Coipel 6.00
2-7-B&W sketch-c by Jae Lee 20.00
... MGC #1 (5/11, $1.00) r/#1 with "Marvel's Greatest Comics" logo on cover 3.00
... Sketchbook (2006, no cover price) pencil art and designs by Lee; coloring process 5.00
Dark Tower: Gunslinger's Guidebook (2007, $3.99) profile pages with Jae Lee-a 4.00
HC (2007, $24.99) r/#1-7; variant covers and sketch pages; Macchio intro. 25.00

DARK TOWER: THE GUNSLINGER - EVIL GROUND (Stephen King's Dark Tower)
Marvel Comics: Jun, 2013 - No. 2, Aug, 2013 ($3.99, limited series)

1,2-Robin Furth & Peter David-s/Richard Isanove-a/c 4.00

DARK TOWER: THE GUNSLINGER - SHEEMIE'S TALE (Stephen King's Dark Tower)
Marvel Comics: Mar, 2013 - No. 2, Apr, 2013 ($3.99, limited series)

1,2-Robin Furth-s/Richard Isanove-a/c 4.00

DARK TOWER: THE GUNSLINGER - SO FELL LORD PERTH (Stephen King's Dark Tower)
Marvel Comics: Sept, 2013 ($3.99, one-shot)

1-Robin Furth & Peter David-s/Richard Isanove-a/c 4.00

DARK TOWER: THE GUNSLINGER - THE BATTLE OF TULL (Stephen King's Dark Tower)
Marvel Comics: Aug, 2011 - No. 5, Dec, 2011 ($3.99, limited series)

1-5-Peter David & Robin Furth-s/Michael Lark-a/c 4.00

DARK TOWER: THE GUNSLINGER - THE JOURNEY BEGINS (Stephen King's Dark Tower)
Marvel Comics: Jul, 2010 - No. 5, Nov, 2010 ($3.99, limited series)

1-Peter David & Robin Furth-s/Sean Phillips-a/c 4.00
1-Variant cover by Jae Lee 5.00

DARK TOWER: THE GUNSLINGER - THE LITTLE SISTERS OF ELURIA (Stephen King)
Marvel Comics: Feb, 2011 - No. 5, Jun, 2011 ($3.99, limited series)

1-5: 1-Peter David & Robin Furth-s/Luke Ross-a/c 4.00

DARK TOWER: THE GUNSLINGER - THE MAN IN BLACK (Stephen King)
Marvel Comics: Aug, 2012 - No. 5, Dec, 2012 ($3.99, limited series)

1-5-Peter David & Robin Furth-s/Maleev-a/c 4.00

DARK TOWER: THE GUNSLINGER - THE WAY STATION (Stephen King)
Marvel Comics: Feb, 2012 - No. 5, Jun, 2012 ($3.99, limited series)

1-5-Peter David & Robin Furth-s/Laurence Campbell-a/c 4.00

DARK TOWER: THE LONG ROAD HOME (Based on Stephen King's Dark Tower series)
Marvel Comics: May, 2008 - No. 5, Sept, 2008 ($3.99, limited series)

1-Peter David & Robin Furth-s/Jae Lee & Richard Isanove-a 4.00
1-Variant cover by Deodato 6.00
1-Sketch cover variant by Jae Lee 40.00
2-5-Jae Lee-c 4.00
2-5: 2-Variant-c by Quesada. 3-Djurdjevic var-c. 4-Garney var-c. 5-Bermejo var-c 6.00
2-5-B&W sketch-c by Jae Lee 20.00
2-Second printing with variant-c by Lee 4.00
Dark Tower: End-World Almanac (2008, $3.99) guide to locations and inhabitants 4.00

DARK TOWER: THE SORCEROR (Based on Stephen King's Dark Tower)
Marvel Comics: June, 2009 ($3.99, one-shot)

1-Robin Furth-s/Richard Isanove-a/c; the story of Marten Broadcloak 4.00

DARK TOWER: TREACHERY (Based on Stephen King's Dark Tower series)
Marvel Comics: Nov, 2008 - No. 6, Apr, 2009 ($3.99, limited series)

1-6-Peter David & Robin Furth-s/Jae Lee & Richard Isanove-a 4.00
1-Variant cover by Dell'otto 10.00

DARKWING DUCK (TV cartoon) (Also see Cartoon Tales)
Disney Comics: Nov, 1991 - No. 4, Feb, 1992 ($1.50, limited series)

1-4: Adapts hour-long premiere TV episode 3.00

DARKWING DUCK (TV cartoon)
BOOM! Studios (KABOOM!): Jun, 2010 - No. 18, Nov, 2011 ($3.99)

1-Brill-s/Silvani-a; Launchpad McQuack app.; 3 covers 5.00
2-18-Multiple covers on all. 7-Batman #1 cover swipe. 8-Detective #31 cover swipe 4.00
Annual 1 (3/11, $4.99) Three covers; Quackerjack app. 5.00
... Free Comic Book Day Edition (5/11) Flip book with Chip 'N' Dale Rescue Rangers 3.00

DARK WOLVERINE (See Wolverine 2003 series)

DARK X-MEN (See Dark Avengers and the Dark Reign mini-series)
Marvel Comics: Jan, 2010 - No. 5, May, 2010 ($3.99, limited series)

1-5-Cornell-s/Kirk-a. 1-3-Bianchi-c. 1-Nate Grey returns 4.00
...: The Confession (11/09, $3.99) Cansino-a; Paquette-c 4.00

DARK X-MEN: THE BEGINNING (See Dark Avengers and the Dark Reign mini-series)
Marvel Comics: Sept, 2009 - No. 3, Oct, 2009 ($3.99, limited series)

1-3: 1-Cornell-s/Kirk-a; Jae Lee-c on all. 2-Daken app. 3-Mystique app.; Jock-a 4.00

DARLING LOVE
Close Up/Archie Publ. (A Darling Magazine): Oct-Nov, 1949 - No. 11, 1952 (no month) (52 pgs.)(Most photo-c)

	GD 2.0	VG 4.0	FN 6.0	VF 8.0	VF/NM 9.0	NM- 9.2
1-Photo-c	22	44	66	132	216	300
2-Photo-c	14	28	42	80	115	150
3-8,10,11: 3-6-photo-c	12	24	36	67	94	120
9-Krigstein-a	13	26	39	72	101	130

DARLING ROMANCE
Close Up (MLJ Publications): Sept-Oct, 1949 - No. 7, 1951 (All photo-c)

	GD 2.0	VG 4.0	FN 6.0	VF 8.0	VF/NM 9.0	NM- 9.2
1-(52 pgs.)-Photo-c	24	48	72	144	237	330
2	14	28	42	80	115	150
3-7	12	24	36	67	94	120

DARQUE PASSAGES (See Master Darque)
Acclaim (Valiant): April, 1998 ($2.50)

1-Christina Z.-s/Manco-c/a 3.00

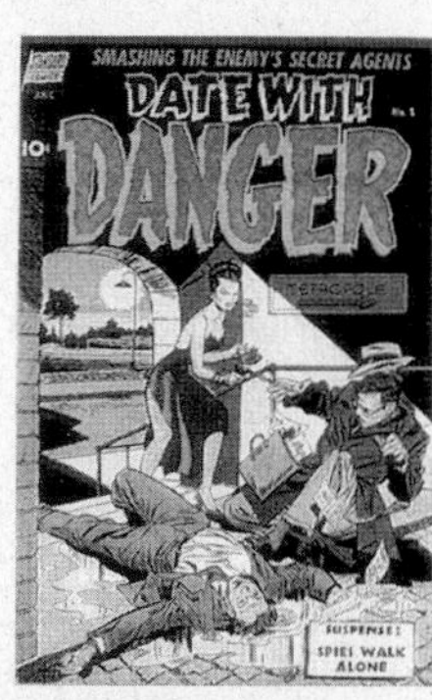

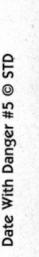

Date With Danger #5 © STD

Dawn of the Dead #1 © MKR Group

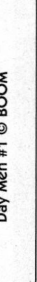

Day Men #1 © BOOM

DART (Also see Freak Force & Savage Dragon)
Image Comics (Highbrow Entertainment): Feb, 1996 - No. 3, May, 1996 ($2.50, lim. series)

	GD 2.0	VG 4.0	FN 6.0	VF 8.0	VF/NM 9.0	NM- 9.2
1-3						3.00

DASTARDLY & MUTTLEY (See Fun-In No. 1-4, 6 and Kite Fun Book)

DATE WITH DANGER
Standard Comics: No. 5, Dec, 1952 - No. 6, Feb, 1953

	GD 2.0	VG 4.0	FN 6.0	VF 8.0	VF/NM 9.0	NM- 9.2
5,6-Secret agent stories: 6-Atom bomb story	9	18	27	52	69	85

DATE WITH DEBBI (Also see Debbi's Dates)
National Periodical Publ.: Jan-Feb, 1969 - No. 17, Sept-Oct, 1971; No. 18, Oct-Nov, 1972

	GD 2.0	VG 4.0	FN 6.0	VF 8.0	VF/NM 9.0	NM- 9.2
1-Teenage	6	12	18	41	76	110
2-5,17-(52 pgs) James Taylor sty.	4	8	12	25	40	55
6-12,18-Last issue	4	8	12	23	37	50
13-16-(68 pgs.): 14-1 pg. story on Jack Wild. 15-Marlo Thomas/"That Girl" story	4	8	12	27	44	60

DATE WITH JUDY, A (Radio/TV, and 1948 movie)
National Periodical Publications: Oct-Nov, 1947 - No. 79, Oct-Nov, 1960 (No. 1-25: 52 pgs.)

	GD 2.0	VG 4.0	FN 6.0	VF 8.0	VF/NM 9.0	NM- 9.2
1-Teenage	31	62	93	182	296	410
2	15	30	45	86	133	180
3-10	14	28	42	76	108	140
11-20	10	20	30	58	79	100
21-40	10	20	30	54	72	90
41-45: 45-Last pre-code (2-3/55)	9	18	27	50	65	80
46-79: 79-Drucker-c/a	8	16	24	44	57	70

DATE WITH MILLIE, A (Life With Millie No. 8 on)(Teenage)
Atlas/Marvel Comics (MPC): Oct, 1956 - No. 7, Aug, 1957; Oct, 1959 - No. 7, Oct, 1960

	GD 2.0	VG 4.0	FN 6.0	VF 8.0	VF/NM 9.0	NM- 9.2
1(10/56)-(1st Series)-Dan DeCarlo-a in #1-7	32	64	96	188	307	425
2	18	36	54	103	162	220
3-7	15	30	45	83	124	165
1(10/59)-(2nd Series)	18	36	54	103	162	220
2-7	12	24	36	69	97	125

DATE WITH PATSY, A (Also see Patsy Walker)
Atlas Comics: Sept, 1957 (One-shot)

	GD 2.0	VG 4.0	FN 6.0	VF 8.0	VF/NM 9.0	NM- 9.2
1-Starring Patsy Walker	14	28	42	82	121	160

DAUGHTERS OF THE DRAGON (See Heroes For Hire)
Marvel Comics: 2005; Mar, 2006 - No. 6, Aug, 2006 ($2.99, limited series)

	GD 2.0	VG 4.0	FN 6.0	VF 8.0	VF/NM 9.0	NM- 9.2
1-6-Palmiotti & Gray-s/Evans-a. 1-Rhino app. 5,6-Iron Fist app.						3.00
... Deadly Hands Special (2005, $3.99) reprints app. from Deadly Hands of Kung Fu #32,33 & Bizarre Adventures #25; Claremont-s/Rogers-a; new Rogers-c & interview						4.00
...: Samurai Bullets TPB (2006, $15.99) r/#1-6						16.00

DAVID AND GOLIATH (Movie)
Dell Publishing Co.: No. 1205, July, 1961

	GD 2.0	VG 4.0	FN 6.0	VF 8.0	VF/NM 9.0	NM- 9.2
Four Color 1205-Photo-c	6	12	18	38	69	100

DAVID BORING (See Eightball)
Pantheon Books: 2000 ($24.95, hardcover w/dust jacket)

	GD 2.0	VG 4.0	FN 6.0	VF 8.0	VF/NM 9.0	NM- 9.2
Hardcover - reprints David Boring stories from Eightball; Clowes-s/a						25.00

DAVID CASSIDY (TV)(See Partridge Family, Swing With Scooter #33 & Time For Love #30)
Charlton Comics: Feb, 1972 - No. 14, Sept, 1973

	GD 2.0	VG 4.0	FN 6.0	VF 8.0	VF/NM 9.0	NM- 9.2
1-Most have photo covers	6	12	18	38	69	100
2-5	4	8	12	25	40	55
6-14	4	8	12	23	37	50

DAVID LADD'S LIFE STORY (See Movie Classics)

DAVY CROCKETT (See Dell Giants, Fightin..., Frontier Fighters, It's Game Time, Power Record Comics, Western Tales & Wild Frontier)

DAVY CROCKETT (Frontier Fighter...)
Avon Periodicals: 1951

	GD 2.0	VG 4.0	FN 6.0	VF 8.0	VF/NM 9.0	NM- 9.2
nn-Tuska?, Reinman-a; Fawcette-c	18	36	54	107	169	230

DAVY CROCKETT (...King of the Wild Frontier No. 1,2)(TV)
Dell Publishing Co./Gold Key: 5/55 - No. 671, 12/55; No. 1, 12/63; No. 2, 11/69 (Walt Disney)

	GD 2.0	VG 4.0	FN 6.0	VF 8.0	VF/NM 9.0	NM- 9.2
Four Color 631(#1)-Fess Parker photo-c	14	28	42	96	211	325
Four Color 639-Photo-c	11	22	33	76	163	260
Four Color 664,671(Marsh-a)-Photo-c	11	22	33	75	160	245
1(12/63-Gold Key)-Fess Parker photo-c; reprints	7	14	21	46	86	125
2(11/69)-Fess Parker photo-c; reprints	4	8	12	28	44	60

DAVY CROCKETT (...Frontier Fighter #1,2; Kid Montana #9 on)
Charlton Comics: Aug, 1955 - No. 8, Jan, 1957

	GD 2.0	VG 4.0	FN 6.0	VF 8.0	VF/NM 9.0	NM- 9.2
1	10	20	30	58	79	100
2	7	14	21	37	46	55
3-8	6	12	18	28	34	40

DAWN
Sirius Entertainment/Image Comics: June, 1995 - No. 6, 1996 ($2.95)

	GD 2.0	VG 4.0	FN 6.0	VF 8.0	VF/NM 9.0	NM- 9.2
1/2-w/certificate	1	2	3	5	6	8
1/2-Variant-c	2	4	6	10	14	18
1-Linsner-c/a	1	2	3	5	6	8
1-Black Light Edition	2	4	6	9	13	16
1-White Trash Edition	3	6	9	16	23	30
1-Look Sharp Edition	3	6	9	18	28	38
2-4: Linsner-c/a						4.50
2-Variant-c, 3-Limited Edition	2	4	6	13	18	22
4-6-Vibrato-c						3.50
4, 5-Limited Edition	2	4	6	8	10	12
6-Limited Edition	2	4	6	8	10	12
...Convention Sketchbook (Image Comics, 2002, $2.95) pin-ups						3.00
...2003 Convention Sketchbook (Image Comics, 3/03, $2.95) pin-ups						3.00
...2004 Convention Sketchbook (Image Comics, 4/04, $2.95) pin-ups						3.00
...2005 Convention Sketchbook (Image Comics, 5/05, $2.95) pin-ups						3.00
Genesis Edition ('99, Wizard supplement) previews Return of the Goddess						3.00
Lucifer's Halo TPB (11/97, $19.95) r/Drama, Dawn #1-6 plus 12 pages of new artwork						20.00
...: Not to Touch The Earth (9/10, $5.99) Linsner-s/c/a; pin-ups by various incl. Turner						6.00
...: Tenth Anniversary Special (9/99, $2.95) Interviews						3.00
The Portable Dawn ($9.95, 5"x4", 64 pgs.) Pocket-sized cover gallery						10.00
...: The Swordmaster's Daughter & Other Stories (2013, $3.99) Linsner-s/c/a						4.00

DAWN OF THE DEAD (George A. Romaro's...)
IDW Publishing: Apr, 2004 - No. 3, Jun, 2004 ($3.99, limited series)

	GD 2.0	VG 4.0	FN 6.0	VF 8.0	VF/NM 9.0	NM- 9.2
1-3-Adaptation of the 2004 movie; Niles-s						4.00
TPB (9/04, $17.99) r/#1-3; intro. by George A. Romero						18.00

DAWN: THE RETURN OF THE GODDESS
Sirius Entertainment: Apr, 1999 - No. 4, July, 2000 ($2.95, limited series)

	GD 2.0	VG 4.0	FN 6.0	VF 8.0	VF/NM 9.0	NM- 9.2
1-4-Linsner-s/a						3.00
TPB (4/02, $12.95) r/#1-4; intro. by Linsner						13.00

DAWN: THREE TIERS
Image Comics: Jun, 2003 - No. 6, Aug, 2005 ($2.95, limited series)

	GD 2.0	VG 4.0	FN 6.0	VF 8.0	VF/NM 9.0	NM- 9.2
1-6-Linsner-s/a. 2-Preview of Vampire's Christmas						3.00

DAYDREAMERS (See Generation X)
Marvel Comics: Aug, 1997 - No. 3, Oct, 1997 ($2.50, limited series)

	GD 2.0	VG 4.0	FN 6.0	VF 8.0	VF/NM 9.0	NM- 9.2
1-3-Franklin Richards, Howard the Duck, Man-Thing app.						3.00

DAY MEN
BOOM! Studios: Jul, 2013 - Present ($3.99)

	GD 2.0	VG 4.0	FN 6.0	VF 8.0	VF/NM 9.0	NM- 9.2
1-Stelfreeze-a/c; Gagnon & Nelson-s						5.00
2,3: 2-Covers by Stelfreeze & Pérez						4.00

DAY OF JUDGMENT
DC Comics: Nov, 1999 - No. 5, Nov, 1999 ($2.95/$2.50, limited series)

	GD 2.0	VG 4.0	FN 6.0	VF 8.0	VF/NM 9.0	NM- 9.2
1-($2.95) Spectre possessed; Matt Smith-a						3.00
2-5: Parallax returns. 5-Hal Jordan becomes the Spectre						3.00
...Secret Files 1 (11/99, $4.95) Harris-c						5.00

DAY OF VENGEANCE (Prelude to Infinite Crisis)(Also see Birds of Prey #76 for 1st app. of Black Alice)
DC Comics: June, 2005 - No. 6, Nov, 2005 ($2.50, limited series)

	GD 2.0	VG 4.0	FN 6.0	VF 8.0	VF/NM 9.0	NM- 9.2
1-6: 1-Jean Loring becomes Eclipso; Spectre, Ragman, Enchantress, Detective Chimp, Shazam app.; Justiniano-a. 2,3-Capt. Marvel app. 4-6-Black Alice app.						3.00
...: Infinite Crisis Special 1 (3/06, $4.99) Justiniano-a/Simonson-c						5.00
TPB (2005, $12.99) r/series & Action #826, Advs. of Superman #639, Superman #216						13.00

DAYS OF THE DEFENDERS (See Defenders, The)
Marvel Comics: Mar, 2001 ($3.50, one-shot)

	GD 2.0	VG 4.0	FN 6.0	VF 8.0	VF/NM 9.0	NM- 9.2
1-Reprints early team-ups of members, incl. Marvel Feature #1; Larsen-c						3.50

DAYS OF THE MOB (See In the Days of the Mob)

DAYTRIPPER
DC Comics (Vertigo): Feb, 2010 - No. 10, Nov, 2010 ($2.99, limited series)

	GD 2.0	VG 4.0	FN 6.0	VF 8.0	VF/NM 9.0	NM- 9.2
1-10-Gabriel Bá & Fábio Moon-s/a						3.00
TPB (2010, $19.99) r/#1-10; sketch art pages						20.00

DAZEY'S DIARY
Dell Publishing Co.: June-Aug, 1962

Dazzler #35 © MAR

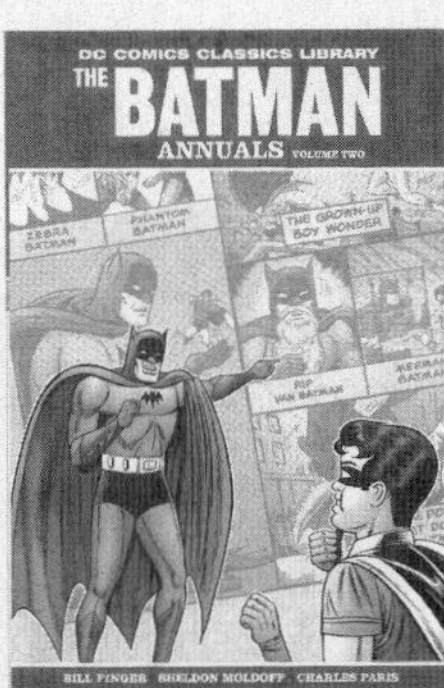

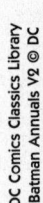

DC Comics Classics Library Batman Annuals V2 © DC

DC Comics Presents: Green Lantern #1 © DC

GD	VG	FN	VF	VF/NM	NM-
2.0	4.0	6.0	8.0	9.0	9.2

01-174-208: Bill Woggon-c/a 4 8 12 27 44 60

DAZZLER, THE (Also see Marvel Graphic Novel & X-Men #130)
Marvel Comics Group: Mar, 1981 - No. 42, Mar, 1986

1,21,22,24,27,28,38,42: 1-X-Men app. 21-Double size; photo-c. 22 (12/82)-vs. Rogue Battle-c/sty. 24-Full app. Rogue w/Powerman (Iron Fist). 27-Rogue app. 28-Full app. Rogue; Mystique app. 38-Wolverine-c/app.; X-Men app. 42-Beast-c/app. 4.00
2-20,23,25,26,29-32,34-37,39-41: 2-X-Men app. 10,11-Galactus app. 23-Rogue/Mystique 1 pg. app. 26-Jusko-c. 40-Secret Wars II 3.00
33-Michael Jackson "Thriller" swipe-c/sty 4.00
One-shot (7/10, $3.99) Andrasofszky-a/c; Arcade app. 4.00
NOTE: *No. 1 distributed only through comic shops.* ***Alcala*** *a-1i, 2i.* ***Chadwick*** *a-38-42p; c(p)-39, 41, 42.* ***Guice*** *a-38i, 42i; c-38, 40.*

DC CHALLENGE (Most DC superheroes appear)
DC Comics: Nov, 1985 - No. 12, Oct, 1986 ($1.25/$2.00, maxi-series)

1-11: 1-Colan-a. 2,8-Batman-c/app. 4-Gil Kane-c/a 3.00
12-($2.00-c) Giant; low print 4.00
NOTE: *Batman app. in 1-4, 6-12. Joker app. in 7.* ***Infantino*** *a-3.* ***Ordway*** *c-12.* ***Swan/Austin*** *c-10.*

DC COMICS CLASSICS LIBRARY (Hardcover collections of classic DC stories)
DC Comics: 2009 - Present ($39.99, hardcover with dustjacket)

Batman: A Death in the Family ('09)- r/Batman #426-429, 440-442, New Titans #60,61 40.00
Batman Annuals ('09)- r/Batman Annual #1-3; afterword by Richard Bruning 40.00
Batman Annuals Volume 2 ('10)- r/Batman Annual #4-7; intro. by Michael Uslan 40.00
Flash of Two Worlds ('09)- r/Flash #123,129,137,151,170&173 team-ups with G.A. Flash 40.00
Justice League of America by George Pérez ('09) r/J.L.of A. #184-186, 192-194 40.00
Justice League of America by George Pérez Vol. 2 ('10) r/J.L.of A. #195-197,200 40.00
Legion of Super-Heroes: The Life and Death of Ferro Lad ('09) - r/Adventure Comics # 346, 347,352-355,357; intro. by Paul Levitz; afterword by Jim Shooter 40.00
Roots of the Swamp Thing ('09)- r/House of Secrets #92 & Swamp Thing #1-13; Wein intro. 40.00
Superman: Kryptonite Nevermore ('09)- r/Superman #233-238,240-242; afterword by Denny O'Neil 40.00

DC COMICS ESSENTIALS
DC Comics: ($1.00, flipbooks with DC Graphic Novel catalog of recommended titles)

...: Action Comics #1 (2/14, $1.00) Reprints Action #1 (2011) with flipbook of DC GNs 3.00
...: Batman #1 (12/13, $1.00) Reprints Batman #1 (2011) with flipbook of DC GNs 3.00
...: Green Lantern #1 (1/14, $1.00) Reprints Green Lantern #1 (2011) with flipbook 3.00
...: Justice League #1 (1/14, $1.00) Reprints Justice League #1 (2011) with flipbook 3.00
...: Watchmen #1 (2/14, $1.00) Reprints Watchmen #1 (1986) with flipbook 3.00
...: Wonder Woman #1 (12/13, $1.00) Reprints Wonder Woman #1 (2011) with flipbook 3.00

DC COMICS MEGA SAMPLER
DC Comics: 2009; Jul, 2010 (6-1/4" x 9-1/2", FCBD giveaways)

1, 2010- Short stories of kid-friendly titles; Tiny Titans, Billy Batson, Super Friends app. 3.00

DC COMICS PRESENTS
DC Comics: July-Aug, 1978 - No. 97, Sept, 1986 (Superman team-ups in all)

1-4th Superman/Flash race 4 8 12 28 47 65
1-(Whitman variant) 5 10 15 31 53 75
2-Part 2 of Superman/Flash race 3 6 9 15 22 28
2-(Whitman variant) 3 6 9 17 26 35
3,4,9-12,14-16,19,21,22-(Whitman variants, low print run, none have issue # on cover) 3 6 9 14 20 25
3-10: 3-Adam Strange. 4-Metal Men. 5-Aquaman. 6-Green Lantern. 7-Red Tornado. 8-Swamp Thing. 9-Wonder Woman. 10-Sgt. Rock 2 4 6 8 10 12
11-25,27-40: 12-Mister Miracle. 13-Legion of Super-Heroes. 19-Batgirl. 21-Elongated Man. 23-Dr. Fate. 24-Deadman. 30-Black Canary. 31-Robin. 34-Marvel Family. 35-Man-Bat. 36-Starman. 37-Hawkgirl. 38-The Flash 6.00
26-(10/80)-Green Lantern; intro Cyborg, Starfire, Raven (1st app. New Teen Titans in 16 pg. preview); Starlin-c/a; Sargon the Sorcerer back-up 5 10 15 34 60 85
41,72,77,78,97: 41-Superman/Joker-c/story. 72-Joker/Phantom Stranger-c/story. 77,78-Animal Man app. (77-c also). 97-Phantom Zone 6.00
42-46,48-50,52-71,73-76,79-83: 42-Sandman. 43,80-Legion of Super-Heroes. 52-Doom Patrol; 1st app. Ambush Bug. 58-Robin. 82-Adam Strange. 83-Batman & Outsiders 4.00
47-He-Man-c/s (1st app. in comics) 3 6 9 17 26 35
51-Preview insert (16 pgs.) of He-Man (2nd app.) 2 4 6 9 12 15
84-Challengers of the Unknown; Kirby-c/s. 6.00
85-Swamp Thing; Alan Moore scripts 6.00
86,88-96: 86-88-Crisis x-over. 88-Creeper 4.00
87-Origin/1st app. Superboy of Earth Prime 1 3 4 6 8 10
Annual 1,4: 1(9/82)-G.A. Superman; 1st app. Alexander Luthor. 4(10/85)-Superwoman 4.00
Annual 2,3: 2(7/83)-Intro/origin Superwoman. 3(9/84)-Shazam 4.00
NOTE: ***Adkins*** *a-2, 54; c-2.* ***Buckler*** *a-33, 34; c-30, 33, 34.* ***Giffen*** *a-39; c-59.* ***Gil Kane*** *a-28, 35, Annual 3; c-48p, 56, 58, 60, 62, 64, 68, Annual 2, 3.* ***Kirby*** *c/a-84.* ***Kubert*** *c/a-66.* ***Morrow*** *c/a-65.* ***Newton*** *c/a-54p.* ***Orlando*** *c-53i.* ***Perez*** *a-26p, 61p; c-38, 61, 94.* ***Starlin*** *a-26-29p, 36p, 37p; c-26-29, 36, 37, 93.* ***Toth*** *a-84.* ***Williamson*** *i-79, 85, 87.*

GD	VG	FN	VF	VF/NM	NM-
2.0	4.0	6.0	8.0	9.0	9.2

DC COMICS PRESENTS: ...(Julie Schwartz tribute series of one-shots based on classic covers)
DC Comics: Sept, 2004 - Oct, 2004 ($2.50)

The Atom -(Based on cover of Atom #10) Gibbons-s/Oliffe-a; Waid-s/Jurgens-a; Bolland-c 3.00
Batman -(Batman #183) Johns-s/Infantino-a; Wein-s/Kuhn-a; Hughes-c 3.00
The Flash -(Flash #163) Loeb-s/McGuinness-a; O'Neil-s/Mahnke-a; Ross-c 3.00
Green Lantern -(Green Lantern #31) Azzarello-s/Breyfogle-a; Pasko-s/McDaniel-a; Bolland-c 3.00
Hawkman -(Hawkman #6) Bates-s/Byrne-a; Busiek-s/Simonson-a; Garcia-Lopez-c 3.00
Justice League of America -(J.L. of A. #53) Ellison & David-s/Giella-a; Wolfman-s/Nguyen-a; Garcia-Lopez-c 3.00
Mystery in Space -(M.I.S. #82) Maggin-s/Williams-a; Morrison-s/Ordway-a; Ross-c 3.00
Superman -(Superman #264) Stan Lee-s/Cooke-a; Levitz-s/Giffen-a; Hughes-c 3.00

DC COMICS PRESENTS: ...
DC Comics: Dec, 2010 - Present ($7.99, squarebound, one-shot reprints)

The Atom 1 (3/11) r/Legends of the DC Universe #28,29,40,41; Gil Kane-a 8.00
Batman 1 (12/10) r/Batman #582-585,600 8.00
Batman 2 (1/11) r/Batman #591-594 8.00
Batman 3 (2/11) r/Batman #595-598 8.00
Batman: Arkham 1 (6/11) r/Batman Chronicles #6, Batman; Arkham Asylum - Tales of Madness #1, Batman Villains Secret Files #1 & Justice Leagues: J.L. of Arkham #1 8.00
Batman - Bad 1 (1/12) r/Batman: Legends of the D.K. #146-148 8.00
Batman Beyond 1 (2/11) r/Batman Beyond #13,14,21,22 8.00
Batman: Blaze of Glory 1 (2/12) r/Batman: Legends of the D.K. #197-199,212 8.00
Batman - Blink 1 (12/11) r/Batman: Legends of the D.K. #156-158 8.00
Batman/Catwoman 1 (12/10) r/Batman and Catwoman: Trail of the Gun 8.00
Batman - Conspiracy 1 (4/11) r/Batman: Legends of the D.K. #86-88; Detective #821 8.00
Batman - Dark Knight, Dark City 1 (7/11) r/Batman #452-454; Detective #633 8.00
Batman - Don't Blink 1 (1/12) r/Batman: Legends of the D.K. #164-167 8.00
Batman: Gotham Noir 1 (9/11) r/Batman: Gotham Noir #1 & Batman #604 8.00
Batman - Irresistible 1 (5/11) r/Batman: Legends of the D.K. #169-171; Hourman #22 8.00
Batman - The Demon Laughs 1 (12/11) r/Batman: Legends of the D.K. #142-145; Aparo-a 8.00
Batman: The Secret City 1 (2/12) r/Batman: Legends of the D.K. #180,181,190,191 8.00
Batman: Urban Legends 1 (2/12) r/Batman: Legends of the D.K. #168,177-179 8.00
Brightest Day 1 (12/10) r/Strange Advs. #205, Hawkman #27,34,36, Solo #8, DC Hol. '09 8.00
Brightest Day 2 (1/11) r/Firestorm #11-13 & Martian Manhuner #11,24 8.00
Brightest Day 3 (2/11) r/Legends of the DC Univ. #25-27 & Teen Titans #27,28 8.00
Captain Atom 1 (2/12) r/back-up stories from Action Comics #879-889 8.00
Catwoman - Guardian of Gotham 1 (12/11) r/Catwoman: Guardian of Gotham #1,2 8.00
Chase 1 (1/11) r/Chase #1,6-8 8.00
Elseworlds 80-Page Giant 1 (1/12) r/Elseworlds 80-Page Giant (pulled from distribution) 8.00
Flash 1 (7/11) r/Showcase #4,14 and Flash #125,130,139 8.00
Flash/Green Lantern: Faster Friends (1/11) r/G.L./Flash: Faster Friends & Flash/G.L. : FF 8.00
Green Lantern 1 (12/10) r/Green Lantern #137-140 (2001) 8.00
Green Lantern - Fear Itself 1 (4/11) r/Green Lantern: Fear Itself GN 8.00
Green Lantern - Willworld 1 (7/11) r/Green Lantern: Willworld GN 8.00
Harley Quinn 1 (4/14) r/Batman: Harley Quinn #1, Joker's Asylum II: HQ #1 and others 8.00
Impulse 1 (8/11) r/Impulse #50-53 8.00
Jack Kirby Omnibus Sampler 1 (12/11) r/Kirby art stories from 1957,1958 8.00
JLA 1 (2/11) r/JLA #90-93 8.00
JLA - Age of Wonder 1 (12/11) r/JLA: Age of Wonder 8.00
JLA: Black Baptism 1 (8/11) r/JLA: Black Baptism #1-4 8.00
JLA Heaven's Ladder 1 (10/11) comic-sized reprint; and r/Green Lantern #1,000,000 8.00
Legion of Super-Heroes 1 (6/11) r/Legion of Super-Heroes #122,123 & Legionnaires 79,80 8.00
Legion of Super-Heroes 2 (2/12) r/Adv. #247 and recent Legion short stories 8.00
Lobo 1 (3/11) r/Lobo #63,64 & DC First: Superman/Lobo #1 8.00
Metal Men 1 (4/11) r/Doom Patrol ('09) #1-7 and Silver Age: The Brave and the Bold #1 8.00
Night Force 1 (4/11) r/Night Force #1-4; Gene Colan-a 8.00
Ninja Boy 1 (6/11) r/Ninja Boy #1-4 8.00
Shazam! 1,2 (9/11,10/11) 1-r/Power of Shazam #38-41. 2-r/ #42-46 8.00
Son of Superman 1 (7/11) r/Son of Superman GN 8.00
Superboy's Legion 1 (12/11) r/Superboy's Legion #1,2 (Elseworlds) 8.00
Superman 1 (12/10) r/Superman: The Man of Steel #121 & Superman #179,180,185 8.00
Superman 2 (1/11) r/Action #798, Superman: The Man of Steel #133, Superman #189 & Advs. of Superman #611 8.00
Superman 3 (2/11) r/Superman #177,178,181,182 8.00
Superman 4 (9/11) r/Action #768,771-773 8.00
Superman Adventures 1 (8/12) r/Superman Adventures #16,19,22,23 8.00
Superman/Doomsday 1 (5/11) r/Doomsday Annual #1 & Superman #175 8.00
Superman - Infestation 1 (8/11) r/Action #778, Advs. of Superman #591, Superman #169 and Superman: The Man of Steel #113 8.00
Superman - Secret Identity 1 (12/11) r/Superman: Secret Identity #1,2 8.00
Superman - Secret Identity 2 (1/12) r/Superman: Secret Identity #3,4 8.00
Superman - Sole Survivor 1 (3/11) r/Legends of the DC Universe #1-3,39 8.00
Superman - The Kents 1,2 (1/12, 2/12) 1-r/The Kents #1-4. 2-The Kents #5-8 8.00

DC Countdown #1 © DC

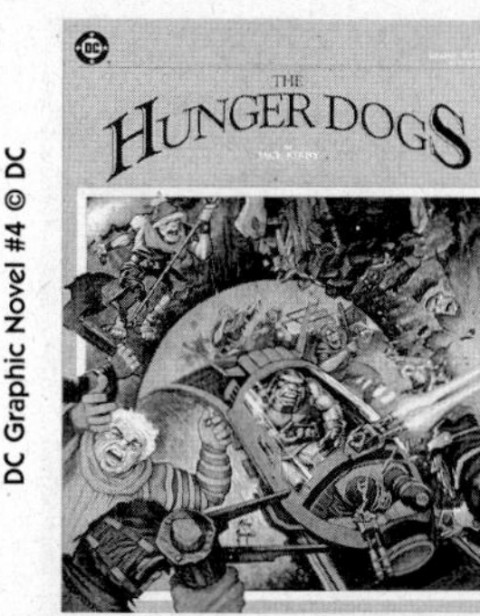

DC Graphic Novel #4 © DC

DC One Million #4 © DC

GD VG FN VF VF/NM NM-
2.0 4.0 6.0 8.0 9.0 9.2

Teen Titans 1 (10/11) Teen Titans Lost Annual #1 and Solo #7; Allred-a 8.00
The Life Story of the Flash 1 (1/12) r/The Life Story of the Flash GN 8.00
T.H.U.N.D.E.R. Agents 1 (2/11) r/T.H.U.N.D.E.R. Agents #1,2,7 (1966) 8.00
Wonder Woman 1 (4/11) r/Wonder Woman #139-142 (1998) 8.00
Wonder Woman Adventures 1 (9/12) r/Advs. in the DC Universe #1,3,11,19 8.00
Young Justice 1 (12/10) r/JLA World Without Grownups #1,2 8.00
Young Justice 2 (1/11) r/Y.J: The Secret, Y.J. Secret Files #1, Y.J. In No Man's Land 8.00
Young Justice 3 (2/11) r/Young Justice #7 & Y.J Secret Origins 80-Page Giant #1 8.00

DC COMICS - THE NEW 52 FCBD SPECIAL EDITION
DC Comics: Jun, 2012 (giveaway one-shot)

1-Origin of The Trinity of Sin (Pandora, The Question, Phantom Stranger); Justice League app.; Jim Lee, Reis, Ha, Rocafort-a; previews Earth 2, G.I. Combat, Ravagers 3.00

DC COMICS THE NEW 52 PRESENTS: ...
DC Comics: Mar, 2012 - Present ($7.99, squarebound, one-shot reprints)

The Dark 1 (3/12) r/Animal Man #1, Swamp Thing #1, I, Vampire #1, and J.L. Dark #1 8.00

DC COUNTDOWN (To Infinite Crisis)
DC Comics: May, 2005 ($1.00, 80 pages, one-shot)

1-Death of Blue Beetle; prelude to OMAC Project, Day of Vengeance, Rann/Thanagar War and Villains United mini-series; s/a by various; Jim Lee/Alex Ross-c 4.00

DC FIRST: ...(series of one-shots)
DC Comics: July, 2002 ($3.50)

Batgirl/Joker 1-Sienkiewicz & Terry Moore-a; Nowlan-c 3.50
Green Lantern/Green Lantern 1-Alan Scott & Hal Jordan vs. Krona 3.50
Flash/Superman 1-Superman races Jay Garrick; Abra Kadabra app. 3.50
Superman/Lobo 1-Giffen-s; Nowlan-c 3.50

DC GOES APE
DC Comics: 2008 ($19.99, trade paperback)

Vol. 1 - Reprints app. of Grodd, Beppo, Titano and other monkey tales; Art Adams-c 20.00

DC GRAPHIC NOVEL (Also see DC Science Fiction...)
DC Comics: Nov, 1983 - No. 7, 1986 ($5.95, 68 pgs.)

1-3,5,7: 1-Star Raiders. 2-Warlords; not from regular Warlord series. 3-The Medusa Chain; Ernie Colon story/a. 5-Me and Joe Priest; Chaykin-c. 7-Space Clusters; Nino-c/a
2 4 6 9 12 15
4-The Hunger Dogs by Kirby; Darkseid kills Himon from Mister Miracle & destroys New Genesis 5 10 15 31 53 75
6-Metalzoic; Sienkiewicz-c ($6.95) 2 4 6 9 12 15

DC HOLIDAY SPECIAL '09
DC Comics: Feb, 2010 ($5.99, one-shot)

1-Christmas short stories by various incl. Dragotta, Tucci, Chaykin; Dustin Nguyen-c 6.00

DC INFINITE HALLOWEEN SPECIAL
DC Comics: Dec, 2007 ($5.99, one-shot)

1-Halloween short stories by various incl. Dini, Waid, Hairsine, Kelley Jones; Gene Ha-c 6.00

DC KIDS MEGA SAMPLER
DC Comics: June, 2009 (Free Comic Book Day giveaway, one-shot)

1-Tiny Titans, Batman: The Brave and the Bold, Billy Batson/Shazam short stories 3.00

DC/MARVEL: ALL ACCESS (Also see DC Versus Marvel & Marvel Versus DC)
DC Comics: 1996 - No. 4, 1997 ($2.95, limited series)

1-4: 1-Superman & Spider-Man app. 2-Robin & Jubilee app. 3-Dr. Strange & Batman-c/app., X-Men, JLA app. 4-X-Men vs. JLA-c/app. rebirth of Amalgam 3.00

DC/MARVEL: CROSSOVER CLASSICS
DC Comics: 1998; 2003 ($14.95, TPB)

Vol. II-Reprints Batman/Punisher: Lake of Fire, Punisher/Batman: Deadly Knights, Silver Surfer/Superman, Batman & Capt. America 15.00
Vol. 4 (2003, $14.95) Reprints Green Lantern/Silver Surfer: Unholy Alliances, Darkseid/Galactus: The Hunger, Batman & Spider-Man, and Superman/Fantastic Four 15.00

DC NATION FCBD SUPER SAMPLER
DC Comics: (Giveaway)

.../ Superman Adventures Flip Book (6/12) stories from Superman Family Adventures, Young Justice, Green Lantern: The Animated Series 3.00
... (7/13) Stories from Beware the Batman and Teen Titans Go! 3.00

DC 100 PAGE SUPER SPECTACULAR
(Title is 100 Page... No. 14 on)(Square bound) (Reprints, 50¢)
National Periodical Publications: No. 4, Summer, 1971 - No. 13, 6/72; No. 14, 2/73 - No. 22, 11/73 (No #1-3)

4-Weird Mystery Tales; Johnny Peril & Phantom Stranger; cover & splashes by Wrightson; origin Jungle Boy of Jupiter 23 46 69 161 356 550
5-Love Stories; Wood inks (7 pgs.)(scarcer) 46 92 138 340 770 1200
6- "World's Greatest Super-Heroes"; JLA, JSA, Spectre, Johnny Quick, Vigilante & Hawkman; contains unpublished Wildcat story; N. Adams wrap-around-c; r/JLA #21,22
17 34 51 119 265 410
6-Replica Edition (2004, $6.95) complete reprint w/wraparound-c 7.00
7-(Also listed as Superman #245) Air Wave, Kid Eternity, Hawkman-r; Atom-r/Atom #3
9 18 27 60 120 180
8-(Also listed as Batman #238) Batman, Legion, Aquaman-r; G.A. Atom, Sargon (r/Sensation #57), Plastic Man (r/Police #14) stories; Doom Patrol origin-r; Neal Adams wraparound-c 12 24 36 82 179 275
9-(Also listed as Our Army at War #242) Kubert-c 9 18 27 58 114 170
10-(Also listed as Adventure Comics #416) Golden Age-reprints; r/1st app. Black Canary from Flash #86; no Zatanna 10 20 30 68 144 220
11-(Also listed as Flash #214) origin Metal Men-r/Showcase #37; never before published G.A. Flash story. 8 16 24 54 102 150
12,14: 12-(Also listed as Superboy #185) Legion-c/story; Teen Titans, Kid Eternity (r/Hit #46), Star Spangled Kid-r(S.S. #55). 14-Batman-r/Detective #31,32,156; Atom-r/Showcase #34
7 14 21 46 86 125
13-(Also listed as Superman #252) Ray(r/Smash #17), Black Condor, (r/Crack #18), Hawkman(r/Flash #24); Starman-r/Adv. #67; Dr. Fate & Spectre-r/More Fun #57; Neal Adams-c 10 20 30 66 138 210
15,16,18,19,21,22: 15-r/2nd Boy Commandos/Det. #64. 16-Sgt. Rock. 18-Superman. 21-Superboy; r/Brave & the Bold #54. 22-r/All-Flash #13
6 12 18 37 66 95
17,20: 17-JSA-r/All Star #37 (10-11/47, 38 pgs.), Sandman-r/Adv. #65 (8/41), JLA #23 (11/63) & JLA #43 (3/66). 20-Batman-r/Det. #66,68, Spectre; origin Two-Face
6 12 18 38 69 100
... : Love Stories Replica Edition (2000, $6.95) reprints #5 7.00

NOTE: ***Anderson*** *r-11, 14, 18i, 22.* ***B. Baily*** *r-18, 20.* ***Burnley*** *r-18, 20.* ***Crandall*** *r-14p, 20.* ***Drucker*** *r-4.* ***Grandenetti*** *a-22(2)r.* ***Heath*** *a-22r.* ***Infantino*** *r-17, 20, 22.* ***G. Kane*** *r-18.* ***Kirby*** *r-15.* ***Kubert*** *r-6, 7, 16, 17; c-16, 19.* ***Manning*** *a-19r.* ***Meskin*** *r-4, 22.* ***Mooney*** *r-15, 21.* ***Toth*** *r-17, 20.*

DC ONE MILLION (Also see crossover #1,000,000 issues and JLA One Million TPB)
DC Comics: Nov, 1998 - No. 4, Nov, 1998 ($2.95/$1.99, weekly lim. series)

1-($2.95) JLA travels to the 853rd century; Morrison-s 4.00
2-4-($1.99) 3.00
... Eighty-Page Giant (8/99, $4.95) 5.00
TPB ('99, $14.95) r/#1-4 and several x-over stories 15.00

DC RETROACTIVE (New stories done in old style plus reprint from decade)
DC Comics: Sept, 2011 - Oct, 2011 ($4.99, series of one-shots)

...: Batman - The '70s (9/11, $4.99) Len Wein-s/Tom Mandrake-a; r/Batman #307 5.00
...: Batman - The '80s (10/11, $4.99) Mike Barr-s/Jerry Bingham-a; The Reaper app. 5.00
...: Batman - The '90s (10/11, $4.99) Grant-s/Breyfogle-a; Scarface & Ventriloquist app. 5.00
...: Flash - The '70s (9/11, $4.99) Bates-s/Gallego-a; r/DC Comics Presents #1,2 5.00
...: Flash - The '80s (10/11, $4.99) Messner-Loebs-s/LaRocque-a; r/Flash v2 #18 5.00
...: Flash - The '90s (10/11, $4.99) Augustyn-s/Bowden-a; r/Flash v2 #142 5.00
...: Green Lantern - The '70s (9/11, $4.99) O'Neil-s/Grell-a; r/Green Lantern #76 5.00
...: Green Lantern - The '80s (10/11, $4.99) Wein-s/Staton-a; r/Green Lantern #172 5.00
...: Green Lantern - The '90s (10/11, $4.99) Marz-s/Banks-a; r/Green Lantern v3 #78 5.00
...: JLA - The '70s (9/11, $4.99) Bates-s; Adam Strange app.; r/J.L. of A. #123 5.00
...: JLA - The '80s (10/11, $4.99) Conway-s/Randall-a; Felix Faust app.; r/J.L.of A. #239 5.00
...: JLA - The '90s (10/11, $4.99) Giffen & DeMatteis-s/Maguire-a; r/J.L.A. #6 5.00
...: Superman - The '70s (9/11, $4.99) Pasko-s/Barreto-a; r/Action Comics #484 5.00
...: Superman - The '80s (10/11, $4.99) Wolfman-s/Cariello-a; r/Superman #352 5.00
...: Superman - The '90s (10/11, $4.99) L. Simonson-s/Bogdanove-a; Guardian app. 5.00
...: Wonder Woman - The '70s (9/11, $4.99) O'Neil-s/J. Bone-a; r/Wonder Woman #201 5.00
...: Wonder Woman - The '80s (10/11, $4.99) Thomas-s/Buckler-a; r/W.W. #288 5.00
...: Wonder Woman - The '90s (10/11, $4.99) Messner-Loebs-s/Moder-a; r/W.W. v2 #66 5.00

DC SCIENCE FICTION GRAPHIC NOVEL
DC Comics: 1985 - No. 7, 1987 ($5.95)

SF1-SF7: SF1-Hell on Earth by Robert Bloch; Giffen-p. SF2-Nightwings by Robert Silverberg; G. Colan-p. SF3-Frost & Fire by Bradbury. SF4-Merchants of Venus. SF5-Demon With A Glass Hand by Ellison; M. Rogers-a. SF6-The Magic Goes Away by Niven. SF7-Sandkings by George R.R. Martin 2 4 6 8 11 14

DC SILVER AGE CLASSICS
DC Comics: 1992 ($1.00, all reprints)

...Action Comics #252-r/1st Supergirl. Adventure Comics #247-r/1st Legion of Super-Heroes. The Brave and the Bold #28-r/1st JLA. Detective Comics #225-r/1st Martian Manhunter. Detective Comics #327-r/1st new look Batman. Green Lantern #76-r/1st Green Lantern/Green Arrow. House of Secrets #92-r/1st Swamp Thing. Showcase #4-r/1st S.A. Flash. Showcase #22-r/1st S.A. Green Lantern 4.00
...Sugar and Spike #99; includes 2 unpublished stories 5.00

DC SPECIAL (Also see Super DC Giant)

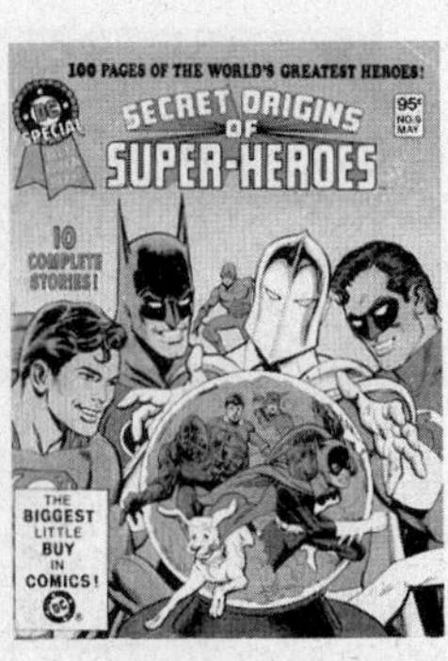
DC Special Blue Ribbon Digest #9 © DC

DC Special Series #22 © DC

DC Super-Stars #7 © DC

GD VG FN VF VF/NM NM-
2.0 4.0 6.0 8.0 9.0 9.2

National Per. Publ.: 10-12/68 - No. 15, 11-12/71; No. 16, Spr/75 - No. 29, 8-9/77

1-All Infantino issue; Flash, Batman, Adam Strange-r; begin 68 pg. issues, end #21
8 16 24 54 102 150
2-Teen humor; Binky, Buzzy, Harvey app. 9 18 27 62 126 190
3-All-Girl issue; unpubl. GA Wonder Woman story 9 18 27 57 111 165
4,11: 4-Horror (1st Abel, brief). 11-Monsters 5 10 15 33 57 80
5-10,12-15: 5-All Kubert issue; Viking Prince, Sgt. Rock-r. 6-Western. 7,9,13-Strangest Sports. 12-Viking Prince; Kubert-c/a (r/B&B almost entirely). 15-G.A. Plastic Man origin-r/Police #1; origin Woozy by Cole; 14,15-(52 pgs.)
4 8 12 27 44 60
16-27: 16-Super Heroes Battle Super Gorillas; r/Capt. Storm #1, 1st Johnny Cloud/All-Amer. Men of War #82. 17-Early S.A. Green Lantern-r. 22-Origin Robin Hood. 26-Enemy Ace. 27-Captain Comet story 3 6 9 16 23 30
28-Earth Shattering Disaster Stories; Legion of Super-Heroes story
3 6 9 16 24 32
29-New "The Untold Origin of the Justice Society"; Staton-a/Neal Adams-c; Hitler app. in story and on cover 5 10 15 31 53 75

NOTE: ***N. Adams** c-3, 4, 6, 11, 29. **Grell** a-20; c-17, 20. **Heath** a-12r. **G. Kane** a-6p, 13r, 17r, 19-21r. **Kirby** a-4,11. **Kubert** a-6r, 12r, 22. **Meskin** a-10. **Moreira** a-10. **Staton** a-29p. **Toth** a-13, 20r. #1-15: 25¢; 16-27: 50¢; 28, 29: 60¢. #1-13, 16-21: 68 pgs.; 14, 15: 52 pgs.; 25-27: oversized.*

DC SPECIAL BLUE RIBBON DIGEST
DC Comics: Mar-Apr, 1980 - No. 24, Aug, 1982

1,2,4,5: 1-Legion reprints. 2-Flash. 4-Green Lantern. 5-Secret Origins; new Zatara and Zatanna 2 4 6 8 11 14
3-Justice Society 2 4 6 10 14 18
6,8-10: 6-Ghosts. 8-Legion. 9-Secret Origins. 10-Warlord-"The Deimos Saga"-Grell-s/c/a
2 4 6 8 11 14
7-Sgt. Rock's Prize Battle Tales 2 4 6 13 18 22
11,16: 11-Justice League. 16-Green Lantern/Green Arrow-r; all Adams-a
2 4 6 11 16 20
12-Haunted Tank; reprints 1st app. 2 4 6 13 18 22
13-15,17-19: 13-Strange Sports Stories. 14-UFO Invaders; Adam Strange app. 15-Secret Origins of Super Villains; JLA app. 17-Ghosts. 18-Sgt. Rock; Kubert front & back-c. 19-Doom Patrol; new Perez-c 2 4 6 9 13 16
20-Dark Mansion of Forbidden Love (scarce) 4 8 12 28 47 65
21-Our Army at War 3 6 9 15 22 28
22-24: 22-Secret Origins. 23-Green Arrow, w/new 7 pg. story. 24-House of Mystery; new Kubert wraparound-c 2 4 6 13 18 22

NOTE: ***N. Adams** a-16(6)r, 17r, 23r; c-16. **Aparo** a-6r, 24r; c-23. **Grell** a-8, 10; c-10. **Heath** a-14. **Infantino** a-15r. **Kaluta** a-17r. **Gil Kane** a-15r, 22r. **Kirby** a-5, 9, 23r. **Kubert** a-3, 18r, 21r; c-7, 12, 14, 17, 18, 21, 24. **Morrow** a-24r. **Orlando** a-17r, 22r; c-1, 20. **Toth** a-21r, 24r. **Wood** a-3, 17r, 24r. **Wrightson** a-16r, 17r, 24r.*

DC SPECIAL: CYBORG (From Teen Titans) (See Teen Titans 2003 series for TPB collection)
DC Comics: Jul, 2008 - No. 6, Dec, 2008 ($2.99, limited series)

1-6: 1-Sable-s/Lashley-a; origin re-told. 3-6-Magno-a 3.00

DC SPECIAL: RAVEN (From Teen Titans) (See Teen Titans 2003 series for TPB collection)
DC Comics: May, 2008 - No. 5, Sept, 2008 ($2.99, limited series)

1-5-Marv Wolfman-s/Damion Scott-a 3.00

DC SPECIAL SERIES
National Periodical Publications/DC Comics: 9/77 - No. 16, Fall, 1978; No. 17, 8/79 - No. 27, Fall, 1981 (No. 18, 19, 23, 24 - digest size, 100 pgs.; No. 25-27 - Treasury sized)

1-"5-Star Super-Hero Spectacular 1977"; Batman, Atom, Flash, Green Lantern, Aquaman, in solo stories, Kobra app.; N. Adams-c 4 8 12 28 47 65
2(#1)-"The Original Swamp Thing Saga 1977"-r/Swamp Thing #1&2 by Wrightson; new Wrightson wraparound-c. 2 4 6 11 16 20
3,4,6-8: 3-Sgt Rock. 4-Unexpected. 6-Secret Society of Super Villains, Jones-a. 7-Ghosts Special. 8-Brave and Bold w/ new Batman, Deadman & Sgt Rock team-up
2 4 6 13 18 22
5-"Superman Spectacular 1977"-(84 pg, $1.00)-Superman vs. Brainiac & Lex Luthor, new 63 pg. story 3 6 9 15 22 28
9-Wonder Woman; Ditko-a (11 pgs.) 3 6 9 15 22 28
10-"Secret Origins of Superheroes Special 1978"-(52 pgs.)-Dr. Fate, Lightray & Black Canary on-c/new origin stories; Staton, Newton-a 3 6 9 14 20 26
11-"Flash Spectacular 1978"-(84 pgs.) Flash, Kid Flash, GA Flash & Johnny Quick vs. Grodd; Wood-i on Kid Flash chapter 2 4 6 13 18 22
12-"Secrets of Haunted House Special Spring 1978" 2 4 6 13 18 22
13-"Sgt. Rock Special Spring 1978", 50 pg new story 3 6 9 14 19 24
14,17,20-"Original Swamp Thing Saga", Wrightson-a: 14-Sum '78, r/#3,4. 17-Sum '79 r/#5-7. 20-Jan/Feb '80, r/#8-10 2 4 6 9 13 16
15-"Batman Spectacular Summer 1978", Ra's Al Ghul-app.; Golden-a. Rogers-a/front & back-c 4 8 12 23 37 50
16-"Jonah Hex Spectacular Fall 1978"; death of Jonah Hex, Heath-a; Bat Lash and Scalphunter stories 6 12 18 37 66 95

GD VG FN VF VF/NM NM-
2.0 4.0 6.0 8.0 9.0 9.2

18,19-Digest size: 18-"Sgt. Rock's Prize Battle Tales Fall 1979". 19-"Secret Origins of Super-Heroes Fall 1979"; origins Wonder Woman (new-a),r/Robin, Batman-Superman team, Aquaman, Hawkman and others 2 4 6 13 18 22
21-"Super-Star Holiday Special Spring 1980", Frank Miller-a in "Batman--Wanted Dead or Alive" (1st Batman story); Jonah Hex, Sgt. Rock, Superboy & LSH and House of Mystery/ Witching Hour-c/stories 4 8 12 27 44 60
22-"G.I. Combat Sept. 1980", Kubert-c. Haunted Tank-s 3 6 9 14 19 24
23,24-Digest size: 23-World's Finest-r. 24-Flash 2 4 6 11 16 20
V5#25-($2.95)-"Superman II, the Adventure Continues Summer 1981"; photos from movie & photo-c (see All-New Coll. Ed. C-62) 3 6 9 14 19 24
26-($2.50)-"Superman and His Incredible Fortress of Solitude Summer 1981"
3 6 9 14 19 24
27-($2.50)-"Batman vs. The Incredible Hulk Fall 1981" 4 8 12 23 37 50

NOTE: ***Aparo** c-8. **Heath** a-12i, 16. **Infantino** a-19r. **Kirby** a-23, 19r. **Kubert** c-13, 19r. **Nasser/Netzer** a-1, 10i, 15. **Newton** a-10. **Nino** a-4, 7. **Starlin** c-12. **Staton** a-1. **Tuska** a-19r. #25 & 26. were advertised as All-New Collectors' Edition C-63, C-64. #26 was originally planned as All-New Collectors' Ed. C-30?; has C-630 & A.N.C.E. on cover.*

DC SPECIAL: THE RETURN OF DONNA TROY
DC Comics: Aug, 2005 - No. 4, Late Oct, 2005 ($2.99, limited series)

1-4-Jimenez-s/Garcia-Lopez-a(p)/Pérez-i 3.00

DC SUPER-STARS
National Periodical Publications/DC Comics: March, 1976 - No. 18, Winter, 1978 (No. 3-18: 52 pgs.)

1-(68 pgs.)-Re-intro Teen Titans (predates T. T. #44 (11/76); tryout iss.) plus r/Teen Titans; W.W. as girl was original Wonder Girl 3 6 9 19 30 40
2-7,9,11,12,16: 2,4,6,8-Adam Strange; 2-(68 pgs.)-r/1st Adam Strange/Hawkman team-up from Mystery in Space #90 plus Atomic Knights origin-r. 3-Legion issue. 4-r/Tales/Unexpected #45 2 4 6 8 11 14
8-r/1st Space Ranger from Showcase #15, Adam Strange-r/Mystery in Space #89 & Star Rovers-r/M.I.S. #80 2 4 6 9 13 16
10-Strange Sports Stories; Batman/Joker-c/story 2 4 6 10 14 18
13-Sergio Aragonés Special 3 6 9 15 22 28
14,15,18: 15-Sgt. Rock 2 4 6 9 13 16
17-Secret Origins of Super-Heroes (origin of The Huntress); origin Green Arrow by Grell; Legion app.; Earth II Batman & Catwoman marry (1st revealed; also see B&B #197 & Superman Family #211) 5 10 15 34 60 85

NOTE: ***M. Anderson** r-2, 4, 6. **Aparo** c-7, 14, 18. **Austin** a-11i. **Buckler** a-14p; c-10. **Grell** a-17. **G. Kane** a-1r, 10r. **Kubert** c-15. **Layton** c/a-16i, 17i. **Mooney** a-4r, 6r. **Morrow** c/a-11r. **Nasser** a-11. **Newton** c/a-16p. **Staton** a-17; c-17. No. 10, 12-18 contain all new material; the rest are reprints. #1 contains new and reprint material.*

DC: THE NEW FRONTIER (Also see Justice League: The New Frontier Special)
DC Comics: Mar, 2004 - No. 6, Nov, 2004 ($6.95, limited series)

1-6-DCU in the 1940s-60s; Darwyn Cooke-c/s/a in all. 1-Hal Jordan and The Losers app. 2-Origin Martian Manhunter; Barry Allen app. 3-Challengers of the Unknown 7.00
...Volume One (2004, $19.95, TPB) r/#1-3; cover gallery & intro. by Paul Levitz 20.00
...Volume Two (2005, $19.99, TPB) r/#4-6; cover gallery & afterword by Cooke 20.00

DC TOP COW CROSSOVERS
DC Comics/Top Cow Productions: 2007 ($14.99, TPB)

SC-r/The Darkness/Batman; JLA/Witchblade; The Darkness/Superman; JLA/Cyberforce 15.00

DC 2000
DC Comics: 2000 - No. 2, 2000 ($6.95, limited series)

1,2-JLA visit 1941 JSA; Semeiks-a 7.00

DCU BRAVE NEW WORLD (See Infinite Crisis and tie-ins)
DC Comics: Aug, 2006 ($1.00, 80 pgs., one-shot)

1-Previews 2006 series Martian Manhunter, OMAC, The Creeper, The All-New Atom, The Trials of Shazam, and Uncle Sam and the Freedom Fighters; the Monitor app. 4.00

DCU (Halloween and Christmas one-shot anthologies)
DC Comics

... Halloween Special '09 (12/09, $5.99) Ha-c; art from Bagley, Tucci, K. Jones, Nguyen 6.00
... Halloween Special 2010 (12/10, $4.99) Ha-c; art from Tucci, Garbett; I...Vampire app. 5.00
... Holiday Special (2/09, $5.99) Christmas by various incl. Dini, Maguire, Reis; Quitely-c 6.00
... Holiday Special 2010 (2/11, $4.99) Jonah Hex, Spectre, Legion of S.H., Anthro app. 5.00
... Infinite Halloween Special (12/08, $5.99) Ralph & Sue Dibny app.; Gene Ha-c 6.00
... Infinite Holiday Special (2/07, $4.99) by various; Batwoman app.; Porter-c 5.00

DCU HEROES SECRET FILES
DC Comics: Feb, 1999 ($4.95, one-shot)

1-Origin-s and pin-ups; new Star Spangled Kid app. 5.00

DCU: LEGACIES
DC Comics: Jul, 2010 - No. 10, Apr, 2011 ($3.99, limited series)

1-10: 1,2-Andy Kubert-c; JSA app.; two covers on each. 3-JLA app.; Garcia-Lopez-a. 4-Sgt. Rock back-up; Joe Kubert-a. 5-Pérez-a. 8-Back-up Quitely-a 4.00

DC Universe Presents #10 © DC

Dead Boy Detectives #1 © DC

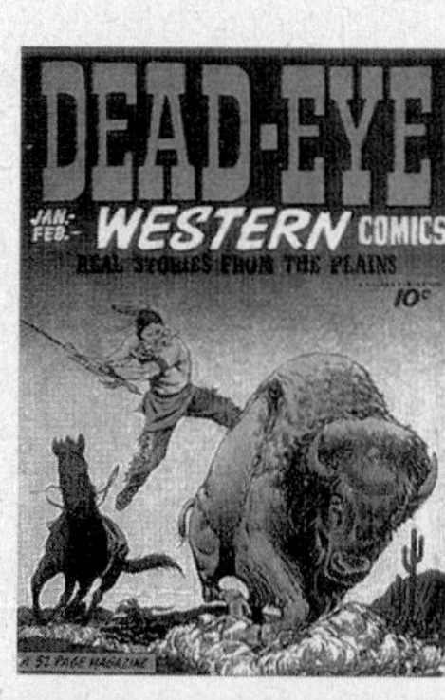

Dead-Eye Western Comics #2 © HILL

	GD 2.0	VG 4.0	FN 6.0	VF 8.0	VF/NM 9.0	NM- 9.2

DC UNIVERSE CHRISTMAS, A
DC Comics: 2000 ($19.95)

TPB-Reprints DC Christmas stories by various 20.00

DC UNIVERSE: DECISIONS
DC Comics: Early Nov, 2008 - No. 4, Late Dec, 2008 ($2.99, limited series)

1-4-Assassination plot in the Presidential election; Winick & Willingham-s/Porter-a 3.00

DC UNIVERSE HOLIDAY BASH
DC Comics: 1997- 1999 ($3.95)

I,II-(X-mas '96,'97) Christmas stories by various 5.00
III (1999, for Christmas '98, $4.95) 5.00

DC UNIVERSE ILLUSTRATED BY NEAL ADAMS (Also see Batman Illustrated by Neal Adams HC Vol. 1-3)
DC Comics: 2008 ($39.99, hardcover with dustjacket)

Vol. 1 - Reprints Adams' non-Batman/non-Green Lantern work from 1967-1972; incl. Teen Titans, DC war, Enemy Ace, Superman and PSAs; promo art; Levitz foreword 40.00

DC UNIVERSE: LAST WILL AND TESTAMENT
DC Comics: Oct, 2008 ($3.99, one-shot)

1-Geo-Force vs. Deathstroke; DC heroes prepare for Final Crisis; Brad Meltzer-s; Adam Kubert & Joe Kubert-a; two covers 4.00

DC UNIVERSE ONLINE LEGENDS (Based on the online game)
DC Comics: Early Apr. 2011 - Late May, 2012 ($2.99)

1-26: 1-Wolfman & Bedard-s/Porter-a; DC heroes & Luthor vs. Brainiac. 1-Wraparound-c 3.00

DC UNIVERSE: ORIGINS
DC Comics: 2009 ($14.99, TPB)

nn-Reprints 2-page origins of DC characters from back-ups in 52, Countdown and Justice League: Cry For Justice #1-3; s/a by various; Alex Ross-c 15.00

DC UNIVERSE PRESENTS (DC New 52)
DC Comics: Nov, 2011 - No. 19, Jun, 2013 ($2.99)

1-5-Deadman. 1-Deadman origin re-told; Jenkins-s/Chang-a/Sook-c 3.00
6-8-Challengers of the Unknown; DiDio-s/Ordway-a/Sook-c 3.00
9-19: 9-11-Savage; Chang-a. 12-Kid Flash. 13-16-Black Lightning & Blue Devil 3.00
#0 (11/12, $5.99) O.M.A.C., Mr. Terrific, Hawk & Dove, Blackhawks, Deadman origins 6.00

DC UNIVERSE SPECIAL
DC Comics: July, 2008 - Aug, 2008 ($4.99, collection of reprints related to Final Crisis)

...: Justice League of America (7/08) r/J.L. of A. #111,166-168 & Detective #274; Sook-c 5.00
...: Reign in Hell (8/08) r/Blaze/Satanus War x-over; Sook-c 5.00
...: Superman (7/08) r/Mongul app. in Superman #32, Showcase '95 #7,8, Flash #102 5.00

DC UNIVERSE: THE STORIES OF ALAN MOORE (Also see Across the Universe:...)
DC Comics: 2006 ($19.99)

TPB-Reprints Batman: The Killing Joke, "Whatever Happened to the Man of Tomorrow", "For The Man Who Has Everything, and other classic Moore DC stories; Bolland-c 20.00

DC UNIVERSE: TRINITY
DC Comics: Aug, 1993 - No. 2, Sept, 1993 ($2.95, 52 pgs, limited series)

1,2-Foil-c; Green Lantern, Darkstars, Legion app. 4.00

DC UNIVERSE VS. MASTERS OF THE UNIVERSE
DC Comics: Oct, 2013 - No. 6, May, 2014 ($2.99, limited series)

1-6: 1-3-Giffen-s/Soy-a/Benes-c; Constantine app. 4-6-Mhan-a 3.00

DCU VILLAINS SECRET FILES
DC Comics: Apr, 1999 ($4.95, one-shot)

1-Origin-s and profile pages 5.00

DC VERSUS MARVEL (See Marvel Versus DC) (Also see Amazon, Assassins, Bruce Wayne: Agent of S.H.I. E. L.D., Bullets & Bracelets, Doctor Strangefate, JLX, Legend of the Dark Claw, Magneto & The Magnetic Men, Speed Demon, Spider-Boy, Super Soldier, X-Patrol)
DC Comics: No. 1, 1996, No. 4, 1996 ($3.95, limited series)

1,4: 1-Marz script, Jurgens-a(p); 1st app. of Access. 5.00
.../Marvel Versus DC ($12.95, trade paperback) r/1-4 13.00

DC/WILDSTORM DREAMWAR
DC Comics: Jun, 2008 - No. 6, Nov, 2008 ($2.99, limited series)

1-6-Giffen-s; Silver Age JLA, Teen Titans, JSA, Legion app. on WildStorm Earth 3.00
1-Variant-c of Superman & Midnighter by Garbett 6.00
TPB (2009, $19.99) r/series 20.00

DC: WORLD WAR III (See 52/WWIII)

D-DAY (Also see Special War Series)
Charlton Comics (no No. 3): Sum/63; No. 2, Fall/64; No. 4, 9/66; No. 5, 10/67; No. 6, 11/68

	GD 2.0	VG 4.0	FN 6.0	VF 8.0	VF/NM 9.0	NM- 9.2
1,2: 1(1963)-Montes/Bache-c. 2(Fall '64)-Wood-a(4)	3	6	9	21	33	45
4-6('66-'68)-Montes/Bache-a #5	3	6	9	14	20	25

DEAD AIR
Slave Labor Graphics: July, 1989 ($5.95, graphic novel)

nn-Mike Allred's 1st published work	1	2	3	5	6	8

DEAD BOY DETECTIVES
DC Comics (Vertigo): Feb, 2014 - Present ($2.99, limited series)

1-4-Litt-s/Buckingham-a. 1-Covers by Buckingham & Chiang 3.00

DEAD CORPSE
DC Comics (Helix): Sept, 1998 - No. 4, Dec, 1998 ($2.50, limited series)

1-4-Pugh-a/Hinz-s 3.00

DEAD END CRIME STORIES
Kirby Publishing Co.: April, 1949 (52 pgs.)

nn-(Scarce)-Powell, Roussos-a; painted-c	55	110	165	352	601	850

DEAD ENDERS
DC Comics (Vertigo): Mar, 2000 - No. 16, June, 2001 ($2.50)

1-16-Brubaker-s/Pleece & Case-a 3.00
Stealing the Sun (2000, $9.95, TPB) r/#1-4, Vertigo Winter's Edge #3 10.00

DEAD-EYE WESTERN COMICS
Hillman Periodicals: Nov-Dec, 1948 - V3#1, Apr-May, 1953

V1#1-(52 pgs.)-Krigstein, Roussos-a	20	40	60	117	189	260
V1#2,3-(52 pgs.)	13	26	39	72	101	130
V1#4-12-(52 pgs.)	9	18	27	50	65	80
V2#1,2,5-8,10-12: 1-7-(52 pgs.)	8	16	24	42	54	65
3,4-Krigstein-a	9	18	27	47	61	75
9-One pg. Frazetta ad	8	16	24	42	54	65
V3#1	8	16	24	42	54	65

NOTE: *Briefer a-V1#8. Kinstleresque stories by McCann-12, V2#1, 2, V3#1. McWilliams a-V1#5. Ed Moore a-V1#4.*

DEADFACE: DOING THE ISLANDS WITH BACCHUS
Dark Horse Comics: July, 1991 - No. 3, Sept, 1991 ($2.95, B&W, lim. series)

1-3: By Eddie Campbell 3.00

DEADFACE: EARTH, WATER, AIR, AND FIRE
Dark Horse Comics: July, 1992 - No. 4, Oct, 1992 ($2.50, B&W, limited series; British-r)

1-4: By Eddie Campbell 3.00

DEAD IN THE WEST
Dark Horse Comics: Oct, 1993 - No. 2, Mar, 1994 ($3.95, B&W, 52 pgs.)

1,2-Timothy Truman-c 4.00

DEAD IRONS
Dynamite Entertainment: 2009 - No. 4, 2009 ($3.99)

1-4-Kuhoric-s/Alexander-a/Jae Lee-c 4.00

DEADLANDER (Becomes Dead Rider for #2)
Dark Horse Comics: Oct, 2007 - No. 4, ($2.99, limited series)

1-2-Kevin Ferrara-s/a 3.00

DEADLANDS (Old West role playing game)
Image Comics: Jul, 2011; Aug, 2011; Jan, 2012 ($2.99, one-shots)

...: Black Water (1/12) Mariotte-s/Brook Turner-a 3.00
...: Death Was Silent (8/11) Marz-s/Sears-a/c 3.00
...: Massacre at Red Wing (7/11) Palmiotti & Gray-s/Moder-a/c 3.00

DEADLIEST HEROES OF KUNG FU (Magazine)
Marvel Comics Group: Summer, 1975 (B&W)(76 pgs.)

1-Bruce Lee vs. Carradine painted-c; TV Kung Fu, 4pgs. photos/article; Enter the Dragon, 24 pgs. photos/article w/ Bruce Lee; Bruce Lee photo pinup	5	10	15	31	53	75

DEADLINE
Marvel Comics: June, 2002 - No. 4, Sept, 2002 ($2.99, limited series)

1-4: 1-Intro. Kat Farrell; Bill Rosemann-s/Guy Davis-a; Horn painted-c 3.00
TPB (2002. $9.99) r/#1-4 10.00

DEADLY DUO, THE
Image Comics (Highbrow Entertainment): Nov, 1994 - No. 3, Jan, 1995 ($2.50, lim. series)

1-3: 1-1st app. of Kill Cat 3.00

DEADLY DUO, THE
Image Comics (Highbrow Entertainment): June, 1995 - No. 4, Oct, 1995 ($2.50, lim. series)

1-4: 1-Spawn app. 2-Savage Dragon app. 3-Gen 13 app. 3.00

Deadly Foes of Spider-Man #2 © MAR

Deadman (2006 series) #8 © DC

Deadpool #51 © MAR

GD 2.0 | VG 4.0 | FN 6.0 | VF 8.0 | VF/NM 9.0 | NM- 9.2

DEADLY FOES OF SPIDER-MAN (See Lethal Foes of...)
Marvel Comics: May, 1991 - No. 4, Aug, 1991 ($1.00, limited series)

1-4: 1-Punisher, Kingpin, Rhino app. 3.00

DEADLY HANDS OF KUNG FU, THE (See Master of Kung Fu)
Marvel Comics Group: April, 1974 - No. 33, Feb, 1977 (75¢) (B&W, magazine)

1(V1#4 listed in error)-Origin Sons of the Tiger; Shang-Chi, Master of Kung Fu begins (ties w/Master of Kung Fu #17 as 3rd app. Shang-Chi); Bruce Lee painted-c by Neal Adams; 2pg. memorial photo pinup w/8 pgs. photos/articles; TV Kung Fu, 9 pgs. photos/articles; 15 pgs. Starlin-a 5 10 15 35 63 90
2-Adams painted-c; 1st time origin of Shang-Chi, 34 pgs. by Starlin. TV Kung Fu, 6 pgs. photos & article w/2 pg. pinup. Bruce Lee, 11 pgs. ph/a
4 8 12 28 47 65
3,4,7,10: 3-Adams painted-c; Gulacy-a. Enter the Dragon, photos/articles, 8 pgs. 4-TV Kung Fu painted-c by Neal Adams; TV Kung Fu 7 pg. article/art; Fu Manchu; Enter the Dragon, 10 pg. photos/article w/Bruce Lee. 7-Bruce Lee painted-c & 9 pgs. photos/articles-Return of Dragon plus 1 pg. photo pinup. 10-(3/75)-Iron Fist painted-c & 34 pg. sty-Early app.
3 6 9 21 33 45
5,6: 5-1st app. Manchurian, 6 pgs. Gulacy-a. TV Kung Fu, 4 pg. article; reprints books w/Barry Smith-a. Capt. America-sty, 10 pgs. Kirby-a(r). 6-Bruce Lee photos/article, 6 pgs.; 15 pgs. early Perez-a 3 6 9 20 31 42
8,9,11: 9-Iron Fist, 2 pg. Preview pinup; Nebres-a. 11-Billy Jack painted-c by Adams; 17 pgs. photos/article 3 6 9 18 28 38
12,13: 12-James Bond painted-c by Adams; 14 pg. photos/article. 13-16 pgs. early Perez-a; Piers Anthony, 7 pgs. photos/article 3 6 9 17 26 35
14-Classic Bruce Lee painted-c by Adams. Lee pinup by Chaykin. Lee 16 pg. photos/article w/2 pgs. Green Hornet TV 6 12 18 37 66 95
15,19: 15-Sum, '75 Giant Annual #1. 20pgs. Starlin-a. Bruce Lee photo pinup & 3 pg. photos/ article re book; Man-Thing app. Iron Fist-c/sty; Gulacy-a 18pgs. 19-Iron Fist painted-c & series begins; 1st White Tiger 3 6 9 18 28 38
16,18,20: 16-1st app. Corpse Rider, a Samurai w/Sanho Kim-a. 20-Chuck Norris painted-c & 16 pgs. interview w/photos/article; Bruce Lee vs. C. Norris pinup by Ken Barr. Origin The White Tiger, Perez-a 3 6 9 16 24 32
17-Bruce Lee painted-c by Adams; interview w/R. Clouse, director Enter Dragon 7 pgs. w/B. Lee app. 1st Giffen-a (1pg. 11/75) 4 8 12 28 47 65
21-Bruce Lee 1pg. photos/article 3 6 9 16 24 32
22-1st brief app. Jack of Hearts. 1st Giffen sty-a (along w/Amazing Adv. #35, 3/76)
3 6 9 19 30 40
23-1st full app. Jack of Hearts 4 8 12 23 37 50
24-26,29: 24-Iron Fist-c & centerfold pinup. early Zeck-a; Shang Chi pinup; 6 pgs. Piers Anthony text sty w/Perez/Austin-a; Jack of Hearts app. early Giffen-a. 25-1st app. Shimuru, "Samurai", 20 pgs. Mantlo-sty/Broderick-a; "Swordquest"-c & begins 17 pgs. sty by Sanho Kim; 11 pg. photos/article; partly Bruce Lee. 26-Bruce Lee painted-c & pinup; 16 pgs. interviews w/Kwon & Clouse; talk about Bruce Lee re-filming of Lee legend. 29-Ironfist vs. Shang Chi battle-c/sty; Jack of Hearts app. 3 6 9 18 28 38
27 3 6 9 15 22 28
28-All Bruce Lee Special Issue; (1st time in comics). Bruce Lee painted-c by Ken Barr & pinup. 36 pgs. comics chronicaling Bruce Lee's life; 15 pgs. B. Lee photos/article (Rare in high grade) 7 14 21 46 86 125
30-32: 30-Swordquest-c/sty & conclusion; Jack of Hearts app. 31-Jack of Hearts app; Staton-a. 32-1st Daughters of the Dragon-c/sty, 21 pgs. M. Rogers-a/Claremont-sty; Iron Fist pinup 3 6 9 16 23 30
33-Shang Chi-c/sty; Classic Daughters of the Dragon, 21 pgs. M. Rogers-a/Claremont-story with nudity; Bob Wall interview, photos/article, 14 pgs.
3 6 9 20 31 42
...Special Album Edition 1(Summer, '74)-Iron Fist-c/story (early app., 3rd?); 10 pgs. Adams-i; Shang Chi/Fu Manchu, 10 pgs.; Sons of Tiger, 11 pgs.; TV Kung Fu, 6 pgs. photos/article
4 8 12 23 37 50

NOTE: ***Bruce Lee:** 1-7, 14, 15, 17, 25, 26, 28. **Kung Fu (TV):** 1, 2, 4. **Jack of Hearts**: 22, 23, 29-33. **Shang Chi Master of Kung Fu**: 1-9, 11-18, 29, 31, 33. **Sons of Tiger:** 1, 3, 4, 6-14, 16-19. **Swordquest:** 25-27, 29-33. **White Tiger:** 19-24, 26, 27, 29-33. **N. Adams** a-1i(part), 27i; c-1, 2-4, 11, 12, 14, 17. **Giffen** a-22p, 24p. **G. Kane** a-23p. **Kirby** a-5r. **Nasser** a-27p, 28. **Perez** a(p)-6-14, 16, 17, 19, 21. **Rogers** a-26, 32, 33. **Starlin** a-1, 2r, 15r. **Staton** a-28p, 31, 32.*

DEADMAN (See The Brave and the Bold & Phantom Stranger #39)
DC Comics: May, 1985 - No. 7, Nov, 1985 ($1.75, Baxter paper)

1-7: 1-Deadman-r by Infantino, N. Adams in all. 5-Batman-c/story-r/Strange Adventures. 7-Batman-r 4.00
... Book One TPB (2011, $19.99) r/apps. in Strange Adventures #205-213 20.00

DEADMAN
DC Comics: Mar, 1986 - No. 4, June, 1986 (75¢, limited series)

1-4: Lopez-c/a. 4-Byrne-c(p) 4.00

DEADMAN
DC Comics: Feb, 2002 - No. 9, Oct, 2002 ($2.50)

1-9: 1-4-Vance-s/Beroy-a. 3,4-Mignola-c. 5,6-Garcia-Lopez-a 3.00

DEADMAN
DC Comics (Vertigo): Oct, 2006 - No. 13, Oct, 2007 ($2.99)

1-13: 1-Bruce Jones-s/John Watkiss-a/c; intro Brandon Cayce 3.00
...: Deadman Walking TPB (2007, $9.99) r/#1-5 10.00

DEADMAN: DEAD AGAIN (Leads into 2002 series)
DC Comics: Oct, 2001 - No. 5, Oct, 2001 ($2.50, weekly limited series)

1-5: Deadman at the deaths of the Flash, Robin, Superman, Hal Jordan 3.00

DEADMAN: EXORCISM
DC Comics: 1992 - No. 2, 1992 ($4.95, limited series, 52 pgs.)

1,2: Kelley Jones-c/a in both 5.00

DEADMAN: LOVE AFTER DEATH
DC Comics: 1989 - No. 2, 1990 ($3.95, 52 pgs., limited series, mature)

Book One, Two: Kelley Jones-c/a in both. 1-Contains nudity 5.00

DEAD MAN'S RUN
Aspen MLT: No. 0, Dec, 2011 - No. 6, Jul, 2013 ($2.50/$3.50)

0-($2.50) Greg Pak-s/Tony Parker-a; 3 covers; bonus design sketch art 3.00
1-6: 1-(2/12, $3.50) Greg Pak-s/Tony Parker-a; 2 covers 3.50

DEAD OF NIGHT
Marvel Comics Group: Dec, 1973 - No. 11, Aug, 1975

1-Horror reprints 4 8 12 23 37 50
2-10: 10-Kirby-a. 6-Jack the Ripper-c/s 3 6 9 16 23 30
11-Intro Scarecrow; Kane/Wrightson-c 4 8 12 25 40 55

NOTE: ***Ditko** r-7, 10. **Everett** c-2. **Sinnott** r-1.*

DEAD OF NIGHT FEATURING DEVIL-SLAYER
Marvel Comics (MAX): Nov, 2008 - No. 4, Feb, 2009 ($3.99, limited series)

1-4-Keene-s/Samnee-a/Andrews-c 4.00

DEAD OF NIGHT FEATURING MAN-THING
Marvel Comics (MAX): Apr, 2008 - No. 4, July, 2008 ($3.99, limited series)

1-4: 1-Man-Thing origin re-told; Kano-a. 2-4-Jennifer Kale app. 4.00

DEAD OF NIGHT FEATURING WEREWOLF BY NIGHT
Marvel Comics (MAX): Mar, 2009 - No. 4, Jun, 2009 ($3.99, limited series)

1-4: 1-Werewolf By Night origin re-told; Swierczynski-s/Suayan-a 4.00

DEAD OR ALIVE - A CYBERPUNK WESTERN
Image Comics (Shok Studio): Apr, 1998 - No. 4, July, 1998 ($2.50, limited series)

1-4 3.00

DEADPOOL (See New Mutants #98 for 1st app.)
Marvel Comics: Aug, 1994 - No. 4, Nov, 1994 ($2.50, limited series)

1-Mark Waid's 1st Marvel work; Ian Churchill-c/a 1 3 4 6 8 10
2-4 6.00

DEADPOOL (... : Agent of Weapon X on cover #57-60) (title becomes Agent X)
Marvel Comics: Jan, 1997 - No. 69, Sept, 2002 ($2.95/$1.95/$1.99)

1-($2.95)-Wraparound-c 4 8 12 23 37 50
2-Begin-$1.95-c. 6.00
3-10,12-22,24: 4-Hulk-c/app. 12-Variant-c. 14-Begin McDaniel-a. 22-Cable app. 5.00
11-($3.99)-Deadpool replaces Spider-Man from Amazing Spider-Man #47; Kraven, Gwen Stacy app. 1 2 3 5 6 8
23,25-($2.99); 23-Dead Reckoning pt. 1; wraparound-c 6.00
26-40: 27-Wolverine-c/app. 37-Thor app. 4.00
41-53,56-60: 41-Begin $2.25-c. 44-Black Panther-c/app. 46-49-Chadwick-a 51-Cover swipe of Detective #38. 57-60-BWS-c 3.00
54,55-Punisher-c/app. 54-Dillon-c. 55-Bradstreet-c 3.00
61-69: 61-64-Funeral For a Freak on cover. 65-69-Udon Studios-a. 67-Dazzler-c/app. 3.00
#(-1) Flashback (7/97) Lopresti-a; Wade Wilson's early days 3.00
.../Death '98 Annual ($2.99) Kelly-s, ... Team-Up (12/98, $2.99) Widdle Wade-c/app., Baby's First Deadpool Book (12/98, $2.99), Encyclopædia Deadpoolica (12/98, $2.99) Synopses 4.00
.../GLI - Summer Fun Spectacular #1 (9/07, $3.99) short stories; Pelletier-c 4.00
... Classic Vol. 1 TPB (2008, $29.99) r/#1, New Mutants #98, Deadpool: The Circle Chase #1-4 and Deadpool (1994 series) #1-4 30.00
Mission Improbable TPB (9/98, $14.95) r/#1-5 15.00
Wizard #0 ('98, bagged with Wizard #87) 3.00

DEADPOOL
Marvel Comics: Nov, 2008 - No. 63, Dec, 2012 ($3.99/$2.99)

1-($3.99) Medina-a; Secret Invasion x-over; 2 covers by Crain & Liefeld 5.00
2-24,26-33, 33.1,34-49-($2.99) Variant covers for most. 4-20-Pearson-c. 8,9-Thunderbolts

Deadpool (2013 series) #7 © MAR

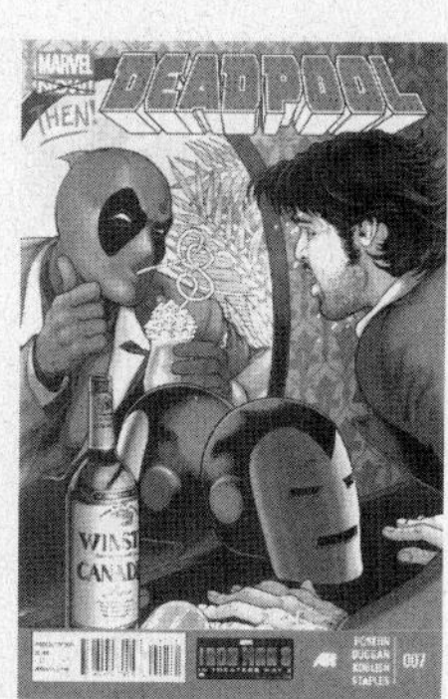

Deadpool Team-Up #1 © MAR

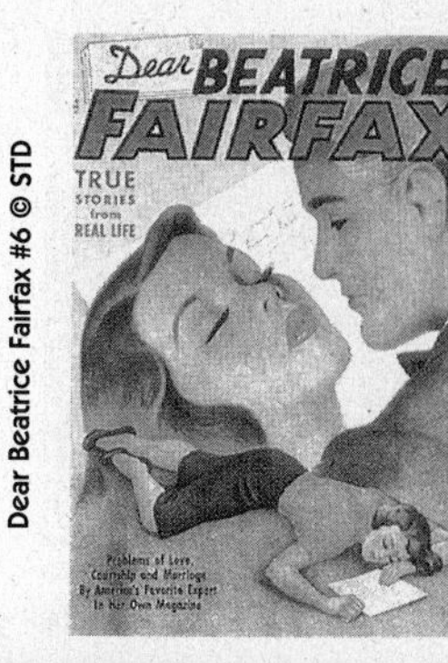

Dear Beatrice Fairfax #6 © STD

GD 2.0 | VG 4.0 | FN 6.0 | VF 8.0 | VF/NM 9.0 | NM- 9.2

x-over. 10-Dark Reign. 16-18-X-Men app. 19-21-Spider-Man & Hit-Monkey app. 26-Ghost Rider app. 27-29-Secret Avengers app. 30,31-Curse of the Mutants. 37-39-Hulk app. 3.00
25-($3.99) 3-D cover, fake 3-D glasses on back-c; back-up story w/Bond-a 4.00
49.1, 51-63 ($2.99) 49-McCrea-a. 51-Garza-a. 61-Hit-Monkey app. 3.00
50-($3.99) Uncanny X-Force & Kingpin app.; Barberi-a 4.00
900-(12/09, $4.99) Stories by various incl. Liefeld, Baker; wraparound-c by Johnson 5.00
1000-(10/10, $4.99) Stories by various; gallery of variant covers; Johnson-c 5.00
Annual 1 (7/11, $3.99) "Identity Wars" crossover; Spider-Man & Hulk app. 4.00
... & Cable #26 (4/11, $3.99) Swierczynski-s/Fernandez-a 4.00
... Family 1 (6/11, $3.99) short stories by various; Pearson-c 4.00
...: Games of Death 1 (5/09, $3.99) Benson-s/Crystal-a/Land-c 4.00
... MCG (7/10, $1.00) r/#1 with "Marvel's Greatest Comics" logo on cover 3.00

DEADPOOL
Marvel Comics: Jan, 2013 - Present ($2.99)
1-Posehn & Duggan-s/Tony Moore-a/Darrow-c; Deadpool vs. Zombie ex-Presidents 3.00
2-26: 7-Iron Man app.; spoof in 1980s style; Koblish-a/Maguire-c. 10-Spider-Man app. 13-Spoof in 1970s style; Heroes For Hire app. 15-19-Wolverine & Capt. America app. 3.00
27-($9.99) Wedding of Deadpool; wraparound-c with 236 characters 10.00
Annual 1 (1/14, $4.99) Madcap and Avengers app.; Acker & Blacker-s/Shaner-a 5.00
...: The Gauntlet (3/14, giveaway) printing of Marvel digital comics content; Cho-c 3.00
... vs Carnage 1 (6/14, $3.99) Bunn-s/Espin-a/Fabry-c 4.00

DEADPOOL CORPS (Continues from Prelude to Deadpool Corps series)
Marvel Comics: Jun, 2010 - No. 12, May, 2011 ($3.99/$2.99)
1-($3.99) Liefeld-a/c; Gischler-s; 2 covers by Liefeld 4.00
2-12-($2.99) 2-5,7,9-Liefeld-a. 6-Mychaels-a 3.00
...: Rank and Foul 1 (5/10, $3.99) Handbook-style profile pages of allies and enemies 4.00

DEADPOOL KILLS DEADPOOL
Marvel Comics: Sept, 2013 - No. 4, Dec, 2013 ($2.99, limited series)
1-4-Bunn-s/Espin-a; Deadpool Corps app. 3.00

DEADPOOL KILLS THE MARVEL UNIVERSE
Marvel Comics: Oct, 2012 - No. 4, Oct, 2012 ($2.99, weekly limited series)
1-4-Bunn-s/Talajic-a/Andrews-c 5.00

DEADPOOL KILLUSTRATED
Marvel Comics: Mar, 2013 - No. 4, JUn, 2013 ($2.99, limited series)
1-4-Bunn-s/Lolli-a/Del Mundo-c; stories/covers styled like Classics Illustrated 3.00

DEADPOOL MAX
Marvel Comics (MAX): Dec, 2010 - No. 12, Nov, 2011 ($3.99)
1-12: 1-8,10-12-David Lapham-s/Kyle Baker-a/c. 6,7-Domino app. 9-Crystal-a 4.00
... X-Mas Special 1 (2/12, $4.99) Lapham-s; art by Lapham, Baker & Crystal; Baker-c 5.00

DEADPOOL MAX 2
Marvel Comics (MAX): Dec, 2011 - No. 6, May, 2012 ($3.99)
1-6: 1,2-David Lapham-s/Kyle Baker-a/c. 3-Crystal-a 4.00

DEADPOOL: MERC WITH A MOUTH
Marvel Comics: Sept, 2009 - No. 13, Sept, 2010 ($3.99/$2.99)
1-($3.99) Suydam-c/Dazo-a; Zombie-head Deadpool & Ka-Zar app.; r/Deadpool #4 ('97) 4.00
2-6,8-12-($2.99) Suydam-c on all. 8-Deadpool goes to Zombie dimension 3.00
7-13-($3.99) 7-Covers by Suydam & Liefeld; art by Liefeld, Baker, Pastoras, Dazo 4.00

DEADPOOL PULP
Marvel Comics: Nov, 2010 - No. 4, Feb, 2011 ($3.99, limited series)
1-4-Alternate Deadpool in 1955; Glass & Benson-s/Laurence Campbell-a/Jae Lee-c 4.00

DEADPOOL: SUICIDE KINGS
Marvel Comics: Jun, 2009 - No. 5, Oct, 2009 ($3.99, limited series)
1-5-Barberi-a; Punisher, Daredevil, & Spider-Man app. 4.00

DEADPOOL TEAM-UP
Marvel Comics: No. 899, Jan, 2010 - No. 883, May, 2011 ($2.99, numbering runs in reverse)
899-883: 899-Hercules app.; Ramos-c. 897-Ghost Rider app. 894-Franken-Castle app. 887-Thor app. 883-Galactus & Silver Surfer app. 3.00

DEADPOOL: THE CIRCLE CHASE (See New Mutants #98)
Marvel Comics: Aug, 1993 - No. 4, Nov, 1993 ($2.00, limited series)

	GD	VG	FN	VF	VF/NM	NM-
1-($2.50)-Embossed-c	1	3	4	6	8	10
2-4						6.00

DEADPOOL: WADE WILSON'S WAR
Marvel Comics: Aug, 2010 - No. 4, Nov, 2010 ($3.99, limited series)
1-4-Swierczynski-s/Pearson-a/c; Bullseye, Domino & Silver Sable app. 4.00

DEAD RIDER (See Deadlander)

DEAD RISING: ROAD TO FORTUNE (Based on the CAPCOM videogame)
IDW Publishing: Oct, 2011 - Present ($3.99, limited series)
1-2-Tom Waltz-s/Kenneth Loh-a 4.00

DEAD ROMEO
DC Comics: June, 2009 - No. 6, Nov, 2009 ($2.99, limited series)
1-6-Ryan Benjamin-a/Jesse Snider-s 3.00
TPB (2010, $19.99) r/#1-6; cover gallery 20.00

DEAD, SHE SAID
IDW Publishing: May, 2008 - No. 3, Sept, 2008 ($3.99, limited series)
1-3-Bernie Wrightson-a/Steve Niles-s 4.00

DEADSHOT (See Batman #59, Detective Comics #474, & Showcase '93 #8)
DC Comics: Nov, 1988 - No. 4, Feb, 1989 ($1.00, limited series)
1-4 4.00

DEADSHOT
DC Comics: Feb, 2005 - No. 5, June 2005 ($2.95, limited series)
1-5-Zeck-c/Gage-s/Cummings-a. 3-Green Arrow app. 3.00

DEAD SPACE (Based on the Electronics Arts videogame)
Image Comics: Mar, 2008 - No. 6, Sept, 2008 ($2.99, limited series)
1-6-Templesmith-a/Johnston-s 3.00
... Extraction (9/09, $3.50) Templesmith-a/Johnston-s 3.50

DEAD WHO WALK, THE (See Strange Mysteries-Super Reprint #15,16 {1963-64})
Realistic Comics: 1952 (one-shot)

	GD	VG	FN	VF	VF/NM	NM-
nn	60	120	180	381	653	925

DEADWORLD (Also see The Realm)
Arrow Comics/Caliber Comics: Dec, 1986 - No. 26 ($1.50/$1.95/#15-28: $2.50, B&W)
1-4 4.00
5-26-Graphic cover version 4.00
5-26-Tame cover version 3.00
...Archives 1-3 (1992, $2.50) 3.00

DEAN MARTIN & JERRY LEWIS (See Adventures of...)

DEAR BEATRICE FAIRFAX
Best/Standard Comics (King Features): No. 5, Nov, 1950 - No. 9, Sept, 1951
(Vern Greene art)

	GD	VG	FN	VF	VF/NM	NM-
5-All have Schomburg air brush-c	15	30	45	86	133	180
6-9	12	24	36	67	94	120

DEAR HEART (Formerly Lonely Heart)
Ajax: No. 15, July, 1956 - No. 16, Sept, 1956

	GD	VG	FN	VF	VF/NM	NM-
15,16	8	16	24	44	57	70

DEAR LONELY HEART (...Illustrated No. 1-6)
Artful Publications: Mar, 1951; No. 2, Oct, 1951 - No. 8, Oct, 1952

	GD	VG	FN	VF	VF/NM	NM-
1	19	38	57	111	176	240
2	11	22	33	60	85	105
3-Matt Baker Jungle Girl story	21	42	63	122	199	275
4-8	10	20	30	56	76	95

DEAR LONELY HEARTS (Lonely Heart #9 on)
Harwell Publ./Mystery Publ. Co. (Comic Media): Aug, 1953 -No. 8, Oct, 1954

	GD	VG	FN	VF	VF/NM	NM-
1	15	30	45	83	124	165
2-8	11	22	33	62	86	110

DEARLY BELOVED
Ziff-Davis Publishing Co.: Fall, 1952

	GD	VG	FN	VF	VF/NM	NM-
1-Photo-c	18	36	54	107	169	230

DEAR NANCY PARKER
Gold Key: June, 1963 - No. 2, Sept, 1963

	GD	VG	FN	VF	VF/NM	NM-
1-Painted-c on both	4	8	12	23	37	50
2	3	6	9	17	26	35

DEATH, THE ABSOLUTE... (From Neil Gaiman's Sandman titles)
DC Comics (Vertigo): 2009 ($99.99, oversized hardcover in slipcase)
nn-Reprints 1st app. in Sandman #8, Sandman #20, Death: The High Cost of Living #1-3, Death: the Time of Your Life #1-3, Death Talks About Life; short stories and pin-ups; merchandise pics; script and sketch art for Sandman #8; Gaiman afterword 100.00

DEATH: AT DEATH'S DOOR (See Sandman: The Season of Mists)
DC Comics (Vertigo): 2003 ($9.95, graphic novel one-shot, B&W, 7-1/2" x 5")
1-Jill Thompson-s/a/c; manga-style; Morpheus and the Endless app. 10.00

Deathblow #16 © WSP

Deathlok #7 © MAR

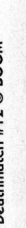

Deathmatch #12 © BOOM

GD 2.0	VG 4.0	FN 6.0	VF 8.0	VF/NM 9.0	NM- 9.2

DEATHBLOW (Also see Batman/Deathblow and Darker Image)
Image Comics (WildStorm Productions): May (Apr. inside), 1993 - No. 29, Aug, 1996 ($1.75/$1.95/$2.50)

0-(8/96, $2.95, 32 pgs.)-r/Darker Image w/new story & art; Jim Lee & Trevor Scott-a; new Jim Lee-c 3.00
1-($2.50)-Red foil stamped logo on black varnish-c; Jim Lee-c/a; flip-book side has Cybernary -c/story (#2 also) 4.00
1-($1.95)-Newsstand version w/o foil-c & varnish 3.00
2-29: 2-(8/93)-Lee-a; with bound-in poster. 2-($1.75)-Newsstand version w/o poster. 4-Jim Lee-c/Tim Sale-a begin. 13-W/pinup poster by Tim Sale & Jim Lee. 16-($1.95 Newsstand & $2.50 Direct Market editions)-Wildstorm Rising Pt. 6. 17-Variant "Chicago Comicon" edition exists. 20,21-Gen 13 app. 23-Backlash-c/app. 24,25-Grifter-c/app; Gen 13 & Dane from Wetworks app. 28-Deathblow dies. 29-Memorial issue 3.00
5-Alternate Portacio-c (Forms larger picture when combined with alternate-c for Gen 13 #5, Kindred #3, Stormwatch #10, Team 7 #1, Union #0, Wetworks #2 & WildC.A.T.S #11) 6.00
...:Sinners and Saints TPB ('99, $19.95) r/#1-12; Sale-c 20.00

DEATHBLOW (Volume 2)
DC Comics (WildStorm): Dec, 2006 - No. 9, Apr, 2008 ($2.99)

1-9: 1-Azzarello-s/D'Anda-a; two covers by D'Anda & Platt 3.00
...: And Then You Live! TPB (2008, $19.99) r/#1-9 20.00

DEATHBLOW BY BLOWS
DC Comics (WildStorm): Nov, 1999 - No. 3, Jan, 2000 ($2.95, limited series)

1-3-Alan Moore-s/Jim Baikie-a 3.00

DEATHBLOW/WOLVERINE
Image Comics (WildStorm Productions)/ Marvel Comics: Sept, 1996 - No. 2, Feb, 1997 ($2.50, limited series)

1,2: Wiesenfeld-s/Bennett-a 3.00
TPB (1997, $8.95) r/#1,2 9.00

DEATH DEALER (Also see Frank Frazetta's...)
Verotik: July, 1995 - No. 4, July, 1997 ($5.95)

1-Frazetta-c; Bisley-a 1 2 3 5 6 8
1-2nd print, 2-4-($6.95)-Frazetta-c; embossed logo 1 2 3 4 5 7

DEATH-DEFYING 'DEVIL, THE (Also see Project Superpowers)
Dynamite Entertainment: 2008 - No. 4, 2009 ($3.50, limited series)

1-4-Casey & Ross-s/Salazar-a; multiple covers; the Dragon app. 3.50

DEATH, JR.
Image Comics: Apr, 2005 - No. 3, Aug, 2005 ($4.99, squarebound, limited series)

1-3-Gary Whitta-s/Ted Naifeh-a 5.00
Vol. 1 TPB (2005, $14.99) r/series; concept and promotional art 15.00

DEATH, JR. (Volume 2)
Image Comics: Jul, 2006 - No. 3, May, 2007 ($4.99, squarebound, limited series)

1-3-Gary Whitta-s/Ted Naifeh-a. 1-Dan Brereton-c 5.00
Vol. 2 TPB (2007, $14.99) r/series; Halloween story w/Guy Davis-a; promotional art 15.00

DEATHLOK (Also see Astonishing Tales #25)
Marvel Comics: July, 1990 - No. 4, Oct, 1990 ($3.95, limited series, 52 pgs.)

1-4: 1,2-Guice-a(p). 3,4-Denys Cowan-a, c-4 5.00

DEATHLOK
Marvel Comics: July, 1991 - No. 34, Apr, 1994 ($1.75)

1-Silver ink cover; Denys Cowan-c/a(p) begins 4.00
2-18,20-24,26-34: 2-Forge (X-Men) app. 3-Vs. Dr. Doom. 5-X-Men & F.F. x-over. 6,7-Punisher x-over. 9,10-Ghost Rider-c/story. 16-Infinity War x-over. 17-Jae Lee-c. 22-Black Panther app. 27-Siege app. 3.00
19-($2.25)-Foil-c 4.00
25-($2.95, 52 pgs.)-Holo-grafx foil-c 4.00
Annual 1 (1992, $2.25, 68 pgs.)-Guice-p; Quesada-c(p) 4.00
Annual 2 (1993, $2.95, 68 pgs.)-Bagged w/card; intro Tracer 4.00
NOTE: *Denys Cowan a(p)-9-13, 15, Annual 1; c-9-12, 13p, 14. Guice/Cowan c-8.*

DEATHLOK
Marvel Comics: Sept, 1999 - No. 11, June, 2000 ($1.99)

1-11: 1-Casey-s/Manco-a. 2-Two covers. 4-Canete-a 3.00

DEATHLOK (... The Demolisher on cover)
Marvel Comics: Jan, 2010 - No. 7, Jul, 2010 ($3.99, limited series)

1-7-Huston-s/Medina-a/Peterson-c 4.00

DEATHLOK SPECIAL
Marvel Comics: May, 1991 - No. 4, June, 1991 ($2.00, bi-weekly lim. series)

1-4: r/1-4(1990) w/new Guice-c #1,2; Cowan c-3,4 3.00
1-2nd printing w/white-c 3.00

DEATHMASK
Future Comics: Mar, 2003 - No. 3, June, 2003 ($2.99)

1-3-Giordano-a(p)/Michelinie & Layton-s 3.00

DEATHMATCH
BOOM! Studios: Dec, 2012 - No. 12, Nov, 2013 ($2.99)

1-($1.00) Jenkins-s/Magno-a; multiple covers 3.00
2-12 ($3.99) Multiple covers on each 4.00

DEATHMATE
Valiant (Prologue/Yellow/Blue)/Image Comics (Black/Red/Epilogue): Sept, 1993 - Epilogue (#6), Feb, 1994 ($2.95/$4.95, limited series)

Preview-(7/93, 8 pgs.) 3.00
Prologue (#1)–Silver foil; Jim Lee/Layton-c; B. Smith/Lee-a; Liefeld-a(p) 3.00
Prologue–Special gold foil ed. of silver ed. 4.00
Black (#2)-(9/93, $4.95, 52 pgs.)-Silvestri/Jim Lee-c; pencils by Peterson/Silvestri/Capullo/ Jim Lee/Portacio; 1st story app. Gen 13 telling their rebellion against the Troika (see WildC.A.T.S. Trilogy) 6.00
Black-Special gold foil edition 7.00
Yellow (#3)-(10/93, $4.95, 52 pgs)-Yellow foil-c; Indicia says Prologue Sept 1993 by mistake; 3rd app. Ninjak; Thibert-c(i) 5.00
Yellow-Special gold foil edition 6.00
Blue (#4)-(10/93, $4.95, 52 pgs.)-Thibert blue foil-c(i); Reese-a(i) 5.00
Blue-Special gold foil edition 6.00
Red (#5), Epilogue (#6)-(2/94, $2.95)-Silver foil Quesada/Silvestri-c; Silvestri-a(p) 3.00

DEATH METAL
Marvel Comics UK: Jan, 1994 - No. 4, Apr, 1994 ($1.95, limited series)

1-4: 1-Silver ink-c. Alpha Flight app. 3.00

DEATH METAL VS. GENETIX
Marvel Comics UK: Dec, 1993 - No. 2, Jan, 1994 (Limited series)

1-($2.95)-Polybagged w/2 trading cards 3.00
2-($2.50)-Polybagged w/2 trading cards 3.00

DEATH OF CAPTAIN MARVEL (See Marvel Graphic Novel #1)

DEATH OF DRACULA
Marvel Comics: Aug, 2010 ($3.99, one shot)

1-Gischler-s/Camuncoli-a/c 4.00

DEATH OF MR. MONSTER, THE (See Mr. Monster #8)

DEATH OF SUPERMAN (See Superman, 2nd Series)

DEATH OF THE NEW GODS (Tie-in to the Countdown series)
DC Comics: Early Dec, 2007 - No. 8, Jun, 2008 ($3.50, limited series)

1-8-Jim Starlin-s/a/c. 1-Barda killed. 6-Orion dies. 7-Scott Free and Metron die 3.50
TPB (2009, $19.99) r/#1-8; Starlin intro.; cover gallery 20.00

DEATH RACE 2020
Roger Corman's Cosmic Comics: Apr, 1995 - No. 8, Nov, 1995 ($2.50)

1-8: Sequel to the Movie 3.00

DEATH RATTLE (Formerly an Underground)
Kitchen Sink Press: V2#1, 10/85 - No. 18, 1988, 1994 ($1.95, Baxter paper, mature); V3#1, 11/95 - No. 5, 6/96 ($2.95, B&W)

V2#1-7,9-18: 1-Corben-c. 2-Unpubbed Spirit story by Eisner. 5-Robot Woman-r by Wolverton. 6-B&W issues begin. 10-Savage World-r by by Williamson/Torres/ Krenkel/Frazetta from Witzend #1. 16-Wolverton Spacehawk-r 5.00
8-(12/86)-1st app. Mark Schultz's Xenozoic Tales/Cadillacs & Dinosaurs 2 4 6 9 12 15
8-(1994)-r plus interview w/Mark Schultz 3.50
V3#1-5 ($2.95-c) 3.50

DEATH SENTENCE
Titan Comics: Nov, 2003 - No. 6, Apr, 2014 ($3.99)

1-6-Montynero-s/c; Dowling-a 4.00

DEATH'S HEAD (See Daredevil #56, Dragon's Claws #5 & Incomplete...)(See Amazing Fantasy (2004) for Death's Head 3.0)
Marvel Comics: Dec, 1988 - No. 10, Sept, 1989 ($1.75)

1-Dragon's Claws spin-off 3.00
2-Fantastic Four app.; Dragon's Claws x-over 3.00
3-10: 8-Dr. Who app. 9-F. F. x-over; Simonson-c(p) 3.00

DEATH'S HEAD II (Also see Battletide)
Marvel Comics UK, Ltd.: Mar, 1992 - No. 4, June (May inside), 1992 ($1.75, color, lim. series)

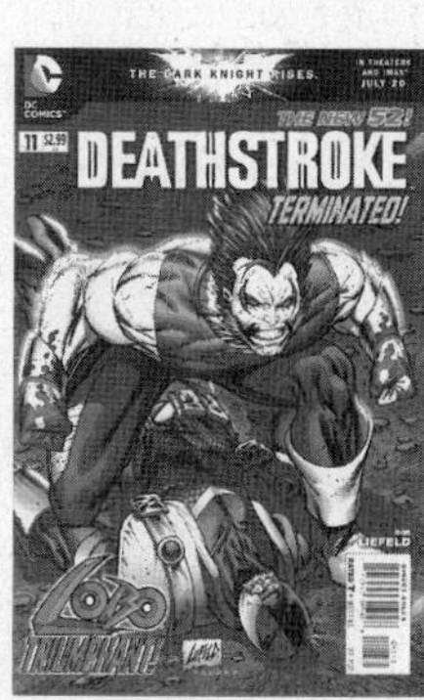

Deathstroke #11 © DC

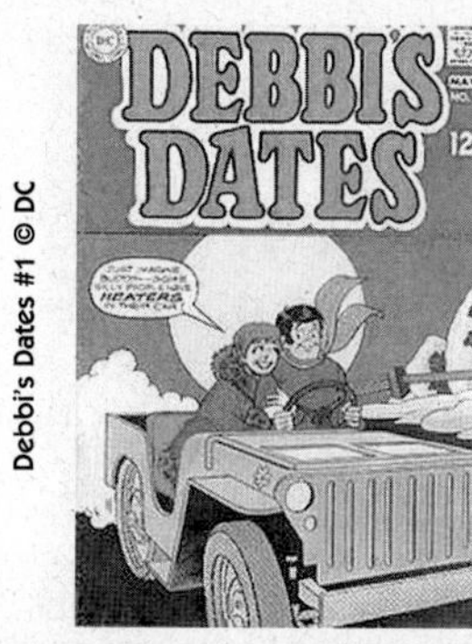

Debbi's Dates #1 © DC

The Defenders #15 © MAR

GD VG FN VF VF/NM NM-
2.0 4.0 6.0 8.0 9.0 9.2

1-4: 2-Fantastic Four app. 4-Punisher, Spider-Man, Daredevil, Dr. Strange, Capt. America & Wolverine in the year 2020 3.00
1,2-Silver ink 2nd printiings 3.00

DEATH'S HEAD II (Also see Battletide)
Marvel Comics UK, Ltd.: Dec, 1992 - No. 16, Mar, 1994 ($1.75/$1.95)

V2#1-13,15,16: 1-Gatefold-c. 1-4-X-Men app.15-Capt. America & Wolverine app. 3.00
14-($2.95)-Foil flip-c w/Death's Head II Gold #0 4.00
...Gold 1 (1/94, $3.95, 68 pgs.)-Gold foil-c 4.00

DEATH'S HEAD II & THE ORIGIN OF DIE CUT
Marvel Comics UK, Ltd.: Aug, 1993 - No. 2, Sept, 1993 (limited series)

1-($2.95)-Embossed-c 4.00
2 ($1.75) 3.00

DEATHSTROKE (DC New 52)
DC Comics: Nov, 2011 - No. 20, Jul, 2013 ($2.99)

1-20: 1-Higgins-s/Bennett-a/Bisley-c. 4-Blackhawks app. 9-12-Liefeld-s/a/c; Lobo app. 3.00
#0 (11/12, $2.99) Origin story, Team 7 app.; Liefeld-s/a/c 3.00

DEATHSTROKE: THE TERMINATOR (Deathstroke: The Hunted #0-47; Deathstroke #48-60) (Also see Marvel & DC Present, New Teen Titans #2, New Titans, Showcase '93 #7,9 & Tales of the Teen Titans #42-44)
DC Comics: Aug, 1991 - No. 60, June, 1996 ($1.75-$2.25)

1-New Titans spin-off; Mike Zeck c-1-28 4.00
1-Gold ink 2nd printing ($1.75) 3.00
2 3.00
3-40,0(10/94),41(11/94)-49,51-60: 6,8-Batman cameo. 7,9-Batman-c/story. 9-1st brief app. new Vigilante (female). 10-1st full app. new Vigilante; Perez-i. 13-Vs. Justice League; Team Titans cameo on last pg. 14-Total Chaos, part 1; Team Titans-c/story cont'd in New Titans #90. 40-(9/94). 0-(10/94)-Begin Deathstroke, The Hunted, ends #47. 3.00
50 ($3.50) 4.00
Annual 1-4 ('92-'95, 68 pgs.): 1-Nightwing & Vigilante app.; minor Eclipso app. 2-Bloodlines Deathstorm; 1st app. Gunfire. 3-Elseworlds story. 4-Year One story 4.00
NOTE: *Golden a-12. Perez a-11i. Zeck c-Annual 1, 2.*

DEATH: THE HIGH COST OF LIVING (See Sandman #8) (Also see the Books of Magic limited & ongoing series)
DC Comics (Vertigo): Mar, 1993 - No. 3, May, 1993 ($1.95, limited series)

1-Bachalo/Buckingham-a; Dave McKean-c; Neil Gaiman scripts in all 6.00
1-Platinum edition 40.00
2 3.50
3-Pgs. 19 & 20 had wrong placement 3.00
3-Corrected version w/pgs. 19 & 20 facing each other; has no-c & ads for Sebastion O & The Geek added 4.00
Death Talks About Life-giveaway about AIDS prevention 5.00
Hardcover (1994, $19.95)-r/#1-3 & Death Talks About Life; intro. by Tori Amos 20.00
Trade paperback (6/94, $12.95, Titan Books)-r/#1-3 & Death Talks About Life; prism-c 13.00

DEATH: THE TIME OF YOUR LIFE (See Sandman #8)
DC Comics (Vertigo): Apr, 1996 - No. 3, July, 1996 ($2.95, limited series)

1-3: Neil Gaiman story & Bachalo/Buckingham-a; Dave McKean-c. 2-(5/96) 3.00
Hardcover (1997, $19.95)-r/#1-3 w/3 new pages & gallery art by various 20.00
TPB (1997, $12.95)-r/#1-3 & Visions of Death gallery; Intro. by Claire Danes 13.00

DEATH 3
Marvel Comics UK: Sept, 1993 - No. 4, Dec, 1993 ($1.75, limited series)

1-($2.95)-Embossed-c 4.00
2-4 3.00

DEATH VALLEY (Cowboys and Indians)
Comic Media: Oct, 1953 - No. 6, Aug, 1954

1-Billy the Kid; Morisi-a; Andru/Esposito-c/a 21 42 63 126 206 285
2-Don Heck-c 14 28 42 80 115 150
3-6: 3,5-Morisi-a. 5-Discount-a 13 26 39 74 105 135

DEATH VALLEY (Becomes Frontier Scout, Daniel Boone No.10-13)
Charlton Comics: No. 7, 6/55 - No. 9, 10/55 (Cont'd from Comic Media series)

7-9: 8-Wolverton-a (half pg.) 10 20 30 58 79 100

DEATHWISH
DC Comics (Milestone Media): Dec, 1994 - No. 4, Mar, 1995 (2.50, lim. series)

1-4 3.00

DEATH WRECK
Marvel Comics UK: Jan, 1994 - No. 4, Apr, 1994 ($1.95, limited series)

1-4: 1-Metallic ink logo; Death's Head II app. 3.00

DEBBIE DEAN, CAREER GIRL
Civil Service Publ.: April, 1945 - No. 2, July, 1945

1,2-Newspaper reprints by Bert Whitman 14 28 42 76 108 140

DEBBI'S DATES (Also see Date With Debbi)
National Periodical Publications: Apr-May, 1969 - No. 11, Dec-Jan, 1970-71

1 6 12 18 40 73 105
2,3,5,7-11: 2-Last 12¢ issue 4 8 12 23 37 50
4-Neal Adams text illo 4 8 12 27 44 60
6-Superman cameo 5 10 15 35 63 90

DECADE OF DARK HORSE, A
Dark Horse Comics: Jul, 1996 - No. 4, Oct, 1996 ($2.95, B&W/color, lim. series)

1-4: 1-Sin City-c/story by Miller; Grendel by Wagner; Predator. 2-Star Wars wraparound-c. 3-Aliens-c/story; Nexus, Mask stories 3.00

DECAPITATOR (Randy Bowen's...)
Dark Horse Comics: Jun, 1998 - No. 4, ($2.95)

1-4-Bowen-s/art by various. 1-Mahnke-c. 3-Jones-c 4.00

DECEPTION, THE
Image Comics (Flypaper Press): 1999 - No. 3, 1999 ($2.95, B&W, mini-series)

1-3-Horley painted-c 3.00

DECIMATION: THE HOUSE OF M
Marvel Comics: Jan, 2006 ($3.99)

... - The Day After (one-shot) Claremont-s/Green-a 4.00

DECISION 2012 (Biographies of the main 2012 presidential candidates)
BOOM! Studios: Nov, 2011 - Present ($3.99, series of one-shots)

...: Barack Obama 1 (11/11, $3.99) biography; Damian Couceiro-a; 2 covers 4.00
...: Michelle Bachman 1 (11/11) biography; Aaron McConnell-a; 2 covers 4.00
...: Ron Paul 1 (11/11) biography; Dean Kotz-a; 2 covers 4.00
...: Sarah Palin 1 (11/11) biography; Damian Couceiro-a; 2 covers 4.00

DEEP, THE (Movie)
Marvel Comics Group: Nov, 1977 (Giant)

1-Infantino-c/a 1 3 4 6 8 10

DEEP SLEEPER
Oni Press/Image Comics: Feb, 2004 - No. 4, Sept, 2004 ($3.50/$2.95, B&W, limited series)

1,2-(Oni Press, $3.50)-Hester-s/Huddleston-a 3.50
3,4-(Image Comics, $2.95) 3.00
... Omnibus (Image, 8/04, $5.95) r/#1,2 6.00
... Vol. 1 TPB (2005, $12.95) r/#1-4; cover gallery 13.00

DEFCON 4
Image Comics (WildStorm Productions): Feb, 1996 - No. 4, Sept, 1996 ($2.50, lim. series)

1/2 1 2 3 5 7 9
1/2 Gold-(1000 printed) 14.00
1-Main Cover by Mat Broome & Edwin Rosell 3.00
1-Hordes of Cymulants variant-c by Michael Golden 5.00
1-Backs to the Wall variant-c by Humberto Ramos & Alex Garner 5.00
1-Defcon 4-Way variant-c by Jim Lee 1 2 3 4 5 7
2-4 3.00

DEFENDERS, THE (TV)
Dell Publishing Co.: Sept-Nov, 1962 - No. 2, Feb-Apr, 1963

12-176-211(#1) 4 8 12 25 40 55
12-176-304(#2) 3 6 9 20 31 42

DEFENDERS, THE (Also see Giant-Size..., Marvel Feature, Marvel Treasury Edition, Secret Defenders & Sub-Mariner #34, 35; The New...#140-on)
Marvel Comics Group: Aug, 1972 - No. 152, Feb, 1986

1-The Hulk, Doctor Strange, Sub-Mariner begin 12 24 36 79 170 260
2-Silver Surfer x-over 6 12 18 41 76 110
3-5: 3-Silver Surfer x-over. 4-Valkyrie joins 5 10 15 30 50 70
6,7: 6-Silver Surfer x-over 3 6 9 21 33 45
8,9,11: 8-11-Defenders vs. the Avengers (Crossover with Avengers #115-118)
8,11-Silver Surfer x-over 4 8 12 27 44 60
10-Hulk vs. Thor battle 8 16 24 52 99 145
12-14: 12-Last 20¢ issue 3 6 9 14 19 24
15,16-Magneto & Brotherhood of Evil Mutants app. from X-Men 3 6 9 16 23 30
17-20: 17-Power Man x-over (11/74) 2 4 6 8 11 14
21-25: 24,25-Son of Satan app. 1 2 3 5 7 9
26,27,29-Guardians of the Galaxy app. (#26 is 8/75; pre-dates Marvel Presents #3).
29-Starhawk joins Guardians 2 4 6 9 12 15
28-1st full app. Starhawk (1st brief app. #27); Guardians of the Galaxy app.

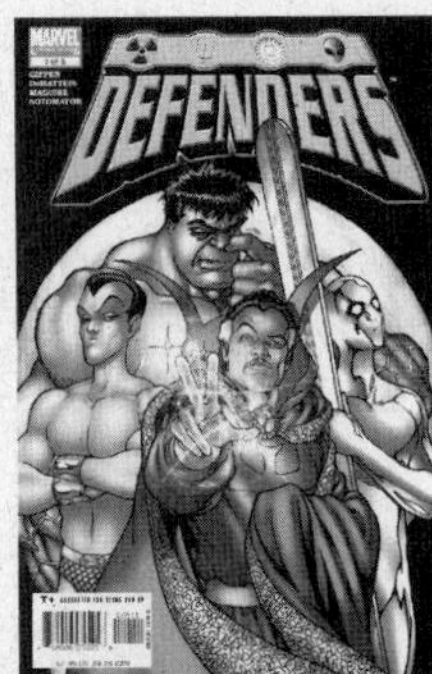

The Defenders (2005) #1 © MAR

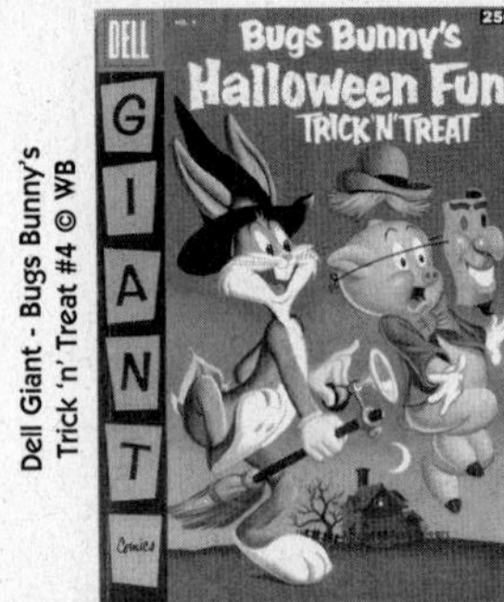

Dell Giant - Bugs Bunny's Trick 'n' Treat #4 © WB

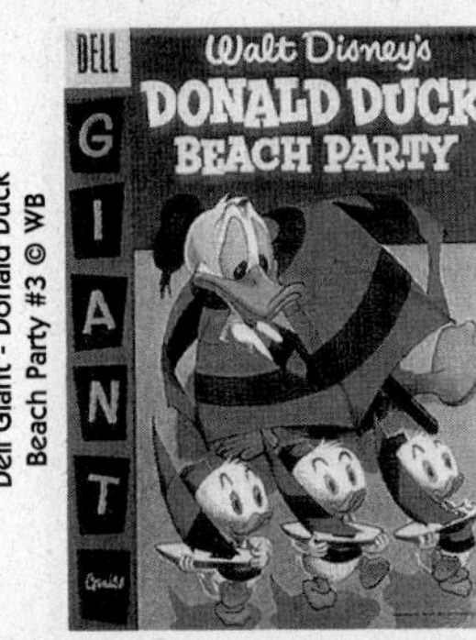

Dell Giant - Donald Duck Beach Party #3 © WB

GD VG FN VF VF/NM NM-
2.0 4.0 6.0 8.0 9.0 9.2

3 6 9 19 30 40

30-33,39-50: 31,32-Origin Nighthawk. 44-Hellcat joins. 45-Dr. Strange leaves. 47-49-Early Moon Knight app. (5/77). 48-50-(Reg. 30¢-c) 6.00

34-38-(Regular 25¢ editions): 35-Intro New Red Guardian 6.00

34-38-(30¢-c variants, limited distribution)(4-8/76) 3 6 9 19 30 40

48-52-(35¢-c variants, limited distribution)(6-10/77) 4 8 12 27 44 60

51-60: 51,52-(Reg. 30¢-c). 53-1st brief app. Lunatik (Lobo lookalike). 55-Origin Red Guardian; Lunatik cameo. 56-1st full Lunatik story 5.00

61-75: 61-Lunatik & Spider-Man app. 70-73-Lunatik (origin #71). 73-75-Foolkiller II app. (Greg Salinger). 74-Nighthawk resigns 4.00

76-93,95,97-99,102-119,123,124,126-149,151: 77-Origin Omega. 78-Original Defenders return thru #101. 104-The Beast joins. 105-Son of Satan joins. 106-Death of Nighthawk. 129-New Mutants cameo (3/84, early x-over) 3.00

94-1st Gargoyle 1 2 3 5 6 8

96-Ghost Rider app. 4.00

100-(52 pgs.)-Hellcat (Patsy Walker) revealed as Satan's daughter 5.00

101,120-122: 101-Silver Surfer-c & app. 120,121-Son of Satan-c/stories. 122-Final app. Son of Satan (2 pgs.) 4.00

125,150: 125-(52 pgs.)-Intro new Defenders. 150-(52 pgs.)-Origin Cloud 4.00

152-(52 pgs.)-Ties in with X-Factor & Secret Wars II 6.00

Annual 1 (1976, 52 pgs.)-New book-length story 3 6 9 19 30 40

NOTE: ***Art Adams*** *c-142p.* ***Austin*** *a-53i; c-65i, 119i, 145i.* ***Frank Bolle*** *a-7i, 10i, 11i.* ***Buckler*** *c(p)-34, 38, 76, 77, 79-86, 90, 91.* ***J. Buscema*** *c-66.* ***Giffen*** *a-42-49p, 50, 51-54p.* ***Golden*** *a-53p, 54p; c-94, 96.* ***Guice*** *c-129.* ***G. Kane*** *c(p)-13, 16, 18, 19, 21-26, 31-33, 35-37, 40, 41, 52, 55.* ***Kirby*** *c-42-45.* ***Mooney*** *a-3i, 31-34i, 62i, 63i, 85i.* ***Nasser*** *c-88p.* ***Perez*** *c(p)-51, 53, 54.* ***Rogers*** *c-98.* ***Starlin*** *c-110.* ***Tuska*** *a-57p. Silver Surfer in No. 2, 3, 6, 8-11, 92, 98-101, 107, 112-115, 122-125.*

DEFENDERS, THE (Volume 2) (Continues in The Order)
Marvel Comics: Mar, 2001 - No. 12, Feb, 2002 ($2.99/$2.25)

1-Busiek & Larsen-s/Larsen & Janson-a/c 3.00
2-11: 2-Two covers by Larsen & Art Adams; Valkyrie app. 4-Frenz-a 3.00
12-($3.50) 'Nuff Said issue; back-up-s Reis-a 4.00
...: From the Vault (9/11, $2.99) Previously unpublished story; Bagley-a 3.00

DEFENDERS, THE
Marvel Comics: Sept, 2005 - No. 5, Jan, 2006 ($2.99, limited series)

1-5-Giffen & DeMatteis-s/Maguire-a. 2-Dormammu app. 3.00
...: Indefensible HC (2006, $19.99, dust jacket) r/#1-5; Giffen & Maguire sketch page 20.00
...: Indefensible SC (2007, $13.99) r/#1-5; Giffen & Maguire sketch page 14.00

DEFENDERS, THE
Marvel Comics: Feb, 2012 - No. 12, Jan, 2013 ($3.99)

1-12: 1-Dr. Strange, Namor, Silver Surfer, Red She-Hulk, Iron Fist team; Dodson-a 4.00
...: Strange Heroes 1 (2/12, $4.99) Handbook-style profiles of team members and foes 5.00
...: The Coming of the Defenders 1 (2/12, $5.99) r/Marvel Feature #1-3; recolored-c of #1 6.00
...: Tournament of Heroes 1 (3/12, $5.99) r/Defenders #62-65 (1978); recolored-c of #62 6.00

DEFENDERS OF DYNATRON CITY
Marvel Comics: Feb, 1992 - No. 6, July, 1992 ($1.25, limited series)

1-6-Lucasarts characters. 2-Origin 3.00

DEFENDERS OF THE EARTH (TV)
Marvel Comics (Star Comics): Jan, 1987 - No. 4, July, 1987

1-4: The Phantom, Mandrake The Magician, Flash Gordon begin. 3-Origin Phantom. 4-Origin Mandrake 4.00

DEFEX
Devil's Due Publ.: Oct, 2004 - No. 6, Apr, 2005 ($2.95)

1-6: 1-Wolfman-s/Caselli-a. 6-Pérez-c 3.00

DEFIANCE
Image Comics: Feb, 2002 - No. 8, Jun, 2003 ($2.95)

Preview Edition (12/01) 3.00
1-8-Barré-s/Kang & Suh-a 3.00

DEFINITIVE DIRECTORY OF THE DC UNIVERSE, THE (See Who's Who...)

DEJAH THORIS AND THE GREEN MEN OF MARS (Warlord of Mars)
Dynamite Entertainment: 2013 - Present ($3.99)

1-12: 1-8-Rahner-s/Antonio-a; multiple covers on each. 9-12-Morales-a 4.00

DEJAH THORIS AND THE WHITE APES OF MARS (Warlord of Mars)
Dynamite Entertainment: 2012 - No. 3, 2012 ($3.99)

1-3-Rahner-s/Antonio-a; 2 covers by Peterson & Garza 4.00

DELECTA OF THE PLANETS (See Don Fortune & Fawcett Miniatures)

DELICATE CREATURES
Image Comics (Top Cow): 2001 ($16.95, hardcover with dust jacket)

nn-Fairy tale storybook; J. Michael Straczynski-s; Michael Zulli-a 17.00

GD VG FN VF VF/NM NM-
2.0 4.0 6.0 8.0 9.0 9.2

DELIRIUM'S PARTY: A LITTLE ENDLESS STORYBOOK (Characters from The Sandman titles and The Little Endless Storybook)
DC Comics: 2011 ($14.99, hardcover, one-shot)

HC-Jill Thompson-s/painted-a/c; Little Delirium throws a party; watercolor page process 15.00

DELLA VISION (...The Television Queen) (Patty Powers #4 on)
Atlas Comics: April, 1955 - No. 3, Aug, 1955

1-Al Hartley-c 18 36 54 103 162 220
2,3 12 24 36 69 97 125

DELLEC
Aspen MLT.: Aug, 2009 - No. 6, Oct, 2011 ($2.50)

1-6-Gunnell-a/c 3.00

DELL GIANT COMICS

Dell Publishing began to release square bound comics in 1949 with a 132-page issue called Christmas Parade #1. The covers were of a heavier stock to accommodate the increased number of pages. The books proved profitable at 25 cents, but the average number of pages was quickly reduced to 100. Ten years later they were converted to a numbering system similar to the Four Color Comics, for greater ease in distribution and the page counts cut back to mostly 84 pages. The label "Dell Giant" began to appear on the covers in 1954. Because of the size of the books and the heavier, less pliant cover stock, they are rarely found in high grade condition, and with the exception of a small quantity of copies released from Western Publishing's warehouse–are almost never found in near mint.

Abraham Lincoln Life Story 1(3/58) 8 16 24 64 107 150
Bugs Bunny Christmas Funnies 1(11/50, 116pp) 21 42 63 168 289 410
...Christmas Funnies 2(11/51, 116pp) 12 24 36 96 171 245
...Christmas Funnies 3-5(11/52-11/54,)-Becomes Christmas Party #6
10 20 30 80 140 200
...Christmas Funnies 7-9(12/56-12/58) 9 18 27 72 124 175
...Christmas Party 6(11/55)-Formerly Bugs Bunny Christmas Funnies
9 18 27 72 124 175
...County Fair 1(9/57) 11 22 33 88 149 210
...Halloween Parade 1(10/53) 12 24 36 96 166 235
...Halloween Parade 2(10/54)-Trick 'N' Treat Halloween Fun #3 on
10 20 30 80 135 190
...Trick 'N' Treat Halloween Fun 3,4(10/55-10/56)-Formerly Halloween Parade #2
9 18 27 72 129 185
...Vacation Funnies 1(7/51, 112pp) 19 38 57 152 269 385
...Vacation Funnies 2('52) 13 26 39 104 180 255
...Vacation Funnies 3-5('53-'55) 10 20 30 80 138 195
...Vacation Funnies 6,7,9('56-'59) 9 18 27 72 124 175
...Vacation Funnies 8('58) 1st app. Beep Beep the Road Runner, Wile E. Coyote (1st meeting), Mathilda (Mrs. Beep Beep) and their 3 children who hatch from eggs; one month before Four Color #918 11 22 33 88 157 225
Cadet Gray of West Point 1(4/58)-Williamson-a, 10pgs.; Buscema-a; photo-c
8 16 24 64 107 150
Christmas In Disneyland 1(12/57)-Barks-a, 18 pgs. 25 50 75 200 350 500
Christmas Parade 1(11/49)(132 pgs.)(1st Dell Giant)-Donald Duck (25 pgs. by Barks, r-in G.K. Christmas Parade #5); Mickey Mouse & other film oriented stories; Cinderella (prior to movie), 7 Dwarfs, Bambi & Thumper, So Dear To My Heart, Flying Mouse, Dumbo, Cookieland & others 63 126 189 504 877 1250
Christmas Parade 2('50)-Donald Duck (132 pgs.)(25 pgs. by Barks, r-in Gold Key's Christmas Parade #6). Mickey, Pluto, Chip & Dale, etc. Contents shift to a holiday expansion of W.D. C&S type format 42 84 126 336 588 840
Christmas Parade 3-7('51-'55, #3-116pgs; #4-7, 100 pgs.)
14 28 42 112 196 280
Christmas Parade 8(12/56)-Barks-a, 8 pgs. 22 44 66 176 306 435
Christmas Parade 9(12/58)-Barks-a, 20 pgs. 25 50 75 200 350 500
Christmas Treasury, A 1(11/54) 9 18 27 72 126 180
Davy Crockett, King Of The Wild Frontier 1(9/55)-Fess Parker photo-c; Marsh-a
19 38 57 152 269 385
Disneyland Birthday Party 1(10/58)-Barks-a, 16 pgs. r-by Gladstone
25 50 75 200 350 500
Donald and Mickey In Disneyland 1(5/58) 11 22 33 88 157 225
Donald Duck Beach Party 1(7/54)-Has an Uncle Scrooge story (not by Barks) that prefigures the later rivalry with Flintheart Glomgold and tells of Scrooge's wild rivalry with another millionaire 16 32 48 128 224 320
...Beach Party 2(1955)-Lady & Tramp 11 22 33 88 157 225
...Beach Party 3-5(1956-58) 11 22 33 88 152 215
...Beach Party 6(8/59, 84pp)-Stapled 8 16 24 64 115 165
Donald Duck Fun Book 1,2 (1953 & 10/54)-Games, puzzles, comics & cut-outs (very rare in unused condition)(most copies commonly have defaced interior pgs.)
63 126 189 504 877 1250
Donald Duck In Disneyland 1(9/55)-1st Disneyland Dell Giant

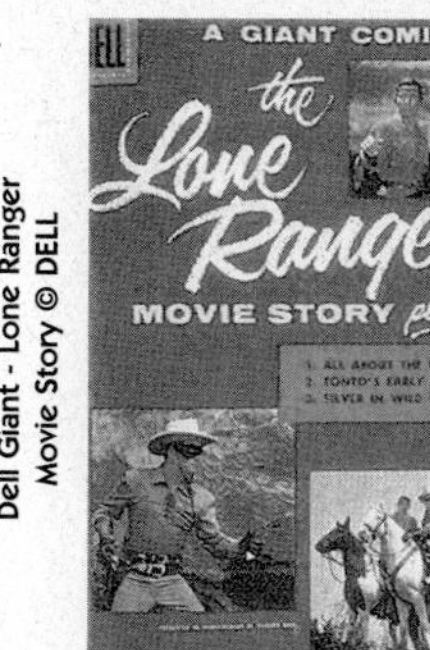

Dell Giant - Lone Ranger Movie Story © DELL

Dell Giant - Western Roundup #11 © DELL

Dell Giant #26 © DIS

	GD 2.0	VG 4.0	FN 6.0	VF 8.0	VF/NM 9.0	NM- 9.2
	15	30	45	120	210	300
Golden West Rodeo Treasury 1(10/57)	10	20	30	80	135	190
Huey, Dewey and Louie Back To School 1(9/58)	9	18	27	72	126	180
Lady and The Tramp 1(6/55)	17	34	51	136	233	330
Life Stories of American Presidents 1(11/57)-Buscema-a	8	16	24	64	107	150
Lone Ranger Golden West 3(8/55)-Formerly Lone Ranger Western Treasury	18	36	54	144	255	365
Lone Ranger Movie Story nn(3/56)-Origin Lone Ranger in text; Clayton Moore photo-c	36	72	108	288	507	725
...Western Treasury 1(9/53)-Origin Lone Ranger, Silver, & Tonto; painted cover	23	46	69	184	325	465
...Western Treasury 2(8/54)-Becomes Lone Ranger Golden West #3	18	36	54	144	255	365
Marge's Little Lulu & Alvin Story Telling Time 1(3/59)-r/#2,5,3,11,30,10,21,17,8, 14,16; Stanley-a	14	28	42	112	196	280
...& Her Friends 4(3/56)-Tripp-a	14	28	42	112	191	270
...& Her Special Friends 3(3/55)-Tripp-a	15	30	45	120	210	300
...& Tubby At Summer Camp 5,2: 5(10/57)-Tripp-a. 2(10/58)-Tripp-a	13	26	39	104	182	260
...& Tubby Halloween Fun 6,2: 6(10/57)-Tripp-a. 2(10/58)-Tripp-a	13	26	39	104	182	260
...& Tubby In Alaska 1(7/59)-Tripp-a	13	26	39	104	177	250
...On Vacation 1(7/54)-r/4C-110,14,4C-146,5,4C-97,4,4C-158,3,1;Stanley-a	25	50	75	200	350	500
...& Tubby Annual 1(3/53)-r/4C-165,4C-74,4C-146,4C-97,4C-158, 4C-139, 4C-131; Stanley-a (1st Lulu Dell Giant)	30	60	90	240	420	600
...& Tubby Annual 2('54)-r/4C-139,6,4C-115,4C-74,5,4C-97,3,4C-146,18; Stanley-a	25	50	75	200	350	500
Marge's Tubby & His Clubhouse Pals 1(10/56)-1st app. Gran'pa Feeb;1st app. Janie; written by Stanley; Tripp-a	15	30	45	120	210	300
Mickey Mouse Almanac 1(12/57)-Barks-a, 8pgs.	27	54	81	216	378	540
...Birthday Party 1(9/53)-r/entire 48pgs. of Gottfredson's "Mickey Mouse in Love Trouble" from WDC&S 36-39. Quality equal to original. Also reprints one story each from Four Color 27, 79, & 181 plus 6 panels of highlights in the career of Mickey Mouse	31	62	93	248	434	620
...Club Parade 1(12/55)-r/4-Color 16 with some death trap scenes redrawn by Paul Murry & recolored with night turned into day; quality less than original	22	44	66	176	308	440
...In Fantasy Land 1(5/57)	13	26	39	104	180	255
...In Frontier Land 1(5/56)-Mickey Mouse Club iss.	13	26	39	104	180	255
...Summer Fun 1(8/58)-Mobile cut-outs on back-c; becomes Summer Fun with #2; Canadian version exists with 30¢-c price	13	26	39	104	180	255
Moses & The Ten Commandments 1(8/57)-Not based on movie; Dell's adaptation; Sekowsky-a; variant version has "Gods of Egypt" comic back-c	8	16	24	64	107	150
Nancy & Sluggo Travel Time 1(9/58)	8	16	24	64	115	165
Peter Pan Treasure Chest 1(1/53, 212pp)-Disney; contains 54-page movie adaptation & other Peter Pan stories; plus Donald & Mickey stories w/P. Pan; a 32-page retelling of "D. Duck Finds Pirate Gold" with yellow beak, called "Capt. Hook & the Buried Treasure"	135	270	405	1080	1890	2700
Picnic Party 6,7(7/55-6/56)(Formerly Vacation Parade)-Uncle Scrooge, Mickey & Donald	12	24	36	96	166	235
Picnic Party 8(7/57)-Barks-a, 6pgs	21	42	63	168	289	410
Pogo Parade 1(9/53)-Kelly-a(r-/Pogo from Animal Comics in this order: #11,13,21,14,27,16,23,9,18,15,17)	25	50	75	200	350	500
Raggedy Ann & Andy 1(2/55)	16	32	48	128	224	320
Santa Claus Funnies 1(11/52)-Dan Noonan -A Christmas Carol adaptation	9	18	27	72	126	180
Silly Symphonies 1(9/52)-Redrawing of Gotfredson's Mickey Mouse strip of "The Brave Little Tailor;" 2 Good Housekeeping pages (from 1943); Lady and the Two Siamese Cats, three years before "Lady & the Tramp;" a retelling of Donald Duck's first app. in "The Wise Little Hen" & other stories based on 1930's Silly Symphony cartoons	32	64	96	256	448	640
Silly Symphonies 2(9/53)-M. Mouse in "The Sorcerer's Apprentice", 2 Good Housekeeping pages (from 1944); The Pelican & the Snipe, Elmer Elephant, Peculiar Penguins, Little Hiawatha, & others	24	48	72	192	339	485
Silly Symphonies 3(2/54)-r/Mickey & The Beanstalk (4-Color #157, 39pgs.), Little Minnehaha, Pablo, The Flying Gauchito, Pluto, & Bongo, & 2 Good Housekeeping pages (1944)	20	40	60	160	275	390
Silly Symphonies 4(8/54)-r/Dumbo (4-Color 234), Morris The Midget Moose, The Country Cousin, Bongo, & Clara Cluck	20	40	60	160	275	390
Silly Symphonies 5-8: 5(2/55)-r/Cinderella (4-Color 272), Bucky Bug, Pluto, Little Hiawatha, The 7 Dwarfs & Dumbo, Pinocchio. 6(8/55)-r/Pinocchio (WDC&S 63), The 7 Dwarfs & Thumper (WDC&S 45), M. Mouse "Adventures With Robin Hood" (40 pgs.), Johnny Appleseed, Pluto & Peter Pan, & Bucky Bug; Cut-out on back-c. 7(2/57)-r/Reluctant Dragon, Ugly Duckling, M. Mouse & Peter Pan, Jiminy Cricket, Peter & The Wolf, Brer Rabbit, Bucky Bug; Cut-out on back-c. 8(2/58)-r/Thumper Meets The 7 Dwarfs (4-Color #19), Jiminy Cricket, Niok, Brer Rabbit; Cut-out on back-c	16	32	48	128	224	320
Silly Symphonies 9(2/59)-r/Paul Bunyan, Humphrey Bear, Jiminy Cricket, The Social Lion, Goliath II; cut-out on back-c	15	30	45	120	210	300
Sleeping Beauty 1(4/59)	25	50	75	200	350	500
Summer Fun 2(8/59, 84pp, stapled binding)(Formerly Mickey Mouse...)-Barks-a(2), 24 pgs.	24	48	72	192	336	480
Tarzan's Jungle Annual 1(8/52)-Lex Barker photo on-c of #1,2	15	30	45	120	210	300
...Annual 2(8/53)	11	22	33	88	152	215
...Annual 3-7('54-9/58)(two No. 5s)-Manning-a-No. 3,5-7; Marsh-a in No. 1-7 plus painted-c 1-7	9	18	27	72	124	175
Tom And Jerry Back To School 1(9/56) 2 different back-c, variant has "Apple for the Teacher" cut-out	12	24	36	96	168	240
...Picnic Time 1(7/58)	10	20	30	80	135	190
...Summer Fun 1(7/54)-Droopy written by Barks	15	30	45	120	205	290
...Summer Fun 2-4(7/55-7/57)	8	16	24	64	107	150
...Toy Fair 1(6/58)	9	18	27	72	126	180
...Winter Carnival 1(12/52)-Droopy written by Barks	20	40	60	160	280	400
...Winter Carnival 2(12/53)-Droopy written by Barks	16	32	48	128	224	320
...Winter Fun 3(12/54)	8	16	24	64	115	165
...Winter Fun 4-7(12/55-11/58)	7	14	21	56	101	145
Treasury of Dogs, A 1(10/56)	7	14	21	56	101	145
Treasury of Horses, A (9/55)	7	14	21	56	101	145
Uncle Scrooge Goes To Disneyland 1(8/57p)-Barks-a, 20 pgs. r-by Gladstone; 2 different back-c; variant shows 6 snapshots of Scrooge	26	52	78	208	359	510
Vacation In Disneyland 1(8/58)	11	22	33	88	157	225
Vacation Parade 1(7/50, 132pp)-Donald Duck & Mickey Mouse; Barks-a, 55 pgs.	95	190	285	760	1330	1900
Vacation Parade 2(7/51,116pp)	25	50	75	200	350	500
Vacation Parade 3-5(7/52-7/54)-Becomes Picnic Party No. 6 on. #4-Robin Hood Advs.	14	28	42	112	194	275
Western Roundup 1(6/52)-Photo-c; Gene Autry, Roy Rogers, Johnny Mack Brown, Rex Allen, & Bill Elliott begin; photo back-c begin, end No. 14,16,18	25	50	75	200	350	500
Western Roundup 2(2/53)-Photo-c	14	28	42	112	196	280
Western Roundup 3-5(7-9/53 - 1-3/54)-Photo-c	11	22	33	88	157	225
Western Roundup 6-10(4-6/54 - 4-6/55)-Photo-c	11	22	33	88	149	210
Western Roundup 11-17,25: 11-17-Photo-c; 11-13,16,17-Manning-a. 11-Flying A's Range Rider, Dale Evans begin	9	18	27	72	129	185
Western Roundup 18-Toth-a; last photo-c; Gene Autry ends	11	22	33	88	149	210
Western Roundup 19-24-Manning-a. 19-Buffalo Bill Jr. begins (7-9/57; early app.). 19,20,22-Toth-a. 21-Rex Allen, Johnny Mack Brown end. 22-Jace Pearson's Texas Rangers, Rin Tin Tin, Tales of Wells Fargo (2nd app., 4-6/58) & Wagon Train (2nd app.) begin	9	18	27	72	129	185
Woody Woodpecker Back To School 1(10/52)	10	20	30	80	140	200
...Back To School 2-4,6('53-10/57)-County Fair No. 5	8	16	24	64	112	160
...County Fair 5(9/56)-Formerly Back To School	8	16	24	64	112	160
...County Fair 2(11/58)	7	14	21	56	101	145

DELL GIANTS (Consecutive numbering)

Dell Publishing Co.: No. 21, Sept, 1959 - No. 55, Sept, 1961 (Most 84 pgs., 25¢)

	GD 2.0	VG 4.0	FN 6.0	VF 8.0	VF/NM 9.0	NM- 9.2
21-(#1)-M.G.M.'s Tom & Jerry Picnic Time (84pp, stapled binding)-Painted-c	11	22	33	88	157	225
22-Huey, Dewey & Louie Back to School (Disney; 10/59, 84pp, square binding begins)	9	18	27	72	129	185
23-Marge's Little Lulu & Tubby Halloween Fun (10/59)-Tripp-a	12	24	36	96	168	240
24-Woody Woodpecker's Family Fun (11/59)(Walter Lantz)	8	16	24	64	112	160
25-Tarzan's Jungle World(11/59)-Marsh-a; painted-c	11	22	33	88	152	215
26-Christmas Parade(Disney; 12/59)-Barks-a, 16pgs.; Barks draws himself on wanted poster on pg. 13	21	42	63	168	289	410
27-Walt Disney's Man in Space (10/59) r-/4-Color 716,866, & 954 (100 pgs., 35¢)(TV)	9	18	27	72	129	185
28-Bugs Bunny's Winter Fun (2/60)	9	18	27	72	126	180
29-Marge's Little Lulu & Tubby in Hawaii (4/60)-Tripp-a	12	24	36	96	166	235
30-Disneyland USA(Disney; 6/60)	9	18	27	72	124	175
31-Huckleberry Hound Summer Fun (7/60)(TV)(HannaBarbera)-Yogi Bear & Pixie & Dixie app.	12	24	36	96	173	250

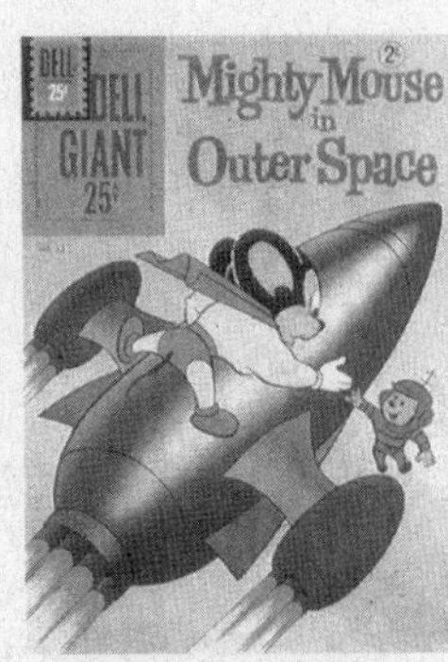

Dell Giant #43 © MGM

Demon Knights #15 © DC

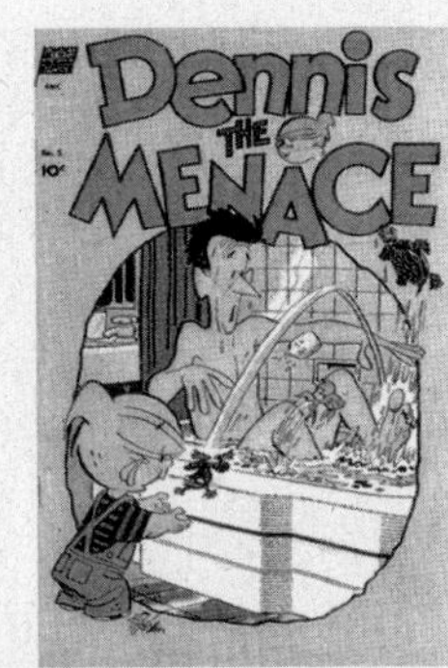

Dennis the Menace #5 © FAW

	GD 2.0	VG 4.0	FN 6.0	VF 8.0	VF/NM 9.0	NM- 9.2
32-Bugs Bunny Beach Party	7	14	21	56	101	145
33-Daisy Duck & Uncle Scrooge Picnic Time (Disney; 9/60)	9	18	27	72	124	175
34-Nancy & Sluggo Summer Camp (8/60)	7	14	21	56	101	145
35-Huey, Dewey & Louie Back to School (Disney; 10/60)-1st app. Daisy Duck's Nieces, April, May & June	12	24	36	96	163	230
36-Marge's Little Lulu & Witch Hazel Halloween Fun (10/60)-Tripp-a	11	22	33	88	157	225
37-Tarzan, King of the Jungle (11/60)-Marsh-a; painted-c	9	18	27	72	129	185
38-Uncle Donald & His Nephews Family Fun (Disney; 11/60)-Cover painting based on a pencil sketch by Barks	12	24	36	96	173	250
39-Walt Disney's Merry Christmas (Disney; 12/60)-Cover painting based on a pencil sketch by Barks	12	24	36	96	173	250
40-Woody Woodpecker Christmas Parade (12/60)(Walter Lantz)	6	12	18	48	87	125
41-Yogi Bear's Winter Sports (12/60)(TV)(Hanna-Barbera)-Huckleberry Hound, Pixie & Dixie, Augie Doggie app.	12	24	36	96	173	250
42-Marge's Little Lulu & Tubby in Australia (4/61)	11	22	33	88	157	225
43-Mighty Mouse in Outer Space (5/61)	18	36	54	144	252	360
44-Around the World with Huckleberry and His Friends (7/61)(TV)(Hanna-Barbera)-Yogi Bear, Pixie & Dixie, Quick Draw McGraw, Augie Doggie app.; 1st app. Yakky Doodle	13	26	39	104	182	260
45-Nancy & Sluggo Summer Camp (8/61)	7	14	21	56	96	135
46-Bugs Bunny Beach Party (8/61)	7	14	21	56	96	135
47-Mickey & Donald in Vacationland (Disney; 8/61)	8	16	24	64	115	165
48-The Flintstones (No. 1)(Bedrock Bedlam)(7/61)(TV)(Hanna-Barbera) 1st app. in comics	21	42	63	168	289	410
49-Huey, Dewey & Louie Back to School (Disney; 9/61)	9	18	27	72	124	175
50-Marge's Little Lulu & Witch Hazel Trick 'N' Treat (10/61)	11	22	33	88	157	225
51-Tarzan, King of the Jungle by Jesse Marsh (11/61)-Painted-c	8	16	24	64	110	155
52-Uncle Donald & His Nephews Dude Ranch (Disney; 11/61)	8	16	24	64	115	165
53-Donald Duck Merry Christmas (Disney; 12/61)	8	16	24	64	112	160
54-Woody Woodpecker's Christmas Party (12/61)-Issued after No. 55	7	14	21	56	98	140
55-Daisy Duck & Uncle Scrooge Showboat (Disney; 9/61)	8	16	24	64	117	170

NOTE: All issues printed with & without ad on back cover.

DELL JUNIOR TREASURY
Dell Publishing Co.: June, 1955 - No. 10, Oct, 1957 (15¢) (All painted-c)

	GD 2.0	VG 4.0	FN 6.0	VF 8.0	VF/NM 9.0	NM- 9.2
1-Alice in Wonderland; r/4-Color #331 (52 pgs.)	8	16	24	54	102	150
2-Aladdin & the Wonderful Lamp	6	12	18	41	76	110
3-Gulliver's Travels (1/56)	6	12	18	37	66	95
4-Adventures of Mr. Frog & Miss Mouse	6	12	18	38	69	100
5-The Wizard of Oz (7/56)	6	12	18	41	76	110
6-10: 6-Heidi (10/56). 7-Santa and the Angel. 8-Raggedy Ann and the Camel with the Wrinkled Knees. 9-Clementina the Flying Pig. 10-Adventures of Tom Sawyer	6	12	18	37	66	95

DEMOLITION MAN
DC Comics: Nov, 1993 - No. 4, Feb, 1994 ($1.75, color, limited series)

	GD 2.0	VG 4.0	FN 6.0	VF 8.0	VF/NM 9.0	NM- 9.2
1-4-Movie adaptation						3.00

DEMON, THE (See Detective Comics No. 482-485)
National Periodical Publications: Aug-Sept, 1972 - V3#16, Jan, 1974

	GD 2.0	VG 4.0	FN 6.0	VF 8.0	VF/NM 9.0	NM- 9.2
1-Origin; Kirby-c/a in all	8	16	24	54	102	150
2-5	4	8	12	27	44	60
6-16	3	6	9	19	30	40

DEMON, THE (1st limited series)(Also see Cosmic Odyssey #2)
DC Comics: Nov, 1986 - No. 4, Feb, 1987 (75¢, limited series)(#2 has #4 of 4 on-c)

	GD 2.0	VG 4.0	FN 6.0	VF 8.0	VF/NM 9.0	NM- 9.2
1-4: Matt Wagner-a(p) & scripts in all. 4-Demon & Jason Blood become separate entities.						4.00

DEMON, THE (2nd Series)
DC Comics: July, 1990 - No. 58, May, 1995 ($1.50/$1.75/$1.95)

	GD 2.0	VG 4.0	FN 6.0	VF 8.0	VF/NM 9.0	NM- 9.2
1-Grant scripts begin, ends #39: 1-4-Painted-c						5.00
2-18,20-27,29-39,41,42: 3,8-Batman app. (cameo #4). 12-Bisley painted-c. 12-15,21-Lobo app. (1 pg. cameo #11). 23-Robin app. 29-Superman app. 31,33-39-Lobo app.						3.00
19-($2.50, 44 pgs.)-Lobo poster stapled inside						5.00
28,40: 28-Superman-c/story; begin $1.75-c. 40-Garth Ennis scripts begin						4.00
43-45-Hitman app.	1	2	3	5	7	9
46-48 Return of The Haunted Tank-c/s. 48-Begin $1.95-c.						5.00
49,51,0-(10/94),55-58: 51-(9/94)						3.00
50 ($2.95, 52 pgs.)						4.00
52-54-Hitman-s						5.00
Annual 1 (1992, $3.00, 68 pgs.)-Eclipso-c/story						4.00
Annual 2 (1993, $3.50, 68 pgs.)-1st app. of Hitman	2	4	6	9	13	16

NOTE: ***Alan Grant*** *scripts in #1-16, 20, 21, 23-25, 30-39, Annual 1.* ***Wagner*** *a/scripts-22.*

DEMON DREAMS
Pacific Comics: Feb, 1984 - No. 2, May, 1984

	GD 2.0	VG 4.0	FN 6.0	VF 8.0	VF/NM 9.0	NM- 9.2
1,2-Mostly r-/Heavy Metal						3.00

DEMON: DRIVEN OUT
DC Comics: Nov, 2003 - No. 6, Apr, 2004 ($2.50, limited series)

	GD 2.0	VG 4.0	FN 6.0	VF 8.0	VF/NM 9.0	NM- 9.2
1-6-Dysart-s/Mhan-a						3.00

DEMON-HUNTER
Seaboard Periodicals (Atlas): Sept, 1975

	GD 2.0	VG 4.0	FN 6.0	VF 8.0	VF/NM 9.0	NM- 9.2
1-Origin/1st app. Demon-Hunter; Buckler-c/a	2	4	6	11	16	20

DEMON KNIGHT: A GRIMJACK GRAPHIC NOVEL
First Publishing: 1990 ($8.95, 52 pgs.)

	GD 2.0	VG 4.0	FN 6.0	VF 8.0	VF/NM 9.0	NM- 9.2
nn-Flint Henry-a						9.00

DEMON KNIGHTS (New DC 52) (Set in the Dark Ages)
DC Comics: Nov, 2011 - No. 23, Oct, 2013 ($2.99)

	GD 2.0	VG 4.0	FN 6.0	VF 8.0	VF/NM 9.0	NM- 9.2
1-23: 1-Cornell-s/Neves-a/Daniel-c; Etrigan, Madame Xanadu & The Shining Knight app.						3.00
#0 (11/12, $2.99) Origin of Etrigan The Demon; Merlin app.; Cornell-s/Chang-a						3.00

DENNIS THE MENACE (TV with 1959 issues) (Becomes ...Fun Fest Series; See The Best of... & The Very Best of...)(...Fun Fest on-c only to #156-166)
Standard Comics/Pines No.15-31/Hallden (Fawcett) No.32 on: 8/53 - #14, 1/56; #15, 3/56 - #31, 11/58; #32, 1/59 - #166, 11/79

	GD 2.0	VG 4.0	FN 6.0	VF 8.0	VF/NM 9.0	NM- 9.2
1-1st app. Dennis, Mr. & Mrs. Wilson, Ruff & Dennis' mom & dad; Wiseman-a, written by Fred Toole-most issues	142	284	426	909	1555	2200
2	45	90	135	284	480	675
3-10: 8-Last pre-code issue	24	48	72	142	234	325
11-20	16	32	48	94	147	200
21,23-30	12	24	36	69	97	125
22-1st app. Margaret w/blonde hair	15	30	45	85	130	175
31-1st app. Joey	15	30	45	85	130	175
32-38,40(1/60): 37-A-Bomb blast panel	9	18	27	50	65	80
39-1st app. Gina (11/59)	10	20	30	58	79	100
41-60(7/62)	4	8	12	22	34	45
61-80(9/65),100(1/69)	3	6	9	14	20	25
81-99	2	4	6	11	16	20
101-117: 102-Last 12¢ issue	2	4	6	9	12	15
118(1/72)-131 (All 52 pages)	2	4	6	10	14	18
132(1/74)-142,144-160	1	2	3	5	7	9
143(3/76) Olympic-c/s; low print	2	4	6	10	14	18
161-166	1	3	4	6	8	10

NOTE: ***Wiseman*** *c/a-1-46, 53, 68, 69.*

DENNIS THE MENACE (Giants) (No. 1 titled Giant Vacation Special; becomes Dennis the Menace Bonus Magazine No. 76 on)
(#1-8,18,23,25,30,38: 100 pgs.; rest to #41: 84 pgs.; #42-75: 68 pgs.)
Standard/Pines/Hallden(Fawcett): Summer, 1955 - No. 75, Dec, 1969

	GD 2.0	VG 4.0	FN 6.0	VF 8.0	VF/NM 9.0	NM- 9.2
nn-Giant Vacation Special(Summ/55-Standard)	18	36	54	103	162	220
nn-Christmas issue (Winter '55)	15	30	45	88	137	185
2-Giant Vacation Special (Summer '56-Pines)	14	28	42	78	112	145
3-Giant Christmas issue (Winter '56-Pines)	13	26	39	72	101	130
4-Giant Vacation Special (Summer '57-Pines)	12	24	36	67	94	120
5-Giant Christmas issue (Winter '57-Pines)	12	24	36	67	94	120
6-In Hawaii (Giant Vacation Special)(Summer '58-Pines)	11	22	33	62	86	110
6-In Hawaii (Summer '59-Hallden)-2nd printing; says 3rd large printing on-c 6-In Hawaii (Summer '60)-3rd printing; says 4th large printing on-c 6-In Hawaii (Summer '62)-4th printing; says 5th large printing on-c each....	8	16	24	42	54	65
6-Giant Christmas issue (Winter '58)	11	22	33	62	86	110
7-In Hollywood (Winter '59-Hallden)	5	10	15	30	50	70
7-In Hollywood (Summer '61)-2nd printing	3	6	9	20	31	42
8-In Mexico (Winter '60, 100 pgs.-Hallden/Fawcett)	5	10	15	30	50	70
8-In Mexico (Summer '62, 2nd printing)	3	6	9	20	31	42
9-Goes to Camp (Summer '61, 84 pgs.)-1st CCA approved issue	5	10	15	30	50	70

Dennis the Menace (1981) #7 © MAR

Desperado #2 © LEV

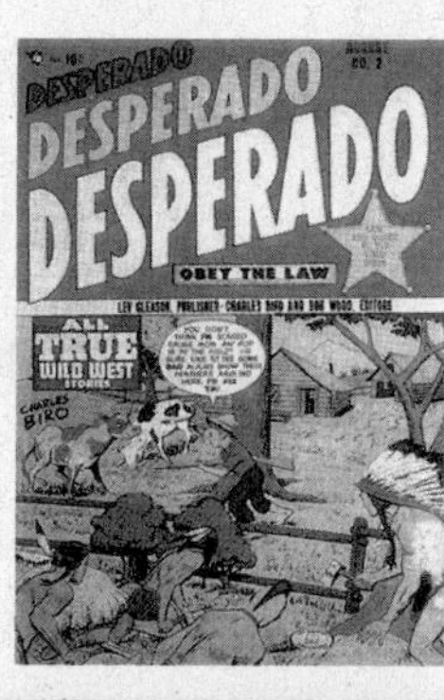

Desperadoes #1 © Aegis

	GD 2.0	VG 4.0	FN 6.0	VF 8.0	VF/NM 9.0	NM- 9.2
9-Goes to Camp (Summer '62)-2nd printing	3	6	9	20	31	42
10-12: 10-X-Mas issue (Winter '61), 11-Giant Christmas issue (Winter '62), 12-Triple Feature (Winter '62)	5	10	15	33	57	80
13-17: 13-Best of Dennis the Menace (Spring '63)-Reprints, 14-And His Dog Ruff (Summer '63), 15-In Washington, D.C. (Summer '63), 16-Goes to Camp (Summer '63)-Reprints No. 9, 17-& His Pal Joey (Winter '63)	4	8	12	23	37	50
18-In Hawaii (Reprints No. 6)	3	6	9	19	30	40
19-Giant Christmas issue (Winter '63)	4	8	12	23	37	50
20-Spring Special (Spring '64)	4	8	12	23	37	50
21-40 (Summer '66): 30-r/#6. #35-Xmas spec.Wint,'65	3	6	9	17	26	35
41-60 (Fall '68)	3	6	9	14	19	24
61-75 (12/69): 68-Partial-r/#6	2	4	6	11	16	20

NOTE: ***Wiseman*** *c/a-1-8, 12, 14, 15, 17, 20, 22, 27, 28, 31, 35, 36, 41, 49.*

DENNIS THE MENACE
Marvel Comics Group: Nov, 1981 - No. 13, Nov, 1982

	GD	VG	FN	VF	VF/NM	NM-
1-New-a	2	4	6	9	12	15
2-13: 2-New art. 3-Part-r. 4,5-r. 5-X-Mas-c & issue, 7-Spider Kid-c/sty	1	2	3	4	5	7

NOTE: ***Hank Ketcham*** *c-most; a-3, 12.* ***Wiseman*** *a-4, 5.*

DENNIS THE MENACE AND HIS DOG RUFF
Halldén/Fawcett: Summer, 1961

	GD	VG	FN	VF	VF/NM	NM-
1-Wiseman-c/a	5	10	15	34	60	85

DENNIS THE MENACE AND HIS FRIENDS
Fawcett Publ.: 1969; No. 5, Jan, 1970 - No. 46, April, 1980 (All reprints)

	GD	VG	FN	VF	VF/NM	NM-
Dennis the Menace & Joey No. 2 (7/69)	2	4	6	13	18	22
Dennis the Menace & Ruff No. 2 (9/69)	2	4	6	13	18	22
Dennis the Menace & Mr. Wilson No. 1 (10/69)	3	6	9	15	22	28
Dennis & Margaret No. 1 (Winter '69)	3	6	9	15	22	28
5-12: 5-Dennis the Menace & Margaret. 6-...& Joey. 7-...& Ruff. 8-...& Mr. Wilson	2	4	6	8	11	14
13-21-(52 pg Giants): 13-(1/72). 21-(1/74)	2	4	6	10	14	18
22-37	1	3	4	6	8	10
38-46 (Digest size, 148 pgs., 4/78, 95¢)	2	4	6	8	11	14

NOTE: *Titles rotate every four issues, beginning with No. 5. Joey issues: #2(7/69),6,10,14,18,22,26,30,34. Ruff issues: #2(9/69), 7,11,15,19,23,27,31,35. Mr. Wilson issues: #1(10/69),8,12,16,20,24,28,32,36. Margaret issues: #1(Wint./69),5,9,13,17,21,25,29,33,37.*

DENNIS THE MENACE AND HIS PAL JOEY
Fawcett Publ.: Summer, 1961 (10¢) (See Dennis the Menace Giants No. 45)

	GD	VG	FN	VF	VF/NM	NM-
1-Wiseman-c/a	5	10	15	34	60	85

DENNIS THE MENACE AND THE BIBLE KIDS
Word Books: 1977 (36 pgs.)

	GD	VG	FN	VF	VF/NM	NM-
1-6: 1-Jesus. 2-Joseph. 3-David. 4-The Bible Girls. 5-Moses. 6-More About Jesus	2	4	6	9	12	15
7-9-Low print run: 7-The Lord's Prayer. 8-Stories Jesus told. 9-Paul, God's Traveller	3	6	9	19	30	40
10-Low print run; In the Beginning	5	10	15	33	57	80

NOTE: ***Ketcham*** *c/a in all.*

DENNIS THE MENACE BIG BONUS SERIES
Fawcett Publications: No. 10, Feb, 1980 - No. 11, Apr, 1980

	GD	VG	FN	VF	VF/NM	NM-
10,11	1	2	3	5	6	8

DENNIS THE MENACE BONUS MAGAZINE (Formerly Dennis the Menace Giants Nos. 1-75)
(...Big Bonus Series on-c for #174-194)
Fawcett Publications: No. 76, 1/70 - No. 95, 7/71; No. 95, 7/71; No. 97, '71; No. 194, 10/79; (No. 76-124: 68 pgs.; No. 125-163: 52 pgs.; No. 164 on: 36 pgs.)

	GD	VG	FN	VF	VF/NM	NM-
76-90(3/71)	2	4	6	10	14	18
91-95, 97-110(10/72): Two #95's with same date(7/71) A-Summer Games, and B-That's Our Boy. No #96	2	4	6	9	13	16
111-124	2	4	6	8	10	12
125-163-(52 pgs.)	2	4	6	8	10	12
164-194: 166-Indicia printed backwards	1	2	3	4	5	7

DENNIS THE MENACE COMICS DIGEST
Marvel Comics Group: April, 1982 - No. 3, Aug, 1982 ($1.25, digest-size)

	GD	VG	FN	VF	VF/NM	NM-
1-3-Reprints	1	3	4	6	8	10
1-Mistakenly printed with DC emblem on cover	2	4	6	10	12	15

NOTE: ***Ketcham*** *c-all.* ***Wiseman*** *a-all. A few thousand #1's were published with a DC emblem on cover.*

DENNIS THE MENACE FUN BOOK
Fawcett Publications/Standard Comics: 1960 (100 pgs.)

	GD	VG	FN	VF	VF/NM	NM-
1-Part Wiseman-a	5	10	15	35	63	90

DENNIS THE MENACE FUN FEST SERIES (Formerly Dennis the Menace #166)
Halldén (Fawcett): No. 16, Jan, 1980 - No. 17, Mar, 1980 (40¢)

	GD	VG	FN	VF	VF/NM	NM-
16,17-By Hank Ketcham	1	2	3	4	5	7

DENNIS THE MENACE POCKET FULL OF FUN!
Fawcett Publications (Halldén): Spring, 1969 - No. 50, March, 1980 (196 pgs.) (Digest size)

	GD	VG	FN	VF	VF/NM	NM-
1-Reprints in all issues	5	10	15	33	57	80
2-10	4	8	12	23	37	50
11-20	3	6	9	15	22	28
21-28	2	4	6	11	16	20
29-50: 35,40,46-Sunday strip-r	2	4	6	8	11	14

NOTE: *No. 1-28 are 196 pgs.; No. 29-36: 164 pgs.; No. 37: 148 pgs.; No. 38 on: 132 pgs. No. 8, 11, 15, 21, 25, 29 all contain strip reprints.*

DENNIS THE MENACE TELEVISION SPECIAL
Fawcett Publ. (Halldén Div.): Summer, 1961 - No. 2, Spring, 1962 (Giant)

	GD	VG	FN	VF	VF/NM	NM-
1	5	10	15	34	60	85
2	3	6	9	21	33	45

DENNIS THE MENACE TRIPLE FEATURE
Fawcett Publications: Winter, 1961 (Giant)

	GD	VG	FN	VF	VF/NM	NM-
1-Wiseman-c/a	5	10	15	34	60	85

DEPUTY, THE (TV)
Dell Publishing Co.: No. 1077, Feb-Apr, 1960 - No. 1225, Oct-Dec, 1961 (all-Henry Fonda photo-c)

	GD	VG	FN	VF	VF/NM	NM-
Four Color 1077 (#1)-Buscema-a	10	20	30	64	132	200
Four Color 1130 (9-11/60)-Buscema-a,1225	8	16	24	54	102	150

DEPUTY DAWG (TV) (Also see New Terrytoons)
Dell Publishing Co./Gold Key: Oct-Dec, 1961 - No. 1299, 1962; No. 1, Aug, 1965

	GD	VG	FN	VF	VF/NM	NM-
Four Color 1238,1299	9	18	27	63	129	195
1(10164-508)(8/65)-Gold Key	9	18	27	63	129	195

DEPUTY DAWG PRESENTS DINKY DUCK AND HASHIMOTO-SAN (TV)
Gold Key: August, 1965

	GD	VG	FN	VF	VF/NM	NM-
1(10159-508)	9	18	27	57	111	165

DESERT GOLD (See Zane Grey 4-Color 467)

DESIGN FOR SURVIVAL (Gen. Thomas S. Power's...)
American Security Council Press: 1968 (36 pgs. in color) (25¢)

	GD	VG	FN	VF	VF/NM	NM-
nn-Propaganda against the Threat of Communism-Aircraft cover; H-Bomb panel	3	6	9	17	26	35
Twin Circle Edition-Cover shows panels from inside	2	4	6	13	18	22

DESOLATION JONES
DC Comics (WildStorm): July, 2005 - Present ($2.95/$2.99)

1-8: 1-6-Warren Ellis-s/J.H. Williams-a. 7,8-Zezelj-a 3.00

DESPERADO (Becomes Black Diamond Western No. 9 on)
Lev Gleason Publications: June, 1948 - No. 8, Feb, 1949 (All 52 pgs.)

	GD	VG	FN	VF	VF/NM	NM-
1-Biro-c on all; contains inside photo-c of Charles Biro, Lev Gleason & Bob Wood	15	30	45	90	140	190
2	10	20	30	56	76	95
3-Story with over 20 killings	10	20	30	58	79	100
4-8	8	16	24	44	57	70

NOTE: ***Barry*** *a-2.* ***Fuje*** *a-4, 8.* ***Guardineer*** *a-5-7.* ***Kida*** *a-3-7.* ***Ed Moore*** *a-4, 6.*

DESPERADO PRIMER
Image Comics (Desperado): Apr, 2005 ($1.99, one-shot)

1-Previews of Roundeye, World Traveler, A Mirror To The Soul; Bolland-c 3.00

DESPERADOES
Image Comics (Homage): Sept, 1997 - No. 5, June, 1998 ($2.50/$2.95)

1-5-Mariotte-s/Cassaday-c/a: 1-($2.50-c). 2-5-($2.95) 3.00
...: A Moment's Sunlight TPB ('98, $16.95) r/#1-5 17.00
...: Epidemic! (11/99, $5.95) Mariotte-s 6.00

DESPERADOES: BANNERS OF GOLD
IDW Publishing: Dec, 2004 - No. 5, Apr, 2005 ($3.99, limited series)

1-5: Mariotte-s/Haun-a. 1-Cassaday-c 4.00

DESPERADOES: BUFFALO DREAMS
IDW Publishing: Jan, 2007 - No. 4, Apr, 2007 ($3.99, limited series)

1-4: Mariotte-s/Dose-a/c 4.00

DESPERADOES: QUIET OF THE GRAVE
DC Comics (Homage): Jul, 2001 - No. 5, Nov, 2001 ($2.95)

1-5-Jeff Mariotte-s/John Severin-c/a 3.00

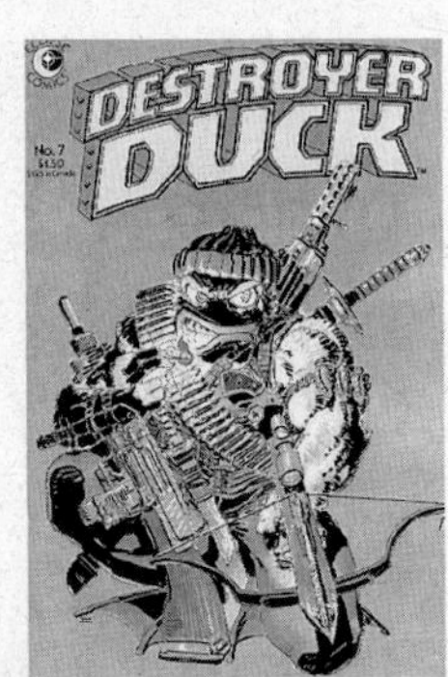

Destroyer Duck #7 © Gerber & Kirby

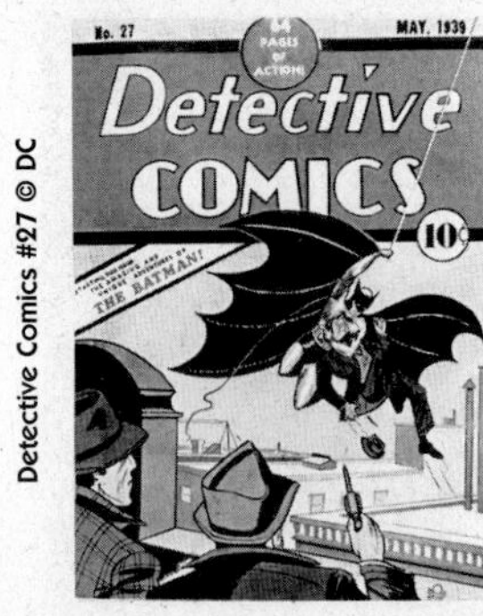

Detective Comics #27 © DC

Detective Comics #73 © DC

GD 2.0 | VG 4.0 | FN 6.0 | VF 8.0 | VF/NM 9.0 | NM- 9.2

GD 2.0 | VG 4.0 | FN 6.0 | VF 8.0 | VF/NM 9.0 | NM- 9.2

TPB (2002, $14.95) r/#1-5; intro. by Brian Keene 15.00

DESPERATE TIMES (See Savage Dragon)
Image Comics: Jun, 1998 - No. 4, Dec, 1998; Nov, 2000 - No. 4, July, 2001 ($2.95, B&W)

1-4-Chris Eliopoulos-s/a 3.00
(Vol. 2) 1-4 3.00
(Vol. 3) 0-(1/04, $3.50) Pages read sideways 3.50
(Vol. 3) 1-Pages read sideways 3.00

DESTINATION MOON (See Fawcett Movie Comics, Space Adventures #20, 23, & Strange Adventures #1)

DESTINY: A CHRONICLE OF DEATHS FORETOLD (See Sandman)
DC Comics (Vertigo): 1997 - No.3, 1998 ($5.95, limited series)

1-3-Alisa Kwitney-s in all: 1-Kent Williams & Michael Zulli-a, Williams painted-c. 2-Williams & Scott Hampton-painted-c/a. 3-Williams & Guay-a 6.00
TPB (2000, $14.95) r/series 15.00

DESTROY!!
Eclipse Comics: 1986 ($4.95, B&W, magazine-size, one-shot)

1 5.00
3-D Special 1-r-/#1 ($2.50) 5.00

DESTROYER
Marvel Comics: June, 2009 - No. 5, Oct, 2009 ($3.99, limited series)

1-5-Kirkman-s/Walker-a/Pearson-c 4.00

DESTROYER, THE
Marvel Comics (MAX): Nov, 1989 - No. 9, Jun, 1990 ($2.25, B&W, magazine, 52 pgs.)

1-Based on Remo Williams movie, paperbacks 6.00
2-9: 2-Williamson part inks. 4-Ditko-a 4.00

DESTROYER, THE
Marvel Comics: V2#1, March, 1991 ($1.95, 52 pgs.)
V3#1, Dec, 1991 - No. 4, Mar, 1992 ($1.95, mini-series)

V2#1,V3#1-4: Based on Remo Williams paperbacks. V3#1-4-Simonson-c. 3-Morrow-a 4.00

DESTROYER, THE (Also see Solar, Man of the Atom)
Valiant: Apr, 1995 ($2.95, color, one-shot)

0-Indicia indicates #1 3.00

DESTROYER DUCK
Eclipse Comics: Feb, 1982 - No. 7, May, 1984 (#2-7: Baxter paper) ($1.50)

1-Origin Destroyer Duck; 1st app. Groo; Kirby-c/a(p) 1 3 4 6 8 10
2-5: 2-Starling back-up begins; Kirby-c/a(p) thru #5 5.00
6,7 4.00
NOTE: ***Neal Adams** c-1i. **Kirby** c/a-1-5p. **Miller** c-7.*

DESTRUCTOR, THE
Atlas/Seaboard: February, 1975 - No. 4, Aug, 1975

1-Origin/1st app.; Ditko/Wood-a; Wood-c(i) 2 4 6 13 18 22
2-4: 2-Ditko/Wood-a. 3,4-Ditko-a(p) 2 4 6 9 13 16

DETECTIVE COMICS (Also see other Batman titles)
National Periodical Publications/DC Comics: Mar, 1937 - No. 881, Oct, 2011

1-(Scarce)-Slam Bradley & Spy by Siegel & Shuster, Speed Saunders by Stoner and Flessel, Cosmo, the Phantom of Disguise, Buck Marshall, Bruce Nelson begin; Chin Lung in 'Claws of the Red Dragon' serial begins; Vincent Sullivan-c
12,700 25,400 38,100 94,000 - -
2 (Rare)-Creig Flessel-c begin; new logo 4450 8900 13,350 32,000 - -
3 (Rare) 3450 6900 10,350 25,000 - -
4,5: 5-Larry Steele begins 1750 3500 5250 9625 13,563 17,500
6,7,9,10 1200 2400 3600 6600 9300 12,000
8-Mister Chang-c; classic-c 1750 3500 5250 9625 13,563 17,500
11-17,19: 15,16-Have interior ad for Action Comics #1. 17-1st app. Fu Manchu in Detective
950 1900 2850 5225 7363 9500
18-Fu Manchu-c; last Flessel-c 1550 3100 4650 8525 12,013 15,500
20-The Crimson Avenger begins (1st app.) 1150 2300 3450 6325 8913 11,500
21,23-25 800 1600 2400 4400 6200 8000
22-1st Crimson Avenger-c by Chambers (12/38) 970 1940 2910 5335 7518 9700
26 830 1660 2490 4565 6433 8300
27-The Bat-Man & Commissioner Gordon begin (1st app.), created by Bill Finger & Bob Kane (5/39); Batman-c (1st)(by Kane). Bat-Man's secret identity revealed as Bruce Wayne in six pg. story. Signed Rob't Kane (also see Det. Picture Stories #5 & Funny Pages V3#1)
100,000 200,000 300,000 750,000 1,200,000 1,650,000
27-Reprint, Oversize 13-1/2x10". WARNING: This comic is an exact duplicate reprint of the original except for its size. DC published it in 1974 with a second cover titling it as Famous First Edition. There have been many reported cases of the outer cover being removed and the interior sold as the original edition. The reprint with the new outer cover removed is practically worthless; see Famous First Edition for value.
28-2nd app. The Batman (6 pg. story); non-Bat-Man-c; signed Rob't Kane
4500 9000 13,500 32,000 56,000 80,000
29-1st app. Doctor Death-c/story, Batman's 1st name villain. 1st 2 part story (10 pgs.).
2nd Batman-c by Kane 9000 18,000 27,000 65,000 110,000 155,000
30-Dr. Death app. Story concludes from issue #29. Classic Batman splash panel by Kane.
1467 2934 4400 11,000 18,500 26,000
31-Classic Batman over castle cover; 1st app. The Monk & 1st Julie Madison (Bruce Wayne's 1st love interest); 1st Batplane (Bat-Gyro) and Batarang; 2nd 2-part Batman adventure. Gardner Fox takes over script from Bill Finger. 1st mention of locale (New York City) where Batman lives 11,000 22,000 33,000 82,500 133,750 185,000
32-Batman story concludes from issue #31. 1st app. Dala (Monk's assistant). Batman uses gun for 1st time to slay The Monk and Dala. This was the 1st time a costumed hero used a gun in comic books. 1st Batman head logo on cover
1200 2400 3600 9000 16,000 23,000
33-Origin The Batman (2 pgs.)(1st told origin); Batman gun holster-c; Batman w/smoking gun panel at end of story. Batman story now 12 pgs. Classic Batman-c
7000 14,000 21,000 52,500 93,750 135,000
34-2nd Crimson Avenger-c by Creig Flessel and last non Batman-c. Story from issue #32 x-over as Bruce Wayne sees Julie Madison off to America from Paris. Classic Batman splash panel used later in Batman #1 for origin story. Steve Malone begins
900 1800 2700 6750 11,875 17,000
35-Classic Batman hypodermic needle-c that reflects story in issue #34. Classic Batman with smoking .45 automatic splash panel. Batman-c begin
5335 10,667 16,000 40,000 65,000 90,000
36-Batman-c that reflects adventure in issue #35. Origin/1st app. of Dr. Hugo Strange (1st major villain, 2/40). 1st finned-gloves worn by Batman
2100 4200 6300 15,750 26,875 38,000
37-Last solo Golden-Age Batman adventure in Detective Comics. Panel at end of story reflects solo Batman adventure in Batman #1 that was originally planned for Detective #38. Cliff Crosby begins 1750 3500 5250 13,000 22,500 32,000
38-Origin/1st app. Robin the Boy Wonder (4/40); Batman and Robin-c begin; cover by Kane
5200 10,400 15,600 39,000 67,000 95,000
39-Opium story; Clayface app. in 1 panel ad at the end of the Batman story
838 1676 2514 6117 10,809 15,500
40-Origin & 1st app. Clayface (Basil Karlo); 1st Joker cover app. (6/40); Joker story intended for this issue was used in Batman #1 instead; cover is similar to splash page in 2nd Joker story in Batman #1 1000 2000 3000 7300 12,900 18,500
41-Robin's 1st solo 432 864 1296 3154 5577 8000
42-44: 44-Crimson Avenger-new costume 343 686 1029 2400 4200 6000
45-1st Joker story in Det. (3rd book app. & 4th story app. over all, 11/40)
432 864 1296 3154 5577 8000
46-50: 46-Death of Hugo Strange. 48-1st time car called Batmobile (2/41); Gotham City 1st mention in Detective (1st mentioned in Wow #1; also see Batman #4).
49-Last Clayface 309 618 927 2163 3782 5400
51-57 239 478 717 1530 2615 3700
58-1st Penguin app. (12/41); last Speed Saunders; Fred Ray-c
568 1136 1704 4146 7323 10,500
59,60: 59-Last Steve Malone; 2nd Penguin; Wing becomes Crimson Avenger's aide.
60-Intro. Air Wave; Joker app. (2nd in Det.) 245 490 735 1568 2684 3800
61,63: 63-Last Cliff Crosby; 1st app. Mr. Baffle 219 438 657 1402 2401 3400
62-Joker-c/story (2nd Joker-c, 4/42) 432 864 1296 3154 5577 8000
64-Origin & 1st app. Boy Commandos by Simon & Kirby (6/42); Joker app.
421 842 1263 2947 5174 7400
65-1st Boy Commandos-c (S&K-a on Boy Commandos & Ray/Robinson-a on Batman & Robin on-c; 4 artists on one-c) 303 606 909 2121 3711 5300
66-Origin & 1st app. Two-Face (originally named Harvey Kent)
649 1298 1947 4738 8369 12,000
67-1st Penguin-c (9/42) 326 652 978 2282 3991 5700
68-Two-Face-c/story; 1st Two-Face-c 300 600 900 2010 3505 5000
69-Joker-c/story 371 742 1113 2600 4550 6500
70 206 412 618 1318 2259 3200
71-Joker-c/story 309 618 927 2163 3782 5400
72,74,75: 74-1st Tweedledum & Tweedledee plus-c; S&K-a
168 336 504 1075 1838 2600
73-Scarecrow-c/story (1st Scarecrow-c) 300 600 900 2010 3505 5000
76-Newsboy Legion & The Sandman x-over in Boy Commandos; S&K-a; Joker-c/story 271 542 813 1734 2967 4200
77-79: All S&K-a 148 296 444 947 1624 2300
80-Two-Face-c/sty; S&K-a 187 374 561 1197 2049 2900
81,82,84,86-90: 81-1st Cavalier-c & app. 87-Penguin app. 89-Last Crimson Avenger; 2nd Cavalier-c & app. 119 238 357 762 1306 1850
83-1st "skinny" Alfred (1/44)(see Batman #21; last S&K Boy Commandos (also #92,128); most issues #84 on signed S&K are not by them
126 252 378 806 1378 1950
85-Joker-c/story; last Spy; Kirby/Klech Boy Commandos

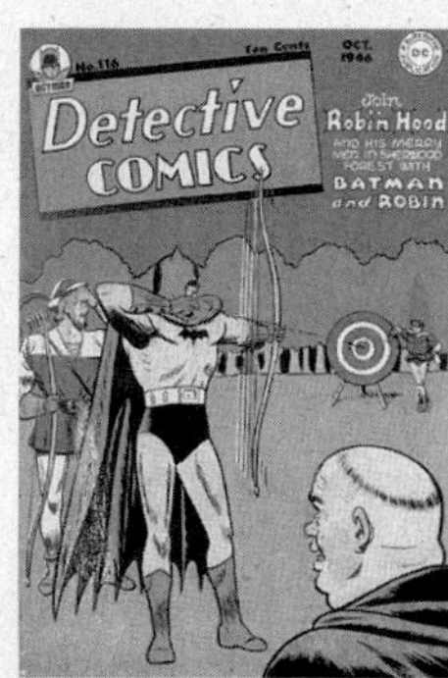

Detective Comics #116 © DC

Detective Comics #321 © DC

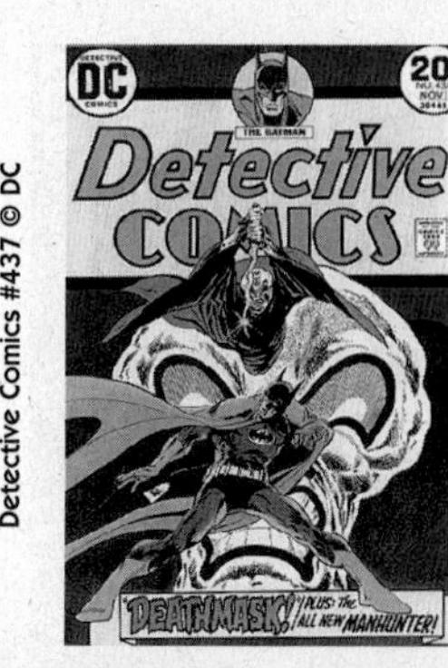

Detective Comics #437 © DC

	GD 2.0	VG 4.0	FN 6.0	VF 8.0	VF/NM 9.0	NM- 9.2
	213	426	639	1363	2332	3300
91,102,109-Joker-c/stories	200	400	600	1280	2190	3100
92-98: 96-Alfred's last name 'Beagle' revealed, later changed to 'Pennyworth' in #214	97	194	291	621	1061	1500
99-Penguin-c/story	161	322	483	1030	1765	2500
100 (6/45)	135	270	405	864	1482	2100
101,103-108,110-113,115-117,119: 108-1st Bat-signal-c (2/46)	90	180	270	576	988	1400
114,118-Joker-c/stories. 114-1st small logo (8/46)	181	362	543	1158	1979	2800
120-Penguin-c/story	168	336	504	1075	1838	2600
121,123,125,127,129,130	84	168	252	538	919	1300
122-1st Catwoman-c (4/47)	245	490	735	1568	2684	3800
124,128-Joker-c/stories	161	322	483	1030	1765	2500
126-Penguin-c	142	284	426	909	1555	2200
131-134,136,139	81	162	243	518	884	1250
135-Frankenstein-c/story	100	200	300	635	1093	1550
137-Joker-c/story; last Air Wave	148	296	444	947	1624	2300
138-Origin Robotman (see Star Spangled #7 for 1st app.); series ends #202	123	246	369	787	1344	1900
140-The Riddler-c/story (1st app., 10/48)	838	1676	2514	6117	10,809	15,500
141,143-148,150: 150-Last Boy Commandos	81	162	243	518	884	1250
142-2nd Riddler-c/story	226	452	678	1446	2473	3500
149-Joker-c/story	142	284	426	909	1555	2200
151-Origin & 1st app. Pow Wow Smith, Indian lawman (9/49) & begins series	90	180	270	576	988	1400
152,154,155,157-160: 152-Last Slam Bradley	81	162	243	518	884	1250
153-1st app. Roy Raymond TV Detective (11/49); origin The Human Fly	84	168	252	538	919	1300
156(2/50)-The new classic Batmobile	123	246	369	787	1344	1900
161-167,169,170,172-176: Last 52 pg. issue	77	154	231	493	847	1200
168-Origin the Joker	595	1190	1785	4350	7675	11,000
171-Penguin-c	107	214	321	680	1165	1650
177-179,181-186,188,189,191,192,194-199,201,202,204,206-210,212,214-216: 184-1st app. Fire Fly. 185-Secret of Batman's utility belt. 202-Last Robotman & Pow Wow Smith. 215-1st app. of Batmen of all Nations. 216-Last precode (2/55)	74	148	222	470	810	1150
180,193-Joker-c/story	110	220	330	704	1202	1700
187-Two-Face-c/story	103	206	309	659	1130	1600
190-Origin Batman retold	97	194	291	621	1061	1500
200(10/53), 205: 205-Origin Batcave	90	180	270	576	988	1400
203,211-Catwoman-c/stories	103	206	309	659	1130	1600
213-Origin & 1st app. Mirror Man	86	172	258	546	936	1325
217-224: 218-Batman Jr. & Robin Sr. app.	63	126	189	403	689	975
225-(11/55)-1st app. Martian Manhunter (J'onn J'onzz); origin begins; also see Batman #78	450	900	1350	4100	8300	12,500
226-Origin Martian Manhunter cont'd (2nd app.)	181	362	543	1158	1979	2800
227-229: Martian Manhunter stories in all	76	152	228	486	831	1175
230-1st app. Mad Hatter; brief recap origin of Martian Manhunter	82	164	246	528	902	1275
231-Brief origin recap Martian Manhunter	57	114	171	362	619	875
232,234,237,238,240	54	108	162	343	574	825
233-Origin & 1st app. Batwoman (7/56)	245	490	735	1568	2684	3800
235-Origin Batman & his costume; tells how Bruce Wayne's father (Thomas Wayne) wore Bat costume & fought crime (reprinted in Batman #255)	86	172	258	546	936	1325
236-1st S.A. issue; J'onn J'onzz talks to parents and Mars-1st since being stranded on Earth; 1st app. Bat-Tank?	57	114	171	362	619	875
239-Early DC grey tone-c	58	116	174	371	636	900
241-260: 246-Intro. Diane Meade, John Jones' girl. 249-Batwoman-c/app. 253-1st app. The Terrible Trio. 254-Bat-Hound-c/story. 257-Intro. & 1st app. Whirly Bats. 259-1st app. The Calendar Man	42	84	126	265	450	635
261-264,266,268-271: 261-J. Jones tie-in to sci/fi movie "Incredible Shrinking Man"; 1st app. Dr. Double X. 262-Origin Jackal. 268,271-Manhunter origin recap	36	72	108	216	351	485
265-Batman's origin retold with new facts	48	96	144	302	514	725
267-Origin & 1st app. Bat-Mite (5/59)	71	142	213	454	777	1100
272,274,275,277-280	31	62	93	186	303	420
273-J'onn J'onzz i.d. revealed for 1st time	32	64	96	192	314	435
276-2nd app. Bat-Mite	40	80	120	246	411	575
281-292, 294-297: 286,292-Batwoman-c/app. 287-Origin J'onn J'onzz retold. 289-Bat-Mite-c/story. 292-Last Roy Raymond. 297-Last 10¢ issue (11/61)	24	48	72	144	237	330
293-(7/61)-Aquaman begins (pre #1); ends #300	25	50	75	150	245	340
298-(12/61)-1st modern Clayface (Matt Hagen)	27	54	81	194	435	675

	GD 2.0	VG 4.0	FN 6.0	VF 8.0	VF/NM 9.0	NM- 9.2
299, 300-(2/62)-Aquaman ends	13	26	39	89	195	300
301-(3/62)-J'onn J'onzz returns to Mars (1st time since stranded on Earth six years before)	10	20	30	69	147	225
302-310,312-317,319-321,323,324,326,329,330: 302,307-Batwoman-c/app. 321-2nd Terrible Trio. 326-Last J'onn J'onzz, story cont'd in House of Mystery #143; intro. Idol-Head of Diabolu	9	18	27	62	125	190
311-1st app. Cat-Man; intro. Zook in John Jones	10	20	30	66	138	210
318,322,325: 318,325-Cat-Man-c/story (2nd & 3rd app.); also 1st & 2nd app. Batwoman as the Cat-Woman. 322-Bat-Girl's 1st/only app. in Det. (6th in all); Batman cameo in J'onn J'onzz (only hero to app. in series)	10	20	30	66	138	210
327-(5/64)-Elongated Man begins, ends #383; 1st new look Batman with new costume; Infantino/Giella new look-a begins; Batman with gun	13	26	39	91	201	310
328-Death of Alfred; Bob Kane biog, 2 pgs.	12	24	36	79	170	260
331,333-340: 334-1st app. The Outsider	8	16	24	54	102	150
332,341,365-Joker-c/stories	10	20	30	66	138	210
342-358,360,361,366-368: 345-Intro Block Buster. 347-"What If" theme story (1/66). 350-Elongated Man new costume. 355-Zatanna x-over in Elongated Man. 356-Alfred brought back in Batman, early SA app.	7	14	21	48	89	130
359-Intro/origin Batgirl (Barbara Gordon)-c/story (1/67); 1st Silver Age app. Killer Moth	70	140	280	550	900	1250
362,364-S.A. Riddler app. (early)	9	18	27	57	111	165
363-2nd app. new Batgirl	11	22	33	73	157	240
369(11/67)-N. Adams-a (Elongated Man); 3rd app. S.A. Catwoman (cameo; leads into Batman #197); 4th app. new Batgirl	11	22	33	76	163	250
370-1st Neal Adams-a on Batman (cover only, 12/67)	8	16	24	56	108	160
371-(1/68) 1st new Batmobile from TV show; classic Batgirl-c	10	20	30	66	138	210
372-376,378-386,389,390: 375-New Batmobile-c	6	12	18	38	69	100
377-S.A. Riddler-c/sty	7	14	21	44	82	120
387-r/1st Batman story from #27 (30th anniversary, 5/69); Joker-c; last 12¢ issue	9	18	27	57	111	165
388-Joker-c/story	9	18	27	57	111	165
391-394,396,398,399,401,403,406,409: 392-1st app. Jason Bard. 401-2nd Batgirl/Robin team-up	6	12	18	37	66	95
395,397,402,404,407,408,410-Neal Adams-a. 404-Tribute to Enemy Ace	10	20	30	66	138	210
400-(6/70)-Origin & 1st app. Man-Bat; 1st Batgirl/Robin team-up (cont'd in #401); Neal Adams-a	22	44	66	154	340	525
405-Debut League of Assassins	9	18	27	57	111	165
411-(5/71) Intro. Talia, daughter of Ra's al Ghul (Ra's mentioned, but doesn't appear until Batman #232 (6/71); Bob Brown-a	15	30	45	103	227	350
412-413: 413-Last 15¢ issue	5	10	15	35	63	90
414-424: All-25¢, 52 pgs. 418-Creeper x-over. 424-Last Batgirl.	6	12	18	37	66	95
425-436: 426,430,436-Elongated Man app. 428,434-Hawkman begins, ends #467	5	10	15	30	50	70
437-New Manhunter begins (10-11/73, 1st app.) by Simonson, ends #443	5	10	15	34	60	85
438-445 (All 100 Page Super Spectaculars): 438-Kubert Hawkman-r. 439-Origin Manhunter. 440-G.A. Manhunter(Adv. #79) by S&K, Hawkman, Dollman, Green Lantern; Toth-a. 441-G.A. Plastic Man, Batman, Ibis-r. 442-G.A. Newsboy Legion, Black Canary, Elongated Man, Dr. Fate-r. 443-Origin The Creeper-r; death of Manhunter; G.A. Green Lantern, Spectre-r; Batman-r/Batman #18. 444-G.A. Kid Eternity-r. 445-G.A. Dr. Midnite-r	6	12	18	38	69	100
446-460: 457-Origin retold & updated	3	6	9	17	26	35
461-465,470,480: 480-(44 pgs.). 463-1st app. Black Spider. 464-2nd app. Black Spider 470-Intro. Silver St. Cloud.	3	6	9	16	23	30
466-468,471-474,478,479-Rogers-a in all: 466-1st app. Signalman since Batman #139. 470,471-1st modern app. Hugo Strange. 474-1st app. new Deadshot. 478-1st app. 3rd Clayface (Preston Payne). 479-(44 pgs.)	4	8	12	25	40	55
469-Intro/origin Dr. Phosphorous; Simonson-a	4	8	12	23	37	50
475,476-Joker-c/stories; Rogers-a	7	14	21	46	86	125
477-Neal Adams-a(r); Rogers-a (3 pgs.)	4	8	12	23	37	50
481-(Combined with Batman Family, 12-1/78-79, begin $1.00, 68 pg. issues, ends #495); 481-495-Batgirl, Robin solo stories	3	6	9	17	26	35
482-Starlin/Russell, Golden-a; The Demon begins (origin-r), ends #485 (by Ditko #483-485)	3	6	9	14	20	25
483-40th Anniversary issue; origin retold; Newton Batman begins	3	6	9	15	22	28
484-495 (68 pgs): 484-Origin Robin. 485-Death of Batwoman. 486-Killer Moth app. 487-The Odd Man by Ditko. 489-Robin/Batgirl team-up. 490-Black Lightning begins. 491-(#492 on inside). 493-Intro. The Swashbuckler	2	4	6	9	13	16
496-499: 496-Clayface app.	2	4	6	8	10	12

Detective Comics #524 © DC

Detective Comics #864 © DC

Detective Comics (2011 series) #23.2 © DC

GD VG FN VF VF/NM NM-
2.0 4.0 6.0 8.0 9.0 9.2

500-($1.50, 52 pgs.)-Batman/Deadman team-up with Infantino-a; new Hawkman story by Joe Kubert; incorrectly says 500th Anniv. of Det. 2 4 6 13 18 22
501-503,505-523: 509-Catman-c. 510-Mad Hatter-c. 512-2nd app. new Dr. Death. 519-Last Batgirl. 521-Green Arrow series begins. 523-Solomon Grundy app.; 1st Killer Croc (cameo) 1 2 3 5 6 8
504-Joker-c/story 2 4 6 9 13 16
524-2nd app. Jason Todd (cameo)(3/83) 2 4 6 8 10 12
525-3rd app. Jason Todd (See Batman #357) 2 4 6 8 10 12
526-Batman's 500th app. in Detective Comics ($1.50, 68 pgs.); Death of Jason Todd's parents, Joker-c/story (55 pgs.); Bob Kane pin-up 3 6 9 15 22 28
527-531,533,534,536-568,571,573: 538-Cat-Man-c/story cont'd from Batman #371. 542-Jason Todd quits as Robin (becomes Robin again #547). 549,550-Alan Moore scripts (Green Arrow). 554-1st new Black Canary (9/85). 566-Batman villains profiled. 567-Harlan Ellison scripts. 6.00
532,569,570-Joker-c/stories 2 4 6 9 13 16
535-Intro new Robin (Jason Todd)-1st appeared in Batman 1 3 4 6 8 10
572-(3/87, $1.25, 60 pgs.)-50th Anniv. of Det. Comics 1 3 4 6 8 10
574-Origin Batman & Jason Todd retold 2 4 6 8 10 12
575-Year 2 begins, ends #578 3 6 9 15 22 28
576-578: McFarlane-c/a; The Reaper app. 3 6 9 15 22 28
579-597,599,601-610: 579-New bat wing logo. 583-1st app. villains Scarface & Ventriloquist. 589-595-(52 pgs.)-Each contain free 16 pg. Batman stories. 604-607-Mudpack storyline; 604,607-Contain Batman mini-posters. 610-Faked death of Penguin; artists names app. on tombstone on-c 4.00
598-($2.95, 84 pgs.)- "Blind Justice" storyline begins by Batman movie writer Sam Hamm, ends #600 6.00
600-(5/89, $2.95, 84 pgs.)-50th Anniv. of Batman in Det.; 1 pg. Neal Adams pin-up, among other artists 6.00
611-626,628-658: 612-1st new look Cat-Man; Catwoman app. 615- "The Penguin Affair" part 2 (See Batman #448,449). 617-Joker-c/story. 624-1st new Catwoman (w/death) & 1st new Batwoman. 626-Batman's 600th app. in Detective. 642-Return of Scarface, part 2. 644-Last $1.00-c. 652,653-Huntress-c/story w/new costume plus Charest-c on both 4.00
627-($2.95, 84 pgs.)-Batman's 601st app. in Det.; reprints 1st story/#27 plus 3 versions (2 new) of same story 6.00
659-664: 659-Knightfall part 2; Kelley Jones-c. 660-Knightfall part 4; Bane-c by Sam Kieth. 661-Knightfall part 6; brief Joker & Riddler app. 662-Knightfall part 8; Riddler app.; Sam Kieth-c. 663-Knightfall part 10; Kelley Jones-c. 664-Knightfall part 12; Bane-c/story; Joker app.; continued in Showcase 93 #7 & 8; Jones-c 6.00
665-675: 665,666-Knightfall parts 16 & 18; 666-Bane-c/story. 667-Knightquest: The Crusade & new Batman begins (1st app. in Batman #500). 669-Begin $1.50-c; Knightquest, cont'd in Robin #1. 671,673-Joker app. 4.00
675-($2.95)-Collectors edition w/foil-c 5.00
676-($2.50, 52 pgs.)-KnightsEnd pt. 3 5.00
677,678: 677-KnightsEnd pt. 9. 678-(9/94)-Zero Hour tie-in. 4.00
679-685: 679-(11/94). 682-Troika pt. 3 3.00
682-($2.50) Embossed-c Troika pt. 3 4.00
686-699,701-719: 686-Begin $1.95-c. 693,694-Poison Ivy-c/app. 695-Contagion pt. 2; Catwoman, Penguin app. 696-Contagion pt. 8. 698-Two-Face-c/app. 701-Legacy pt. 6; Batman vs. Bane-c/app. 702-Legacy Epilogue. 703-Final Night x-over. 705-707-Riddler-app. 714,715-Martian Manhunter-app. 3.00
700-($4.95, Collectors Edition)-Legacy pt. 1; Ra's Al Ghul-c/app; Talia & Bane app; book displayed at shops in envelope 6.00
700-($2.95, Regular Edition)-Different-c 4.00
720-740: 720,721-Cataclysm pts. 5,14. 723-Green Arrow app. 730-740-No Man's Land stories 3.00
741-($2.50) Endgame; Joker-c/app. 4.00
742-749,751-765: 742-New look Batman begins; 1st app. Crispus Allen (who later becomes the Spectre). 751,752-Poison Ivy app. 756-Superman-c/app. 759-762-Catwoman back-up 3.00
750-($4.95, 64 pgs.) Ra's al Ghul-c 6.00
766-772: 766,767-Bruce Wayne: Murderer pt. 1,8. 769-772-Bruce Wayne: Fugitive pts. 4,8,12,16 3.00
773,774,776-799: 773-Begin $2.75-c; Sienkiewicz-c. 777-784-Sale-c. 784-786-Alan Scott app. 787-Mad Hatter app. 793-Begin $2.95-c. 797-799-War Games 3.00
775-($3.50) Sienkiewicz-c 4.00
800-($3.50) Jock-c; aftermath of War Games; back-up by Lapham 4.00
801-816: 801-814-Lapham-s. 804-Mr. Freeze app. 809-War Crimes 3.00
817-849,851,852: 817-820: One Year Later 8-part x-over with Batman #651-654; Robinson-s/ Bianchi-c. 819-Begin $2.99-c. 820-Dini-s/Williams III-a. 825-Doctor Phosphorus app. 827-Debut of new Scarface. 831-Harley app.; Dini-s. 833,834-Zatanna & Joker app. 838,839-Resurrection of Ra's al Ghul x-over. 846-847-Batman R.I.P. x-over 3.00
817,818,838,839-2nd printings. 817-Combo-c of #817̳ cover images. 818-Combo-c of #818 and Batman #653 cover images. 838-Andy Kubert variant-c. 839-Red bkgd-c 3.00
850-($3.99) Batman vs. Hush; Dini-s/Nguyen-a 4.00

GD VG FN VF VF/NM NM-
2.0 4.0 6.0 8.0 9.0 9.2

853-($3.99) Gaiman-s/Andy Kubert-a; continued from Batman #686; Kubert sketch pgs. 4.00
853-Variant-c with red background by Andy Kubert 12.00
854-872-($3.99) 854-Batwoman features begin; Rucka-a/J.H. Williams-a/c; The Question back-ups begin. 858-860-Batwoman origin 4.00
854,858,859,860-Variant-c: 854-JG Jones. 858-Hughes. 859-Jock. 860-Alex Ross 6.00
854-Special Edition (8/10, $1.00) reprints issue with "What's Next?" logo on cover 3.00
873-880-($2.99) 874,875,879-Francavilla-a. 880-Jock-a 3.00
881-(10/11) Last issue of first volume; Snyder-s/Jock & Francavilla-a 3.00
#0-(10/94) Zero Hour tie-in, released between #678 & 679 3.00
#1,000,000 (11/98) 853rd Century x-over 3.00
Annual 1 (1988, $1.50) 5.00
Annual 2-7,9 ('89-'94, '96, 68 pgs.)-4-Painted-c. 5-Joker-c/story (54 pgs.) continued in Robin Annual #1; Sam Kieth-c; Eclipso app. 6-Azrael as Batman in new costume; intro Geist the Twilight Man; Bloodlines storyline. 7-Elseworlds story. 9-Legends of the Dead Earth story 5.00
Annual 8 (1995, $3.95, 68 pgs.)-Year One story 5.00
Annual 10 (1997, $3.95)-Pulp Heroes story 5.00
Annual 11 (12/09, $4.99)-Azrael & The Question app.; continued from Batman Ann. #27 5.00
Annual 12 (2/11, $4.99)-Nightrunner & The Question app.; continued in Batman Ann. #28 5.00

NOTE: ***Neal Adams*** *c-370, 372, 385, 389, 391, 392, 394-422, 439.* ***Aparo*** *a-437, 438, 444-446, 500, 625-632p, 638-643p; c-430, 437, 440-446, 448, 468-470, 480, 484(back), 492-502,508, 509, 515, 518-522, 641, 716, 719, 722, 724.* ***Austin*** *a(i)-450, 451, 463-468, 471-476; c(i)-474-476, 478.* ***Baily*** *a-443r.* ***Buckler*** *a-434, 446p, 479p; c(p)-467, 482, 505-507, 511, 513-516, 518.* ***Burnley*** *a(Batman)-65, 75, 78, 83, 100, 103, 125; c-62i, 63i, 64, 73i, 78, 83p, 96p, 103p, 105p, 106, 108, 121p, 123p, 125p.* ***Chaykin*** *a-441.* ***Colan*** *a(p)-510, 512, 517, 523, 528-538, 540-546, 555-567; c(p)-510, 512, 528, 530-535, 537, 538, 540, 541, 543-545, 556-558, 560-564.* ***J. Craig*** *a-488.* ***Ditko*** *a-443r, 483-485, 487.* ***Golden*** *a-482p; c-625, 626, 628-631, 633, 644-646.* ***Alan Grant*** *scripts-584-597, 601-621, 641, 642, Annual 5.* ***Grell*** *a-445, 455, 463p, 464p; c-455.* ***Guardineer*** *c-23, 24, 26, 28, 30, 32.* ***Gustavson*** *a-441r.* ***Infantino*** *a-354, 442(2)r, 500, 572.* ***Infantino/Anderson*** *c-333, 337-340, 343, 344, 347, 351, 352, 359, 361-368, 371.* ***Kelley Jones*** *c-651, 657i, 658i, 659, 661, 663-675.* ***Kaluta*** *c-423, 424, 426-428, 431, 434, 438, 484, 486, 572.* ***Bob Kane*** *a-Most early issues #27 on, 297r, 356r, 438-440r, 442r, 443r.* ***Kane/Robinson*** *c-33.* ***Gil Kane*** *a(p)-368, 370-374, 384, 385, 388-407, 438r, 439r, 520.* ***Kane/Anderson*** *c-369.* ***Sam Kieth*** *c-654-656 (657, 658 w/****Kelley Jones****), 660, 662, Annual #5.* ***Kubert*** *a-438r, 439r, 500; c-348-350.* ***McFarlane*** *c/a(p)-576-578.* ***Meskin*** *a-420r.* ***Mignola*** *c-583.* ***Moldoff*** *c-233-354, 259, 266, 267, 275, 287, 289, 290, 297, 300.* ***Moldoff/Giella*** *a-328, 330, 332, 334, 336, 338, 340, 342, 344, 346, 348, 350, 352, 354, 356.* ***Mooney*** *a-444r.* ***Moreira*** *a-153-300, 419r, 444r, 445r.* ***Nasser/Netzer*** *a-654, 655, 657, 658.* ***Newton*** *a(p)-480, 481, 483-499, 501-509, 511, 513-516, 518-520, 524, 526, 539; c-526p.* ***Irv Novick*** *c-375-377, 383.* ***Robbins*** *a-426p, 429p.* ***Robinson*** *a-part: 66, 68, 71-73; all: 74-76, 79, 80; c-62, 64, 66, 68-74, 76, 79, 82, 86, 88, 442r, 443r.* ***Rogers*** *a-466-468, 471-479p, 481p; c-471p, 472p, 473, 474-479p.* ***Roussos*** *Airwave-76-105(most); c(i)-71, 72, 74-76, 79, 107.* ***Russell*** *a-481i, 482i.* ***Simon/Kirby*** *a-440r, 442r.* ***Simonson*** *a-437-443, 450, 469, 470, 500.* ***Dick Sprang*** *c-77, 82, 84, 85, 87, 89-93, 95-100, 102, 103i, 104i, 106, 108, 114, 117, 118, 122, 123, 128, 129, 131, 133, 135, 141, 148, 149, 168, 622-624.* ***Starlin*** *a-481p, 482p; c-503, 504, 567p.* ***Starr*** *a-444r.* ***Toth*** *a-442; r-414, 416, 418, 424, 440-441, 443, 444.* ***Tuska*** *a-486p, 490p.* ***Matt Wagner*** *c-647-649.* ***Wrightson*** *c-425.*

DETECTIVE COMICS (DC New 52)
DC Comics: Nov, 2011 - Present ($2.99/$3.99)

1-Joker app.; Tony Daniel-s/a/c 20.00
2-7: 2-Intro of The Dollmaker. 5-7-Penguin app. 3.00
8,10-14,16-18: 8-($3.99) Catwoman & Scarecrow app.; back-up Two-Face story begins 4.00
9-Night of the Owls 5.00
15-Die-cut Joker cover; Death of the Family tie-in 8.00
19-(6/13, $7.99) 900th issue of Detective; bonus back-up stories and pin-up art 8.00
20-24,26: 21-23-Man-Bat back-up story. 26-Man-Bat app. 4.00
23.1, 23.2, 23.3, 23.4 (11/13, $2.99, regular covers) 3.00
23.1 (11/13, $3.99, 3-D cover) "Poison Ivy #1" on cover; Fridolfs-s/Pina-a 8.00
23.2 (11/13, $3.99, 3-D cover) "Harley Quinn #1" on cover; Googe-a/Kindt-s; origin 12.00
23.3 (11/13, $3.99, 3-D cover) "Scarecrow #1" on cover; Kudranski-a 5.00
23.4 (11/13, $3.99, 3-D cover) "Man-Bat #1" on cover; Tieri-s/Eaton-a 5.00
25-($3.99) Zero Year focus on Lt. Gordon; Fabok-a/c; Man-Bat back-up 4.00
27-($7.99) Start of Gothtopia; short stories by Meltzer, Hitch, Neal Adams, Francavilla, Murphy 8.00
28-30: 28,29-Gothtopia. 30-Manupul-a 4.00
#0 (11/12, $3.99) Flashback to training and return to Alfred 4.00
Annual 1 (10/12, $4.99) Black Mask app.; Daniel-s/c; Molenaar-a 5.00
Annual 2 (9/13, $4.99) The Wrath app.; Eaton-a/Clarke-c 5.00

DETECTIVE DAN, SECRET OP. 48 (Also see Adventures of Detective Ace King and Bob Scully, The Two-Fisted Hick Detective)
Humor Publ. Co. (Norman Marsh): 1933 (10¢, 10x13", 36 pgs., B&W, one-shot) (3 color, cardboard-c)

nn-By Norman Marsh, 1st comic w/ original-a; 1st newsstand-c; Dick Tracy look-alike; forerunner of Dan Dunn. (Title and Wu Fang character inspired Detective Comics #1 four years later.) (1st comic of a single theme) 1750 3500 5250 10,500 - -

DETECTIVE EYE (See Keen Detective Funnies)
Centaur Publications: Nov, 1940 - No. 2, Dec, 1940

1-Air Man (see Keen Detective) & The Eye Sees begins; The Masked Marvel & Dean Denton app. 252 504 756 1613 2757 3900
2-Origin Don Rance and the Mysticape; Binder-a; Frank Thomas-c 135 270 405 864 1482 2100

Devi #8 © Virgin Comics

Devil Dinosaur #6 © MAR

Dexter #1 © Jeff Lindsay

GD VG FN VF VF/NM NM-
2.0 4.0 6.0 8.0 9.0 9.2

DETECTIVE PICTURE STORIES (Keen Detective Funnies No. 8 on?)
Comics Magazine Company: Dec, 1936 - No. 5, Apr, 1937
1 (All issues are very scarce) 580 1160 1740 3306 4803 6300
2-The Clock app. (1/37, early app.) 250 500 750 1425 2113 2800
3,4: 4-Eisner-a 170 340 510 969 1485 2000
5-The Clock-c/story (4/37); 1st detective/adventure art by Bob Kane; Bruce Wayne prototype app.(see Funny Pages V3/1) 195 390 585 1112 1681 2250

DETECTIVES, THE (TV)
Dell Publishing Co.: No. 1168, Mar-May, 1961 - No. 1240, Oct-Dec, 1961
Four Color 1168 (#1)-Robert Taylor photo-c 9 18 27 57 111 165
Four Color 1219-Robert Taylor, Adam West photo-c 8 16 24 52 99 145
Four Color 1240-Tufts-a; Robert Taylor photo-c; 2 different back-c 7 14 21 48 89 130

DETECTIVES, INC. (See Eclipse Graphic Album Series)
Eclipse Comics: Apr, 1985 - No. 2, Apr, 1985 ($1.75, both w/April dates)
1,2: 2-Nudity 3.00

DETECTIVES, INC.: A TERROR OF DYING DREAMS
Eclipse Comics: Jun, 1987 - No. 3, Dec, 1987 ($1.75, B&W& sepia)
1-3: Colan-a 3.00
TPB ('99, $19.95) r/series 20.00

DETENTION COMICS
DC Comics: Oct, 1996 ($3.50, 56 pgs., one-shot)
1-Robin story by Dennis O'Neil & Norm Breyfogle; Superboy story by Ron Marz & Ron Lim; Warrior story by Ruben Diaz & Joe Phillips; Phillips-c 5.00

DETHKLOK (Based on the animated series Metalocalypse)
Dark Horse Comics: Oct, 2010 - No. 3, Feb, 2011 ($3.99, limited series)
1-3-Small & Schnepp-s; covers by Schnepp & Eric Powell 4.00
...: Versus the Goon 1-(7/09, $3.50) Powell-s/a/c; Dethklok visits the Goon universe 3.50
...: Versus the Goon 1-Variant cover by Jon Schnepp 5.00
HC (7/11, $19.99) r/#1-3 & Dethklok: Versus the Goon 20.00

DETONATOR (Mike Baron's...)
Image Comics: Nov, 2004 - No. 4 ($2.50/$2.95)
1-4-Mike Baron-s/Mel Rubi-a 3.00

DEUS EX (Based on the Square Enix videogame)
DC Comics: Apr, 2011 - No. 6, Sept, 2011 ($2.99, limited series)
1-6-Robbie Morrison-s/Trevor Hairsine-a 3.00

DEVASTATOR
Image Comics/Halloween: 1998 - No. 3 ($2.95, B&W, limited series)
1,2-Hudnall-s/Horn-c/a 3.00

DEVI (Shekhar Kapur's...)
Virgin Comics: July, 2006 - No. 20, Jun, 2008 ($2.99)
1-20: 1-Mukesh Singh-a/Siddharth Kotian-s. 2-Greg Horn-c 3.00
.../Witchblade (4/08, $2.99) Singh-a/Land-c; continued from Witchblade/Devi 3.00
... Vol. 1 TPB (5/07, $14.99) r/#1-5 and Story from Virgin Comics Preview #0 15.00
... Vol. 2 TPB (9/07, $14.99) r/#6-10; character and cover sketches 15.00

DEVIL CHEF
Dark Horse Comics: July, 1994 ($2.50, B&W, one-shot)
nn 3.00

DEVIL DINOSAUR
Marvel Comics Group: Apr, 1978 - No. 9, Dec, 1978
1-Kirby/Royer-a in all; all have Kirby-c 3 6 9 16 23 30
2-9: 4-7-UFO/sci. fic. 8-Dinoriders-c/sty 2 4 6 9 13 16
... By Jack Kirby Omnibus HC (2007, $29.99, dustjacket) r/#1-9; intro. by Brevoort 30.00

DEVIL DINOSAUR SPRING FLING
Marvel Comics: June, 1997 ($2.99. one-shot)
1-(48 pgs.) Moon-Boy-c/app. 4.00

DEVIL-DOG DUGAN (Tales of the Marines No. 4 on)
Atlas Comics (OPI): July, 1956 - No. 3, Nov, 1956
1-Severin-c 15 30 45 86 133 180
2-Iron Mike McGraw x-over; Severin-c 10 20 30 56 76 95
3 9 18 27 52 69 85

DEVIL DOGS
Street & Smith Publishers: 1942
1-Boy Rangers, U.S. Marines 32 64 96 192 314 435

GD VG FN VF VF/NM NM-
2.0 4.0 6.0 8.0 9.0 9.2

DEVILINA (Magazine)
Atlas/Seaboard: Feb, 1975 - No. 2, May, 1975 (B&W)
1-Art by Reese, Marcos; "The Tempest" adapt. 4 8 12 27 44 60
2 (Low printing) 4 8 12 28 47 65

DEVIL KIDS STARRING HOT STUFF
Harvey Publications (Illustrated Humor): July, 1962 - No. 107, Oct, 1981 (Giant-Size #41-55)
1 (12¢ cover price #1-#41-9/69) 24 48 72 168 372 575
2 10 20 30 69 147 225
3-10 (1/64) 8 16 24 51 96 140
11-20 5 10 15 33 57 80
21-30 4 8 12 25 40 55
31-40: 40-(6/69) 3 6 9 19 30 40
41-50: All 68 pg. Giants 3 6 9 21 33 45
51-55: All 52 pg. Giants 3 6 9 19 30 40
56-70 2 4 6 11 16 20
71-90 2 4 6 8 11 14
91-107 1 2 3 5 6 8

DEVIL'S DUE FREE COMIC BOOK DAY
Devil's Due Publ.: May, 2005 (Free Comic Book Day giveaway)
nn-Short stories of G.I. Joe, Defex and Darkstalkers; Darkstalkers flip cover 3.00

DEVIL'S FOOTPRINTS, THE
Dark Horse Comics: March, 2003 - No. 4, June, 2003 ($2.99, limited series)
1-4-Paul Lee-c/a; Scott Allie-s 3.00

DEXTER (Character from the novels and Showtime series)
Marvel Comics: Sept, 2013 - No. 5, Jan, 2014 ($3.99, limited series)
1-5-Jeff Linsday-s/Dalibor Talajic-a/Mike Del Mundo-c 4.00

DEXTER COMICS
Dearfield Publ.: Summer, 1948 - No. 5, July, 1949
1-Teen-age humor 14 28 42 76 108 140
2-Junie Prom app. 9 18 27 52 69 85
3-5 8 16 24 44 57 70

DEXTER DOWN UNDER (Character from the novels and Showtime series)
Marvel Comics: Apr, 2014 - No. 5 ($3.99, limited series)
1,2-Jeff Linsday-s/Dalibor Talajic-a/Mike Del Mundo-c 4.00

DEXTER'S LABORATORY (Cartoon Network)
DC Comics: Sept, 1999 - No. 34, Apr, 2003 ($1.99/$2.25)
1 4.00
2-10: 2-McCracken-s 3.00
11-24, 26-34: 31-Begin $2.25-c. 32-34-Wray-c 3.00
25-(50¢-c) Tartakovsky-s/a; Action Hank-c/app. 3.00

DEXTER THE DEMON (Formerly Melvin The Monster)(See Cartoon Kids & Peter the Little Pest)
Atlas Comics (HPC): No. 7, Sept, 1957
7 9 18 27 52 69 85

DHAMPIRE: STILLBORN
DC Comics (Vertigo): 1996 ($5.95, one-shot, mature)
1-Nancy Collins script; Paul Lee-c/a 6.00

DIABLO
DC Comics: Jan, 2012 - No. 5, Oct, 2012 ($2.99, limited series)
1-5-Aaron Williams-s/Joseph Lacroix-a/c 3.00

DIAL H (Dial H for HERO)(Also see Justice League #23.3)
DC Comics: Jul, 2012 - No. 15, Oct, 2013 ($2.99/$4.99)
1-14: 1-6-China Miéville-s/Mateus Santolouco-a/Brian Bolland-c. 1-Variant-c by Finch 3.00
15-($4.99) Mieville-s/Ponticelli-a/Bolland-c 5.00
#0 (11/12, $2.99) Origin of the dial; Miéville-s/Burchielli-a/Bolland-c 3.00

DIARY CONFESSIONS (Formerly Ideal Romance)
Stanmor/Key Publ.(Medal Comics): No. 9, May, 1955 - No. 14, Apr, 1955
9 10 20 30 54 72 90
10-14 8 16 24 44 57 70

DIARY LOVES (Formerly Love Diary #1; G. I. Sweethearts #32 on)
Quality Comics Group: No. 2, Nov, 1949 - No. 31, April, 1953
2-Ward-c/a, 9 pgs. 20 40 60 114 182 250
3 (1/50)-Photo-c begin, end #27? 11 22 33 64 90 115
4-Crandall-a 13 26 39 72 101 130
5-7,10 10 20 30 58 79 100
8,9-Ward-a 6,8 pgs. 8-Gustavson-a; Esther Williams photo-c

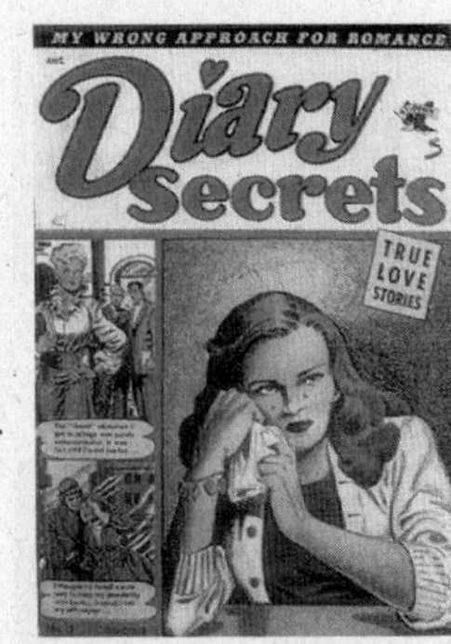

Diary Secrets #12 © STJ

Dick Cole #6 © STAR

Dick Tracy #24 © KFS

	GD 2.0	VG 4.0	FN 6.0	VF 8.0	VF/NM 9.0	NM- 9.2
	15	30	45	83	124	165
11,13,14,17-20	10	20	30	56	76	95
12,15,16-Ward-a 9,7,8 pgs.	14	28	42	80	115	150
21-Ward-a, 7 pgs.	13	26	39	74	105	135
22-31: 31-Whitney-a	10	20	30	54	72	90

NOTE: *Photo c-3-10, 12-27.*

DIARY OF HORROR
Avon Periodicals: December, 1952

	GD 2.0	VG 4.0	FN 6.0	VF 8.0	VF/NM 9.0	NM- 9.2
1-Hollingsworth-c/a; bondage-c	53	106	159	334	567	800

DIARY SECRETS (Formerly Teen-Age Diary Secrets)(See Giant Comics Ed.)
St. John Publishing Co.: No. 10, Feb, 1952 - No. 30, Sept, 1955

	GD 2.0	VG 4.0	FN 6.0	VF 8.0	VF/NM 9.0	NM- 9.2
10-Baker-c/a most issues	39	78	117	240	395	550
11-16,18,19	34	68	102	199	325	450
17,20: Kubert-r/Hollywood Confessions #1. 17-r/Teen Age Romances #9	34	68	102	199	325	450
21-30: 22,27-Signed stories by Estrada. 28-Last precode (3/55)	26	52	78	154	252	350
nn-(25¢ giant, nd (1950?)-Baker-c & rebound St. John comics	103	206	309	659	1130	1600

DICK COLE (Sport Thrills No. 11 on)(See Blue Bolt & Four Most #1)
Curtis Publ./Star Publications: Dec-Jan, 1948-49 - No. 10, June-July, 1950

	GD 2.0	VG 4.0	FN 6.0	VF 8.0	VF/NM 9.0	NM- 9.2
1-Sgt. Spook; L. B. Cole-c; McWilliams-a; Curt Swan's 1st work	34	68	102	199	325	450
2,5	15	30	45	92	144	195
3,4,6-10: All-L.B. Cole-c. 10-Joe Louis story	22	44	66	130	213	295
Accepted Reprint #7(V1#6 on-c)(1950's)-Reprints #7; L.B. Cole-c	9	18	27	47	61	75
Accepted Reprint #9(nd)-(Reprints #9 & #8-c)	9	18	27	47	61	75

NOTE: ***L. B. Cole** c-1, 3, 4, 6-10. **Al McWilliams** a-6. Dick Cole in 1-9. Baseball c-10. Basketball c-9. Football c-8.*

DICKIE DARE
Eastern Color Printing Co.: 1941 - No. 4, 1942 (#3 on sale 6/15/42)

	GD 2.0	VG 4.0	FN 6.0	VF 8.0	VF/NM 9.0	NM- 9.2
1-Caniff-a, bondage-c by Everett	62	124	186	394	677	960
2	29	58	87	170	278	385
3,4-Half Scorchy Smith by Noel Sickles who was very influential in Milton Caniff's development	31	62	93	182	296	410

DICK POWELL (Also see A-1 Comics)
Magazine Enterprises: No. 22, 1949 (one shot)

	GD 2.0	VG 4.0	FN 6.0	VF 8.0	VF/NM 9.0	NM- 9.2
A-1 22-Photo-c	22	44	66	132	216	300

DICK QUICK, ACE REPORTER (See Picture News #10)

DICKS
Caliber Comics: 1997 - No. 4, 1998 ($2.95, B&W)

	NM- 9.2
1-4-Ennis-s/McCrea-c/a; r/Fleetway	3.00
TPB ('98, $12.95) r/series	13.00

DICK'S ADVENTURES
Dell Publishing Co.: No. 245, Sept, 1949

	GD 2.0	VG 4.0	FN 6.0	VF 8.0	VF/NM 9.0	NM- 9.2
Four Color 245	6	12	18	37	66	95

DICK TRACY (See Famous Feature Stories, Harvey Comics Library, Limited Collectors' Ed., Mammoth Comics, Merry Christmas, The Original..., Popular Comics, Super Book No. 1, 7, 13, 25, Super Comics & Tastee-Freez)

DICK TRACY
David McKay Publications: May, 1937 - Jan, 1938

	GD 2.0	VG 4.0	FN 6.0	VF 8.0	VF/NM 9.0	NM- 9.2
Feature Books nn - 100 pgs., partially reprinted as 4-Color No. 1 (appeared before Large Feature Comics, 1st Dick Tracy comic book) (Very Rare-five known copies; two incomplete)	1200	2400	3600	9000	16,500	24,000
Feature Books 4 - Reprints nn issue w/new-c	145	290	435	921	1586	2250
Feature Books 6,9	103	206	309	659	1130	1600

DICK TRACY (...Monthly #1-24)
Dell Publishing Co.: 1939 - No. 24, Dec, 1949

	GD 2.0	VG 4.0	FN 6.0	VF 8.0	VF/NM 9.0	NM- 9.2
Large Feature Comic 1 (1939) -Dick Tracy Meets The Blank	206	412	618	1318	2259	3200
Large Feature Comic 4,8	107	214	321	680	1165	1650
Large Feature Comic 11,13,15	97	194	291	621	1061	1500
Four Color 1(1939)('35-r)	1050	2100	3150	7800	14,650	21,500
Four Color 6(1940)('37-r)-(Scarce)	239	478	717	1530	2615	3700
Four Color 8(1940)('38-'39-r)	119	238	357	762	1306	1850
Large Feature Comic 3(1941, Series II)	90	180	270	576	988	1400
Four Color 21('41)('38-r)	87	174	261	553	952	1350
Four Color 34('43)('39-'40-r)	37	74	111	274	612	950
Four Color 56('44)('40-r)	33	66	99	238	532	825
Four Color 96('46)('40-r)	22	44	66	154	340	525
Four Color 133('47)('40-'41-r)	17	34	51	117	259	400
Four Color 163('47)('41-r)	15	30	45	103	227	350
1(1/48)('34-r)	36	72	108	266	596	925
2,3	19	38	57	131	291	450
4-10	16	32	48	112	249	385
11-18: 13-Bondage-c	12	24	36	84	185	285
19-1st app. Sparkle Plenty, B.O. Plenty & Gravel Gertie in a 3-pg. strip not by Gould	13	26	39	89	195	300
20-1st app. Sam Catchem; c/a not by Gould	12	24	36	81	176	270
21-24-Only 2 pg. Gould-a in each	12	24	36	79	170	260

NOTE: *No. 19-24 have a 2 pg. biography of a famous villain illustrated by **Gould**: 19-Little Face; 20-Flattop; 21-Breathless Mahoney; 22-Measles; 23-Itchy; 24-The Brow.*

DICK TRACY (Continued from Dell series)(...Comics Monthly #25-140)
Harvey Publications: No. 25, Mar, 1950 - No. 145, April, 1961

	GD 2.0	VG 4.0	FN 6.0	VF 8.0	VF/NM 9.0	NM- 9.2
25-Flat Top-c/story (also #26,27)	11	22	33	76	163	250
26-28,30: 28-Bondage-c. 28,29-The Brow-c/stories	9	18	27	61	123	185
29-1st app. Gravel Gertie in a Gould-r	10	20	30	69	147	225
31,32,34,35,37-40: 40-Intro/origin 2-way wrist radio (6/51)	8	16	24	52	99	145
33- "Measles the Teen-Age Dope Pusher"	9	18	27	61	123	185
36-1st app. B.O. Plenty in a Gould-r	9	18	27	61	123	185
41-50	7	14	21	46	86	125
51-56,58-80: 51-2pgs Powell-a	6	12	18	40	73	105
57-1st app. Sam Catchem in a Gould-r	7	14	21	46	86	125
81-99,101-140: 99-109-Painted-c	6	12	18	37	66	95
100, 141-145 (25¢)(titled "Dick Tracy")	6	12	18	40	73	105

NOTE: ***Powell** a(1-2pgs.)-43, 44, 104, 108, 109, 145. No. 110-120, 141-145 are all reprints from earlier issues.*

DICK TRACY ("Reuben Award" series)
Blackthorne Publishing: 12/84 - No. 24, 6/89 (1-12: $5.95; 13-24: $6.95, B&W, 76 pgs.)

	NM- 9.2
1-8-1st printings; hard-c ed. ($14.95)	20.00
1-3-2nd printings, 1986; hard-c ed.	20.00
1-12-1st & 2nd printings; squarebound, thick-c	12.00
13-24 ($6.95): 21,22-Regular-c & stapled	14.00

NOTE: ***Gould** daily & Sunday strip-r in all. 1-12 r-12/31/45-4/5/49; 13-24 r-7/13/41-2/20/44.*

DICK TRACY (Disney)
WD Publications: 1990 - No. 3, 1990 (color) (Book 3 adapts 1990 movie)

	NM- 9.2
Book One ($3.95, 52pgs.)-Kyle Baker-c/a	6.00
Book Two, Three ($5.95, 68pgs.)-Direct sale	6.00
Book Two, Three ($2.95, 68pgs.)-Newsstand	4.00

DICK TRACY ADVENTURES
Gladstone Publishing: May, 1991 ($4.95, 76 pgs.)

	NM- 9.2
1-Reprints strips 2/1/42-4/18/42	5.00

DICK TRACY, EXPLOITS OF
Rosdon Books, Inc.: 1946 ($1.00, hard-c strip reprints)

	GD 2.0	VG 4.0	FN 6.0	VF 8.0	VF/NM 9.0	NM- 9.2
1-Reprints the near complete case of "The Brow" from 6/12/44 to 9/24/44 (story starts a few weeks late)	25	50	75	147	241	335
with dust jacket...	39	78	117	240	395	550

DICK TRACY MONTHLY/WEEKLY
Blackthorne Publishing: May, 1986 - No. 99, 1989 ($2.00, B&W)
(Becomes Weekly #26 on)

	GD 2.0	VG 4.0	FN 6.0	VF 8.0	VF/NM 9.0	NM- 9.2
1-60: Gould-r. 30,31-Mr. Crime app.						4.00
61-90						4.00
91-95						6.00
96-99-Low print	1	2	3	5	7	9

NOTE: *#1-10 reprint strips 3/10/40-7/13/41; #10(pg.8)-51 reprint strips 4/6/49-12/31/55; #52-99 reprint strips 12/26/56-4/26/64.*

DICK TRACY SPECIAL
Blackthorne Publ.: Jan, 1988 - No. 3, Aug. (no month), 1989 ($2.95, B&W)

	NM- 9.2
1-3: 1-Origin D. Tracy; 4/strips 10/12/31-3/30/32	4.00

DICK TRACY: THE EARLY YEARS
Blackthorne Publishing: Aug, 1987 - No. 4, Aug (no month) 1989 ($6.95, B&W, 76 pgs.)

	GD 2.0	VG 4.0	FN 6.0	VF 8.0	VF/NM 9.0	NM- 9.2
1-3: 1-4-r/strips 10/12/31(1st daily)-8/31/32 & Sunday strips 6/12/32-8/28/32; Big Boy apps. in #1-3	1	2	3	4	5	7
4 ($2.95, 52pgs.)						4.00

DICK TRACY UNPRINTED STORIES
Blackthorne Publishing: Sept, 1987 - No. 4, June, 1988 ($2.95, B&W)

	NM- 9.2
1-4: Reprints strips 1/1/56-12/25/56	4.00

DICK TURPIN (See Legend of Young...)

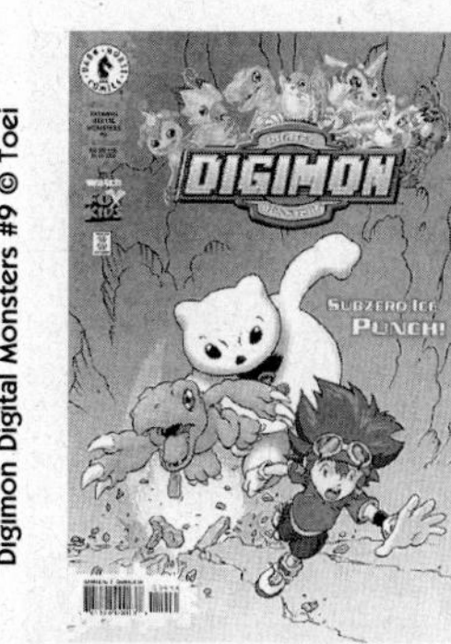

Digimon Digital Monsters #9 © Toei

Dinosaurs Attack! #3 © Topps

Dirty Pair #2 © ECL

	GD 2.0	VG 4.0	FN 6.0	VF 8.0	VF/NM 9.0	NM- 9.2

GD VG FN VF VF/NM NM- 2.0 4.0 6.0 8.0 9.0 9.2

DIE-CUT
Marvel Comics UK, Ltd: Nov, 1993 - No. 4, Feb, 1994 ($1.75, limited series)
1-4: 1-Die-cut-c; The Beast app. 3.00

DIE-CUT VS. G-FORCE
Marvel Comics UK, Ltd: Nov, 1993 - No. 2, Dec, 1993 ($2.75, limited series)
1,2-($2.75)-Gold foil-c on both 4.00

DIE HARD: YEAR ONE (Based on the John McClane character)
BOOM! Studios: Aug, 2009 - No. 8, Mar, 2010 ($3.99, limited series)
1-8-Chaykin-s; Officer McClane in 1976 NYC; multiple covers on each 4.00

DIE, MONSTER, DIE (See Movie Classics)

DIGIMON DIGITAL MONSTERS (TV)
Dark Horse Comics: May, 2000 - No. 12, Nov, 2000 ($2.95/$2.99)
1-12 3.00

DIGITEK
Marvel UK, Ltd: Dec, 1992 - No. 4, Mar, 1993 ($1.95/$2.25, mini-series)
1-4: 3-Deathlock-c/story 3.00

DILLY (Dilly Duncan from Daredevil Comics; see Boy Comics #57)
Lev Gleason Publications: May, 1953 - No. 3, Sept, 1953

	GD	VG	FN	VF	VF/NM	NM-
1-Teenage; Biro-c	7	14	21	37	46	55
2,3-Biro-c	5	10	15	24	30	35

DILTON'S STRANGE SCIENCE (See Pep Comics #78)
Archie Comics: May, 1989 - No. 5, May, 1990 (75¢/$1.00)
1-5 3.00

DIME COMICS
Newsbook Publ. Corp.: 1945; 1951

	GD	VG	FN	VF	VF/NM	NM-
1-Silver Streak/Green Dragon-c/sty; Japanese WWII-c by L. B. Cole (Rare)	168	336	504	1075	1838	2600
1(1951)	16	32	48	94	147	200

DINGBATS (See 1st Issue Special)

DING DONG
Compix/Magazine Enterprises: Summer?, 1946 - No. 5, 1947 (52 pgs.)

	GD	VG	FN	VF	VF/NM	NM-
1-Funny animal	32	64	96	188	307	425
2 (9/46)	15	30	45	86	133	180
3 (Wint '46-'47) - 5	14	28	42	76	108	140

DINKY DUCK (Paul Terry's...) (See Approved Comics, Blue Ribbon, Giant Comics Edition #5A & New Terrytoons)
St. John Publishing Co./Pines No. 16 on: Nov, 1951 - No. 16, Sept, 1955; No. 16, Fall, 1956; No. 17, May, 1957 - No. 19, Summer, 1958

	GD	VG	FN	VF	VF/NM	NM-
1-Funny animal	14	28	42	76	108	140
2	8	16	24	44	57	70
3-10	6	12	18	31	38	45
11-16(9/55)	6	12	18	28	34	40
16 (Fall, '56) - 19	5	10	15	23	28	32

DINKY DUCK & HASHIMOTO-SAN (See Deputy Dawg Presents...)

DINO (TV)(The Flintstones)
Charlton Publications: Aug, 1973 - No. 20, Jan, 1977 (Hanna-Barbera)

	GD	VG	FN	VF	VF/NM	NM-
1	3	6	9	17	26	35
2-10	2	4	6	10	14	18
11-20	2	4	6	8	10	12
Digest nn (w/Xerox Pub., 1974) (low print run)	2	4	6	11	16	20

DINO ISLAND
Mirage Studios: Feb, 1994 - No. 2, Mar, 1994 ($2.75, limited series)
1,2-By Jim Lawson 3.00

DINO RIDERS
Marvel Comics: Feb, 1989 - No. 3, 1989 ($1.00)
1-3: Based on toys 3.00

DINOSAUR REX
Upshot Graphics (Fantagraphics): 1986 - No. 3, 1986 ($2.00, limited series)
1-3 3.00

DINOSAURS, A CELEBRATION
Marvel Comics (Epic): Oct, 1992 - No. 4, Oct, 1992 ($4.95, lim. series, 52 pgs.)
1-4: 2-Bolton painted-c 5.00

DINOSAURS ATTACK! (Based on Topps trading card set)
IDW Publishing: Jul, 2013 - No. 5, Nov, 2013 ($3.99, limited series)
1-5: 1,2-Remastered version of 1991 graphic novel. 3-5-New continuation of story 4.00

DINOSAURS ATTACK! THE GRAPHIC NOVEL
Eclipse Comics: 1991 ($3.95, coated stock, stiff-c)
Book One- Based on Topps trading cards 5.00

DINOSAURS FOR HIRE
Malibu Comics: Feb, 1993 - No. 12, Feb, 1994 ($1.95/$2.50)
1-12: 1,10-Flip bk. 8-Bagged w/Skycap; Staton-c. 10-Flip book 3.00

DINOSAURS GRAPHIC NOVEL (TV)
Disney Comics: 1992 - No. 2, 1993 ($2.95, 52 pgs.)
1,2-Staton-a; based on Dinosaurs TV show 4.00

DINOSAURUS
Dell Publishing Co.: No. 1120, Aug, 1960

	GD	VG	FN	VF	VF/NM	NM-
Four Color 1120-Movie, painted-c	7	14	21	48	89	130

DIPPY DUCK
Atlas Comics (OPI): October, 1957

	GD	VG	FN	VF	VF/NM	NM-
1-Maneely-a; code approved	11	22	33	62	86	110

DIRECTORY TO A NONEXISTENT UNIVERSE
Eclipse Comics: Dec, 1987 ($2.00, B&W)
1 3.00

DIRTY DOZEN (See Movie Classics)

DIRTY PAIR (Manga)
Eclipse Comics: Dec, 1988 - No. 4, Apr, 1989 ($2.00, B&W, limited series)
1-4: Japanese manga with original stories 3.00
...: Start the Violence (Dark Horse, 9/99, $2.95) r/B&W stories in color from Dark Horse Presents #132-134; covers by Warren & Pearson 3.00

DIRTY PAIR: FATAL BUT NOT SERIOUS (Manga)
Dark Horse Comics: July, 1995 - No. 5, Nov, 1995 ($2.95, limited series)
1-5 3.00

DIRTY PAIR: RUN FROM THE FUTURE (Manga)
Dark Horse Comics: Jan, 2000 - No. 4, Mar, 2000 ($2.95, limited series)
1-4-Warren-s/c/a. Var.-c by Hughes(1), Stelfreeze(2), Timm(3), Ramos(4) 3.00

DIRTY PAIR: SIM HELL (Manga)
Dark Horse Comics: May, 1993 - No. 4, Aug, 1993 ($2.50, B&W, limited series)
1-4 3.00
...Remastered #1-4 (5/01 - 8/01) reprints in color, with pin-up gallery 3.00

DIRTY PAIR II (Manga)
Eclipse Comics: June, 1989 - No. 5, Mar, 1990 ($2.00, B&W, limited series)
1-5: 3-Cover is misnumbered as #1 3.00

DIRTY PAIR III, THE (A Plague of Angels) (Manga)
Eclipse Comics: Aug, 1990 - No. 5, Aug, 1991 ($2.00/$2.25, B&W, lim. series)
1-5 3.00

DISHMAN
Eclipse Comics: Sept, 1988 ($2.50, B&W, 52 pgs.)
1 4.00

DISNEY AFTERNOON, THE (TV)
Marvel Comics: Nov, 1994 - No. 10?, Aug, 1995 ($1.50)
1-10: 3-w/bound-in Power Ranger Barcode Card 3.00

DISNEY COMIC ALBUM
Disney Comics: 1990(no month, year) - No. 8, 1991 ($6.95/$7.95)
1,2 ($6.95): 1-Donald Duck and Gyro Gearloose by Barks(r). 2-Uncle Scrooge by Barks(r); Jr. Woodchucks app. 9.00
3-8: 3-Donald Duck-r/F.C. 308 by Barks; begin $7.95-c. 4-Mickey Mouse Meets the Phantom Blot; r/M.M Club Parade (censored 1956 version of story). 5-Chip 'n' Dale Rescue Rangers; new-a. 6-Uncle Scrooge. 7-Donald Duck in Too Many Pets; Barks-r(4) including F.C. #29. 8-Super Goof; r/S.G. #1, D.D. #102 9.00

DISNEY COMIC HITS
Marvel Comics: Oct, 1995 - No. 16, Jan, 1997 ($1.50/$2.50)
1-16: 4-Toy Story. 6-Aladdin. 7-Pocahontas. 10-The Hunchback of Notre Dame (Same story in Disney's The Hunchback of Notre Dame). 13-Aladdin and the Forty Thieves 4.00

DISNEY COMICS
Disney Comics: June, 1990
Boxed set of #1 issues includes Donald Duck Advs., Ducktales, Chip 'n Dale Rescue Rangers,

Disney's Aladdin #10 © DIS

A Distant Soil #24 © Colleen Doran

Division 13 #1 © DH

	GD 2.0	VG 4.0	FN 6.0	VF 8.0	VF/NM 9.0	NM- 9.2

Roger Rabbit, Mickey Mouse Advs. & Goofy Advs.; limited to 10,000 sets 2 4 6 11 16 20

DISNEY KINGDOMS: SEEKERS OF THE WEIRD
Marvel Comics: Mar, 2014 - Present ($3.99)
1-3: 1-Seifert-s/Moline-a/Del Mundo-c. 3-Andrade-a 4.00

DISNEYLAND BIRTHDAY PARTY (Also see Dell Giants)
Gladstone Publishing Co.: Aug, 1985 ($2.50)
1-Reprints Dell Giant with new-photo-c 2 4 6 8 10 12
...Comics Digest #1-(Digest) 2 4 6 8 11 14

DISNEYLAND MAGAZINE
Fawcett Publications: Feb. 15, 1972 - ? (10-1/4"x12-5/8", 20 pgs, weekly)
1-One or two page painted art features on Dumbo, Snow White, Lady & the Tramp, the Aristocats, Brer Rabbit, Peter Pan, Cinderella, Jungle Book, Alice & Pinocchio. Most standard characters app. 3 6 9 16 23 30

DISNEYLAND, USA (See Dell Giant No. 30)

DISNEY MOVIE BOOK
Walt Disney Productions (Gladstone): 1990 ($7.95, 8-1/2"x11", 52 pgs.) (w/pull-out poster)
1-Roger Rabbit in Tummy Trouble; from the cartoon film strips adapted to the comic format. Ron Dias-c 2 4 6 8 10 12

DISNEY'S ACTION CLUB
Acclaim Books: 1997 - No. 4 ($4.50, digest size)
1-4: 1-Hercules. 4-Mighty Ducks 4.50

DISNEY'S ALADDIN (Movie)
Marvel Comics: Oct, 1994 - No. 11, 1995 ($1.50)
1-11 3.00

DISNEY'S BEAUTY AND THE BEAST (Movie)
Marvel Comics: Sept, 1994 - No. 13, 1995 ($1.50)
1-13 3.00

DISNEY'S BEAUTY AND THE BEAST HOLIDAY SPECIAL
Acclaim Books: 1997 ($4.50, digest size, one-shot)
1-Based on The Enchanted Christmas video 4.50

DISNEY'S COLOSSAL COMICS COLLECTION
Disney Comics: 1991 - No. 10, 1993 ($1.95, digest-size, 96/132 pgs.)
1-10: Ducktales, Talespin, Chip 'n Dale's Rescue Rangers. 4-r/Darkwing Duck #1-4. 6-Goofy begins. 8-Little Mermaid 5.00

DISNEY'S COMICS IN 3-D
Disney Comics: 1992 ($2.95, w/glasses, polybagged)
1-Infinity-c; Barks, Rosa, Gottfredson-r 5.00

DISNEY'S ENCHANTING STORIES
Acclaim Books: 1997 - No. 5 ($4.50, digest size)
1-5: 1-Hercules. 2-Pocahontas 4.50

DISNEY'S HERO SQUAD
BOOM! Studios: Jan, 2010 - No. 8, Aug, 2010 ($2.99)
1-8: 1-3-Phantom Blot app. 1-Back-up reprint of Super Goof #1 3.00

DISNEY'S NEW ADVENTURES OF BEAUTY AND THE BEAST (Also see Beauty and the Beast & Disney's Beauty and the Beast)
Disney Comics: 1992 - No. 2, 1992 ($1.50, limited series)
1,2-New stories based on movie 3.00

DISNEY'S POCAHONTAS (Movie)
Marvel Comics: 1995 ($4.95, one-shot)
1-Movie adaptation 1 2 3 4 5 7

DISNEY'S TALESPIN LIMITED SERIES: "TAKE OFF" (TV) (See Talespin)
W. D. Publications (Disney Comics): Jan, 1991 - No. 4, Apr, 1991 ($1.50, lim. series, 52 pgs.)
1-4: Based on animated series; 4 part origin 4.00

DISNEY'S TARZAN (Movie)
Dark Horse Comics: June, 1999 - No. 2, July, 1999 ($2.95, limited series)
1,2: Movie adaptation 3.00

DISNEY'S THE LION KING (Movie)
Marvel Comics: July, 1994 - No. 2, July, 1994 ($1.50, limited series)
1,2: 2-part movie adaptation 3.00
1-($2.50, 52 pgs.)-Complete story 5.00

DISNEY'S THE LITTLE MERMAID (Movie)
Marvel Comics: Sept, 1994 - No. 12, 1995 ($1.50)
1-12 4.00

DISNEY'S THE LITTLE MERMAID LIMITED SERIES (Movie)
Disney Comics: Feb, 1992 - No. 4, May, 1992 ($1.50, limited series)
1-4: Peter David scripts 4.00

DISNEY'S THE LITTLE MERMAID: UNDERWATER ENGAGEMENTS
Acclaim Books: 1997 ($4.50, digest size)
1-Flip book 4.50

DISNEY'S THE HUNCHBACK OF NOTRE DAME (Movie)(See Disney's Comic Hits #10)
Marvel Comics: July, 1996 ($4.95, squarebound, one-shot)
1-Movie adaptation. 1 2 3 4 5 7
NOTE: A different edition of this series was sold at Wal-Mart stores with new covers depicting scenes from the 1989 feature film. Inside contents and price were identical.

DISNEY'S THE THREE MUSKETEERS (Movie)
Marvel Comics: Jan, 1994 - No. 2, Feb, 1994 ($1.50, limited series)
1,2-Morrow-c; Spiegle-a; Movie adaptation 3.00

DISNEY'S TOY STORY (Movie)
Marvel Comics: Dec, 1995 ($4.95, one-shot)
nn-Adaptation of film 1 2 3 4 5 7

DISTANT SOIL, A (1st Series)
WaRP Graphics: Dec, 1983 - No. 9, Mar 1986 ($1.50, B&W)
1-Magazine size 6.00
2-9: 2-4 are magazine size 4.00
NOTE: Second printings exist of #1, 2, 3 & 6.

DISTANT SOIL, A
Donning (Star Blaze): Mar, 1989 ($12.95, trade paperback)
nn-new material 13.00

DISTANT SOIL, A (2nd Series)
Aria Press/Image Comics (Highbrow Entertainment) #15 on:
June, 1991 - Present ($1.75/$2.50/$2.95/$3.50/$3.95, B&W)
1-27: 13-$2.95-c begins. 14-Sketchbook. 15-(8/96)-1st Image issue 4.00
29-33,35,37-($3.95) 4.00
34-($4.95, 64 pages) includes sketchbook pages 5.00
36,38-($4.50) 36-Back-up story by Darnall & Doran. 38-Includes sketch pages 4.50
39-42-($3.50) 3.50
The Aria ('01, $16.95,TPB) r/#26-31 17.00
The Ascendant ('98, $18.95,TPB) r/#13-25 19.00
The Gathering ('97, $18.95,TPB) r/#1-13; intro. Neil Gaiman 19.00
Vol. 4: Coda (2005, $17.99, TPB) r/#32-38 18.00
NOTE: Four separate printings exist for #1 and are clearly marked. Second printings exist of #2-4 and are also clearly marked.

DISTANT SOIL, A: IMMIGRANT SONG
Donning (Star Blaze): Aug, 1987 ($6.95, trade paperback)
nn-new material 7.00

DISTRICT X (Also see X-Men titles) (Also see Mutopia X)
Marvel Comics: July, 2004 - No. 14, Aug, 2005 ($2.99)
1-14: 1-3-Bishop app.; Yardin-a/Hine-s 3.00
...Vol. 1: Mr. M (2005, $14.99) r/#1-6; sketch page by Yardin 15.00
...Vol. 2: Underground (2005, $19.99) r/#7-14; prologue from X-Men Unlimited #2 20.00

DIVER DAN (TV)
Dell Publishing Co.: Feb-Apr, 1962 - No. 2, June-Aug, 1962
Four Color 1254(#1), 2 5 10 15 31 53 75

DIVINE RIGHT
Image Comics (WildStorm Prod.): Sept, 1997 - No. 12, Nov, 1999 ($2.50)
Preview 5.00
1,2: 1-Jim Lee-s/a(p)/c, 1-Variant-c by Charest 4.00
1-($3.50)-Voyager Pack w/Stormwatch preview 4.00
1-American Entertainment Ed. 6.00
2-Variant-c of Exotica & Blaze 5.00
3-Chromium-c by Jim Lee 5.00
3-12: 3-5-Fairchild & Lynch app. 4-American Entertainment Ed. 8-Two covers. 9-1st DC issue. 11,12-Divine Intervention pt. 1,4 3.00
5-Pacific Comicon Ed. 6.00
6-Glow in the dark variant-c, European Tour Edition 20.00
...Book One TPB (2002, $17.95) r/#1-7 18.00
...Book Two TPB (2002, $17.95) r/#8-12 & Divine Intervention Gen13, ...Wildcats 18.00
...Collected Edition #1-3 ($5.95, TPB) 1-r/#1,2. 2-r/#3,4. 3-r/#5,6 6.00
Divine Intervention/Gen 13 (11/99, $2.50) Part 3; D'Anda-a 3.00

Dixie Dugan #3 © McNaught

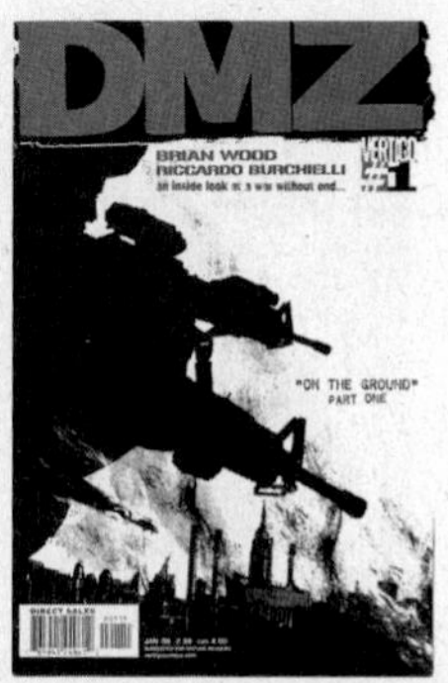

DMZ #1 © Wood & Burchelli

Doc Frankenstein #1 © Burlyman

	GD	VG	FN	VF	VF/NM	NM-
	2.0	4.0	6.0	8.0	9.0	9.2

Divine Intervention/Wildcats (11/99, $2.50) Part 2; D'Anda-a 3.00

DIVISION 13 (See Comic's Greatest World)
Dark Horse Comics: Sept, 1994 - Jan, 1995 ($2.50, color)

1-4: Giffen story in all. 1-Art Adams-c 3.00

DIXIE DUGAN (See Big Shot, Columbia Comics & Feature Funnies)
McNaught Syndicate/Columbia/Publication Ent.: July, 1942 - No. 13, 1949
(Strip reprints in all)

1-Joe Palooka x-over by Ham Fisher	27	54	81	160	263	365
2	15	30	45	86	133	180
3	12	24	36	69	97	125
4,5(1945-46)-Bo strip-r	10	20	30	54	72	90
6-13(1/47-49): 6-Paperdoll cut-outs	9	18	27	47	61	75

DIXIE DUGAN
Prize Publications (Headline): V3#1, Nov, 1951 - V4#4, Feb, 1954

V3#1	10	20	30	54	72	90
2-4	7	14	21	35	43	50
V4#1-4(#5-8)	6	12	18	28	34	40

DIZZY DAMES
American Comics Group (B&M Distr. Co.): Sept-Oct, 1952 - No. 6, Jul-Aug, 1953

1-Whitney-c	20	40	60	114	182	250
2	12	24	36	69	97	125
3-6	10	20	30	56	76	95

DIZZY DON COMICS
F. E. Howard Publications/Dizzy Don Ent. Ltd (Canada): 1942 - No. 22, Oct, 1946; No. 3, Apr, 1947 - No. 4, Sept./Oct., 1947 (Most B&W)

1 (B&W)	26	52	78	154	252	350
2 (B&W)	14	28	42	82	121	160
4-21 (B&W)	13	26	39	72	101	130
22-Full color, 52 pgs.	26	52	78	154	252	350
3 (4/47), 4 (9-10/47)-Full color, 52 pgs.	26	52	78	154	252	350

DIZZY DUCK (Formerly Barnyard Comics)
Standard Comics: No. 32, Nov, 1950 - No. 39, Mar, 1952

32-Funny animal	10	20	30	56	76	95
33-39	7	14	21	35	43	50

DJANGO UNCHAINED (Adaptation of the 2012 movie)
DC Comics (Vertigo): Feb, 2013 - No. 7, Oct, 2013 ($3.99, limited series)

1-Adaptation of Quentin Tarantino's script; Guéra-a; Tarantino foreword; sketch pages 20.00
1-Variant-c by Jim Lee 80.00
2-Cowan-c; bonus concept art and cover sketch art 8.00
2-Variant-c by Mark Chiarello 35.00
3-7: 5-Quitely-c. 7-Alex Ross-c 5.00

DMZ
DC Comics (Vertigo): Jan, 2006 - No. 72, Feb, 2012 ($2.99)

1-Brian Wood-s/Riccardo Burchielli-a 4.00
1-(2008, no cover price) Convention Exclusive promotional edition 3.00
2-49,51-72: 2-10-Brian Wood-s/Riccardo Burchielli-a. 11-Donaldson-a. 12-Wood-s/a 3.00
50-($3.99) Short stories by various incl. Risso, Moon, Gibbons, Bermejo, Jim Lee 4.00
...: Blood in the Game TPB (2009, $12.99) r/#29-34; intro. by Greg Palast 13.00
...: Body of a Journalist TPB (2007, $12.99) r/#6-12; intro. by D. Randall Blythe 13.00
...: Collective Punishment TPB (2011, $14.99) r/#55-59 15.00
...: Friendly Fire TPB (2008, $12.99) r/#18-22; intro. by Sgt. John G. Ford 13.00
...: Hearts and Minds TPB (2010, $16.99) r/#42-49; intro. by Morgan Spurlock 17.00
...: M.I.A. TPB (2011, $14.99) r/#50-54 15.00
...: On the Ground TPB (2006, $9.99) r/#1-5; intro. by Brian Azzarello 10.00
...: Public Works TPB (2007, $12.99) r/#13-17; intro. by Cory Doctorow 13.00
...: The Hidden War TPB (2008, $12.99) r/#23-28 13.00
...: War Powers TPB (2009, $14.99) r/#35-41 15.00

DNAGENTS (The New DNAgents V2/1 on)(Also see Surge)
Eclipse Comics: March, 1983 - No. 24, July, 1985 ($1.50, Baxter paper)

1-Origin. 4.00
2-23: 4-Amber app. 8-Infinity-c 3.00
24-Dave Stevens-c 1 2 3 5 6 8
... Industrial Strength Edition TPB (Image, 2008, $24.99) B&W r/#1-14; Evanier intro. 25.00

DOBERMAN (See Sgt. Bilko's Private...)

DOBIE GILLIS (See The Many Loves of...)

DOC CHAOS: THE STRANGE ATTRACTOR
Vortex Comics: Apr, 1990 - No. 3, 1990 ($3.00, 32 pgs.)

1-3: The Lust For Order 3.00

DOC FRANKENSTEIN
Burlyman Entertainment: Nov, 2004 - No. 6 ($3.50)

1-6-Wachowski brothers-s/Skroce-a 3.50

DOCK WALLOPER (Ed Burns' ...)
Virgin Comics: Nov, 2007 - No. 5, Jun, 2008 ($2.99)

1-5-Burns & Palmiotti-s/Siju Thomas-a; Prohibition time 3.00

DOC MACABRE
IDW Publishing: Dec, 2010 - No. 3, Feb, 2011 ($3.99)

1-3-Steve Niles-s/Bernie Wrightson-a/c 4.00

DOC SAMSON (Also see Incredible Hulk)
Marvel Comics: Jan, 1996 - No. 4, Apr, 1996 ($1.95, limited series)

1-4: 1-Hulk c/app. 2-She-Hulk-c/app. 3-Punisher-c/app. 4-Polaris-c/app. 3.00

DOC SAMSON (Incredible Hulk)
Marvel Comics: Mar, 2006 - No. 5, July, 2006 ($2.99, limited series)

1-5: 1-DiFilippo-s/Fiorentino-a. 3-Conner-c 3.00

DOC SAVAGE
Gold Key: Nov, 1966

1-Adaptation of the Thousand-Headed Man; James Bama c-r/1964 Doc Savage paperback	10	20	30	69	147	225

DOC SAVAGE (Also see Giant-Size...)
Marvel Comics Group: Oct, 1972 - No. 8, Jan, 1974

1	3	6	9	21	33	45
2,3-Steranko-c	3	6	9	15	22	28
4-8	2	4	6	9	13	16

...: The Man of Bronze TPB (DC Comics, 2010, $17.99) r/#1-8 18.00
NOTE: ***Gil Kane** c-5, 6. **Mooney** a-1i. No. 1, 2 adapts pulp story "The Man of Bronze"; No. 3, 4 adapts "Death in Silver"; No. 5, 6 adapts "The Monsters"; No. 7, 8 adapts "The Brand of The Werewolf".*

DOC SAVAGE (Magazine) (See Showcase Presents for reprint)
Marvel Comics Group: Aug, 1975 - No. 8, Spring, 1977 ($1.00, B&W)

1-Cover from movie poster; Ron Ely photo-c	3	6	9	15	22	28
2-5: 3-Buscema-a. 5-Adams-a(1 pg.), Rogers-a(1 pg)	2	4	6	9	13	16
6-8	2	4	6	10	14	18

DOC SAVAGE
DC Comics: Nov, 1987 - No. 4, Feb, 1988 ($1.75, limited series)

1-4: Dennis O'Neil-s/Adam & Andy Kubert-a/c in all 4.00
...: The Silver Pyramid TPB (2009, $19.99) r/#1-4 20.00

DOC SAVAGE
DC Comics: Nov, 1988 - No. 24, Oct, 1990 ($1.75/$2.00: #13-24)

1-16,19-24 4.00
17,18-Shadow x-over 5.00
Annual 1 (1989, $3.50, 68 pgs.) 5.00

DOC SAVAGE (First Wave)
DC Comics: Jun, 2010 - No. 18, Nov, 2011 ($3.99/$2.99)

1-9: 1-4-Malmont-s/Porter-a/J.G. Jones-c. Justice Inc. back-up; S. Hampton-a 4.00
1-6-Variant covers by Cassaday 5.00
10-17-($2.99) 10,16,17-Winslade-a 3.00

DOC SAVAGE
Dynamite Entertainment: 2013 - Present ($3.99)

1-4: 1-Roberson-s/Evely-a; covers by Ross & Cassaday 4.00

DOC SAVAGE COMICS (Also see Shadow Comics)
Street & Smith Publ.: May, 1940 - No. 20, Oct, 1943 (1st app. in Doc Savage pulp, 3/33)

1-Doc Savage, Cap Fury, Danny Garrett, Mark Mallory, The Whisperer, Captain Death, Billy the Kid, Sheriff Pete & Treasure Island begin; Norgil, the Magician app.	514	1028	1542	3750	6625	9500
2-Origin & 1st app. Ajax, the Sun Man; Danny Garrett, The Whisperer end; classic sci-fi cover	213	426	639	1363	2332	3300
3	139	278	417	883	1517	2150
4-Treasure Island ends; Tuska-a	108	216	324	686	1181	1675
5-Origin & 1st app. Astron, the Crocodile Queen, not in #9 & 11; Norgi the Magician app.; classic-c	97	194	291	621	1061	1500
6-10: 6-Cap Fury ends; origin & only app. Red Falcon in Astron story. 8-Mark Mallory ends; Charlie McCarthy app. on-c plus true life story. 9-Supersnipe app. 10-Origin & only app. The Thunderbolt	61	122	183	390	670	950
11,12	52	104	156	328	557	785

V2#1-6,8(#13-18,20): 15-Origin of Ajax the Sun Man; Jack Benny on-c; Hitler app. 16-The

Doctor Kildare #1 © MGM

Doctor Mid-Nite #3 © DC

Doctor Spectrum #1 © MAR

GD VG FN VF VF/NM NM-
2.0 4.0 6.0 8.0 9.0 9.2

Pulp Hero, The Avenger app.; Fanny Brice story. 17-Sun Man ends; Nick Carter begins; Duffy's Tavern part photo-c & story. 18-Huckleberry Finn part-c/story. 19-Henny Youngman part photo-c & life story. 20-Only all funny-c w/Huckleberry Finn
47 94 141 296 498 700
V2#7-Classic Devil-c 52 104 156 328 557 785

DOC SAVAGE: CURSE OF THE FIRE GOD
Dark Horse Comics: Sept, 1995 - No. 4, Dec, 1995 ($2.95, limited series)
1-4 3.00

DOC SAVAGE: THE MAN OF BRONZE
Skylark Pub: Mar, 1979, 68pgs. (B&W comic digest, 5-1/4x7-5/8")(low print)
15406-0: Whitman-a, 60 pgs., new comics 4 8 12 23 37 50

DOC SAVAGE: THE MAN OF BRONZE
Millennium Publications: 1991 - No. 4, 1991 ($2.50, limited series)
1-4: 1-Bronze logo 3.00
...: The Manual of Bronze 1 ($2.50, B&W, color, one-shot)-Unpublished proposed Doc Savage strip in color, B&W strip-r 3.00

DOC SAVAGE: THE MAN OF BRONZE, DOOM DYNASTY
Millennium Publ.: 1992 (Says 1991) - No. 2, 1992 ($2.50, limited series)
1,2 3.00

DOC SAVAGE: THE MAN OF BRONZE - REPEL
Innovation Publishing: 1992 ($2.50)
1-Dave Dorman painted-c 3.00

DOC SAVAGE: THE MAN OF BRONZE THE DEVIL'S THOUGHTS
Millennium Publ.: 1992 (Says 1991) - No. 3, 1992 ($2.50, limited series)
1-3 3.00

DOC STEARN...MR. MONSTER (See Mr. Monster)

DR. ANTHONY KING, HOLLYWOOD LOVE DOCTOR
Minoan Publishing Corp./Harvey Publications No. 4: 1952(Jan) - No. 3, May, 1953; No. 4, May, 1954
1 15 30 45 88 137 185
2-4: 4-Powell-a 10 20 30 54 72 90

DR. ANTHONY'S LOVE CLINIC (See Mr. Anthony's...)

DR. BOBBS
Dell Publishing Co.: No. 212, Jan, 1949
Four Color 212 5 10 15 35 63 90

DOCTOR CYBORG
Attention! Publishing: 1996 - No. 5 ($2.95, B&W)
1-5 3.00
The Clone Conspiracy TPB (1998, $14.95) r/#1-5 15.00

DOCTOR DOOM AND THE MASTERS OF EVIL (All ages title)
Marvel Comics: Mar, 2009 - No. 4, Jun, 2009 ($2.99)
1-4: 1-Sinister Six app. 4-Magneto app. 3.00

DR. DOOM'S REVENGE
Marvel Comics: 1989 (Came w/computer game from Paragon Software)
V1#1-Spider-Man & Captain America fight Dr. Doom 3.00

DR. FATE (See 1st Issue Special, The Immortal..., Justice League, More Fun #55, & Showcase)

DOCTOR FATE
DC Comics: July, 1987 - No. 4, Oct, 1987 ($1.50, limited series, Baxter paper)
1-4: Giffen-c/a in all 4.00

DOCTOR FATE
DC Comics: Winter, 1988-'89 - No. 41, June, 1992 ($1.25/$1.50 #5 on)
1,15: 15-Justice League app. 4.00
2-14 3.00
16-41: 25-1st new Dr. Fate. 36-Original Dr. Fate returns 3.00
Annual 1(1989, $2.95, 68 pgs.)-Sutton-a 4.00

DOCTOR FATE
DC Comics: Oct, 2003 - No. 5, Feb, 2004 ($2.50, limited series)
1-5-Golden-s/Kramer-a 3.00

DR. FU MANCHU (See The Mask of...)
I.W. Enterprises: 1964
1-r/Avon's "Mask of Dr. Fu Manchu"; Wood-a 6 12 18 41 76 110

DR. GIGGLES (See Dark Horse Presents #64-66)
Dark Horse Comics: Oct, 1992 - No. 2, Oct, 1992 ($2.50, limited series)

GD VG FN VF VF/NM NM-
2.0 4.0 6.0 8.0 9.0 9.2

1,2-Based on movie 3.00

DOCTOR GRAVES (Formerly The Many Ghosts of...)
Charlton Comics: No. 73, Sept, 1985 - No. 75, Jan, 1986
73-75-Low print run. 73,74-Ditko-a 1 2 3 5 6 8
... Magic Book nn (Charlton Press/Xerox Education, 1977, 68 pgs., digest) Ditko-c/a; Staton-a
4 8 12 23 37 50

DR. HORRIBLE (Based on Joss Whedon's internet feature)
Dark Horse Comics: Nov, 2009 ($3.50, one-shot)
1-Zack Whedon-s/Joëlle Jones-a; Captain Hammer pin-up by Gene Ha; 3 covers 3.50
... and other Horrible Stories TPB (9/10, $9.99) r/#1 and 3 stories from MySpace DHP 10.00

DR. JEKYLL AND MR. HYDE (See A Star Presentation & Supernatural Thrillers #4)

DR. KILDARE (TV)
Dell Publishing Co.: No. 1337, 4-6/62 - No. 9, 4-6/65 (All Richard Chamberlain photo-c)
Four Color 1337(#1, 1962) 7 14 21 49 92 135
2-9 6 12 18 37 66 95

DR. MASTERS (See The Adventures of Young...)

DOCTOR MID-NITE (Also see All-American #25)
DC Comics: 1999 - No. 3, 1999 ($5.95, square-bound, limited series)
1-3-Matt Wagner-s/John K. Snyder III-painted art 6.00
TPB (2000, $19.95) r/series 20.00

DOCTOR OCTOPUS: NEGATIVE EXPOSURE
Marvel Comics: Dec, 2003 - No. 5, Apr, 2004 ($2.99, limited series)
1-5-Vaughan-s/Staz Johnson-a; Spider-Man app. 3.00
Spider-Man/Doctor Octopus: Negative Exposure TPB (2004, $13.99) r/series 14.00

DR. ROBOT SPECIAL
Dark Horse Comics: Apr, 2000 ($2.95, one-shot)
1-Bernie Mireault-s/a; some reprints from Madman Comics #12-15 3.00

DOCTOR SOLAR, MAN OF THE ATOM (See The Occult Files of Dr. Spektor #14 & Solar)
Gold Key/Whitman No. 28 on: 10/62 - No. 27, 4/69; No. 28, 4/81 - No. 31, 3/82 (1-27 have painted-c)
1-(#10000-210)-Origin/1st app. Dr. Solar (1st original Gold Key character)
21 42 63 147 324 500
2-Prof. Harbinger begins 9 18 27 61 123 185
3,4 6 12 18 42 79 115
5-Intro. Man of the Atom in costume 7 14 21 44 82 120
6-10 5 10 15 33 57 80
11-14,16-20 4 8 12 27 44 60
15-Origin retold 4 8 12 28 47 65
21-23: 23-Last 12¢ issue 4 8 12 23 37 50
24-27 3 6 9 21 33 45
28-31: 29-Magnus Robot Fighter begins. 31-(3/82)The Sentinel app.
3 6 9 14 20 25
Hardcover Volume One (Dark Horse Books, 2004, $49.95) r/#1-7; creator bios 50.00
Hardcover Volume Two (Dark Horse Books, 6/05, $49.95) r/#8-14; Jim Shooter foreword 50.00
Hardcover Volume Three (Dark Horse Books, 9/05, $49.95) r/#15-22; Mike Baron foreword 50.00
Hardcover Volume Four (Dark Horse Books, 11/07, $49.95) r/#23-31 and The Occult Files of Dr. Spektor #14; Batton Lash foreword 50.00
NOTE: ***Frank Bolle** a-6-19, 29-31; c-29i, 30i.* ***Bob Fugitani** a-1-5.* ***Spiegle** a-29-31.* ***Al McWilliams** a-20-23.*

DOCTOR SOLAR, MAN OF THE ATOM
Valiant Comics: 1990 - No. 2, 1991 ($7.95, card stock-c, high quality, 96 pgs.)
1,2: Reprints Gold Key series 1 2 3 5 6 8

DOCTOR SOLAR, MAN OF THE ATOM
Dark Horse Comics: Jul, 2010 - No. 8, Sept, 2011 ($3.50)
1-(48 pgs.) Shooter-s/Calero-a; back-up reprint of origin/1st app. in D.S. #1 (1962) 4.00
2-8: 2-7-Roger Robinson-a 3.50
Free Comic Book Day Doctor Solar, Man of the Atom & Magnus, Robot Fighter (5/10, free) short story re-intros of Solar & Magnus; Shooter-s/Swanland-c; Calero & Reinhold-a 3.00

DOCTOR SPECTRUM (See Supreme Power)
Marvel Comics: Oct, 2004 - No. 6, Mar, 2005 ($2.99, limited series)
1-6-Origin; Sara Barnes-s/Travel Foreman-a 3.00
TPB (2005, $16.99) r/#1-6 17.00

DOCTOR SPEKTOR (See The Occult Files of..., & Spine-Tingling Tales)

DOCTOR STRANGE (Formerly Strange Tales #1-168) (Also see The Defenders, Giant-Size..., Marvel Fanfare, Marvel Graphic Novel, Marvel Premiere, Marvel Treasury Edition, Strange & Strange Tales, 2nd Series)
Marvel Comics Group: No. 169, 6/68 - No. 183, 11/69; 6/74 - No. 81, 2/87

Doctor Strange #37 © MAR

Doctor Strange, Sorceror Supreme #69 © MAR

Doctor Who (2009 series) #3 © BBC

GD VG FN VF VF/NM NM-
2.0 4.0 6.0 8.0 9.0 9.2

169(#1)-Origin retold; panel swipe/M.D. #1-c 14 28 42 94 207 320
170-177: 177-New costume 5 10 15 33 57 80
178-183: 178-Black Knight app. 179-Spider-Man story-r. 180-Photo montage-c.
181-Brunner-c(part-i), last 12¢ issue 5 10 15 31 53 75
1(6/74, 2nd series)-Brunner-c/a 8 16 24 56 108 160
2 5 10 15 31 53 75
3-5 3 6 9 17 26 35
6-10 2 4 6 10 14 18
11-13,15-20: 13,15-17-(Regular 25¢ editions) 1 3 4 6 8 10
13,15-17-(30¢-c variants, limited distribution) 3 6 9 21 33 45
14-(5/76) Dracula app.; (regular 25¢ edition) 2 4 6 10 14 18
14-(30¢-c variant, limited distribution) 5 10 15 30 50 70
21-40: 21-Origin-r/Doctor Strange #169. 23-25-(Regular 30¢ editions). 31-Sub-Mariner-c/story 6.00
23-25-(35¢-c variants, limited distribution)(6,8,10/77) 2 4 6 8 10 12
41-57,63-77,79-81: 56-Origin retold 4.00
58-62: 58-Re-intro Hannibal King (cameo). 59-Hannibal King full app. 59-62-Dracula app. (Darkhold storyline). 61,62-Doctor Strange, Blade, Hannibal King & Frank Drake team-up to battle. Dracula. 62-Death of Dracula & Lilith 6.00
78-New costume 5.00
Annual 1(1976, 52 pgs.)-New Russell-a (35 pgs.) 3 6 9 14 20 25
...: From the Marvel Vault (4/11, $2.99) Stern-s/Vokes-a 3.00
.../Silver Dagger Special Edition 1 (3/83, $2.50)-r/#1,2,4,5; Wrightson-c 4.00
... Vs. Dracula TPB (2006, $19.99) r/#14,58-62 and Tomb of Dracula #44 20.00
...What Is It That Disturbs You, Stephen? #1 (10/97, $5.99, 48 pgs.) Russell-a/Andreyko & Russell-s, retelling of Annual #1 story 6.00

NOTE: ***Adkins** a-169, 170, 171i; c-169-171, 172i, 173. **Adams** a-4i. **Austin** a(i)-48-60, 66, 68, 70, 73; c(i)-38, 47-53, 55, 58-60, 70. **Brunner** a-1-5p; c-1-6, 22, 28-30, 33. **Colan** a(p)-172-178, 180-183, 6-18, 36-45, 47; c(p)-172, 174-183, 11-21, 23, 27, 35, 36, 47. **Ditko** a-179r, 3r. **Everett** c-183i. **Golden** a-46p, 55p; c-42-44, 46, 55p. **G. Kane** c(p)-8-10. **Miller** c-46p. **Nebres** a-20, 22, 23, 24i, 26i, 32i; c-32i, 34. **Rogers** a-48-53p; c-47p-53p. **Russell** a-34i, 46i, Annual 1. **B. Smith** c-179. **Paul Smith** a-54p, 56p, 65, 66p, 68p, 69, 71-73; c-56, 65, 66, 68, 71. **Starlin** a-23p, 26; c-25, 26. **Sutton** a-27-29p, 31i, 33, 34p. Painted c-62, 63.*

DOCTOR STRANGE (Volume 2)
Marvel Comics: Feb, 1999 - No. 4, May, 1999 ($2.99, limited series)

1-4: 1,2-Tony Harris-a/painted cover. 3,4-Chadwick-a 3.00

DOCTOR STRANGE CLASSICS
Marvel Comics Group: Mar, 1984 - No. 4, June, 1984 ($1.50, Baxter paper)

1-4: Ditko-r; Byrne-c. 4-New Golden pin-up 4.00
NOTE: ***Byrne** c-1i, 2-4.*

DOCTOR STRANGEFATE (See Marvel Versus DC #3 & DC Versus Marvel #4)
DC Comics (Amalgam): Apr, 1996 ($1.95)

1-Ron Marz script w/Jose Garcia-Lopez-(p) & Kevin Nowlan-(i). Access & Charles Xavier app. 3.00

DOCTOR STRANGE MASTER OF THE MYSTIC ARTS (See Fireside Book Series)

DOCTOR STRANGE, SORCERER SUPREME
Marvel Comics (Midnight Sons imprint #60 on): Nov, 1988 - No. 90, June, 1996 ($1.25/$1.50/$1.75/$1.95, direct sales only, Mando paper)

1 ($1.25) 5.00
2-9,12-14,16-25,27,29-40,42-49,51-64: 3-New Defenders app. 5-Guice-c/a begins. 14-18-Morbius story line. 31-36-Infinity Gauntlet x-overs. 31-Silver Surfer app. 33-Thanos-c & cameo. 36-Warlock app. 37-Silver Surfer app. 40-Daredevil x-over. 42-47-Infinity War x-overs. 47-Gamora app. 52,53-Morbius-c/stories. 60,61-Siege of Darkness pt. 7 & 15. 60-Spot varnish-c. 61-New Doctor Strange begins (cameo, 1st app.). 62-Dr. Doom & Morbius app. 3.00
10,11,26,28,41: 10-Re-intro Morbius w/new costume (11/89). 11-Hobgoblin app. 26-Werewolf by Night app. 28-Ghost Rider-s cont'd from G.R. #12; published at same time as Doctor Strange/Ghost Rider Special #1(4/91). 41-Wolverine-c/story 4.00
15-Unauthorized Amy Grant photo-c 5.00
50-($2.95, 52 pgs.)-Holo-grafx foil-c; Hulk, Ghost Rider & Silver Surfer app.; leads into new Secret Defenders series 4.00
65-74, 76-90: 65-Begin $1.95-c; bound-in card sheet. 72-Silver ink-c. 80-82- Ellis-s. 84-DeMatteis story begins. 87-Death of Baron Mordo 3.00
75 ($2.50) 4.00
75 ($3.50)-Foil-c 5.00
Annual 2-4 ('92-'94, 68 pgs.)-2-Defenders app. 3-Polybagged w/card 4.00
Ashcan (1995, 75¢) 3.00
.../Ghost Rider Special 1 (4/91, $1.50)-Same book as D.S.S.S. #28 3.00
...Vs. Dracula 1 (3/94, $1.75, 52 pgs.)-r/Tomb of Dracula #44 & Dr. Strange #14 4.00
NOTE: ***Colan** c/a-19. **Golden** c-28. **Guice** a-5-16, 18, 20-24; c-5-12, 20-24. See 1st series for Annual #1.*

DOCTOR STRANGE: THE OATH
Marvel Comics: Dec, 2006 - No. 5, Apr, 2007 ($2.99, limited series)

1-5-Vaughan-s/Martin-a; Night Nurse app. 3.00

GD VG FN VF VF/NM NM-
2.0 4.0 6.0 8.0 9.0 9.2

TPB (2007, $13.99) r/#1-5; sketch pages and promotional art 14.00

DR. TOM BRENT, YOUNG INTERN
Charlton Publications: Feb, 1963 - No. 5, Oct, 1963

1 3 6 9 16 23 30
2-5 2 4 6 11 16 20

DR. TOMORROW
Acclaim Comics (Valiant): Sept, 1997 - No. 12 ($2.50)

1-12: 1-Mignola-c 3.00

DR. VOLTZ (See Mighty Midget Comics)

DOCTOR VOODOO: AVENGER OF THE SUPERNATURAL
Marvel Comics: Dec, 2009 - No. 5, Apr, 2010 ($2.99, limited series)

1-5-Dr. Doom, Son of Satan & Ghost Rider app.; Palo-a 3.00
Doctor Voodoo: The Origin of Jericho Drumm (1/10, $4.99) r/Strange Tales #169,170 5.00

DR. WEIRD
Big Bang Comics: Oct, 1994 - No. 2, May, 1995 ($2.95, B&W)

1,2: 1-Frank Brunner-c 4.00

DR. WEIRD SPECIAL
Big Bang Comics: Feb, 1994 ($3.95, B&W, 68 pgs.)

1-Origin-r by Starlin; Starlin-c. 4.00

DOCTOR WHO (Also see Marvel Premiere #57-60)
Marvel Comics Group: Oct, 1984 - No. 23, Aug, 1986 ($1.50, direct sales, Baxter paper)

1-British-r 1 3 4 6 8 10
2-15-British-r 5.00
16-23 6.00
Graphic Novel Voyager (1985, $8.95) color reprints of B&W comic pages from Doctor Who Magazine #88-99; Colin Baker afterword 15.00

DOCTOR WHO (Based on the 2005 TV series with David Tennant)
IDW Publishing: Jan, 2008 - No. 6, Jun, 2008 ($3.99)

1-6: 1-Nick Roche-a/Gary Russell-s; two covers 4.00

DOCTOR WHO (Based on the 2005 TV series with David Tennant)
IDW Publishing: Jul, 2009 - No. 16, Oct, 2010 ($3.99)

1-16-Grist-c on all. 3-5,13-16-Art by Matt Smith (not the actor) 4.00
... Annual 2010 (7/10, $7.99) short stories by various; Yates-c; cameo by 11th Doctor 8.00
...: Autopia (6/09, $3.99) Ostrander-s; Yates-a/c; variant photo-c 4.00
...: Black Death White Life (9/09, $3.99) Mandrake-a; Guy Davis- c; variant photo-c 4.00
...: Cold-Blooded War (8/09, $3.99) Salmon-a/c; variant photo-c 4.00
...: Room With a Déjà View (6/09, $3.99) Eric J-a; Mandrake-c; variant photo-c 4.00
...: The Whispering Gallery (2/09, $3.99) Moore & Reppion-s; Templesmith-a/2 covers 4.00
...: Time Machination (5/09, $3.99) Paul Grist-a/c; variant photo-c 4.00

DOCTOR WHO (Based on the 2010 TV series with Matt Smith)
IDW Publishing: Jan, 2011 - No. 12, Apr, 2012 ($3.99)

1-16: 1-Edwards & photo-c; Currie-a. 5-Buckingham-a. 12-Grist-a 4.00
Annual 2011 (8/11, $7.99) short stories by Fialkov, Shedd, Smith, McDaid and others 8.00
... Convention Special (7/11, no cover price, BBC America Shop Exclusive) The Doctor, Amy, and Rory at the San Diego Comic-Con; Matthew Dow Smith-s/Domingues-a 15.00
... 100 Page Spectacular 1 (7/12, $7.99) Short story reprints from various eras 8.00

DOCTOR WHO (Volume 3)(Based on the 2010 TV series with Matt Smith)
IDW Publishing: Sept, 2012 - No. 16, Dec, 2013 ($3.99)

1-16-Regular & photo-c on each: 1,2-Diggle-s/Buckingham-a. 3,4-Bond-a 4.00
... Special 2012 (8/12, $7.99) Short stories by various incl. Wein, Diggle; Buckingham-c 8.00
... Special 2013 (12/13, $7.99) Cornell-s/Broxton-a; The Doctor visits the real world 8.00

DOCTOR WHO: A FAIRYTALE LIFE (Based on the 2010 TV series with Matt Smith)
IDW Publishing: Apr, 2011 - No. 4, Jul, 2011 ($3.99, limited series)

1-4: 1-Sturges-s/Yeates-a; covers by Buckingham & Mebberson. 3-Shearer-a 4.00

DR. WHO & THE DALEKS (See Movie Classics)

DOCTOR WHO CLASSICS
IDW Publishing: Nov, 2005 - Present ($3.99)

1-10: Reprints from Doctor Who Weekly (1979); art by Gibbons, Neary and others 4.00
Series 2 (12/08 - No. 12, 11/09, $3.99) 1-12 4.00
Series 3 (3/10 - No. 6, 8/10, $3.99) 1-6 4.00
Series 4 (2/12 - No. 6, 7/12, $3.99) 1-6: Colin Baker era 4.00
Series 5 (3/13 - Present, $3.99) 1-5: Sylvester McCoy era 4.00
...: The Seventh Doctor (2/11, $3.99) 1-5: 1-Furman-s/Ridgway-a; Sylvester McCoy-era 4.00

DOCTOR WHO: PRISONERS OF TIME
IDW Publishing: Feb, 2013 - No. 12, Nov, 2013 ($3.99, limited series)

Doctor Zero #1 © MAR

Doll Man Quarterly #6 © QUA

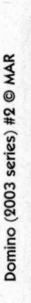

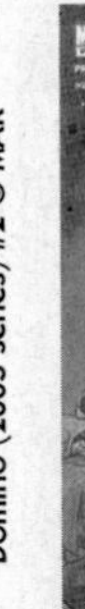
Domino (2003 series) #2 © MAR

	GD 2.0	VG 4.0	FN 6.0	VF 8.0	VF/NM 9.0	NM- 9.2
1-50th Anniversary series with each issue spotlighting one Doctor; Francavilla-c						6.00
1-12-Photo covers						5.00
2-12: Francavilla-c on all. 5-12-Dave Sim variant-c. 8-Langridge-a						4.00

DOCTOR WHO: THE FORGOTTEN (Based on the 2005 TV series with David Tennant)
IDW Publishing: Aug, 2008 - No. 6, Jan, 2009 ($3.99)

	GD 2.0	VG 4.0	FN 6.0	VF 8.0	VF/NM 9.0	NM- 9.2
1-6: 1,2-Pia Guerra-a/Tony Lee-s; two covers						4.00

DR. WONDER
Old Town Publishing: June, 1996 - No. 5 ($2.95, B&W)

	GD 2.0	VG 4.0	FN 6.0	VF 8.0	VF/NM 9.0	NM- 9.2
1-5: 1-Intro & origin of Dr. Wonder; Dick Ayers-c/a; Irwin Hasen-a						3.00

DOCTOR ZERO
Marvel Comics (Epic Comics): Apr, 1988 - No. 8, Aug, 1989 ($1.25/$1.50)

	GD 2.0	VG 4.0	FN 6.0	VF 8.0	VF/NM 9.0	NM- 9.2
1-8: 1-Sienkiewicz-c. 6,7-Spiegle-a						3.00

NOTE: ***Sienkiewicz** a-3i, 4i; c-1. **Spiegle** a-6, 7.*

DO-DO (Funny Animal Circus Stories)
Nation-Wide Publishers: 1950 - No. 7, 1951 (5¢, 5x7-1/4" Miniature)

	GD 2.0	VG 4.0	FN 6.0	VF 8.0	VF/NM 9.0	NM- 9.2
1 (52 pgs.)	28	56	84	165	270	375
2-7	16	32	48	94	147	200

DODO & THE FROG, THE (Formerly Funny Stuff; also see It's Game Time #2)
National Periodical Publications: No. 80, 9-10/54 - No. 88, 1-2/56; No. 89, 8-9/56; No. 90, 10-11/56; No. 91, 9/57; No. 92, 11/57 (See Comic Cavalcade and Captain Carrot)

	GD 2.0	VG 4.0	FN 6.0	VF 8.0	VF/NM 9.0	NM- 9.2
80-1st app. Doodles Duck by Sheldon Mayer	20	40	60	114	182	250
81-91: Doodles Duck by Mayer in #81,83-90	14	28	42	76	108	140
92-(Scarce)-Doodles Duck by S. Mayer	18	36	54	105	165	225

DOGFACE DOOLEY
Magazine Enterprises: 1951 - No. 5, 1953

	GD 2.0	VG 4.0	FN 6.0	VF 8.0	VF/NM 9.0	NM- 9.2
1(A-1 40)	8	16	24	40	50	60
2(A-1 43), 3(A-1 49), 4(A-1 53), 5(A-1 64)	6	12	18	28	34	40
I.W. Reprint #1('64), Super Reprint #17	2	4	6	9	13	16

DOG MOON
DC Comics (Vertigo): 1996 ($6.95, one-shot)

	GD 2.0	VG 4.0	FN 6.0	VF 8.0	VF/NM 9.0	NM- 9.2
1-Robert Hunter-scripts; Tim Truman-c/a.						7.00

DOG OF FLANDERS, A
Dell Publishing Co.: No. 1088, Mar, 1960

	GD 2.0	VG 4.0	FN 6.0	VF 8.0	VF/NM 9.0	NM- 9.2
Four Color 1088-Movie, photo-c	4	8	12	28	47	65

DOGPATCH (See Al Capp's... & Mammy Yokum)

DOGS OF WAR (Also see Warriors of Plasm)
Defiant: Apr, 1994 - No. 5, Aug, 1994 ($2.50)

	GD 2.0	VG 4.0	FN 6.0	VF 8.0	VF/NM 9.0	NM- 9.2
1-5						3.00

DOGS-O-WAR
Crusade Comics: June, 1996 - No. 3, Jan, 1997 ($2.95, B&W, limited series)

	GD 2.0	VG 4.0	FN 6.0	VF 8.0	VF/NM 9.0	NM- 9.2
1-3: 1,2-Photo-c						3.00

DOLLFACE & HER GANG (Betty Betz'...)
Dell Publishing Co.: No. 309, Jan, 1951

	GD 2.0	VG 4.0	FN 6.0	VF 8.0	VF/NM 9.0	NM- 9.2
Four Color 309	5	10	15	33	57	80

DOLLHOUSE
Dark Horse Comics: Mar, 2011; Jul, 2011 - No. 5, Nov, 2011 ($3.50, limited series)

	GD 2.0	VG 4.0	FN 6.0	VF 8.0	VF/NM 9.0	NM- 9.2
1-5-Richards-a; two covers on each						4.00
...: Epitaphs (3/11, $3.50) reprints story from DVD collection; covers by Noto & Morris						4.00

DOLLMAN (Movie)
Eternity Comics: Sept, 1991 - No. 4, Dec, 1991 ($2.50, limited series)

	GD 2.0	VG 4.0	FN 6.0	VF 8.0	VF/NM 9.0	NM- 9.2
1-4: Adaptation of film						3.00

DOLL MAN QUARTERLY, THE (Doll Man #17 on; also see Feature Comics #27 & Freedom Fighters)
Quality Comics: Fall, 1941 - No. 7, Fall, '43; No. 8, Spr, '46 - No. 47, Oct, 1953

	GD 2.0	VG 4.0	FN 6.0	VF 8.0	VF/NM 9.0	NM- 9.2
1-Dollman (by Cassone), Justin Wright begin	331	662	993	2317	4059	5800
2-The Dragon begins; Crandall-a(5)	145	290	435	921	1586	2250
3,4	89	178	267	565	970	1375
5-Crandall-a	86	172	258	546	936	1325
6,7(1943)	54	108	162	343	574	825
8(1946)-1st app. Torchy by Bill Ward	165	330	495	1048	1799	2550
9(Summer 1946)	53	106	159	334	567	800
10-20	41	82	123	256	428	600
21-30: 28-Vs. The Flame	37	74	111	222	361	500
31-36,38,40: 31-(12/50)-Intro Elmo, the wonder dog (Dollman's faithful dog). 32-34-Jeb Rivers app.; 34 by Crandall(p)	36	72	108	216	351	485
37-Origin & 1st app. Dollgirl; Dollgirl bondage-c	50	100	150	315	533	750
39- "Narcotics...the Death Drug" c-/story	39	78	117	240	395	550
41-47	25	50	75	150	245	340
Super Reprint #11('64, r/#20),15(r/#23),17(r/#28): 15,17-Torchy app.; Andru/Esposito-c	3	6	9	20	30	40

NOTE: ***Ward** Torchy in 8, 9, 11, 12, 14-24, 27; by Fox-#26, 30, 35-47. **Crandall** a-2, 5, 10, 13 & Super #11, 17, 18. **Crandall/Cuidera** c-40-42. **Guardineer** a-3. Bondage c-27, 37, 38, 39.*

DOLLY
Ziff-Davis Publ. Co.: No. 10, July-Aug, 1951 (Funny animal)

	GD 2.0	VG 4.0	FN 6.0	VF 8.0	VF/NM 9.0	NM- 9.2
10-Painted-c	9	18	27	52	69	85

DOLLY DILL
Marvel Comics/Newsstand Publ.: 1945

	GD 2.0	VG 4.0	FN 6.0	VF 8.0	VF/NM 9.0	NM- 9.2
1	19	38	57	112	179	245

DOLLZ, THE
Image Comics: Apr, 2001 - No. 2, June, 2001 ($2.95)

	GD 2.0	VG 4.0	FN 6.0	VF 8.0	VF/NM 9.0	NM- 9.2
1,2: 1-Four covers; Sniegoski & Green-s/Green-a						3.00

DOMINATION FACTOR
Marvel Comics: Nov, 1999 - 4.8, Feb, 2000 ($2.50, interconnected mini- series)

	GD 2.0	VG 4.0	FN 6.0	VF 8.0	VF/NM 9.0	NM- 9.2
1.1, 2.3, 3.5, 4.7-Fantastic Four; Jurgens-s/a						3.00
1.2, 2.4, 3.6, 4.8-Avengers; Ordway-s/a						3.00

DOMINIC FORTUNE
Marvel Comics (MAX): Oct, 2009 - No. 4, Jan, 2010 ($3.99, limited series)

	GD 2.0	VG 4.0	FN 6.0	VF 8.0	VF/NM 9.0	NM- 9.2
1-4-Howard Chaykin-s/a/c						4.00

DOMINION
Image Comics: Jan, 2003 - No. 2 ($2.95)

	GD 2.0	VG 4.0	FN 6.0	VF 8.0	VF/NM 9.0	NM- 9.2
1,2-Keith Giffen-s/a						3.00

DOMINION (Manga)
Eclipse Comics: Dec, 1990 - No. 6., July, 1990 ($2.00, B&W, limited series)

	GD 2.0	VG 4.0	FN 6.0	VF 8.0	VF/NM 9.0	NM- 9.2
1-6						3.00

DOMINION: CONFLICT 1 (Manga)
Dark Horse Comics: Mar, 1996 - No. 6, Aug, 1996 ($2.95, B&W, limited series)

	GD 2.0	VG 4.0	FN 6.0	VF 8.0	VF/NM 9.0	NM- 9.2
1-6: Shirow-c/a/scripts						3.00

DOMINIQUE LAVEAU: VOODOO CHILD
DC Comics (Vertigo): May, 2012 - No. 7, Nov, 2012 ($2.99, limited series)

	GD 2.0	VG 4.0	FN 6.0	VF 8.0	VF/NM 9.0	NM- 9.2
1-7-Selwyn Seyfu Hinds-s/Denys Cowan-a						3.00

DOMINO (See X-Force)
Marvel Comics: Jan, 1997 - No. 3, Mar, 1997 ($1.95, limited series)

	GD 2.0	VG 4.0	FN 6.0	VF 8.0	VF/NM 9.0	NM- 9.2
1-3: 2-Deathstrike-c/app.						3.00

DOMINO (See X-Force)
Marvel Comics: June, 2003 - No. 4, Aug, 2003 ($2.50, limited series)

	GD 2.0	VG 4.0	FN 6.0	VF 8.0	VF/NM 9.0	NM- 9.2
1-4-Stelfreeze-c/a; Pruett-s.						3.00

DOMINO CHANCE
Chance Enterprises: May-June, 1982 - No. 9, May, 1985 (B&W)

	GD 2.0	VG 4.0	FN 6.0	VF 8.0	VF/NM 9.0	NM- 9.2
1-9: 7-1st app. Gizmo, 2 pgs. 8-1st full Gizmo story. 1-Reprint, May, 1985						4.00

DONALD AND MICKEY IN DISNEYLAND (See Dell Giants)

DONALD AND SCROOGE
Disney Comics: 1992 ($8.95, squarebound, 100 pgs.)

	GD 2.0	VG 4.0	FN 6.0	VF 8.0	VF/NM 9.0	NM- 9.2
nn-Don Rosa reprint special; r/U.S., D.D. Advs.	1	3	4	6	8	10
1-3 (1992, $1.50)-r/D.D. Advs. (Disney) #1,22,24 & U.S. #261-263,269						3.00

DONALD AND THE WHEEL (Disney)
Dell Publishing Co.: No. 1190, Nov, 1961

	GD 2.0	VG 4.0	FN 6.0	VF 8.0	VF/NM 9.0	NM- 9.2
Four Color 1190-Movie, Barks-c	7	14	21	46	86	125

DONALD DUCK (See Adventures of Mickey Mouse, Cheerios, Donald & Mickey, Ducktales, Dynabrite Comics, Gladstone Comic Album, Mickey & Donald, Mickey Mouse Mag., Story Hour Series, Uncle Scrooge, Walt Disney's Comics & Stories, W. D.'s Donald Duck, Wheaties & Whitman Comic Books, Wise Little Hen, The)

DONALD DUCK
Whitman Publishing Co./Grosset & Dunlap/K.K.: 1935, 1936 (All pages on heavy linen-like finish cover stock in color;1st book ever devoted to Donald Duck; see Advs. of Mickey Mouse for 1st app.) (9-1/2x13")

	GD 2.0	VG 4.0	FN 6.0	VF 8.0	VF/NM 9.0	NM- 9.2
978(1935)-16 pgs.; Illustrated text story book	206	412	618	1318	2259	3200
nn(1936)-36 pgs.plus hard cover & dust jacket. Story completely rewritten with B&W illos added. Mickey appears and his nephews are named Morty & Monty						
Book only	194	388	582	1242	2121	3000
Dust jacket only....	39	78	117	240	395	550

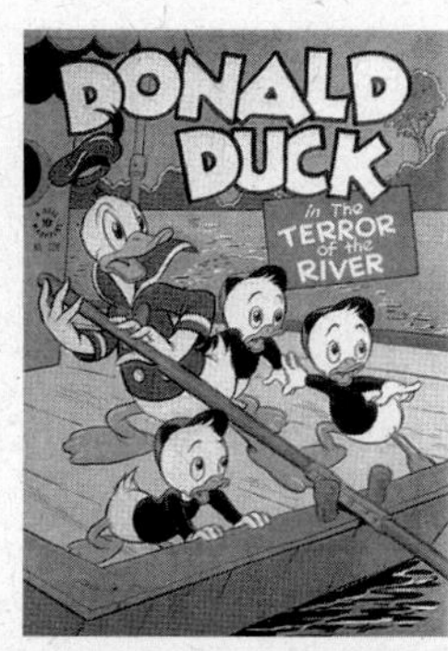

Donald Duck FC #108 © DIS

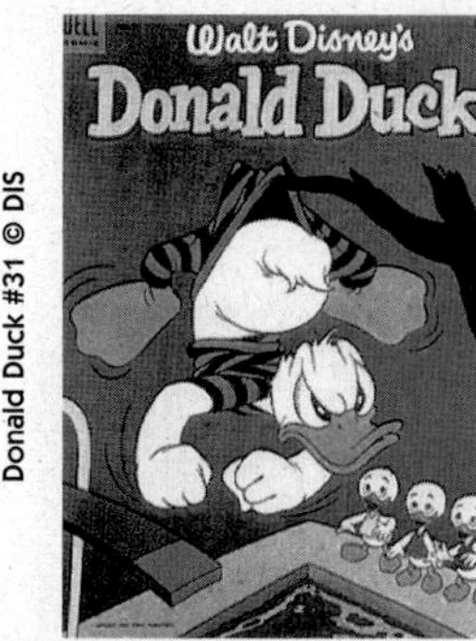

Donald Duck #31 © DIS

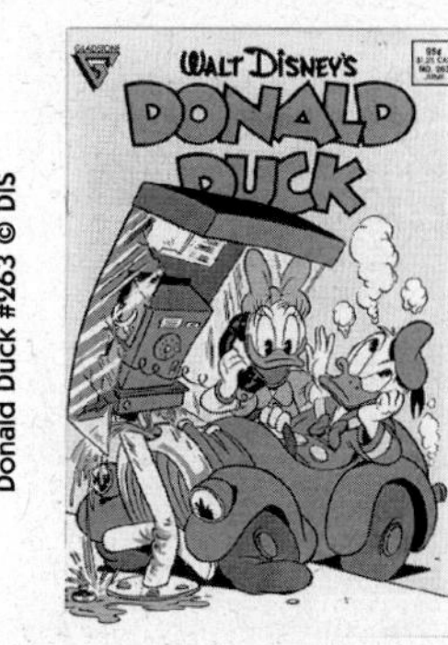

Donald Duck #263 © DIS

	GD	VG	FN	VF	VF/NM	NM-
	2.0	4.0	6.0	8.0	9.0	9.2

DONALD DUCK (Walt Disney's) (10¢)
Whitman/K.K. Publications: 1938 (8-1/2x11-1/2", B&W, cardboard-c)
(Has D. Duck with bubble pipe on-c)

nn-The first Donald Duck & Walt Disney comic book; 1936 & 1937 Sunday strip-r(in B&W); same format as the Feature Books; 1st strips with Huey, Dewey & Louie from 10/17/37 — 284 568 852 1818 3109 4400

DONALD DUCK (Walt Disney's...#262 on; see 4-Color listings for titles & Four Color No. 1109 for origin story)
Dell Publ. Co./Gold Key #85-216/Whitman #217-245/Gladstone #246 on: 1940 - No. 84, Sept-Nov, 1962; No. 85, Dec, 1962 - No. 245, July, 1984; No. 246, Oct, 1986 - No. 279, May, 1990; No. 280, Sept, 1993 - No. 307, Mar,1998

Four Color 4(1940)-Daily 1939 strip-r by Al Taliaferro — 1800 3600 5400 13,500 22,750 32,000
Large Feature Comic 16(1/41?)-1940 Sunday strips-r in B&W — 757 1514 2271 5526 9763 14,000
Large Feature Comic 20('41)-Comic Paint Book, r-single panels from Large Feature #16 at top of each pg. to color; daily strip-r across bottom of each pg. (Rare) — 811 1622 2433 5920 10,460 15,000
Four Color 9('42)- "Finds Pirate Gold"; 64 pgs. by Carl Barks & Jack Hannah (pgs. 1,2,5,12-40 are by Barks, his 1st Donald Duck comic book art work; © 8/17/42) — 1000 2000 3000 7600 13,800 20,000
Four Color 29(9/43)- "Mummy's Ring" by Barks; reprinted in Uncle Scrooge & Donald Duck #1('65), W. D. Comics Digest #44('73) & Donald Duck Advs. #14 — 784 1568 2352 5723 10,112 14,500
Four Color 62(1/45)- "Frozen Gold"; 52 pgs. by Barks, reprinted in The Best of W.D. Comics & Donald Duck Advs. #4 — 207 414 621 1708 3854 6000
Four Color 108(1946)- "Terror of the River"; 52 pgs. by Carl Barks; reprinted in Gladstone Comic Album #2 — 145 290 435 1196 2698 4200
Four Color 147(5/47)-in "Volcano Valley" by Barks — 100 200 300 800 1800 2800
Four Color 159(8/47)-in "The Ghost of the Grotto";52 pgs. by Carl Barks; reprinted in Best of Uncle Scrooge & Donald Duck #1 ('66) & The Best of W.D. Comics & D.D. Advs. #9; two Barks stories — 86 172 258 688 1544 2400
Four Color 178(12/47)-1st app. Uncle Scrooge by Carl Barks; reprinted in Gold Key Christmas Parade #3 & The Best of Walt Disney Comics — 118 236 354 944 2122 3300
Four Color 189(6/48)-by Carl Barks; reprinted in Best of Donald Duck & Uncle Scrooge #1('64) & D.D. Advs. #19 — 73 146 219 584 1317 2050
Four Color 199(10/48)-by Carl Barks; mentioned in Love and Death; r/in Gladstone Comic Album #5 — 79 158 237 632 1416 2200
Four Color 203(12/48)-by Barks; reprinted as Gold Key Christmas Parade #4 — 55 110 165 440 995 1550
Four Color 223(4/49)-by Barks; reprinted as Best of Donald Duck #1 & Donald Duck Advs. #3 — 71 142 213 568 1284 2000
Four Color 238(8/49)-in "Voodoo Hoodoo" by Barks — 54 108 162 432 966 1500
Four Color 256(12/49)-by Barks; reprinted in Best of Donald Duck & Uncle Scrooge #2('67), Gladstone Comic Album #16 & W.D. Comics Digest 44('73) — 46 92 138 359 805 1250
Four Color 263(2/50)-Two Barks stories; r-in D.D. #278 — 46 92 138 340 770 1200
Four Color 275(5/50), 282(7/50), 291(9/50), 300(11/50)-All by Carl Barks; 275, 282 reprinted in W.D. Comics Digest #44('73). #275 r/in Gladstone Comic Album #10. #291 r/in D. Duck Advs. #16 — 45 90 135 333 754 1175
Four Color 308(1/51), 318(3/51)-by Barks; #318-reprinted in W.D. Comics Digest #34 & D.D. Advs. #2,19 — 42 86 126 311 706 1100
Four Color 328(5/51)-by Carl Barks — 41 82 123 303 689 1075
Four Color 339(7-8/51), 379-2nd Uncle Scrooge-c; art not by Barks. — 13 26 39 89 195 300
Four Color 348(9-10/51), 356,394-Barks-c only — 20 40 60 141 313 485
Four Color 367(1-2/52)-by Barks; reprinted as Gold Key Christmas Parade #2 & #8 — 33 66 99 238 532 825
Four Color 408(7-8/52), 422(9-10/52)-All by Carl Barks. #408-r-in Best of Donald Duck & Uncle Scrooge #1('64) & Gladstone Comic Album #13 — 33 66 99 238 532 825
26(11-12/52)-In "Trick or Treat" (Barks-a, 36pgs.) 1st story r-in Walt Disney Digest #16 & Gladstone C.A. #23 — 32 64 96 230 515 800
27-30-Barks-c only — 12 24 36 79 170 260
31-44,47-50 — 7 14 21 46 86 125
45-Barks-a (6 pgs.) — 13 26 39 89 195 300
46- "Secret of Hondorica" by Barks, 24 pgs.; reprinted in Donald Duck #98 & 154 — 17 34 51 119 265 410
51-Barks-a,1/2 pg. — 7 14 21 46 86 125
52- "Lost Peg-Leg Mine" by Barks, 10 pgs. — 13 26 39 89 195 300
53,55-59 — 6 12 18 38 69 100
54- "Forbidden Valley" by Barks, 26 pgs. (10¢ & 15¢ versions exist) — 14 28 42 98 217 335
60- "Donald Duck & the Titanic Ants" by Barks, 20 pgs. plus 6 more pgs. — 14 28 42 98 217 335
61-67,69,70 — 5 10 15 34 60 85
68-Barks-a, 5 pgs. — 9 18 27 62 126 190
71-Barks-r, 1/2 pg. — 5 10 15 34 60 85
72-78,80,82-97,99,100: 96-Donald Duck Album — 5 10 15 33 57 80
79,81-Barks-a, 1pg. — 5 10 15 34 60 85
98-Reprints #46 (Barks) — 5 10 15 34 60 85
101,103-111,113-135: 120-Last 12¢ issue. 134-Barks-r/#52 & WDC&S 194. 135-Barks-r/WDC&S 198, 19 pgs. — 4 8 12 22 35 48
102-Super Goof. 112-1st Moby Duck — 4 8 12 23 37 50
136-153,155,156,158: 149-20¢-c begin — 3 6 9 14 20 26
154-Barks-r(#46) — 3 6 9 16 24 32
157,159,160,164: 157-Barks-r(#45); 25¢-c begin. 159-Reprints/WDC&S #192 (10 pgs.). 160-Barks-r(#26). 164-Barks-r(#79) — 3 6 9 14 20 26
161-163,165-173,175-187,189-191: 175-30¢-c begin. 187-Barks r/#68. — 2 4 6 13 18 22
174,188: 174-r/4-Color #394. — 3 6 9 14 19 24
192-Barks-r(40 pgs.) from Donald Duck #60 & WDC&S #226,234 (52 pgs.) — 3 6 9 15 22 28
193-200,202-207,209-211,213-216 — 2 4 6 9 13 16
201,208,212: 201-Barks-r/Christmas Parade #26, 16pgs. 208-Barks-r/#60 (6 pgs.). 212-Barks-r/WDC&S #130 — 2 4 6 9 13 16
217-219: 217 has 216 on-c. 219-Barks-r/WDC&S #106,107, 10 pgs. ea. — 2 4 6 10 14 18
220,225-228: 228-Barks-r/F.C. #275 — 2 4 6 13 18 22
221,223,224: Scarce; only sold in pre-packs. 221(8/80), 223(11/80), 224(12/80) — 5 10 15 34 60 85
222-(9-10/80)-(Very low distribution) — 15 30 45 103 227 350
229-240: 229-Barks-r/F.C. #282. 230-Barks-r/ #52 & WDC&S #194. 236(2/82), 237(2-3/82), 238(3/82), 239(4/82), 240(5/82) — 2 4 6 9 13 16
241-245: 241(4/83), 242(5/83), 243(3/84), 244(4/84), 245(7/84)(low print) — 3 6 9 14 19 24
246-(1st Gladstone issue)-Barks-r/FC #422 — 3 6 9 15 21 26
247-249,251: 248,249-Barks-r/DD #54 & 26. 251-Barks-r/1945 Firestone — 2 4 6 9 13 16
250-($1.50, 68 pgs.)-Barks-r/4-Color #9 — 2 4 6 10 14 18
252-277,280: 254-Barks-r/FC #328. 256-Barks-r/FC #147. 257-($1.50, 52 pgs.)-Barks-r/ Vacation Parade #1. 261-Barks-r/FC #300. 275-Kelly-r/FC #92. 280 (#1, 2nd Series) — 1 2 3 5 6 8
278,279,286: 278,279 ($1.95, 68 pgs.): 278-Rosa-a; Barks-r/FC #263. 279-Rosa-c; Barks-r/MOC #4. 286-Rosa-a — 1 2 3 5 7 9
281,282,284 — 1 2 3 4 5 7
283-Don Rosa-a, part-c & scripts — 1 2 3 5 6 8
285,287-307 — 5.00
286 ($2.95, 68 pgs.)-Happy Birthday, Donald — 6.00
Mini-Comic #1(1976)-(3-1/4x6-1/2"); r/D.D. #150 — 2 4 6 8 11 14

NOTE: ***Carl Barks** wrote all issues he illustrated, but #117, 126, 138 contain his script only. Issues 4-Color #189, 199, 203, 223, 238, 256, 263, 275, 282, 308, 348, 356, 367, 394, 408, 422, 26-30, 35, 44, 46, 52, 55, 57, 60, 65, 70-73, 77-80, 83, 101, 103, 105, 106, 111, 126, 246r, 266r, 268r, 271r, 275r, 278r(F.C. 263) all have **Barks** covers. **Barks** r-263-267, 269-278-282, 284, 285. #96 titled "Comic Album", #99-"Christmas Album". New art issues (not reprints)-106-46, 148-63, 167, 169, 170, 172, 173, 175, 178, 179, 196, 209, 223, 225, 236. **Taliaferro** daily newspaper strips #258-260, 264, 284, 285; Sunday strips #247, 280-283.*

DONALD DUCK (Numbering continues from Donald Duck and Friends #362)
BOOM! Studios (Kaboom!): No. 363, Feb, 2011 - No. 367, Jun, 2011 ($3.99)

363-367: 363-Barks reprints incl. "Mystery of the Loch". 364-Rosa-c — 4.00

DONALD DUCK ADVENTURES (See Walt Disney's Donald Duck Adventures)

DONALD DUCK ALBUM (See Comic Album No. 1,3 & Duck Album)
Dell Publishing Co./Gold Key: 5-7/59 - F.C. No. 1239, 10-12/61; 1962; 8/63 - No. 2, Oct, 1963

Four Color 995 (#1) — 6 12 18 37 66 95
Four Color 1099,1140,1239-Barks-c — 6 12 18 38 69 100
Four Color 1182, 01204-207 (1962-Dell) — 5 10 15 30 50 70
1(8/63-Gold Key)-Barks-c — 5 10 15 34 60 85
2(10/63) — 4 8 12 28 47 65

DONALD DUCK AND FRIENDS (Numbering continues from Walt Disney's ...)
BOOM! Studios: No. 347, Oct, 2009 - No. 362, Jan, 2011 ($2.99)

347-362: Two covers on most. Retitled "Donald Duck" with #363 — 3.00

DONALD DUCK AND THE BOYS (Also see Story Hour Series)
Whitman Publishing Co.: 1948 (5-1/4x5-1/2", 100pgs., hard-c; art & text)

845-(49) new illos by Barks based on his Donald Duck 10-pager in WDC&S #74,

Don Fortune Magazine #1 © Don Fortune Pub.

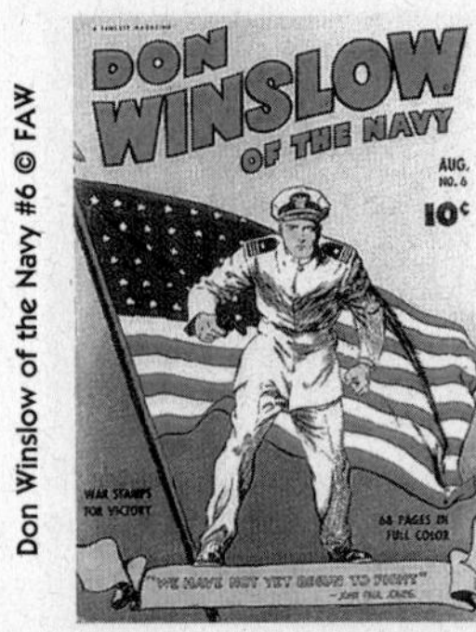

Don Winslow of the Navy #6 © FAW

Doom Patrol #109 © DC

	GD	VG	FN	VF	VF/NM	NM-
	2.0	4.0	6.0	8.0	9.0	9.2

Expanded text not written by Barks; Cover not by Barks
50 100 150 350 600 850
(Prices vary widely on this book)

DONALD DUCK AND THE CHRISTMAS CAROL
Whitman Publishing Co.: 1960 (A Little Golden Book, 6-3/ "x7-5/8", 28 pgs.)
nn-Story book pencilled by Carl Barks with the intended title "Uncle Scrooge's Christmas Carol." Finished art adapted by Norman McGary. (Rare)-Reprinted in Uncle Scrooge in Color. 20 40 60 100 185 270

DONALD DUCK BEACH PARTY (Also see Dell Giants)
Gold Key: Sept, 1965 (12¢)
1(#10158-509)-Barks-r/WDC&S #45; painted-c 6 12 18 37 66 95

DONALD DUCK BOOK (See Story Hour Series)

DONALD DUCK COMICS DIGEST
Gladstone Publishing: Nov, 1986 - No. 5, July, 1987 ($1.25/$1.50, 96 pgs.)
1,3: 1-Barks-c/a-r 1 3 4 6 8 10
2,4,5: 4,5-$1.50-c 6.00

DONALD DUCK FUN BOOK (See Dell Giants)

DONALD DUCK IN DISNEYLAND (See Dell Giants)

DONALD DUCK MARCH OF COMICS (See March of Comics #4,20,41,56,69,263)

DONALD DUCK MERRY CHRISTMAS (See Dell Giant No. 53)

DONALD DUCK PICNIC PARTY (See Picnic Party listed under Dell Giants)

DONALD DUCK TELLS ABOUT KITES (See Kite Fun Book)

DONALD DUCK, THIS IS YOUR LIFE (Disney, TV)
Dell Publishing Co.: No. 1109, Aug-Oct, 1960
Four Color 1109-Gyro flashback to WDC&S #141; origin Donald Duck (1st told)
12 24 36 79 170 260

DONALD DUCK XMAS ALBUM (See regular Donald Duck No. 99)

DONALD IN MATHMAGIC LAND (Disney)
Dell Publishing Co.: No. 1051, Oct-Dec, 1959 - No. 1198, May-July, 1961
Four Color 1051 (#1)-Movie 8 16 24 54 102 150
Four Color 1198-Reprint of above 6 12 18 37 66 95

DONATELLO, TEENAGE MUTANT NINJA TURTLE
Mirage Studios: Aug, 1986 ($1.50, B&W, one-shot, 44 pgs.)
1 2 4 6 9 12 15

DONDI
Dell Publishing Co.: No. 1176, Mar-May, 1961 - No. 1276, Dec, 1961
Four Color 1176 (#1)-Movie; origin, photo-c 5 10 15 33 57 80
Four Color 1276 4 8 12 23 37 50

DON FORTUNE MAGAZINE
Don Fortune Publishing Co.: Aug, 1946 - No. 6, Feb, 1947
1-Delecta of the Planets by C.C. Beck in all 28 56 84 165 270 375
2 15 30 45 85 130 175
3-6: 3-Bondage-c 14 28 42 76 108 140

DONG XOAI, VIETNAM 1965
DC Comics: 2010 ($19.95, B&W graphic novel)
SC-Joe Kubert-s/a/c; includes report of actual events that inspired the story 20.00

DONKEY KONG (See Blip #1)

DONNA MATRIX
Reactor, Inc.: Aug, 1993 ($2.95, 52 pgs.)
1-Computer generated-c/a by Mike Saenz; 3-D effects 4.00

DON NEWCOMBE
Fawcett Publications: 1950 (Baseball)
nn-Photo-c 47 94 141 296 498 700

DON ROSA'S COMICS AND STORIES
Fantagraphics Books (CX Comics): 1983 ($2.95)
1,2: 1-(68 pgs.) Reprints Rosa's The Pertwillaby Papers episodes #128-133. 2-(60 pgs.) Reprints episodes #134-138 2 4 6 11 16 20

DON SIMPSON'S BIZARRE HEROES (Also see Megaton Man)
Fiasco Comics: May, 1990 - No. 17, Sept, 1996 ($2.50/$2.95, B&W)
1-10,0,11-17: 0-Begin $2.95-c; r/Bizarre Heroes #1. 17-(9/96)-Indicia also reads Megaton Man #0; intro Megaton Man and the Fiascoverse to new readers 3.00

DON'T GIVE UP THE SHIP
Dell Publishing Co.: No. 1049, Aug, 1959

	GD	VG	FN	VF	VF/NM	NM-
	2.0	4.0	6.0	8.0	9.0	9.2

Four Color 1049-Movie, Jerry Lewis photo-c 8 16 24 55 105 155

DON WINSLOW OF THE NAVY
Merwil Publishing Co.: Apr, 1937 - No. 2, May, 1937 (96 pgs.)(A pulp/comic book cross; stapled spine)
V1#1-Has 16 pgs. comics in color. Captain Colorful & Jupiter Jones by Sheldon Mayer; complete Don Winslow novel 653 1306 1959 4900 - -
2-Sheldon Mayer-a 177 354 531 1325 - -

DON WINSLOW OF THE NAVY (See Crackajack Funnies, Famous Feature Stories, Popular Comics & Super Book #5,6)
Dell Publishing Co.: No. 2, Nov, 1939 - No. 22, 1941
Four Color 2 (#1)-Rare 210 420 630 1334 2292 3250
Four Color 22 50 100 150 315 533 750

DON WINSLOW OF THE NAVY (See TV Teens; Movie, Radio, TV) (Fightin' Navy No. 74 on)
Fawcett Publications/Charlton No. 70 on: 2/43 - #64, 12/48; #65, 1/51 - #69, 9/51; #70, 3/55 - #73, 9/55
1-(68 pgs.)-Captain Marvel on cover 116 232 348 742 1271 1800
2 43 86 129 271 461 650
3 34 68 102 204 332 460
4-6: 6-Flag-c 27 54 81 158 259 360
7-10: 8-Last 68 pg. issue? 20 40 60 117 189 260
11-20 16 32 48 94 147 200
21-40 15 30 45 85 130 175
41-43,45-64: 51,60-Singapore Sal (villain) app. 64-(12/48)
14 28 42 82 121 160
44-Classic spider-c 34 68 102 199 325 450
65(1/51)-Flying Saucer attack; photo-c 21 42 63 126 206 285
66 - 69(9/51): All photo-c. 66-sci-fi story 14 28 42 82 121 160
70(3/55)-73: 70-73 r-/#26,58 & 59 9 18 27 52 69 85

DOOM
Marvel Comics: Oct, 2000 - No. 3, Dec, 2000 ($2.99, limited series)
1-3-Dr. Doom; Dixon-s/Manco-a 3.00

DOOM FORCE SPECIAL
DC Comics: July, 1992 ($2.95, 68 pgs., one-shot, mature) (X-Force parody)
1-Morrison scripts; Simonson, Steacy, & others-a; Giffen/Mignola-c 4.00

DOOM PATROL, THE (Formerly My Greatest Adventure No. 1-85; see Brave and the Bold, DC Special Blue Ribbon Digest 19, Official... Index & Showcase No. 94-96)
National Periodical Publ.: No. 86, 3/64 - No. 121, 9-10/68; No. 122, 2/73 - No. 124, 6-7/73
86-1 pg. origin (#86-121 are 12¢ issues) 10 20 30 68 144 220
87-98: 88-Origin The Chief. 91-Intro. Mento 8 16 24 51 96 140
99-Intro. Beast Boy (later becomes the Changeling in New Teen Titans)
9 18 27 61 123 185
100-Origin Beast Boy; Robot-Maniac series begins (12/65)
9 18 27 59 117 175
101-110: 102-Challengers of the Unknown app. 104-Wedding issue. 105-Robot-Maniac series ends. 106-Negative Man begins (origin) 6 12 18 37 66 95
111-120 5 10 15 31 53 75
121-Death of Doom Patrol; Orlando-c. 10 20 30 64 132 200
122-124: All reprints 2 4 6 8 11 14

DOOM PATROL
DC Comics (Vertigo imprint #64 on): Oct, 1987 - No, 87, Feb, 1995 (75¢-$1.95, new format)
1-Wraparound-c; Lightle-a 6.00
2-18: 3-1st app. Lodestone. 4-1st app. Karma. 8,15,16-Art Adams-c(i). 18-Invasion tie-in 4.00
19-(2/89)-Grant Morrison scripts begin, ends #63; 1st app Crazy Jane; $1.50-c & new format begins. 1 2 3 5 6 8
20-30: 29-Superman app. 30-Night Breed fold-out 5.00
31-34,37-41,45-49,51-56,58-60: 39-World Without End preview 3.00
35-1st brief app. of Flex Mentallo 5.00
36-1st full app. of Flex Mentallo 6.00
42-44-Origin of Flex Mentallo 4.00
50,57 ($2.50, 52 pgs.) 4.00
61-87: 61,70-Photo-c. 73-Death cameo (2 panels) 3.00
...And Suicide Squad 1 (3/88, $1.50, 52 pgs.)-Wraparound-c 4.00
Annual 1 (1988, $1.50, 52 pgs.) 4.00
Annual 2 (1994, $3.95, 68 pgs.)-Children's Crusade tie-in. 4.00
...: Crawling From the Wreckage TPB (2004, $19.95) r/#19-25; Morrison-s 20.00
...: Down Paradise Way TPB (2005, $19.99) r/#35-41; Morrison-s 20.00
...: Magic Bus TPB (2007, $19.99) r/#51-57; Morrison-s; new Bolland-c 20.00
...: Musclebound TPB (2006, $19.99) r/#42-50; Morrison-s; new Bolland-c 20.00
...: Planet Love TPB (2008, $19.99) r/#58-63 & Doom Force Special #1; Morrison-s 20.00
...: The Painting That Ate Paris TPB (2004, $19.95) r/#26-34; Morrison-s 20.00

Doom Patrol (2009 series) #12 © DC

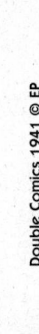

Doom 2099 #16 © MAR

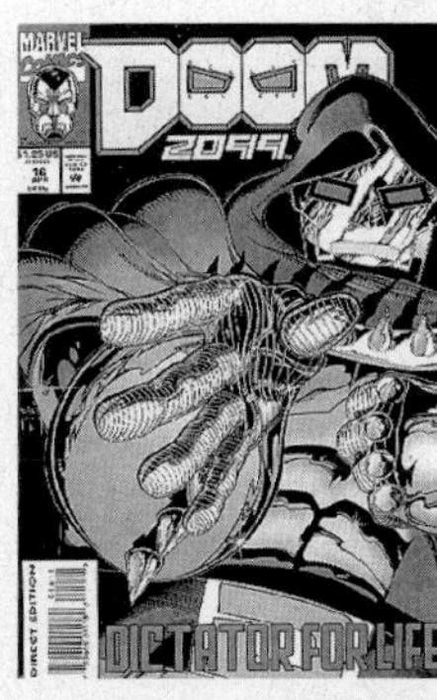

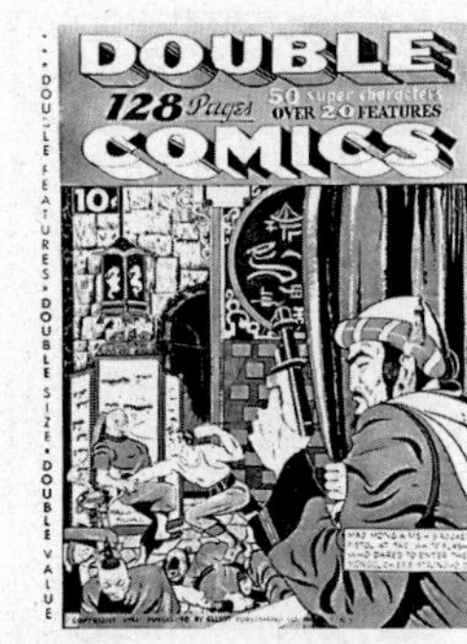

Double Comics 1941 © EP

GD VG FN VF VF/NM NM-
2.0 4.0 6.0 8.0 9.0 9.2

NOTE: *Bisley painted c-26-48, 55-58. Bolland c-64, 75. Dringenberg a-42(p). Steacy a-53.*

DOOM PATROL
DC Comics: Dec, 2001 - No. 22, Sept, 2003 ($2.50)

1-Intro. new team with Robotman; Tan Eng Huat-c/a; John Arcudi-s 4.00
2-22: 4,5-Metamorpho & Elongated Man app. 13,14-Fisher-a. 20-Geary-a 3.00

DOOM PATROL (see JLA #94-99)
DC Comics: Aug, 2004 - No. 18, Jan, 2006 ($2.50)

1-18-John Byrne-s/a. 1-Green Lantern, Batman app. 3.00

DOOM PATROL
DC Comics: Oct, 2009 - No. 22, Jul, 2011 ($3.99/$2.99)

1-7: 1-Giffen-s/Clark-a; back-up Metal Men feature w/Maguire-a. 1-Two covers. 4-5-Blackest Night. 6-Negative Man origin re-told 4.00
8-22-($2.99) 11,12-Ambush Bug app. 16-Giffen-a. 21-Robotman origin retold 3.00
...: Brotherhood TPB (2011, $17.99) r/#7-13 18.00
...: We Who Are About to Die TPB (2010, $14.99) r/#1-6; cover gallery; design art 15.00

DOOM PATROL (See Tangent Comics/ Doom Patrol)

DOOMSDAY
DC Comics: 1995 ($3.95, one-shot)

1-Year One story by Jurgens, L. Simonson, Ordway, and Gil Kane; Superman app. 5.00

DOOMSDAY + 1 (Also see Charlton Bullseye)
Charlton Comics: July, 1975 - No. 6, June, 1976; No. 7, June, 1978 - No. 12, May, 1979

1: #1-5 are 25¢ issues 3 6 9 15 22 28
2-6: 4-Intro Lor. 5-Ditko-a(1 pg.) 6-Begin 30¢-c 2 4 6 10 14 18
V3#7-12 (reprints #1-6) 6.00
5 (Modern Comics reprint, 1977) 6.00
NOTE: *Byrne c/a-1-12; Painted covers-2-7.*

DOOMSDAY.1
IDW Publishing: May, 2013 - No. 4, Aug, 2013 ($3.99)

1-4-John Byrne-s/a/c 4.00

DOOMSDAY SQUAD, THE
Fantagraphics Books: Aug, 1986 - No. 7, 1987 ($2.00)

1,2,4-7: Byrne-a in all. 1,2-New Byrne-c. 4-Neal Adams-c. 5-7-Gil Kane-c 4.00
3-Usagi Yojimbo app. (1st in color); new Byrne-c 6.00

DOOM'S IV
Image Comics (Extreme): July, 1994 - No.4, Oct, 1994 ($2.50, limited series)

1-4-Liefeld story 3.00
1,2-Two alternate Liefeld-c each, 4 covers form 1 picture 5.00

DOOM: THE EMPEROR RETURNS
Marvel Comics: Jan, 2002 - No. 3, Mar, 2002 ($2.50, limited series)

1-3-Dixon-s/Manco-a; Franklin Richards app. 3.00

DOOM 2099 (See Marvel Comics Presents #118 & 2099: World of Tomorrow)
Marvel Comics: Jan, 1993 - No. 44, Aug, 1996 ($1.25/$1.50/$1.95)

1-Metallic foil stamped-c 4.00
1-2nd printing 3.00
2-24,26-44: 4-Ron Lim-c(p). 17-bound-in trading card sheet. 40-Namor & Doctor Strange app. 41-Daredevil app., Namor-c/app. 44-Intro The Emissary; story contin'd in 2099: World of Tomorrow 3.00
18-Variant polybagged with Sega Sub-Terrania poster 4.00
25 ($2.25, 52 pgs.) 4.00
25 ($2.95, 52pgs.) Foil embossed cover 5.00
29 ($3.50)-acetate-c. 4.00

DOOMWAR
Marvel Comics: Apr, 2010 - No. 6, Sept, 2010 ($3.99, limited series)

1-6-Doctor Doom invades Wakanda; Black Panther & X-Men app.; Romita Jr.-c/Eaton-a 4.00

DOORWAY TO NIGHTMARE (See Cancelled Comic Cavalcade and Madame Xanadu)
DC Comics: Jan-Feb, 1978 - No. 5, Sept-Oct, 1978

1-Madame Xanadu in all 2 4 6 11 16 20
2-5: 4-Craig-a 2 4 6 8 11 14
NOTE: *Kaluta covers on all. Merged into The Unexpected with No. 190.*

DOPEY DUCK COMICS (Wacky Duck No. 3) (See Super Funnies)
Timely Comics (NPP): Fall, 1945 - No. 2, Apr, 1946

1-Casper Cat, Krazy Krow 34 68 102 199 325 450
2-Casper Cat, Krazy Krow 28 56 84 165 270 375

DORK
Slave Labor: June, 1993 - Present ($2.50-$3.50, B&W, mature)

GD VG FN VF VF/NM NM-
2.0 4.0 6.0 8.0 9.0 9.2

1-7,9-11: Evan Dorkin-c/a/scripts in all. 1(8/95),2(1/96)-(2nd printings). 1(3/97) (3rd printing). 1-Milk & Cheese app. 3-Eltingville Club starts. 6-Reprints 1st Eltingville Club app. from Instant Piano #1 3.00
8-($3.50) 4.00
Who's Laughing Now? TPB (2001, $11.95) reprints most of #1-5 12.00
The Collected Dork, Vol. 2: Circling the Drain (6/03, $13.95) r/most of #7-10 & other-s 14.00

DOROTHY & THE WIZARD IN OZ (Adaptation of the original 1908 L. Frank Baum book) (Also see Wonderful Wizard of Oz, Marvelous Land of Oz, and Ozma of Oz)
Marvel Comics: Nov, 2011 - No. 8, Aug, 2012 ($3.99, limited series)

1-8-Eric Shanower-a/Skottie Young-a/c 4.00

DOROTHY LAMOUR (Formerly Jungle Lil)(Stage, screen, radio)
Fox Features Syndicate: No. 2, June, 1950 - No. 3, Aug, 1950

2,3-Wood-a(3) each, photo-c 28 56 84 165 270 375

DOROTHY OF OZ PREQUEL
IDW Publishing: Mar, 2012 - No. 4, Aug, 2012 ($3.99, limited series)

1-4-Tipton-s/Shedd-a 4.00

DOT DOTLAND (Formerly Little Dot Dotland)
Harvey Publications: No. 62, Sept, 1974 - No. 63, Nov, 1974

62,63 2 4 6 9 12 15

DOTTY (...& Her Boy Friends)(Formerly Four Teeners; Glamorous Romances No. 41 on)
Ace Magazines (A. A. Wyn): No. 35, June, 1948 - No. 40, May, 1949

35-Teen-age 9 18 27 52 69 85
36-40: 37-Transvestism story 7 14 21 37 46 55

DOTTY DRIPPLE (Horace & Dotty Dripple No. 25 on)
Magazine Ent.(Life's Romances)/Harvey No. 3 on: 1946 - No. 24, June, 1952 (Also see A-1 No. 1, 3-8, 10)

1 (nd) (10¢) 13 26 39 72 101 130
2 8 16 24 42 54 65
3-10: 3,4-Powell-a 7 14 21 35 43 50
11-24 6 12 18 28 34 40

DOTTY DRIPPLE AND TAFFY
Dell Publishing Co.: No. 646, Sept, 1955 - No. 903, May, 1958

Four Color 646 (#1) 5 10 15 31 53 75
Four Color 691,718,746,801,903 4 8 12 23 37 50

DOUBLE ACTION COMICS
National Periodical Publications: No. 2, Jan, 1940 (68 pgs., B&W)

2-Contains original stories(?); pre-hero DC contents; same cover as Adventure No. 37. (seven known copies, four in high grade) (not an ashcan) 2400 4800 7200 14,400 19,200 24,000
NOTE: *The cover to this book was probably reprinted from Adventure #37. #1 exists as an ash can copy with B&W cover; contains a coverless comic on inside with 1st & last page missing. There is proof of at least limited newsstand distribution. #2 cover proof only sold in 2005 for $4,000.*

DOUBLE COMICS
Elliot Publications: 1940 - 1944 (132 pgs.)

1940 issues; Masked Marvel-c & The Mad Mong vs. The White Flash covers known 290 580 870 1856 3178 4500
1941 issues; Tornado Tim-c, Nordac-c, & Green Light covers known 184 368 552 1168 2009 2850
1942 issues 132 264 396 838 1444 2050
1943,1944 issues 110 220 330 704 1202 1700
NOTE: *Double Comics consisted of an almost endless combination of pairs of remaindered, unsold issues of comics representing most publishers and usually mixed publishers in the same book; e.g., a Captain America with a Silver Streak, or a Feature with a Detective, etc., could appear inside the same cover. The actual contents would have to determine its price. Prices listed are for average contents. Any containing rare origin or first issues are worth much more. Covers also vary in same year. Value would be approximately 50 percent of contents.*

DOUBLE-CROSS (See The Crusaders)

DOUBLE-DARE ADVENTURES
Harvey Publications: Dec, 1966 - No. 2, Mar, 1967 (35¢/25¢, 68 pgs.)

1-Origin Bee-Man, Glowing Gladiator, & Magic-Master; Simon/Kirby-a 6 12 18 37 66 95
2-Torres-a; r/Alarming Adv. #3('63) 4 8 12 28 47 65
NOTE: *Powell a-1. Simon/Sparling c-1, 2.*

DOUBLE DRAGON
Marvel Comics: July, 1991 - No. 6, Dec, 1991 ($1.00, limited series)

1-6: Based on video game. 2-Art Adams-c 3.00

DOUBLE EDGE
Marvel Comics: Alpha, 1995; Omega, 1995 ($4.95, limited series)

Alpha ($4.95)- Punisher story, Nick Fury app. 5.00

Double Life of Private Strong #2 © AP

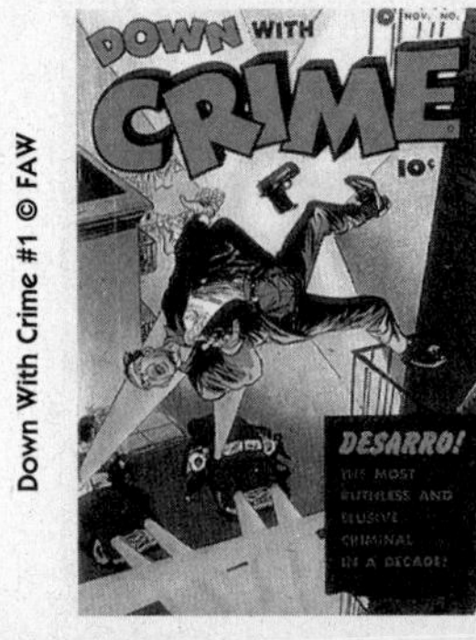

Down With Crime #1 © FAW

Dracula: Vlad the Impaler #1 © Topps

	GD	VG	FN	VF	VF/NM	NM-
	2.0	4.0	6.0	8.0	9.0	9.2

Omega ($4.95)-Punisher, Daredevil, Ghost Rider app. Death of Nick Fury 5.00

DOUBLE IMAGE
Image Comics: Feb, 2001 - No. 5, July, 2001 ($2.95)

1-5: 1-Flip covers of Codeflesh (Casey-s/Adlard-a) and The Bod (Young-s). 2-Two covers. 5-"Trust in Me" begins; Chaudhary-a 3.00

DOUBLE LIFE OF PRIVATE STRONG, THE
Archie Publications/Radio Comics: June, 1959 - No. 2, Aug, 1959

1-Origin & re-intro The Shield; Simon & Kirby-c/a, their re-entry into the super-hero genre; intro./1st app. The Fly; 1st S.A. super-hero for Archie Publ. 30 60 90 216 483 750
2-S&K-c/a; Tuska-a; The Fly app. (2nd or 3rd?) 18 36 54 124 275 425

DOUBLE TROUBLE
St. John Publishing Co.: Nov, 1957 - No. 2, Jan-Feb, 1958

1,2: Tuffy & Snuffy by Frank Johnson; dubbed "World's Funniest Kids" 6 12 18 31 38 45

DOUBLE TROUBLE WITH GOOBER
Dell Publishing Co.: No. 417, Aug, 1952 - No. 556, May, 1954

Four Color 417 4 8 12 28 47 65
Four Color 471,516,556 4 8 12 23 37 50

DOUBLE UP COMICS
Elliott Publications: 1941 (Pocket size, 192 pgs., 10¢)

1-Contains rebound copies of digest sized issues of Pocket Comics, Speed Comics, & Spitfire Comics; Japanese WWII-c 100 200 300 635 1093 1550

DOVER & CLOVER (See All Funny & More Fun Comics #93)

DOVER BOYS (See Adventures of the...)

DOVER THE BIRD
Famous Funnies Publishing Co.: Spring, 1955

1-Funny animal; code approved 7 14 21 35 43 50

DOWN
Image Comics (Top Cow): Dec, 2005 - No. 4, Mar, 2006 ($2.99)

1-4-Warren Ellis-s. 1-Tony Harris-a/c. 2-4-Cully Hamner-a 3.00
Down & Top Cow's Best of Warren Ellis TPB (6/06, $15.99) r/#1-4 & Tales of the Witchblade #3,4; Ellis-s; script for Down #1 with Harris sketch pages 16.00

DOWN WITH CRIME
Fawcett Publications: Nov, 1952 - No. 7, Nov, 1953

1 37 74 111 222 361 500
2,4,5: 2,4-Powell-a in each. 5-Bondage-c 19 38 57 111 176 240
3-Used in **POP**, pg. 106; "H is for Heroin" drug story 21 42 63 126 206 285
6,7: 6-Used in **POP**, pg. 80 18 36 54 105 165 225

DO YOU BELIEVE IN NIGHTMARES?
St. John Publishing Co.: Nov, 1957 - No. 2, Jan, 1958

1-Mostly Ditko-c/a 55 110 165 352 601 850
2-Ayers-a 32 64 96 192 314 435

D.P. 7
Marvel Comics Group (New Universe): Nov, 1986 - No. 32, June, 1989

1-20, 3.00
21-32-Low print 4.00
Annual #1 (11/87)-Intro. The Witness 4.00
... Classic Vol. 1 TPB (2007, $24.99) r/#1-9; Mark Gruenwald-s/Paul Ryan-a in all 25.00
NOTE: ***Williamson*** *a-9i, 11i; c-9i.*

DRACULA (See Bram Stoker's Dracula, Giant-Size..., Little Dracula, Marvel Graphic Novel, Requiem for Dracula, Spider-Man Vs...., Stoker's..., Tomb of... & Wedding of...; also see Movie Classics under Universal Presents as well as Dracula)

DRACULA (See Movie Classics for #1)(Also see Frankenstein & Werewolf)
Dell Publ. Co.: No. 2, 11/66 - No. 4, 3/67; No. 6, 7/72 - No. 8, 7/73 (No #5)

2-Origin & 1st app. Dracula (11/66) (super hero) 4 8 12 28 47 65
3,4: 4-Intro. Fleeta ('67) 3 6 9 19 30 40
6-('72)-r/#2 w/origin 3 6 9 15 21 26
7,8-r/#3, #4 2 4 6 11 16 20

DRACULA (Magazine)
Warren Publishing Co.: 1979 (120 pgs., full color)

Book 1-Maroto art; Spanish material translated into English (mail order only) 6 12 18 37 66 95

DRACULA
Marvel Comics: Jul, 2010 - No. 4, Sept, 2010 ($3.99, limited series)

1-4-Colored reprint of Bram Stoker's Classic Dracula adapt. from Dracula Lives!, Legion of Monsters and Stoker's Dracula; Thomas-s/Giordano-a; J. Djurdjevic-c 4.00

DRACULA CHRONICLES
Topps Comics: Apr, 1995 - No. 3, June, 1995 ($2.50, limited series)

1-3-Linsner-c 3.00

DRACULA LIVES! (Magazine)(Also see Tomb of Dracula) (Reprinted in Stoker's Dracula)
Marvel Comics Group: 1973(no month) - No. 13, July, 1975 (75¢, B&W) (76 pgs.)

1-Boris painted-c 8 16 24 51 96 140
2 (7/73)-1st time origin Dracula; Adams, Starlin-a 5 10 15 31 53 75
3-1st app. Robert E. Howard's Soloman Kane; Adams-c/a 5 10 15 31 53 75
4,5: 4-Ploog-a. 5(V2#1)-Bram Stoker's Classic Dracula adapt. begins 4 8 12 23 37 50
6-9: 6-8-Bram Stoker adapt. 9-Bondage-c 4 8 12 23 37 50
10 (1/75)-16 pg. Lilith solo (1st?) 4 8 12 27 44 60
11-13: 11-21 pg. Lilith solo sty. 12-31 pg. Dracula sty 4 8 12 23 37 50
Annual 1(Summer, 1975, $1.25, 92 pgs.)-Morrow painted-c; 6 Dracula stys. 25 pgs. Adams-a(r) 4 8 12 25 40 55
NOTE: ***N. Adams*** *a-2, 3i, 10i, Annual 1r(2, 3i).* ***Alcala*** *a-9.* ***Buscema*** *a-3p, 6p, Annual 1p.* ***Colan*** *a(p)-1, 2, 5, 6, 8.* ***Evans*** *a-7.* ***Gulacy*** *a-9.* ***Heath*** *a-1r, 13.* ***Pakula*** *a-6r. Sutton a-13.****Weiss*** *r-Annual 1p. 4* ***Dracula*** *stories each in 1, 609; 3* ***Dracula*** *stories each in 2, 4, 5,, 13.*

DRACULA: LORD OF THE UNDEAD
Marvel Comics: Dec, 1998 - No. 3, Dec, 1998 ($2.99, limited series)

1-3-Olliffe & Palmer-a 3.00

DRACULA: RETURN OF THE IMPALER
Slave Labor Graphics: July, 1993 - No. 4, Oct, 1994 ($2.95, limited series)

1-4 3.00

DRACULA'S REVENGE
IDW Publishing: Apr, 2004 - No. 3 ($3.99, limited series)

1,2-Forbeck-s/Kudranski-a 4.00

DRACULA: THE COMPANY OF MONSTERS
BOOM! Studios: Aug, 2010 - No. 12, Jul, 2011 ($3.99)

1-12: 1-5-Busiek & Gregory-s/Godlewski-a. 1-Two covers by Brereton and Salas 4.00

DRACULA VERSUS ZORRO
Topps Comics: Oct, 1993 - No. 2, Nov, 1993 ($2.95, limited series)

1,2: 1-Spot varnish & red foil-c. 2-Polybagged w/16 pg. Zorro #0 4.00

DRACULA VERSUS ZORRO
Dark Horse Comics: Sept, 1998 - No. 2, Oct, 1998 ($2.95, limited series)

1,2 3.00

DRACULA: VLAD THE IMPALER (Also see Bram Stoker's Dracula)
Topps Comics: Feb, 1993 - No. 3, Apr, 1993 ($2.95, limited series)

1-3-Polybagged with 3 trading cards each; Maroto-c/a 4.00

DRAFT, THE
Marvel Comics: 1988 ($3.50, one-shot, squarebound)

1-Sequel to "The Pitt" 4.00

DRAFTED: ONE HUNDRED DAYS
Devil's Due Publishing: June, 2009 ($5.99, one-shot)

1-Barack Obama on a post-galactic-war Earth; Powers-s 6.00

DRAG 'N' WHEELS (Formerly Top Eliminator)
Charlton Comics: No. 30, Sept, 1968 - No. 59, May, 1973

30 4 8 12 27 44 60
31-40-Scot Jackson begins 3 6 9 18 28 38
41-50 3 6 9 16 24 32
51-59: Scot Jackson 2 4 6 13 18 22
Modern Comics Reprint 58('78) 5.00

DRAGON, THE (Also see The Savage Dragon)
Image Comics (Highbrow Ent.): Mar, 1996 - No. 5, July, 1996 (99¢, lim. series)

1-5: Reprints Savage Dragon limited series w/new story & art. 5-Youngblood app; includes 5 pg. Savage Dragon story from 1984 3.00

DRAGON AGE (Based on the EA videogame)
IDW Publishing (EA Comics): Mar, 2010 - No. 6, Nov, 2010 ($3.99)

1-6-Orson Scott Card & Aaron Johnston-s; Ramos-c 4.00

DRAGON AGE: THOSE WHO SPEAK (Based on the EA videogame)
Dark Horse Comics: Aug, 2012 - No. 3, Nov, 2012 ($3.50, limited series)

1-3-Gaider-s/Hardin-a/Palumbo-c 3.50

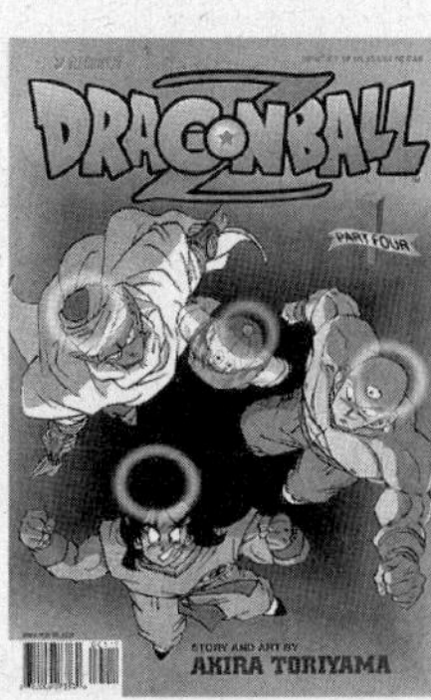

Dragon Ball Z pt. 4 #1 © Bird Studios

Dragon Lines #2 © MAR

Drax the Destroyer #4 © MAR

GD 2.0 | VG 4.0 | FN 6.0 | VF 8.0 | VF/NM 9.0 | NM- 9.2

DRAGON ARCHIVES, THE (Also see The Savage Dragon)
Image Comics: Jun, 1998 - No. 4, Jan, 1999 ($2.95, B&W)
1-4: Reprints early Savage Dragon app. 3.00

DRAGON BALL
Viz Comics: Mar, 1998 - Part 6: #2, Feb, 2003($2.95, B&W, Manga reprints read right to left)
Part 1: 1-Akira Toriyama-s/a 2 4 6 8 10 12
2-12 6.00
1-12 (2nd & 3rd printings) 4.00
Part 2: 1-15: 15-($3.50-c) 5.00
Part 3: 1-14 4.00
Part 4: 1-10 4.00
Part 5: 1-7 4.00
Part 6: 1,2 4.00

DRAGON BALL Z
Viz Comics: Mar, 1998 - Part 5: #10, Oct, 2002 ($2.95, B&W, Manga reprints read right to left)
Part 1: 1-Akira Toriyama-s/a 2 4 6 8 10 12
2-9 6.00
1-9 (2nd & 3rd printings) 4.00
Part 2: 1-14 5.00
Part 3: 1-10 4.00
Part 4: 1-15 4.00
Part 5: 1-10 4.00

DRAGON, THE: BLOOD & GUTS (Also see The Savage Dragon)
Image Comics (Highbrow Entertainment): Mar, 1995 - No. 3, May, 1995 ($2.50, lim. series)
1-3: Jason Pearson-c/a/scripts 3.00

DRAGON CHIANG
Eclipse Books: 1991 ($3.95, B&W, squarebound, 52 pgs.)
nn-Timothy Truman-c/a(p) 4.00

DRAGONFLIGHT
Eclipse Books: Feb, 1991 - No. 3, 1991 ($4.95, 52 pgs.)
Book One - Three: Adapts 1968 novel 5.00

DRAGONFLY (See Americomics #4)
Americomics: Sum, 1985 - No. 8, 1986 ($1.75/$1.95)
1 4.00
2-8 3.00

DRAGONFORCE
Aircel Publishing: 1988 - No. 13, 1989 ($2.00)
1-Dale Keown-c/a/scripts in #1-12 4.00
2-13: 13-No Keown-a 3.00
...Chronicles Book 1-5 ($2.95, B&W, 60 pgs.): Dale Keown-r/Dragonring & Dragonforce 4.00

DRAGONHEART (Movie)
Topps Comics: May, 1996 - No. 2, June, 1996 ($2.95/$4.95, limited series)
1-($2.95, 24 pgs.)-Adaptation of the film; Hildebrandt Bros-c; Lim-a. 3.00
2-($4.95, 64 pgs.) 5.00

DRAGONLANCE (Also see TSR Worlds)
DC Comics: Dec, 1988 - No. 34, Sept, 1991 ($1.25/$1.50, Mando paper)
1-Based on TSR game 4.00
2-34: Based on TSR game. 30-32-Kaluta-c 3.00

DRAGONLANCE: CHRONICLES
Devil's Due Publ.: Aug, 2005 - No. 8, Mar, 2006 ($2.95)
1-8-Dabb-s/Kurth-a 3.00
...: Dragons of Autumn Twilight TPB (2006, $17.95) r/#1-8 18.00

DRAGONLANCE: CHRONICLES (Volume 2)
Devil's Due Publ.: July, 2006 - No. 4, Jan, 2007 ($4.95/$4.99, 48 pgs.)
1-4-Dragons of Winter Night; Dabb-s/Kurth-a 5.00
...: Dragons of Winter Night TPB (3/07, $18.99) r/#1-4; cover gallery 19.00

DRAGONLANCE: CHRONICLES (Volume 3)
Devil's Due Publ.: Mar, 2007 - No. 12, ($3.50)
1-11-Dragons of Spring Dawning; Dabb-s/Cope-a 3.50

DRAGONLANCE: THE LEGEND OF HUMA
Devil's Due Publ.: Jan, 2004 - No. 6, Oct, 2005 ($2.95)
1-6-Mike Miller & Rael-a 3.00

DRAGON LINES
Marvel Comics (Epic Comics/Heavy Hitters): May, 1993 - No. 4, Aug, 1993 ($1.95, limited series)
1-($2.50)-Embossed-c; Ron Lim-c/a in all 4.00
2-4 3.00

DRAGON LINES: WAY OF THE WARRIOR
Marvel Comics (Epic Comics/ Heavy Hitters): Nov, 1993 - No. 2, Jan, 1994 ($2.25, limited series)
1,2-Ron Lim-c/a(p) 3.00

DRAGON PRINCE
Image Comics (Top Cow): Sept, 2008 - No. 4, Jan, 2009 ($2.99)
1-4-Marz-s/Moder-a; two covers 3.00

DRAGONQUEST
Silverwolf Comics: Dec, 1986 - No. 2, 1987 ($1.50, B&W, 28 pgs.)
1,2-Tim Vigil-c/a in all 5.00

DRAGONRING
Aircel Publishing: 1986 - V2#15, 1988 ($1.70/$2.00, B&W/color)
1-6: 6-Last B&W issue, V2#1-15($2.00, color) 3.00

DRAGON'S CLAWS
Marvel UK, Ltd.: July, 1988 - No. 10, Apr, 1989 ($1.25/$1.50/$1.75, British)
1-10: 3-Death's Head 1 pg. strip on back-c (1st app.). 4-Silhouette of Death's Head on last pg. 5-1st full app. new Death's Head 3.00

DRAGON'S LAIR: SINGE'S REVENGE (Based on the Don Bluth video game)
CrossGen Comics: Sept, 2003 - No. 3 ($2.95, limited series)
1-3-Mangels-s/Laguna-a 3.00

DRAGONSLAYER (Movie)
Marvel Comics Group: October, 1981 - No. 2, Nov, 1981
1,2-Paramount Disney movie adaptation 4.00

DRAGOON WELLS MASSACRE
Dell Publishing Co.: No. 815, June, 1957
Four Color 815-Movie, photo-c 6 12 18 42 79 115

DRAGSTRIP HOTRODDERS (World of Wheels No. 17 on)
Charlton Comics: Sum, 1963; No. 2, Jan, 1965 - No. 16, Aug, 1967
1 6 12 18 41 76 110
2-5 4 8 12 25 40 55
6-16 3 6 9 21 33 45

DRAIN
Image Comics: Nov, 2006 - No. 6, Mar, 2008 ($2.99)
1-6: 1-Cebulski-s/Takeda-a; two covers by Takeda and Finch 3.00
Vol. 1 TPB (2008, $16.99) r/#1-6; cover gallery and Takeda sketch art gallery 17.00

DRAKUUN
Dark Horse Comics: Feb, 1997 - No. 25, Mar, 1999 ($2.95, B&W, manga)
1-25; 1-6- Johji Manabe-s/a in all. Rise of the Dragon Princess series. 7-12-Revenge of Gustav. 13-18-Shadow of the Warlock. 19-25-The Hidden War 3.00

DRAMA
Sirius: June, 1994 ($2.95, mature)
1-1st full color Dawn app. in comics 1 3 4 6 8 10
1-Limited edition (1400 copies); signed & numbered; fingerprint authenticity 3 6 9 14 20 25
NOTE: *Dawn's 1st full color app. was a pin-up in Amazing Heroes' Swimsuit Special #5.*

DRAMA OF AMERICA, THE
Action Text: 1973 ($1.95, 224 pgs.)
1- "Students' Supplement to History" 1 3 4 6 8 10

DRAWING ON YOUR NIGHTMARES
Dark Horse Comics: Oct, 2003 ($2.99, one-shot)
1-Short stories; The Goon, Criminal Macabre, Tales of the Vampires; Templesmith-c 3.00

DRAX THE DESTROYER (Guardians of the Galaxy)
Marvel Comics: Nov, 2005 - No. 4, Feb, 2006 ($2.99, limited series)
1-4-Giffen-s/Breitweiser-a 3.00
...: Earthfall TPB (2006, $10.99) r/#1-4; character design page 11.00

DREADLANDS (Also see Epic)
Marvel Comics (Epic Comics): 1992 - No. 4, 1992 ($3.95, lim. series, 52 pgs.)
1-4: Stiff-c 4.00

DREADSTAR (See Epic Illustrated #3 for 1st app. and Eclipse Graphic Album Series #5)
Marvel Comics (Epic Comics)/First Comics No. 27 on: Nov, 1982 - No. 64, Mar, 1991
1 6.00

Dreadstar #33 © FC

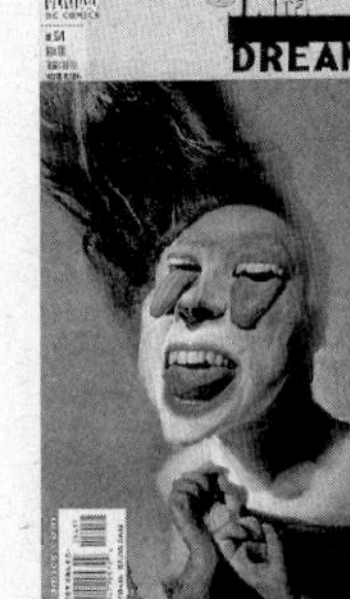

The Dreaming #54 © DC

Duck Album FC #492 © DIS

GD VG FN VF VF/NM NM-
2.0 4.0 6.0 8.0 9.0 9.2

2-5,8-49 4.00
6,7,51-64: 6,7-1st app. Interstellar Toybox; 8pgs. ea.; Wrightson-a. 51-64-Lower print run 5.00
50 6.00
Annual 1 (12/83)-r/The Price (Eclipse Graphic Album Series #5) 5.00

DREADSTAR
Malibu Comics (Bravura): Apr, 1994 - No. 6, Jan, 1995 ($2.50, limited series)
1-6-Peter David scripts: 1,2-Starlin-c 3.00
NOTE: *Issues 1-6 contain Bravura stamps.*

DREADSTAR AND COMPANY
Marvel Comics (Epic Comics): July, 1985 - No. 6, Dec, 1985
1-6: 1,3,6-New Starlin-a: 2-New Wrightson-c; reprints of Dreadstar series 3.00

DREAM BOOK OF LOVE (Also see A-1 Comics)
Magazine Enterprises: No. 106, June-July, 1954 - No. 123, Oct-Nov, 1954
A-1 106 (#1)-Powell, Bolle-a; Montgomery Clift, Donna Reed photo-c
16 32 48 94 147 200
A-1-114 (#2)-Guardineer, Bolle-a; Piper Laurie, Victor Mature photo-c
13 26 39 72 101 130
A-1 123 (#3)-Movie photo-c 12 24 36 67 94 120

DREAM BOOK OF ROMANCE (Also see A-1 Comics)
Magazine Enterprises: No. 92, 1954 - No. 124, Oct-Nov, 1954
A-1 92 (#5)-Guardineer-a; photo-c 15 30 45 84 127 170
A-1 101 (#6)(4-6/54)-Marlon Brando photo-c; Powell, Bolle, Guardineer-a
26 52 78 154 252 350
A-1 109,110,124: 109 (#7)(7-8/54)-Powell-a; movie photo-c. 110 (#8)(1/54)-Movie photo-c. 124 (#9)(10-11/54) 12 24 36 67 94 120

DREAMER, THE
Kitchen Sink Press: 1986 ($6.95, B&W, graphic novel)
nn-Will Eisner-s/a 15.00
DC Comics Reprint ($7.95, 6/00) 8.00

DREAMERY, THE
Eclipse Comics: Dec, 1986 - No. 14, Feb, 1989 ($2.00, B&W, Baxter paper)
1-14: 2-7-Alice In Wonderland adapt. 3.00

DREAMING, THE (See Sandman, 2nd Series)
DC Comics (Vertigo): June, 1996 - No. 60, May, 2001 ($2.50)
1-McKean-c on all.; LaBan scripts & Snejbjerg-a 4.00
2-30,32-60: 2,3-LaBan scripts & Snejbjerg-a. 4-7-Hogan scripts; Parkhouse-a. 8-Zulli-a. 9-11-Talbot-s/Taylor-a(p). 41-Previews Sandman: The Dream Hunters. 50-Hempel, Fegredo, McManus, Totleben-a 3.00
31-($3.95) Art by various 4.00
...Beyond The Shores of Night TPB ('97, $19.95) r/#1-8 20.00
...Special (7/98, $5.95, one-shot) Trial of Cain 6.00
...Through The Gates of Horn and Ivory TPB ('99, $19.95) r/#15-19,22-25 20.00

DREAM OF LOVE
I. W. Enterprises: 1958 (Reprints)
1,2,8: 1-r/Dream Book of Love #1; Bob Powell-a. 2-r/Great Lover's Romances #10. 8-Great Lover's Romances #1; also contains 2 Jon Juan stories by Siegel & Schomburg; Kinstler-c. 2 4 6 11 16 20
9-Kinstler-c; 1pg. John Wayne interview & Frazetta illo from John Wayne Adv. Comics #2
2 4 6 11 16 20

DREAM POLICE
Marvel Comics (Icon): Aug, 2005 ($3.99)
1-Straczynski-s/Deodato-a/c 4.00

DREAMS OF THE DARKCHYLDE
Darkchylde Entertainment: Oct, 2000 - No. 6, Sept, 2001 ($2.95)
1-6-Randy Queen-s in all. 1-Brandon Peterson-c/a 3.00

DREAM TEAM (See Battlezones: Dream Team 2)
Malibu Comics (Ultraverse): July, 1995 ($4.95, one-shot)
1-Pin-ups teaming up Marvel & Ultraverse characters by various artists including Allred, Romita, Darrow, Balent, Quesada & Palmiotti 5.00

DREAM THIEF
Dark Horse Comics: May, 2013 - No. 5, Sept, 2013 ($3.99, limited series)
1-5-Nitz-s/Smallwood-a. 1-Alex Ross-c, 2-Ryan Sook-c. 4-Dan Brereton-c 4.00

DREAMWAVE PRODUCTIONS PREVIEW
Dreamwave Productions: May, 2002 ($1.00, one-shot)
nn-Previews Arkanium, Transformers: The War Within and other series 3.00

DRESDEN FILES (See Jim Butcher's...)

GD VG FN VF VF/NM NM-
2.0 4.0 6.0 8.0 9.0 9.2

DRIFT FENCE (See Zane Grey 4-Color 270)

DRIFT MARLO
Dell Publishing Co.: May-July, 1962 - No. 2, Oct-Dec, 1962 (Painted-c)
01-232-207 (#1) 5 10 15 30 50 70
2 (12-232-212) 4 8 12 27 44 60

DRISCOLL'S BOOK OF PIRATES
David McKay Publ. (Not reprints): 1934 (B&W, hardcover; 124 pgs, 7x9")
nn-"Pieces of Eight" strip by Montford Amory 24 48 72 144 237 330

DRIVER: CROSSING THE LINE (Based on the Ubisoft videogame)
DC Comics: Oct, 2011 ($2.99, one-shot)
1-David Lapham-s/Greg Scott-a/ Jock-c; bonus character design art 3.00

DROIDS (Based on Saturday morning cartoon) (Also see Dark Horse Comics)
Marvel Comics (Star Comics): April, 1986 - No. 8, June, 1987
1-R2D2 & C-3PO from Star Wars app. in all 2 4 6 11 16 20
2-8: 2,5,7,8-Williamson-a(i) 2 4 6 8 10 12
NOTE: *Romita a-3p. Sinnott a-3i.*

DROOPY (see Tom & Jerry #60)

DROOPY (Tex Avery's...)
Dark Horse Comics: Oct, 1995 - No. 3, Dec, 1995 ($2.50, limited series)
1-3: Characters created by Tex Avery; painted-c 3.00

DROPSIE AVENUE: THE NEIGHBORHOOD
Kitchen Sink Press: June, 1995 ($15.95/$24.95, B&W)
nn-Will Eisner (softcover) 16.00
nn-Will Eisner (hardcover) 25.00

DROWNED GIRL, THE
DC Comics (Piranha Press): 1990 ($5.95, 52 pgs, mature)
nn 6.00

DRUG WARS
Pioneer Comics: 1989 ($1.95)
1-Grell-c 3.00

DRUID
Marvel Comics: May, 1995 - No. 4, Aug, 1995 ($2.50, limited series)
1-4: Warren Ellis scripts. 3.00

DRUM BEAT
Dell Publishing Co.: No. 610, Jan, 1955
Four Color 610-Movie, Alan Ladd photo-c 8 16 24 51 96 140

DRUMS OF DOOM
United Features Syndicate: 1937 (25¢)(Indian)(Text w/color illos.)
nn-By Lt. F.A. Methot; Golden Thunder app.; Tip Top Comics ad in comic; nice-c
39 78 117 231 378 525

DRUNKEN FIST
Jademan Comics: Aug, 1988 - No. 54, Jan, 1993 ($1.50/$1.95, 68 pgs.)
1 5.00
2-50 4.00
51-54 4.00

DUCK ALBUM (See Donald Duck Album)
Dell Publishing Co.: No. 353, Oct, 1951 - No. 840, Sept, 1957
Four Color 353 (#1)-Barks-c; 1st Uncle Scrooge-c (also appears on back-c).
9 18 27 62 126 190
Four Color 450-Barks-c 7 14 21 44 82 120
Four Color 492,531,560,586,611,649,686, 6 12 18 38 69 100
Four Color 726,782,840 5 10 15 33 57 80

DUCKMAN
Dark Horse Comics: Sept, 1990 ($1.95, B&W, one-shot)
1-Story & art by Everett Peck 4.00

DUCKMAN
Topps Comics: Nov, 1994 - No. 5, May, 1995; No. 0, Feb, 1996 ($2.50)
0 (2/96, $2.95, B&W)-r/Duckman #1 from Dark Horse Comics 3.00
1-5: 1-w/ coupon #A for Duckman trading card. 2-w/Duckman 1st season episode guide 3.00

DUCKMAN: THE MOB FROG SAGA
Topps Comics: Nov, 1994 - No. 3, Feb, 1995 ($2.50, limited series)
1-3: 1-w/coupon #B for Duckman trading card, S. Shaw!-c 3.00

DUCKTALES

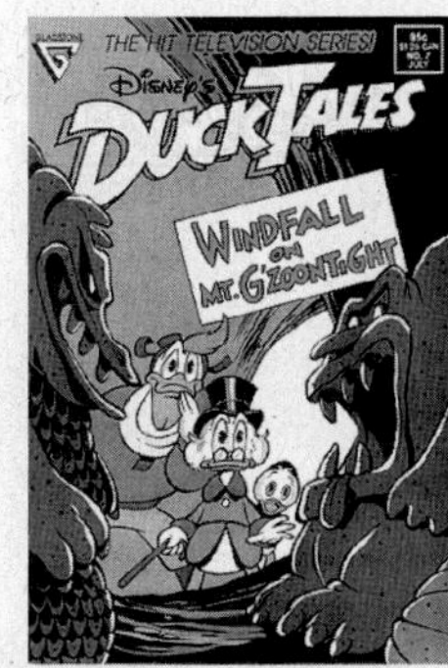

Duck Tales #7 © DIS

Durango Kid #4 © ME

DV8 #11 © WSP

	GD 2.0	VG 4.0	FN 6.0	VF 8.0	VF/NM 9.0	NM- 9.2

Gladstone Publ.: Oct, 1988 - No. 13, May, 1990 (1,2,9-11: $1.50; 3-8: 95¢)
1-Barks-r 6.00
2-11: 2-7,9-11-Barks-r 4.00
12,13 ($1.95, 68 pgs.)-Barks-r; 12-r/F.C. #495 5.00
Disney Presents Carl Barks' Greatest DuckTales Stories Vol. 1 (Gemstone Publ., 2006, $10.95) r/stories adapted for the animated TV series including "Back to the Klondike" 11.00
Disney Presents Carl Barks' Greatest DuckTales Stories Vol. 2 (Gemstone Publ., 2006, $10.95) r/stories adapted for the animated TV series; "Robot Robbers" app. 11.00

DUCKTALES (TV)
Disney Comics: June, 1990 - No. 18, Nov, 1991 ($1.50)
1-All new stories; Marv Wolfman-s 4.00
2-18 3.00
Disney's DuckTales by Marv Wolfman: Scrooge's Quest TPB (Gemstone, 9/07, $15.99) r/#1-7; intro. by Wolfman 16.00
Disney's DuckTales: The Gold Odyssey TPB (Gemstone, 10/08, $15.99) 16.00
The Movie nn (1990, $7.95, 68 pgs.)-Graphic novel adapting animated movie 8.00

DUCKTALES (TV)
Boom Entertainment (KABOOM!): May, 2011 - No. 4, Aug, 2011 ($3.99)
1-6: 1-4-Three covers on each; Spector-s/Massaroli-a. 5,6-Two covers; Crossover with Darkwing Duck #17,18 4.00

DUDLEY (Teen-age)
Feature/Prize Publications: Nov-Dec, 1949 - No. 3, Mar-Apr, 1950
1-By Boody Rogers 15 30 45 88 137 185
2,3 10 20 30 56 76 95

DUDLEY DO-RIGHT (TV)
Charlton Comics: Aug, 1970 - No. 7, Aug, 1971 (Jay Ward)
1 8 16 24 52 99 145
2-7 6 12 18 37 66 95

DUEL MASTERS (Based on a trading card game) (Also see Free Comic Book Day Edition in the Promotional Comics section)
Dreamwave Productions: Nov, 2003 - No. 8, Sept, 2004 ($2.95)
1-8: 1-Bagged with card; Augustyn-s 3.00

DUKE NUKEM: GLORIOUS BASTARD (Based on the video game)
IDW Publishing: Jul, 2011 - No. 4, Nov, 2011 ($3.99)
1-4: 1-Three covers; Waltz-s/Xermanico-a 4.00

DUKE OF THE K-9 PATROL
Gold Key: Apr, 1963
1 (10052-304) 4 8 12 23 37 50

DUMBO (Disney; see Movie Comics, & Walt Disney Showcase #12)
Dell Publishing Co.: No. 17, 1941 - No. 668, Jan, 1958
Four Color 17 (#1)-Mickey Mouse, Donald Duck, Pluto app. 268 536 804 1702 2926 4150
Large Feature Comic 19 ('41)-Part-r 4-Color 17 300 600 900 1905 4230 4650
Four Color 234 ('49) 12 24 36 83 182 280
Four Color 668 (12/55)-1st of two printings. Dumbo on-c with starry sky. Same-c as #234 9 18 27 61 123 185
Four Color 668 (1/58)-2nd printing. Same cover altered with Timothy Mouse added. Same contents 6 12 18 38 69 100

DUMBO COMIC PAINT BOOK (See Dumbo, Large Feature Comic No. 19)

DUNC AND LOO (#1-3 titled "Around the Block with Dunc and Loo")
Dell Publishing Co.: Oct-Dec, 1961 - No. 8, Oct-Dec, 1963
1 5 10 15 35 63 90
2 4 8 12 27 44 60
3-8 3 6 9 21 33 45
NOTE: *Written by* ***John Stanley; Bill Williams*** *art.*

DUNE (Movie)
Marvel Comics: Apr, 1985 - No. 3, June, 1985
1-3-r/Marvel Super Special; movie adaptation 4.00

DUNGEONS & DRAGONS
IDW Publishing: No. 0, Aug, 2010 - No. 15, Jan, 2012($1.00/$3.99)
0-(8/10, $1.00) Five covers; previews D&D series and Dark Sun mini-series 3.00
1-15: 1-(11/10, $3.99) Di Vito-a/Rogers-s; two covers. 2-Two covers 4.00
Annual 2012: Eberron (3/12, $7.99) Crilley-s/Diaz & Rojo-a 8.00
... 100 Page Spectacular (1/12, $7.99) Reprints by various incl. Duursema & Morales 8.00

DUNGEONS & DRAGONS: CUTTER
IDW Publishing: Apr, 2013 - No. 5, Sept, 2013 ($3.99)
1-5-R.A. & Geno Salvatore-s/Baldeon-a; 2 covers on each 4.00

DUNGEONS & DRAGONS: FORGOTTEN REALMS
IDW Publishing: Apr, 2012 - No. 5, Sept, 2012 ($3.99, limited series)
1-5-Greenwood-s/Ferguson-a 4.00
... 100 Page Spectacular (4/12, $7.99) Reprints by various incl. Rags Morales 8.00

DUNGEONS & DRAGONS: THE LEGEND OF DRIZZT: NEVERWINTER TALES
IDW Publishing: Aug, 2011 - No. 5, Dec, 2011 ($3.99, limited series)
1-5-R.A. & Geno Salvatore-s/Agustin Padilla-a 4.00

DURANGO KID, THE (Also see Best of the West, Great Western & White Indian)
(Charles Starrett starred in Columbia's Durango Kid movies)
Magazine Enterprises: Oct-Nov, 1949 - No. 41, Oct-Nov, 1955 (All 36 pgs.)
1-Charles Starrett photo-c; Durango Kid & his horse Raider begin; Dan Brand & Tipi (origin) begin by Frazetta & continue through #16 73 146 219 467 796 1125
2-Starrett photo-c. 34 68 102 199 325 450
3-5-All have Starrett photo-c. 29 58 87 172 281 390
6-10: 7-Atomic weapon-c/story 16 32 48 94 147 200
11-16-Last Frazetta issue 14 28 42 80 115 150
17-Origin Durango Kid 16 32 48 94 147 200
18-30: 18-Fred Meagher-a on Dan Brand begins.19-Guardineer-c/a(3) begins, end #41. 23-Intro. The Red Scorpion 10 20 30 54 72 90
31-Red Scorpion returns 9 18 27 52 69 85
32-41-Bolle/Frazetta*ish*-a (Dan Brand; true in later issues?) 9 18 27 50 65 80
NOTE: *#6, 8, 14, 15 contain* ***Frazetta*** *art not reprinted in White Indian.* ***Ayers*** *c-18.* ***Guardineer*** *a(3)-19-41; c-19-41.* ***Fred Meagher*** *a-18-29 at least.*

DURANGO KID, THE
AC Comics: 1990 - #2, 1990 ($2.50,$2.75, half-color)
1,2: 1-Starrett photo front/back-c; Guardineer-r. 2-B&W)-Starrett photo-c; White Indian-r by Frazetta; Guardineer-r (50th anniversary of films) 3.00

DUSTCOVERS: THE COLLECTED SANDMAN COVERS 1989-1997
DC Comics (Vertigo): 1997 ($39.95, Hardcover)
Reprints Dave McKean's Sandman covers with Gaiman text 40.00
Softcover (1998, $24.95) 25.00

DUSTY STAR
Image Comics (Desperado Studios): No. 0, Apr, 1997 - No. 1 ($2.95, B&W)
0,1-Pruett-s/Robinson-a 3.00

DUSTY STAR
Image Comics (Desperado Publishing): June, 2006 ($3.50)
1-Pruett-s/Robinson-s/a 3.50

DV8 (See Gen 13)
Image Comics (WildStorm Productions): Aug, 1996 - No. 25, Dec, 1998;
DC Comics (WildStorm Prod.): No. 0, Apr, 1999 - No. 32, Nov, 1999 ($2.50)
1/2 6.00
1-Warren Ellis scripts & Humberto Ramos-c/a(p) 4.00
1-(7-variant covers, w/1 by Jim Lee) ...each 4.00
2-4: 3-No Ramos-a 3.00
5-32: 14-Regular-c, 14-Variant-c by Charest. 26-(5/99)-McGuinness-c 3.00
14-($3.50) Voyager Pack w/Danger Girl preview 5.00
0-(4/99, $2.95) Two covers (Rio and McGuinness) 3.00
Annual 1 (1/98, $2.95) 4.00
Annual 1999 ($3.50) Slipstream x-over with Gen13 4.00
Rave-(7/96, $1.75)-Ramos-c; pinups & interviews 3.00
...: Neighborhood Threat TPB (2002, $14.95) r/#1-6 & #1/2; Ellis intro.; Ramos-c 15.00

DV8: GODS AND MONSTERS
DC Comics (WildStorm): June, 2010 - No. 8, Jan, 2011 ($2.99, limited series)
1-8-Wood-s/Issacs-a 3.00
TPB (2011, $17.99) r/#1-8 18.00

DV8 VS. BLACK OPS
Image Comics (WildStorm): Oct, 1997 - No. 3, Dec, 1997 ($2.50, limited series)
1-3-Bury-s/Norton-a 3.00

DWIGHT D. EISENHOWER
Dell Publishing Co.: December, 1969
01-237-912 - Life story 4 8 12 28 47 65

DYNABRITE COMICS
Whitman Publishing Co.: 1978 - 1979 (69¢, 10x7-1/8", 48 pgs., cardboard-c)
(Blank inside covers)
11350 - Walt Disney's Mickey Mouse & the Beanstalk (4-C 157). 11350-1 - Mickey Mouse Album (4-C 1057, 1151,1246). 11351 - Mickey Mouse & His Sky Adventure (4-C 214, 343). 11354 - Goofy: A Gaggle of Giggles.

Dynamic Comics #1 © CHES

Dynamo 5 #1 © Faerber & Asrar

Earth 2 #17 © DC

	GD	VG	FN	VF	VF/NM	NM-
	2.0	4.0	6.0	8.0	9.0	9.2

11354-1 - Super Goof Meets Super Thief. 11356 - (?). 11359 - Bugs Bunny-r. 11360 - Winnie the Pooh Fun and Fantasy (Disney-r).
each.... 2 4 6 9 12 15
11352 - Donald Duck (4-C 408, Donald Duck 45,52)-Barks-a. 11352-1 - Donald Duck (4-C 318, 10 pg. Barks/WDC&S 125,128)-Barks-c(r). 11353 - Daisy Duck's Diary (4-C 1055,1150) Barks-a. 11355 - Uncle Scrooge (Barks-a/U.S. 12,33). 11355-1 - Uncle Scrooge (Barks-a/U.S. 13,16) - Barks-c(r). 11357 - Star Trek (r/-Star Trek 33,41). 11358 - Star Trek (r/-Star Trek 34,36). 11361 - Gyro Gearloose & the Disney Ducks (r/4-C 1047,1184)-Barks-c(r)
each.... 2 4 6 10 14 18

DYNAMIC ADVENTURES
I. W. Enterprises: No. 8, 1964 - No. 9, 1964
8-Kayo Kirby-r by Baker?/Fight Comics 53. 3 6 9 14 20 25
9-Reprints Avon's "Escape From Devil's Island"; Kinstler-c
3 6 9 16 23 30
nn (no date)-Reprints Risks Unlimited with Rip Carson, Senorita Rio; r/Fight #53
3 6 9 16 22 28

DYNAMIC CLASSICS (See Cancelled Comic Cavalcade)
DC Comics: Sept-Oct, 1978 (44 pgs.)
1-Neal Adams Batman, Simonson Manhunter-r 2 4 6 8 10 12

DYNAMIC COMICS (No #4-7)
Harry 'A' Chesler: Oct, 1941 - No. 3, Feb, 1942; No. 8, Mar, 1944 - No. 25, May, 1948
1-Origin Major Victory by Charles Sultan (reprinted in Major Victory #1), Dynamic Man & Hale the Magician; The Black Cobra only app.; Major Victory & Dynamic Man begin
232 464 696 1485 2543 3600
2-Origin Dynamic Boy & Lady Satan; intro. The Green Knight & sidekick Lance Cooper
110 220 330 704 1202 1700
3-1st small logo, resumes with #10 103 206 309 659 1130 1600
8-Classic-c; Dan Hastings, The Echo, The Master Key, Yankee Boy begin; Yankee Doodle Jones app.; hypo story 194 388 582 1242 2121 3000
9-Mr. E begins; Mac Raboy-c 94 188 282 597 1024 1450
10-Small logo begins 77 154 231 493 847 1200
11-Classic-c 81 162 243 518 884 1250
12-16: 15-The Sky Chief app. 16-Marijuana story 65 130 195 416 708 1000
17(1/46)-Illustrated in **SOTI**, "The children told me what the man was going to do with the hot poker," but Wertham saw this in Crime Reporter #2
74 148 222 470 810 1150
18-Classic Airplanehead monster-c 61 122 183 390 670 950
19-Classic puppeteer-c by Gattuso 65 130 195 416 708 1000
20-Bare-breasted woman-c 103 206 309 659 1130 1600
21,22,25: 21-Dinosaur-c; new logo 47 94 141 296 498 700
23,24-(68 pgs.): 23-Yankee Girl app. 43 86 129 271 461 650
I.W. Reprint #1,8('64): 1-r/#23. 8-Exist? 3 6 9 17 26 35
NOTE: *Kinstler c-IW #1. Tuska art in many issues, #3, 9, 11, 12, 16, 19. Bondage c-16.*

DYNAMITE (Becomes Johnny Dynamite No. 10 on)
Comic Media/Allen Hardy Publ.: May, 1953 - No. 9, Sept, 1954
1-Pete Morisi-a; Don Heck-c; r-as Danger #6 40 80 120 246 411 575
2 21 42 63 124 202 280
3-Marijuana story; Johnny Dynamite (1st app.) begins by Pete Morisi(c/a); Heck text-a; man shot in face at close range 27 54 81 158 259 360
4-Injury-to-eye, prostitution; Morisi-c/a 24 48 72 142 234 325
5-9-Morisi-c/a in all. 7-Prostitute story & reprints 20 40 60 117 189 260

DYNAMO (Also see Tales of Thunder & T.H.U.N.D.E.R. Agents)
Tower Comics: Aug, 1966 - No. 4, June, 1967 (25¢)
1-Crandall/Wood, Ditko/Wood-a; Weed series begins; NoMan & Lightning cameos; Wood-c/a 8 16 24 54 105 150
2-4: Wood-c/a in all 5 10 15 34 60 85
NOTE: *Adkins/Wood a-2. Ditko a-4?. Tuska a-2, 3.*

DYNAMO 5 (See Noble Causes: Extended Family #2 for debut of Captain Dynamo)
Image Comics: Jan, 2007 - No. 25, Oct, 2009 ($3.50/$2.99)
1-Intro. the offspring of Captain Dynamo; Faerber-s/Asrar-a 8.00
2 5.00
3-7,11-24 : 5-Intro. Synergy. 13-Origin of Myriad. 21-Firebird app. 3.50
8-10-($2.99) 3.50
25-($4.99) Back-up short stories of team members 5.00
Annual #1 (4/08, $5.99) r/Captain Dynamo app. in Nobel Causes: Extended Family #2 and three new stories by Faerber & various; pin-up gallery 6.00
#0 (2/09, 99¢) short story leading into #20; text synopsis of story so far 3.00
...: Holiday Special 2010 (12/10, $3.99) Faerber-s/Takara-a 4.00
... Vol. 1: Post-Nuclear Family TPB (2007, $9.99) r/#1-7; Kirkman intro. 10.00
... Vol. 2: Moments of Truth TPB (2008, $14.99) r/#8-13 15.00

	GD	VG	FN	VF	VF/NM	NM-
	2.0	4.0	6.0	8.0	9.0	9.2

DYNAMO 5: SINS OF THE FATHER
Image Comics: Jun, 2010 - No. 5, Oct, 2010 ($3.99, limited series)
1-5-Faerber-s/Brilha-a. 2-4-Invincible app. 4.00

DYNAMO JOE (Also see First Adventures & Mars)
First Comics: May, 1986 - No. 15, Jan, 1988 (#12-15: $1.75)
1-15: 4-Cargonauts begin, Special 1(1/87)-Mostly-r/Mars 3.00

DYNOMUTT (TV)(See Scooby-Doo (3rd series))
Marvel Comics Group: Nov, 1977 - No. 6, Sept, 1978 (Hanna-Barbera)
1-The Blue Falcon, Scooby Doo in all 4 8 12 27 44 60
2-6-All newsstand only 3 6 9 17 26 35

EAGLE, THE (1st Series) (See Science Comics & Weird Comics #8)
Fox Features Syndicate: July, 1941 - No. 4, Jan, 1942
1-The Eagle begins; Rex Dexter of Mars app. by Briefer; all issues feature German war covers 194 388 582 1242 2121 3000
2-The Spider Queen begins (origin) 92 184 276 584 1005 1425
3,4: 3-Joe Spook begins (origin) 73 146 219 467 796 1125

EAGLE COMICS (2nd Series)
Rural Home Publ.: Feb-Mar, 1945 - No. 2, Apr-May, 1945
1-Aviation stories 52 104 156 328 552 775
2-Lucky Aces 28 56 84 165 270 375
NOTE: *L. B. Cole c/a in each.*

EARTH 4 (Also see Urth 4)
Continuity Comics: Dec, 1993 - No. 4, Jan, 1994 ($2.50)
1-4: 1-3 all listed as Dec, 1993 in indicia 3.00

EARTH 4 DEATHWATCH 2000
Continuity Comics: Apr, 1993 - No. 3, Aug, 1993 ($2.50)
1-3 3.00

EARTH MAN ON VENUS (An...) (Also see Strange Planets)
Avon Periodicals: 1951
nn-Wood-a (26 pgs.); Fawcette-c 152 304 456 965 1658 2350

EARTH 2
DC Comics: Jul, 2012 - Present ($3.99/$2.99)
1-($3.99) James Robinson-s/Nicola Scott-a/Ivan Reis-c; 4.00
1-Variant-c by Hitch 6.00
2-15-($2.99) 2-New Flash. 3-New Green Lantern. 4-New Atom 3.00
15.1, 15.2 (11/13, $2.99, regular covers) 3.00
15.1 (11/13, $3.99, 3-D cover) "Desaad #1" on cover; Levitz-s/Cinar-a 5.00
15.2 (11/13, $3.99, 3-D cover) "Solomon Grundy #1" on cover; Kindt-s/Lopresti-a 5.00
16-22: 16-Superman returns. 17-Batman returns. 20-Jae Lee-c 3.00
#0 (11/12, $2.99) Superman, Batman, Wonder Woman, Terry Sloan app.; Giorello-a 3.00
Annual 1 (7/13, $4.99) Robinson-s/Cafu-a; new Batman app. 5.00
Annual 2 (3/14, $4.99) Taylor-s/Rocha-a; origin of new Batman 5.00

EARTHWORM JIM (TV, cartoon)
Marvel Comics: Dec, 1995 - No. 3, Feb, 1996 ($2.25)
1-3: Based on video game and toys 3.00

EARTH X
Marvel Comics: No. 0, Mar, 1999 - No. 12, Apr, 2000 ($3.99/$2.99, lim. series)
nn- (Wizard supplement) Alex Ross sketchbook; painted-c 6.00
Sketchbook (2/99) New sketches and previews 6.00
0-(3/99)-Prelude; Leon-a(p)/Ross-c 1 2 3 4 5 7
1-(4/99)-Leon-a(p)/Ross-c 1 2 3 4 5 7
1-2nd printing 4.00
2-12 4.00
#1/2 (Wizard) Nick Fury on cover; Reinhold-a 6.00
#X (6/00, $3.99) 4.00
... Trilogy Companion TPB (2008, $29.99) r/#1/2; artwork and content from the Earth X, Paradise X and Universe X series; gallery of variant covers and promotional art 30.00
HC (2005, $49.99) r/#0,1-12, #1/2, X; foreward by Joss Whedon; Ross sketch pages 50.00
TPB (12/00, $24.95) r/#0,1-12, X; foreward by Joss Whedon 25.00

EASTER BONNET SHOP (See March of Comics No. 29)

EASTER WITH MOTHER GOOSE
Dell Publishing Co.: No. 103, 1946 - No. 220, Mar, 1949
Four Color 103 (#1)-Walt Kelly-a 15 30 45 105 233 360
Four Color 140 ('47)-Kelly-a 12 24 36 84 185 285
Four Color 185 ('48), 220-Kelly-a 11 22 33 76 163 250

EAST MEETS WEST

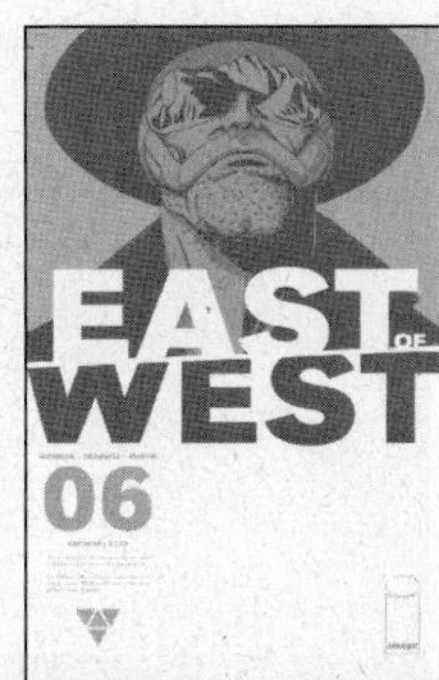

East of West #6 © Hickman & Dragotta

Echo #2 © Dreamwave

Eclipse Graphic Album #35 © ECL

GD 2.0 | VG 4.0 | FN 6.0 | VF 8.0 | VF/NM 9.0 | NM- 9.2

Innovation Publishing: Apr, 1990 - No. 2, 1990 ($2.50, limited series, mature)

1,2: 1-Stevens part-i; Redondo-c(i). 2-Stevens-c(i); 1st app. Cheech & Chong in comics 3.00

EAST OF WEST
Image Comics: Mar, 2013 - Present ($3.50)

1-11-Hickman-s/Dragotta-a 3.50

EC ARCHIVES
Gemstone Publishing/Dark Horse Books: 2006 - Present ($49.95, hardcover with dustjacket)

Crime SuspenStories Vol. 1 - Recolored reprints of #1-6; foreward by Max Allan Collins 50.00
Frontline Combat Vol. 1 - Recolored reprints of #1-6; foreward by Henry G. Franke III 50.00
Shock SuspenStories Vol. 1 - Recolored reprints of #1-6; foreward by Steven Spielberg 50.00
Shock SuspenStories Vol. 2 - Recolored reprints of #7-12; foreward by Dean Kamen 50.00
Tales From the Crypt Vol. 1 - Recolored reprints of Crypt of Terror #17-19 and Tales From the Crypt #20-22; foreward by John Carpenter; Al Feldstein behind-the-scenes info 100.00
Tales From the Crypt Vol. 2 - Recolored reprints of #23-28; foreward by Joe Dante 50.00
Tales From the Crypt Vol. 3 - Recolored reprints of #29-34; foreward by Bob Overstreet 50.00
Tales From the Crypt Vol. 4 - (DH) Recolored reprints of #35-40; foreward by Russ Cochran 50.00
Two-Fisted Tales Vol. 1 - Recolored reprints of #18-23; foreward by Stephen Geppi 50.00
Two-Fisted Tales Vol. 2 - Recolored reprints of #24-29; foreward by Rocco Versaci, Ph.D. 50.00
Vault of Horror Vol. 1 - Recolored reprints of #12-17; foreward by R.L. Stine 50.00
Weird Fantasy Vol. 1 - (DH) Recolored reprints of #13-17; foreward by Walt Simonson 50.00
Weird Science Vol. 1 - Recolored reprints of #1-6; foreward by George Lucas 75.00
Weird Science Vol. 2 - Recolored reprints of #7-12; foreward by Paul Levitz 50.00
Weird Science Vol. 3 - Recolored reprints of #13-18; foreward by Jerry Weist 50.00

E. C. CLASSIC REPRINTS
East Coast Comix Co.: May, 1973 - No. 12, 1976 (E.C. Comics reprinted in color minus ads)

1-The Crypt of Terror #1 (Tales from the Crypt #46) 2 4 6 11 16 20
2-12: 2-Weird Science #15('52). 3-Shock SuspenStories #12. 4-Haunt of Fear #12. 5-Weird Fantasy #13('52). 6-Crime SuspenStories #25. 7-Vault of Horror #26. 8-Shock SuspenStories #6. 9-Two-Fisted Tales #34. 10-Haunt of Fear #23. 11-Weird Science 12(#1). 12-Shock SuspenStories #2 2 4 6 8 11 14

EC CLASSICS
Russ Cochran: Aug, 1985 - No. 12, 1986? (High quality paper; each-r 8 stories in color) (#2-12 were resolicited in 1990)($4.95, 56 pgs., 8x11")

1-12: 1-Tales From the Crypt. 2-Weird Science. 3-Two-Fisted Tales (r/31); Frontline Combat (r/9). 4-Shock SuspenStories. 5-Weird Fantasy. 6-Vault of Horror. 7-Weird Science-Fantasy (r/23,24). 8-Crime SuspenStories (r/17,18). 9-Haunt of Fear (r/14,15). 10-Panic (r/1,2). 11-Tales From the Crypt (r/23,24). 12-Weird Science (r/20,22) 1 2 3 4 5 7

ECHO
Image Comics (Dreamwave Prod.): Mar, 2000 - No. 5, Sept, 2000 ($2.50)

1-5: 1-3-Pat Lee-c 3.00
0-(7/00) 3.00

ECHO
Abstract Studio: Mar, 2008 - No. 30, May, 2011 ($3.50)

1-Terry Moore-s/a/c 8.00
2-30 3.50
Terry Moore's Echo: Moon Lake TPB (2008, $15.95) r/#1-5; Moore sketch pages 16.00

ECHO OF FUTUREPAST
Pacific Comics/Continuity Com.: May, 1984 - No. 9, Jan, 1986 ($2.95, 52 pgs.)

1-9: Neal Adams-c/a in all? 6.00
NOTE: ***N. Adams*** *a-1-6,7i,9i; c-1-3, 5p,7i,8,9i.* ***Golden*** *a-1-6 (Bucky O'Hare); c-6.* ***Toth*** *a-6,7.*

ECLIPSE GRAPHIC ALBUM SERIES
Eclipse Comics: Oct, 1978 - 1989 (8-1/2x11") (B&W #1-5)

1-Sabre (10/78, B&W, 1st print.); Gulacy-a; 1st direct sale graphic novel 16.00
1-Sabre (2nd printing, 1/79) 8.00
1-Sabre (3rd printing, $5.95) 6.00
1-Sabre 30th Anniversary Edition (2008, $14.99, 9x6" HC) new McGregor & Gulacy intros. original script with sketch art 15.00
2,6,7: 2-Night Music (11/79, B&W)-Russell-a. 6-I Am Coyote (11/84, color)-Rogers-c/a. 7-The Rocketeer (2nd print, $7.95). 7-The Rocketeer (3rd print, 1991, $8.95) 10.00
3,4: 3-Detectives, Inc. (5/80, B&W, $6.95)-Rogers-a. 4-Stewart The Rat (1980, B&W) -G. Colan-a 10.00
5-The Price (10/81, B&W)-Starlin-a 18.00
7-The Rocketeer (9/85, color)-Dave Stevens-a (r/chapters 1-5)(see Pacific Presents & Starslayer); has 7 pgs. new-a 20.00
7-The Rocketeer, signed & limited HC 85.00
7-The Rocketeer, hardcover (1986, $19.95) 40.00
7-The Rocketeer, unsigned HC (3rd, $32.95) 33.00
8-Zorro In Old California ('86, color) 14.00
8,12-Hardcover 18.00
9,10: 9-Sacred And The Profane ('86)-Steacy-a. 10-Somerset Holmes ('86, $15.95)-Adults, soft-c 16.00
9,10,12-Hardcover ($24.95). 12-signed & #'d 25.00
11-Floyd Farland, Citizen of the Future ('87, $2.95, B&W) Chris Ware-s/a 7.00
12,28,31,35: 12-Silverheels ('87, $7.95, color). 28-Miracleman Book I ($5.95). 31-Pigeons From Hell by R. E. Howard (11/88). 35-Rael: Into The Shadow of the Sun ('88, $7.95) 10.00
13-The Sisterhood of Steel ('87, $8.95, color) 10.00
14,16,18,20,23,24: 14-Samurai, Son of Death ('87, $4.95, B&W). 16,18,20,23-See Airfighters Classics #1-4. 24-Heartbreak ($4.95, B&W) 7.00
14 (2nd pr.),17,21: 14-Samurai, Son of Death ($3.95, 2nd printing). 17-Valkyrie, Prisoner of the Past SC ('88, $3.95, color). 21-XYR-Multiple ending comic ('88, $3.95, B&W) 6.00
15,22,27: 15-Twisted Tales (11/87, color)-Dave Stevens-c. 22-Alien Worlds #1 (5/88, $3.95, 52 pgs.)-Nudity. 27-Fast Fiction (She) ($5.95, B&W) 8.00
17-Valkyrie, Prisoner of the Past S&N Hardcover ('88, $19.95) 25.00
19-Scout: The Four Monsters ('88, $14.95, color)-r/Scout #1-7; soft-c 15.00
25,30,32-34: 25-Alex Toth's Zorro Vol. 1 ,2($10.95, B&W). 30-Brought To Light; Alan Moore scripts ('89). 32-Teenaged Dope Slaves and Reform School Girls. 33-Bogie. 34-Air Fighters Classics #5 12.00
29-Real Love: Best of Simon & Kirby Romance Comics (10/88, $12.95) 15.00
30,31: Limited hardcover ed. ($29.95). 31-signed 30.00
36-Dr. Watchstop: Adventures in Time and Space ('89, $8.95) 10.00

ECLIPSE MAGAZINE (Becomes Eclipse Monthly)
Eclipse Publishing: May, 1981 - No. 8, Jan, 1983 ($2.95, B&W, magazine)

1-8: 1-1st app. Cap'n Quick and a Foozle by Rogers, Ms. Tree by Beatty, and Dope by Trina Robbins. 2-1st app. I Am Coyote by Rogers. 7-1st app. Masked Man by Boyer 4.00
NOTE: ***Colan*** *a-3, 5, 8.* ***Golden*** *c/a-2.* ***Gulacy*** *a-6, c-1, 6.* ***Kaluta*** *c/a-5.* ***Mayerik*** *a-2, 3.* ***Rogers*** *a-1-8.* ***Starlin*** *a-1.* ***Sutton*** *a-6.*

ECLIPSE MONTHLY
Eclipse Comics: Aug, 1983 - No. 10, Jul, 1984 (Baxter paper, $2.00/$1.50/$1.75)

1-10: ($2.00, 52 pgs.)-Cap'n Quick and a Foozle by Rogers, Static by Ditko, Dope by Trina Robbins, Rio by Wildey, The Masked Man by Boyer begin. 3-Ragamuffins begins 4.00
NOTE: ***Boyer*** *c-6.* ***Ditko*** *a-1-3.* ***Rogers*** *a-1-4; c-2, 4, 7.* ***Wildey*** *a-1, 2, 5, 9, 10; c-5, 10.*

ECLIPSO (See Brave and the Bold #64, House of Secrets #61 & Phantom Stranger, 1987)
DC Comics: Nov, 1992 - No. 18, Apr, 1994 ($1.25)

1-18: 1-Giffen plots/breakdowns begin. 10-Darkseid app. Creeper in #3-6,9,11-13. 18-Spectre-c/s 3.00
Annual 1 (1993, $2.50, 68 pgs.)-Intro Prism 4.00
...: The Music of the Spheres TPB (2009, $19.99) r/stories from Countdown to Mystery #1-8 20.00

ECLIPSO: THE DARKNESS WITHIN
DC Comics: July, 1992 - No. 2, Oct, 1992 ($2.50, 68 pgs.)

1,2: 1-With purple gem attached to-c, 1-Without gem; Superman, Creeper app., 2-Concludes Eclipso storyline from annuals 4.00

EC SAMPLER - FREE COMIC BOOK DAY
Gemstone Publishing: May, 2008

Reprinted stories with restored color from Weird Science #6, Two-Fisted Tales #22, Crypt of Terror #17, Shock Suspenstories #6 3.00

E. C. 3-D CLASSICS (See Three Dimensional...)

ECTOKID (See Razorline)
Marvel Comics: Sept, 1993 - No. 9, May, 1994 ($1.75/$1.95)

1-($2.50)-Foil embossed-c; created by C. Barker 4.00
2-9: 2-Origin. 5-Saint Sinner x-over 3.00
...: Unleashed! 1 (10/94, $2.95, 52 pgs.) 4.00

ED "BIG DADDY" ROTH'S RATFINK COMIX (Also see Ratfink)
World of Fandom/ Ed Roth: 1991 - No. 3, 1991 ($2.50)

1-3: Regular Ed., 1-Limited double cover 1 3 4 6 8 10

EDDIE CAMPBELL'S BACCHUS
Eddie Campbell Comics: May, 1995 - No. 60, May, 2001 ($2.95, B&W)

1-Cerebus app. 1 2 3 5 6 8
1-2nd printing (5/97) 3.00
2-10: 9-Alex Ross back-c 5.00
11-60 3.00
Doing The Islands With Bacchus ('97, $17.95) 18.00
Earth, Water, Air & Fire ('98, $9.95) 10.00
King Bacchus ('99, $12.95) 13.00
The Eyeball Kid ('98, $8.50) 8.50

EDDIE STANKY (Baseball Hero)
Fawcett Publications: 1951 (New York Giants)

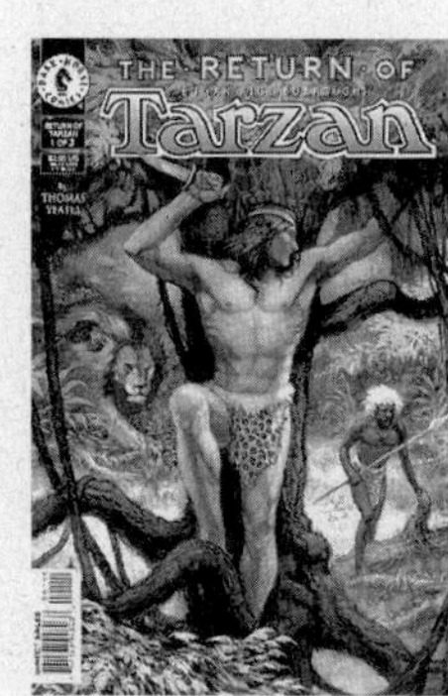

E.R.B.'s Tarzan: The Return of Tarzan #1 © ERB

Eerie #4 © AVON

Eerie #15 © WP

GD 2.0 | VG 4.0 | FN 6.0 | VF 8.0 | VF/NM 9.0 | NM- 9.2

nn-Photo-c 36 72 108 216 351 485

EDEN'S TRAIL
Marvel Comics: Jan, 2003 - No. 5, May 2003 ($2.99, unfinished lim. series, printed sideways)

1-5-Chuck Austen-s/Steve Uy-a 3.00

EDGAR ALLAN POE'S THE CONQUEROR WORM
Dark Horse Comics: Nov, 2012 ($3.99, one-shot)

1-Adaptation of Poe's poem; story and art by Richard Corben; Corben sketch pages 4.00

EDGAR ALLAN POE'S THE FALL OF THE HOUSE OF USHER
Dark Horse Comics: May, 2013 - No. 2, Jun, 2013 ($3.99, limited series)

1,2-Adaptation of Poe's poem; story and art by Richard Corben; Corben sketch pages 4.00

EDGAR ALLAN POE'S - THE FALL OF THE HOUSE OF USHER AND OTHER TALES OF HORROR
Catlan Communications Pub.: Sept. 1985 (hardcover graphic novel)

nn-Reprints of Poe story issues from Warren comic mags; all Richard Corben-a; numbered edition of 350 signed by Corben; 60 pgs. 130.00
nn-Softcover edition 60.00

EDGAR ALLAN POE'S THE PREMATURE BURIAL
Dark Horse Comics: Apr, 2014 ($3.99, one-shot)

1-Adaptation of The Premature Burial and The Cask of Amontillado; Corben-s/a/c 4.00

EDGAR ALLAN POE'S THE RAVEN AND THE RED DEATH
Dark Horse Comics: Oct, 2013 ($3.99, one-shot)

1-Adaptation of The Raven and The Masque of the Red Death; Corben-s/a/c 4.00

EDGAR BERGEN PRESENTS CHARLIE McCARTHY
Whitman Publishing Co. (Charlie McCarthy Co.): No. 764, 1938 (36 pgs.; 15x10-1/2"; color)

764 79 158 237 502 864 1225

EDGAR RICE BURROUGHS' TARZAN: A TALE OF MUGAMBI
Dark Horse Comics: 1995 ($2.95, one-shot)

1 3.00

EDGAR RICE BURROUGHS' TARZAN: IN THE LAND THAT TIME FORGOT AND THE POOL OF TIME
Dark Horse Comics: 1996 ($12.95, trade paperback)

nn-r/Russ Manning-a 13.00

EDGAR RICE BURROUGHS' TARZAN OF THE APES
Dark Horse Comics: May, 1999 ($12.95, trade paperback)

nn-reprints 13.00

EDGAR RICE BURROUGHS' TARZAN: THE LOST ADVENTURE
Dark Horse Comics: Jan, 1995 - No. 4, Apr, 1995 ($2.95, B&W, limited series)

1-4: ERB's last Tarzan story, adapted by Joe Lansdale 3.00
Hardcover (12/95, $19.95) 20.00
Limited Edition Hardcover ($99.95)-signed & numbered 100.00

EDGAR RICE BURROUGHS' TARZAN: THE RETURN OF TARZAN
Dark Horse Comics: May, 1997 - No. 3, July, 1997 ($2.95, limited series)

1-3 3.00

EDGAR RICE BURROUGHS' TARZAN: THE RIVERS OF BLOOD
Dark Horse Comics: Nov, 1999 - No. 4, Feb, 2000 ($2.95, limited series)

1-4-Kordey-c/a 3.00

EDGE
Malibu Comics (Bravura): July, 1994 - No. 3, Apr, 1995 ($2.50/$2.95, unfinished lim.series)

1,2-S. Grant-story & Gil Kane-c/a; w/Bravura stamp 3.00
3-($2.95-c) 3.00

EDGE (Re-titled as Vector starting with #13)
CrossGeneration Comics: May, 2002 - No. 12, Apr, 2003 ($9.95/$11.95/$7.95, TPB)

1-3: Reprints from various CrossGen titles 10.00
4-8-($11.95) 12.00
9-12-($7.95, 8-1/4" x 5-1/2") digest-sized reprints 8.00

EDGE OF CHAOS
Pacific Comics: July, 1983 - No. 3, Jan, 1984 (Limited series)

1-3-Morrow c/a; all contain nudity 3.00

EDGE OF DOOM (Horror anthology)
IDW Publishing: Oct, 2010 - No. 4, Mar, 2011 ($3.99)

1-5-Steve Niles-s/Kelley Jones-a 4.00

ED WHEELAN'S JOKE BOOK STARRING FAT & SLAT (See Fat & Slat)

GD 2.0 | VG 4.0 | FN 6.0 | VF 8.0 | VF/NM 9.0 | NM- 9.2

EERIE (Strange Worlds No. 18 on)
Avon Per.: No. 1, Jan, 1947; No. 1, May-June, 1951 - No. 17, Aug-Sept, 1954

1(1947)-1st supernatural comic; Kubert, Fugitani-a; bondage-c
541 1082 1623 3950 6975 10,000
1(1951)-Reprints story from 1947 #1 90 180 270 576 988 1400
2-Wood-c/a; bondage-c 92 184 276 584 1005 1425
3-Wood-c; Kubert, Wood/Orlando-a 90 180 270 576 988 1400
4,5-Wood-c 68 136 204 435 743 1050
6,8,13,14: 8-Kinstler-a; bondage-c; Phantom Witch Doctor story
40 80 120 246 411 575
7-Wood/Orlando-c; Kubert-a 53 106 159 334 567 800
9-Kubert-a; Check-c 42 84 126 265 445 625
10,11: 10-Kinstler-a. 11-Kinstlerish-a by McCann 40 80 120 246 411 575
12-Dracula story from novel, 25 pgs. 43 86 129 271 461 650
15-Reprints No. 1('51) minus-c(bondage) 28 56 84 165 270 375
16-Wood-a r-/No. 2 28 56 84 165 270 375
17-Wood/Orlando & Kubert-a; reprints #3 minus inside & outside Wood-c
28 56 84 165 270 375

NOTE: ***Hollingsworth** a-9-11; c-10, 11.*

EERIE
I. W. Enterprises: 1964

I.W. Reprint #1('64)-Wood-c(r); r-story/Spook #1 3 6 9 21 33 45
I.W. Reprint #2,6,8: 8-Dr. Drew by Grandenetti from Ghost #9
3 6 9 19 30 40
I.W. Reprint #9-r/Tales of Terror #1(Toby); Wood-c 4 8 12 23 37 50

EERIE (Magazine)(See Warren Presents)
Warren Publ. Co.: No. 1, Sept, 1965; No. 2, Mar, 1966 - No. 139, Feb, 1983

1-24 pgs., black & white, small size (5-1/4x7-1/4"), low distribution; cover from inside back cover of Creepy No. 2; stories reprinted from Creepy No. 7, 8. At least three different versions exist.
First Printing - B&W, 5-1/4" wide x 7-1/4" high, evenly trimmed. On page 18, panel 5, in the upper left-hand corner, the large rear view of a bald headed man blends into solid black and is unrecognizable. Overall printing quality is poor.
43 86 129 318 722 1125
Second Printing - B&W, 5-1/4x7-1/4", with uneven, untrimmed edges (if one of these were trimmed evenly, the size would be less than as indicated). The figure of the bald headed man on page 18, panel 5 is clear and discernible. The staples have a 1/4" blue stripe.
14 28 42 96 211 325

Other unauthorized reproductions for comparison's sake would be practically worthless. One known version was probably shot off a first printing copy with some loss of detail; the finer lines tend to disappear in this version which can be determined by looking at the lower right-hand corner of page one, first story. The roof of the house is shaded with straight lines. These lines are sharp and distinct on original, but broken on this version.

NOTE: ***The Overstreet Comic Book Price Guide** recommends that, before buying a 1st issue, you consult an expert.*

2-Frazetta-c; Toth-a; 1st app. host Cousin Eerie 10 20 30 66 138 210
3-Frazetta-c & half pg. ad (rerun in #4); Toth, Williamson, Ditko-a
8 16 24 56 108 160
4-7: 4-Frazetta-a (1/2 pg. ad). 5,7-Frazetta-c. Ditko-a in all.
6 12 18 37 66 95
8-Frazetta-c; Ditko-a 7 14 21 44 82 120
9-11,25: 9,10-Neal Adams-a, Ditko-a. 11-Karloff Mummy adapt.-Wood-s/a. 25-Steranko-c
6 12 18 38 69 100
12-16,18-22,24,32-35,40,45: 12,13,20-Poe-s. 12-Bloch-s. 12,15-Jones-a. 13-Lovecraft-s. 14,16-Toth-a. 16,19,24-Stoker-s. 16,32,33,43-Corben-a. 34-Early Boris-c. 35-Early Brunner-a. 35,40-Early Ploog-a. 40-Frankenstein; Ploog-a (6/72, 6 months before Marvel's series) 4 8 12 28 47 65
17-(low distribution) 19 38 57 131 291 450
23-Frazetta-c; Adams-a(reprint) 8 16 24 54 102 150
26-31,36-38,43,44 4 8 12 25 40 55
39,41: 39-1st Dax the Warrior; Maroto-a. 41-(low distribution)
5 10 15 30 50 70
42,51: 42-('73 Annual, 84 pgs.) Spooktacular; Williamson-a. 51-('74 Annual, 76 pgs.) Color poster insert; Toth-a 4 8 12 28 47 65
46,48: 46-Dracula series by Sutton begins; 2pgs. Vampirella. 48-Begin "Mummy Walks" and "Curse of the Werewolf" series (both continue in #49,50,52,53)
4 8 12 25 40 55
47,49,50,52,53: 47-Lilith. 49-Marvin the Dead Thing. 50-Satanna, Daughter of Satan. 52-Hunter by Neary begins. 53-Adams-a 4 8 12 23 37 50
54,55-Color insert Spirit story by Eisner, reprints sections 12/21/47 & 6/16/46
54-Dr. Archaeus series begins 3 6 9 19 30 40
56,57,59,63,69,77,78: All have 8 pg. slick color insert. 56,57,77-Corben-a. 59-(100 pgs.) Summer Special, all Dax issue. 69-Summer Special, all Hunter issue, Neary-a.
78-All Mummy issue 3 6 9 19 30 40
58,60,62,68,72,: 8 pg. slick color insert & Wrightson-a in all. 58,60,62-Corben-a. 60-Summer Giant (9/74, $1.25) 1st Exterminator One; Wood-a. 62-Mummies Walk. 68-Summer Special (84 pgs.) 3 6 9 21 33 45
61,64-67,71: 61-Mummies Walk-s, Wood-a. 64-Corben-a. 64,65,67-Toth-a. 65,66-El Cid.

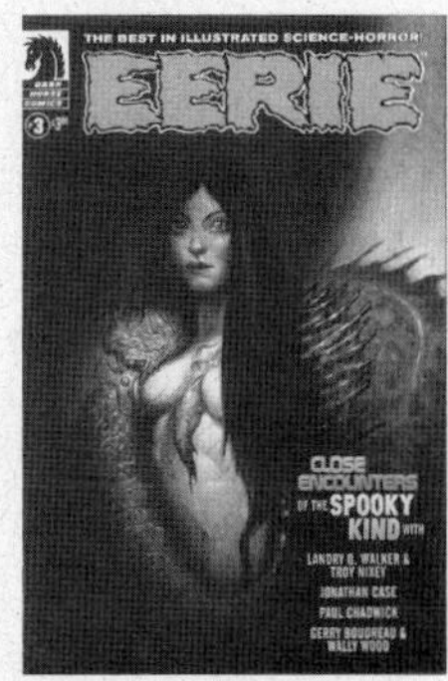

Eerie (2012 series) #3 © NCC

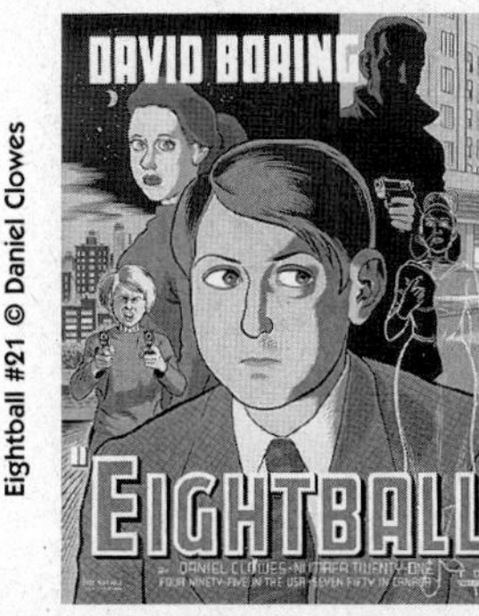

Eightball #21 © Daniel Clowes

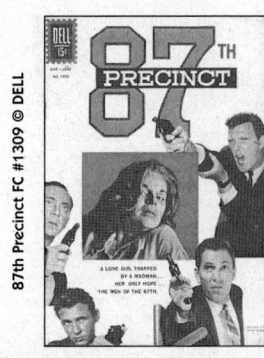

87th Precinct FC #1309 © DELL

GD VG FN VF VF/NM NM-
2.0 4.0 6.0 8.0 9.0 9.2

67-Hunter II. 71-Goblin-c/1st app. 3 6 9 17 26 35
70,73-75 3 6 9 14 20 26
76-1st app. Darklon the Mystic by Starlin-s/a 3 6 9 20 31 42
79,80-Origin Darklon the Mystic by Starlin 3 6 9 17 26 35
81,86,97: 81-Frazetta-c, King Kong; Corben-a. 86-(92 pgs.) All Corben issue. 97-Time Travel/ Dinosaur issue; Corben,Adams-a 3 6 9 16 23 30
82-Origin/1st app. The Rook 3 6 9 18 28 38
83,85,88,89,91-93,98,99: 98-Rook (31 pgs.). 99-1st Horizon Seekers. 2 4 6 10 14 18
84,87,90,96,100: 84,100-Starlin-a. 87-Hunter 3; Nino-a. 87,90-Corben-a. 96-Summer Special (92 pgs.). 100-(92 pgs.) Anniversary issue; Rook (30 pgs.) 2 4 6 13 18 22
94,95-The Rook & Vampirella team-up. 95-Vampirella-c; 1st MacTavish 3 6 9 16 24 32
101,106,112,115,118,120,121,128: 101-Return of Hunter II, Starlin-a. 106-Hard John Nuclear Hit Parade Special, Corben-a. 112-All Maroto issue, Luana-s. 115-All José Ortiz issues. 118-1st Haggarth. 120-1st Zud Kamish. 121-Hunter/Darklon. 128-Starlin-a, Hsu-a 2 4 6 10 14 18
102-105,107-111,113,114,116,117,119,122-124,126,127,129: 103-105,109-111-Gulacy-a. 104-Beast World. 2 4 6 9 13 16
125-(10/81, 84 pgs.) all Neal Adams issue 3 6 9 14 19 24
130-(76 pgs.) Vampirella-c/sty (54 pgs.); Pantha, Van Helsing, Huntress, Dax, Schreck, Hunter, Exterminator One, Rook app. 3 6 9 16 23 30
131-(Lower distr.); all Wood issue 3 6 9 14 20 26
132-134,136: 132-Rook returns. 133-All Ramon Torrents-a issue. 134,136-Color comic insert 2 4 6 10 14 18
135-(Lower distr., 10/82, 100 pgs.) All Ditko issue 3 6 9 14 20 26
137-139 (lower distr.):137-All Super-Hero issue. 138-Sherlock Holmes. 138,139-Color comic insert 2 4 6 13 18 22
Yearbook '70-Frazetta-c 5 10 15 33 57 80
Annual '71, '72-Reprints in both 4 8 12 25 40 55
... Archives - Volume One HC (Dark Horse, 3/09, $49.95, dustjacket) r/#1-5 50.00
... Archives - Volume Two HC (Dark Horse, 9/09, $49.95, dustjacket) r/#6-10; interview with Frank Frazetta from 1985 50.00

NOTE: *The above books contain art by many good artists:* **N. Adams, Brunner, Corben, Craig (Taycee), Crandall, Ditko, Eisner, Evans, Jeff Jones, Krenkel, McWilliams, Morrow, Orlando, Ploog, Severin, Starlin, Torres, Toth, Williamson, Wood,** *and* **Wrightson**; *covers by* **Bode', Corben, Davis, Frazetta, Morrow**, *and* **Orlando**. **Frazetta** *c-2, 3, 7, 8, 23. Annuals from 1973-on are included in regular numbering. 1970-74 Annuals are complete reprints. Annuals from 1975-on are in the format of the regular issues.*

EERIE
Dark Horse Comics: Jul, 2012 - Present ($2.99, B&W)

1-4-Sci-fi anthology by various. 2-Allred-a. 3-Wood-a(r). 4-Kelley Jones-a 3.00

EERIE ADVENTURES (Also see Weird Adventures)
Ziff-Davis Publ. Co.: Winter, 1951 (Painted-c)

1-Powell-a(2), McCann-a; used in **SOTI;** bondage-c; Krigstein back-c 61 122 183 390 670 950

NOTE: *Title dropped due to similarity to Avon's Eerie & legal action.*

EERIE TALES (Magazine)
Hastings Associates: 1959 (Black & White)

1-Williamson, Torres, Tuska-a, Powell(2), & Morrow(2)-a 17 34 51 98 154 210

EERIE TALES
Super Comics: 1963-1964

Super Reprint No. 10,11,12,18: 10('63)-r/Spook #27. Purple Claw in #11,12 ('63); #12-r/Avon's Eerie #1('51)-Kida-r 3 6 9 16 24 32
15-Wolverton-a, Spacehawk-r/Blue Bolt Weird Tales #113; Disbrow-a 4 8 12 28 47 65

EGBERT
Arnold Publications/Quality Comics Group: Spring, 1946 - No. 20, Aug, 1950

1-Funny animal; intro Egbert & The Count 20 40 60 117 189 260
2 11 22 33 64 90 115
3-10 9 18 27 50 65 80
11-20 8 16 24 40 50 60

EGON
Dark Horse Comics: Jan, 1998 - No.2, Feb, 1998 ($2.95, limited series)

1,2-Horley-painted-c 3.00

EGYPT
DC Comics (Vertigo): Aug, 1995 - No.7, Feb, 1996 ($2.50, lim. series, mature)

1-7: Milligan scripts in all. 3.00

EH! (...Dig This Crazy Comic) (From Here to Insanity No. 8 on)
Charlton Comics: Dec, 1953 - No. 7, Nov-Dec, 1954 (Satire)

1-Davis-*ish*-c/a by Ayers, Wood-*ish*-a by Giordano; Atomic Mouse app. 39 78 117 240 395 550
2-Ayers-c/a 23 46 69 136 223 310
3,5,7 21 42 63 122 199 275
4,6: Sexual innuendo-c. 6-Ayers-a 22 44 66 128 209 290

EIGHTBALL (Also see David Boring)
Fantagraphics Books: Oct, 1989 - Present ($2.75/$2.95/$3.95, semi-annually, mature)

1 (1st printing) Daniel Clowes-s/a in all 2 4 6 8 10 12
2,3 1 2 3 5 6 8
4-8 6.00
9-19: 17-(8/96) 4.00
20-($4.50) 4.50
21-($4.95) Concludes David Boring 3-parter 5.00
22-($5.95) 29 short stories 6.00
23-($7.00, 9" x 12") The Death Ray 7.00
Twentieth Century Eightball (2002, $19.00) r/Clowes strips 19.00

EIGHTH WONDER, THE
Dark Horse Comics: Nov, 1997 ($2.95, one-shot)

nn-Reprints stories from Dark Horse Presents #85-87 3.00

EIGHT IS ENOUGH KITE FUN BOOK (See Kite Fun Book 1979 in the Promotional Comics section)

EIGHT LEGGED FREAKS
DC Comics (WildStorm): 2002 ($6.95, one-shot, squarebound)

nn-Adaptation of 2002 mutant spider movie; Joe Phillips-a; intro by Dean Devlin 7.00

80 PAGE GIANT (...Magazine No. 2-15)
National Periodical Publications: 8/64 - No. 15, 10/65; No. 16, 11/65 - No. 89, 7/71 (25¢) (All reprints) (#1-56: 84 pgs.; #57-89: 68 pgs.)

1-Superman Annual; originally planned as Superman Annual #9 (8/64) 34 68 102 243 542 840
2-Jimmy Olsen 18 36 54 124 275 425
3,4: 3-Lois Lane. 4-Flash-G.A.-r; Infantino-a 15 30 45 100 220 340
5-Batman; has Sunday newspaper strip; Catwoman-r; Batman's Life Story-r (25th anniversary special) 15 30 45 100 220 340
6-Superman 13 26 39 87 191 295
7-Sgt. Rock's Prize Battle Tales; Kubert-c/a 21 42 63 147 324 500
8-More Secret Origins-origins of JLA, Aquaman, Robin, Atom, & Superman; Infantino-a 26 52 78 182 404 625
9-15: 9-Flash (r/Flash #106,117,123 & Showcase #14); Infantino-a. 10-Superboy. 11-Superman; all Luthor issue. 12-Batman; has Sunday newspaper strip. 13-Jimmy Olsen. 14-Lois Lane. 15-Superman and Batman; Joker-c/story 12 24 36 82 179 275

Continued as part of regular series under each title in which that particular book came out, a Giant being published instead of the regular size. Issues No. 16 to No. 89 are listed for your information. See individual titles for prices. 16-JLA #39 (11/65), 17-Batman #176, 18-Superman #183, 19-Our Army at War #164, 20-Action #334, 21-Flash #160, 22-Superboy #129, 23-Superman #187, 24-Batman #182, 25-Jimmy Olsen #95, 26-Lois Lane #68, 27-Batman #185, 28-World's Finest #161, 29-JLA #48, 30-Batman #187, 31-Superman #193, 32-Our Army at War #177, 33-Action #347, 34-Flash #169, 35-Superboy #138, 36-Superman #197, 37-Batman #193, 38-Jimmy Olsen #104, 39-Lois Lane #77, 40-World's Finest #170, 41-JLA #58, 42-Superman #202, 43-Batman #198, 44-Our Army at War #190, 45-Action #360, 46-Flash #178, 47-Superboy #147, 48-Superman #207, 49-Batman #203, 50-Jimmy Olsen #113, 51-Lois Lane #86, 52-World's Finest #179, 53-JLA #67, 54-Superman #212, 55-Batman #208, 56-Our Army at War #203, 57-Action #373, 58-Flash #187, 59-Superboy #156, 60-Superman #217, 61-Batman #213, 62-Jimmy Olsen #122, 63-Lois Lane #95, 64-World's Finest #188, 65-JLA #76, 66-Superman #222, 67-Batman #218, 68-Our Army at War #216, 69-Adventure #390, 70-Flash #196, 71-Superboy #165, 72-Superman #227, 73-Batman #223, 74-Jimmy Olsen #131, 75-Lois Lane #104, 76-World's Finest #197, 77-JLA #85, 78-Superman #232, 79-Batman #228, 80-Our Army at War #229, 81-Adventure #403, 82-Flash #205, 83-Superboy #174, 84-Superman #239, 85-Batman #233, 86-Jimmy Olsen #140, 87-Lois Lane #113, 88-World's Finest #206, 89-JLA #93.

87TH PRECINCT (TV) (Based on the Ed McBain novels)
Dell Publishing Co.: Apr-June, 1962 - No. 2, July-Sept, 1962

Four Color 1309(#1)-Krigstein-a 9 18 27 57 111 165
2-Photo-c 7 14 21 43 89 130

EL BOMBO COMICS
Standard Comics/Frances M. McQueeny: 1946

nn(1946), 1(no date) 15 30 45 85 130 175

EL CAZADOR
CrossGen Comics: Oct, 2003 - No. 6, Jun, 2004 ($2.95)

1-Dixon-s/Epting-a 5.00
2-6: 5-Lady Death preview 3.00
...: The Bloody Ballad of Blackjack Tom 1 (4/04, $2.95, one-shot) Cariello-a 3.00

EL CID
Dell Publishing Co.: No. 1259, 1961

Four Color 1259-Movie, photo-c 6 12 18 41 76 110

Electric Warrior #8 © DC

Elektra #19 © MAR

Elephantmen #54 © Active Images

	GD	VG	FN	VF	VF/NM	NM-
	2.0	4.0	6.0	8.0	9.0	9.2

EL DIABLO (See All-Star Western #2 & Weird Western Tales #12)
DC Comics: Aug, 1989 - No. 16, Jan, 1991 ($1.50-$1.75, color)

1 ($2.50, 52pgs.)-Masked hero 4.00
2-16 3.00

EL DIABLO
DC Comics (Vertigo): Mar, 2001 - No. 4, Jun, 2001 ($2.50, limited series)

1-4-Azzarello-s/Zezelj-a/Sale-c 3.00
TPB (2008, $12.99) r/#1-4 13.00

EL DIABLO
DC Comics: Nov, 2008 - No. 6, Apr, 2009 ($2.99, limited series)

1-6-Nitz-s/Hester-a/c. 4,5-Freedom Fighters app. 3.00
...: The Haunted Horseman TPB (2009, $17.99) r/#1-6 18.00

EL DORADO (See Movie Classics)

ELECTRIC ANT
Marvel Comics: Jun, 2010 - No. 5, Oct, 2010 ($3.99, Baxter paper)

1-5-Based on a Philip K. Dick story; David Mack-s/Pascal Alixe-a; Paul Pope-c 4.00

ELECTRIC UNDERTOW (See Strikeforce Morituri: Electric Undertow)

ELECTRIC WARRIOR
DC Comics: May, 1986 - No. 18, Oct, 1987 ($1.50, Baxter paper)

1-18 3.00

ELECTROPOLIS
Image Comics: May, 2001 - No. 4, Jan, 2003 ($2.95/$5.95)

1-3-Dean Motter-s/a. 3-(12/01) 3.00
4-(1/03, $5.95, 72 pages) The Infernal Machine pts. 4-6 6.00

ELEKTRA (Also see Daredevil #319-325)
Marvel Comics: Mar, 1995 - No. 4, June, 1995 ($2.95, limited series)

1-4-Embossed-c; Scott McDaniel-a 4.00

ELEKTRA (Also see Daredevil)
Marvel Comics: Nov, 1996 - No. 19, Jun, 1998 ($1.95)

1-Peter Milligan scripts; Deodato-c/a 4.00
1-Variant-c 6.00
2-19: 4-Dr. Strange-c/app. 10-Logan-c/app. 3.00
#(-1) Flashback (7/97) Matt Murdock-c/app.; Deodato-c/a 3.00
.../Cyblade (Image, 3/97,$2.95) Devil's Reign pt. 7 3.00

ELEKTRA (Vol. 2) (Marvel Knights)
Marvel Comics: Sept, 2001 - No. 35, Jun, 2004 ($3.50/$2.99)

1-Bendis-s/Austen-a/Horn-c 4.00
2-6: 2-Two covers (Sienkiewicz and Horn) 3,4-Silver Samurai app. 3.00
3-Initial printing with panel of nudity; most copies pulped 30.00
7-35: 7-Rucka-s begin. 9,10,17-Bennett-a. 19-Meglia-a. 23-25-Chen-a; Sienkiewicz-c 3.00
...Vol. 1: Introspect TPB (2002, $16.99) r/#10-15; Marvel Knights: Double Shot #3 17.00
...Vol. 2: Everything Old is New Again TPB (2003, $16.99) r/#16-22 17.00
...Vol. 3: Relentless TPB (2004, $14.99) r/#23-28 15.00
...Vol. 4: Frenzy TPB (2004, $17.99) r/#29-35 18.00

ELEKTRA & WOLVERINE: THE REDEEMER
Marvel Comics: Jan, 2002 - No. 3, Mar, 2002 ($5.95, square-bound, lim. series)

1-3-Greg Rucka-s/Yoshitaka Amano-a/c 6.00
HC (5/02, $29.95, with dustjacket) r/#1-3, interview with Greg Rucka 30.00

ELEKTRA: ASSASSIN (Also see Daredevil)
Marvel Comics (Epic Comics): Aug, 1986 - No. 8, June, 1987 (Limited series, mature)

1,8-Miller scripts in all; Sienkiewicz-c/a. 6.00
2-7 5.00
Signed & numbered hardcover (Graphitti Designs, $39.95, 2000 print run)- reprints 1-8 60.00
TPB (2000, $24.95) 25.00

ELEKTRA: GLIMPSE & ECHO
Marvel Comics: Sept, 2002 - No. 4, Dec, 2002 ($2.99, limited series)

1-4-Scott Morse-s/painted-a 3.00

ELEKTRA LIVES AGAIN (Also see Daredevil)
Marvel Comics (Epic Comics): 1990 ($24.95, oversize, hardcover, 76 pgs.)(Produced by Graphitti Designs)

nn-Frank Miller-c/a/scripts; Lynn Varley painted-a; Matt Murdock & Bullseye app. 40.00
2nd printing (9/02, $24.99) 25.00

ELEKTRA MEGAZINE
Marvel Comics: Nov, 1996 - No. 2, Dec, 1996 ($3.95, 96 pgs., reprints, limited series)

1,2: Reprints Frank Miller's Elektra stories in Daredevil 4.00

	GD	VG	FN	VF	VF/NM	NM-
	2.0	4.0	6.0	8.0	9.0	9.2

ELEKTRA SAGA, THE
Marvel Comics Group: Feb, 1984 - No. 4, June, 1984 ($2.00, limited series, Baxter paper)

1-4-r/Daredevil 168-190; Miller-c/a 5.00

ELEKTRA: THE HAND
Marvel Comics: Nov, 2004 - No. 5, Feb, 2005 ($2.99, limited series)

1-5-Gossett-a/Sienkiewicz-c/Yoshida-s; origin of the Hand in the 16th century 3.00

ELEKTRA: THE MOVIE
Marvel Comics: Feb, 2005 ($5.99)

1-Movie adaptation; McKeever-s/Perkins-a; photo-c 6.00
TPB (2005, $12.95) r/movie adaptation, Daredevil #168, 181 & Elektra #(-1) 13.00

ELEMENTALS, THE (See The Justice Machine & Morningstar Spec.)
Comico The Comic Co. : June, 1984 - No. 29, Sept, 1988; V2#1, Mar, 1989 - No. 28, 1994? ($1.50/$2.50, Baxter paper); V3#1, Dec, 1995 - No. 3 ($2.95)

1-Willingham-c/a, 1-8 5.00
2-29, V2#1-28: 9-Bissette-a(p). 10-Photo-c. V2#6-1st app. Strike Force America. 18-Prelude to Avalon mini-series. 27-Prequel to Strike Force America series 3.00
V3#1-3: 1-Daniel-a(p), bagged w/gaming card 3.00
Lingerie (5/96, $2.95) 3.00
Special 1,2 (3/86, 1/89)-1-Willingham-a(p) 3.00

ELEMENTALS: (Title series), **Comico**

--GHOST OF A CHANCE, 12/95 ($5.95)-graphic novel, nn-Ross-c. 6.00
--HOW THE WAR WAS WON, 6/96 - No. 2, 8/96 ($2.95) 1,2-Tony Daniel-a, & 1-Variant-c; no logo 3.00
--SEX SPECIAL, 1991 - No. 4, Feb, 1993 ($2.95, color) 2 covers for each 3.00
--SEX SPECIAL, 5/97 - No. 2, 6/97 ($2.95, B&W) 1-Tony Daniel, Jeff Moy-a, 2-Robb Phipps, Adam McDaniel-a 3.00
--SWIMSUIT SPECTACULAR 1996, 6/96 ($2.95), 1-pin-ups, 1-Variant-c; no logo 3.00
--THE VAMPIRE'S REVENGE, 6/96 - No. 2 8/96 ($2.95) 1,2-Willingham-s, 1-Variant-c; no logo 3.00

ELEPHANTMEN
Image Comics: July, 2006 - Present ($2.99/$3.50/$3.99) (Flip covers on most)

1-16: 1-Starkings-s/Moritat-a/Ladronn-c. 6-Campbell flip-c. 15-Sale flip-c 4.00
17-30-($3.50) 25-Flip book preview of Marineman 4.00
31-49,51-55-($3.99) 32-Conan/Red Sonja homage. 33-Shaky Kane-c/a. 42-44-Dave Sim-a (5 pgs.) 4.00
50-($5.99) Flip book with reprint of #1; cover gallery 6.00
...: Man and Elephantman 1 (3/11, $3.99) Three covers 4.00
...: The Pilot (5/07, $2.99) short stories and pin-ups by various incl. Sale, Jim Lee, Jae Lee 4.00
...: War Toys (11/07 - No. 3, 4/08, $2.99) 1-3-Mappo war; Starkings-s/Moritat-a/Ladronn-c 4.00
... War Toys: Yvette (7/09, $3.50) Starkings-s/Moritat-a 4.00
Giant-Size Elephantmen 1 (10/11, $5.99) r/#31,32 & Man and Elephantman; Campbell-c 6.00

1111 (ELEVEN ELEVEN)
Crusade Entertainment: Oct, 1996 ($2.95, B&W, one-shot)

1-Wrightson-c/a 4.00

ELEVEN OR ONE
Sirius: Apr, 1995 ($2.95)

	GD	VG	FN	VF	VF/NM	NM-
1-Linsner-c/a	1	3	4	6	8	10
1-(6/96) 2nd printing						3.50

ELFLORD
Nightwind Productions: Jun, 1980 - Vol. 2 #1, 1982 (B&W, magazine-size)

	GD	VG	FN	VF	VF/NM	NM-
1-1st Barry Blair-s/c/a in comics; B&W-c; limited print run for all	10	20	30	64	132	200
2-5-B&W-c	5	10	15	31	53	75
6-14: 9-14-Color-c	4	8	12	27	44	60
Vol. 2 #1 (1982)	4	8	12	23	37	50

ELFLORD
Aircel Publ.: 1986 - No. 6, Oct, 1989 ($1.70, B&W); V2#1- V2#31, 1995 ($2.00)

1 4.00
2-4,V2#1-20,22-30: 4-6: Last B&W issue. V2#1-Color-a begin. 22-New cast. 25-Begin B&W 3.00
1,2-2nd printings 3.00
21-Double size ($4.95) 5.00

ELFLORD
Warp Graphics: Jan, 1997-No.4, Apr, 1997 ($2.95, B&W, mini-series)

1-4 3.00

ElfQuest #23 © Warp Graphics

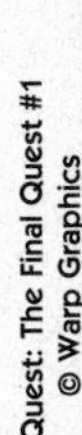
ElfQuest: The Final Quest #1 © Warp Graphics

Ellery Queen #2 © Z-D

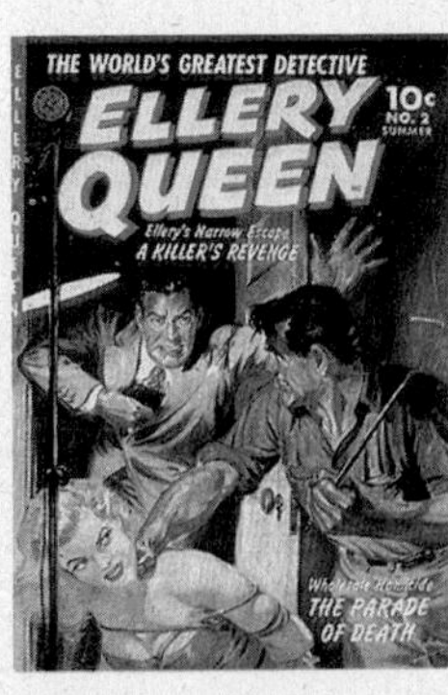

GD VG FN VF VF/NM NM-
2.0 4.0 6.0 8.0 9.0 9.2

ELFLORD (CUTS LOOSE) (Vol. 2)
Warp Graphics: Sept, 1997 - No. 7, Apr, 1998 ($2.95, B&W, mini-series)
1-7 3.00

ELFLORD: DRAGON'S EYE
Night Wynd Enterprises: 1993 ($2.50, B&W)
1 3.00

ELFLORD: THE RETURN
Mad Monkey Press: 1996 ($6.95, magazine size)
1 7.00

ELFQUEST (Also see Fantasy Quarterly & Warp Graphics Annual)
Warp Graphics, Inc.: No. 2, Aug, 1978 - No. 21, Feb, 1985 (All magazine size)
No. 1, Apr, 1979
NOTE: ***Elfquest*** was originally published as one of the stories in **Fantasy Quarterly** #1. When the publisher went out of business, the creative team, Wendy and Richard Pini, formed WaRP Graphics and continued the series, beginning with **Elfquest** #2. **Elfquest** #1, which reprinted the story from **Fantasy Quarterly**, was published about the same time **Elfquest** #4 was released. Thereafter, most issues were reprinted as demand warranted, until Marvel announced it would reprint the entire series under its Epic imprint (Aug., 1985).

1(4/79)-Reprints Elfquest story from Fantasy Quarterly No. 1
1st printing ($1.00-c) 5 10 15 35 63 90
2nd printing ($1.25-c) 2 4 6 9 12 15
3rd printings ($1.50-c) 1 2 3 5 6 8
4th printing; different-c ($1.50-c) 5.00
2(8/78) 1st printing ($1.00-c) 3 6 9 27 44 60
2nd printings ($1.25-c) 6.00
3rd & 4th printings ($1.50-c)(all 4th prints 1989) 5.00
3-5: 1st printings ($1.00-c) 3 6 9 16 23 30
6-9: 1st printings ($1.25-c) 3 6 9 14 20 25
2nd & 3rd printings ($1.50-c) 5.00
10-21: ($1.50-c); 16-8pg. preview of A Distant Soil 2 4 6 11 16 20
10-14: 2nd printings ($1.50) 5.00

ELFQUEST
Marvel Comics (Epic Comics): Aug, 1985 - No. 32, Mar, 1988
1-Reprints in color the Elfquest epic by Warp Graphics 5.00
2-32 4.00

ELFQUEST
DC Comics: 2003 - 2005
Archives Vol. 1 (2003, $49.95, HC) r/#1-5 50.00
Archives Vol. 2 (2005, $49.95, HC) r/#6-10 & Epic Illustrated #1 50.00
25th Anniversary Special (2003, $2.95) r/Elfquest #1 (Apr, 1979); interview w/Pinis 4.00

ELFQUEST (Title series), Warp Graphics
'89 - No. 4, '89 ($1.50, B&W) 1-4: R-original Elfquest series 4.00

ELFQUEST (Volume 2),**Warp Graphics:** V2#1, 5/96 - No. 33, 2/99 ($4.95/$2.95, B&W)
V2#1-31: 1,3,5,8,10,12,13,18,21,23,25-Wendy Pini-c 6.00
32,33-($2.95-c) 4.00

--BLOOD OF TEN CHIEFS, 7/93 - No. 20, 9/95 ($2.00/$2.50)
1-20-By Richard & Wendy Pini 4.00

--HIDDEN YEARS, 5/92 - No. 29, 3/96 ($2.00/$2.25)1-9,9 1/2, 10-29 4.00

--JINK, 11/94 - No. 12, 2/6 ($2.25/$2.50) 1-12-W. Pini/John Byrne-back-c 4.00

--KAHVI, 10/95 - No. 6,3/96 ($2.25, B&W) 1-6 4.00

--KINGS CROSS, 11/97 - No. 2, 12/97 ($2.95, B&W) 1,2 4.00

--KINGS OF THE BROKEN WHEEL, 6/90 - No. 9, 2/92 ($2.00, B&W) (3rd Elfquest saga)
1-9: By R. & W. Pini; 1-Color insert 5.00
1-2nd printing 4.00

--METAMORPHOSIS, 4/96 ($2.95, B&W) 1 4.00

--NEW BLOOD (...Summer Special on-c #1 only), 8/92 - No. 35, 1/96 ($2.00-$2.50, color/B&W) 1-($3.95, 68 pgs.,...Summer Special on-c)-Byrne-a/scripts (16 pgs.) 5.00
2-35: Barry Blair-a in all 4.00
1993 Summer Special ($3.95) Byrne-a/scripts 5.00

--SHARDS, 8/94 - No. 16, 3/96 ($2.25/$2.50) 1-16 4.00

--SIEGE AT BLUE MOUNTAIN, WaRP Graphics/Apple 3/87 - No. 8, 12/88 (1.75/ $1.95, B&W)
1-Staton-a(i) in all; 2nd Elfquest saga 1 2 3 5 6 8
1-3-2nd printing 4.00
2-8 5.00

--THE REBELS, 11/94 - No. 12, 3/96 ($2.25/$2.50, B&W/color) 1-12 4.00

--TWO-SPEAR, 10/95 - No. 5, 2/96 ($2.25, B&W) 1-5 4.00

--WAVE DANCERS, 12/93 - No. 6, 3/96, 1-6: 1-Foil-c & poster 4.00
Special 1 ($2.95) 4.00

GD VG FN VF VF/NM NM-
2.0 4.0 6.0 8.0 9.0 9.2

--WORLDPOOL, 7/97 ($2.95, B&W) 1-Richard Pini-s/Barry Blair-a 4.00

ELFQUEST: THE DISCOVERY
DC Comics: Mar, 2006 - No. 4, Sept, 2006 ($3.99, limited series)
1-4-Wendy Pini-a/Wendy & Richard Pini-s 5.00
TPB (2006, $14.99) r/#1-4 15.00

ELFQUEST: THE FINAL QUEST
Dark Horse Comics: Oct, 2013; No. 1, Jan, 2014 - Present ($3.50)
1,2-Wendy Pini-a/Wendy & Richard Pini-s 3.50
... Special (10/13, $5.99) Wendy Pini-a/Wendy & Richard Pini-s; prologue to series 6.00

ELFQUEST: THE GRAND QUEST
DC Comics: 2004 - No. 14, 2006 ($9.95/$9.99, B&W, digest-size)
Vol. 1-6 ('04)1-r/Elfquest #1-5; new W. Pini-c. 2-r/#5-8. 3-r/#8-11. 4-r/#11-15. 5-r/#15-18 6-r/#18-20 10.00
Vol. 7-9 ('05) 1-r/Siege At Blue Mountain #1-3. 8-r/SABM #3-5. 9-r/SABM #6-8 10.00
Vol. 10-14 ('05) 10-r/Kings of the Broken Wheel #1-3. 11-KotBW #5-7 & Frazetta Fant. Ill. 12-r/Kings of the Broken Wheel #8&9. 13-r/Elfquest V2 #4-18. 14-r/Hidden Years #4-9 1/2 10.00

ELFQUEST: THE SEARCHER AND THE SWORD
DC Comics: 2004 ($24.95/$14.99, graphic novel)
HC (2004, $24.95, with dust jacket)-Wendy and Richard Pini-s/a/c 25.00
SC (2004, $14.99) 15.00

ELFQUEST: WOLFRIDER
DC Comics: 2003 - No. 2, 2003 ($9.95, digest-size)
Volume 1 ('03, $9.95, digest-size) r/Elfquest V2#19,21,23,25,27,29,31; Blood of Ten Chiefs #2; Hidden Years #5; New Blood Special #1; New Blood 1993 Special #1; new W. Pini-c 10.00
Volume 2 ('03, $9.95, digest-size) r/Elfquest V2#33; Blood of Ten Chiefs #10,11,19; Warp Graphics Annual #1 10.00

ELF-THING
Eclipse Comics: March, 1987 ($1.50, B&W, one-shot)
1 3.00

ELIMINATOR (Also see The Solution #16 & The Night Man #16)
Malibu Comics (Ultraverse): Apr, 1995 - No. 3, Jul, 1995 ($2.95/$2.50, lim. series)
0-Mike Zeck-a in all 3.00
1-3-($2.50): 1-1st app. Siren 3.00
1-($3.95)-Black cover edition 4.00

ELIMINATOR FULL COLOR SPECIAL
Eternity Comics: Oct, 1991 ($2.95, one-shot)
1-Dave Dorman painted-c 3.00

ELLA CINDERS (See Comics On Parade, Comics Revue #1,4, Famous Comics Cartoon Book, Giant Comics Editions, Sparkler Comics, Tip Top & Treasury of Comics)

ELLA CINDERS
United Features Syndicate: 1938 - 1940
Single Series 3(1938) 41 82 123 256 428 600
Single Series 21(#2 on-c, #21 on inside), 28('40) 36 72 108 216 351 485

ELLA CINDERS
United Features Syndicate: Mar, 1948 - No. 5, Mar, 1949
1-(#2 on cover) 14 28 42 82 121 160
2 10 20 30 56 76 95
3-5 8 16 24 42 54 65

ELLERY QUEEN
Superior Comics Ltd.: May, 1949 - No. 4, Nov, 1949
1-Kamen-c; L.B. Cole-a; r-in Haunted Thrills 52 104 156 328 557 785
2-4: 3-Drug use stories(2) 39 78 117 240 395 550
NOTE: *Iger shop art in all issues.*

ELLERY QUEEN (TV)
Ziff-Davis Publishing Co.: 1-3/52 (Spring on-c) - No. 2, Summer/52 (Saunders painted-c)
1-Saunders-c 47 94 141 296 498 700
2-Saunders bondage, torture-c 39 78 117 231 378 525

ELLERY QUEEN (Also see Crackajack Funnies No. 23)
Dell Publishing Co.: No. 1165, Mar-May, 1961 - No.1289, Apr, 1962
Four Color 1165 (#1) 9 18 27 58 114 175
Four Color 1243 (11/61-1/62), 1289 7 14 21 48 89 130

ELMER FUDD (Also see Camp Comics, Daffy, Looney Tunes #1 & Super Book #10, 22)
Dell Publishing Co.: No. 470, May, 1953 - No. 1293, Mar-May, 1962
Four Color 470 (#1) 9 18 27 58 114 170
Four Color 558,628,689('56) 5 10 15 34 60 85

Elseworlds 80-Page Giant #1 © DC

E-Man #3 © CC

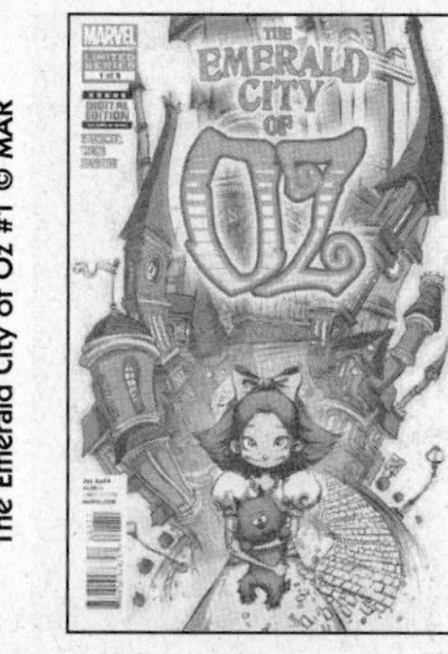

The Emerald City of Oz #1 © MAR

	GD 2.0	VG 4.0	FN 6.0	VF 8.0	VF/NM 9.0	NM- 9.2

Four Color 725,783,841,888,938,977,1032,1081,1131,1171,1222,1293('62)
4 8 12 28 47 65

ELMO COMICS
St. John Publishing Co.: Jan, 1948 (Daily strip-r)

1-By Cecil Jensen 11 22 33 60 83 105

ELONGATED MAN (See Flash #112 & Justice League of America #105)
DC Comics: Jan, 1992 - No. 4, Apr, 1992 ($1.00, limited series)

1-4: 3-The Flash app. 3.00

ELRIC (Of Melnibone)(See First Comics Graphic Novel #6 & Marvel Graphic Novel #2)
Pacific Comics: Apr, 1983 - No. 6, Apr, 1984 ($1.50, Baxter paper)

1-6: Russell-c/a(i) in all 3.00

ELRIC
Topps Comics: 1996 ($2.95, one-shot)

0-One Life: Russell-c/a; adapts Neil Gaiman's short story "One Life--Furnished in Early Moorcock." 3.00

ELRIC, SAILOR ON THE SEAS OF FATE
First Comics: June, 1985 - No. 7, June, 1986 ($1.75, limited series)

1-7: Adapts Michael Moorcock's novel 3.00

ELRIC, STORMBRINGER
Dark Horse Comics/Topps Comics: 1997 - No. 7, 1997 ($2.95, limited series)

1-7: Russell-c/s/a; adapts Michael Moorcock's novel 3.00

ELRIC: THE BALANCE LOST
BOOM! Studios: Jul, 2011 - No. 12, Jun, 2012 ($3.99)

1-12: 1-Roberson-s/Biagini-a; four covers. 2-11-Three covers 4.00

ELRIC: THE BANE OF THE BLACK SWORD
First Comics: Aug, 1988 - No. 6, June, 1989 ($1.75/$1.95, limited series)

1-6: Adapts Michael Moorcock's novel 3.00

ELRIC: THE VANISHING TOWER
First Comics: Aug, 1987 - No. 6, June, 1988 ($1.75, limited series)

1-6: Adapts Michael Moorcock's novel 3.00

ELRIC: WEIRD OF THE WHITE WOLF
First Comics: Oct, 1986 - No. 5, June, 1987 ($1.75, limited series)

1-5: Adapts Michael Moorcock's novel 3.00

EL SALVADOR - A HOUSE DIVIDED
Eclipse Comics: March, 1989 ($2.50, B&W, Baxter paper, stiff-c, 52 pgs.)

1-Gives history of El Salvador 4.00

ELSEWHERE PRINCE, THE (Moebius' Airtight Garage)
Marvel Comics (Epic): May, 1990 - No. 6, Oct, 1990 ($1.95, limited series)

1-6: Moebius scripts & back-up-a in all 3.00

ELSEWORLDS 80-PAGE GIANT (See DC Comics Presents: ... for reprint)
DC Comics: Aug, 1999 ($5.95, one-shot)

1-Most copies destroyed by DC over content of the "Superman's Babysitter" story; some UK shipments sold before recall 11 22 33 76 163 250

ELSEWORLD'S FINEST
DC Comics: 1997 - No. 2, 1997 ($4.95, limited series)

1,2: Elseworld's story-Superman & Batman in the 1920's 5.00

ELSEWORLD'S FINEST: SUPERGIRL & BATGIRL
DC Comics: 1998 ($5.95, one-shot)

1-Haley-a 6.00

ELSIE THE COW
D. S. Publishing Co.: Oct-Nov, 1949 - No. 3, July-Aug, 1950

1-(36 pgs.) 27 54 81 158 259 360
2,3 19 38 57 109 172 235

ELSINORE
Alias Entertainment: Apr, 2005 - No. 5, Apr, 2006 (75¢/$2.99/$3.25)

1-5: 1-(75¢-c) Brian Denham-a/Kenneth Lillie-Paetz-s. 2-($2.99-c). 4-($3.25-c) 5-Sparacio-a 3.25

ELSON'S PRESENTS
DC Comics: 1981 (100 pgs., no cover price)

Series 1-6: Repackaged 1981 DC comics; 1-DC Comics Presents #29, Flash #303, Batman #331. 2-Superman #335, Ghosts #96, Justice League of America #186. 3-New Teen Titans #3, Secrets of Haunted House #32, Wonder Woman #275. 4-Secrets of the LSH #1, Brave & the Bold #170, New Adv. of Superboy #13. 5-LSH #271, Green Lantern #136, Super Friends #40. 6-Action #515, Mystery in Space #115, Detective #498
2 4 6 11 16 20

ELVEN (Also see Prime)
Malibu Comics (Ultraverse): Oct, 1994 - No. 4, Feb, 1995 ($2.50, lim. series)

0 ($2.95)-Prime app. 3.00
1-4: 2,4-Prime app. 3-Primevil app. 3.00
1-Limited Foil Edition- no price on cover 4.00

ELVIRA MISTRESS OF THE DARK
Marvel Comics: Oct, 1988 ($2.00, B&W, magazine size)

1-Movie adaptation 5.00

ELVIRA MISTRESS OF THE DARK
Claypool Comics (Eclipse): May, 1993 - No. 166, Feb, 2007 ($2.50, B&W)

1-Austin-a(i). Spiegle-a 6.00
2-6: Spiegle-a 4.00
7-99,101-166-Photo-c: 3.00
100-(8/01) Kurt Busiek back-up-s; art by DeCarlo and others 4.00
TPB ($12.95) 13.00

ELVIRA'S HOUSE OF MYSTERY
DC Comics: Jan, 1986 - No. 11, Jan, 1987

1,11: 11-Dave Stevens-c 2 4 6 8 10 12
2-10: 9-Photo-c, Special 1 (3/87, $1.25) 6.00

ELVIS MANDIBLE, THE
DC Comics (Piranha Press): 1990 ($3.50, 52 pgs., B&W, mature)

nn 4.00

ELVIS PRESLEY (See Career Girl Romances #32, Go-Go, Howard Chaykin's American Flagg #10, Humbug #8, I Love You #60 & Young Lovers #18)

EL ZOMBO FANTASMA
Dark Horse Comics (Rocket Comics): Apr, 2004 - No. 3, June, 2004 ($2.99)

1-3-Wilkins-s&a/Munroe-s 3.00

E-MAN
Charlton Comics: Oct, 1973 - No. 10, Sept, 1975 (Painted-c No. 7-10)

1-Origin & 1st app. E-Man; Staton c/a in all 3 6 9 16 23 30
2-5: 2,4,5-Ditko-a. 3-Howard-a. 5-Miss Liberty Belle app. by Ditko
2 4 6 9 12 15
6-10: 6,7,9,10-Early Byrne-a (#6 is 1/75). 6-Disney parody. 8-Full-length story; Nova begins as E-Man's partner 2 4 6 11 16 20
1-4,9,10 (Modern Comics reprints, '77) 5.00

NOTE: *Killjoy app.-No. 2, 4. Liberty Belle app.-No. 5. Rog 2000 app.-No. 6, 7, 9, 10. Travis app.-No. 3.* ***Sutton*** *a-1.*

E-MAN
Comico: Sept, 1989 ($2.75, one-shot, no ads, high quality paper)

1-Staton-c/a; Michael Mauser story 3.00

E-MAN
Comico: V4#1, Jan, 1990 - No. 3, Mar, 1990 ($2.50, limited series)

1-3: Staton-c/a 3.00

E-MAN
Alpha Productions: Oct, 1993 ($2.75)

V5#1-Staton-c/a; 20th anniversary issue 3.00

E-MAN COMICS (Also see Michael Mauser & The Original E-Man)
First Comics: Apr, 1983 - No. 25, Aug, 1985 ($1.00/$1.25, direct sales only)

1-25: 2-X-Men satire. 3-X-Men/Phoenix satire. 6-Origin retold. 8-Cutey Bunny app. 10-Origin Nova Kane. 24-Origin Michael Mauser 3.00

NOTE: ***Staton*** *a-1-5, 6-25p; c-1-25.*

E-MAN RETURNS
Alpha Productions: 1994 ($2.75, B&W)

1-Joe Staton-c/a(p) 3.00

EMERALD CITY OF OZ, THE (Dorothy Gale from Wonderful Wizard of Oz)
Marvel Comics: Sept, 2013 - No. 5, Feb, 2014 ($3.99, limited series)

1-5-Eric Shanower-s/Skottie Young-a/c 4.00

EMERALD DAWN
DC Comics: 1991 ($4.95, trade paperback)

nn-Reprints Green Lantern: Emerald Dawn #1-6 1 2 3 5 6 8

EMERALD DAWN II (See Green Lantern...)

EMERGENCY (Magazine)

Emma Frost #2 © MAR

Enchanting Love #3 © Kirby Publ.

Enigma #8 © DC

	GD 2.0	VG 4.0	FN 6.0	VF 8.0	VF/NM 9.0	NM- 9.2

Charlton Comics: June, 1976 - No. 4, Jan, 1977 (B&W)

1-Neal Adams-c/a; Heath, Austin-a	4	8	12	23	37	50
2,3: 2-N. Adams-c. 3-N. Adams-a.	3	6	9	18	28	38
4-Alcala-a	3	6	9	14	20	25

EMERGENCY (TV)
Charlton Comics: June, 1976 - No. 4, Dec, 1976

1-Staton-c; early Byrne-a (22 pages)	3	6	9	19	30	40
2-4: 2-Staton-c. 2,3-Byrne text illos.	3	6	9	14	20	25

EMERGENCY DOCTOR
Charlton Comics: Summer, 1963 (one-shot)

1	3	6	9	18	28	38

EMIL & THE DETECTIVES (See Movie Comics)

EMISSARY (Jim Valentino's...)
Image Comics (Shadowline): May, 2006 - No. 6 ($3.50)

1-6: 1-Rand-s/Ferreyra-a. 4-6-Long-s 3.50

EMMA (Adaptation of the Jane Austen novel)
Marvel Comics: May, 2011 - No. 5, Sept, 2011 ($3.99)

1-5-Nancy Butler-s/Janet K. Lee-a 4.00

EMMA FROST
Marvel Comics: Aug, 2003 - No. 18, Feb, 2005 ($2.50/$2.99)

1-7-Emma in high school; Bollers-s/Green-a/Horn-c 3.00
8-18-($2.99) 3.00
... Vol. 1: Higher Learning TPB (2004, $7.99, digest size) r/#1-6 8.00
... Vol. 2: Mind Games TPB (2005, $7.99, digest size) r/#7-12 8.00
... Vol. 3: Bloom TPB (2005, $7.99, digest size) r/#13-18 8.00

EMMA PEEL & JOHN STEED (See The Avengers)

EMPEROR'S NEW CLOTHES, THE
Dell Publishing Co.: 1950 (10¢, 68 pgs., 1/2 size, oblong)

nn - (Surprise Books series)	6	12	18	28	34	40

EMPIRE
Image Comics (Gorilla): May, 2000 - No. 2, Sept, 2000 ($2.50)
DC Comics: No. 0, Aug, 2003; Sept, 2003 - No. 6, Feb, 2004 ($4.95/$2.50, limited series)

1,2: 1 (5/00)-Waid-s/Kitson-a; w/Crimson Plague prologue 3.00
0-(8/03) reprints #1,2 5.00
1-6: 1-(9/03) new Waid-s/Kitson-a/c 3.00
TPB (DC, 2004, $14.95) r/series; Kitson sketch pages; Waid intro. 15.00

EMPIRE OF THE DEAD: ACT ONE (George Romero's...)
Marvel Comics: Mar, 2014 - Present ($3.99)

1-3-George Romero-s/Alex Maleev-a/c; zombies & vampires 4.00

EMPIRE STRIKES BACK, THE (See Marvel Comics Super Special #16 & Marvel Special Edition)

EMPTY LOVE STORIES
Slave Labor #1 & 2/Funny Valentine Press: Nov, 1994 - Present ($2.95, B&W)

1,2: Steve Darnall scripts in all. 1-Alex Ross-c. 2-(8/96)-Mike Allred-c 4.00
1,2-2nd printing (Funny Valentine Press) 3.00
... 1999-Jeff Smith-c; Doran-a 3.00
..."Special" (2.95) Ty Templeton-c 3.00

ENCHANTED APPLES OF OZ, THE (See First Comics Graphic Novel #5)

ENCHANTER
Eclipse Comics: Apr, 1987 - No. 3, Aug. 1987 ($2.00, B&W, limited series)

1-3 3.00

ENCHANTING LOVE
Kirby Publishing Co.: Oct, 1949 - No. 6, July, 1950 (All 52 pgs.)

1-Photo-c	18	36	54	107	169	230
2-Photo-c; Powell-a	11	22	33	64	90	115
3,4,6: 3-Jimmy Stewart photo-c. 4-Photo-c	11	22	33	62	86	110
5-Ingels-a, 9 pgs.; photo-c	17	34	51	98	154	210

ENCHANTMENT VISUALETTES (Magazine)
World Editions: Dec, 1949 - No. 5, Apr, 1950 (Painted c-1)

1-Contains two romance comic strips each	18	36	54	103	162	220
2	14	28	42	76	108	140
3-5	11	22	33	62	86	110

ENDER IN EXILE (Orson Scott Card's...)
Marvel Comics: Aug, 2010 - No. 5, Dec, 2010 ($3.99, limited series)

1-5-Sequel to Ender's Game; Johnston-s/Mhan-a/Fiumara-c 4.00

ENDER'S GAME: BATTLE SCHOOL
Marvel Comics: Dec, 2008 - No. 5, Jun, 2009 ($3.99, limited series)

1-5-Adaptation of Orson Scott Card novel Ender's Game; Yost-s/Ferry-a. 1-Two covers 4.00
Ender's Game: Mazer in Prison Special (4/10, $3.99) Johnston-s/Mhan-a 4.00
Ender's Game: Recruiting Valentine (8/09, $3.99) Timothy Green-a 4.00
Ender's Game: The League War (6/10, $3.99) Aaron Johnston-s/Timothy Green-a 4.00
Ender's Game: War of Gifts Special (2/10, $4.99) Timothy Green-a 5.00

ENDER'S GAME: COMMAND SCHOOL
Marvel Comics: Nov, 2009 - No. 5, Apr, 2010 ($3.99, limited series)

1-5-Adaptation of Orson Scott Card novel Ender's Game; Yost-s/Ferry-a 4.00

ENDER'S SHADOW: BATTLE SCHOOL
Marvel Comics: Feb, 2009 - No. 5, Jun, 2009 ($3.99, limited series)

1-5-Adaptation of O.S. Card novel Ender's Shadow; Carey-s/Fiumara-a. 1-Two covers 4.00

ENDER'S SHADOW: COMMAND SCHOOL
Marvel Comics: Nov, 2009 - No. 5, Apr, 2010 ($3.99, limited series)

1-5-Adaptation of O.S. Card novel Ender's Shadow; Carey-s/Fiumara-a 4.00

END LEAGUE, THE
Dark Horse Comics: Dec, 2007 - No. 9, Nov, 2009 ($2.99/$3.99)

1-8: 1-Broome-c/a; Remender-s. 5,6-Canete-a 3.00
9-($3.99) MacDonald-a/Canete-c 4.00

END OF NATIONS
DC Comics: Jan, 2012 - No. 4, Apr, 2012 ($2.99, limited series)

1-4-Based on the Trion Worlds videogame; Sanchez-s/Guichet-a/Sprouse-c 3.00

END TIMES OF BRAM AND BEN
Image Comics: Jan, 2013 - No. 4, Apr, 2013 ($2.99, limited series)

1-4: 1-Rapture parody; Asmus & Festante-s/Broo-a. 1-Mahfood-c 3.00

ENEMY ACE SPECIAL (Also see Our Army at War #151, Showcase #57, 58 & Star Spangled War Stories #138)
DC Comics: 1990 ($1.00, one-shot)

1-Kubert-r/Our Army #151,153; c-r/Showcase 57 5.00

ENEMY ACE: WAR IDYLL
DC Comics: 1990 (Graphic novel)

Hardcover-George Pratt-s/painted-a/c 30.00
Softcover (1991, $14.95) 15.00

ENEMY ACE: WAR IN HEAVEN
DC Comics: 2001 - No. 2, 2001 ($5.95, squarebound, limited series)

1,2-Ennis-s; Von Hammer in WW2. 1-Weston & Alamy-a. 2-Heath-a 6.00
TPB (2003, $14.95) r/#1,2 & Star Spangled War Stories #139; Jim Dietz-painted-c 15.00

ENGINEHEAD
DC Comics: June, 2004 - No. 6, Nov, 2004 ($2.50, limited series)

1-6-Joe Kelly-s/Ted McKeever-a/c. 6-Metal Men app. 3.00

ENIGMA
DC Comics (Vertigo): Mar, 1993 - No. 8, Oct, 1993 ($2.50, limited series)

1-8: Milligan scripts 3.00
Trade paperback ($19.95)-reprints 20.00

ENO AND PLUM (Also see Cud Comics)
Oni Press: Mar, 1998 ($2.95, B&W)

1-Terry LaBan-s/c/a 3.00

ENSIGN O'TOOLE (TV)
Dell Publishing Co.: Aug-Oct, 1963

1	3	6	9	19	30	40

ENSIGN PULVER (See Movie Classics)

ENTER THE HEROIC AGE
Marvel Comics: July, 2010 ($3.99, one-shot)

1-Short stories of Avengers Academy, Atlas, Black Widow, Thunderbolts; Hitch-c 4.00

EPIC
Marvel Comics (Epic Comics): 1992 - Book 4, 1992 ($4.95, lim. series, 52 pgs.)

Book One-Four: 2-Dorman painted-c 5.00
NOTE: *Alien Legion in #3. Cholly & Flytrap by* ***Burden****(scripts) &* ***Suydam****(art) in 3, 4. Dinosaurs in #4. Dreadlands in #1. Hellraiser in #1. Nightbreed in #2. Sleeze Brothers in #2. Stalkers in #1-4. Wild Cards in #1-4.*

EPIC ANTHOLOGY
Marvel Comics (Epic Comics): Apr, 2004 ($5.99)

1-Short stories by various 6.00

Epic Illustrated #14 © MAR

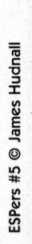

ESPers #5 © James Hudnall

Essential Hulk Vol. 1 © MAR

EPIC ILLUSTRATED (Magazine)
Marvel Comics Group: Spring, 1980 - No. 34, Feb, 1986 ($2.00/$2.50, B&W/color, mature)

1-Frazetta-c; Silver Surfer/Galactus-sty; Wendy Pini-s/a; Suydam-s/a; Metamorphosis Odyssey begins (thru #9) Starlin-a 2 4 6 11 16 20
2-10: 2-Bissette/Veitch-a; Goodwin-s. 3-1st app. Dreadstar. 4-Ellison 15 pg. story w/Steacy-a; Hempel-s/a; Veitch-s/a. 5-Hildebrandts-c/interview; Jusko-a; Vess-s/a. 6-Ellison-s (26 pgs). 7-Adams-s/a(16 pgs.); BWS interview. 8-Suydam-s/a; Vess-s/a. 9-Conrad-c. 10-Marada the She-Wolf-c/sty(21 pgs.) by Claremont/Bolton 1 3 4 6 8 10
11-20: 11-Wood-a; Jusko-a. 12-Wolverton Spacehawk-r edited & recolored w/article on him; Muth-a. 13-Blade Runner preview by Williamson. 14-Elric of Melnibone by Russell; Revenge of the Jedi preview. 15-Vallejo-c & interview; 1st Dreadstar solo story (cont'd in Dreadstar #1). 16-B. Smith-c/a(2); Sim-s/a. 17-Starslammers preview. 18-Go Nagai; Williams-a. 19-Jabberwocky w/Hampton-a; Cheech Wizard-s. 20-The Sacred & the Profane begins by Ken Steacy; Elric by Gould; Williams-a 1 3 4 6 8 10
21-30: 21-Vess-s/a. 22-Frankenstein w/Wrightson-a. 26-Galactus series begins (thru #34); Cerebus the Aardvark story by Dave Sim. 27-Groo. 28-Cerebus. 29-1st Sheeva. 30-Cerebus; History of Dreadstar, Starlin-s/a; Williams-a; Vess-a 2 4 6 8 10 12
31-33: 31-Bolton-c/a. 32-Cerebus portfolio. 2 4 6 8 11 14
34-R.E.Howard tribute by Thomas-s/Plunkett-a; Moore-s/Veitch-a; Cerebus; Cholly & Flytrap w/Suydam-a; BWS-a 2 4 6 10 14 18
Sampler (early 1980 8 pg. preview giveaway) same cover as #1 with "Sampler" text 6.00

NOTE: ***N. Adams** a-7; c-6. **Austin** a-15-20i. **Bode** a-19, 23, 27r. **Bolton** a-7, 10-12, 15, 18, 22-25; c-10, 18, 22, 23. **Boris** c/a-15. **Brunner** c-12. **Buscema** a-1p, 9p, 11-13p. **Byrne/Austin** a-26-34. **Chaykin** a-2; c-8. **Conrad** a-2-5, 7-9, 25-34; c-17. **Corben** a-15; c-2. **Frazetta** c-1. **Golden** a-3r. **Gulacy** c/a-3. **Jeff Jones** c-25. **Kaluta** a-17r, 21, 24r, 26; c-4, 28. **Nebres** a-1. **Reese** a-12. **Russell** a-2-4, 9, 14, 33; c-14. **Simonson** a-17. **B. Smith** c/a-7, 16. **Starlin** a-1-9, 14, 15, 34. **Steranko** c-19. **Williamson** a-13, 27, 34. **Wrightson** a-13p, 22, 25, 27, 34; c-30.*

EPIC LITE
Marvel Comics (Epic Comics): Sept, 1991 ($3.95, 52 pgs., one-shot)

1-Bob the Alien, Normalman by Valentino 4.00

EPICURUS THE SAGE
DC Comics (Piranha Press): Vol. 1, 1991 - Vol. 2, 1991 ($9.95, 8-1/8x10-7/8")

Volume 1,2-Sam Kieth-c/a; Messner-Loebs-s 12.00
TPB (2003, $19.95) r/ #1,2, Fast Forward Rising the Sun; new story 20.00

EPILOGUE
IDW Publishing: Sept, 2008 - No. 4, Dec, 2008 ($3.99)

1-4-Steve Niles-s/Kyle Hotz-a/c 4.00

ERADICATOR
DC Comics: Aug, 1996 - No. 3, Oct, 1996 ($1.75, limited series)

1-3: Superman app. 3.00

ERNIE COMICS (Formerly Andy Comics #21; All Love Romances #26 on)
Current Books/Ace Periodicals: No. 22, Sept, 1948 - No. 25, Mar, 1949

nn (9/48,11/48; #22,23)-Teenage humor 9 18 27 47 61 75
24,25 7 14 21 37 46 55

ESCAPADE IN FLORENCE (See Movie Comics)

ESCAPE FROM DEVIL'S ISLAND
Avon Periodicals: 1952

1-Kinstler-c; r/as Dynamic Adventures #9 41 82 123 256 428 600

ESCAPE FROM THE PLANET OF THE APES (See Power Record Comics)

ESCAPE TO WITCH MOUNTAIN (See Walt Disney Showcase No. 29)

ESCAPISTS, THE (See Michael Chabon Presents The Amazing Adventures of the Escapist)
Dark Horse Comics: July, 2006 - No. 6, Dec, 2006 ($1.00/$2.99, limited series)

1-($1.00) Frank Miller-c; r/Vaughan story from Michael Chabon... #8 3.00
2-6($2.99) Vaughan-s/Rolston & Alexander-a. 2-James Jean-c. 3-Cassaday-c 3.00

ESPERS (Also see Interface)
Eclipse Comics: July, 1986 - No. 5, Apr, 1987 ($1.25/$1.75, Mando paper)

1-5-James Hudnall story & David Lloyd-a. 3.00

ESPERS
Halloween Comics: V2#1, 1996 - No. 6, 1997 ($2.95, B&W) (1st Halloween Comics series)

V2#1-6: James D. Hudnall scripts 3.00
Undertow TPB ('98, $14.95) r/#1-6 15.00

ESPERS
Image Comics: V3#1, 1997 - Present ($2.95, B&W, limited series)

V3#1-7: James D. Hudnall scripts 3.00
Black Magic TPB ('98, $14.95) r/#1-4 15.00

ESPIONAGE (TV)
Dell Publishing Co.: May-July, 1964

1 3 6 9 19 30 40

ESSENTIAL (Title series), **Marvel Comics**

--ANT-MAN, '02 (B&W- r) V1-Reprints app. from Tales To Astonish #27, #35-69; Kirby-c 15.00

--AVENGERS, '98 (B&W- r) V1-R-Avengers #1-24; new Immonen-c 15.00
V2(6/00)-Reprints Avengers #25-46, King-Size Special #1; Immonen-c 15.00
V3(3/01)-Reprints Avengers #47-68, Annual #2; Immonen-c 15.00
V4('04)-Reprints Avengers #69-97, Incredible Hulk #140; Neal Adams-c 17.00
V5('06)-Reprints Avengers #98-119, Daredevil #99, Defenders #8-11 17.00
V6('08)-Reprints Avengers #120-140, Giant Size #1-4, Capt. Marvel #33 & FF #150 17.00

--CAPTAIN AMERICA, '00 (B&W- r) V1-Reprints stories from Tales of Suspense #59-99, Captain America #100-102; new Romita & Milgrom-c 15.00
V2(1/02)-Reprints #103-126; Steranko-c 15.00
V3('06)-Reprints #127-153 17.00
V4('07)-Reprints #157-186 17.00

--CLASSIC X-MEN, '06 - Present (B&W- r) (See Essential Uncanny X-Men for V1)
V2-($16.99) R-X-Men #25-53 & Avengers #53; Gil Kane-c 17.00

--CONAN, '00 (B&W- r) V1-R-Conan the Barbarian#1-25; new Buscema-c 15.00

--DAREDEVIL, '02 - Present (B&W-r)
V1-R-Daredevil #1-25 15.00
V2-($16.99) R-Daredevil #26-48, Special #1, Fantastic Four #73 17.00
V3-($16.99) R-Daredevil #49-74, Iron Man #35-38 17.00
V4-($16.99) R-Daredevil #75-101, Avengers #111 17.00

--DAZZLER, '07 (B&W- r) V1-R/#1-21, X-Men #130-131, Amaz. Spider-Man #203 17.00

--DEFENDERS, '05 (B&W-r) V1-Reprints Doctor Strange #183, Sub-Mariner #22,34,35, Incredible Hulk #126, Marvel Feature #1-3, Defenders #1-14, Avengers #115-118 17.00
V2-($16.99) R- Defenders #15-30, Giant-Size Defenders #1-4, Marvel Two-In-One #6,7, Marvel Team-Up #33-35 and Marvel Treasury Edition #12 17.00
V3-($16.99) R- Defenders #31-60 and Annual #1 17.00

--DOCTOR STRANGE, '04 - Present (B&W-r)
V1-($15.95) Reprints Strange Tales #110,111,114-168 17.00
V1 (2nd printing)-(2006, $16.99) Reprints Strange Tales #110,111,114-168 17.00
V2-($16.99) R-Doctor Strange #169-178,180-183; Avengers #61, Sub-Mariner #22 Marvel Feature #1, Incredible Hulk #126 and Marvel Premiere #3-14 17.00
V3-($16.99) R-Doctor Strange #1-29 & Annual #1;Tomb of Dracula #44,45 17.00

--FANTASTIC FOUR, '98 - Present (B&W-r)
V1-Reprints FF #1-20, Annual #1; new Alan Davis-c; multiple printings exist 17.00
V2-Reprints FF #21-40, Annual #2; Davis and Farmer-c 15.00
V3-Reprints FF #41-63, Annual #3,4; Davis-c 15.00
V4-Reprints FF #64-83, Annual #5,6 17.00
V5-Reprints FF #84-110 17.00
V6-Reprints FF #111-137 17.00

--GHOST RIDER, '05 (B&W-r) V1-Reprints Marvel Spotlight #5-12, Ghost Rider #1-20 and Daredevil #138 17.00
V2-Reprints Ghost Rider #21-50 17.00

--GODZILLA, '06 (B&W-r) V1-Godzilla #1-24 20.00

--HOWARD THE DUCK, '02 (B&W- r) V1-Reprints #1-27, Annual #1; plus stories from Marvel Treasury Ed. #12, Man-Thing #1, Giant-Size Man-Thing #4,5, Fear #19; Bolland-c 15.00

--HULK, '99 (B&W-r) V1-R-Incred. Hulk #1-6, Tales To Astonish stories; new Timm-c 15.00
V2-Reprints Tales To Astonish #102-117, Annual #1 15.00
V3-Reprints Incredible Hulk #118-142, Capt. Marvel #20&21, Avengers #88 17.00
V4-Reprints Incredible Hulk #143-170 17.00
V5-Reprints Incredible Hulk #171-200, Annual #5 17.00

--HUMAN TORCH, '03 (B&W-r) V1-Strange Tales #101-134 & Ann. 2; Kirby-c 15.00

--IRON MAN, '00 - Present (B&W-r)
V1-Reprints Tales Of Suspense #39-72; new Timm-c and back-c 15.00
V2-Reprints Tales Of Suspense #73-99, Tales To Astonish #82 & Iron Man #1-11 17.00
V3-Reprints Iron Man #12-38 & Daredevil #73 17.00

--KILLRAVEN, '05 (B&W-r) V1-Reprints Amazing Adventures V2 #18-39, Marvel Team-Up #45, Marvel Graphic Novel #7, Killraven #1 (2001) 17.00

--LUKE CAGE, POWER MAN, '05 (B&W-r) V1-Hero For Hire #1-16 & Power Man #17-27 17.00
V2-Reprints Power Man #28-49 & Annual #1 17.00

--MAN-THING, '06 (B&W-r) V1-Reprints Savage Tales #1, Astonishing Tales #12-13, Adventure Into Fear #10-19, Man-Thing #1-14, Giant-Size Man-Thing #1-2 & Monsters Unleashed #5,8,9 17.00
V2-R/Man-Thing #15-22 & #1-11 ('79 series), Giant-Size Man-Thing #3-5, Rampaging Hulk #7, Marvel Team-Up #68, Marvel Two-In-One #43 & Doctor Strange #41 17.00

--MARVEL HORROR, '06 (B&W-r) V1-R/#Ghost Rider #1-2, Marvel Spotlight #12-24, Son of

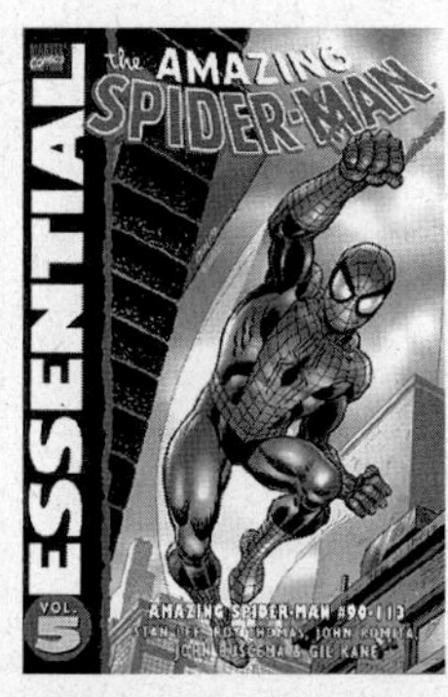

Essential Spider-Man Vol. 5 © MAR

The Establishment #1 © DC

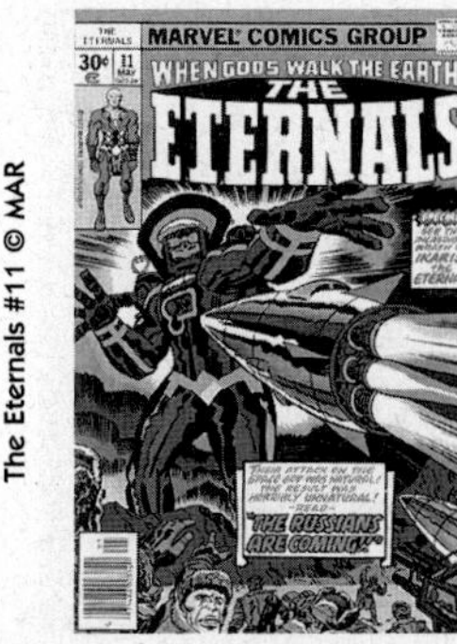

The Eternals #11 © MAR

	GD 2.0	VG 4.0	FN 6.0	VF 8.0	VF/NM 9.0	NM- 9.2

Satan #1-8, Marvel Two-In-One #14, Marvel Team-Up #32,80,81, Vampire Tales #2-3, Haunt of Horror #2,4,5, Marvel Premiere #27, & Marvel Preview #7 17.00

--MARVEL SAGA, '08 (B&W-r) V1-R/#1-12 17.00

--MARVEL TEAM-UP, '02 - Present (B&W-r) V1('02, '06)-R/#1-24 17.00
V2-R/#25-51 and Marvel Two-In-One #17 17.00

--MARVEL TWO-IN-ONE, '05 - Present (B&W-r)
V1-Reprints Marvel Feature #11&12, Marvel Two-In-One #1-20,22-25 & Annual #1, Marvel Team-Up #47 and Fantastic Four Ann. #11 17.00
V2-R/#26-52 & Annual #2,3 17.00

--MONSTER OF FRANKENSTEIN, '04 (B&W-r) V1-Reprints Monster of Frankenstein #1-5, Frankenstein Monster #6-18, Giant-Size Werewolf #2, Monsters Unleashed #2,4-10 & Legion of Monsters #1 17.00

--MOON KNIGHT, '06 (B&W-r) V1-Reprints Moon Knight #1-10 and early apps. 17.00
V2-R/#11-30 17.00

--MS. MARVEL, '07 (B&W-r) V1-Reprints Ms. Marvel #1-23, Marvel Super-Heroes Magazine #10,11, and Avengers Annual #10 17.00

--NOVA, '06 (B&W-r) V1-Reprints Nova #1-25, AS-M #171, Marvel Two-In-One Ann. #3 17.00

--OFFICIAL HANDBOOK OF THE MARVEL UNIVERSE, '06 (B&W-r) V1-Reprints #1-15 profiling Abomination through Zzzax; dead and inactive characters; weapons & hardware; wraparound-c by Byrne 17.00

--OFFICIAL HANDBOOK OF THE MARVEL UNIVERSE - DELUXE EDITION, '06 (B&W-r)
V1-Reprints #1-7 profiling Abomination through Magneto; wraparound-c by Byrne 17.00
V2-Reprints #8-14 profiling Magus through Wolverine; wraparound-c by Byrne 17.00
V3-Reprints #15-20 profiling Wonder Man through Zzzax & Book of the Dead 17.00

--OFFICIAL HANDBOOK OF THE MARVEL UNIVERSE - MASTER EDITION, '08 (B&W-r)
V1-Reprints profiling Abomination through Gargoyle 17.00
V2-Reprints profiles 17.00

--OFFICIAL HANDBOOK OF THE MARVEL UNIVERSE - UPDATE '89, '06 (B&W-r)
V1-Reprints #1-8; wraparound-c by Frenz 17.00

--PETER PARKER, THE SPECTACULAR SPIDER-MAN, '05 (B&W-r) V1-Reprints #1-31 17.00
V2-Reprints #32-53 & Annual #1,2; Amazing Spider-Man Annual #13 17.00
V3-Reprints #54-74 & Annual #3; Frank Miller-c 17.00

--POWER MAN AND IRON FIST, '07 (B&W-r) V1-R/#50-72,74-75 17.00

--PUNISHER, '04, '06 - Present (B&W-r) V1-Reprints early app. in Amazing Spider-Man, Captain America, Daredevil, Marvel Preview and Punisher #1-5 (2 printings) 17.00
V2-Punisher #1-20, Annual #1 and Daredevil #257 17.00
V3-Punisher #21-40, Annual #2,3 17.00

--RAMPAGING HULK, '08 (B&W-r) V1-R/#1-9, The Hulk! #10-15 & Incredible Hulk #269 17.00

--SAVAGE SHE-HULK, '06 (B&W-r) V1-R/#1-25 17.00

--SILVER SURFER, '98 - Present (B&W-r)
V1-R-material from SS#1-18 and Fantastic Four Ann. #5 15.00
V2-R-SS#1(1982), SS#1-18 & Ann#1(1987), Epic Illustrated #1, Marvel Fanfare #51 17.00

--SPIDER-MAN, '96 - Present (B&W-r)
V1-R-AF #15, Amaz. S-M #1-20, Ann. #1 (2 printings) 15.00
V2-R-Amaz. Spider-Man #21-43, Annual #2,3 15.00
V3-R-Amaz. Spider-Man #44-68 15.00
V4-R-Amaz. Spider-Man #69-89; Annual #4,5; new Timm-f&b-c 15.00
V5-R-Amaz. Spider-Man #90-113; new Romita-c 15.00
V6-R-Amaz. Spider-Man #114-137, Giant-Size Super-Heroes #1 G-S S-M #1,2 17.00
V7-R-Amaz. Spider-Man #138-160, Annual #10; Giant-Size Spider-Man #3-5 17.00
V8-R-Amaz. Spider-Man #161-185, Annual #11; G-S Spider-Man #6; Nova #12 17.00

--SPIDER-WOMAN, '05 (B&W-r) V1-Reprints Marvel Spotlight #32, Marvel Two-In-One #29-33, Spider-Woman #1-25 17.00
V2-R-Spider-Woman #26-50, Marvel Team-Up #97 & Uncanny X-Men #148 17.00

--SUPER-VILLAIN TEAM-UP, '04 (B&W-r) V1-r/S-V T-U #1-14 & 16-17, Giant-Size S-V T-U #1,2; Avengers #154-156; Champions #16, & Astonishing Tales #1-8 17.00

--TALES OF THE ZOMBIE, '06 (B&W-r) V1-($16.99) r/#1-10 & Dracula Lives #1,2 17.00

--THOR, '01 (B&W-r) V1-R-Journey Into Mystery #83-112 15.00
V2-($16.99) R-Thor #113-136 & Annual #1,2 17.00
V3-($16.99) R-Thor #137-166 17.00

--TOMB OF DRACULA, '03 - Present (B&W-r) V1-R-Tomb of Dracula #1-25, Werewolf By Night #15, Giant-Size Chillers #1 15.00
V2-($16.99) R-Tomb of Dracula #26-49, Giant-Size Dracula #2-5, Dr. Strange #14 17.00
V3-($16.99) R-Tomb of Dracula #50-70, Tomb of Dracula Magazine #1-4 17.00
V4-($16.99) R/Stories from Tomb of Dracula Magazine #2-6, Dracula Lives! #1-13, and Frankenstein Monster #7-9 17.00

--UNCANNY X-MEN, '99 - Present (B&W reprints) (See Essential Classic X-Men for V2)
V1-Reprints X-Men (1st series) #1-24; Timm-c 15.00

ESSENTIAL VERTIGO: THE SANDMAN
DC Comics (Vertigo): Aug, 1996 - No. 32, Mar, 1999 ($1.95/$2.25, reprints)

1-13,15-31: Reprints Sandman, 2nd series 3.00
14-($2.95) 3.50
32-($4.50) Reprints Sandman Special #1 4.50

ESSENTIAL VERTIGO: SWAMP THING
DC Comics: Nov, 1996 - No. 24, Oct, 1998 ($1.95/$2.25,B&W, reprints)

1-11,13-24: 1-9-Reprints Alan Moore's Swamp Thing stories 3.00
12-($3.50) r/Annual #2 4.00

ESSENTIAL WEREWOLF BY NIGHT
Marvel Comics: 2005 - Present (B&W reprints)

V1-($16.99) r/Marvel Spotlight #2-4, Werewolf By Night 1-23, Marvel Team-Up #12, Tomb of Dracula #18, Giant-Size Creatures #1 17.00
V2-R/#22-43, Giant-Size Werewolf #2-5 and Marvel Premiere #28 17.00

ESSENTIAL WOLVERINE
Marvel Comics: 1999 - Present (B&W reprints)

V1-r/#1-23, V2-r/#24-47, V3-R/#48-69, V4-R/#70-90 17.00

ESSENTIAL X-FACTOR
Marvel Comics: 2005 - Present (B&W reprints)

V1-($16.99) r/X-Factor #1-16 & Annual #1, Avengers #262, Fantastic Four #286, Thor #373&374 and Power Pack #27 17.00
V2-Reprints X-Factor #17-35 & Annual #2, Thor #378 17.00

ESSENTIAL X-MEN
Marvel Comics: 1996 - Present (B&W reprints)

V1-V4: V1-R/Giant Size X-Men #1, X-Men #94-119. V2-R-X-Men #120-144. V3-R-Uncanny X-Men #145-161, Ann. #3-5. V4-Uncanny X-Men #162-179, Ann. #6 15.00
V5-($16.99) R/Uncanny X-Men #180-198, Ann. #7-8 17.00
V6-($16.99) R/Uncanny X-Men #199-213, Ann. #9, New Mutants Special Edition #1, X-Factor #9-11, New Mutants #46, Thor #373-374 and Power Pack #27 17.00
V7-($16.99) R/Uncanny X-Men #214-228, Ann. #10,11, and F.F. vs. The X-Men #1-4 17.00
V8-($16.99) R/Uncanny X-Men #229-243, Ann. #12 & X-Factor #36-39 17.00

ESTABLISHMENT, THE (Also see The Authority and The Monarchy)
DC Comics (WildStorm): Nov, 2001 - No. 13, Nov, 2002 ($2.50)

1-13-Edginton-s/Adlard-a 3.00

ETERNAL, THE
Marvel Comics (MAX): Aug, 2003 - No. 6, Jan, 2004 ($2.99, mature)

1-6-Austen-s/Walker-a 3.00

ETERNAL BIBLE, THE
Authentic Publications: 1946 (Large size) (16 pgs. in color)

	GD	VG	FN	VF	VF/NM	NM-
1	15	30	45	90	140	190

ETERNALS, THE
Marvel Comics Group: July, 1976 - No. 19, Jan, 1978

	GD	VG	FN	VF	VF/NM	NM-
1-(Regular 25¢ edition)-Origin & 1st app. Eternals	3	6	9	16	23	30
1-(30¢-c variant, limited distribution)	4	8	12	22	34	45
2-(Reg. 25¢ edition)-1st app. Ajak & The Celestials	2	4	6	9	12	15
2-(30¢-c variant, limited distribution)	2	4	6	14	20	25
3-19: 14,15-Cosmic powered Hulk-c/story	2	4	6	8	10	12
12-16-(35¢-c variants, limited distribution)	2	4	6	10	14	18
Annual 1(10/77)	2	4	6	9	12	15

Eternals by Jack Kirby HC (2006, $75.00, dust jacket) r/#1-19 & Annual #1; intro by Royer; letter pages from #1,2,Annual #1; afterwords by Robert Greenberger 75.00
NOTE: *Kirby c/a(p) in all.*

ETERNALS, THE
Marvel Comics: Oct, 1985 - No. 12, Sept, 1986 (Maxi-series, mando paper)

1,12 (52 pgs.): 12-Williamson-a(i) 5.00
2-11 4.00

ETERNALS
Marvel Comics: Aug, 2006 - No. 7, Mar, 2007 ($3.99, limited series)

1-7-Neil Gaiman-s/John Romita Jr.-a/Rick Berry-c 4.00
1-7-Variant covers by Romita Jr. 4.00
1-Variant cover by Coipel 4.00
... Sketchbook (2006, $1.99, B&W) character sketches and sketch pages from #1 3.00
HC (2007, $29.99, dustjacket) r/#1-7; gallery of variant covers; sketches, Gaiman interview, Gaiman's original proposal; background essay on Kirby's Eternals 30.00

Eternal Warrior (2013 series) #3 © VAL

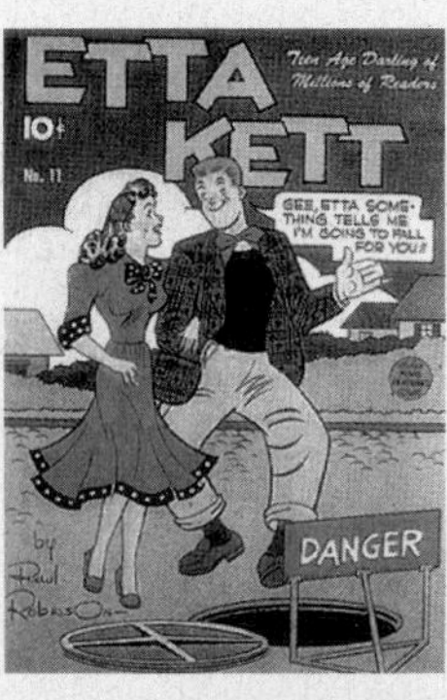

Etta Kett #11 © KING

Evil Ernie (2012 series) #2 © Dynamite Ent.

GD 2.0 | VG 4.0 | FN 6.0 | VF 8.0 | VF/NM 9.0 | NM- 9.2

ETERNALS
Marvel Comics: Aug, 2008 - No. 9, May, 2009 ($2.99)

1-9: 1-6-Acuña-a/c; Knauf-s. 2,4-Iron Man app. 7,8-Nguyen-a; X-Men app. 3.00
Annual 1 (1/09, $3.99) Alixe-a/McGuinness-c; & reprint from Eternals #7 ('77) Kirby-s/a 4.00

ETERNALS: THE HEROD FACTOR
Marvel Comics: Nov, 1991 ($2.50, 68 pgs.)

1 4.00

ETERNAL WARRIOR (See Solar #10 & 11)
Valiant/Acclaim Comics (Valiant): Aug, 1992 - No. 50, Mar, 1996 ($2.25/$2.50)

1-Unity x-over; Miller-c; origin Eternal Warrior & Aram (Armstrong) 6.00
1-($2.25-c) Gold logo 2 4 6 9 12 15
1-Gold foil logo on embossed cover; no cover price 3 6 9 14 20 25
2-8: 2-Unity x-over; Simonson-c. 3-Archer & Armstrong x-over. 4-1st brief app. Bloodshot (last pg.); see Rai #0 for 1st full app.; Cowan-c. 5-2nd full app. Bloodshot (12/92; see Rai #0). 6,7: 6-2nd app. Master Darque. 8-Flip book w/Archer & Armstrong #8 4.00
9-25,27-34: 9-1st Book of Geomancer. 14-16-Bloodshot app. 18-Doctor Mirage cameo. 19-Doctor Mirage app. 22-W/bound-in trading card. 25-Archer & Armstrong app.; cont'd from A&A #25 3.00
26-($2.75, 44 pgs.)-Flip book w/Archer & Armstrong 4.00
35-50: 35-Double-c; $2.50-c begins. 50-Geomancer app. 3.00
Special 1 (2/96, $2.50)-Wings of Justice; Art Holcomb script 3.00
Yearbook 1 (1993, $3.95), 2(1994, $3.95) 4.00

ETERNAL WARRIOR
Valiant Entertainment: Sept, 2013 - Present ($3.99)

1-7: 1-Pak-s/Hairsine-a; 2 covers. 2-Hairsine & Crain-a 4.00

ETERNAL WARRIORS: BLACKWORKS
Acclaim Comics (Valiant Heroes): Mar, 1998 ($3.50, one-shot)

1 3.50

ETERNAL WARRIORS: DIGITAL ALCHEMY
Acclaim Comics (Valiant Heroes): Vol. 2, Sep, 1997 ($3.95, one-shot, 64 pgs.)

Vol. 2-Holcomb-s/Eaglesham-a(p) 4.00

ETERNAL WARRIORS: FIST AND STEEL
Acclaim Comics (Valiant): May, 1996 - No. 2, June, 1996 ($2.50, lim. series)

1,2: Geomancer app. in both. 1-Indicia reads "June." 2-Bo Hampton-a 3.00

ETERNAL WARRIORS: TIME AND TREACHERY
Acclaim Comics (Valiant Heroes): Vol. 1, Jun, 1997 ($3.95, one-shot, 48 pgs.)

Vol. 1-Reintro Aram, Archer, Ivar the Timewalker, & Gilad the Warmaster; 1st app. Shalla Redburn; Art Holcomb script 4.00

ETERNITY SMITH
Renegade Press: Sept, 1986 - No. 5, May, 1987 ($1.25/$1.50, 36 pgs.)

1-5: 1st app. Eternity Smith. 5-Death of Jasmine 3.00

ETERNITY SMITH
Hero Comics: Sept, 1987 - No. 9, 1988 ($1.95)

V2#1-9: 8-Indigo begins 3.00

ETTA KETT
King Features Syndicate/Standard: No. 11, Dec, 1948 - No. 14, Sept, 1949

11-Teenage 14 28 42 76 108 140
12-14 10 20 30 54 72 90

EVA: DAUGHTER OF THE DRAGON
Dynamite Entertainment: 2007 ($4.99, one-shot)

1-Two covers by Jo Chen and Edgar Salazar; Jerwa-s/Salazar-a 5.00

EVANGELINE (Also see Primer)
Comico/First Comics V2#1 on/Lodestone Publ.: 1984 - #2, 6/84; V2#1, 5/87 - V2#12, Mar, 1989 (Baxter paper)

1,2, V2#1 (5/87) - 12, Special #1 (1986, $2.00)-Lodestone Publ. 3.00

EVA THE IMP
Red Top Comic/Decker: 1957 - No. 2, Nov, 1957

1,2 5 10 14 20 24 28

EVEN MORE FUND COMICS (Benefit book for the Comic Book Legal Defense Fund) (Also see More Fund Comics)
Sky Dog Press: Sept, 2004 ($10.00, B&W, trade paperback)

nn-Anthology of short stories and pin-ups by various; Spider-Man-c by Cho 10.00

E.V.E. PROTOMECHA
Image Comics (Top Cow): Mar, 2000 - No. 6, Sept, 2000 ($2.50)

Preview ($5.95) Flip book w/Soul Saga preview 2 4 6 8 10 12
1-6: 1-Covers by Finch, Madureira, Garza. 2-Turner var-c 3.00
1-Another Universe variant-c 5.00
TPB (5/01, $17.95) r/#1-6 plus cover galley and sketch pages 18.00

EVERQUEST: ... (Based on online role-playing game)
DC Comics (WildStorm): 2002 ($5.95, one-shots)

The Ruins of Kunark - Jim Lee & Dan Norton-a; McQuaid & Lee-s; Lee-c 6.00
Transformations - Philip Tan-a; Devin Grayson-s; Portacio-c 6.00

EVERYBODY'S COMICS (See Fox Giants)

EVERYMAN, THE
Marvel Comics (Epic Comics): Nov, 1991 ($4.50, one-shot, 52 pgs.)

1-Mike Allred-a 1 2 3 4 5 7

EVERYTHING HAPPENS TO HARVEY
National Periodical Publications: Sept-Oct, 1953 - No. 7, Sept-Oct, 1954

1 31 62 93 186 303 420
2 17 34 51 100 158 215
3-7 15 30 45 84 127 170

EVERYTHING'S ARCHIE
Archie Publications: May, 1969 - No. 157, Sept, 1991 (Giant issues No. 1-20)

1-(68 pages) 7 14 21 49 92 135
2-(68 pages) 4 8 12 28 47 65
3-5-(68 pages) 4 8 12 25 40 55
6-13-(68 pages) 3 6 9 17 26 35
14-31-(52 pages) 2 4 6 13 18 22
32 (7/74)-50 (8/76) 2 4 6 8 10 12
51-80 (12/79),100 (4/82) 1 2 3 5 6 8
81-99 6.00
101-103,105,106,108-120 5.00
104,107-Cheryl Blossom app. 1 2 3 4 5 7
121-156: 142,148-Gene Colan-a 4.00
157-Last issue 5.00

EVERYTHING'S DUCKY (Movie)
Dell Publishing Co.: No. 1251, 1961

Four Color 1251 5 10 15 30 50 70

EVIL DEAD, THE (Movie)
Dark Horse Comics: Jan, 2008 - No. 4, Apr, 2008 ($2.99, limited series)

1-4-Adaptation of the Sam Raimi/Bruce Campbell movie; Bolton painted-a/c 3.00

EVIL ERNIE
Eternity Comics: Dec, 1991 - No. 5, 1992 ($2.50, B&W, limited series)

1-1st app. Lady Death by Steven Hughes (12,000 print run); Lady Death app. in all issues 6 12 18 41 76 110
2,3: 2-1st Lady Death-c. 2,3-(7,000 print run) 4 8 12 28 47 65
4-(8,000 print run) 3 6 9 19 30 40
5 2 4 6 11 16 20
Special Edition 1 3 6 9 16 23 30
Youth Gone Wild! ($9.95, trade paperback)-r/#1-5 2 4 6 8 10 12
Youth Gone Wild! Director's Cut ($4.95)-Limited to 15,000, shows the making of the comic 6.00

EVIL ERNIE (Monthly series)
Chaos! Comics: July, 1998 - No. 10, Apr, 1999 ($2.95)

1-10-Pulido & Nutman-s/Brewer-a 3.00
1-($10.00) Premium Ed. 10.00
... Baddest Battles (1/97, $1.50) Pin-ups; 2 covers 3.00
... Pieces of Me (11/00, $2.95, B&W) Flashback story; Pulido-s/Beck-a 3.00
... Relentless (5/02, $4.99, B&W) Pulido-s/Beck, Bonk, & Brewer-a 5.00
... Returns (10/01, $3.99, B&W) Pulido-s/Beck-a 4.00

EVIL ERNIE
Dynamite Entertainment: 2012 - No. 6, 2013 ($3.99)

1-6: 1-Origin re-told; Snider-s/Craig-a; covers by Brereton, Seeley, Syaf & Bradshaw 4.00

EVIL ERNIE: DEPRAVED
Chaos! Comics: Jul, 1999 - No. 3, Sept, 1999 ($2.95, limited series)

1-3-Pulido-s/Brewer-a 3.00

EVIL ERNIE: DESTROYER
Chaos! Comics: Oct, 1997 - No. 9, Jun, 1998 ($2.95, limited series)

Preview ($2.50), 1-9-Flip cover 3.00

EVIL ERNIE: IN SANTA FE
Devil's Due Publ.: Sept, 2005 - No. 4, Mar, 2006 ($2.95, limited series)

Evil Eye #4 © Richard Sala

Excalibur #116 © MAR

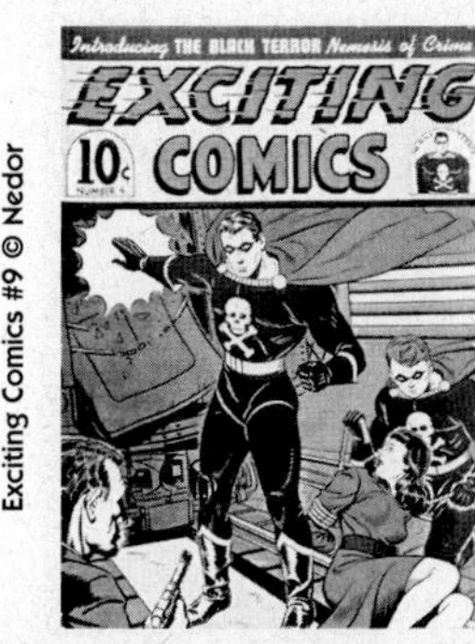

Exciting Comics #9 © Nedor

GD VG FN VF VF/NM NM-
2.0 4.0 6.0 8.0 9.0 9.2

1-4-Alan Grant-s/Tommy Castillo-a/Alex Horley-c 3.00

EVIL ERNIE: REVENGE
Chaos! Comics: Oct, 1994 - No. 4, Feb, 1995 ($2.95, limited series)
1-Glow-in-the-dark-c; Lady Death app. 1-3-flip book w. Kilzone Preview (series of 3) 5.00
1-Commemorative-(4000 print run) 1 3 4 6 8 10
2-4 4.00
Trade paperback (10/95, $12.95) 13.00

EVIL ERNIE: STRAIGHT TO HELL
Chaos! Comics: Oct, 1995 - No. 5, May, 1996 ($2.95, limited series)
1-5: 1-fold-out-c 4.00
1,3:1-($19.95) Chromium Ed. 3-Chastity Chase-c-(4000 printed) 20.00
Special Edition (10,000) 20.00

EVIL ERNIE: THE RESURRECTION
Chaos! Comics: 1993 - No. 4, 1994 (Limited series)
0 5.00
1 2 4 6 8 10 12
1A-Gold 3 6 9 16 23 30
2-4 1 2 3 5 6 8

EVIL ERNIE VS. THE MOVIE MONSTERS
Chaos! Comics: Mar, 1997 ($2.95, one-shot)
1 4.00
1-Variant-"Chaos-Scope•Terror Vision" card stock-c 6.00

EVIL ERNIE VS. THE SUPER HEROES
Chaos! Comics: Aug, 1995; Sept, 1998 ($2.95)
1-Lady Death poster 4.00
1-Foil-c variant (limited to 10,000) 2 4 6 11 16 20
1-Limited Edition (1000) 2 4 6 11 16 20
2-(9/98) Ernie vs. JLA and Marvel parodies 4.00

EVIL ERNIE: WAR OF THE DEAD
Chaos! Comics: Nov, 1999 - No. 3, Jan, 2000 ($2.95, limited series)
1-3-Pulido & Kaminski-s/Brewer-a. 3-End of Evil Ernie 3.00

EVIL EYE
Fantagraphics Books: June, 1998 - No. 12, Jun, 2004 ($2.95/$3.50/$3.95, B&W)
1-7-Richard Sala-s/a 4.00
8-10-($3.50) 4.00
11,12-($3.95) 4.00

EVO (Crossover from Tomb Raider #25 & Witchblade #60)
Image Comics (Top Cow): Feb, 2003 ($2.99, one-shot)
1-Silvestri-c/a(p); Endgame x-over pt. 3; Sara Pezzini & Lara Croft app. 3.00

EWOKS (Star Wars) (TV) (See Star Comics Magazine)
Marvel Comics (Star Comics): June, 1985 - No. 14, Jul, 1987 (75¢/$1.00)
1,10: 10-Williamson-a (From Star Wars) 2 4 6 10 14 18
2-9 2 4 6 8 10 12
11-14: 14-($1.00-c) 2 4 6 9 12 15

EXCALIBUR (Also see Marvel Comics Presents #31)
Marvel Comics: Apr, 1988; Oct, 1988 - No. 125, Oct, 1998 ($1.50/$1.75/$1.99)
Special Edition nn (The Sword is Drawn)(4/88, $3.25)-1st Excalibur comic
1 2 3 5 6 8
Special Edition nn (4/88)-no price on-c 2 4 6 8 10 12
Special Edition nn (2nd & 3rd print, 10/88, 12/89) 5.00
...The Sword is Drawn (Apr, 1992, $4.50) 5.00
1($1.50, 10/88)-X-Men spin-off; Nightcrawler, Shadowcat(Kitty Pryde), Capt. Britain, Phoenix & Meggan begin 6.00
2-4 5.00
5-10 4.00
11-49,51-70,72-74,76: 10,11-Rogers/Austin-a. 21-Intro Crusader X. 22-Iron Man x-over. 24-John Byrne app. in story. 26-Ron Lim-c/a. 27-B. Smith-a(p). 37-Dr. Doom & Iron Man app. 41-X-Men (Wolverine) app.; Cable cameo. 49-Neal Adams c-swipe. 52,57-X-Men (Cyclops, Wolverine) app. 53-Spider-Man-c/story. 58-X-Men (Wolverine, Gambit, Cyclops, etc.)-c/story. 61-Phoenix returns. 68-Starjammers-c/story 3.00
50-($2.75, 56 pgs.)-New logo 4.00
71-($3.95, 52 pgs.)-Hologram on-c; 30th anniversary 5.00
75-($3.50, 52 pgs.)-Holo-grafx foil-c 5.00
75-($2.25, 52 pgs.)-Regular edition 4.00
77-81,83-86: 77-Begin $1.95-c; bound-in trading card sheet. 83-86-Deluxe Editions and Standard Editions. 86-1st app. Pete Wisdom 3.00
82-($2.50)-Newsstand edition 4.00
82-($3.50)-Enhanced edition 5.00
87-89,91-99,101-110: 87-Return from Age of Apocalypse. 92-Colossus-c/app. 94-Days of Future Tense 95-X-Man-c/app. 96-Sebastian Shaw & the Hellfire Club app. 99-Onslaught app. 101-Onslaught tie-in. 102-w/card insert. 103-Last Warren Ellis scripts; Belasco app. 104,105-Hitch & Neary-c/a. 109-Spiral-c/app. 3.00
90,100-($2.95)-double-sized. 100-Onslaught tie-in; wraparound-c 4.00
111-124: 111-Begin $1.99-c, wraparound-c. 119-Calafiore-a 3.00
125-($2.99) Wedding of Capt. Britain and Meggan 4.00
Annual 1,2 ('93, '94, 68 pgs.)-1st app. Khaos. 2-X-Men & Psylocke app. 4.00
#(-1) Flashback (7/97) 3.00
...Air Apparent nn (12/91, $4.95)-Simonson-c 6.00
...Mojo Mayhem nn (12/89, $4.50)-Art Adams/Austin-c/a 6.00
...: The Possession nn (7/91, $2.95, 52 pgs.) 4.00
...: XX Crossing (7/92, 5/92-inside, $2.50)-vs. The X-Men 4.00
...Classic Vol. 1: The Sword is Drawn TPB (2005, $19.99) r/#1-5 & Special Edition nn (The Sword is Drawn) 20.00
...Classic Vol. 2: Two-Edged Sword TPB (2006, $24.99) r/#6-11 25.00
...Classic Vol. 3: Cross-Time Caper Book 1 TPB (2007, $24.99) r/#12-20 25.00
...Classic Vol. 4: Cross-Time Caper Book 2 TPB (2007, $24.99) r/#21-28 25.00
...Classic Vol. 5 TPB (2008, $24.99) r/#29-34 & Marvel GN Excalibur: Weird War III 25.00

EXCALIBUR
Marvel Comics: Feb, 2001 - No. 4, May, 2001 ($2.99)
1-4-Return of Captain Britain; Raimondi-a 3.00

EXCALIBUR (X-Men Reloaded title) (Leads into House of M series, then New Excalibur)
Marvel Comics: July, 2004 - No. 14, July, 2005 ($2.99)
1-14: 1-Claremont-s/Lopresti-a/Park-c; Magneto returns. 6-11-Beast app. 13,14-Prelude to House of M; Dr. Strange app. 3.00
House of M Prelude: Excalibur TPB (2005, $11.99) r/#11-14 12.00
... Vol. 1: Forging the Sword (2004, $9.99) r/#1-4 10.00
... Vol. 2: Saturday Night Fever (2005, $14.99) r/#5-10 15.00

EXCITING COMICS
Nedor/Better Publications/Standard Comics: Apr, 1940 - No. 69, Sept, 1949
1-Origin & 1st app. The Mask, Jim Hatfield, Sgt. Bill King, Dan Williams begin; early Robot-c (see Smash #1) 443 886 1329 3234 5717 8200
2-The Sphinx begins; The Masked Rider app.; Son of the Gods begins, ends #8
213 426 639 1363 2332 3300
3-Robot-c 161 322 483 1030 1765 2500
4-6 103 206 309 659 1130 1600
7,8 77 154 231 493 847 1200
9-Origin/1st app. of The Black Terror & sidekick Tim, begin series (5/41)
(Black Terror c-9-21,23-52,54,55) 1100 2200 3300 8250 15,625 23,000
10-2nd app. Black Terror (6/41) 343 686 1029 2400 4200 6000
11 206 412 618 1318 2259 3200
12,13 135 270 405 864 1482 2100
14-Last Sphinx, Dan Williams 110 220 330 704 1202 1700
15-The Liberator begins (origin) 148 296 444 947 1624 2300
16-20: 20-The Mask ends 87 174 261 553 952 1350
21,23,24 71 142 213 454 777 1100
22-Origin The Eaglet; The American Eagle begins 84 168 252 538 919 1300
25-Robot-c 81 162 243 518 884 1250
26-Schomburg-c begin; Nazi WWII-c 148 296 444 947 1624 2300
27,30-Japanese WWII-c 135 270 405 864 1482 2100
28-(Scarce) Crime Crusader begins, ends #58; Nazi WWII-c
290 580 870 1856 3178 4500
29-Nazi WWII-c 135 270 405 864 1482 2100
31,35,36-Japanese WWII-c. 35-Liberator ends, not in 31-33
116 232 348 742 1271 1800
32-34,37-Nazi WWII-c 116 232 348 742 1271 1800
38 Gangster-c 97 194 291 621 1061 1500
39-WWII-c; Nazis giving poison candy to kids on cover; origin Kara, Jungle Princess
284 568 852 1818 3109 4400
40,41-Last WWII covers in this title; Japanese WWII-c
110 220 330 704 1202 1700
42-50: 42-The Scarab begins. 45-Schomburg Robot-c. 49-Last Kara, Jungle Princess. 50-Last American Eagle 69 138 207 442 759 1075
51-Miss Masque begins (1st app.) 77 154 231 493 847 1200
52-54: Miss Masque ends. 53-Miss Masque-c 61 122 183 390 670 950
55-58: 55-Judy of the Jungle begins (origin), ends #69; 1 pg. Ingels-a; Judy of the Jungle c-56-66. 57,58-Airbrush-c 61 122 183 390 670 950
59-Frazetta art in Caniff style; signed Frank Frazeta (one t), 9 pgs.
63 126 189 403 689 975
60-66: 60-Rick Howard, the Mystery Rider begins. 66-Robinson/Meskin-a
58 116 174 371 636 900

Exiles #78 © MAR

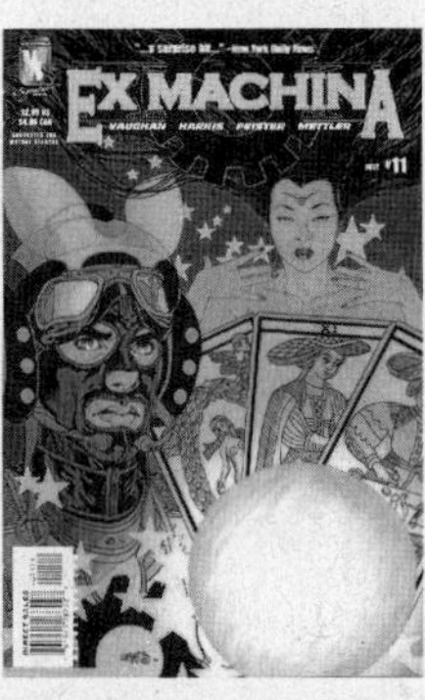
Ex Machina #11 © Vaughan & Harris

Ex-Mutants #18 © MAL

	GD 2.0	VG 4.0	FN 6.0	VF 8.0	VF/NM 9.0	NM- 9.2
67-69-All western covers	21	42	63	126	206	285

NOTE: ***Schomburg (Xela)*** *c-26-68; airbrush c-57-66. Black Terror by* ***R. Moreira****-#65.* ***Roussos*** *a-62. Bondage-c 9, 12, 13, 20, 23, 25, 30, 59.*

EXCITING ROMANCES
Fawcett Publications: 1949 (nd); No. 2, Spring, 1950 - No. 5, 10/50; No. 6 (1951, nd); No. 7, 9/51 -No. 12, 1/53 (Photo-c on #1-3)

1,3: 1(1949). 3-Wood-a	14	28	42	82	121	160
2,4,5-(1950)	10	20	30	56	76	95
6-12	9	18	27	50	65	80

NOTE: ***Powell*** *a-8-10.* ***Marcus Swayze*** *a-5, 6, 9. Photo c-1-7, 10-12.*

EXCITING ROMANCE STORIES (See Fox Giants)

EXCITING WAR (Korean War)
Standard Comics (Better Publ.): No. 5, Sept, 1952 - No. 8, May, 1953; No. 9, Nov, 1953

5	13	26	39	74	105	135
6-Flamethrower/burning body-c	17	34	51	98	154	210
7,9	10	20	30	54	72	90
8-Toth-a	10	20	30	58	79	100

EXCITING X-PATROL
Marvel Comics (Amalgam): June, 1997 ($1.95, one-shot)

1-Barbara Kesel-s/ Bryan Hitch-a 3.00

EXECUTIONER, THE (Don Pendleton's...)
IDW Publishing: Apr, 2008 - No. 5, Aug, 2008 ($3.99)

1-5-Mack Bolan origin re-told; Gallant-a/Wojtowicz-s 4.00

EXECUTIVE ASSISTANT: ASSASSINS
Aspen MLT: Jul, 2012 - No. 18, Feb, 2014 ($3.99)

1-18: 1-Five covers; Hernandez-s/Gunderson-a 4.00

EXECUTIVE ASSISTANT: IRIS
Aspen MLT: No. 0, Apr, 2009 - No. 6, Nov, 2010 ($2.50/$2.99)

0-($2.50) Wohl-s/Francisco-a; 3 covers 3.00
1-6-($2.99) Multiple covers on each 3.00

EXECUTIVE ASSISTANT: IRIS (Volume 2) (The Hit List Agenda x-over)
Aspen MLT: No. 0, Jul, 2011 - No. 5, Dec, 2011 ($2.50/$2.99/$3.50)

0-($2.50) Wohl-s/Francisco-a; sketch page art; 3 covers 3.00
1-4-($2.99) Multiple covers on each. 1-Francisco-a. 2-4-Odagawa-a 3.00
5-($3.50) Odagawa-a 3.50

EXECUTIVE ASSISTANT: IRIS (Volume 3) (See All New Executive Assistant: Iris for Vol. 4)
Aspen MLT: Dec, 2012 - No. 5, Sept, 2013 ($3.99)

1-5-Multiple covers on each. 1-Wohl-s/Lei-a 4.00

EXECUTIVE ASSISTANT: LOTUS (The Hit List Agenda x-over)
Aspen MLT: Aug, 2011 - No. 3, Oct, 2011 ($2.99, limited series)

1-3-Multiple covers on each. Hernandez-s/Nome-a 3.00

EXECUTIVE ASSISTANT: ORCHID (The Hit List Agenda x-over)
Aspen MLT: Aug, 2011 - No. 3, Oct, 2011 ($2.99, limited series)

1-3: 1-Lobdell-s/Gunnell-a; multiple covers 3.00

EXECUTIVE ASSISTANT: VIOLET (The Hit List Agenda x-over)
Aspen MLT: Aug, 2011 - No. 3, Oct, 2011 ($2.99, limited series)

1-3: 1-Andreyko-s/Mhan-a; multiple covers 3.00

EXILED (Part 1 of x-over with Journey Into Mystery #637,638 & New Mutants #42,43)
Marvel Comics: July, 2012 ($2.99, one-shot)

1-Thor, Loki and New Mutants app.; DiGiandomenico-a 3.00

EXILE ON THE PLANET OF THE APES
BOOM! Studios: Mar, 2012 - No. 4 ($3.99, limited series)

1-3-Bechko & Hardman-s/Laming-a 4.00

EXILES (Also see Break-Thru)
Malibu Comics (Ultraverse): Aug, 1993 - No. 4, Nov, 1993 ($1.95)

1,2,4: 1,2-Bagged copies of each exist. 4-Team dies; story cont'd in Break-Thru #1 3.00
3-($2.50, 40 pgs.)-Rune flip-c/story by B. Smith (3 pgs.) 4.00
1-Holographic-c edition 1 2 3 5 6 8

EXILES (All New, The) (2nd Series) (Also see Black September)
Malibu Comics (Ultraverse): Sept, 1995 - V2#11, Aug, 1996 ($1.50)

Infinity (9/95, $1.50)-Intro new team including Marvel's Juggernaut & Reaper 3.00
Infinity (2000 signed), V2#1 (2000 signed) 1 3 4 6 8 10
V2 #1-(10/95, 64 pgs.)-Reprint of Ultraforce V2#1 follows lead story 4.00
V2#2-4,6-11: 2-1st app. Hellblade. 8-Intro Maxis. 11-Vs. Maxis; Ripfire app.; cont'd in Ultraforce #12 3.00
V2#5-($2.50) Juggernaut returns to the Marvel Universe. 4.00

EXILES (Also see X-Men titles) (Leads into New Exiles series)
Marvel Comics: Aug, 2001 - No. 100, Feb, 2008 ($2.99/$2.25)

1-($2.99) Blink and parallel world X-Men; Winick-s/McKone & McKenna-a
1 2 3 4 5 7
2-10-($2.25) 2-Two covers (McKone & JH Williams III). 5-Alpha Flight app. 4.00
11-24: 22-Blink leaves; Magik joins. 23,24-Walker-a; alternate Weapon-X app. 3.00
25-99: 25-Begin $2.99-c; Inhumans app.; Walker-a. 26-30-Austen-s. 33-Wolverine app. 35-37-Fantastic Four app. 37-Sunfire dies, Blink returns. 38-40-Hyperion app. 69-71-House of M. 77,78-Squadron Supreme app. 85,86-Multiple Wolverines. 90-Claremont-s begin; Psylocke app. 97-Shadowcat joins 3.00
100-($3.99) Last issue; Blink leaves; continues in Exiles (Days of Then and Now); r/#1 4.00
Annual 1 (2/07, $3.99) Bedard-s/Raney-a/c 4.00
Exiles #1 (Days of Then and Now) (3/08, $3.99) short stories by various 4.00
TPB (3/02, $12.95) r/#1-4 13.00
...: A World Apart TPB (7/02, $14.99) r/#5-11 15.00
...: Vol. 3: Out of Time TPB (2003, $17.99) r/#12-19 18.00
...: Vol. 4: Legacy TPB (2003, $12.99) r/#20-25 13.00
...: Vol. 5: Unnatural Instinct TPB (2003, $14.99) r/#26-30 15.00
...: Vol. 6: Fantastic Voyage TPB (2004, $17.99) r/#31-37 18.00
...: Vol. 7: A Blink in Time TPB (2004, $19.99) r/#38-45 20.00
...: Vol. 8: Earn Your Wings TPB (2004, $14.99) r/#46-51 15.00
...: Vol. 9: Bump in the Night TPB (2005, $17.99) r/#52-58 18.00
...: Vol. 10: Age of Apocalypse TPB ('05, $12.99) r/#59-61 & Official Handbook:AoA 2005 13.00
...: Vol. 11: Time Breakers TPB (2006, $17.99) r/#62-68 18.00
...: Vol. 12: World Tour Book 1 TPB (2006, $16.99) r/#69-74 17.00
...: Vol. 13: World Tour Book 2 TPB (2006, $23.99) r/#75-83 24.00
...: Vol. 14: The New Exiles TPB (2007, $14.99) r/#84-89 and Annual #1 15.00
...: Vol. 15: Enemy of the Stars TPB (2007, $13.99) r/#90-94 14.00
...: Vol. 16: Starting Over TPB (2008, $14.99) r/#95-100 & ...: Days of Then and Now 15.00

EXILES
Marvel Comics: Jun, 2009 - No. 6, Nov, 2009 ($2.99/$3.99)

1,6-($3.99) Blink and parallel world Scarlet Witch, Beast and others; Bullock-c 4.00
2-5-($2.99) 3.00

EXILES VS. THE X-MEN
Malibu Comics (Ultraverse): Oct, 1995 (one-shot)

0-Limited Super Premium Edition; signed w/certificate; gold foil logo,
0-Limited Premium Edition 1 3 4 6 8 10

EX MACHINA
DC Comics: Aug, 2004 - No. 50, Sept, 2010 ($2.95/$2.99)

1-Intro. Mitchell Hundred; Vaughan-s/Harris-a/c 4.00
1-Special Edition (6/10, $1.00) Reprints #1 with "What's Next?" logo on cover 3.00
2-49: 12-Intro. Automaton. 33-Mitchell meets the Pope 3.00
50-($4.99) Wraparound-c 5.00
...: The Deluxe Edition Book One HC (2008, $29.99, dustjacket) r/#1-11; Vaughan's original proposal, Harris sketch pages; Brad Meltzer intro. 30.00
...: The Deluxe Edition Book Two HC (2009, $29.99, dustjacket) r/#12-20; Special #1,2; script and pencil art for #20; Wachowski Bros. intro. 30.00
...: The Deluxe Edition Book Three HC (2010, $29.99, dustjacket) r/#21-29; Special #3 and Ex Machina: Inside the Machine 30.00
...: The Deluxe Edition Book Four HC (2010, $29.99, dustjacket) r/#30-40; cover gallery 30.00
...: The Deluxe Edition Book Five HC (2011, $29.99, dustjacket) r/#41-50; Special #4 30.00
...: Inside the Machine (4/07, $2.99) script pages and Harris art and cover process 3.00
...: Masquerade Special (#3) (10/07, $3.50) John Paul Leon-a; Harris-c 3.50
... Special 1,2 (6/06 - No. 2, 8/06, $2.99) Sprouse-a; flashback to the Great Machine 3.00
... Special 4 (5/09, $3.99) Leon-a; Great Machine flashback; covers by Harris & Leon 4.00
...: Dirty Tricks TPB (2009, $12.99) r/#35-39 and Masquerade Special #3 13.00
...: Ex Cathedra TPB (2008, $12.99) r/#30-34 13.00
...: March To War TPB (2006, $12.99) r/#17-20 and Special #1,2 13.00
...: Power Down TPB (2008, $12.99) r/#26-29 & ...: Inside the Machine 13.00
...: Ring Out the Old TPB (2010, $14.99) r/#40-44 and Special #4 15.00
...: Smoke Smoke TPB (2007, $12.99) r/#21-25 13.00
...: The First Hundred Days TPB ('05, $9.95) r/#1-5; photo reference and sketch pages 10.00
...: Tag TPB (2005, $12.99) r/#6-10; Harris sketch pages 13.00
...: Term Limits TPB (2010, $14.99) r/#45-50 15.00

EX-MUTANTS
Malibu Comics: Nov, 1992 - No. 18, Apr, 1994 ($1.95/$2.25/$2.50)

1-18: 1-Polybagged w/Skycap; prismatic cover 3.00

EXORCISTS (See The Crusaders)

EXOSQUAD (TV)

Explorers of the Unknown #5 © AP

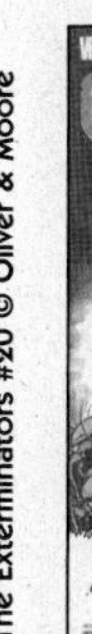
The Exterminators #20 © Oliver & Moore

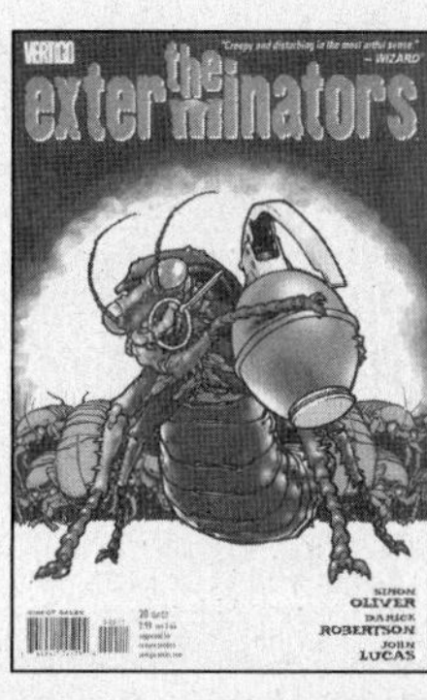

Fables #33 © Willingham & DC

	GD 2.0	VG 4.0	FN 6.0	VF 8.0	VF/NM 9.0	NM- 9.2

Topps Comics: No. 0, Jan, 1994 ($1.00)
0-($1.00, 20 pgs.)-1st app.; Staton-a(p); wraparound-c 3.00

EXOTIC ROMANCES (Formerly True War Romances)
Quality Comics Group (Comic Magazines): No. 22, Oct, 1955-No. 31, Nov, 1956

22	14	28	42	80	115	150
23-26,29	10	20	30	54	72	90
27,31-Baker-c/a	18	36	54	105	165	225
28,30-Baker-a	14	28	42	82	121	160

EXPENDABLES, THE (Movie)
Dynamite Entertainment: 2010 - No. 4, 2010 ($3.99, limited series)
1-4-Chuck Dixon-s/Esteve Polls-a/Lucio Parrillo-c; prelude to the 2010 movie 4.00

EXPLOITS OF DANIEL BOONE
Quality Comics Group: Nov, 1955 - No. 6, Oct, 1956

1-All have Cuidera-c(i)	20	40	60	114	182	250
2 (1/56)	14	28	42	82	121	160
3-6	13	26	39	74	105	135

EXPLOITS OF DICK TRACY (See Dick Tracy)

EXPLORER JOE
Ziff-Davis Comic Group (Approved Comics): Win, 1951 - No. 2, Oct-Nov, 1952

1-2: Saunders painted covers; 2-Krigstein-a	14	28	42	76	108	140

EXPLORERS OF THE UNKNOWN (See Archie Giant Series #587, 599)
Archie Comics: June, 1990 - No. 6, Apr, 1991 ($1.00)
1-6: Featuring Archie and the gang 3.00

EXPOSED (...True Crime Cases; ...Cases in the Crusade Against Crime #5-9)
D. S. Publishing Co.: Mar-Apr, 1948 - No. 9, July-Aug, 1949

1	28	56	84	165	270	375
2-Giggling killer story with excessive blood; two injury-to-eye panels; electrocution panel	36	72	108	211	343	475
3,8,9	15	30	45	86	133	180
4-Orlando-a	15	30	45	90	140	190
5-Breeze Lawson, Sky Sheriff by E. Good	15	30	45	90	140	190
6,7: 6-Ingels-a; used in **SOTI**, illo. "How to prepare an alibi" 7-Illo. in **SOTI**, "Diagram for housebreakers;" used by N.Y. Legis. Committee	36	72	108	216	351	485

EXTERMINATION
BOOM! Studios: Jun, 2012 - No. 8, Jan, 2013 ($1.00/$3.99)
1-($1.00) Nine covers; Spurrier-s/Jeffrey Edwards-a 3.00
2-8-($3.99) 4.00

EXTERMINATORS, THE
DC Comics (Vertigo): Mar, 2006 - No. 30, Aug, 2008 ($2.99)
1-30: Simon Oliver-s/Tony Moore-a in most. 11,12-Hawthorne-a 3.00
...: Bug Brothers TPB (2006, $9.99) r/#1-5; intro. by screenwriter Josh Olson 10.00
...: Bug Brothers Forever TPB (2008, $14.99) r/#24-30; intro. by Simon Oliver 15.00
...: Crossfire and Collateral TPB (2008, $14.99) r/#17-23 15.00
...: Insurgency TPB (2007, $12.99) r/#6-10 13.00
...: Lies of Our Fathers TPB (2007, $14.99) r/#11-16 15.00

EXTINCT!
New England Comics Press: Wint, 1991-92 - No. 2, Fall, 1992 ($3.50, B&W)
1,2-Reprints and background info of "perfectly awful" Golden Age stories 4.00

EXTINCTION EVENT
DC Comics (WildStorm): Sept, 2003 - No. 5, Jan, 2004 ($2.50, limited series)
1-5-Booth-a/Weinberg-s 3.00

EXTINCTION PARADE, THE
Avatar Press: May, 2013 - Present ($3.99)
1-5-Max Brooks-s/Raulo Caceres-a 4.00

EXTRA!
E. C. Comics: Mar-Apr, 1955 - No. 5, Nov-Dec, 1955

1-Not code approved	21	42	63	168	264	360
2-5	13	26	39	104	167	230

NOTE: ***Craig, Crandall, Severin*** *art in all.*

EXTRA!
Gemstone Publishing: Jan, 2000 - No. 5, May, 2000 ($2.50)
1-5-Reprints E.C. series 4.00

EXTRA COMICS
Magazine Enterprises: 1948 (25¢, 3 comics in one)

1-Giant; consisting of rebound ME comics. Two versions known; (1)-Funnyman by Siegel & Shuster, Space Ace, Undercover Girl, Red Fox by L.B. Cole, Trail Colt & (2)-All Funnyman	60	120	180	381	653	925

EXTREME
Image Comics (Extreme Studios): Aug, 1993 (Giveaway)
0 3.00

EXTREME DESTROYER
Image Comics (Extreme Studios): Jan, 1996 ($2.50)
Prologue 1-Polybagged w/card; Liefeld-c, Epilogue 1-Liefeld-c 3.00

EXTREME JUSTICE
DC Comics: No. 0, Jan, 1995 - No. 18, July, 1996 ($1.50/$1.75)
0-18 3.00

EXTREMELY YOUNGBLOOD
Image Comics (Extreme Studios): Sept, 1996 ($3.50, one-shot)
1 3.50

EXTREME SACRIFICE
Image Comics (Extreme Studios): Jan, 1995 ($2.50, limited series)
Prelude (#1)-Liefeld wraparound-c; polybagged w/ trading card 3.00
Epilogue (#2)-Liefeld wraparound-c; polybagged w/trading card 3.00
Trade paperback (6/95, $16.95)-Platt-a 17.00

EXTREME SUPER CHRISTMAS SPECIAL
Image Comics (Extreme Studios): Dec, 1994 ($2.95, one-shot)
1 3.00

EXTREMIST, THE
DC Comics (Vertigo): Sept, 1993 - No. 4, Dec, 1993 ($1.95, limited series)
1-4-Peter Milligan scripts; McKeever-c/a 3.00
1-Platinum Edition 5.00

EYE OF THE STORM
Rival Productions: Dec, 1994 - No. 7, June, 1995? ($2.95)
1-7: Computer generated comic 3.00

EYE OF THE STORM
DC Comics (WildStorm): Sept, 2003 ($4.95)
Annual 1-Short stories by various incl. Portacio, Johns, Coker, Pearson, Arcudi 5.00

FABLES
DC Comics (Vertigo): July, 2002 - Present ($2.50/$2.75/$2.99)
1-Willingham-s/Medina-a; two covers by Maleev & Jean 40.00
1: Special Edition (12/06, 25¢) r/#1 with preview of 1001 Nights of Snowfall 3.00
1: Special Edition (9/09, $1.00) r/#1 with preview of Peter & Max 3.00
1-Special Edition (8/10, $1.00) Reprints #1 with "What's Next?" logo on cover 3.00
2-Medina-a 6.00
3-5 5.00
6-37: 6-10-Buckingham-a. 11-Talbot-a. 18-Medley-a. 26-Preview of The Witching 4.00
6-RRP Edition wraparound variant-c; promotional giveaway for retailers (200 printed) 90.00
38-49,51-74,76-99,101-139: 38-Begin $2.75-c. 49-Begin $2.99-c. 57,58,76-Allred-a. 83-85-X-over with Jack of Fables & The Literals. 101-Shanower-a. 107-Terry Moore-a 113-Back-up art by Russell, Cannon, Hughes 3.00
50-($3.99) Wedding of Snow White and Bigby Wolf; preview of Jack of Fables series 5.00
75-($4.99) Geppetto surrenders; pin-up gallery by Powell, Nowlan, Cooke & others 5.00
100-(1/11, $9.99, squarebound) Buckingham-a; short stories art by Hughes & others 10.00
Animal Farm (2003, $12.95, TPB) r/#6-10; sketch pages by Buckingham & Jean 13.00
...: Arabian Nights (And Days) (2006, $14.99, TPB) r/#42-47 15.00
...: Homelands (2005, $14.99, TPB) r/#34-41 15.00
Legends in Exile (2002, $9.95, TPB) r/#1-5; new short story Willingham-s/a 15.00
...: March of the Wooden Soldiers (2004, $17.95, TPB) r/#19-21 & ...: The Last Castle 18.00
...: 1001 Nights of Snowfall HC (2006, $19.99) short stories by Willingham with art by various incl. Bolton, Kaluta, Jean, McPherson, Thompson, Vess, Wheatley, Buckingham 20.00
...: 1001 Nights of Snowfall (2008, $14.99, TPB) short stories with art by various 15.00
...: Rose Red (2011, $17.99, TPB) r/#94-100; Buckingham design and sketch pages 18.00
...: Sons of Empire (2007, $17.99, TPB) r/#52-59 18.00
...: Storybook Love (2004, $14.95, TPB) r/#11-18 15.00
...: The Dark Ages (2009, $17.99, TPB) r/#76-82 18.00
...: The Deluxe Edition Book One HC (2009, $29.99, DJ) r/#1-10; character sketch-a 30.00
...: The Deluxe Edition Book Two HC (2010, $29.99, DJ) r/#11-18 & ...: The Last Castle 30.00
...: The Good Prince (2008, $17.99, TPB) r/#60-69 18.00
...: The Great Fables Crossover (2010, $17.99, TPB) r/#83-85, Jack of Fables #33-35 and The Literals #1-3; sneak preview of Peter & Max: A Fables Novel 18.00
...: The Last Castle (2003, $5.95) Hamilton-a/Willingham-s; prequel to title 6.00
...: The Mean Seasons (2005, $14.99, TPB) r/#22,28-33 15.00
...: War and Pieces (2008, $17.99, TPB) r/#70-75; sketch and pin-up pages 18.00

Factor X #2 © MAR

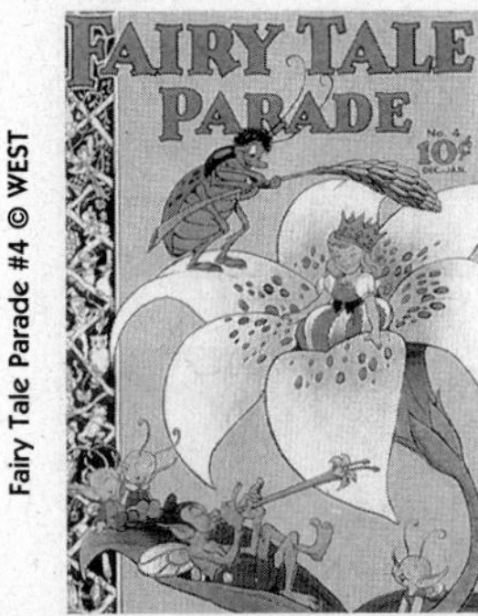

Fairy Tale Parade #4 © WEST

The Falcon #3 © MAR

	GD 2.0	VG 4.0	FN 6.0	VF 8.0	VF/NM 9.0	NM- 9.2
...: Witches (2010, $17.99, TPB) r/#86-93						18.00
...: Wolves (2006, $17.99, TPB) r/#48-51; script to #50						18.00

FACE, THE (Tony Trent, the Face No. 3 on) (See Big Shot Comics)
Columbia Comics Group: 1941 - No. 2, 1943

	GD	VG	FN	VF	VF/NM	NM-
1-The Face; Mart Bailey-c	94	188	282	597	1024	1450
2-Bailey-c	53	106	159	334	567	800

FACES OF EVIL
DC Comics: Mar, 2009 ($2.99, series of one-shots)

...: Deathstroke 1 - Jeanty-a/Ladronn-c; Ravager app. 3.00
...: Kobra 1 - Jason Burr returns; Julian Lopez-a 3.00
...: Prometheus 1 - Gates-s/Dallacchio-a; origin re-told; Anima killed 3.00
...: Solomon Grundy 1 - Johns-s/Kolins-a; leads into Solomon Grundy mini-series 3.00

FACTOR X
Marvel Comics: Mar, 1995 - No. 4, July, 1995 ($1.95, limited series)

1-Age of Apocalypse 4.00
2-4 3.00

FACULTY FUNNIES
Archie Comics: June, 1989 - No. 5, May, 1990 (75¢/95¢ #2 on)

1-5: 1,2-The Awesome Four app. 3.00

FADE FROM GRACE
Beckett Comics: Aug, 2004 - No. 5, Mar, 2005 (99¢/$1.99)

1-(99¢) Jeff Amano-a/c; Gabriel Benson-s; origin of Fade 3.00
2-5-($1.99) 3.00
TPB (2005, $14.99) r/#1-5; cover gallery, afterword by David Mack 15.00

FAFHRD AND THE GREY MOUSER (Also see Sword of Sorcery & Wonder Woman #202)
Marvel Comics: Oct, 1990 - No. 4, 1991 ($4.50, 52 pgs., squarebound)

1-4: Mignola/Williamson-a; Chaykin scripts 5.00

FAGIN THE JAW
Doubleday: Oct, 2003 ($15.95, softcover graphic novel)

nn-Will Eisner-s/a; story of Fagin from Dickens' Oliver Twist 16.00

FAIREST (Characters from Fables)
DC Comics (Vertigo): May, 2012 - Present ($2.99)

1-25: 1-6-Willingham-s/Jimenez-a. 1-Wraparound-c by Hughes & variant-c by Jimenez 3.00
...: In All The Land HC (2013, $24.99, dustjacket) New short stories by various; Hughes-c 25.00

FAIRY QUEST: OUTLAWS
BOOM! Studios: Feb, 2013 - No. 2, Mar, 2013 ($3.99, limited series)

1,2-Jenkins-s/Ramos-a/c 4.00

FAIRY TALE PARADE (See Famous Fairy Tales)
Dell Publishing Co.: June-July, 1942 - No. 121, Oct, 1946 (Most by Walt Kelly)

	GD	VG	FN	VF	VF/NM	NM-
1-Kelly-a begins	86	172	258	688	1544	2400
2(8-9/42)	38	76	114	285	641	1000
3-5 (10-11/42 - 2-4/43)	29	58	87	196	441	685
6-9 (5-7/43 - 11-1/43-44)	22	44	66	154	340	525
Four Color 50('44), 69('45), 87('45)	21	42	63	147	324	500
Four Color 104, 114('46)-Last Kelly issue	16	32	48	112	249	385
Four Color 121('46)-Not by Kelly	10	20	30	69	147	225

NOTE: *#1-9, 4-Color #50, 69 have* ***Kelly*** *c/a; 4-Color #87, 104, 114-****Kelly*** *art only. #9 has a redrawn version of The Reluctant Dragon. This series contains all the classic fairy tales from Jack In The Beanstalk to Cinderella.*

FAIRY TALES
Ziff-Davis Publ. Co. (Approved Comics): No. 10, Apr-May, 1951 - No. 11, June-July, 1951

	GD	VG	FN	VF	VF/NM	NM-
10,11-Painted-c	21	42	63	122	199	275

FAITH
DC Comics (Vertigo): Nov, 1999 - No. 5, Mar, 2000 ($2.50, limited series)

1-5-Ted McKeever-s/c/a 3.00

FAITHFUL
Marvel Comics/Lovers' Magazine: Nov, 1949 - No. 2, Feb, 1950 (52 pgs.)

	GD	VG	FN	VF	VF/NM	NM-
1,2-Photo-c	14	28	42	76	108	140

FAKER
DC Comics (Vertigo): Sept, 2007 - No. 6, Feb, 2008 ($2.99, limited series)

1-6-Mike Carey-s/Jock-a/c 3.00
TPB (2008, $14.99) r/#1-6; Jock sketch pages 15.00

FALCON (See Marvel Premiere #49, Avengers #181 & Captain America #117 & 133)
Marvel Comics Group: Nov, 1983 - No. 4, Feb, 1984 (Mini-series)

	GD	VG	FN	VF	VF/NM	NM-
1-Paul Smith-c/a(p)	1	3	4	6	8	10
2-4: 2-Paul Smith-c/Mark Bright-a. 3-Kupperberg-c						6.00

FALLEN ANGEL
DC Comics: Sept, 2003 - No. 20, July, 2005 ($2.50/$2.95)

1-9-Peter David-s/David Lopez-a/Stelfreeze-c; intro. Lee 3.00
10-20: 10-Begin $2.95-c. 13,17-Kaluta-c. 20-Last issue; Pérez-c 3.00
TPB (2004, $12.95) r/#1-6; intro. by Harlan Ellison 13.00
Down to Earth TPB (2007, $14.99) r/#7-12 15.00

FALLEN ANGEL
IDW Publ.: Dec, 2005 - No. 33, Dec, 2008 ($3.99)

1-33: 1-14-Peter David-s/J.K Woodward-a. Retailer variant-c for each. 15-Donaldson-a. 17-Flip cover with Shi story; Tucci-a. 25-Wraparound-c; character gallery 4.00
... Reborn 1-4 (7/09 - No. 4, 10/09, $3.99) David-s/Woodward-a; Illyria (from Angel) app. 4.00
... Return of the Son 1-4 (1/11 - No. 4, 4/11, $3.99) David-s/Woodward-a; 4.00
...: To Serve in Heaven TPB (8/06, $19.99) r/#1-5; gallery of reg & variant covers 20.00

FALLEN ANGEL ON THE WORLD OF MAGIC: THE GATHERING
Acclaim (Armada): May, 1996 ($5.95, one-shot)

1-Nancy Collins story 6.00

FALLEN ANGELS
Marvel Comics Group: April, 1987 - No. 8, Nov, 1987 (Limited series)

1-8 4.00

FALLEN SON: THE DEATH OF CAPTAIN AMERICA
Marvel Comics: June, 2007 - No. 5, Aug, 2007 ($2.99, limited series)

1-5: Loeb-s in all. 1-Wolverine; Yu-a/c. 2-Avengers; McGuinness-a/c. 3-Captain America; Romita Jr.-a/c; Hawkeye app. 4-Spider-Man; Finch-c/a. 5-Cassaday-c/a 3.00
1-5-Variant covers by Turner 3.00
HC (2007, $19.99, dustjacket) r/#1-5 20.00
TPB (2008, $13.99) r/#1-5 14.00

FALLING IN LOVE
Arleigh Pub. Co./National Per. Pub.: Sept-Oct, 1955 - No. 143, Oct-Nov, 1973

	GD	VG	FN	VF	VF/NM	NM-
1	41	82	123	256	428	600
2	22	44	66	132	216	300
3-10	15	30	45	86	133	180
11-20	14	28	42	76	108	140
21-40	11	22	33	62	86	110
41-47: 47-Last 10¢ issue	10	20	30	56	76	95
48-70	5	10	15	31	53	75
71-99,108: 108-Wood-a (4 pgs., 7/69)	3	6	9	21	33	45
100 (7/68)	4	8	12	25	40	55
101-107,109-124	3	6	9	15	22	28
134-143	3	6	9	14	19	24
125-133: 52 pgs.	3	6	9	21	33	45

NOTE: ***Colan*** *c/a-75, 81. 52 pgs.-#125-133.*

FALLING MAN, THE
Image Comics: Feb, 1998 ($2.95)

1-McCorkindale-s/Hester-a 3.00

FALL OF THE HOUSE OF USHER, THE (See A Corben Special & Spirit section 8/22/48)

FALL OF THE HULKS (Also see Hulk and Incredible Hulk)
Marvel Comics: Feb, 2010 - July, 2010 ($3.99, one-shots & limited series)

Alpha (2/10) Pelletier-a; The Leader, Dr. Doom, MODOK and The Thinker app. 4.00
Gamma (2/10) Romita Jr. -a; funeral for General Ross 4.00
Red Hulk (3/10 - No. 4, 6/10) 1-4: 1-A-Bomb app. 4.00
Savage She-Hulks (5/10 - No. 3, 7/10) 1-3: Cover tryptich by Campbell; Espin-a 4.00

FALL OF THE ROMAN EMPIRE (See Movie Comics)

FALL OUT TOY WORKS
Image Comics: Sept, 2009 - No. 5, Jun, 2010 ($3.99)

1-5-Co-created by Pete Wentz of the band Fall Out Boy; Basri-a. 5-Lau-c 4.00

FAMILY AFFAIR (TV)
Gold Key: Feb, 1970 - No. 4, Oct, 1970 (25¢)

	GD	VG	FN	VF	VF/NM	NM-
1-With pull-out poster; photo-c	5	10	15	34	60	85
1-With poster missing	3	6	9	17	26	35
2-4-Photo-c	3	6	9	20	31	42

FAMILY DYNAMIC, THE
DC Comics: Oct, 2008 - No. 3, Dec, 2008 ($2.25)

1-3-J. Torres-s/Tim Levins-a 3.00

FAMILY FUNNIES
Parents' Magazine Institute: No. 9, Aug-Sept, 1946

	GD	VG	FN	VF	VF/NM	NM-
9	6	12	18	28	34	40

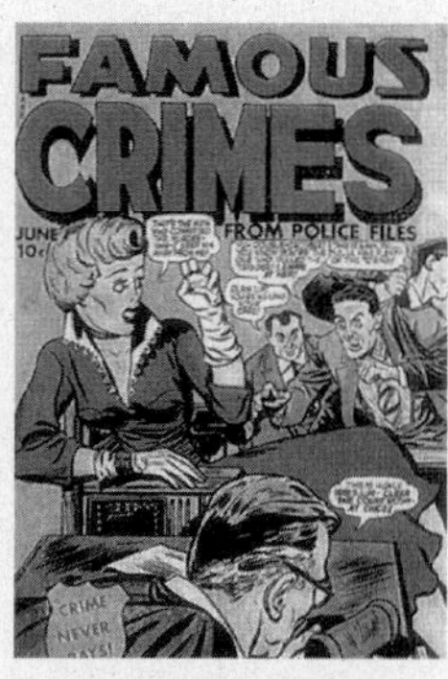

Famous Crimes #10 © FOX

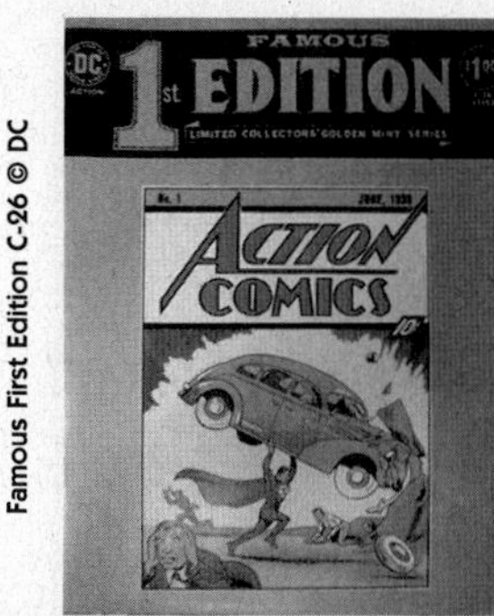

Famous First Edition C-26 © DC

Famous Funnies #6 © EAS

GD VG FN VF VF/NM NM-
2.0 4.0 6.0 8.0 9.0 9.2

FAMILY FUNNIES (Tiny Tot Funnies No. 9)
Harvey Publications: Sept, 1950 - No. 8, Apr, 1951

1-Mandrake (has over 30 King Feature strips) 10 20 30 58 79 100
2-Flash Gordon, 1 pg. 8 16 24 40 50 60
3-8: 4,5,7-Flash Gordon, 1 pg. 6 12 18 31 38 45

FAMILY GUY (TV)
Devil's Due Publ.: 2006 ($6.95)

nn-101 Ways to Kill Lois; 2-Peter Griffin's Guide to Parenting; 3-Books Don't Taste Very Good 7.00
... A Big Book o' Crap TPB (10/06, $16.95) r/nn,2,3 17.00

FAMILY MATTER
Kitchen Sink Press: 1998 ($24.95/$15.95, graphic novel)

Hardcover ($24.95) Will Eisner-s/a 25.00
Softcover ($15.95) 16.00

FAMOUS AUTHORS ILLUSTRATED (See Stories by...)

FAMOUS CRIMES
Fox Features Syndicate/M.S. Dist. No. 51,52: June, 1948 - No. 19, Sept, 1950; No. 20, Aug, 1951; No. 51, 52, 1953

1-Blue Beetle app. & crime story-r/Phantom Lady #16
58 116 174 371 636 900
2-Has woman dissolved in acid; lingerie-c/panels 45 90 135 284 480 675
3-Injury-to-eye story used in **SOTI**, pg. 112; has two electrocution stories
54 108 162 343 574 825
4-6 27 54 81 158 259 360
7- "Tarzan, the Wyoming Killer" (**SOTI**, pg. 44) 43 86 129 271 461 650
8-20: 17-Morisi-a. 20-Same cover as #15 20 40 60 118 192 265
51 (nd, 1953) 17 34 51 98 154 210
52 (Exist?) 17 34 51 98 154 210

FAMOUS FEATURE STORIES
Dell Publishing Co.: 1938 (7-1/2x11", 68 pgs.)

1-Tarzan, Terry & the Pirates, King of the Royal Mtd., Buck Jones, Dick Tracy, Smilin' Jack, Dan Dunn, Don Winslow, G-Man, Tailspin Tommy, Mutt & Jeff, Little Orphan Annie reprints - all illustrated text 64 128 192 406 696 985

FAMOUS FIRST EDITION (See Limited Collectors' Edition)
National Periodical Publications/DC Comics: ($1.00, 10x13-1/2", 72 pgs.) (No.6-8, 68 pgs.) 1974 - No. 8, Aug-Sept, 1975; C-61, 1979
(Hardbound editions with dust jackets are from Lyle Stuart, Inc.)

C-26-Action Comics #1; gold ink outer-c 5 10 15 35 63 90
C-26-Hardbound edition w/dust jacket 15 30 45 103 227 350
C-28-Detective #27; silver ink outer-c 5 10 15 35 63 90
C-28-Hardbound edition w/dust jacket 15 30 45 103 227 350
C-30-Sensation #1(1974); bronze ink outer-c 4 8 12 28 47 65
C-30-Hardbound edition w/dust jacket 13 26 39 86 188 290
F-4-Whiz Comics #2(#1)(10-11/74)-Cover not identical to original (dropped "Gangway for Captain Marvel" from cover); gold ink on outer-c 4 8 12 28 47 65
F-4-Hardbound edition w/dust jacket 13 26 39 86 188 290
F-5-Batman #1(F-6 inside); silver ink on outer-c 5 10 15 31 53 75
F-5-Hardbound edition w/dust jacket 13 26 39 86 188 290
V2#F-6-Wonder Woman #1 4 8 12 28 47 65
F-6-Wonder Woman #1 Hardbound w/dust jacket 13 26 39 86 188 290
F-7-All-Star Comics #3 4 8 12 28 47 65
F-8-Flash Comics #1(8-9/75) 4 8 12 28 47 65
V8#C-61-Superman #1(1979, $2.00) 4 8 12 25 40 55
V8#C-61 (Whitman variant) 4 8 12 27 44 60
V8#C-61 (SC in slipcase, edition of 250 copies) Each signed by Jerry Siegel and Joe Shuster 550.00

Warning: The above books are almost **exact** reprints of the originals that they represent except for the Giant-Size format. None of the originals are Giant-Size. The first five issues and C-61 were printed with two covers. Reprint information can be found on the outside cover, but not on the inside cover which was reprinted exactly like the original (inside and out).

FAMOUS FUNNIES
Eastern Color: 1934; July, 1934 - No. 218, July, 1955

A Carnival of Comics (See Promotional Comics section)

Series 1-(Very rare)(nd-early 1934)(68 pgs.) No publisher given (Eastern Color PrintingCo.); sold in chain stores for 10¢. 35,000 print run. Contains Sunday strip reprints of Mutt & Jeff, Reg'lar Fellers, Nipper, Hairbreadth Harry, Strange As It Seems, Joe Palooka, Dixie Dugan, The Nebbs, Keeping Up With the Jones, and others. Inside front and back covers and pages 1-16 of Famous Funnies Series 1, #s 49-64 reprinted from **Famous Funnies, A Carnival of Comics**, and most of pages 17-48 reprinted from **Funnies on Parade**.
4600 9200 13,800 34,000 - -

No. 1 (Rare)(7/34-on stands 5/34) - Eastern Color Printing Co. First monthly newsstand comic book. Contains Sunday strip reprints of Toonerville Folks, Mutt & Jeff, Hairbreadth Harry, S'Matter Pop, Nipper, Dixie Dugan, The Bungle Family, Connie, Ben Webster, Tailspin Tommy, The Nebbs, Joe Palooka, & others.
3200 6400 9600 24,000 - -
2 (Rare, 9/34) 747 1494 2241 5600 - -
3-Buck Rogers Sunday strip-r by Rick Yager begins, ends #218; not in #191-208; 1st comic book app. of Buck Rogers; the number of the 1st strip reprinted is pg. 190, Series No. 1
933 1866 2799 7000 - -
4 307 614 921 2300 - -
5-1st Christmas-c on a newsstand comic 340 680 1020 2550 - -
6-10 213 426 639 1600 - -
11,12,18-Four pgs. of Buck Rogers in each issue, completes stories in Buck Rogers #1 which lacks these pages. 18-Two pgs. of Buck Rogers reprinted in Daisy Comics #1
102 204 306 612 1106 1600
13-17,19,20: 14-Has two Buck Rogers panels missing. 17-2nd Christmas-c on a newsstand comic (12/35) 79 158 237 474 887 1300
21,23-30: 27-(10/36)-War on Crime begins (4 pgs.); 1st true crime in comics (reprints); part photo-c. 29-X-Mas-c (12/36) 60 120 180 360 655 950
22-Four pgs. of Buck Rogers needed to complete stories in Buck Rogers #1
63 126 189 378 677 975
31,33,34,36,37,39,40: 33-Careers of Baby Face Nelson & John Dillinger traced
42 84 126 252 464 675
32-(3/37) 1st app. the Phantom Magician (costume hero) in Advs. of Patsy
46 92 138 276 501 725
35-Two pgs. Buck Rogers omitted in Buck Rogers #2
46 92 138 276 501 725
38-Full color portrait of Buck Rogers 44 88 132 264 482 700
41-60: 41,53-X-Mas-c. 55-Last bottom panel, pg. 4 in Buck Rogers redrawn in Buck Rogers #3 36 72 108 211 343 475
61,63,64,66,67,69,70 25 50 75 150 245 340
62,65,68,73-78-Two pgs. Kirby-a "Lightnin' & the Lone Rider". 65,77-X-Mas-c
27 54 81 160 263 365
71,79,80: 80-(3/41)-Buck Rogers story continues from Buck Rogers #5
20 40 60 118 192 265
72-Speed Spaulding begins by Marvin Bradley (artist), ends #88. This series was written by Edwin Balmer & Philip Wylie (later appeared as film & book "When Worlds Collide")
22 44 66 132 216 300
81-Origin & 1st app. Invisible Scarlet O'Neil (4/41); strip begins #82, ends #167; 1st non-funny-c (Scarlet O'Neil) 24 48 72 142 234 325
82-Buck Rogers-c 26 52 78 154 252 350
83-87,90: 86-Connie vs. Monsters on the Moon-c (sci/fi). 87 has last Buck Rogers full page-r. 90-Bondage-c 19 38 57 111 176 240
88,89: 88-Buck Rogers in "Moon's End" by Calkins, 2 pgs.(not reprints). Beginning with #88, all Buck Rogers pgs. have rearranged panels. 89-Origin & 1st app. Fearless Flint, the Flint Man 20 40 60 114 182 250
91-93,95,96,98-99,101,103-110: 105-Series 2 begins (Strip Page #1)
15 30 45 90 140 190
94-Buck Rogers in "Solar Holocaust" by Calkins, 3 pgs.(not reprints)
17 34 51 98 154 210
97-War Bond promotion, Buck Rogers by Calkins, 2 pgs.(not reprints)
17 34 51 98 154 210
100-1st comic to reach #100; 100th Anniversary cover features 11 major Famous Funnies characters, including Buck Rogers 22 44 66 128 209 290
102-Chief Wahoo vs. Hitler,Tojo & Mussolini-c (1/43) 79 158 237 502 864 1225
111-130 (5/45): 113-X-Mas-c 13 26 39 74 105 135
131-150 (1/47): 137-Strip page No. 110 omitted. 144-(7/46) 12th Anniversary cover
12 24 36 67 94 120
151-162,164-168 11 22 33 62 86 110
163-St. Valentine's Day-c 11 22 33 64 90 115
169,170-Two text illos. by Al Williamson, his 1st comic book work
14 28 42 78 112 145
171-190: 171-Strip pgs. 227,229,230, Series 2 omitted. 172-Strip Pg. 232 omitted. 173-Christmas-c. 190-Buck Rogers ends with start of strip pg. 302, Series 2; Oaky Doaks-c/story 10 20 30 58 79 100
191-197,199,201,203,206-208: No Buck Rogers. 191-Barney Carr, Space detective begins, ends #192. 10 20 30 56 76 95
198,200,202,205-One pg. Frazetta ads; no B. Rogers 10 20 30 58 79 100
204-Used in **POP**, pg. 79,99; war-c begin, end #208 11 22 33 60 83 105
209-216: Frazetta-c. 209-Buck Rogers begins (12/53) with strip pg. 480, Series 2; 211-Buck Rogers ads by Anderson begins, ends #217. #215-Contains B. Rogers strip pg. 515-518, series 2 followed by pgs.179-181, Series 3 155 310 465 992 1696 2400
217,218-B. Rogers ends with pg. 199, Series 3. 218-Wee Three-c/story
10 20 30 58 79 100

NOTE: *Rick Yager did the Buck Rogers Sunday strips reprinted in Famous Funnies. The Sundays were formerly done by Russ Keaton and Lt. Dick Calkins did the dailies, but would sometimes assist Yager on a panel or two from time to time. Strip No. 169 is Yager's first full Buck Rogers page. Yager did the strip until 1958 when* **Murphy Anderson** *took over.* **Tuska** *art from 4/26/59 - 1965. Virtually every panel was rewritten for Famous Funnies. Not*

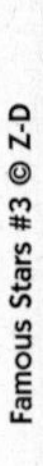
Famous Stars #3 © Z-D

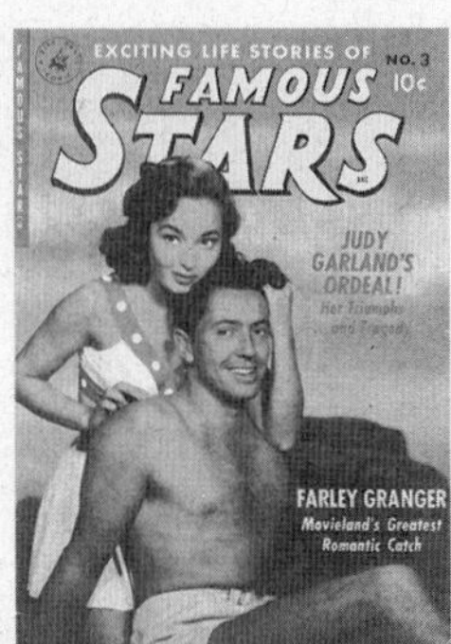

Fanboys vs. Zombies #2 © BOOM

Fantastic Comics #4 © FOX

identical to the original Sunday page. The Buck Rogers reprints run continuously through Famous Funnies issue No. 190 (Strip No. 302) with no break in story line. The story line has no continuity after No. 190. The Buck Rogers newspaper strips came out in four series: Series 1, 3/30/30 - 9/21/41 (No. 1 - 600); Series 2, 9/28/41 -10/21/51 (No. 1 -525)(Strip No. 110-1/2 (1/2 pg.) published in only a few newspapers); Series 3, 10/28/51 -2/9/58 (No. 100-428)(No No.1-99); Series 4, 2/16/58 - 6/13/65 (No numbers, dates only). ***Everett*** *c-85, 86.* ***Moulton*** *a-100. Chief Wahoo c-93, 97, 102, 116, 136, 139, 151. Dickie Dare c-83, 88. Fearless Flint c-89. Invisible Scarlet O'Neil c-81, 87, 95, 121(part), 132. Scorchy Smith c-84, 90.*

FAMOUS FUNNIES
Super Comics: 1964

Super Reprint Nos. 15-18:17-r/Double Trouble #1. 18-Space Comics #? 2 4 6 9 12 15

FAMOUS GANGSTERS (Crime on the Waterfront No. 4)
Avon Periodicals/Realistic No. 3: Apr, 1951 - No. 3, Feb, 1952

1-3: 1-Capone, Dillinger; c-/Avon paperback #329. 2-Dillinger Machine Gun Killer; Wood-c/a (1 pg.); r/Saint #7 & retitled "Mike Strong". 3-Lucky Luciano & Murder, Inc; c-/Avon paperback #66 37 74 111 222 361 500

FAMOUS INDIAN TRIBES
Dell Publishing Co.: July-Sept, 1962; No. 2, July, 1972

12-264-209(#1) (The Sioux) 3 6 9 15 21 26
2(7/72)-Reprints above 1 3 4 6 8 10

FAMOUS STARS
Ziff-Davis Publ. Co.: Nov-Dec, 1950 - No. 6, Spring, 1952 (All have photo-c)

1-Shelley Winters, Susan Peters, Ava Gardner, Shirley Temple; Jimmy Stewart & Shelley Winters photo-c; Whitney-a 39 78 117 231 378 525
2-Betty Hutton, Bing Crosby, Colleen Townsend, Gloria Swanson; Betty Hutton photo-c; Everett-a(2) 25 50 75 150 245 340
3-Farley Granger, Judy Garland's ordeal (life story; she died 6/22/69 at the age of 47), Alan Ladd; Farley Granger photo-c; Whitney-a 32 64 96 188 307 425
4-Al Jolson, Bob Mitchum, Ella Raines, Richard Conte, Vic Damone; Jane Russell and Bob Mitchum photo-c; Crandall-a, 6pgs. 22 44 66 132 216 300
5-Liz Taylor, Betty Grable, Esther Williams, George Brent, Mario Lanza; Liz Taylor photo-c; Krigstein-a 48 96 144 302 514 725
6-Gene Kelly, Hedy Lamarr, June Allyson, William Boyd, Janet Leigh, Gary Cooper; Gene Kelly photo-c 20 40 60 118 192 265

FAMOUS STORIES (...Book No. 2)
Dell Publishing Co.: 1942 - No. 2, 1942

1,2: 1-Treasure Island. 2-Tom Sawyer 30 60 90 177 289 400

FAMOUS TV FUNDAY FUNNIES
Harvey Publications: Sept, 1961 (25¢ Giant)

1-Casper the Ghost, Baby Huey, Little Audrey 5 10 15 34 60 85

FAMOUS WESTERN BADMEN (Formerly Redskin)
Youthful Magazines: No. 13, Dec, 1952 - No. 15, Apr, 1953

13-Redskin story 15 30 45 83 124 165
14,15: 15-The Dalton Boys story 11 22 33 62 86 110

FAN BOY
DC Comics: Mar, 1999 - No. 6, Aug, 1999 ($2.50, limited series)

1-6: 1-Art by Aragonés and various in all. 2-Green Lantern-c/a by Gil Kane. 3-JLA. 4-Sgt. Rock art by Heath, Marie Severin. 5-Batman art by Sprang, Adams, Miller, Timm. 6-Wonder Woman; art by Rude, Grell 3.00
TPB (2001, $12.95) r/#1-6 13.00

FANBOYS VS. ZOMBIES
BOOM! Studios: Apr, 2012 - No. 20, Nov, 2013 ($1.00/$3.99)

1-($1.00) Eight covers; Humphries-s/Gaylord-a; zombies at San Diego Comic-Con 3.00
2-20-($3.99) 2-12-Multiple covers on each. 17-Bryan Turner-a 4.00

FANTASTIC (Formerly Captain Science; Beware No. 10 on)
Youthful Magazines: No. 8, Feb, 1952 - No. 9, Apr, 1952

8-Capt. Science by Harrison 45 90 135 284 480 675
9-Harrison-a; decapitation, shrunken head panels 37 74 111 222 361 500

FANTASTIC ADVENTURES
Super Comics: 1963 - 1964 (Reprints)

9,10,12,15,16,18: 9-r/? 10-r/He-Man #2(Toby). 11-Disbrow-a. 12-Unpublished Chesler material? 15-r/Spook #23. 16-r/Dark Shadows #2(Steinway); Briefer-a.18-r/Superior Stories #1 3 6 9 17 26 35
11-Wood-a; r/Blue Bolt #118 4 8 12 23 37 50
17-Baker-a(2) r/Seven Seas #6 4 8 12 23 37 50

FANTASTIC COMICS
Fox Features Syndicate: Dec, 1939 - No. 23, Nov, 1941

1-Intro/origin Samson; Stardust, The Super Wizard, Sub Saunders (by Kiefer), Space Smith, Capt. Kidd begin 524 1048 1572 3825 6763 9700
2-Powell text illos 290 580 870 1856 3178 4500
3-Classic Lou Fine Robot-c; Powell text illos 2500 5000 7500 12,000 16,000 20,000
4-Lou Fine-c 258 516 774 1651 2826 4000
5-Classic Lou Fine-c 300 600 900 1950 3375 4800
6,7-Simon-c 194 388 582 1242 2121 3000
8-10: 10-Intro/origin David, Samson's aide 116 232 348 742 1271 1800
11-17,19,20: 16-Stardust ends 90 180 270 576 988 1400
18,23: 18-1st app. Black Fury & sidekick Chuck; ends #23. 23-Origin The Gladiator 94 188 282 597 1024 1450
21-The Banshee begins(origin); ends #23; Hitler-c 135 270 405 864 1482 2100
22-Hitler-c (likeness of Hitler as furnace on cover) 148 296 444 947 1624 2300

NOTE: ***Lou Fine*** *c-1-5.* ***Tuska*** *a-3-5, 8. Bondage c-6, 8, 9. Issue #11 has indicia to Mystery Men Comics #15. All issues feature Samson covers.*

FANTASTIC COMICS (Imagining of a 1941 issue by modern creators in Golden Age style)
Image Comics: No. 24, Jan, 2008 ($5.99, Golden Age sized, one-shot)

24-Samson, Yank Wilson, Stardust, Sub Saunders, Space Smith, Capt. Kidd app.; Larsen-c/a; art by Allred, Sienkiewicz, Yeates, Scioli, Hembeck, Ashley Wood & others 6.00

FANTASTIC COMICS (Fantastic Fears #1-9; Becomes Samson #12)
Ajax/Farrell Publ.: No. 10, Nov-Dec, 1954 - No. 11, Jan-Feb, 1955

10 (#1) 24 48 72 142 234 325
11-Robot-c 30 60 90 177 289 400

FANTASTIC FABLES
Silverwolf Comics: Feb, 1987 - No. 2, 1987 ($1.50, 28 pgs., B&W)

1,2: 1-Tim Vigil-a (6 pgs.). 2-Tim Vigil-a (7 pgs.) 4.00

FANTASTIC FEARS (Formerly Captain Jet) (Fantastic Comics #10 on)
Ajax/Farrell Publ.: No. 7, May, 1953 - No. 9, Sept-Oct, 1954

7(#1, 5/53)-Tales of Stalking Terror 53 106 159 334 567 800
8(#2, 7/53) 40 80 120 244 402 560
3,4 34 68 102 199 325 450
5-(1-2/54)-Ditko story (1st drawn) is written by Bruce Hamilton; r-in Weird V2#8 (1st pro work for Ditko but Daring Love #1 was published 1st) 148 296 444 947 1624 2300
6-Decapitation-girl's head w/paper cutter (classic) 79 158 237 502 864 1225
7(5-6/54), 9(9-10/54) 32 64 96 192 314 435
8(7-8/54)-Contains story intended for Jo-Jo; name changed to Kaza; decapitation story 34 68 102 199 325 450

FANTASTIC FIVE
Marvel Comics: Oct, 1999 - No. 5, Feb, 2000 ($1.99)

1-5: 1-M2 Universe; recaps origin; Ryan-a. 2-Two covers 3.00
Spider-Girl Presents Fantastic Five: In Search of Doom (2006, $7.99, digest) r/#1-5 8.00

FANTASTIC FIVE
Marvel Comics: Sept, 2007 - No. 5, Nov, 2007 ($2.99, limited series)

1-5-DeFalco-s/Lim-a; Dr. Doom returns vs. the future Fantastic Five 3.00
...: The Final Doom TPB (2007, $13.99) r/#1-5; cover sketches with inks 14.00

FANTASTIC FORCE
Marvel Comics: Nov, 1994 - No. 18, Apr, 1996 ($1.75)

1-($2.50)-Foil wraparound-c; intro Fantastic Force w/Huntara, Delvor, Psi-Lord & Vibraxas 4.00
2-18: 13-She-Hulk app. 3.00

FANTASTIC FORCE (See Fantastic Four #558, Nu-World heroes from 500 years in the future)
Marvel Comics: Jun, 2009 - No. 4, Sept, 2009 ($3.99/$2.99, limited series)

1-($3.99)-Ahearne-s/Kurth-a/Hitch-c; Fantastic Four app. 4.00
2-4-($2.99) 3,4-Ego the Living Planet app. 3.00

FANTASTIC FOUR (See America's Best TV..., Fireside Book Series, Giant-Size..., Giant Size Super-Stars, Marvel Age..., Marvel Collectors Item Classics, Marvel Knights 4, Marvel Milestone Edition, Marvel's Greatest, Marvel Treasury Edition, Marvel Triple Action, Official Marvel Index to..., Power Record Comics & Ultimate...)

FANTASTIC FOUR (See Volume Three for issues #500-611)
Marvel Comics Group: Nov, 1961 - No. 416, Sept, 1996 (Created by Stan Lee & Jack Kirby)

1-Origin & 1st app. The Fantastic Four (Reed Richards: Mr. Fantastic, Johnny Storm: The Human Torch, Sue Storm: The Invisible Girl, & Ben Grimm: The Thing–Marvel's 1st super-hero group since the G.A.; 1st app. S.A. Human Torch); origin/1st app. The Mole Man. 2100 4200 8000 28,000 69,000 110,000
1-Golden Record Comic Set Reprint (1966)-cover not identical to original 21 42 63 147 324 500
with Golden Record 28 56 84 203 439 750
2-Vs. The Skrulls (last 10¢ issue) 410 820 1230 3700 7850 12,800
3-Fantastic Four don costumes & establish Headquarters; brief 1pg. origin; intro. The Fantasti-Car; Human Torch drawn w/two left hands on-c 350 700 1050 3100 6800 11,500

Fantastic Four #4 © MAR

Fantastic Four #201 © MAR

Fantastic Four #391 © MAR

	GD 2.0	VG 4.0	FN 6.0	VF 8.0	VF/NM 9.0	NM- 9.2
4-1st S. A. Sub-Mariner app. (5/62)	360	720	1080	3300	7600	12,800
5-Origin & 1st app. Doctor Doom	520	1040	1820	5600	11,800	18,000
6-Sub-Mariner, Dr. Doom team up; 1st Marvel villain team-up (2nd S.A. Sub-Mariner app.	217	434	651	1790	4045	6300
7-10: 7-1st app. Kurrgo. 8-1st app. Puppet-Master & Alicia Masters. 9-3rd Sub-Mariner app. 10-Stan Lee & Jack Kirby app. in story	141	282	423	1163	2632	4100
11-Origin/1st app. The Impossible Man (2/63)	139	278	417	1112	2506	3900
12-Fantastic Four vs. The Hulk (1st meeting); 1st Hulk x-over & ties w/Amazing Spider-Man #1 as 1st Marvel x-over; (3/63)	340	680	1020	3100	7400	12,000
13-Intro. The Watcher; 1st app. The Red Ghost	100	200	300	800	1800	2800
14,15,17,19: 14-Sub-Mariner x-over. 15-1st app. Mad Thinker. 19-Intro. Rama-Tut	52	104	156	411	931	1450
16-1st Ant-Man x-over (7/63); Wasp cameo	68	136	204	544	1222	1900
18-Origin/1st app. The Super Skrull	75	150	225	600	1350	2100
20-Origin/1st app. The Molecule Man	54	108	162	432	966	1500
21-Intro. The Hate Monger; 1st Sgt. Fury x-over (12/63)	46	92	138	340	770	1200
22-24: 22-Sue Storm gains more powers	34	68	102	241	541	840
25,26-The Hulk vs. The Thing (their 1st battle). 25-3rd Avengers x-over (1st time w/Captain America)(cameo, 4/64); 2nd S.A. app. Cap (takes place between Avengers #4 & 5.) 26-4th Avengers x-over	63	126	189	504	1140	1775
27-1st Doctor Strange x-over (6/64)	38	76	114	281	628	975
28-Early X-Men x-over (7/64); same date as X-Men #6	47	94	141	367	821	1275
29,30: 30-Intro. Diablo	27	54	81	194	435	675
31-40: 31-Early Avengers x-over (10/64). 33-1st app. Attuma; part photo-c. 35-Intro/1st app. Dragon Man. 36-Intro/1st app. Madam Medusa & the Frightful Four (Sandman, Wizard, Paste Pot Pete). 39-Wood inks on Daredevil (early x-over)	22	44	66	154	340	525
41-44,47: 41-43-Frightful Four app. 44-Intro. Gorgon	14	28	42	96	211	325
45-Intro/1st app. The Inhumans (c/story, 12/65); also see Incredible Hulk Special #1 & Thor #146, & 147	27	54	81	189	420	650
46-1st Black Bolt-c (Kirby) & 1st full app.	17	34	51	117	259	400
48-Partial origin/1st app. The Silver Surfer & Galactus (3/66) by Lee & Kirby; Galactus brief app. in last panel; 1st of 3 part story	61	122	183	488	1094	1700
49-2nd app./1st cover Silver Surfer & Galactus	40	80	120	296	673	1050
50-Silver Surfer battles Galactus; full S.S.-c	49	98	147	382	866	1350
51-Classic "This Man...This Monster" story	19	38	57	131	291	450
52-1st app. The Black Panther (7/66)	42	84	126	311	706	1100
53-Origin & 2nd app. The Black Panther	17	34	51	117	259	400
54-Inhumans cameo	12	24	36	80	173	265
55-Thing battles Silver Surfer; 4th app. Silver Surfer	21	42	63	147	324	500
56-Silver Surfer cameo	12	24	36	79	170	260
57-60: Dr. Doom steals Silver Surfer's powers (also see Silver Surfer: Loftier Than Mortals). 59,60-Inhumans cameo	10	20	30	64	132	200
61-65,68-71: 61-Silver Surfer cameo; Sandman-c/s	8	16	24	54	102	150
66-Begin 2 part origin of Him (Warlock); does not app. (9/67)	12	24	36	82	179	275
66,67-2nd printings (1994)	2	4	6	8	10	12
67-Origin/1st brief app. Him (Warlock); 1 page; see Thor #165,166 for 1st full app.	12	24	36	82	179	275
72-Silver Surfer-c/story (pre-dates Silver Surfer #1)	12	24	36	84	185	285
73-Spider-Man, D.D., Thor x-over; cont'd from Daredevil #38	10	20	30	69	147	225
74-77: Silver Surfer app.(#77 is same date/S.S. #1)	9	18	27	62	126	190
78-80	6	12	18	41	76	110
81-88: 81-Crystal joins & dons costume. 82,83-Inhumans app. 84-87-Dr. Doom app. 88-Last 12¢ issue	6	12	18	40	73	105
89-99,101: 94-Intro. Agatha Harkness.	6	12	18	37	66	95
100 (7/70) F.F. vs Thinker and Puppet-Master	9	18	27	62	126	190
102-104: F.F. vs. Sub-Mariner. 104-Magneto-c/story	6	12	18	37	66	95
105-109,111: 108-Last Kirby issue (not in #103-107)	5	10	15	35	63	90
110-Initial version w/green Thing and blue faces and pink uniforms on-c	10	20	30	64	132	200
110-Corrected-c w/accurately colored faces and uniforms and orange Thing	6	12	18	38	69	100
112-Hulk Vs. Thing (7/71)	18	36	54	124	275	425
113-115: 115-Last 15¢ issue	5	10	15	30	50	70
116 (52 pgs.)	6	12	18	41	76	110
117-120	4	8	12	28	47	65
121-123-Silver Surfer-c/stories. 122,123-Galactus	5	10	15	31	53	75
124,125,127,129-140: 129-Intro. Thundra. 130-Sue leaves F.F. 131-Quicksilver app. 132-Medusa joins. 133-Thundra Vs. Thing	4	8	12	23	37	50
126-Origin F.F. retold; cover swipe of F.F. #1	4	8	12	27	44	60
128-Four pg. insert of F.F. Friends & Foes	4	8	12	25	40	55
141-149: 142-Kirbyish-a by Buckler begins. 143-Dr. Doom-c/story. 147-Sub-Mariner	3	6	9	21	33	45
150-Crystal & Quicksilver's wedding	4	8	12	25	40	55
151-154,158-160: 151-Origin Thundra. 159-Medusa leaves; Sue rejoins	3	6	9	15	22	28
155-157: Silver Surfer in all	3	6	9	19	30	40
161-165,168,174-180: 164-The Crusader (old Marvel Boy) revived (origin #165); 1st app. Frankie Raye. 168-170-Cage app. 176-Re-intro Impossible Man; Marvel artists app. 180-r/#101 by Kirby	2	4	6	10	14	18
166,167-vs. Hulk	3	6	9	16	24	32
169-173-(Regular 25¢ edition)(4-8/75)	2	4	6	10	14	18
169-173-(30¢-c, limited distribution)	3	6	9	18	27	36
181-199: 189-G.A. Human Torch app. & origin retold. 190,191-Fantastic Four break up	2	4	6	8	10	12
183-187-(35¢-c variants, limited dist.)(6-10/77)	4	8	12	23	37	50
200-(11/78, 52 pgs.)-F.F. re-united vs. Dr. Doom	2	4	6	10	14	18
201-208,219,222-231: 207-Human Torch vs. Spider-Man-c/story. 224-Contains unused alternate-c for FF #3 and pin-ups						6.00
209,210,212-216,218,220,221-Byrne-a. 209-1st Herbie the Robot. 220-Brief origin	1	2	3	5	6	8
211-1st app. Terrax	1	3	4	6	8	10
217-Early app. Dazzler (4/80); by Byrne	1	2	3	5	6	8
232-Byrne-a begins	1	2	3	5	6	8
233-235,237-249,251-260: All Byrne-a. 238-Origin Frankie Raye. 244-Frankie Raye becomes Nova, Herald of Galactus. 252-Reads sideways; Annihilus app.; contains skin "Tattooz" decals (no "Tattooz" were included in the Canadian edition)						6.00
236-20th Anniversary issue(11/81, 68 pgs., $1.00)-Brief origin F.F.; Byrne-c(p)/a; new Kirby-a(p); Marvel Heroes and Stan Lee app. on cover	1	2	3	5	6	8
250-(52 pgs)-Spider-Man x-over; Byrne-a; Skrulls impersonate New X-Men	1	2	3	5	6	8
261-285: 261-Silver Surfer. 262-Origin Galactus; Byrne writes & draws himself into story. 264-Swipes-c of F.F. #1. 274-Spider-Man's alien costume app. (4th app., 1/85, 2 pgs.)						4.00
286-2nd app. X-Factor continued from Avengers #263; story continues in X-Factor #1	1	2	3	5	6	8
287-295: 291-Action Comcis #1 cover swipe. 292-Nick Fury app. 293-Last Byrne-a						4.00
296-($1.50)-Barry Smith-c/a; Thing rejoins						5.00
297-318,321-330: 300-Johnny Storm & Alicia Masters wed. 306-New team begins (9/87). 311-Re-intro The Black Panther. 327-Mr. Fantastic & Invisible Girl return						3.00
319,320: 319-Double size. 320-Thing vs. Hulk						6.00
331-346,351-357,359,360: 334-Simonson-c/scripts begin. 337-Simonson-a begins. 342-Spider-Man cameo. 356-F.F. vs. The New Warriors; Paul Ryan-c/a begins. 360-Last $1.00-c						3.00
347-Ghost Rider, Wolverine, Spider-Man, Hulk-c/stories thru #349; Arthur Adams-c/a(p) in each						5.00
347,348-Gold 2nd printing						5.00
348-350: 350-($1.50, 52 pgs.)-Dr. Doom app.						4.00
358-(11/91, $2.25, 88 pgs.)-30th anniversary issue; gives history of F.F.; die cut-c; Art Adams back-up story-a						5.00
361-368,372-374,376-380,382-386: 362-Spider-Man app. 367-Wolverine app. (brief). 374-Secret Defenders (Ghost Rider, Hulk, Wolverine) x-over						3.00
369,370-Infinity War x-over; Thanos app. 370-Magus app.						4.00
371-All white embossed-c ($2.00)						4.00
371-All red 2nd printing ($2.00)						3.00
375-($2.95, 52 pgs.)-Holo-grafx foil-c; ann. issue						5.00
376-($2.95)-Variant polybagged w/Dirt Magazine #4 and music tape						5.00
381-Death of Reed Richards (Mister Fantastic) & Dr. Doom						4.00
387-Newsstand ed. ($1.25)						3.00
387-($2.95)-Collector's Ed. w/Die-cut foil-c						4.00
388-393,395-397: 388-bound-in trading card sheet. 394-($1.50-c)						3.00
394,398,399: 394 ($2.95)-Collector's Edition-polybagged w/16 pg. Marvel Action Hour book and acetate print; pink logo. 398,399-Rainbow Foil-c						4.00
400-Rainbow-Foil-c						5.00
401-415: 401,402-Atlantis Rising. 407,408-Return of Reed Richards. 411-Inhumans app. 414-Galactus vs. Hyperstorm. 415-Onslaught tie-in; X-Men app.						3.00
416-($2.50)-Onslaught tie-in; Dr. Doom app.; wraparound-c						4.00
#500-up (See Fantastic Four Vol. 3; series resumed original numbering after Vol. 3 #70)						
Annual 1('63)-Origin F.F.; Ditko-i; early Spidey app.	70	140	210	555	1253	1950
Annual 2('64)-Dr. Doom origin & c/story	36	72	108	266	596	925
Annual 3('65)-Reed & Sue wed; r/#6,11	18	36	54	126	281	435
Special 4(11/66)-G.A. Torch x-over (1st S.A. app.) & origin retold; r/#25,26 (Hulk vs. Thing); Torch vs. Torch battle	12	24	36	80	173	265
Special 5(11/67)-New art; Intro. Psycho-Man; early Black Panther, Inhumans & Silver Surfer (1st solo story) app.	12	24	36	82	179	275

Fantastic Four V2 #6 © MAR

Fantastic Four V3 #2 © MAR

Fantastic Four #500 © MAR

	GD	VG	FN	VF	VF/NM	NM-
	2.0	4.0	6.0	8.0	9.0	9.2

Special 6(11/68)-Intro. Annihilus; birth of Franklin Richards; new 48 pg. movie length epic; last non-reprint annual 9 18 27 59 117 175
Special 7(11/69)-r/F.F. #1,2; Marvel staff photos 5 10 15 33 57 80
Special 8-10: All reprints. 8(12/70)-F.F. vs. Sub-Mariner plus gallery of F.F. foes. 9(12/71). 10('73) 3 6 9 21 33 45
Annual 11-14: 11(1976)-New art begins again. 12(1978). 13(1978). 14(1979) 2 4 6 8 10 12
Annual 15-17: 15('80, 68 pgs.). 16-Ditko-a/c. 17(1983)-Byrne-c/a 6.00
Annual 18-27: 21(1988)-Evolutionary War x-over. 22-Atlantis Attacks x-over; Sub-Mariner & The Avengers app.; Buckler-a. 23-Byrne-c; Guice-p. 24-2 pg. origin recap of Fantastic Four; Guardians of the Galaxy x-over. 25-Moondragon story. 26-Bagged w/card 4.00
Best of the Fantastic Four Vol. 1 HC (2005, $29.99) oversized reprints of classic stories from FF#1,39,40,51,100,116,176,236,267, Ann.2, V3#56,60 and more; Brevoort intro. 30.00
Maximum Fantastic Four HC (2005, $49.99, dust jacket) r/Fantastic Four #1 with super-sized art; historical background from Walter Mosley and Mark Evanier; dust jacket unfolds to a poster: giant FF#1 cover on one side, gallery of interior pages on other 50.00
...: Monsters Unleashed nn (1992, $5.95)-r/F.F. #347-349 w/new Arthur Adams-c 1 2 3 5 6 8
...: Nobody Gets Out Alive (1994, $15.95) TPB r/ #387-392 16.00
... Omnibus Vol. 1 HC (2005, $99.99) r/#1-30 & Annual 1 plus letter pages; 3 intros. and a 1974 essay by Stan Lee; original plot synopsis for FF #1; essays and Kirby art 100.00
... Omnibus Vol. 2 HC (2007, $99.99) r/#31-60, Annual 2-4 and Not Brand Echh #1 plus letter pages and essays by Stan Lee, Reginald Hudlin, Roy Thomas and others 100.00
Special Edition 1(5/84)-r/Annual #1; Byrne-c/a 5.00
...: The Lost Adventure (4/08, $4.99) Lee & Kirby story partially used in flashback in FF #108 completed with additional art by Frenz & Sinnott; plus reprint of FF #108 5.00
... Visionaries: George Pérez Vol. 1 (2005, $19.99) r/#164-167,170,176-178,184-186 20.00
... Visionaries: George Pérez Vol. 2 (2006, $19.99) r/#187-188,191-192, Annual #14-15, Marvel Two-In-One #60 and back-up story from Adventures of the Thing #3 20.00
... Visionaries (11/01, $19.95) r/#232-240 by John Byrne 20.00
... Visionaries Vol. 2 (2004, $24.99) r/#241-250 by John Byrne 25.00
... Visionaries John Byrne Vol. 3 (2004, $24.99) r/#251-257; Annual #17; Avengers #233 and Thing #2 25.00
... Visionaries John Byrne Vol. 4 (2005, $24.99) r/#258-267; Alpha Flight #4 & Thing #10 25.00
... Visionaries John Byrne Vol. 5 (2005, $24.99) r/#268-275; Annual #18 & Thing #19 25.00
... Visionaries John Byrne Vol. 6 ('06, $24.99) r/#276-284; Secret Wars II #2 & Thing #23 25.00
... Visionaries John Byrne Vol. 7 ('07, $24.99) r/#285,286, Ann. #19, Avengers #263 & Ann. #14, and X-Factor #1 25.00
... Visionaries John Byrne Vol. 8 ('07, $24.99) r/#287-295 25.00
... Visionaries: Walter Simonson Vol. 1 (2007, $19.99) r/#334-341 20.00

NOTE: ***Arthur Adams*** *c/a-347-349p.* ***Austin*** *c(i)-232-236, 238, 240-242, 250i, 286i.* ***Buckler*** *c-151, 168.* ***John Buscema*** *a(p)-107, 108(w/**Kirby, Sinnott** & **Romita**),109-130, 132, 134-141, 160, 173-175, 202, 296-309p, Annual 11, 13; c(p)-107-122, 124-129, 133-139, 202, Annual 12p, Special 10.* ***Byrne*** *a-209-218p, 220p, 221p, 232-265, 266i, 267-273, 274-293p, Annual 17, 19; c-211-214p, 220p, 232-236p, 237, 238p, 239, 240-242p, 243-249, 250p, 251-267, 269-277, 278-281p, 283p, 284, 285, 286p, 288-293, Annual 17, 18.* ***Ditko*** *a-13i, 14i(w/**Kirby**-p), Annual 16.* ***G. Kane*** *c-145p, 146p, 150p, 160p.* ***Kirby*** *a-1-102p, 108p, 180r, 189r, 236p, Special 1-10; c-1-101, 164, 167, 171-177, 180, 181, 190, 200, Annual 11, Special 1-7, 9.* ***Marcos*** *a-Annual 14i.* ***Mooney*** *a-118i, 152i.* ***Perez*** *a(p)-164-167, 170-172, 176-178, 184-188, 191p, 192p. Annual 14p, 15p; c(p)-183-188, 191, 192, 194-197.* ***Simonson*** *a-337-341, 343, 344p, 345p, 346, 350p, 352-354; c-212, 334-341, 342p, 343-346, 350, 353, 354.* ***Steranko*** *c-130-132p.* ***Williamson*** *c-357i.*

FANTASTIC FOUR (Volume Two)
Marvel Comics: V2#1, Nov, 1996 - No. 13, Nov, 1997 ($2.95/$1.95/$1.99) (Produced by WildStorm Productions)

1-($2.95)-Reintro Fantastic Four; Jim Lee-c/a; Brandon Choi scripts; Mole Man app. 5.00
1-($2.95)-Variant-c 1 2 3 4 5 7
2-9: 2-Namor-c/app. 3-Avengers-c/app. 4-Two covers; Dr. Doom cameo 3.00
10,11,13: All $1.99-c. 13-"World War 3"-pt. 1, x-over w/Image 3.00
12-($2.99) "Heroes Reunited"-pt. 1 4.00
...: Heroes Reborn (7/00, $17.95, TPB) r/#1-6 18.00
Heroes Reborn: Fantastic Four (2006, $29.99, TPB) r/#1-12; Jim Lee intro.; pin-ups 30.00

FANTASTIC FOUR (Volume Three)
Marvel Comics: V3#1, Jan, 1998 - No. 588, Apr, 2011 ($2.99/$1.99/$2.25)
No. 600, Jan, 2012 - No. 611, Dec, 2012 (Issues #589-#599 do not exist, see FF series)

1-($2.99)-Heroes Return; Lobdell-s/Davis & Farmer-a 1 2 3 5 6 8
1-Alternate Heroes Return-c 1 3 4 6 8 10
2-4,12: 2-2-covers. 4-Claremont-s/Larroca-a begin; Silver Surfer c/app.
12-($2.99) Wraparound-c by Larroca 5.00
5-11: 6-Heroes For Hire app. 9-Spider-Man-c/app. 4.00
13-24: 13,14-Ronan-c/app. 3.00
25-($2.99) Dr. Doom returns 4.00
26-49: 27-Dr. Doom marries Sue. 30-Begin $2.25-c. 32,42-Namor-c/app. 35-Regular cover; Pacheco-s/a begins. 37-Super-Skrull-c/app. 38-New Baxter Building 3.00
35-($3.25) Variant foil enhanced-c; Pacheco-s/a begins 4.00
50-($3.99, 64 pgs.) BWS-c; Grummett, Pacheco, Rude, Udon-a 4.00
51-53,55-59: 51-53-Bagley-a(p)/Wieringo-c; Inhumans app. 55,56-Immonen-a
57-59-Warren-s/Grant-a 3.00
54-($3.50, 100 pgs.) Birth of Valeria; r/Annual #6 birth of Franklin 4.00
60-(9¢-c) Waid-s/Wieringo-a begin 3.00
60-($2.25 newsstand edition)(also see Promotional Comics section) 3.00
61-70: 62-64-FF vs. Modulus. 65,66-Buckingham-a. 68-70-Dr. Doom app. 3.00
(After #70 [Aug, 2003] numbering reverted back to original Vol. 1 with #500, Sept, 2003)
500-($3.50) Regular edition; concludes Dr. Doom app.; Dr. Strange app.; Rivera painted-c 4.00
500-($4.99) Director's Cut Edition; chromium-c by Wieringo; sketch and script pages 8.00
501-516: 501,502-Casey Jones-a. 503-508-Porter-a. 509-Wieringo-c/a resumes. 512,513-Spider-Man app. 514-516-Ha-c/Medina-a 3.00
517-537: 517-Begin $2.99-c. 519-523-Galactus app. 527-Straczynski-s begins. 537-Dr. Doom. 3.00
527-Variant Edition with different McKone-c 3.00
527-Wizard World Philadelphia Edition with B&W McKone sketch-c 3.00
536-Variant cover by Bryan Hitch 5.00
537-B&W variant cover 5.00
538-542-Civil War. 538-Don Blake reclaims Thor's hammer 4.00
543-45th Anniversary; Black Panther and Storm replace Reed and Sue; Granov-c 4.00
544-553: 544-546-Silver Surfer app.; Turner-c 3.00
554-568-Millar-s/Hitch-a/c. 558-561-Doctor Doom-c/app. 562-Funeral & proposal 3.00
554-Variant-c by Bianchi 6.00
554-Variant Skrull-c by Suydam 30.00
569-($3.99) Wraparound-c; Immonen-a; Dr. Doom app. 4.00
570-586: 570-572,575-578-Eaglesham-a. 574-Spider-Man app. 584-586-Galactus app. 3.00
587-(3/11, $3.99) Death of Human Torch; Epting-a; issue is in black polybag; Davis-c 4.00
587-Variant-c by Cassaday 10.00
588-($3.99) Last issue; Dragotta-a; preview of FF #1; back-up w/Spider-Man; Davis-c 4.00
589-599-**Do not exist**; story continues in FF series
600-(1/12, $7.99) Avengers app.; Human Torch returns, back-up short stories; Dell'Otto-c 8.00
600-Variant-c by John Romita, Jr. 10.00
600-Variant-c by Art Adams 15.00
601-603,605,605.1, 606-611: 601-603-Johnny Storm & Avengers app. 602,603-Galactus app. 605.1-Alternate origin; Choi-a. 607,608-Black Panther app. 611-Doctor Doom app. 3.00
604-($3.99) Future Franklin and Valeria app. 4.00
...'98 Annual ($3.50) Immonen-a 4.00
...'99 Annual ($3.50) Ladronn-a 4.00
...'00 Annual ($3.50) Larocca-a; Marvel Girl back-up story 4.00
...'01 Annual ($2.99) Maguire-a; Thing back-up w/Yu-a 4.00
... Annual 32 (8/10, $4.99) Hitch-a/c 5.00
... Annual 33 (9/12, $4.99) Alan Davis-s/a/c; Dr. Strange & Clan Destine app. 5.00
... : A Death in the Family (7/06, $3.99, one-shot) Weeks-a/c; and r/F.F. #245 4.00
... By J. Michael Straczynski Vol. 1 (2005, $19.99, HC) r/#527-532 20.00
Civil War: Fantastic Four TPB (2007, $17.99) r/#538-543; 45th Anniversary Toasts 18.00
... Cosmic-Size Special 1 (2/09, $4.99) Cary Bates-s/Bing Cansino-a; r/F.F. #237 5.00
Fantastic 4th Voyage of Sinbad (9/01, $5.95) Claremont-s/Ferry-a 6.00
Flesh and Stone (8/01, $12.95, TPB) r/#35-39 13.00
... Giant-Size Adventures 1 (8/09, $3.99) Cifuentes & Coover-a; Egghead app. 4.00
... In...Ataque del M.O.D.O.K.! (11/10, $3.99) English & Spanish editions; Beland-s/Doe-a 4.00
... /Inhumans TPB (2007, $19.99) r/#51-54 and Inhumans ('00) #1-4 20.00
...: Isla De La Muerte! (2/08, $3.99) English & Spanish editions; Beland-s/Doe-a 4.00
... MGC #570 (7/11, $1.00) r/#570 with "Marvel's Greatest Comics" cover banner 3.00
... Presents: Franklin Richards 1 (11/05, $2.99) r/back-up stories from Power Pack #1-4 plus new 5 pg. story; Sumerak-s/Eliopoulos-a (Also see Franklin Richards) 3.00
...Special (2/06, $2.99) McDuffie-s/Casey Jones-a; dinner with Dr. Doom 3.00
...Tales Vol. 1 (2005, $7.99, digest) r/Marvel Age: FF Tales #1, Tales of the Thing #1-3, and Spider-Man Team-Up Special 8.00
...: The Last Stand (8/11, $4.99) r/#574, 587 & 588 (death of Johnny Storm) 5.00
...: The New Fantastic Four HC (2007, $19.99) r/#544-550; variant covers & sketch pgs. 20.00
...: The New Fantastic Four SC (2008, $15.99) r/#544-550; variant covers & sketch pgs. 16.00
... : The Wedding Special 1 (1/06, $5.00) 40th Anniversary new story & r/FF Annual #3 5.00
... Vol. 1 HC (2004, $29.99, dust jacket) oversized reprint /#60-70, 500-502; Mark Waid intro and series proposal; cover gallery 30.00
... Vol. 2 HC (2005, $29.99, d.j.) oversized r/#503-513; Waid intro.; deleted scenes 30.00
... Vol. 3 HC (2005, $29.99, d.j.) oversized r/#514-524; Waid commentaries; cover sketches 30.00
... Vol. 1: Imaginauts (2003, $17.99, TPB) r/#56,60-66; Mark Waid's series proposal 18.00
... Vol. 2: Unthinkable (2003, $17.99, TPB) r/#67-70,500-502; #500 Director's Cut extras 18.00
... Vol. 3: Authoritative Action (2004, $12.99, TPB) r/#503-508 13.00
... Vol. 4: Hereafter (2004, $11.99, TPB) r/#509-513 12.00
... Vol. 5: Disassembled (2004, $14.99, TPB) r/#514-519 15.00
... Vol. 6: Rising Storm (2005, $13.99, TPB) r/#520-524 14.00
...: The Beginning of the End TPB (2008, $14.99) r/#525,526,551-553 & Fantastic Four: Isla De La Muerte! one-shot 15.00
...: The Life Fantastic TPB (2006, $16.99) r/#533-535; The Wedding Special, Special (2/06) and A Death in the Family one-shots 17.00

Fantastic Four (2014 series) #1 © MAR

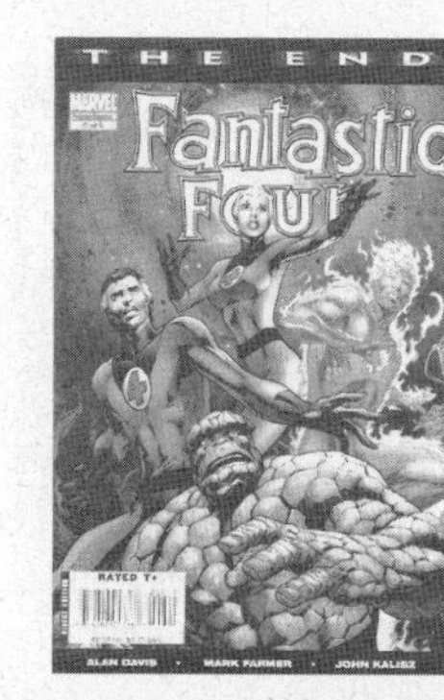

Fantastic Four: The End #6 © MAR

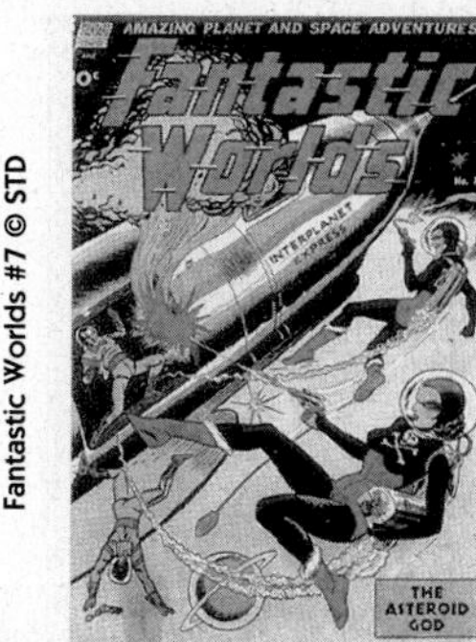

Fantastic Worlds #7 © STD

GD VG FN VF VF/NM NM-
2.0 4.0 6.0 8.0 9.0 9.2

Wizard #1/2 -Lim-a 10.00

FANTASTIC FOUR (Volume Four) (Marvel NOW!) (Also see FF)
Marvel Comics: Jan, 2013 - No. 16, Mar, 2014 ($2.99)

1-5-Fraction-s/Bagley-a/c 3.00
5AU-(5/13, $3.99) Age of Ultron tie-in; Fraction-s/Araújo-a/Bagley-c 4.00
6-15: 6,7-Blastaar app. 9,13-15-Dr. Doom app. 14,15-Ienco-a 3.00
16-($3.99) Fantastic Four vs. Doom, The Annihilating Conqueror; back-up w/Quinones-a 4.00

FANTASTIC FOUR (Volume Five) (All-New Marvel NOW!)
Marvel Comics: Apr, 2014 - Present ($3.99)

1,2-Robinson-s/Kirk-a 4.00

FANTASTIC FOUR AND POWER PACK
Marvel Comics: Sept, 2007 - No. 4, Dec, 2007 ($2.99, limited series)

1-4-Gurihiru-a/Van Lente-s; the Wizard app. 3.00
...: Favorite Son TPB (2008, $7.99, digest size) r/#1-4 8.00

FANTASTIC FOUR: ATLANTIS RISING
Marvel Comics: June, 1995 - No. 2, July, 1995 ($3.95, limited series)

1,2: Acetate-c 5.00
Collector's Preview (5/95, $2.25, 52 pgs.) 4.00

FANTASTIC FOUR: BIG TOWN
Marvel Comics: Jan, 2001 - No. 4, Apr, 2001 ($2.99, limited series)

1-4:"What If?" story; McKone-a/Englehart-s 3.00

FANTASTIC FOUR: FIREWORKS
Marvel Comics: Jan, 1999 - No. 3, Mar, 1999 ($2.99, limited series)

1-3-Remix; Jeff Johnson-a 3.00

FANTASTIC FOUR: FIRST FAMILY
Marvel Comics: May, 2006 - No. 6, Oct, 2006 ($2.99, limited series)

1-6-Casey-s/Weston-a; flashback to the days after the accident 3.00
TPB (2006, $15.99) r/#1-6 16.00

FANTASTIC FOUR: FOES
Marvel Comics: Mar, 2005 - No. 6, Aug, 2005 ($2.99, limited series)

1-6-Kirkman-s/Rathburn-a. 1-Puppet Master app. 3-Super-Skrull app. 4-Mole Man app. 3.00
TPB (2005, $16.99) r/#1-6 17.00

FANTASTIC FOUR: HOUSE OF M (Reprinted in House of M: Fantastic Four/ Iron Man TPB)
Marvel Comics: Sept, 2005 - No. 3, Nov, 2005 ($2.99, limited series)

1-3: Fearsome Four, led by Doom; Scot Eaton-a 3.00

FANTASTIC FOUR INDEX (See Official...)

FANTASTIC FOUR/ IRON MAN: BIG IN JAPAN
Marvel Comics: Dec, 2005 - No. 4, Mar, 2006 ($3.50, limited series)

1-4-Seth Fisher-a/c; Zeb Wells-s; wraparound-c on each 3.50
TPB (2006, $12.99) r/#1-4 and Seth Fisher illustrated story from Spider-Man Unlimited #8 13.00

FANTASTIC FOUR: 1 2 3 4
Marvel Comics: Oct, 2001 - No. 4, Jan, 2002 ($2.99, limited series)

1-4-Morrison-s/Jae Lee-a. 2-4-Namor-c/app. 3.00
TPB (2002, $9.99) r/#1-4 10.00

FANTASTIC FOUR ROAST
Marvel Comics Group: May, 1982 (75¢, one-shot, direct sales)

1-Celebrates 20th anniversary of F.F.#1; X-Men, Ghost Rider & many others cameo; Golden, Miller, Buscema, Rogers, Byrne, Anderson art; Hembeck/Austin-c 5.00

FANTASTIC FOUR: THE END
Marvel Comics: Jan, 2007 - No. 6, May, 2007 ($2.99, limited series)

1-6-Alan Davis-s/a; last adventure of the future FF. 1-Dr. Doom-c/app. 3.00
Roughcut #1 ($3.99) B&W pencil art for full story and text script; B&W sketch cover 4.00
HC (2007, $19.99, dustjacket) r/#1-6 20.00
SC (2008, $14.99) r/#1-6 15.00

FANTASTIC FOUR: THE LEGEND
Marvel Comics: Oct, 1996 ($3.95, one-shot)

1-Tribute issue 4.00

FANTASTIC FOUR: THE MOVIE
Marvel Comics: Aug, 2005 ($4.99/$12.99, one-shot)

1-($4.99) Movie adaptation; Jurgens-a; behind the scenes feature; Doom origin; photo-c 5.00
TPB-($12.99) Movie adaptation, r/Fantastic Four #5 & 190, and FF Vol. 3 #60, photo-c 13.00

FANTASTIC FOUR: TRUE STORY
Marvel Comics: Sept, 2008 - No. 4, Jan, 2009 ($2.99, limited series)

1-4-Cornell-s/Domingues-a/Henrichon-c 3.00

FANTASTIC FOUR 2099
Marvel Comics: Jan, 1996 - No. 8, Aug, 1996 ($3.95/$1.95)

1-($3.95)-Chromium-c; X-Nation preview 4.00
2-8: 4-Spider-Man 2099-c/app. 5-Doctor Strange app. 7-Thibert-c 3.00
NOTE: *Williamson a-1i; c-1i.*

FANTASTIC FOUR UNLIMITED
Marvel Comics: Mar, 1993 - No. 12, Dec, 1995 ($3.95, 68 pgs.)

1-12: 1-Black Panther app. 4-Thing vs. Hulk. 5-Vs. The Frightful Four. 6-Vs. Namor. 7, 9-12-Wraparound-c 4.00

FANTASTIC FOUR UNPLUGGED
Marvel Comics: Sept, 1995 - No. 6, Aug 1996 (99¢, bi-monthly)

1-6 3.00

FANTASTIC FOUR - UNSTABLE MOLECULES
(Indicia for #1 reads STARTLING STORIES: ... ; #2 reads UNSTABLE MOLECULES)
Marvel Comics: Mar, 2003 - No. 4, June, 2003 ($2.99, limited series)

1-4-Guy Davis-c/a 3.00
Fantastic Four Legends Vol. 1 TPB (2003, $13.99) r/#1-4, origin from FF #1 (1963) 14.00
TPB (2005, $13.99) r/#1-4 14.00

FANTASTIC FOUR VS. X-MEN
Marvel Comics: Feb, 1987 - No. 4, June, 1987 (Limited series)

1-4: 4-Austin-a(i) 4.00

FANTASTIC FOUR: WORLD'S GREATEST COMICS MAGAZINE
Marvel Comics: Feb, 2001 - No. 12 (Limited series)

1-12: Homage to Lee & Kirby era of F.F.; s/a by Larsen & various. 5-Hulk-c/app. 10-Thor app. 3.00

FANTASTIC GIANTS (Formerly Konga #1-23)
Charlton Comics: V2#24, Sept, 1966 (25¢, 68 pgs.)

V2#24-Special Ditko issue; origin Konga & Gorgo reprinted plus two new Ditko stories 6 12 18 38 69 100

FANTASTIC TALES
I. W. Enterprises: 1958 (no date) (Reprint, one-shot)

1-Reprints Avon's "City of the Living Dead" 3 6 9 19 30 40

FANTASTIC VOYAGE (See Movie Comics)
Gold Key: Aug, 1969 - No. 2, Dec, 1969

1 (TV) 4 8 12 27 44 60
2-Cover has the text "Civilian Miniaturized Defense Force" in yellow bar at top; back cover has painted art 3 6 9 19 30 40
2-Variant cover has text "In This Issue Sweepstakes..." along top; ad on back-c 4 8 12 23 37 50

FANTASTIC VOYAGES OF SINDBAD, THE
Gold Key: Oct, 1965 - No. 2, June, 1967

1-Painted-c on both 6 12 18 37 66 95
2 5 10 15 30 50 70

FANTASTIC WORLDS
Standard Comics: No. 5, Sept, 1952 - No. 7, Jan, 1953

5-Toth, Anderson-a 37 74 111 222 361 500
6-Toth-c/a 30 60 90 177 289 400
7 21 42 63 122 199 275

FANTASY FEATURES
Americomics: 1987 - No. 2, 1987 ($1.75)

1,2 3.00

FANTASY ILLUSTRATED
New Media Publ.: Spring 1982 ($2.95, B&W magazine)

1-P. Craig Russell-c/a; art by Ditko, Sekowsky, Sutton; Englehart-s 1 2 3 4 5 7

FANTASY MASTERPIECES (Marvel Super Heroes No. 12 on)
Marvel Comics Group: Feb, 1966 - No. 11, Oct, 1967; V2#1, Dec, 1979 - No. 14, Jan, 1981

1-Photo of Stan Lee (12¢-c #1,2) 8 16 24 56 108 160
2-r/1st Fin Fang Foom from Strange Tales #89 5 10 15 34 60 85
3-8: 3-G.A. Capt. America-r begin, end #11; 1st 25¢ Giant; Colan-r. 3-6-Kirby-c(p). 4-Kirby-c(p)(i). 7-Begin G.A. Sub-Mariner, Torch-r/M. Mystery. 8-Torch battles the Sub-Mariner-r/Marvel Mystery #9 5 10 15 35 63 90
9-Origin Human Torch-r/Marvel Comics #1 6 12 18 37 66 95
10,11: 10-r/origin & 1st app. All Winners Squad from All Winners #19. 11-r/origin of Toro

Fantomex MAX #1 © MAR

Fast Fiction #1 © Seaboard

Fatale #15 © Basement Gang

	GD 2.0	VG 4.0	FN 6.0	VF 8.0	VF/NM 9.0	NM- 9.2
(H.T. #1) & Black Knight #1	5	10	15	34	60	85
V2#1(12/79, 75¢, 52 pgs.)-r/origin Silver Surfer from Silver Surfer #1 with editing plus reprints cover; J. Buscema-a	2	4	6	9	12	15
2-14-Reprints Silver Surfer #2-14 w/covers						6.00

NOTE: ***Buscema** c-V2#7-9(in part). **Ditko** r-1-3, 7, 9. **Everett** r-1,7-9. **Matt Fox** r-9i. **Kirby** r-1-11; c(p)-3, 4i, 5, 6. **Starlin** r-8-13. Some direct sale V2#14's had a 50¢ cover price. #3-11 contain Capt. America-r/Capt. America #3-10. #7-11 contain G.A.Human Torch & Sub-Mariner-r.*

FANTASY QUARTERLY (Also see Elfquest)
Independent Publishers Syndicate: Spring, 1978 (B&W)

	GD	VG	FN	VF	VF/NM	NM-
1-1st app. Elfquest; Dave Sim-a (6 pgs.)	8	16	24	54	102	150

FANTOMAN (Formerly Amazing Adventure Funnies)
Centaur Publications: No. 2, Aug, 1940 - No. 4, Dec, 1940

	GD	VG	FN	VF	VF/NM	NM-
2-The Fantom of the Fair, The Arrow, Little Dynamite-r begin; origin The Ermine by Filchock; Fantoman app. in 2-4; Burgos, J. Cole, Ernst, Gustavson-a	115	230	345	730	1253	1775
3,4: Gustavson-r. 4-Red Blaze story	89	178	267	565	970	1375

FANTOMEX MAX
Marvel Comics: Dec, 2013 - No. 4, Mar, 2014 ($3.99)

1-4-Hope-s/Crystal-a/Francavilla-c 4.00

FAREWELL MOONSHADOW (See Moonshadow)
DC Comics (Vertigo): Jan, 1997 ($7.95, one-shot)

nn-DeMatteis-s/Muth-c/a 8.00

FARGO KID (Formerly Justice Traps the Guilty)(See Feature Comics #47)
Prize Publications: V11#3(#1), June-July, 1958 - V11#5, Oct-Nov, 1958

	GD	VG	FN	VF	VF/NM	NM-
V11#3(#1)-Origin Fargo Kid, Severin-c/a; Williamson-a(2); Heath-a	18	36	54	105	165	225
V11#4,5-Severin-c/a	13	26	39	74	105	135

FARMER'S DAUGHTER, THE
Stanhall Publ./Trojan Magazines: Feb-Mar, 1954 - No. 3, June-July, 1954; No. 4, Oct, 1954

	GD	VG	FN	VF	VF/NM	NM-
1-Lingerie, nudity panel	61	122	183	390	670	950
2-4(Stanhall)	42	84	126	265	445	625

FARSCAPE (Based on TV series)
BOOM! Studios: Nov, 2008 - No. 4, Feb, 2009 ($3.99)

1-4-O'Bannon-s/Patterson-a; multiple covers 4.00

FARSCAPE (Based on TV series)
BOOM! Studios: Nov, 2009 - No. 24, Oct, 2011 ($3.99)

	NM-
1-24-O'Bannon-s/Sliney-a; multiple covers	4.00
...: D'Argo's Lament 1-4 (4/09 - No. 4, 7/09, $3.99) Edwards-a; three covers on each	4.00
...: D'Argo's Quest 1-4 (12/09 - No. 4, 3/10, $3.99) Cleveland-a; three covers on each	4.00
...: D'Argo's Trial 1-4 (8/09 - No. 4, 11/09, $3.99) Cleveland-a; multiple covers on each	4.00
...: Gone and Back 1-4 (7/09 - No. 4, 10/09, $3.99) Patterson-a; multiple covers on each	4.00
...: Scorpius 0-7 (4/10 - No. 7, 2010, $3.99) 0-3-Ruiz-a; multiple-c. 4-7-Purcell-a	4.00
...: Strange Detractors 1-4 (3/09 - No. 4, 6/09, $3.99) Sliney-a; three covers on each	4.00

FARSCAPE: WAR TORN (Based on TV series)
DC Comics (WildStorm): Apr, 2002 - No. 2, May, 2002 ($4.95, limited series)

1,2-Teranishi-a/Wolfman-s; photo-c 5.00

FASHION IN ACTION
Eclipse Comics: Aug, 1986 - Feb, 1987 (Baxter paper)

Summer Special 1 , Winter Special 1, each Snyder III-c/a 3.00

FASTBALL EXPRESS (Major League Baseball)
Ultimate Sports Force: 2000 ($3.95, one-shot)

1-Polybagged with poster; Johnson, Maddux, Park, Nomo, Clemens app. 4.00

FASTEST GUN ALIVE, THE (Movie)
Dell Publishing Co.: No. 741, Sept, 1956 (one-shot)

	GD	VG	FN	VF	VF/NM	NM-
Four Color 741-Photo-c	6	12	18	40	73	105

FAST FICTION (...Action) (Stories by Famous Authors Illustrated #6 on)
Seaboard Publ./Famous Authors Ill.: Oct, 1949 - No. 5, Mar, 1950
(All have Kiefer-c)(48 pgs.)

	GD	VG	FN	VF	VF/NM	NM-
1-Scarlet Pimpernel; Jim Lavery-c/a	28	56	84	135	270	375
2-Captain Blood; H. C. Kiefer-c/a	24	48	72	142	234	325
3-She, by Rider Haggard; Vincent Napoli-a	30	60	90	177	289	400
4-(1/50, 52 pgs.)-The 39 Steps; Lavery-c/a	19	38	57	112	176	240
5-Beau Geste; Kiefer-c/a	19	38	57	112	176	240

NOTE: ***Kiefer** a-2, 5; c-2, 3,5. **Lavery** c/a-1, 4. **Napoli** a-3.*

FAST FORWARD
DC Comics (Piranha Press): 1992 - No. 3, 1993 ($4.95, 68 pgs.)

1-3: 1-Morrison scripts; McKean-c/a. 3-Sam Kieth-a 5.00

FAST WILLIE JACKSON
Fitzgerald Periodicals, Inc.: Oct, 1976 - No. 7, 1977

	GD	VG	FN	VF	VF/NM	NM-
1	3	6	9	19	30	40
2-7	3	6	9	14	20	25

FAT ALBERT (...& the Cosby Kids) (TV)
Gold Key: Mar, 1974 - No. 29, Feb, 1979

	GD	VG	FN	VF	VF/NM	NM-
1	4	8	12	25	40	55
2-10	3	6	9	15	22	28
11-29	2	4	6	10	14	18

FATALE (Also see Powers That Be #1 & Shadow State #1,2)
Broadway Comics: Jan, 1996 - No. 6, Aug, 1996 ($2.50)

1-6: J.G. Jones-c/a in all, Preview Edition 1 (11/95, B&W) 3.00

FATALE
Image Comics: Jan, 2012 - Present ($3.50)

	NM-
1-Brubaker-s/Phillips-a/c	5.00
1-Variant-c of Demon with machine gun	8.00
1-Second through Fifth printings	4.00
2-21-Brubaker-s/Phillips-a/c in all	3.50

FAT AND SLAT (Ed Wheelan) (Becomes Gunfighter No. 5 on)
E. C. Comics: Summer, 1947 - No. 4, Spring, 1948

	GD	VG	FN	VF	VF/NM	NM-
1-Intro/origin Voltage, Man of Lightning; "Comics" McCormick, the World's No. 1 Comic Book Fan begins, ends #4	39	78	117	240	395	550
2-4: 4-Comics McCormick-c feature	26	52	78	154	252	350

FAT AND SLAT JOKE BOOK
All-American Comics (William H. Wise): Summer, 1944 (52 pgs., one-shot)

	GD	VG	FN	VF	VF/NM	NM-
nn-by Ed Wheelan	30	60	90	177	289	400

FATE (See Hand of Fate & Thrill-O-Rama)

FATE
DC Comics: Oct, 1994 - No. 22, Sept, 1996 ($1.95/$2.25)

0,1-22: 8-Begin $2.25-c. 11-14-Alan Scott (Sentinel) app. 10,14-Zatanna app. 21-Phantom Stranger app. 22-Spectre app. 3.00

FATHOM
Comico: May, 1987 - No. 3, July, 1987 ($1.50, limited series)

1-3 3.00

FATHOM
Image Comics (Top Cow Prod.): Aug, 1998 - No. 14, May, 2002 ($2.50)

	NM-
Preview	12.00
0-Wizard supplement	7.00
0-($6.95) DF Alternate	7.00
1/2 (Wizard) origin of Cannon; Turner-a	6.00
1/2 (3/03, $2.99) origin of Cannon	3.00
1-Turner-s/a; three covers; alternate story pages	6.00
1-Wizard World Ed.	9.00
2-14: 12-14-Witchblade app. 13,14-Tomb Raider app.	3.00
9-Green foil-c edition	15.00
9,12-Holofoil editions	18.00
12,13-DFE alternate-c	6.00
13,14-DFE Gold edition	8.00
14-DFE Blue	15.00
... Collected Edition 1 (3/99, $5.95) r/Preview & all three #1's	6.00
... Collected Edition 2-4 (3-12/99, $5.95) 2-r/#2,3. 3-r/#4,5. 4-r/#6,7	6.00
... Collected Edition 5 (4/00, $5.95) 5-r/#8,9	6.00
... Primer (6/11, $1.00) Comic style summary of Volume 1; text summaries of Vol. 2 & 3	3.00
... Swimsuit Special (5/99, $2.95) Pin-ups by various	3.00
... Swimsuit Special 2000 (12/00, $2.95) Pin-ups by various; Turner-c	3.00
Michael Turner's Fathom HC ('01, $39.95) r/#1-9, black-c w/silver foil	40.00
Michael Turner's Fathom SC ('01, $24.95) r/#1-9, new Turner-c	25.00
Michael Turner's Fathom The Definitive Edition ('08, $49.95) r/Preview, #0,1/2,1-14, Swimsuit Special 1999 & 2000; cover gallery; foreword by Geoff Johns	50.00

FATHOM (MICHAEL TURNER'S...) (Volume 2)
Aspen MLT, Inc.: No. 0, Apr, 2005 - No. 11, Dec, 2006 ($2.50/$2.99)

	NM-
0-($2.50) Turnbull-a/Turner-c	3.00
1-11-($2.99) 1-Five covers. 2-Two covers. 4-Six covers	3.00
... Beginnings (2005, $1.99) Two covers; Turnbull-a	3.00
...: Killian's Vessel 1 (7/07, $2.99) 3 covers; Odagawa-a	3.00
... Prelude (6/05, $2.99) Seven covers; Garza-a	3.00

Fathom V4 #6 © Aspen MLT

Fauntleroy Comics #2 © AP

Fawcett Movie Comic #17 © FAW

FATHOM (MICHAEL TURNER'S...) (Volume 3)
Aspen MLT, Inc.: No. 0, Jun, 2008 - No. 10, Feb, 2010 ($2.50/$2.99)

	GD 2.0	VG 4.0	FN 6.0	VF 8.0	VF/NM 9.0	NM- 9.2
0-($2.50) Garza-a/c						3.00
1-10-($2.99) Garza-a; multiple covers on each						3.00

FATHOM (MICHAEL TURNER'S...) (Volume 4)
Aspen MLT, Inc.: No. 0, Jun, 2011 - No. 9, May, 2013 ($2.50/$2.99/$3.50)

	GD 2.0	VG 4.0	FN 6.0	VF 8.0	VF/NM 9.0	NM- 9.2
0-($2.50) Lobdell-s/Konat-a/c; interview with Lobdell; sketch art						3.00
1-3-($2.99) 1-Five covers						3.00
4-9-($3.50)						3.50

FATHOM (MICHAEL TURNER'S...) (Volume 5)
Aspen MLT, Inc.: Jul, 2013 - Present ($1.00/$3.99)

	GD 2.0	VG 4.0	FN 6.0	VF 8.0	VF/NM 9.0	NM- 9.2
1-($1.00) Wohl-s/Konat-a; multiple covers						3.00
2-5-($3.99) Multiple covers on all						4.00

FATHOM: BLUE DESCENT (MICHAEL TURNER'S...)
Aspen MLT, Inc.: Jun, 2010 - No. 4, Feb, 2012 ($2.50/$2.99, limited series)

	GD 2.0	VG 4.0	FN 6.0	VF 8.0	VF/NM 9.0	NM- 9.2
0-($2.50) Scott Clark-a; covers by Clark & Benitez						3.00
1-4-($2.99) Alex Sanchez-a. 1-Covers by Clark & Finch						3.00

FATHOM: CANNON HAWKE (MICHAEL TURNER'S...)
Aspen MLT, Inc.: Nov, 2005 - No. 5, Feb, 2006 ($2.99)

	GD 2.0	VG 4.0	FN 6.0	VF 8.0	VF/NM 9.0	NM- 9.2
1-5-To-a/Turner-c						3.00
... Prelude (11/05, $2.50) Turner-c						3.00

FATHOM: DAWN OF WAR (MICHAEL TURNER'S...)
Aspen MLT, Inc.: Oct, 2004 - No. 3, Dec, 2004 ($2.99, limited series)

	GD 2.0	VG 4.0	FN 6.0	VF 8.0	VF/NM 9.0	NM- 9.2
0-Caldwell-a						3.00
1-3-Caldwell-a						3.00
...: Cannon Hawke #0 ('04, $2.50) Turner-c						3.00
... The Complete Saga Vol. 1 (2005, $9.99) r/series with cover gallery						10.00

FATHOM: KIANI (MICHAEL TURNER'S...)
Aspen MLT, Inc.: No. 0, Feb, 2007 - No. 4, Dec, 2007 ($2.99, limited series)

	GD 2.0	VG 4.0	FN 6.0	VF 8.0	VF/NM 9.0	NM- 9.2
0-4-Marcus To-a. 1-Six covers						3.00
Vol. 2 (4/12, $2.50) 0-Four covers						3.00
Vol. 2 (5/12 - No. 4, 11/12, $3.50) 1-4-Hernandez-s/Nome-a; multiple covers on each						3.50
Vol. 3 (3/14, $3.99) 1-Multiple covers						4.00

FATHOM: KILLIAN'S TIDE
Image Comics (Top Cow Prod.): Apr, 2001 - No. 4, Nov, 2001 ($2.95)

	GD 2.0	VG 4.0	FN 6.0	VF 8.0	VF/NM 9.0	NM- 9.2
1-4-Caldwell-a(p); two covers by Caldwell and Turner. 2-Flip-book preview of Universe						3.00
1-DFE Blue, 1-Holographic logo						12.00
4-Foil-c						12.00

FATHOM: THE ELITE SAGA (MICHAEL TURNER'S...)
Aspen MLT, Inc.: Jun, 2013 - No. 5, Jul, 2013 ($3.99, weekly limited series)

	GD 2.0	VG 4.0	FN 6.0	VF 8.0	VF/NM 9.0	NM- 9.2
1-5-Hernandez-s/Marion-a; multiple covers; leads into Fathom Volume 5						4.00

FATIMA...CHALLENGE TO THE WORLD (Also see Our Lady of Fatima)
Catechetical Guild: 1951, 36 pgs. (15¢)

	GD 2.0	VG 4.0	FN 6.0	VF 8.0	VF/NM 9.0	NM- 9.2
nn (not same as 'Challenge to the World')	6	12	18	29	36	42

FATMAN, THE HUMAN FLYING SAUCER
Lightning Comics(Milson Publ. Co.): April, 1967 - No. 3, Aug-Sept, 1967 (68 pgs.) (Written by Otto Binder)

	GD 2.0	VG 4.0	FN 6.0	VF 8.0	VF/NM 9.0	NM- 9.2
1-Origin/1st app. Fatman & Tinman by Beck	5	10	15	35	63	90
2-C. C. Beck-a	4	8	12	25	40	55
3-(Scarce)-Beck-a	6	12	18	37	66	95

FAULTLINES
DC Comics (Vertigo): May, 1997 - No. 6, Oct, 1997 ($2.50, limited series)

	GD 2.0	VG 4.0	FN 6.0	VF 8.0	VF/NM 9.0	NM- 9.2
1-6-Lee Marrs-s/Bill Koeb-a in all						3.00

FAUNTLEROY COMICS (Super Duck Presents...)
Close-Up/Archie Publications: 1950; No. 2, 1951; No. 3, 1952

	GD 2.0	VG 4.0	FN 6.0	VF 8.0	VF/NM 9.0	NM- 9.2
1-Super Duck-c/stories by Al Fagaly in all	10	20	30	54	72	90
2,3	6	12	18	31	38	45

FAUST
Northstar Publishing/Rebel Studios #7 on: 1989 - No 13, 1997 ($2.00/$2.25, B&W, mature themes)

	GD 2.0	VG 4.0	FN 6.0	VF 8.0	VF/NM 9.0	NM- 9.2
1-Decapitation-c; Tim Vigil-c/a in all	3	6	9	14	19	24
1-2nd - 4th printings						4.00
2	2	4	6	8	10	12
2-2nd & 3rd printings, 3,5-2nd printing						4.00
3	1	3	4	6	8	10
4-10: 7-Begin Rebel Studios series						5.00
11-13-Scarce	2	4	6	8	10	12

FAWCETT MOTION PICTURE COMICS (See Motion Picture Comics)

FAWCETT MOVIE COMIC
Fawcett Publications: 1949 - No. 20, Dec, 1952 (All photo-c)

	GD 2.0	VG 4.0	FN 6.0	VF 8.0	VF/NM 9.0	NM- 9.2
nn- "Dakota Lil"; George Montgomery & Rod Cameron (1949)	20	40	60	114	182	250
nn- "Copper Canyon"; Ray Milland & Hedy Lamarr (1950)	15	30	45	86	133	180
nn- "Destination Moon" (1950)	61	122	183	390	670	950
nn- "Montana"; Errol Flynn & Alexis Smith (1950)	15	30	45	86	133	180
nn- "Pioneer Marshal"; Monte Hale (1950)	15	30	45	86	133	180
nn- "Powder River Rustlers"; Rocky Lane (1950)	20	40	60	114	182	250
nn- "Singing Guns"; Vaughn Monroe, Ella Raines & Walter Brennan (1950)	14	28	42	82	121	160
7- "Gunmen of Abilene"; Rocky Lane; Bob Powell-a (1950)	16	32	48	92	144	195
8- "King of the Bullwhip"; Lash LaRue; Bob Powell-a (1950)	21	42	63	126	206	285
9- "The Old Frontier"; Monte Hale; Bob Powell-a (2/51; mis-dated 2/50)	15	30	45	90	140	190
10- "The Missourians"; Monte Hale (4/51)	15	30	45	90	140	190
11- "The Thundering Trail"; Lash LaRue (6/51)	19	38	57	111	176	240
12- "Rustlers on Horseback"; Rocky Lane (8/51)	15	30	45	90	140	190
13- "Warpath"; Edmond O'Brien & Forrest Tucker (10/51)	14	28	42	80	115	150
14- "Last Outpost"; Ronald Reagan (12/51)	32	64	96	188	307	425
15-(Scarce)- "The Man From Planet X"; Robert Clark; Schaffenberger-a (2/52)	245	490	735	1568	2684	3800
16- "Ten Tall Men"; Burt Lancaster	13	26	39	74	105	135
17- "Rose of Cimarron"; Jack Buetel & Mala Powers	10	20	30	58	79	100
18- "The Brigand"; Anthony Dexter & Anthony Quinn; Schaffenberger-a	10	20	30	58	79	100
19- "Carbine Williams"; James Stewart; Costanza-a; James Stewart photo-c	11	22	33	62	86	110
20- "Ivanhoe"; Robert Taylor & Liz Taylor photo-c	18	36	54	105	165	225

FAWCETT'S FUNNY ANIMALS (No. 1-26, 80-on titled "Funny Animals"; becomes Li'l Tomboy No. 92 on?)
Fawcett Publications/Charlton Comics No. 84 on: 12/42 - #79, 4/53; #80, 6/53 - #83, 12?/53; #84, 4/54 - #91, 2/56

	GD 2.0	VG 4.0	FN 6.0	VF 8.0	VF/NM 9.0	NM- 9.2
1-Capt. Marvel on cover; intro. Hoppy The Captain Marvel Bunny, cloned from Capt. Marvel; Billy the Kid & Willie the Worm begin	58	116	174	371	636	900
2-Xmas-c	36	72	108	211	343	475
3-5: 3(2/43)-Spirit of '43-c	25	50	75	150	245	340
6,7,9,10	15	30	45	88	137	185
8-Flag-c	16	32	48	92	144	195
11-20: 14-Cover is a 1944 calendar	12	24	36	69	97	125
21-40: 25-Xmas-c. 26-St. Valentine's Day-c	10	20	30	54	72	90
41-86,90,91	9	18	27	47	61	75
87-89(10-54-2/55)-Merry Mailman ish (TV/Radio)-part photo-c	10	20	30	54	72	90

NOTE: *Marvel Bunny in all issues to at least No. 68 (not in 49-54).*

FAZE ONE FAZERS
AC Comics: 1986 - No. 4, Sept, 1986 (Limited series)

	GD 2.0	VG 4.0	FN 6.0	VF 8.0	VF/NM 9.0	NM- 9.2
1-4						3.00

F.B.I., THE
Dell Publishing Co.: Apr-June, 1965

	GD 2.0	VG 4.0	FN 6.0	VF 8.0	VF/NM 9.0	NM- 9.2
1-Sinnott-a	3	6	9	17	26	35

F.B.I. STORY, THE (Movie)
Dell Publishing Co.: No. 1069, Jan-Mar, 1960

	GD 2.0	VG 4.0	FN 6.0	VF 8.0	VF/NM 9.0	NM- 9.2
Four Color 1069-Toth-a; James Stewart photo-c	8	16	24	54	102	150

FBP: FEDERAL BUREAU OF PHYSICS (Titled Collider for issue #1)
DC Comics (Vertigo): Sept, 2013 - Present ($2.99)

	GD 2.0	VG 4.0	FN 6.0	VF 8.0	VF/NM 9.0	NM- 9.2
Collider #1- Simon Oliver-s/Robbi Rodriguez-a/Nathan Fox-c						3.00
2-8: 2-(10/13)						3.00

FEAR (Adventure into...)
Marvel Comics Group: Nov, 1970 - No. 31, Dec, 1975

	GD 2.0	VG 4.0	FN 6.0	VF 8.0	VF/NM 9.0	NM- 9.2
1-Fantasy & Sci-Fi-r in early issues; 68 pg. Giant size; Kirby-a(r)	7	14	21	46	86	125
2-6: 2-4-(68 pgs.). 5,6-(52 pgs.) Kirby-a(r)	4	8	12	27	44	60

Fear Agent #1 © Remender, Moore & Walker

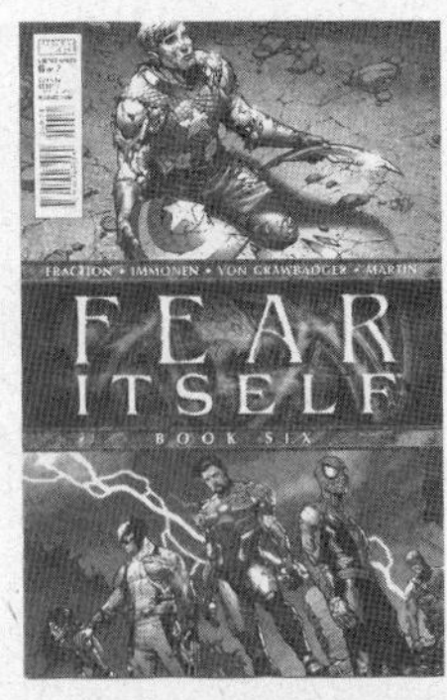

Fear Itself #6 © MAR

Fearless Defenders #11 © MAR

	GD 2.0	VG 4.0	FN 6.0	VF 8.0	VF/NM 9.0	NM- 9.2
7-9-Kirby-a(r)	3	6	9	17	26	35
10-Man-Thing begins (10/72, 4th app.), ends #19; see Savage Tales #1 for 1st app.; 1st solo series; Chaykin/Morrow-c/a;	5	10	15	33	57	80
11,12: 11-N. Adams-c. 12-Starlin/Buckler-a	3	6	9	16	23	30
13,14,16-18: 17-Origin/1st app. Wundarr	3	6	9	14	20	26
15-1st full-length Man-Thing story (8/73)	3	6	9	16	24	32
19-Intro. Howard the Duck; Val Mayerik-a (12/73)	5	10	15	31	53	75
20-Morbius, the Living Vampire begins, ends #31; has history recap of Morbius with X-Men & Spider-Man	5	10	15	31	53	75
21-23,25	3	6	9	14	20	26
24-Blade-c/sty	3	6	9	21	33	45
26-31	2	4	6	10	14	18

NOTE: ***Bolle** a-13i. **Brunner** c-15-17. **Buckler** a-11p, 12i. **Chaykin** a-10i. **Colan** a-23r. **Craig** a-10p. **Ditko** a-6-8r. **Evans** a-30. **Everett** a-9, 10i, 21r. **Gulacy** a-20p. **Heath** a-12r. **Heck** a-8r, 13r. **Gil Kane** a-21p; c(p)-20, 21, 23-28, 31. **Kirby** a-1-9r. **Maneely** a-24r. **Mooney** a-11i, 26r. **Morrow** a-11i. **Paul Reinman** a-14r. **Robbins** a(p)-25-27, 31. **Russell** a-23p, 24p. **Severin** c-8. **Starlin** c-12p.*

FEAR AGENT
Image Comics (#1-11)/Dark Horse Comics.: Oct, 2005 - No. 32, Nov, 2011 ($2.99/$3.50)

1-11: 1-Remender-s/Moore-a. 5-Opeña-a begins. 11-Francavilla-a 3.00
... The Last Goodbye 1-4 (Dark Horse, 6/07 - No. 4, 9/07) (#12-15) 3.00
Tales of the Fear Agent: Twelve Steps in One (#16), 17-27 3.00
28-32-($3.50) Hawthorne & Moore-a/Moore-c 3.50
... Vol 1.: Re-Ignition TPB (2006, $9.99) r/#1-4 10.00
... Vol 2.: My War TPB (Dark Horse Books, 2007, $14.95) r/#5-10; Opeña sketch pages 15.00

FEARBOOK
Eclipse Comics: April, 1986 ($1.75, one-shot, mature)

1-Scholastic Mag-r; Bissette-a 4.00

FEAR EFFECT (Based on the video game)
Image Comics (Top Cow): May, 2000; March, 2001 ($2.95)

Retro Helix 1 (3/01), Special 1 (5/00) 3.00

FEAR IN THE NIGHT (See Complete Mystery No. 3)

FEAR ITSELF
Marvel Comics: Jun, 2011 - No. 7, Dec, 2011 ($3.99/$4.99, limited series)

1-6-Fraction-s/Immonen-a/McNiven-c. 3-Bucky apparently killed 4.00
1-Blank cover 4.00
7-($4.99) Thor perishes; previews of ...: The Fearless, Incredible Hulk #1, Defenders #1 5.00
7.1 Captain America (1/12, $3.99) Brubaker-s/Guice-a; Bucky's fate 4.00
7.2 Thor (1/12, $3.99) Fraction-s/Adam Kubert-a/c; Thor's funeral; Tanarus returns 4.00
7.3 Iron Man (1/12, $3.99) Fraction-s/Larroca-a/c; Odin app. 4.00
...: Black Widow (8/11, $3.99) Peter Nguyen-a; Peregrine app. 4.00
...: Book of the Skull (5/11, $3.99) prequel to series; WWII flashback, Red Skull app. 4.00
...: Fellowship of Fear (10/11, $3.99) profiles of hammer-wielders and fear thrivers 4.00
...: FF (9/11, $2.99) Reed & Sue vs. Ben Grimm; Grummett-a/Dell'Otto-c 3.00
...: Sin's Past (6/11, $4.99) r/Captain America #355-357; Sisters of Sin app. 5.00
... Spotlight (6/11, $3.99) Interviews with Fraction and Immonen; feature articles 4.00
...: The Monkey King (11/11, $2.99) Joshua Fialkov-s/Juan Doe-a 3.00
...: The Worthy (9/11, $3.99) Origins of the hammer wielders; s/a by various 4.00

FEAR ITSELF: DEADPOOL
Marvel Comics: Aug, 2011 - No. 3, Oct, 2011 ($2.99, limited series)

1-3-Hastings-s/Dazo-a 3.00

FEAR ITSELF: FEARSOME FOUR
Marvel Comics: Aug, 2011 - No. 4, Nov, 2011 ($2.99, limited series)

1-4-Art by Bisley and others; Man-Thing, She-Hulk & Howard the Duck app. 3.00

FEAR ITSELF: HULK VS. DRACULA
Marvel Comics: Nov, 2011 - No. 3, Dec, 2011 ($2.99, limited series)

1-3-Gischler-s/Stegman-a; Dell'Otto-c 3.00

FEAR ITSELF: SPIDER-MAN
Marvel Comics: Jul, 2011 - No. 3, Sept, 2011 ($2.99, limited series)

1-3-Yost-s/McKone-a; Vermin app. 3.00

FEAR ITSELF: THE DEEP
Marvel Comics: Aug, 2011 - No. 4, Nov, 2011 ($2.99, limited series)

1-4-Bunn-s/Garbett-a; Sub-Mariner vs. Attuma; Doctor Strange & Silver Surfer app. 3.00

FEAR ITSELF: THE FEARLESS (Follows Fear Itself #7)
Marvel Comics: Dec, 2011 - No. 12, Jun, 2012 ($2.99, limited series)

1-12: 1-Fate of the Hammers; Bagley & Pelletier-a; Art Adams-c. 7-Wolverine app. 3.00

FEAR ITSELF: THE HOME FRONT
Marvel Comics: Jun, 2011 - No. 7, Dec, 2011 ($3.99, limited series)

1-7-Short story anthology; Speedball w/Mayhew-a in all; Chaykin-a; Djurdjevic-c 4.00

FEAR ITSELF: UNCANNY X-FORCE
Marvel Comics: Sept, 2011 - No. 3, Nov, 2011 ($2.99, limited series)

1-3-Bianchi-a/c 3.00

FEAR ITSELF: WOLVERINE
Marvel Comics: Sept, 2011 - No. 3, Nov, 2011 ($2.99, limited series)

1-3-Boschi-a; Wolverine vs. S.T.R.I.K.E. 1-Acuña-c. 2,3-Molina-c 3.00

FEAR ITSELF: YOUTH IN REVOLT
Marvel Comics: Jul, 2011 - No. 6, Dec, 2011 ($2.99, limited series)

1-6-Firestar and The Initiative app.; McKeever-s/Norton-a 3.00

FEARLESS DEFENDERS (Marvel NOW!)
Marvel Comics: Apr, 2013 - No. 12, Feb, 2014 ($2.99/3.99)

1-4,5-7: 1-Valkyrie & Misty Knight team-up; Bunn-s/Sliney-a. 2-Dani Moonstar app. 3.00
4AU-(7/13, $3.99) Age of Ultron tie-in; Dr. Doom & Ares app. 4.00
8-12-($3.99) 4.00

FEARLESS FAGAN
Dell Publishing Co.: No. 441, Dec, 1952 (one-shot)

	GD 2.0	VG 4.0	FN 6.0	VF 8.0	VF/NM 9.0	NM- 9.2
Four Color 441	4	8	12	25	40	55

FEATURE BOOK (Dell) (See Large Feature Comic)

FEATURE BOOKS (Newspaper-r, early issues)
David McKay Publications: May, 1937 - No. 57, 1948 (B&W)
(Full color, 68 pgs. begin #26 on)

Note: See individual alphabetical listings for prices

nn-Popeye & the Jeep (#1, 100 pgs.); reprinted as Feature Books #3(Very Rare; only 3 known copies, 1-VF, 2-in low grade)
nn-Dick Tracy (#1)-Reprinted as Feature Book #4 (100 pgs.) & in part as 4-Color #1 (Rare, less than 10 known copies)

NOTE: *Above books were advertised together with different covers from Feat. Books #3 & 4.*

1-King of the Royal Mtd. (#1)
3-Popeye (7/37) by Segar;
4-Dick Tracy (8/37)-Same as nn issue but a new cover added
6-Dick Tracy (10/37)
8-Secret Agent X-9 (12/37) -Not by Raymond
9-Dick Tracy (1/38)
11-Little Annie Rooney (#1, 3/38)
13-Inspector Wade (5/38)
15-Barney Baxter (#1) (7/38)
17-Gangbusters (#1, 9/38) (1st app.)
20-Phantom (#1, 12/38)
22-Phantom
24-Lone Ranger (1941)
26-Prince Valiant (1941)-Hal Foster-c/a; newspaper strips reprinted, pgs. 1-28,30-63; color & 68 pg. issues begin; Foster cover is only original comic book artwork by him
36('43),38,40('44),42,43, 45,47-Blondie
39-Phantom
46-Mandrake in the Fire World-(58 pgs.)
48-Maltese Falcon by Dashiell Hammett('46)
51,54-Rip Kirby; Raymond-c/s; origin-#51
53,56,57-Phantom
2-Popeye (6/37) by Segar same as nn issue but a new cover added
5-Popeye (9/37) by Segar
7-Little Orphan Annie (#1, 11/37) (Rare)-Reprints strips from 12/31/34 to 7/17/35
10-Popeye (2/38)
12-Blondie (#1) (4/38) (Rare)
14-Popeye (6/38) by Segar
16-Red Eagle (8/38)
18,19-Mandrake
21-Lone Ranger
23-Mandrake
25-Flash Gordon (#1)-Reprints not by Raymond
27-29,31,34-Blondie
30-Katzenjammer Kids (#1, 1942)
32,35,41,44-Katzenjammer Kids
33(nn)-Romance of Flying; World War II photos
37-Katzenjammer Kids; has photo & biog. of Harold H. Knerr (1883-1949) who took over strip from Rudolph Dirks in 1914
49,50-Perry Mason; based on Gardner novels
52,55-Mandrake

NOTE: *All Feature Books through #25 are over-sized 8-1/2x11-3/8" comics with color covers and black and white interiors. The covers are rough, heavy stock. The page counts, including covers, are as follows: nn, #3, 4-100 pgs.; #1, 2-52 pgs.; #5-25 are all 76 pgs. #33 was found in bound set from publisher. Reprints from 1980s exist.*

FEATURE COMICS (Formerly Feature Funnies)
Quality Comics Group: No. 21, June, 1939 - No. 144, May, 1950

	GD 2.0	VG 4.0	FN 6.0	VF 8.0	VF/NM 9.0	NM- 9.2
21-The Clock, Jane Arden & Mickey Finn continue from Feature Funnies	56	112	168	356	608	860
22-26: 23-Charlie Chan begins (8/39, 1st app.)	41	82	123	250	418	585
26-(nn, nd)-Cover in one color, (10¢, 36 pgs.; issue No. blanked out. Two variations exist, each contain half of the regular #26)	41	82	123	250	418	585
27-(12/39, Rare)-Origin/1st app. Doll Man by Eisner (scripts) & Lou Fine (art); Doll Man begins, ends #139	584	1168	1752	4263	7532	10,800
28-(1/40, Rare)-2nd app. Doll Man by Lou Fine	216	432	648	1372	2361	3350

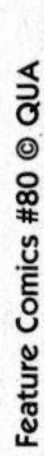
Feature Comics #80 © QUA

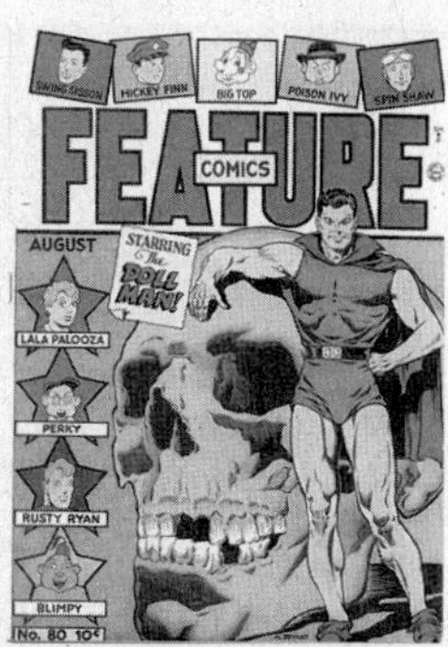

Feature Funnies #9 © QUA

Felix the Cat #19 © KING

	GD 2.0	VG 4.0	FN 6.0	VF 8.0	VF/NM 9.0	NM- 9.2
29	113	226	339	718	1084	1750
30-1st Doll Man-c	200	400	600	1280	2190	3100
31-Last Clock & Charlie Chan issue (4/40); Charlie Chan moves to Big Shot #1 following month (5/40)	76	152	228	486	831	1175
32,34,36: Dollman covers. 32-Rusty Ryan & Samar begin. 34-Captain Fortune app.	76	152	228	486	831	1175
33,35,37: 37-Last Fine Doll Man	48	96	144	302	514	725

NOTE: *A 15¢ Canadian version of Feature Comics #37, made in the US, exists.*

	GD	VG	FN	VF	VF/NM	NM-
38,40-Dollman covers. 38-Origin the Ace of Space. 40-Bruce Blackburn in costume	57	114	171	362	619	875
39,41: 39-Origin The Destroying Demon, ends #40; X-Mas-c.	40	80	120	242	401	560
42,46,48,50-Dollman covers. 42-USA, the Spirit of Old Glory begins. 46-Intro. Boyville Brigadiers in Rusty Ryan. 48-USA ends	43	86	129	271	461	650
43,45,47,49: 47-Fargo Kid begins	30	60	90	177	289	400
44-Doll Man by Crandall begins, ends #63; Crandall-a(2)	55	110	165	352	601	850
51,53,55,57,59: 57-Spider Widow begins	22	44	66	128	209	290
52,54,56,58,60-Dollman covers. 56-Marijuana story in Swing Sisson strip. 60-Raven begins, ends #71	31	62	93	186	303	420
61,63,65,67	20	40	60	114	182	250
62,64,66,68-Dollman covers. 68-(5/43)	28	56	84	165	270	375
69,71-Phantom Lady x-over in Spider Widow	22	44	66	128	209	290
70-Dollman-c; Phantom Lady x-over	30	60	90	177	289	400
72,74,77-80,100-Dollman covers. 72-Spider Widow ends	22	44	66	132	216	300
73,75,76	17	34	51	98	154	210
81-99-All Dollman covers	17	34	51	98	154	210
101-144: 139-Last Doll Man & last Doll Man cover. 140-Intro. Stuntman Stetson (Stuntman Stetson c-140-144)	15	30	45	84	127	170

NOTE: ***Celardo** a-37-43. **Crandall** a-44-60, 62, 63-on(most). **Gustavson** a-(Rusty Ryan)- 32-134. **Powell** a-34, 64-73. The Clock c-25, 28, 29. Doll Man c-30, 32, 34, 36, 38, 40, 42, 44, 46, 48, 50, 52, 54, 56, 58, 60, 62, 64, 66, 68, 70, 72, 74, 77-139. Joe Palooka c-21, 24, 27.*

FEATURE FILMS
National Periodical Publ.: Mar-Apr, 1950 - No. 4, Sept-Oct, 1950 (All photo-c)

	GD	VG	FN	VF	VF/NM	NM-
1- "Captain China" with John Payne, Gail Russell, Lon Chaney & Edgar Bergen	66	132	198	416	701	985
2- "Riding High" with Bing Crosby	69	138	207	435	735	1035
3- "The Eagle & the Hawk" with John Payne, Rhonda Fleming & D. O'Keefe	66	132	198	416	701	985
4- "Fancy Pants"; Bob Hope & Lucille Ball	72	144	216	454	770	1085

FEATURE FUNNIES (Feature Comics No. 21 on)(Earliest Quality Comics title)
Comic Favorites Inc./Quality Comics Group: Oct, 1937 - No. 20, May, 1939

	GD	VG	FN	VF	VF/NM	NM-
1(V9#1-indicia)-Joe Palooka, Mickey Finn (1st app.), The Bungles, Jane Arden, Dixie Dugan (1st app.), Big Top, Ned Brant, Strange As It Seems, & Off the Record strip reprints begin	322	644	966	1770	2635	3500
2-The Hawk app. (11/37); Goldberg-c	150	300	450	825	1213	1600
3-Hawks of Seas begins by Eisner, ends #12; The Clock begins; Christmas-c	117	234	351	644	947	1250
4,5	86	172	258	473	699	925
6-12: 11-Archie O'Toole by Bud Thomas begins, ends #22	67	134	201	369	542	715
13-Espionage, Starring Black X begins by Eisner, ends #20	71	142	213	391	578	765
14-20	50	100	150	275	408	540

NOTE: *Joe Palooka covers 1, 6, 9, 12, 15, 18.*

FEATURE PRESENTATION, A (Feature Presentations Magazine #6)
(Formerly Women in Love) (Also see Startling Terror Tales #11)
Fox Features Syndicate: No. 5, April, 1950

	GD	VG	FN	VF	VF/NM	NM-
5(#1)-Black Tarantula (scarce)	61	122	183	390	670	950

FEATURE PRESENTATIONS MAGAZINE (Formerly A Feature Presentation #5; becomes Feature Stories Magazine #3 on)
Fox Features Syndicate: No. 6, July, 1950

	GD	VG	FN	VF	VF/NM	NM-
6(#2)-Moby Dick; Wood-c	34	68	102	199	325	450

FEATURE STORIES MAGAZINE (Formerly Feature Presentations Mag. #6)
Fox Features Syndicate: No. 3, Aug, 1950

	GD	VG	FN	VF	VF/NM	NM-
3-Jungle Lil, Zegra stories; bondage-c	41	82	123	250	418	585

FEDERAL MEN COMICS
DC Comics: 1936

nn-Ashcan comic, not distributed to newsstands, only for in house use (no known sales)

FEDERAL MEN COMICS (See Adventure Comics #32, The Comics Magazine, New Adventure Comics, New Book of Comics, New Comics & Star Spangled Comics #91)
Gerard Publ. Co.: No. 2, 1945 (DC reprints from 1930's)

	GD	VG	FN	VF	VF/NM	NM-
2-Siegel/Shuster-a; cover redrawn from Det. #9	37	74	111	218	354	490

FELICIA HARDY: THE BLACK CAT
Marvel Comics: July, 1994 - No. 4, Oct, 1994 ($1.50, limited series)

1-4: 1,4-Spider-Man app. 3.00

FELIX'S NEPHEWS INKY & DINKY
Harvey Publications: Sept, 1957 - No. 7, Oct, 1958

	GD	VG	FN	VF	VF/NM	NM-
1-Cover shows Inky's left eye with 2 pupils	10	20	30	58	79	100
2-7	7	14	21	37	46	55

NOTE: ***Messmer** art in 1-6. **Oriolo** a-1-7.*

FELIX THE CAT (See Cat Tales 3-D, The Funnies, March of Comics #24,36,51, New Funnies & Popular Comics)
Dell Publ. No. 1-19/Toby No. 20-61/Harvey No. 62-118/Dell No. 1-12:
1943 - No. 118, Nov, 1961; Sept-Nov, 1962 - No. 12, July-Sept, 1965

	GD	VG	FN	VF	VF/NM	NM-
Four Color 15	71	142	213	568	1284	2000
Four Color 46('44)	36	72	108	266	596	925
Four Color 77('45)	34	68	102	245	548	850
Four Color 119('46)-All new stories begin	29	58	87	209	467	725
Four Color 135('46)	20	40	60	141	313	485
Four Color 162(9/47)	15	30	45	105	233	360
1(2-3/48)(Dell)	24	48	72	168	372	575
2	12	24	36	79	170	260
3-5	9	18	27	62	126	190
6-19(2-3/51-Dell)	8	16	24	51	96	140
20-30,32,33,36,38-61(6/55)-All Messmer issues.(Toby): 28-(2/52)-Some copies have #29 on cover, #28 on inside (Rare in high grade)	14	28	42	93	204	315
31,34,35-No Messmer-a; Messmer-c only 31,34	8	16	24	51	96	140
37-(100 pgs., 25 ¢, 1/15/53, X-Mas-c, Toby; daily & Sunday-r (rare)	34	68	102	242	541	840
62(8/55)-80,100 (Harvey)	4	8	12	27	44	60
81-99	4	8	12	23	37	50
101-118(11/61): 101-117-Reprints. 118-All new-a	3	6	9	17	26	35
12-269-211(#1, 9-11/62)(Dell)-No Messmer	4	8	12	28	47	65
2-12(7-9/65)(Dell, TV)-No Messmer	4	8	12	23	37	50
3-D Comic Book 1(1953-One Shot, 25¢)-w/glasses	34	68	102	199	325	450
Summer Annual nn ('53, 25¢, 100 pgs., Toby)-Daily & Sunday-r	45	90	135	284	480	675
Winter Annual 2 ('54, 25¢, 100 pgs., Toby)-Daily & Sunday-r	42	84	126	265	445	625

(Special note: Despite the covers on Toby 37 and the Summer Annual above proclaiming "all new stories," they were actually reformatted newspaper strips)

NOTE: ***Otto Messmer** went to work for Universal Film as an animator in 1915 and then worked for the Pat Sullivan animation studio in 1916. He created a black cat in the cartoon short, Feline Follies in 1919 that became known as Felix in the early 1920s. The Felix Sunday strip began Aug. 14, 1923 and continued until Sept. 19, 1943 whjen **Messmer** took the character to Dell (Western Publishing) and began doing Felix comic books, first adapting strips to the comic format. The first all new Felix comic was Four Color #119 in 1946 (#4 in the Dell run). The daily Felix was begun on May 9, 1927 by another artist, but by the following year, **Messmer** did it too. King Features took the daily away from **Messmer** in 1954 and he began to do some of his most dynamic art for Toby Press. The daily was continued by **Joe Oriolo** who drew it until it was discontinued Jan. 9, 1967. **Oriolo** was **Messmer's** assistant for many years and inked some of **Messmer's** pencils through the Toby run, as well as doing some of the stories by himself. Though **Messmer** continued to work for Harvey, his contirubitons were limited, and no all **Messmer** stories appeared after the Toby run until some early Toby reprints were published in the 1990s Harvey revival of the title. 4-Color No. 15, 46, 77 and the Toby Annuals are all daily or Sunday newspaper reprints from the 1930's-1940's drawn by **Otto Messmer**. #101-r/#64; 102-r/#65; 103-r/#67; 104-117-r/#68-81. **Messmer**-a in all Dell/Toby/Harvey issues except #31, 34, 35, 97, 98, 100, 118. **Oriolo** a-20, 31-on.*

FELIX THE CAT (Also see The Nine Lives of...)
Harvey Comics/Gladstone: Sept, 1991 - No. 7, Jan, 1993 ($1.25/$1.50, bi-monthly)

1: 1950s-r/Toby issues by Messmer begins. 1-Inky and Dinky back-up story (produced by Gladstone) 4.00
2-7, Big Book, V2#1 (9/92, $1.95, 52 pgs.) 4.00

FELIX THE CAT AND FRIENDS
Felix Comics: 1992 - No. 5, 1993 ($1.95)

1-5: 1-Contains Felix trading cards 3.00

FELIX THE CAT & HIS FRIENDS (Pat Sullivan's...)
Toby Press: Dec, 1953 - No. 3, 1954 (Indicia title for #2&3 as listed)

	GD	VG	FN	VF	VF/NM	NM-
1 (Indicia title, "Felix and His Friends," #1 only)	29	58	87	170	278	385
2-3	18	36	54	105	165	225

FELIX THE CAT DIGEST MAGAZINE
Harvey Comics: July, 1992 ($1.75, digest-size, 98 pgs.)

1-Felix, Richie Rich stories 6.00

FELIX THE CAT KEEPS ON WALKIN'

FF (2013 series) #12 © MAR

52 #46 © DC

Fight Against Crime #6 © Story

GD VG FN VF VF/NM NM-
2.0 4.0 6.0 8.0 9.0 9.2

GD VG FN VF VF/NM NM-
2.0 4.0 6.0 8.0 9.0 9.2

Hamilton Comics: 1991 ($15.95, 8-1/2"x11", 132 pgs.)
nn-Reprints 15 Toby Press Felix the Cat and Felix and His Friends stories in new color 16.00

FELL
Image Comics: Sept, 2005 - No. 9, Jan, 2008 ($1.99)
1-9-Warren Ellis-s/Ben Templesmith-a 3.00
..., Vol. 1: Feral City TPB (2007, $14.99) r/#1-8 15.00

FELON
Image Comics (Minotaur Press): Nov, 2001 - No. 4, Apr, 2002 ($2.95, B&W)
1-4-Rucka-s/Clark-a/c 3.00

FEM FANTASTIQUE
AC Comics: Aug, 1988 ($1.95, B&W)
V2#1-By Bill Black; Bettie Page pin-up 4.00

FEMFORCE (Also see Untold Origin of the Femforce)
Americomics: Apr, 1985 - No. 109 (1.75-/2.95, B&W #16-56)
1-Black-a in most; Nightveil, Ms. Victory begin 1 3 4 6 8 10
2-10 4.00
11-43: 25-Origin/1st app. new Ms. Victory. 28-Colt leaves. 29,30-Camilla-r by Mayo from Jungle Comics. 36-(2.95, 52 pgs.) 4.00
44,64: 44-W/mini-comic, Catman & Kitten #0. 64-Re-intro Black Phantom 5.00
45-49,51-63,65-99: 51-Photo-c from movie. 57-Begin color issues. 95-Photo-c 3.00
50 ($2.95, 52 pgs.)-Contains flexi-disc; origin retold; most AC characters app. 4.00
100-($3.95) 5.00
100-($6.90)-Polybagged 1 2 3 5 6 8
101-109-($4.95) 5.00
Special 1 (Fall, '84)(B&W, 52pgs.)-1st app. Ms. Victory, She-Cat, Blue Bulleteer, Rio Rita & Lady Luger 4.00
Bad Girl Backlash-(12/95, $5.00) 5.00
Frightbook 1 ('92, $2.95, B&W)-Halloween special, In the House of Horror 1 ('89, 2.50, B&W), Night of the Demon 1 ('90, 2.75, B&W), Out of the Asylum Special 1 ('87, B&W, $1.95), Pin-Up Portfolio 4.00
Pin-Up Portfolio (5 issues) 4.00

FEMFORCE UP CLOSE
AC Comics: Apr, 1992 - No. 11, 1995 ($2.75, quarterly)
1-11: 1-Stars Nightveil; inside f/c photo from Femforce movie. 2-Stars Stardust. 3-Stars Dragonfly. 4-Stars She-Cat 4.00

FERDINAND THE BULL (See Mickey Mouse Magazine V4#3)(Walt Disney's)
Dell Publishing Co.: 1938 (10¢, large size (9-1/2" x 10"), some color w/rest B&W)
nn 20 40 60 118 192 265

FERRET
Malibu Comics: Sept, 1992; May, 1993 - No. 10, Feb, 1994 ($1.95)
1-(1992, one-shot) 3.00
1-10: 1-Die-cut-c. 2-4-Collector's Ed. w/poster. 5-Polybagged w/Skycap 3.00
2-4-($1.95)-Newsstand Edition w/different-c 3.00

FERRYMAN
DC Comics (WildStorm): Early Dec, 2008 - No. 5, Mar, 2009 ($3.50)
1-5-Andreyko-s/Wayshak-a 3.50

FEVER RIDGE: A TALE OF MACARTHUR'S JUNGLE WAR
IDW Publishing: Feb, 2013 - No. 4, Oct, 2013 ($3.99)
1-4-Heimos-s/Runge-a/DeStefano-l; 1940s War stories on New Guinea 4.00

FF (Fantastic Four after Human Torch's death)
Marvel Comics: May, 2011 - No. 23, Dec, 2012 ($3.99)
1-Hickman-s/Epting-a; Spider-Man joins 4.00
1-Blank variant cover 4.00
1-Variant-c by Daniel Acuña 8.00
1-Variant-c by Stan Goldberg 6.00
2-23-($2.99) 2-Dr. Doom joins. 4,5-Kitson-a. 5-7-Black Bolt returns. 10,11-Avengers app. 3.00
...: Fifty Fantastic Years 1 (11/11, $4.99) Handbook format profiles of heroes and foes 5.00

FF (Marvel NOW!)
Marvel Comics: Jan, 2013 - No. 16, Mar, 2014 ($2.99)
1-15: 1-Fraction-s/Allred-a; new team forms (Ant-Man, She-Hulk, Medusa, Ms. Thing) 6,9-Quinones-a. 7,8,12-15-Dr. Doom app. 11-Impossible Man app. 3.00
16-($3.99) Ant-Man vs. Doom; back-up w/Quinones-a; Uatu & Silver Surfer app. 4.00

F5
Image Comics/Dark Horse: Jan, 2000 - No. 4, Oct, 2000 ($2.50/$2.95)
Preview (1/00, $2.50) Character bios and b&w pages; Daniel-s/a 3.00
1-($2.95, 48 pages) Tony Daniel-s/a 4.00
1-($20.00) Variant bikini-c 20.00
2-4-($2.50) 3.00
F5 Origin (Dark Horse Comics, 11/01, $2.99) w/cover gallery & sketches 3.00

FIBBER McGEE & MOLLY (Radio)(Also see A-1 Comics)
Magazine Enterprises: No. 25, 1949 (one-shot)
A-1 25 12 24 36 69 97 125

FICTION ILLUSTRATED
Byron Preiss Visual Publ./Pyramid: No. 1, Jan, 1975 - No. 4, Jan, 1977 ($1.00, #1,2 are digest size, 132 pgs.; #3,4 are graphic novels for mail order and specialty bookstores only)
1,2: 1-Schlomo Raven; Sutton-a. 2-Starfawn; Stephen Fabian-a. 2 4 6 13 18 22
3-($1.00-c, 4 3/4 x 6 1/2" digest size) Chandler; new Steranko-a 3 6 9 14 20 26
3-($4.95-c, 8 1/2 x 11" graphic novel; low print) same contents and indicia, but "Chandler" is the cover feature title 5 10 15 31 53 75
4-($4.95-c, 8 1/2 x 11" graphic novel; low print) Son of Sherlock Holmes; Reese-a 4 8 12 27 44 60

FIELD, THE
Image Comics: Apr, 2014 - Present ($3.50)
1-Brisson-s/Roy-a 3.50

FIERCE
Dark Horse Comics (Rocket Comics): July, 2004 - No. 4, Dec, 2004 ($2.99, limited series)
1-4-Jeremy Love-s/Robert Love-a 3.00

15-LOVE
Marvel Comics: Aug, 2011 - No. 3, Oct, 2011 ($4.99, limited series)
1-3-Tennis academy story; Andi Watson-s/Tommy Ohtsuka-a/c; Sho Murase-c 5.00

50 GIRLS 50
Image Comics: Jun, 2011 - No. 4, Sept, 2011 ($2.99, limited series)
1-4-Frank Cho-c; Cho & Murray-s/Medellin-a 3.00

52 (Leads into Countdown series)
DC Comics: Week One, July, 2006 - Week Fifty-Two, Jul, 2007 ($2.50, weekly series)
1-Chronicles the year after Infinite Crisis; Johns, Morrison, Rucka & Waid-s; JG Jones-c 4.00
2-10: 2-History of the DC Universe back-up thru #11. 7-Intro. Kate Kane. 10-Supernova 3.00
11-Batwoman debut (single panel cameo in #9) 4.00
12-52: 12-Isis gains powers; back-up 2 pg. origins begin. 15-Booster Gold killed. 17-Lobo returns. 30-Batman-c/Robin & Nightwing app. 37-Booster Gold returns. 38-The Question dies. 42-Ralph Dibny dies. 44-Isis dies. 48-Renee becomes The Question. 50-World War III. 51-Mister Mind evolves. 52-The Multiverse is re-formed; wraparound-c 3.00
...: The Companion TPB (2007, $19.99) r/solo stories of series' prominent characters 20.00
...: Volume One TPB (2007, $19.99) r/#1-13; sample of page development; cover gallery 20.00
...: Volume Two TPB (2007, $19.99) r/#14-26; creator notes and sketches; cover gallery 20.00
...: Volume Three TPB (2007, $19.99) r/#27-39; notes and sketches; cover gallery 20.00
...: Volume Four TPB (2007, $19.99) r/#40-52; creator commentary; cover gallery 20.00

52 AFTERMATH: THE FOUR HORSEMEN (Takes place during 52 Week Fifty)
DC Comics: Oct, 2007 - No. 6, Mar, 2008 ($2.99, limited series)
1-6-Giffen-s/Olliffe-a; Superman, Batman & Wonder Woman app. 2-4,6-Van Sciver-c 3.00
TPB (2008, $19.99) r/#1-6 20.00

52/WWIII (Takes place during 52 Week Fifty)
DC Comics: Part One, Jun, 2007 - Part Four, Jun, 2007 ($2.50, 4 issues came out same day)
Part One - Part Four: Van Sciver-c; heroes vs. Black Adam. 3-Terra dies 3.00
DC: World War III TPB (2007, $17.99) r/Part One - Four and 52 Week 50 18.00

55 DAYS AT PEKING (See Movie Comics)

FIGHT AGAINST CRIME (Fight Against the Guilty #22, 23)
Story Comics: May, 1951 - No. 21, Sept, 1954
1-True crime stories #1-4 44 88 132 277 469 660
2 26 52 78 154 252 350
3,5: 5-Frazetta-a, 1 pg.; content change to horror & suspense 23 46 69 136 223 310
4-Drug story "Hopped Up Killers" 25 50 75 150 245 340
6,7: 6-Used in **POP**, pgs. 83,84 22 44 66 128 209 290
8-Last crime format issue 21 42 63 122 199 275
NOTE: *No. 9-21 contain violent, gruesome stories with blood, dismemberment, decapitation, E.C. style plot twists and several E.C. swipes. Bondage c-4, 6, 18, 19.*
9-11,13 48 96 144 302 514 725
12-Morphine drug story "The Big Dope" 52 104 156 328 552 775
14-Tothish art by Ross Andru; electrocution-c 52 104 156 328 552 775
15-B&W & color illos in **POP** 50 100 150 315 533 750
16-E.C. story swipe/Haunt of Fear #19; Tothish-a by Ross Andru;

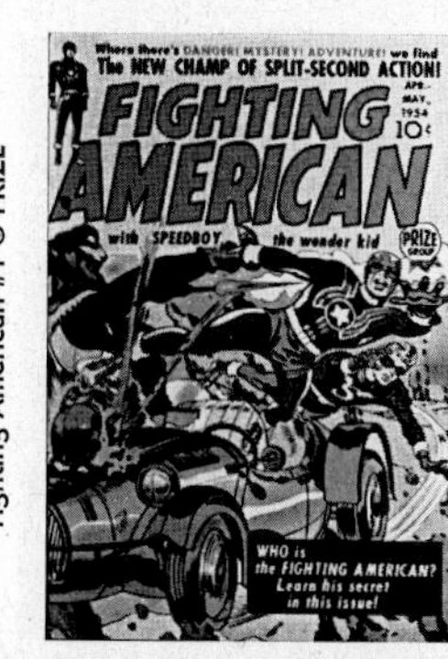

Fight Comics #29 © FH

Fighting American #1 © PRIZE

Fightin' Army #17 © CC

	GD 2.0	VG 4.0	FN 6.0	VF 8.0	VF/NM 9.0	NM- 9.2
bondage-c	52	104	156	328	552	775
17-Wildey E.C. story swipe/Shock SuspenStories #9; knife through neck-c (1/54)	55	110	165	352	601	850
18,19: 19-Bondage/torture-c	48	96	144	302	514	725
20-Decapitation cover; contains hanging, ax murder, blood & violence	181	362	543	1158	1979	2800
21-E.C. swipe	40	80	120	246	411	575

NOTE: ***Cameron** a-4, 5, 8. **Hollingsworth** a-3-7, 9, 10, 13. **Wildey** a-6, 15, 16.*

FIGHT AGAINST THE GUILTY (Formerly Fight Against Crime)
Story Comics: No. 22, Dec, 1954 - No. 23, Mar, 1955

	GD 2.0	VG 4.0	FN 6.0	VF 8.0	VF/NM 9.0	NM- 9.2
22-Tothish-a by Ross Andru; Ditko-a; E.C. story swipe; electrocution-c (Last pre-code)	41	82	123	250	418	585
23-Hollingsworth-a	27	54	81	160	263	365

FIGHT COMICS
Fiction House Magazines: Jan, 1940 - No. 83, 11/52; No. 84, Wint, 1952-53; No. 85, Spring, 1953; No. 86, Summer, 1954

	GD 2.0	VG 4.0	FN 6.0	VF 8.0	VF/NM 9.0	NM- 9.2
1-Origin Spy Fighter, Starring Saber; Jack Dempsey life story; Shark Brodie & Chip Collins begin; Fine-c; Eisner-a	377	754	1131	2639	4620	6600
2-Joe Louis life story; Fine/Eisner-c	135	270	405	864	1482	2100
3-Rip Regan, the Power Man begins (3/40); classic-c	135	270	405	864	1482	2100
4,5: 4-Fine-c	74	148	222	470	810	1150
6-10: 6,7-Powell-c	61	122	183	390	670	950
11-14: Rip Regan ends	58	116	174	371	636	900
15-1st app. Super American plus-c (10/41)	71	142	213	454	777	1100
16-Captain Fight begins (12/41); Spy Fighter ends	71	142	213	454	777	1100
17,18: Super American ends	55	110	165	352	601	850
19-Japanese WWII-c; Captain Fight ends; Senorita Rio begins (6/42, origin & 1st app.); Rip Carson, Chute Trooper begins	58	116	174	371	636	900
20-Bondage/torture-c	55	110	165	352	601	850
21-30: 21-24,26-28-Japanese WWII-c	47	94	141	296	498	700
31-Classic Japanese WWII decapitation-c	181	362	543	1158	1979	2800
32-Tiger Girl begins (6/44, 1st app.?); Nazi WWII-c	53	106	159	334	567	800
33-44: 42-Last WWII-c (2/46). 44-Capt. Fight returns.	41	82	123	256	428	600
45-50: 48-Used in Love and Death by Legman. 49-Jungle-c begin, end #81	37	74	111	222	361	500
51-Origin Tiger Girl; Patsy Pin-Up app.	40	80	120	244	402	560
52-60,62-64-Last Baker issue	26	52	78	154	252	350
61-Origin Tiger Girl retold	27	54	81	158	259	360
65-78: 78-Used in **POP**, pg. 99	21	42	63	122	199	275
79-The Space Rangers app.	21	42	63	126	206	285
80-85: 81-Last jungle-c. 82-85-War-c/stories	19	38	57	109	172	235
86-Two Tigerman stories by Evans-r/Rangers Comics #40,41; Moreira-r/Rangers Comics #45	19	38	57	109	172	235

NOTE: *Bondage covers, Lingerie, headlights panels are common. Captain Fight by **Kamen**-51-66. Kayo Kirby by **Baker**-#43-64, 67(not by Baker). Senorita Rio by **Kamen**-#57-64; by **Grandenetti**-#65, 66. Tiger Girl by **Baker**-#36-60, 62-64; **Eisner** c-1-3, 5, 10, 11. **Kamen** a-54?, 57? **Tuska** a-1, 5, 8, 10, 21, 29, 34. **Whitman** c-73-84. **Zolnerwich** c-16, 17, 22. Power Man c-5, 6, 9. Super American c-15-17. Tiger Girl c-49-81.*

FIGHT FOR LOVE
United Features Syndicate: 1952 (no month)

	GD 2.0	VG 4.0	FN 6.0	VF 8.0	VF/NM 9.0	NM- 9.2
nn-Abbie & Slats newspaper-r	9	18	27	47	61	75

FIGHT FOR TOMORROW
DC Comics (Vertigo): Nov, 2002 - No. 6, Apr, 2003 ($2.50, limited series)

	GD 2.0	VG 4.0	FN 6.0	VF 8.0	VF/NM 9.0	NM- 9.2
1-6-Denys Cowan-a/Brian Wood-s. 1-Jim Lee-c. 5-Jo Chen-c						3.00
TPB (2008, $14.99) r/#1-6						15.00

FIGHTING AIR FORCE (See United States Fighting Air Force)

FIGHTIN' AIR FORCE (Formerly Sherlock Holmes?; Never Again? War and Attack #54 on)
Charlton Comics: No. 3, Feb, 1956 - No. 53, Feb-Mar, 1966

	GD 2.0	VG 4.0	FN 6.0	VF 8.0	VF/NM 9.0	NM- 9.2
V1#3	10	20	30	54	72	90
4-10	7	14	21	35	43	50
11(3/58, 68 pgs.)	9	18	27	47	61	75
12 (100 pgs.)-U.S. Nukes Russia	14	28	42	76	108	140
13-30: 13,24-Glanzman-a. 24-Glanzman-c. 27-Area 51, UFO story	3	6	9	19	30	40
31-50,52,53: 50-American Eagle begins	3	6	9	15	22	28
51-Hitler-c/story	3	6	9	17	26	35

FIGHTING AMERICAN
Headline Publ./Prize (Crestwood): Apr-May, 1954 - No. 7, Apr-May, 1955

	GD 2.0	VG 4.0	FN 6.0	VF 8.0	VF/NM 9.0	NM- 9.2
1-Origin & 1st app. Fighting American & Speedboy (Capt. America & Bucky clones); S&K-c/a(3); 1st super hero satire series	174	348	522	1114	1907	2700
2-S&K-a(3)	81	162	243	518	884	1250
3-5: 3,4-S&K-a(3). 5-S&K-a(2); Kirby/?-a	62	124	186	394	680	965
6-Origin-r (4 pgs.) plus 2 pgs. by S&K	59	118	177	375	643	910
7-Kirby-a	53	106	159	334	567	800

NOTE: ***Simon** & **Kirby** covers on all. 6 is last pre-code issue.*

FIGHTING AMERICAN
Harvey Publications: Oct, 1966 (25¢)

	GD 2.0	VG 4.0	FN 6.0	VF 8.0	VF/NM 9.0	NM- 9.2
1-Origin Fighting American & Speedboy by S&K-r; S&K-c/a(3); 1 pg. Neal Adams ad	5	10	15	33	57	80

FIGHTING AMERICAN
DC Comics: Feb, 1994 - No. 6, 1994 ($1.50, limited series)

	GD 2.0	VG 4.0	FN 6.0	VF 8.0	VF/NM 9.0	NM- 9.2
1-6						3.00

FIGHTING AMERICAN (Vol. 3)
Awesome Entertainment: Aug, 1997 - No. 2, Oct, 1997 ($2.50)

	GD 2.0	VG 4.0	FN 6.0	VF 8.0	VF/NM 9.0	NM- 9.2
Preview-Agent America (pre-lawsuit)	1	2	3	5	6	7
1-Four covers by Liefeld, Churchill, Platt, McGuinness						3.00
1-Platinum Edition, 1-Gold foil Edition						10.00
1-Comic Cavalcade Edition, 2-American Ent. Spice Ed.						4.00
2-Platt-c, 2-Liefeld variant-c						3.00

FIGHTING AMERICAN: DOGS OF WAR
Awesome-Hyperwerks: Sept, 1998 - No. 3, May, 1999 ($2.50)

	GD 2.0	VG 4.0	FN 6.0	VF 8.0	VF/NM 9.0	NM- 9.2
Limited Convention Special (7/98, B&W) Platt-a						3.00
1-3-Starlin-s/Platt-a/c						3.00

FIGHTING AMERICAN: RULES OF THE GAME
Awesome Entertainment: Nov, 1997 - No. 3, Mar, 1998 ($2.50, lim. series)

	GD 2.0	VG 4.0	FN 6.0	VF 8.0	VF/NM 9.0	NM- 9.2
1-3: 1-Loeb-s/McGuinness-a/c. 2-Flip book with Swat! preview						3.00
1-Liefeld SPICE variant-c, 1-Dynamic Forces Ed.; McGuinness-c						3.00
1-Liefeld Fighting American & cast variant-c						3.00

FIGHTIN' ARMY (Formerly Soldier and Marine Comics) (See Captain Willy Schultz)
Charlton Comics: No. 16, 1/56 - No. 127, 12/76; No. 128, 9/77 - No. 172, 11/84

	GD 2.0	VG 4.0	FN 6.0	VF 8.0	VF/NM 9.0	NM- 9.2
16	9	18	27	52	69	85
17-19,21-23,25-30	7	14	21	35	43	50
20-Ditko-a	9	18	27	50	65	80
24 (3/58, 68 pgs.)	8	16	24	44	57	70
31-45	3	6	9	18	28	38
46-50,52-60	3	6	9	16	23	30
51-Hitler-c	3	6	9	17	26	35
61-75	3	6	9	14	19	24
76-1st The Lonely War of Willy Schultz	3	6	9	17	26	35
77-80: 77-92-The Lonely War of Willy Schultz. 79-Devil Brigade	3	6	9	14	19	24
81-88,91,93-99: 82,83-Devil Brigade	2	4	6	10	14	18
89,90,92-Ditko-a	3	6	9	14	20	26
100	2	4	6	13	18	22
101-127	2	4	6	8	11	14
128-140	1	2	3	5	7	9
141-165	1	2	3	4	5	7
166-172-Low print run	1	2	3	5	6	8
108 (Modern Comics-1977)-Reprint						5.00

NOTE: ***Aparo** c-154. **Glanzman** a-77-88. **Montes/Bache** a-48, 49, 51, 69, 75, 76, 170r.*

FIGHTING CARAVANS (See Zane Grey 4-Color 632)

FIGHTING DANIEL BOONE
Avon Periodicals: 1953

	GD 2.0	VG 4.0	FN 6.0	VF 8.0	VF/NM 9.0	NM- 9.2
nn-Kinstler-c/a, 22 pgs.	19	38	57	109	172	235
I.W. Reprint #1-Reprints #1 above; Kinstler-c/a; Lawrence/Alascia-a	3	6	9	14	19	24

FIGHTING DAVY CROCKETT (Formerly Kit Carson)
Avon Periodicals: No. 9, Oct-Nov, 1955

	GD 2.0	VG 4.0	FN 6.0	VF 8.0	VF/NM 9.0	NM- 9.2
9-Kinstler-c	10	20	30	56	76	95

FIGHTIN' FIVE, THE (Formerly Space War) (Also see The Peacemaker)
Charlton Comics: July, 1964 - No. 41, Jan, 1967; No. 42, Oct, 1981 - No. 49, Dec, 1982

	GD 2.0	VG 4.0	FN 6.0	VF 8.0	VF/NM 9.0	NM- 9.2
V2#28-Origin/1st app. Fightin' Five; Montes/Bache-a	5	10	15	35	63	90
29-39-Montes/Bache-a in all	3	6	9	21	33	45
40-Peacemaker begins (1st app.)	6	12	18	37	66	95
41-Peacemaker (2nd app.); Montes/Bache-a	4	8	12	28	47	65
42-49: Reprints						5.00

FIGHTING FRONTS!
Harvey Publications: Aug, 1952 - No. 5, Jan, 1953

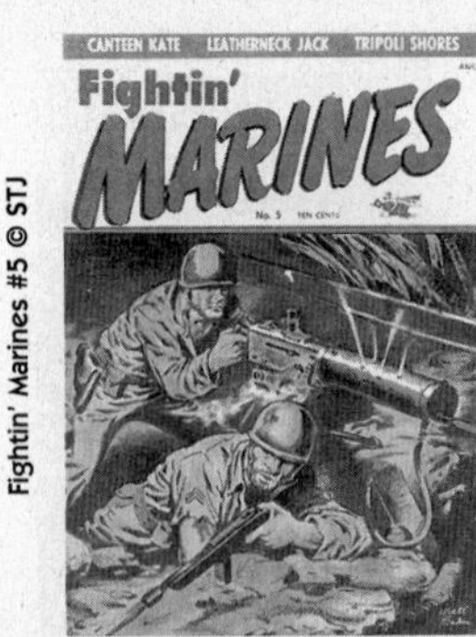

Fightin' Marines #5 © STJ

Fighting Yank #18 © Nedor

Final Crisis #7 © DC

	GD 2.0	VG 4.0	FN 6.0	VF 8.0	VF/NM 9.0	NM- 9.2
1	10	20	30	54	72	90
2-Extreme violence; Nostrand/Powell-a	11	22	33	60	83	105
3-5: 3-Powell-a	7	14	21	37	46	55

FIGHTING INDIAN STORIES (See Midget Comics)

FIGHTING INDIANS OF THE WILD WEST!
Avon Periodicals: Mar, 1952 - No. 2, Nov, 1952

	GD 2.0	VG 4.0	FN 6.0	VF 8.0	VF/NM 9.0	NM- 9.2
1-Geronimo, Chief Crazy Horse, Chief Victorio, Black Hawk begin; Larsen-a; McCann-a(2)	18	36	54	105	165	225
2-Kinstler-c & inside-c only; Larsen, McCann-a	13	26	39	74	105	135
100 Pg. Annual (1952, 25¢)-Contains three comics rebound; Geronimo, Chief Crazy Horse, Chief Victorio; Kinstler-c	39	78	117	231	378	525

FIGHTING LEATHERNECKS
Toby Press: Feb, 1952 - No. 6, Dec, 1952

	GD 2.0	VG 4.0	FN 6.0	VF 8.0	VF/NM 9.0	NM- 9.2
1- "Duke's Diary"; full pg. pin-ups by Sparling	15	30	45	84	127	170
2-5: 2- "Duke's Diary" full pg. pin-ups. 3-5- "Gil's Gals"; full pg. pin-ups	10	20	30	56	76	95
6-(Same as No. 3-5?)	10	20	30	56	76	95

FIGHTING MAN, THE (War)
Ajax/Farrell Publications(Excellent Publ.): May, 1952 - No. 8, July, 1953

	GD 2.0	VG 4.0	FN 6.0	VF 8.0	VF/NM 9.0	NM- 9.2
1	15	30	45	84	127	170
2	9	18	27	52	69	85
3-8	8	16	24	42	54	65
Annual 1 (1952, 25¢, 100 pgs.)	28	56	84	165	270	375

FIGHTIN' MARINES (Formerly The Texan; also see Approved Comics)
St. John(Approved Comics)/Charlton Comics No. 14 on:
No. 15, 8/51 - No. 12, 3/53; No. 14, 5/55 - No. 132, 11/76; No. 133, 10/77 - No. 176, 9/84 (No #13?) (Korean War #1-3)

	GD 2.0	VG 4.0	FN 6.0	VF 8.0	VF/NM 9.0	NM- 9.2
15(#1)-Matt Baker c/a "Leatherneck Jack"; slightly large size; Fightin' Texan No. 16 & 17?	48	96	144	302	514	725
2-1st Canteen Kate by Baker; slightly large size; partial Baker-c	57	114	171	362	619	875
3-9,11-Canteen Kate by Baker; Baker c-#2,3,5-11; 4-Partial Baker-c	34	68	102	204	332	460
10-Matt Baker-c	18	36	54	105	165	225
12-No Baker-a; Last St. John issue?	10	20	30	54	72	90
14 (5/55; 1st Charlton issue; formerly?)-Canteen Kate by Baker; all stories reprinted from #2	19	38	57	111	176	240
15-Baker-c	12	24	36	69	97	125
16,18-20-Not Baker-c	7	14	21	37	46	55
17-Canteen Kate by Baker	15	30	45	86	133	180
21-24	7	14	21	35	43	50
25-(68 pgs.)(3/58)-Check-a?	10	20	30	56	76	95
26-(100 pgs.)(8/58)-Check-a(5)	14	28	42	82	121	160
27-50	3	6	9	18	28	38
51-81: 78-Shotgun Harker & the Chicken series begin	3	6	9	15	22	28
82-85: 85-Last 12¢ issue	3	6	9	14	20	25
86-94: 94-Last 15¢ issue	2	4	6	10	14	18
95-100,122: 122-(1975) Pilot issue for "War" title (Fightin' Marines Presents War)	2	4	6	9	13	16
101-121	2	4	6	8	10	12
123-140: 132 Hitler-c	1	2	3	5	7	9
141-170						6.00
171-176-Low print run	1	2	3	5	6	8
120(Modern Comics reprint, 1977)						5.00

NOTE: *No. 14 & 16 (CC) reprint St. John issues; No. 16 reprints St. John insignia on cover.* ***Colan*** *a-3, 7.* ***Glanzman*** *c/a-92, 94.* ***Montes/Bache*** *a-48, 53, 55, 64, 65, 72-74, 77-83, 176r.*

FIGHTING MARSHAL OF THE WILD WEST (See The Hawk)

FIGHTIN' NAVY (Formerly Don Winslow)
Charlton Comics: No. 74, 1/56 - No. 125, 4-5/66; No. 126, 8/83 - No. 133, 10/84

	GD 2.0	VG 4.0	FN 6.0	VF 8.0	VF/NM 9.0	NM- 9.2
74	5	10	15	34	60	85
75-81	4	8	12	23	37	50
82-Sam Glanzman-a (68 pg. Giant)	5	10	15	31	53	75
83-(100 pgs.)	6	12	18	41	76	110
84-99,101: 101-UFO-c/story	3	6	9	17	26	35
100	3	6	9	18	28	38
102-105,106-125('66)	3	6	9	14	21	26
126-133 (1984)-Low print run	1	2	3	5	6	8

NOTE: ***Montes/Bache*** *a-109.* ***Glanzman*** *a-82, 92, 96, 98, 100, 131r.*

FIGHTING PRINCE OF DONEGAL, THE (See Movie Comics)

FIGHTIN' TEXAN (Formerly The Texan & Fightin' Marines?)
St. John Publishing Co.: No. 16, Sept, 1952 - No. 17, Dec, 1952

	GD 2.0	VG 4.0	FN 6.0	VF 8.0	VF/NM 9.0	NM- 9.2
16,17: Tuska-a each. 17-Cameron-c/a	9	18	27	50	65	80

FIGHTING UNDERSEA COMMANDOS (See Undersea Fighting...)
Avon Periodicals: May, 1952 - No. 5, April, 1953 (U.S. Navy frogmen)

	GD 2.0	VG 4.0	FN 6.0	VF 8.0	VF/NM 9.0	NM- 9.2
1-Cover title is Undersea Fighting... #1 only	15	30	45	88	137	185
2	10	20	30	56	76	95
3-5: 1,3-Ravielli-c. 4-Kinstler-c	9	18	27	50	65	80

FIGHTING WAR STORIES
Men's Publications/Story Comics: Aug, 1952 - No. 5, 1953

	GD 2.0	VG 4.0	FN 6.0	VF 8.0	VF/NM 9.0	NM- 9.2
1	13	26	39	74	105	135
2-5	8	16	24	42	54	65

FIGHTING YANK (See America's Best Comics & Startling Comics)
Nedor/Better Publ./Standard: Sept, 1942 - No. 29, Aug, 1949

	GD 2.0	VG 4.0	FN 6.0	VF 8.0	VF/NM 9.0	NM- 9.2
1-The Fighting Yank begins; Mystico, the Wonder Man app; bondage-c	309	618	927	2163	3782	5400
2	148	296	444	947	1624	2300
3,4: Nazi WWII-c. 4-Schomburg-c begin	119	238	357	762	1306	1850
5,8-10: 5,10-Nazi-c. 8-Japan War-c	110	220	330	704	1202	1700
6-Classic Japanese WWII-c	116	232	348	742	1271	1800
7-Classic Hitler special bomb-c; Grim Reaper app.	161	322	483	1030	1765	2500
11,14,15: 11-The Oracle app. 15-Bondage/torture-c	71	142	213	454	777	1100
12-Hirohito bondage Japanese WWII-c	116	232	348	742	1271	1800
13-Last War-c (Japanese)	77	154	231	493	847	1200
16-20: 18-The American Eagle app.	57	114	171	362	619	875
21-Kara, Jungle Princess app.; lingerie-c	81	162	243	518	884	1250
22-Miss Masque-c/story	60	120	180	381	653	925
23-Classic Schomburg hooded vigilante-c	97	194	291	621	1061	1500
24-Miss Masque app.	54	108	162	343	574	825
25-Robinson/Meskin-a; strangulation, lingerie panel; The Cavalier app.	57	114	171	362	619	875
26-29: All-Robinson/Meskin-a. 28-One pg. Williamson-a	46	92	138	290	488	685

NOTE: ***Schomburg (Xela)*** *c-4-29; airbrush-c 28, 29. Bondage c-1, 4, 8, 10, 11, 12, 15, 17.*

FIGHTMAN
Marvel Comics: June, 1993 ($2.00, one-shot, 52 pgs.)

	GD 2.0	VG 4.0	FN 6.0	VF 8.0	VF/NM 9.0	NM- 9.2
1						4.00

FIGHT THE ENEMY
Tower Comics: Aug, 1966 - No. 3, Mar, 1967 (25¢, 68 pgs.)

	GD 2.0	VG 4.0	FN 6.0	VF 8.0	VF/NM 9.0	NM- 9.2
1-Lucky 7 & Mike Manly begin	4	8	12	27	44	60
2-1st Boris Vallejo comic art; McWilliams-a	3	6	9	21	33	45
3-Wood-a (1/2 pg.); McWilliams, Bolle-a	3	6	9	21	33	45

FILM FUNNIES
Marvel Comics (CPC): Nov, 1949 - No. 2, Feb, 1950 (52 pgs.)

	GD 2.0	VG 4.0	FN 6.0	VF 8.0	VF/NM 9.0	NM- 9.2
1-Krazy Krow, Wacky Duck	20	40	60	120	195	270
2-Wacky Duck	15	30	45	85	130	175

FILM STARS ROMANCES
Star Publications: Jan-Feb, 1950 - No. 3, May-June, 1950 (True life stories of movie stars)

	GD 2.0	VG 4.0	FN 6.0	VF 8.0	VF/NM 9.0	NM- 9.2
1-Rudy Valentino & Gregory Peck stories; L. B. Cole-c; lingerie panels	44	88	132	277	469	660
2-Liz Taylor/Robert Taylor photo-c & true life story	58	116	174	371	636	900
3-Douglas Fairbanks story; photo-c	27	54	81	158	259	360

FILTH, THE
DC Comics (Vertigo): Aug, 2002 - No. 13, Oct, 2003 ($2.95, limited series)

	GD 2.0	VG 4.0	FN 6.0	VF 8.0	VF/NM 9.0	NM- 9.2
1-13-Morrison-s/Weston & Erskine-a						3.00
TPB (2004, $19.95) r/#1-13						20.00

FINAL CRISIS
DC Comics: July, 2008 - No. 7, Mar, 2009 ($3.99, limited series)

	GD 2.0	VG 4.0	FN 6.0	VF 8.0	VF/NM 9.0	NM- 9.2
1-Grant Morrison-s/J.G. Jones-a/c; Martian Manhunter killed; 2 covers						4.00
1-Director's Cut (10/08, $4.99) B&W printing of #1 with creator commentary						5.00
2-7: 2-Barry Allen-c/cameo; intro Big Science Action; two covers. 6-Batman zapped						4.00
SC (2010, $19.99) r/#1-7, FC: Superman Beyond #1,2, FC: Submit & FC Sketchbook						20.00
...: Rage of the Red Lanterns (12/08, $3.99) Atrocitus app.; intro. Blue Lantern; 3 covers						4.00
...: Requiem (9/08, $3.99) History, death and funeral of the Martian Manhunter; 2 covers						4.00
...: Resist (12/08, $3.99) Checkmate app; Rucka & Trautman-s/Sook-a; 2 covers						4.00
...: Secret Files (2/09, $3.99) origin of Libra; Wein-s/Shasteen-a; JG Jones sketch-a						4.00
... Sketchbook (7/08, $2.99) Jones development sketches with Morrison commentary						3.00
...: Submit (12/08, $3.99) Black Lightning & Tattooed Man team up; Morrison-s; 2 covers						4.00

Fire #1 © Brian Bendis

Firearm #8 © MAL

Firehair Comics #4 © FH

GD 2.0 | VG 4.0 | FN 6.0 | VF 8.0 | VF/NM 9.0 | NM- 9.2

FINAL CRISIS: DANCE (Final Crisis Aftermath)
DC Comics: Jul, 2009 - No. 6, Dec, 2009 ($2.99, limited series)

1-6-Super Young Team; Joe Casey-s/Chriscross-a/Stanley Lau-c 3.00
TPB (2009, $17.99) r/#1-6 18.00

FINAL CRISIS: ESCAPE (Final Crisis Aftermath)
DC Comics: Jul, 2009 - No. 6, Dec, 2009 ($2.99, limited series)

1-6-Nemesis & Cameron Chase app.; Ivan Brandon-s/Marco Rudy-a/Scott Hampton-c 3.00
TPB (2010, $17.99) r/#1-6 18.00

FINAL CRISIS: INK (Final Crisis Aftermath)
DC Comics: Jul, 2009 - No. 6, Dec, 2009 ($2.99, limited series)

1-6-The Tattooed Man; Eric Wallace-s/Fabrizio Florentino-a/Brian Stelfreeze-c 3.00
TPB (2010, $17.99) r/#1-6 18.00

FINAL CRISIS: LEGION OF THREE WORLDS
DC Comics: Oct, 2008 - No. 5, Sept, 2009 ($3.99, limited series)

1-Johns-s/Pérez-a; R.J. Brande killed; Time Trapper app.; two covers on each issue 5.00
2-5-Three Legions meet; two covers. 3-Bart Allen returns. 4-Superboy (Conner) returns 4.00
HC (2009, $19.99) r/#1-5; variant covers 20.00
SC (2010, $14.99) r/#1-5; variant covers 15.00

FINAL CRISIS: REVELATIONS
DC Comics: Oct, 2008 - No. 5, Feb, 2009 ($3.99, limited series)

1-5-Spectre and The Question; 2 covers on each. 1-Dr. Light killed; Rucka-s/Tan-a 4.00
HC (2009, $19.99, d.j.) r/#1-5; variant covers 20.00
SC (2010, $14.99) r/#1-5; variant covers 15.00

FINAL CRISIS: ROGUE'S REVENGE
DC Comics: Sept, 2008 - No. 3, Nov, 2008 ($3.99, limited series)

1-3-Johns-s/Kolins-a; Flash's Rogues, Zoom and Inertia app. 4.00
HC (2009, $19.99, d.j.) r/#1-3 & Flash #182,197; variant covers 20.00
SC (2010, $14.99) r/#1-3 & Flash #182,197; variant covers 15.00

FINAL CRISIS: RUN (Final Crisis Aftermath)
DC Comics: Jul, 2009 - No. 6, Dec, 2009 ($2.99, limited series)

1-6-The Human Flame on the run; Sturges-s/Williams-a/Kako-c 3.00
TPB (2010, $17.99) r/#1-6 18.00

FINAL CRISIS: SUPERMAN BEYOND
DC Comics: Oct, 2008 - No. 2, Mar, 2009 ($4.50, limited series)

1,2-Morrison-s/Mahnke-a; parallel-Earth Supermen app.; 3-D pages and glasses 4.50

FINAL NIGHT, THE (See DC related titles and Parallax: Emerald Night)
DC Comics: Nov, 1996 - No. 4, Nov, 1996 ($1.95, weekly limited series)

1-4: Kesel-s/Immonen-a(p) in all. 4-Parallax's final acts 4.00
Preview 3.00
TPB-(1998, $12.95) r/#1-4, Parallax: Emerald Night #1, and preview 13.00

FINALS (See Vertigo Resurrected:... for collected reprint)
DC Comics (Vertigo): Sept, 1999 - No. 4, Dec, 1999 ($2.95, limited series)

1-4-Will Pfeifer-s/Jill Thompson-a 3.00

FINDING NEMO (Based on the Pixar movie)
BOOM! Studios: Jul, 2010 - No. 4, Oct, 2010 ($2.99, limited series)

1-4-Michael Raicht & Brian Smith-s/Jake Myler-a.1-Three covers 3.00

FINDING NEMO: REEF RESCUE (Based on the Pixar movie)
BOOM! Studios: May, 2009 - No. 4, Aug, 2009 ($2.99, limited series)

1-4-Marie Croall-s/Erica Leigh Currey-a; 2 covers 3.00

FIN FANG FOUR RETURN!
Marvel Comics: Jul, 2009 ($3.99, one-shot)

1-Fin Fang Foom, Googam, Elektro, Gorgilla and Doc Samson app. 5.00

FIRE
Caliber Press: 1993 - No. 2, 1993 ($2.95, B&W, limited series, 52 pgs.)

1,2-Brian Michael Bendis-s/a 4.00
TPB (1999, 2001, $9.95) Restored reprints of series 10.00

FIREARM (Also see Codename: Firearm, Freex #15, Night Man #4 & Prime #10)
Malibu Comics (Ultraverse): Sept, 1993 - No. 18, Mar, 1995 ($1.95/$2.50)

0 ($14.95)-Came w/ video containing 1st half of story (comic contains 2nd half); 1st app. Duet 15.00
1,3-6: 1-James Robinson scripts begin; Cully Hamner-a; Chaykin-c; 1st app. Alec Swan. 3-Intro The Sportsmen; Chaykin-c. 4-Break-Thru x-over; Chaykin-c. 5-1st app. Ellen (Swan's girlfriend); 2 pg. origin of Prime. 6-Prime app. (story cont'd in Prime #10); Brereton-c 3.00
1-($2.50)-Newsstand edition polybagged w/card 3.50
1-Ultra Limited silver foil-c 1 2 3 5 6 8
2 ($2.50, 44 pgs.)-Hardcase app.;Chaykin-c; Rune flip-c/story by B. Smith (3 pgs.) 4.00
7-10,12-17: 12-The Rafferty Saga begins, ends #18; 1st app. Rafferty. 15-Night Man & Freex app. 17-Swan marries Ellen 3.00
11-($3.50, 68 pgs.)-Flip book w/Ultraverse Premiere #5 4.00
18-Death of Rafferty; Chaykin-c 4.00
NOTE: ***Brereton*** *c-6.* ***Chaykin*** *c-1-4, 14, 16, 18.* ***Hamner*** *a-1-4.* ***Herrera*** *a-12.* ***James Robinson*** *scripts-0-18.*

FIRE BALL XL5 (See Steve Zodiac & The ...)

FIREBIRDS (See Noble Causes)
Image Comics: Nov, 2004 ($5.95)

1-Faerber-s/Ponce-a/c; intro. Firebird 6.00

FIREBRAND (Also see Showcase '96 #4)
DC Comics: Feb, 1996 - No. 9, Oct, 1996 ($1.75)

1-9: Brian Augustyn scripts; Velluto-c/a in all. 9-Daredevil #319-c/swipe 3.00

FIREBREATHER
Image Comics: Jan, 2003 - No. 4, Apr, 2003 ($2.95)

1-4-Hester-s/Kuhn-a 3.00
...: The Iron Saint (12/04, $6.95, squarebound) Hester-s/Kuhn-a 7.00
TPB (7/04, $13.95) r/#1-4; foreword by Brad Meltzer; gallery and sketch pages 14.00

FIREBREATHER
Image Comics: Jun, 2008 - No. 4, Feb, 2009 ($2.99)

1-4-Hester-s/Kuhn-a 3.00

FIREBREATHER (Vol.3): HOLMGANG
Image Comics: Nov, 2010 - No. 4, ($3.99, limited series)

1,2-Hester-s/Kuhn-a 4.00

FIRE FROM HEAVEN
Image Comics (WildStorm Productions): Mar, 1996 ($2.50)

1,2-Moore-s 3.00

FIREHAIR COMICS (Formerly Pioneer West Romances #3-6; also see Rangers Comics)
Fiction House Magazines (Flying Stories): Winter/48-49; No. 2, Wint/49-50; No. 7, Spr/51 - No. 11, Spr/52

	GD 2.0	VG 4.0	FN 6.0	VF 8.0	VF/NM 9.0	NM- 9.2
1-Origin Firehair	34	68	102	199	325	450
2-Continues as Pioneer West Romances for #3-6	18	36	54	105	165	225
7-11	14	28	42	80	115	150
I.W. Reprint 8-(nd)-Kinstler-c; reprints Rangers #57; Dr. Drew story by Grandenetti	3	6	9	16	23	30

FIRESIDE BOOK SERIES (Hard and soft cover editions)
Simon and Schuster: 1974 - 1980 (130-260 pgs.), Square bound, color

		GD 2.0	VG 4.0	FN 6.0	VF 8.0	VF/NM 9.0	NM- 9.2
Amazing Spider-Man, The, 1979,	HC	7	14	21	48	89	130
130 pgs., $3.95, Bob Larkin-c	SC	5	10	15	33	57	80
America At War–The Best of DC War	HC	10	20	30	64	132	200
Comics, 1979, $6.95, 260 pgs, Kubert-c	SC	6	12	18	42	79	115
Best of Spidey Super Stories (Electric	HC	9	18	27	57	111	165
Company) 1978, $3.95,	SC	6	12	18	37	66	95
Bring On The Bad Guys (Origins of the	HC	7	14	21	46	86	125
Marvel Comics Villains) 1976, $6.95, 260 pgs.; Romita-c	SC	5	10	15	31	53	75
Captain America, Sentinel of Liberty,1979,	HC	7	14	21	48	89	130
130 pgs., $12.95, Cockrum-c	SC	5	10	15	33	57	80
Doctor Strange Master of the Mystic	HC	7	14	21	48	89	130
Arts, 1980, 130 pgs.	SC	5	10	15	33	57	80
Fantastic Four, The, 1979, 130 pgs.	HC	7	14	21	46	86	125
	SC	5	10	15	31	53	75
Heart Throbs–The Best of DC Romance	HC	13	26	39	86	188	290
Comics, 1979, 260 pgs., $6.95	SC	8	16	24	56	108	160
Incredible Hulk, The, 1978, 260 pgs.	HC	7	14	21	46	86	125
(8 1/4" x 11")	SC	5	10	15	31	53	75
Marvel's Greatest Superhero Battles,	HC	9	18	27	57	111	165
1978, 260 pgs., $6.95, Romita-c	SC	6	12	18	37	66	95
Mysteries in Space, 1980, $7,95,	HC	8	16	24	52	99	145
Anderson-c. r-DC sci/fi stories	SC	5	10	15	34	60	85
Origins of Marvel Comics, 1974, 260 pgs., $5.95. r-covers & origins of Fantastic							
Four, Hulk, Spider-Man, Thor,	HC	7	14	21	46	86	125
& Doctor Strange	SC	5	10	15	31	53	75
Silver Surfer, The, 1978, 130 pgs.,	HC	7	14	21	48	89	130

Firestorm (2004 series) #23 © DC

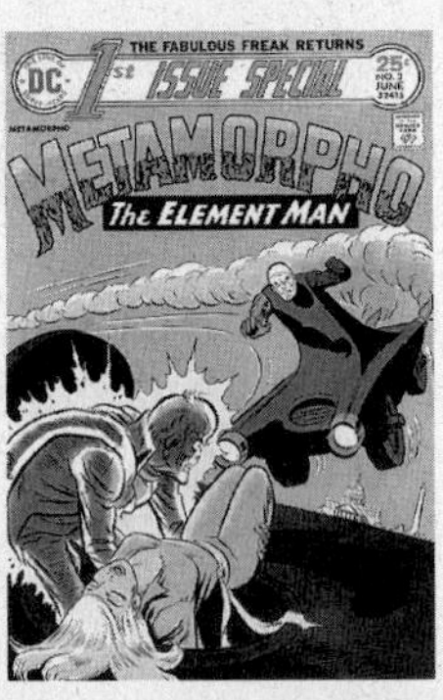

First Issue Special #3 © DC

First Love Illustrated #11 © HARV

	GD 2.0	VG 4.0	FN 6.0	VF 8.0	VF/NM 9.0	NM- 9.2

$4.95, Norem-c SC 5 10 15 34 60 85

Son of Origins of Marvel Comics, 1975, 260 pgs., $6.95, Romita-c. Reprints
covers & origins of X-Men, Iron Man, HC 7 14 21 46 86 125
Avengers, Daredevil, Silver Surfer SC 5 10 15 31 53 75

Superhero Women, The–Featuring the HC 9 18 27 57 111 165
Fabulous Females of Marvel Comics, SC 6 12 18 37 66 95
1977, 260 pgs., $6.95, Romita-c

Note: Prices listed are for 1st printings. Later printings have lesser value.

FIRESTAR
Marvel Comics Group: Mar, 1986 - No. 4, June, 1986 (75¢)(From Spider-Man TV series)

1,2: 1-X-Men & New Mutants app. 2-Wolverine-c (not real Wolverine?); Art Adams-a(p) 6.00
3,4: 3-Art Adams/Sienkiewicz-c. 4-B. Smith-c 4.00
X-Men: Firestar Digest (2006, $7.99, digest-size) r/#1-4; profile pages 8.00
1 (Jun, 2010, $3.99) Sean McKeever-s/Emma Rios-a 4.00

FIRESTONE (See Donald And Mickey Merry Christmas)

FIRESTORM (Also see The Fury of Firestorm, Cancelled Comic Cavalcade, DC Comics Presents, Flash #289, & Justice League of America #179)
DC Comics: March, 1978 - No. 5, Oct-Nov, 1978

1,5: 1-Origin & 1st app. 2 4 6 9 12 15
2-4: 2-Origin Multiplex. 3-Origin & 1st app. Killer Frost. 4-1st app. Hyena
1 2 3 5 7 9
...: The Nuclear Man TPB (2011, $17.99) r/#1-5 and stories from Flash #289-293, plus story from Cancelled Comic Cavalcade (uncolored) 18.00

FIRESTORM
DC Comics: July, 2004 - No. 35, June, 2007 ($2.50/$2.99)

1-24: 1-Intro. Jason Rusch; Jolley-s/ChrisCross-a. 6-Identity Crisis tie-in. 7-Bloodhound x-over. 8-Killer Frost returns. 9-Ronnie Raymond returns. 17-Villains United tie-in. 21-Infinite Crisis. 24-One Year Later; Killer Frost app. 3.00
25-35: 25-Begin $2.99-c; Mr. Freeze app. 33-35-Mister Miracle & Orion app. 3.00
...: Reborn TPB (2007, $14.99) r/#23-27 15.00

FIRESTORM, THE NUCLEAR MAN (Formerly Fury of Firestorm)
DC Comics: No. 65, Nov, 1987 - No. 100, Aug, 1990

65-99: 66-1st app. Zuggernaut; Firestorm vs. Green Lantern. 67,68-Millennium tie-ins. 71-Death of Capt. X. 83-1st new look 3.00
100-($2.95, 68 pgs.) 4.00
Annual 5 (10/87)-1st app. new Firestorm 4.00

FIRST, THE
CrossGeneration Comics: Jan, 2001 - No. 37, Jan, 2004 ($2.95)

1-3: 1-Barbara Kesel-s/Bart Sears & Andy Smith-a 5.00
4-10 4.00
11-37 3.00
Preview (11/00, free) 8 pg. intro 3.00
Two Houses Divided Vol. 1 TPB (11/01, $19.95) r/#1-7; new Moeller-c 20.00
Magnificent Tension Vol. 2 TPB (2002, $19.95) r/#8-13 20.00
Sinister Motives Vol. 3 TPB (2003, $15.95) r/#14-19 16.00
Vol. 4 Futile Endeavors (2003, $15.95) r/#20-25 16.00
Vol. 5 Liquid Alliances (2003, $15.95) r/#26-31 16.00
Vol. 6 Ragnarok (2004, $15.95) r/#32-37 16.00

FIRST ADVENTURES
First Comics: Dec, 1985 - No. 5, Apr, 1986 ($1.25)

1-5: Blaze Barlow, Whisper & Dynamo Joe in all 3.00

FIRST AMERICANS, THE
Dell Publishing Co.: No. 843, Sept, 1957

Four Color 843-Marsh-a 7 14 21 48 89 130

FIRST BORN (See Witchblade and Darkness titles)
Image Comics (Top Cow): Aug, 2007 - No. 3 ($2.99, limited series)

... First Look (6/07, 99¢) Preview; The Darkness app.; Sejic-a; 2 covers (color & B&W) 3.00
1-3-($2.99) Two covers; Marz-s/Sejic-a. 3-Sara's baby is born 3.00
1-B&W variant Sejic cover 5.00
...: Aftermath (5/08, $3.99) short stories; Magdalena app.; two covers by Sook & Sejic 4.00

FIRST CHRISTMAS, THE (3-D)
Fiction House Magazines (Real Adv. Publ. Co.): 1953 (25¢, 8-1/4x10-1/4", oversize)(Came w/glasses)

nn-(Scarce)-Kelly Freas painted-c; Biblical theme, birth of Christ; Nativity-c
34 68 102 206 336 465

FIRST COMICS GRAPHIC NOVEL
First Comics: Jan, 1984 - No. 21? (52 pgs./176 pgs., high quality paper)

1,2: 1-Beowulf ($5.95)(both printings). 2-Time Beavers 10.00
3($11.95, 100 pgs.)-American Flagg! Hard Times (2nd printing exists) 15.00
4-Nexus ($6.95)-r/B&W 1-3 15.00
5,7: 5-The Enchanted Apples of Oz ($7.95, 52 pgs.)-Intro by Harlan Ellison (1986). 7-The Secret Island Of Oz ($7.95) 10.00
6-Elric of Melnibone ($14.95, 176 pgs.)-Reprints with new color 18.00
8,10,14,18: Teenage Mutant Ninja Turtles Book I -IV ($9.95, 132 pgs.)-8-r/TMNT #1-3 in color w/12 pgs. new-a; origin. 10-r/TMNT #4-6 in color. 14-r/TMNT #7,8 in color plus new 12 pg. story. 18-r/TMNT #10,11 plus 3 pg. fold-out 11.00
9-Time 2: The Epiphany by Chaykin (11/86, $7.95, 52pgs. - indicia says #8) 10.00
11-Sailor On The Sea of Fate ($14.95) 16.00
nn-Time 2: The Satisfaction of Black Mariah (9/87) 10.00
12-American Flagg! Southern Comfort (10/87, $11.95) 15.00
13,16,17,21: 13-The Ice King Of Oz. 16-The Forgotten Forest of Oz ($8.95). 17-Mazinger (68 pgs., $8.95). 21-Elric, The Weird of the White Wolf; r/#1-5 10.00
15,19: 15-Hex Breaker: Badger ($7.95). 19-The Original Nexus Graphic Novel ($7.95, 104 pgs.)-Reprints First Comics Graphic Novel #4 12.00
20-American Flagg!: State of the Union ($11.95, 96 pgs.); r/A.F. #7-9 15.00

NOTE: *Most or all issues have been reprinted.*

1ST FOLIO (The Joe Kubert School Presents...)
Pacific Comics: Mar, 1984 ($1.50, one-shot)

1-Joe Kubert-c/a(2 pgs.); Adam & Andy Kubert-a 3.00

1ST ISSUE SPECIAL
National Periodical Publications: Apr, 1975 - No. 13, Apr, 1976 (Tryout series)

1,6: 1-Intro. Atlas; Kirby-c/a/script. 6-Dingbats 2 4 6 11 16 20
2,12: 2-Green Team (see Cancelled Comic Cavalcade). 12-Origin/1st app. "Blue" Starman (2nd app. in Starman, 2nd Series #3); Kubert-c 2 4 6 8 11 14
3-Metamorpho by Ramona Fradon 2 4 6 8 11 14
4,10,11: 4-Lady Cop. 10-The Outsiders. 11-Code Name: Assassin; Grell-c
1 3 4 6 8 10
5-Manhunter; Kirby-c/a/script 3 6 9 14 20 26
7,9: 7-The Creeper by Ditko (c/a). 9-Dr. Fate; Kubert-c/Simonson-a.
2 4 6 11 16 20
8-Origin/1st app. The Warlord; Grell-c/a (11/75) 5 10 15 31 53 75
13-Return of the New Gods; Darkseid app.; 1st new costume Orion; predates New Gods #12 by more than a year 3 6 9 19 30 40

FIRST KISS
Charlton Comics: Dec, 1957 - No. 40, Jan, 1965

V1#1 4 8 12 28 47 65
V1#2-10 3 6 9 18 28 38
11-40 3 6 9 14 19 24

FIRST LOVE ILLUSTRATED
Harvey Publications(Home Comics)(True Love): 2/49 - No. 9, 6/50; No. 10, 1/51 - No. 86, 3/58; No. 87, 9/58 - No. 88, 11/58; No. 89, 11/62, No. 90, 2/63

1-Powell-a(2) 20 40 60 114 182 250
2-Powell-a 12 24 36 69 97 125
3-"Was I Too Fat To Be Loved" story 15 30 45 83 124 165
4-10 9 18 27 52 69 85
11-30: 13-"I Joined a Teen-age Sex Club" story. 30-Lingerie panel
8 16 24 42 54 65
31-34,37,39-49: 49-Last pre-code (2/55) 7 14 21 37 46 55
35-Used in **SOTI**, illo "The title of this comic book is First Love"
20 40 60 117 189 260
36-Communism story, "Love Slaves" 12 24 36 69 97 125
38-Nostrand-a 9 18 27 47 61 75
50-66,71-90 6 12 18 31 38 45
67-70-Kirby-c 8 16 24 42 54 65

NOTE: ***Disbrow** a-13. **Orlando** c-87. **Powell** a-1, 3-5, 7, 10, 11, 13-17, 19-24, 26-29, 33,35-41, 43, 45, 46, 50, 54, 55, 57, 58, 61-63, 65, 71-73, 76, 79r, 82, 84, 88.*

FIRST MEN IN THE MOON (See Movie Comics)

FIRST ROMANCE MAGAZINE
Home Comics(Harvey Publ.)/True Love: 8/49 - #6, 6/50; #7, 6/51 - #50, 2/58; #51, 9/58 - #52, 11/58

1 18 36 54 103 162 220
2 11 22 33 62 86 110
3-5 9 18 27 52 69 85
6-10,28: 28-Nostrand-a(Powell swipe) 8 16 24 42 54 65
11-20 7 14 21 37 46 55
21-27,29-32: 32-Last pre-code issue (2/55) 7 14 21 35 43 50
33-40,44-52 6 12 18 31 38 45
41-43-Kirby-c 8 16 24 42 54 65

NOTE: ***Powell** a-1-5, 8-10, 14, 18, 20-22, 24, 25, 28, 36, 46, 48, 51.*

The First X-Men #1 © MAR

The Flame #1 © FOX

The Flash #107 © DC

GD 2.0 VG 4.0 FN 6.0 VF 8.0 VF/NM 9.0 NM- 9.2

FIRST TRIP TO THE MOON (See Space Adventures No. 20)

FIRST WAVE (Based on Sci-Fi Channel TV series)
Andromeda Entertainment: Dec, 2000 - No. 4, Jun, 2001 ($2.99)

1-4-Kuhoric-s/Parsons-a/Busch-c 3.00

FIRST WAVE (Also see Batman/Doc Savage Special #1)
DC Comics: May, 2010 - No. 6, Mar, 2011 ($3.99, limited series)

1-6-Batman, Doc Savage and The Spirit app.; Azzarello-s/Morales-a/JG Jones-c 4.00
... Special 1 (6/11, $3.99) Winslade-a/Jones-c 4.00
HC (2011, $29.99, dustjacket) r/#1-6 & Batman/Doc Savage Special #1; sketch art 30.00

FIRST X-MEN
Marvel Comics: Oct, 2012 - No. 5, Mar, 2013 ($3.99, limited series)

1-5: 1-Neal Adams-a/c; Adams & Gage-s; Wolverine & Sabretooth 1st meet Xavier 4.00

FISH POLICE (Inspector Gill of the...#2, 3)
Fishwrap Productions/Comico V2#5-17/Apple Comics #18 on:
Dec, 1985 - No. 11, Nov, 1987 ($1.50, B&W); V2#5, April, 1988 - V2#17, May, 1989 ($1.75, color) No. 18, Aug, 1989 - No. 26, Dec, 1990 ($2.25, B&W)

1-11, 1(5/86),2-2nd print, V2#5-17-(Color): V2#5-11. 12-17, new-a, 18-26 ($2.25-c, B&W). 18-Origin Inspector Gill 3.00
Special 1($2.50, 7/87, Comico) 3.00
Graphic Novel: Hairballs (1987, $9.95, TPB) r/#1-4 in color 10.00

FISH POLICE
Marvel Comics: V2#1, Oct, 1992 - No. 6, Mar, 1993 ($1.25)

V2#1-6: 1-Hairballs Saga begins; r/#1 (1985) 3.00

5 CENT COMICS (Also see Whiz Comics)
Fawcett Publ.: Feb, 1940 (8 pgs., reg. size, B&W)

nn - 1st app. Dan Dare. Ashcan comic, not distributed to newsstands, only for in-house use. A CGC certified 9.6 copy sold for $10,800 in 2003, and a CGC 9.4 sold for $11,500 in 2005.

5 RONIN (Marvel characters in Samurai setting)
Marvel Comics: May, 2011 - No. 5, May, 2011 ($2.99, weekly limited series)

1-Wolverine. 2-Hulk. 3-Punisher. 4-Psylocke; Mack-c. 5-Deadpool 3.00

5-STAR SUPER-HERO SPECTACULAR (See DC Special Series No. 1)

FIVE WEAPONS
Image Comics: Feb, 2013 - Present ($3.50, limited series)

1-7-Jimmie Robinson-s/a/c 3.50

FLAME, THE (See Big 3 & Wonderworld Comics)
Fox Features Synd.: Sum, 1940 - No. 8, Jan, 1942 (#1,2: 68 pgs; #3-8: 44 pgs.)

1-Flame stories reprinted from Wonderworld #5-9; origin The Flame; Lou Fine-a (36 pgs.), 320 640 960 2240 3920 5600
2-Fine-a(2); Wing Turner by Tuska; r/Wonderworld #3,10 126 252 378 806 1378 1950
3-8: 3-Powell-a 84 168 252 538 919 1300

FLAME, THE (Formerly Lone Eagle)
Ajax/Farrell Publications (Excellent Publ.): No. 5, Dec-Jan, 1954-55 - No. 3, April-May, 1955

5(#1)-1st app. new Flame 52 104 156 328 552 775
2,3 32 64 96 188 307 425

FLAMING CARROT COMICS (Also see Junior Carrot Patrol)
Killian Barracks Press: Summer-Fall, 1981 ($1.95, one shot) (Lg size, 8-1/2x11")

1-Bob Burden-c/a/scripts; serially #'ed to 6500 5 10 15 34 60 85

FLAMING CARROT COMICS (See Anything Goes, Cerebus, Teenage Mutant Ninja Turtles/Flaming Carrot Crossover & Visions)
Aardvark-Vanaheim/Renegade Press #6-17/Dark Horse #18-31:
May, 1984 - No. 5, Jan, 1985; No. 6, Mar, 1985 - No. 31, Oct, 1994 ($1.70/$2.00, B&W)

1-Bob Burden story/art 4 8 12 28 47 65
2 3 6 9 16 23 30
3 2 4 6 10 16 20
4-6 2 4 6 9 12 15
7-9 1 3 4 6 8 10
10-12 6.50
13-15 4.00
15-Variant without cover price 6.00
16-(6/87) 1st app. Mystery Men 1 2 3 5 6 8
17-20: 18-1st Dark Horse issue 4.00
21-23,25: 25-Contains trading cards; TMNT app. 3.00
24-(2.50, 52 pgs.)-10th anniversary issue 4.00
26-28: 26-Begin $2.25-c. 26,27-Teenage Mutant Ninja Turtles x-over. 27-McFarlane-c 3.00
29-31-(2.50-c) 3.00

Annual 1(1/97, $5.00) 5.00
... & Reid Fleming, World's Toughest Milkman (12/02, $3.99) listed as #32 in indicia 4.00
... :Fortune Favors the Bold (1998, $16.95, TPB) r/#19-24 17.00
... :Men of Mystery (7/97, $12.95, TPB) r/#1-3, + new material 13.00
... 's Greatest Hits (4/98, $17.95, TPB) r/#12-18, + new material 18.00
... :The Wild Shall Wild Remain (1997, $17.95, TPB) r/#4-11, + new s/a 18.00

FLAMING CARROT COMICS
Image Comics (Desperado): Dec, 2004 - 2006 ($2.95/$3.50, B&W)

1-3-Bob Burden story/art 3.00
4-($3.50-c) 3.50
... Special #1 (3/06, $3.50) All Photo comic 3.50
... Vol. 6 (2006, $14.99) r/1-4 & Special #1; intro. by Brian Bolland 15.00

FLAMING LOVE
Quality Comics Group (Comic Magazines): Dec, 1949 - No. 6, Oct, 1950 (Photo covers #2-6) (52 pgs.)

1-Ward-c/a (9 pgs.) 41 82 123 256 428 600
2 20 40 60 117 189 260
3-Ward-a (9 pgs.); Crandall-a 29 58 87 170 278 385
4-6: 4-Gustavson-a 17 34 51 98 154 210

FLAMING WESTERN ROMANCES (Formerly Target Western Romances)
Star Publications: No. 3, Mar-Apr, 1950

3-Robert Taylor, Arlene Dahl photo on-c with biographies inside; L. B. Cole-c 34 68 102 199 325 450

FLARE (Also see Champions for 1st app. & League of Champions)
Hero Comics/Hero Graphics Vol. 2 on: Nov, 1988 - No. 3, Jan, 1989 ($2.75, color, 52 pgs); V2#1, Nov, 1990 - No. 7, Nov, 1991 ($2.95/$3.50, color, mature, 52 pgs.);V2#8, Oct, 1992 - No. 16, Feb, 1994 ($3.50/$3.95, B&W, 36 pgs.)

V1#1-3, V2#1-16: 5-Eternity Smith returns. 6-Intro The Tigress 4.00
Annual 1(1992, $4.50, B&W, 52 pgs.)-Champions-r 4.50

FLARE ADVENTURES
Hero Graphics: Feb, 1992 - No. 12, 1993? ($3.50/$3.95)

1 (90¢, color, 20 pgs.) 4.00
2-12-Flip books w/Champions Classics 4.00

FLASH, THE (See Adventure Comics, The Brave and the Bold, Crisis On Infinite Earths, DC Comics Presents, DC Special, DC Special Series, DC Super-Stars, The Greatest Flash Stories Ever Told, Green Lantern, Impulse, JLA, Justice League of America, Showcase, Speed Force, Super Team Family, Titans & World's Finest)

FLASH, THE (1st Series)(Formerly Flash Comics)(See Showcase #4,8,13,14)
National Periodical Publ./DC: No. 105, Feb-Mar, 1959 - No. 350, Oct, 1985

105-(2-3/59)-Origin Flash(retold), & Mirror Master (1st app.) 500 1000 1750 6000 14,000 22,000
106-Origin Grodd & Pied Piper; Flash's 1st visit to Gorilla City; begin Grodd the Super Gorilla trilogy (Scarce) 200 400 600 1650 3725 5800
107-Grodd trilogy, part 2 114 228 342 912 2056 3200
108-Grodd trilogy ends 96 192 288 768 1734 2700
109-2nd app. Mirror Master 79 158 237 632 1416 2200
110-Intro/origin Kid Flash who later becomes Flash in Crisis On Infinite Earths #12; begin Kid Flash trilogy, ends #112 (also in #114,116,118); 1st app. & origin of The Weather Wizard 166 332 498 1370 3085 4800
111-2nd Kid Flash tryout; Cloud Creatures 56 112 168 448 999 1550
112-Origin & 1st app. Elongated Man (4-5/60); also apps. in #115,119,130 64 128 192 512 1156 1800
113-Origin & 1st app. Trickster 50 100 150 390 870 1350
114-Captain Cold app. (see Showcase #8) 41 82 123 303 689 1075
115,116,118-120: 119-Elongated Man marries Sue Dearborn. 120-Flash & Kid Flash team-up for 1st time 35 70 105 252 564 875
117-Origin & 1st app. Capt. Boomerang; 1st & only S.A. app. Winky Blinky & Noddy 37 74 111 274 612 950
121,122: 122-Origin & 1st app. The Top 27 54 81 194 435 675
123-(9/61)-Re-intro. Golden Age Flash; origins of both Flashes; 1st mention of an Earth II where DC G. A. heroes live 166 332 498 1370 3085 4800
124-Last 10¢ issue 22 44 66 154 340 525
125-128,130: 127-Return of Grodd-c/story. 128-Origin & 1st app. Abra Kadabra. 130-(7/62)-1st Gauntlet of Super-Villains (Mirror Master, Capt. Cold, The Top, Capt. Boomerang & Trickster) 20 40 60 141 313 485
129-2nd G.A. Flash x-over; J.S.A. cameo in flashback (1st S.A. app. G.A. Green Lantern, Hawkman, Atom, Black Canary & Dr. Mid-Nite. Wonder Woman (1st S.A. app.?) appears) 27 54 81 189 420 650
131-136,138,140: 131-Early Green Lantern x-over (9/62). 135-1st app. of Kid Flash's yellow costume (3/63). 136-1st Dexter Miles. 140-Origin & 1st app. Heat Wave 15 30 45 103 227 350

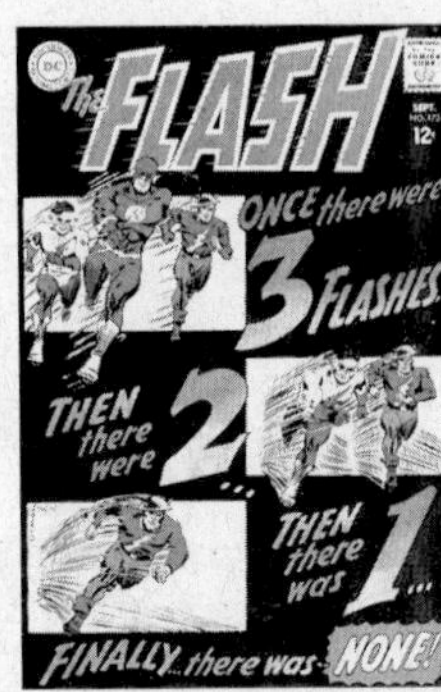

The Flash #173 © DC

The Flash #233 © DC

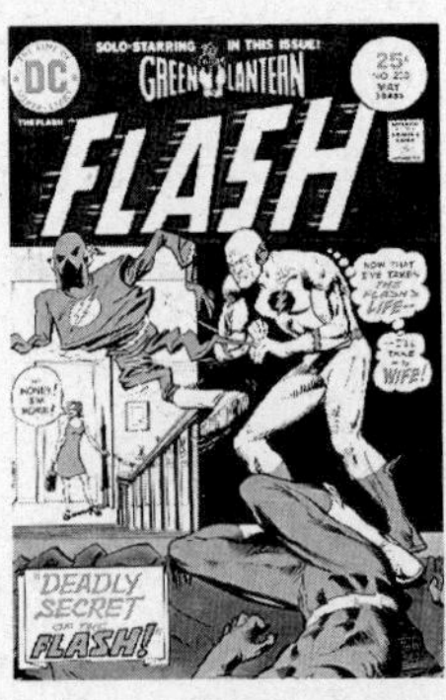

The Flash (2nd series) #149 © DC

GD 2.0 VG 4.0 FN 6.0 VF 8.0 VF/NM 9.0 NM- 9.2

137-G.A. Flash x-over; J.S.A. cameo (1st S.A. app.)(1st real app. since 2-3/51); 1st S.A. app. Vandal Savage & Johnny Thunder; JSA team decides to re-form 36 72 108 259 580 900
139-Origin & 1st app. Prof. Zoom 25 50 75 175 388 600
141-150: 142-Trickster app. 147-2nd Prof. Zoom 11 22 33 76 163 250
151-Engagement of Barry Allen & Iris West; G.A. Flash vs. The Shade. 12 24 36 82 179 275
152-159: 159-Dr. Mid-Nite cameo 10 20 30 64 132 200
160-(80-Pg. Giant G-21); G.A. Flash & Johnny Quick-r 11 22 33 73 157 240
161-164,166,167: 167-New facts about Flash's origin 8 16 24 54 102 150
165-Barry Allen weds Iris West 8 16 24 56 108 160
168,170: 168-Green Lantern-c/app. 170-Dr. Mid-Nite, Dr. Fate, G.A. Flash x-over 8 16 24 54 102 150
169-(80-Pg. Giant G-34)-New facts about origin 9 18 27 57 111 165
171,172,174,176,177,179,180: 171-JLA, Green Lantern, Atom flashbacks. 174-Barry Allen reveals I.D. to wife. 179-(5/68)-Flash travels to Earth-Prime and meets DC editor Julie Schwartz; 1st unnamed app. Earth-Prime (See Justice League of America #123 for 1st named app. & 3rd app. overall) 7 14 21 46 86 125
173-G.A. Flash x-over 8 16 24 54 102 150
175-2nd Superman/Flash race (12/67) (See Superman #199 & World's Finest #198,199); JLA cameo; gold kryptonite used (on J'onn J'onzz impersonating Superman) 16 32 48 112 249 385
178-(80-Pg. Giant G-46) 8 16 24 52 99 145
181-186,188,189: 186-Re-intro. Sargon. 189-Last 12¢-c 5 10 15 34 60 85
187,196: (68-Pg. Giants G-58, G-70) 6 12 18 40 73 105
190-195,197-199 4 8 12 27 44 60
200 5 10 15 30 50 70
201-204,206,207: 201-New G.A. Flash story. 206-Elongated Man begins 207-Last 15¢ issue 3 6 9 21 33 45
205-(68-Pg. Giant G-82) 6 12 18 41 76 110
208-213-(52 pg.): 211-G.A. Flash origin-r/#104; Roller Derby-c. 213-Reprints #137 4 8 12 25 40 55
214-DC 100 Page Super Spectacular DC-11; origin Metal Men-r/Showcase #37; never before published G.A. Flash story 8 16 24 54 102 150
215 (52 pgs.)-Flash-r/Showcase #4; G.A. Flash x-over, continued in #216 4 8 12 27 44 60
216,220: 220-1st app. Turtle since Showcase #4 3 6 9 17 26 35
217-219: Neal Adams-a in all. 217-Green Lantern/Green Arrow series begins (9/72); 2nd G.L. & G.A. team-up series (see Green Lantern #76). 219-Last Green Arrow 4 8 12 28 47 65
221-225,227,228,230,231,233: 222-G. Lantern x-over. 228-(7-8/74)-Flash writer Cary Bates travels to Earth-One & meets Flash, Iris Allen & Trickster; 2nd unnamed app. Earth-Prime (See Justice League of America #123 for 1st named app. & 3rd app. overall) 3 6 9 14 19 24
226-Neal Adams-p 3 6 9 16 24 32
229,232-(100 pg. issues)-G.A. Flash-r & new-a 54 8 12 28 47 65
234-250: 235-Green Lantern x-over. 243-Death of The Top. 245-Origin The Floronic Man in Green Lantern back-up, ends #246. 246-Last Green Lantern. 247-Jay Garrick app. 250-Intro Golden Glider 2 4 6 10 14 18
251-274: 256-Death of The Top retold. 265-267-(44 pgs.). 267-Origin of Flash's uniform. 270-Intro The Clown 2 4 6 8 10 12
268,273,274,278,283,286-(Whitman variants; low print run; no issue #s shown on covers) 2 4 6 8 11 14
275,276-Iris Allen dies 2 4 6 10 14 18
275,276-(Whitman variants; low print run; no issue #s shown on covers) 2 4 6 11 16 20
277-288,290: 286-Intro/origin Rainbow Raider 1 2 3 5 6 8
289-1st Pérez DC art (Firestorm); new Firestorm back-up series begins (9/80), ends #304 2 3 4 6 8 10
291-299,301-305: 291-1st app. Saber-Tooth (villain). 295-Gorilla Grodd-c/story. 298-Intro & origin new Shade. 301-Atomic bomb-c. 303-The Top returns. 304-Intro/origin Colonel Computron; 305-G.A. Flash x-over 6.00
300-(8/81, 52 pgs.)-25th Anniversary issue; Flash's origin and life story retold; wraparound-c by Infantino; no ads 1 2 3 5 6 8
306-313-Dr. Fate by Giffen. 309-Origin Flash retold 6.00
314-322,325-340: 318-323-Creeper back-ups. 328-Iris West Allen's death retold. 329-JLA app. 340-Trial of the Flash begins 5.00
323,324-Two part Flash vs. Flash story. 323-Creeper back-up. 324-Death of Reverse Flash (Professor Zoom) 1 3 4 6 8 10
341-349: 344-Origin Kid Flash 6.00
350-Double size ($1.25) Final issue 1 2 3 5 6 8
Annual 1 (10-12/63, 84 pgs.)-Origin Elongated Man & Kid Flash-r; origin Grodd; G.A. Flash-r 32 64 96 230 515 800
Annual 1 Replica Edition (2001, $6.95)-Reprints the entire 1963 Annual 7.00
...Chronicles SC Vol. 1 (2009, $14.99)-r/Showcase #4,8,13,14 and Flash #105,106 15.00
...Chronicles SC Vol. 2 (2010, $14.99)-r/Flash #107-112 15.00
The Flash Spectacular (See DC Special Series No. 11)
The Flash vs. The Rogues TPB (2009, $14.99) r/1st app. of classic rogues in Showcase #8 and Flash #105,106,110,113,117,122,140,155; new Van Sciver-c 15.00
The Life Story of the Flash (1997, $19.95, Hardcover) "Iris Allen's" chronicle of Barry Allen's life; comic panels w/additional text; Waid & Augustyn-s/ Kane & Staton-a/Orbik painted-c 20.00
The Life Story of the Flash (1998, $12.95, Softcover) New Orbik-c 13.00

NOTE: ***N. Adams*** *c-194, 195, 203, 204, 206-208, 211, 213, 215, 226p, 246.* ***M. Anderson*** *c-165, a(i)-195, 200-204, 206-208.* ***Austin*** *a-233i, 234i, 246i.* ***Buckler*** *a-271p, 272p; c(p)-247-250, 252, 253p, 255, 256p, 258, 262, 265-267, 269-271.* ***Giffen*** *a-306-313p; c-310p, 315.* ***Giordano*** *a-226i.* ***Sid Greene*** *a-167-174i, 229i(r).* ***Grell*** *a-237p, 238p, 240-243p; c-236.* ***Heck*** *a-198p.* ***Infantino/Anderson*** *a-135. c-135, 170-174, 192, 200, 201, 328-330.* ***Infantino/Giella*** *c-105-112, 163, 164, 166-168.* ***G. Kane*** *a-195p, 197-199p, 229r, 232r; c-197-199, 312p.* ***Kubert*** *a-108p, 215i(r); c-189-191.* ***Lopez*** *c-272.* ***Meskin*** *a-229r, 232r.* ***Perez*** *a-289-293p; c-293.* ***Starlin*** *a-294-296p.* ***Staton*** *c-263p, 264p. Green Lantern x-over-131, 143, 168, 171, 191.*

FLASH (2nd Series)(See Crisis on Infinite Earths #12 and All Flash #1)
DC Comics: June, 1987 - No. 230, Mar, 2006; No. 231, Oct, 2007 - No. 247, Feb, 2009

1-Guice-c/a begins; New Teen Titans app. 2 4 6 8 10 12
2-10: 3-Intro. Kilgore. 5-Intro. Speed McGee. 7-1st app. Blue Trinity. 8,9-Millennium tie-ins. 9-1st app. The Chunk 5.00
11-61: 12-Free extra 16 pg. Dr. Light story. 19-Free extra 16 pg. Flash story. 28-Capt. Cold app. 29-New Phantom Lady app. 40-Dr. Alchemy app. 50-($1.75, 52 pgs.) 4.00
62-78,80: 62-Flash: Year One begins, ends #65. 65-Last $1.00-c. 66-Aquaman app. 69,70-Green Lantern app. 70-Gorilla Grodd story ends. 73-Re-intro Barry Allen & begin saga ("Barry Allen's" true ID revealed in #78). 76-Re-intro of Max Mercury (Quality Comics' Quicksilver), not in uniform until #77. 80-($1.25-c) Regular Edition 4.00
79,80 ($2.50): 79-(68 pgs.) Barry Allen saga ends. 80-Foil-c 5.00
81-91,93,94,0,95-99,101: 81,82-Nightwing & Starfire app. 84-Razer app. 94-Zero Hour. 0-(10/94). 95-"Terminal Velocity" begins, ends #100. 96,98,99-Kobra app. 97-Origin Max Mercury; Chillblaine app. 4.00
92-1st Impulse 1 3 4 6 8 10
100 ($2.50)-Newstand edition; Kobra & JLA app. 4.00
100 ($3.50)-Foil-c edition; Kobra & JLA app. 5.00
102-131: 102-Mongul app.; begin-$1.75-c. 105-Mirror Master app. 107-Shazam app. 108-"Dead Heat" begins; 1st app. Savitar. 109-"Dead Heat" Pt. 2 (cont'd in Impulse #10). 110-"Dead Heat" Pt. 4 (cont'd in Impulse #11). 111-"Dead Heat" finale; Savitar disappears into the Speed Force; John Fox cameo (2nd app.). 112-"Race Against Time" begins, ends #118; re-intro John Fox. 113-Tornado Twins app. 119-Final Night x-over. 127-129-Rogue's Gallery & Neron. 128,129-JLA-app.130-Morrison & Millar-s begin 3.50
132-149: 135-GL & GA app. 142-Wally almost marries Linda; Waid-s return. 144-Cobalt Blue origin. 145-Chain Lightning begins.147-Professor Zoom app. 149-Barry Allen app. 3.00
150-($2.95) Final showdown with Cobalt Blue 4.00
151-162: 151-Casey-s. 152-New Flash-c. 154-New Flash ID revealed. 159-Wally marries Linda. 162-Last Waid-s. 3.00
163-187,189-196,198,199,201-206: 163-Begin $2.25-c. 164-186-Bolland-c. 183-New Trickster. 196-Winslade-a. 201-Dose-a begins. 205-Batman-c/app. 3.00
188-($2.95) Mirror Master, Weather Wizard, Trickster app. 4.00
197-Origin of Zoom (6/03) 1 3 4 6 8 10
200-($3.50) Flash vs. Zoom; Barry Allen & Hal Jordan app.; wraparound-c 5.00
207-230: 207-211-Turner-c/Porter-a. 209-JLA app. 210-Nightwing app. 212-Origin Mirror Master. 214-216-Identity Crisis x-over. 219-Wonder Woman app. 220-Rogue War 224-Zoom & Prof. Zoom app. 225-Twins born; Barry Allen app.; last Johns-s 3.00
231-247: 231-(10/07) Waid-s/Acuña-a. 240-Grodd app.; "Dark Side Club" 3.00
#1,000,000 (11/98) 853rd Century x-over 3.00
Annual 1-7,9: 2-('87-'94,'96, 68 pgs). 3-Gives history of G.A.,S.A., & Modern Age Flash in text. 4-Armageddon 2001. 5-Eclipso-c/story. 7-Elseworlds story. 9-Legends of the Dead Earth story; J.H. Williams-a(p); Mick Gray-a(i) 4.00
Annual 8 (1995, $3.50)-Year One story 4.00
Annual 10 (1997, $3.95)-Pulp Heroes stories 4.00
Annual 11,12 ('98, '99)-11-Ghosts; Wrightson-c. 12-JLApe; Art Adams-c 4.00
Annual 13 ('00, $3.50) Planet DC; Alcatena-c/a 4.00
...: Blitz (2004, $19.95, TPB)-r/#192-200; Kolins-c 20.00
...: Blood Will Run (2002, 2008; $17.95, TPB)-r/#170-176, Secret Files #3, Iron Heights 18.00
...: Crossfire (2004, $17.95, TPB)-r/#183-191 & parts of Flash Secret Files #3 18.00
Dead Heat (2000, $14.95, TPB)-r/#108-111, Impulse #10,11 15.00
...80-Page Giant (8/98, $4.95) Flash family stories by Waid, Millar and others; Mhan-c 5.00
...80-Page Giant 2 (4/99, $4.95) Stories of Flash family, future Kid Flash, original Teen Titans and XS 5.00
...: Emergency Stop (2008, $12.99, TPB)-r/#130-135; Morrison & Millar-s 13.00
...: Ignition (2005, $14.95, TPB)-r/#201-206 15.00
...: Iron Heights (2001, $5.95)-Van Sciver-c/a; intro. Murmur 6.00
...: Mercury Falling (2009, $14.99, TPB)-r/Impulse #62-67 15.00

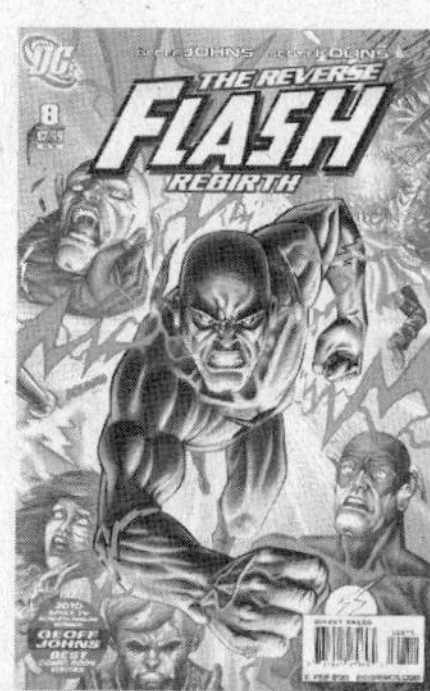

The Flash (2010 series) #8 © DC

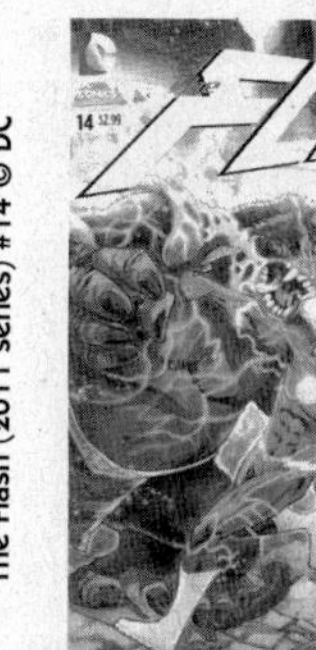

The Flash (2011 series) #14 © DC

Flash Comics #36 © DC

	GD 2.0	VG 4.0	FN 6.0	VF 8.0	VF/NM 9.0	NM- 9.2

...: Our Worlds at War 1 (10/01, $2.95)-Jae Lee-c; Black Racer app. 3.00
...Plus 1 (1/1997, $2.95)-Nightwing-c/app. 4.00
Race Against Time (2001, $14.95, TPB)-r/#112-118 15.00
...: Rogues (2003, $14.95, TPB)-r/#177-182 15.00
...: Rogue War (2006, $17.99, TPB)-r/#1/2,212,218,220-225; cover gallery 18.00
...Secret Files 1 (11/97, $4.95) Origin-s & pin-ups 5.00
...Secret Files 2 (11/99, $4.95) Origin of Replicant 5.00
...Secret Files 3 (11/01; $4.95) Intro. Hunter Zolomon (who later becomes Zoom) 5.00
Special 1 (1990, $2.95, 84 pgs.)-50th anniversary issue; Kubert-c; 1st Flash story by Mark Waid; 1st app. John Fox (27th Century Flash) 5.00
Terminal Velocity (1996, $12.95, TPB)-r/#95-100. 1[illegible].00
...: The Greatest Stories Ever Told (2007, $19.99, TPB) reprints; Ross-c/Waid intro. [illegible].00
The Return of Barry Allen (1996, $12.95, TPB)-r/#74-79 13.00
The Secret of Barry Allen (2005, $19.99, TPB)-r/#207-211,213-217; Turner sketch page 20.00
...: The Wild Wests HC (2008, $24.99, dustjacket)-r/#231-237 25.00
...: Time Flies (2002, $5.95)-Seth Fisher-c/a; Rozum-s 6.00
TV Special 1 (1991, $3.95, 76 pgs.)-Photo-c plus behind the scenes photos of TV show; Saltares-a, Byrne scripts 5.00
Wizard #1/2 (2005) prelude to Rogue Wars; Justiano-a 10.00
...: Wonderland TPB (2007, $12.99, TPB)-r/#164-169 13.00

NOTE: *Guice a-1-9p, 11p, Annual 1p; c-1-9p, Annual 1p.* ***Perez*** *c-15-17, Annual 2i.* ***Charest*** *c/a-Annual 5p.*

FLASH, THE (Brightest Day)(Leads into Flashpoint series)
DC Comics: Jun, 2010 - No. 12, Jul, 2011 ($3.99/$2.99)

1-($3.99) Barry Allen vs. the 25th Century Rogues; Johns-s/Manapul-a/c 4.00
1-Variant-c by Tony Harris 10.00
2-12-($2.99) Capt. Boomerang app. 8-Reverse Flash origin retold 3.00
2-12-Variant covers. 2-Sook. 3-Horn. 4-Kolins. 5-Sook. 6-Garza. 7-Cooke 5.00
...: Secret Files and Origins 1 (5/10, $3.99) Johns-s/Kolins-a; profiles of the Rogues 4.00
...: The Dastardly Death of the Rogues HC (2011, $19.99, dj) r/#1-7 & Secret Files 20.00

FLASH (New DC 52)
DC Comics: Nov, 2011 - Present ($2.99)

1-24: 1-Manapul & Buccellato-s/Manapul-a/c. 6,7-Captain Cold app. 8,9,13-17-Grodd app. 17-24-Reverse Flash app. 18-Takara-a. 21-Kid Flash app. 3.00
23.1, 23.2, 23.3 (11/13, $2.99, regular-c) 3.00
23.1 (11/13, $3.99, 3-D cover) "Grodd #1" on cover; Batista-a/Manapul-c 5.00
23.2 (11/13, $3.99, 3-D cover) "Reverse Flash #1" on cover; origin; Hepburn-a/Manapul-c 5.00
23.3 (11/13, $3.99, 3-D cover) "The Rogues #1" on cover; Zircher-a/Manapul-c 5.00
25-($3.99) Zero Year; Sprouse & Manapul-a; first meeting of Barry and Iris 4.00
26-29: 26-Googe-a. 27-Buccellato-s begin. 28-Deadman app. 3.00
#0 (11/12, $2.99) Barry's childhood and origin re-told; Manapul-a/c 3.00
Annual #1 (10/12, $4.99) Continued from #12; origin of Glider; Kolins-a 5.00
Annual #2 (9/13, $4.99) Green Lantern app.; Basri-a 5.00

FLASH: REBIRTH
DC Comics: Jun, 2009 - No. 6, Apr, 2010 ($3.99/$2.99, limited series)

1-($3.99) Barry Allen's return; Johns-s/Van Sciver-a; Flash-c by Van Sciver 4.00
1-Variant Barry Allen-c by Van Sciver 10.00
1-Second thru fourth printings 4.00
1-Special Edition (8/10, $1.00) reprints #1 with "What's Next?" logo on cover 3.00
2-6-($2.99) 3-Max Mercury returns 3.00
2-6-Variant covers by Van Sciver 8.00
HC (2010, $19.99, dustjacket) r/#1-6; Johns original proposal; sketch art; cover gallery 20.00
SC (2011, $14.99) r/#1-6; Johns original proposal; sketch art; cover gallery 15.00

FLASH: THE FASTEST MAN ALIVE (3rd Series)(See Infinite Crisis)
DC Comics: Aug, 2006 - No. 13, Aug, 2007 ($2.99)

1-Bart Allen becomes the Flash; Lashley-a/Bilson & Demeo-s 3.00
1-Variant-c by Joe and Andy Kubert 5.00
2-12: 5-Cyborg app. 7-Inertia returns. 10-Zoom app. 3.00
13-Bart Allen dies; 2 covers 3.00
13-DC Nation Edition from the 2007 San Diego Comic-Con 8.00
...: Full Throttle TPB (2007, $12.99) r/#7-13, All-Flash #1, DCU Infinite Holiday Spec. story 13.00
...: Lightning in a Bottle TPB (2007, $12.99) r/#1-6 13.00

FLASH, THE (See Tangent Comics/ The Flash)

FLASH AND GREEN LANTERN: THE BRAVE AND THE BOLD
DC Comics: Oct, 1999 - No. 6, Mar, 2000 ($2.50, limited series)

1-6-Waid & Peyer-s/Kitson-a. 4-Green Arrow app.; Grindberg-a(p) 3.00
TPB (2001, $12.95) r/#1-6 13.00

FLASH COMICS
DC Comics:. Dec. 1939

1-Ashcan comic, not distributed to newsstands, only for in-house use. Cover art is Adventure Comics #41 and interior from All-American Comics #8. A CGC certified 9.6 sold for $11,500 in 2004. A CGC certified 9.4 sold for $6,572.50 in 2008. A CGC certified 9.6 sold for $8,513 in 2013.

FLASH COMICS (Whiz Comics No. 2 on)
Fawcett Publications: Jan, 1940 (12 pgs., B&W, regular size)
(Not distributed to newsstands; printed for in-house use)

NOTE: ***Whiz Comics*** *#2 was preceded by two books,* ***Flash Comics*** *and* ***Thrill Comics****, both dated Jan, 1940, (12 pgs, B&W, regular size) and were not distributed. These two books are identical except for the title, and were sent out to major distributors as ad copies to promote sales. It is believed that the complete 68 page issue of Fawcett's* ***Flash*** *and* ***Thrill Comics*** *#1 was finished and ready for publication with the January date. Since DC Comics was also about to publish a book with the same date and title, Fawcett hurriedly printed up the black and white version of* ***Flash Comics*** *to secure copyright before DC. The inside covers are blank, with the covers and inside pages printed on a high quality uncoated paper stock. The eight page origin story of Captain Thunder is composed of pages 1-7 and 13 of the Captain Marvel story essentially as they appeared in the first issue of* ***Whiz Comics****. The balloon dialogue on page thirteen was relettered to tie the story into the end of page seven in* ***Flash*** *and* ***Thrill Comics*** *to produce a shorter version of the origin story for copyright purposes. Obviously, DC acquired the copyright and Fawcett dropped* ***Flash*** *as well as* ***Thrill*** *and came out with* ***Whiz Comics*** *a month later. Fawcett never used the cover to* ***Flash*** *and* ***Thrill*** *#1, designing a new cover for* ***Whiz Comics****. Fawcett also must have discovered that Captain Thunder had already been used by another publisher (Captain Terry Thunder by Fiction House). All references to Captain Thunder were relettered to Captain Marvel before appearing in* ***Whiz****.*

1 (nn on-c, #1 on inside)-Origin & 1st app. Captain Thunder. Cover by C.C. Beck. Eight copies of Flash and three copies of Thrill exist. All 3 copies of Thrill sold in 1986 for between $4,000-$10,000 each. A NM copy of Thrill sold in 1987 for $12,000. A VG copy of Thrill sold in 1987 for $9000 cash. A VF(8.0) copy of Thrill sold in 2003 for $11,400. A CGC certified 9.0 copy of the Flash Comics version sold for $10,117.50 in 2006. A CGC certified 9.4 copy of the Flash Comics version sold for $14,340 in 2008. A CGC certified 9.0 copy of the Thrill Comics version sold for $20,315 in 2008. A CGC certified 8.0 copy sold for $12,999 in 2012.

FLASH COMICS (The Flash No. 105 on) (Also see All-Flash)
National Periodical Publ./All-American: Jan, 1940 - No. 104, Feb, 1949

	GD 2.0	VG 4.0	FN 6.0	VF 8.0	VF/NM 9.0	NM- 9.2
1-The Flash (origin/1st app.) by Harry Lampert, Hawkman (origin/1st app.) by Gardner Fox, The Whip, & Johnny Thunder (origin/1st app.) by Stan Asch; Cliff Cornwall by Moldoff, Flash Picture Novelets (later Minute Movies w/#12) begin; Moldoff (Shelly) cover; 1st app. Shiera Sanders who later becomes Hawkgirl, #24; reprinted in Famous First Edition (on sale 11/10/39); The Flash-c	8500	17,000	25,500	66,000	123,000	180,000

1-Reprint, Oversize 13-1/2x10". **WARNING:** This comic is an exact reprint of the original except for its size. DC published it in 1974 with a second cover titling it as a Famous First Edition. There have been many reported cases of the outer cover being removed and the interior sold as the original edition. The reprint with the new outer cover removed is practically worthless. See Famous First Edition for value.

	GD 2.0	VG 4.0	FN 6.0	VF 8.0	VF/NM 9.0	NM- 9.2
2-Rod Rian begins, ends #11; Hawkman-c	935	1870	2805	6826	12,063	17,300
3-King Standish begins (1st app.), ends #41 (called The King #16-37,39-41); E.E. Hibbard-a begins on Flash	459	918	1377	3350	5925	8500
4-Moldoff (Shelly) Hawkman begins; The Whip-c	314	628	942	2198	3849	5500
5-The King-c	258	516	774	1651	2826	4000
6-2nd Flash-c (alternates w/Hawkman #6 on)	638	1276	1914	4657	8229	11,800
7-2nd Hawkman-c; 1st Moldoff Hawkman-c	584	1168	1752	4263	7532	10,800
8-New logo begins; classic Moldoff Flash-c	371	742	1113	2600	4550	6500
9,10: 9-Moldoff Hawkman-c; 10-Classic Moldoff Flash-c	383	766	1149	2681	4691	6700
11-13,15-20: 12-Les Watts begins; "Sparks" #16 on. 13-Has full page ad for All Star Comics #3. 17-Last Cliff Cornwall	242	484	726	1537	2644	3750
14-World War II cover	284	568	852	1818	3109	4400
21-Classic Hawkman-c	232	464	696	1485	2543	3600
22,23	213	426	639	1363	2332	3300
24-Shiera becomes Hawkgirl (12/41); see All-Star Comics #5 for 1st app.	245	490	735	1568	2684	3800
25-28,30: 28-Last Les Sparks.	139	278	417	883	1517	2150
29-Ghost Patrol begins (origin/1st app.), ends #104	142	284	426	909	1555	2200
31,33-Classic Hawkman-c. 33-Origin Shade	155	310	465	992	1696	2400
32,34-40: 36-1st app. Rag Doll	132	264	396	838	1444	2050
41-50	113	226	339	718	1234	1750
51-61: 52-1st computer in comics, c/s (4/44). 59-Last Minute Movies. 61-Last Moldoff Hawkman	95	190	285	603	1039	1475
62-Hawkman by Kubert begins	116	232	348	742	1271	1800
63-85: 66-68-Hop Harrigan in all. 70-Mutt & Jeff app. 80-Atom begins, ends #104	86	172	258	546	936	1325
86-Intro. The Black Canary in Johnny Thunder (8/47); see All-Star #38.	300	600	900	2040	3570	5100
87,88,90: 87-Intro. The Foil. 88-Origin Ghost.	129	258	387	826	1413	2000
89-Intro villain The Thorn (scarce)	232	464	696	1485	2543	3600
91,93-99: 98-Atom & Hawkman don new costumes	135	270	405	864	1482	2100
92-1st solo Black Canary plus-c; rare in Mint due to black ink smearing on white-c	377	754	1131	2639	4620	6600
100 (10/48),103(Scarce)-52 pgs. each	300	600	900	1950	3375	4800
101,102(Scarce)	274	548	822	1740	2995	4250

Flash Gordon (2014 series) #1 © KING

Flat-Top #1 © HARV

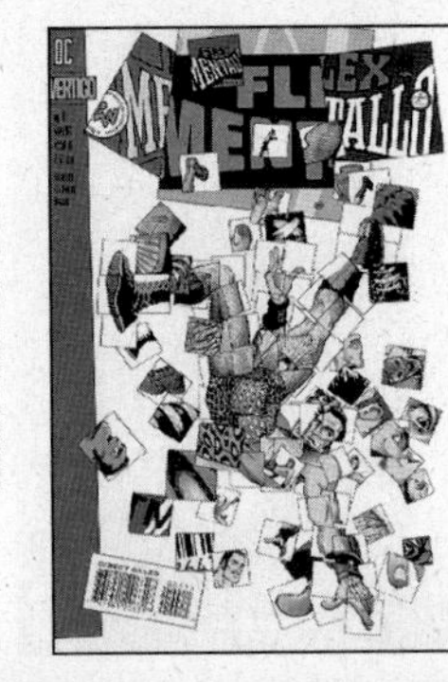
Flex Mentallo #4 © DC

	GD 2.0	VG 4.0	FN 6.0	VF 8.0	VF/NM 9.0	NM- 9.2

104-Origin The Flash retold (Scarce) 719 1438 2157 5249 9275 13,300

NOTE: ***Irwin Hasen** a-Wheaties Giveaway. c-97, Wheaties Giveaway. **E.E. Hibbard** c-6, 12, 20, 24, 26, 28, 30, 44, 46, 48, 50, 62, 66, 68, 69, 72, 74, 76, 78, 80, 82. **Infantino** a-86p, 90, 93-95, 99-104; c-90, 92, 93, 97, 99, 101, 103. **Kinstler** a-87, 89(Hawkman); c-87. **Chet Kozlak** c-77, 79, 81. **Krigstein** a-94. **Kubert** a-62-76, 83, 85, 86, 88-104; c-63, 65, 67, 70, 71, 73, 75, 83, 85, 86, 88, 89, 91, 94, 96, 98, 100, 104. **Moldoff** a-3; c-3, 7-11, 13-17, plus odd #'s 19-61. **Martin Naydell** c-52, 54, 56, 58, 60, 64, 84.*

FLASH DIGEST, THE (See DC Special Series #24)

FLASH GORDON (See Defenders Of The Earth, Eat Right to Work..., Giant Comic Album, King Classics, King Comics, March of Comics #118, 133, 142, The Phantom #18, Street Comix & Wow Comics, 1st series)

FLASH GORDON
Dell Publishing Co.: No. 25, 1941; No. 10, 1943 - No. 512, Nov, 1953

Feature Books 25 (#1)(1941))-r-not by Raymond 148 296 444 947 1624 2300
Four Color 10(1942)-by Alex Raymond; reprints "The Ice Kingdom" 84 168 252 672 1511 2350
Four Color 84(1945)-by Alex Raymond; reprints "The Fiery Desert" 40 80 120 296 673 1050
Four Color 173 19 38 57 131 291 450
Four Color 190-Bondage-c; "The Adventures of the Flying Saucers"; 5th Flying Saucer story (6/48)- see The Spirit 9/28/47(1st), Shadow Comics V7#10 (2nd, 1/48), Captain Midnight #60 (3rd, 2/48) & Boy Commandos #26 (4th, 3-4/48) 21 42 63 147 324 500
Four Color 204,247 15 30 45 103 227 350
Four Color 424-Painted-c 11 22 33 72 154 235
2(5-7/53-Dell)-Painted-c; Evans-a? 9 18 27 59 117 175
Four Color 512-Painted-c 9 18 27 59 117 175

FLASH GORDON (See Tiny Tot Funnies)
Harvey Publications: Oct, 1950 - No. 4, April, 1951

1-Alex Raymond-a; bondage-c; reprints strips from 7/14/40 to 12/8/40 41 82 123 256 428 600
2-Alex Raymond-a; r/strips 12/15/40-4/27/41 26 52 78 154 252 350
3,4-Alex Raymond-a; 3-bondage-c; r/strips 5/4/41-9/21/41. 4-r/strips 10/24/37-3/27/38 24 48 72 142 234 325
5-(Rare)-Small size-5-1/2x8-1/2"; B&W; 32 pgs.; Distributed to some mail subscribers only 84 168 252 538 919 1300
(Also see All-New No. 15, Boy Explorers No. 2, and Stuntman No. 3)

FLASH GORDON
Gold Key: June, 1965

1 (1947 reprint)-Painted-c 6 12 18 41 76 110

FLASH GORDON (Also see Comics Reading Libraries in the Promotional Comics section)
King #1-11/Charlton #12-18/Gold Key #19-23/Whitman #28 on:
9/66 - #11, 12/67; #12, 2/69 - #18, 1/70; #19, 9/78 - #37, 3/82 (Painted covers No. 19-30, 34)

1-1st S.A. app Flash Gordon; Williamson c/a(2); E.C. swipe/Incredible S.F. #32; Mandrake story 7 14 21 49 92 135
1-Army giveaway(1968)("Complimentary" on cover)(Same as regular #1 minus Mandrake story & back-c) 4 8 12 28 47 65
2-8: 2-Bolle, Gil Kane-c; Mandrake story. 3-Williamson-c. 4-Secret Agent X-9 begins, Williamson-c/a(3). 5-Williamson-c/a(2). 6,8-Crandall-a. 7-Raboy-a (last in comics?). 8-Secret Agent X-9-r 4 8 12 28 47 65
9-13: 9,10-Raymond-r. 10-Buckler's 1st pro work (11/67). 11-Crandall-a. 12-Crandall-c/a. 13-Jeff Jones-a (15 pgs.) 4 8 12 27 44 60
14,15: 15-Last 12¢ issue 3 6 9 19 30 40
16,17: 17-Brick Bradford story 3 6 9 16 24 32
18-Kaluta-a (3rd pro work?)(see Teen Confessions) 3 6 9 21 33 45
19(9/78, G.K.), 20-26 2 4 6 8 10 12
27-29,34-37: 34-37-Movie adaptation 2 4 6 8 11 14
30 (10/80) (scarce, from Whitman 3-pack only, 40¢-c) 4 8 12 23 37 50
30 (7/81; re-issue, 50¢-c), 31-33-single issues 2 4 6 11 16 20
31-33 (Bagged 3-pack): Movie adaptation; Williamson-a. 60.00

NOTE: ***Aparo** a-8. **Bolle** a-21, 22. **Boyette** a-14-18. **Briggs** c-10. **Buckler** a-10. **Crandall** c-6. **Estrada** a-3. **Gene Fawcette** a-29, 30, 34, 37. **McWilliams** a-31-33, 36.*

FLASH GORDON
DC Comics: June, 1988 - No. 9, Holiday, 1988-'89 ($1.25, mini-series)

1-9: 1,5-Painted-c 4.00

FLASH GORDON
Marvel Comics: June, 1995 - No. 2, July, 1995 ($2.95, limited series)

1,2: Schultz scripts; Williamson-a 3.00

FLASH GORDON (The Mercy Wars)
Ardden Entertainment: Aug, 2008 - No. 6, Jul, 2009 ($3.99)

1-6: 1-Deneen-s/Green-a; two covers 4.00
...: The Mercy Wars #0 (4/09, $2.99) 3.00

FLASH GORDON
Dynamite Entertainment: 2014 ($3.99)

1-Parker-s/Shaner-a; six covers 4.00

FLASH GORDON: INVASION OF THE RED SWORD
Ardden Entertainment: Jan, 2011 - No. 6, Nov, 2011 ($3.99)

1-6-Deneen-s/Garcia-a. 1-Two covers 4.00

FLASH GORDON THE MOVIE
Western Publishing Co.: 1980 (8-1/4 x 11", $1.95, 68 pgs.)

11294-Williamson-c/a; adapts movie 2 4 6 10 14 18
13743-Hardback edition 3 6 9 15 21 26

FLASH GORDON: ZEITGEIST
Dynamite Entertainment: 2011 - No. 10, 2013 ($1.00/$3.99)

1-($1.00) Flash, Dale and Zarkov head to Mongo; 4 covers by Ross, Renaud & others 3.00
2-10-($3.99) 2-8-Three covers. 9,10-Ross-c 4.00

FLASH/ GREEN LANTERN: FASTER FRIENDS (See Green Lantern/Flash...)
DC Comics: No. 2, 1997 ($4.95, continuation of Green Lantern/Flash: Faster Friends #1)

2-Waid/Augustyn-s 5.00

FLASHPOINT (Elseworlds Flash)
DC Comics: Dec, 1999 - No. 3, Feb, 2000 ($2.95, limited series)

1-3-Paralyzed Barry Allen; Breyfogle-a/McGreal-s 3.00

FLASHPOINT (Leads into DC New 52 relaunches)
DC Comics: Jul, 2011 - No. 5, Late Oct, 2011 ($3.99, limited series)

1-5-Johns-s/Andy Kubert-a; 2 covers on each. 2-4-Bonus design art. 5-New timeline 4.00
...: Abin Sur - The Green Lantern 1-3 (8/11 - No. 3, 10/11, $2.99) Massaferra-a/c 3.00
...: Batman Knight of Vengeance 1-3 (8/11 - No. 3, 10/11, $2.99) Risso-a/Johnson-c 3.00
...: Canterbury Cricket, The (8/11, $2.99, one-shot) Carlin-s/Morales-a 3.00
...: Citizen Cold 1-3 (8/11 - No. 3, 10/11, $2.99) Scott Kolins-s/a/c 3.00
...: Deadman and the Flying Grayson 1-3 (8/11 - No. 3, 10/11, $2.99) Chiang-c 3.00
...: Deathstroke & The Curse of the Ravager 1-3 (8/11 - No. 3, 10/11, $2.99) Bennett-a 3.00
...: Emperor Aquaman 1-3 (8/11 - No. 3, 10/11, $2.99) Bedard-s/Syaf-c 3.00
...: Frankenstein and the Creatures of the Unknown 1-3 (8/11 - No. 3, 10/11, $2.99) 3.00
...: Green Arrow Industries (8/11, $2.99, one-shot) Kalvachev-c 3.00
...: Grodd of War (8/11, $2.99, one-shot) Manapul-c 3.00
...: Hal Jordan 1-3 (8/11 - No. 3, 10/11, $2.99) 1-Oliver-a. 2,3-Richards-a 3.00
...: Kid Flash Lost 1-3 (8/11 - No. 3, 10/11, $2.99) Gates-s/Manapul-c; Brainiac app. 3.00
...: Legion of Doom 1-3 (8/11 - No. 3, 10/11, $2.99) Glass-s/Sepulveda-c 3.00
...: Lois Lane and the Resistance 1-3 (8/11 - No. 3, 10/11, $2.99) Abnett & Lanning-s 3.00
...: Outsider, The 1-3 (8/11 - No. 3, 10/11, $2.99) Robinson-s/Nowlan-c 3.00
...: Project Superman 1-3 (8/11 - No. 3, 10/11, $2.99) Gene Ha-c/a 3.00
...: Reverse Flash (8/11, $2.99, one-shot) Kolins-s/Gomez-a 3.00
...: Secret Seven 1-3 (8/11 - No. 3, 10/11, $2.99) Pérez-c on all. 1-Pérez-a. 3.00
...: Wonder Woman and The Furies 1-3 (8/11 - No. 3, 10/11, $2.99) Aquaman app. 3.00
...: World of Flashpoint 1-3 (8/11 - No. 3, 10/11, $2.99) Traci 13 app. 3.00

FLAT-TOP
Mazie Comics/Harvey Publ.(Magazine Publ.) No. 4 on: 11/53 - No. 3, 5/54; No. 4, 3/55 - No. 7, 9/55

1-Teenage; Flat-Top, Mazie, Mortie & Stevie begin 10 20 30 56 76 95
2,3 6 12 18 31 38 45
4-7 6 12 18 28 34 40

FLESH & BLOOD
Brainstorm Comics: Dec, 1995 ($2.95, B&W, mature)

1-Balent-c; foil-c. 3.00

FLESH AND BONES
Upshot Graphics (Fantagraphics Books): June, 1986 - No. 4, Dec, 1986 (Limited series)

1-4: Alan Moore scripts (r) & Dalgoda by Fujitake 3.00

FLESH CRAWLERS
Kitchen Sink Press: Aug, 1993 - No. 3, 1995 ($2.50, B&W, limited series, mature)

1-3 3.00

FLEX MENTALLO (Man of Muscle Mystery) (See Doom Patrol, 2nd Series)
DC Comics (Vertigo): Jun, 1996 - No. 4, Sept, 1996 ($2.50, lim. series, mature)

1-4: Grant Morrison scripts & Frank Quitely-c/a in all; banned from reprints due to Charles Atlas legal action 2 4 6 9 13 16

FLINCH (Horror anthology)
DC Comics (Vertigo): Jun, 1999 - No. 16, Jan, 2001 ($2.50)

1-16: 1-Art by Jim Lee, Quitely, and Corben. 5-Sale-c. 11-Timm-a 3.00

FLINTSTONE KIDS, THE (TV) (See Star Comics Digest)

Flintstones and the Jetsons #12 © H-B

Flip #2 © HARV

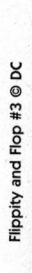

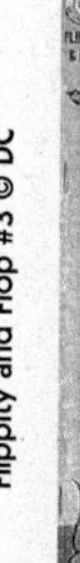
Flippity and Flop #3 © DC

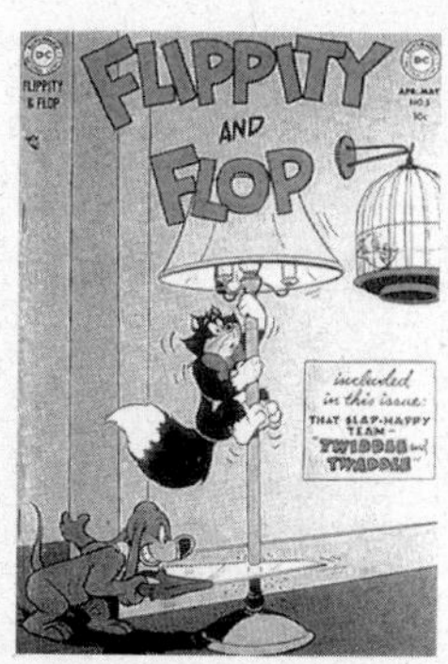

	GD 2.0	VG 4.0	FN 6.0	VF 8.0	VF/NM 9.0	NM- 9.2

Star Comics/Marvel Comics #5 on: Aug, 1987 - No. 11, Apr, 1989

1	1	2	3	5	6	8
2-11						5.00

FLINTSTONES, THE (TV)(See Dell Giant #48 for No. 1)
Dell Publ. Co./Gold Key No. 7 (10/62) on: No. 2, Nov-Dec, 1961 - No. 60, Sept, 1970 (Hanna-Barbera)

2-2nd app. (TV show debuted on 9/30/60); 1st app. of Cave Kids; 15¢-c thru #5	9	18	27	59	117	175
3-6(7-8/62): 3-Perry Gunnite begins. 6-1st 12¢-c	6	12	18	38	69	100
7 (10/62; 1st GK)	6	12	18	38	69	100
8-10	5	10	15	33	57	80
11-1st app. Pebbles (6/63)	8	16	24	51	96	140
12-15,17-20	4	8	12	28	47	65
16-1st app. Bamm-Bamm (1/64)	7	14	21	46	86	130
21-23,25-30,33: 26,27-2nd & 3rd app. The Grusomes. 30-1st app. Martian Mopheads (10/65). 33-Meet Frankenstein & Dracula	4	8	12	27	44	60
24-1st app. The Grusomes	5	10	15	35	63	90
31,32,35-40: 31-Xmas-c. 36-Adaptation of "the Man Called Flintstone" movie. 39-Reprints	4	8	12	23	37	50
34-1st app. The Great Gazoo	5	10	15	35	63	90
41-60: 46-Last 12¢ issue	3	6	9	20	31	42
At N. Y. World's Fair ('64)-J.W. Books (25¢)-1st printing; no date on-c (29¢ version exists, 2nd print?) Most H-B characters app.; including Yogi Bear, Top Cat, Snagglepuss and the Jetsons	5	10	15	31	53	75
At N. Y. World's Fair (1965 on-c; re-issue; Warren Pub.) NOTE: Warehouse find in 1984	2	4	6	10	14	18
Bigger & Boulder 1(#30013-211) (Gold Key Giant, 11/62, 25¢, 84 pgs.)	7	14	21	46	86	125
Bigger & Boulder 2-(1966, 25¢)-Reprints B&B No. 1	4	8	12	23	37	50
...On the Rocks (9/61, $1.00, 6-1/4x9", cardboard-c, high quality paper,116 pgs.) B&W new material	8	16	24	54	102	150
...With Pebbles & Bamm Bamm (100 pgs., G.K.)-30028-511 (paper-c, 25¢) (11/65)	6	12	18	38	69	100

NOTE: *(See Comic Album #16, Bamm-Bamm & Pebbles Flintstone, Dell Giant 48, Golden Comics Digest, March of Comics #229, 243, 271, 289, 299, 317, 327, 341, Pebbles Flintstone, Top Comics #2-4, and Whitman Comic Book.)*

FLINTSTONES, THE (TV)(...& Pebbles)
Charlton Comics: Nov, 1970 - No. 50, Feb, 1977 (Hanna-Barbera)

1	7	14	21	44	82	120
2	4	8	12	27	44	60
3-7,9,10	3	6	9	19	30	40
8- "Flintstones Summer Vacation" (Summer, 1971, 52 pgs.)	5	10	15	31	53	75
11-20,36: 36-Mike Zeck illos (early work)	3	6	9	16	23	30
21-35,38-41,43-45	3	6	9	14	19	24
37-Byrne text illos (early work; see Nightmare #20)	3	6	9	16	23	30
42-Byrne-a (2 pgs.)	3	6	9	16	23	30
46-50	2	4	6	13	18	22
Digest nn (1972, B&W, 100 pgs.) (low print run)	3	6	9	19	30	40

(Also see Barney & Betty Rubble, Dino, The Great Gazoo, & Pebbles & Bamm-Bamm)

FLINTSTONES, THE (TV)(See Yogi Bear, 3rd series) (Newsstand sales only)
Marvel Comics Group: October, 1977 - No. 9, Feb, 1979 (Hanna-Barbera)

1,7-9: 1-(30¢-c). 7-9-Yogi Bear app.	3	6	9	19	30	40
1-(35¢-c variant, limited distribution)	8	16	24	51	96	140
2,3,5,6: Yogi Bear app.	3	6	9	15	22	28
4-The Jetsons app.	3	6	9	16	24	32

FLINTSTONES, THE (TV)
Harvey Comics: Sept, 1992 - No. 13, Jun, 1994 ($1.25/$1.50) (Hanna-Barbera)

V2#1-13						4.00
...Big Book 1,2 (11/92, 3/93; both $1.95, 52 pgs.)						5.00
...Giant Size 1-3 (10/92, 4/93, 11/93; $2.25, 68 pgs.)						5.00

FLINTSTONES, THE (TV)
Archie Publications: Sept, 1995 - No. 22, June, 1997 ($1.50)

1-22						3.00

FLINTSTONES AND THE JETSONS, THE (TV)
DC Comics: Aug, 1997 - No. 21, May, 1999 ($1.75/$1.95/$1.99)

1						6.00
2-21: 19-Bizarro Elroy-c						3.00

FLINTSTONES CHRISTMAS PARTY, THE (See The Funtastic World of Hanna-Barbera No. 1)

FLIP
Harvey Publications: April, 1954 - No. 2, June, 1954 (Satire)

1,2-Nostrand-a each. 2-Powell-a	22	44	66	128	209	290

FLIPPER (TV)
Gold Key: Apr, 1966 - No. 3, Nov, 1967 (All have photo-c)

1	6	12	18	38	69	100
2,3	4	8	12	28	47	65

FLIPPITY & FLOP
National Per. Publ. (Signal Publ. Co.): 12-1/51-52 - No. 46, 8-10/59; No. 47, 9-11/60

1-Sam dog & his pets Flippity The Bird and Flop The Cat begin; Twiddle and Twaddle begin	29	58	87	170	278	385
2	15	30	45	90	140	190
3-5	14	28	42	80	115	150
6-10	12	24	36	69	97	125
11-20: 20-Last precode (3/55)	10	20	30	58	79	100
21-47	9	18	27	52	69	85

FLOATERS
Dark Horse Comics: Sept, 1993 - No. 5, Jan, 1994 ($2.50, B&W, lim. series)

1-5						3.00

FLOYD FARLAND (See Eclipse Graphic Album Series #11)

FLY, THE (Also see Adventures of..., Blue Ribbon Comics & Flyman)
Archie Enterprises, Inc.: May, 1983 - No. 9, Oct, 1984

1,2: 1-Mr. Justice app; origin Shield; Kirby-a; Steranko-c. 2-Ditko-a; Flygirl app.						6.00
3-5: Ditko-a in all. 4,5-Ditko-c(p)						5.00
6-9: Ditko-a in all. 6-8-Ditko-c(p)						6.00

NOTE: *Ayers c-9. Buckler a-1, 2. Kirby a-1. Nebres c-3, 4, 5i, 6, 7i. Steranko c-1, 2.*

FLY, THE
Impact Comics (DC): Aug, 1991 - No. 17, Dec, 1992 ($1.00)

1						4.00
2-17: 4-Vs. The Black Hood. 9-Trading card inside						3.00
Annual 1 ('92, $2.50, 68 pgs.)-Impact trading card						4.00

FLYBOY (Flying Cadets)(Also see Approved Comics #5)
Ziff-Davis Publ. Co. (Approved): Spring, 1952 - No. 2, Oct-Nov, 1952

1-Saunders painted-c	20	40	60	114	182	250
2-(10-11/52)-Saunders painted-c	14	28	42	80	115	150

FLYING ACES (Aviation stories)
Key Publications: July, 1955 - No. 5, Mar, 1956

1	9	18	27	52	69	85
2-5: 2-Trapani-a	6	12	18	28	34	40

FLYING A'S RANGE RIDER, THE (TV)(See Western Roundup under Dell Giants)
Dell Publishing Co.: #404, 6-7/52; #2, June-Aug, 1953 - #24, Aug, 1959 (All photo-c)

Four Color 404(#1)-Titled "The Range Rider"	9	18	27	57	111	165
2	5	10	15	35	63	90
3-10	5	10	15	31	53	75
11-16,18-24	4	8	12	28	47	65
17-Toth-a	5	10	15	33	57	80

FLYING CADET (WW II Plane Photos)
Flying Cadet Publ. Co.; Jan, 1943 - V2#8, Nov, 1944 (Half photos, half comics)

V1#1-Painted-c	17	34	51	98	154	210
2-Photo-c, P-47 Thunderbolt	11	22	33	60	83	105
3-9 (Two #6's, Sept. & Oct.): 4,5,6a,6b-Photo-c	10	20	30	56	76	95
V2#1-7 (1/44-9/44)(#10-16): 1,2,4-7-Photo-c	9	18	27	52	69	85
7 (#17 on cover)-Bare-breasted woman-c	24	48	72	142	234	325

FLYING COLORS 10th ANNIVERSARY SPECIAL
Flying Colors Comics: Fall 1998 ($2.95, one-shot)

1-Dan Brereton-c; pin-ups by Jim Lee and Jeff Johnson						3.00

FLYIN' JENNY
Pentagon Publ. Co./Leader Enterprises #2: 1946 - No. 2, 1947 (1945 strip-r)

nn-Marcus Swayze strip-r (entire insides)	18	36	54	105	165	225
2-Baker-c; Swayze strip reprints	26	52	78	154	252	350

FLYING MODELS
H-K Publ. (Health-Knowledge Publs.): V61#3, May, 1954 (5¢, 16 pgs.)

V61#3 (Rare)	9	18	27	50	65	80

FLYING NUN (TV)
Dell Publishing Co.: Feb, 1968 - No. 4, Nov, 1968

1-Sally Field photo-c	6	12	18	38	69	100

Fly Man #37 © AP

Foodini #2 © HOKE

Forbidden Love #4 © QUA

GD 2.0 VG 4.0 FN 6.0 VF 8.0 VF/NM 9.0 NM- 9.2

2-4: 2-Sally Field photo-c 4 8 12 27 44 60

FLYING NURSES (See Sue & Sally Smith...)

FLYING SAUCERS (See The Spirit 9/28/47(1st app.), Shadow Comics V7#10 (2nd, 1/48), Captain Midnight #60 (3rd, 2/48), Boy Commandos #26 (4th, 3-4/48) & Flash Gordon Four Color 190 (5th, 6/48))

FLYING SAUCERS (See Out of This World Adventures #2)
Avon Periodicals/Realistic: 1950; 1952; 1953

1(1950)-Wood-a, 21 pgs.; Fawcette-c 94 188 282 597 1024 1450
nn(1952)-Cover altered plus 2 pgs. of Wood-a not in original
50 100 150 315 533 750
nn(1953)-Reprints above (exist?) 50 100 150 315 533 750

FLYING SAUCERS (Comics)
Dell Publishing Co.: April, 1967 - No. 4, Nov, 1967; No. 5, Oct, 1969

1-(12¢-c) 4 8 12 27 44 60
2-5: 5-Has same cover as #1, but with 15¢ price 3 6 9 19 30 40

FLY MAN (Formerly Adventures of The Fly; Mighty Comics #40 on)
Mighty Comics Group (Radio Comics) (Archie): No. 32, July, 1965 - No. 39, Sept, 1966 (Also see Mighty Crusaders)

32,33-Comet, Shield, Black Hood, The Fly & Flygirl x-over. 33-Re-intro Wizard, Hangman (1st S.A. appearances) 5 10 15 34 60 85
34-39: 34-Shield begins. 35-Origin Black Hood. 36-Hangman x-over in Shield; re-intro. & origin of Web (1st S.A. app.). 37-Hangman, Wizard x-over in Flyman; last Shield issue. 38-Web story. 39-Steel Sterling (1st S.A. app.) 4 8 12 27 44 60

FOLLOW THE SUN (TV)
Dell Publishing Co.: May-July, 1962 - No. 2, Sept-Nov, 1962 (Photo-c)

01-280-207(No.1) 5 10 15 30 50 70
12-280-211(No.2) 4 8 12 27 44 60

FOODANG
Continum Comics: July, 1994 ($1.95, B&W, bi-monthly)

1 3.00

FOODINI (TV)(The Great...; see Jingle Dingle & Pinhead &...)
Continental Publ. (Holyoke): March, 1950 - No. 4, Aug, 1950 (All have 52 pgs.)

1-Based on TV puppet show (very early TV comic) 22 44 66 132 216 300
2-Jingle Dingle begins 14 28 42 80 115 150
3,4 10 20 30 58 79 100

FOOEY (Magazine) (Satire)
Scoff Publishing Co.: Feb, 1961 - No. 4, May, 1961

1 4 8 12 28 47 65
2-4 3 6 9 19 30 40

FOOFUR (TV)
Marvel Comics (Star Comics)/Marvel No. 5 on: Aug, 1987 - No. 6, Jun, 1988

1-6 5.00

FOOLKILLER (Also see The Amazing Spider-Man #225, The Defenders #73, Man-Thing #3 & Omega the Unknown #8)
Marvel Comics: Oct, 1990 - No. 10, Oct, 1991 ($1.75, limited series)

1-10: 1-Origin 3rd Foolkiller; Greg Salinger app; DeZuniga-a(i) in 1-4. 8-Spider-Man x-over 3.00

FOOLKILLER
Marvel Comics: Dec, 2007 - No. 5, Jul, 2008 ($3.99, limited series)

1-5-Hurwitz-s/Medina-a. 2-Origin 4.00

FOOLKILLER: WHITE ANGELS
Marvel Comics: Sept, 2008 - No. 5, Jan, 2009 ($3.99, limited series)

1-5-Hurwitz-s/Azaceta-a 4.00

FOOM (Friends Of Ol' Marvel)
Marvel Comics: 1973 - No. 22, 1979 (Marvel fan magazine)

1 8 16 24 54 102 150
2-Hulk-c by Steranko 5 10 15 35 63 90
3,4 5 10 15 34 60 85
5-11: 11-Kirby-a and interview 5 10 15 31 53 75
12-15: 12-Vision-c. 13-Daredevil-c. 14-Conan. 15-Howard the Duck
5 10 15 31 53 75
16-20: 16-Marvel bullpen. 17-Stan Lee issue. 19-Defenders
4 8 12 28 47 65
21-Star Wars 5 10 15 30 50 70
22-Spider-Man-c; low print run final issue 6 12 18 38 69 100

FOOTBALL THRILLS (See Tops In Adventure)
Ziff-Davis Publ. Co.: Fall-Winter, 1951-52 - No. 2, Fall, 1952 (Edited by "Red" Grange)

1-Powell a(2); Saunders painted-c; Red Grange, Jim Thorpe stories
27 54 81 158 259 360
2-Saunders painted-c 18 36 54 105 165 225

FOOT SOLDIERS, THE
Dark Horse Comics: Jan, 1996 - No. 4, Apr, 1996 ($2.95, limited series)

1-4: Krueger story & Avon Oeming-a. in all. 1-Alex Ross-c. 4-John K. Snyder, III-c 3.00

FOOT SOLDIERS, THE (Volume Two)
Image Comics: Sept, 1997 - No. 5, May, 1998 ($2.95, limited series)

1-5: 1-Yeowell-a. 2-McDaniel, Hester, Sienkiewicz, Giffen-a 3.00

FOR A NIGHT OF LOVE
Avon Periodicals: 1951

nn-Two stories adapted from the works of Emile Zola; Astarita, Ravielli-a; Kinstler-c
34 68 102 206 336 465

FORBIDDEN KNOWLEDGE: ADVENTURE BEYOND THE DOORWAY TO SOULS WITH RADICAL DREAMER (Also see Radical Dreamer)
Mark's Giant Economy Size Comics: 1996 ($3.50, B&W, one-shot, 48 pgs.)

nn-Max Wrighter app.; Wheatley-c/a/script; painted infinity-c 4.00

FORBIDDEN LOVE
Quality Comics Group: Mar, 1950 - No. 4, Sept, 1950 (52 pgs.)

1-(Scarce)-Classic photo-c; Crandall-a 97 194 291 621 1061 1500
2-(Scarce)-Classic photo-c 74 148 222 470 810 1150
3-(Scarce)-Photo-c 50 100 150 315 533 750
4-(Scarce)-Ward/Cuidera-a; photo-c 53 106 159 334 567 800

FORBIDDEN LOVE (See Dark Mansion of...)

FORBIDDEN PLANET
Innovation Publishing: May, 1992 - No. 4, 1992 ($2.50, limited series)

1-4: Adapts movie; painted-c 3.00

FORBIDDEN TALES OF DARK MANSION (Formerly Dark Mansion of Forbidden Love #1-4)
National Periodical Publ.: No. 5, May-June, 1972 - No. 15, Feb-Mar, 1974

5-(52 pgs.) 5 10 15 34 60 85
6-15: 13-Kane/Howard-a 3 6 9 17 26 35

NOTE: ***N. Adams*** *c-9.* ***Alcala*** *a-9-11, 13.* ***Chaykin*** *a-7,15.* ***Evans*** *a-14.* ***Heck*** *a-5.* ***Kaluta*** *a-7i, 8-12; c-7, 8, 13.* ***G. Kane*** *a-13.* ***Kirby*** *a-6.* ***Nino*** *a-8, 12, 15.* ***Redondo*** *a-14.*

FORBIDDEN WORLDS
American Comics Group: 7-8/51 - No. 34, 10-11/54; No. 35, 8/55 - No. 145, 8/67 (No. 1-5: 52 pgs.; No. 6-8: 44 pgs.)

1-Williamson/Frazetta-a (10 pgs.) 168 336 504 1075 1838 2600
2 68 136 204 438 749 1060
3-Williamson/Wood-a (7 pgs.); Frazetta (1 panel) 69 138 207 442 759 1075
4 45 90 135 283 477 670
5-Krenkel/Williamson-a (8 pgs.) 54 108 162 346 591 835
6-Harrison/Williamson-a (8 pgs.) 49 98 147 309 522 735
7,8,10: 7-1st monthly issue 34 68 102 204 332 460
9-A-Bomb explosion story 38 76 114 228 369 510
11-20 23 46 69 136 223 310
21-33: 24-E.C. swipe by Landau 19 38 57 111 176 240
34(10-11/54)(Scarce)(becomes Young Heroes #35 on)-Last pre-code issue; A-Bomb explosion story 21 42 63 124 202 280
35(8/55)-Scarce 20 40 60 120 195 270
36-62 14 28 42 76 108 140
63,69,76,78-Williamson-a in all; w/Krenkel #69 14 28 42 78 112 145
64,66-68,70-72,74,75,77,79-85,87-90 10 20 30 56 76 95
65- "There's a New Moon Tonight" listed in #114 as holding 1st record fan mail response
14 28 42 78 112 145
73-1st app. Herbie by Ogden Whitney 47 94 141 296 498 700
86-Flying saucer-c by Schaffenberger 11 22 33 62 86 110
91-93,95-100 5 10 15 31 53 75
94-Herbie (2nd app.) 10 20 30 69 147 225
101-109,111-113,115,117-120 4 8 12 28 44 60
110,116-Herbie app. 116-Herbie goes to Hell 7 14 21 49 92 135
114-1st Herbie-c; contains list of editor's top 20 ACG stories
9 18 27 61 123 185
121-123 3 6 9 21 33 45
124,127-130: 124-Magic Agent app. 4 8 12 23 37 50
125-Magic Agent app.; intro. & origin Magicman series, ends #141; Herbie app.
5 10 15 31 53 75
126-Herbie app. 4 8 12 27 44 60
131-139: 133-Origin/1st app. Dragonia in Magicman (1-2/66); returns in #138. 136-Nemesis x-over in Magicman 3 6 9 21 33 45

Force Works #11 © MAR

Forever Evil #1 © DC

47 Ronin #5 © DH

	GD 2.0	VG 4.0	FN 6.0	VF 8.0	VF/NM 9.0	NM- 9.2
140-Mark Midnight app. by Ditko	4	8	12	23	37	50
141-145	3	6	9	19	30	40

NOTE: ***Buscema** a-75, 79, 81, 82, 140r. **Cameron** a-5. **Disbrow** a-10. **Ditko** a-137p, 138, 140. **Landau** a-24, 27-29, 31-34, 48, 86r, 96, 143-45. **Lazarus** a-18, 23, 24, 57. **Moldoff** a-27, 31, 139r. **Reinman** a-93. **Whitney** a-70, 115, 116, 137; c-40, 46, 57, 60, 68, 70, 78, 79, 90, 93, 94, 100, 102, 103, 106-108, 114, 129.*

FORCE, THE (See The Crusaders)

FORCE MAJEURE: PRAIRIE BAY (Also see Wild Stars)
Little Rocket Publications: May, 2002 ($2.95, B&W)

1-Tierney-s/Gil-c/a 3.00

FORCE OF BUDDHA'S PALM THE
Jademan Comics: Aug, 1988 - No. 55, Feb, 1993 ($1.50/$1.95, 68 pgs.)

1,55-Kung Fu stories in all 5.00
2-54 4.00

FORCE WORKS
Marvel Comics: July, 1994 - No. 22, Apr, 1996 ($1.50)

1-($3.95)-Fold-out pop-up-c; Iron Man, Wonder Man, Spider-Woman, U.S. Agent & Scarlet Witch (new costume) 4.00
2-11, 13-22: 5-Blue logo & pink logo versions. 9-Intro Dreamguard. 13-Avengers app. 3.00
5-Pink logo ($2.95)-polybagged w/ 16pg. Marvel Action Hour Preview & acetate print 4.00
12 ($2.50)-Flip book w/War Machine. 4.00

FORD ROTUNDA CHRISTMAS BOOK (See Christmas at the Rotunda)

FOREIGN INTRIGUES (Formerly Johnny Dynamite; becomes Battlefield Action #16 on)
Charlton Comics: No. 14, 1956 - No. 15, Aug, 1956

	GD	VG	FN	VF	VF/NM	NM-
14,15-Johnny Dynamite continues	8	16	24	44	57	70

FOREMOST BOYS (See 4Most)

FOREVER AMBER
Image Comics: July, 1999 - Oct, 1999 ($2.95, B&W)

1-4-Don Hudson-s/a 3.00

FOREVER DARLING (Movie)
Dell Publishing Co.: No. 681, Feb, 1956

	GD	VG	FN	VF	VF/NM	NM-
Four Color 681-w/Lucille Ball & Desi Arnaz; photo-c	10	20	30	66	138	210

FOREVER EVIL (See Justice League #23 (2013))
DC Comics: Nov, 2013 - No. 7, Jul, 2014 ($3.99, limited series)

1-Earth Three Crime Syndicate takes over; Nightwing unmasked; Johns-s/Finch-a 4.00
1-Director's Cut 1 (12/13, $5.99) Pencil artwork with full script 6.00
2-6: 2-Luthor dons the green battlesuit. 4-Sinestro returns 4.00
7-($4.99) 5.00

FOREVER EVIL: A.R.G.U.S.
DC Comics: Dec, 2013 - No. 6, May, 2014 ($2.99, limited series)

1-6-Gates-s. Steve Trevor in search of missing heroes. 1,2-Deathstroke app. 3.00

FOREVER EVIL: ARKHAM WAR
DC Comics: Dec, 2013 - No. 6, May, 2014 ($2.99, limited series)

1-6-Tomasi-s/Eaton-a; Bane and the Arkham inmates. 4-6-The Talons app. 3.00

FOREVER EVIL: ROGUES REBELLION
DC Comics: Dec, 2013 - No. 6, May, 2014 ($2.99, limited series)

1-6-Buccellato-s/Hepburn-a/Shalvey-c. 2-Deathstorm & Power Ring app. 6-Grodd app. 3.00

FOREVER MAELSTROM
DC Comics: Jan, 2003 - No. 6, Jun, 2003 ($2.95, limited series)

1-6-Chaykin & Tischman-s/Lucas & Barreto-a 3.00

FOREVER PEOPLE, THE
National Periodical Publications: Feb-Mar, 1971 - No. 11, Oct-Nov, 1972 (Fourth World)
(#1-3, 10-11 are 36 pgs; #4-9 are 52 pgs.)

	GD	VG	FN	VF	VF/NM	NM-
1-1st app. Forever People; Superman x-over; Kirby-c/a begins; 1st full app. Darkseid (3rd anywhere, 3 weeks before New Gods #1); Darkseid storyline begins, ends #8 (app. in 1-4,6,8; cameos in 5,11)	6	12	18	41	76	110
2-9: 4-G.A. reprints thru #9. 9,10-Deadman app.	4	8	12	25	40	55
10,11	3	6	9	19	30	40

Jack Kirby's Forever People TPB ('99, $14.95, B&W&Grey) r/#1-11 plus cover gallery 15.00
NOTE: ***Kirby** c/a(p)-1-11; #4-9 contain Sandman reprints from Adventure #85, 84, 75, 80, 77, 74 in that order.*

FOREVER PEOPLE
DC Comics: Feb, 1988 - No. 6, July, 1988 ($1.25, limited series)

1-6 4.00

FORGE
CrossGeneration Comics: Feb, 2002 - No. 13, May, 2003 ($9.95/$11.95/$7.95, TPB)

1-3: Reprints from various CrossGen titles 10.00

4-8-($11.95) 12.00
9-13-($7.95, 8-1/4" x 5-1/2") digest-sized reprints 8.00

FOR GIRLS ONLY
Bernard Baily Enterprises: 11/53 - No. 2, 6/54 (100 pgs., digest size, 25¢)

	GD	VG	FN	VF	VF/NM	NM-
1-25% comic book, 75% articles, illos, games	22	44	66	132	216	300
2-Eddie Fisher photo & story.	16	32	48	94	147	200

FORGOTTEN FOREST OF OZ, THE (See First Comics Graphic Novel #16)

FORGOTTEN REALMS (Also see Avatar & TSR Worlds)
DC Comics: Sept, 1989 - No. 25, Sept, 1991 ($1.50/$1.75)

1, Annual 1 (1990, $2.95, 68 pgs.) 4.00
2-25: Based on TSR role-playing game. 18-Avatar story 3.00

FORGOTTEN REALMS (Based on Wizards of the Coast game)
Devil's Due Publ.: June, 2005 - No. 3, Aug, 2005 ($4.95)

1-3-Salvatore-s/Seeley-a 5.00
...Exile (11/05 - No. 3, 1/06, $4.95) 1-3-Daab-s/Seeley-a. 1-Flip cover 5.00
...: Legacy (2/08 - No. 3, 6/08, $5.50) 1-3-Daab-s/Atkins-a 5.50
The Legend of Drizzt Book II: Exile (2006, $14.95, TPB) r/#1-3 15.00
...Sojourn (3/06 - No. 3, 6/06, $4.95) 1-3-Daab-s/Seeley-a 5.00
...: Streams of Silver (12/06 - No. 3, $5.50) 1-3-Daab-s/Semeiks-a 5.50
...The Crystal Shard (8/06 - No. 3, 12/06, $4.95) 1-3-Daab-s/Semeiks-a 5.00
...The Halfling's Gem (8/07 - No. 3, 12/07, $5.50) 1-3-Daab-s/Seeley-a; two covers 5.50

FORLORN RIVER (See Zane Grey Four Color 395)

FOR LOVERS ONLY (Formerly Hollywood Romances)
Charlton Comics: No. 60, Aug, 1971 - No. 87, Nov, 1976

	GD	VG	FN	VF	VF/NM	NM-
60	3	6	9	19	30	40
61-80,82-87: 67-Morisi-a	2	4	6	11	16	20
81-Psychedelic cover	3	6	9	16	23	30

FORMERLY KNOWN AS THE JUSTICE LEAGUE
DC Comics: Sept, 2003 - No. 6, Feb, 2004 ($2.50, limited series)

1-Giffen & DeMatteis-s/Maguire-a; Booster Gold, Blue Beetle, Captain Atom, Mary Marvel, Fire, and Elongated Man app. 4.00
2-6: 3,4-Roulette app. 6-JLA app. 3.00
TPB (2004, $12.95) r/#1-6 13.00

FORMIC WARS: BURNING EARTH
Marvel Comics: Apr, 2011 - No. 7, Sept, 2011 ($3.99, limited series)

1-7-Prequel to Orson Scott Card's novel Ender's Game. 1-Covers by Larroca & Hitch 4.00

FORMIC WARS: SILENT STRIKE (Follows Burning Earth limited series)
Marvel Comics: Feb, 2012 - No. 5, Jun, 2012 ($3.99, limited series)

1-5-Johnston-s/Caracuzzo-a/Camuncoli-c 4.00

FORT: PROPHET OF THE UNEXPLAINED
Dark Horse Comics: June, 2002 - No. 4, Sept, 2002 ($2.99, B&W, limited series)

1-4-Peter Lenkov-s/Frazer Irving-c/a 3.00
TPB (2003, $9.95) r/#1-4 10.00

FORTUNE AND GLORY
Oni Press: Dec, 1999 - No. 3, Apr, 2000 ($4.95, B&W, limited series)

1-3-Brian Michael Bendis in Hollywood 5.00
TPB ($14.95) 15.00

40 BIG PAGES OF MICKEY MOUSE
Whitman Publ. Co.: No. 945, Jan, 1936 (10-1/4x12-1/2", 44 pgs., cardboard-c)

	GD	VG	FN	VF	VF/NM	NM-
945-Reprints Mickey Mouse Magazine #1, but with a different cover; ads were eliminated and some illustrated stories had expanded text. The book is 3/4" shorter than Mickey Mouse Mag. #1, but the reprints are same size (Rare)	164	328	492	1025	1688	2350

40 oz. COLLECTED
Image Comics: Nov, 2003 ($9.95, digest-size, B&W)

Vol. 1-Reprints Jim Mahfood's mini-comics plus 20 pgs. new material; Grrl Scouts app. 10.00

47 RONIN
Dark Horse Comics: Nov, 2012 - No. 5, Jul, 2013 ($3.99, limited series)

1-5-Mike Richardson-s/Stan Sakai-a/c; 18th century samurai legend 4.00

FOR YOUR EYES ONLY (See James Bond...)

FOUNTAIN, THE (Companion graphic novel to the Darren Aronofsky film)
DC Comics (Vertigo): 2005 ($39.99, hardcover with dust jacket)

1-Darren Aronofsky-s/Kent Williams-a 40.00

FOUR (Fantastic Four; See Marvel Knights 4 #28-30)

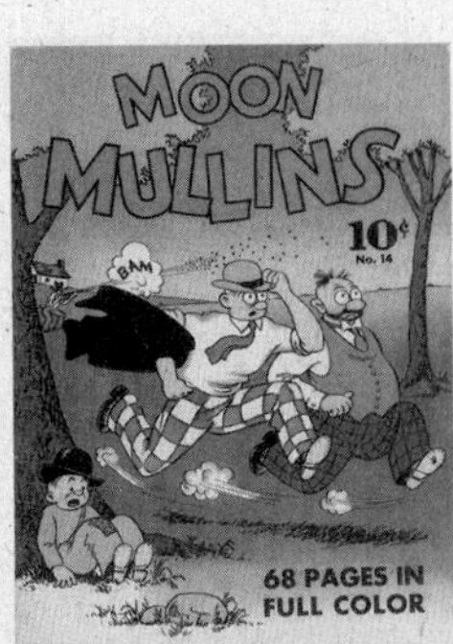

Four Color Comics Series 1 #14 © DELL

Four Color Comics Series 2 #49 © DIS

Four Color Comics #79 © DIS

	GD 2.0	VG 4.0	FN 6.0	VF 8.0	VF/NM 9.0	NM- 9.2

FOUR COLOR
Dell Publishing Co.: Sept?, 1939 - No. 1354, Apr-June, 1962
(Series I are all 68 pgs.)

NOTE: *Four Color only appears on issues #19-25, 1-99,101. Dell Publishing Co. filed these as Series I, #1-25, and Series II, #1-1354. Issues beginning with #710? were printed with and without ads on back cover. Issues without ads are worth more.*

SERIES I:

Issue	GD 2.0	VG 4.0	FN 6.0	VF 8.0	VF/NM 9.0	NM- 9.2
1(nn)-Dick Tracy	1050	2100	3150	7800	14,650	21,500
2(nn)-Don Winslow of the Navy (#1) (Rare) (11/39?)	210	420	630	1334	2292	3250
3(nn)-Myra North (1/40)	100	200	300	640	1095	1550
4-Donald Duck by Al Taliaferro (1940)(Disney)(3/40?)	1800	3600	5400	13,500	22,750	32,000
(Prices vary widely on this book)						
5-Smilin' Jack (#1) (5/40?)	77	154	231	493	847	1200
6-Dick Tracy (Scarce)	239	478	717	1530	2615	3700
7-Gang Busters	53	106	159	334	567	800
8-Dick Tracy	119	238	357	762	1306	1850
9-Terry and the Pirates-r/Super #9-29	71	142	213	454	777	1100
10-Smilin' Jack	65	130	195	416	708	1000
11-Smitty (#1)	48	96	144	302	514	725
12-Little Orphan Annie; reprints strips from 12/19/37 to 6/4/38	61	122	183	390	670	950
13-Walt Disney's Reluctant Dragon('41)-Contains 2 pgs. of photos from film; 2 pg. foreword to Fantasia by Leopold Stokowski; Donald Duck, Goofy, Baby Weems & Mickey Mouse (as the Sorcerer's Apprentice) app. (Disney)	219	438	657	1402	2401	3400
14-Moon Mullins (#1)	47	94	141	296	498	700
15-Tillie the Toiler (#1)	50	100	150	315	533	750
16-Mickey Mouse (#1) (Disney) by Gottfredson	1250	2500	3750	16,500	-	-
17-Walt Disney's Dumbo, the Flying Elephant (#1)(1941)-Mickey Mouse, Donald Duck, & Pluto app. (Disney)	268	536	804	1702	2926	4150
18-Jiggs and Maggie (#1)(1936-38-r)	50	100	150	315	533	750
19-Barney Google and Snuffy Smith (#1)-(1st issue with Four Color on the cover)	48	96	144	302	514	725
20-Tiny Tim	39	78	117	231	378	525
21-Dick Tracy	87	174	261	553	952	1350
22-Don Winslow	50	100	150	315	533	750
23-Gang Busters	41	82	123	260	435	610
24-Captain Easy	52	104	156	328	552	775
25-Popeye (1942)	94	188	282	602	1026	1450

SERIES II:

Issue	GD 2.0	VG 4.0	FN 6.0	VF 8.0	VF/NM 9.0	NM- 9.2
1-Little Joe (1942)	54	108	162	432	966	1500
2-Harold Teen	27	54	81	194	435	675
3-Alley Oop (#1)	44	88	132	326	738	1150
4-Smilin' Jack	35	70	105	252	564	875
5-Raggedy Ann and Andy (#1)	44	88	132	326	738	1150
6-Smitty	19	38	57	131	291	450
7-Smokey Stover (#1)	24	48	72	170	378	585
8-Tillie the Toiler	21	42	63	147	324	500
9-Donald Duck Finds Pirate Gold, by Carl Barks & Jack Hannah (Disney) (© 8/17/42)	1000	2000	3000	7600	13,800	20,000
10-Flash Gordon by Alex Raymond; reprinted from "The Ice Kingdom"	84	168	252	672	1511	2350
11-Wash Tubbs	24	48	72	168	372	575
12-Walt Disney's Bambi (#1)	46	92	138	340	770	1200
13-Mr. District Attorney (#1)-See The Funnies #35 for 1st app.	24	48	72	168	372	575
14-Smilin' Jack	27	54	81	194	435	675
15-Felix the Cat (#1)	71	142	213	568	1284	2000
16-Porky Pig (#1)(1942)- "Secret of the Haunted House"	82	164	246	656	1478	2300
17-Popeye	40	80	120	296	673	1050
18-Little Orphan Annie's Junior Commandos; Flag-c; reprints strips from 6/14/42 to 11/21/42	32	64	96	230	515	800
19-Walt Disney's Thumper Meets the Seven Dwarfs (Disney); reprinted in Silly Symphonies	41	82	123	303	689	1075
20-Barney Baxter	23	46	69	164	362	560
21-Oswald the Rabbit (#1)(1943)	38	76	114	282	634	985
22-Tillie the Toiler	15	30	45	105	233	360
23-Raggedy Ann and Andy	31	62	93	223	499	775
24-Gang Busters	25	50	75	175	388	600
25-Andy Panda (#1) (Walter Lantz)	46	92	138	354	797	1240
26-Popeye	40	80	120	296	673	1050
27-Walt Disney's Mickey Mouse and the Seven Colored Terror	71	142	213	568	1284	2000
28-Wash Tubbs	16	32	48	110	243	375
29-Donald Duck and the Mummy's Ring, by Carl Barks (Disney) (9/43)	784	1568	2352	5723	10,112	14,500
30-Bambi's Children (1943)-Disney	40	80	120	296	673	1050
31-Moon Mullins	15	30	45	103	227	350
32-Smitty	14	28	42	94	207	320
33-Bugs Bunny "Public Nuisance #1"	96	192	288	768	1734	2700
34-Dick Tracy	37	74	111	274	612	950
35-Smokey Stover	14	28	42	96	211	325
36-Smilin' Jack	20	40	60	138	307	475
37-Bringing Up Father	17	34	51	117	259	400
38-Roy Rogers (#1, © 4/44)-1st western comic with photo-c (see Movie Comics #3)	152	306	456	1216	2733	4250
39-Oswald the Rabbit (1944)	26	52	78	182	404	625
40-Barney Google and Snuffy Smith	18	36	54	126	281	435
41-Mother Goose and Nursery Rhyme Comics (#1)-All by Walt Kelly	20	40	60	135	300	465
42-Tiny Tim (1934-r)	15	30	45	100	220	340
43-Popeye (1938-'42-r)	27	54	81	189	420	650
44-Terry and the Pirates (1938-r)	30	60	90	216	483	750
45-Raggedy Ann	25	50	75	175	388	600
46-Felix the Cat and the Haunted Castle	36	72	108	266	596	925
47-Gene Autry (copyright 6/16/44)	30	60	90	216	483	750
48-Porky Pig of the Mounties by Carl Barks (7/44)	86	172	258	688	1544	2400
49-Snow White and the Seven Dwarfs (Disney)	46	92	138	340	770	1200
50-Fairy Tale Parade-Walt Kelly art (1944)	21	42	63	147	324	500
51-Bugs Bunny Finds the Lost Treasure	32	64	96	230	515	800
52-Little Orphan Annie; reprints strips from 6/18/38 to 11/19/38	23	46	69	164	362	560
53-Wash Tubbs	12	24	36	82	179	275
54-Andy Panda	25	50	75	175	388	600
55-Tillie the Toiler	12	24	36	79	170	260
56-Dick Tracy	33	66	99	238	532	825
57-Gene Autry	27	54	81	194	435	675
58-Smilin' Jack	20	40	60	138	307	475
59-Mother Goose and Nursery Rhyme Comics-Kelly-c/a	16	32	48	110	243	375
60-Tiny Folks Funnies	13	26	39	89	195	300
61-Santa Claus Funnies(11/44)-Kelly art	20	40	60	141	313	485
62-Donald Duck in Frozen Gold, by Carl Barks (Disney) (1/45)	207	414	621	1708	3854	6000
63-Roy Rogers; color photo-all 4 covers	37	74	111	274	612	950
64-Smokey Stover	11	22	33	76	163	250
65-Smitty	11	22	33	76	163	250
66-Gene Autry	27	54	81	194	435	675
67-Oswald the Rabbit	15	30	45	103	227	350
68-Mother Goose and Nursery Rhyme Comics, by Walt Kelly	16	32	48	110	243	375
69-Fairy Tale Parade, by Walt Kelly	21	42	63	147	324	500
70-Popeye and Wimpy	19	38	57	133	297	460
71-Walt Disney's Three Caballeros, by Walt Kelly (© 4/45)-(Disney)	56	112	168	450	1013	1575
72-Raggedy Ann	20	40	60	141	313	485
73-The Gumps (#1)	10	20	30	69	147	225
74-Marge's Little Lulu (#1)	155	310	465	1279	2890	4500
75-Gene Autry and the Wildcat	22	44	66	154	340	525
76-Little Orphan Annie; reprints strips from 2/28/40 to 6/24/40	19	38	57	131	291	450
77-Felix the Cat	34	68	102	245	548	850
78-Porky Pig and the Bandit Twins	23	46	69	161	356	550
79-Walt Disney's Mickey Mouse in The Riddle of the Red Hat by Carl Barks (8/45)	88	176	264	704	1577	2450
80-Smilin' Jack	13	26	39	86	188	290
81-Moon Mullins	10	20	30	64	132	200
82-Lone Ranger	35	70	105	252	564	875
83-Gene Autry in Outlaw Trail	22	44	66	154	340	525
84-Flash Gordon by Alex Raymond-Reprints from "The Fiery Desert"	40	80	120	296	673	1050
85-Andy Panda and the Mad Dog Mystery	15	30	45	100	220	340
86-Roy Rogers; photo-c	27	54	81	189	420	650
87-Fairy Tale Parade by Walt Kelly; Dan Noonan-c	21	42	63	147	324	500
88-Bugs Bunny's Great Adventure (Sci/fi)	21	42	63	147	324	500

Four Color Comics #125 © L.R. Inc.

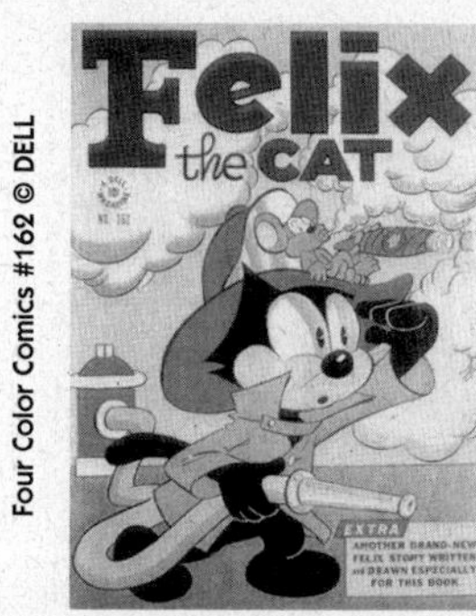

Four Color Comics #162 © DELL

Four Color Comics #173 © KING

	GD 2.0	VG 4.0	FN 6.0	VF 8.0	VF/NM 9.0	NM- 9.2
89-Tillie the Toiler	12	24	36	79	170	260
90-Christmas with Mother Goose by Walt Kelly (11/45)	15	30	45	103	227	350
91-Santa Claus Funnies by Walt Kelly (11/45)	15	30	45	105	233	360
92-Walt Disney's The Wonderful Adventures Of Pinocchio (1945); Donald Duck by Kelly, 16 pgs. (Disney)	46	92	138	340	770	1200
93-Gene Autry in The Bandit of Black Rock	18	36	54	126	281	435
94-Winnie Winkle (1945)	11	22	33	73	157	240
95-Roy Rogers Comics; photo-c	27	54	81	189	420	650
96-Dick Tracy	22	44	66	154	340	525
97-Marge's Little Lulu (1946)	59	118	177	472	1061	1650
98-Lone Ranger, The	26	52	78	182	404	625
99-Smitty	9	18	27	62	126	190
100-Gene Autry Comics; 1st Gene Autry photo-c	21	42	63	147	324	500
101-Terry and the Pirates	19	38	57	131	291	450

NOTE: *No. 101 is last issue to carry "Four Color" logo on cover; all issues beginning with No. 100 are marked "...O. S." (One Shot) which can be found in the bottom left-hand panel on the first page; the numbers following "O. S." relate to the year/month issued.*

	GD 2.0	VG 4.0	FN 6.0	VF 8.0	VF/NM 9.0	NM- 9.2
102-Oswald the Rabbit-Walt Kelly art, 1 pg.	12	24	36	84	185	285
103-Easter with Mother Goose by Walt Kelly	15	30	45	105	233	360
104-Fairy Tale Parade by Walt Kelly	16	32	48	112	249	385
105-Albert the Alligator and Pogo Possum (#1) by Kelly (4/46)	49	98	147	382	854	1325
106-Tillie the Toiler (5/46)	9	18	27	60	120	180
107-Little Orphan Annie; reprints strips from 11/16/42 to 3/24/43	16	32	48	112	249	385
108-Donald Duck in The Terror of the River, by Carl Barks (Disney) (© 4/16/46)	145	290	435	1196	2698	4200
109-Roy Rogers Comics; photo-c	20	40	60	138	307	475
110-Marge's Little Lulu	38	76	114	285	641	1000
111-Captain Easy	11	22	33	76	163	250
112-Porky Pig's Adventure in Gopher Gulch	14	28	42	96	211	325
113-Popeye; all new Popeye stories begin	12	24	36	82	179	275
114-Fairy Tale Parade by Walt Kelly	16	32	48	112	249	385
115-Marge's Little Lulu	38	76	114	281	628	975
116-Mickey Mouse and the House of Many Mysteries (Disney)	24	48	72	168	372	575
117-Roy Rogers Comics; photo-c	16	32	48	110	243	375
118-Lone Ranger, The	26	52	78	182	404	625
119-Felix the Cat; all new Felix stories begin	29	58	87	209	467	725
120-Marge's Little Lulu	32	64	96	230	515	800
121-Fairy Tale Parade-(not Kelly)	10	20	30	69	147	225
122-Henry (#1) (10/46)	13	26	39	89	195	300
123-Bugs Bunny's Dangerous Venture	15	30	45	100	220	340
124-Roy Rogers Comics; photo-c	16	32	48	110	243	375
125-Lone Ranger, The	17	34	51	119	265	410
126-Christmas with Mother Goose by Walt Kelly (1946)	11	22	33	76	163	250
127-Popeye	12	24	36	82	179	275
128-Santa Claus Funnies- "Santa & the Angel" by Gollub; "A Mouse in the House" by Kelly	12	24	36	84	185	285
129-Walt Disney's Uncle Remus and His Tales of Brer Rabbit (#1) (1946)-Adapted from Disney movie "Song of the South"	22	44	66	156	346	535
130-Andy Panda (Walter Lantz)	10	20	30	67	141	215
131-Marge's Little Lulu	32	64	96	230	515	800
132-Tillie the Toiler (1947)	9	18	27	60	120	180
133-Dick Tracy	17	34	51	117	259	400
134-Tarzan and the Devil Ogre; Marsh-c/a	53	106	159	413	932	1450
135-Felix the Cat	20	40	60	141	313	485
136-Lone Ranger, The	17	34	51	119	265	410
137-Roy Rogers Comics; photo-c	16	32	48	110	243	375
138-Smitty	8	16	24	56	108	160
139-Marge's Little Lulu (1947)	31	62	93	223	499	775
140-Easter with Mother Goose by Walt Kelly	12	24	36	84	185	285
141-Mickey Mouse and the Submarine Pirates (Disney)	20	40	60	140	310	485
142-Bugs Bunny and the Haunted Mountain	15	30	45	100	220	340
143-Oswald the Rabbit & the Prehistoric Egg	8	16	24	56	108	160
144-Roy Rogers Comics (1947)-Photo-c	16	32	48	110	243	375
145-Popeye	12	24	36	82	179	275
146-Marge's Little Lulu	31	62	93	223	499	775
147-Donald Duck in Volcano Valley, by Carl Barks (Disney) (5/47)	100	200	300	800	1800	2800
148-Albert the Alligator and Pogo Possum by Walt Kelly (5/47)	38	76	114	281	628	975
149-Smilin' Jack	9	18	27	61	123	185
150-Tillie the Toiler (6/47)	8	16	24	56	108	160
151-Lone Ranger, The	15	30	45	103	227	350
152-Little Orphan Annie; reprints strips from 1/2/44 to 5/6/44	11	22	33	73	157	240
153-Roy Rogers Comics; photo-c	15	30	45	100	220	340
154-Walter Lantz Andy Panda	10	20	30	67	141	215
155-Henry (7/47)	9	18	27	61	123	185
156-Porky Pig and the Phantom	10	20	30	69	147	225
157-Mickey Mouse & the Beanstalk (Disney)	20	40	60	140	310	485
158-Marge's Little Lulu	31	62	93	223	499	775
159-Donald Duck in the Ghost of the Grotto, by Carl Barks (Disney) (8/47)	86	172	258	688	1544	2400
160-Roy Rogers Comics; photo-c	15	30	45	100	220	340
161-Tarzan and the Fires Of Tohr; Marsh-c/a	43	86	129	318	722	1125
162-Felix the Cat (9/47)	15	30	45	105	233	360
163-Dick Tracy	15	30	45	103	227	350
164-Bugs Bunny Finds the Frozen Kingdom	15	30	45	100	220	340
165-Marge's Little Lulu	31	62	93	223	499	775
166-Roy Rogers Comics (52 pgs.)-Photo-c	15	30	45	100	220	340
167-Lone Ranger, The	15	30	45	103	227	350
168-Popeye (10/47)	12	24	36	82	179	275
169-Woody Woodpecker (#1)- "Manhunter in the North"; drug use story	17	34	51	117	259	400
170-Mickey Mouse on Spook's Island (11/47)(Disney)-reprinted in Mickey Mouse #103	17	34	51	119	265	410
171-Charlie McCarthy (#1) and the Twenty Thieves	22	44	66	154	340	525
172-Christmas with Mother Goose by Walt Kelly (11/47)	11	22	33	76	163	250
173-Flash Gordon	19	38	57	131	291	450
174-Winnie Winkle	8	16	24	51	96	140
175-Santa Claus Funnies by Walt Kelly (1947)	12	24	36	84	185	285
176-Tillie the Toiler (12/47)	8	16	24	56	108	160
177-Roy Rogers Comics-(36 pgs.); Photo-c	14	28	42	94	207	320
178-Donald Duck "Christmas on Bear Mountain" by Carl Barks; 1st app. Uncle Scrooge (Disney)(12/47)	118	236	354	944	2122	3300
179-Uncle Wiggily (#1)-Walt Kelly-c	13	26	39	89	195	300
180-Ozark Ike (#1)	9	18	27	59	117	175
181-Walt Disney's Mickey Mouse in Jungle Magic	17	34	51	119	265	410
182-Porky Pig in Never-Never Land (2/48)	10	20	30	69	147	225
183-Oswald the Rabbit (Lantz)	8	16	24	56	108	160
184-Tillie the Toiler	8	16	24	56	108	160
185-Easter with Mother Goose by Walt Kelly (1948)	11	22	33	76	163	250
186-Walt Disney's Bambi (4/48)-Reprinted as Movie Classic Bambi #3 (1956)	14	28	42	96	211	325
187-Bugs Bunny and the Dreadful Dragon	11	22	33	73	157	240
188-Woody Woodpecker (Lantz, 5/48)	10	20	30	68	144	220
189-Donald Duck in The Old Castle's Secret, by Carl Barks (Disney) (6/48)	73	146	219	584	1317	2050
190-Flash Gordon (6/48); bondage-c; "The Adventures of the Flying Saucers"; 5th Flying Saucer story- see The Spirit 9/28/47(1st), Shadow Comics V7#10 (2nd, 1/48),Captain Midnight #60 (3rd, 2/48) & Boy Commandos #26 (4th, 3-4/48)	21	42	63	147	324	500
191-Porky Pig to the Rescue	10	20	30	69	147	225
192-The Brownies (#1)-by Walt Kelly (7/48)	12	24	36	82	179	275
193-M.G.M. Presents Tom and Jerry (#1)(1948)	22	44	66	154	340	525
194-Mickey Mouse in The World Under the Sea (Disney)-Reprinted in Mickey Mouse #101	17	34	51	119	265	410
195-Tillie the Toiler	7	14	21	46	86	125
196-Charlie McCarthy in The Haunted Hide-Out; part photo-c	14	28	42	94	207	320
197-Spirit of the Border (#1) (Zane Grey) (1948)	10	20	30	66	138	210
198-Andy Panda	10	20	30	67	141	215
199-Donald Duck in Sheriff of Bullet Valley, by Carl Barks; Barks draws himself on wanted poster, last page; used in Love & Death (Disney) (10/48)	79	158	237	632	1416	2200
200-Bugs Bunny, Super Sleuth (10/48)	11	22	33	73	157	240
201-Christmas with Mother Goose by W. Kelly	10	20	30	64	132	200
202-Woody Woodpecker	8	16	24	54	102	150
203-Donald Duck in the Golden Christmas Tree, by Carl Barks (Disney) (12/48)	55	110	165	440	995	1550
204-Flash Gordon (12/48)	15	30	45	103	227	350
205-Santa Claus Funnies by Walt Kelly	11	22	33	76	163	250

Four Color Comics #235 © News Synd.

Four Color Comics #260 © WB

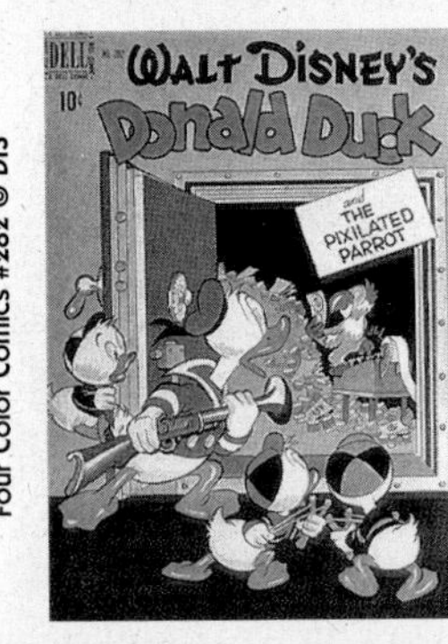

Four Color Comics #282 © DIS

	GD 2.0	VG 4.0	FN 6.0	VF 8.0	VF/NM 9.0	NM- 9.2
206-Little Orphan Annie; reprints strips from 11/10/40 to 1/11/41	7	14	21	48	89	130
207-King of the Royal Mounted (#1) (12/48)	12	24	36	79	170	260
208-Brer Rabbit Does It Again (Disney) (1/49)	10	20	30	66	138	210
209-Harold Teen	5	10	15	34	60	90
210-Tippie and Cap Stubbs	5	10	15	35	63	90
211-Little Beaver (#1)	8	16	24	51	96	140
212-Dr. Bobbs	5	10	15	35	63	90
213-Tillie the Toiler	7	14	21	46	86	125
214-Mickey Mouse and His Sky Adventure (2/49)(Disney)-Reprinted in Mickey Mouse #105	13	26	39	91	201	310
215-Sparkle Plenty (Dick Tracy-r by Gould)	10	20	30	68	144	220
216-Andy Panda and the Police Pup (Lantz)	8	16	24	51	96	140
217-Bugs Bunny in Court Jester	11	22	33	73	157	240
218-Three Little Pigs and the Wonderful Magic Lamp (Disney) (3/49)(#1)	9	18	27	61	123	185
219-Swee'pea	8	16	24	51	96	140
220-Easter with Mother Goose by Walt Kelly	11	22	33	76	163	250
221-Uncle Wiggily-Walt Kelly cover in part	8	16	24	56	108	160
222-West of the Pecos (Zane Grey)	6	12	18	41	76	110
223-Donald Duck "Lost in the Andes" by Carl Barks (Disney-4/49) (square egg story)	71	142	213	568	1284	2000
224-Little Iodine (#1), by Hatlo (4/49)	11	22	33	73	157	240
225-Oswald the Rabbit (Lantz)	6	12	18	40	73	105
226-Porky Pig and Spoofy, the Spook	9	18	27	59	117	175
227-Seven Dwarfs (Disney)	9	18	27	58	114	170
228-Mark of Zorro, The (#1) (1949)	18	36	54	122	271	420
229-Smokey Stover	6	12	18	38	69	100
230-Sunset Pass (Zane Grey)	6	12	18	41	76	110
231-Mickey Mouse and the Rajah's Treasure (Disney)	13	26	39	91	201	310
232-Woody Woodpecker (Lantz, 6/49)	8	16	24	54	102	150
233-Bugs Bunny, Sleepwalking Sleuth	11	22	33	73	157	240
234-Dumbo in Sky Voyage (Disney)	12	24	36	83	182	280
235-Tiny Tim	5	10	15	35	63	90
236-Heritage of the Desert (Zane Grey) (1949)	6	12	18	41	76	110
237-Tillie the Toiler	7	14	21	46	86	125
238-Donald Duck in Voodoo Hoodoo, by Carl Barks (Disney) (8/49)	54	108	162	432	966	1500
239-Adventure Bound (8/49)	5	10	15	34	60	85
240-Andy Panda (Lantz)	8	16	24	51	96	140
241-Porky Pig, Mighty Hunter	9	18	27	59	117	175
242-Tippie and Cap Stubbs	4	8	12	28	47	65
243-Thumper Follows His Nose (Disney)	10	20	30	66	138	210
244-The Brownies by Walt Kelly	9	18	27	60	120	180
245-Dick's Adventures (9/49)	6	12	18	37	66	95
246-Thunder Mountain (Zane Grey)	5	10	15	31	53	75
247-Flash Gordon	15	30	45	103	227	350
248-Mickey Mouse and the Black Sorcerer (Disney)	13	26	39	91	201	310
249-Woody Woodpecker in the "Globetrotter" (10/49)	8	16	24	54	102	150
250-Bugs Bunny in Diamond Daze; used in **SOTI**, pg. 309	11	22	33	76	163	250
251-Hubert at Camp Moonbeam	8	16	24	54	102	150
252-Pinocchio (Disney)-not by Kelly; origin	10	20	30	66	138	210
253-Christmas with Mother Goose by W. Kelly	10	20	30	64	132	200
254-Santa Claus Funnies by Walt Kelly; Pogo & Albert story by Kelly (11/49)	11	22	33	76	163	250
255-The Ranger (Zane Grey) (1949)	5	10	15	31	53	75
256-Donald Duck in "Luck of the North" by Carl Barks (Disney) (12/49)-Shows #257 on inside	46	92	138	359	805	1250
257-Little Iodine	8	16	24	51	96	140
258-Andy Panda and the Balloon Race (Lantz)	8	16	24	51	96	140
259-Santa and the Angel (Gollub art-condensed from #128) & Santa at the Zoo (12/49) -two books in one	5	10	15	33	57	80
260-Porky Pig, Hero of the Wild West (12/49)	9	18	27	59	117	175
261-Mickey Mouse and the Missing Key (Disney)	13	26	39	91	201	310
262-Raggedy Ann and Andy	9	18	27	57	111	165
263-Donald Duck in "Land of the Totem Poles" by Carl Barks (Disney) (2/50)-Has two Barks stories	46	92	138	340	770	1200
264-Woody Woodpecker in the Magic Lantern (Lantz)	8	16	24	54	102	150
265-King of the Royal Mounted (Zane Grey)	8	16	24	51	96	140
266-Bugs Bunny on the "Isle of Hercules" (2/50)-Reprinted in Best of Bugs Bunny #1	9	18	27	60	120	180

	GD 2.0	VG 4.0	FN 6.0	VF 8.0	VF/NM 9.0	NM- 9.2
267-Little Beaver; Harmon-c/a	5	10	15	33	57	80
268-Mickey Mouse's Surprise Visitor (1950)(Disney)	12	24	36	84	185	285
269-Johnny Mack Brown (#1)-Photo-c	18	36	54	124	275	425
270-Drift Fence (Zane Grey) (3/50)	5	10	15	31	53	75
271-Porky Pig in Phantom of the Plains	9	18	27	59	117	175
272-Cinderella (Disney) (4/50)	11	22	33	76	163	250
273-Oswald the Rabbit (Lantz)	6	12	18	40	73	105
274-Bugs Bunny, Hare-brained Reporter	9	18	27	60	120	180
275-Donald Duck in "Ancient Persia" by Carl Barks (Disney) (5/50)	45	90	135	333	754	1175
276-Uncle Wiggily	7	14	21	46	86	125
277-Porky Pig in Desert Adventure (5/50)	9	18	27	59	117	175
278-(Wild) Bill Elliott Comics (#1)-Photo-c	11	22	33	73	157	240
279-Mickey Mouse and Pluto Battle the Giant Ants (Disney); reprinted in Mickey Mouse #102 & 245	10	20	30	68	144	220
280-Andy Panda in The Isle Of Mechanical Men (Lantz)	8	16	24	51	96	140
281-Bugs Bunny in The Great Circus Mystery	9	18	27	60	120	180
282-Donald Duck and the Pixilated Parrot by Carl Barks (Disney) (© 5/23/50)	45	90	135	333	754	1175
283-King of the Royal Mounted (7/50)	8	16	24	51	96	140
284-Porky Pig in The Kingdom of Nowhere	9	18	27	59	117	175
285-Bozo the Clown & His Minikin Circus (#1) (TV)	17	34	51	114	252	390
286-Mickey Mouse in The Uninvited Guest (Disney	10	20	30	68	144	220
287-Gene Autry's Champion in The Ghost Of Black Mountain; photo-c	10	20	30	66	138	210
288-Woody Woodpecker in Klondike Gold (Lantz)	8	16	24	54	102	150
289-Bugs Bunny in "Indian Trouble"	9	18	27	60	120	180
290-The Chief (#1) (8/50)	7	14	21	44	82	120
291-Donald Duck in "The Magic Hourglass" by Carl Barks (Disney) (9/50)	45	90	135	333	754	1175
292-The Cisco Kid Comics (#1)	19	38	57	133	297	460
293-The Brownies-Kelly-c/a	9	18	27	60	120	180
294-Little Beaver	5	10	15	33	57	80
295-Porky Pig in President Porky (9/50)	9	18	27	59	117	175
296-Mickey Mouse in Private Eye for Hire (Disney)	10	20	30	68	144	220
297-Andy Panda in The Haunted Inn (Lantz, 10/50)	8	16	24	51	96	140
298-Bugs Bunny in Sheik for a Day	9	18	27	60	120	180
299-Buck Jones & the Iron Horse Trail (#1)	11	22	33	76	163	250
300-Donald Duck in "Big-Top Bedlam" by Carl Barks (Disney) (11/50)	45	90	135	333	754	1175
301-The Mysterious Rider (Zane Grey)	5	10	15	31	53	75
302-Santa Claus Funnies (11/50)	6	12	18	41	76	110
303-Porky Pig in The Land of the Monstrous Flies	7	14	21	46	86	125
304-Mickey Mouse in Tom-Tom Island (Disney) (12/50)	10	20	30	64	132	200
305-Woody Woodpecker (Lantz)	6	12	18	38	69	100
306-Raggedy Ann	7	14	21	44	82	120
307-Bugs Bunny in Lumber Jack Rabbit	8	16	24	54	102	150
308-Donald Duck in "Dangerous Disguise" by Carl Barks (Disney) (1/51)	42	86	126	311	706	1100
309-Betty Betz' Dollface and Her Gang (1951)	5	10	15	33	57	80
310-King of the Royal Mounted (1/51)	6	12	18	38	69	100
311-Porky Pig in Midget Horses of Hidden Valley	7	14	21	46	86	125
312-Tonto (#1)	10	20	30	66	138	210
313-Mickey Mouse in The Mystery of the Double-Cross Ranch (#1) (Disney) (2/51)	10	20	30	64	132	200

Note: Beginning with the above comic in 1951 Dell/Western began adding #1 in small print on the covers of several long running titles with the evident intention of switching these titles to their own monthly numbers, but when the conversions were made, there was no connection. It is thought that the post office may have stepped in and decreed the sequences should commence as though the first four colors printed had each begun with number one, or the first issues sold by subscription. Since the regular series' numbers don't correctly match to the numbers of earlier issues published, it's not known whether or not the numbering was in error.

	GD 2.0	VG 4.0	FN 6.0	VF 8.0	VF/NM 9.0	NM- 9.2
314-Ambush (Zane Grey)	5	10	15	31	53	75
315-Oswald the Rabbit (Lantz)	5	10	15	35	63	90
316-Rex Allen (#1)-Photo-c; Marsh-a	12	24	36	80	173	265
317-Bugs Bunny in Hair Today Gone Tomorrow (#1)	8	16	24	54	102	150
318-Donald Duck in "No Such Varmint" by Carl Barks (#1)-Indicia shows #317 (Disney, © 1/23/51)	42	86	126	311	706	1100
319-Gene Autry's Champion; painted-c	6	12	18	37	66	95
320-Uncle Wiggily (#1)	7	14	21	46	86	125
321-Little Scouts (#1) (3/51)	5	10	15	31	53	75
322-Porky Pig in Roaring Rockets (#1 on-c)	7	14	21	46	86	125

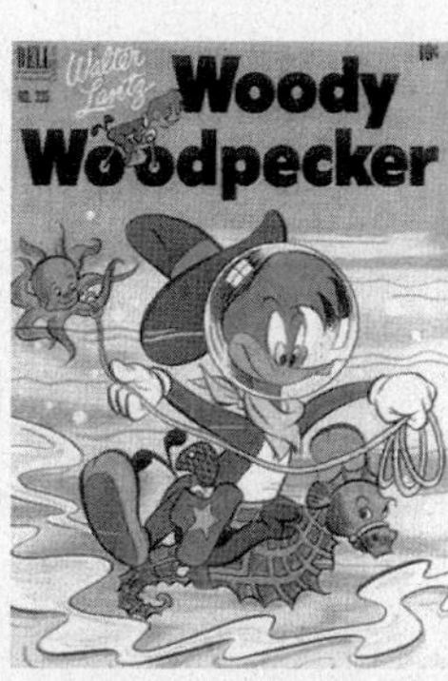

Four Color Comics #336 © W. Lantz

Four Color Comics #362 © DIS

Four Color Comics #406 © WB

	GD 2.0	VG 4.0	FN 6.0	VF 8.0	VF/NM 9.0	NM- 9.2
323-Susie Q. Smith (#1) (3/51)	5	10	15	31	53	75
324-I Met a Handsome Cowboy (3/51)	7	14	21	48	89	130
325-Mickey Mouse in The Haunted Castle (#2) (Disney) (4/51)	10	20	30	64	132	200
326-Andy Panda (#1) (Lantz)	6	12	18	38	69	100
327-Bugs Bunny and the Rajah's Treasure (#2)	8	16	24	54	102	150
328-Donald Duck in Old California (#2) by Carl Barks-Peyote drug use issue (Disney) (5/51)	41	82	123	303	689	1075
329-Roy Roger's Trigger (#1)(5/51)-Painted-c	12	24	36	84	185	285
330-Porky Pig Meets the Bristled Bruiser (#2)	7	14	21	46	86	125
331-Alice in Wonderland (Disney) (1951)	13	26	39	86	188	290
332-Little Beaver	5	10	15	33	57	80
333-Wilderness Trek (Zane Grey) (5/51)	5	10	15	31	53	75
334-Mickey Mouse and Yukon Gold (Disney) (6/51)	10	20	30	64	132	200
335-Francis the Famous Talking Mule (#1, 6/51)-1st Dell non animated movie comic (all issues based on movie)	9	18	27	62	126	190
336-Woody Woodpecker (Lantz)	6	12	18	38	69	100
337-The Brownies-not by Walt Kelly	5	10	15	34	60	85
338-Bugs Bunny and the Rocking Horse Thieves	8	16	24	54	102	150
339-Donald Duck and the Magic Fountain-not by Carl Barks (Disney) (7-8/51)	13	26	39	89	195	300
340-King of the Royal Mounted (7/51)	6	12	18	38	69	100
341-Unbirthday Party with Alice in Wonderland (Disney) (7/51)	13	26	39	86	188	290
342-Porky Pig the Lucky Peppermint Mine; r/in Porky Pig #3	6	12	18	37	66	95
343-Mickey Mouse in The Ruby Eye of Homar-Guy-Am (Disney)-Reprinted in Mickey Mouse #104	8	16	24	56	108	160
344-Sergeant Preston from Challenge of The Yukon (#1) (TV)	10	20	30	69	147	225
345-Andy Panda in Scotland Yard (8-10/51) (Lantz)	6	12	18	38	69	100
346-Hideout (Zane Grey)	5	10	15	31	53	75
347-Bugs Bunny the Frigid Hare (8-9/51)	8	16	24	54	102	150
348-Donald Duck "The Crocodile Collector"; Barks-c only (Disney) (9-10/51)	20	40	60	141	313	485
349-Uncle Wiggily	6	12	18	38	69	100
350-Woody Woodpecker (Lantz)	6	12	18	38	69	100
351-Porky Pig & the Grand Canyon Giant (9-10/51)	6	12	18	37	66	95
352-Mickey Mouse in The Mystery of Painted Valley (Disney)	8	16	24	56	108	160
353-Duck Album (#1)-Barks-c (Disney)	9	18	27	62	126	190
354-Raggedy Ann & Andy	7	14	21	44	82	120
355-Bugs Bunny Hot-Rod Hare	8	16	24	54	102	150
356-Donald Duck in "Rags to Riches"; Barks-c only	20	40	60	141	313	485
357-Comeback (Zane Grey)	4	8	12	28	47	65
358-Andy Panda (Lantz) (11-1/52)	6	12	18	38	69	100
359-Frosty the Snowman (#1)	8	16	24	56	108	160
360-Porky Pig in Tree of Fortune (11-12/51)	6	12	18	37	66	95
361-Santa Claus Funnies	6	12	18	41	76	110
362-Mickey Mouse and the Smuggled Diamonds (Disney)	8	16	24	56	108	160
363-King of the Royal Mounted	5	10	15	35	63	90
364-Woody Woodpecker (Lantz)	5	10	15	34	60	85
365-The Brownies-not by Kelly	5	10	15	34	60	85
366-Bugs Bunny Uncle Buckskin Comes to Town (12-1/52)	8	16	24	54	102	150
367-Donald Duck in "A Christmas for Shacktown" by Carl Barks (Disney) (1-2/52)	33	66	99	238	532	825
368-Bob Clampett's Beany and Cecil (#1)	20	40	60	138	307	475
369-The Lone Ranger's Famous Horse Hi-Yo Silver (#1); Silver's origin	9	18	27	62	126	190
370-Porky Pig in Trouble in the Big Trees	6	12	18	37	66	95
371-Mickey Mouse in The Inca Idol Case (1952) (Disney)	8	16	24	56	108	160
372-Riders of the Purple Sage (Zane Grey)	4	8	12	28	47	65
373-Sergeant Preston (TV)	7	14	21	46	86	125
374-Woody Woodpecker (Lantz)	5	10	15	34	60	85
375-John Carter of Mars (E. R. Burroughs)-Jesse Marsh-a; origin	27	54	81	189	420	650
376-Bugs Bunny, "The Magic Sneeze"	8	16	24	54	102	150
377-Susie Q. Smith	4	8	12	27	44	60
378-Tom Corbett, Space Cadet (#1) (TV)-McWilliams-a	15	30	45	103	227	350
379-Donald Duck in "Southern Hospitality"; Not by Barks (Disney)	13	26	39	89	195	300
380-Raggedy Ann & Andy	7	14	21	44	82	120
381-Marge's Tubby (#1)	17	34	51	119	265	410
382-Snow White and the Seven Dwarfs (Disney)-origin; partial reprint of Four Color #49 (Movie)	9	18	27	59	117	175
383-Andy Panda (Lantz)	5	10	15	33	57	80
384-King of the Royal Mounted (3/52)(Zane Grey)	5	10	15	35	63	90
385-Porky Pig in The Isle of Missing Ships (3-4/52)	6	12	18	37	66	95
386-Uncle Scrooge (#1)-by Carl Barks (Disney) in "Only a Poor Old Man" (3/52)	179	358	537	1477	3339	5200
387-Mickey Mouse in High Tibet (Disney) (4-5/52)	8	16	24	56	108	160
388-Oswald the Rabbit (Lantz)	5	10	15	35	63	90
389-Andy Hardy Comics (#1)	5	10	15	31	53	75
390-Woody Woodpecker (Lantz)	5	10	15	34	60	85
391-Uncle Wiggily	6	12	18	38	69	100
392-Hi-Yo Silver	6	12	18	37	66	95
393-Bugs Bunny	8	16	24	54	102	150
394-Donald Duck in Malayalaya-Barks-c only (Disney)	20	40	60	141	313	485
395-Forlorn River(Zane Grey)-First Nevada (5/52)	4	8	12	28	47	65
396-Tales of the Texas Rangers(#1)(TV)-Photo-c	9	18	27	62	126	190
397-Sergeant Preston of the Yukon (TV) (5/52)	7	14	21	46	86	125
398-The Brownies-not by Kelly	5	10	15	34	60	85
399-Porky Pig in The Lost Gold Mine	6	12	18	37	66	95
400-Tom Corbett, Space Cadet (TV)-McWilliams-c/a	9	18	27	61	123	185
401-Mickey Mouse and Goofy's Mechanical Wizard (Disney) (6-7/52)	7	14	21	48	89	130
402-Mary Jane and Sniffles	7	14	21	44	82	120
403-Li'l Bad Wolf (Disney) (6/52)(#1)	6	12	18	41	76	110
404-The Range Rider (#1) (Flying A's...)(TV)-Photo-c	9	18	27	57	111	165
405-Woody Woodpecker (Lantz) (6-7/52)	5	10	15	34	60	85
406-Tweety and Sylvester (#1)	11	22	33	73	157	240
407-Bugs Bunny, Foreign-Legion Hare	7	14	21	46	86	125
408-Donald Duck and the Golden Helmet by Carl Barks (Disney) (7-8/52)	33	66	99	238	532	825
409-Andy Panda (7-9/52)	5	10	15	33	57	80
410-Porky Pig in The Water Wizard (7/52)	6	12	18	37	66	95
411-Mickey Mouse and the Old Sea Dog (Disney) (8-9/52)	7	14	21	48	89	130
412-Nevada (Zane Grey)	4	8	12	28	47	65
413-Robin Hood (Disney-Movie) (8/52)-Photo-c (1st Disney movie Four Color book)	9	18	27	58	114	170
414-Bob Clampett's Beany and Cecil (TV)	12	24	36	82	179	275
415-Rootie Kazootie (#1) (TV)	9	18	27	57	111	165
416-Woody Woodpecker (Lantz)	5	10	15	34	60	85
417-Double Trouble with Goober (#1) (8/52)	4	8	12	28	47	65
418-Rusty Riley, a Boy, a Horse, and a Dog (#1)-Frank Godwin-a (strip reprints) (8/52)	5	10	15	31	53	75
419-Sergeant Preston (TV)	7	14	21	46	86	125
420-Bugs Bunny in The Mysterious Buckaroo (8-9/52)	7	14	21	46	86	125
421-Tom Corbett, Space Cadet(TV)-McWilliams-a	9	18	27	61	123	185
422-Donald Duck and the Gilded Man, by Carl Barks (Disney) (9-10/52) (#423 on inside)	33	66	99	238	532	825
423-Rhubarb, Owner of the Brooklyn Ball Club (The Millionaire Cat) (#1)-Painted cover	5	10	15	35	63	90
424-Flash Gordon-Test Flight in Space (9/52)	11	22	33	72	154	235
425-Zorro, the Return of	10	20	30	68	144	220
426-Porky Pig in The Scalawag Leprechaun	6	12	18	37	66	95
427-Mickey Mouse and the Wonderful Whizzix (Disney) (10-11/52)-Reprinted in Mickey Mouse #100	7	14	21	48	89	130
428-Uncle Wiggily	5	10	15	33	57	80
429-Pluto in "Why Dogs Leave Home" (Disney) (10/52)(#1)	9	18	27	60	120	180
430-Marge's Tubby, the Shadow of a Man-Eater	10	20	30	69	147	225
431-Woody Woodpecker (10/52) (Lantz)	5	10	15	34	60	85
432-Bugs Bunny and the Rabbit Olympics	7	14	21	46	86	125
433-Wildfire (Zane Grey) (11-1/52-53)	4	8	12	28	47	65
434-Rin Tin Tin "In Dark Danger" (#1) (TV) (11/52)-Photo-c	13	26	39	89	195	300
435-Frosty the Snowman (11/52)	5	10	15	34	60	85
436-The Brownies-not by Kelly (11/52)	5	10	15	33	57	80
437-John Carter of Mars (E.R. Burroughs)-Marsh-a	15	30	45	103	227	350
438-Annie Oakley (#1) (TV)	12	24	36	82	179	275
439-Little Hiawatha (Disney) (12/52)j(#1)	6	12	18	37	66	95
440-Black Beauty (12/52)	5	10	15	30	50	70

Four Color Comics #468 © DIS

Four Color Comics #521 © KING

Four Color Comics #534 © DELL

	GD 2.0	VG 4.0	FN 6.0	VF 8.0	VF/NM 9.0	NM- 9.2
441-Fearless Fagan	4	8	12	25	40	55
442-Peter Pan (Disney) (Movie)	9	18	27	61	123	185
443-Ben Bowie and His Mountain Men (#1)	8	16	24	54	102	150
444-Marge's Tubby	10	20	30	69	147	225
445-Charlie McCarthy	6	12	18	37	66	95
446-Captain Hook and Peter Pan (Disney)(Movie)(1/53)	8	16	24	54	102	150
447-Andy Hardy Comics	4	8	12	25	40	55
448-Bob Clampett's Beany and Cecil (TV)	12	24	36	82	179	275
449-Tappan's Burro (Zane Grey) (2-4/53)	4	8	12	28	47	65
450-Duck Album; Barks-c (Disney)	7	14	21	44	82	120
451-Rusty Riley-Frank Godwin-a (strip-r) (2/53)	4	8	12	25	40	55
452-Raggedy Ann & Andy (1953)	7	14	21	44	82	120
453-Susie Q. Smith (2/53)	4	8	12	27	44	60
454-Krazy Kat Comics; not by Herriman	5	10	15	31	53	75
455-Johnny Mack Brown Comics(3/53)-Photo-c	6	12	18	40	73	105
456-Uncle Scrooge Back to the Klondike (#2) by Barks (3/53) (Disney)	88	176	264	704	1577	2450
457-Daffy (#1)	10	20	30	70	150	230
458-Oswald the Rabbit (Lantz)	5	10	15	31	53	75
459-Rootie Kazootie (TV)	6	12	18	41	76	110
460-Buck Jones (4/53)	6	12	18	38	69	100
461-Marge's Tubby	10	20	30	64	132	200
462-Little Scouts	4	8	12	25	40	55
463-Petunia (4/53)	4	8	12	28	47	65
464-Bozo (4/53)	9	18	27	57	111	165
465-Francis the Famous Talking Mule	6	12	18	37	66	95
466-Rhubarb, the Millionaire Cat; painted-c	5	10	15	33	57	80
467-Desert Gold (Zane Grey) (5-7/53)	4	8	12	28	47	65
468-Goofy (#1) (Disney)	10	20	30	68	144	220
469-Beetle Bailey (#1) (5/53	11	22	33	76	163	250
470-Elmer Fudd	9	18	27	58	114	170
471-Double Trouble with Goober	4	8	12	23	37	50
472-Wild Bill Elliott (6/53)-Photo-c	5	10	15	33	57	80
473-Li'l Bad Wolf (Disney) (6/53)(#2)	5	10	15	31	53	75
474-Mary Jane and Sniffles	6	12	18	41	76	110
475-M.G.M.'s The Two Mouseketeers (#1)	7	14	21	49	92	135
476-Rin Tin Tin (TV)-Photo-c	8	16	24	51	96	140
477-Bob Clampett's Beany and Cecil (TV)	12	24	36	82	179	275
478-Charlie McCarthy	6	12	18	37	66	95
479-Queen of the West Dale Evans (#1)-Photo-c	16	32	48	107	236	365
480-Andy Hardy Comics	4	8	12	25	40	55
481-Annie Oakley And Tagg (TV)	8	16	24	56	108	160
482-Brownies-not by Kelly	5	10	15	33	57	80
483-Little Beaver (7/53)	5	10	15	30	50	70
484-River Feud (Zane Grey) (8-10/53)	4	8	12	28	47	65
485-The Little People-Walt Scott (#1)	7	14	21	46	86	125
486-Rusty Riley-Frank Godwin strip-r	4	8	12	25	40	55
487-Mowgli, the Jungle Book (Rudyard Kipling's)	5	10	15	35	63	90
488-John Carter of Mars (Burroughs)-Marsh-a; painted-c	15	30	45	103	227	350
489-Tweety and Sylvester	7	14	21	44	82	120
490-Jungle Jim (#1)	7	14	21	44	82	120
491-Silvertip (#1) (Max Brand)-Kinstler-a (8/53)	7	14	21	46	86	125
492-Duck Album (Disney)	6	12	18	38	69	100
493-Johnny Mack Brown; photo-c	6	12	18	40	73	105
494-The Little King (#1)	8	16	24	52	99	145
495-Uncle Scrooge (#3) (Disney)-by Carl Barks (9/53)	59	118	177	472	1061	1650
496-The Green Hornet; painted-c	23	46	69	161	356	550
497-Zorro (Sword of...)-Kinstler-a	11	22	33	72	154	235
498-Bugs Bunny's Album (9/53)	6	12	18	37	66	95
499-M.G.M.'s Spike and Tyke (#1) (9/53)	6	12	18	42	79	115
500-Buck Jones	6	12	18	38	69	100
501-Francis the Famous Talking Mule	5	10	15	31	53	75
502-Rootie Kazootie (TV)	6	12	18	41	76	110
503-Uncle Wiggily (10/53)	5	10	15	33	57	80
504-Krazy Kat; not by Herriman	5	10	15	31	53	75
505-The Sword and the Rose (Disney) (10/53)(Movie)-Photo-c	7	14	21	49	92	135
506-The Little Scouts	4	8	12	25	40	55
507-Oswald the Rabbit (Lantz)	5	10	15	31	53	75
508-Bozo (10/53)	9	18	27	57	111	165
509-Pluto (Disney) (10/53)	6	12	18	37	66	95

	GD 2.0	VG 4.0	FN 6.0	VF 8.0	VF/NM 9.0	NM- 9.2
510-Son of Black Beauty	4	8	12	27	44	60
511-Outlaw Trail (Zane Grey)-Kinstler-a	5	10	15	31	53	75
512-Flash Gordon (11/53)	9	18	27	59	117	175
513-Ben Bowie and His Mountain Men	5	10	15	31	53	75
514-Frosty the Snowman (11/53)	5	10	15	34	60	85
515-Andy Hardy	4	8	12	25	40	55
516-Double Trouble With Goober	4	8	12	23	37	50
517-Chip 'N' Dale (#1) (Disney)	10	20	30	66	138	210
518-Rivets (11/53)	4	8	12	25	40	55
519-Steve Canyon (#1)-Not by Milton Caniff	7	14	21	49	92	135
520-Wild Bill Elliott-Photo-c	5	10	15	33	57	80
521-Beetle Bailey (12/53)	7	14	21	44	82	120
522-The Brownies	5	10	15	33	57	80
523-Rin Tin Tin (TV)-Photo-c (12/53)	8	16	24	51	96	140
524-Tweety and Sylvester	7	14	21	44	82	120
525-Santa Claus Funnies	6	12	18	41	76	110
526-Napoleon	4	8	12	25	40	55
527-Charlie McCarthy	6	12	18	37	66	95
528-Queen of the West Dale Evans; photo-c	9	18	27	59	117	175
529-Little Beaver	5	10	15	30	50	70
530-Bob Clampett's Beany and Cecil (TV) (1/54)	12	24	36	82	179	275
531-Duck Album (Disney)	6	12	18	38	69	100
532-The Rustlers (Zane Grey) (2-4/54)	4	8	12	28	47	65
533-Raggedy Ann and Andy	7	14	21	44	82	120
534-Western Marshal (Ernest Haycox's)-Kinstler-a	5	10	15	35	63	90
535-I Love Lucy (#1) (TV) (2/54)-Photo-c	40	80	120	296	673	1050
536-Daffy (3/54)	6	12	18	42	79	115
537-Stormy, the Thoroughbred... (Disney-Movie) on top 2/3 of each page; Pluto story on bottom 1/3 of each page (2/54)	5	10	15	30	50	70
538-The Mask of Zorro; Kinstler-a	11	22	33	72	154	235
539-Ben and Me (Disney) (3/54)	4	8	12	27	44	60
540-Knights of the Round Table (3/54) (Movie)-Photo-c	6	12	18	40	73	105
541-Johnny Mack Brown; photo-c	6	12	18	40	73	105
542-Super Circus Featuring Mary Hartline (TV) (3/54)	6	12	18	41	76	110
543-Uncle Wiggily (3/54)	5	10	15	33	57	80
544-Rob Roy (Disney-Movie)-Manning-a; photo-c	7	14	21	44	82	120
545-The Wonderful Adventures of Pinocchio-Partial reprint of Four Color #92 (Disney-Movie)	7	14	21	44	82	120
546-Buck Jones	6	12	18	38	69	100
547-Francis the Famous Talking Mule	5	10	15	31	53	75
548-Krazy Kat; not by Herriman (4/54)	5	10	15	30	50	70
549-Oswald the Rabbit (Lantz)	5	10	15	31	53	75
550-The Little Scouts	4	8	12	25	40	55
551-Bozo (4/54)	9	18	27	57	111	165
552-Beetle Bailey	7	14	21	44	82	120
553-Susie Q. Smith	4	8	12	27	44	60
554-Rusty Riley (Frank Godwin strip-r)	4	8	12	25	40	55
555-Range War (Zane Grey)	4	8	12	28	47	65
556-Double Trouble With Goober (5/54)	4	8	12	23	37	50
557-Ben Bowie and His Mountain Men	5	10	15	31	53	75
558-Elmer Fudd (5/54)	5	10	15	34	60	85
559-I Love Lucy (#2) (TV)-Photo-c	24	48	72	170	379	585
560-Duck Album (Disney) (5/54)	6	12	18	38	69	100
561-Mr. Magoo (5/54)	9	18	27	58	114	170
562-Goofy (Disney)(#2)	6	12	18	41	76	110
563-Rhubarb, the Millionaire Cat (6/54)	5	10	15	33	57	80
564-Li'l Bad Wolf (Disney)(#3)	5	10	15	31	53	75
565-Jungle Jim	5	10	15	30	50	70
566-Son of Black Beauty	4	8	12	27	44	60
567-Prince Valiant (#1)-By Bob Fuje (Movie)-Photo-c	9	18	27	62	126	190
568-Gypsy Colt (Movie) (6/54)	5	10	15	31	53	75
569-Priscilla's Pop	4	8	12	27	44	60
570-Bob Clampett's Beany and Cecil (TV)	12	24	36	82	179	275
571-Charlie McCarthy	6	12	18	37	66	95
572-Silvertip (Max Brand) (7/54); Kinstler-a	5	10	15	30	50	70
573-The Little People by Walt Scott	5	10	15	31	53	75
574-The Hand of Zorro; Kinstler-a	11	22	33	72	154	235
575-Annie Oakley and Tagg (TV)-Photo-c	8	16	24	56	108	160
576-Angel (#1) (8/54)	4	8	12	25	40	55
577-M.G.M.'s Spike and Tyke	5	10	15	31	53	75
578-Steve Canyon (8/54)	5	10	15	31	53	75

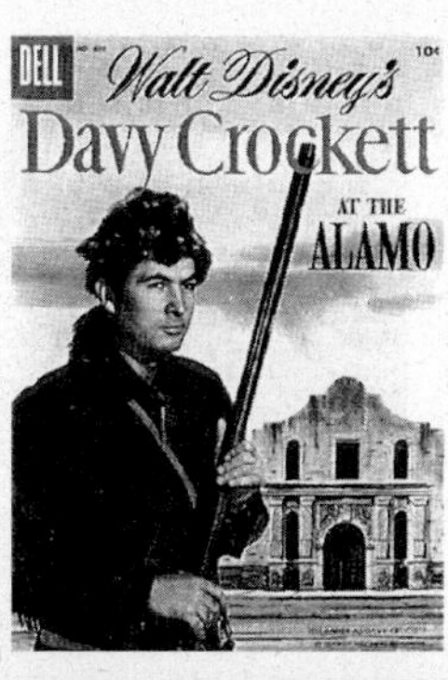

Four Color Comics #639 © DIS

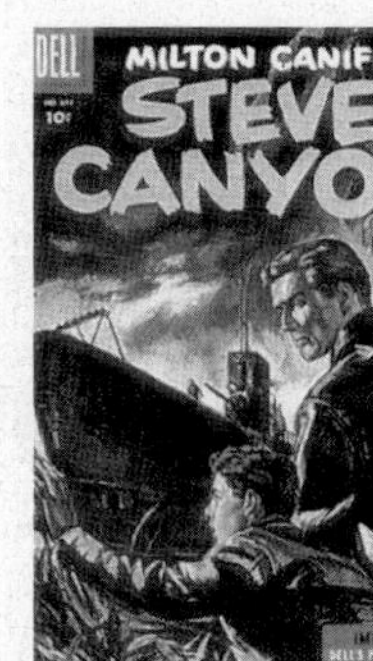

Four Color Comics #641 © DELL

Four Color Comics #676 © DELL

	GD 2.0	VG 4.0	FN 6.0	VF 8.0	VF/NM 9.0	NM- 9.2
579-Francis the Famous Talking Mule	5	10	15	31	53	75
580-Six Gun Ranch (Luke Short-8/54)	4	8	12	28	47	65
581-Chip 'N' Dale (#2) (Disney)	6	12	18	38	69	100
582-Mowgli Jungle Book (Kipling) (8/54)	5	10	15	30	50	70
583-The Lost Wagon Train (Zane Grey)	4	8	12	28	47	65
584-Johnny Mack Brown-Photo-c	6	12	18	40	73	105
585-Bugs Bunny's Album	6	12	18	37	66	95
586-Duck Album (Disney)	6	12	18	38	69	100
587-The Little Scouts	4	8	12	25	40	55
588-King Richard and the Crusaders (Movie) (10/54) Matt Baker-a; photo-c	8	16	24	54	102	150
589-Buck Jones	6	12	18	38	69	100
590-Hansel and Gretel; partial photo-c	6	12	18	37	66	95
591-Western Marshal (Ernest Haycox's)-Kinstler-a	5	10	15	33	57	80
592-Super Circus (TV)	6	12	18	37	66	95
593-Oswald the Rabbit (Lantz)	5	10	15	31	53	75
594-Bozo (10/54)	9	18	27	57	111	165
595-Pluto (Disney)	5	10	15	31	53	75
596-Turok, Son of Stone (#1)	63	126	189	504	1127	1750
597-The Little King	5	10	15	33	57	80
598-Captain Davy Jones	5	10	15	30	50	70
599-Ben Bowie and His Mountain Men	5	10	15	31	53	75
600-Daisy Duck's Diary (#1) (Disney) (11/54)	7	14	21	44	82	120
601-Frosty the Snowman	5	10	15	34	60	85
602-Mr. Magoo and Gerald McBoing-Boing	9	18	27	58	114	170
603-M.G.M.'s The Two Mouseketeers	5	10	15	35	63	90
604-Shadow on the Trail (Zane Grey)	4	8	12	28	47	65
605-The Brownies-not by Kelly (12/54)	5	10	15	33	57	80
606-Sir Lancelot (not TV)	6	12	18	41	76	110
607-Santa Claus Funnies	6	12	18	41	76	110
608-Silvertip- "Valley of Vanishing Men" (Max Brand)-Kinstler-a	5	10	15	30	50	70
609-The Littlest Outlaw (Disney-Movie) (1/55)-Photo-c	6	12	18	37	66	95
610-Drum Beat (Movie); Alan Ladd photo-c	8	16	24	51	96	140
611-Duck Album (Disney)	6	12	18	38	69	100
612-Little Beaver (1/55)	5	10	15	30	50	70
613-Western Marshal (Ernest Haycox's) (2/55)-Kinstler-a	5	10	15	33	57	80
614-20,000 Leagues Under the Sea (Disney) (Movie) (2/55)-Painted-c	8	16	24	51	96	140
615-Daffy	6	12	18	42	79	115
616-To the Last Man (Zane Grey)	4	8	12	28	47	65
617-The Quest of Zorro	10	20	30	68	144	220
618-Johnny Mack Brown; photo-c	6	12	18	40	73	105
619-Krazy Kat; not by Herriman	5	10	15	30	50	70
620-Mowgli Jungle Book (Kipling)	5	10	15	30	50	70
621-Francis the Famous Talking Mule (4/55)	4	8	12	28	47	65
622-Beetle Bailey	7	14	21	44	82	120
623-Oswald the Rabbit (Lantz)	4	8	12	28	47	65
624-Treasure Island(Disney-Movie)(4/55)-Photo-c	7	14	21	46	86	125
625-Beaver Valley (Disney-Movie)	5	10	15	35	63	90
626-Ben Bowie and His Mountain Men	5	10	15	31	53	75
627-Goofy (Disney) (5/55)	6	12	18	41	76	110
628-Elmer Fudd	5	10	15	34	60	85
629-Lady and the Tramp with Jock (Disney)	6	12	18	41	76	110
630-Priscilla's Pop	4	8	12	27	44	60
631-Davy Crockett, Indian Fighter (#1) (Disney) (5/55) (TV)-Fess Parker photo-c	14	28	42	96	211	325
632-Fighting Caravans (Zane Grey)	4	8	12	28	47	65
633-The Little People by Walt Scott (6/55)	5	10	15	31	53	75
634-Lady and the Tramp Album (Disney) (6/55)	5	10	15	31	53	75
635-Bob Clampett's Beany and Cecil (TV)	12	24	36	82	179	275
636-Chip 'N' Dale (Disney)	6	12	18	38	69	100
637-Silvertip (Max Brand)-Kinstler-a	5	10	15	30	50	70
638-M.G.M.'s Spike and Tyke (8/55)	5	10	15	31	53	75
639-Davy Crockett at the Alamo (Disney) (7/55) (TV)-Fess Parker photo-c	11	22	33	76	163	260
640-Western Marshal(Ernest Haycox's)-Kinstler-a	5	10	15	33	57	80
641-Steve Canyon (1955)-by Caniff	5	10	15	31	53	75
642-M.G.M.'s The Two Mouseketeers	5	10	15	35	63	90
643-Wild Bill Elliott; photo-c	5	10	15	30	50	70
644-Sir Walter Raleigh (5/55)-Based on movie "The Virgin Queen"; photo-c	6	12	18	40	73	105

	GD 2.0	VG 4.0	FN 6.0	VF 8.0	VF/NM 9.0	NM- 9.2
645-Johnny Mack Brown; photo-c	6	12	18	40	73	105
646-Dotty Dripple and Taffy (#1)	5	10	15	31	53	75
647-Bugs Bunny's Album (9/55)	6	12	18	37	66	95
648-Jace Pearson of the Texas Rangers (TV)-Photo-c	6	12	18	37	66	95
649-Duck Album (Disney)	6	12	18	38	69	100
650-Prince Valiant; by Bob Fuje	7	14	21	44	82	120
651-King Colt (Luke Short) (9/55)-Kinstler-a	4	8	12	28	47	65
652-Buck Jones	5	10	15	31	53	75
653-Smokey the Bear (#1) (10/55)	9	18	27	62	126	190
654-Pluto (Disney)	5	10	15	31	53	75
655-Francis the Famous Talking Mule	4	8	12	28	47	65
656-Turok, Son of Stone (#2) (10/55)	31	62	93	223	499	775
657-Ben Bowie and His Mountain Men	5	10	15	31	53	75
658-Goofy (Disney)	6	12	18	41	76	110
659-Daisy Duck's Diary (Disney)(#2)	5	10	15	35	63	90
660-Little Beaver	5	10	15	30	50	70
661-Frosty the Snowman	5	10	15	34	60	85
662-Zoo Parade (TV)-Marlin Perkins (11/55)	5	10	15	30	50	70
663-Winky Dink (TV)	7	14	21	48	89	130
664-Davy Crockett in the Great Keelboat Race (TV) (Disney) (11/55)-Fess Parker photo-c	11	22	33	75	160	245
665-The African Lion (Disney-Movie) (11/55)	5	10	15	33	57	80
666-Santa Claus Funnies	6	12	18	41	76	110
667-Silvertip and the Stolen Stallion (Max Brand) (12/55)-Kinstler-a	5	10	15	30	50	70
668-Dumbo (Disney) (12/55)-First of two printings. Dumbo on cover with starry sky. Reprints 4-Color #234?; same-c as #234	9	18	27	61	123	185
668-Dumbo (Disney) (1/58)-Second printing. Same cover altered, with Timothy Mouse added. Same contents as above	6	12	18	38	69	100
669-Robin Hood (Disney-Movie) (12/55)-Reprints #413 plus-c; photo-c	5	10	15	34	60	85
670-M.G.M's Mouse Musketeers (#1) (1/56)-Formerly the Two Mouseketeers	5	10	15	33	57	80
671-Davy Crockett and the River Pirates (TV) (Disney) (12/55)-Jesse Marsh-a; Fess Parker photo-c	11	22	33	75	160	245
672-Quentin Durward (1/56) (Movie)-Photo-c	6	12	18	38	69	100
673-Buffalo Bill, Jr. (#1) (TV)-James Arness photo-c	8	16	24	52	99	145
674-The Little Rascals (#1) (TV)	8	16	24	54	102	150
675-Steve Donovan, Western Marshal (#1) (TV)-Kinstler-a; photo-c	7	14	21	46	86	125
676-Will-Yum!	4	8	12	27	44	60
677-Little King	5	10	15	33	57	80
678-The Last Hunt (Movie)-Photo-c	6	12	18	38	69	100
679-Gunsmoke (#1) (TV)-Photo-c	15	30	45	100	220	340
680-Out Our Way with the Worry Wart (2/56)	4	8	12	25	40	55
681-Forever Darling (Movie) with Lucille Ball & Desi Arnaz (2/56)-; photo-c	10	20	30	66	138	210
682-The Sword & the Rose (Disney-Movie)-Reprint of #505; Renamed When Knighthood Was in Flower for the novel; photo-c	6	12	18	40	73	105
683-Hi and Lois (3/56)	5	10	15	30	50	70
684-Helen of Troy (Movie)-Buscema-a; photo-c	8	16	24	56	108	160
685-Johnny Mack Brown; photo-c	6	12	18	40	73	105
686-Duck Album (Disney)	6	12	18	38	69	100
687-The Indian Fighter (Movie)-Kirk Douglas photo-c	7	14	21	44	82	120
688-Alexander the Great (Movie) (5/56)-Buscema-a; photo-c	6	12	18	41	76	110
689-Elmer Fudd (3/56)	5	10	15	34	60	85
690-The Conqueror (Movie) - John Wayne photo-c	14	28	42	94	207	320
691-Dotty Dripple and Taffy	4	8	12	23	37	50
692-The Little People-Walt Scott	5	10	15	31	53	75
693-Song of the South (Disney) (1956)-Partial reprint of #129	7	14	21	49	92	135
694-Super Circus (TV)-Photo-c	6	12	18	37	66	95
695-Little Beaver	5	10	15	30	50	70
696-Krazy Kat; not by Herriman (4/56)	5	10	15	30	50	70
697-Oswald the Rabbit (Lantz)	4	8	12	28	47	65
698-Francis the Famous Talking Mule (4/56)	4	8	12	28	47	65
699-Prince Valiant-by Bob Fuje	7	14	21	44	82	120
700-Water Birds and the Olympic Elk (Disney-Movie) (4/56)	5	10	15	31	53	75
701-Jiminy Cricket (#1) (Disney) (5/56)	7	14	21	48	89	130
702-The Goofy Success Story (Disney)	6	12	18	41	76	110
703-Scamp (#1) (Disney)	8	16	24	51	96	140

Four Color Comics #760 © DIS

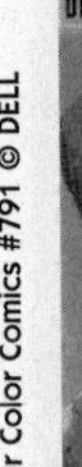
Four Color Comics #791 © DELL

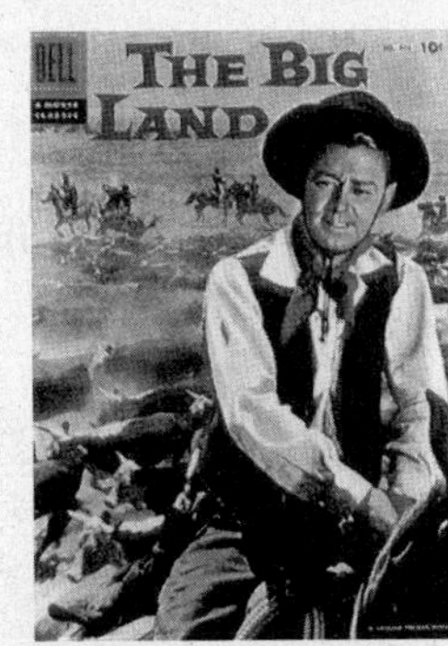

Four Color Comics #812 © WB

	GD 2.0	VG 4.0	FN 6.0	VF 8.0	VF/NM 9.0	NM- 9.2
704-Priscilla's Pop (5/56)	4	8	12	27	44	60
705-Brave Eagle (#1) (TV)-Photo-c	6	12	18	38	69	100
706-Bongo and Lumpjaw (Disney) (6/56)	5	10	15	33	57	80
707-Corky and White Shadow (Disney) (5/56)-Mickey Mouse Club (TV); photo-c	6	12	18	40	73	105
708-Smokey the Bear	6	12	18	37	66	95
709-The Searchers (Movie) - John Wayne photo-c	20	40	60	138	307	475
710-Francis the Famous Talking Mule	4	8	12	28	47	65
711-M.G.M's Mouse Musketeers	4	8	12	27	44	60
712-The Great Locomotive Chase (Disney-Movie) (9/56)-Photo-c	6	12	18	40	73	105
713-The Animal World (Movie) (8/56)	4	8	12	25	40	55
714-Spin and Marty (#1) (TV) (Disney)-Mickey Mouse Club (6/56); photo-c	10	20	30	69	147	225
715-Timmy (8/56)	5	10	15	30	50	70
716-Man in Space (Disney)(A science feature from Tomorrowland)	7	14	21	48	89	130
717-Moby Dick (Movie)-Gregory Peck photo-c	7	14	21	48	89	130
718-Dotty Dripple and Taffy	4	8	12	23	37	50
719-Prince Valiant; by Bob Fuje (8/56)	7	14	21	44	82	120
720-Gunsmoke (TV)-James Arness photo-c	8	16	24	54	102	150
721-Captain Kangaroo (TV)-Photo-c	13	26	39	86	188	290
722-Johnny Mack Brown-Photo-c	6	12	18	40	73	105
723-Santiago (Movie)-Kinstler-a (9/56); Alan Ladd photo-c	8	16	24	54	102	150
724-Bugs Bunny's Album	5	10	15	33	57	80
725-Elmer Fudd (9/56)	4	8	12	28	47	65
726-Duck Album (Disney) (9/56)	5	10	15	33	57	80
727-The Nature of Things (TV) (Disney)-Jesse Marsh-a	5	10	15	31	53	75
728-M.G.M's Mouse Musketeers	4	8	12	27	44	60
729-Bob Son of Battle (11/56)	4	8	12	23	37	50
730-Smokey Stover	5	10	15	31	53	75
731-Silvertip and The Fighting Four (Max Brand)-Kinstler-a	5	10	15	30	50	70
732-Zorro, the Challenge of (10/56)	10	20	30	68	144	220
733-Buck Jones	5	10	15	31	53	75
734-Cheyenne (#1) (TV) (10/56)-Clint Walker photo-c	12	24	36	84	185	285
735-Crusader Rabbit (#1) (TV)	21	42	63	147	324	500
736-Pluto (Disney)	5	10	15	31	53	75
737-Steve Canyon-Caniff-a	5	10	15	31	53	75
738-Westward Ho, the Wagons (Disney-Movie)-Fess Parker photo-c	8	16	24	54	102	150
739-Bounty Guns (Luke Short)-Drucker-a	4	8	12	27	44	60
740-Chilly Willy (#1) (Walter Lantz)	7	14	21	44	82	120
741-The Fastest Gun Alive (Movie)(9/56)-Photo-c	6	12	18	40	73	105
742-Buffalo Bill, Jr. (TV)-Photo-c	5	10	15	35	63	90
743-Daisy Duck's Diary (Disney) (11/56)	5	10	15	35	63	90
744-Little Beaver	5	10	15	30	50	70
745-Francis the Famous Talking Mule	4	8	12	28	47	65
746-Dotty Dripple and Taffy	4	8	12	23	37	50
747-Goofy (Disney)	6	12	18	41	76	110
748-Frosty the Snowman (11/56)	5	10	15	31	53	75
749-Secrets of Life (Disney-Movie)-Photo-c	5	10	15	30	50	70
750-The Great Cat Family (Disney-TV/Movie)-Pinocchio & Alice app.	6	12	18	37	66	95
751-Our Miss Brooks (TV)-Photo-c	6	12	18	42	79	115
752-Mandrake, the Magician	9	18	27	60	120	180
753-Walt Scott's Little People (11/56)	5	10	15	31	53	75
754-Smokey the Bear	6	12	18	37	66	95
755-The Littlest Snowman (12/56)	5	10	15	31	53	75
756-Santa Claus Funnies	6	12	18	41	76	110
757-The True Story of Jesse James (Movie)-Photo-c	8	16	24	51	96	140
758-Bear Country (Disney-Movie)	5	10	15	31	53	75
759-Circus Boy (TV)-The Monkees' Mickey Dolenz photo-c (12/56)	10	20	30	69	147	225
760-The Hardy Boys (#1) (TV) (Disney)-Mickey Mouse Club; photo-c	9	18	27	59	117	175
761-Howdy Doody (TV) (1/57)	9	18	27	61	123	185
762-The Sharkfighters (Movie) (1/57); Buscema-a; photo-c	7	14	21	44	82	120
763-Grandma Duck's Farm Friends (#1) (Disney)	7	14	21	44	82	120
764-M.G.M's Mouse Musketeers	4	8	12	27	44	60
765-Will-Yum!	4	8	12	27	44	60
766-Buffalo Bill, Jr. (TV)-Photo-c	5	10	15	35	63	90
767-Spin and Marty (TV) (Disney)-Mickey Mouse Club (2/57)	8	16	24	54	102	150
768-Steve Donovan, Western Marshal (TV)-Kinstler-a; photo-c	6	12	18	37	66	95
769-Gunsmoke (TV)-James Arness photo-c	8	16	24	54	102	150
770-Brave Eagle (TV)-Photo-c	4	8	12	27	44	60
771-Brand of Empire (Luke Short)(3/57)-Drucker-a	4	8	12	27	44	60
772-Cheyenne (TV)-Clint Walker photo-c	8	16	24	51	96	140
773-The Brave One (Movie)-Photo-c	5	10	15	31	53	75
774-Hi and Lois (3/57)	4	8	12	25	40	55
775-Sir Lancelot and Brian (TV)-Buscema-a; photo-c	8	16	24	56	108	160
776-Johnny Mack Brown; photo-c	6	12	18	40	73	105
777-Scamp (Disney) (3/57)	6	12	18	37	66	95
778-The Little Rascals (TV)	5	10	15	35	63	90
779-Lee Hunter, Indian Fighter (3/57)	5	10	15	33	57	80
780-Captain Kangaroo (TV)-Photo-c	11	22	33	73	157	240
781-Fury (#1) (TV) (3/57)-Photo-c	7	14	21	44	82	120
782-Duck Album (Disney)	5	10	15	33	57	80
783-Elmer Fudd	4	8	12	28	47	65
784-Around the World in 80 Days (Movie) (2/57)-Photo-c	6	12	18	42	79	115
785-Circus Boy (TV) (4/57)-The Monkees' Mickey Dolenz photo-c	9	18	27	59	117	175
786-Cinderella (Disney) (3/57)-Partial-r of #272	6	12	18	41	76	110
787-Little Hiawatha (Disney) (4/57)(#2)	5	10	15	30	50	70
788-Prince Valiant; by Bob Fuje	6	12	18	41	76	110
789-Silvertip-Valley Thieves (Max Brand) (4/57)-Kinstler-a	5	10	15	30	50	70
790-The Wings of Eagles (Movie) (John Wayne)-Toth-a; John Wayne photo-c; 10¢ & 15¢ editions exist	12	24	36	79	170	260
791-The 77th Bengal Lancers (TV)-Photo-c	6	12	18	40	73	105
792-Oswald the Rabbit (Lantz)	4	8	12	28	47	65
793-Morty Meekle	4	8	12	25	40	55
794-The Count of Monte Cristo (5/57) (Movie)-Buscema-a	7	14	21	48	89	130
795-Jiminy Cricket (Disney)(#2)	6	12	18	37	66	95
796-Ludwig Bemelman's Madeleine and Genevieve	4	8	12	25	40	55
797-Gunsmoke (TV)-Photo-c	8	16	24	54	102	150
798-Buffalo Bill, Jr. (TV)-Photo-c	5	10	15	35	63	90
799-Priscilla's Pop	4	8	12	27	44	60
800-The Buccaneers (TV)-Photo-c	6	12	18	40	73	105
801-Dotty Dripple and Taffy	4	8	12	23	37	50
802-Goofy (Disney) (5/57)	6	12	18	41	76	110
803-Cheyenne (TV)-Clint Walker photo-c	8	16	24	51	96	140
804-Steve Canyon-Caniff-a (1957)	5	10	15	31	53	75
805-Crusader Rabbit (TV)	16	32	48	111	246	380
806-Scamp (Disney) (6/57)	6	12	18	37	66	95
807-Savage Range (Luke Short)-Drucker-a	4	8	12	27	44	60
808-Spin and Marty (TV)(Disney)-Mickey Mouse Club; photo-c	8	16	24	54	102	150
809-The Little People (Walt Scott)	5	10	15	31	53	75
810-Francis the Famous Talking Mule	4	8	12	27	44	60
811-Howdy Doody (TV) (7/57)	9	18	27	61	123	185
812-The Big Land (Movie); Alan Ladd photo-c	8	16	24	51	96	140
813-Circus Boy (TV)-The Monkees' Mickey Dolenz photo-c	9	18	27	59	117	175
814-Covered Wagons, Ho! (Disney)-Donald Duck (TV) (6/57); Mickey Mouse app.	5	10	15	31	53	75
815-Dragoon Wells Massacre (Movie)-photo-c	6	12	18	42	79	115
816-Brave Eagle (TV)-photo-c	4	8	12	27	44	60
817-Little Beaver	5	10	15	30	50	70
818-Smokey the Bear (6/57)	6	12	18	37	66	95
819-Mickey Mouse in Magicland (Disney) (7/57)	5	10	15	35	63	90
820-The Oklahoman (Movie)-Photo-c	7	14	21	49	92	135
821-Wringle Wrangle (Disney)-Based on movie "Westward Ho, the Wagons"; Marsh-a; Fess Parker photo-c	7	14	21	46	86	125
822-Paul Revere's Ride with Johnny Tremain (TV) (Disney)-Toth-a	7	14	21	49	92	135
823-Timmy	4	8	12	27	44	60
824-The Pride and the Passion (Movie) (8/57)-Frank Sinatra & Cary Grant photo-c	8	16	24	56	108	160
825-The Little Rascals (TV)	5	10	15	35	63	90

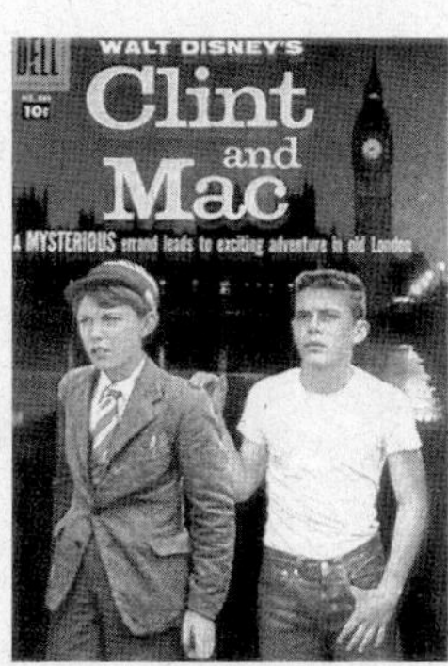

Four Color Comics #887 © DIS

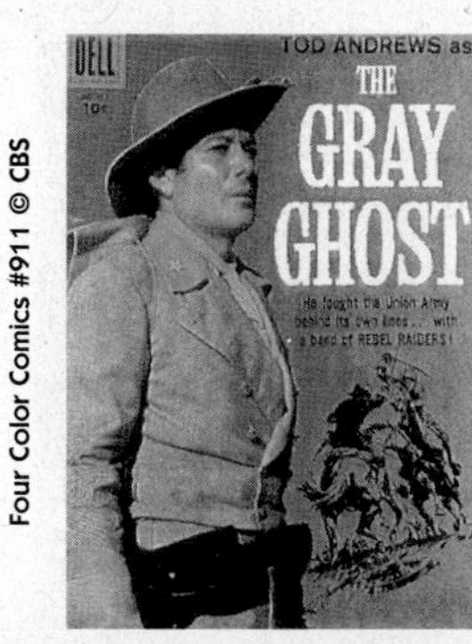

Four Color Comics #911 © CBS

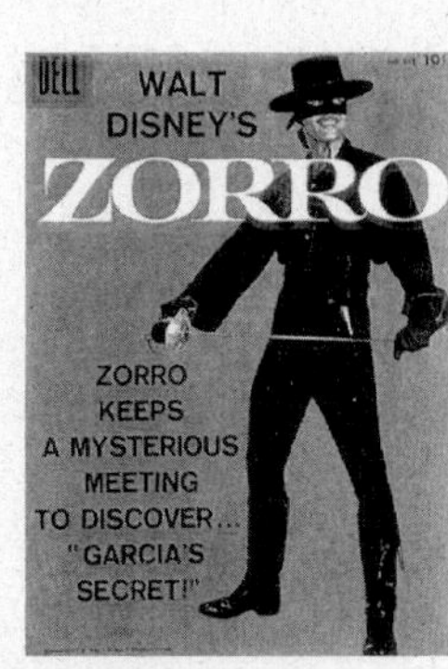

Four Color Comics #933 © DIS

	GD 2.0	VG 4.0	FN 6.0	VF 8.0	VF/NM 9.0	NM- 9.2
826-Spin and Marty and Annette (TV) (Disney)-Mickey Mouse Club; Annette Funicello photo-c	18	36	54	124	275	425
827-Smokey Stover (8/57)	5	10	15	31	53	75
828-Buffalo Bill, Jr. (TV)-Photo-c	5	10	15	35	63	90
829-Tales of the Pony Express (TV) (8/57)-Painted-c	5	10	15	30	50	70
830-The Hardy Boys (TV) (Disney)-Mickey Mouse Club (8/57); photo-c	8	16	24	51	96	140
831-No Sleep 'Til Dawn (Movie)-Karl Malden photo-c	6	12	18	37	66	95
832-Lolly and Pepper (#1)	5	10	15	31	53	75
833-Scamp (Disney) (9/57)	6	12	18	37	66	95
834-Johnny Mack Brown; photo-c	6	12	18	40	73	105
835-Silvertip-The False Rider (Max Brand)	5	10	15	30	50	70
836-Man in Flight (Disney) (TV) (9/57)	6	12	18	40	73	105
837-Cotton Woods, (All-American Athlete...)	4	8	12	25	40	55
838-Bugs Bunny's Life Story Album (9/57)	5	10	15	33	57	80
839-The Vigilantes (Movie)	6	12	18	41	76	110
840-Duck Album (Disney) (9/57)	5	10	15	33	57	80
841-Elmer Fudd	4	8	12	28	47	65
842-The Nature of Things (Disney-Movie) ('57)-Jesse Marsh-a (TV series)	5	10	15	31	53	75
843-The First Americans (Disney) (TV)-Marsh-a	7	14	21	48	89	130
844-Gunsmoke (TV)-Photo-c	8	16	24	54	102	150
845-The Land Unknown (Movie)-Alex Toth-a	10	20	30	64	132	200
846-Gun Glory (Movie)-by Alex Toth; photo-c	8	16	24	51	96	140
847-Perri (squirrels) (Disney-Movie)-Two different covers published	5	10	15	33	57	80
848-Marauder's Moon (Luke Short)	4	8	12	27	44	60
849-Prince Valiant; by Bob Fuje	6	12	18	41	76	110
850-Buck Jones	5	10	15	31	53	75
851-The Story of Mankind (Movie) (1/58)-Hedy Lamarr & Vincent Price photo-c	6	12	18	41	76	110
852-Chilly Willy (2/58) (Lantz)	5	10	15	30	50	70
853-Pluto (Disney) (10/57)	5	10	15	31	53	75
854-The Hunchback of Notre Dame (Movie)-Photo-c	10	20	30	70	150	230
855-Broken Arrow (TV)-Photo-c	5	10	15	33	57	80
856-Buffalo Bill, Jr. (TV)-Photo-c	5	10	15	35	63	90
857-The Goofy Adventure Story (Disney) (11/57)	6	12	18	41	76	110
858-Daisy Duck's Diary (Disney) (11/57)	5	10	15	31	53	75
859-Topper and Neil (TV) (11/57)	5	10	15	30	50	70
860-Wyatt Earp (#1) (TV)-Manning-a; photo-c	9	18	27	57	111	165
861-Frosty the Snowman	5	10	15	31	53	75
862-The Truth About Mother Goose (Disney-Movie) (11/57)	6	12	18	41	76	110
863-Francis the Famous Talking Mule	4	8	12	27	44	60
864-The Littlest Snowman	5	10	15	31	53	75
865-Andy Burnett (TV) (Disney) (12/57)-Photo-c	7	14	21	49	92	135
866-Mars and Beyond (Disney-TV)(A science feature from Tomorrowland)	7	14	21	48	89	130
867-Santa Claus Funnies	6	12	18	41	76	110
868-The Little People (12/57)	5	10	15	31	53	75
869-Old Yeller (Disney-Movie)-Photo-c	5	10	15	33	57	80
870-Little Beaver (1/58)	5	10	15	30	50	70
871-Curly Kayoe	4	8	12	25	40	55
872-Captain Kangaroo (TV)-Photo-c	11	22	33	73	157	240
873-Grandma Duck's Farm Friends (Disney)	5	10	15	33	57	80
874-Old Ironsides (Disney-Movie with Johnny Tremain) (1/58)	6	12	18	38	69	100
875-Trumpets West (Luke Short) (2/58)	4	8	12	27	44	60
876-Tales of Wells Fargo (#1)(TV)(2/58)-Photo-c	8	16	24	51	96	140
877-Frontier Doctor with Rex Allen (TV)-Alex Toth-a; Rex Allen photo-c	8	16	24	54	102	150
878-Peanuts (#1)-Schulz-c only (2/58)	50	100	150	400	900	1400
879-Brave Eagle (TV) (2/58)-Photo-c	4	8	12	27	44	60
880-Steve Donovan, Western Marshal-Drucker-a (TV)-Photo-c	5	10	15	30	50	70
881-The Captain and the Kids (2/58)	4	8	12	28	44	60
882-Zorro (Disney)-1st Disney issue; by Alex Toth (TV) (2/58); photo-c	13	26	39	86	188	290
883-The Little Rascals (TV)	5	10	15	34	60	85
884-Hawkeye and the Last of the Mohicans (TV) (3/58); photo-c	6	12	18	40	73	105
885-Fury (TV) (3/58)-Photo-c	5	10	15	35	63	90
886-Bongo and Lumpjaw (Disney) (3/58)	4	8	12	28	47	65
887-The Hardy Boys (Disney) (TV)-Mickey Mouse Club (1/58)-Photo-c	8	16	24	51	96	140
888-Elmer Fudd (3/58)	4	8	12	28	47	65
889-Clint and Mac (Disney) (TV) (3/58)-Alex Toth-a; photo-c	10	20	30	64	132	200
890-Wyatt Earp (TV)-by Russ Manning; photo-c	6	12	18	41	76	110
891-Light in the Forest (Disney-Movie) (3/58)-Fess Parker photo-c	6	12	18	42	79	115
892-Maverick (#1) (TV) (4/58)-James Garner photo-c	18	36	54	124	275	425
893-Jim Bowie (TV)-Photo-c	5	10	15	35	63	90
894-Oswald the Rabbit (Lantz)	4	8	12	28	47	65
895-Wagon Train (#1) (TV) (3/58)-Photo-c	9	18	27	61	123	185
896-The Adventures of Tinker Bell (Disney)	8	16	24	54	102	150
897-Jiminy Cricket (Disney)	6	12	18	37	66	95
898-Silvertip (Max Brand)-Kinstler-a (5/58)	5	10	15	30	50	70
899-Goofy (Disney) (5/58)	5	10	15	31	53	75
900-Prince Valiant; by Bob Fuje	6	12	18	41	76	110
901-Little Hiawatha (Disney)	5	10	15	30	50	70
902-Will-Yum!	4	8	12	27	44	60
903-Dotty Dripple and Taffy	4	8	12	23	37	50
904-Lee Hunter, Indian Fighter	4	8	12	27	44	60
905-Annette (Disney) (TV) (5/58)-Mickey Mouse Club; Annette Funicello photo-c	21	42	63	147	324	500
906-Francis the Famous Talking Mule	4	8	12	27	44	60
907-Sugarfoot (#1) (TV)Toth-a; photo-c	10	20	30	67	141	215
908-The Little People and the Giant-Walt Scott (5/58)	5	10	15	31	53	75
909-Smitty	4	8	12	23	37	50
910-The Vikings (Movie)-Buscema-a; Kirk Douglas photo-c	7	14	21	48	89	130
911-The Gray Ghost (TV)-Photo-c	7	14	21	48	89	130
912-Leave It to Beaver (#1) (TV)-Photo-c	13	26	39	89	195	300
913-The Left-Handed Gun (Movie) (7/58); Paul Newman photo-c	8	16	24	54	102	150
914-No Time for Sergeants (Movie)-Andy Griffith photo-c; Toth-a	9	18	27	57	111	165
915-Casey Jones (TV)-Alan Hale photo-c	5	10	15	33	57	80
916-Red Ryder Ranch Comics (7/58)	4	8	12	28	47	65
917-The Life of Riley (TV)-Photo-c	9	18	27	59	117	175
918-Beep Beep, the Roadrunner (#1) (7/58)-Published with two different back covers	11	22	33	73	157	240
919-Boots and Saddles (#1) (TV)-Photo-c	6	12	18	42	79	115
920-Zorro (Disney) (TV) (6/58)Toth-a; photo-c	10	20	30	66	138	210
921-Wyatt Earp (TV)-Manning-a; photo-c	6	12	18	41	76	110
922-Johnny Mack Brown by Russ Manning; photo-c	6	12	18	41	76	110
923-Timmy	4	8	12	27	44	60
924-Colt .45 (#1) (TV) (8/58)-W. Preston photo-c	9	18	27	60	120	180
925-Last of the Fast Guns (Movie) (8/58)-Photo-c	6	12	18	37	66	95
926-Peter Pan (Disney)-Reprint of #442	4	8	12	28	47	65
927-Top Gun (Luke Short) Buscema-a	4	8	12	27	44	60
928-Sea Hunt (#1) (9/58) (TV)-Lloyd Bridges photo-c	10	20	30	64	132	200
929-Brave Eagle (TV)-Photo-c	4	8	12	27	44	60
930-Maverick (TV) (7/58)-James Garner photo-c	9	18	27	62	126	190
931-Have Gun, Will Travel (#1) (TV)-Photo-c	11	22	33	73	157	240
932-Smokey the Bear (His Life Story)	6	12	18	37	66	95
933-Zorro (Disney, 9/58) (TV)-Alex Toth-a; photo-c	10	20	30	66	138	210
934-Restless Gun (#1) (TV)-Photo-c	9	18	27	61	123	185
935-King of the Royal Mounted	4	8	12	27	44	60
936-The Little Rascals (TV)	5	10	15	34	60	85
937-Ruff and Reddy (#1) (9/58) (TV) (1st Hanna-Barbera comic book)	10	20	30	67	141	215
938-Elmer Fudd (9/58)	4	8	12	28	47	65
939-Steve Canyon - not by Caniff	5	10	15	31	53	75
940-Lolly and Pepper (10/58)	4	8	12	23	37	50
941-Pluto (Disney) (10/58)	4	8	12	28	47	65
942-Pony Express (Tales of the ...) (TV)	5	10	15	30	50	70
943-White Wilderness (Disney-Movie) (10/58)	6	12	18	37	66	95
944-The 7th Voyage of Sinbad (Movie) (9/58)-Buscema-a; photo-c	10	20	30	70	150	230
945-Maverick (TV)-James Garner/Jack Kelly photo-c	9	18	27	62	126	190
946-The Big Country (Movie)-Photo-c	6	12	18	40	73	105
947-Broken Arrow (TV)-Photo-c (11/58)	5	10	15	30	50	70
948-Daisy Duck's Diary (Disney) (11/58)	5	10	15	31	53	75
949-High Adventure(Lowell Thomas')(TV)-Photo-c	5	10	15	33	57	80

Four Color Comics #1016 © DELL

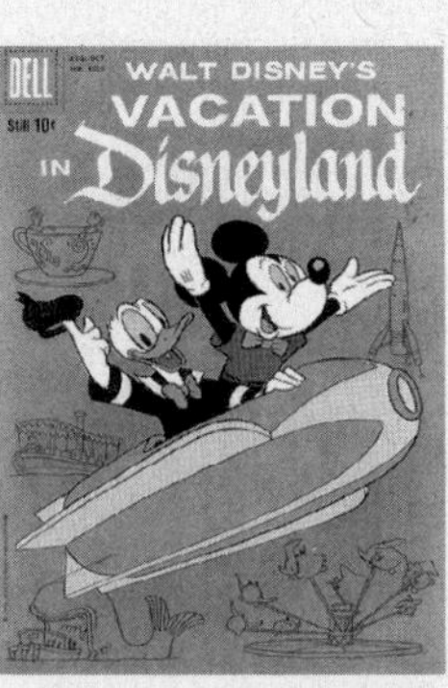

Four Color Comics #1025 © DIS

Four Color Comics #1055 © DIS

	GD 2.0	VG 4.0	FN 6.0	VF 8.0	VF/NM 9.0	NM- 9.2
950-Frosty the Snowman	5	10	15	31	53	75
951-The Lennon Sisters Life Story (TV)-Toth-a, 32 pgs.; photo-c	11	22	33	73	157	240
952-Goofy (Disney) (11/58)	5	10	15	31	53	75
953-Francis the Famous Talking Mule	4	8	12	27	44	60
954-Man in Space-Satellites (TV)	6	12	18	40	73	105
955-Hi and Lois (11/58)	4	8	12	25	40	55
956-Ricky Nelson (#1) (TV)-Photo-c	15	30	45	100	220	340
957-Buffalo Bee (#1) (TV)	8	16	24	51	96	140
958-Santa Claus Funnies	6	12	18	37	66	95
959-Christmas Stories-(Walt Scott's Little People) (1951-56 strip reprints)	5	10	15	31	53	75
960-Zorro (Disney) (TV) (12/58)-Toth art; photo-c	10	20	30	66	138	210
961-Jace Pearson's Tales of the Texas Rangers (TV)-Spiegle-a; photo-c	5	10	15	33	57	80
962-Maverick (TV) (1/59)-James Garner/Jack Kelly photo-c	9	18	27	62	126	190
963-Johnny Mack Brown; photo-c	6	12	18	40	73	105
964-The Hardy Boys (TV) (Disney) (1/59)-Mickey Mouse Club; photo-c	8	16	24	51	96	140
965-Grandma Duck's Farm Friends (Disney)(1/59)	5	10	15	30	50	70
966-Tonka (starring Sal Mineo; Disney-Movie)-Photo-c	8	16	24	51	96	140
967-Chilly Willy (2/59) (Lantz)	5	10	15	30	50	70
968-Tales of Wells Fargo (TV)-Photo-c	7	14	21	48	89	130
969-Peanuts (2/59)	19	38	57	131	291	450
970-Lawman (#1) (TV)-Photo-c	10	20	30	69	147	225
971-Wagon Train (TV)-Photo-c	6	12	18	40	73	105
972-Tom Thumb (Movie)-George Pal (1/59)	8	16	24	51	96	140
973-Sleeping Beauty and the Prince(Disney)(5/59)	10	20	30	64	132	200
974-The Little Rascals (TV) (3/59)	5	10	15	34	60	85
975-Fury (TV)-Photo-c	5	10	15	35	63	90
976-Zorro (Disney) (TV)-Toth-a; photo-c	10	20	30	66	138	210
977-Elmer Fudd (3/59)	4	8	12	28	47	65
978-Lolly and Pepper	4	8	12	23	37	50
979-Oswald the Rabbit (Lantz)	4	8	12	28	47	65
980-Maverick (TV) (4-6/59)-James Garner/Jack Kelly photo-c	9	18	27	62	126	190
981-Ruff and Reddy (TV) (Hanna-Barbera)	7	14	21	44	82	120
982-The New Adventures of Tinker Bell (TV) (Disney)	8	16	24	51	96	140
983-Have Gun, Will Travel (TV) (4-6/59)-Photo-c	8	16	24	51	96	140
984-Sleeping Beauty's Fairy Godmothers (Disney)	8	16	24	54	102	150
985-Shaggy Dog (Disney-Movie)-Photo-all four covers; Annette on back-c(5/59)	6	12	18	42	79	115
986-Restless Gun (TV)-Photo-c	7	14	21	46	86	125
987-Goofy (Disney) (7/59)	5	10	15	31	53	75
988-Little Hiawatha (Disney)	5	10	15	30	50	70
989-Jiminy Cricket (Disney) (5-7/59)	6	12	18	37	66	95
990-Huckleberry Hound (#1)(TV)(Hanna-Barbera); 1st app. Huck, Yogi Bear, & Pixie & Dixie & Mr. Jinks	10	20	30	70	150	230
991-Francis the Famous Talking Mule	4	8	12	27	44	60
992-Sugarfoot (TV)-Toth-a; photo-c	9	18	27	63	129	195
993-Jim Bowie (TV)-Photo-c	5	10	15	33	57	80
994-Sea Hunt (TV)-Lloyd Bridges photo-c	7	14	21	46	86	125
995-Donald Duck Album (Disney) (5-7/59)(#1)	6	12	18	37	66	95
996-Nevada (Zane Grey)	4	8	12	28	47	65
997-Walt Disney Presents-Tales of Texas John Slaughter (#1) (TV) (Disney)-Photo-c; photo of W. Disney inside-c	6	12	18	41	76	110
998-Ricky Nelson (TV)-Photo-c	15	30	45	100	220	340
999-Leave It to Beaver (TV)-Photo-c	11	22	33	76	163	250
1000-The Gray Ghost (TV) (6-8/59)-Photo-c	7	14	21	48	89	130
1001-Lowell Thomas' High Adventure (TV) (8-10/59)-Photo-c	5	10	15	31	53	75
1002-Buffalo Bee (TV)	6	12	18	40	73	105
1003-Zorro (TV) (Disney)-Toth-a; photo-c	10	20	30	66	138	210
1004-Colt .45 (TV) (6-8/59)-Photo-c	7	14	21	48	89	130
1005-Maverick (TV)-James Garner/Jack Kelly photo-c	9	18	27	62	126	190
1006-Hercules (Movie)-Buscema-a; photo-c	8	16	24	51	96	140
1007-John Paul Jones (Movie)-Robert Stack photo-c	5	10	15	33	57	80
1008-Beep Beep, the Road Runner (7-9/59)	7	14	21	44	82	120
1009-The Rifleman (#1) (TV)-Photo-c	18	36	54	126	281	435
1010-Grandma Duck's Farm Friends (Disney)-by Carl Barks	10	20	30	69	147	225
1011-Buckskin (#1) (TV)-Photo-c	6	12	18	41	76	110
1012-Last Train from Gun Hill (Movie) (7/59)-Photo-c	7	14	21	48	89	130
1013-Bat Masterson (#1) (TV) (8/59)-Gene Barry photo-c	10	20	30	66	138	210
1014-The Lennon Sisters (TV)-Toth-a; photo-c	10	20	30	69	147	225
1015-Peanuts-Schulz-c	19	38	57	131	291	450
1016-Smokey the Bear Nature Stories	4	8	12	28	47	65
1017-Chilly Willy (Lantz)	5	10	15	30	50	70
1018-Rio Bravo (Movie)(6/59)-John Wayne; Toth-a; John Wayne, Dean Martin & Ricky Nelson photo-c	20	40	60	138	307	475
1019-Wagon Train (TV)-Photo-c	6	12	18	40	73	105
1020-Jungle Jim-McWilliams-a	4	8	12	25	40	55
1021-Jace Pearson's Tales of the Texas Rangers (TV)-Photo-c	5	10	15	33	57	80
1022-Timmy	4	8	12	27	44	60
1023-Tales of Wells Fargo (TV)-Photo-c	7	14	21	48	89	130
1024-Darby O'Gill and the Little People (Disney-Movie)-Toth-a; photo-c	9	18	27	57	111	165
1025-Vacation in Disneyland (8-10/59)-Carl Barks-a(24pgs.) (Disney)	14	28	42	93	204	315
1026-Spin and Marty (TV) (Disney) (9-11/59)-Mickey Mouse Club; photo-c	7	14	21	44	82	120
1027-The Texan (#1)(TV)-Photo-c	7	14	21	48	89	130
1028-Rawhide (#1) (TV) (9-11/59)-Clint Eastwood photo-c; Tufts-a	20	40	60	138	307	475
1029-Boots and Saddles (TV) (9/59)-Photo-c	5	10	15	31	53	75
1030-Spanky and Alfalfa, the Little Rascals (TV)	5	10	15	34	60	85
1031-Fury (TV)-Photo-c	5	10	15	35	63	90
1032-Elmer Fudd	4	8	12	28	47	65
1033-Steve Canyon-not by Caniff; photo-c	5	10	15	31	53	75
1034-Nancy and Sluggo Summer Camp (9-11/59)	5	10	15	30	50	70
1035-Lawman (TV)-Photo-c	7	14	21	46	86	125
1036-The Big Circus (Movie)-Photo-c	6	12	18	37	66	95
1037-Zorro (Disney) (TV)-Tufts-a; Annette Funicello photo-c	12	24	36	81	176	270
1038-Ruff and Reddy (TV)(Hanna-Barbera)(1959)	7	14	21	44	82	120
1039-Pluto (Disney) (11-1/60)	4	8	12	28	47	65
1040-Quick Draw McGraw (#1) (TV) (Hanna-Barbera) (12-2/60)	11	22	33	76	163	250
1041-Sea Hunt (TV) (10-12/59)-Toth-a; Lloyd Bridges photo-c	7	14	21	46	86	125
1042-The Three Chipmunks (Alvin, Simon & Theodore) (#1) (TV) (10-12/59)	8	16	24	56	108	160
1043-The Three Stooges (#1)-Photo-c	21	42	63	147	324	500
1044-Have Gun, Will Travel (TV)-Photo-c	8	16	24	51	96	140
1045-Restless Gun (TV)-Photo-c	7	14	21	46	86	125
1046-Beep Beep, the Road Runner (11-1/60)	7	14	21	44	82	120
1047-Gyro Gearloose (#1) (Disney)-All Barks-c/a	14	28	42	97	214	330
1048-The Horse Soldiers (Movie) (John Wayne)-Sekowsky-a; painted cover featuring John Wayne	11	22	33	73	157	240
1049-Don't Give Up the Ship (Movie) (8/59)-Jerry Lewis photo-c	8	16	24	55	105	155
1050-Huckleberry Hound (TV) (Hanna-Barbera) (10-12/59)	7	14	21	49	92	135
1051-Donald in Mathmagic Land (Disney-Movie)	8	16	24	54	102	150
1052-Ben-Hur (Movie) (11/59)-Manning-a	9	18	27	58	114	170
1053-Goofy (Disney) (11-1/60)	5	10	15	31	53	75
1054-Huckleberry Hound Winter Fun (TV) (Hanna-Barbera) (12/59)	7	14	21	49	92	135
1055-Daisy Duck's Diary (Disney)-by Carl Barks (11-1/60)	8	16	24	54	102	150
1056-Yellowstone Kelly (Movie)-Clint Walker photo-c	5	10	15	34	60	85
1057-Mickey Mouse Album (Disney)	5	10	15	33	57	80
1058-Colt .45 (TV)-Photo-c	7	14	21	48	89	130
1059-Sugarfoot (TV)-Photo-c	7	14	21	49	92	135
1060-Journey to the Center of the Earth (Movie)-Pat Boone & James Mason photo-c	9	18	27	61	123	185
1061-Buffalo Bee (TV)	6	12	18	40	73	105
1062-Christmas Stories (Walt Scott's Little People strip-r)	5	10	15	31	53	75
1063-Santa Claus Funnies	6	12	18	37	66	95
1064-Bugs Bunny's Merry Christmas (12/59)	5	10	15	33	57	80
1065-Frosty the Snowman	5	10	15	31	53	75

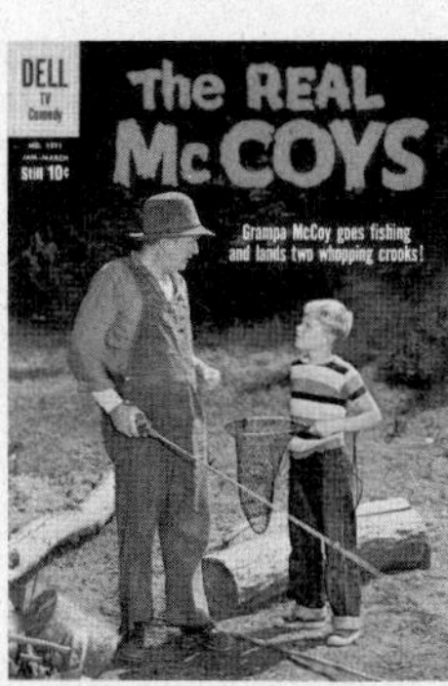

Four Color Comics #1071 © W. Brennan

Four Color Comics #1102 © Four Star

Four Color Comics #1173 © CBS

	GD 2.0	VG 4.0	FN 6.0	VF 8.0	VF/NM 9.0	NM- 9.2
1066-77 Sunset Strip (#1) (TV)-Toth-a (1-3/60)-Efrem Zimbalist, Jr. & Edd "Kookie" Byrnes photo-c	9	18	27	60	120	180
1067-Yogi Bear (#1) (TV) (Hanna-Barbera)	11	22	33	73	157	240
1068-Francis the Famous Talking Mule	4	8	12	27	44	60
1069-The FBI Story (Movie)-Toth-a; James Stewart photo on-c	8	16	24	54	102	150
1070-Solomon and Sheba (Movie)-Sekowsky-a; photo-c	8	16	24	51	96	140
1071-The Real McCoys (#1) (TV) (1-3/60)-Toth-a; Walter Brennan photo-c	8	16	24	51	96	140
1072-Blythe (Marge's)	5	10	15	33	57	80
1073-Grandma Duck's Farm Friends-Barks-c/a (Disney)	10	20	30	69	147	225
1074-Chilly Willy (Lantz)	5	10	15	30	50	70
1075-Tales of Wells Fargo (TV)-Photo-c	7	14	21	48	89	130
1076-The Rebel (#1) (TV)-Sekowsky-a; photo-c	9	18	27	57	111	165
1077-The Deputy (#1) (TV)-Buscema-a; Henry Fonda photo-c	10	20	30	64	132	200
1078-The Three Stooges (2-4/60)-Photo-c	10	20	30	70	150	230
1079-The Little Rascals (TV) (Spanky & Alfalfa)	5	10	15	34	60	85
1080-Fury (TV) (2-4/60)-Photo-c	5	10	15	35	63	90
1081-Elmer Fudd	4	8	12	28	47	65
1082-Spin and Marty (Disney) (TV)-Photo-c	7	14	21	44	82	120
1083-Men into Space (TV)-Anderson-a; photo-c	5	10	15	31	53	75
1084-Speedy Gonzales	5	10	15	34	60	85
1085-The Time Machine (H.G. Wells) (Movie) (3/60)-Alex Toth-a; Rod Taylor photo-c	12	24	36	80	173	265
1086-Lolly and Pepper	4	8	12	23	37	50
1087-Peter Gunn (TV)-Photo-c	7	14	21	49	92	135
1088-A Dog of Flanders (Movie)-Photo-c	4	8	12	28	47	65
1089-Restless Gun (TV)-Photo-c	7	14	21	46	86	125
1090-Francis the Famous Talking Mule	4	8	12	27	44	60
1091-Jacky's Diary (4-6/60)	5	10	15	30	50	70
1092-Toby Tyler (Disney-Movie)-Photo-c	6	12	18	37	66	95
1093-MacKenzie's Raiders (Movie/TV)-Richard Carlson photo-c from TV show	6	12	18	37	66	95
1094-Goofy (Disney)	5	10	15	31	53	75
1095-Gyro Gearloose (Disney)-All Barks-c/a	9	18	27	57	111	165
1096-The Texan (TV)-Rory Calhoun photo-c	7	14	21	44	82	120
1097-Rawhide (TV)-Manning-a; Clint Eastwood photo-c	12	24	36	84	185	285
1098-Sugarfoot (TV)-Photo-c	7	14	21	49	92	135
1099-Donald Duck Album (Disney) (5-7/60)-Barks-c	6	12	18	38	69	100
1100-Annette's Life Story (Disney-Movie) (5/60)-Annette Funicello photo-c	17	34	51	117	259	400
1101-Robert Louis Stevenson's Kidnapped (Disney-Movie) (5/60); photo-c	6	12	18	37	66	95
1102-Wanted: Dead or Alive (#1) (TV) (5-7/60); Steve McQueen photo-c	10	20	30	69	147	225
1103-Leave It to Beaver (TV)-Photo-c	11	22	33	76	163	250
1104-Yogi Bear Goes to College (TV) (Hanna-Barbera) (6-8/60)	7	14	21	48	89	130
1105-Gale Storm (Oh! Susanna) (TV)-Toth-a; photo-c	9	18	27	63	129	195
1106-77 Sunset Strip(TV)(6-8/60)-Toth-a; photo-c	7	14	21	49	92	135
1107-Buckskin (TV)-Photo-c	6	12	18	38	69	100
1108-The Troubleshooters (TV)-Keenan Wynn photo-c	5	10	15	33	57	80
1109-This Is Your Life, Donald Duck (Disney) (TV) (8-10/60)-Gyro flashback to WDC&S #141; origin Donald Duck (1st told)	12	24	36	79	170	260
1110-Bonanza (#1) (TV) (6-8/60)-Photo-c	29	58	87	203	444	685
1111-Shotgun Slade (TV)-Photo-c	6	12	18	37	66	95
1112-Pixie and Dixie and Mr. Jinks (#1) (TV) (Hanna-Barbera) (7-9/60)	7	14	21	44	82	120
1113-Tales of Wells Fargo (TV)-Photo-c	7	14	21	48	89	130
1114-Huckleberry Finn (Movie) (7/60)-Photo-c	5	10	15	33	57	80
1115-Ricky Nelson (TV)-Manning-a; photo-c	12	24	36	80	173	265
1116-Boots and Saddles (TV) (8/60)-Photo-c	5	10	15	31	53	75
1117-Boy and the Pirates (Movie)-Photo-c	6	12	18	37	66	95
1118-The Sword and the Dragon (Movie) (6/60)-Photo-c	7	14	21	44	82	120
1119-Smokey the Bear Nature Stories	4	8	12	28	47	65
1120-Dinosaurus (Movie)-Painted-c	7	14	21	48	89	130
1121-Hercules Unchained (Movie) (8/60)-Crandall/Evans-a	8	16	24	51	96	140
1122-Chilly Willy (Lantz)	5	10	15	30	50	70
1123-Tombstone Territory (TV)-Photo-c	7	14	21	49	92	135
1124-Whirlybirds (#1) (TV)-Photo-c	7	14	21	48	89	130
1125-Laramie (#1) (TV)-Photo-c; G. Kane/Heath-a	7	14	21	49	92	135
1126-Hotel Deparee - Sundance (TV) (8-10/60)-Earl Holliman photo-c	6	12	18	37	66	95
1127-The Three Stooges-Photo-c (8-10/60)	10	20	30	70	150	230
1128-Rocky and His Friends (#1) (TV) (Jay Ward) (8-10/60)	25	50	75	175	388	600
1129-Pollyanna (Disney-Movie)-Hayley Mills photo-c	7	14	21	44	82	120
1130-The Deputy (TV)-Buscema-a; Henry Fonda photo-c	8	16	24	54	102	150
1131-Elmer Fudd (9-11/60)	4	8	12	28	47	65
1132-Space Mouse (Lantz) (8-10/60)	4	8	12	28	47	65
1133-Fury (TV)-Photo-c	5	10	15	35	63	90
1134-Real McCoys (TV)-Toth-a; photo-c	8	16	24	51	96	140
1135-M.G.M.'s Mouse Musketeers (9-11/60)	4	8	12	25	40	55
1136-Jungle Cat (Disney-Movie)-Photo-c	6	12	18	37	66	95
1137-The Little Rascals (TV)	5	10	15	34	60	85
1138-The Rebel (TV)-Photo-c	7	14	21	49	92	135
1139-Spartacus (Movie) (11/60)-Buscema-a; Kirk Douglas photo-c	10	20	30	69	147	225
1140-Donald Duck Album (Disney)-Barks-c	6	12	18	38	69	100
1141-Huckleberry Hound for President (TV) (Hanna-Barbera) (10/60)	7	14	21	44	82	120
1142-Johnny Ringo (TV)-Photo-c	6	12	18	40	73	105
1143-Pluto (Disney) (11-1/61)	4	8	12	28	47	65
1144-The Story of Ruth (Movie)-Photo-c	7	14	21	49	92	135
1145-The Lost World (Movie)-Gil Kane-a; photo-c; 1 pg. Conan Doyle biography by Torres	8	16	24	55	105	155
1146-Restless Gun (TV)-Photo-c; Wildey-a	7	14	21	46	86	125
1147-Sugarfoot (TV)-Photo-c	7	14	21	49	92	135
1148-I Aim at the Stars-the Werner Von Braun Story (Movie) (11-1/61)-Photo-c	6	12	18	40	73	105
1149-Goofy (Disney) (11-1/61)	5	10	15	31	53	75
1150-Daisy Duck's Diary (Disney) (12-1/61) by Carl Barks	8	16	24	54	102	150
1151-Mickey Mouse Album (Disney) (11-1/61)	5	10	15	33	57	80
1152-Rocky and His Friends (TV) (Jay Ward) (12-2/61)	16	32	48	107	236	365
1153-Frosty the Snowman	5	10	15	31	53	75
1154-Santa Claus Funnies	6	12	18	37	66	95
1155-North to Alaska (Movie)-John Wayne photo-c	14	28	42	96	211	325
1156-Walt Disney Swiss Family Robinson (Movie) (12/60)-Photo-c	6	12	18	42	79	115
1157-Master of the World (Movie) (7/61)	6	12	18	40	73	105
1158-Three Worlds of Gulliver (2 issues exist with different covers) (Movie)-Photo-c	6	12	18	40	73	105
1159-77 Sunset Strip (TV)-Toth-a; photo-c	7	14	21	49	92	135
1160-Rawhide (TV)-Clint Eastwood photo-c	12	24	36	84	185	285
1161-Grandma Duck's Farm Friends (Disney) by Carl Barks (2-4/61)	10	20	30	69	147	225
1162-Yogi Bear Joins the Marines (TV) (Hanna-Barbera) (5-7/61)	7	14	21	48	89	130
1163-Daniel Boone (3-5/61); Marsh-a	5	10	15	31	53	75
1164-Wanted: Dead or Alive (TV)-Steve McQueen photo-c	8	16	24	54	102	150
1165-Ellery Queen (#1) (3-5/61)	9	18	27	58	114	175
1166-Rocky and His Friends (TV) (Jay Ward)	16	32	48	107	236	365
1167-Tales of Wells Fargo (TV)-Photo-c	7	14	21	44	82	120
1168-The Detectives (TV)-Robert Taylor photo-c	9	18	27	57	111	165
1169-New Adventures of Sherlock Holmes	12	24	36	79	170	260
1170-The Three Stooges (3-5/61)-Photo-c	10	20	30	70	150	230
1171-Elmer Fudd	4	8	12	28	47	65
1172-Fury (TV)-Photo-c	5	10	15	35	63	90
1173-The Twilight Zone (#1) (TV) (5/61)-Crandall/Evans-c/a; Crandall tribute to Ingles	18	36	54	128	284	440
1174-The Little Rascals (TV)	5	10	15	30	50	70
1175-M.G.M.'s Mouse Musketeers (3-5/61)	4	8	12	25	40	55
1176-Dondi (Movie)-Origin; photo-c	5	10	15	33	57	80
1177-Chilly Willy (Lantz) (4-6/61)	5	10	15	30	50	70
1178-Ten Who Dared (Disney-Movie) (12/60)-Painted-c; cast member photo on back-c	6	12	18	41	76	110

Four Color Comics #1180 © Danny Thomas

Four Color Comics #1195 © DIS

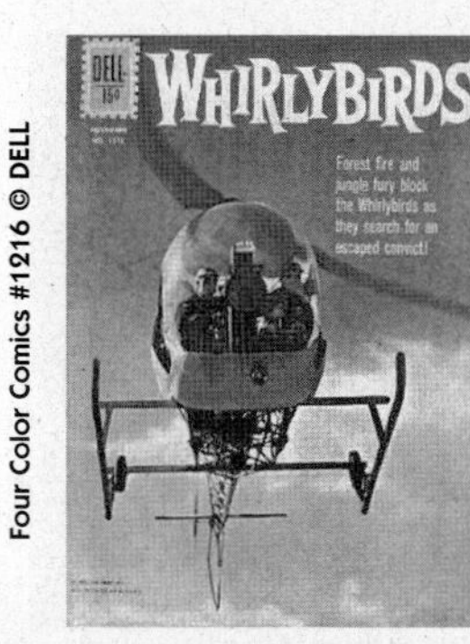

Four Color Comics #1216 © DELL

	GD 2.0	VG 4.0	FN 6.0	VF 8.0	VF/NM 9.0	NM- 9.2
1179-The Swamp Fox (TV) (Disney)-Leslie Nielsen photo-c	7	14	21	48	89	130
1180-The Danny Thomas Show (TV)-Toth-a; photo-c	13	26	39	89	195	300
1181-Texas John Slaughter (TV) (Walt Disney Presents...) (4-6/61)-Photo-c	5	10	15	34	60	85
1182-Donald Duck Album (Disney) (5-7/61)	5	10	15	30	50	70
1183-101 Dalmatians (Disney-Movie) (3/61)	9	18	27	59	117	175
1184-Gyro Gearloose; All Barks-c/a (Disney) (5-7/61) Two variations exist	9	18	27	57	111	165
1185-Sweetie Pie	5	10	15	30	50	70
1186-Yak Yak (#1) by Jack Davis (2 versions - one minus 3-pg. Davis-c/a)	8	16	24	51	96	140
1187-The Three Stooges (6-8/61)-Photo-c	10	20	30	70	150	230
1188-Atlantis, the Lost Continent (Movie) (5/61)-Photo-c	9	18	27	58	114	170
1189-Greyfriars Bobby (Disney-Movie) (11/61)-Photo-c (scarce)	6	12	18	41	76	110
1190-Donald and the Wheel (Disney-Movie) (11/61); Barks-c	7	14	21	46	86	125
1191-Leave It to Beaver (TV)-Photo-c	11	22	33	76	163	250
1192-Ricky Nelson (TV)-Manning-a; photo-c	12	24	36	80	173	265
1193-The Real McCoys (TV) (6-8/61)-Photo-c	7	14	21	48	89	130
1194-Pepe (Movie) (4/61)-Photo-c	4	8	12	25	40	55
1195-National Velvet (#1) (TV)-Photo-c	6	12	18	41	76	110
1196-Pixie and Dixie and Mr. Jinks (TV) (Hanna-Barbera) (7-9/61)	5	10	15	34	60	85
1197-The Aquanauts (TV) (5-7/61)-Photo-c	6	12	18	40	73	105
1198-Donald in Mathmagic Land (Disney-Movie)-Reprint of #1051	6	12	18	37	66	95
1199-The Absent-Minded Professor (Disney-Movie) (4/61)-Photo-c	6	12	18	42	79	115
1199-Shaggy Dog & The Absent-Minded Professor (Disney-Movie) (8/67)-Photo-c	6	12	18	42	79	115
1200-Hennessey (TV) (8-10/61)-Gil Kane-a; photo-c	6	12	18	40	73	105
1201-Goofy (Disney) (8-10/61)	5	10	15	31	53	75
1202-Rawhide (TV)-Clint Eastwood photo-c	12	24	36	84	185	285
1203-Pinocchio (Disney) (3/62)	5	10	15	35	63	90
1204-Scamp (Disney)	4	8	12	27	44	60
1205-David and Goliath (Movie) (7/61)-Photo-c	6	12	18	38	69	100
1206-Lolly and Pepper (9-11/61)	4	8	12	23	37	50
1207-The Rebel (TV)-Sekowsky-a; photo-c	7	14	21	49	92	135
1208-Rocky and His Friends (Jay Ward) (TV)	16	32	48	107	236	365
1209-Sugarfoot (TV)-Photo-c (10-12/61)	7	14	21	49	92	135
1210-The Parent Trap (Disney-Movie) (8/61)-Hayley Mills photo-c	8	16	24	52	99	145
1211-77 Sunset Strip (TV)-Manning-a; photo-c	7	14	21	46	86	125
1212-Chilly Willy (Lantz) (7-9/61)	5	10	15	30	50	70
1213-Mysterious Island (Movie)-Photo-c	7	14	21	48	89	130
1214-Smokey the Bear	4	8	12	28	47	65
1215-Tales of Wells Fargo (TV) (10-12/61)-Photo-c	7	14	21	44	82	120
1216-Whirlybirds (TV)-Photo-c	7	14	21	44	82	120
1218-Fury (TV)-Photo-c	5	10	15	35	63	90
1219-The Detectives (TV)-Robert Taylor & Adam West photo-c	8	16	24	52	99	145
1220-Gunslinger (TV)-Photo-c	7	14	21	49	92	135
1221-Bonanza (TV) (9-11/61)-Photo-c	15	30	45	100	220	340
1222-Elmer Fudd (9-11/61)	4	8	12	28	47	65
1223-Laramie (TV)-Gil Kane-a; photo-c	6	12	18	37	66	95
1224-The Little Rascals (TV) (10-12/61)	5	10	15	30	50	70
1225-The Deputy (TV)-Henry Fonda photo-c	8	16	24	54	102	150
1226-Nikki, Wild Dog of the North (Disney-Movie) (9/61)-Photo-c	5	10	15	31	53	75
1227-Morgan the Pirate (Movie)-Photo-c	6	12	18	42	79	115
1229-Thief of Baghdad (Movie)-Crandall/Evans-a; photo-c	6	12	18	40	73	105
1230-Voyage to the Bottom of the Sea (#1) (Movie)-Photo insert on-c	9	18	27	62	126	190
1231-Danger Man (TV) (9-11/61)-Patrick McGoohan photo-c	9	18	27	61	123	185
1232-On the Double (Movie)	5	10	15	30	50	70
1233-Tammy Tell Me True (Movie) (1961)	6	12	18	37	66	95
1234-The Phantom Planet (Movie) (1961)	6	12	18	40	73	105
1235-Mister Magoo (#1) (12-2/62)	7	14	21	48	89	130
1235-Mister Magoo (3-5/65) 2nd printing; reprint of 12-2/62 issue	5	10	15	35	63	90
1236-King of Kings (Movie)-Photo-c	6	12	18	42	79	115
1237-The Untouchables (#1) (TV)-Not by Toth; photo-c	17	34	51	114	252	390
1238-Deputy Dawg (TV)	9	18	27	63	129	195
1239-Donald Duck Album (Disney) (10-12/61)-Barks-c	6	12	18	38	69	100
1240-The Detectives (TV)-Tufts-a; Robert Taylor photo-c	7	14	21	48	89	130
1241-Sweetie Pie	4	8	12	25	40	55
1242-King Leonardo and His Short Subjects (#1) (TV) (11-1/62)	10	20	30	67	141	215
1243-Ellery Queen	7	14	21	48	89	130
1244-Space Mouse (Lantz) (11-1/62)	4	8	12	28	47	65
1245-New Adventures of Sherlock Holmes	10	20	30	70	150	230
1246-Mickey Mouse Album (Disney)	5	10	15	33	57	80
1247-Daisy Duck's Diary (Disney) (12-2/62)	5	10	15	31	53	75
1248-Pluto (Disney)	4	8	12	28	47	65
1249-The Danny Thomas Show (TV)-Manning-a; photo-c	12	24	36	80	173	265
1250-The Four Horsemen of the Apocalypse (Movie)-Photo-c	6	12	18	37	66	95
1251-Everything's Ducky (Movie) (1961)	5	10	15	30	50	70
1252-The Andy Griffith Show (TV)-Photo-c; 1st show aired 10/3/60	33	66	99	238	532	825
1253-Space Man (#1) (1-3/62)	7	14	21	44	82	120
1254-"Diver Dan" (#1) (TV) (2-4/62)-Photo-c	5	10	15	31	53	75
1255-The Wonders of Aladdin (Movie) (1961)	6	12	18	37	66	95
1256-Kona, Monarch of Monster Isle (#1) (2-4/62)-Glanzman-a	8	16	24	56	108	160
1257-Car 54, Where Are You? (#1) (TV) (3-5/62)-Photo-c	7	14	21	49	92	135
1258-The Frogmen (#1)-Evans-a	7	14	21	46	86	125
1259-El Cid (Movie) (1961)-Photo-c	6	12	18	41	76	110
1260-The Horsemasters (TV, Movie) (Disney) (12-2/62)-Annette Funicello photo-c	10	20	30	69	147	225
1261-Rawhide (TV)-Clint Eastwood photo-c	12	24	36	84	185	285
1262-The Rebel (TV)-Photo-c	7	14	21	49	92	135
1263-77 Sunset Strip (TV) (12-2/62)-Manning-a; photo-c	7	14	21	46	86	125
1264-Pixie and Dixie and Mr. Jinks (TV) (Hanna-Barbera)	5	10	15	34	60	85
1265-The Real McCoys (TV)-Photo-c	7	14	21	48	89	130
1266-M.G.M.'s Spike and Tyke (12-2/62)	4	8	12	25	40	55
1267-Gyro Gearloose; Barks-c/a, 4 pgs. (Disney) (12-2/62)	7	14	21	46	86	125
1268-Oswald the Rabbit (Lantz)	4	8	12	28	47	65
1269-Rawhide (TV)-Clint Eastwood photo-c	12	24	36	84	185	285
1270-Bullwinkle and Rocky (#1) (TV) (Jay Ward) (3-5/62)	16	32	48	110	243	375
1271-Yogi Bear Birthday Party (TV) (Hanna-Barbera) (11/61) (Given away for 1 box top from Kellogg's Corn Flakes)	5	10	15	35	63	90
1272-Frosty the Snowman	5	10	15	31	53	75
1273-Hans Brinker (Disney-Movie)-Photo-c (2/62)	6	12	18	37	66	95
1274-Santa Claus Funnies (12/61)	6	12	18	37	66	95
1275-Rocky and His Friends (TV) (Jay Ward)	16	32	48	107	236	365
1276-Dondi	4	8	12	23	37	50
1278-King Leonardo and His Short Subjects (TV)	10	20	30	67	141	215
1279-Grandma Duck's Farm Friends (Disney)	5	10	15	30	50	70
1280-Hennesey (TV)-Photo-c	6	12	18	37	66	95
1281-Chilly Willy (Lantz) (4-6/62)	5	10	15	30	50	70
1282-Babes in Toyland (Disney-Movie) (1/62); Annette Funicello photo-c	12	24	36	81	176	270
1283-Bonanza (TV) (2-4/62)-Photo-c	15	30	45	100	220	340
1284-Laramie (TV)-Heath-a; photo-c	6	12	18	37	66	95
1285-Leave It to Beaver (TV)-Photo-c	11	22	33	76	163	250
1286-The Untouchables (TV)-Photo-c	12	24	36	80	173	265
1287-Man from Wells Fargo (TV)-Photo-c	5	10	15	33	57	80
1288-Twilight Zone (TV) (4/62)-Crandall/Evans-c/a	10	20	30	69	147	225
1289-Ellery Queen	7	14	21	48	89	130
1290-M.G.M.'s Mouse Musketeers	4	8	12	25	40	55
1291-77 Sunset Strip (TV)-Manning-a; photo-c	7	14	21	46	86	125
1293-Elmer Fudd (3-5/62)	4	8	12	28	47	65

Four Color Comics #1289 © DELL

Four Favorites #3 © ACE

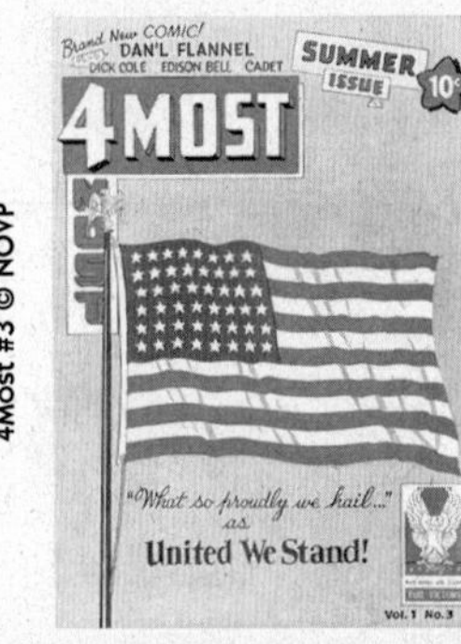

4Most #3 © NOVP

	GD 2.0	VG 4.0	FN 6.0	VF 8.0	VF/NM 9.0	NM- 9.2
1294-Ripcord (TV)	6	12	18	40	73	105
1295-Mister Ed, the Talking Horse (#1) (TV) (3-5/62)-Photo-c	10	20	30	69	147	225
1296-Fury (TV) (3-5/62)-Photo-c	5	10	15	35	63	90
1297-Spanky, Alfalfa and the Little Rascals (TV)	5	10	15	30	50	70
1298-The Hathaways (TV)-Photo-c	4	8	12	28	47	65
1299-Deputy Dawg (TV)	9	18	27	63	129	195
1300-The Comancheros (Movie) (1961)-John Wayne photo-c	13	26	39	86	188	290
1301-Adventures in Paradise (TV) (2-4/62)	5	10	15	34	60	85
1302-Johnny Jason, Teen Reporter (2-4/62)	4	8	12	23	37	50
1303-Lad: A Dog (Movie)-Photo-c	4	8	12	28	47	65
1304-Nellie the Nurse (3-5/62)-Stanley-a	6	12	18	41	76	110
1305-Mister Magoo (3-5/62)	7	14	21	48	89	130
1306-Target: The Corruptors (#1) (TV) (3-5/62)-Photo-c	5	10	15	33	57	80
1307-Margie (TV) (3-5/62)	5	10	15	34	60	85
1308-Tales of the Wizard of Oz (TV) (3-5/62)	10	20	30	66	138	210
1309-87th Precinct (#1) (TV) (4-6/62)-Krigstein-a; photo-c	9	18	27	57	111	165
1310-Huck and Yogi Winter Sports (TV) (Hanna-Barbera) (3/62)	7	14	21	49	92	135
1311-Rocky and His Friends (TV) (Jay Ward)	16	32	48	107	236	365
1312-National Velvet (TV)-Photo-c	4	8	12	27	44	60
1313-Moon Pilot (Disney-Movie)-Photo-c	6	12	18	40	73	105
1328-The Underwater City (Movie) (1961)-Evans-a; photo-c	6	12	18	41	76	110
1329-See Gyro Gearloose #01329-207						
1330-Brain Boy (#1)-Gil Kane-a	10	20	30	64	132	200
1332-Bachelor Father (TV)	6	12	18	42	79	115
1333-Short Ribs (4-6/62)	5	10	15	33	57	80
1335-Aggie Mack (4-6/62)	4	8	12	28	47	65
1336-On Stage; not by Leonard Starr	5	10	15	30	50	70
1337-Dr. Kildare (#1) (TV) (4-6/62)-Photo-c	7	14	21	49	92	135
1341-The Andy Griffith Show (TV) (4-6/62)-Photo-c	30	60	90	216	483	750
1348-Yak Yak (#2)-Jack Davis-c/a	7	14	21	46	86	125
1349-Yogi Bear Visits the U.N. (TV) (Hanna-Barbera) (1/62)-Photo-c	7	14	21	49	92	135
1350-Comanche (Disney-Movie)(1962)-Reprints 4-Color #966 (title change from "Tonka" to "Comanche") (4-6/62)-Sal Mineo photo-c	5	10	15	31	53	75
1354-Calvin & the Colonel (#1) (TV) (4-6/62)	8	16	24	51	96	140

NOTE: *Missing numbers probably do not exist.*

4-D MONKEY, THE (Adventures of... #? on)
Leung's Publications: 1988 - No. 11, 1990 ($1.80/$2.00, 52 pgs.)

1-11: 1-Karate Pig, Ninja Flounder & 4-D Monkey (48 pgs., centerfold is a Christmas card). 2-4 (52 pgs.) 4.00

FOUR FAVORITES (Crime Must Pay the Penalty No. 33 on)
Ace Magazines: Sept, 1941 - No. 32, Dec, 1947

	GD	VG	FN	VF	VF/NM	NM-
1-Vulcan, Lash Lightning (formerly Flash Lightning in Sure-Fire), Magno the Magnetic Man & The Raven begin; flag/Hitler-c	219	438	657	1402	2401	3400
2-The Black Ace only app.	74	148	222	470	810	1150
3-Last Vulcan	61	122	183	390	670	950
4,5: 4-The Raven & Vulcan end; Unknown Soldier begins (see Our Flag), ends #28. 5-Captain Courageous begins (5/42), ends #28 (moves over from Captain Courageous #6); not in #6	55	110	165	352	601	850
6-8: 6-The Flag app.; Mr. Risk begins (7/42)	53	106	159	334	567	800
9-Kurtzman-a (Lash Lightning); robot-c	58	116	174	371	636	900
10-Classic Kurtzman-c/a (Magno & Davey)	81	162	243	518	884	1250
11-Kurtzman-a; Hitler, Mussolini, Hirohito-c; L.B. Cole-a; Unknown Soldier by Kurtzman	129	258	387	826	1413	2000
12-L.B. Cole-a	52	104	156	328	552	775
13-L.B. Cole-c (his first cover?)	84	168	252	538	919	1300
14-20: 18,20-Palais-c/a	41	82	123	256	428	600
21-No Unknown Soldier; The Unknown app.	34	68	102	199	325	450
22-26: 22-Captain Courageous drops costume. 23-Unknown Soldier drops costume. 25-29-Hap Hazard app. 26-Last Magno	32	64	96	188	307	425
27-29: Hap Hazard app. in all	22	44	66	132	216	300
30-32: 30-Funny-c begin (teen humor), end #32	15	30	45	88	137	185

NOTE: ***Dave Berg** c-5. **Jim Mooney** a-6; c-1-3. **Palais** a-18-20; c-18-25. Torture chamber c-5.*

FOUR HORSEMEN, THE (See The Crusaders)

FOUR HORSEMEN
DC Comics (Vertigo): Feb, 2000 - No. 4, May, 2000 ($2.50, limited series)

1-4-Esad Ribic-c/a; Robert Rodi-s 3.00

FOUR HORSEMEN OF THE APOCALYPSE, THE (Movie)
Dell Publishing Co.: No. 1250, Jan-Mar, 1962 (one-shot)

	GD	VG	FN	VF	VF/NM	NM-
Four Color 1250-Photo-c	6	12	18	37	66	95

4MOST (Foremost Boys No. 32-40; becomes Thrilling Crime Cases #41 on)
Novelty Publications/Star Publications No. 37-on:
Winter, 1941-42 - V8#5(#36), 9-10/49; #37, 11-12/49 - #40, 4-5/50

	GD	VG	FN	VF	VF/NM	NM-
V1#1-The Target by Sid Greene, The Cadet & Dick Cole begin with origins retold; produced by Funnies Inc.; quarterly issues begin, end V6#3; German WWII-c	168	336	504	1075	1838	2600
2-Last Target (Spr/42); WWII cover	66	132	198	419	722	1025
3-Dan'l Flannel begins; flag-c	49	98	147	309	522	735
4-1pg. Dr. Seuss (signed) (Aut/42); fish in the face-c	52	104	156	328	552	775
V2#1-3	20	40	60	118	192	265
4-Hitler, Tojo & Mussolini app. as pumpkins on-c	48	96	144	302	514	725
V3#1-4	15	30	45	90	140	190
V4#1-4: 2-Walter Johnson-c	14	28	42	76	108	140
V5#1-4: 1-The Target & Targeteers app.	11	22	33	64	90	115
V6#1-4	10	20	30	56	76	95
5-L. B. Cole-c	20	40	60	114	182	250
V7#1,3,5, V8#1, 37	10	20	30	56	76	95
2,4,6-L. B. Cole-c. 6-Last Dick Cole	20	40	60	114	182	250
V8#2,3,5-L. B. Cole-c/a	22	44	66	132	216	300
4-L. B. Cole-a	15	30	45	83	124	165
38-40: 38-Johnny Weismuller (Tarzan) life story & Jim Braddock (boxer) life story. 38-40-L.B. Cole-c. 40-Last White Rider	17	34	51	98	154	210
Accepted Reprint 38-40 (nd): 40-r/Johnny Weismuller life story; all have L.B. Cole-c	10	20	30	56	76	95

411
Marvel Comics: June, 2003 - No. 3 ($3.50, limited series)

1,2-Tributes to peacemakers; s/a by various. 1-Millar, Quitely, Mack, Winslade & others-s/a. 2-Harris, Phillips, Manco, Bruce Jones. 3.50

FOUR-STAR BATTLE TALES
National Periodical Publications: Feb-Mar, 1973 - No. 5, Nov-Dec, 1973

	GD	VG	FN	VF	VF/NM	NM-
1-Reprints begin	3	6	9	16	24	32
2-5	2	4	6	11	16	20

NOTE: ***Drucker** r-1, 3-5. **Heath** r-2, 5; c-1. **Krigstein** r-5. **Kubert** r-4; c-2.*

FOUR STAR SPECTACULAR
National Periodical Publications: Mar-Apr, 1976 - No. 6, Jan-Feb, 1977

	GD	VG	FN	VF	VF/NM	NM-
1-Includes G.A. Flash story with new art	2	4	6	11	16	20
2-6: Reprints in all. 2-Infinity cover	2	4	6	8	10	12

NOTE: *All contain DC Superhero reprints. #1 has 68 pgs.; #2-6, 52 pgs.. #1, 4-Hawkman app.; #2-Kid Flash app.; #3-Green Lantern app; #2, 4, 5-Wonder Woman, Superboy app; #5-Green Arrow, Vigilante app; #6-Blackhawk G.A.-r.*

FOUR TEENERS (Formerly Crime Must Pay The Penalty; Dotty No. 35 on)
A. A. Wyn: No. 34, April, 1948 (52 pgs.)

	GD	VG	FN	VF	VF/NM	NM-
34-Teen-age comic; Dotty app.; Curly & Jerry continue from Four Favorites	11	22	33	64	90	115

FOURTH WORLD GALLERY, THE (Jack Kirby's...)
DC Comics: 1996 (9/96) ($3.50, one-shot)

nn-Pin-ups of Jack Kirby's Fourth World characters (New Gods, Forever People & Mister Miracle) by John Byrne, Rick Burchett, Dan Jurgens, Walt Simonson & others 4.00

FOUR WOMEN
DC Comics (Homage): Dec, 2001 - No. 5, Apr, 2002 ($2.95, limited series)

1-5-Sam Kieth-s/a 3.00
TPB (2002, $17.95) r/series; foreward by Kieth 18.00

FOX, THE
Archie Comic Publication (Red Circle Comics): Dec, 2013 - No. 5, Apr, 2014 ($2.99)

1-5-Dean Haspiel-a/Haspiel and Mark Waid-s. 1-Three covers. 2-Two covers 3.00

FOX AND THE CROW (Stanley & His Monster No. 109 on) (See Comic Cavalcade & Real Screen Comics)
National Periodical Publications: Dec-Jan, 1951-52 - No. 108, Feb-Mar, 1968

	GD	VG	FN	VF	VF/NM	NM-
1	127	254	381	807	1391	1975
2(Scarce)	56	112	168	356	611	865
3-5	37	74	111	222	361	500
6-10	26	52	78	154	252	350
11-20	20	40	60	114	182	250

Fox and the Crow #89 © DC

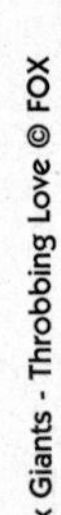
Fox Giants - Throbbing Love © FOX

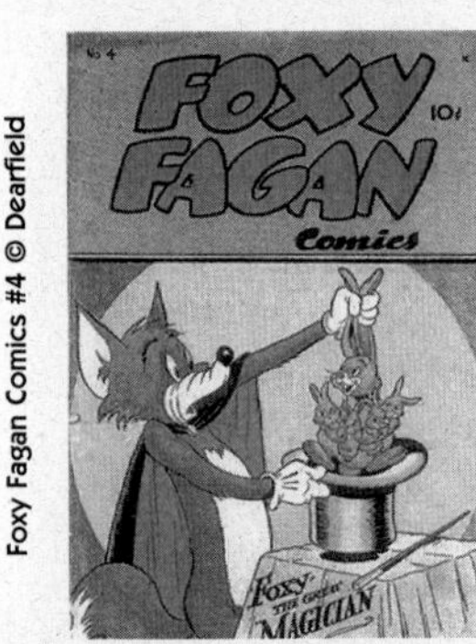

Foxy Fagan Comics #4 © Dearfield

	GD 2.0	VG 4.0	FN 6.0	VF 8.0	VF/NM 9.0	NM- 9.2
21-30: 22-Last precode issue (2/55)	15	30	45	83	124	165
31-40	12	24	36	69	97	125
41-60	6	12	18	37	66	95
61-80	5	10	15	31	53	75
81-94: 94-(11/65)-The Brat Finks begin	4	8	12	25	40	55
95-Stanley & His Monster begins (origin & 1st app)	5	10	15	33	57	80
96-99,101-108	3	6	9	19	30	40
100 (10-11/66)	3	6	9	21	33	45

NOTE: *Many later covers by* ***Mort Drucker.***

FOX AND THE HOUND, THE (Disney)(Movie)
Whitman Publishing Co.: Aug, 1981 - No. 3, Oct, 1981

	GD	VG	FN	VF	VF/NM	NM-
11292- Golden Press Graphic Novel	2	4	6	8	10	12
1-3-Based on animated movie	1	2	3	5	7	9

FOXFIRE (See The Phoenix Resurrection)
Malibu Comics (Ultraverse): Feb, 1996 - No. 4, May, 1996 ($1.50)

	GD	VG	FN	VF	VF/NM	NM-
1-4: Sludge, Ultraforce app. 4-Punisher app.						3.00

FOX GIANTS (Also see Giant Comics Edition)
Fox Features Syndicate: 1944 - 1950 (25¢, 132 - 196 pgs.)

	GD	VG	FN	VF	VF/NM	NM-
Album of Crime nn(1949, 132p)	57	114	171	362	619	875
Album of Love nn(1949, 132p)	57	114	171	362	619	875
All Famous Crime Stories nn('49, 132p)	57	114	171	362	619	875
All Good Comics 1(1944, 132p)(R.W. Voigt)-The Bouncer, Purple Tigress,Rick Evans, Puppeteer, Green Mask; Infinity-c	65	130	195	416	708	1000
All Great nn(1944, 132p)-Capt. Jack Terry, Rick Evans, Jaguar Man	47	94	141	296	498	700
All Great nn(Chicago Nite Life News)(1945, 132p)-Green Mask, Bouncer, Puppeteer, Rick Evans, Rocket Kelly	45	90	135	284	480	675
All-Great Confession Magazine nn(1949, 132p)	57	114	171	362	619	875
All-Great Confessions nn(1949, 132p)	57	114	171	362	619	875
All Great Crime Stories nn('49, 132p)	57	114	171	362	619	875
All Great Jungle Adventures nn('49, 132p)	65	130	195	416	708	1000
All Real Confession Magazine 3 (3/49, 132p)	55	110	165	352	601	850
All Real Confession Magazine 4 (4/49, 132p)	55	110	165	352	601	850
All Your Comics 1(1944, 132p)-The Puppeteer, Red Robbins, & Merciless the Sorcerer	47	94	141	296	498	700
Almanac Of Crime nn(1948, 148p)-Phantom Lady	65	130	195	416	708	1000
Almanac Of Crime 1(1950, 132p)	55	110	165	352	601	850
Book Of Love nn(1950, 132p)	54	108	162	343	574	825
Burning Romances 1(1949, 132p)	61	122	183	390	670	950
Crimes Incorporated nn(1950, 132p)	53	106	159	334	567	800
Daring Love Stories nn(1950, 132p)	54	108	162	343	574	825
Everybody's Comics 1(1944, 50¢, 196p)-The Green Mask, The Puppeteer, The Bouncer, Rocket Kelly, Rick Evans	58	116	174	371	636	900
Everybody's Comics 1(1946, 196p)-Green Lama, The Puppeteer	47	94	141	296	498	700
Everybody's Comics 1(1946, 196p)-Same as 1945 Ribtickler	37	74	111	222	361	500
Everybody's Comics nn(1947, 132p)-Jo-Jo, Purple Tigress, Cosmo Cat, Bronze Man	47	94	141	296	498	700
Exciting Romance Stories nn(1949, 132p)	57	114	171	362	619	875
Famous Love nn(1950, 132p)-Photo-c	55	110	165	352	601	850
Intimate Confessions nn(1950, 132p)	54	108	162	343	574	825
Journal Of Crime nn(1949, 132p)	57	114	171	362	619	875
Love Problems nn(1949, 132p)	57	114	171	362	619	875
Love Thrills nn(1950, 132p)	54	108	162	343	574	825
March of Crime nn('48, 132p)-Female w/rifle-c	58	116	174	371	636	900
March of Crime nn('49, 132p)-Cop w/pistol-c	54	108	162	343	574	825
March of Crime nn(1949, 132p)-Coffin & man w/machine-gun-c	54	108	162	343	574	825
Revealing Love Stories nn(1950, 132p)	54	108	162	343	574	825
Ribtickler nn(1945, 50¢, 196p)-Chicago Nite Life News; Marvel Mutt, Cosmo Cat, Flash Rabbit, The Nebbs app.	42	84	126	265	445	625
Romantic Thrills nn(1950, 132p)	54	108	162	343	574	825
Secret Love Stories nn(1949, 132p)	57	114	171	362	619	875
Strange Love nn(1950, 132p)-Photo-c	68	136	204	435	743	1050
Sweetheart Scandals nn(1950, 132p)	54	108	162	343	574	825
Teen-Age Love nn(1950, 132p)	54	108	162	343	574	825
Throbbing Love nn(1950, 132p)-Photo-c; used in **POP**, pg. 107	68	136	204	435	743	1050
Truth About Crime nn(1949, 132p)	57	114	171	362	619	875
Variety Comics 1(1946, 132p)-Blue Beetle, Jungle Jo	48	96	144	302	514	725
Variety Comics nn(1950, 132p)-Jungle Jo, My Secret Affair (w/Harrison/Wood-a), Crimes by Women & My Story	45	90	135	284	480	675
Western Roundup nn('50, 132p)-Hoot Gibson; Cody of the Pony Express app.	41	82	123	256	428	600

NOTE: *Each of the above usually contain four remaindered Fox books minus covers. Since these missing covers often had the first page of the first story, most Giants therefore are incomplete. Approximate values are listed. Books with appearances of Phantom Lady, Rulah, Jo-Jo, etc. could bring more.*

FOXHOLE (Becomes Never Again #8?)
Mainline/Charlton No. 5 on: 9-10/54 - No. 4, 3-4/55; No. 5, 7/55 - No. 7, 3/56

	GD	VG	FN	VF	VF/NM	NM-
1-Classic Kirby-c	57	114	171	362	619	875
2-Kirby-c/a(2); Kirby scripts based on his war time experiences	39	78	117	240	395	550
3-5-Simon/Kirby-c only	26	52	78	154	252	350
6-Kirby-c/a(2)	36	72	108	211	343	475
7-Simon & Kirby-c	15	30	45	83	124	165
Super Reprints #10,15-17: 10-r/? 15,16-r/United States Marines #5,8. 17-r/Monty Hall #?	2	4	6	11	16	20
11,12,18-r/Foxhole #1,2,3; Kirby-c	3	6	9	17	26	35

NOTE: ***Kirby*** *a(r)-Super #11, 12.* ***Powell*** *a(r)-Super #15, 16. Stories by actual veterans.*

FOXY FAGAN COMICS (Funny Animal)
Dearfield Publishing Co.: Dec, 1946 - No. 7, Summer, 1948

	GD	VG	FN	VF	VF/NM	NM-
1-Foxy Fagan & Little Buck begin	13	26	39	74	105	135
2	8	16	24	42	54	65
3-7: 6-Rocket ship-c	7	14	21	37	46	55

FRACTION
DC Comics (Focus): June, 2004 - No. 6, Nov, 2004 ($2.50, limited series)

	GD	VG	FN	VF	VF/NM	NM-
1-6-David Tischman-s/Timothy Green II-a						3.00
SC (2011, $17.99) r/#1-6; cover gallery						18.00

FRACTURED FAIRY TALES (TV)
Gold Key: Oct, 1962 (Jay Ward)

	GD	VG	FN	VF	VF/NM	NM-
1 (10022-210)-From Bullwinkle TV show	9	18	27	60	120	180

FRAGGLE ROCK (TV)
Marvel Comics (Star Comics)/Marvel V2#1 on: Apr, 1985 - No. 8, Sept, 1986; V2#1, Apr, 1988 - No. 5, Aug, 1988

	GD	VG	FN	VF	VF/NM	NM-
1-6 (75¢-c)						5.00
7,8						6.00
V2#1-5-($1.00): Reprints 1st series						3.00

FRANCIS, BROTHER OF THE UNIVERSE
Marvel Comics Group: 1980 (75¢, 52 pgs., one-shot)

	GD	VG	FN	VF	VF/NM	NM-
nn-John Buscema/Marie Severin-a; story of Francis Bernadone, celebrating his 800th birthday in 1982						6.00

FRANCIS THE FAMOUS TALKING MULE (All based on movie)
Dell Publishing Co.: No. 335 (#1), June, 1951 - No. 1090, March, 1960

	GD	VG	FN	VF	VF/NM	NM-
Four Color 335 (#1)	9	18	27	62	126	190
Four Color 465	6	12	18	37	66	95
Four Color 501,547,579	5	10	15	31	53	75
Four Color 621,655,698,710,745	4	8	12	28	47	65
Four Color 810,863,906,953,991,1068,1090	4	8	12	27	44	60

FRANK
Nemesis Comics (Harvey): Apr (Mar inside), 1994 - No. 4, 1994 ($1.75/$2.50, limited series)

	GD	VG	FN	VF	VF/NM	NM-
1-4-($2.50, direct sale): 1-Foil-c Edition						3.50
1-4-($1.75)-Newsstand Editions; Cowan-a in all						3.00

FRANK
Fantagraphics Books: Sept, 1996 ($2.95, B&W)

	GD	VG	FN	VF	VF/NM	NM-
1-Woodring-c/a/scripts						3.00

FRANK BUCK (Formerly My True Love)
Fox Features Syndicate: No. 70, May, 1950 - No. 3, Sept, 1950

	GD	VG	FN	VF	VF/NM	NM-
70-Wood a(p)(3 stories)-Photo-c	36	72	108	211	343	475
71-Wood-a (9 pgs.); photo/painted-c	19	38	57	109	172	235
3: 3-Photo/painted-c	14	28	42	82	121	160

NOTE: *Based on "Bring 'Em Back Alive" TV show.*

FRANKEN-CASTLE (See The Punisher, 2009 series)

FRANKENSTEIN (See Dracula, Movie Classics & Werewolf)
Dell Publishing Co.: Aug-Oct, 1964; No. 2, Sept, 1966 - No. 4, Mar, 1967

	GD	VG	FN	VF	VF/NM	NM-
1(12-283-410)(1964)(2nd printing; see Movie Classics for 1st printing)	5	10	15	31	53	75
2-Intro. & origin super-hero character (9/66)	4	8	12	28	47	65
3,4	3	6	9	21	33	45

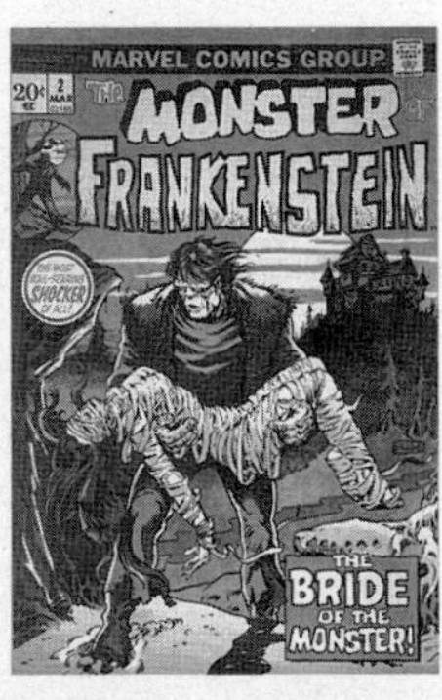

Frankenstein #2 © MAR

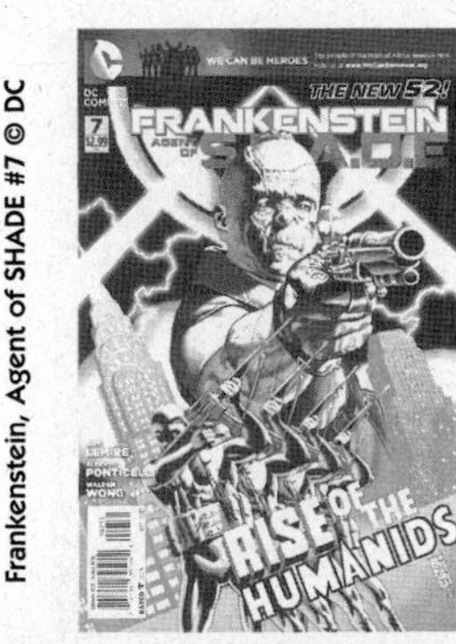

Frankenstein, Agent of SHADE #7 © DC

Fray #1 © Joss Whedon

	GD 2.0	VG 4.0	FN 6.0	VF 8.0	VF/NM 9.0	NM- 9.2

	GD 2.0	VG 4.0	FN 6.0	VF 8.0	VF/NM 9.0	NM- 9.2

FRANKENSTEIN (The Monster of...; also see Monsters Unleashed #2, Power Record Comics, Psycho & Silver Surfer #7)
Marvel Comics Group: Jan, 1973 - No. 18, Sept, 1975

	GD	VG	FN	VF	VF/NM	NM-
1-Ploog-c/a begins, ends #6	7	14	21	46	86	125
2	4	8	12	27	44	60
3-5	3	6	9	21	33	45
6,7,10: 7-Dracula cameo	3	6	9	17	26	35
8,9-Dracula c/sty. 9-Death of Dracula	4	8	12	28	47	65
11-17	3	6	9	15	22	28
18-Wrightson-c(i)	3	6	9	16	24	32

NOTE: ***Adkins** c-17i. **Buscema** a-7-10p. **Ditko** a-12r. **G. Kane** c-15p. **Orlando** a-8r. **Ploog** a-1-3, 4p, 5p, 6; c-1-6. **Wrightson** c-18i.*

FRANKENSTEIN (Mary Wollstonecraft Shelley's...; A Marvel Illustrated Novel)
Marvel Pub.: 1983 ($8.95, B&W, 196 pgs., 8x11" TPB)

	GD	VG	FN	VF	VF/NM	NM-
nn-Wrightson-a; 4 pg. intro. by Stephen King	5	10	15	30	50	70
Limited HC Edition						175.00

FRANKENSTEIN, AGENT OF S.H.A.D.E. (New DC 52)
DC Comics: Nov, 2011 - No. 16, Mar, 2013 ($2.99)

	GD	VG	FN	VF	VF/NM	NM-
1-16: 1-Lemire-s/Ponticelli-a/J.G. Jones-c; Ray Palmer & The Creature Commandos app. 5-Crossover with OMAC #5. 13-15-Rotworld						3.00
#0 (11/12, $2.99) Kindt-s/Ponticelli-a; Frankenstein's origin						3.00

FRANKENSTEIN ALIVE, ALIVE
IDW Publishing: May, 2012 - Present ($3.99, B&W)

	GD	VG	FN	VF	VF/NM	NM-
1,2-Niles-s/Wrightson-a; interview with creators; excerpt from M.W. Shelley writings						4.00

FRANKENSTEIN COMICS (Also See Prize Comics)
Prize Publ. (Crestwood/Feature): Sum, 1945 - V5#5(#33), Oct-Nov, 1954

	GD	VG	FN	VF	VF/NM	NM-
1-Frankenstein begins by Dick Briefer (origin); Frank Sinatra parody	161	322	483	1030	1765	2500
2	63	126	189	403	689	975
3-5	47	94	141	296	498	700
6-10: 7-S&K a(r)/Headline Comics. 8(7-8/47)-Superman satire	40	80	120	246	411	575
11-17(1-2/49)-11-Boris Karloff parody-c/story. 17-Last humor issue	37	74	111	222	361	500
18(3/52)-New origin, horror series begins	53	106	159	334	567	800
19,20(V3#4, 8-9/52)	36	72	108	211	343	475
21(V3#5), 22(V3#6), 23(V4#1) - #28(V4#6)	33	66	99	194	317	440
29(V5#1) - #33(V5#5)	32	64	96	188	307	425

NOTE: ***Briefer** c/a-all. **Meskin** a-21, 29.*

FRANKENSTEIN/DRACULA WAR, THE
Topps Comics: Feb, 1995 - No. 3, May, 1995 ($2.50, limited series)

	GD	VG	FN	VF	VF/NM	NM-
1-3						3.00

FRANKENSTEIN, JR. (...& the Impossibles) (TV)
Gold Key: Jan, 1966 (Hanna-Barbera)

	GD	VG	FN	VF	VF/NM	NM-
1-Super hero (scarce)	10	20	30	64	132	200

FRANKENSTEIN MOBSTER
Image Comics: No. 0, Oct, 2003 - No. 7, Dec, 2004 ($2.95)

	GD	VG	FN	VF	VF/NM	NM-
0-7: 0-Two covers by Wheatley and Hughes; Wheatley-s/a. 1-Variant-c by Wieringo						3.00

FRANKENSTEIN: OR THE MODERN PROMETHEUS
Caliber Press: 1994 ($2.95, one-shot)

	GD	VG	FN	VF	VF/NM	NM-
1						3.00

FRANK FRAZETTA FANTASY ILLUSTRATED (Magazine)
Quantum Cat Entertainment: Spring 1998 - No. 8 ($5.95, quarterly)

	GD	VG	FN	VF	VF/NM	NM-
1-Anthology; art by Corben, Horley, Jusko	1	2	3	4	5	7
1-Linsner variant-c						10.00
2-Battle Chasers by Madureira; Harris-a						8.00
2-Madureira Battle Chasers variant-c						12.00
3-8-Frazetta-c						6.00
3-Tony Daniel variant-c						15.00
5,6-Portacio variant-c, 7,8-Alex Nino variant-c						10.00
8-Alex Ross Chicago Comicon variant-c						10.00

FRANK FRAZETTA'S DEATH DEALER
Image Comics: Mar, 2007 - No. 6, Jan, 2008 ($3.99)

	GD	VG	FN	VF	VF/NM	NM-
1-6-Nat Jones-a; 3 covers (Frazetta, Jones, Jones sketch)						4.00

FRANK FRAZETTA'S...
Fantagraphics Books/Image Comics: one-shots

	GD	VG	FN	VF	VF/NM	NM-
... Creatures 1 (Image Comics, 7/08, $3.99) Bergting-a; covers by Frazetta & Bergting						4.00
... Dark Kingdom 1-4 (Image, 4/08 - No. 4, 1/10, $3.99) Vigil-a; covers by Frazetta & Vigil						4.00
... Dracula Meets the Wolfman 1 (Image, 8/08, $3.99) Francavilla-a; 2 covers						4.00
... Moon Maid 1 (Image, 1/09, $3.99) Tim Vigil-a; covers by Frazetta & Vigil						4.00
... Neanderthal 1 (Image, 4/09, $3.99) Fotos & Vigil-a; covers by Frazetta & Fotos						4.00
... Sorcerer 1 (Image, 8/09, $3.99) Medors-a; covers by Frazetta & Medors						4.00
... Swamp Demon 1 (Image, 7/08, $3.99) Medors-a; covers by Frazetta & Medors						4.00
... Thun'da Tales 1 (Fantagraphics Books, 1987, $2.00) Frazetta-r						6.00
... Untamed Love 1 (Fantagraphics Books, 11/87, $2.00) r/1950's romance comics						6.00

FRANKIE COMICS (...& Lana No. 13-15) (Formerly Movie Tunes; becomes Frankie Fuddle No. 16 on)
Marvel Comics (MgPC): No. 4, Wint, 1946-47 - No. 15, June, 1949

	GD	VG	FN	VF	VF/NM	NM-
4-Mitzi, Margie, Daisy app.	19	38	57	111	176	240
5-9	13	26	39	74	105	135
10-15: 13-Anti-Wertham editorial	12	24	36	67	94	120

FRANKIE DOODLE (See Sparkler, both series)
United Features Syndicate: No. 7, 1939

	GD	VG	FN	VF	VF/NM	NM-
Single Series 7	34	68	102	199	325	450

FRANKIE FUDDLE (Formerly Frankie & Lana)
Marvel Comics: No. 16, Aug, 1949 - No. 17, Nov, 1949

	GD	VG	FN	VF	VF/NM	NM-
16,17	12	24	36	67	94	120

FRANKLIN RICHARDS (Fantastic Four)
Marvel Comics: April, 2006 - Present ($2.99/$3.99, one-shots)

	GD	VG	FN	VF	VF/NM	NM-
...: April Fools (6/09, $3.99) Eliopoulos-s/a						4.00
...: Collected Chaos (2008, $8.99, digest) reprints various one-shots						9.00
...: Fall Football Fiasco (1/08, $2.99) Eliopoulos-a/Sumerak-s						3.00
...: Happy Franksgiving (1/07, $2.99) Thanksgiving stories by Eliopoulos-a/Sumerak-s						3.00
...: It's Dark Reigning Cats & Dogs (4/09, $3.99) Eliopoulos-s/a						4.00
...: Lab Brat (2007, $7.99, digest) reprints one-shots and Masked Marvel back-ups						8.00
...: March Madness (5/07, $2.99) More science gone wrong by Eliopoulos-a/Sumerak-s						3.00
...: Monster Mash (11/07, $2.99) Science mishaps by Eliopoulos-a/Sumerak-s						3.00
...: Not-So-Secret Invasion (7/08, $2.99) Skrull cover; The Wizard app.						3.00
... One Shot (4/06, $2.99) short stories by Eliopoulos-a/Sumerak-s						3.00
...: School's Out (4/09, $3.99) Eliopoulos-s/a; Katie Power app.						4.00
...: Sons of Geniuses (1/09, $3.99) parallel dimension alternate version hijinks						4.00
...: Spring Break (5/08, $2.99) short stories by Eliopoulos-a/Sumerak-s						3.00
...: Summer Smackdown (10/08, $2.99) short stories by Eliopoulos-a/Sumerak-s						3.00
...: Super Summer Spectacular (9/06, $2.99) short stories by Eliopoulos-a/Sumerak-s						3.00
...: World Be Warned (8/07, $2.99) short stories by Eliopoulos-a/Sumerak-s; Hulk app.						3.00

FRANK LUTHER'S SILLY PILLY COMICS (See Jingle Dingle...)
Children's Comics (Maltex Cereal): 1950 (10¢)

	GD	VG	FN	VF	VF/NM	NM-
1-Characters from radio, records, & TV	9	18	27	50	65	80

NOTE: *Also printed as a promotional comic for Maltex cereal.*

FRANK MERRIWELL AT YALE (Speed Demons No. 5 on?)
Charlton Comics: June, 1955 - No. 4, Jan, 1956 (Also see Shadow Comics)

	GD	VG	FN	VF	VF/NM	NM-
1	7	14	21	37	46	55
2-4	5	10	15	24	30	35

FRANTIC (Magazine) (See Ratfink & Zany)
Pierce Publishing Co.: Oct, 1958 - V2#2, Apr, 1959 (Satire)

	GD	VG	FN	VF	VF/NM	NM-
V1#1	14	28	42	80	115	150
2	10	20	30	56	76	95
V2#1,2: 1-Burgos-a, Severin-c/a; Powell-a?	9	18	27	47	61	75

FRAY (Also see Buffy the Vampire Slayer "season eight" #16-19)
Dark Horse Comics: June, 2001 - No. 8, July, 2003 ($2.99, limited series)

	GD	VG	FN	VF	VF/NM	NM-
1-Joss Whedon-s/Moline & Owens-a	1	2	3	5	6	8
1-DF Gold edition	2	4	6	9	12	15
2-8: 6-(3/02). 7-(4/03)						4.00
TPB (11/03, $19.95) r/#1-8; intros by Whedon & Loeb; Moline sketch pages						20.00

FREAK FORCE (Also see Savage Dragon)
Image Comics (Highbrow Ent.): Dec, 1993 - No. 18, July, 1995 ($1.95/$2.50)

	GD	VG	FN	VF	VF/NM	NM-
1-18-Superpatriot & Mighty Man in all; Erik Larsen scripts in all. 4-Vanguard app. 8-Begin $2.50-c. 9-Cyberforce-c & app. 13-Variant-c						3.00

FREAK FORCE (Also see Savage Dragon)
Image Comics: Apr, 1997 - No. 3, July, 1997 ($2.95)

	GD	VG	FN	VF	VF/NM	NM-
1-3-Larsen-s						3.00

FREAK OUT, USA (See On the Scene Presents...)

FREAK SHOW
Image Comics (Desperado): 2006 ($5.99, B&W, one-shot)

Freckles and His Friends #5 © STD

Freedom Fighters #3 © DC

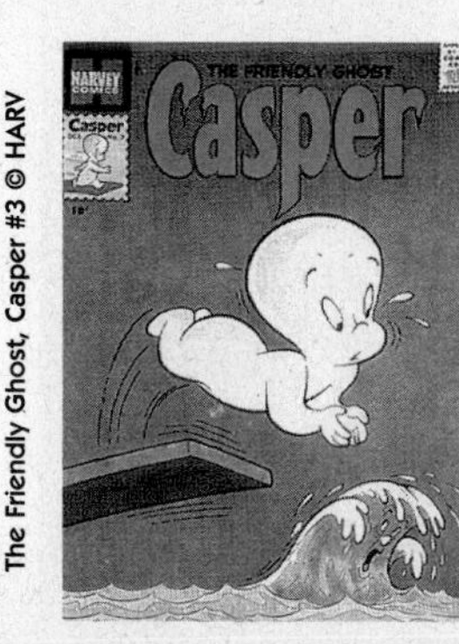

The Friendly Ghost, Casper #3 © HARV

GD 2.0 | VG 4.0 | FN 6.0 | VF 8.0 | VF/NM 9.0 | NM- 9.2

GD 2.0 | VG 4.0 | FN 6.0 | VF 8.0 | VF/NM 9.0 | NM- 9.2

nn-Bruce Jones-s/Bernie Wrightson-c/a 6.00

FREAKS OF THE HEARTLAND
Dark Horse Comics: Jan, 2004 - No. 6, Nov, 2004 ($2.99)

1-6-Steve Niles-s/Greg Ruth-a 3.00

FRECKLES AND HIS FRIENDS (See Crackajack Funnies, Famous Comics Cartoon Book, Honeybee Birdwhistle... & Red Ryder)

FRECKLES AND HIS FRIENDS
Standard Comics/Argo: No. 5, 11/47 - No. 12, 8/49; 11/55 - No. 4, 6/56

5-Reprints 9 18 27 50 65 80
6-12-Reprints. 7-9-Airbrush-c (by Schomburg?). 11-Lingerie panels
7 14 21 35 43 50

NOTE: *Some copies of No. 8 & 9 contain a printing oddity. The negatives were elongated in the engraving process, probably to conform to page dimensions on the filler pages. Those pages only look normal when viewed at a 45 degree angle.*

1(Argo,'55)-Reprints (NEA Service) 6 12 18 28 34 40
2-4 4 8 12 18 22 25

FREDDY (Formerly My Little Margie's Boy Friends) (Also see Blue Bird)
Charlton Comics: V2#12, June, 1958 - No. 47, Feb, 1965

V2#12-Teenage 3 6 9 21 33 45
13-15 3 6 9 15 22 28
16-47 2 4 6 11 16 20

FREDDY
Dell Publishing Co.: May-July, 1963 - No. 3, Oct-Dec, 1964

1 3 6 9 18 28 38
2,3 3 6 9 14 20 26

FREDDY KRUEGER'S A NIGHTMARE ON ELM STREET
Marvel Comics: Oct, 1989 - No. 2, Dec, 1989 ($2.25, B&W, movie adaptation, magazine)

1,2: Origin Freddy Krueger; Buckler/Alcala-a 1 3 4 6 8 10

FREDDY'S DEAD: THE FINAL NIGHTMARE
Innovation Publishing: Oct, 1991 - No. 3, Dec 1991 ($2.50, color mini-series, adapts movie)

1-3: Dismukes (film poster artist) painted-c 3.00

FREDDY VS. JASON VS. ASH (Freddy Krueger, Friday the 13th, Army of Darkness)
DC Comics (WildStorm): Early Jan, 2008 - No. 6, May, 2008 ($2.99, limited series)

1-Three covers by J. Scott Campbell; Kuhoric-s/Craig-a 5.00
1-Second printing with 3 covers combined sideways 4.00
2-6: 2-4-Eric Powell-c. 5,6-Richard Friend-c 4.00
2-4-Second printings with B&W covers 3.00
TPB (2008, $17.99) r/#1-6; creators' interview afterword 18.00

FREDDY VS. JASON VS. ASH: THE NIGHTMARE WARRIORS
DC Comics (WildStorm): Aug, 2009 - No. 6, Jan, 2010 ($3.99, limited series)

1-6-Katz & Kuhoric-s/Craig-a. 1-Suydam-c 4.00
TPB (2010, $17.99) r/#1-6; cover gallery 18.00

FRED HEMBECK DESTROYS THE MARVEL UNIVERSE
Marvel Comics: July, 1989 ($1.50, one-shot)

1-Punisher app.; Staton-i (5 pgs.) 4.00

FRED HEMBECK SELLS THE MARVEL UNIVERSE
Marvel Comics: Oct, 1990 ($1.25, one-shot)

1-Punisher, Wolverine parodies; Hembeck/Austin-c 4.00

FREE COMIC BOOK DAY
Various publishers

2013 (Avengers/Hulk)(Marvel, 5/13) Hulk and Avengers Assemble animated series 3.00
...: R.I.P.D. and The True Lives of the Fabulous Killjoys (Dark Horse, 5/13) Flipbook with Mass Effect 3.00

FREEDOM AGENT (Also see John Steele)
Gold Key: Apr, 1963 (12¢)

1 (10054-304)-Painted-c 4 8 12 25 40 55

FREEDOM FIGHTERS (See Justice League of America #107,108)
National Periodical Publ./DC Comics: Mar-Apr, 1976 - No. 15, July-Aug, 1978

1-Uncle Sam, The Ray, Black Condor, Doll Man, Human Bomb, & Phantom Lady begin (all former Quality characters) 3 6 9 14 19 24
2-9: 4,5-Wonder Woman x-over. 7-1st app. Crusaders 2 4 6 9 12 15
10-15: 10-Origin Doll Man; Cat-Man-c/story (4th app; 1st revival since Detective #325). 11-Origin The Ray. 12-Origin Firebrand. 13-Origin Black Condor. 14-Batgirl & Batwoman app. 15-Batgirl & Batwoman app.; origin Phantom Lady
2 4 6 9 13 16

NOTE: ***Buckler** c-5-11p, 13p, 14p.*

FREEDOM FIGHTERS (Also see "Uncle Sam and the Freedom Fighters")
DC Comics: Nov, 2010 - No. 9, Jul, 2011 ($2.99)

1-9-Travis Moore-a. 1-6-Dave Johnson-c 3.00

FREEDOM FORCE
Image Comics: Jan, 2005 - No. 6, June, 2005 ($2.95)

1-6-Eric Dieter-s/Tom Scioli-a 3.00

FREELANCERS
BOOM! Studios: Oct, 2012 - No. 6, Mar, 2013 ($1.00/$3.99)

1-($1.00) Brill-s/Covey-a; eight covers; back-up origin of Valerie & Cassie 3.00
2-6-($3.99) Multiple covers on each 4.00

FREEMIND
Future Comics: No. 0, Aug, 2002; Nov, 2002 - No. 7, June, 2003 ($3.50)

0-($2.25) Two covers by Giordano & Layton 3.00
1-7 ($3.50) 1-Two covers by Giordano & Layton; Giordano-a thru #3. 4,5-Leeke-a 3.50

FREEREALMS
DC Comics (WildStorm): Sept, 2009 - No. 12, Oct, 2010 ($3.99, limited series)

1-12-Based on the online game; Jon Buran-a 4.00
... Book One TPB (2010, $19.99) r/#1-6 20.00
... Book Two TPB (2010, $19.99) r/#7-12 20.00

FREEX
Malibu Comics (Ultraverse): July, 1993 - No. 18, Mar, 1995 ($1.95)

1-3,5-14,16-18: 1-Polybagged w/trading card. 2-Some were polybagged w/card. 6-Nightman-c/story. 7-2 pg. origin Hardcase by Zeck. 17-Rune app. 3.00
1-Holographic-c edition 8.00
1-Ultra 5,000 limited silver ink-c 5.00
4-($2.50, 48 pgs.)-Rune flip-c/story by B. Smith (3 pgs.); 3 pg. Night Man preview 4.00
15 ($3.50)-w/Ultraverse Premiere #9 flip book; Alec Swan & Rafferty app. 4.00
Giant Size 1 (1994, $2.50)-Prime app. 4.00

NOTE: ***Simonson** c-1.*

FRENEMY OF THE STATE
Oni Press: May, 2010 - No. 5, Dec, 2011 ($3.99)

1-5-Rashida Jones, Christina Weir & Nunzio DeFilippis-s 4.00

FRENZY (Magazine) (Satire)
Picture Magazine: Apr, 1958 - No. 6, Mar, 1959

1-Painted-c 13 26 39 74 105 135
2-6 8 16 24 44 57 70

FRESHMEN
Image Comics: Jul, 2005 - No. 6, Mar, 2006 ($2.99)

1-Sterbakov-s/Kirk-a; co-created by Seth Green; covers by Pérez, Migliari, Linsner 3.00
2-6-Migliari-c 3.00
... Yearbook (1/06, $2.99) profile pages of characters; art by various incl. Chaykin, Kirk 3.00
... Vol. 1 (3/06, $16.99, TPB) r/#1-6 & Yearbook; cover gallery with concept art 17.00

FRESHMEN (Volume 2)
Image Comics: Nov, 2006 - No. 6, Aug, 2007 ($2.99)

1-6: 1-Sterbakov-s/Conrad-a; 4 covers 3.00
...: Summer Vacation Special (7/08, $4.99) Sterbakov-s; bonus pin-ups by various 5.00
... Vol. 2 Fundamentals of Fear (6/07, $16.99, TPB) r/#1-6; cover gallery, journals 17.00

FRIDAY FOSTER
Dell Publishing Co.: October, 1972

1 4 8 12 25 40 55

FRIDAY THE 13TH (Based on the horror movie franchise)
DC Comics (WildStorm): Feb, 2007 - No. 6, July, 2007 ($2.99, mature)

1-6: 1-Two covers by Sook and Bradstreet; Gray & Palmiotti-s 3.00
...: Abuser and The Abused (6/08, $3.50) Fialkov-s/Andy B. -a 3.50
...: Bad Land 1,2 (3/08 - No. 2, 4/08, $2.99) Marz-s/Huddleston-a/McKone-c 3.00
...: How I Spent My Summer Vacation 1,2 (11/07 - No. 2, 12/07, $2.99) Aaron-s/Archer-a 3.00
...: Pamela's Tale 1,2 (9/07 - No. 2, 10/07, $2.99) Andreyko-s/Moll-a/Nguyen-c 3.00

FRIENDLY GHOST, CASPER, THE (Becomes Casper... #254 on)
Harvey Publications: Aug, 1958 - No. 224, Oct, 1982; No. 225, Oct, 1986 - No. 253, June, 1990

1-Infinity-c 46 92 138 340 770 1200
2 18 36 54 124 275 425
3-6: 6-X-Mas-c 10 20 30 66 138 210
7-10 8 16 24 56 108 160
11-20: 18-X-Mas-c 7 14 21 46 86 125
21-30 5 10 15 31 53 75
31-50 4 8 12 23 37 50

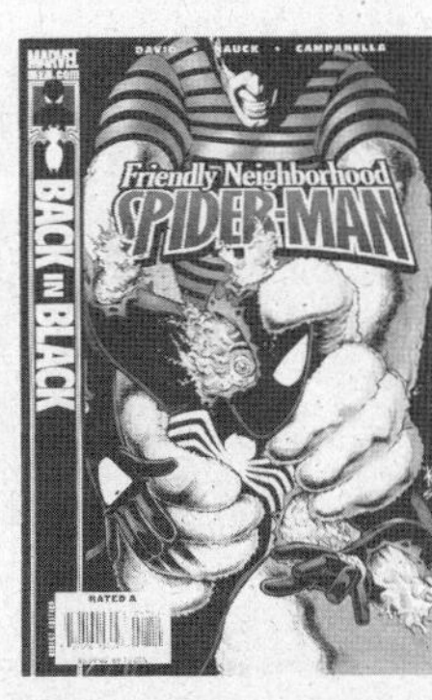

Friendly Neighborhood Spider-Man #17 © MAR

Frisky Fables V3 #6 © STAR

Frogman Comics #5 © HILL

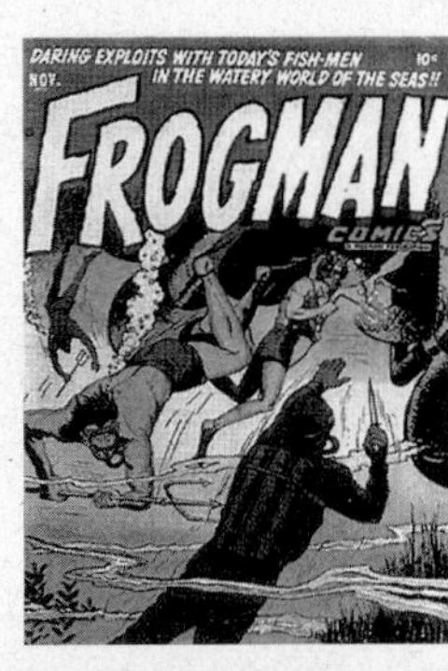

	GD 2.0	VG 4.0	FN 6.0	VF 8.0	VF/NM 9.0	NM- 9.2
51-70,100: 54-X-Mas-c	3	6	9	19	30	40
71-99	3	6	9	16	23	30
101-131: 131-Last 12¢ issue	3	6	9	14	20	26
132-159	2	4	6	11	16	20
160-163: All 52 pg. Giants	3	6	9	14	20	26
164-199: 173,179,185-Cub Scout Specials	2	4	6	8	10	12
200	2	4	6	8	11	14
201-224	1	2	3	5	7	9
225-237: 230-X-mas-c. 232-Valentine's-c						5.00
238-253: 238-Begin $1.00-c. 238,244-Halloween-c. 243-Last new material						4.00

FRIENDLY NEIGHBORHOOD SPIDER-MAN
Marvel Comics: Dec, 2005 - No. 24, Nov, 2007 ($2.99)

	GD 2.0	VG 4.0	FN 6.0	VF 8.0	VF/NM 9.0	NM- 9.2
1-Evolve or Die pt. 1; Peter David-s/Mike Wieringo-a; Morlun app.						4.00
1-Variant Wieringo-c with regular costume						5.00
2-4: 2-New Avengers app. 3-Spider-Man dies						3.00
2-4-var-c: 2-Bag-Head Fantastic Four costume. 3-Captain Universe. 4-Wrestler						5.00
5-10: 6-Red & gold costume. 8-10-Uncle Ben app.						3.00
11-23: 17-Black costume; Sandman app.						3.00
24-($3.99) "One More Day" part 2; Quesada-a; covers by Quesada & Djurdjevic						4.00
Annual 1 (7/07, $3.99) Origin of The Sandman; back-up w/Doran-a						4.00
... Vol. 1: Derailed (2006, $14.99) r/#5-10; Wieringo sketch pages						15.00
... Vol. 2: Mystery Date (2007, $13.99) r/#11-16						14.00

FRIENDS OF MAXX (Also see Maxx)
Image Comics (I Before E): Apr, 1996 - No. 3, Mar, 1997 ($2.95)

	GD 2.0	VG 4.0	FN 6.0	VF 8.0	VF/NM 9.0	NM- 9.2
1-3: Sam Kieth-c/a/scripts. 1-Featuring Dude Japan						3.00

FRIGHT
Atlas/Seaboard Periodicals: June, 1975 (Aug. on inside)

	GD 2.0	VG 4.0	FN 6.0	VF 8.0	VF/NM 9.0	NM- 9.2
1-Origin/1st app. The Son of Dracula; Frank Thorne-c/a	3	6	9	14	19	24

FRIGHT NIGHT
Now Comics: Oct, 1988 - No. 22, 1990 ($1.75)

	GD 2.0	VG 4.0	FN 6.0	VF 8.0	VF/NM 9.0	NM- 9.2
1-22: 1,2 Adapts movie. 8, 9-Evil Ed horror photo-c from movie						3.00

FRIGHT NIGHT II
Now Comics: 1989 ($3.95, 52 pgs.)

	GD 2.0	VG 4.0	FN 6.0	VF 8.0	VF/NM 9.0	NM- 9.2
1-Adapts movie sequel						4.00

FRINGE (Based on the 2008 FOX television series)
DC Comics (WildStorm): Oct, 2008 - No. 6, Aug, 2009 ($2.99, limited series)

	GD 2.0	VG 4.0	FN 6.0	VF 8.0	VF/NM 9.0	NM- 9.2
1-6-Anthology by various. 1-Mandrake & Coleby-a						3.00
TPB (2009, $19.99) r/#1-6; intro. by TV series co-creators Kurtzman & Orci						20.00

FRINGE: TALES FROM THE FRINGE (Based on the 2008 FOX television series)
DC Comics (WildStorm): Aug, 2010 - No. 6, Jan, 2011 ($3.99, limited series)

	GD 2.0	VG 4.0	FN 6.0	VF 8.0	VF/NM 9.0	NM- 9.2
1-6-Anthology by various; LaTorre-c. 1-Reg & photo-c						4.00
2-6-Variant covers from parallel world. 2-Death of Batman. 3-Superman/Dark Knight Returns. 4-Crisis #7 Supergirl holding dead Superman. 5-Justice League #1 w/Jonah Hex. 6-Red Lantern/Red Arrow #76						10.00
TPB (2011, $14.99) r/#1-6 with variant cover gallery and sketch art						15.00

FRISKY ANIMALS (Formerly Frisky Fables; Super Cat #56 on)
Star Publications: No. 44, Jan, 1951 - No. 55, Sept, 1953

	GD 2.0	VG 4.0	FN 6.0	VF 8.0	VF/NM 9.0	NM- 9.2
44-Super Cat; L.B. Cole	20	40	60	114	182	250
45-Classic L. B. Cole-c	28	56	84	165	270	375
46-51,53-55: Super Cat. 54-Super Cat-c begin	19	38	57	109	172	235
52-L. B. Cole-c/a, 3 1/2 pgs.; X-Mas-c	20	40	60	114	182	250

NOTE: *All have* ***L. B. Cole****-c. No. 47-No Super Cat.* ***Disbrow*** *a-49, 52.* ***Fago*** *a-51.*

FRISKY ANIMALS ON PARADE (Formerly Parade Comics; becomes Superspook)
Ajax-Farrell Publ. (Four Star Comic Corp.): Sept, 1957 - No. 3, Dec-Jan, 1957-1958

	GD 2.0	VG 4.0	FN 6.0	VF 8.0	VF/NM 9.0	NM- 9.2
1-L. B. Cole-c	17	34	51	98	154	210
2-No L. B. Cole-c	10	20	30	56	76	95
3-L. B. Cole-c	15	30	45	85	130	175

FRISKY FABLES (Frisky Animals No. 44 on)
Premium Group/Novelty Publ./Star Publ. V5#4 on: Spring, 1945 - No. 43, Oct, 1950

	GD 2.0	VG 4.0	FN 6.0	VF 8.0	VF/NM 9.0	NM- 9.2
V1#1-Funny animal; Al Fago-c/a #1-38	22	44	66	132	216	300
2,3(Fall & Winter, 1945)	14	28	42	76	108	140
V2#1(#4, 4/46) - 9,11,12(#15, 3/47): 4-Flag-c	10	20	30	58	79	100
10-Christmas-c. 12-Valentine's-c	11	22	33	60	83	105
V3#1(#16, 4/47) - 12(#27, 3/48): 4-Flag-c. 7,9-Infinity-c. 10-X-Mas-c. 12-Washington crossing the Delaware parody-c	9	18	27	50	65	80
V4#1(#28, 4/48) - 7(#34, 2-3/49)	9	18	27	47	61	75
V5#1(#35, 4-5/49) - 4(#38, 10-11/49)	9	18	27	47	61	75
39-43-L. B. Cole-c; 40-Xmas-c	20	40	60	114	182	250
Accepted Reprint No. 43 (nd); L.B. Cole-c	10	20	30	54	72	90

FRITZI RITZ (See Comics On Parade, Single Series #5, 1(reprint), Tip Top & United Comics)

FRITZI RITZ (United Comics No. 8-26) (Also see Tip Topper for early Peanuts by Schulz)
United Features Synd./St. John No. 37-55/Dell No. 56 on:
1939; Fall, 1948; No. 3, 1949 - No. 7, 1949; No. 27, 3-4/53 - No. 36, 9-10/54; No. 37 - No. 55, 9-11/57; No. 56, 12-2/57-58 - No. 59, 9-11/58

	GD 2.0	VG 4.0	FN 6.0	VF 8.0	VF/NM 9.0	NM- 9.2
Single Series #5 (1939)	36	72	108	211	343	475
nn(1948)-Special Fall issue; by Ernie Bushmiller	18	36	54	107	169	230
3(#1)	14	28	42	76	108	140
4-7(1949): 6-Abbie & Slats app.	10	20	30	54	72	90
27(1953)-33,37-50,57-59-Early Peanuts (1-4 pgs.) by Schulz. 29-Five pg. Abbie & Slats; 1 pg. Mamie by Russell Patterson. 38(9/55)-41(4/56)-Low print run	15	30	45	83	124	165
34-36,51-56: 36-1 pg. Mamie by Patterson	8	16	24	44	57	70

NOTE: *Abbie & Slats in #6,7, 27-31. Li'l Abner in #32-36.*

FROGMAN COMICS
Hillman Periodicals: Jan-Feb, 1952 - No. 11, May, 1953

	GD 2.0	VG 4.0	FN 6.0	VF 8.0	VF/NM 9.0	NM- 9.2
1	16	32	48	94	147	200
2	10	20	30	58	79	100
3,4,6-11: 4-Meskin-a	9	18	27	47	61	75
5-Krigstein-a	9	18	27	52	69	85

FROGMEN, THE
Dell Publishing Co.: No. 1258, Feb-Apr, 1962 - No. 11, Nov-Jan, 1964-65 (Painted-c)

	GD 2.0	VG 4.0	FN 6.0	VF 8.0	VF/NM 9.0	NM- 9.2
Four Color 1258(#1)-Evans-a	7	14	21	46	86	125
2,3-Evans-a; part Frazetta inks in #2,3	5	10	15	33	57	80
4,6-11	4	8	12	23	37	50
5-Toth-a	4	8	12	27	44	60

FROM BEYOND THE UNKNOWN
National Periodical Publications: 10-11/69 - No. 25, 11-12/73

	GD 2.0	VG 4.0	FN 6.0	VF 8.0	VF/NM 9.0	NM- 9.2
1	5	10	15	33	57	80
2-6	3	6	9	19	30	40
7-11: (64 pgs.) 7-Intro Col. Glenn Merrit	3	6	9	21	33	45
12-17: (52 pgs.) 13-Wood-a(i)(r). 17-Pres. Nixon-c	3	6	9	17	26	35
18-25: Star Rovers-r begin #18,19. Space Museum in #23-25	2	4	6	13	18	22

NOTE: ***N. Adams*** *c-3, 6, 8, 9.* ***Anderson*** *c-2, 4, 5, 10, 11i, 15-17, 22; reprints-3, 4, 6-8, 10, 11, 13-16, 24, 25.* ***Infantino*** *r-1-5, 7-19, 23-25; c-11p.* ***Kaluta*** *c-18, 19.* ***Gil Kane*** *a-9r.* ***Kubert*** *c-1, 7, 12-14.* ***Toth*** *a-2r.* ***Wood*** *a-13i. Photo c-22.*

FROM DUSK TILL DAWN (Movie)
Big Entertainment: 1996 ($4.95, one-shot)

	GD 2.0	VG 4.0	FN 6.0	VF 8.0	VF/NM 9.0	NM- 9.2
nn-Adaptation of the film; Brereton-c						5.00
nn-($9.95)Deluxe Ed. w/ new material						10.00

FROM HELL
Mad Love/Tundra Publishing/Kitchen Sink: 1991 - No. 11, Sept, 1998 (B&W)

	GD 2.0	VG 4.0	FN 6.0	VF 8.0	VF/NM 9.0	NM- 9.2
1-Alan Moore and Eddie Campbell's Jack The Ripper story collected from the Taboo anthology series	2	4	6	11	16	20
1-(2nd printing)	2	4	6	8	10	12
1-(3rd printing)	1	2	3	4	5	7
2	1	2	3	5	6	8
2-(2nd printing)						6.00
2-(3rd printing)						4.00
3-1st Kitchen Sink Press issue	1	2	3	5	6	8
3-(2nd printing)						5.00
4-10: 10-(8/96)	1	2	3	4	5	7
11-Dance of the Gull Catchers (9/98, $4.95) Epilogue	2	4	6	9	12	15
Tundra Publishing reprintings 1-5 ('92)	1	2	3	4	5	7
HC						125.00
HC Ltd. Edition of 1,000 (signed and numbered)						225.00
TPB-1st printing (11/99)						60.00
TPB-2nd printing (3/00)						50.00
TPB-3rd printing (11/00)						40.00
TPB-4th printing (7/01) Regular and movie covers						35.00
TPB-5th printing - Regular and movie covers						35.00

FROM HERE TO INSANITY (Satire) (Formerly Eh! #1-7) (See Frantic & Frenzy)
Charlton Comics: No. 8, Feb, 1955 - V3#1, 1956

	GD 2.0	VG 4.0	FN 6.0	VF 8.0	VF/NM 9.0	NM- 9.2
8	20	40	60	114	182	250
9	18	36	54	105	165	225
10-Ditko-c/a (3 pgs.)	28	56	84	165	270	375
11-All Kirby except 4 pgs.	37	74	111	222	361	500

Frontier Fighters #7 © DC

Frontline Combat #2 © WMG

Fun Comics #9 © STAR

GD 2.0 | VG 4.0 | FN 6.0 | VF 8.0 | VF/NM 9.0 | NM- 9.2

12-(Mag. size) Marilyn Monroe, Jackie Gleason-c; all Kirby except 4 pgs. 39 78 117 240 395 550
V3#1(1956)-Ward-c/a(2) (signed McCartney); 5 pgs. Wolverton-a; 3 pgs. Ditko-a; magazine format (cover says "Crazy, Man, Crazy" and becomes Crazy, Man, Crazy with V2#2) 42 84 126 267 451 660

FROM THE PIT
Fantagor Press: 1994 ($4.95, one-shot, mature)
1-R. Corben-a; HP Lovecraft back-up story 1 2 3 5 6 8

FRONTIER DOCTOR (TV)
Dell Publishing Co.: No. 877, Feb, 1958 (one-shot)
Four Color 877-Toth-a, Rex Allen photo-c 8 16 24 54 102 150

FRONTIER FIGHTERS
National Periodical Publications: Sept-Oct, 1955 - No. 8, Nov-Dec, 1956
1-Davy Crockett, Buffalo Bill (by Kubert), Kit Carson begin (Scarce) 55 110 165 352 601 850
2 37 74 111 222 361 500
3-8 34 68 102 199 325 450
NOTE: *Buffalo Bill by **Kubert** in all.*

FRONTIER ROMANCES
Avon Periodicals/I. W.: Nov-Dec, 1949 - No. 2, Feb-Mar, 1950 (Painted-c)
1-Used in **SOTI**, pg. 180 (General reference) & illo. "Erotic spanking in a western comic book" 53 106 159 334 567 800
2 (Scarce)-Woodish-a by Stallman 39 78 117 234 385 535
I.W. Reprint #1-Reprints Avon's #1 3 6 9 21 33 45
I.W. Reprint #9-Reprints ? 3 6 9 15 22 28

FRONTIER SCOUT: DAN'L BOONE (Formerly Death Valley; The Masked Raider No. 14 on)
Charlton Comics: No. 10, Jan, 1956 - No. 13, Aug, 1956; V2#14, Mar, 1965
10 10 20 30 54 72 90
11-13(1956) 6 12 18 31 38 45
V2#14(3/65) 3 6 9 15 22 28

FRONTIER TRAIL (The Rider No. 1-5)
Ajax/Farrell Publ.: No. 6, May, 1958
6 6 12 18 28 34 40

FRONTIER WESTERN
Atlas Comics (PrPI): Feb, 1956 - No. 10, Aug, 1957
1-The Pecos Kid rides 20 40 60 117 189 260
2,3,6-Williamson-a, 4 pgs. each 14 28 42 81 118 155
4,7,9,10: 10-Check-a 10 20 30 58 79 100
5-Crandall, Baker, Davis-a; Williamson text illos 14 28 42 78 112 145
8-Crandall, Morrow, & Wildey-a 11 22 33 60 83 105
NOTE: ***Baker** a-9. **Colan** a-2, 6. **Drucker** a-3, 4. **Heath** c-5. **Maneely** c/a-2, 7, 9. **Maurera** a-2. **Romita** a-7. **Severin** c-6, 8, 10. **Tuska** a-2. **Wildey** a-5, 8. Ringo Kid in No. 4.*

FRONTLINE COMBAT
E. C. Comics: July-Aug, 1951 - No. 15, Jan, 1954
1-Severin/Kurtzman-a 76 152 258 608 967 1325
2 39 78 117 312 499 685
3 31 62 93 248 392 535
4-Used in **SOTI**, pg. 257; contains "Airburst" by Kurtzman which is his personal all-time favorite story 29 58 87 232 371 510
5-John Severin and Bill Elder bios. 24 48 72 192 309 425
6-10: 6-Kurtzman bio. 9-Civil War issue 21 42 63 168 272 375
11-15: 11-Civil War issue 17 34 51 136 213 290
NOTE: ***Davis** a-in all; c-11, 12. **Evans** a-10-15. **Heath** a-1. **Kubert** a-14. **Kurtzman** a-1-5; c-1-9. **Severin** a-5-7, 9, 13, 15. **Severin/Elder** a-2-11; c-10. **Toth** a-8, 12. **Wood** a-1-4, 6-10, 12-15; c-13-15. Special issues: No. 7 (Iwo Jima), No. 9 (Civil War), No. 12 (Air Force).*
(Canadian reprints known; see Table of Contents.)

FRONTLINE COMBAT
Russ Cochran/Gemstone Publishing: Aug, 1995 - No. 14 ($2.00/$2.50)
1-14-E.C. reprints in all 4.00

FRONT PAGE COMIC BOOK
Front Page Comics (Harvey): 1945
1-Kubert-a; intro. & 1st app. Man in Black by Powell; Fuje-c 43 86 129 271 461 650

FROST AND FIRE (See DC Science Fiction Graphic Novel)

FROSTY THE SNOWMAN
Dell Publishing Co.: No. 359, Nov, 1951 - No. 1272, Dec-Feb?/1961-62
Four Color 359 (#1) 8 16 24 56 108 160
Four Color 435,514,601,661 5 10 15 34 60 85
Four Color 748,861,950,1065,1153,1272 5 10 15 31 53 75

FRUITMAN SPECIAL (See Bunny #2 for 1st app.)
Harvey Publications: Dec, 1969 (68 pgs.)
1-Funny super hero 4 8 12 23 37 50

F-TROOP (TV)
Dell Publishing Co.: Aug, 1966 - No. 7, Aug, 1967 (All have photo-c)
1 8 16 24 55 105 155
2-7 5 10 15 34 60 85

FUGITIVES FROM JUSTICE (True Crime Stories)
St. John Publishing Co.: Feb, 1952 - No. 5, Oct, 1952
1 24 48 72 140 230 320
2-Matt Baker-r/Northwest Mounties #2; Vic Flint strip reprints begin 23 46 69 136 223 310
3-Reprints panel from Authentic Police Cases that was used in **SOTI** with changes; Tuska-a 22 44 66 132 216 300
4 14 28 42 78 112 145
5-Last Vic Flint-r; bondage-c 15 30 45 83 124 165

FUGITOID
Mirage Studios: 1985 (B&W, magazine size, one-shot)
1-Ties into Teenage Mutant Ninja Turtles #5 2 4 6 11 16 20

FULL OF FUN
Red Top (Decker Publ.)(Farrell)/I. W. Enterprises: Aug, 1957 - No. 2, Nov, 1957; 1964
1(1957)-Funny animal; Dave Berg-a 7 14 21 37 46 55
2-Reprints Bingo, the Monkey Doodle Boy 5 10 15 22 26 30
8-I.W. Reprint('64) 2 4 6 9 12 15

FUN AT CHRISTMAS (See March of Comics No. 138)

FUN CLUB COMICS (See Interstate Theatres...)

FUN COMICS (Formerly Holiday Comics #1-8; Mighty Bear #13 on)
Star Publications: No. 9, Jan, 1953 - No. 12, Oct, 1953
9-(25¢ Giant)-L. B. Cole X-Mas-c; X-Mas issue 22 44 66 132 216 300
10-12-L. B. Cole-c. 12-Mighty Bear-c/story 18 36 54 105 165 225

FUNDAY FUNNIES (See Famous TV..., and Harvey Hits No. 35,40)

FUN-IN (TV)(Hanna-Barbera)
Gold Key: Feb, 1970 - No. 10, Jan, 1972; No. 11, 4/74 - No. 15, 12/74
1-Dastardly & Muttley in Their Flying Machines; Perils of Penelope Pitstop in #1-4; It's the Wolf in all 6 12 18 41 76 110
2-4,6-Cattanooga Cats in 2-4 3 6 9 21 33 45
5,7-Motormouse & Autocat, Dastardly & Muttley in both; It's the Wolf in #7 4 8 12 23 37 50
8,10-The Harlem Globetrotters, Dastardly & Muttley in #10 4 8 12 23 37 50
9-Where's Huddles?, Dastardly & Muttley, Motormouse & Autocat app. 4 8 12 23 37 50
11-Butch Cassidy 3 6 9 19 30 40
12-15: 12,15-Speed Buggy. 13-Hair Bear Bunch. 14-Inch High Private Eye 3 6 9 19 30 40

FUNKY PHANTOM, THE (TV)
Gold Key: Mar, 1972 - No. 13, Mar, 1975 (Hanna-Barbera)
1 5 10 15 31 53 75
2-5 3 6 9 18 28 38
6-13 3 6 9 15 22 28

FUNLAND
Ziff-Davis (Approved Comics): No date (1940s) (25¢)
nn-Contains games, puzzles, cut-outs, etc. 19 38 57 112 179 245

FUNLAND COMICS
Croyden Publishers: 1945
1-Funny animal 15 30 45 90 140 190

FUNNIES, THE (New Funnies No. 65 on)
Dell Publishing Co.: Oct, 1936 - No. 64, May, 1942
1-Tailspin Tommy, Mutt & Jeff, Alley Oop (1st app?), Capt. Easy (1st app.), Don Dixon begin 400 800 1200 2300 3650 5000
2 (11/36)-Scribbly by Mayer begins (see Popular Comics #6 for 1st app.) 180 360 540 1035 1643 2250
3 124 248 372 713 1132 1550
4,5: 4(1/37)-Christmas-c 92 184 276 529 840 1150
6-10 70 140 210 403 639 875

The Funnies #61 © DELL

Funny Folks #11 © DC

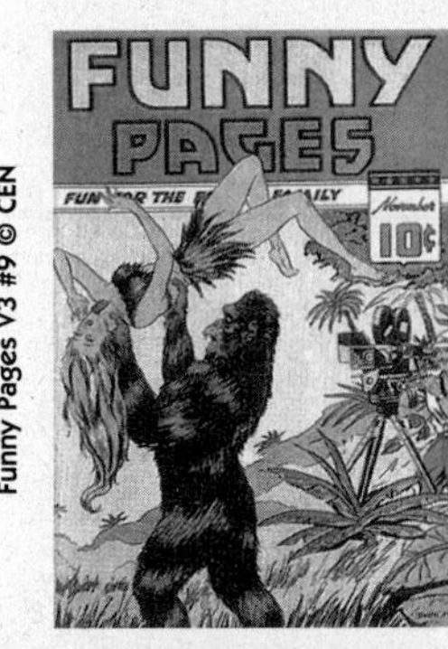

Funny Pages V3 #9 © CEN

GD 2.0 | VG 4.0 | FN 6.0 | VF 8.0 | VF/NM 9.0 | NM- 9.2

11-20: 16-Christmas-c 65 130 195 374 597 820
21-29: 25-Crime Busters by McWilliams(4pgs.) 52 104 156 299 475 650
30-John Carter of Mars (origin/1st app.) begins by Edgar Rice Burroughs; Jim Gary-a
Warner Bros.' Bosko-c (4/39) 168 336 504 1075 1838 2600
31-34,36-44: 31,32-Gary-a. 33-John Coleman Burroughs art begins on John Carter.
34-Last funny-c 86 172 258 546 936 1325
35-(9/39)-Mr. District Attorney begins; based on radio show; 1st cover app. John Carter
of Mars 107 214 321 680 1165 1650
45-Origin/1st app. Phantasmo, the Master of the World (Dell's 1st super-hero, 7/40) & his
sidekick Whizzer McGee 95 190 285 603 1039 1475
46-50: 46-The Black Knight begins, ends #62 58 116 174 371 636 900
51-56-Last ERB John Carter of Mars 47 94 141 296 498 700
57-Intro. & origin Captain Midnight (7/41) 354 708 1062 2478 4339 6200
58-60: 58-Captain Midnight-c begin, end #63 87 174 261 553 952 1350
61-Andy Panda begins by Walter Lantz; WWII-c 108 216 324 686 1181 1675
62,63: 63-Last Captain Midnight-c; bondage-c 68 136 204 435 743 1050
64-Format change; Oswald the Rabbit, Felix the Cat, Li'l Eight Ball app.; origin & 1st app.
Woody Woodpecker in Oswald; last Capt. Midnight; Oswald, Andy Panda, Li'l Eight Ball-c
168 336 504 1075 1838 2600

NOTE: ***Mayer*** *c-26, 48.* ***McWilliams*** *art in many issues on "Rex King of the Deep". Alley Oop c-17, 20. Captain Midnight c-57(i/2), 58-63. John Carter c-35-37, 40. Phantasmo c-45-56, 57(1/2), 58-61(part). Rex King c-38, 39, 42. Tailspin Tommy c-41.*

FUNNIES ANNUAL, THE
Avon Periodicals: 1959 ($1.00, approx. 7x10", B&W; tabloid-size)

1-(Rare)-Features the best newspaper comic strips of the year: Archie, Snuffy Smith, Beetle Bailey, Henry, Blondie, Steve Canyon, Buz Sawyer, The Little King, Hi & Lois, Popeye, & others. Also has a chronological history of the comics from 2000 B.C. to 1959.
48 96 144 302 514 725

FUNNIES ON PARADE (See Promotional Comics section)

FUNNY ANIMALS (See Fawcett's Funny Animals)
Charlton Comics: Sept, 1984 - No. 2, Nov, 1984

1,2-Atomic Mouse-r; low print 6.00

FUNNYBONE (... The Laugh-Book of Comical Comics)
La Salle Publishing Co.: 1944 (25¢, 132 pgs.)

nn 30 60 90 177 289 400

FUNNY BOOK (...Magazine for Young Folks) (Hocus Pocus No. 9)
Parents' Magazine Press (Funny Book Publishing Corp.):
Dec, 1942 - No. 9, Aug-Sept, 1946 (Comics, stories, puzzles, games)

1-Funny animal; Alice In Wonderland app. 15 30 45 86 133 180
2-Gulliver in Giant-Land 10 20 30 56 76 95
3-9: 4-Advs. of Robin Hood. 9-Hocus-Pocus strip 9 18 27 47 61 75

FUNNY COMICS
Modern Store Publ.: 1955 (7¢, 5x7", 36 pgs.)

1-Funny animal 4 8 12 23 37 50

FUNNY COMIC TUNES (See Funny Tunes)

FUNNY FABLES
Decker Publications (Red Top Comics): Aug, 1957 - V2#2, Nov, 1957

V1#1 6 12 18 31 38 45
V1#2,V2#1,2: V1#2 (11/57)-Reissue of V1#1 5 10 14 20 24 28

FUNNY FILMS (Features funny animal characters from films)
American Comics Group(Michel Publ./Titan Publ.): Sept-Oct, 1949 - No. 29, May-June, 1954 (No. 1-4: 52 pgs.)

1-Puss An' Boots, Blunderbunny begin 18 36 54 105 165 225
2 11 22 33 62 86 110
3-10: 3-X-Mas-c 9 18 27 47 61 75
11-20 7 14 21 35 43 50
21-29 6 12 18 28 34 40

FUNNY FOLKS
DC Comics: Feb, 1946

nn-Ashcan comic, not distributed to newsstands, only for in house use (no known sales)

FUNNY FOLKS (Hollywood... on cover only No. 16-26; becomes Hollywood Funny Folks No. 27 on)
National Periodical Publ.: April-May, 1946 - No. 26, June-July, 1950 (52 pgs., #15 on)

1-Nutsy Squirrel begins (1st app.) by Rube Grossman;
Grossman-a in most issues 39 78 117 240 395 550
2 20 40 60 114 182 250
3-5: 4-1st Nutsy Squirrel-c 15 30 45 84 127 170
6-10: 6,9-Nutsy Squirrel-c begin 11 22 33 62 86 110
11-26: 15-Begin 52 pg. issues (8-9/48) 10 20 30 54 72 90

NOTE: ***Sheldon Mayer*** *a-in some issues.* ***Post*** *a-18. Christmas c-12.*

FUNNY FROLICS
Timely/Marvel Comics (SPI): Summer, 1945 - No. 5, Dec, 1946

1-Sharpy Fox, Puffy Pig, Krazy Krow 28 56 84 168 274 380
2-(Fall 1945) 15 30 45 90 140 190
3,4: 3-(Spring 1946) 14 28 42 76 112 145
5-Kurtzman-a 14 28 42 82 121 160

FUNNY FUNNIES
Nedor Publishing Co.: April, 1943 (68 pgs.)

1-Funny animals; Peter Porker app. 20 40 60 114 182 250

FUNNYMAN (Also see Cisco Kid Comics & Extra Comics)
Magazine Enterprises: Dec, 1947; No. 1, Jan, 1948 - No. 6, Aug, 1948

nn(12/47)-Prepublication B&W undistributed copy by Siegel & Shuster-(5-3/4x8"), 16 pgs.;
Sold at auction in 1997 for $575.00
1-Siegel & Shuster-a in all; Dick Ayers 1st pro work (as assistant) on 1st few issues
47 94 141 296 498 700
2 28 56 84 165 270 375
3-6 24 48 72 142 234 325

FUNNY MOVIES (See 3-D Funny Movies)

FUNNY PAGES (Formerly The Comics Magazine)
Comics Magazine Co./Ultem Publ.(Chesler)/Centaur Publications:
No. 6, Nov, 1936 - No. 42, Oct, 1940

V1#6 (nn, nd)-The Clock begins (2 pgs., 1st app.), ends #11; The Clock is the 1st masked
comic book hero 300 600 900 1950 3375 4800
7-11: 11-(6/37) 129 258 387 826 1413 2000
V2#1-V2#3: V2#1 (9/37)(V2#2 on-c; V2#1 in indicia). V2#2 (10/37)(V2#3 on-c; V2#2 in indicia).
V2#3(11/37)-5 94 188 282 597 1024 1450
6(1st Centaur, 3/38) 110 220 330 704 1202 1700
7-9 94 188 282 597 1024 1450
10(Scarce, 9/38)-1st app. of The Arrow by Gustavson (Blue costume)
423 846 1269 3000 5250 7500
11,12 145 290 435 921 1586 2250
V3#1-Bruce Wayne prototype in "Case of the Missing Heir," by Bob Kane, 3 months before
app. Batman (See Det. Pic. Stories #5) 174 348 522 1114 1907 2700
2-6,8: 6,8-Last funny covers 129 258 387 826 1413 2000
7-1st Arrow-c (9/39) 354 708 1062 2478 4339 6200
9-Tarpe Mills jungle-c 145 290 435 921 1586 2250
10-2nd Arrow-c 300 600 900 2070 3635 5200
V4#1(1/40, Arrow-c)-(Rare)-The Owl & The Phantom Rider app.; origin Mantoka, Maker of
Magic by Jack Cole. Mad Ming begins, ends #42; Tarpe Mills-a
343 686 1029 2400 4200 6000
35-Classic Arrow-c (Scarce) 343 686 1029 2400 4200 6000
36-38-Mad Ming-c 148 296 444 947 1624 2300
39-41-Arrow-c 265 530 795 1694 2897 4100
42 (Scarce,10/40)-Last Arrow; Arrow-c 271 542 813 1734 2967 4200

NOTE: ***Biro*** *c-V2#9.* ***Burgos*** *c-V3#10.* ***Jack Cole*** *a-V2#3, 7, 8, 10, 11, V3#2, 6, 9, 10, V4#1, 37; c-V3#2, 4.* ***Eisner*** *a-V1#7, 8?, 10.* ***Ken Ernst*** *a-V1#7, 8.* ***Everett*** *a-V2#11 (illos).* ***Filchock*** *c-V2#10, V3#6.* ***Gill Fox*** *a-V2#11.* ***Sid Greene*** *a-39.* ***Guardineer*** *a-V2#2, 3, 5.* ***Gustavson*** *a-V2#5, 11, 12, V3#1-10, 35, 38-42; c-V3#7, 35, 39-42.* ***Bob Kane*** *a-V3#1.* ***McWilliams*** *a-V2#12, V3#1, 3-6.* ***Tarpe Mills*** *a-V3#8-10, V4#1; c-V3#9.* ***Ed Moore Jr.*** *a-V2#12.* ***Schwab*** *c-V3#1.* ***Bob Wood*** *a-V2#2, 3, 8, 11, V3#6, 9, 10; c-V2#6, 7. Arrow c-V3#7, 10, V4#1, 35, 40-42.*

FUNNY PICTURE STORIES (Comic Pages V3#4 on)
Comics Magazine Co./Centaur Publications: Nov, 1936 - V3#3, May, 1939

V1#1-The Clock begins (c-feature)(see Funny Pages for 1st app.)
400 800 1200 2800 4900 7000
2 161 322 483 1030 1765 2500
3-6(4/37): 4-Eisner-a; X-Mas-c. 113 226 339 718 1234 1750
7-(6/37) (Rare) Racial humor-c 271 542 813 1734 2967 4200
V2#1 (9/37; V1#10 on-c; V2#1 in indicia)-Jack Strand begins
74 148 222 470 810 1150
2 (10/37; V1#11 on-c; V2#2 in indicia) 74 148 222 470 810 1150
3-5,7-11(11/38): 4-Xmas-c 68 136 204 435 743 1050
6-(1st Centaur, 3/38) 89 178 267 565 970 1375
V3#1(1/39)-3 65 130 195 416 708 1000

NOTE: ***Biro*** *c-V2#1, 8, 9, 11.* ***Guardineer*** *a-V1#11; c-V2#6, V3#5.* ***Bob Wood*** *c/a-V1#11, V2#2; c-V2#3, 5.*

FUNNY STUFF (Becomes The Dodo & the Frog No. 80)
All-American/National Periodical Publications No. 7 on: Summer, 1944 - No. 79, July-Aug, 1954 (#1-7 are quarterly)

1-The Three Mouseketeers (ends #28) & The "Terrific Whatzit" begin;
Sheldon Mayer-a; Grossman-a in most issues 89 178 267 565 970 1375
2-Sheldon Mayer-a 42 84 126 265 445 625

Funny Tunes #3 © AVON

Fury MAX #12 © MAR

Futurama Comics #67 © Bongo

	GD 2.0	VG 4.0	FN 6.0	VF 8.0	VF/NM 9.0	NM- 9.2
3-5: 3-Flash parody. 5-All Mayer-a/scripts issue	30	60	90	177	289	400
6-10 10-(6/46)	20	40	60	114	182	250
11-17,19	15	30	45	90	140	190
18-The Dodo & the Frog (2/47, 1st app?) begin?; X-Mas-c	27	54	81	160	263	365
19-1st Dodo & the Frog-c (3/47)	18	36	54	105	165	225
20-2nd Dodo & the Frog-c (4/47)	14	28	42	80	115	150
21,23-30: 24-Infinity-c. 30-Christmas-c	11	22	33	62	86	110
22-Superman cameo	37	74	111	222	361	500
31-79: 70-1st Bo Bunny by Mayer & begins	10	20	30	56	76	95

NOTE: *Mayer a-1-8, 55, 57, 58, 61, 62, 64, 65, 68, 70, 72, 74-79; c-2, 5, 6, 8.*

FUNNY STUFF STOCKING STUFFER
DC Comics: Mar, 1985 ($1.25, 52 pgs.)

1-Almost every DC funny animal featured 4.00

FUNNY 3-D
Harvey Publications: December, 1953 (25¢, came with 2 pair of glasses)

	GD 2.0	VG 4.0	FN 6.0	VF 8.0	VF/NM 9.0	NM- 9.2
1-Shows cover in 3-D on inside	11	22	33	62	86	110

FUNNY TUNES (Animated Funny Comic Tunes No. 16-22; Funny Comic Tunes No. 23, on covers only; Oscar No. 24 on)
U.S.A. Comics Magazine Corp. (Timely): No. 16, Summer, 1944 - No. 23, Fall, 1946

	GD 2.0	VG 4.0	FN 6.0	VF 8.0	VF/NM 9.0	NM- 9.2
16-Silly Seal, Ziggy Pig, Krazy Krow begin	20	40	60	117	189	260
17 (Fall/44)-Becomes Gay Comics #18 on?	15	30	45	88	137	185
18-22: 21-Super Rabbit app.	14	28	42	82	121	160
23-Kurtzman-a	15	30	45	85	130	175

FUNNY TUNES (Becomes Space Comics #4 on)
Avon Periodicals: July, 1953 - No. 3, Dec-Jan, 1953-54

	GD 2.0	VG 4.0	FN 6.0	VF 8.0	VF/NM 9.0	NM- 9.2
1-Space Mouse, Peter Rabbit, Merry Mouse, Spotty the Pup, Cicero the Cat begin; all continue in Space Comics	11	22	33	62	86	110
2,3	8	16	24	44	57	70

FUNNY WORLD
Marbak Press: 1947 - No. 3, 1948

	GD 2.0	VG 4.0	FN 6.0	VF 8.0	VF/NM 9.0	NM- 9.2
1-The Berrys, The Toodles & other strip-r begin	9	18	27	47	61	75
2,3	6	12	18	31	38	45

FUNTASTIC WORLD OF HANNA-BARBERA, THE (TV)
Marvel Comics Group: Dec, 1977 - No. 3, June, 1978 ($1.25, oversized)

	GD 2.0	VG 4.0	FN 6.0	VF 8.0	VF/NM 9.0	NM- 9.2
1-3: 1-The Flintstones Christmas Party(12/77). 2-Yogi Bear's Easter Parade(3/78). 3-Laff-a-lympics(6/78)	4	8	12	25	40	55

FUN TIME
Ace Periodicals: Spring, 1953; No. 2, Sum, 1953; No. 3(nn), Fall, 1953; No. 4, Wint, 1953-54

	GD 2.0	VG 4.0	FN 6.0	VF 8.0	VF/NM 9.0	NM- 9.2
1-(25¢, 100 pgs.)-Funny animal	20	40	60	114	182	250
2-4 (All 25¢, 100 pgs.)	15	30	45	88	137	185

FUN WITH SANTA CLAUS (See March of Comics No. 11, 108, 325)

FURIOUS
Dark Horse Comics: Jan, 2014 - Present ($3.99)

1-4: 1-Glass-s/Santos-a 4.00

FURTHER ADVENTURES OF CYCLOPS AND PHOENIX (Also see Adventures of Cyclops and Phoenix, Uncanny X-Men & X-Men)
Marvel Comics: June, 1996 - No. 4, Sept, 1996 ($1.95, limited series)

1-4: Origin of Mr. Sinister; Milligan scripts; John Paul Leon-c/a(p). 2-4-Apocalypse app. 3.00
Trade Paperback (1997, $14.99) r/1-4 15.00

FURTHER ADVENTURES OF INDIANA JONES, THE (Movie) (Also see Indiana Jones and the Last Crusade & Indiana Jones and the Temple of Doom)
Marvel Comics Group: Jan, 1983 - No. 34, Mar, 1986

1-Byrne/Austin-a; Austin-c 6.00
2-34: 2-Byrne/Austin-c/a 4.00

NOTE: *Austin a-1i, 2i, 6i, 9i; c-1, 2i, 6i, 9i. Byrne a-1p, 2p; c-2p. Chaykin a-6p; c-6p, 8p-10p. Ditko a-21p, 25-28, 34. Golden c-24, 25. Simonson c-9. Painted c-14.*

FURTHER ADVENTURES OF NYOKA, THE JUNGLE GIRL, THE (See Nyoka)
AC Comics: 1988 - No. 5, 1989 ($1.95, color; $2.25/$2.50, B&W)

1-5 : 1,2-Bill Black-a plus reprints. 3-Photo-c. 5-(B&W)-Reprints plus movie photos 3.00

FURY (Straight Arrow's Horse...) (See A-1 No. 119)

FURY (TV) (See March Of Comics #200)
Dell Publishing Co./Gold Key: No. 781, Mar, 1957 - Nov, 1962 (All photo-c)

	GD 2.0	VG 4.0	FN 6.0	VF 8.0	VF/NM 9.0	NM- 9.2
Four Color 781	7	14	21	44	82	120
Four Color 885,975,1031,1080,1133,1172,1218,1296	5	10	15	35	63	90
01292-208(#1-'62), 10020-211(11/62-G.K.)	5	10	15	33	57	80

FURY
Marvel Comics: May, 1994 ($2.95, one-shot)

1-Iron Man, Red Skull, FF, Hatemonger, Logan app.; Origin Nick Fury 3.00

FURY (Volume 3)
Marvel Comics (MAX): Nov, 2001 - No. 6, Apr, 2002 ($2.99, mature content)

1-6-Ennis-s/Robertson-a 3.00

FURY/ AGENT 13
Marvel Comics: June, 1998 - No. 2, July, 1998 ($2.99, limited series)

1,2-Nick Fury returns 3.00

FURY MAX (Nick Fury)("My War Gone By" on cover)
Marvel Comics (MAX): Jul, 2012 - No. 13, Aug, 2013 ($3.99, mature content)

1-13: 1-Ennis-s/Parlov-a/Johnson-c; Nick Fury in 1954 Indochina. 7-9-Frank Castle app. 4.00

FURY OF FIRESTORM, THE (Becomes Firestorm The Nuclear Man on cover with #50, in indicia with #65) (Also see Firestorm)
DC Comics: June, 1982 - No. 64, Oct, 1987 (75¢ on)

	GD 2.0	VG 4.0	FN 6.0	VF 8.0	VF/NM 9.0	NM- 9.2
1-Intro The Black Bison; brief origin						6.00
2-40,43-64: 4-JLA x-over. 17-1st app. Firehawk. 21-Death of Killer Frost. 22-Origin. 23-Intro. Byte. 24-(6/84)-1st app. Blue Devil & Bug (origin); origin Byte. 34-1st app./origin Killer Frost II. 39-Weasel's ID revealed. 48-Intro. Moonbow. 53-Origin/1st app. Silver Shade. 55,56-Legends x-over. 58-1st app./origin new Parasite						3.00
41,42-Crisis x-over						4.00
61-Test cover variant; Superman logo	3	6	9	21	33	45
Annual 1-4: 1(1983), 2(1984), 3(1985), 4(1986)						4.00

NOTE: *Colan a-19p, Annual 4p. Giffen a-Annual 4p. Gil Kane c-30. Nino a-37. Tuska a-(p)-17, 18, 32, 45.*

FURY OF FIRESTORM: THE NUCLEAR MEN (New DC 52)
DC Comics: Nov, 2011 - No. 20, Jul, 2013 ($2.99)

1-20: 1-Van Sciver & Simone-s/Cinar-a/Van Sciver-c. 7,8-Van Sciver-a. 9-JLI app. 3.00
#0 (11/12, #2.99) Cinar-a/c 3.00

FURY OF SHIELD
Marvel Comics: Apr, 1995 - No. 4, July, 1995 ($2.50/$1.95, limited series)

1 ($2.50)-Foil-c 4.00
2-4: 4-Bagged w/ decoder 3.00

FURY: PEACEMAKER
Marvel Comics: Apr, 2006 - No. 6, Sept, 2006 ($3.50, limited series)

1-6-Flashback to WW2; Ennis-s/Robertson-a. 1-Deodato-c. 2-Texeira-c. 5-Dillon-c 3.50
TPB (2006, $17.99) r/#1-6 18.00

FUSED
Image Comics: Mar, 2002 - No. 4, Jan, 2003 ($2.95)

1-4-Steve Niles-s. 1,2-Paul Lee-a. 3-Brad Rader-a. 4-Templesmith-a 3.00
Canned Heat TPB (Dark Horse, 6/04, $12.95) r/series; Dan Wickline intro. 13.00

FUSED
Dark Horse Comics: Dec, 2003 - No. 4, Mar, 2004 ($2.95)

1-4-Steve Niles-s/Josh Medors-a. 1-Powell-c 3.00

FUSION
Eclipse Comics: Jan, 1987 - No. 17, Oct, 1989 ($2.00, B&W, Baxter paper)

1-17: 11-The Weasel Patrol begins (1st app.?) 3.00

FUSION
Image Comics (Top Cow): May, 2009 - No. 3, Jul, 2009 ($2.99, limited series)

1-3-Avengers, Thunderbolts, Cyberforce and Hunter-Killer meet; Kirkham-a 3.00

FUTURAMA (TV)
Bongo Comics: 2000 - Present ($2.50/$2.99, bi-monthly)

1-Based on the FOX-TV animated series; Groening/Morrison-c 4.00
1-San Diego Comic-Con Premiere Edition 5.00
2-70: 8-CGC cover spoof; X-Men parody. 40,64-Santa app. 50-55-Poster included 3.00
Futurama Adventures TPB (2004, $14.95) r/#5-9 15.00
Futurama Conquers the Universe TPB (2007, $14.95) r/#10-13 15.00
Futurama-O-Rama TPB (2002, $12.95) r/#1-4; sketch pages of Fry's development 13.00
...: The Time Bender Trilogy TPB (2006, $14.95) r/#16-19; cover gallery 15.00

FUTURAMA/SIMPSONS INFINITELY SECRET CROSSOVER CRISIS (TV) (See Simpsons/ Futurama Crossover Crisis II for sequel)
Bongo Comics: 2002 - No. 2, 2002 ($2.50, limited series)

1,2-Evil Brain Spawns put Futurama crew into the Simpsons' Springfield 3.00

FUTURE COMICS
David McKay Publications: June, 1940 - No. 4, Sept, 1940

Future Comics #4 © DMP

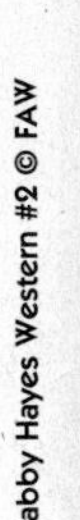
Gabby Hayes Western #2 © FAW

Gambit V2 #11 © MAR

	GD 2.0	VG 4.0	FN 6.0	VF 8.0	VF/NM 9.0	NM- 9.2

1-(6/40, 64 pgs.)-Origin The Phantom (1st in comics) (4 pgs.); The Lone Ranger (8 pgs.) & Saturn Against the Earth (4 pgs.) begin 300 600 900 1950 3375 4800
2 123 246 369 787 1344 1900
3,4 90 180 270 576 988 1400

FUTURE COP L.A.P.D. (Electronic Arts video game) (Also see Promotional Comics section)
DC Comics (WildStorm): Jan, 1999 ($4.95, magazine sized)
1-Stories & art by various 5.00

FUTURE SHOCK
Image Comics: 2006 (Free Comic Book Day giveaway)
...: FCBD 2006 Edition; Spawn, Invincible, Savage Dragon & others short stories 3.00

FUTURE WORLD COMICS
George W. Dougherty: Summer, 1946 - No. 2, Fall, 1946
1,2: H. C. Kiefer-c; preview of the World of Tomorrow 29 58 87 170 278 385

FUTURE WORLD COMIX (Warren Presents...)
Warren Publications: Sept, 1978 (B&W magazine, 84 pgs.)
1-Corben, Maroto, Morrow, Nino, Sutton-a; Todd-c/a; contains nudity panels 2 4 6 8 11 14

FUTURIANS, THE (See Marvel Graphic Novel #9)
Lodestone Publishing/Eternity Comics: Sept, 1985 - No. 3, 1985 ($1.50)
1-3: Indicia title "Dave Cockrum's..." 3.00
Graphic Novel 1 ($9.95, Eternity)-r/#1-3, plus never published #4 issue 10.00

FX
IDW Publishing: Mar, 2008 - No. 6, Aug, 2008 ($3.99)
1-6-John Byrne-a/c; Wayne Osborne-s 4.00

G-8 (Listed at G-Eight)

GABBY (Formerly Ken Shannon) (Teen humor)
Quality Comics Group: No. 11, Jul, 1953; No. 2, Sep, 1953 - No. 9, Sep, 1954
11(#1)(7/53) 9 18 27 47 61 75
2 6 12 18 31 38 45
3-9 5 10 15 24 30 35

GABBY GOB (See Harvey Hits No. 85, 90, 94, 97, 100, 103, 106, 109)

GABBY HAYES ADVENTURE COMICS
Toby Press: Dec, 1953
1-Photo-c 15 30 45 88 137 185

GABBY HAYES WESTERN (Movie star)(See Monte Hale, Real Western Hero & Western Hero)
Fawcett Publications/Charlton Comics No. 51 on: Nov, 1948 - No. 50, Jan, 1953; No. 51, Dec, 1954 - No. 59, Jan, 1957
1-Gabby & his horse Corker begin; photo front/back-c begin 40 80 120 246 411 575
2 20 40 60 118 192 265
3-5 15 30 45 88 137 185
6-10: 9-Young Falcon begins 14 28 42 78 112 145
11-20: 19-Last photo back-c 11 22 33 64 90 115
21-49: 20,22,24,26,28,29-(52 pgs.) 9 18 27 52 69 85
50-(1/53)-Last Fawcett issue; last photo-c? 10 20 30 58 79 100
51-(12/54)-1st Charlton issue; photo-c 11 22 33 60 83 105
52-59(1955-57): 53,55-Photo-c. 58-Swayze-a 8 16 24 42 54 65

GAGS
United Features Synd./Triangle Publ. No. 9 on: Jul, 1937 - V3#10, Oct, 1944 (13-3/4x10-3/4")
1(7/37)-52 pgs.; 20 pgs. Grin & Bear It, Fellow Citizen 14 28 42 76 108 140
V1#9 (36 pgs.) (7/42) 8 16 24 42 54 65
V3#10 8 16 24 40 50 60

GALACTA: DAUGHTER OF GALACTUS
Marvel Comics: July, 2010 ($3.99, one-shot)
1-Adam Warren-s/Hector Sevilla-a; Warren & Sevilla-c : Wolverine and the FF app. 4.00

GALACTICA 1980 (Based on the Battlestar Galactica TV series)
Dynamite Entertainment: 2009 - No. 4, 2009 ($3.50)
1-4-Guggenheim-s/Razek-a 3.50

GALACTICA: THE NEW MILLENNIUM
Realm Press: Sept, 1999 ($2.99)
1-Stories by Shooter, Braden, Kuhoric 3.00

GALACTIC GUARDIANS
Marvel Comics: July, 1994 - No. 4, Oct, 1994 ($1.50, limited series)
1-4 3.00

GALACTIC WARS COMIX (Warren Presents... on cover)
Warren Publications: Dec, 1978 (B&W magazine, 84 pgs.)
nn-Wood, Williamson-r; Battlestar Galactica/Flash Gordon photo/text stories 2 4 6 8 11 14

GALACTUS THE DEVOURER
Marvel Comics: Sept, 1999 - No. 6, Mar, 2000 ($3.50/$2.50, limited series)
1-($3.50) L. Simonson-s/Muth & Sienkiewicz-a 4.00
2-5-($2.50) Buscema & Sienkiewicz-a 3.00
6-($3.50) Death of Galactus; Buscema & Sienkiewicz-a 4.00

GALAXIA (Magazine)
Astral Publ.: 1981 ($2.50, B&W, 52 pgs.)
1-Buckler/Giordano-c; Texeira/Guice-a; 1st app. Astron, Sojourner, Bloodwing, Warlords; Buckler-s/a 2 4 6 9 13 16

GALAXY QUEST: GLOBAL WARNING! (Based on the 1999 movie)
IDW Publishing: Aug, 2008 - No. 5, Dec, 2008 ($3.99)
1-5-Lobdell-s/Kyriazis-a 4.00

GALLANT MEN, THE (TV)
Gold Key: Oct, 1963 (Photo-c)
1(1008-310)-Manning-a 3 6 9 21 33 45

GALLEGHER, BOY REPORTER (Disney, TV)
Gold Key: May, 1965
1(10149-505)-Photo-c 3 6 9 17 26 35

GAMBIT (See X-Men #266 & X-Men Annual #14)
Marvel Comics: Dec, 1993 - No. 4, Mar, 1994 ($2.00, limited series)
1-($2.50)-Lee Weeks-c/a in all; gold foil stamped-c 2 4 6 8 10 12
1 (Gold) 3 6 9 15 22 28
2-4 6.00

GAMBIT
Marvel Comics: Sept, 1997 - No. 4, Dec, 1997 ($2.50, limited series)
1-4-Janson-a/Mackie & Kavanagh-s 4.00

GAMBIT
Marvel Comics: Feb, 1999 - No. 25, Feb, 2001 ($2.99/$1.99)
1-($2.99) Five covers; Nicieza-a/Skroce-a 5.00
2-11,13-16-($1.99): 2-Two covers (Skroce & Adam Kubert) 3.00
12-($2.99) 4.00
17-24: 17-Begin $2.25-c. 21-Mystique-c/app. 3.00
25-($2.99) Leads into "Gambit & Bishop" 4.00
...1999 Annual ($3.50) Nicieza-s/McDaniel-a 4.00
...2000 Annual ($3.50) Nicieza-s/Derenick & Smith-a 4.00

GAMBIT
Marvel Comics: Nov, 2004 - No. 12, Aug, 2005 ($2.99)
1-12: 1-Jeanty-a/Land-c/Layman-s. 5-Wolverine-c/app. 9-Brother Voodoo-c/app. 3.00
... and the Champions: From the Marvel Vault 1 (10/11, $2.99) George Tuska's last art 3.00
...: Hath No Fury TPB (2005, $14.99) r/#7-12 15.00
...: House of Cards TPB (2005, $14.99) r/#1-6; Land cover sketches; unused covers 15.00

GAMBIT
Marvel Comics: Oct, 2012 - No. 17, Nov, 2013 ($2.99)
1-17: 1-Asmus-s/Mann-a; covers by Mann & Bachalo. 6,7-Pete Wisdom app. 3.00

GAMBIT & BISHOP (... : Sons of the Atom on cover)
Marvel Comics: Feb, 2001 - No. 6, May, 2001 ($2.25, bi-weekly limited series)
Alpha (2/01) Prelude to series; Nord-a 3.00
1-6-Jeanty-a/Williams-c 3.00
Genesis (3/01, $3.50) reprints their first apps. and first meeting 4.00

GAMBIT AND THE X-TERNALS
Marvel Comics: Mar, 1995 - No. 4, July, 1995 ($1.95, limited series)
1-4-Age of Apocalypse 4.00

GAMEBOY (Super Mario covers on all)
Valiant: 1990 - No. 5 ($1.95, coated-c)
1-5: 3,4-Layton-c. 4-Morrow-a. 5-Layton-c(i) 8.00

GAMEKEEPER (Guy Ritchie's...)
Virgin Comics: Mar, 2007 - No. 5, Sept, 2007; Mar, 2008 - No. 5, Jul, 2008 ($2.99)
1-5-Andy Diggle-s/Mukesh Singh-a; 2 covers on each 3.00
1-Extended Edition (6/07, $2.99) r/#1 with script excerpt and sketch art 3.00

A Game of Thrones #18 © G.R.R. Martin

Garfield #16 © Jim Davis

Gay Comics #18 © MAR

	GD 2.0	VG 4.0	FN 6.0	VF 8.0	VF/NM 9.0	NM- 9.2
Series 2 (3/08 - No. 5, 7/08) 1-5-Parker-s/Randle-a						3.00
Vol. 1 TPB (10/07, $14.99) r/#1-5; script and sketch pages; Guy Ritchie intro.						15.00

GAME OF THRONES, A (George R.R. Martin's...) (Based on *A Song of Fire and Ice*)
Dynamite Entertainment: 2011 - Present ($3.99)

	GD	VG	FN	VF	VF/NM	NM-
1-Covers by Alex Ross and Mike Miller	1	2	3	5	6	8
2-19: 2-Covers by Alex Ross and Mike Miller						4.00

GAMERA
Dark Horse Comics: Aug, 1996 - No. 4, Nov, 1996 ($2.95, limited series)

	GD	VG	FN	VF	VF/NM	NM-
1-4						3.00

GAMMARAUDERS
DC Comics: Jan, 1989 - No. 10, Dec, 1989 ($1.25/$1.50/$2.00)

	GD	VG	FN	VF	VF/NM	NM-
1-10-Based on TSR game						3.00

GAMORRA SWIMSUIT SPECIAL
Image Comics (WildStorm Productions): June, 1996 ($2.50, one-shot)

	GD	VG	FN	VF	VF/NM	NM-
1-Campbell wraparound-c; pinups						3.00

GANDY GOOSE (Movies/TV)(See All Surprise, Giant Comics Edition #5A &10, Paul Terry's Comics & Terry-Toons)
St. John Publ. Co./Pines No. 5,6: Mar, 1953 - No. 5, Nov, 1953; No. 5, Fall, 1956 - No. 6, Sum/58

	GD	VG	FN	VF	VF/NM	NM-
1-All St. John issues are pre-code	10	20	30	58	79	100
2	7	14	21	35	43	50
3-5(1953)(St. John)	6	12	18	31	38	45
5,6(1956-58)(Pines)-CBS Television Presents...	5	10	15	24	30	35

GANG BUSTERS (See Popular Comics #38)
David McKay/Dell Publishing Co.: 1938 - 1943

	GD	VG	FN	VF	VF/NM	NM-
Feature Books 17(McKay)('38)-1st app.	71	142	213	454	777	1100
Large Feature Comic 10('39)-(Scarce)	71	142	213	454	777	1100
Large Feature Comic 17('41)	50	100	150	315	533	750
Four Color 7(1940)	53	106	159	334	567	800
Four Color 23('42)	41	82	123	260	435	610
Four Color 24('43)	25	50	75	175	388	600

GANG BUSTERS (Radio/TV)(Gangbusters #14 on)
National Periodical Publ.: Dec-Jan, 1947-48 - No. 67, Dec-Jan, 1958-59 (No. 1-23: 52 pgs.)

	GD	VG	FN	VF	VF/NM	NM-
1	84	168	252	538	919	1300
2	39	78	117	240	395	550
3-5	28	56	84	165	270	375
6-10: 9-Dan Barry-a. 9,10-Photo-c	21	42	63	122	199	275
11-13-Photo-c	17	34	51	100	158	215
14,17-Frazetta-a, 8 pgs. each. 14-Photo-c	36	72	108	211	343	475
15,16,18-20,26: 26-Kirby-a	15	30	45	85	130	175
21-25,27-30	14	28	42	76	108	140
31-44: 44-Last Pre-code (2-3/55)	12	24	36	67	94	120
45-67	10	20	30	54	72	90

NOTE: ***Barry** a-6, 8, 10. **Drucker** a-51. **Moreira** a-48, 50, 59. **Roussos** a-8.*

GANGLAND
DC Comics (Vertigo): Jun, 1998 - No. 4, Sept, 1998 ($2.95, limited series)

	GD	VG	FN	VF	VF/NM	NM-
1-4:Crime anthology by various. 2-Corben-a						3.00
TPB-(2000, $12.95) r/#1-4; Bradstreet-c						13.00

GANGSTERS AND GUN MOLLS
Avon Per./Realistic Comics: Sept, 1951 - No. 4, June, 1952 (Painted c-1-3)

	GD	VG	FN	VF	VF/NM	NM-
1-Wood-a, 1 pg; c-/Avon paperback #292	53	106	159	334	567	800
2-Check-a, 8 pgs.; Kamen-a; Bonnie Parker story	41	82	123	256	428	600
3-Marijuana mentioned; used in **POP**, pg. 84,85	39	78	117	242	401	560
4-Syd Shores-c	34	68	102	199	325	450

GANGSTERS CAN'T WIN
D. S. Publishing Co.: Feb-Mar, 1948 - No. 9, June-July, 1949 (All 52 pgs?)

	GD	VG	FN	VF	VF/NM	NM-
1-True crime stories	39	78	117	236	388	540
2-Skull-c	21	42	63	126	206	285
3,5,6	19	38	57	111	176	240
4-Acid in face story	24	48	72	142	234	325
7-9	15	30	45	90	140	190

NOTE: ***Ingles** a-5, 6. **McWilliams** a-5, 7, 8. **Reinman** c-6.*

GANG WORLD
Standard Comics: No. 5, Nov, 1952 - No. 6, Jan, 1953

	GD	VG	FN	VF	VF/NM	NM-
5-Bondage-c	19	38	57	109	172	235
6	15	30	45	83	124	165

GARFIELD (Newspaper/cartoon cat)
Boom Entertainment (KaBOOM!): May, 2012 - Present ($3.99)

	GD	VG	FN	VF	VF/NM	NM-
1-24-Evanier-s. 1-Two covers by Barker. 8-Christmas-c. 13,20-Pet Force app.						4.00
1-4-First Appearance Variants by Jim Davis. 1-Garfield. 2-Odie. 3-Jon. 4-Nermal						10.00
...: Pet Force Special 1 (8/13, $4.99) Cover swipe of Amazing Spider-Man #50						5.00

GARGOYLE (See The Defenders #94)
Marvel Comics Group: June, 1985 - No. 4, Sept, 1985 (75¢, limited series)

	GD	VG	FN	VF	VF/NM	NM-
1-Wrightson-c; character from Defenders						5.00
2-4						4.00

GARGOYLES (TV cartoon)
Marvel Comics: Feb, 1995 - No. 11, Dec, 1995 ($2.50)

	GD	VG	FN	VF	VF/NM	NM-
1-11: Based on animated series						3.00

GARRISON
DC Comics (WildStorm): Jun, 2010 - No. 6, Nov, 2010 ($2.99)

	GD	VG	FN	VF	VF/NM	NM-
1-6-Mariotte-s/Francavilla-a/c						3.00

GARRISON'S GORILLAS (TV)
Dell Publishing Co.: Jan, 1968 - No. 4, Oct, 1968; No. 5, Oct, 1969 (Photo-c)

	GD	VG	FN	VF	VF/NM	NM-
1	4	8	12	28	47	65
2-5: 5-Reprints #1	3	6	9	19	30	40

GARY GIANNI'S THE MONSTERMEN
Dark Horse Comics: Aug, 1999 ($2.95, one-shot)

	GD	VG	FN	VF	VF/NM	NM-
1-Gianni-s/c/a; back-up Hellboy story by Mignola						4.00

GASM (Sci-Fi, Horror, Fantasy comics magazine)(Mature content)
Stories, Layouts & Press, Inc.: Nov, 1977 - nn (No. 5), Jun, 1978 (B&W/color)

	GD	VG	FN	VF	VF/NM	NM-
1-Mark Wheatley-s/a; Gene Day-s/a; Workman-a	3	6	9	14	19	24
2 (12/77) Wheatley-a; Winnick-s/a; Workman-a	2	4	6	11	16	20
nn(#3, 2/78) Day-s/a; Wheatley-a; Workman-a	2	4	6	10	14	18
nn(#4, 4/78) Day-s/a; Wheatley-a; Corben-a	3	6	9	14	20	26
nn(#5, 6/78) Hempel-a; Howarth-a; Corben-a	3	6	9	15	22	28

GASOLINE ALLEY (Top Love Stories No. 3 on?)
Star Publications: Sept-Oct, 1950 - No. 2, Dec, 1950 (Newspaper-r)

	GD	VG	FN	VF	VF/NM	NM-
1-Contains 1 pg. intro. history of the strip (The Life of Skeezix); reprints 15 scenes of highlights from 1921-1935, plus an adventure from 1935 and 1936 strips; a 2-pg. filler is included on the life of the creator Frank King, with photo of the cartoonist.	20	40	60	115	185	255
2-(1936-37 reprints)-L. B. Cole-c	22	44	66	128	209	290

(See Super Book No. 21)

GASP!
American Comics Group: Mar, 1967 - No. 4, Aug, 1967 (12¢)

	GD	VG	FN	VF	VF/NM	NM-
1	5	10	15	31	53	75
2-4	3	6	9	21	33	45

GATECRASHER
Black Bull Entertainment: Mar, 2000 - No. 4, Jun, 2000 ($2.50, limited series)

	GD	VG	FN	VF	VF/NM	NM-
1,2-Waid-s/Conner & Palmiotti-c/a; 1,2-variant-c by J.G. Jones						3.00
3,4: 3-Jusko var-c. 4-Linsner-c						3.00
... Ring of Fire TPB (11/00, $12.95) r/#1-4; Hughes-c; Ennis intro.						13.00

GATECRASHER (Regular series)
Black Bull Entertainment: Aug, 2000 - No. 6, Jan, 2001 ($2.50, limited series)

	GD	VG	FN	VF	VF/NM	NM-
1-6-Waid-s/Conner & Palmiotti-c/a; 1-3-Variant-c by Fabry. 4-Hildebrandts variant-c. 5-Art Adams var-c. 6-Texeira var-c						3.00

GAY COMICS (Honeymoon No. 41)
Timely Comics/USA Comic Mag. Co. No. 18-24: Mar, 1944 (no month); No. 18, Fall, 1944 - No. 40, Oct, 1949

	GD	VG	FN	VF	VF/NM	NM-
1-Wolverton's Powerhouse Pepper; Tessie the Typist begins; 1st app. Willie (one shot)	61	122	183	390	670	950
18-(Formerly Funny Tunes #17?)-Wolverton-a	41	82	123	256	428	600
19-29: Wolverton-a in all. 21,24-6 pg., 7 pg. Powerhouse Pepper; additional 2 pg. story in 24). 23-7 pg Wolverton story & 2 two pg stories(total of 11pgs.). 24,29-Kurtzman-a (24-"Hey Look"(2))	39	78	117	240	395	550
30,33,36,37-Kurtzman's "Hey Look"	17	34	51	98	154	210
31-Kurtzman's "Hey Look" (1), Giggles 'N' Grins (1-1/2)	17	34	51	98	154	210
32,35,38-40: 35-Nellie The Nurse begins?	16	32	48	92	144	195
34-Three Kurtzman's "Hey Look"	18	36	54	103	162	220

GAY COMICS (Also see Smile, Tickle, & Whee Comics)
Modern Store Publ.: 1955 (7¢, 5x7-1/4", 52 pgs.)

	GD	VG	FN	VF	VF/NM	NM-
1	4	8	12	23	37	50

Gemini Blood #2 © DC

Gene Autry Comics #73 © DELL

Generation X #35 © MAR

	GD	VG	FN	VF	VF/NM	NM-
	2.0	4.0	6.0	8.0	9.0	9.2

GAY PURR-EE (See Movie Comics)

GEARS OF WAR (Based on the video game)
DC Comics (WildStorm): Dec, 2008 - No. 24, Aug, 2012 ($3.99/$2.99)

1-15: 1-Liam Sharp-a/Joshua Ortega-s. 1-Two covers 4.00
16-24-($2.99) 16-Traviss-s/Gopez-a. 18-20-Mhan-a. 19-24-Prelude to Gears of War 3 3.00
... Reader (4/09, $3.99) r/#1 & 2 in flipbook 4.00
... Sourcebook (8/09, $3.99) character pin-ups by various; Platt-c 4.00
Book One HC (2009, $19.99, dustjacket) r/#1-6 & Sourcebook 20.00
Book One SC (2010, $14.99) r/#1-6 & Sourcebook 15.00
Book Two HC (2011, $24.99, dustjacket) r/#7-13 25.00

GEAR STATION, THE
Image Comics: Mar, 2000 - No. 5, Nov, 2000 ($2.50)

1-Four covers by Ross, Turner, Pat Lee, Fraga 3.00
1-($6.95) DF Cover 7.00
2-5: 2-Two covers by Fraga and Art Adams 3.00

GEEK, THE (See Brother Power... & Vertigo Visions)

GEEKSVILLE (Also see 3 Geeks, The)
3 Finger Prints/ Image: Aug, 1999 - No. 6, Mar, 2001 ($2.75/$2.95, B&W)

1,2,4-6-The 3 Geeks by Koslowski; Innocent Bystander by Sassaman 3.00
3-Includes "Babes & Blades" mini-comic 5.00
0-(3/00) First Image issue 3.00
(Vol. 2) 1-4-($2.95) 3-Mini-comic insert by the Geeks. 4-Steve Borock app. 3.00

G-8 AND HIS BATTLE ACES (Based on pulps)
Gold Key: Oct, 1966

1 (10184-610)-Painted-c 4 8 12 25 40 55

G-8 AND HIS BATTLE ACES
Blazing Comics: 1991 ($1.50, one-shot)

1-Glanzman-a; Truman-c 3.00
NOTE: *Flip book format with "The Spider's Web" #1 on other side w/**Glanzman**-a, **Truman**-c.*

GEM COMICS
Spotlight Publishers: Apr, 1945 (52 pgs)

1-Little Mohee, Steve Strong app.; Jungle bondage-c
55 110 165 352 601 850

GEMINAR
Image Comics: July, 2000 ($4.95, B&W)

1-(72-Page Special) Terry Collins-s/Al Bigley-a 5.00

GEMINI BLOOD
DC Comics (Helix): Sept, 1996 - No. 9, May, 1997 ($2.25, limited series)

1-9: 5-Simonson-c 3.00

GEN ACTIVE
DC Comics (WildStorm): May, 2000 - No. 6, Aug, 2001 ($3.95)

1-6: 1-Covers by Campbell and Madureira; Gen 13 & DV8 app. 5-Mahfood-a; Quitely and Stelfreeze-c. 6-Portacio-a/c 4.00

GENE AUTRY (See March of Comics No. 25, 28, 39, 54, 78, 90, 104, 120, 135, 150 in the Promotional Comics section & Western Roundup under Dell Giants)

GENE AUTRY COMICS (Movie, Radio star; singing cowboy)
Fawcett Publications: Jan, 1942 (On sale 12/17/41) - No. 10, 1943 (68 pgs.)
(Dell takes over with No. 11)

1 (Scarce)-Gene Autry & his horse Champion begin; photo back-c
423 846 1269 3000 5250 7500
2-(1942) 90 180 270 576 988 1400
3-5: 3-(11/1/42) 50 100 150 315 533 750
6-10 41 82 123 256 428 600

GENE AUTRY COMICS (...& Champion No. 102 on)
Dell Publishing Co.: No. 11, 1943 - No. 121, Jan-Mar, 1959 (TV - later issues)

11 (1943, 60 pgs.)-Continuation of Fawcett series; photo back-c; first Dell issue
32 64 96 230 515 800
12 (2/44, 60 pgs.) 28 56 84 202 451 700
Four Color 47 (1944, 60 pgs.) 30 60 90 216 483 750
Four Color 57 (11/44),66('45)(52 pgs. each) 27 54 81 194 435 675
Four Color 75,83 ('45, 36 pgs. each) 22 44 66 154 340 525
Four Color 93 ('45, 36 pgs.) 18 36 54 126 281 435
Four Color 100 ('46, 36 pgs.) First Gene Autry photo-c
21 42 63 147 324 500
1 (5-6/46, 52 pgs.) 29 58 87 209 467 725
2 (7-8/46)-Photo-c begin, end #111 14 28 42 96 211 325
3-5: 4-Intro Flapjack Hobbs 11 22 33 76 163 250
6-10 10 20 30 64 132 200
11-20: 20-Panhandle Pete begins 9 18 27 60 120 180
21-29 (36 pgs.) 8 16 24 52 99 145
30-40 (52 pgs.) 7 14 21 44 82 120
41-56 (52 pgs.) 6 12 18 38 69 100
57-66 (36 pgs.): 58-X-mas-c 5 10 15 34 60 85
67-80 (52 pgs.): 70-X-mas-c 5 10 15 34 60 85
81-90 (52 pgs.): 82-X-mas-c. 87-Blank inside-c 5 10 15 31 53 75
91-99 (36 pgs. No. 91-on). 94-X-mas-c 4 8 12 28 47 65
100 5 10 15 30 50 70
101-111-Last Gene Autry photo-c 4 8 12 27 44 60
112-121-All Champion painted-c, most by Savitt 4 8 12 25 40 55
NOTE: *Photo back covers 4-18, 20-45, 48-65. **Manning** a-118. **Jesse Marsh** art: 4-Color No. 66, 75, 93, 100, No. 1-25, 27-37, 39, 40.*

GENE AUTRY'S CHAMPION (TV)
Dell Publ. Co.: No. 287, 8/50; No. 319, 2/51; No. 3, 8-10/51 - No. 19, 8-10/55

Four Color 287(#1)('50, 52 pgs.)-Photo-c 10 20 30 66 138 210
Four Color 319(#2, '51), 3: 2-Painted-c begin, most by Sam Savitt
6 12 18 37 66 95
4-19: 19-Last painted-c 4 8 12 28 47 65

GENE COLAN TRIBUTE BOOK (Produced for The Hero Initiative)
Marvel Comics: 2008 ($9.99, one-shot)

1-Spotlighted stories from Tales of Suspense #89,90, Doctor Strange #174 and others 10.00

GENE DOGS
Marvel Comics UK: Oct, 1993 - No. 4, Jan, 1994 ($1.75, limited series)

1-($2.75)-Polybagged w/4 trading cards 4.00
2-4: 2-Vs. Genetix 3.00

GENE POOL
IDW Publishing: Oct, 2003 ($6.99, squarebound)

nn-Wein & Wolfman-s/Cummings-a 7.00

GENERAL DOUGLAS MACARTHUR
Fox Features Syndicate: 1951

nn-True life story 20 40 60 114 182 250

GENERIC COMIC, THE
Marvel Comics Group: Apr, 1984 (one-shot)

1 3.00

GENERATION HEX
DC Comics (Amalgam): June, 1997 ($1.95, one-shot)

1-Milligan-s/ Pollina & Morales-a 3.00

GENERATION HOPE (See X-Men titles and Cable)
Marvel Comics: Jan, 2011 - No. 17, May, 2012 ($3.99/$2.99)

1-($3.99) Gillen-s/Espin-a; Coipel-c; back-up bio of Hope Summers 4.00
1-Variant-c by Greg Land 8.00
2-17-($2.99) 5,9-McKelvie-a. 10,11-Seeley-a. 11-X-Men: Schism tie-in 3.00

GENERATION M (Follows House of M x-over)
Marvel Comics: Jan, 2006 - No. 5, May, 2006 ($2.99, limited series)

1-5-Jenkins-s/Bachs-a. 1-Chamber app. 2-Jubilee app. 3-Blob-c. 4-Angel-c 3.00
Decimation: Generation M TPB (2006, $13.99) r/#1-5 14.00

GENERATION NEXT
Marvel Comics: Mar, 1995 - No. 4, June, 1995 ($1.95, limited series)

1-4-Age of Apocalypse; Scott Lobdell scripts & Chris Bachalo-c/a 3.00

GENERATION X (See Gen [13]/ Generation X)
Marvel Comics: Oct, 1994 - No. 75, June, 2001 ($1.50/$1.95/$1.99/$2.25)

Collectors Preview ($1.75), "Ashcan" Edition 3.00
-1(7/97) Flashback story 3.00
1/2 (San Diego giveaway) 2 4 6 8 10 12
1-($3.95)-Wraparound chromium-c; Scott Lobdell scripts & Chris Bachalo-a begins 6.00
2-($1.95)-Deluxe edition, Bachalo-a 4.00
3,4-($1.95)-Deluxe Edition; Bachalo-a 4.00
2-10: 2-4-Standard Edition. 5-Returns from "Age of Apocalypse," begin $1.95-c. 6-Bachalo-a(p) ends, returns #17. 7-Roger Cruz-a(p). 10-Omega Red-c/app. 3.00
11-24, 26-28: 13,14-Bishop-app. 17-Stan Lee app. (Stan Lee scripts own dialogue); Bachalo/Buckingham-a; Onslaught update. 18-Toad cameo. 20-Franklin Richards app; Howard the Duck cameo. 21-Howard the Duck app. 22-Nightmare app. 3.00
25-($2.99)-Wraparound-c. Black Tom, Howard the Duck app. 4.00
29-37: 29-Begin $1.99-c, "Operation Zero Tolerance". 33-Hama-s 3.00
38-49: 38-Dodson-a begins. 40-Penance ID revealed. 49-Maggott app. 3.00

Gen 12 #1 © DC

Gen 13 #25 © WSP

Gen 13 V4 #1 © WSP

GD 2.0 | VG 4.0 | FN 6.0 | VF 8.0 | VF/NM 9.0 | NM- 9.2

50,57-($2.99): 50-Crossover w/X-Man #50 4.00
51-56, 58-62: 59-Avengers & Spider-Man app. 3.00
63-74: 63-Ellis-s begin. 64-Begin $2.25-c. 69-71-Art Adams-c 3.00
75-($2.99) Final issue; Chamber joins the X-Men; Lim-a 4.00
'95 Special-($3.95) 4.00
'96 Special-($2.95)-Wraparound-c; Jeff Johnson-c/a 4.00
'97 Special-($2.99)-Wraparound-c; 4.00
'98 Annual-($3.50)-vs. Dracula 4.00
'99 Annual-($3.50)-Monet leaves 4.00
75¢ Ashcan Edition 3.00
...Holiday Special 1 (2/99, $3.50) Pollina-a 4.00
...Underground Special 1 (5/98, $2.50, B&W) Mahfood-a 3.00

GENERATION X/ GEN 13 (Also see Gen 13/ Generation X)
Marvel Comics: 1997 ($3.99, one-shot)

1-Robinson-s/Larroca-a(p) 4.00

GENE RODDENBERRY'S LOST UNIVERSE
Tekno Comix: Apr, 1995 - No. 7, Oct, 1995 ($1.95)

1-7: 1-3-w/ bound-in game piece & trading card. 4-w/bound-in trading card 3.00

GENE RODDENBERRY'S XANDER IN LOST UNIVERSE
Tekno Comix: No. 0, Nov, 1995; No. 1, Dec, 1995 - No. 8, July, 1996 ($2.25)

0,1-8: 1-5-Jae Lee-c. 4-Polybagged. 8-Pt. 5 of The Big Bang x-over 3.00

GENESIS (See DC related titles)
DC Comics: Oct, 1997 - No. 4, Oct, 1997 ($1.95, weekly limited series)

1-4: Byrne-s/Wagner-a(p) in all. 3.00

GENESIS: THE #1 COLLECTION (WildStorm Archives)
WildStorm Productions: 1998 ($9.99, TPB, B&W)

nn-Reprints #1 issues of WildStorm titles and pin-ups 10.00

GENETIX
Marvel Comics UK: Oct, 1993 - No. 6, Mar, 1994 ($1.75, limited series)

1-($2.75)-Polybagged w/4 cards; Dark Guard app. 4.00
2-6: 2-Intro Tektos. 4-Vs. Gene Dogs 3.00

GENEXT (Next generation of X-Men)
Marvel Comics: July, 2008 - No. 5, Nov, 2008 ($3.99, limited series)

1-5: 1-Claremont-s/Scherberger-a; character profile pages 4.00

GENEXT: UNITED
Marvel Comics: July, 2009 - No. 5, Dec, 2009 ($3.99, limited series)

1-5: 1-Claremont-s/Meyers-a; Beast app. 4.00

GEN 12 (Also see Gen13 and Team 7)
Image Comics (WildStorm Productions): Feb, 1998 - No. 5, June, 1998 ($2.50, lim. series)

1-5: 1-Team 7 & Gen13 app.; wraparound-c 3.00

GEN 13 (Also see Wild C.A.T.S. #1 & Deathmate Black #2)
Image Comics (WildStorm Productions): Feb, 1994 - No. 5, July 1994 ($1.95, limited series)

0 (8/95, $2.50)-Ch. 1 w/Jim Lee-p; Ch. 4 w/Charest-p 4.00
1/2 1 2 3 4 5 7
1-($2.50)-Created by Jim Lee 1 3 4 6 8 10
1-2nd printing 3.00
1-"3-D" Edition (9/97, $4.95)-w/glasses 5.00
2-($2.50) 1 2 3 4 5 7
3-Pitt-c & story 4.00
4-Pitt-c & story; wraparound-c 4.00
5 4.00
5-Alternate Portacio-c; see Deathblow #5 6.00
...Collected Edition ('94, $12.95)-r/#1-5 13.00
...Rave ($1.50, 3/95)-wraparound-c 4.00
...: Who They Are And How They Came To Be... (2006, $14.99) r/#1-5; sketch gallery 15.00
NOTE: *Issues 1-4 contain coupons redeemable for the ashcan edition of Gen 13 #0. Price listed is for a complete book.*

GEN 13
Image Comics (WildStorm Productions): Mar, 1995 - No. 36, Dec, 1998;
DC Comics (WildStorm): No. 37, Mar, 1999 - No. 77, Jul, 2002 ($2.95/$2.50)

1-A (Charge)-Campbell/Garner-c 5.00
1-B (Thumbs Up)-Campbell/Garner-c 5.00
1-C-1-F,1-I-1-M: 1-C (Lil' GEN 13)-Art Adams-c. 1-D (Barbari-GEN)-Simon Bisley-c. 1-E (Your Friendly Neighborhood Grunge)-Cleary-c. 1-F (GEN 13 Goes Madison Ave.)-Golden-c. 1-I (That's the way we became GEN 13)-Campbell/Gibson-c. 1-J (All Dolled Up)-Campbell/ McWeeney-c. 1-K (Verti-GEN)-Dunn-c. 1-L (Picto-Fiction). 1-M (Do it Yourself Cover) 1 2 3 4 5 7
1-G (Lin-GEN-re)-Michael Lopez-c 3 6 9 14 20 25
1-H (GEN-et Jackson)-Jason Pearson-c 2 4 6 8 10 12
1-Chromium-c by Campbell 4 8 12 27 44 60
1-Chromium-c by Jim Lee 5 10 15 33 57 80
1-"3-D" Edition (2/98, $4.95)-w/glasses 5.00
2 ($1.95, Newsstand)-WildStorm Rising Pt. 4; bound-in card 3.00
2-12: 2-($2.50, Direct Market)-WildStorm Rising Pt. 4, bound-in card. 6,7-Jim Lee-c/a(p). 9-Ramos-a. 10,11-Fire From Heaven Pt. 3. & Pt.9 4.00
11-($4.95)-Special European Tour Edition; chromium-c 2 4 6 10 14 18
13A,13B,13C-($1.30, 13 pgs.): 13A-Archie & Friends app. 13B-Bone-c/app.; Teenage Mutant Ninja Turtles, Madman, Spawn & Jim Lee app. 4.00
14-24: 20-Last Campbell-a 3.00
25-($3.50)-Two covers by Campbell and Charest 4.00
25-($3.50)-Voyager Pack w/Danger Girl preview 5.00
25-Foil-c 10.00
26-32,34: 26-Arcudi-s/Frank-a begins. 34-Back-up story by Art Adams 3.00
33-Flip book w/Planetary preview 4.00
35-49: 36,38,40-Two covers. 37-First DC issue. 41-Last Frank-a 3.00
50-($3.95) Two covers by Lee and Benes; art by various 4.00
51-76: 51-Moy-a; Fairchild loses her powers. 60-Warren-s/a. 66-Art by various incl. Campbell (3 pgs.). 70,75,76-Mays-a. 76-Original team dies 3.00
77-($3.50) Mays, Andrews, Warren-a 4.00
Annual 1 (1997, $2.95) Ellis-s/ Dillon-c/a. 4.00
Annual 1999 ($3.50, DC) Slipstream x-over w/ DV8 4.00
Annual 2000 ($3.50) Devil's Night x-over w/WildStorm titles; Bermejo-c 4.00
...: A Christmas Caper (1/00, $5.95, one-shot) McWeeney-s/a 6.00
... Archives (4/98, $12.99) B&W reprints of mini-series, #0,1/2,1-13ABC; includes cover gallery and sourcebook 13.00
...: Carny Folk (2/00, $3.50) Collect back-up stories 3.50
... European Vacation TPB ($6.95) r/#6,7 7.00
.../ Fantastic Four (2001, $5.95) Maguire-s/c/a(p) 6.00
...: Going West (6/99, $2.50, one-shot) Pruett-s 3.00
...: Grunge Saves the World (5/99, $5.95, one-shot) Altieri-c/a 6.00
... I Love New York TPB ($9.95) r/part #25, 26-29; Frank-c 10.00
... London, New York, Hell TPB ($6.95) r/Annual #1 & Bootleg Ann. #1 7.00
... Lost in Paradise TPB ($6.95) r/#3-5 7.00
.../ Maxx (12/95, $3.50, one-shot) Messner-Loebs-s, 1st Coker-c/a. 4.00
...: Meanwhile (2003, $17.95) r/#43,44,66-70; all Warren-s; art by various 18.00
...: Medicine Song (2001, $5.95) Brent Anderson-c/a(p)/Raab-s 6.00
... Science Friction (2001, $5.95) Haley & Lopresti-a 6.00
... Starting Over TPB ($14.95) r/#1-7 15.00
... Superhuman Like You TPB ($12.95) r/#60-65; Warren-c 13.00
... #13 A,B&C Collected Edition ($6.95, TPB) r/#13A,B&C 7.00
... 3-D Special (1997, $4.95, one-shot) Art Adams-s/a(p) 5.00
...: The Unreal World (7/96, $2.95, one-shot) Humberto Ramos-c/a 3.00
... We'll Take Manhattan TPB ($14.95) r/#45-50; new Benes-c 15.00
...: Wired (4/99, $2.50, one-shot) Richard Bennett-c/a 3.00
... Yearbook 1997 (6/97, $2.50) College-themed stories and pin-ups by various 3.00
...: 'Zine (12/96, $1.95, B&W, digest size) Campbell/Garner-c 3.00
Variant Collection-Four editions (all 13 variants w/Chromium variant-limited, signed) 100.00

GEN 13
DC Comics (WildStorm): No. 0, Sept, 2002 - No. 16, Feb, 2004 ($2.95)

0-(13¢-c) Intro. new team; includes previews of 21 Down & The Resistance 3.00
1-Claremont-s/Garza-c/a; Fairchild app. 3.00
2-16: 8-13-Bachs-a. 16-Original team returns 3.00
...: September Song TPB (2003, $19.95) r/#0-6; Garza sketch pages 20.00

GEN 13 (Volume 4)
DC Comics (WildStorm): Dec, 2006 - No. 39, Feb, 2011 ($2.99)

1-39: 1-Simone-s/Caldwell-a; re-intro the original team; Caldwell-c. 8-The Authority app. 3.00
1-Variant-c by J. Scott Campbell 5.00
...: Armageddon (1/08, $2.99) Gage-s/Meyers-a; future Gen13 app. 3.00
...: Best of a Bad Lot TPB (2007, $14.99) r/#1-6 15.00
...: 15 Minutes TPB (2008, $14.99) r/#14-20 15.00
...: Road Trip TPB (2008, $14.99) r/#7-13 15.00
...: World's End TPB (2009, $17.99) r/#21-26 18.00

GEN 13 BOOTLEG
Image Comics (WildStorm): Nov, 1996 - No. 20, Jul, 1998 ($2.50)

1-Alan Davis-a; alternate costumes-c 3.00
1-Team falling variant-c 4.00
2-7: 2-Alan Davis-a. 5,6-Terry Moore-s. 7-Robinson-s/Scott Hampton-a 3.00
8-10-Adam Warren-s/a 4.00

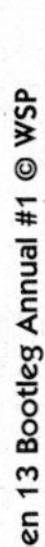

Ghost (2012 series) #2 © DC

	GD 2.0	VG 4.0	FN 6.0	VF 8.0	VF/NM 9.0	NM- 9.2

11-20: 11,12-Lopresti-s/a & Simonson-s. 13-Wieringo-s/a. 14-Mariotte-s/Phillips-a. 15,16-Strnad-s/Shaw-a. 18-Altieri-s/a(p)/c, 18-Variant-c by Bruce Timm 3.00
Annual 1 (2/98, $2.95) Ellis-s/Dillon-c/a 4.00
... Grunge: The Movie (12/97, $9.95) r/#8-10, Warren-c 10.00
...Vol. 1 TPB (10/98, $11.95) r/#1-4 12.00

GEN 13/ GENERATION X (Also see Generation X / Gen 13)
Image Comics (WildStorm Publications): July, 1997 ($2.95, one-shot)

1-Choi-s/ Art Adams-p/Garner-i. Variant covers by Adams/Garner and Campbell/McWeeney 3.00
1-($4.95) 3-D Edition w/glasses; Campbell-c 5.00

GEN 13 INTERACTIVE
Image Comics (WildStorm): Oct, 1997 - No. 3, Dec, 1997 ($2.50, lim. series)

1-3-Internet voting used to determine storyline 3.00
... Plus! (7/98, $11.95) r/series & 3-D Special (in 2-D) 12.00

GEN 13 : MAGICAL DRAMA QUEEN ROXY
Image Comics (WildStorm): Oct, 1998 - No. 3, Dec, 1998 ($3.50, lim. series)

1-3-Adam Warren-s/c/a; manga style, 2-Variant-c by Hiroyuki Utatane 3.50
1-($6.95) Dynamic Forces Ed. w/Variant Warren-c 7.00

GEN 13 /MONKEYMAN & O'BRIEN
Image Comics (WildStorm): Jun, 1998 - No. 2, July, 1998 ($2.50, lim. series)

1,2-Art Adams-s/a(p); 1-Two covers 3.00
1-($4.95) Chromium-c 5.00
1-($6.95) Dynamic Forces Ed. 7.00

GEN 13: ORDINARY HEROES
Image Comics (WildStorm Publications): Feb, 1996 - No. 2, July, 1996 ($2.50, lim. series)

1,2-Adam Hughes-c/a/scripts 3.00
TPB (2004, $14.95) r/series, Gen13 Bootleg #1&2 and Wildstorm Thunderbook; new Hughes-c and art pages 15.00

GENTLE BEN (TV)
Dell Publishing Co.: Feb, 1968 - No. 5, Oct, 1969 (All photo-c)

1 4 8 12 25 40 55
2-5: 5-Reprints #1 3 6 9 16 23 30

GEOMANCER (Also see Eternal Warrior: Fist & Steel)
Valiant: Nov, 1994 - No. 8, June, 1995 ($3.75/$2.25)

1 ($3.75)-Chromium wraparound-c; Eternal Warrior app. 4.00
2-8 3.00

GEORGE OF THE JUNGLE (TV)(See America's Best TV Comics)
Gold Key: Feb, 1969 - No. 2, Oct, 1969 (Jay Ward)

1 8 16 24 56 108 160
2 5 10 15 35 63 90

GEORGE PAL'S PUPPETOONS (Funny animal puppets)
Fawcett Publications: Dec, 1945 - No. 18, Dec, 1947; No. 19, 1950

1-Captain Marvel-c 42 84 126 265 445 625
2 23 46 69 136 223 310
3-10 15 30 45 86 133 180
11-19 13 26 39 74 105 135

GEORGIE COMICS (...& Judy Comics #20-35?; see All Teen & Teen Comics)
Timely Comics/GPI No. 1-34: Spr, 1945 - No. 39, Oct, 1952 (#1-3 are quarterly)

1-Dave Berg-a 37 74 111 222 361 500
2 20 40 60 114 182 250
3-5,7,8 17 34 51 98 154 210
6-Georgie visits Timely Comics 20 40 60 114 182 250
9,10-Kurtzman's "Hey Look" (1 & ?); Millie the Model & Margie app. 18 36 54 103 162 220
11,12: 11-Margie, Millie app. 14 28 42 81 118 155
13-Kurtzman's "Hey Look", 3 pgs. 15 30 45 83 124 165
14-Wolverton-a(1 pg.); Kurtzman's "Hey Look" 15 30 45 85 130 175
15,16,18-20 14 28 42 78 112 145
17,29-Kurtzman's "Hey Look", 1 pg. 14 28 42 81 118 155
21-24,27,28,30-39: 21-Anti-Wertham editorial. 33-38-Hy Rosen-c 13 26 39 74 105 135
25-Painted-c by classic pin-up artist Peter Driben 15 30 45 86 133 180
26-Logo design swipe from Archie Comics 14 28 42 76 108 140

GERALD McBOING-BOING AND THE NEARSIGHTED MR. MAGOO (TV)
(Mr. Magoo No. 6 on)
Dell Publishing Co.: Aug-Oct, 1952 - No. 5, Aug-Oct, 1953

1 9 18 27 62 126 190
2-5 8 16 24 54 102 150

GERONIMO (See Fighting Indians of the Wild West!)
Avon Periodicals: 1950 - No. 4, Feb, 1952

1-Indian Fighter; Maneely-a; Texas Rangers-r/Cowpuncher #1; Fawcette-c 19 38 57 111 176 240
2-On the Warpath; Kit West app.; Kinstler-c/a 14 28 42 76 108 140
3-And His Apache Murderers; Kinstler-c/a(2); Kit West-r/Cowpuncher #6 14 28 42 76 108 140
4-Savage Raids of; Kinstler-c & inside front-c; Kinstlerish-a by McCann(3) 13 26 39 72 101 130

GERONIMO JONES
Charlton Comics: Sept, 1971 - No. 9, Jan, 1973

1 2 4 6 13 18 22
2-9 2 4 6 8 10 12
Modern Comics Reprint #7('78) 5.00

GETALONG GANG, THE (TV)
Marvel Comics (Star Comics): May, 1985 - No. 6, Mar, 1986

1-6: Saturday morning TV stars 5.00

GET LOST
Mikeross Publications/New Comics: Feb-Mar, 1954 - No. 3, June-July, 1954 (Satire)

1-Andru/Esposito-a in all? 34 68 102 199 325 450
2-Andru/Esposito-c; has 4 pg. E.C. parody featuring "The Sewer Keeper" 22 44 66 132 216 300
3-John Wayne 'Hondo' parody 19 38 57 111 176 240
1,2 (10,12/87-New Comics)-B&W r-original 4.00

GET SMART (TV)
Dell Publ. Co.: June, 1966 - No. 8, Sept, 1967 (All have Don Adams photo-c)

1 9 18 27 59 117 175
2,3-Ditko-a 6 12 18 40 73 105
4-8: 8-Reprints #1 (cover and insides) 5 10 15 33 57 80

GHOST (...Comics #9)
Fiction House Magazines: 1951(Winter) - No. 11, Summer, 1954

1-Most covers by Whitman 89 178 267 565 970 1375
2-Ghost Gallery & Werewolf Hunter stories 48 96 144 302 514 725
3-9: 3,6,7,9-Bondage-c. 9-Abel, Discount-a 41 82 123 256 428 600
10,11-Dr. Drew by Grandenetti in each, reprinted from Rangers; 11-Evans-r/Rangers #39; Grandenetti-r/Rangers #49 32 64 96 188 307 425

GHOST (See Comic's Greatest World)
Dark Horse Comics: Apr, 1995 - No. 36, Apr, 1998 ($2.50/$2.95)

1-Adam Hughes-a 1 2 3 5 6 8
2,3-Hughes-a 4.00
4-24: 4-Barb Wire app. 5,6-Hughes-c. 12-Ghost/Hellboy preview. 15,21-X app. 18,19-Barb Wire app. 3.00
25-($3.50)-48 pgs. special 4.00
26-36: 26-Begin $2.95-c. 29-Flip book w/Timecop. 33-36-Jade Cathedral; Harris painted-c 3.00
Special 1 (7/94, $3.95, 48 pgs.) 1 2 3 4 5 7
Special 2 (6/98, $3.95) Barb Wire app. 4.00
... Black October (1/99, $14.95, trade paperback)-r/#6-9,26,27 15.00
... Nocturnes (1996, $9.95, trade paperback)-r/#1-3 & 5 10.00
... Omnibus Vol. 1 (10/08, $24.95, 9x6") r/#1-12; Special 1 and Decade of Dark Horse #2 25.00
... Stories (1995, $9.95, trade paperback)-r/Early Ghost app. 10.00

GHOST (Volume 2)
Dark Horse Comics: Sept, 1998 - No. 22, Aug, 2000 ($2.95)

1-22: 1-4-Ryan Benjamin-c/Zanier-a 3.00
Handbook (8/99, $2.95) guide to issues and characters 3.00
Special 3 (12/98, $3.95) 4.00

GHOST (3rd series)
Dark Horse Comics: No. 0, Sept, 2012 - No. 4, Mar, 2013 ($2.99)

0-4-DeConnick-s/Noto-a. 0-Frison-c. 1,2-Covers by Noto & Alex Ross 3.00

GHOST (4th series)
Dark Horse Comics: Dec, 2013 - Present ($2.99)

1,2-DeConnick & Sebela-s/Sook-a/Dodson-c 3.00

GHOST AND THE SHADOW
Dark Horse Comics: Dec, 1995 ($2.95, one-shot)

1-Moench scripts 3.00

GHOST/BATGIRL
Dark Horse Comics: Aug, 2000 - No. 4, Dec, 2000 ($2.95, limited series)

Ghostbusters (2013 series) #12 © Columbia Picts.

Ghostly Haunts #20 © DC

Ghost Manor #15 © DC

	GD 2.0	VG 4.0	FN 6.0	VF 8.0	VF/NM 9.0	NM- 9.2
1-4-New Batgirl; Oracle & Bruce Wayne app.; Benjamin-c/a						3.00

GHOST/HELLBOY
Dark Horse Comics: May, 1996 - No. 2, June, 1996 ($2.50, limited series)

	GD 2.0	VG 4.0	FN 6.0	VF 8.0	VF/NM 9.0	NM- 9.2
1,2: Mike Mignola-c/scripts & breakdowns; Scott Benefiel finished-a						4.00

GHOST BREAKERS (Also see Racket Squad in Action, Red Dragon & (CC) Sherlock Holmes Comics)
Street & Smith Publications: Sept, 1948 - No. 2, Dec, 1948 (52 pgs.)

	GD 2.0	VG 4.0	FN 6.0	VF 8.0	VF/NM 9.0	NM- 9.2
1-Powell-c/a(3); Dr. Neff (magician) app.	42	84	126	265	445	625
2-Powell-c/a(2); Maneely-a	34	68	102	206	336	465

GHOSTBUSTERS (TV) (Also, see Real...and Slimer)
First Comics: Feb, 1987 - No. 6, Aug, 1987 ($1.25)

	GD 2.0	VG 4.0	FN 6.0	VF 8.0	VF/NM 9.0	NM- 9.2
1-6: Based on new animated TV series						3.00

GHOSTBUSTERS
IDW Publishing: Sept, 2011 - No. 16, Dec, 2012 ($3.99)

	GD 2.0	VG 4.0	FN 6.0	VF 8.0	VF/NM 9.0	NM- 9.2
1-16-Burnham-s/Schoening-a; multiple covers						4.00
...: 100-Page Spooktacular (10/12, $7.99) reprints of IDW stories						8.00

GHOSTBUSTERS
IDW Publishing: (one-shots)

	GD 2.0	VG 4.0	FN 6.0	VF 8.0	VF/NM 9.0	NM- 9.2
...: Con-Volution (6/10, $3.99) Josh Howard-a						4.00
...: Tainted Love (2/10, $3.99) Salgood Sam-a						4.00
...: What in Samhain Just Happened? (10/10, $3.99) Peter David-s/Dan Schoening-a						4.00

GHOSTBUSTERS
IDW Publishing: Feb, 2013 - Present ($3.99)

	GD 2.0	VG 4.0	FN 6.0	VF 8.0	VF/NM 9.0	NM- 9.2
1-14-Janine & the female Ghostbuster crew; Burnham-s/Schoening-a; multiple covers						4.00

GHOSTBUSTERS: DISPLACED AGGRESSION
IDW Publishing: Sept, 2009 - No. 4, Dec, 2009 ($3.99)

	GD 2.0	VG 4.0	FN 6.0	VF 8.0	VF/NM 9.0	NM- 9.2
1-3-Lobdell-s/Kyriazis-a						4.00
Hundred Penny Press: Ghostbusters: Displaced Aggression (3/11, $1.00) r/#1						3.00

GHOSTBUSTERS: INFESTATION (Zombie x-over with Star Trek, G.I. Joe & Transformers)
IDW Publishing: Mar, 2011 - No. 2, Mar, 2011 ($3.99, limited series)

	GD 2.0	VG 4.0	FN 6.0	VF 8.0	VF/NM 9.0	NM- 9.2
1,2-Kyle Hotz-a; covers by Hotz and Snyder III						4.00

GHOSTBUSTERS: LEGION (Movie)
88 MPH Studios: Feb, 2004 - No. 4, May, 2004 ($2.95/$3.50)

	GD 2.0	VG 4.0	FN 6.0	VF 8.0	VF/NM 9.0	NM- 9.2
1-4-Steve Kurth-a/Andrew Dabb-s						3.00
1-3-($3.50) Brereton variant-c						3.50

GHOSTBUSTERS: THE OTHER SIDE
IDW Publishing: Oct, 2008 - No. 4, Jan, 2009 ($3.99)

	GD 2.0	VG 4.0	FN 6.0	VF 8.0	VF/NM 9.0	NM- 9.2
1-4-Champagne-s/Nguyen-a						4.00

GHOSTBUSTERS II
Now Comics: Oct, 1989 - No. 3, Dec, 1989 ($1.95, mini-series)

	GD 2.0	VG 4.0	FN 6.0	VF 8.0	VF/NM 9.0	NM- 9.2
1-3: Movie Adaptation						3.00

GHOST CASTLE (See Tales of...)

GHOSTED
Image Comics (Skybound): Jul, 2013 - Present ($2.99)

	GD 2.0	VG 4.0	FN 6.0	VF 8.0	VF/NM 9.0	NM- 9.2
1-8: 1-Williamson-s/Sudzuka-a/Phillips-c. 6-8-Gianfelice-a						3.00

GHOST IN THE SHELL (Manga)
Dark Horse: Mar, 1995 - No. 8, Oct, 1995 ($3.95, B&W/color, lim. series)

	GD 2.0	VG 4.0	FN 6.0	VF 8.0	VF/NM 9.0	NM- 9.2
1,2	3	6	9	14	20	25
3	2	4	6	9	12	15
4-8	1	3	4	6	8	10

GHOST IN THE SHELL 2: MAN-MADE INTERFACE (Manga)
Dark Horse Comics: Jan, 2003 - No. 11, Dec, 2003 ($3.50, color/B&W, lim. series)

	GD 2.0	VG 4.0	FN 6.0	VF 8.0	VF/NM 9.0	NM- 9.2
1-11-Masamune Shirow-s/a. 5-B&W						5.00

GHOSTLY HAUNTS (Formerly Ghost Manor)
Charlton Comics: #20, 9/71 - #53, 12/76; #54, 9/77 - #55, 10/77; #56, 1/78 - #58, 4/78

	GD 2.0	VG 4.0	FN 6.0	VF 8.0	VF/NM 9.0	NM- 9.2
20	3	6	9	18	28	38
21	2	4	6	13	18	22
22-25,27,31-34,36-Ditko-c/a. 27-Dr. Graves x-over. 32-New logo. 33-Back to old logo	3	6	9	15	22	28
26,29,30,35-Ditko-c	2	4	6	13	18	22
28,37-40-Ditko-a. 39-Origin & 1st app. Destiny Fox	2	4	6	11	16	20
41,42: 41-Sutton-c; Ditko-a. 42-Newton-c/a	2	4	6	13	18	22
43-46,48,50,52-Ditko-a	2	4	6	10	14	18
47,54,56-Ditko-c/a. 56-Ditko-a(r).	3	6	9	14	19	24
49,51,53,55,57	2	4	6	8	10	12
58 (4/78) Last issue	3	6	9	14	19	24
40,41(Modern Comics-r, 1977, 1978)						6.00

NOTE: ***Ditko** a-22-25, 27, 28, 31-34, 36-41, 43-48, 50, 52, 54, 56r; c-22-27, 29, 30, 33-36, 47, 54, 56. **Glanzman** a-20. **Howard** a-27, 30, 35, 40-43, 48, 54, 57. **Kim** a-38, 41, 57. **Larson** a-48, 50. **Newton** c/a-42. **Staton** a-32, 35; c-28, 46. **Sutton** c-33, 37, 39, 41.*

GHOSTLY TALES (Formerly Blue Beetle No. 50-54)
Charlton Comics: No. 55, 4-5/66 - No. 124, 12/76; No. 125, 9/77 - No. 169, 10/84

	GD 2.0	VG 4.0	FN 6.0	VF 8.0	VF/NM 9.0	NM- 9.2
55-Intro. & origin Dr. Graves; Ditko-a	8	16	24	54	102	150
56-58,60,61,70,71,72,75-Ditko-a. 70-Dr. Graves ends. 75-Last 12¢ issue	5	10	15	30	50	70
59,62-66,68	4	8	12	23	37	50
67,69-Ditko-c/a	5	10	15	33	57	80
73,77,78,83,84,86-90,92-95,97,99-Ditko-c/a	3	6	9	21	33	45
74,91,98,119,123,124,127-130: 127,130-Sutton-a	2	4	6	13	18	22
76,79-82,85-Ditko-a	3	6	9	16	24	32
96-Ditko-c	3	6	9	16	24	32
100-Ditko-c; Sutton-a	3	6	9	17	26	35
101,103-105-Ditko-a	3	6	9	14	19	24
102,109-Ditko-c/a	3	6	9	16	23	30
110,113-Sutton-c; Ditko-a	3	6	9	14	19	24
106-Ditko & Sutton-a; Sutton-c	3	6	9	14	19	24
107-Ditko, Wood, Sutton-a	3	6	9	14	20	26
108,116,117,126-Ditko-a	3	6	9	14	19	24
111,118,120-122,125-Ditko-c/a	3	6	9	16	23	30
112,114,115: 112,114-Ditko, Sutton-a. 114-Newton-a. 115-Newton, Ditko-a.	3	6	9	14	19	24
131-134,151,157,163-Ditko-c/a	2	4	6	13	18	22
135,142,145-150,153,154,156,158-160	1	2	3	5	7	9
136-141,143,144,152,155-Ditko-a	2	4	6	8	10	12
161,162,164-168-Lower print run. 162-Nudity panel	2	4	6	9	12	15
169 (10/84) Last issue; lower print run	2	4	6	11	16	20

NOTE: ***Aparo** a-65, 66, 68, 72, 137, 141r, 142r; c-71, 72, 74-76, 81, 146r, 149. **Ditko** a-55-58, 60, 61, 67, 69-73, 75-90, 92-95, 97, 99-118, 120-122, 125r, 126r, 131-141r, 143r, 144r, 146, 147, 149-152, 154-157, 159-161, 163; c-67, 69, 73, 77, 78, 83, 84, 86-90, 92-97, 99, 102, 109, 111, 118, 120-122, 125, 131-133, 147, 148, 151, 157-160, 163. **Glanzman** a-167. **Howard** a-95, 98, 99, 108, 117, 129, 131; c-98, 107, 120, 121, 161. **Larson** a-117, 119, 136, 159; c-136. **Morisi** a-83, 84, 86. **Newton** a-114; c-115(painted). **Palais** a-61. **Staton** a-161; c-117. **Sutton** a-106, 107, 111-114, 127, 130, 162; c-100, 106, 110, 113(painted). **Wood** a-107.*

GHOSTLY WEIRD STORIES (Formerly Blue Bolt Weird)
Star Publications: No. 120, Sept, 1953 - No. 124, Sept, 1954

	GD 2.0	VG 4.0	FN 6.0	VF 8.0	VF/NM 9.0	NM- 9.2
120-Jo-Jo-r	43	86	129	271	461	650
121-124: 121-Jo-Jo-r. 122-The Mask-r/Capt. Flight #5; Rulah-r; has 1pg. story 'Death and the Devil Pills'-r/Western Outlaws #17. 123-Jo-Jo; Disbrow-a(2). 124-Torpedo Man	40	80	120	246	411	575

NOTE: ***Disbrow** a-120-124. **L. B. Cole** covers-all issues (#122 is a sci-fi cover).*

GHOST MANOR (Ghostly Haunts No. 20 on)
Charlton Comics: July, 1968 - No. 19, July, 1971

	GD 2.0	VG 4.0	FN 6.0	VF 8.0	VF/NM 9.0	NM- 9.2
1	7	14	21	44	82	120
2-6: 6-Last 12¢ issue	4	8	12	27	44	60
7-12,17: 17-Morisi-a	3	6	9	19	30	40
13,14,16-Ditko-a	4	8	12	22	35	48
15,18,19-Ditko-c/a	4	8	12	28	47	65

GHOST MANOR (2nd Series)
Charlton Comics: Oct, 1971-No. 32, Dec, 1976; No. 33, Sept, 1977-No. 77, 11/84

	GD 2.0	VG 4.0	FN 6.0	VF 8.0	VF/NM 9.0	NM- 9.2
1	5	10	15	30	50	70
2,3,5-7,9-Ditko-c	3	6	9	17	26	35
4,10-Ditko-c/a	3	6	9	21	33	45
8-Wood, Ditko-a; Sutton-c	3	6	9	19	30	40
11,14-Ditko-c/a	3	6	9	16	24	32
12,17,27,30	2	4	6	9	13	16
13,15,16,23-26,29: 13-Ditko-a. 15,16-Ditko-c. 23-Sutton-a. 24-26,29-Ditko-a. 26-Early Zeck-a; Boyette-c	2	4	6	13	18	22
18-(3/74) Newton 1st pro art; Ditko-a; Sutton-c	3	6	9	15	22	28
19-21: 19-Newton, Sutton-a; nudity panels. 20-Ditko-a. 21-E-Man, Blue Beetle, Capt. Atom cameos; Ditko-a.	2	4	6	13	18	22
22-Newton-c/a; Ditko-a	3	6	9	14	19	24
25,28,31,37,38-Ditko-c/a: 28-Nudity panels	3	6	9	14	19	24
32-36,39,41,45,48-50,53: 34-Black Cat by Kim	2	4	6	8	10	12
40-Ditko-a; torture & drug use	2	4	6	13	18	22
42,43,46,47,51,52,60,62,69-Ditko-c/a	2	4	6	11	16	20
44,54,71-Ditko-a	2	4	6	8	11	14
55,56,58,59,61,63,65-68,70	1	2	3	5	7	9
57-Wood, Ditko, Howard-a	2	4	6	9	12	15

Ghost Rider #10 © MAR

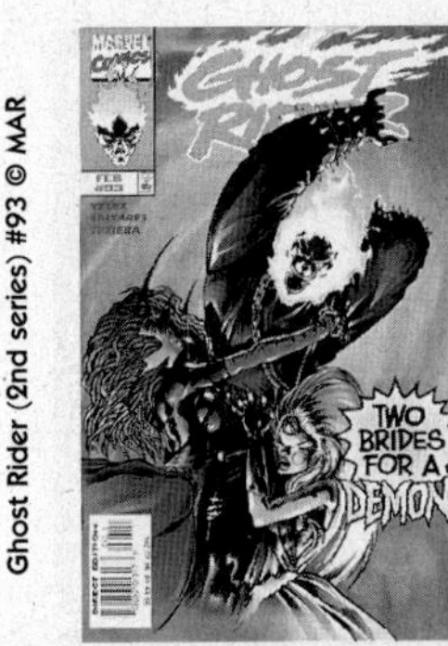

Ghost Rider (2nd series) #93 © MAR

Ghost Rider (2011 series) #2 © MAR

GD VG FN VF VF/NM NM-
2.0 4.0 6.0 8.0 9.0 9.2

64-Ditko & Newton-a 2 4 6 8 11 14
71-76 (low print) 2 3 4 6 8 10
77-(11/84) Last issue Aparo-r/Space Adventures V3#60 (Paul Mann)
2 4 6 9 13 16
19 (Modern Comics reprint, 1977) 6.00

NOTE: ***Ditko*** *a-4, 8, 10, 11(2), 13, 14, 18, 20-22, 24-26, 28, 29, 31, 37r, 38r, 40r, 42-44r, 46r, 47, 51r, 52r, 54r, 57, 60, 62(4), 64r, 69, 71; c-2-7, 9-11, 14-16, 28, 31, 37, 38, 42, 43, 46, 47, 51, 52, 60, 62, 64.* ***Howard*** *a-4, 8, 12, 17, 19-21, 31, 41, 45, 57.* ***Newton*** *a-18-20, 22, 64; c-22.* ***Staton*** *a-13, 38, 44, 45.* ***Sutton*** *a-19, 23, 25, 45;c-8, 18.*

GHOST RIDER (See A-1 Comics, Best of the West, Black Phantom, Bobby Benson, Great Western, Red Mask & Tim Holt)
Magazine Enterprises: 1950 - No. 14, 1954

NOTE: *The character was inspired by Vaughn Monroe's "Ghost Riders in the Sky", and Disney's movie "The Headless Horseman".*

1(A-1 #27)-Origin Ghost Rider 116 232 348 742 1271 1800
2-5: 2(A-1 #29), 3(A-1 #31), 4(A-1 #34), 5(A-1 #37)-All Frazetta-c only
81 162 243 518 884 1250
6,7: 6(A-1 #44)-Loco weed story, 7(A-1 #51) 37 74 111 222 361 500
8,9: 8(A-1 #57)-Drug use story, 9(A-1 #69) 32 64 96 192 314 435
10(A-1 #71)-Vs. Frankenstein 36 72 108 216 351 485
11-14: 11(A-1 #75). 12(A-1 #80)-Bondage-c; one-eyed Devil-c. 13(A-1 #84).
14(A-1 #112) 27 54 81 160 263 365

NOTE: ***Dick Ayers*** *art in all; c-1, 6-14.*

GHOST RIDER, THE (See Night Rider & Western Gunfighters)
Marvel Comics Group: Feb, 1967 - No. 7, Nov, 1967 (Western hero)(12¢)

1-Origin & 1st app. Ghost Rider; Kid Colt-reprints begin
9 18 27 60 120 180
2 5 10 15 35 63 90
3-7: 6-Last Kid Colt-r; All Ayers-c/a(p) 5 10 15 33 57 80

GHOST RIDER (See The Champions, Marvel Spotlight #5, Marvel Team-Up #15, 58, Marvel Treasury Edition #18, Marvel Two-In-One #8, The Original Ghost Rider & The Original Ghost Rider Rides Again)
Marvel Comics Group: Sept, 1973 - No. 81, June, 1983 (Super-hero)

1-Johnny Blaze, the Ghost Rider begins; 1st brief app. Daimon Hellstrom (Son of Satan)
15 30 45 105 233 360
2-1st full app. Daimon Hellstrom; gives glimpse of costume (1 panel); story continues in Marvel Spotlight #12 6 12 18 42 79 115
3-5: 3-Ghost Rider gains power to make cycle of fire; Son of Satan app.
5 10 15 31 53 75
6-10: 10-Hulk on cover; reprints origin/1st app. from Marvel Spotlight #5; Ploog-a
3 6 9 21 33 45
11-16: 11-Hulk app. 3 6 9 14 20 25
17,19-(Reg. 25¢ editions)(4,8/76) 3 6 9 14 20 25
17,19-(30¢-c variants, limited distribution) 4 8 12 27 44 60
18-(Reg. 25¢ edition)(6/76). Spider-Man-c & app. 3 6 9 15 22 28
18-(30¢-c variant, limited distribution) 5 10 15 30 50 70
20-Daredevil x-over; ties into D.D. #138; Byrne-a 3 6 9 17 26 35
21-30: 22-1st app. Enforcer. 29,30-Vs. Dr. Strange 2 4 6 9 12 15
24-26-(35¢-c variants, limited distribution) 4 8 12 25 40 55
31-34,36-49 2 3 4 6 8 10
35-Death Race classic; Starlin-c/a/sty 2 4 6 10 14 18
50-Double size 2 4 6 9 12 15
51-76: 68-Origin retold 6.00
77-80: 77-Origin retold. 80-Brief origin recap 1 2 3 5 6 8
81-Death of Ghost Rider (Demon leaves Blaze) 3 6 9 17 26 35
... Team Up TPB (2007, $15.99) r/#27, 50, Marvel Team-Up #91, Marvel Two-In-One #80, Avengers #214 and Marvel Premiere #28; Night Rider app.; cover gallery 16.00

NOTE: ***Anderson*** *c-64p.* ***Infantino*** *a(p)-43, 44, 51.* ***G. Kane*** *a-21p; c(p)-1, 2, 4, 5, 8, 9, 11-13, 19, 20, 24, 25.* ***Kirby*** *c-21-23.* ***Mooney*** *a-2-9p, 30i.* ***Nebres*** *c-26i.* ***Newton*** *a-23i.* ***Perez*** *c-26p.* ***Shores*** *a-2i. J.* ***Sparling*** *a-62p, 64p, 65p.* ***Starlin*** *a(p)-35.* ***Sutton*** *a-1p, 44i, 64i, 65i, 66, 67i.* ***Tuska*** *a-13p, 14p, 16p.*

GHOST RIDER (Volume 2) (Also see Doctor Strange/Ghost Rider Special, Marvel Comics Presents & Midnight Sons Unlimited)
Marvel Comics (Midnight Sons imprint #44 on): V2#1, May, 1990 - No. 93, Feb, 1998 ($1.50/$1.75/$1.95)

1-($1.95, 52 pgs.)-Origin/1st app. new Ghost Rider; Kingpin app.
2 4 6 8 10 12
1-2nd printing (not gold) 4.00
2-5: 3-Kingpin app. 5-Punisher app.; Jim Lee-c 5.00
5-Gold background 2nd printing 4.00
6-14,16-24,29,30,32-39: 6-Punisher app. 6,17-Spider-Man/Hobgoblin-c/story. 9-X-Factor app. 10-Reintro Johnny Blaze on the last pg. 11-Stroman-c/a(p). 12,13-Dr. Strange x-over cont'd in D.S. #28. 13-Painted-c. 14-Johnny Blaze vs. Ghost Rider; origin recap 1st Ghost Rider (Blaze). 18-Painted-c by Nelson. 29-Wolverine-c/story. 32-Dr. Strange x-over; Johnny Blaze app. 34-Williamson-a(i). 36-Daredevil app. 37-Archangel app. 3.00

GD VG FN VF VF/NM NM-
2.0 4.0 6.0 8.0 9.0 9.2

15-Glow in the dark-c 4.00
25-27: 25-($2.75)-Contains pop-up scene insert. 26,27-X-Men x-over; Lee/Williams-c on both 4.00
28,31-($2.50, 52 pgs.)-Polybagged w/poster; part 1 & part 6 of Rise of the Midnight Sons storyline (see Ghost Rider/Blaze #1) 4.00
40-Outer-c is Darkhold envelope made of black parchment w/gold ink; Midnight Massacre; Demogoblin app. 4.00
41-48: 41-Lilith & Centurious app.; begin $1.75-c. 41-43-Neon ink-c. 43-Has free extra 16 pg. insert on Siege of Darkness. 44,45-Siege of Darkness parts 2 & 10. 44-Spot varnish-c. 46-Intro new Ghost Rider. 48-Spider-Man app. 3.00
49,51-60,62-74: 49-Begin $1.95-c; bound-in trading card sheet; Hulk app. 55-Werewolf by Night app. 65-Punisher app. 67,68-Gambit app. 68-Wolverine app. 73,74-Blaze, Vengeance app. 3.00
50,61: 50-($2.50, 52 pgs.)-Regular edition 4.00
50-($2.95, 52 pgs.)-Collectors Ed. die cut foil-c 5.00
75-89: 76-Vs. Vengeance. 77,78-Dr. Strange-app. 78-New costume 3.00
90-92 6.00
93-($2.99)-Last issue; Saltares & Texeira-a 2 4 6 8 10 12
(#94, see Ghost Rider Finale for unpublished story)
#(-1) Flashback (7/97) Saltares-a 3.00
Annual 1,2 ('93, '94, $2.95, 68 pgs.) 1-Bagged w/card 4.00
...And Cable 1 (9/92, $3.95, stiff-c, 68 pgs.)-Reprints Marvel Comics Presents #90-98 w/new Kieth-c 4.00
...:Crossroads (11/95, $3.95) Die cut cover; Nord-a 5.00
... Cycle of Vengeance 1 (3/12, $5.99) r/Marvel Spotlight #5, Ghost Rider (1990) #1 and Ghost Rider (2006) #1; Leinil Yu-c 6.00
... Finale (2007, $3.99) r/#93 and the story meant for the unpublished #94; Saltares-a 4.00
Highway to Hell (2001, $3.50) Reprints origin from Marvel Spotlight #5 3.50
...: Resurrected TPB (2001, $12.95) r/#1-7 13.00

NOTE: ***Andy & Joe Kubert*** *c/a-28-31.* ***Quesada*** *c-21.* ***Williamson*** *a(i)-33-35; c-33i.*

GHOST RIDER (Volume 3)
Marvel Comics: Aug, 2001 - No. 6, Jan, 2002 ($2.99, limited series)

1-6-Grayson-s/Kaniuga-a/c 3.00
...: The Hammer Lane TPB (6/02, $15.95) r/#1-6 16.00

GHOST RIDER
Marvel Comics: Nov, 2005 - No. 6, Apr, 2006 ($2.99, limited series)

1-6-Garth Ennis-s/Clayton Crain-a/c. 1-Origin retold 3.00
1 (Director's Cut) (2005, $3.99) r/#1 with Ennis pitch and script and Crain art process 4.00
...: Road to Damnation HC (2006, $19.99, dust jacket) r/#1-6; variant covers & concept-a 20.00
...: Road to Damnation SC (2007, $14.99) r/#1-6; variant covers & concept-a 15.00

GHOST RIDER
Marvel Comics: Sept, 2006 - No. 35, Jul, 2009 ($2.99)

1-11: 1-Daniel Way-s/Saltares & Texeira-a. 2-4-Dr. Strange app. 6,7-Corben-a 3.00
12-27,29-35: 12,13-World War Hulk; Saltares-a/Dell'Otto-c. 23-Danny Ketch returns 3.00
28-($3.99) Silvestri-c/Huat-a; back-up history of Danny Ketch 4.00
Annual 1 (1/08, $3.99) Ben Oliver-a/c/Stuart Moore-s 4.00
Annual 2 (10/08, $3.99) Spurrier-s/Robinson-a; r/Ghost Rider #35 (1979) 4.00
... Vol. 1: Vicious Cycle TPB (2007, $13.99) r/#1-5 14.00
... Vol. 2: The Life and Death of Johnny Blaze TPB (2007, $13.99) r/#6-11 14.00
... Vol. 3: Apocalypse Soon TPB (2008, $10.99) r/#12,13 & Annual #1 11.00
... Vol. 4: Revelations TPB (2008, $14.99) r/#14-19 15.00

GHOST RIDER
Marvel Comics: No. 0.1, Aug, 2011 - No. 9, May 2012 ($2.99/$3.99)

0.1-($2.99) Johnny Blaze gets rid of the Spirit of Vengeance; Matthew Clark-a 3.00
1-($3.99) Adam Kubert-c; Fear Itself tie-in; new female Ghost Rider; Mephisto app. 4.00
2-9: 2-4-($2.99) Fear Itself tie-in. 5-Garbett-a. 7,8-Hawkeye app. 3.00

GHOST RIDER/BALLISTIC
Marvel Comics: Feb, 1997 ($2.95, one-shot)

1-Devil's Reign pt. 3 3.00

GHOST RIDER/BLAZE: SPIRITS OF VENGEANCE (Also see Blaze)
Marvel Comics (Midnight Sons imprint #17 on): Aug, 1992 - No. 23, June, 1994 ($1.75)

1-($2.75, 52 pgs.)-Polybagged w/poster; part 2 of Rise of the Midnight Sons storyline; Adam Kubert-c/a begins 4.00
2-11,14-21: 4-Art Adams & Joe Kubert-p. 5,6-Spirits of Venom parts 2 & 4 cont'd from Web of Spider-Man #95,96 w/Demogoblin. 14-17-Neon ink-c. 15-Intro Blaze's new costume & power. 17,18-Siege of Darkness parts 8 & 13. 17-Spot varnish-c 3.00
12-($2.95)-Glow-in-the-dark-c 4.00
13-($2.25)-Outer-c is Darkhold envelope made of black parchment w/gold ink; Midnight Massacre x-over 4.00
22,23: 22-Begin $1.95-c; bound-in trading card sheet 3.00

NOTE: ***Adam & Joe Kubert*** *c-7, 8.* ***Adam Kubert/Steacy*** *c-6.* ***J. Kubert*** *a-13p(6 pgs.)*

Ghost Rider 2099 #1 © MAR

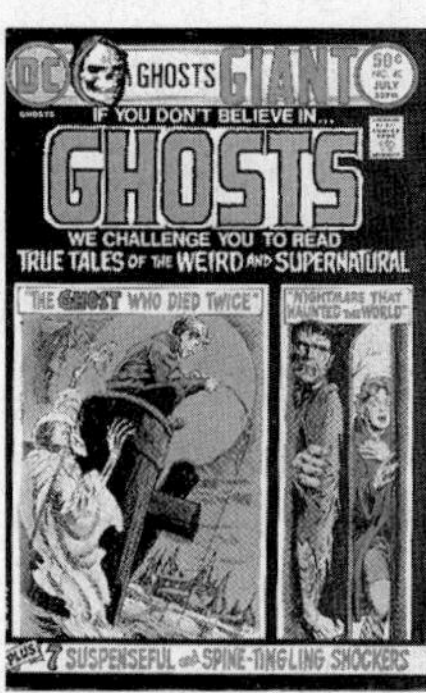

Ghosts #40 © DC

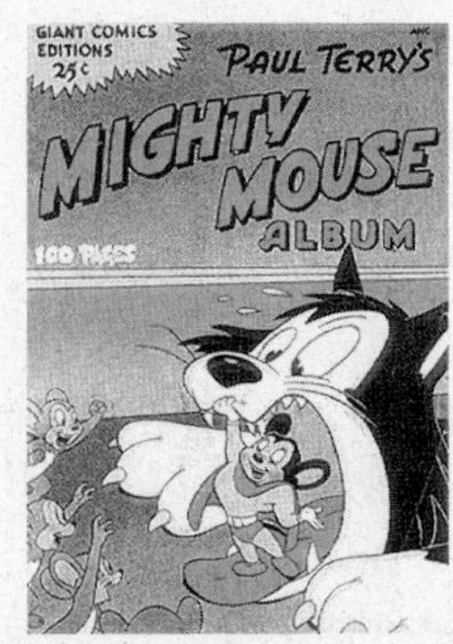

Giant Comics Editions #17 © STJ

GD VG FN VF VF/NM NM-
2.0 4.0 6.0 8.0 9.0 9.2

GHOST RIDER/CAPTAIN AMERICA: FEAR
Marvel Comics: Oct, 1992 ($5.95, 52 pgs.)
nn-Wraparound gatefold-c; Williamson inks 6.00

GHOST RIDER: DANNY KETCH
Marvel Comics: Dec, 2008 - No. 5, Apr, 2009 ($3.99, limited series)
1-5-Saltares-a 4.00

GHOST RIDER: HEAVEN'S ON FIRE
Marvel Comics: Oct, 2009 - No. 6, Mar, 2010 ($3.99, limited series)
1-6: 1-Jae Lee-c/Boschi-a/Aaron-s; Hellstorm app.; r/pages from Ghost Rider #1 ('73) 4.00

GHOST RIDER: TRAIL OF TEARS
Marvel Comics: Apr, 2007 - No. 6, Sept, 2007 ($2.99, limited series)
1-6-Garth Ennis-s/Clayton Crain-a/c; Civil War era tale 3.00
HC (2007, $19.99) r/series 20.00
SC (2008, $14.99) r/series 15.00

GHOST RIDER 2099
Marvel Comics: May, 1994 - No. 25, May, 1996 ($1.50/$1.95)
1 ($2.25)-Collector's Edition w/prismatic foil-c 4.00
1 ($1.50)-Regular Edition; bound-in trading card sheet 3.00
2-24: 7-Spider-Man 2099 app. 3.00
2-(Variant; polybagged with Sega Sub-Terrania poster) 5.00
25 ($2.95) 4.00

GHOST RIDER, WOLVERINE, PUNISHER: THE DARK DESIGN
Marvel Comics: Dec, 1994 ($5.95, one-shot)
nn-Gatefold-c 6.00

GHOST RIDER; WOLVERINE; PUNISHER: HEARTS OF DARKNESS
Marvel Comics: Dec, 1991 ($4.95, one-shot, 52 pgs.)
1-Double gatefold-c; John Romita, Jr.-c/a(p) 6.00

GHOSTS (See The World Around Us #24)

GHOSTS (Ghost No. 1)
National Periodical Publications/DC Comics: Sept-Oct, 1971 - No. 112, May, 1982 (No. 1-5: 52 pgs.)

	GD	VG	FN	VF	VF/NM	NM-
1-Aparo-a	11	22	33	76	163	250
2-Wood-a(i)	7	14	21	44	82	120
3-5-(52 pgs.)	6	12	18	38	69	100
6-10	4	8	12	27	44	60
11-20	3	6	9	14	20	25
21-39	2	4	6	9	13	16
40-(68 pgs.)	3	6	9	16	23	30
41-60	2	4	6	8	10	12
61-96	1	2	3	5	6	8
97-99-The Spectre vs. Dr. 13 by Aparo. 97,98-Spectre-c by Aparo.	2	4	6	10	14	18
100-Infinity-c	2	3	4	6	8	10
101-112	1	2	3	5	6	8

NOTE: ***B. Baily** a-77. **Buckler** c-99, 100. **J. Craig** a-108. **Ditko** a-77, 111. **Giffen** a-104p, 106p, 111p. **Glanzman** a-2. **Golden** a-88. **Infantino** a-8. **Kaluta** c-7, 93, 101. **Kubert** a-8; c-89, 105-108, 111. **Mayer** a-111. **McWilliams** a-99. **Win Mortimer** a-89, 91, 94. **Nasser/Netzer** a-97. **Newton** a-92p, 94p. **Nino** a-35, 37, 57. **Orlando** a-74i; c-80. **Redondo** a-8, 13, 45. **Sparling** a(p)-90, 93, 94. **Spiegle** a-103, 105. **Tuska** a-2i. Dr. 13, the Ghostbreaker back-ups in 95-99, 101.*

GHOSTS
DC Comics (Vertigo): Dec, 2012 ($7.99, one-shot)
1-Short stories by various incl. Johns, Lemire, Pope, Lapham; Joe Kubert's last work 8.00

GHOSTS SPECIAL (See DC Special Series No. 7)

GHOST STORIES (See Amazing Ghost Stories)

GHOST STORIES
Dell Publ. Co.: Sept-Nov, 1962; No. 2, Apr-June, 1963 - No. 37, Oct, 1973

	GD	VG	FN	VF	VF/NM	NM-
12-295-211(#1)-Written by John Stanley	6	12	18	38	69	100
2	4	8	12	23	37	50
3-10: Two No. 6's exist with different c/a(12-295-406 & 12-295-503) #12-295-503 is actually #9 with indicia to #6	3	6	9	19	30	40
11-21: 21-Last 12¢ issue	3	6	9	16	23	30
22-37	2	4	6	13	18	22

NOTE: *#21-34, 36, 37 all reprint earlier issues.*

GHOST WHISPERER (Based on the CBS television series)
IDW Publishing: Mar, 2008 - No. 5, July, 2008 ($3.99)
1-5: 1-Two covers by Casagrande & Ho; Casagrande-a 4.00

GHOST WHISPERER: THE MUSE
IDW Publishing: Dec, 2008 - No. 4, Mar, 2009 ($3.99)
1-4-Two covers (photo & art) for each; Barbara Kesel-s/ Adriano Loyola-a 4.00

GD VG FN VF VF/NM NM-
2.0 4.0 6.0 8.0 9.0 9.2

GHOUL, THE
IDW Publishing: Nov, 2009 - No. 3, Mar, 2010 ($3.99, limited series)
1-3-Niles-s/Wrightson-a 4.00

GHOUL TALES (Magazine)
Stanley Publications: Nov, 1970 - No. 5, July, 1971 (52 pgs.) (B&W)

	GD	VG	FN	VF	VF/NM	NM-
1-Aragon pre-code reprints; Mr. Mystery as host; bondage-c	8	16	24	52	99	145
2,3: 2-(1/71)Reprint/Climax #1. 3-(3/71)	5	10	15	30	50	70
4-(5/71)Reprints story "The Way to a Man's Heart" used in **SOTI**	5	10	15	33	57	80
5-ACG reprints	4	8	12	25	40	55

NOTE: *No. 1-4 contain pre-code Aragon reprints.*

GIANT BOY BOOK OF COMICS (Also see Boy Comics)
Newsbook Publications (Gleason): 1945 (240 pgs., hard-c)

	GD	VG	FN	VF	VF/NM	NM-
1-Crimebuster & Young Robin Hood; Biro-c	100	200	300	635	1093	1550

GIANT COMIC ALBUM
King Features Syndicate: 1972 (59¢, 11x14", 52 pgs., B&W, cardboard-c)

	GD	VG	FN	VF	VF/NM	NM-
Newspaper reprints: Barney Google, Lil Iodine, Katzenjammer Kids, Henry, Beetle Bailey, Blondie, & Snuffy Smith each...	3	6	9	19	30	40
Flash Gordon ('68-69 Dan Barry)	4	8	12	25	40	55
Mandrake the Magician ('59 Falk), Popeye	4	8	12	23	37	50

GIANT COMICS
Charlton Comics: Summer, 1957 - No. 3, Winter, 1957 (25¢, 96 pgs., not rebound material)

	GD	VG	FN	VF	VF/NM	NM-
1-Atomic Mouse, Lil Genius, Lil Tomboy app.	23	46	69	136	223	310
2-(Fall '57) Romance	22	44	66	132	216	300
3-Christmas Book; Atomic Mouse, Atomic Rabbit, Li'l Genius, Li'l Tomboy & Atom the Cat stories	18	36	54	103	162	220

GIANT COMICS (See Wham-O Giant Comics)

GIANT COMICS EDITION (See Terry-Toons) (Also see Fox Giants)
St. John Publishing Co.: 1947 - No. 17, 1950 (25¢, 100-164 pgs.)

	GD	VG	FN	VF	VF/NM	NM-
1-Mighty Mouse	54	108	162	346	591	835
2-Abbie & Slats	32	64	96	188	307	425
3-Terry-Toons Album; 100 pgs.	42	84	126	265	445	625
4-Crime comics; contains Red Seal No. 16, used & illo. in **SOTI**	65	130	195	416	708	1000
5-Police Case Book (4/49, 132 pgs.)-Contents varies; contains remaindered St. John books - some volumes contain 5 copies rather than 4, with 160 pages; Matt Baker-c	66	132	198	419	722	1025
5A-Terry-Toons Album (132 pgs.)-Mighty Mouse, Heckle & Jeckle, Gandy Goose & Dinky stories	39	78	117	240	395	550
6-Western Picture Stories; Baker-c/a(3); Tuska-a; The Sky Chief, Blue Monk, Ventrilo app., 132 pgs.	55	110	165	352	601	850
7-Contains a teen-age romance plus 3 Mopsy comics	47	94	141	296	498	700
8-The Adventures of Mighty Mouse (10/49)	39	78	117	240	395	550
9-Romance and Confession Stories; Kubert-a(4); Baker-a; photo-c (132 pgs.)	116	232	348	742	1271	1800
10-Terry-Toons Album (132 pgs.)-Mighty Mouse, Heckle & Jeckle, Gandy Goose stories	39	78	117	240	395	550
11-Western Picture Stories-Baker-c/a(4); The Sky Chief, Desperado, & Blue Monk app.; another version with Son of Sinbad by Kubert (132 pgs.)	55	110	165	352	601	850
12-Diary Secrets; Baker prostitute-c; 4 St. John romance comics; Baker-a	432	864	1296	3154	5577	8000
13-Romances; Baker, Kubert-a	103	206	309	659	1130	1600
14-Mighty Mouse Album (132 pgs.)	39	78	117	231	378	525
15-Romances (4 love comics)-Baker-c	116	232	348	742	1271	1800
16-Little Audrey; Abbott & Costello, Casper	47	94	141	296	498	700
17(nn)-Mighty Mouse Album (nn, no date, but did follow No. 16); 100 pgs. on cover but has 148 pgs.	39	78	117	231	378	525

NOTE: *The above books contain remaindered comics and contents could vary with each issue. No. 11, 12 have part photo magazine insides.*

GIANT COMICS EDITIONS
United Features Syndicate: 1940's (132 pgs.)

	GD	VG	FN	VF	VF/NM	NM-
1-Abbie & Slats, Abbott & Costello, Jim Hardy, Ella Cinders, Iron Vic, Gordo, & Bill Bumlin	41	82	123	256	428	600
2-Jim Hardy, Ella Cinders, Elmo & Gordo	30	60	90	177	289	400

NOTE: *Above books contain rebound copies; contents can vary.*

Giantkiller #1 © Dan Brereton

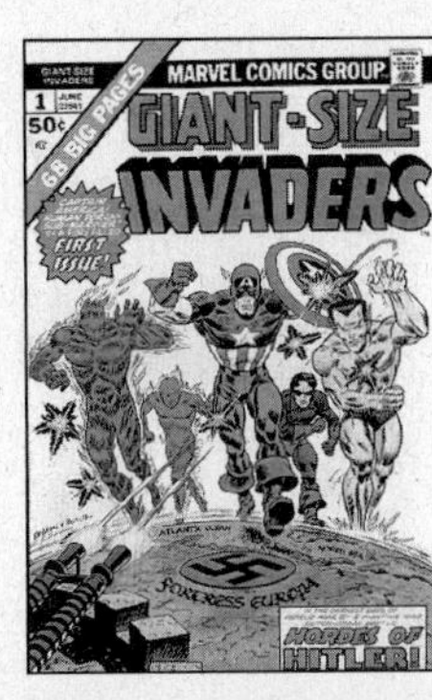

Giant-Size Invaders #1 © MAR

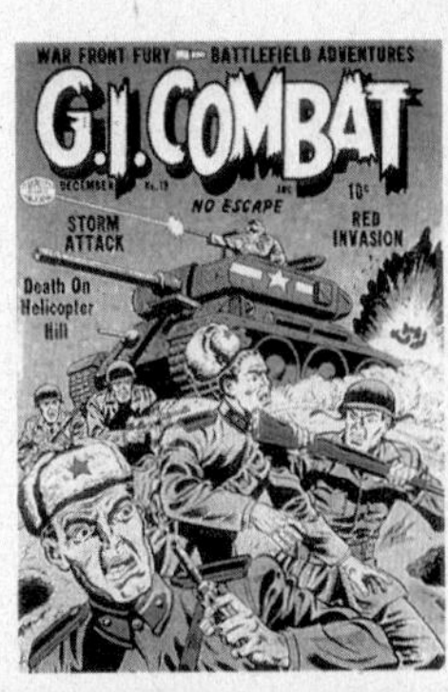

G.I. Combat #19 © QUA

GD 2.0 | VG 4.0 | FN 6.0 | VF 8.0 | VF/NM 9.0 | NM- 9.2

GIANT GRAB BAG OF COMICS (See Archie All-Star Specials under Archie Comics)

GIANTKILLER
DC Comics: Aug, 1999 - No. 6, Jan, 2000 ($2.50, limited series)
1-6-Story and painted art by Dan Brereton 3.00
...A to Z: A Field Guide to Big Monsters (8/99) 3.00
...Vol. 1 TPB (Image Comics, 2006, $14.99) r/#1-6 & A-Z; gallery of concept art 15.00

GIANTS (See Thrilling True Story of the Baseball...)

GIANT-SIZE ATOM
DC Comics: May, 2011 ($4.99, one-shot)
1-Gary Frank-c; Hawkman app.; Lemire-s/Asrar-a 5.00

GIANT-SIZE...
Marvel Comics Group: May, 1974 - Dec, 1975 (35/50¢, 52/68 pgs.)
(Some titles quarterly) (Scarce in strict NM or better due to defective cutting, gluing and binding; warping, splitting and off-center pages are common)

Avengers 1(8/74)-New-a plus G.A. H. Torch-r; 1st modern app. The Whizzer; 1st modern app. Miss America; 2nd app. Invaders; Kang, Rama-Tut, Mantis app. 6 12 18 37 66 95
Avengers 2,3,5: 2(11/74)-Death of the Swordsman; origin of Rama-Tut. 3(2/75). 5(12/75)-Reprints Avengers Special #1 4 8 12 25 40 55
Avengers 4 (6/75)-Vision marries Scarlet Witch. 5 10 15 30 50 70
Captain America 1(12/75)-r/stories T.O.S. 59-63 by Kirby (#63 reprints origin) 4 8 12 27 44 60
Captain Marvel 1(12/75)-r/Capt. Marvel #17, 20, 21 by Gil Kane (p) 4 8 12 22 35 48
Chillers 1(6/74, 52 pgs)-Curse of Dracula; origin/1st app. Lilith, Dracula's daughter; Heath-r, Colan-c/a(p); becomes Giant-Size Dracula #2 on 5 10 15 35 63 90
Chillers 1(2/75, 50¢, 68 pgs.)-Alcala-a 4 8 12 23 37 50
Chillers 2(5/75)-All-r; Everett-r from Advs. into Weird Worlds 3 6 9 18 28 38
Chillers 3(8/75)-Wrightson-c(new)/a(r); Colan, Kirby, Smith-r 4 8 12 23 37 50
Conan 1(9/74)-B. Smith-r/#3; start adaptation of Howard's "Hour of the Dragon" (ends #4); 1st app. Belit; new-a begins 4 8 12 22 35 48
Conan 2(12/74)-B. Smith-r/#5; Sutton-a(i)(#1 also); Buscema-c 3 6 9 18 28 38
Conan 3-5: 3(4/75)-B. Smith-r/#6; Sutton-a(i). 4(6/75)-B. Smith-r/#7. 5(1975)-B. Smith-r/#14,15; Kirby-c 3 6 9 16 24 32
Creatures 1(5/74, 52 pgs.)-Werewolf app; 1st app. Tigra (formerly Cat); Crandall-r; becomes Giant-Size Werewolf w/#2 4 8 12 28 47 65
Daredevil 1(1975)-Reprints Daredevil Annual #1 3 6 9 20 31 42
Defenders 1(7/74)-Silver Surfer app.; Starlin-a; Ditko, Everett & Kirby reprints 5 10 15 30 50 70
Defenders 2(10/74, 68 pgs.)-New G. Kane-c/a(p); Son of Satan app.; Sub-Mariner-r by Everett; Ditko-r/Strange Tales #119 (Dr. Strange); Maneely-r 4 8 12 22 35 48
Defenders 3-5: 3(1/75)-1st app. Korvac.; Newton, Starlin-a; Ditko, Everett-r. 4(4/75)-Ditko, Everett-r; G. Kane-c. 5-(7/75)-Guardians app. 3 6 9 20 31 42
Doc Savage 1(1975, 68 pgs.)-r/#1,2; Mooney-r 3 6 9 16 24 32
Doctor Strange 1(11/75)-Reprints stories from Strange Tales #164-168; Lawrence, Tuska-r 3 6 9 18 28 38
Dracula 2(9/74, 50¢)-Formerly Giant-Size Chillers 4 8 12 22 35 48
Dracula 3(12/74)-Fox-r/Uncanny Tales #6 3 6 9 20 31 42
Dracula 4(3/75)-Ditko-r(2) 3 6 9 20 31 42
Dracula 5(6/75)-1st Byrne art at Marvel 5 10 15 33 57 80
Fantastic Four 2-4: 2(8/74)-Formerly Giant-Size Super-Stars; Ditko-r. 2,4-Buscema-a. 3(11/74)-Buckler-a. 4(2/75)-1st Madrox. 4 8 12 25 40 55
Fantastic Four 5,6: 5(5/75)-All-r; Kirby, G. Kane-r. 6(10/75)-All-r; Kirby-r 3 6 9 20 31 42
Hulk 1(1975) r/Hulk Special #1 4 8 12 22 35 48
Invaders 1(6/75, 50¢, 68 pgs.)-Origin; G.A. Sub-Mariner-r/Sub-Mariner #1; intro Master Man 4 8 12 27 44 60
Iron Man 1(1975)-Ditko reprint 4 8 12 22 35 48
Kid Colt 1-3: 1(1/75). 2(4/75). 3(7/75)-new Ayers-a 7 14 21 48 89 130
Man-Thing 1(8/74)-New Ploog-c/a (25 pgs.); Ditko-r/Amazing Adv. #11; Kirby-r/Strange Tales Ann. #2 & T.O.S. #15; (#1-5 all have new Man-Thing stories, pre-hero-r & are 68 pgs.) 4 8 12 27 44 60
Man-Thing 2,3: 2(11/74)-Buscema-c/a(p); Kirby, Powell-r. 3(2/75)-Alcala-a; Ditko, Kirby, Sutton-r; Gil Kane-c 3 6 9 20 31 42
Man-Thing 4,5: 4(5/75)-Howard the Duck by Brunner-c/a; Ditko-r. 5(8/75)-Howard the Duck by Brunner (p); Dracula cameo in Howard the Duck; Buscema-a(p); Sutton-a(i); G. Kane-c 4 8 12 27 44 60
Marvel Triple Action 1,2: 1(5/75). 2(7/75) 3 6 9 16 24 32
Master of Kung Fu 1(9/74)-Russell-a; Yellow Claw-r in #1-4; Gulacy-a in #1,2 4 8 12 25 40 55
Master of Kung Fu 2-4: 2-(12/74)-r/Yellow Claw #1. 3(3/75)-Gulacy-a; Kirby-a. 4(6/75)-Kirby-a 3 6 9 20 31 42
Power Man 1(1975) 3 6 9 18 28 38
Spider-Man 1(7/74)-Spider-Man /Human Torch-r by Kirby/Ditko; Byrne-r plus new-a (Dracula-c/story) 6 12 18 40 73 105
Spider-Man 2,3: 2(10/74)-Shang-Chi-c/app. 3(1/75)-Doc Savage-c/app.; Daredevil/Spider-Man-r w/Ditko-a 4 8 12 27 44 60
Spider-Man 4(4/75)-3rd Punisher app.; Byrne, Ditko-r 10 20 30 66 138 210
Spider-Man 5,6: 5(7/75)-Man-Thing/Lizard-c. 6(9/75) 4 8 12 23 37 50
Super-Heroes Featuring Spider-Man 1(6/74, 35¢, 52 pgs.)-Spider-Man vs. Man-Wolf; Morbius, the Living Vampire app.; Ditko-r; G. Kane-a(p); Spidey villains app. 6 12 18 37 66 95
Super-Stars 1(5/74, 35¢, 52 pgs.)-Fantastic Four; Thing vs. Hulk; Kirbyish-c/a by Buckler/Sinnott; F.F. villains profiled; becomes Giant-Size Fantastic Four #2 on 5 10 15 35 63 90
Super-Villain Team-Up 1(3/75, 68 pgs.)-Craig-r(i) (Also see Fantastic Four #6 for 1st super-villain team-up) 3 6 9 20 31 42
Super-Villain Team-Up 2(6/75, 68 pgs.)-Dr. Doom, Sub-Mariner app.; Spider-Man-r from Amazing Spider-Man #8 by Ditko; Sekowsky-a(p) 3 6 9 17 26 35
Thor 1(7/75) 4 8 12 25 40 55
Werewolf 2(10/74, 68 pgs.)-Formerly Giant-Size Creatures; Ditko-r; Frankenstein app. 3 6 9 19 30 40
Werewolf 3,5: 3(1/75, 68 pgs.). 5(7/75, 68 pgs.) 3 6 9 19 30 40
Werewolf 4(4/75, 68 pgs.)-Morbius the Living Vampire app. 3 6 9 21 33 45
X-Men 1(Summer, 1975, 50¢, 68 pgs.)-1st app. new X-Men; intro. Nightcrawler, Storm, Colossus & Thunderbird; 2nd full app. Wolverine after Incredible Hulk #181 100 200 300 600 975 1350
X-Men 2 (11/75)-N. Adams-r (51 pgs) 8 16 24 56 108 160
Giant Size Marvel TPB (2005, $24.99) reprints stories from Giant-Size Avengers #1, G-S Fantastic Four #4, G-S Defenders #4, G-S Super-Heroes #1, G-S Invaders #1, G-S X-Men #1 and Giant-Size Creatures #1 25.00

GIANT-SIZE...
Marvel Comics: 2005 - 2008 ($4.99/$3.99)
Astonishing X-Men 1 (7/08, $4.99) Concludes story from Astonishing X-Men #24; Whedon-s/Cassaday-a/wraparound-c; Spider-Man, FF, Dr. Strange app.; variant cover gallery 5.00
Astonishing X-Men 1 (7/08, $4.99) Variant B&W cover 5.00
Avengers 1 (2/08, $4.99) new short stories and r/Avengers #58, 201; Hitch-c 5.00
Avengers/Invaders 1 ('08, $3.99) r/Avengers #71; Invaders #10, Ann. 1 & G-S #2 4.00
Hulk 1 (8/06, $4.99)-2 new stories; Planet Hulk (David-s/Santacruz-a) & Hulk vs. The Champions (Pak-s/Lopresti-a; r/Incredible Hulk: The End) 5.00
Incredible Hulk 1 (7/08, $3.99)-1 new story; r/Incredible Hulk Annual #7; Frank-c 4.00
Invaders 2 ('05, $4.99)-new Thomas-s/Weeks-a; r/Invaders #1&2 & All-Winners #1&2 5.00
Marvel Adventures The Avengers (9/07, $3.99) Agents of Atlas and Kang app.; Kirk-a: reprint of 1st Namora app. from Marvel Mystery Comics #82; reprint from Venus #1 4.00
Spider-Woman ('05, $4.99)-new Bendis-s/Mays-a; r/Marvel Spotlight #32 & S-W #1,37,38 5.00
Wolverine (12/06, $4.99)-new Lapham-s/Aja-a; r/X-Men #6,7 5.00
X-Men 3 ('05, $4.99)-new Whedon-s/N. Adams-a; r/team-ups; Cockrum & Cassaday-c 5.00

GIANT SPECTACULAR COMICS (See Archie All-Star Special under Archie Comics)

GIANT SUMMER FUN BOOK (See Terry-Toons...)

G. I. COMBAT
Quality Comics Group: Oct, 1952 - No. 43, Dec, 1956

	GD 2.0	VG 4.0	FN 6.0	VF 8.0	VF/NM 9.0	NM- 9.2
1-Crandall-c; Cuidera a-1-43i	107	214	321	680	1165	1650
2	46	92	138	290	488	685
3-5,10-Crandall-c/a	41	82	123	250	418	585
6-Crandall-a	39	78	117	231	378	525
7-9	36	72	108	211	343	475
11-20	26	52	78	154	252	350
21-31,33,35-43: 41-1st S.A. issue	24	48	72	142	234	325
32-Nuclear attack-c/story "Atomic Rocket Assault"	27	54	81	160	263	365
34-Crandall-a	25	50	75	150	245	340

G. I. COMBAT (See DC Special Series #22)
National Periodical Publ./DC Comics: No. 44, Jan, 1957 - No. 288, Mar, 1987

	GD 2.0	VG 4.0	FN 6.0	VF 8.0	VF/NM 9.0	NM- 9.2
44-Grey tone-c	75	150	225	600	1350	2100
45	35	70	105	252	564	875
46-50	30	60	90	216	483	750
51-Grey tone-c	38	76	114	281	628	975
52-54,59,60	27	54	81	194	435	675
55-Minor Sgt. Rock prototype by Finger	29	58	87	209	467	725

G.I. Combat (2012 series) #0 © DC

Giggle Comics #1 © ACG

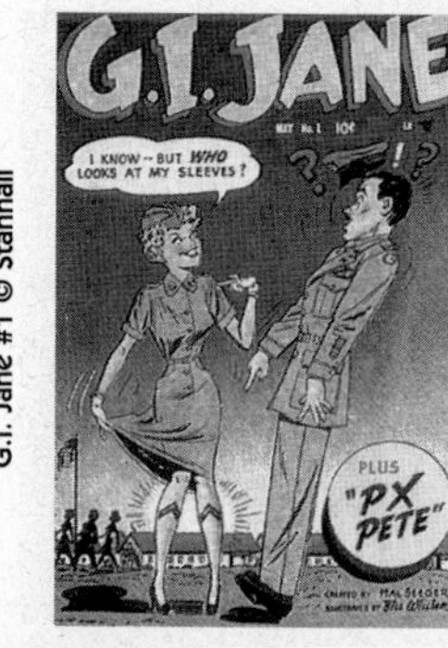

G.I. Jane #1 © Stanhall

	GD 2.0	VG 4.0	FN 6.0	VF 8.0	VF/NM 9.0	NM- 9.2
56-Sgt. Rock prototype by Kanigher/Kubert	36	72	108	266	596	925
57,58-Pre-Sgt. Rock Easy Co. stories	33	66	99	238	532	825
61-65,70-73	21	42	63	147	324	500
66-Pre-Sgt. Rock Easy Co. story	30	60	90	216	483	750
67-1st Tank Killer	37	74	111	274	612	950
68-(1/59) "The Rock" - Sgt. Rock prototype. Part of lead-up trio to 1st definitive Sgt. Rock. Character named Jimmy referred to as "The Rock" appears as a sergeant on the cover and as a private in the story. In reprint (Our Army at War #242) DC edits Jimmy's name out; also see Our Army at War #81-84	141	282	423	1142	2571	4000
69-Grey tone-c	36	72	108	259	580	900
74-American flag-c	24	48	72	168	372	575
75-80: 75-Grey tone-c begin, end #109	31	62	93	223	499	775
81,82,84-86-Grey tone-c	27	54	81	194	435	675
83-1st Big Al, Little Al, & Charlie Cigar; grey tone-c	34	68	102	245	548	850
87-(4-5/61) 1st Haunted Tank; series begins; classic Heath washtone-c	145	290	435	1196	2698	4200
88-(6-7/61) 2nd Haunted Tank; Grey tone-c	44	88	132	326	738	1150
89,90: 90-Last 10¢ issue; Grey tone-c	28	56	84	202	451	700
91-(12/61-1/62)1st Haunted Tank-c; Grey tone-c	56	112	168	448	1000	1550
92-95,99-Grey tone-c	24	48	72	170	378	585
96-98-Grey tone-c	18	36	54	126	281	435
100,108: 100-(6-7/63). 108-1st Sgt. Rock x-over; Grey tone-c	20	40	60	138	307	475
101-103,105-107-Grey tone-c	15	30	45	105	233	360
104,109-Grey tone-c	19	38	57	133	297	460
110-112,115-118,120	12	24	36	82	179	275
113-Grey tone-c	16	32	48	110	243	375
114-Origin Haunted Tank	33	66	99	238	532	825
119-Grey tone-c	15	30	45	103	227	350
121-136: 121-1st app. Sgt. Rock's father. 125-Sgt. Rock app. 136-Last 12¢ issue	8	16	24	56	108	160
137,139,140	5	10	15	35	63	90
138-Intro. The Losers (Capt. Storm, Gunner/Sarge, Johnny Cloud) in Haunted Tank (10-11/69)	12	24	36	80	173	265
141-143	4	8	12	25	40	55
144-148 (68 pgs.)	5	10	15	30	50	70
149,151-154 (52 pgs.): 151-Capt. Storm story. 151,153-Medal of Honor series by Maurer	4	8	12	25	40	55
150- (52 pgs.) Ice Cream Soldier story (tells how he got his name); Death of Haunted Tank-c/s	5	10	15	30	50	70
155-167,169,170	3	6	9	14	20	25
168-Neal Adams-c	3	6	9	17	26	35
171-192,194-199: 195-Haunted Tank & War That Time Forgot	2	4	6	11	16	20
193-(10/76) Haunted Tank meets War That Time Forgot; Dinosaur-c/s; Kubert-a	3	6	9	14	20	25
200-(3/77) Haunted Tank-c/s; Sgt. Rock and the Losers app.; Kubert-c	3	6	9	16	23	30
201,202 ($1.00 size) Neal Adams-c	3	6	9	16	23	30
203-210 ($1.00 size)	3	6	9	14	20	25
211-230 ($1.00 size)	2	4	6	11	16	20
231-259 ($1.00 size).232-Origin Kana the Ninja. 244-Death of Slim Stryker; 1st app. The Mercenaries. 246-(76 pgs., $1.50)-30th Anniversary issue. 257-Intro. Stuart's Raiders	2	4	6	9	13	16
260-281: 260-Begin $1.25, 52 pg. issues, end #281. 264-Intro Sgt. Bullet; origin Kana. 269-Intro. The Bravos of Vietnam. 274-Cameo of Monitor from Crisis on Infinite Earths	2	4	6	8	10	12
282-288 (75¢): 282-New advs. begin	1	2	3	5	7	9

NOTE: ***N. Adams** c-168, 201, 202. **Check** a-168, 173. **Drucker** a-48, 61, 63, 66, 71, 72, 76, 134, 140, 141, 144, 147, 148, 153. **Evans** a-135, 138, 158, 164, 166, 201, 202, 204, 205, 215, 256. **Giffen** a-267. **Glanzman** a-most issues. **Kubert/Heath** a-most issues; **Kubert** covers most issues. **Morrow** a-159-161(2 pgs.). **Redondo** a-189, 240i, 243i. **Sekowsky** a-162p. **Severin** a-147, 152, 154. **Simonson** c-169. **Thorne** a-152, 156. **Wildey** a-153. Johnny Cloud app.-112, 115, 120. Mlle. Marie app.-123, 132, 200. Sgt. Rock app.-111-113, 115, 120, 125, 141, 146, 147, 149, 200. USS Stevens by **Glanzman**-145, 150-153, 157. **Grandenetti** c-44-48.*

G. I. COMBAT
DC Comics: Nov, 2010 ($3.99, one-shot)

	GD 2.0	VG 4.0	FN 6.0	VF 8.0	VF/NM 9.0	NM- 9.2
1-Haunted Tank and General J.E.B. Stuart app.; Sturges-s/Winslade-a/Darrow-c						4.00

G. I. COMBAT
DC Comics: Jul, 2012 - No. 7, Feb, 2013 ($3.99)

	GD 2.0	VG 4.0	FN 6.0	VF 8.0	VF/NM 9.0	NM- 9.2
1-7: 1-War That Time Forgot; Olivetti-a; Unknown Soldier; Panosian-a; two covers						4.00
#0 (11/12, $3.99) Unknown Soldiers through history; War That Time Forgot; Olivetti-a						4.00

GIDGET (TV)
Dell Publishing Co.: Apr, 1966 - No. 2, Dec, 1966

	GD 2.0	VG 4.0	FN 6.0	VF 8.0	VF/NM 9.0	NM- 9.2
1-Sally Field photo-c	8	16	24	51	96	140
2	6	12	18	37	66	95

GIFT COMICS
Fawcett Publications: 1942 - No. 4, 1949 (50¢/25¢, 324 pgs./152 pgs.)

	GD 2.0	VG 4.0	FN 6.0	VF 8.0	VF/NM 9.0	NM- 9.2
1-Captain Marvel, Bulletman, Golden Arrow, Ibis the Invincible, Mr. Scarlet, & Spy Smasher begin; not rebound, remaindered comics, printed at same time as originals; 50¢-c & 324 pgs. begin, end #3.	300	600	900	1980	3440	4900
2-Commando Yank, Phantom Eagle, others app.	181	362	543	1158	1979	2800
3-(50¢, 324 pgs.)	126	252	378	806	1378	1950
4-(25¢, 152 pgs.)-The Marvel Family, Captain Marvel, etc.; each issue can vary in contents	76	152	228	486	831	1175

GIFTS FROM SANTA (See March of Comics No. 137)

GIFTS OF THE NIGHT
DC Comics (Vertigo): Feb, 1999 - No. 4, May, 1999 ($2.95, limited series)

	GD 2.0	VG 4.0	FN 6.0	VF 8.0	VF/NM 9.0	NM- 9.2
1-4-Bolton-c/a; Chadwick-s						3.00

GIGANTIC
Dark Horse Comics: Nov, 2008 - No. 5, Jan, 2010 ($3.50, limited series)

	GD 2.0	VG 4.0	FN 6.0	VF 8.0	VF/NM 9.0	NM- 9.2
1-5-Remender-s/Nguyen-a; Earth as a reality show						3.50

GIGGLE COMICS (Spencer Spook No. 100) (Also see Ha Ha Comics)
Creston No.1-63/American Comics Group No. 64 on; Oct, 1943 - No. 99, Jan-Feb, 1955

	GD 2.0	VG 4.0	FN 6.0	VF 8.0	VF/NM 9.0	NM- 9.2
1-Funny animal	37	74	111	222	361	500
2	19	38	57	111	176	240
3-5: Ken Hultgren-a begins?	15	30	45	84	127	170
6-9: 9-1st Superkatt (6/44)	13	26	39	72	101	130
10-Superkatt shoots Japanese plane & fights Nazi robot	14	28	42	78	112	145
11-20	11	22	33	60	83	105
21-40: 22-Spencer Spook 2nd app. 32-Patriotic-c. 37-X-Mas-c	10	20	30	54	72	90
41-54,56-59,62-99: Spencer Spook app. in many. 44-Mussel-Man app. (Superman parody). 45-Witch Hazel 1st app. 46-Bob Hope & Bing Crosby app. 49,69-X-Mas-c.	9	18	27	50	65	80
55,60,61-Milt Gross-a. 61-X-Mas-c	11	22	33	60	83	105

G-I IN BATTLE (G-I No. 1 only)
Ajax-Farrell Publ./Four Star: Aug, 1952 - No. 9, July, 1953; Mar, 1957 - No. 6, May, 1958

	GD 2.0	VG 4.0	FN 6.0	VF 8.0	VF/NM 9.0	NM- 9.2
1	15	30	45	84	127	170
2	9	18	27	52	69	85
3-9	9	18	27	47	61	75
Annual 1(1952, 25¢, 100 pgs.)	29	58	87	170	278	385
1(1957-Ajax)	8	16	24	42	54	70
2-6	6	12	18	28	34	40

G. I. JANE
Stanhall/Merit No. 11: May, 1953 - No. 11, Mar, 1955 (Misdated 3/54)

	GD 2.0	VG 4.0	FN 6.0	VF 8.0	VF/NM 9.0	NM- 9.2
1-PX Pete begins; Bill Williams-c/a	16	32	48	94	147	200
2-7(5/54)	10	20	30	58	79	100
8-10(12/54, Stanhall)	10	20	30	54	72	90
11 (3/55, Merit)	10	20	30	54	72	90

G. I. JOE (Also see Advs. of..., Showcase #53, 54 & The Yardbirds)
Ziff-Davis Publ. Co. (Korean War): No. 10, 1950; No. 11, 4-5/51 - No. 51, 6/57(52pgs.: 10-14,6-17?)

	GD 2.0	VG 4.0	FN 6.0	VF 8.0	VF/NM 9.0	NM- 9.2
10(#1, 1950)-Saunders painted-c begin	19	38	57	109	172	235
11-14(#2-5, 10/51): 11-New logo. 12-New logo	13	26	39	72	101	130
V2#6(12/51)-17-(11/52; Last 52 pgs.?)	11	22	33	62	86	110
18-(25¢, 100 pg. Giant, 12-1/52-53)	27	54	81	158	259	360
19-30: 20-22,24,28-31-The Yardbirds app.	10	20	30	56	76	95
31-47,49-51	10	20	30	54	72	90
48-Atom bomb story	10	20	30	56	76	95

NOTE: ***Powell** a-V2#7, 8, 11. **Norman Saunders** painted c-10-14, V2#6-14, 26, 30, 31, 35, 38, 39. **Tuska** a-7. Bondage c-29, 35, 38.*

G. I. JOE (America's Movable Fighting Man)
Custom Comics: 1967 (5-1/8x8-3/8", 36 pgs.)

	GD 2.0	VG 4.0	FN 6.0	VF 8.0	VF/NM 9.0	NM- 9.2
nn-Schaffenberger-a; based on Hasbro toy	3	6	9	21	33	45

G.I. JOE
Dark Horse Comics: Dec, 1995 - No. 4, Apr, 1996 ($1.95, limited series)

	GD 2.0	VG 4.0	FN 6.0	VF 8.0	VF/NM 9.0	NM- 9.2
1-4: Mike W. Barr scripts. 1-Three Frank Miller covers with title logos in red, white and blue. 2-Breyfogle-c. 3-Simonson-c						4.00

G.I. JOE
Dark Horse Comics: V2#1, June, 1996 - V2#4, Sept, 1996 ($2.50)

G.I. Joe #8 © Hasbro

G.I. Joe (2009 series) #1 © Hasbro

G.I. Joe, A Real American Hero #152 © Hasbro

GD 2.0 | VG 4.0 | FN 6.0 | VF 8.0 | VF/NM 9.0 | NM- 9.2

V2#1-4: Mike W. Barr scripts. 4-Painted-c 4.00

G.I. JOE
Image Comics/Devil's Due Publishing: 2001 - No. 43, May, 2005 ($2.95)

1-Campbell-c; back-c painted by Beck; Blaylock-s 2 4 6 8 10 12
1-2nd printing with front & back covers switched 6.00
2,3 5.00
4-($3.50) 5.00
5-20,22-41: 6-SuperPatriot preview. 18-Brereton-c. 31-33-Wraith back-up; Caldwell-a 3.00
21-Silent issue; Zeck-a; two covers by Campbell and Zeck 4.00
42,43-($4.50)-Dawn of the Red Shadows; leads into G.I. Joe Vol. 2 4.50
...:Cobra Reborn (1/04, $4.95) Bradstreet-c/Jenkins-s 5.00
...:G.I. Joe Reborn (2/04, $4.95) Bradstreet-c/Bennett & Saltares-a 5.00
...: Malfunction (2003, $15.95) r/#11-15 16.00
... M. I. A. (2002, $4.95) r/#1&2; Beck back-c from #1 on cover 5.00
...: Players & Pawns (11/04, $12.95) r/#28-33; cover gallery 13.00
...: Reborn (2004, $9.95) r/Cobra Reborn & G.I. Joe Reborn 10.00
...: Reckonings (2002, $12.95) r/#6-9; Zeck-c 13.00
...: Reinstated (2002, $14.95) r/#1-4 15.00
...: The Return of Serpentor (9/04, $12.95) r/#16,22-25; cover gallery 13.00
...Vol. 8: The Rise of the Red Shadows (1/06, $14.95) r/#42,43 & prologue pgs. from #37-41 15.00

G.I. JOE (Volume 2) (Also see Snake Eyes: Declassified)
Devil's Due Publishing: No. 0, June, 2005 - No. 36, June, 2008 (25¢/$2.95/$3.50/$4.50)

0-(25¢-c) Casey-s/Caselli-a 3.00
1-4,7-19 ($2.95): 1-Four covers; Casey-s/Caselli-a. 4-R. Black-c 3.00
5,6-($4.50) 6-Wraparound-c 4.50
20-29,31-35-($3.50) 25-Wraparound-c World War III part 1 3.50
30,36-($5.50) 30-Double-sized World War III part 6. 36-Double-sized WW III part 12 5.50
...America's Elite Vol. 1: The Newest War TPB ('06, $14.95) r/#0-5; cover gallery 15.00
...America's Elite Vol. 2: The Ties That Bind TPB (8/06, $15.95) r/#6-12; cover gallery 16.00
...America's Elite Vol. 3: In Sheep's Clothing TPB (2007, $18.99) r/#13-18; cover gallery 19.00
...America's Elite Vol. 4: Truth and Consequences TPB (9/07, $18.99) r/#19-24; covers 19.00
... Data Desk Handbook (10/05, $2.95) character profile pages 3.00
... Data Desk Handbook A-M (10/07, $5.50) character profile pages 5.50
... Data Desk Handbook N-Z (11/07, $3.50) character profile pages 3.50
...: Scarlett: Declassified (7/06, $4.95) Scarlett's childhood and training; Noto-c/a 5.00
... Special Missions (2/06, $4.95) short stories and profile pages by various 5.00
... Special Missions Antarctica (12/06, $4.95) short stories and profile pages by various 5.00
... Special Missions Brazil (4/07, $5.50) short stories and profile pages by various 5.50
... Special Missions: The Enemy (9/07, $5.50) two stories and profile pages by various 5.50
... Special Missions Tokyo (9/06, $4.95) short stories and profile pages by various 5.00
...: The Hunt For Cobra Commander (5/06, 25¢) short story and character profiles 3.00

G.I. JOE
IDW Publishing: No. 0, Oct, 2008; No. 1, Jan, 2009 - No. 27, Feb, 2011 ($1.00/$3.99)

0-($1.00) Short stories by Dixon & Hama; creator interviews and character sketches 3.00
1-27-($3.99) 1-Dixon-s/Atkins-a; covers by Johnson, Atkins and Dell'Otto 4.00
...: Cobra Commander Tribute - 100-Page Spectacular 1 (4/11, $7.99) reprints 8.00
...: Special - Helix (8/09, $3.99) Reed-s/Suitor-a 4.00

G.I. JOE, VOLUME 2 (Prelude in G.I. Joe: Cobra Civil War #0) (Season 2 in indicia)
IDW Publishing: May, 2011 - No. 21, Jan, 2013 ($3.99)

1-21: 1-Dixon-s/Saltares-a; three covers by Howard. 9-Cobra Command Part 1 4.00

G.I. JOE VOLUME 3
IDW Publishing: Feb, 2013 - Present ($3.99)

1-14-Van Lente-s/Kurth-a in most; multiple covers. 6-Igle-a. 12-14-Allor-s 4.00

G.I. JOE AND THE TRANSFORMERS
Marvel Comics Group: Jan, 1987 - No. 4, Apr, 1987 (Limited series)

1 2 4 6 9 12 15
2-4 1 2 3 5 6 8

G.I. JOE, A REAL AMERICAN HERO (...Starring Snake-Eyes on-c #135 on)
Marvel Comics Group: June, 1982 - No. 155, Dec, 1994

1-Printed on Baxter paper; based on Hasbro toy 4 8 12 23 37 50
2-Printed on regular paper; 1st app. Kwinn 3 6 9 19 30 40
3-10: 6-1st app. Oktober Guard 3 6 9 14 20 25
11-20: 11-Intro Airborne. 13-1st Destro (cameo). 14-1st full app. Destro. 15-1st app. Major Blood. 16-1st app. Cover Girl and Trip-Wire 2 4 6 10 14 18
21-1st app. Storm Shadow; silent issue 5 10 15 33 57 80
22-1st app. Duke and Roadblock 2 4 6 11 16 20
23,24,28-30,60: 60-Todd McFarlane-a 2 3 4 6 8 10
25-1st full app. Zartan, 1st app of Cutter, Deep Six, Mutt and Junkyard, and The Dreadnoks 3 6 9 14 20 25
26,27-Origin Snake-Eyes parts 1 & 2 3 6 9 14 20 26
31-50: 31-1st Spirit Iron-Knife. 32-1st Blowtorch, Lady J, Recondo, Ripcord. 33-New headquarters. 40-1st app. of Shipwreck, Barbecue. 48-1st app. Sgt. Slaughter. 49-1st app. of Lift-Ticket, Slipstream, Leatherneck, Serpentor 6.00
51-59,61-90 5.00
91,92,94-99: 94-96-Snake Eyes Trilogy 6.00
93-Snake-Eyes' face first revealed 2 4 6 13 18 22
100,135-138: 135-138-($1.75)-Bagged w/trading card. 138-Transformers app. 2 4 6 9 13 16
101-134: 101-New Oktober Guard app. 110-1st Garney-a. 117- Debut G.I. Joe Ninja Force 2 3 4 6 8 10
139-142-New Transformers app. 2 4 6 13 18 22
143,145-149: 145-Intro. G.I. Joe Star Brigade 2 4 6 9 13 16
144-Origin Snake-Eyes 3 6 9 14 19 24
150-Low print thru #155 3 6 9 19 30 40
151-154: 152-30th Anniversary (of doll) issue, original G.I. Joe General Joseph Colton app. (also app. in #151) 3 6 9 18 28 38
155-Last issue 5 10 15 34 60 85
All 2nd printings 4.00
Special #1 (2/95, $1.50) r/#60 w/McFarlane-a. Cover swipe from Spider-Man #1 4 8 12 27 44 60
Special Treasury Edition (1982)-r/#1 3 6 9 19 30 40
Volume 1 TPB (4/02, $24.95) r/#1-10; new cover by Michael Golden 25.00
Volume 2 TPB (6/02, $24.95) r/#11-20; new cover by J. Scott Campbell 25.00
Volume 3 TPB (2002, $24.99) r/#21-30; new cover by J. Scott Campbell 25.00
Volume 4 TPB (2002, $25.99) r/#31-40; new cover by J. Scott Campbell 26.00
Volume 5 TPB (2002, $24.99) r/#42-50; new cover by J. Scott Campbell 25.00
Yearbook 1-4: (3/85-3/88)-r/#1; Golden-c. 2-Golden-c/a 5.00
NOTE: ***Garney*** *a(p)-110.* ***Golden*** *c-23, 29, 34, 36.* ***Heath*** *a-24.* ***Rogers*** *a(p)-75, 77-82, 84, 86; c-77.*

G. I. JOE, A REAL AMERICAN HERO
IDW Publishing: No. 156, Jul, 2010 - Present ($3.99)

156-199-Continuation of story from Marvel series #155 (1994); Hama-s 4.00
200-(3/14, $5.99) Multiple covers; bonus interview with artist SL Gallant 6.00
Annual 2012 (2/12, $7.99) Hama-s; Frenz, Wagner & Trimpe-a 8.00
Hundred Penny Press: G.I. Joe: Real American Hero #1 (3/11, $1.00) r/#1 (1982) 3.00

G.I. JOE: BATTLE FILES
Image Comics: 2002 - No. 3, 2002 ($5.95)

1-3-Profile pages of characters and history; Beck-c 6.00

G.I. JOE: COBRA (#5-on is continuation of G.I. Joe: Cobra II #4, not G.I. Joe: Cobra #4)
IDW Publishing: Mar, 2009 - No. 13, Feb, 2011 ($3.99)

1-4,5-13: 1-4-Gage & Costa-s/Fuso-a/covers by Chaykin & Fuso. 5-8-Carrera-a 4.00
Hundred Penny Press: G.I. Joe: Cobra #1 (4/11, $1.00) r/#1 with Chaykin-c 3.00
... Special (9/09, $3.99) Costa-s/Fuso-a 4.00
... Special 2 - Chameleon (9/10, $3.99) Costa-s/Fuso-a 4.00
... II (1/10 - No. 4, 4/10, $3.99) 1-4-Gage & Costa-s/Fuso-a/covers by Chaykin & Fuso 4.00

G.I. JOE: COBRA CIVIL WAR
IDW Publishing: No. 0, Apr, 2011 ($3.99)

0-Prelude to G.I. Joe, Cobra & Snake Eyes Civil War series; four covers 4.00
0-Muzzle Flash Edition (6/11, price not shown) r/#0 in B&W and partial color 4.00

G.I. JOE: COBRA VOLUME 2 (Prelude in G.I. Joe: Cobra Civil War #0)
IDW Publishing: May, 2011 - No. 9, Jan, 2012 ($3.99)(Re-named Cobra with #10)

1-9: Multiple covers on all. 1-4-Costa-s/Fuso-a 4.00

G. I. JOE COMICS MAGAZINE
Marvel Comics Group: Dec, 1986 - No. 13, 1988 ($1.50, digest-size)

1-G.I. Joe reprints 2 4 6 11 16 20
2-13: G.I. Joe-r 2 4 6 8 10 12

G.I. JOE DECLASSIFIED
Devil's Due Publishing: June, 2006 - No. 3 ($4.95, bi-monthly)

1-3-New "early" adventures of the team; Hama-s; Quinn & DeLandro-a; var-c for each 5.00
TPB (1/07, $18.99) r/#1-3; cover gallery 19.00

G.I. JOE DREADNOKS: DECLASSIFIED
Devil's Due Publishing: Nov, 2006 - No. 3, Mar, 2007 ($4.95/$4.99/$5.50, bi-monthly)

1,2-Secret history of the team; Blaylock-s; var-c for each 5.00
3-($5.50) 5.50

G.I. JOE EUROPEAN MISSIONS (Action Force in indicia) (Series reprints Action Force)
Marvel Comics Ltd. (British): Jun, 1988 - No. 15, Dec, 1989 ($1.50/$1.75)

1,3-Snake Eyes & Storm Shadow-c/s 2 4 6 8 10 12
2,4-15 6.00

G.I. JOE: FRONT LINE

G.I. Joe Special Missions #10 © Hasbro

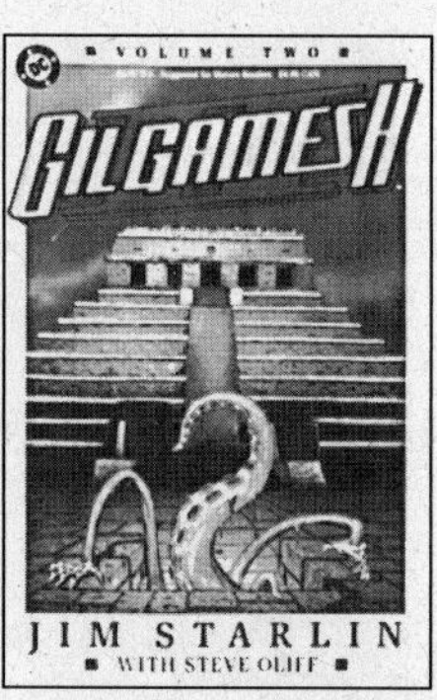

Gilgamesh II #2 © DC

Ginger Comics #8 © AP

	GD 2.0	VG 4.0	FN 6.0	VF 8.0	VF/NM 9.0	NM- 9.2

Image Comics: 2002 - No. 18, Dec, 2003 ($2.95)

1-18: 1-Jurgens-a/Hama-s. 1-Two covers by Dorman & Sharpe. 7,8-Harris-c 3.00
...Vol. 1 - The Mission That Never Was TPB (2003, $14.95) r/ #1-4; script pages 15.00
...Vol. 2 - Icebound TPB (3/04, $12.95) r/ #5-8 13.00
...Vol. 3 - History Repeating TPB (4/04, $9.95) r/#11-14 10.00
...Vol. 4 - One-Shots TPB (5/04, $15.95) r/#9,10,15-18 16.00

G.I. JOE: FUTURE NOIR SPECIAL
IDW Publishing: Nov, 2010 - No. 2, Dec, 2010 ($3.99, limited series, greytone art)

1,2-Schmidt-s/Bevilacqua-a 4.00

G. I. JOE: HEARTS & MINDS
IDW Publishing: May, 2010 - No. 5, Sept, 2010 ($3.99)

1-5: Short origin stories; Brooks-s; Chaykin & Fuso-a 4.00

G. I. JOE: INFESTATION (Zombie x-over with Star Trek, Ghostbusters & Transformers)
IDW Publishing: Mar, 2011 - No. 2, Mar, 2011 ($3.99, limited series)

1,2-Timpano-a; covers by Timpano and Snyder III 4.00

G.I. JOE: MASTER & APPRENTICE
Image Comics: May, 2004 - No. 4, Aug, 2004 ($2.95)

1-4-Caselli-a/Jerwa-s 3.00

G.I. JOE: MASTER & APPRENTICE 2
Image Comics: Feb, 2005 - No. 4, May, 2005 ($2.95, limited series)

1-4: Stevens & Vedder-a/Jerwa-s 3.00

G.I. JOE MOVIE PREQUEL...
IDW Publishing: Mar, 2009 - No. 4, June, 2009 ($3.99, limited series)

1-4-Two covers on each: 1-Duke. 2-Destro. 3-The Baroness. 4-SnakeEyes 4.00

G.I. JOE: OPERATION HISS
IDW Publishing: Feb, 2010 - No. 5, Jun, 2010 ($3.99, limited series)

1-5: 1-4-Reed-s/Padilla-a; covers by Corroney & Padilla. 5-Guglotta-a 4.00

G. I. JOE ORDER OF BATTLE, THE
Marvel Comics Group: Dec, 1986 - No. 4, Mar, 1987 (limited series)

1-4 6.00

G.I. JOE: ORIGINS
IDW Publishing: Feb, 2009 - No. 23, Jan, 2011 ($3.99)

1-23: 1-Origin of Snake Eyes; Hama-s. 12-Templesmith-a. 19-Benitez-a 4.00

G.I. JOE: RELOADED
Image Comics: Mar, 2004 -No. 14, Apr, 2005 ($2.95)

1-14: 1-3-Granov-c/Ney Rieber-s. 5,6-Rieber-s/Saltares-a. 8-Origin of the Baroness 3.00
Vol. 1 In the Name of Patriotism (11/04, $12.95) r/#1-6; cover gallery 13.00

G.I. JOE: RISE OF COBRA MOVIE ADAPTATION
IDW Publishing: July, 2009 - No. 4, July, 2009 ($3.99, weekly limited series)

1-4-Tipton-s/Maloney-a; two covers 4.00

G.I. JOE SIGMA 6 (Based on the cartoon TV series)
Devil's Due Publishing: Dec, 2005 - No. 6, May, 2006 ($2.95, limited series)

1-6-Andrew Daab-s 3.00
TPB Vol. 1 (10/06, $10.95, 8-1/4" x 5-3/4") r/#1-6; cover gallery 11.00

G.I. JOE: SNAKE EYES
IDW Publishing: Oct, 2009 - No. 4, Jan, 2010 ($3.99, limited series)

1-4-Ray Park & Kevin VanHook-s/Lee Ferguson-a; two covers 4.00

G.I. JOE: SNAKE EYES, VOLUME 2 (Continues as Snake Eyes #8)
IDW Publishing: May, 2011 - No. 7, Nov, 2011 ($3.99)

1-7: 1-Dixon-s/Atkins & Padilla-a; two covers 4.00

G. I. JOE SPECIAL MISSIONS (Indicia title: Special Missions)
Marvel Comics Group: Oct, 1986 - No. 28, Dec, 1989 ($1.00)

1-20 5.00
21-28 6.00

G. I. JOE: SPECIAL MISSIONS
IDW Publishing: Mar, 2013 - Present ($3.99)

1-12: 1-4-Dixon-s/Gulacy-a; covers by Chen and Gulacy. 5-7-Rosado-a. 10-12-Gulacy-a 4.00

G. I. JOE: THE COBRA FILES
IDW Publishing: Apr, 2013 - No. 9, Dec, 2013 ($3.99)

1-9: 1-Costa-s/Fuso-a; multiple covers. 5,6-Dell'edera-a 4.00

G.I. JOE 2 MOVIE PREQUEL...
IDW Publishing: Feb, 2012 - No. 4, Apr, 2012 ($3.99, limited series)

1-4-Barber-s/Navarro & Rojo-a 4.00

G.I. JOE VS. THE TRANSFORMERS
Image Comics: Jun, 2003 - No. 6, Nov, 2003 ($2.95, limited series)

1-Blaylock-s/Mike Miller-a; three covers by Miller, Campbell & Andrews 4.00
1-2nd printing; black cover with logo; back-c by Campbell 3.00
2-6: 2-Two covers by Miller & Brooks 3.00
TPB (3/04, $15.95) r/series; sketch pages 16.00

G.I. JOE VS. THE TRANSFORMERS (Volume 2)
Devil's Due Publ.: Sept, 2004 - No. 4, Dec, 2004 ($4.95/$2.95, limited series)

1-($4.95) Three covers; Jolley-s/Su & Seeley-a 5.00
2-4-($2.95) Two covers by Su & Pollina 3.00
Vol. 2 TPB (4/05, $14.95) r/series; interview with creators; sketch pages and covers 15.00

G.I. JOE VS. THE TRANSFORMERS (Volume 3) THE ART OF WAR
Devil's Due Publ.: Mar, 2006 - No. 5, July, 2006 ($2.95, limited series)

1-5: 1-Three covers; Seeley-s/Ng-a 3.00
TPB (8/06, $14.95) r/series; cover gallery 15.00

G.I. JOE VS. THE TRANSFORMERS (Volume 4) BLACK HORIZON
Devil's Due Publ.: Jan, 2007 - No. 2, Feb, 2007 ($5.50, limited series)

1,2: 1-Three covers; Seeley-s/Wildman-a. 2-Two covers 5.50

G. I. JUNIORS (See Harvey Hits No. 86,91,95,98,101,104,107,110,112,114,116,118,120,122)

GILGAMESH II
DC Comics: 1989 - No. 4, 1989 ($3.95, limited series, prestige format, mature)

1-4: Starlin-c/a/scripts 5.00

GIL THORP
Dell Publishing Co.: May-July, 1963

	GD 2.0	VG 4.0	FN 6.0	VF 8.0	VF/NM 9.0	NM- 9.2
1-Caniff-*ish* art	4	8	12	23	37	50

GINGER
Archie Publications: 1951 - No. 10, Summer, 1954

	GD 2.0	VG 4.0	FN 6.0	VF 8.0	VF/NM 9.0	NM- 9.2
1-Teenage humor	15	30	45	90	140	190
2-(1952)	10	20	30	56	76	95
3-6: 6-(Sum/53)	9	18	27	50	65	80
7-10-Katy Keene app.	10	20	30	56	76	95

GINGER FOX (Also see The World of Ginger Fox)
Comico: Sept, 1988 - No. 4, Dec, 1988 ($1.75, limited series)

1-4: Part photo-c on all 3.00

G.I. R.A.M.B.O.T.
Wonder Color Comics/Pied Piper #2: Apr, 1987 - No. 2? ($1.95)

1,2: 2-Exist? 3.00

GIRL
DC Comics (Vertigo Verite): Jul, 1996 - No. 3, 1996 ($2.50, lim. series, mature)

1-3: Peter Milligan scripts; Fegredo-c/a 3.00

GIRL COMICS (Becomes Girl Confessions No. 13 on)
Marvel/Atlas Comics(CnPC): Oct, 1949 - No. 12, Jan, 1952 (#1-4: 52 pgs.)

	GD 2.0	VG 4.0	FN 6.0	VF 8.0	VF/NM 9.0	NM- 9.2
1-Photo-c	25	50	75	150	245	340
2-Kubert-a; photo-c	15	30	45	84	127	170
3-Everett-a; Liz Taylor photo-c	36	72	108	211	343	475
4-11: 4-Photo-c. 10-12-Sol Brodsky-c	13	26	39	74	105	135
12-Krigstein-a; Al Hartley-c	14	28	42	78	112	145

GIRL COMICS
Marvel Comics: May, 2010 - No. 3, Sept, 2010 ($4.99, limited series)

1-3-Anthology of short stories by women creators. 1-Conner-c. 2-Thompson-c. 3-Chen-c 5.00

GIRL CONFESSIONS (Formerly Girl Comics)
Atlas Comics (CnPC/ZPC): No. 13, Mar, 1952 - No. 35, Aug, 1954

	GD 2.0	VG 4.0	FN 6.0	VF 8.0	VF/NM 9.0	NM- 9.2
13-Everett-a	14	28	42	81	118	155
14,15,19,20	11	22	33	62	86	110
16-18-Everett-a	13	26	39	72	101	130
21-35: Robinson-a	10	20	30	54	72	90

GIRL CRAZY
Dark Horse Comics: May, 1996 - No. 3, July, 1996 ($2.95, B&W, limited series)

1-3: Gilbert Hernandez-a/scripts. 3.00

GIRL FROM U.N.C.L.E., THE (TV) (Also see The Man From...)
Gold Key: Jan, 1967 - No. 5, Oct, 1967

	GD 2.0	VG 4.0	FN 6.0	VF 8.0	VF/NM 9.0	NM- 9.2
1-McWilliams-a; Stephanie Powers photo front/back-c & pin-ups (no ads, 12¢)	7	14	21	46	86	125

Girls #24 © Luna Brothers

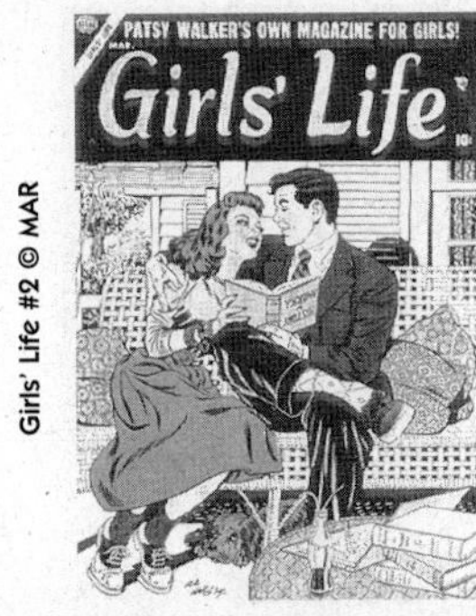

Girls' Life #2 © MAR

Girls' Romances #1 © DC

	GD 2.0	VG 4.0	FN 6.0	VF 8.0	VF/NM 9.0	NM- 9.2
2-5-Leonard Swift-Courier No. 5. 4-Back-c pin-up	5	10	15	33	57	80

GIRLS
Image Comics: May, 2005 - No. 24, Apr, 2007 ($2.95/$2.99)

	GD 2.0	VG 4.0	FN 6.0	VF 8.0	VF/NM 9.0	NM- 9.2
1-Luna Brothers-s/a/c						4.00
2-24						3.00
Image Firsts: Girls #1 (4/10, $1.00) r/#1 with "Image Firsts" cover logo						3.00
... Vol. 1: Conception TPB (2005, $14.99) r/#1-6						15.00
... Vol. 2: Emergence TPB (2006, $14.99) r/#7-12						15.00
... Vol. 3: Survival TPB (2006, $14.99) r/#13-18						15.00
... Vol. 4: Extinction TPB (2007, $14.99) r/#19-24						15.00

GIRLS' FUN & FASHION MAGAZINE (Formerly Polly Pigtails)
Parents' Magazine Institute: V5#44, Jan, 1950 - V5#48, Sept., 1950

	GD 2.0	VG 4.0	FN 6.0	VF 8.0	VF/NM 9.0	NM- 9.2
V5#44	8	16	24	40	50	60
45-48	6	12	18	28	34	40

GIRLS IN LOVE
Fawcett Publications: May, 1950 - No. 2, July, 1950

	GD 2.0	VG 4.0	FN 6.0	VF 8.0	VF/NM 9.0	NM- 9.2
1-Photo-c	12	24	36	69	97	125
2-Photo-c	10	20	30	54	72	90

GIRLS IN LOVE (Formerly G. I. Sweethearts No. 45)
Quality Comics Group: No. 46, Sept, 1955 - No. 57, Dec, 1956

	GD 2.0	VG 4.0	FN 6.0	VF 8.0	VF/NM 9.0	NM- 9.2
46	10	20	30	56	76	95
47-53,55,56	8	16	24	42	54	65
54- 'Commie' story	10	20	30	54	72	90
57-Matt Baker-c/a	14	28	42	80	115	150

GIRLS IN WHITE (See Harvey Comics Hits No. 58)

GIRLS' LIFE (Patsy Walker's Own Magazine For Girls!)
Atlas Comics (BFP): Jan, 1954 - No. 6, Nov, 1954

	GD 2.0	VG 4.0	FN 6.0	VF 8.0	VF/NM 9.0	NM- 9.2
1	15	30	45	90	140	190
2-Al Hartley-c	10	20	30	56	76	95
3-6	9	18	27	52	69	85

GIRLS' LOVE STORIES
National Comics(Signal Publ. No. 9-65/Arleigh No. 83-117): Aug-Sept, 1949 - No. 180, Nov-Dec, 1973 (No. 1-13: 52 pgs.)

	GD 2.0	VG 4.0	FN 6.0	VF 8.0	VF/NM 9.0	NM- 9.2
1-Toth, Kinstler-a, 8 pgs. each; photo-c	55	100	165	352	601	850
2-Kinstler-a?	31	62	93	182	296	410
3-10: 1-9-Photo-c	21	42	63	122	199	275
11-20	16	32	48	94	147	200
21-33: 21-Kinstler-a. 33-Last pre-code (1-2/55)	13	26	39	72	101	130
34-50	11	22	33	60	83	105
51-70	10	20	30	54	72	90
71-99: 83-Last 10¢ issue	5	10	15	30	50	70
100	5	10	15	31	53	75
101-146: 113-117-April O'Day app.	3	6	9	19	30	40
147-151- "Confessions" serial. 150-Wood-a	3	6	9	20	31	42
152-160,171-179	3	6	9	15	22	28
161-170 (52 pgs.)	3	6	9	21	33	45
180 Last issue	3	6	9	19	30	40
Ashcan (8-9/49) not distributed to newsstands	(a FN/VF copy sold for $836.50 in 2012)					

GIRLS' ROMANCES
National Periodical Publ.(Signal Publ. No. 7-79/Arleigh No. 84): Feb-Mar, 1950 - No. 160, Oct, 1971 (No. 1-11: 52 pgs.)

	GD 2.0	VG 4.0	FN 6.0	VF 8.0	VF/NM 9.0	NM- 9.2
1-Photo-c	53	106	159	334	567	800
2-Photo-c; Toth-a	30	60	90	177	289	400
3-10: 3-6-Photo-c	21	42	63	122	199	275
11,12,14-20	15	30	45	86	133	180
13-Toth-c	15	30	45	90	140	190
21-31: 31-Last pre-code (2-3/55)	13	26	39	72	101	130
32-50	6	12	18	38	69	100
51-99: 80-Last 10¢ issue	5	10	15	30	50	70
100	5	10	15	31	53	75
101-108,110-120	3	6	9	19	30	40
109-Beatles-c/story	11	22	33	73	157	240
121-133,135-140	3	6	9	17	26	35
134-Neal Adams-c (splash pg. is same as-c)	5	10	15	31	53	75
141-158	3	6	9	15	22	28
159,160-52 pgs.	3	6	9	21	33	45

GIRL WHO WOULD BE DEATH, THE
DC Comics (Vertigo): Dec, 1998 - No. 4, March, 1999 ($2.50, lim. series)

	GD 2.0	VG 4.0	FN 6.0	VF 8.0	VF/NM 9.0	NM- 9.2
1-4-Kiernan-s/Ormston-a						3.00

GIRL WITH THE DRAGON TATTOO, THE
DC Comics (Vertigo): Book One, 2012; Book Two, 2013 ($19.99, HC graphic novels)

	GD 2.0	VG 4.0	FN 6.0	VF 8.0	VF/NM 9.0	NM- 9.2
Book One HC-First part of the adaptation of the novel; Mina-s/Manco-a/Bermejo-c						20.00
Book Two HC-Second part of the adaptation; Mina-s/Manco-a/Bermejo-c						20.00

G. I. SWEETHEARTS (Formerly Diary Loves; Girls In Love #46 on)
Quality Comics Group: No. 32, June, 1953 - No. 45, May, 1955

	GD 2.0	VG 4.0	FN 6.0	VF 8.0	VF/NM 9.0	NM- 9.2
32	11	22	33	62	86	110
33-45: 44-Last pre-code (3/55)	9	18	27	47	61	75

G.I. TALES (Formerly Sgt. Barney Barker No. 1-3)
Atlas Comics (MCI): No. 4, Feb, 1957 - No. 6, July, 1957

	GD 2.0	VG 4.0	FN 6.0	VF 8.0	VF/NM 9.0	NM- 9.2
4-Severin-a(4)	11	22	33	60	83	105
5	8	16	24	44	57	70
6-Orlando, Powell, & Woodbridge-a	9	18	27	47	81	75

GIVE ME LIBERTY (Also see Dark Horse Presents Fifth Anniversary Special, Dark Horse Presents #100-4, Happy Birthday Martha Washington, Martha Washington Goes to War, Martha Washington Stranded In Space & San Diego Comicon Comics #2)
Dark Horse Comics: June, 1990 - No. 4, 1991 ($4.95, limited series, 52 pgs.)

	GD 2.0	VG 4.0	FN 6.0	VF 8.0	VF/NM 9.0	NM- 9.2
1-4: 1st app. Martha Washington; Frank Miller scripts, Dave Gibbons-c/a in all						6.00

G. I. WAR BRIDES
Superior Publishers Ltd.: Apr, 1954 - No. 8, June, 1955

	GD 2.0	VG 4.0	FN 6.0	VF 8.0	VF/NM 9.0	NM- 9.2
1	12	24	36	67	94	120
2	9	18	27	47	61	75
3-8: 4-Kamen*esque*-a; lingerie panels	8	16	24	42	54	65

G. I. WAR TALES
National Periodical Publications: Mar-Apr, 1973 - No. 4, Oct-Nov, 1973

	GD 2.0	VG 4.0	FN 6.0	VF 8.0	VF/NM 9.0	NM- 9.2
1-Reprints in all; dinosaur-c/s	3	6	9	17	26	35
2-N. Adams-a(r)	2	4	6	13	18	22
3,4: 4-Krigstein-a(r)	2	4	6	11	16	20

NOTE: ***Drucker*** *a-3r, 4r.* ***Heath*** *a-4r.* ***Kubert*** *a-2, 3; c-4r.*

GIZMO (Also see Domino Chance)
Chance Ent.: May-June, 1985 (B&W, one-shot)

	GD 2.0	VG 4.0	FN 6.0	VF 8.0	VF/NM 9.0	NM- 9.2
1						6.00

GIZMO
Mirage Studios: 1986 - No. 6, July, 1987 ($1.50, B&W)

	GD 2.0	VG 4.0	FN 6.0	VF 8.0	VF/NM 9.0	NM- 9.2
1-6						4.00

G.L.A. (Great Lakes Avengers)(Also see GLX-Mas Special)
Marvel Comics: June, 2005 - No. 4, Sept, 2005 ($2.99, limited series)

	GD 2.0	VG 4.0	FN 6.0	VF 8.0	VF/NM 9.0	NM- 9.2
1-4-Slott-s/Pelletier-a						3.00
...: Misassembled TPB (2005, $14.99) r/#1-4, West Coast Avengers #46 (1st app.) and Marvel Super-Heroes #8 (1st app. Squirrel Girl; Ditko-a)						15.00

GLADSTONE COMIC ALBUM
Gladstone: 1987 - No. 28, 1990 ($5.95/$9.95, 8-1/2x11")(All Mickey Mouse albums are by Gottfredson)

	GD 2.0	VG 4.0	FN 6.0	VF 8.0	VF/NM 9.0	NM- 9.2
1-10: 1-Uncle Scrooge; Barks-r; Beck-c. 2-Donald Duck; r/F.C. #108 by Barks. 3-Mickey Mouse-r by Gottfredson. 4-Uncle Scrooge; r/F.C. #456 by Barks w/unedited story. 5-Donald Duck Advs.; r/F.C. #199. 6-Uncle Scrooge-r by Barks. 7-Donald Duck-r by Barks. 8-Mickey Mouse-r. 9-Bambi; r/F.C. #186? 10-Donald Duck Advs.; r/F.C. #275	1	3	4	6	8	10
11-20: 11-Uncle Scrooge; r/U.S. #4. 12-Donald And Daisy; r/F.C. #1055, WDC&S. 13-Donald Duck Advs.; r/F.C. #408. 14-Uncle Scrooge; Barks-r/U.S #21. 15-Donald And Gladstone; Barks-r. 16-Donald Duck Advs.; r/F.C. #238. 17-Mickey Mouse strip-r (The World of Tomorrow, The Pirate Ghost Ship). 18-Donald Duck and the Junior Woodchucks; Barks-r. 19-Uncle Scrooge; r/U.S. #12; Rosa-c. 20-Uncle Scrooge; r/F.C. #386; Barks-c/a(r)	1	3	4	6	8	10
21-25: 21-Donald Duck Family; Barks-c/a(r). 22-Mickey Mouse strip-r. 23-Donald Duck; Barks-r/D.D. #26 w/unedited story. 24-Uncle Scrooge; Barks-r; Rosa-c. 25-D. Duck; Barks-c/a-r/F.C. #367	1	3	4	6	8	10
26-28: All have $9.95-c. 26-Mickey & Donald; Gottfredson-c/a(r). 27-Donald Duck; r/WDC&S by Barks; Barks painted-c. 28-Uncle Scrooge & Donald Duck; Rosa-c/a (4 stories)	1	3	4	6	8	10
Special 1-7: 1 ('89-'90, $9.95/13.95)-1-Donald Duck Finds Pirate Gold; r/F.C. #9. 2 ('89, $8.95)-Uncle Scrooge and Donald Duck; Barks-r/Uncle Scrooge #5; Rosa-c. 3 ('89, $8.95)-Mickey Mouse strip-r. 4 ('89, $11.95)-Uncle Scrooge; Rosa-c/a-r/Son of the Sun from U.S. #219 plus Barks-r/U.S. 5 ('90, $11.95)-Donald Duck Advs.; Barks-r/F.C. #282 & 422 plus Barks painted-c. 6 ('90, $12.95)-Uncle Scrooge; Barks-c/a-r/Uncle Scrooge. 7 ('90, $13.95)-Mickey Mouse; Gottfredson strip-r	2	4	6	9	11	14

GLADSTONE COMIC ALBUM (2nd Series)(Also see The Original Dick Tracy)
Gladstone Publishing: 1990 ($5.95, 8-1/2 x 11," stiff-c, 52 pgs.)

Glamorous Romances #45 © ACE

Goddess #1 © Ennis & Winslade

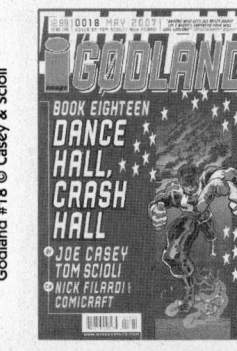

Godland #18 © Casey & Scioli

GD VG FN VF VF/NM NM-
2.0 4.0 6.0 8.0 9.0 9.2

1,2-The Original Dick Tracy. 2-Origin of the 2-way wrist radio 6.00
3-D Tracy Meets the Mole-r by Gould ($6.95). 1 2 3 5 6 8

GLAMOROUS ROMANCES (Formerly Dotty)
Ace Magazines (A. A. Wyn): No. 41, July, 1949 - No. 90, Oct, 1956 (Photo-c 68-90)

41-Dotty app. 14 28 42 76 108 140
42-72,74-80: 44-Begin 52 pg. issues. 45,50-61-Painted-c. 80-Last pre-code (2/55) 10 20 30 56 76 95
73-L.B. Cole-r/All Love #27 10 20 30 58 79 100
81-90 10 20 30 54 72 90

GLAMOURPUSS
Aardvark-Vanaheim Inc.: Apr, 2008 - No. 26, Jul, 2012 ($3.00, B&W)

1-26: 1-Two covers; Dave Sim-s/a/c. 9,10-Gene Colan-c. 11-Heath-c. 19-Allred-c 3.00
1-Comics Industry Preview Edition (Diamond Dateline supplement) 4.00

GLOBAL FREQUENCY
DC Comics (WildStorm): Dec, 2002 - No. 12, Aug, 2004 ($2.95, limited series)

1-12-Warren Ellis-s. 1-Leach-a. 2-Fabry-a. 3-Dillon-a. 5-Muth-a. 7-Bisley-a. 12-Ha-a 3.00
1-RRP Edition variant-c; promotional giveaway for retailers (200 printed) 10.00
...: Detonation Radio TPB (2005, $14.95) r/#7-12 15.00
...: Planet Ablaze TPB (2003, $14.95) r/#1-6 15.00

GLORY
Image Comics (Extreme Studios)/Maximum Press: Mar, 1995 - No. 22, Apr, 1997 ($2.50)

0-Deodato-c/a, 1-(3/95)-Deodato-a 4.00
1A-Variant-c 5.00
2-11,13-22: 4-Variant-c by Quesada & Palmiotti. 5-Bagged w/Youngblood gaming card. 7,8-Deodato-c/a(p). 8-Babewatch x-over. 9-Cruz-c; Extreme Destroyer Pt. 5; polybagged w/card. 10-Angela-c/app. 11-Deodato-c. 3.00
12-($3.50)-Photo-c 4.00
... & Friends Christmas Special (12/95, $2.50) Deodato-c 3.00
... & Friends Lingerie Special (9/95, $2.95) Pin-ups w/photos; photo-c; variant-c exists 3.00
... /Angela: Angels in Hell (4/96, $2.50) Flip book w/Darkchylde #1 4.00
... /Avengelyne (10/95, $3.95) 1-Chromium-c, 1-Regular-c 4.00
Trade Paperback (1995, $9.95)-r/#1-4 10.00

GLORY (Continues numbering from the 1995-1997 series)
Image Comics: Feb, 2012 - No. 34, Apr, 2013 ($2.99/$3.99)

23-28-Joe Keatinge-s/Ross Campbell-a. 23-Supreme app. 3.00
29-34-($3.99) 4.00

GLORY
Awesome Comics: Mar, 1999 ($2.50)

0-Liefeld-c; story and sketch pages 3.00

GLORY (ALAN MOORE'S...)
Avatar Press: Dec, 2001 - No. 2 ($3.50)

Preview-(9/01, $1.99) B&W pages and cover art; Alan Moore-s 3.00
0-Four regular covers 3.50
1,2: 1-Alan Moore-s/Mychaels & Gebbie-a; nine covers by various. 2-Five covers 3.50

GLORY & FRIENDS BIKINI FEST
Image Comics (Extreme): Sept, 1995 - No. 2, Oct, 1995 ($2.50, limited series)

1,2: 1-Photo-c; centerfold photo; pin-ups 4.00

GLORY/CELESTINE: DARK ANGEL
Image Comics/Maximum Press (Extreme Studios): Sept, 1996 - No. 3, Nov, 1996 ($2.50)

1-3 3.00

GLX-MAS SPECIAL (Great Lakes Avengers)
Marvel Comics: Feb, 2006 ($3.99, one-shot)

1-Christmas themed stories by various incl. Haley, Templeton, Grist, Wieringo 4.00

G-MAN: CAPE CRISIS
Image Comics: Aug, 2009 - No. 5, Jan, 2010 ($2.99, limited series)

1-5-Chris Giarrusso-s/a; back-up short strips by various 3.00

GNOME MOBILE, THE (See Movie Comics)

GOBBLEDYGOOK
Mirage Studios: 1984 - No. 2, 1984 (B&W)(1st Mirage comics, published at same time)

1-(24 pgs.)-(distribution of approx. 50) Teenage Mutant Ninja Turtles app. on full page back-c ad; Teenage Mutant Ninja Turtles do not appear inside. 1st app of Fugitoid 197 394 591 1625 3663 5700
2-(24 pgs.)-Teenage Mutant Ninja Turtles on full page back-c ad 77 154 231 616 1383 2150

NOTE: Counterfeit copies exist. Originals feature both black & white covers and interiors. Signed and numbered copies do not exist.

GD VG FN VF VF/NM NM-
2.0 4.0 6.0 8.0 9.0 9.2

GOBBLEDYGOOK
Mirage Studios: Dec, 1986 ($3.50, B&W, one-shot, 100 pgs.)

1-New 8 pg. TMNT story plus a Donatello/Michaelangelo 7 pg. story & a Gizmo story; Corben-i(r)/TMNT #7 2 4 6 11 16 20

GOBLIN, THE
Warren Publishing Co.: June, 1982 - No. 3, Dec, 1982 ($2.25, B&W magazine with 8 pg. color insert comic in all)

1-The Gremlin app. Philo Photon & the Troll Patrol, Micro-Buccaneers & Wizard Wormglow begin & app. in all. Tin Man app. Golden-a(p). Nebres-c/a in all 2 4 6 13 18 22
2,3: 2-1st Hobgoblin. 3-Tin Man app. 2 4 6 9 12 15

NOTE: *Bermejo a-1-3. Elias a-1-3. Laxamana a-1-3. Nino a-3.*

GOD COMPLEX
Image Comics: Dec, 2009 - No. 7, Jun, 2010 ($2.99)

1-7-Oeming & Berman-s/Broglia-a/Oeming-c 3.00

GODDESS
DC Comics (Vertigo): June, 1995 - No. 8, Jan, 1996 ($2.95, limited series)

1-Garth Ennis scripts; Phil Winslade-c/a in all 5.00
2-8 4.00
TPB (2002, $19.95) r/#1-8; foreword and sketch pages by Winslade 20.00

GODFATHERS, THE (See The Crusaders)

GOD IS
Spire Christian Comics (Fleming H. Revell Co.): 1973, 1975 (35-49¢)

nn-(1973) By Al Hartley 3 6 9 14 19 24
nn-(1975) 2 4 6 10 14 18

GOD IS DEAD
Avatar Press: Aug, 2013 - Present ($3.99)

1-10: 1-5-Hickman & Costa-s/Amorim-a 4.00

GODLAND
Image Comics: July, 2005 - Finale, Dec, 2013 ($2.99)

1-15,17-35-Joe Casey-s; Kirby-esque art by Tom Scioli. 13-Var-c by Giffen & Larsen. 33-"Dogland" on cover 3.00
16-(60¢-c) Re-cap/origin issue 3.00
36-($3.99) 4.00
... Finale (12/13, $6.99) Final issue 7.00
Image Firsts: Godland #1 (9/10, $1.00) r/#1 with "Image Firsts" cover logo 3.00
...: Celestial Edition One HC (2007, $34.99) r/#1-12 and story from Image Holiday Special; intro. by Grant Morrison; cover gallery, developmental art and original story pitches 35.00

GOD OF WAR (Based on the Sony videogame)
DC Comics (WildStorm): May, 2010 - No. 6, Mar, 2011 ($3.99/$2.99, limited series)

1-6-Wolfman-s/Sorrentino-a/Park-c. 6-($2.99) 4.00
TPB (2011, $14.99) r/#1-6; cover gallery 15.00

GOD SAVE THE QUEEN
DC Comics (Vertigo): 2007 ($19.99, hardcover with dustjacket, graphic novel)

HC-Mike Carey-s/John Bolton-painted art 20.00
SC-(2008, $12.99) Different painted-c by Bolton 13.00

GOD'S COUNTRY (Also see Marvel Comics Presents)
Marvel Comics: 1994 ($6.95)

nn-P. Craig Russell-a; Colossus story; r/Marvel Comics Presents #10-17 7.00

GOD'S HEROES IN AMERICA
Catechetical Guild Educational Society: 1956 (nn) (25¢/35¢, 68 pgs.)

307 3 6 9 16 23 30

GOD'S SMUGGLER (Religious)
Spire Christian Comics/Fleming H. Revell Co.: 1972 (35¢/39¢/40¢)

1-Three variations exist 3 6 9 14 19 24

GODWHEEL
Malibu Comics (Ultraverse): No. 0, Jan, 1995 - No. 3, Feb, 1995 ($2.50, limited series)

0-3: 0-Flip-c. 1-1st app. of Primevil; Thor cameo (1 panel). 3-Perez-a in Chapter 3, Thor app. 3.00

GODZILLA (Movie)
Marvel Comics : August, 1977 - No. 24, July, 1979 (Based on movie series)

1-(Regular 30¢ edition)-Mooney-i 3 6 9 21 33 45
1-(35¢-c variant, limited distribution) 6 12 18 41 76 110

Godzilla #17 © Toho

Go-Go #6 © CC

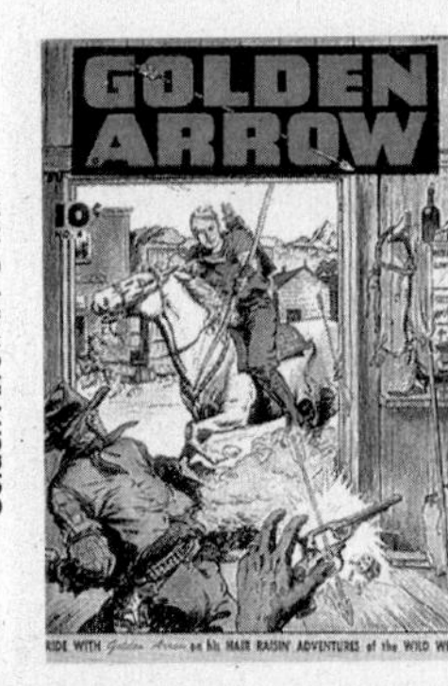

Golden Arrow #4 © FAW

	GD 2.0	VG 4.0	FN 6.0	VF 8.0	VF/NM 9.0	NM- 9.2
2-(Regular 30¢ edition)-Tuska-i.	2	4	6	10	14	18
2,3-(35¢-c variant, limited distribution)	4	8	12	27	44	60
3-(30¢-c) Champions app.(w/o Ghost Rider)	2	4	6	11	16	20
4-10: 4,5-Sutton-a	2	4	6	9	13	16
11-23: 14-Shield app. 20-F.F. app. 21,22-Devil Dinosaur app.	2	4	6	8	11	14
24-Last issue	2	4	6	10	14	18

GODZILLA (Movie)
Dark Horse Comics: May, 1988 - No. 6, 1988 ($1.95, B&W, limited series) (Based on movie series)

	GD	VG	FN	VF	VF/NM	NM-
1	2	4	6	8	10	12
2-6	1	2	3	5	6	8
...Collection (1990, $10.95)-r/1-6 with new-c						14.00
...Color Special 1 (Sum, 1992, $3.50, color, 44 pgs.)-Arthur Adams wraparound-c/a & part scripts	1	2	3	5	6	8
...King Of The Monsters Special (8/87, $1.50)-Origin; Bissette-c/a	1	2	3	5	6	8
...Vs. Barkley nn (12/93, $2.95, color)-Dorman painted-c	1	2	3	5	6	8

GODZILLA (King of the Monsters) (Movie)
Dark Horse Comics: May, 1995 - No. 16, Sept, 1996 ($2.50) (Based on movies)

0-16: 0-r/Dark Horse Comics #10,11. 1-3-Kevin Maguire scripts. 3-8-Art Adams-c 5.00
...Vs. Hero Zero ($2.50) 5.00

GODZILLA
IDW Publishing: May, 2012 - May, 2013 ($3.99)

1-13: 1-5,7,8,10-Swierczynski-s/Gane-a; multiple covers on each. 6-Wachter-a 4.00

GODZILLA: GANGSTERS AND GOLIATHS
IDW Publishing: Jun, 2011 - No. 5, Oct, 2011 ($3.99, limited series)

1-5-Layman-s/Ponticelli-a; Mothra app. 1-Darrow-c 4.00

GODZILLA: KINGDOM OF MONSTERS
IDW Publishing: Mar, 2011 - No. 12, Feb, 2012 ($3.99)

1-12: 1-Hester-a; covers by Ross & Powell. 2,3-Covers by Hester & Powell 4.00
...: 100 Cover Charity Spectacular (8/11, $7.99) Variant covers for Japan Disaster Relief 8.00

GODZILLA LEGENDS (Spotlight on other monsters)
IDW Publishing: Nov, 2011 - No. 5, Mar, 2012 ($3.99, limited series)

1-5-Art Adams-c. 1-Anguirus. 2-Rodan. 3-Titanosaurus. 4-Hedorah. 5-Kumonga 4.00

GODZILLA: RULERS OF EARTH
IDW Publishing: Jun, 2013 - Present ($3.99, limited series)

1-10: 1-8-Chris Mowry-s/Matt Frank-a 4.00

GODZILLA: THE HALF-CENTURY WAR
IDW Publishing: Aug, 2012 - No. 5, Feb, 2013 ($3.99, limited series)

1-5-James Stokoe-s/a 4.00

GOG (VILLAINS) (See Kingdom Come)
DC Comics: Feb, 1998 ($1.95, one-shot)

1-Waid-s/Ordway-a(p)/Pearson-c 3.00

GO GIRL!
Image Comics: Aug, 2000 - No. 5 ($3.50, B&W, quarterly)

1-5-Trina Robbins-s/Anne Timmons-a; pin-up gallery 3.50

GO-GO
Charlton Comics: June, 1966 - No. 9, Oct, 1967

	GD	VG	FN	VF	VF/NM	NM-
1-Miss Bikini Luv begins w/Jim Aparo's 1st published work; Rolling Stones, Beatles, Elvis, Sonny & Cher, Bob Dylan, Sinatra, parody; Herman's Hermits pin-ups; D'Agostino-c/a in #1-8	7	14	21	49	92	135
2-Ringo Starr, David McCallum & Beatles photos on cover; Beatles story and photos; Blooperman & parody of JLA heroes	7	14	21	49	92	135
3,4: 3-Blooperman, ends #6; 1 pg. Batman & Robin satire; full pg. photo pin-ups Lovin' Spoonful & The Byrds	5	10	15	31	53	75
5,7,9: 5 (2/67)-Super Hero & TV satire by Jim Aparo & Grass Green begins. 6-8-Aparo-a. 7-Photo of Brian Wilson of Beach Boys on-c & Beach Boys photo inside f/b-c. 9-Aparo-c/a	5	10	15	35	55	75
6-Parody of JLA & DC heroes vs. Marvel heroes; Aparo-a; Elvis parody; Petula Clark photo-c	5	10	15	34	60	85
8-Monkees photo on-c & photo inside f/b-c	6	12	18	37	66	95

GO-GO AND ANIMAL (See Tippy's Friends...)

GOING STEADY (Formerly Teen-Age Temptations)
St. John Publ. Co.: No. 10, Dec, 1954 - No. 13, June, 1955; No. 14, Oct, 1955

	GD	VG	FN	VF	VF/NM	NM-
10(1954)-Matt Baker-c/a	37	74	111	222	361	500
11(2/55, last precode), 12(4/55)-Baker-c	22	44	66	132	216	300
13(6/55)-Baker-c/a	30	60	90	177	289	400
14(10/55)-Matt Baker-c/a, 25 pgs.	34	68	102	199	325	450

GOING STEADY (Formerly Personal Love)
Prize Publications/Headline: V3#3, Feb, 1960 - V3#6, Aug, 1960; V4#1, Sept-Oct, 1960

	GD	VG	FN	VF	VF/NM	NM-
V3#3-6, V4#1	3	6	9	21	33	45

GOING STEADY WITH BETTY (Becomes Betty & Her Steady No. 2)
Avon Periodicals: Nov-Dec, 1949 (Teen-age)

	GD	VG	FN	VF	VF/NM	NM-
1-Partial photo-c	18	36	54	105	165	225

GOLDEN AGE, THE (TPB also reprinted in 2005 as JSA: The Golden Age)
DC Comics (Elseworlds): 1993 - No. 4, 1994 ($4.95, limited series)

1-4: James Robinson scripts; Paul Smith-c/a; gold foil embossed-c 6.00
Trade Paperback (1995, $19.95) intro by Howard Chaykin 20.00

GOLDEN AGE SECRET FILES
DC Comics: Feb, 2001 ($4.95, one-shot)

1-Origins and profiles of JSA members and other G.A. heroes; Lark-c 5.00

GOLDEN ARROW (See Fawcett Miniatures, Mighty Midget & Whiz Comics)

GOLDEN ARROW (...Western No. 6)
Fawcett Publications: Spring, 1942 - No. 6, Spring, 1947 (68 pgs.)

	GD	VG	FN	VF	VF/NM	NM-
1-Golden Arrow begins	47	94	141	296	498	700
2-(1943)	22	44	66	132	216	300
3-5: 3-(Win/45-46). 4-(Spr/46). 5-(Fall/46)	15	30	45	90	140	190
6-Krigstein-a	16	32	48	94	147	200

Ashcan (1942) not distributed to newsstands, only for in house use. A CGC certified 9.0 sold for $3,734.38 in 2008.

GOLDEN COMICS DIGEST
Gold Key: May, 1969 - No. 48, Jan, 1976

NOTE: *Whitman editions exist of many titles and are generally valued the same.*

	GD	VG	FN	VF	VF/NM	NM-
1-Tom & Jerry, Woody Woodpecker, Bugs Bunny	5	10	15	33	57	80
2-Hanna-Barbera TV Fun Favorites; Space Ghost, Flintstones, Atom Ant, Jetsons, Yogi Bear, Banana Splits, others app.	6	12	18	41	76	110
3-Tom & Jerry, Woody Woodpecker	3	6	9	16	24	32
4-Tarzan; Manning & Marsh-a	4	8	12	28	47	65
5,8-Tom & Jerry, W. Woodpecker, Bugs Bunny	3	6	9	16	23	30
6-Bugs Bunny	3	6	9	16	23	30
7-Hanna-Barbera TV Fun Favorites	5	10	15	33	57	80
9-Tarzan	4	8	12	28	47	65
10,12-17: 10-Bugs Bunny. 12-Tom & Jerry, Bugs Bunny, W. Woodpecker Journey to the Sun. 13-Tom & Jerry. 14-Bugs Bunny Fun Packed Funnies. 15-Tom & Jerry, Woody Woodpecker, Bugs Bunny. 16-Woody Woodpecker Cartoon Special. 17-Bugs Bunny	3	6	9	16	23	30
11-Hanna-Barbera TV Fun Favorites	5	10	15	34	60	85
18-Tom & Jerry; Barney Bear-r by Barks	3	6	9	16	24	32
19-Little Lulu	4	8	12	25	40	55
20-22: 20-Woody Woodpecker Falltime Funtime. 21-Bugs Bunny Showtime. 22-Tom & Jerry Winter Wingding	3	6	9	16	23	30
23-Little Lulu & Tubby Fun Fling	4	8	12	25	40	55
24-26,28: 24-Woody Woodpecker Fun Festival. 25-Tom & Jerry. 26-Bugs Bunny Halloween Hulla-Boo-Loo; Dr. Spektor article, also #25. 28-Tom & Jerry	3	6	9	14	20	26
27-Little Lulu & Tubby in Hawaii	4	8	12	24	38	52
29-Little Lulu & Tubby	4	8	12	24	38	52
30-Bugs Bunny Vacation Funnies	3	6	9	14	20	26
31-Turok, Son of Stone; r/4-Color #596,656; c-r/#9	4	8	12	27	44	60
32-Woody Woodpecker Summer Fun	3	6	9	14	20	26
33,36: 33-Little Lulu & Tubby Halloween Fun; Dr. Spektor app. 36-Little Lulu & Her Friends	4	8	12	24	38	52
34,35,37-39: 34-Bugs Bunny Winter Funnies. 35-Tom & Jerry Snowtime Funtime. 37-Woody Woodpecker County Fair. 39-Bugs Bunny Summer Fun	3	6	9	14	20	26
38-The Pink Panther	3	6	9	16	24	32
40,43: 40-Little Lulu & Tubby Trick or Treat; all by Stanley. 43-Little Lulu in Paris	4	8	12	24	38	52
41,42,44,47: 41-Tom & Jerry Winter Carnival. 42-Bugs Bunny. 44-Woody Woodpecker Family Fun Festival. 47-Bugs Bunny	3	6	9	14	20	25
45-The Pink Panther	3	6	9	16	24	32
46-Little Lulu & Tubby	4	8	12	21	33	45
48-The Lone Ranger	3	6	9	17	26	35

NOTE: *#1-30, 164 pgs.; #31 on, 132 pgs..*

Golden Lad #4 © Spark

Gomer Pyle #1 © GK

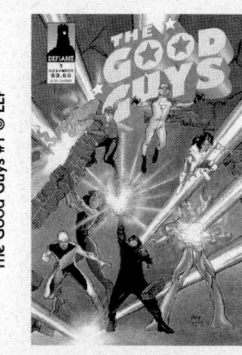

The Good Guys #1 © EEP

GD VG FN VF VF/NM NM-
2.0 4.0 6.0 8.0 9.0 9.2

GD VG FN VF VF/NM NM-
2.0 4.0 6.0 8.0 9.0 9.2

GOLDEN LAD
Spark/Fact & Fiction Publ.: July, 1945 - No. 5, June, 1946 (#4, 5: 52 pgs.)

1-Origin & 1st app. Golden Lad & Swift Arrow; Sandusky and the Senator begins
60 120 180 381 653 925
2-Mort Meskin-c/a 30 60 90 177 289 400
3,4-Mort Meskin-c/a 27 54 81 158 259 360
5-Origin & 1st app. Golden Girl; Shaman & Flame app.
30 60 90 177 289 400

NOTE: *All have **Robinson,** and **Roussos** art plus **Meskin** covers and art.*

GOLDEN LEGACY
Fitzgerald Publishing Co.: 1966 - 1972 (Black History) (25¢)

1-12,14-16: 1-Toussaint L'Ouverture (1966), 2-Harriet Tubman (1967), 3-Crispus Attucks & the Minutemen (1967), 4-Benjamin Banneker (1968), 5-Matthew Henson (1969), 6-Alexander Dumas & Family (1969), 7-Frederick Douglass, Part 1 (1969), 8-Frederick Douglass, Part 2 (1970), 9-Robert Smalls (1970), 10-J. Cinque & the Amistad Mutiny (1970), 11-Men in Action: White, Marshall J. Wilkins (1970), 12-Black Cowboys (1972), 14-The Life of Alexander Pushkin (1971), 15-Ancient African Kingdoms (1972), 16-Black Inventors (1972) each.... 4 8 12 23 37 50
13-The Life of Martin Luther King, Jr. (1972) 4 8 12 28 47 65
1-10,12,13,15,16(1976)-Reprints 2 4 6 9 12 15

GOLDEN LOVE STORIES (Formerly Golden West Love)
Kirby Publishing Co.: No. 4, April, 1950

4-Powell-a; Glenn Ford/Janet Leigh photo-c 17 34 51 98 154 210

GOLDEN PICTURE CLASSIC, A
Western Printing Co. (Simon & Shuster): 1956-1957 (Text stories w/illustrations in color; 100 pgs. each)

CL-401: Treasure Island 11 22 33 64 90 115
CL-402,403: 402: Tom Sawyer. 403: Black Beauty 10 20 30 54 72 90
CL-404, 405: CL-404: Little Women. CL-405: Heidi 10 20 30 54 72 90
CL-406: Ben Hur 8 16 24 44 57 70
CL-407: Around the World in 80 Days 8 16 24 44 57 70
CL-408: Sherlock Holmes 9 18 27 50 65 80
CL-409: The Three Musketeers 8 16 24 44 57 70
CL-410: The Merry Advs. of Robin Hood 8 16 24 44 57 70
CL-411,412: 411: Hans Brinker. 412: The Count of Monte Cristo
9 18 27 50 65 80
(Both soft & hardcover editions are valued the same)

NOTE: *Recent research has uncovered new information. Apparently #s 1-6 were issued in 1956 and #7-12 in 1957. But they can be found in five different series listings: CL-1 to CL-12 (softbound); CL-401 to CL-412 (also softbound); CL-101 to CL-112 (hardbound); plus two new series discoveries: A Golden Reading Adventure, publ. by Golden Press; edited down to 60 pages and reduced in size to 6x9"; only #s discovered so far are #381 (CL-4), #382 (CL-6) & #387 (CL-3). They have no reorder list and some have covers different from GPC. There have also been found British hardbound editions of GPC with dust jackets. Copies of all five listed series vary from scarce to very rare. Some editions of some series have not yet been found at all.*

GOLDEN PICTURE STORY BOOK
Racine Press (Western): Dec, 1961 (50¢, Treasury size, 52 pgs.) (All are scarce)

ST-1-Huckleberry Hound (TV); Hokey Wolf, Pixie & Dixie, Quick Draw McGraw, Snooper and Blabber, Augie Doggie app. 15 30 45 103 227 350
ST-2-Yogi Bear (TV); Snagglepuss, Yakky Doodle, Quick Draw McGraw, Snooper and Blabber, Augie Doggie app. 15 30 45 103 227 350
ST-3-Babes in Toyland (Walt Disney's...)-Annette Funicello photo-c
19 38 57 131 291 450
ST-4-(...of Disney Ducks)-Walt Disney's Wonderful World of Ducks (Donald Duck, Uncle Scrooge, Donald's Nephews, Grandma Duck, Ludwig Von Drake, & Gyro Gearloose stories) 19 38 57 131 291 450

GOLDEN RECORD COMIC (See Amazing Spider-Man #1, Avengers #4, Fantastic Four #1, Journey Into Mystery #83) (Also see Superman Record Comic and Batman Record Comic in the Promotional section)

GOLDEN STORY BOOKS
Western Printing Co. (Simon & Shuster): 1949-1950 (Heavy covers, digest size, 128 pgs.) (Illustrated text in color)

7-Walt Disney's Mystery in Disneyville, a book-length adventure starring Donald and Nephews, Mickey and Nephews, and with Minnie, Daisy and Goofy. Art by Dick Moores & Manuel Gonzales (scarce) 30 60 90 177 289 400
10-Bugs Bunny's Treasure Hunt, a book-length adventure starring Bugs & Porky Pig, with Petunia Pig & Nephew, Cicero. Art by Tom McKimson (scarce)
21 42 63 122 199 275
11,12 ('50): 11-M-G-M's Tom & Jerry. 12-Walt Disney's "So Dear My Heart"
20 40 60 114 182 250

GOLDEN WEST LOVE (Golden Love Stories No. 4)
Kirby Publishing Co.: Sept-Oct, 1949 - No. 3, Feb, 1950 (All 52 pgs.)

1-Powell-a in all; Roussos-a; painted-c 22 44 66 128 209 290
2,3: Photo-c 17 34 51 98 154 210

GOLDEN WEST RODEO TREASURY (See Dell Giants)

GOLDFISH (See A.K.A. Goldfish)

GOLDILOCKS (See March of Comics No. 1)

GOLD KEY CHAMPION
Gold Key: Mar, 1978 - No. 2, May, 1978 (50¢, 52pgs.)

1,2: 1-Space Family Robinson; half-r. 2-Mighty Samson; half-r
1 3 4 6 8 10

GOLD KEY SPOTLIGHT
Gold Key: May, 1976 - No. 11, Feb, 1978

1-Tom, Dick & Harriet 2 4 6 8 11 14
2-11: 2-Wacky Advs. of Cracky. 3-Wacky Witch. 4-Tom, Dick & Harriet. 5-Wacky Advs. of Cracky. 6-Dagar the Invincible; Santos-a; origin Demonomicon. 7-Wacky Witch & Greta Ghost. 8-The Occult Files of Dr. Spektor, Simbar, Lu-sai; Santos-a. 9-Tragg. 10-O. G. Whiz. 11-Tom, Dick & Harriet 2 4 6 8 10 12

GOLD MEDAL COMICS
Cambridge House: 1945 (25¢, one-shot, 132 pgs.)

nn-Captain Truth by Fugitani as well as Stallman and Howie Post, Crime Detector, The Witch of Salem, Luckyman, others app. 34 68 102 199 325 450

GOMER PYLE (TV)
Gold Key: July, 1966 - No. 3, Oct, 1967

1-Photo front/back-c 7 14 21 46 86 125
2,3-Photo-c 5 10 15 34 60 85

GON
DC Comics (Paradox Press): July, 1996 - No. 4, Oct, 1996; No. 5, 1997 ($5.95, B&W, digest-size, limited series)

1-5: Misadventures of baby dinosaur; 1-Gon. 2-Gon Again. 3-Gon: Here Today, Gone Tomorrow. 4-Gon: Going, Going...Gon. 5-Gon Swimmin'. Tanaka-c/a/scripts in all
1 2 3 5 6 8

GON COLOR SPECTACULAR
DC Comics (Paradox Press): 1998 ($5.95, square-bound)

nn-Tanaka-c/a/scripts 1 2 3 5 6 8

GON ON SAFARI
DC Comics (Paradox Press): 2000 ($7.95, B&W, digest-size)

nn-Tanaka-c/a/scripts 1 2 3 5 6 8

GON UNDERGROUND
DC Comics (Paradox Press): 1999 ($7.95, B&W, digest-size)

nn-Tanaka-c/a/scripts 1 2 3 5 6 8

GON WILD
DC Comics (Paradox Press): 1997 ($9.95, B&W, digest-size)

nn-Tanaka-c/a/scripts in all. (Rep. Gon #3,4) 1 3 4 6 8 10

GOODBYE, MR. CHIPS (See Movie Comics)

GOOD GIRL ART QUARTERLY
AC Comics: Summer, 1990 - No. 15, Spring, 1994 (B&W/color, 52 pgs.)

1,3-15 ($3.50)-All have one new story (often FemForce) & rest reprints by Baker, Ward & other "good girl" artists 4.00
2 ($3.95) 4.00

GOOD GIRL COMICS (Formerly Good Girl Art Quarterly)
AC Comics: No. 16, Summer, 1994 - No. 18, 1995 (B&W)

16-18 4.00

GOOD GUYS, THE
Defiant: Nov, 1993 - No. 9, July, 1994 ($2.50/$3.25/$3.50)

1-($3.50, 52 pgs.)-Glory x-over from Plasm 4.00
2,3,5-9: 9-Pre-Schism issue 3.00
4-($3.25, 52 pgs.) 4.00

GOOD, THE BAD AND THE UGLY, THE (Also see Man With No Name)
Dynamite Entertainment: 2009 - No. 8 ($3.50)

1-8: 1-Character from the 1966 Clint Eastwood movie; Dixon-s/Polls-a; three covers 3.50

GOOD TRIUMPHS OVER EVIL! (Also see Narrative Illustration)
M.C. Gaines: 1943 (12 pgs., 7-1/4"x10", B&W) (not a comic book) (Rare)

nn-A pamphlet, sequel to Narrative Illustration 129 258 387 826 1413 2000

NOTE: ***Print, A Quarterly Journal of the Graphic Arts** Vol. 3 No. 3 (64 pg. square bound) features 1st printing of Good Triumphs Over Evil! A VG copy sold for $350 in 2005.*

GOOFY (Disney)(See Dynabrite Comics, Mickey Mouse Magazine V4#7, Walt Disney

Goofy Comics #26 © STD

Goon Noir #3 © Eric Powell

Gotham Central #38 © DC

GD 2.0 | VG 4.0 | FN 6.0 | VF 8.0 | VF/NM 9.0 | NM- 9.2

Showcase #35 & Wheaties)
Dell Publishing Co.: No. 468, May, 1953 - Sept-Nov, 1962

Four Color 468 (#1) 10 20 30 68 144 220
Four Color 562,627,658,702,747,802,857 6 12 18 41 76 110
Four Color 899,952,987,1053,1094,1149,1201 5 10 15 31 53 75
12-308-211(Dell, 9-11/62) 5 10 15 31 53 75

GOOFY ADVENTURES
Disney Comics: June, 1990 - No. 17, 1991 ($1.50)

1-17: Most new stories. 2-Joshua Quagmire-a w/free poster. 7-WDC&S-r plus new-a. 9-Gottfredson-r. 14-Super Goof story. 15-All Super Goof issue. 17-Gene Colan-a(p) 3.00

GOOFY ADVENTURE STORY (See Goofy No. 857)

GOOFY COMICS (Companion to Happy Comics)(Not Disney)
Nedor Publ. Co. No. 1-14/Standard No. 14-48: June, 1943 - No. 48, 1953
(Animated Cartoons)

1-Funny animal; Oriolo-c 34 68 102 199 325 450
2 18 36 54 105 165 225
3-10 15 30 45 83 124 165
11-19 12 24 36 67 94 120
20-35-Frazetta text illos in all 13 26 39 74 105 135
36-48 10 20 30 56 76 95

GOOFY SUCCESS STORY (See Goofy No. 702)

GOON, THE
Avatar Press: Mar, 1999 - No. 3, July, 1999 ($3.00, B&W)

1-Eric Powell-s/a 10 20 30 64 132 200
2,3 4 8 12 23 37 60
...: Rough Stuff (Albatross, 1/03, $15.95) r/Avatar Press series #1-3 20.00
...: Rough Stuff (Dark Horse, 2/04, $12.95) r/Avatar Press series #1-3 newly colored 15.00

GOON, THE (2nd series)
Albatross Exploding Funny Books: Oct, 2002 - No. 4, Feb, 2003 ($2.95)

1-Eric Powell-s/a 4 8 12 23 37 50
2-4 2 4 6 11 16 20
...Color Special 1 (8/02) 3 6 9 14 20 25
...: Nothin' But Misery Vol. 1 (Dark Horse, 7/03, $15.95, TPB) - Reprints The Goon #1-4 (Albatross series), Color Special, and story from DHP #157 18.00

GOON, THE (3rd series) (Also see Dethklok Versus the Goon)
Dark Horse Comics: June, 2003 - No. 44, Nov, 2013 ($2.99/$3.50)

1-Eric Powell-s/a in all 2 4 6 11 16 20
2-4 1 2 3 5 6 8
5-31: 7-Hellboy-c/app; framing seq. by Mignola 14-Two covers 4.00
32-($3.99, 3/09) Tenth Anniversary issue; with sketch pages and pin-ups 5.00
33-44-($3.50) 33-Silent issue. 35-Dorkin-s. 39-Gimmick issue. 41-43-Buckingham-a. 44-Spanish issue 3.50
... 25¢ Edition (9/05, 25¢) 3.00
...: Chinatown and the Mystery of Mr. Wicker HC (11/07, $19.95) original GN; Powell-s/a 20.00
...: Fancy Pants Edition HC (10/05, $24.95, dust jacket) r/#1,2 of 2nd series & #1,3,5,9 of 3rd series; Powell intro.; sketch pages and cover gallery 25.00
...: Heaps of Ruination (5/05, $12.95, TPB) r/#5-8; intro. by Frank Darabont 13.00
...: My Murderous Childhood (And Other Grievous Yarns) (5/04, $13.95, TPB) r/#1-4 and short story from Drawing on Your Nightmares one-shot; intro. by Frank Cho 14.00
...: One For One (8/10, $1.00) r/#1 with red cover frame 3.00
...: Virtue and the Grim Consequences Thereof (2/06, $16.95) r/#9-13 17.00
...: Wicked Inclinations (12/06, $14.95) r/#14-18; intro. by Mike Allred 15.00

GOON NOIR, THE (Dwight T. Albatross's...)
Dark Horse Comics: Sept, 2006 - No. 3, Jan, 2007 ($2.99, B&W, limited series)

1-3-Anthology 1-Oswalt-s/Ploog-a; Sniegoski-s/Powell-a; Morrison-s/a; Niles-s/Sook-a. 2-Nowlan, Barta-a. 3-Ramos, Guy Davis-a; Nelson, Posehn, Thomas Lennon-s 4.00
TPB (7/07, $12.95) r/#1-3; sketch pages; intros by "Dwight" 13.00

GOOSE (Humor magazine)
Cousins Publ. (Fawcett): Sept, 1976 - No. 3, 1976 (75¢, 52 pgs., B&W)

1-Nudity in all 3 6 9 16 23 30
2,3: 2-(10/76) Fonz-c/s; Lone Ranger story. 3-Wonder Woman, King Kong, Six Million Dollar Man stories 2 4 6 11 16 20

GORDO (See Comics Revue No. 5 & Giant Comics Edition)

GORGO (Based on M.G.M. movie) (See Return of...)
Charlton Comics: May, 1961 - No. 23, Sept, 1965

1-Ditko-a, 22 pgs. 22 44 66 156 346 535
2,3-Ditko-c/a 12 24 36 82 179 275
4-Ditko-c 9 18 27 59 117 175

GD 2.0 | VG 4.0 | FN 6.0 | VF 8.0 | VF/NM 9.0 | NM- 9.2

5-11,13-16: 11,13-16-Ditko-a. 11-Ditko-c 8 16 24 51 96 140
12,17-23: 12-Reptisaurus x-over. 17-23-Montes/Bache-a. 20-Giordano-c 5 10 15 35 63 90
Gorgo's Revenge('62)-Becomes Return of... 6 12 18 42 79 115

GORILLA MAN (From Agents of Atlas)
Marvel Comics: Sept, 2010 - No. 3, Nov, 2010 ($3.99, limited series)

1-3-Parker-s/Caracuzzo-a. 1-Johnson-c. 3-Dell'Otto-c 4.00

GOSPEL BLIMP, THE
Spire Christian Comics (Fleming H. Revell Co.): 1974, 1975 (35¢/39¢, 36 pgs.)

nn-(1974) 3 6 9 14 19 24
nn-(1975) 2 4 6 9 13 16

GOTHAM BY GASLIGHT (A Tale of the Batman)(See Batman: Master of...)
DC Comics: 1989 ($3.95, one-shot, squarebound, 52 pgs.)

nn-Mignola/Russell-a; intro by Robert Bloch 1 2 3 5 6 8

GOTHAM CENTRAL
DC Comics: Early Feb, 2003 - No. 40, Apr, 2006 ($2.50)

1-40-Stories of Gotham City Police. 1-Brubaker & Rucka-s/Lark-c/a. 10-Two-Face app. 13,15-Joker-c. 18-Huntress app. 27-Catwoman-c. 32-Poison Ivy app. 34-Teen Titans-c/app. 38-Crispus Allen killed (becomes The Spectre in Infinite Crisis #5) 3.00
... Book One: In the Line of Duty HC (2008, $29.99, dustjacket) r/#1-10; sketch pages 30.00
... Book One: In the Line of Duty SC (2008, $19.99) r/#1-10; sketch pages 20.00
... Book Two: Jokers and Madmen HC (2009, $29.99, dustjacket) r/#11-22 30.00
... Book Two: Jokers and Madmen SC (2011, $19.99) r/#11-22 20.00
... Book Three: On the Freak Beat HC (2010, $29.99, dustjacket) r/#23-31 30.00
... Book Four: Corrigan HC (2011, $29.99, dustjacket) r/#32-40 30.00
...: Dead Robin (2007, $17.99, TPB) r/#33-40; cover gallery 18.00
...: Half a Life (2005, $14.99, TPB) r/#6-10, Batman Chronicles #16 and Detective #747 15.00
...: In The Line of Duty (2004, $9.95, TPB) r/#1-5, cover gallery & sketch pages 10.00
...: The Quick and the Dead TPB (2006, $14.99) r/#23-25,28-31 15.00
...: Unresolved Targets (2006, $14.99, TPB) r/#12-15,19-22, cover gallery 15.00

GOTHAM CITY SIRENS (Batman: Reborn)
DC Comics: Aug, 2009 - No. 26, Oct, 2011 ($2.99)

1-Catwoman, Harley Quinn and Poison Ivy; Dini-s/March-a/c 2 4 6 9 12 15
1-Variant-c by JG Jones 2 4 6 9 12 15
2-5 5.00
6-26 3.00
...: Song of the Sirens HC (2010, $19.99, dustjacket) r/#8-13 & Catwoman #83 20.00
...: Union HC (2010, $19.99, dustjacket) r/#1-7 20.00
...: Union SC (2011, $17.99) r/#1-7 18.00

GOTHAM GAZETTE (Battle For The Cowl crossover in Batman titles)
DC Comics: May, 2009; Jul, 2009 ($2.99, one-shots)

1-Short stories of Gotham without Batman; Nguyen, March, ChrisCross & others-a 3.00
...: Batman Alive? (7/09) Vicki Vale app.; Nguyen, March, ChrisCross & others-a 3.00

GOTHAM GIRLS
DC Comics: Oct, 2002 - No. 5, Feb, 2003 ($2.25, limited series)

1-5-Catwoman, Batgirl, Poison Ivy, Harley Quinn from animated series 1 3 4 6 8 10
2,4,5 6.00
3-Harley Quinn-c 2 4 6 11 16 20

GOTHAM NIGHTS (See Batman: Gotham Nights II)
DC Comics: Mar, 1992 - No. 4, June, 1992 ($1.25, limited series)

1-4: Featuring Batman 3.00

GOTHAM UNDERGROUND
DC Comics: Dec, 2007 - No. 9, Aug, 2008 ($2.99, limited series)

1-9-Nine covers interlock for single image; Tieri-s/Calafiore-a/c. 7,8-Vigilante app. 3.00
Batman: Gotham Underground TPB (2008, $19.99) r/#1-9; interlocked image cover 20.00

GOTHIC ROMANCES (Also see My Secrets)
Atlas/Seaboard Publ.: Dec, 1974 (75¢, B&W, magazine, 76 pgs.)

1-Text w/ illos by N. Adams, Chaykin, Heath (2 pgs. ea.); painted cover from Ravenwood Gothic paperback "The Conservatory"(scarce) 23 46 69 161 356 550

GOTHIC TALES OF LOVE (Magazine)
Marvel Comics: Apr, 1975 - No. 3, 1975 (B&W, 76 pgs.)

1-3-Painted-c/a (scarce) 25 50 75 175 388 600

GOVERNOR & J. J., THE (TV)
Gold Key: Feb, 1970 - No. 3, Aug, 1970 (Photo-c)

Grackle #3 © ACC

Great Comics #1 © Novack

Great Gazoo #1 © H-B

	GD 2.0	VG 4.0	FN 6.0	VF 8.0	VF/NM 9.0	NM- 9.2

1 4 8 12 25 40 55
2,3 3 6 9 18 28 38

GRACKLE, THE
Acclaim Comics: Jan, 1997 - No. 4, Apr, 1997 ($2.95, B&W)
1-4: Mike Baron scripts & Paul Gulacy-c/a. 1-4-Doublecross 3.00

GRAFIK MUSIK
Caliber Press: Nov, 1990 - No. 4, Aug, 1991 ($3.50/$2.50)
1-($3.50, 48 pgs., color) Mike Allred-c/a/scripts-1st app. in color of Frank Einstein (Madman)
3 6 9 14 20 25
2-($2.50, 24 pgs., color) 2 4 6 9 12 15
3,4-($2.50, 24 pgs., B&W) 2 4 6 8 10 12

GRANDMA DUCK'S FARM FRIENDS(See Walt Disney's C&S 293 & Wheaties)
Dell Publishing Co.: No. 763, Jan, 1957 - No. 1279, Feb, 1962 (Disney)
Four Color 763 (#1) 7 14 21 44 82 120
Four Color 873 5 10 15 33 57 80
Four Color 965,1279 5 10 15 30 50 70
Four Color 1010,1073,1161-Barks-a; 1073,1161-Barks-c/a
10 20 30 69 147 225

GRAND PRIX (Formerly Hot Rod Racers)
Charlton Comics: No. 16, Sept, 1967 - No. 31, May, 1970
16-Features Rick Roberts 3 6 9 21 33 45
17-20 3 6 9 17 26 35
21-31 3 6 9 16 23 30

GRAPHIQUE MUSIQUE
Slave Labor Graphics: Dec, 1989 - No. 3, May, 1990 ($2.95, 52 pgs.)
1-Mike Allred-c/a/scripts 3 6 9 19 30 40
2,3 3 6 9 16 23 30

GRAVESLINGER
Image Comics (Shadowline): Oct, 2007 - No. 4, Mar, 2008 ($3.50, limited series)
1-4-Denton & Mariotte-s/Cboins-a 3.50

GRAVE TALES
Hamilton Comics: Oct, 1991 - No. 3, Feb, 1992 ($3.95, B&W, mag., 52 pgs.)
1-Staton-c/a 2 3 4 6 8 10
2,3: 2-Staton-a; Morrow-c 1 2 3 5 6 8

GRAVITY (Also see Beyond! limited series)
Marvel Comics: Aug, 2005 - No. 5, Dec, 2005 ($2.99, limited series)
1-5: 1-Intro. Gravity; McKeever-s/Norton-a. 2-Rhino-c/app. 5-Spider-Man app. 3.00
...: Big-City Super Hero (2005, $7.99, digest) r/#1-5 8.00

GRAY AREA, THE
Image Comics: Jun, 2004 - No. 3, Oct, 2004 ($5.95/$3.95, limited series)
1,3-($5.95) Romita, Jr.-a/Brunswick-s; sketch pages and script pages. 3-Pin-up pages 6.00
2-($3.95) 4.00
...Vol. 1: All Of This Can Be Yours (2005, $14.95) r/series & sketch,script & pin-up pages 15.00

GRAY GHOST, THE
Dell Publishing Co.: No. 911, July, 1958; No. 1000, June-Aug, 1959
Four Color 911 (#1), 1000-Photo-c each 7 14 21 48 89 130

GREAT ACTION COMICS
I. W. Enterprises: 1958 (Reprints with new covers)
1-Captain Truth reprinted from Gold Medal #1 3 6 9 16 23 30
8,9-Reprints Phantom Lady #15 & 23 6 12 18 41 76 110

GREAT AMERICAN COMICS PRESENTS - THE SECRET VOICE
Peter George 4-Star Publ./American Features Syndicate: 1945 (10¢)
1-Anti-Nazi; "What Really Happened to Hitler" 50 100 150 315 533 750

GREAT AMERICAN WESTERN, THE
AC Comics: 1987 - No. 4, 1990? ($1.75/$2.95/$3.50, B&W with some color)
1-4: 1-Western-r plus Bill Black-a. 2-Tribute to ME comics; Durango Kid photo-c 3-Tribute to Tom Mix plus Roy Rogers, Durango Kid; Billy the Kid-r by Severin; photo-c. 4- ($3.50, 52 pgs., 16 pgs. color)-Tribute to Lash LaRue; photo-c & interior photos; Fawcett-r 4.00
...Presents 1 (1991, $5.00) New Sunset Carson; film history 5.00

GREAT CAT FAMILY, THE (Disney-TV/Movie)
Dell Publishing Co.: No. 750, Nov, 1956 (one-shot)
Four Color 750-Pinocchio & Alice app. 6 12 18 37 66 95

GREAT COMICS
Great Comics Publications: Nov, 1941 - No. 3, Jan, 1942
1-Origin/1st app. The Great Zarro; Madame Strange & Guy Gorham, Wizard of Science & The Great Zarro begin 135 270 405 864 1482 2100
2-Buck Johnson, Jungle Explorer app.; X-Mas-c 68 136 204 435 743 1050
3-Futuro Takes Hitler to Hell-c/s; "The Lost City" movie story (starring William Boyd); continues in Choice Comics #3 (scarce) 1000 2000 3000 4000 7000 10,000

GREAT COMICS
Novack Publishing Co./Jubilee Comics/Knockout/Barrel O' Fun: 1945
1-(Four publ. variations: Barrel O-Fun, Jubilee, Knockout & Novack)-The Defenders, Capt. Power app.; L. B. Cole-c 32 64 96 188 307 425
1-(Jubilee)-Same cover; Boogey Man, Satanas, & The Sorcerer & His Apprentice
26 52 78 154 252 350
1-(Barrel O' Fun)-L. B. Cole-c; Barrel O' Fun overprinted in indicia; Li'l Cactus, Cuckoo Sheriff (humorous) 20 40 60 114 182 250

GREAT DOGPATCH MYSTERY (See Mammy Yokum & the...)

GREATEST AMERICAN HERO (Based on the 1981-1986 TV series)
Catastrophic Comics: Dec, 2008 - No. 3, May, 2009 ($3.50/$3.95)
1-3-Origin re-told; William Katt and others-s. 3-Obama-c/app. 4.00

GREATEST BATMAN STORIES EVER TOLD, THE
DC Comics
Hardcover ($24.95) 50.00
Softcover ($15.95) "Greatest DC Stories Vol. 2" on spine 20.00
Vol. 2 softcover (1992, $16.95) "Greatest DC Stories Vol. 7" on spine 20.00

GREATEST FLASH STORIES EVER TOLD, THE
DC Comics: 1991
nn-Hardcover ($29.95); Infantino-c 45.00
nn-Softcover ($14.95) 20.00

GREATEST GOLDEN AGE STORIES EVER TOLD, THE
DC Comics: 1990 ($24.95, hardcover)
nn-Ordway-c 60.00

GREATEST HITS
DC Comics (Vertigo): Dec, 2008 - No. 6, Apr, 2009 ($2.99, limited series)
1-6-Intro. The Mates superhero team in 1967 England; Tischman-s/Fabry-a/c 3.00

GREATEST JOKER STORIES EVER TOLD, THE (See Batman)
DC Comics: 1983
Hardcover ($19.95)-Kyle Baker painted-c 50.00
Softcover ($14.95) 20.00
Stacked Deck...Expanded Edition (1992, $29.95)-Longmeadow Press Publ. 35.00

GREATEST 1950s STORIES EVER TOLD, THE
DC Comics: 1990
Hardcover ($29.95)-Kubert-c 55.00
Softcover ($14.95) "Greatest DC Stories Vol. 5" on spine 22.00

GREATEST TEAM-UP STORIES EVER TOLD, THE
DC Comics: 1989
Hardcover ($24.95)-DeVries and Infantino painted-c 55.00
Softcover ($14.95) "Greatest DC Stories Vol. 4" on spine; Adams-c 22.00

GREATEST SUPERMAN STORIES EVER TOLD, THE
DC Comics: 1987
Hardcover ($24.95) 50.00
Softcover ($15.95) 22.00

GREAT EXPLOITS
Decker Publ./Red Top: Oct, 1957
1-Krigstein-a(2) (re-issue on cover); reprints Daring Advs. #6 by Approved Comics
6 12 18 31 38 45

GREAT FOODINI, THE (See Foodini)

GREAT GAZOO, THE (The Flintstones)(TV)
Charlton Comics: Aug, 1973 - No. 20, Jan, 1977 (Hanna-Barbera)
1 4 8 12 23 37 50
2-10 3 6 9 14 19 24
11-20 2 4 6 10 14 18

GREAT GRAPE APE, THE (TV)(See TV Stars #1)
Charlton Comics: Sept, 1976 - No. 2, Nov, 1976 (Hanna-Barbera)
1 3 6 9 21 33 45
2 3 6 9 14 20 25

GREAT LOCOMOTIVE CHASE, THE (Disney)
Dell Publishing Co.: No. 712, Sept, 1956 (one-shot)

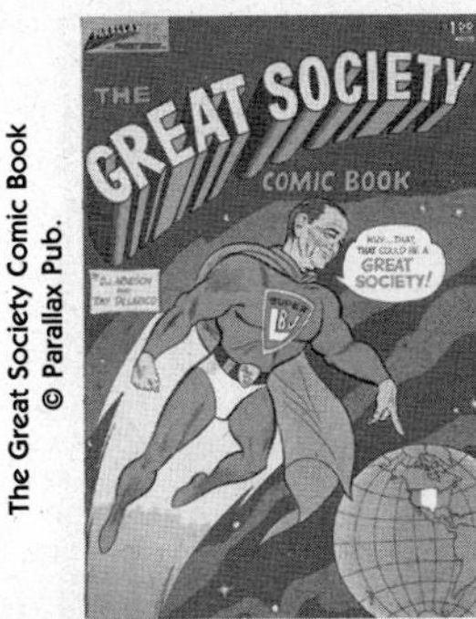

The Great Society Comic Book © Parallax Pub.

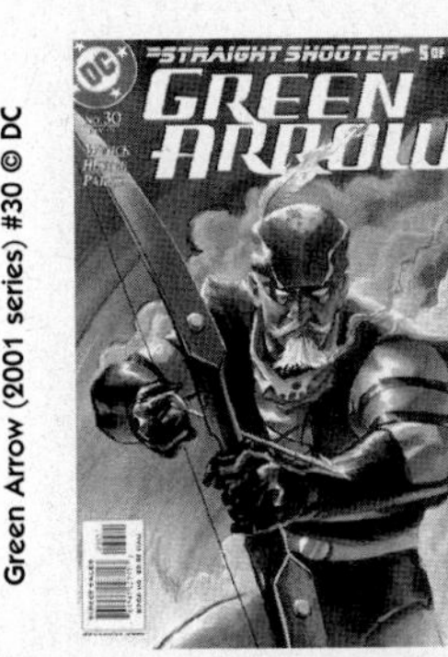

Green Arrow (2001 series) #30 © DC

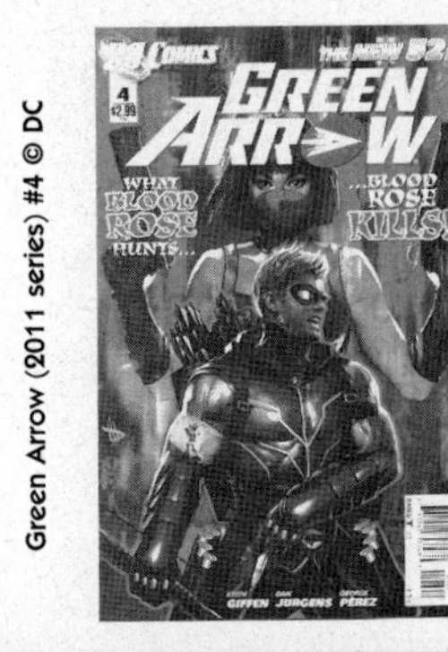

Green Arrow (2011 series) #4 © DC

GD 2.0 | VG 4.0 | FN 6.0 | VF 8.0 | VF/NM 9.0 | NM- 9.2

Four Color 712-Movie, photo-c 6 12 18 40 73 105

GREAT LOVER ROMANCES (Young Lover Romances #4,5)
Toby Press: 3/51; #2, 1951(nd); #3, 1952 (nd); #6, Oct?, 1952 - No. 22, May, 1955 (Photo-c #1-5, 10 ,13, 15, 17) (no #4, 5)
1-Jon Juan story-r/Jon Juan #1 by Schomburg; Dr. Anthony King app. 20 40 60 120 195 270
2-Jon Juan, Dr. Anthony King app. 13 26 39 74 105 135
3,7,9-14,16-22: 10-Rita Hayworth photo-c. 17-Rita Hayworth & Aldo Ray photo-c 10 20 30 58 79 100
6-Kurtzman-a (10/52) 13 26 39 72 101 130
8-Five pgs. of "Pin-Up Pete" by Sparling 13 26 39 72 101 130
15-Liz Taylor photo-c (scarce) 43 86 129 271 461 650

GREAT RACE, THE (See Movie Classics)

GREAT SCOTT SHOE STORE (See Bulls-Eye)

GREAT SOCIETY COMIC BOOK, THE (Political parody)
Pocket Books Inc./Parallax Pub.: 1966 ($1.00, 36 pgs., 7"x10", one-shot)
nn-Super-LBJ-c/story; 60s politicians app. as super-heroes; Tallarico-a 3 6 9 17 26 35

GREAT TEN, THE (Characters from Final Crisis)
DC Comics: Jan, 2010 - No. 9, Sept, 2010 ($2.99, limited series)
1-9-Super team of China; Bedard-s/McDaniel-a/Stanley Lau-c 3.00

GREAT WEST (Magazine)
M. F. Enterprises: 1969 (B&W, 52 pgs.)
V1#1 2 4 6 10 14 18

GREAT WESTERN
Magazine Enterprises: No. 8, Jan-Mar, 1954 - No. 11, Oct-Dec, 1954
8(A-1 93)-Trail Colt by Guardineer; Powell Red Hawk-r/Straight Arrow begins, ends #11; Durango Kid story 18 36 54 103 162 220
9(A-1 105), 11(A-1 127)-Ghost Rider, Durango Kid app. in each. 9-Red Mask-c, but no app. 15 30 45 83 124 165
10(A-1 113)-The Calico Kid by Guardineer-r/Tim Holt #8; Straight Arrow, Durango Kid app. 12 24 36 69 97 125
I.W. Reprint #1,2 9: 1,2-r/Straight Arrow #36,42. 9-r/Straight Arrow #? 3 6 9 15 22 28
I.W. Reprint #8-Origin Ghost Rider(r/Tim Holt #11); Tim Holt app.; Bolle-a 3 6 9 16 24 32
NOTE: ***Guardineer** c-8. **Powell** a(r)-8-11 (from Straight Arrow).*

GREEK STREET
DC Comics (Vertigo): Sept, 2009 - No. 16, Dec, 2010 ($1.00/$2.99)
1-16: 1-($1.00) Milligan-s/Gianfelice-a. 2: Begin $2.99-c 3.00
...: Blood Calls For Blood SC (2010, $9.99) r/#1-5; Mike Carey intro.; sketch art 10.00
...: Cassandra Complex SC (2010, $14.99) r/#6-11 15.00

GREEN ARROW (See Action #440, Adventure, Brave & the Bold, DC Super Stars #17, Detective #521, Flash #217, Green Lantern #76, Justice League of America #4, Leading Comics, More Fun #73 (1st app.), Showcase '95 #9 & World's Finest Comics)

GREEN ARROW
DC Comics: May, 1983 - No. 4, Aug, 1983 (limited series)
1-Origin; Speedy cameo; Mike W. Barr scripts, Trevor Von Eeden-c/a 2 4 6 9 12 15
2-4 1 2 3 5 6 8

GREEN ARROW
DC Comics: Feb, 1988 - No. 137, Oct, 1998 ($1.00-$2.50) (Painted-c #1-3)
1-Mike Grell scripts begin, ends #80 1 2 3 5 6 8
2-49,51-74,76-86: 27,28-Warlord app. 35-38-Co-stars Black Canary; Bill Wray-i. 40-Grell-a. 47-Begin $1.50-c. 63-No longer has mature readers on-c. 63-66-Shado app. 81-Aparo-a begins, ends #100; Nuklon app. 82-Intro & death of Rival. 83-Huntress-c/story. 84, 85-Deathstroke app. 86-Catwoman-c/story w/Jim Balent layouts 4.00
50,75-($2.50, 52 pgs.): Anniversary issues. 75-Arsenal (Roy Harper) & Shado app. 5.00
0,87-96: 87-$1.95-c begins. 88-Guy Gardner, Martian Manhunter, & Wonder Woman-c/app.; Flash-c. 89-Anarky app. 90-(9/94)-Zero Hour tie-in. 0-(10/94)-1st app. Connor Hawke; Aparo-a(p). 91-(11/94). 93-1st app. Camorouge. 95-Hal Jordan cameo. 96-Intro new Force of July; Hal Jordan (Parallax) app; Oliver Queen learns that Connor Hawke is his son 3.00
97-99,102-109: 97-Begin $2.25-c; no Aparo-a. 97-99-Arsenal app. 102,103-Underworld Unleashed x-over. 104-GL(Kyle Rayner)-c/app. 105-Robin-c/app. 107-109-Thorn app. 109-Lois Lane cameo; Weeks-c. 3.00
100-($3.95)-Foil-c; Superman app. 1 3 4 6 8 10
101-Death of Oliver Queen; Superman app. 3 6 9 16 23 30
110,111-124: 110,111-GL x-over. 110-Intro Hatchet. 114-Final Night. 115-117-Black Canary & Oracle app. 3.00
125-($3.50, 48 pgs)-GL x-over cont. in GL #92 4.00
126-136: 126-Begin $2.50-c. 130-GL & Flash x-over. 132,133-JLA app. 134,135-Brotherhood of the Fist pts. 1,5. 136-Hal Jordan-c/app. 3.00
137-Last issue; Superman app.; last panel cameo of Oliver Queen 2 4 6 9 12 15
#1,000,000 (11/98) 853rd Century x-over 3.00
Annual 1-6 ('88-'94, 68 pgs.)-1-No Grell scripts. 2-No Grell scripts; recaps origin Green Arrow, Speedy, Black Canary & others. 3-Bill Wray-a. 4-50th anniversary issue. 5-Batman, Eclipso app. 6-Bloodlines; Hook app. 4.00
Annual 7-('95, $3.95)-Year One story 4.00
NOTE: ***Aparo** a-0, 81-85, 86 (partial),87p, 88p, 91-95, 96i, 98-100p, 109p; c-81,98-100p. **Austin** c-96i. **Balent** layouts-86. **Burchett** c-91-95. **Campanella** a-100-108i, 110-113i; c-99i, 101-108i,110-113i. **Denys Cowan** a-39p, 41-43p, 47p, 48p, 60p; c-41-43. **Damaggio** a(p)-97p, 100-108p, 110-112p; c-97-99p, 101-108p, 110-113p. **Mike Grell** c-1-4, 10p, 11, 39, 40, 44, 45, 47-80, Annual 4, 5. **Nasser/Netzer** a-89, 96. **Sienkiewicz** a-109i. **Springer** a-67, 68. **Weeks** c-109.*

GREEN ARROW
DC Comics: Apr, 2001 - No. 75, Aug, 2007 ($2.50/$2.99)
1-Oliver Queen returns; Kevin Smith-s/Hester-a/Wagner-painted-c 2 4 6 9 13 16
1-2nd-4th printings 3.00
2-Batman cameo 1 2 3 4 5 7
2-2nd printing 3.00
3-5: 4-JLA app. 5.00
6-15: 7-Barry Allen & Hal Jordan app. 9,10-Stanley & his Monster app. 10-Oliver regains his soul. 12-Hawkman-c/app. 4.00
16-25: 16-Brad Meltzer-s begin; The Shade app. 18-Solomon Grundy-c/app. 19-JLA app. 22-Beatty-s; Count Vertigo app. 23-25-Green Lantern app.; Raab-s/Adlard-a 3.00
26-49: 26-Winick-s begin. 35-37-Riddler app. 43-Mia learns she's HIV+. 45-Mia becomes the new Speedy. 46-Teen Titans app. 49-The Outsiders app. 3.00
50-($3.50) Green Arrow's team and the Outsiders vs. The Riddler and Drakon 4.00
51-59: 51-Anarky app. 52-Zatanna-c/app. 55-59-Dr. Light app. 3.00
60-74: 60-One Year Later starts. 62-Begin $2.99-c; Deathstroke app. 69-Batman app. 3.00
75-($3.50) Ollie proposes to Dinah (see Black Canary mini-series); JLA app. 4.00
...: City Walls SC (2005, $17.95) r/#32, 34-39 18.00
...: Crawling Through the Wreckage SC (2007, $12.99) r/#60-65 13.00
...: Heading Into the Light SC (2006, $12.99) r/#52,54-59 13.00
...: Moving Targets SC (2006, $17.99) r/#40-50 18.00
...: Quiver HC (2002, $24.95) r/#1-10; Smith intro. 25.00
...: Quiver SC (2003, $17.95) r/#1-10; Smith intro. 18.00
...: Road to Jericho SC (2007, $17.99) r/#66-75 18.00
...Secret Files & Origins 1-(12/02, $4.95) Origin stories & profiles; Wagner-c 5.00
...: Sounds of Violence HC (2003, $19.95) r/#11-15; Hester intro. & sketch pages 20.00
...: Sounds of Violence SC (2003, $12.95) r/#11-15; Hester intro. & sketch pages 13.00
...: Straight Shooter SC (2004, $12.95) r/#26-31 13.00
...: The Archer's Quest HC (2003, $19.95) r/#16-21; pitch, script and sketch pages 20.00
...: The Archer's Quest SC (2004, $14.95) r/#16-21; pitch, script and sketch pages 15.00

GREEN ARROW (Brightest Day)
DC Comics: Aug, 2010 - No. 15, Oct, 2011 ($3.99/$2.99)
1-Oliver Queen in the Star City forest; Green Lantern app.; Neves-a/Cascioli-c 5.00
1-Variant-c by Van Sciver 8.00
2-15-($2.99) 2-Green Lantern app. 7-Mayhew-a. 8-11-The Demon app. 12-Swamp Thing 3.00
...: Into the Woods HC (2011, $22.99) r/#1-7; variant cover gallery 23.00

GREEN ARROW (DC New 52)
DC Comics: Nov, 2011 - Present ($2.99)
1-24: 1-Krul-s/Jurgens & Pérez-a/Wilkins-c. 4,5-Giffen-s. 13,14-Hawkman app. 17-24-Lemire-s/Sorrentino-a/c. 22-Count Vertigo app. 23,24-Richard Dragon app. 3.00
25-($3.99) Zero Year tie-in; Batman app.; back-up with Cowan-a 4.00
26-30-Outsiders War; Lemire-s/Sorrentino-a/c 3.00
#0 (11/12) Origin story re-told; Nocenti-s/Williams II-a 3.00

GREEN ARROW/BLACK CANARY (Titled Green Arrow for #30-32)
DC Comics: Dec, 2007 - No. 32, Jun, 2010 ($3.50/$2.99)
1-($3.50) Connor Hawke & Black Canary; follows Wedding Special; Winick-s/Chang-a 4.00
2-21-($2.99) 3-Two covers; Connor shot. 5-Dinah & Ollie's real wedding 3.00
22-30-($3.99) Back-up stories begin. 28-Origin of Cupid. 30-Blackest Night 4.00
30-Variant cover by Mike Grell 8.00
31-32-($2.99) Rise and Fall; Dallocchio-a 3.00
...: A League of Their Own TPB (2009, $17.99) r/#11-14 & G.A. Secret Files & Origins 18.00
...: Big Game TPB (2010, $19.99) r/#21-26 20.00
...: Enemies List TPB (2009, $17.99) r/#15-20 18.00
...: Family Business TPB (2008, $17.99) r/#5-10 18.00
...: Five Stages TPB (2010, $17.99) r/#27-30 18.00
...: Road To The Altar TPB (2008, $17.99) r/proposal pages from Green Arrow #75, Birds of Prey #109, Black Canary #1-4 and Black Canary Wedding Planner #1 18.00

Green Goblin #4 © MAR

Green Hornet Comics #4 © HARV

Green Hornet Strikes #4 © GHI

	GD 2.0	VG 4.0	FN 6.0	VF 8.0	VF/NM 9.0	NM- 9.2

...: The Wedding Album HC (2008, $19.99, dustjacket) r/#1-5 & Wedding Special #1 20.00
...: The Wedding Album SC (2009, $17.99) r/#1-5 & Wedding Special #1 18.00
... Wedding Special 1 (11/07, $3.99) Winick-s/Conner-a/c; Dinah & Ollie's "wedding" 5.00
... Wedding Special 1 (11/07, $3.99) 2nd printing with Ryan Sook variant-c 4.00

GREEN ARROW: THE LONG BOW HUNTERS
DC Comics: Aug, 1987 - No. 3, Oct, 1987 ($2.95, limited series, mature)

1-Grell-c/a in all 1 3 4 6 8 10
1,2-2nd printings 4.00
2,3 6.00
Trade paperback (1989, $12.95)-r/#1-3 15.00

GREEN ARROW: THE WONDER YEAR
DC Comics: Feb, 1993 - No. 4, May, 1993 ($1.75, limited series)

1-4: Mike Grell-a(p)/scripts & Gray Morrow-a(i) 4.00

GREEN ARROW: YEAR ONE
DC Comics: Early Sept, 2007 - No. 6, Late Nov, 2007 ($2.99, bi-weekly limited series)

1-6-Origin re-told; Diggle-s/Jock-a 3.00
HC (2008, $24.99) r/#1-6; intro. by Brian K. Vaughan; script and sketch pages 25.00
SC (2009, $14.99) r/#1-6; intro. by Brian K. Vaughan; script and sketch pages 15.00

GREEN BERET, THE (See Tales of...)

GREEN GIANT COMICS (Also see Colossus Comics)
Pelican Publ. (Funnies, Inc.): 1940 (No price on cover; distributed in New York City only)

1-Dr. Nerod, Green Giant, Black Arrow, Mundoo & Master Mystic app.; origin Colossus (Rare) 1200 2400 3600 9000 17,500 26,000

NOTE: *The idea for this book came from George Kapitan. Printed by Moreau Publ. of Orange, N.J. as an experiment to see if they could profitably use the idle time of their 40-page Hoe color press. The experiment failed due to the difficulty of obtaining good quality color registration and Mr. Moreau believes the book never reached the stands. The book has no price or date which lends credence to this. Contains five pages reprinted from Motion Picture Funnies Weekly.*

GREEN GOBLIN
Marvel Comics: Oct, 1995 - No. 13, Oct, 1996 ($2.95/$1.95)

1-($2.95)-Scott McDaniel-c/a begins, ends #7; foil-c 4.00
2-13: 2-Begin $1.95-c. 4-Hobgoblin-c/app; Thing app. 6-Daredevil-c/app. 8-Robertson-a; McDaniel-c. 12,13-Onslaught x-over. 13-Green Goblin quits; Spider-Man app. 3.00

GREENHAVEN
Aircel Publishing: 1988 - No. 3, 1988 ($2.00, limited series, 28 pgs.)

1-3 3.00

GREEN HORNET, THE (TV)
Dell Publishing Co./Gold Key: Sept, 1953; Feb, 1967 - No. 3, Aug, 1967

Four Color 496-Painted-c. 23 46 69 161 356 550
1-Bruce Lee photo-c and back-c pin-up 16 32 48 112 249 385
2,3-Bruce Lee photo-c 10 20 30 70 150 230

GREEN HORNET, THE (Also see Kato of the... & Tales of the...)
Now Comics: Nov, 1989 - No. 14, Feb, 1991 ($1.75)
V2#1, Sept, 1991 - V2#40, Jan, 1995 ($1.95)

1 ($2.95, double-size)-Steranko painted-c; G.A. Green Hornet 6.00
1,2: 1-2nd printing ('90, $3.95)-New Butler-c 4.00
3-14: 5-Death of original ('30s) Green Hornet. 6-Dave Dorman painted-c. 11-Snyder-c 4.00
V2#1-11,13-21,24-26,28-30,32-37: 1-Butler painted-c. 9-Mayerik-c 3.00
12-($2.50)-Color Green Hornet button polybagged inside 4.00
22,23-($2.95)-Bagged w/color hologravure card 4.00
27-($2.95)-Newsstand ed. polybagged w/multi-dimensional card (1993 Anniversary Special on cover), 27-($2.95)-Direct Sale ed. polybagged w/multi-dimensional card; cover variations 4.00
31,38: 31-($2.50)-Polybagged w/trading card 4.00
39,40-Low print run 6.00
1-($2.50)-Polybagged w/button (same as #12) 4.00
2,3-($1.95)-Same as #13 & 14 3.00
Annual 1 (12/92, $2.50), Annual 1994 (10/94, $2.95) 4.00

GREEN HORNET (Becomes Green Hornet: Legacy with #34)
Dynamite Entertainment: 2010 - No. 33, 2013 ($3.99)

1-Kevin Smith-s/Jonathan Lau-a; multiple covers by Alex Ross, Cassaday, Campbell and Segovia 4.00
2-33-Multiple covers by Ross and others on each. 11-Hester-s begins 4.00
Annual 1 (2010, $5.99) Hester-s/Netzer & Rafael-a 6.00
Annual 2 (2012, $4.99) Hester-c/Rahner-s/Cliquet-a; back-up r/G.H. Comics #1 (1940) 5.00
... FCBD Edition; 5 previews of various new Green Hornet series; Cassaday-c 3.00

GREEN HORNET
Dynamite Entertainment: 2013 - Present ($3.99)

1-11: 1-Set in 1941; Mark Waid-s/Daniel Indro-a; 2 covers by Alex Ross & Paolo Rivera 4.00

GREEN HORNET: AFTERMATH
Dynamite Entertainment: 2011 - No. 4, 2011 ($1.99/$3.99, limited series)

1-Nitz-s/Raynor-a; Green Hornet & Kato after the 2011 movie 3.00
2-4-($3.99) 4.00

GREEN HORNET: BLOOD TIES
Dynamite Entertainment: 2010 - No. 4, 2011 ($3.99)

1-4-Ande Parks-s/Johnny Desjardins-a; original Green Hornet & Kato 4.00

GREEN HORNET COMICS (...Racket Buster #44) (Radio, movies)
Helnit Publ. Co.(Holyoke) No. 1-6/Family Comics(Harvey) No. 7-on:
Dec, 1940 - No. 47, Sept, 1949 (See All New #13,14)(Early issues: 68 pgs.)

	GD 2.0	VG 4.0	FN 6.0	VF 8.0	VF/NM 9.0	NM- 9.2
1-1st app. Green Hornet & Kato; origin of Green Hornet on inside front-c; intro the Black Beauty (Green Hornet's car); painted-c	649	1298	1947	4738	8369	12,000
2-(3/41) Early issues based on radio adventures	245	490	735	1568	2684	3800
3	161	322	483	1030	1765	2500
4-6: 6-(8/41)	142	284	426	909	1555	2200
7 (6/42)-Origin The Zebra & begins; Robin Hood, Spirit of '76, Blonde Bomber & Mighty Midgets begin; new logo	116	232	348	742	1271	1800
8,10	100	200	300	635	1093	1550
9-Kirby-c	129	258	387	826	1413	2000
11,12,14-Mr. Q in all	95	190	285	603	1039	1475
13-1st Nazi-c; shows Hitler poster on-c	135	270	405	864	1482	2100
15-19-WWII-c; 15,17-Nazi; 16,18,19-Japanese	81	162	243	518	884	1250
20-Classic-c	100	200	300	635	1093	1550
21-23	58	116	174	371	636	900
24-Japanese WWII rocket-c	61	122	183	390	670	950
25,27,28,30	47	94	141	298	504	710
26-(9/45) Japanese WWII-c	48	96	144	302	514	725
29-Jerry Robinson skull-c	48	96	144	302	514	725
31-The Man in Black Called Fate begins (11-12/45, early app.)	51	102	153	320	543	765
32-36	36	72	108	216	351	485
37,38: Shock Gibson app. by Powell. 37-S&K Kid Adonis reprinted from Stuntman #3. 38-Kid Adonis app.	36	72	108	211	343	475
39-Stuntman story by S&K	39	78	117	236	388	540
40-47: 42-47-Kerry Drake in all. 45-Boy Explorers on-c only. 46- "Case of the Marijuana Racket" cover/story; Kerry Drake app. 27	54	81	160	263	365	

NOTE: *Fuje a-23, 24, 26.* ***Henkle*** *c-7-9.* ***Kubert*** *a-20, 30.* ***Powell*** *a-7-10, 12, 14, 16-21, 30, 31(2), 32(3), 33, 34(3), 35, 36, 37(2), 38.* ***Robinson*** *a-27.* ***Schomburg*** *c-17-23. Kirbyish c-7, 15. Bondage c-8, 14, 18, 26, 36.*

GREEN HORNET: DARK TOMORROW
Now Comics: Jun, 1993 - No. 3, Aug, 1993 ($2.50, limited series)

1-3: Future Green Hornet 3.00

GREEN HORNET: GOLDEN AGE RE-MASTERED
Dynamite Entertainment: 2010 - No. 8, 2011 ($3.99)

1-8-Re-colored reprints of 1940's Green Hornet Comics; new Rubenstein-c 4.00

GREEN HORNET: LEGACY (Numbering continues from Green Hornet 2010-2013 series)
Dynamite Entertainment: No. 34, 2013 - No. 42, 2013 ($3.99)

34-42: 34-Jai Nitz-s/Jethro Morales-a 4.00

GREEN HORNET: PARALLEL LIVES
Dynamite Entertainment: 2010 - No. 5, 2010 ($3.99, limited series)

1-5-Jai Nitz-s/Nigel Raynor-a; semi-prequel to the 2011 movie; Kato's origin 4.00

GREEN HORNET: SOLITARY SENTINEL, THE
Now Comics: Dec, 1992 - No. 3, 1993 ($2.50, limited series)

1-3 3.00

GREEN HORNET STRIKES!
Dynamite Entertainment: 2010 - No. 10, 2012 ($3.99, limited series)

1-10: 1-Matthews-s/Padilla-a/Cassaday-c; future Green Hornet 4.00

GREEN HORNET: YEAR ONE
Dynamite Entertainment: 2010 - No. 12, 2011 ($3.99, limited series)

1-12-Matt Wagner-s/Aaron Campbell-a; 1940s' Green Hornet & Kato. 1-5-Cassaday-c 4.00
...: Special 1 (2013, $4.99) Crosby-s/Menna-a/Chen-c 5.00

GREEN JET COMICS, THE (See Comic Books, Series 1 in the Promotional Comics section)

GREEN LAMA (Also see Comic Books, Series 1, Daring Adventures #17 & Prize Comics #7)
Spark Publications/Prize No. 7 on: Dec, 1944 - No. 8, Mar, 1946

1-Intro. Lt. Hercules & The Boy Champions; Mac Raboy-c/a #1-8 121 242 363 768 1322 1875
2-Lt. Hercules borrows the Human Torch's powers for one panel

Green Lantern #11 © DC

Green Lantern (2nd series) #92 © DC

Green Lantern (3rd series) #53 © DC

	GD 2.0	VG 4.0	FN 6.0	VF 8.0	VF/NM 9.0	NM- 9.2

65 130 195 416 708 1000

3-5,8: 4-Dick Tracy take-off in Lt. Hercules story by H. L. Gold (science fiction writer); Japanese WWII-c. 5-Nazi WWII-c; Hitler story; Lt. Hercules story; Little Orphan Annie, Smilin' Jack & Snuffy Smith take-off (5/45) 52 104 156 327 556 785

6-Classic Raboy swastika-c 56 112 168 356 608 860

7-X-mas-c; Raboy craft tint-c/a (note: a small quantity of NM copies surfaced) 34 68 102 199 325 450

... Archives Featuring the Art of Mac Raboy Vol. 1 HC (Dark Horse Books, 4/08, $49.95) r/#1-4 including back-up features; foreward by Chuck Rozanski 50.00

... Archives Featuring the Art of Mac Raboy Vol. 2 HC (Dark Horse Books, 1/09, $49.95) r/#5-8; foreward by Chuck Rozanski 50.00

NOTE: ***Robinson** a-3-5, 8. **Roussos** a-8. Formerly a pulp hero who began in 1940.*

GREEN LANTERN (1st Series) (See All-American, All Flash Quarterly, All Star Comics, The Big All-American & Comic Cavalcade)
National Periodical Publications/All-American: Fall, 1941 - No. 38, May-June, 1949 (#1-18 are quarterly)

	GD	VG	FN	VF	VF/NM	NM-
1-Origin retold; classic Purcell-c	2700	5400	8100	22,000	38,000	67,000
2-1st book-length story	676	1352	2028	4935	8718	12,500
3-Classic German war-c by Mart Nodell	622	1244	1866	4541	8021	11,500
4-Green Lantern & Doiby Dickles join the Army	400	800	1200	2800	4900	7000
5-WWII-c	309	618	927	2163	3782	5400
6,8: 8-Hop Harrigan begins; classic-c	284	568	852	1818	3109	4400
7-Classic robot-c	300	600	900	1980	3440	4900
9,10: 10-Origin/1st app. Vandal Savage	232	464	696	1485	2543	3600
11-15: 12-Origin/1st app. Gambler	165	330	495	1048	1799	2550
16-Classic jungle-c (scarce in high grade)	177	354	531	1124	1937	2750
17,19,20	135	270	405	864	1482	2100
18-Christmas-c	184	368	552	1168	2009	2850
21-26,28: 28-1st Sportsmaster (Crusher Crock)	132	264	396	838	1444	2050
27-Origin/1st app. Sky Pirate	161	322	483	1030	1765	2500
29-All Harlequin issue; classic Harlequin-c	181	362	543	1158	1979	2800
30-Origin/1st app. Streak the Wonder Dog by Toth (2-3/48) (Rare)	343	686	1029	2400	4200	6000
31-35: 35-Kubert-c. 35-38-New logo	118	236	354	749	1287	1825
36-38: 37-Sargon the Sorcerer app.	132	264	396	838	1444	2050

NOTE: *Book-length stories #2-7. **Mayer/Moldoff** c-9. **Mayer/Purcell** c-8. **Purcell** c-1. **Mart Nodell** c-2, 3, 7. **Paul Reinman** c-11, 12, 15-22. **Toth** a-28, 30, 31, 34-38; c-28, 30, 34p, 36-38p. Cover to #8 says Fall while the indicia says Summer Issue. Streak the Wonder Dog c-30 (w/Green Lantern), 34, 36, 38.*

GREEN LANTERN (See Action Comics Weekly, Adventure Comics, Brave & the Bold, Day of Judgment, DC Special, DC Special Series, Flash, Guy Gardner, Guy Gardner Reborn, JLA, JSA, Justice League of America, Parallax: Emerald Night, Showcase, Showcase '93 #12 & Tales of The...Corps)

GREEN LANTERN (2nd Series)(Green Lantern Corps #206 on) (See Showcase #22-24)
National Periodical Publ./DC Comics: Jul/Aug. 1960 - No. 89, Apr/May 1972; No. 90, Aug/Sept. 1976 - No. 205, Oct, 1986

	GD	VG	FN	VF	VF/NM	NM-
1-(7-8/60)-Origin retold; Gil Kane-c/a continues; 1st app. Guardians of the Universe	450	900	1350	4200	9850	15,500
2-1st Pieface	82	164	246	656	1478	2300
3-Contains readers poll	47	94	141	364	820	1275
4,5: 5-Origin/1st app. Hector Hammond	39	78	117	289	657	1025
6-Intro Tomar-Re the alien G.L.	38	76	114	281	628	975
7-Origin/1st app. Sinestro (7-8/61)	64	128	192	512	1156	1800
8-1st 5700 A.D. story; grey tone-c	35	70	105	252	564	875
9-1st Sinestro-c; 1st Jordan Brothers; last 10¢-c	32	64	96	230	515	800
10	30	60	90	216	483	750
11,12	21	42	63	147	324	500
13-Flash x-over	32	64	96	230	515	800
14,15,17-20: 14-Origin/1st app. Sonar. 20-Flash x-over	17	34	51	117	259	400
16-Origin & 1st app. (Silver Age) Star Sapphire	28	56	84	202	451	700
21,22,24-28,30: 21-Origin & 1st app. Dr. Polaris. 24-Origin & 1st app. Shark	12	24	36	81	176	270
23-1st Tattooed Man	13	26	39	89	195	300
29-JLA cameo; 1st Blackhand	13	26	39	91	201	310
31-39: 37-1st app. Evil Star (villain)	10	20	30	69	147	225
40-Origin of Infinite Earths (10/65); 2nd solo G.A. Green Lantern in Silver Age (see Showcase #55); origin The Guardians; Doiby Dickles app.	46	92	138	335	760	1185
41-44,46-50: 42-Zatanna x-over. 43-Flash x-over	9	18	27	60	120	180
45-2nd S.A. app. G.A. Green Lantern in title (6/66)	13	26	39	91	201	310
51,53-58	8	16	24	51	96	140
52-G.A. Green Lantern x-over; Sinestro app.	10	20	30	64	132	200
59-1st app. Guy Gardner (3/68)	16	32	48	112	249	385
60,62-69: 69-Wood inks; last 12¢ issue	6	12	18	38	69	100
61-G.A. Green Lantern x-over	7	14	21	44	82	120
70-75	5	10	15	34	60	85
76-(4/70)-Begin Green Lantern/Green Arrow series (by Neal Adams #76-89) ends #122 (see Flash #217 for 2nd series)	96	192	288	768	1734	2700
77	11	22	33	76	163	250
78-80	10	20	30	66	138	210
81-84: 82-Wrightson-i(1 pg.). 83-G.L. reveals i.d. to Carol Ferris. 84-N. Adams/Wrightson-a (22 pgs.); last 15¢-c; partial photo-c	9	18	27	59	117	175
85,86-(52 pgs.)-Anti-drug issues. 86-G.A. Green Lantern-r; Toth-a	11	22	33	72	154	235
87-(52 pgs.): 2nd app. Guy Gardner (cameo); 1st app. John Stewart (12-1/71-72) (becomes 3rd Green Lantern in #182)	10	20	30	66	138	210
88-(2-3/72, 52 pgs.)-Unpubbed G.A. Green Lantern story; Green Lantern-r/Showcase #23. N. Adams-c/a (1 pg.)	6	12	18	42	79	115
89-(4-5/72, 52 pgs.)-G.A. Green Lantern-r; Green Lantern & Green Arrow move to Flash #217 (2nd team-up series)	8	16	24	55	105	155
90 (8-9/76)-Begin 3rd Green Lantern/Green Arrow team-up series; Mike Grell-c/a begins, ends #111	3	6	9	17	26	35
91-99	2	4	6	10	16	20
100-(1/78, Giant)-1st app. Air Wave II	3	6	9	16	23	30
101-107,111,113-115,117-119: 107-1st Tales of the G.L. Corps story	2	4	6	8	11	14
108-110-(44 pgs)-G.A. Green Lantern back-ups in each. 111-Origin retold; G.A. Green Lantern app.	2	4	6	10	14	18
112-G.A. Green Lantern origin retold	2	4	6	13	18	22
116-1st app. Guy Gardner as a G.L. (5/79)	4	8	12	27	44	60
116-Whitman variant; issue # on cover	5	10	15	31	53	75
117-119,121-(Whitman variants; low print run; none have issue # on cover)	2	4	6	10	14	18
120-122,124-150: 122-Last Green Lantern/Green Arrow team-up. 130-132-Tales of the G.L. Corps. 132-Adam Strange series begins, ends147. 136,137-1st app. Citadel; Space Ranger app. 141-1st app. Omega Men (6/81). 142,143-Omega Men app.;Perez-c. 144-Omega Men cameo. 148-Tales of the G.L. Corps begins, ends #173. 150-Anniversary issue, 52 pgs.; no G.L. Corps	1	2	3	5	7	9
123-Green Lantern back to solo action; 2nd app. Guy Gardner as Green Lantern	2	4	6	9	12	15
151-180,183,184,186,187: 159-Origin Evil Star. 160,161-Omega Men app.						6.00
181,182,185,188,191: 181-Hal Jordan resigns as G.L. 182-John Stewart becomes new G.L.; origin recap of Hal Jordan as G.L. 185-Origin new G.L. (John Stewart).188-I.D. revealed; Alan Moore back-up scripts. 191-Re-intro Star Sapphire (cameo)	1	2	3	5	6	8
189,190,193,196-199,202-205: 194,198-Crisis x-over. 199-Hal Jordan returns as a member of G.L. Corps (3 G.L.s now).						5.00
192-Re-intro & origin of Star Sapphire (1st full app.)	2	4	6	9	13	16
194-Hal Jordan/Guy Gardner battle; Guardians choose Guy Gardner to become new Green Lantern	1	2	3	5	6	8
195-Guy Gardner becomes Green Lantern; Crisis on Infinite Earths x-over	2	4	6	9	13	16
200-Double-size						6.00
201-Green Lantern Corps begins (is cover title, says premiere issue); intro. Kilowog	2	4	6	9	12	15
Annual 1 (Listed as Tales Of The Green Lantern Corps Annual 1)						
Annual 2,3 (See Green Lantern Corps Annual #2,3)						5.00
Special 1 (1988), 2 (1989)-(Both $1.50, 52 pgs.)						5.00
... Chronicles TPB (2009, $14.99) r/Showcase #22-24 & Green Lantern #1-3						15.00
... Chronicles Vol. 2 TPB (2009, $14.99) r/Green Lantern #4-9						15.00
... Chronicles Vol. 3 TPB (2010, $14.99) r/Green Lantern #10-14 and Flash #131						15.00

NOTE: ***N. Adams** a-76, 77-87p, 89; c-63, 76-89. **M. Anderson** a-137i. **Austin** a-93i, 94i, 171i. **Chaykin** c-196. **Greene** a-39-49i, 58-63i; c-54-58i. **Grell** a-90-100, 106, 108-111; c-90-106, 108-112. **Heck** a-120-122p. **Infantino** a-137p, 145-147p, 151, 152p. **Gil Kane** a-1-49p, 50-57, 58-61p, 68-75p, 85p(r), 87p(r), 88p(r), 156, 177, 184p; c-1-52, 54-61p, 67-75, 123, 154, 156, 165-171, 177, 184. **Newton** a-148p, 149p, 181. **Perez** c-132p, 141-144. **Sekowsky** a-65p, 170p. **Simonson** c-200. **Sparling** a-63p. **Starlin** c-129, 133. **Staton** a-117p, 123-127p, 128, 129-131p, 132-139, 140p, 141-146, 147p, 148-150, 151-155p; c-107p, 117p, 135(i), 136p, 145p, 146, 147, 148-152p, 155p. **Toth** a-86r, 171p. **Tuska** a-166-168p, 170p.*

GREEN LANTERN (3rd Series)
DC Comics: June, 1990 - No. 181, Nov, 2004 ($1.00/$1.25/$1.50/$1.75/$1.95/$1.99/$2.25)

	NM-
1-Hal Jordan, John Stewart & Guy Gardner return; Batman & JLA app.	6.00
2-18,20-26: 9-12-Guy Gardner solo story. 13-(52 pgs.). 18-Guy Gardner solo story. 25-($1.75, 52 pgs.)-Hal Jordan/Guy Gardner battle	4.00
19-($1.75, 52 pgs.)-50th anniversary issue; Mart Nodell (original G.A. artist) part-p on G.A. Green Lantern; G. Kane-c	5.00
27-45,47: 30,31-Gorilla Grodd-c/story(see Flash #69). 38,39-Adam Strange-c/story. 42-Deathstroke-c/s. 47-Green Arrow x-over	4.00
46,48,49,50: 46-Superman app. cont'd in Superman #82. 48-Emerald Twilight part 1. 50-($2.95, 52 pgs.)-Glow-in-the-dark-c	6.00
0, 51-62: 51-1st app. New Green Lantern (Kyle Rayner) with new costume. 53-Superman-c/story. 55-(9/94)-Zero Hour. 0-(10/94). 56-(11/94)	4.00

Green Lantern (3rd series) #150 © DC

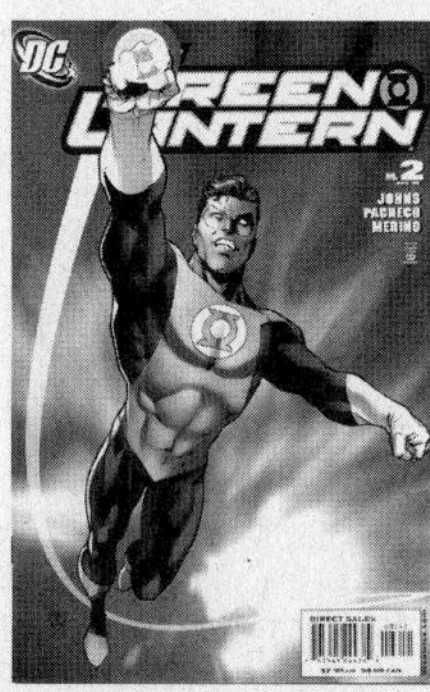

Green Lantern (2005 series) #2 © DC

Green Lantern (2011 series) #18 © DC

GD VG FN VF VF/NM NM-
2.0 4.0 6.0 8.0 9.0 9.2

63,64-Kyle Rayner vs. Hal Jordan. 4.00
65-80,82-92: 63-Begin $1.75-c. 65-New Titans app. 66,67-Flash app. 71-Batman & Robin app. 72-Shazam!-c/app. 73-Wonder Woman-c/app. 73-75-Adam Strange app. 76,77-Green Arrow x-over. 80-Final Night. 87-JLA app. 91-Genesis x-over. 92-Green Arrow x-over 3.00
81-(Regular Ed.)-Memorial for Hal Jordan (Parallax); most DC heroes app. 5.00
81-($3.95, Deluxe Edition)-Embossed prism-c 6.00
93-99: 93-Begin $1.95-c; Deadman app. 94-Superboy app. 95-Starlin-a(p). 98,99-Legion of Super-Heroes-c/app. 3.00
100-($2.95) Two covers (Jordan & Rayner); vs. Sinestro 6.00
101-106: 101-106-Hal Jordan-c/app. 103-JLA-c/app. 104-Green Arrow app. 105,106-Parallax app. 3.00
107-126: 107-Jade becomes a Green Lantern. 119-Hal Jordan/Spectre app. 125-JLA app. 3.00
127-149: 127-Begin $2.25-c. 129-Winick-s begin. 134-136-JLA-c/app. 143-Joker: Last Laugh; Lee-c. 145-Kyle becomes The Ion. 149-Superman-c/app. 3.00
150-($3.50) Jim Lee-c; Kyle becomes Green Lantern again; new costume 4.00
151-181: 151-155-Jim Lee-c: 154-Terry attacked. 155-Spectre-c/app. 162-164-Crossover with Green Arrow #23-25. 165-Raab-s begin. 169-Kilowog returns 3.00
#1,000,000 (11/98) 853rd Century x-over; Hitch & Neary-a/c 3.00
Annual 1-3: ('92-'94, 68 pgs.)-1-Eclipso app. 2 -Intro Nightblade. 3-Elseworlds story 4.00
Annual 4 (1995, $3.50)-Year One story 4.00
Annual 5,7,8 ('96, '98, '99, $2.95): 5-Legends of the Dead Earth. 7-Ghosts; Wrightson-c. 8-JLApe; Art Adams-c 4.00
Annual 6 (1997, $3.95)-Pulp Heroes story 5.00
Annual 9 (2000, $3.50) Planet DC 4.00
...80 Page Giant (12/98, $4.95) Stories by various 5.00
...80 Page Giant 2 (6/99, $4.95) Team-ups 5.00
...80 Page Giant 3 (8/00, $5.95) Darkseid vs. the GL Corps 6.00
...: 1001 Emerald Nights (2001, $6.95) Elseworlds; Guay-a/c; LaBan-s 7.00
...3-D #1 (12/98, $3.95) Jeanty-a 4.00
...: A New Dawn TPB (1998, $9.95)-r/#50-55 10.00
...: Baptism of Fire TPB (1999, $12.95)-r/#59,66,67,70-75 13.00
...: Brother's Keeper (2003, $12.95)-r/#151-155; Green Lantern Secret Files #3 13.00
...: Emerald Allies TPB (2000, $14.95)-r/GL/GA team-ups 15.00
...: Emerald Knights TPB (1998, $12.95)-r/Hal Jordan's return 13.00
...: Emerald Twilight nn (1994, $5.95)-r/#48-50 6.00
...: Emerald Twilight/New Dawn TPB (2003, $19.95)-r/#48-55 20.00
...: Ganthet's Tale nn (1992, $5.95, 68 pgs.)-Silver foil logo; Niven scripts; Byrne-c/a 6.00
.../Green Arrow Vol. 1 (2004, $12.95) -r/GL #76-82; intro. by O'Neil 13.00
.../Green Arrow Vol. 2 (2004, $12.95) -r/GL #83-87,89 & Flash #217-219, 226; cover gallery with 1983-84 GL/GA covers #1-7; intro. by Giordano 13.00
.../Green Arrow Collection, Vol. 2-r/GL #84-87,89 & Flash #217-219 & GL/GA #5-7 by O'Neil/Adams/Wrightson 13.00
...: New Journey, Old Path TPB (2001, $12.95)-r/#129-136 13.00
... : Our Worlds at War (8/01, $2.95) Jae Lee-c; prelude to x-over 3.00
...: Passing The Torch (2004, $12.95, TPB) r/#156,158-161 & GL Secret Files #2 13.00
...Plus 1 (12/1996, $2.95)-The Ray & Polaris-c/app. 4.00
...Secret Files 1-3 (7/98-7/02, $4.95)1-Origin stories & profiles. 2-Grell-c 5.00
.../Superman: Legend of the Green Flame (2000, $5.95) 1988 unpub. Neil Gaiman story of Hal Jordan with new art by various; Frank Miller-c 6.00
...: The Power of Ion (2003, $14.95, TPB) r/#142-150 15.00
...The Road Back nn (1992, $8.95)-r/1-8 w/covers 9.00
...: Traitor TPB (2001, $12.95) r/Legends of the DCU #20,21,28,29,37,38 13.00
...: Willworld (2001, $24.95, HC) Seth Fisher-a/J.M. DeMatteis-s; Hal Jordan 25.00
...: Willworld (2003, $17.95, SC) Seth Fisher-a/J.M. DeMatteis-s; Hal Jordan 18.00
NOTE: ***Staton*** *a(p)-9-12; c-9-12.*

GREEN LANTERN (See Tangent Comics/ Green Lantern)

GREEN LANTERN (4th Series) (Follows Hal Jordan's return in Green Lantern: Rebirth)
DC Comics: July, 2005 - No. 67, Aug, 2011 ($3.50/$2.99)

1-($3.50) Two covers by Pacheco and Ross; Johns-s/Van Sciver and Pacheco-a 5.00
2-20-($2.99) 2-4-Manhunters app. 6-Bianchi-a. 7,8-Green Arrow app. 8-Bianchi-c. 9-Batman app.; two covers by Bianchi and Van Sciver. 10,11-Reis-a. 17-19-Star Sapphire returns. 18-Acuna-a; Sinestro Corps back-ups begin 3.00
8-Variant-c by Neal Adams 8.00
21-Sinestro Corps War pt. 2 5.00
21-2nd printing with variant green hued background-c 3.00
22-24: 22-Sinestro Corps War pt. 4; green hued-c. 23-Part 6. 24-Part 8 4.00
22,23-2nd printings. 22-Yellow hued-c. 23-B&W Hal Jordan with colored rings 3.00
25-($4.99) Sinestro Corps War conclusion; Ivan Reis-c 6.00
25-($4.99) Variant cover by Gary Frank; Sinestro Corps War conclusion 8.00
26-28,30-43: 26-Alpha Lanterns. 30-35-Childhood & origin re-told; Sinestro app. 41-Origin Larfleeze. 43-Prologue to Blackest Night, origin of Black Hand; Mahnke-a 3.00
29-Childhood & origin re-told 5.00
29-Special Edition (6/10, $1.00) reprints #29 with "What's Next?" logo on cover 3.00
29-Special Edition (2010 San Diego Comic-Con giveaway) reprints #29 with new Van Sciver cover and Geoff Johns intro on inside front cover 3.00
39-43-Variant covers: 39,40-Migliari. 41-42-Barrows 12.00
44-49,51,52-Blackest Night. 44-Flash app. 46-Sinestro vs. Mongul. 47-Black Lantern Abin Sur. 49-Art by Benes & Ordway; Atom and Mera app. 51-Nekron app. 3.00
44-49,51-Variant covers: 44-Tan. 45-Manapul. 46. Andy Kubert. 47-Benes. 48-Morales. 49-Migliari. 51-Horn. 52-Shane Davis 8.00
50-($3.99)-Black Lantern Spectre & Parallax app.; Mahnke-a/c 4.00
50-Variant-c by Jim Lee 12.00
53-67: 53-62-Brightest Day. 54,55-Lobo app. 58-60-Flash app. 60-Krona returns. 64-67-War of the Green Lanterns x-over. 67-Sinestro becomes a Green Lantern 3.00
FCBD 2011 Green Lantern Flashpoint Special Edition (6/11, giveaway) r/#30 and previews Flashpoint x-over; Andy Kubert-a 3.00
...: Larfleeze Christmas Special 1 (2/11, $3.99) Johns-s/Booth-a/Ha-c 4.00
.../Plastic Man: Weapons of Mass Deception (2/11, $4.99) Brent Anderson-a 5.00
...Secret Files and Origins 2005 (6/05, $4.99) Johns-s/Cooke & Van Sciver-a; profiles with art by various incl. Chaykin, Gibbons, Gleason, Igle; Pacheco-c 5.00
.../Sinestro Corps: Secret Files 1 (2/08, $4.99) Profiles of Green Lanterns and Corps info 5.00
...: Agent Orange HC (2009, $19.99) r/#38-42 & Blackest Night #0; sketch art 20.00
...: Agent Orange SC (2010, $14.99) r/#38-42 & Blackest Night #0; sketch art 15.00
Blackest Night: Green Lantern HC (2010, $24.99) r/#43-52; variant covers; sketch art 25.00
Blackest Night: Green Lantern SC (2011, $19.99) r/#43-52; variant covers; sketch art 20.00
...: Brightest Day HC (2011, $22.99) r/#53-62; variant cover gallery 23.00
...: In Brightest Day SC (2008, $19.99) r/stories selected by Geoff Johns w/commentary 20.00
...: No Fear HC (2006, $24.99) r/#1-6 & Secret Files and Origins 25.00
...: No Fear SC (2008, $12.99) r/#1-6 & Secret Files and Origins 13.00
...: Rage of the Red Lanterns HC (2009, $24.99) r/#26-28,36-38 & Final Crisis: Rage... 25.00
...: Rage of the Red Lanterns SC (2010, $14.99) r/#26-28,36-38 & Final Crisis: Rage... 15.00
...: Revenge of the Green Lanterns HC (2006, $19.99) r/#7-13; variant cover gallery 20.00
...: Revenge of the Green Lanterns SC (2008, $12.99) r/#7-13; variant cover gallery 13.00
...: Secret Origin HC (2008, $19.99) r/#29-35 20.00
...: Secret Origin (New Edition) HC (2010, $19.99) r/#29-35; intro. by Ryan Reynolds 20.00
...: Secret Origin SC (2008, $14.99) r/#29-35 15.00
...: Secret Origin (New Edition) SC (2011, $14.99) r/#29-35; intro. by Ryan Reynolds; photo-c of Reynolds from movie; movie preview photo gallery 15.00
... Super Spectacular (1/12, $7.99, magazine-size) r/Blackest Night #0,1, Green Lantern #76 from 1970 and Brave and the Bold #30 from 2009 8.00
...: Tales of the Sinestro Corps HC (2008, $29.99, d.j.) r/back-up stories from #18-20, Tales of the Sinestro Corps series, Green Lantern: Sinestro Corps Special and Sinestro Corps: Secret Files 30.00
...: Tales of the Sinestro Corps SC (2009, $14.99) same contents as HC 15.00
...: The Sinestro Corps War Vol. 1 HC (2008, $24.99, d.j.) r/#21-23, Green Lantern Corps #14-15 and Green Lantern: Sinestro Corps Special 25.00
...: The Sinestro Corps War Vol. 1 SC (2009, $14.99) same contents as HC 15.00
...: The Sinestro Corps War Vol. 2 HC (2008, $24.99, d.j.) r/#24,25, Green Lantern Corps #16-19; interview with the creators and sketch art 25.00
... - Wanted: Hal Jordan HC (2007, $19.99) r/#14-20 without Sinestro Corps back-ups 20.00
... - Wanted: Hal Jordan SC (2008, $14.99) r/#14-20 without Sinestro Corps back-ups 15.00

GREEN LANTERN (DC New 52)
DC Comics: Nov, 2011 - Present ($2.99)

1-19: 1-Sinestro as Green Lantern; Johns-s/Mahnke-a/Reis-c (1st & 2nd print). 6-Choi-a. 9-Origin of the Indigo tribe. 14-Justice League app. 17-19-Wrath of the First Lantern 3.00
1-9-Variant-c. 1-Capullo. 2-Finch. 3-Van Sciver. 4-Manapul. 5-Choi. 6-Reis. 8-Keown 4.00
8-Combo pack ($3.99) polybagged with digital code 4.00
20-($7.99, squarebound) Conclusion of "Wrath of the First Lantern"; last Johns-s 8.00
21-23: 21-Venditti-s/Tan-a begin 3.00
23.1, 23.2, 23.3, 23.4 (11/13, $2.99, regular covers) 3.00
23.1 (11/13, $3.99, 3-D cover) "Relic #1" on cover; origin of Relic; Morales-a 6.00
23.2 (11/13, $3.99, 3-D cover) "Mongul #1" on cover; origin; Starlin-s/Porter-a 5.00
23.3 (11/13, $3.99, 3-D cover) "Black Hand #1" on cover; Soule-s/Ponticelli-a 5.00
23.4 (11/13, $3.99, 3-D cover) "Sinestro #1" on cover; origin; Kindt-s/Eaglesham-a 5.00
24-27,29,30: 24-Lights Out pt. 1; Relic app.; Central Battery destroyed 3.00
28-Flip-book with Red Lanterns #28; Red Lantern Supergirl app. 3.00
#0 (11/12, $2.99) Simon Baz becomes a Green Lantern; Mahnke-a 3.00
Annual 1 (10/12, $4.99) 1st print w/black-c; Rise of the Third Army prologue 5.00
Annual 2 (12/13, $4.99) Lights Out pt. 5; Sean Chen-a 5.00

GREEN LANTERN ANNUAL NO. 1, 1963
DC Comics: 1998 ($4.95, one-shot)

1-Reprints Golden Age & Silver Age stories in 1963-style 80 pg. Giant format; new Gil Kane sketch art 5.00

GREEN LANTERN: BRIGHTEST DAY; BLACKEST NIGHT
DC Comics: 2002 ($5.95, squarebound, one-shot)

nn-Alan Scott vs. Solomon Grundy in 1944; Snyder III-c/a; Seagle-s

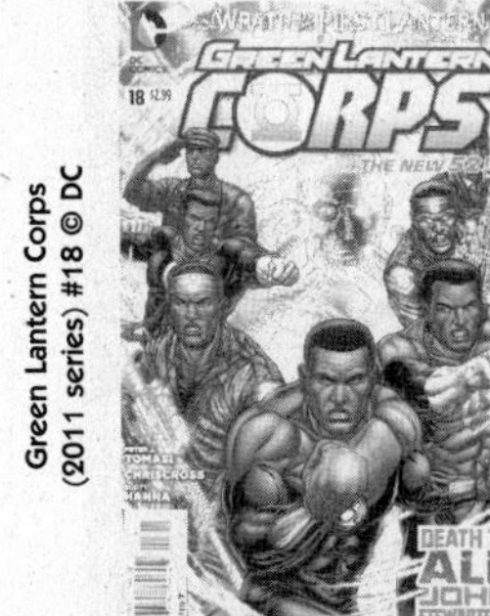

Green Lantern Corps (2011 series) #18 © DC

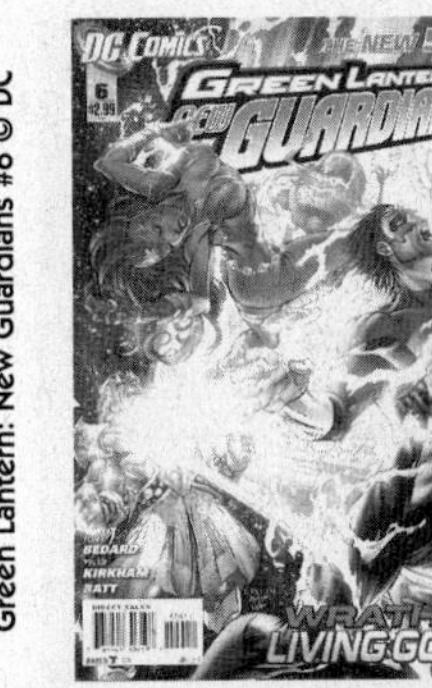

Green Lantern: New Guardians #6 © DC

Green Lantern: Rebirth #2 © DC

GD	VG	FN	VF	VF/NM	NM-
2.0	4.0	6.0	8.0	9.0	9.2
1	2	3	5	6	8

GREEN LANTERN: CIRCLE OF FIRE
DC Comics: Early Oct, 2000 - No. 2, Late Oct, 2000 (limited series)

1-($4.95) Intro. other Green Lanterns 5.00
2-($3.75) 4.00
Green Lantern (x-overs)- .../Adam Strange; .../Atom; .../Firestorm; ... /Green Lantern, Winick-s; .../Power Girl (all $2.50-c) 3.00
TPB (2002, $17.95) r/#1,2 & x-overs 18.00

GREEN LANTERN CORPS, THE (Formerly Green Lantern; see Tales of...)
DC Comics: No. 206, Nov, 1986 - No. 224, May, 1988

206-223: 212-John Stewart marries Katma Tui. 220,221-Millennium tie-ins 4.00
224-Double-size last issue 5.00
...Corps Annual 2,3- (12/86,8/87) 1-Formerly Tales of ...Annual #1; Alan Moore scripts. 3-Indicia says Green Lantern Annual #3; Moore scripts; Byrne-a 5.00

NOTE: ***Austin** a-Annual 3i. **Gil Kane** a-223, 224p; c-223, 224, Annual 2. **Russell** a-Annual 3i. **Staton** a-207-213p, 217p, 221p, 222p, Annual 3; c-207-213p, 217p, 221p, 222p. **Willingham** a-213p, 219p, 220p, 218p, 219p, Annual 2, 3p; c-218p, 219p.*

GREEN LANTERN CORPS
DC Comics: Aug, 2006 - No. 63, Oct, 2011 ($2.99)

1,14-19: 1-Gibbons-s. 14-19-Sinestro Corps War pts. 3,5,7,9,10, Epilogue 4.00
2-13: 2-6,10,11-Gibbons-s. 9-Darkseid app. 3.00
20-38: 20-Mongul app. 3.00
20-Second printing with sketch-c 3.00
34-38: 34-37-Variant covers by Migliari. 38-Fabry var-c 10.00
39-45-Blackest Night. 43-45-Red Lantern Guy Gardner 3.00
39-45-Variant covers: 39-Jusko. 40-Tucci. 41,42,44-Horn. 43-Ladronn. 45 Bolland 8.00
46,47-($3.99) 46-Blackest Night. 47-Brightest Day 4.00
48-61-($2.99) 48-Migliari-c; Ganthet joins the Corps. 49-52-Cyborg Superman app. 58-60-War of the Green Lanterns x-over. 60-Mogo destroyed 3.00
Blackest Night: Green Lantern Corps HC (2010, $24.99, d.j.) r/#39-47, cover gallery 25.00
Blackest Night: Green Lantern Corps SC (2011, $19.99) r/#39-47, cover gallery 20.00
...: Emerald Eclipse HC (2009, $24.99) r/#33-39; gallery of variant covers 25.00
...: Emerald Eclipse SC (2010, $14.99) r/#33-39; gallery of variant covers 15.00
...: Revolt of the Alpha-Lanterns HC (2011, $22.99) r/#21,22,48-52 23.00
...: Ring Quest TPB (2008, $14.99) r/#19,20,23-26 15.00
...: The Dark Side of Green TPB (2007, $12.99) r/#7-13 13.00
...: To Be a Lantern TPB (2007, $12.99) r/#1-6 13.00

GREEN LANTERN CORPS (DC New 52)
DC Comics: Nov, 2011 - Present ($2.99)

1-23: 1-Tomasi-s/Pasarin-a/Mahnke-c; John Stewart & Guy Gardner. 4-6-Andy Kubert-c 3.00
24-29: 24-Lights Out pt. 2; Oa destroyed. 25-Year Zero 3.00
#0 (11/12, $2.99) Origin of Guy Gardner; Tomasi-s/Pasarin-a 3.00
Annual 1 (3/13, $4.99) Rise of the Third Army conclusion; Mogo returns 5.00
Annual 2 (3/14, $4.99) Villains United; Evil Star, Bolphunga, Kanjar Ro app. 5.00

GREEN LANTERN CORPS QUARTERLY
DC Comics: Summer, 1992 - No. 8, Spring, 1994 ($2.50/$2.95, 68 pgs.)

1-G.A. Green Lantern story; Staton-a(p) 5.00
2-8: 2-G.A. G.L.-c/story; Austin-c(i); Gulacy-a(p). 3-G.A. G.L. story. 4-Austin-i. 7-Painted-c; Tim Vigil-a. 8-Lobo-c/s 4.00

GREEN LANTERN CORPS: RECHARGE
DC Comics: Nov, 2005 - No. 5, Mar, 2006 ($3.50/$2.99, limited series)

1-($3.50) Kyle Rayner, Guy Gardner & Kilowog app.; Gleason-a 4.00
2-5-($2.99) 3.00
TPB (2006, $12.99) r/series 13.00

GREEN LANTERN: DRAGON LORD
DC Comics: 2001 - No. 3, 2001 ($4.95, squarebound, limited series)

1-3: A G.L. in ancient China; Moench-s/Gulacy-c/a 5.00

GREEN LANTERN: EMERALD DAWN (Also see Emerald Dawn)
DC Comics: Dec, 1989 - No. 6, May, 1990 ($1.00, limited series)

1-Origin retold; Giffen plots in all 6.00
2-6: 4-Re-intro. Tomar-Re 4.00

GREEN LANTERN: EMERALD DAWN II (Emerald Dawn II #1 & 2)
DC Comics: Apr, 1991 - No. 6, Sept, 1991 ($1.00, limited series)

1-6 3.00
TPB (2003, $12.95) r/#1-6; Alan Davis-c 13.00

GREEN LANTERN: EMERALD WARRIORS
DC Comics: Oct, 2010 - No. 13, Oct, 2011 ($3.99/$2.99)

1-5-($3.99) Guy Gardner's exploits; Migliari-c. 1-Bermejo variant-c. 2-5-Massaferra var-c 4.00
6-13-($2.99) 6,7-Covers by Migliari & Massaferra. 8-10-War of the Green Lanterns x-over 3.00

GREEN LANTERN: EVIL'S MIGHT (Elseworlds)
DC Comics: 2002 - No. 3 ($5.95, squarebound, limited series)

1-3-Kyle Rayner in 19th century NYC; Rogers-a; Chaykin & Tischman-s 6.00

GREEN LANTERN: FEAR ITSELF
DC Comics: 1999 (Graphic novel)

Hardcover ($24.95) Ron Marz-s/Brad Parker painted-a 25.00
Softcover ($14.95) 15.00

GREEN LANTERN/FLASH: FASTER FRIENDS (See Flash/Green Lantern...)
DC Comics: 1997 ($4.95, limited series)

1-Marz-s 5.00

GREEN LANTERN GALLERY
DC Comics: Dec, 1996 ($3.50, one-shot)

1-Wraparound-c; pin-ups by various 3.50

GREEN LANTERN/GREEN ARROW (Also see The Flash #217)
DC Comics: Oct, 1983 - No. 7, April, 1984 (52-60 pgs.)

1-7- r-Green Lantern #76-89 5.00

NOTE: ***Neal Adams** r-1-7; c-1-4. **Wrightson** r-4, 5.*

GREEN LANTERN • LEGACY: THE LAST WILL & TESTAMENT OF HAL JORDAN
DC Comics: 2002 ($24.95, hardcover graphic novel)

Hardcover-Anderson & Sienkiewicz-a/c; Kelly-s; Return of Oa 25.00
Softcover (2004, $17.95) 18.00

GREEN LANTERN: MOSAIC (Also see Cosmic Odyssey #2)
DC Comics: June, 1992 - No. 18, Nov, 1993 ($1.25)

1-18: Featuring John Stewart. 1-Painted-c by Cully Hamner 3.00

GREEN LANTERN MOVIE PREQUEL (2011 movie)
DC Comics: July, 2011; Oct, 2011 ($2.99, one-shots)

...: Abin Sur 1 - Green-s/Gleason-a; movie photo-c 3.00
...: Hal Jordan 1 - Johns & Berlanti-s/Ordway-a; movie photo-c; Sinestro & Tomar-Re app. 3.00
...: Kilowog 1 - Tomasi-s/Ferreira-a; movie photo-c 3.00
...: Sinestro 1 (10/11) - Johns-s/Tolibao, Richards & Ordway-a; movie photo-c 3.00
...: Tomar-Re 1 - Guggenheim-s/Richards-a; movie photo-c 3.00

GREEN LANTERN: NEW GUARDIANS (DC New 52)
DC Comics: Nov, 2011 - Present ($2.99)

1-Bedard-s/Kirkham-a/c; Kyle origin flashback; Fatality app. 6.00
2-23: 13-16-Third Army. 21-Relic freed. 22,23-Kyle vs. Relic. 23-Blue Lanterns destroyed 3.00
24-29: 24-Lights Out pt. 3 3.00
#0 (11/12, $2.99) Bedard-s/Kuder-a; Zamarons app. 3.00
Annual 1 (3/13, $4.99) Giffen-s/Kolins-a/c 5.00

GREEN LANTERN: REBIRTH
DC Comics: Dec, 2004 - No. 6, May, 2005 ($2.95, limited series)

1-Johns-s/Van Sciver-a; Hal Jordan as The Spectre on-c 8.00
1-2nd printing; Hal Jordan as Green Lantern on-c 4.00
1-3rd printing; B&W-c version of 1st printing 3.00
1 Special Edition (9/09, $1.00) r/#1 with "After Watchmen" cover frame 3.00
2-Guy Gardner becomes a Green Lantern again; JLA app. 5.00
2-2nd & 3rd printings 3.00
3-6: 3-Sinestro returns. 4-6-JLA & JSA app. 3.00
HC (2005, $24.99, dust jacket) r/series & Wizard preview; intro. by Brad Meltzer 25.00
SC (2007, 2010, $14.99) r/series & Wizard preview; intro. by Brad Meltzer 15.00

GREEN LANTERN/SENTINEL: HEART OF DARKNESS
DC Comics: Mar, 1998 - No. 3, May, 1998 ($1.95, limited series)

1-3-Marz-s/Pelletier-a 3.00

GREEN LANTERN/SILVER SURFER: UNHOLY ALLIANCES
DC Comics: 1995 ($4.95, one-shot)(Prelude to DC Versus Marvel)

nn-Hal Jordan app. 6.00

GREEN LANTERN SINESTRO CORPS SPECIAL (Continues in Green Lantern #21)
DC Comics: Aug, 2007 ($4.99, one-shot)

1-Kyle Rayner becomes Parallax; Cyborg Superman & Earth-Prime Superboy app.; Johns-s; Van Sciver-a/c; back-up story origin of Sinestro; Gibbons-a; Sinestro on cover 8.00
1-(2nd printing) Kyle Rayner as Parallax on cover 6.00
1-(3rd printing) Sinestro cover with muted colors 5.00

GREEN LANTERN: THE ANIMATED SERIES (Based on the Cartoon Network series)
DC Comics: No. 0, Jan, 2012 - No. 14, Sept, 2013 ($2.99)

0-14: 0-Baltazar & Franco-s/Brizuela-a; Kilowog and Red Lanterns app. 13-Lobo app. 3.00

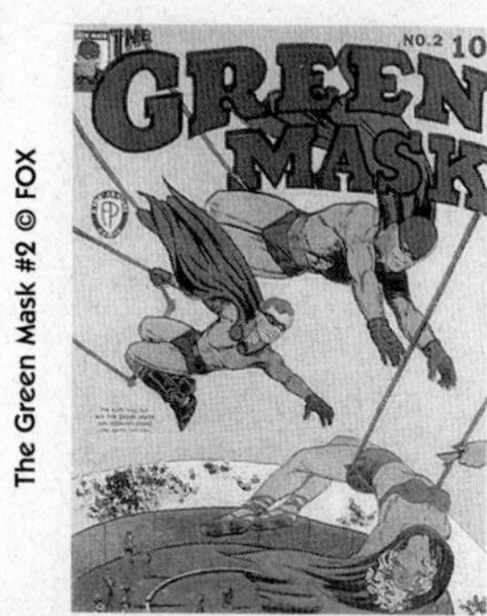

The Green Mask #2 © FOX

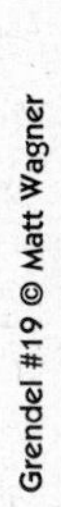
Grendel #19 © Matt Wagner

Grifter (2011 series) #1 © DC

	GD 2.0	VG 4.0	FN 6.0	VF 8.0	VF/NM 9.0	NM- 9.2

GREEN LANTERN: THE GREATEST STORIES EVER TOLD
DC Comics: 2006 ($19.99, TPB)
SC-Reprints Showcase #22; G.L. #1,31,74,87,172; ('90 series) #3, and others; Ross-c 20.00

GREEN LANTERN: THE NEW CORPS
DC Comics: 1999 - No. 2, 1999 ($4.95, limited series)
1,2-Kyle recruits new GLs; Eaton-a 5.00

GREEN LANTERN VS. ALIENS
Dark Horse Comics: Sept, 2000 - No. 4, Dec, 2000 ($2.95, limited series)
1-4: 1-Hal Jordan and GL Corps vs. Aliens; Leonardi-p. 2-4-Kyle Rayner 3.00

GREEN MASK, THE (See Mystery Men)
Summer, 1940 - No. 9, 2/42; No. 10, 8/44 - No. 11, 11/44;
Fox Features Syndicate: V2#1, Spring, 1945 - No. 6, 10-11/46

	GD 2.0	VG 4.0	FN 6.0	VF 8.0	VF/NM 9.0	NM- 9.2
V1#1-Origin The Green Mask & Domino; reprints/Mystery Men #1-3,5-7; Lou Fine-c	300	600	900	1950	3375	4800
2-Zanzibar The Magician by Tuska	116	232	348	742	1271	1800
3-Powell-a; Marijuana story	84	168	252	538	919	1300
4-Navy Jones begins, ends #6	65	130	195	416	708	1000
5	53	106	159	334	567	800
6-The Nightbird begins, ends #9; bondage/torture-c	47	94	141	296	498	700
7-9: 9(2/42)-Becomes The Bouncer #10(nn) on? & Green Mask #10 on	39	78	117	231	378	525
10,11: 10-Origin One Round Hogan & Rocket Kelly	30	60	90	177	289	400
V2#1	23	46	69	136	223	310
2-6	19	38	57	112	179	245

GREEN PLANET, THE
Charlton Comics: 1962 (one-shot) (12¢)

	GD 2.0	VG 4.0	FN 6.0	VF 8.0	VF/NM 9.0	NM- 9.2
nn-Giordano-c; sci-fi	6	12	18	42	79	115

GREEN TEAM (See Cancelled Comic Cavalcade & 1st Issue Special)

GREEN TEAM: TEEN TRILLIONAIRES
DC Comics: Jul, 2013 - No. 8, Mar, 2014 ($2.99)
1-8-Baltazar & Franco-s/Guara-a. 1-3-Conner-c. 3-Deathstroke app. 8-Teen Titans app. 3.00
1-Variant-c by Chiang 3.00

GREEN WOMAN, THE
DC Comics (Vertigo): 2010 ($24.99, HC graphic novel)
HC-John Bolton-a/Peter Straub & Michael Easton-s 25.00

GREETINGS FROM SANTA (See March of Comics No. 48)

GRENDEL (Also see Primer #2, Mage and Comico Collection)
Comico: Mar, 1983 - No. 3, Feb, 1984 ($1.50, B&W)(#1 has indicia to Skrog #1)

	GD 2.0	VG 4.0	FN 6.0	VF 8.0	VF/NM 9.0	NM- 9.2
1-Origin Hunter Rose	9	18	27	62	126	190
2,3: 2-Origin Argent	7	14	21	46	86	125

GRENDEL
Comico: Oct, 1986 - No. 40, Feb, 1990 ($1.50/$1.95/$2.50, mature)

	GD 2.0	VG 4.0	FN 6.0	VF 8.0	VF/NM 9.0	NM- 9.2
1	1	2	3	5	7	9
1,2: 2nd printings						3.00
2,3,5-15: 13-15-Ken Steacy-c.						4.00
4,16: 4-Dave Stevens-c(i). 16-Re-intro Mage (series begins, ends #19)						6.00
17-40: 24-25,27-28,30-31-Snyder-c/a						3.00
Devil by the Deed (Graphic Novel, 10/86, $5.95, 52 pgs.)-r/Grendel back-ups/ Mage 6-14; Alan Moore intro.	1	3	4	6	8	10
Devil's Legacy ($14.95, 1988, Graphic Novel)	2	4	6	9	12	15
Devil's Vagary (10/87, B&W & red)-No price; included in Comico Collection	2	4	6	8	10	12

GRENDEL (Title series): **Dark Horse Comics**
--ARCHIVES, 5/07 ($14.95, HC) r/1st apps. in Primer #2 and Grendel #1-3; Wagner intro. 15.00
--BEHOLD THE DEVIL, No. 0, 7/07 - No. 8, 6/08 ($3.50/50¢, B&W&Red)
0-(50¢-c) Prelude to series; Matt Wagner-s/a; interview with Wagner 3.00
1-8-Matt Wagner-s/a/c in all 3.50
--BLACK, WHITE, AND RED, 11/98 - No. 4, 2/99 ($3.95, anthology)
1-Wagner-s in all. Art by Sale, Leon and others 5.00
2-4: 2-Mack, Chadwick-a. 3-Allred, Kristensen-a. 4-Pearson, Sprouse-a 4.00
--CLASSICS, 7/95 - 8/95 ($3.95, mature) 1,2-reprints; new Wagner-c 4.00
--CYCLE, 10/95 ($5.95) 1-nn-history of Grendel by M. Wagner & others 6.00
--DEVIL BY THE DEED, 7/93 ($3.95, varnish-c) 1-nn-M. Wagner-c/a/scripts; r/Grendel back-ups from Mage #6-14 6.00
Reprint (12/97, $3.95) w/pin-ups by various 4.00
Hardcover (2007, $12.95) reprint recolored to B&W&red; includes covers and intros from previously reprinted editions 13.00
--DEVIL CHILD, 6/99 - No. 2, 7/99 ($2.95, mature) 1,2-Sale & Kristiansen-a/Schutz-s 3.00
--DEVIL QUEST, 11/95 ($4.95) 1-nn-Prequel to Batman/Grendel II; M. Wagner story & art; r/back-up story from Grendel Tales series. 5.00
--DEVILS AND DEATHS, 10/94 - 11/94 ($2.95, mature) 1,2 3.00
: DEVIL'S LEGACY, 3/00 - No. 12, 2/01 ($2.95, reprints 1986 series, recolored)
1-12-Wagner-s/c; Pander Bros.-a 3.00
: DEVIL'S REIGN, 5/04 - No. 7, 12/04 ($3.50, repr. 1989 series #34-40, recolored)
1-7-Sale-c/a. 3.50
: GOD AND THE DEVIL, No. 0, 1/03 - No. 10, 12/03 ($3.50/$4.99, repr. 1986 series, recolored)
0-9: 0-Sale-c/a; r/#23. 1-9-Snyder-c 3.50
10-($4.99) Double-sized; Snyder-c 5.00
--RED, WHITE & BLACK, 9/02 - No. 4, 12/02 ($4.99, anthology)
1-4-Wagner-s in all. 1-Art by Thompson, Sakai, Mahfood and others. 2-Kelley Jones, Watson, Brereton, Hester & Parks-a. 3-Oeming, Noto, Cannon, Ashley Wood, Huddleston-a 4-Chiang, Dalrymple, Robertson, Snyder III and Zulli-a 5.00
TPB (2005, $19.95) r/#1-4; cover gallery, artist bios 20.00
--TALES: DEVIL'S CHOICES, 3/95 - 6/95 ($2.95, mature) 1-4 3.00
--TALES: FOUR DEVILS, ONE HELL, 8/93 - 1/94 ($2.95, mature)
1-6-Wagner painted-c 3.00
TPB (12/94, $17.95) r/#1-6 18.00
--TALES: HOMECOMING, 12/94 - 2/95 ($2.95, mature) 1-3 3.00
--TALES: THE DEVIL IN OUR MIDST, 5/94 - 9/95 ($2.95, mature) 1-5-Wagner painted-c 3.00
--TALES: THE DEVIL MAY CARE, 12/95 - No. 6, 5/96 ($2.95, mature)
1-6-Terry LaBan scripts. 5-Batman/Grendel II preview 3.00
--TALES: THE DEVIL'S APPRENTICE, 9/97 - No. 3, 11/97 ($2.95, mature)
1-3 3.00
: THE DEVIL INSIDE, 9/01 - No. 3, 11/01 ($2.99)
1-3-r/#13-15 with new Wagner-c 3.00
: WAR CHILD, 8/92 - No. 10, 6/93 ($2.50, lim. series, mature)
1-9: 1-4-Bisley painted-c; Wagner-i & scripts in all 3.00
10-($3.50, 52 pgs.) Wagner-c 4.00
Limited Edition Hardcover ($99.95) 100.00

GREYFRIARS BOBBY (Disney)(Movie)
Dell Publishing Co.: No. 1189, Nov, 1961 (one-shot)

	GD 2.0	VG 4.0	FN 6.0	VF 8.0	VF/NM 9.0	NM- 9.2
Four Color 1189-Photo-c (scarce)	6	12	18	41	76	110

GREYLORE
Sirius: 12/85 - No. 5, Sept, 1986 ($1.50/$1.75, high quality paper)
1-5: Bo Hampton-a in all 3.00

GREYSHIRT: INDIGO SUNSET (Also see Tomorrow Stories)
America's Best Comics: Dec, 2001 - No. 6, Aug, 2002 ($3.50, limited series)
1-6-Veitch-s/a. 4-Back-up w/John Severin-a. 6-Cho-a 3.50
TPB (2002, $19.95) r/#1-6; preface by Alan Moore 20.00

GRIDIRON GIANTS
Ultimate Sports Ent.: 2000 - No. 2 ($3.95, cardstock covers)
1,2-NFL players Sanders, Marino, Plummer, T. Davis battle evil 4.00

GRIFFIN, THE
DC Comics: 1991 - No. 6, 1991 ($4.95, limited series, 52 pgs.)
Book 1-6: Matt Wagner painted-c 5.00

GRIFTER (Also see Team 7 & WildC.A.T.S)
Image Comics (WildStorm Prod.): May, 1995 - No. 10, Mar, 1996 ($1.95)
1 ($1.95, Newsstand)-WildStorm Rising Pt. 5 3.00
1-10:1 ($2.50, Direct)-WildStorm Rising Pt. 5, bound-in trading card 3.00
...: One Shot (1/95, $4.95) Flip-c 5.00

GRIFTER
Image Comics (WildStorm Prod.): V2#1, July, 1996 - No. 14, Aug, 1997 ($2.50)
V2#1-14: Steven Grant scripts 3.00

GRIFTER (DC New 52)
DC Comics: Nov, 2011 - No. 16, Mar, 2013 ($2.99)
1-16: 1-Grifter in the new DC universe; Edmonson-s/Cafu-a/c. 4-Green Arrow app. 3.00
#0 (11/12, $2.99) Liefeld-s/c; Clark-a 3.00

GRIFTER & MIDNIGHTER

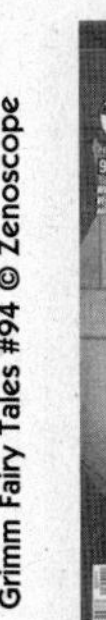

Grimm #1 © Universal

Grimm Fairy Tales #94 © Zenoscope

Groo #1 © Sergio Aragonés

GD VG FN VF VF/NM NM-
2.0 4.0 6.0 8.0 9.0 9.2

DC Comics (WildStorm Prod.): May, 2007 - No. 6, Oct, 2007 ($2.99, limited series)

1-6-Dixon-s/Benjamin-a/c. 1,3-The Authority app. 3.00
TPB (2008, $17.99) r/#1-6 18.00

GRIFTER AND THE MASK
Dark Horse Comics: Sept, 1996 - No. 2, Oct, 1996 ($2.50, limited series)
(1st Dark Horse Comics/Image x-over)

1,2: Steve Seagle scripts 3.00

GRIFTER/BADROCK (Also see WildC.A.T.S & Youngblood)
Image Comics (Extreme Studios): Oct, 1995 - No.2, Nov, 1995 ($2.50, unfinished lim. series)

1,2: 2-Flip book w/Badrock #2 3.00

GRIFTER/SHI
Image Comics (WildStorm Productions): Apr, 1996 - No. 2, May, 1996 ($2.95, limited series)

1,2: 1-Jim Lee-c/a(p); Travis Charest-a(p). 2-Billy Tucci-c/a(p); Travis Charest-a(p) 3.00

GRIM GHOST, THE
Atlas/Seaboard Publ.: Jan, 1975 - No. 3, July, 1975

1-3: Fleisher-s in all. 1-Origin. 2-Son of Satan; Colan-a. 3-Heath-c
2 4 6 11 16 20

GRIM GHOST
Ardden Entertainment (Atlas Comics): Mar, 2011 - Present ($2.99)

1-5-Isabella & Susco-s/Kelley Jones-a. 1-Re-intro. Matthew Dunsinane 3.00
... Issue Zero - NY Comicon Edtion (10/10, $2.99) Qing Ping Mui-a; prequel to #1 3.00

GRIMJACK (Also see Demon Knight & Starslayer)
First Comics: Aug, 1984 - No. 81, Apr, 1991 ($1.00/$1.95/$2.25)

1-John Ostrander scripts & Tim Truman-c/a begins. 5.00
2-25: 20-Sutton-c/a begins. 22-Bolland-a. 3.00
26-2nd color Teenage Mutant Ninja Turtles 6.00
27-74,76-81 (Later issues $1.95, $2.25): 30-Dynamo Joe x-over; 31-Mandrake-c/a begins. 73,74-Kelley Jones-a 3.00
75-($5.95, 52 pgs.)-Fold-out map; coated stock 6.00
The Legend of Grimjack Vol. 1 (IDW Publishing, 2004, $19.99) r/Starslayer #10-18; 8 new pages & art 20.00
The Legend of Grimjack Vol. 2 (IDW, 2005, $19.99) r/#1-7; unpublished art 20.00
The Legend of Grimjack Vol. 3 (IDW, 2005, $19.99) r/#8-14; cover gallery 20.00
The Legend of Grimjack Vol. 4 (IDW, 2005, $24.99) r/#15-21; cover gallery 25.00
The Legend of Grimjack Vol. 5 (IDW, 5/06, $24.99) r/#22-30; cover gallery 25.00
The Legend of Grimjack Vol. 6 (IDW, 1/07, $24.99) r/#31-37; cover gallery 25.00
The Legend of Grimjack Vol. 7 (IDW, 4/07, $24.99) r/#38-46; covers; "Rough Trade" 25.00
NOTE: ***Truman** c/a-1-17.*

GRIMJACK CASEFILES
First Comics: Nov, 1990 - No. 5, Mar, 1991 ($1.95, limited series)

1-5 Reprints 1st stories from Starslayer #10 on 3.00

GRIMJACK: KILLER INSTINCT
IDW Publ.: Jan, 2005 - No. 6, June, 2005 ($3.99, limited series)

1-6-Ostrander-s/Truman-a 4.00

GRIMJACK: THE MANX CAT
IDW Publ.: Aug, 2009 - No. 6, Jan, 2010 ($3.99, limited series)

1-6-Ostrander-s/Truman-a 4.00

GRIMM (Based on the NBC TV series)
Dynamite Entertainment.: 2013 - No. 12, 2014 ($3.99)

1-11: 1-Two covers (Alex Ross & photo). 2-11-Pararillo & photo-c on each 4.00
12-($4.99) Gaffen & McVey-s/Rodolfo-a; Pararillo & photo-c 5.00
#0 (2013, Free Comic Book Day giveaway) Prequel to issue #1; Portacio-c 3.00
...: The Warlock 1-4 (2013 - No. 4, 2014, $3.99) Nitz-s/Malaga-a 4.00

GRIMM FAIRY TALES
Zenescope Entertainment: Jun, 2005 - Present ($2.99)

1-Al Rio-c; Little Red Riding Hood app.; multiple variant covers
5 10 15 31 53 75
2-Multiple variant covers 3 6 9 16 23 30
3-6-Multiple variant covers 2 4 6 9 12 15
7-12: Multiple covers on each 6.00
13-74,76-84,86-96: Multiple covers on each 3.00
75-(7/12, $5.99) Covers by Campbell, Sejic, Michaels and others 6.00
85-(5/13, $5.99) Unleashed part 2 6.00
... Animated One Shot (10/12, $3.99) Schnepp-c; bonus design art 4.00
... Halloween Special 1,2, 2013 (10/09, 10/10, 10/13, $5.99) Multiple covers on each 6.00
... Presents Wounded Warriors (7/13, $6.99) Multiple military-themes covers 7.00
... The Dark Queen One Shot (1/14, $5.99) Sharma-a; 4 covers 6.00

GRIMM FAIRY TALES PRESENTS ALICE IN WONDERLAND
Zenescope Entertainment: Jan, 2012 - No. 6, May, 2012 ($2.99)

1-Multiple variant covers 2 4 6 9 12 15
2-6: Multiple covers on each 6.00

GRIMM FAIRY TALES MYTHS & LEGENDS
Zenescope Entertainment: Jan, 2011 - Present ($2.99)

1-Campbell-c; multiple variant covers 1 3 4 6 8 10
2-5 5.00
6-24 3.00
25-(2/13, $5.99) Multiple variant covers 6.00

GRIMM FAIRY TALES PRESENTS WONDERLAND
Zenescope Entertainment: Jul, 2012 - Present ($2.99)

1-Campbell-c; multiple variant covers 1 3 4 6 8 10
2,3 5.00
4-21 3.00

GRIMM'S GHOST STORIES (See Dan Curtis)
Gold Key/Whitman No. 55 on: Jan, 1972 - No. 60, June, 1982 (Painted-c #1-42,44,46-56)

1 3 6 9 21 33 45
2-5,8: 5,8-Williamson-a 2 4 6 13 18 22
6,7,9,10 2 4 6 11 16 20
11-20 2 4 6 8 11 14
21-42,45-54: 32,34-Reprints. 45-Photo-c 1 3 4 6 8 10
43,44,55-60: 43,44-(52 pgs.). 43-Photo-c. 58(2/82). 59(4/82)-Williamson-a(r/#8). 60(6/82)
2 4 6 8 11 14
Mini-Comic No. 1 (3-1/4x6-1/2", 1976) 1 3 4 6 8 10
NOTE: *Reprints-#32?, 34?, 39, 43, 44, 47?, 53; 56-60(1/3).* ***Bolle** a-8, 17, 22-25, 27, 29(2), 33, 35, 41, 43r, 45(2), 48(2), 50, 52, 57.* ***Celardo** a-17, 26, 28p, 30, 31, 43(2), 45.* ***Lopez** a-24, 25.* ***McWilliams** a-33, 44r, 48, 54(2), 57, 58.* ***Win Mortimer** a-31, 33, 49, 51, 55, 56, 58(2), 59, 60.* ***Roussos** a-25, 30.* ***Sparling** a-23, 24, 28, 30, 31, 33, 43r, 44, 45, 51(2), 52, 56-58, 59(2), 60.* ***Spiegle** a-44.*

GRIN (The American Funny Book) (Satire)
APAG House Pubs: Nov, 1972 - No. 3, April, 1973 (Magazine, 52 pgs.)

1-Parodies-Godfather, All in the Family 3 6 9 16 24 32
2,3 2 4 6 11 16 20

GRIN & BEAR IT (See Gags)
Dell Publishing Co.: No. 28, 1941

Large Feature Comic 28 17 34 51 98 154 210

GRINDHOUSE: DOORS OPEN AT MIDNIGHT
Dark Horse Comics: Oct, 2013 - Present ($3.99)

1-7: 1-Francavilla-c/DeCampi-s. 1,2-Bee Vixens From Mars. 3,4-Prison Ship Antares 4.00

GRIPS (Extreme violence)
Silverwolf Comics: Sept, 1986 - No. 4, Dec, 1986 ($1.50, B&W, mature)

1-Tim Vigil-c/a in all 6.00
2-4 4.00

GRIP: THE STRANGE WORLD OF MEN
DC Comics (Vertigo): Jan, 2002 - No. 5, May, 2002 ($2.50, limited series)

1-4-Gilbert Hernandez-s/a 3.00

GRIT GRADY (See Holyoke One-Shot No. 1)

GROO (Also see Sergio Aragonés' Groo...)

GROO (Sergio Aragonés'...)
Image Comics: Dec, 1994 - No. 12, Dec, 1995 ($1.95)

1-12: 2-Indicia reads #1, Jan, 1995; Aragonés-c/a in all 4.00

GROO (Sergio Aragonés'...)
Dark Horse Comics: Jan, 1998 - No. 4, Apr, 1998 ($2.95)

1-4: Aragonés-c/a in all 4.00
...: One For One (9/10, $1.00) reprints #1 with red cover frame 3.00

GROO CHRONICLES, THE (Sergio Aragonés)
Marvel Comics (Epic Comics): June, 1989 - No. 6, Feb, 1990 ($3.50)

Book 1-6: Reprints early Pacific issues 5.00

GROO SPECIAL
Eclipse Comics: Oct, 1984 ($2.00, 52 pgs., Baxter paper)

1-Aragonés-c/a 3 6 9 15 22 28

GROO THE WANDERER (See Destroyer Duck #1 & Starslayer #5)
Pacific Comics: Dec, 1982 - No. 8, Apr, 1984

1-Aragonés-c/a(p) in all; Aragonés bio., photo 3 6 9 15 22 28

Gross Point #7 © DC

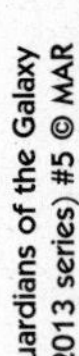

Guardians of the Galaxy (2013 series) #5 © MAR

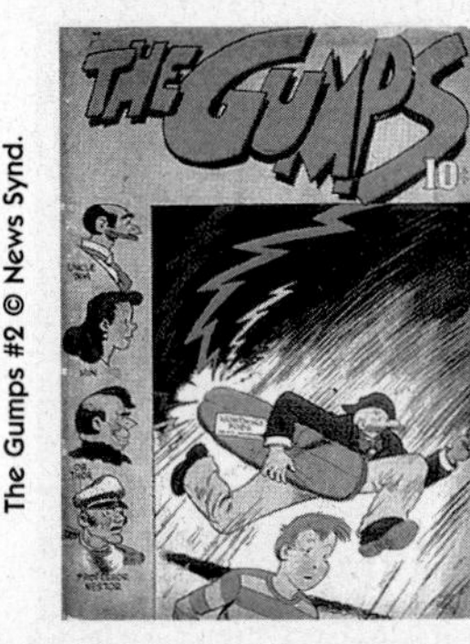

The Gumps #2 © News Synd.

	GD 2.0	VG 4.0	FN 6.0	VF 8.0	VF/NM 9.0	NM- 9.2
2-5: 5-Deluxe paper (1.00-c)	2	4	6	9	13	16
6-8	2	4	6	10	14	18

GROO THE WANDERER (Sergio Aragonés'...) (See Marvel Graphic Novel #32)
Marvel Comics (Epic Comics): March, 1985 - No. 120, Jan, 1995

	GD	VG	FN	VF	VF/NM	NM-
1-Aragonés-c/a in all	2	4	6	10	14	18
2-10	1	2	3	5	6	8
11-20,50-($1.50, double size)						5.00
21-49,51-99: 87-direct sale only, high quality paper						3.00
100-($2.95, 52 pgs.)						5.00
101-120						4.00
Groo Carnival, The (12/91, $8.95)-r/#9-12						11.00
Groo Garden, The (4/94, $10.95)-r/#25-28						11.00

GROOVY (Cartoon Comics - not CCA approved)
Marvel Comics Group: March, 1968 - No. 3, July, 1968

	GD	VG	FN	VF	VF/NM	NM-
1-Monkees, Ringo Starr, Sonny & Cher, Mamas & Papas photos	8	16	24	52	99	145
2,3	5	10	15	35	63	90

GROSS POINT
DC Comics: Aug, 1997 - No. 14, Aug, 1998 ($2.50)

1-14: 1-Waid/Augustyn-s 3.00

GROUNDED
Image Comics: July, 2005 - No. 6, May, 2006 ($2.95/$2.99, limited series)

1-6-Mark Sable-s/Paul Azaceta-a. 1-Mike Oeming-c 3.00
Vol. 1: Powerless TPB (2006, $14.99) r/#1-6; sketch pages and creator bios 15.00

GRRL SCOUTS (Jim Mahfood's...) (Also see 40 oz. Collected)
Oni Press: Mar,1999 - No. 4, Dec, 1999 ($2.95, B&W, limited series)

1-4-Mahfood-s/c/a 3.00
TPB (2003, $12.95) r/#1-4; pin-ups by Warren, Winick, Allred, Fegredo and others 13.00

GRRL SCOUTS: WORK SUCKS
Image Comics: Feb, 2003 - No. 4, May, 2003 ($2.95, B&W, limited series)

1-4-Mahfood-s/c/a 3.00
TPB (2004, $12.95) r/#1-4; pin-ups by Oeming, Dwyer, Tennapel and others 13.00

GUADALCANAL DIARY (See American Library)

GUARDIAN ANGEL
Image Comics: May, 2002 - No. 2, July, 2002 ($2.95)

1,2-Peterson-s/Wiesenfeld-a 3.00

GUARDIANS
Marvel Comics: Sept, 2004 - No. 5, Dec, 2004 ($2.99, limited series)

1-5-Sumerak-s/Casey Jones-a 3.00

GUARDIANS OF METROPOLIS
DC Comics: Nov, 1995 - Feb, 1995 ($1.50, limited series)

1-4: 1-Superman & Granny Goodness app. 3.00

GUARDIANS OF THE GALAXY (Also see The Defenders #26, Marvel Presents #3, Marvel Super-Heroes #18, Marvel Two-In-One #5)
Marvel Comics: June, 1990 - No. 62, July, 1995 ($1.00/$1.25)

	GD	VG	FN	VF	VF/NM	NM-
1-Valentino-c/a(p) begin.	2	4	6	9	12	15
2-5: 2-Zeck-c(i). 5-McFarlane-c(i)						6.00
6-15: 7-Intro Malevolence (Mephisto's daughter); Perez-c(i). 8-Intro Rancor (descendant of Wolverine) in cameo. 9-1st full app. Rancor; Rob Liefeld-c(i). 10-Jim Lee-c(i). 13,14-1st app. Spirit of Vengeance (futuristic Ghost Rider). 14-Spirit of Vengeance vs. The Guardians. 15-Starlin-c(i)						4.00
16-($1.50, 52 pgs.)-Starlin-c(i)						5.00
17-24,26-38,40-47: 17-20-31st century Punishers storyline. 20-Last $1.00-c. 21-Rancor app. 22-Reintro Starhawk. 24-Silver Surfer-c/story; Ron Lim-c. 26-Origin retold. 27-28-Infinity War x-over; 27-Inhumans app. 43-Intro Wooden (son of Thor)						3.00
25-($2.50)-Prism foil-c; Silver Surfer/Galactus-c/s						5.00
25-($2.50)-Without foil-c; newsstand edition						4.00
39-($2.95, 52 pgs.)-Embossed & holo-grafx foil-c; Dr. Doom vs. Rancor						4.00
48,49,51-56: 48-bound-in trading card sheet						4.00
50-($2.00, 52 pgs.)-Newsstand edition						4.00
50-($2.95, 52 pgs.)-Collectors ed. w/foil embossed-c						5.00
57-61	1	2	3	5	6	8
62	2	4	6	8	10	12
Annual 1-4: ('91-'94, 68 pgs.)-1-Origin. 2-Spirit of Vengeance-c/story. 3,4-Bagged w/card						4.00

GUARDIANS OF THE GALAXY (See Annihilation series)
Marvel Comics: July, 2008 - No. 25, Jun, 2010 ($2.99)

	GD	VG	FN	VF	VF/NM	NM-
1-Pelletier-a/Abnett & Lanning-s	5	10	15	31	53	75
1-Second printing	2	4	6	11	16	20
2,3	2	4	6	9	12	15
4-24: 24-Thanos returns						6.00
25	2	4	6	9	12	15

GUARDIANS OF THE GALAXY (Marvel NOW!) (Also see the 2013 Nova series) (See Incredible Hulk #271, Iron Man #55, Marvel Preview #4,7, Strange Tales #180 and Tales to Astonish #13 for 1st app. of 2014 movie characters)
Marvel Comics: No. 0.1, Apr, 2013; No. 1, May, 2013 - Present ($3.99)

	GD	VG	FN	VF	VF/NM	NM-
0.1-(4/13) Origin of Star-Lord; Bendis-s/McNiven-a						5.00
1-Bendis-s/McNiven-a; Iron Man app.; at least 15 variant covers exist	1	3	4	6	8	10
2-4: Iron Man app.						6.00
5-Angela & Thanos app.						5.00
6-13: 8,9-Infinity tie-in; Francavilla-a/c. 10-Maguire-a. 11-13-Trial of Jean Grey						4.00
14-($4.99) Venom and Captain Marvel app.; Bradshaw-a; Guardians of 3014 app.						5.00
Marvel's Guardians of the Galaxy Prelude 1 (6/14 - No. 2, $2.99) Gamora & Nebula						3.00
...: Tomorrow's Avengers 1 (9/13, $4.99) Short stories; art by various						5.00

GUARDING THE GLOBE (See Invincible)
Image Comics: Aug, 2010 - No. 6, Oct, 2011 ($3.50)

1-6-Kirkman & Cereno-s/Getty-a. 1-Back-c swipe of Avengers #4 w/Obama 3.50

GUARDING THE GLOBE (2nd series) (See Invincible Universe)
Image Comics: Sept, 2012 - No. 6, Feb, 2013 ($2.99)

1-6: 1-Wraparound-c; Hester-s/Nauck-a 3.00

GUERRILLA WAR (Formerly Jungle War Stories)
Dell Publishing Co.: No. 12, July-Sept, 1965 - No. 14, Mar, 1966

	GD	VG	FN	VF	VF/NM	NM-
12-14	3	6	9	15	22	28

GUILD, THE (Based on the web-series)
Dark Horse Comics: Mar, 2010 - No. 3, May, 2010 ($3.50, limited series)

1-3-Felicia Day-s/Jim Rugg-a; two covers on each 3.50
... Bladezz 1 (6/11, $3.50) Currie-a/Kerschl-c; variant-c by Dalrymple 3.50
... Clara 1 (9/11, $3.50) Chan-a/Chaykin-c; variant-c by Aronowitz 3.50
... Fawkes 1 (5/12, $3.50) Day & Wheaton-s/McKelvie-a; variant-c by Rios 3.50
... Tink 1 (3/11, $3.50) art by Donaldson, Warren, Seeley & others; variant-c by Bagge 3.50
... Vork 1 (12/10, $3.50) Robertson-a/c; variant-c by Hernandez 3.50
... Zaboo 1 (12/11, $3.50) Cloonan-a/Dorkin-c; variant-c by Jeanty 3.50

GUILTY (See Justice Traps the Guilty)

GULLIVER'S TRAVELS (See Dell Jr. Treasury No. 3)
Dell Publishing Co.: Sept-Nov, 1965

	GD	VG	FN	VF	VF/NM	NM-
1	5	10	15	31	53	75

GUMBY
Wildcard Ink: July, 2006 - No. 3 ($3.99)

1-3-Bob Burden & Rick Geary-s&a 4.00

GUMBY'S SUMMER FUN SPECIAL
Comico: July, 1987 ($2.50)

1-Art Adams-c/a; B. Burden scripts 5.00

GUMBY'S WINTER FUN SPECIAL
Comico: Dec, 1988 ($2.50, 44 pgs.)

1-Art Adams-c/a 5.00

GUMPS, THE (See Merry Christmas..., Popular & Super Comics)
Dell Publ. Co./Bridgeport Herald Corp.: No. 73, 1945; Mar-Apr, 1947 - No. 5, Nov-Dec, 1947

	GD	VG	FN	VF	VF/NM	NM-
Four Color 73 (Dell)(1945)	10	20	30	69	147	225
1 (3-4/47)	15	30	45	88	137	185
2-5	11	22	33	60	83	105

GUN CANDY (Also see The Ride)
Image Comics: July, 2005 - No. 2 ($5.99)

1,2-Stelfreeze-c/a; flip book with The Ride (1-Pearson-c. 2-Noto-c) 6.00

GUNFIGHTER (Fat & Slat #1-4) (Becomes Haunt of Fear #15 on)
E. C. Comics (Fables Publ. Co.): No. 5, Sum, 1948 - No. 14, Mar-Apr, 1950

	GD	VG	FN	VF	VF/NM	NM-
5,6-Moon Girl in each	55	110	165	352	601	850
7-14: 14-Bondage-c	41	82	123	250	418	585

NOTE: ***Craig** & **H. C. Kiefer** art in most issues. **Craig** c-5, 6, 13, 14. **Feldstein/Craig** a-10. **Feldstein** a-7-11. **Harrison/Wood** a-13, 14. **Ingels** a-5-14; c-7-12.*

GUNFIGHTERS, THE
Super Comics (Reprints): 1963 - 1964

10-12,15,16,18: 10,11-r/Billy the Kid #s? 12-r/The Rider #5(Swift Arrow). 15-r/Straight Arrow

Gunhawks #1 © MAR

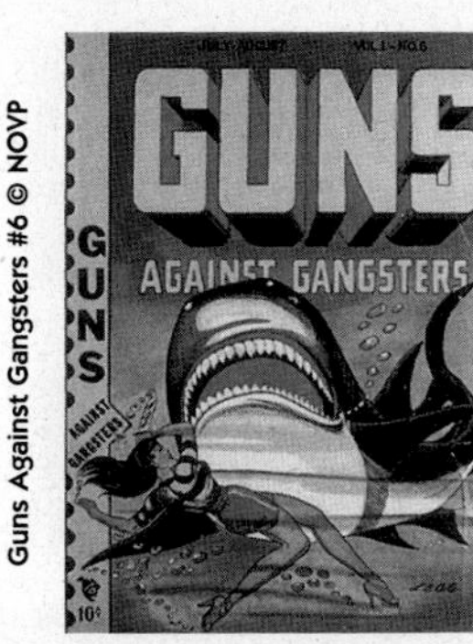

Guns Against Gangsters #6 © NOVP

Gunsmoke #14 © WEST

	GD 2.0	VG 4.0	FN 6.0	VF 8.0	VF/NM 9.0	NM- 9.2
#42; Powell-r. 16-r/Billy the Kid #?(Toby). 18-r/The Rider #3; Severin-c	2	4	6	10	14	18

GUNFIGHTERS, THE (Formerly Kid Montana)
Charlton Comics: No. 51, 10/66 - No. 52, 10/67; No. 53, 6/79 - No. 85, 7/84

	GD	VG	FN	VF	VF/NM	NM-
51,52	2	4	6	11	16	20
53,54,56:53,54-Williamson/Torres-r/Six Gun Heroes #47,49. 56-Williamson/Severin-c; Severin-r/Sheriff of Tombstone #1	1	3	4	6	8	10
55,57-80						6.00
81-84-Lower print run	1	2	3	5	6	8
85-S&K-r/1955 Bullseye	1	3	4	6	8	10

GUNFIRE (See Deathstroke Annual #2 & Showcase 94 #1,2)
DC Comics: May, 1994 - No. 13, June, 1995 ($1.75/$2.25)

	GD	VG	FN	VF	VF/NM	NM-
1-5,0,6-13: 2-Ricochet-c/story. 5-(9/94). 0-(10/94). 6-(11/94)						3.00

GUN GLORY (Movie)
Dell Publishing Co.: No. 846, Oct, 1957 (one-shot)

	GD	VG	FN	VF	VF/NM	NM-
Four Color 846-Toth-a, photo-c.	8	16	24	51	96	140

GUNHAWK, THE (Formerly Whip Wilson)(See Wild Western)
Marvel Comics/Atlas (MCI): No. 12, Nov, 1950 - No. 18, Dec, 1951
(Also see Two-Gun Western #5)

	GD	VG	FN	VF	VF/NM	NM-
12	19	38	57	111	176	240
13-18: 13-Tuska-a. 16-Colan-a. 18-Maneely-c	14	28	42	80	115	150

GUNHAWKS (Gunhawk No. 7)
Marvel Comics Group: Oct, 1972 - No. 7, October, 1973

	GD	VG	FN	VF	VF/NM	NM-
1,6: 1-Reno Jones, Kid Cassidy; Shores-c/a(p). 6-Kid Cassidy dies	3	6	9	16	23	30
2-5,7: 7-Reno Jones solo	2	4	6	11	16	20

GUNMASTER (Becomes Judo Master #89 on)
Charlton Comics: 9/64 - No. 4, 1965; No. 84, 7/65 - No. 88, 3-4/66; No. 89, 10/67

	GD	VG	FN	VF	VF/NM	NM-
V1#1	3	6	9	21	33	45
2,4, V5#84-86: 84-Formerly Six-Gun Heroes	3	6	9	15	22	28
V5#87-89	2	4	6	11	16	20

NOTE: *Vol. 5 was originally cancelled with #88 (3-4/66). #89 on, became Judo Master, then later in 1967, Charlton issued #89 as a Gunmaster one-shot.*

GUN RUNNER
Marvel Comics UK: Oct, 1993 - No. 6, Mar, 1994 ($1.75, limited series)

	GD	VG	FN	VF	VF/NM	NM-
1-($2.75)-Polybagged w/4 trading cards; Spirits of Vengeance app.						4.00
2-6: 2-Ghost Rider & Blaze app.						3.00

GUNS AGAINST GANGSTERS (True-To-Life Romances #8 on)
Curtis Publications/Novelty Press: Sept-Oct, 1948 - No. 6, July-Aug, 1949; V2#1, Sept-Oct, 1949

	GD	VG	FN	VF	VF/NM	NM-
1-Toni & Greg Gayle begins by Schomburg; L.B. Cole-c	40	80	120	246	411	575
2-L.B. Cole-c	29	58	87	170	278	385
3-6, V2#1: 6-Toni Gayle-c by Cole	26	52	78	154	252	350

NOTE: ***L. B. Cole** c-1-6, V2#1, 2; a-1, 2, 3(2), 4-6.*

GUNSLINGER
Dell Publishing Co.: No. 1220, Oct-Dec, 1961 (one-shot)

	GD	VG	FN	VF	VF/NM	NM-
Four Color 1220-Photo-c	7	14	21	49	92	135

GUNSLINGER (Formerly Tex Dawson...)
Marvel Comics Group: No. 2, Apr, 1973 - No. 3, June, 1973

	GD	VG	FN	VF	VF/NM	NM-
2,3	2	4	6	13	18	22

GUNSLINGERS
Marvel Comics: Feb, 2000 ($2.99)

	GD	VG	FN	VF	VF/NM	NM-
1-Reprints stories of Two-Gun Kid, Rawhide Kid and Caleb Hammer						3.00

GUNSMITH CATS: (Title series), **Dark Horse Comics**

	GD	VG	FN	VF	VF/NM	NM-
--BAD TRIP (Manga), 6/98 - No. 6, 11/98 ($2.95, B&W) 1-6						3.00
--BEAN BANDIT (Manga), 1/99 - No. 9 ($2.95, B&W, limited series) 1-9						3.00
--GOLDIE VS. MISTY (Manga), 11/97 - No. 7, 5/98 ($2.95, B&W) 1-7						3.00
--KIDNAPPED (Manga), 11/99 - No. 10, 8/00 ($2.95, B&W) 1-10						3.00
--MISTER V (Manga), 10/00 - No. 11, 8/01 ($3.50/$2.99), B&W) 1-11						3.50
--THE RETURN OF GRAY (Manga), 8/96 - No. 7, 2/97 ($2.95, B&W) 1-7						3.00
--SHADES OF GRAY (Manga), 5/97 - No. 5, 9/97 ($2.95, B&W) 1-5						3.00
--SPECIAL (Manga) Nov, 2001 ($2.99, B&W, one-shot)						3.00

GUNSMOKE (Blazing Stories of the West)
Western Comics (Youthful Magazines): Apr-May, 1949 - No. 16, Jan, 1952

	GD	VG	FN	VF	VF/NM	NM-
1-Gunsmoke & Masked Marvel begin by Ingels; Ingels bondage-c	50	100	150	315	533	750
2-Ingels-c/a(2)	32	64	96	192	314	435
3-Ingels bondage-c/a	28	56	84	165	270	375
4-6: Ingels-c	22	44	66	132	216	300
7-10	15	30	45	85	130	175
11-16: 15,16-Western/horror stories	15	30	45	83	124	165

NOTE: ***Stallman** a-11, 14. **Wildey** a-15, 16.*

GUNSMOKE (TV)
Dell Publishing Co./Gold Key (All have James Arness photo-c): No. 679, Feb, 1956 - No. 27, Feb, 1969 - No. 6, Feb, 1970

	GD	VG	FN	VF	VF/NM	NM-
Four Color 679(#1)	15	30	45	100	220	340
Four Color 720,769,797,844 (#2-5),6(11-1/57-58)	8	16	24	54	102	150
7,8,9,11,12-Williamson-a in all, 4 pgs. each	8	16	24	54	102	150
10-Williamson/Crandall-a, 4 pgs.	8	16	24	54	102	150
13-27	7	14	21	44	82	120
1 (Gold Key)	5	10	15	35	63	90
2-6('69-70)	3	6	9	21	33	45

GUNSMOKE TRAIL
Ajax-Farrell Publ./Four Star Comic Corp.: June, 1957 - No. 4, Dec, 1957

	GD	VG	FN	VF	VF/NM	NM-
1	11	22	33	60	83	105
2-4	7	14	21	35	43	50

GUNSMOKE WESTERN (Formerly Western Tales of Black Rider)
Atlas Comics No. 32-35(CPS/NPI); Marvel No. 36 on: No. 32, Dec, 1955 - No. 77, July, 1963

	GD	VG	FN	VF	VF/NM	NM-
32-Baker & Drucker-a	20	40	60	114	182	250
33,35,36-Williamson-a in each: 5,6 & 4 pgs. plus Drucker-a #33. 33-Kinstler-a?	15	30	45	85	130	175
34-Baker-a, 4 pgs.; Severin-c	15	30	45	85	130	175
37-Davis-a(2); Williamson text illo	13	26	39	72	101	130
38,39: 39-Williamson text illo (unsigned)	10	20	30	58	79	100
40-Williamson/Mayo-a (4 pgs.)	11	22	33	62	86	110
41,42,45,46,48,49,52-54,57,58,60: 49,52-Kid from Texas story. 57-1st Two Gun Kid by Severin. 60-Sam Hawk app. in Kid Colt	9	18	27	50	65	80
43,44-Torres-a	9	18	27	50	65	80
47,51,59,61: 47,51,59-Kirby-a. 61-Crandall-a	10	20	30	56	76	95
50-Kirby, Crandall-a	11	22	33	62	86	110
55,56-Matt Baker-a	11	22	33	62	86	110
62-67,69,71-73,77-Kirby-a. 72-Origin Kid Colt	5	10	15	34	60	85
68,70,74-76: 68-(10¢-c)	5	10	15	30	50	70
68-(10¢ cover price blacked out, 12¢ printed on)	8	16	24	56	108	160

NOTE: ***Colan** a-35-37, 39, 72, 76. **Davis** a-37, 52, 54, 55; c-50, 54. **Ditko** a-66; c-56p. **Drucker** a-32-34. **Heath** c-33. **Jack Keller** a-34, 35, 40, 51, 53, 55, 56, 60, 61, 65, 68, 71, 72, 74, 75, 77; c-72. **Kirby** a-47, 50, 51, 59, 62(3), 63-67, 69, 71, 73, 77; c-56(w/**Ditko**), 57, 58, 60, 61(w/**Ayers**), 62, 63, 65, 66, 68, 69, 71-77. **Maneely** a-53; c-45. **Robinson** a-35. **Severin** a-35, 59-61; c-34, 35, 39, 42, 43. **Tuska** a-34. **Wildey** a-10, 37, 42, 56, 57. Kid Colt in all. Two-Gun Kid in No. 57, 59, 60-63. Wyatt Earp in No. 45, 48, 49, 51-56, 58.*

GUNS OF FACT & FICTION (Also see A-1 Comics)
Magazine Enterprises: No. 13, 1948 (one-shot)

	GD	VG	FN	VF	VF/NM	NM-
A-1 13-Used in **SOTI**, pg. 19; Ingels & J. Craig-a	28	56	84	165	270	375

GUNS OF THE DRAGON
DC Comics: Oct, 1998 - No. 4, Jan, 1999 ($2.50, limited series)

	GD	VG	FN	VF	VF/NM	NM-
1-4-DCU in the 1920's; Enemy Ace & Bat Lash app.						3.00

GUNWITCH, THE : OUTSKIRTS OF DOOM (See The Nocturnals)
Oni Press: June, 2001 - No. 3, Oct, 2001 ($2.95, B&W, limited series)

	GD	VG	FN	VF	VF/NM	NM-
1-3-Brereton-s/painted-c/Naifeh-s						3.00

GUY GARDNER (Guy Gardner: Warrior #17 on)(Also see Green Lantern #59)
DC Comics: Oct, 1992 - No. 44, July, 1996 ($1.25/$1.50/$1.75)

	GD	VG	FN	VF	VF/NM	NM-
1-Staton-c/a(p) begins						4.00
2-24,0,26-30: 6-Guy vs. Hal Jordan. 8-Vs. Lobo-c/story. 15-JLA x-over, begin $1.50-c. 18-Begin 4-part Emerald Fallout story; splash page x-over GL #50. 18-21-Vs. Hal Jordan. 24-(9/94)-Zero Hour. 0-(10/94)						3.00
25 (11/94, $2.50, 52 pgs.)						4.00
29 ($2.95)-Gatefold-c						4.00
29-Variant-c (Edward Hopper's Nighthawks)						3.00
31-44: 31-$1.75-c begins. 40-Gorilla Grodd-c/app. 44-Parallax-app. (1 pg.)						3.00
Annual 1 (1995, $3.50)-Year One story						4.00
Annual 2 (1996, $2.95)-Legends of the Dead Earth story						4.00

GUY GARDNER: COLLATERAL DAMAGE
DC Comics: 2006 - No. 2 ($5.99, square-bound, limited series)

	GD	VG	FN	VF	VF/NM	NM-
1,2-Howard Chaykin-s/a						6.00

Hack / Slash #19 © H/S Inc.

Ha Ha Comics #10 © ACG

Halo: Escalation #1 © MS

GD VG FN VF VF/NM NM- 2.0 4.0 6.0 8.0 9.0 9.2

GUY GARDNER REBORN
DC Comics: 1992 - Book 3, 1992 ($4.95, limited series)

1-3: Staton-c/a(p). 1-Lobo-c/cameo. 2,3-Lobo-c/s 6.00

GYPSY COLT
Dell Publishing Co.: No. 568, June, 1954 (one-shot)

	GD 2.0	VG 4.0	FN 6.0	VF 8.0	VF/NM 9.0	NM- 9.2
Four Color 568-Movie	5	10	15	31	53	75

GYRO GEARLOOSE (See Dynabrite Comics, Walt Disney's C&S #140 & Walt Disney Showcase #18)
Dell Publishing Co.: No. 1047, Nov-Jan/1959-60 - May-July, 1962 (Disney)

	GD 2.0	VG 4.0	FN 6.0	VF 8.0	VF/NM 9.0	NM- 9.2
Four Color 1047 (No. 1)-All Barks-c/a	14	28	42	97	214	330
Four Color 1095,1184-All by Carl Barks	9	18	27	57	111	165
Four Color 1267-Barks c/a, 4 pgs.	7	14	21	46	86	125
01329-207 (#1, 5-7/62)-Barks-c only (intended as 4-Color 1329?)	5	10	15	35	63	90

HACKER FILES, THE
DC Comics: Aug, 1992 - No. 12, July, 1993 ($1.95)

1-12: 1-Sutton-a(p) begins; computer generated-c 3.00

HACK/SLASH
Devil's Due Publishing: Apr. 2004 - No. 32, Mar, 2010 ($3.25/$4.95)

	GD 2.0	VG 4.0	FN 6.0	VF 8.0	VF/NM 9.0	NM- 9.2
1-Seeley-s/Caselli-a/c	3	6	9	14	20	25

...: (The Series) 1-24,26-32 (5/07-No. 32, 3/10, $3.50) Flashack to Cassie's childhood and origin. 12-Milk & Cheese cameo. 15-Re-Animator app. 3.50
25-($5.50) Double sized issue; Baugh-a; two covers 5.50
...: Comic Book Carnage (3/05) Manfredi-a/Seeley-s; Robert Kirkman & Steve Niles app. 5.00
...: First Cut TPB (10/05, $14.95) r/one-shots with sketch pages, designs, interviews 15.00
...: Girls Gone Dead (10/04, $4.95) Manfredi-a/Seeley-s 5.00
...: Land of Lost Toys 1-3 (11/05 - No. 3, 1/06, $3.25) Crossland-a/Seeley-s 3.25
...: New Reader Halloween Treat #1 (10/08, $3.50) origin retold; Cassie's diary pages 3.50
...: The Final Revenge of Evil Ernie (6/05, $4.95) Salman-a/Seeley-s; two covers 5.00
...: Trailers (2/05, $3.25) short stories by Seeley; art by various; three covers 3.25
...: Slice Hard (12/05, $4.95) Seeley-s 5.00
...: Slice Hard Pre-Sliced 25¢ Special (2/06, 25¢) origin story by Seeley; sketch pages 3.00
...: Vs Chucky (3/07, $5.50) Seeley-s/Merhoff-a; 3 covers 5.50
...: Vol. 2 Death By Sequel TPB (1/07, $18.99) r/Land of Lost Toys #1-3, Trailers, Slice Hard 19.00
...: Vol. 3 Friday the 31st TPB (10/07, $18.99) r/The Series #1-4 & ... Vs Chucky 19.00

HACK/SLASH
Image Comics: Jun, 2010 - Present ($3.50)

1-25: 1-(2/11, $3.50) Seeley-s/Leister-a. 5-Esquejo-c. 9-11-Bomb Queen app. 3.50
... Annual 2010: Murder Messiah (10/10, $5.99) Seeley-s/Morales-a 6.00
... Annual 2011: Hatchet/Slash (11/11, $5.99) 6.00
.../ Eva: Monster's Ball 1-4 (Dynamite Ent., 2011 - No. 4, 2011, $3.99) Jerwa-s/Razek-a 4.00
...: Me Without You (1/11, $3.50) Leister-a/Seeley-s; 2 covers 3.50
...: My First Maniac 1-4 (6/10- No. 4, 9/10) Leister-a/Seeley-s 3.50
...: Trailers #2 (11/10, $6.99) short stories; story & art by various; Seeley-c 7.00
Image Firsts: Hack/Slash #1 (10/10, $1.00) r/#1 (2004) with "Image Firsts" cover frame 3.00

HACKTIVIST
Archaia Black Label: Jan, 2014 - No. 4, Apr, 2014 ($3.99)

1-4-Kelly & Lanzing-s/To-a; created by Alyssa Milano 4.00

HAGAR THE HORRIBLE (See Comics Reading Libraries in the Promotional Comics section)

HA HA COMICS (Teepee Tim No. 100 on; also see Giggle Comics)
Scope Mag.(Creston Publ.) No. 1-80/American Comics Group: Oct, 1943 - No. 99, Jan, 1955

	GD 2.0	VG 4.0	FN 6.0	VF 8.0	VF/NM 9.0	NM- 9.2
1-Funny animal	37	74	111	222	361	500
2	19	38	57	111	176	240
3-5: Ken Hultgren-a begins?	14	28	42	82	121	160
6-10	13	26	39	72	101	130
11-20: 14-Infinity-c	11	22	33	62	86	110
21-40	10	20	30	54	72	90
41-43,45-94,97-99: 49,61-X-Mas-c	9	18	27	50	65	80
44-1st Tee-Pee Tim app.; begin series; Little Black Sambo app.	10	20	30	54	72	90
95,96-3-D effect-c/story	17	34	51	98	154	210

HAIR BEAR BUNCH, THE (TV) (See Fun-In No. 13)
Gold Key: Feb, 1972 - No. 9, Feb, 1974 (Hanna-Barbera)

	GD 2.0	VG 4.0	FN 6.0	VF 8.0	VF/NM 9.0	NM- 9.2
1	4	8	12	23	37	50
2-9	3	6	9	16	24	32

HALCYON
Image Comics: Nov, 2010 - No. 5, May, 2011 ($2.99)

1-5-Guggenheim & Butters-s/Bodenheim-a 3.00

HALF PAST DANGER
IDW Publishing: May, 2013 - No. 6, Oct, 2013 ($3.99, limited series)

1-6: Dinosuars and Nazis in 1943; Stephen Mooney-s/a/c 4.00

HALLELUJAH TRAIL, THE (See Movie Classics)

HALL OF FAME FEATURING THE T.H.U.N.D.E.R. AGENTS
JC Productions(Archie Comics Group): May, 1983 - No. 3, Dec, 1983

1-3: Thunder Agents-r(Crandall, Kane, Tuska, Wood-a). 2-New Ditko-c 4.00

HALLOWEEN (Movie)
Chaos! Comics: Nov, 2000; Apr, 2001 ($2.95/$2.99, one-shots)

1-Brewer-a; Michael Myers childhood at the Sanitarium 3.00
...II: The Blackest Eyes (4/01, $2.99) Beck-a 3.00
...III: The Devil's Eyes (11/01, $2.99) Justiniano-a 3.00

HALLOWEEN (Halloween Nightdance on cover)(Movie)
Devils Due Publishing: Mar, 2008 - No. 4, May, 2008 ($3.50, limited series)

1-4-Seeley-a/Hutchinson-s; multiple covers on each 3.50
...: 30 Years of Terror (8/08, $5.50) short stories by various incl. Seeley 5.50

HALLOWEEN EVE
Image Comics: Oct, 2012 ($3.99, one-shot)

One-Shot - Brandon Montclare-s/Amy Reeder-a; two covers by Reeder 4.00

HALLOWEEN HORROR
Eclipse Comics: Oct, 1987 (Seduction of the Innocent #7)($1.75)

1-Pre-code horror-r 5.00

HALLOWEEN MEGAZINE
Marvel Comics: Dec, 1996 ($3.95, one-shot, 96 pgs.)

1-Reprints Tomb of Dracula 4.00

HALO GRAPHIC NOVEL (Based on video game)
Marvel Publishing Inc.: 2006 ($24.99, hardcover with dust jacket)

HC-Anthology set in the Halo universe; art by Bisley, Moebius and others; pin-up gallery by various incl. Darrow, Pratt, Williams and Van Fleet; Phil Hale painted-c 25.00

HALO: BLOOD LINE (Based on video game)
Marvel Comics: Feb, 2010 - No. 5, Jul, 2010 ($3.99, limited series)

1-5-Van Lente-s/Portela-a 4.00

HALO: ESCALATION (Based on video game)
Dark Horse Comics: Dec, 2013 - Present ($3.99, limited series)

1-4-Chris Schlerf-s/Sergio Ariño-a 4.00

HALO: FALL OF REACH - BOOT CAMP (Based on video game)
Marvel Comics: Nov, 2010 - No. 4, Apr, 2011 ($3.99, limited series)

1-4-Reed-s/Ruiz-a 4.00

HALO: FALL OF REACH - COVENANT (Based on video game)
Marvel Comics: Jun, 2011 - No. 4, Dec, 2011 ($3.99, limited series)

1-4-Reed-s/Ruiz-a 4.00

HALO: FALL OF REACH - INVASION (Based on video game)
Marvel Comics: Mar, 2012 - No. 4, Aug, 2012 ($3.99, limited series)

1-4-Reed-s/Ruiz-a 4.00

HALO: HELLJUMPER (Based on video game)
Marvel Comics: Sept, 2009 - No. 5, Jan, 2010 ($3.99, limited series)

1-5-Peter David-s/Eric Nguyen-a 4.00

HALO: INITIATION (Based on video game)
Dark Horse Comics: Aug, 2013 - No. 3, Oct, 2013 ($3.99, limited series)

1-3-Brian Reed-s/Marco Castiello-a 4.00

HALO: UPRISING (Based on video game) (Also see Marvel Spotlight: Halo)
Marvel Comics: Oct, 2007 - No. 4, Jun, 2009 ($3.99, limited series)

1-4-Bendis-s/Maleev-a; takes place between the *Halo 2* and *Halo 3* video games 4.00

HALO JONES (See The Ballad of...)

HAMMER, THE
Dark Horse Comics: Oct, 1997 - No. 4, Jan, 1998 ($2.95, limited series)

1-4-Kelley Jones-s/c/a, ...: Uncle Alex (8/98, $2.95) 3.00

HAMMER, THE: THE OUTSIDER
Dark Horse Comics: Feb, 1999 - No. 3, Apr, 1999 ($2.95, limited series)

1-3-Kelley Jones-s/c/a 3.00

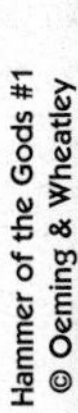
Hammer of the Gods #1 © Oeming & Wheatley

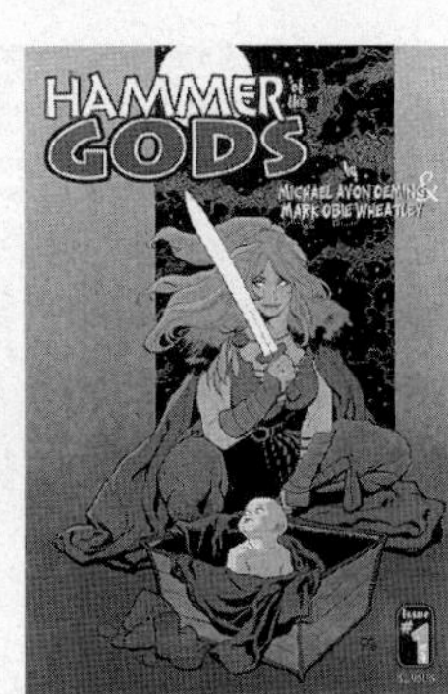

Hangman Comics #6 © MLJ

Hap Hazard Comics #3 © ACE

	GD 2.0	VG 4.0	FN 6.0	VF 8.0	VF/NM 9.0	NM- 9.2

HAMMERLOCKE
DC Comics: Sept, 1992 - No. 9, May, 1993 ($1.75, limited series)

1-($2.50, 52 pgs.)-Chris Sprouse-c/a in all 4.00
2-9 3.00

HAMMER OF GOD (Also see Nexus)
First Comics: Feb, 1990 - No. 4, May, 1990 ($1.95, limited series)

1-4 3.00

HAMMER OF GOD: BUTCH
Dark Horse Comics: May, 1994 - No. 4, Aug, 1994 ($2.50, limited series)

1-3 3.00

HAMMER OF GOD: PENTATHLON
Dark Horse Comics: Jan, 1994 ($2.50, one shot)

1-Character from Nexus 3.00

HAMMER OF GOD: SWORD OF JUSTICE
First Comics: Feb 1991 - Mar 1991 ($4.95, lim. series, squarebound, 52 pgs.)

V2#1,2 5.00

HAMMER OF THE GODS
Insight Studio Groups: 2001 - No. 5, 2001 ($2.95, limited series)

1-Michael Oeming & Mark Wheatley-s/a; Frank Cho-c 6.00
1-(IDW, 7/11, $1.00) reprints #1 with "Hundred Penny Press" logo on Oeming cover 3.00
2-5: 3-Hughes-c. 5-Dave Johnson-c 3.00
The Color Saga (2002, $4.95) r/"Enemy of the Gods" internet strip 5.00
Mortal Enemy TPB (2002, $18.95) r/#1-5; intro. by Peter David; afterword by Raven 19.00

HAMMER OF THE GODS: HAMMER HITS CHINA
Image Comics: Feb, 2003 - No. 3, Sept, 2003 ($2.95, limited series)

1-3-Oeming & Wheatley-s/a; Oeming-c. 2-Frankenstein Mobster by Wheatley 3.00

HANDBOOK OF THE CONAN UNIVERSE, THE
Marvel Comics: June, 1985; Jan, 1986 ($1.25, one-shot)

1-(6/85) Kaluta-c (2 printings) 6.00
1-(1/86) Kaluta-c 6.00
nn-(no date, circa '87-88, B&W, 36 pgs.) reprints '86 with changes; new painted cover
1 2 3 5 6 8

HAND OF FATE (Formerly Men Against Crime)
Ace Magazines: No. 8, Dec, 1951 - No. 25, Dec, 1954 (Weird/horror stories) (Two #25's)

8-Surrealistic text story 47 94 141 296 498 700
9,10,21-Necronomicon sty; drug belladonna used 30 60 90 177 289 400
11-18,20,22,23 24 48 72 144 237 330
19-Bondage, hypo needle scenes 26 52 78 154 252 350
24-Electric chair-c 36 72 108 216 351 485
25a(11/54), 25b(12/54)-Both have Cameron-a 20 40 60 117 189 260

NOTE: ***Cameron*** *a-9, 10, 19-25a, 25b; c-13.* ***Sekowsky*** *a-8, 9, 13, 14.*

HAND OF FATE
Eclipse Comics: Feb, 1988 - No. 3, Apr, 1988 ($1.75/$2.00, Baxter paper)

1-3; 3-B&W 4.00

HANDS OF THE DRAGON
Seaboard Periodicals (Atlas): June, 1975

1-Origin/1st app.; Craig-a(p)/Mooney inks 2 4 6 11 16 20

HANGMAN COMICS (Special Comics No. 1; Black Hood No. 9 on)
(Also see Flyman, Mighty Comics, Mighty Crusaders & Pep Comics)
MLJ Magazines: No. 2, Spring, 1942 - No. 8, Fall, 1943

2-The Hangman, Boy Buddies begin 271 542 813 1734 2967 4200
3-Beheading splash pg.; 1st Nazi war-c 258 516 774 1651 2826 4000
4-Classic Nazi WWII hunchback torture-c 245 490 735 1568 2684 3800
5-1st Japan war-c 161 322 483 1030 1765 2500
6-8: 8-2nd app. Super Duck (ties w/Jolly Jingles #11)
155 310 465 992 1696 2400

NOTE: ***Fuje*** *a-7(3), 8(3); c-3.* ***Reinman*** *c/a-3. Bondage c-3.* ***Sahle*** *c-6.*

HANK
Pentagon Publishing Co.: 1946

nn-Coulton Waugh's newspaper reprint 9 18 27 47 61 75

HANNA-BARBERA (See Golden Comics Digest No. 2, 7, 11)

HANNA-BARBERA ALL-STARS
Archie Publications: Oct, 1995 - No. 4, Apr, 1996 ($1.50, bi-monthly)

1-4 4.00

HANNA-BARBERA BANDWAGON (TV)
Gold Key: Oct, 1962 - No. 3, Apr, 1963

1-Giant, 84 pgs. 1-Augie Doggie app.; 1st app. Lippy the Lion, Touché Turtle & Dum Dum, Wally Gator, Loopy de Loop, 10 20 30 69 147 225
2-Giant, 84 pgs.; Mr. & Mrs. J. Evil Scientist (1st app.) in Snagglepuss story; Yakky Doodle, Ruff and Reddy and others app. 8 16 24 51 96 140
3-Regular size; Mr. & Mrs. J. Evil Scientist app. (pre-#1), Snagglepuss, Wally Gator and others app. 6 12 18 40 73 105

HANNA-BARBERA GIANT SIZE
Harvey Comics: Oct, 1992 - No. 3 ($2.25, 68 pgs.)

V2#1-3:Flintstones, Yogi Bear, Magilla Gorilla, Huckleberry Hound, Quick Draw McGraw, Yakky Doodle & Chopper, Jetsons & others 6.00

HANNA-BARBERA HI-ADVENTURE HEROES (See Hi-Adventure...)

HANNA-BARBERA PARADE (TV)
Charlton Comics: Sept, 1971 - No. 10, Dec, 1972

1 6 12 18 41 76 110
2,4-10 4 8 12 25 40 55
3-(52 pgs.)- "Summer Picnic" 5 10 15 33 57 80

NOTE: *No. 4 (1/72) went on sale late in 1972 with the January 1973 issues.*

HANNA-BARBERA PRESENTS
Archie Publications: Nov, 1995 - No. 8 ($1.50, bi-monthly)

1-8: 1-Atom Ant & Secret Squirrel. 2-Wacky Races. 3-Yogi Bear. 4-Quick Draw McGraw & Magilla Gorilla. 5-A Pup Named Scooby-Doo. 6-Superstar Olympics. 7-Wacky Races. 8-Frankenstein Jr. & the Impossibles 4.00

HANNA-BARBERA SPOTLIGHT (See Spotlight)

HANNA-BARBERA SUPER TV HEROES (TV)
Gold Key: Apr, 1968 - No. 7, Oct, 1969 (Hanna-Barbera)

1-The Birdman, The Herculoids (ends #6; not in #3), Moby Dick, Young Samson & Goliath (ends #2,4), and The Mighty Mightor begin; Spiegle-a in all
11 22 33 76 163 250
2-The Galaxy Trio app.; Shazzan begins; 12¢ & 15¢ versions exist
8 16 24 56 108 160
3,6,7-The Space Ghost app. 8 16 24 51 96 140
4,5 7 14 21 44 82 120

NOTE: *Birdman in #1,2,4,5. Herculoids in #2,4-7. Mighty Mightor in #1,2,4-7. Moby Dick in all. Shazzan in #2-5. Young Samson & Goliath in #1,3.*

HANNA-BARBERA TV FUN FAVORITES (See Golden Comics Digest #2,7,11)

HANNA-BARBERA (TV STARS) (See TV Stars)

HANS BRINKER (Disney)
Dell Publishing Co.: No. 1273, Feb, 1962 (one-shot)

Four Color 1273-Movie, photo-c 6 12 18 37 66 95

HANS CHRISTIAN ANDERSEN
Ziff-Davis Publ. Co.: 1953 (100 pgs., Special Issue)

nn-Danny Kaye (movie)-Photo-c; fairy tales 17 34 51 98 154 210

HANSEL & GRETEL
Dell Publishing Co.: No. 590, Oct, 1954 (one-shot)

Four Color 590-Partial photo-c 6 12 18 37 66 95

HANSI, THE GIRL WHO LOVED THE SWASTIKA
Spire Christian Comics (Fleming H. Revell Co.): 1973, 1976 (39¢/49¢)

1973 edition with 39¢-c 8 16 24 56 108 160
1976 edition with 49¢-c 7 14 21 44 82 120

HAP HAZARD COMICS (Real Love No. 25 on)
Ace Magazines (Readers' Research): Summer, 1944 - No. 24, Feb, 1949
(#1-6 are quarterly issues)

1 15 30 45 86 133 180
2 10 20 30 54 72 90
3-10 9 18 27 47 61 75
11-13,15-24 8 16 24 42 54 65
14-Feldstein-c (4/47) 10 20 30 56 76 95

HAP HOPPER (See Comics Revue No. 2)

HAPPIEST MILLIONAIRE, THE (See Movie Comics)

HAPPI TIM (See March of Comics No. 182)

HAPPY
Image Comics: Sept, 2012 - No. 4, Feb, 2013 ($2.99, limited series)

1-4-Grant Morrison-s/Darick Robertson-a. 1-Covers by Robertson & Allred 5.00

HAPPY BIRTHDAY MARTHA WASHINGTON (Also see Give Me Liberty,

Happy Comics #8 © STD

Harbinger Wars #1 © VAL

Hardware #21 © Milestone

GD VG FN VF VF/NM NM-
2.0 4.0 6.0 8.0 9.0 9.2

Martha Washington Goes To War, & Martha Washington Stranded In Space)
Dark Horse Comics: Mar, 1995 ($2.95, one-shot)

1-Miller script; Gibbons-c/a 3.00

HAPPY COMICS (Happy Rabbit No. 41 on)
Nedor Publ./Standard Comics (Animated Cartoons): Aug, 1943 - No. 40, Dec, 1950
(Companion to Goofy Comics)

1-Funny animal 28 56 84 168 274 380
2 15 30 45 90 140 190
3-10 13 26 39 72 101 130
11-19 10 20 30 58 79 100
20-31,34-37-Frazetta text illos in all (2 in #34&35, 3 in #27,28,30). 27-Al Fago-a
12 24 36 67 94 120
32-Frazetta-a, 7 pgs. plus 2 text illos; Roussos-a 21 42 63 122 199 275
33-Frazetta-a(2), 6 pgs. each (Scarce) 29 58 87 170 278 385
38-40 9 18 27 52 69 85

HAPPYDALE: DEVILS IN THE DESERT
DC Comics (Vertigo): 1999 - No. 2, 1999 ($6.95, limited series)

1,2-Andrew Dabb-s/Seth Fisher-a 7.00

HAPPY DAYS (TV)(See Kite Fun Book)
Gold Key: Mar, 1979 - No. 6, Feb, 1980

1-Photo-c of TV cast; 35¢-c 3 6 9 16 23 30
2-6-(40¢-c) 2 4 6 9 12 15

HAPPY HOLIDAY (See March of Comics No. 181)

HAPPY HOULIHANS (Saddle Justice No. 3 on; see Blackstone, The Magician Detective)
E. C. Comics: Fall, 1947 - No. 2, Winter, 1947-48

1-Origin Moon Girl (same date as Moon Girl #1) 58 116 174 371 636 900
2 34 68 102 199 325 450

HAPPY JACK
Red Top (Decker): Aug, 1957 - No. 2, Nov, 1957

V1#1,2 5 10 15 22 26 30

HAPPY JACK HOWARD
Red Top (Farrell)/Decker: 1957

nn-Reprints Handy Andy story from E. C. Dandy Comics #5, renamed "Happy Jack"
5 10 15 22 26 30

HAPPY RABBIT (Formerly Happy Comics)
Standard Comics (Animated Cartoons): No. 41, Feb, 1951 - No. 48, Apr, 1952

41-Funny animal 9 18 27 50 65 80
42-48 8 16 24 40 50 60

HARBINGER (Also see Unity)
Valiant: Jan, 1992 - No. 41, June, 1995 ($1.95/$2.50)

0-Prequel to the series; available by redeeming coupons in #1-6; cover image has pink sky;
title logo is blue 4 8 12 25 40 55
0-(2nd printing) cover has blue sky & red logo 1 2 3 5 6 8
1-1st app. 4 8 12 28 47 65
2-4: 4-Low print run 2 4 6 11 16 20
5,6: 5-Solar app. 6-Torque dies 2 4 6 9 12 15
7-10: 8,9-Unity x-overs. 8-Miller-c. 9-Simonson-c. 10-1st app. H.A.R.D Corps (10/92)
1 2 3 5 6 8
11-24,26-41: 14-1st app. Stronghold. 18-Intro Screen. 19-1st app. Stunner. 22-Archer & Armstrong app. 24-Cover similar to #1. 26-Intro New Harbingers. 29-Bound-in trading card. 30-H.A.R.D. Corps app. 32-Eternal Warrior app. 33-Dr. Eclipse app. 4.00
25-($3.50, 52 pgs.)-Harada vs. Sting 5.00
...Files 1,2 (8/94,2/95 $2.50) 4.00
...: The Beginning HC (2007, $24.95) recolored reprints #0-7 and Story of Harada from coupons from #1-6; new "Origin of Harada" story by Shooter and Bob Hall 30.00
Trade paperback nn (11/92, $9.95)-Reprints #1-4 & comes polybagged with a copy of Harbinger #0 w/new-c. Price for TPB only 15.00
NOTE: *Issues 1-6 have coupons with origin of Harada and are redeemable for Harbinger #0.*

HARBINGER
Valiant Entertainment: Jun, 2012 - Present ($3.99)(#0 released between #8 & #9)

1-Dysart-s/Khari Evans-a; covers by Lozzi and Suayan (Pullbox variant) 4.00
1-Variant cover by Braithwaite 10.00
1-QR voice variant cover by Jelena Djurdjevic 30.00
2-21-Two covers on each (standard & pullbox). 2-Origin continues. 11-14-Harbinger Wars tie-in 4.00
#0 (2/13, $3.99) Origin of Harada; Suayan & Pere Pérez-a; covers by Crain & Suayan 4.00
#0-Variant gatefold-c by Lewis Larosa 15.00
... Bleeding Monk #0 (3/14, $3.99) Dysart-s; art by Evans, Suayan, Segovia & LaRosa 4.00

HARBINGER WARS
Valiant Entertainment: Apr, 2013 - No. 4, Jul, 2013 ($3.99, limited series)

1-4: 1-Dysart-s/Henry, Crain & Suayan-a; covers by Larosa & Henry (Pullbox) 4.00
1-Variant cover by Crain 8.00
1-Variant cover by Zircher 25.00

HARD BOILED
Dark Horse Comics: Sept, 1990 - No. 3, Mar, 1992 ($4.95/$5.95, 8 1/2x11", lim. series)

1-3-Miller-s; Darrow-c/a; sexually explicit & violent 2 4 6 8 10 12
TPB (5/93, $15.95) 20.00
Big Damn Hard Boiled (12/97, $29.95, B&W) r/#1-3 30.00

HARDCASE (See Break Thru, Flood Relief & Ultraforce, 1st Series)
Malibu Comics (Ultraverse): June, 1993 - No. 26, Aug, 1995 ($1.95/$2.50)

1-Intro Hardcase; Dave Gibbons-c; has coupon for Ultraverse Premiere #0; Jim Callahan-a(p) begin, ends #3 4.00
1-With coupon missing 2.00
1-Platinum Edition 6.00
1-Holographic Cover Edition; 1st full-c holograph tied w/Prime 1 & Strangers 1 8.00
1-Ultra Limited silver foil-c 6.00
2,3-Callahan-a, 2-($2.50)-Newsstand edition bagged w/trading card 3.00
4,6-15, 17-19: 4-Strangers app. 7-Break-Thru x-over. 8-Solution app. 9-Vs. Turf. 12-Silver foil logo, wraparound-c. 17-Prime app. 3.00
5-($2.50, 48 pgs.)-Rune flip-c/story by B. Smith (3 pgs.) 4.00
16 ($3.50, 68 pgs.)-Rune pin-up 4.00
20-26: 23-Loki app. 3.00
NOTE: *Perez a-8(2); c-20i.*

HARDCORE
Image Comics: May, 2012 ($2.99)

1-Kirkman-s/Stelfreeze-a/Silvestri-c 3.00

HARDCORE STATION
DC Comics: July, 1998 - No. 6, Dec, 1998 ($2.50, limited series)

1-6-Starlin-s/a(p). 3-Green Lantern-c/app. 5,6-JLA-c/app. 3.00

H.A.R.D. CORPS, THE (See Harbinger #10)
Valiant: Dec, 1992 - No. 30, Feb, 1995 ($2.25) (Harbinger spin-off)

1-($2.50)-Gatefold-c by Jim Lee & Bob Layton 5.00
1-Gold variant 10.00
2-30: 5-Bloodshot-c/story cont'd from Bloodshot #3. 5-Variant edition; came w/Comic Defense System. 10-Turok app. 17-vs. Armorines. 18-Bound-in trading card. 20-Harbinger app. 3.00

HARD TIME
DC Comics (Focus): Apr, 2004 - No. 12, Mar, 2005 ($2.50)

1-12-Gerber-s/Hurtt-a; 1-Includes previews of other DC Focus series 3.00
...: 50 to Life (2004, $9.95, TPB) r/#1-6; cover gallery with sketches 10.00

HARD TIME: SEASON TWO
DC Comics: Feb, 2006 - No. 7, Aug, 2006 ($2.50/$2.99)

1-5-Gerber-s/Hurtt-a 3.00
6,7-($2.99) 7-Ethan paroled in 2053 3.00

HARDWARE
DC Comics (Milestone): Apr, 1993 - No. 50, Apr, 1997 ($1.50/$1.75/$2.50)

1-($2.95)-Collector's Edition polybagged w/poster & trading card (direct sale only) 4.00
1-Platinum Edition 6.00
1-15,17-19: 11-Shadow War x-over. 11,14-Simonson-c. 12-Buckler-a(p). 17-Worlds Collide Pt. 2. 18-Simonson-c; Worlds Collide Pt. 9. 15-1st Humberto Ramos DC work 3.00
16,25: 16-($2.50, 52 pgs.)-Newsstand Ed. 25-($2.95, 52 pgs.) 4.00
16,50-($3.95, 52 pgs.)-16-Collector's Edition w/gatefold 2nd cover by Byrne; new armor; Icon app. 5.00
20-24,26-49: 49-Moebius-c 3.00
...: The Man in the Machine TPB (2010, $19.99) r/#1-8 20.00

HARDY BOYS, THE (Disney
Dell Publ. Co.: No. 760, Dec, 1956 - No. 964, Jan, 1959 (Mickey Mouse Club)

Four Color 760 (#1)-Photo-c 9 18 27 59 117 175
Four Color 830(8/57), 887(1/58), 964-Photo-c 8 16 24 51 96 140

HARDY BOYS, THE (TV)
Gold Key: Apr, 1970 - No. 4, Jan, 1971

1 4 8 12 27 44 60
2-4 3 6 9 17 26 35

HARLAN ELLISON'S DREAM CORRIDOR
Dark Horse Comics: Mar, 1995 - No. 5, July, 1995 ($2.95, anthology)

Harley Quinn (2014 series) #1 © DC

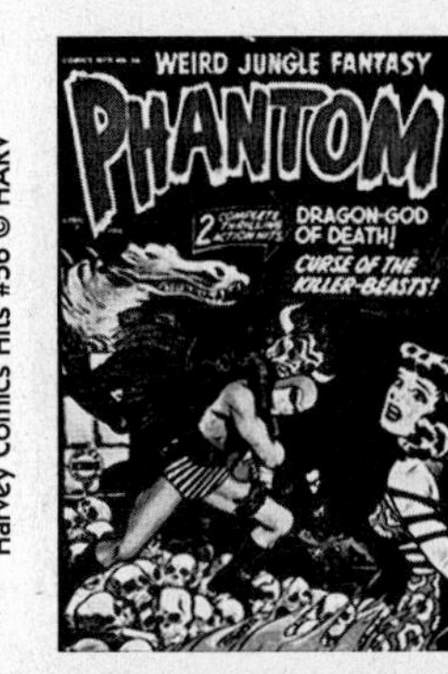

Harvey Comics Hits #56 © HARV

Harvey Hits #10 © HARV

	GD 2.0	VG 4.0	FN 6.0	VF 8.0	VF/NM 9.0	NM- 9.2
1-5: Adaptation of Ellison stories. 1-4-Byrne-a.						4.00
Special (1/95, $4.95)						6.00
Trade paperback-(1996, $18.95, 192 pgs)-r/#1-5 & Special #1						19.00

HARLAN ELLISON'S DREAM CORRIDOR QUARTERLY
Dark Horse Comics: V2#1, Aug, 1996 ($5.95, anthology, squarebound)

	GD 2.0	VG 4.0	FN 6.0	VF 8.0	VF/NM 9.0	NM- 9.2
V2#1-Adaptations of Ellison's stories w/new material; Neal Adams-a						6.00
Volume 2 TPB (3/07, $19.95) r/V2#1 and unpublished material incl. last Swan-a						20.00

HARLEM GLOBETROTTERS (TV) (See Fun-In No. 8, 10)
Gold Key: Apr, 1972 - No. 12, Jan, 1975 (Hanna-Barbera)

	GD 2.0	VG 4.0	FN 6.0	VF 8.0	VF/NM 9.0	NM- 9.2
1	4	8	12	25	40	55
2-5	3	6	9	15	22	28
6-12	2	4	6	13	18	22

NOTE: *#4, 8, and 12 contain 16 extra pages of advertising.*

HARLEQUIN ROMANCE
Dark Horse Comics: Nov, 2001 ($10.95, hardcover, one-shot)

	GD 2.0	VG 4.0	FN 6.0	VF 8.0	VF/NM 9.0	NM- 9.2
nn-Neil Gaiman-s; painted-a/c by John Bolton						11.00

HARLEY QUINN (Also see Gotham City Sirens)
DC Comics: Dec, 2000 - No. 38, Jan, 2004 ($2.95/$2.25/$2.50)

	GD 2.0	VG 4.0	FN 6.0	VF 8.0	VF/NM 9.0	NM- 9.2
1-Joker and Poison Ivy app.; Terry & Rachel Dodson-a/c	3	6	9	19	30	40
2,3-($2.25): 2-Two-Face-c/app. 3-Slumber party	1	3	4	6	8	10
4-9,11-($2.25). 6,7-Riddler app.						6.00
10-Batgirl-c/s	2	4	6	9	12	15
12-($2.95) Batman app.	2	4	6	8	10	12
13-24,26-37: 13-Joker: Last Laugh. 17,18-Bizarro-c/app. 23-Begin $2.50-c. 23,24-Martian Manhunter app.						5.00
25-Classic Joker-c/s	3	6	9	14	20	25
32-Joker-c/app.	2	4	6	11	16	20
Harley & Ivy: Love on the Lam (2001, $5.95) Winick-s/Chiodo-c/a	1	3	4	6	8	10
...: Our Worlds at War (10/01, $2.95) Jae Lee-c; art by various	2	4	6	8	10	12

HARLEY QUINN (DC New 52)
DC Comics: No. 0, Jan, 2014 - Present ($2.99)

	GD 2.0	VG 4.0	FN 6.0	VF 8.0	VF/NM 9.0	NM- 9.2
0-Conner & Palmiotti-s; art by Conner & various; Conner-c						4.00
0-Variant-c by Stephane Roux						12.00
1-(2/14) Chad Hardin-a; Conner-c						5.00
2-4: 2-Poison Ivy app. 4-Roux-a						3.00
1-Variant-c by Adam Hughes						20.00

HAROLD TEEN (See Popular Comics, & Super Comics)
Dell Publishing Co.: No. 2, 1942 - No. 209, Jan, 1949

	GD 2.0	VG 4.0	FN 6.0	VF 8.0	VF/NM 9.0	NM- 9.2
Four Color 2	27	54	81	194	435	675
Four Color 209	5	10	15	34	60	90

HARROWERS, THE (See Clive Barker's...)

HARSH REALM (Inspired 1999 TV series)
Harris Comics: 1993- No. 6, 1994 ($2.95, limited series)

	GD 2.0	VG 4.0	FN 6.0	VF 8.0	VF/NM 9.0	NM- 9.2
1-6: Painted-c. Hudnall-s/Paquette & Ridgway-a						4.00
TPB (2000, $14.95) r/series						15.00

HARVEY
Marvel Comics: Oct, 1970; No. 2, 12/70; No. 3, 6/72 - No. 6, 12/72

	GD 2.0	VG 4.0	FN 6.0	VF 8.0	VF/NM 9.0	NM- 9.2
1	10	20	30	64	132	200
2-6	7	14	21	44	82	120

HARVEY COLLECTORS COMICS (Titled Richie Rich Collectors Comics on cover of #6-on)
Harvey Publ.: Sept, 1975 - No. 15, Jan, 1978; No. 16, Oct, 1979 (52 pgs.)

	GD 2.0	VG 4.0	FN 6.0	VF 8.0	VF/NM 9.0	NM- 9.2
1-Reprints Richie Rich #1,2	2	4	6	13	18	22
2-10: 7-Splash pg. shows cover to Friendly Ghost Casper #1	2	4	6	8	11	14
11-16: 16-Sad Sack-r	1	2	3	5	7	9

NOTE: *All reprints: Casper-#2, 7, Richie Rich-#1, 3, 5, 6, 8-15, Sad Sack-#16. Wendy-#4.*

HARVEY COMICS HITS (Formerly Joe Palooka #50)
Harvey Publications: No. 51, Oct, 1951 - No. 62, Apr, 1953

	GD 2.0	VG 4.0	FN 6.0	VF 8.0	VF/NM 9.0	NM- 9.2
51-The Phantom	31	62	93	186	303	420
52-Steve Canyon's Air Power(Air Force sponsored)	13	26	39	72	101	130
53-Mandrake the Magician	20	40	60	114	182	250
54-Tim Tyler's Tales of Jungle Terror	13	26	39	74	105	135
55-Love Stories of Mary Worth	11	22	33	62	86	110
56-The Phantom; bondage-c	26	52	78	154	252	350
57-Rip Kirby Exposes the Kidnap Racket; entire book by Alex Raymond	15	30	45	85	130	175
58-Girls in White (nurses stories)	11	22	33	62	86	110
59-Tales of the Invisible featuring Scarlet O'Neil	12	24	36	67	94	120
60-Paramount Animated Comics #1 (9/52) (3rd app. Baby Huey); 2nd Harvey app. Baby Huey & Casper the Friendly Ghost (1st in Little Audrey #25 (8/52)); 1st app. Herman & Catnip (c/story) & Buzzy the Crow	48	96	144	302	514	725
61-Casper the Friendly Ghost #6 (3rd Harvey Casper, 10/52)-Casper-c	47	94	141	296	498	700
62-Paramount Animated Comics #2; Herman & Catnip, Baby Huey & Buzzy the Crow	17	34	51	98	154	210

HARVEY COMICS LIBRARY
Harvey Publications: Apr, 1952 - No. 2, 1952

	GD 2.0	VG 4.0	FN 6.0	VF 8.0	VF/NM 9.0	NM- 9.2
1-Teen-Age Dope Slaves as exposed by Rex Morgan, M.D.; drug propaganda story; used in **SOTI**, pg. 27	206	412	618	1318	2259	3200
2-Dick Tracy Presents Sparkle Plenty in "Blackmail Terror"	20	40	60	114	182	250

HARVEY COMICS SPOTLIGHT
Harvey Comics: Sept, 1987 - No. 4, Mar, 1988 (75¢/$1.00)

	GD 2.0	VG 4.0	FN 6.0	VF 8.0	VF/NM 9.0	NM- 9.2
1-New material; begin 75¢, ends #3; Sand Sack						5.00
2-4: 2,4-All new material. 2-Baby Huey. 3-Little Dot; contains reprints w/5 pg. new story. 4-$1.00-c; Little Audrey						4.00

NOTE: No. 5 was advertised but not published.

HARVEY HITS (Also see Tastee-Freez Comics in the Promotional Comics section)
Harvey Publications: Sept, 1957 - No. 122, Nov, 1967

	GD 2.0	VG 4.0	FN 6.0	VF 8.0	VF/NM 9.0	NM- 9.2
1-The Phantom	24	48	72	168	372	575
2-Rags Rabbit (10/57)	5	10	15	31	53	75
3-Richie Rich (11/57)-r/Little Dot; 1st book devoted to Richie Rich; see Little Dot for 1st app.	132	264	396	1056	2378	3700
4-Little Dot's Uncles (12/57)	14	28	42	96	211	325
5-Stevie Mazie's Boy Friend (1/58)	4	8	12	27	44	60
6-The Phantom (2/58); 2pg. Powell-a	15	30	45	103	227	350
7-Wendy the Good Little Witch (3/58, pre-dates Wendy #1; 1st book devoted to Wendy)	30	60	90	216	483	750
8-Sad Sack's Army Life; George Baker-c	7	14	21	44	82	120
9-Richie Rich's Golden Deeds; (2nd book devoted to Richie Rich) reprints Richie Rich story from Tastee-Freez #1	56	112	168	448	999	1550
10-Little Lotta's Lunch Box	10	20	30	66	138	210
11-Little Audrey Summer Fun (7/58)	8	16	24	51	96	140
12-The Phantom; 2pg. Powell-a (8/58)	12	24	36	83	182	280
13-Little Dot's Uncles (9/58); Richie Rich 1pg.	10	20	30	64	132	200
14-Herman & Katnip (10/58, TV/movies)	4	8	12	28	44	60
15-The Phantom (12/58)-1 pg. origin	12	24	36	83	182	280
16-Wendy the Good Little Witch (1/59); Casper app.	10	20	30	68	144	220
17-Sad Sack's Army Life (2/59)	5	10	15	34	66	85
18-Buzzy & the Crow	4	8	12	25	40	55
19-Little Audrey (4/59)	5	10	15	33	57	80
20-Casper & Spooky	7	14	21	44	82	120
21-Wendy the Witch	7	14	21	44	82	120
22-Sad Sack's Army Life	4	8	12	28	47	65
23-Wendy the Witch (8/59)	7	14	21	44	82	120
24-Little Dot's Uncles (9/59); Richie Rich 1pg.	8	16	24	51	96	140
25-Herman & Katnip (10/59)	3	6	9	21	33	45
26-The Phantom (11/59)	9	18	27	62	126	190
27-Wendy the Good Little Witch (12/59)	6	12	18	42	79	115
28-Sad Sack's Army Life (1/60)	4	8	12	25	40	55
29-Harvey-Toon (No.1)('60); Casper, Buzzy	5	10	15	31	53	75
30-Wendy the Witch (3/60)	6	12	18	42	79	115
31-Herman & Katnip (4/60)	3	6	9	19	30	40
32-Sad Sack's Army Life (5/60)	3	6	9	21	33	45
33-Wendy the Witch (6/60)	6	12	18	40	73	105
34-Harvey-Toon (7/60)	4	8	12	23	37	50
35-Funday Funnies (8/60)	3	6	9	19	30	40
36-The Phantom (1960)	9	18	27	59	117	175
37-Casper & Nightmare	5	10	15	33	57	80
38-Harvey-Toon	4	8	12	23	37	50
39-Sad Sack's Army Life (12/60)	3	6	9	20	31	42
40-Funday Funnies (1/61)	3	6	9	16	24	32
41-Herman & Katnip	3	6	9	16	24	32
42-Harvey-Toon (3/61)	3	6	9	18	28	38
43-Sad Sack's Army Life (4/61)	3	6	9	18	28	38
44-The Phantom (5/61)	8	16	24	57	111	165
45-Casper & Nightmare	4	8	12	28	47	65
46-Harvey-Toon (7/61)	3	6	9	16	24	32

Hate #20 © Peter Bagge

Haunted #38 © CC

Haunted Tank #4 © DC

	GD 2.0	VG 4.0	FN 6.0	VF 8.0	VF/NM 9.0	NM- 9.2
47-Sad Sack's Army Life (8/61)	3	6	9	16	24	32
48-The Phantom (9/61)	9	18	27	57	111	165
49-Stumbo the Giant (1st app. in Hot Stuff)	8	16	24	56	108	160
50-Harvey-Toon (11/61)	3	6	9	16	23	30
51-Sad Sack's Army Life (12/61)	3	6	9	16	23	30
52-Casper & Nightmare	4	8	12	27	44	60
53-Harvey-Toons (2/62)	3	6	9	16	23	30
54-Stumbo the Giant	5	10	15	31	53	75
55-Sad Sack's Army Life (4/62)	3	6	9	16	23	30
56-Casper & Nightmare	4	8	12	25	40	55
57-Stumbo the Giant	5	10	15	31	53	75
58-Sad Sack's Army Life	3	6	9	16	23	30
59-Casper & Nightmare (7/62)	4	8	12	25	40	55
60-Stumbo the Giant (9/62)	5	10	15	31	53	75
61-Sad Sack's Army Life	3	6	9	15	22	28
62-Casper & Nightmare	4	8	12	22	35	48
63-Stumbo the Giant	4	8	12	27	44	60
64-Sad Sack's Army Life (1/63)	3	6	9	15	22	28
65-Casper & Nightmare	4	8	12	22	35	48
66-Stumbo The Giant (3/63)	4	8	12	27	44	60
67-Sad Sack's Army Life (4/63)	3	6	9	15	22	28
68-Casper & Nightmare	4	8	12	22	35	48
69-Stumbo the Giant (6/63)	4	8	12	27	44	60
70-Sad Sack's Army Life (7/63)	3	6	9	15	22	28
71-Casper & Nightmare (8/63)	3	6	9	20	31	42
72-Stumbo the Giant	4	8	12	27	44	60
73-Little Sad Sack (10/63)	3	6	9	15	22	28
74-Sad Sack's Muttsy... (11/63)	3	6	9	15	22	28
75-Casper & Nightmare	3	6	9	18	28	38
76-Little Sad Sack	3	6	9	15	22	28
77-Sad Sack's Muttsy...	3	6	9	15	22	28
78-Stumbo the Giant (3/64); JFK caricature	4	8	12	28	44	60
79-87: 79-Little Sad Sack (4/64). 80-Sad Sack's Muttsy... (5/64). 81-Little Sad Sack. 82-Sad Sack's Muttsy... 83-Little Sad Sack(8/64). 84-Sad Sack's Muttsy... 85-Gabby Gob (#1) (10/64). 86-G. I. Juniors (#1)(11/64). 87-Sad Sack's Muttsy... (12/64)	3	6	9	15	22	28
88-Stumbo the Giant (1/65)	4	8	12	27	44	60
89-122: 89-Sad Sack's Muttsy... 90-Gabby Gob. 91-G. I. Juniors. 92-Sad Sack's Muttsy... (5/65). 93-Sadie Sack (6/65). 94-Gabby Gob. 95-G. I. Juniors (8/65). 96-Sad Sack's Muttsy... (9/65). 97-Gabby Gob (10/65). 98-G. I. Juniors (11/65). 99-Sad Sack's Muttsy... (12/65). 100-Gabby Gob(1/66). 101-G. I. Juniors (2/66). 102-Sad Sack's Muttsy... (3/66). 103-Gabby Gob. 104- G. I. Juniors. 105-Sad Sack's Muttsy... 106-Gabby Gob (7/66). 107-G. I. Juniors (8/66). 108-Sad Sack's Muttsy...109-Gabby Gob. 110-G. I. Juniors (11/66). 111-Sad Sack's Muttsy... (12/66). 112-G. I. Juniors. 113-Sad Sack's Muttsy... 114-G. I. Juniors. 115-Sad Sack's Muttsy... 116-G. I. Juniors (5/67). 117-Sad Sack's Muttsy... 118-G. I. Juniors. 119-Sad Sack's Muttsy... (8/67). 120-G. I. Juniors (9/67). 121-Sad Sack's Muttsy... (10/67). 122-G. I. Juniors (11/67)	2	4	6	10	14	18

HARVEY HITS COMICS
Harvey Publications: Nov, 1986 - No. 6, Oct, 1987

	GD	VG	FN	VF	VF/NM	NM-
1-Little Lotta, Little Dot, Wendy & Baby Huey	1	2	3	4	5	7
2-6: 3-Xmas-c						4.50

HARVEY POP COMICS (Rock Happening) (Teen Humor)
Harvey Publications: Oct, 1968 - No. 2, Nov, 1969 (Both are 68 pg. Giants)

	GD	VG	FN	VF	VF/NM	NM-
1-The Cowsills	5	10	15	34	60	85
2-Bunny	5	10	15	31	53	75

HARVEY 3-D HITS (See Sad Sack)

HARVEY-TOON (...S) (See Harvey Hits No. 29, 34, 38, 42, 46, 50, 53)

HARVEY WISEGUYS (...Digest #? on)
Harvey Comics: Nov, 1987; #2, Nov, 1988; #3, Apr, 1989 - No. 4, Nov, 1989 (98 pgs., digest-size, $1.25/$1.75)

	GD	VG	FN	VF	VF/NM	NM-
1-Hot Stuff, Spooky, etc.	2	3	4	6	8	10
2-4: 2 (68 pgs.)	1	2	3	4	5	7

HATARI (See Movie Classics)

HATE
Fantagraphics Books: Spr, 1990 - No. 30, 1998 ($2.50/$2.95, B&W/color)

	GD	VG	FN	VF	VF/NM	NM-
1	2	4	6	10	12	15
2-3	1	2	3	5	6	8
4-10						5.00
11-20: 16- color begins						4.00
21-29						3.00
30-($3.95) Last issue						4.00
Annual 1 (2/01, $3.95) Peter Bagge-s/a						5.00
Annual 2-9 (12/01-Present; $4.95) Peter Bagge-s/a						5.00
Buddy Bites the Bullet! (2001, $16.95) r/Buddy stories in color						17.00
Buddy Go Home! (1997, $16.95) r/Buddy stories in color						17.00
Hate-Ball Special Edition ($3.95, giveaway)-reprints						4.00
Hate Jamboree (10/98, $4.50) old & new cartoons						4.50

HATHAWAYS, THE (TV)
Dell Publishing Co.: No. 1298, Feb-Apr, 1962 (one-shot)

	GD	VG	FN	VF	VF/NM	NM-
Four Color 1298-Photo-c	4	8	12	28	47	65

HAUNTED (See This Magazine Is Haunted)

HAUNT
Image Comics: Oct, 2009 - Present ($2.99)

	GD	VG	FN	VF	VF/NM	NM-
1-McFarlane & Kirkman-s/Capullo & Ottley-a/McFarlane-a(i)/c; two variant-c						6.00
2-28: 2-Two covers. 13-($1.99). 19-Casey-s/Fox-a begins						3.00
Image Firsts: Haunt #1 (10/10, $1.00) r/#1 with "Image First" cover logo						3.00

HAUNTED (Baron Weirwulf's Haunted Library on-c #21 on)
Charlton Comics: 9/71 - No. 30, 11/76; No. 31, 9/77 - No. 75, 9/84

	GD	VG	FN	VF	VF/NM	NM-
1-All Ditko issue	5	10	15	33	57	80
2-7-Ditko-c/a	3	6	9	19	30	40
8,12,28-Ditko-a	2	4	6	13	18	22
9,19	2	4	6	8	11	14
10,20,15,18: 10,20-Sutton-a. 15-Sutton-c	2	4	6	8	11	14
11,13,14,16-Ditko-c/a	3	6	9	15	22	28
17-Sutton-c/a; Newton-a	2	4	6	9	12	15
21-Newton-c/a; Sutton-a; 1st Baron Weirwulf	3	6	9	16	24	32
22-Newton-c/a; Sutton-a	2	4	6	9	13	16
23,24-Sutton-c; Ditko-a	2	4	6	9	13	16
25-27,29,32,33	1	3	4	6	8	10
30,41,47,49-52,60,74-Ditko-c/a: 51-Reprints #1	2	4	6	11	16	20
31,35,37,38-Sutton-a	1	3	4	6	8	10
34,36,39,40,42,57-Ditko-a	2	4	6	8	10	12
43-46,48,53-56,58,59,61-73: 59-Newton-a. 64-Sutton-c. 71-73-Low print	1	2	3	5	6	8
75-(9/84) Last issue; low print	2	4	6	9	13	16

NOTE: ***Aparo** c-45. **Ditko** a-1-8, 11-16, 18, 23, 24, 28, 30, 34r, 36r, 39-42r, 47r, 49-52r, 57, 60, 74. c-1-7, 11, 13, 14, 16, 30, 41, 47, 49-52, 74. **Howard** a-6, 9, 18, 22, 25, 32. **Kim** a-9, 19. **Morisi** a-13. **Newton** a-17, 21, 59r; c-21, 22(painted). **Staton** a-11; 12, 18, 21, 22, 30, 33, 35, 38; c-18, 33, 38. **Sutton** a-10, 17, 20-22, 31, 35, 37, 38; c-15, 17, 18, 23(painted), 24(painted), 27, 64r. #49 reprints Tales of the Mysterious Traveler #4.*

HAUNTED, THE
Chaos! Comics: Jan, 2002 - No. 4, Apr, 2002 ($2.99, limited series)

	GD	VG	FN	VF	VF/NM	NM-
1-4-Peter David-s/Nat Jones-a						3.00
...: Gray Matters (7/02, $2.99) David-s/Jones-a						3.00

HAUNTED CITY
Aspen MLT: No. 0, Aug, 2011 - Present ($2.50)

	GD	VG	FN	VF	VF/NM	NM-
0-($2.50)-Taylor & Johnson-s/Michael Ryan-a; four covers						3.00
1,2-($3.50) 1-Taylor & Johnson-s/Michael Ryan-a; four covers						3.50

HAUNTED LOVE
Charlton Comics: Apr, 1973 - No. 11, Sept, 1975

	GD	VG	FN	VF	VF/NM	NM-
1-Tom Sutton-a (16 pgs.)	5	10	15	33	57	80
2,3,6,7,10,11	3	6	9	17	26	35
4,5-Ditko-a	3	6	9	21	33	45
8,9-Newton-c	3	6	9	18	28	38
Modern Comics #1(1978)	2	3	4	6	8	10

NOTE: ***Howard** a-8i. **Kim** a-7-9. **Newton** c-8, 9. **Staton** a-1-6. **Sutton** a-1, 3-5, 10, 11.*

HAUNTED TANK, THE
DC Comics (Vertigo): Feb, 2009 - No. 5, June, 2009 ($2.99, limited series)

	GD	VG	FN	VF	VF/NM	NM-
1-5-Marraffino-s/Flint-a. 1-Two covers by Flint and Joe Kubert						3.00
TPB (2010, $14.99) r/#1-5						15.00

HAUNTED THRILLS (Tales of Horror and Terror)
Ajax/Farrell Publications: June, 1952 - No. 18, Nov-Dec, 1954

	GD	VG	FN	VF	VF/NM	NM-
1-r/Ellery Queen #1	68	136	204	435	743	1050
2-L. B. Cole-a r-/Ellery Queen #1	41	82	123	256	428	600
3,4: 3-Drug use story	39	78	117	240	395	550
5-Classic skull-c	58	116	174	371	636	900
6-8,10,12: 7-Hitler story.	39	78	117	231	378	525
9-Classic decapitated heads-c	50	100	150	315	533	750
11-Nazi death camp story	39	78	117	240	395	550
13-18: 14-Jesus Christ apps. in story by Webb. 15-Jo-Jo-r. 18-Lingerie panels; skull-c	34	68	102	199	325	450

NOTE: ***Kamenish** art in most issues. **Webb** a-12.*

Haunt of Fear #15 © WMG

Haven: The Broken City #6 © DC

Hawk and the Dove #6 © DC

GD	VG	FN	VF	VF/NM	NM-
2.0	4.0	6.0	8.0	9.0	9.2

HAUNT OF FEAR (Formerly Gunfighter)
E. C. Comics: No. 15, May-June, 1950 - No. 28, Nov-Dec, 1954

15(#1, 1950)(Scarce) 303 606 909 2424 3862 5300
16-1st app. "The Witches Cauldron" & the Old Witch (by Kamen); begin series as hostess of Haunt of Fear 126 252 378 1008 1604 2200
17-Origin of Crypt of Terror, Vault of Horror, & Haunt of Fear; used in **SOTI**, pg. 43; last pg. Ingels-a used by N.Y. Legis. Comm.; story "Monster Maker" based on Frankenstein. Old Witch by Feldstein 126 252 378 1008 1604 2200
4-Ingels becomes regular artist for Old Witch. 1st Vault Keeper & Crypt Keeper app. in HOF; begin series 80 160 240 640 1020 1400
5-Injury-to-eye panel, pg. 4 of Wood story 69 138 207 552 876 1200
6,7,9,10: 6-Crypt Keeper by Feldstein begins. 9-Crypt Keeper by Davis begins. 10-Ingels biog. 51 102 153 408 654 900
8-Classic Feldstein Shrunken Head-c 56 112 168 448 712 975
11,12: Classic Ingels-c; 11-Kamen biog. 12-Feldstein biog. 44 88 132 352 564 775
13,15,16,20: 16-Ray Bradbury adaptation. 20-Feldstein-r/Vault of Horror #12 41 82 123 328 527 725
14-Origin Old Witch by Ingels; classic-Ingels-c 54 108 162 432 691 950
17-Classic Ingels-c 51 102 153 408 654 900
18-Old Witch-c; Ray Bradbury adaptation & biography 43 86 129 344 552 760
19-Used in **SOTI**, ill. "A comic book baseball game" & Senate investigation on juvenile delinq. bondage/decapitation-c 50 100 150 400 638 875
21-27: 23-EC version of the Hansel and Gretel story; **SOTI**, pg. 241 discusses the original Grimm tale in relation to comics. 24-Used in Senate Investigative Report, pg.8. 26-Contains anti-censorship editorial, 'Are you a Red Dupe?' 27-Cannibalism story; Vault Keeper shown reading **SOTI** 30 60 90 240 383 525
28-Low distribution 38 76 114 304 482 660

NOTE: *(Canadian reprints known; see Table of Contents).* ***Craig*** *a-15-17, 5, 7, 10, 12, 13; c-15-17, 5-7.* ***Crandall*** *a-20, 21, 26, 27.* ***Davis*** *a-4-26, 28.* ***Evans*** *a-15-19, 22-25, 27.* ***Feldstein*** *a-15-17, 20; c-4, 8-10.* ***Ingels*** *a-16, 17, 4-28; c-11-28.* ***Kamen*** *a-16, 4, 6, 7, 9-11, 13-19, 21-28.* ***Krigstein*** *a-28.* ***Kurtzman*** *a-15(#1), 17(#3).* ***Orlando*** *a-9, 12.* ***Wood*** *a-15, 16, 4-6.*

HAUNT OF FEAR, THE
Gladstone Publishing: May, 1991 - No. 2, July, 1991 ($2.00, 68 pgs.)

1,2: 1-Ghastly Ingels-c(r); 2-Craig-c(r) 4.00

HAUNT OF FEAR
Russ Cochran/Gemstone Publ.: Sept, 1991 - No. 5, 1992 ($2.00, 68 pgs.); Nov, 1992 - No. 28, Aug, 1998 ($1.50/$2.00/$2.50)

1-28: 1-Ingels-c(r). 1-3-r/HOF #15-17 with original-c. 4,5-r/HOF #4,5 with original-c 4.00
Annual 1-5: 1- r/#1-5. 2- r/#6-10. 3- r/#11-15. 4- r/#16-20. 5- r/#21-25 14.00
Annual 6-r/#26-28 9.00

HAUNT OF HORROR, THE (Digest)
Marvel Comics: Jun, 1973 - No. 2, Aug, 1973 (164 pgs.; text and art)

1-Morrow painted skull-c; stories by Ellison, Howard, and Leiber; Brunner-a 4 8 12 23 37 50
2-Kelly Freas painted bondage-c; stories by McCaffrey, Goulart, Leiber, Ellison; art by Simonson, Brunner, and Buscema 3 6 9 16 24 32

HAUNT OF HORROR, THE (Magazine)
Cadence Comics Publ. (Marvel): May, 1974 - No. 5, Jan, 1975 (75¢) (B&W)

1,2: 2-Origin & 1st app. Gabriel the Devil Hunter; Satana begins 3 6 9 14 20 26
3-5: 4-Neal Adams-a. 5-Evans-a(2) 3 6 9 17 26 35

NOTE: ***Alcala*** *a-2.* ***Colan*** *a-2p.* ***Heath*** *r-1.* ***Krigstein*** *r-3.* ***Reese*** *a-1.* ***Simonson*** *a-1.*

HAUNT OF HORROR: EDGAR ALLAN POE
Marvel Comics (MAX): July, 2006 - No. 3, Sept, 2006 ($3.99, B&W, limited series)

1-3- Poe-inspired/adapted stories with Richard Corben-a 4.00
HC (2006, $19.99) r/series; cover sketches 20.00

HAUNT OF HORROR: LOVECRAFT
Marvel Comics (MAX): Aug, 2008 - No. 3, Oct, 2008 ($3.99, B&W, limited series)

1-3-Lovecraft-inspired/adapted stories with Richard Corben-a 4.00

HAVE GUN, WILL TRAVEL (TV)
Dell Publishing Co.: No. 931, 8/58 - No. 14, 7-9/62 (All Richard Boone photo-c)

Four Color 931 (#1) 11 22 33 73 157 240
Four Color 983,1044 (#2,3) 8 16 24 51 96 140
4 (1-3/60) - 10 7 14 21 46 86 125
11-14 7 14 21 44 82 120

HAVEN: THE BROKEN CITY (See JLA/Haven: Arrival and JLA/Haven: Anathema)
DC Comics: Feb, 2002 - No. 9, Oct, 2002 ($2.50, limited series)

1-9-Olivetti-c/a: 1- JLA app. Series concludes in JLA/Haven: Anathema 3.00

HAVOK & WOLVERINE - MELTDOWN (See Marvel Comics Presents #24)
Marvel Comics (Epic Comics): Mar, 1989 - No. 4, Oct, 1989 ($3.50, mini-series, square-bound, mature)

1-4: Art by Kent Williams & Jon J. Muth; story by Walt & Louise Simonson 6.00

HAWAIIAN DICK
Image Comics: Dec, 2002 - No. 3, Feb, 2003 ($2.95, limited series)

1-3-B. Clay Moore-s/Steven Griffin-a 3.00
...: Byrd of Paradise TPB (8/03, $14.95) r/#1-3, script & sketch pages 15.00

HAWAIIAN DICK: SCREAMING BLACK THUNDER
Image Comics: Nov, 2007 - No. 5, Oct, 2008 ($2.99, limited series)

1-5-B. Clay Moore-s/Scott Chantler-a 3.00

HAWAIIAN DICK: THE LAST RESORT
Image Comics: Aug, 2004 - No. 4, June, 2006 ($2.95/$2.99, limited series)

1-4-B. Clay Moore-s/Steven Griffin-a 3.00
Vol. 2 TPB (10/06, $14.99) r/#1-4 & the original series pitch 15.00

HAWAIIAN EYE (TV)
Gold Key: July, 1963 (Troy Donahue, Connie Stevens photo-c)

1 (10073-307) 5 10 15 31 53 75

HAWAIIAN ILLUSTRATED LEGENDS SERIES
Hogarth Press: 1975 (B&W)(Cover printed w/blue, yellow, and green)

1-Kalelealuaka, the Mysterious Warrior 5.00

HAWK, THE (Also see Approved Comics #1, 7 & Tops In Adventure)
Ziff-Davis/St. John Publ. Co. No. 4 on: Wint/51 - No. 3, 11-12/52; No. 4, 1-2/53; No. 8, 9/54 - No. 12, 5/55 (Painted c-1-4)(#5-7 don't exist)

1-Anderson-a 20 40 60 120 195 270
2 (Sum, '52)-Kubert, Infantino-a 13 26 39 74 105 135
3-4 11 22 33 60 83 105
8-12: 8(9/54)-Reprints #3 w/different-c by Baker. 9-Baker-c/a; Kubert-a(r)/#2. 10-Baker-c/a; r/one story from #2. 11-Baker-c; Buckskin Belle & The Texan app. 12-Baker-c/a; Buckskin Belle app. 16 32 48 94 147 200
3-D 1(11/53, 25¢)-Came w/glasses; Baker-c 33 66 99 194 317 440

NOTE: ***Baker*** *c-8-12.* ***Larsen*** *a-10.* ***Tuska*** *a-1, 9, 12. Painted c-1, 4, 7.*

HAWK AND THE DOVE, THE (See Showcase #75 & Teen Titans) (1st series)
National Periodical Publications: Aug-Sept, 1968 - No. 6, June-July, 1969

1-Ditko-c/a 8 16 24 53 89 125
2-6: 5-Teen Titans cameo 5 10 15 32 51 70

NOTE: ***Ditko*** *c/a-1, 2.* ***Gil Kane*** *a-3p, 4p, 5, 6p; c-3-6.*

HAWK AND DOVE (2nd Series)
DC Comics: Oct, 1988 - No. 5, Feb, 1989 ($1.00, limited series)

1-Rob Liefeld-c/a(p) in all 4.00
2-5 3.00
Trade paperback ('93, $9.95)-Reprints #1-5 12.00

HAWK AND DOVE
DC Comics: June, 1989 - No. 28, Oct, 1991 ($1.00)

1-28 3.00
Annual 1,2 ('90, '91; $2.00) 1-Liefeld pin-up. 2-Armageddon 2001 x-over 4.00

HAWK AND DOVE
DC Comics: Nov, 1997 - No. 5, Mar, 1998 ($2.50, limited series)

1-5-Baron-s/Zachary & Giordano-a 3.00

HAWK AND DOVE (DC New 52)
DC Comics: Nov, 2011 - No. 8, Jun, 2012 ($2.99)

1-8: 1-Gates-s/Liefeld-a/c; Deadman app. 6-Batman & Robin app.; Liefeld-s/a/c 3.00

HAWK AND WINDBLADE (See Elflord)
Warp Graphics: Aug, 1997 - No.2, Sept, 1997 ($2.95, limited series)

1,2-Blair-s/Chan-c/a 3.00

HAWKEN: MELEE (Based on the computer game Hawken)
Archaia Black Label: Dec, 2013 - No. 5 ($3.99, limited series)

1,2: 1-Abnett-s/Dallocchio-a. 2-Jim Mahfood-s/a 4.00

HAWKEYE (See The Avengers #16 & Tales Of Suspense #57)
Marvel Comics Group: Sept, 1983 - No. 4, Dec, 1983 (limited series)

1-Mark Gruenwald-a/scripts in all; origin Hawkeye 2 4 6 9 12 15
2-4: 3-Origin Mockingbird. 4-Hawkeye & Mockingbird elope 1 2 3 5 6 8

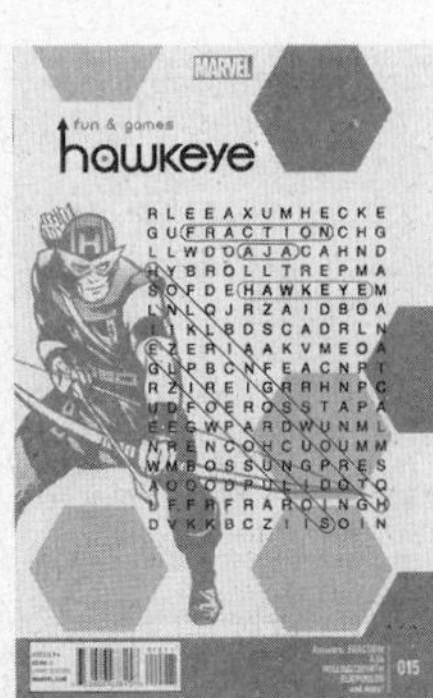

Hawkeye (2012 series) #15 © MAR

Hawkman #2 © DC

Hawkmoon: The Runestaff #1 © FC

GD 2.0 | VG 4.0 | FN 6.0 | VF 8.0 | VF/NM 9.0 | NM- 9.2

GD 2.0 | VG 4.0 | FN 6.0 | VF 8.0 | VF/NM 9.0 | NM- 9.2

HAWKEYE
Marvel Comics: Jan, 1994 - No. 4, Apr, 1994 ($1.75, limited series)

1-4 5.00

HAWKEYE (Volume 2)
Marvel Comics: Dec, 2003 - No. 8, Aug, 2004 ($2.99)

1-8: 1-6-Nicieza-s/Raffaele-a. 7,8-Bennett-a; Black Widow app. 4.00

HAWKEYE
Marvel Comics: Oct, 2012 - Present ($2.99)

1-Fraction-s/Aja-a; Kate Bishop app. 2 4 6 11 16 20
2,3 1 3 4 6 8 10
4-8: 7-Lieber & Hamm-a 6.00
9-18: 10,12-Francavilla-a. 11-Dog issue. 16-Released before #15 4.00
Annual 1 (9/13, $4.99) Pulido-a; Kate Bishop in L.A.; Madame Mask app. 5.00

HAWKEYE AND MOCKINGBIRD (Avengers) (Leads into Widowmaker mini-series)
Marvel Comics: Aug, 2010 - No. 6, Jan, 2011 ($3.99/$2.99)

1-($3.99) Heroic Age; Jim McCann-s/David Lopez-a; history of the characters 4.00
2-6-($2.99) Phantom Rider, Dominic Fortune & Crossfire app. 3.00

HAWKEYE & THE LAST OF THE MOHICANS (TV)
Dell Publishing Co.: No. 884, Mar, 1958 (one-shot)

Four Color 884-Lon Chaney Jr. photo-c 6 12 18 40 73 105

HAWKEYE: BLINDSPOT (Avengers)
Marvel Comics: Apr, 2011 - No. 4, Jul, 2011 ($2.99, limited series)

1-4: 1-McCann-s/Diaz-a; Zemo app. 2-Diaz & Dragotta-a 3.00

HAWKEYE: EARTH'S MIGHTIEST MARKSMAN
Marvel Comics: Oct, 1998 ($2.99, one-shot)

1-Justice and Firestar app.; DeFalco-s 5.00

HAWKGIRL (Title continued from Hawkman #49, Apr, 2006)
DC Comics: No. 50, May, 2006 - No. 66, Sept, 2007 ($2.50/$2.99)

50-66: 50-Chaykin-a/Simonson-s begin; One Year Later. 52-Begin $2.99-c. 57,58-Bennett-a. 59-Blackfire app. 63-Batman app. 64-Superman app. 3.00
...: Hath-Set TPB (2008, $17.99) r/#61-66 18.00
...: Hawkman Returns TPB (2007, $17.99) r/#57-60 & JSA Classified #21,22 18.00
...: The Maw TPB (2007, $17.99) r/#50-56 18.00

HAWKMAN (See Atom & Hawkman, The Brave & the Bold, DC Comics Presents, Detective Comics, Flash Comics, Hawkworld, JSA, Justice League of America #31, Legend of the Hawkman, Mystery in Space, Savage Hawkman, Shadow War Of..., Showcase, & World's Finest #256)

HAWKMAN (1st Series) (Also see The Atom #7 & Brave & the Bold #34-36, 42-44, 51)
National Periodical Publications: Apr-May, 1964 - No. 27, Aug-Sept, 1968

1-(4-5/64)-Anderson-c/a begins, ends #21 53 106 159 424 950 1475
2 20 40 60 141 313 485
3,5: 5-2nd app. Shadow Thief 13 26 39 89 195 300
4-Origin & 1st app. Zatanna (10-11/64) 18 36 54 124 275 425
6 10 20 30 66 138 210
7 9 18 27 60 120 180
8-10: 9-Atom cameo; Hawkman & Atom learn each other's I.D.; 3rd app. Shadow Thief 8 16 24 54 102 150
11-15 6 12 18 40 73 105
16-27: 18-Adam Strange x-over (cameo #19). 25-G.A. Hawkman-r by Moldoff. 26-Kirby-a(r). 27-Kubert-c 5 10 15 33 57 80

HAWKMAN (2nd Series)
DC Comics: Aug, 1986 - No. 17, Dec, 1987

1-17: 10-Byrne-c, Special #1 (1986, $1.25) 4.00
Trade paperback (1989, $19.95)-r/Brave and the Bold #34-36,42-44 by Kubert; Kubert-c 20.00

HAWKMAN (4th Series)(See both Hawkworld limited & ongoing series)
DC Comics: Sept, 1993 - No. 33, July, 1996 ($1.75/$1.95/$2.25)

1-($2.50)-Gold foil embossed-c; storyline cont'd from Hawkworld ongoing series; new costume & powers. 4.00
2-13,0,14-33: 2-Green Lantern x-over. 3-Airstryke app. 4,6-Wonder Woman app. 13-(9/94)-Zero Hour. 0-(10/94). 14-(11/94). 15-Aquaman-c & app. 23-Wonder Woman app. 25-Kent Williams-c. 29,30-Chaykin-c. 32-Breyfogle-c 3.00
Annual 1 (1993, $2.50, 68 pgs.)-Bloodlines Earthplague 4.00
Annual 2 (1995, $3.95)-Year One story 4.00

HAWKMAN (Title continues as Hawkgirl #50-on) (See JSA #23 for return)
DC Comics: May, 2002 - No. 49, Apr, 2006 ($2.50)

1-Johns & Robinson-s/Morales-a 5.00
1-2nd printing 3.00
2-40: 2-4-Shadow Thief app. 5,6-Green Arrow-c/app. 8-Atom-c/app. 13-Van Sciver-a. 14-Gentleman Ghost app. 15-Hawkwoman app. 16-Byth returns. 23-25-Black Reign x-over with JSA #56-58. 26-Byrne-c/a. 29,30-Land-c. 37-Golden Eagle returns 3.00
41-49: 41-Hawkman killed. 43-Golden Eagle origin. 46-49-Adam Kubert-c 3.00
...: Allies & Enemies TPB (2004, $14.95) r/#7-14 & pages from Secret Files and Origins 15.00
...: Endless Flight TPB (2003, $12.95) r/#1-6 & Secret Files and Origins 13.00
...: Rise of the Golden Eagle TPB (2006, $17.99) r/#37-45 18.00
... Secret Files and Origins (10/02, $4.95) profiles and pin-ups by various 5.00
... Special 1 (10/08, $3.50) Tie-in to Rann-Thanagar Holy War series; Starlin-s/a(p) 3.50
...: Wings of Fury TPB (2005, $17.99) r/#15-22 18.00

HAWKMOON: THE JEWEL IN THE SKULL
First Comics: May, 1986 - No. 4, Nov, 1986 ($1.75, limited series, Baxter paper)

1-4: Adapts novel by Michael Moorcock 3.00

HAWKMOON: THE MAD GOD'S AMULET
First Comics: Jan, 1987 - No. 4, July, 1987 ($1.75, limited series, Baxter paper)

1-4: Adapts novel by Michael Moorcock 3.00

HAWKMOON: THE RUNESTAFF
First Comics: Jun, 1988 -No. 4, Dec, 1988 ($1.75-$1.95, lim. series, Baxter paper)

1-4: ($1.75) Adapts novel by Michael Moorcock. 3,4 ($1.95) 3.00

HAWKMOON: THE SWORD OF DAWN
First Comics: Sept, 1987 - No. 4, Mar, 1988 ($1.75, lim. series, Baxter paper)

1-4: Dorman painted-c; adapts Moorcock novel 3.00

HAWKS OF THE SEAS (WILL EISNER'S...)
Dark Horse Comics: July, 2003 ($19.95, B&W, hardcover)

nn-Reprints 1937-1939 weekly Pirate serial by Will Eisner; Williamson intro. 20.00

HAWKWORLD
DC Comics: 1989 - No. 3, 1989 ($3.95, prestige format, limited series)

Book 1-3: 1-Tim Truman story & art in all; Hawkman dons new costume; reintro Byth 5.00
TPB (1991, $16.95) r/#1-3 17.00

HAWKWORLD (3rd Series)
DC Comics: June, 1990 - No. 32, Mar, 1993 ($1.50/$1.75)

1-Hawkman spin-off; story cont'd from limited series. 4.00
2-32: 15,16-War of the Gods x-over. 22-J'onn J'onzz app. 3.00
Annual 1-3 ('90-'92, $2.95, 68 pgs.), 2-2nd printing with silver ink-c 4.00
NOTE: *Truman a-30-32; c-27-32, Annual 1.*

HAYWIRE
DC Comics: Oct, 1988 - No. 13, Sept, 1989 ($1.25, mature)

1-13 3.00

HAZARD
Image Comics (WildStorm Prod.): June, 1996 - No. 7, Nov, 1996 ($1.75)

1-7: 1-Intro Hazard; Jeff Mariotte scripts begin; Jim Lee-c(p) 3.00

HEADHUNTERS
Image Comics: Apr, 1997 - No. 3, June, 1997 ($2.95, B&W)

1-3: Chris Marrinan-s/a 3.00

HEADLINE COMICS
DC Comics: Jan. 1942

nn - Ashcan comic, not distributed to newsstands, only for in-house use. Cover art is More Fun Comics #73, interior being Star Spangled Comics #2 (a FN copy sold for $2270.50 in 2012)

HEADLINE COMICS (...For the American Boy) (...Crime No. 32-39)
Prize Publ./American Boys' Comics: Feb, 1943 - No. 22, Nov-Dec, 1946; No. 23, 1947 - No. 77, Oct, 1956

1-Junior Rangers-c/stories begin; Yank & Doodle x-over in Junior Rangers (Junior Rangers are Uncle Sam's nephews) 68 136 204 435 743 1050
2 39 78 117 231 378 525
3-Used in **POP**, pg. 84 28 56 84 165 270 375
4-7,9,10: 4,9,10-Hitler stories in each 24 48 72 140 230 320
8-Classic Hitler-c 258 516 774 1651 2826 4000
11,12 20 40 60 118 192 265
13-15-Blue Streak in all 22 42 63 122 199 275
16-Origin & 1st app. Atomic Man (11-12/45) 32 64 96 188 307 425
17,18,20,21: 21-Atomic Man ends (9-10/46) 18 36 54 107 169 230
19-S&K-a 34 68 102 199 325 450
22-Last Junior Rangers; Kiefer-c 15 30 45 88 137 185
23,24: (All S&K-a). 23-Valentine's Day Massacre story; content changes to true crime. 24-Dope-crazy killer story 34 68 102 199 325 450
25-35-S&K-c/a. 25-Powell-a 29 58 87 172 281 390
36-S&K-a; photo-c begin 21 42 63 126 206 285

Headline Comics #4 © Prize

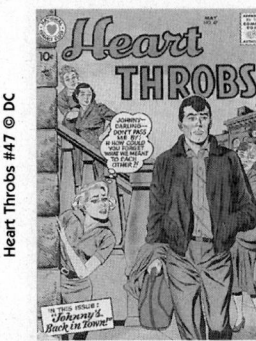

Heart Throbs #47 © DC

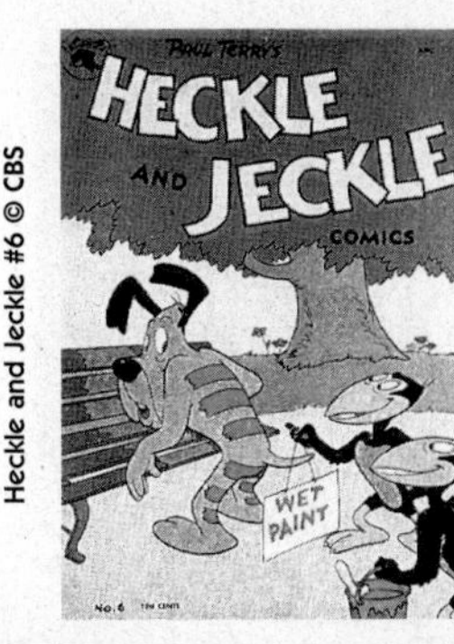

Heckle and Jeckle #6 © CBS

	GD 2.0	VG 4.0	FN 6.0	VF 8.0	VF/NM 9.0	NM- 9.2
37-1 pg. S&K, Severin-a; rare Kirby photo-c app.	23	46	69	136	223	310
38,40-Meskin-a	11	22	33	64	90	115
39,41-43,46-56: 41-J. Edgar Hoover 26th Anniversary Issue with photo on-c. 43,49-Meskin-a. 48-Meskin-c	10	20	30	56	76	95
44,45-S&K-c; Severin/Elder, Meskin-a	15	30	45	86	133	180
57-77: 70-Roller Derby-c. 72-Meskin-c/a(i)	9	18	27	50	65	80

NOTE: ***Hollingsworth** a-30. Photo c-36-43. **H. C. Kiefer** c-12-16, 22. Atomic Man c-17-19.*

HEADMAN
Innovation Publishing: 1990 ($2.50, mature)

	GD	VG	FN	VF	VF/NM	NM-
1-Sci/fi						3.00

HEAP, THE
Skywald Publications: Sept, 1971 (52 pgs.)

	GD	VG	FN	VF	VF/NM	NM-
1-Kinstler-r/Strange Worlds #8; new-s w/Sutton-a	4	8	12	28	47	65

HEART AND SOUL
Mikeross Publications: April-May, 1954 - No. 2, June-July, 1954

	GD	VG	FN	VF	VF/NM	NM-
1,2	10	20	30	56	76	95

HEARTBREAKERS (Also see Dark Horse Presents)
Dark Horse Comics: Apr, 1996 - No. 4, July, 1996 ($2.95, limited series)

	GD	VG	FN	VF	VF/NM	NM-
1-4: 1-W/paper doll & pin-up. 2-Alex Ross pin-up. 3-Evan Dorkin pin-ups. 4-Brereton-c; Matt Wagner pin-up						3.00
...Superdigest (7/98, $9.95, digest-size) new stories						10.00

HEARTLAND (See Hellblazer)
DC Comics (Vertigo): Mar, 1997 ($4.95, one-shot, mature)

	GD	VG	FN	VF	VF/NM	NM-
1-Garth Ennis-s/Steve Dillon-c/a						5.00

HEART OF DARKNESS
Hardline Studios: 1994 ($2.95)

	GD	VG	FN	VF	VF/NM	NM-
1-Brereton-c						3.00

HEART OF EMPIRE
Dark Horse Comics: Apr, 1999 - No. 9, Dec, 1999 ($2.95, limited series)

	GD	VG	FN	VF	VF/NM	NM-
1-9-Bryan Talbot-s/a						3.00

HEART OF THE BEAST, THE
DC Comics (Vertigo): 1994 ($19.95, hardcover, mature)

	GD	VG	FN	VF	VF/NM	NM-
1-Dean Motter scripts						20.00

HEARTS OF DARKNESS (See Ghost Rider; Wolverine; Punisher: Hearts of...)

HEART THROBS (Love Stories No. 147 on)
Quality Comics/National Periodical #47(4-5/57) on (Arleigh #48-101): 8/49 - No. 8, 10/50; No. 9, 3/52 - No. 146, Oct, 1972

	GD	VG	FN	VF	VF/NM	NM-
1-Classic Ward-c, Gustavson-a, 9 pgs.	45	90	135	284	480	675
2-Ward-c/a (9 pgs); Gustavson-a	28	56	84	165	270	375
3-Gustavson-a	14	28	42	82	121	160
4,6,8-Ward-a, 8-9 pgs.	18	36	54	103	162	220
5,7	12	24	36	69	97	125
9-Robert Mitchum, Jane Russell photo-c	15	30	45	83	124	165
10,15-Ward-a	15	30	45	83	124	165
11-14,16-20: 12 (7/52)	10	20	30	58	79	100
21-Ward-c	14	28	42	81	118	155
22,23-Ward-a(p)	11	22	33	62	86	110
24-33: 33-Last pre-code (3/55)	10	20	30	56	76	95
34-39,41-44,46 (12/56; last Quality issue)	10	20	30	54	72	90
40-Ward-a; r-7 pgs./#21	10	20	30	58	79	100
45-Baker-a	6	12	18	40	73	105
47-(4-5/57; 1st DC issue)	18	36	54	128	284	440
48-60, 100	9	18	27	57	111	165
61-70	6	12	18	41	76	110
71-99: 74-Last 10 cent issue	6	12	18	37	66	95
101-The Beatles app. on-c	12	24	36	82	179	275
102-119: 102-123-(Serial)-Three Girls, Their Lives, Their Loves	4	8	12	27	44	60
120-(6-7/69) Neal Adams-c	4	8	12	28	47	65
121-132,143-146	3	6	9	21	33	45
133-142-(52 pgs.)	4	8	12	27	44	60

NOTE: ***Gustavson** a-8. **Tuska** a-128. Photo c-4, 5, 8-10, 15, 17.*

HEART THROBS - THE BEST OF DC ROMANCE COMICS (See Fireside Book Series)

HEART THROBS
DC Comics (Vertigo): Jan, 1999 - No. 4, Apr, 1999 ($2.95, lim. series)

	GD	VG	FN	VF	VF/NM	NM-
1-4-Romance anthology. 1-Timm-c. 3-Corben-a						3.00

HEATHCLIFF (See Star Comics Magazine)
Marvel Comics (Star Comics)/Marvel Comics No. 23 on: Apr, 1985 - No. 56, Feb, 1991 (#16-on, $1.00)

	GD	VG	FN	VF	VF/NM	NM-
1-Post-a most issues	1	2	3	4	5	7
2-10,47: 47-Batman parody (Catman vs. the Soaker)						5.00
11-46,48-56: 43-X-Mas issue						4.00
Annual 1 ('87)						4.00

HEATHCLIFF'S FUNHOUSE
Marvel Comics (Star Comics)/Marvel No. 6 on: May, 1987 - No. 10, 1988

	GD	VG	FN	VF	VF/NM	NM-
1						5.00
2-10						4.00

HEAVEN'S DEVILS
Image Comics: Sept, 2003 - No. 4, July, 2004 ($2.95/$3.50, B&W, limited series)

	GD	VG	FN	VF	VF/NM	NM-
1-3-($2.95) Jai Nitz-s/Zach Howard-a						3.00
4-($3.50) Kevin Sharpe-a						3.50

HEAVY HITTERS
Marvel Comics (Epic Comics): 1993 ($3.75, 68 pgs.)

	GD	VG	FN	VF	VF/NM	NM-
1-Bound w/trading card; Lawdog, Feud, Alien Legion, Trouble With Girls, & Spyke						4.00

HEAVY LIQUID
DC Comics (Vertigo): Oct, 1999 - No. 5, Feb, 2000 ($5.95, limited series)

	GD	VG	FN	VF	VF/NM	NM-
1-5-Paul Pope-s/a; flip covers						6.00
TPB (2001, $29.95) r/#1-5						30.00
TPB (2009, $24.95) r/#1-5; development sketches and cover gallery; new cover						25.00
HC (2008, $39.99, dustjacket) r/#1-5; development sketches and cover gallery						40.00

HECKLE AND JECKLE (Paul Terry's...)(See Blue Ribbon, Giant Comics Edition #5A & 10, Paul Terry's, Terry-Toons Comics)
St. John Publ. Co. No. 1-24/Pines No. 25 on: No. 3, 2/52 - No. 24, 10/55; No. 25, Fall/56 - No. 34, 6/59

	GD	VG	FN	VF	VF/NM	NM-
3(#1)-Funny animal	24	48	72	142	234	325
4(6/52), 5	14	28	42	76	108	140
6-10(4/53)	9	18	27	52	69	85
11-20	8	16	24	40	50	60
21-34: 25-Begin CBS Television Presents on-c	7	14	21	35	43	50

HECKLE AND JECKLE (TV) (See New Terrytoons)
Gold Key/Dell Publ. Co.: 11/62 - No. 4, 8/63; 5/66; No. 2, 10/66; No. 3, 8/67

	GD	VG	FN	VF	VF/NM	NM-
1 (11/62; Gold Key)	6	12	18	37	66	95
2-4	3	6	9	21	33	45
1 (5/66; Dell)	4	8	12	25	40	55
2,3	3	6	9	18	28	38

(See March of Comics No. 379, 472, 484)

HECKLE AND JECKLE 3-D
Spotlight Comics: 1987 - No. 2?, 1987 ($2.50)

	GD	VG	FN	VF	VF/NM	NM-
1,2						5.00

HECKLER, THE
DC Comics: Sept, 1992 - No. 6, Feb, 1993 ($1.25)

	GD	VG	FN	VF	VF/NM	NM-
1-6-T&M Bierbaum-s/Keith Giffen-c/a						3.00

HECTIC PLANET
Slave Labor Graphics 1998 ($12.95/$14.95)

	GD	VG	FN	VF	VF/NM	NM-
Book 1,2-r-Dorkin-s/a from Pirate Corp$ Vol. 1 & 2						15.00

HECTOR COMICS (The Keenest Teen in Town)
Key Publications: Nov, 1953 - No. 3, 1954

	GD	VG	FN	VF	VF/NM	NM-
1-Teen humor	7	14	21	37	46	55
2,3	5	10	15	22	26	30

HECTOR HEATHCOTE (TV)
Gold Key: Mar, 1964

	GD	VG	FN	VF	VF/NM	NM-
1 (10111-403)	6	12	18	40	73	105

HECTOR THE INSPECTOR (See Top Flight Comics)

HEDGE KNIGHT, THE
Image Comics: Aug, 2003 - No. 6, Apr, 2004 ($2.95, limited series)

	GD	VG	FN	VF	VF/NM	NM-
1-6-George R.R. Martin-s/Mike S. Miller-a. 1-Two covers by Kaluta and Miller						3.00
George R.R. Martin's The Hedge Knight HC (Marvel, 2006, $19.99) r/series; 2 covers						20.00
George R.R. Martin's The Hedge Knight SC (Marvel, 2007, $14.99) r/series						15.00
TPB (2004, $14.95) r/series plus new short story						15.00

HEDGE KNIGHT II: SWORN SWORD
Marvel Comics (Dabel Brothers): Jun, 2007 - No. 6, Jun, 2008 ($2.99, limited series)

	GD	VG	FN	VF	VF/NM	NM-
1-6-George R.R. Martin-s/Mike Miller-a. 1-Two covers by Yu & Miller, plus Miller B&W-c						3.00

Hedy Devine Comics #29 © MAR

Hellblazer #128 © DC

Hellblazer #293 © DC

	GD 2.0	VG 4.0	FN 6.0	VF 8.0	VF/NM 9.0	NM- 9.2
... HC (2008, $19.99) r/series; 2 covers						20.00
HEDY DEVINE COMICS (Formerly All Winners #21? or Teen #22?(6/47); Hedy of Hollywood #36 on; also see Annie Oakley, Comedy & Venus) **Marvel Comics (RCM)/Atlas #50:** No. 22, Aug, 1947 - No. 50, Sept, 1952						
22-1st app. Hedy Devine (also see Joker #32)	39	78	117	231	378	525
23,24,27-30: 23-Wolverton-a, 1 pg; Kurtzman's "Hey Look", 2 pgs. 24,27-30- "Hey Look" by Kurtzman, 1-3 pgs.	22	44	66	132	216	300
25-Classic "Hey Look" by Kurtzman, "Optical Illusion"	24	48	72	142	234	325
26- "Giggles 'n' Grins" by Kurtzman	20	40	60	117	189	260
31-34,36-50: 32-Anti-Wertham editorial	15	30	45	83	124	165
35-Four pgs. "Rusty" by Kurtzman	18	36	54	103	162	220
HEDY-MILLIE-TESSIE COMEDY (See Comedy Comics)						
HEDY WOLFE (Also see Patsy & Hedy & Miss America Magazine V1#2) **Atlas Publishing Co. (Emgee):** Aug, 1957						
1-Patsy Walker's rival; Al Hartley-c	14	28	42	80	115	150
HEE HAW (TV) **Charlton Press:** July, 1970 - No. 7, Aug, 1971						
1	4	8	12	27	44	60
2-7	3	6	9	18	28	38
HEIDI (See Dell Jr. Treasury No. 6)						
HEIDI SAHA (AN ILLUSTRATED HISTORY OF...) **Warren Publishing:** 1973 (500 printed)						
nn-Photo-c; an early Vampirella model for Warren (a FN/VF copy sold in 2011 for $776.75)						
HELEN OF TROY (Movie) **Dell Publishing Co.:** No. 684, Mar, 1956 (one-shot)						
Four Color 684-Buscema-a, photo-c	8	16	24	56	108	160
HELL **Dark Horse Comics:** July, 2003 - No. 4, Mar, 2004 ($2.99, limited series)						
1-4-Augustyn-s/Demong-a/Meglia-c						3.00
HELLBLAZER (John Constantine) (See Saga of Swamp Thing #37 & 2013 Constantine title) (Also see Books of Magic limited series) **DC Comics (Vertigo #63 on):** Jan, 1988 - No. 300, Apr, 2013 ($1.25-$2.99)						
1-(44 pgs.)-John Constantine; McKean-c thru #21	2	4	6	11	16	20
1-Special Edition (7/10, $1.00) r/#1 with "What's Next?" cover logo						3.00
2-5	1	2	3	5	7	9
6-8,10: 10-Swamp Thing cameo						6.00
9,19: 9-X-over w/Swamp Thing #76. 19-Sandman app.	1	2	3	5	6	8
11-18,20						6.00
21-26,28-30: 22-Williams-c. 24-Contains bound-in Shocker movie poster. 25,26-Grant Morrison scripts.						5.00
27-Gaiman scripts; Dave McKean-a; low print run	2	4	6	10	12	15
31-39: 36-Preview of World Without End.						4.00
40-($2.25, 52 pgs.)-Dave McKean-a & colors; preview of Kid Eternity						5.00
41-Ennis scripts begin; ends #83						5.00
42-49,51-74,76-99,101-119: 44,45-Sutton-a(i). 52-Glenn Fabry painted-c begin. 62-Special Death insert by McKean. 63-Silver metallic ink on-c. 77-Totleben-c. 84-Sean Phillips-c/a begins; Delano story. 85-88-Eddie Campbell story. 89-Paul Jenkins scripts begin						3.50
50,75,100,120: 50-($3.00, 52 pgs.). 75-($2.95, 52 pgs.). 100,120 ($3.50,48 pgs.)						4.00
121-199, 201-249, 251-274,276-299: 129-Ennis-s. 141-Bradstreet-a. 146-150-Corben-a. 151-Azzarello-s begin. 175-Carey-s begin; Dillon-a. 176-Begin $2.75-c. 182,183-Bermejo-a. 216-Mina-s begins. 220-Begin $2.99-c. 229-Carey-s/Leon-a. 234-Initial printing (white title logo) has missing text; corrected printing has lt. blue title logo. 265,266,271-274-Bisley-a. 268-271-Shade the Changing Man app.						3.00
200-($4.50) Carey-s/Dillon, Frusin, Manco-a						5.00
250-($3.99) Short stories by various; art by Lloyd, Phillips, Milligan; Bermejo-c						4.00
275-($4.99) Constantine's wedding; Bisley-c						5.00
300-($4.99) Last issue; Bisley-c						5.00
Annual 1 (1989, $2.95, 68 pgs.)-Bryan Talbot's 1st work in American comics						6.00
Annual 1 (Annual 2011 on cover, 2/12, $4.99)-Milligan-s/Bisley-a/c						5.00
Special 1 (1993, $3.95, 68 pgs.)-Ennis story; w/pin-ups.						5.00
...Black Flowers (2005, $14.99, TPB) r/#181-186						15.00
...Bloodlines (2007, $19.99, TPB) r/#47-50,52-55,59-61						20.00
...Damnation's Flame (1999, $16.95, TPB) r/#72-77						17.00
...Dangerous Habits (1997, $14.95, TPB) r/#41-46						15.00
...Fear and Loathing (1997, $14.95, TPB) r/#62-67						18.00
...Fear and Loathing (2nd printing, $17.95)						18.00
...: Freezes Over (2003, $14.95, TPB) r/#157-163						15.00

	GD 2.0	VG 4.0	FN 6.0	VF 8.0	VF/NM 9.0	NM- 9.2
...Good Intentions (2002, $12.95, TPB) r/#151-156						13.00
...Hard Time (2001, $9.95, TPB) r/#146-150						10.00
...Haunting (2003, $12.95, TPB) r/#134-139						13.00
...Highwater (2004, $19.95, TPB) r/#164-174						20.00
John Constantine Hellblazer: All His Engines HC (2005, $24.95, with dustjacket) new graphic novel; Mike Carey-s/Leonardo Manco-a						25.00
John Constantine Hellblazer: All His Engines SC (2006, $14.99) new graphic novel						15.00
John Constantine Hellblazer: Bloody Carnations SC (2011, $19.99) r/#267-275						20.00
John Constantine Hellblazer: Empathy is the Enemy SC (2006, $14.99) r/#216-222						15.00
John Constantine Hellblazer: Hooked SC (2010, $14.99) r/#256-260						15.00
John Constantine Hellblazer: India SC (2010, $14.99) r/#261-266						15.00
John Constantine Hellblazer: Joyride SC (2008, $14.99) r/#230-237						15.00
John Constantine Hellblazer: Pandemonium HC (2010, $24.99,with dustjacket) new graphic novel; Jamie Delano-s/Jock-a						25.00
John Constantine Hellblazer: Pandemonium SC (2011, $7.99) new graphic novel						18.00
John Constantine Hellblazer: Scab SC (2009, $14.99) r/#250-255						15.00
John Constantine Hellblazer: The Devil You Know SC (2007, $19.99) r/#10-13, Annual #1 and The Horrorist miniseries #1,2						20.00
John Constantine Hellblazer: The Family Man SC (2008, $19.99, TPB) r/#23,24,28-33						20.00
John Constantine Hellblazer: The Fear Machine SC (2008, $19.99, TPB) r/#14-22						20.00
John Constantine Hellblazer: The Red Right Hand SC (2007, $14.99) r/#223-228						15.00
John Const. Hellblazer: The Roots of Coincidence SC ('09, $14.99) r/#243,244,247-249						15.00
...Original Sins (1993, $19.95, TPB) r/#1-9						20.00
...Original Sins (2011, $19.99, TPB) r/#1-9						20.00
...Rake at the Gates of Hell (2003, $19.95, TPB) r/#78-83; Heartland #1						20.00
...: Rare Cuts (2005, $14.95, TPB) r/#11,25,26,35,56,84 & Vertigo Secret Files: Hellblazer						15.00
...: Reasons To Be Cheerful (2007, $14.99, TPB) r/#201-206						15.00
...: Red Sepulchre (2005, $12.99, TPB) r/#175-180						13.00
...: Setting Sun (2004, $12.95, TPB) r/#140-143						13.00
...: Son of Man (2004, $12.95, TPB) r/#129-133						13.00
...: Stations of the Cross (2006, $14.99, TPB) r/#194-200						15.00
...: Staring At The Wall (2005, $14.99, TPB) r/#187-193						15.00
...Tainted Love (1998, $16.95, TPB) r/#68-71, Vertigo Jam #1 and Hellblazer Special #1						17.00
NOTE: *Alcala a-8i, 9i, 18-22i.* ***Gaiman*** *scripts-27.* ***McKean*** *a-27,40; c-1-21.* ***Sutton*** *a-44i, 45i.* ***Talbot*** *a-Annual 1.*						
HELLBLAZER: CITY OF DEMONS **DC Comics (Vertigo):** Early Dec, 2010 - No. 5, Feb, 2011 ($2.99, limited series)						
1-5-Si Spencer-s/Sean Murphy-a/c						3.00
TPB (2011, $14.99) r/#1-5 & story from Vertigo Winter's Edge #3						15.00
HELLBLAZER SPECIAL: BAD BLOOD **DC Comics (Vertigo):** Sept, 2000 - No. 4, Dec, 2000 ($2.95, limited series)						
1-4-Delano-s/Bond-a; Constantine in 2025 London						3.00
HELLBLAZER SPECIAL: CHAS **DC Comics (Vertigo):** Sept, 2008 - No. 5, Jan, 2009 ($2.99, limited series)						
1-5-Story of Constantine's cab driver; Oliver-s/Sudzuka-a/Fabry-c						3.00
... - The Knowledge TPB (2009, $14.99) r/#1-5						15.00
HELLBLAZER SPECIAL: LADY CONSTANTINE **DC Comics (Vertigo):** Feb, 2003 - No. 4, May, 2003 ($2.95, limited series)						
1-4-Story of Johanna Constantine in 1785; Diggle-s/Sudzuka-a/Noto-c						3.00
HELLBLAZER/THE BOOKS OF MAGIC **DC Comics (Vertigo):** Dec, 1997 - No. 2, Jan, 1998 ($2.50, limited series)						
1,2-John Constantine and Tim Hunter						3.00
HELLBOY (Also see Batman/Hellboy/Starman, Danger Unlimited #4, Dark Horse Presents, Gen[13] #13B, Ghost/Hellboy, John Byrne's Next Men, San Diego Comic Con #2, & Savage Dragon)						
HELLBOY **Dark Horse Comics:** Apr, 2008						
... : Free Comic Book Day; Three short stories; Mignola-c; art by Fegredo, Davis, Azaceta						3.00
HELLBOY: ALMOST COLOSSUS **Dark Horse Comics (Legend):** Jun, 1997 - No. 2, Jul, 1997 ($2.95, lim. series)						
1,2-Mignola-s/a						5.00
HELLBOY/BEASTS OF BURDEN **Dark Horse Comics:** Oct, 2010 ($3.50, one-shot)						
... Sacrifice - Evan Dorkin & Mignola-s/Jill Thompson-a						3.50
HELLBOY: BEING HUMAN **Dark Horse Comics:** May, 2011 ($3.50, one-shot)						
nn-Mignola-s; Richard Corben-a/c; Roger app.						3.50
HELLBOY: BOX FULL OF EVIL **Dark Horse Comics:** Aug, 1999 - No. 2, Sept, 1999 ($2.95, lim. series)						
1,2-Mignola-s/a; back-up story w/ Matt Smith-a						4.00

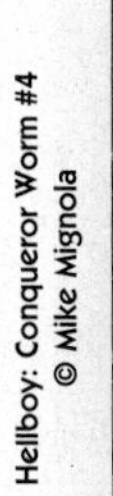
Hellboy: Conqueror Worm #4
© Mike Mignola

Hellboy: Wake the Devil #3
© Mike Mignola

Hellboy: Weird Tales #6
© Mike Mignola

	GD 2.0	VG 4.0	FN 6.0	VF 8.0	VF/NM 9.0	NM- 9.2

HELLBOY: BUSTER OAKLEY GETS HIS WISH
Dark Horse Comics: Apr, 2011 ($3.50, one-shot)
nn-Mignola-s; Kevin Nowlan-a; two covers by Mignola & Nowlan 3.50

HELLBOY CHRISTMAS SPECIAL
Dark Horse Comics: Dec, 1997 ($3.95, one-shot)
nn-Christmas stories by Mignola, Gianni, Darrow, Purcell 6.00

HELLBOY: CONQUEROR WORM
Dark Horse Comics: May, 2001 - No. 4, Aug, 2001 ($2.99, lim. series)
1-4-Mignola-s/a/c 4.00

HELLBOY: DARKNESS CALLS
Dark Horse Comics: Apr, 2007 - No. 6, Nov, 2007 ($2.99, lim. series)
1-6-Mignola-s/Fegredo-a 3.00

HELLBOY: DOUBLE FEATURE OF EVIL
Dark Horse Comics: Nov, 2010 ($3.50, one-shot)
1-Mignola-s; Corben-a/c 3.50

HELLBOY: HOUSE OF THE LIVING DEAD
Dark Horse Comics: Nov, 2011 ($14.99, hardcover graphic novel)
1-Mignola-s; Corben-a/c; Hellboy and Lucha Libre 15.00

HELLBOY IN HELL (Follows Hellboy's death in Hellboy: The Fury)
Dark Horse Comics: Dec, 2012 - No. 5, Dec, 2013($2.99)
1-5-Mignola-s/a/c 3.00
1-Variant "Year in Monsters" cover 5.00

HELLBOY IN MEXICO
Dark Horse Comics: May, 2010 ($3.50, one-shot)
1-Mignola-s; Corben-a/c; Mexican wrestlers vs. monsters 3.50

HELLBOY: IN THE CHAPEL OF MOLOCH
Dark Horse Comics: Oct, 2008 ($2.99, one-shot)
nn-Mignola-s/a/c 3.00

HELLBOY, JR.
Dark Horse Comics: Oct, 1999 - No. 2, Nov, 1999 ($2.95, limited series)
1,2-Stories and art by various 4.00
TPB (1/04, $14.95) r/#1&2, Halloween; sketch pages; intro. by Steve Niles; Bill Wray-c 15.00

HELLBOY, JR., HALLOWEEN SPECIAL
Dark Horse Comics: Oct, 1997 ($3.95, one-shot)
nn-"Harvey" style renditions of Hellboy characters; Bill Wray, Mike Mignola & various-s/a; wraparound-c by Wray 5.00

HELLBOY: MAKOMA, OR A TALE TOLD...
Dark Horse Comics: Feb, 2006 - No. 2, Mar, 2006 ($2.99, lim. series)
1,2-Mignola-s/c; Mignola & Corben-a 3.00

HELLBOY PREMIERE EDITION
Dark Horse Comics (Wizard): 2004 (no price, one-shot)
nn- Two covers by Mignola & Davis; Mignola-s/a; BPRD story w/Arcudi-s/Davis-a 5.00
Wizard World Los Angeles-Movie photo-c; Mignola-s/a; BPRD story w/Arcudi-s/Davis-a 10.00

HELLBOY: SEED OF DESTRUCTION (First Hellboy series)
Dark Horse Comics (Legend): Mar, 1994 - No. 4, Jun, 1994 ($2.50, lim. series)

	GD	VG	FN	VF	VF/NM	NM-
1-Mignola-c/a w/Byrne scripts; Monkeyman & O'Brien back-up story (origin) by Art Adams.	3	6	9	16	23	30
2-4	1	3	4	6	8	10

Hellboy: One for One (8/10, $1.00) r/#1 Hellboy story with red cover frame 3.00
Trade paperback (1994, $17.95)-collects all four issues plus r/Hellboy's 1st app. in San Diego Comic Con #2 & pin-ups 18.00
Limited edition hardcover (1995, $99.95)-includes everything in trade paperback plus additional material. 100.00

HELLBOY STRANGE PLACES
Dark Horse Books: Apr, 2006 ($17.95, TPB)
SC - Reprints Hellboy: The Third Wish #1,2 and Hellboy: The Island #1,2; sketch pages 18.00

HELLBOY: THE BRIDE OF HELL
Dark Horse Comics: Dec, 2009 ($3.50, one-shot)
1-Mignola-s/c; Corben-a; preview of The Marquis: Inferno 3.50

HELLBOY: THE CHAINED COFFIN AND OTHERS
Dark Horse Comics (Legend): Aug, 1998 ($17.95, TPB)
nn-Mignola-c/a/s; reprints out-of-print one shots; pin-up gallery 18.00

HELLBOY: THE COMPANION
Dark Horse Books: May, 2008 ($14.95, 9"x6", TPB)
nn-Overview of Hellboy history, characters, stories, mythology; text with Mignola panels 15.00

HELLBOY: THE CORPSE
Dark Horse Comics: Mar, 2004 (25¢, one-shot)
nn-Mignola-c/a/scripts; reprints "The Corpse" serial from Capitol City's Advance Comics catalog; development sketches and photos of the Corpse from the Hellboy movie 3.00

HELLBOY: THE CORPSE AND THE IRON SHOES
Dark Horse Comics (Legend): Jan, 1996 ($2.95, one-shot)
nn-Mignola-c/a/scripts; reprints "The Corpse" serial w/new story 5.00

HELLBOY: THE CROOKED MAN
Dark Horse Comics: Jul, 2008 - No. 3, Sept, 2008 ($2.99, lim. series)
1-3-Mignola-s/Corben-a/c 3.00

HELLBOY: THE FURY
Dark Horse Comics: Jun, 2011 - No. 3, Aug, 2011 ($2.99, lim. series)
1-3-Mignola-s/c; Fegredo-a. 1-Variant-c by Fegredo. 3-Hellboy dies 3.00

	GD	VG	FN	VF	VF/NM	NM-
3-Retailer Incentive Variant	20	40	60	100	150	200

HELLBOY: THE GOLDEN ARMY
Dark Horse Comics: Jan, 2008 (no cover price)
nn-Prelude to the 2008 movie; Del Toro & Mignola-s/Velasco-a; 3 photo covers 3.00

HELLBOY: THE ISLAND
Dark Horse Comics: June, 2005 - No. 2, July, 2005 ($2.99, lim. series)
1,2: Mignola-c/a & scripts 4.00

HELLBOY: THE MIDNIGHT CIRCUS
Dark Horse Books: Oct, 2013 ($14.99, hardcover graphic novel)
nn-Mignola-s/c; Fegredo-a; young Hellboy runs away from BPRD in 1948 15.00

HELLBOY: THE RIGHT HAND OF DOOM
Dark Horse Comics (Legend): Apr, 2000 ($17.95, TPB)
nn-Mignola-c/a/s; reprints 18.00

HELLBOY: THE SLEEPING AND THE DEAD
Dark Horse Comics: Dec, 2010 - No. 2, Feb, 2011 ($3.50, lim. series)
1,2-Mignola-s/Scott Hampton-a 3.50

HELLBOY: THE STORM
Dark Horse Comics: Jul, 2010 - No. 3, Sept, 2010 ($2.99, lim. series)
1-3-Mignola-s/Fegredo-a 3.00

HELLBOY: THE THIRD WISH
Dark Horse Comics (Maverick): July, 2002 - No. 2, Aug, 2002 ($2.99, limited series)
1,2-Mignola-c/a/s 4.00

HELLBOY THE TROLL WITCH AND OTHERS
Dark Horse Books: Nov, 2007 ($17.95, TPB)
SC - Reprints Hellboy: Makoma, Hellboy Premiere Edition and stories from Dark Horse Book of Hauntings, DHB of Witchcraft, DHB of the Dead, DHB of Monsters 18.00

HELLBOY: THE WILD HUNT
Dark Horse Comics: Dec, 2008 - No. 8, Nov, 2009 ($2.99, lim. series)
1-8: Mignola-c/s; Fegredo-a 3.00

HELLBOY: THE WOLVES OF ST. AUGUST
Dark Horse Comics (Legend): 1995 ($4.95, squarebound, one-shot)
nn-Mignola--c/a/scripts; r/Dark Horse Presents #88-91 with additional story 6.00

HELLBOY: WAKE THE DEVIL (Sequel to Seed of Destruction)
Dark Horse Comics (Legend): Jun, 1996 - No. 5, Oct, 1996 ($2.95, lim. series)
1-5: Mignola-c/a & scripts; The Monstermen back-up story by Gary Gianni 6.00
TPB (1997, $17.95) r/#1-5 18.00

HELLBOY: WEIRD TALES
Dark Horse Comics: Feb, 2003 - No. 8, Apr, 2004 ($2.99, limited series, anthology)
1-8-Hellboy stories from other creators. 1-Cassaday-c/s/a; Watson-s/a. 6-Cho-c 4.00
... Vol. 1 (2004, 17.95) r/#1-4 18.00
... Vol. 2 (2004, 17.95) r/#5-8 and Lobster Johnson serial from #1-8 18.00

HELLCAT
Marvel Comics: Sept, 2000 - No. 3, Nov, 2000 ($2.99)
1-3-Englehart-s/Breyfogle-a; Hedy Wolfe app. 3.00

HELLCOP
Image Comics (Avalon Studios): Aug, 1998 - No. 4, Mar, 1999 ($2.50)
1-4: 1-(Oct. on-c) Casey-s 3.00

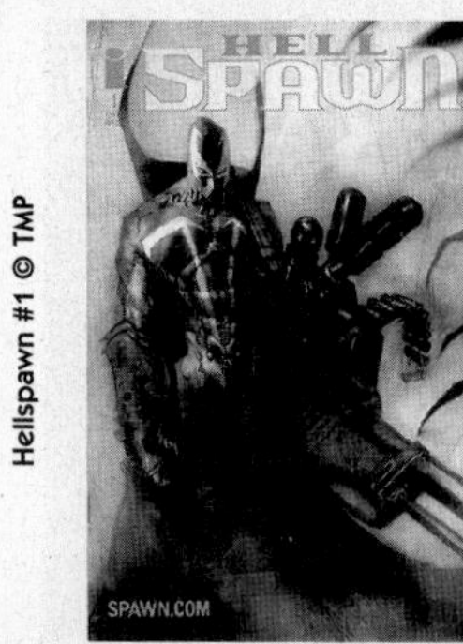

Hellspawn #1 © TMP

Helmet of Fate: Black Alice #1 © DC

Henry #2 © KING

	GD 2.0	VG 4.0	FN 6.0	VF 8.0	VF/NM 9.0	NM- 9.2

HELL ETERNAL
DC Comics (Vertigo Verité): 1998 ($6.95, squarebound, one-shot)

1-Delano-s/Phillips-a 7.00

HELLGATE: LONDON (Based on the video game)
Dark Horse Comics: No. 0, May 2006 - No. 3, Mar, 2007 ($2.99)

0-3-Edginton-s/Pugh-a/Briclot-c 3.00

HELLHOUNDS (...: Panzer Cops #3-6)
Dark Horse Comics: 1994 - No. 6, July, 1994 ($2.50, B&W, limited series)

1-6: 1-Hamner-c. 3-(4/94). 2-Joe Phillips-c 3.00

HELLHOUND, THE REDEMPTION QUEST
Marvel Comics (Epic Comics): Dec, 1993 - No. 4, Mar, 1994 ($2.25, lim. series, coated stock)

1-4 3.00

HELLO BUDDIES
Harvey Publications: 1953 (25¢, small size)

1	3	6	9	17	26	35

HELLO, I'M JOHNNY CASH
Spire Christian Comics (Fleming H. Revell Co.): 1976 (39¢/49¢)

nn-(39¢-c)	3	6	9	16	23	30
nn-(49¢-c)	2	4	6	11	16	20

HELL ON EARTH (See DC Science Fiction Graphic Novel)

HELLO PAL COMICS (Short Story Comics)
Harvey Publications: Jan, 1943 - No. 3, May, 1943 (Photo-c)

1-Rocketman & Rocketgirl begin; Yankee Doodle Jones app.; Mickey Rooney photo-c	63	126	189	403	689	975
2-Charlie McCarthy photo-c (scarce)	56	112	168	349	595	840
3-Bob Hope photo-c (scarce)	60	120	180	384	660	935

HELLRAISER (See Clive Barker's...)

HELLRAISER/NIGHTBREED – JIHAD (Also see Clive Barker's...)
Epic Comics (Marvel Comics): 1991 - Book 2, 1991 ($4.50, 52 pgs.)

Book 1,2 5.00

HELL-RIDER (Motorcycle themed magazine)
Skywald Publications: Aug, 1971 - No. 2, Oct, 1971 (B&W, 68 pgs.)

1-Origin & 1st app.; Butterfly & the Wild Bunch begin; 1st Hell-Rider by Andru, Esposito and Friedrich	5	10	15	35	63	90
2-Andru, Ayers, Buckler, Shores-a	4	8	12	27	44	60

NOTE: *#3 advertised in Psycho #5 but did not come out.* ***Buckler*** *a-1, 2.* ***Rosenbaum*** *c-1,2.*

HELL'S ANGEL (Becomes Dark Angel #6 on)
Marvel Comics UK: July, 1992 - No. 5, Nov, 1993 ($1.75)

1-5: X-Men (Wolverine, Cyclops)-c/stories. 1-Origin. 3-Jim Lee cover swipe 3.00

HELLSHOCK
Image Comics: July, 1994 - No. 4, Nov, 1994 ($1.95, limited series)

1-4-Jae Lee-c/a & scripts. 4-Variant-c. 3.00

HELLSHOCK
Image Comics: Jan, 1997 - No. 3, Jan, 1998 ($2.95/$2.50, limited series)

1-($2.95)-Jae Lee-c/s/a, Villarrubia-painted-a 4.00
2-($2.50) 3.00
Book 3: The Science of Faith (1/98, $2.50) Jae Lee-c/s/a, Villarrubia-painted-a 3.00
Vol. 1 HC (2006, $49.99) r/#1-3 re-colored, with unpublished 22 pg. conclusion; cover gallery and sketches; alternate opening art; intro. by Jim Lee 50.00

HELLSPAWN
Image Comics: Aug, 2000 - No. 16, Apr, 2003 ($2.50)

1-Bendis-s/Ashley Wood-c/a; Spawn and Clown app. 3.00
2-9: 6-Last Bendis-s; Mike Moran (Miracleman app.). 7-Niles-s 3.00
10-16-Templesmith-a 3.00
...: The Ashley Wood Collection Vol. 1 (4/06, $24.95, TPB) r/#1-10; sketch & cover gallery 25.00

HELLSTORM: PRINCE OF LIES (See Ghost Rider #1 & Marvel Spotlight #12)
Marvel Comics: Apr, 1993 - No. 21, Dec, 1994 ($2.00)

1-($2.95)-Parchment-c w/red thermographic ink 4.00
2-21: 14-Bound-in trading card sheet. 18-P. Craig Russell-c 3.00

HELLSTORM: SON OF SATAN
Marvel Comics (MAX): Dec, 2006 - No. 5, Apr, 2007 ($3.99, limited series)

1-5-Suydam-c/Irvine-s/Braun & Janson-a 4.00
... - Equinox TPB (2007, $17.99) r/#1-5; interviews with the creators 18.00

HELL YEAH
Image Comics: Mar, 2012 - Present ($2.99/$3.50)

1-5-Joe Keatinge-s/Andre Szymanowicz-a 3.00
6-($3.50) 3.50

HELMET OF FATE, THE (Series of one-shots following Doctor Fate's helmet)
DC Comics: Mar, 2007 - May 2007 ($2.99, one-shots)

...: Black Alice (5/07) Simone-s/Rouleau-a/c 3.00
...: Detective Chimp (3/07) Willingham-s/McManus-a/Bolland-c 3.00
...: Ibis the Invincible (3/07) Williams-s/Winslade-a; the Ibistick returns 3.00
...: Sargon the Sorcerer (4/07) Niles-s/Scott Hampton-s; debut new Sargon 3.00
...: Zauriel (4/07) Gerber-s/Snejbjerg-a/Kaluta-c; leads into new Doctor Fate series 3.00
TPB (2007, $14.99) r/one-shots 15.00

HE-MAN (See Masters Of The Universe)

HE-MAN (Also see Tops In Adventure)
Ziff-Davis Publ. Co. (Approved Comics): Fall, 1952

1-Kinstler painted-c; Powell-a	16	32	48	94	147	200

HE-MAN
Toby Press: May, 1954 - No. 2, July, 1954 (Painted-c by B. Safran)

1-Gorilla-c	15	30	45	88	137	185
2-Shark-c	15	30	45	85	130	175

HE-MAN AND THE MASTERS OF THE UNIVERSE
DC Comics: Sept, 2012 - No. 6, Mar, 2013 ($2.99)

1-6: 1-James Robinson-s/Philip Tan-a/c; Skeletor app. 5-Adam gets the sword 3.00

HE-MAN AND THE MASTERS OF THE UNIVERSE
DC Comics: Jun, 2013 - Present ($2.99)

1-11: 1-Giffen-s/Mhan-a/Benes-c. 7,8-Abnett-s/Kayanan-a 3.00

HENNESSEY (TV)
Dell Publishing Co.: No. 1200, Aug-Oct, 1961 - No. 1280, Mar-May, 1962

Four Color 1200-Gil Kane-a, photo-c	6	12	18	40	73	105
Four Color 1280-Photo-c	6	12	18	37	66	95

HENRY (Also see Little Annie Rooney)
David McKay Publications: 1935 (52 pgs.) (Daily B&W strip reprints)(10"x10" cardboard-c)

1-By Carl Anderson	40	80	120	244	402	560

HENRY (See King Comics & Magic Comics)
Dell Publishing Co.: No. 122, Oct, 1946 - No. 65, Apr-June, 1961

Four Color 122-All new stories begin	13	26	39	89	195	300
Four Color 155 (7/47), 1 (1-3/48)-All new stories	9	18	27	61	123	185
2	6	12	18	37	66	95
3-10	5	10	15	33	57	80
11-20: 20-Infinity-c	4	8	12	28	47	65
21-30	4	8	12	23	37	50
31-40	3	6	9	19	30	40
41-65	3	6	9	16	24	32

HENRY (See Giant Comic Album and March of Comics No. 43, 58, 84, 101, 112, 129, 147, 162, 178, 189)

HENRY ALDRICH COMICS (TV)
Dell Publishing Co.: Aug-Sept, 1950 - No. 22, Sept-Nov, 1954

1-Part series written by John Stanley; Bill Williams-a	9	18	27	58	114	170
2	5	10	15	34	60	85
3-5	5	10	15	30	50	70
6-10	4	8	12	27	44	60
11-22	4	8	12	23	37	50

HENRY BREWSTER
Country Wide (M.F. Ent.): Feb, 1966 - V2#7, Sept, 1967 (All 25¢ Giants)

1	3	6	9	18	28	38
2-6(12/66), V2#7-Powell-a in most	2	4	6	13	18	22

HEPCATS
Antarctic Press: Nov, 1996 - No. 12 ($2.95, B&W)

0-12-Martin Wagner-c/s/a: 0-color 3.00
0-($9.95) CD Edition 10.00

HERALDS
Marvel Comics: Aug, 2010 - No. 5, Aug, 2010 ($2.99, weelky limited series)

1-5-Kathryn Immonen-s/Zonjic & Harren-a; She-Hulk, Hellcat, Emma Frost, Photon app. 3.00

HERBIE (See Forbidden Worlds #73,94,110,114,116 & Unknown Worlds #20)
American Comics Group: April-May, 1964 - No. 23, Feb, 1967 (All 12¢)

Herbie #7 © ACG

Here's Howie Comics #9 © DC

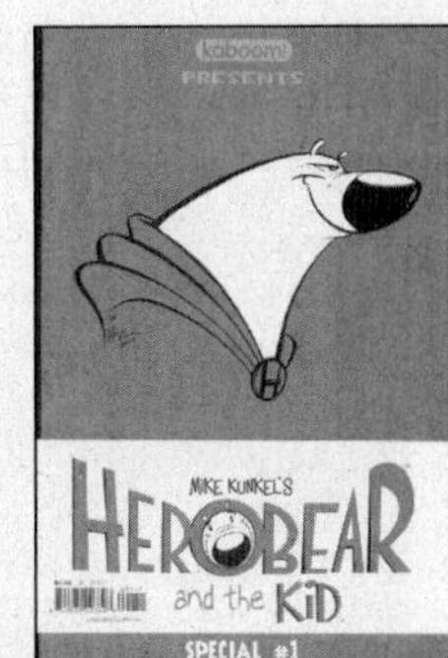

Herobear and the Kid Special #1 © Mike Kunkel

	GD 2.0	VG 4.0	FN 6.0	VF 8.0	VF/NM 9.0	NM- 9.2
1-Whitney-c/a in most issues	15	30	45	105	233	360
2-4	8	16	24	56	108	160
5-Beatles parody (10 pgs.), Dean Martin, Frank Sinatra app. (10-11/64)	9	18	27	61	123	185
6,7,9,10	7	14	21	48	89	130
8-Origin & 1st app. The Fat Fury	8	16	24	55	105	155
11-23: 14-Nemesis & Magicman app. 17-r/2nd Herbie from Forbidden Worlds #94. 23-r/1st Herbie from F.W. #73	6	12	18	37	66	95

... Archives Volume One HC (Dark Horse, 8/08, $49.95, dust jacket) r/earliest apps. in Forbidden Worlds, Unknown Worlds, and Herbie #1-5; Scott Shaw intro. 50.00

HERBIE
Dark Horse Comics: Oct, 1992 - No. 12, 1993 ($2.50, limited series)

1-Whitney-r plus new-c/a in all; Byrne-c/a & scripts 4.00
2-6: 3-Bob Burden-c/a. 4-Art Adams-c 3.00

HERBIE GOES TO MONTE CARLO, HERBIE RIDES AGAIN (See Walt Disney Showcase No. 24, 41)

HERC (Hercules from the Avengers)
Marvel Comics: Jun, 2011 - No. 10, Jan, 2012 ($2.99)

1-6, (6.1), 7-10: 1-Pak & Van Lente-s; Hobgoblin app. 3-6-Fear Itself tie-in. 6.1-Grell-a 7,8-Spider-Island tie-in; Herc gets Spider-powers. 10-Elektra app. 3.00

HERCULES (See Hit Comics #1-21, Journey Into Mystery Annual, Marvel Graphic Novel #37, Marvel Premiere #26 & The Mighty...)

HERCULES (See Charlton Classics)
Charlton Comics: Oct, 1967 - No. 13, Sept, 1969; Dec, 1968

	GD	VG	FN	VF	VF/NM	NM-
1-Thane of Bagarth begins; Glanzman-a in all	4	8	12	27	44	60
2-13: 1-5,7-10-Aparo-a. 8-(12¢-c)	4	8	12	23	37	50
4-Magazine format (low distribution)	8	16	24	54	102	150
8-Magazine format (low distribution)(12/68, 35¢, B&W); new Hercules story plus-r story/#1; Thane-r/#1-3	5	10	15	33	57	80

Modern Comics reprint 10('77), 11('78) 6.00

HERCULES (Prince of Power) (Also see The Champions)
Marvel Comics Group: V1#1, Sept, 1982 - V1#4, Dec, 1982; V2#1, Mar, 1984 - V2#4, Jun, 1984 (color, both limited series)

1-4, V2#1-4: Layton-c/a. 4-Death of Zeus. 4.00
NOTE: *Layton a-1, 2, 3p, 4p, V2#1-4; c-1-4, V2#1-4.*

HERCULES
Marvel Comics: Jun, 2005 - No. 5, Sept, 2005 ($2.99, limited series)

1-5-Texeira-a/c; Tieri-s. 4-Capt. America, Wolverine and New Avengers app. 3.00
...: New Labors of Hercules TPB (2005, $13.99) r/#1-5 14.00

HERCULES: HEART OF CHAOS
Marvel Comics: Aug, 1997 - No. 3, Oct, 1997 ($2.50, limited series)

1-3-DeFalco-s, Frenz-a 3.00

HERCULES: OFFICIAL COMICS MOVIE ADAPTION
Acclaim Books: 1997 ($4.50, digest size)

nn-Adaption of the Disney animated movie 4.50

HERCULES: THE LEGENDARY JOURNEYS (TV)
Topps Comics: June, 1996 - No. 5, Oct, 1996 ($2.95)

	GD	VG	FN	VF	VF/NM	NM-
1-2: 1-Golden-c.						3.00
3-Xena-c/app.	1	2	3	4	5	7
3-Variant-c	2	4	6	9	12	15
4,5: Xena-c/app.						5.00

HERCULES UNBOUND
National Periodical Publications: Oct-Nov, 1975 - No. 12, Aug-Sept, 1977

	GD	VG	FN	VF	VF/NM	NM-
1-Wood-i begins	2	4	6	9	13	16
2-12: 7-Adams ad. 10-Atomic Knights x-over	2	3	4	6	8	10

NOTE: ***Buckler** c-7p. **Layton** inks-No. 9, 10. **Simonson** a-7-10p, 11, 12; c- 8p, 9-12. **Wood** a-1-8i; c-7i, 8i.*

HERCULES (...Unchained #1121) (Movie)
Dell Publishing Co.: No. 1006, June-Aug, 1959 - No.1121, Aug, 1960

	GD	VG	FN	VF	VF/NM	NM-
Four Color 1006-Buscema-a, photo-c	8	16	24	51	96	140
Four Color 1121-Crandall/Evans-a	8	16	24	51	96	140

HERCULES: FALL OF AN AVENGER (Continues in Heroic Age: Prince of Power)
Marvel Comics: May, 2010 - No. 2, June, 2010 ($3.99, limited series)

1,2-Follows Hercules' demise in Incredible Hercules #141; Olivetti-c/a 4.00

HERCULES: TWILIGHT OF A GOD
Marvel Comics: Aug, 2010 - No. 4, Nov, 2010 ($3.99, limited series)

1-4-Layton-s/a(i); Lim-a; Galactus app. 4.00

HERCULIAN
Image Comics: Mar, 2011 ($4.99, oversized, one-shot)

1-Golden Age style superhero stories and humor pages; Erik Larsen-s/a/c 5.00

HERE COMES SANTA (See March of Comics No. 30, 213, 340)

HERE'S HOWIE COMICS
National Periodical Publications: Jan-Feb, 1952 - No. 18, Nov-Dec, 1954

	GD	VG	FN	VF	VF/NM	NM-
1	30	60	90	177	289	400
2	16	32	48	94	147	200
3-5: 5-Howie in the Army issues begin (9-10/52)	14	28	42	80	115	150
6-10	12	24	36	69	97	125
11-18	11	22	33	64	90	115

Ashcan (1,2/51) not distributed to newsstands (a FN copy sold for $836.50 in 2012)

HERETIC, THE
Dark Horse (Blanc Noir): Nov, 1996 - No. 4, Mar, 1997 ($2.95, lim. series)

1-4:-w/back-up story 3.00

HERITAGE OF THE DESERT (See Zane Grey, 4-Color 236)

HERMAN & KATNIP (See Harvey Comics Hits #60 & 62, Harvey Hits #14,25,31,41 & Paramount Animated Comics #1)

HERMES VS. THE EYEBALL KID
Dark Horse Comics: Dec, 1994 - No. 3,Feb, 1995 ($2.95, B&W, limited series)

1-3: Eddie Campbell-c/a/scripts 3.00

H-E-R-O (Dial H For HERO)
DC Comics: Apr, 2003 - No. 22, Jan, 2005 ($2.50)

1-Will Pfeiffer-s/Kano-a/Van Fleet-c 3.50
2-22: 2-6-Kano-a. 7,8-Gleason-a. 12-14-Kirk-a. 15-22-Robby Reed app. 3.00
...: Double Feature (6/03, $4.95) r/#1&2 5.00
...: Powers and Abilities (2003, $9.95) r/#1-6; intro. by Geoff Johns 10.00

HERO (Warrior of the Mystic Realms)
Marvel Comics: May, 1990 - No. 6, Oct, 1990 ($1.50, limited series)

1-6: 1-Portacio-i 3.00

HERO ALLIANCE, THE
Sirius Comics: Dec, 1985 - No. 2, Sept, 1986 (B&W)

1,2: 2-($1.50), Special Edition 1 (7/86, color) 3.00

HERO ALLIANCE
Wonder Color Comics: May, 1987 ($1.95)

1-Ron Lim-a 3.00

HERO ALLIANCE
Innovation Publishing: V2#1, Sept, 1989 - V2#17, Nov, 1991 ($1.95, 28 pgs.)

V2#1-17: 1,2-Ron Lim-a 3.00
Annual 1 (1990, $2.75, 36 pgs.)-Paul Smith-c/a 3.00
Special 1 (1992, $2.50, 32 pgs.)-Stuart Immonen-a (10 pgs.) 3.00

HERO ALLIANCE: END OF THE GOLDEN AGE
Innovation Publ.: July, 1989 - No. 3, Aug, 1989 ($1.75, bi-weekly lim. series)

1-3: Bart Sears & Ron Lim-c/a; reprints & new-a 3.00

HEROBEAR AND THE KID
Boom Entertainment (KaBOOM!)

... 2013 Annual 1 (10/13, $3.99) Halloween-themed story 4.00
... Special (6/13, $3.99) Mike Kunkel-s/a/c 4.00
...: The Inheritance (8/13 - No. 5, 12/13, $3.99) 1-5-Mike Kunkel-s/a/c; origin re-told 4.00

HERO COMICS (Hero Initiative benefit book)
IDW Publishing: 2009, 2011 ($3.99)

1-Short story anthology by various incl. Colan, Chaykin; covers by Wagner & Campbell 4.00
2011-Covers by Campbell & Hughes; Gaiman-s/Kieth-a; Chew & Elephantmen app. 4.00
2012-Cover by Campbell; TMNT by Eastman; art by Heath, Sim, Kupperberg, & others 4.00

HEROES
Marvel Comics: Dec, 2001 ($3.50, magazine-size, one-shot)

1-Pin-up tributes to the rescue workers of the Sept. 11 tragedy; art and text by various; cover by Alex Ross 6.00
1-2nd and 3rd printings 4.00

HEROES (Also see Shadow Cabinet & Static)
DC Comics (Milestone): May, 1996 - No. 6, Nov, 1996 ($2.50, limited series)

1-6: 1-Intro Heroes (Iota, Donner, Blitzen, Starlight, Payback & Static) 3.00

HEROES (Based on the NBC TV series)
DC Comics (WildStorm): 2007; 2009 ($29.99, hardcover with dustjacket)

Vol. 1 - Collects 34 installments of the online graphic novel; art by various; two covers by

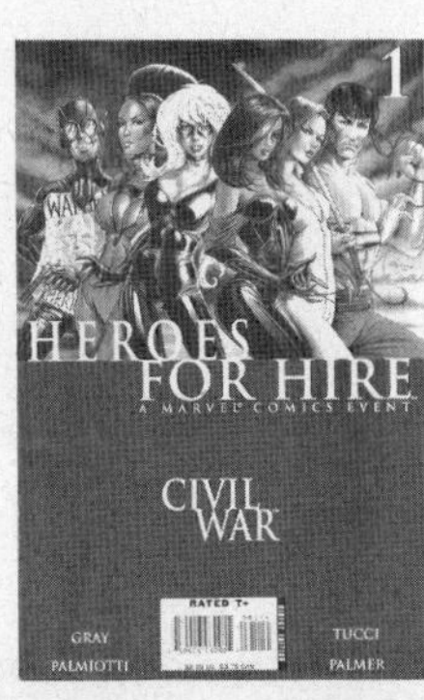

Heroes For Hire (2006 series) #1 © MAR

Hero For Hire #1 © MAR

Heroic Comics #18 © EAS

	GD 2.0	VG 4.0	FN 6.0	VF 8.0	VF/NM 9.0	NM- 9.2

Jim Lee and Alex Ross; intro. by Masi Oka; Jeph Loeb interview 30.00
Vol. 2 - (2009) Collects 46 installments of the online graphic novel; art by various incl. Gaydos, Grummett, Gunnell, Odagawa; two covers by Tim Sale and Gene Ha 30.00

HER-OES
Marvel Comics: Jun, 2010 - No. 4, Sept, 2010 ($2.99, limited series)
1-4-Randolph-s/Rousseau-a; Wasp, She-Hulk, Namora as teenagers 3.00

HEROES AGAINST HUNGER
DC Comics: 1986 ($1.50; one-shot for famine relief)
1-Superman, Batman app.; Neal Adams-c(p); includes many artists work; Jeff Jones assist (2 pg.) on B. Smith-a; Kirby-a 5.00

HEROES ALL CATHOLIC ACTION ILLUSTRATED
Heroes All Co.: 1943 - V6#5, Mar 10, 1948 (paper covers)
V1#1-(16 pgs., 8x11") 24 48 72 142 234 325
V1#2-(16 pgs., 8x11") 19 38 57 111 176 240
V2#1(1/44)-3(3/44)-(16 pgs., 8x11") 15 30 45 94 147 200
V3#1(1/45)-10(12/45)-(16 pgs., 8x11") 15 30 45 85 130 175
V4#1-35 (12/20/46)-(16 pgs.) 14 28 42 80 115 150
V5#1(1/10/47)-8(2/28/47)-(16 pgs.), V5#9(3/7/47)-20(11/25/47)-(32 pgs.), V6#1(1/10/48)-5(3/10/48)-(32 pgs.) 12 24 36 69 97 125

HEROES ANONYMOUS
Bongo Comics: 2003 - No. 6, 2004 ($2.99, limited series)
1-6-($2.99)-Bill Morrison-c. 2-Guerra-a. 3-Pepoy-a 3.00

HEROES FOR HIRE
Marvel Comics: July, 1997 - No. 19, Jan, 1999 ($2.99/$1.99)
1-($2.99)-Wraparound cover 5.00
2-19: 2-Variant cover. 7-Thunderbolts app. 9-Punisher-c/app. 10,11-Deadpool-c/app. 18,19-Wolverine-c/app. 3.00
.../Quicksilver '98 Annual ($2.99) Siege of Wundagore pt.5 4.00

HEROES FOR HIRE
Marvel Comics: Oct, 2006 - No. 15, Dec, 2007 ($2.99)
1-5-Tucci-a/c; Black Cat, Shang-Chi, Tarantula, Humbug & Daughters of the Dragon app. 3.00
6-15: 6-8-Sparacio-c. 9,10-Golden-c. 11-13-World War Hulk x-over. 13-Takeda-c 3.00
... Vol. 1: Civil War (2007, $13.99) r/#1-5 14.00
... Vol. 2: Ahead of the Curve (2007, $13.99) r/#6-10 14.00
... Vol. 3: World War Hulk (2008, $13.99) r/#11-15 14.00

HEROES FOR HIRE
Marvel Comics: Feb, 2011 - No. 12, Nov, 2011 ($3.99/$2.99)
1-($3.99) Abnett & Lanning-s/Walker-a; back-up history of the various teams 4.00
2-12-($2.99) 2-Silver Sable & Ghost Rider app. 5-Punisher app. 9-11-Fear Itself tie-in 3.00

HEROES FOR HOPE STARRING THE X-MEN
Marvel Comics Group: Dec, 1985 ($1.50, one-shot, 52 pgs., proceeds donated to famine relief)
1-Stephen King scripts; Byrne, Miller, Corben-a; Wrightson/J. Jones-a (3 pgs.); Art Adams-c; Starlin back-c 1 2 3 5 6 8

HEROES, INC. PRESENTS CANNON
Wally Wood/CPL/Gang Publ.: 1969 - No. 2, 1976 (Sold at Army PXs)
nn-Ditko, Wood-a; Wood-c; Reese-a(p) 2 4 6 9 12 15
2-Wood-c; Ditko, Byrne, Wood-a; 8-1/2x10-1/2"; B&W; $2.00 3 6 9 16 23 30
NOTE: *First issue not distributed by publisher; 1,800 copies were stored and 900 copies were stolen from warehouse. Many copies have surfaced in recent years.*

HEROES OF THE WILD FRONTIER (Formerly Baffling Mysteries)
Ace Periodicals: No. 27, Jan, 1956 - No. 2, Apr, 1956
27(#1),2-Davy Crockett, Daniel Boone, Buffalo Bill 6 12 18 29 36 42

HEROES REBORN (one-shots)
Marvel Comics: Jan, 2000 ($1.99)
...:Ashema; ...:Doom; ...:Doomsday; ...:Masters of Evil; ...:Rebel; ...:Remnants; ...:Young Allies 3.00

HEROES REBORN: THE RETURN (Also see Avengers, Fantastic Four, Iron Man & Captain America titles for issues and TPBs)
Marvel Comics: Dec, 1997 - No. 4 ($2.50, weekly mini-series)
1-4-Avengers, Fantastic Four, Iron Man & Captain America rejoin regular Marvel Universe; Peter David-s/Larocca-c/a 4.00
1-4-Variant-c for each 6.00
Wizard 1/2 1 2 3 5 7 9
Return of the Heroes TPB ('98, $14.95) r/#1-4 15.00

HERO FOR HIRE (Power Man No. 17 on; also see Cage)
Marvel Comics Group: June, 1972 - No. 16, Dec, 1973
1-Origin & 1st app. Luke Cage; Tuska-a(p) 15 30 45 103 227 350
2-Tuska-a(p) 6 12 18 38 69 100
3-5: 3-1st app. Mace. 4-1st app. Phil Fox of the Bugle 4 8 12 28 47 65
6-10: 8,9-Dr. Doom app. 9-F.F. app. 3 6 9 19 30 40
11-16: 14-Origin retold. 15-Everett Sub-Mariner-r('53). 16-Origin Stilletto; death of Rackham 3 6 9 16 23 30

HERO HOTLINE (1st app. in Action Comics Weekly #637)
DC Comics: April, 1989 - No. 6, Sept, 1989 ($1.75, limited series)
1-6: Super-hero humor; Schaffenberger-i 3.00

HEROIC ADVENTURES (See Adventures)

HEROIC AGE
Marvel Comics: Nov, 2010 ($3.99, limited series)
... Heroes 1 (11/10, $3.99) profile of heroes, bios, pros, cons, "power grid"; Raney-c 4.00
... Villains 1 (1/11, $3.99) profile of villains, bios, pros, cons, "power grid"; Jae Lee-c 4.00
... X-Men 1 (2/11, $3.99) profile of members in Steve Rogers journal entries,; Jae Lee-c 4.00

HEROIC AGE: PRINCE OF POWER (Continued from Hercules: Fall of an Avenger)
Marvel Comics: Jul, 2010 - No. 4, Oct, 2010 ($3.99, limited series)
1-4-Van Lente & Pak-s; Thor app.; leads into Chaos War #1 4.00

HEROIC COMICS (Reg'lar Fellers...#1-15; New Heroic #41 on)
Eastern Color Printing Co./Famous Funnies (Funnies, Inc. No. 1):
Aug, 1940 - No. 97, June, 1955
1-Hydroman (origin) by Bill Everett, The Purple Zombie (origin) & Mann of India by Tarpe Mills begins (all 1st apps.) 206 412 618 1318 2259 3200
2 84 168 252 538 919 1300
3,4 53 106 159 334 567 800
5,6 45 90 135 284 480 675
7-Origin & 1st app. Man O'Metal (1 pg.) 47 94 141 298 504 710
8-10: 10-Lingerie panels 36 72 108 216 351 485
11,13 34 68 102 199 325 450
12-Music Master (origin/1st app.) begins by Everett, ends No. 31; last Purple Zombie & Mann of India 38 76 114 226 368 510
14,15-Hydroman x-over in Rainbow Boy. 14-Origin & 1st app. Rainbow Boy (super hero). 15-1st app. Downbeat 36 72 108 216 351 485
16-20: 16-New logo. 17-Rainbow Boy x-over in Hydroman. 19-Rainbow Boy x-over in Hydroman & vice versa 25 50 75 147 241 335
21-30:25-Rainbow Boy x-over in Hydroman. 28-Last Man O'Metal. 29-Last Hydroman 19 38 57 111 176 240
31,34,38 9 18 27 50 65 80
32,36,37-Toth-a (3-4 pgs. each) 10 20 30 56 76 95
33,35-Toth-a (8 & 9 pgs.) 10 20 30 58 79 100
39-42-Toth, Ingels-a 10 20 30 58 79 100
43,46,47,49-Toth-a (2-4 pgs.). 47-Ingels-a 10 20 30 54 72 90
44,45,50-Toth-a (6-9 pgs.) 10 20 30 56 76 95
48,53,54 9 18 27 47 61 75
51-Williamson-a 10 20 30 56 76 95
52-Williamson-a (3 pg. story) 9 18 27 50 65 80
55-Toth-a 10 20 30 54 72 90
56-60: 60-Everett-a 9 18 27 50 65 80
61-Everett-a 9 18 27 47 61 75
62,64-Everett-c/a 10 20 30 54 72 90
63-Everett-c 9 18 27 52 69 85
65-Williamson/Frazetta-a; Evans-a (2 pgs.) 13 26 39 72 101 130
66,75,94-Frazetta-a (2 pgs. each) 9 18 27 52 69 85
67,73-Frazetta-a (4 pgs. each) 11 22 33 60 83 105
68,74,76-80,84,85,88-93,95-97: 95-Last pre-code 9 18 27 47 61 75
69,72-Frazetta-a (6 & 8 pgs. each); 1st (?) app. Frazetta Red Cross ad 13 26 39 72 101 130
70,71,86,87-Frazetta, 3-4 pgs. each; 1 pg. ad by Frazetta in #70 10 20 30 56 76 95
81,82-Frazetta art (1 pg. each): 81-1st (?) app. Frazetta Boy Scout ad (tied w/ Buster Crabbe #9 9 18 27 50 65 80
83-Frazetta-a (1/2 pg.) 9 18 27 50 65 80
NOTE: ***Evans** a-64, 65. **Everett** a-(Hydroman-c/a-No. 1-9), 44, 60-64; c-1-9, 62-64. **Harvey Fuller** c-28-35. **Sid Greene** a-38-43, 46. **Guardineer** a-42(3), 43, 44, 45(2), 49(3), 50, 60, 61(2), 65, 67(2) 70-72. **Ingels** c-41. **Kiefer** a-46, 48; c-19-22, 24, 44, 46, 48, 51-53, 65, 67-69, 71-74, 76, 77, 79, 80, 82, 85, 86, 88, 89, 94, 95. **Mort Lawrence** a-45. **Tarpe Mills** a-2(2), 3(2), 10. **Ed Moore** a-49, 52-54, 56-63, 65-69, 72-74, 76, 77. **H.G. Peter** a-58-74, 76, 77, 87. **Paul Reinman** a-49. **Rico** a-31. Captain Tootsie by **Beck**-31, 32. Painted-c #16 on. Hydroman c-1-11. Music Master c-12, 13, 15. Rainbow Boy c-14.*

HERO INITIATIVE: MIKE WIERINGO BOOK (Also see Hero Comics)

Hickory #6 © QUA

Hi-Ho Comics #1 © Four Star

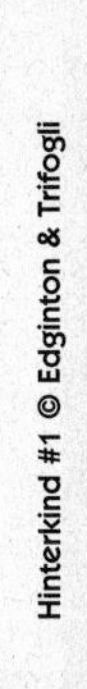
Hinterkind #1 © Edginton & Trifogli

	GD 2.0	VG 4.0	FN 6.0	VF 8.0	VF/NM 9.0	NM- 9.2

Marvel Comics: Aug, 2008 ($4.99)

1-The "What If" Fantastic Four story with Wieringo-a (7 pgs.) finished by other artists after his passing; art by Davis, Immonen, Ramos, Kitson and others; written tributes						5.00

HERO WORSHIP
Avatar Press: Jun, 2012 - No. 6, Nov, 2012 ($3.99)

1-6: 1-Zak Penn & Scott Murphy-s/Michael DiPascale-a; 2 covers						4.00

HERO ZERO (Also see Comics' Greatest World & Godzilla Versus Hero Zero)
Dark Horse Comics: Sept, 1994 ($2.50)

0						3.00

HEX (Replaces Jonah Hex)
DC Comics: Sept, 1985 - No. 18, Feb, 1987 (Story cont'd from Jonah Hex # 92)

1-Hex in post-atomic war world; origin	2	4	6	8	10	12
2-10,14-18: 6-Origin Stiletta	1	2	3	4	5	7
11-13: All contain future Batman storyline. 13-Intro The Dogs of War (origin #15)	1	3	4	6	8	10

NOTE: ***Giffen** a(p)-15-18; c(p)-15,17,18. **Texeira** a-1, 2p, 3p, 5-7p, 9p, 11-14p; c(p)-1, 2, 4-7, 12.*

HEXBREAKER (See First Comics Graphic Novel #15)

HEY THERE, IT'S YOGI BEAR (See Movie Comics)

HI-ADVENTURE HEROES (TV)
Gold Key: May, 1969 - No. 2, Aug, 1969 (Hanna-Barbera)

1-Three Musketeers, Gulliver, Arabian Knights	5	10	15	30	50	70
2-Three Musketeers, Micro-Venture, Arabian Knights	4	8	12	27	44	60

HI AND LOIS
Dell Publishing Co.: No. 683, Mar, 1956 - No. 955, Nov, 1958

Four Color 683 (#1)	5	10	15	30	50	70
Four Color 774(3/57),955	4	8	12	25	40	55

HI AND LOIS
Charlton Comics: Nov, 1969 - No. 11, July, 1971

1	3	6	9	14	20	25
2-11	2	4	6	9	12	15

HICKORY (See All Humor Comics)
Quality Comics Group: Oct, 1949 - No. 6, Aug, 1950

1-Sahl-c/a in all; Feldstein?-a	20	40	60	118	192	265
2	13	26	39	72	101	130
3-6	11	22	33	60	83	105

HIDDEN CREW, THE (See The United States Air Force Presents:...)

HIDE-OUT (See Zane Grey, Four Color No. 346)

HIDING PLACE, THE
Spire Christian Comics (Fleming H. Revell Co.): 1973 (39¢/49¢)

nn	2	4	6	13	18	22

HIGH ADVENTURE
Red Top(Decker) Comics (Farrell): Oct, 1957

1-Krigstein-r from Explorer Joe (re-issue on-c)	5	10	15	23	28	32

HIGH ADVENTURE (TV)
Dell Publishing Co.: No. 949, Nov, 1958 - No. 1001, Aug-Oct, 1959 (Lowell Thomas)

Four Color 949 (#1)-Photo-c	5	10	15	33	57	80
Four Color 1001-Lowell Thomas'...(#2)	5	10	15	31	53	75

HIGH CHAPPARAL (TV)
Gold Key: Aug, 1968 (Photo-c)

1 (10226-808)-Tufts-a	5	10	15	35	63	90

HIGHLANDER
Dynamite Entertainment: No. 0, 2006 - No. 12, 2007 (25¢/$2.99)

0-(25¢-c) Takes place after the first movie; photo-c and Dell'Otto painted-c						3.00
1-12: 1-($2.99) Three covers; Moder-a/Jerwa & Oeming-s. 2-Three covers						3.00
... Origins: The Kurgan 1,2 (2009 - No. 2, 2009, $4.99) Three covers; Rafael-a						5.00
...: Way of the Sword (2007 - No. 4, 2008, $3.50) Two interlocking covers for each						3.50

HIGH ROADS
DC Comics (Cliffhanger): June, 2002 - No. 6, Nov, 2002 ($2.95, limited series)

1-6-Leinil Yu-c/a; Lobdell-s						3.00
TPB (2003, $14.95) r/#1-6; sketch pages						15.00

HIGH SCHOOL CONFIDENTIAL DIARY (Confidential Diary #12 on)
Charlton Comics: June, 1960 - No. 11, Mar, 1962

1	4	8	12	27	44	60
2-11	3	6	9	17	26	35

HIGHWAYMEN
DC Comics (WildStorm): Aug, 2007 - No. 5, Dec, 2007 ($2.99)

1-5-Bernardin & Freeman-s/Garbett-a						3.00
TPB (2008, $17.99) r/#1-5						18.00

HIGH WAYS, THE
IDW Publishing: Dec, 2012 - No. 4, Apr, 2013 ($3.99, limited series)

1-4-John Byrne-s/a/c						4.00

HI HI PUFFY AMIYUMI (Based on Cartoon Network animated series)
DC Comics: Apr, 2006 - No. 3, June, 2006 ($2.25, limited series)

1-3-Phil Moy-a						3.00

HI-HO COMICS
Four Star Publications: nd (2/46?) - No. 3, 1946

1-Funny Animal; L. B. Cole-c	37	74	111	222	361	500
2,3: 2-L. B. Cole-c	21	42	63	122	199	275

HI-JINX (Teen-age Animal Funnies)
La Salle Publ. Co./B&I Publ. Co. (American Comics Group)/Creston: 1945; July-Aug, 1947 - No. 7, July-Aug, 1948

nn-(© 1945, 25 cents, 132 Pgs.)(La Salle)	28	56	84	165	270	375
1-Teen-age, funny animal	20	40	60	114	182	250
2,3	14	28	42	76	108	140
4-7-Milt Gross. 4-X-Mas-c	19	38	57	111	176	240

HI-LITE COMICS
E. R. Ross Publishing Co.: Fall, 1945

1-Miss Shady	21	42	63	122	199	275

HILLBILLY COMICS
Charlton Comics: Aug, 1955 - No. 4, July, 1956 (Satire)

1-By Art Gates	9	18	27	52	69	85
2-4	7	14	21	35	43	50

HILLY ROSE'S SPACE ADVENTURES
Astro Comics: May, 1995 - No. 9 ($2.95, B&W)

1	1	2	3	5	7	9
2-9						5.00
Trade Paperback (1996, $12.95)-r/#1-5						13.00

HINTERKIND
DC Comics (Vertigo): Dec, 2013 - Present ($2.99)

1-6: 1-Ian Edginton-s/Francesco Trifogli-a/Greg Tocchini-c						3.00

HIP FLASK (Also see Elephantmen)
Active Images/Image Comics

...: Ouroborous (12/12, $4.99) Starkings-s/Ladronn-a						5.00
... Unnatural Selection (9/02, $2.99) Casey & Starkings-s/Ladronn-a; var.-c by Madureira, Campbell, Churchill						3.00

HIP-IT-TY HOP (See March of Comics No. 15)

HIRE, THE (BMWfilms.com's...)
Dark Horse Comics: July, 2004 - No. 6 ($2.99)

1-4: 1-Matt Wagner-s/Wagner & Velasco-a. 2-Bruce Campbell-s/Plunkett-a. 3-Waid-s						3.00
TPB (4/06, $17.95) r/#1-4						18.00

HI-SCHOOL ROMANCE (...Romances No. 41 on)
Harvey Publ./True Love(Home Comics): Oct, 1949 - No. 5, June, 1950; No. 6, Dec, 1950 - No. 73, Mar, 1958; No. 74, Sept, 1958 - No. 75, Nov, 1958

1-Photo-c	15	30	45	90	140	190
2-Photo-c	10	20	30	56	76	95
3-9: 3-5-Photo-c	9	18	27	47	61	75
10-Rape story	10	20	30	56	76	95
11-20	8	16	24	40	50	60
21-31	6	12	18	31	38	45
32- "Unholy passion" story	9	18	27	50	65	80
33-36: 36-Last pre-code (2/55)	6	12	18	29	36	42
37-53,59-72,74,75	5	10	15	24	30	35
54-58,73-Kirby-c	6	12	18	31	38	45

NOTE: ***Powell** a-1-3, 5, 8, 12-16, 18, 21-23, 25-27, 30-34, 36, 37, 39, 45-48, 50-52, 57, 58, 60, 64, 65, 67, 69.*

HI-SCHOOL ROMANCE DATE BOOK
Harvey Publications: Nov, 1962 - No. 3, Mar, 1963 (25¢ Giants)

1-Powell, Baker-a	5	10	15	35	63	90
2,3	3	6	9	21	33	45

Hit Comics #13 © QUA

Hit-Girl #5 © Millarworld & John Romita Jr.

Holiday Comics #5 © STAR

GD 2.0 | VG 4.0 | FN 6.0 | VF 8.0 | VF/NM 9.0 | NM- 9.2

HIS NAME IS SAVAGE (Magazine format)
Adventure House Press: June, 1968 (35¢, 52 pgs.)
1-Gil Kane-a 5 10 15 31 53 75

HI-SPOT COMICS (Red Ryder No. 1 & No. 3 on)
Hawley Publications: No. 2, Nov, 1940
2-David Innes of Pellucidar; art by J. C. Burroughs; written by Edgar Rice Burroughs
145 290 435 921 1586 2250

HISTORY OF THE DC UNIVERSE (Also see Crisis on Infinite Earths)
DC Comics: Sept, 1986 - No. 2, Nov, 1986 ($2.95, limited series)
1,2: 1-Perez-c/a 5.00
Limited Edition hardcover 4 8 12 26 41 55
Softcover (2002, $9.95) new Alex Ross wraparound-c 13.00
Softcover (2009, $12.99) Alex Ross wraparound-c 13.00

HISTORY OF VIOLENCE, A (Inspired the 2005 movie)
DC Comics (Paradox Press) 1997 ($9.95, B&W graphic novel)
nn-Paperback ($9.95) John Wagner-s/Vince Locke-a 15.00

HIT
BOOM! Studios: Sept, 2013 - No. 4, Dec, 2013 ($3.99, limited series)
1-4-Bryce Carlson-s/Vanesa R. Del Ray-a/Ryan Sook-c 4.00

HITCHHIKERS GUIDE TO THE GALAXY (See Life, the Universe and Everything & Restaurant at the End of the Universe)
DC Comics: 1993 - No. 3, 1993 ($4.95, limited series)
1-3: Adaptation of Douglas Adams book 5.00
TPB (1997, $14.95) r/#1-3 15.00

HIT COMICS
Quality Comics Group: July, 1940 - No. 65, July, 1950
1-Origin/1st app. Neon, the Unknown & Hercules; intro. The Red Bee; Bob & Swab, Blaze Barton, the Strange Twins, X-5 Super Agent, Casey Jones & Jack & Jill (ends #7) begin
811 1622 2433 5920 10,460 15,000
2-The Old Witch begins, ends #14 303 606 909 2121 3711 5300
3-Casey Jones ends; transvestism story "Jack & Jill"
300 600 900 2070 3635 5200
4-Super Agent (ends #17), & Betty Bates (ends #65) begin; X-5 ends
284 568 852 1818 3109 4400
5-Classic Lou Fine cover 811 1622 2433 5920 10,460 15,000
6-10: 10-Old Witch by Crandall (4 pgs.); 1st work in comics (4/41)
232 464 696 1485 2543 3600
11-Classic cover 271 542 813 1734 2967 4200
12-17: 13-Blaze Barton ends. 17-Last Neon; Crandall Hercules in all; Last Lou Fine-c
139 278 417 883 1517 2150
18-Origin & 1st app. Stormy Foster, the Great Defender (12/41); The Ghost of Flanders begins; Crandall-c 145 290 435 921 1586 2250
19,20 116 232 348 742 1271 1800
21-24: 21-Last Hercules. 24-Last Red Bee & Strange Twins
113 226 339 718 1234 1750
25-Origin & 1st app. Kid Eternity and begins by Moldoff (12/42); 1st app. The Keeper (Kid Eternity's aide) 210 420 630 1334 2292 3250
26-Blackhawk x-over in Kid Eternity 100 200 300 635 1093 1550
27-29 52 104 156 328 552 775
30,31- "Bill the Magnificent" by Kurtzman, 11 pgs. in each
47 94 141 296 498 700
32-40: 32-Plastic Man x-over. 34-Last Stormy Foster
31 62 93 182 296 410
41-50 22 44 66 128 209 290
51-60-Last Kid Eternity 21 42 63 122 199 275
61-63-Crandall-c/a; 61-Jeb Rivers begins 21 42 63 126 206 285
64,65-Crandall-a 21 42 63 122 199 275
NOTE: ***Crandall*** *a-11-17(Hercules), 23, 24(Stormy Foster); c-18-20, 23, 24.* ***Fine*** *c-1-14, 16, 17(most).* ***Ward*** *c-33. Bondage c-7, 64. Hercules c-3, 10-17. Jeb Rivers c-61-65. Kid Eternity c-25-60 (w/Keeper-28-34, 36, 39-43, 45-55). Neon the Unknown c-2, 4, 8, 9. Red Bee c-1, 5-7. Stormy Foster c-18-24.*

HIT-GIRL (Also see Kick-Ass)
Marvel Comics (Icon): Aug, 2012 - No. 5, Apr, 2013 ($2.99, limited series)
1-5-Takes place between Kick-Ass & Kick Ass 2 series; Millar-s/Romita Jr.-a/c 3.00

HITLER'S ASTROLOGER (See Marvel Graphic Novel #35)

HITMAN (Also see Bloodbath #2, Batman Chronicles #4, Demon #43-45 & Demon Annual #2)
DC Comics: May, 1996 - No. 60, Apr, 2001 ($2.25/$2.50)
1-Garth Ennis-s & John McCrea-c/a begin; Batman app.
2 4 6 8 10 12
2-Joker-c;Two Face, Mad Hatter, Batman app. 1 2 3 5 6 8

GD 2.0 | VG 4.0 | FN 6.0 | VF 8.0 | VF/NM 9.0 | NM- 9.2

3-5: 3-Batman-c/app.; Joker app. 4-1st app. Nightfist 5.00
6-20: 8-Final Night x-over. 10-GL cameo. 11-20: 11,12-GL-c/app. 15-20-"Ace of Killers". 16-18-Catwoman app. 17-19-Demon-app. 4.00
21-59: 34-Superman-c/app. 3.00
60-($3.95) Final issue; includes pin-ups by various 4.00
#1,000,000 (11/98) Hitman goes to the 853rd Century 3.00
Annual 1 (1997, $3.95) Pulp Heroes 5.00
.../Lobo: That Stupid Bastich (7/00, $3.95) Ennis-s/Mahnke-a 4.00
TPB-(1997, $9.95) r/#1-3, Demon Ann. #2, Batman Chronicles #4 10.00
Ace of Killers TPB ('00/'11, $17.95/$17.99) r/#15-22 18.00
Local Heroes TPB ('99, $17.95) r/#9-14 & Annual #1 18.00
10,000 Bullets TPB ('98, $9.95) r/#4-8 10.00
Ten Thousand Bullets TPB ('10, $17.99) r/#4-8 & Annual #1; intro, by Kevin Smith 18.00
Who Dares Wins TPB ('01, $12.95) r/#23-28 13.00

HIT-MONKEY (See Deadpool)
Marvel Comics: Apr, 2010; Sept, 2010 - No. 3, Nov, 2010 ($3.99/$2.99)
1-(4/10, $3.99) Printing of story from Marvel Digital Comics; Frank Cho-c; origin revealed 4.00
1-3-Daniel Way-s/Talajic-a/Johnson-c; Bullseye app. 3.00

HI-YO SILVER (See Lone Ranger's Famous Horse... and The Lone Ranger; and March of Comics No. 215 in the Promotional Comics section)

HOBBIT, THE
Eclipse Comics: 1989 - No. 3, 1990 ($4.95, squarebound, 52 pgs.)
Book 1-3: Adapts novel; Wenzel-a 1 3 4 6 8 10
Book 1-Second printing 5.00
Graphic Novel (1990, Ballantine)-r/#1-3 25.00

HOCUS POCUS (See Funny Book #9)

HOGAN'S HEROES (TV) (Also see Wild!)
Dell Publishing Co.: June, 1966 - No. 8, Sept, 1967; No. 9, Oct, 1969
1: Photo-c on #1-7 7 14 21 48 89 130
2,3-Ditko-a(p) 5 10 15 33 57 80
4-9: 9-Reprints #1 4 8 12 28 47 65

HOKUM & HEX (See Razorline)
Marvel Comics (Razorline): Sept, 1993 - No. 9, May, 1994 ($1.75/$1.95)
1-($2.50)-Foil embossed-c; by Clive Barker 4.00
2-9: 5-Hyperkind x-over 3.00

HOLIDAY COMICS
Fawcett Publications: 1942 (25¢, 196 pgs.)
1-Contains three Fawcett comics plus two page portrait of Captain Marvel; Capt. Marvel, Jungle Girl #1, & Whiz. Not rebound, remaindered comics; printed at the same time as originals (scarce in high grade) 300 600 900 2100 3800 5500

HOLIDAY COMICS (Becomes Fun Comics #9-12)
Star Publications: Jan, 1951 - No. 8, Oct, 1952
1-Funny animal contents (Frisky Fables) in all; L. B. Cole X-Mas-c
29 58 87 170 278 385
2-Classic L. B. Cole-c 31 62 93 186 303 420
3-8: 5,8-X-Mas-c; all L.B. Cole-c 19 38 57 109 172 235
Accepted Reprint 4 (nd)-L.B. Cole-c 10 20 30 58 79 100

HOLIDAY DIGEST
Harvey Comics: 1988 ($1.25, digest-size)
1 1 2 3 5 7 9

HOLIDAY PARADE (Walt Disney's...)
W. D. Publications (Disney): Winter, 1990-91(no year given) - No. 2, Winter, 1990-91 ($2.95, 68 pgs.)
1-Reprints 1947 Firestone by Barks plus new-a 5.00
2-Barks-r plus other stories 4.00

HOLI-DAY SURPRISE (Formerly Summer Fun)
Charlton Comics: V2#55, Mar, 1967 (25¢ Giant)
V2#55 4 8 12 23 37 50

HOLLYWOOD COMICS
New Age Publishers: Winter, 1944 (52 pgs.)
1-Funny animal 18 36 54 107 169 230

HOLLYWOOD CONFESSIONS
St. John Publishing Co.: Oct, 1949 - No. 2, Dec, 1949
1-Kubert-c/a (entire book) 37 74 111 222 361 500
2-Kubert-c/a (entire book) (Scarce) 39 78 117 231 378 525

HOLLYWOOD DIARY

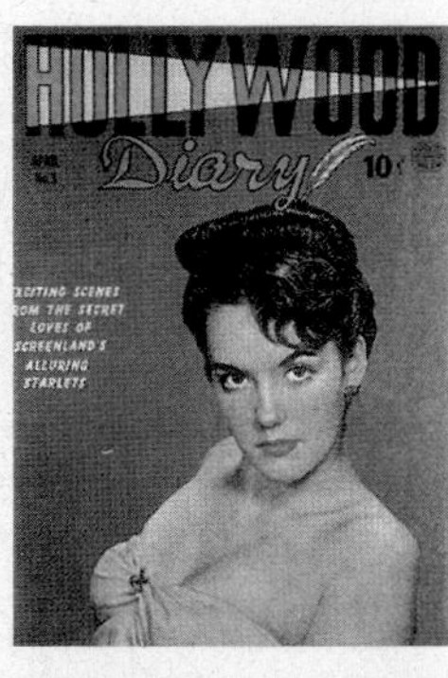

Hollywood Diary #3 © QUA

Homer Hooper #3 © MAR

Honeymoon Romance #2 © Artful

	GD 2.0	VG 4.0	FN 6.0	VF 8.0	VF/NM 9.0	NM- 9.2

Quality Comics Group: Dec, 1949 - No. 5, July-Aug, 1950

1-No photo-c	24	48	72	142	234	325
2-Photo-c	15	30	45	88	137	185
3-5-Photo-c. 3-Betty Carlin photo-c. 5-June Allyson/Peter Lawford photo-c	14	28	42	82	121	160

HOLLYWOOD FILM STORIES
Feature Publications/Prize: April, 1950 - No. 4, Oct, 1950 (All photo-c; "Fumetti" type movie comic)

1-June Allyson photo-c	21	42	63	124	202	280
2-4: 2-Lizabeth Scott photo-c. 3-Barbara Stanwick photo-c. 4-Betty Hutton photo-c	15	30	45	88	137	185

HOLLYWOOD FUNNY FOLKS (Formerly Funny Folks; Becomes Nutsy Squirrel #61 on)
National Periodical Publ.: No. 27, Aug-Sept, 1950 - No. 60, July-Aug, 1954

27-Nutsy Squirrel continues	14	28	42	76	108	140
28-40	10	20	30	54	72	90
41-60	9	18	27	47	61	75

NOTE: ***Rube Grossman** a-most issues.* ***Sheldon Mayer** a-27-35, 37-40, 43-46, 48-51, 53, 56, 57, 60.*

HOLLYWOOD LOVE DOCTOR (See Doctor Anthony King...)

HOLLYWOOD PICTORIAL (...Romances on cover)
St. John Publishing Co.: No. 3, Jan, 1950

3-Matt Baker-a; photo-c	32	64	96	188	307	425

(Becomes a movie magazine - Hollywood Pictorial Western with No. 4.)

HOLLYWOOD ROMANCES (Formerly Brides In Love; becomes For Lovers Only #60 on)
Charlton Comics: V2#46, 11/66; #47, 10/67; #48, 11/68;V3#49,11/69-V3#59, 6/71

V2#46-Rolling Stones-c/story	8	16	24	56	108	160
V2#47-V3#59: 56- "Born to Heart Break" begins	3	6	9	14	19	24

HOLLYWOOD SECRETS
Quality Comics Group: Nov, 1949 - No. 6, Sept, 1950

1-Ward-c/a (9 pgs.)	39	78	117	231	378	525
2-Crandall-a, Ward-c/a (9 pgs.)	26	52	78	154	252	350
3-6: All photo-c. 5-Lex Barker (Tarzan)-c	15	30	45	85	130	175
...of Romance, I.W. Reprint #9; r/#2 above w/Kinstler-c	2	4	6	11	16	20

HOLLYWOOD SUPERSTARS
Marvel Comics (Epic Comics): Nov, 1990 - No. 5, Apr, 1991 ($2.25)

1-($2.95, 52 pgs.)-Spiegle-c/a in all; Aragonés-a, inside front-c plus 2-4 pgs.						4.00
2-5 ($2.25)						3.00

HOLO-MAN (See Power Record Comics)

HOLYOKE ONE-SHOT
Holyoke Publishing Co. (Tem Publ.): 1944 - No. 10, 1945 (All reprints)

1,2: 1-Grit Grady (on cover only), Miss Victory, Alias X (origin)-All reprints from Captain Fearless. 2-Rusty Dugan (Corporal); Capt. Fearless (origin), Mr. Miracle (origin) app.	32	64	96	188	307	425
3-Miss Victory; r/Crash #4; Cat Man (origin), Solar Legion by Kirby app.; Miss Victory on cover only (1945)	47	94	141	296	498	700
4,6,8: 4-Mr. Miracle; The Blue Streak app. 6-Capt. Fearless, Alias X, Capt. Stone (splash used as-c to #10); Diamond Jim & Rusty Dugan (splash from cover of #2). 8-Blue Streak, Strong Man (story matches cover to #7)-Crash reprints	28	56	84	165	270	375
5,7: 5-U.S. Border Patrol Comics (Sgt. Dick Carter of the...), Miss Victory (story matches cover to #3), Citizen Smith, & Mr. Miracle app. 7-Secret Agent Z-2, Strong Man, Blue Streak (story matches cover to #8); Reprints from Crash #2	29	58	87	172	281	390
9-Citizen Smith, The Blue Streak, Solar Legion by Kirby & Strongman, the Perfect Human app.; reprints from Crash #4 & 5; Citizen Smith on cover only-from story in #5 (1944-before #3)	32	64	96	188	307	425
10-Captain Stone; r/Crash; Solar Legion by S&K	32	64	96	188	307	425

HOLY TERROR
Legendary Comics: Sept, 2011 ($29.95, HC graphic novel, 12-1/4" wide x 9-1/4" tall)

HC-Frank Miller-s/a/c; B&W art with spot color; The Fixer vs. Al-Qaeda in Empire City						30.00

HOMECOMING
Aspen MLT: Aug, 2012 - No. 4, Sept, 2013 ($3.99)

1-4: 1-Wohl-s/Laiso-a; covers by Michael Turner and Mike DeBalfo						4.00

HOMER COBB (See Adventures of...)

HOMER HOOPER
Atlas Comics: July, 1953 - No. 4, Dec, 1953

1-Teenage humor	12	24	36	67	94	120
2-4	8	16	24	44	57	70

HOMER, THE HAPPY GHOST (See Adventures of...)
Atlas(ACI/PPI/WPI)/Marvel: 3/55 - No. 22, 11/58; V2#1, 11/69 - V2#4, 5/70

V1#1-Dan DeCarlo-c/a begins, ends #22	26	52	78	154	252	350
2-1st code approved issue	15	30	45	85	130	175
3-10	14	28	42	82	121	160
11-22	14	28	42	76	108	140
V2#1 (11/69)	10	20	30	70	150	230
2-4	6	12	18	42	79	115

HOME RUN (Also see A-1 Comics)
Magazine Enterprises: No. 89, 1953 (one-shot)

A-1 89 (#3)-Powell-a; Stan Musial photo-c	15	30	45	88	137	185

HOMICIDE (Also see Dark Horse Presents)
Dark Horse Comics: Apr, 1990 ($1.95, B&W, one-shot)

1-Detective story						3.00

HONEYMOON (Formerly Gay Comics)
A Lover's Magazine(USA) (Marvel): No. 41, Jan, 1950

41-Photo-c; article by Betty Grable	14	28	42	76	108	140

HONEYMOONERS, THE (TV)
Lodestone: Oct, 1986 ($1.50)

1-Photo-c						6.00

HONEYMOONERS, THE (TV)
Triad Publications: Sept, 1987 - No. 13? ($2.00)

1-13						5.00

HONEYMOON ROMANCE
Artful Publications (Canadian): Apr, 1950 - No. 2, July, 1950 (25¢, digest size)

1,2-(Rare)	140	280	420	700	1050	1400

HONEY WEST (TV)
Gold Key: Sept, 1966 (Photo-c)

1 (10186-609)	8	16	24	54	102	150

HONEY WEST (TV)
Moonstone: 2010 - Present ($5.99/$3.99)

1-($5.99) Trina Robbins-s/Cynthia Martin-a; two art covers & two photo covers						6.00
2-4-($3.99)						4.00

HONG KONG PHOOEY (TV)
Charlton Comics: June, 1975 - No. 9, Nov, 1976 (Hanna-Barbera)

1	5	10	15	31	53	75
2	3	6	9	18	28	38
3-9	3	6	9	15	22	28

HONG ON THE RANGE
Image/Flypaper Press: Dec, 1997 - No. 3, Feb, 1998 ($2.50, lim. series)

1-3: Wu-s/Lafferty-a						3.00

HOOD, THE
Marvel Comics (MAX): Jul, 2002 - No. 6, Dec, 2002 ($2.99, limited series)

1-6-Vaughan-s/Hotz-c/a						3.00
Vol. 1 Blood From Stones HC (2007, $19.99, dustjacket) r/#1-6; production sketch art						20.00
Vol. 1 Blood From Stones TPB (2003, $14.99) r/#1-6						15.00

HOODED HORSEMAN, THE (Formerly Blazing West)
American Comics Group (Michel Publ.): No. 21, 1-2/52 - No. 27, 1-2/54; No. 18, 12-1/54-55 - No. 22, 8-9/55

21(1-2/52)-Hooded Horseman, Injun Jones cont.	15	30	45	83	124	165
22	10	20	30	56	76	95
23,24,27(1-2/54)	9	18	27	50	65	80
25 (9-10/53)-Cowboy Sahib on cover only; Hooded Horseman i.d. revealed	9	18	27	52	69	85
26-Origin/1st app. Cowboy Sahib by L. Starr	11	22	33	62	86	110
18(12-1/54-55)(Formerly Out of the Night)	10	20	30	54	72	90
19,21,22: 19-Last precode (1-2/55)	8	16	24	44	57	70
20-Origin Johnny Injun	9	18	27	50	65	80

NOTE: ***Whitney** c/a-21('52), 20-22.*

HOODED MENACE, THE (Also see Daring Adventures)
Realistic/Avon Periodicals: 1951 (one-shot)

nn-Based on a band of hooded outlaws in the Pacific Northwest, 1900-1906; reprinted in Daring Advs. #15	52	104	156	327	556	785

HOODS UP (See the Promotional Comics section)

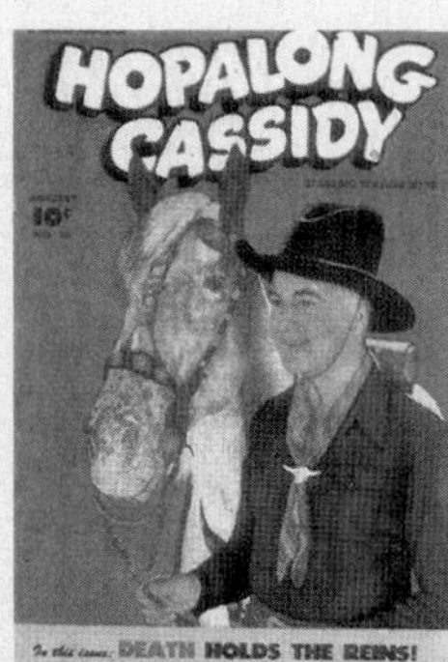

Hopalong Cassidy #15 © FAW

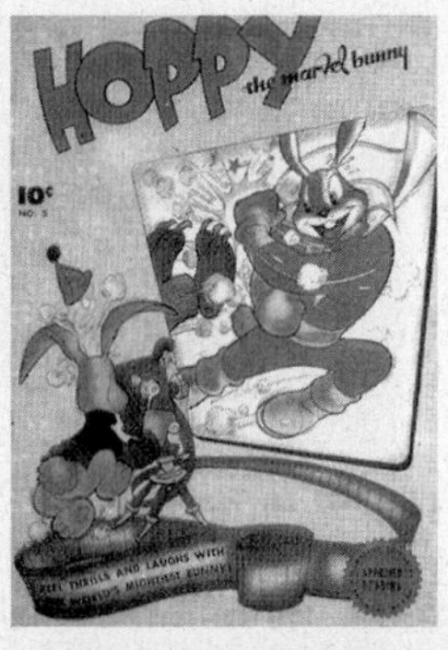

Hoppy the Marvel Bunny #5 © FAW

Horrific #5 © Comic Media

	GD 2.0	VG 4.0	FN 6.0	VF 8.0	VF/NM 9.0	NM- 9.2

HOOK (Movie)
Marvel Comics: Early Feb, 1992 - No. 4, Late Mar, 1992 ($1.00, limited series)

Issue	GD 2.0	VG 4.0	FN 6.0	VF 8.0	VF/NM 9.0	NM- 9.2
1-4: Adapts movie; Vess-c; 1-Morrow-a(p)						3.00
nn (1991, $5.95, 84 pgs.)-Contains #1-4; Vess-c						6.00
1 (1991, $2.95, magazine, 84 pgs.)-Contains #1-4; Vess-c (same cover as nn issue)						4.00

HOOT GIBSON'S WESTERN ROUNDUP (See Western Roundup under Fox Giants)

HOOT GIBSON WESTERN (Formerly My Love Story)
Fox Features Syndicate: No. 5, May, 1950 - No. 3, Sept, 1950

Issue	GD 2.0	VG 4.0	FN 6.0	VF 8.0	VF/NM 9.0	NM- 9.2
5,6(#1,2): 5-Photo-c. 6-Photo/painted-c	21	42	63	123	197	270
3-Wood-a; painted-c	22	44	66	131	211	290

HOPALONG CASSIDY (Also see Bill Boyd Western, Master Comics, Real Western Hero, Six Gun Heroes & Western Hero; Bill Boyd starred as Hopalong Cassidy in movies, radio & TV)
Fawcett Publications: Feb, 1943; No. 2, Summer, 1946 - No. 85, Nov, 1953

Issue	GD 2.0	VG 4.0	FN 6.0	VF 8.0	VF/NM 9.0	NM- 9.2
1 (1943, 68 pgs.)-H. Cassidy & his horse Topper begin (on sale 1/8/43)-Captain Marvel app. on-c	290	580	870	1856	3178	4500
2-(Sum, '46)	41	82	123	256	428	600
3,4: 3-(Fall, '46, 52 pgs. begin)	20	40	60	114	182	250
5- "Mad Barber" story mentioned in **SOTI**, pgs. 308,309; photo-c	19	38	57	111	176	240
6-10: 8-Photo-c	16	32	48	94	147	200
11-19: 11,13-19-Photo-c	14	28	42	80	115	150
20-29 (52 pgs.)-Painted/photo-c	12	24	36	69	97	125
30,31,33,34,37-39,41 (52 pgs.)-Painted-c	11	22	33	60	83	105
32,40 (36pgs.)-Painted-c	10	20	30	54	72	90
35,42,43,45-47,49-51,53,54,56 (52 pgs.)-Photo-c	10	20	30	56	76	95
36,44,48 (36 pgs.)-Photo-c	9	18	27	52	69	85
52,55,57-70 (36 pgs.)-Photo-c	9	18	27	47	61	75
71-84-Photo-c	8	16	24	42	54	65
85-Last Fawcett issue; photo-c	9	18	27	52	69	85

NOTE: *Line-drawn c-1-4, 6, 7, 9, 10, 12.*

Issue	GD 2.0	VG 4.0	FN 6.0	VF 8.0	VF/NM 9.0	NM- 9.2
... & The 5 Men of Evil (AC Comics, 1991, $12.95) r/newspaper strips and Fawcett story "Signature of Death"						13.00

HOPALONG CASSIDY
National Periodical Publications: No. 86, Feb, 1954 - No. 135, May-June, 1959 (All-36 pgs.)

Issue	GD 2.0	VG 4.0	FN 6.0	VF 8.0	VF/NM 9.0	NM- 9.2
86-Gene Colan-a begins, ends #117; photo covers continue	36	72	108	216	351	485
87	20	40	60	118	189	260
88-91: 91-1 pg. Superboy-sty (7/54)	15	30	45	83	124	165
92-99 (98 has #93 on-c; last precode issue, 2/55). 95-Reversed photo-c to #52. 98-Reversed photo-c to #61. 99-Reversed photo-c to #60	14	28	42	76	108	140
100-Same cover as #50	15	30	45	83	124	165
101-108: 105-Same photo-c as #54. 107-Same photo-c as #51. 108-Last photo-c	6	12	18	38	69	100
109-130: 118-Gil Kane-a begins. 123-Kubert-a (2 pgs.). 124-Grey tone-c	5	10	15	35	63	90
131-135	6	12	18	37	66	95

HOPELESS SAVAGES (Also see Too Much Hopeless Savages)
Oni Press: Aug, 2001 - No. 4, Nov, 2001 ($2.95, B&W, limited series)

Issue	GD 2.0	VG 4.0	FN 6.0	VF 8.0	VF/NM 9.0	NM- 9.2
1-4-Van Meter-s/Norrie-a/Clugston-Major-a/Watson-c						3.00
Free Comic Book Day giveaway (5/02) r/#1 with "Free Comic Book Day" banner on-c						3.00
TPB (2002, $13.95, 8" x 5.75") r/#1-4; plus color stories; Watson-c						14.00

HOPELESS SAVAGES: GROUND ZERO
Oni Press: June, 2002 - No. 4, Oct, 2002 ($2.95, B&W, limited series)

Issue	GD 2.0	VG 4.0	FN 6.0	VF 8.0	VF/NM 9.0	NM- 9.2
1-4-Van Meter-s/O'Malley-a/Dodson-c. 1-Watson-a						3.00
TPB (2003, $11.95, 8" x 5.75") r/#1-4; Dodson-c						12.00

HOPE SHIP
Dell Publishing Co.: June-Aug, 1963

Issue	GD 2.0	VG 4.0	FN 6.0	VF 8.0	VF/NM 9.0	NM- 9.2
1	3	6	9	15	22	28

HOPPY THE MARVEL BUNNY (See Fawcett's Funny Animals)
Fawcett Publications: Dec, 1945 - No. 15, Sept, 1947

Issue	GD 2.0	VG 4.0	FN 6.0	VF 8.0	VF/NM 9.0	NM- 9.2
1	28	56	84	165	270	375
2	14	28	42	82	121	160
3-15: 7-Xmas-c	12	24	36	67	94	120

HORACE & DOTTY DRIPPLE (Dotty Dripple No. 1-24)
Harvey Publications: No. 25, Aug, 1952 - No. 43, Oct, 1955

Issue	GD 2.0	VG 4.0	FN 6.0	VF 8.0	VF/NM 9.0	NM- 9.2
25-43	4	9	13	18	22	26

HORIZONTAL LIEUTENANT, THE (See Movie Classics)

HOROBI
Viz Premiere Comics: 1990 - No. 8, 1990 ($3.75, B&W, mature readers, 84 pgs.) V2#1, 1990 - No. 7, 1991 ($4.25, B&W, 68 pgs.)

Issue	GD 2.0	VG 4.0	FN 6.0	VF 8.0	VF/NM 9.0	NM- 9.2
1-8: Japanese manga, Part Two, #1-7						5.00

HORRIFIC (Terrific No. 14 on)
Artful/Comic Media/Harwell/Mystery: Sept, 1952 - No. 13, Sept, 1954

Issue	GD 2.0	VG 4.0	FN 6.0	VF 8.0	VF/NM 9.0	NM- 9.2
1	77	154	231	493	847	1200
2	47	94	141	296	498	700
3-Bullet in head-c	110	220	330	704	1202	1700
4,5,7,9,10: 4-Shrunken head-c. 7-Guillotine-c	42	84	126	265	445	625
6-Jack The Ripper story	43	86	129	271	461	650
8-Origin & 1st app. The Teller (E.C. parody)	47	94	141	296	498	700
11-13: 11-Swipe/Witches Tales #6,27; Devil-c	37	74	111	222	361	500

NOTE: *Don Heck a-8; c-3-13.* ***Hollingsworth*** *a-4.* ***Morisi*** *a-8.* ***Palais*** *a-5, 7-12.*

HORRORCIDE
IDW Publishing: Sept, 2004 ($6.99)

Issue	GD 2.0	VG 4.0	FN 6.0	VF 8.0	VF/NM 9.0	NM- 9.2
1-Steve Niles short stories; art by Templesmith, Medors and Chee						7.00

HORROR FROM THE TOMB (Mysterious Stories No. 2 on)
Premier Magazine Co.: Sept, 1954

Issue	GD 2.0	VG 4.0	FN 6.0	VF 8.0	VF/NM 9.0	NM- 9.2
1-Woodbridge/Torres, Check-a; The Keeper of the Graveyard is host	48	96	144	302	514	725

HORRORIST, THE (Also see Hellblazer)
DC Comics (Vertigo): Dec, 1995 - No. 2, Jan, 1996 ($5.95, lim. series, mature)

Issue	GD 2.0	VG 4.0	FN 6.0	VF 8.0	VF/NM 9.0	NM- 9.2
1,2: Jamie Delano scripts, David Lloyd-c/a; John Constantine (Hellblazer) app.						6.00

HORROR OF COLLIER COUNTY
Dark Horse Comics: Oct, 1999 - No. 5, Feb, 2000 ($2.95, B&W, limited series)

Issue	GD 2.0	VG 4.0	FN 6.0	VF 8.0	VF/NM 9.0	NM- 9.2
1-5-Rich Tommaso-s/a						3.00

HORRORS, THE (Formerly Startling Terror Tales #10)
Star Publications: No. 11, Jan, 1953 - No. 15, Apr, 1954

Issue	GD 2.0	VG 4.0	FN 6.0	VF 8.0	VF/NM 9.0	NM- 9.2
11-Horrors of War; Disbrow-a(2)	31	62	93	182	296	410
12-Horrors of War; color illo in **POP**	29	58	87	170	278	385
13-Horrors of Mystery; crime stories	27	54	81	158	259	360
14,15-Horrors of the Underworld; crime stories	29	58	87	170	278	385

NOTE: *All have* ***L. B. Cole*** *covers; a-12.* ***Hollingsworth*** *a-13.* ***Palais*** *a-13r.*

HORROR TALES (Magazine)
Eerie Publications: V1#7, 6/69 - V6#6, 12/74; V7#1, 2/75; V7#2, 5/76 - V8#5, 1977; V9#1-3, 8/78; V10#1(2/79) (V1-V6: 52 pgs.; V7, V8#2: 112 pgs.; V8#4 on: 68 pgs.) (No V5#3, V8#1,3)

Issue	GD 2.0	VG 4.0	FN 6.0	VF 8.0	VF/NM 9.0	NM- 9.2
V1#7	7	14	21	48	89	130
V1#8,9	5	10	15	33	57	80
V2#1-6('70), V3#1-6('71), V4#1-3,5-7('72)	5	10	15	30	50	70
V4#4-LSD story reprint/Weird V3#5	5	10	15	35	63	90
V5#1,2,4,5(6/73),5(10/73),6(12/73),V6#1-6('74),V7#1,2,4('76),V7#3('76)-Giant issue, V8#2,4,5('77)	5	10	15	30	50	70
V9#1-3(11/78, $1.50), V10#1(2/79)	5	10	15	31	53	75

NOTE: *Bondage-c-V6#1, 3, V7#2.*

HORSE FEATHERS COMICS
Lev Gleason Publ.: Nov, 1945 - No. 4, July(Summer on-c), 1948 (52 pgs.) (#2,3 are oversized)

Issue	GD 2.0	VG 4.0	FN 6.0	VF 8.0	VF/NM 9.0	NM- 9.2
1-Wolverton's Scoop Scuttle, 2 pgs.	19	38	57	109	172	235
2	11	22	33	60	83	105
3,4: 3-(5/48)	9	18	27	47	61	75

HORSEMAN
Crusade Comics/Kevlar Studios: Mar, 1996 - No. 3, Nov, 1997 ($2.95)

Issue	GD 2.0	VG 4.0	FN 6.0	VF 8.0	VF/NM 9.0	NM- 9.2
0-1st Kevlar Studios issue, 1-(3/96)-Crusade issue; Shi-c/app., 1-(11/96)-3-(11/97)-Kevlar Studios						3.00

HORSEMASTERS, THE (Disney)(TV, Movie)
Dell Publishing Co.: No. 1260, Dec-Feb, 1961/62

Issue	GD 2.0	VG 4.0	FN 6.0	VF 8.0	VF/NM 9.0	NM- 9.2
Four Color 1260-Annette Funicello photo-c	10	20	30	69	147	225

HORSE SOLDIERS, THE
Dell Publishing Co.: No. 1048, Nov-Jan, 1959/60 (John Wayne movie)

Issue	GD 2.0	VG 4.0	FN 6.0	VF 8.0	VF/NM 9.0	NM- 9.2
Four Color 1048-Painted-c, Sekowsky-a	11	22	33	73	157	240

HORSE WITHOUT A HEAD, THE (See Movie Comics)

HOT DOG
Magazine Enterprises: June-July, 1954 - No. 4, Dec-Jan, 1954-55

Issue	GD 2.0	VG 4.0	FN 6.0	VF 8.0	VF/NM 9.0	NM- 9.2
1(A-1 #107)	9	18	27	47	61	75
2,3(A-1 #115),4(A-1 #136)	6	12	18	31	38	45

HOT DOG (See Jughead's Pal, Hotdog)

HOTEL DEPAREE - SUNDANCE (TV)

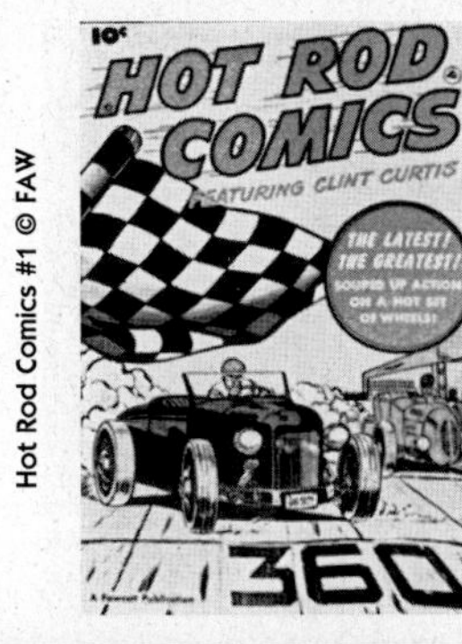

Hot Rod Comics #1 © FAW

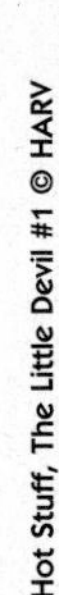
Hot Stuff, The Little Devil #1 © HARV

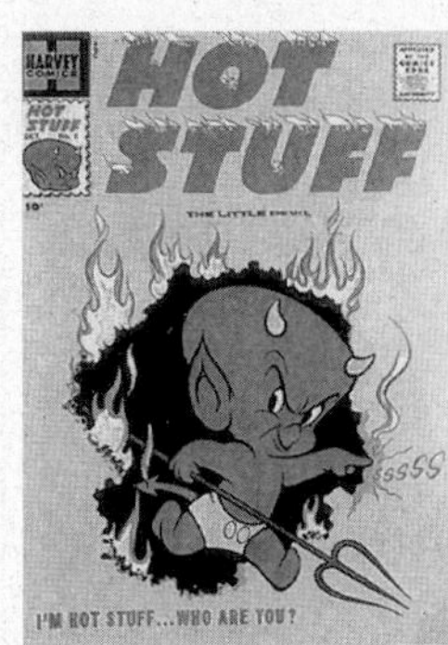

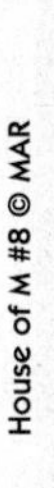
House of M #8 © MAR

	GD 2.0	VG 4.0	FN 6.0	VF 8.0	VF/NM 9.0	NM- 9.2
Dell Publishing Co.: No. 1126, Aug-Oct, 1960 (one-shot)						
Four Color 1126-Earl Holliman photo-c	6	12	18	37	66	95

HOT ROD AND SPEEDWAY COMICS
Hillman Periodicals: Feb-Mar, 1952 - No. 5, Apr-May, 1953

	GD	VG	FN	VF	VF/NM	NM-
1	27	54	81	158	259	360
2-Krigstein-a	18	36	54	105	165	225
3-5	13	26	39	72	101	130

HOT ROD COMICS (...Featuring Clint Curtis) (See XMas Comics)
Fawcett Publications: Nov, 1951 (no month given) - V2#7, Feb, 1953

	GD	VG	FN	VF	VF/NM	NM-
nn (V1#1)-Powell-c/a in all	29	58	87	170	278	385
2 (4/52)	15	30	45	90	140	190
3-6, V2#7	13	26	39	72	101	130

HOT ROD KING (Also see Speed Smith the Hot Rod King)
Ziff-Davis Publ. Co.: Fall, 1952

	GD	VG	FN	VF	VF/NM	NM-
1-Giacoia-a; Saunders painted-c	25	50	75	150	245	340

HOT ROD RACERS (Grand Prix No. 16 on)
Charlton Comics: Dec, 1964 - No. 15, July, 1967

	GD	VG	FN	VF	VF/NM	NM-
1	7	14	21	46	86	125
2-5	5	10	15	30	50	70
6-15	4	8	12	23	37	50

HOT RODS AND RACING CARS
Charlton Comics (Motor Mag. No. 1): Nov, 1951 - No. 120, June, 1973

	GD	VG	FN	VF	VF/NM	NM-
1-Speed Davis begins; Indianapolis 500 story	28	56	84	165	270	375
2	15	30	45	86	133	180
3-10	12	24	36	67	94	120
11-20	10	20	30	54	72	90
21-33,36-40	8	16	24	44	57	70
34, 35 (? & 6/58, 68 pgs.)	11	22	33	60	83	105
41-60	7	14	21	37	46	55
61-80	3	6	9	19	30	40
81-100	3	6	9	16	23	30
101-120	3	6	9	14	19	24

HOT SHOT CHARLIE
Hillman Periodicals: 1947 (Lee Elias)

	GD	VG	FN	VF	VF/NM	NM-
1	13	26	39	74	105	135

HOT SHOTS: AVENGERS
Marvel Comics: Oct, 1995 ($2.95, one-shot)

	GD	VG	FN	VF	VF/NM	NM-
nn-pin-ups						3.00

HOTSPUR
Eclipse Comics: Jun, 1987 - No. 3, Sep, 1987 ($1.75, lim. series, Baxter paper)

	GD	VG	FN	VF	VF/NM	NM-
1-3						3.00

HOT STUFF (See Stumbo Tinytown)
Harvey Comics: V2#1, Sept, 1991 - No. 12, June, 1994 ($1.00)

	GD	VG	FN	VF	VF/NM	NM-
V2#1-Stumbo back-up story						5.00
2-12 ($1.50)						4.00
...Big Book 1 (11/92), 2 (6/93) (Both $1.95, 52 pgs.)						5.00

HOT STUFF CREEPY CAVES
Harvey Publications: Nov, 1974 - No. 7, Nov, 1975

	GD	VG	FN	VF	VF/NM	NM-
1	3	6	9	21	33	45
2-7	3	6	9	15	21	26

HOT STUFF DIGEST
Harvey Comics: July, 1992 - No. 5, Nov, 1993 ($1.75, digest-size)

	GD	VG	FN	VF	VF/NM	NM-
V2#1-Hot Stuff, Stumbo, Richie Rich stories						6.00
2-5						4.00

HOT STUFF GIANT SIZE
Harvey Comics: Oct, 1992 - No. 3, Oct, 1993 ($2.25, 68 pgs.)

	GD	VG	FN	VF	VF/NM	NM-
V2#1-Hot Stuff & Stumbo stories						5.00
2,3						4.00

HOT STUFF SIZZLERS
Harvey Publications: July, 1960 - No. 59, Mar, 1974; V2#1, Aug, 1992

	GD	VG	FN	VF	VF/NM	NM-
1- 84 pgs. begin, ends #5; Hot Stuff, Stumbo begin	14	28	42	96	211	325
2-5	7	14	21	49	92	135
6-10: 6-68 pgs. begin, ends #45	5	10	15	35	63	90
11-20	4	8	12	27	44	60
21-45	3	6	9	19	30	40
46-52: 52 pgs. begin	3	6	9	16	23	30
53-59	2	4	6	10	14	18
V2#1-(8/92, $1.25)-Stumbo back-up						5.00

HOT STUFF, THE LITTLE DEVIL (Also see Devil Kids & Harvey Hits)
Harvey Publications (Illustrated Humor): 10/57 - No. 141, 7/77; No. 142, 2/78 - No. 164, 8/82; No. 165, 10/86 - No. 171, 11/87; No. 172, 11/88; No. 173, Sept, 1990 - No. 177, 1/91

	GD	VG	FN	VF	VF/NM	NM-
1-UFO story	64	128	192	512	1156	1800
2-Stumbo-like giant 1st app. (12/57)	24	48	72	170	378	585
3-Stumbo the Giant debut (2/58)	19	38	57	133	297	460
4,5	17	34	51	117	259	400
6-10	10	20	30	66	138	210
11-20	8	16	24	51	96	140
21-40	5	10	15	34	60	85
41-60	4	8	12	25	40	55
61-80	3	6	9	19	30	40
81-105	3	6	9	15	22	28
106-112: All 52 pg. Giants	3	6	9	17	26	35
113-125	2	4	6	9	12	15
126-141	1	2	3	5	7	9
142-177: 172-177-($1.00)						6.00
Harvey Comics Classics Vol. 3 TPB (Dark Horse Books, 3/08, $19.95) Reprints Hot Stuff's earliest appearances in this title and Devil Kids, mostly B&W with some color stories; history, early concept drawings; foreword by Mark Arnold						20.00

HOT WHEELS (TV)
National Periodical Publications: Mar-Apr, 1970 - No. 6, Jan-Feb, 1971

	GD	VG	FN	VF	VF/NM	NM-
1	9	18	27	58	114	170
2,4,5	5	10	15	34	60	85
3-Neal Adams-c	6	12	18	41	76	110
6-Neal Adams-c/a	7	14	21	49	92	135

NOTE: *Toth a-1p, 2-5; c-1p, 5.*

HOURMAN (Justice Society member, see Adventure Comics #48)

HOURMAN (See JLA and DC One Million)
DC Comics: Apr, 1999 - No. 25, Apr, 2001 ($2.50)

	GD	VG	FN	VF	VF/NM	NM-
1-25: 1-JLA app.; McDaniel-c. 2-Tomorrow Woman-c/app. 6,7-Amazo app. 11-13-Justice Legion A app. 16-Silver Age flashback. 18,19-JSA-c/app. 22-Harris-c/a. 24-Hourman Vs. Rex Tyler						3.00

HOUSE OF FUN
Dark Horse Comics: Dec, 2012 ($3.50)

	GD	VG	FN	VF	VF/NM	NM-
0-Reprints Evan Dorkin humor strips from Dark Horse Presents #10-12						3.50

HOUSE OF GOLD AND BONES
Dark Horse Comics: Apr, 2013 - No. 4, Jul, 2013 ($3.99, limited series)

	GD	VG	FN	VF	VF/NM	NM-
1-4-Corey Taylor-s/Richard Clark-a; 2 covers on each						4.00

HOUSE OF M (Also see miniseries with Fantastic Four, Iron Man and Spider-Man)
Marvel Comics: Aug, 2005 - No. 8, Dec, 2005 ($2.99, limited series)

	GD	VG	FN	VF	VF/NM	NM-
1-Bendis-s/Coipel-a/Ribic-c; Scarlet Witch changes reality; Quesada variant-c						3.00
2-8-Variant covers for each. 3-Hawkeye returns						3.00
... MGC #1 (6/11, $1.00) r/#1 with "Marvel's Greatest Comics" logo on cover						3.00
Secrets Of The House Of M (2005, $3.99, one-shot) profile pages and background info						4.00
... Sketchbook (6/05) B&W preview sketches by Coipel, Davis, Hairsine, Quesada						3.00
TPB (2006, $24.99) r/#1-8 and The Pulse: House of M Special Edition newspaper						25.00
...: Fantastic Four/ Iron Man TPB (2006, $13.99) r/ both House of M mini-series						14.00
...: World of M Featuring Wolverine TPB (2006, $13.99) r/2005 x-over issues Wolverine #33-35, Black Panther #7, Captain America #10 and The Pulse #10						14.00
HC (2008, $29.99, oversized with d.j.) r/#1-8, The Pulse: House of M Special Edition newspaper and Secrets Of The House Of M one-shot; script pages; cover gallery						30.00

HOUSE OF M: AVENGERS
Marvel Comics: Jan, 2008 - No. 5, Apr, 2008 ($2.99, limited series)

	GD	VG	FN	VF	VF/NM	NM-
1-5-Gage-s/Perkins-a; Luke Cage, Iron Fist, Hawkeye, Tigra, Misty Knight, Shang-Chi						3.00

HOUSE OF M: MASTERS OF EVIL
Marvel Comics: Oct, 2009 - No. 4, Jan, 2010 ($3.99, limited series)

	GD	VG	FN	VF	VF/NM	NM-
1-4-Gage-s/Garcia-a/Perkins-c; The Hood app.						4.00

HOUSE OF MYSTERY
DC Comics: Dec/Jan. 1951

nn - Ashcan comic, not distributed to newsstands, only for in-house use. Cover art is Danger Trail #3 with interior being Star Spangled Comics #109. A VG+ copy sold for $2,357.50 in 2002.

HOUSE OF MYSTERY (See Brave and the Bold #93, Elvira's House of Mystery, Limited Collectors' Edition & Super DC Giant)

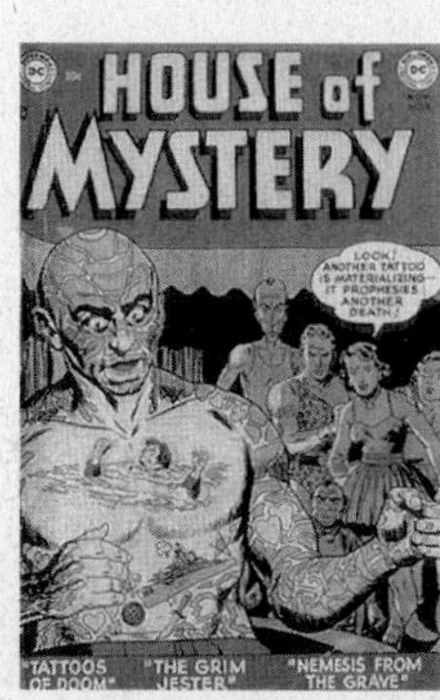

House of Mystery #8 © DC

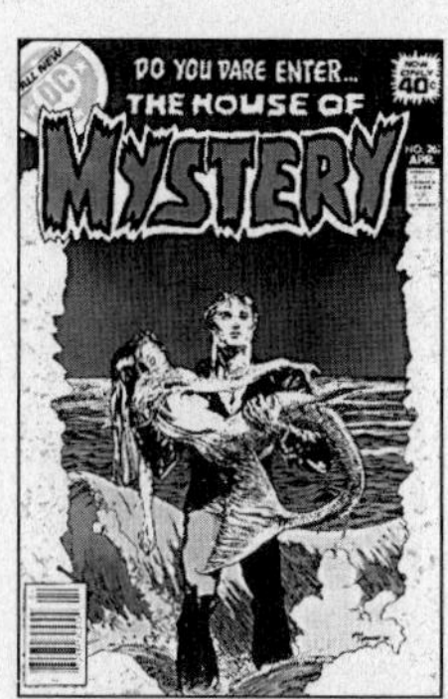

House of Mystery #267 © DC

House of Secrets #76 © DC

HOUSE OF MYSTERY, THE

National Periodical Publications/DC Comics: Dec-Jan, 1951-52 - No. 321, Oct, 1983 (No. 194-203: 52 pgs.)

	GD 2.0	VG 4.0	FN 6.0	VF 8.0	VF/NM 9.0	NM- 9.2
1-DC's first horror comic	258	516	774	1651	2826	4000
2	97	194	291	621	1061	1500
3	66	132	198	419	722	1025
4,5	54	108	162	343	574	825
6-10	48	96	144	302	514	725
11-15	41	82	123	250	418	585
16(7/53)-25	34	68	102	204	332	460
26-35(2/55)-Last pre-code issue; 30-Woodish-a	27	54	81	158	259	360
36-50: 50-Text story of Orson Welles' War of the Worlds broadcast	13	26	39	91	201	310
51-60: 55-1st S.A. issue	12	24	36	79	170	260
61,63,65,66,69,70,72,76,85-Kirby-a	13	26	39	86	188	290
62,64,67,68,71,73-75,77-83,86-99	10	20	30	70	150	230
84-Prototype of Negative Man (Doom Patrol)	13	26	39	89	195	300
100 (7/60)	11	22	33	76	163	250
101-116: 109-Toth, Kubert-a. 116-Last 10¢ issue	10	20	30	64	132	200
117-130: 117-Swipes-c to HOS #20. 120-Toth-a	9	18	27	59	117	175
131-142	8	16	24	54	102	150
143-J'onn J'onzz, Manhunter begins (6/64), ends #173; story continues from Detective #326; intro. Idol-Head of Diabolu	17	34	51	117	259	400
144	8	16	24	51	96	140
145-155,157-159: 149-Toth-a. 155-The Human Hurricane app. (12/65), Red Tornado prototype. 158-Origin Diabolu Idol-Head	5	10	15	35	63	90
156-Robby Reed begins (origin/1st app.), ends #173	7	14	21	44	82	120
160-(7/66)-Robby Reed becomes Plastic Man in this issue only; 1st S.A. app. Plastic Man; intro Marco Xavier (Martian Manhunter) & Vulture Crime Organization; ends #173	8	16	24	56	108	160
161-173: 169-Origin/1st app. Gem Girl	4	8	12	28	47	65
174-Mystery format begins.	12	24	36	82	179	275
175-1st app. Cain (House of Mystery host); Adams-c	10	20	30	64	132	200
176,177-Neal Adams-c	9	18	27	58	114	170
178-Neal Adams-c/a (2/69)	9	18	27	61	123	185
179-Neal Adams/Orlando, Wrightson-a (1st pro work, 3 pgs.); Adams-c	11	22	33	73	157	240
180,181,183: Wrightson-a (3,10, & 3 pgs.); Adams-c. 180-Last 12¢ issue; Kane/Wood-a(2). 183-Wood-a	8	16	24	56	108	160
182,184-Adams-c. 182-Toth-a. 184-Kane/Wood, Toth-a	6	12	18	41	76	110
185-Williamson/Kaluta-a; Howard-a (3 pgs.); Adams-c	7	14	21	44	82	120
186-N. Adams-c/a; Wrightson-a (10 pgs.)	9	18	27	59	117	175
187,190: Adams-c. 187-Toth-a. 190-Toth-a(r)	6	12	18	40	73	105
188-Wrightson-a (8 & 3pgs.); Adams-c	7	14	21	49	92	135
189,192,197: Adams-c on all. 189-Wood-a(i). 192-Last 15¢-c	6	12	18	40	73	105
191-Wrightson-a (8 & 3pgs.); Adams-c	7	14	21	49	92	135
193-Wrightson-c	6	12	18	40	73	105
194-Wrightson-c; 52 pgs begin, end #203; Toth,Kirby-a	8	16	24	51	96	140
195: Wrightson-c. Swamp creature story by Wrightson similar to Swamp Thing (10 pgs.)(10/71)	9	18	27	59	117	175
196,198	5	10	15	35	63	90
199-Adams-c; Wood-a(8pgs.); Kirby-a	6	12	18	42	79	115
200-(25¢, 52 pgs.)-One third-r (3/72)	6	12	18	41	76	110
201-203-(25¢, 52 pgs.)-One third-r	5	10	15	33	57	80
204-Wrightson-c/a, 9 pgs.	5	10	15	35	63	90
205,206,208,210,212,215,216,218	4	8	12	23	37	50
207-Wrightson-c/a; Starlin, Redondo-a	5	10	15	35	63	90
209,211,213,214,217,219-Wrightson-c	5	10	15	31	53	75
220,222,223	3	6	9	21	33	45
221-Wrightson/Kaluta-a(8 pgs.); Wrightson-c	5	10	15	34	60	85
224-229: 224-Wrightson-r from Spectre #9; Dillin/Adams-r from House of Secrets #82; begin 100 pg. issues; Phantom Stranger-r. 225,227-(100 pgs.): 225-Spectre app. 226-Wrightson/Redondo-a Phantom Stranger-r. 228-N. Adams inks; Wrightson-r. 229-Wrightson-a(r); Toth-r; last 100 pg. issue	5	10	15	35	63	90
230,232-235,237-250	3	6	9	15	22	28
231-Classic Wrightson-c	5	10	15	34	60	85
236-Wrightson-c; Ditko-a(p); N. Adams-i	4	8	12	28	47	65
251-254-(84 pgs.)-Adams-c. 251-Wood-a	4	8	12	27	44	60
255,256-(84 pgs.)-Wrightson-c	4	8	12	27	44	60
257-259-(84 pgs.)	3	6	9	18	28	38
260-289: 282-(68 pgs.)-Has extra story "The Computers That Saved Metropolis" Radio Shack giveaway by Jim Starlin	2	4	6	8	10	12
290-1st "I, Vampire"	3	6	9	17	26	35
291-299: 291,293,295-299- "I, Vampire"	2	4	6	10	14	18
300,319-"I, Vampire"	2	4	6	11	16	20
301-318,320: 301-318-"I, Vampire"	2	4	6	10	14	18
321-Death of "I, Vampire"	3	6	9	14	20	25

Welcome to the House of Mystery (7/98, $5.95) reprints stories with new framing story by Gaiman and Aragonés 6.00

NOTE: ***Neal Adams*** *a-236i; c-175-192, 197, 199, 251-254.* ***Alcala*** *a-209, 217, 219, 224, 227.* ***M. Anderson*** *a-212; c/a-37.* ***Aparo*** *a-209.* ***Aragones*** *a-185, 186, 194, 196, 200, 202, 229, 251.* ***Baily*** *a-279p.* ***Cameron*** *a-76, 79.* ***Colan*** *a-202r.* ***Craig*** *a-263, 275, 295, 300.* ***Dillin/Adams*** *r-224.* ***Ditko*** *a-236p, 247, 254, 258, 276; c-277.* ***Drucker*** *a-37.* ***Evans*** *c-218.* ***Fradon*** *a-251.* ***Giffen*** *a-284.* ***Giunta*** *a-199, 227r.* ***Golden*** *a-257, 259.* ***Heath*** *a-194r; c-203.* ***Howard*** *a-182, 185, 187, 196, 229r, 247i, 254, 279i.* ***Kaluta*** *a-195, 200, 250r; c-200-202, 210, 212, 233, 260, 261, 263, 265, 267, 268, 273, 276, 284, 287, 288, 293-295, 300, 302, 304, 305, 309-319, 321.* ***Bob Kane*** *a-84.* ***Gil Kane*** *a-196p, 253p, 300p.* ***Kirby*** *a-194r, 199r; c-65, 76, 78, 79, 85.* ***Kubert*** *c-282, 283, 285, 286, 289-292, 297-299, 301, 303, 306-308.* ***Maneely*** *a-68, 227r.* ***Mayer*** *a-317p.* ***Meskin*** *a-52-144 (most), 195r, 224r, 229r; c-63, 66, 124, 127.* ***Mooney*** *a-24, 159, 160.* ***Moreira*** *a-3, 4, 20-50, 58, 59, 62, 68, 77, 79, 90, 108, 113, 123, 201r, 228; c-4-28, 44, 47, 50, 54, 59, 62, 64, 68, 70, 73.* ***Morrow*** *a-192, 196, 255, 320i.* ***Mortimer*** *a-204(3 pgs.).* ***Nasser*** *a-276.* ***Newton*** *a-259, 272.* ***Nino*** *a-204, 212, 213, 220, 224, 225, 245, 250, 252-256, 283.* ***Orlando*** *a-175(2 pgs.), 178, 240i; c-240, 258p, 262, 264p, 270p, 271, 272, 274, 275, 278, 296i.* ***Redondo*** *a-194, 195, 197, 202, 203, 207, 211, 214, 217, 219, 226, 227, 229, 235, 241, 287(layout), 302p, 303i, 308; c-229.* ***Reese*** *a-195, 200, 205i.* ***Rogers*** *a-254, 274, 277.* ***Roussos*** *a-65, 84, 224i.* ***Sekowsky*** *a-282p.* ***Sparling*** *a-203.* ***Starlin*** *a-207(2 pgs.), 282p; c-281.* ***Leonard Starr*** *a-9.* ***Staton*** *a-300p.* ***Sutton*** *a-189, 271, 290, 291, 293, 295, 297-299, 302, 303, 306-309, 310-313i, 314.* ***Tuska*** *a-293p, 294p, 316p.* ***Wrightson*** *c-193-195, 204, 207, 209, 211, 213, 214, 217, 219, 221, 231, 236, 255, 256; r-224.*

HOUSE OF MYSTERY

DC Comics (Vertigo): Jul, 2008 - No. 42, Dec, 2011 ($2.99)

	NM- 9.2
1-12,14-42: 1-Cain & Abel app.; Rossi-a/Weber-c. 9-Wrightson-a (6 pgs.). 16-Corben-a	3.00
1-Variant-c by Bernie Wrightson	5.00
13-Art by Neal Adams, Ralph Reese, Eric Powell, Sergio Aragonés	3.00
13-Variant-c by Neal Adams	5.00
... Halloween Annual #1 (12/09, $4.99) short stories by various incl. Hadley, Allred, Nowlan	5.00
... Halloween Annual #2 (12/10, $4.99) short stories by various incl. Carey, Allred, Gross	5.00
...: Love Stories for Dead People TPB (2009, $14.99) r/#6-10	15.00
...: Room and Boredom TPB (2008, $9.99) r/#1-5	10.00
...: Safe as Houses TPB (2011, $14.99) r/#26-30	15.00
...: The Beauty of Decay TPB (2010, $17.99) r/#16-20 & Halloween Annual #1	18.00
...: The Space Between TPB (2010, $14.99) r/#11-15; sketch pages	15.00
...: Under New Management TPB (2011, $14.99) r/#20-25	15.00

HOUSE OF NIGHT (Based on the series of novels by P.C. Cast and Kristin Cast)

Dark Horse Comics: Nov, 2011 - No. 5, Mar, 2012 ($1.00/$2.99, limited series)

	NM- 9.2
1-($1.00) Cast, Cast & Dalian-s/Joëlle Jones & Kerschl-a; Frison-c	3.00
1-($1.00) Variant-c by Steve Morris	4.00
2-5-($2.99) Jones-a; two covers by Jones & Ryan Hill on each	3.00

HOUSE OF SECRETS (Combined with The Unexpected after #154)

National Periodical Publications/DC Comics: 11-12/56 - No. 80, 9-10/66; No. 81, 8-9/69 - No. 140, 2-3/76; No. 141, 8-9/76 - No. 154, 10-11/78

	GD 2.0	VG 4.0	FN 6.0	VF 8.0	VF/NM 9.0	NM- 9.2
1-Drucker-a; Moreira-c	114	228	342	912	2056	3200
2-Moreira-a	40	80	120	296	673	1050
3-Kirby-c/a	35	70	105	252	564	875
4-Kirby-a	26	52	78	182	404	625
5-7	19	38	57	131	291	450
8-Kirby-a	20	40	60	141	313	485
9-11: 11-Lou Cameron-a (unsigned)	17	34	51	117	259	400
12-Kirby-c/a; Lou Cameron-a	18	36	54	124	275	425
13-15: 14-Flying saucer-c	13	26	39	89	195	300
16-20	12	24	36	82	179	275
21,22,24-30	11	22	33	73	157	240
23-1st app. Mark Merlin & begin series (8/59)	12	24	36	79	170	260
31-50: 48-Toth-a. 50-Last 10¢ issue	10	20	30	66	138	210
51-60: 58-Origin Mark Merlin	8	16	24	56	108	160
61-First Eclipso (7-8/63) and begin series	16	32	48	110	243	375
62	7	14	21	46	86	125
63-65-Toth-a on Eclipso (see Brave and the Bold #64)	6	12	18	37	66	95
66-1st Eclipso-c (also #67,70,78,79); Toth-a	7	14	21	46	86	125
67,73: 67-Toth-a on Eclipso. 73-Mark Merlin becomes Prince Ra-Man (1st app.)	6	12	18	37	66	95
68-72,74-80: 76-Prince Ra-Man vs. Eclipso. 80-Eclipso, Prince Ra-Man end	5	10	15	34	60	85
81-Mystery format begins; 1st app. Abel (House Of Secrets host); (cameo in DC Special #4)	12	24	36	82	179	275
82-84: 82-Neal Adams-c(i)	7	14	21	49	92	135
85,90: 85-N. Adams-a(i). 90-Buckler (early work)/N. Adams-a(i)	8	16	24	51	96	140
86,88,89,91	7	14	21	44	82	120

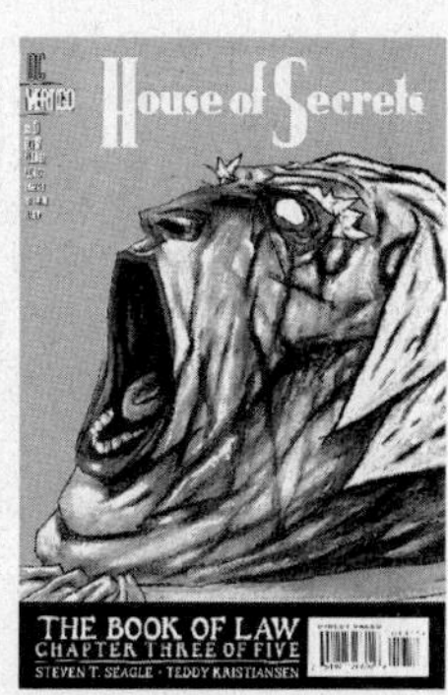

House of Secrets #13 © Seagle & Kristiansen

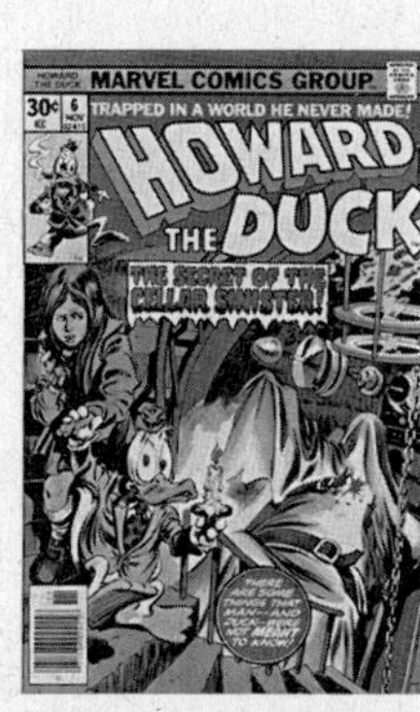

Howard the Duck #6 © MAR

Howdy Doody #10 © CNP

	GD 2.0	VG 4.0	FN 6.0	VF 8.0	VF/NM 9.0	NM- 9.2

87-Wrightson & Kaluta-a 8 16 24 52 99 145
92-1st app. Swamp Thing-c/story (8 pgs.)(6-7/71) by Berni Wrightson(p)
w/JeffJones/Kaluta/Weiss ink assists; classic-c. 46 92 138 350 788 1225
93,94,96-(52 pgs.)-Wrightson-c. 94-Wrightson-a(i); 96-Wood-a
7 14 21 46 86 125
95,97,98-(52 pgs.) 5 10 15 35 63 90
99-Wrightson splash pg. 5 10 15 34 60 85
100-Classic Wrightson-c 7 14 21 49 92 135
101,102,104,105,108-111,113-120 3 6 9 19 30 40
103,106,107-Wrightson-c 5 10 15 33 57 80
112-Grey tone-c 4 8 12 23 37 50
121-133 2 4 6 11 16 20
134-Wrightson-a 3 6 9 17 26 35
135,136,139-Wrightson-a/c 3 6 9 20 31 42
137,138,141-153 2 4 6 8 10 12
140-1st solo origin of the Patchworkman (see Swamp Thing #3)
3 6 9 16 23 30
154 (10-11/78, 44 pgs.) Last issue 2 4 6 9 13 16

NOTE: ***Neal Adams*** *c-81, 82, 84-88, 90, 91.* ***Alcala*** *a-104-107.* ***Anderson*** *a-91. Aparo a-93, 97, 105.* ***B. Bailey*** *a-107.* ***Cameron*** *a-13, 15.* ***Colan*** *a-63.* ***Ditko*** *a-139p, 148.* ***Elias*** *a-58.* ***Evans*** *a-118.* ***Finlay*** *a-7r(Real Fact?).* ***Glanzman*** *a-91.* ***Golden*** *a-151.* ***Heath*** *a-31.* ***Heck*** *a-85.* ***Kaluta*** *a-87, 98, 99; c-98, 99, 101, 102, 105, 149, 151, 154.* ***Bob Kane*** *a-18, 21.* ***G. Kane*** *a-85p.* ***Kirby*** *c-3, 11, 12.* ***Kubert*** *a-39.* ***Meskin*** *a-2-68 (most), 94r; c-55-60.* ***Moreira*** *a-7, 8, 51, 54, 102-104, 106, 108, 113, 116, 118, 121, 123, 127; c-1, 2, 4-10, 13-20.* ***Morrow*** *a-86, 89, 90; c-89, 146-148.* ***Nino*** *a-101, 103, 106, 109, 115, 117, 126, 128, 131, 147, 153.* ***Redondo*** *a-95, 99, 102, 104p, 113, 116, 134, 136, 139, 140.* ***Reese*** *a-85.* ***Severin*** *a-91.* ***Starlin*** *c-150.* ***Sutton*** *a-154.* ***Toth*** *a-63-67, 83, 93r, 94r, 96r-98r, 123.* ***Tuska*** *a-90, 104.* ***Wrightson*** *a-134; c-92-94, 96, 100, 103, 106, 107, 135, 136, 139.*

HOUSE OF SECRETS
DC Comics (Vertigo): Oct, 1996 - No. 25, Dec, 1998 ($2.50) (Creator-owned series)

1-Steven Seagle-s/Kristiansen-c/a. 3.50
2-25: 5,7-Kristiansen-c/a. 6-Fegrado-a 3.00
TPB-(1997, $14.95) r/1-5 15.00

HOUSE OF SECRETS: FACADE
DC Comics (Vertigo): 2001 - No. 2, 2001 ($5.95, limited series)

1,2-Steven Seagle-s/Teddy Kristiansen-c/a. 6.00

HOUSE OF TERROR (3-D)
St. John Publishing Co.: Oct, 1953 (25¢, came w/glasses)

1-Kubert, Baker-a 27 54 81 158 259 360

HOUSE OF YANG, THE (See Yang)
Charlton Comics: July, 1975 - No. 6, June, 1976; 1978

1-Sanho Kim-a in all 2 4 6 13 18 22
2-6 2 4 6 8 10 12
Modern Comics #1,2(1978) 6.00

HOUSE ON THE BORDERLAND
DC Comics (Vertigo): 2000 ($29.95, hardcover, one-shot)

HC-Adaptation of William Hope Hodgson book; Corben-a 30.00
SC (2003, $19.95) 20.00

HOUSE II: THE SECOND STORY
Marvel Comics: Oct, 1987 (One-shot)

1-Adapts movie 4.00

HOWARD CHAYKIN'S AMERICAN FLAGG (See American Flagg!)
First Comics: V2#1, May, 1988 - V2#12, Apr, 1989 ($1.75/$1.95, Baxter paper)

V2#1-9,11,12-Chaykin-c(p) in all 3.00
10-Elvis Presley photo-c 4.00

HOWARD THE DUCK (See Bizarre Adventures #34, Crazy Magazine, Fear, Man-Thing, Marvel Treasury Edition & Sensational She-Hulk #14-17)
Marvel Comics Group: Jan, 1976 - No. 31, May, 1979; No. 32, Jan, 1986; No. 33, Sept, 1986

1-Brunner-c/a; Spider-Man x-over (low distr.) 4 8 12 28 47 65
2-Brunner-c/a 2 4 6 11 16 20
3,4-(Regular 25¢ edition). 3-Buscema-a(p), (7/76) 2 4 6 8 11 14
3,4-(30¢-c, limited distribution) 3 6 9 15 22 28
5 2 4 6 8 11 14
6-11: 8-Howard The Duck for president. 9-1st Sgt. Preston Dudley of RCMP.
10-Spider-Man-c/sty 1 2 3 5 7 9
12-1st brief app. Kiss (3/77) 4 8 12 23 37 50
13-(30¢-c) 1st full app. Kiss (6/77); Daimon Hellstrom app. plus cameo of
Howard as Son of Satan 4 8 12 27 44 60
13-(35¢-c, limited distribution) 8 16 24 56 108 160
14-32: 14-17-(Regular 30¢-c). 14-Howard as Son of Satan-c/story; Son of Satan app.
16-Album issue; 3 pgs. comics. 22,23-Man-Thing-c/stories; Star Wars parody.
30,32-P. Smith-a 6.00

	GD 2.0	VG 4.0	FN 6.0	VF 8.0	VF/NM 9.0	NM- 9.2

14-17-(35¢-c, limited distribution) 3 6 9 14 20 25
33-Last issue; low print run 1 2 3 5 6 8
Annual 1(1977, 52 pgs.)-Mayerik-a 2 3 4 6 8 10
... Omnibus HC (2008, $99.99, dustjacket) r/#1-33 & Annual #1, Adventure Into Fear #19,
Man-Thing #1, Giant-Size Man-Thing #4&5, Marvel Treasury Ed. #12, Marvel Team-Up
#96 and FOOM #15; Gerber foreword; creator interviews; bonus art; 2 covers 100.00

NOTE: ***Austin*** *c-29i.* ***Bolland*** *c-33.* ***Brunner*** *a-1p, 2p; c-1, 2.* ***Buckler*** *c-3p.* ***Buscema*** *a-3p.* ***Colan*** *a(p)-4-15, 17-20, 24-27, 30, 31; c(p)-4-31, Annual 1p.* ***Leialoha*** *a-1-13i; c(i)-3-5, 8-11.* ***Mayerik*** *a-22, 23, 33.* ***Paul Smith*** *a-30p, 32. Man-Thing app. in #22, 23.*

HOWARD THE DUCK (Magazine)
Marvel Comics Group: Oct, 1979 - No. 9, Mar, 1981 (B&W, 68 pgs.)

1-Art by Colan, Janson, Golden. Kidney Lady app. 2 4 6 8 10 12
2,3,5-9 (nudity in most): 2-Mayerick-c. 3-Xmas issue; Jack Davis-c; Duck World flashback.
5-Dracula app. 6-1st Street People back-up story. 7-Has pin-up by Byrne; Man-Thing-c/s (46 pgs.). 8-Batman parody w/Marshall Rogers-a; Dave Sim-a (1 pg.). 9-Marie Severin-a;
John Pound painted-c 6.00
4-Beatles, John Lennon, Elvis, Kiss & Devo cameos; Hitler app.
2 4 6 9 12 15

NOTE: ***Buscema*** *a-4p.* ***Colan*** *a-1-5p, 7-9p.* ***Jack Davis*** *c-3.* ***Golden*** *a(p)-1, 5, 6(51pgs.).* ***Rogers*** *a-7, 8.* ***Simonson*** *a-7.*

HOWARD THE DUCK (Volume 2)
Marvel Comics: Mar, 2002 - No. 6, Aug, 2002 ($2.99)

1-Gerber-s/Winslade-a/Fabry-c 4.00
2-6: 2,4-6-Gerber-s/Winslade-a/Fabry-c. 3-Fabry-a/c 3.00
TPB (9/02, $14.99) r/#1-6 15.00

HOWARD THE DUCK (Volume 3)
Marvel Comics: Dec, 2007 - No. 4, Feb, 2008 ($2.99, limited series)

1-4-Templeton-s/Bobillo-a/c; She-Hulk app. 3.00
...: Media Duckling TPB (2008, $11.99) r/#1-4; Howard the Duck #1 (1/76) and pages from
Civil War: Choosing Sides 12.00

HOWARD THE DUCK HOLIDAY SPECIAL
Marvel Comics: Feb, 1997 ($2.50, one-shot)

1-Wraparound-c; Hama-s 4.00

HOWARD THE DUCK: THE MOVIE
Marvel Comics Group: Dec, 1986 - No. 3, Feb, 1987 (Limited series)

1-3: Movie adaptation; r/Marvel Super Special 4.00

HOW BOYS AND GIRLS CAN HELP WIN THE WAR
The Parents' Magazine Institute: 1942 (10¢, one-shot)

1-All proceeds used to buy war bonds 31 62 93 182 296 410

HOWDY DOODY (TV)(See Jackpot of Fun-- & Poll Parrot)(Some have stories by John Stanley)
Dell Publishing Co.: 1/50 - No. 38, 7-9/56; No. 761, 1/57; No. 811, 7/57

1-(Scarce)-Photo-c; 1st TV comic 71 142 213 568 1284 2000
2-Photo-c 34 68 102 241 541 840
3-5: All photo-c 19 38 57 133 297 460
6-Used in **SOTI**, pg. 309; classic-c; painted covers begin
21 42 63 147 324 500
7-10 12 24 36 84 185 285
11-20: 13-X-Mas-c 10 20 30 70 150 230
21-38, Four Color 761,811 9 18 27 61 123 185

HOW IT BEGAN
United Features Syndicate: No. 15, 1939 (one-shot)

Single Series 15 34 68 102 199 325 450

HOW SANTA GOT HIS RED SUIT (See March of Comics No. 2)

HOW THE WEST WAS WON (See Movie Comics)

HOW TO DRAW FOR THE COMICS
Street and Smith: No date (1942?) (10¢, 64 pgs., B&W & color, no ads)

nn-Art by Robert Winsor McCay (recreating his father's art), George Marcoux (Supersnipe artist), Vernon Greene (The Shadow artist), Jack Binder (with biog.), Thorton Fisher, Jon Small, & Jack Farr; has biographies of each artist
32 64 96 192 314 435

H. P. LOVECRAFT'S CTHULHU
Millennium Publications: Dec, 1991 - No. 3, May, 1992 ($2.50, limited series)

1-3: 1-Contains trading cards on thin stock 3.00

H. R. PUFNSTUF (TV) (See March of Comics #360)
Gold Key: Oct, 1970 - No. 8, July, 1972

1-Photo-c 10 20 30 64 132 200
2-8-Photo-c on all. 6-8-Both Gold Key and Whitman editions exist

Huckleberry Hound #5 © H-B

Hulk #29 © MAR

Hulk and Power Pack #1 © MAR

GD VG FN VF VF/NM NM-
2.0 4.0 6.0 8.0 9.0 9.2

GD VG FN VF VF/NM NM-
2.0 4.0 6.0 8.0 9.0 9.2

7 14 21 46 86 125

HUBERT AT CAMP MOONBEAM
Dell Publishing Co.: No. 251, Oct, 1949 (one shot)

Four Color 251 8 16 24 54 102 150

HUCK & YOGI JAMBOREE (TV)
Dell Publishing Co.: Mar, 1961 ($1.00, 6-1/4x9", 116 pgs., cardboard-c, high quality paper) (B&W original material)

nn (scarce) 8 16 24 54 102 150

HUCK & YOGI WINTER SPORTS (TV)
Dell Publishing Co.: No. 1310, Mar, 1962 (Hanna-Barbara) (one-shot)

Four Color 1310 7 14 21 49 92 135

HUCK FINN (See The New Adventures of... & Power Record Comics)

HUCKLEBERRY FINN (Movie)
Dell Publishing Co.: No. 1114, July, 1960

Four Color 1114-Photo-c 5 10 15 33 57 80

HUCKLEBERRY HOUND (See Dell Giant #31,44, Golden Picture Story Book, Kite Fun Book, March of Comics #199, 214, 235, Spotlight #1 & Whitman Comic Books)

HUCKLEBERRY HOUND (TV)
Dell/Gold Key No. 18 (10/62) on: No. 990, 5-7/59 - No. 43, 10/70 (Hanna-Barbera)

Four Color 990(#1)-1st app. Huckleberry Hound, Yogi Bear, & Pixie & Dixie & Mr. Jinks
10 20 30 70 150 230
Four Color 1050,1054 (12/59) 7 14 21 49 92 135
3(1-2/60) - 7 (9-10/60), Four Color 1141 (10/60) 7 14 21 44 82 120
8-10 6 12 18 37 66 95
11,13-17 (6-8/62) 5 10 15 30 50 70
12-1st Hokey Wolf & Ding-a-Ling 5 10 15 33 57 80
18,19 (84pgs.; 18-20 titled ...Chuckleberry Tales) 7 14 21 44 82 120
20-Titled Chuckleberry Tales 4 8 12 28 47 65
21-30: 28-30-Reprints 4 8 12 23 37 50
31-43: 31,32,35,37-43-Reprints 3 6 9 19 30 40

HUCKLEBERRY HOUND (TV)
Charlton Comics: Nov, 1970 - No. 8, Jan, 1972 (Hanna-Barbera)

1 5 10 15 30 50 70
2-8 3 6 9 17 26 35

HUEY, DEWEY, & LOUIE (See Donald Duck, 1938 for 1st app. Also see Mickey Mouse Magazine V4#2, V5#7 & Walt Disney's Junior Woodchucks Limited Series)

HUEY, DEWEY, & LOUIE BACK TO SCHOOL (See Dell Giant #22, 35, 49 & Dell Giants)

HUEY, DEWEY, AND LOUIE JUNIOR WOODCHUCKS (Disney)
Gold Key No. 1-61/Whitman No. 62 on: Aug, 1966 - No. 81, July, 1984
(See Walt Disney's Comics & Stories #125)

1 5 10 15 35 63 90
2,3(12/68) 3 6 9 21 33 45
4,5(4/70)-r/two WDC&S D.Duck stories by Barks 3 6 9 19 30 40
6-17 3 6 9 17 26 35
18,27-30 3 6 9 15 21 26
19-23,25-New storyboarded scripts by Barks, 13-25 pgs. per issue
3 6 9 18 28 38
24,26: 26-r/Barks Donald Duck WDC&S stories 3 6 9 16 23 30
31-57,60,61: 35,41-r/Barks J.W. scripts 2 4 6 8 11 14
58,59: 58-r/Barks Donald Duck WDC&S stories 2 4 6 9 13 16
62-64 (Whitman) 2 4 6 9 13 16
65-(9/80), 66 (Pre-pack? scarce) 4 8 12 23 37 50
67 (1/81),68 2 4 6 9 13 16
67-40¢ cover variant 4 8 12 17 21 24
69-74: 72(2/82), 73(2-3/82), 74(3/82) 2 4 6 8 11 14
75-81 (all #90183; pre-pack; nd, nd code; scarce): 75(4/83), 76(5/83), 77(7/83), 78(8/83), 79(4/84), 80(5/84), 81(7/84) 3 6 9 15 22 28

HUGGA BUNCH (TV)
Marvel Comics (Star Comics): Oct, 1986 - No. 6, Aug, 1987

1-6 5.00

HULK (Magazine)(Formerly The Rampaging Hulk)(Also see The Incredible Hulk)
Marvel Comics: No. 10, Aug., 1978 - No. 27, June, 1981 ($1.50)

10-18: 10-Bill Bixby interview. 11-Moon Knight begins. 12-15,17,18-Moon Knight stories. 12-Lou Ferrigno interview. 2 4 6 10 14 18
19-27: 20-Moon Knight story. 23-Last full color issue; Banner is attacked. 24-Part color, Lou Ferrigno interview. 25-Part color. 26,27-are B&W
2 4 6 9 12 15

NOTE: #10-20 have fragile spines which split easily. ***Alcala*** *a(i)-15, 17-20, 22, 24-27.* ***Buscema*** *a-23; c-26.* ***Chaykin*** *a-21-25.* ***Colan*** *a(p)-11, 19, 24-27.* ***Jusko*** *painted c-12.* ***Nebres*** *a-16.* ***Severin*** *a-19i. Moon Knight by* ***Sienkiewicz*** *in 13-15, 17, 18, 20.* ***Simonson*** *a-27; c-23. Dominic Fortune appears in #21-24.*

HULK (Becomes Incredible Hulk Vol. 2 with issue #12) (Also see Marvel Age Hulk)
Marvel Comics: Apr, 1999 - No. 11, Feb, 2000 ($2.99/$1.99)

1-($2.99) Byrne-s/Garney-a 5.00
1-Variant-c 1 3 4 6 8 10
1-DFE Remarked-c 50.00
1-Gold foil variant 10.00
2-7-($1.99): 2-Two covers. 5-Art by Jurgens, Buscema & Texeira. 7-Avengers app. 4.00
8-Hulk battles Wolverine 7.00
9-11: 11-She-Hulk app. 3.00
1999 Annual ($3.50) Chapter One story; Byrne-s/Weeks-a 4.00
Hulk Vs. The Thing (12/99, $3.99, TPB) reprints their notable battles 4.00

HULK (Also see Fall of the Hulks and King-Size Hulk) (Becomes Red She-Hulk with #58)
Marvel Comics: Mar, 2008 - No. 57, Oct, 2012 ($2.99/$3.99)

1-Red Hulk app.; Abomination killed; Loeb-s/McGuinness-a/c
1 2 3 5 6 8
1-Variant-c by Acuña 10.00
1-Variant-c with Incredible Hulk #1 cover swipe by McGuinness 20.00
1,2-2nd printings with wraparound McGuinness variant-c 3.00
2-22: 2-Iron Man app.; Rick Jones becomes the new Abomination. 4,6-Red Hulk vs. green Hulk; two covers (each Hulk); Thor app. 7-9-Art Adams & Cho-a (2 covers) 10-Defenders re-form. 14,15-X-Force, Elektra & Deadpool app. 15-Red She-Hulk app. 19-21-Fall of the Hulks x-over. 19-FF app. 22-World War Hulks 4.00
2-9: 2-Variant-c by Djurdjevic. 3-Var-c by Finch. 5-Var-c by Coipel. 6,7-Var-c by Turner 8-Var-c by Sal Buscema. 9-Two covers w/Hulks as Santa 6.00
23-($4.99) Origin of the Red Hulk; art by Sale, Romita, Deodato, Trimpe, Yu, others 5.00
24-31-($3.99): 24-World war Hulks. 25,26-Iron Man app. 26-Thor app. 4.00
30.1, 32-49 ($2.99): 34-Planet Red Hulk begins. 37-38-Fear Itself tie-in 3.00
50-($3.99) Haunted Hulk; Dr. Strange app.; back-up w/Brereton-a; Pagulayan-c 4.00
50-Variant covers by Art Adams, Humberto Ramos & Walt Simonson 10.00
51-57: 53-57-Eaglesham-a; Alpha Flight app. 3.00
... Family: Green Genes 1 (2/09, $4.99) new She-Hulk, Scorpion, Skaar & Mr. Fixit stories 5.00
... Let the Battle Begin 1 (5/10, $3.99) Snider-s/Kurth-a; Del Mundo-c; McGuinness-a 4.00
... MGC #1 (6/10, $1.00) r/#1 with "Marvel's Greatest Comics" logo on cover 3.00
... Monster-Size Special (12/08, $3.99) monster-themed stories by Niles, David & others 4.00
...: Raging Thunder 1 (8/08, $3.99) Hulk vs. Thundra; Breitweiser-a; r/FF #133; Land-c 4.00
Hulk-Sized Mini-Hulks ('11, $2.99) Red, Green & Blue Hulks all-ages humor; Giarrusso-a 3.00
... Vs. Fin Fang Foom (2/08, $3.99) new re-telling of first meeting; r/Strange Tales #89 4.00
... Vs. Hercules (6/08, $3.99) Djurdjevic-c; new story w/art by various; r/Tales To Ast. #79 4.00
...: Winter Guard (2/10, $3.99) Darkstar, Crimson Dynamo app. Steve Ellis-a/c 4.00
Hulk 100 Project (2008, $10.00, SC, charity book for the HERO Initiative) collection of 100 variant covers by Adams, Romita Sr. & Jr., Cho, McGuinness and more 10.00

HULK AND POWER PACK (All ages series)
Marvel Comics: May, 2007 - No. 4, Aug, 2007 ($2.99, limited series)

1-4-Sumerak-s. 1,2,4-Williams-a. 1-Absorbing Man app. 3-Kuhn-a; Abomination app. 3.00
...: Pack Smash! (2007, $6.99, digest) r/#1-4 7.00

HULK & THING: HARD KNOCKS
Marvel Comics: Nov, 2004 - No. 4, Feb, 2005 ($3.50, limited series)

1-4-Bruce Jones-s/Jae Lee-a/c 3.50
TPB (2005, $13.99) r/#1-4 and Giant-Size Super-Stars #1 14.00

HULK: BROKEN WORLDS
Marvel Comics: May, 2009 -No. 2, July, 2009 ($3.99, limited series)

1,2-Short stories of alternate world Hulks by various, incl. Trimpe, David, Warren 4.00

HULK CHRONICLES: WWH
Marvel Comics: Oct, 2008 - No. 6, Mar, 2009 ($4.99, limited series)

1-6-Reprints stories from World War Hulk x-over. 1-R/Inc. Hulk #106 & WWH Prologue 5.00

HULK: DESTRUCTION
Marvel Comics: Sept, 2005 - No. 4, Dec, 2005 ($2.99, limited series)

1-4-Origin of the Abomination; Peter David-s/Jim Muniz-a 3.00

HULKED-OUT HEROES
Marvel Comics: Jun, 2010 - No. 2, Jun, 2010 ($3.99, limited series)

1,2-World War Hulks tie-in; Deadpool app.; Ramos-a 4.00

HULK: FUTURE IMPERFECT
Marvel Comics: Jan, 1993 - No. 2, Dec, 1992 (In error) ($5.95, 52 pgs., squarebound, limited series)

1,2: Embossed-c; Peter David story & George Perez-c/a. 1-1st app. Maestro.
1 2 3 5 6 8

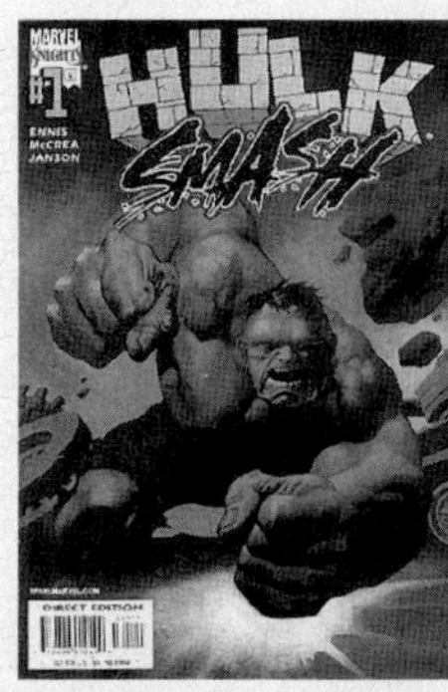

Hulk Smash #1 © MAR

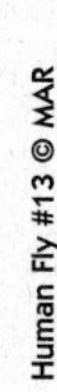
Human Fly #13 © MAR

The Human Torch #11 © MAR

GD 2.0 | VG 4.0 | FN 6.0 | VF 8.0 | VF/NM 9.0 | NM- 9.2

HULK: GRAY
Marvel Comics: Dec, 2003 - No. 6, Apr, 2004 ($3.50, limited series)
1-6-Hulk's origin & early days; Loeb-s/Sale-a/c 3.50
HC (2004, $21.99, with dust jacket) oversized r/#1-6 22.00
SC (2005, $19.99) r/#1-6 20.00

HULK: NIGHTMERICA
Marvel Comics: Aug, 2003 - No. 6, May, 2004 ($2.99, limited series)
1-6-Brian Ashmore painted-a/c 3.00

HULK/ PITT
Marvel Comics: 1997 ($5.99, one-shot)
1-David-s/Keown-c/a 6.00

HULK: SEASON ONE
Marvel Comics: 2012 ($24.99, hardcover graphic novel)
HC - Origin and early days; Van Lente-s/Fowler-a/Tedesco painted-c 25.00

HULK SMASH
Marvel Comics: Mar, 2001 - No. 2, Apr, 2001 ($2.99, limited series)
1,2-Ennis-s/McCrea & Janson-a/Nowlan painted-c 3.00

HULK SMASH AVENGERS
Marvel Comics: Jul, 2012 - No. 5, July, 2012 ($2.99, weekly limited series)
1-5-Hulk vs. Avengers from various points in Marvel History. 1-Frenz-a. 5-Oeming-a 3.00

HULK: THE MOVIE
Marvel Comics
...Adaptation (8/03, $3.50) Bruce Jones-s/Bagley-a/Keown-c 3.50
TPB (2003, $12.99) r/Adaptation, Ultimates #5, Inc. Hulk #34, Ult. Marvel Team-Up #2&3 13.00

HULK 2099
Marvel Comics: Dec, 1994 - No. 10, Sept, 1995 ($1.50/$1.95)
1-($2.50)-Green foil-c 4.00
2-10: 2-A. Kubert-c 3.00

HULK/WOLVERINE: 6 HOURS
Marvel Comics: Mar, 2003 - No. 4, May, 2003 ($2.99, limited series)
1-4-Bruce Jones-s/Scott Kolins-a; Bisley-c 3.00
Hulk Legends Vol. 1: Hulk/Wolverine: 6 Hours (2003, $13.99, TPB) r/#1-4 & 1st Wolverine app. from Incredible Hulk #181 14.00

HUMAN BOMB
DC Comics: Feb, 2013 - No. 4, May, 2013 ($2.99, limited series)
1-4: 1-Re-intro/origin; Gray & Palmiotti-s/Ordway-a/c 3.00

HUMAN DEFENSE CORPS
DC Comics: Jul, 2003 - No. 6, Dec, 2003 ($2.50, limited series)
1-6-Ty Templeton-s/Sauve, Jr & Vlasco-a. 1-Lois Lane app. 3.00

HUMAN FLY
I.W. Enterprises/Super: 1963 - 1964 (Reprints)
I.W. Reprint #1-Reprints Blue Beetle #44('46) 2 4 6 13 18 22
Super Reprint #10-R/Blue Beetle #46('47) 2 4 6 13 18 22

HUMAN FLY, THE
Marvel Comics Group: Sept, 1977 - No. 19, Mar, 1979
1,2,9,19: 1,2-(Regular 30¢-c). 1-Origin; Spider-Man x-over. 2-Ghost Rider app. 9-Daredevil x-over; Byrne-c(p). 19-Last issue 2 3 4 6 8 10
1,2-(35¢-c, limited distribution) 3 6 9 19 30 40
3-8,10-18 5.00
NOTE: ***Austin*** *c-4i, 9i.* ***Elias*** *a-1, 3p, 4p, 7p, 10-12p, 15p, 18p, 19p.* ***Layton*** *c-19.*

HUMANKIND
Image Comics (Top Cow): Sept, 2004 - No. 5, Mar, 2005 ($2.99, limited series)
1-5-Tony Daniel-a. 1-Three covers by Daniel, Silvestri, and Land 3.00

HUMAN RACE, THE
DC Comics: May, 2005 - No. 7, Nov, 2005 ($2.99, limited series)
1-7-Raab-s/Justiniano-a/c 3.00

HUMAN TARGET
DC Comics (Vertigo): Apr, 1999 - No. 4, July, 1999 ($2.95, limited series)
1-4-Milligan-s/Bradstreet-c/Biuković-a 3.00
1-Special Edition (6/10, $1.00) r/#1 with "What's Next?" logo on cover 3.00
TPB (2000, $12.95) new Bradstreet-c 13.00
...: Chance Meetings TPB (2010, $14.99) r/#1-4 and Human Target: Final Cut GN 15.00

HUMAN TARGET
DC Comics (Vertigo): Oct, 2003 - No. 21, June, 2005 ($2.95)
1-21: 1-5-Milligan-s/Pulido-a/c. 6-Chiang-a 3.00
...: Living in Amerika TPB (2004, $14.95) r/#6-10; Chiang sketch pages 15.00
...: Second Chances TPB (2011, $19.99) r/#1-10; Chiang sketch pages 20.00
...: Strike Zones TPB (2004, $9.95) r/#1-5 10.00

HUMAN TARGET (Based on the Fox TV series)
DC Comics: Apr, 2010 - No. 6, Sept, 2010 ($2.99, limited series)
1-6-Wein-s/Redondo-a; back-up stories by various. 1-Bermejo-c. 5-Sook-c 3.00
TPB (2010, $17.99) r/#1-6 18.00

HUMAN TARGET: FINAL CUT
DC Comics (Vertigo): 2002 ($29.95/$19.95, graphic novel)
Hardcover (2002, $29.95) Milligan-s/Pulido-a/c 30.00
Softcover (2003, $19.95) 20.00

HUMAN TARGET SPECIAL (TV)
DC Comics: Nov, 1991 ($2.00, 52 pgs., one-shot)
1 4.00

HUMAN TORCH, THE (Red Raven #1)(See All-Select, All Winners, Marvel Mystery, Men's Adventures, Mystic Comics (2nd series), Sub-Mariner, USA & Young Men)
Timely/Marvel Comics (TP 2,3/TCI 4-9/SePI 10/SnPC 11-25/CnPC 26-35/Atlas Comics (CPC 36-38)): No. 2, Fall, 1940 - No. 15, Spring, 1944; No. 16, Fall, 1944 - No. 35, Mar, 1949 (Becomes Love Tales #36 on); No. 36, April, 1954 - No. 38, Aug, 1954
2(#1)-Intro & Origin Toro; The Falcon, The Fiery Mask, Mantor the Magician, & Microman only app.; Human Torch by Burgos, Sub-Mariner by Everett begin (origin of each in text) 3000 6000 9000 21,000 44,500 68,000
3(#2)-40 pg. H.T. story; H.T. & S.M. battle over who is best artist in text-Everett or Burgos 595 1190 1785 4350 7675 11,000
4(#3)-Origin The Patriot in text; last Everett Sub-Mariner; Sid Greene-a 476 952 1428 3475 6138 8800
5(#4)-The Patriot app; Angel x-over in Sub-Mariner (Summer, 1941); 1st Nazi war-c this title; back-c ad for Young Allies #1 with diff. cover-a 421 842 1263 2947 5174 7400
5-Human Torch battles Sub-Mariner (Fall, '41); 60 pg. story 665 1330 1995 4855 8578 12,300
6-Schomburg hooded villain bondage-c 343 686 1029 2400 4200 6000
7-1st Japanese war-c 360 720 1080 2520 4410 6300
8-Human Torch battles Sub-Mariner; 52 pg. story; Wolverton-a, 1 pg.; Nazi WWII-c 449 898 1347 3278 5789 8300
9-Classic Human Torch vs. Gen. Rommel, "The Desert Rat"; Nazi WWII-c 366 732 1098 2562 4481 6400
10-Human Torch battles Sub-Mariner, 45 pg. story; Wolverton-a, 1 pg. 400 800 1200 2800 4900 7000
11,13-15: 11-Nazi WWII-c. 13-Japanese WWII-c. 14-1st Atlas Globe logo (Winter, 1943-44; see All Winners #11 also) 300 600 900 1950 3375 4800
12-Classic Japanese WWII-c 514 1028 1542 3750 6625 9500
16-20: 16-18,20-Japanese WWII-c. 20-Last War issue 213 426 639 1363 2332 3300
21,22,24-30: 27-2nd app. (1st-c) Asbestos Lady (see Capt. America Comics #63 for 1st app.) 165 330 495 1048 1799 2550
23 (Sum/46)-Becomes Junior Miss 24? Classic Schomburg Robot-c 206 412 618 1318 2259 3200
31,32: 31-Namora x-over in Sub-Mariner (also #30); last Toro. 32-Sungirl, Namora app.; Sungirl-c 145 290 435 921 1586 2250
33-Capt. America x-over 148 296 444 947 1624 2300
34-Sungirl solo 135 270 405 864 1482 2100
35-Captain America & Sungirl app. (1949) 139 278 417 883 1517 2150
36-38(1954)-Sub-Mariner in all 113 226 339 718 1234 1750
NOTE: ***Ayers*** *Human Torch in 36(3).* ***Brodsky*** *c-25, 31-33?, 37, 38.* ***Burgos*** *c-36.* ***Everett*** *a-1-3, 27, 28, 30, 37, 38.* ***Powell*** *a-36(Sub-Mariner).* ***Schomburg*** *c-1-3, 5-8, 10-23.* ***Sekowsky*** *c-28, 34?, 35?* ***Shores*** *c-24, 26, 27, 29, 30.* ***Mickey Spillane*** *text 4-6. Bondage c-2, 12, 19.*

HUMAN TORCH, THE (Also see Avengers West Coast, Fantastic Four, The Invaders, Saga of the Original... & Strange Tales #101)
Marvel Comics Group: Sept, 1974 - No. 8, Nov, 1975
1: 1-8-r/stories from Strange Tales #101-108 3 6 9 19 30 40
2-8: 1st H.T. title since G.A. 7-vs. Sub-Mariner 3 6 9 14 20 25
NOTE: *Golden Age & Silver Age Human Torch-r #1-8.* ***Ayers*** *r-6, 7.* ***Kirby/Ayers*** *r-1-5, 8.*

HUMAN TORCH (From the Fantastic Four)
Marvel Comics: June, 2003 - No. 12, Jun, 2004 ($2.50/$2.99)
1-7-Skottie Young-c/a; Karl Kesel-s 3.00
8-12-($2.99) 8,10-Dodd-a. 9-Young-a. 11-Porter-a. 12-Medina-a 3.00
... Vol. 1: Burn TPB (2005, $7.99, digest size) r/#1-6 8.00

HUMAN TORCH COMICS 70TH ANNIVERSARY SPECIAL
Marvel Comics: July, 2009 ($3.99, one-shot)

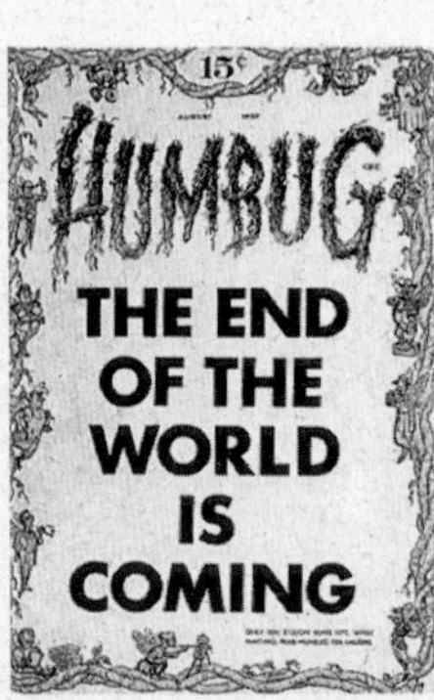

Humbug #1 © Harvey Kurtzman

Hunger #1 © MAR

Hyper Mystery Comics #2 © Hyper Mystery

	GD	VG	FN	VF	VF/NM	NM-
	2.0	4.0	6.0	8.0	9.0	9.2

GD VG FN VF VF/NM NM-
2.0 4.0 6.0 8.0 9.0 9.2

1-Covers by Granov and Martin; new story and r/1st app Toro from Human Torch #2 5.00

HUMBUG (Satire by Harvey Kurtzman)
Humbug Publications: Aug, 1957 - No. 9, May, 1958; No. 10, June, 1958; No. 11, Oct, 1958

	GD	VG	FN	VF	VF/NM	NM-
1-Wood-a (intro pgs. only)	27	54	81	158	259	360
2	15	30	45	85	130	175
3-9: 8-Elvis in Jailbreak Rock	14	28	42	76	108	140
10,11-Magazine format. 10-Photo-c	15	30	45	90	140	190
Bound Volume(#1-9)(extremely rare)	65	130	195	416	708	1000

NOTE: ***Davis** a-1-11. **Elder** a-2-4, 6-9, 11. **Heath** a-2, 4-8, 10. **Jaffee** a-2, 4-9. **Kurtzman** a-11.*

HUMDINGER (Becomes White Rider and Super Horse #3 on?)
Novelty Press/Premium Group: May-June, 1946 - V2#2, July-Aug, 1947

	GD	VG	FN	VF	VF/NM	NM-
1-Jerkwater Line, Mickey Starlight by Don Rico, Dink begin	36	72	108	216	351	485
2	16	32	48	94	147	200
3-6, V2#1,2	12	24	36	69	97	125

HUMONGOUS MAN
Alternative Press (Ikon Press): Sept, 1997 -No. 3 ($2.25, B&W)

1-3-Stepp & Harrison-c/s/a. 3.00

HUMOR (See All Humor Comics)

HUMPHREY COMICS (Joe Palooka Presents...; also see Joe Palooka)
Harvey Publications: Oct, 1948 - No. 22, Apr, 1952

	GD	VG	FN	VF	VF/NM	NM-
1-Joe Palooka's pal (r); (52 pgs.)-Powell-a	14	28	42	80	115	150
2,3: Powell-a	9	18	27	47	61	75
4-Boy Heroes app.; Powell-a	9	18	27	50	65	80
5-8,10: 5,6-Powell-a. 7-Little Dot app.	8	16	24	40	50	60
9-Origin Humphrey	9	18	27	47	61	75
11-22	7	14	21	37	46	55

HUNCHBACK OF NOTRE DAME, THE
Dell Publishing Co.: No. 854, Oct, 1957 (one shot)

	GD	VG	FN	VF	VF/NM	NM-
Four Color 854-Movie, photo-c	10	20	30	70	150	230

HUNGER (See Age of Ultron and Cataclysm titles)
Marvel Comics: Sept, 2013 - No. 4, Dec, 2013 ($3.99, limited series)

1-4-Fialkov-s/Kirk-a/Granov-c; Galactus in the Ultimate Universe. 2-4-Silver Surfer app. 4.00
1-Variant-c by Neal Adams 15.00

HUNGER, THE
Speakeasy Comics: May, 2005 ($2.99)

1-Andy Bradshaw-s/a; Eric Powell-c 3.00

HUNGER DOGS, THE (See DC Graphic Novel #4)

HUNK
Charlton Comics: Aug, 1961 - No. 11, 1963

	GD	VG	FN	VF	VF/NM	NM-
1	4	8	12	23	37	50
2-11	3	6	9	14	20	25

HUNTED (Formerly My Love Memoirs)
Fox Features Syndicate: No. 13, July, 1950; No. 2, Sept, 1950

	GD	VG	FN	VF	VF/NM	NM-
13(#1)-Used in **SOTI**, pg. 42 & illo. "Treating police contemptuously" (lower left); Hollingsworth bondage-c	39	78	117	231	378	525
2	19	38	57	111	176	240

HUNTER-KILLER
Image Comics (Top Cow): Nov, 2004 - No. 12, Mar, 2007 ($2.99)

0-(11/04, 25¢) Prelude with Silvestri sketch page and Waid afterword 3.00
1-12: 1-(3/05, $2.99) Waid-s/Silvestri-a; four covers. 2-Linsner variant-c 3.00
... Collected Edition Vol. 1 (9/05, $4.99) r/#0-3 5.00
...Dossier 1 (9/05, $2.99) character profiles with art by various; Migliari-c 3.00
... Volume 1 TPB (1/08, $24.99) r/#0-12; Dossier and Script Book; variant covers 25.00

HUNTER: THE AGE OF MAGIC (See Books of Magic)
DC Comics (Vertigo): Sept, 2001 - No. 25, Sept, 2003 ($2.50/$2.75)

1-25: Horrocks-s/Case-a. 1-8-Bolton-c. 14-Begin $2.75-c. 19-Bachalo-c 3.00

HUNTRESS, THE (See All-Star Comics #69, Batman Family, DC Super Stars #17, Detective #652, Infinity, Inc. #1 & Wonder Woman #271)
DC Comics: Apr, 1989 - No. 19, Oct, 1990 ($1.00, mature)

1-16: Staton-c/a(p) in all 3.00
17-19-Batman-c/stories 3.00
...: Darknight Daughter TPB (2006, $19.99) r/origin & early apps. in DC Super Stars #17, Batman Family #18-20 & Wonder Woman #271-287,289,290,294,295; Bolland-c 20.00

HUNTRESS, THE
DC Comics: June, 1994 - No. 4, Sept, 1994 ($1.50, limited series)

1-4-Netzer-c/a: 2-Batman app. 3.00

HUNTRESS (Leads into 2012 World's Finest series)
DC Comics: Dec, 2011 - No. 6, May, 2012 ($2.99, limited series)

1-6-Levitz-s/To-a/March-c 3.00

HUNTRESS: YEAR ONE
DC Comics: Early July, 2008 - No. 6, Late Sept, 2008 ($2.99, limited series)

1-6-Origin re-told; Cliff Richards-a/Ivory Madison-s 3.00
TPB (2009, $17.99) r/#1-6; intro. by Paul Levitz 18.00

HURRICANE COMICS
Cambridge House: 1945 (52 pgs.)

	GD	VG	FN	VF	VF/NM	NM-
1-(Humor, funny animal)	24	48	72	140	230	320

HUSK
Marvel Comics (Soleil): May, 2010 - No. 2, Jun, 2010 ($5.99, limited series)

1,2-English version of French comic; L'Homme-s/Boudoiron-a 6.00

HYBRIDS
Continuity Comics: Jan, 1994 ($2.50, one-shot)

1-Neal Adams-c(p) & part-a(i); embossed-c. 4.00

HYBRIDS DEATHWATCH 2000
Continuity Comics: Apr, 1993 - No. 3, Aug, 1993 ($2.50)

0-(Giveaway)-Foil-c; Neal Adams-c(i) & plots (also #1,2) 4.00
1-3: 1-Polybagged w/card; die-cut-c. 2-Thermal-c. 3-Polybagged w/card; indestructible-c; Adams plot 4.00

HYBRIDS ORIGIN
Continuity Comics: 1993 - No. 5, Jan, 1994 ($2.50)

1-5: 2,3-Neal Adams-c. 4,5-Valeria the She-Bat app. Adams-c(i) 4.00

HYDE
IDW Publ.: Oct, 2004 ($7.49, one-shot)

1-Steve Niles-s/Nick Stakal 7.50

HYDE-25
Harris Publications: Apr, 1995 ($2.95, one-shot)

0-Coupon for poster; r/Vampirella's 1st app. 3.00

HYDROMAN (See Heroic Comics)

HYPERKIND (See Razorline)
Marvel Comics: Sept, 1993 - No. 9, May, 1994 ($1.75/$1.95)

1-($2.50)-Foil embossed-c; by Clive Barker 4.00
2-9 3.00
...Unleashed 1 (8/94, $2.95, 52 pgs., one-shot) 4.00

HYPER MYSTERY COMICS
Hyper Publications: May, 1940 - No. 2, June, 1940 (68 pgs.)

	GD	VG	FN	VF	VF/NM	NM-
1-Hyper, the Phenomenal begins; Calkins-a	226	452	678	1446	2473	3500
2	113	226	339	718	1234	1750

HYPERNATURALS
BOOM! Studios: Jul, 2012 - No. 12, Jun, 2013 ($3.99)

1-12: 1-Abnett & Lanning-s/Walker & Guinaldo-a; at least eight covers. 2-Two printings 4.00
... Free Comic Book Day Edition (5/12) Prelude to issue #1 3.00

HYPERSONIC
Dark Horse Comics: Nov, 1997 - No. 4, Feb, 1998 ($2.95, limited series)

1-4: Abnett & White-s/Erskine-a 3.00

I AIM AT THE STARS (Movie)
Dell Publishing Co.: No. 1148, Nov-Jan/1960-61 (one-shot)

	GD	VG	FN	VF	VF/NM	NM-
Four Color 1148-The Werner Von Braun Sty-photo-c	6	12	18	40	73	105

I AM AN AVENGER (See Avengers, Young Avengers and Pet Avengers)
Marvel Comics: Nov, 2010 - No. 5, Mar, 2011 ($3.99, limited series)

1-5-Short stories by various. 1-Yu-c. 2-Land-c. 2-4-Mayhew-a. 3-Noto-c. 4-Acuña-c 4.00

I AM CAPTAIN AMERICA
Marvel Comics: Jan, 2012 ($3.99, one-shot)

1-Collection of Captain America-themed 70th Anniversary covers with artist profiles 4.00

I AM COYOTE (See Eclipse Graphic Album Series & Eclipse Magazine #2)

I AM LEGEND
Eclipse Books: 1991 - No. 4, 1991 ($5.95, B&W, squarebound, 68 pgs.)

	GD	VG	FN	VF	VF/NM	NM-
1-4: Based on 1954 novel by Richard Matheson	1	2	3	5	6	8

I AM LEGION (English version of French graphic novel Je Suis Légion)

Ibis, The Invincible #3 © FAW

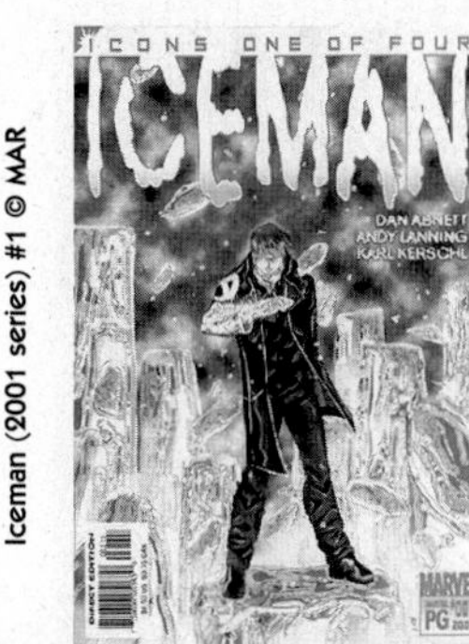

Iceman (2001 series) #1 © MAR

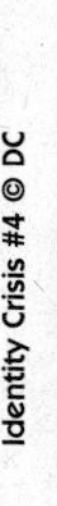
Identity Crisis #4 © DC

	GD 2.0	VG 4.0	FN 6.0	VF 8.0	VF/NM 9.0	NM- 9.2

Devils Due Publishing: Jan, 2009 - No. 6, July, 2009 ($3.50)

1-6-John Cassaday-a/Fabien Nury-s; two covers 3.50

IBIS, THE INVINCIBLE (See Fawcett Miniatures, Mighty Midget & Whiz)
Fawcett Publications: 1942 (Fall?); #2, Mar.,1943; #3, Wint, 1945 - #5, Fall, 1946; #6, Spring, 1948

	GD	VG	FN	VF	VF/NM	NM-
1-Origin Ibis; Raboy-c; on sale 1/2/43	271	542	813	1734	2967	4200
2-Bondage-c (on sale 2/5/43)	113	226	339	718	1234	1750
3-Wolverton-a #3-6 (4 pgs. each)	77	154	231	493	847	1200
4-6: 5-Bondage-c	53	106	159	334	567	800

NOTE: ***Mac Raboy** c(p)-3-5. **Schaffenberger** c-6.*

I-BOTS (See Isaac Asimov's I-BOTS)

ICE AGE ON THE WORLD OF MAGIC: THE GATHERING (See Magic The Gathering)

ICE KING OF OZ, THE (See First Comics Graphic Novel #13)

ICEMAN (Also see The Champions & X-Men #94)
Marvel Comics Group: Dec, 1984 - No. 4, June, 1985 (Limited series)

1,2,4: Zeck covers on all 4.00
3-The Defenders, Champions (Ghost Rider) & the original X-Men x-over 5.00

ICEMAN (X-Men)
Marvel Comics: Dec, 2001 - No. 4, Mar, 2002 ($2.50, limited series)

1-4-Abnett & Lanning-s/Kerschl-a 3.00

ICEMAN AND ANGEL (X-Men)
Marvel Comics: May, 2011 ($2.99, one-shot)

1-Brian Clevinger-s/Juan Doe-a; Goom & Googam app. 3.00

ICON
DC Comics (Milestone): May, 1993 - No. 42, Feb, 1997($1.50/$1.75/$2.50)

1-($2.95)-Collector's Edition polybagged w/poster & trading card (direct sale only) 4.00
1-24,30-42: 9-Simonson-c. 15,16-Worlds Collide Pt. 4 & 11. 15-Superboy app.
16-Superman-c/story. 40-Vs. Blood Syndicate 3.00
25-($2.95, 52 pgs.) 4.00
... A Hero's Welcome SC (2009, $19.99) r/#1-8; intro. by Reginald Hudlin 20.00
...: Mothership Connection SC (2010, $24.99) r/#13,19-22,24-27,30 25.00

IDAHO
Dell Publishing Co.: June-Aug, 1963 - No. 8, July-Sept, 1965

	GD	VG	FN	VF	VF/NM	NM-
1	3	6	9	16	24	32
2-8: 5-7-Painted-c	2	4	6	9	13	16

IDEAL (... a Classical Comic) (2nd Series) (Love Romances No. 6 on)
Timely Comics: July, 1948 - No. 5, March, 1949 (Feature length stories)

	GD	VG	FN	VF	VF/NM	NM-
1-Antony & Cleopatra	37	74	111	222	361	500
2-The Corpses of Dr. Sacotti	31	62	93	186	303	420
3-Joan of Arc; used in **SOTI**, pg. 310 'Boer War'	29	58	87	172	281	390
4-Richard the Lion-hearted; titled "...the World's Greatest Comics"; The Witness story	40	80	120	246	411	575
5-Ideal Love & Romance; change to love; photo-c	20	40	60	117	189	260

IDEAL COMICS (1st Series) (Willie Comics No. 5 on)
Timely Comics (MgPC): Fall, 1944 - No. 4, Spring, 1946

	GD	VG	FN	VF	VF/NM	NM-
1-Funny animal; Super Rabbit in all	34	68	102	199	325	450
2	18	36	54	105	165	225
3,4	16	32	48	94	147	200

IDEAL LOVE & ROMANCE (See Ideal, A Classical Comic)

IDEAL ROMANCE (Formerly Tender Romance)
Key Publ.: No. 3, April, 1954 - No. 8, Feb, 1955 (Diary Confessions No. 9 on)

	GD	VG	FN	VF	VF/NM	NM-
3-Bernard Baily-c	10	20	30	54	72	90
4-8: 4-6-B. Baily-c	8	16	24	40	50	60

IDEALS (Secret Stories)
Ideals Publ., USA: 1981 (68 pgs, graphic novels, 7x10", stiff-c)

	GD	VG	FN	VF	VF/NM	NM-
Captain America - Star Spangled Super Hero	3	6	9	17	26	35
Fantastic Four - Cosmic Quartet	3	6	9	17	26	35
Incredible Hulk - Gamma Powered Goliath	3	6	9	17	26	35
Spider-Man - World Famous Wall Crawler	3	6	9	21	33	45

IDENTITY CRISIS
DC Comics: Aug, 2004 - No. 7, Feb, 2005 ($3.95, limited series)

1-Meltzer-s/Morales-a/Turner-c in all; Sue Dibny murdered 5.00
1-(Second printing) black-c with white sketch lines 5.00
1-(3rd & 4th) 3rd-Bloody broken photo glass image-c by Morales. 4th-Turner red-c 4.00
1-Diamond Retailer Summit Edition with sketch-c 30.00
1-Special Edition (6/09, $1.00) r/#1 with "After Watchmen" cover frame 3.00
2-7: 2-4-Deathstroke app. 5-Firestorm, Jack Drake, Capt. Boomerang killed 4.00
2-(Second printing) new Morales sketch-c 4.00
Final printings for all issues with red background variant covers 4.00
HC (2005, $24.99, dust jacket) r/series; Director's Cut extras; cover gallery; Whedon intro.;
2 covers: Direct Market-c by Turner, Bookstore-c with Morales-a 25.00
SC (2006, $14.99) r/series; Director's Cut extras; cover gallery; Whedon intro 15.00

IDENTITY DISC
Marvel Comics: Aug, 2004 - No. 5, Dec, 2004 ($2.99, limited series)

1-5-Sabretooth, Bullseye, Sandman, Vulture, Deadpool, Juggernaut app.; Higgins-a 4.00
TPB (2004, $13.99) r/#1-5 14.00

IDES OF BLOOD
DC Comics (WildStorm): Oct, 2010 - No. 6, Mar, 2011 ($3.99/$2.99, limited series)

1-6-Stuart Paul-s/Christian Duce-a/Michael Geiger-c; Roman Empire vampires 4.00

I DIE AT MIDNIGHT (Vertigo V2K)
DC Comics (Vertigo): 2000 ($6.95, prestige format, one-shot)

1-Kyle Baker-s/a 7.00

IDOL
Marvel Comics (Epic Comics): 1992 - No. 3, 1992 ($2.95, mini-series, 52 pgs.)

Book 1-3 4.00

IDOLIZED
Aspen MLT: No. 0, Jun, 2012 - No. 5, Apr, 2013 ($2.50/$3.99)

0-($2.50) Schwartz-s/Gunnell-a; regular & photo covers; Superhero Idol background 3.00
1-5-($3.99) 1-Art Adams & photo covers; origin of Joule 4.00

I DREAM OF JEANNIE (TV)
Dell Publishing Co.: Apr, 1965 - No. 2, Dec, 1966 (Photo-c)

	GD	VG	FN	VF	VF/NM	NM-
1-Barbara Eden photo-c, each	12	24	36	79	170	260
2	9	18	27	63	129	195

I FEEL SICK
Slave Labor Graphics: Aug, 1999 - No. 2, May, 2000 ($3.95, limited series)

1,2-Jhonen Vasquez-s/a 4.00

I HATE GALLANT GIRL
Image Comics (Shadowline): Nov, 2008 - No. 3, Jan, 2009 ($3.50, limited series)

1-3-Kat Cahill-s/Seth Damoose-a 3.50

I (heart) MARVEL
Marvel Comics: Apr, 2006; May, 2006 ($2.99, one-shots)

...: Marvel AI 1 (4/06) Cebulski-s; manga art by various; Vision, Daredevil, Elektra app. 3.00
...: Masked Intentions 1 (5/06) Squirrel Girl, Speedball, Firestar, Justice app.; Nicieza-s 3.00
...: My Mutant Heart 1 (4/06) Wolverine, Cannonball, Doop app. 3.00
...: Outlaw Love 1 (4/06) Bullseye, The Answer, Ruby Thursday app.; Nicieza-s 3.00
...: Web of Romance 1 (4/06) Spider-Man, Mary Jane, The Avengers app. 3.00

ILLEGITIMATES, THE
IDW Publishing: Dec, 2013 - Present ($3.99)

1-4: 1-Taran Killam & Marc Andreyko-a/Kevin Sharpe-a; covers by Ordway & Willingham 4.00

ILLUMINATOR
Marvel Comics/Nelson Publ.: 1993 - No. 4, 1993 ($4.99/$2.95, 52 pgs.)

1,2-($4.99) Religious themed 5.00
3,4 4.00

ILLUSTRATED GAGS
United Features Syndicate: No. 16, 1940

	GD	VG	FN	VF	VF/NM	NM-
Single Series 16	18	36	54	107	169	230

ILLUSTRATED LIBRARY OF..., AN (See Classics Illustrated Giants)

ILLUSTRATED STORIES OF THE OPERAS
Baily (Bernard) Publ. Co.: 1943 (16 pgs.; B&W) (25 cents) (cover-B&W & red)

	GD	VG	FN	VF	VF/NM	NM-
nn-(Rare)(4 diff. issues)-Faust (part-r in Cisco Kid #1, 2 cover versions: 25¢ & no price) nn-Aida, nn-Carmen; Baily-a, nn-Rigoleito	63	126	189	403	689	975

ILLUSTRATED STORY OF ROBIN HOOD & HIS MERRY MEN, THE (See Classics Giveaways, 12/44)

ILLUSTRATED TARZAN BOOK, THE (See Tarzan Book)

I LOVED (Formerly Rulah; Colossal Features Magazine No. 33 on)
Fox Features Syndicate: No. 28, July, 1949 - No. 32, Mar, 1950

	GD	VG	FN	VF	VF/NM	NM-
28	15	30	45	85	130	175
29-32	12	24	36	67	94	120

I LOVE LUCY
Eternity Comics : 6/90 - No. 6, 1990;V2#1, 11/90 - No. 6, 1991 ($2.95, B&W, mini-series)

I, Lusiphur #1 © Drew Hayes

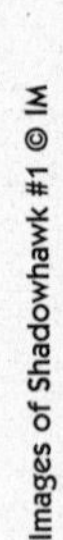
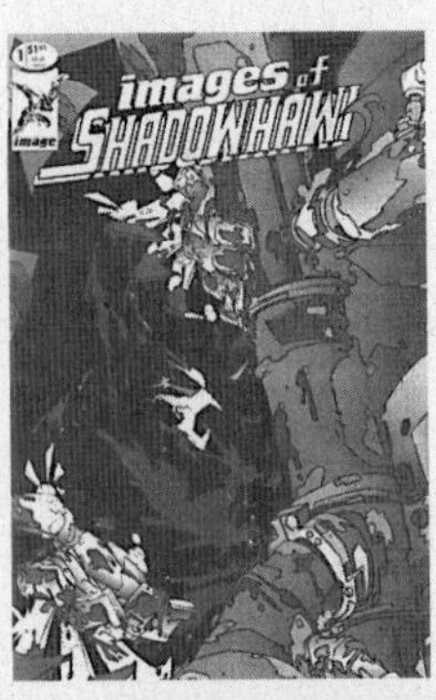

Images of Shadowhawk #1 © IM

Imagine Agents #1 © BOOM

GD 2.0 | VG 4.0 | FN 6.0 | VF 8.0 | VF/NM 9.0 | NM- 9.2

1-6: Reprints 1950s comic strip; photo-c 4.00
Book II #1-6: Reprints comic strip; photo-c 4.00
...In Full Color 1 (1991, $5.95, 52 pgs.)-Reprints I Love Lucy Comics #4,5,8,16; photo-c with embossed logo (2 versions exist, one with pgs. 18 & 19 reversed, the other corrected) 1 2 3 5 6 8
...In 3-D 1 (1991, $3.95, w/glasses)-Reprints I Love Lucy Comics; photo-c; bagged 6.00

I LOVE LUCY COMICS (TV) (Also see The Lucy Show)
Dell Publishing Co.: No. 535, Feb, 1954 - No. 35, Apr-June, 1962 (Lucille Ball photo-c on all)

Four Color 535(#1) 40 80 120 296 673 1050
Four Color 559(#2, 5/54) 24 48 72 170 379 585
3 (8-10/54) - 5 15 30 45 103 227 350
6-10 12 24 36 82 179 275
11-20 10 20 30 64 132 200
21-35 8 16 24 56 108 160

I LOVE NEW YORK
Linsner.com: 2002 ($2.95, B&W, one-shot)
1-Linsner-s/a; benefit book for the Sept. 11 charities 3.00

I LOVE TROUBLE
Image Comics: Dec, 2012 - No. 6, Aug, 2013 ($2.99)
1-6: 1-5-Kel Symons-s/Mark Robinson-a. 6-Nathan Stockman-a 3.00

I LOVE YOU
Fawcett Publications: June, 1950 (one-shot)
1-Photo-c 15 30 45 84 127 170

I LOVE YOU (Formerly In Love)
Charlton Comics: No. 7, 9/55 - No. 121, 12/76; No. 122, 3/79 - No. 130, 5/80

7-Kirby-c; Powell-a 8 16 24 54 102 150
8-10 5 10 15 30 50 70
11-16,18-20 4 8 12 27 44 60
17-(68 pg. Giant) 6 12 18 41 76 110
21-50: 26-No Torres-a 3 6 9 20 31 42
51-59 3 6 9 16 23 30
60-(1/66)-Elvis Presley line drawn c/story 14 28 42 96 211 325
61-85 2 4 6 11 16 20
86-90,92-98,100-110 2 4 6 8 10 12
91-(5/71) Ditko-a (5 pgs.) 2 4 6 13 18 22
99-David Cassidy pin-up 2 4 6 10 14 18
111-113,115-130 1 3 4 6 8 10
114-Psychedelic cover 3 6 9 17 26 35

I, LUSIPHUR (Becomes Poison Elves, 1st series #8 on)
Mulehide Graphics: 1991 - No. 7, 1992 (B&W, magazine size)

1-Drew Hayes-c/a/scripts 4 8 12 25 40 55
2,4,5 3 6 9 14 20 25
3-Low print run 4 8 12 27 44 60
6,7 2 4 6 8 11 14
Poison Elves: Requiem For An Elf (Sirius Ent., 6/96, $14.95, trade paperback) -Reprints I, Lusiphur #1,2 as text, and 3-6 15.00

I'M A COP
Magazine Enterprises: 1954 - No. 3, 1954
1(A-1 #111)-Powell-c/a in all 15 30 45 88 137 185
2(A-1 #126), 3(A-1 #128) 10 20 30 56 76 95

IMAGE COMICS HARDCOVER
Image Comics: 2005 ($24.99, hardcover with dust jacket)
Vol. 1-New Spawn by McFarlane-s/a; Savage Dragon origin by Larsen; CyberForce by Silvestri; ShadowHawk by Valentino; intro by Marder; Image timeline 25.00

IMAGE COMICS SUMMER SPECIAL
Image Comics: July, 2004 (Free Comic Book Day giveaway)
1-New short stories of Spawn, Invincible, Savage Dragon and Witchblade 3.00

IMAGE FIRST
Image Comics: 2005 ($6.99, TPB)
Vol. 1 (2005) r/Strange Girl #1, Sea of Red #1, The Walking Dead #1 and Girls #1 2 4 6 11 16 20

IMAGE GRAPHIC NOVEL
Image Int.: 1984 ($6.95)(Advertised as Pacific Comics Graphic Novel #1)
1-The Seven Samuroid; Brunner-c/a 12.00

IMAGE HOLIDAY SPECIAL 2005
Image Comics: 2005 ($9.99, TPB)
nn-Holiday-themed short stories by various incl. Larsen, Kurtz, Kirkman, Valentino 10.00

IMAGE INTRODUCES...
Image Comics: Oct, 2001 - June, 2002 ($2.95, anthology)
Believer #1-Schamberger-s/Thurman & Molder-a; Legend of Isis preview 3.00
Cryptopia #1-Raab-s/Quinn-a 3.00
Dog Soldiers #1-Hunter-s/Pachoumis-a 3.00
Legend of Isis #1-Valdez-a 3.00
Primate #1-Two covers; Beau Smith & Bernhardt-s/Byrd-a 3.00

IMAGES OF A DISTANT SOIL
Image Comics: Feb, 1997 ($2.95, B&W, one-shot)
1-Sketches by various 3.00

IMAGES OF SHADOWHAWK (Also see Shadowhawk)
Image Comics: Sept, 1993 - No. 3, 1994 ($1.95, limited series)
1-3: Keith Giffen-c/a; Trencher app. 3.00

IMAGE 20 (FREE COMIC BOOK DAY 2012...)
Image Comics: May, 2012 (giveaway, one-shot)
nn-Previews of Revival, Guarding the Globe, It-Girl and the Atomics, Near Death 3.00

IMAGE TWO-IN-ONE
Image Comics: Mar, 2001 ($2.95, 48 pgs., B&W, one-shot)
1-Two stories; 24 pages produced in 24 hrs. by Larsen and Eliopoulos 4.00

IMAGE UNITED
Image Comics: No. 0, Mar, 2010; Nov, 2009 - No. 6 ($3.99, limited series)
0-(3/10, $2.99) Fortress and Savage Dragon app. 3.00
1-3-($3.99) Image character crossover; Kirkman-s; art by Larsen, Liefeld, McFarlane, Portacio, Silvestri and Valentino; Spawn, Witchblade, Savage Dragon, Youngblood, Cyberforce and Shadowhawk app. Multiple covers on each 4.00
1-Jim Lee variant-c 8.00

IMAGE ZERO
Image Comics: 1993 (Received through mail w/coupons from Image books)
0-Savage Dragon, StormWatch, Shadowhawk, Strykeforce; 1st app. Troll; 1st app. McFarlane's Freak, Blotch, Sweat and Bludd 5.00

IMAGINARIES, THE
Image Comics: Mar, 2005 - No. 4, June, 2005 ($2.95, limited series)
1-4-Mike S. Miller & Ben Avery-s; Miller & Titus-a 3.00

IMAGINE AGENTS
BOOM! Studios: Oct, 2013 - No. 4, Jan, 2014 ($3.99, limited series)
1-4-Brian Joines-s/Bachan-a 4.00

I'M DICKENS - HE'S FENSTER (TV)
Dell Publishing Co.: May-July, 1963 - No. 2, Aug-Oct, 1963 (Photo-c)
1 5 10 15 33 57 80
2 5 10 15 30 50 70

I MET A HANDSOME COWBOY
Dell Publishing Co.: No. 324, Mar, 1951
Four Color 324 7 14 21 48 89 130

IMMORTAL DOCTOR FATE, THE
DC Comics: Jan, 1985 - No. 3, Mar, 1985 ($1.25, limited series)
1-3: 1-Simonson-c/a. 2-Giffen-c/a(p) 4.00

IMMORTAL IRON FIST, THE (Also see Iron Fist)
Marvel Comics: Jan, 2007 - No. 27, Aug, 2009 ($2.99/$3.99)
1-Brubaker & Fraction-s/Aja-c/a; origin retold; intro. Orson Randall 5.00
1-Variant-c by Dell'Otto 8.00
1-Director's Cut ($3.99) r/#1 and 8-page story from Civil War: Choosing Sides; script excerpt; character designs; sketch and inks art; cover variant and concepts 4.00
2-13,15-26: 6,17-20-Flashback-a by Heath. 21-Green-a 3.00
14,27: 14-($3.99) Heroes For Hire app. 27-Last issue; 2 covers; Foreman & Lapham-a 4.00
Annual 1 (11/07, $3.99) Brubaker & Fraction-s/Chaykin, Brereton & J. Djurdjevic-a 4.00
... Orson Randall and the Death Queen of California (11/08, $3.99) art by Camuncoli 4.00
... Orson Randall and the Green Mist of Death (4/08, $3.99) art by Heath and various 4.00
...: The Origin of Danny Rand (2008, $3.99) r/Marvel Premiere #15-16 recolored 4.00
... Vol. 1: The Last Iron Fist Story HC (2007, $19.99, dustjacket) r/#1-6, story from Civil War: Choosing Sides; sketch pages 20.00
... Vol. 1: The Last Iron Fist Story SC (2007, $14.99) same content as HC 15.00
... Vol. 2: The Seven Capital Cities HC (2008, $24.99, dustjacket) r/#8-14 & Annual #1 25.00

IMMORTALIS (See Mortigan Goth: Immortalis)

IMMORTAL II

Impact #2 © WMG

Impulse #56 © DC

Incredible Hulk #181 © MAR

GD 2.0 | VG 4.0 | FN 6.0 | VF 8.0 | VF/NM 9.0 | NM- 9.2

Image Comics: Apr, 1997 - No. 5, Feb, 1998 ($2.50, B&W&Grey, limited series)
1-5: 1-B&W w/ color pull-out poster 3.00

IMMORTAL WEAPONS (Also see Immortal Iron Fist)
Marvel Comics: Sept, 2009 - No. 5, Jan, 2010 ($3.99, limited series)
1-5: Back-up Iron Fist stories in all. 1-Origin of Fat Cobra. 2-Brereton-a 4.00

IMPACT
E. C. Comics: Mar-Apr, 1955 - No. 5, Nov-Dec, 1955
1-Not code approved 20 40 60 160 255 350
1-Variant printed by Charlton. Title logo is white instead of yellow and print quality is inferior. Distributed to newsstands before being destroyed & reprinted (scarce) 26 52 78 208 329 450
2 13 26 39 104 162 220
3-5: 4-Crandall-a 11 22 33 88 137 185
NOTE: ***Crandall** a-1-4. **Davis** a-2-4; c-1-5. **Evans** a-1, 4, 5. **Ingels** a-in all. **Kamen** a-3. **Krigstein** a-1, 5. **Orlando** a-2, 5.*

IMPACT
Gemstone Publishing: Apr, 1999 - No. 5, Aug, 1999 ($2.50)
1-5-Reprints E.C. series 4.00

IMPACT CHRISTMAS SPECIAL
DC Comics (Impact Comics): 1991 ($2.50, 68 pgs.)
1-Gift of the Magi by Infantino/Rogers; The Black Hood, The Fly, The Jaguar, & The Shield stories 4.00

IMPERIAL GUARD
Marvel Comics: Jan, 1997 - No. 3, Mar, 1997 ($1.95, limited series)
1-3: Augustyn-s in all; 1-Wraparound-c 3.00

IMPOSSIBLE MAN SUMMER VACATION SPECTACULAR, THE
Marvel Comics: Aug, 1990; No. 2, Sept, 1991 ($2.00, 68 pgs.) (See Fantastic Four#11)
1-Spider Man, Quasar, Dr. Strange, She-Hulk, Punisher & Dr. Doom stories; Barry Crain, Guice-a; Art Adams-c(i) 4.00
2-Ka Zar & Thor app.; Cable Wolverine-c app. 4.00

IMPULSE (See Flash #92, 2nd Series for 1st app.) (Also see Young Justice)
DC Comics: Apr, 1995 - No. 89, Oct, 2002 ($1.50/$1.75/$1.95/$2.25/$2.50)
1-Mark Waid scripts & Humberto Ramos-c/a(p) begin; brief retelling of origin 6.00
2-12: 9-XS from Legion (Impulse's cousin) comes to the 20th Century, returns to the 30th Century in #12. 10-Dead Heat Pt. 3 (cont'd in Flash #110). 11-Dead Heat Pt. 4 (cont'd in Flash #111); Johnny Quick dies. 4.00
13-25: 14-Trickster app. 17-Zatanna-c/app. 21-Legion-c/app. 22-Jesse Quick-c/app. 24-Origin; Flash app. 25-Last Ramos-a. 3.00
26-55: 26-Rousseau-a begins. 28-1st new Arrowette (see World's Finest #113). 30-Genesis x-over. 47-Superman-c/app. 50-Batman & Joker-c/app. Van Sciver-a begins 3.00
56-62: 56-Young Justice app. 3.00
63-89: 63-Begin $2.50-c. 66-JLA,JSA-c/app. 68,69-Adam Strange, GL app. 77-Our Worlds at War x-over; Young Justice-c/app. 85-World Without Young Justice x-over pt. 2. 3.00
#1,000,000 (11/98) John Fox app. 3.00
Annual 1 (1996, $2.95)-Legends of the Dead Earth; Parobeck-a 4.00
Annual 2 (1997, $3.95)-Pulp Heroes stories; Orbik painted-c 4.00
.../Atom Double-Shot 1(2/98, $1.95) Jurgens-s/Mhan-a 3.00
...: Bart Saves the Universe (4/99, $5.95) JSA app. 6.00
...Plus (9/97, $2.95) w/Gross Out (Scare Tactics)-c/app. 4.00
...Reckless Youth (1997, $14.95, TPB) r/Flash #92-94, Impulse #1-6 15.00

INCAL, THE
Marvel Comics (Epic): Nov, 1988 - No. 3, Jan, 1989 ($10.95/$12.95, mature)
1-3: Moebius-c/a in all; sexual content 16.00

INCOGNEGRO
DC Comics (Vertigo): 2008 ($19.99, B&W, hardcover graphic novel with dustjacket)
HC-Mat Johnson-s/Warren Pleece-a 20.00

INCOGNITO
Marvel Comics (Icon): Dec, 2008 - No. 6, Aug, 2009 ($3.50/$3.99, limited series)
1-5-Brubaker-s/Phillips-a/c; pulp noir-style 3.50
6-($3.99) Bonus history of the Zeppelin pulps 4.00
...: Bad Influences (10/10 - No. 5, 4/11, $3.50) 1-5 Brubaker-s/Phillips-a/c 3.50

INCOMPLETE DEATH'S HEAD (Also see Death's Head)
Marvel Comics UK: Jan, 1993 - No. 12, Dec, 1993 ($1.75, limited series)
1-($2.95, 56 pgs.)-Die-cut cover 4.00
2-11: 2-Re-intro original Death's Head. 3-Original Death's Head vs. Dragon's Claws 3.00
12-($2.50, 52 pgs.)-She Hulk app. 4.00

INCORRUPTIBLE (Also see Irredeemable)
BOOM! Studios: Dec, 2000 - No. 30, May, 2012 ($3.99)
1-30: 1-Waid-s/Diaz-a; 3 covers 4.00
1-Artist Edition (12/11, $3.99) r/#1 in B&W with bonus sketch and design art 4.00

INCREDIBLE HERCULES (Continued from Incredible Hulk #112, Jan, 2008)
Marvel Comics: No. 113, Feb, 2008 - No. 141, Apr, 2010 ($2.99/$3.99)
113-125: 113-Ares and Wonder Man app.; Art Adams-c. 116-Romita Jr-c; Eternals app. 3.00
113-Variant-c by Pham 5.00
126-($3.99) Hercules origin retold; back-up story w/Miyazawa-a 4.00
127-137: 128-Dark Avengers app. 132-Replacement Thor. 136-Thor app. 3.00
138-141-($3.99) Assault on New Olympus; Avengers app. 4.00

INCREDIBLE HULK, THE (See Aurora, The Avengers #1, The Defenders #1, Giant-Size..., Hulk, Marvel Collectors Item Classics, Marvel Comics Presents #26, Marvel Fanfare, Marvel Treasury Edition, Power Record Comics, Rampaging Hulk, She-Hulk, 2099 Unlimited & World War Hulk)

INCREDIBLE HULK, THE
Marvel Comics: May, 1962 - No. 6, Mar, 1963; No. 102, Apr, 1968 - No. 474, Mar, 1999
1-Origin & 1st app. (skin is grey colored); Kirby pencils begin, end #5 2400 4800 7200 32,000 76,000 120,000
2-1st green skinned Hulk; Kirby/Ditko-a 317 634 951 2695 6098 9500
3-Origin retold; 1st app. Ringmaster (9/62) 217 434 651 1790 4045 6300
4,5: 4-Brief origin retold 162 324 486 1337 3019 4700
6-(3/63) Intro. Teen Brigade; all Ditko-a 169 338 507 1394 3147 4900
102-(4/68) (Formerly Tales to Astonish)-Origin retold; story continued from Tales to Astonish #101 22 44 66 154 340 525
103 10 20 30 64 132 200
104-Rhino app. 10 20 30 64 132 200
105-108: 105-1st Missing Link. 107-Mandarin app.(9/68). 108-Mandarin & Nick Fury app. (10/68) 7 14 21 46 86 125
109,110: 109-Ka-Zar app. 6 12 18 40 73 105
111-117: 117-Last 12¢ issue 5 10 15 33 57 80
118-Hulk vs. Sub-Mariner 6 12 18 40 73 105
119,120,123-125 4 8 12 27 44 60
121-1st app. The Glob 5 10 15 31 53 75
122-Hulk battles Thing (12/69) 8 16 24 54 102 150
126-1st Barbara Norriss (Valkyrie) 4 8 12 28 47 65
127-139: 131-Hulk vs. Iron Man; 1st Jim Wilson, Hulk's new sidekick. 136-1st Xeron, The Star-Slayer 3 6 9 19 30 40
140-Written by Harlan Ellison; 1st Jarella, Hulk's love 3 6 9 21 35 45
140-2nd printing (1994) 2 4 6 8 10 12
141-1st app. Doc Samson (7/71) 9 18 27 59 117 175
142-144: 144-Last 15¢ issue 3 6 9 18 28 38
145-(52 pgs.)-Origin retold 4 8 12 28 47 65
146-160: 149-1st app. The Inheritor. 155-1st app. Shaper. 158-Warlock cameo(12/72) 3 6 9 16 24 32
161-The Mimic dies; Beast app. 4 8 12 28 47 65
162-1st app. The Wendigo (4/73); Beast app. 7 14 21 46 86 125
163-171,173-176: 163-1st app. The Gremlin. 164-1st Capt. Omen & Colonel John D. Armbruster. 166-1st Zzzax. 168-1st The Harpy; nudity panels of Betty Ross. 169-1st app. Bi-Beast.176-Warlock cameo (2 panels only); same date as Strange Tales #178 (6/74) 3 6 9 14 20 26
172-X-Men cameo; origin Juggernaut retold 4 8 12 27 44 60
177-1st actual death of Warlock (last panel only) 3 6 9 16 24 32
178-Rebirth of Warlock 3 6 9 16 24 32
179 3 6 9 14 19 24
180-(10/74)-1st brief app. Wolverine (last pg.) 19 38 57 131 291 450
181-(11/74)-1st full Wolverine story; Trimpe-a 200 400 600 1000 1500 2000
182-Wolverine cameo; see Giant-Size X-Men #1 for next app.; 1st Crackajack Jackson 10 20 30 69 147 225
183-199: 185-Death of Col. Armbruster. 195,196-Abomination app. 197,198-Man-Thing-c/s 2 4 6 10 14 18
198,199, 201,202-(30¢-c variants, lim. distribution) 3 6 9 17 26 35
200-(25¢-c) Silver Surfer app.; anniversary issue 3 6 9 19 30 40
200-(30¢-c variant, limited distribution)(6/76) 5 10 15 34 60 85
201-220: 201-Conan swipe-c/sty. 212-1st app. The Constrictor 1 2 3 5 7 9
212-216-(35¢-c variant, limited distribution) 4 8 12 23 37 50
221-249: 227-Original Avengers app. 232-Capt. America x-over from C.A. #230. 233-Marvel Man app. 234-(4/79)-1st app. Quasar (formerly called Marvel Man. 243-Cage app. 1 2 3 4 5 7
250-Giant size; Silver Surfer app. 2 4 6 9 12 15
251-270,272-277,280-299: 272-Sasquatch & Wendigo app.; Wolverine & Alpha Flight cameo in flashback. 282-284-She-Hulk app. 293-F.F. app. 5.00
271-(5/82) 2nd app. & 1st full app. Rocket Raccoon (see Marvel Preview #7 for debut) 8 16 24 54 102 150

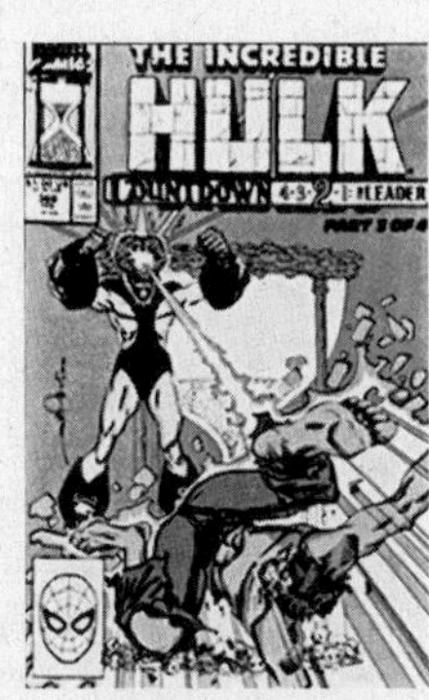

Incredible Hulk #366 © MAR

Incredible Hulk #474 © MAR

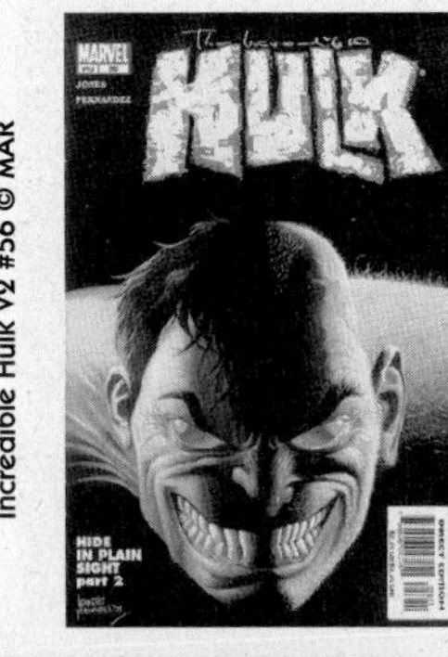

Incredible Hulk V2 #56 © MAR

GD VG FN VF VF/NM NM-
2.0 4.0 6.0 8.0 9.0 9.2

278,279-Most Marvel characters app. (Wolverine in both). 279-X-Men & Alpha Flight cameos 6.00
300-(11/84, 52 pgs.)-Spider-Man app in new black costume on-c & 2 pg. cameo 1 2 3 5 6 8
301-313: 312-Origin Hulk retold 4.00
314-Byrne-c/a begins, ends #319 6.00
315-319: 319-Bruce Banner & Betty Talbot wed 5.00
320-323,325,327-329 4.00
324-1st app. Grey Hulk since #1 (c-swipe of #1) 2 4 6 8 10 12
326-Grey vs. Green Hulk 6.00
330,331: 330-1st McFarlane ish (4/87); Thunderbolt Ross dies. 331-Grey Hulk series begins 3 6 9 17 26 35
332-334,336-339: 336,337-X-Factor app. 2 4 6 9 12 15
335-No McFarlane-a 6.00
340-Hulk battles Wolverine by McFarlane 4 8 12 27 44 60
341-346: 345-($1.50, 52 pgs.). 346-Last McFarlane issue 2 4 6 8 10 12
347-349,351-358,360-366: 347-1st app. Marlo 3.00
350-Hulk/Thing battle 6.00
359-Wolverine app. (illusion only) 3.00
367,372,377: 367-1st Dale Keown-a on Hulk (3/90). 372-Green Hulk app.;Keown-c/a. 377-1st all new Hulk; fluorescent-c; Keown-c/a 1 2 3 5 6 8
368-371,373-376: 368-Sam Kieth-c/a, 1st app. Pantheon. 369,370-Dale Keown-c/a. 370,371-Original Defenders app. 371,373-376: Keown-c/a. 376-Green vs. Grey Hulk 5.00
377-Fluorescent green logo 2nd printing 3.00
378,380,389: No Keown-a. 380-Doc Samson app. 3.00
379,381-388,390-392-Keown-a. 385-Infinity Gauntlet x-over. 389-Last $1.00-c. 392-X-Factor app. 4.00
393-($2.50, 72 pgs.)-30th anniversary issue; green foil stamped-c; swipes-c to #1; has pin-ups of classic battles; Keown-c/a 6.00
393,400-2nd printings: 400-2nd print-Diff. color foil-c. 4.00
394-399: 394-No Keown-c/a; intro Trauma. 395,396-Punisher-c/stories; Keown-c/a. 397-Begin "Ghost of the Past" 4-part sty; Keown c/a. 398-Last Keown-c/a 3.00
400-($2.50, 68 pgs.)-Holo-grafx foil-c & r/TTA #63 5.00
401-416: 402-Return of Doc Samson 3.00
417-424: 417-Begin $1.50-c; Rick Jones' bachelor party; Hulk returns from "Future Imperfect"; bound-in trading card sheet. 418-(Regular edition)-Rick Jones marries Marlo; includes cameo apps of various Marvel characters as well as DC's Death & Peter David. 420-Death of Jim Wilson 3.00
418-($2.50)-Collector's Edition w/gatefold die-cut-c 4.00
425 ($2.25, 52 pgs.) 4.00
425 ($3.50, 52 pgs.)-Holographic-c 5.00
426-434, 436-442: 426-Begin $1.95-c. 427, 428-Man-Thing app. 431,432-Abomination app. 434-Funeral for Nick Fury. 436-Ghosts of the Future begins, ends #440. 439-Hulk becomes Maestro, Avengers app. 440-Thor-c/app. 441,442-She-Hulk-c/app. 3.00
435 ($2.50)-Rhino-app; excerpt from "What Savage Beast" 4.00
443,446-448: 443-Begin $1.50-c; re-app. of Hulk. 446-w/card insert. 447-Begin Deodato-c/a(p) 3.00
444,445: 444-Cable-c/app.; "Onslaught". 445-"Onslaught" 4.00
447-Variant cover 4.00
449-1st app. Thunderbolts 6.00
450-($2.95)-Thunderbolts app.; 2 stories; Heroes Reborn-c/app. 5.00
451-470: 455-X-Men-c/app. 460-Bruce Banner returns. 464-Silver Surfer-c/app. 466,467: Betty dies. 467-Last Peter David-s/Kubert-a. 468-Casey-s/Pulido-a begin 3.00
471-473 4.00
474-($2.99) Last issue; Abomination app. 5.00
#(-1) Flashback (7/97) Kubert-a 3.00
Special 1 (10/68, 25¢, 68 pg.)-New 51 pg. story, Hulk battles The Inhumans (early app.); Steranko-c. 11 22 33 72 154 235
Special 2 (10/69, 25¢, 68 pg.)-Origin retold 6 12 18 38 69 100
Special 3,4: 3-(1/71, 25¢, 68 pg.). 4-(1/72, 52pgs.) 4 8 12 23 37 50
Annual 5 (1976) 2 4 6 10 14 18
Annual 6,8 ('77,'79): 8-Book-length Sasquatch-c/sty 2 4 6 8 10 12
Annual 7('78)-Byrne/Layton-c/a; Iceman & Angel app. in book-length story 2 4 6 11 16 20
Annual 9,10: 9('80). 10 ('81) 6.00
Annual 11('82)-Doc Samson back-up by Miller(p)(5 pgs.); Spider-Man & Avengers app. Buckler-a(p) 6.00
Annual 12-17: 12 ('83). 13('84). 14('85). 15('86). 16('90, $2.00, 68 pgs.)-She-Hulk app. 17(1991, $2.00)-Origin retold 5.00
Annual 18-20 ('92-'94 68 pgs.)-18-Return of the Defenders, Pt. I; no Keown-c/a 19-Bagged w/card 4.00
...'97 ($2.99) Pollina-c 4.00
...And Wolverine 1 (10/86, $2.50)-r/1st app. (#180-181) 2 4 6 9 12 15

GD VG FN VF VF/NM NM-
2.0 4.0 6.0 8.0 9.0 9.2

...: Beauty and the Behemoth ('98, $19.95, TPB) r/Bruce & Betty stories 20.00
...Ground Zero ('95, $12.95) r/#340-346 13.00
...Hercules Unleashed (10/96, $2.50) David-s/Deodato-c/a 4.00
... Omnibus Vol. 1 HC (2008, $99.99, dustjacket) r/#1-6 & 102, Tales To Astonish #59-101 bonus art, cover reprints; afterword by Peter David; Kirby cover from #1 130.00
... Omnibus Vol. 1 HC (2008, $99.99, dustjacket) Variant-c swipe of #1 by Alex Ross 110.00
.../Sub-Mariner '98 Annual ($2.99) 4.00
...Versus Quasimodo 1 (3/83, one-shot)-Based on Saturday morning cartoon 4.00
...Vs. Superman 1 (7/99, $5.95, one-shot)-painted-c by Rude 6.00
...Versus Venom 1 (4/94, $2.50, one-shot)-Embossed-c; red foil logo 4.00
... Visionaries: Peter David Vol. 1 (2005, $19.99) r/#331-339 written by Peter David 20.00
... Visionaries: Peter David Vol. 2 (2005, $19.99) r/#340-348 20.00
... Visionaries: Peter David Vol. 3 (2006, $19.99) r/#349-354, Web of Spider-Man #44, and Fantastic Four #320 20.00
... Visionaries: Peter David Vol. 4 (2007, $19.99) r/#355-363 and Marvel Comics Presents #26,45 20.00
... Visionaries: Peter David Vol. 5 (2008, $19.99) r/#364-372 and Annual #16 20.00
Wizard #1 Ace Edition - Reprints #1 with new Andy Kubert-c 14.00
Wizard #181 Ace Edition - Reprints #181 with new Chen-c 14.00
(Also see titles listed under **Hulk**)

NOTE: ***Adkins*** *a-111-116i.* ***Austin*** *a(i)-350, 351, 353, 354; c-302i, 350i.* ***Ayers*** *a-3-5i.* ***Buckler*** *a-Annual 5; c-252.* ***John Buscema*** *c-202p.* ***Byrne*** *a-314-319p; c-314-316, 318, 319, 359, Annual 14i.* ***Colan*** *c-363.* ***Ditko*** *a-2i, 6, 249, Annual 2r(5), 3r, 9p; c-2i, 6, 235, 249.* ***Everett*** *c-133i.* ***Golden*** *c-248, 251.* ***Kane*** *c(p)-193, 194, 196, 198.* ***Dale Keown*** *a(p)-367, 369-377, 379, 381-388, 390-393, 395-398; c-369-377p, 381, 382p, 384, 385, 386, 387p, 388, 390p, 391-393, 395p, 396, 397p, 398.* ***Kirby*** *a-1-5p, Special 2, 3p, Annual 5p; c-1-5, Annual 5.* ***McFarlane*** *a-330-334p, 336-339p, 340-343, 344-346p; c-330p, 340p, 341-343, 344p, 345, 346p.* ***Mignola*** *c-302, 305, 313.* ***Miller*** *c-258p, 261, 264, 268.* ***Mooney*** *a-230p, 287i, 288i.* ***Powell*** *a-Special 3r(2).* ***Romita*** *a-Annual 17p.* ***Severin*** *a(i)-108-110, 131-133, 141-151, 153-155; c(i)-109, 110, 132, 142, 144-155.* ***Simonson*** *c-283, 364-367.* ***Starlin*** *a-222p; c-217.* ***Staton*** *a(i)-187-189, 191-209.* ***Tuska*** *a-102i, 105i, 106i, 218p.* ***Williamson*** *a-310i; c-310i, 311i.* ***Wrightson*** *c-197.*

INCREDIBLE HULK (Vol. 2) (Formerly Hulk #1-11; becomes Incredible Hercules with #113) (Re-titled Incredible Hulks #612-on)(Also see World War Hulk)
Marvel Comics: No. 12, Mar, 2000 - No. 112, Jan, 2008 ($1.99-$3.50)
No. 600, Sept, 2009 - No. 625, Oct, 2011 ($3.99/$4.99)

12-Jenkins-s/Garney & McKone-a 4.00
13,14-($1.99) Garney & Buscema-a 3.00
15-24,26-32: 15-Begin $2.25-c. 21-Maximum Security x-over. 24-($1.99-c) 3.00
25-($2.99) Hulk vs. The Abomination; Romita Jr.-a 4.00
33-($3.50, 100 pgs.) new Bogdanove-a/Priest-s; reprints 4.00
34-Bruce Jones-s begin; Romita Jr.-a 5.00
35-49,51-54: 35-39-Jones-s/Romita Jr.-a. 40-43-Weeks-a. 44-49-Immonen-a 3.00
50-($3.50) Deodato-a begins; Abomination app. thru #54 4.00
55-74,77-91: 55(25¢-c) Absorbing Man returns; Fernandez-a. 60-65,70-72-Deodato-a. 66-69-Braithwaite-a. 71-74-Iron Man app. 77-($2.99-c) Peter David-s begin/Weeks-a. 80-Wolverine-c. 82-Jae Lee-c/a. 83-86-House of M x-over. 87-Scorpion app. 3.00
75,76-($3.50) The Leader app. 75-Robertson-a/Frank-c. 76-Braithwaite-a 4.00
92-Planet Hulk begins; Ladronn-c 5.00
92-2nd printing with variant-c by Bryan Hitch 4.00
93-99,101-105 Planet Hulk; Ladronn-c 3.00
100-($3.99) Planet Hulk continues; back-up w/Frank-a; r/#152,153; Ladronn-c 5.00
100-($3.99) Green Hulk variant-c by Michael Turner 10.00
100-($3.99) Gray Hulk variant-c by Michael Turner 30.00
106-World War Hulk begins; Gary Frank-a/c 6.00
106-2nd printing with new cover of Hercules and Angel 3.00
107-112: 107-Hercules vs. Hulk. 108-Rick Jones app. 112-Art Adams-c 3.00
600-(9/09, $4.99) Covers by Ross, Sale and wraparound-c by McGuinness; back-up with Stan Lee-s; r/Hulk: Gray #1; cover gallery 5.00
601-611-($3.99): 601-605-Olivetti-a. 603-Wolverine app. 606-608-Fall of the Hulks 4.00
(Title becomes Incredible Hulks with #612, Nov, 2010)
612-621: 612-617-Dark Son. 618-620-Chaos War. 621-Hercules app. 4.00
622-634-($2.99) 623-625-Ka-Zar app.; Eaglesham-a. 626-629-Grummett-a 3.00
635-($3.99) Fin Fang Foom & Dr. Strange app.; Greg Pak interview 4.00
Annual 2000 ($3.50) Texeira-a/Jenkins-s; Avengers app. 4.00
Annual 2001 ($2.99) Thor-c/app.; Larsen-s/Williams III-c 4.00
Annual 1 (8/11, $3.99) Identity Wars; Spider-Man and Deadpool app.; Barrionuevo-a 4.00
... & The Human Torch: From the Marvel Vault 1 (8/11, $2.99) unpublished story w/Ditko-a 3.00
... : Boiling Point (Volume 2, 2002, $8.99, TPB) r/#40-43; Andrews-c 9.00
Dogs of War (6/01, $19.95, TPB) r/#12-20 20.00
House of M (2006, $13.99) r/House of M tie-in issues Incredible Hulk #83-87 14.00
Hulk: Planet Hulk HC (2007, $39.99, dustjacket) oversized r/#92-105, Planet Hulk: Gladiator Guidebook, stories from Amazing Fantasy (2004) #15 and Giant-Size Hulk #1 40.00
Hulk: Planet Hulk SC (2008, $34.99) same content as HC 35.00
Planet Hulk: Gladiator Guidebook (2006, $3.99) bios of combatants and planet history 4.00
...: Prelude to Planet Hulk (2006, $13.99, TPB) r/#88-91 & Official Handbook: Hulk 2004 14.00
...: Return of the Monster (7/02, $12.99, TPB) r/#34-39 13.00

The Incredibles #1 © DIS & Pixar

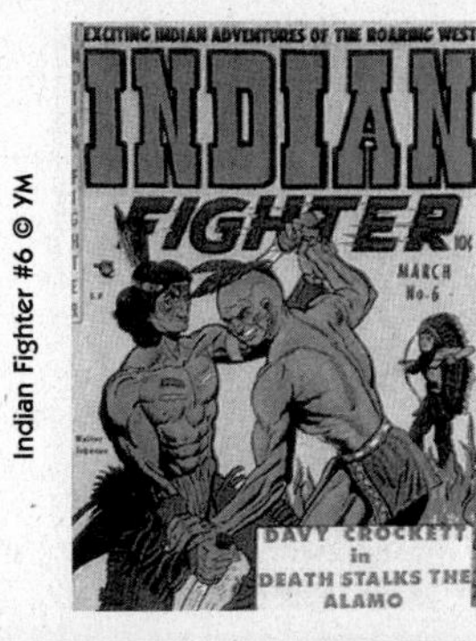

Indian Fighter #6 © YM

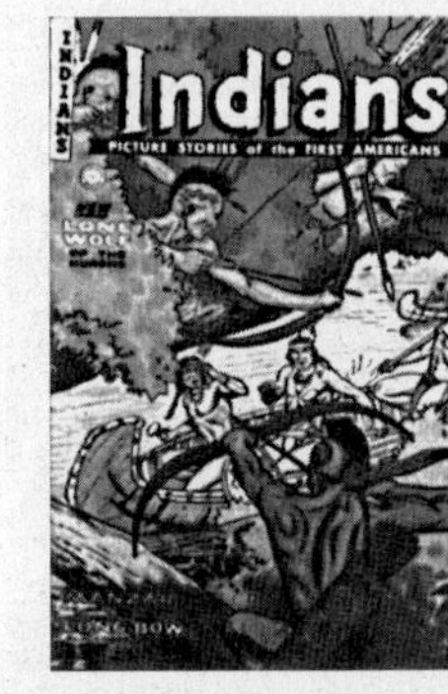

Indians #12 © FH

GD 2.0 | VG 4.0 | FN 6.0 | VF 8.0 | VF/NM 9.0 | NM- 9.2

...: The End (8/02, $5.95) David-s/Keown-a; Hulk in the far future 6.00
...: The End HC (2008, $19.99, dustjacket) r/The End and Hulk: Future Imperfect #1-2 20.00
...Volume 1 HC (2002, $29.99, oversized) r/#34-43 & Startling Stories: Banner #1-4 30.00
...Volume 2 HC (2003, $29.99, oversized) r/#44-54; sketch pages and cover gallery 30.00
Volume 3: Transfer of Power (2003, $12.99, TPB) r/#44-49 13.00
Volume 4: Abominable (2003, $11.99, TPB) r/#50-54; Abomination app.; Deodato-a 12.00
Volume 5: Hide in Plain Sight (2003, $11.99, TPB) r/#55-59; Fernandez-a 12.00
Volume 6: Split Decisions (2004, $12.99, TPB) r/#60-65; Deodato-a 13.00
Volume 7: Dead Like Me (2004, $12.99, TPB) r/#66-69 & Hulk Smash #1&2 13.00
Volume 8: Big Things (2004, $17.99, TPB) r/#70-76; Iron Man app. 18.00
Volume 9: Tempest Fugit (2005, $14.99, TPB) r/#77-82 15.00

INCREDIBLE HULK (Also see Indestructible Hulk)
Marvel Comics: Dec, 2011 - No. 15, Dec, 2012 ($3.99)

1-Aaron-s/Silvestri-a; bonus interview with Aaron; cover by Silvestri 4.00
1-Variant covers by Neal Adams, Whilce Portacio & Ladronn 8.00
2-7: 2-Silvestri, Portacio & Tan-a. 7-Hulk & Banner merge; Portacio-a 4.00
7.1-(7/12, $2.99) Palo-a/Komarck-c; Red She-Hulk app. 3.00
8-15: 8-Punisher app.; Dillon-a. 12-Wolverine & The Thing app. 4.00

INCREDIBLE HULKS: ENIGMA FORCE
Marvel Comics: Nov, 2010 - No. 3, Jan, 2011 ($3.99, limited series)

1-3-Reed-s/Munera-a/Pagulayan-c; Bug app. 4.00

INCREDIBLE MR. LIMPET, THE (See Movie Classics)

INCREDIBLES, THE
Image Comics: Nov, 2004 - No. 4, Feb, 2005 ($2.99, limited series)

1-4-Adaptation of 2004 Pixar movie; Ricardo Curtis-a 3.00
TPB (2005, $12.95) r/#1-4; cover gallery 13.00

INCREDIBLES, THE (Pixar characters)
BOOM! Studios: No. 0, Jul, 2009 - Present ($2.99)

0-15: 0-3-City of Incredibles; Waid & Walker-s. 0,1-Wagner-c. 8-15-Walker-s 3.00
...: Family Matters 1-4 (3/09 - No. 4, 6/09) Waid-s/Takara-a. 1-Five covers 3.00

INCREDIBLE SCIENCE FICTION (Formerly Weird Science-Fantasy)
E. C. Comics: No. 30, July-Aug, 1955 - No. 33, Jan-Feb, 1956

	GD	VG	FN	VF	VF/NM	NM-
30-Davis-c begin, end #32	41	82	123	328	519	710
31-Williamson/Krenkel-a, Wood-a(2)	41	82	123	328	524	720
32-Williamson/Krenkel-a	41	82	123	328	524	720
33-Classic Wood-c; "Judgment Day" story-r/Weird Fantasy #18; final issue & last E.C. comic book	42	84	126	336	538	740

NOTE: *Davis a-30, 32, 33; c-30-32.* ***Krigstein*** *a-in all.* ***Orlando*** *a-30, 32, 33.* ***Wood*** *a-30, 31, 33; c-33.*

INCREDIBLE SCIENCE FICTION (Formerly Weird Science-Fantasy)
Russ Cochran/Gemstone Publ.: No. 8, Aug, 1994 - No. 11, May, 1995 ($2.00)

8-11: Reprints #30-33 of E.C. series 4.00

INDEPENDENCE DAY (Movie)
Marvel Comics: No. 0, June, 1996 - No. 2, Aug, 1996 ($1.95, limited series)

0-Special Edition; photo-c 5.00
0-2 3.00

INDESTRUCTIBLE
IDW (Darby Pop): Dec, 2013 - Present ($3.99)

1-5: 1-Kline-s/Garron & Garcia-a 4.00

INDESTRUCTIBLE HULK (Marvel NOW!)(Follows Incredible Hulk 2011-2012 series)
Marvel Comics: Jan, 2013 - No. 20, May, 2014 ($3.99)

1-Waid-s/Yu-a; Banner hired by SHIELD; Maria Hill app. 4.00
2-20: 2-Iron Man app. 4,5-Attuma app. 6-8-Thor app.; Simonson-a/c. 9,10-Daredevil app. 12-Two-Gun Kid, Kid Colt, and Rawhide Kid app. 17,18-Iron Man app. 4.00
Annual 1 (2/14, $4.99) Parker-s/Asrar-a; Iron Man app. 5.00
... Special 1 (12/13, $4.99) Original X-Men and Superior Spider-Man app. 5.00

INDIANA JONES (Title series), **Dark Horse Comics**

--ADVENTURES, 6/08 ($6.95, digest-sized) Vol. 1 - new all-ages adventures; Beavers-a 7.00
--AND THE ARMS OF GOLD, 2/94 - 5/94 ($2.50) 1-4 3.00
--AND THE FATE OF ATLANTIS, 3/91 - 9/91 ($2.50) 1-4-Dorman painted-c on all; contain trading cards (#1 has a 2nd printing, 10/91) 3.00
--AND THE GOLDEN FLEECE, 6/94 - 7/94 ($2.50) 1,2 3.00
--AND THE IRON PHOENIX, 12/94 - 3/95 ($2.50) 1-4 3.00

INDIANA JONES AND THE KINGDOM OF THE CRYSTAL SKULL
Dark Horse Comics: May, 2008 - No. 2, May, 2008 ($5.99, limited series, movie adaptation)

1,2-Luke Ross-a/John Jackson Miller-adapted-s; two covers by Struzan & Fleming 6.00
TPB (5/08, $12.95) r/#1,2; Struzan-c 13.00

INDIANA JONES AND THE LAST CRUSADE
Marvel Comics: 1989 - No. 4, 1989 ($1.00, limited series, movie adaptation)

1-4: Williamson-i assist 3.00
1-(1989, $2.95, B&W mag., 80 pgs.) 4.00

--AND THE SHRINE OF THE SEA DEVIL: Dark Horse, 9/94 ($2.50, one shot)
1-Gary Gianni-a 3.00
--AND THE SARGASSO PIRATES: Dark Horse, 12/95 - 3/96 ($2.50) 1-4: 1,2-Ross-c 3.00
--AND THE SPEAR OF DESTINY: Dark Horse, 4/95 - 8/95 ($2.50) 1-4 3.00
--AND THE TOMB OF THE GODS, 6/08 - No. 4, 3/09 ($2.99) 1-4: 1-Tony Harris-c 3.00
--THUNDER IN THE ORIENT: Dark Horse, 9/93 - '94 ($2.50)
1-6: Dan Barry story & art in all; 1-Dorman painted-c 3.00

INDIANA JONES AND THE TEMPLE OF DOOM
Marvel Comics Group: Sept, 1984 - No. 3, Nov, 1984 (Movie adaptation)

1-3-r/Marvel Super Special; Guice-a 4.00

INDIANA JONES OMNIBUS
Dark Horse Books: Feb, 2008; June 2008; Feb, 2009 ($24.95, digest-size)

Volume One - Reprints Indiana Jones and the Fate of Atlantis, Indiana Jones: Thunder in the Orient; and Indiana Jones and the Arms of Gold mini-series 25.00
Volume Two - Reprints I.J. and the Golden Fleece, I.J. and the Shrine of the Sea Devil, I.J. and the Iron Phoenix, I.J. and the Spear of Destiny, I.J. and the Sargasso Pirates 25.00
The Further Adventures Volume One - (2/09) r/Raiders of the Lost Ark #1-3 & The Further Adventures of Indiana Jones #1-12 25.00

INDIAN BRAVES (Baffling Mysteries No. 5 on)
Ace Magazines: March, 1951 - No. 4, Sept, 1951

	GD	VG	FN	VF	VF/NM	NM-
1-Green Arrowhead begins, apps. in all	15	30	45	86	133	180
2	10	20	30	54	72	90
3,4	9	18	27	47	61	75
I.W. Reprint #1 (nd)-r/Indian Braves #4	2	4	6	9	13	16

INDIAN CHIEF (White Eagle...) (Formerly The Chief, Four Color 290)
Dell Publ. Co.: No. 3, July-Sept, 1951 - No. 33, Jan-Mar, 1959 (All painted-c)

	GD	VG	FN	VF	VF/NM	NM-
3	5	10	15	33	57	80
4-11: 6-White Eagle app.	4	8	12	28	47	65
12-1st White Eagle (10-12/53)-Not same as earlier character	5	10	15	33	57	80
13-29	4	8	12	23	37	50
30-33-Buscema-a	4	8	12	25	40	55

INDIAN CHIEF (See March of Comics No. 94, 110, 127, 140, 159, 170, 187)

INDIAN FIGHTER, THE (Movie)
Dell Publishing Co.: No. 687, May, 1956 (one-shot)

	GD	VG	FN	VF	VF/NM	NM-
Four Color 687-Kirk Douglas photo-c	7	14	21	44	82	120

INDIAN FIGHTER
Youthful Magazines: May, 1950 - No. 11, Jan, 1952

	GD	VG	FN	VF	VF/NM	NM-
1	16	32	48	94	147	200
2-Wildey-a/c(bondage)	12	24	36	67	94	120
3-11: 3,4-Wildey-a	10	20	30	54	72	90

NOTE: ***Hollingsworth*** *a-5.* ***Walter Johnson*** *c-1, 3, 4, 6.* ***Palais*** *a-10.* ***Stallman*** *a-5-8.* ***Wildey*** *a-2-4; c-2, 5.*

INDIAN LEGENDS OF THE NIAGARA (See American Graphics)

INDIANS
Fiction House Magazines (Wings Publ. Co.): Spring, 1950 - No. 17, Spr, 1953 (1-8: 52 pgs.)

	GD	VG	FN	VF	VF/NM	NM-
1-Manzar The White Indian, Long Bow & Orphan of the Storm begin	30	60	90	177	289	400
2-Starlight begins	15	30	45	90	140	190
3-5: 5-17-Most-c by Whitman	14	28	42	81	118	155
6-10	13	26	39	72	101	130
11-17	11	22	33	64	90	115

INDIANS OF THE WILD WEST
I. W. Enterprises: Circa 1958? (no date) (Reprints)

	GD	VG	FN	VF	VF/NM	NM-
9-Kinstler-c; Whitman-a; r/Indians #?	2	4	6	10	14	18

INDIANS ON THE WARPATH
St. John Publishing Co.: No date (Late 40s, early 50s) (132 pgs.)

	GD	VG	FN	VF	VF/NM	NM-
nn-Matt Baker-c; contains St. John comics rebound. Many combinations possible	40	80	120	246	411	575

INDIAN TRIBES (See Famous Indian Tribes)

INDIAN WARRIORS (Formerly White Rider and Super Horse; becomes Western Crime Cases #9)
Star Publications: No. 7, June, 1951 - No. 8, Sept, 1951

Inferior Five #2 © DC

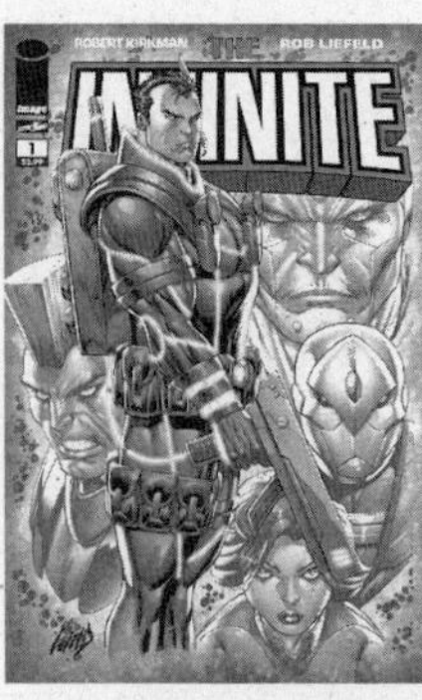

The Infinite #1 © Kirkman & Liefeld

Infinity Inc. #25 © DC

GD VG FN VF VF/NM NM-
2.0 4.0 6.0 8.0 9.0 9.2

7-White Rider & Superhorse continue; "Last of the Mohicans" serial begins;
L.B. Cole-c 18 36 54 105 165 225
8-L.B. Cole-c 17 34 51 98 154 210
3-D 1(12/53, 25¢)-Came w/glasses; L.B. Cole-c 34 68 102 199 325 450
Accepted Reprint(nn)(inside cover shows White Rider & Superhorse #11)-r/cover to #7;
origin White Rider &...; L.B. Cole-c 8 16 24 40 50 60
Accepted Reprint #8 (nd); L.B. Cole-c (r-cover to #8) 8 16 24 40 50 60

INDOORS-OUTDOORS (See Wisco)

INDOOR SPORTS
National Specials Co.: nd (6x9", 64 pgs., B&W-r, hard-c)
nn-By Tad 5 10 15 24 30 35

INDUSTRIAL GOTHIC
DC Comics (Vertigo): Dec, 1995 - No. 5, Apr, 1996 ($2.50, limited series)
1-5: Ted McKeever-c/a/scripts 3.00

INFAMOUS (Based on the Sony videogame)
DC Comics: Early May, 2011 - No. 6, Late July, 2011 ($2.99, limited series)
1-6: 1-William Harms-s/Eric Nguyen-a/Doug Mahnke-c. 3-6-Benes-c 3.00

INFERIOR FIVE, THE (Inferior 5 #11, 12) (See Showcase #62, 63, 65)
National Periodical Publications (#1-10: 12¢): 3-4/67 - No. 10, 9-10/68; No. 11, 8-9/72 - No. 12, 10-11/72
1-(3-4/67)-Sekowsky-a(p); 4th app. 5 10 15 33 57 80
2-5: 2-Plastic Man, F.F. app. 4-Thor app. 3 6 9 19 30 40
6-9: 6-Stars DC staff 3 6 9 16 23 30
10-Superman x-over; F.F., Spider-Man & Sub-Mariner app.
3 6 9 18 28 38
11,12: Orlando-c/a; both r/Showcase #62,63 2 4 6 11 16 20

INFERNAL MAN-THING (Sequel to story in Man-Thing #12 [1974])
Marvel Comics: Sept, 2012 - No. 3, Oct, 2012 ($3.99, limited series)
1-3-Gerber-s; painted-a by Nowlan; Art Adams-c. 1,2-Bonus reprint of Man-Thing #12 4.00

INFERNO
Caliber Comics: 1995 - No. 5 ($2.95, B&W)
1-5 3.00

INFERNO (See Legion of Super-Heroes)
DC Comics: Oct, 1997 - No. 4, Feb, 1998 ($2.50, limited series)
1-Immonen-s/c/a in all 4.00
2-4 3.00

INFERNO: HELLBOUND
Image Comics (Top Cow): Jan, 2002 - No. 3 ($2.50/$2.99)
1,2: 1-Seven covers; Silvestri-a/Silvestri and Wohl-s 3.00
3-($2.99) Tan-a 3.00
#0 (7/02, $3.00) Tan-a 3.00
Wizard #0- Previews series; bagged with Wizard Top Cow Special mag 3.00

INFESTATION (Zombie crossover with G.I. Joe, Star Trek, Transformers and Ghostbusters)
IDW Publishing: Jan, 2011 - No. 2, Apr, 2011 ($3.99, limited series)
1,2-Abnett & Lanning-s/Messina-a; two covers by Messina & Snyder III 4.00
...: Outbreak 1-4 (6/11 - No. 4, 9/11, $3.99) Messina-a; Covert Vampiric Operations app. 4.00

INFESTATION 2 (IDW characters vs. H.P. Lovecraft's Elder Gods)
IDW Publishing: Jan, 2012 - No. 2, Apr, 2012 ($3.99, limited series)
1,2-Swierczynski-s/Messina-a; three covers by Garner, Ramondelli & Messina 4.00
...: Dungeons & Dragons 1,2 (2/12 - No. 2, 2/12, $3.99) 3 covers 4.00
...: G.I. Joe 1,2 (3/12 - No. 2, 3/12, $3.99) Raicht-s/De Landro-a; 3 covers 4.00
...: Team-Up 1 (2/12, $3.99) Ryall-s/Robinson-a; covers by Powell & Morrison 4.00
...: Teenage Mutant Ninja Turtles 1,2 (3/12 - No. 2, 3/12, $3.99) Mark Torres-a; 3 covers 4.00
...: 30 Days of Night 1 (4/12, $3.99) Swierczynski-s/Sayger-a; 3 covers 4.00
...: Transformers 1,2 (2/12 - No. 2, 2/12, $3.99) Dixon-s/Guidi-a; 3 covers 4.00

INFINITE, THE
Image Comics (SkyBound): Aug, 2011 - No. 4, Nov, 2011 ($2.99)
1-4: 1-Robert Kirkman-s/Rob Liefeld-a; at least 11 covers. 2-Six covers 3.00

INFINITE CRISIS
DC Comics: Dec, 2005 - No. 7, Jun, 2006 ($3.99, limited series)
1-Johns-s/Jimenez-a; two covers by Jim Lee and George Pérez 5.00
1-RRP Edition with Jim Lee sketch-c 150.00
2-7: 4-New Spectre; Earth-2 returns. 5-Earth-2 Lois dies; new Blue Beetle debut. 6-Superboy killed, new Earth formed. 7-Earth-2 Superman dies 4.00
HC (2006, $24.99, dustjacket) r/#1-7; DiDio intro.; sketch cover gallery; interview/commentary with Johns, Jimenez and editors; sketch art 25.00

GD VG FN VF VF/NM NM-
2.0 4.0 6.0 8.0 9.0 9.2

... Companion TPB (2006, $14.99) r/Day of Vengeance: Infinite Crisis Special #1, Rann-Thanagar War: ICS #1, The Omac Project: ICS #1, Villains United: ICS #1 15.00
... Secret Files 2006 (4/06, $5.99) tie-in story with Earth-2 Lois and Superman, Earth-Prime Superboy and Alexander Luthor; art by various; profile pages 6.00

INFINITE CRISIS AFTERMATH (See Crisis Aftermath:...)

INFINITE VACATION
Image Comics (Shadowline): Jan, 2011 - No. 5, Jan, 2013 ($3.50/$5.99)
1-4-Nick Spencer-s/Christian Ward-a/c 3.50
5-($5.99) Conclusion; gatefold centerfold 6.00

INFINITY (Crossover with the Avengers titles)
Marvel Comics: Oct, 2013 - No. 6, Jan, 2014 ($4.99/$3.99/$5.99, limited series)
1-($4.99) Avengers, Inhumans and Thanos app.; Hickman-s/Cheung-a/Adam Kubert-c 5.00
2-5-($3.99) Opeña-a. 3-Terragen bomb triggered 4.00
6-($5.99) Cheung-a 6.00
Free Comic Book Day 2013 (Infinity) 1 (5/13, giveaway) Previews series; Cheung-a 3.00

INFINITY ABYSS (Also see Marvel Universe: The End)
Marvel Comics: Aug, 2002 - No. 6, Oct, 2002 ($2.99, limited series)
1-5-Starlin-s/a; Thanos, Captain Marvel, Spider-Man, Dr. Strange app. 4.00
6-($3.50) 4.00
Thanos Vol. 2: Infinity Abyss TPB (2003, $17.99) r/ #1-6 25.00

INFINITY CRUSADE
Marvel Comics: June, 1993 - No. 6, Nov, 1993 ($3.50/$2.50, limited series, 52 pgs.)
1-6: By Jim Starlin & Ron Lim. 1-($3.50). 2-6-($2.99) 6.00

INFINITY GAUNTLET (The... #2 on; see Infinity Crusade, The Infinity War & Warlock & the Infinity Watch)
Marvel Comics: July, 1991 - No. 6, Dec, 1991 ($2.50, limited series)
1-Thanos-c/stories in all; Starlin scripts in all 3 6 9 14 20 25
2-6: 5,6-Ron Lim-c/a 1 3 4 6 8 10
TPB (4/99, $24.95) r/#1-6 30.00
NOTE: ***Lim** a-3p(part), 5p, 6p; c-5i, 6i.* ***Perez** a-1-3p, 4p(part); c-1(painted), 2-4, 5i, 6i.*

INFINITY: HEIST (Tie-in to the Infinity crossover)
Marvel Comics: Nov, 2013 - No. 4, Feb, 2014 ($3.99, limited series)
1-4-Tieri-s/Barrionuevo-a; Spymaster, Titanium Man, Whirlwind app. 4.00

INFINITY, INC. (See All-Star Squadron #25)
DC Comics: Mar, 1984 - No. 53, Aug, 1988 ($1.25, Baxter paper, 36 pgs.)
1-Brainwave, Jr., Fury, The Huntress, Jade, Northwind, Nuklon, Obsidian, Power Girl, Silver Scarab & Star Spangled Kid begin 4.00
2-13,38-49,51-53: 2-Dr. Midnite, G.A. Flash, W. Woman, Dr. Fate, Hourman, Green Lantern, Wildcat app. 5-Nudity panels. 46,47-Millennium tie-ins 3.00
14-Todd McFarlane-a (5/85, 2nd full story) 1 2 3 6 8 9
15-37-McFarlane-a (20,23,24: 5 pgs. only; 33: 2 pgs.); 18-24-Crisis x-over. 21-Intro new Hourman & Dr. Midnight. 26-New Wildcat app. 31-Star Spangled Kid becomes Skyman. 32-Green Fury becomes Green Flame. 33-Origin Obsidian. 35-1st modern app. G.A. Fury 4.00
50 ($2.50, 52 pgs.) 4.00
Annual 1,2: 1(12/85)-Crisis x-over. 2('88, $2.00), Special 1 ('87, $1.50) 4.00
...: The Generations Saga Volume One HC (2011, $39.99) r/#1-4, All-Star Squadron #25,26 & All-Star Squadron Annual #2 40.00
NOTE: ***Kubert** r-4.* ***McFarlane** a-14-37p, Annual 1p; c(p)-14-19, 22, 25, 26, 31-33, 37, Annual 1.* ***Newton** a-12p, 13p(last work 4/85).* ***Tuska** a-11p. JSA app. 3-10.*

INFINITY, INC. (See 52)
DC Comics: Nov, 2007 - No. 12, Oct, 2008 ($2.99)
1-12: 1-Milligan-s; Steel app. 3.00
...: Luthor's Monsters TPB (2008, $14.99) r/#1-5 15.00
...: The Bogeyman TPB (2008, $14.99) r/#6-10 15.00

INFINITY: THE HUNT (Tie-in to the Infinity crossover)
Marvel Comics: Nov, 2013 - No. 4, Jan, 2014 ($3.99, limited series)
1-4-Kindt-s/Sanders-a; Avengers Academy, Wolverine & She-Hulk app. 4.00

INFINITY WAR, THE (Also see Infinity Gauntlet & Warlock and the Infinity...)
Marvel Comics: June, 1992 - No. 6, Nov, 1992 ($2.50, mini-series)
1-Starlin scripts, Lim-c/a(p), Thanos app. in all 6.00
2-6: All have wraparound gatefold covers 6.00
TPB (2006, $29.99) r/#1-6, Marvel Comics Presents #108-111, Warlock and the Infinity Watch #7-10; cover gallery and synopses of Infinity War crossovers 30.00

INFORMER, THE
Feature Television Productions: April, 1954 - No. 5, Dec, 1954
1-Sekowsky-a begins 12 24 36 69 97 125

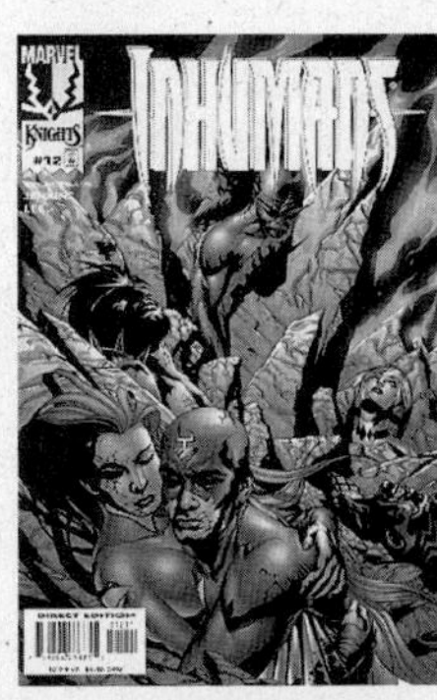
Inhumans V2 #12 © MAR

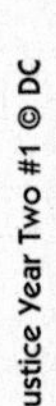
Injustice Year Two #1 © DC

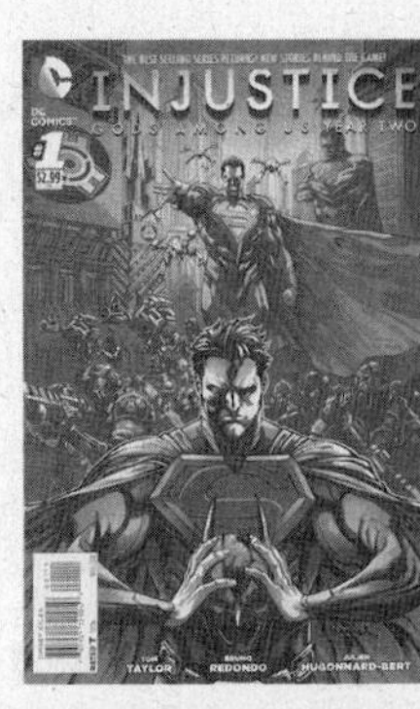

The Inspector #3 © GK

	GD 2.0	VG 4.0	FN 6.0	VF 8.0	VF/NM 9.0	NM- 9.2
2	9	18	27	47	61	75
3-5	8	16	24	42	54	65

IN HIS STEPS
Spire Christian Comics (Fleming H. Revell Co.): 1973, 1977 (39/49¢)

	GD	VG	FN	VF	VF/NM	NM-
nn	2	4	6	11	16	20

INHUMAN
Marvel Comics: Jun, 2014 - Present ($3.99)

	GD	VG	FN	VF	VF/NM	NM-
1-Soule-s/Madureira-a; Medusa app.						4.00

INHUMANITY
Marvel Comics: Feb, 2014 - No. 2, Mar, 2014 ($3.99)

	GD	VG	FN	VF	VF/NM	NM-
1,2: 1-After the fall of Attilan, origin of the Inhumans retold; Fraction-s/Coipel-a						4.00
...: Superior Spider-Man 1 (3/14, $3.99) Gage-s/Hans-a/c						4.00
...: The Awakening 1,2 (2/14 - No. 2, 3/14, $3.99) Kindt-s/Davidson-a						4.00

INHUMANOIDS, THE (TV)
Marvel Comics (Star Comics): Jan, 1987 - No. 4, July 1987

	GD	VG	FN	VF	VF/NM	NM-
1-4: Based on Hasbro toys						4.00

INHUMANS, THE (See Amazing Adventures, Fantastic Four #54 & Special #5, Incredible Hulk Special #1, Marvel Graphic Novel & Thor #146)
Marvel Comics Group: Oct, 1975 - No. 12, Aug, 1977

	GD	VG	FN	VF	VF/NM	NM-
1: #1-4,6 are 25¢ issues	3	6	9	19	30	40
2-4-Peréz-a	2	4	6	10	14	18
5-12: 9-Reprints Amazing Adventures #1,2('70). 12-Hulk app.	2	4	6	8	10	12
4-(30¢-c variant, limited distribution)(4/76) Peréz-a	3	6	9	17	26	35
6-(30¢-c variant, limited distribution)(8/76)	3	6	9	17	26	35
11,12-(35¢-c variants, limited distribution)	4	8	12	25	40	55
Special 1(4/90, $1.50, 52 pgs.)-F.F. cameo						4.00
...: The Great Refuge (5/95, $2.95)						4.00

NOTE: ***Buckler** c-2-4p, 5. **Gil Kane** a-5-7p; c-1p, 7p, 8p. **Kirby** a-9r. **Mooney** a-11i. **Perez** a-1-4p, 8p.*

INHUMANS (Marvel Knights)
Marvel Comics: Nov, 1998 - No. 12, Oct, 1999 ($2.99, limited series)

	GD	VG	FN	VF	VF/NM	NM-
1-Jae Lee-c/a; Paul Jenkins-s						10.00
1-($6.95) DF Edition; Jae Lee variant-c						7.00
2-Two covers by Lee and Darrow						4.00
3-12						3.00
TPB (10/00, $24.95) r/#1-12						25.00

INHUMANS (Volume 3)
Marvel Comics: Jun, 2000 - No. 4, Oct, 2000 ($2.99, limited series)

	GD	VG	FN	VF	VF/NM	NM-
1-4-Ladronn-c/Pacheco & Marin-s. 1-3-Ladronn-a. 4-Lucas-a						3.00

INHUMANS (Volume 6)
Marvel Comics: Jun, 2003 - No. 12, Jun, 2004 ($2.50/$2.99)

	GD	VG	FN	VF	VF/NM	NM-
1-12: 1-6-McKeever-s/Clark-a/JH Williams III-c. 7-Begin $2.99-c. 7,8-Teranishi-a						3.00
Vol. 1: Culture Shock (2005, $7.99, digest) r/#1-6; story pitch and sketch pages						8.00

INHUMANS 2099
Marvel Comics: Nov, 2004 ($2.99, one-shot)

	GD	VG	FN	VF	VF/NM	NM-
1-Kirkman-s/Rathburn-a/Pat Lee-c						3.00

INJUSTICE: GODS AMONG US (Based on the video game)
DC Comics: Mar, 2013 - No. 12, Feb, 2014 ($3.99)

	GD	VG	FN	VF	VF/NM	NM-
1-Lois Lane dies; Joker app.	3	6	9	16	23	30
1-Variant-c	3	6	9	17	26	35
1-Second printing						6.00
2-Joker killed						10.00
3-12: 6-Nightwing dies						4.00
Annual 1 (1/14, $4.99) Harley Quinn & Lobo app.; Ryp-c						5.00

INJUSTICE YEAR TWO (Based on the video game)
DC Comics: Mar, 2014 - Present ($2.99)

	GD	VG	FN	VF	VF/NM	NM-
1-3-Sinestro app.						3.00

INKY & DINKY (See Felix's Nephews...)

IN LOVE (...Magazine on-c; I Love You No. 7 on)
Mainline/Charlton No. 5 (5/55)-on: Aug-Sept, 1954 - No. 6, July, 1955 ('Adult Reading' on-c)

	GD	VG	FN	VF	VF/NM	NM-
1-Simon & Kirby-a; book-length novel in all issues	43	86	129	271	461	650
2,3-S&K-a. 3-Last pre-code (12-1/54-55)	28	56	84	165	270	375
4-S&K-a.(Rare)	31	62	93	182	296	410
5-S&K-c only	16	32	48	94	147	200
6-No S&K-a	11	22	33	62	86	110

INNOVATION SPECTACULAR
Innovation Publishing: 1991 - No. 2, 1991 ($2.95, squarebound, 100 pgs.)

	GD	VG	FN	VF	VF/NM	NM-
1,2: Contains rebound comics w/o covers						4.00

INNOVATION SUMMER FUN SPECIAL
Innovation Publishing: 1991 ($3.50, B&W/color, squarebound)

	GD	VG	FN	VF	VF/NM	NM-
1-Contains rebound comics (Power Factory)						4.00

IN SEARCH OF THE CASTAWAYS (See Movie Comics)

INSIDE CRIME (Formerly My Intimate Affair)
Fox Features Syndicate (Hero Books): No. 3, July, 1950 - No. 2, Sept, 1950

	GD	VG	FN	VF	VF/NM	NM-
3-Wood-a (10 pgs.); L. B. Cole-c	30	60	90	177	289	400
2-Used in **SOTI**, pg. 182,183; r/Spook #24	23	46	69	136	223	310
nn(no publ. listed, nd)	11	22	33	62	86	110

INSPECTOR, THE (TV) (Also see The Pink Panther)
Gold Key: July, 1974 - No. 19, Feb, 1978

	GD	VG	FN	VF	VF/NM	NM-
1	3	6	9	18	28	38
2-5	2	4	6	13	18	22
6-9	2	4	6	10	14	18
10-19: 11-Reprints	2	4	6	8	10	12

INSPECTOR GILL OF THE FISH POLICE (See Fish Police)

INSPECTOR WADE
David McKay Publications: No. 13, May, 1938

	GD	VG	FN	VF	VF/NM	NM-
Feature Books 13	30	60	90	177	289	400

INSTANT PIANO
Dark Horse Comics: Aug, 1994 - No. 4, Feb, 1995 ($3.95, B&W, bimonthly, mature)

	GD	VG	FN	VF	VF/NM	NM-
1-4						4.00

INSURGENT
DC Comics: Mar, 2013 - No. 6 ($2.99, limited series)

	GD	VG	FN	VF	VF/NM	NM-
1-3-DeSanto & Farmer-s/Dallocchio-a						3.00

INTERFACE
Marvel Comics (Epic Comics): Dec, 1989 - No. 8, Dec, 1990 ($1.95, mature, coated paper)

	GD	VG	FN	VF	VF/NM	NM-
1-8: Cont. from 1st ESPers series; painted-c/a						3.00
Espers: Interface TPB ('98, $16.95) r/#1-6						17.00

INTERNATIONAL COMICS (...Crime Patrol No. 6)
E. C. Comics: Spring, 1947 - No. 5, Nov-Dec, 1947

	GD	VG	FN	VF	VF/NM	NM-
1-Schaffenberger-a begins, ends #4	68	136	204	435	743	1050
2	45	90	135	284	480	675
3-5	41	82	123	250	418	585

INTERNATIONAL CRIME PATROL (Formerly International Comics #1-5; becomes Crime Patrol No. 7 on)
E. C. Comics: No. 6, Spring, 1948

	GD	VG	FN	VF	VF/NM	NM-
6-Moon Girl app.	68	136	204	435	743	1050

IN THE DAYS OF THE MOB (Magazine)
Hampshire Dist. Ltd. (National): Fall, 1971 (B&W)

	GD	VG	FN	VF	VF/NM	NM-
1-Kirby-a; John Dillinger wanted poster inside (1/2 value if poster is missing)	7	14	21	44	82	120

IN THE PRESENCE OF MINE ENEMIES
Spire Christian Comics/Fleming H. Revell Co.: 1973 (35/49¢)

	GD	VG	FN	VF	VF/NM	NM-
nn	2	4	6	10	14	18

IN THE SHADOW OF EDGAR ALLAN POE
DC Comics (Vertigo): 2002 (Graphic novel)

	GD	VG	FN	VF	VF/NM	NM-
Hardcover (2002, $24.95) Fuqua-s/Phillips and Parke photo-a						25.00
Softcover (2003, $17.95)						18.00

INTIMATE
Charlton Comics: Dec, 1957 - No. 3, May, 1958

	GD	VG	FN	VF	VF/NM	NM-
1	6	12	18	28	34	40
2,3	4	8	12	18	22	25

INTIMATE CONFESSIONS (See Fox Giants)

INTIMATE CONFESSIONS
Country Press Inc.: 1942

nn-Ashcan comic, not distributed to newsstands, only for in house use. A VF copy sold for $1,000 in 2007, and a VF+ copy sold for $1,525 in 2007.

INTIMATE CONFESSIONS
Realistic Comics: July-Aug, 1951 - No. 7, Aug, 1952; No. 8, Mar, 1953 (All painted-c)

	GD	VG	FN	VF	VF/NM	NM-
1-Kinstler-a; c/Avon paperback #222	142	284	426	909	1555	2200

Intimate Confessions #3 © REAL

The Invaders #19 © MAR

Invincible #100 © Kirkman & Walker

	GD 2.0	VG 4.0	FN 6.0	VF 8.0	VF/NM 9.0	NM- 9.2
2	39	78	117	231	378	525
3-c/Avon paperback #250; Kinstler-c/a	40	80	120	246	411	575
4-8: 4-c/Avon paperback #304; Kinstler-c. 6-c/Avon paperback #120. 8-c/Avon paperback #375; Kinstler-a	37	74	111	222	361	500

INTIMATE CONFESSIONS
I. W. Enterprises/Super Comics: 1964

I.W. Reprint #9,10, Super Reprint #10,12,18	2	4	6	13	18	22

INTIMATE LOVE
Standard Comics: No. 5, 1950 - No. 28, Aug, 1954

5-8: 6-8-Severin/Elder-a	12	24	36	67	94	120
9	9	18	27	50	65	80
10-Jane Russell, Robert Mitchum photo-c	15	30	45	84	127	170
11-18,20,23,25,27,28	9	18	27	47	61	75
19,21,22,24,26-Toth-a	10	20	30	54	72	90

NOTE: ***Celardo** a-8, 10. **Colletta** a-23. **Moreira** a-13(2). Photo-c-6, 7, 10, 12, 14, 15, 18-20, 24, 26, 27.*

INTIMATES, THE
DC Comics (WildStorm): Jan, 2005 - No. 12, Dec, 2005 ($2.95/$2.99)

1-12: 1-Joe Casey-s/Jim Lee-c/Lee and Giuseppe Camuncoli-a — 3.00

INTIMATE SECRETS OF ROMANCE
Star Publications: Sept, 1953 - No. 2, Apr, 1954

1,2-L. B. Cole-c	19	38	57	111	176	240

INTRIGUE
Quality Comics Group: Jan, 1955

1-Horror; Jack Cole reprint/Web of Evil	34	68	102	204	332	460

INTRIGUE
Image Comics: Aug, 1999 - No. 3, Feb, 2000 ($2.50/$2.95)

1,2: 1-Two covers (Andrews, Wieringo); Shum-s/Andrews-a — 3.00
3-($2.95) — 3.00

INTRUDER
TSR, Inc.: 1990 - No. 10, 1991 ($2.95, 44 pgs.)

1-10 — 4.00

INVADERS, THE (TV)(Aliens From a Dying Planet)
Gold Key: Oct, 1967 - No. 4, Oct, 1968 (All have photo-c)

1-Spiegle-a in all	8	16	24	51	96	140
2-4: 2-Pin-up on back-c	5	10	15	35	63	90

INVADERS, THE (Also see The Avengers #71, Giant-Size Invaders, and All-New Invaders)
Marvel Comics Group: August, 1975 - No. 40, May, 1979; No. 41, Sept, 1979

1-Captain America & Bucky, Human Torch & Toro, & Sub-Mariner begin; cont'd. from Giant Size Invaders #1; #1-7 are 25¢ issues	6	12	18	37	66	95
2-5: 2-1st app. Brain-Drain. 3-Battle issue; Cap vs. Namor vs. Torch; intro U-Man	3	6	9	17	26	35
6-10: 6,7-(Regular 25¢ edition). 6-(7/76) Liberty Legion app. 7-Intro Baron Blood & intro/1st app. Union Jack; Human Torch origin retold. 8-Union Jack-c/story. 9-Origin Baron Blood. 10-G.A. Capt. America-r/C.A #22	2	4	6	11	16	20
6,7-(30¢-c variants, limited distribution)	4	8	12	23	37	50
11-19: 11-Origin Spitfire; intro The Blue Bullet. 14-1st app. The Crusaders. 16-Re-intro The Destroyer. 17-Intro Warrior Woman. 18-Re-intro The Destroyer w/new origin. 19-Hitler-c/story	2	4	6	8	11	14
17-19,21-(35¢-c variants, limited distribution)	4	8	12	27	44	60
20-(Regular 30¢-c) Reprints origin/1st app. Sub-Mariner from Motion Picture Funnies Weekly with color added & brief write-up about MPFW; 1st app. new Union Jack II	2	4	6	10	14	18
20-(35¢-c variant, limited distribution)	5	10	15	30	50	70
21-(Regular 30¢ edition)-r/Marvel Mystery #10 (battle issue)	2	4	6	9	13	16
22-30,34-40: 22-New origin Toro. 24-r/Marvel Mystery #17 (team-up issue; all-r). 25-All new-a begins. 28-Intro new Human Top & Golden Girl. 29-Intro Teutonic Knight. 34-Mighty Destroyer joins. 35-The Whizzer app.	1	2	3	5	7	9
31-33: 31-Frankenstein-c/sty. 32,33-Thor app.	2	4	6	8	11	14
41-Double size last issue	3	6	9	14	19	24
Annual 1 (9/77)-Schomburg, Rico stories (new); Schomburg-c/a (1st for Marvel in 30 years); Avengers app.; re-intro The Shark & The Hyena	5	10	15	31	53	75
... Classic Vol. 1 TPB (2007, $24.99) r/#1-9, Giant-Size Invaders #1 and Marvel Premiere #29,30; cover pencils and cover inks						25.00

NOTE: ***Buckler** a-5. **Everett** r-20('39), 21(1940), 24, Annual 1. **Gil Kane** c(p)-13, 17, 18, 20-27. **Kirby** c(p)-3-12, 14-16, 32, 33. **Mooney** a-5i, 16, 22. **Robbins** a-1-4, 6-9, 10(3 pg.), 11-15, 17-21, 23, 25-28; c-28.*

INVADERS (See Namor, the Sub-Mariner #12)
Marvel Comics Group: May, 1993 - No. 4, Aug, 1993 ($1.75, limited series)

1-4 — 3.00

INVADERS (2004 title - see New Invaders)

INVADERS FROM HOME
DC Comics (Piranha Press): 1990 - No. 6, 1990 ($2.50, mature)

1-6 — 3.00

INVADERS NOW! (See Avengers/Invaders and The Torch series)
Marvel Comics: Nov, 2010 - No. 5, Mar, 2011 ($3.99, limited series)

1-5-Alex Ross-c; Steve Rogers, Bucky, Human Torch & Toro, Sub-Mariner app. — 4.00

INVASION
DC Comics: Holiday, 1988-'89 - No. 3, Jan, 1989 ($2.95, lim. series, 84 pgs.)

1-3:1-McFarlane/Russell-a. 2-McFarlane/Russell & Giffen/Gordon-a — 5.00
Invasion! TPB (2008, $24.99) r/#1-3 — 25.00

INVINCIBLE (Also see The Pact #4)
Image Comics: Jan, 2003 - Present ($2.95/$2.99)

	GD 2.0	VG 4.0	FN 6.0	VF 8.0	VF/NM 9.0	NM- 9.2
1-Kirkman-s/Walker-a	6	12	18	38	69	100
2,3-Kirkman-s/Walker-a	3	6	9	19	30	40
4-8: 4-Preview of The Moth	2	4	6	10	14	18
9-14: 11-Origin of Omni-Man. 14-Cho-c	1	2	3	5	6	8
15-24,26-41,43-49: 33-Tie-in w/Marvel Team-Up #14						5.00
25-($4.95) Science Dog app.; back-up stories w/origins of Science Dog and teammates						6.00
42-($1.99) Includes re-cap of the entire series						5.00
50-(6/08, $4.99) Two covers; back-up origin of Cecil Stedman; Science Dog app.						6.00
51-59,61-74: 51-Jim Lee-c; new costumes. 57-Continues in Astounding Wolf-Man #11. 71-74-Viltrumite War						4.00
76-99,101-109: 89-Intro. Zandale. 97-Origin of Bulletproof						3.00
60-($3.99) Invincible War; Witchblade, Savage Dragon, Spawn, Youngblood app.	1	2	3	5	6	8
75-($5.99) Viltrumite War; Science Dog back-up; 2 covers	1	2	3	4	5	7
100-(1/13, $3.99) "The Death of Everyone" conclusion; multiple covers						5.00
110-Rape issue						6.00
#0-(4/05, 50¢) Origin of Invincible; Ottley-a						3.00
Image Firsts: Invincible #1 (4/10, $1.00) r/#1 with "Image Firsts" cover logo						3.00
Official Handbook of the Invincible Universe 1,2 (11/06, 1/07, $4.99) profile pages						5.00
Official Handbook of the Invincible Universe Vol. 1 (2007, $12.99) r/#1-2; sketch pages						13.00
... Presents Atom Eve 1,2 (12/07, 3/08, $2.99) origin of Atom Eve; Bellegarde-a						3.00
... Presents Atom Eve & Rex Splode 1-3 (10/09 - 2/10, $2.99) origin of Rex						3.00
... Returns (4/10, $3.99) Leads into Viltrumite War in #71; 4 covers						4.00
... Universe Primer 1 (5/08, $5.99) r/Invincible #1, Brit #1, Astounding Wolf-Man #1						6.00
The Complete Invincible Library Vol. 1 Slipcase HC (2006, $125.00) oversized r/#1-24, #0 and story from Image Comics Summer Special (FCBD 2004); sketch pages; script for #1						125.00
..., Ultimate Collection Vol. 1 HC (2005, $34.95) oversized r/#1-13; sketch pages						35.00
..., Ultimate Collection Vol. 2 HC (2006, $34.99) oversized r/#14-24, #0 and story from Image Comics Summer Special (FCBD 2004); sketch pages and script for #23; intro by Damon Lindelof; afterword by Robert Kirkman						35.00
..., Ultimate Collection Vol. 3 HC (2007, $34.95) oversized r/#25-35 & The Pact #4; sketch pages and script for #28; afterword by Robert Kirkman						35.00
..., Ultimate Collection Vol. 4 HC (2008, $34.99) oversized r/#36-47; sketch & script pgs.						35.00
Vol. 1: Family Matters TPB (8/03, $12.95) r/#1-4; intro. by Busiek; sketch pages						13.00
Vol. 2: Eight in Enough TPB (3/04, $12.95) r/#5-8; intro. by Larsen; sketch pages						13.00
Vol. 3: Perfect Strangers TPB (2004, $12.95) r/#9-12; intro. by Brevoort; sketch pages						13.00
Vol. 4: Head of the Class TPB (1/05, $14.95) r/#14-19; intro. by Waid; sketch pages						15.00
Vol. 5: The Facts of Life TPB (2005, $14.99) r/#0,20-24; intro. by Wieringo; sketch pages						15.00
Vol. 6: A Different World TPB (2006, $14.99) r/#25-30; intro. by Brubaker; sketch pages						15.00
Vol. 7: Three's Company TPB (2006, $14.99) r/#31-35 & The Pact #4; sketch pages						15.00
Vol. 8: My Favorite Martian TPB (2007, $14.99) r/#36-41; sketch pages						15.00
Vol. 9: Out of This World TPB (2008, $14.99) r/#42-47; sketch pages						15.00

INVINCIBLE FOUR OF KUNG FU & NINJA
Leung Publications: April, 1988 - No. 6, 1989 ($2.00)

1-($2.75) — 4.00
2-6: 2-Begin $2.00-c — 3.00

INVINCIBLE IRON MAN
Marvel Comics: July, 2008 - No. 33, Feb, 2011;
No. 500, Mar, 2011 - No. 527, Dec, 2012 ($2.99/$3.99)

1-Fraction-s/Larroca-a; covers by Larroca & Quesada — 4.00
1-Downey movie photo wraparound — 5.00
1-Secret Movie Variant white-c with movie cast — 30.00
2-18: 2-War Machine and Thor app. 7-Spider-Man app. 8-10-Dark Reign. 11-War Machine app.; Pepper gets her armor suit. 12-Namor app. — 3.00
19,20-($3.99) 20-Stark Disassembled starts; back-up synopsis of recent storylines — 4.00

Invincible Iron Man #518 © MAR

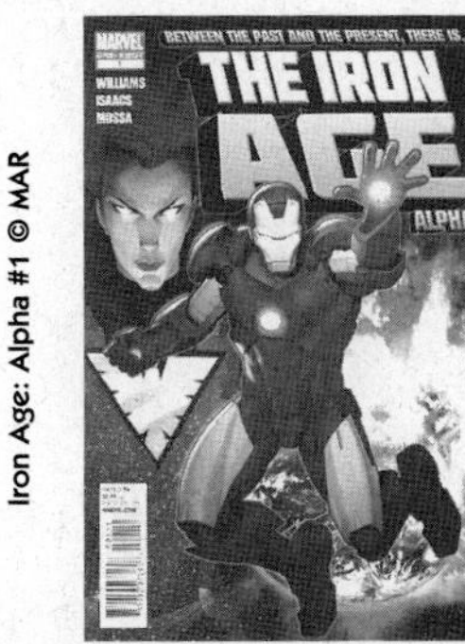

Iron Age: Alpha #1 © MAR

Iron Fist (1998 series) #3 © MAR

	GD 2.0	VG 4.0	FN 6.0	VF 8.0	VF/NM 9.0	NM- 9.2

21-24-Covers by Larocca and Zircher: 21-Thor & Capt. America app. 22-Dr. Strange app. 3.00
25-($3.99) Fraction-s/Larroca-a; new armor 4.00
26-31-($2.99) 29-New Rescue armor 3.00
32,33-($3.99)-War Machine app.; back-up w/McKelvie-a 4.00
(After #33, numbering reverts to original Vol. 1 as #500)
500-(3/11, $4.99) Two covers by Larroca; Mandarin & Spider-Man app.; cover gallery 5.00
500-Variant-c by Romita Jr. 10.00
500.1 (4/11, $2.99) Histroy re-told; Fraction-s/Larroca-a/c 3.00
501-527-($3.99) 501-503-Doctor Octopus app. 503-Back-up w/Chaykin-a. 504-509-Fear Itself tie-in; Grey Gargoyle app. 517-New War Machine armor 4.00
Annual 1 (8/10, $4.99) Larroca-c; history of the Mandarin; Di Giandomenico-a 5.00
...MGC #1 (4/10, free) r/#1 with "Marvel's Greatest Comics" cover logo 3.00

INVINCIBLE UNIVERSE (Characters from Invincible)
Image Comics: Apr, 2013 - No. 12, Apr, 2014 ($2.99)

1-12-Hester-s/Nauck-a. 1-Wraparound-c 3.00

INVISIBLE BOY (See Approved Comics)

INVISIBLE MAN, THE (See Superior Stories #1 & Supernatural Thrillers #2)

INVISIBLE PEOPLE
Kitchen Sink Press: 1992 (B&W, lim. series)

Book One: Sanctum; Book Two: "The Power": Will Eisner-s/a in all 4.00
Book Three: "Mortal Combat" 4.00
Hardcover ($34.95) 35.00
TPB (DC Comics, 9/00, $12.95) reprints series 13.00

INVISIBLES, THE (1st Series)
DC Comics (Vertigo): Sept, 1994 - No. 25, Oct, 1996 ($1.95/$2.50, mature)

1-($2.95, 52 pgs.)-Intro King Mob, Ragged Robin, Boy, Lord Fanny & Dane (Jack Frost); Grant Morrison scripts in all 6.00
2-8: 4-Includes bound-in trading cards. 5-1st app. Orlando; brown paper-c 4.00
9-25: 10-Intro Jim Crow. 13-15-Origin Lord Fanny. 19-Origin King Mob; polybagged. 20-Origin Boy. 21-Mister Six revealed. 25-Intro Division X 3.00
Apocalipstick (2001, $19.95, TPB)-r/#9-16; Bolland-c 20.00
Entropy in the U.K. (2001, $19.95, TPB)-r/#17-25; Bolland-c 20.00
Say You Want A Revolution (1996, $17.50, TPB)-r/#1-8 18.00
NOTE: ***Buckingham** a-25p. **Rian Hughes** c-1, 5. **Phil Jimenez** a-17p-19p. **Paul Johnson** a-16, 21. **Sean Phillips** c-2-4, 6-25. **Weston** a-10p. **Yeowell** a-1p-4p, 22p-24p.*

INVISIBLES, THE (2nd Series)
DC Comics (Vertigo): V2#1, Feb, 1997 - No. 22, Feb, 1999 ($2.50, mature)

1-Intro Jolly Roger; Grant Morrison scripts, Phil Jimenez-a, & Brian Bolland-c begins 4.00
2-22: 9,14-Weston-a 3.00
Bloody Hell in America TPB ('98, $12.95) r/#1-4 13.00
Counting to None TPB ('99, $19.95) r/#5-13 20.00
Kissing Mr. Quimper TPB ('00, $19.95) r/#14-22 20.00

INVISIBLES, THE (3rd Series) (Issue #'s go in reverse from #12 to #1)
DC Comics (Vertigo): V3#12, Apr, 1999 - No. 1, June, 2000 ($2.95, mature)

1-12-Bolland-c; Morrison-s on all. 1-Quitely-a. 2-4-Art by various. 5-8-Phillips-a. 9-12-Phillip Bond-a. 3.00
The Invisible Kingdom TPB ('02, $19.95) r/#12-1; new Bolland-c 20.00

INVISIBLE SCARLET O'NEIL (Also see Famous Funnies #81 & Harvey Comics Hits #59)
Famous Funnies (Harvey): Dec, 1950 - No. 3, Apr, 1951 (2-3 pgs. of Powell-a in each issue.)

	GD	VG	FN	VF	VF/NM	NM-
1	15	30	45	86	133	180
2,3	12	24	36	67	94	120

ION (Green Lantern Kyle Rayner) (See Countdown)
DC Comics: Jun, 2006 - No. 12, May, 2007 ($2.99)

1-12: 1-Marz-s/Tocchini-a. 3-Mogo app. 9,10-Tangent Green Lantern app. 12-Monitor app. 3.00
...: The Torchbearer TPB (2007, $14.99) r/#1-6 15.00

I, PAPARAZZI
DC Comics (Vertigo): 2001 ($29.95, HC, digitally manipulated photographic art)

nn-Pat McGreal-s/Steven Parke-digital-a/Stephen John Phillips-photos 30.00

IRON AGE
Marvel Comics: Aug, 2011 - No. 3, Oct, 2011 ($4.99, limited series)

1-3-Iron Man time travels. 1-Avengers. 2-Fantastic Four. 3-Dazzler & X-Men 5.00
...: Alpha (8/11, $2.99) First part of the series; Dark Phoenix app.; Issacs-a 3.00
...: Omega (10/11, $2.99) Conclusion of the series; Olivetti-c/Issacs-a 3.00

IRON AND THE MAIDEN
Aspen MLT: Sept, 2007 - No. 4, Dec, 2007 ($3.99)

1-4: 1-Two covers by Manapul and Madureira/Matsuda; Jason Rubin-s 4.00
...: Brutes, Bims and the City (2/08, $2.99) character backgrounds/development art 3.00

IRON CORPORAL, THE (See Army War Heroes #22)
Charlton Comics: No. 23, Oct, 1985 - No. 25, Feb, 1986

23-25: Glanzman-a(r); low print 6.00

IRON FIST (See Immortal Iron Fist, Deadly Hands of Kung Fu, Marvel Premiere & Power Man)
Marvel Comics: Nov, 1975 - No. 15, Sept, 1977

	GD	VG	FN	VF	VF/NM	NM-
1-Iron Fist battles Iron Man (#1-6: 25¢)	7	14	21	46	86	125
2	4	8	12	25	40	55
3-10: 4-6-(Regular 25¢ edition)(4-6/76). 8-Origin retold	3	6	9	19	30	40
4-6-(30¢-c variant, limited distribution)	5	10	15	35	63	90
11,13: 13-(30¢-c)	3	6	9	16	24	32
12-Capt. America app.	3	6	9	21	33	45
13-(35¢-c variant, limited distribution)	7	14	21	44	82	120
14-1st app. Sabretooth (8/77)(see Power Man)	15	30	45	103	227	350
14-(35¢-c variant, limited distribution)	79	158	237	632	1416	2200
15-(Regular 30¢ ed.) X-Men app., Byrne-a	6	12	18	41	76	110
15-(35¢-c variant, limited distribution)	17	34	51	117	259	400

NOTE: ***Adkins** a-8p, 10i, 13i; c-8i. **Byrne** a-1-15p; c-8p, 15p. **G. Kane** c-4-6p. **McWilliams** a-1i.*

IRON FIST
Marvel Comics: Sept, 1996 - No. 2, Oct, 1996 ($1.50, limited series)

1,2 3.00

IRON FIST
Marvel Comics: Jul, 1998 - No. 3, Sept, 1998 ($2.50, limited series)

1-3: Jurgens-s/Guice-a 3.00

IRON FIST (Also see Immortal Iron Fist)
Marvel Comics: May, 2004 - No. 6, Oct, 2004 ($2.99)

1-6: 1-4,6-Kevin Lau-c/a. 5-Mays-c/a 3.00

IRON FIST: THE LIVING WEAPON
Marvel Comics: Jun, 2014 - Present ($3.99)

1-Kaare Andrews-s/a/c 4.00

IRON FIST: WOLVERINE
Marvel Comics: Nov, 2000 - No. 4, Feb, 2001 ($2.99, limited series)

1-4-Igle-c/a; Kingpin app. 2-Iron Man app. 3,4-Capt. America app. 3.00

IRON GHOST
Image Comics: Apr, 2005 - No. 6, Mar, 2006 ($2.95/$2.99, limited series)

1-6-Chuck Dixon-s/Sergio Cariello-a; flip cover on each 3.00

IRONHAND OF ALMURIC (Robert E. Howard's...)
Dark Horse Comics: Aug, 1991 - No. 4, 1991 ($2.00, B&W, mini-series)

1-4: 1-Conrad painted-c 3.00

IRON HORSE (TV)
Dell Publishing Co.: March, 1967 - No. 2, June, 1967

	GD	VG	FN	VF	VF/NM	NM-
1-Dale Robertson photo covers on both	3	6	9	17	26	35
2	3	6	9	15	21	26

IRONJAW (Also see The Barbarians)
Atlas/Seaboard Publ.: Jan, 1975 - No. 4, July, 1975

	GD	VG	FN	VF	VF/NM	NM-
1,2-Neal Adams-c. 1-1st app. Iron Jaw; Sekowsky-a(p); Fleisher-s	3	6	9	14	20	25
3,4-Marcos. 4-Origin	2	4	6	9	13	16

IRON LANTERN
Marvel Comics (Amalgam): June, 1997 ($1.95, one-shot)

1-Kurt Busiek-s/Paul Smith & Al Williamson-a 3.00

IRON MAN (Also see The Avengers #1, Giant-Size..., Marvel Collectors Item Classics, Marvel Double Feature, Marvel Fanfare, Tales of Suspense #39 & Uncanny Tales #52)
Marvel Comics: May, 1968 - No. 332, Sept, 1996

	GD	VG	FN	VF	VF/NM	NM-
1-Origin; Colan-c/a(p); story continued from Iron Man & Sub-Mariner #1	75	150	225	450	775	1100
2	13	26	39	89	195	300
3-Iron Man vs. The Freak	10	20	30	64	132	200
4,5: 4-Unicorn app.	8	16	24	54	102	150
6-10: 7,8-Gladiator app. 9-Iron Man battles green Hulk-like android. 9,10-The Mandarin app.	7	14	21	44	82	120
11-15: 10,11-Mandarin app. 13-1st app. Controller. 15-Last 12c issue; vs Unicorn and the Red Ghost	6	12	18	38	69	100
16-20: 16-Vs. Unicorn and the Red Ghost. 17-1st Midas (Mordecai Midas). 18-Avengers app. 19-Captain America app.	5	10	15	31	53	75

21-24,26-30: 21-Crimson Dynamo app. 22-Death of Janice Cord; Crimson Dynamo app.

Iron Man #61 © MAR

Iron Man #286 © MAR

Iron Man #308 © MAR

GD 2.0 | VG 4.0 | FN 6.0 | VF 8.0 | VF/NM 9.0 | NM- 9.2

27-Intro Firebrand. 28-Controller app. 4 8 12 25 40 55
25-Iron Man battles Sub-Mariner 4 8 12 28 47 65
31-42: 33-1st app. Spymaster. 35-Daredevil & Nick Fury vs. Zodiak; x-over w/Daredevil #73. 36-Daredevil & Nick Fury vs Zodiak. 39-Avengers app. 42-Last 15c issue 3 6 9 21 33 45
43-Intro the Guardsman (25¢ Giant, 52 pgs); Giant-Man back-up (r) from TTA #52 5 10 15 30 50 70
44-46,48-53: 44-Capt. America app; back-up Ant-Man w/Andru-a. 46-The Guardsman dies. 48-Firebrand app. 49-Super-Adaptoid app. 50-Princess Python app. 53-1st Black Lama; Starlin part pencils 3 6 9 18 30 40
47-Origin retold; Barry Smith-a(p) 4 8 12 28 47 65
54-Iron Man battles Sub-Mariner; 1st app. Moondragon (1/73) as Madame MacEvil; Everett part-c 5 10 15 34 60 85
55-1st app. Thanos, Drax the Destroyer, Mentor, Starfox & Kronos (2/73); Starlin-c/a 75 150 225 450 650 850
56-Starlin-a 5 10 15 33 57 80
57-63: 57,58-Mandarin and Unicorn app. 59-Firebrand app. 60,61-Vs. the Masked Marauder. 62-Whiplash app. 63-Vs. Dr. Spectrum 3 6 9 16 24 32
64,65,67-70: 64,65-Dr. Spectrum app; origin is #65; Thor brief app. 67-Last 20c issue. 68-Sunfire, Mandarin and Unicorn app. 69,70-Mandarin, Yellow Claw & Ultimo app. 3 6 9 14 20 25
66-Iron Man vs. Thor. 3 6 9 21 33 45
71-84: 71-Yellow Claw & Black Lama app. 72-Black Lama app; Iron Man at the San Diego Comic Con. 73-Vs. Crimson Dynamo & Radioactive Man; Stark Industries renamed Stark International. 74-Modok vs. Mad-Thinker; Black Lama app in "War of the Super-Villains". 75-Black Lama & Yellow Claw app. 76-r/#9. 77-Conclusion of the "War of the Super-Villains"; Black Lama app. 80-Origin of Black Lama. 81-Black Lama & Firebrand app. 82,83-Red Ghost app. 2 4 6 10 14 18
85-89-(Regular 25¢ editions): 86-1st app. Blizzard. 87-Origin Blizzard. 88-Brief Thanos cameo. 89-Daredevil app.; last 25¢-c 2 4 6 10 14 18
85-89-(30¢-c variants, limited distribution)(4-8/76) 4 8 12 23 37 50
90-99: 90,91-Blood Brothers & Controller app. 92-Vs. Melter. 95-Ultimo app. 96-1st new Guardsman (Michael O' Brien). 98,99-Mandarin & Sunfire app. 2 4 6 9 12 15
99,101-103-(35¢-c variants, limited dist.) 4 8 12 28 47 65
100-(7/77)-Starlin-c; Iron Man vs. The Mandarin 3 6 9 21 33 45
100-(35¢-c variant, limited dist.) 8 16 24 54 102 150
101-117: 101-Intro DreadKnight; Frankenstein app. 103-Jack of Hearts app; guest stars through issue #113. 104-107-Vs. Midas. 109-1st app. New Crimson Dynamo; 1st app. Vanguard. 110-Origin Jack of Hearts retold; death of Count Nefaria. 113,114-Unicorn and Titanium Man app. 114,115-Avengers app; 1st John Romita Jr. pencils on Iron Man (10/78). 116-1st David Michelinie & Bob Layton issue 2 4 6 8 10 12
118-Byrne-a(p); 1st app. Jim Rhodes 4 8 12 23 37 50
119,122-125,127: 122-Origin. 123-128-Tony treated for alcohol problem. 123,124-Vs. Blizzard, Melter & Whiplash; Justine Hammer app. 125-Avengers & Ant-Man (Scott Lang) app. 127-Vs. Justin Hammer's "Super-Villain army" 2 4 6 11 16 20
120-121,126: 120-121-Sub-Mariner app. 126-Classic Tony becoming Iron Man-c 2 4 6 13 19 25
128-(11/79) Classic Tony Stark alcoholism cover 5 10 15 30 50 70
129,130,134-149: 134,135-Titanium Man app. 137-139-Spymaster app. 142-Intro. Space Armor. 143-1st app. Sunturion. 146 Backlash app. (formally Whiplash). 148-Captain America app. 149-Dr. Doom app. 1 2 3 5 7 9
131-133: 131,132-Hulk x-over. 133-Hulk/Ant Man-c 2 4 6 8 10 12
150-Double size; Dr. Doom; Merlin & Camelot 2 4 6 10 14 18
151-168: 151-Ant-Man (Scott Lang) app. 152-1st app stealth armor. 153-Living Laser app; last Layton co-plot (returns in #215). 154-Unicorn app. 156-Intro the Mauler; last Michelinie plot (returns in issue #215); last Romita Jr. art (p). 159-Paul Smith-a(p); Fantastic Four app. 160-Serpent Squad app. 161-Moon Knight app. 163-Intro. Obadiah Stane (hand only). 166-1st full app. Obadiah Stane. 167-Tony Stark alcohol problem resurfaces. 168-Machine Man app. 6.00
169-New Iron Man (Jim Rhodes replaces Tony Stark) 2 4 6 9 12 15
170,171 6.00
172-199: 172-Captain America x-over. 173-Stark International becomes Stane International. 179-Radioactive Man app. 180-181-Vs. Mandarin. 186-Intro. Vibro. 188-Brother Grimm app. 189-Intro. Termite. 190-Scarlet Witch app. 191-198-Tony Stark returns as original Iron Man. 191-192-Vibro app. 192-Tony Stark Iron Man vs. James Rhodes Iron Man. 193-West Coast Avengers app; unofficial 'Godzilla' app. 194-Intro. Scourge; kills the Enforcer. 195-West Coast Avengers & Shaman from Alpha Flight app. 197-Secret Wars II x-over; Byrne-c 5.00
200-(11/85, $1.25, 52 pgs.)-Tony Stark returns as new Iron Man (red & white armor) thru #230 1 2 3 5 6 8
201-213,215-224: 206-Hawkeye & Mockingbird app. 211-Vs. the Melter. 213-Intro. New Dominic Fortune. 215-Return of Michelinie/Layton creative team; James Rhodes app. (as Iron Man – also in #216). 219-Intro. The Ghost. 220-Spymaster & Ghost app. 221-Vs. Ghost. 222-Force app. 223-Intro. new Blizzard (Donald Gil). 224-Vs. Beetle, Backlash, Blizzard & Justin Hammer 4.00
214-Spider-Woman (Julia Carpenter) app. in new black costume (1/87) 6.00
225-(12/87, $1.25, 40 pgs)- Armor Wars begins; Ant-Man app. 1 3 4 6 8 10
226-227,229-230: Armor Wars in all. 226-West Coast Avengers app. 227-Beetle app.; Iron Man vs SHIELD Mandroids. 229-Vs. Crimson Dynamo & Titanium Man. 230-Armor Wars conclusion; vs Firepower 5.00
228-Armor Wars; Iron Man vs. Captain America (as the Captain) 6.00
231,234,247: 231-Intro. new Iron Man armor. 234-Spider-Man x-over. 247-Hulk x-over 5.00
232,233,235-243,245,246,248,249: 232-Barry Windsor Smith co-plot and (p). 233-Ant-Man app. 235,236-Vs. Grey Gargoyle. 238-Rhino & Capt. America app. 239,240-Vs. Justin Hammer. 241,242-Mandarin app. 243-Tony Stark loses use of legs. 249-Dr. Doom app. 3.00
244-($1.50, 52 pgs.)-New Armor makes him walk 4.00
250-($1.50, 52 pgs.)-Dr. Doom-c/story; Acts of Vengeance x-over; last Michelinie/Layton issue 4.00
251-274,276-281,283,285-287,289,292-299: 251,252-Acts of Vengeance x-over. 255-Intro new Crimson Dynamo (Valenyine Shatalov). 258-Byrne script & Romita Jr.-a(p) begins. 259-Armor Wars II begins; ends #266. 260-Vs. Living Laser. 261-Fin Fang Foom app. 261-264-Mandarin & Fin Fang Foom app. 266-Last Romita Jr.-a(p). 267,268-Origin expanded; Mandarin added to origin. 270-275-Dragon seed story w/Mandarin and Fin Fang Foom. 276-Black Widow app. 277-Last Byrne-s. 278-279-Operation Galactic Storm x-overs. 281-Intro. Masters of Silence. 285,286-Beetle, Backlash & Blizzard app. 287-West Coast Avengers app. 287-Intro Atom Smasher. 289-Vs. Living Laser. 290-James Rhodes retains the War Machine armor. 292-Capt. America app. 295-Infinity Crusade x-over. 296,297-Omega Red app. 298,299-Return of Ultimo 3.00
275-($1.50, 52 pgs.) Mandarin & Fin Fang Foom app. 4.00
282-1st full app. War Machine (7/92) 3 6 9 17 26 35
284-Death of Iron Man (Tony Stark); James Rhodes becomes War Machine 6.00
288-($2.50, 52pg.)-Silver foil stamped-c; Iron Man's 350th app. in comics 5.00
290-($2.95, 52pg.)-Gold foil stamped-c; 30th ann. 5.00
291-Iron Man & War Machine team-up 5.00
300-($3.95, 68 pgs.)-Collector's Edition w/embossed foil-c; anniversary issue; War Machine-c/story 5.00
300-($2.50, 68 pgs.)-Newsstand Edition 1 2 3 5 6 8
301,303,304: 301-Venom cameo. 303-Captain America app. 304-Thunderstrike app; begin $1.50-c; bound-in-trading card sheet 4.00
302-Venom-c/story; Captain America app. 6.00
305-Hulk-c/story 1 3 4 6 8 10
306-309-Mandarin app. 309-War Machine app. 3.00
310-($2.95) Polybagged w/16 pg Marvel Action Hour preview & acetate print 6.00
310-($1.50) Regular edition; white logo; "Hands of the Mandarin" x-over w/Force Works and War Machine 4.00
311,312- "Hands of the Mandarin" x-over w/Force Works and War Machine. 312-w/bound-in Power Ranger card 4.00
313,315,316,318: 315-316-Black Widow app. 316-Crimson Dynamo & Titanium Man app. 5.00
314-Crossover w/Captain America; Henry Pym app. 6.00
317-($2.50)-Flip book; Black Widow app; death of Titanium Man; Hawkeye, War Machine & USAgent app. 6.00
319-Intro. new Iron Man armor; Force Works app; prologue to "The Crossing" story 6.00
320,321: 321-w/Overpower card insert 5.00
322-324-Avengers app; x-over w/Avengers and Force Works 1 2 3 5 6 8
325-($2.95)-Wraparound-c; Tony Stark Iron Man vs "Teen" Tony Iron Man; Avengers & Force Works x-over; continued in Avengers #395 1 2 3 5 7 9
326- "Teen" Tony app. as Iron Man thru #332; Avengers, Thor & Cap America x-over 6.00
327-330: 330-War Machine & Stockpile app; return of Morgan Stark 4.00
331-War Machine app; leads into the "Onslaught" x-over 5.00
332-(9/96) Onslaught x-over; last issue 6.00
Special 1 (8/70)-Sub-Mariner x-over; Everett-c 5 10 15 33 57 80
Special 2 (11/71, 52 pgs.)-r/TOS #81,82,91 (all-r) 3 6 9 19 30 40
Annual 3 (1976)-Man-Thing app. 3 6 9 14 20 25
King Size 4 (8/77)-The Champions (w/Ghost Rider) app.; Newton-a(i) 2 4 6 11 16 20
Annual 5 ('82) Black Panther & Mandarin app. 1 2 3 5 6 8
Annual 6-9: ('83-'86) 6-New Iron Man (J. Rhodes) app. 8-X-Factor app. 5.00
Annual 10 ('89) Atlantis Attacks x-over; P. Smith-a; Layton/Guice-a; Sub-Mariner app. 4.00
Annual 11-14 ('90-'93): 11-Terminus Factor pt. 2; origin of Mrs. Arbogast by Ditko (p&i). 12-1 pg. origin recap; Ant-Man back-up-s; Subterranean Wars Pt. 4. 13-Darkhawk & Avengers West Coast app.; Colan/Williamson-a. 14-Bagged w/card; 1st app. Face Thief 4.00
Annual 15 ('94)- Iron Man vs. the Controller 4.00
...: Armor Wars TPB (2007, $24.99) r/#225-232; Michelinie intro. 25.00
Manual 1 (1993, $1.75)-Operations handbook 3.00
Graphic Novel: Crash (1988, $12.95, Adults, 72 pgs.)-Computer generated art & color;

Iron Man V3 #2 © MAR

Iron Man (2005 series) #5 © MAR

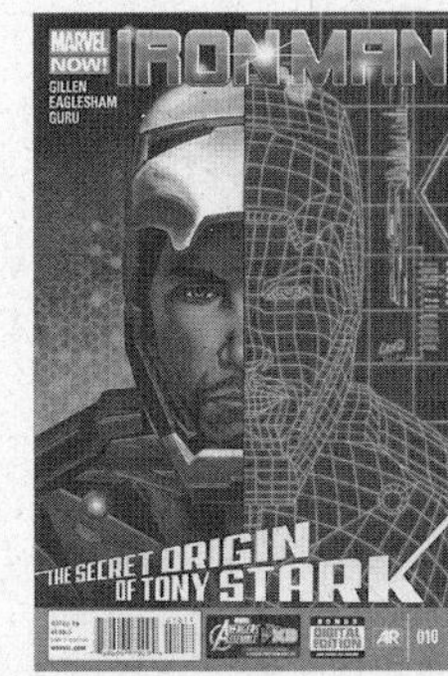

Iron Man (2013 series) #10 © MAR

GD VG FN VF VF/NM NM-
2.0 4.0 6.0 8.0 9.0 9.2

violence & nudity 13.00
...Collector's Preview 1(11/94, $1.95)-wraparound-c; text & illos-no comics 3.00
...: Demon in a Bottle HC (2008, $24.99) r/#120-128; two covers 25.00
...: Demon in a Bottle TPB (2006, $24.99) r/#120-128 25.00
...: Many Armors of Iron Man (2008, $24.99) r/#47, 142-144, 152-153, 200, 218 25.00
...Vs. Dr. Doom (12/94, $12.95)-r/#149-150, 249,250. Julie Bell-c 13.00
...Vs. Dr. Doom: Doomquest HC (2008, $19.99, dustjacket)-r/#149-150, 249,250; new Michelinie intro.; bonus art 20.00
...: War Machine TPB (2008, $29.99) r/#280-291 30.00
The Invincible Iron Man Omnibus Vol. 1 HC (2008, $99.99, dustjacket) r/Iron Man stories from Tales of Suspense #39-83 & Tales To Astonish #82; 1992 intro. by Stan Lee; 1975 essay by Lee; 2008 essay by Layton; gallery of original art and covers; creator bios 100.00

NOTE: ***Austin*** *c-105i, 109-111i, 151i.* ***Byrne*** *a-118p; c-109p, 197, 253.* ***Colan*** *a-1p, 253, Special 1p(3); c-1p.* ***Craig*** *a-1i, 2-4, 5-13i, 14, 15-19i, 24p, 25p, 26-28i; c-2-4.* ***Ditko*** *a-160p.* ***Everett*** *c-29.* ***Guice*** *a-233-241p.* ***G. Kane*** *c(p)-52-54, 63, 67, 72-75, 77-79, 88, 98.* ***Kirby*** *a-Special 1p; 80p, 90, 92-95.* ***Mooney*** *a-40i, 43i, 47i.* ***Perez*** *c-103p.* ***Simonson*** *c-Annual 8.* ***B. Smith*** *a-232p, 243i; c-232.* ***P. Smith*** *a-159p, 245p, Annual 10p; c-159.* ***Starlin*** *a-53p(part), 55p, 56p; c-55p, 160, 163.* ***Tuska*** *a-5-13p, 15-23p, 24i, 32p, 38-46p, 48-54p, 57-61p, 63-69p, 70-72p, 78p, 86-92p, 95-106p, Annual 4p.* ***Wood*** *a-Special 1i.*

IRON MAN (The Invincible...) (Volume Two)
Marvel Comics: Nov, 1996 - No. 13, Nov, 1997 ($2.95/$1.95/$1.99)
(Produced by WildStorm Productions)

V2#1-3-Heroes Reborn begins; Scott Lobdell scripts & Whilce Portacio-c/a begin; new origin Iron Man & Hulk. 2-Hulk app. 3-Fantastic Four app. 4.00
1-Variant-c 5.00
4-11: 4-Two covers. 6-Fantastic Four app.; Industrial Revolution; Hulk app. 7-Return of Rebel. 11-($1.99) Dr. Doom-c/app. 3.00
12-($2.99) "Heroes Reunited"-pt. 3; Hulk-c/app. 4.00
13-($1.99) "World War 3"-pt. 3, x-over w/Image 3.00
Heroes Reborn: Iron Man (2006, $29.99, TPB) r/#1-12; Heroes Reborn #1/2; pin-ups 30.00

IRON MAN (The Invincible...) (Volume Three)
Marvel Comics: Feb, 1998 - No. 89, Dec, 2004 ($2.99/$1.99/$2.25)

V3#1-($2.99)-Follows Heroes Return; Busiek scripts & Chen-c/a begin; Deathsquad app. 6.00
1-Alternate Ed. 1 2 3 5 7 9
2-12: 2-Two covers. 6-Black Widow-c/app. 7-Warbird-c/app. 8-Black Widow app. 9-Mandarin returns 4.00
13-($2.99) battles the Controller 5.00
14-24: 14-Fantastic Four-c/app. 3.00
25-($2.99) Iron Man and Warbird battle Ultimo; Avengers app. 4.00
26-30-Quesada-s. 28-Whiplash killed. 29-Begin $2.25-c. 3.00
31-45,47-49,51-54: 35-Maximum Security x-over; FF-c/app. 41-Grant-a begins. 44-New armor debut. 48-Ultron-c/app. 3.00
46-($3.50, 100 pgs.) Sentient armor returns; r/V1#78,140,141 4.00
50-($3.50) Grell-s begin; Black Widow app. 4.00
55-($3.50) 400th issue; Asamiya-c; back-up story Stark reveals ID; Grell-a 4.00
56-66: 56-Reis-a. 57,58-Ryan-a. 59-61-Grell-c/a. 62,63-Ryan-a. 64-Davis-a; Thor-c/app. 3.00
67-89: 67-Begin $2.99-c; Gene Ha-c. 75-83-Granov-c. 84-Avengers Disassembled prologue 85-89-Avengers Disassembled. 85-88-Harris-a. 86-89-Pat Lee-c. 87-Rumiko killed 3.00
.../Captain America '98 Annual ($3.50) vs. Modok 4.00
1999, 2000 Annual ($3.50) 4.00
2001 Annual ($2.99) Claremont-s/Ryan-a 4.00
Avengers Disassembled: Iron Man TPB (2004, $14.99) r/#84-89 15.00
Mask in the Iron Man (5/01, $14.95, TPB) r/#26-30, #1/2 15.00

IRON MAN (The Invincible...)
Marvel Comics: Jan, 2005 - No. 35, Jan, 2009 ($3.50/$2.99)

1-($3.50-c) Warren Ellis-s/Adi Granov-c/a; start of Extremis storyline 5.00
2-6-($2.99): 5-Flashback to origin; Stark gets new abilities 4.00
7-14: 7-Knauf-s/Zircher-a. 13,14-Civil War 3.00
15-24,26,27,29-35: 15-Stark becomes Director of S.H.I.E.L.D. 19,20-World War Hulk. 33-Secret Invasion; War Machine app. 34,35-War Machine title logo 3.00
25,28-($3.99) 25-Includes movie preview & armor showcase. 28-Red & white armor 4.00
All-New Iron Manual (2/08, $4.99) Handbook-style guide to characters & armor suits 5.00
... By Design 1 (11/10, $3.99) Gallery of 2010 variant covers with artist commentary 4.00
.../Captain America: Casualities of War (2/07, $3.99) two covers; flashbacks 4.00
...: Director of S.H.I.E.L.D. Annual 1 (1/08, $3.99) Madame Hydra app.; Cheung-c 4.00
Free Comic Book Day 2010 (Iron Man: Supernova) #1 (5/10, 9-1/2" x 6-1/4") Nova app. 3.00
Free Comic Book Day 2010 (Iron Man/Thor) #1 (5/10, 9-1/2" x 6-1/4") Romita Jr.-a/c 3.00
...Golden Avenger 1 (11/08, $2.99) Santacruz-a; movie photo-c 3.00
.../Hulk/Fury 1 (2/09, $3.99) crossover of movie-version characters 4.00
Indomitable Iron Man (4/10, $3.99) B&W stories; Chaykin-s/a; Rosado-a; Parrillo-c 4.00
Iron Manual Mark 3 (6/10, $3.99) Handbook-format profiles of characters 4.00
...: Iron Protocols (12/09, $3.99) Olivetti-c/Nelson-a 4.00
...: Kiss and Kill (8/10, $3.99) Black Widow and Wolverine app. 4.00
...: Requiem (2009, $4.99) r/TOS #39, Iron Man #144 (1981); armor profiles 5.00

GD VG FN VF VF/NM NM-
2.0 4.0 6.0 8.0 9.0 9.2

...: The End (1/09, $4.99) future Tony Stark retires; Michelinie-s/Chang & Layton-a 5.00
...: Titanium! 1 (12/10, $4.99) short stories by various; Yardin-c 5.00
Civil War: Iron Man TPB (2007, $11.99) r/#13,14, .../Captain America: Casualities of War, and Civil War: The Confession 12.00
HC (2006, $19.99, dust jacket) r/#1-6 and Granov covers from Iron Man V3 #75-83 20.00
...: Director of S.H.I.E.L.D. TPB (2007, $14.99) r/#15-18; Strange Tales #135 (1965) and Iron Man #129; profile pages for Iron Man and S.H.I.E.L.D.; creator interviews 15.00
...: Extremis SC (2007, $14.99) r/#1-6 and Granov covers from Iron Man V3 #75-83 15.00
...: Execute Program SC (2007, $14.99) r/#7-12; cover layouts and sketches 15.00

IRON MAN (Marvel Now!)
Marvel Comics: Jan, 2013 - Present ($3.99)

1-24: 1-8-Gillen-s/Land-c/a. 5-Stark heads out to space. 9-17-Secret Origin of Tony Stark. 9-12-Eaglesham-a. 17-Arno Stark revealed. 23,24-Malekith app. 4.00
20.INH (3/12, $3.99) Inhumanity tie-in; origin The Exile; Padilla-a 4.00
Annual 1 (4/14, $4.99) Gillen-s/Martinez, Padilla & Marz-a 5.00

IRON MAN (The Armor Wars)
Marvel Comics: No. 258.1, Jul, 2013 - No. 258.4, Jul, 2013 ($3.99, weekly limited series)

258.1-258.4 - Set after Iron Man #258 (1990); Michelinie-s/Dave Ross & Bob Layton-a 4.00

IRON MAN AND POWER PACK
Marvel Comics: Jan, 2008 - No. 4, Apr, 2008 ($2.99, limited series)

1-4-Gurihiru-c/Sumerak-s; Puppet Master app.; Mini Marvels back-ups in each 3.00
...: Armored and Dangerous TPB (2008, $7.99, digest size) r/series 8.00

IRON MAN & SUB-MARINER
Marvel Comics Group: Apr, 1968 (12¢, one-shot) (Pre-dates Iron Man #1 & Sub-Mariner #1)

1-Iron Man story by Colan/Craig continued from Tales of Suspense #99 & continued in Iron Man #1; Sub-Mariner story by Colan continued from Tales to Astonish #101 & continued in Sub-Mariner #1; Colan/Everett-c 15 30 45 103 227 350

IRON MAN AND THE ARMOR WARS
Marvel Comics: Oct, 2009 - No. 4, Jan, 2010 ($2.99, limited series)

1-4-Rousseau-a; Crimson Dynamo & Omega Red app. 3.00

IRON MAN: ARMORED ADVENTURES
Marvel Comics: Sept, 2009 ($3.99, one-shot)

1-Based on the 2009 cartoon; Brizuela-a; Nick Fury & Living Laser app. 4.00

IRON MAN: BAD BLOOD
Marvel Comics: Sept, 2000 - No. 4, Dec, 2000 ($2.99, limited series)

1-4-Micheline-s/Layton-a 3.00

IRON MAN: ENTER THE MANDARIN
Marvel Comics: Nov, 2007 - No. 6, Apr, 2008 ($2.99, limited series)

1-6-Casey-s/Canete-a; retells first meeting 3.00
TPB (2008, $14.99) r/#1-6 15.00

IRON MAN: EXTREMIS DIRECTOR'S CUT
Marvel Comics: Jun, 2010 - No. 6, Sept, 2010 ($3.99, limited series)

1-6-Reprints Iron Man #1-6 (2005 series) with script pages and design art 4.00

IRON MAN: HOUSE OF M (Also see House of M and related x-overs)
(Reprinted in House of M: Fantastic Four/ Iron Man TPB)
Marvel Comics: Sept, 2005 - No. 3, Nov, 2005 ($2.99, limited series)

1-3-Pat Lee-a/c; Greg Pak-s 3.00

IRON MAN: HYPERVELOCITY
Marvel Comics: Mar, 2007 - No. 6, Aug, 2007 ($2.99, limited series)

1-6-Adam Warren-s/Brian Denham-a/c 3.00
TPB (2007, $14.99) r/#1-6; layout pages and armor design sketches 15.00

IRON MAN: I AM IRON MAN
Marvel Comics: Mar, 2010 - No. 2, Apr, 2010 ($3.99, limited series)

1,2-Adaptation of the first movie; Peter David-s/Sean Chen-a/Adi Granov-c 4.00

IRON MAN: INEVITABLE
Marvel Comics: Feb, 2006 - No. 6, July, 2006 ($2.99, limited series)

1-6-Joe Casey-s/Frazer Irving; Spymaster and the Living Laser app. 3.00
TPB (2006, $14.99) r/#1-6; cover sketches 15.00

IRON MAN: LEGACY
Marvel Comics: Jun, 2010 - No. 11, Apr, 2011 ($3.99/$2.99)

1-Van Lente-s/Kurth-a; Dr. Doom app.; back-up r/debut in Tales of Suspense #39 4.00
2-11-($2.99) 4-Titanium Man & Crimson Dynamo app. 6-The Pride app. 3.00

IRON MAN: LEGACY OF DOOM
Marvel Comics: Jun, 2008 - No. 4, Sept, 2008 ($2.99, limited series)

Iron Man: The Iron Age #1 © MAR

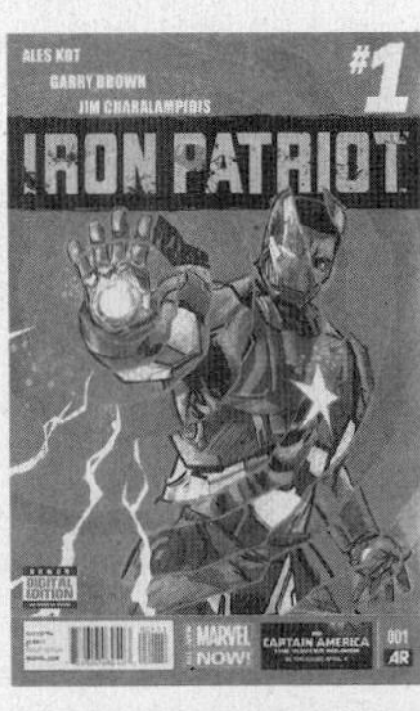

Iron Patriot #1 © MAR

Isis #3 © Filmation

GD VG FN VF VF/NM NM-
2.0 4.0 6.0 8.0 9.0 9.2

GD VG FN VF VF/NM NM-
2.0 4.0 6.0 8.0 9.0 9.2

1-4-Michelinie-s/Lim & Layton-a; Dr. Doom app. 3.00

IRON MAN NOIR
Marvel Comics: Jun, 2010 - No. 4, Sept, 2010 ($3.99, limited series)
1-4-Pulp-style set in 1939; Snyder-s/Garcia-a 4.00

IRON MAN: RAPTURE
Marvel Comics: Jan, 2011 - No. 4, Feb, 2011 ($3.99, limited series)
1-4-Irvine-s/Medina-a/Bradstreet-c. 3,4-War Machine app. 4.00

IRON MAN: SEASON ONE
Marvel Comics: 2013 ($24.99, hardcover graphic novel)
HC - Origin story and early days; Chaykin-s/Parel-a/Tedesco painted-c 25.00

IRON MAN: THE COMING OF THE MELTER
Marvel Comics: Jul, 2013 ($3.99, one-shot)
1-Movie version; Ron Lim-a; back-up reprint of Iron Man #72 (1/75); 3 covers 4.00

IRON MAN: THE IRON AGE
Marvel Comics: Aug, 1998 - No. 2, Sept, 1998 ($5.99, limited series)
1,2-Busiek-s; flashback story from gold armor days 6.00

IRON MAN: THE LEGEND
Marvel Comics: Sept, 1996 ($3.95, one-shot)
1-Tribute issue 5.00

IRON MAN/ THOR
Marvel Comics: Jan, 2011 - No. 4, Apr, 2011 ($3.99, limited series)
1-4-Eaton-a; Crimson Dynamo & Diablo app. 4.00

IRON MAN 2: ... (Follows the first movie)
Marvel Comics: Jun, 2010 - Nov, 2010 ($3.99, limited series)
Agents of S.H.I.E.L.D. 1 (11/10, $3.99) Nick Fury, Agent Coulson & Black Widow app. 4.00
Public Identity (6/10 - No. 3, 7/10, $3.99) 1-3-Kitson & Lim-a/Granov-c 4.00
Spotlight (4/10, $3.99) Interviews with Granov, Guggenheim, Fraction, Ellis, Michelinie 4.00

IRON MAN 2 ADAPTATION, (MARVEL'S...)
Marvel Comics: Jan, 2013 - No. 2, Feb, 2013 ($2.99, limited series)
1,2-Photo-c; Rosanas-a 3.00

IRON MAN 2.0
Marvel Comics: Apr, 2011 - No. 12, Feb, 2012 ($3.99/$2.99)
1-($3.99) Spencer-s/Kitson-c; back-up history of War Machine 4.00
1-Variant-c by Djurdjevic 6.00
2-7,(7.1),8-12-($2.99) 2,3-Kitson, Kano & Di Giandomenico-a. 5-7-Fear Itself tie-in 3.00
...: Modern Warfare 1 (10/11, $4.99) r/#1-3 with variant covers 5.00

IRON MAN 3 PRELUDE, (MARVEL'S...)
Marvel Comics: Mar, 2013 - No. 2, Apr, 2013 ($2.99, limited series)
1,2-Photo-c; Gage-s/Kurth-a; War Machine app. 3.00

IRON MAN 2020 (Also see Machine Man limited series)
Marvel Comics: June, 1994 ($5.95, one-shot)
nn 6.00

IRON MAN: VIVA LAS VEGAS
Marvel Comics: Jul, 2008 - No. 2 ($3.99, unfinished limited series)
1,2-Jon Favreau-s/Adi Granov-a/c 4.00

IRON MAN VS WHIPLASH
Marvel Comics: Jan, 2010 - No. 4, Apr, 2010 ($3.99, limited series)
1-4-Briones-a/Peterson-c; origin of new Whiplash 4.00

IRON MAN/X-O MANOWAR: HEAVY METAL (See X-O Manowar/Iron Man: In Heavy Metal)
Marvel Comics: Sept, 1996 ($2.50, one-shot) (1st Marvel/Valiant x-over)
1-Pt. II of Iron Man/X-O Manowar x-over; Fabian Nicieza scripts; 1st app. Rand Banion 4.00

IRON MARSHALL
Jademan Comics: July, 1990 - No. 32, Feb, 1993 ($1.75, plastic coated-c)
1,32: Kung Fu stories. 1-Poster centerfold 4.00
2-31-Kung Fu stories in all 3.00

IRON PATRIOT (Marvel Now!)
Marvel Comics: May, 2014 - Present ($3.99)
1-James Rhodes in the armor; Ales Kot-s/Garry Brown-a/c 4.00

IRON VIC (See Comics Revue No. 3 & Giant Comics Editions)
United Features Syndicate/St. John Publ. Co.: 1940
Single Series 22 34 68 102 199 325 450

IRONWOLF
DC Comics: 1986 ($2.00, one shot)
1-r/Weird Worlds #8-10; Chaykin story & art 4.00

IRONWOLF: FIRES OF THE REVOLUTION (See Weird Worlds #8-10)
DC Comics: 1992 ($29.95, hardcover)
nn-Chaykin/Moore story, Mignola-a w/Russell inks. 30.00

IRREDEEMABLE (Also see Incorruptible)
BOOM! Studios: Apr, 2009 - No. 37, May, 2012 ($3.99)
1-37: 1-Waid-s/Krause-a; 3 covers; Grant Morrison afterword. 2-32-Three covers 4.00
1-Artist Edition (12/11, $3.99) r/#1 in B&W with bonus sketch and design art 4.00
... Special 1 (4/10, $3.99) Art by Azaceta, Rios & Chaykin; three covers 4.00

IRREDEEMABLE ANT-MAN, THE
Marvel Comics: Dec, 2006 - No. 12, Nov, 2007 ($2.99)
1-12-Kirkman-s/Hester-a/c; intro. Eric O'Grady as the new Ant-Man. 7-Ms. Marvel app. 10-World War Hulk x-over 3.00
... Vol. 1: Lowlife (2007, $9.99, digest) r/#1-6 10.00
... Vol. 2: Small-Minded (2007, $9.99, digest) r/#7-12 10.00

ISAAC ASIMOV'S I-BOTS
Tekno Comix: Dec, 1995 - No. 7, May, 1996 ($1.95)
1-7: 1-6-Perez-c/a. 2-Chaykin variant-c exists. 3-Polybagged. 7-Lady Justice-c/app. 3.00

ISAAC ASIMOV'S I-BOTS
BIG Entertainment: V2#1, June, 1996 - No. 9, Feb, 1997 ($2.25)
V2#1-9: 1-Lady Justice-c/app. 6-Gil Kane-c 3.00

ISIS (TV) (Also see Shazam)
National Per.l Publ./DC Comics: Oct-Nov, 1976 - No. 8, Dec-Jan, 1977-78
1-Wood inks 2 4 6 10 14 18
2-8: 5-Isis new look. 7-Origin 2 3 4 6 8 10

ISLAND AT THE TOP OF THE WORLD (See Walt Disney Showcase #27)

ISLAND OF DR. MOREAU, THE (Movie)
Marvel Comics Group: Oct, 1977 (52 pgs.)
1-Gil Kane-c 1 2 3 5 6 8

I SPY (TV)
Gold Key: Aug, 1966 - No. 6, Sept, 1968 (All have photo-c)
1-Bill Cosby, Robert Culp photo covers 10 20 30 66 138 210
2-6: 3,4-McWilliams-a. 5-Last 12¢-c 6 12 18 38 69 100

IT! (See Astonishing Tales No. 21-24 & Supernatural Thrillers No. 1)

ITCHY & SCRATCHY COMICS (The Simpsons TV show)
Bongo Comics: 1993 - No. 3, 1993 ($1.95)
1-3: 1-Bound-in jumbo poster. 3-w/decoder screen trading card 1 2 3 5 6 8
Holiday Special ('94, $1.95) 1 2 3 5 6 8

IT GIRL (Also see Atomics, and Madman Comics)
Oni Press: May, 2002 ($2.95, one-shot)
1-Allred-s/Clugston-Major-c/a; Atomics and Madman app. 3.00

IT GIRL! AND THE ATOMICS (Also see Atomics, and Madman Comics)
Image Comics: Aug, 2012 - No. 12, Jul, 2013 ($2.99)
1-12: 1-Rich-s/Norton-a/Allred-c. 2-Two covers (Allred & Cooke). 6-Clugston Flores-a 3.00

IT REALLY HAPPENED
William H. Wise No. 1,2/Standard (Visual Editions): 1944 - No. 11, Oct, 1947
1-Kit Carson & Ben Franklin stories 26 52 78 154 252 350
2,3-Nazi WWII-c 15 30 45 85 130 175
4,6,9,11: 4-D-Day story. 6-Ernie Pyle WWII-c; Joan of Arc story. 9-Captain Kidd & Frank Buck stories 14 28 42 76 108 140
5-Lou Gehrig & Lewis Carroll stories 18 36 54 107 169 230
7-Teddy Roosevelt story 15 30 45 83 124 165
8-Story of Roy Rogers 17 34 51 98 154 210
10-Honus Wagner & Mark Twain stories 15 30 45 90 140 190
NOTE: *Guardineer a-7(2), 8(2), 10, 11. Schomburg c-1-7, 9-11.*

IT RHYMES WITH LUST (Also see Bold Stories & Candid Tales)
St. John Publishing Co.: 1950 (Digest size, 128 pgs., 25¢)
nn (Rare)-Matt Baker & Ray Osrin-a 194 388 582 1242 2121 3000

IT'S A BIRD...
DC Comics: 2004 ($24.95, hardcover with dust jacket)
HC-Semi-autobiographical story of Steven Seagle writing Superman; Kristiansen-a 25.00

I, Vampire #14 © DC

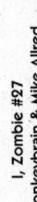

I, Zombie #27 © Monkeybrain & Mike Allred

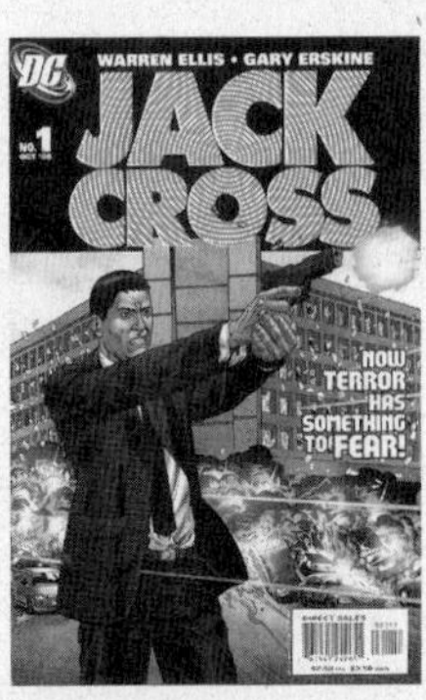

Jack Cross #1 © Ellis & DC

	GD 2.0	VG 4.0	FN 6.0	VF 8.0	VF/NM 9.0	NM- 9.2
SC-($17.95)						18.00

IT'S ABOUT TIME (TV)
Gold Key: Jan, 1967

	GD 2.0	VG 4.0	FN 6.0	VF 8.0	VF/NM 9.0	NM- 9.2
1 (10195-701)-Photo-c	4	8	12	27	44	60

IT'S A DUCK'S LIFE
Marvel Comics/Atlas(MMC): Feb, 1950 - No. 11, Feb, 1952

	GD 2.0	VG 4.0	FN 6.0	VF 8.0	VF/NM 9.0	NM- 9.2
1-Buck Duck, Super Rabbit begin	17	34	51	98	154	210
2	11	22	33	60	83	105
3-11	10	20	30	56	76	95

IT'S GAMETIME
National Periodical Publications: Sept-Oct, 1955 - No. 4, Mar-Apr, 1956

	GD 2.0	VG 4.0	FN 6.0	VF 8.0	VF/NM 9.0	NM- 9.2
1-(Scarce)-Infinity-c; Davy Crockett app. in puzzle	94	188	282	597	1024	1450
2,3 (Scarce): 2-Dodo & The Frog	66	132	198	419	722	1025
4 (Rare)	69	138	207	442	759	1075

IT'S LOVE, LOVE, LOVE
St. John Publishing Co.: Nov, 1957 - No. 2, Jan, 1958 (10¢)

	GD 2.0	VG 4.0	FN 6.0	VF 8.0	VF/NM 9.0	NM- 9.2
1,2	8	16	24	40	50	60

IT! THE TERROR FROM BEYOND SPACE
IDW Publishing: Jul, 2010 - No. 3, Sept, 2010 ($3.99, limited series)

	GD 2.0	VG 4.0	FN 6.0	VF 8.0	VF/NM 9.0	NM- 9.2
1-3-Naraghi-s/Dos Santos-a/Mannion-c						4.00

ITTY BITTY HELLBOY
Dark Horse Comics: Aug, 2013 - No. 5, Dec, 2013 ($2.99, limited series)

	GD 2.0	VG 4.0	FN 6.0	VF 8.0	VF/NM 9.0	NM- 9.2
1-5-All-ages humor stories of kid-version Hellboy characters by Art Baltazar & Franco						3.00

I, VAMPIRE (DC New 52)
DC Comics: Nov, 2011 - No. 19, Jun, 2013 ($2.99)

	GD 2.0	VG 4.0	FN 6.0	VF 8.0	VF/NM 9.0	NM- 9.2
1-19: 1-Fialkov-s/Sorrentino-a/Frison-c. 4-Constantine app. 5-7-Batman app. 7,8-Crossover with Justice League Dark #7,8. 12-Stormwatch app. 16-19-Constantine app.						3.00
#0-(11/12, $2.99) Origin of Andrew Bennett; Fialkov-s/Sorrentino-a/Crain-c						3.00

IVANHOE (See Fawcett Movie Comics No. 20)

IVANHOE
Dell Publishing Co.: July-Sept, 1963

	GD 2.0	VG 4.0	FN 6.0	VF 8.0	VF/NM 9.0	NM- 9.2
1 (12-372-309)	3	6	9	20	31	42

IWO JIMA (See Spectacular Features Magazine)

I, ZOMBIE (Also see House of Mystery Halloween Annual #1)
DC Comics (Vertigo): July, 2010 - No. 28, Oct, 2012 ($1.00/$2.99)

	GD 2.0	VG 4.0	FN 6.0	VF 8.0	VF/NM 9.0	NM- 9.2
1-($1.00) Allred-a/Roberson-s; 2 covers by Allred & Cooke	1	2	3	5	6	8
2-28-($2.99) Allred-c/a in most. 12-Gilbert Hernandez-a. 18-Jay Stephens-a. 25-Rugg-a						3.00
...: Dead to the World TPB (2011, $14.99) r/#1-5 & House of Mystery Hall. Ann. #1						15.00

JACE PEARSON OF THE TEXAS RANGERS (Radio/TV)(4-Color #396 is titled Tales of the Texas Rangers; ...'s Tales of ... #11-on)(See Western Roundup under Dell Giants)
Dell Publishing Co.: No. 396, 5/52 - No. 1021, 8-10/59 (No #10) (All-Photo-c)

	GD 2.0	VG 4.0	FN 6.0	VF 8.0	VF/NM 9.0	NM- 9.2
Four Color 396 (#1)	9	18	27	62	126	190
2(5-7/53) - 9(2-4/55)	6	12	18	40	73	105
Four Color 648(#10, 9/55)	6	12	18	37	66	95
11(11-2/55-56) - 14,17-20(6-8/58)	5	10	15	33	57	80
15,16-Toth-a	5	10	15	34	60	85
Four Color 961,1021: 961-Spiegle-a	5	10	15	33	57	80

NOTE: *Joel McCrea photo c-1-9, F.C. 648 (starred on radio show only); Willard Parker photo c-11-on (starred on TV series).*

JACK ARMSTRONG (Radio)(See True Comics)
Parents' Institute: Nov, 1947 - No. 9, Sept, 1948; No. 10, Mar, 1949 - No. 13, Sept, 1949

	GD 2.0	VG 4.0	FN 6.0	VF 8.0	VF/NM 9.0	NM- 9.2
nn (6/47) Ashcan edition; full color slick cover (a FN/VF sold for $485 in 2011)						
1-(Scarce) (odd size) Cast intro. inside front-c; Vic Hardy's Crime Lab begins	45	90	135	284	480	675
2	20	40	60	117	189	260
3-5	15	30	45	85	130	175
6-13	14	28	42	76	108	140

JACK AVARICE IS THE COURIER
IDW Publishing: Nov, 2012 - No. 5, Nov, 2012 ($3.99, weekly limite series)

	GD 2.0	VG 4.0	FN 6.0	VF 8.0	VF/NM 9.0	NM- 9.2
1-5-Chriss Madden-s/a/c						4.00

JACK CROSS
DC Comics: Oct, 2005 - No. 4, Jan, 2006 ($2.50)

	GD 2.0	VG 4.0	FN 6.0	VF 8.0	VF/NM 9.0	NM- 9.2
1-4-Warren Ellis-s/Gary Erskine-a						3.00
DC Comics Presents: Jack Cross #1 (12/10, $7.99, squarebound) r/#1-4						8.00

JACK HUNTER
Blackthorne Publishing: July, 1987 - No. 3 ($1.25)

	GD 2.0	VG 4.0	FN 6.0	VF 8.0	VF/NM 9.0	NM- 9.2
1-3						3.00

JACKIE CHAN'S SPARTAN X
Topps Comics: May, 1997 - No. 3 ($2.95, limited series)

	GD 2.0	VG 4.0	FN 6.0	VF 8.0	VF/NM 9.0	NM- 9.2
1-3-Michael Golden-s/a; variant photo-c						3.00

JACKIE CHAN'S SPARTAN X: HELL BENT HERO FOR HIRE
Image Comics (Little Eva Ink): Mar, 1998 - No. 3 ($2.95, B&W)

	GD 2.0	VG 4.0	FN 6.0	VF 8.0	VF/NM 9.0	NM- 9.2
1-3-Michael Golden-s/a: 1-variant photo-c						3.00

JACKIE GLEASON (TV) (Also see The Honeymooners)
St. John Publishing Co.: Sept, 1955 - No. 4, Dec, 1955?

	GD 2.0	VG 4.0	FN 6.0	VF 8.0	VF/NM 9.0	NM- 9.2
1(1955)(TV)-Photo-c	68	136	204	435	743	1050
2-4	45	90	135	284	480	675

JACKIE GLEASON AND THE HONEYMOONERS (TV)
National Periodical Publications: June-July, 1956 - No. 12, Apr-May, 1958

	GD 2.0	VG 4.0	FN 6.0	VF 8.0	VF/NM 9.0	NM- 9.2
1-1st app. Ralph Kramden	100	200	300	635	1093	1550
2	57	114	171	362	619	875
3-11: 8-Statue of Liberty-c	45	90	135	284	480	675
12 (Scarce)	63	126	189	403	689	975

JACKIE JOKERS (Became Richie Rich &...)
Harvey Publications: March, 1973 - No. 4, Sept, 1973 (#5 was advertised, but not published)

	GD 2.0	VG 4.0	FN 6.0	VF 8.0	VF/NM 9.0	NM- 9.2
1-1st app.	3	6	9	16	22	28
2-4: 2-President Nixon app.	2	4	6	8	11	14

JACKIE ROBINSON (Famous Plays of...) (Also see Negro Heroes #2 & Picture News #4)
Fawcett Publications: May, 1950 - No. 6, 1952 (Baseball hero) (All photo-c)

	GD 2.0	VG 4.0	FN 6.0	VF 8.0	VF/NM 9.0	NM- 9.2
nn	97	194	291	621	1061	1500
2	55	110	165	352	601	850
3-6	47	94	141	296	498	700

JACK IN THE BOX (Formerly Yellowjacket Comics #1-10; becomes Cowboy Western Comics #17 on)
Frank Comunale/Charlton Comics No. 11 on: Feb, 1946; No. 11, Oct, 1946 - No. 16, Nov-Dec, 1947

	GD 2.0	VG 4.0	FN 6.0	VF 8.0	VF/NM 9.0	NM- 9.2
1-Stitches, Marty Mouse & Nutsy McKrow	20	40	60	120	195	270
11-Yellowjacket (early Charlton comic)	24	48	72	140	230	320
12,14,15	15	30	45	84	127	170
13-Wolverton-a	23	46	69	136	223	310
16-12 pg. adapt. of Silas Marner; Kiefer-a	15	30	45	88	137	185

JACK KIRBY OMNIBUS, THE
DC Comics: 2011 ($49.99, hardcover with dustjacket)

	GD 2.0	VG 4.0	FN 6.0	VF 8.0	VF/NM 9.0	NM- 9.2
Vol. 1 ('11) Recolored reprints of Kirby's DC work from 1946, 1957-1959; Evanier intro						50.00

JACK KIRBY'S FOURTH WORLD (See Mister Miracle & New Gods, 3rd Series)
DC Comics: Mar, 1997 - No. 20, Oct, 1998 ($1.95/$2.25)

	GD 2.0	VG 4.0	FN 6.0	VF 8.0	VF/NM 9.0	NM- 9.2
1-20: 1-Byrne-a/scripts & Simonson-c begin; story cont'd from New Gods, 3rd Series #15; retells "The Pact" (New Gods, 1st Series #7); 1st brief DC app. Thor. 2-Thor vs. Big Barda; "Apokolips Then" back-up begins; Kirby-c/swipe (Thor #126) 8-Genesis x-over. 10-Simonson-s/a 13-Simonson back-up story. 20-Superman-c/app.						3.00

JACK KIRBY'S FOURTH WORLD OMNIBUS
DC Comics: 2007 - Vol. 4, 2008 ($49.99, hardcovers with dustjackets)

	GD 2.0	VG 4.0	FN 6.0	VF 8.0	VF/NM 9.0	NM- 9.2
Vol. 1 ('07) Recolored reprints in chronological order of Superman's Pal, Jimmy Olsen #133-139, Forever People #1-3, New Gods #1-3, and Mister Miracle #1-3; Morrison intro, bonus art						50.00
Vol. 2 ('07) r/Jimmy Olsen #141-145, F.P. #4-6, N.G. #4-6 & M.M. #4-6; bonus art						50.00
Vol. 3 ('07) r/Jimmy Olsen #146-148, F.P. #7-10, N.G. #7-10 & M.M. #7-9; bonus art						50.00
Vol. 4 ('08) r/F.P. #11, M.M. #10-18, N.G. #11 & reprint series #6, & DC Graphic Novel #6 (The Hunger Dogs); Levitz intro.; Evanier afterword; character profile pages						50.00

JACK KIRBY'S GALACTIC BOUNTY HUNTERS
Marvel Comics (Icon): July, 2006 - No. 6, Nov, 2007 ($3.99)

	GD 2.0	VG 4.0	FN 6.0	VF 8.0	VF/NM 9.0	NM- 9.2
1-6-Based on a Kirby concept; Mike Thibodeaux-a; Lisa Kirby, Thibodeaux and others-s						4.00
HC (2007, $24.99) r/series; pin-ups and supplemental art and interviews						25.00

JACK KIRBY'S SECRET CITY SAGA
Topps Comics (Kirbyverse): No. 0, Apr, 1993; No. 1, May, 1993 - No. 4, Aug, 1993 ($2.95, limited series)

	GD 2.0	VG 4.0	FN 6.0	VF 8.0	VF/NM 9.0	NM- 9.2
0-(No cover price, 20 pgs.)-Simonson-c/a						3.00
0-Red embossed-c (limited ed.)						5.00
1-4-Bagged w/3 trading cards; Ditko-c/a: 1-Ditko/Art Adams-c. 2-Ditko/Byrne-c; has coupon for Pres. Clinton holo-foil trading card. 3-Dorman poster; has coupon for Gore holo-foil trading card. 4-Ditko/Perez-c						3.00

Jack of Fables #2 © DC & Bill Willingham

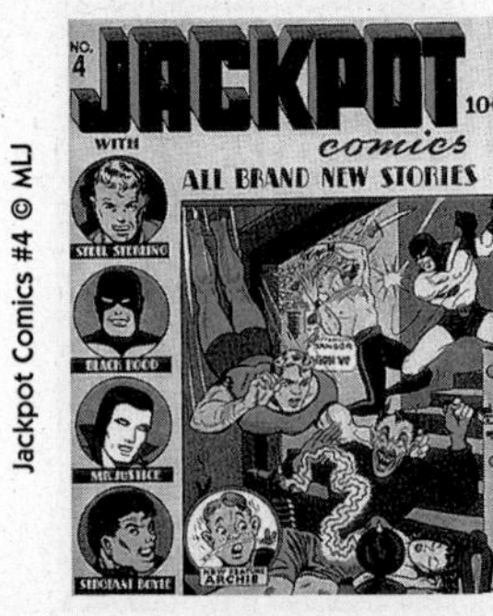
Jackpot Comics #4 © MLJ

James Bond Jr. #3 © Eon

GD 2.0 | VG 4.0 | FN 6.0 | VF 8.0 | VF/NM 9.0 | NM- 9.2

NOTE: *Issues #1-4 contain coupons redeemable for Kirbychrome version of #1*

JACK KIRBY'S SILVER STAR (Also see Silver Star)
Topps Comics (Kirbyverse): Oct, 1993 ($2.95)(Intended as a 4-issue limited series)
1-Silver ink-c; Austin-c/a(i); polybagged w/3 cards 3.00

JACK KIRBY'S TEENAGENTS (See Satan's Six)
Topps Comics (Kirbyverse): Aug, 1993 - No. 4, Nov, 1993 ($2.95, limited series)
1-4: Bagged with/3 trading cards; Busiek-s/Austin-c(i): 3-Liberty Project app. 3.00

JACK OF FABLES (See Fables)
DC Comics (Vertigo): Sept, 2006 - No. 50, Apr, 2011 ($2.99)
1-49: 1-Willingham & Sturges-s/Akins-a. 33-35-Crossover with Fables and The Literals 3.00
50-($4.99) Akins & Braun-a; Bolland-c 5.00
1-Special Edition (8/10, $1.00) r/#1 with "What's Next?" logo on cover 3.00
...: Americana TPB (2008, $14.99) r/#17-21 15.00
...: Jack of Hearts TPB (2007, $14.99) r/#6-11 15.00
...: The Bad Prince TPB (2008, $14.99) r/#12-16 15.00
...: The Big Book of War TPB (2009, $14.99) r/#28-32 15.00
...: The End TPB (2011, $17.99) r/#46-50 18.00
...: The Fulminate Blade TPB (2011, $14.99) r/#41-45 15.00
...: The (Nearly) Great Escape TPB (2007, $14.99) r/#1-5; Akins sketch pages 15.00
...: The New Adventures of Jack and Jack TPB (2010, $14.99) r/#36-40 15.00
...: Turning Pages TPB (2009, $14.99) r/#22-27 15.00

JACK OF HEARTS (Also see The Deadly Hands of Kung Fu #22 & Marvel Premiere #44)
Marvel Comics Group: Jan, 1984 - No. 4, Apr, 1984 (60¢, limited series)
1-4 4.00

JACKPOT COMICS (Jolly Jingles #10 on)
MLJ Magazines: Spring, 1941 - No. 9, Spring, 1943
1-The Black Hood, Mr. Justice, Steel Sterling & Sgt. Boyle begin; Biro-c 331 662 993 2317 4059 5800
2-S. Cooper-c 155 310 465 992 1696 2400
3-Hubbell-c 119 238 357 762 1306 1850
4-Archie begins; (his face appears on cover in small circle) (Win/41; on sale 12/41)-(also see Pep Comics #22); 1st app. Mrs. Grundy, the principal; Novick-c 1500 3000 4500 9000 14,000 19,000
5-Hitler, Tojo, Mussolini-c by Montana; 1st definitive Mr. Weatherbee; 1st brief app. Reggie in 1 panel 300 600 900 1950 3375 4800
6-9: 6,7-Bondage-c by Novick. 8,9-Sahle-c 142 284 426 909 1555 2200

JACK Q FROST (See Unearthly Spectaculars)

JACK STAFF (Vol. 2; previously published in Britain)
Image Comics: Feb, 2003 - No. 20, May, 2009 ($2.95/$3.50)
1-5-Paul Grist-s/a 3.50
6-20-($3.50) 6-Flashback to the WW2 Freedom Fighters 3.50
... Special 1 (1/08, $3.50) Molachi the Immortal app. 3.50
The Weird World of Jack Staff King Size Special 1 (7/07, $5.99, B&W) r/story serialized in Comics International magazine; afterword by Grist 6.00
Vol. 1: Everything Used to Be Black and White TPB (12/03, $19.95) r/British issues 20.00
Vol. 2: Soldiers TPB (2005, $15.95) r/#1-5; cover gallery 16.00
Vol. 3: Echoes of Tomorrow TPB (2006, $16.99) r/#6-12; cover gallery 17.00

JACK THE GIANT KILLER (See Movie Classics)

JACK THE GIANT KILLER (New Adventures of...)
Bimfort & Co.: Aug-Sept, 1953
V1#1-H. C. Kiefer-c/a 26 52 78 154 252 350

JACKY'S DIARY
Dell Publishing Co.: No. 1091, Apr-June, 1960 (one-shot)
Four Color 1091 5 10 15 30 50 70

JADEMAN COLLECTION
Jademan Comics: Dec, 1989 - No. 3, 1990 ($2.50, plastic coated-c, 68 pgs.)
1-3: 1-Wraparound-c w/fold-out poster 4.00

JADEMAN KUNG FU SPECIAL
Jademan Comics: 1988 ($1.50, 64 pgs.)
1 4.00

JADE WARRIORS (Mike Deodato's...)
Image Comics (Glass House Graphics): Nov, 1999 - No. 3, 2000 ($2.50)
1-3-Deodato-a 3.00
1-Variant-c 3.00

JAGUAR, THE (Also see The Adventures of...)
Impact Comics (DC): Aug, 1991 - No. 14, Oct, 1992 ($1.00)
1-14: 4-The Black Hood x-over. 7-Sienkiewicz-c. 9-Contains Crusaders trading card 3.00
Annual 1 (1992, $2.50, 68 pgs.)-With trading card 4.00

JAGUAR GOD
Verotik: Mar, 1995 - No. 7, June, 1997 ($2.95, mature)
0 (2/96, $3.50)-Embossed Frazetta-c; Bisley-a; w/pin-ups. 5.00
1-Frazetta-c. 5.00
2-7: 2-Frazetta-c. 3-Bisley-c. 4-Emond-c. 7-($2.95)-Frazetta-c 4.00

JAKE THRASH
Aircel Publishing: 1988 - No. 3, 1988 ($2.00)
1-3 3.00

JAM, THE (...Urban Adventure)
Slave Labor Nos. 1-5/Dark Horse Comics Nos. 6-8/Caliber Comics No. 9 on: Nov, 1989 - No. 14, 1997 ($1.95/$2.50/$2.95, B&W)
1-14: Bernie Mireault-c/a/scripts. 6-1st Dark Horse issue. 9-1st Caliber issue 3.00

JAMBOREE COMICS
Round Publishing Co.: Feb, 1946(no month given) - No. 3, Apr, 1946
1-Funny animal 21 42 63 122 199 275
2,3 15 30 45 85 130 175

JAMES BOND 007: A SILENT ARMAGEDDON
Dark Horse Comics/Acme Press: Mar, 1993 - Apr 1993 (limited series)
1,2 4.00

JAMES BOND 007: GOLDENEYE (Movie)
Topps Comics: Jan, 1996 ($2.95, unfinished limited series of 3)
1-Movie adaptation; Stelfreeze-c 3.00

JAMES BOND 007: SERPENT'S TOOTH
Dark Horse Comics/Acme Press: July 1992 - Aug 1992 ($4.95, limited series)
1-3-Paul Gulacy-c/a 5.00

JAMES BOND 007: SHATTERED HELIX
Dark Horse Comics: Jun 1994 - July 1994 ($2.50, limited series)
1,2 3.00

JAMES BOND 007: THE QUASIMODO GAMBIT
Dark Horse Comics: Jan 1995 - May 1995 ($3.95, limited series)
1-3 4.50

JAMES BOND FOR YOUR EYES ONLY
Marvel Comics Group: Oct, 1981 - No. 2, Nov, 1981
1,2-Movie adapt.; r/Marvel Super Special #19 6.00

JAMES BOND JR. (TV)
Marvel Comics: Jan, 1992 - No. 12, Dec, 1992 (#1: $1.00, #2-on: $1.25)
1-12: Based on animated TV show 3.00

JAMES BOND: LICENCE TO KILL (See Licence To Kill)

JAMES BOND: PERMISSION TO DIE
Eclipse Comics/ACME Press: 1989 - No. 3, 1991 ($3.95, lim. series, squarebound, 52 pgs.)
1-3: Mike Grell-c/a/scripts in all. 3-($4.95) 5.00

JAM, THE: SUPER COOL COLOR INJECTED TURBO ADVENTURE #1 FROM HELL!
Comico: May, 1988 ($2.50, 44 pgs., one-shot)
1 4.00

JANE ARDEN (See Feature Funnies & Pageant of Comics)
St. John (United Features Syndicate): Mar, 1948 - No. 2, June, 1948
1-Newspaper reprints 15 30 45 88 137 185
2 12 24 36 67 94 120

JANE WIEDLIN'S LADY ROBOTIKA
Image Comics: Jul, 2010 - No. 2, Aug, 2010 ($3.50, unfinished limited series)
1,2-Wiedlin & Bill Morrison-s. 1-Morrison & Rodriguez-a. 2-Moy-a 3.50

JANN OF THE JUNGLE (Jungle Tales No. 1-7)
Atlas Comics (CSI): No. 8, Nov, 1955 - No. 17, June, 1957
8(#1) 39 78 117 240 395 550
9,11-15 22 44 66 132 216 300
10-Williamson/Colletta-c 23 46 69 136 223 310
16,17-Williamson/Mayo-a(3), 5 pgs. each 24 48 72 140 230 320
NOTE: *Everett c-15-17.* ***Heck*** *a-8, 15, 17.* ***Maneely*** *c-11.* ***Shores*** *a-8.*

JASON & THE ARGOBOTS
Oni Press: Aug, 2002 - No. 4, Dec, 2002 ($2.95, B&W, limited series)

Jay & Silent Bob #3 © View Askew

Jennifer Blood #11 © Spitfire

Jesse James #6 © AVON

GD 2.0 | VG 4.0 | FN 6.0 | VF 8.0 | VF/NM 9.0 | NM- 9.2

1-4-Torres-s/Norton-c/a 3.00
Vol. 1 Birthquake TPB (6/03, $11.95, digest size) r/#1-4, Sunday comic strips 12.00
Vol. 2 Machina Ex Deus TPB (9/03, $11.95, digest size) new story 12.00

JASON & THE ARGONAUTS (See Movie Classics)

JASON GOES TO HELL: THE FINAL FRIDAY (Movie)
Topps Comics: July, 1993 - No. 3, Sept, 1993 ($2.95, limited series)
1-3: Adaptation of film. 1-Glow-in-the-dark-c 3.00

JASON'S QUEST (See Showcase #88-90)

JASON VS. LEATHERFACE
Topps Comics: Oct, 1995 - No. 3, Jan, 1996 ($2.95, limited series)
1-3: Collins scripts; Bisley-c 5.00

JAWS 2 (See Marvel Comics Super Special, A)

JAY & SILENT BOB (See Clerks, Oni Double Feature, and Tales From the Clerks)
Oni Press: July, 1998 - No. 4, Oct, 1999 ($2.95, B&W, limited series)
1-Kevin Smith-s/Fegredo-a; photo-c & Quesada/Palmiotti-c 8.00
1-San Diego Comic Con variant covers (2 different covers, came packaged with action figures) 10.00
1-2nd & 3rd printings, 2-4: 2-Allred-c. 3-Flip-c by Jaime Hernandez 3.00
Chasing Dogma TPB (1999, $11.95) r/#1-4; Alanis Morissette intro. 13.00
Chasing Dogma TPB (2001, $12.95) r/#1-4 in color; Morissette intro. 13.00
Chasing Dogma HC (1999, $69.95, S&N) r/#1-4 in color; Morissette intro. 70.00

JCP FEATURES
J.C. Productions (Archie): Feb, 1982-c; Dec, 1981-indicia ($2.00, one-shot, B&W magazine)
1-T.H.U.N.D.E.R. Agents; Black Hood by Morrow & Neal Adams; Texeira-a; 2 pgs. S&K-a from Fly #1 2 4 6 8 10 12

JEANIE COMICS (Formerly All Surprise; Cowgirl Romances #28)
Marvel Comics/Atlas(CPC): No. 13, April, 1947 - No. 27, Oct, 1949
13-Mitzi, Willie begin 24 48 72 144 237 330
14,15 17 34 51 98 154 210
16-Used in Love and Death by Legman; Kurtzman's "Hey Look" 20 40 60 117 189 260
17-19,21,22-Kurtzman's "Hey Look" (1-3 pgs. each) 15 30 45 85 130 175
20,23-27 14 28 42 82 121 160

JEEP COMICS (Also see G.I. Comics and Overseas Comics)
R. B. Leffingwell & Co.: Winter, 1944, No. 2, Spring, 1945 - No. 3, Mar-Apr, 1948
1-Capt. Power, Criss Cross & Jeep & Peep (costumed) begin 69 138 207 442 759 1075
2- Jeep & Peep-c 43 86 129 271 461 650
3-L. B. Cole dinosaur-c 54 108 162 343 574 825

JEFF JORDAN, U.S. AGENT
D. S. Publishing Co.: Dec, 1947 - Jan, 1948
1 16 32 48 94 147 200

JEMM, SON OF SATURN
DC Comics: Sept, 1984 - No. 12, Aug, 1985 (Maxi-series, mando paper)
1-12: 3-Origin 4.00
NOTE: ***Colan** a-1-12p; c-1-5, 7-12p.*

JENNIFER BLOOD
Dynamite Entertainment: 2011 - No. 36, 2014 ($3.99)
1-36: 1-3-Garth Ennis-s/Adriano Batista-a; four covers on each. 4-The Ninjettes app. 4.00
Annual 1 (2012, $4.99) Al Ewing-s/Igor Vitorino-a/Sean Chen-c; origin 5.00

JENNIFER BLOOD: FIRST BLOOD
Dynamite Entertainment: 2011 - No. 6, 2013 ($3.99)
1-6-Mike Carroll-s/Igor Vitorino-a/Mike Mayhew-c; origin & training 4.00

JENNIFER'S BODY (Based on the 2009 movie)
BOOM! Studios: Aug, 2009 ($24.99, hardcover graphic novel)
HC-Short stories of Jennifer and her victims; Spears-s/art by various; pin-up art 25.00

JENNY FINN
Oni Press: June, 1999 - No. 2, Sept, 1999 ($2.95, B&W, unfinished lim. series)
1,2-Mignola & Nixey-s/Nixey-a/Mignola-c 3.00
...: Doom (Atomeka, 2005, $6.99, TPB) r/#1 & 2 with new supplemental material 7.00

JENNY SPARKS: THE SECRET HISTORY OF THE AUTHORITY
DC Comics (WildStorm): Aug, 2000 - No. 5, Mar, 2001 ($2.50, limited series)
1-Millar-s/McCrea & Hodgkins-a/Hitch & Neary-c 4.00
1-Variant-c by McCrea 1 3 4 6 8 10
2-5: 2-Apollo & Midnighter. 3-Jack Hawksmoor. 4-Shen. 5-Engineer 3.00

TPB (2001, $14.95) r/#1-5; Ellis intro. 15.00

JERICHO (Based on the TV series)
Devil's Due Publishing/IDW Publishing: Oct, 2009 - Present ($3.99)
... Redux (IDW, 2/11, $7.99) r/Season 3: Civil War #1-3 8.00
... Season 3: Civil War 1-4: 1-Story by the show's writing staff 4.00
... Season 4: 1-5: 1-(7/12) Photo-c & Bradstreet-c 4.00

JERRY DRUMMER (Boy Heroes of the Revolutionary War) (Formerly Soldier & Marine V2#9)
Charlton Comics: V3#10, Apr, 1957 - V3#12, Oct, 1957
V3#10-12: 11-Whitman-c/a 6 12 18 29 36 42

JERRY IGER'S... (All titles, Blackthorne/First)(Value: cover or less)

JERRY LEWIS (See The Adventures of...)

JERSEY GODS
Image Comics: Feb, 2009 - No. 12, May, 2010 ($3.50)
1-11: 1-Brunswick-s/McDaid-a; two covers by McDaid and Allred 3.50
12-($4.99) Wraparound cover swipe of Superman #252 by Allred 5.00

JESSE JAMES (The True Story Of..., also seeThe Legend of...)
Dell Publishing Co.: No. 757, Dec, 1956 (one shot)
Four Color 757-Movie, photo-c 8 16 24 51 96 140

JESSE JAMES (See Badmen of the West & Blazing Sixguns)
Avon Periodicals: 8/50 - No. 9, 11/52; No. 15, 10/53 - No. 29, 8-9/56
1-Kubert Alabam-r/Cowpuncher #1 18 36 54 105 165 225
2-Kubert-a(3) 14 28 42 82 121 160
3-Kubert Alabam-r/Cowpuncher #2 14 28 42 80 115 150
4,9-No Kubert 9 18 27 50 65 80
5,6-Kubert Jesse James-a(3); 5-Wood-a(1pg.) 14 28 42 80 115 150
7-Kubert Jesse James-a(2) 13 26 39 72 101 130
8-Kinstler-a(3) 10 20 30 54 72 90
15-Kinstler-r/#3 8 16 24 44 57 70
16-Kinstler-r/#3 & story-r/Butch Cassidy #1 9 18 27 47 61 75
17-19,21: 17-Jesse James-r/#4; Kinstler-c idea from Kubert splash in #6. 18-Kubert Jesse James-r/#5. 19-Kubert Jesse James-r/#6. 21-Two Jesse James-r/#4, Kinstler-r/#4 8 16 24 42 54 65
20-Williamson/Frazetta-a; r/Chief Vic. Apache Massacre; Kubert Jesse James-r/#6; Kit West story by Larsen 14 28 42 82 121 160
22-29: 22,23-No Kubert. 24-New McCarty strip by Kinstler; Kinstler-r. 25-New McCarty Jesse James strip by Kinstler; Jesse James-r/#7,9. 26,27-New McCarty Jesse James strip plus a Kinstler/McCann Jesse James-r. 28-Reprints most of Red Mountain, Featuring Quantrells Raiders 8 16 24 42 54 65
Annual nn (1952; 25¢, 100 pgs.)- "...Brings Six-Gun Justice to the West"- 3 earlier issues rebound; Kubert, Kinstler-a(3) 31 62 93 186 303 420
NOTE: *Mostly reprints #10 on.* ***Fawcett** c-1, 2.* ***Kida** a-5.* ***Kinstler** a-3, 4, 7-9, 15r, 16r(2), 21-27; c-3, 4, 9, 17-27. Painted c-5-8. 22 has 2 stories r/Sheriff Bob Dixon's Chuck Wagon #1 with name changed to Sheriff Bob Trent.*

JESSE JAMES
Realistic Publications: July, 1953
nn-Reprints Avon's #1; same-c, colors different 10 20 30 56 76 95

JEST (Formerly Snap; becomes Kayo #12)
Harry 'A' Chesler: No. 10, 1944; No. 11, 1944
10-Johnny Rebel & Yankee Boy app. in text 19 38 57 111 176 240
11-Little Nemo in Adventure Land 19 38 57 111 176 240

JESTER
Harry 'A' Chesler: No. 10, 1945
10 18 36 54 103 162 220

JESUS
Spire Christian Comics (Fleming H. Revell Co.): 1979 (49¢)
nn 2 4 6 11 16 20

JET (See Jet Powers)

JET (Crimson from Wildcore & Backlash)
DC Comics (WildStorm): Nov, 2000 - No. 4, Feb, 2001 ($2.50, limited series)
1-4-Nguyen-a/Abnett & Lanning-s 3.00

JET ACES
Fiction House Magazines: 1952 - No. 4, 1953
1- Sky Advs. of American War Aces (on sale 6/20/52) 19 38 57 111 176 240
2-4 12 24 36 69 97 125

JETCAT CLUBHOUSE (Also see Land of Nod, The)
Oni Press: Apr, 2001 - No. 3, Aug, 2001 ($3.25)

The Jetsons #24 © H-B

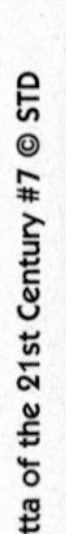
Jetta of the 21st Century #7 © STD

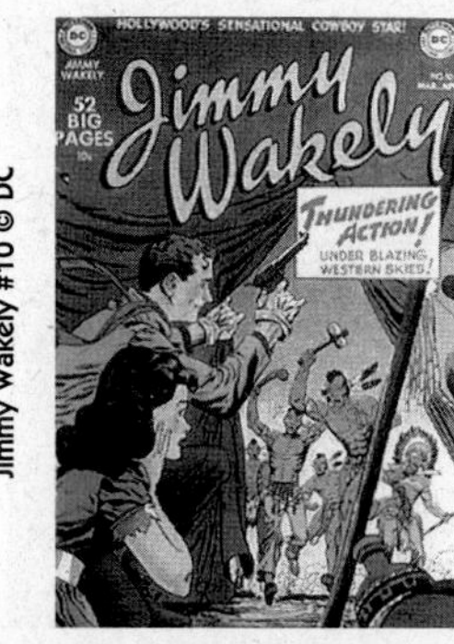

Jimmy Wakely #10 © DC

	GD 2.0	VG 4.0	FN 6.0	VF 8.0	VF/NM 9.0	NM- 9.2
1-3-Jay Stephens-s/a. 1-Wraparound-c						3.25
TPB (8/02, $10.95, 8 3/4" x 5 3/4") r/#1-3 & stories from Nickelodeon mag. & other						11.00

JET DREAM (...and Her Stunt-Girl Counterspies)(See The Man from Uncle #7)
Gold Key: June, 1968 (12¢)

	GD 2.0	VG 4.0	FN 6.0	VF 8.0	VF/NM 9.0	NM- 9.2
1-Painted-c	3	6	9	21	33	45

JET FIGHTERS (Korean War)
Standard Magazines: No. 5, Nov, 1952 - No. 7, Mar, 1953

	GD 2.0	VG 4.0	FN 6.0	VF 8.0	VF/NM 9.0	NM- 9.2
5,7-Toth-a. 5-Toth-c	14	28	42	78	112	145
6-Celardo-a	9	18	27	52	69	85

JET POWER
I.W. Enterprises: 1963

	GD 2.0	VG 4.0	FN 6.0	VF 8.0	VF/NM 9.0	NM- 9.2
I.W. Reprint 1,2-r/Jet Powers #1,2	3	6	9	16	24	32

JET POWERS (American Air Forces No. 5 on)
Magazine Enterprises: 1950 - No. 4, 1951

	GD 2.0	VG 4.0	FN 6.0	VF 8.0	VF/NM 9.0	NM- 9.2
1(A-1 #30)-Powell-c/a begins	38	76	114	226	368	510
2(A-1 #32) Classic Powell dinosaur-c/a	38	76	114	226	368	510
3(A-1 #35)-Williamson/Evans-a	40	80	120	244	407	570
4(A-1 #38)-Williamson/Wood-a; "The Rain of Sleep" drug story	40	80	120	244	407	570

JET PUP (See 3-D Features)

JETSONS, THE (TV) (See March of Comics #276, 330, 348 & Spotlight #3)
Gold Key: Jan, 1963 - No. 36, Oct, 1970 (Hanna-Barbera)

	GD 2.0	VG 4.0	FN 6.0	VF 8.0	VF/NM 9.0	NM- 9.2
1-1st comic book app.	20	40	60	141	313	485
2	10	20	30	66	138	210
3-10: 9-Flintstones x-over	8	16	24	51	96	140
11-22	6	12	18	40	73	105
23-36-Reprints	4	8	12	27	44	60

JETSONS, THE (TV) (Also see Golden Comics Digest)
Charlton Comics: Nov, 1970 - No. 20, Dec, 1973 (Hanna-Barbera)

	GD 2.0	VG 4.0	FN 6.0	VF 8.0	VF/NM 9.0	NM- 9.2
1	7	14	21	48	89	130
2	4	8	12	28	47	65
3-10: Flintstones x-over	3	6	9	20	31	42
11-20	3	6	9	16	24	32
nn (1973, digest, 60¢, 100 pgs.) B&W one page gags	4	8	12	23	37	50

JETSONS, THE (TV)
Harvey Comics: V2#1, Sept, 1992 - No. 5, Nov, 1993 ($1.25/$1.50) (Hanna-Barbera)

	GD 2.0	VG 4.0	FN 6.0	VF 8.0	VF/NM 9.0	NM- 9.2
V2#1-5						5.00
...Big Book V2#1,2,3 ($1.95, 52 pgs.): 1-(11/92). 2-(4/93). 3-(7/93)						5.00
...Giant Size 1,2,3 ($2.25, 68 pgs): 1-(10/92). 2-(4/93). 3-(10/93)						5.00

JETSONS, THE (TV)
Archie Comics: Sept, 1995 - No. 8, Apr, 1996 ($1.50)

	GD 2.0	VG 4.0	FN 6.0	VF 8.0	VF/NM 9.0	NM- 9.2
1-8						3.00

JETTA OF THE 21ST CENTURY
Standard Comics: No. 5, Dec, 1952 - No. 7, Apr, 1953 (Teen-age Archie type)

	GD 2.0	VG 4.0	FN 6.0	VF 8.0	VF/NM 9.0	NM- 9.2
5-Dan DeCarlo-a	24	48	72	140	230	320
6,7: 6-Robot-c	15	30	45	85	130	175
TPB (Airwave Publ., 2006, $9.99) B&W reprint of series; Bill Morrison intro./back-c						10.00

JEW GANGSTER
DC Comics: 2005 ($14.99, SC graphic novel)

	GD 2.0	VG 4.0	FN 6.0	VF 8.0	VF/NM 9.0	NM- 9.2
SC-Joe Kubert-s/a						15.00

JEZEBEL JADE (Hanna-Barbara)
Comico: Oct, 1988 - No. 3, Dec, 1988 ($2.00, mini-series)

	GD 2.0	VG 4.0	FN 6.0	VF 8.0	VF/NM 9.0	NM- 9.2
1-3: Johnny Quest spin-off						3.00

JEZEBELLE (See Wildstorm 2000 Annuals)
DC Comics (WildStorm): Mar, 2001 - No. 6, Aug, 2001 ($2.50, limited series)

	GD 2.0	VG 4.0	FN 6.0	VF 8.0	VF/NM 9.0	NM- 9.2
1-6-Ben Raab-s/Steve Ellis-a						3.00

JIGGS & MAGGIE
Dell Publishing Co.: No. 18, 1941 (one shot)

	GD 2.0	VG 4.0	FN 6.0	VF 8.0	VF/NM 9.0	NM- 9.2
Four Color 18 (#1)-(1936-38-r)	50	100	150	315	533	750

JIGGS & MAGGIE
Standard Comics/Harvey Publications No. 22 on: No. 11, 1949 (June) - No. 21, 2/53; No. 22, 4/53 - No. 27, 2-3/54

	GD 2.0	VG 4.0	FN 6.0	VF 8.0	VF/NM 9.0	NM- 9.2
11	18	36	54	105	165	225
12-15,17-21	12	24	36	69	97	125
16-Wood text illos.	13	26	39	72	101	130
22-24-Little Dot app.	11	22	33	64	90	115
25,27	10	20	30	56	76	95
26-Four pgs. partially in 3-D	14	28	42	81	118	155

NOTE: *Sunday page reprints by McManus loosely blended into story continuity. Based on Bringing Up Father strip. Advertised on covers as "All New."*

JIGSAW (Big Hero Adventures)
Harvey Publ. (Funday Funnies): Sept, 1966 - No. 2, Dec, 1966 (36 pgs.)

	GD 2.0	VG 4.0	FN 6.0	VF 8.0	VF/NM 9.0	NM- 9.2
1-Origin & 1st app.; Crandall-a (5 pgs.)	3	6	9	21	33	45
2-Man From S.R.A.M.	3	6	9	15	22	28

JIGSAW OF DOOM (See Complete Mystery No. 2)

JIM BOWIE (Formerly Danger?; Black Jack No. 20 on)
Charlton Comics: No. 16, Mar, 1956 - No. 19, Apr, 1957

	GD 2.0	VG 4.0	FN 6.0	VF 8.0	VF/NM 9.0	NM- 9.2
16	8	16	24	42	54	65
17-19: 18-Giordano-c	6	12	18	29	36	42

JIM BOWIE (TV, see Western Tales)
Dell Publishing Co.: No. 893, Mar, 1958 - No. 993, May-July, 1959

	GD 2.0	VG 4.0	FN 6.0	VF 8.0	VF/NM 9.0	NM- 9.2
Four Color 893 (#1)	5	10	15	35	63	90
Four Color 993-Photo-c	5	10	15	33	57	80

JIM BUTCHER'S THE DRESDEN FILES: FOOL MOON (Based on the Dresden Files novels)
Dynamite Entertainment: 2011 - No. 8, 2012 ($3.99, limited series)

	GD 2.0	VG 4.0	FN 6.0	VF 8.0	VF/NM 9.0	NM- 9.2
1-8: 1-Jim Butcher & Mark Powers-s/Chase Conley-a/Brett Booth-c						4.00

JIM BUTCHER'S THE DRESDEN FILES: GHOUL GOBLIN
Dynamite Entertainment: 2012 - No. 6, 2013 ($3.99, limited series)

	GD 2.0	VG 4.0	FN 6.0	VF 8.0	VF/NM 9.0	NM- 9.2
1-6: 1-Jim Butcher & Mark Powers-s/Joseph Cooper-a; Syaf-c						4.00

JIM BUTCHER'S THE DRESDEN FILES: STORM FRONT (Based on the Dresden Files novels)
Dabel Bros. Productions: Oct, 2008 (Nov. on-c) - No. 4, Apr, 2009 ($3.99, limited series)

	GD 2.0	VG 4.0	FN 6.0	VF 8.0	VF/NM 9.0	NM- 9.2
1-4-Jim Butcher & Mark Powers-s/Ardian Syaf-a; covers by Syaf & Tsai						4.00
Vol. 2: 1,2 (7/09 - No. 4)						4.00

JIM BUTCHER'S THE DRESDEN FILES: WELCOME TO THE JUNGLE
Dabel Bros. Productions: Mar, 2008 (Apr. on-c) - No. 4, Jul, 2008 ($3.99, limited series)

	GD 2.0	VG 4.0	FN 6.0	VF 8.0	VF/NM 9.0	NM- 9.2
1-Jim Butcher-s/Ardian Syaf-a; Ardian Syaf-c						5.00
1-Variant-c by Chris McGrath						8.00
1-New York Comic-Con 2008 variant-c						15.00
1-Second printing						4.00
2-4-Two covers on each						4.00
HC (2008, $19.95, dustjacket) r/#1-4; Butcher intro.; concept art pages						20.00

JIM DANDY
Dandy Magazine (Lev Gleason): May, 1956 - No. 3, Sept, 1956 (Charles Biro)

	GD 2.0	VG 4.0	FN 6.0	VF 8.0	VF/NM 9.0	NM- 9.2
1-Jim Dandy adventures w/Cup, an alien & his flying saucer (both invisible) from the planet Zikalug begins; ends #3. Biro-c. 1,2-Bammy Boozle app.	10	20	30	58	79	100
2,3: 2-Two pg. actual flying saucer reports	8	16	24	40	50	60

JIM HARDY (See Giant Comics Eds., Sparkler & Treasury of Comics #2 & 5)
United Features Syndicate/Spotlight Publ.: 1939; 1942; 1947 - No. 2, 1947

	GD 2.0	VG 4.0	FN 6.0	VF 8.0	VF/NM 9.0	NM- 9.2
Single Series 6 ('39)	41	82	123	256	428	600
Single Series 27('42)	36	72	108	211	343	475
1('47)-Spotlight Publ.	15	30	45	85	130	175
2	10	20	30	54	72	90

JIM HARDY
Spotlight/United Features Synd.: 1944 (25¢, 132 pgs.) (Tip Top, Sparkler-r)

	GD 2.0	VG 4.0	FN 6.0	VF 8.0	VF/NM 9.0	NM- 9.2
nn-Origin Mirror Man; Triple Terror app.	39	78	117	231	378	525

JIMINY CRICKET (Disney,, see Mickey Mouse Mag. V5#3 & Walt Disney Showcase #37)
Dell Publishing Co.: No. 701, May, 1956 - No. 989, May-July, 1959

	GD 2.0	VG 4.0	FN 6.0	VF 8.0	VF/NM 9.0	NM- 9.2
Four Color 701	7	14	21	48	89	130
Four Color 795, 897, 989	6	12	18	37	66	95

JIM LEE SKETCHBOOK
DC Comics (WildStorm): 2002 (no price, 16 pgs.)

	GD 2.0	VG 4.0	FN 6.0	VF 8.0	VF/NM 9.0	NM- 9.2
nn-Various DC and WildStorm character sketches by Lee						8.00

JIMMY CORRIGAN (See Acme Novelty Library)

JIMMY DURANTE (Also see A-1 Comics)
Magazine Enterprises: No. 18, Oct, 1949 - No. 20, Winter 1949-50

	GD 2.0	VG 4.0	FN 6.0	VF 8.0	VF/NM 9.0	NM- 9.2
A-1 18,20-Photo-c (scarce)	51	102	153	318	539	760

JIMMY OLSEN (See Superman's Pal...)

JIMMY OLSEN
DC Comics: May, 2011 ($5.99, one-shot)

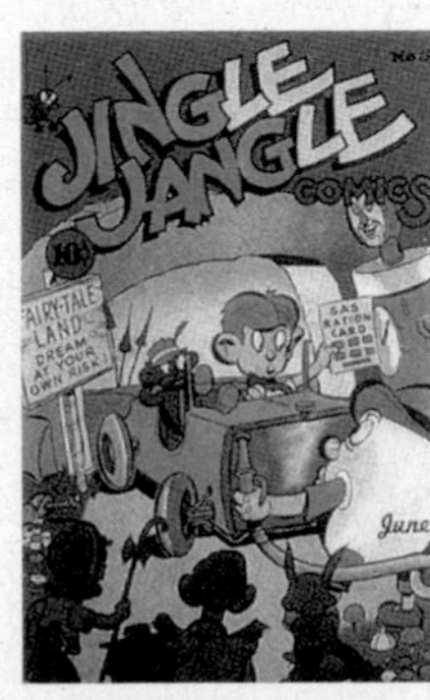

Jingle Jangle Comics #15 © EAS

Jirni #3 © Aspen MLT

JLA #15 © DC

GD VG FN VF VF/NM NM-
2.0 4.0 6.0 8.0 9.0 9.2

1-Reprints back-up feature from Action Comics #893-896 plus new material; Conner-c 6.00

JIMMY OLSEN: ADVENTURES BY JACK KIRBY
DC Comics: 2003, 2004 ($19.95, TPB)

nn-(2003) Reprints Jack Kirby's early issues of Superman's Pal Jimmy Olsen #133-139,141; Mark Evanier intro.; cover by Kirby and Steve Rude 20.00
Vol. 2 (2004) Reprints #142-148; Evanier intro.; cover gallery and sketch pages 20.00

JIMMY WAKELY (Cowboy movie star)
National Per. Publ.: Sept-Oct, 1949 - No. 18, July-Aug, 1952 (1-13: 52pgs.)

1-Photo-c, 52 pgs. begin; Alex Toth-a; Kit Colby Girl Sheriff begins 41 82 123 256 428 600
2-Toth-a 18 36 54 105 165 225
3,4,6,7-Frazetta-a in all, 3 pgs. each; Toth-a in all. 7-Last photo-c. 4-Kurtzman "Pot-Shot Pete", 1 pg; Toth-a 21 42 63 122 199 275
5,8-15-Toth-a; 12,14-Kubert-a (3 & 2 pgs.) 16 32 48 94 147 200
16-18 15 30 45 83 124 165

NOTE: ***Gil Kane*** *c-10-18p.*

JIM RAY'S AVIATION SKETCH BOOK
Vital Publishers: Mar-Apr, 1946 - No. 2, May-June, 1946 (15¢)

1-Picture stories of planes and pilots; atomic explosion panel 39 78 117 231 378 525
2-Story of General "Nap" Arnold 25 50 75 147 241 335

JIM SOLAR (See Wisco/Klarer in the Promotional Comics section)

JINGLE BELLE (Paul Dini's...)
Oni Press/Top Cow: Nov, 1999 - No. 2, Dec, 1999 ($2.95, B&W, limited series)

1,2-Paul Dini-s. 2-Alex Ross flip-c 3.00
Jingle Belle: Dash Away All (12/03, $11.95, digest-size) Dini-s/Garibaldi-a 12.00
Jingle Belle: Gift-Wrapped (Top Cow, 12/11, $3.99) Dini-s/Gladden-a 4.00
Jingle Belle: Santa Claus vs. Frankenstein (Top Cow, 12/08, $2.99) Dini-s/Gladden-a 3.00
Jingle Belle's Cool Yule (11/02, $13.95,TPB) r/All-Star Holiday Hullabaloo, The Mighty Elves, and Jubilee; internet strips and a color section w/DeStefano-a 14.00
Paul Dini's Jingle Belle Jubilee (11/01, $2.95) Dini-s; art by Rolston, DeCarlo, Morrison and Bone; pin-ups by Thompson and Aragonés 3.00
Paul Dini's Jingle Belle's All-Star Holiday Hullabaloo (11/00, $4.95) stories by various including Dini, Aragonés, Jeff Smith, Bill Morrison; Frank Cho-c 5.00
Paul Dini's Jingle Belle: The Fight Before Christmas (12/05, $2.99) Dini-s/Bone & others-a 3.00
Paul Dini's Jingle Belle: The Mighty Elves (7/01, $2.95) Dini-s/Bone-a 3.00
Paul Dini's Jingle Belle Winter Wingding (11/02, $2.95) Dini-s/Clugston-Major-c 3.00
The Bakers Meet Jingle Belle (12/06, $2.99) Dini-s/Kyle Baker-a 3.00
TPB (10/00, $8.95) r/#1&2, and app. from Oni Double Feature #13 9.00

JINGLE BELLE (Paul Dini's...)
Dark Horse Comics: Nov, 2004 - No. 4, Apr, 2005 ($2.99, limited series)

1-4-Paul Dini-s/Jose Garibaldi-a 3.00
TPB (9/05, $12.95) r/#1-4 13.00

JINGLE BELLS (See March of Comics No. 65)

JINGLE DINGLE CHRISTMAS STOCKING COMICS (See Foodini #2)
Stanhall Publications: V2#1, 1951 (no date listed) (25¢, 100 pgs.; giant-size) (Publ. annually)

V2#1-Foodini & Pinhead, Silly Pilly plus games & puzzles 21 42 63 124 202 280

JINGLE JANGLE COMICS (Also see Puzzle Fun Comics)
Eastern Color Printing Co.: Feb, 1942 - No. 42, Dec, 1949

1-Pie-Face Prince of Old Pretzleburg, Jingle Jangle Tales by George Carlson, Hortense, & Benny Bear begin 45 90 135 284 480 675
2-4: 2,3-No Pie-Face Prince. 4-Pie-Face Prince-c 21 42 63 122 199 275
5 (10/42) 19 38 57 111 176 240
6-10: 8-No Pie-Face Prince 15 30 45 85 130 175
11-15 12 24 36 69 97 125
16-30: 17,18-No Pie-Face Prince. 24,30-XMas-c 10 20 30 56 76 95
31-42: 36,42-Xmas-c 9 18 27 52 69 85

NOTE: ***George Carlson*** *a-(2) in all except No. 2, 3, 8; c-1-6.* ***Carlson*** *1 pg. puzzles in 9, 10, 12-15, 18, 20.* ***Carlson*** *illustrated a series of Uncle Wiggily books in 1930's.*

JING PALS
Victory Publishing Corp.: Feb, 1946 - No. 4, Aug?, 1946 (Funny animal)

1-Wishing Willie, Puggy Panda & Johnny Rabbit begin 15 30 45 88 137 185
2-4 10 20 30 54 72 90

JINKS, PIXIE, AND DIXIE (See Kite Fun Book & Whitman Comic Books)

JINX
Caliber Press: 1996 - No. 7, 1996 ($2.95, B&W, 32 pgs.)

1-7: Brian Michael Bendis-c/a/scripts. 2-Photo-c 3.00

JINX (Volume 2)
Image Comics: 1997 - No. 5, 1998 ($2.95, B&W, bi-monthly)

1-4: Brian Michael Bendis-c/a/scripts. 3.00
5-($3.95) Brereton-c 4.00
...Buried Treasures ('98, $3.95) short stories, ...Confessions ('98, $3.95) short stories, ...Pop Culture Hoo-Hah ('98, $3.95) humor shorts 4.00
TPB (1997, $10.95) r/Vol 1,#1-4 11.00
...: The Definitive Collection ('01, $24.95) remastered #1-5, sketch pages, art gallery, script excerpts, Mack intro. 25.00

JINX: TORSO
Image Comics: 1998 - No. 6, 1999 ($3.95/$4.95, B&W)

1-6-Based on Eliot Ness' pursuit of America's first serial killer; Brian Michael Bendis & Marc Andreyko-s/Bendis-a. 3-6-($4.95) 5.00
Softcover (2000, $24.95) r/#1-6; intro. by Greg Rucka; photo essay of the actual murders and police documents 25.00
Hardcover (2000, $49.95) signed & numbered 50.00

JIRNI
Aspen MLT: Apr, 2013 - No. 5, Oct, 2013 ($1.00/$3.99)

1-($1.00) J.T. Krul-s/Paolo Pantalena-a; multiple covers 3.00
2-5-($3.99) Multiple covers on each 4.00

JLA (See Justice League of America and Justice Leagues)
DC Comics: Jan, 1997 - No. 125, Apr, 2006 ($1.95/$1.99/$2.25/$2.50)

1-Morrison-s/Porter & Dell-a. The Hyperclan app. 2 4 6 9 12 15
2 1 3 4 6 8 10
3,4 1 2 3 5 7 9
5-Membership drive; Tomorrow Woman app. 6.00
6-9: 8-Green Arrow joins. 6.00
10-21: 10-Rock of Ages begins. 11-Joker and Luthor-c/app. 15-($2.95) Rock of Ages concludes. 16-New members join; Prometheus app. 17,20-Jorgensen-a. 18-21-Waid-s. 20,21-Adam Strange c/app. 5.00
22-40: 22-Begin $1.99-c; Sandman (Daniel) app. 27-Amazo app. 28-31-JSA app. 35-Hal Jordan/Spectre app. 36-40-World War 3 3.00
41-($2.99) Conclusion of World War 3; last Morrison-s 4.00
42-46: 43-Waid-s; Ra's al Ghul app. 44-Begin $2.25-c. 46-Batman leaves 3.00
47-49: 47-Hitch & Neary-a begins; JLA battles Queen of Fables 3.00
50-($3.75) JLA vs. Dr. Destiny; art by Hitch & various 4.00
51-74: 52-55-Hitch-a. 59-Joker: Last Laugh. 61-68-Kelly-s/Mahnke-a. 69-73-Hunt for Aquaman; bi-monthly with alternating art by Mahnke and Guichet 3.00
75-(1/03, $3.95) leads into Aquaman (4th series) #1 4.00
76-93: 76-Firestorm app. 77-Banks-a. 79-Kanjar Ro app. 91-93-O'Neil-s/Huat-a 3.00
94-99-Byrne & Ordway-a/Claremont-s; Doom Patrol app. 3.00
100-($3.50) Intro. Vera Black; leads into Justice League Elite #1 4.00
101-114: 101-106-Austen-s/Garney-a/c. 107-114-Crime Syndicate app.; Busiek-s 3.00
115-125: 115-Begin $2.50-c; Johns & Heinberg-s;Secret Society of Super-Villains app. 3.00
#1,000,000 (11/98) 853rd Century x-over 3.00
Annual 1 (1997, $3.95) Pulp Heroes; Augustyn-s/Olivetti & Ha-a 4.00
Annual 2 (1998, $2.95) Ghosts; Wrightson-c 4.00
Annual 3 (1999, $2.95) JLApe; Art Adams-c 4.00
Annual 4 (2000, $3.50) Planet DC x-over; Steve Scott-c/a 4.00
... American Dreams (1998, $7.95, TPB) r/#5-9 8.00
...: Crisis of Conscience TPB (2006, $12.99) r/#115-119 13.00
.../ Cyberforce (DC/Top Cow, 2005, $5.99) Kelly-s/Mahnke-a/Silvestri-c 6.00
Divided We Fall (2001, $17.95, TPB) r/#47-54 18.00
...80-Page Giant 1 (7/98, $4.95) stories & art by various 6.00
...80-Page Giant 2 (11/99, $4.95) Green Arrow & Hawkman app. Hitch-c 6.00
...80-Page Giant 3 (10/00, $5.95) Pariah & Harbinger; intro. Moon Maiden 6.00
...Foreign Bodies (1999, $5.95, one-shot) Kobra app.; Semeiks-a 6.00
...Gallery (1997, $2.95) pin-ups by various; Quitely-c 3.00
...God & Monsters (2001, $6.95, one-shot) Benefiel-a/c 7.00
Golden Perfect (2003, $12.95, TPB) r/#61-65 13.00
.../ Haven: Anathema (2002, $6.95) Concludes the Haven: The Broken City series 7.00
.../ Haven: Arrival (2001, $6.95) Leads into the Haven: The Broken City series 7.00
...In Crisis Secret Files 1 (11/98, $4.95) recap of JLA in DC x-overs 5.00
...: Island of Dr. Moreau, The (2002, $6.95, one-shot) Elseworlds; Pugh-c/a; Thomas-s 7.00
.../ JSA Secret Files & Origins (1/03, $4.95) prelude to JLA/JSA: Virtue & Vice; short stories and pin-ups by various; Pacheco-c 5.00
.../ JSA: Virtue and Vice HC (2002, $24.95) Teams battle Despero & Johnny Sorrow; Goyer & Johns-s/Pacheco-a/c 25.00
.../ JSA: Virtue and Vice SC (2003, $17.95) 18.00

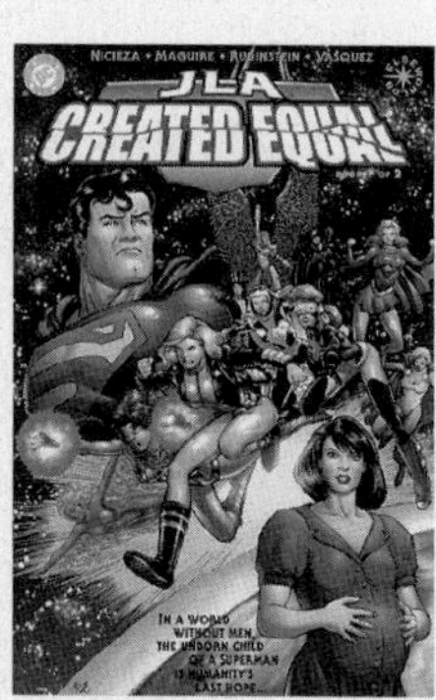

JLA: Created Equal #1 © DC

JLA / Titans #1 © DC

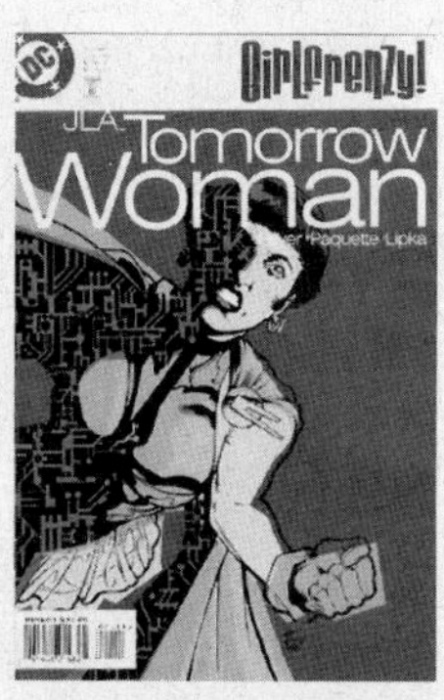

JLA: Tomorrow Woman #1 © DC

GD 2.0 | VG 4.0 | FN 6.0 | VF 8.0 | VF/NM 9.0 | NM- 9.2

Justice For All (1999, $14.95, TPB) r/#24-33 15.00
New World Order (1997, $5.95, TPB) r/#1-4 6.00
...: Obsidian Age Book One, The (2003, $12.95) r/#66-71 13.00
...: Obsidian Age Book Two, The (2003, $12.95) r/#72-76 13.00
One Million (2004, $19.95, TPB) r/#DC One Million #1-4 and other #1,000,000 x-overs 20.00
...: Our Worlds at War (9/01, $2.95) Jae Lee-c; Aquaman presumed dead 3.00
...: Pain of the Gods (2005, $12.99) r/#101-106 13.00
...Primeval (1999, $5.95, one-shot) Abnett & Lanning-s/Olivetti-a 6.00
...: Riddle of the Beast HC (2001, $24.95) Grant-s/painted-a by various; Sweet-c 25.00
...: Riddle of the Beast SC (2003, $14.95) Grant-s/painted-a by various; Kaluta-c 15.00
Rock of Ages (1998, $9.95, TPB) r/#10-15 10.00
Rules of Engagement (2004, $12.95, TPB) r/#77-82 13.00
...: Seven Caskets (2000, $5.95, one-shot) Brereton-s/painted-c/a 6.00
...: Shogun of Steel (2002, $6.95, one-shot) Elseworlds; Justiniano-c/a 7.00
...Showcase 80-Page Giant (2/00, $4.95) Hitch-c 5.00
Strength in Numbers (1998, $12.95, TPB) r/#16-23, Secret Files #2 and Prometheus #1 13.00
...Superpower (1999, $5.95, one-shot) Arcudi-s/Eaton-a; Mark Antaeus joins 6.00
Syndicate Rules (2005, $17.99, TPB) r/#107-114, Secret Files #4 18.00
Terror Incognita (2002, $12.95, TPB) r/#55-60 13.00
...: The Deluxe Edition Vol. 1 HC (2008, $29.99, dustjacket) oversized r/#1-9 and JLA Secret Files #1 30.00
...: The Deluxe Edition Vol. 2 HC (2009, $29.99, dustjacket) oversized r/#10-17, JLA/Wildcats, and Prometheus #1 30.00
...: The Deluxe Edition Vol. 3 HC (2010, $29.99, dustjacket) oversized r/#22-26, 28-31 & #1,000,000 30.00
...: The Deluxe Edition Vol. 4 HC (2010, $34.99, dustjacket) oversized r/#34, 36-41, JLA Classified #1-3 and JLA: Earth 2 GN 35.00
The Tenth Circle (2004, $12.95, TPB) r/#94-99 13.00
...: The Greatest Stories Ever Told TPB (2006, $19.99) r/Justice League of America #19,71,122, 166-168,200, Justice League #1, JLA Secret Files #1 and JLA #61; Alex Ross-c 20.00
Tower of Babel (2001, $12.95, TPB) r/#42-46, Secret Files #3, 80-Page Giant #1 13.00
Trial By Fire (2004, $12.95, TPB) r/#84-89 13.00
...Vs. Predator (DC/Dark Horse, 2000, $5.95, one-shot) Nolan-c/a 6.00
...: Welcome to the Working Week (2003, $6.95, one-shot) Patton Oswalt-s 7.00
...: World War III (2000, $12.95, TPB) r/#34-41 13.00
...: World Without a Justice League (2006, $12.99, TPB) r/#120-125 13.00
...: Zatanna's Search (2003, $12.95, TPB) rep. Zatanna's early app. & origin; Bolland-c 13.00

JLA: ACT OF GOD
DC Comics: 2000 - No. 3, 2001 ($4.95, limited series)
1-3-Elseworlds; metahumans lose their powers; Moench-s/Dave Ross-a 5.00

JLA: AGE OF WONDER
DC Comics: 2003 - No. 2, 2003 ($5.95, limited series)
1,2-Elseworlds; Superman and the League of Science during the Industrial Revolution 6.00

JLA: A LEAGUE OF ONE
DC Comics: 2000 (Graphic novel)
Hardcover ($24.95) Christopher Moeller-s/painted-a 25.00
Softcover (2002, $14.95) 15.00

JLA/AVENGERS (See Avengers/JLA for #2 & #4)
Marvel Comics: Sept, 2003; No. 3, Dec, 2003 ($5.95, limited series)
1-Busiek-s/Pérez-a; wraparound-c; Krona, Starro, Grandmaster, Terminus app. 6.00
3-Busiek-s/Pérez-a; wraparound-c; Phantom Stranger app. 6.00
SC (2008, $19.99) r/4-issue series; cover gallery; intros by Stan Lee & Julius Schwartz 20.00

JLA: BLACK BAPTISM
DC Comics: May, 2001 - No. 4, Aug, 2001 ($2.50, limited series)
1-4-Saiz-a(p)/Bradstreet-c; Zatanna app. 3.00

JLA: CLASSIFIED
DC Comics: Jan, 2005 - No. 54, May, 2008 ($2.95/$2.99)
1-3-Morrison-s/McGuinness-a/c; Ultramarines app. 3.00
4-9-"I Can't Believe It's Not The Justice League," Giffen & DeMatteis-s/Maguire-a 3.00
10-31,33-54: 10-15-New Maps of Hell; Ellis-s/Guice-a. 16-21-Garcia-Lopez-a. 22-25-Detroit League & Royal Flush Gang app.; Englehart-s. 26-28-Chaykin-s. 37-41-Kid Amazo. 50-54-Byrne-a/Middleston-c 3.00
32-($3.99) Dr. Destiny app.; Jurgens-a 4.00
I Can't Believe It's Not The Justice League TPB (2005, $12.99) r/#4-9 13.00
...: Kid Amazo TPB (2007, $12.99) r/#37-41 13.00
...: New Maps of Hell TPB (2006, $12.99) r/#10-15 13.00
...: That Was Now, This Is Then TPB (2008, $14.99) r/#50-54 15.00
...: The Hypothetical Woman TPB (2008, $12.99) r/#16-21 13.00
...: Ultramarine Corps TPB (2007, $14.99) r/#1-3, JLA/WildC.A.T.s #1 and JLA Secret Files 2004 #1 15.00

JLA CLASSIFIED: COLD STEEL
DC Comics: 2005 - No. 2, 2006 ($5.99, limited series, prestige format)
1,2-Chris Moeller-s/a; giant robot Justice League 6.00

JLA: CREATED EQUAL
DC Comics: 2000 - No. 2, 2000 ($5.95, limited series, prestige format)
1,2-Nicieza-s/Maguire-a; Elseworlds-Superman as the last man on Earth 6.00

JLA: DESTINY
DC Comics: 2002 - No. 4, 2002 ($5.95, prestige format, limited series)
1-4-Elseworlds; Arcudi-s/Mandrake-a 6.00

JLA: EARTH 2
DC Comics: 2000 (Graphic novel)
Hardcover ($24.95) Morrison-s/Quitely-a; Crime Syndicate app. 25.00
Softcover ($14.95) 15.00

JLA: GATEKEEPER
DC Comics: 2001 - No. 3, 2001 ($4.95, prestige format, limited series)
1-3-Truman-s/a 5.00

JLA: HEAVEN'S LADDER
DC Comics: 2000 ($9.95, Treasury-size one-shot)
nn-Bryan Hitch & Paul Neary-c/a; Mark Waid-s 10.00

JLA/HITMAN (Justice League/Hitman in indicia)
DC Comics: Nov, 2007 - No. 2, Dec, 2007 ($3.99, limited series)
1,2-Ennis-s/McCrea-a; Bloodlines creatures return 4.00

JLA: INCARNATIONS
DC Comics: Jul, 2001 - No. 7, Feb, 2002 ($3.50, limited series)
1-7-Ostrander-s/Semeiks-a; different eras of the Justice League 4.00

JLA: LIBERTY AND JUSTICE
DC Comics: Nov, 2003 ($9.95, Treasury-size one-shot)
nn-Alex Ross-c/a; Paul Dini-s; story of the classic Justice League 10.00

JLA PARADISE LOST
DC Comics: Jan, 1998 - No. 3, Mar, 1998 ($1.95, limited series)
1-3-Millar-s/Olivetti-a 3.00

JLA: SCARY MONSTERS
DC Comics: May, 2003 - No. 6, Oct, 2003 ($2.50, limited series)
1-6-Claremont-s/Art Adams-c 3.00

JLA SECRET FILES
DC Comics: Sept, 1997 - 2004 ($4.95)
1-Standard Ed. w/origin-s & pin-ups 5.00
1-Collector's Ed. w/origin-s & pin-ups; cardstock-c 6.00
2,3: 2-(8/98) origin-s of JLA #16's newer members. 3-(12/00) 5.00
... 2004 (11/04) Justice League Elite app.; Mahnke & Byrne-a; Crime Syndicate app. 5.00

JLA: SECRET ORIGINS
DC Comics: Nov, 2002 ($7.95, Treasury-size one-shot)
nn-Alex Ross 2-page origins of Justice League members; text by Paul Dini 8.00

JLA: SECRET SOCIETY OF SUPER-HEROES
DC Comics: 2000 - No. 2, 2000 ($5.95, limited series, prestige format)
1,2-Elseworlds JLA; Chaykin and Tischman-s/McKone-a 6.00

JLA /SPECTRE: SOUL WAR
DC Comics: 2003 - No. 2, 2003 ($5.95, limited series, prestige format)
1,2-DeMatteis-s/Banks & Neary-a 6.00

JLA: THE NAIL (Elseworlds) (Also see Justice League of America: Another Nail)
DC Comics: Aug, 1998 - No. 3, Oct, 1998 ($4.95, prestige format)
1-3-JLA in a world without Superman; Alan Davis-s/a(p) 5.00
TPB ('98, $12.95) r/series w/new Davis-c 13.00

JLA / TITANS
DC Comics: Dec, 1998 - No. 3, Feb, 1999 ($2.95, limited series)
1-3-Grayson-s; P. Jimenez-c/a 3.00
...:The Technis Imperative ('99, $12.95, TPB) r/#1-3; Titans Secret Files 13.00

JLA: TOMORROW WOMAN (Girlfrenzy)
DC Comics: June, 1998 ($1.95, one-shot)
1-Peyer-s; story takes place during JLA #5 3.00

JLA / WILDC.A.T.S
DC Comics: 1997 ($5.95, one-shot, prestige format)

Joe Kubert Presents #1 © DC

Joe Palooka #6 © VJIB

John Byrne's Next Men #21 © DH

GD 2.0 | VG 4.0 | FN 6.0 | VF 8.0 | VF/NM 9.0 | NM- 9.2

1-Morrison-s/Semeiks & Conrad-a 6.00

JLA /WITCHBLADE
DC Comics/Top Cow: 2000 ($5.95, prestige format, one-shot)
1-Pararillo-c/a 6.00

JLA / WORLD WITHOUT GROWN-UPS (See Young Justice)
DC Comics: Aug, 1998 - No. 2, Sept, 1998 ($4.95, prestige format)
1,2-JLA, Robin, Impulse & Superboy app.; Ramos & McKone-a 6.00
TPB ('98, $9.95) r/series & Young Justice: The Secret #1 10.00

JLA: YEAR ONE
DC Comics: Jan, 1998 - No. 12, Dec, 1998 ($2.95/$1.95, limited series)
1-($2.95)-Waid & Augustyn-s/Kitson-a 5.00
1-Platinum Edition 10.00
2-8-($1.95): 5-Doom Patrol-c/app. 7-Superman app. 4.00
9-12 3.00
TPB ('99,'09; $19.95/$19.99) r/#1-12; Busiek intro. 20.00

JLA-Z
DC Comics: Nov, 2003 - No. 3, Jan, 2004 ($2.50, limited series)
1-3-Pin-ups and info on current and former JLA members and villains; art by various 3.00

JLX
DC Comics (Amalgam): Apr, 1996 ($1.95, one-shot)
1-Mark Waid scripts 3.00

JLX UNLEASHED
DC Comics (Amalgam): June, 1997 ($1.95, one-shot)
1-Priest-s/ Oscar Jimenez & Rodriquez/a 3.00

JOAN OF ARC (Also see A-1 Comics, Classics Illustrated #78, and Ideal a Classical Comic)
Magazine Enterprises: No. 21, 1949 (one shot)
A-1 21-Movie adaptation; Ingrid Bergman photo-covers & interior photos;
Whitney-a 29 58 87 170 278 385

JOE COLLEGE
Hillman Periodicals: Fall, 1949 - No. 2, Wint, 1950 (Teen-age humor, 52 pgs.)
1-Powell-a; Briefer-a 14 28 42 76 108 140
2-Powell-a 10 20 30 54 72 90

JOE JINKS
United Features Syndicate: No. 12, 1939
Single Series 12 31 62 93 182 296 410

JOE KUBERT PRESENTS
DC Comics: Dec, 2012 - No. 6, May, 2013 ($4.99, limited series)
1-6: Anthology of short stories by Kubert, Buniak & Glanzman. 1-Hawkman app. 5.00

JOE LOUIS (See Fight Comics #2, Picture News #6 & True Comics #5)
Fawcett Publications: Sept, 1950 - No. 2, Nov, 1950 (Photo-c) (Boxing champ) (See Dick Cole #10)
1-Photo-c; life story 55 110 165 352 601 850
2-Photo-c 39 78 117 240 395 550

JOE PALOOKA (1st Series)(Also see Big Shot Comics, Columbia Comics & Feature Funnies)
Columbia Comic Corp. (Publication Enterprises): 1942 - No. 4, 1944
1-1st to portray American president; gov't permission required
116 232 348 742 1271 1800
2 (1943)-Hitler-c 84 168 252 538 919 1300
3-Nazi Sub-c 43 86 129 271 461 650
4 36 72 108 216 351 485

JOE PALOOKA (2nd Series) (Battle Adv. #68-74; ...Advs. #75, 77-81, 83-85, 87; Champ of the Comics #76, 82, 86, 89-93) (See All-New)
Harvey Publications: Nov, 1945 - No. 118, Mar, 1961
1-By Ham Fisher 51 102 153 318 539 760
2 25 50 75 147 241 335
3,4,6,7-1st Flyin' Fool, ends #25 16 32 48 94 147 200
5-Boy Explorers by S&K (7-8/46) 21 42 63 122 199 275
8-10 14 28 42 80 115 150
11-14,16,18-20: 14-Black Cat text-s(2). 18-Powell-a.; Little Max app. 19-Freedom Train-c
11 22 33 64 90 115
15-Origin & 1st app. Humphrey (12/47); Super-heroine Atoma app. by Powell
15 30 45 90 140 190
17-Humphrey vs. Palooka-c/s; 1st app. Little Max 15 30 45 90 140 190
21-26,29,30: 22-Powell-a. 30-Nude female painting 10 20 30 56 76 95
27-Little Max app.; Howie Morenz-s 10 20 30 58 79 100
28-Babe Ruth 4 pg. sty. 10 20 30 58 79 100
31,39,51: 31-Dizzy Dean 4 pg. sty. 39-(12/49) Humphrey & Little Max begin; Sonny Baugh football-s; Sherlock Max-s. 51-Babe Ruth 2 pg. sty; Jake Lamotta 1/2 pg. sty
9 18 27 50 65 80
32-38,40-50,52-61: 35-Little Max-c/story(4 pgs.); Joe Louis 1 pg. sty. 36-Humphrey story. 41-Bing Crosby photo on-c. 44-Palooka marries Ann Howe. 50-(11/51)-Becomes Harvey Comics Hits #51 8 16 24 44 57 70
62-S&K Boy Explorers-r 9 18 27 50 65 80
63-65,73-80,100: 79-Story of 1st meeting with Ann 8 16 24 40 50 60
66,67-'Commie' torture story "Drug-Diet Horror" 12 24 36 67 94 120
68,70-72: 68,70-Joe vs. "Gooks"-c. 71-Bloody bayonets-c. 72-Tank-c
11 22 33 64 90 115
69-1st "Battle Adventures" issue; torture & bondage 12 24 36 67 94 120
81-99,101-115: 104,107-Humphrey & Little Max-s 7 14 21 37 46 55
116-S&K Boy Explorers-r (Giant, '60) 9 18 27 47 61 75
117-(84 pg. Giant) r/Commie issues #66,67; Powell-a 9 18 27 52 69 85
118-(84 pg. Giant) Jack Dempsey 2 pg. sty, Powell-a 9 18 27 47 61 75
...**Visits the Lost City** nn (1945)(One Shot)(50¢)-164 page continuous story strip reprint. Has biography & photo of Ham Fisher; possibly the single longest comic book story published in that era (159 pgs.?) (scarce) 213 426 639 1363 2332 3300
NOTE: ***Nostrand/Powell** a-73. **Powell** a-7, 8, 10, 12, 14, 17, 19, 26-45, 47-53, 70, 73 at least. Black Cat text stories #8, 12, 13, 19.*

JOE PALOOKA
IDW Publishing: Dec, 2012 - No. 6, May, 2013 ($3.99, limited series)
1-6: 1-Bullock-s/Peniche-a; Joe Palooka updated as a MMA fighter 4.00

JOE PSYCHO & MOO FROG
Goblin Studios: 1996 - No. 5, 1997 ($2.50, B&W)
1-5: 4-Two covers 3.00
...Full Color Extravagarbonzo ($2.95, color) 3.00

JOE THE BARBARIAN
DC Comics (Vertigo): Mar, 2010 - No. 8, May, 2011 ($1.00/$2.99/$3.99)
1-($1.00) Grant Morrison-s/Sean Murphy-a 3.00
2-7-($2.99) 3.00
8-($3.99) 4.00

JOE YANK (Korean War)
Standard Comics (Visual Editions): No. 5, Mar, 1952 - No. 16, 1954
5-Toth, Celardo, Tuska-a 10 20 30 58 79 100
6-Toth, Severin/Elder-a 10 20 30 56 76 95
7-Pinhead Perkins by Dan DeCarlo (in all?) 8 16 24 44 57 70
8-Toth-c 9 18 27 50 65 80
9-16: 9-Andru-c. 12-Andru-a 8 16 24 42 54 65

JOHN BOLTON'S HALLS OF HORROR
Eclipse Comics: June, 1985 - No. 2, June, 1985 ($1.75, limited series)
1,2-British-r; Bolton-c/a 4.00

JOHN BOLTON'S STRANGE WINK
Dark Horse Comics: Mar, 1998 - No. 3, May, 1998 ($2.95, B&W, limited series)
1-3-Anthology; Bolton-s/c/a 3.00

JOHN BYRNE'S NEXT MEN (See Dark Horse Presents #54)
Dark Horse Comics (Legend imprint #19 on): Jan, 1992 - No. 30, Dec, 1994 ($2.50, mature)
1-Silver foil embossed-c; Byrne-c/a/scripts in all 4.00
1-4: 1-2nd printing with gold ink logo 3.00
0-(2/92)-r/chapters 1-4 from DHP w/new Byrne-c 3.00
5-20,22-30: 7-10-MA #1-4 mini-series on flip side. 16-Origin of Mark IV. 17-Miller-c. 19-22-Faith storyline. 23-26-Power storyline. 27-30-Lies storyline Pt. 1-4 3.00
21-(12/93) 2nd Hellboy; cover and Hellboy pages by Mike Mignola; Byrne other pages (see San Diego Comic Con Comics #2 for 1st app.) 4 8 12 28 47 65
...Parallel, Book 2 ($16.95)-TPB; r/#7-12 17.00
...Fame, Book 3($16.95)-TPB r/#13-18 17.00
...Faith, Book 4($14.95)-TPB r/#19-22 15.00
NOTE: *Issues 1 through 6 contain certificates redeemable for an exclusive Next Men trading card set by Byrne. Prices are for complete books. **Cody** painted c-23-26. **Mignola** a-21(part); c-21.*

JOHN BYRNE'S NEXT MEN (Continues in Next Men: Aftermath #40)
IDW Publishing: Dec, 2010 - No. 9, Aug, 2011 ($3.99)
1-9-John Byrne-s/a/c in all. 1-Origin retold. 6,7-Abraham Lincoln app. 4.00

JOHN BYRNE'S 2112
Dark Horse Comics (Legend): Oct, 1991 ($9.95, TPB)
1-Byrne-c/a/s 10.00

JOHN CARTER OF MARS (See The Funnies & Tarzan #207)
Dell Publishing Co.: No. 375, Mar-May, 1952 - No. 488, Aug-Oct, 1953
(Edgar Rice Burroughs)

John Carter, Warlord of Mars #17 © ERB

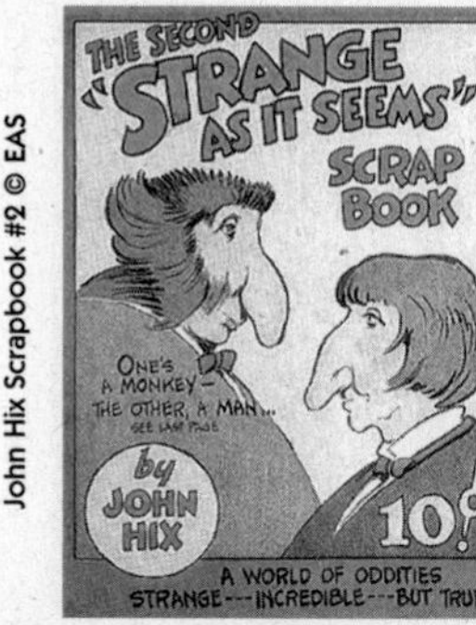

John Hix Scrapbook #2 © EAS

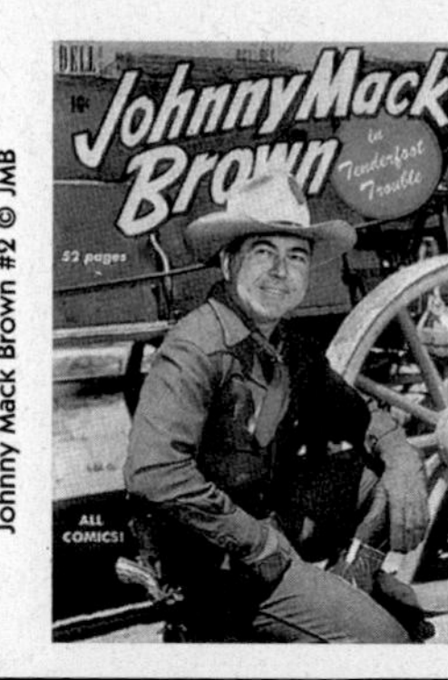

Johnny Mack Brown #2 © JMB

	GD 2.0	VG 4.0	FN 6.0	VF 8.0	VF/NM 9.0	NM- 9.2
Four Color 375 (#1)-Origin; Jesse Marsh-a	27	54	81	189	420	650
Four Color 437, 488-Painted-c	15	30	45	103	227	350

JOHN CARTER OF MARS
Gold Key: Apr, 1964 - No. 3, Oct, 1964

1(10104-404)-r/4-Color #375; Jesse Marsh-a	6	12	18	38	69	100
2(407), 3(410)-r/4-Color #437 & 488; Marsh-a	4	8	12	28	47	65

JOHN CARTER OF MARS
House of Greystroke: 1970 (10-1/2x16-1/2", 72 pgs., B&W, paper-c)

1941-42 Sunday strip-r; John Coleman Burroughs-a	4	8	12	23	37	50

JOHN CARTER OF MARS: A PRINCESS OF MARS
Marvel Comics: Nov, 2011 - No. 5, Mar, 2012 ($2.99, limited series)

1-5: 1-Langridge-s/Andrade-a; covers by Young and Andrade. 2-4-Young-c 3.00

JOHN CARTER: THE GODS OF MARS
Marvel Comics: May, 2012 - No. 5, Sept, 2012 ($3.99, limited series)

1-5-Sam Humphries-s/Ramón Pérez-a; Carter's 2nd trip to Mars 4.00

JOHN CARTER: THE WORLD OF MARS
Marvel Comics: Dec, 2011 - No. 4, Mar, 2012 ($3.99, limited series)

1-4-Movie prequel; Peter David-s/Luke Ross-a. 1-Ribic-c. 4-Olivetti-c 4.00

JOHN CARTER, WARLORD OF MARS (Also see Tarzan #207-209 and Weird Worlds)
Marvel Comics: June, 1977 - No. 28, Oct, 1979

1,18: 1-Origin. 18-Frank Miller-a(p)(1st publ. Marvel work)	3	6	9	14	20	25
1-(35¢-c variant, limited dist.)	5	10	15	31	53	75
2-5-(35¢-c variants, limited dist.)	4	8	12	23	37	50
2-17,19-28: 11-Origin Dejah Thoris	1	3	4	6	8	10
Annuals 1-3: 1(1977). 2(1978). 3(1979)-All 52 pgs. with new book-length stories	1	3	4	6	8	10

Edgar Rice Burroughs' John Carter of Mars: Weird Worlds TPB (Dark Horse Books, Jan. 2011, $14.99) r/stories from Tarzan #207-209 and Weird Worlds #1-7; Marv Wolfman intro. 15.00

NOTE: ***Austin** c-24i. **Gil Kane** a-1-10p; c-1p, 2p, 3, 4-9p, 10, 15p, Annual 1p. **Layton** a-17i. **Miller** c-25, 26p. **Nebres** a-2-4i, 8-16i; c(i)-6-9, 11-22, 25, Annual 1. **Perez** c-24p. **Simonson** a-15p. **Sutton** a-7i.*

JOHN CONSTANTINE - HELLBLAZER SPECIAL: PAPA MIDNITE
DC Comics (Vertigo): April, 2005 - No. 5, Aug, 2005 ($2.95/$2.99, limited series)

1-5-Origin of Papa Midnite; Akins-a/Johnson-s 3.00

JOHN F. KENNEDY, CHAMPION OF FREEDOM
Worden & Childs: 1964 (no month) (25¢)

nn-Photo-c	7	14	21	49	92	135

JOHN F. KENNEDY LIFE STORY
Dell Publishing Co.: Aug-Oct, 1964; Nov, 1965; June, 1966 (12¢)

12-378-410-Photo-c	7	14	21	44	82	120
12-378-511 (reprint, 11/65)	3	6	9	21	33	45
12-378-606 (reprint, 6/66)	3	6	9	19	30	40

JOHN FORCE (See Magic Agent)

JOHN HIX SCRAP BOOK, THE
Eastern Color Printing Co. (McNaught Synd.): Late 1930's (no date) (10¢, 68 pgs., regular size)

1-Strange As It Seems (resembles Single Series books)	40	80	120	244	402	560
2-Strange As It Seems	27	54	81	158	259	360

JOHN JAKES' MULLKON EMPIRE
Tekno Comix: Sept, 1995 - No. 6, Feb, 1996 ($1.95)

1-6 3.00

JOHN LAW DETECTIVE (See Smash Comics #3)
Eclipse Comics: April, 1983 ($1.50, Baxter paper)

1-Three Eisner stories originally drawn in 1948 for the never published John Law #1; original cover pencilled in 1948 & inked in 1982 by Eisner 4.00

JOHN McCAIN (See Presidential Material: John McCain)

JOHNNY APPLESEED (See Story Hour Series)

JOHNNY CASH (See Hello, I'm...)

JOHNNY DANGER (See Movie Comics, 1946)
Toby Press: 1950 (Based on movie serial)

1-Photo-c; Sparling-a	20	40	60	118	192	265

JOHNNY DANGER PRIVATE DETECTIVE
Toby Press: Aug, 1954 (Reprinted in Danger #11 by Super)

	GD 2.0	VG 4.0	FN 6.0	VF 8.0	VF/NM 9.0	NM- 9.2
1-Photo-c; Opium den story	18	36	54	105	165	225

JOHNNY DYNAMITE (Formerly Dynamite #1-9; Foreign Intrigues #14 on)
Charlton Comics: No. 10, June, 1955 - No. 12, Oct, 1955

10-12	13	26	39	74	105	135

JOHNNY DYNAMITE
Dark Horse Comics: Sept, 1994 - Dec, 1994 ($2.95, B&W & red, limited series)

1-4: Max Allan Collins scripts in all; Terry Beatty-a 3.00
...: Underworld GN (AiT/Planet Lar, 3/03, $12.95, B&W) r/#1-4 in B&W without red 13.00

JOHNNY HAZARD
Best Books (Standard Comics) (King Features): No. 5, Aug, 1948 - No. 8, May, 1949; No. 35, date?

5-Strip reprints by Frank Robbins (c/a)	18	36	54	105	165	225
6,8-Strip reprints by Frank Robbins	15	30	45	88	137	185
7,35: 7-New art, not Robbins	12	24	36	67	94	120

JOHNNY JASON (...Teen Reporter)
Dell Publishing Co.: Feb-Apr, 1962 - No. 2, June-Aug, 1962

Four Color 1302, 2(01380-208)	4	8	12	23	37	50

JOHNNY LAW, SKY RANGER
Good Comics (Lev Gleason): Apr, 1955 - No. 3, Aug, 1955; No. 4, Nov, 1955

1-Edmond Good-c/a	10	20	30	56	76	95
2-4	7	14	21	35	43	50

JOHNNY MACK BROWN (Western star; see Western Roundup under Dell Giants)
Dell Publishing Co.: No. 269, Mar, 1950 - No. 963, Feb, 1959 (All Photo-c)

Four Color 269(#1)(3/50, 52pgs.)-Johnny Mack Brown & his horse Rebel begin; photo front/back-c begin; Marsh-a in #1-9	18	36	54	124	275	425
2(10-12/50, 52pgs.)	10	20	30	64	132	200
3(1-3/51, 52pgs.)	8	16	24	54	102	150
4-10 (9-11/52)(36pgs.), Four Color 455,493,541,584,618,645,685,722,776,834,963	6	12	18	40	73	105
Four Color 922-Manning-a	6	12	18	41	76	110

JOHNNY NEMO
Eclipse Comics: Sept, 1985 - No. 3, Feb, 1986 (Mini-series)

1-3 4.00

JOHNNY PERIL (See Comic Cavalcade #15, Danger Trail #5, Sensation Comics #107 & Sensation Mystery)

JOHNNY RINGO (TV)
Dell Publishing Co.: No. 1142, Nov-Jan, 1960/61 (one shot)

Four Color 1142-Photo-c	6	12	18	40	73	105

JOHNNY STARBOARD (See Wisco)

JOHNNY THE HOMICIDAL MANIAC (Also see Squee)
Slave Labor Graphics: Aug, 1995 - No. 7, Jan, 1997 ($2.95, B&W, lim. series)

1-Jhonen Vasquez-c/s/a (1995)	4	8	12	27	44	60
1-Special Signed & numbered edition of 2,000 (1996)	3	6	9	16	23	30
2,3: 2-(11/95). 3-(2/96)	1	2	3	5	6	8
4-7: 4-(5-96). 5-(8/96)						4.00
Hardcover-($29.95) r/#1-7						35.00
TPB-($19.95)						25.00

JOHNNY THUNDER
National Periodical Publications: Feb-Mar, 1973 - No. 3, July-Aug, 1973

1-Johnny Thunder & Nighthawk-r. in all	2	4	6	13	18	22
2,3: 2-Trigger Twins app.	2	4	6	8	11	14

NOTE: *All contain 1950s DC reprints from All-American Western. **Drucker** r-2, 3. **G. Kane** r-2, 3. **Moreira** r-1. **Toth** r-1, 3; c-1r, 3r. Also see All-American, All-Star Western, Flash Comics, Western Comics, World's Best & World's Finest.*

JOHN PAUL JONES
Dell Publishing Co.: No. 1007, July-Sept, 1959 (one-shot)

Four Color 1007-Movie, Robert Stack photo-c	5	10	15	33	57	80

JOHN ROMITA JR. 30TH ANNIVERSARY SPECIAL
Marvel Comics: 2006 ($3.99, one-shot)

nn-r/1st story in Amazing Spider-Man Annual #11; timeline, sketch pages, interviews 4.00

JOHN STEED & EMMA PEEL (See The Avengers, Gold Key series)

JOHN STEELE SECRET AGENT (Also see Freedom Agent)
Gold Key: Dec, 1964

1-Freedom Agent	5	10	15	33	57	80

JOHN WAYNE ADVENTURE COMICS (Movie star; See Big Tex, Oxydol-Dreft, Tim McCoy, &

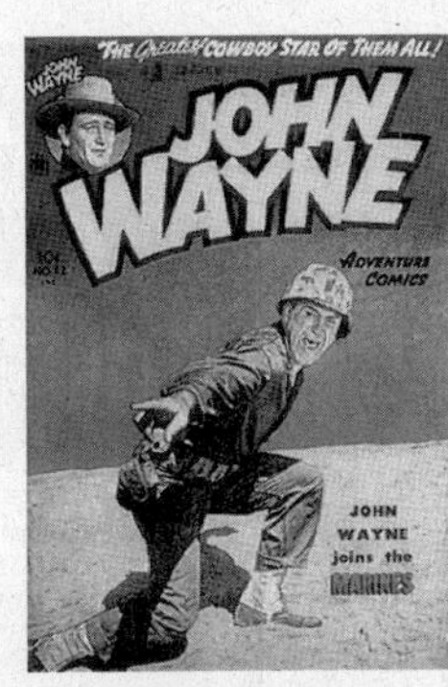

John Wayne Adventure Comics #12 © TOBY

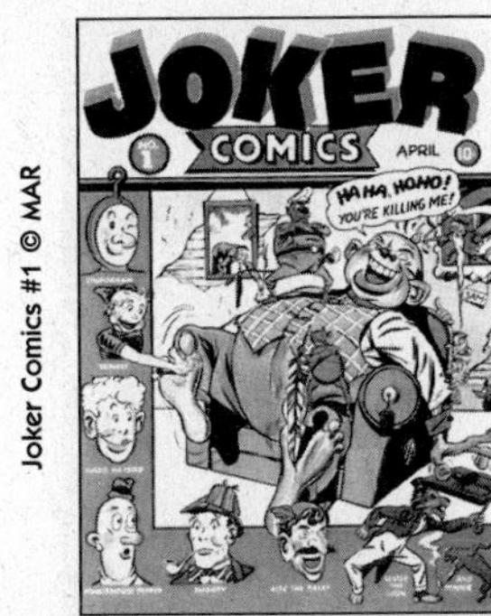

Joker Comics #1 © MAR

Jonah Hex (2006 series) #13 © DC

GD 2.0 | VG 4.0 | FN 6.0 | VF 8.0 | VF/NM 9.0 | NM- 9.2

With The Marines...#1)
Toby Press: Winter, 1949-50 - No. 31, May, 1955 (Photo-c: 1-12,17,25-on)

1 (36pgs.)-Photo-c begin (1st time in comics on-c) 213 426 639 1363 2332 3300
2-4: 2-(4/50, 36pgs.)-Williamson/Frazetta-a(2) 6 & 2 pgs. (one story-r/Billy the Kid #1); photo back-c. 3-(36pgs.)-Williamson/Frazetta-a(2), 16 pgs. total; photo back-c. 4-(52pgs.)-Williamson/Frazetta-a(2), 16 pgs. total 77 154 231 493 847 1200
5 (52pgs.)-Kurtzman-a-(Alfred "L" Newman in Potshot Pete) 57 114 171 362 619 875
6 (52pgs.)-Williamson/Frazetta-a (10 pgs.); Kurtzman-a "Pot-Shot Pete", (5 pgs.); & "Genius Jones", (1 pg.) 68 136 204 435 743 1050
7 (52pgs.)-Williamson/Frazetta-a (10 pgs.) 58 116 174 371 636 900
8 (36pgs.)-Williamson/Frazetta-a(2) (12 & 9 pgs.) 71 142 213 454 777 1100
9-11: Photo western-c 41 82 123 256 428 600
12,14-Photo war-c. 12-Kurtzman-a(2 pg.) "Genius" 41 82 123 260 435 610
13,15: 13,15-Line-drawn-c begin, end #24 37 74 111 222 361 500
16-Williamson/Frazetta-r/Billy the Kid #1 39 78 117 236 388 540
17-Photo-c 39 78 117 236 388 540
18-Williamson/Frazetta-a (r/#4 & 8, 19 pgs.) 41 82 123 256 428 600
19-24: 23-Evans-a? 33 66 99 194 317 440
25-Photo-c resume; end #31; Williamson/Frazetta-r/Billy the Kid #3 41 82 123 256 428 600
26-28,30-Photo-c 37 74 111 222 361 500
29,31-Williamson/Frazetta-a in each (r/#4, 2) 40 80 120 244 402 560
NOTE: *Williamsonish art in later issues by* ***Gerald McCann.***

JO-JO COMICS (...Congo King #7-29; My Desire #30 on)(Also see Fantastic Fears and Jungle Jo)
Fox Feature Syndicate: 1945 - No. 29, July, 1949 (Two No.7's; no #13)

nn(1945)-Funny animal, humor 21 42 63 126 206 285
2(Sum,'46)-6(4-5/47): Funny animal. 2-Ten pg. Electro story (Fall/46) 15 30 45 85 130 175
7(7/47)-Jo-Jo, Congo King begins (1st app.); Bronze Man & Purple Tigress app. 97 194 291 621 1061 1500
7(#8) (9/47) 69 138 207 442 759 1075
8(#9) Classic Kamen mountain of skulls-c; Tanee begins 68 136 204 435 743 1050
9,10(#10,11) 60 120 180 381 653 925
11,12(#12,13),14,16: 11,16-Kamen bondage-c 53 106 159 334 567 800
15,17: 15-Cited by Dr. Wertham in 5/47 Saturday Review of Literature. 17-Kamen bondage-c 54 108 162 343 574 825
18-20 52 104 156 328 552 775
21-29: 21-Hollingsworth-a(4 pgs.; 23-1 pg.) 42 84 126 265 445 625
NOTE: *Many bondage-c/a by* ***Baker/Kamen/Feldstein/Good.*** *No. 7's have Princesses Gwenna, Geesa, Yolda, & Safra before settling down on Tanee.*

JOKEBOOK COMICS DIGEST ANNUAL (...Magazine No. 5 on)
Archie Publications: Oct, 1977 - No. 13, Oct, 1983 (Digest Size)

1(10/77)-Reprints; Neal Adams-a 2 4 6 13 18 22
2(4/78)-5 2 4 6 9 12 15
6-13 1 3 4 6 8 10

JOKER
DC Comics: 2008 ($19.99, hardcover graphic novel with dustjacket)

HC-Joker is released from Arkham; Azzarello-s/Bermejo-a 20.00

JOKER, THE (See Batman #1, Batman: The Killing Joke, Brave & the Bold, Detective, Greatest Joker Stories & Justice League Annual #2)
National Periodical Publications: May, 1975 - No. 9, Sept-Oct, 1976

1-Two-Face app. 5 10 15 35 63 90
2,3: 3-The Creeper app. 3 6 9 21 33 45
4-9: 4-Green Arrow-c/sty. 6-Sherlock Holmes-c/sty. 7-Lex Luthor-c/story. 8-Scarecrow-c/story. 9-Catwoman-c/story 3 6 9 17 26 35
...: The Greatest Stories Ever Told TPB (2008, $19.99) r/Batman #1 and other apps. 20.00

JOKER, THE (See Tangent Comics/ The Joker)

JOKER COMICS (Adventures Into Terror No. 43 on)
Timely/Marvel Comics No. 36 on (TCI/CDS): Apr, 1942 - No. 42, Aug, 1950

1-(Rare)-Powerhouse Pepper (1st app.) begins by Wolverton; Stuporman app. from Daring Comics 300 600 900 2070 3635 5200
2-Wolverton-a; 1st app. Tessie the Typist & begin series 110 220 330 704 1202 1700
3-5-Wolverton-a 61 122 183 390 670 950
6-10-Wolverton-a. 6-Tessie-c begin 45 90 135 284 480 675
11-20-Wolverton-a 41 82 123 256 428 600
21,22,24-27,29,30-Wolverton cont'd. & Kurtzman's "Hey Look" in #23-27 37 74 111 222 361 500
23-1st "Hey Look" by Kurtzman; Wolverton-a 39 78 117 231 378 525
28,32,34,37-41: 28-Millie the Model begins. 32-Hedy begins. 41-Nellie the Nurse app. 18 36 54 105 165 225
31-Last Powerhouse Pepper; not in #28 31 62 93 186 303 420
33,35,36-Kurtzman's "Hey Look" 19 38 57 109 172 235
42-Only app. 'Patty Pinup,' clone of Millie the Model 19 38 57 109 172 235

JOKER: DEVIL'S ADVOCATE
DC Comics: 1996 ($24.95/$12.95, one-shot)

nn-(Hardcover)-Dixon scripts/Nolan & Hanna-a 30.00
nn-(Softcover) 15.00

JOKER: LAST LAUGH (See Batman: The Joker's Last Laugh for TPB)
DC Comics: Dec, 2001 - No. 6, Jan, 2002 ($2.95, weekly limited series)

1-6: 1,6-Bolland-c 3.00
...Secret Files (12/01, $5.95) Short stories by various; Simonson-c 6.00

JOKER / MASK
Dark Horse Comics: May, 2000 - No. 4, Aug, 2000 ($2.95, limited series)

1-4-Batman, Harley Quinn, Poison Ivy app. 3.00

JOKER'S ASYLUM
DC Comics: Sept, 2008 ($2.99, weekly limited series of one-shots)

...: Joker - Andy Kubert-c, Sanchez-a; ...: Penguin - Pearson-c/a; ...: Poison Ivy - Guillem March-c/a; ...: Scarecrow - Juan Doe-c/a; ...: Two-Face - Andy Clarke-c/a 3.00
Batman: The Joker's Asylum TPB (2008, $14.99) r/one-shots 15.00

JOKER'S ASYLUM II
DC Comics: Aug, 2010 ($2.99, weekly limited series of one-shots)

...: Clayface - Kelley Jones-c/a; ; ...: Killer Croc - Mattina-c; Mad Hatter - Giffen & Sienkiewicz-a, Sienkiewicz-c; ...: Riddler - Van Sciver-c 3.00
...: Harley Quinn - Quinones-a 1 3 4 6 8 10
Batman: The Joker's Asylum Volume 2 TPB (2011, $14.99) r/one-shots 15.00

JOLLY CHRISTMAS, A (See March of Comics No. 269)

JOLLY COMICS: **Four Star Publishing Co.:** 1947 (Advertised, not published)

JOLLY JINGLES (Formerly Jackpot Comics)
MLJ Magazines: No. 10, Sum, 1943 - No. 16, Wint, 1944/45

10-Super Duck begins (origin & 1st app.); Woody The Woodpecker begins (not same as Lantz character) 48 96 144 302 514 725
11 (Fall, '43)-2nd Super Duck(see Hangman #8) 26 52 78 154 252 350
12-Hitler-c 53 106 159 334 567 800
13-16: 13-Sahle-c. 15,16-Vigoda-c 18 36 54 105 165 225

JONAH HEX (See All-Star Western, Hex and Weird Western Tales)
National Periodical Pub./DC Comics: Mar-Apr, 1977 - No. 92, Aug, 1985

1 10 20 30 69 147 225
2 6 12 18 38 69 100
3,4,9: 9-Wrightson-c. 5 10 15 33 57 80
5,6,10: 5-Rep 1st app. from All-Star Western #10 5 10 15 30 50 70
7,8-Explains Hex's face disfigurement (origin) 5 10 15 35 63 90
11-20: 12-Starlin-c 3 6 9 19 30 40
21-32: 31,32-Origin retold 2 4 6 13 18 22
33-50 2 4 6 8 11 14
51-80 1 2 3 5 7 9
81-91: 89-Mark Texeira-a. 91-Cover swipe from Superman #243 (hugging a mystery woman) 2 4 6 8 10 12
92-Story cont'd in Hex #1 3 6 9 19 30 40
NOTE: ***Ayers*** *a(p)-35-37, 40, 41, 44-53, 56, 58-82.* ***Buckler*** *a-11; c-11, 13-16.* ***Kubert*** *c-43-46.* ***Morrow*** *a-90-92; c-10.* ***Spiegle(Tothish)*** *a-34, 38, 40, 49, 52.* ***Texeira*** *a-89p. Batlash back-ups in 49, 52. El Diablo back-ups in 48, 56-60, 73-75. Scalphunter back-ups in 40, 41, 45-47.*

JONAH HEX (Also see All Star Western [2011 DC New 52 title])
DC Comics: Jan, 2006 - No. 70, Oct, 2011 ($2.99)

1-Justin Gray & Jimmy Palmiotti-s/Luke Ross-a/Quitely-c 5.00
1-Special Edition (7/10, $1.00) r/#1 with "What's Next?" logo on cover 3.00
2-49,51-70: 3-Bat Lash app. 10,16,17,19,20,22-Noto-a. 11-El Diablo app.; Beck-a. 13-15-Origin retold. 21,23,27,30,32,37,38,42,52,54,57,59,61,63,67-Bernet-a. 33-Darwyn Cooke-a/c. 34-Sparacio-a. 51-Giordano-c. 53-Tucci-c/a. 62-Risso-a 3.00
50-($3.99) Darwyn Cooke-a/c 4.00
...: Bullets Don't Lie TPB (2009, $14.99) r/#31-36 15.00
...: Counting Corpses TPB (2010, $14.99) r/#43,50-54 15.00
...: Face Full of Violence TPB (2006, $12.99) r/#1-6 13.00
...: Guns of Vengeance TPB (2007, $12.99) r/#7-12 13.00
...: Lead Poisoning TPB (2009, $14.99) r/#37-42 15.00
...: Luck Runs Out TPB (2008, $12.99) r/#25-30 13.00
...: No Way Back HC (2010, $19.99) new GN; Gray & Palmiotti-s/DeZuniga-a 20.00

Jon Juan #1 © TOBY

Jon Sable, Freelance #23 © FC

Journey Into Mystery #5 © MAR

GD 2.0 | VG 4.0 | FN 6.0 | VF 8.0 | VF/NM 9.0 | NM- 9.2

...: No Way Back SC (2011, $14.99) new GN; Gray & Palmiotti-s/DeZuniga-a 15.00
...: Only the Good Die Young TPB (2008, $12.99) r/#19-24 13.00
...: Origins TPB (2007, $12.99) r/#13-18 13.00
...: Tall Tales TPB (2011, $14.99) r/#55-60 15.00
...: The Six Gun War TPB (2010, $14.99) r/#44-49 15.00
...: Welcome to Paradise TPB (2010, $17.99) r/debut in All-Star Western #10 plus early apps. in Weird Western Tales and Jonah Hex #2,4 (1977 series) 18.00

JONAH HEX AND OTHER WESTERN TALES (Blue Ribbon Digest)
DC Comics: Sept-Oct, 1979 - No. 3, Jan-Feb, 1980 (100 pgs.)
1-3: 1-Origin Scalphunter-r, Ayers/Evans, Neal Adams-a.; painted-c. 2-Weird Western Tales-r; Neal Adams, Toth, Aragones-a. 3-Outlaw-r, Scalphunter-r; Gil Kane, Wildey-a 2 4 6 11 16 20

JONAH HEX: RIDERS OF THE WORM AND SUCH
DC Comics (Vertigo): Mar, 1995 - No. 5, July, 1995 ($2.95, limited series)
1-5-Lansdale story, Truman -a 4.00

JONAH HEX: SHADOWS WEST
DC Comics (Vertigo): Feb, 1999 - No. 3, Apr, 1999 ($2.95, limited series)
1-3-Lansdale-s/Truman -a 4.00

JONAH HEX SPECTACULAR (See DC Special Series No. 16)

JONAH HEX: TWO-GUN MOJO
DC Comics (Vertigo): Aug, 1993 - No. 5, Dec, 1993 ($2.95, limited series)
1-Lansdale scripts in all; Truman/Glanzman-a in all w/Truman-c 6.00
1-Platinum edition with no price on cover 20.00
2-5 4.00
TPB-(1994, $12.95) r/#1-5 13.00

JONESY (Formerly Crack Western)
Comic Favorite/Quality Comics Group: No. 85, Aug, 1953; No. 2, Oct, 1953 - No. 8, Oct, 1954
85(#1)-Teen-age humor 9 18 27 50 65 80
2 6 12 18 29 36 42
3-8 6 12 18 27 33 38

JON JUAN (Also see Great Lover Romances)
Toby Press: Spring, 1950
1-All Schomburg-a (signed Al Reid on-c); written by Siegel; used in **SOTI**, pg. 38 (Scarce) 68 132 204 435 743 1050

JONNI THUNDER (...A.K.A. Thunderbolt)
DC Comics: Feb, 1985 - No. 4, Aug, 1985 (75¢, limited series)
1-4: 1-Origin & 1st app. 4.00

JONNY DOUBLE
DC Comics (Vertigo): Sept, 1998 - No. 4, Dec, 1998 ($2.95, limited series)
1-4-Azzarello-s 3.00
TPB (2002, $12.95) r/#1-4; Chiarello-c 13.00

JONNY QUEST (TV)
Gold Key: Dec, 1964 (Hanna-Barbera)
1 (10139-412) 29 58 87 209 467 725

JONNY QUEST (TV)
Comico: June 1986 - No. 31, Dec, 1988 ($1.50/$1.75)(Hanna-Barbera)
1,3,5: 3,5-Dave Stevens-c 6.00
2,4,6-31: 30-Adapts TV episode 4.00
Special 1(9/88, $1.75), 2(10/88, $1.75) 4.00
NOTE: ***M. Anderson*** *a-9.* ***Mooney*** *a-Special 1.* ***Pini*** *a-2.* ***Quagmire*** *a-31p.* ***Rude*** *a-1; c-2i.* ***Sienkiewicz*** *c-11.* ***Spiegle*** *a-7, 12, 21; c-21* ***Staton*** *a-2i, 11p.* ***Steacy*** *c-8.* ***Stevens*** *a-4i; c-3,5.* ***Wildey*** *a-1, c-1, 7, 12.* ***Williamson*** *a-4i; c-4i.*

JONNY QUEST CLASSICS (TV)
Comico: May, 1987 - No. 3, July, 1987 ($2.00) (Hanna-Barbera)
1-3: Wildey-c/a; 3-Based on TV episode 4.00

JON SABLE, FREELANCE (Also see Mike Grell's Sable & Sable)
First Comics: 6/83 - No. 56, 2/88 (#1-17, $1; #18-33, $1.25, #34-on, $1.75)
1-Mike Grell-c/a/scripts 5.00
2-56: 3-5-Origin, parts 1-3. 6-Origin, part 4. 11-1st app. of Maggie the Cat. 14-Mando paper begins. 16-Maggie the Cat. app. 25-30-Shatter app. 34-Deluxe format begins ($1.75) 3.00
The Complete Jon Sable, Freelance: Vol. 1 (IDW, 2005, $19.99) r/#1-6 20.00
The Complete Jon Sable, Freelance: Vol. 2 (IDW, 2005, $19.99) r/#7-11 20.00
The Complete Jon Sable, Freelance: Vol. 3 (IDW, 2005, $19.99) r/#12-16 20.00
The Complete Jon Sable, Freelance: Vol. 4 (IDW, 2005, $19.99) r/#17-21 20.00
NOTE: ***Aragones*** *a-33; c-33(part).* ***Grell*** *a-1-43;c-1-52, 53p, 54-56.*

JON SABLE, FREELANCE
IDW Publ.: (Limited series)
...: Ashes of Eden 1-5 (2009 - No. 5, 2/10, $3.99) Mike Grell-c/a/scripts 4.00
...: Bloodtrail 1-6 (4/05 - No. 6, 11/05, $3.99) Mike Grell-c/a/scripts 4.00
...: Bloodtrail TPB (4/06, $19.99) r/#1-6; cover gallery 20.00

JOSEPH & HIS BRETHREN (See The Living Bible)

JOSIE (She's... #1-16) (...& the Pussycats #45 on) (See Archie's Pals 'n' Gals #23 for 1st app.) (Also see Archie Giant Series Magazine #528, 540, 551, 562, 571, 584, 597, 610, 622)
Archie Publ./Radio Comics: Feb, 1963; No. 2, Aug, 1963 - No. 106, Oct, 1982
1 14 28 42 97 214 330
2 9 18 27 57 111 165
3-5 6 12 18 41 76 110
6-10: 6-(5/64) Book length Haunted Mansion-c/s. 7-(8/64) 1st app. Alexandra Cabot? 5 10 15 30 50 70
11-20 4 8 12 23 37 50
21, 23-30 3 6 9 18 28 38
22 (9/66)-Mighty Man & Mighty (Josie Girl) app. 4 8 12 25 40 55
31-44 3 6 9 16 23 30
45 (12/69)-Josie and the Pussycats begins (Hanna Barbera TV cartoon); 1st app. of the Pussycats 11 22 33 76 163 250
46-2nd app./1st cover Pussycats 8 16 24 54 102 150
47-3rd app. of the Pussycats 5 10 15 35 63 90
48,49-Pussycats band-c/s 6 12 18 38 69 100
50-J&P-c; go to Hollywood, meet Hanna & Barbera 6 12 18 42 79 115
51-54 3 6 9 18 28 38
55-74 (2/74)(52 pg. issues). 73-Pussycats band-c 3 6 9 18 28 38
75-90(8/76) 2 4 6 13 18 22
91-99 2 4 6 10 14 18
100 (10/79) 2 4 6 13 18 22
101-106: 103-Pussycats band-c 2 4 6 11 16 20

JOSIE & THE PUSSYCATS (TV)
Archie Comics: 1993 - No. 2, 1994 ($2.00, 52 pgs.)(Published annually)
1,2-Bound-in pull-out poster in each. 2-(Spr/94) 5.00

JOURNAL OF CRIME (See Fox Giants)

JOURNEY
Aardvark-Vanaheim #1-14/Fantagraphics Books #15-on: 1983 - No. 14, Sept, 1984; No. 15, Apr, 1985 - No. 27, July, 1986 (B&W)
1 4.00
2-27: 20-Sam Kieth-a 3.00

JOURNEY INTO FEAR
Superior-Dynamic Publications: May, 1951 - No. 21, Sept, 1954
1-Baker-r(2) 73 146 219 467 796 1125
2 48 96 144 302 514 725
3,4 41 82 123 256 428 600
5-10,15: 15-Used in **SOTI**, pg. 389 34 68 102 206 336 465
11-14,16-21 32 64 96 188 307 425
NOTE: Kamenish 'headlight'-a most issues. ***Robinson*** *a-10.*

JOURNEY INTO MYSTERY (1st Series) (Thor Nos. 126-502)
Atlas(CPS No. 1-48/AMI No. 49-68/Marvel No. 69 (6/61) on): 6/52 - No. 48, 8/57; No. 49, 11/58 - No. 125, 2/66; 503, 11/96 - No. 521, June, 1998
1-Weird/horror stories begin 432 864 11296 3154 5577 8000
2 155 310 465 992 1696 2400
3,4 116 232 348 742 1271 1800
5-11 90 180 270 576 988 1400
12-20,22: 15-Atomic explosion panel. 22-Davis*esque*-a; last pre-code issue (2/55) 68 136 204 435 743 1050
21-Kubert-a; Tothish-a by Andru 69 138 207 442 759 1075
23-32,35-38,40: 24-Torres?-a. 38-Ditko-a 53 106 159 334 567 800
33-Williamson-a; Ditko-a (his 1st for Atlas?) 55 110 165 352 601 850
34,39: 34-Krigstein-a. 39-1st S.A. issue; Wood-a 54 108 162 343 574 825
41-Crandall-a; Frazetta*esque*-a by Morrow 26 52 76 182 404 625
42,46,48: 42,48-Torres-a. 46-Torres & Krigstein-a 25 50 75 175 388 600
43,44-Williamson/Mayo-a in both. 43-Invisible Woman prototype 26 52 78 182 404 625
45,47 24 48 72 170 378 585
49-Matt Fox, Check-a 25 50 75 175 388 600
50,52-54: Ditko/Kirby-a. 50-Davis-a. 54-Williamson-a 32 64 96 230 515 800
51-Kirby/Wood-a 33 66 99 238 532 825
55-61,63-65,67-69,71,72,74,75: 74-Contents change to Fantasy. 75-Last 10¢ issue 30 60 90 216 483 750

Journey Into Mystery #112 © MAR

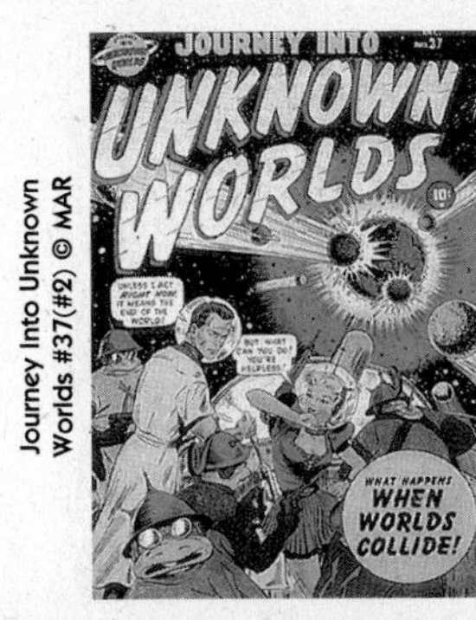

Journey Into Unknown Worlds #37(#2) © MAR

JSA #50 © DC

GD VG FN VF VF/NM NM-
2.0 4.0 6.0 8.0 9.0 9.2

GD VG FN VF VF/NM NM-
2.0 4.0 6.0 8.0 9.0 9.2

62-Prototype ish. (The Hulk); 1st app. Xemnu (Titan) called "The Hulk"
42 84 126 311 706 1100
66-Prototype ish. (The Hulk)-Return of Xemnu "The Hulk"
38 76 114 285 641 1000
70-Prototype ish. (The Sandman)(7/61); similar to Spidey villain
33 66 99 238 532 825
73-Story titled "The Spider" where a spider is exposed to radiation & gets powers of a human and shoots webbing; a reverse prototype of Spider-Man's origin
46 92 138 340 770 1200
76,77,80-82: 80-Anti-communist propaganda story 27 54 81 189 420 650
76-(10¢ cover price blacked out, 12¢ printed on) 38 76 114 285 641 1000
78-The Sorceror (Dr. Strange prototype) app. (3/62) 32 64 96 230 515 800
79-Prototype issue. (Mr. Hyde) 29 58 87 209 467 725
83-Origin & 1st app. The Mighty Thor by Kirby (8/62) and begin series; Thor-c also begin
1200 2400 4200 13,000 32,000 55,000
83-Reprint from the Golden Record Comic Set 17 34 51 117 259 400
With the record (1966) 25 50 75 175 388 600
84-2nd app. Thor 224 448 672 1848 4174 6500
85-1st app. Loki & Heimdall; 1st brief app. Odin (1 panel); 1st app. Asgard
186 372 558 1535 3468 5400
86-1st full app. Odin 88 176 264 704 1577 2450
87-89: 89-Origin Thor retold 70 140 210 560 1255 1950
90-No Kirby-a 56 112 168 448 999 1550
91,92,94,96-Sinnott-a 43 86 129 318 722 1125
93,97-Kirby-a; Tales of Asgard series begins #97 (origin which concludes in #99); origin/1st app. Lava Man 46 92 138 359 805 1250
95-Sinnott-a; Thor vs. Thor 46 92 138 364 820 1275
98,99-Kirby/Heck-a. 98-Origin/1st app. The Human Cobra. 99-1st app. Surtur & Mr. Hyde
35 70 105 252 564 875
100-Kirby/Heck-a; Thor battles Mr. Hyde 34 68 102 245 548 850
101,108: 101-(2/64)-2nd Avengers x-over (w/o Capt. America); see Tales Of Suspense #49 for 1st x-over. 108-(9/64)-Early Dr. Strange & Avengers x-over; ten extra pgs. Kirby-a
25 50 75 175 388 600
102,104-107,110: 102-(3/64) 1st app. Sif. 105-109-Ten extra pgs. Kirby-a in each. 107-1st app. Grey Gargoyle. 110,111-Two part battle vs. The Human Cobra & Mr. Hyde
23 46 69 161 356 550
103-1st app. Enchantress 34 68 102 245 548 850
109-Magneto-c & app. (1st x-over, 10/64) 43 86 129 318 722 1125
111,113: 113-Origin Loki 18 36 54 124 275 425
112-Thor Vs. Hulk (1/65); Origin Loki 54 108 162 432 966 1500
114-Origin/1st app. Absorbing Man 24 48 72 170 378 585
115-Detailed origin of Loki 20 40 60 138 307 475
116,117,120-123,125 14 28 42 96 211 325
118-1st app. Destroyer 21 42 63 147 324 500
119-Intro Hogun, Fandral, Volstagg; 2nd Destroyer 17 34 51 117 259 400
124-Hercules-c/story 15 30 45 100 220 340
503-521: 503-(11/96, $1.50)-The Lost Gods begin; Tom DeFalco scripts & Deodato Studios-c/a. 505-Spider-Man-c/app. 509-Loki-c/app. 514-516-Shang-Chi 3.00
#(-1) Flashback (7/97) Tales of Asgard Donald Blake app. 3.00
Annual 1(1965, 25¢, 72 pgs.)-New Thor vs. Hercules(1st app.)-c/story (see Incredible Hulk #3); Kirby-c/a; r/#85,93,95,97 24 48 72 168 372 575

NOTE: ***Ayers** a-14, 39, 64i, 71i, 74i, 80i. **Bailey** a-43. **Briefer** a-5, 12. **Cameron** a-35. **Check** a-17. **Colan** a-23, 81; c-14. **Ditko** a-33, 38, 50-96; c-58, 67, 71, 88i. **Kirby/Ditko** a-50-83. **Everett** a-20, 48; c-4-7, 9, 36, 37, 39-42, 44, 45, 47. **Forte** a-19, 35, 40, 53. **Heath** a-4-6, 11, 14; c-1, 8, 11, 15, 51. **Heck** a-53, 73. **Kirby** a(p)-51, 52, 56, 57-60, 62-64, 66, 67, 69-89, 93, 97, 98, 100(w/**Heck**), 101-125; c-50-57, 59-66, 68-70, 72-82, 88(w/**Ditko**), 83 & 84(w/**Sinnott**), 85-96(w/**Ayers**), 97-125p. **Leiber/Fox** a-93, 98-102. **Maneely** c-20-22. **Morisi** a-42. **Morrow** a-41, 42. **Orlando** a-30, 45, 57. **Mac Pakula** (Tothish) a-9, 35, 41. **Powell** a-20, 27, 34. **Reinman** a-39, 70, 87, 92, 96i. **Robinson** a-9. **Roussos** a-39. **Robert Sale** a-14. **Severin** a-27; c-30. **Sinnott** a-41; c-50. **Tuska** a-11. **Wildey** a-16.*

JOURNEY INTO MYSTERY (Series and numbering continue from Thor #621)
Marvel Comics: No. 622, Jun, 2011 - No. 655, Oct, 2013 ($3.99/$2.99)

622-Reincarnated young Loki; Thor app.; Braithwaite-a; Hans-c 4.00
622-Variant covers by Art Adams and Lee Weeks 6.00
623-626, 626.1, 627-630-($2.99) Fear Itself tie-in. 628,629-Portacio-a 3.00
631-655: 631-Portacio-a; Aftermath. 632-Hellstrom app. 637,638-Exiled x-over with New Mutants #41-43. 642-644-Crossover with Mighty Thor #19-21. 646-Features Sif 3.00

JOURNEY INTO MYSTERY (2nd Series)
Marvel Comics: Oct, 1972 - No. 19, Oct, 1975

1-Robert Howard adaptation; Starlin/Ploog-a 4 8 12 27 44 60
2-5: 2,3,5-Bloch adapt. 4-H. P. Lovecraft adapt. 3 6 9 17 26 35
6-19: Reprints 3 6 9 16 23 30

NOTE: ***N. Adams** a-2i. **Ditko** r-7, 10, 12, 14, 15, 19; c-10. **Everett** r-9, 14. **G. Kane** a-1p, 2p; c-1-3p. **Kirby** r-7, 13, 15, 18, 19; c-7. **Mort Lawrence** r-2. **Maneely** r-3. **Orlando** r-16. **Reese** a-1, 2i. **Starlin** a-1p, 3p. **Torres** r-16. **Wildey** r-9, 14.*

JOURNEY INTO UNKNOWN WORLDS (Formerly Teen)
Atlas Comics (WFP): No. 36, Sept, 1950 - No. 38, Feb, 1951; No. 4, Apr, 1951 - No. 59, Aug, 1957

36(#1)-Science fiction/weird; "End Of The Earth" c/story
275 550 825 1750 3175 4600
37(#2)-Science fiction; "When Worlds Collide" c/story; Everett-c/a; Hitler story
116 232 348 742 1271 1800
38(#3)-Science fiction 97 194 291 621 1061 1500
4-6,8,10-Science fiction/weird 60 120 180 381 653 925
7-Wolverton-a "Planet of Terror", 6 pgs; electric chair c-inset/story
97 194 291 621 1061 1500
9-Giant eyeball story 77 154 231 493 847 1200
11,12-Krigstein-a 45 90 135 284 480 675
13,16,17,20 40 80 120 246 411 575
14-Wolverton-a "One of Our Graveyards Is Missing", 4 pgs; Tuska-a
73 146 219 467 796 1125
15-Wolverton-a "They Crawl by Night", 5 pgs.; 2 pg. Maneely s/f story
73 146 219 467 796 1125
18,19-Matt Fox-a 45 90 135 284 480 675
21-33: 21-Decapitation-c. 24-Sci/fic story. 26-Atom bomb panel. 27-Sid Check-a. 33-Last pre-code (2/55) 32 64 96 192 314 435
34-Kubert, Torres-a 25 50 75 147 241 335
35-Torres-a 23 46 69 136 223 310
36-45,48,50,53,55,59: 43-Krigstein-a. 44-Davis-a. 45,55,59-Williamson-a in all; with Mayo #55,59. 55-Crandall-a. 48,53-Crandall-a (4 pgs. #48). 48-Check-a. 50-Davis, Crandall-a
22 44 66 132 216 300
46,47,49,52,54,56-58: 54-Torres-a 21 42 63 122 199 275
51-Ditko, Wood-a 24 48 72 142 234 325

NOTE: ***Ayers** a-24, 43, **Berg** a-38(#3), 43. **Lou Cameron** a-33. **Colan** a-37(#2), 6, 17, 19, 20, 23, 39. **Ditko** a-45, 51. **Drucker** a-35, 58. **Everett** a-37(#2), 11, 14, 41, 55, 56; c-37(#2), 11, 13, 14, 17, 22, 47, 48, 50, 53-55, 59. **Forte** a-49. **Fox** a-21i. **Heath** a-36(#1), 4, 6-8, 17, 20, 22, 36i; c-18. **Keller** a-15. **Mort Lawrence** a-38, 39. **Maneely** a-7, 8, 15, 16, 22, 49, 58; c-19, 25, 52. **Morrow** a-48. **Orlando** a-44, 57. **Pakula** a-36. **Powell** a-42, 53, 54. **Reinman** a-8. **Rico** a-21. **Robert Sale** a-24, 49. **Sekowsky** a-4, 5, 9. **Severin** a-38, 51; c-38, 48i, 56. **Sinnott** a-9, 21, 24. **Tuska** a-38(#3), 14. **Wildey** a-25, 43, 44.*

JOURNEYMAN
Image Comics: Aug, 1999 - No. 3, Oct, 1999 ($2.95, B&W, limited series)

1-3-Brandon McKinney-s/a 3.00

JOURNEY TO THE CENTER OF THE EARTH (Movie)
Dell Publishing Co.: No. 1060, Nov-Jan, 1959/60 (one-shot)

Four Color 1060-Pat Boone & James Mason photo-c 9 18 27 61 123 185

JSA (Justice Society of America) (Also see All Star Comics)
DC Comics: Aug, 1999 - No. 87, Sept, 2006 ($2.50/$2.99)

1-Robinson and Goyer-s; funeral of Wesley Dodds 2 4 6 8 10 12
2-5: 4-Return of Dr. Fate 6.00
6-24: 6-Black Adam-c/app. 11,12-Kobra. 16-20-JSA vs. Johnny Sorrow. 19,20-Spectre app. 22-Hawkgirl origin. 23-Hawkman returns 4.00
25-($3.75) Hawkman rejoins the JSA 1 2 3 5 7 9
26-36, 38-49: 27-Capt. Marvel app. 29-Joker: Last Laugh. 31,32-Snejbjerg-a. 33-Ultra-Humanite. 34-Intro. new Crimson Avenger and Hourman. 42-G.A. Mr. Terrific and the Freedom Fighters app. 46-Eclipso returns 3.00
37-($3.50) Johnny Thunder merges with the Thunderbolt; origin new Crimson Avenger 4.00
50-($3.95) Wraparound-c by Pacheco; Sentinel becomes Green Lantern again 4.00
51-74,76-82: 51-Kobra killed. 54-JLA app. 55-Ma Hunkle (Red Tornado) app. 56-58-Black Reign x-over with Hawkman #23-25. 64-Sand returns. 67-Identity Crisis tie-in; Gibbons-a. 68,69,72-81-Ross-c. 73,74-Day of Vengeance tie-in. 76-OMAC tie-in. 82-Infinite Crisis x-over; Levitz-s/Pérez-a 3.00
75-($2.99) Day of Vengeance tie-in; Alex Ross Spectre-c 4.00
83-87: One Year Later; Pérez-c. 83-85,87-Morales-a; Gentleman Ghost app. 85-Begin $2.99-c; Earth-2 Batman, Atom, Sandman, Mr. Terrific app. 86,87-Ordway-a. 3.00
Annual 1 (10/00, $3.50) Planet DC; intro. Nemesis 4.00
...: Black Reign TPB (2005, $12.99) r/#56-58, Hawkman #23-25; Watson cover gallery 13.00
...: Black Vengeance TPB (2006, $19.99) r/#66-75 20.00
...: Darkness Falls TPB (2002, $19.95) r/#6-15 20.00
...: Fair Play TPB (2003, $14.95) r/#26-31 & Secret Files #2 15.00
...: Ghost Stories TPB (2006, $14.99) r/#82-87 15.00
...: Justice Be Done TPB (2000, $14.95) r/Secret Files & #1-5 15.00
...: Lost TPB (2005, $19.99) r/#59-67 20.00
...: Mixed Signals TPB (2006, $14.99) r/#76-81 15.00
...: Our Worlds at War 1 (9/01, $2.95) Jae Lee-c; Saltares-a 3.00
... Presents Green Lantern TPB (2008, $14.99) r/JSA Classified #25,32,33 and Green Lantern: Brightest Day, Blackest Night 15.00
...: Princes of Darkness TPB (2005, $19.95) r/#46-55 20.00
...: Savage Times TPB (2004, $14.95) r/#39-45 15.00
... Secret Files 1 (8/99, $4.95) Origin stories and pin-ups; death of Wesley Dodds

JSA: Classified #2 © DC

J2 #5 © MAR

Judge Dredd (2012 series) #9 © Rebellion

(G.A. Sandman); intro new Hawkgirl 5.00
... Secret Files 2 (9/01, $4.95) Short stories and profile pages 5.00
...: Stealing Thunder TPB (2003, $14.95) r/#32-38; JSA vs. The Ultra-Humanite 15.00
...: The Golden Age TPB (2005, $19.99) r/"The Golden Age" Elseworlds mini-series 20.00
...: The Return of Hawkman TPB (2002, $19.95) r/#16-26 & Secret Files #1 20.00

JSA: ALL STARS
DC Comics: July, 2003 - No. 8, Feb, 2004 ($2.50/$3.50, limited series, back-up stories in Golden Age style)

1-6,8-Goyer & Johns-s/Cassaday-c. 1-Velluto-a; intro. Legacy. 2-Hawkman by Loeb/Sale 3-Dr. Fate by Cooke. 4-Starman by Robinson/Harris. 5-Hourman by Chaykin. 6-Dr. Mid-nite by Azzarello/Risso 3.00
7-($3.50) Mr. Terrific back-up story by Chabon; Lark-a 4.00
TPB (2004, $14.95) r/#1-8 15.00

JSA: ALL STARS
DC Comics: Feb, 2010 - No. 18, Jul, 2011 ($3.99/$2.99)

1-13-Younger JSA members form team. 1-Covers by Williams and Sook 4.00
14-18-($2.99) 3.00
...: Constellations TPB (2010, $14.99) r/#1-6 and sketch art 15.00
...: Glory Days TPB (2011, $17.99) r/#7-13 18.00

JSA: CLASSIFIED (Issues #1-4 reprinted in Power Girl TPB)
DC Comics: Sept, 2005 - No. 39, Aug, 2008 ($2.50/$2.99)

1-(1st printing) Conner-c/a; origin of Power Girl 4.00
1-(1st printing) Adam Hughes variant-c 5.00
1-(2nd & 3rd printings) 2nd-Hughes B&W sketch-c. 3rd-Close-up of Conner-c 3.00
2-11: 2-LSH app. 4-Leads into Infinite Crisis #2. 5-7-Injustice Society app. 10-13-Vandal Savage origin retold; Gulacy-a/c 3.00
12-39: 12-Begin $2.99-c. 17,18-Bane app. 19,20-Morales-a. 21,22-Simonson-s/a 3.00
...: Honor Among Thieves TPB (2007, $14.99) r/#5-9 15.00

JSA LIBERTY FILES: THE WHISTLING SKULL
DC Comics: Feb, 2013 - No. 6, Jul, 2013 ($2.99, limited series)

1-6-Dr. Mid-Nite and Hourman in 1940; B. Clay Moore-s/Tony Harris-c/a 3.00

JSA STRANGE ADVENTURES
DC Comics: Oct, 2004 - No. 6, Mar, 2005 ($3.50, limited series)

1-6-Johnny Thunder as pulp writer; Kitson-a/Watson-c/ Kevin Anderson-s 3.50
TPB (2010, $14.99) r/#1-6 15.00

JSA: THE LIBERTY FILE (Elseworlds)
DC Comics: Feb, 2000 - No. 2, Mar, 2000 ($6.95, limited series)

1,2-Batman, Dr. Mid-Nite and Hourman vs. WW2 Joker; Tony Harris-c/a 7.00
JSA: The Liberty Files TPB (2004, $19.95) r/The Liberty File and The Unholy Three series 20.00

JSA: THE UNHOLY THREE (Elseworlds)(Sequel to JSA: The Liberty File)
DC Comics: 2003 - No. 2, 2003 ($6.95, limited series)

1,2-Batman, Superman and Hourman; Tony Harris-c/a 7.00

JSA VS. KOBRA
DC Comics: Aug, 2009 - No. 6, Jan, 2010 ($2.99, limited series)

1-6-Kramer-a/Ha-c; Jason Burr app. 3.00
TPB (2010, $14.99) r/#1-6; cover gallery 15.00

J2 (Also see A-Next and Juggernaut)
Marvel Comics: Oct, 1998 - No. 12, Sept, 1999 ($1.99)

1-12:1-Juggernaut's son; Lim-a. 2-Two covers; X-People app. 3-J2 battles the Hulk 3.00
Spider-Girl Presents Juggernaut Jr. Vol.1: Secrets & Lies (2006, $7.99, digest) r/#1-6 8.00

JUBILEE (X-Men)
Marvel Comics: Nov, 2004 - No. 6, Apr, 2005 ($2.99)

1-6: 1-Jubilee in a Los Angeles high school; Kirkman-s; Casey Jones-c 3.00

JUDAS COIN, THE
DC Comics: 2012 ($22.99, hardcover graphic novel with dust jacket)

HC-Walt Simonson-s/a/c; Batman, Two-Face, Golden Gladiator, Viking Prince, Captain Fear, Bat Lash, Manhunter 2070 app.; bonus sketch gallery 23.00

JUDENHASS
Aardvark-Vanaheim Press: 2008 ($4.00, B&W, squarebound)

nn-Dave Sim-writer/artist; The Shoah and Jewish persecution through history 4.00

JUDE, THE FORGOTTEN SAINT
Catechetical Guild Education Soc.: 1954 (16 pgs.; 8x11"; full color; paper-c)

nn 6 12 18 28 34 40

J.U.D.G.E.: THE SECRET RAGE
Image Comics: Mar, 2000 - No. 3, May, 2000 ($2.95)

1-3-Greg Horn-s/c/a 3.00

JUDGE COLT
Gold Key: Oct, 1969 - No. 4, Sept, 1970 (Painted cover)

1 3 6 9 16 23 30
2-4 2 4 6 9 13 16

JUDGE DREDD (...Classics #62 on; also see Batman - Judge Dredd, The Law of Dredd & 2000 A.D. Monthly)
Eagle Comics/IPC Magazines Ltd./Quality Comics #34-35, V2#1-37/ Fleetway #38 on: Nov, 1983 - No. 35, 1986; V2#1, Oct, 1986 - No. 77, 1993

1-Bolland-c/a 3 6 9 16 23 30
2-5 1 2 3 5 6 8
6-35 5.00
V2#1-('86)-New look begins 5.00
2-10 4.00
11-77: 20-Begin $1.50-c. 21/22, 23/24-Two issue numbers in one. 28-1st app. Megaman (super-hero). 39-Begin $1.75-c. 51-Begin $1.95-c. 53-Bolland-a. 57-Reprints 1st published Judge Dredd story 3.00
Special 1 5.00
NOTE: *Bolland a-1-6, 8, 10; c-1-10, 15. Guice c-V2#23/24, 26, 27.*

JUDGE DREDD (3rd Series)
DC Comics: Aug, 1994 - No. 18, Jan, 1996 ($1.95)

1-18: 12-Begin $2.25-c 3.00
nn ($5.95)-Movie adaptation, Sienkiewicz-c 6.00

JUDGE DREDD
IDW Publishing: Nov, 2012 - Present ($3.99)

1-17: 1-Swierczynski-s; six covers 4.00

JUDGE DREDD CLASSICS (Reprints)
IDW Publishing: Jul, 2013 - Present ($3.99)

1-6-Wagner & Grant-s 4.00
Free Comic Book Day 2013 (5/13, free) Judge Death app.; Walter the Wobot back-ups 3.00

JUDGE DREDD: LEGENDS OF THE LAW
DC Comics: Dec, 1994 - No. 13, Dec, 1995 ($1.95)

1-13: 1-5-Dorman-c 3.00

JUDGE DREDD: MEGA-CITY TWO
IDW Publishing: Jan, 2014 - Present ($3.99)

1,2-Wolk-s/Farinas-a 4.00

JUDGE DREDD'S CRIME FILE
Eagle Comics: Aug, 1985 - No. 6, Feb, 1986 ($1.25, limited series)

1-6: 1-Byrne-a 5.00

JUDGE DREDD: THE EARLY CASES
Eagle Comics: Feb, 1986 - No. 6, Jul, 1986 ($1.25, Mega-series, Mando paper)

1-6: 2000 A.D.-r 5.00

JUDGE DREDD: THE JUDGE CHILD QUEST (Judge Child in indicia)
Eagle Comics: Aug, 1984 - No. 5, Oct, 1984 ($1.25, Lim. series, Baxter paper)

1-5: 2000A.D.-r; Bolland-c/a 6.00

JUDGE DREDD: THE MEGAZINE
Fleetway/Quality: 1991 - No. 3 ($4.95, stiff-c, squarebound, 52 pgs.)

1-3 5.00

JUDGE DREDD VS. ALIENS: INCUBUS
Dark Horse Comics: March, 2003 - No. 4, June, 2003 ($2.99, limited series)

1-4-Flint-a/Wagner & Diggle-s 3.00

JUDGE DREDD: YEAR ONE
IDW Publishing: Mar, 2013 - No. 4, Jul, 2013 ($3.99)

1-4-Matt Smith-s/Simon Coleby-a 4.00

JUDGE PARKER
Argo: Feb, 1956 - No. 2, 1956

1-Newspaper strip reprints 7 14 21 35 43 50
2 5 10 15 24 30 35

JUDGMENT DAY
Awesome Entertainment: June, 1997 - No. 3, Oct, 1997 ($2.50, limited series)

1-3: 1 Alpha-Moore-s/Liefeld-c/a(p) flashback art by various in all. 2 Omega. 3 Final Judgment. All have a variant cover by Dave Gibbons 3.00
...Aftermath-($3.50) Moore-s/Kane-a; Youngblood, Glory, New Men, Maximage, Allies and Spacehunter short stories. Also has a variant cover by Dave Gibbons 4.00
TPB (Checker Books, 2003, $16.95) r/series 17.00

Judomaster #94 © CC

Jughead's Double Digest #62 © AP

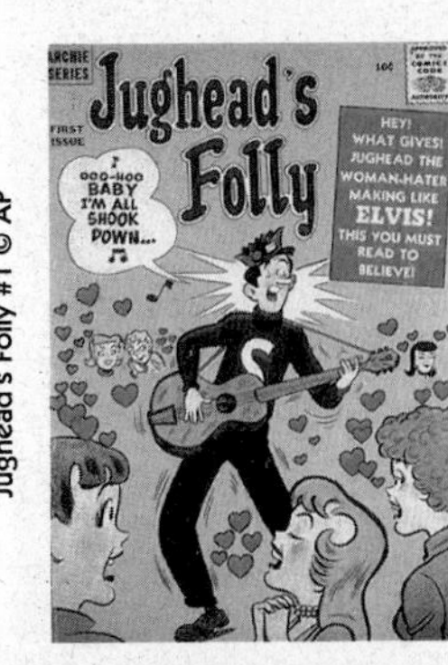

Jughead's Folly #1 © AP

JUDO JOE
Jay-Jay Corp.: Aug, 1953 - No. 3, Dec, 1953 (Judo lessons in each issue)

	GD 2.0	VG 4.0	FN 6.0	VF 8.0	VF/NM 9.0	NM- 9.2
1-Drug ring story	12	24	36	67	94	120
2,3: 3-Hypo needle story	8	16	24	44	57	70

JUDOMASTER (Gun Master #84-89) (Also see Crisis on Infinite Earths, Sarge Steel #6, Special War Series, & Thunderbolt)
Charlton Comics: No. 89, May-June, 1966 - No. 98, Dec, 1967 (Two No. 89's)

	GD 2.0	VG 4.0	FN 6.0	VF 8.0	VF/NM 9.0	NM- 9.2
89-3rd app. Judomaster	4	8	12	25	40	55
90-Origin of Thunderbolt	4	8	12	23	37	50
91-Sarge Steel begins	3	6	9	21	33	45
92-98: 93-Intro. Tiger	3	6	9	20	31	42
93,94,96,98 (Modern Comics reprint, 1977)						6.00

NOTE: *Morisi Thunderbolt #90. #91 has 1 pg. biography on writer/artist Frank McLaughlin.*

JUDY CANOVA (Formerly My Experience) (Stage, screen, radio)
Fox Features Syndicate: No. 23, May, 1950 - No. 3, Sept, 1950

	GD 2.0	VG 4.0	FN 6.0	VF 8.0	VF/NM 9.0	NM- 9.2
23(#1)-Wood-c,a(p)?	25	50	75	150	245	340
24-Wood-a(p)	24	48	72	144	237	330
3-Wood-c; Wood/Orlando-a	27	54	81	158	259	360

JUDY GARLAND (See Famous Stars)

JUDY JOINS THE WAVES
Toby Press: 1951 (For U.S. Navy)

	GD 2.0	VG 4.0	FN 6.0	VF 8.0	VF/NM 9.0	NM- 9.2
nn	7	14	21	37	46	55

JUGGERNAUT (See X-Men)
Marvel Comics: Apr, 1997, Nov, 1999 ($2.99, one-shots)

	GD 2.0	VG 4.0	FN 6.0	VF 8.0	VF/NM 9.0	NM- 9.2
1-(4/97) Kelly-s/ Rouleau-a						3.00
1-(11/99) Casey-s; Eighth Day x-over; Thor, Iron Man, Spidey app.						3.00

JUGHEAD (Formerly Archie's Pal...)
Archie Publications: No. 127, Dec, 1965 - No. 352, June, 1987

	GD 2.0	VG 4.0	FN 6.0	VF 8.0	VF/NM 9.0	NM- 9.2
127-130: 129-LBJ on cover	3	6	9	17	26	35
131,133,135-160(9/68)	3	6	9	15	22	28
132,134: 132-Shield-c; The Fly & Black Hood app.; Shield cameo. 134-Shield-c	4	8	12	27	44	60
161-180	2	4	6	13	18	22
181-199	2	4	6	9	13	16
200(1/72)	2	4	6	11	16	20
201-240(5/75)	2	4	6	8	10	12
241-270(11/77)	1	2	3	5	7	9
271-299	1	2	3	4	5	7
300(5/80)-Anniversary issue; infinity-c	1	2	3	5	6	8
301-320(1/82)						5.00
321-324,326-352						4.00
325-(10/82) Cheryl Blossom app. (not on cover); same month as intro. (cover & story) in Archie's Girls, Betty & Veronica #320; Jason Blossom app.; DeCarlo-a	4	8	12	27	44	60

JUGHEAD (2nd Series)(Becomes Archie's Pal Jughead Comics #46 on)
Archie Enterprises: Aug, 1987 - No. 45, May, 1993 (.75/$1.00/$1.25)

	GD 2.0	VG 4.0	FN 6.0	VF 8.0	VF/NM 9.0	NM- 9.2
1	1	2	3	4	5	7
2-10						4.00
11-45: 4-X-Mas issue. 17-Colan-c/a						3.00

JUGHEAD AND ARCHIE DOUBLE DIGEST
Archie Comic Publ.: Jun, 2014 - Present ($3.99, digest-size)

	GD 2.0	VG 4.0	FN 6.0	VF 8.0	VF/NM 9.0	NM- 9.2
1-Reprints; That Wilkin Boy app.						4.00

JUGHEAD & FRIENDS DIGEST MAGAZINE
Archie Publ.: June, 2005 - No. 38, Aug, 2010 ($2.39/$2.49/$2.69, digest-size)

	GD 2.0	VG 4.0	FN 6.0	VF 8.0	VF/NM 9.0	NM- 9.2
1-38: 1-That Wilkin Boy app.						3.00

JUGHEAD AS CAPTAIN HERO (See Archie as Pureheart the Powerful, Archie Giant Series Magazine #142 & Life With Archie)
Archie Publications: Oct, 1966 - No. 7, Nov, 1967

	GD 2.0	VG 4.0	FN 6.0	VF 8.0	VF/NM 9.0	NM- 9.2
1-Super hero parody	6	12	18	41	76	110
2	4	8	12	28	47	65
3-7	4	8	12	25	40	55

JUGHEAD COMICS. NIGHT AT GEPPI'S ENTERTAINMENT MUSEUM
Archie Comic Publ. Inc: 2008

	GD 2.0	VG 4.0	FN 6.0	VF 8.0	VF/NM 9.0	NM- 9.2
Free Comic Book Day giveaway - New story; Archie gang visits GEM; Steve Geppi app.						3.00

JUGHEAD JONES COMICS DIGEST, THE (...Magazine No. 10-64; Jughead Jones Digest Magazine #65)
Archie Publ.: June, 1977 - No. 100, May, 1996 ($1.35/$1.50/$1.75, digest-size, 128 pgs.)

	GD 2.0	VG 4.0	FN 6.0	VF 8.0	VF/NM 9.0	NM- 9.2
1-Neal Adams-a; Capt. Hero-r	3	6	9	20	31	42
2(9/77)-Neal Adams-a	3	6	9	15	22	28
3-6,8-10	2	4	6	11	16	20
7-Origin Jaguar-r; N. Adams-a.	2	4	6	13	18	22
11-20: 13-r/1957 Jughead's Folly	2	4	6	8	10	12
21-50	1	2	3	4	5	7
51-70						5.00
71-100						3.00

JUGHEAD'S BABY TALES
Archie Comics: Spring, 1994 - No. 2, Wint. 1994 ($2.00, 52 pgs.)

	GD 2.0	VG 4.0	FN 6.0	VF 8.0	VF/NM 9.0	NM- 9.2
1,2: 1-Bound-in pull-out poster						4.00

JUGHEAD'S DINER
Archie Comics: Apr, 1990 - No. 7, Apr, 1991 ($1.00)

	GD 2.0	VG 4.0	FN 6.0	VF 8.0	VF/NM 9.0	NM- 9.2
1						4.00
2-7						3.00

JUGHEAD'S DOUBLE DIGEST (...Magazine #5)
Archie Comics: Oct, 1989 - No. 200, Apr, 2014 ($2.25 - $3.99/$5.99)

	GD 2.0	VG 4.0	FN 6.0	VF 8.0	VF/NM 9.0	NM- 9.2
1	2	4	6	8	10	12
2-10: 2,5-Capt. Hero stories	1	2	3	5	6	8
11-25						5.00
26-195: 58-Begin $2.99-c. 66-Begin $3.19-c. 91-Begin $3.59-c. 138-Reprints entire Jughead #1 (1949). 139-142-"New Look" Jughead; Staton-a. 148-Begin $3.99-c						4.00
196-200-($5.99) Titled "Jughead's Double Double Digest"						6.00
Archie New Look Series Book 2, Jughead "The Matchmakers" TPB (2009, $10.95) r/new look series in #139-142; new cover by Staton & Milgrom						11.00

JUGHEAD'S EAT-OUT COMIC BOOK MAGAZINE (See Archie Giant Series Magazine No. 170)

JUGHEAD'S FANTASY
Archie Publications: Aug, 1960 - No. 3, Dec, 1960

	GD 2.0	VG 4.0	FN 6.0	VF 8.0	VF/NM 9.0	NM- 9.2
1	15	30	45	105	233	360
2	10	20	30	66	138	210
3	9	18	27	57	111	165

JUGHEAD'S FOLLY
Archie Publications (Close-Up): 1957 (36 pgs.)(one-shot)

	GD 2.0	VG 4.0	FN 6.0	VF 8.0	VF/NM 9.0	NM- 9.2
1-Jughead a la Elvis (Rare) (1st reference to Elvis in comics?)	57	114	171	362	619	875

JUGHEAD'S JOKES
Archie Publications: Aug, 1967 - No. 78, Sept, 1982
(No. 1-8, 38 on: reg. size; No. 9-23: 68 pgs.; No. 24-37: 52 pgs.)

	GD 2.0	VG 4.0	FN 6.0	VF 8.0	VF/NM 9.0	NM- 9.2
1	6	12	18	37	66	95
2	4	8	12	23	37	50
3-8	3	6	9	16	24	32
9,10 (68 pgs.)	3	6	9	18	28	38
11-23(4/71) (68 pgs.)	3	6	9	16	23	30
24-37(1/74) (52 pgs.)	2	4	6	11	16	20
38-50(9/76)	1	3	4	6	8	10
51-78						6.00

JUGHEAD'S PAL HOT DOG (See Laugh #14 for 1st app.)
Archie Comics: Jan, 1990 - No. 5, Oct, 1990 ($1.00)

	GD 2.0	VG 4.0	FN 6.0	VF 8.0	VF/NM 9.0	NM- 9.2
1						4.00
2-5						3.00

JUGHEAD'S SOUL FOOD
Spire Christian Comics (Fleming H. Revell Co.): 1979 (49¢/59¢)

	GD 2.0	VG 4.0	FN 6.0	VF 8.0	VF/NM 9.0	NM- 9.2
nn-Low print run	3	6	9	15	22	28

JUGHEAD'S TIME POLICE
Archie Comics: July, 1990 - No. 6, May, 1991 ($1.00, bi-monthly)

	GD 2.0	VG 4.0	FN 6.0	VF 8.0	VF/NM 9.0	NM- 9.2
1						4.00
2-6: Colan a-3-6p; c-3-6						3.00

JUGHEAD WITH ARCHIE DIGEST (...Plus Betty & Veronica & Reggie Too No. 1,2; ...Magazine #33-?, 101-on; ...Comics Digest Mag.)
Archie Pub.: Mar, 1974 - No. 200, May, 2005 ($1.00-$2.39)

	GD 2.0	VG 4.0	FN 6.0	VF 8.0	VF/NM 9.0	NM- 9.2
1	5	10	15	31	53	75
2	3	6	9	21	33	45
3-10	3	6	9	17	26	35
11-13,15-17,19,20: Capt. Hero-r in #14-16; Capt. Pureheart #17,19	2	4	6	10	14	18
14,18,21,22-Pureheart the Powerful in #18,21,22	2	4	6	11	16	20
23-30: 29-The Shield-r. 30-The Fly-r	1	3	4	6	8	10

Jumbo Comics #27 © FH

Jungle Action #12 © MAR

Jungle Comics #82 © FH

	GD 2.0	VG 4.0	FN 6.0	VF 8.0	VF/NM 9.0	NM- 9.2
31-50,100	1	2	3	5	6	8
51-99	1	2	3	4	5	7
101-121						4.00
122-200: 156-Begin $2.19-c. 180-Begin $2.39-c						3.00

JUICE SQUEEZERS
Dark Horse Comics: Jan, 2014 - No. 4, Apr, 2014 ($3.99, limited series)

	GD	VG	FN	VF	VF/NM	NM-
1-4-David Lapham-s/a/c						4.00

JUKE BOX COMICS
Famous Funnies: Mar, 1948 - No. 6, Jan, 1949

	GD	VG	FN	VF	VF/NM	NM-
1-Toth-c/a; Hollingsworth-a	37	74	111	222	361	500
2-Transvestism story	22	44	66	132	216	300
3-6: 3-Peggy Lee story. 4-Jimmy Durante line drawn-c. 6-Features Desi Arnaz plus Arnaz line drawn-c	18	36	54	105	165	225

JUMBO COMICS (Created by S.M. Iger)
Fiction House Magazines (Real Adv. Publ. Co.): Sept, 1938 - No. 167, Mar, 1953 (No. 1-3: 68 pgs.; No. 4-8: 52 pgs.)(No. 1-8 oversized-10-1/2x14-1/2"; black & white)

	GD	VG	FN	VF	VF/NM	NM-
1-(Rare)-Sheena Queen of the Jungle(1st app.) by Meskin, Hawks of the Seas (The Hawk #10 on; see Feature Funnies #3) by Eisner, The Hunchback by Dick Briefer (ends #8), Wilton of the West (ends #24), Inspector Dayton (ends #67) & ZX-5 (ends #140) begin; 1st comic art by Jack Kirby (Count of Monte Cristo & Wilton of the West); Mickey Mouse appears (1 panel) with brief biography of Walt Disney; 1st app. Peter Pupp by Bob Kane. Note: Sheena was created by Iger for publication in England as a newspaper strip. The early issues of Jumbo contain Sheena strip-r; multiple panel-c 1,2,7	3000	6000	9000	24,000	-	-
2-(Rare)-Origin Sheena. Diary of Dr. Hayward by Kirby (also #3) plus 2 other stories; contains strip from Universal Film featuring Edgar Bergen & Charlie McCarthy plus-c (preview of film)	1000	2000	3000	7500	-	-
3-Last Kirby issue	750	1500	2250	6000	-	-
4-(Scarce)-Origin The Hawk by Eisner; Wilton of the West by Fine (ends #14)(1st comic work); Count of Monte Cristo by Fine (ends #15); The Diary of Dr. Hayward by Fine (cont'd #8,9)	700	1400	2100	5600	-	-
5-Christmas-c	625	1250	1875	5000	-	-
6-8-Last B&W issue. #8 was a 1939 N. Y. World's Fair Special Edition; Frank Buck's Jungleland story	550	1100	1650	4400	-	-
9-Stuart Taylor begins by Fine (ends #140); Fine-c; 1st color issue (8-9/39)-1st Sheena (jungle) cover; 8-1/4x10-1/4" (oversized in width only)	700	1400	2100	5600	-	-
10-Regular size 68 pg. issues begin; Sheena dons new costume w/origin costume; Stuart Taylor sci/fi-c; classic Lou Fine-c.	400	800	1200	2800	4900	7000
11-13: 12-The Hawk-c by Eisner. 13-Eisner-c	177	354	531	1124	1937	2750
14-Intro. Lightning (super-hero) on-c only	181	362	543	1158	1979	2800
15-1st Lightning story and begins, ends #41	135	270	405	864	1482	2100
16-Lightning-c	148	296	444	947	1624	2300
17,18,20: 17-Lightning part-c	110	220	330	704	1202	1700
19-Classic Sheena Giant Ape-c by Powell	129	258	387	826	1413	2000
21-30: 22-1st Tom, Dick & Harry; origin The Hawk retold. 25-Midnight the Black Stallion begins, ends #65	74	148	222	470	810	1150
31-(9/41)-1st app. Mars God of War in Stuart Taylor story (see Planet Comics #15.)	71	142	213	454	777	1100
32-40: 35-Shows V2#11 (correct number does not appear)	57	114	171	362	619	875
41-50: 42-Ghost Gallery begins, ends #167	43	86	129	271	461	650
51-60: 52-Last Tom, Dick & Harry	39	78	117	240	395	550
61-70: 68-Sky Girl begins, ends #130; not in #79	34	68	102	199	325	450
71-93,95-99: 89-ZX5 becomes a private eye.	26	52	78	154	252	350
94-Used in Love and Death by Legman	28	56	84	165	270	375
100	28	56	84	165	270	375
101-121	22	44	66	132	216	300
121-140,150-158: 155-Used in **POP**, pg. 98	20	40	60	118	192	265
141-149-Two Sheena stories. 141-Long Bow, Indian Boy begins, ends #160	21	42	63	122	199	275
159-163: Space Scouts serial in all. 160-Last jungle-c (6/52). 161-Ghost Gallery covers begin, end #167. 163-Suicide Smith app.	20	40	60	114	182	250
164-The Star Pirate begins, ends #165	20	40	60	114	182	250
165-167: 165,167-Space Rangers app.	20	40	60	114	182	250

NOTE: *Bondage covers, negligee panels, torture, etc. are common in this series. Hawks of the Seas, Inspector Dayton, Spies in Action, Sports Shorts, & Uncle Otto by Eisner, #1-7. Hawk by* ***Eisner****-#10-15.* ***Eisner*** *c-1-8, 12-14. 1pg. Patsy pin-ups in 92-97, 99-101. Sheena by* ***Meskin****-#1, 4; by* ***Powell****-#2, 3, 5-28;* ***Powell*** *c-14, 16, 17, 19.* ***Powell/Eisner*** *c-15. Sky Girl by* ***Matt Baker****-#69-78, 80-130. ZX-5 & Ghost Gallery by* ***Kamen****-#90-130.* ***Bailey*** *a-3-8.* ***Briefer*** *a-1-8, 10.* ***Fine*** *a-14; c-9-11.* ***Kamen*** *a-101, 105, 123, 132; c-105, 121-145.* ***Bob Kane*** *a-1-8.* ***Whitman*** *c-146-167(most). Jungle c-9, 13, 15, 17 on.*

JUMPER: JUMPSCARS
Oni Press: Jan, 2008 ($14.95, graphic novel)

	GD	VG	FN	VF	VF/NM	NM-
SC-Prelude to 2008 movie Jumper; Brian Hurtt-a/c						15.00

JUNGLE ACTION
Atlas Comics (IPC): Oct, 1954 - No. 6, Aug, 1955

	GD	VG	FN	VF	VF/NM	NM-
1-Leopard Girl begins by Al Hartley (#1,3); Jungle Boy by Forte; Maneely-a in all	41	82	123	256	428	600
2-(3-D effect cover)	40	80	120	246	411	575
3-6: 3-Last precode (2/55)	27	54	81	158	259	360

NOTE: ***Maneely*** *c-1, 2, 5, 6.* ***Romita*** *a-3, 6.* ***Shores*** *a-3, 6; c-3, 4?.*

JUNGLE ACTION (...& Black Panther #18-21?)
Marvel Comics Group: Oct, 1972 - No. 24, Nov, 1976

	GD	VG	FN	VF	VF/NM	NM-
1-Lorna, Jann-r (All reprints in 1-4)	3	6	9	14	20	25
2-4	2	4	6	9	12	15
5-Black Panther begins (r/Avengers #62)	3	6	9	21	33	45
6-New solo Black Panther stories begin	3	6	9	21	33	45
7,9,10: 9-Contains pull-out centerfold ad by Mark Jewelers	2	4	6	13	18	22
8-Origin Black Panther	3	6	9	16	23	30
11-20,23,24: 19-23-KKK x-over. 23-r/#22. 24-1st Wind Eagle; story contd in Marvel Premiere #51-#53	2	4	6	9	13	16
21,22-(Regular 25¢ edition)(5,7/76)	2	4	6	9	13	16
21,22-(30¢-c variant, limited distribution)	3	6	9	19	30	40

NOTE: ***Buckler*** *a-6-9p, 22; c-8p, 12p.* ***Buscema*** *a-5p; c-22.* ***Byrne*** *c-23.* ***Gil Kane*** *a-8p; c-2, 4, 10p, 11p, 13-17, 19, 24.* ***Kirby*** *c-18.* ***Maneely*** *r-1.* ***Russell*** *a-13i.* ***Starlin*** *c-3p.*

JUNGLE ADVENTURES
Super Comics: 1963 - 1964 (Reprints)

	GD	VG	FN	VF	VF/NM	NM-
10,12,15,17,18: 10-r/Terrors of the Jungle #4 & #10(Rulah). 12-r/Zoot #14(Rulah).15-r/Kaanga from Jungle #152 & Tiger Girl. 17-All Jo-Jo-r. 18-Reprints/White Princess of the Jungle #1; no Kinstler-a; origin of both White Princess & Cap'n Courage	3	6	9	18	28	38

JUNGLE ADVENTURES
Skywald Comics: Mar, 1971 - No. 3, June, 1971 (25¢, 52 pgs.) (Pre-code reprints & new-s)

	GD	VG	FN	VF	VF/NM	NM-
1-Zangar origin; reprints of Jo-Jo, Blue Gorilla(origin)/White Princess #3, Kinstler-r/White Princess #2	3	6	9	19	30	40
2,3: 2-Zangar, Sheena-r/Sheena #17 & Jumbo #162, Jo-Jo, origin Slave Girl-r. 3-Zangar, Jo-Jo, White Princess, Rulah-r	3	6	9	15	22	28

JUNGLE BOOK (See King Louie and Mowgli, Movie Comics, Mowgli..., Walt Disney Showcase #45 & Walt Disney's The Jungle Book)

JUNGLE CAT (Disney)
Dell Publishing Co.: No. 1136, Sept-Nov, 1960 (one shot)

	GD	VG	FN	VF	VF/NM	NM-
Four Color 1136-Movie, photo-c	6	12	18	37	66	95

JUNGLE COMICS
Fiction House Magazines: 1/40 - No. 157, 3/53; No. 158, Spr, 1953 - No. 163, Summer, 1954

	GD	VG	FN	VF	VF/NM	NM-
1-Origin The White Panther, Kaanga, Lord of the Jungle, Tabu, Wizard of the Jungle; Wambi, the Jungle Boy, Camilla & Capt. Terry Thunder begin (all 1st app.). Lou Fine-c	514	1028	1542	3750	6625	9500
2-Fantomah, Mystery Woman of the Jungle begins, ends #51; The Red Panther begins, ends #26	181	362	543	1158	1979	2800
3,4	145	290	435	921	1586	2250
5-Classic Eisner-c	168	336	504	1075	1838	2600
6-10: 7,8-Powell-c	84	168	252	538	919	1300
11-Classic dinosaur-c	77	154	231	493	847	1200
12-20: 13-Tuska-c	58	116	174	371	636	900
21-30: 25-Shows V2#1 (correct number does not appear). #27-New origin Fantomah, Daughter of the Pharoahs; Camilla dons new costume	50	100	150	315	533	750
31-40	40	80	120	244	402	560
41,43-50	36	72	108	216	351	485
42-Kaanga by Crandall, 12 pgs.	38	76	114	228	369	510
51-60	32	64	96	190	310	430
61-70: 67-Cover swipes Crandall splash pg. in #42	28	56	84	165	270	375
71-80: 79-New origin Tabu	24	48	72	142	234	325
81-97,99	23	46	69	136	223	310
98-Used in **SOTI**, pg. 185 & illo "In ordinary comic books, there are pictures within pictures for children who know how to look;" used by N.Y. Legis. Comm.	36	72	108	211	343	475
100	27	54	81	160	263	365
101-110: 104-In Camilla story, villain is Dr. Wertham	22	44	66	132	216	300
111-120: 118-Clyde Beatty app.	21	42	63	124	202	280
121-130	20	40	60	118	192	265

131-163: 135-Desert Panther begins in Terry Thunder (origin), not in #137; ends (dies) #138.

Jungle Jim #13 © STD

Jungle Tales #1 © MAR

Junior Comics #11 © FOX

GD 2.0 | VG 4.0 | FN 6.0 | VF 8.0 | VF/NM 9.0 | NM- 9.2

139-Last 52 pg. issue. 141-Last Tabu. 143,145-Used in **POP**, pg. 99. 151-Last Camilla & Terry Thunder. 152-Tiger Girl begins. 158-Last Wambi; Sheena app. 19 38 57 111 176 240
I.W. Reprint #1,9: 1-r/? 9-r/#151 3 6 9 16 24 32

NOTE: *Bondage covers, negligee panels, torture, etc. are common to this series. Camilla by* **Fran Hopper**-*#70-92; by* **Baker**-*#69, 100-113, 115, 116; by* **Lubbers**-*#97-99 by* **Tuska**-*#63, 65. Kaanga by* **John Celardo**-*#80-113; by* **Larsen**-*#71, 75-79; by* **Moreira**-*#58, 60, 61, 63-70, 72-74; by* **Tuska**-*#37, 62; by* **Whitman**-*#114-163. Tabu by* **Larsen**-*#59-75, 82-92; by* **Whitman**-*#93-115. Terry Thunder by* **Hopper**-*#71, 72; by* **Celardo**-*#78, 79; by* **Lubbers**-*#80-85. Tiger Girl-r by* **Baker**-*#152, 153, 155-157, 159. Wambi by* **Baker**-*#62-67, 74.* **Astarita** *c-45, 46.* **Celardo** *a-78; c-98-113.* **Crandall** *c-67 from splash pg.* **Eisner** *c-2, 5, 6.* **Fine** *c-1.* **Larsen** *a-65, 66, 71, 72, 74, 75, 79, 83, 84, 87-90.* **Moreira** *c-43, 44.* **Morisi** *a-51.* **Powell** *c-7, 8.* **Sultan** *c-3, 4.* **Tuska** *c-13.* **Whitman** *c-132-163(most).* **Zolnerowich** *c-11, 12, 18-41.*

JUNGLE COMICS
Blackthorne Publishing: May, 1988 - No. 4 ($2.00, B&W/color)
1-Dave Stevens-c; B. Jones scripts in all 2 4 6 10 14 18
2-4: 2-B&W-a begins 4.00

JUNGLE GIRL (See Lorna, the...)

JUNGLE GIRL (Nyoka, Jungle Girl No. 2 on)
Fawcett Publications: Fall, 1942 (one-shot)(No month listed)
1-Bondage-c; photo of Kay Aldridge who played Nyoka in movie serial app. on-c. Adaptation of the classic Republic movie serial Perils of Nyoka. 1st comic to devote entire contents to a movie serial adaptation 132 264 396 838 1444 2050

JUNGLE GIRL
Dynamite Entertainment: No. 0, 2007 - 2009 (25¢/$2.99/$3.50)
0-(25¢-c) Eight page preview; preview of Superpowers w/Alex Ross-a 3.00
1-5-Frank Cho-plot/cover; Batista-a/variant-c 3.00
... Season 2 ($3.50) 1-5-Two covers by Cho & Batista 3.50

JUNGLE GIRLS
AC Comics: 1989 - No. 16, 1993 (B&W)
1-16: 1-4,10,13-16-New story & "good girl" reprints. 5-9,11,12-All g.g. reprints (Baker, Powell, Lubbers, others) 3.00

JUNGLE JIM (Also see Ace Comics)
Standard Comics (Best Books): No. 11, Jan, 1949 - No. 20, Apr, 1951
11 12 24 36 67 94 120
12-20 8 16 24 44 57 70

JUNGLE JIM
Dell Publishing Co.: No. 490, 8/53 - No. 1020, 8-10/59 (Painted-c)
Four Color 490(#1) 7 14 21 44 82 120
Four Color 565(#2, 6/54) 5 10 15 30 50 70
3(10-12/54)-5 4 8 12 27 44 60
6-19(1-3/59), Four Color 1020(#20) 4 8 12 25 40 55

JUNGLE JIM
King Features Syndicate: No. 5, Dec, 1967
5-Reprints Dell #5; Wood-c 2 4 6 10 14 18

JUNGLE JIM (Continued from Dell series)
Charlton Comics: No. 22, Feb, 1969 - No. 28, Feb, 1970 (#21 was an overseas edition only)
22-Dan Flagg begins; Ditko/Wood-a 3 6 9 20 31 42
23-26: 23-Last Dan Flagg; Howard-c. 24-Jungle People begin 3 6 9 15 21 26
27,28: 27-Ditko/Howard-a. 28-Ditko-a 3 6 9 16 24 32
NOTE: *Ditko cover of #22 reprints story panels*

JUNGLE JO
Fox Feature Syndicate (Hero Books): Mar, 1950 - No. 3, Sept, 1950
nn-Jo-Jo blanked out in titles of interior stories, leaving Congo King; came out after Jo-Jo #29 (intended as Jo-Jo #30?) 54 108 162 343 574 825
1-Tangi begins; part Wood-a 57 114 171 362 619 875
2,3 42 84 126 265 445 625

JUNGLE LIL (Dorothy Lamour #2 on; also see Feature Stories Magazine)
Fox Feature Syndicate (Hero Books): April, 1950
1 47 94 141 296 498 700

JUNGLE TALES (Jann of the Jungle No. 8 on)
Atlas Comics (CSI): Sept, 1954 - No. 7, Sept, 1955
1-Jann of the Jungle 41 82 123 256 428 600
2-7: 3-Last precode (1/55) 30 60 90 177 289 400
NOTE: **Heath** *c-5.* **Heck** *a-6, 7.* **Maneely** *a-2; c-1, 3.* **Shores** *a-5-7; c-4, 6.* **Tuska** *a-2.*

JUNGLE TALES OF TARZAN
Charlton Comics: Dec, 1964 - No. 4, July, 1965
1 5 10 15 33 57 80
2-4 4 8 12 22 37 50
NOTE: **Giordano** *c-3p.* **Glanzman** *a-1-3.* **Montes/Bache** *a-4.*

JUNGLE TERROR (See Harvey Comics Hits No. 54)

JUNGLE THRILLS (Formerly Sports Thrills; Terrors of the Jungle #17 on)
Star Publications: No. 16, Feb, 1952; Dec, 1953; No. 7, 1954
16-Phantom Lady & Rulah story-reprint/All Top No. 15; used in **POP**, pg. 98,99; L. B. Cole-c 53 106 159 334 567 800
3-D 1(12/53, 25¢)-Came w/glasses; Jungle Lil & Jungle Jo appear; L. B. Cole-c 53 106 159 334 567 800
7-Titled 'Picture Scope Jungle Adventures;' (1954, 36 pgs, 15¢)-3-D effect c/stories; story & coloring book; Disbrow-a/script; L.B. Cole-c 53 106 159 334 567 800

JUNGLE TWINS, THE (Tono & Kono)
Gold Key/Whitman No. 18: Apr, 1972 - No. 17, Nov, 1975; No. 18, May, 1982
1-All painted covers 3 6 9 16 23 30
2-5 2 4 6 9 12 15
6-18: 18(Whitman, 5/82)-Reprints 1 3 4 6 8 10
NOTE: *UFO c/story No. 13. Painted-c No. 1-17.* **Spiegle** *c-18.*

JUNGLE WAR STORIES (Guerrilla War No. 12 on)
Dell Publishing Co.: July-Sept, 1962 - No. 11, Apr-June, 1965 (Painted-c)
01-384-209 (#1) 4 8 12 23 37 50
2-11 3 6 9 16 24 32

JUNIE PROM (Also see Dexter Comics)
Dearfield Publishing Co.: Winter, 1947-48 - No. 7, Aug, 1949
1-Teen-age 15 30 45 90 140 190
2 10 20 30 56 76 95
3-7 9 18 27 50 65 80

JUNIOR
Fantagraphics Books: June, 2000 - No. 5, Jan, 2001 ($2.95, B&W)
1-5-Peter Bagge-s/a 3.00

JUNIOR CARROT PATROL (Jr. Carrot Patrol #2)
Dark Horse Comics: May, 1989; No. 2, Nov, 1990 ($2.00, B&W)
1,2-Flaming Carrot spin-off. 1-Bob Burden-c(i) 3.00

JUNIOR COMICS (Formerly Li'l Pan; becomes Western Outlaws with #17)
Fox Feature Syndicate: No. 9, Sept, 1947 - No. 16, July, 1948
9-Feldstein-c/a; headlights-c 148 296 444 947 1624 2300
10-16: 10-12,14-16-Feldstein-c/a; headlights-c 135 270 405 864 1482 2100

JUNIOR FUNNIES (Formerly Tiny Tot Funnies No. 9)
Harvey Publ. (King Features Synd.): No. 10, Aug, 1951 - No. 13, Feb, 1952
10-Partial reprints in all; Blondie, Dagwood, Daisy, Henry, Popeye, Felix, Katzenjammer Kids 6 12 18 28 34 40
11-13 5 10 15 24 30 35

JUNIOR HOPP COMICS
Stanmor Publ.: Feb, 1952 - No. 3, July, 1952
1-Teenage humor 11 22 33 62 86 110
2,3: 3-Dave Berg-a 7 14 21 37 46 55

JUNIOR MEDICS OF AMERICA, THE
E. R. Squire & Sons: No. 1359, 1957 (15¢)
1359 4 8 12 17 21 24

JUNIOR MISS
Timely/Marvel (CnPC): Wint, 1944; No. 24, Apr, 1947 - No. 39, Aug, 1950
1-Frank Sinatra & June Allyson life story 36 72 108 211 343 475
24-Formerly The Human Torch #23? 18 36 54 103 162 220
25-38: 29,31,34-Cindy-c/stories (others?) 12 24 36 67 94 120
39-Kurtzman-a 14 28 42 76 108 140
NOTE: *Painted-c 35-37. 35, 37-all romance. 36, 38-mostly teen humor.* **Louise Alston** *c-36.*

JUNIOR PARTNERS (Formerly Oral Roberts' True Stories)
Oral Roberts Evangelistic Assn.: No. 120, Aug, 1959 - V3#12, Dec, 1961
120(#1) 4 8 12 23 37 50
2(9/59) 3 6 9 16 24 32
3-12(7/60) 2 4 6 13 18 22
V2#1(8/60)-5(12/60) 2 4 6 9 13 16
V3#1(1/61)-12 2 4 6 8 10 12

JUNIOR TREASURY (See Dell Junior...)

JUNIOR WOODCHUCKS GUIDE (Walt Disney's...)
Danbury Press: 1973 (8-3/4"x5-3/4", 214 pgs., hardcover)

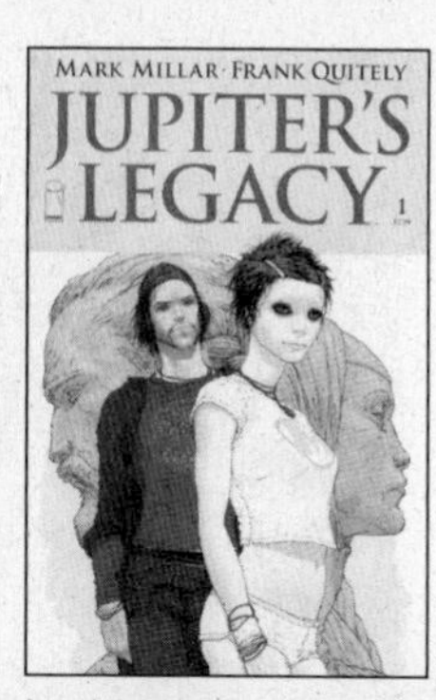

Jupiter's Legacy #1
© Millarworld & Frank Quitely

Justice #4 © DC

Justice Comics #5 © MAR

	GD 2.0	VG 4.0	FN 6.0	VF 8.0	VF/NM 9.0	NM- 9.2

nn-Illustrated text based on the long-standing J.W. Guide used by Donald Duck's nephews Huey, Dewey & Louie by Carl Barks. The guidebook was a popular plot device to enable the nephews to solve problems facing their uncle or Scrooge McDuck (scarce) 5 10 15 31 53 75

JUNIOR WOODCHUCKS LIMITED SERIES (Walt Disney's...)
W. D. Publications (Disney): July, 1991 - No. 4, Oct, 1991 ($1.50, limited series; new & reprint-a)

1-4: 1-The Beagle Boys app.; Barks-r 3.00

JUNIOR WOODCHUCKS (See Huey, Dewey & Louie...)

JUPITER'S LEGACY
Image Comics: Apr, 2013 - Present ($2.99)

1-4-Mark Millar-s/Frank Quitely-a/c 3.00
1-Variant-c by Hitch 4.00
1-Studio Edition (12/13, $4.99) Quitely's B&W art and Millar's script; design art 5.00

JURASSIC PARK
Topps Comics: June, 1993 - No. 4, Aug, 1993; No. 5, Oct, 1994 - No. 10, Feb, 1995

1-($2.50)-Newsstand Edition; Kane/Perez-a in all; 1-4: movie adaptation 3.00
1-($2.95)-Collector's Ed.; polybagged w/3 cards 4.00
1-Amberchrome Edition w/no price or ads 1 2 3 4 5 7
2-4-($2.50)-Newsstand Edition 3.00
2,3-($2.95)-Collector's Ed.; polybagged w/3 cards 4.00
4-10: 4-($2.95)-Collector's Ed.; polybagged w/1 of 4 different action hologram trading card; Gil Kane/Perez-a. 5-becomes Advs. of 3.00
Annual 1 ($3.95, 5/95) 4.00
Trade paperback (1993, $9.95)-r/#1-4; bagged w/#0 10.00

JURASSIC PARK
IDW Publishing: Jun, 2010 - No. 5, Oct, 2010 ($3.99, limited series)

1-5: Takes place 13 years after the first movie; Schreck-s. 1-Covers by Yeates & Miller 4.00

JURASSIC PARK: DANGEROUS GAMES
IDW Publishing: Sept, 2011 - No. 5, Jan, 2012 ($3.99, limited series)

1-5-Erik Bear-s/Jorge Jimenez-a, 1-Covers by Darrow & Zornow 4.00

JURASSIC PARK: RAPTOR
Topps Comics: Nov, 1993 - No. 2, Dec, 1993 ($2.95, limited series)

1,2: 1-Bagged w/3 trading cards & Zorro #0; Golden c-1,2 4.00

JURASSIC PARK: RAPTORS ATTACK
Topps Comics: Mar, 1994 - No. 4, June, 1994 ($2.50, limited series)

1-4-Michael Golden-c/frontispiece 3.00

JURASSIC PARK: RAPTORS HIJACK
Topps Comics: July, 1994 - No. 4, Oct, 1994 ($2.50, limited series)

1-4: Michael Golden-c/front piece 3.00

JURASSIC PARK: THE DEVILS IN THE DESERT
IDW Publishing: Jan, 2011 - No. 4, Apr, 2011 ($3.99, limited series)

1-4-John Byrne-s/a/c 4.00

JUST A PILGRIM
Black Bull Entertainment: May, 2001 - No. 5, Sept, 2001 ($2.99)

Limited Preview Edition (12/00, $7.00) Ennis & Ezquerra interviews 7.00
1-Ennis-s/Ezquerra-a; two covers by Texeira & JG Jones 3.00
2-5: 2-Fabry-c. 3-Nowlan-c. 4-Sienkiewicz-c 3.00
TPB (11/01, $12.99) r/#1-5; Waid intro. 13.00

JUST A PILGRIM: GARDEN OF EDEN
Black Bull Entertainment: May, 2002 - No. 4, Aug, 2002 ($2.99, limited series)

Limited Preview Ed. (1/02, $7.00) Ennis & Ezquerra interviews; Jones-c 7.00
1-4-Ennis-s/Ezquerra-a 3.00
TPB (11/02, $12.99) r/#1-4; Gareb Shamus intro. 13.00

JUSTICE
Marvel Comics Group (New Universe): Nov, 1986 - No. 32, June, 1989

1-32: 26-32-$1.50-c (low print run) 3.00

JUSTICE
DC Comics: Oct, 2005 - No. 12, Aug, 2007 ($2.99/$3.50/$3.99, bi-monthly maxi-series)

1-Classic Justice League vs. The Legion of Doom; Alex Ross & Doug Braithwaite-a; Jim Krueger-s; two covers by Ross; Ross sketch pages 5.00
1-2nd & 3rd printings 4.00
2-($3.50) 4.00
2 (2nd printing), 3-11-($3.50) 3.50
12-($3.99) Two covers (Heroes & Villains) 4.00
Absolute Justice HC (2009, $99.99, slipcased book with dustjacket) oversized r/#1-12; afterwords by creators; Ross sketch and design art; photo gallery of action figures 100.00
HC (2011, $39.99, dustjacket) r/#1-12 40.00
... Volume One HC (2006, $19.99, dustjacket) r/#1-4; Krueger intro.; sketch pages 20.00
... Volume One SC (2008, $14.99) r/#1-4; Krueger intro.; sketch pages 15.00
... Volume Two HC (2007, $19.99, dustjacket) r/#5-8; Krueger intro.; sketch pages 20.00
... Volume Two SC (2008, $14.99) r/#5-8; Krueger intro.; sketch pages 15.00
... Volume Three HC (2007, $19.99, dustjacket) r/#9-12; Ross intro.; sketch pages 20.00
... Volume Three SC (2007, $14.99) r/#9-12; Ross intro.; sketch pages 15.00

JUSTICE COMICS (Formerly Wacky Duck; Tales of Justice #53 on)
Marvel/Atlas Comics (NPP 7-9,4-19/CnPC 20-23/MjMC 24-38/Male 39-52:
No. 7, Fall/47 - No. 9, 6/48; No. 4, 8/48 - No. 52, 3/55

	GD 2.0	VG 4.0	FN 6.0	VF 8.0	VF/NM 9.0	NM- 9.2
7(#1, 1947)	31	62	93	186	303	420
8(#2)-Kurtzman-a "Giggles 'n' Grins" (3)	21	42	63	122	199	275
9(#3, 6/48)	19	38	57	111	176	240
4	17	34	51	98	154	210
5(9/48)-9: 8-Anti-Wertham editorial	15	30	45	85	130	175
10-15-Photo-c	13	26	39	74	105	135
16-30	12	24	36	67	94	120
31-40,42-52: 35-Gene Colan-a. 48-Last precode; Pakula & Tuska-a. 50-Ayers-a	11	22	33	62	86	110
41-Electrocution-c	18	36	54	105	165	225

NOTE: ***Hartley*** *a-48.* ***Heath*** *a-24.* ***Maneely*** *c-44, 52.* ***Pakula*** *a-43, 45, 47, 48.* ***Louis Ravielli*** *a-39, 47.* ***Robinson*** *a-22, 25, 41.* ***Sale*** *c-45.* ***Shores*** *c-7(#1), 8(#2)?* ***Tuska*** *a-41, 48.* ***Wildey*** *a-52.*

JUSTICE: FOUR BALANCE
Marvel Comics: Sept, 1994 - No. 4, Dec, 1994 ($1.75, limited series)

1-4: 1-Thing & Firestar app. 3.00

JUSTICE, INC. (The Avenger) (Pulp)
National Periodical Publications: May-June, 1975 - No. 4, Nov-Dec, 1975

1-McWilliams-a, Kubert-c; origin	2	4	6	11	16	20
2-4: 2-4-Kirby-a(p), c-2,3p. 4-Kubert-c	2	4	6	11	16	20

NOTE: *Adapted from Kenneth Robeson novel, creator of Doc Savage.*

JUSTICE, INC. (Pulp)
DC Comics: 1989 - No. 2, 1989 ($3.95, 52 pgs., squarebound, mature)

1,2: Re-intro The Avenger; Andrew Helfer scripts & Kyle Baker-c/a 5.00

JUSTICE LEAGUE (...International #7-25; ...America #26 on)
DC Comics: May, 1987 - No. 113, Aug, 1996 (Also see Legends #6)

1-Batman, Green Lantern (Guy Gardner), Blue Beetle, Mr. Miracle, Capt. Marvel & Martian Manhunter begin 1 2 3 5 6 8
2,3: 3-Regular-c (white background) 5.00
3-Limited-c (yellow background, Superman logo) 4 8 12 23 37 50
4-6,8-10: 4-Booster Gold joins. 5-Origin Gray Man; Batman vs. Guy Gardner; Creeper app. 9,10-Millennium x-over 4.00
7-($1.25, 52 pgs.)-Capt. Marvel & Dr. Fate resign; Capt. Atom & Rocket Red join 5.00
11-17,22,23,25-49,51-68,71-82: 16-Bruce Wayne-c/story. 31,32-J. L. Europe x-over. 58-Lobo app. 61-New team begins; swipes-c to J.L. of A. #1('60). 70-Newsstand version w/o outer-c. 71-Direct sales version w/black outer-c. 71-Newsstand version w/o outer-c. 80-Intro new Booster Gold. 82,83-Guy Gardner-c/stories 3.00
18-21,24,50: 18-21-Lobo app. 24-($1.50)-1st app. Justice League Europe. 50-($1.75, 52 pgs.) 4.00
69-Doomsday tie-in; takes place between Superman: The Man of Steel #18 & Superman #74 6.00
69,70-2nd printings 3.00
70-Funeral for a Friend part 1; red 3/4 outer-c 5.00
83-99,101-113: 92-(9/94)-Zero Hour x-over; Triumph app. 113-Green Lantern, Flash & Hawkman app. 3.00
100 ($3.95)-Foil-c; 52 pgs. 5.00
100 ($2.95)-Newstand 4.00
#0-(10/94) Zero Hour (publ between #92 & #93); new team begins (Hawkman, Flash, Wonder Woman, Metamorpho, Nuklon, Crimson Fox, Obsidian & Fire) 3.00
Annual 1-8,10 ('87-'94, '96, 68 pgs.): 2-Joker-c/story; Batman cameo. 5-Armageddon 2001 x-over; Silver ink 2nd print. 7-Bloodlines x-over. 8-Elseworlds story. 10-Legends of the Dead Earth 4.00
Annual 9 (1995, $3.50)-Year One story 4.00
Special 1,2 ('90,'91, 52 pgs.): 1-Giffen plots. 2-Staton-a(p) 4.00
Spectacular 1 (1992, $1.50, 52 pgs.)-Intro new JLI & JLE teams; ties into JLI #61 & JLE #37; two interlocking covers by Jurgens 4.00
A New Beginning Trade Paperback (1989, $12.95)-r/#1-7 13.00
... International Vol. 1 HC (2008, $24.99) r/#1-7; new intro. by Giffen 25.00
... International Vol. 1 SC (2009, $17.99) r/#1-7; new intro. by Giffen 18.00
... International Vol. 2 HC (2008, $24.99) r/#8-13, Annual #1 and Suicide Squad #13 25.00
... International Vol. 2 SC (2009, $17.99) r/#8-13, Annual #1 and Suicide Squad #13 18.00
... International Vol. 3 SC (2009, $19.99) r/#14-22 20.00

Justice League (2011 series) #12 © DC

Justice League Dark #3 © DC

Justice League of America #55 © DC

GD VG FN VF VF/NM NM-
2.0 4.0 6.0 8.0 9.0 9.2

GD VG FN VF VF/NM NM-
2.0 4.0 6.0 8.0 9.0 9.2

... International Vol. 4 SC (2010, $17.99) r/#23-30 18.00
... International Vol. 5 SC (2011, $19.99) r/#Annual #2,3 & Justice League Europe #1-6 20.00
... International Vol. 6 SC (2011, $24.99) r/#31-35 & Justice League Europe #7-11 25.00
NOTE: ***Anderson*** *c-61i.* ***Austin*** *a-1i, 60i; c-1i.* ***Giffen*** *a-13; c-21p.* ***Guice*** *a-62i.* ***Maguire*** *a-1-12, 16-19, 22, 23.* ***Russell*** *a-Annual 1i; c-54i.* ***Willingham*** *a-30p, Annual 2.*

JUSTICE LEAGUE (DC New 52)
DC Comics: Oct, 2011 - Present ($3.99)
1-Johns-s/Jim Lee-a/c; Batman, Green Lantern & Superman app.; orange background-c
2 4 6 9 12 15
1-Combo-Pack edition ($4.99) polybagged with digital download code; blue background-c
1 3 4 6 8 10
1-Variant-c by Finch 25.00
1-Second printing 25.00
2-11,13-23: 3-Wonder Woman & Aquaman arrive. 4-Darkseid arrives. 6-Pandora back-up. 7-Gene Ha-a; back-up Shazam origin begins; Frank-a. 8-D'Anda-a. 13,14-Cheetah app. 15-17-Throne of Atlantis. 22,23-Trinity War. 23-Crime Syndicate arrives 4.00
12-Superman/Wonder Woman kiss-c 4.00
23.1, 23.2, 23.3, 23.4 (11/13, $2.99, regular-c) 3.00
23.1 (11/13, $3.99, 3-D cover) "Darkseid #1" on cover; origin; Kaiyo app.; Reis-c 5.00
23.2 (11/13, $3.99, 3-D cover) "Lobo #1" on cover; Bennett-s/Oliver-a/Kuder-c 5.00
23.3 (11/13, $3.99, 3-D cover) "Dial E #1" on cover; Miéville-s; art by various 5.00
23.4 (11/13, $3.99, 3-D cover) "Secret Society #1" on cover; Owlman app.; Kudranski-a 5.00
24-29-Forever Evil. 24-Origin of Ultraman. 25-Origin of Owlman. 27-Cyborg upgraded. 28,29-Metal Men return 4.00
#0-(11/12, $3.99) Origin of Shazam; back-up with Pandora 4.00
...: Trinity War Director's Cut 1 (10/13, $5.99) r/#22 pencil art and script 6.00

JUSTICE LEAGUE ADVENTURES (Based on Cartoon Network series)
DC Comics: Jan, 2002 - No. 34, Oct, 2004 ($1.99/$2.25)
1-Timm & Ross-c 4.00
2-32: 3-Nicieza-s. 5-Starro app. 10-Begin $2.25-c. 14-Includes 16 pg. insert for VERB with Haberlin CG-art. 15,29-Amancio-a. 16-McCloud-s. 20-Psycho Pirate app. 25,26-Adam Strange-c/app. 28-Legion of Super-Heroes app. 30-Kamandi app. 3.00
Free Comic Book Day giveaway - (5/02) r/#1 with "Free Comic Book Day" banner on-c 3.00
TPB (2003, $9.95) r/#1,3,6,10-13; Timm/Ross-c from #1 10.00
...Vol. 1: The Magnificent Seven (2004, $6.95) digest-size reprints #3,6,10-12 7.00
...Vol. 2: Friends and Foes (2004, $6.95) digest-size reprints #13,14,16,19,20 7.00

JUSTICE LEAGUE: A MIDSUMMER'S NIGHTMARE
DC Comics: Sept, 1996 - No. 3, Nov, 1996 ($2.95, limited series, 38 pgs.)
1-3: Re-establishes Superman, Batman, Green Lantern, The Martian Manhunter, Flash, Aquaman & Wonder Woman as the Justice League; Mark Waid & Fabian Nicieza co-scripts; Jeff Johnson & Darick Robertson-a(p); Kevin Maguire-c 5.00
TPB-(1997, $8.95) r/1-3 9.00

JUSTICE LEAGUE: CRY FOR JUSTICE
DC Comics: Sept, 2009 - No. 7, Apr, 2010 ($3.99, limited series)
1-7-James Robinson-s/Mauro Cascioli-a/c. 1-Two covers; Congorilla origin 4.00
HC (2010, $24.99, d.j.) r/#1-7, Face of Evil: Prometheus 25.00
SC (2011, $19.99) r/#1-7, Face of Evil: Prometheus 20.00

JUSTICE LEAGUE DARK (DC New 52)
DC Comics: Nov, 2011 - Present ($2.99)
1-23: 1-Milligan-s; Deadman, Madame Xanadu, Zatanna, Shade, John Constantine app. 7,8-Crossover with I,Vampire #6,7. 7-Batgirl app. 9-Black Orchid joins. 11,12-Tim Hunter app. 13-Leads into J.L. Dark Annual #1. 19-21-Flash app. 22,23-Trinity War 3.00
23.1, 23.2 (11/13, $2.99, regular-c) 3.00
23.1 (11/13, $3.99, 3-D cover) "The Creeper #1" on cover; origin; Nocenti-s/Janin-c 5.00
23.2 (11/13, $3.99, 3-D cover) "Eclipso #1" on cover; origin; Tan-a/Janin-c 5.00
24-29-Forever Evil tie-ins
#0-(11/12, $2.99) Constantine and Zatanna's 1st meeting; Garbett-a/Sook-c 3.00
Annual #1 (12/12, $4.99) Continued from #13; Frankenstein & Amethyst app. 5.00

JUSTICE LEAGUE ELITE (See JLA #100 and JLA Secret Files 2004)
DC Comics: Sept, 2004 - No. 12, Aug, 2005 ($2.50)
1-12-Flash, Green Arrow, Vera Black and others; Kelly-s/Mahnke-a. 5,6-JSA app. 3.00
JL Elite TPB (2005, $19.99) r/#1-4, Action #775, JLA #100, JLA Secret Files 2004 20.00
... Vol. 2 TPB (2007, $19.99) r/#5-12 20.00

JUSTICE LEAGUE EUROPE (Justice League International #51 on)
DC Comics: Apr, 1989 - No. 68, Sept., 1994 (75¢/$1.00/$1.25/$1.50)
1-Giffen plots in all, breakdowns in #1-8,13-30; Justice League #1-c/swipe 4.00
2-10: 7-9-Batman app. 7,8-JLA x-over. 8,9-Superman app. 3.00
11-49: 12-Metal Men app. 20-22-Rogers-c/a(p). 33,34-Lobo vs. Despero. 37-New team begins; swipes-c to JLA #9; see JLA Spectacular 3.00
50-($2.50, 68 pgs.)-Battles Sonar 4.00
51-68: 68-Zero Hour x-over; Triumph joins Justice League Task Force (See JLTF #17) 3.00
Annual 1-5 ('90-'94, 68 pgs.)-1-Return of the Global Guardians; Giffen plots/breakdowns. 2-Armageddon 2001; Giffen-a(p); Rogers-a(p); Golden-a(i). 5-Elseworlds story 4.00
NOTE: ***Phil Jimenez*** *a-68p.* ***Rogers*** *c/a-20-22.* ***Sears*** *a-1-12, 14-19, 23-29; c-1-10, 12, 14-19, 23-29.*

JUSTICE LEAGUE: GENERATION LOST (Brightest Day)
DC Comics: Early July, 2010 - No. 24, Early Jun, 2011 ($2.99, bi-weekly limited series)
1-23: 1-Maxwell Lord's return; Winick & Giffen-s. 1-5,7-Harris-c. 13-Magog killed 3.00
24-($4.99) Wonder Woman vs. Omac Prime; Lopresti-a/Nguyen-c 5.00
... Volume One HC (2010, $39.99, dustjacket) r/#1-12; cover gallery 40.00

JUSTICE LEAGUE INTERNATIONAL (See Justice League Europe)

JUSTICE LEAGUE INTERNATIONAL (DC New 52)
DC Comics: Nov, 2011 - No. 12, Oct, 2012 ($2.99)
1-12: 1-Jurgens-s/Lopresti-a/c; Batman, Booster Gold, Guy Gardner, Vixen, Fire, Ice. 8-Batwing joins; OMAC app. 3.00
Annual 1 (10/12, $4.99) Fabok-a/c; JLI vs. OMAC; Blue Beetle joins 5.00

JUSTICE LEAGUE OF AMERICA (See Brave & the Bold #28-30, Mystery In Space #75 & Official... Index) (See Crisis on Multiple Earths TPBs for reprints of JLA/JSA crossovers)
National Periodical Publ./DC Comics: Oct-Nov, 1960 - No. 261, Apr, 1987 (#91-99,139-157: 52 pgs.)
1-(10-11/60)-Origin & 1st app. Despero; Aquaman, Batman, Flash, Green Lantern, J'onn J'onzz, Superman & Wonder Woman continue from Brave and the Bold
425 850 1275 4700 12,350 20,000
2 107 214 321 856 1928 3000
3-Origin/1st app. Kanjar Ro (see Mystery in Space #75)(scarce in high grade due to black-c)
100 200 300 800 1800 2800
4-Green Arrow joins JLA 64 128 192 512 1156 1800
5-Origin & 1st app. Dr. Destiny 53 106 159 416 933 1450
6-8,10: 6-Origin & 1st app. Prof. Amos Fortune. 7-(10-11/61)-Last 10¢ issue. 10-(3/62)-Origin & 1st app. Felix Faust; 1st app. Lord of Time 41 82 123 303 689 1075
9-(2/62)-Origin JLA (1st origin) 46 92 138 368 834 1300
11-15: 12-(6/62)-Origin & 1st app. Dr. Light. 13-(8/62)-Speedy app. 14-(9/62)-Atom joins JLA. 27 54 81 189 420 650
16-20: 17-Adam Strange flashback 23 46 69 161 356 550
21-(8/63)-"Crisis on Earth-One"; re-intro. of JSA in this title (see Flash #129) (1st S.A. app. Hourman & Dr. Fate) 38 76 114 285 641 1000
22- "Crisis on Earth-Two"; JSA x-over (story continued from #21)
31 62 93 223 499 775
23-28: 24-Adam Strange app. 27-Robin app. 16 32 48 112 249 385
29-"Crisis on Earth-Three"; JSA x-over; 1st app. Crime Syndicate of America (Ultraman, Owlman, Superwoman, Power Ring, Johnny Quick); 1st S.A. app. Starman
20 40 60 140 310 485
30-JSA x-over; Crime Syndicate app. 19 38 57 131 291 450
31-Hawkman joins JLA, Hawkgirl cameo (11/64) 13 26 39 91 201 310
32,34: 32-Intro & Origin Brain Storm. 34-Joker-c/sty 10 20 30 69 147 225
33,35,36,40,41: 40-3rd S.A. Penguin app. 41-Intro & origin The Key
10 20 30 66 138 210
37-39: 37,38-JSA x-over. 37-1st S.A. app. Mr. Terrific; Batman cameo. 38-"Crisis on Earth-A". 39-Giant G-16; r/B&B #28,30 & JLA #5 12 24 36 81 176 270
42-45: 42-Metamorpho app. 43-Intro. Royal Flush Gang
8 16 24 56 108 160
46-JSA x-over; 1st S.A. app. Sandman; 3rd S.A. app. of G.A. Spectre (8/66)
11 22 33 76 163 250
47-JSA x-over; 4th S.A. app of G.A. Spectre. 9 18 27 60 120 180
48-Giant G-29; r/JLA #2,3 & B&B #29 9 18 27 58 114 170
49-54,57,59,60 7 14 21 46 86 125
55-Intro. Earth 2 Robin (1st G.A. Robin in S.A.) 9 18 27 57 111 165
56-JLA vs. JSA (1st G.A. Wonder Woman in S.A.) 8 16 24 52 99 145
58-Giant G-41; r/JLA #6,8,1 8 16 24 52 99 145
61-63,66,68-72: 69-Wonder Woman quits. 71-Manhunter leaves. 72-Last 12¢ issue
5 10 15 35 63 90
64,65-JSA story. 64-(8/68)-Origin/1st app. S.A. Red Tornado
6 12 18 37 66 95
67-Giant G-53; r/JLA #4,14,31 7 14 21 48 89 130
73-1st S.A. app. of G.A. Superman 6 12 18 40 73 105
74-Black Canary joins; Larry Lance dies; 1st meeting of G.A. & S.A. Superman; Neal Adams-c 7 14 21 44 82 120
75-2nd app. Green Arrow in new costume (see Brave & the Bold #85)
8 16 24 54 102 150
76-Giant G-65 6 12 18 38 69 100
77-80: 78-Re-intro Vigilante (1st S.A. app?) 4 8 12 28 47 65
81-84,86-90: 82-1st S.A. app. of G.A. Batman (cameo). 83-Apparent death of The Spectre. 90-Last 15¢ issue 4 8 12 27 44 60

Justice League of America #94 © DC

Justice League of America (2006 series) #8 © DC

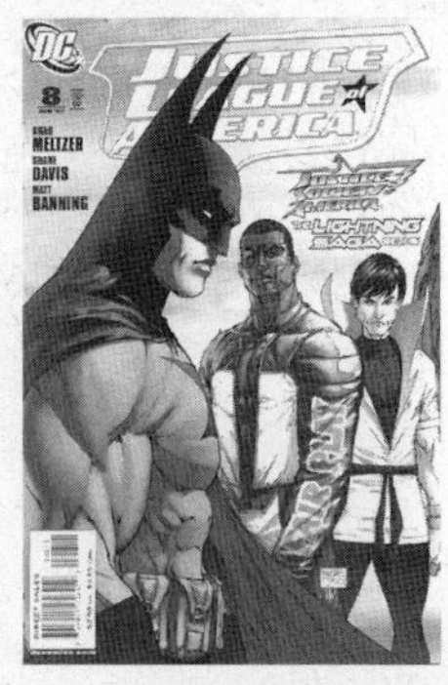

Justice League of America (2011 series) #7 © DC

GD 2.0 | VG 4.0 | FN 6.0 | VF 8.0 | VF/NM 9.0 | NM- 9.2

85,93-(Giant G-77,G-89; 68 pgs.) 5 10 15 31 53 75
91,92: 91-1st meeting of the G.A. & S.A. Robin; begin 25¢, 52 pgs. issues, ends #99.
92-S.A. Robin tries on costume that is similar to that of G.A. Robin in All Star Comics #58 4 8 12 28 47 65
94-Reprints 1st Sandman story (Adv. #40) & origin/1st app. Starman (Adventure #61); Deadman x-over; N. Adams-a (4 pgs.) 8 16 24 52 99 145
95,96: 95-Origin Dr. Fate & Dr. Midnight -r/ More Fun #67, All-American #25).
96-Origin Hourman (Adv. #48); Wildcat-r 5 10 15 30 50 70
97-99: 97-Origin JLA retold; Sargon, Starman-r. 98-G.A. Sargon, Starman-r.
99-G.A. Sandman, Atom-r; last 52 pg. issue 4 8 12 27 44 60
100-(8/72)-1st meeting of G.A. & S.A. W. Woman 5 10 15 33 57 80
101,102: JSA x-overs. 102-Red Tornado destroyed 4 8 12 27 44 60
103-106,109: 103-Rutland Vermont Halloween x-over; Phantom Stranger joins. 105-Elongated Man joins. 106-New Red Tornado joins. 109-Hawkman resigns 3 6 9 19 30 40
107,108-JSA x-over; 1st revival app. of G.A. Uncle Sam, Black Condor, The Ray, Dollman, Phantom Lady & The Human Bomb 3 6 9 21 33 45
110,112-116: All 100 pgs. 112-Amazo app; Crimson Avenger, Vigilante-r; origin Starman-r/ Adv. #81. 115-Martian Manhunter app. 5 10 15 31 53 75
111-JLA vs. Injustice Gang; intro. Libra (re-appears in 2008's Final Crisis); Shining Knight, Green Arrow-r 5 10 15 34 60 85
117-122,125-134: 117-Hawkman rejoins. 120,121-Adam Strange app. 125,126-Two-Face-app. 128-Wonder Woman rejoins. 129-Destruction of Red Tornado 3 6 9 16 23 30
123-(10/75),124: JLA/JSA x-over. DC editor Julie Schwartz & JLA writers Cary Bates & Elliot S! Maggin appear in story as themselves. 1st named app. Earth-Prime (3rd app. after Flash; 1st Series #179 & 228) 3 6 9 17 26 35
135-136: 135-137-G.A. Bulletman, Bulletgirl, Spy Smasher, Mr. Scarlet, Pinky & Ibis x-over, 1st appearances since G.A. 3 6 9 17 26 35
137-Superman battles G.A. Capt. Marvel 3 6 9 20 31 42
138-Adam Strange app. w/c by Neal Adams; 1st app. Green Lantern of the 73rd Century 3 6 9 16 24 32
139-157: 139-157-(52 pgs.): 139-Adam Strange app. 144-Origin retold; origin J'onn J'onzz. 145-Red Tornado resurrected. 147,148-Legion of Super-Heroes x-over 2 4 6 10 14 18
158-160-(44 pgs.) 2 4 6 8 11 14
158,160-162,169,171,172,173,176,179,181-(Whitman variants; low print run, none show issue # on cover) 2 4 6 10 14 18
161-165,169-182: 161-Zatanna joins & new costume. 171,172-JSA x-over. 171-Mr. Terrific murdered. 178-Cover similar to #1; J'onn J'onzz app. 179-Firestorm joins. 181-Green Arrow leaves JLA 1 2 3 5 6 8
166-168- "Identity Crisis (2004)" precursor; JSA app. vs. Secret Society of Super-Villains 3 6 9 16 23 30
166-168-Whitman variants (no issue # on covers) 4 8 12 23 37 50
183-185-JSA/New Gods/Darkseid/Mr. Miracle x-over 2 4 6 8 10 12
186-194,198,199: 192,193-Real origin Red Tornado. 193-1st app. All-Star Squadron as free 16 pg. insert 6.00
195-197-JSA app. vs. Secret Society of Super-Villains 1 2 3 5 6 8
200 ($1.50, Anniversary issue, 76 pgs.)-JLA origin retold; Green Arrow rejoins; Bolland, Aparo, Giordano, Gil Kane, Infantino, Kubert-a; Pérez-c/a 1 3 4 6 8 10
201-206,209-243,246-259: 203-Intro/origin new Royal Flush Gang. 219,220-True origin Black Canary. 228-Re-intro Martian Manhunter. 228-230-War of the Worlds storyline; JLA Satellite destroyed by Martians. 233-Story cont'd from Annual #2. 243-Aquaman leaves. 250-Batman rejoins. 253-Origin Despero. 258-Death of Vibe. 258-261-Legends x-over 5.00
207,208-JSA, JLA, & All-Star Squadron team-up 1 2 3 4 5 7
244,245-Crisis x-over 6.00
260-Death of Steel 1 2 3 4 5 7
261-Last issue 1 3 4 6 8 10
Annual 1-3 ('83-'85), 2-Intro new J.L.A. (Aquaman, Martian Manhunter, Steel, Gypsy, Vixen, Vibe, Elongated Man & Zatanna). 3-Crisis x-over 5.00
... Hereby Elects (2006, $14.99, TPB) reprints issues where new members joined; JLofA #4,75,105,106,146,161,173 &174; roster of various incarnations; Ordway-c 15.00

NOTE: ***Neal Adams** c-63, 66, 67, 70, 74, 79, 81, 82, 86-89, 91, 92, 94, 96-98, 138, 139. **M. Anderson** c-1-4, 6, 7, 10, 12-14. **Aparo** a-200. **Austin** a-200i. **Baily** a-96r. **Bolland** a-200. **Buckler** c-158, 163, 164. **Burnley** r-94, 98, 99. **Greene** a-46-61i, 64-73i, 110i(r). **Grell** c-117, 122. **Kaluta** c-154p. **Gil Kane** a-200. **Krigstein** a-96(r/Sensation #84). **Kubert** a-200; c-72, 73. **Nino** a-228i, 230i. **Orlando** c-151i. **Perez** a-184-186p, 192-197p, 200p; c-184p, 186, 192-195, 196p, 197p, 199, 200, 201p, 202, 203-205p, 207-209, 212-215, 217, 219, 220. **Reinman** r-97. **Roussos** a-62i. **Sekowsky** a-37, 38, 44-63p, 110-112p(r); c-46-48p, 51p. **Sekowsky/Anderson** c-5, 8, 9, 11, 15. **B. Smith** c-185i. **Starlin** c-178-180, 183, 185p. **Staton** a-244p; c-157p, 244p. **Toth** r-110. **Tuska** a-153, 228p, 241-243p. JSA x-overs-21, 22, 29, 30, 37, 38, 46, 47, 55, 56, 64, 65, 73, 74, 82, 83, 91, 92, 100, 101, 102, 107, 108, 110, 113, 115, 123, 124, 135-137, 147, 148, 159, 160, 171, 172, 183-185, 195-197, 207-209, 219, 220, 231, 232, 244.*

JUSTICE LEAGUE OF AMERICA
DC Comics: No. 0, Sept, 2006 - No. 60, Oct, 2011 ($2.99/$3.99)

GD 2.0 | VG 4.0 | FN 6.0 | VF 8.0 | VF/NM 9.0 | NM- 9.2

0-Meltzer-s; history of the JLA; art by various incl. Lee, Giordano, Benes; Turner-c 5.00
0-Variant-c by Campbell 8.00
1-($3.99) Two interlocking covers by Benes; Benes-a 5.00
1-Variant-c by Turner 8.00
1-RRP Edition; sideways composite of both Benes covers 50.00
1-Second printing; Benes cover image between black bars 4.00
2-5-($2.99) Turner-c 4.00
2-5: Variant-c: 2-Jimenez. 3-Sprouse. 4-JG Jones. 5-Art Adams 5.00
6,7-($3.50) 6-JLA vs. Amazo; covers by Turner and Hughes. 7-Roster picked, new HQs; two Benes covers and Turner cover. 4.00
8-11,13-24,26-38-($2.99) 8-11-JLA/JSA team-up; covers by Turner & Jimenez. 10-Wally West returns. 13-Two covers. 13-15-Injustice Gang. 16-Tangent Flash. 20-Queen Bee app. 21-Libra app.; leads into Final Crisis #1. 35,36-Royal Flush Gang app. 38-Bagley-a begins 3.00
12-($3.50) Two Ross covers; origin retold with Wight-a; Benes-a 4.00
25-($3.99) McDuffie-s/art by various; Benes-c 4.00
39-49,51,52-($3.99) 39,40-Blackest Night. 41-New team; 2 covers. 44-48-Justice Society app. 44-Jade returns. 4.00
50-($4.99) Crime Syndicate app.; Bagley-a; wraparound-c by Van Sciver 5.00
50-Variant-c by Bagley, swipe of Quitely's JLA: Earth 2 cover 8.00
50-Variant-c by Jim Lee; swipe of Brave and the Bold #28 Starro cover 12.00
53-60-($2.99) 54-Booth-a; Eclipso returns. 55-Doomsday app. 3.00
... 80 Page Giant (11/09, $5.99) Anacleto-c; short stories by various; Ra's al Ghul app. 6.00
... 80 Page Giant 2011 (6/11, $5.99) Lau-c; chapters by various; JLA goes to Hell 6.00
Free Comic Book Day giveaway - (2007) r/#0 with "Free Comic Book Day" banner on-c 3.00
Justice League Wedding Special 1 (11/07, $3.99) McKone-a; Injustice League forms 4.00
...: Dark Things HC (2011, $24.99, dustjacket) r/#44-48 & J.S.A. #41,42 25.00
...: The Injustice Gang HC (2008, $19.99, dustjacket) r/#13-16; Wedding Special 20.00
...: The Lightning Saga HC (2008, $24.99, dustjacket) r/#0,8-12 & Justice Society of America #5,6; intro. by Patton Oswalt 25.00
...: The Lightning Saga SC (2008, $17.99) r/#0,8-12 & J.S.A. #5,6; intro. by Oswalt 18.00
...: Sanctuary SC (2009, $14.99) r/#17-21 15.00
...: Second Coming HC (2009, $19.99, dustjacket) r/#22-26 20.00
...: Second Coming SC (2010, $17.99) r/#22-26 18.00
...: Team History HC (2010, $19.99, dustjacket) r/#38-43 20.00
...: The Tornado's Path HC (2007, $24.99, dustjacket) r/#1-7; variant cover gallery; Lindelof intro.; commentary by Meltzer & Benes 25.00
...: The Tornado's Path SC (2008, $17.99) r/#1-7; variant cover gallery; Lindelof intro.; commentary by Meltzer & Benes 18.00
...: When Worlds Collide HC (2009, $24.99, dustjacket) r/#27,28,30-34 25.00
...: When Worlds Collide SC (2010, $14.99) r/#27,28,30-34 15.00

JUSTICE LEAGUE OF AMERICA (DC New 52)
DC Comics: Apr, 2013 - Present ($3.99)
1-Johns-s/Finch-a/c; Green Arrow, Catwoman, Martian Manhunter, Katana & others team; variants covers with U.S. flag and each of the 50 state flags plus DC and Puerto Rico 4.00
2-Covers by Finch and Ryp 4.00
3-7: 3-5-Martian Manhunter back-up. 4,5-Shaggy Man app. 6,7-Trinity War 4.00
7.1, 7.2, 7.3, 7.4 (11/13, $2.99, regular-c) 3.00
7.1 (11/13, $3.99, 3-D cover) "Deadshot #1" on cover; origin; Kindt-s/Daniel-c 5.00
7.2 (11/13, $3.99, 3-D cover) "Killer Frost #1" on cover; origin; Gates-s/Santacruz-a 5.00
7.3 (11/13, $3.99, 3-D cover) "Shadow Thief #1" on cover; origin; Hardin-a/Daniel-c 5.00
7.4 (11/13, $3.99, 3-D cover) "Black Adam #1" on cover; Black Adam returns 5.00
8-13-Forever Evil. 10-Stargirl origin. 11,12-Despero app. 4.00

JUSTICE LEAGUE OF AMERICA : ANOTHER NAIL (Elseworlds) (Also see JLA: The Nail)
DC Comics: 2004 - No. 3, 2004 ($5.95, prestige format)
1-3-Sequel to JLA: The Nail; Alan Davis-s/a(p) 6.00
TPB (2004, $12.95) r/series 13.00

JUSTICE LEAGUE OF AMERICA SUPER SPECTACULAR
DC Comics: 1999 ($5.95, mimics format of DC 100 Page Super Spectaculars)
1-Reprints Silver Age JLA and Golden Age JSA 6.00

JUSTICE LEAGUE OF AMERICA'S VIBE (DC New 52)
DC Comics: Apr, 2013 - No. 10, Feb, 2014 ($2.99)
1-10: 1,2-Johns & Kreisberg-s/Woods-a/Finch-c; origin. 5-Suicide Squad app. 3.00

JUSTICE LEAGUE OF AMERICA/ THE 99
DC Comics: Dec, 2010 - No. 6, May, 2011 ($3.99/$2/99, limited series)
1-3-($3.99) Derenick-a/Massaferra-c; JLA meets Teshkeel Comics characters 4.00
4-6-($2.99) Starro app. 3.00

JUSTICE LEAGUE QUARTERLY (...International Quarterly #6 on)
DC Comics: Winter, 1990-91 - No. 17, Winter, 1994 ($2.95/$3.50, 84 pgs.)
1-12,14-17: 1-Intro The Conglomerate (Booster Gold, Praxis, Gypsy, Vapor, Echo, Maxi-Man,

Justice League Unlimited #1 © DC

Justice Society of America (2007 series) #22 © DC

Justice Traps the Guilty #2 © Prize

GD VG FN VF VF/NM NM-
2.0 4.0 6.0 8.0 9.0 9.2

GD VG FN VF VF/NM NM-
2.0 4.0 6.0 8.0 9.0 9.2

& Reverb); Justice League #1-c/swipe. 1,2-Keith Giffen plots/breakdowns. 3-Giffen plot; 72 pg. story. 4-Rogers/Russell-a in back-up. 5,6-Mark Waid scripts. 8,17-Global Guardians app. 4.00
13-Linsner-c 6.00
NOTE: ***Phil Jimenez** a-17p. **Sprouse** a-1p.*

JUSTICE LEAGUE: RISE AND FALL
DC Comics: 2010, 2011

Justice League: The Rise and Fall Special #1 (5/10, $3.99) Hunt for Green Arrow 4.00
HC-(2011, $24.99) Reprints Justice League of America #43, Justice League: The Rise and Fall Special #1, Green Arrow #31,32 and Justice League: The Rise of Arsenal #1-4 25.00

JUSTICE LEAGUES...
DC Comics: Mar, 2001 ($2.50, limited series)

JL?, Justice League of Amazons, Justice League of Atlantis, Justice League of Arkham, Justice League of Aliens, JLA: JLA split by the Advance Man; Perez-c in all; s&a by various 3.00

JUSTICE LEAGUE TASK FORCE
DC Comics: June, 1993 - No. 37, Aug, 1996 ($1.25/$1.50/$1.75)

1-16,0,17-37: Aquaman, Nightwing, Flash, J'onn J'onzz, & Gypsy form team. 5,6-Knight-quest tie-ins (new Batman cameo #5, 1 pg.). 15-Triumph cameo. 16-(9/94)-Zero Hour x-over; Triumph app. 0-(10/94). 17-(11/94)-Triumph becomes part of Justice League Task Force (See JLE #68). 26-Impulse app. 35-Warlord app. 37-Triumph quits team 3.00

JUSTICE LEAGUE: THE NEW FRONTIER SPECIAL (Also see DC: The New Frontier)
DC Comics: May, 2008 ($4.99, one-shot)

1-Short stories by Darwyn Cooke, J.Bone and Dave Bullock; bonus storyboards from the movie 5.00

JUSTICE LEAGUE: THE RISE OF ARSENAL (Follows Justice League: Cry For Justice)
DC Comics: May, 2010 - No. 4, Aug, 2010 ($3.99, limited series)

1-4-Horn-c/Borges-a/Krul-s. 2,3-Cheshire app. 4.00

JUSTICE LEAGUE 3000
DC Comics: Feb, 2014 - Present ($2.99)

1-4-Justice League of the 31st century; Giffen & DeMatteis-s/Porter-a/c 3.00

JUSTICE LEAGUE UNLIMITED (Based on Cartoon Network animated series)
DC Comics: Nov, 2004 - No. 46, Aug, 2008 ($2.25)

1-46: 1-Zatanna app. 2,23,42-Royal Flush Gang app. 4-Adam Strange app. 10-Creeper app. 17-Freedom Fighters app. 18-Space Cabby app. 27-Black Lightning app. 34-Zod app. 3.00
Free Comic Book Day giveaway (5/06) r/#1 with "Free Comic Book Day" banner on-c 3.00
Jam Packed Action (2005, $7.99, digest) adaptations of two TV episodes 8.00
... Vol. 1: United They Stand (2005, $6.99, digest) r/#1-5 7.00
... Vol. 2: World's Greatest Heroes (2006, $6.99, digest) r/#6-10 7.00
... Vol. 3: Champions of Justice (2006, $6.99, digest) r/#11-15 7.00
...: Heroes (2009, $12.99, full-size) r/#23-29 13.00
...: The Ties That Bind (2008, $12.99, full-size) r/#16-22 13.00

JUSTICE MACHINE, THE
Noble Comics: June, 1981 - No. 5, Nov, 1983 ($2.00, nos. 1-3 are mag. size)

	GD 2.0	VG 4.0	FN 6.0	VF 8.0	VF/NM 9.0	NM- 9.2
1-Byrne-c(p)	3	6	9	15	21	26
2-Austin-c(i)	2	4	6	9	12	15
3	1	3	4	6	8	10

4,5, Annual 1: Ann. 1-(1/84, 68 pgs.)(published by Texas Comics); 1st app. The Elementals; Golden-c(p); new Thunder Agents story (43 pgs.) 6.00

JUSTICE MACHINE (Also see The New Justice Machine)
Comico/Innovation Publishing: Jan, 1987 - No. 29, May 1989 ($1.50/$1.75)

1-29 3.00
Annual 1(6/89, $2.50, 36 pgs.)-Last Comico ish. 3.00
Summer Spectacular 1 ('89, $2.75)-Innovation Publ.; Byrne/Gustovich-c 3.00

JUSTICE MACHINE, THE
Innovation Publishing: 1990 - No. 4, 1990 ($1.95/$2.25, deluxe format, mature)

1-4: Gustovich-c/a in all 3.00

JUSTICE MACHINE FEATURING THE ELEMENTALS
Comico: May, 1986 - No. 4, Aug, 1986 ($1.50, limited series)

1-4 3.00

JUSTICE RIDERS
DC Comics: 1997 ($5.95, one-shot, prestige format)

1-Elseworlds; Dixon-s/Williams & Gray-a 6.00

JUSTICE SOCIETY
DC Comics: 2006; 2007 ($14.99, TPB)

Vol. 1 - Rep. from 1976 revival in All Star Comics #58-67 & DC Special #29; Bolland-c 15.00
Vol. 2 - R/All Star Comics #68-74 & Adventure Comics #461-466; new Bolland-c 15.00

JUSTICE SOCIETY OF AMERICA (See Adventure #461 & All-Star #3)
DC Comics: April, 1991 - No. 8, Nov, 1991 ($1.00, limited series)

1-8: 1-Flash. 2-Black Canary. 3-Green Lantern. 4-Hawkman. 5-Flash/Hawkman. 6-Green Lantern/Black Canary. 7-JSA 3.00

JUSTICE SOCIETY OF AMERICA (Also see Last Days of the... Special)
DC Comics: Aug, 1992 - No. 10, May, 1993 ($1.25)

1-10 3.00

JUSTICE SOCIETY OF AMERICA (Follows JSA series)
DC Comics: Feb, 2007 - No. 54, Oct, 2011 ($3.99/$2.99)

1-($3.99) New team selected; intro. Maxine Hunkle; Alex Ross-c 4.00
1-Variant-c by Eaglesham 6.00
2-49,51-54: 1-Covers by Ross & Eaglesham. 3,4-Vandal Savage app. 5,6-JLA/JSA team-up. 9-22-Kingdom Come Superman app.18-Magog app. 22-Superman returns to Kingdom Come Earth; Ross partial art. 23-25-Ordway-a. 26-Triptych cover by Ross. 33-Team splits. 34,35-Mordru app. 41,42-Justice League x-over. 52-54-Challengers of the Unknown app. 54-Darwyn Cooke-c 3.00
50-($4.99) Degaton app.; art by Derenick, Chaykin, Williams II, and Pérez; Massafera-c 5.00
JSA Annual 1 (9/08, $3.99) Power Girl on Earth-2; Ross-c/Ordway-a 5.00
JSA Annual 2 (4/10, $4.99) All Star team app.; Magog quits; Williams-a 5.00
... 80 Page Giant (1/10, $5.99) short stories by various incl. Ordway, S. Hampton 6.00
... 80 Page Giant 2010 (12/10, $5.99) short stories by various 6.00
... 80 Page Giant 2011 (8/11, $5.99) short stories by various incl. Chaykin, Hampton 6.00
... Special (11/10, $4.99) Scott Kolins-s/a; spotlight on Magog 5.00
...: Axis of Evil SC (2010, $14.99) r/#34-40 15.00
...: Black Adam and Isis HC (2009, $19.99, d.j.) r/#23-28 20.00
...: Black Adam and Isis SC (2010, $14.99) r/#23-28 15.00
... Kingdom Come Special: Magog (1/09, $3.99) Pasarin-a; origin re-told; 2 covers 4.00
... Kingdom Come Special: Superman (1/09, $3.99) Lois' death re-told; Alex Ross-s/a/c; thumbnails, photo references, sketch art 4.00
... Kingdom Come Special: Superman (1/09, $3.99) Eaglesham variant cover 8.00
... Kingdom Come Special: The Kingdom (1/09, $3.99) Pasarin-a; 2 covers 4.00
...: The Bad Seed SC (2010, $14.99) r/#29-33 15.00
...: The Next Age SC (2008, $14.99) r/#1-4; Ross and Eaglesham sketch pages 15.00
...: Thy Kingdom Come Part One HC (2008, $19.99, d.j.) r/#7-12; Ross sketch pages 20.00
...: Thy Kingdom Come Part One SC (2009, $14.99) r/#7-12; Ross sketch pages 15.00
...: Thy Kingdom Come Part Two HC (2008, $24.99, d.j.) r/#13-18 & Annual #1; Ross sketch pages 25.00
...: Thy Kingdom Come Part Two SC (2009, $19.99) r/#13-18 & Ann. #1; Ross sketch-a 20.00
...: Thy Kingdom Come Part Three HC (2009, $24.99, d.j.) r/#19-22 & K.C. Specials - Superman, Magog and The Kingdom; Ross sketch pages 25.00
...: Thy Kingdom Come Part Three SC (2010, $19.99) same contents as HC 20.00

JUSTICE SOCIETY OF AMERICA 100-PAGE SUPER SPECTACULAR
DC Comics: 2000 ($6.95, mimics format of DC 100 Page Super Spectaculars)

1-"1975 Issue" reprints Flash team-up and Golden Age JSA 7.00

JUSTICE SOCIETY RETURNS, THE (See All Star Comics (1999) for related titles)
DC Comics: 2003 ($19.95, TPB)

TPB-Reprints 1999 JSA x-over from All-Star Comics #1,2 and related one-shots 20.00

JUSTICE TRAPS THE GUILTY (Fargo Kid V11#3 on)
Prize/Headline Publications: Oct-Nov, 1947 - V11#2(#92), Apr-May, 1958 (True FBI Cases)

	GD 2.0	VG 4.0	FN 6.0	VF 8.0	VF/NM 9.0	NM- 9.2
V2#1-S&K-c/a; electrocution-c	61	122	183	390	670	950
2-S&K-c/a	36	72	108	216	351	485
3-5-S&K-c/a	34	68	102	199	325	450
6-S&K-c/a; Feldstein-a	36	72	108	211	343	475
7,9-S&K-c/a. 7-9-V2#1-3 in indicia; #7-9 on-c	30	60	90	177	289	400
8-Krigstein-a; S&K-c; electric chair-c	27	54	81	160	263	365
10-Krigstein-a; S&K-c/a	30	60	90	177	289	400
11,18,19-S&K-c	17	34	51	98	154	210
12,14-17,20-No S&K. 14-Severin/Elder-a (8pg.)	11	22	33	62	86	110
13-Used in **SOTI**, pg. 110-111	13	26	39	74	105	135
21,30-S&K-c/a	18	36	54	103	162	220
22,23-S&K-c	14	28	42	78	112	145
24-26,27,29,31-50: 32-Meskin story	11	22	33	60	83	105
28-Kirby-c	13	26	39	74	105	135
51-55,57,59-70	10	20	30	54	72	90
56-Ben Oda, Joe Simon, Joe Genola, Mort Meskin & Jack Kirby app. in police line-up on classic-c	14	28	42	82	121	160
58-Illo. in **SOTI**, "Treating police contemptuously" (top left); text on heroin	26	52	78	154	252	350

Ka'a'nga Comics #10 © FH

Kabuki #8 © David Mack

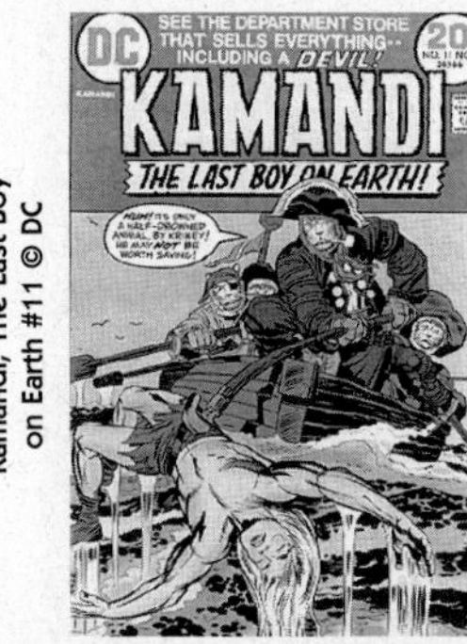

Kamandi, The Last Boy on Earth #11 © DC

	GD 2.0	VG 4.0	FN 6.0	VF 8.0	VF/NM 9.0	NM- 9.2
71-92: 76-Orlando-a	8	16	24	44	57	70

NOTE: ***Bailey** a-12, 13. **Elder** a-8. **Kirby** a-19p. **Meskin** a-22, 27, 63, 64; c-45, 46. **Robinson/Meskin** a-5, 19. **Severin** a-8, 11p. Photo c-12, 15-17.*

JUST IMAGINE STAN LEE WITH... (Stan Lee re-invents DC icons)
DC Comics: 2001 - 2002 ($5.95, prestige format, one-shots)
(Adam Hughes back-c on all)(Michael Uslan back-up stories in all, diff. artists)

	GD 2.0	VG 4.0	FN 6.0	VF 8.0	VF/NM 9.0	NM- 9.2
Scott McDaniel Creating **Aquaman**- Back-up w/Fradon-a						6.00
Joe Kubert Creating **Batman**- Back-up w/Kaluta-a						6.00
Chris Bachalo Creating **Catwoman**- Back-up w/Cooke & Allred-a						6.00
John Cassaday Creating **Crisis**- no back-up story						6.00
Kevin Maguire Creating **The Flash**- Back-up w/Aragonés-a						6.00
Dave Gibbons Creating **Green Lantern**- Back-up w/Giordano-a						6.00
Jerry Ordway Creating **JLA**						6.00
John Byrne Creating **Robin**- Back-up w/John Severin-a						6.00
Walter Simonson Creating **Sandman**- Back-up w/Corben-a						6.00
Gary Frank Creating **Shazam!**- Back-up w/Kano-a						6.00
John Buscema Creating **Superman**- Back-up w/Kyle Baker-a						6.00
Jim Lee Creating **Wonder Woman**- Back-up w/Gene Colan-a						6.00
Secret Files and Origins #1 (3/02, $4.95) Crisis prologue; Jurgens-a						5.00
TPB -Just Imagine Stan Lee Creating the DC Universe: Book One (2002, $19.95) r/Batman, Wonder Woman, Superman, Green Lantern						20.00
TPB -Just Imagine Stan Lee Creating the DC Universe: Book Two (2003, $19.95) r/Flash, JLA, Secret Files and Origins, Robin, Shazam; sketch pages						20.00
TPB -Just Imagine Stan Lee Creating the DC Universe: Book Three (2004, $19.95) r/Aquaman, Catwoman, Sandman, Crisis; profile pages						20.00

JUST MARRIED
Charlton Comics: January, 1958 - No. 114, Dec, 1976

	GD 2.0	VG 4.0	FN 6.0	VF 8.0	VF/NM 9.0	NM- 9.2
1	5	10	15	35	63	90
2	3	6	9	21	33	45
3-10	3	6	9	17	26	35
11-30	3	6	9	14	20	26
31-50	2	4	6	11	16	20
51-70	2	4	6	9	13	16
71-78,80-89	2	4	6	8	11	14
79-Ditko-a (7 pages)	2	4	6	10	14	18
90-Susan Dey and David Cassidy full page poster	2	4	6	11	16	20
91-114	2	4	6	8	10	12

KA'A'NGA COMICS (...Jungle King)(See Jungle Comics)
Fiction House Magazines (Glen-Kel Publ. Co.): Spring, 1949 - No. 20, Summer, 1954

	GD 2.0	VG 4.0	FN 6.0	VF 8.0	VF/NM 9.0	NM- 9.2
1-Ka'a'nga, Lord of the Jungle begins	54	108	162	343	574	825
2 (Winter, '49-'50)	32	64	96	188	307	425
3,4	24	48	72	142	234	325
5-Camilla app.	22	44	66	132	216	300
6-10: 7-Tuska-a. 9-Tabu, Wizard of the Jungle app. 10-Used in **POP**, pg. 99	16	32	48	94	147	200
11-15: 15-Camilla-r by Baker/Jungle #106	14	28	42	80	115	150
16-Sheena app.	14	28	42	82	121	160
17-20	13	26	39	74	105	135
I.W. Reprint #1,8: 1-r/#18; Kinstler-c. 8-r/#10	3	6	9	14	20	25

NOTE: ***Celardo** c-1. **Whitman** c-8-20(most).*

KABOOM
Awesome Entertainment: Sept, 1997 - No. 3, Nov, 1997 ($2.50)

	GD 2.0	VG 4.0	FN 6.0	VF 8.0	VF/NM 9.0	NM- 9.2
1-3: 1-Matsuda-a/Loeb-s; 4 covers exist (Matsuda, Sale, Pollina and McGuinness), 1-Dynamic Forces Edition, 2-Regular, 2-Alicia Watcher variant-c, 2-Gold logo variant-c, 3-Two covers by Liefeld & Matsuda, 3-Dynamic Forces Ed., Prelude Ed.						3.00
Prelude Gold Edition						4.00

KABOOM (2nd series)
Awesome Entertainment: July, 1999 - No. 3, Dec, 1999 ($2.50)

	GD 2.0	VG 4.0	FN 6.0	VF 8.0	VF/NM 9.0	NM- 9.2
1-3: 1-Grant-a(p); at least 4 variant covers						3.00

KABOOM! SUMMER BLAST FREE COMIC BOOK DAY EDITION
Boom Entertainment (KaBOOM!): May 2013 (free giveaway)

	GD 2.0	VG 4.0	FN 6.0	VF 8.0	VF/NM 9.0	NM- 9.2
nn-Short stories of Adventure TIme, Regular Show, Herobear, Garfield, Peanuts, Ice Age						3.00

KABUKI
Caliber: Nov, 1994 ($3.50, B&W, one-shot)

	GD 2.0	VG 4.0	FN 6.0	VF 8.0	VF/NM 9.0	NM- 9.2
nn-(Fear The Reaper) 1st app.; David Mack-c/a/s	1	2	3	5	6	8
Color Special (1/96, $2.95)-Mack-c/a/scripts; pin-ups by Tucci, Harris & Quesada						4.00
Gallery (8/95, $2.95)- pinups from Mack, Bradstreet, Paul Pope & others						3.00

KABUKI
Image Comics: Oct, 1997 - No. 9, Mar, 2000 ($2.95, color)

	GD 2.0	VG 4.0	FN 6.0	VF 8.0	VF/NM 9.0	NM- 9.2
1-David Mack-c/s/a						5.00
1-($10.00)-Dynamic Forces Edition	1	3	4	6	8	10
2-5						4.00
6-9						3.00
#1/2 (9/01, $2.95) r/Wizard 1/2; Eklipse Mag. article; bio						3.00
...Classics (2/99, $3.95) Reprints Fear the Reaper						4.00
...Classics 2 (3/99, $3.95) Reprints Dance of Dance						4.00
...Classics 3-5 (3-6/99, $4.95) Reprints Circle of Blood-Acts 1-3						5.00
...Classics 6-12 (7/99-3/00, $3.25) Various reprints						3.25
...Images (6/98, $4.95) r/#1 with new pin-ups						5.00
...Images 2 (1/99, $4.95) r/#1 with new pin-ups						5.00
...Metamorphosis TPB (10/00, $24.95) r/#1-9; Sienkiewicz intro.; 2nd printing exists						25.00
...Reflections 1-4 (7/98-5/02; $4.95) new story plus art techniques						5.00
... The Ghost Play (11/02, $2.95) new story plus interview						3.00

KABUKI
Marvel Comics (Icon): July, 2004 - Present ($2.99, color)

	GD 2.0	VG 4.0	FN 6.0	VF 8.0	VF/NM 9.0	NM- 9.2
1-9: 1-David Mack-c/s/a in all; variant-c by Alex Maleev. 4-Variant-c by Adam Hughes. 6-Variant-c by Mignola. 8-Variant-c by Kent Williams. 9-Allred var-c						3.00
...: The Alchemy HC (2008, $29.99, dust jacket) oversized r/#1-9; bonus art & content						30.00
... Reflections 5-15 (7/05-10/09, $5.99) paintings & sketches of recent work; photos						6.00

KABUKI AGENTS (SCARAB)
Image Comics: Aug, 1999 - No. 8, Aug, 2001 ($2.95, B&W)

	GD 2.0	VG 4.0	FN 6.0	VF 8.0	VF/NM 9.0	NM- 9.2
1-8-David Mack-s/Rick Mays-a						3.00
Lost in Translation HC (3/02, $29.95) r/#1-8; intro. by Paul Pope						30.00
Lost in Translation SC (3/02, $19.95) r/#1-8; intro. by Paul Pope						20.00

KABUKI: CIRCLE OF BLOOD
Caliber Press: Jan, 1995 - No. 6, Nov, 1995 ($2.95, B&W)

	GD 2.0	VG 4.0	FN 6.0	VF 8.0	VF/NM 9.0	NM- 9.2
1-David Mack story/a in all						5.00
2-6: 3-#1 on inside indicia.						3.00
6-Variant-c						3.00
TPB ($16.95) r/#1-6, intro. by Steranko						17.00
TPB (1997, $17.95) Image Edition-r/#1-6, intro. by Steranko						18.00
TPB ($24.95) Deluxe Edition						25.00

KABUKI: DANCE OF DEATH
London Night Studios: Jan, 1995 ($3.00, B&W, one-shot)

	GD 2.0	VG 4.0	FN 6.0	VF 8.0	VF/NM 9.0	NM- 9.2
1-David Mack-c/a/scripts	1	2	3	5	6	8

KABUKI: DREAMS
Image Comics: Jan, 1998 ($4.95, TPB)

	GD 2.0	VG 4.0	FN 6.0	VF 8.0	VF/NM 9.0	NM- 9.2
nn-Reprints Color Special & Dreams of the Dead						5.00

KABUKI: DREAMS OF THE DEAD
Caliber: July, 1996 ($2.95, one-shot)

	GD 2.0	VG 4.0	FN 6.0	VF 8.0	VF/NM 9.0	NM- 9.2
nn-David Mack-c/a/scripts						3.00

KABUKI FAN EDITION
Gemstone Publ./Caliber: Feb, 1997 (mail-in offer, one-shot)

	GD 2.0	VG 4.0	FN 6.0	VF 8.0	VF/NM 9.0	NM- 9.2
nn-David Mack-c/a/scripts						4.00

KABUKI: MASKS OF THE NOH
Caliber: May, 1996 - No. 4, Feb, 1997 ($2.95, limited series)

	GD 2.0	VG 4.0	FN 6.0	VF 8.0	VF/NM 9.0	NM- 9.2
1-4: 1-Three-c (1A-Quesada, 1B-Buzz, &1C-Mack). 3-Terry Moore pin-up						3.00
TPB-(4/98, $10.95) r/#1-4; intro by Terry Moore						11.00

KABUKI: SKIN DEEP
Caliber Comics: Oct, 1996 - No. 3, May, 1997 ($2.95)

	GD 2.0	VG 4.0	FN 6.0	VF 8.0	VF/NM 9.0	NM- 9.2
1-3:David Mack-c/a/scripts. 2-Two-c (1-Mack, 1-Ross)						3.00
TPB-(5/98, $9.95) r/#1-3; intro by Alex Ross						10.00

KAMANDI: AT EARTH'S END
DC Comics: June, 1993 - No. 6, Nov, 1993 ($1.75, limited series)

	GD 2.0	VG 4.0	FN 6.0	VF 8.0	VF/NM 9.0	NM- 9.2
1-6: Elseworlds storyline						3.00

KAMANDI, THE LAST BOY ON EARTH (Also see Alarming Tales #1, Brave and the Bold #120 & 157, Cancelled Comic Cavalcade & Wednesday Comics)
National Periodical Publ./DC Comics: Oct-Nov, 1972 - No. 59, Sept-Oct, 1978

	GD 2.0	VG 4.0	FN 6.0	VF 8.0	VF/NM 9.0	NM- 9.2
1-Origin & 1st app. Kamandi	7	14	21	46	86	125
2,3	4	8	12	28	47	65
4,5: 4-Intro. Prince Tuftan of the Tigers	4	8	12	25	40	55
6-10	3	6	9	18	28	38
11-20	3	6	9	15	22	28
21-28,30,31,33-40: 24-Last 20¢ issue. 31-Intro Pyra.	2	4	6	13	18	22
29,32: 29-Superman x-over. 32-(68 pgs.)-r/origin from #1 plus one new story; 4 pg. biog. of Jack Kirby with B&W photos	3	6	9	14	20	26

Kaos Moon #3 © David Boller

Katana #6 © DC

Katy Keene #4 © AP

	GD 2.0	VG 4.0	FN 6.0	VF 8.0	VF/NM 9.0	NM- 9.2
41-57	2	4	6	10	14	18
58-Karate Kid x-over from LSH (see Karate Kid #15)	3	6	9	14	19	24
59-(44 pgs.)-Story cont'd in Brave and the Bold #157; The Return of Omac back-up by Starlin-c/a(p)	3	6	9	16	23	30

NOTE: *Ayers a(p)-48-59 (most). **Giffen** a-44p, 45p. **Kirby** a-1-40p; c-1-33. **Kubert** c-34-41. **Nasser** a-45p, 46p. **Starlin** a-59p; c-57, 59p.*

KAMUI (Legend Of...#2 on)
Eclipse Comics/Viz Comics: May 12, 1987 - No. 37, Nov. 15, 1988 ($1.50, B&W, bi-weekly)

	GD 2.0	VG 4.0	FN 6.0	VF 8.0	VF/NM 9.0	NM- 9.2
1-37: 1-3 have 2nd printings						3.00

KANE & LYNCH (Based on the video games)
DC Comics (WildStorm): Oct, 2010 - No. 6, Apr, 2011 ($3.99/$2.99, limited series)

	GD 2.0	VG 4.0	FN 6.0	VF 8.0	VF/NM 9.0	NM- 9.2
1-4-($3.99) Templesmith-c/Edginton-s/Mitten-a						4.00
5,6-($2.99)						3.00
TPB (2011, $17.99) r/#1-6; cover gallery						18.00

KAOS MOON (Also see Negative Burn #34)
Caliber Comics: 1996 - No. 4, 1997 ($2.95, B&W)

	GD 2.0	VG 4.0	FN 6.0	VF 8.0	VF/NM 9.0	NM- 9.2
1-4-David Boller-s/a						3.00
3,4-Limited Alternate-c						4.00
3,4-Gold Alternate-c, Full Circle TPB ($5.95) r/#1,2						6.00

KARATE KID (See Action, Adventure, Legion of Super-Heroes, & Superboy)
National Periodical Publications/DC Comics: Mar-Apr, 1976 - No. 15, July-Aug, 1978
(Legion of Super-Heroes spin-off)

	GD 2.0	VG 4.0	FN 6.0	VF 8.0	VF/NM 9.0	NM- 9.2
1,15: 1-Meets Iris Jacobs; Estrada/Staton-a. 15-Continued into Kamandi #58	2	4	6	11	16	20
2-14: 2-Major Disaster app. 14-Robin x-over	2	3	4	6	8	10

NOTE: ***Grell** c-1-4, 5p, 6p, 7, 8. **Staton** a-1-9i. Legion x-over-No. 1, 2, 4, 6, 10, 12, 13. Princess Projectra x-over-#8, 9.*

KATANA (DC New 52) (From Justice League Of America 2013 series)
DC Comics: Apr, 2013 - No. 10, Feb, 2014 ($2.99)

	GD 2.0	VG 4.0	FN 6.0	VF 8.0	VF/NM 9.0	NM- 9.2
1-10: 1,2-Nocenti-s/Sanchez-a/Finch-c; origin. 2-Steve Trevor app. 3-6-Creeper app.						3.00

KATHY
Standard Comics: Sept, 1949 - No. 17, Sept, 1955

	GD 2.0	VG 4.0	FN 6.0	VF 8.0	VF/NM 9.0	NM- 9.2
1-Teen-age	16	32	48	94	147	200
2-Schomburg-c	13	26	39	72	101	130
3-5	10	20	30	54	72	90
6-17: 17-Code approved	9	18	27	50	65	80

KATHY (The Teenage Tornado)
Atlas Comics/Marvel (ZPC): Oct, 1959 - No. 27, Feb, 1964 (most issues contain paper dolls and pin-up pages)

	GD 2.0	VG 4.0	FN 6.0	VF 8.0	VF/NM 9.0	NM- 9.2
1-The Teen-age Tornado; Goldberg-c/a in all	9	18	27	58	114	170
2	5	10	15	35	63	90
3-15	5	10	15	31	53	75
16-23,25,27	4	8	12	25	40	55
24-(8/63) Frank Sinatra, Cary Grant, Ed Sullivan & Liz Taylor-c	5	10	15	31	53	75
26-(12/63) Kathy becomes a model; Millie app.	4	8	12	27	44	60

KAT KARSON
I. W. Enterprises: No date (Reprint)

	GD 2.0	VG 4.0	FN 6.0	VF 8.0	VF/NM 9.0	NM- 9.2
1-Funny animals	2	4	6	10	12	15

KATO (Also see The Green Hornet)
Dynamite Entertainment: 2010 - No. 14, 2011 ($3.99)

	GD 2.0	VG 4.0	FN 6.0	VF 8.0	VF/NM 9.0	NM- 9.2
1-14: 1-Kato and daughter origin; Garza-a/Parks-s. 2-10 Bernard-a						4.00
Annual 1 (2011, $4.99) Parks-s/Salazar-a						5.00

KATO OF THE GREEN HORNET (Also see The Green Hornet)
Now Comics: Nov, 1991 - No. 4, Feb, 1992 ($2.50, mini-series)

	GD 2.0	VG 4.0	FN 6.0	VF 8.0	VF/NM 9.0	NM- 9.2
1-4: Brent Anderson-c/a						3.00

KATO OF THE GREEN HORNET II (Also see The Green Hornet)
Now Comics: Nov, 1992 - No. 2, Dec, 1993 ($2.50, mini-series)

	GD 2.0	VG 4.0	FN 6.0	VF 8.0	VF/NM 9.0	NM- 9.2
1,2-Baron-s/Mayerik & Sherman-a						3.00

KATO ORIGINS (Also see The Green Hornet: Year One)
Dynamite Entertainment: 2010 - No. 11, 2011 ($3.99)

	GD 2.0	VG 4.0	FN 6.0	VF 8.0	VF/NM 9.0	NM- 9.2
1-11-Kato in 1942; Jai Nitz-s/Colton Worley-a; covers by Worley & Francavilla						4.00

KATY KEENE (Also see Kasco Komics, Laugh, Pep, Suzie, & Wilbur)
Archie Publ./Close-Up/Radio Comics: 1949 - No. 4, 1951; No. 5, 3/52 - No. 62, Oct, 1961
(50-53-Adventures of...on-c) (Cut and missing pages are common)

	GD 2.0	VG 4.0	FN 6.0	VF 8.0	VF/NM 9.0	NM- 9.2
1-Bill Woggon-c/a begins; swipes-c to Mopsy #1	184	368	552	1168	2009	2850
2-(1950)	63	126	189	403	689	975
3-5: 3-(1951). 4-(1951). 5-(3/52)	52	104	156	322	549	775
6-10	39	78	117	231	378	525
11,13-21: 21-Last pre-code issue (3/55)	32	64	96	188	307	425
12-(Scarce)	39	78	117	231	378	525
22-40	22	44	66	132	216	300
41-60: 54-Wedding Album plus wedding pin-up	18	36	54	105	165	225
61,62: 62-Robot-c	20	40	60	117	189	260
Annual 1('54, 25¢)-All new stories; last pre-code	55	110	165	352	601	850
Annual 2-6('55-59, 25¢)-All new stories	32	64	96	188	307	425
3-D 1(1953, 25¢, large size)-Came w/glasses	39	78	117	231	378	525
Charm 1(9/58)-Woggon-c/a; new stories, and cut-outs	29	58	87	170	278	385
Glamour 1(1957)-Puzzles, games, cut-outs	29	58	87	170	278	385
Spectacular 1('56)	30	60	90	177	289	400

NOTE: *Debby's Diary in #45, 47-49, 52, 57.*

KATY KEENE COMICS DIGEST MAGAZINE
Close-Up, Inc. (Archie Ent.): 1987 - No. 10, July, 1990 ($1.25/$1.35/$1.50, digest size)

	GD 2.0	VG 4.0	FN 6.0	VF 8.0	VF/NM 9.0	NM- 9.2
1	2	4	6	10	14	18
2-10	1	3	4	6	8	10

NOTE: *Many used copies are cut-up inside.*

KATY KEENE FASHION BOOK MAGAZINE
Radio Comics/Archie Publications: 1955 - No. 13, Sum, '56 - N. 23, Wint, '58-59 (nn 3-10)

	GD 2.0	VG 4.0	FN 6.0	VF 8.0	VF/NM 9.0	NM- 9.2
1-Bill Woggon-c/a	54	108	162	343	574	825
2	31	62	93	182	296	410
11-18: 18-Photo Bill Woggon	22	44	66	132	216	300
19-23	19	38	57	111	176	240

KATY KEENE HOLIDAY FUN (See Archie Giant Series Magazine No. 7, 12)

KATY KEENE MODEL BEHAVIOR
Archie Comic Publications: 2008 ($10.95, TPB)

	GD 2.0	VG 4.0	FN 6.0	VF 8.0	VF/NM 9.0	NM- 9.2
Vol. 1 - New story and reprinted apps./pin-ups from Archie & Friends #101-112						11.00

KATY KEENE PINUP PARADE
Radio Comics/Archie Publications: 1955 - No. 15, Summer, 1961 (25¢)
(Cut-out & missing pages are common)

	GD 2.0	VG 4.0	FN 6.0	VF 8.0	VF/NM 9.0	NM- 9.2
1-Cut-outs in all?; last pre-code issue	54	108	162	343	574	825
2-(1956)	31	62	93	182	296	410
3-5: 3-(1957)	26	52	78	154	252	350
6-10,12-14: 8-Mad parody. 10-Bill Woggon photo	22	44	66	128	209	290
11-Story of how comics get CCA approved, narrated by Katy	27	54	81	158	259	360
15(Rare)-Photo artist & family	41	82	123	251	418	585

KATY KEENE SPECIAL (Katy Keene #7 on; see Laugh Comics Digest)
Archie Ent.: Sept, 1983 - No. 33, 1990 (Later issues published quarterly)

	GD 2.0	VG 4.0	FN 6.0	VF 8.0	VF/NM 9.0	NM- 9.2
1-10: 1-Woggon-r; new Woggon-c. 3-Woggon-r						5.00
11-25: 12-Spider-Man parody						6.00
26-32-(Low print run)	1	2	3	5	7	9
33	2	4	6	8	10	12

KATZENJAMMER KIDS, THE (See Captain & the Kids & Giant Comic Album)
David McKay Publ./Standard No. 12-21(Spring/'50 - 53)/Harvey No. 22, 4/53 on: 1945-1946; Summer, 1947 - No. 27, Feb-Mar, 1954

	GD 2.0	VG 4.0	FN 6.0	VF 8.0	VF/NM 9.0	NM- 9.2
Feature Books 30	20	40	60	117	189	260
Feature Books 32,35('45),41,44('46)	18	36	54	105	165	225
Feature Book 37-Has photos & biography of Harold Knerr	19	38	57	111	176	240
1(1947)-All new stories begin	19	38	57	111	176	240
2	12	24	36	67	94	120
3-11	10	20	30	54	72	90
12-14(Standard)	8	16	24	44	57	70
15-21(Standard)	8	16	24	42	54	65
22-25,27(Harvey): 22-24-Henry app.	7	14	21	35	43	50
26-Half in 3-D	16	32	48	94	147	200

KAYO (Formerly Bullseye & Jest; becomes Carnival Comics)
Harry 'A' Chesler: No. 12, Mar, 1945

	GD 2.0	VG 4.0	FN 6.0	VF 8.0	VF/NM 9.0	NM- 9.2
12-Green Knight, Capt. Glory, Little Nemo (not by McCay)	21	42	63	122	199	275

KA-ZAR (Also see Marvel Comics #1, Savage Tales #6 & X-Men #10)
Marvel Comics Group: Aug, 1970 - No. 3, Mar, 1971 (Giant-Size, 68 pgs.)

	GD 2.0	VG 4.0	FN 6.0	VF 8.0	VF/NM 9.0	NM- 9.2
1-Reprints earlier Ka-Zar stories; Avengers x-over in Hercules; Daredevil, X-Men app.; hidden profanity-c	4	8	12	27	44	60

Ka-Zar #12 © MAR

Keen Detective Funnies #10 © CEN

Ken Shannon #6 © QUA

GD VG FN VF VF/NM NM-
2.0 4.0 6.0 8.0 9.0 9.2

2,3-Daredevil-r. 2-r/Daredevil #13 w/Kirby layouts; Ka-Zar origin, Angel-r from X-Men by Tuska. 3-Romita & Heck-a (no Kirby) 3 6 9 17 26 35
NOTE: *Buscema r-2. Colan a-1p(r). Kirby c/a-1, 2. #1-Reprints X-Men #10 & Daredevil #24.*

KA-ZAR
Marvel Comics Group: Jan, 1974 - No. 20, Feb, 1977 (Regular Size)

1 3 6 9 14 19 24
2-10 2 4 6 8 10 12
11-14,16,18-20: 16-Only a 30 ¢ edition exists 1 2 3 5 6 8
15,17-(Regular 25¢ edition)(8/76) 1 2 3 5 6 8
15,17-(30¢-c variants, limited distribution) 3 6 9 15 22 28
NOTE: *Alcala a-6i, 8i. Brunner c-4. J. Buscema a-6-10p; c-1, 5, 7. Heath a-12. G. Kane c(p)-3, 5, 8-11, 15, 20. Kirby c-12p. Reinman a-1p.*

KA-ZAR (Volume 2)
Marvel Comics: May, 1997 - No. 20, Dec, 1998 ($1.95/$1.99)

1-Waid-s/Andy Kubert-c/a. thru #4 4.00
1-2nd printing; new cover 3.00
2,4: 2-Two-c 3.00
3-Alpha Flight #1 preview 4.00
5-13,15-20: 8-Includes Spider-Man Cybercomic CD-ROM. 9-11-Thanos app. 15-Priest-s/Martinez & Rodriguez-a begin; Punisher app. 3.00
14-($2.99) Last Waid/Kubert issue; flip book with 2nd story previewing new creative team of Priest-s/Martinez & Rodriguez-a 4.00
'97 Annual ($2.99)-Wraparound-c 4.00

KA-ZAR
Marvel Comics: Aug, 2011 - No. 5, Dec, 2011 ($2.99, limited series)

1-5-Jenkins-s/Alixe-a/c 3.00

KA-ZAR OF THE SAVAGE LAND
Marvel Comics: Feb, 1997 ($2.50, one-shot)

1-Wraparound-c 4.00

KA-ZAR: SIBLING RIVALRY
Marvel Comics: July, 1997 ($1.95, one-shot)

(# -1) Flashback story w/Alpha Flight #1 preview 3.00

KA-ZAR THE SAVAGE (See Marvel Fanfare)
Marvel Comics Group: Apr, 1981 - No. 34, Oct, 1984 (Regular size)(Mando paper #10 on)

1 5.00
2-20,24,27,28,30-34: 11-Origin Zabu. 12-One of two versions with panel missing on pg. 10. 20-Kraven the Hunter-c/story (also apps. in #21) 3.00
12-Version with panel on pg. 10 (1600 printed) 1 2 3 5 6 8
21-23, 25,26-Spider-Man app. 26-Photo-c. 4.00
29-Double size; Ka-Zar & Shanna wed 4.00
NOTE: *B. Anderson a-1-15p, 18, 19; c-1-17, 18p, 20(back). G. Kane a(back-up)-11, 12, 14.*

KEEN DETECTIVE FUNNIES (Formerly Detective Picture Stories?)
Centaur Publications: No. 8, July, 1938 - No. 24, Sept, 1940

V1#8-The Clock continues-r/Funny Picture Stories #1; Roy Crane-a (1st?) 300 600 900 1950 3375 4800
9-Tex Martin by Eisner; The Gang Buster app. 145 290 435 921 1586 2250
10,11: 11-Dean Denton story (begins?) 135 270 405 864 1482 2100
V2#1,2-The Eye Sees by Frank Thomas begins; ends #23(Not in V2#3&5). 2-Jack Cole-a 110 220 330 704 1202 1700
3-6: 3-TNT Todd begins. 4-Gabby Flynn begins. 5,6-Dean Denton story 103 206 309 659 1130 1600
7-The Masked Marvel by Ben Thompson begins (7/39, 1st app.)(scarce) 277 554 831 1776 3038 4300
8-Nudist ranch panel w/four girls 110 220 330 704 1202 1700
9-11 97 194 291 621 1061 1500
12(12/39)-Origin The Eye Sees by Frank Thomas; death of Masked Marvel's sidekick ZL 119 238 357 762 1306 1850
V3#1,2 90 180 270 576 988 1400
18-Bondage/torture-c 113 226 339 718 1234 1750
19,21,22 90 180 270 576 988 1400
20-Classic Eye Sees-c by Thomas 155 310 465 992 1696 2400
23-Air Man begins (intro); Air Man-c 123 246 369 787 1344 1900
24-(scarce) Air Man-c 129 258 387 826 1413 2000
NOTE: *Burgos a-V2#2. Jack Cole a-V2#2. Eisner a-10, V2#6r. Ken Ernst a-V2#4-7, 9, 10, 19, 21; c-V2#4. Everett a-V2#6, 7, 9, 11, 12, 20. Guardineer a-V2#5, 66. Gustavson a-V2#4-6. Simon c-V3#1. Thompson c-V2#7, 9, 10, 22.*

KEEN KOMICS
Centaur Publications: V2#1, May, 1939 - V2#3, Nov, 1939

V2#1(Large size)-Dan Hastings (s/f), The Big Top, Bob Phantom the Magician, The Mad Goddess app. 129 258 387 826 1413 2000

GD VG FN VF VF/NM NM-
2.0 4.0 6.0 8.0 9.0 9.2

V2#2(Reg. size)-The Forbidden Idol of Machu Picchu; Cut Carson by Burgos begins 74 148 222 470 810 1150
V2#3-Saddle Sniffl by Jack Cole, Circus Pays, Kings Revenge app. 74 148 222 470 810 1150
NOTE: *Binder a-V2#2. Burgos a-V2#2, 3. Ken Ernst a-V2#3. Gustavson a-V2#2. Jack Cole a-V2#3.*

KEEN TEENS (Girls magazine)
Life's Romances Publ./Leader/Magazine Ent.: 1945; nn, 1946; No. 3, Feb-Mar, 1947 - No. 6, Aug-Sept, 1947

nn (#1)-14 pgs. Claire Voyant (cont'd. in other nn issue) movie photos, Dotty Dripple, Gertie O'Grady & Sissy; Van Johnson, Sinatra photo-c 41 82 123 256 428 600
nn (#2, 1946)-16 pgs. Claire Voyant & 16 pgs. movie photos 31 62 93 182 296 410
3-6: 4-Glenn Ford photo-c. 5-Perry Como-c 15 30 45 90 140 190

KELLYS, THE (Formerly Rusty Comics; Spy Cases No. 26 on)
Marvel Comics (HPC): No. 23, Jan, 1950 - No. 25, June, 1950 (52 pgs.)

23-Teenage 15 30 45 84 127 170
24,25: 24-Margie app. 10 20 30 58 79 100

KEN MAYNARD WESTERN (Movie star)(See Wow Comics, 1936)
Fawcett Publ.: Sept, 1950 - No. 8, Feb, 1952 (All 36 pgs; photo front/back-c)

1-Ken Maynard & his horse Tarzan begin 28 56 84 165 270 375
2 17 34 51 98 154 210
3-8: 6-Atomic bomb explosion panel 14 28 42 76 108 140

KEN SHANNON (Becomes Gabby #11 on) (Also see Police Comics #103)
Quality Comics Group: Oct, 1951 - No. 10, Apr, 1953 (A private eye)

1-Crandall-a 42 84 126 265 445 625
2-Crandall c/a(2) 32 64 96 192 314 435
3-Horror-c; Crandall-a 36 72 108 216 351 485
4,5-Crandall-a 24 48 72 140 230 320
6-Crandall-c/a; "The Weird Vampire Mob"-c/s 37 74 111 222 361 500
7-"The Ugliest Man Alive"-c; Crandall-a 32 64 96 188 307 425
8,9: 8-Opium den drug use story 20 40 60 117 189 260
10-Crandall-c 20 40 60 120 195 270
NOTE: *Crandall/Cuidera c-1-10. Jack Cole a-1-9. #1-15 published after title change to Gabby.*

KEN STUART
Publication Enterprises: Jan, 1949 (Sea Adventures)

1-Frank Borth-c/a 10 20 30 56 76 95

KENT BLAKE OF THE SECRET SERVICE (Spy)
Marvel/Atlas Comics (20CC): May, 1951 - No. 14, July, 1953

1-Injury to eye, bondage, torture; Brodsky-c 24 48 72 140 230 320
2-Drug use w/hypo scenes; Brodsky-c 17 34 51 98 154 210
3-14: 8-R.Q. Sale-a (2 pgs.) 12 24 36 67 94 120
NOTE: *Heath c-5, 7, 8. Infantino c-12. Maneely c-3. Sinnott a-2(3). Tuska a-8(3pg.).*

KENTS, THE
DC Comics: Aug, 1997 - No. 12, July, 1998 ($2.50, limited series)

1-12-Ostrander-s/art by Truman and Bair (#1-8), Mandrake (#9-12) 3.00
TPB ($19.95) r/#1-12 20.00

KERRY DRAKE (Also see A-1 Comics)
Argo: Jan, 1956 - No. 2, March, 1956

1,2-Newspaper-r 8 16 24 44 57 70

KERRY DRAKE DETECTIVE CASES (...Racket Buster No. 32,33)
(Also see Chamber of Clues & Green Hornet Comics #42-47)
Life's Romances/Com/Magazine Ent. No.1-5/Harvey No.6 on: 1944 - No. 5, 1944; No. 6, Jan, 1948 - No. 33, Aug, 1952

nn(1944)(A-1 Comics)(slightly over-size) 31 62 93 182 296 410
2 19 38 57 111 176 240
3-5(1944) 15 30 45 90 140 190
6,8(1948): Lady Crime by Powell. 8-Bondage-c 12 24 36 67 94 120
7-Kubert-a; biog of Andriola (artist) 13 26 39 74 105 135
9,10-Two-part marijuana story; Kerry smokes marijuana in #10 15 30 45 88 137 185
11-15 10 20 30 58 79 100
16-33 9 18 27 50 65 80
NOTE: *Andiola c-6-9. Berg a-5. Powell a-10-23, 28, 29.*

KEVIN KELLER (Also see Veronica #202 for 1st app. & #207-210 for first mini-series)
Archie Comics Publications: Apr, 2012 - Present ($2.99)

1-13-Two covers on each. 5-Action #1 swipe-c. 6-George Takei app. 3.00

KEWPIES
Will Eisner Publications: Spring, 1949

Kick-Ass #3 © Millarworld & JR Jr.

Kid Colt #2 © MAR

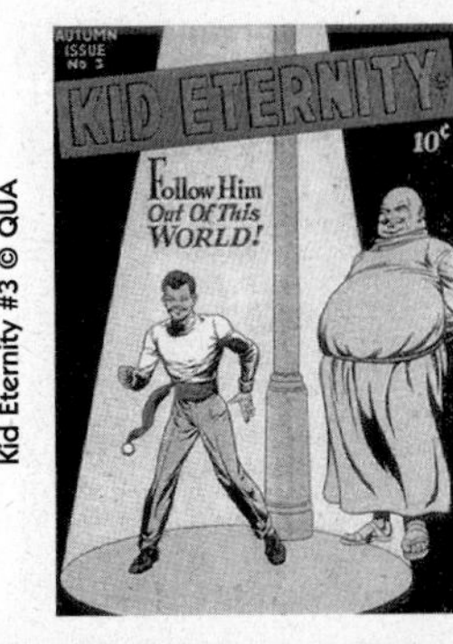

Kid Eternity #3 © QUA

GD 2.0 | VG 4.0 | FN 6.0 | VF 8.0 | VF/NM 9.0 | NM- 9.2

1-Feiffer-a; Kewpie Doll ad on back cover; used in **SOTI**, pg. 35
52 104 156 328 552 775

KEY COMICS
Consolidated Magazines: Jan, 1944 - No. 5, Aug, 1946
1-The Key, Will-O-The-Wisp begin 45 90 135 284 480 675
2 (3/44) 25 50 75 147 241 335
3,4: 3 (Winter 45/46). 4-(5/46)-Origin John Quincy The Atom (begins); Walter Johnson c-3-5
22 44 66 128 209 290
5-4pg. Faust Opera adaptation; Kiefer-a; back-c advertises "Masterpieces Illustrated" by Lloyd Jacquet after he left Classic Comics (no copies of Masterpieces Illustrated known)
28 56 84 165 270 375

KEY OF Z
BOOM! Studios: Oct, 2011 - No. 4, Jan, 2012 ($3.99, limited series)
1-4: 1-Claudio Sanchez & Chondra Echert-s/Aaron Kuder-a; covers by Fox & Moore 4.00

KEY RING COMICS
Dell Publishing Co.: 1941 (16 pgs.; two colors) (sold 5 for 10¢)
1-Sky Hawk, 1-Features Sleepy Samson, 1-Origin Greg Gilday; r/War Comics #2
10 20 30 58 79 100
1-Radior (Super hero) 13 26 39 72 101 130
1-Viking Carter (WWII Nazi-c) 12 24 36 67 94 120
NOTE: *Each book has two holes in spine to put in binder.*

KICK-ASS
Marvel Comics (Icon): April, 2008 - No. 8, Mar, 2010 ($2.99)
1-Mark Millar-s/John Romita Jr.-a/c 18.00
1-Red variant cover by McNiven 25.00
1-2nd printing 4.00
1-Director's Cut (8/08, $3.99) r/#1 with script and sketch pages; Millar afterword 5.00
2 8.00
3-8: 5-Intro. Red Mist 4.00
NOTE: *Multiple printings exist for most issues.*

KICK-ASS 2
Marvel Comics (Icon): Dec, 2010 - No. 7, May, 2012 ($2.99/$4.99)
1-6-Mark Millar-s/John Romita Jr.-a/c. 1-Five printings 3.00
1-6-Variant covers. 1-Edwards. 2-Yu. 5-Photo & Hitch. 6-Photo-c 5.00
7-($4.99) Extra-sized finale; bonus preview of Secret Service #1 5.00
7-($4.99) Variant photo-c 7.00

KICK-ASS 3
Marvel Comics (Icon): Jul, 2013 - No. 8 ($2.99/$3.99/$4.99)
1-5-($2.99) Mark Millar-s/John Romita Jr.-a/c 3.00
1-5-Variant covers. 1-Hughes. 2-Fegredo. 3-Mack. 5-Bond 5.00
6-($4.99) Secret origin of Hit-Girl 5.00
7-($3.99) 4.00

KID CARROTS
St. John Publishing Co.: September, 1953
1-Funny animal 9 18 27 50 65 80

KID COLT ONE-SHOT
Marvel Comics: Sept, 2009 ($3.99)
1-DeFalco-s/Burchett-a/Luke Ross-c 4.00

KID COLT OUTLAW (Kid Colt #1-4; ...Outlaw #5-on)(Also see All Western Winners, Best Western, Black Rider, Giant-Size..., Two-Gun Kid, Two-Gun Western, Western Winners, Wild Western, Wisco)
Marvel Comics(LCC) 1-16; Atlas(LMC) 17-102; Marvel 103-on: 8/48 - No. 139, 3/68; No. 140, 11/69 - No. 229, 4/79
1-Kid Colt & his horse Steel begin. 148 296 444 947 1624 2300
2 65 130 195 416 708 1000
3-5: 4-Anti-Wertham editorial; Tex Taylor app. 5-Blaze Carson app.
53 106 159 334 567 800
6-8: 6-Tex Taylor app; 7-Nimo the Lion begins, ends #10
34 68 102 206 336 465
9,10 (52 pgs.) 34 68 102 206 336 465
11-Origin (10/50) 39 78 117 236 388 540
12-20 23 46 69 136 223 310
21-32 20 40 60 114 182 250
33-45: Black Rider in all 16 32 48 94 147 200
46,47,49,50 15 30 45 83 124 165
48-Kubert-a 15 30 45 84 127 170
51-53,55,56 13 26 39 72 101 130
54-Williamson/Maneely-c 14 28 42 76 108 140
57-60,66: 4-pg. Williamson-a in all 8 16 24 52 99 145
61-63,67-78,80-86: 70-Severin-c. 69,73-Maneely-c. 86-Kirby-a(r).
6 12 18 42 79 115
64,65-Crandall-a 7 14 21 44 82 120
79,87: 79-Origin retold. 87-Davis-a(r) 7 14 21 44 82 120
88,89-Williamson-a in both (4 pgs.). 89-Redrawn Matt Slade #2
7 14 21 46 86 125
90-99,101-106,108,109: 91-Kirby/Ayers-c. 95-Kirby/Ayers-c/story. 102-Last 10¢ issue
6 12 18 40 73 105
100 7 14 21 46 86 125
107-Only Kirby sci-fi cover of title 17 34 51 117 259 400
110-(5/63)-1st app. Iron Mask (Iron Man type villain) 7 14 21 49 92 135
111-120: 114-(1/64)-2nd app. Iron Mask 6 12 18 37 66 95
121-129,133-139: 121-Rawhide Kid x-over. 125-Two-Gun Kid x-over. 139-Last 12¢ issue
5 10 15 31 53 75
130-132 (68 pgs.)-one new story each. 130-Origin 6 12 18 37 66 95
140-155: 140-Reprints begin (later issues mostly-r). 155-Last 15¢ issue
3 6 9 16 23 30
156-Giant; reprints (52 pgs.) 3 6 9 20 31 42
157-180,200: 170-Origin retold. 3 6 9 14 20 25
181-199 2 4 6 11 16 20
201-229: 201-New material w/Rawhide Kid app; Kane-c. 229-Rawhide Kid-r
2 4 6 10 14 18
205-209-(30¢-c variants, limited dist.) 5 10 15 34 60 85
218-220-(35¢-c variants, limited dist.) 8 16 24 54 102 150
...Album (no date; 1950's; Atlas Comics)-132 pgs.; cardboard cover, B&W stories; (Rare)
116 232 348 742 1271 1800
NOTE: ***Ayers** a-many. **Colan** a-52, 53, 84, 112, 114; c(p)-223, 228, 229. **Crandall** a-140r, 167r. **Everett** a-90, 137i, 225i(r). **Heath** a-8(2); c-34, 35, 39, 44, 46, 48, 49, 57, 64. **Heck** a-135, 139. **Jack Keller** a-25(2), 26-68(3-4), 73, 78, 84, 85, 88, 92, 94p, 98, 99, 101, 102, 106-108, 110-112, 114, 115, 117-127, 129, 130, 132, 140-150r. **Kirby** a-86r, 93, 96, 119, 176(part); c-87, 92-95, 97, 99-112, 114-117, 121-123, 197r; w/**Ditko** c-89. **Maneely** a-12, 68, 81; c-17, 19, 40-43, 47, 52, 53, 62, 65, 68, 73, 78, 81, 142r, 150r. **Morrow** a-173r, 216r. **Rico** a-13, 18. **Severin** c-55, 58, 59, 84, 143, 148, 149i. **Shores** a-39, 41-43, 143r; c-1-10(most), 24. **Sutton** a-136, 137p, 225p(r). **Wildey** a-47, 54, 82, 144r. **Williamson** r-147, 170, 172, 216. **Woodbridge** a-64, 81. Black Rider in #33-45, 74, 86. Iron Mask in #110, 114, 121, 127. Sam Hawk in #80, 84, 101, 111, 121, 146, 174, 181, 188.*

KID COWBOY (Also see Approved Comics #4 & Boy Cowboy)
Ziff-Davis Publ./St. John (Approved Comics) #11,14: 1950 - No. 11, Wint, '52-'53; No. 13, April 1953; No. 14, June, 1954 (No #12) (Painted covers #1-10,13,14)
1-Lucy Belle & Red Feather begin 18 36 54 103 162 220
2-Maneely-c 12 24 36 67 94 120
3-11,13,14: (#3, spr. '51). 5-Berg-a. 14-Code approved
11 22 33 60 83 105

KID DEATH & FLUFFY HALLOWEEN SPECIAL
Event Comics: Oct, 1997 ($2.95, B&W, one-shot)
1-Variant-c by Cebollero & Quesada/Palmiotti 3.00

KID DEATH & FLUFFY SPRING BREAK SPECIAL
Event Comics: July, 1996 ($2.50, B&W, one-shot)
1-Quesada & Palmiotti-c/scripts 3.00

KIDDIE KAPERS
Kiddie Kapers Co., 1945/Decker Publ. (Red Top-Farrell): 1945?(nd); Oct, 1957; 1963 - 1964
1(nd, 1945-46?, 36 pgs.)-Infinity-c; funny animal 10 20 30 58 79 100
1(10/57)(Decker)-Little Bit-r from Kiddie Karnival 5 10 15 22 26 30
Super Reprint #7, 10('63), 12, 14('63), 15,17('64), 18('64): 10, 14-r/Animal Adventures #1. 15-Animal Advs. #? 17-Cowboys 'N' Injuns #? 2 4 6 8 11 14

KIDDIE KARNIVAL
Ziff-Davis Publ. Co. (Approved Comics): 1952 (25¢, 100 pgs.) (One Shot)
nn-Rebound Little Bit #1,2; painted-c 36 72 108 216 351 485

KID ETERNITY (Becomes Buccaneers) (See Hit Comics)
Quality Comics Group: Spring, 1946 - No. 18, Nov, 1949
1 90 180 270 576 988 1400
2 39 78 117 240 395 550
3-Mac Raboy-a 40 80 120 246 411 575
4-10 25 50 75 147 241 335
11-18 19 38 57 112 179 245

KID ETERNITY
DC Comics: 1991 - No. 3, Nov, 1991 ($4.95, limited series)
1-3: Grant Morrison scripts/Duncan Fegredo-a/c 6.00
TPB (2006, $14.99) r/#1-3 15.00

KID ETERNITY
DC Comics (Vertigo): May, 1993 - No. 16, Sept, 1994 ($1.95, mature)

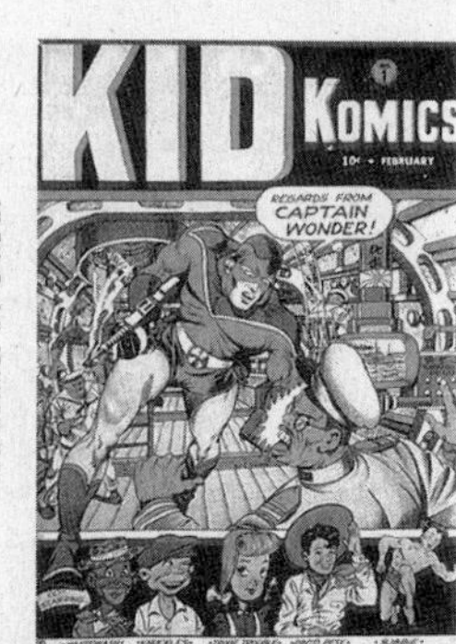

Kid Komics #1 © MAR

The Killers #1 © ME

Kilroy V2 #1 © Joe Pruett

	GD 2.0	VG 4.0	FN 6.0	VF 8.0	VF/NM 9.0	NM- 9.2
1-16: 1-Gold ink-c. 6-Photo-c. All Sean Phillips-c/a except #15 (Phillips-c/i only)						3.00

KID FROM DODGE CITY, THE
Atlas Comics (MMC): July, 1957 - No. 2, Sept, 1957

	GD	VG	FN	VF	VF/NM	NM-
1-Don Heck-c	11	22	33	62	86	110
2-Everett-c	8	16	24	42	54	65

KID FROM TEXAS, THE (A Texas Ranger)
Atlas Comics (CSI): June, 1957 - No. 2, Aug, 1957

	GD	VG	FN	VF	VF/NM	NM-
1-Powell-a; Severin-c	11	22	33	62	86	110
2	8	16	24	42	54	65

KID KOKO
I. W. Enterprises: 1958

	GD	VG	FN	VF	VF/NM	NM-
Reprint #1,2-(r/M.E.'s Koko & Kola #4, 1947)	2	4	6	8	11	14

KID KOMICS (Kid Movie Komics No. 11)
Timely Comics (USA 1,2/FCI 3-10): Feb, 1943 - No. 10, Spring, 1946

	GD	VG	FN	VF	VF/NM	NM-
1-Origin Captain Wonder & sidekick Tim Mullrooney, & Subbie; intro the Sea-Going Lad, Pinto Pete, & Trixie Trouble; Knuckles & Whitewash Jones (from Young Allies) app.; Wolverton-a (7 pgs.)	541	1082	1623	3950	6975	10,000
2-The Young Allies, Red Hawk, & Tommy Tyme begin; last Captain Wonder & Subbie; Schomburg Japanese WWII bondage-c	258	516	774	1651	2826	4000
3-The Vision, Daredevils & Red Hawk app.	174	348	522	1114	1907	2700
4-The Destroyer begins; Sub-Mariner app.; Red Hawk & Tommy Tyme end; classic Schomburg WWII human meat grinder-c	213	426	639	1363	2332	3300
5,6: 5-Tommy Tyme begins, ends #10	113	226	339	723	1237	1750
7-10: 7,10-The Whizzer app. Destroyer not in #7,8. 10-Last Destroyer, Young Allies & Whizzer	97	194	291	621	1061	1500

NOTE: ***Brodsky*** *c-5.* ***Schomburg*** *c-2-4, 6-10.* ***Shores*** *c-1. Captain Wonder c-1, 2. The Young Allies c-3-10.*

KID MONTANA (Formerly Davy Crockett Frontier Fighter; The Gunfighters No. 51 on)
Charlton Comics: V2#9, Nov, 1957 - No. 50, Mar, 1965

	GD	VG	FN	VF	VF/NM	NM-
V2#9 (#1)	4	8	12	27	44	60
10	3	6	9	19	30	40
11,12,14-20	3	6	9	15	22	28
13-Williamson-a	3	6	9	19	30	40
21-35: 25,31-Giordano-c. 32-Origin Kid Montana. 34-Geronimo-c/s. 35-Snow Monster-c/s	2	4	6	11	16	20
36-50: 36-Dinosaur-c/s. 37,48-Giordano-c	2	4	6	9	12	15

NOTE: *Title change to Montana Kid on cover only #44 & 45; remained Kid Montana on inside.* ***Chasal*** *a-29,30.* ***Giordano*** *c-25,31,37,48.* ***Giordano/Alascia*** *c-12.* ***Mastroserio*** *a-9,11,13,14,22; c-11,14.* ***Masulli/Mastroserio*** *c-13.* ***Montes/Bache*** *c-42.* ***Morisi*** *c-16,32-34,36?,40,41,44,46; a-13,15;16,31-50.* ***Nicholas/Alascia*** *a-44,48.*

KID MOVIE KOMICS (Formerly Kid Komics; Rusty Comics #12 on)
Timely Comics: No. 11, Summer, 1946

	GD	VG	FN	VF	VF/NM	NM-
11-Silly Seal & Ziggy Pig; 2 pgs. Kurtzman "Hey Look" plus 6 pg. "Pigtales" story	28	56	84	165	270	375

KIDNAPPED (See Marvel Illustrated: Kidnapped)

KIDNAPPED (Robert Louis Stevenson's...also see Movie Comics)(Disney)
Dell Publishing Co.: No. 1101, May, 1960

	GD	VG	FN	VF	VF/NM	NM-
Four Color 1101-Movie, photo-c	6	12	18	37	66	95

KIDNAP RACKET (See Harvey Comics Hits No. 57)

KID SLADE GUNFIGHTER (Formerly Matt Slade...)
Atlas Comics (SPI): No. 5, Jan, 1957 - No. 8, July, 1957

	GD	VG	FN	VF	VF/NM	NM-
5-Maneely, Roth, Severin-a in all; Maneely-c	13	26	39	74	105	135
6,8-Severin-c	9	18	27	47	61	75
7-Williamson/Mayo-a, 4 pgs.; Maneely-c	10	20	30	58	79	100

KID SUPREME (See Supreme)
Image Comics (Extreme Studios): Mar, 1996 - No. 3, July, 1996 ($2.50)

	GD	VG	FN	VF	VF/NM	NM-
1-3: Fraga-a/scripts. 3-Glory-c/app.						3.00

KID TERRIFIC
Image Comics: Nov, 1998 ($2.95, B&W)

	GD	VG	FN	VF	VF/NM	NM-
1-Snyder & Diliberto-s/a						3.00

KID ZOO COMICS
Street & Smith Publications: July, 1948 (52 pgs.)

	GD	VG	FN	VF	VF/NM	NM-
1-Funny Animal	32	64	96	188	307	425

KILL ALL PARENTS
Image Comics: June, 2008 ($3.99, one-shot)

	GD	VG	FN	VF	VF/NM	NM-
1-Marcelo Di Chiara-a/Mark Andrew Smith-s						4.00

KILLAPALOOZA
DC Comics (WildStorm): July, 2009 - No. 6, Dec, 2009 ($2.99, limited series)

	GD 2.0	VG 4.0	FN 6.0	VF 8.0	VF/NM 9.0	NM- 9.2
1-6: 1-Beechen-s/Hairsine-a/c						3.00
TPB (2010, $19.99) r/#1-6						20.00

KILLER (...Tales By Timothy Truman)
Eclipse Comics: March, 1985 ($1.75, one-shot, Baxter paper)

	GD	VG	FN	VF	VF/NM	NM-
1-Timothy Truman-c/a						3.00

KILLER INSTINCT (Video game)
Acclaim Comics: June, 1996 - No. 6 ($2.50, limited series)

	GD	VG	FN	VF	VF/NM	NM-
1-6: 1-Bart Sears-a(p). 4-Special #1. 5-Special #2. 6-Special #3						3.00

KILLERS, THE
Magazine Enterprises: 1947 - No. 2, 1948 (No month)

	GD	VG	FN	VF	VF/NM	NM-
1-Mr. Zin, the Hatchet Killer; mentioned in **SOTI**, pgs. 179,180; used by N.Y. Legis. Comm.; L. B. Cole-c	139	278	417	890	1520	2150
2-(Scarce)-Hashish smoking story; "Dying, Dying, Dead" drug story; Whitney, Ingels-a; Whitney hanging-c	113	226	339	723	1237	1750

KILLING GIRL
Image Comics: Aug, 2007 - No. 5, Dec, 2007 ($2.99, limited series)

	GD	VG	FN	VF	VF/NM	NM-
1-5: 1-Frank Espinosa-a/Glen Brunswick-s; covers by Espinosa and Frank Cho						3.00

KILLING JOKE, THE (See Batman: The Killing Joke under Batman one-shots)

KILLPOWER: THE EARLY YEARS
Marvel Comics UK: Sept, 1993 - No. 4, Dec, 1993 ($1.75, mini-series)

	GD	VG	FN	VF	VF/NM	NM-
1-($2.95)-Foil embossed-c						4.00
2-4: 2-Genetix app. 3-Punisher app.						3.00

KILLRAVEN (See Amazing Adventures #18 (5/73))
Marvel Comics: Feb, 2001 ($2.99, one-shot)

	GD	VG	FN	VF	VF/NM	NM-
1-Linsner-s/a/c						3.00

KILLRAVEN
Marvel Comics: Dec, 2002 - No. 6, May, 2003 ($2.99, limited series)

	GD	VG	FN	VF	VF/NM	NM-
1-6-Alan Davis-s/a(p)/Mark Farmer-i						3.00
HC (2007, $19.99) r/#1-6; cover gallery, pencil art; foreward by Alan Davis						20.00

KILLRAZOR
Image Comics (Top Cow Productions): Aug, 1995 ($2.50, one-shot)

	GD	VG	FN	VF	VF/NM	NM-
1						3.00

KILL YOUR BOYFRIEND
DC Comics (Vertigo): June, 1995 ($4.95, one-shot)

	GD	VG	FN	VF	VF/NM	NM-
1-Grant Morrison story						6.00
1 ($5.95, 1998) 2nd printing						6.00

KILROY (Volume 2)
Caliber Press: 1998 ($2.95, B&W)

	GD	VG	FN	VF	VF/NM	NM-
1-Pruett-s						3.00

KILROY IS HERE
Caliber Press: 1995 ($2.95, B&W)

	GD	VG	FN	VF	VF/NM	NM-
1-10						3.00

KILROYS, THE
B&I Publ. Co. No. 1-19/American Comics Group: June-July, 1947 - No. 54, June-July, 1955

	GD	VG	FN	VF	VF/NM	NM-
1	24	48	72	140	230	320
2	14	28	42	82	121	160
3-5: 5-Gross-a	14	28	42	76	108	140
6-10: 8-Milt Gross's Moronica	11	22	33	60	83	105
11-20: 14-Gross-a	10	20	30	54	72	90
21-30	9	18	27	50	65	80
31-47,50-54	9	18	27	47	61	75
48,49-(3-D effect-c/stories)	18	36	54	105	165	225

KILROY: THE SHORT STORIES
Caliber Press: 1995 ($2.95, B&W)

	GD	VG	FN	VF	VF/NM	NM-
1						3.00

KIN
Image Comics (Top Cow): Mar, 2000 - No. 6, Sept, 2000 ($2.95)

	GD	VG	FN	VF	VF/NM	NM-
1-5-Gary Frank-s/c/a						3.00
1-($6.95) DF Alternate footprint cover						7.00
6-($3.95)						4.00
... Descent of Man TPB (2002, $19.95) r/ #1-6						20.00

KINDRED, THE
Image Comics (WildStorm Productions): Mar, 1994 - No. 4, July, 1995 ($1.95, lim. series)

	GD	VG	FN	VF	VF/NM	NM-
1-($2.50)-Grifter & Backlash app. in all; bound-in trading card						4.00

Kinetic #8 © Purepop

King Comics #23 © DMP

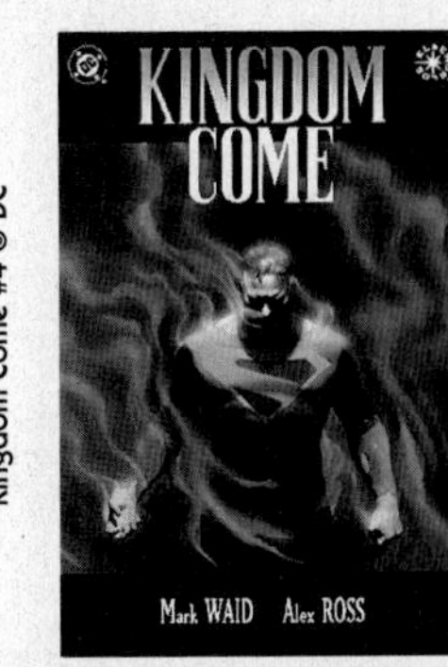

Kingdom Come #4 © DC

	GD 2.0	VG 4.0	FN 6.0	VF 8.0	VF/NM 9.0	NM- 9.2
2-4						3.00
2,3: 2-Variant-c. 3-Alternate-c by Portacio, see Deathblow #5						4.00
Trade paperback (2/95, $9.95)						10.00

NOTE: ***Booth** c/a-1-4. The first four issues contain coupons redeemable for a Jim Lee Grifter/Backlash print.*

KINDRED II, THE
DC Comics (WildStorm): Mar, 2002 - No. 4, June, 2002 ($2.50, limited series)

1-4-Booth-s/Booth & Regla-a 3.00

KINETIC
DC Comics (Focus): May, 2004 - No. 8, Dec, 2004 ($2.50)

1-8-Puckett-s/Pleece-a/c 3.00
TPB (2005, $9.99) r/#1-8; cover gallery and sketch pages 10.00

KING (Magazine)
Skywald Publ.: Mar, 1971 - No. 2, July, 1971

	GD 2.0	VG 4.0	FN 6.0	VF 8.0	VF/NM 9.0	NM- 9.2
1-Violence; semi-nudity; Boris Vallejo-a (2 pgs.)	5	10	15	31	53	75
2-Photo-c	3	6	9	21	33	45

KING ARTHUR AND THE KNIGHTS OF JUSTICE
Marvel Comics UK: Dec, 1993 - No. 3, Feb, 1994 ($1.25, limited series)

1-3: TV adaptation 3.00

KING CLASSICS
King Features : 1977 (36 pgs., cardboard-c) (Printed in Spain for U.S. distr.)

1-Connecticut Yankee, 2-Last of the Mohicans, 3-Moby Dick, 4-Robin Hood, 5-Swiss Family Robinson, 6-Robinson Crusoe, 7-Treasure Island, 8-20,000 Leagues, 9-Christmas Carol, 10-Huck Finn, 11-Around the World in 80 Days, 12-Davy Crockett, 13-Don Quixote, 14-Gold Bug, 15-Ivanhoe, 16-Three Musketeers, 17-Baron Munchausen, 18-Alice in Wonderland, 19-Black Arrow, 20-Five Weeks in a Balloon, 21-Great Expectations, 22-Gulliver's Travels, 23-Prince & Pauper, 24-Lawrence of Arabia (Originals, 1977-78)

	GD 2.0	VG 4.0	FN 6.0	VF 8.0	VF/NM 9.0	NM- 9.2
each....	2	4	6	10	14	18
Reprints (1979; HRN-24)	2	4	6	8	10	12

NOTE: *The first eight issues were not numbered. Issues No. 25-32 were advertised but not published. The 1977 originals have HRN 32a; the 1978 originals have HRN 32b.*

KING COLT (See Luke Short's Western Stories)

KING COMICS (Strip reprints)
David McKay Publications/Standard #156-on: 4/36 - No. 155, 11-12/49; No. 156, Spr/50 - No. 159, 2/52 (Winter on-c)

	GD 2.0	VG 4.0	FN 6.0	VF 8.0	VF/NM 9.0	NM- 9.2
1-1st app. Flash Gordon by Alex Raymond; Brick Bradford (1st app.), Popeye, Henry (1st app.) & Mandrake the Magician (1st app.) begin; Popeye-c begin	1300	2600	3900	10,400	-	-
2	360	720	1080	1980	2840	3700
3	245	490	735	1348	1924	2500
4	190	380	570	1045	1498	1950
5	140	280	420	770	1110	1450
6-10: 9-X-Mas-c	95	190	285	523	749	975
11-20	75	150	225	413	587	760
21-30: 21-X-Mas-c	55	110	165	303	432	560
31-40: 33-Last Segar Popeye	45	90	135	248	354	460
41-50: 46-Text illos by Marge Buell contain characters similar to Lulu, Alvin & Tubby. 50-The Lone Ranger begins	31	62	93	186	303	420
51-60: 52-Barney Baxter begins?	26	52	78	154	252	350
61-The Phantom begins	27	54	81	158	259	360
62-80: 76-Flag-c. 79-Blondie begins	18	36	54	105	165	225
81-99	14	28	42	82	121	160
100	16	32	48	94	147	200
101-114: 114-Last Raymond issue (1 pg.); Flash Gordon by Austin Briggs begins, ends #155	14	28	42	76	108	140
115-145: 117-Phantom origin retold	10	20	30	56	76	95
146,147-Prince Valiant in both	9	18	27	50	65	80
148-155: 155-Flash Gordon ends (11-12/49)	9	18	27	50	65	80
156-159: 156-New logo begins (Standard)	9	18	27	47	61	75

NOTE: *Marge Buell text illos in No. 24-46 at least.*

KING CONAN (Conan The King No. 20 on)
Marvel Comics Group: Mar, 1980 - No. 19, Nov, 1983 (52 pgs.)

	GD 2.0	VG 4.0	FN 6.0	VF 8.0	VF/NM 9.0	NM- 9.2
1	1	2	3	5	6	8
2-19: 4-Death of Thoth Amon. 7-1st Paul Smith-a, 1 pg. pin-up (9/81)						5.00

NOTE: ***J. Buscema** a-1-9p, 17p; c(p)-1-5, 7-9, 14, 17. **Kaluta** c-19. **Nebres** a-17i, 18, 19i. **Severin** c-18. **Simonson** c-6.*

KING CONAN: THE CONQUEROR
Dark Horse Comics: Feb, 2014 - No. 6 ($3.50, limited series)

1,2-Truman-s/Giorello-a/c 3.50

KING CONAN: THE HOUR OF THE DRAGON
Dark Horse Comics: May, 2013 - No. 6, Oct, 2013 ($3.50, limited series)

1-6-Truman-s/Giorello-a/Parel-c 3.50

KING CONAN: THE PHOENIX ON THE SWORD
Dark Horse Comics: Jan, 2012 - No. 4, Apr, 2012 ($3.50, limited series)

1-4-Truman-s/Giorello-a/Robinson-c. 1-Variant-c by Parel 3.50

KING CONAN: THE SCARLET CITADEL
Dark Horse Comics: Feb, 2011 - No. 4, May, 2011 ($3.50, limited series)

1-4-Truman-s/Giorello-a/Robertson-c. 1-Variant-c by Parel 3.50

KING DAVID
DC Comics (Vertigo): 2002 ($19.95, 8 1/2" x 11")

nn-Story of King David; Kyle Baker-s/a 20.00

KINGDOM, THE
DC Comics: Feb, 1999 - No. 2, Feb, 1999 ($2.95/$1.99, limited series)

1,2-Waid-s; sequel to Kingdom Come; introduces Hypertime 4.00
...: Kid Flash 1 (2/99, $1.99) Waid-s/Pararillo-a, ...: Nightstar 1 (2/99, $1.99) Waid-s/Haley-a, ...: Offspring 1 (2/99, $1.99) Waid-s/Quitely-a, ...: Planet Krypton 1 (2/99, $1.99) Waid-s/Kitson-a, ...: Son of the Bat 1 (2/99, $1.99) Waid-s/Apthorp-a 3.00

KINGDOM COME (Also see Justice Society of America #9-22)
DC Comics: 1996 - No. 4, 1996 ($4.95, painted limited series)

	GD 2.0	VG 4.0	FN 6.0	VF 8.0	VF/NM 9.0	NM- 9.2
1-Mark Waid scripts & Alex Ross-painted c/a in all; tells the last days of the DC Universe; 1st app. Magog	1	3	4	6	8	10
2-Superman forms new Justice League	1	2	3	5	6	8
3-Return of Captain Marvel	1	2	3	5	6	8
4-Final battle of Superman and Captain Marvel	1	3	4	6	8	10
Deluxe Slipcase Edition-($89.95) w/Revelations companion book, 12 new story pages, foil stamped covers, signed and numbered						120.00
Hardcover Edition-($29.95)-Includes 12 new story pages and artwork from Revelations, new cover artwork with gold foil inlay						40.00
Hardcover 2nd printing						30.00
Softcover Ed.-($14.95)-Includes 12 new story pgs. & artwork from Revelations, new c-artwork						20.00
Softcover Ed.-(2008, $17.99)-New wraparound gatefold cover by Ross						18.00

KING KONG (See Movie Comics)

KING KONG: THE 8TH WONDER OF THE WORLD (Adaptation of 2005 movie)
Dark Horse Comics: Dec, 2005 ($3.99, planned limited series completed in TPB)

1-Photo-c; Dustin Weaver-a/Christian Gossett-s 4.00
TPB (11/06, $12.95) r/#1 and unpublished parts 2&3; photo-c; Dorman paintings 13.00

KING LEONARDO & HIS SHORT SUBJECTS (TV)
Dell Publishing Co./Gold Key: Nov-Jan, 1961-62 - No. 4, Sept, 1963

	GD 2.0	VG 4.0	FN 6.0	VF 8.0	VF/NM 9.0	NM- 9.2
Four Color 1242,1278	10	20	30	67	141	215
01390-207(5-7/62)(Dell)	8	16	24	52	99	145
1 (10/62)	9	18	27	60	120	180
2-4	7	14	21	48	89	130

KING LOUIE & MOWGLI (See Jungle Book under Movie Comics)
Gold Key: May, 1968 (Disney)

	GD 2.0	VG 4.0	FN 6.0	VF 8.0	VF/NM 9.0	NM- 9.2
1 (#10223-805)-Characters from Jungle Book	3	6	9	19	30	40

KING OF DIAMONDS (TV)
Dell Publishing Co.: July-Sept, 1962

	GD 2.0	VG 4.0	FN 6.0	VF 8.0	VF/NM 9.0	NM- 9.2
01-391-209-Photo-c	4	8	12	25	40	55

KING OF KINGS (Movie)
Dell Publishing Co.: No. 1236, Oct-Nov, 1961

	GD 2.0	VG 4.0	FN 6.0	VF 8.0	VF/NM 9.0	NM- 9.2
Four Color 1236-Photo-c	6	12	18	42	79	115

KING OF THE BAD MEN OF DEADWOOD
Avon Periodicals: 1950 (See Wild Bill Hickok #16)

	GD 2.0	VG 4.0	FN 6.0	VF 8.0	VF/NM 9.0	NM- 9.2
nn-Kinstler-c; Kamen/Feldstein-r/Cowpuncher #2	16	32	48	94	147	200

KING OF THE ROYAL MOUNTED (See Famous Feature Stories, King Comics, Red Ryder #3 & Super Book #2, 6)

KING OF THE ROYAL MOUNTED (Zane Grey's...)
David McKay/Dell Publishing Co.: No. 1, May, 1937; No. 9, 1940; No. 207, Dec, 1948 - No. 935, Sept-Nov, 1958

	GD 2.0	VG 4.0	FN 6.0	VF 8.0	VF/NM 9.0	NM- 9.2
Feature Books 1 (5/37)(McKay)	100	200	300	640	1095	1550
Large Feature Comic 9 (1940)	50	100	150	315	533	750
Four Color 207(#1, 12/48)	12	24	36	79	170	260
Four Color 265,283	8	16	24	51	96	140
Four Color 310,340	6	12	18	38	69	100
Four Color 363,384, 8(6-8/52)-10	5	10	15	35	63	90
11-20	5	10	15	31	53	75
21-28(3-5/58), Four Color 935(9-11/58)	4	8	12	27	44	60

NOTE: *4-Color No. 207, 265, 283, 310, 340, 363, 384 are all newspaper reprints with **Jim Gary** art. No. 8 on are*

Kings Watch #1 © KFS

KISS Solo #1 © KISS Catalog

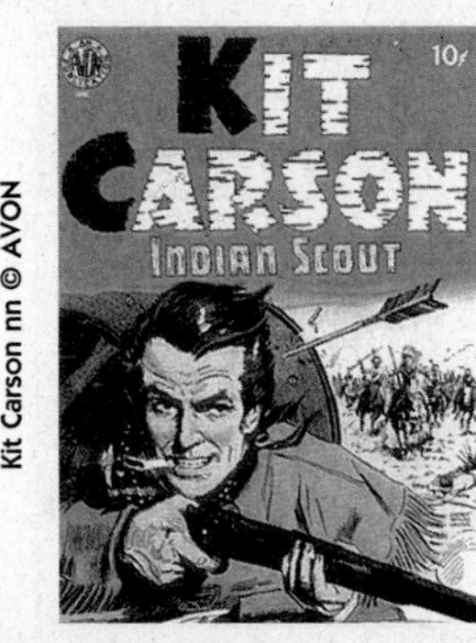

Kit Carson nn © AVON

GD 2.0 VG 4.0 FN 6.0 VF 8.0 VF/NM 9.0 NM- 9.2

all Dell originals. Painted c-No. 9-on.

KINGPIN
Marvel Comics: Nov, 1997 ($5.99, squarebound, one-shot)
nn-Spider-Man & Daredevil vs. Kingpin; Stan Lee-s/ John Romita Sr.-a 6.00

KINGPIN
Marvel Comics: Aug, 2003 - No. 7, Jan, 2004 ($2.50/$2.99, limited series)
1-6-Bruce Jones-s/Sean Phillips & Klaus Janson-a 3.00
7-($2.99) 3.00

KING RICHARD & THE CRUSADERS
Dell Publishing Co.: No. 588, Oct, 1954
Four Color 588-Movie, Matt Baker-a, photo-c 8 16 24 54 102 150

KING-SIZE CABLE SPECTACULAR (Takes place between Cable (2008 series) #6 & #7)
Marvel Comics: Nov, 2008 ($4.99, one-shot)
1-Lashley-a; Deadpool #1 preview; cover gallery of variants from 2008 series 5.00

KING-SIZE HULK (Takes place between Hulk (2008 series) #3 & #4)
Marvel Comics: July, 2008 ($4.99, one-shot)
1-Art Adams, Frank Cho, & Herb Trimpe-a; double-c by Cho & Adams; Red Hulk, She-Hulk & Wendigo app.; origin Abomination; r/Incr. Hulk #180,181 & Avengers #83 5.00

KING-SIZE SPIDER-MAN SUMMER SPECIAL
Marvel Comics: Oct, 2008 ($4.99, one-shot)
1-Short stories by various; Falcon app.; Burchett, Giarrusso & Coover-a 5.00

KINGS OF THE NIGHT
Dark Horse Comics: 1990 - No. 2, 1990 ($2.25, limited series)
1,2-Robert E. Howard adaptation; Bolton-c 3.00

KING SOLOMON'S MINES (Movie)
Avon Periodicals: 1951
nn (#1 on 1st page) 41 82 123 250 418 585

KINGS WATCH
Dynamite Entertainment: 2013 - No. 5, 2014 ($3.99)
1-5-Flash Gordon, Mandrake and The Phantom team up; Parker-s/Laming-a 4.00

KIPLING, RUDYARD (See Mowgli, The Jungle Book)

KIRBY: GENESIS
Dynamite Entertainment: No. 0, 2011 - No. 8, 2012 ($1.00/$3.99)
0-($1.00) Busiek-s; art by Alex Ross & Jack Herbert; series preview, sketch-a 3.00
1-8-($3.99) Ross & Herbert-a. 1-Seven covers. 2-8-Covers by Ross & Sook 4.00

KIRBY: GENESIS - CAPTAIN VICTORY
Dynamite Entertainment: 2011 - No. 6, 2012 ($3.99)
1-6: 1-Origin retold; four covers; Sterling Gates-s/Wagner Reis-a 4.00

KIRBY: GENESIS - DRAGONSBANE
Dynamite Entertainment: 2012 - No. 4, 2013 ($3.99, unfinished limited series)
1-4-Rodi & Ross-s/Casas-a; covers by Ross and Herbert 4.00

KIRBY: GENESIS - SILVER STAR
Dynamite Entertainment: 2011 - No. 6, 2012 ($3.99)
1-6-Jai Nitz-s/Johnny Desjardins-a. 1-Four covers. 2-6-Three covers 4.00

KISS (See Crazy Magazine, Howard the Duck #12, 13, Marvel Comics Super Special #1, 5, Rock Fantasy Comics #10 & Rock N' Roll Comics #9)

KISS
Dark Horse Comics: June, 2002 - No. 13, Sept, 2003 ($2.99, limited series)
1-Photo-c and J. Scott Campbell-c; Casey-s 5.00
2-13: 2-Photo-c and J. Scott Campbell-c. 3-Photo-c and Leinil Yu-c 4.00
...: Men and Monsters TPB (9/03, $12.95) r/#7-10 13.00
...: Rediscovery TPB (2003, $9.95) r/#1-3 10.00
...: Return of the Phantom TPB (2003, $9.95) r/#4-6 10.00
...: Unholy War TPB (2004, $9.95) r/#11-13 10.00

KISS
IDW Publishing: June, 2012 - No. 8, Jan, 2013 ($3.99)
1-8-Multiple covers on each. 1,2-Ryall-s/Igle-a 4.00

KISS 4K
Platinum Studios Comics: May, 2007 - No. 6, Apr, 2008 ($3.99/$2.99)
1-Sprague-s/Crossley & Campos-a/Migliari-c 4.00
1-B&W sketch-c 6.00
1-Destroyer Edition ($50.00, 30"x18", edition of 5000) 50.00
2-6-($2.99) 3.00

GD 2.0 VG 4.0 FN 6.0 VF 8.0 VF/NM 9.0 NM- 9.2

KISSMAS (12/07, $4.99) Christmas-themed issue; re-cap of issues #1-4 5.00

KISS KIDS
IDW Publishing: Aug, 2013 - No. 4, Nov, 2013 ($3.99, limited series)
1-4-Short stories of KISS members as grade-school kids; Ryall & Waltz-s 4.00

KISS SOLO
IDW Publishing: Mar, 2013 - No. 4, Jun, 2013 ($3.99, limited series)
1-4-Multiple covers on each. 1-Ryall-s/Medina-a. 2-Waltz-s/Rodriguez-a 4.00

KISS: THE PSYCHO CIRCUS
Image Comics: Aug, 1997 - No. 31, June, 2000 ($1.95/$2.25/$2.50)
1-Holguin-s/Medina-a(p) 1 3 4 6 8 10
1-2nd & 3rd printings 3.00
2 6.00
3,4: 4-Photo-c 5.00
5-8: 5-Begin $2.25-c 4.00
9-29 4.00
30,31: 30-Begin $2.50-c 4.00
Book 1 TPB ('98, $12.95) r/#1-6 13.00
Book 2 Destroyer TPB (8/99, $9.95) r/#10-13 10.00
Book 3 Whispered Scream TPB ('00, $9.95) r/#7-9,18 10.00
...Magazine 1 ($6.95) r/#1-3 plus interviews 7.00
...Magazine 2-5 ($4.95) 2-r/#4,5 plus interviews. 3-r/#6,7. 4-r/#8,9 5.00
Wizard Edition ('98, supplement) Bios, tour preview and interviews 3.00

KISSING CHAOS
Oni Press: Sept, 2001 - No. 8, Mar, 2002 ($2.25, B&W, 6" x 9", limited series)
1-8-Arthur Dela Cruz-s/a 3.00
...: Nine Lives (12/03, $2.99, regular comic-sized) 3.00
...: 1000 Words (7/03, $2.99, regular comic-sized) 3.00
TPB (9/02, $17.95) r/#1-8 18.00

KISSING CHAOS: NONSTOP BEAUTY
Oni Press: Oct, 2002 - No. 4, March, 2003 ($2.95, B&W, 6" x 9", limited series)
1-4-Arthur Dela Cruz-s/a 3.00
TPB (9/03, $11.95) r/#1-4 12.00

KISS KISS BANG BANG
CrossGen Comics: Feb, 2004 - No. 5, Jun, 2004 ($2.95)
1-5-Bedard-s/Perkins-a 3.00

KISS ME, SATAN
Dark Horse Comics: Sept, 2013 - No. 5, Jan, 2014 ($3.99, limited series)
1-5-Gischler-s/Ferreyra-a; Dave Johnson-c 4.00

KISSYFUR (TV)
DC Comics: 1989 (Sept.) ($2.00, 52 pgs., one-shot)
1-Based on Saturday morning cartoon 4.00

KIT CARSON (Formerly All True Detective Cases No. 4; Fighting Davy Crockett No. 9; see Blazing Sixguns & Frontier Fighters)
Avon Periodicals: 1950; No. 2, 8/51 - No. 3, 12/51; No. 5, 11-12/54 - No. 8, 9/55 (No #4)
nn(#1) (1950)- "...Indian Scout" ; r-Cowboys 'N' Injuns #? 14 28 42 80 115 150
2(8/51) 10 20 30 58 79 100
3(12/51)- "...Fights the Comanche Raiders" 9 18 27 52 69 85
5-6,8(11-12/54-9/55): 5-Formerly All True Detective Cases (last pre-code); titled "...and the Trail of Doom" 9 18 27 50 65 80
7-McCann-a? 9 18 27 50 65 80
I.W. Reprint #10('63)-r/Kit Carson #1; Severin-c 2 4 6 11 16 20
NOTE: *Kinstler c-1-3, 5-8.*

KIT CARSON & THE BLACKFEET WARRIORS
Realistic: 1953
nn-Reprint; Kinstler-c 9 18 27 52 69 85

KIT KARTER
Dell Publishing Co.: May-July, 1962
1 3 6 9 18 28 38

KITTY
St. John Publishing Co.: Oct, 1948
1-Teenage; Lily Renee-c/a 10 20 30 56 76 95

KITTY PRYDE, AGENT OF S.H.I.E.L.D. (Also see Excalibur and Mekanix)
Marvel Comics: Dec, 1997 - No. 3, Feb, 1998 ($2.50, limited series)
1-3-Hama-s 3.00

KITTY PRYDE AND WOLVERINE (Also see Uncanny X-Men & X-Men)

Klaws of the Panther #4 © MAR

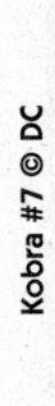

Kobra #7 © DC

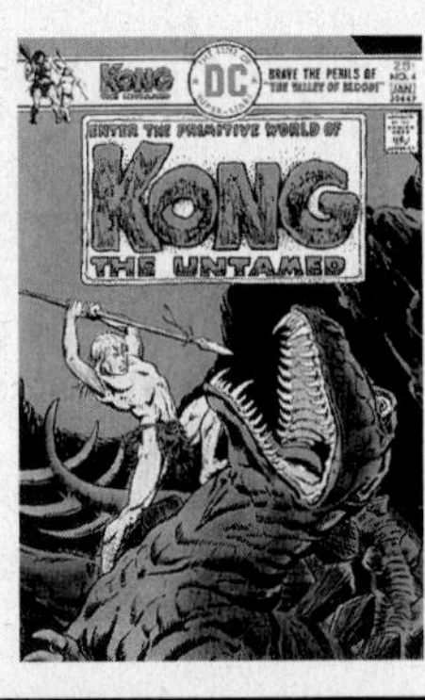

Kong the Untamed #4 © DC

GD 2.0 VG 4.0 FN 6.0 VF 8.0 VF/NM 9.0 NM- 9.2

Marvel Comics Group: Nov, 1984 - No. 6, Apr, 1985 (Limited series)

1-6: Characters from X-Men 5.00
X-Men: Kitty Pryde and Wolverine HC (2008, $19.99) r/series 20.00

KLARER GIVEAWAYS (See Wisco in the Promotional Comics section)

KLAWS OF THE PANTHER (Also see Black Panther)
Marvel Comics: Dec, 2010 - No. 4, Feb, 2011 ($3.99, limited series)

1-4-Maberry-s/Gugliotta-a/Del Mundo-c. 1-Ka-Zar & Shanna app. 3-Spider-Man app. 4.00

KNIGHT AND SQUIRE (Also see Batman #667-669)
DC Comics: Dec, 2010 - No. 6, May, 2011 ($2.99, limited series)

1-6-Cornell-s/Broxton-a. 1-Two covers by Paquette & Tucci. 5,6-Joker app. 3.00
TPB (2011, $14.99) r/#1-6; sketch and design art 15.00

KNIGHTHAWK
Acclaim Comics (Windjammer): Sept, 1995 - No. 6, Nov, 1995 ($2.50, lim. series)

1-6: 6-origin 3.00

KNIGHTMARE
Antarctic Press: July, 1994 - May, 1995 ($2.75, B&W, mature readers)

1-6 3.00

KNIGHTMARE
Image Comics (Extreme Studios): Feb, 1995 - No. 5, June, 1995 ($2.50)

0 ($3.50) 4.00
1-5: 4-Quesada & Palmiotti variant-c, 5-Flip book w/Warcry 3.00

KNIGHTS 4 (See Marvel Knights 4)

KNIGHTS OF PENDRAGON, THE (Also see Pendragon)
Marvel Comics Ltd.: July, 1990 - No. 18, Dec, 1991 ($1.95)

1-18: 1-Capt. Britain app. 2,8-Free poster inside. 9,10-Bolton-c. 11,18-Iron Man app. 3.00

KNIGHTS OF THE ROUND TABLE
Dell Publishing Co.: No. 540, Mar, 1954

Four Color 540-Movie, photo-c 6 12 18 40 73 105

KNIGHTS OF THE ROUND TABLE
Pines Comics: No. 10, April, 1957

10-Features Sir Lancelot 5 10 15 24 30 35

KNIGHTS OF THE ROUND TABLE
Dell Publishing Co.: Nov-Jan, 1963-64

1 (12-397-401)-Painted-c 3 6 9 20 31 42

KNIGHTSTRIKE (Also see Operation: Knightstrike)
Image Comics (Extreme Studios): Jan, 1996 ($2.50)

1-Rob Liefeld & Eric Stephenson story; Extreme Destroyer Part 6. 3.00

KNIGHT WATCHMAN (See Big Bang Comics & Dr. Weird)
Image Comics: June, 1998 - No. 4, Oct, 1998 ($2.95/$3.50, B&W, lim. series)

1-3-Ben Torres-c/a in all 3.00
4-($3.50) 3.50

KNIGHT WATCHMAN: GRAVEYARD SHIFT
Caliber Press: 1994 ($2.95, B&W)

1,2-Ben Torres-a 3.00

KNOCK KNOCK (...Who's There?)
Dell Publ./Gerona Publications: No. 801, 1936 (52 pgs.) (8x9", B&W)

801-Joke book; Bob Dunn-a 12 24 36 69 97 125

KNOCKOUT ADVENTURES
Fiction House Magazines: Winter, 1953-54

1-Reprints Fight Comics #53 w/Rip Carson-c/s 14 28 42 76 108 140

KNUCKLES (Spin-off of Sonic the Hedgehog)
Archie Publications: Apr, 1997 - No. 32, Feb, 2000 ($1.50/$1.75/$1.79)

1-32 4.00

KNUCKLES' CHAOTIX
Archie Publications: Jan, 1996 ($2.00, annual)

1 5.00

KOBALT
DC Comics (Milestone): June, 1994 - No. 16, Sept, 1995 ($1.75/$2.50)

1-16: 1-Byrne-c. 4-Intro Page. 16-Kent Williams-c 3.00

KOBRA (Unpublished #8 appears in DC Special Series No. 1)
National Periodical Publications: Feb-Mar, 1976 - No. 7, Mar-Apr, 1977

GD 2.0 VG 4.0 FN 6.0 VF 8.0 VF/NM 9.0 NM- 9.2

1-1st app.; Kirby-a redrawn by Marcos; only 25¢-c 2 4 6 10 14 18
2-7: (All 30¢ issues) 3-Giffen-a 1 3 4 6 8 10
...: Resurrection TPB (2010, $19.99) r/#1, DC Special Series No. 1 and later apps. in Checkmate #23-25, Faces of Evil: Kobra #1 and various Who's Who issues 20.00

NOTE: *Austin a-3i. Buckler a-5p; c-5p. Kubert c-4. Nasser a-6p, 7; c-7.*

KOKEY KOALA (...and the Magic Button)
Toby Press: May, 1952

1-Funny animal 13 26 39 74 105 135

KOKO AND KOLA (Also see A-1 Comics #16 & Tick Tock Tales)
Com/Magazine Enterprises: Fall, 1946 - No. 5, May, 1947; No. 6, 1950

1-Funny animal 14 28 42 80 115 150
2-X-Mas-c 10 20 30 56 76 95
3-6: 6(A-1 28) 9 18 27 50 65 80

KO KOMICS
Gerona Publications: Oct, 1945 (scarce)

1-The Duke of Darkness & The Menace (hero); Kirby-c 77 154 231 493 847 1200

KOLCHAK: THE NIGHT STALKER (TV)
Moonstone: 2002 - Present ($6.50/$6.95)

1-($6.50) Jeff Rice-s/Gordon Purcell-a 6.50
... Black & White & Read All Over (2005, $4.95) short stories by various; 2 covers 5.00
... Devil in the Details (2003, $6.95) Trevor Von Eeden-a 7.00
... Eve of Terror (2005, $5.95) Gentile-s/Figueroa-a/Beck-c 6.00
... Fever Pitch (2002, $6.95) Christopher Jones-a 7.00
... Get of Belial (2002, $6.95) Art Nichols-a 7.00
... Lambs to the Slaughter (2003, $6.95) Trevor Von Eeden-a 7.00
... Pain Most Human (2004, $6.95) Greg Scott-a 7.00
... Tales: The Frankenstein Agenda 1 (2007 - No. 3, $3.50) Michelinie-s 3.50
... Tales of the Night Stalker 1-7 (2003-Present, $3.50) two covers by Moore & Ulanski 3.50
TPB (2004, $17.95) r/#1, Get of Belial & Fever Pitch 18.00
Vol. 2: Terror Within TPB (2006, $16.95) r/Pain Most Human, Pain Without Tears & Devil in the Details 17.00

KOMIC KARTOONS
Timely Comics (EPC): Fall, 1945 - No. 2, Winter, 1945

1,2-Andy Wolf, Bertie Mouse 25 50 75 150 245 340

KOMIK PAGES (Formerly Snap; becomes Bullseye #11)
Harry 'A' Chesler, Jr. (Our Army, Inc.): Apr, 1945 (All reprints)

10(#1 on inside)-Land O' Nod by Rick Yager (2 pgs.), Animal Crackers, Foxy GrandPa, Tom, Dick & Mary, Cheerio Minstrels, Red Starr plus other 1-2 pg. strips; Cole-a 24 48 72 142 234 325

KONA (...Monarch of Monster Isle)
Dell Publishing Co.: Feb-Apr, 1962 - No. 21, Jan-Mar, 1967 (Painted-c)

Four Color 1256 (#1) 8 16 24 56 108 160
2-10: 4-Anak begins. 6-Gil Kane-c 5 10 15 33 57 80
11-21 4 8 12 28 47 65

NOTE: *Glanzman a-all issues.*

KONGA (Fantastic Giants No. 24) (See Return of...)
Charlton Comics: 1960; No. 2, Aug, 1961 - No. 23, Nov, 1965

1(1960)-Based on movie; Giordano-c 21 42 63 147 324 500
2-5: 2-Giordano-c; no Ditko-a 10 20 30 66 138 210
6-9-Ditko-c/a 9 18 27 58 114 170
10-15 8 16 24 54 102 150
16-23 5 10 15 35 63 90

NOTE: *Ditko a-1, 3-15; c-4, 6-9, 11. Glanzman a-12. Montes & Bache a-16-23.*

KONGA'S REVENGE (Formerly Return of...)
Charlton Comics: No. 2, Summer, 1963 - No. 3, Fall, 1964; Dec, 1968

2,3: 2-Ditko-c/a 7 14 21 44 82 120
1(12/68)-Reprints Konga's Revenge #3 3 6 9 16 24 32

KONG THE UNTAMED
National Periodical Publications: June-July, 1975 - V2#5, Feb-Mar, 1976

1-1st app. Kong; Wrightson-c; Alcala-a 2 4 6 13 18 22
2-Wrightson-c; Alcala-a 2 4 6 10 14 18
3-5: 3-Alcala-a 1 3 4 6 8 10

KOOKABURRA K
Marvel Comics (Soleil): 2009 - No. 3, 2010 ($5.99, limited series)

1-3-Humbertos Ramos-a/c 6.00

KOOKIE

Krampus #1 © Joines & Kotz

Krazy Komics #8 © MAR

Kull the Conqueror #4 © MAR

	GD	VG	FN	VF	VF/NM	NM-
	2.0	4.0	6.0	8.0	9.0	9.2

GD VG FN VF VF/NM NM-
2.0 4.0 6.0 8.0 9.0 9.2

Dell Publishing Co.: Feb-Apr, 1962 - No. 2, May-July, 1962 (15 cents)
1-Written by John Stanley; Bill Williams-a 7 14 21 46 86 125
2 6 12 18 41 76 110

KOOSH KINS
Archie Comics: Oct, 1991 - No. 3, Feb, 1992 ($1.00, bi-monthly, limited series)
1-3 4.00
NOTE: *No. 4 was planned, but cancelled.*

KORAK, SON OF TARZAN (Edgar Rice Burroughs)(See Tarzan #139)
Gold Key: Jan, 1964 - No. 45, Jan, 1972 (Painted-c No. 1-?)
1-Russ Manning-a 8 16 24 56 108 160
2-5-Russ Manning-a 5 10 15 33 57 80
6-11-Russ Manning-a 5 10 15 30 50 70
12-23: 12,13-Warren Tufts-a. 14-Jon of the Kalahari ends. 15-Mabu, Jungle Boy begins.
21-Manning-a. 23-Last 12¢ issue 4 8 12 27 44 60
24-30 3 6 9 21 33 45
31-45 3 6 9 17 26 35

KORAK, SON OF TARZAN (Tarzan Family #60 on; see Tarzan #230)
National Periodical Publications: V9#46, May-June, 1972 - V12#56, Feb-Mar, 1974; No. 57, May-June, 1975 - No. 59, Sept-Oct, 1975 (Edgar Rice Burroughs)
46-(52 pgs.)-Carson of Venus begins (origin), ends #56; Pellucidar feature; Weiss-a
3 6 9 15 22 28
47-59: 49-Origin Korak retold 2 4 6 8 11 14
NOTE: *All have covers by **Joe Kubert**. **Manning** strip reprints-No. 57-59. **Murphy Anderson** a-52. **Michael Kaluta** a-46-56. **Frank Thorne** a-46-51.*

KORE
Image Comics: Apr, 2003 - No. 5, Sept, 2003 ($2.95)
1-5: 1-Two covers by Capullo and Seeley; Seeley-a (p) 3.00

KORG: 70,000 B. C. (TV)
Charlton Publications: May, 1975 - No. 9, Nov, 1976 (Hanna-Barbera)
1,2: 1-Boyette-c/a. 2-Painted-c; Byrne text illos 2 4 6 11 16 20
3-9 2 4 6 8 11 14

KORNER KID COMICS: Four Star Publications: 1947 (Advertised, not pub.)

KRAMPUS
Image Comics: Dec, 2013 - Present ($2.99)
1-4-Sinterklaas' assistant; Joines-s/Kotz-a 3.00

KRAZY KAT
Holt: 1946 (Hardcover)
Reprints daily & Sunday strips by Herriman 55 110 165 352 601 850
dust jacket only 42 84 126 265 450 635

KRAZY KAT (See Ace Comics & March of Comics No. 72, 87)

KRAZY KAT COMICS (...& Ignatz the Mouse early issues)
Dell Publ. Co./Gold Key: May-June, 1951 - F.C. #696, Apr, 1956; Jan, 1964 (None by Herriman)
1(1951) 8 16 24 56 108 160
2-5 (#5, 8-10/52) 5 10 15 33 57 80
Four Color 454,504 5 10 15 31 53 75
Four Color 548,619,696 (4/56) 5 10 15 30 50 70
1(10098-401)(1/64-Gold Key)(TV) 4 8 12 25 40 55

KRAZY KOMICS (1st Series) (Cindy Comics No. 27 on) (Also see Ziggy Pig)
Timely Comics (USA No. 1-21/JPC No. 22-26): July, 1942 - No. 26, Spr, 1947
1-Toughy Tomcat, Ziggy Pig (by Jaffee) & Silly Seal begin
110 220 330 704 1202 1700
2 41 82 123 256 428 600
3-8,10 30 60 90 177 289 400
9-Hitler parody-c 41 82 123 256 428 600
11,13,14 20 40 60 117 189 260
12-Timely's entire art staff drew themselves into a Creeper story
32 64 96 188 307 425
15-(8-9/44)-Has "Super Soldier" by Pfc. Stan Lee 20 40 60 120 195 270
16-24,26: 16-(10-11/44). 26-Super Rabbit-c/story 17 34 51 98 154 210
25-Wacky Duck-c/story & begin; Kurtzman-a (6pgs.) 20 40 60 117 189 260

KRAZY KOMICS (2nd Series)
Timely/Marvel Comics: Aug, 1948 - No. 2, Nov, 1948
1-Wolverton (10 pgs.) & Kurtzman (8 pgs.)-a; Eustice Hayseed begins (Li'l Abner swipe)
48 96 144 302 514 725
2-Wolverton-a (10 pgs.); Powerhouse Pepper cameo
34 68 102 204 332 460

KRAZY KROW (Also see Dopey Duck, Film Funnies, Funny Frolics & Movie Tunes)
Marvel Comics (ZPC): Summer, 1945 - No. 3, Wint, 1945/46
1 25 50 75 150 245 340
2,3 16 32 48 94 147 200
I.W. Reprint #1('57), 2('58), 7 2 4 6 11 16 20

KRAZYLIFE (Becomes Nutty Life #2)
Fox Feature Syndicate: 1945 (no month)
1-Funny animal 24 48 72 142 234 325

KREE/SKRULL WAR STARRING THE AVENGERS, THE
Marvel Comics: Sept, 1983 - No. 2, Oct, 1983 ($2.50, 68 pgs., Baxter paper)
1,2 6.00
NOTE: ***Neal Adams** p-1r, 2. **Buscema** a-1r, 2r. **Simonson** a-1p; c-1p.*

KROFFT SUPERSHOW (TV)
Gold Key: Apr, 1978 - No. 6, Jan, 1979
1-Photo-c 3 6 9 17 26 35
2-6: 6-Photo-c 3 6 9 14 19 24

KRULL
Marvel Comics Group: Nov, 1983 - No. 2, Dec, 1983
1,2-Adaptation of film; r/Marvel Super Special. 1-Photo-c from movie 4.00

KRUSTY COMICS (TV)(See Simpsons Comics)
Bongo Comics: 1995 - No. 3, 1995 ($2.25, limited series)
1-3 3.00

KRYPTON CHRONICLES
DC Comics: Sept, 1981 - No. 3, Nov, 1981
1-3: 1-Buckler-c(p) 4.00

KRYPTO THE SUPERDOG (TV)
DC Comics: Nov, 2006 - No. 6, Apr, 2007 ($2.25)
1-6-Based on Cartoon Network series. 1-Origin retold 3.00

KULL
Dark Horse Comics: Nov, 2008 - No. 6, May, 2009 ($2.99)
1-6: 1-Nelson-s/Conrad-a; two covers by Andy Brase and Joe Kubert 3.00

KULL AND THE BARBARIANS
Marvel Comics: May, 1975 - No. 3, Sept, 1975 ($1.00, B&W, magazine)
1-(84 pgs.) Andru/Wood-r/Kull #1; 2 pgs. Neal Adams; Gil Kane(p),
Marie & John Severin-a(r); Krenkel text illo. 3 6 9 16 24 32
2,3: 2-(84 pgs.) Red Sonja by Chaykin begins; Solomon Kane by Weiss/Adams; Gil Kane-a; Solomon Kane pin-up by Wrightson. 3-(76 pgs.) Origin Red Sonja by Chaykin; Adams-a; Solomon Kane app. 3 6 9 14 19 24

KULL: THE CAT AND THE SKULL
Dark Horse Comics: Oct, 2011 - No. 4, Jan, 2012 ($3.50, limited series)
1-4-Lapham-s/Guzman-a/Chen-c. 1-Variant-c by Hans 3.50

KULL THE CONQUEROR (...the Destroyer #11 on; see Conan #1, Creatures on the Loose #10, Marvel Preview, Monsters on the Prowl)
Marvel Comics Group: June, 1971 - No. 2, Sept, 1971; No. 3, July, 1972 - No. 15, Aug, 1974; No. 16, Aug, 1976 - No. 29, Oct, 1978
1-Andru/Wood-a; 2nd app. & origin Kull; 15¢ issue 6 12 18 37 66 95
2-5: 2-3rd Kull app. Last 15¢ iss. 3-13: 20¢ issues. 3-Thulsa Doom-c/app.
3 6 9 17 26 35
6-10: 7-Thulsa Doom-c/app 2 4 6 10 14 18
11-15: 11-15-Ploog-a. 14,15: 25¢ issues 2 4 6 8 11 14
16-(Regular 25¢ edition)(8/76) 2 3 4 6 8 10
16-(30¢-c variant, limited distribution) 3 6 9 16 23 30
17-29: 21-23-(Reg. 30¢ editions) 2 3 4 6 8 10
21-23-(35¢-c variants, limited distribution) 4 8 12 28 47 65
NOTE: *No. 1, 2, 7-9, 11 are based on Robert E. Howard stories. **Alcala** a-17p, 18-20i; c-24. **Ditko** a-12r, 15r. **Gil Kane** c-15p, 21. **Nebres** a-22i-27i; c-25i, 27i. **Ploog** c-11, 12p, 13. **Severin** a-2-9i; c-2-10i, 19. **Starlin** c-14.*

KULL THE CONQUEROR
Marvel Comics Group: Dec, 1982 - No. 2, Mar, 1983 (52 pgs., Baxter paper)
1,2: 1-Buscema-a(p) 4.00

KULL THE CONQUEROR (No. 9,10 titled "Kull")
Marvel Comics Group: 5/83 - No. 10, 6/85 (52 pgs., Baxter paper)
V3#1-10: Buscema-a in #1-3,5-10 4.00
NOTE: *Bolton a-4. Golden painted c-3-8. Guice a-4p. Sienkiewicz a-4; c-2.*

KULL: THE HATE WITCH
Dark Horse Comics: Nov, 2010 - No. 4, Feb, 2011 ($3.50)

Kung-Fu Panda #5 © Dreamworks

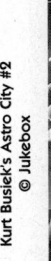

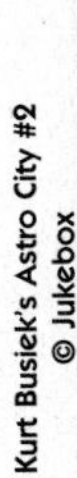
Kurt Busiek's Astro City #2 © Jukebox

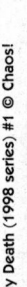

Lady Death (1998 series) #1 © Chaos!

	GD 2.0	VG 4.0	FN 6.0	VF 8.0	VF/NM 9.0	NM- 9.2
1-4-Lapham-s/Guzman-a/Fleming-c						3.50

KUNG FU (See Deadly Hands of..., & Master of...)

KUNG FU FIGHTER (See Richard Dragon...)

KUNG FU PANDA 2
Ape Entertainment: 2011 - No. 6, 2012 ($3.95/$3.99, limited series)

1-6-Short stories by various 4.00

KURT BUSIEK'S ASTRO CITY (Limited series) (Also see Astro City: Local Heroes)
Image Comics (Juke Box Productions): Aug, 1995 - No. 6, Jan, 1996 ($2.25)

1-Kurt Busiek scripts, Brent Anderson-a & Alex Ross front & back-c begins; 1st app. Samaritan & Honor Guard (Cleopatra, MHP, Beautie, The Black Rapier, Quarrel & N-Forcer) 2 4 6 8 10 12
2-6: 2-1st app. The Silver Agent, The Old Soldier, & the "original" Honor Guard (Max O'Millions, Starwoman, the "original" Cleopatra, the "original" N-Forcer, the Bouncing Beatnik, Leopardman & Kitkat). 3-1st app. Jack-in-the-Box & The Deacon. 4-1st app. Winged Victory (cameo), The Hanged Man & The First Family. 5-1st app. Crackerjack, The Astro City Irregulars, Nightingale & Sunbird. 6-Origin Samaritan; 1st full app. Winged Victory 1 3 4 6 8 10
Life In The Big City-(8/96, $19.95, trade paperback)-r/Image Comics limited series w/sketchbook & cover gallery; Ross-c 20.00
Life In The Big City-(8/96, $49.95, hardcover, 1000 print run)-r/Image Comics limited series w/sketchbook & cover gallery; Ross-c 50.00

KURT BUSIEK'S ASTRO CITY (1st Homage Comics series)
Image Comics (Homage Comics): V2#1, Sept, 1996 - No. 15, Dec, 1998;
DC Comics (Homage Comics): No. 16, Mar, 1999 - No. 22, Aug, 2000 ($2.50)

1/2-(10/96)-The Hanged Man story; 1st app. The All-American & Slugger, The Lamplighter, The Time-Keeper & Eterneon 1 3 4 6 8 10
1/2-(1/98) 2nd printing w/new cover 3.00
1- Kurt Busiek scripts, Alex Ross-c, Brent Anderson-p & Will Blyberg-i begin; intro The Gentleman, Thunderhead & Helia. 1 2 3 5 6 8
1-(12/97, $4.95) "3-D Edition" w/glasses 5.00
2-Origin The First Family; Astra story 1 2 3 4 5 7
3-5: 4-1st app. The Crossbreed, Ironhorse, Glue Gun & The Confessor (cameo) 6.00
6-10 5.00
11-22: 14-20-Steeljack story arc. 16-(3/99) First DC issue 3.00
TPB-($19.95) Ross-c, r/#4-9, #1/2 w/sketchbook 20.00
Family Album TPB ($19.95) r/#1-3,10-13 20.00
The Tarnished Angel HC ($29.95) r/#14-20; new Ross dust jacket; sketch pages by Anderson & Ross; cover gallery with reference photos 30.00
The Tarnished Angel SC ($19.95) r/#14-20; new Ross-c 20.00

LABMAN
Image Comics: Nov, 1996 ($3.50, one-shot)

1-Allred-c 4.00

LAB RATS
DC Comics: June, 2002 - No. 8, Jan, 2003 ($2.50)

1-8-John Byrne-s/a. 5,6-Superman app. 3.00

LABYRINTH
Marvel Comics Group: Nov, 1986 - No. 3, Jan, 1987 (Limited series)

1-3: David Bowie movie adaptation; r/Marvel Super Special #40 1 2 3 5 6 8

LA COSA NOSTROID (See Scud: The Disposible Assassin)
Fireman Press: Mar, 1996 - No. 9, 1998 ($2.95, B&W)

1-9-Dan Harmon-s/Rob Schrab-c/a 3.00

LAD: A DOG (Movie)
Dell Publishing Co.: 1961 - No. 2, July-Sept, 1962

Four Color 1303 4 8 12 28 47 65
2 4 8 12 23 37 50

LADY AND THE TRAMP (Disney, See Dell Giants & Movie Comics)
Dell Publishing Co.: No. 629, May, 1955 - No. 634, June, 1955

Four Color 629 (#1)-..with Jock 6 12 18 41 76 110
Four Color 634-...Album 5 10 15 31 53 75

LADY COP (See 1st Issue Special)

LADY DEADPOOL
Marvel Comics: Sept, 2010 ($3.99, one-shot)

1-Land-c/Lashley-a 4.00

LADY DEATH (See Evil Ernie)
Chaos! Comics: Jan, 1994 - No. 3, Mar, 1994 ($2.75, limited series)

1/2-S. Hughes-c/a in all, 1/2 Velvet 1 2 3 4 5 7
1/2 Gold 1 3 4 6 8 10
1/2 Signed Limited Edition 2 4 6 8 10 12
1-($3.50)-Chromium-c 2 4 6 10 14 18
1-Commemorative 2 4 6 9 13 16
1-(9/96, $2.95) "Encore Presentation"; r/#1 3.00
2 1 2 3 5 6 8
3 5.00
... And Jade (4/02, $2.99) Augustyn-s/Reis-a 3.00
...And The Women of Chaos! Gallery #1 (11/96, $2.25) pin-ups by various 3.00
.../Bad Kitty (9/01, $2.99) Mota-c/a 3.00
.../Bedlam (6/02, $2.99) Augustyn-s/Reis-c 3.00
...By Steven Hughes (6/00, $2.95) Tribute issue to Steven Hughes 3.00
...By Steven Hughes Deluxe Edition(6/00, $15.95) 16.00
.../Chastity (1/02, $2.99) Mota-c/a; Augustyn-s 3.00
...Death Becomes Her #0 (11/97, $2.95) Hughes-c/a 3.00
...FAN Edition: All Hallow's Eve #1 (1/97, mail-in) 5.00
...In Lingerie #1 (8/95, $2.95) pin-ups, wraparound-c 3.00
...In Lingerie #1-Leather Edition (10,000) 12.00
...In Lingerie #1-Micro Premium Edition; Lady Demon-c (2,000) 35.00
...: Love Bites (3/01, $2.99) Kaminski-s/Luke Ross-a 3.00
.../Medieval Witchblade (8/01, $3.50) covers by Molenaar and Silvestri 3.50
.../Medieval Witchblade Preview Ed. (8/01, $1.99) Molenaar-c 3.00
...: Mischief Night (11/01, $2.99) Ostrander-s/Reis-a 3.00
...: Re-Imagined (7/02, $2.99) Gossett-c 3.00
...: River of Fear (4/01, $2.99) Bennett-a(p)/Cleavenger-c 3.00
...Swimsuit Special #1-($2.50)-Wraparound-c 3.00
...Swimsuit Special #1-Red velvet-c 14.00
...Swimsuit 2001 #1-(2/01, $2.99)-Reis-c; art by various 3.00
...: The Reckoning (7/94, $6.95)-r/#1-3 7.00
...: The Reckoning (8/95, $12.95)- new printing including Lady Death 1/2 & Swimsuit Special #1 13.00
.../Vampirella (3/99, $3.50) Hughes-c/a 3.50
.../Vampirella 2 (3/00, $3.50) Deodato-c/a 3.50
... Vs. Purgatori (12/99, $3.50) Deodato-a 3.50
... Vs. Vampirella Preview (2/00, $1.00) Deodato-a/c 3.00

LADY DEATH (Ongoing series)
Chaos! Comics: Feb, 1998 - No. 16, May, 1999 ($2.95)

1-16: 1-4: Pulido-s/Hughes-c/a. 5-8,13-16-Deodato-a. 9-11-Hughes-a 3.00
...Retribution (8/98, $2.95) Jadsen-a 3.00
...Retribution Premium Ed. 6.00

LADY DEATH
Boundless Comics: No. 0, Nov, 2010 - Present ($3.99)

0-25-Pulido & Wolfer-s/Mueller-a on most; multiple covers on all. 25-Borstel-a 4.00
... Free Comic Book Day 2012 (5/12, free) "The Beginning" on cover; Mueller-a 3.00
... Origins Annual 1 (8/11, $4.99) Martin-a/Pulido-s 5.00
... Premiere (7/10, free) previews series; five covers 3.00

LADY DEATH: ALIVE
Chaos! Comics: May, 2001 - No. 4, Aug, 2001 ($2.99, limited series)

1-4-Ivan Reis-a; Lady Death becomes mortal 3.00

LADY DEATH: A MEDIEVAL TALE (Brian Pulido's...)
CG Entertainment: Mar, 2003 - No. 12, Apr, 2004 ($2.95)

1-12: 1-Brian Pulido-s/Ivan Reis-a; Lady Death in the CrossGen Universe 3.00
Vol.1 TPB (2003, $9.95) digest-sized reprint of #1-6 10.00

LADY DEATH: DARK ALLIANCE
Chaos! Comics: July, 2002 - No. 5, ($2.99, limited series)

1-3-Reis-a/Ostrander-s 3.00

LADY DEATH: DARK MILLENNIUM
Chaos! Comics: Feb, 2000 - No. 3, Apr, 2000 ($2.95, limited series)

Preview (6/00, $5.00) 5.00
1-3-Ivan Reis-a 3.00

LADY DEATH: GODDESS RETURNS
Chaos! Comics: Jun, 2002 - No. 2, Aug, 2002 ($2.99, limited series)

1,2-Mota-a/Ostrander-s 3.00

LADY DEATH: HEARTBREAKER
Chaos! Comics: Mar, 2002 - No. 4, ($2.99, limited series)

1-Molenaar-a/Ostrander-s 3.00

LADY DEATH: JUDGEMENT WAR
Chaos! Comics: Nov, 1999 - No. 3, Jan, 2000 ($2.95, limited series)

Lady Pendragon V2 #1 © Matt Hawkins

Lady Rawhide (2013 series) #1 © Zorro Prods.

Lana #3 © MAR

	GD 2.0	VG 4.0	FN 6.0	VF 8.0	VF/NM 9.0	NM- 9.2

Prelude (10/99) two covers 3.00
1-3-Ivan Reis-a 3.00

LADY DEATH: LAST RITES
Chaos! Comics: Oct, 2001 - No. 4, Feb, 2001 ($2.99, limited series)
1-4-Ivan Reis-a/Ostrander-s 3.00

LADY DEATH ORIGINS: CURSED
Boundless Comics: Mar, 2012 - No. 3, May, 2012 ($4.99/$3.99, limited series)
1-($4.99)-Pulido-s/Guzman-a; multiple covers 5.00
2,3-($3.99) 4.00

LADY DEATH: THE CRUCIBLE
Chaos! Comics: Nov, 1996 - No. 6, Oct, 1997 ($3.50/$2.95, limited series)
1/2 4.00
1/2 Cloth Edition 8.00
1-Wraparound silver foil embossed-c 4.00
2-6-($2.95) 3.00

LADY DEATH: THE GAUNTLET
Chaos! Comics: Apr, 2002 - No. 2, May, 2002 ($2.99, limited series)
1,2: 1-J. Scott Campbell-c/redesign of Lady Death's outfit; Mota-a 3.00

LADY DEATH: THE ODYSSEY
Chaos! Comics: Apr, 1996 - No. 4, Aug, 1996 ($3.50/$2.95)
1-($1.50)-Sneak Peek Preview 3.00
1-($1.50)-Sneak Peek Preview Micro Premium Edition (2500 print run)
2 4 6 8 10 12
1-($3.50)-Embossed, wraparound goil foil-c 5.00
1-Black Onyx Edition (200 print run) 5 10 15 33 57 80
1-($19.95)-Premium Edition (10,000 print run) 20.00
2-4-($2.95) 3.00

LADY DEATH: THE RAPTURE
Chaos! Comics: Jun, 1999 - No. 4, Sept, 1999 ($2.95, limited series)
1-4-Ivan Reis-c/a; Pulido-s 3.00

LADY DEATH: THE WILD HUNT (Brian Pulido's...)
CG Entertainment: Apr, 2004 - No. 2, May, 2005 ($2.95)
1-2: 1-Brian Pulido-s/Jim Cheung-a 3.00

LADY DEATH: TRIBULATION
Chaos! Comics: Dec, 2000 - No. 4, Mar, 2001 ($2.95, limited series)
1-4-Ivan Reis-a; Kaminski-s 3.00

LADY DEATH II: BETWEEN HEAVEN & HELL
Chaos! Comics: Mar, 1995 - No. 4, July, 1995 ($3.50, limited series)
1-Chromium wraparound-c; Evil Ernie cameo 5.00
1-Commemorative (4,000), 1-Black Velvet-c 2 4 6 10 14 18
1-Gold 1 3 4 6 8 10
1-"Refractor" edition (5,000) 2 4 6 11 16 20
2-4 3.50
4-Lady Demon variant-c 1 2 3 5 7 9
Trade paperback-($12.95)-r/#1-4 13.00

LADY DEMON
Chaos! Comics: Mar, 2000 - No. 3, May, 2000 ($2.95, limited series)
1-3-Kaminski-s/Brewer-a 3.00

LADY FOR A NIGHT (See Cinema Comics Herald)

LADY JUSTICE (See Neil Gaiman's...)

LADY LUCK (Formerly Smash #1-85) (Also see Spirit Sections #1)
Quality Comics Group: No. 86, Dec, 1949 - No. 90, Aug, 1950
86(#1) 97 194 291 621 1061 1500
87-90 66 132 198 419 722 1025

LADY MECHANIKA
Aspen MLT: No. 0, Oct, 2010 - Present ($2.50/$2.99)
0-Joe Benitez-s/a; two covers; Benitez interview and sketch pages 3.00
1-(1/11, $2.99) Multiple covers 10.00
2,3-Multiple covers on each 5.00

LADY PENDRAGON
Maximum Press: Mar, 1996 ($2.50)
1-Matt Hawkins script 3.00

LADY PENDRAGON
Image Comics: Nov, 1998 - No. 3, Jan, 1999 ($2.50, mini-series)
Preview (6/98) Flip book w/ Deity preview 3.00
1-3: 1-Matt Hawkins-s/Stinsman-a 3.00
1-($6.95) DF Ed. with variant-c by Jusko 7.00
2-($4.95)Variant edition 5.00
0-(3/99) Origin; flip book 3.00

LADY PENDRAGON (Volume 3)
Image Comics: Apr, 1999 - No. 9, Mar, 2000 ($2.50, mini-series)
1,2,4-6,8-10: 1-Matt Hawkins-s/Stinsman-a. 2-Peterson-c 3.00
3-Flip book w/Alley Cat preview (1st app.) 4.00
7-($3.95) Flip book; Stinsman-a/Cleavenger painted-a 4.00
Gallery Edition (10/99, $2.95) pin-ups 3.00
...Merlin (1/00, $2.95) Stinsman-a 3.00
.../ More Than Mortal (5/99, $2.50) Scott-s/Norton-a; 2 covers by Norton & Finch 3.00
.../ More Than Mortal Preview (2/99) Diamond Dateline supplement 3.00
Pilot Season: Lady Pendragon (5/08, $3.99) Hawkins-s/Eru-a; wraparound-c by Struzan 4.00

LADY RAWHIDE
Topps Comics: July, 1995 - No. 5, Mar, 1996 ($2.95, bi-monthly, limited series)
1-5: Don McGregor scripts & Mayhew-a. in all. 2-Stelfreeze-c. 3-Hughes-c. 4-Golden-c. 5-Julie Bell-c. 3.00
It Can't Happen Here TPB (8/99, $16.95) r/#1-5 17.00
Mini Comic 1 (7/95) Maroto-a; Zorro app. 3.00
Special Edition 1 (6/95, $3.95)-Reprints 4.00

LADY RAWHIDE (Volume 2)
Topps Comics: Oct, 1996 -No. 5, June, 1997 ($2.95, limited series)
1-5: 1-Julie Bell-c. 3.00

LADY RAWHIDE (Volume 1)
Dynamite Entertainment: 2013 - No. 5, 2014 ($3.99)
1-5-Trautmann-s/Estevam-a/Linsner-c 4.00

LADY RAWHIDE OTHER PEOPLE'S BLOOD (ZORRO'S ...)
Image Comics: Mar, 1999 - No. 5, July, 1999 ($2.95, B&W)
1-5-Reprints Lady Rawhide series in B&W 3.00

LADY SUPREME (See Asylum)(Also see Supreme & Kid Supreme)
Image Comics (Extreme): May, 1996 - No. 2, June, 1996 ($2.50, limited series)
1,2-Terry Moore -s: 1-Terry Moore-c. 2-Flip book w/Newmen preview 3.00

LAFF-A-LYMPICS (TV)(See The Funtastic World of Hanna-Barbera)
Marvel Comics: Mar, 1978 - No. 13, Mar, 1979 (Newsstand sales only)
1-Yogi Bear, Scooby Doo, Pixie & Dixie, etc. 3 6 9 17 26 35
2-8 3 6 9 14 19 24
9-13: 11-Jetsons x-over; 1 pg. illustrated bio of Mighty Mightor, Herculoids, Shazzan, Galaxy Trio & Space Ghost 3 6 9 16 23 30

LAFFY-DAFFY COMICS
Rural Home Publ. Co.: Feb, 1945 - No. 2, Mar, 1945
1-Funny animal 12 24 36 67 94 120
2-Funny animal 11 22 33 60 83 105

LANA (Little Lana No. 8 on)
Marvel Comics (MjMC): Aug, 1948 - No. 7, Aug, 1949 (Also see Annie Oakley)
1-Rusty, Millie begin 41 82 123 256 428 600
2-Kurtzman's "Hey Look" (1); last Rusty 21 42 63 122 199 275
3-7: 3-Nellie begins 15 30 45 85 130 175

LANCELOT & GUINEVERE (See Movie Classics)

LANCELOT LINK, SECRET CHIMP (TV)
Gold Key: Apr, 1971 - No. 8, Feb, 1973
1-Photo-c 5 10 15 35 63 90
2-8: 2-Photo-c 4 8 12 23 37 50

LANCELOT STRONG (See The Shield)

LANCE O'CASEY (See Mighty Midget & Whiz Comics)
Fawcett Publications: Spring, 1946 - No. 3, Fall, 1946; No. 4, Summer, 1948
1-Captain Marvel app. on-c 26 52 78 154 252 350
2 16 32 48 94 147 200
3,4 14 28 42 80 115 150
NOTE: *The cover for the 1st issue was done in 1942 but was not published until 1946. The cover shows 68 pages but actually has only 36 pages.*

LANCER (TV)(Western)
Gold Key: Feb, 1969 - No. 3, Sept, 1969 (All photo-c)
1 4 8 12 23 37 50
2,3 3 6 9 17 26 35

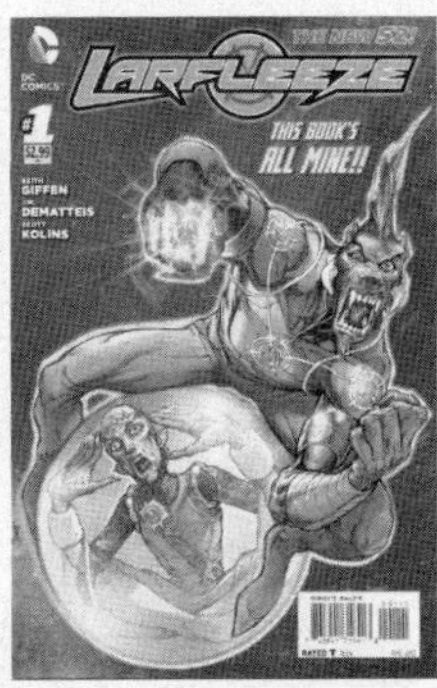

Larfleeze #1 © DC

Large Feature Comic #3 © LR Inc.

Lash Larue Western #9 © FAW

GD VG FN VF VF/NM NM-
2.0 4.0 6.0 8.0 9.0 9.2

LAND OF NOD, THE
Dark Horse Comics: July, 1997 - No. 3, Feb, 1998 ($2.95, B&W)

1-3-Jetcat; Jay Stephens-s/a 3.00

LAND OF OZ
Arrow Comics: 1998 - No. 9 ($2.95, B&W)

1-9-Bishop-s/Bryan-s/a 3.00

LAND OF THE DEAD (George A. Romaro's...)
IDW Publishing: Aug, 2005 - No. 5 ($3.99, limited series)

1-4-Adaptation of 2005 movie; Ryall-s/Rodriguez-a 4.00
TPB (3/06, $19.99) r/#1-5; cover gallery 20.00

LAND OF THE GIANTS (TV)
Gold Key: Nov, 1968 - No. 5, Sept, 1969 (All have photo-c)

	GD	VG	FN	VF	VF/NM	NM-
1	6	12	18	37	66	95
2-5	4	8	12	25	40	55

LAND OF THE LOST COMICS (Radio)
E. C. Comics: July-Aug, 1946 - No. 9, Spring, 1948

	GD	VG	FN	VF	VF/NM	NM-
1	40	80	120	246	411	575
2	25	50	75	150	245	340
3-9	22	44	66	128	209	290

LAND UNKNOWN, THE (Movie)
Dell Publishing Co.: No. 845, Sept, 1957

	GD	VG	FN	VF	VF/NM	NM-
Four Color 845-Alex Toth-a	10	20	30	64	132	200

LA PACIFICA
DC Comics (Paradox Press): 1994/1995 ($4.95, B&W, limited series, digest size, mature)

1-3 5.00

LARAMIE (TV)
Dell Publishing Co.: Aug, 1960 - July, 1962 (All photo-c)

	GD	VG	FN	VF	VF/NM	NM-
Four Color 1125-Gil Kane/Heath-a	7	14	21	49	92	135
Four Color 1223,1284, 01-418-207 (7/62)	6	12	18	37	66	95

LAREDO (TV)
Gold Key: June, 1966

	GD	VG	FN	VF	VF/NM	NM-
1 (10179-606)-Photo-c	3	6	9	21	33	45

LARFLEEZE (Orange Lantern) (Story continued from back-ups in Threshold #1-5)
DC Comics: Aug, 2013 - Present ($2.99)

1-9: 1-Giffen & DeMatteis-s/Kolins-a/Porter-c; origin told 3.00

LARGE FEATURE COMIC (Formerly called Black & White in previous guides)
Dell Publishing Co.: 1939 - No. 13, 1943

Note: See individual alphabetical listings for prices

1 (Series I)-Dick Tracy Meets the Blank
2-Terry and the Pirates (#1)
3-Heigh-Yo Silver! The Lone Ranger (text & ill.)(76 pgs.); also exists as a Whitman #710; based on radio
4-Dick Tracy Gets His Man
5-Tarzan of the Apes (#1) by Harold Foster (origin); reprints 1st Tarzan dailies from 1929
6-Terry & the Pirates & The Dragon Lady; reprints dailies from 1936
7-(Scarce, 52 pgs.)-Hi-Yo Silver the Lone Ranger to the Rescue; also exists as a Whitman #715, based on radio program
8-Dick Tracy the Racket Buster
9-King of the Royal Mounted (Zane Grey's...)
10-(Scarce)-Gang Busters (No. appears on inside front cover); first slick cover (based on radio program)
11-Dick Tracy Foils the Mad Doc Hump
12-Smilin' Jack; no number on-c
13-Dick Tracy and Scottie of Scotland Yard
14-Smilin' Jack Helps G-Men Solve a Case!
15-Dick Tracy and the Kidnapped Princes
16-Donald Duck; 1st app. Daisy Duck on back cover (6/41-Disney)
17-Gang Busters (1941)
18-Phantasmo (see The Funnies #45)
19-Dumbo Comic Paint Book (Disney); partial-r from 4-Color #17
20-Donald Duck Comic Paint Book (rarer than #16) (Disney)
21,22: 21-Private Buck. 22-Nuts & Jolts
23-The Nebbs
24-Popeye in "Thimble Theatre" by Segar
25-Smilin' Jack-1st issue to show title on-c
26-Smitty
27-Terry and the Pirates; Caniff-c/a
28-Grin and Bear It
29-Moon Mullins
30-Tillie the Toiler
1 (Series II)-Peter Rabbit by Harrison Cady; arrival date-3/27/42
2-Winnie Winkle (#1)
3-Dick Tracy
4-Tiny Tim (#1)
5-Toots and Casper
6-Terry and the Pirates; Caniff-a
7-Pluto Saves the Ship (#1) (Disney)-Written by Carl Barks, Jack Hannah, & Nick George (Barks' 1st comic book work)
8-Bugs Bunny (#1)('42)
9-Bringing Up Father
10-Popeye (Thimble Theatre)
11-Barney Google and Snuffy Smith
12-Private Buck
13-(nn)-1001 Hours Of Fun; puzzles & games; by A. W. Nugent. This book was bound as #13 with Large Feature Comics in publisher's files

NOTE: The Black & White Feature Books are oversized 8-1/2x11-3/8" comics with color covers and black and white interiors. The first nine issues all have rough, heavy stock covers and, except for #7, all have 76 pages, including covers. #7 and #10-on all have 52 pages. Beginning with #10 the covers are slick and thin and, because of their size, are difficult to handle without damaging. For this reason, they are seldom found in fine to mint condition. The paper stock, unlike Wow #1 and Capt. Marvel #1, is itself not unstable ...just thin. Many issues were reprinted in the early 1980s, identical except for the copyright notice on the first page.

LARRY DOBY, BASEBALL HERO
Fawcett Publications: 1950 (Cleveland Indians)

	GD	VG	FN	VF	VF/NM	NM-
nn-Bill Ward-a; photo-c	79	158	237	502	864	1225

LARRY HARMON'S LAUREL AND HARDY (...Comics)
National Periodical Publ.: July-Aug, 1972 (Digest advertised, not published)

	GD	VG	FN	VF	VF/NM	NM-
1-Low print run	9	18	27	57	111	165

LARS OF MARS
Ziff-Davis Publishing Co.: No. 10, Apr-May, 1951 - No. 11, July-Aug, 1951 (Painted-c)
(Created by Jerry Siegel, editor)

	GD	VG	FN	VF	VF/NM	NM-
10-Origin; Anderson-a(3) in each; classic robot-c	97	194	291	621	1061	1500
11-Gene Colan-a; classic-c	77	154	231	493	847	1200

LARS OF MARS 3-D
Eclipse Comics: Apr, 1987 ($2.50)

1-r/Lars of Mars #10,11 in 3-D plus new story 4.00
2-D limited edition (B&W, 100 copies) 10.00

LASER ERASER & PRESSBUTTON (See Axel Pressbutton & Miracle Man 9)
Eclipse Comics: Nov, 1985 - No. 6, 1987 (95¢/$2.50, limited series)

1-6: 5,6-(95¢) 3.00
...In 3-D 1 (8/86, $2.50) 4.00
2-D 1 (B&W, limited to 100 copies signed & numbered) 10.00

LASH LARUE WESTERN (Movie star; King of the bullwhip)(See Fawcett Movie Comic, Motion Picture Comics & Six-Gun Heroes)
Fawcett Publications: Sum, 1949 - No. 46, Jan, 1954 (36 pgs., 1-6,9,13,16-on)

	GD	VG	FN	VF	VF/NM	NM-
1-Lash & his horse Black Diamond begin; photo front/back-c begin	58	116	174	371	636	900
2(11/49)	28	56	84	165	270	375
3-5	21	42	63	126	206	285
6,9: 6-Last photo back-c; intro. Frontier Phantom (Lash's twin brother)	19	38	57	109	172	235
7,8,10 (52pgs.)	20	40	60	114	182	250
11,12,14,15 (52pgs.)	15	30	45	84	127	170
13,16-20 (36pgs.)	14	28	42	80	115	150
21-30: 21-The Frontier Phantom app.	12	24	36	69	97	125
31-45	11	22	33	60	83	105
46-Last Fawcett issue & photo-c	11	22	33	64	90	115

LASH LARUE WESTERN (Continues from Fawcett series)
Charlton Comics: No. 47, Mar-Apr, 1954 - No. 84, June, 1961

	GD	VG	FN	VF	VF/NM	NM-
47-Photo-c	14	28	42	80	115	150
48	11	22	33	60	83	105
49-60, 67,68-(68 pgs.). 68-Check-a	9	18	27	52	69	85
61-66,69,70: 52-r/#8; 53-r/#22	9	18	27	47	61	75
71-83	8	16	24	40	50	60
84-Last issue	9	18	27	47	61	75

LASH LARUE WESTERN
AC Comics: 1990 ($3.50, 44 pgs) (24 pgs. of color, 16 pgs. of B&W)

1-Photo covers; r/Lash #6; r/old movie posters 4.00
Annual 1 (1990, $2.95, B&W, 44 pgs.)-Photo covers 4.00

LASSIE (TV)(M-G-M's... #1-36; see Kite Fun Book)
Dell Publ. Co./Gold Key No. 59 (10/62) on: June, 1950 - No. 70, July, 1969

	GD	VG	FN	VF	VF/NM	NM-
1 (52 pgs.)-Photo-c; inside lists One Shot #282 in error	19	38	57	131	291	450
2-Painted-c begin	8	16	24	54	102	150
3-10	6	12	18	37	66	95
11-19: 12-Rocky Langford (Lassie's master) marries Gerry Lawrence. 15-1st app. Timbu	5	10	15	30	50	70
20-22-Matt Baker-a	5	10	15	33	57	80

The Last American #1 © MAR

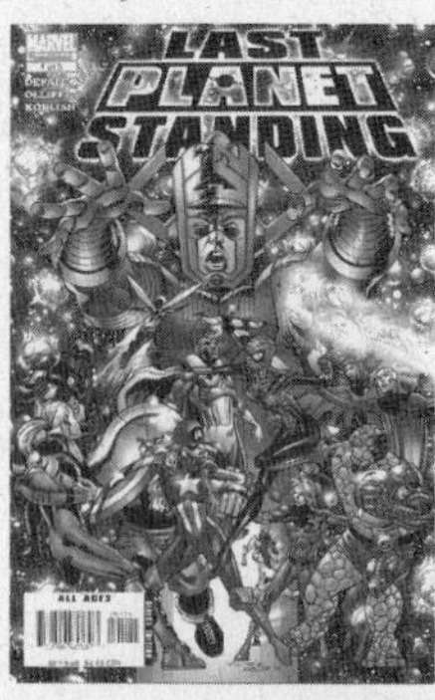

Last Planet Standing #1 © MAR

Laugh V2 #21 © AP

GD VG FN VF VF/NM NM-
2.0 4.0 6.0 8.0 9.0 9.2

23-38: 33-Robinson-a. 4 8 12 28 47 65
39-1st app. Timmy as Lassie picks up her TV family; photo-c
5 10 15 35 63 90
40-50-Photo-c on all 4 8 12 28 47 65
51-58-Photo-c on all 4 8 12 27 44 60
59 (10/62)-1st Gold Key 4 8 12 28 47 65
60-70: 63-Last Timmy (10/63). 64-r/#19. 65-Forest Ranger Corey Stuart begins, ends #69. 70-Forest Rangers Bob Ericson & Scott Turner app. (Lassie's new masters)
4 8 12 25 40 55
11193(1978, $1.95, 224 pgs., Golden Press)-Baker-r (92 pgs.)
4 8 12 25 40 55
NOTE: *Also see March of Comics #210, 217, 230, 254, 266, 278, 296, 308, 324,334, 346, 358, 370, 381, 394, 411, 432.*

LAST AMERICAN, THE
Marvel Comics (Epic): Dec, 1990 - No. 4, March, 1991 ($2.25, mini-series)
1-4: Alan Grant scripts 3.00

LAST AVENGERS STORY, THE (Last Avengers #1)
Marvel Comics: Nov, 1995 - No. 2, Dec, 1995 ($5.95, painted, limited series) (Alterniverse)
1,2: Peter David story; acetate-c in all. 1-New team (Hank Pym, Wasp, Human Torch, Cannonball, She-Hulk, Hotshot, Bombshell, Tommy Maximoff, Hawkeye & Mockingbird) forms to battle Ultron 59, Kang the Conqueror, The Grim Reaper & Oddball 6.00

LAST BATTLE, THE
Image Comics: Dec, 2011 ($7.99, square-bound, one-shot)
1-Facari-s/Brereton-painted art/c; Roman gladiator story; bonus Brereton sketch pages 8.00

LAST CHRISTMAS, THE
Image Comics: May, 2006 - No. 5, Oct, 2006 ($2.99, limited series)
1-5-Gerry Duggan & Brian Posehn-s/Rick Remender & Hilary Barta-a 3.00
TPB (2006, $14.99) r/#1-5; Patton Oswalt intro.; sketch pages and art 15.00

LAST DAY IN VIETNAM
Dark Horse Books: July, 2000 ($10.95, graphic novel)
nn-Will Eisner-s/a/c 11.00

LAST DAYS OF ANIMAL MAN, THE
DC Comics: July, 2009 - No. 6, Dec, 2009 ($2.99, limited series)
1-6: 1-Conway-s/Batista-a/Bolland-c. 3,4-Starfire app. 5,6-Future Justice League app. 3.00
TPB (2010, $17.99) r/#1-6 18.00

LAST DAYS OF THE JUSTICE SOCIETY SPECIAL
DC Comics: 1986 ($2.50, one-shot, 68 pgs.)
1-62 pg. JSA story plus unpubbed G.A. pg. 2 4 6 8 10 12

LAST DEFENDERS, THE
Marvel Comics: May, 2008 - No. 6, Oct, 2008 ($2.99, limited series)
1-6-Nighthawk, She-Hulk, Colossus, and Blazing Skull; Muniz-a. 2-Deodato-c 3.00

LAST FANTASTIC FOUR STORY, THE
Marvel Comics: Oct, 2007 ($4.99, one-shot)
1-Stan Lee-s/John Romita, Jr.-a/c; Galactus app. 5.00

LAST GENERATION, THE
Black Tie Studios: 1986 - No. 5, 1989 ($1.95, B&W, high quality paper)
1-5 3.00
Book 1 (1989, $6.95)-By Caliber Press 7.00

LAST HERO STANDING (Characters from Spider-Girl's M2 universe)
Marvel Comics: Aug, 2005 - No. 5, Aug, 2005 ($2.99, weekly limited series)
1-5: 1-DeFalco-s/Olliffe-a. 4-Thor app. 5-Capt. America dies 3.00
TPB (2005, $13.99) r/#1-5 14.00

LAST HUNT, THE
Dell Publishing Co.: No. 678, Feb, 1956
Four Color 678-Movie, photo-c 6 12 18 38 69 100

LAST KISS
ACME Press (Eclipse): 1988 ($3.95, B&W, squarebound, 52 pgs.)
1-One story adapts E.A. Poe's The Black Cat 4.00

LAST OF THE COMANCHES (Movie) (See Wild Bill Hickok #28)
Avon Periodicals: 1953
nn-Kinstler-c/a, 21pgs.; Ravielli-a 16 32 48 92 144 195

LAST OF THE ERIES, THE (See American Graphics)

LAST OF THE FAST GUNS, THE
Dell Publishing Co.: No. 925, Aug, 1958
Four Color 925-Movie, photo-c 6 12 18 37 66 95

LAST OF THE MOHICANS (See King Classics & White Rider and...)

LAST OF THE VIKING HEROES, THE (Also see Silver Star #1)
Genesis West Comics: Mar, 1987 - No. 12 ($1.50/$1.95)
1-4,5A,5B,6-12: 4-Intro The Phantom Force, 1-Signed edition ($1.50), 5A-Kirby/Stevens-c. 5B,6 ($1.95). 7-Art Adams-c. 8-Kirby back-c. 4.00
Summer Special 1-3: 1-(1988)-Frazetta-c & illos. 2 (1990, $2.50)-A TMNT app. 3 (1991, $2.50)-Teenage Mutant Ninja Turtles 4.00
Summer Special 1-Signed edition (sold for $1.95) 4.00
NOTE: ***Art Adams** c-7. **Byrne** c-3. **Kirby** c-1p, 5p. **Perez** c-2i. **Stevens** c-5Ai.*

LAST ONE, THE
DC Comics (Vertigo): July, 1993 - No. 6, Dec, 1993 ($2.50, lim. series, mature)
1-6 3.00

LAST PHANTOM, THE (Lee Falk's Phantom)
Dynamite Entertainment: 2010 - No. 12, 2012 ($3.99)
1-12-Beatty-s/Ferigato-a; 1-Two covers by Alex Ross; Neves & Prado var. covers 4.00
Annual 1 (2011, $4.99) Beatty-s/Desjardins-a; two covers by Desjardins & Ross 5.00

LAST PLANET STANDING
Marvel Comics: July, 2006 - No. 5, Sept, 2006 ($2.99, limited series)
1-5-Galactus threatens Spider-Girl & Fantastic Five's M2 Earth; Avengers app.; Olliffe-a 3.00
TPB (2006, $13.99) r/series 14.00

LAST SHOT
Image Comics: Aug, 2001 - No. 4, Mar, 2002 ($2.95, limited series)
1-4: 1-Wraparound-c; by Studio XD 3.00
...: First Draw (5/01, $2.95) Introductory one-shot 3.00

LAST STARFIGHTER, THE
Marvel Comics Group: Oct, 1984 - No. 3, Dec, 1984 (75¢, movie adaptation)
1-3: r/Marvel Super Special; Guice-c 4.00

LAST TEMPTATION, THE
Marvel Comics: 1994 - No. 3, 1994 ($4.95, limited series)
1-3-Alice Cooper story; Neil Gaiman scripts; McKean-c; Zulli-a: 1-Two covers 5.00
HC (Dark Horse Comics, 2005, $14.95) r/#1-3; Gaiman intro. 15.00

LAST TRAIN FROM GUN HILL
Dell Publishing Co.: No. 1012, July, 1959
Four Color 1012-Movie, photo-c 7 14 21 48 89 130

LAST TRAIN TO DEADSVILLE: A CAL McDONALD MYSTERY (See Criminal Macabre)
Dark Horse Comics: May, 2004 - No. 4, Sept, 2004 ($2.99, limited series)
1-4-Steve Niles-s/Kelley Jones-a/c 3.00
TPB (2005, $14.95) r/series 15.00

LATEST ADVENTURES OF FOXY GRANDPA (See Foxy Grandpa)

LATEST COMICS (Super Duper No. 3?)
Spotlight Publ./Palace Promotions (Jubilee): Mar, 1945 - No. 2, 1945?
1-Super Duper 17 34 51 98 154 210
2-Bee-29 (nd); Jubilee in indicia blacked out 14 28 42 76 108 140

LAUGH
Archie Enterprises: June, 1987 - No. 29, Aug, 1991 (75¢/$1.00)
V2#1 5.00
2-10,14,24: 5-X-Mas issue. 14-1st app. Hot Dog. 24-Re-intro Super Duck 4.00
11-13,15-23,25-29: 19-X-Mas issue 3.00

LAUGH COMICS (Teenage) (Formerly Black Hood #9-19) (Laugh #226 on)
Archie Publications (Close-Up): No. 20, Fall, 1946 - No. 400, Apr, 1987
20-Archie begins; Katy Keene & Taffy begin by Woggon; Suzie & Wilbur also begin; Archie covers begin 123 246 369 787 1344 1900
21-23,25 48 96 144 302 514 725
24- "Pipsy" by Kirby (6 pgs.) 49 98 147 309 522 735
26-30 34 68 102 204 332 460
31-40 24 48 72 140 230 320
41-60: 41,54-Debbi by Woggon 17 34 51 98 154 210
61-80: 67-Debbi by Woggon 13 26 39 72 101 130
81-99 6 12 18 41 76 110
100 7 14 21 44 82 120
101-105,110,112,114-126: 125-Debbi app. 5 10 15 33 57 80
106-109,111,113-Neal Adams-a (1 pg.) in each 5 10 15 34 60 85
127-144: Super-hero app. in all (see note) 6 12 18 37 66 95
145-(4/63) Josie by DeCarlo begins 6 12 18 37 66 95
146-149-early Josie app. by DeCarlo 4 8 12 28 47 65

Laugh Digest Magazine #167 © AP

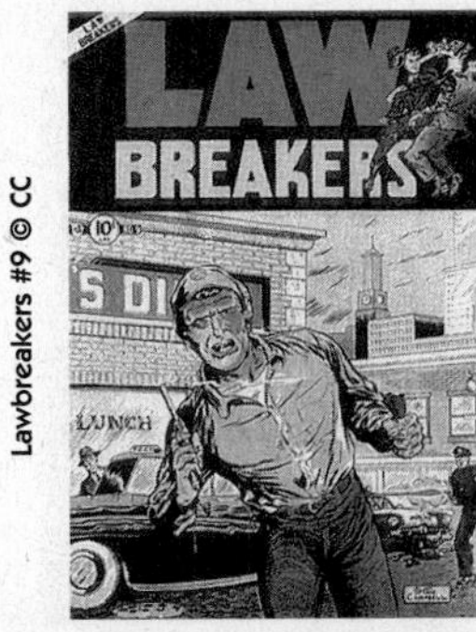

Lawbreakers #9 © CC

Lazarus #1 © Rucka & Lark

GD VG FN VF VF/NM NM-
2.0 4.0 6.0 8.0 9.0 9.2

150,162,163,165,167,169,170-No Josie 3 6 9 19 30 40
151-161,164,168-Josie app. by DeCarlo 4 8 12 25 40 55
166-Beatles-c (1/65) 6 12 18 37 66 95
171-180, 200 (12/67) 3 6 9 16 24 32
181-199 3 6 9 14 20 26
201-240(3/71) 2 4 6 11 16 20
241-280(7/74) 2 4 6 9 13 16
281-299 2 4 6 8 10 12
300(3/76) 2 4 6 8 11 14
301-340 (7/79) 1 2 3 5 7 9
341-370 (1/82) 1 2 3 4 5 7
371-379,385-399 5.00
380-Cheryl Blossom app. 1 3 4 6 8 10
381-384,400: 381-384-Katy Keene app.; by Woggon-381,382 6.00

NOTE: *The Fly app. in 128, 129, 132, 134, 138, 139. Flygirl app. in 136, 137, 143. Flyman app. in 137. The Jaguar app. in 127, 130, 131, 133, 135, 140-142, 144. Josie app. in 145-149, 151-161, 164, 168. Katy Keene app. in 20-125, 129, 130, 133. Horror/Sci-Fi covers on 128-135, 137, 139. Many issues contain paper dolls.* ***Al Fagaly*** *c-20-29.* ***Montana*** *c-33, 36, 37, 42.* ***Bill Vigoda*** *c-30, 50.*

LAUGH COMICS DIGEST (...Magazine #23-89; Laugh Digest Mag. #90 on)
Archie Publ. (Close-Up No. 1, 3 on): 8/74; No. 2, 9/75; No. 3, 3/76 - No. 200, Apr, 2005 (Digest-size) (Josie and Sabrina app. in most issues)

1-Neal Adams-a 5 10 15 31 53 75
2,7,8,19-Neal Adams-a 3 6 9 19 30 40
3-6,9,10 3 6 9 15 22 28
11-18,20 2 4 6 11 16 20
21-40 2 4 6 9 13 16
41-60 1 3 4 6 8 10
61-80 1 2 3 5 6 8
81-99 5.00
100 6.00
101-138 4.00
139-200: 139-Begin $1.95-c. 148-Begin $1.99-c. 156-Begin $2.19-c. 180-Begin $2.39-c 3.00

NOTE: *Katy Keene in 23, 25, 27, 32-38, 40, 45-48, 50. The Fly-r in 19, 20. The Jaguar-r in 25, 27. Mr. Justice-r in 21. The Web-r in 23.*

LAUGH COMIX (Laugh Comics inside)(Formerly Top Notch Laugh; Suzie Comics No. 49 on)
MLJ Magazines: No. 46, Summer, 1944 - No. 48, Winter, 1944-45

46-Wilbur & Suzie in all; Harry Sahle-c 27 54 81 158 259 360
47,48: 47-Sahle-c. 48-Bill Vigoda-c 19 38 57 112 179 240

LAUGH-IN MAGAZINE (TV)(Magazine)
Laufer Publ. Co.: Oct, 1968 - No. 12, Oct, 1969 (50¢) (Satire)

V1#1 5 10 15 30 50 70
2-12 3 6 9 21 33 45

LAUREL & HARDY (See Larry Harmon's... & March of Comics No. 302, 314)

LAUREL AND HARDY (...Comics)
St. John Publ. Co.: 3/49 - No. 3, 9/49; No. 26, 11/55 - No. 28, 3/56 (No #4-25)

1 77 154 231 493 847 1200
2 41 82 123 250 418 585
3 32 64 96 192 314 435
26-28 (Reprints) 16 32 48 94 147 200

LAUREL AND HARDY (TV)
Dell Publishing Co.: Oct, 1962 - No. 4, Sept-Nov, 1963

12-423-210 (8-10/62) 6 12 18 38 69 100
2-4 (Dell) 4 8 12 27 44 60

LAUREL AND HARDY (Larry Harmon's...)
Gold Key: Jan, 1967 - No. 2, Oct, 1967

1-Photo back-c 4 8 12 27 44 60
2 4 8 12 21 33 45

LAUREL AND HARDY DIGEST: DC Comics. 1972 (Advertised, not published)

L.A.W., THE (LIVING ASSAULT WEAPONS)
DC Comics: Sept, 1999 - No. 6, Feb, 2000 ($2.50, limited series)

1-6-Blue Beetle, Question, Judomaster, Capt. Atom app.; Giordano-a. 5-JLA app. 3.00

LAW AGAINST CRIME (Law-Crime on cover)
Essenkay Publishing Co.: April, 1948 - No. 3, Aug, 1948 (Real Stories from Police Files)

1-(#1-3 are half funny animal, half crime stories)-L. B. Cole-c/a in all; electrocution-c
81 162 243 518 884 1250
2-L. B. Cole-c/a 58 116 174 371 636 900
3-Used in **SOTI**, pg. 180,181 & illo "The wish to hurt or kill couples in lovers' lanes;" reprinted in All-Famous Crime #9 74 148 222 470 810 1150

LAW AND ORDER

GD VG FN VF VF/NM NM-
2.0 4.0 6.0 8.0 9.0 9.2

Maximum Press: Sept, 1995 - No. 2, 1995 ($2.50, unfinished limited series)

1,2 3.00

LAWBREAKERS (...Suspense Stories No. 10 on)
Law and Order Magazines (Charlton): Mar, 1951 - No. 9, Oct-Nov, 1952

1 41 82 123 256 428 600
2 24 48 72 142 234 325
3,5,6,8,9: 6-Anti-Wertham editorial 20 40 60 118 192 265
4- "White Death" junkie story 29 58 87 170 278 385
7- "The Deadly Dopesters" drug story 29 58 87 170 278 385

LAWBREAKERS ALWAYS LOSE!
Marvel Comics (CBS): Spring, 1948 - No. 10, Oct, 1949

1-2pg. Kurtzman-a, "Giggles 'n' Grins" 39 78 117 231 378 525
2 20 40 60 118 192 265
3-5: 4-Vampire story 16 32 48 94 147 200
6(2/49)-Has editorial defense against charges of Dr. Wertham
18 36 54 105 165 225
7-Used in **SOTI**, illo "Comic-book philosophy" 32 64 96 192 314 435
8-10: 9,10-Photo-c 15 30 45 85 130 175

NOTE: ***Brodsky*** *c-4, 5.* ***Shores*** *c-1-3, 6-8.*

LAWBREAKERS SUSPENSE STORIES (Formerly Lawbreakers; Strange Suspense Stories No. 16 on)
Capitol Stories/Charlton Comics: No. 10, Jan, 1953 - No. 15, Nov, 1953

10 45 90 135 284 480 675
11 (3/53)-Severed tongues-c/story & woman negligee scene
213 426 639 1363 2332 3300
12-14: 13-Giordano-c begin, end #15 32 64 96 188 307 425
15-Acid-in-face-c/story; hands dissolved in acid story
68 136 204 435 743 1050

LAW-CRIME (See Law Against Crime)

LAWDOG
Marvel Comics (Epic Comics): May, 1993 - No. 10, Feb, 1993

1-10 3.00

LAWDOG/GRIMROD: TERROR AT THE CROSSROADS
Marvel Comics (Epic Comics): Sept, 1993 ($3.50)

1 4.00

LAWMAN (TV)
Dell Publishing Co.: No. 970, Feb, 1959 - No. 11, Apr-June, 1962 (All photo-c)

Four Color 970(#1) 10 20 30 69 147 225
Four Color 1035('60), 3(2-4/60)-Toth-a 7 14 21 46 86 125
4-11 6 12 18 37 66 95

LAW OF DREDD, THE (Also see Judge Dredd)
Quality Comics/Fleetway #8 on: 1989 - No. 33, 1992 ($1.50/$1.75)

1-33: Bolland a-1-6,8,10-12,14(2 pg),15,19 3.00

LAWRENCE (See Movie Classics)

LAZARUS
Image Comics: Jun, 2013 - Present ($2.99)

1-7-Rucka-s/Lark-a/c 3.00

LAZARUS CHURCHYARD
Tundra Publishing: June, 1992 - No. 3, 1992 ($3.95/$4.50, 44 pgs., coated stock)

1-3 5.00
The Final Cut (Image, 1/01, $14.95, TPB) Reprints Ellis/D'Israeli strips 15.00

LAZARUS FIVE
DC Comics: July, 2000 - No. 5, Nov, 2000 ($2.50, limited series)

1-5-Harris-c/Abell-a(p) 3.00

LEADING COMICS
DC Comics: Jan. 1942

nn - Ashcan comic, not distributed to newsstands, only for in-house use. Cover art is Detective Comics #57, interior of Star Spangled Comics #2 (a FN+ copy sold for $1015.75 in 2012)

LEADING COMICS (...Screen Comics No. 42 on)
National Periodical Publications: Winter, 1941-42 - No. 41, Feb-Mar, 1950

1-Origin The Seven Soldiers of Victory; Green Arrow & Speedy, Crimson Avenger, Shining Knight, The Vigilante, Star Spangled Kid & Stripesy begin; The Dummy (Vigilante villain) 1st app.; 1st Green Arrow-c 343 686 1029 2400 4200 6000
2-Meskin-a; Fred Ray-c 116 232 348 742 1271 1800
3 90 180 270 576 988 1400

Leading Comics #7 © DC

Leave It to Binky #5 © DC

Leave It to Chance #11 © Robinson & Smith

	GD 2.0	VG 4.0	FN 6.0	VF 8.0	VF/NM 9.0	NM- 9.2
4,5	65	130	195	416	708	1000
6-10	50	100	150	315	533	750
11,12,14(Spring, 1945)	39	78	117	240	395	550
13-Classic robot-c	94	188	282	602	1026	1450
15-(Sum,'45)-Contents change to funny animal	26	52	78	154	252	350
16-22,24-30: 16-Nero Fox-c begin, end #22	14	28	42	80	115	150
23-1st app. Peter Porkchops by Otto Feuer & begins	26	52	78	154	252	350
31,32,34-41: 34-41-Leading Screen... on-c only	12	24	36	67	94	120
33-(Scarce)	20	40	60	114	182	250

NOTE: *Otto Feuer-a most #15-on; **Rube Grossman**-a most #15-on;c-15-41. **Post** a-23-37, 39, 41.*

LEADING MAN
Image Comics: June, 2006 - No. 5, Feb, 2007 ($3.50, limited series)

	GD	VG	FN	VF	VF/NM	NM-
1-5-B. Clay Moore-s/Jeremy Haun-a						3.50
TPB (2/07, $14.95) r/#1-5; sketch gallery						15.00

LEADING SCREEN COMICS (Formerly Leading Comics)
National Periodical Publ.: No. 42, Apr-May, 1950 - No. 77, Aug-Sept, 1955

	GD	VG	FN	VF	VF/NM	NM-
42-Peter Porkchops-c/stories continue	12	24	36	67	94	120
43-77	11	22	33	60	83	105

NOTE: ***Grossman** a-most. **Mayer** a-45-48, 50, 54-57, 60, 62-74, 75(3), 76, 77.*

LEAGUE OF CHAMPIONS, THE (Also see The Champions)
Hero Graphics: Dec, 1990 - No. 12, 1992 ($2.95, 52 pgs.)

	GD	VG	FN	VF	VF/NM	NM-
1-12: 1-Flare app. 2-Origin Malice						4.00

LEAGUE OF EXTRAORDINARY GENTLEMEN, THE
America's Best Comics: Mar, 1999 - No. 6, Sept, 2000 ($2.95, limited series)

	GD	VG	FN	VF	VF/NM	NM-
1-Alan Moore-s/Kevin O'Neill-a	2	4	6	8	10	12
1-DF Edition ($10.00) O'Neill-c	2	4	6	9	12	15
2,3						6.00
4-6: 5-Revised printing with "Amaze 'Whirling Spray' Syringe" parody ad						4.00
5-Initial printing recalled because of "Marvel Co. Syringe" parody ad	12	24	36	81	176	270
... Compendium 1,2: 1-r/#1,2. 2-r/#3,4						6.00
Hardcover (2000, $24.95) r/#1-6 plus cover gallery						25.00

LEAGUE OF EXTRAORDINARY GENTLEMEN, THE (Volume 2)
America's Best Comics: Sept, 2002 - No. 6, Nov, 2003 ($3.50, limited series)

	GD	VG	FN	VF	VF/NM	NM-
1-6-Alan Moore-s/Kevin O'Neill-a						5.00
... Bumper Compendium 1,2: 1-r/#1,2. 2-r/#3,4						6.00
... Black Dossier (HC, 2007, $29.99) new graphic novel; 3-D section with glasses; extras						30.00

LEAGUE OF EXTRAORDINARY GENTLEMEN
Top Shelf Productions/Knockabout Comics: 2009; 2011; 2012 ($7.95/$9.95, squarebound)

	GD	VG	FN	VF	VF/NM	NM-
... Century: 1910 (2009, $7.95) Alan Moore-s/Kevin O'Neill-a						8.00
... Century #2 "1969" (2011, $9.95) Alan Moore-s/Kevin O'Neill-a						10.00
... Century #3 "2009" (2012, $9.95) Alan Moore-s/Kevin O'Neill-a						10.00

LEAGUE OF JUSTICE
DC Comics (Elseworlds): 1996 - No. 2, 1996 ($5.95, 48 pgs., squarebound)

	GD	VG	FN	VF	VF/NM	NM-
1,2: Magic-based alternate DC Universe story; Giordano-i						6.00

LEATHERFACE
Arpad Publishing: May (April on-c), 1991 - No. 4, May, 1992 ($2.75, painted-c)

	GD	VG	FN	VF	VF/NM	NM-
1-4-Based on Texas Chainsaw movie; Dorman-c	1	2	3	5	7	9

LEATHERNECK THE MARINE (See Mighty Midget Comics)

LEAVE IT TO BEAVER (TV)
Dell Publishing Co.: No. 912, June, 1958; May-July, 1962 (All photo-c)

	GD	VG	FN	VF	VF/NM	NM-
Four Color 912	13	26	39	89	195	300
Four Color 999,1103,1191,1285, 01-428-207	11	22	33	76	163	250

LEAVE IT TO BINKY (Binky No. 72 on) (Super DC Giant) (No. 1-22: 52 pgs.)
National Periodical Publications: 2-3/48 - #60, 10/58; #61, 6-7/68 - #71, 2-3/70 (Teen-age humor)

	GD	VG	FN	VF	VF/NM	NM-
1-Lucy wears Superman costume	39	78	117	240	395	550
2	21	42	63	124	202	280
3,4	15	30	45	86	135	180
5-Superman cameo	20	40	60	114	182	250
6-10	14	28	42	76	108	140
11-14,16-22: Last 52 pg. issue	12	24	36	67	94	120
15-Scribbly story by Mayer	14	28	42	76	108	140
23-28,30-45: 45-Last pre-code (2/55)	10	20	30	56	76	95
29-Used in **POP**, pg. 78	10	20	30	58	79	100
46-60: 60-(10/58)	5	10	15	35	63	90
61 (6-7/68) 1950's reprints with art changes	5	10	15	34	60	85
62-69: 67-Last 12¢ issue	4	8	12	27	44	60
70-7pg. app. Bus Driver who looks like Ralph from Honeymooners	5	10	15	30	50	70
71-Last issue	4	8	12	28	47	65

NOTE: ***Aragones**-a-61, 62, 67. **Drucker** a-28. **Mayer** a-1, 2, 15. Created by **Mayer**.*

LEAVE IT TO CHANCE
Image Comics (Homage Comics): Sept, 1996 - No. 11, Sept, 1998; No. 13, July, 2002
DC Comics (Homage Comics): No. 12, Jun, 1999 ($2.50/$2.95/$4.95)

	GD	VG	FN	VF	VF/NM	NM-
1-3: 1-Intro Chance Falconer & St. George; James Robinson scripts & Paul Smith-c/a						5.00
4-12: 12-(6/99)						3.00
13-(7/02, $4.95) includes sketch pages and pin-ups						5.00
Free Comic Book Day Edition (2003) - James Robinson-s/Paul Smith-a						3.00
Shaman's Rain TPB (1997, $9.95) r/#1-4						10.00
Shaman's Rain HC (2002, $14.95, over-sized 8 1/4" x 12") r/#1-4						15.00
Trick or Threat TPB (1997, $12.95) r/#5-8						13.00
Trick or Threat HC (2002, $14.95, over-sized 8 1/4" x 12") r/#5-8						15.00
Vol. 3: Monster Madness and Other Stories HC (2003, $14.95, 8 1/4" x 12") r/#9-11						15.00

LEE HUNTER, INDIAN FIGHTER
Dell Publishing Co.: No. 779, Mar, 1957; No. 904, May, 1958

	GD	VG	FN	VF	VF/NM	NM-
Four Color 779 (#1)	5	10	15	33	57	80
Four Color 904	4	8	12	27	44	60

LEFT-HANDED GUN, THE (Movie)
Dell Publishing Co.: No. 913, July, 1958

	GD	VG	FN	VF	VF/NM	NM-
Four Color 913-Paul Newman photo-c	8	16	24	54	102	150

LEGACY
Majestic Entertainment: Oct, 1993 - No. 2, Nov, 1993; No. 0, 1994 ($2.25)

	GD	VG	FN	VF	VF/NM	NM-
1-2,0: 1-Glow-in-the-dark-c. 0-Platinum						3.00

LEGACY
Image Comics: May, 2003 - No. 4, Feb, 2004 ($2.95)

	GD	VG	FN	VF	VF/NM	NM-
1-4: 1-Francisco-a/Treffiletti-s						3.00

LEGACY OF KAIN (Based on the Eidos video game)
Top Cow Productions: Oct, 1999; Jan, 2004 ($2.99)

	GD	VG	FN	VF	VF/NM	NM-
...Defiance 1 (1/04, $2.99) Cha-c; Kirkham-a						3.00
...Soul Reaver 1 (10/99, Diamond Dateline supplement) Benitez-c						3.00

LEGEND
DC Comics (WildStorm): Apr, 2005 - No. 4, July, 2005 ($5.95/$5.99, limited series)

	GD	VG	FN	VF	VF/NM	NM-
1-4-Howard Chaykin-s/Russ Heath-a; inspired by Philip Wylie's novel "Gladiator"						6.00

LEGENDARY TALESPINNERS
Dynamite Entertainment: 2010 - No. 3, 2010 ($3.99)

	GD	VG	FN	VF	VF/NM	NM-
1-3-Kuhoric-s/Bond-a; two covers						4.00

LEGENDERRY: A STEAMPUNK ADVENTURE
Dynamite Entertainment: 2014 - Present ($3.99)

	GD	VG	FN	VF	VF/NM	NM-
1-3-Willingham-s/Davila-a/Benitez-c						4.00

LEGEND OF CUSTER, THE (TV)
Dell Publishing Co.: Jan, 1968

	GD	VG	FN	VF	VF/NM	NM-
1-Wayne Maunder photo-c	3	6	9	17	26	35

LEGEND OF ISIS
Alias Entertainment: May, 2005 - No. 5 ($2.99)

	GD	VG	FN	VF	VF/NM	NM-
1-5: 1-Three covers; Ottney-s/Fontana-a						3.00
...: Beginnings TPB (5/05, $9.99) Ottney-s						10.00

LEGEND OF JESSE JAMES, THE (TV)
Gold Key: Feb, 1966

	GD	VG	FN	VF	VF/NM	NM-
10172-602-Photo-c	3	6	9	17	26	35

LEGEND OF KAMUI, THE (See Kamui)

LEGEND OF LOBO, THE (See Movie Comics)

LEGEND OF LUTHER STRODE, THE (Sequel to Strange Talent of Luther Strode)
Image Comics: Dec, 2012 - No. 6, Aug, 2013 ($3.50, limited series)

	GD	VG	FN	VF	VF/NM	NM-
1-5: Justin Jordan-s/Tradd Moore-a						3.50

LEGEND OF OZ: THE WICKED WEST
Big Dog Press: Oct, 2011 - No. 6, Aug, 2012; Oct, 2012 - Present ($3.50)

	GD	VG	FN	VF	VF/NM	NM-
1-12-Multiple covers on all						3.50
Vol. 2 1-6-Multiple covers on all						3.50

LEGEND OF SUPREME
Image Comics (Extreme): Dec, 1994 - No. 3, Feb, 1995 ($2.50, limited series)

	GD	VG	FN	VF	VF/NM	NM-
1-3						3.00

Legend of the Elflord #1 © DavDez

Legends of Red Sonja #1 © RS LLC

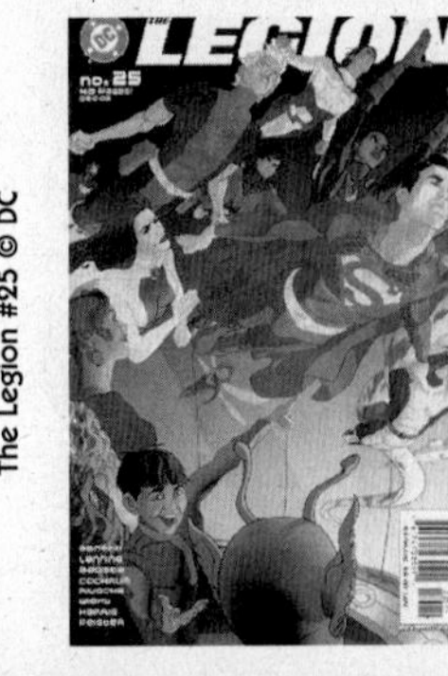

The Legion #25 © DC

GD 2.0 VG 4.0 FN 6.0 VF 8.0 VF/NM 9.0 NM- 9.2

LEGEND OF THE ELFLORD
DavDez Arts: July, 1998 - No. 2, Sept, 1998 ($2.95)
1,2-Barry Blair & Colin Chin-s/a 3.00

LEGEND OF THE HAWKMAN
DC Comics: 2000 - No. 3, 2000 ($4.95, limited series)
1-3-Raab-s/Lark-c/a 5.00

LEGEND OF THE SHADOW CLAN
Aspen MLT: Feb, 2013 - No. 5, Jul, 2013 ($1.00/$3.99)
1-($1.00) David Wohl-s/Cory Smith-a; mutiple covers 3.00
2-5-($3.99) 4.00

LEGEND OF THE SHIELD, THE
DC Comics (Impact Comics): July, 1991 - No. 16, Oct, 1992 ($1.00)
1-16: 6,7-The Fly x-over. 12-Contains trading card 4.00
Annual 1 (1992, $2.50, 68 pgs.)-Snyder-a; w/trading card 4.00

LEGEND OF WONDER WOMAN, THE
DC Comics: May, 1986 - No. 4, Aug, 1986 (75¢, limited series)
1-4 4.00

LEGEND OF YOUNG DICK TURPIN, THE (Disney)(TV)
Gold Key: May, 1966
1 (10176-605)-Photo/painted-c 3 6 9 17 26 35

LEGEND OF ZELDA, THE (Link: The Legend... in indicia)
Valiant Comics: 1990 - No. 4, 1990 ($1.95, coated stiff-c) V2#1, 1990 - No. 5, 1990 ($1.50)
1-4: 4-Layton-c(i) 1 3 4 6 8 10
V2#1-5 1 2 3 5 6 8

LEGENDS
DC Comics: Nov, 1986 - No. 6, Apr, 1987 (75¢, limited series)
1-5: 1-Byrne-c/a(p) in all; 1st app. new Capt. Marvel. 3-1st app. new Suicide Squad; death of Blockbuster 6.00
6-1st app. new Justice League 1 3 4 6 8 10

LEGENDS OF DANIEL BOONE, THE (...Frontier Scout)
National Periodical Publications: Oct-Nov, 1955 - No. 8, Dec-Jan, 1956-57
1 (Scarce)-Nick Cardy c-1-8 54 108 162 346 591 835
2 (Scarce) 40 80 120 246 411 575
3-8 (Scarce) 34 68 102 199 325 450

LEGENDS OF NASCAR, THE
Vortex Comics: Nov, 1990 - No. 14, 1992? (#1 3rd printing (1/91) says 2nd printing inside)
1-Bill Elliott biog.; Trimpe-a ($1.50) 5.00
1-2nd printing (11/90, $2.00) 3.00
1-3rd print; contains Maxx racecards ($3.00) 3.00
2-14: 2-Richard Petty. 3-Ken Schrader (7/91). 4-Bobby Allison; Spiegle-a(p); Adkins part-i. 5-Sterling Marlin. 6-Bill Elliott. 7-Junior Johnson; Spiegle-c/a. 8-Benny Parsons; Heck-a 3.00
1-13-Hologram cover versions. 2-Hologram shows Bill Elliott's car by mistake (all are numbered & limited) 5.00
2-Hologram corrected version 5.00
Christmas Special ($5.95) 6.00

LEGENDS OF RED SONJA
Dynamite Entertainment: 2013 - Present ($3.99)
1-5-Short stories by various incl. Simone, Grayson; covers by Anacleto & Thorne 4.00

LEGENDS OF THE DARK CLAW
DC Comics (Amalgam): Apr, 1996 ($1.95)
1-Jim Balent-c/a 3.00

LEGENDS OF THE DARK KNIGHT (See Batman: ...)

LEGENDS OF THE DARK KNIGHT
DC Comics: Dec, 2012 - Present ($3.99, printings of stories first released online)
1-13: 1-Lindelof-s. 2-4-Joker app. 5-Hester-a 4.00
... 100 Page Super Spectacular (2/14, $9.99) Online chapters #42-47,49,50 10.00
... 100 Page Super Spectacular 2 (5/14, $9.99) Online chapters #38-40,51,53-55,59,60 10.00

LEGENDS OF THE DC UNIVERSE
DC Comics: Feb, 1998 - No. 41, June, 2001 ($1.95/$1.99/$2.50)
1-13,15-21: 1-3-Superman; Robinson-s/Semeiks-a/Orbik-painted-c. 4,5-Wonder Woman; Deodato-a/Rude painted-c. 8-GL/GA, O'Neil-s. 10,11-Batgirl; Dodson-a. 12,13-Justice League. 15-17-Flash. 18-Kid Flash; Guice-a. 19-Impulse; prelude to JLApe Annuals. 20,21-Abin Sur 4.00
14-($3.95) Jimmy Olsen; Kirby-esque-c by Rude 5.00
22-27,30: 22,23-Superman; Rude-c/Ladronn-a. 26,27-Aquaman/Joker 3.00
28,29: Green Lantern & the Atom; Gil Kane-a; covers by Kane and Ross 3.00
31,32: 32-Begin $2.50-c; Wonder Woman; Texeira-c 3.00
33-36-Hal Jordan as The Spectre; DeMatteis-s/Zulli-a; Hale painted-c 3.00
37-41: 37,38-Kyle Rayner. 39-Superman. 40,41-Atom; Harris-c 3.00
... Crisis on Infinite Earths 1 (2/99, $4.95) Untold story during and after Crisis on Infinite Earths #4; Wolfman-s/Ryan-a/Orbik-c 5.00
... 80 Page Giant 1 (9/98, $4.95) Stories and art by various incl. Ditko, Perez, Gibbons, Mumy; Joe Kubert-c 5.00
... 80 Page Giant 2 (1/00, $4.95) Stories and art by various incl. Challengers by Art Adams; Sean Phillips-c 5.00
... 3-D Gallery (12/98, $2.95) Pin-ups w/glasses 3.00

LEGENDS OF THE LEGION (See Legion of Super-Heroes)
DC Comics: Feb, 1998 - No. 4, May, 1998 ($2.25, limited series)
1-4:1-Origin-s of Ultra Boy. 2-Spark. 3-Umbra. 4-Star Boy 3.00

LEGENDS OF THE STARGRAZERS (See Vanguard Illustrated #2)
Innovation Publishing: Aug, 1989 - No. 6, 1990 ($1.95, limited series, mature)
1-6: 1-Redondo part inks 3.00

LEGENDS OF THE WORLD'S FINEST (See World's Finest)
DC Comics: 1994 - No. 3, 1994 ($4.95, squarebound, limited series)
1-3: Simonson scripts; Brereton-c/a; embossed foil logos 6.00
TPB-(1995, $14.95) r/#1-3 15.00

L.E.G.I.O.N. (The # to right of title represents year of print)(Also see Lobo & R.E.B.E.L.S.)
DC Comics: Feb, 1989 - No. 70, Sept, 1994 ($1.50/$1.75)
1-Giffen plots/breakdowns in #1-12,28 5.00
2-22,24-47: 3-Lobo app. #3 on. 4-1st Lobo-c this title. 5-Lobo joins L.E.G.I.O.N. 13-Lar Gand app. 16-Lar Gand joins L.E.G.I.O.N., leaves #19. 31-Capt. Marvel app. 35-L.E.G.I.O.N. '92 begins 3.00
23,70-($2.50, 52 pgs.)-L.E.G.I.O.N. '91 begins. 70-Zero Hour 4.00
48,49,51-69: 48-Begin $1.75-c. 63-L.E.G.I.O.N. '94 begins; Superman x-over 3.00
50-($3.50, 68 pgs.) 4.00
Annual 1-5 ('90-94, 68 pgs.): 1-Lobo, Superman app. 2-Alan Grant scripts. 5-Elseworlds story; Lobo app. 4.00
NOTE: *Alan Grant scripts in #1-39, 51, Annual 1, 2.*

LEGION, THE (Continued from Legion Lost & Legion Worlds)
DC Comics: Dec, 2001 - No. 38, Oct, 2004 ($2.50)
1-Abnett & Lanning-s; Coipel & Lanning-c/a 4.00
2-24: 3-8-Ra's al Ghul app. 5-Snejbjerg-a. 9-DeStefano-a. 12-Legion vs. JLA. 16-Fatal Five app.; Walker-a 17,18-Ra's al Ghul app. 20-23-Universo app. 3.00
25-($3.95) Art by Harris, Cockrum, Rivoche; teenage Clark Kent app.; Harris-c 4.00
26-38-Superboy in classic costume. 26-30-Darkseid app. 31-Giffen-a. 35-38-Jurgens-a 3.00
...Secret Files 3003 (1/04, $4.95) Kirk-a, Harris-c/a; Superboy app. 5.00
...Foundations TPB (2004, $19.95) r/#25-30 & Secret Files 3003; Harris-c 20.00

LEGION LOST (Continued from Legion of Super-Heroes [4th series] #125)
DC Comics: May, 2000 - No. 12, Apr, 2001 ($2.50, limited series)
1-Abnett & Lanning-s. Coipel & Lanning-c/a 1 2 3 4 5 7
2-12-Abnett & Lanning-s. Coipel & Lanning-c/a in most. 4,9-Alixe-a 3.00
HC (2011, $39.99, dustjacket) r/#1-12 40.00

LEGION LOST (DC New 52)
DC Comics: Nov, 2011 - No. 16, Mar, 2013 ($2.99)
1-16: 1-Nicieza-s/Woods/a/c; Legionnaires trapped in the 21st century. 7,8-DeFalco-s. 8-Prelude to The Culling; Ravagers app. 9-The Culling x-over with Teen Titans. 14-16-Superboy & the Ravagers app. 3.00
#0 (11/12, $2.99) Origin of Timber Wolf; DeFalco-s/Woods-a 3.00

LEGIONNAIRES (See Legion of Super-Heroes #40, 41 & Showcase 95 #6)
DC Comics: Apr, 1992 - No. 81, Mar, 2000 ($1.25/$1.50/$2.25)
0-(10/94)-Zero Hour restart of Legion; released between #18 & #19 3.00
1-49,51-77: 1-(4/92)-Chris Sprouse-c/a; polybagged w/SkyBox trading card. 11-Kid Quantum joins. 18-(9/94)-Zero Hour. 19(11/94). 37-Valor (Lar Gand) becomes M'onel (5/96). 43-Legion tryouts; reintro Princess Projectra, Shadow Lass & others. 47-Forms one cover image with LSH #91. 60-Karate Kid & Kid Quantum join. 61-Silver Age & 70's Legion app. 76-Return of Wildfire. 79,80-Coipel-c/a; Legion vs. the Blight 3.00
50-($3.95) Pullout poster by Davis/Farmer 4.00
#1,000,000 (11/98) Sean Phillips-a 3.00
Annual 1,3 ('94,'96 $2.95)-1-Elseworlds-s. 3-Legends of the Dead Earth-s 4.00
Annual 2 (1995, $3.95)-Year One-s 4.50

LEGIONNAIRES THREE
DC Comics: Jan, 1986 - No. 4, May, 1986 (75¢, limited series)
1-4 4.00

Legion of Monsters (2011 series) #1 © MAR

Legion of Super-Heroes (4th series) #110 © DC

Legion of Super-Heroes (2011 series) #14 © DC

	GD 2.0	VG 4.0	FN 6.0	VF 8.0	VF/NM 9.0	NM- 9.2

LEGION OF MONSTERS (Also see Marvel Premiere #28 & Marvel Preview #8)
Marvel Comics Group: Sept, 1975 ($1.00, B&W, magazine, 76 pgs.)

1-Origin & 1st app. Legion of Monsters; Neal Adams-c; Morrow-a; origin & only app. The Manphibian; Frankenstein by Mayerik; Bram Stoker's Dracula adaptation; Reese-a; painted-c (#2 was advertised with Morbius & Satana, but was never published) 5 10 15 34 60 85

LEGION OF MONSTERS (One-shots)
Marvel Comics: Apr, 2007 - Sept, 2007 ($2.99)

... Man-Thing (5/07) Huston-s/Janson-a/Land-c; Simon Garth: Zombie by Ted McKeever 3.00
... Morbius (9/07) Cahill-s/Gaydos-a/Land-c; Dracula w/Finch-a/Cebulski-s 3.00
... Satana (8/07) Furth-s/Andrasofszky-a/Land-c; Living Mummy by Hickman 3.00
... Werewolf By Night (4/07) Carey-s/Land-a/c; Monster of Frankenstein by Skottie Young 3.00
HC (2007, $24.99, dustjacket) oversized r/series and classic stories; sketch pages 25.00

LEGION OF MONSTERS
Marvel Comics: Dec, 2011 - No. 4, Mar, 2012 ($3.99, limited series)

1-4-Hopeless-s/Doe-a/c; Morbius, Manphibian, Elsa Bloodstone app. 4.00

LEGION OF NIGHT, THE
Marvel Comics: Oct, 1991 - No. 2, Oct, 1991 ($4.95, 52 pgs.)

1,2-Whilce Portacio-c/a(p) 5.00

LEGION OF SUBSTITUTE HEROES SPECIAL (See Adventure Comics #306)
DC Comics: July, 1985 ($1.25, one-shot, 52 pgs.)

1-Giffen-c/a(p) 4.00

LEGION OF SUPER-HEROES (See Action Comics, Adventure, All New Collectors Edition, Legionnaires, Legends of the Legion, Limited Collectors Edition, Secrets of the..., Superboy & Superman)
National Periodical Publications: Feb, 1973 - No. 4, July-Aug, 1973

1-Legion & Tommy Tomorrow reprints begin 3 6 9 17 26 35
2-4: 2-Forte-r. 3-r/Adv. #340. Action #240. 4-r/Adv. #341, Action #233; Mooney-r 2 4 6 11 16 20

LEGION OF SUPER-HEROES, THE (Formerly Superboy and...; Tales of The Legion #314 on)
DC Comics: No. 259, Jan, 1980 - No. 313, July, 1984

259(#1)-Superboy leaves Legion 2 4 6 8 11 14
260-270,285-289: 265-Contains 28 pg. insert "Superman & the TRS-80 computer"; origin Tyroc; Tyroc leaves Legion 6.00
261,263,264,266-(Whitman variants; low print run; no cover #'s) 2 4 6 8 11 14
271-284: 272-Blok joins; origin; 20 pg. insert-Dial 'H' For Hero. 277-Intro. Reflecto. 280-Superboy re-joins Legion. 282-Origin Reflecto. 283-Origin Wildfire 6.00
290-294-Great Darkness saga. 294-Double size (52 pgs.) 1 2 3 5 7 9
295-299,301-313: 297-Origin retold. 298-Free 16 pg. Amethyst preview. 306-Brief origin Star Boy (Swan art). 311-Colan-a 4.00
300-(68 pgs., Mando paper)-Anniversary issue; has c/a by almost everyone at DC 5.00
Annual 1-3(82-84, 52 pgs.)-1-Giffen-c/a; 1st app./origin new Invisible Kid who joins Legion. 2-Karate Kid & Princess Projectra wed & resign 4.00
...The Great Darkness Saga (1989, $17.95, 196 pgs.)-r/LSH #287,290-294 & Annual #3; Giffen-c/a 2 4 6 10 14 18
...The Great Darkness Saga The Deluxe Edition HC (2010, $39.99, dj)-r/LSH #284-296 & Annual #1; new intro. by Levitz, script for #290, Giffen design sketches 40.00
NOTE: ***Aparo** c-282, 283, 300(part). **Austin** c-268i. **Buckler** c-273p, 274p, 276p. **Colan** a-311p. **Ditko** a(p)-267, 268, 272, 274, 276, 281. **Giffen** a-285-313p, Annual 1p; c-287p, 288p, 289, 290p, 291p, 292, 293, 294-299p, 300, 301-313p, Annual 1p, 2p. **Perez** c-268p, 277-280, 281p. **Starlin** a-265. **Staton** a-259p, 260p, 280. **Tuska** a-308p.*

LEGION OF SUPER-HEROES (3rd Series) (Reprinted in Tales of the Legion)
DC Comics: Aug, 1984 - No. 63, Aug, 1989 ($1.25/$1.75, deluxe format)

1-Silver ink logo 6.00
2-36,39-44,46-49,51-62: 4-Death of Karate Kid. 5-Death of Nemesis Kid. 12-Cosmic Boy, Lightning Lad, & Saturn Girl resign. 14-Intro new members: Tellus, Sensor Girl, Quislet. 15-17-Crisis tie-ins. 18-Crisis x-over. 25-Sensor Girl i.d. revealed as Princess Projectra. 35-Saturn Girl rejoins. 42,43-Millennium tie-ins. 44-Origin Quislet 3.00
37,38-Death of Superboy 2 4 6 9 13 16
45,50: 45 ($2.95, 68 pgs.)-Anniversary ish. 50-Double size ($2.50-c) 4.00
63-Final issue 4.00
Annual 1-4 (10/85-'88, 52 pgs.)-1-Crisis tie-in 4.00
...: An Eye For An Eye TPB (2007, $17.99)-r/#1-6; intro by Paul Levitz; cover gallery 18.00
...: The More Things Change TPB (2008, $17.99)-r/#7-13; cover gallery 18.00
NOTE: ***Byrne** c-36p. **Giffen** a(p)-1, 2, 50-55, 57-63, Annual 1p, 2; c-1-5p, 54p, Annual 1. **Orlando** a-6p. **Steacy** c-45-50, Annual 3.*

LEGION OF SUPER-HEROES (4th Series)
DC Comics: Nov, 1989 - No. 125, Mar, 2000 ($1.75/$1.95/$2.25)

0-(10/94)-Zero Hour restart of Legion; released between #61 & #62 3.00
1-Giffen-c/a(p)/scripts begin (4 pg.-a only #18) 6.00
2-20,26-49,51-53,55-58: 4-Mon-El (Lar Gand) destroys Time Trapper, changes reality. 5-Alt. reality story where Mordru rules all; Ferro Lad app. 6-1st app. of Laurel Gand (Lar. Gand's cousin). 8-Origin. 13-Free poster by Giffen showing new costumes. 15-(2/91)-1st reference of Lar Gand as Valor. 26-New map of headquarters. 34-Six pg. preview of Timber Wolf mini-series. 40-Minor Legionnaires app. 41-(3/93)-SW6 Legion renamed Legionnaires w/new costumes and some new code-names 4.00
21-25: 21-24-Lobo & Darkseid storyline. 24-Cameo SW6 younger Legion duplicates. 25-SW6 Legion full intro. 5.00
50-($3.50, 68 pgs.) 5.00
54-($2.95)-Die-cut & foil stamped-c 5.00
59-99: 61-(9/94)-Zero Hour. 62-(11/94). 75-XS travels back to the 20th Century (cont'd in Impulse #9). 77-Origin of Brainiac 5. 81-Reintro Sun Boy. 85-Half of the Legion sent to the 20th century, Superman-c/app. 86-Final Night. 87-Deadman-c/app. 88-Impulse-c/app. Adventure Comics #247 cover swipe. 91-Forms one cover image with Legionnaires #47. 96-Wedding of Ultra Boy and Apparition. 99-Robin, Impulse, Superboy app. 3.00
100-($5.95, 96 pgs.)-Legionnaires return to the 30th Century; gatefold-c; 5 stories-art by Simonson, Davis and others 1 2 3 4 5 7
101-121: 101-Armstrong-a(p) begins. 105-Legion past & present vs. Time Trapper. 109-Moder-a. 110-Thunder joins. 114,115-Bizarro Legion. 120,121-Fatal Five. 3.00
122-124: 122,123-Coipel-c/a. 124-Coipel-c 4.00
125-Leads into "Legion Lost" maxi-series; Coipel-c 5.00
#1,000,000 (11/98) Giffen-a 3.00
Annual 1-5 (1990-1994, $3.50, 68 pgs.): 4-Bloodlines. 5-Elseworlds story 4.00
Annual 6 (1995,$3.95)-Year One story 4.00
Annual 7 (1996, $3.50, 48 pgs.)-Legends of the Dead Earth story; intro 75th Century Legion of Super-Heroes; Wildfire app. 4.00
Legion: Secret Files 1 (1/98, $4.95) Retold origin & pin-ups 5.00
Legion: Secret Files 2 (6/99, $4.95) Story and profile pages 5.00
The Beginning of Tomorrow TPB ('99, $17.95) r/post-Zero Hour reboot 18.00
NOTE: ***Giffen** a-1-24; breakdowns-26-32, 34-36; c-1-7, 8(part), 9-24. **Brandon Peterson** a(p)-15(1st for DC), 16, 18, Annual 2(54 pgs.); c-Annual 2p. **Swan/Anderson** c-8(part).*

LEGION OF SUPER-HEROES (5th Series) (Title becomes Supergirl and the Legion of Super-Heroes #16-36) (Intro. in Teen Titans/Legion Special)
DC Comics: Feb, 2005 - No. 15, Apr, 2006; No. 37, Feb, 2008 - No. 50, Mar, 2009 ($2.95/$2.99)

1-15: 1-Waid-s/Kitson-a/c. 4-Kirk & Gibbons-a. 9-Jeanty-a. 15-Dawnstar, Tyroc, Blok-c 3.00
37-50: 37-Shooter-s/Manapul-a begin; two interlocking covers. 50-Wraparound cover 3.00
44-Variant-c by Neal Adams 5.00
... Death of a Dream TPB ('06, $14.99) r/#7-13 15.00
... Enemy Manifest HC ('09, $24.99, dustjacket) r/#45-50 25.00
... Enemy Manifest SC ('10, $14.99) r/#45-50 15.00
... Enemy Rising HC ('08, $19.99, dustjacket) r/#37-44 20.00
... Enemy Rising SC ('09, $14.99) r/#37-44 15.00
...: 1050 Years of the Future TPB ('08, $19.99) r/greatest tales of their 50 year history 20.00
... Teenage Revolution TPB ('05, $14.99) r/#1-6 & Teen Titans/Legion Spec.; sketch pages 15.00

LEGION OF SUPER-HEROES (6th Series)
DC Comics: Jul, 2010 - No. 16, Oct, 2011 ($3.99/$2.99)

1-9: 1-Earth-Man app.; Titan destroyed; Levitz-s/Cinar-a/c. 6-Jimenez back-up-a 4.00
1-6-Variant covers by Jim Lee 8.00
10-16-($2.99) 12-16-Legion of Super-Villains app. 3.00
Annual 1 (2/11, $4.99) New Emerald Empress; Levitz-s/Giffen-a 5.00
...: The Choice HC (2011, $24.99, dustjacket) r/#1-6; variant-c gallery and Cinar art 25.00

LEGION OF SUPER-HEROES (DC New 52)(Also see Legion Lost)
DC Comics: Nov, 2011 - No. 23, Oct, 2013 ($2.99)

1-23: 1-4-Levitz-s/Portela-a. 5-Simonson-c/a. 8-Lightle-a. 17-Giffen-a. 23-Maguire-a 3.00
#0 (11/12, $2.99) Story of Brainiac 5 joining the Legion; Levitz-s/Kolins-a 3.00

LEGION OF SUPER-HEROES IN THE 31ST CENTURY (Based on the animated series)
DC Comics: June, 2007 - No. 20, Jan, 2009 ($2.25)

1-20: 1-Chynna Clugston-a; Fatal Five app. 6-Green Lantern Corps app. 15-Impulse app. 3.00
1-(6/07) Free Comic Book Day giveaway 3.00
...: Tomorrow's Heroes (2008, $14.99) r/#1-7; cover gallery 15.00

LEGION OF SUPER-VILLAINS
DC Comics: May, 2011 ($4.99, one-shot)

1-Levitz-s/Portela-a; Saturn Queen, Lightning Lord, Sun-Killer, Micro Lad app. 5.00

LEGION: PROPHETS (Prelude to 2010 movie)
IDW Publishing: Nov, 2009 - No. 4, Dec, 2009 ($3.99, limited series)

1-4: Stewart & Waltz-s. 1-Muriel-a. 2-Holder-a. 3-Paronzini-a. 4-Gaydos-a 4.00

LEGION: SCIENCE POLICE (See Legion of Super-Heroes)
DC Comics: Aug, 1998 - No. 4, Nov, 1998 ($2.25, limited series)

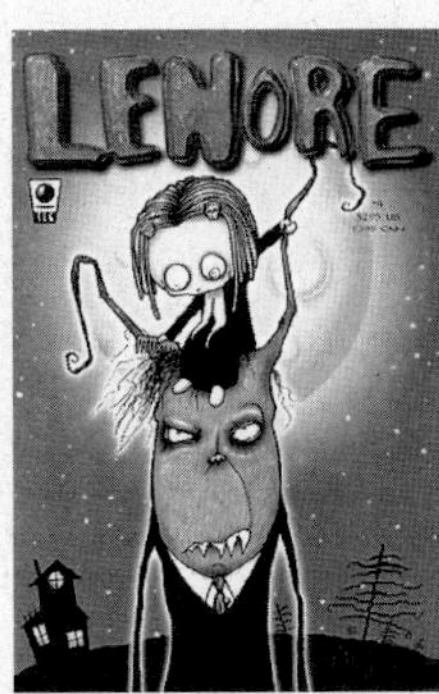

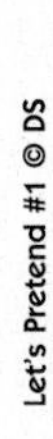

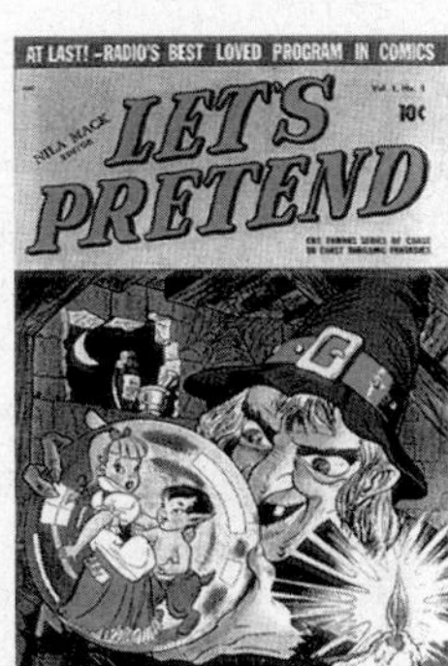

Letter 44 #1 © Charles Soule

GD 2.0 | VG 4.0 | FN 6.0 | VF 8.0 | VF/NM 9.0 | NM- 9.2

GD 2.0 | VG 4.0 | FN 6.0 | VF 8.0 | VF/NM 9.0 | NM- 9.2

1-4-Ryan-a 3.00

LEGION: SECRET ORIGIN (Legion of Super-Heroes)
DC Comics: Dec, 2011 - No. 6, May, 2012 ($2.99, limited series)

1-6-Levitz-s/Batista-a; formation of the Legion retold 3.00

LEGION WORLDS (Follows Legion Lost series)
DC Comics: Jun, 2001 - No. 6, Nov, 2001 ($3.95, limited series)

1-6-Abnett & Lanning-s; art by various. 5-Dillon-a. 6-Timber Wolf app. 4.00

LEMONADE KID, THE (See Bobby Benson's B-Bar-B Riders)
AC Comics: 1990 ($2.50, 28 pgs.)

1-Powell-c(r); Red Hawk-r by Powell; Lemonade Kid-r/Bobby Benson by Powell (2 stories) 3.00

LENNON SISTERS LIFE STORY, THE
Dell Publishing Co.: No. 951, Nov, 1958 - No. 1014, Aug, 1959

Four Color 951 (#1)-Toth-a, 32pgs, photo-c 11 22 33 73 157 240
Four Color 1014-Toth-a, photo-c 10 20 30 69 147 225

LENORE
Slave Labor Graphics: Feb, 1998 - Present ($2.95/$3.95, B&W, color #13-on)

1-12: 1-Roman Dirge-s/a, 1,2-2nd printing 4.00
13-($3.95, color) 4.00
Vol. 2 (8/09 - Present) 1-9: 1-1st and 2nd printings; Lenore's origin 4.00
...: Cooties TPB (3/06, $13.95) r/#9-12; pin-ups by various 14.00
...: Noogies TPB ($11.95) r/#1-4 12.00
...: Purple Nurples HC (8/13, $17.95) Vol. 2 #4-7 18.00
...: Swirlies HC (8/12, $17.95) r/#13 & Vol. 2 #1-3 18.00
...: Wedgies TPB (2000, $13.95) r/#5-8 14.00

LEONARD NIMOY'S PRIMORTALS
Tekno Comix: Mar, 1995 - No. 15, May, 1996 ($1.95)

1-15: Concept by Leonard Nimoy & Isaac Asimov 1-3-w/bound-in game piece & trading card. 4-w/Teknophage Steel Edition coupon. 13,14-Art Adams-c. 15-Simonson-c 3.00

LEONARD NIMOY'S PRIMORTALS
BIG Entertainment: V2#0, June, 1996 - No. 8, Feb, 1997 ($2.25)

V2#0-8: 0-Includes Pt. 9 of "The Big Bang" x-over. 0,1-Simonson-c. 3-Kelley Jones-c 3.00

LEONARD NIMOY'S PRIMORTALS ORIGINS
Tekno Comix: Nov, 1995 - No. 2, Dec, 1995 ($2.95, limited series)

1,2: Nimoy scripts; Art Adams-c; polybagged 3.00

LEONARDO (Also see Teenage Mutant Ninja Turtles)
Mirage Studios: Dec, 1986 ($1.50, B&W, one-shot)

1 2 4 6 9 12 15

LEO THE LION
I. W. Enterprises: No date(1960s) (10¢)

1-Reprint 2 4 6 9 13 16

LEROY (Teen-age)
Standard Comics: Nov, 1949 - No. 6, Nov, 1950

1 15 30 45 90 140 190
2-Frazetta text illo. 11 22 33 62 86 110
3-6: 3-Lubbers-a 10 20 30 56 76 95

LETHAL (Also see Brigade)
Image Comics (Extreme Studios): Feb, 1996 ($2.50, unfinished limited series)

1-Marat Mychaels-c/a. 3.00

LETHAL FOES OF SPIDER-MAN (Sequel to Deadly Foes of Spider-Man)
Marvel Comics: Sept, 1993 - No. 4, Dec, 1993 ($1.75, limited series)

1-4 3.00

LETHARGIC LAD
Crusade Ent.: June, 1996 - No. 3, Sept, 1996 ($2.95, B&W, limited series)

1,2 3.00
3-Alex Ross-c/swipe (Kingdom Come) 4.00
...Jumbo Sized Annual #1 (Summer 2002, $3.99) prints comic stories from internet 4.00

LETHARGIC LAD ADVENTURES
Crusade Ent./Destination Ent.#3 on: Oct, 1997 - No. 12, Sept./Oct. 1999 ($2.95, B&W)

1-12-Hyland-s/a. 9-Alex Ross sketch page & back-c 3.00

LET ME IN: CROSSROADS (Based on the 2010 movie Let Me In)
Dark Horse Comics: Dec, 2010 - No. 4, Mar, 2011 ($3.99, limited series)

1-4-Prelude to the film; Andreyko-s/Reynolds-a/Phillips-c 4.00
1-4 Variant photo-c 8.00

LET'S PRETEND (CBS radio)
D. S. Publishing Co.: May-June, 1950 - No. 3, Sept-Oct, 1950

1 18 36 54 105 165 225
2,3 14 28 42 82 121 160

LET'S READ THE NEWSPAPER
Charlton Press: 1974

nn-Features Quincy by Ted Sheares 1 3 4 6 8 10

LET'S TAKE A TRIP (TV) (CBS Television Presents)
Pines Comics: Spring, 1958

1-Marv Levy-c/a 5 10 15 23 28 32

LETTER 44
Oni Press: Oct, 2013 - Present ($1.00/$3.99)

1-($1.00)-Soule-a/Alburquerque-a 5.00
2-5-($3.99) 4.00

LETTERS TO SANTA (See March of Comics No. 228)

LEX LUTHOR: MAN OF STEEL
DC Comics: May, 2005 - No. 5, Sept, 2005 ($2.99, limited series)

1-5: 1-Azzarello-s/Bermejo-a/c in all. 3-Batman-c/app. 3.00
TPB (2005, $12.99) r/series 13.00
Luthor HC (2010, $19.99, d.j.) r/#1-5 with 10 new story pages; cover gallery & sketch-a 20.00

LEX LUTHOR: THE UNAUTHORIZED BIOGRAPHY
DC Comics: 1989 ($3.95, 52 pgs., one-shot, squarebound)

1-Painted-c; Clark Kent app. 6.00

LIBERTY COMICS (Miss Liberty No. 1)
Green Publishing Co.: No. 5, May, 1945 - No. 15, July, 1946 (MLJ & other-r)

5 (5/45)-The Prankster app; Starr-a 24 48 72 140 230 320
10-Hangman & Boy Buddies app.; reprints 3 Hangman stories, incl. Hangman #8 23 46 69 136 223 310
11 (V2#2, 1/46)-Wilbur in women's clothes 18 36 54 105 165 225
12 (V2#4)-Black Hood & Suzie app.; classic Skull-c 63 126 189 403 689 975
14,15-Patty of Airliner; Starr-a in both 20 40 60 120 195 270

LIBERTY COMICS (The CBLDF Presents...)
Image Comics: July, 2008; Oct, 2009 ($3.99/$4.99, Comic Book Legal Defense Fund benefit)

1-Two covers by Campbell & Mignola; art by Cooke, Aragones, A. Adams & others 4.00
1-(12/08) Second printing with Thor-c by Simonson 4.00
2-(10/09, $4.99) two covers by Romita Jr. & Sale; art by Allred, Templesmith, Jim Lee 5.00
Liberty Annual 2010 (10/10, $4.99) Covers by Gibbons & Robertson 5.00
Liberty Annual 2011 (10/11, $4.99) Covers by Wagner & Cassaday 5.00
Liberty Annual 2012 (10/12, $4.99) Covers by Dodson & Bá; Walking Dead story 5.00
Liberty Annual 2013 (10/13, $4.99) Covers by Corben & Marquez 5.00

LIBERTY COMICS
Heroic Publishing: Sept, 2007 ($4.50)

1-Mark Sparacio-c 4.50

LIBERTY GIRL
Heroic Publishing: Aug, 2006 - No. 3, May, 2007 ($3.25/$2.99)

1-3-Mark Sparacio-c/a 3.25

LIBERTY GUARDS
Chicago Mail Order: No date (1946?)

nn-Reprints Man of War #1 with cover of Liberty Scouts #1; Gustavson-c 37 74 111 222 361 500

LIBERTY MEADOWS
Insight Studios Group/Image Comics #27 on: 1999 - Present ($2.95, B&W)

1-Frank Cho-s/a; reprints newspaper strips 3 6 9 14 20 25
1-2nd & 3rd printings 1 2 3 4 5 7
2,3 2 4 6 8 11 14
4-10 1 2 3 4 5 7
11-25,27-37: 20-Adam Hughes-c. 22-Evil Brandy vs. Brandy. 27-1st Image issue, printed sideways 3.00
..., Cover Girl HC (Image, 2006, $24.99, with dustjacket) r/color covers of #1-19,21-37 along with B&W inked versions, sketches and pin-up art 25.00
...: Eden Book 1 SC (Image, 2002, $14.95) r/#1-9; sketch gallery 15.00
...: Eden Book 1 SC 2nd printing (Image, 2004, $19.95) r/#1-9; sketch gallery 20.00
...: Eden Book 1 HC (Image, 2003, $24.95, with dustjacket) r/#1-9; sketch gallery 25.00
...: Creature Comforts Book 2 HC (Image, 2004, $24.95, with d.j.) r/#10-18; sketch gallery 25.00
...: Creature Comforts Book 2 SC (Image, 12/04, $14.95) r/#10-18; sketch gallery 15.00
...Book 3: Summer of Love HC (Image, 12/04, $24.95) r/#19-27; sketch gallery 25.00

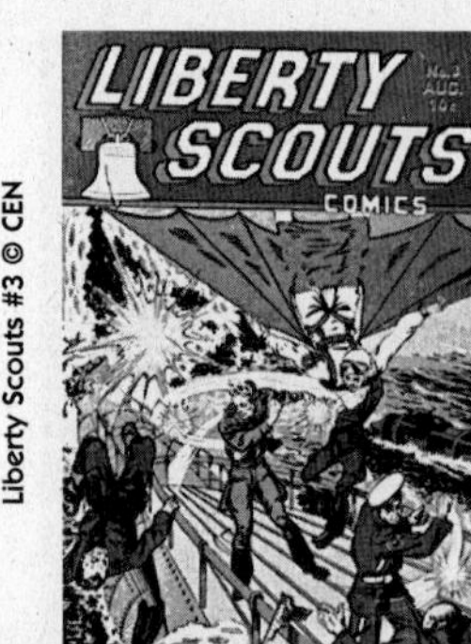

Liberty Scouts #3 © CEN

Life of Captain Marvel #4 © MAR

Life Story #45 © FAW

	GD 2.0	VG 4.0	FN 6.0	VF 8.0	VF/NM 9.0	NM- 9.2
...Book 3: Summer of Love SC (Image, 7/05, $14.95) r/#19-27; sketch gallery						15.00
...Book 4: Cold, Cold Heart HC (Image, 9/05, $24.95) r/#28-36; sketch gallery						25.00
...Book 4: Cold, Cold Heart SC (Image, 2006, $14.99) r/#28-36; sketch gallery						15.00
Image Firsts: Liberty Meadows #1 (9/10, $1.00) r/#1						3.00
... Sourcebook (5/04, $4.95) character info and unpublished strips						5.00
... Wedding Album (#26) (2002, $2.95)						3.00

LIBERTY PROJECT, THE
Eclipse Comics: June, 1987 - No. 8, May, 1988 ($1.75, color, Baxter paper)

	GD	VG	FN	VF	VF/NM	NM-
1-8: 6-Valkyrie app.						3.00

LIBERTY SCOUTS (See Liberty Guards & Man of War)
Centaur Publications: No. 2, June, 1941 - No. 3, Aug, 1941

	GD	VG	FN	VF	VF/NM	NM-
2(#1)-Origin The Fire-Man, Man of War; Vapo-Man & Liberty Scouts begin; intro Liberty Scouts; Gustavson-c/a in both	145	290	435	928	1589	2250
3(#2)-Origin & 1st app. The Sentinel	100	200	300	640	1095	1550

LICENCE TO KILL (James Bond 007) (Movie)
Eclipse Comics: 1989 ($7.95, slick paper, 52 pgs.)

	GD	VG	FN	VF	VF/NM	NM-
nn-Movie adaptation; Timothy Dalton photo-c	1	2	3	5	6	8
Limited Hardcover ($24.95)						25.00

LIDSVILLE (TV)
Gold Key: Oct, 1972 - No. 5, Oct, 1973

	GD	VG	FN	VF	VF/NM	NM-
1-Photo-c on all	5	10	15	31	53	75
2-5	3	6	9	21	33	45

LIEUTENANT, THE (TV)
Dell Publishing Co.: April-June, 1964

	GD	VG	FN	VF	VF/NM	NM-
1-Photo-c	3	6	9	17	26	35

LIEUTENANT BLUEBERRY (Also see Blueberry)
Marvel Comics (Epic Comics): 1991 - No. 3, 1991 (Graphic novel)

	GD	VG	FN	VF	VF/NM	NM-
1,2 ($8.95)-Moebius-a in all	2	4	6	11	16	20
3 ($14.95)	3	6	9	15	22	28

LT. ROBIN CRUSOE, U.S.N. (See Movie Comics & Walt Disney Showcase #26)

LIFE EATERS, THE
DC Comics (WildStorm): 2003 ($29.95, hardcover with dust jacket)

	GD	VG	FN	VF	VF/NM	NM-
HC-David Brin-s; Scott Hampton-painted-a/c; Norse Gods team with the Nazis						30.00
SC-(2004, $19.95)						20.00

LIFE OF CAPTAIN MARVEL, THE
Marvel Comics Group: Aug, 1985 - No. 5, Dec, 1985 ($2.00, Baxter paper)

	GD	VG	FN	VF	VF/NM	NM-
1-5: 1-All reprint Starlin issues of Iron Man #55, Capt. Marvel #25-34 plus Marvel Feature #12 (all with Thanos). 4-New Thanos back-c by Starlin						6.00

LIFE OF CHRIST, THE
Catechetical Guild Educational Society: No. 301, 1949 (35¢, 100 pgs.)

	GD	VG	FN	VF	VF/NM	NM-
301-Reprints from Topix(1949)-V5#11,12	9	18	27	50	65	80

LIFE OF CHRIST: THE CHRISTMAS STORY, THE
Marvel Comics/Nelson: Feb, 1993 ($2.99, slick stock)

	GD	VG	FN	VF	VF/NM	NM-
nn						5.00

LIFE OF CHRIST: THE EASTER STORY, THE
Marvel Comics/Nelson: 1993 ($2.99, slick stock)

	GD	VG	FN	VF	VF/NM	NM-
nn						5.00

LIFE OF CHRIST VISUALIZED
Standard Publishers: 1942 - No. 3, 1943

	GD	VG	FN	VF	VF/NM	NM-
1-3: All came in cardboard case, each...	9	18	27	50	65	80
Case only.....	10	20	30	54	72	90

LIFE OF CHRIST VISUALIZED
The Standard Publ. Co.: 1946? (48 pgs. in color)

	GD	VG	FN	VF	VF/NM	NM-
nn	7	14	21	37	46	55

LIFE OF ESTHER VISUALIZED
The Standard Publ. Co.: No. 2062, 1947 (48 pgs. in color)

	GD	VG	FN	VF	VF/NM	NM-
2062	7	14	21	37	46	55

LIFE OF JOSEPH VISUALIZED
The Standard Publ. Co.: No. 1054, 1946 (48 pgs. in color)

	GD	VG	FN	VF	VF/NM	NM-
1054	7	14	21	37	46	55

LIFE OF PAUL (See The Living Bible)

LIFE OF POPE JOHN PAUL II, THE
Marvel Comics Group: Jan, 1983 ($1.50/$1.75)

	GD 2.0	VG 4.0	FN 6.0	VF 8.0	VF/NM 9.0	NM- 9.2
1	2	4	6	8	10	12

LIFE OF RILEY, THE (TV)
Dell Publishing Co.: No. 917, July, 1958

	GD	VG	FN	VF	VF/NM	NM-
Four Color 917-Photo-c	9	18	27	59	117	175

LIFE ON ANOTHER PLANET
Kitchen Sink Press: 1978 (B&W, graphic novel, magazine size)

	GD	VG	FN	VF	VF/NM	NM-
nn-Will Eisner-s/a						20.00
Reprint (DC Comics, 5/00, $12.95)						13.00

LIFE'S LIKE THAT
Croyden Publ. Co.: 1945 (25¢, B&W, 68 pgs.)

	GD	VG	FN	VF	VF/NM	NM-
nn-Newspaper Sunday strip-r by Neher	7	14	21	35	43	50

LIFE STORIES OF AMERICAN PRESIDENTS (See Dell Giants)

LIFE STORY
Fawcett Publications: Apr, 1949 - V8#46, Jan, 1953; V8#47, Apr, 1953 (All have photo-c?)

	GD	VG	FN	VF	VF/NM	NM-
V1#1	15	30	45	90	140	190
2	10	20	30	56	76	95
3-6, V2#7-12 (3/50)	9	18	27	50	65	80
V3#13-Wood-a (4/50)	15	30	45	86	133	180
V3#14-18, V4#19-24, V5#25-30, V6#31-35	8	16	24	44	57	70
V6#36- "I sold drugs" on-c	14	28	42	78	112	145
V7#37,40-42, V8#44,45	8	16	24	42	54	65
V7#38, V8#43-Evans-a	8	16	24	44	57	70
V7#39-Drug Smuggling & Junkie story	11	22	33	64	90	115
V8#46,47 (Scarce)	10	20	30	54	72	90

NOTE: *Powell a-13, 23, 24, 26, 28, 30, 32, 39. **Marcus Swayze** a-1-3, 10-12, 15, 16, 20, 21, 23-25, 31, 35, 37, 40, 44, 46.*

LIFE, THE UNIVERSE AND EVERYTHING (See Hitchhikers Guide to the Galaxy & Restaurant at the End of the Universe)
DC Comics: 1996 - No. 3, 1996 ($6.95, squarebound, limited series)

	GD	VG	FN	VF	VF/NM	NM-
1-3: Adaptation of novel by Douglas Adams.	1	2	3	4	5	7

LIFE WITH ARCHIE
Archie Publications: Sept, 1958 - No. 286, Sept, 1991

	GD	VG	FN	VF	VF/NM	NM-
1	28	56	84	202	451	700
2-(9/59)	13	26	39	89	195	300
3-5: 3-(7/60)	9	18	27	61	123	185
6-8,10	8	16	24	52	99	145
9,11-Horror/SciFi-c	9	18	27	61	123	185
12-20	6	12	18	38	69	100
21(7/63)-30	5	10	15	33	57	80
31-34,36-38,40,41	4	8	12	28	47	65
35,39-Horror/Sci-Fi-c	6	12	18	38	69	100
42-Pureheart begins (1st app.-c/s, 10/65)	8	16	24	52	99	145
43,44	5	10	15	34	60	85
45(1/66) 1st Man From R.I.V.E.R.D.A.L.E.	6	12	18	41	76	110
46-Origin Pureheart	5	10	15	35	63	90
47-49	4	8	12	28	47	65
50-United Three begin: Pureheart (Archie), Superteen (Betty), Captain Hero (Jughead)	6	12	18	37	66	95
51-59: 59-Pureheart ends	4	8	12	27	44	60
60-Archie band begins, ends #66	5	10	15	33	57	80
61-66: 61-Man From R.I.V.E.R.D.A.L.E.-c/s	4	8	12	23	37	50
67-80	3	6	9	16	24	32
81-99	3	6	9	15	22	28
100 (8/70), 113-Sabrina & Salem app.	3	6	9	18	28	38
101-112, 114-130(2/73), 139(11/73)-Archie Band c/s	2	4	6	11	16	20
131,134-138,140-146,148-161,164-170(6/76)	2	4	6	9	12	15
132,133,147,163-all horror-c/s	3	6	9	14	20	26
162-UFO c/s	3	6	9	14	19	24
171,173-175,177-184,186,189,191-194,196	2	3	4	6	8	10
172,185,197 : 172-(9/77)-Bi-Cent. spec. ish, 185-2nd 24th cent.-c/s, 197-Time machine/SF-c/s	2	4	6	8	10	12
176(12/76)-1st app. Capt. Archie of Starship Rivda, in 24th century c/s; 1st app. Stella the Robot	3	6	9	14	19	24
187,188,195,198,199-all horror-c/s	2	4	6	9	13	16
190-1st Dr. Doom-c/s	2	4	6	9	13	16
200 (12/78) Maltese Pigeon-s	2	4	6	8	11	14
201-203,205-237,239,240(1/84): 208-Reintro Veronica	1	2	3	5	6	8
204-Flying saucer-c/s	2	3	4	6	8	10
238-(9/83)-25th anniversary issue; Ol' Betsy (jalopy) replaced	1	2	3	5	7	9

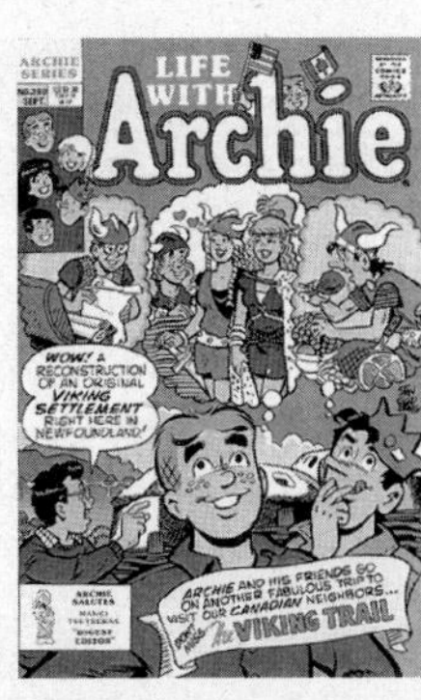

Life With Archie #280 © AP

Linda #1 © AJAX

Lionheart #2 © Awesome

GD 2.0 | VG 4.0 | FN 6.0 | VF 8.0 | VF/NM 9.0 | NM- 9.2

241-278,280-285: 250-Comic book convention-s 5.00
279,286: 279-Intro Mustang Sally ($1.00, 7/90) 6.00
NOTE: *Gene Colan a-272-279, 285, 286. Horror/Sci-Fi-c 9, 11, 35, 39, 162.*

LIFE WITH ARCHIE (The Married Life) (Magazine)
Archie Publications: Sept, 2010 - No. 37 ($3.99, magazine-size)
1-15,17-34: Continuation of Married Life stories from Archie #600-605; articles/interviews 4.00
16-Kevin Keller gay wedding 10.00

LIFE WITH MILLIE (Formerly A Date With Millie) (Modeling With Millie #21 on)
Atlas/Marvel Comics Group: No. 8, Dec, 1960 - No. 20, Dec, 1962
8-Teenage 9 18 27 58 114 170
9-11 6 12 18 41 76 110
12-20 6 12 18 38 69 100

LIFE WITH SNARKY PARKER (TV)
Fox Feature Syndicate: Aug, 1950
1-Early TV comic; photo-c from TV puppet show 29 58 87 170 278 385

LIGHT AND DARKNESS WAR, THE
Marvel Comics (Epic Comics): Oct, 1988 - No. 6, Dec, 1989 ($1.95, lim. series)
1-6 3.00

LIGHT BRIGADE, THE
DC Comics: 2004 - No. 4, 2004 ($5.95, limited series)
1-4-Archangels in World War II; Tomasi-s/Snejbjerg-a 6.00
TPB (2005, 2009, $19.99) r/series; cover galery 20.00

LIGHT FANTASTIC, THE (Terry Pratchett's)
Innovation Publishing: June, 1992 - No. 4, Sept, 1992 ($2.50, mini-series)
1-4: Adapts 2nd novel in Discworld series 3.00

LIGHT IN THE FOREST (Disney)
Dell Publishing Co.: No. 891, Mar, 1958
Four Color 891-Movie, Fess Parker photo-c 6 12 18 42 79 115

LIGHTNING COMICS (Formerly Sure-Fire No. 1-3)
Ace Magazines: No. 4, Dec, 1940 - No. 13(V3#1), June, 1942
4-Characters continue from Sure-Fire 110 220 330 704 1202 1700
5,6: 6-Dr. Nemesis begins 74 148 222 470 810 1150
V2#1-6: 2- "Flash Lightning" becomes "Lash..." 58 116 174 371 636 900
V3#1-Intro. Lightning Girl & The Sword 58 116 174 371 636 900
NOTE: ***Anderson** a-V2#6. **Mooney** c-V1#5, 6, V2#1-6, V3#1. Bondage c-V2#6. Lightning-c on all.*

LIGHTNING COMICS PRESENTS
Lightning Comics: May, 1994 ($3.50)
1-Red foil-c distr. by Diamond Distr., 1-Black/yellow/blue-c distrib. by Capital Distr., 1-Red/yellow-c distributed by H. World, 1-Platinum 3.50

LI'L ... (These titles are listed under Little ...)

LILI
Image Comics: No. 0, 1999 ($4.95, B&W)
0-Bendis & Yanover-s 5.00

LILLITH (See Warrior Nun...)
Antarctic Press: Sept, 1996 - No. 3, Feb, 1997 ($2.95, limited series)
1-3: 1-Variant-c 3.00

LIMITED COLLECTORS' EDITION (See Famous First Edition, Marvel Treasury #28, Rudolph The Red-Nosed Reindeer, & Superman Vs. The Amazing Spider-Man; becomes All-New Collectors' Edition)
National Periodical Publications/DC Comics:
(#21-34,51-59: 84 pgs.; #35-41: 68 pgs.; #42-50: 60 pgs.)
C-21, Summer, 1973 - No. C-59, 1978 ($1.00) (10x13-1/2")
(Rudolph...C-20 (implied), 12/72)-See Rudolph The Red-Nosed Reindeer
C-21: Shazam (TV); r/Captain Marvel Jr. #11 by Raboy; C.C. Beck-c, biog. & photo 3 6 9 19 30 40
C-22: Tarzan; complete origin reprinted from #207-210; all Kubert-c/a; Joe Kubert biography & photo inside 3 6 9 16 24 32
C-23: House of Mystery; Wrightson, N. Adams/Orlando, G. Kane/Wood, Toth, Aragones, Sparling reprints 4 8 12 23 37 50
C-24: Rudolph The Red-Nosed Reindeer 6 12 18 38 69 100
C-25: Batman; Neal Adams-c/a(r); G.A. Joker-r; Batman/Enemy Ace-r; Novick-a(r); has photos from TV show 4 8 12 25 40 55
C-26: See Famous First Edition C-26 (same contents)
C-27,C-29,C-31: C-27: Shazam (TV); G.A. Capt. Marvel & Mary Marvel-r; Beck-r. C-29: Tarzan; reprints "Return of Tarzan" from #219-223 by Kubert; Kubert-c. C-31: Superman; origin-r; Giordano-a; photos of George Reeves from 1950s TV show on inside b/c; Burnley, Boring-r 3 6 9 16 23 30
C-32: Ghosts (new-a) 3 6 9 21 33 45
C-33: Rudolph The Red-Nosed Reindeer(new-a) 5 10 15 35 63 90
C-34: Christmas with the Super-Heroes; unpublished Angel & Ape story by Oksner & Wood; Batman & Teen Titans-r 3 6 9 16 23 30
C-35: Shazam (TV); photo cover features TV's Captain Marvel, Jackson Bostwick; Beck-r; TV photos inside b/c 3 6 9 15 22 28
C-36: The Bible; all new adaptation beginning with Genesis by Kubert, Redondo & Mayer; Kubert-c 3 6 9 15 22 28
C-37: Batman; r-1946 Sundays; inside b/c photos of Batman TV show villains (all villain issue; r/G.A. Joker, Catwoman, Penguin, Two-Face, & Scarecrow stories plus 1946 Sundays-r) 3 6 9 17 26 35
C-38: Superman; 1 pg. N. Adams; part photo-c; photos from TV show on inside back-c 3 6 9 15 22 28
C-39: Secret Origins of Super-Villains; N. Adams-i(r); collection reprints 1950's Joker origin, Luthor origin from Adv. Comics #271, Captain Cold origin from Showcase #8 among others; G.A. Batman-r; Beck-r 3 6 9 15 22 28
C-40: Dick Tracy by Gould featuring Flattop; newspaper-r from 12/21/43 - 5/17/44; biog. of Chester Gould 3 6 9 15 22 28
C-41: Super Friends (TV); JLA-r(1965); Toth-c/a 3 6 9 16 23 30
C-42: Rudolph 4 8 12 27 44 60
C-43-C-47: C-43: Christmas with the Super-Heroes; Wrightson, S&K, Neal Adams-a. C-44: Batman; N. Adams-p(r) & G.A.-r; painted-c. C-45: More Secret Origins of Super-Villains; Flash-r/#105; G.A. Wonder Woman & Batman/Catwoman-r. C-46: Justice League of America(1963-r); 3 pgs. Toth-a C-47: Superman Salutes the Bicentennial (Tomahawk interior); 2 pgs. new-a 3 6 9 14 20 26
C-48,C-49: C-48: Superman Vs. The Flash (Superman/Flash race); swipes-c to Superman #199; r/Superman #199 & Flash #175; 6 pgs. Neal Adams-a. C-49: Superboy & the Legion of Super-Heroes 3 6 9 16 23 30
C-50: Rudolph The Red-Nosed Reindeer; contains poster (1/2 price if poster is missing) 4 8 12 27 44 60
C-51: Batman; Neal Adams-c/a 3 6 9 16 24 32
C-52,C-57: C-52: The Best of DC; Neal Adams-c/a; Toth, Kubert-a. C-57: Welcome Back, Kotter-r(TV)(5/78) includes unpublished #11 3 6 9 15 22 28
C-53 thru C-56, C-58, C-60 thru C-62 (See All-New Collectors' Edition)
C-59: Batman's Strangest Cases; N. Adams-r; Wrightson-r/Swamp Thing #7; N. Adams/Wrightson-c 3 6 9 15 22 28
NOTE: *All-r with exception of some special features and covers. **Aparo** a-52r; c-37. **Grell** c-49. **Infantino** a-25, 39, 44, 45, 52. **Bob Kane** r-25. **Robinson** r-25, 44. **Sprang** r-44. Issues #21-31, 35-39, 45, 48 have back cover cut-outs.*

LINDA (Everybody Loves...) (Phantom Lady No. 5 on)
Ajax-Farrell Publ. Co.: Apr-May, 1954 - No. 4, Oct-Nov, 1954
1-Kamenish-a 15 30 45 85 130 175
2-Lingerie panel 13 26 39 72 101 130
3,4 10 20 30 56 76 95

LINDA CARTER, STUDENT NURSE
Atlas Comics (AMI): Sept, 1961 - No. 9, Jan, 1963
1-Al Hartley-c 6 12 18 41 76 110
2-9 5 10 15 31 53 75

LINDA LARK
Dell Publishing Co.: Oct-Dec, 1961 - No. 8, Aug-Oct, 1963
1 3 6 9 18 28 38
2-8 3 6 9 14 19 24

LINE OF DEFENSE 3000AD (Based on the video game)
DC Comics: No. 0, 2012 (no price)
0-Brian Ching-a 3.00

LINUS, THE LIONHEARTED (TV)
Gold Key: Sept, 1965
1 (10155-509) 6 12 18 38 69 100

LION, THE (See Movie Comics)

LIONHEART
Awesome Comics: Sept, 1999 - No. 2, Dec, 1999 ($2.99/$2.50)
1-Ian Churchill-story/a, Jeph Loeb-s; Coven app. 3.50
2-Flip book w/Coven #4 3.00

LION OF SPARTA (See Movie Classics)

LIPPY THE LION AND HARDY HAR HAR (TV)
Gold Key: Mar, 1963 (12¢) (See Hanna-Barbera Band Wagon #1)
1 (10049-303) 7 14 21 46 86 125

LISA COMICS (TV)(See Simpsons Comics)

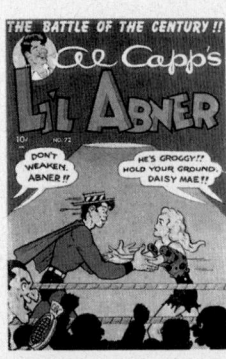

Li'l Abner #72 © TOBY

Little Archie #40 © AP

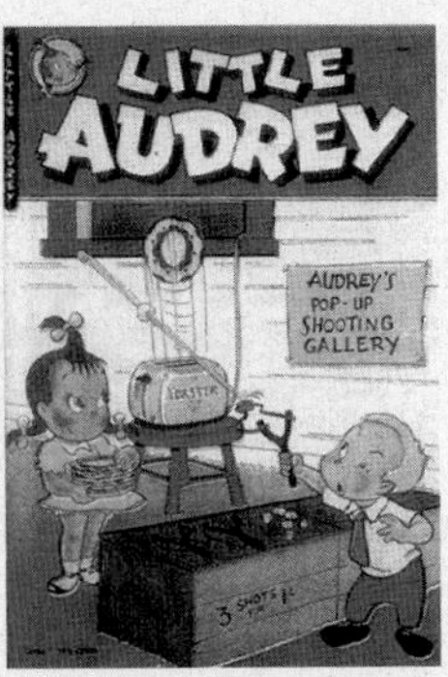

Little Audrey #5 © HARV

Bongo Comics: 1995 ($2.25)

	GD 2.0	VG 4.0	FN 6.0	VF 8.0	VF/NM 9.0	NM- 9.2
1-Lisa in Wonderland						4.00

LITERALS, THE (See Fables and Jack of Fables)
DC Comics (Vertigo): June, 2009 - No. 3, Aug, 2009 ($2.99)

	GD	VG	FN	VF	VF/NM	NM-
1-3-Crossover with Fables #83-85 and Jack of Fables #33-35; Buckingham-c/a						3.00

LI'L ABNER (See Comics on Parade, Sparkle, Sparkler Comics, Tip Top Comics & Tip Topper)
United Features Syndicate: 1939 - 1940

	GD	VG	FN	VF	VF/NM	NM-
Single Series 4 ('39)	84	168	252	538	919	1300
Single Series 18 ('40) (#18 on inside, #2 on-c)	63	126	189	403	689	975

LI'L ABNER (Al Capp's; continued from Comics on Parade #58)
Harvey Publ. No. 61-69 (2/49)/Toby Press No. 70 on: No. 61, Dec, 1947 - No. 97, Jan, 1955 (See Oxydol-Dreft in Promotional Comics section)

	GD	VG	FN	VF	VF/NM	NM-
61(#1)-Wolverton & Powell-a	23	46	69	136	223	310
62-65: 63-The Wolf Girl app. 65-Powell-a	15	30	45	85	130	175
66,67,69,70	14	28	42	82	121	160
68-Full length Fearless Fosdick-c/story	15	30	45	88	137	185
71-74,76,80	13	26	39	74	105	135
75,77-79,86,91-All with Kurtzman art; 86-Sadie Hawkins Day. 91-r/#77	15	30	45	83	124	165
81-85,87-90,92-94,96,97: 83-Evil-Eye Fleegle & Double Whammy app. 88-Cousin Weakeyes goes hunting. 94-Six lessons from Adam Lazonga. 96-Football issue	12	24	36	69	97	125
95-Full length Fearless Fosdick story	14	28	42	76	108	140

LI'L ABNER
Toby Press: 1951

	GD	VG	FN	VF	VF/NM	NM-
1	18	36	54	103	162	220

LI'L ABNER'S DOGPATCH (See Al Capp's...)

LITTLE AL OF THE F.B.I.
Ziff-Davis Publications: No. 10, 1950 (no month) - No. 11, Apr-May, 1951 (Saunders painted-c)

	GD	VG	FN	VF	VF/NM	NM-
10(1950)	17	34	51	98	154	210
11(1951)	14	28	42	80	115	150

LITTLE AL OF THE SECRET SERVICE
Ziff-Davis Publications: No. 10, 7-8/51; No, 2, 9-10/51; No. 3, Winter, 1951 (Saunders painted-c)

	GD	VG	FN	VF	VF/NM	NM-
10(#1)	16	32	48	92	144	195
2,3	14	28	42	76	108	140

LITTLE AMBROSE
Archie Publications: September, 1958

	GD	VG	FN	VF	VF/NM	NM-
1-Bob Bolling-c	15	30	45	88	137	185

LITTLE ANGEL
Standard (Visual Editions)/Pines: No. 5, Sept, 1954; No. 6, Sept, 1955 - No. 16, Sept, 1959

	GD	VG	FN	VF	VF/NM	NM-
5-Last pre-code issue	8	16	24	40	50	60
6-16	5	10	15	24	30	35

LITTLE ANNIE ROONEY (Also see Henry)
David McKay Publ.: 1935 (25¢, B&W dailies, 48 pgs.)(10"x10", cardboard-c)

	GD	VG	FN	VF	VF/NM	NM-
Book 1-Daily strip-r by Darrell McClure	38	76	114	226	368	510

LITTLE ANNIE ROONEY (See King Comics & Treasury of Comics)
David McKay/St. John/Standard: 1938; Aug, 1948 - No. 3, Oct, 1948

	GD	VG	FN	VF	VF/NM	NM-
Feature Books 11 (McKay, 1938)	39	78	117	231	378	525
1 (St. John)	15	30	45	88	137	185
2,3	10	20	30	54	72	90

LITTLE ARCHIE (The Adventures of... #13-on) (See Archie Giant Series Mag. #527, 534, 538, 545, 549, 556, 560, 566, 570, 583, 594, 596, 607, 609, 619)
Archie Publications: 1956 - No. 180, Feb, 1983 (Giants No. 3-84)

	GD	VG	FN	VF	VF/NM	NM-
1-(Scarce)	75	150	225	600	1350	2100
2 (1957)	27	54	81	189	420	650
3-5: 3-(1958)-Bob Bolling-c & giant issues begin	15	30	45	103	227	350
6-10	11	22	33	76	163	250
11-17,19,21 (84 pgs.)	9	18	27	57	111	165
18,20,22 (84 pgs.)-Horror/Sci-Fi-c	10	20	30	69	147	225
23-39 (68 pgs.)	6	12	18	40	73	105
40 (Fall/66)-Intro. Little Pureheart-c/s (68 pgs.)	6	12	18	42	79	115
41,44-Little Pureheart (68 pgs.)	6	12	18	37	66	95
42-Intro The Little Archies Band, ends #66 (68 pgs.)	6	12	18	40	73	105
43-1st Boy From R.I.V.E.R.D.A.L.E. (68 pgs.)	6	12	18	38	69	100
45-58 (68 pgs.)	5	10	15	31	53	75
59 (68 pgs.)-Little Sabrina begins	7	14	21	48	89	130
60-66 (68 pgs.)	4	8	12	27	44	60
67(9/71)-84: 84-Last 52pg. Giant-Size (2/74)	3	6	9	17	26	35
85-99	2	4	6	10	14	18
100	2	4	6	13	18	22
101-112,114-116,118-129	2	4	6	8	10	12
113,117,130: 113-Halloween Special issue(12/76). 117-Donny Osmond-c cameo 130-UFO cover (5/78)	2	4	6	9	13	16
131-150(1/80), 180(Last issue, 2/83)	1	2	3	5	7	9
151-179						5.00
...In Animal Land 1 (1957)	17	34	51	117	259	400
...In Animal Land 17 (Winter, 1957-58)-19 (Summer,1958)-Formerly Li'l Jinx	8	16	24	56	108	160
Archie Classics - The Adventures of Little Archie Vol. 1 TPB (2004, $10.95) reprints						11.00
Vol. 2 TPB (2008, $9.95) reprints plus new 22 pg. story with Bolling-s/a						10.00

NOTE: *Little Archie Band app. 42-66. Little Sabrina in 59-78,80-180*

LITTLE ARCHIE CHRISTMAS SPECIAL (See Archie Giant Series #581)

LITTLE ARCHIE COMICS DIGEST ANNUAL (...Magazine #5 on)
Archie Publications: 10/77 - No. 48, 5/91 (Digest-size, 128 pgs., later issues $1.35-$1.50)

	GD	VG	FN	VF	VF/NM	NM-
1(10/77)-Reprints	3	6	9	19	30	40
2(4/78,3(11/78)-Neal Adams-a. 3-The Fly-r by S&K	3	6	9	14	20	26
4(4/79) - 10	2	4	6	10	14	18
11-20	2	4	6	8	10	12
21-30: 28-Christmas-c	1	2	3	5	6	8
31-48: 40,46-Christmas-c						5.00

NOTE: *Little Archie, Little Jinx, Little Jughead & Little Sabrina in most issues.*

LITTLE ARCHIE DIGEST MAGAZINE
Archie Comics: July, 1991 - No. 21, Mar, 1998 ($1.50/$1.79/$1.89, digest size, bi-annual)

	GD	VG	FN	VF	VF/NM	NM-
V2#1						6.00
2-10						4.00
11-21						3.00

LITTLE ARCHIE MYSTERY
Archie Publications: Aug, 1963 - No. 2, Oct, 1963 (12¢ issues)

	GD	VG	FN	VF	VF/NM	NM-
1	10	20	30	68	144	220
2	6	12	18	41	76	110

LITTLE ASPIRIN (See Little Lenny & Wisco)
Marvel Comics (CnPC): July, 1949 - No. 3, Dec, 1949 (52 pgs.)

	GD	VG	FN	VF	VF/NM	NM-
1-Oscar app.; Kurtzman-a (4 pgs.)	18	36	54	107	169	230
2-Kurtzman-a (4 pgs.)	11	22	33	64	90	115
3-No Kurtzman-a	9	18	27	52	69	85

LITTLE AUDREY (Also see Playful...)
St. John Publ.: Apr, 1948 - No. 24, May, 1952

	GD	VG	FN	VF	VF/NM	NM-
1-1st app. Little Audrey	77	154	231	493	847	1200
2	32	64	96	188	307	425
3-5	21	42	63	122	199	275
6-10	15	30	45	88	137	185
11-20: 16-X-Mas-c	12	24	36	69	97	125
21-24	11	22	33	60	83	105

LITTLE AUDREY (See Harvey Hits #11, 19)
Harvey Publications: No. 25, Aug, 1952 - No. 53, April, 1957

	GD	VG	FN	VF	VF/NM	NM-
25-(Paramount Pictures Famous Star... on-c); 1st Harvey Casper and Baby Huey (1 month earlier than Harvey Comic Hits #60(9/52))	14	28	42	94	207	320
26-30: 26-28-Casper app.	7	14	21	49	92	135
31-40: 32-35-Casper app.	6	12	18	40	73	105
41-53	5	10	15	31	53	75
...Clubhouse 1 (9/61, 68 pg. Giant)-New stories & reprints	8	16	24	51	96	140

LITTLE AUDREY
Harvey Comics: Aug, 1992 - No. 8, July, 1994 ($1.25/$1.50)

	GD	VG	FN	VF	VF/NM	NM-
V2#1						4.00
2-8						3.00

LITTLE AUDREY (...Yearbook)
St. John Publishing Co.: 1950 (50¢, 260 pgs.)

	GD	VG	FN	VF	VF/NM	NM-
Contains 8 complete 1949 comics rebound; Casper, Alice in Wonderland, Little Audrey, Abbott & Costello, Pinocchio, Moon Mullins, Three Stooges (from Jubilee), Little Annie Rooney app. (Rare)	148	296	444	947	1624	2300

(Also see All Good & Treasury of Comics)

NOTE: *This book contains remaindered St. John comics; many variations possible.*

LITTLE AUDREY & MELVIN (Audrey & Melvin No. 62)

Little Dot #20 © HARV

Little Endless Storybook © DC

Little Giant Comics #3 © CEN

Harvey Publications: May, 1962 - No. 61, Dec, 1973

	GD 2.0	VG 4.0	FN 6.0	VF 8.0	VF/NM 9.0	NM- 9.2
1	9	18	27	58	114	170
2-5	4	8	12	25	40	55
6-10	3	6	9	21	33	45
11-20	3	6	9	16	23	30
21-40: 22-Richie Rich app.	2	4	6	13	18	22
41-50,55-61	2	4	6	9	13	16
51-54: All 52 pg. Giants	2	4	6	13	18	22

LITTLE AUDREY TV FUNTIME
Harvey Publ.: Sept, 1962 - No. 33, Oct, 1971 (#1-31: 68 pgs.; #32,33: 52 pgs.)

	GD 2.0	VG 4.0	FN 6.0	VF 8.0	VF/NM 9.0	NM- 9.2
1-Richie Rich app.	9	18	27	58	114	170
2,3: Richie Rich app.	4	8	12	27	44	60
4,5: 5-25¢ & 35¢ issues exist	4	8	12	23	37	50
6-10	3	6	9	17	26	35
11-20	3	6	9	14	19	24
21-33	2	4	6	11	16	20

LITTLE BAD WOLF (Disney; see Walt Disney's C&S #52, Walt Disney Showcase #21 & Wheaties)
Dell Publishing Co.: No. 403, June, 1952 - No. 564, June, 1954

	GD 2.0	VG 4.0	FN 6.0	VF 8.0	VF/NM 9.0	NM- 9.2
Four Color 403 (#1)	6	12	18	41	76	110
Four Color 473 (6/53), 564	5	10	15	31	53	75

LI'L BATTLESTAR GALACTICA (Classic 1978 TV series)
Dynamite Entertainment: 2014 ($3.99, one-shot)

	GD 2.0	VG 4.0	FN 6.0	VF 8.0	VF/NM 9.0	NM- 9.2
1-Kid version spoof by Franco & Art Baltazar; covers by Baltazar & Garbowska						4.00

LITTLE BEAVER
Dell Publishing Co.: No. 211, Jan, 1949 - No. 870, Jan, 1958 (All painted-c)

	GD 2.0	VG 4.0	FN 6.0	VF 8.0	VF/NM 9.0	NM- 9.2
Four Color 211('49)-All Harman-a	8	16	24	51	96	140
Four Color 267,294,332(5/51)	5	10	15	33	57	80
3(10-12/51)-8(1-3/53)	5	10	15	30	50	70
Four Color 483(8-10/53),529	5	10	15	30	50	70
Four Color 612,660,695,744,817,870	5	10	15	30	50	70

LI'L BIONIC KIDS (Six Million Dollar Man and Bionic Woman)
Dynamite Entertainment: 2014 ($3.99, one-shot)

	GD 2.0	VG 4.0	FN 6.0	VF 8.0	VF/NM 9.0	NM- 9.2
1-Kid version spoof; Bigfoot app.; Jerwa-s/McGinty-a; covers by Baltazar & Garbowska						4.00

LITTLE BIT
Jubilee/St. John Publishing Co.: Mar, 1949 - No. 2, June, 1949

	GD 2.0	VG 4.0	FN 6.0	VF 8.0	VF/NM 9.0	NM- 9.2
1-Kid humor	11	22	33	62	86	110
2	9	18	27	47	61	75

LI'L DEPRESSED BOY
Image Comics: Feb, 2011 - No. 16, Apr, 2013 ($2.99/$3.99)

	GD 2.0	VG 4.0	FN 6.0	VF 8.0	VF/NM 9.0	NM- 9.2
1-12-S. Steven Struble-s/Sina Grace-a. 5-Guillory-c. 6-Adlard-c. 10-Childish Gambino app.						3.00
13-16-($3.99)						4.00
Vol. 0 (12/11, $9.99) reprints earlier stories from webcomics & anthologies; various-a						10.00

LITTLE DOT (See Humphrey, Li'l Max, Sad Sack, and Tastee-Freez Comics)
Harvey Publications: Sept, 1953 - No. 164, Apr, 1976

	GD 2.0	VG 4.0	FN 6.0	VF 8.0	VF/NM 9.0	NM- 9.2
1-Intro./1st app. Richie Rich & Little Lotta	423	846	1269	3000	5250	7500
2-1st app. Freckles & Pee Wee (Richie Rich's poor friends)	129	258	387	826	1413	2000
3	77	154	231	493	847	1200
4	71	142	213	454	777	1100
5-Origin dots on Little Dot's dress	74	148	222	470	810	1150
6-Richie Rich, Little Lotta, & Little Dot all on cover; 1st Richie Rich cover featured	103	206	309	659	1130	1600
7-10: 9-Last pre-code issue (1/55)	43	86	129	271	461	650
11-20	29	58	87	170	278	385
21-30	18	36	54	105	165	225
31-40	14	28	42	80	115	150
41-50	11	22	33	62	86	110
51-60	9	18	27	52	69	85
61-80	4	8	12	27	44	60
81-100	3	6	9	19	30	40
101-141	3	6	9	16	23	30
142-145: All 52 pg. Giants	3	6	9	17	26	35
146-164	2	4	6	11	16	20

NOTE: *Richie Rich & Little Lotta in all.*

LITTLE DOT
Harvey Comics: Sept, 1992 - No. 7, June, 1994 ($1.25/$1.50)

	GD 2.0	VG 4.0	FN 6.0	VF 8.0	VF/NM 9.0	NM- 9.2
V2#1-Little Dot, Little Lotta, Richie Rich in all						4.00
2-7 ($1.50)						3.00

LITTLE DOT DOTLAND (Dot Dotland No. 62, 63)
Harvey Publications: July, 1962 - No. 61, Dec, 1973

	GD 2.0	VG 4.0	FN 6.0	VF 8.0	VF/NM 9.0	NM- 9.2
1-Richie Rich begins	11	22	33	76	163	250
2,3	7	14	21	44	82	120
4,5	5	10	15	35	63	90
6-10	5	10	15	30	50	70
11-20	4	8	12	23	37	50
21-30	3	6	9	17	26	35
31-50	3	6	9	16	23	30
51-54: All 52 pg. Giants	3	6	9	17	26	35
55-61	2	4	6	11	16	20

LITTLE DOT'S UNCLES & AUNTS (See Harvey Hits No. 4, 13, 24)
Harvey Enterprises: Oct, 1961; No. 2, Aug, 1962 - No. 52, Apr, 1974

	GD 2.0	VG 4.0	FN 6.0	VF 8.0	VF/NM 9.0	NM- 9.2
1-Richie Rich begins; 68 pgs. begin	13	26	39	86	188	290
2,3	8	16	24	51	96	140
4,5	5	10	15	35	63	90
6-10	5	10	15	31	53	75
11-20	4	8	12	23	37	50
21-37: Last 68 pg. issue	3	6	9	18	28	38
38-52: All 52 pg. Giants	3	6	9	16	23	30

LITTLE DRACULA
Harvey Comics: Jan, 1992 - No. 3, May, 1992 ($1.25, quarterly, mini-series)

	GD 2.0	VG 4.0	FN 6.0	VF 8.0	VF/NM 9.0	NM- 9.2
1-3						3.00

LITTLE ENDLESS STORYBOOK, THE (See The Sandman titles and Delirium's Party)
DC Comics: 2001 ($5.95, Prestige format, one-shot)

	GD 2.0	VG 4.0	FN 6.0	VF 8.0	VF/NM 9.0	NM- 9.2
nn-Jill Thompson-s/painted-a/c; puppy Barnabas searches for Delirium						20.00
HC (2011, $14.99) r/story plus original character sketches and merchandise design						15.00

LI'L ERNIE (Evil Ernie)
Dynamite Entertainment: 2014 ($3.99, one-shot)

	GD 2.0	VG 4.0	FN 6.0	VF 8.0	VF/NM 9.0	NM- 9.2
1-Kid version spoof; Roger Langridge-s/a; covers by Baltazar & Garbowska						4.00

LITTLE EVA
St. John Publishing Co.: May, 1952 - No. 31, Nov, 1956

	GD 2.0	VG 4.0	FN 6.0	VF 8.0	VF/NM 9.0	NM- 9.2
1	17	34	51	98	154	210
2	11	22	33	60	83	105
3-5	9	18	27	47	61	75
6-10	8	16	24	42	54	65
11-31	7	14	21	37	46	55
3-D 1,2(10/53, 11/53, 25¢)-Both came w/glasses. 1-Infinity-c	18	36	54	107	169	230
I.W. Reprint #1-3,6-8: 1-r/Little Eva #28. 2-r/Little Eva #29. 3-r/Little Eva #24	2	4	6	8	11	14
Super Reprint #10,12('63),14,16,18('64): 18-r/Little Eva #25.	2	4	6	8	11	14

LI'L GENIUS (Formerly Super Brat; Summer Fun No. 54) (See Blue Bird & Giant Comics #3)
Charlton Comics: No. 6, 1954 - No. 52, 1/65; No. 53, 10/65; No. 54, 10/85 - No. 55, 1/86

	GD 2.0	VG 4.0	FN 6.0	VF 8.0	VF/NM 9.0	NM- 9.2
6 (#1)	11	22	33	62	86	110
7-10	7	14	21	37	46	55
11-1st app. Li'l Tomboy (10/56); same month as 1st issue of Li'l Tomboy (V14#92)	8	16	24	40	50	60
12-15,19,20	6	12	18	29	36	42
16,17-(68 pgs.)	8	16	24	40	50	60
18-(100 pgs., 10/58)	11	22	33	60	83	105
21-35: 34-Atomic bomb explosion	3	6	9	15	22	28
36-53	2	4	6	10	14	18
54,55 (Low print)						6.00

LI'L GHOST
St. John Publ. Co./Fago No. 1 on: 2/58; No. 2,1/59 - No. 3, Mar, 1959

	GD 2.0	VG 4.0	FN 6.0	VF 8.0	VF/NM 9.0	NM- 9.2
1(St. John)	10	20	30	54	72	90
2,3	6	12	18	31	38	45

LITTLE GIANT COMICS
Centaur Publications: 7/38 - No. 3, 10/38; No. 4, 2/39 (132 pgs.) (6-3/4x4-1/2")

	GD 2.0	VG 4.0	FN 6.0	VF 8.0	VF/NM 9.0	NM- 9.2
1-B&W with color-c; stories, puzzles, magic	174	348	522	1114	1907	2700
2,3-B&W with color-c	123	246	369	787	1344	1900
4 (6-5/8x9-3/8")(68 pgs., B&W inside)	123	246	369	787	1344	1900

NOTE: *Filchock c-2, 4.* ***Gustavson*** *a-1.* ***Pinajian*** *a-4.* ***Bob Wood*** *a-1.*

LITTLE GIANT DETECTIVE FUNNIES

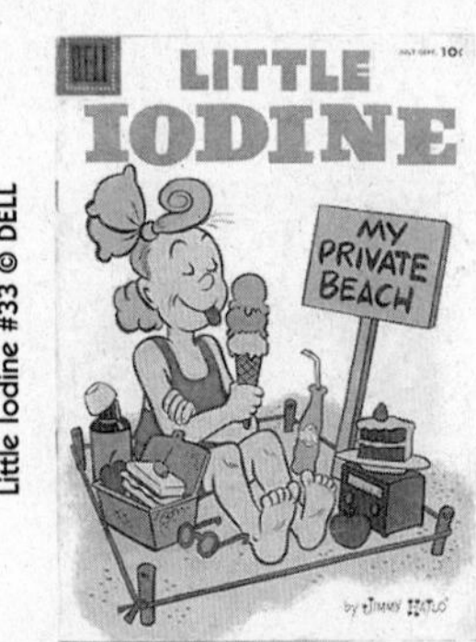

Little Iodine #33 © DELL

Little Jack Frost #1 © AVON

Li'l Menace #1 © Fago

Centaur Publ.: Oct, 1938; No. 4, Jan, 1939 (6-3/4x4-1/2", 132 pgs., B&W)

	GD 2.0	VG 4.0	FN 6.0	VF 8.0	VF/NM 9.0	NM- 9.2
1-B&W with color-c	174	348	522	1114	1907	2700
4(1/39, B&W; color-c; 68 pgs., 6-1/2x9-1/2")-Eisner-r	123	246	369	787	1344	1900

LITTLE GIANT MOVIE FUNNIES
Centaur Publ.: Aug, 1938 - No. 2, Oct, 1938 (6-3/4x4-1/2", 132 pgs., B&W)

	GD 2.0	VG 4.0	FN 6.0	VF 8.0	VF/NM 9.0	NM- 9.2
1-Ed Wheelan's "Minute Movies" reprints	174	348	522	1114	1907	2700
2-Ed Wheelan's "Minute Movies" reprints	123	246	369	787	1344	1900

LITTLE GROUCHO (...the Red-Headed Tornado; ...Grouchy No. 2)
Reston Publ. Co.: No. 16; Feb-Mar, 1955 - No. 2, June-July, 1955 (See Tippy Terry)

	GD 2.0	VG 4.0	FN 6.0	VF 8.0	VF/NM 9.0	NM- 9.2
16, 1 (2-3/55)	8	16	24	44	57	70
2(6-7/55)	6	12	18	28	34	40

LITTLE HIAWATHA (Disney; see Walt Disney's C&S #143)
Dell Publishing Co.: No. 439, Dec, 1952 - No. 988, May-July, 1959

	GD 2.0	VG 4.0	FN 6.0	VF 8.0	VF/NM 9.0	NM- 9.2
Four Color 439 (#1)	6	12	18	37	66	95
Four Color 787 (4/57), 901 (5/58), 988	5	10	15	30	50	70

LITTLE IKE
St. John Publishing Co.: April, 1953 - No. 4, Oct, 1953

	GD 2.0	VG 4.0	FN 6.0	VF 8.0	VF/NM 9.0	NM- 9.2
1-Kid humor	10	20	30	58	79	100
2	7	14	21	35	43	50
3,4	6	12	18	28	34	40

LITTLE IODINE (See Giant Comic Album)
Dell Publ. Co.: No. 224, 4/49 - No. 257, 1949; 3-5/50 - No. 56, 4-6/62 (1-4-52pgs.)

	GD 2.0	VG 4.0	FN 6.0	VF 8.0	VF/NM 9.0	NM- 9.2
Four Color 224-By Jimmy Hatlo	11	22	33	73	157	240
Four Color 257	8	16	24	51	96	140
1(3-5/50)	9	18	27	60	120	180
2-5	5	10	15	35	63	90
6-10	5	10	15	30	50	70
11-20	4	8	12	27	44	60
21-30: 27-Xmas-c	4	8	12	23	37	50
31-40	3	6	9	21	33	45
41-56	3	6	9	19	30	40

LITTLE JACK FROST
Avon Periodicals: 1951

	GD 2.0	VG 4.0	FN 6.0	VF 8.0	VF/NM 9.0	NM- 9.2
1	13	26	39	72	101	130

LI'L JINX (Little Archie in Animal Land #17) (Also see Pep Comics #62)
Archie Publications: No. 1(#11), Nov, 1956 - No. 16, Sept, 1957

	GD 2.0	VG 4.0	FN 6.0	VF 8.0	VF/NM 9.0	NM- 9.2
1(#11)-By Joe Edwards; "First Issue" on cover	14	28	42	82	121	160
12(1/57)-16	10	20	30	56	76	95

LI'L JINX (See Archie Giant Series Magazine No. 223)

LI'L JINX CHRISTMAS BAG (See Archie Giant Series Mag. No. 195, 206, 219)

LI'L JINX GIANT LAUGH-OUT (See Archie Giant Series Mag. No. 176, 185)
Archie Publications: No. 33, Sept, 1971 - No. 43, Nov, 1973 (52 pgs.)

	GD 2.0	VG 4.0	FN 6.0	VF 8.0	VF/NM 9.0	NM- 9.2
33-43 (52 pgs.)	2	4	6	13	18	22

LITTLE JOE (See Popular Comics & Super Comics)
Dell Publishing Co.: No. 1, 1942

	GD 2.0	VG 4.0	FN 6.0	VF 8.0	VF/NM 9.0	NM- 9.2
Four Color 1	54	108	162	432	966	1500

LITTLE JOE
St. John Publishing Co.: Apr, 1953

	GD 2.0	VG 4.0	FN 6.0	VF 8.0	VF/NM 9.0	NM- 9.2
1	7	14	21	35	43	50

LI'L KIDS (Also see Li'l Pals)
Marvel Comics Group: 8/70 - No. 2, 10/70; No. 3, 11/71 - No. 12, 6/73

	GD 2.0	VG 4.0	FN 6.0	VF 8.0	VF/NM 9.0	NM- 9.2
1	7	14	21	49	92	135
2-9	4	8	12	28	47	65
10-12-Calvin app.	5	10	15	30	50	70

LITTLE KING
Dell Publishing Co.: No. 494, Aug, 1953 - No. 677, Feb, 1956

	GD 2.0	VG 4.0	FN 6.0	VF 8.0	VF/NM 9.0	NM- 9.2
Four Color 494 (#1)	8	16	24	52	99	145
Four Color 597, 677	5	10	15	33	57	80

LITTLE LANA (Formerly Lana)
Marvel Comics (MjMC): No. 8, Nov, 1949; No. 9, Mar, 1950

	GD 2.0	VG 4.0	FN 6.0	VF 8.0	VF/NM 9.0	NM- 9.2
8,9	14	28	42	82	121	160

LITTLE LENNY
Marvel Comics (CDS): June, 1949 - No. 3, Nov, 1949

	GD 2.0	VG 4.0	FN 6.0	VF 8.0	VF/NM 9.0	NM- 9.2
1-Little Aspirin app.	14	28	42	80	115	150
2,3	9	18	27	50	65	80

LITTLE LIZZIE
Marvel Comics (PrPI)/Atlas (OMC): 6/49 - No. 5, 4/50; 9/53 - No. 3, Jan, 1954

	GD 2.0	VG 4.0	FN 6.0	VF 8.0	VF/NM 9.0	NM- 9.2
1-Kid humor	15	30	45	86	133	180
2-5	10	20	30	54	72	90
1 (9/53, 2nd series by Atlas)-Howie Post-c	11	22	33	62	86	110
2,3	9	18	27	47	61	75

LITTLE LOTTA (See Harvey Hits No. 10)
Harvey Publications: 11/55 - No. 110, 11/73; No. 111, 9/74 - No. 120, 5/76
V2#1, Oct, 1992 - No. 4, July, 1993 ($1.25)

	GD 2.0	VG 4.0	FN 6.0	VF 8.0	VF/NM 9.0	NM- 9.2
1-Richie Rich (r) & Little Dot begin	46	92	138	359	805	1250
2,3	16	32	48	110	243	375
4,5	10	20	30	69	147	225
6-10	7	14	21	46	86	125
11-20	5	10	15	35	63	90
21-40	4	8	12	23	37	50
41-60	3	6	9	18	28	38
61-80: 62-1st app. Nurse Jenny	3	6	9	15	22	28
81-99	2	4	6	11	16	20
100-103: All 52 pg. Giants	3	6	9	14	19	24
104-120	2	4	6	8	10	12
V2#1-4 (1992-93)						4.00

NOTE: *No. 121 was advertised, but never released.*

LITTLE LOTTA FOODLAND
Harvey Publications: 9/63 - No. 14, 10/67; No. 15, 10/68 - No. 29, Oct, 1972

	GD 2.0	VG 4.0	FN 6.0	VF 8.0	VF/NM 9.0	NM- 9.2
1-Little Lotta, Little Dot, Richie Rich, 68 pgs. begin	11	22	33	73	157	240
2,3	6	12	18	38	69	100
4,5	5	10	15	30	50	70
6-10	4	8	12	23	37	50
11-20	3	6	9	16	23	30
21-26: 26-Last 68 pg. issue	3	6	9	14	20	25
27,28: Both 52 pgs.	2	4	6	11	16	20
29-(36 pgs.)	2	4	6	8	11	14

LITTLE LULU (Formerly Marge's Little Lulu)
Gold Key 207-257/Whitman 258 on: No. 207, Sept, 1972 - No. 268, Mar, 1984

	GD 2.0	VG 4.0	FN 6.0	VF 8.0	VF/NM 9.0	NM- 9.2
207,209,220-Stanley-r. 207-1st app. Henrietta	2	4	6	13	18	22
208,210-219: 208-1st app. Snobbly, Wilbur's butler	2	4	6	9	13	16
221-240,242-249, 250(r/#166), 251-254(r/#206)	2	4	6	8	10	12
241,263-Stanley-r	2	4	6	8	11	14
255-257(Gold Key): 256-r/#212	1	3	4	6	8	10
258,259,262(50¢-c),264(2/82),265(3/82) (Whitman)	2	4	6	11	16	20
260-(9/80)(Whitman pre-pack only - low distribution)	13	26	39	89	195	300
261-(11/80)(Whitman pre-pack only)	5	10	15	31	53	75
262-(1/81) Variant 40¢-c price error (reg. ed. 50¢-c)	3	6	9	15	22	28
266-268 (All #90028 on-c; no date, no date code; 3-pack): 266(7/83). 267(8/83). 268(3/84)-Stanley-r	3	6	9	17	26	35

LITTLE MARY MIXUP (See Comics On Parade)
United Features Syndicate: No. 10, 1939, - No. 26, 1940

	GD 2.0	VG 4.0	FN 6.0	VF 8.0	VF/NM 9.0	NM- 9.2
Single Series 10, 26	34	68	102	204	332	460

LITTLE MAX COMICS (Joe Palooka's Pal; see Joe Palooka)
Harvey Publications: Oct, 1949 - No. 73, Nov, 1961

	GD 2.0	VG 4.0	FN 6.0	VF 8.0	VF/NM 9.0	NM- 9.2
1-Infinity-c; Little Dot begins; Joe Palooka on-c	23	46	69	136	223	310
2-Little Dot app.; Joe Palooka on-c	14	28	42	81	118	155
3-Little Dot app.; Joe Palooka on-c	10	20	30	58	79	100
4-10: 5-Little Dot app., 1pg.	9	18	27	47	61	75
11-20	8	16	24	40	50	60
21-40: 23-Little Dot app. 38-r/#20	6	12	18	31	38	45
41-62,66	3	6	9	17	26	35
63-65,67-73-Include new five pg. Richie Rich stories. 70-73-Little Lotta app.	3	6	9	18	28	38

LI'L MENACE
Fago Magazine Co.: Dec, 1958 - No. 3, May, 1959

	GD 2.0	VG 4.0	FN 6.0	VF 8.0	VF/NM 9.0	NM- 9.2
1-Peter Rabbit app.	9	18	27	47	61	75
2-Peter Rabbit (Vincent Fago's)	7	14	21	35	43	50
3	6	12	18	28	34	40

LITTLE MERMAID, THE (Walt Disney's...; also see Disney's...)
W. D. Publications (Disney): 1990 (no date given)($5.95, no ads, 52 pgs.)

	GD 2.0	VG 4.0	FN 6.0	VF 8.0	VF/NM 9.0	NM- 9.2
nn-Adapts animated movie	1	2	3	4	5	7

Little Miss Muffet #11 © STD

Li'l Pan #2 © FOX

Li'l Vampi #1 © Dynamite

	GD 2.0	VG 4.0	FN 6.0	VF 8.0	VF/NM 9.0	NM- 9.2
nn-Comic version ($2.50)						4.00
LITTLE MERMAID, THE						
Disney Comics: 1992 - No. 4, 1992 ($1.50, mini-series)						
1-4: Based on movie						4.00
1-4: 2nd printings sold at Wal-Mart w/different-c						4.00
LITTLE MISS MUFFET						
Best Books (Standard Comics)/King Features Synd.: No. 11, Dec, 1948 - No. 13, March, 1949						
11-Strip reprints; Fanny Cory-c/a	9	18	27	52	69	85
12,13-Strip reprints; Fanny Cory-c/a	7	14	21	37	46	55
LITTLE MISS SUNBEAM COMICS						
Magazine Enterprises/Quality Bakers of America: June-July, 1950 - No. 4, Dec-Jan, 1950-51						
1	15	30	45	94	147	200
2-4	10	20	30	56	76	95
...Advs. In Space ('55)	7	14	21	35	43	50
LITTLE MONSTERS, THE (See March of Comics #423, Three Stooges #17)						
Gold Key: Nov, 1964 - No. 44, Feb, 1978						
1	5	10	15	33	57	80
2	3	6	9	19	30	40
3-10	3	6	9	16	24	32
11-20	3	6	9	15	21	26
21-30: 19-21-Reprints	2	4	6	11	16	20
31-44: 34-39,43-Reprints	2	4	6	8	11	14
LITTLE MONSTERS (Movie)						
Now Comics: 1989 - No. 6, June, 1990 ($1.75)						
1-6: Photo-c from movie						3.00
LITTLE NEMO (See Cocomalt, Future Comics, Help, Jest, Kayo, Punch, Red Seal, & Superworld; most by Winsor McCay Jr., son of famous artist) (Other McCay books: see Little Sammy Sneeze & Dreams of the Rarebit Fiend)						
LITTLE NEMO (...in Slumberland)						
McCay Features/Nostalgia Press('69): 1945 (11x7-1/4", 28 pgs., B&W)						
1905 & 1911 reprints by Winsor McCay	10	20	30	56	76	95
1969-70 (Exact reprint)	2	4	6	9	12	15
LITTLE ORPHAN ANNIE (See Annie, Famous Feature Stories, Marvel Super Special, Merry Christmas..., Popular Comics, Super Book #7, 11, 23 & Super Comics)						
LITTLE ORPHAN ANNIE						
David McKay Publ./Dell Publishing Co.: No. 7, 1937 - No. 3, Sept-Nov, 1948; No. 206, Dec, 1948						
Feature Books(McKay) 7-(1937) (Rare)	107	214	321	685	1168	1650
Four Color 12(1941)	61	122	183	390	670	950
Four Color 18(1943)-Flag-c	32	64	96	230	515	800
Four Color 52(1944)	23	46	69	164	362	560
Four Color 76(1945)	19	38	57	131	291	450
Four Color 107(1946)	16	32	48	112	249	385
Four Color 152(1947)	11	22	33	73	157	240
1(3-5/48)-r/strips from 5/7/44 to 7/30/44	10	20	30	69	147	225
2-r/strips from 7/21/40 to 9/9/40	8	16	24	51	96	140
3-r/strips from 9/10/40 to 11/9/40	8	16	24	51	96	140
Four Color 206(12/48)	7	14	21	48	89	130
LI'L PALS (Also see Li'l Kids)						
Marvel Comics Group: Sept, 1972 - No. 5, May, 1973						
1	7	14	21	44	82	120
2-5	5	10	15	30	50	70
LI'L PAN (Formerly Rocket Kelly; becomes Junior Comics with #9)(Also see Wotalife Comics)						
Fox Features Syndicate: No. 6, Dec-Jan, 1946-47 - No. 8, Apr-May, 1947						
6	12	24	36	67	94	120
7,8: 7-Atomic bomb story; robot-c	10	20	30	54	72	90
LITTLE PEOPLE (Also see Darby O'Gill & the...)						
Dell Publishing Co.: No. 485, Aug-Oct, 1953 - No. 1062, Dec, 1959 (Walt Scott's)						
Four Color 485 (#1)	7	14	21	46	86	125
Four Color 573(7/54), 633(6/55)	5	10	15	31	53	75
Four Color 692(3/56),753(11/56),809(7/57),868(12/57),908(5/58), 959(12/58), 1062	5	10	15	31	53	75
LITTLE RASCALS						
Dell Publishing Co.: No. 674, Jan, 1956 - No. 1297, Mar-May, 1962						
Four Color 674 (#1)	8	16	24	54	102	150
Four Color 778(3/57),825(8/57)	5	10	15	35	63	90
Four Color 883(3/58),936(9/58),974(3/59),1030(9/59),1079(2-4/60),1137(9-11/60)	5	10	15	34	60	85
Four Color 1174(3-5/61),1224(10-12/61),1297	5	10	15	30	50	70
LI'L RASCAL TWINS (Formerly Nature Boy)						
Charlton Comics: No. 6, 1957 - No. 18, Jan, 1960						
6-Li'l Genius & Tomboy in all	6	12	18	29	36	42
7-18: 7-Timmy the Timid Ghost app.	4	8	12	18	22	25
LITTLE RED HOT: (CHANE OF FOOLS)						
Image Comics: Feb, 1999 - No. 3, Apr, 1999 ($2.95/$3.50, B&W, limited series)						
1-3-Dawn Brown-s/a. 2,3-($3.50-c)						3.50
The Foolish Collection TPB ($12.95) r/#1-3						13.00
LITTLE RED HOT: BOUND						
Image Comics: July, 2001 - No. 3, Nov, 2001 ($2.95, color, limited series)						
1-3-Dawn Brown-s/a.						3.00
LITTLE ROQUEFORT COMICS (See Paul Terry's Comics #105)						
St. John Publishing Co.(all pre-code)/Pines No. 10: June, 1952 - No. 9, Oct, 1953; No. 10, Summer, 1958						
1-By Paul Terry; Funny Animal	10	20	30	58	79	100
2	7	14	21	35	43	50
3-10: 10-CBS Television Presents on-c	6	12	18	28	34	40
LITTLE SAD SACK (See Harvey Hits No. 73, 76, 79, 81, 83)						
Harvey Publications: Oct, 1964 - No. 19, Nov, 1967						
1-Richie Rich app. on cover only	5	10	15	31	53	75
2-10	3	6	9	17	26	35
11-19	3	6	9	15	22	28
LITTLE SCOUTS						
Dell Publishing Co.: No. 321, Mar, 1951 - No. 587, Oct, 1954						
Four Color 321 (#1, 3/51)	5	10	15	31	53	75
2(10-12/51) - 6(10-12/52)	4	8	12	25	40	55
Four Color 462,506,550,587	4	8	12	25	40	55
LITTLE SHOP OF HORRORS SPECIAL (Movie)						
DC Comics: Feb, 1987 ($2.00, 68 pgs.)						
1-Colan-c/a						5.00
LI'L SONJA (Red Sonja)						
Dynamite Entertainment: 2014 ($3.99, one-shot)						
1-Kid version spoof; Jim Zub-s/Joel Carroll-a; covers by Baltazar & Garbowska						4.00
LITTLE SPUNKY						
I. W. Enterprises: No date (1958) (10¢)						
1-r/Frisky Fables #1	2	4	6	8	11	14
LITTLE STAR						
Oni Press: Feb, 2005 - No. 6, Dec, 2005 ($2.99, B&W, limited series)						
1-6-Andi Watson-s/a						3.00
TPB (4/06, $19.95) r/#1-6						20.00
LITTLE STOOGES, THE (The Three Stooges' Sons)						
Gold Key: Sept, 1972 - No. 7, Mar, 1974						
1-Norman Maurer cover/stories in all	3	6	9	18	28	38
2-7	2	4	6	13	18	22
LITTLEST OUTLAW (Disney)						
Dell Publishing Co.: No. 609, Jan, 1955						
Four Color 609-Movie, photo-c	6	12	18	37	66	95
LITTLEST SNOWMAN, THE						
Dell Publishing Co.: No. 755, 12/56; No. 864, 12/57; 12-2/1963-64						
Four Color 755,864, 1(1964)	5	10	15	31	53	75
LI'L TOMBOY (Formerly Fawcett's Funny Animals; see Giant Comics #3)						
Charlton Comics: V14#92, Oct, 1956; No. 93, Mar, 1957 - No. 107, Feb, 1960						
V14#92-Ties as 1st app. with Li'l Genius #11	6	12	18	27	33	38
93-107: 97-Atomic Bunny app.	5	10	14	20	24	28
LI'L VAMPI (Vampirella)						
Dynamite Entertainment: 2014 ($3.99, one-shot)						
1-Kid version spoof; Trautmann-s/Garbowska-a; covers by Baltazar & Garbowska						4.00
LI'L WILLIE COMICS (Formerly & becomes Willie Comics #22 on)						
Marvel Comics (MgPC): No. 20, July, 1949 - No. 21, Sept, 1949						
20,21: 20-Little Aspirin app.	14	28	42	82	121	160

The Living Bible #2 © LBC

Lobo #24 © DC

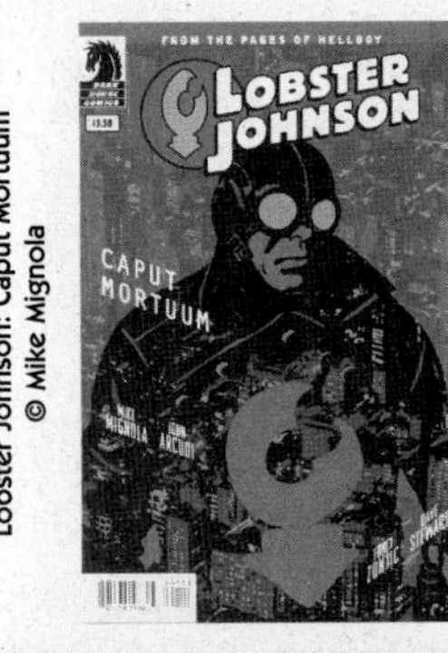

Lobster Johnson: Caput Mortuum © Mike Mignola

	GD 2.0	VG 4.0	FN 6.0	VF 8.0	VF/NM 9.0	NM- 9.2

LITTLE WOMEN (See Power Record Comics)

LIVE IT UP
Spire Christian Comics (Fleming H. Revell Co.): 1973, 1974,1976 (39-49 cents)
nn-1973 Edition 2 4 6 13 18 22
nn-1974,1976 Editions 2 4 6 8 11 14

LIVEWIRES
Marvel Comics: Apr, 2005 - No. 6, Sept, 2005 ($2.99, limited series)
1-6-Adam Warren-s/c; Rick Mays-a 3.00
...: Clockwork Thugs, Yo (2005, $7.99, digest) r/#1-6 8.00

LIVING BIBLE, THE
Living Bible Corp.: Fall, 1945 - No. 3, Spring, 1946
1-The Life of Paul; all have L. B. Cole-c 39 78 117 235 385 535
2-Joseph & His Brethren; Jonah & the Whale 27 54 81 160 263 365
3-Chaplains At War (classic-c) 41 82 123 250 418 585

LIVING WITH THE DEAD
Dark Horse Comics: Oct, 2007 - No. 3, Nov, 2007 ($2.99, limited series)
1-3-Zombies; Mike Richardson-s/Ben Stenbeck-a/Richard Corben-c 3.00

LOADED BIBLE
Image Comics: Apr, 2006; May, 2007; Feb, 2008 ($4.99)
...: Jesus vs. Vampires (4/06) Tim Seeley-s/Nate Bellegarde-a 5.00
...2: Blood of Christ (5/07) Seeley-s/Mike Norton-a. ...3: Communion (2/08) 5.00

LOBO
Dell Publishing Co.: Dec, 1965; No. 2, Oct, 1966
1-1st black character to have his own title 7 14 21 46 86 125
2 5 10 15 31 53 75

LOBO (Also see Action #650, Adventures of Superman, Demon (2nd series), Justice League, L.E.G.I.O.N., Mister Miracle, Omega Men #3 & Superman #41)
DC Comics: Nov, 1990 - No. 4, Feb, 1991 ($1.50, color, limited series)
1-(99¢)-Giffen plots/Breakdowns in all 6.00
1-2nd printing 3.00
2-4: 2-Legion '89 spin-off. 1-4 have Bisley painted covers & art 4.00
...: Blazing Chain of Love 1 (9/92, $1.50)-Denys Cowan-c/a; Alan Grant scripts, ...Convention Special 1 (1993, $1.75), ...: Portrait of a Victim 1 (1993, $1.75) 3.00
... Paramilitary Christmas Special 1 (1991, $2.39, 52 pgs.) Bisley-c/a 4.00
...: Portrait of a Bastich TPB (2008, $19.99) r/#1-4 & Lobo's Back #1-4 20.00

LOBO (Also see Showcase '95 #9)
DC Comics: Dec, 1993 - No. 64, Jul, 1999 ($1.75/$1.95/$2.25/$2.50, mature)
1 ($2.95)-Foil enhanced-c; Alan Grant scripts begin 4.00
2-9,0,10-64: 2-7-Alan Grant scripts. 9-(9/94). 0-(10/94)-Origin retold. 50-Lobo vs. the DCU. 58-Giffen-a 3.00
#1,000,000 (11/98) 853rd Century x-over 3.00
Annual 1 (1993, $3.50, 68 pgs.)-Bloodlines x-over 4.00
Annual 2 (1994, $3.50)-21 artists (20 listed on-c); Alan Grant script; Elseworlds story 4.00
Annual 3 (1995, $3.95)-Year One story 4.00
.../Authority: Holiday Hell TPB (2006, $17.99) r/Lobo Paramilitary Christmas Special; Authority/Lobo: Jingle Hell and Spring Break Massacre; WildStorm Winter Special 18.00
...Big Babe Spring Break Special (Spr, '95, $1.95)-Balent-a 3.00
...Bounty Hunting for Fun and Profit ('95)-Bisley-c 5.00
... Chained (5/97, $2.50)-Alan Grant story 3.00
.../Deadman: The Brave And The Bald (2/95, $3.50) 4.00
.../Demon: Helloween (12/96, $2.25)-Giarrano-a 3.00
...Fragtastic Voyage 1 ('97, $5.95)-Mejia painted-c/a 6.00
...Gallery (9/95, $3.50)-pin-ups. 3.50
...In the Chair 1 (8/94, $1.95, 36 pgs.), ...I Quit-(12/95, $2.25) 3.00
.../Judge Dredd ('95, $4.95). 5.00
...Lobocop 1 (2/94, $1.95)-Alan Grant scripts; painted-c 3.00

LOBO: (Title Series), DC Comics
--A CONTRACT ON GAWD, 4/94 - 7/94 (mature) 1-4: Alan Grant scripts. 3-Groo cameo 3.00
--DEATH AND TAXES, 10/96 - No. 4, 1/97, 1-4-Giffen/Grant scripts 3.00
--GOES TO HOLLYWOOD, 8/96 ($2.25), 1-Grant scripts 3.00
--HIGHWAY TO HELL, 1/10 - No. 2, 2/10 ($6.99), 1,2-Scott Ian-s/Sam Kieth-a/c 7.00
TPB (2010, $19.99) r/#1,2; intro. by Scott Ian; Kieth B&W art pages 20.00
--INFANTICIDE, 10/92 - 1/93 ($1.50, mature), 1-4-Giffen-c/a; Grant scripts 3.00
--/ MASK, 2/97 - No. 2, 3/97 ($5.95), 1,2 6.00
--'S BACK, 5/92 - No. 4, 11/92 ($1.50, mature), 1-4: 1-Has 3 outer covers. Bisley painted-c 1,2; a-1-3. 3-Sam Kieth-c; all have Giffen plots/breakdown & Grant scripts 4.00
Trade paperback (1993, $9.95)-r/1-4 10.00
--THE DUCK, 6/97 ($1.95), 1-A. Grant-s/V. Semeiks & R. Kryssing-a 3.00
--UNAMERICAN GLADIATORS, 6/93 - No. 4, 9/93 ($1.75, mature), 1-4-Mignola-c; Grant/Wagner scripts 4.00
--UNBOUND, 8/03 - No. 6, 5/04 ($2.95), 1-6-Giffen-s/Horley-c/a. 4-6-Ambush Bug app. 3.00

LOBSTER JOHNSON (One-shots) (See B.P.R.D. and Hellboy titles)
Dark Horse Comics
...: Caput Mortuum (9/12, $3.50) Mignola & Arcudi-s; Zonjic-c/a 3.50
...: Satan Smells a Rat (5/13, $3.50) Mignola & Arcudi-s; Nowlan-c/a 3.50

LOBSTER JOHNSON: A SCENT OF LOTUS (See B.P.R.D. and Hellboy titles)
Dark Horse Comics: Jul, 2013 - No. 2, Aug, 2013 ($3.50, limited series)
1,2-Mignola & Arcudi-s; Fiumara-a/Zonjic-c 3.50

LOBSTER JOHNSON: GET THE LOBSTER
Dark Horse Comics: Feb, 2014 - Present ($3.99, limited series)
1-3-Mignola & Arcudi-s; Zonjic-a/c 4.00

LOBSTER JOHNSON: THE BURNING HAND
Dark Horse Comics: Jan, 2012 - No. 5, May, 2012 ($3.50, limited series)
1-5-Mignola & Arcudi-s; Zonjic-a. 1-Two covers by Dave Johnson & Mignola 3.50

LOBSTER JOHNSON: THE IRON PROMETHEUS
Dark Horse Comics: Sept, 2007 - No. 5, Jan, 2008 ($2.99, limited series)
1-5-Mignola-s/c; Armstrong-a 3.00

LOCKE & KEY
IDW Publ.: Feb, 2008 - No. 6, July, 2008 ($3.99, limited series)
1-Joe Hill-s/Gabriel Rodriguez-a 25.00
1-Second printing 5.00
2 10.00
3-6 5.00
...: Free Comic Book Day Edition (5/11) r/story from Crown of Shadows 3.00
...: Grindhouse (8/12, $3.99) EC-style; Hill-s/Rodriguez-a; bonus Guide to the Keyhouse 4.00
...: Guide to the Known Keys (1/12, $3.99) Key to the Moon; bonus Guide to the Keys 4.00
...: Welcome to Lovecraft Legacy Edition #1 (8/10, $1.00) r/#1; synopsis of later issues 3.00
...: Welcome to Lovecraft Special Edition #1 SC (9/09, $5.99) Hill-s/Rodriguez-a; script; back-up story with final art from Seth Fisher 6.00

LOCKE & KEY: ALPHA
IDW Publ.: Aug, 2013 - No. 2, Oct, 2013 ($7.99, limited series)
1,2-Series conclusion; Joe Hill-s/Gabriel Rodriguez-a 8.00

LOCKE & KEY: CLOCKWORKS
IDW Publ.: Jun, 2011 - No. 6, Apr, 2012 ($3.99, limited series)
1-6: 1-Hill-s/Rodriguez-a; set in 1776 4.00

LOCKE & KEY: CROWN OF SHADOWS
IDW Publ.: Nov, 2009 - No. 6, Apr, 2010 ($3.99, limited series)
1-6-Joe Hill-s/Gabriel Rodriguez-a 4.00

LOCKE & KEY: HEAD GAMES
IDW Publ.: Jan, 2009 - No. 6, Jun, 2009 ($3.99, limited series)
1-6-Joe Hill-s/Gabriel Rodriguez-a. 3-EC style-c 4.00

LOCKE & KEY: KEYS TO THE KINGDOM
IDW Publ.: Sept, 2010 - No. 6, Mar, 2011 ($3.99, limited series)
1-6-Joe Hill-s/Gabriel Rodriguez-a 4.00

LOCKE & KEY: OMEGA
IDW Publ.: Nov, 2012 - No. 5, May, 2013 ($3.99, limited series)
1-5-Next to Final series; Joe Hill-s/Gabriel Rodriguez-a 4.00

LOCKJAW AND THE PET AVENGERS (Also see Tails of the Pet Avengers)
Marvel Comics: July, 2009 - No. 4, Oct, 2009 ($2.99, limited series)
1-4-Lockheed, Frog Thor, Zabu, Lockjaw and Redwing team up; 2 covers on each 3.00

LOCKJAW AND THE PET AVENGERS UNLEASHED
Marvel Comics: May, 2010 - No. 4, Aug, 2010 ($2.99, limited series)
1-4-Eliopoulos-s/Guara-a; 2 covers on each 3.00

LOCO (Magazine) (Satire)
Satire Publications: Aug, 1958 - V1#3, Jan, 1959
V1#1-Chic Stone-a 9 18 27 47 61 75
V1#2,3-Severin-a, 2 pgs. Davis; 3-Heath-a 7 14 21 35 43 50

LOGAN (Wolverine)
Marvel Comics: May, 2008 - No. 3, Jul, 2008 ($3.99, limited series)

Logan's Run #5 © MAR

Loki: Agent of Asgard #3 © MAR

The Lone Ranger (2006 series) #14 © Classic Media

1-3-Vaughan-s/Risso-a/c; regular & B&W editions for each 4.00

LOGAN: PATH OF THE WARLORD
Marvel Comics: Feb, 1996 ($5.95, one-shot)

1-John Paul Leon-a 6.00

LOGAN: SHADOW SOCIETY
Marvel Comics: 1996 ($5.95, one-shot)

1 6.00

LOGAN'S RUN
Marvel Comics Group: Jan, 1977 - No. 7, July, 1977

1: 1-5-Based on novel & movie 2 4 6 9 12 15
2-5,7: 6,7-New stories adapted from novel 1 3 4 6 8 10
6-1st Thanos solo story (back-up) by Zeck (6/77)(See Iron Man #55 for debut) 4 8 12 27 44 60
6-(35¢-c variant, limited distribution) 8 16 24 54 102 150
7-(35¢-c variant, limited distribution) 3 6 9 21 33 45

NOTE: ***Austin** a-6i. **Gulacy** c-6. **Kane** c-7p. **Perez** a-1-5p; c-1-5p. **Sutton** a-6p, 7p.*

LOIS & CLARK, THE NEW ADVENTURES OF SUPERMAN
DC Comics: 1994 ($9.95, one-shot)

1-r/Man of Steel #2, Superman Ann. 1, Superman #9 & 11, Action #600 & 655, Adventures of Superman #445, 462 & 466 1 3 4 6 8 10

LOIS LANE (Also see Daring New Adventures of Supergirl, Showcase #9,10 & Superman's Girlfriend...)
DC Comics: Aug, 1986 - No. 2, Sept, 1986 ($1.50, 52 pgs.)

1,2-Morrow-c/a in each 4.00

LOKI (Thor)
Marvel Comics: Sept, 2004 - No. 4, Nov, 2004 ($3.50)

1-4-Rodi-s/Ribic-a/c 3.50
HC (2005, $17.99, with dustjacket) oversized r/#1-4; original proposal and sketch pages 18.00
SC (2007, $12.99) r/#1-4; original proposal and sketch pages 13.00

LOKI (Thor)
Marvel Comics: Dec, 2010 - No. 4, May, 2011 ($3.99, limited series)

1-4-Aguirre-Sacasa-s/Fiumara-a. 2-Balder dies 4.00

LOKI: AGENT OF ASGARD (Thor)
Marvel Comics: Apr, 2014 - Present ($2.99)

1-3: 1-Ewing-s/Garbett-a/Frison-c; Avengers app. 3.00

LOKI: RAGNAROK AND ROLL (not Thor)
BOOM! Studios: Feb, 2014 - No. 4 ($3.99, limited series)

1,2-Esquivel-s/Gaylord-a/Ziritt-c 4.00

LOLA XOXO
Aspen MLT: Apr, 2014 - Present ($3.99)

1-Siya Oum-s/a; multiple covers 4.00

LOLLY AND PEPPER
Dell Publishing Co.: No. 832, Sept, 1957 - July, 1962

Four Color 832(#1) 5 10 15 31 53 75
Four Color 940,978,1086,1206 4 8 12 23 37 50
01-459-207 (7/62) 3 6 9 17 26 35

LOMAX (See Police Action)

LONDON'S DARK
Escape/Titan: 1989 ($8.95, B&W, graphic novel)

nn-James Robinson script; Paul Johnson-c/a 1 2 3 5 7 9

LONE
Dark Horse Comics: Sept, 2003 - No. 6, Mar, 2004 ($2.99)

1-6-Stuart Moore-s/Jerome Opeña-a/Templesmith-c 3.00

LONE EAGLE (The Flame No. 5 on)
Ajax/Farrell Publications: Apr-May, 1954 - No. 4, Oct-Nov, 1954

1 13 26 39 74 105 135
2-4: 3-Bondage-c 9 18 27 50 65 80

LONE GUNMEN, THE (From the X-Files)
Dark Horse Comics: June, 2001 ($2.99, one-shot)

1-Paul Lee-a; photo-c 3.00

LONELY HEART (Formerly Dear Lonely Hearts; Dear Heart #15 on)
Ajax/Farrell Publ. (Excellent Publ.): No. 9, Mar, 1955 - No. 14, Feb, 1956

9-Kamen*esque*-a; (Last precode) 12 24 36 67 94 120
10-14 9 18 27 47 61 75

LONE RANGER, THE (See Ace Comics, Aurora, Dell Giants,Future Comics, Golden Comics Digest #48, King Comics, Magic Comics & March of Comics #165, 174, 193, 208, 225, 238, 310, 322, 338, 350)

LONE RANGER, THE
Dell Publishing Co.: No. 3, 1939 - No. 167, Feb, 1947

Large Feature Comic 3(1939)-Heigh-Yo Silver; text with illus. by Robert Weisman; also exists as a Whitman #710 (scarce) 226 452 678 1446 2473 3500
Large Feature Comic 7(1939)-Illustr. by Henry Vallely; Hi-Yo Silver the Lone Ranger to the Rescue; also exists as Whitman #715 (scarce) 206 412 618 1318 2259 3200
Feature Book 21(1940), 24(1941) 95 190 285 608 1042 1475
Four Color 82(1945) 35 70 105 252 564 875
Four Color 98(1945),118(1946) 26 52 78 182 404 625
Four Color 125(1946),136(1947) 17 34 51 119 265 410
Four Color 151,167(1947) 15 30 45 103 227 350

LONE RANGER, THE (Movie, radio & TV; Clayton Moore starred as Lone Ranger in the movies; No. 1-37: strip reprints)(See Dell Giants)
Dell Publishing Co.: Jan-Feb, 1948 - No. 145, May-July, 1962

1 (36 pgs.)-The Lone Ranger, his horse Silver, companion Tonto & his horse Scout begin 57 114 171 456 1028 1600
2 (52 pgs. begin, end #41) 26 52 78 182 404 625
3-5 20 40 60 138 307 475
6,7,9,10 16 32 48 110 243 375
8-Origin retold; Indian back-c begin, end #35 18 36 54 126 281 435
11-20: 11- "Young Hawk" Indian boy serial begins, ends #145 12 24 36 79 170 260
21,22,24-31: 51-Reprint. 31-1st Mask logo 10 20 30 64 132 200
23-Origin retold 12 24 36 79 170 260
32-37: 32-Painted-c begin. 36-Animal photo back-c begin, end #49. 37-Last newspaper-r issue; new outfit; red shirt becomes blue; most known copies show the blue shirt on-c & inside 9 18 27 57 111 165
37-Variant issue; Long Ranger wears a red shirt on-c and inside. A few copies of the red shirt outfit were printed before catching the mistake and changing the color to blue (rare) 15 30 45 105 233 360
38-41 (All 52 pgs.) 38-Paul S. Newman-s (wrote most of the stories #38-on) 8 16 24 54 102 150
42-50 (36 pgs.) 7 14 21 46 86 125
51-74 (52 pgs.): 56-One pg. origin story of Lone Ranger & Tonto. 71-Blank inside-c 6 12 18 42 79 115
75,77-99: 79-X-mas-c 6 12 18 40 73 105
76-Classic flag-c 6 12 18 42 79 115
100 7 14 21 46 86 125
101-111: Last painted-c 6 12 18 37 66 95
112-Clayton Moore photo-c begin, end #145 15 30 45 103 227 350
113-117: 117-10¢ &15¢-c exist 9 18 27 60 120 180
118-Origin Lone Ranger, Tonto, & Silver retold; Dan Reid origin; Special Silver anniversary issue 19 38 57 131 291 450
119-140: 139-Fran Striker-s 8 16 24 56 108 160
141-145 9 18 27 58 114 170

NOTE: ***Hank Hartman** painted c(signed)-65, 66, 70, 75, 82; unsigned-64?, 67-69?, 71, 72, 73?, 74?, 76-78, 80, 81, 83-91, 92?, 93-111. **Ernest Nordli** painted c(signed)-42, 50, 52, 53, 56, 59, 60; unsigned-39-41, 44-49, 51, 54, 55, 57, 58, 61-63?*

LONE RANGER, THE
Gold Key (Reprints in #13-20): 9/64 - No. 16, 12/69; No. 17, 11/72; No. 18, 9/74 - No. 28, 3/77

1-Retells origin 5 10 15 35 63 90
2 3 6 9 21 33 45
3-10: Small Bear-r in #6-12. 10-Last 12¢ issue 3 6 9 19 30 40
11-17 3 6 9 15 22 28
18-28 2 4 6 11 16 20
Golden West 1(30029-610, 10/66)-Giant; r/most Golden West #3 including Clayton Moore photo front/back-c 6 12 18 38 69 100

LONE RANGER
Dynamite Entertainment: 2006 - No. 25, 2011 ($2.99/$3.50/$3.99)

1-Retells origin; Carriello-a/Matthews-s; badge cover by Cassaday 4.00
1-Variant mask cover by Cassaday 5.00
1-Baltimore Comic-Con 2006 variant cover with masked face and horse silhouette 12.00
1-Directors' Cut ($4.99) r/#1 with comments at page bottoms, script and sketches 5.00
2-23: 2-Origin continues; Tonto app. 3.50
24-($3.99) 4.00
25-($4.99) Carriello-a 5.00
... and Tonto 1-4 (200-2010, $4.99) Cassaday-c 5.00
... Volume 1: Now and Forever TPB (2007, $19.99) r/#1-6; sketch pages 20.00

LONE RANGER, THE (Volume 2)
Dynamite Entertainment: 2012 - Present ($3.99)

Lone Rider #18 © SUPR

Lone Wolf 2100 #1 © DH & Koike Shoin

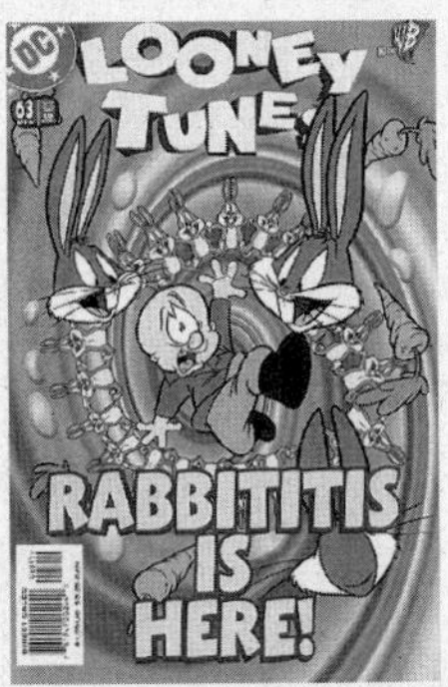

Looney Tunes #63 © WB

	GD	VG	FN	VF	VF/NM	NM-
	2.0	4.0	6.0	8.0	9.0	9.2

1-23: 1-Parks-s/Polls-a; two covers by Ross & Francavilla. 2-21-Francavilla-c 4.00
Annual 2013 ($4.99) Denton-s/Triano-a/Worley-c 5.00

LONE RANGER AND TONTO, THE
Topps Comics: Aug, 1994 - No. 4, Nov, 1994 ($2.50, limited series)

1-4: 3-Origin of Lone Ranger; Tonto leaves; Lansdale story, Truman-c/a in all. 3.00
1-4: Silver logo. 1-Signed by Lansdale and Truman 6.00
Trade paperback (1/95, $9.95) 10.00

LONE RANGER AND ZORRO: THE DEATH OF ZORRO, THE
Dynamite Entertainment: 2011 - No. 5, 2011 ($3.99, limited series)

1-5: 1-Four covers by Alex Ross and others; Parks-s/Polls-a 4.00

LONE RANGER'S COMPANION TONTO, THE (TV)
Dell Publishing Co.: No. 312, Jan, 1951 - No. 33, Nov-Jan/58-59 (All painted-c)

Four Color 312(#1, 1/51) 10 20 30 66 138 210
2(8-10/51),3: (#2 titled "Tonto") 6 12 18 40 73 105
4-10 5 10 15 35 63 90
11-20 5 10 15 31 53 75
21-33 4 8 12 28 47 65

NOTE: ***Ernest Nordli*** *painted c(signed)-2, 7; unsigned-3-6, 8-11, 12?, 13, 14, 18?, 22-24? See Aurora Comic Booklets.*

LONE RANGER'S FAMOUS HORSE HI-YO SILVER, THE (TV)
Dell Publishing Co.: No. 369, Jan, 1952 - No. 36, Oct-Dec, 1960 (All painted-c, most by Sam Savitt) (Lone Ranger appears in most issues)

Four Color 369(#1)-Silver's origin as told by The Lone Ranger
9 18 27 62 126 190
Four Color 392(#2, 4/52) 6 12 18 37 66 95
3(7-9/52)-10(4-6/52) 5 10 15 31 53 75
11-36 4 8 12 27 44 60

LONE RANGER, THE : SNAKE OF IRON
Dynamite Entertainment: 2012 - No. 4, 2013 ($3.99, limited series)

1-3: 1-Dixon-s/Polls-a/Calero-c 4.00

LONE RIDER (Also see The Rider)
Superior Comics(Farrell Publ.): Apr, 1951 - No. 26, Jul, 1955 (#3-on: 36 pgs.)

1 (52 pgs.)-The Lone Rider & his horse Lightnin' begin; Kamenish-a begins
32 64 96 188 307 425
2 (52 pgs.)-The Golden Arrow begins (origin) 20 40 60 120 195 220
3-6: 6-Last Golden Arrow 17 34 51 98 154 210
7-Golden Arrow becomes Swift Arrow; origin of his shield
20 40 60 120 195 220
8-Origin Swift Arrow 18 36 54 107 169 230
9,10 12 24 36 69 97 125
11-14 10 20 30 54 72 90
15-Golden Arrow origin-r from #2, changing name to Swift Arrow
10 20 30 58 79 100
16-20,22-26: 23-Apache Kid app. 9 18 27 50 65 80
21-3-D effect-c 16 32 48 94 147 200

LONERS, THE
Marvel Comics: June, 2007 - No. 6, Jan, 2008 ($2.99, limited series)

1-6-Cebulski-s/Moline-a/Pearson-c; Lightspeed, Spider-Woman, Ricochet app. 3.00
...: The Secret Lives of Super Heroes TPB (2008, $14.99) r/#1-6; sketch pages 15.00

LONE WOLF AND CUB
First Comics: May, 1987 - No. 45, Apr, 1991 ($1.95-$3.25, B&W, deluxe size)

1-Frank Miller-c & intro.; reprints manga series by Koike & Kojima
1 2 3 6 8 10
1-2nd print, 3rd print, 2-2nd print 4.00
2-12: 6-72 pgs. origin issue 6.00
13-38,40: 40-Ploog-c 4.00
39-($5.95, 120 pgs.)-Ploog-c 1 2 3 4 5 7
41-44: 41-($3.95, 84 pgs.)-Ploog-c. 42-Ploog-c 6.00
45-Last issue; low print 2 4 6 8 10 12
Deluxe Edition ($19.95, B&W) 20.00

NOTE: ***Sienkiewicz*** *c-13-24.* ***Matt Wagner*** *c-25-30.*

LONE WOLF AND CUB (Trade paperbacks)
Dark Horse Comics: Aug, 2000 - No. 28 ($9.95, B&W, 4" x 6", approx. 300 pgs.)

1-Collects First Comics reprint series; Frank Miller-c 18.00
1-(2nd printing) 12.00
1-(3rd-5th printings) 10.00
2,3-(1st printings) 12.00
2,3-(2nd printings) 10.00
4-28 10.00

LONE WOLF 2100 (Also see Reveal)
Dark Horse Comics: May, 2002 - No. 11, Dec, 2003 ($2.99, color)

1-New homage to Lone Wolf and Cub; Kennedy-s/Velasco-a 4.00
2-11 3.00
...: The Red File (1/03, $2.99) character and story background files 3.00
... Vol. 1 - Shadows on Saplings TPB (2003, $12.95, 6" x 9") r/#1-4 13.00
... Vol. 2 - The Language of Chaos TPB (2003, $12.95, 6" x 9") r/#5-8, Dirty Tricks short story from Reveal 13.00

LONG BOW (...Indian Boy)(See Indians & Jumbo Comics #141)
Fiction House Mag. (Real Adventures Publ.): 1951 - No. 8, Fall, 1952; No. 9, Spring, 1953

1-Most covers by Maurice Whitman 18 36 54 105 165 225
2 11 22 33 62 86 110
3-9 10 20 30 56 76 95

LONG HOT SUMMER, THE
DC Comics (Milestone): Jul, 1995 - No. 3, Sept, 1995 ($2.95/$2.50, lim. series)

1-3: 1-($2.95-c). 2,3-($2.50-c) 3.00

LONG JOHN SILVER & THE PIRATES (Formerly Terry & the Pirates)
Charlton Comics: No. 30, Aug, 1956 - No. 32, March, 1957 (TV)

30-32: Whitman-c 10 20 30 54 72 90

LONGSHOT (Also see X-Men, 2nd Series #10)
Marvel Comics: Sept, 1985 - No. 6, Feb, 1986 (60¢, limited series)

1,6: 1-Art Adams/Whilce Portacio-c/a in all. 6-Double size
2 4 6 11 16 20
2-5: 4-Spider-Man app. 2 4 6 8 10 12
Trade Paperback (1989, $16.95)-r/#1-6 17.00

LONGSHOT
Marvel Comics: Feb, 1998 ($3.99, one-shot)

1-DeMatteis-s/Zulli-a 4.00

LONGSHOT SAVES THE MARVEL UNIVERSE
Marvel Comics: Jan, 2014 - No. 4, Feb, 2014 ($2.99, limited series)

1-4-Hastings-s/Camagni-a/Nakayama-c. 3,4-Superior Spider-Man app. 3.00

LOOKING GLASS WARS: HATTER M
Image Comics (Desperado): Dec, 2005 - No. 4, Nov, 2006 ($3.99)

1-4-Templesmith-a/c 4.00

LOONEY TUNES (2nd Series) (TV)
Gold Key/Whitman: April, 1975 - No. 47, June, 1984

1-Reprints 3 6 9 21 33 45
2-10: 2,4-reprints 2 4 6 13 18 22
11-20: 16-reprints 2 4 6 9 12 15
21-30 2 3 4 6 8 10
31,32,36-42(2/82) 1 2 3 5 6 8
33-(8/80)-35 (Whitman pre-pack only, scarce) 3 6 9 17 26 35
43(4/82),44(6/83) (low distribution) 2 4 6 9 13 16
45-47 (All #90296 on-c; nd, nd code, pre-pack) 45(8/83), 46(3/84), 47(6/84)
3 6 9 14 20 26

LOONEY TUNES (3rd Series) (TV)
DC Comics: Apr, 1994 - Present ($1.50/$1.75/$1.95/$1.99/$2.25/$2.50/$2.99)

1-10,120: 1-Marvin Martian-c/sty; Bugs Bunny, Roadrunner, Daffy begin. 120-($2.95-C) 4.00
11-119,121-187: 23-34-($1.75-c). 35-43-($1.95-c). 44-Begin $1.99-c. 93-Begin $2.25-c. 100-Art by various incl. Kyle Baker, Marie Severin, Darwyn Cooke, Jill Thompson 3.00
188-218: 188-Begin $2.99-c; Scooby-Doo spoof. 193-Christmas-c 3.00
...Back In Action Movie Adaptation (12/03, $3.95) photo-c 4.00

LOONEY TUNES AND MERRIE MELODIES COMICS ("Looney Tunes" #166(8/55) on) (Also see Porky's Duck Hunt)
Dell Publishing Co.: 1941 - No. 246, July-Sept, 1962

1-Porky Pig, Bugs Bunny, Daffy Duck, Elmer Fudd, Mary Jane & Sniffles, Pat Patsy and Pete begin (1st comic book app. of each). Bugs Bunny story by Win Smith (early Mickey Mouse artist) 1150 2300 3450 8800 16,900 25,000
2 (11/41) 162 324 486 1337 3019 4700
3-Kandi the Cave Kid begins by Walt Kelly; also in #4-6,8,11,15
111 222 333 888 1994 3100
4-Kelly-a 111 222 333 888 1994 3100
5-Bugs Bunny The Super-Duper Rabbit story (1st funny animal super hero, 3/42; also see Coo Coo); Kelly-a 80 160 240 640 1445 2250
6,8-Kelly-a 63 126 189 504 1127 1750
7,9,10: 9-Painted-c. 10-Flag-c 46 92 138 368 834 1300
11,15-Kelly-a; 15-X-Mas-c 49 98 147 382 854 1325

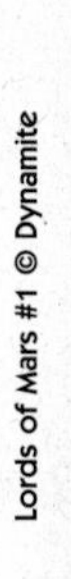
Looney Tunes and Merrie Melodies #27 © WB

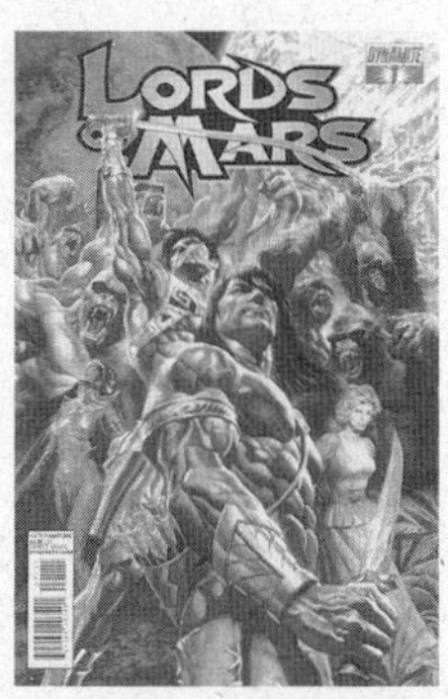

Lords of Mars #1 © Dynamite

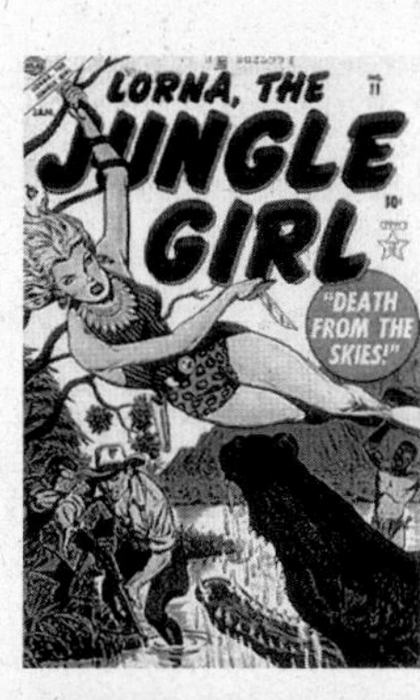

Lorna, The Jungle Girl #11 © MAR

	GD 2.0	VG 4.0	FN 6.0	VF 8.0	VF/NM 9.0	NM- 9.2
12-14,16-19	36	72	108	266	596	925
20-25: Pat, Patsy & Pete by Walt Kelly in all. 20-War Bonds-c	30	60	90	216	483	750
26-30	23	46	69	158	349	540
31-40: 33-War Bonds-c. 39-X-Mas-c	18	36	54	126	281	435
41-50: 45-War Bonds-c	14	28	42	96	211	325
51-60	11	22	33	76	163	250
61-80	8	16	24	56	108	160
81-99: 87-X-Mas-c	7	14	21	49	92	135
100	8	16	24	52	99	145
101-120	6	12	18	40	73	105
121-150	5	10	15	35	63	90
151-200: 159-X-Mas-c	5	10	15	33	57	80
201-240	5	10	15	31	53	75
241-246	5	10	15	33	57	80

LOONY SPORTS (Magazine)
3-Strikes Publishing Co.: Spring, 1975 (68 pgs.)

1-Sports satire	2	4	6	8	11	14

LOOSE CANNON (Also see Action Comics Annual #5 & Showcase '94 #5)
DC Comics: June, 1995 - No. 4, Sept, 1995 ($1.75, limited series)

1-4: Adam Pollina-a. 1-Superman app. 3.00

LOOY DOT DOPE
United Features Syndicate: No. 13, 1939

Single Series 13	31	62	93	182	296	410

LORD JIM (See Movie Comics)

LORD OF THE JUNGLE
Dynamite Entertainment: 2012 - No. 15, 2013 ($1.00/$3.99)

1-($1.00) Retelling of Tarzan's origin; Nelson-s/Castro-a; four covers 3.00
2-15-($3.99) 2-6-Three covers. 7-13-Two covers 4.00
Annual 1 (2012, $4.99) Rahner-s/Davila-a/Parrillo-c 5.00

LORD PUMPKIN
Malibu Comics (Ultraverse): Oct, 1994 ($2.50, one-shot)

0-Two covers 3.00

LORD PUMPKIN/NECROMANTRA
Malibu Comics (Ultraverse): Apr, 1995 - No. 4, July, 1995 ($2.95, limited series, flip book)

1-4 3.00

LORDS OF AVALON: KNIGHT OF DARKNESS
Marvel Comics: Jan, 2008 - No. 6, July, 2009 ($3.99, limited series)

1-6-($3.99)-Kenyon & Furth-s; Ohtsuka-a/c 4.00

LORDS OF AVALON: SWORD OF DARKNESS
Marvel Comics: Apr, 2008 - No. 6, Sept, 2008 ($3.99/$2.99, limited series)

1-($3.99)-Adaptation of Sherrilyn Kenyon's Arthurian fantasy; Ohtsuka-a/c 4.00
2-6-($2.99) 3.00
HC (2008, $19.99) r/#1-6; two covers 20.00

LORDS OF MARS
Dynamite Entertainment: 2013 - No. 6, 2014 ($3.99, limited series)

1-6-Tarzan and Jane meet John Carter on Mars; Nelson-s/Castro-a; multiple covers 4.00

LORNA, RELIC WRANGLER
Image Comics: Mar, 2011 ($3.99, one-shot)

1-Micah Harris-s; J. Bone-c 4.00

LORNA THE JUNGLE GIRL (...Jungle Queen #1-5)
Atlas Comics (NPI 1/OMC 2-11/NPI 12-26): July, 1953 - No. 26, Aug, 1957

1-Origin & 1st app.	42	84	126	265	445	625
2-Intro. & 1st app. Greg Knight	22	44	66	132	216	300
3-5	20	40	60	114	182	250
6-11: 11-Last pre-code (1/55)	16	32	48	94	147	200
12-17,19-26: 14-Colletta & Maneely-c	15	30	45	84	127	170
18-Williamson/Colletta-c	15	30	45	86	133	180

NOTE: ***Brodsky** c-1-3, 5, 9. **Everett** c-21, 23-26. **Heath** c-6, 7. **Maneely** c-12, 15. **Romita** a-18, 20, 22, 24, 26. **Shores** a-14-16, 18, 24, 26; c-11, 13, 16. **Tuska** a-6.*

LOSERS (Inspired the 2010 movie)
DC Comics (Vertigo): Aug, 2003 - No. 32, Mar, 2006 ($2.95/$2.99)

1-Andy Diggle-s/Jock-a 4.00
1-Special Edition (6/10, $1.00) r/#1 with "What's Next?" logo on cover 3.00
2-32: 15-Bagged with Sky Captain CD. 20-Oliver-a. 27-Wilson-a 3.00
...: Ante Up TPB (2004, $9.95) r/#1-6 10.00
...: Book Two TPB (2010, $24.99) r/#13-32; Ian Rankin intro.; preliminary art pages 25.00
...: Close Quarters TPB (2005, $14.99) r/#20-25 15.00
...: Double Down TPB (2004, $12.95) r/#7-12 13.00
...: Endgame TPB (2006, $14.99) r/#26-32 15.00
...: Trifecta TPB (2005, $14.99) r/#13-19 15.00
...: Volumes One and Two TPB (2010, $19.99) r/#1-12; new intro. by Diggle 20.00

LOSERS SPECIAL (See Our Fighting Forces #123)(Also see G.I. Combat & Our Fighting Forces)
DC Comics: Sept, 1985 ($1.25, one-shot)

1-Capt. Storm, Gunner & Sarge; Crisis on Infinite Earths x-over 6.00

LOST, THE
Chaos! Comics: Dec, 1997 - No. 3 ($2.95, B&W, unfinished limited series)

1-3-Andreyko-script: 1-Russell back-c 3.00

LOST BOYS: REIGN OF FROGS (Based on the 1987 vampire movie)
DC Comics (WildStorm): Jul, 2008 - No. 4, Oct, 2008 ($3.50, limited series)

1-4-Rodionoff-s/Gomez-a; Edgar Frog app. 3.50
TPB (2009, $12.99) r/#1-4 13.00

LOST CONTINENT
Eclipse Int'l: Sept, 1990 - No. 6, 1991 ($3.50, B&W, squarebound, 60 pgs.)

1-6: Japanese story translated to English 4.00

LOST IN SPACE (Movie)
Dark Horse Comics: Apr, 1998 - No. 3, July, 1998 ($2.95, limited series)

1-3-Continuation of 1998 movie; Erskine-c 3.00

LOST IN SPACE (TV)(Also see Space Family Robinson)
Innovation Publishing: Aug, 1991 - No. 12, Jan, 1993 ($2.50, limited series)

1-12: Bill Mumy (Will Robinson) scripts in #1-9. 9-Perez-c 3.00
1,2-Special Ed.; r/#1,2 plus new art & new-c 3.00
Annual 1,2 (1991, 1992, $2.95, 52 pgs.) 4.00
...: Project Robinson (11/93, $2.50) 1st & only part of intended series 3.00

LOST IN SPACE: VOYAGE TO THE BOTTOM OF THE SOUL
Innovation Publishing: No. 13, Aug, 1993 - No. 18, 1994 ($2.50, limited series)

13(V1#1, $2.95)-Embossed silver logo edition; Bill Mumy scripts begin; painted-c 3.00
13(V1#1, $4.95)-Embossed gold logo edition bagged w/poster 5.00
14-18: Painted-c 3.00
NOTE: *Originally intended to be a 12 issue limited series.*

LOST ONES, THE
Image Comics: Mar, 2000 ($2.95)

1-Ken Penders-s/a 3.00

LOST PLANET
Eclipse Comics: 5/87 - No. 5, 2/88; No. 6, 3/89 (Mini-series, Baxter paper)

1-6-Bo Hampton-c/a in all 3.00

LOST WAGON TRAIN, THE (See Zane Grey Four Color 583)

LOST WORLD, THE
Dell Publishing Co.: No. 1145, Nov-Jan, 1960-61

Four Color 1145-Movie, Gil Kane-a, photo-c; 1pg. Conan Doyle biography by Torres	8	16	24	55	105	155

LOST WORLD, THE (See Jurassic Park)
Topps Comics: May, 1997 - No. 4, Aug, 1997 ($2.95, limited series)

1-4-Movie adaption 3.00

LOST WORLDS (Weird Tales of the Past and Future)
Standard Comics: No. 5, Oct, 1952 - No. 6, Dec, 1952

5- "Alice in Terrorland" by Alex Toth; J. Katz-a	47	94	141	296	498	700
6-Toth-a	39	78	117	231	378	525

LOTS 'O' FUN COMICS
Robert Allen Co.: 1940s? (5¢, heavy stock, blue covers)

nn-Contents can vary; Felix, Planet Comics known; contents would determine value. Similar to Up-To-Date Comics. Remainders - re-packaged.

LOT 13
DC Comics: Dec, 2012 - No. 5, Apr, 2013 ($2.99, limited series)

1-5-Niles-s/Fabry-a/c 3.00

LOU GEHRIG (See The Pride of the Yankees)

LOVE ADVENTURES (Actual Confessions #13)
Marvel (IPS)/Atlas Comics (MPI): Oct, 1949; No. 2, Jan, 1950; No. 3, Feb, 1951 - No. 12, Aug, 1952

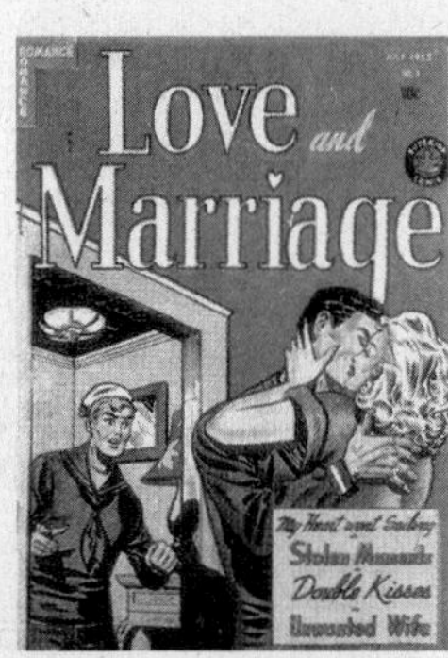

Love and Marriage #3 © SUP

Love Confessions #2 © QUA

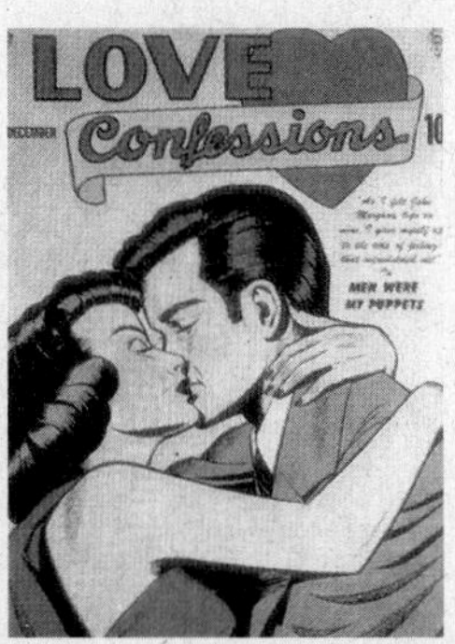

Love Journal #11 © Our Pub. Co.

	GD 2.0	VG 4.0	FN 6.0	VF 8.0	VF/NM 9.0	NM- 9.2
1-Photo-c	21	42	63	122	199	275
2-Powell-a; Tyrone Power, Gene Tierney photo-c	16	32	48	94	147	200
3-8,10-12: 8-Robinson-a	11	22	33	64	90	115
9-Everett-a	12	24	36	67	94	120

LOVE AND MARRIAGE
Superior Comics Ltd. (Canada): Mar, 1952 - No. 16, Sept, 1954

	GD 2.0	VG 4.0	FN 6.0	VF 8.0	VF/NM 9.0	NM- 9.2
1	17	34	51	98	154	210
2	11	22	33	60	83	105
3-10	10	20	30	54	72	90
11-16	9	18	27	50	65	80
I.W. Reprint #1,2,8,11,14: 8-r/Love and Marriage #3. 11-r/Love and Marriage #11	2	4	6	10	14	18
Super Reprint #10('63),15,17('64):15-Love and Marriage #?	2	4	6	10	14	18

NOTE: *All issues have* ***Kamenish*** *art.*

LOVE AND ROCKETS
Fantagraphics Books: July, 1982 - No. 50, May, 1996 ($2.95/$2.50/$4.95, B&W, mature)

	GD 2.0	VG 4.0	FN 6.0	VF 8.0	VF/NM 9.0	NM- 9.2
1-B&W-c (6/82, $2.95; small size, publ. by Hernandez Bros.)(800 printed)	6	12	18	38	69	100
1 (Fall, '82; color-c)	4	8	12	23	37	50
1-2nd & 3rd printing, 2-11,29-31: 2nd printings						4.00
2	2	4	6	13	18	22
3-10	1	3	4	6	8	10
11-49: 30 ($2.95, 52 pgs.)						5.00
50-($4.95)						6.00

LOVE AND ROCKETS (Volume 2)
Fantagraphics Books: Spring, 2001 - Present ($3.95-$7.99, B&W, mature)

	GD 2.0	VG 4.0	FN 6.0	VF 8.0	VF/NM 9.0	NM- 9.2
1-9-Gilbert, Jaime and Mario Hernandez-s/a						5.00
10-($5.95)						6.00
11-19-($4.50)						4.50
20-($7.99)						8.00

LOVE AND ROMANCE
Charlton Comics: Sept, 1971 - No. 24, Sept, 1975

	GD 2.0	VG 4.0	FN 6.0	VF 8.0	VF/NM 9.0	NM- 9.2
1	3	6	9	17	26	35
2-5,7-10	2	4	6	10	14	18
6-David Cassidy pin-up; grey-tone cover	3	6	9	14	19	24
11,13-24	2	4	6	8	10	12
12-Susan Dey poster	2	4	6	10	14	18

LOVE AT FIRST SIGHT
Ace Magazines (RAR Publ. Co./Periodical House): Oct, 1949 - No. 43, Nov, 1956 (Photo-c: 18-42)

	GD 2.0	VG 4.0	FN 6.0	VF 8.0	VF/NM 9.0	NM- 9.2
1-Painted-c	20	40	60	114	182	250
2-Painted-c	12	24	36	69	97	125
3-10: 4,7-Painted-c	11	22	33	60	83	105
11-20	10	20	30	56	76	95
21-33: 33-Last pre-code	10	20	30	54	72	90
34-43	9	18	27	52	69	85

LOVE BUG, THE (See Movie Comics)

LOVEBUNNY AND MR. HELL
Devil's Due Publ./Image Comics: 2002 - 2004 ($2.95, B&W, one-shots)

	GD 2.0	VG 4.0	FN 6.0	VF 8.0	VF/NM 9.0	NM- 9.2
1-Tim Seeley-s						3.00
...: A Day in the Lovelife (Image, 2003) Blaylock-a						3.00
...: Savage Love (Image, 2003) Seeley-s/a; Savage Dragon app.; Seeley & Larsen-c						3.00
TPB (4/04, $9.95, digest-sized) reprints						10.00

LOVE CLASSICS
A Lover's Magazine/Marvel: Nov, 1949 - No. 2, Feb, 1950 (Photo-c, 52 pgs.)

	GD 2.0	VG 4.0	FN 6.0	VF 8.0	VF/NM 9.0	NM- 9.2
1,2: 2-Virginia Mayo photo-c; 30 pg. story "I Turned Into a Small-Town Flirt"	18	36	54	107	169	230

LOVE CONFESSIONS
Quality Comics: Oct, 1949 - No. 54, Dec, 1956 (Photo-c: 3,4,6,7,9,11-18,21,24,25)

	GD 2.0	VG 4.0	FN 6.0	VF 8.0	VF/NM 9.0	NM- 9.2
1-Ward-c/a, 9 pgs; Gustavson-a	36	72	108	211	343	475
2-Gustavson-a; Ward-c	18	36	54	107	169	230
3	13	26	39	74	105	135
4-Crandall-a	14	28	42	80	115	150
5-Ward-a, 7 pgs.	15	30	45	84	127	170
6,7,9,11-13,15,16,18: 7-Van Johnson photo-c. 8-Robert Mitchum & Jane Russell photo-c	11	22	33	60	83	105
8,10-Ward-a (2 stories in #10)	15	30	45	83	124	165
14,17,19,22-Ward-a; 17-Faith Domerque photo-c	14	28	42	81	118	155
20-Ward-a(2)	15	30	45	83	124	165
21,23-28,30-38,40-42: Last precode, 4/55	10	20	30	54	72	90
29-Ward-a	14	28	42	78	112	145
39,53-Matt Baker-a	12	24	36	69	97	125
43,44,46,47,50-52,54: 47-Ward-c?	9	18	27	52	69	85
45,48-Ward-a	11	22	33	60	83	105
49-Baker-c/a	14	28	42	81	118	155

LOVECRAFT
DC Comics: 2003 (graphic novel)

	GD 2.0	VG 4.0	FN 6.0	VF 8.0	VF/NM 9.0	NM- 9.2
Hardcover ($24.95) Rodionoff & Giffen-s/Breccia-a; intro. by John Carpenter						25.00
Softcover ($17.95)						18.00

LOVE DIARY
Our Publishing Co./Toytown/Patches: July, 1949 - No. 48, Oct, 1955 (Photo-c: 1-24,27-29) (52 pgs. #1-11?)

	GD 2.0	VG 4.0	FN 6.0	VF 8.0	VF/NM 9.0	NM- 9.2
1-Krigstein-a	23	46	69	136	223	310
2,3-Krigstein & Mort Leav-a in each	15	30	45	86	133	180
4-8	12	24	36	67	94	120
9,10-Everett-a	13	26	39	72	101	130
11-15,17-20	11	22	33	60	83	105
16- Mort Leav-a, 3 pg. Baker-sty. Leav-a	11	22	33	64	90	115
21-30,32-48: 45-Leav-a. 47-Last precode(12/54)	10	20	30	56	76	95
31-John Buscema headlights-c	14	28	42	76	108	140

LOVE DIARY (Diary Loves #2 on; title change due to previously published title)
Quality Comics Group: Sept, 1949

	GD 2.0	VG 4.0	FN 6.0	VF 8.0	VF/NM 9.0	NM- 9.2
1-Ward-c/a, 9 pgs.	36	72	108	211	343	475

LOVE DIARY
Charlton Comics: July, 1958 - No. 102, Dec, 1976

	GD 2.0	VG 4.0	FN 6.0	VF 8.0	VF/NM 9.0	NM- 9.2
1	11	22	33	62	86	110
2	8	16	24	40	50	60
3-5,7-10: 10-Photo-c	7	14	21	35	43	50
6-Torres-a	7	14	21	37	46	55
11-20: 20-Photo-c	3	6	9	17	26	35
21-40	3	6	9	15	22	28
41-60	2	4	6	13	18	22
61-78,80,100-102	2	4	6	9	13	16
79-David Cassidy pin-up	2	4	6	13	18	22
81,83,84,86-99	2	4	6	8	10	12
82,85: 82-Partridge Family poster. 85-Danny poster	2	4	6	10	14	18

LOVE DOCTOR (See Dr. Anthony King...)

LOVE DRAMAS (True Secrets No. 3 on?)
Marvel Comics (IPS): Oct, 1949 - No. 2, Jan, 1950

	GD 2.0	VG 4.0	FN 6.0	VF 8.0	VF/NM 9.0	NM- 9.2
1-Jack Kamen-a; photo-c	21	42	63	122	199	275
2-Photo-c	15	30	45	85	130	175

LOVE EXPERIENCES (Challenge of the Unknown No. 6)
Ace Periodicals (A.A. Wyn/Periodical House): Oct, 1949 - No. 5, June, 1950; No. 6, Apr, 1951 - No. 38, June, 1956

	GD 2.0	VG 4.0	FN 6.0	VF 8.0	VF/NM 9.0	NM- 9.2
1-Painted-c	19	38	57	111	176	240
2	12	24	36	67	94	120
3-5: 5-Painted-c	11	22	33	60	83	105
6-10	10	20	30	56	76	95
11-30: 30-Last pre-code (2/55)	9	18	27	52	69	85
31-38: 38-Indicia date-6/56; c-date-8/56	9	18	27	50	65	80

NOTE: ***Anne Brewster*** *a-15. Photo c-4, 15-35, 38.*

LOVE FIGHTS
Oni Press: June, 2003 - No. 12, Aug, 2004 ($2.99, B&W)

	GD 2.0	VG 4.0	FN 6.0	VF 8.0	VF/NM 9.0	NM- 9.2
1-12-Andi Watson-s/a						3.00
Vol. 1 TPB (4/04, $14.95, digest-size) r/#1-6						15.00

LOVE JOURNAL
Our Publishing Co.: No. 10, Oct, 1951 - No. 25, July, 1954

	GD 2.0	VG 4.0	FN 6.0	VF 8.0	VF/NM 9.0	NM- 9.2
10	16	32	48	94	147	200
11-15,17-25: 19-Mort Leav-a	12	24	36	67	94	120
16-Buscema headlight-c	14	28	42	82	121	160

LOVELAND
Mutual Mag./Eye Publ. (Marvel): Nov, 1949 - No. 2, Feb, 1950 (52 pgs.)

	GD 2.0	VG 4.0	FN 6.0	VF 8.0	VF/NM 9.0	NM- 9.2
1,2-Photo-c	15	30	45	83	124	165

LOVELESS
DC Comics: Dec, 2005 - No. 24, Jun, 2008 ($2.99)

	GD 2.0	VG 4.0	FN 6.0	VF 8.0	VF/NM 9.0	NM- 9.2
1-24: 1-Azzarello-s/Frusin-a. 6-8,15,22,23,24-Zezelj-a. 11,12,16-21-Dell'Edera-a						3.00

Love Lessons #1 © HARV

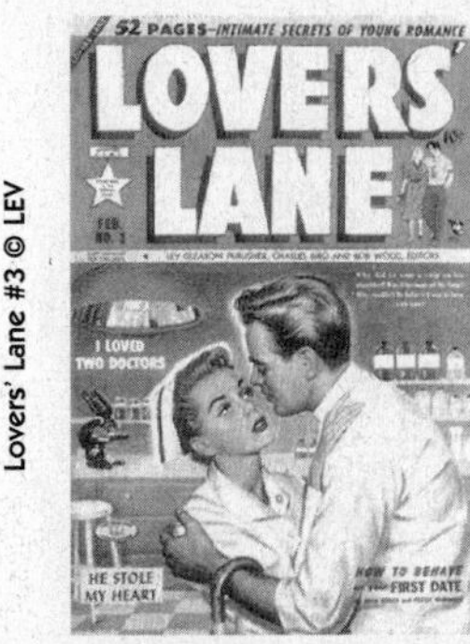

Lovers' Lane #3 © LEV

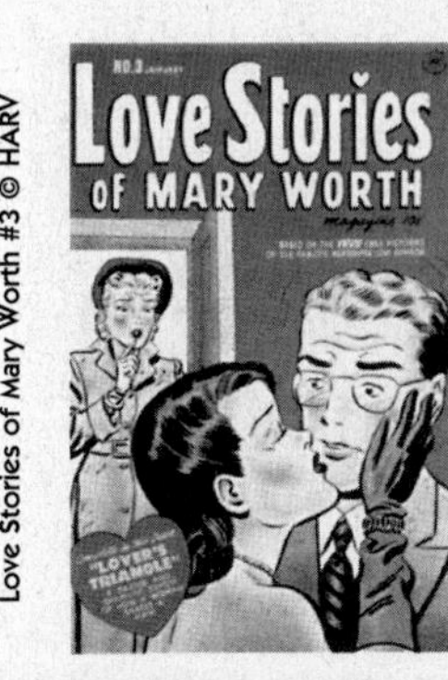

Love Stories of Mary Worth #3 © HARV

	GD 2.0	VG 4.0	FN 6.0	VF 8.0	VF/NM 9.0	NM- 9.2
...: A Kin of Homecoming TPB (2006, $9.99) r/#1-5						10.00
...: Blackwater Falls TPB (2008, $19.99) r/#13-24						20.00
...: Thicker Than Blackwater TPB (2007, $14.99) r/#6-12						15.00

LOVE LESSONS
Harvey Comics/Key Publ. No. 5: Oct, 1949 - No. 5, June, 1950

	GD	VG	FN	VF	VF/NM	NM-
1-Metallic silver-c printed over the cancelled covers of Love Letters #1; indicia title is "Love Letters"	15	30	45	86	133	180
1-Non-metallic version	15	30	45	86	133	180
2-Powell-a; photo-c	9	18	27	52	69	85
3-5: 3,4-Photo-c	8	16	24	42	54	65

LOVE LETTERS (10/49, Harvey; advertised but never published; covers were printed before cancellation and were used as the cover to Love Lessons #1)

LOVE LETTERS (Love Secrets No. 32 on)
Quality Comics: 11/49 - #6, 9/50; #7, 3/51 - #31, 6/53; #32, 2/54 - #51, 12/56

	GD	VG	FN	VF	VF/NM	NM-
1-Ward-c, Gustavson-a	27	54	81	158	259	360
2-Ward-c, Gustavson-a	21	42	63	126	206	285
3-Gustavson-a	15	30	45	90	140	190
4-Ward-a, 9 pgs.; photo-c	20	40	60	114	182	250
5-8,10	12	24	36	67	94	120
9-One pg. Ward "Be Popular with the Opposite Sex"; Robert Mitchum photo-c	13	26	39	74	105	135
11-Ward-r/Broadway Romances #2 & retitled	13	26	39	74	105	135
12-15,18-20	11	22	33	60	83	105
16,17-Ward-a; 16-Anthony Quinn photo-c. 17-Jane Russell photo-c	15	30	45	86	133	180
21-29	10	20	30	58	79	100
30,31(6/53)-Ward-a	12	24	36	67	94	120
32(2/54)-39: 37-Ward-a. 38-Crandall-a. 39-Last precode (4/55)	10	20	30	54	72	90
40-48	9	18	27	50	65	80
49-51: 49,50-Baker-a. 51-Baker-c	14	28	42	78	112	145

NOTE: *Photo-c on most 3-28.*

LOVE LIFE
P. L. Publishing Co.: Nov, 1951

	GD	VG	FN	VF	VF/NM	NM-
1	12	24	36	67	94	120

LOVELORN (Confessions of the Lovelorn #52 on)
American Comics Group (Michel Publ./Regis Publ.): Aug-Sept, 1949 - No. 51, July, 1954 (No. 1-26: 52 pgs.)

	GD	VG	FN	VF	VF/NM	NM-
1	19	38	57	111	176	240
2	12	24	36	67	94	120
3-10	10	20	30	58	79	100
11-20,22-48: 18-Drucker-a(2 pgs.). 46-Lazarus-a	9	18	27	52	69	85
21-Prostitution story	12	24	36	69	97	125
49-51-Has 3-D effect-c/stories	17	34	51	98	154	210

LOVE MEMORIES
Fawcett Publications: 1949 (no month) - No. 4, July, 1950 (All photo-c)

	GD	VG	FN	VF	VF/NM	NM-
1	15	30	45	90	140	190
2-4: 2-(Win/49-50)	10	20	30	56	76	95

LOVE ME TENDERLOIN: A CAL McDONALD MYSTERY
Dark Horse Comics: Jan, 2004 ($2.99, one-shot)

	GD	VG	FN	VF	VF/NM	NM-
1-Niles-s/Templesmith-a/c						3.00

LOVE MYSTERY
Fawcett Publications: June, 1950 - No. 3, Oct, 1950 (All photo-c)

	GD	VG	FN	VF	VF/NM	NM-
1-George Evans-a	21	42	63	124	202	280
2,3-Evans-a. 3-Powell-a	16	32	48	92	144	195

LOVE PROBLEMS (See Fox Giants)

LOVE PROBLEMS AND ADVICE ILLUSTRATED (see True Love...)

LOVE ROMANCES (Formerly Ideal #5)
Timely/Marvel/Atlas(TCI No. 7-71/Male No. 72-106): No. 6, May, 1949 - No. 106, July, 1963

	GD	VG	FN	VF	VF/NM	NM-
6-Photo-c	21	42	63	122	199	275
7-Photo-c; Kamen-a	14	28	42	80	115	150
8-Kubert-a; photo-c	14	28	42	80	115	150
9-20: 9-12-Photo-c	13	26	39	74	105	135
21,24-Krigstein-a	14	28	42	76	108	140
22,23,25-35,37,39,40	12	24	36	69	97	125
36,38-Krigstein-a	13	26	39	72	101	130
41-44,46,47: Last precode (2/55)	12	24	36	67	94	120
45,57-Matt Baker-a	14	28	42	80	115	150
48,50-52,54-56,58-74	6	12	18	40	73	105
49,53-Toth-a, 6 & ? pgs.	6	12	18	42	79	115
75,77,82-Matt Baker-a	8	16	24	51	96	140
76,78-81,86,88-90,92-95: 80-Heath-c. 95-Last 10¢-c?	6	12	18	38	69	100
83,84,87,91,106-Kirby-c. 83-Severin-a	7	14	21	48	89	130
85,96,97,99-105-Kirby-c/a. 97-10¢ cover price blacked out, 12¢ printed on cover	8	16	24	54	102	150
98-Kirby-c/a	8	16	24	54	102	150

NOTE: ***Anne Brewster** a-67, 72. **Colletta** a-37, 40, 42, 44, 46, 67(2); c-42, 44, 46, 49, 54, 80. **Everett** c-70. **Hartley** c-20, 21, 30, 31. **Heath** a-87. **Kirby** c-80, 85, 88. **Robinson** a-29.*

LOVERS (Formerly Blonde Phantom)
Marvel Comics No. 23,24/Atlas No. 25 on (ANC): No. 23, May, 1949 - No. 86, Aug?, 1957

	GD	VG	FN	VF	VF/NM	NM-
23-Photo-c begin, end #29	21	42	63	122	199	275
24-Toth-*ish* plus Robinson-a	14	28	42	76	108	140
25,30-Kubert-a; 7, 10 pgs.	14	28	42	78	112	145
26-29,31-36,39,40: 35-Maneely-c	12	24	36	69	97	125
37,38-Krigstein-a	14	28	42	76	108	140
41-Everett-a(2)	14	28	42	76	108	140
42,44-65: 65-Last pre-code (1/55)	11	22	33	60	83	105
43-Frazetta 1 pg. ad	11	22	33	62	86	110
66,68-80,82-86	10	20	30	58	79	100
67-Toth-a	11	22	33	62	86	110
81-Baker-a	12	24	36	67	94	120

NOTE: ***Anne Brewster** a-86. **Colletta** a-54, 59, 62, 64, 65, 69, 85; c-61, 64, 65, 75. **Hartley** c-37, 53, 54. **Heath** a-61. **Maneely** a-57. **Powell** a-27, 30. **Robinson** a-42, 54, 56.*

LOVERS' LANE
Lev Gleason Publications: Oct, 1949 - No. 41, June, 1954 (No. 1-18: 52 pgs.)

	GD	VG	FN	VF	VF/NM	NM-
1-Biro-c	17	34	51	98	154	210
2-Biro-c	11	22	33	60	83	105
3-20: 3,4-Painted-c. 20-Frazetta 1 pg. ad	10	20	30	56	76	95
21-38,40,41	9	18	27	50	65	80
39-Story narrated by Frank Sinatra	11	22	33	62	86	110

NOTE: ***Briefer** a-6, 13, 21. **Esposito** a-5. **Fuje** a-4, 16; c-many. **Guardineer** a-1, 3. **Kinstler** c-41. **Sparling** a-3. **Tuska** a-6. Painted c-3-18. Photo c-19-22, 26-28.*

LOVE SCANDALS
Quality Comics: Feb, 1950 - No. 5, Oct, 1950 (Photo-c #2-5) (All 52 pgs.)

	GD	VG	FN	VF	VF/NM	NM-
1-Ward-c/a, 9 pgs.	29	58	87	170	278	385
2,3: 2-Gustavson-a	14	28	42	82	121	160
4-Ward-a, 18 pgs; Gil Fox-a	22	44	66	128	209	290
5-C. Cuidera-a; tomboy story "I Hated Being a Woman"	16	32	48	94	147	200

LOVE SECRETS
Marvel Comics(IPC): Oct, 1949 - No. 2, Jan, 1950 (52 pgs., photo-c)

	GD	VG	FN	VF	VF/NM	NM-
1	19	38	57	111	176	240
2	14	28	42	76	108	140

LOVE SECRETS (Formerly Love Letters #31)
Quality Comics Group: No. 32, Aug, 1953 - No. 56, Dec, 1956

	GD	VG	FN	VF	VF/NM	NM-
32	14	28	42	80	115	150
33,35-39	10	20	30	58	79	100
34-Ward-a	14	28	42	80	115	150
40-Matt Baker-c	14	28	42	80	115	150
41-43: 43-Last precode (3/55)	10	20	30	58	79	100
44,47-50,53,54	9	18	27	52	69	85
45-Ward-a	12	24	36	67	94	120
46-Ward-a; Baker-a	14	28	42	76	108	140
51,52-Ward(r). 52-r/Love Confessions #17	10	20	30	58	79	100
55,56: 55-Baker-a. 56-Baker-c	13	26	39	72	101	130

LOVE STORIES (See Top Love Stories)

LOVE STORIES (Formerly Heart Throbs)
National Periodical Publ.: No. 147, Nov, 1972 - No. 152, Oct-Nov, 1973

	GD	VG	FN	VF	VF/NM	NM-
147-152	3	6	9	14	20	26

LOVE STORIES OF MARY WORTH (See Harvey Comics Hits #55 & Mary Worth)
Harvey Publications: Sept, 1949 - No. 5, May, 1950

	GD	VG	FN	VF	VF/NM	NM-
1-1940's newspaper reprints-#1-4	9	18	27	47	61	75
2-5: 3-Kamen/Baker-a?	6	12	18	31	38	45

LOVE TALES (Formerly The Human Torch #35)
Marvel/Atlas Comics (ZPC No. 36-50/MMC No. 67-75): No. 36, 5/49 - No. 58, 8/52; No. 59, date? - No. 75, Sept, 1957

	GD	VG	FN	VF	VF/NM	NM-
36-Photo-c	20	40	60	117	189	260

Lucifer #25 © DC

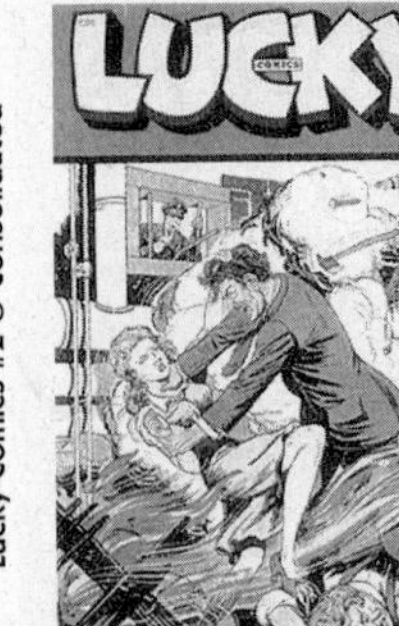

Lucky Comics #2 © Consolidated

Lumberjanes #1 © BOOM

	GD 2.0	VG 4.0	FN 6.0	VF 8.0	VF/NM 9.0	NM- 9.2
37	13	26	39	72	101	130
38-44,46-50: 39-41-Photo-c	12	24	36	67	94	120
45,51,52,69: 45-Powell-a. 51,69-Everett-a. 52-Krigstein-a	12	24	36	69	97	125
53-60: 60-Last pre-code (2/55)	10	20	30	58	79	100
61-68,70-75: 75-Brewster, Cameron, Colletta-a	10	20	30	56	76	95

LOVE THRILLS (See Fox Giants)

LOVE TRAILS (Western romance)
A Lover's Magazine (CDS)(Marvel): Dec, 1949 - No. 2, Mar, 1950 (52 pgs.)

	GD 2.0	VG 4.0	FN 6.0	VF 8.0	VF/NM 9.0	NM- 9.2
1,2: 1-Photo-c	15	30	45	90	140	190

LOWELL THOMAS' HIGH ADVENTURE (See High Adventure)

LT. (See Lieutenant)

LUCIFER (See The Sandman #4)
DC Comics (Vertigo): Jun, 2000 - No. 75, Aug, 2006 ($2.50/$2.75)

	GD 2.0	VG 4.0	FN 6.0	VF 8.0	VF/NM 9.0	NM- 9.2
1-Carey-s/Weston-a/Fegredo-c						8.00
2,3-Carey-s/Weston-a/Fegredo-c						5.00
4-10: 4-Pleece-a. 5-Gross-a						4.00
11-49,51-73: 16-Moeller-c begin. 25,26-Death app. 45-Naifeh-a. 53-Kaluta-c begin. 62-Doran-a. 63-Begin $2.75-c						3.00
50-($3.50) P. Craig Russell-a; Mazikeen app.						4.00
74-($2.99) Kaluta-c						3.00
75-($3.99) Last issue; Lucifer's origins retold; Morpheus app.; Gross-a/Moeller-c						4.00
Preview-16 pg. flip book w/Swamp Thing Preview						3.00
...: A Dalliance With the Damned TPB ('02, $14.95) r/#14-20						15.00
...: Children and Monsters TPB ('01, $17.95) r/#5-13						18.00
...: Crux TPB (2006, $14.99) r/#55-61						15.00
...: Devil in the Gateway TPB ('01, $14.95) r/#1-4 & Sandman Presents:..#1-3						15.00
...: Evensong TPB (2007, $14.99) r/#70-75 & Lucifer: Nirvana one-shot						15.00
...: Exodus TPB (2005, $14.95) r/#42-44,46-49						15.00
...: Inferno TPB (2003, $14.95) r/#29-35						15.00
...: Mansions of the Silence TPB (2004, $14.95) r/#36-41						15.00
...: Morningstar TPB (2006, $14.99) r/#62-69						15.00
...: Nirvana (2002, $5.95) Carey-s/Muth-painted-c/a; Daniel app.						6.00
...: The Divine Comedy TPB (2003, $17.95) r/#21-28						18.00
...: The Wolf Beneath the Tree TPB (2005, $14.99) r/#45,50-54						15.00

LUCIFER'S HAMMER (Larry Niven & Jerry Pournelle's...)
Innovation Publishing: Nov, 1993 - No. 6, 1994 ($2.50, painted, limited series)

	GD 2.0	VG 4.0	FN 6.0	VF 8.0	VF/NM 9.0	NM- 9.2
1-6: Adaptatin of novel, painted-c & art						3.00

LUCKY COMICS
Consolidated Magazines: Jan, 1944; No. 2, Sum, 1945 - No. 5, Sum, 1946

	GD 2.0	VG 4.0	FN 6.0	VF 8.0	VF/NM 9.0	NM- 9.2
1-Lucky Starr & Bobbie begin	24	48	72	144	237	330
2-5: 5-Devil-c by Walter Johnson	15	30	45	83	124	165

LUCKY DUCK
Standard Comics (Literary Ent.): No. 5, Jan, 1953 - No. 8, Sept, 1953

	GD 2.0	VG 4.0	FN 6.0	VF 8.0	VF/NM 9.0	NM- 9.2
5-Funny animal; Irving Spector-a	11	22	33	60	83	105
6-8-Irving Spector-a	10	20	30	54	72	90

NOTE: *Harvey Kurtzman tried to hire Spector for Mad #1.*

LUCKY "7" COMICS
Howard Publishers Ltd.: 1944 (No date listed)

	GD 2.0	VG 4.0	FN 6.0	VF 8.0	VF/NM 9.0	NM- 9.2
1-Pioneer, Sir Gallagher, Dick Royce, Congo Raider, Punch Powers; bondage-c	41	82	123	256	428	600

LUCKY STAR (Western)
Nation Wide Publ. Co.: 1950 - No. 7, 1951; No. 8, 1953 - No. 14, 1955 (5x7-1/4"; full color, 5¢)

	GD 2.0	VG 4.0	FN 6.0	VF 8.0	VF/NM 9.0	NM- 9.2
nn (#1)-(5¢, 52 pgs.)-Davis-a	20	40	60	114	182	250
2,3-(5¢, 52 pgs.)-Davis-a	14	28	42	76	108	140
4-7-(5¢, 52 pgs.)-Davis-a	13	26	39	72	101	130
8-14-(36 pgs.)(Exist?)	13	26	39	72	101	130
Given away with Lucky Star Western Wear by the Juvenile Mfg. Co.	7	14	21	35	43	50

LUCY SHOW, THE (TV) (Also see I Love Lucy)
Gold Key: June, 1963 - No. 5, June, 1964 (Photo-c: 1,2)

	GD 2.0	VG 4.0	FN 6.0	VF 8.0	VF/NM 9.0	NM- 9.2
1	10	20	30	69	147	225
2	6	12	18	41	76	110
3-5: Photo back c-1,2,4,5	6	12	18	37	66	95

LUCY, THE REAL GONE GAL (Meet Miss Pepper #5 on)
St. John Publishing Co.: June, 1953 - No. 4, Dec, 1953

	GD 2.0	VG 4.0	FN 6.0	VF 8.0	VF/NM 9.0	NM- 9.2
1-Negligee panels	18	36	54	103	162	220
2	11	22	33	62	86	110
3,4: 3-Drucker-a	10	20	30	56	76	95

LUDWIG BEMELMAN'S MADELEINE & GENEVIEVE
Dell Publishing Co.: No. 796, May, 1957

	GD 2.0	VG 4.0	FN 6.0	VF 8.0	VF/NM 9.0	NM- 9.2
Four Color 796	4	8	12	25	40	55

LUDWIG VON DRAKE (TV)(Disney)(See Walt Disney's C&S #256)
Dell Publishing Co.: Nov-Dec, 1961 - No. 4, June-Aug, 1962

	GD 2.0	VG 4.0	FN 6.0	VF 8.0	VF/NM 9.0	NM- 9.2
1	6	12	18	38	69	100
2-4	5	10	15	30	50	70

LUFTWAFFE: 1946 (Volume 1)
Antarctic Press: July, 1996 - No. 4, Jan, 1997 ($2.95, B&W, limited series)

	GD 2.0	VG 4.0	FN 6.0	VF 8.0	VF/NM 9.0	NM- 9.2
1-4-Ben Dunn & Ted Nomura-s/a, ...Special Ed.						3.00

LUFTWAFFE: 1946 (Volume 2)
Antarctic Press: Mar, 1997 - No. 18 ($2.95/$2.99, B&W, limited series)

	GD 2.0	VG 4.0	FN 6.0	VF 8.0	VF/NM 9.0	NM- 9.2
1-18: 8-Reviews Tigers of Terra series						3.00
Annual 1 (4/98, $2.95)-Reprints early Nomura pages						4.00
...Color Special (4/98)						3.00
...Technical Manual 1,2 (2/98, 4/99)						4.00

LUGER
Eclipse Comics: Oct, 1986 - No. 3, Feb, 1987 ($1.75, miniseries, Baxter paper)

	GD 2.0	VG 4.0	FN 6.0	VF 8.0	VF/NM 9.0	NM- 9.2
1-3: Bruce Jones scripts; Yeates-c/a						3.00

LUKE CAGE (See Cage & Hero for Hire)

LUKE CAGE NOIR
Marvel Comics: Oct, 2009 - No. 4, Jan, 2010 ($3.99, limited series)

	GD 2.0	VG 4.0	FN 6.0	VF 8.0	VF/NM 9.0	NM- 9.2
1-4-Glass & Benson-a/Martinbrough-a; covers by Bradstreet and Calero						4.00

LUKE SHORT'S WESTERN STORIES
Dell Publishing Co.: No. 580, Aug, 1954 - No. 927, Aug, 1958

	GD 2.0	VG 4.0	FN 6.0	VF 8.0	VF/NM 9.0	NM- 9.2
Four Color 580(8/54), 651(9/55)-Kinstler-a	4	8	12	28	47	65
Four Color 739,771,807,848,875,927	4	8	12	27	44	60

LUMBERJANES
BOOM! Box: Apr, 2014 - Present ($3.99)

	GD 2.0	VG 4.0	FN 6.0	VF 8.0	VF/NM 9.0	NM- 9.2
1-Noelle Stevenson & Grace Ellis-s/Brooke Allen-a; multiple covers						4.00

LUNA MOON-HUNTER
WaterWalker Studios: Jul, 2012 - No. 2, Aug, 2012 ($5.95, limited series)

	GD 2.0	VG 4.0	FN 6.0	VF 8.0	VF/NM 9.0	NM- 9.2
1,2-Rob Hughes-s/Jeff Slemons-a. 1-Posada-c. 2-Buzz-c						6.00
SC-($24.95, 180 pgs.) Painted-c by Buzz & Parrillo; art by Slemons, Buzz & LaRocque						25.00
HC-($49.95, limited edition of 1000) Signed by Hughes & Slemons; 2 bonus articles						50.00

LUNATIC FRINGE, THE
Innovation Publishing: July, 1989 - No. 2, 1989 ($1.75, deluxe format)

	GD 2.0	VG 4.0	FN 6.0	VF 8.0	VF/NM 9.0	NM- 9.2
1,2						3.00

LUNATICKLE (Magazine) (Satire)
Whitstone Publ.: Feb, 1956 - No. 2, Apr, 1956

	GD 2.0	VG 4.0	FN 6.0	VF 8.0	VF/NM 9.0	NM- 9.2
1,2-Kubert-a (scarce)	9	18	27	47	61	75

LUNATIK
Marvel Comics: Dec, 1995 - No. 3, Feb, 1996 ($1.95, limited series)

	GD 2.0	VG 4.0	FN 6.0	VF 8.0	VF/NM 9.0	NM- 9.2
1-3						3.00

LURKERS, THE
IDW Publ.: Oct, 2004 - No. 4, Jan, 2005 ($3.99)

	GD 2.0	VG 4.0	FN 6.0	VF 8.0	VF/NM 9.0	NM- 9.2
1-4-Niles-s/Casanova-a						4.00

LUST FOR LIFE
Slave Labor Graphics: Feb, 1997 - No. 4, Jan, 1998 ($2.95, B&W)

	GD 2.0	VG 4.0	FN 6.0	VF 8.0	VF/NM 9.0	NM- 9.2
1-4: 1-Jeff Levin-s/a						3.00

LUTHOR (See Lex Luthor: Man of Steel)

LYCANTHROPE LEO
Viz Communications: 1994 - No. 7($2.95, B&W, limited series, 44 pgs.)

	GD 2.0	VG 4.0	FN 6.0	VF 8.0	VF/NM 9.0	NM- 9.2
1-7						4.00

LYNCH (See Gen 13)
Image Comics (WildStorm Productions): May, 1997 ($2.50, one-shot)

	GD 2.0	VG 4.0	FN 6.0	VF 8.0	VF/NM 9.0	NM- 9.2
1-Helmut-c/app.						3.00

LYNCH MOB
Chaos! Comics: June, 1994 - No. 4, Sept, 1994 ($2.50, limited series)

	GD 2.0	VG 4.0	FN 6.0	VF 8.0	VF/NM 9.0	NM- 9.2
1-4						5.00
1-Special edition full foil-c	1	2	3	5	6	8

Machine Man #11 © MAR

Mad #15 © EC Pub.

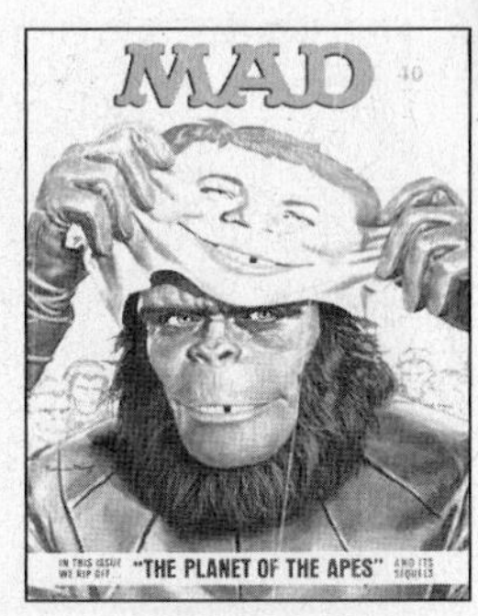

Mad #157 © EC Publ.

	GD 2.0	VG 4.0	FN 6.0	VF 8.0	VF/NM 9.0	NM- 9.2
LYNDON B. JOHNSON						
Dell Publishing Co.: Mar, 1965						
12-445-503-Photo-c	3	6	9	19	30	40
M						
Eclipse Books: 1990 - No. 4, 1991 ($4.95, painted, 52 pgs.)						
1-Adapts movie; contains flexi-disc ($5.95)						6.00
2-4						5.00
MACE GRIFFIN BOUNTY HUNTER (Based on video game)						
Image Comics (Top Cow): May, 2003 ($2.99, one-shot)						
1-Nocon-a						3.00
MACGYVER: FUGITIVE GAUNTLET (Based on TV series)						
Image Comics: Oct, 2012 - No. 5, Feb, 2013 ($3.50, limited series)						
1-5-Lee Zlotoff & Tony Lee-s/Will Sliney-a						3.50
MACHETE (Based on the Robert Rodriguez movie)						
IDW Publishing: No. 0, Sept, 2010 ($3.99)						
0-Origin story; Rodriguez & Kaufman-s/Sayger-a; 3 covers						4.00
MACHINE, THE						
Dark Horse Comics: Nov, 1994 - No. 4, Feb, 1995 ($2.50, limited series)						
1-4						3.00
MACHINE MAN (Also see 2001, A Space Odyssey)						
Marvel Comics Group: Apr, 1978 - No. 9, Dec, 1978; No. 10, Aug, 1979 - No. 19, Feb, 1981						
1-Jack Kirby-c/a/scripts begin; end #9	3	6	9	19	30	40
2-9-Kirby-c/a/s. 9-(12/78)	2	4	6	9	12	15
10-17: 10-(8/79) Marv Wolfman scripts & Ditko-a begins	1	3	4	6	8	10
18-Wendigo, Alpha Flight-ties into X-Men #140	3	6	9	16	23	30
19-Intro/1st app. Jack O'Lantern (Macendale), later becomes 2nd Hobgoblin	3	6	9	16	23	30
NOTE: ***Austin** c-7i, 19i. **Buckler** c-17p, 18p. **Byrne** c-14p. **Ditko** a-10-19; c-10-13, 14i, 15, 16. **Kirby** a-1-9p; c-1-5, 7-9p. **Layton** c-7i. **Miller** c-19p. **Simonson** c-6.*						
MACHINE MAN (Also see X-51)						
Marvel Comics Group: Oct, 1984 - No. 4, Jan, 1985 (limited series)						
1-4-Barry Smith-c/a(i) & colors in all						5.00
TPB (1988, $6.95) r/ #1-4; Barry Smith-c						10.00
.../Bastion '98 Annual ($2.99) wraparound-c						4.00
MACHINE MAN 2020						
Marvel Comics: Aug, 1994 - Nov, 1994 ($2.00, 52 pgs., limited series)						
1-4: Reprints Machine Man limited series; Barry Windsor-Smith-c/i(r)						4.00
MACHINE TEEN						
Marvel Comics: July, 2005 - No. 5, Nov, 2005 ($2.99, limited series)						
1-5-Sumerak-s/Hawthorne-a. 1-James Jean-c						3.00
...: History (2005, $7.99, digest) r/#1-5						8.00
MACK BOLAN: THE EXECUTIONER (Don Pendleton's...)						
Innovation Publishing: July, 1993 ($2.50)						
1-3-($2.50)						3.00
1-($3.95)-Indestructible Cover Edition						4.00
1-($2.95)-Collector's Gold Edition; foil stamped						4.00
1-($3.50)-Double Cover Edition; red foil outer-c						4.00
MACKENZIE'S RAIDERS (Movie, TV)						
Dell Publishing Co.: No. 1093, Apr-June, 1960						
Four Color 1093-Richard Carlson photo-c from TV show	6	12	18	37	66	95
MACROSS (Becomes Robotech: The Macross Saga #2 on)						
Comico: Dec, 1984 ($1.50)(Low print run)						
1-Early manga app.	3	6	9	21	33	45
MACROSS II						
Viz Select Comics: 1992 - No. 10, 1993 ($2.75, B&W, limited series)						
1-10: Based on video series						4.00
MAD (Tales Calculated to Drive You...)						
E. C. Comics (Educational Comics): Oct-Nov, 1952 - Present (No. 24-on are magazine format) (Kurtzman editor No. 1-28, Feldstein No. 29 - No. ?)						
1-Wood, Davis, Elder start as regulars	417	834	1251	3336	5318	7300
2-Dick Tracy cameo	110	220	330	880	1403	1925
3,4: 3-Stan Lee mentioned. 4-Reefer mention story "Flob Was a Slob" by Davis; Superman parody	80	160	240	640	1020	1400

	GD 2.0	VG 4.0	FN 6.0	VF 8.0	VF/NM 9.0	NM- 9.2
5-W.M. Gaines biog.	160	320	480	1280	2040	2800
6-11: 6-Popeye cameo. 7,8- "Hey Look" reprints by Kurtzman. 11-Wolverton-a; Davis story was-r/Crime Suspenstories #12 w/new Kurtzman dialogue	60	120	180	480	765	1050
12-15: 12-Archie parody. 15,18-Pot Shot Pete-r by Kurtzman	48	96	144	384	612	840
16-23(5/55): 18-Alice in Wonderland by Jack Davis. 21-1st app. Alfred E. Neuman on-c in fake ad. 22-All by Elder plus photo-montages by Kurtzman. 23-Special cancel announcement	40	80	120	320	510	700
24(7/55)-1st magazine issue (25¢); Kurtzman logo & border on-c; 1st "What? Me Worry?" on-c; 2nd printing exists	94	188	282	752	1201	1650
25-Jaffee starts as regular writer	44	88	132	352	564	775
26,27: 27-Jaffee starts as story artist; new logo	39	78	117	312	499	685
28-Last issue edited by Kurtzman; (three cover variations exist with different wording on contents banner on lower right of cover; value of each the same)	36	72	108	216	351	485
29-Kamen-a; Don Martin starts as regular; Feldstein editing begins	36	72	108	216	351	485
30-1st A. E. Neuman cover by Mingo; last Elder-a; Bob Clarke starts as regular; Disneyland & Elvis Presley spoof	51	102	153	321	541	760
31-Freas starts as regular; last Davis-a until #99	32	64	96	192	314	435
32,33: 32-Orlando, Drucker, Woodbridge start as regulars; Wood back-c. 33-Orlando back-c	27	54	81	162	266	370
34-Berg starts as regular	22	44	66	132	216	300
35-Mingo wraparound-c; Crandall-a	22	44	66	132	216	300
36-40 (7/58): 39-Beall-c	18	36	54	105	165	225
41-50: 42-Danny Kaye-s. 44-Xmas-c. 47-49-Sid Caesar-s. 48-Uncle Sam-c. 50 (10/59)-Peter Gunn-s	15	30	45	90	140	190
51-59: 52-Xmas-c; 77 Sunset Strip. 53-Rifleman-s. 54-Jaffee-a begins. 55-Sid Caesar-s. 59-Strips of Superman, Flash Gordon, Donald Duck & others. 59-Halloween/Headless Horseman-c	14	28	42	80	115	150
60 (1/61)-JFK/Nixon flip-c; 1st Spy vs. Spy by Prohias, who starts as regular	15	30	45	86	133	180
61-70: 64-Rickard starts as regular. 65-JFK-s. 66-JFK-c. 68-Xmas-c by Martin. 70-Route 66-s	6	12	18	41	76	110
71-75,77-80 (7/63): 72-10th Anniv. special; 1/3 pg. strips of Superman, Tarzan & others. 73-Bonanza-s. 74-Dr. Kildare-s	5	10	15	31	53	75
76-Aragonés starts as regular	5	10	15	34	60	85
81-85: 81-Superman strip. 82-Castro-c. 85-Lincoln-c	4	8	12	28	47	65
86-1st Fold-in; commonly creased back covers makes these and later issues scarcer in NM	5	10	15	33	57	80
87,88	5	10	15	31	53	75
89,90: 89-One strip by Walt Kelly; Frankenstein-c; Fugitive-s. 90-Ringo back-c by Frazetta; Beatles app.	5	10	15	33	57	80
91,94,96,100: 94-King Kong-c. 96-Man From U.N.C.L.E. 100-(1/66)-Anniversary issue	4	8	12	28	47	65
92,93,95,97-99: 99-Davis-a resumes	4	8	12	27	44	60
101,104,106,108,114,115,119,121: 101-Infinity-c; Voyage to the Bottom of the Sea-s. 104-Lost in Space-s. 106-Tarzan back-c by Frazetta; 2 pg. Batman by Aragonés. 108-Hogan's Heroes by Davis. 114-Rat Patrol-s. 115-Star Trek. 119-Invaders (TV). 121-Beatles-c; Ringo pin-up; flip-c of Sik-Teen; Flying Nun-s	3	6	9	20	31	42
102,103,107,109-113,116-118,120(7/68): 118-Beatles cameo	3	6	9	18	28	38
105-Batman-c/s, TV show parody (9/66)	4	8	12	23	37	50
122,124,126,128,129,131-134,136,137,139,140: 122-Ronald Reagan photo inside; Drucker & Mingo-c. 126-Family Affair-s. 128-Last Orlando. 131-Reagan photo back-c. 132-Xmas-c. 133-John Wayne/True Grit. 136-Room 222	3	6	9	15	22	28
123-Four different covers	3	6	9	16	23	30
125,127,130,135,138: 125-2001 Space Odyssey; Hitler back-c. 127-Mod Squad-c/s. 130-Land of the Giants-s; Torres begins as reg. 135-Easy Rider-c by Davis. 138-Snoopy-c; MASH-s	3	6	9	16	24	32
141-149,151-156,158-165,167-170: 141-Hawaii Five-0. 147-All in the Family-s. 153-Dirty Harry-s. 155-Godfather-c/s. 156-Columbo-s. 159-Clockwork Orange-c/s. 161-Tarzan-s. 164-Kung Fu (TV)-s. 165-James Bond-s; Dean Martin-c. 169-Drucker-c; McCloud-s. 170-Exorcist-s	3	6	9	14	19	24
150-(4/72) Partridge Family-s	3	6	9	15	21	26
157-(3/73) Planet of the Apes-c/s	3	6	9	16	23	30
166-(4/74) Classic finger-c	3	6	9	16	23	30
171-185,187,189-192,194,195,198,199: 172-Six Million Dollar Man-s; Hitler back-c. 178-Godfather II-c/s. 180-Jaws-c/s (1/76). 182-Bob Jones starts as regular.185-Starsky & Hutch-s. 187-Fonz/Happy Days-c/s; Harry North starts as regular. 189-Travolta/Kotter-c/s. 190-John Wayne-c/s. 192-King Kong-c/s. 194-Rocky-c/s; Laverne & Shirley-s. 199-James Bond-s	2	4	6	10	14	18
186,188,197,200: 186-Star Trek-c/s. 188-Six Million Dollar Man/ Bionic Woman. 197-Spock-s;						

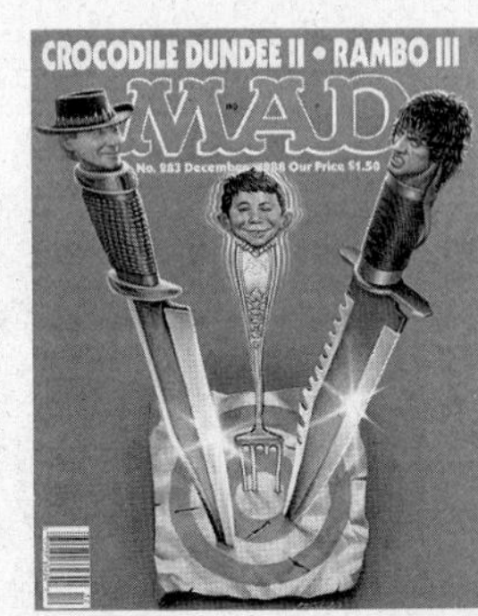

Mad #283 © EC Publ.

Madame Mirage #5 © Paul Dini & TCOW

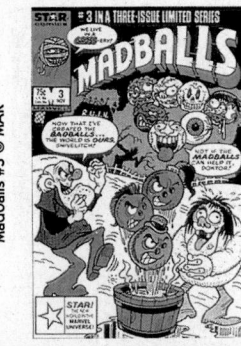

Madballs #3 © MAR

	GD 2.0	VG 4.0	FN 6.0	VF 8.0	VF/NM 9.0	NM- 9.2
Star Wars-s. 200-Close Encounters	2	4	6	13	18	22
193,196: 193-Farrah/Charlie's Angels-c/s. 196-Star Wars-c/s	3	6	9	14	19	24
201,203,205,220: 201-Sat. Night Fever-c/s. 203-Star Wars. 205-Travolta/Grease. 220-Yoda-c, Empire Strikes Back-s	2	4	6	9	13	16
202,204,206,207,209,211-219,221-227,229,230: 204-Hulk TV show. 206-Tarzan. 208-Superman movie. 209-Mork & Mindy. 212-Spider-Man-s; Alien (movie)-s. 213-James Bond, Dracula, Rocky II-s 216-Star Trek. 219-Martin-c. 221-Shining-s. 223-Dallas-c/s. 225-Popeye. 226-Superman II. 229-James Bond. 230-Star Wars	1	3	4	6	8	10
208,228: 208-Superman movie-c/s; Battlestar Galactica-s. 228-Raiders of the Lost Ark-c/s	2	4	6	9	12	15
210-Lord of the Rings	2	4	6	9	13	16
231-235,237-241,243-249,251-260: 233-Pac-Man-c. 234-MASH-c/s. 235-Flip-c with Rocky III & Conan; Boris-a. 239-Mickey Mouse-c. 241-Knight Rider-s. 243-Superman III. 245- Last Rickard-a. 247-Seven Dwarfs-c. 253-Supergirl movie-s; Prince/Purple Rain-s. 254-Rock stars-s. 255-Reagan-c; Cosby-s. 256-Last issue edited by Feldstein; Dynasty, Bev. Hills Cop. 259-Rambo. 260-Back to the Future-c/s; Honeymooners-s	1	2	3	5	6	8
236,242,250: 236-E.T.-c/s;Star Trek II-s. 242-Star Wars/A-Team-c/s. 250-Temple of Doom-c/s; Tarzan-s	1	2	3	5	7	9
261-267,269-276,278-288,290-297: 261-Miami Vice. 262-Rocky IV-c/s, Leave It To Beaver-s. 263-Young Sherlock Holmes-s. 264-Hulk Hogan-c; Rambo-s. 267-Top Gun. 271-Star Trek IV-c/s. 272-ALF-c; Get Smart-s. 273-Pee Wee Herman-c/s. 274-Last Martin-a. 281-California Raisins-c. 282-Star Trek:TNG-s; ALF-s. 283-Rambo III-c/s. 284-Roger Rabbit-c/s. 285-Hulk Hogan-c. 287-3 pgs. Eisner-a. 291-TMNT-c; Indiana Jones-s. 292-Super Mario Bros.-c; Married with Children-s. 295-Back to the Future II. 297-Mike Tyson-c	1	2	3	4	5	7
268,277,289,298-300: 268-Aliens-c/s. 277-Michael Jackson-c/s; Robocop-s. 289-Batman movie parody. 298-Gremlins II-c/s; Robocop II. Batman-s. 299-Simpsons-c/story; Total Recall-s. 300(1/91) Casablanca-s, Dick Tracy-s, Wizard of Oz-s, Gone With The Wind-s	1	2	3	5	6	8
300-303 (1/91-6/91)-Special Hussein Asylum Editions; only distributed to the troops in the Middle East (see Mad Super Spec.)	2	4	6	13	18	22
301-310,312,313,315-320,322,324,326-334,337-349: 303-Home Alone-c/s. 305-Simpsons-s. 306-TMNT II movie. 308-Terminator II. 315-Tribute to William Gaines. 316-Photo-c. 319-Dracula-c/s. 320-Disney's Aladdin-s. 322-Batman Animated series. 327-Seinfeld-s; X-Men-s. 331-Flintstones-c/s. 332-O.J. Simpson-c/s; Simpsons app. in Lion King. 334-Frankenstein-c/s. 338-Judge Dredd-c by Frazetta. 341-Pocahontas-s. 345-Beatles app. (1 pg.) 347-Broken Arrow & Mission Impossible						5.00
311,314,321,323,325,335,336,350,354,358: 311-Addams Family-c/story, Home Improvement-s. 314-Batman Returns-c/story. 321-Star Trek DS9-c/s. 323-Jurassic Park-c/s. 325,336-Beavis & Butthead-c/s. 335-X-Files-s; Pulp Fiction-s; Interview with the Vampire-s. 336-Lois & Clark-s. 350-Polybagged w/CD Rom. 354-Star Wars; Beavis & Butthead-s. 358-X-Files						6.00
351-353,355-357,359-500						5.00
501-527-($5.99)						6.00
Mad About Super Heroes (2002, $9.95) r/super hero app.; Alex Ross-c						10.00

NOTE: **Aragones** *c-210, 293.* **Beall** *c-39.* **Davis** *c-2, 27, 135, 139, 173, 178, 212, 213, 219, 246, 260, 296, 308.* **Drucker** *a-35-62; c-122, 169, 176, 225, 234, 264, 266, 274, 280, 285, 297, 299, 303, 314, 315, 321.* **Elder** *c-5, 259, 261, 268.* **Elder/Kurtzman** *a-258-274.* **Jules Feiffer** *a(r)-42.* **Freas** *c-40-59, 62-67, 69-70, 72, 74.* **Heath** *a-14, 27.* **Jaffee** *c-199, 217, 224, 258.* **Kamen** *a-29.* **Krigstein** *a-12, 17, 24, 26.* **Kurtzman** *c-1, 3, 4, 6-10, 13, 16, 18.* **Martin** *a-29-62; c-68, 165, 229.* **Mingo** *c-30-37, 61, 71, 75-80, 82-114, 117-124, 126, 129, 131, 133, 134, 136, 140, 143-148, 150-162, 164, 166-168, 171, 172, 174, 175, 177, 179, 181, 183, 185, 198, 206, 209, 211, 214, 218, 221, 222, 300.* **John Severin** *a-1-6, 9, 10.* **Wolverton** *c-11; a-11, 17, 29, 31, 36, 40, 82, 137.* **Wood** *a-1-21, 23-62; c-26, 28, 29.* **Woodbridge** *a-35-62. Issues 1-23 are 36 pgs.; 24-28 are 58 pgs.; 29 on are 52 pgs.*

MAD (See Mad Follies, ...Special, More Trash from..., and The Worst from...)

MAD ABOUT MILLIE (Also see Millie the Model)
Marvel Comics Group: April, 1969 - No. 16, Nov, 1970

	GD 2.0	VG 4.0	FN 6.0	VF 8.0	VF/NM 9.0	NM- 9.2
1-Giant issue	9	18	27	60	120	180
2,3 (Giants)	6	12	18	40	73	105
4-10	5	10	15	31	53	75
11-16: 16-r	5	10	15	30	50	70
Annual 1(11/71, 52 pgs.)	5	10	15	31	53	75

MADAME MIRAGE
Image Comics (Top Cow): June, 2007 - No. 6, May, 2008 ($2.99)

	GD 2.0	VG 4.0	FN 6.0	VF 8.0	VF/NM 9.0	NM- 9.2
1-6: 1-Paul Dini-s/Kenneth Rocafort-a; two covers by Horn and Rocafort						3.00
... First Look (5/07, 99¢) preview of series; Dini interview; cover gallery						3.00
Volume 1 TPB (7/08, $14.99) r/#1-6; cover gallery; cover and design sketches						15.00

MADAME XANADU
DC Comics: July, 1981 ($1.00, no ads, 36 pgs.)

	GD 2.0	VG 4.0	FN 6.0	VF 8.0	VF/NM 9.0	NM- 9.2
1-Marshall Rogers-a (25 pgs.); Kaluta-c/a (2pgs.); pin-up	1	2	3	5	6	8

MADAME XANADU (Also see Doorway to Nightmare)
DC Comics (Vertigo): Aug, 2008 - No. 29, Jan, 2011 ($2.99)

	GD 2.0	VG 4.0	FN 6.0	VF 8.0	VF/NM 9.0	NM- 9.2
1-Matt Wagner-s/Amy Reeder Hadley-a/c; Phantom Stranger app.						4.00
1,2-Variant covers. 1-Wagner. 2-Kaluta						5.00
2-29: 2-10-Amy Reeder Hadley-a/c; Phantom Stranger app. 6-Death (from The Sandman) app.; covers by Hadley & Quitely. 9-Zatara app. 10-Jim Corrigan becomes The Spectre. 11-15-Kaluta-a. 14,15-Sandman (Wesley Dodds) app. 16-18-Hadley-a; Det. Jones app.						3.00
...: Broken House of Cards TPB (2011, $17.99) r/#16-23 and story from House of Mystery Halloween Annual #1						18.00
...: Disenchanted TPB (2009, $12.99) r/#1-10; James Robinson intro.; Hadley sketch-a						13.00
...: Exodus TPB (2010, $12.99) r/#11-15; Chris Roberson intro.						13.00
...: Extra-Sensory TPB (2011, $17.99) r/#24-29						18.00

MADBALLS
Star Comics/Marvel Comics #9 on: Sept, 1986 - No. 3, Nov, 1986; No. 4, June, 1987 - No. 10, June, 1988

	GD 2.0	VG 4.0	FN 6.0	VF 8.0	VF/NM 9.0	NM- 9.2
1-10: Based on toys. 9-Post-a						5.00

MAD DISCO
E.C. Comics: 1980 (one-shot, 36 pgs.)

	GD 2.0	VG 4.0	FN 6.0	VF 8.0	VF/NM 9.0	NM- 9.2
1-Includes 30 minute flexi-disc of Mad disco music	2	4	6	11	16	20

MAD-DOG
Marvel Comics: May, 1993 - No. 6, Oct, 1993 ($1.25)

	GD 2.0	VG 4.0	FN 6.0	VF 8.0	VF/NM 9.0	NM- 9.2
1-6-Flip book w/2nd story "created" by Bob Newhart's character from his TV show "Bob" set at a comic book company; actual s/a-Ty Templeton						3.00

MAD DOGS
Eclipse Comics: Feb, 1992 - No. 3, July, 1992 ($2.50, B&W, limited series)

	GD 2.0	VG 4.0	FN 6.0	VF 8.0	VF/NM 9.0	NM- 9.2
1-3						3.00

MAD 84 (Mad Extra)
E.C. Comics: 1984 (84 pgs.)

	GD 2.0	VG 4.0	FN 6.0	VF 8.0	VF/NM 9.0	NM- 9.2
1	1	3	4	6	8	10

MAD FOLLIES (Special)
E. C. Comics: 1963 - No. 7, 1969

	GD 2.0	VG 4.0	FN 6.0	VF 8.0	VF/NM 9.0	NM- 9.2
nn(1963)-Paperback book covers	19	38	57	129	287	445
2(1964)-Calendar	15	30	45	100	220	340
3(1965)-Mischief Stickers	11	22	33	76	163	250
4(1966)-Mobile; Frazetta-r/back-c Mad #90	9	18	27	57	111	165
5,6: 5(1967)-Stencils. 6(1968)-Mischief Stickers	7	14	21	44	82	120
7(1969)-Nasty Cards	7	14	21	44	82	120

(If bonus is missing, issue is half price)
NOTE: **Clarke** *c-4.* **Frazetta** *r-4, 6 (1 pg. ea.).* **Mingo** *c-1-3.* **Orlando** *a-5.*

MAD HATTER, THE (Costumed Hero)
O. W. Comics Corp.: Jan-Feb, 1946; No. 2, Sept-Oct, 1946

	GD 2.0	VG 4.0	FN 6.0	VF 8.0	VF/NM 9.0	NM- 9.2
1-Freddy the Firefly begins; Giunta-c/a	77	154	231	493	847	1200
2-Has ad for E.C.'s Animal Fables #1	40	80	120	246	411	575

MADHOUSE
Ajax/Farrell Publ. (Excellent Publ./4-Star): 3-4/54 - No. 4, 9-10/54; 6/57 - No. 4, Dec?, 1957

	GD 2.0	VG 4.0	FN 6.0	VF 8.0	VF/NM 9.0	NM- 9.2
1(1954)	36	72	108	211	343	475
2,3	20	40	60	114	182	250
4-Surrealistic-c	26	52	78	154	252	350
1(1957, 2nd series)	15	30	45	85	130	175
2-4 (#4 exist?)	10	20	30	58	79	100

MAD HOUSE (Formerly Madhouse Glads; ...Comics #104? on)
Red Circle Productions/Archie Publications: No. 95, 9/74 - No. 97, 1/75; No. 98, 8/75 - No. 130, 10/82

	GD 2.0	VG 4.0	FN 6.0	VF 8.0	VF/NM 9.0	NM- 9.2
95,96-Horror stories through #97; Morrow-c	2	4	6	11	16	20
97-Intro. Henry Hobson; Morrow-a/c, Thorne-a	2	4	6	10	14	18
98,99,101-120-Satire/humor stories. 110-Sabrina app.,1pg.	1	3	4	6	8	10
100	2	4	6	8	10	12
121-129	2	4	6	8	10	12
130	2	4	6	9	13	16
Annual 8(1970-71)-Formerly Madhouse Ma-ad Annual; Sabrina app. (6 pgs.)	4	8	12	25	40	55
Annual 9-12(1974-75): 11-Wood-a(r)	3	6	9	14	20	25
...Comics Digest 1('75-76) r/1st & 2nd Sabrina app.	2	4	6	10	14	18
2-8(8/82)(...Mag. #5 on)-Sabrina in many	2	4	6	8	11	14

NOTE: **B. Jones** *a-96.* **McWilliams** *a-97.* **Wildey** *a-95, 96. See Archie Comics Digest #1, 13.*

MADHOUSE GLADS (Formerly ...Ma-ad; Madhouse #95 on)
Archie Publ.: No. 73, May, 1970 - No. 94, Aug, 1974 (No. 78-92: 52 pgs.)

	GD 2.0	VG 4.0	FN 6.0	VF 8.0	VF/NM 9.0	NM- 9.2
73-77,93,94: 74-1 pg. Sabrina	2	4	6	9	13	16

Madman Comics #12 © Mike Allred

The Magdalena V3 #11 © TCOW

Mage #9 © Matt Wagner

	GD 2.0	VG 4.0	FN 6.0	VF 8.0	VF/NM 9.0	NM- 9.2
78-92 (52 pgs.)	2	4	6	11	16	20

MADHOUSE MA-AD (...Jokes #67-70; ...Freak-Out #71-74)
(Formerly Archie's Madhouse) (Becomes Madhouse Glads #73 on)
Archie Publications: No. 67, April, 1969 - No. 72, Jan, 1970

	GD 2.0	VG 4.0	FN 6.0	VF 8.0	VF/NM 9.0	NM- 9.2
67-71: 70-1 pg. Sabrina	3	6	9	15	22	28
72-6 pgs. Sabrina	4	8	12	25	40	55
...Annual 7(1969-70)-Formerly Archie's Madhouse Annual; becomes Madhouse Annual; 6 pgs. Sabrina	4	8	12	27	44	60

MADMAN (See Creatures of the Id #1)
Tundra Publishing: Mar, 1992 - No. 3, 1992 ($3.95, duotone, high quality, lim. series, 52 pgs.)

	GD 2.0	VG 4.0	FN 6.0	VF 8.0	VF/NM 9.0	NM- 9.2
1-Mike Allred-c/a in all	2	4	6	8	10	12
1-2nd printing						4.00
2,3						6.00

MADMAN ADVENTURES
Tundra Publishing: 1992 - No. 3, 1993 ($2.95, limited series)

	GD 2.0	VG 4.0	FN 6.0	VF 8.0	VF/NM 9.0	NM- 9.2
1-Mike Allred-c/a in all	1	3	4	6	8	10
2,3						5.00
TPB (Oni Press, 2002, $14.95) r/#1-3 & first app. of Frank Einstein from Creatures of the Id in color; gallery pages						15.00

MADMAN ATOMIC COMICS (Also see The Atomics)
Image Comics: Apr, 2007 - Present ($2.99/$3.50)

	NM- 9.2
1-12-Mike Allred-s/c/a. 1-Origin re-told; pin-ups by Rivoche and Powell. 3-Sale back-c	3.50
13-17-($3.50) Wraparound-c. 14-Back up w/Darwyn Cooke-a	3.50
All-New Giant-Size Super Ginchy Special (4/11, $5.99) Allred-s/a; back-ups/pin-ups	6.00
... Vol. 1 (2008, $19.99) r/#1-7; bonus art; Jamie Rich intro.	20.00

MADMAN COMICS (Also see The Atomics)
Dark Horse Comics (Legend No. 2 on): Apr, 1994 - No. 20, Dec, 2000 ($2.95/$2.99)

	GD 2.0	VG 4.0	FN 6.0	VF 8.0	VF/NM 9.0	NM- 9.2
1-Allred-c/a; F. Miller back-c.	1	2	3	5	6	8
2-3: 3-Alex Toth back-c.						5.00
4-11: 4-Dave Stevens back-c. 6,7-Miller/Darrow's Big Guy app. 6-Bruce Timm back-c. 7-Darrow back-c. 8-Origin?; Bagge back-c. 10-Allred/Ross-c; Ross back-c. 11-Frazetta back-c						4.00
12-16: 12-(4/99)						3.50
17-20: 17-The G-Men From Hell #1 on cover; Brereton back-c. 18-(#2). 19,20-($2.99-c). 20-Clowes back-c						3.50
... Boogaloo TPB (6/99, $8.95) r/Nexus Meets Madman & Madman/The Jam						9.00
... Gargantua! (2007, $125.00, HC with dustjacket) r/Madman#1-3, Madman Adventures #1-3, Madman Comics #1-20 and Madman King-Size Super Groovy Special; pin-ups						125.00
Image Firsts: Madman #1 (10/10, $1.00) r/#1						3.00
Ltd. Ed. Slipcover (1997, $99.95, signed and numbered) w/Vol.1 & Vol. 2. Vol.1- reprints #1-5; Vol. 2- reprints #6-10						100.00
The Complete Madman Comics: Vol. 2 (11/96, $17.95, TPB) r/#6-10 plus new material						18.00
Madman King-Size Super Groovy Special (Oni Press, 7/03, $6.95) new short stories by Allred, Derington, Krall and Weissman						7.00
Madman Picture Exhibition No. 1-4 (4-7/02, $3.95) pin-ups by various						4.00
Madman Picture Exhibition Limited Edition (10/02, $29.95) Hardcover collects MPE #1-4						30.00
... Volume 2 SC (2007, $17.99) r/#1-11; Erik Larsen intro.						18.00
... Volume 3 SC (2007, $17.99) r/#12-20 and story from King-Size Groovy; Allred intro.						18.00
Yearbook '95 (1996, $17.95, TPB)-r/#1-5, intro by Teller						18.00

MADMAN / THE JAM
Dark Horse Comics: Jul, 1998 - No. 2, Aug, 1998 ($2.95, mini-series)

	NM- 9.2
1,2-Allred & Mireault-s/a	4.00

MAD MONSTER PARTY (See Movie Classics)

MADNESS IN MURDERWORLD
Marvel Comics: 1989 (Came with computer game from Paragon Software)

	NM- 9.2
V1#1-Starring The X-Men	5.00

MADRAVEN HALLOWEEN SPECIAL
Hamilton Comics: Oct, 1995 ($2.95, one-shot)

	NM- 9.2
nn-Morrow-a	3.00

MADROX (from X-Factor)
Marvel Comics (Marvel Knights): Nov, 2004 - No. 5, Mar, 2005 ($2.99)

	NM- 9.2
1-5-Peter David-s/Pablo Raimondi-a; Strong Guy app.	3.00
...: Multiple Choice TPB (2005, $13.99) r/#1-5	14.00
X-Factor: Madrox - Multiple Choice HC (2008, $19.99) r/#1-5	20.00

MAD SPECIAL (...Super Special)
E. C. Publications, Inc.: Fall, 1970 - No. 141, Nov, 1999 (84 - 116 pgs.)
(If bonus is missing, issue is one half price)

	GD 2.0	VG 4.0	FN 6.0	VF 8.0	VF/NM 9.0	NM- 9.2
Fall 1970(#1)-Bonus-Voodoo Doll; contains 17 pgs. new material	9	18	27	58	114	170
Spring 1971(#2)-Wall Nuts; 17 pgs. new material	5	10	15	33	57	80
3-Protest Stickers	5	10	15	33	57	80
4-8: 4-Mini Posters. 5-Mad Flag. 6-Mad Mischief Stickers. 7-Presidential candidate posters, Wild Shocking Message posters. 8-TV Guise	5	10	15	30	50	70
9(1972)-Contains Nostalgic Mad #1 (28 pgs.)	4	8	12	25	40	55
10-13: 10-Nonsense Stickers (Don Martin). 13-Sickie Stickers; 3 pgs. Wolverton-r/Mad #137. 11-Contains 33-1/3 RPM record. 12-Contains Nostalgic Mad #2 (36 pgs.); Davis, Wolverton-a	3	6	9	19	30	40
14,16-21,24: 4-Vital Message posters & Art Depreciation paintings. 16-Mad-hesive Stickers. 17-Don Martin posters. 20-Martin Stickers. 18-Contains Nostalgic Mad #4 (36 pgs.). 21,24-Contains Nostalgic Mad #5 (28 pgs.) & #6 (28 pgs.)	3	6	9	16	23	30
15-Contains Nostalgic Mad #3 (28 pgs.)	3	6	9	16	24	32
22,23,25,27-29,30: 22-Diplomas. 23-Martin Stickers. 25-Martin Posters. 27-Mad Shock-Sticks. 28-Contains Nostalgic Mad #7 (36 pgs.). 29-Mad Collectable-Connectables Posters. 30-The Movies	2	4	6	9	13	16
26-Has 33-1/3 RPM record	2	4	6	13	18	22
31,33-35,37-50	2	4	6	8	11	14
32-Contains Nostalgic Mad #8. 36-Has 96 pgs. of comic book & comic strip spoofs: titles "The Comics" on-c	2	4	6	9	13	16
51-70	1	3	4	6	8	10
71-88,90-100: 71-Batman parodies-r by Wood, Drucker. 72-Wolverton-c r-from 1st panel in Mad #11; Wolverton-s r/new dialogue. 83-All Star Trek spoof issue	1	2	3	5	6	8
76-(Fall, 1991)-Special Hussein Asylum Edition; distributed only to the troops in the Middle East (see Mad #300-303)	2	4	6	13	18	22
89-($3.95)-Polybaged w/1st of 3 Spy vs. Spy hologram trading cards (direct sale only issue) (other cards came w/card set)	1	3	4	6	8	10
101-141: 117-Sci-Fi parodies-r.						4.00

NOTE: *#28-30 have no number on cover.* ***Freas*** *c-76.* ***Mingo*** *c-9, 11, 15, 19, 23.*

MAGDALENA, THE (See The Darkness #15-18)
Image Comics (Top Cow): Apr, 2000 - No. 3, Jan, 2001 ($2.50)

	NM- 9.2
Preview Special ('00, $4.95) Flip book w/Blood Legacy preview	5.00
1-Benitez-c/a; variant covers by Silvestri & Turner	3.00
2,3: 2-Two covers	3.00
.../Angelus #1/2 (11/01, $2.95) Benitez-c/Ching-a	3.00
...Blood Divine (2002, $9.95) r/#1-3 & #1/2; cover gallery	10.00
.../Vampirella (7/03, $2.99) Wohl-s/Benitez-a; two covers	3.00

MAGDALENA, THE (Volume 2)
Image Comics (Top Cow): Aug, 2003 - No. 4, Dec, 2003 ($2.99)

	NM- 9.2
Preview (6/03) B&W preview; Wizard World East logo on cover	3.00
1-4-Holguin-s/Basaldua-a	3.00
1-Variant-c by Jim Silke benefitting ACTOR charity	5.00
TPB Volume 1 (12/06, $19.99) r/both series, Darkness #15-18 & Magdalena/Angelus	20.00
.../Daredevil (5/08, $3.99) Phil Hester-s/a; Hester & Sejic-c	4.00
.../Vampirella (12/04, $2.99) Kirkman-s/Manapul-a; two covers by Manapul and Bachalo	3.00
... Vs. Dracula Monster War 2005 (6/05, $2.99) four covers; Joyce Chin-a	3.00

MAGDALENA, THE (Volume 3)
Image Comics (Top Cow): Apr, 2010 - No. 12, May, 2012 ($3.99)

	NM- 9.2
1-12: 1-Marz-s/Blake-a/Sook-c. 7,8-Keu Cha-a	4.00

MAGE (The Hero Discovered...; also see Grendel #16)
Comico: Feb, 1984 (no month) - No. 15, Dec, 1986 ($1.50, Mando paper)

	GD 2.0	VG 4.0	FN 6.0	VF 8.0	VF/NM 9.0	NM- 9.2
1-Comico's 1st color comic	2	4	6	8	11	14
2-5: 3-Intro Edsel						6.00
6-Grendel begins (1st in color)	3	6	9	14	20	25
7-1st new Grendel story	2	4	6	8	10	12
8-14: 13-Grendel dies. 14-Grendel story ends						6.00
15-($2.95) Double size w/pullout poster	1	2	3	5	6	8
Image Firsts: Mage - The Hero Discovered #1 (10/10, $1.00) r/#1 w/"Image Firsts" logo						3.00
TPB Volume 1-4 (Image, $5.95) 1- r/#1,2. 2- r/#3,4. 3- r/#5,6. 4- r/#7,8						7.00
TPB Volume 5-7 (Image, $6.95) 5- r/#9,10. 6- r/#11,12. 7- r/#13,14						7.00
TPB Volume 8 (Image, 9/99, $7.50) r/#15						7.50
..., Vol. 1 TPB (Image, 2004, $29.99) r/#1-15; cover gallery, promo artwork, bonus art						30.00

MAGE (The Hero Defined) (Volume 2)
Image Comics: July, 1997 - No. 15, Oct, 1999 ($2.50)

	NM- 9.2
0-(7/97, $5.00) American Ent. Ed.	5.00
1-14:Matt Wagner-c/s/a in all. 13-Three covers	3.00
1-"3-D Edition" (2/98, $4.95) w/glasses	5.00
15-($5.95) Acetate cover	6.00

Magic Comics #11 © DMP

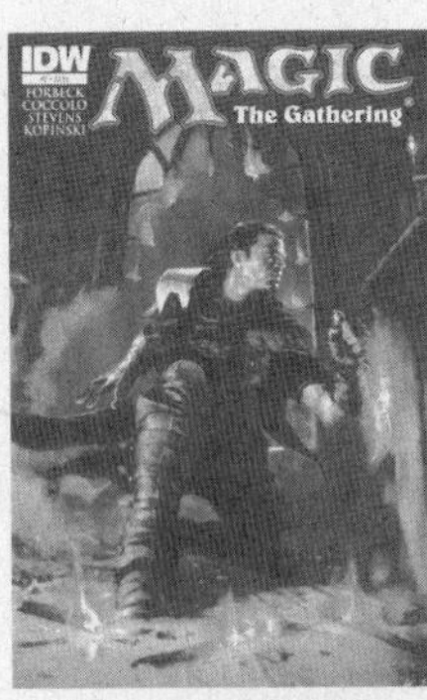

Magic: The Gathering #2 © WOTC

Magneto (2014 series) #1 © MAR

GD 2.0 | VG 4.0 | FN 6.0 | VF 8.0 | VF/NM 9.0 | NM- 9.2

Volume 1,2 TPB ('98,'99, $9.95) 1- r/#1-4. 2-r/#5-8 10.00
Volume 3 TPB ('00, $12.95) r/#9-12 13.00
Volume 4 TPB ('01, $14.95) r/#13-15 15.00
Hardcover Vol. 2 (2005, $49.95) r/#1-15; cover gallery, character design & sketch pages 50.00

MAGE KNIGHT: STOLEN DESTINY (Based on the fantasy game Mage Knight)
Idea + Design Works: Oct, 2002 - No. 5, Feb, 2003 ($3.50, limited series)

1-5: 1-J. Scott Campbell-c; Cabrera-a/Dezago-s, 2-Dave Johnson-c 3.50

MAGGIE AND HOPEY COLOR SPECIAL (See Love and Rockets)
Fantagraphics Books: May, 1997 ($3.50, one-shot)

1 4.00

MAGGIE THE CAT (Also see Jon Sable, Freelance #11 & Shaman's Tears #12)
Image Comics (Creative Fire Studio): Jan, 1996 - No. 2, Feb, 1996 ($2.50, unfinished limited series)

1,2: Mike Grell-c/a/scripts 3.00

MAGICA DE SPELL (See Walt Disney Showcase #30)

MAGIC AGENT (See Forbidden Worlds & Unknown Worlds)
American Comics Group: Jan-Feb, 1962 - No. 3, May-June, 1962

	GD	VG	FN	VF	VF/NM	NM-
1-Origin & 1st app. John Force	4	8	12	25	40	55
2,3	3	6	9	18	28	38

MAGICAL POKÉMON JOURNEY
Viz Comics: 2000 - Present ($4.95, B&W, magazine-size)

1-4 5.00
Part 2: 1-3; Part 3: 1-4: 1-Includes color poster; Part 4: 1-4; Part 5: 1-4; Part 6: 1-4 5.00

MAGIC COMICS
David McKay Publications: Aug, 1939 - No. 123, Nov-Dec, 1949

	GD	VG	FN	VF	VF/NM	NM-
1-Mandrake the Magician, Henry, Popeye , Blondie, Barney Baxter, Secret Agent X-9 (not by Raymond), Bunky by Billy DeBeck & Thornton Burgess text stories illustrated by Harrison Cady begin; Henry covers begin	356	712	1068	2065	3433	4800
2	126	252	378	731	1216	1700
3	93	186	279	539	895	1250
4	74	148	222	429	715	1000
5	62	124	186	360	598	835
6-10: 8-11,21-Mandrake/Henry funny covers	50	100	150	290	483	675
11-16,18,20: 12-20,22-24-Serious Mandrake mystery covers	48	96	144	278	464	650
17-The Lone Ranger begins	56	112	168	325	538	750
19-Classic robot-c (scarce)	119	238	357	690	1145	1600
21-24	37	74	111	222	361	500
25-1st Blondie-c	39	78	117	231	378	525
26-30: 26-Dagwood-c begin	30	60	90	177	289	400
31-40: 36-Flag-c	21	42	63	122	199	275
41-50	16	32	48	94	147	200
51-60	14	28	42	80	115	150
61-70	11	22	33	64	90	115
71-99, 107,108-Flash Gordon app; not by Raymond	10	20	30	54	72	90
100	10	20	30	58	79	100
101-106,109-123: 123-Last Dagwood-c	9	18	27	50	65	80

MAGIC FLUTE, THE (See Night Music #9-11)

MAGICIAN: APPRENTICE
Dabel Brothers/Marvel Comics (Dabel Brothers) #3 on: Mar, 2007 - No. 12, Dec, 2007 ($2.95/$2.99)

1-12-Adaptation of the Raymond E. Feist Riftwar Saga series 3.00
1,2-($5.95) 1-Wraparound variant-c by Maitz. 2-Wraparound variant-c by Booth 6.00
Collected Edition (10/06, $3.99) r/#1&2 4.00
Vol. 1 HC (2007, $19.99, dustjacket) r/#1-6; foreword by Feist 20.00
Vol. 1 SC (2007, $15.99) r/#1-6; foreword by Feist 16.00
Vol. 2 HC (2008, $19.99, dustjacket) r/#7-12 20.00

MAGIC PICKLE
Oni Press: Sept, 2001 - No. 4, Dec, 2001 ($2.95, limited series)

1-4-Scott Morse-s/a; Mahfood-a (2 pgs.) 3.00

MAGIC SWORD, THE (See Movie Classics)

MAGIC THE GATHERING (Title Series), **Acclaim Comics (Armada)**

...ANTIQUITIES WAR,11/95 - 2/96 ($2.50), 1-4-Paul Smith-a(p) 3.00
...ARABIAN NIGHTS, 12/95 - 1/96 ($2.50), 1,2 3.00
...COLLECTION ,'95 ($4.95), 1,2-polybagged 5.00
...CONVOCATIONS, '95 ($2.50), 1-nn-pin-ups 3.00
...ELDER DRAGONS ,'95 ($2.50), 1,2-Doug Wheatley-a 3.00
...FALLEN ANGEL ,'95 ($5.95), nn 6.00
...FALLEN EMPIRES ,9/95 - 10/95 ($2.75), 1,2 3.00
...Collection ($4.95)-polybagged 5.00
...HOMELANDS ,'95 ($5.95), nn-polybagged w/card; Hildebrandts-c 6.00
... ICE AGE (On The World of...) ,7/5 -11/95 ($2.50), 1-4: 1,2-bound-in Magic Card. 3,4-bound-in insert 3.00
...LEGEND OF JEDIT OJANEN, '96 ($2.50), 1,2 3.00
...NIGHTMARE, '95 ($2.50, one shot), 1 3.00
...THE SHADOW MAGE, 7/95 - 10/95 ($2.50), 1-4-bagged w/Magic The Gathering card 3.00
...Collection 1,2 (1995, $4.95)-Trade paperback; polybagged 5.00
...SHANDALAR ,'96 ($2.50), 1,2 3.00
...WAYFARER ,11/95 - 2/96 ($2.50), 1-5 3.00

MAGIC: THE GATHERING
IDW Publishing: Dec, 2011 - No. 4, Mar, 2012 ($3.99, limited series)

1-4-Forbeck-s/Cóccolo-a 4.00

MAGIC: THE GATHERING: GERRARD'S QUEST
Dark Horse Comics: Mar, 1998 - No. 4, June, 1998 ($2.95, limited series)

1-4: Grell-s/Mhan-a 3.00

MAGIC: THE GATHERING - PATH OF VENGEANCE
IDW Publishing: Oct, 2012 - No. 4, Feb, 2013 ($4.99, limited series, bagged with card)

1-4-Forbeck-s/Cóccolo-a 5.00

MAGIC: THE GATHERING - THEROS
IDW Publishing: Oct, 2013 - Present ($4.99, limited series, bagged with card)

1-5-Ciaramella-s/Cóccolo-a 5.00

MAGIC: THE GATHERING - THE SPELL THIEF
IDW Publishing: May, 2012 - No. 4, Aug, 2012 ($4.99, limited series, bagged with card)

1-4-Forbeck-s/Cóccolo-a 5.00

MAGIK (Illyana and Storm Limited Series)
Marvel Comics Group: Dec, 1983 - No. 4, Mar, 1984 (60¢, limited series)

1-4: 1-Characters from X-Men; Inferno begins; X-Men cameo (Buscema pencils in #1,2; c-1p. 2-4: 2-Nightcrawler app. & X-Men cameo 5.00

MAGIK (See Black Sun mini-series)
Marvel Comics: Dec, 2000 - No. 4, Mar, 2001 ($2.99, limited series)

1-4-Liam Sharp-a/Abnett & Lanning-s; Nightcrawler app. 3.00

MAGILLA GORILLA (TV) (See Kite Fun Book)
Gold Key: May, 1964 - No. 10, Dec, 1968 (Hanna-Barbera)

	GD	VG	FN	VF	VF/NM	NM-
1-1st comic app.	8	16	24	56	108	160
2-4: 3-Vs. Yogi Bear for President. 4-1st Punkin Puss & Mushmouse, Ricochet Rabbit & Droop-a-Long	5	10	15	33	57	80
5-10: 10-Reprints	4	8	12	28	47	65

MAGILLA GORILLA (TV)(See Spotlight #4)
Charlton Comics: Nov, 1970 - No. 5, July, 1971 (Hanna-Barbera)

	GD	VG	FN	VF	VF/NM	NM-
1	5	10	15	31	53	75
2-5	3	6	9	21	33	45

MAGNETIC MEN FEATURING MAGNETO
Marvel Comics (Amalgam): June, 1997 ($1.95, one-shot)

1-Tom Peyer-s/Barry Kitson & Dan Panosian-a 3.00

MAGNETO (See X-Men #1)
Marvel Comics: nd (Sept, 1993) (Giveaway) (one-shot)

0-Embossed foil-c by Sienkiewicz; r/Classic X-Men #19 & 12 by Bolton 5.00

MAGNETO
Marvel Comics: Nov, 1996 - No. 4, Feb, 1997 ($1.95, limited series)

1-4: Peter Milligan scripts & Kelley Jones-a(p) 3.00

MAGNETO
Marvel Comics: Mar, 2011 ($2.99, one-shot)

1-Howard Chaykin-s/a; Roger Cruz-c 3.00

MAGNETO
Marvel Comics: May, 2014 - Present ($3.99)

1,2: 1-Bunn-s/Walta-a/Rivera-c 4.00

MAGNETO AND THE MAGNETIC MEN
Marvel Comics (Amalgam): Apr, 1996 ($1.95, one-shot)

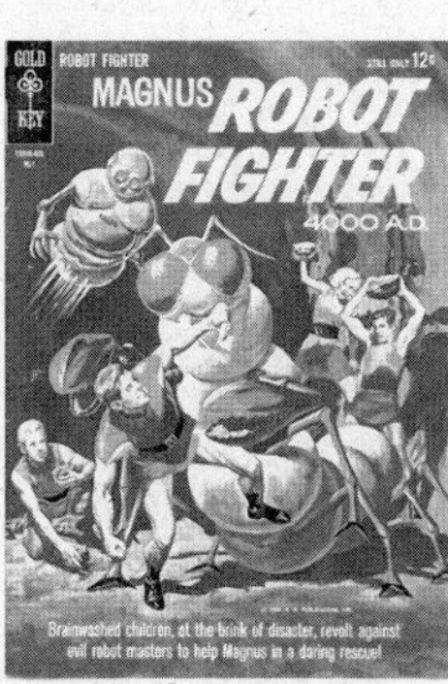

Magnus, Robot Fighter #20 © GK

Magog #12 © DC

Major Victory Comics #1 © CHES

	GD	VG	FN	VF	VF/NM	NM-
	2.0	4.0	6.0	8.0	9.0	9.2

1-Jeff Matsuda-a(p) 3.00

MAGNETO ASCENDANT
Marvel Comics: May, 1999 ($3.99, squarebound one-shot)

1-Reprints early Magneto appearances 4.00

MAGNETO: DARK SEDUCTION
Marvel Comics: Jun, 2000 - No. 4, Sept, 2000 ($2.99, limited series)

1-4: Nicieza-s/Cruz-a. 3,4-Avengers-c/app. 3.00

MAGNETO: NOT A HERO (X-Men Regenesis)
Marvel Comics: Jan, 2012 - No. 4, Apr, 2012 ($2.99, limited series)

1-4-Skottie Young-s/Clay Mann-a; Joseph returns 3.00

MAGNETO REX
Marvel Comics: Apr, 1999 - No. 3, July, 1999 ($2.50, limited series)

1-3-Rogue, Quicksilver app.; Peterson-a(p) 3.00

MAGNUS, ROBOT FIGHTER (...4000 A.D.)(See Doctor Solar)
Gold Key: Feb, 1963 - No. 46, Jan, 1977 (All painted covers except #5,30,31)

1-Origin & 1st app. Magnus; Aliens (1st app.) series begins 26 52 78 182 404 625
2,3 10 20 30 69 147 225
4-10: 10-Simonson fan club illo (5/65, 1st-a?) 7 14 21 46 86 125
11-20 5 10 15 33 57 80
21,24-28: 28-Aliens ends 4 8 12 25 40 55
22,23: 22-Origin-r/#1; last 12¢ issue 4 8 12 27 44 60
29-46-Mostly reprints 3 6 9 14 20 25
...: One For One (Dark Horse Comics, 9/10, $1.00) r/#1 3.00
Russ Manning's Magnus Robot Fighter - Vol. 1 HC (Dark Horse, 2004, $49.95) r/#1-7 70.00
Russ Manning's Magnus Robot Fighter - Vol. 2 HC (DH, 6/05, $49.95) r/#8-14; forward by Steve Rude 50.00
Russ Manning's Magnus Robot Fighter - Vol. 3 HC (Dark Horse, 10/06, $49.95) r/#15-21 50.00
NOTE: ***Manning** a-1-22, 28-43(r). **Spiegle** a-23, 44r.*

MAGNUS ROBOT FIGHTER (Also see Vintage Magnus)
Valiant/Acclaim Comics: May, 1991 - No. 64, Feb, 1996 ($1.75/$1.95/$2.25/$2.50)

1-Nichols/Layton-c/a; 1-8 have trading cards 2 4 6 9 12 15
2-4,6,8: 4-Rai cameo. 6-1st Solar x-over. 1 2 3 5 6 8
5-Origin & 1st full app. Rai (10/91); #5-8 are in flip book format and back-c & half of book are Rai #1-4 mini-series 2 4 6 8 10 12
7-Magnus vs. Rai-c/story; 1st X-O Armor 2 4 6 8 10 12
0-Origin issue; Layton-a; ordered through mail w/coupons from 1st 8 issues plus 50¢; B. Smith trading card 3 6 9 16 23 30
0-Sold thru comic shops without trading card 2 4 6 10 14 18
9-11 6.00
12-(3.25, 44 pgs.)-Turok-c/story (1st app. in Valiant universe, 5/92); has 8 pg. Magnus story insert 3 6 9 16 23 30
13-24,26-48: 14-1st app. Isak. 15,16-Unity x-overs. 15-Miller-c. 16-Birth of Magnus. 21-New direction & new logo. 21-Gold ink variant. 24-Story cont'd in Rai & the Future Force #9. 33-Timewalker app.36-Bound-in trading cards. 37-Rai & Starwatchers app. 44-Bound-in sneak peek card. 4.00
25-($2.95)-Embossed silver foil-c; new costume 5.00
49-63 4.00
64-($2.50): 64-Magnus dies? 1 2 3 5 6 8
...Invasion (1994, $9.95)-r/Rai #1-4 & Magnus #5-8 12.00
Magnus Steel Nation (1994, $9.95) r/#1-4 12.00
Yearbook (1994, $3.95, 52 pgs.) 5.00
NOTE: ***Ditko/Reese** a-18. **Layton** a(i)-5; c-6-9i, 25; back(i)-5-8. **Reese** a(i)-22, 25, 28; c(i)-22, 24, 28. **Simonson** c-16. Prices for issues 1-8 are for trading cards and coupons intact.*

MAGNUS ROBOT FIGHTER
Acclaim Comics (Valiant Heroes): V2#1, May, 1997 - No. 18, Jun, 1998 ($2.50)

1-18: 1-Reintro Magnus; Donavon Wylie (X-O Manowar) cameo; Tom Peyer scripts & Mike McKone-c/a begin; painted variant-c exists 3.00

MAGNUS ROBOT FIGHTER
Dark Horse Comics: Aug, 2010 - No. 4, May, 2011 ($3.50)

1-4: 1-Shooter-s/Reinhold-a; covers by Swanland & Reinhold; back-up r/#1 (1963) 3.50

MAGNUS ROBOT FIGHTER
Dynamite Entertainment: 2014 - Present ($3.99)

1,2-Fred Van Lente-s/Cory Smith-a; multiple covers on each 4.00

MAGNUS ROBOT FIGHTER/NEXUS
Valiant/Dark Horse Comics: Dec, 1993 - No. 2, Apr, 1994 ($2.95, lim. series)

1,2: Steve Rude painted-c & pencils in all 4.00

MAGOG (See Justice Society of America 2007 series)(Continues in Justice Society Special #1)
DC Comics: Nov, 2009 - No.12, Ot. 2010 ($2.99)

1-12: 1-Giffen-s/Porter-a/Fabry-c; variant-c by Porter. 7-Zatanna app. 3.00
...: Lethal Force TPB (2010, $14.99) r/#1-5 15.00

MAID OF THE MIST (See American Graphics)

MAI, THE PSYCHIC GIRL
Eclipse Comics: May, 1987 - No. 28, July, 1989 ($1.50, B&W, bi-weekly, 44pgs.)

1-28, 1,2-2nd print 4.00

MAJESTIC (Mr. Majestic from WildCATS)
DC Comics: Oct, 2004 - No. 4, Jan, 2005 ($2.95, limited series)

1-4-Kerschl-a/Abnett & Lanning-s. 1-Superman app.; Superman #1 cover swipe 3.00
...: Strange New Visitor TPB (2005, $14.99) r/#1-4 & Action #811, Advs. of Superman #624 & Superman #201 15.00

MAJESTIC (Mr. Majestic from WildCATS)
DC Comics (WildStorm): Mar, 2005 - No. 17, July, 2006 ($2.95/$2.99)

1-17: 1-Googe-a/Abnett & Lanning-s; Superman app. 9-Jeanty-a; Zealot app. 3.00
...: Meanwhile, Back on Earth... TPB (2006, $14.99) r/#8-12 15.00
...: The Final Cut TPB (2007, $14.99) r/#13-17 & story fro WildStorm Winter Special 15.00
...: While You Were Out TPB (2006, $12.99) r/#1-7 13.00

MAJOR BUMMER
DC Comics: Aug, 1997 - No. 15, Oct, 1998 ($2.50)

1-15: 1-Origin and 1st app. Major Bummer 3.00

MAJOR HOOPLE COMICS (See Crackajack Funnies)
Nedor Publications: nd (Jan, 1943)

1-Mary Worth, Phantom Soldier app. by Moldoff 38 76 114 219 352 485

MAJOR VICTORY COMICS (Also see Dynamic Comics)
H. Clay Glover/Service Publ./Harry 'A' Chesler: 1944 - No. 3, Summer, 1945

1-Origin Major Victory (patriotic hero) by C. Sultan (reprint from Dynamic #1); 1st app. Spider Woman 71 142 213 454 777 1100
2-Dynamic Boy app. 42 84 126 265 445 625
3-Rocket Boy app. 40 80 120 246 411 575

MALIBU ASHCAN: RAFFERTY (See Firearm #12)
Malibu Comics (Ultraverse): Nov, 1994 (99¢, B&W w/color-c; one-shot)

1-Previews "The Rafferty Saga" storyline in Firearm; Chaykin-c 3.00

MALTESE FALCON
David McKay Publications: No. 48, 1946

Feature Books 48-by Dashiell Hammett 90 180 270 576 988 1400

MALU IN THE LAND OF ADVENTURE
I. W. Enterprises: 1964 (See White Princess of Jungle #2)

1-r/Avon's Slave Girl Comics #1; Severin-c 4 8 12 28 47 65

MAMMOTH COMICS
Whitman Publishing Co.(K. K. Publ.): 1938 (84 pgs.) (B&W, 8-1/2x11-1/2")

1-Alley Oop, Terry & the Pirates, Dick Tracy, Little Orphan Annie, Wash Tubbs, Moon Mullins, Smilin' Jack, Tailspin Tommy, Don Winslow, Dan Dunn, Smokey Stover & other reprints (scarce) 219 438 657 1402 2401 3400

MAN AGAINST TIME
Image Comics (Motown Machineworks): May, 1996 - No. 4, Aug, 1996 ($2.25, lim. series)

1-4: 1-Simonson-c. 2,3-Leon-c. 4-Barreto & Leon-c 3.00

MAN-BAT (See Batman Family, Brave & the Bold, & Detective #400)
National Periodical Publ./DC Comics: Dec-Jan, 1975-76 - No. 2, Feb-Mar, 1976; Dec, 1984

1-Ditko-a(p); Aparo-c; Batman app.; 1st app. She-Bat? 3 6 9 16 23 30
2-Aparo-c 2 4 6 10 14 18
1 (12/84)-N. Adams-r(3)/Det.(Vs. Batman on-c) 6.00

MAN-BAT
DC Comics: Feb, 1996 - No. 3, Apr, 1996 ($2.25, limited series)

1-3: Dixon scripts in all. 2-Killer Croc-c/app. 3.00

MAN-BAT
DC Comics: Jun, 2006 - No. 5, Oct, 2006 ($2.99, limited series)

1-5: Bruce Jones-s/Mike Huddleston-a/c. 1-Hush app. 3.00

MAN CALLED A-X, THE
Malibu Comics (Bravura): Nov, 1994 - No. 4, Jun, 1995 ($2.95, limited series)

0-4: Marv Wolfman scripts & Shawn McManus-c/a. 0-(2/95). 1-"1A" on cover 3.00

MAN CALLED A-X, THE

Man Comics #10 © MAR

Man From Atlantis #4 © SOLOW

Manhunt! #4 © ME

	GD 2.0	VG 4.0	FN 6.0	VF 8.0	VF/NM 9.0	NM- 9.2

DC Comics: Oct, 1997 - No. 8, May, 1998 ($2.50)

1-8: Marv Wolfman scripts & Shawn McManus-c/a. 3.00

MAN CALLED KEV, A (See The Authority)
DC Comics (WildStorm): Sept, 2006 - No. 5, Feb, 2007 ($2.99, limited series)

1-5-Ennis-s/Ezquerra-a/Fabry-c 3.00
TPB (2007, $14.99) r/#1-5; cover gallery 15.00

MAN COMICS
Marvel/Atlas Comics (NPI): Dec, 1949 - No. 28, Sept, 1953 (#1-6: 52 pgs.)

	GD	VG	FN	VF	VF/NM	NM-
1-Tuska-a	27	54	81	158	259	360
2-Tuska-a	15	30	45	88	137	185
3-6	14	28	42	78	112	145
7,8	13	26	39	74	105	135
9-13,15: 9-Format changes to war	11	22	33	62	86	110
14-Henkel (3 pgs.); Pakula-a	11	22	33	64	90	115
16-21,23-28: 28-Crime issue (Bob Brant)	10	20	30	58	79	100
22-Krigstein-a, 5 pgs.	12	24	36	67	94	120

NOTE: ***Berg** a-14, 15, 19. **Colan** a-9, 21, 23. **Everett** a-8, 22; c-22, 25. **Heath** a-11, 13, 16, 17, 21. **Kubertish** a-by **Bob Brown**-3. **Maneely** a-11-13; c-10, 11, 16. **Reinman** a-11. **Robinson** a-7, 10, 14. **Robert Sale** a-9, 11. **Sinnott** a-22, 23. **Tuska** a-14, 23.*

MANDRAKE THE MAGICIAN (See Defenders Of The Earth, 123, 46, 52, 55, Giant Comic Album, King Comics, Magic Comics, The Phantom #21, Tiny Tot Funnies & Wow Comics, '36)

MANDRAKE THE MAGICIAN (See Harvey Comics Hits #53)
David McKay Publ./Dell/King Comics (All 12¢): 1938 - 1948; Sept, 1966 - No. 10, Nov, 1967

	GD	VG	FN	VF	VF/NM	NM-
Feature Books 18,19,23 (1938)	87	174	261	553	952	1350
Feature Books 46	52	104	156	328	552	775
Feature Books 52,55	42	84	126	265	445	625
Four Color 752 (11/56)	9	18	27	60	120	180
1-Begin S.O.S. Phantom, ends #3	5	10	15	34	60	85
2-7,9: 4-Girl Phantom app. 5-Flying Saucer-c/story. 5,6-Brick Bradford app. 7-Origin Lothar. 9-Brick Bradford app.	3	6	9	21	33	45
8-Jeff Jones-a (4 pgs.)	4	8	12	23	37	50
10-Rip Kirby app.; Raymond-a (14 pgs.)	4	8	12	27	44	60

MANDRAKE THE MAGICIAN
Marvel Comics: Apr, 1995 - No. 2, May, 1995 ($2.95, unfinished limited series)

1,2: Mike Barr scripts 3.00

MAN-EATING COW (See Tick #7,8)
New England Comics: July, 1992 - No. 10, 1994? ($2.75, B&W, limited series)

1-10 3.00
Man-Eating Cow Bonanza (6/96, $4.95, 128 pgs.)-r/#1-4. 5.00

MAN FROM ATLANTIS (TV)
Marvel Comics: Feb, 1978 - No. 7, Aug, 1978

	GD	VG	FN	VF	VF/NM	NM-
1-(84 pgs.)-Sutton-a(p), Buscema-c; origin & cast photos	2	4	6	8	12	15
2-7						6.00

MAN FROM PLANET X, THE
Planet X Productions: 1987 (no price; probably unlicensed)

1-Reprints Fawcett Movie Comic 3.00

MAN FROM U.N.C.L.E., THE (TV) (Also see The Girl From Uncle)
Gold Key: Feb, 1965 - No. 22, Apr, 1969 (All photo-c)

	GD	VG	FN	VF	VF/NM	NM-
1	11	22	33	73	157	240
2-Photo back c-2-8	6	12	18	42	79	115
3-10: 7-Jet Dream begins (1st app., also see Jet Dream) (all new stories)	5	10	15	33	57	80
11-22: 19-Last 12¢ issue. 21,22-Reprint #10 & 7	5	10	15	30	50	70

MAN FROM U.N.C.L.E., THE (TV)
Entertainment Publishing: 1987 - No. 11 ($1.50/$1.75, B&W)

1-7 ($1.50), 8-11 ($1.75) 4.00

MAN FROM WELLS FARGO (TV)
Dell Publishing Co.: No. 1287, Feb-Apr, 1962 - May-July, 1962 (Photo-c)

	GD	VG	FN	VF	VF/NM	NM-
Four Color 1287, #01-495-207	5	10	15	33	57	80

MANGA DARKCHYLDE (Also see Darkchylde titles)
Dark Horse Comics: Feb, 2005 - No. 5 ($2.99, limited series)

1,2-Randy Queen-s/a; manga-style pre-teen Ariel Chylde 3.00

MANGA SHI (See Tomoe)
Crusade Entertainment: Aug, 1996 ($2.95)

1-Printed back to front (manga-style) 3.00

MANGA SHI 2000
Crusade Entertainment: Feb, 1997 - No. 3, June, 1997 ($2.95, mini-series)

1-3: 1-Two covers 3.00

MANGA ZEN (Also see Zen Intergalactic Ninja)
Zen Comics (Fusion Studios): 1996 - No. 3, 1996 ($2.50, B&W)

1-3 3.00

MANGAZINE
Antarctic Press: Aug, 1985 - No. 4, Sept, 1986 (B&W)

	GD	VG	FN	VF	VF/NM	NM-
1-Soft paper-c	2	4	6	11	16	20
2-4	2	4	6	8	11	14

MANHATTAN PROJECTS, THE
Image Comics: Mar, 2012 - Present ($3.50)

1-Hickman-s/Pitarra-a; intro. Robert and Joseph Oppenheimer 40.00
2 20.00
3 10.00
4-6 8.00
7-19: 10,15,19-Browne-a 4.00

MANHUNT! (Becomes Red Fox #15 on)
Magazine Enterprises: 10/47 - No. 11, 8/48; #13,14, 1953 (no #12)

	GD	VG	FN	VF	VF/NM	NM-
1-Red Fox by L. B. Cole, Undercover Girl by Whitney, Space Ace begin (1st app.); negligee panels	60	120	180	381	653	925
2-Electrocution-c	47	94	141	296	498	700
3-6: 6-Bondage-c	39	78	117	231	378	525
7-10: 7-Space Ace ends. 8-Trail Colt begins (intro/1st app., 5/48) by Guardineer; Trail Colt-c. 10-G. Ingels-a	34	68	102	199	325	450
11(8/48)-Frazetta-a, 7 pgs.; The Duke, Scotland Yard begin	43	86	129	271	461	650
13(A-1 #63)-Frazetta, r-/Trail Colt #1, 7 pgs.	39	78	117	240	395	550
14(A-1 #77)-Bondage/hypo-c; last L. B. Cole Red Fox; Ingels-a	50	100	150	315	533	750

NOTE: ***Guardineer** a-1-5; c-8. **Whitney** a-2-14; c-1-6, 10. Red Fox by **L. B. Cole**-#1-14. #15 was advertised but came out as Red Fox #15.*

MANHUNTER (See Adventure #58, 73, Brave & the Bold, Detective Comics, 1st Issue Special, House of Mystery #143 and Justice League of America)
DC Comics: 1984 ($2.50, 76 pgs; high quality paper)

1-Simonson-c/a(r)/Detective; Batman app. 4.00

MANHUNTER
DC Comics: July, 1988 - No. 24, Apr, 1990 ($1.00)

1-24: 8,9-Flash app. 9-Invasion. 17-Batman-c/sty 3.00

MANHUNTER
DC Comics: No. 0, Nov, 1994 - No. 12, Nov, 1995 ($1.95/$2.25)

0-12 3.00

MANHUNTER (Also see Batman: Streets of Gotham)
DC Comics: Oct, 2004 - No. 38, Mar, 2009 ($2.50/$2.99)

1-21: 1-Intro. Kate Spencer; Saiz-a/Jae Lee-c/Andreyko-s. 2,3 Shadow Thief app. 13,14-Omac x-over. 20-One Year Later 3.00
22-30: 22-Begin $2.99-c. 23-Sandra Knight app. 27-Chaykin-c. 28-Batman app. 3.00
31-38: 31-(8/08) Gaydos-a. 33,34-Suicide Squad app. 3.00
...: Forgotten (2009, $17.99) r/#31-38 18.00
...: Origins (2007, $17.99) r/#15-23 18.00
...: Street Justice (2005, $12.99) r/#1-5; Andreyko intro. 13.00
...: Trial By Fire (2007, $17.99) r/#6-14 18.00
...: Unleashed (2008, $17.99) r/#24-30 18.00

MANHUNTER: ...
DC Comics: 1979, 1999

The Complete Saga TPB (1979) Reprints stories from Detective Comics #437-443 by Goodwin and Simonson 40.00
The Special Edition TPB (1999, $9.95) r/stories from Detective Comics #437-443 12.00

MANIFEST ETERNITY
DC Comics: Aug, 2006 - No. 6, Jan, 2007 ($2.99)

1-6-Lobdell-s/Nguyen-a/c 3.00

MAN IN BLACK (See Thrill-O-Rama) (Also see All New Comics, Front Page, Green Hornet #31, Strange Story & Tally-Ho Comics)
Harvey Publications: Sept, 1957 - No. 4, Mar, 1958

	GD	VG	FN	VF	VF/NM	NM-
1-Bob Powell-c/a	18	36	54	105	165	225
2-4: Powell-c/a	14	28	42	80	115	150

MAN IN BLACK
Lorne-Harvey Publications (Recollections): 1990 - No. 2, July, 1991 (B&W)

Man of War #8 © MAL

Man-Thing V3 #6 © MAR

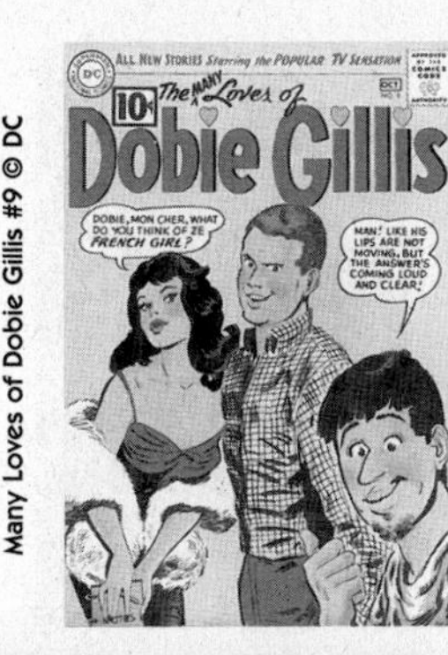

Many Loves of Dobie Gillis #9 © DC

GD 2.0 | VG 4.0 | FN 6.0 | VF 8.0 | VF/NM 9.0 | NM- 9.2

1,2 4.00

MAN IN FLIGHT (Disney, TV)
Dell Publishing Co.: No. 836, Sept, 1957
Four Color 836 6 12 18 40 73 105

MAN IN SPACE (Disney, TV, see Dell Giant #27)
Dell Publishing Co.: No. 716, Aug, 1956 - No. 954, Nov, 1958
Four Color 716-A science feat. from Tomorrowland 7 14 21 48 89 130
Four Color 954-Satellites 6 12 18 40 73 105

MANKIND (WWF Wrestling)
Chaos Comics: Sept, 1999 ($2.95, one-shot)
1-Regular and photo-c 3.00
1-Premium Edition ($10.00) Dwayne Turner & Danny Miki-c 10.00

MANN AND SUPERMAN
DC Comics: 2000 ($5.95, prestige format, one-shot)
nn-Michael T. Gilbert-s/a 6.00

MAN OF STEEL, THE (Also see Superman: The Man of Steel)
DC Comics: 1986 (June release) - No. 6, 1986 (75¢, limited series)
1-6: 1-Silver logo; Byrne-c/a/scripts in all; origin, 1-Alternate-c for newsstand sales,1-Distr. to toy stores by So Much Fun, 2-6: 2-Intro. Lois Lane, Jimmy Olsen. 3-Intro/origin Magpie; Batman-c/story. 4-Intro. new Lex Luthor 1 2 3 5 6 8
1-6-Silver Editions (1993, $1.95)-r/1-6 3.00
...The Complete Saga nn (SC)-Contains #1-6, given away in contest; limited edition 4 8 12 28 47 65
NOTE: *Issues 1-6 were released between Action #583 (9/86) & Action #584 (1/87) plus Superman #423 (9/86) & Advs. of Superman #424 (1/87).*

MAN OF THE ATOM (See Solar, Man of the Atom Vol. 2)

MAN OF WAR (See Liberty Guards & Liberty Scouts)
Centaur Publications: Nov, 1941 - No. 2, Jan, 1942
1-The Fire-Man, Man of War, The Sentinel, Liberty Guards, & Vapo-Man begin; Gustavson-c/a; Flag-c 187 374 561 1197 2049 2900
2-Intro The Ferret; Gustavson-c/a 132 264 396 845 1448 2050

MAN OF WAR
Eclipse Comics: Aug, 1987 - No. 3, Feb, 1988 ($1.75, Baxter paper)
1-3: Bruce Jones scripts 3.00

MAN OF WAR (See The Protectors)
Malibu Comics: 1993 - No, 8, Feb, 1994 ($1.95/$2.50/$2.25)
1-5 ($1.95)-Newsstand Editions w/different-c 3.00
1-8: 1-5-Collector's Edi. w/poster. 6-8 ($2.25): 6-Polybagged w/Skycap. 8-Vs. Rocket Rangers 4.00

MAN O' MARS
Fiction House Magazines: 1953; 1964
1-Space Rangers; Whitman-c 50 100 150 315 533 750
I.W. Reprint #1-r/Man O'Mars #1 & Star Pirate; Murphy Anderson-a 5 10 15 35 63 90

MANTECH ROBOT WARRIORS
Archie Enterprises, Inc.: Sept, 1984 - No. 4, Apr, 1985 (75¢)
1-4: Ayers-c/a(p). 1-Buckler-c(i) 4.00

MAN-THING (See Fear, Giant-Size..., Marvel Comics Presents, Marvel Fanfare, Monsters Unleashed, Power Record Comics & Savage Tales)
Marvel Comics Group: Jan, 1974 - No. 22, Oct, 1975; V2#1, Nov, 1979 - V2#11, July, 1981
1-Howard the Duck(2nd app.) cont'd/Fear #19 6 12 18 38 69 100
2 3 6 9 17 26 35
3-1st app. original Foolkiller 3 6 9 15 22 28
4-Origin Foolkiller; last app. 1st Foolkiller 3 6 9 14 20 26
5-11-Ploog-a. 11-Foolkiller cameo (flashback) 3 6 9 14 20 26
12-22: 19-1st app. Scavenger. 20-Spidey cameo. 21-Origin Scavenger, Man-Thing. 22-Howard the Duck cameo 2 4 6 9 13 16
V2#1(1979) 2 4 6 8 10 12
V2#2-11: 4-Dr. Strange-c/app. 11-Mayerik-a 6.00
NOTE: ***Alcala** a-14. **Brunner** c-1. J. **Buscema** a-12p, 13p, 16p. **Gil Kane** c-4p, 10p, 12-20p, 21. **Mooney** a-17, 18, 19p, 20-22, V2#1-3p. **Ploog** Man-Thing-5p, 6p, 7, 8, 9-11p; c-5, 6, 8, 9, 11. **Sutton** a-13i. No. 19 says #10 in indicia.*

MAN-THING (Volume Three, continues in Strange Tales #1 (9/98))
Marvel Comics: Dec, 1997 - No. 8, July, 1998 ($2.99)
1-8-DeMatteis-s/Sharp-a. 2-Two covers. 6-Howard the Duck-c/app. 3.00

MAN-THING (Prequel to 2005 movie)
Marvel Comics: Sept, 2004 - No. 3, Nov, 2004 ($2.99, limited series)
1-3-Hans Rodionoff-s/Kyle Hotz-a 3.00
...: Whatever Knows Fear... (2005, $12.99, TPB) r/#1-3, Savage Tales #1, Adv. Into Fear #16 13.00

MANTRA
Malibu Comics (Ultraverse): July, 1993 - No. 24, Aug, 1995 ($1.95/$2.50)
1-Polybagged w/trading card & coupon 5.00
1-Newsstand edition w/o trading card or coupon 3.00
1-Full cover holographic edition 2 4 6 8 10 12
1-Ultra-limited silver foil-c 1 2 3 5 6 8
2,3,5-9,11-24: 2-($2.50-Newsstand edition bagged w/card. 3-Intro Warstrike & Kismet. 6-Break-Thru x-over. 7-Prime app.; origin Prototype by Jurgens/Austin (2 pgs.). 11-New costume. 17-Intro NecroMantra & Pinnacle; prelude to Godwheel 3.00
4-($2.50, 48 pgs.)-Rune flip-c/story by B. Smith (3 pgs.) 4.00
10-($3.50, 68 pgs.)-Flip-c w/Ultraverse Premiere #2 4.00
Giant Size 1 (7/94, $2.50, 44 pgs.) 4.00
...Spear of Destiny 1,2 (4/95, $2.50, 36pgs.) 3.00

MANTRA (2nd Series) (Also See Black September)
Malibu Comics (Ultraverse): Infinity, Sept, 1995 - No. 7, Apr, 1996 ($1.50)
Infinity (9/95, $1.50)-Black September x-over, Intro new Mantra 3.00
1-7: 1-(10/95). 5-Return of Eden (original Mantra). 6,7-Rush app. 3.00

MAN WITH NO NAME, THE (Based on the Clint Eastwood gunslinger character)
Dynamite Entertainment: 2008 - No. 11, 2009 ($3.50)
1-11: 1-Gage-s/Dias-a/Isanove-c. 7-Bernard-a 3.50

MAN WITH THE SCREAMING BRAIN (Based on screenplay by Bruce Campbell & David Goodman)
Dark Horse Comics: Apr, 2005 - No. 4, July, 2005 ($2.99, limited series)
1-4-Campbell & Goodman-s; Remender-a/c. 1-Variant-c by Noto. 3-Powell var-c. 4-Mignola var-c 3.00
TPB (11/05, $13.95) r/#1-4; David Goodman intro.; cover gallery 14.00

MAN WITH THE X-RAY EYES, THE (See X,... under Movie Comics)

MANY GHOSTS OF DR. GRAVES, THE (Doctor Graves #73 on)
Charlton Comics: 5/67 - No. 60, 12/76; No. 61, 9/77 - No. 62, 10/77; No. 63, 2/78 - No. 65, 4/78; No. 66, 6/81 - No. 72, 5/82
1-Ditko-a; Palais-a; early issues 12¢-c 7 14 21 44 82 120
2-6,8,10 3 6 9 19 30 40
7,9-Ditko-a 4 8 12 23 37 50
11-13,16-18-Ditko-c/a 3 6 9 19 30 40
14,19,23,25 2 4 6 10 14 18
15,20,21-Ditko-a 3 6 9 14 20 25
22,24,26,27,29-35,38,40-Ditko-c/a 3 6 9 15 22 28
28-Ditko-c 3 6 9 14 20 25
36,46,56,57,59,61,66,67,69,71 2 4 6 8 10 12
37,41,43,51,60-Ditko-a 2 4 6 9 13 16
39,58-Ditko-c. 39-Sutton-a. 58-Ditko-a 2 4 6 9 13 16
42,44,53-Sutton-c; Ditko-a. 42-Sutton-a 2 4 6 9 13 16
45-(5/74) 2nd Newton comic work (8 pgs.); new logo; Sutton-c 2 4 6 11 16 20
47-Newton, Sutton, Ditko-a 2 4 6 10 14 18
48-Ditko, Sutton-a 2 4 6 9 13 16
49-Newton-c/a; Sutton-a. 2 4 6 8 11 14
50-Sutton-a 2 4 6 8 10 12
52-Newton-c; Ditko-a 2 4 6 9 13 16
54-Early Byrne-c; Ditko-a 2 4 6 10 14 18
55-Ditko-c; Sutton-a 2 4 6 9 13 16
62-65,68-Ditko-c/a. 65-Sutton-a 2 4 6 11 16 20
70,72-Ditko-a 2 4 6 10 14 18
Modern Comics Reprint 12,25 (1978) 6.00
NOTE: ***Aparo** a-4, 5, 7, 8, 66r, 69r; c-8, 14, 19, 66r, 67r. **Byrne** c-54. **Ditko** a-1, 7, 9, 11-13, 15-18, 20-22, 24, 26, 27, 29, 30-35, 37, 38, 40-44, 47, 48, 51-54, 58, 60r-65r, 70, 72; c-11-13, 16-18, 22, 24, 26-35, 38, 40, 55, 58, 62-65. **Howard** a-38, 39, 45i, 65; c-48. **Kim** a-36, 46, 52. **Larson** a-58. **Morisi** a-13, 14, 23, 26. **Newton** a-45, 47p, 49p; c-49, 52. **Staton** a-36, 37, 41, 43. **Sutton** a-39, 42, 47-50, 55, 65; c-42, 44, 45; painted c-53. **Zeck** a-56, 59.*

MANY LOVES OF DOBIE GILLIS (TV)
National Periodical Publications: May-June, 1960 - No. 26, Oct, 1964
1-Most covers by Bob Oskner 22 44 66 154 340 525
2-5 12 24 36 79 170 260
6-10: 10-Last 10¢-c 9 18 27 57 111 165
11-26: 20-Drucker-a. 24-(3-4/64). 25-(9/64) 8 16 24 51 96 140

MANY WORLDS OF TESLA STRONG, THE (Also see Tom Strong)
America's Best Comics: July, 2003 ($5.95, one-shot)
1-Two covers by Timm & Art Adams; art by various incl. Campbell, Cho, Noto, Hughes 6.00

MARA

Marc Spector: Moon Knight #15 © MAR

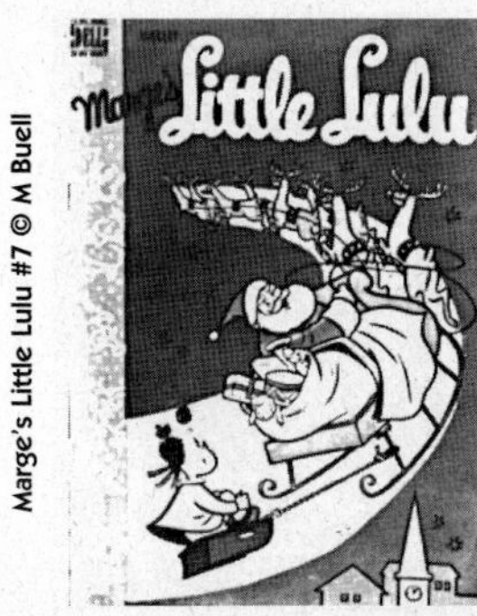

Marge's Little Lulu #7 © M Buell

Marines in Battle #1 © ATLAS

Image Comics: Dec, 2012 - No. 6, Oct, 2013 ($2.99)

	GD 2.0	VG 4.0	FN 6.0	VF 8.0	VF/NM 9.0	NM- 9.2
1-6-Brian Wood-s/Ming Doyle-a						3.00

MARAUDER'S MOON (See Luke Short, Four Color #848)

MARCH OF COMICS (See Promotional Comics section)

MARCH OF CRIME (Formerly My Love Affair #1-6) (See Fox Giants)
Fox Features Synd.: No. 7, July, 1950 - No. 2, Sept, 1950; No. 3, Sept, 1951

	GD 2.0	VG 4.0	FN 6.0	VF 8.0	VF/NM 9.0	NM- 9.2
7(#1)(7/50)-True crime stories; Wood-a	42	84	126	265	445	625
2(9/50)-Wood-a (exceptional)	41	82	123	256	428	600
3(9/51)	22	44	66	128	209	290

MARCO POLO (Also see Classic Comics #27
Charlton Comics Group: 1962 (Movie classic)

	GD 2.0	VG 4.0	FN 6.0	VF 8.0	VF/NM 9.0	NM- 9.2
nn (Scarce)-Glanzman-c/a (25 pgs.)	9	18	27	61	123	185

MARC SILVESTRI SKETCHBOOK
Image Comics (Top Cow): Jan, 2004 ($2.99, one-shot)

	GD 2.0	VG 4.0	FN 6.0	VF 8.0	VF/NM 9.0	NM- 9.2
1-Character sketches, concept artwork, storyboards of Witchblade, Darkness & others						3.00

MARC SPECTOR: MOON KNIGHT (Also see Moon Knight)
Marvel Comics: June, 1989 - No. 60, Mar, 1994 ($1.50/$1.75, direct sales)

	GD 2.0	VG 4.0	FN 6.0	VF 8.0	VF/NM 9.0	NM- 9.2
1-24,26-49,51-54,58,59: 4-Intro new Midnight. 8,9-Punisher app. 15-Silver Sable app. 19-21-Spider-Man & Punisher app. 32,33-Hobgoblin II (Macendale) & Spider-Man (in black costume) app. 35-38-Punisher story. 42-44-Infinity War x-over. 46-Demogoblin app. 51,53-Gambit app. 55-New look. 57-Spider-Man-c/story. 60-Moon Knight dies						3.00
25,50: 25-(52 pgs.)-Ghost Rider app. 50-(56 pgs.)-Special die-cut-c						4.00
55-57,60-Platt a						4.00
...: Divided We Fall ($4.95, 52 pgs.)						5.00
Special 1 (1992, $2.50)						4.00

NOTE: *Cowan c(p) 20-23. Guice c-20. Heath c/a-4. Platt -a 55-57,60; c-55-60.*

MARGARET O'BRIEN (See The Adventures of...)

MARGE'S LITTLE LULU (Continues as Little Lulu from #207 on)
Dell Publishing Co./Gold Key #165-206: No. 74, 6/45 - No. 164, 7-9/62; No. 165, 10/62 - No. 206, 8/72

Marjorie Henderson Buell, born in Philadelphia, Pa., in 1904, created Little Lulu, a cartoon character that appeared weekly in the Saturday Evening Post from Feb. 23, 1935 through Dec. 30, 1944. She was not responsible for any of the comic books. **John Stanley** did pencils only on all Little Lulu comics through at least #135 (1959). He did pencils and inks on Four Color #74 & 97. **Irving Tripp** began inking stories from #1 on, and remained the comic's illustrator throughout its entire run. **Stanley** did storyboards (layouts), pencils, and scripts in all cases and inking only on covers. His word balloons were written in cursive. **Tripp** and occasionally other artists at Western Publ. in Poughkeepsie, N.Y. blew up the pencilled pages, inked the blowups, and lettered them. **Arnold Drake** did storyboards, pencils and scripts starting with #197 (1970) on, amidst reprinted issues. **Buell** sold her rights exclusively to Western Publ. in Dec., 1971. The earlier issues had to be approved by **Buell** prior to publication.

	GD 2.0	VG 4.0	FN 6.0	VF 8.0	VF/NM 9.0	NM- 9.2
Four Color 74('45)-Intro Lulu, Tubby & Alvin	155	310	465	1279	2890	4500
Four Color 97(2/46)	59	118	177	472	1061	1650
(Above two books are all John Stanley - cover, pencils, and inks.)						
Four Color 110('46)-1st Alvin Story Telling Time; 1st app. Willy; variant cover exists	38	76	114	285	641	1000
Four Color 115-1st app. Boys' Clubhouse	38	76	114	281	628	975
Four Color 120, 131: 120-1st app. Eddie	32	64	96	230	515	800
Four Color 139('47),146,158	31	62	93	223	499	775
Four Color 165 (10/47)-Smokes doll hair & has wild hallucinations. 1st Tubby detective story	31	62	93	223	499	775
1(1-2/48)-Lulu's Diary feature begins	69	138	207	552	1239	1925
2-1st app. Gloria; 1st app. Miss Feeny	30	60	90	216	483	750
3-5	27	54	81	194	435	675
6-10: 7-1st app. Annie; Xmas-c	21	42	63	150	330	510
11-20: 18-X-Mas-c. 19-1st app. Wilbur. 20-1st app. Mr. McNabbem	17	34	51	114	252	390
21-30: 26-r/F.C. 110. 30-Xmas-c	15	30	45	100	220	340
31-38,40: 35-1st Mumday story	12	24	36	81	176	270
39-Intro. Witch Hazel in "That Awful Witch Hazel"	12	24	36	82	179	275
41-60: 42-Xmas-c. 45-2nd Witch Hazel app. 49-Gives Stanley & others credit	10	20	30	69	147	225
61-80: 63-1st app. Chubby (Tubby's cousin). 68-1st app. Prof. Cleff. 78-Xmas-c. 80-Intro. Little Itch (2/55)	9	18	27	57	111	165
81-99: 90-Xmas-c	7	14	21	46	86	125
100	7	14	21	49	92	135
101-130: 123-1st app. Fifi	6	12	18	37	66	95
131-164: 135-Last Stanley-p	5	10	15	33	57	80
165-Giant; ...in Paris ('62)	9	18	27	61	123	185
166-Giant; ...Christmas Diary (1962 - '63)	9	18	27	61	123	185
167-169	4	8	12	28	47	65
170,172,175,176,178-196,198-200-Stanley-r. 182-1st app. Little Scarecrow Boy	3	6	9	17	26	35
171,173,174,177,197	3	6	9	16	23	30
201,203,206-Last issue to carry Marge's name	3	6	9	14	20	26
202,204,205-Stanley-r	3	6	9	16	23	30
...Summer Camp 1(8/67-G.K.-Giant) '57-58-r	5	10	15	35	63	90
...Trick 'N' Treat 1(12¢)(12/62-Gold Key)	6	12	18	40	73	105
Marge's Lulu and Tubby in Japan (15¢)(5-7/62) 01476-207	7	14	21	44	82	120

NOTE: *See Dell Giant Comics #23, 29, 36, 42, 50, & Dell Giants for annuals. All Giants not by Stanley from L.L. on Vacation (7/54) on. Irving Tripp a-#1-on. Christmas c-7, 18, 30, 42, 78, 90, 126, 166, 250. Summer Camp issues #173, 177, 181, 189, 197, 201, 206.*

MARGE'S LITTLE LULU (See Golden Comics Digest #19, 23, 27, 29, 33, 36, 40, 43, 46, & March of Comics #251, 267, 275, 293, 307, 323, 335, 349, 355, 369, 385, 406, 417, 427, 439, 456, 468, 475, 488)

MARGE'S TUBBY (Little Lulu)(See Dell Giants)
Dell Publishing Co./Gold Key: No. 381, Aug, 1952 - No. 49, Dec-Feb, 1961-62

	GD 2.0	VG 4.0	FN 6.0	VF 8.0	VF/NM 9.0	NM- 9.2
Four Color 381(#1)-Stanley script; Irving Tripp-a	17	34	51	119	265	410
Four Color 430,444-Stanley-a	10	20	30	69	147	225
Four Color 461 (4/53)-1st Tubby & Men From Mars story; Stanley-a	10	20	30	64	132	200
5 (7-9/53)-Stanley-a	8	16	24	54	102	150
6-10	7	14	21	44	82	120
11-20	5	10	15	34	60	85
21-30	5	10	15	30	50	70
31-49	4	8	12	27	44	60
...& the Little Men From Mars No. 30020-410(10/64-G.K.)-25¢, 68 pgs.	7	14	21	44	82	120

NOTE: ***John Stanley** did all storyboards & scripts through at least #35 (1959). **Lloyd White** did all art except F.C. 381, 430, 444, 461 & #5.*

MARGIE (See My Little...)

MARGIE (TV)
Dell Publ. Co.: No. 1307, Mar-May, 1962 - No. 2, July-Sept, 1962 (Photo-c)

	GD 2.0	VG 4.0	FN 6.0	VF 8.0	VF/NM 9.0	NM- 9.2
Four Color 1307(#1)	5	10	15	34	60	85
2	4	8	12	28	47	65

MARGIE COMICS (Formerly Comedy Comics; Reno Browne #50 on)
(Also see Cindy Comics & Teen Comics)
Marvel Comics (ACI): No. 35, Winter, 1946-47 - No. 49, Dec, 1949

	GD 2.0	VG 4.0	FN 6.0	VF 8.0	VF/NM 9.0	NM- 9.2
35	21	42	63	122	199	275
36-38,42,45,47-49	14	28	42	76	108	140
39,41,43(2),44,46-Kurtzman's "Hey Look"	14	28	42	81	118	155
40-Three "Hey Looks", three "Giggles 'n' Grins" by Kurtzman	15	30	45	85	130	175

MARINEMAN (Ian Churchill's...)
Image Comics: Dec, 2010 - No. 6, Jun, 2011 ($3.99/$4.99)

	GD 2.0	VG 4.0	FN 6.0	VF 8.0	VF/NM 9.0	NM- 9.2
1-5-Ian Churchill-s/a/c						4.00
6-($4.99) Origin revealed						5.00

MARINES (See Tell It to the...)

MARINES ATTACK
Charlton Comics: Aug, 1964 - No. 9, Feb-Mar, 1966

	GD 2.0	VG 4.0	FN 6.0	VF 8.0	VF/NM 9.0	NM- 9.2
1-Glanzman-a begins	4	8	12	23	37	50
2-9: 8-1st Vietnam war-c/story	3	6	9	16	23	30

MARINES AT WAR (Formerly Tales of the Marines #4)
Atlas Comics (OPI): No. 5, Apr, 1957 - No. 7, Aug, 1957

	GD 2.0	VG 4.0	FN 6.0	VF 8.0	VF/NM 9.0	NM- 9.2
5-7	12	24	36	67	94	120

NOTE: ***Colan** a-5. **Drucker** a-5. **Everett** a-5. **Maneely** a-5. **Orlando** a-7. **Severin** c-5.*

MARINES IN ACTION
Atlas News Co.: June, 1955 - No. 14, Sept, 1957

	GD 2.0	VG 4.0	FN 6.0	VF 8.0	VF/NM 9.0	NM- 9.2
1-Rock Murdock, Boot Camp Brady begin	15	30	45	86	133	180
2-14	12	24	36	67	94	120

NOTE: ***Berg** a-2, 8, 9, 11, 14. **Heath** c-2, 9. **Maneely** c-1, 3. **Severin** a-4; c-7-11, 14.*

MARINES IN BATTLE
Atlas Comics (ACI No. 1-12/WPI No. 13-25): Aug, 1954 - No. 25, Sept, 1958

	GD 2.0	VG 4.0	FN 6.0	VF 8.0	VF/NM 9.0	NM- 9.2
1-Heath-c; Iron Mike McGraw by Heath; history of U.S. Marine Corps. begins	28	56	84	165	270	375
2-Heath-c	15	30	45	88	137	185
3-6,8-10: 4-Last precode (2/55); Romita-a	13	26	39	74	105	135
7-Kubert/Moskowitz-a (6 pgs.)	14	28	42	76	108	140
11-16,18-21,24	12	24	36	69	97	125
17-Williamson-a (3 pgs.)	14	28	42	78	112	145
22,25-Torres-a	12	24	36	69	97	125
23-Crandall-a; Mark Murdock app.	13	26	39	72	101	130

NOTE: ***Berg** a-22. **G. Colan** a-22, 23. **Drucker** a-6. **Everett** a-4, 15; c-21. **Heath** c-1, 2, 4. **Maneely** c-23, 24. **Orlando** a-14. **Pakula** a-6, 23. **Powell** a-16. **Severin** a-22; c-12. **Sinnott** a-23. **Tuska** a-15.*

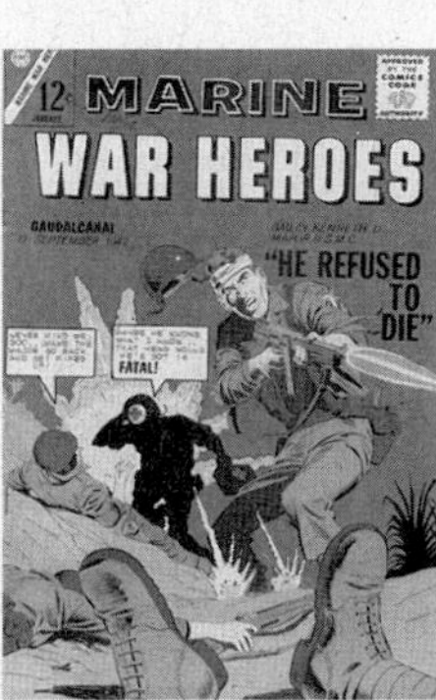

Marine War Heroes #1 © CC

Mark Trail #5 © Hall Synd.

Mars Attacks (2012 series) #4 © Topps

GD VG FN VF VF/NM NM-
2.0 4.0 6.0 8.0 9.0 9.2

GD VG FN VF VF/NM NM-
2.0 4.0 6.0 8.0 9.0 9.2

MARINE WAR HEROES (Charlton Premiere #19 on)
Charlton Comics: Jan, 1964 - No. 18, Mar, 1967
1-Montes/Bache-c/a 4 8 12 23 37 50
2-16,18: 11-Vietnam sty w/VC tunnels & moles.14,18-Montes/Bache-a 3 6 9 16 23 30
17-Tojo's plan to bomb Pearl Harbor & 1st Atomic bomb blast on Japan 3 6 9 19 30 40

MARK, THE (Also see Mayhem)
Dark Horse Comics: Dec, 1993 - No. 4, Mar, 1994 ($2.50, limited series)
1-4 3.00

MARK HAZZARD: MERC
Marvel Comics Group: Nov, 1986 - No. 12, Oct, 1987 (75¢)
1-12: Morrow-a 3.00
Annual 1 (11/87, $1.25) 4.00

MARK OF CHARON (See Negation)
CG Entertainment: Apr, 2003 - No. 5, Aug, 2003 ($2.95, limited series)
1-5-Bedard-s/Bennett-a 3.00

MARK OF ZORRO (See Zorro, Four Color #228)

MARK 1 COMICS (Also see Shaloman)
Mark 1 Comics: Apr, 1988 - No. 3, Mar, 1989 ($1.50)
1-3: Early Shaloman app. 2-Origin 3.00

MARKSMAN, THE (Also see Champions)
Hero Comics: Jan, 1988 - No. 5, 1988 ($1.95)
1-5: 1-Rose begins. 1-3-Origin The Marksman 3.00
Annual 1 ('88, $2.75, 52 pgs.)-Champions app. 4.00

MARK TRAIL
Standard Magazines (Hall Syndicate)/Fawcett Publ. No. 5: Oct, 1955; No. 5, Summer, 1959
1(1955)-Sunday strip-r 7 14 21 37 46 55
5(1959) By Ed Dodd 5 10 15 22 26 30
...Adventure Book of Nature 1 (Summer, 1958, 25¢, Pines)-100 pg. Giant; Special Camp Issue; contains 78 Sunday strip-r by Ed Dodd 9 18 27 52 69 85

MARMADUKE MONK
I. W. Enterprises/Super Comics: No date; 1963 (10¢)
I.W. Reprint 1 (nd) 2 4 6 8 11 14
Super Reprint 14 (1963)-r/Monkeyshines Comics #? 2 4 6 8 10 12

MARMADUKE MOUSE
Quality Comics Group (Arnold Publ.): Spring, 1946 - No. 65, Dec, 1956 (Early issues: 52 pgs.)
1-Funny animal 18 36 54 107 169 230
2 11 22 33 64 90 115
3-10 9 18 27 52 69 85
11-30 8 16 24 40 50 60
31-65: Later issues are 36 pgs. 7 14 21 35 43 50
Super Reprint #14(1963) 2 4 6 9 12 15

MARQUIS, THE
Oni Press
...: A Sin of One ($2.99, 5/03) Guy Davis-s/a; Michael Gaydos-c 3.00
...: Intermezzo TPB ($11.95, 12/03) r/A Sin of One and Hell's Courtesan #1,2 12.00

MARQUIS, THE: DANSE MACABRE
Oni Press: May, 2000 - No. 5, Feb, 2001 ($2.95, B&W, limited series)
1-5-Guy Davis-s/a. 1-Wagner-c. 2-Mignola-c. 3-Vess-c. 5-K. Jones-c 3.00
TPB (8/2001, $18.95) r/1-5 & Les Preludes; Seagle intro. 19.00

MARQUIS, THE: DEVIL'S REIGN: HELL'S COURTESAN
Oni Press: Feb, 2002 - No. 2, Apr, 2002 ($2.95, B&W, limited series)
1,2-Guy Davis-s/a 3.00

MARRIAGE OF HERCULES AND XENA, THE
Topps Comics: July, 1998 ($2.95, one-shot)
1-Photo-c; Lopresti-a; Alex Ross pin-up, 1-Alex Ross painted-c 3.00
1-Gold foil logo-c 5.00

MARRIED ... WITH CHILDREN (TV)(Based on Fox TV show)
Now Comics: June, 1990 - No. 7, Feb, 1991(12/90 inside) ($1.75)
V2#1, Sept, 1991 - No. 7, Apr, 1992 ($1.95)
1-7: 2-Photo-c, 1,2-2nd printing, V2#1-7: 1,4,6-Photo-c 3.00
...Buck's Tale (6/94, $1.95) 3.00
...1994 Annual nn (2/94, $2.50, 52 pgs.)-Flip book format 4.00
Special 1 (7/92, $1.95)-Kelly Bundy photo-c/poster 3.00

MARRIED ... WITH CHILDREN: KELLY BUNDY
Now Comics: Aug, 1992 - No. 3, Oct, 1992 ($1.95, limited series)
1-3: Kelly Bundy photo-c & poster in each 3.00

MARRIED ... WITH CHILDREN: QUANTUM QUARTET
Now Comics: Oct, 1993 - No. 4, 1994, ($1.95, limited series)
1-4: Fantastic Four parody 3.00

MARRIED ... WITH CHILDREN: 2099
Now Comics: June, 1993 - No. 3, Aug, 1993 ($1.95, limited series)
1-3 3.00

MARS
First Comics: Jan, 1984 - No. 12, Jan, 1985 ($1.00, Mando paper)
1-12: Marc Hempel & Mark Wheatley story & art. 2-The Black Flame begins. 10-Dynamo Joe begins 3.00
TPB (IDW Publ., 8/05, $39.99) r/#1-12, creator commentary; bonus art; new Hempel-c 40.00

MARS & BEYOND (Disney, TV)
Dell Publishing Co.: No. 866, Dec, 1957
Four Color 866-A Science feat. from Tomorrowland 7 14 21 48 89 130

MARS ATTACKS
Topps Comics: May, 1994 - No. 5, Sept, 1994 ($2.95, limited series)
1-5-Giffen story; flip books 2 4 6 8 10 12
Special Edition 2 4 6 9 12 15
Trade paperback (12/94, $12.95)-r/limited series plus new 8 pg. story 15.00

MARS ATTACKS
Topps Comics: V2#1, 8/95 - V2#3, 10/95; V2#4, 1/96 - No. 7, 5/96($2.95, bi-monthly #6 on)
V2#1-7: 1-Counterstrike storyline begins. 4-(1/96). 5-(1/96). 5,7-Brereton-c. 6-(3/96)-Simonson-c. 7-Story leads into Baseball Special #1 5.00
Baseball Special 1 (6/96, $2.95)-Bisley-c. 5.00

MARS ATTACKS
IDW Publishing: Jun, 2012 - No. 10, May, 2013 ($3.99, issues #6-10 polybagged with card)
1-10: 1-Layman-s/McCrea-a; 58 covers including all 54 cards from 1962 set 4.00
...: Classics Obliterated (6/13, $7.99) Spoofs of Moby Dick, Jeckll & Hyde, Robinson Crusoe 8.00
... KISS (1/13, $3.99) Ryall-s/Robinson-a; 2 variant-c with Judge Dredd & Star Slammers 4.00
... Popeye (1/13, $3.99) Beatty-a; 2 variant-c with Miss Fury & Opus 4.00
... The Holidays (10/12, $7.99) short stories for Halloween-Christmas; 5 covers 8.00
... The Real Ghostbusters (1/13, $3.99) Holder-a; 2 variant-c with Chew & Madman 4.00
... : The Transformers (1/13, $3.99) 2 variant-c with Spike & Strangers in Paradise 4.00
... Zombie vs. Robots (1/13, $3.99) Ryall-s; 2 variant-c with Rog-2000 & Cerebus 4.00

MARS ATTACKS HIGH SCHOOL
Topps Comics: May, 1997 - No. 2, Sept, 1997 ($2.95, B&W, limited series)
1,2-Stelfreeze-c 4.00

MARS ATTACKS JUDGE DREDD
IDW Publishing: Sept, 2013 - No. 4, Dec, 2013 ($3.99, limited series)
1-4-Al Ewing-s/John McCrea-a/Greg Staples-c 4.00

MARS ATTACKS IMAGE
Topps Comics: Dec, 1996 - No. 4, Mar, 1997 ($2.50, limited series)
1-4-Giffen-s/Smith/Sienkiewicz-a 4.00

MARS ATTACKS THE SAVAGE DRAGON
Topps Comics: Dec, 1996 - No. 4, Mar, 1997 ($2.95, limited series)
1-4: 1-w/bound-in card 4.00

MARSHAL BLUEBERRY (See Blueberry)
Marvel Comics (Epic Comics): 1991 ($14.95, graphic novel)
1-Moebius-a 3 6 9 14 19 24

MARSHAL LAW (Also see Crime And Punishment: Marshall Law...)
Marvel Comics (Epic Comics): Oct, 1987 - No. 6, May, 1989 ($1.95, mature)
1-6 3.00

M.A.R.S. PATROL TOTAL WAR (Formerly Total War #1,2)
Gold Key: No. 3, Sept, 1966 - No. 10, Aug, 1969 (All-Painted-c except #7)
3-Wood-a; aliens invade USA 5 10 15 35 63 90
4-10 4 8 12 23 37 50
Wally Wood's M.A.R.S. Patrol Total War TPB (Dark Horse, 9/04, $12.95) r/#3 & Total War #1&2; foreward by Batton Lash; afterword by Dan Adkins 13.00

MARTHA WASHINGTON (Also see Dark Horse Presents Fifth Anniversary Special, Dark Horse Presents #100-4, Give Me Liberty, Happy Birthday Martha Washington & San Diego Comicon Comics #2)

Martian Manhunter (2006 series) #5 © DC

Marvel Adventures #18 © MAR

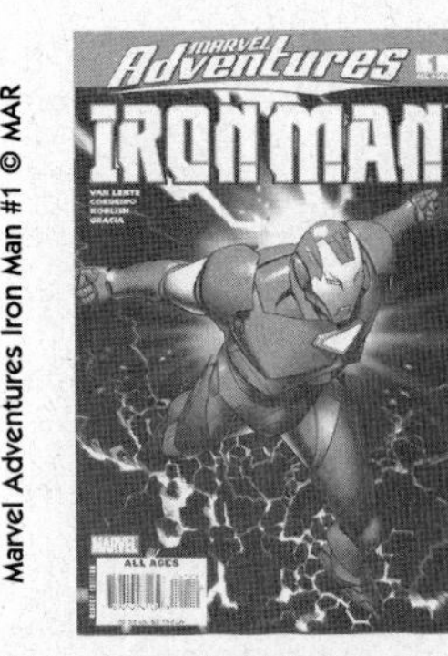

Marvel Adventures Iron Man #1 © MAR

GD	VG	FN	VF	VF/NM	NM-
2.0	4.0	6.0	8.0	9.0	9.2

MARTHA WASHINGTON... (one-shots)
Dark Horse Comics (Legend): ($2.95/$3.50, one-shots)

... Dies (7/07, $3.50) Miller-s/Gibbons-a; r/Miller's original outline for Give Me Liberty 4.00
... Stranded in Space (11/95, $2.95) Miller-s/Gibbons-a; Big Guy app. 5.00

MARTHA WASHINGTON GOES TO WAR
Dark Horse Comics (Legend): May, 1994 - No. 5, Sep, 1994 ($2.95, lim. series)

1-5-Miller scripts; Gibbons-c/a 5.00
TPB ($17.95) r/#1-5 18.00

MARTHA WASHINGTON SAVES THE WORLD
Dark Horse Comics: Dec, 1997 - No. 3, Feb, 1998 ($2.95/$3.95, lim. series)

1,2-Miller scripts; Gibbons-c/a in all 5.00
3-($3.95) 5.00

MARTHA WAYNE (See The Story of...)

MARTIAN MANHUNTER (See Detective Comics & Showcase '95 #9)
DC Comics: May, 1988 - No. 4, Aug,. 1988 ($1.25, limited series)

1-4: 1,4-Batman app. 2-Batman cameo 4.00
Special 1-(1996, $3.50) 4.00

MARTIAN MANHUNTER (See JLA)
DC Comics: No. 0, Oct, 1998 - No. 36, Nov, 2001 ($1.99)

0-(10/98) Origin retold; Ostrander-s/Mandrake-c/a 3.00
1-36: 1-(12/98). 6-9-JLA app. 18,19-JSA app. 24-Mahnke-a 3.00
#1,000,000 (11/98) 853rd Century x-over 3.00
Annual 1,2 (1998,1999; $2.95) 1-Ghosts; Wrightson-c. 2-JLApe 4.00

MARTIAN MANHUNTER (See DCU Brave New World)
DC Comics: Oct, 2006 - No. 8, May, 2007 ($2.99, limited series)

1-8-Lieberman-s/Barrionuevo-a/c 3.00
...: The Others Among Us TPB (2007, $19.99) r/#1-8 & story from DCU Brave New World 20.00

MARTIAN MANHUNTER: AMERICAN SECRETS
DC Comics: 1992 - Book Three, 1992 ($4.95, limited series, prestige format)

1-3: Barreto-a 5.00

MARTIN KANE (William Gargan as... Private Eye)(Stage/Screen/Radio/TV)
Fox Features Syndicate (Hero Books): No. 4, June, 1950 - No. 2, Aug, 1950 (Formerly My Secret Affair)

	GD	VG	FN	VF	VF/NM	NM-
4(#1)-True crime stories; Wood-c/a(2); used in **SOTI**, pg. 160; photo back-c	34	68	102	199	325	450
2-Wood/Orlando story, 5 pgs; Wood-a(2)	25	50	75	147	241	335

MARTIN LUTHER KING AND THE MONTGOMERY STORY (See Promotional Comics section)

MARTIN MYSTERY
Dark Horse (Bonelli Comics): Mar, 1999 - No. 6, Aug, 1999 ($4.95, B&W, digest size)

1-6-Reprints Italian series in English; Gibbons-c on #1-3 5.00

MARTY MOUSE
I. W. Enterprises: No date (1958?) (10¢)

	GD	VG	FN	VF	VF/NM	NM-
1-Reprint	2	4	6	9	12	15

MARVEL ACTION HOUR FEATURING IRON MAN (TV cartoon)
Marvel Comics: Nov, 1994 - No. 8, June, 1995 ($1.50/$2.95)

1-8: Based on cartoon series 3.00
1 ($2.95)-Polybagged w/16 pg Marvel Action Hour Preview & acetate print 4.00

MARVEL ACTION HOUR FEATURING THE FANTASTIC FOUR (TV cartoon)
Marvel Comics: Nov, 1994 - No. 8, June, 1995 ($1.50/$2.95)

1-8: Based on cartoon series 3.00
1-($2.95)-Polybagged w/ 16 pg. Marvel Action Hour Preview & acetate print 4.00

MARVEL ACTION UNIVERSE (TV cartoon)
Marvel Comics: Jan, 1989 ($1.00, one-shot)

1-r/Spider-Man And His Amazing Friends 4.00

MARVEL ADVENTURES
Marvel Comics: Apr, 1997 - No. 18, Sept, 1998 ($1.50)

1-18-"Animated style": 1,4,7-Hulk-c/app. 2,11-Spider-Man. 3,8,15-X-Men. 5-Spider-Man & X-Men. 6-Spider-Man & Human Torch. 9,12-Fantastic Four. 10,16-Silver Surfer. 13-Spider-Man & Silver Surfer. 14-Hulk & Dr. Strange. 18-Capt. America 3.00

MARVEL ADVENTURES...
Marvel Comics: 2007, 2008 (Free Comic Book Day giveaways)

... Free Comic Book Day 2007 (6/07) 1-Iron Man, Hulk and Franklin Richards app. 3.00
... Free Comic Book Day 2008 - Iron Man, Hulk, Ant-Man and Spider-Man app. 3.00

MARVEL ADVENTURES FANTASTIC FOUR (All ages title)
Marvel Comics: No. 0, July, 2005 - No. 48, July, 2009 ($1.99/$2.50/$2.99)

0-($1.99) Movie version characters; Dr. Doom app.; Eaton-a 3.00
1-10-($2.50) 1-Skrulls app.; Pagulayan-a. 7-Namor app. 3.00
11-48-($2.99) 12,42-Dr. Doom app. 24-Namor app. 26,28-Silver Surfer app. 3.00
... Vol. 1: Family of Heroes (2005, $6.99, digest) r/#1-4 7.00
... Vol. 2: Fantastic Voyages (2006, $6.99, digest) r/#5-8 7.00
... Vol. 3: World's Greatest (2006, $6.99, digest) r/#9-12 7.00
... Vol. 4: Cosmic Threats (2006, $6.99, digest) r/#13-16 7.00
... Vol. 5: All 4 One, 4 For All (2007, $6.99, digest) r/#17-20 7.00
... Vol. 6: Monsters & Mysteries (2007, $6.99, digest) r/#21-24 7.00
... Vol. 7: The Silver Surfer (2007, $6.99, digest) r/#25-28 7.00
... Vol. 8: Monsters, Moles, Cowboys & Coupons (2008, $7.99, digest) r/#29-32 8.00

MARVEL ADVENTURES FLIP MAGAZINE (All ages title)
Marvel Comics: Aug, 2005 - No. 26, Sept, 2007 ($3.99/$4.99)

1-11: 1-10-Rep. Marvel Advs. Fantastic Four and Marvel Advs. Spider-Man in flip format 4.00
12-14-($4.99) Reprints Marvel Advs. Spider-Man & X-Men/Power Pack in flip format 5.00
15-26-Rep. Marvel Advs. Fantastic Four and Marvel Advs. Spider-Man in flip format 5.00

MARVEL ADVENTURES HULK (All ages title)
Marvel Comics: Sept, 2007 - No. 16, Dec, 2008 ($2.99)

1-16: 1-New version of Hulk's origin; Pagulayan-c. 2-Jamie Madrox app. 13-Mummies 3.00
... Vol. 1: Misunderstood Monster (2007, $6.99, digest) r/#1-4 7.00

MARVEL ADVENTURES IRON MAN (All ages title)
Marvel Comics: July, 2007 - No. 13, Jul, 2008 ($2.99)

1-13: 1-4-Michael Golden-c. 1-New version of Iron Man's origin. 2-Intro. the Mandarin 3.00
... Vol. 1: Heart of Steel (2007, $6.99, digest) r/#1-4 7.00
... Vol. 2: Iron Armory (2008, $7.99, digest) r/#5-8 8.00

MARVEL ADVENTURES SPIDER-MAN (All ages title)
Marvel Comics: May, 2005 - No. 61, May, 2010 ($2.50/$2.99)

1-13-Lee & Ditko stories retold with new art. 13-Conner-c 3.00
14-48: 14-Begin $2.99-c. 14-16-Conner-c. 22,23-Black costume. 35-Venom app. 3.00
50-($3.99) Sinister Six app.; back-up w/Sonny Liew-a 4.00
51-61: 53-Emma Frost becomes a regular; intro. Chat; Skottie Young-c begin 3.00
... Vol. 1 HC (2006, $19.99, with dustjacket) r/#1-8; plot for #7; sketch pages from #6,8 20.00
... Vol. 1: The Sinister Six (2005, $6.99, digest) r/#1-4 7.00
... Vol. 2: Power Struggle (2005, $6.99, digest) r/#5-8 7.00
... Vol. 3: Doom With a View (2006, $6.99, digest) r/#9-12 7.00
... Vol. 4: Concrete Jungle (2006, $6.99, digest) r/#13-16 7.00
... Vol. 5: Monsters on the Prowl (2007, $6.99, digest) r/#17-20 7.00
... Vol. 6: The Black Costume (2007, $6.99, digest) r/#21-24 7.00
... Vol. 7: Secret Identity (2007, $6.99, digest) r/#25-28 7.00
... Vol. 8: Forces of Nature (2008, $7.99, digest) r/#29-32 8.00
... Vol. 9: Fiercest Foes (2008, $7.99, digest) r/#33-36 8.00

MARVEL ADVENTURES SPIDER-MAN (All ages title)
Marvel Comics: June, 2010 - No. 24, May, 2012 ($3.99/$2.99)

1-($3.99) Tobin-s; Franklin Richards back-up 4.00
2-23-($2.99): 3,7-Wolverine app. 3,4-Bullseye app. 6-Doctor Octopus app. 3.00

MARVEL ADVENTURES STARRING DAREDEVIL (...Adventure #3 on)
Marvel Comics Group: Dec, 1975 - No. 6, Oct, 1976

	GD	VG	FN	VF	VF/NM	NM-
1	2	4	6	11	16	20
2-6-r/Daredevil #22-27 by Colan. 3-5-(25¢-c)	1	3	4	6	8	10
3-5-(30¢-c variants, limited distribution)(4,6,8/76)	3	6	9	14	20	25

MARVEL ADVENTURES SUPER HEROES (All ages title)
Marvel Comics: Sept, 2008 - No. 21, May, 2010 ($2.99)

1-21: 1-4: Spider-Man, Hulk and Iron Man team-ups. 1-Hercules app. 5-Dr. Strange app. 6-Ant-Man origin re-told. 7-Thor. 8,12-Capt. America. 17-Avengers begin 3.00

MARVEL ADVENTURES SUPER HEROES (All ages title)
Marvel Comics: June, 2010 - No. 24, May, 2012 ($3.99/$2.99)

1-($3.99) Iron Man and Avengers vs. Magneto 4.00
2-24-($2.99) 4-Deadpool app. 5-Rhino app. 11,12,22-Hulk app. 13,14,19-Thor 3.00

MARVEL ADVENTURES THE AVENGERS (All ages title)
Marvel Comics: July, 2006 - No. 39, Oct, 2009 ($2.99)

1-39-Spider-Man, Wolverine, Hulk, Iron Man, Capt. America, Storm, Giant-Girl app. 3.00
... Vol. 1: Heroes Assembled (2006, $6.99, digest) r/#1-4 7.00
... Vol. 2: Mischief (2007, $6.99, digest) r/#5-8 7.00
... Vol. 3: Bizarre Adventures (2007, $6.99, digest) r/#9-12 7.00
... Vol. 4: The Dream Team (2007, $6.99, digest) r/#13-15 & Giant-Size #1 7.00
... Vol. 5: Some Assembling Required (2008, $7.99, digest) r/#16-19 8.00

MARVEL ADVENTURES TWO-IN-ONE

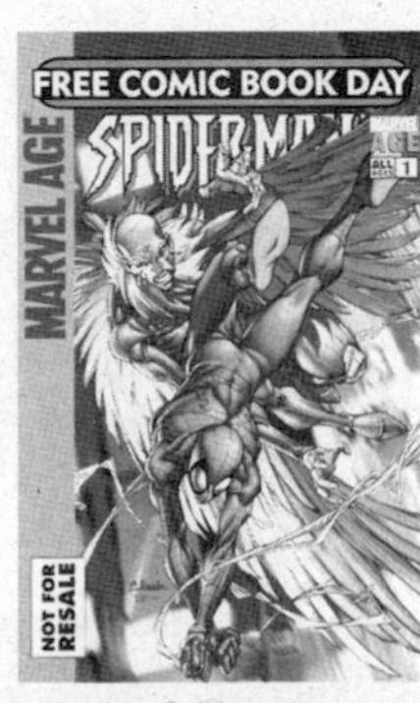

Marvel Age Spider-Man FCBD © MAR

Marvel Boy (2000 series) #4 © MAR

Marvel Collectors' Item Classics #8 © MAR

GD VG FN VF VF/NM NM-
2.0 4.0 6.0 8.0 9.0 9.2

Marvel Comics: Oct, 2007 - No. 18 ($4.99, bi-weekly)
1-18: 1-9-Reprints Marvel Adventures Spider-Man and Fantastic Four stories. 10-Hulk 5.00

MARVEL AGE FANTASTIC FOUR (All ages title)
Marvel Comics: Jun, 2004 - No. 12, Mar, 2005 ($2.25)
1-12-Lee & Kirby stories retold with new art by various. 11-Impossible Man app. 3.00
...Tales (4/05, $2.25) retells first meeting with the Black Panther; O'Hare & Lim-a 3.00
Vol. 1: All For One TPB (2004, $5.99, digest size) r/#1-4 6.00
Vol. 2: Doom TPB (2004, $5.99, digest size) r/#5-8 6.00
Vol. 3: The Return of Doctor Doom TPB (2005, $5.99, digest size) r/#9-12 6.00

MARVEL AGE HULK (All ages title)
Marvel Comics: Nov, 2004 - No. 4, Feb, 2005 ($1.75)
1-3-Lee & Kirby stories retold with new art by various 3.00
Vol. 1: Incredible TPB (2005, $5.99, digest size) r/#1-4 6.00
Vol. 2: Defenders (2008, $7.99, digest) r/#5-8 8.00

MARVEL AGE SPIDER-MAN (All ages title)
Marvel Comics: May, 2004 - No. 20, Mar, 2005 ($2.25)
1-20-Lee & Ditko stories retold with new art. 4-Doctor Doom app. 5-Lizard app. 3.00
1-(Free Comic Book Day giveaway, 8/04) Spider-Man vs. The Vulture; Brooks-a 3.00
Vol. 1 TPB (2004, $5.99, digest) 1-r/#1-4 6.00
Vol. 2: Everyday Hero TPB (2004, $5.99, digest) r/#5-8 6.00
Vol. 3: Swingtime TPB (2004, $5.99, digest) r/#9-12 6.00
Spidey Strikes Back TPB (2005, 5.99, digest) r/#17-20 6.00

MARVEL AGE SPIDER-MAN TEAM-UP (Marvel Adventures on cover)
Marvel Comics: June, 2005 (Free Comic Book Day giveaway)
1-Spider-Man meets the Fantastic Four 3.00

MARVEL AGE TEAM-UP (All ages Spider-Man team-ups) (Also see Free Comic Book Day edition in the Promotional Comics section)
Marvel Comics: Nov, 2004 - No. 5, Apr, 2005 ($1.75)
1-5-Stories retold with new art by various. 1-Fantastic Four app. 3-Kitty Pryde app. 3.00
... Vol. 1: A Little Help From My Friends (2005, $7.99, digest) r/#1-5 8.00

MARVEL AND DC PRESENT FEATURING THE UNCANNY X-MEN AND THE NEW TEEN TITANS
Marvel Comics/DC Comics: 1982 ($2.00, 68 pgs., one-shot, Baxter paper)
1-3rd app. Deathstroke the Terminator; Darkseid app.; Simonson/Austin-c/a
2 4 6 13 18 22

MARVEL APES
Marvel Comics: Nov, 2008 - No. 4, Dec, 2008 ($3.99, limited series)
1-4: 1-Kesel-s/Bachs-a; back-up history story with Peyer-s/Kitson-a; two covers 4.00
1-($10.00) Hero Initiative edition with Daredevil gorilla cover by Mike Wieringo 10.00
#0-(2008, $3.99) r/Amazing Spider-Man #110,111; gallery of Marvel Apes variant covers 4.00
...: Amazing Spider-Monkey Special 1 (6/09, $3.99) Sandmonk and the Apevengers app. 4.00
...: Grunt Line 1 (7/09, $3.99) Kesel-s; Charles Darwin app. 4.00
...: Speedball Special 1 (5/09, $3.99) Bachs & Hardin-a 4.00

MARVEL ASSISTANT-SIZED SPECTACULAR
Marvel Comics: Jun, 2009 - No. 2, Jun, 2009 ($3.99, limited series)
1,2-Short stories by various incl. Isanove, Giarrusso, Nauck, Wyatt Cenak, Warren 4.00

MARVEL ATLAS (Styled after the Official Marvel Handbooks)
Marvel Comics: 2007 - No. 2, 2008 ($3.99, limited series)
1,2-Profiles and maps of countries in the Marvel Universe 4.00

MARVEL BOY (Astonishing #3 on; see Marvel Super Action #4)
Marvel Comics (MPC): Dec, 1950 - No. 2, Feb, 1951
1-Origin Marvel Boy by Russ Heath 123 246 369 787 1344 1900
2-Everett-a; Washington DC under attack 84 168 252 538 919 1300

MARVEL BOY (Marvel Knights)
Marvel Comics: Aug, 2000 - No. 6, Mar, 2001 ($2.99, limited series)
1-Intro. Marvel Boy; Morrison-s/J.G. Jones-c/a 4.00
1-DF Variant-c 5.00
2-6 3.00
TPB (6/01, $15.95) 16.00

MARVEL BOY: THE URANIAN (Agents of Atlas)
Marvel Comics: Mar, 2010 - No. 3, May, 2010 ($3.99, limited series)
1-3-Origin re-told; back-up reprints from 1950s; Heath & Everett-a 4.00

MARVEL CHILLERS (Also see Giant-Size Chillers)
Marvel Comics Group: Oct, 1975 - No. 7, Oct, 1976 (All 25¢ issues)
1-Intro. Modred the Mystic, ends #2; Kane-c(p) 3 6 9 14 19 24
2,4,5,7: 4-Kraven app. 5,6-Red Wolf app. 7-Kirby-c; Tuska-p
2 4 6 8 11 14
3-Tigra, the Were-Woman begins (origin), ends #7 (see Giant-Size Creatures #1). Chaykin/Wrightson-c. 3 6 9 17 26 35
4-6-(30¢-c variants, limited distribution)(4-8/76) 3 6 9 19 30 40
6-Byrne-a(p); Buckler-c(p) 2 4 6 11 16 20
NOTE: *Bolle a-1. Buckler c-2. Kirby c-7.*

MARVEL CLASSICS COMICS SERIES FEATURING...
(Also see Pendulum Illustrated Classics)
Marvel Comics Group: 1976 - No. 36, Dec, 1978 (52 pgs., no ads)
1-Dr. Jekyll and Mr. Hyde 2 4 6 10 14 18
2-10,28: 28-1st Golden-c/a; Pit and the Pendulum 2 4 6 8 10 12
11-27,29-36 1 2 3 5 7 9
NOTE: ***Adkins** c-1i, 4i, 12i. **Alcala** a-34i; c-34. **Bolle** a-35. **Buscema** c-17p, 19p, 26p. **Golden** c/a-28. **Gil Kane** c-1-16p, 21p, 22p, 24p, 32p. **Nebres** a-5; c-24i. **Nino** a-2, 8, 12. **Redondo** a-1, 9. No. 1-12 were reprinted from Pendulum Illustrated Classics.*

MARVEL COLLECTIBLE CLASSICS: AVENGERS
Marvel Comics: 1998 ($10.00, reprints with chromium wraparound-c)
1-Reprints Avengers Vol.3, #1; Perez-c 2 4 6 11 16 20

MARVEL COLLECTIBLE CLASSICS: SPIDER-MAN
Marvel Comics: 1998 ($10.00, reprints with chromium wraparound-c)
1-Reprints Amazing Spider-Man #300; McFarlane-c 9 18 27 59 117 175
2-Reprints Spider-Man #1; McFarlane-c 8 16 24 54 102 150

MARVEL COLLECTIBLE CLASSICS: X-MEN
Marvel Comics: 1998 ($10.00, reprints with chromium wraparound-c)
1-Reprints (Uncanny) X-Men #1 & 2; Adam Kubert-c 2 4 6 11 16 20
2-6: 2-Reprints Uncanny X-Men #141 & 142; Byrne-c. 3-Reprints (Uncanny) X-Men #137; Larroca-c. 4-Reprints X-Men #25; Andy Kubert-c. 5-Reprints Giant Size X-Men #1; Gary Frank-c. 6-Reprints X-Men V2#1; Ramos-c 2 4 6 8 10 12

MARVEL COLLECTOR'S EDITION
Marvel Comics: 1992 (Ordered thru mail with Charleston Chew candy wrapper)
1-Flip-book format; Spider-Man, Silver Surfer, Wolverine (by Sam Kieth), & Ghost Rider stories; Wolverine back-c by Kieth 1 2 3 5 6 8

MARVEL COLLECTORS' ITEM CLASSICS (Marvel's Greatest #23 on)
Marvel Comics Group(ATF): Feb, 1965 - No. 22, Aug, 1969 (25¢, 68 pgs.)
1-Fantastic Four, Spider-Man, Thor, Hulk, Iron Man-r begin
10 20 30 69 147 225
2 (4/66) 6 12 18 41 76 110
3,4 5 10 15 35 63 90
5-10 5 10 15 33 57 80
11-22: 22-r/The Man in the Ant Hill/TTA #27 4 8 12 28 47 65
NOTE: *All reprints; **Ditko, Kirby** art in all.*

MARVEL COMICS (Marvel Mystery Comics #2 on)
Timely Comics (Funnies, Inc.): Oct, Nov, 1939
NOTE: The first issue was originally dated October 1939. Most copies have a black circle stamped over the date (on cover and inside) with "November" printed over it. However, some copies do not have the November overprint and could have a higher value. Most No. 1's have printing defects, i.e., tilted pages which caused trimming into the panels usually on right side and bottom. Covers exist with and without gloss finish.
1-Origin Sub-Mariner by Bill Everett(1st newsstand app.); 1st 8 pgs. were produced for Motion Picture Funnies Weekly #1 which was probably not distributed outside of advance copies; intro Human Torch by Carl Burgos, Kazar the Great (1st Tarzan clone), & Jungle Terror(only app.); intro. The Angel by Gustavson, The Masked Raider & his horse Lightning (ends #12); cover by sci/fi pulp illustrator Frank R. Paul
22,500 45,000 67,500 145,000 245,000 500,000

MARVEL COMICS
Marvel Comics: 1990 ($17.95, hardcover)
1-Reprint of entire Marvel Comics #1 3 6 9 16 23 30

MARVEL COMICS 70th ANNIVERARY SPECIAL
Marvel Comics: Oct, 2009 ($4.99, one-shot)
1-Re-colored reprint of entire Marvel Comics #1; cover swipe by Jelena Djurdjevic 6.00

MARVEL COMICS PRESENTS
Marvel Comics (Midnight Sons imprint #143 on): Early Sept, 1988 - No. 175, Feb, 1995 ($1.25/$1.50/$1.75, bi-weekly)
1-Wolverine by Buscema in #1-10 1 3 4 6 8 10
2-5 6.00
6-10: 6-Sub-Mariner app. 10-Colossus begins 4.00
11-47,51-71: 17-Cyclops begins. 19-1st app. Damage Control. 24-Havok begins. 25-Origin/1st app. Nth Man. 26-Hulk begins by Rogers. 29-Quasar app. 31-Excalibur begins by Austin (i). 32-McFarlane-a(p). 33-Capt. America; Jim Lee-a. 37-Devil-Slayer app.

Marvel Comics Presents #52 © MAR

Marvel Double Feature #19 © MAR

The Marvel Family #7 © FAW

GD VG FN VF VF/NM NM-
2.0 4.0 6.0 8.0 9.0 9.2

38-Wolverine begins by Buscema; Hulk app. 39-Spider-Man app. 46-Liefeld Wolverine-c. 51-53-Wolverine by Rob Liefeld. 54-61-Wolverine/Hulk story: 54-Werewolf by Night begins; The Shroud by Ditko. 58-Iron Man by Ditko. 59-Punisher. 62-Deathlok & Wolverine stories 63-Wolverine. 64-71-Wolverine/Ghost Rider 8-part story. 70-Liefeld Ghost Rider/ Wolverine-c 3.00
48-50-Wolverine & Spider-Man team-up by Erik Larsen-c/a. 48-Wasp app. 49,50-Savage Dragon prototype app. by Larsen. 50-Silver Surfer. 50-53-Comet Man; Mumy scripts 5.00
72-Begin 13-part Weapon-X story (Wolverine origin) by B. Windsor-Smith (prologue) 5.00
73-Weapon-X part 1; Black Knight, Sub-Mariner 4.00
74-84: 74-Weapon-X part 2; Black Knight, Sub-Mariner. 76-Death's Head story. 77-Mr. Fantastic story. 78-Iron Man by Steacy. 80,81-Capt. America by Ditko/Austin. 81-Daredevil by Rogers/Williamson. 82-Power Man. 83-Human Torch by Ditko(a&scripts); $1.00-c direct, $1.25 newsstand. 84-Last Weapon-X (24 pg. conclusion) 3.00
85-Begin 8-part Wolverine story by Sam Kieth (c/a); 1st Kieth-a on Wolverine; begin 8-part Beast story by Jae Lee(p) with Liefeld part pencils #85,86; 1st Jae Lee-a (assisted w/Liefeld, 1991) 4.00
86-90: 86-89-Wolverine, Beast stories continue. 90-Begin 8-part Ghost Rider & Cable story, ends #97; begin flip book format w/two-c 3.00
91-175: 93-Begin 6-part Wolverine story, ends #98. 98-Begin 2-part Ghost Rider story. 99-Spider-Man story. 100-Full-length Ghost Rider/Wolverine story by Sam Kieth w/Tim Vigil assists; anniversary issue, non flip-book. 101-Begin 6-part Ghost Rider/Dr. Strange story & begin 8-part Wolverine/Nightcrawler story by Colan/Williamson; Punisher story. 107-Begin 6-part Ghost Rider/Werewolf by Night story. 109-Begin 8 part Wolverine/Typhoid Mary story. 111-Iron Fist. 113-Begin 6-part Giant-Man & begin 6-part Ghost Rider/Iron Fist stories. 117-Preview of Ravage 2099 (1st app.); begin 6 part Wolverine/Venom story w/Kieth-a. 118-Preview of Doom 2099 (1st app.). 119-Begin Ghost Rider/Cloak & Dagger by Colan. 120,136,138-Spider-Man. 123-Begin 8-part Ghost Rider/Typhoid Mary story; begin 4-part She Hulk story; begin 8-part Wolverine/Lynx story. 125-Begin 6-part Iron Fist story. 130-Begin 6-part Ghost Rider/ Cage story. 136-Daredevil. 137-Begin 6-part Wolverine story & 6-part Ghost Rider story. 147-Begin 2-part Vengeance-c/story w/new Ghost Rider. 149-Vengeance-c/story w/new Ghost Rider. 150-Silver ink-c; begin 2-part Bloody Mary story w/Typhoid Mary,Wolverine, Daredevil, new Ghost Rider; intro Steel Raven. 152-Begin 4-part Wolverine, 4-part War Machine, 4-part Vengeance, 3-part Moon Knight stories; same date as War Machine #1. 143-146: Siege of Darkness parts 3,6,11,14; all have spot-varnished-c. 143-Ghost Rider/Scarlet Witch; intro new Werewolf. 144-Begin 2-part Morbius story. 145-Begin 2-part Nightstalkers story. 153-155-Bound-in Spider-Man trading card sheet 3.00
...Colossus: God's Country (1994, $6.95) r/#10-17 1 2 3 4 5 7
...: Wolverine Vol. 1 TPB (2005, $12.99) r/Wolverine stories from #1-10 13.00
...: Wolverine Vol. 2 TPB (2006, $12.99) r/from #39-50 and Marvel Age Annual #4 13.00
...: Wolverine Vol. 3 TPB (2006, $12.99) r/from #51-61 13.00
...: Wolverine Vol. 4 TPB (2006, $12.99) r/from #62-71 13.00

NOTE: **Austin** a-31-37i; c(i)-48, 50, 99, 122. **Buscema** a-1-10, 38-47; c-6. **Byrne** a-79; c-71. **Colan** a(p)-36, 37. **Colan/Williamson** a-101-108. **Ditko** a-7p, 10, 56p, 58, 80, 81, 83. **Guice** a-62. **Sam Kieth** a-85-92, 117-122; c-85-98, 99p, 100-108, 117, 118, 120-122; back c-109-113, 117. **Jae Lee** c-129(back). **Liefeld** a-51, 52, 53p(2), 85p; c-46, 70. **McFarlane** c-32. **Mooney** a-73. **Rogers** a-26, 38, 46i, 81p. **Russell** a-10-14,16,17i; c-4,19, 30,31i. **Saltares** a-8p(early), 38-45p. **Simonson** c-1. **B. Smith** a-72-84; c-72-84. **P. Smith** c-34. **Sparling** a-33. **Starlin** a-89i. **Staton** a-74. **Steacy** a-78. **Sutton** a-101-105. **Williamson** c-62i. Two Gun Kid by **Gil Kane** in #116, 122.

MARVEL COMICS PRESENTS
Marvel Comics: Nov, 2007 - No. 12, Oct, 2008 ($3.99)

1-12-Short stories by various. 1-Wraparound-c by Campbell 4.00

MARVEL COMICS SUPER SPECIAL, A (Marvel Super Special #5 on)
Marvel Comics: Sept, 1977 - No. 41(?), Nov, 1986 (nn 7) ($1.50, magazine)

1-Kiss, 40 pgs. comics plus photos & features; John Buscema-a(p); also see Howard the Duck #12; ink contains real KISS blood; Dr. Doom, Spider-Man, Avengers, Fantastic Four, Mephisto app. 12 24 36 80 173 265
2-Conan (1978) 3 6 9 14 20 25
3-Close Encounters of the Third Kind (1978); Simonson-a
2 4 6 11 16 20
4-The Beatles Story (1978)-Perez/Janson-a; has photos & articles
5 10 15 35 63 90
5-Kiss (1978)-Includes poster 12 24 36 80 173 265
6-Jaws II (1978) 2 4 6 9 13 16
7-Sgt. Pepper; Beatles movie adaptation; withdrawn from U.S. distribution (French ed. exists)
8-Battlestar Galactica; tabloid size ($1.50, 1978); adapts TV show
2 4 6 13 18 20
8-Modern-r of tabloid size 2 4 6 10 14 18
8-Battlestar Galactica; publ. in regular magazine format; low distribution ($1.50, 8-1/2x11")
3 6 9 14 20 25
9-Conan 2 4 6 11 16 20
10-Star-Lord 4 8 12 27 44 60
11-13-Weirdworld begins #11; 25 copy special press run of each with gold seal and signed by artists (Proof quality), Spring-June, 1979 8 16 24 54 102 150
11-15: 11-13-Weirdworld (regular issues): 11-Fold-out centerfold. 14-Miller-c(p); adapts movie "Meteor." 15-Star Trek with photos & pin-ups ($1.50-c)
1 3 4 6 8 10
15-With $2.00 price; the price was changed at tail end of a 200,000 press run
2 4 6 8 10 12
16-Empire Strikes Back adaptation; Williamson-a 3 6 9 17 26 35
17-20 (Movie adaptations): 17-Xanadu. 18-Raiders of the Lost Ark. 19-For Your Eyes Only (James Bond). 20-Dragonslayer 6.00
21,23-26,28-30 (Movie adaptations): 21-Conan. 23-Annie. 24-The Dark Crystal. 25-Rock and Rule-w/photos; artwork is from movie. 26-Octopussy (James Bond). 28-Krull; photo-c. 29-Tarzan of the Apes (Greystoke movie). 30-Indiana Jones and the Temple of Doom
1 2 3 4 5 7
22-Blade Runner; Williamson-a/Steranko-c 2 4 6 8 10 12
27,31-41: 27-Return of the Jedi. 31-The Last Star Fighter. 32-The Muppets Take Manhattan. 33-Buckaroo Banzai. 34-Sheena. 35-Conan The Destroyer. 36-Dune. 37-2010. 38-Red Sonja. 39-Santa Claus:The Movie. 40-Labyrinth. 41-Howard The Duck
1 2 3 5 7 9

NOTE: **J. Buscema** a-1, 2, 9, 11-13, 18p, 21, 35, 40; c-11(part), 12. **Chaykin** a-9, 19p; c-18, 19. **Colan** a(p)-6, 10, 14. **Morrow** a-34; c-1i, 34. **Nebres** a-11. **Spiegle** a-29. **Stevens** a-27. **Williamson** a-27. #22-28 contain photos from movies.

MARVEL COMICS: 2001
Marvel Comics: 2001 (no cover price, one-shot)

1-Previews new titles for Fall 2001; Wolverine-c 3.00

MARVEL DABEL BROTHERS SAMPLER
Marvel Comics: Dec, 2006 (no cover price, one-shot)

1-Profiles and sample pages of Anita Blake, Magician: Apprentice, Red Prophet, Ptolus 3.00

MARVEL DIVAS
Marvel Comics: Sept, 2009 - No. 4, Dec, 2009 ($3.99, limited series)

1-4-Black Cat, Firestar, Hellcat and Photon app. 1-Campbell-c 4.00

MARVEL DOUBLE FEATURE
Marvel Comics Group: Dec, 1973 - No. 21, Mar, 1977

1-Capt. America, Iron Man-r/T.O.S. begin 3 6 9 15 22 28
2-10: 3-Last 20¢ issue 2 4 6 8 10 12
11-17,20,21:17-Story-r/Iron Man & Sub-Mariner #1; last 25¢ issue
1 2 3 5 7 9
15-17-(30¢-c variants, limited distribution)(4,6,8/76) 2 4 6 11 16 20
18,19-Colan/Craig-r from Iron Man #1 in both 2 4 6 8 10 12

NOTE: **Colan** r-1-19p. **Craig** r-17-19i. **G. Kane** r-15p; c-15p. **Kirby** r-1-16p, 20, 21; c-17-20.

MARVEL DOUBLE SHOT
Marvel Comics: Jan, 2003 - No. 4, April, 2003 ($2.99, limited series)

1-4: 1-Hulk by Haynes; Thor w/Asamiya-a; Jusko-c. 2-Dr. Doom by Rivera; Simpsons-style Avengers by Bill Morrison 3.00

MARVEL FAMILY (Also see Captain Marvel Adventures No. 18)
Fawcett Publications: Dec, 1945 - No. 89, Jan, 1954

1-Origin Captain Marvel, Captain Marvel Jr., Mary Marvel, & Uncle Marvel retold; origin/1st app. Black Adam 181 362 543 1158 1979 2800
2-The 3 Lt. Marvels & Uncle Marvel app. 77 154 231 493 847 1200
3 54 108 162 346 591 835
4,5 45 90 135 284 480 675
6-10: 7-Shazam app. 39 78 117 231 378 525
11-20 31 62 93 182 296 410
21-30 27 54 81 158 259 360
31-40 23 46 69 136 223 310
41-46,48-50 20 40 60 117 189 260
47-Flying Saucer-c/story (5/50) 26 52 78 154 252 350
51-76 19 38 57 111 176 240
77-Communist Threat-c 30 60 90 177 289 400
78,81-Used in **POP**, pg. 92,93. 21 42 63 124 202 280
79,80,82-88: 79-Horror satire-c 20 40 60 120 195 270
89-Last issue; last Fawcett Captain Marvel app. (low distribution)
27 54 81 158 259 360

MARVEL FANFARE (1st Series)
Marvel Comics Group: Mar, 1982 - No. 60, Jan, 1992 ($1.25/$2.25, slick paper, direct sales)

1-Spider-Man/Angel team-up; 1st Paul Smith-a (1st full story; see King Conan #7); Daredevil app. (many copies were printed missing the centerfold)
1 3 4 6 8 10
2-Spider-Man, Ka-Zar, The Angel. F.F. origin retold 1 2 3 5 6 8
3,4-X-Men & Ka-Zar. 4-Deathlok, Spidey app. 6.00
5-14: 5-Dr. Strange, Capt. America. 6-Spider-Man, Scarlet Witch. 7-Incredible Hulk; D.D. back-up(also 15). 8-Dr. Strange; Wolf Boy begins. 9-Man-Thing. 10-13-Black Widow. 14-The Vision 4.00

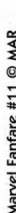

Marvel Fanfare #11 © MAR

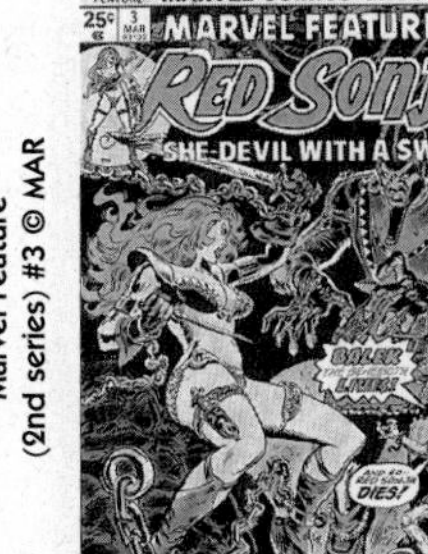

Marvel Feature (2nd series) #3 © MAR

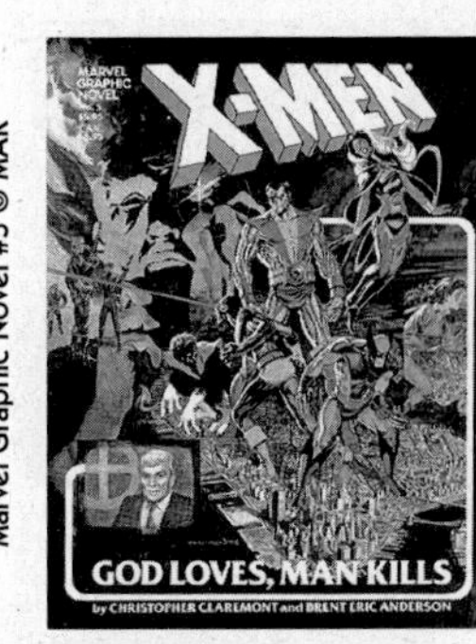

Marvel Graphic Novel #5 © MAR

GD VG FN VF VF/NM NM-
2.0 4.0 6.0 8.0 9.0 9.2

15,24,33: 15-The Thing by Barry Smith, c/a. 24-Weirdworld; Wolverine back-up. 33-X-Men, Wolverine app.; Punisher pin-up 5.00
16-23,25-32,34-44,46-50: 16,17-Skywolf. 16-Sub-Mariner back-up. 17-Hulk back-up. 18-Capt. America by Miller. 19-Cloak and Dagger. 20-Thing/Dr. Strange. 21-Thing/Dr. Strange /Hulk. 22,23-Iron Man vs. Dr. Octopus. 25,26-Weirdworld. 27-Daredevil/Spider-Man. 28-Alpha Flight. 29-Hulk. 30-Moon Knight. 31,32-Captain America. 34-37-Warriors Three. 38-Moon Knight/Dazzler. 39-Moon Knight/Hawkeye. 40-Angel/Rogue & Storm. 41-Dr. Strange. 42-Spider-Man. 43-Sub-Mariner/Human Torch. 44-Iron Man vs. Dr. Doom by Ken Steacy. 46-Fantastic Four. 47-Hulk. 48-She-Hulk/Vision. 49-Dr. Strange/Nick Fury. 50-X-Factor 3.00
45-All pin-up issue by Steacy, Art Adams & others 5.00
51-($2.95, 52 pgs.)-Silver Surfer; Fantastic Four & Capt. Marvel app.; 51,52-Colan/Williamson back-up (Dr. Strange) 4.00
52,53,56-60: 52,53-Black Knight; 53-Iron Man back up. 56-59-Shanna the She-Devil. 58-Vision & Scarlet Witch back-up. 60-Black Panther/Rogue/Daredevil stories 3.00
54,55-Wolverine back-ups. 54-Black Knight. 55-Power Pack 4.00
... Vol. 1 TPB (2008, $24.99) r/#1-7 25.00

NOTE: ***Art Adams*** *c-13.* ***Austin*** *a-1i, 4i, 33i, 38i; c-8i, 33i.* ***Buscema*** *a-51p.* ***Byrne*** *a-1p, 29, 48; c-29.* ***Chiodo*** *painted c-56-59.* ***Colan*** *a-51p.* ***Cowan/Simonson*** *c/a-60.* ***Golden*** *a-1, 2, 4p, 47; c-1, 2, 47.* ***Infantino*** *c/a(p)-8.* ***Gil Kane*** *a-8-11p.* ***Miller*** *a-18; c-1(Back-c), 18.* ***Perez*** *a-10, 11p, 12, 13p; c-10-13p.* ***Rogers*** *a-5p; c-5p.* ***Russell*** *a-5i, 6i, 8-11i, 43i; c-5i, 6.* ***Paul Smith*** *a-1p, 4p, 32, 60; c-4p. Staton c/a-50(p).* ***Williamson*** *a-30i, 51i.*

MARVEL FANFARE (2nd Series)
Marvel Comics: Sept, 1996 - No. 6, Feb, 1997 (99¢)

1-6: 1-Capt. America & The Falcon-c/story; Deathlok app. 2-Wolverine & Hulk-c/app. 3-Ghost Rider & Spider-Man-c/app. 5-Longshot-c/app. 6-Sabretooth, Power Man, & Iron Fist-c/app 3.00

MARVEL FEATURE (See Marvel Two-In-One)
Marvel Comics Group: Dec, 1971 - No. 12, Nov, 1973 (1,2: 25¢, 52 pg. giants) (#1-3: quarterly)

1-Origin/1st app. The Defenders (Sub-Mariner, Hulk & Dr. Strange); see Sub-Mariner #34,35 for prequel; Dr. Strange solo story (predates Dr. Strange #1) plus 1950s Sub-Mariner-r; Neal Adams-c 16 32 48 110 243 375
2-2nd app. Defenders; 1950s Sub-Mariner-r. Rutland, Vermont Halloween x-over 9 18 27 57 111 165
3-Defenders ends 6 12 18 40 73 105
4-Re-intro Antman (1st app. since 1960s), begin series; brief origin; Spider-Man app. 6 12 18 38 69 100
5-7,9,10: 6-Wasp app. & begins team-ups. 9-Iron Man app. 10-Last Antman 3 6 9 21 33 45
8-Origin Antman & Wasp-r/TTA #44; Kirby-a 4 8 12 23 37 50
11-Thing vs. Hulk; 1st Thing solo book (9/73); origin Fantastic Four retold 7 14 21 49 92 135
12-Thing/Iron Man; early Thanos app.; occurs after Capt. Marvel #33; Starlin-a(p) 5 10 15 33 57 80

NOTE: ***Bolle*** *a-9i.* ***Everett*** *a-1i, 3i.* ***Hartley*** *r-10.* ***Kane*** *c-3p, 7p.* ***Russell*** *a-7-10p.* ***Starlin*** *a-8, 11, 12; c-8.*

MARVEL FEATURE (Also see Red Sonja)
Marvel Comics: Nov, 1975 - No. 7, Nov, 1976 (Story cont'd in Conan #68)

1,7: 1-Red Sonja begins (pre-dates Red Sonja #1); adapts Howard short story; Adams-r/Savage Sword of Conan #1. 7-Battles Conan 2 4 6 13 18 22
2-6: Thorne-c/a in #2-7. 4,5-(Regular 25¢ edition)(5,7/76) 1 3 4 6 8 10
4,5-(30¢-c variants, limited distribution) 3 6 9 17 26 35

MARVEL FRONTIER COMICS UNLIMITED
Marvel Frontier Comics: Jan, 1994 ($2.95, 68 pgs.)

1-Dances with Demons, Immortalis, Children of the Voyager, Evil Eye, The Fallen stories 4.00

MARVEL FUMETTI BOOK
Marvel Comics Group: Apr, 1984 ($1.00, one-shot)

1-All photos; Stan Lee photo-c; Art Adams touch-ups 5.00

MARVEL FUN & GAMES
Marvel Comics Group: 1979/80 (color comic for kids)

1,11: 1-Games, puzzles, etc. 11-X-Men-c 2 3 4 6 8 10
2-10,12,13: (beware marked pages) 1 2 3 4 5 7

MARVEL GIRL
Marvel Comics: Apr, 2011 ($2.99, one-shot)

1-Early X-Men days of Jean Grey; Fialkov-s/Plati-a/Cruz-c 3.00

MARVEL GRAPHIC NOVEL
Marvel Comics Group (Epic Comics): 1982 - No. 38, 1990? ($5.95/$6.95)

1-Death of Captain Marvel (2nd Marvel graphic novel); Capt. Marvel battles Thanos by Jim Starlin (c/a/scripts) 3 6 9 17 26 35
1 (2nd & 3rd printings) 2 4 6 8 10 12

GD VG FN VF VF/NM NM-
2.0 4.0 6.0 8.0 9.0 9.2

2-Elric: The Dreaming City 2 4 6 9 12 15
3-Dreadstar; Starlin-c/a, 52 pgs. 2 4 6 11 16 20
4-Origin/1st app. The New Mutants (1982) 2 4 6 13 18 22
4,5-2nd printings 2 4 6 8 10 12
5-X-Men; book-length story (1982) 3 6 9 17 26 35
6-15,20,23,25,30,31: 6-The Star Slammers. 7-Killraven. 8-Super Boxers; Byrne scripts. 9-The Futurians. 10-Heartburst. 11-Void Indigo. 12-Dazzler. 13-Starstruck. 14-The Swords Of The Swashbucklers. 15-The Raven Banner (a Tale of Asgard). 20-Greenberg the Vampire. 23-Dr. Strange. 25-Alien Legion. 30-A Sailor's Story. 31-Wolfpack 1 3 4 6 8 10
16,17,21,29: 16-The Aladdin Effect (Storm, Tigra, Wasp, She-Hulk). 17-Revenge Of The Living Monolith (Spider-Man, Avengers, FF app.). 21-Marada the She-Wolf. 29-The Big Chance (Thing vs. Hulk) 2 4 6 8 10 12
18,19,26-28: 18-She Hulk. 19-Witch Queen of Acheron (Conan). 26-Dracula. 27-Avengers (Emperor Doom). 28-Conan the Reaver 2 4 6 9 12 15
22-Amaz. Spider-Man in Hooky by Wrightson 2 4 6 11 16 20
24-Love and War (Daredevil); Miller scripts 2 4 6 10 14 18
32-Death of Groo 2 4 6 10 14 18
32-2nd printing ($5.95) 1 3 4 6 8 10
33,34,36,37: 33-Thor. 34-Predator & Prey (Cloak & Dagger). 36-Willow (movie adapt.). 37-Hercules 1 3 4 6 8 10
35-Hitler's Astrologer (The Shadow, $12.95, HC) 2 4 6 10 14 18
35-Soft-c reprint (1990, $10.95) 2 4 6 8 10 12
38-Silver Surfer (Judgement Day)($14.95, HC) 2 4 6 11 16 20
38-Soft-c reprint (1990, $10.95) 2 4 6 8 11 14
nn-Abslom Daak: Dalek Killer (1990, $8.95) Dr. Who 2 4 6 8 11 14
nn-Arena by Bruce Jones (1989, $5.95) Dinosaurs 1 3 4 6 8 10
nn- A-Team Storybook Comics Illustrated (1983) r/ A-Team mini-series #1-3 1 3 4 6 8 10
nn-Ax (1988, $5.95) Ernie Colan-s/a 1 3 4 6 8 10
nn-Black Widow Coldest War (4/90, $9.95) 2 4 6 8 11 14
nn-Chronicles of Genghis Grimtoad (1990, $8.95)-Alan Grant-s 1 3 4 6 8 10
nn-Conan the Barbarian in the Horn of Azoth (1990, $8.95) 2 4 6 8 11 16
nn-Conan of Isles ($8.95) 2 4 6 8 11 16
nn-Conan Ravagers of Time (1992, $9.95) Kull & Red Sonja app. 2 4 6 8 11 16
nn-Conan -The Skull of Set 2 4 6 8 11 16
nn-Doctor Strange and Doctor Doom Triumph and Torment (1989, $17.95, HC) 2 4 6 13 18 22
nn-Dreamwalker (1989, $6.95)-Morrow-a 1 3 4 6 8 10
nn-Excalibur Weird War III (1990, $9.95) 2 4 6 8 10 12
nn-G.I. Joe - The Trojan Gambit (1983, 68 pgs.) 2 4 6 9 12 15
nn-Harvey Kurtzman Strange Adventures (Epic, $19.95, HC) Aragonés, Crumb 3 6 9 14 20 25
nn-Hearts and Minds (1990, $8.95) Heath-a 1 3 4 6 8 10
nn-Inhumans (1988, $7.95)-Williamson-i 1 3 4 6 8 10
nn-Jhereg (Epic, 1990, $8.95) 1 3 4 6 8 10
nn-Kazar-Guns of the Savage Land (7/90, $8.95) 1 3 4 6 8 10
nn-Kull-The Vale of Shadow ('89, $6.95) 2 4 6 8 10 12
nn-Last of the Dragons (1988, $6.95) Austin-a(i) 1 3 4 6 8 10
nn-Nightraven: House of Cards (1991, $14.95) 2 4 6 10 14 18
nn-Nightraven: The Collected Stories (1990, $9.95) Bolton-r/British Hulk mag.; David Lloyd-c/a 2 4 6 8 10 12
nn-Original Adventures of Cholly and Flytrap (Epic, 1991, $9.95) Suydam-s/c/a 2 4 6 9 12 15
nn-Rick Mason Agent (1989, $9.95) 2 4 6 8 10 12
nn-Roger Rabbit In The Resurrection Of Doom (1989, $8.95) 2 4 6 8 10 12
nn-A Sailor's Story Book II: Winds, Dreams and Dragons ('86, $6.95, softcover) Glansman-s/c/a 1 3 4 6 8 10
nn-Squadron Supreme: Death of a Universe (1989, $9.95) Gruenwald-s; Ryan & Williamson-a 3 6 9 14 20 25
nn-Who Framed Roger Rabbit (1989, $6.95) 2 4 6 8 10 12

NOTE: ***Aragones*** *a-27, 32.* ***Buscema*** *a-38.* ***Byrne*** *c/a-18.* ***Heath*** *a-35i.* ***Kaluta*** *a-13, 35p; c-13.* ***Miller*** *a-24p.* ***Simonson*** *a-6; c-6.* ***Starlin*** *c/a-1,3.* ***Williamson*** *a-34.* ***Wrightson*** *c-29i.*

MARVEL HEARTBREAKERS
Marvel Comics: Apr, 2010 ($3.99, one-shot)

1-Romance short stories; Spider-Man, MJ & Gwen app.; Casagrande-a; Beast app. 4.00

MARVEL - HEROES & LEGENDS
Marvel Comics: Oct, 1996; 1997 ($2.95)

nn-Wraparound-c, ...1997 ($2.99) -Original Avengers story 3.00

Marvel Knights #5 © MAR

Marvel Knights: X-Men #1 © MAR

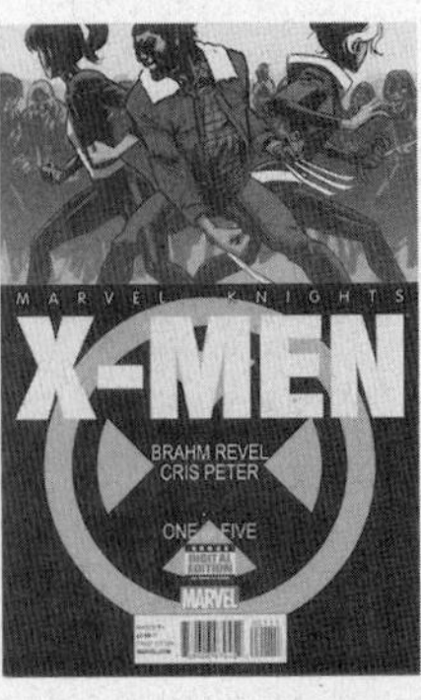

Marvel Mangaverse #3 © MAR

	GD	VG	FN	VF	VF/NM	NM-
	2.0	4.0	6.0	8.0	9.0	9.2

MARVEL HEROES FLIP MAGAZINE
Marvel Comics: Aug, 2005 - No. 26, Sept, 2007 ($3.99/$4.99)

1-11-Reprints New Avengers and Captain America (2005 series) in flip format thru #13 4.00
12-26: 14-19-Reprints New Avengers and Young Avengers in flip format. 20-Ghost Rider 5.00

MARVEL HOLIDAY SPECIAL
Marvel Comics: No. 1, 1991 ($2.25, 84 pgs.) - Present

1-X-Men, Fantastic Four, Punisher, Thor, Capt. America, Ghost Rider, Capt. Ultra, Spidey stories; Art Adams-c/a 4.00
nn (1/93)-Wolverine, Thanos (by Starlin/Lim/Austin) 4.00
nn (1994)-Capt. America, X-Men, Silver Surfer 4.00
... 1996-Spider-Man by Waid & Olliffe; X-Men, Silver Surfer 4.00
... 2004-Spider-Man by DeFalco & Miyazawa; X-Men, Fantastic Four 4.00
... 2004 TPB ($15.99) r/M.H.S. 2004 & past Christmas-themed stories 16.00
1 (1/06, $3.99) new Christmas-themed stories by various; Immonen-c 4.00
... 2006 (2/07, $3.99) Fin Fang Foom, Hydra, AIM app.; gallery of past covers; Irving-c 4.00
... 2007 (2/08, $3.99) Spider-Man & Wolverine stories; Hembeck-a 4.00
... 2011 (2/12, $3.99) Seeley-c; Spider-Man, Wolverine, Nick Fury, The Thing app. 4.00
Marvel Holiday (2006, $7.99, digest) reprints from M.H.S. 2004, 2006 & TPB 8.00
Marvel Holiday Spectacular Magazine (2009, $9.99, magazine) reprints from M.H.S. '93, '94, & Amazing Spider-Man #166; and new material w/Doe, Semeiks & Nauck-a 10.00
NOTE: *Art Adams c-'93. Golden a-'93. Perez c-'94.*

MARVEL ILLUSTRATED...
Marvel Comics: 2007 ($2.99)

...Jungle Book - reprints from Marvel Fanfare #8-11; Gil Kane-s/a(p); P. Craig Russell-i 3.00

MARVEL ILLUSTRATED: KIDNAPPED (Title changes to Kidnapped with #5)
Marvel Comics: Jan, 2009 - No. 5, May, 2009 ($3.99, limited series)

1-5-Adaptation of the Stevenson novel; Roy Thomas-s/Mario Gully-a/Parel-c 4.00

MARVEL ILLUSTRATED: LAST OF THE MOHICANS
Marvel Comics: July, 2007 - No. 6, Dec, 2007 ($2.99, limited series)

1-6-Adaptation of the Cooper novel; Roy Thomas-s/Steve Kurth-a. 1-Jo Chen-c 3.00
HC (2008, $19.99) r/#1-6 20.00

MARVEL ILLUSTRATED: MOBY DICK
Marvel Comics: Apr, 2008 - No. 6, Sept, 2008 ($2.99, limited series)

1-6-Adaptation of the Melville novel; Roy Thomas-s/Alixe-a/Watson-c 3.00

MARVEL ILLUSTRATED: PICTURE OF DORIAN GRAY
Marvel Comics: Jan, 2008 - No. 6, July, 2008 ($2.99, limited series)

1-6-Adaptation of the Wilde novel; Roy Thomas-s/Fiumara-a. 1-Parel-c 3.00

MARVEL ILLUSTRATED: SWIMSUIT ISSUE (Also see Marvel Swimsuit Special)
Marvel Comics: 1991 ($3.95, magazine, 52 pgs.)

V1#1-Parody of Sports Illustrated swimsuit issue; Mary Jane Parker centerfold pin-up by Jusko; 2nd print exists 1 3 4 6 8 10

MARVEL ILLUSTRATED: THE ILIAD
Marvel Comics: Feb, 2008 - No. 8, Sept, 2008 ($2.99, limited series)

1-8-Adaptation of Homer's Epic Poem; Roy Thomas-s/Sepulveda-a/Rivera-c 3.00

MARVEL ILLUSTRATED: THE MAN IN THE IRON MASK
Marvel Comics: Sept, 2007 - No. 6, Feb, 2008 ($2.99, limited series)

1-6-Adaptation of the Dumas novel; Roy Thomas-s/Hugo Petrus-a. 1-Djurdjevic-c 3.00
HC (2008, $19.99) r/#1-6 20.00

MARVEL ILLUSTRATED: THE ODYSSEY (Title changes to The Odyssey with #7)
Marvel Comics: Nov, 2008 - No. 8, June, 2009 ($3.99, limited series)

1-8-Adaptation of Homer's Epic Poem; Roy Thomas-s/Greg Tocchini-a/c 4.00

MARVEL ILLUSTRATED: THE THREE MUSKETEERS
Marvel Comics: Aug, 2008 - No. 6, Jan, 2009 ($3.99, limited series)

1-6-Adaptation of the Dumas novel; Roy Thomas-s/Hugo Petrus-a/Parel-c 4.00

MARVEL ILLUSTRATED: TREASURE ISLAND
Marvel Comics: Aug, 2007 - No. 6, Jan, 2008 ($2.99, limited series)

1-6-Adaptation of the Stevenson novel; Roy Thomas-s/Mario Gully-a/Greg Hildebrandt-c 3.00
HC (2008, $19.99) r/#1-6 20.00

MARVEL KNIGHTS (See Black Panther, Daredevil, Inhumans, & Punisher)
Marvel Comics: 1998 (Previews for upcoming series)

Sketchbook-Wizard suppl.; Quesada & Palmiotti-c 3.00
Tourbook-($2.99) Interviews and art previews 3.00

MARVEL KNIGHTS
Marvel Comics: July, 2000 - No. 15, Sept, 2001 ($2.99)

1-Daredevil, Punisher, Black Widow, Shang-Chi, Dagger app. 4.00
2-15: 2-Two covers by Barreto & Quesada 3.00
.../Marvel Boy Genesis Edition (6/00) Sketchbook preview 3.00
...: Millennial Visions (2/02, $3.99) Pin-ups by various; Harris-c 4.00

MARVEL KNIGHTS (Volume 2)
Marvel Comics: May, 2002 - No. 6, Oct, 2002 ($2.99)

1-6-Daredevil, Punisher, Black Widow app.; Ponticelli-a 3.00

MARVEL KNIGHTS: DOUBLE SHOT
Marvel Comics: June, 2002 - No. 4, Sept, 2002 ($2.99, limited series)

1-4: 1-Punisher by Ennis & Quesada; Daredevil by Haynes; Fabry-c 3.00

MARVEL KNIGHTS 4 (Fantastic Four) (Issues #1&2 are titled **Knights 4**) (#28-30 titled **Four**)
Marvel Comics: Apr, 2004 - No. 30, July, 2006 ($2.99)

1-30: 1-7-McNiven-c/a; Aguirre-Sacasa-a. 8,9-Namor app. 13-Cho-c. 14-Land-c. 21-Flashback meeting with Black Panther. 30-Namor app. 3.00
...Vol. 1: The Wolf at the Door (2004, $16.99, TPB) r/#1-7 17.00
...Vol. 2: The Stuff of Nightmares (2005, $13.99, TPB) r/#8-12 14.00
...Vol. 3: Divine Time (2005, $14.99, TPB) r/#13-18 15.00
...Vol. 4: Impossible Things Happen Every Day (2006, $14.99, TPB) r/#19-24 15.00
Fantastic Four: The Resurrection of Nicholas Scratch TPB (2006, $14.99) r/#25-30 15.00

MARVEL KNIGHTS: HULK
Marvel Comics: Feb, 2014 - No. 4, May, 2104 ($3.99, limited series)

1-4-Keatinge-s/Kowalski-a; Banner in Paris 4.00

MARVEL KNIGHTS MAGAZINE
Marvel Comics: May, 2001 - No. 6, Oct, 2001 ($3.99, magazine size)

1-6-Reprints of recent Daredevil, Punisher, Black Widow, Inhumans 4.00

MARVEL KNIGHTS SPIDER-MAN (Title continues in Sensational Spider-Man #23)
Marvel Comics: Jun, 2004 - No. 22, Mar, 2006 ($2.99)

1-Wraparound-c by Dodson; Millar-s/Dodson-a; Green Goblin app. 4.00
2-12: 2-Avengers app. 2,3-Vulture & Electro app. 5,8-Cho-c/a. 6-8-Venom app. 3.00
13-18-Reginald Hudlin-s/Billy Tan-a. 13,14,18-New Avengers app. 15-Punisher app. 3.00
19-22-The Other x-over pts. 2,5,8,11; Pat Lee-a 3.00
19-22-var-c: 19-Black costume. 20-Scarlet Spider. 21-Spider-Armor. 22-Peter Parker 5.00
... Vol. 1 HC (2005, $29.99, over-sized with d.j.) r/#1-12; Stan Lee intro.; Dodson & Cho sketch pages 30.00
... Vol. 1: Down Among the Dead Men (2004, $9.99, TPB) r/#1-4 10.00
... Vol. 2: Venomous (2005, $9.99, TPB) r/#5-8 10.00
... Vol. 3: The Last Stand (2005, $9.99, TPB) r/#9-12 10.00
... Vol. 4: Wild Blue Yonder (2005, $14.99, TPB) r/#13-18 15.00

MARVEL KNIGHTS: SPIDER-MAN
Marvel Comics: Dec, 2013 - No. 5, Apr, 2014 ($3.99, limited series)

1-5-Matt Kindt-s/Marco Rudy-a; Arcade app. 4.00

MARVEL KNIGHTS 2099
Marvel Comics: 2005 ($13.99, TPB)

nn-Reprints one shots: Daredevil 2099, Punisher 2099, Black Panther 2099, Inhumans 2099 and Mutant 2099; Pat Lee-c 14.00

MARVEL KNIGHTS: X-MEN
Marvel Comics: Jan, 2014 - No. 5, May, 2014 ($3.99, limited series)

1-4-Brahm Revel-s/Cris Peter-a; Sabretooth app. 4.00

MARVEL LEGACY:...
Marvel Comics: 2006, 2007 ($4.99, one-shots)

... The 1960s Handbook - Profiles of 1960s iconic and minor characters; info thru 1969 5.00
... The 1970s Handbook - Profiles of 1970s iconic and minor characters; info thru 1979 5.00
... The 1980s Handbook - Profiles of 1980s iconic and minor characters; info thru 1989 5.00
... The 1990s Handbook - Profiles of 1990s iconic and minor characters; Lim-c 5.00
...: The 1960s-1990s Handbook TPB (2007, $19.99) r/one-shots 20.00

MARVELMAN CLASSIC
Marvel Comics: 2010 ($34.99, B&W)

HC-(2010, $34.99) Reprints of 1950s British Marvelman stories; character history 35.00
... Primer (8/10, $3.99) Character history; Mick Anglo interview; Quesada-c 4.00

MARVELMAN FAMILY'S FINEST
Marvel Comics: 2010 - No. 6, Jan, 2011 ($3.99, B&W, limited series)

1-6-Reprints of 1950s Marvelman, Young Marvelman and Marvelman Family stories 4.00

MARVEL MANGAVERSE:... (one-shots)
Marvel Comics: March, 2002 ($2.25, manga-inspired one-shots)

Avengers Assemble! - Udon Studio-s/a 3.00
Eternity Twilight ($3.50) - Ben Dunn-s/a/wrap-around-c 4.00
Fantastic Four - Adam Warren-s/Keron Grant-a 3.00

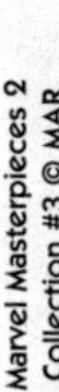
Marvel Masterpieces 2 Collection #3 © MAR

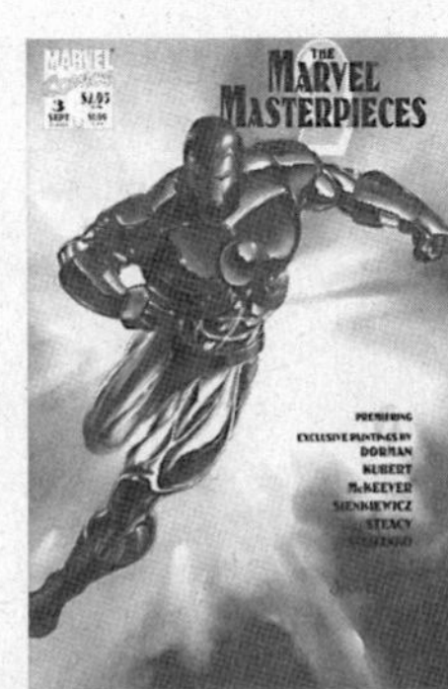

Marvel Monsters: Monsters on the Prowl #1 © MAR

Marvel Mystery Comics #11 © MAR

GD 2.0 | VG 4.0 | FN 6.0 | VF 8.0 | VF/NM 9.0 | NM- 9.2

Ghost Riders - Chuck Austen-s/a 3.00
Punisher - Peter David-s/Lea Hernandez-a 3.00
Spider-Man - Kaare Andrews-s/a 3.00
X-Men - C.B. Cebulski-s/Jeff Matsuda-a 3.00

MARVEL MANGAVERSE (Manga series)
Marvel Comics: June, 2002 - No. 6, Nov., 2002 ($2.25)

1-6: 1-Ben Dunn-s/a; intro. manga Captain Marvel 3.00
Vol. 1 TPB (2002, $24.95) r/one-shots 25.00
Vol. 2 TPB (2002, $12.99) r/#1-6 13.00
Vol. 3: Spider-Man-Legend of the Spider-Clan (2003, $11.99, TPB) r/series 12.00

MARVEL MASTERPIECES COLLECTION, THE
Marvel Comics: May, 1993 - No. 4, Aug, 1993 ($2.95, coated paper, lim. series)

1-4-Reprints Marvel Masterpieces trading cards w/ new Jusko paintings in each; Jusko painted-c/a 3.00

MARVEL MASTERPIECES 2 COLLECTION, THE
Marvel Comics: July, 1994 - No. 3, Sept, 1994 ($2.95, limited series)

1-3: 1-Kaluta-c; r/trading cards; new Steranko centerfold 3.00

MARVEL MILESTONE EDITION
Marvel Comics: 1991 - 1999 ($2.95, coated stock)(r/originals with original ads w/silver ink-c)

...: Amazing Fantasy #15 (3/92); ....:Hulk #181 (8/99, $2.99)
2 4 6 11 16 20
...: Amazing Spider-Man #1 (1/93), ...: Amazing Spider-Man #1 (1/93) variation- no price on-c, ...: Amazing Spider-Man #3 (3/95, $2.95), ...: Amazing Spider-Man #129 (11/92), ...: Avengers #1 (9/93), ...:Avengers #4 (3/95, $2.95), ...: Captain America #1 (3/95, $3.95), ...: Fantastic Four #1 (11/91), ...: Fantastic Four #5 (11/92), ...: Giant Size X-Men #1 (1991, $3.95, 68 pgs.), ...: Incredible Hulk #1 (3/92, says 3/91 by error), ...: Iron Man #55 (11/92), ...: Strange Tales-r/Dr. Strange stories from #110, 111, 114, & 115; ...: Tales of Suspense #39 (3/93), ...: X-Men #1-Reprints X-Men #1 (1991)
2 4 6 8 10 12
...: Amazing Spider-Man #149 (11/94, $2.95), ...: Avengers #16 (10/93), ...: X-Men #9 (10/93), ...:X-Men #28 (11/94, $2.95) 6.00
...: Iron Fist #14 (11/92) 1 3 4 6 8 10

MARVEL MILESTONES
Marvel Comics: 2005 - 2006 ($3.99, coated stock)(r/originals w/silver ink-c)

...: Beast & Kitty Pryde-r/from Amazing Adventures #11 & Uncanny X-Men #153 5.00
...: Black Panther, Storm & Ka-Zar-r/from Black Panther #26, Marvel Team-Up #100 and Marvel Mystery Comics #7 5.00
...: Blade, Man-Thing & Satana-r/from Tomb of Dracula #10, Adv. Into Fear #16 and Vampire Tales #2 5.00
...: Captain Britain, Psylocke & Sub-Mariner-r/from Spect. Spidey #114, Uncanny X-Men #213 and Human Torch #2 5.00
...: Doom, Sub-Mariner & Red Skull -r/from FF Ann. #2, Sub-Mariner Comics #1, Captain America Comics #1 5.00
...: Dragon Lord, Speedball and The Man in the Sky -r/from Marvel Spotlight #5, Speedball #1 and Amazing Adult Fantasy #14; Ditko-a on all 5.00
...: Dr. Strange, Silver Surfer, Sub-Mariner, & Hulk -r/from Marvel Premiere #3, FF Ann. #5, Marvel Comics #1, Incredible Hulk #3 5.00
...: Ghost Rider, Black Widow & Iceman -r/from Marvel Spotlight #5, Daredevil #81, X-Men #47 5.00
...: Iron Man, Ant-Man & Captain America -r/from TOS #39,40, TTA #27, Capt. America #1 5.00
...: Legion of Monsters, Spider-Man and Brother Voodoo -r/Marvel Premiere #28 & others 5.00
...: Millie the Model & Patsy Walker-r/from Millie the Model #100, Defenders #65 5.00
...: Onslaught -r/Onslaught: Marvel; wraparound-c 5.00
...: Rawhide Kid & Two-Gun Kid-r/Two-Gun Kid #60 and Rawhide Kid #17 5.00
...: Special: Bloodstone, X-51 & Captain Marvel II ($4.99) -r/from Marvel Presents #1, Machine Man #1, Amazing Spider-Man Ann. #19, and Bloodstone #1 6.00
...: Star Brand & Quasar -r/from Star Brand #1 & Quasar #1 5.00
...: Ultimate Spider-Man, Ult. X-Men, Microman & Mantor -r/from Ultimate Spider-Man #1/2, Ultimate X-Men #1/2 and Human Torch #2 5.00
...: Venom & Hercules -r/Marvel S-H Secret Wars #8, Journey Into Mystery Ann. #1 5.00
...: Wolverine, X-Men & Tuk: Caveboy -r/from Marvel Comics Presents #1, Uncanny X-Men #201, Capt. America Comics #1,2 5.00
...: (Jim Lee and Chris Claremont) X-Men and the Starjammers Pt. 1 -r/Unc. X-Men #275 5.00
...: X-Men and the Starjammers Pt. 2 -r/Unc. X-Men #276,277 5.00

MARVEL MINI-BOOKS (See Promotional Comics section)

MARVEL MONSTERS:... (one-shots)
Marvel Comics: Dec, 2005 ($3.99)

...Devil Dinosaur 1 - Hulk app.; Eric Powell-c/a; Sniegoski-s; r/Journey Into Mystery #62 5.00
...Fin Fang Four 1 - FF app.; Powell-c; Langridge-s/Gray-a; r/Strange Tales #89 5.00
...From the Files of Ulysses Bloodstone 1 - Guide to classic Marvel monsters; Powell-c 5.00
...Monsters on the Prowl 1 - Niles-s/Fegredo-a/Powell-c; Thing, Hulk, Giant-Man & Beast app. 5.00
...Where Monsters Dwell 1 - Giffen-s/a; David-s/Pander-a; Parker-s/Braun-s; Powell-c 5.00
HC (2006, $20.99, dust jacket) r/one-shots 21.00

MARVEL MOVIE PREMIERE (Magazine)
Marvel Comics Group: Sept, 1975 (B&W, one-shot)

1-Burroughs' "The Land That Time Forgot" adapt. 2 4 6 9 13 16

MARVEL MOVIE SHOWCASE FEATURING STAR WARS
Marvel Comics Group: Nov, 1982 - No. 2, Dec, 1982 ($1.25, 68 pgs.)

1,2-Star Wars movie adaptation; reprints Star Wars #1-6 by Chaykin; 1-Reprints-c to Star Wars #1. 2-Stevens-r 1 2 3 5 6 8

MARVEL MOVIE SPOTLIGHT FEATURING RAIDERS OF THE LOST ARK
Marvel Comics Group: Nov, 1982 ($1.25, 68 pgs.)

1-Edited-r/Raiders of the Lost Ark #1-3; Buscema-c/a(p); movie adapt. 6.00

MARVEL MUST HAVES (Reprints of recent sold-out issues)
Marvel Comics: Dec, 2001 - Present ($2.99/$3.99/$4.99)

1,2,4-6: 1-r/Wolverine: Origin #1, Startling Stories: Banner #1, Tangled Web #4 and Cable #97. 2-Amazing Spider-Man #36 and others. 4-Truth #1, Capt. America V4 #1, and The Ultimates #1. 5-r/Ultimate War #1, Ult. X-Men #26, Ult Spider-Man #33. 6-Ult. Spider-Man #33-36 4.00
3-r/Call of Duty: The Brotherhood #1 & Daredevil #32,33 3.00
Amazing Spider-Man #30-32; Incredible Hulk #34-36; The Ultimates #1-3; Ultimate Spider-Man #1-3; Ultimate X-Men #1-3; (New) X-Men #114-116 each.... 4.00
NYX #1-3; NYX #4-5 with sketch & cover gallery; Ultimates 2 #1-3 each... 5.00
Spider-Man and the Black Cat #1-3; preview of #4 5.00

MARVEL MYSTERY COMICS (Formerly Marvel Comics) (Becomes Marvel Tales No. 93 on)
Timely /Marvel Comics (TP #2-17/TCI #18-54/MCI #55-92): No. 2, Dec, 1939 - No. 92, June, 1949 (Some material from #8-10 reprinted in 2004's Marvel 65th Anniversary Special #1)

2-(Rare)-American Ace begins, ends #3; Human Torch (blue costume) by Burgos, Sub-Mariner by Everett continue; 2 pg. origin recap of Human Torch; Angel-c
3400 6800 10,200 26,000 53,000 80,000
3-New logo from Marvel pulp begins; 1st app. of television in comics? in Human Torch story (1/40); Angel-c 2100 4200 6300 16,000 30,000 44,000
4-Intro. Electro, the Marvel of the Age (ends #19), The Ferret, Mystery Detective (ends #9); 1st Sub-Mariner-c by Schomburg; 2nd German swastika on-c of a comic (2/40); one month after Top-Notch Comics #2 2100 4200 6300 16,000 30,000 44,000
5 Classic Schomburg Torch-c, his 1st ever (Scarce)
2900 5800 8700 22,000 43,500 65,000
6-Angel-c; Gustavson Angel story 1000 2000 3000 7300 12,900 18,500
7-Sub-Mariner attacks N.Y. city & Torch joins police force setting up battle in #8-10. Classic Schomburg Torch-c, his 2nd ever 1,050 2,100 3,150 8000 15,000 22,000
8-1st Human Torch & Sub-Mariner battle(6/40) 1450 2900 4350 11,000 20,500 30,000
9-(Scarce)-Human Torch & Sub-Mariner battle (cover/story); classic-c by Everett
4700 9400 14,100 35,000 62,500 90,000
10-Human Torch & Sub-Mariner battle, conclusion, 1 pg.; Terry Vance, the Schoolboy Sleuth begins, ends #57 1300 2600 3900 9700 18,850 28,000
11-Schomburg Torch-c, his 3rd ever 459 918 1377 3350 5925 8500
12-Classic Angel-c by Kirby 486 972 1458 3550 6275 9000
13-Intro. of The Vision by S&K (11/40); Sub-Mariner dons new costume, ends #15; Schomburg's 4th Human Torch-c 676 1352 2028 4935 8718 12,500
14-16: 14-Shows-c to Human Torch #1 on-c (12/40). 15-S&K Vision, Gustavson Angel story
383 766 1149 2681 4691 6700
17-Human Torch/Sub-Mariner team-up by Burgos/Everett; Human Torch pin-up on back-c; shows-c to Human Torch #2 on-c 400 800 1200 2800 4900 7000
18-1st app. villain "The Cat's Paw" 343 686 1029 2400 4200 6000
19,20: 19-Origin Toro in text; shows-c to Sub-Mariner #1 on-c. 20-Origin The Angel in text
354 708 1062 2478 4339 6200
21-The Patriot begins, (intro. in Human Torch #4 (#3)); not in #46-48; Sub-Mariner pin-up on back-c (7/41) 371 742 1113 2600 4550 6500
22-25: 23-Last Gustavson Angel; origin The Vision in text. 24-Injury-to-eye story
354 708 1062 2478 4339 6200
26-29: 27-Ka-Zar ends; last S&K Vision who battles Satan. 28-Jimmy Jupiter in the Land of Nowhere begins, ends #48; Sub-Mariner vs. The Flying Dutchman
331 662 993 2317 4059 5800
30-"Remember Pearl Harbor" Japanese war-c 366 732 1098 2562 4481 6400
31,32-"Remember Pearl Harbor" Japanese war-c. 31-Sub-Mariner by Everett ends, resumes #84. 32-1st app. The Boboes 331 662 993 2317 4059 5800
33,35,36,38,39 314 629 942 2198 3849 5500
34-Everett, Burgos, Martin Goodman, Funnies, Inc. office appear in story & battles Hitler; last Burgos Human Torch 326 652 978 2282 3991 5700
37-Classic Hitler-c 360 720 1080 2520 4410 6300
40-Classic Zeppelin-c 486 972 1458 3550 6275 9000
41-43,47 300 600 900 2070 3635 5200

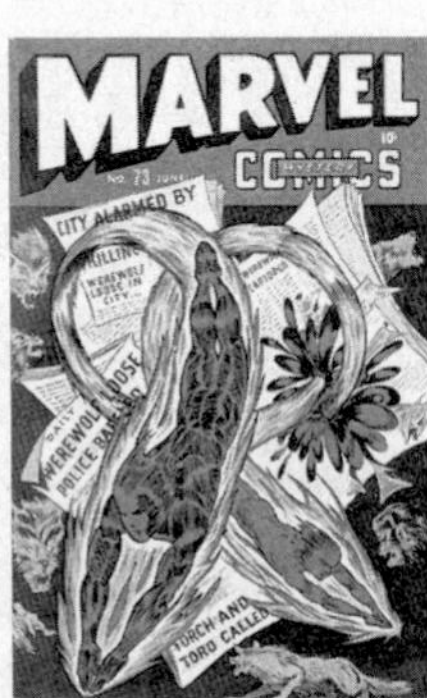

Marvel Mystery Comics #73 © MAR

Marvel Premiere #42 © MAR

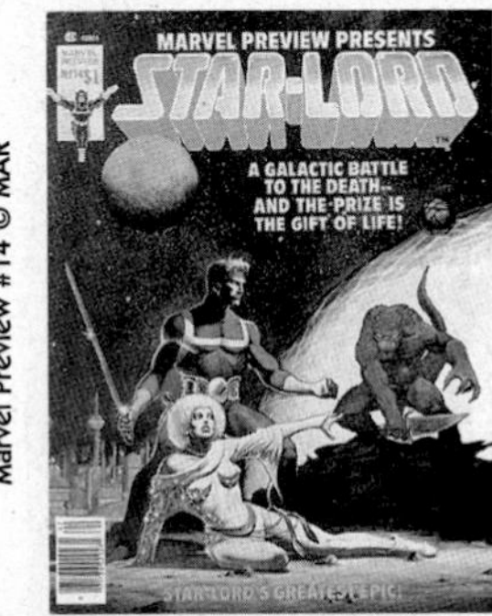

Marvel Preview #14 © MAR

	GD	VG	FN	VF	VF/NM	NM-
	2.0	4.0	6.0	8.0	9.0	9.2

44-Classic Super Plane-c 486 972 1458 3550 6275 9000
45-Red Skull, Nazi hooded Vigilante war-c 354 708 1062 2478 4339 6200
46-Classic Hitler-c 486 972 1458 3550 6275 9000
48-Last Vision; flag-c 303 606 909 2121 3711 5300
49-Origin Miss America 303 606 909 2121 3711 5300
50-Mary becomes Miss Patriot (origin) 300 600 900 1950 3375 4800
51-60: 54-Bondage-c 258 516 774 1651 2826 4000
61,62,64-Last German war-c 239 478 717 1530 2615 3700
63-Classic Hitler War-c; The Villainess Cat-Woman only app. 300 600 900 2010 3505 5000
65,66-Last Japanese War-c 239 478 717 1530 2615 3700
67-78: 74-Last Patriot. 75-Young Allies begin. 76-Ten Chapter Miss America serial begins, ends #85 139 278 417 890 1520 2150
79-New cover format; Super Villains begin on cover; last Angel 161 322 483 1030 1765 2500
80-1st app. Capt. America in Marvel Comics 171 342 513 1094 1872 2650
81-Captain America app. 142 284 426 909 1555 2200
82-Origin & 1st app. Namora (5/47); 1st Sub-Mariner/Namora team-up; Captain America app. 300 600 900 2010 3505 5000
83,85: 83-Last Young Allies. 85-Last Miss America; Blonde Phantom app. 132 264 396 845 1448 2050
84-Blonde Phantom begins (on-c of #84,88,89); Sub-Mariner by Everett begins; Captain America app.; Everett-c 171 342 513 1094 1872 2650
86-Blonde Phantom i.d. revealed; Captain America app.; last Bucky app. 139 278 417 890 1520 2150
87-1st Capt. America/Golden Girl team-up; last Toro app. (8/48) 148 296 444 947 1624 2300
88-Golden Girl, Namora, & Sun Girl (1st in Marvel Comics) x-over; Captain America, Blonde Phantom app. 142 284 426 909 1555 2200
89-1st Human Torch/Sun Girl team-up; 1st Captain America solo; Blonde Phantom app. 140 280 420 896 1536 2175
90,91: 90-Blonde Phantom un-masked; Captain America app. 91-Capt. America app.; Blonde Phantom & Sub-Mariner end; early Venus app. (4/49) (scarce) 194 388 582 1242 2121 3000
92-Feature story on the birth of the Human Torch and the death of Professor Horton (his creator); 1st app. The Witness in Marvel Comics; Captain America app. (scarce) 371 742 1113 2600 4550 6500
132 Pg. issue, B&W, 25¢ (1943-44)-printed in N. Y.; square binding, blank inside covers); has Marvel No. 33-c in color; contains Capt. America #18 & Marvel Mystery Comics #33; same contents as Captain America Annual 7000 14,000 21,500 43,500 - -
132 Pg. issue (with variant contents), B&W, 25¢ (1942-'43)- square binding, blank inside covers; has same Marvel No. 33-c in color but contains Capt. America #22 & Marvel Mystery Comics #41 instead 7000 14,000 21,500 43,500 - -

NOTE: ***Brodsky*** *c-49, 72, 86, 88-92.* ***Crandall*** *a-26i.* ***Everett*** *c-9, 27, 84.* ***Gabrielle*** *c-30-32.* ***Schomburg*** *c-3-11, 13-29, 33-36, 39-48, 50-59, 63-69, 74, 76, 132 pg. issue.* ***Shores*** *c-37, 38, 75p, 77, 78p, 79p, 80, 81p, 82-84, 85p, 87p.* ***Sekowsky*** *c-73. Bondage covers-3, 4, 7, 12, 28, 29, 49, 50, 52, 56, 57, 58, 59, 65. Angel c-2, 3, 8, 12. Remember Pearl Harbor issues-#30-32.*

MARVEL MYSTERY COMICS
Marvel Comics: Dec, 1999 ($3.95, reprints)

1-Reprints original 1940s stories; Schomburg-c from #74 5.00

MARVEL MYSTERY COMICS 70th ANNIVERARY SPECIAL
Marvel Comics: Jul, 2009 ($3.99, one-shot)

1-Rivera-c; new Sub-Mariner/Human Torch team-up set in 1941; reps. from #4 & 5 5.00

MARVEL MYSTERY HANDBOOK: 70th ANNIVERARY SPECIAL
Marvel Comics: 2009 ($4.99, one-shot)

1-Official Handbook-style profile pages of characters from Marvel's first year 5.00

MARVEL NEMESIS: THE IMPERFECTS (EA Games characters)
Marvel Comics: July, 2005 - No. 6, Dec, 2005 ($2.99, limited series)

1-6-Jae Lee-c/Greg Pak-s/Renato Arlem-a; Spider-Man, Thing, Wolverine, Elektra app 3.00
Digest (2005, $7.99) r/#1-6 8.00

MARVEL 1985
Marvel Comics: July, 2008 - No. 6, Dec, 2008 ($3.99, limited series)

1-6: 1-Marvel villains come to the real world; Millar-s/Edwards-a; three covers 4.00
HC (2009, $24.99) r/#1-6; intro. by Lindelof; Edwards production art 25.00

MARVEL NO-PRIZE BOOK, THE (The Official... on-c)
Marvel Comics Group: Jan, 1983 (one-shot, direct sales only)

1-Golden-c; Kirby-a 5.00

MARVEL NOW! POINT ONE
Marvel Comics: Dec, 2012 ($5.99, one-shot)

1-Short story lead-ins to new Marvel Now! series; Nick Fury, Nova, Star-Lord, Ant-Man & others app.; s/a by various; Granov-c and baby variant-c by Skottie Young 6.00

	GD	VG	FN	VF	VF/NM	NM-
	2.0	4.0	6.0	8.0	9.0	9.2

MARVEL: NOW WHAT?!
Marvel Comics: Dec, 2013 ($3.99, one-shot)

1-Short story spoofs; Doct. Octopus, X-Men, Avengers; s/a by various; Skottie Young-c 4.00

MARVELOUS ADVENTURES OF GUS BEEZER
Marvel Comics: May, 2003; Feb, 2004 ($2.99, one-shots)

...: Gus Beezer & Spider-Man 1 - (5/03) Gurihiru-a 3.00
...: Hulk 1 - (5/03) Simone-s/Lethcoe-a; She-Hulk app. 3.00
...: Spider-Man 1 - (5/03) Simone-s/Lethcoe-a; The Lizard & Dr. Doom app. 3.00
...: X-Men 1 - (5/03) Simone-s/Lethcoe-a 3.00

MARVELOUS LAND OF OZ (Sequel to Wonderful Wizard of Oz)
Marvel Comics: Jan, 2010 - No. 8, Sept, 2010 ($3.99, limited series)

1-8-Eric Shanower-a/Skottie Young-a/c. 1-Two covers by Young 4.00
1-Variant Pumpkinhead/Saw-Horse cover by McGuinness 6.00

MARVEL PETS HANDBOOK (Also see "Lockjaw and the Pet Avengers")
Marvel Comics: 2009 ($3.99, one-shot)

1-Official Handbook-style profile pages of animal characters 4.00

MARVEL PREMIERE
Marvel Comics Group: April, 1972 - No. 61, Aug, 1981 (A tryout book for new characters)

1-Origin Warlock (pre-#1) by Gil Kane/Adkins; origin Counter-Earth; Hulk & Thor cameo (#1-14 are 20¢-c) 7 14 21 49 92 135
2-Warlock ends; Kirby Yellow Claw-r 4 8 12 25 40 55
3-Dr. Strange series begins (pre #1, 7/72), B. Smith-c/a(p) 8 16 24 51 96 140
4-Smith/Brunner-a 4 8 12 23 37 50
5-9: 8-Starlin-c/a(p) 3 6 9 16 24 32
10-Death of the Ancient One 3 6 9 18 28 38
11-14: 11-Dr. Strange origin-r by Ditko. 14-Last Dr. Strange (3/74), gets own title 3 months later 2 4 6 13 18 22
15-Origin/1st app. Iron Fist (5/74), ends #25 10 20 30 69 147 225
16,25: 16-2nd app. Iron Fist; origin cont'd from #15; Hama's 1st Marvel-a. 25-1st Byrne Iron Fist (moves to own title next) 4 8 12 28 47 65
17-24: Iron Fist in all 3 6 9 20 31 42
26-Hercules. 2 4 6 8 10 12
27-Satana 2 4 6 10 14 18
28-Legion of Monsters (Ghost Rider, Man-Thing, Morbius, Werewolf) 3 6 9 19 30 40
29-46: 29,30-The Liberty Legion. 29-1st modern app. Patriot. 31-1st app. Woodgod; last 25¢ issue. 32-1st app. Monark Starstalker. 33,34-1st color app. Solomon Kane (Robert E. Howard adaptation "Red Shadows".) 35-Origin/1st app. 3-D Man. 36,37-3-D Man. 38-1st Weirdworld. 39,40-Torpedo. 41-1st Seeker 3000! 42-Tigra. 43-Paladin. 44-Jack of Hearts (1st solo book, 10/78). 45,46-Man-Wolf 1 2 3 5 6 8
29-31-(30¢-c variants, limited distribution)(4,6,8/76) 3 6 9 14 19 24
36-38-(35¢-c variants, limited distribution)(6,8,10/77) 3 6 9 19 30 40
47-Origin/1st app. new Ant-Man (Scott Lang); Byrne-a 6 12 18 38 69 100
48-Ant-Man; Byrne-a 3 6 9 19 30 40
49-The Falcon (1st solo book, 8/79) 1 3 4 6 8 10
50-1st app. Alice Cooper; co-plotted by Alice 2 4 6 9 13 16
51-56,58-60: 51-53-Black Panther. 54-1st Caleb Hammer. 55-Wonder Man. 56-1st color app. Dominic Fortune. 58-60-Dr. Who 6.00
57-Dr. Who (2nd U.S. app.-see Movie Classics) 1 3 4 6 8 10
61-Star Lord 1 3 4 6 8 10

NOTE: ***N. Adams*** *(Crusty Bunkers) part inks-10, 12, 13.* ***Austin*** *a-50i, 56i; c-46i, 50i, 56i, 58.* ***Brunner*** *a-4i, 6p, 9-14p; c-9-14.* ***Byrne*** *a-47p, 48p.* ***Chaykin*** *a-32-34; c-32, 33, 56.* ***Giffen*** *a-31p, 44p; c-44.* ***Gil Kane*** *a(p)-1, 2, 15; c(p)-1, 2, 15, 16, 22-24, 27, 36, 37.* ***Kirby*** *c-26, 29-31, 35.* ***Layton*** *a-47i, 48i; c-47.* ***McWilliams*** *a-25i.* ***Miller*** *c-49p, 53p, 58p.* ***Nebres*** *a-44i; c-38i.* ***Nino*** *a-38i.* ***Perez*** *c/a-38p, 45p, 46p.* ***Ploog*** *a-38; c-5-7.* ***Russell*** *a-7p.* ***Simonson*** *a-60(2pgs.); c-57.* ***Starlin*** *a-8p; c-8.* ***Sutton*** *a-41, 43, 50p, 61; c-50p, 61. #57-60 publ'd w/two different prices on-c.*

MARVEL PRESENTS
Marvel Comics: October, 1975 - No. 12, Aug, 1977 (#1-6 are 25¢ issues)

1-Origin & 1st app. Bloodstone 2 4 6 10 14 18
2-Origin Bloodstone continued; Buckler-c 2 3 4 6 8 10
3-Guardians of the Galaxy (1st solo book, 2/76) begins, ends #12 4 8 12 23 37 50
4-7,9-12: 9,10-Origin Starhawk 2 4 6 8 10 12
4-6-(30¢-c variants, limited distribution)(4-8/76) 3 6 9 19 30 40
8-r/story from Silver Surfer #2 plus 4 pgs. new-a 2 4 6 8 10 12
11,12-(35¢-c variants, limited distribution)(6,8/77) 4 8 12 27 44 60

NOTE: ***Austin*** *a-6i.* ***Buscema*** *r-8p.* ***Chaykin*** *a-5p.* ***Kane*** *c-1p.* ***Starlin*** *layouts-10.*

MARVEL PREVIEW (Magazine) (Bizarre Adventures #25 on)

Marvel Romance Redux: Guys & Dolls © MAR

Marvels Comics: X-Men #1 © MAR

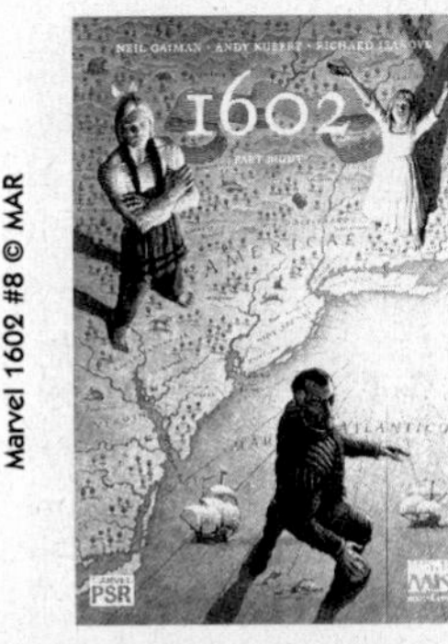

Marvel 1602 #8 © MAR

GD 2.0	VG 4.0	FN 6.0	VF 8.0	VF/NM 9.0	NM- 9.2

Marvel Comics: Feb (no month), 1975 - No. 24, Winter, 1980 (B&W) ($1.00)
1-Man-Gods From Beyond the Stars; Crusty Bunkers (Neal Adams)-a(i) & cover; Nino-a 3 6 9 17 26 35
2-1st origin The Punisher (see Amaz. Spider-Man #129 & Classic Punisher); 1st app. Dominic Fortune; Morrow-c 10 20 30 66 138 210
3,8,10: 3-Blade the Vampire Slayer. 8-Legion of Monsters; Morbius app. 10-Thor the Mighty; Starlin frontispiece 3 6 9 17 26 35
4-Star-Lord & Sword in the Star (origins & 1st app.); Morrow-c 15 30 45 103 227 350
5-Sherlock Holmes 3 6 9 14 19 24
6,9: 6-Sherlock Holmes; N. Adams frontispiece. 9-Man-God; origin Star Hawk, ends #20 2 4 6 11 16 20
7-(Summer/76) Debut of Rocket Raccoon in Sword in the Star story (see Incredible Hulk #271 (5/82) for next app.); Satana on cover 21 42 63 147 324 500
11,14,15,18-Star-Lord. 11-Byrne-a; Starlin frontispiece. 14-Starlin painted-c. 18-Sienkiewicz-a; Veitch & Bissette-a 5 10 15 31 53 75
12,16,19,21,23: 12-Haunt of Horror. 16-Masters of Terror. 19-Kull. 21-Moon Knight (Spr/80)-Predates Moon Knight #1; The Shroud by Ditko. 23-Bizarre Advs.; Miller-a 2 4 6 8 10 12
13,17,20,22,24: 14,15-Star-Lord. 17-Blackmark by G. Kane (see SSOC #1-3). 20-Bizarre Advs. 22-King Arthur. 24-Debut Paradox 1 2 3 5 6 8
NOTE: ***N. Adams*** *(C. Bunkers) r-20i.* ***Buscema*** *a-22, 23.* ***Byrne*** *a-11.* ***Chaykin*** *a-20r; c-20 (new).* ***Colan*** *a-8, 16p(3), 18p, 23p; c-16p.* ***Elias*** *a-18.* ***Giffen*** *a-7.* ***Infantino*** *a-14p.* ***Kaluta*** *a-12; c-15.* ***Miller*** *a-23.* ***Morrow*** *a-8i; c-2-4.* ***Perez*** *a-20p.* ***Ploog*** *a-8.* ***Starlin*** *c-13, 14. Nudity in some issues.*

MARVEL RIOT
Marvel Comics: Dec, 1995 ($1.95, one-shot)
1-"Age of Apocalypse" spoof; Lobdell script 3.00

MARVEL ROMANCE
Marvel Comics: 2006 ($19.99, TPB)
nn-Reprints romance stories from 1960-1972; art by Kirby, Buscema, Colan, Romita 20.00

MARVEL ROMANCE REDUX (Humor stories using art reprinted from Marvel romance comics)
Marvel Comics: Apr, 2006 - Aug, 2006 ($2.99, one-shots)
...: But I Thought He Loved Me Too (4/06) art by Kirby, Colan, Buscema & Romita; Giffen-c 3.00
...: Guys & Dolls (5/06) art by Starlin, Heck, Colan & Buscema; Conner-c 3.00
...: I Should Have Been a Blonde (7/06) art by Brodsky Colletta & Colan; Cho-c 3.00
...: Love is a Four Letter Word (8/06) art by Kirby, Buscema, Colan & Heck; Land-c 3.00
...: Restraining Orders are For Other Girls (6/06) art by Giordano, Kirby; Baker-c 3.00
...: Another Kind of Love TPB (2007, $13.99) r/one-shots 14.00

MARVELS (Also see Marvels: Eye of the Camera)
Marvel Comics: Jan, 1994 - No. 4, Apr, 1994 ($5.95, painted lim. series)
No. 1 (2nd Printing), Apr, 1996 - No. 4 (2nd Printing), July, 1996 ($2.95)
1-4: Kurt Busiek scripts & Alex Ross painted-c/a in all; double-c w/acetate overlay 1 2 3 5 6 8
Marvel Classic Collectors Pack ($11.90)-Issues #1 & 2 boxed (1st printings). 2 4 6 9 13 16
0-(8/94, $2.95)-no acetate overlay. 5.00
1-4-(2nd printing): r/original limited series w/o acetate overlay 3.00
Hardcover (1994, $59.95)-r/#0-4; w/intros by Stan Lee, John Romita, Sr., Kurt Busiek & Scott McCloud. 60.00
...: 10th Anniversary Edition (2004, $49.99, hardcover w/dustjacket) r/#0-4; scripts and commentaries; Ross sketch pages, cover gallery, behind the scenes art 50.00
Trade paperback ($19.95) 20.00

MARVEL SAGA, THE
Marvel Comics Group: Dec, 1985 - No. 25, Dec, 1987
1-25 4.00
NOTE: ***Williamson*** *a(i)-9, 10; c(i)-7, 10-12, 14, 16.*

MARVELS COMICS: ... (Marvel-type comics read in the Marvel Universe)
Marvel Comics: Jul, 2000 ($2.25, one-shots)
...Captain America #1 -Frenz & Sinnott-a; ...Daredevil #1 -Isabella-s/Newell-a; ...Fantastic Four #1 -Kesel-s/Paul Smith-a; Spider-Man #1 -Oliff-a; ...Thor #1 -Templeton-s/Aucoin-a 3.00
...X-Men #1 -Millar-s/ Sean Phillips & Duncan Fegredo-a 3.00
The History of Marvels Comics (no cover price)-Faux history; previews titles 3.00

MARVEL SELECT FLIP MAGAZINE
Marvel Comics: Aug, 2005 - No. 24 ($3.99/$4.99)
1-11-Reprints Astonishing X-Men and New X-Men: Academy X in flip format 4.00
12-24-($4.99) Reprints recent X-Men mini-series in flip format 5.00

MARVEL SELECTS:
Marvel Comics: Jan, 2000 - No. 6, June, 2000 ($2.75/$2.99, reprints)
...Fantastic Four 1-6: Reprints F.F. #107-112; new Davis-c 3.00
...Spider-Man 1,2,4-6: Reprints AS-M #100,101,103,104,93; Wieringo-c 3.00
...Spider-Man 3 ($2.99): Reprints AS-M #102; new Wieringo-c 3.00

MARVELS: EYE OF THE CAMERA (Sequel to Marvels)
Marvel Comics: Feb, 2009 - No. 6, Apr, 2010 ($3.99, limited series)
1-6-Kurt Busiek-s/Jay Anacleto-a; continuing story of photographer Phil Sheldon 4.00
1-6-B&W edition 4.00

MARVEL'S GREATEST COMICS (Marvel Collectors' Item Classics #1-22)
Marvel Comics Group: No. 23, Oct, 1969 - No. 96, Jan, 1981
23-34 (Giants). Begin Fantastic Four-r/#30s?-116 3 6 9 17 26 35
35-37-Silver Surfer-r/Fantastic Four #48-50 2 4 6 9 12 15
38-50: 42-Silver Surfer-r/F.F.(others?) 1 2 3 5 7 9
51-70: 63,64-(25¢ editions) 6.00
63,64-(30¢-c variants, limited distribution)(5,7/76) 3 6 9 14 19 24
71-96: 71-73-(30¢ editions) 5.00
71-73-(35¢-c variants, limited distribution)(7,9-10/77) 3 6 9 19 30 40
...: Fantastic Four #52 (2006, $2.99) reprints entire comic with ads and letter column 4.00
NOTE: *Dr. Strange, Fantastic Four, Iron Man, Watcher-#23, 24. Capt. America, Dr. Strange, Iron Man, Fantastic Four-#25-28. Fantastic Four-#38-96.* ***Buscema*** *r-85-92; c-87-92r.* ***Ditko*** *r-23-28.* ***Kirby*** *r-23-82; c-75, 77p, 80p. #81 reprints Fantastic Four #100.*

MARVEL'S GREATEST SUPERHERO BATTLES (See Fireside Book Series)

MARVEL: SHADOWS AND LIGHT
Marvel Comics: Feb, 1997 ($2.95, B&W, one-shot)
1-Tony Daniel-c 3.00

MARVEL 1602
Marvel Comics: Nov, 2003 - No. 8, June, 2004 ($3.50/$3.99, limited series)
1-7-Neil Gaiman-s; Andy Kubert & Richard Isanove-a 3.50
8-($3.99) 4.00
... MGC #1 (7/10, $1.00) r/#1 with "Marvel's Greatest Comics" logo on cover 3.00
HC (2004, $24.99) r/series; script pages for #1, sketch pages and Gaiman afterword 25.00
SC (2005, $19.99) 20.00

MARVEL 1602: FANTASTICK FOUR
Marvel Comics: Nov, 2006 - No. 5, Mar, 2007s ($3.50, limited series)
1-5-Peter David-s/Pascal Alixe-a/Leinil Yu-c 3.50
TPB (2007, $14.99) r/#1-5; sketch page 15.00

MARVEL 1602: NEW WORLD
Marvel Comics: Oct, 2005 - No. 5, Jan, 2006 ($3.50, limited series)
1-5-Greg Pak-s/Greg Tocchini-a; "Hulk" and "Iron Man" app. 3.50
TPB (2006, $14.99) r/#1-5 15.00

MARVEL 65TH ANNIVERSARY SPECIAL
Marvel Comics: 2004 ($4.99, one-shot)
1-Reprints Sub-Mariner & Human Torch battle from Marvel Mystery Comics #8-10 6.00

MARVELS OF SCIENCE
Charlton Comics: March, 1946 - No. 4, June, 1946
1-A-Bomb story 23 46 69 136 223 310
2-4 14 28 42 80 115 150

MARVEL SPECIAL EDITION FEATURING... (Also see Special Collectors' Ed.)
Marvel Comics Group: 1975 - 1978 (84 pgs.) (Oversized)
1-The Spectacular Spider-Man ($1.50); r/Amazing Spider-Man #6,35, Annual 1; Ditko-a(r) 3 6 9 19 30 40
1,2-Star Wars ('77,'78; r/Star Wars #1-3 & #4-6; regular edition and Whitman variant exist 2 4 6 11 16 20
3-Star Wars ('78, $2.50, 116 pgs.); r/S. Wars #1-6; regular edition and Whitman variant exist 3 6 9 14 20 26
3-Close Encounters of the Third Kind (1978, $1.50, 56 pgs.)-Movie adaptation; Simonson-a(p) 2 4 6 10 14 18
V2#2(Spring, 1980, $2.00, oversized)- "Star Wars: The Empire Strikes Back"; r/Marvel Comics Super Special #16 3 6 9 16 23 30
NOTE: ***Chaykin*** *c/a(r)-1(1977), 2, 3.* ***Stevens*** *a(r)-2i, 3i.* ***Williamson*** *a(r)-V2#2.*

MARVEL SPECTACULAR
Marvel Comics Group: Aug, 1973 - No. 19, Nov, 1975
1-Thor-r from mid-sixties begin by Kirby 2 4 6 10 14 18
2-19 1 3 4 6 8 10

MARVELS: PORTRAITS
Marvel Comics: Mar, 1995 - No. 4, June, 1995 ($2.95, limited series)
1-4:Different artists renditions of Marvel characters 3.00

MARVEL SPOTLIGHT (...& Son of Satan #19, 20, 23, 24)

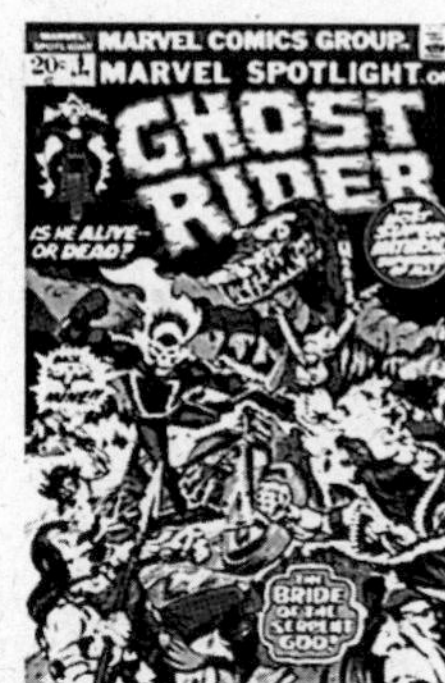

Marvel Spotlight #9 © MAR

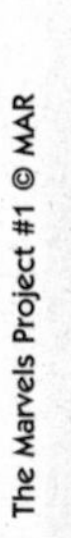
The Marvels Project #1 © MAR

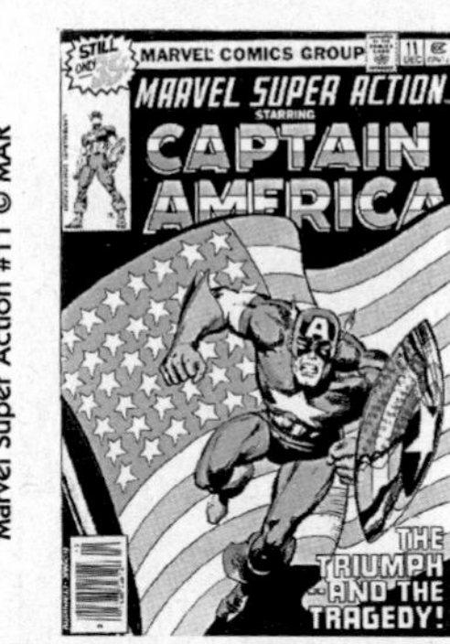

Marvel Super Action #11 © MAR

GD VG FN VF VF/NM NM-
2.0 4.0 6.0 8.0 9.0 9.2

GD VG FN VF VF/NM NM-
2.0 4.0 6.0 8.0 9.0 9.2

Marvel Comics Group: Nov, 1971 - No. 33, Apr, 1977; V2#1, July, 1979 - V2#11, Mar, 1981 (A try-out book for new characters)

1-Origin Red Wolf (western hero)(1st solo book, pre-#1); Wood inks, Neal Adams-c; only 15¢ issue 5 10 15 34 60 85
2-(25¢, 52 pgs.)-Venus-r by Everett; origin/1st app. Werewolf By Night (begins) by Ploog; N. Adams-c 18 36 54 126 281 435
3,4: 4-Werewolf By Night ends (6/72); gets own title 9/72 6 12 18 40 73 105
5-Origin/1st app. Ghost Rider (8/72) & begins 28 56 84 202 451 700
6-8: 6-Origin G.R. retold. 8-Last Ploog issue 8 16 24 52 99 145
9-11-Last Ghost Rider (gets own title next mo.) 6 12 18 37 66 95
12-Origin & 2nd full app. The Son of Satan (10/73); story cont'd from Ghost Rider #2 & into #3; series begins, ends #24 4 8 12 27 44 60
13-24: 13-Partial origin Son of Satan. 14-Last 20¢ issue. 22-Ghost Rider-c & cameo (5 panels). 24-Last Son of Satan (10/75); gets own title 12/75 2 4 6 9 12 15
25,27,30,31: 27-(Regular 25¢-c), Sub-Mariner app. 30-The Warriors Three. 31-Nick Fury 1 2 3 5 6 8
26-Scarecrow 2 4 6 8 10 12
27-(30¢-c variant, limited distribution) 3 6 9 14 20 25
28-(Regular 25¢-c) 1st solo Moon Knight app. 4 8 12 27 44 60
28-(30¢-c variant, limited distribution) 8 16 24 54 102 150
29-(Regular 25¢-c) (8/76) Moon Knight app.; last 25¢ issue 3 6 9 17 26 35
29-(30¢-c variant, limited distribution) 6 12 18 40 73 105
32-1st app./partial origin Spider-Woman (2/77); Nick Fury app. 4 8 12 23 37 50
33-Deathlok; 1st app. Devil-Slayer 2 4 6 8 10 12
V2#1-5,9-11: 1-4-Capt. Marvel. 5-Dragon Lord. 9-11-Capt. Universe (see Micronauts #8) 6.00
1-Variant copy missing issue #1 on cover 2 4 6 10 14 18
6-Star-Lord origin 3 6 9 19 30 40
7-Star-Lord; Miller-c 4 8 12 23 37 50
8-Capt. Marvel; Miller-c/a(p) 2 4 6 8 10 12

NOTE: ***Austin*** *c-V2#2i, 8.* ***J. Buscema*** *c/a-30p.* ***Chaykin*** *a-31; c-26, 31.* ***Colan*** *a-18p, 19p.* ***Ditko*** *a-V2#4, 5, 9-11; c-V2#4, 9-11.* ***Kane*** *c-21p, 32p.* ***Kirby*** *c-29p.* ***McWilliams*** *a-20i.* ***Miller*** *a-V2#8p; c(p)-V2#2, 5, 7, 8.* ***Mooney*** *a-8i, 10i, 14p, 15, 16p, 17p, 24p, 27, 32i.* ***Nasser*** *a-33p.* ***Ploog*** *a-2-5, 6-8p; c-3-9.* ***Romita*** *c-13.* ***Sutton*** *a-9-11p, V2#6, 7. #29-25¢ & 30¢ issues exist.*

MARVEL SPOTLIGHT (Most issues spotlight one Marvel artist and one Marvel writer)
Marvel Comics: 2005 - Present ($2.99/$3.99)

...Brian Bendis/Mark Bagley; Daniel Way/Olivier Coipel; David Finch/Roberto Aguirre-Sacasa; Ed Brubaker/Billy Tan; John Cassaday/Sean McKeever; Joss Whedon/Michael Lark; Laurell K. Hamilton/George R.R. Martin; Neil Gaiman/Salvador Larroca; Robert Kirkman/ Greg Land; Stan Lee/Jack Kirby; Warren Ellis/Jim Cheung each... 3.00
...Steve McNiven/Mark Millar - Civil War 10.00
...: Captain America (2009) interviews with Brubaker & Hitch; Reborn preview 3.00
...: Captain America Remembered (2007) character features; creator interviews 3.00
...: Civil War Aftermath (2007) Top 10 Moments, casualty list, previews of upcoming series 3.00
...: Dark Reign (2009) features on the Avengers, Fury and others; creator interview 4.00
...: Dark Tower (2007) previews the Stephen King adaptation; creator interviews 5.00
...: Deadpool (2009) character features; interviews with Kelly, Way, Medina & Benson 3.00
...: Fantastic Four and Silver Surfer (2007) character features; creator interviews 3.00
...: Ghost Rider (2007) character and movie features; creator interviews 3.00
...: Halo (2007) a World of Halo feature; Bendis & Maleev interviews 3.00
...: Heroes Reborn/Onslaught Reborn (2006) 3.00
...: Hulk Movie (2008) character and movie features; comic & movie creator interviews 3.00
...: Iron Man Movie (2008) character and movie features; Terrence Howard interview 3.00
...: Iron Man 2 (4/10) movie preview; Granov, Fraction interviews; Whiplash profile 4.00
...: Marvel Knights 10th Anniversary (2008) Quesada interview; series synopsis 3.00
...: Marvel Zombies/Mystic Arcana (2008) character features; creator interviews 3.00
...: Marvel Zombies Return (2009) character features; creator interviews 3.00
...: New Mutants (2009) character features; Claremont & McLeod interviews 3.00
...: Punisher Movie (2008) character and movie features; creator interviews 3.00
...: Secret Invasion (2008) features on the Skrulls; Bendis, Reed & Yu interviews 3.00
...: Secret Invasion Aftermath (2008) Skrull profiles; Bendis, Reed & Diggle interviews 4.00
...: Spider-Man (2007) character features; creator interviews; Ditko art showcase 3.00
...: Spider-Man - Brand New Day (2008) storyline features; Romitas interviews 3.00
...: Spider-Man-One More Day/Brand New Day (2008) storyline features; interviews 3.00
...: Summer Events (2009, $3.99) 2009 title previews; creator interviews 4.00
...: Thor (2007) character features; Straczynski interview; Romita Jr. art showcase 3.00
...: Ultimates 3 (2008) character features; Loeb & Madureira interviews 3.00
...: Ultimatum (2008) previews the limited series; Loeb & Bendis interviews 3.00
...: Uncanny X-Men 500 Issues Celebration (2008) creator interviews; timeline 3.00
...: War of Kings (2009) character features; Abnett, Lanning, Pelletier interviews 3.00
...: Wolverine (2009, $3.99) preview of 2009 Wolverine stories; creator interviews 4.00
...: World War Hulk (2007) character features; creator interviews; early art showcase 3.00
...: X-Men: Messiah Complex (2008) X-Men crossover features; creator interviews 3.00

MARVELS PROJECT, THE
Marvel Comics: Oct, 2009 - No. 8, July, 2010 ($3.99, limited series)

1-8-Emergence of Marvel heroes in 1939-40; Brubaker-s/Epting-a; Epting & McNiven-c 4.00
1-8-Variant covers by Parel 5.00

MARVEL'S THE AVENGERS: BLACK WIDOW STRIKES
Marvel Comics: Jul, 2012 - No. 3, Aug, 2012 ($2.99, limited series)

1-3-Prelude to 2012 movie; Van Lente-s. 1,3-Photo-c. 2-Granov-c 3.00

MARVEL'S THE AVENGERS PRELUDE
Marvel Comics: May, 2012 - No. 4, Jun, 2012 ($2.99, limited series)

1-4: 1-Prelude to 2012 movie; Luke Ross & Daniel HDR-a 3.00

MARVEL'S THE AVENGERS: THE AVENGERS INITIATIVE
Marvel Comics: Jul, 2012 ($2.99, one-shot)

1-Prelude to 2012 movie; Van Lente-s/Lim-a 3.00

MARVEL SUPER ACTION (Magazine)
Marvel Comics Group: Jan, 1976 (B&W, 76 pgs.)

1-2nd app. Dominic Fortune (see Marvel Preview); early Punisher app.; Weird World & The Huntress; Evans, Ploog-a 8 16 24 54 102 150

MARVEL SUPER ACTION
Marvel Comics Group: May, 1977 - No. 37, Nov, 1981

1-Reprints Capt. America #100 by Kirby 2 4 6 13 18 22
2-13: 2,3,5-13 reprint Capt. America #101,102,103-111. 4-Marvel Boy-r(origin)/M. Boy #1. 11-Origin-r. 12,13-Classic Steranko-c/a(r). 2 4 6 8 10 12
2,3-(35¢-c variants, limited distribution)(6,8/77) 4 8 12 23 37 50
14-20: r/Avengers #55,56, Annual 2, others 1 2 3 5 6 8
21-37: 30-r/Hulk #6 from U.K. 6.00

NOTE: ***Buscema*** *a(r)-14p, 15p; c-18-20, 22, 35r-37.* ***Everett*** *a-4.* ***Heath*** *a-4r.* ***Kirby*** *r-1-3, 5-11.* ***B. Smith*** *a-27r, 28r.* ***Steranko*** *a(r)-12p, 13p; c-12r, 13r.*

MARVEL SUPER HERO CONTEST OF CHAMPIONS
Marvel Comics Group: June, 1982 - No. 3, Aug, 1982 (Limited series)

1-Features nearly all Marvel characters currently appearing in their comics; 1st Marvel limited series 2 4 6 9 12 15
2,3 1 2 3 5 6 8

MARVEL SUPER HEROES
Marvel Comics Group: October, 1966 (25¢, 68 pgs.) (1st Marvel one-shot)

1-r/origin Daredevil from D.D. #1; r/Avengers #2; G.A. Sub-Mariner-r/Marvel Mystery #8 (Human Torch app.). Kirby-a 11 22 33 72 154 235

MARVEL SUPER-HEROES (Formerly Fantasy Masterpieces #1-11)
(Also see Giant-Size Super Heroes) (#12-20: 25¢, 68 pgs.)
Marvel Comics: No. 12, 12/67 - No. 31, 11/71; No. 32, 9/72 - No. 105, 1/82

12-Origin & 1st app. Capt. Marvel of the Kree; G.A. Human Torch, Destroyer, Capt. America, Black Knight, Sub-Mariner-r (#12-20 all contain new stories and reprints) 14 28 42 96 211 325
13-2nd app. Capt. Marvel; 1st app. of Carol Danvers (later becomes Ms. Marvel); Golden Age Black Knight, Human Torch, Vision, Capt. America, Sub-Mariner-r 13 26 39 89 195 300
14-Amazing Spider-Man (5/68, new-a by Andru/Everett); G.A. Sub-Mariner, Torch, Mercury (1st Kirby-a at Marvel), Black Knight, Capt. America reprints 9 18 27 62 126 190
15-17: 15-Black Bolt cameo in Medusa (new-a); Black Knight, Sub-Mariner, Black Marvel, Capt. America-r. 16-Origin & 1st app. S. A. Phantom Eagle; G.A. Torch, Capt. America, Black Knight, Patriot, Sub-Mariner-r. 17-Origin Black Knight (new-a); G.A. Torch, Sub-Mariner-r; reprint from All-Winners Squad #21 (cover & story) 5 10 15 31 53 75
18-Origin/1st app. Guardians of the Galaxy (1/69); G.A. Sub-Mariner, All-Winners Squad-r 32 64 96 230 515 800
19-Ka-Zar (new-a); G.A. Torch, Marvel Boy, Black Knight, Sub-Mariner reprints; Smith-c(p); Tuska-a(r) 4 8 12 27 44 60
20-Doctor Doom (5/69); r/Young Men #24 w/-c 5 10 15 30 50 70
21-31: All-r issues. 21-X-Men, Daredevil, Iron Man-r begin, end #31. 31-Last Giant issue 3 6 9 17 26 35
32-50: 32-Hulk/Sub-Mariner-r begin from TTA. 1 2 3 6 8 10
51-70,100: 56-r/origin Hulk/Inc. Hulk #102; Hulk-r begin 1 2 3 5 6 8
57,58-(30¢-c variants, limited distribution)(5,7/76) 3 6 9 15 22 28
65,66-(35¢-c variants, limited distribution)(7,9/77) 3 6 9 20 31 42
71-99,101-105 6.00

NOTE: ***Austin*** *a-104.* ***Colan*** *a(p)-12, 13, 15, 18; c-12, 13, 15, 18.* ***Everett*** *a-14i(new); r-14, 15i, 18, 19, 33; c-*

Marvel Super-Heroes #74 © MAR

Marvel Tales #93 © MAR

Marvel Tales (2nd series) #31 © MAR

GD VG FN VF VF/NM NM-
2.0 4.0 6.0 8.0 9.0 9.2

85(r). New ***Kirby*** *c-22, 27, 54.* ***Maneely*** *r-14, 15, 19.* ***Severin*** *r-83-85i, 100-102; c-100-102r.* ***Starlin*** *c-47.* ***Tuska*** *a-19p. Black Knight-r by* ***Maneely*** *in 12-16, 19. Sub-Mariner-r by* ***Everett*** *in 12-20.*

MARVEL SUPER-HEROES
Marvel Comics: May, 1990 - V2#15, Oct, 1993 ($2.95/$2.50, quart., 68-84 pgs.)

1-Moon Knight, Hercules, Black Panther, Magik, Brother Voodoo, Speedball (by Ditko) & Hellcat; Hembeck-a 5.00
2,4,5,V2#3,6-15: 2-Summer Special(7/90); Rogue, Speedball (by Ditko), Iron Man, Falcon, Tigra & Daredevil. 4-Spider-Man/Nick Fury, Daredevil,Speedball, Wonder Man, Spitfire & Black Knight; Byrne-c. 5-Thor, Dr. Strange, Thing & She-Hulk; Speedball by Ditko(p). V2#3-Retells origin Capt. America w/new facts; Blue Shield, Capt. Marvel,Speedball, Wasp; Hulk by Ditko/Rogers V2#6-9: 6-8-$2.25-c. 6,7-X-Men, Cloak & Dagger, The Shroud (by Ditko) & Marvel Boy in each. 8-X-Men, Namor & Iron Man (by Ditko); Larsen-c. 9-West Coast Avengers, Iron Man app.; Kieth-c(p). V2#10-Ms. Marvel/Sabretooth-c/story (intended for Ms. Marvel #24; shows-c to #24); Namor, Vision, Scarlet Witch stories. V2#11,12 :11-Original Ghost Rider-c/story; Giant-Man, Ms. Marvel stories. 12-Dr. Strange, Falcon, Iron Man. V2#13-15 ($2.75, 84 pgs.): 13-All Iron Man 30th anniversary. 15-Iron Man/Thor/Volstagg/Dr. Druid 4.00

MARVEL SUPER-HEROES MEGAZINE
Marvel Comics: Oct, 1994 - No. 6, Mar, 1995 ($2.95, 100 pgs.)

1-6: 1-r/FF #232, DD #159, Iron Man #115, Incred. Hulk #314 4.00

MARVEL SUPER-HEROES SECRET WARS (See Secret Wars II)
Marvel Comics Group: May, 1984 - No. 12, Apr, 1985 (limited series)

1 2 4 6 11 16 20
1-3-(2nd printings, sold in multi-packs) 3.00
2-6,9-11: 6-The Wasp dies 1 2 3 5 6 8
7,12: 7-Intro. new Spider-Woman. 12-($1.00, 52 pgs.) 1 3 4 6 8 10
8-Spider-Man's new black costume explained as alien costume (1st app. Venom as alien costume) 4 8 12 23 37 50
Secret Wars Omnibus HC (2008, $99.99, dustjacket) r/#1-12, Thor #383, She-Hulk (2004) #10 and What If? (1989) #4 & #114; photo gallery of related toys; pencil-a from #1 100.00
NOTE: ***Zeck*** *a-1-12; c-1,3,8-12. Additional artists (John Romita Sr., Art Adams and others) had uncreditted art in #12.*

MARVEL SUPER HERO SQUAD (All ages)
Marvel Comics: Mar, 2009; Nov, 2009 - No. 4, Feb, 2010 ($3.99/$2.99)

1-4-Based on the animated series; back-up humor strips and pin-ups 3.00
...Hero Up! (3/09, $3.99) Collects humor strips from MarvelKids.com; 2 covers 4.00

MARVEL SUPER HERO SQUAD (All ages)
Marvel Comics: Mar, 2010 - No. 12, Feb, 2011 ($2.99)

1-12-Based on the animated series. 1-Wraparound-c 3.00
Super Hero Squad Spectacular 1 (4/11, $3.99) The Beyonder app. 4.00

MARVEL SUPER SPECIAL, A (See Marvel Comics Super...)

MARVEL SWIMSUIT SPECIAL (Also see Marvel Illustrated...)
Marvel Comics: 1992 - No. 4, 1995 ($3.95/$4.50, magazine, 52 pgs.)

1-4-Silvestri-c; pin-ups by diff. artists. 2-Jusko-c. 3-Hughes-c 1 3 4 6 8 10

MARVEL TAILS STARRING PETER PORKER THE SPECTACULAR SPIDER-HAM
(Also see Peter Porker...)
Marvel Comics Group: Nov, 1983 (one-shot)

1-Peter Porker, the Spectacular Spider-Ham, Captain Americat, Goose Rider, Hulk Bunny app. 4.00

MARVEL TALES (Formerly Marvel Mystery Comics #1-92)
Marvel/Atlas Comics (MCI): No. 93, Aug, 1949 - No. 159, Aug, 1957

93-Horror/weird stories begin 181 362 543 1158 1979 2800
94-Everett-a 123 246 369 787 1344 1900
95-New logo 90 180 270 576 988 1400
96,99,101,103,105 65 130 195 416 708 1000
97-Sun Girl, 2 pgs; Kirbyish-a; one story used in N.Y. State Legislative document 86 172 258 546 936 1325
98,100: 98-Krigstein-a 66 132 198 419 722 1025
102-Wolverton-a "The End of the World", (6 pgs.) 87 174 261 553 952 1350
104-Wolverton-a "Gateway to Horror", (6 pgs.) 87 174 261 553 952 1350
106,107-Krigstein-a. 106-Decapitation story 53 106 159 334 567 800
108-120: 116-(7/53) Werewolf By Night story. 118-Hypo-c/panels in End of World story. 120-Jack Katz-a 39 78 117 240 395 550
121,123-131: 128-Flying Saucer-c. 131-Last precode (2/55) 34 68 102 199 325 450
122-Kubert-a 34 68 102 204 332 460
132,133,135-141,143,145 26 52 78 154 252 350
134-Krigstein, Kubert-a; flying saucer-c 29 58 87 170 278 385

GD VG FN VF VF/NM NM-
2.0 4.0 6.0 8.0 9.0 9.2

142-Krigstein-a 27 54 81 158 259 360
144-Williamson/Krenkel-a, 3 pgs. 27 54 81 158 259 360
146,148-151,154-156,158: 150-1st S.A. issue. 156-Torres-a 21 42 63 126 206 285
147,152: 147-Ditko-a. 152-Wood, Morrow-a 24 48 72 140 230 320
153-Everett End of World c/story 26 52 78 154 252 350
157,159-Krigstein-a 22 44 66 132 216 300
NOTE: ***Andru*** *a-103.* ***Briefer*** *a-118.* ***Check*** *a-147.* ***Colan*** *a-102, 105, 107, 118, 120, 121, 127, 131.* ***Drucker*** *a-127, 135, 141, 146, 150.* ***Everett*** *a-98, 104, 106(2), 108(2), 131, 148, 151, 153, 155; c-107, 109, 111, 112, 114, 117, 127, 143, 147-151, 153, 155, 156.* ***Forte*** *a-119, 125, 130, 158.* ***Heath*** *a-110, 113, 118, 119; c-104-106, 110, 130.* ***Gil Kane*** *a-117.* ***Lawrence*** *a-130.* ***Maneely*** *a-111, 126, 129; c-108, 116, 120, 129, 152.* ***Mooney*** *a-114.* ***Morisi*** *a-153.* ***Morrow*** *a-150, 152, 156.* ***Orlando*** *a-149, 151, 157.* ***Pakula*** *a-119, 121, 133, 135, 144, 150, 152, 156.* ***Powell*** *a-136, 137, 150, 154.* ***Ravielli*** *a-117, 123.* ***Rico*** *a-97, 99.* ***Romita*** *a-108.* ***Sekowsky*** *a-96-98.* ***Shores*** *a-110; c-96.* ***Sinnott*** *a-105, 116, 144.* ***Tuska*** *a-114.* ***Whitney*** *a-107.* ***Wildey*** *a-126, 138.*

MARVEL TALES (...Annual #1,2; ...Starring Spider-Man #123 on)
Marvel Comics Group (NPP earlier issues): 1964 - No. 291, Nov, 1994 (No. 1-32: 72 pgs.)
(#1-3 have Canadian variants; back & inside-c are blank, same value)

1-Reprints origins of Spider-Man/Amazing Fantasy #15, Hulk/Inc. Hulk#1, Ant-Man/T.T.A. #35, Giant Man/T.T.A. #49, Iron Man/T.O.S. #39,48, Thor/J.I.M. #83 & r/Sgt. Fury #1 30 60 90 216 483 750
2 ('65)-r/X-Men #1(origin), Avengers #1(origin), origin Dr. Strange-r/Strange Tales #115 & origin Hulk(Hulk #3) 10 20 30 66 138 210
3 (7/66)-Spider-Man, Strange Tales (H. Torch), Journey into Mystery (Thor), Tales to Astonish (Ant-Man)-r begin (r/Strange Tales #101) 6 12 18 40 73 105
4,5 5 10 15 30 50 70
6-8,10: 10-Reprints 1st Kraven/Amaz. S-M #15 3 6 9 21 33 45
9-r/Amazing Spider-Man #14 w/cover 4 8 12 23 37 50
11-33: 11-Spider-Man battles Daredevil-r/Amaz. Spider-Man #16. 13-Origin Marvel Boy-r from M. Boy #1. 22-Green Goblin-c/story-r/Amaz. Spider-Man #27. 30-New Angel story (x-over w/Ka-Zar #2,3). 32-Last 72 pg. iss. 33-(52 pgs.) Kraven-r 3 6 9 16 23 30
34-50: 34-Begin regular size issues 2 3 4 6 8 10
51-65 1 2 3 5 6 8
66-70-(Regular 25¢ editions)(4-8/76) 1 2 3 5 6 8
66-70-(30¢-c variants, limited distribution) 3 6 9 19 30 40
71-105: 75-Origin Spider-Man-r. 77-79-Drug issues-r/Amaz. Spider-Man #96-98. 98-Death of Gwen Stacy-r/Amaz. Spider-Man #121 (Green Goblin). 99-Death Green Goblin-r/Amaz. Spider-Man #122. 100-(52 pgs.)-New Hawkeye/Two Gun Kid story. 101-105-All Spider-Man-r 6.00
80-84-(35¢-c variants, limited distribution)(6-10/77) 3 6 9 17 26 35
106-r/1st Punisher-Amazing Spider-Man #129 2 4 6 8 10 12
107-136: 107-133-All Spider-Man-r. 111,112-r/Spider-Man #134,135 (Punisher). 113,114-r/Spider-Man #136,137(Green Goblin). 126-128-r/clone story from Amazing Spider-Man #149-151. 134-136-Dr. Strange-r begin; SpM stories continue. 134-Dr. Strange-r/Strange Tales #110 5.00
137-Origin-r Dr. Strange; shows original unprinted-c & origin Spider-Man/Amazing Fantasy #15 2 4 6 8 10 12
137-Nabisco giveaway 2 4 6 8 10 12
138-Reprints all Amazing Spider-Man #1; begin reprints of Spider-Man with covers similar to originals 1 2 3 5 7 9
139-144: r/Amazing Spider-Man #2-7 6.00
145-149,151-190,193-199: Spider-Man-r continue w/#8 on. 149-Contains skin "Tattooz" decals. 153-r/1st Kraven/Spider-Man #15. 155-r/2nd Green Goblin/Spider-Man #17. 161,164,165-Gr. Goblin-c/stories-r/Spider-Man #23,26,27. 178,179-Green Goblin-c/story-r/ Spider-Man #39,40. 187,189-Kraven-r. 193-Byrne-r/Marvel Team-Up begin w/scripts 5.00
150,191,192,200: 150-($1.00, 52pgs.)-r/Spider-Man Annual #1(Kraven app.). 191-($1.50, 68 pgs.)-r/Spider-Man #96-98. 192-($1.25, 52 pgs.)-r/Spider-Man #121,122. 200-Double size ($1.25)-Miller-c & r/Annual #14 6.00
201-249,251,252,254-257: 208-Last Byrne-r. 210,211-r/Spidey #134,135. 212,213-r/Giant-Size Spidey #4. 213-r/1st solo Silver Surfer story/F.F. Annual #5. 214,215-r/Spidey #161,162. 222-Reprints origin Punisher/Spect. Spider-Man #83; last Punisher reprint. 209-Reprints 1st app. The Punisher/Amazing Spider-Man #129; Punisher reprints begin, end #222. 223-McFarlane-c begins, end #239. 233-Spider-Man/X-Men team-ups begin; r/X-Men #35. 234-r/Marvel Team-Up #4. 235,236-r/M. Team-Up Annual #1. 237,238-r/M. Team-Up #150. 239,240-r/M. Team-Up #38,90(Beast). 242-r/M.Team-Up #89. 243-r/M. Team-Up #117 (Wolverine). 251-r/Spider-Man #100 (Green Goblin-c/story). 252-r/1st app. Morbius/Amaz. Spider-Man #101. 254-r/M. Team-Up #15(Ghost Rider); new painted-c. 255,256-Spider-Man & Ghost Rider-r/Marvel Team-Up #58,91. 257-Hobgoblin-r begin (r/ASM #238) 3.00
250,253: 250-($1.50, 52 pgs.)-r/1st Karma/M. Team-Up #100. 253-($1.50, 52 pgs.) -r/Amaz. S-M #102 4.00
258-291: 258-261-r/A. Spider-Man #239,249-251(Hobgoblin). 262,263-r/Marv. Team-Up #53,54. 262-New X-Men vs. Sunstroke story. 263-New Woodgod origin story. 264,265-r/Amazing Spider-Man Annual 5. 266-273-Reprints alien costume stories/A. S-M 252-259. 277-r/1st Silver Sable/A. S-M 265. 283-r/A. S-M 275 (Hobgoblin). 284-r/A. S-M 276 (Hobgoblin) 3.00
285-variant w/Wonder-Con logo on c-no price-giveaway 3.00

Marvel Team-Up #94 © MAR

Marvel Team-Up (2nd series) #5 © MAR

Marvel: The Lost Generation #11 © MAR

GD VG FN VF VF/NM NM-
2.0 4.0 6.0 8.0 9.0 9.2

286-($2.95)-p/bagged w/16 page insert & animation print 4.00
NOTE: *All contain reprints; some have new art. #89-97-r/Amazing Spider-Man #110-118; #98-136-r/#121-159; #137-150-r/Amazing Fantasy #15, #1-12 & Annual 1; #151-167-r/#13-28 & Annual 2; #168-186-r/#29-46.* **Austin** *a-100i; c-272i, 273i.* **Byrne** *a(r)-193-198p, 201-208p.* **Ditko** *a-1-30, 83, 100, 137-155.* **G. Kane** *a-71, 81, 98-101p, 249r; c-125-127p, 130p, 137-155.* **Sam Kieth** *c-255, 262, 263.* **Ron Lim** *c-266p-281p, 283p-285p.* **McFarlane** *c-223-239.* **Mooney** *a-63, 95-97i, 103(i).* **Nasser** *a-100p.* **Nebres** *a-242i.* **Perez** *c-259-261.* **Rogers** *c-240, 241, 243-252.*

MARVEL TALES FLIP MAGAZINE
Marvel Comics: Sept, 2005 - No. 25, Sept, 2007 ($3.99/$4.99)

1-6-Reprints Amazing Spider-Man #30-up and Amazing Fantasy (2004) in flip format 4.00
7-10-Reprints Amazing Spider-Man #36-up and Runaways Vol. 2 in flip format 4.00
11-25-($4.99) Reprints Amazing Spider-Man #36-up and Runaways Vol. 2 in flip format 5.00

MARVEL TAROT, THE
Marvel Comics: 2007 ($3.99, one-shot)

1-Marvel characters featured in Tarot deck images; Djurdjevic-c 4.00

MARVEL TEAM-UP (See Marvel Treasury Edition #18 & Official Marvel Index To...)
(Replaced by Web of Spider-Man)
Marvel Comics Group: March, 1972 - No. 150, Feb, 1985
NOTE: *Spider-Man team-ups in all but Nos. 18, 23, 26, 29, 32, 35, 97, 104, 105, 137.*

1-Human Torch 12 24 36 81 176 270
2-Human Torch 5 10 15 35 63 90
3-Spider-Man/Human Torch vs. Morbius (part 1); 3rd app. of Morbius (7/72)
6 12 18 41 76 110
4-Spider-Man/X-Men vs. Morbius (part 2 of story); 4th app. of Morbius
6 12 18 41 76 110
5-10: 5-Vision. 6-Thing. 7-Thor. 8-The Cat (4/73, came out between The Cat #3 & 4). 9-Iron Man. 10-H-T 3 6 9 20 31 42
11,13,14,16-20: 11-Inhumans. 13-Capt. America. 14-Sub-Mariner. 16-Capt. Marvel. 17-Mr. Fantastic. 18-H-T/Hulk. 19-Ka-Zar. 20-Black Panther; last 20¢ issue
2 4 6 13 18 22
12-Werewolf (By Night) (8/73) 3 6 9 19 30 40
15-1st Spider-Man/Ghost Rider team-up (11/73) 3 6 9 20 31 42
21-30: 21-Dr. Strange. 22-Hawkeye. 23-H-T/Iceman (X-Men cameo). 24-Brother Voodoo. 25-Daredevil. 26-H-T/Thor. 27-Hulk. 28-Hercules. 29-H-T/Iron Man. 30-Falcon
2 4 6 8 10 12
31-45,47-50: 31-Iron Fist. 32-H-T/Son of Satan. 33-Nighthawk. 34-Valkyrie. 35-H-T/Dr. Strange. 36-Frankenstein. 37-Man-Wolf. 38-Beast. 39-H-T. 40-Sons of the Tiger/H-T. 41-Scarlet Witch. 42-The Vision. 43-Dr. Doom; retells origin. 44-Moondragon. 45-Killraven. 47-Thing. 48-Iron Man; last 25¢ issue. 49-Dr. Strange; Iron Man app. 50-Iron Man; Dr. Strange app.
1 2 3 5 6 8
44-48-(30¢-c variants, limited distribution)(4-8/76) 4 8 12 23 37 50
46-Spider-Man/Deathlok team-up 1 2 3 5 7 9
51,52,56,57: 51-Iron Man; Dr. Strange app. 52-Capt. America. 56-Daredevil. 57-Black Widow; 2nd app. Silver Samurai 1 2 3 4 5 7
53-Hulk; Woodgod & X-Men app., 1st Byrne-a on X-Men (1/77)
3 6 9 21 33 45
54,55,58-60: 54,59,60: 54-Hulk; Woodgod app. 59-Yellowjacket/The Wasp. 60-The Wasp (Byrne-a in all). 55-Warlock-c/story; Byrne-a. 58-Ghost Rider
2 3 4 6 8 10
58-62-(35¢-c variants, limited distribution)(6-10/77) 5 10 15 31 53 75
61-70: All Byrne-a; 61-H-T. 62-Ms. Marvel; last 30¢ issue. 63-Iron Fist. 64-Daughters of the Dragon. 65-Capt. Britain (1st U.S. app.). 66-Capt. Britain; 1st app. Arcade. 67-Tigra; Kraven the Hunter app. 68-Man-Thing. 69-Havok (from X-Men). 70-Thor
1 2 3 5 7 9
71-74,76-78,80: 71-Falcon. 72-Iron Man. 73-Daredevil. 74-Not Ready for Prime Time Players (Belushi). 76-Dr. Strange. 77-Ms. Marvel. 78-Wonder Man. 80-Dr. Strange/Clea; last 35¢ issue 6.00
75,79,81: Byrne-a(p). 75-Power Man; Cage app. 79-Mary Jane Watson as Red Sonja; Clark Kent cameo (1 panel, 3/79). 81-Death of Satana
1 2 3 5 6 8
82-99: 82-Black Widow. 83-Nick Fury. 84-Shang-Chi. 86-Guardians of the Galaxy. 89-Nightcrawler (from X-Men). 91-Ghost Rider. 92-Hawkeye. 93-Werewolf by Night. 94-Spider-Man vs. The Shroud. 95-Mockingbird (intro.); Nick Fury app. 96-Howard the Duck; last 40¢ issue. 97-Spider-Woman/ Hulk. 98-Black Widow. 99-Machine Man. 85-Shang-Chi/ Black Widow/Nick Fury. 87-Black Panther. 88-Invisible Girl. 90-Beast 5.00
100-(Double-size)-Spider-Man & Fantastic Four story with origin/1st app. Karma, one of the New Mutants; X-Men & Professor X cameo; Miller-c/a(p); Storm & Black Panther story; brief origins; Byrne-a(p) 1 3 4 6 8 10
101-116: 101-Nighthawk(Ditko-a). 102-Doc Samson. 103-Ant-Man. 104-Hulk/Ka-Zar. 105-Hulk/Powerman/Iron Fist. 106-Capt. America. 107-She-Hulk. 108-Paladin; Dazzler cameo. 109-Dazzler; Paladin app. 110-Iron Man. 111-Devil-Slayer. 112-King Kull; last 50¢ issue. 113-Quasar. 114-Falcon. 115-Thor. 116-Valkyrie 4.00
117-Wolverine-c/story 2 4 6 8 10 12
118-140,142-149: 118-Professor X; Wolverine app. (4 pgs.); X-Men cameo. 119-Gargoyle. 120-Dominic Fortune. 121-Human Torch. 122-Man-Thing. 123-Daredevil. 124-The Beast. 125-Tigra. 126-Hulk & Powerman/Son of Satan. 127-The Watcher. 128-Capt. America; Spider-Man/Capt. America photo-c. 129-The Vision. 130-Scarlet Witch. 131-Frogman. 132-Mr. Fantastic. 133-Fantastic Four. 134-Jack of Hearts. 135-Kitty Pryde; X-Men cameo. 136-Wonder Man. 137-Aunt May/Franklin Richards. 138-Sandman. 139-Nick Fury. 140-Black Widow. 142-Capt. Marvel. 143-Starfox. 144-Moon Knight. 145-Iron Man. 146-Nomad. 147-Human Torch; Spider-Man back to old costume. 148-Thor. 149-Cannonball 4.00
141-Daredevil; SpM/Black Widow app. (Spidey in new black costume; ties w/ Amazing Spider-Man #252 for 1st black costume) 3 6 9 16 23 30
150-X-Men ($1.00, double-size); B. Smith-c 6.00
Annual 1 (1976)-Spider-Man/X-Men (early app.) 3 6 9 21 33 45
Annual 2 (1979)-Spider-Man/Hulk 1 3 4 6 8 10
Annuals 3,4: 3 (1980)-Hulk/Power Man/Machine Man/Iron Fist; Miller-c(p). 4 (1981)-Spider-Man /Daredevil/Moon Knight/Power Man/Iron Fist; brief origins of each; Miller-c; Miller scripts on Daredevil 1 2 3 4 5 7
Annuals 5-7: 5 (1982)-SpM/The Thing/Scarlet Witch/Dr. Strange/Quasar. 6 (1983)-Spider-Man/ New Mutants (early app.), Cloak & Dagger. 7(1984)-Alpha Flight; Byrne-c(i) 6.00
NOTE: **Art Adams** *c-141p.* **Austin** *a-79i; c-76i, 79i, 96i, 101i, 112i, 130i.* **Bolle** *a-9i.* **Byrne** *a(p)-53-55, 59-70, 75, 79, 100; c-68p, 70p, 72p, 75, 76p, 79p, 129i, 133i.* **Colan** *a-87p.* **Ditko** *a-101.* **Kane** *a(p)-4-6, 13, 14, 16-19, 23; c(p)-4, 13, 14, 17-19, 23, 25, 26, 32-35, 37, 41, 44, 45, 47, 53, 54.* **Miller** *a-100p; c-95p, 99p, 100p, 102p, 106.* **Mooney** *a-2i, 7i, 8, 10p, 11p, 16i, 24-31p, 72, 93i, Annual 5i.* **Nasser** *a-89p; c-101p.* **Simonson** *c-99i, 148.* **Paul Smith** *c-131, 132.* **Starlin** *c-27.* **Sutton** *a-93p. "H-T" means Human Torch; "SpM" means Spider-Man; "S-M" means Sub-Mariner.*

MARVEL TEAM-UP (2nd Series)
Marvel Comics: Sept, 1997 - No. 11, July, 1998 ($1.99)

1-11: 1-Spider-Man team-ups begin, Generation x-app. 2-Hercules-c/app.; two covers. 3-Sandman. 4-Man-Thing. 7-Blade. 8-Namor team-ups begin, Dr. Strange app. 9-Capt. America. 10-Thing. 11-Iron Man 3.00

MARVEL TEAM-UP
Marvel Comics: Jan, 2005 - No. 25, Dec, 2006 ($2.25/$2.99)

1-7,9: 1,2-Spider-Man & Wolverine; Kirkman-s/Kolins-a. 5,6-X-23 app. 3.00
8,10-25 ($2.99-c) 10-Spider-Man & Daredevil. 12-Origin of Titannus. 14-Invincible app. 3.00
... Vol. 1: The Golden Child TPB (2005, $12.99) r/#1-6 13.00
... Vol. 2: Master of the Ring TPB (2005, $17.99) r/#7-13 18.00
... Vol. 3: League of Losers TPB (2006, $13.99) r/#14-18 14.00
... Vol. 4: Freedom Ring TPB (2007, $17.99) r/#19-25 18.00

MARVEL: THE LOST GENERATION
Marvel Comics: No. 12, Mar, 2000 - No. 1, Feb, 2001 ($2.99, issue #s go in reverse)

1-12-Stern-s/Byrne-s/a; untold story of The First Line. 5-Thor app. 3.00

MARVEL/ TOP COW CROSSOVERS
Image Comics (Top Cow): Nov, 2005 ($24.99, TPB)

Vol. 1-Reprints crossovers with Wolverine, Witchblade, Hulk, Darkness; Devil's Reign 25.00

MARVEL TREASURY EDITION
Marvel Comics Group/Whitman #17,18: 1974; #2, Dec, 1974 - #28, 1981 ($1.50/$2.50, 100 pgs., oversized, new-a &-r)(Also see Amazing Spider-Man, The, Marvel Spec. Ed. Feat.--, Savage Fists of Kung Fu, Superman Vs. , & 2001, A Space Odyssey)

1-Spectacular Spider-Man; story-r/Marvel Super-Heroes #14; Romita-c/a(r); G. Kane, Ditko-r; Green Goblin/Hulk-r 5 10 15 33 57 80
1-1,000 numbered copies signed by Stan Lee & John Romita on front-c & sold thru mail for $5.00; these were the1st 1,000 copies off the press
10 20 30 64 132 200
2-10: 2-Fantastic Four-r/F.F. 6,11,48-50(Silver Surfer). 3-The Mighty Thor-r/Thor #125-130. 4-Conan the Barbarian; Barry Smith-c/a(r)/Conan #11. 5-The Hulk (origin-r/Hulk #3). 6-Dr. Strange. 7-Mighty Avengers. 8-Giant Superhero Holiday Grab-Bag; Spider-Man, Hulk, Nick Fury. 9-Giant; Super-hero Team-up. 10-Thor; r/Thor #154-157
3 6 9 17 26 35
11-20: 11-Fantastic Four. 12-Howard the Duck (r/#H. the Duck #1 & G.S. Man-Thing #4,5) plus new Defenders story. 13-Giant Super-Hero Holiday Grab-Bag. 14-The Sensational Spider-Man; r/1st Morbius from Amazing S-M #101,102 plus #100 & r/Not Brand Echh #6. 15-Conan; B. Smith, Neal Adams-i; r/Conan #24. 16-The Defenders (origin) & Valkyrie; r/Defenders #1,4,13,14. 17-Incredible Hulk; Blob, Havok, Rhino and The Leader app. 18-The Astonishing Spider-Man; r/Spider-Man's 1st team-ups with Iron Fist, The X-Men, Ghost Rider & Werewolf by Night; inside back-c has photos from 1978 Spider-Man TV show. 19-Conan the Barbarian. 20-Hulk 3 6 9 14 20 25
21-24,27: 21-Fantastic Four. 22-Spider-Man. 23-Conan. 24-Rampaging Hulk. 27-Spider-Man
3 6 9 14 20 25
25-Spider-Man vs. The Hulk new story 3 6 9 16 23 30
26-The Hulk; 6 pg. new Wolverine/Hercules-s 3 6 9 15 22 28
28-Spider-Man/Superman; (origin of each) 5 10 15 30 50 70
NOTE: *Reprints-2, 3, 5, 7-9, 13, 14, 16, 17.* **Neal Adams** *a(i)-6, 15.* **Brunner** *a-6, 12; c-6.* **Buscema** *a-15, 19, 28; c-28.* **Colan** *a-6r; c-12p.* **Ditko** *a-1, 6.* **Gil Kane** *c-16p.* **Kirby** *a-1-3, 5, 7, 9-11; c-7.* **Perez** *a-26.* **Romita** *c-1, 5.* **B. Smith** *a-4, 15, 19; c-4, 19.*

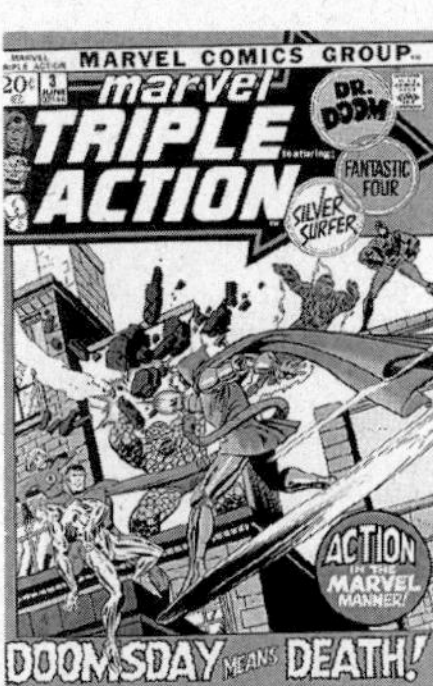

Marvel Triple Action #3 © MAR

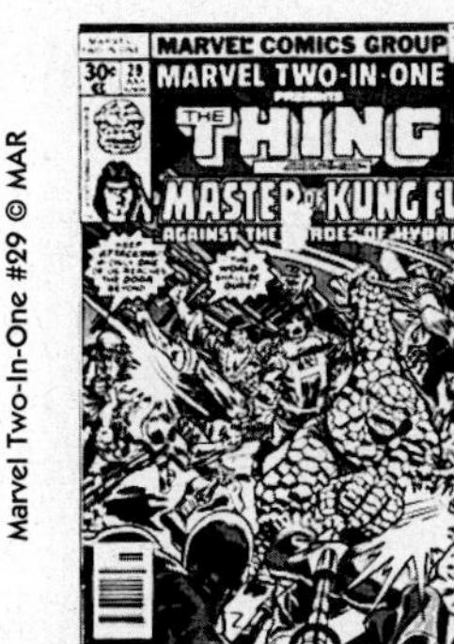

Marvel Two-In-One #29 © MAR

Marvel Universe vs. The Punisher #1 © MAR

GD VG FN VF VF/NM NM-
2.0 4.0 6.0 8.0 9.0 9.2

MARVEL TREASURY OF OZ FEATURING THE MARVELOUS LAND OF OZ
Marvel Comics Group: 1975 ($1.50, oversized) (See MGM's Marvelous...)
1-Roy Thomas-s/Alfredo Alcala-a; Romita-c & bk-c 3 6 9 16 23 30

MARVEL TREASURY SPECIAL (Also see 2001: A Space Odyssey)
Marvel Comics Group: 1974; 1976 ($1.50, oversized, 84 pgs.)
Vol. 1-Spider-Man, Torch, Sub-Mariner, Avengers "Giant Superhero Holiday Grab-Bag"; Wood, Colan/Everett, plus 2 Kirby-r; reprints Hulk vs. Thing from Fantastic Four #25,26 3 6 9 16 24 32
Vol. 1-... Featuring Captain America's Bicentennial Battles (6/76)-Kirby-a; B. Smith inks, 11 pgs. 3 6 9 17 26 35

MARVEL TRIPLE ACTION (See Giant-Size...)
Marvel Comics Group: Feb, 1972 - No. 24, Mar, 1975; No. 25, Aug, 1975 - No. 47, Apr, 1979
1-(25¢ giant, 52 pgs.)-Dr. Doom, Silver Surfer, The Thing begin, end #4 ('66 reprints from Fantastic Four) 4 8 12 23 37 50
2-5 2 4 6 10 14 18
6-10 1 3 4 6 8 10
11-47: 45-r/X-Men #45. 46-r/Avengers #53(X-Men) 1 2 3 5 6 8
29,30-(30¢-c variants, limited distribution)(5,7/76) 3 6 9 16 23 30
36,37-(35¢-c variants, limited distribution)(7,9/77) 3 6 9 21 33 45
NOTE: *#5-44, 46, 47 reprint Avengers #11 thru ?. #40-r/Avengers #48(1st Black Knight).* ***Buscema*** *a(r)-35p, 36p, 38p, 39p, 41, 42, 43p, 44p, 46p, 47p.* ***Ditko*** *a-2r; c-47.* ***Kirby*** *a(r)-1-4p; c-9-19, 22, 24, 29.* ***Starlin*** *c-7.* ***Tuska*** *a(r)-40p, 43i, 46i, 47i. #2 through #17 are 20¢-c.*

MARVEL TRIPLE ACTION
Marvel Comics: May, 2009 - No. 2, Jun, 2009 ($5.99, limited series)
1,2-Reprints stories from Wolverine First Class, Marvel Adventures Avengers & Marvel Super Heroes 6.00

MARVEL TV: GALACTUS - THE REAL STORY
Marvel Comics: Apr, 2009 ($3.99, one-shot)
1-The "hoax" of Galactus, Tieri-s/Santacruz-a; r/Fantastic Four #50 4.00

MARVEL TWO-IN-ONE (...Featuring ... #82 on; also see The Thing)
Marvel Comics Group: January, 1974 - No. 100, June, 1983
1-Thing team-ups begin; Man-Thing 6 12 18 41 76 110
2,3: 2-Sub-Mariner; last 20¢ issue. 3-Daredevil 3 6 9 20 31 42
4,6: 4-Capt. America. 6-Dr. Strange (11/74) 3 6 9 15 22 28
5-Guardians of the Galaxy (9/74, 2nd app.) 4 8 12 23 37 50
7,9,10 2 4 6 10 14 18
8-Early Ghost Rider app. (3/75) 3 6 9 15 22 28
11-14,19,20: 13-Power Man. 14-Son of Satan (early app.) 1 3 4 6 8 10
15-18-(Regular 25¢ editions)(5-7/76) 17-Spider-Man 1 3 4 6 8 10
15-18-(30¢-c variants, limited distribution) 3 6 9 21 33 45
21-29: 27-Deathlok. 29-Master of Kung Fu; Spider-Woman cameo 1 2 3 5 6 8
28,29,31-(35¢-c variants, limited distribution) 4 8 12 25 40 55
30-2nd full app. Spider-Woman (see Marvel Spotlight #32 for 1st app.) 2 4 6 9 13 16
30-(35¢-c variant, limited distribution)(8/77) 5 10 15 35 63 90
31-33-Spider-Woman app. 1 3 4 6 8 10
34-40: 39-Vision 1 2 3 4 5 7
41,42,44,45,47-49: 42-Capt. America. 45-Capt. Marvel 6.00
43,50,53,55-Byrne-a(p). 53-Quasar(7/79, 2nd app.) 1 2 3 5 7 9
46-Thing battles Hulk-c/story 2 4 6 8 10 12
51-The Beast, Nick Fury, Ms. Marvel; Miller-p 1 2 3 5 7 9
52-Moon Knight app. 6.00
54-Death of Deathlok; Byrne-a 2 4 6 8 11 14
56-60,64-68,70-74,76-79,81,82: 60-Intro. Impossible Woman. 68-Angel. 71-1st app. Maelstrom. 76-Iceman 4.00
61-63: 61-Starhawk (from Guardians); "The Coming of Her" storyline begins, ends #63; cover similar to F.F. #67 (Him-c). 62-Moondragon; Thanos & Warlock cameo in flashback; Starhawk app. 63-Warlock revived shortly; Starhawk & Moondragon app. 6.00
69-Guardians of the Galaxy 1 2 3 5 6 8
75-Avengers (52 pgs.) 5.00
80,90,100: 80-Ghost Rider. 90-Spider-Man. 100-Double size, Byrne-s 5.00
83-89,91-99: 83-Sasquatch. 84-Alpha Flight app. 93-Jocasta dies. 96-X-Men-c & cameo 4.00
Annual 1 (1976, 52 pgs.)-Thing/Liberty Legion; Kirby-c 2 4 6 10 14 18
Annual 2 (1977, 52 pgs.)-Thing/Spider-Man; 2nd death of Thanos; end of Thanos saga; Warlock app.; Starlin-c/a 5 10 15 35 63 90
Annual 3,4 (1978-79, 52 pgs.): 3-Nova. 4-Black Bolt 1 2 3 4 5 7
Annual 5-7 (1980-82, 52 pgs.): 5-Hulk. 6-1st app. American Eagle. 7-The Thing/Champion; Sasquatch, Colossus app.; X-Men cameo (1 pg.) 5.00
NOTE: ***Austin*** *c(i)-42, 54, 56, 58, 61, 63, 66.* ***John Buscema*** *a-30p, 45; c-30p.* ***Byrne*** *(p)-43, 50, 53-55; c-43, 53p, 56p, 98i, 99i.* ***Gil Kane*** *a-1p, 2p; c(p)-1-3, 9-11, 14, 28.* ***Kirby*** *c-12, 19p, 20, 25, 27.* ***Mooney*** *a-18i, 38i, 90i.* ***Nasser*** *a-70p.* ***Perez*** *a(p)-56-58, 60, 64, 65; c(p)-32, 33, 42, 50-52, 54, 55, 57, 58, 61-66, 70.* ***Roussos*** *a-Annual 1i.* ***Simonson*** *c-43i, 97p, Annual 6i.* ***Starlin*** *c-6, Annual 1.* ***Tuska*** *a-6p.*

GD VG FN VF VF/NM NM-
2.0 4.0 6.0 8.0 9.0 9.2

MARVEL TWO-IN-ONE
Marvel Comics: Sept, 2007 - No. 17, Jan, 2009 ($4.99, 64 pgs.)
1-8,13-16-Reprints Marvel Adventures Avengers and X-Men: First Class stories 5.00
9-12,17-Reprints Marvel Adventures Iron Man and Avengers stories 5.00

MARVEL UNIVERSE (See Official Handbook Of The...)

MARVEL UNIVERSE (Title on variant covers for newsstand editions of some 2001 Marvel titles. See indicia for actual titles and issue numbers)

MARVEL UNIVERSE
Marvel Comics: June, 1998 - No. 7, Dec, 1998 ($2.99/$1.99)
1-($2.99)-Invaders stories from WW2; Stern-s 4.00
2-7-($1.99): 2-Two covers. 4-7-Monster Hunters; Manley-a/Stern-s 3.00

MARVEL UNIVERSE AVENGERS AND ULTIMATE SPIDER-MAN
Marvel Comics: 2012 (no price, Halloween giveaway)
1-Reprints from Marvel Universe Ultimate Spider-Man #1 & Avengers E.M.H #1 3.00

MARVEL UNIVERSE AVENGERS ASSEMBLE (Based on the Disney XD animated series) (Titled Avengers Assemble for #1,2)
Marvel Comics: Dec, 2013 - Present ($3.99/$2.99)
1-($3.99) Red Skull app.; bonus Lego-style story 4.00
2-7-($2.99) 5-Dracula app. 7-Hyperion app. 3.00

MARVEL UNIVERSE HULK: AGENTS OF S.M.A.S.H (Disney XD animated series)
Marvel Comics: Dec, 2013 - No. 4, Mar, 2014 ($2.99)
1-4: 1-Hulk, A-Bomb, She-Hulk, Red Hulk and Skaar team-up 3.00

MARVEL UNIVERSE: MILLENNIAL VISIONS
Marvel Comics: Feb, 2002 ($3.99, one-shot)
1-Pin-ups by various; wraparound-c by JH Williams & Gray 4.00

MARVEL UNIVERSE: THE END (Also see Infinity Abyss)
Marvel Comics: May, 2003 - No. 6, Aug, 2003 ($3.50/$2.99, limited series)
1-($3.50)-Thanos, X-Men, FF, Avengers, Spider-Man, Daredevil app.; Starlin-s/a(p) 4.00
2-6-($2.99) Akhenaten, Eternity, Living Tribunal app. 3.00
Thanos Vol. 3: Marvel Universe - The End (2003, $16.99) r/#1-6 17.00

MARVEL UNIVERSE VS. THE AVENGERS
Marvel Comics: Dec, 2012 - No. 4, Mar, 2013 ($3.99, limited series)
1-4-Avengers vs. Marvel Zombies; Maberry-s/Fernandez-a/Kuder-c 4.00

MARVEL UNIVERSE VS. THE PUNISHER
Marvel Comics: Oct, 2010 - No. 4, Nov, 2010 ($3.99, limited series)
1-4-Punisher vs. Marvel Zombies; Maberry-s/Parlov-a/c 4.00

MARVEL UNIVERSE VS. WOLVERINE
Marvel Comics: Aug, 2011 - No. 4, Nov, 2011 ($3.99, limited series)
1-4-Wolverine vs. Marvel Zombies; Maberry-s/Laurence Campbell-a/c 4.00

MARVEL UNLIMITED (Title on variant covers for newsstand editions of some 2001 Daredevil issues. See indicia for actual titles and issue numbers)

MARVEL VALENTINE SPECIAL
Marvel Comics: Mar, 1997 ($2.99, one-shot)
1-Valentine stories w/Spider-Man, Daredevil, Cyclops, Phoenix 3.00

MARVEL VERSUS DC (See DC Versus Marvel) (Also see Amazon, Assassins, Bruce Wayne: Agent of S.H.I.E.L.D., Bullets & Bracelets, Doctor Strangefate, JLX, Legend of the Dark Claw, Magneto & The Magnetic Men, Speed Demon, Spider-Boy, Super Soldier, & X-Patrol)
Marvel Comics: No. 2, 1996 - No. 3, 1996 ($3.95, limited series)
2,3: 2-Peter David script. 3-Ron Marz script; Dan Jurgens-a(p). 1st app. of Super Soldier, Spider-Boy, Dr. Doomsday, Doctor Strangefate, The Dark Claw, Nightcreeper, Amazon, Wraith & others. Storyline continues in Amalgam books. 4.00

MARVEL VISIONARIES
Marvel Comics: 2002 - Present (various prices, HC and TPB)
...: Chris Claremont (2005, $29.99) r/X-Men #137, Uncanny X-Men #153,205,268 & Ann. #12, Iron Fist #14, Wolverine #3, New Mutants #21 and other highlights 30.00
...: Gil Kane (8/02, $24.95) r/Amazing Spider-Man #99, Marvel Premiere #1,#15, TOA #76 & others; plus sketch pages and a cover gallery 25.00
...: Jack Kirby HC (2004, $29.99) r/career highlights- Red Raven Comics #1 (1st work), Captain America Comics #1, Avengers #4, Fantastic Four #48-50 and more 30.00
...: Jack Kirby Vol. 2 HC (2006, $34.99) r/career highlights- Captain America, Two-Gun Kid, Fantastic Four, Thor, Fin Fang Foom, Devil Dinosaur, romance and more 35.00
...: Jim Steranko (9/02, $14.95) r/Captain America #110,111,113; X-Men #50,51 and stories from Tower of Shadows #1 and Our Love Story #5; plus a cover gallery 15.00

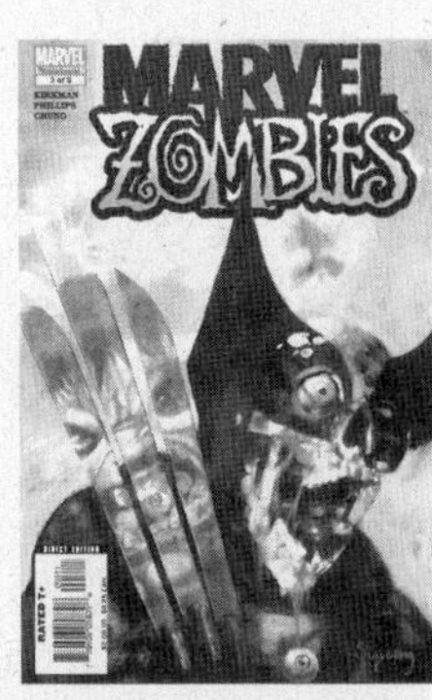

Marvel Zombies #3 © MAR

Mary Marvel Comics #28 © FAW

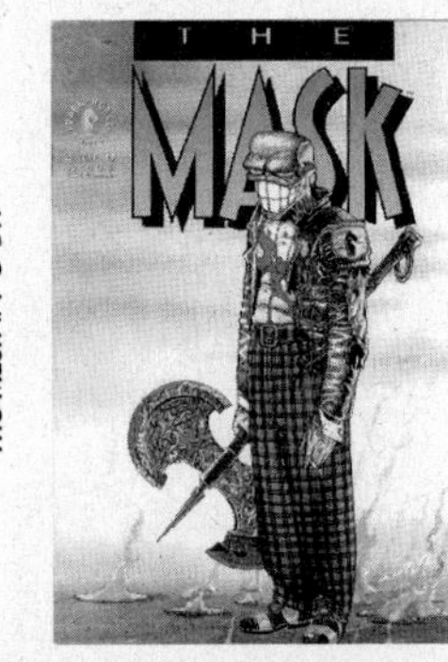

The Mask #4 © DH

GD 2.0 | VG 4.0 | FN 6.0 | VF 8.0 | VF/NM 9.0 | NM- 9.2

...: John Buscema (2007, $34.99) r/career highlights-Avengers, Silver Surfer, Thor, FF, Hulk, Wolverine and others; Roy Thomas intro.; sketch pages and pin-up art 35.00
...: John Romita Jr. (2005, $29.99) r/various stories 1977-2002; debut in AS-M Ann. #11; Iron Man #128, AS-M V2 #36, issues of Hulk, Daredevil: The Man Without Fear, Punisher; sketch pages; intro. by John Romita Sr. 30.00
...: John Romita Sr. (2005, $29.99) r/various stories 1951-1997 including Young Men #24&26, Daredevil #16, ASM #39,42,50; sketch pages; intro. by John Romita Jr. 30.00
...: Roy Thomas (2006, $34.99) r/career highlights; intro. by Stan Lee 35.00
...: Steve Ditko (2005, $29.99) r/various stories 1961-1992; intro. by Blake Bell 30.00
...: Stan Lee HC (2005, $29.99) r/career highlights- Captain America Comics #3 (1st work), and various Spider-Man, FF, Thor, Daredevil stories; 1940-1995; Roy Thomas intro. 30.00

MARVEL WEDDINGS
Marvel Comics: 2005 ($19.99, TPB)

TPB-Reprints weddings of Peter & Mary Jane, Reed & Sue, Scott & Jean, and others 20.00

MARVEL WESTERNS: ...
Marvel Comics: 2006 ($3.99, one-shots)

... Kid Colt and the Arizona Girl 1 (9/06) 2 short stories & 3 Kirby/Ayers reps.; Powell-c 4.00
... Outlaw Files-Profiles and essays about Marvel western characters 4.00
... Strange Westerns Starring The Black Rider 1 (10/06) Englehart-s/Rogers-a & 2 Kirby Rawhide Kid reprints; Rogers-c 4.00
... The Two-Gun Kid 1 (8/06) 2 short stories & a Kirby/Ayers reprint; Powell-c 4.00
... Western Legends 1 (9/06) 2 short stories & r/Rawhide Kid origin by Kirby; Powell-c 4.00
HC (2006, $20.99, dustjacket) r/one-shots 21.00

MARVEL X-MEN COLLECTION, THE
Marvel Comics: Jan, 1994 - No. 3, Mar, 1994 ($2.95, limited series)

1-3-r/X-Men trading cards by Jim Lee 3.00

MARVEL - YEAR IN REVIEW (Magazine)
Marvel Comics: 1989 - No. 3, 1991 (52 pgs.)

1-3: 1-Spider-Man-c by McFarlane. 2-Capt. America-c. 3-X-Men/Wolverine-c 5.00

MARVEL: YOUR UNIVERSE
Marvel Comics: 2008; May, 2009 - No. 3, July, 2009 ($5.99)

1-3-Reprints of 5 recent comics (Ms. Marvel, Nova, Immortal Iron Fist & others) 6.00
...Saga (2008, no cover price) - Re-caps of crossovers (Secret War thru Secret Invasion) 3.00

MARVEL ZOMBIES (See Ultimate Fantastic Four #21-23, 30-32)
Marvel Comics: Feb, 2006 - No. 5, June, 2006 ($2.99, limited series)

1-Zombies vs. Magneto; Kirkman-s/Phillips-a/Suydam-c swipe of A.F. #15 30.00
1-(2nd-4th printings) Variant Suydam-c swipes of Spider-Man #1, Amazing Spider-Man #50 and Incredible Hulk #1 6.00
2-Avengers #4 cover swipe by Suydam 10.00
3-5: 3-Inc. Hulk #340 c-swipe. 4-X-Men #1 c-swipe. 5-AS-M Ann. #21 c-swipe 6.00
3-5-(2nd printings) 3-Daredevil #179 c-swipe. 4-AS-M #39 c-swipe. 5-Silver Surfer #1 4.00
...: Dead Days (7/07, $3.99) Early days of the plaque; Kirkman-s/Phillips-a/Suydam-c 5.00
...: Dead Days HC (2008, $29.99, oversized) r/Dead Days one-shot, Ultimate Fantastic Four #21-23, 30-32, and Black Panther #28-30 30.00
...: Evil Evolution (1/10, $4.99) Apes vs. Zombies; Marcos Martin-c 5.00
... Halloween (12/12, $3.99) Van Lente-s/Vitti-a/Francavilla-c 4.00
... MGC #1 (7/10, $1.00) r/#1 with "Marvel's Greatest Comics" logo on cover 3.00
...: The Book of Angels, Demons and Various Monstrosities (2007, $3.99) profile pages 5.00
...: The Covers HC (2007, $19.99, d.j.) Suydam's covers with originals and commentary 20.00
HC (2006, $19.99) r/#1-5; Kirkman foreword; cover gallery with variants 20.00

MARVEL ZOMBIES 2
Marvel Comics: Dec, 2007 - No. 5, Apr, 2008 ($2.99, limited series)

1-5-Kirkman-s/Phillips-a/Suydam zombie-fied cover swipes 5.00
HC (2008, $19.99) r/#1-5; cover swipe gallery 20.00

MARVEL ZOMBIES 3
Marvel Comics: Dec, 2008 - No. 4, Mar, 2009 ($3.99, limited series)

1-4-Van Lente-s/Walker-a/Land-c; Machine Man, Jocasta and Morbius app. 5.00

MARVEL ZOMBIES 4
Marvel Comics: Jun, 2009 - No. 4, Sept, 2009 ($3.99, limited series)

1-4-Van Lente-s/Walker-a/Land-c; Zombie Deadpool head app. 4.00

MARVEL ZOMBIES 5
Marvel Comics: Jun, 2010 - No. 5, Sept, 2010 ($3.99, limited series)

1-5-Van Lente-s; Machine Man and Howard the Duck app. 3-Kaluta-a 4.00

MARVEL ZOMBIES / ARMY OF DARKNESS
Marvel Comics/Dynamite Entertainment: May, 2007 - No. 5, Aug, 2007($2.99, limited series)

1-Zombies vs. Ash during the start of the plaque; Layman-s/Neves-a/Suydam-c 7.00
1-Second printing with Suydam zombie-fied Captain America Comics #1 cover swipe 4.00
2-5-Suydam zombie-fied cover swipes on all 5.00
HC (2007, $19.99) r/#1-5; cover gallery with variants and non-zombied original covers 20.00

MARVEL ZOMBIES CHRISTMAS CAROL ("Zombies Christmas Carol" on cover)
Marvel Comics: Aug, 2011 - No. 5, Oct, 2011 ($3.99, limited series)

1-5-Adaptation of the Dickens classic with zombies; Kaluta-c/Baldeon-a 4.00

MARVEL ZOMBIES DESTROY!
Marvel Comics: Jul, 2012 - No. 5, Sept, 2012 ($3.99, limited series)

1-5-Howard the Duck, Dum Dum Dugan vs. zombies; Del Mundo-c 4.00

MARVEL ZOMBIES RETURN
Marvel Comics: Nov, 2009 - No. 5, Nov, 2009 ($3.99, weekly limited series)

1-5-Suydam-c. 1-Zombie Spider-Man eats the Earth-Z Sinister Six; Dragotta-a. 4.00

MARVEL ZOMBIES SUPREME
Marvel Comics: May, 2011 - No. 5, Aug, 2011 ($3.99, limited series)

1-5-Zombies in Squadron Supreme dimension; Blanco-a/Komarck-c; Jack of Hearts app. 4.00

MARVILLE
Marvel Comics: Nov, 2002 - No. 7, Jul, 2003 ($2.25, limited series)

1-6-Satire on DC/AOL-Time-Warner; Jemas-a/Bright-a/Horn-c 3.00
1-($3.95) Variant foil cover by Udon Studios; bonus sketch pages and Jemas afterword 4.00
7-($2.99) Intro. to Epic Comics line with submission guidelines 3.00

MARVIN MOUSE
Atlas Comics (BPC): September, 1957

	GD	VG	FN	VF	VF/NM	NM-
1-Everett-c/a; Maneely-a	15	30	45	84	127	170

MARY JANE (Spider-Man) (Also see Spider-Man Loves Mary Jane)
Marvel Comics: Aug, 2004 - No. 4, Nov, 2004 ($2.25, limited series)

1-4-Marvel Age series with teen-age MJ Watson; Miyazawa-c/a; McKeever-s 3.00
... Vol. 1: Circle of Friends (2004, $5.99, digest-size) r/#1-4 6.00

MARY JANE & SNIFFLES (See Looney Tunes)
Dell Publishing Co.: No. 402, June, 1952 - No. 474, June, 1953

	GD	VG	FN	VF	VF/NM	NM-
Four Color 402 (#1)	7	14	21	44	82	120
Four Color 474	6	12	18	41	76	110

MARY JANE: HOMECOMING (Spider-Man)
Marvel Comics: May, 2005 - No. 4, Aug, 2005 ($2.99, limited series)

1-4-Teen-age MJ Watson in high school; Miyazawa-c/a; McKeever-s 3.00
... Vol. 2 (2005, $6.99, digest-size) r/#1-4 7.00

MARY MARVEL COMICS (Monte Hale #29 on) (Also see Captain Marvel #18, Marvel Family, Shazam, & Wow Comics)
Fawcett Publications: Dec, 1945 - No. 28, Sept, 1948

	GD	VG	FN	VF	VF/NM	NM-
1-Captain Marvel introduces Mary on-c; intro/origin Georgia Sivana	161	322	483	1030	1765	2500
2	71	142	213	454	777	1100
3,4: 3-New logo	50	100	150	315	533	750
5-8: 8-Bulletgirl x-over in Mary Marvel; X-Mas-c	40	80	120	246	411	575
9,10	37	74	111	222	361	500
11-20	26	52	78	154	252	350
21-28: 28-Western-c	22	44	66	132	216	300

MARY POPPINS (See Movie Comics & Walt Disney Showcase No. 17)

MARY SHELLEY'S FRANKENSTEIN
Topps Comics: Oct, 1994 - Jan, 1995 ($2.95, limited series)

1-4-polybagged w/3 trading cards 4.00
1-4 ($2.50)-Newstand ed. 3.00

MARY WORTH (See Harvey Comics Hits #55 & Love Stories of...)
Argo: March, 1956 (Also see Romantic Picture Novelettes)

	GD	VG	FN	VF	VF/NM	NM-
1	8	16	24	42	54	65

MASK (TV)
DC Comics: Dec, 1985 - No. 4, Mar, 1986; Feb, 1987 - No. 9, Oct, 1987

1-4; 1-9 (2nd series)-Sat. morning TV show. 4.00

MASK, THE (Also see Mayhem)
Dark Horse Comics: Aug, 1991 - No. 4, Oct, 1991; No. 0, Dec, 1991 ($2.50, 36 pgs., limited series)

1-4: 1-1st app. Lt. Kellaway as The Mask (see Dark Horse Presents #10 for 1st app.) 5.00
0-(12/91, B&W, 56 pgs.)-r/Mayhem #1-4 4.00
...Omnibus Vol. 1 (8/08, $24.95) r/#1-4, Mask Returns and Mask Strikes Back series 25.00
...Omnibus Vol. 2 (4/09, $24.95) r/#1-4, The Hunt For Green October, World Tour, Southern Discomfort, Toys in the Attic series and short stories from DHP 25.00

Masked Marvel #2 © CEN

Masks #6 © Dynamite

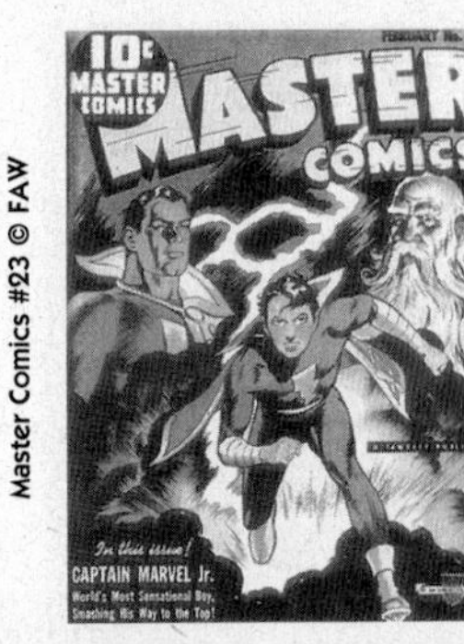

Master Comics #23 © FAW

	GD	VG	FN	VF	VF/NM	NM-
	2.0	4.0	6.0	8.0	9.0	9.2

...: HUNT FOR GREEN OCTOBER July, 1995 - Oct, 1995 ($2.50, lim. series)
1-4-Evan Dorkin scripts 3.00

.../ MARSHALL LAW Feb, 1998 - No. 2, Mar, 1998 ($2.95, lim. series)
1,2-Mills-s/O'Neill-a 3.00

...: OFFICIAL MOVIE ADAPTATION July, 1994 - Aug, 1994 ($2.50, lim. series)
1,2 3.00

... RETURNS Oct, 1992 - No. 4, Mar, 1993 ($2.50, limited series)
1-4 4.00

... SOUTHERN DISCOMFORT Mar, 1996 - No. 4, July, 1996 ($2.50, lim. series)
1-4 3.00

... STRIKES BACK Feb, 1995 - No. 5, Jun, 1995 ($2.50, limited series)
1-5 3.00

... SUMMER VACATION July, 1995 ($10.95, one shot, hard-c)
1-nn-Rick Geary-c/a 11.00

... TOYS IN THE ATTIC Aug, 1998 - No. 4, Nov, 1998 ($2.95, limited series)
1-4-Fingerman-s 3.00

... VIRTUAL SURREALITY July, 1997 ($2.95, one shot)
nn-Mignola, Aragonés, and others-s/a 3.00

... WORLD TOUR Dec, 1995 - No. 4, Mar, 1996 ($2.50, limited series)
1-4: 3-X & Ghost-c/app. 3.00

MASK COMICS
Rural Home Publ.: Feb-Mar, 1945 - No. 2, Apr-May, 1945; No. 2, Fall, 1945

1-Classic L. B. Cole Satan-c/a; Palais-a 331 662 993 2317 4059 5800
2-(Scarce)-Classic L. B. Cole Satan-c; Black Rider, The Boy Magician, & The Collector app. 232 464 696 1485 2543 3600
2-(Fall, 1945)-No publ.-same as regular #2; L. B. Cole-c 181 362 543 1158 1979 2800

MASKED BANDIT, THE
Avon Periodicals: 1952

nn-Kinstler-a 17 34 51 98 154 210

MASKED MAN, THE
Eclipse Comics: 12/84 - #10, 4/86; #11, 10/87; #12, 4/88 ($1.75/$2.00, color/B&W #9 on, Baxter paper)

1-12: 1-Origin retold. 3-Origin Aphid-Man; begin $2.00-c 3.00

MASKED MARVEL (See Keen Detective Funnies)
Centaur Publications: Sept, 1940 - No. 3, Dec, 1940

1-The Masked Marvel begins 168 336 504 1075 1838 2600
2,3: 2-Gustavson, Tarpe Mills-a 110 220 330 704 1202 1700

MASKED RAIDER, THE (Billy The Kid #9 on; Frontier Scout, Daniel Boone #10-13) (Also see Blue Bird)
Charlton Comics: June, 1955 - No. 8, July, 1957; No. 14, Aug, 1958 - No. 30, June, 1961

1-Masked Raider & Talon the Golden Eagle begin; painted-c 13 26 39 72 101 130
2 8 16 24 42 54 65
3-8,15: 8-Billy The Kid app. 15-Williamson-a, 7 pgs. 6 12 18 31 38 45
14,16-30: 22-Rocky Lane app. 5 10 15 24 30 35

MASKED RANGER
Premier Magazines: Apr, 1954 - No. 9, Aug, 1955

1-The Masked Ranger, his horse Streak, & The Crimson Avenger (origin) begin, end #9; Woodbridge/Frazetta-a 41 82 123 250 418 585
2,3 15 30 45 90 140 190
4-8-All Woodbridge-a. 5-Jesse James by Woodbridge. 6-Billy The Kid by Woodbridge. 7-Wild Bill Hickok by Woodbridge. 8-Jim Bowie's Life Story 16 32 48 94 147 200
9-Torres-a; Wyatt Earp by Woodbridge; Says Death of Masked Ranger on-c 18 36 54 103 162 220

NOTE: *Check a-1. Woodbridge c/a-1, 4-9.*

MASK OF DR. FU MANCHU, THE (See Dr. Fu Manchu)
Avon Periodicals: 1951

1-Sax Rohmer adapt.; Wood-c/a (26 pgs.); Hollingsworth-a 107 214 321 685 1168 1650

MASK OF ZORRO, THE
Image Comics: Aug, 1998 - No. 4, Dec, 1998 ($2.95, limited series)

1-4-Movie adapt. Photo variant-c 3.00

MASKS
Dynamite Entertainment: 2012 - No. 8, 2013 ($3.99)

1-Team-up of the Shadow, Green Hornet, Spider; Alex Ross-a; multiple covers 5.00
2-8: 2-Miss Fury and Green Lama app.; Calero-a. 3-Black Terror app. 4.00

MASKS: TOO HOT FOR TV!
DC Comics (WildStorm): Feb, 2004 ($4.95)

1-Short stories by various incl. Thompson, Brubaker, Mahnke, Conner; Fabry-c 5.00

MASQUE OF THE RED DEATH (See Movie Classics)

MASQUERADE (See Project Superpowers)
Dynamite Entertainment: 2009 - No. 4, 2009 ($3.50, limited series)

1-4-Alex Ross & Phil Hester-s/Carlos Paul-a; covers by Ross & others 3.50

MASS EFFECT: EVOLUTION (2nd series based on the EA video game)
Dark Horse Comics: Jan, 2011 - No. 4, Apr, 2011 ($3.50, limited series)

1-4-Walters & Jackson Miller-s/Carnevale-c 3.50

MASS EFFECT: FOUNDATION (Based on the EA video game)
Dark Horse Comics: Jul, 2013 - No. 13 ($3.99, limited series)

1-9: 1-Walters-s/Francia-a. 2-4-Parker-a 4.00

MASS EFFECT: HOMEWORLDS (Based on the EA video game)
Dark Horse Comics: Apr, 2012 - No. 4, Aug, 2012 ($3.50, limited series)

1-4: 1-Walters-s/Francisco-a 3.50

MASS EFFECT: INVASION (3rd series based on the EA video game)
Dark Horse Comics: Oct, 2011 - No. 4, Jan, 2012 ($3.50, limited series)

1-4-Walters & Jackson Miller-s/Carnevale-c 3.50

MASS EFFECT: REDEMPTION (Based on the EA video game)
Dark Horse Comics: Jan, 2010 - No. 4, Apr, 2010 ($3.50, limited series)

1-4-Walters & Jackson Miller-s/Francia-a 3.50

MASSIVE, THE
Dark Horse Comics: Jun, 2012 - Present ($3.50)

1-21: 1-Brian Wood-s/Kristian Donaldson-a. 4-9-Brown-a. 10-Erskine-a 3.50

MASTER COMICS (Combined with Slam Bang Comics #7 on)
Fawcett Publications: Mar, 1940 - No. 133, Apr, 1953 (No. 1-6: oversized issues) (#1-3: 15¢, 52 pgs.; #4-6: 10¢, 36 pgs.; #7-Begin 68 pg. issues)

1-Origin & 1st app. Master Man; The Devil's Dagger, El Carim, Master of Magic, Rick O'Say, Morton Murch, White Rajah, Shipwreck Roberts, Frontier Marshal, Streak Sloan, Mr. Clue begin (all features end #6) 838 1676 2514 6117 10,809 15,500
2 (Rare) 271 542 813 1734 2967 4200
3-6: 6-Last Master Man (Rare) 194 388 582 1242 2121 3000

NOTE: *#1-6 rarely found in near mint or very fine condition due to large-size format.*

7-(10/40)-Bulletman, Zoro, the Mystery Man (ends #22), Lee Granger, Jungle King, & Buck Jones begin; only app. The War Bird & Mark Swift & the Time Retarder; Zoro, Lee Granger, Jungle King & Mark Swift all continue from Slam Bang; Bulletman moves from Nickel 300 600 900 1950 3375 4800
8-The Red Gaucho (ends #13), Captain Venture (ends #22) & The Planet Princess begin 161 322 483 1030 1765 2500
9,10: 10-Lee Granger ends 129 258 387 826 1413 2000
11-Origin & 1st app. Minute-Man (2/41) 277 554 831 1759 3030 4300
12 129 258 387 826 1413 2000
13-Origin & 1st app. Bulletgirl; Hitler-c 232 464 696 1485 2543 3600
14-16: 14-Companions Three begins, ends #31 116 232 348 742 1271 1800
17-20: 17-Raboy-a on Bulletman begins. 20-Captain Marvel cameo app. in Bulletman 110 220 330 704 1202 1700
21-(12/41; Scarce)-Captain Marvel & Bulletman team up against Capt. Nazi; origin & 1st app. Capt. Marvel Jr's most famous nemesis Captain Nazi who will cause creation of Capt. Marvel Jr. in Whiz #25. Part I of trilogy origin of Capt. Marvel Jr.; 1st Mac Raboy-c for Fawcett; Capt. Nazi-c 676 1352 2028 4935 8718 12,500
22-(1/42)-Captain Marvel Jr. moves over from Whiz #25 & teams up with Bulletman against Captain Nazi; part III of trilogy origin of Capt. Marvel Jr. & his 1st cover and adventure 605 1210 1815 4417 7809 11,200
23-Capt. Marvel Jr. c/stories begin (1st solo story); fights Capt. Nazi by himself. 300 600 900 1965 3408 4850
24,25 119 238 357 762 1306 1850
26-28,30-Captain Marvel Jr. vs. Capt. Nazi. 28-Liberty Bell-c. 30-Flag-c 113 226 339 723 1237 1750
29-Hitler & Hirohito-c 194 388 582 1242 2121 3000
31-33,35: 32-Last El Carim & Buck Jones; intro Balbo, the Boy Magician in El Carim story; classic Eagle-c by Raboy. 33-Balbo, the Boy Magician (ends #47), Hopalong Cassidy (ends #49) begins 94 188 282 602 1026 1450
34-Capt. Marvel Jr. vs. Capt. Nazi-c/story; 1st mention of Capt. Nippon 100 200 300 640 1095 1550
36-39 73 146 219 467 796 1125

Master of Kung Fu #71 © MAR

Masters of the Universe #1 © DC

Maverick #6 © MAR

GD VG FN VF VF/NM NM-
2.0 4.0 6.0 8.0 9.0 9.2

40-Classic flag-c 103 206 309 659 1130 1600
41-(8/43)-Bulletman, Capt. Marvel Jr. & Bulletgirl x-over in Minute-Man; only app. Crime Crusaders Club (Capt. Marvel Jr., Minute-Man, Bulletman & Bulletgirl) 76 152 228 486 831 1175
42-47,49: 46-Hitler story. 47-Hitler becomes Corpl. Hitler Jr. 49-Last Minute-Man 45 90 135 284 480 675
48-Intro. Bulletboy; Capt. Marvel cameo in Minute-Man 52 104 156 328 552 775
50-Intro Radar & Nyoka the Jungle Girl & begin series (5/44); Radar also intro in Captain Marvel #35 (same date); Capt. Marvel x-over in Radar; origin Radar; Capt. Marvel & Capt. Marvel, Jr. introduce Radar on-c 46 92 138 290 488 685
51-58 28 56 84 165 270 375
59-62: Nyoka serial "Terrible Tiara" in all; 61-Capt. Marvel Jr. 1st meets Uncle Marvel 30 60 90 177 289 400
63-80 22 44 66 128 209 290
81,83-87,89-91,95-99: 88-Hopalong Cassidy begins (ends #94). 95-Tom Mix begins (cover only in #123, ends #133) 20 40 60 117 189 260
82,88,92-94-Krigstein-a 20 40 60 120 195 270
100 20 40 60 120 195 270
101-106-Last Bulletman (not in #104) 20 40 60 114 182 250
107-120: 118-Mary Marvel 19 38 57 111 176 240
121-131-(lower print run): 123-Tom Mix-c only 20 40 60 117 189 260
132-B&W and color illos in **POP**; last Nyoka 20 40 60 118 192 265
133-Bill Battle app. 25 50 75 150 245 340

NOTE: ***Mac Raboy** a-15-39, 40(part), 42, 58. c-21-49, 51, 52, 54, 56, 58, 68(part), 69(part). Bulletman c-7-11, 13(half), 15, 18(part), 19, 20, 21(w/Capt. Marvel & Capt. Nazi), 22(w/Capt. Marvel, Jr.). Capt. Marvel, Jr. c-23-133. Master Man c-1-6. Minute Man c-12, 13(half), 14, 16, 17, 18(part).*

MASTER DARQUE
Acclaim Comics (Valiant): Feb, 1998 ($3.95)

1-Manco-a/Christina Z.-s 4.00

MASTER DETECTIVE
Super Comics: 1964 (Reprints)

17-r/Criminals on the Loose V4 #2; r/Young King Cole #?; McWilliams-r 2 4 6 8 11 14

MASTER OF KUNG FU (Formerly Special Marvel Edition; see Deadly Hands of Kung Fu & Giant-Size...)
Marvel Comics Group: No. 17, April, 1974 - No. 125, June, 1983

17-Starlin-a; intro Black Jack Tarr; 3rd Shang-Chi (ties w/Deadly Hands #1) 4 8 12 25 40 55
18,20 3 6 9 15 22 28
19-Man-Thing-c/story 3 6 9 17 26 35
21-23,25-30 2 4 6 10 14 18
24-Starlin, Simonson-a 2 4 6 11 16 20
31-50: 33-1st Leiko Wu. 43-Last 25¢ issue 1 3 4 6 8 10
39-43-(30¢-c variants, limited distribution)(5-7/76) 4 8 12 27 44 60
51-75 6.00
53-57-(35¢-c variants, limited distribution)(6-10/77) 5 10 15 30 50 70
76-99 5.00
100,118,125-Double size 6.00
101-117,119-124 4.00
Annual 1(4/76)-Iron Fist app. 3 6 9 17 26 35

NOTE: ***Austin** c-63i, 74i. **Buscema** c-44p. **Gulacy** a(p)-18-20, 22, 25, 29-31, 33-35, 38, 39, 40(p&i), 42-50, 53r(#20); c-51, 55, 64, 67. **Gil Kane** c(p)-20, 38, 39, 42, 45, 59, 63. **Nebres** c-73i. **Starlin** a-17p, 24; c-54. **Sutton** a-42i. #53 reprints #20.*

MASTER OF KUNG-FU, SHANG-CHI:... (2002 series, see Shang Chi:...)

MASTER OF KUNG-FU: BLEEDING BLACK
Marvel Comics: Feb, 1991 ($2.95, 84 pgs., one-shot)

1-The Return of Shang-Chi 4.00

MASTER OF THE WORLD
Dell Publishing Co.: No. 1157, July, 1961

Four Color 1157-Movie based on Jules Verne's "Master of the World" and "Robur the Conqueror" novels; with Vincent Price & Charles Bronson 6 12 18 40 73 105

MASTERS OF TERROR (Magazine)
Marvel Comics Group: July, 1975 - No. 2, Sept, 1975 (B&W) (All reprints)

1-Brunner, Barry Smith-a; Morrow/Steranko-c; Starlin-a(p); Gil Kane-a 3 6 9 17 26 35
2-Reese, Kane, Mayerik-a; Adkins/Steranko-c 2 4 6 13 18 22

MASTERS OF THE UNIVERSE (See DC Comics Presents #47 for 1st app.)
DC Comics: Dec, 1982 - No. 3, Feb, 1983 (Mini-series)

1 2 4 6 10 14 18
2,3: 2-Origin He-Man & Ceril 2 4 6 8 10 12

NOTE: ***Alcala** a-1i,, 2i. **Tuska** a-1-3p; c-1-3p. #2 has 75 & 95 cent cover price.*

MASTERS OF THE UNIVERSE (Comic Album)
Western Publishing Co.: 1984 (8-1/2x11", $2.95, 64 pgs.)

11362-Based on Mattel toy & cartoon 2 4 6 11 16 20

MASTERS OF THE UNIVERSE
Star Comics/Marvel #7 on: May 1986 - No. 13, May, 1988 (75¢/$1.00)

1 2 4 6 9 12 15
2-11: 8-Begin $1.00-c 1 2 3 5 6 8
12-Death of He-Man (1st Marvel app.) 3 6 9 14 20 25
13-Return of He-Man & death of Skeletor 2 4 6 13 18 22
The Motion Picture (11/87, $2.00)-Tuska-p 1 2 3 5 6 8

MASTERS OF THE UNIVERSE
Image Comics: Nov, 2002 - No. 4, March, 2003 ($2.95, limited series)

1-($2.95) Two covers by Santalucia and Campbell; Santalucia-a 4.00
1-($5.95) Variant-c by Norem w/gold foil logo 6.00
2-4($2.95) 2-Two covers by Santalucia and Manapul. 3,4-Two covers 3.00
TPB (CrossGen, 2003, $9.95, 8-1/4" x 5-1/2") digest-sized reprints #1-4 10.00

MASTERS OF THE UNIVERSE (Volume 2)
Image Comics: March, 2003 - No. 6, Aug, 2003 ($2.95)

1-6-($2.95) 1-Santalucia-c. 2-Two covers by Santalucia & JJ Kirby 3.00
1-($5.95) Wraparound variant-c by Struzan w/silver foil logo 6.00
3,4-($5.95) Wraparound variant holofoil-c. 3-By Edwards 4-By Boris Vallejo & Julie Bell 6.00
Volume 2 Dark Reflections TPB (2004, $18.95) r/#1-6 19.00

MASTERS OF THE UNIVERSE (Volume 3)
MVCreations: Apr, 2004 - No. 8, Dec, 2004 ($2.95)

1-8: 1-Santalucia-c 3.00

MASTERS OF THE UNIVERSE...
CrossGen Comics

...Rise of the Snake-Men (Nov, 2003 - No. 3, $2.95) Meyers-a 3.00
...The Power of Fear (12/03, $2.95, one-shot) Santalucia-a 3.00

MASTERS OF THE UNIVERSE, ICONS OF EVIL
Image Comics/CrossGen Comics: 2003 ($4.95, one-shots)

...Beastman -(Image) Origin of Beast Man; Tony Moore-a 5.00
...Mer-Man -(CrossGen) 5.00
...Trapjaw -(CrossGen) 5.00
...Tri-Klops -(CrossGen) Walker-c 5.00
TPB (3/04, $18.95, MVCreations) r/one-shots; sketch pages 19.00

MASTERS OF THE UNIVERSE: ...
DC Comics: Dec, 2012; Mar, 2013; Jul, 2013 ($2.99, one-shots)

... Origin Of He-Man (3/13) Fialkov-s; Ben Oliver-a/c; Prince Adam finds the sword 3.00
... Origin Of Hordak (7/13) Giffen & Keene-s/Giffen-a/c 3.00
... The Origin Of Skeletor (12/12) Fialkov-s; Fraser Irving-a/c; Keldor becomes Skeletor 3.00

MASTERWORKS SERIES OF GREAT COMIC BOOK ARTISTS, THE
Sea Gate Dist./DC Comics: May, 1983 - No. 3, Dec, 1983 (Baxter paper)

1-3: 1,2-Shining Knight by Frazetta r-/Adventure. 2-Tomahawk by Frazetta-r. 3-Wrightson-c/a(r) 6.00

MATADOR
DC Comics (WildStorm): July, 2005 - No. 6, May, 2006 ($2.99, limited series)

1-6-Devin Grayson-s/Brian Stelfreeze-a/c 3.00

MATRIX COMICS, THE (Movie)
Burlyman Entertainment: 2003; 2004 ($21.95, trade paperback)

nn-Short stories by various incl. Wachowskis, Darrow, Gaiman, Sienkiewicz, Bagge 22.00
...Volume One Preview (7/03, no cover price) bios of creators; Chadwick-s/a 3.00
Volume 2-(2004) Short stories by various incl. Wachowskis, Sale, McKeever, Dorman 22.00

MATT SLADE GUNFIGHTER (Kid Slade Gunfighter #5 on; See Western Gunfighters)
Atlas Comics (SPI): May, 1956 - No. 4, Nov, 1956

1-Intro Matt & horse Eagle; Williamson/Torres-a 19 38 57 111 176 240
2-Williamson-a 14 28 42 76 108 140
3,4 10 20 30 56 76 95

NOTE: ***Maneely** a-1, 3, 4; c-1, 2, 4. **Roth** a-2-4. **Severin** a-1, 3, 4. **Maneely** c/a-1. Issue #s stamped on cover after printing.*

MAUS: A SURVIVOR'S TALE (First graphic novel to win a Pulitzer Prize)
Pantheon Books: 1986, 1991 (B&W)

Vol. 1-(...: My Father Bleeds History)(1986) Art Spiegelman-s/a; recounts stories of Spiegelman's father in 1930s-40s Nazi-occupied Poland; collects first six stories serialized

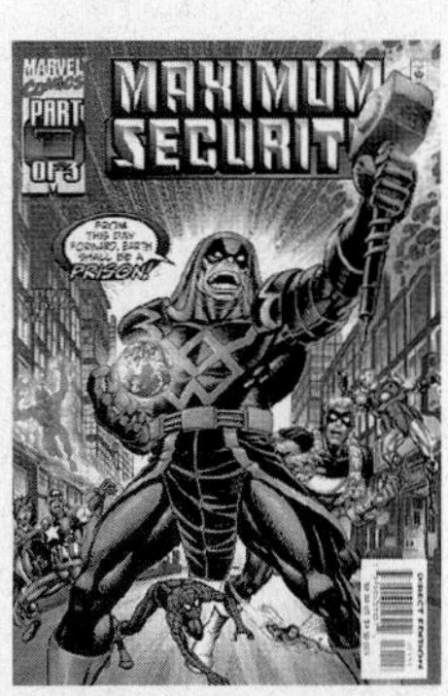

Maximum Security #1 © MAR

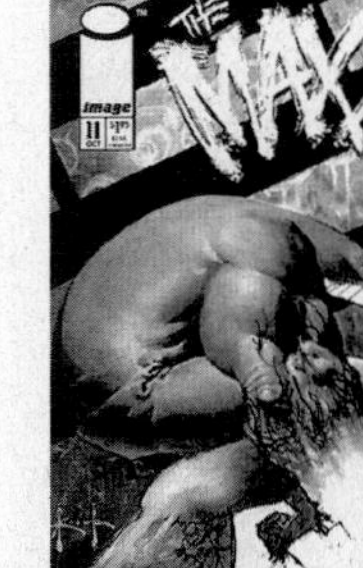

The Maxx #1 © I Before E

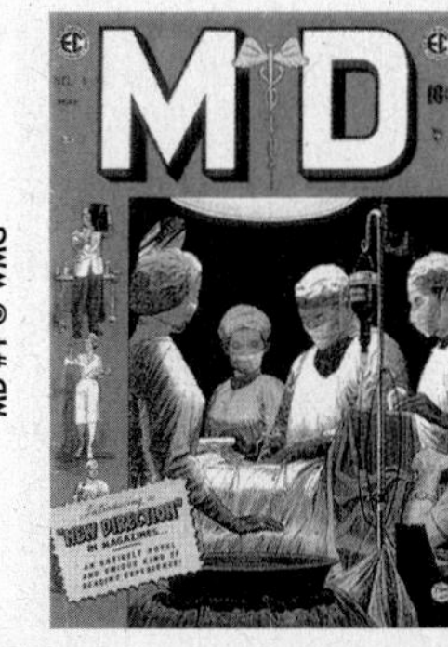

MD #1 © WMG

GD 2.0 | VG 4.0 | FN 6.0 | VF 8.0 | VF/NM 9.0 | NM- 9.2

in Raw Magazine from 1980-1985 30.00
Vol. 2-(...: And Here My Troubles Began)(1991) 25.00
Complete Maus Survivor's Tale -HC Vols. 1& 2 w/slipcase 35.00
Hardcover Vol. 1 (1991) 30.00
Hardcover Vol. 2 (1991) 30.00
TPB (1992, $14.00) Vols. 1& 2 18.00

MAVERICK (TV)
Dell Publishing Co.: No. 892, 4/58 - No. 19, 4-6/62 (All have photo-c)

Four Color 892 (#1)-James Garner photo-c begin 18 36 54 124 275 425
Four Color 930,945,962,980,1005 (6-8/59): 945-James Garner/Jack Kelly photo-c begin 9 18 27 62 126 190
7 (10-12/59) - 14: 11-Variant edition has "Time For Change" comic strip on back-c. 14-Last Garner/Kelly-c 8 16 24 54 102 150
15-18: Jack Kelly/Roger Moore photo-c 7 14 21 44 82 120
19-Jack Kelly photo-c (last issue) 7 14 21 46 86 125

MAVERICK (See X-Men)
Marvel Comics: Jan, 1997 ($2.95, one-shot)

1-Hama-s 4.00

MAVERICK (See X-Men)
Marvel Comics: Sept, 1997 - No. 12, Aug, 1998 ($2.99/$1.99)

1,12: 1-($2.99)-Wraparound-c. 12-($2.99) Battles Omega Red 4.00
2-11: 2-Two covers. 4-Wolverine app. 6,7-Sabretooth app. 3.00

MAVERICK MARSHAL
Charlton Comics: Nov, 1958 - No. 7, May, 1960

1 6 12 18 33 41 48
2-7 5 10 15 23 28 32

MAVERICKS
Daggar Comics Group: Jan, 1994 - No. 5, 1994 (#1-$2.75, #2-5-$2.50)

1-5: 1-Bronze. 1-Gold. 1-Silver 3.00

MAX BRAND (See Silvertip)

MAX HAMM FAIRY TALE DETECTIVE
Nite Owl Comix: 2002 - 2004 ($4.95, B&W, 6 1/2" x 8")

1-(2002) Frank Cammuso-s/a 5.00
Vol. 2 #1-3 (2003-2004) Frank Cammuso-s/a 5.00

MAXIMAGE
Image Comics (Extreme Studios): Dec, 1995 - No. 7, June 1996 ($2.50)

1-7: 1-Liefeld-c. 2-Extreme Destroyer Pt. 2; polybagged w/card. 4-Angela & Glory-c/app. 3.00

MAXIMO
Dreamwave Prods.: Jan, 2004 ($3.95, one-shot)

1-Based on the Capcom video game 4.00

MAXIMUM SECURITY (Crossover)
Marvel Comics: Oct, 2000 - No. 3, Jan, 2001 ($2.99)

1-3-Busiek-s/Ordway-a; Ronan the Accuser, Avengers app. 3.00
...Dangerous Planet 1: Busiek-s/Ordway-a; Ego, the Living Planet 3.00
Thor vs. Ego (11/00, $2.99) Reprints Thor #133,160,161; Kirby-a 3.00

MAXX (Also see Darker Image, Primer #5, & Friends of Maxx)
Image Comics (I Before E): Mar, 1993 - No. 35, Feb, 1998 ($1.95)

1/2 1 3 4 6 8 10
1/2 (Gold) 20.00
1-Sam Kieth-c/a/scripts 5.00
1-Glow-in-the-dark variant 2 4 6 8 10 12
1-"3-D Edition" (1/98, $4.95) plus new back-up story 5.00
2-12: 6-Savage Dragon cameo(1 pg.). 7,8-Pitt-c & story 3.00
13-16 3.00
17-35: 21-Alan Moore-s 3.00
Volume 1 TPB (DC/WildStorm, 2003, $17.95) r/#1-6 18.00
Volume 2 TPB (DC/WildStorm, 2004, $17.95) r/#7-13 18.00
Volume 3 TPB (DC/WildStorm, 2004, $17.95) r/#14-20 18.00
Volume 4 TPB (DC/WildStorm, 2005, $17.95) r/#21-27 18.00
Volume 5 TPB (DC/WildStorm, 2005, $19.99) r/#28-35 20.00
Volume 6 TPB (DC/WildStorm, 2006, $19.99) r/Friends of Maxx #1-3 & The Maxx 3-D 20.00

MAXX: MAXXIMIZED
IDW Publishing: Nov, 2013 - Present ($3.99)

1-4-Remastered, recolored reprint of the original Maxx issues 4.00

MAYA (See Movie Classics)
Gold Key: Mar, 1968

1 (10218-803)(TV) Photo-c 3 6 9 16 24 32

MAYHEM
Dark Horse Comics: May, 1989 - No. 4, Sept, 1989 ($2.50, B&W, 52 pgs.)

1- Four part Stanley Ipkiss/Mask story begins; Mask-c 1 3 4 6 8 10
2-4: 2-Mask 1/2 back-c. 4-Mask-c 1 2 3 5 7 9

MAYHEM (Tyrese Gibson's...)
Image Comics: Aug, 2009 - No. 3, Oct, 2009 ($2.99, limited series)

1-3-Tyrese Gibson co-writer; Tone Rodriguez-a/c 3.00

MAZE AGENCY, THE
Comico/Innovation Publ. #8 on: Dec, 1988 - No. 20, 1991 ($1.95-$2.50, color)

1-20: 9-Ellery Queen app. 7 ($2.50)-Last Comico issue 3.00
Annual 1 (1990, $2.75)-Ploog-c; Spirit tribute ish 4.00
Special 1 (1989, $2.75)-Staton-p (Innovation) 4.00
TPB (IDW Publ., 11/05, $24.99) r/#1-5 25.00

MAZE AGENCY, THE (Vol. 2)
Caliber Comics: July, 1997 - No. 3, 1998 ($2.95, B&W)

1-3: 1-Barr-s/Gonzales-a(p). 3-Hughes-c 3.00

MAZE AGENCY, THE
Caliber Comics: Nov, 2005 - No. 3, Jan, 2006 ($3.99, limited series)

1-3-Barr-s/Padilla-a(p)/c 4.00

MAZIE (...& Her Friends) (See Flat-Top, Mortie, Stevie & Tastee-Freez)
Mazie Comics(Magazine Publ.)/Harvey Publ. No. 13-on: 1953 - #12, 1954; #13, 12/54 - #22, 9/56; #23, 9/57 - #28, 8/58

1-(Teen-age)-Stevie's girlfriend 12 24 36 67 94 120
2 8 16 24 40 50 60
3-10 7 14 21 37 46 55
11-28 6 12 18 31 38 45

MAZIE
Nation Wide Publishers: 1950 - No. 7, 1951 (5¢) (5x7-1/4"-miniature)(52 pgs.)

1-Teen-age 19 38 57 111 176 240
2-7 14 28 42 76 108 140

MAZINGER (See First Comics Graphic Novel #17)

'MAZING MAN
DC Comics: Jan, 1986 - No. 12, Dec, 1986

1-11: 7,8-Hembeck-a 3.00
12-Dark Knight part-c by Miller 4.00
Special 1 ('87), 2 (4/88), 3 ('90)-All $2.00, 52pgs. 4.00

McCANDLESS & COMPANY
Mandalay Books: 2001 ($7.95)

...: Dead Razor - J.C. Vaughn-s/Busch & Sheehan-a; 3 covers 8.00
Crime Scenes: A McCandless & Company Reader TPB (Spring 2006, $17.95) Vaughn-s 18.00

McHALE'S NAVY (TV) (See Movie Classics)
Dell Publ. Co.: May-July, 1963 - No. 3, Nov-Jan, 1963-64 (All have photo-c)

1 6 12 18 38 69 100
2,3 5 10 15 30 50 70

McKEEVER & THE COLONEL (TV)
Dell Publishing Co.: Feb-Apr, 1963 - No. 3, Aug-Oct, 1963

1-Photo-c 5 10 15 34 60 85
2,3-Photo-c 4 8 12 28 47 65

McLINTOCK (See Movie Comics)

MD
E. C. Comics: Apr-May, 1955 - No. 5, Dec-Jan, 1955-56

1-Not approved by code; Craig-c 17 34 51 136 213 290
2-5 11 22 33 88 139 190

NOTE: ***Crandall, Evans, Ingels, Orlando*** *art in all issues;* ***Craig*** *c-1-5.*

MD
Russ Cochran/Gemstone Publishing: Sept, 1999 - No. 5, Jan, 2000 ($2.50)

1-5-Reprints original EC series 4.00
Annual 1 (1999, $13.50) r/#1-5 14.00

MEASLES
Fantagraphics Books: Christmas 1998 - No. 8 ($2.95, B&W, quarterly)

1-8-Anthology: 1-Venus-s by Hernandez 3.00

MECHA (Also see Mayhem)

Meet Merton #2 © TOBY

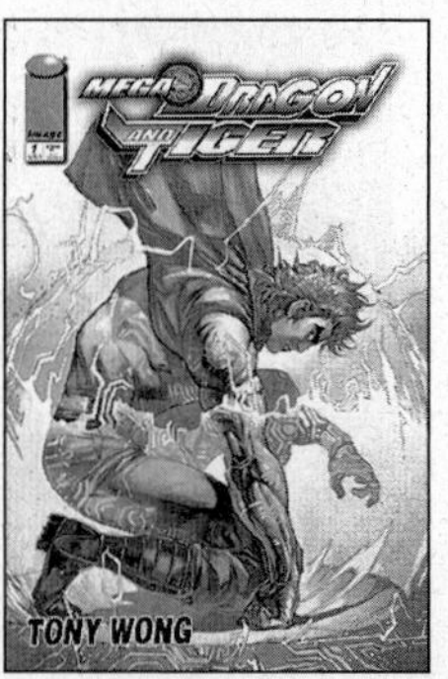

Mega Dragon and Tiger #1 © Jade Dynasty

Mega Morphs #1 © MAR

	GD 2.0	VG 4.0	FN 6.0	VF 8.0	VF/NM 9.0	NM- 9.2

Dark Horse Comics: June, 1987 - No. 6, 1988 ($1.50/$1.95, color/B&W)
1-6: 1,2 ($1.95, color), 3,4-($1.75, B&W), 5,6-($1.50, B&W) 3.00

MECHANIC, THE
Image Comics: 1998 ($5.95, one-shot, squarebound)
1-Chiodo-painted art; Peterson-s 6.00
1-($10.00) DF Alternate Cover Ed. 10.00

MECHA SPECIAL
Dark Horse Comics: May, 1995 ($2.95, one-shot)
1 3.00

MECH DESTROYER
Image Comics: Apr, 2001 - No. 4, Sept, 2001 ($2.95, limited series)
1-4-Jae Kim-c/a; Robert Chong-s 3.00

MEDAL FOR BOWZER, A (See Promotional Comics section)

MEDAL OF HONOR COMICS
A. S. Curtis: Spring, 1946
1-War stories 14 28 42 82 121 160

MEDAL OF HONOR SPECIAL
Dark Horse Comics: 1994 ($2.50, one-shot)
1-Kubert-c/a (first story) 3.00

MEDIA STARR
Innovation Publ.: July, 1989 - No. 3, Sept, 1989 ($1.95, mini-series, 28 pgs.)
1-3: Deluxe format 3.00

MEDIEVAL SPAWN/WITCHBLADE
Image Comics (Top Cow Productions): May, 1996 - No. 3, June, 1996 ($2.95, limited series)
1-3-Garth Ennis scripts in all 6.00
1-Platinum foil-c (500 copies from Pittsburgh Con) 35.00
1-Gold 10.00
1-ETM Exclusive Edition; gold foil logo 7.00
TPB ($9.95) r/#1-3 10.00

MEET ANGEL (Formerly Angel & the Ape)
National Periodical Publications: No. 7, Nov-Dec, 1969
7-Wood-a(i) 3 6 9 19 30 40

MEET CORLISS ARCHER (Radio/Movie)(My Life #4 on)
Fox Features Syndicate: Mar, 1948 - No. 3, July, 1948
1-(Teen-age)-Feldstein-c/a; headlight-c 113 226 339 718 1234 1750
2 58 116 174 371 636 900
3 54 108 162 343 574 825
NOTE: *No. 1-3 used in Seduction of the Innocent, pg. 39.*

MEET HERCULES (See Three Stooges)

MEET MERTON
Toby Press: Dec, 1953 - No. 4, June, 1954
1-(Teen-age)-Dave Berg-c/a 12 24 36 67 94 120
2-Dave Berg-c/a 8 16 24 40 50 60
3,4-Dave Berg-c/a 7 14 21 37 46 55
I.W. Reprint #9, Super Reprint #11('63), 18 2 4 6 8 11 14

MEET MISS BLISS (Becomes Stories Of Romance #5 on)
Atlas Comics (LMC): May, 1955 - No. 4, Nov, 1955
1-Al Hartley-c/a 15 30 45 84 127 170
2-4 11 22 33 60 83 105

MEET MISS PEPPER (Formerly Lucy, The Real Gone Gal)
St. John Publishing Co.: No. 5, April, 1954 - No. 6, June, 1954
5-Kubert/Maurer-a 23 46 69 136 223 310
6-Kubert/Maurer-a; Kubert-c 20 40 60 117 189 260

MEGACITY909
Devil's Due Publ.: Sept, 2004 - No. 8, Aug, 2005 ($2.95)
1-8-Kano Kang & Zack Suh-a 3.00

MEGA DRAGON & TIGER
Image Comics: Mar, 1999 - No. 5 ($2.95)
1-5-Tony Wong-s/a 3.00

MEGAHURTZ
Image Comics: Aug, 1997 - No. 3, Oct, 1997 ($2.95, B&W)
1-3-St. Pierre-s 3.00

MEGALITH (Megalith Deathwatch 2000 #1,2 of second series)
Continuity: 1989 - No. 9, Mar, 1992; No, 0, Apr, 1993 - No. 7, Jan, 1994
1-9-($2.00-c) 1-Neal Adams & Mark Texiera-c/Texiera & Nebres-a 3.00
2nd series: 0-(4/93)-Foil-c; no c-price, giveaway; Adams plot 3.00
1-7: 1-3-Bagged w/card: 1-Gatefold-c by Nebres; Adams plot. 2-Fold-out-c; Adams plot. 3-Indestructible-c. 4-7-Embossed-c: 4-Adams/Nebres-c; Adams part-i. 5-Sienkiewicz-i. 6-Adams part-i. 7-Adams-c(p); Adams plot 3.00

MEGAMAN
Dreamwave Productions: Sept, 2003 - No. 4, Dec, 2003 ($2.95)
1-4-Brian Augustyn-s/Mic Fong-a 3.00
1-($5.95) Chromium wraparound variant-c 6.00

MEGA MAN (Based on the Capcom video game character)
Archie Comics Publications: Jul, 2011 - Present ($2.99)
1-35: 1-Spaziante-a. 20-35-Multiple covers. 24-Worlds Collide x-over begins 3.00
Free Comic Book Day Edition (2012, giveaway) Origin re-told 3.00

MEGAMIND: BAD. BLUE. BRILLIANT (DreamWorks'...) (Based on the 2010 movie)
Ape Entertainment: 2010 - No. 4, 2011 ($3.95, limited series)
1-4: 1-High school flashback 4.00
nn-($6.95, 9x6") Prequel to the movie; Joe Kelly-s 7.00

MEGA MORPHS
Marvel Comics: Oct, 2005 - No. 4, Dec, 2005 ($2.99, limited series)
1-4-Giant robots based on action figures; McKeever-s; Kang-a 3.00
Digest (2006, $7.99) r/#1-4 plus mini-comics 8.00

MEGATON (A super hero)
Megaton Publ.: Nov, 1983; No. 2, Oct, 1985 - No. 8, Aug, 1987 (B&W)
1-($2.00, 68 pgs.)-Erik Larsen's 1st pro work; Vanguard by Larsen begins (1st app.), ends #4; 1st app. Megaton, Berzerker, & Ethrian; Guice-c/a(p); Gustovich-a(p) in #1,2 2 4 6 10 14 18
2-($2.00, 68 pgs.)-1st brief app. The Dragon (1 pg.) by Larsen (later The Savage Dragon in Image Comics); Guice-c/a(p) 2 4 6 9 12 15
3-(44 pgs.)-1st full app. Savage Dragon-c/story by Larsen; 1st comic book work by Angel Medina (pin-up) 3 6 9 16 23 30
4-(52 pgs.)-2nd full app. Savage Dragon by Larsen; 4,5-Wildman by Grass Green 2 4 6 8 10 12
5-1st Liefeld published-a (inside f/c, 6/86) 1 2 3 5 7 9
6,7: 6-Larsen-c 1 2 3 4 5 7
8-1st Liefeld story-a (7 pg. super hero story) plus 1 pg. Youngblood ad 1 3 4 6 8 10
...Explosion (6/87, 16 pg. color giveaway)-1st app. Youngblood by Rob Liefeld (2 pg. spread); shows Megaton heroes 3 6 9 14 20 25
...Holiday Special 1 (1994, $2.95, color, 40 pgs., publ. by Entity Comics)-Gold foil logo; bagged w/Kelley Jones card; Vanguard, Megaton plus shows unpublished-c to 1987 Youngblood #1 by Liefeld/Ordway 5.00
NOTE: *Copies of Megaton Explosion were also released in early 1992 all signed by Rob Liefeld and were made available to retailers.*

MEGATON MAN (See Don Simpson's Bizarre Heroes)
Kitchen Sink Enterprises: Nov, 1984 - No. 10, 1986
1-10, 1-2nd printing (1989) 3.00
...Meets The Uncategorizable X-Thems 1 (4/89, $2.00) 3.00

MEGATON MAN: BOMB SHELL
Image Comics: Jul, 1999 - No. 2 ($2.95, B&W, mini-series)
1-Reprints stories from Megaton Man internet site 3.00

MEGATON MAN: HARD COPY
Image Comics: Feb, 1999 - No. 2, Apr, 1999 ($2.95, B&W, mini-series)
1,2-Reprints stories from Megaton Man internet site 3.00

MEGATON MAN VS. FORBIDDEN FRANKENSTEIN
Fiasco Comics: Apr, 1996 ($2.95, B&W, one-shot)
1-Intro The Tomb Team (Forbidden Frankenstein, Drekula, Bride of the Monster, & Moon Wolf). 3.00

MEK (See Reload/Mek flipbook for TPB reprint)
DC Comics (Homage): Jan, 2003 - No. 3, Mar, 2003 ($2.95, limited series)
1-3-Warren Ellis-s/Steve Rolston-a 3.00

MEKANIX (See X-Men titles) (See X-Treme X-Men Vol. 4 for TPB)
Marvel Comics: Dec, 2002 - No. 6, May, 2003 ($2.99, limited series)
1-6-Kitty Pryde in college; Claremont-s/Bobillo & Sosa-a 3.00

MEL ALLEN SPORTS COMICS (The Voice of the Yankees)
Standard Comics: No. 5, Nov, 1949; No. 6, June, 1950
5(#1 on inside)-Tuska-a 23 46 69 136 223 310

Menace #1 © MAR

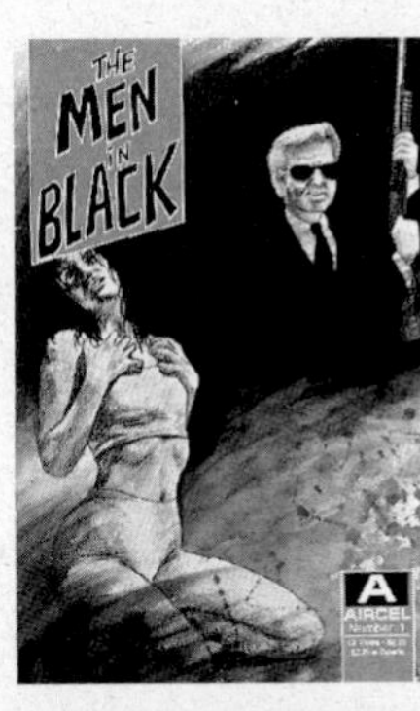

Men in Black #1 © L. Cunningham

Men's Adventures #27 © MAR

	GD 2.0	VG 4.0	FN 6.0	VF 8.0	VF/NM 9.0	NM- 9.2
6(#2)-Lou Gehrig story	16	32	48	94	147	200

MELTDOWN
Image Comics: Dec, 2006 - No. 2, Jan, 2007 ($5.95, squarebound, limited series)

	GD 2.0	VG 4.0	FN 6.0	VF 8.0	VF/NM 9.0	NM- 9.2
1,2-Schwartz-s/Wang-a. 1-Bachalo-c. 2-Horn-c						6.00

MELVIN MONSTER
Dell Publishing Co.: Apr-June, 1965 - No. 10, Oct, 1969

	GD 2.0	VG 4.0	FN 6.0	VF 8.0	VF/NM 9.0	NM- 9.2
1-By John Stanley	6	12	18	40	73	105
2-10-All by Stanley. #10-r/#1	5	10	15	30	50	70

MELVIN THE MONSTER (See Peter, the Little Pest & Dexter The Demon #7)
Atlas Comics (HPC): July, 1956 - No. 6, July, 1957

	GD 2.0	VG 4.0	FN 6.0	VF 8.0	VF/NM 9.0	NM- 9.2
1-Maneely-c/a	15	30	45	85	130	175
2-6: 4-Maneely-c/a	11	22	33	60	83	105

MENACE
Atlas Comics (HPC): Mar, 1953 - No. 11, May, 1954

	GD 2.0	VG 4.0	FN 6.0	VF 8.0	VF/NM 9.0	NM- 9.2
1-Horror & sci/fi stories begin; Everett-c/a	110	220	330	704	1202	1700
2-Post-atom bomb disaster by Everett; anti-Communist propaganda/torture scenes; Sinnott sci/fi story "Rocket to the Moon"	77	154	231	493	847	1200
3,4,6-Everett-a. 4-Sci/fi story "Escape to the Moon". 6-Romita sci/fi story "Science Fiction"	58	116	174	371	636	900
5-Origin & 1st app. The Zombie by Everett (reprinted in Tales of the Zombie #1)(7/53); 5-Sci/fi story "Rocket Ship"	84	168	252	538	919	1300
7,8,10,11: 7-Frankenstein story. 8-End of world story; Heath 3-D art(3 pgs.). 10-H-Bomb panels	47	94	141	296	498	700
9-Everett-a r-in Vampire Tales #1	50	100	150	315	533	750

NOTE: ***Brodsky** c-7, 8, 11. **Colan** a-6; c-9. **Everett** a-1-6, 9; c-1-6. **Heath** a-1-8; c-10. **Katz** a-11. **Maneely** a-3, 5, 7-9. **Powell** a-11. **Romita** a-3, 6, 8, 11. **Shelly** a-10. **Shores** a-7. **Sinnott** a-2, 7. **Tuska** a-1, 2, 5.*

MENACE
Awesome-Hyperwerks: Nov, 1998 ($2.50)

	GD 2.0	VG 4.0	FN 6.0	VF 8.0	VF/NM 9.0	NM- 9.2
1-Jada Pinkett Smith-s/Fraga-a						3.00

MEN AGAINST CRIME (Formerly Mr. Risk; Hand of Fate #8 on)
Ace Magazines: No. 3, Feb, 1951 - No. 7, Oct, 1951

	GD 2.0	VG 4.0	FN 6.0	VF 8.0	VF/NM 9.0	NM- 9.2
3-Mr. Risk app.	11	22	33	62	86	110
4-7: 4-Colan-a; entire book-r as Trapped! #4. 5-Meskin-a	9	18	27	47	61	75

MEN, GUNS, & CATTLE (See Classics Illustrated Special Issue)

MEN IN ACTION (Battle Brady #10 on)
Atlas Comics (IPS): April, 1952 - No. 9, Dec, 1952 (War stories)

	GD 2.0	VG 4.0	FN 6.0	VF 8.0	VF/NM 9.0	NM- 9.2
1-Berg, Reinman-a	20	40	60	120	195	270
2,3: 3-Heath-c/a	13	26	39	74	105	135
4-6,8,9	12	24	36	67	94	120
7-Krigstein-a; Heath-c	13	26	39	74	105	135

NOTE: ***Brodsky** a-3; c-1, 4-6. **Maneely** c-5. **Pakula** a-1, 6. **Robinson** c-8. **Shores** c-9. **Sinnott** a-6.*

MEN IN ACTION
Ajax/Farrell Publications: Apr, 1957 - No. 6, Jun, 1958

	GD 2.0	VG 4.0	FN 6.0	VF 8.0	VF/NM 9.0	NM- 9.2
1	10	20	30	58	79	100
2	7	14	21	37	46	55
3-6	7	14	21	35	43	50

MEN IN BLACK, THE (1st series)
Aircel Comics (Malibu): Jan, 1990 - No. 3 Mar, 1990 ($2.25, B&W, lim. series)

	GD 2.0	VG 4.0	FN 6.0	VF 8.0	VF/NM 9.0	NM- 9.2
1-Cunningham-s/a in all	5	10	15	35	63	90
2,3	3	6	9	17	26	35
Graphic Novel (Jan, 1991) r/#1-3	3	6	9	16	23	30

MEN IN BLACK (2nd series)
Aircel Comics (Malibu): May, 1991 - No. 3, Jul, 1991 ($2.50, B&W, lim. series)

	GD 2.0	VG 4.0	FN 6.0	VF 8.0	VF/NM 9.0	NM- 9.2
1-Cunningham-s/a in all	3	6	9	19	30	40
2,3	2	4	6	11	16	20

MEN IN BLACK: FAR CRY
Marvel Comics: Aug, 1997 ($3.99, color, one-shot)

	GD 2.0	VG 4.0	FN 6.0	VF 8.0	VF/NM 9.0	NM- 9.2
1-Cunningham-s						4.00

MEN IN BLACK: RETRIBUTION
Marvel Comics: Dec, 1997 ($3.99, color, one-shot)

	GD 2.0	VG 4.0	FN 6.0	VF 8.0	VF/NM 9.0	NM- 9.2
1-Cunningham-s; continuation of the movie						4.00

MEN IN BLACK: THE MOVIE
Marvel Comics: Oct, 1997 ($3.99, one-shot, movie adaptation)

	GD 2.0	VG 4.0	FN 6.0	VF 8.0	VF/NM 9.0	NM- 9.2
1-Cunningham-s						4.00

MEN INTO SPACE
Dell Publishing Co.: No. 1083, Feb-Apr, 1960

	GD 2.0	VG 4.0	FN 6.0	VF 8.0	VF/NM 9.0	NM- 9.2
Four Color 1083-Anderson-a, photo-c	5	10	15	31	53	75

MEN OF BATTLE (Also see New Men of Battle)
Catechetical Guild: V1#5, March, 1943 (Hardcover)

	GD 2.0	VG 4.0	FN 6.0	VF 8.0	VF/NM 9.0	NM- 9.2
V1#5-Topix reprints	6	12	18	28	34	40

MEN OF WAR
DC Comics, Inc.: August, 1977 - No. 26, March, 1980 (#9,10: 44 pgs.)

	GD 2.0	VG 4.0	FN 6.0	VF 8.0	VF/NM 9.0	NM- 9.2
1-Enemy Ace, Gravedigger (origin #1,2) begin	3	6	9	16	23	30
2-4,8-10,12-14,19,20: All Enemy Ace stories. 4-1st Dateline Frontline. 9-Unknown Soldier app.	2	4	6	10	14	18
5-7,11,15-18,21-25: 17-1st app. Rosa	2	4	6	8	11	14
26-Sgt. Rock & Easy Co.-c/s	3	6	9	14	19	24

NOTE: ***Chaykin** a-9, 10, 12-14, 19, 20. **Evans** c-25. **Kubert** c-2-23, 24p, 26.*

MEN OF WAR (DC New 52)
DC Comics: Nov, 2011 - No. 8, Jun, 2012 ($3.99)

	GD 2.0	VG 4.0	FN 6.0	VF 8.0	VF/NM 9.0	NM- 9.2
1-8: 1-Sgt. Rock's grandson in modern times; Derenick-a; Navy Seals back-up; Winslade-a 6-Back-up w/Corben-a. 8-Frankenstein & G.I. Robot app.						4.00

MEN'S ADVENTURES (Formerly True Adventures)
Marvel/Atlas Comics (CCC): No. 4, Aug, 1950 - No. 28, July, 1954

	GD 2.0	VG 4.0	FN 6.0	VF 8.0	VF/NM 9.0	NM- 9.2
4(#1)(52 pgs.)	36	72	108	216	351	485
5-Flying Saucer story	24	48	72	140	230	320
6-8: 7-Buried alive story. 8-Sci/fic story	21	42	63	126	206	285
9-20: All war format	15	30	45	85	130	175
21,22,24,26: All horror format	29	58	87	170	278	385
23-Crandall-a; Fox-a(i); horror format	30	60	90	177	289	400
25-Shrunken head-c	40	80	120	246	411	575
27,28-Human Torch & Toro-c/stories; Captain America & Sub-Mariner stories in each (also see Young Men #24-28)	135	270	405	864	1482	2100

NOTE: ***Ayers** a-20, 27(H. Torch). **Berg** a-15, 16. **Brodsky** c-4-9, 11, 12, 16-18, 24. **Burgos** c-27, 28 (Human Torch). **Colan** a-13, 14, 19. **Everett** a-10, 14, 22, 25, 28; c-14, 21-23. **Hartley** a-12. **Heath** a-8, 11, 24; c-13, 20, 26. **Lawrence** a-23; 27(Captain America). **Maneely** a-24; c-10, 15. **Mac Pakula** a-15, 25. **Post** a-23. **Powell** a-27(Sub-Mariner). **Reinman** a-11, 12, 16. **Robinson** c-19. **Romita** a-22. **Sale** a-12, 14. **Shores** c-25. **Sinnott** a-13, 21. **Tuska** a-24. Adventure-#4-8; War-#9-20; Weird/Horror-#21-26.*

MENZ INSANA
DC Comics (Vertigo): 1997 ($7.95, one-shot)

	GD 2.0	VG 4.0	FN 6.0	VF 8.0	VF/NM 9.0	NM- 9.2
nn-Fowler-s/Bolton painted art	1	2	3	5	6	8

MEPHISTO VS... (See Silver Surfer #3)
Marvel Comics Group: Apr, 1987 - No. 4, July, 1987 ($1.50, mini-series)

	GD 2.0	VG 4.0	FN 6.0	VF 8.0	VF/NM 9.0	NM- 9.2
1-4: 1-Fantastic Four; Austin-i. 2-X-Factor. 3-X-Men. 4-Avengers						4.00

MERC (See Mark Hazzard: Merc)

MERCENARIES (Based on the Pandemic video game)
Dynamite Entertainment: 2007 - No. 3, 2008 ($3.99, limited series)

	GD 2.0	VG 4.0	FN 6.0	VF 8.0	VF/NM 9.0	NM- 9.2
1-3-Michael Turner-c; Brian Reed-s/Edgar Salazar-a						4.00

MERCHANTS OF DEATH
Acme Press (Eclipse): Jul, 1988 - No. 4, Nov, 1988 ($3.50, B&W/16 pgs. color, 44 pg. mag.)

	GD 2.0	VG 4.0	FN 6.0	VF 8.0	VF/NM 9.0	NM- 9.2
1-4: 4-Toth-c						4.00

MERCILESS: THE RISE OF MING (Also see Flash Gordon: Zeitgeist)
Dynamite Entertainment: 2012 - No. 4, 2012 ($3.99, limited series)

	GD 2.0	VG 4.0	FN 6.0	VF 8.0	VF/NM 9.0	NM- 9.2
1-4 Ming the Merciless' rise to power; Alex Ross-c; Beatty-c/Adrian-a						4.00

MERCY THOMPSON: HOMECOMING (Patricia Briggs'...)
Dabel Brothers Prods.: Oct, 2008 (Nov. on-c) - No. 4 ($3.99, limited series)

	GD 2.0	VG 4.0	FN 6.0	VF 8.0	VF/NM 9.0	NM- 9.2
1-Characters from the Patricia Briggs werewolf novels; Francis Tsai-a						4.00

MERIDIAN
CrossGeneration Comics: Jul, 2000 - No. 44, Apr, 2004 ($2.95)

	GD 2.0	VG 4.0	FN 6.0	VF 8.0	VF/NM 9.0	NM- 9.2
1-44: Barbara Kesel-s						3.00
Flying Solo Vol. 1 TPB (2001, $19.95) r/#1-7; cover by Steve Rude						20.00
Going to Ground Vol. 2 TPB (2002, $19.95) r/#8-14						20.00
Taking the Skies Vol. 3 TPB (2002, $15.95) r/#15-20						16.00
Vol. 4: Coming Home (12/02, $15.95) r/#21-26						16.00
Vol. 5: Minister of Cadador (7/03, $15.95) r/#27-32						16.00
Vol. 6: Changing Course (1/04, $15.95) r/#33-38						16.00
Traveler Vol. 1-4 ($9.95): Digest-size reprints of TPBs						10.00

MERLIN JONES AS THE MONKEY'S UNCLE (See Movie Comics and The Misadventures of... under Movie Comics)

MERRILL'S MARAUDERS (See Movie Classics)

MERRY CHRISTMAS (See A Christmas Adventure, Donald Duck..., Dell Giant #39, & March of Comics #153 in the Promotional Comics section)

Meta 4 #3 © FC

Metal Men #7 © DC

Metamorpho #9 © DC

	GD 2.0	VG 4.0	FN 6.0	VF 8.0	VF/NM 9.0	NM- 9.2

MERRY COMICS
Carlton Publishing Co.: Dec, 1945 (10¢)

nn-Boogeyman app.	20	40	60	118	192	265

MERRY COMICS: Four Star Publications: 1947 (Advertised, not published)

MERRY-GO-ROUND COMICS
LaSalle Publ. Co./Croyden Publ./Rotary Litho.: 1944 (25¢, 132 pgs.); 1946; 9-10/47 - No. 2, 1948

nn(1944)(LaSalle)-Funny animal; 29 new features	19	38	57	111	176	240
21 (Publisher?)	9	18	27	52	69	85
1(1946)(Croyden)-Al Fago-c; funny animal	11	22	33	64	90	115
V1#1,2(1947-48; 52 pgs.)(Rotary Litho. Co. Ltd., Canada); Ken Hultgren-a	9	18	27	52	69	85

MERRY MAILMAN (See Fawcett's Funny Animals #87-89)

MERRY MOUSE (Also see Funny Tunes & Space Comics)
Avon Periodicals: June, 1953 - No. 4, Jan-Feb, 1954

1-1st app.; funny animal; Frank Carin-c/a	10	20	30	58	79	100
2-4	8	16	24	40	50	60

MERV PUMPKINHEAD, AGENT OF D.R.E.A.M. (See The Sandman)
DC Comics (Vertigo): 2000 ($5.95, one-shot)

1-Buckingham-a(p); Nowlan painted-c 6.00

META-4
First Comics: Feb, 1991 - No. 4, 1991 ($2.25)

1-($3.95, 52pgs.) 4.00
2-4 3.00

METAL GEAR SOLID (Based on the video game)
IDW Publ.: Sept, 2004 - No. 12, Aug, 2005 ($3.99)

1-12: 1-Two covers; Ashley Wood-a/Kris Oprisko-s 4.00
1-Retailer edition with foil cover 15.00

METAL GEAR SOLID: SONS OF LIBERTY
IDW Publ.: Sept, 2005 - No. 12, Sept, 2007 ($3.99)

#0 (9/05) profile pages on characters; Ashley Wood-a 4.00
1-12: 1-Two covers; Ashley Wood-a/Alex Garner-s 4.00

METALLIX
Future Comics: Dec, 2002 - No. 6, June, 2003 ($3.50)

0-6-Ron Lim-a. 0-(6/03) Origin. 1-Layton-c 3.50
1-Collector's Edition with variant cover by Lim 3.50
1-Free Comic Book Day Edition (4/03) Layton-c 3.00

METAL MEN (See Brave & the Bold, DC Comics Presents, and Showcase #37-40)
National Periodical Publications/DC Comics: 4-5/63 - No. 41, 12-1/69-70; No. 42, 2-3/73 - No. 44, 7-8/73; No. 45, 4-5/76 - No. 56, 2-3/78

1-(4-5/63)-5th app. Metal Men	50	100	150	400	900	1400
2	20	40	60	135	300	465
3-5	13	26	39	89	195	300
6-10	9	18	27	59	117	175
11-20: 12-Beatles cameo (2-3/65)	7	14	21	46	86	125
21-Batman, Robin & Flash x-over	6	12	18	37	66	95
22-26,28-30	5	10	15	34	60	85
27-Origin Metal Men retold	6	12	18	42	79	115
31-41(1968-70): 38-Last 12¢ issue. 41-Last 15¢	5	10	15	31	53	75
42-44(1973)-Reprints	2	4	6	10	14	18
45('76)-49-Simonson-a in all: 48,49-Re-intro Eclipso	2	4	6	10	14	18
50-56: 50-Part-r. 54,55-Green Lantern x-over	2	4	6	9	12	15

NOTE: ***Andru/Esposito** c-1-30. **Aparo** c-53-56. **Giordano** c-45, 46. **Kane/Esposito** a-30, 31; c-31. **Simonson** a-45-49; c-47-52. **Staton** a-50-56.*

METAL MEN (Also see Tangent Comics/ Metal Men)
DC Comics: Oct, 1993 - No. 4, Jan, 1994 ($1.25, mini-series)

1-($2.50)-Multi-colored foil-c 4.00
2-4: 2-Origin 3.00

METAL MEN (Also see 52)
DC Comics: Oct, 2007 - No. 8, Jul, 2008 ($2.99, limited series)

1-8-Duncan Rouleau-s/a; origin re-told. 3-Chemo returns 3.00
HC (2008, $24.99, dustjacket) r/#1-8; cover gallery and sketch pages 25.00
SC (2009, $14.99) r/#1-8; cover gallery and sketch pages 15.00

METAMORPHO (See Action Comics #413, Brave & the Bold #57,58, 1st Issue Special, & World's Finest #217)
National Periodical Publications: July-Aug, 1965 - No. 17, Mar-Apr, 1968 (All 12¢ issues)

1-(7-8/65)-3rd app. Metamorpho	12	24	36	81	176	270
2,3	7	14	21	44	82	120
4-6,10:10-Origin & 1st app. Element Girl (1-2/67)	6	12	18	37	66	95
7-9	5	10	15	33	57	80
11-17: 17-Sparling-c/a	5	10	15	30	50	70

NOTE: ***Ramona Fradon** a-B&B 57, 58, 1-4. **Orlando** a-5, 6; c-5-9, 11. **Trapani** a(p)-7-16; i-16.*

METAMORPHO
DC Comics: Aug, 1993 - No. 4, Nov, 1993 ($1.50, mini-series)

1-4 3.00

METAMORPHO: YEAR ONE
DC Comics: Early Dec, 2007 - No. 6, Late Feb, 2008 ($2.99, limited series)

1-6-Origin re-told; Jurgens-s/Jurgens & Delperdang-a/Nowlan-c. 6-Justice League app. 3.00
TPB ('08, $14.99) r/#1-6 15.00

METAPHYSIQUE
Malibu Comics (Bravura): Apr, 1995 - No. 6, Oct, 1995 ($2.95, limited series)

1-6: Norm Breyfogle-c/a/scripts 3.00

METEOR COMICS
L. L. Baird (Croyden): Nov, 1945

1-Captain Wizard, Impossible Man, Race Wilkins app.; origin Baldy Bean, Capt. Wizard's sidekick; bare-breasted mermaids story	41	82	123	250	418	585

METEOR MAN
Marvel Comics: Aug, 1993 - No. 6, Jan, 1994 ($1.25, limited series)

1-6: 1-Regular unbagged. 4-Night Thrasher-c/story. 6-Terry Austin-c(i) 3.00
1-Polybagged w/button & rap newspaper 4.00
...: The Movie (4/93 [7/93 on cover], $2.25) movie adaptation 3.00

METROPOL (See Ted McKeever's...)

METROPOL A.D. (See Ted McKeever's...)

METROPOLIS S.C.U. (Also see Showcase '96 #1)
DC Comics: Nov, 1995 - No. 4, Feb, 1996 ($1.50, limited series)

1-4:1-Superman-c & app. 3.00

MEZZ: GALACTIC TOUR 2494 (Also See Nexus)
Dark Horse Comics: May, 1994 ($2.50, one-shot)

1 3.00

MGM'S MARVELOUS WIZARD OF OZ (See Marvel Treasury of Oz)
Marvel Comics Group/National Periodical Publications: 1975 ($1.50, 84 pgs.; oversize)

1-Adaptation of MGM's movie; J. Buscema-a	3	6	9	16	23	30

M.G.M'S MOUSE MUSKETEERS (Formerly M.G.M.'s The Two Mouseketeers)
Dell Publishing Co.: No. 670, Jan, 1956 - No. 1290, Mar-May, 1962

Four Color 670 (#4)	5	10	15	33	57	80
Four Color 711,728,764	4	8	12	27	44	60
8 (4-6/57) - 21 (3-5/60)	4	8	12	25	40	55
Four Color 1135,1175,1290	4	8	12	25	40	55

M.G.M.'S SPIKE AND TYKE (also see Tom & Jerry #79)
Dell Publishing Co.: No. 499, Sept, 1953 - No. 1266, Dec-Feb, 1961-62

Four Color 499 (#1)	6	12	18	42	79	115
Four Color 577,638	5	10	15	31	53	75
4(12-2/55-56)-10	4	8	12	27	44	60
11-24(12-2/60-61)	4	8	12	23	37	50
Four Color 1266	4	8	12	25	40	55

M.G.M.'S THE TWO MOUSKETEERS
Dell Publishing Co.: No. 475, June, 1953 - No. 642, July, 1955

Four Color 475 (#1)	7	14	21	49	92	135
Four Color 603 (11/54), 642	5	10	15	35	63	90

MICE TEMPLAR, THE
Image Comics: Sept, 2007 - No. 6, Oct, 2008 ($3.99/$2.99)

1-($3.99)-Bryan Glass-s/Michael Avon Oeming-a/c 4.00
2-6-($2.99) 3.00

MICE TEMPLAR, THE , VOLUME 2: DESTINY
Image Comics: July, 2009 - No. 9, May, 2010 ($3.99/$2.99/$4.99)

1,2-($3.99) 1-Bryan Glass-s/Oeming & Santos-a; 2 covers. 2-Santos-a 4.00
3-8-($2.99)-Santos-a; 2 covers by Oeming & Santos 3.00
9-($4.99) 5.00

MICE TEMPLAR, THE , VOLUME 3: A MIDWINTER NIGHT'S DREAM
Image Comics: Dec, 2010 - No. 8, Mar, 2012 ($3.99/$2.99)

1,8-($3.99) 1-Bryan Glass-s/Oeming & Santos-a; 2 covers 4.00

Mice Templar V4 #7 © Oeming & Glass

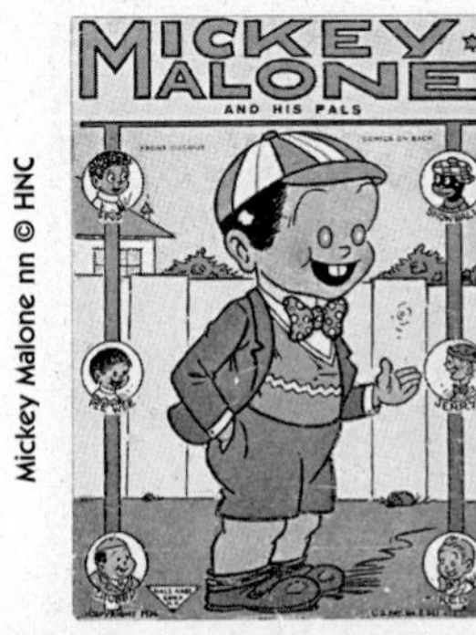

Mickey Malone nn © HNC

Mickey Mouse FC #116 © DIS

GD VG FN VF VF/NM NM-
2.0 4.0 6.0 8.0 9.0 9.2

2-7-($2.99)-Santos-a; 2 covers by Oeming & Santos 3.00

MICE TEMPLAR, THE , VOLUME 4: LEGEND
Image Comics: Mar, 2013 - Present ($3.99/$2.99/$4.99)
1-($3.99)-Bryan Glass-s/Victor Santos-a; 2 covers 4.00
2-7-($2.99)-Santos-a; 2 covers by Oeming & Santos 3.00
8-($4.99) 5.00

MICHAELANGELO CHRISTMAS SPECIAL (See Teenage Mutant Ninja Turtles Christmas Special)

MICHAELANGELO, TEENAGE MUTANT NINJA TURTLE
Mirage Studios: 1986 (One shot) ($1.50, B&W)
1-Christmas-c/story 2 4 6 11 16 20
1-2nd printing ('89, $1.75)-Reprint plus new-a 5.00

MICHAEL CHABON PRESENTS THE AMAZING ADVENTURES OF THE ESCAPIST
Dark Horse Comics: Feb, 2004 - Present ($8.95, squarebound)
1-5,7,8-Short stories by Chabon and various incl. Chaykin, Starlin, Brereton, Baker 9.00
6-Includes 6 pg. Spirit & Escapist story (Will Eisner's last work); Spirit on cover 9.00
... Vol. 1 (5/04, $17.95, digest-size) r/#1&2; wraparound-c by Chris Ware 18.00
... Vol. 2 (11/04, $17.95, digest-size) r/#3&4; wraparound-c by Matt Kindt 18.00
... Vol. 3 (4/06, $14.95, digest-size) r/#5&6; Tim Sale-c 15.00

MICHAEL MOORCOCK'S ELRIC: THE MAKING OF A SORCEROR
DC Comics: 2004 - No. 4, 2006 ($5.95, prestige format, limited series)
1-4-Moorcock-s/Simonson-a 6.00
TPB (2007, $19.99) r/#1-4 20.00

MICHAEL MOORCOCK'S MULTIVERSE
DC Comics (Helix): Nov, 1997 - No. 12, Oct, 1998 ($2.50, limited series)
1-12: Simonson, Reeve & Ridgway-a 3.00
TPB (1999, $19.95) r/#1-12 20.00

MICHAEL TURNER, A TRIBUTE TO...
Aspen MLT: 2008 ($8.99, squarebound)
nn-Pin-ups and tributes from Turner's colleagues and friends; Turner & Ross-c 9.00

MICHAEL TURNER PRESENTS: ASPEN (See Aspen)

MICKEY AND DONALD (See Walt Disney's...)

MICKEY AND DONALD IN VACATIONLAND (See Dell Giant No. 47)

MICKEY & THE BEANSTALK (See Story Hour Series)

MICKEY & THE SLEUTH (See Walt Disney Showcase #38, 39, 42)

MICKEY FINN (Also see Big Shot Comics #74 & Feature Funnies)
Eastern Color 1-4/McNaught Synd. #5 on (Columbia)/Headline V3#2:
Nov?, 1942 - V3#2, May, 1952
1 30 60 90 177 289 400
2 15 30 45 90 140 190
3-Charlie Chan story 12 24 36 69 97 125
4 10 20 30 56 76 95
5-10 9 18 27 47 61 75
11-15(1949): 12-Sparky Watts app. 8 16 24 40 50 60
V3#1,2(1952) 6 12 18 31 38 45

MICKEY MALONE
Hale Nass Corp.: 1936 (Color, punchout-c) (B&W-a on back)
nn - 1pg. of comics 225 450 900 - - -

MICKEY MANTLE (See Baseball's Greatest Heroes #1)

MICKEY MOUSE (See Adventures of Mickey Mouse, The Best of Walt Disney Comics, Cheerios giveaways, Donald and ..., Dynabrite Comics, 40 Big Pages..., Gladstone Comic Album, Merry Christmas From..., Walt Disney's Mickey and Donald, Walt Disney's Comics & Stories, Walt Disney's..., & Wheaties)

MICKEY MOUSE (...Secret Agent #107-109; Walt Disney's... #148-205?)
(See Dell Giants for annuals) (#204 exists from both G.K. & Whitman)
Dell Publ. Co./Gold Key #85-204/Whitman #204-218/Gladstone #219 on:
#16, 1941 - #84, 7-9/62; #85, 11/62 - #218, 6/84; #219, 10/86 - #256, 4/90
Four Color 16(1941)-1st Mickey Mouse comic book; "...vs. the Phantom Blot" by Gottfredson 1250 2500 3750 16,500 - -
Four Color 27(1943)- "7 Colored Terror" 71 142 213 568 1284 2000
Four Color 79(1945)-By Carl Barks (1 story) 88 176 264 704 1577 2450
Four Color 116(1946) 24 48 72 168 372 575
Four Color 141,157(1947) 20 40 60 140 310 485
Four Color 170,181,194('48) 17 34 51 119 265 410
Four Color 214('49),231,248,261 13 26 39 91 201 310
Four Color 268-Reprints/WDC&S #22-24 by Gottfredson ("Surprise Visitor") 12 24 36 84 185 285
Four Color 279,286,296 10 20 30 68 144 220
Four Color 304,313(#1),325(#2),334 10 20 30 64 132 200
Four Color 343,352,362,371,387 8 16 24 56 108 160
Four Color 401,411,427(10-11/52) 7 14 21 48 89 130
Four Color 819-Mickey Mouse in Magicland 5 10 15 35 63 90
Four Color 1057,1151,1246(1959-61)-Album; #1057 has 10¢ & 12¢ editions; back covers are different 5 10 15 33 57 80
28(12-1/52-53)-32,34 6 12 18 40 73 105
33-(Exists with 2 dates, 10-11/53 & 12-1/54) 6 12 18 40 73 105
35-50 5 10 15 35 63 90
51-73,75-80 5 10 15 31 53 75
74-Story swipe "The Rare Stamp Search" from 4-Color #422- "The Gilded Man" 5 10 15 33 57 80
81-105: 93,95-titled "Mickey Mouse Club Album". 100-105: Reprint 4-Color #427,194,279, 170,343,214 in that order 4 8 12 25 40 55
106-120 3 6 9 19 30 40
121-130 3 6 9 16 23 30
131-146 3 6 9 14 20 25
147,148: 147-Reprints "The Phantom Fires" from WDC&S #200-202.148-Reprints "The Mystery of Lonely Valley" from WDC&S #208-210 3 6 9 14 20 25
149-158 2 4 6 10 14 18
159-Reprints "The Sunken City" from WDC&S #205-207 2 4 6 10 14 18
160-178: 162-165,167-170-r 2 4 6 10 14 18
179-(52 pgs.) 2 4 6 11 16 20
180-203: 200-r/Four Color #371 2 4 6 8 10 12
204-(Whitman or G.K.), 205,206 2 4 6 9 13 16
207(8/80), 209(pre-pack?) 5 10 15 31 53 75
208-(8-12/80)-Only distr. in Whitman 3-pack 9 18 27 61 123 185
210(2/81),211-214 2 4 6 9 13 16
215-218: 215(2/82), 216(4/82), 217(3/84), 218(misdated 8/82; actual date 7/84) 2 4 6 10 14 18
219-1st Gladstone issue; The Seven Ghosts serial-r begins by Gottfredson 2 4 6 11 16 20
220,221 2 3 4 6 8 10
222-225: 222-Editor-in Grief strip-r 5.00
226-230 5.00
231-243,246-254: 240-r/March of Comics #27. 245-r/F.C. #279. 250-r/F.C. #248 4.00
244 (1/89, $2.95, 100 pgs.)-Squarebound 60th anniversary issue; gives history of Mickey 5.00
245, 256: 245-r/F.C. #279. 256-$1.95, 68 pgs. 5.00
255 ($1.95, 68 pgs.) 5.00
NOTE: *Reprints #195-197, 198(2/3), 199(1/3), 200-208, 211(1/2), 212, 213, 215(1/3), 216-on.* ***Gottfredson*** *Mickey Mouse serials in #219-239, 241-244, 246-249, 251-253, 255.*
Album 01-518-210(Dell), 1(10082-309)(9/63-Gold Key) 3 6 9 21 33 45
...Club 1(1/64-Gold Key)(TV) 4 8 12 22 35 48
Mini Comic 1(1976)(3-1/4x6-1/2")-Reprints 158 1 2 3 5 6 8
Surprise Party 1(30037-901, G.K.)(1/69)-40th Anniversary (see Walt Disney Showcase #47) 3 6 9 20 31 42
Surprise Party 1(1979)-r/1969 issue 1 2 3 5 6 8

MICKEY MOUSE (Continued from Mickey Mouse and Friends)
BOOM! Studios: No. 304, Jan, 2011 - No. 309, Jun, 2011 ($3.99)
304-309: 304-Peg-Leg Pete app. 309-Continues in Walt Disney's C&S #720 4.00

MICKEY MOUSE ADVENTURES
Disney Comics: June, 1990 - No. 18, Nov, 1991 ($1.50)
1,8,9: 1-Bradbury, Murry-r/M.M. #45,73 plus new-a. 8-Byrne-c. 9-Fantasia 50th ann. issue w/new adapt. of movie 4.00
2-7,10-18: 2-Begin all new stories. 10-r/F.C. #214 3.00

MICKEY MOUSE AND FRIENDS (Continued from Walt Disney's Mickey Mouse and Friends)
(Title continues as Mickey Mouse #304-on)
BOOM! Studios: No. 296, Sept, 2009 - No. 303, Dec, 2010 ($2.99/$3.99)
296-299,301-303: 296-299-Wizards of Mickey stories. 301-Conclusion to story in #300 3.00
300-($3.99, 9/10) Petrucha-s/Pelaez-a; back-up Tanglefoot story w/Gottfredson-a 4.00
300 Deluxe Edition ($6.99) Variant cover by Daan Jippes 7.00

MICKEY MOUSE CLUB FUN BOOK
Golden Press: 1977 (1.95, 228 pgs.)(square bound)
11190-1950s-r; 20,000 Leagues, M. Mouse Silly Symphonys, The Reluctant Dragon, etc. 4 8 12 27 44 60

MICKEY MOUSE CLUB MAGAZINE (See Walt Disney...)

MICKEY MOUSE COMICS DIGEST
Gladstone: 1986 - No. 5, 1987 (96 pgs.)
1 ($1.25-c) 1 2 3 5 6 8

Mickey Mouse Magazine V2 #3 © DIS

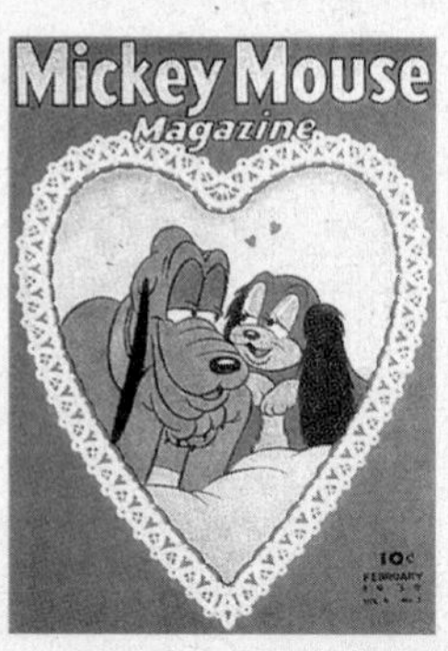

Mickey Mouse Magazine V4 #5 © DIS

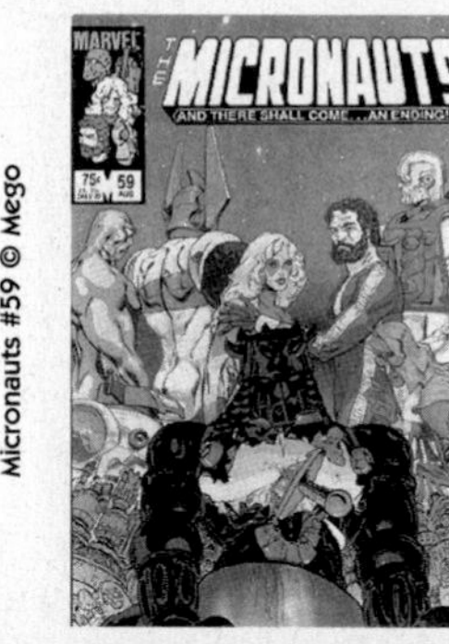

Micronauts #59 © Mego

GD 2.0 | VG 4.0 | FN 6.0 | VF 8.0 | VF/NM 9.0 | NM- 9.2

2-5: 3-5 ($1.50-c) 5.00

MICKEY MOUSE IN COLOR
Another Rainbow/Pantheon: 1988 (Deluxe, 13"x17", hard-c, $250.00)
(Trade, 9-7/8"x11-1/2", hard-c, $39.95)

Deluxe limited edition of 3,000 copies signed by Floyd Gottfredson and Carl Barks, designated as the "Official Mickey Mouse 60th Anniversary" book. Mickey Sunday and daily reprints, plus Barks "Riddle of the Red Hat" from Four Color #79. Comes with 45 r.p.m. record interview with Gottfredson and Barks. 240 pgs. 12 24 36 82 179 275
Deluxe, limited to 100 copies, as above, but with a unique colored pencil original drawing of Mickey Mouse by Carl Barks. 800.00
Pantheon trade edition, edited down & without Barks, 192 pgs. 3 6 9 19 30 40

MICKEY MOUSE MAGAZINE (Becomes Walt Disney's Comics & Stories)(Also see 40 Big Pages of Mickey Mouse)
K. K. Publ./Western Publishing Co.: Summer, 1935 (June-Aug, indicia) - V5#12, Sept, 1940; V1#1-5, V3#11,12, V4#1-3 are 44 pgs; V2#3-100 pgs; V5#12-68 pgs; rest are 36 pgs.(No V3#1, V4#6)

V1#1 (Large size, 13-1/4x10-1/4"; 25¢)-Contains puzzles, games, cels, stories & comics of Disney characters. Promotional magazine for Disney cartoon movies and paraphernalia 1425 2850 4275 9200 19,000 -
Note: *Some copies were autographed by the editors & given away with all early one year subscriptions.*
2 (Size change, 11-1/2x8-1/2"; 10/35; 10¢)-High quality paper begins; Messmer-a 306 612 918 2600 - -
3,4: 3-Messmer-a 176 352 528 1500 - -
5-1st Donald Duck solo-c; 2nd cover app. ever; last 44 pg. & high quality paper issue 329 658 987 2800 - -
6-9: 6-36 pg. issues begin; Donald becomes editor. 8-2nd Donald solo-c. 9-1st Mickey/Minnie-c 159 318 477 1350 - -
10-12, V2#1,2: 11-1st Pluto/Mickey-c; Donald fires himself and appoints Mickey as editor 147 294 441 1250 - -
V2#3-Special 100 pg. Christmas issue (25¢); Messmer-a; Donald becomes editor of Wise Quacks 471 942 1413 4000 - -
4-Mickey Mouse Comics & Roy Ranger (adventure strip) begin; both end V2#9; Messmer-a 129 258 387 1100 - -
5-9: 5-Ted True (adventure strip, ends V2#9) & Silly Symphony Comics (ends V3#3) begin. 6-1st solo Minnie-c. 6-9-Mickey Mouse Movies cut-out in each 60 120 180 381 653 925
10-1st full color issue; Mickey Mouse (by Gottfredson; ends V3#12) & Silly Symphony (ends V3#3) full color Sunday-r, Peter The Farm Detective (ends V5#8) & Ole Of The North (ends V3#3) begins 90 180 270 576 988 1400
11-13: 12-Hiawatha-c & feature story 57 114 171 362 619 875
V3#2-Big Bad Wolf Halloween-c 65 130 195 416 708 1000
3 (12/37)-1st app. Snow White & The Seven Dwarfs (before release of movie) (possibly 1st in print); Mickey X-Mas-c 116 232 348 742 1271 1800
4 (1/38)-Snow White & The Seven Dwarfs serial begins (on stands before release of movie); Ducky Symphony (ends V3#11) begins 95 190 285 608 1042 1475
5-1st Snow White & Seven Dwarfs-c (St. Valentine's Day) 111 222 333 710 1218 1725
6-Snow White serial ends; Lonesome Ghosts app. (2 pp.) 66 132 198 419 722 1025
7-Seven Dwarfs Easter-c 61 122 183 390 670 950
8-10: 9-Dopey-c. 10-1st solo Goofy-c 52 104 156 328 552 775
11,12 (44 pgs; 8 more pgs. color added). 11-Mickey the Sheriff serial (ends V4#3) & Donald Duck strip-r (ends V3#12) begin. Color feature on Snow White's Forest Friends 55 110 165 352 601 850
V4#1 (10/38; 44 pgs.)-Brave Little Tailor-c/feature story, nominated for Academy Award; Bobby & Chip by Otto Messmer (ends V4#2) & The Practical Pig (ends V4#2) begin 54 108 162 343 574 825
2 (44 pgs.)-1st Huey, Dewey & Louie-c 58 116 174 371 636 900
3 (12/38, 44 pgs.)-Ferdinand The Bull-c/feature story, Academy Award winner; Mickey Mouse & The Whalers serial begins, ends V4#12 54 108 162 343 574 825
4-Spotty, Mother Pluto strip-r begin, end V4#8 52 104 156 328 552 775
5-St. Valentine's day-c. 1st Pluto solo-c 57 114 171 362 619 875
7 (3/39)-The Ugly Duckling-c/feature story, Academy Award winner 54 108 162 343 574 825
7 (4/39)-Goofy & Wilbur The Grasshopper classic-c/feature story from 1st Goofy solo cartoon movie; Timid Elmer begins, ends V5#5 57 114 171 362 619 875
8-Big Bad Wolf-c from Practical Pig movie poster; Practical Pig feature story 54 108 162 343 574 825
9-Donald Duck & Mickey Mouse Sunday-r begin; The Pointer feature story, nominated for Academy Award 54 108 162 343 574 825
10-Classic July 4th drum & fife-c; last Donald Sunday-r 74 148 222 470 810 1150
11-1st slick-c; last over-sized issue 53 106 159 334 567 800
12 (9/39; format change, 10-1/4x8-1/4")-1st full color, cover to cover issue; Donald's Penguin-c/feature story 58 116 174 371 636 900
V5#1-Black Pete-c; Officer Duck-c/feature story; Autograph Hound feature story; Robinson Crusoe serial begins 68 136 204 435 743 1050
2-Goofy-c; 1st brief app. Pinocchio 74 148 222 470 810 1150
3 (12/39)-Pinocchio Christmas-c (Before movie release). 1st app. Jiminy Cricket; Pinocchio serial begins 90 180 270 576 988 1400
4,5: 5-Jiminy Cricket-c; Pinocchio serial ends; Donald's Dog Laundry feature story 58 116 174 371 636 900
6,7: 6-Tugboat Mickey feature story; Rip Van Winkle feature begins, ends V5#8. 7-2nd Huey, Dewey & Louie-c 57 114 171 362 619 875
8-Last magazine size issue; 2nd solo Pluto-c; Figaro & Cleo feature story 58 116 174 371 636 900
9-11: 9 (6/40; change to comic book size)-Jiminy Cricket feature story; Donald-c & Sunday-r begin. 10-Special Independence Day issue. 11-Hawaiian Holiday & Mickey's Trailer feature stories; last 36 pg. issue 63 126 189 403 689 975
12 (Format change)-The transition issue (68 pgs.) becoming a comic book. With only a title change to follow, becomes Walt Disney's Comics & Stories #1 with the next issue 476 952 1428 3475 6138 8800
NOTE: ***Otto Messmer**-a is in many issues of the first two-three years. The following story titles and issues have gags created by **Carl Barks:** V4#3(12/38)-'Donald's Better Self' & 'Donald's Golf Game;' V4#4(1/39)-'Donald's Lucky Day;' V4#7(3/39)-'Hockey Champ;' V4#7(4/39)-'Donald's Cousin Gus;' V4#9(6/39)-'Sea Scouts;' V4#12(9/39)-'Donald's Penguin;' V5#9 (6/40)-'Donald's Vacation;' V5#10(7/40)-'Bone Trouble;' V5#12(9/40)-'Window Cleaners.'*

MICKEY MOUSE MAGAZINE (Russian Version)
May 16, 1991 (1st Russian printing of a modern comic book)
1-Bagged w/gold label commemoration in English 10.00

MICKEY MOUSE MARCH OF COMICS (See March of Comics #8,27,45,60,74)

MICKEY MOUSE'S SUMMER VACATION (See Story Hour Series)

MICKEY MOUSE SUMMER FUN (See Dell Giants)

MICKEY SPILLANE'S MIKE DANGER
Tekno Comix: Sept, 1995 - No. 11, May, 1996 ($1.95)
1-11: 1-Frank Miller-c. 7-polybagged; Simonson-c. 8,9-Simonson-c 3.00

MICKEY SPILLANE'S MIKE DANGER
Big Entertainment: V2#1, June, 1996 - No. 10, Apr, 1997 ($2.25)
V2#1-10: Max Allan Collins scripts 3.00

MICKEY'S TWICE UPON A CHRISTMAS (Disney)
Gemstone Publishing: 2004 ($3.95, square-bound, one-shot)
nn-Christmas short stories with Mickey, Minnie, Donald, Uncle Scrooge, Goofy and others 4.00

MICROBOTS, THE
Gold Key: Dec, 1971 (one-shot)
1 (10271-112) Painted-c 3 6 9 15 22 28

MICRONAUTS (Toys)
Marvel Comics Group: Jan, 1979 - No. 59, Aug, 1984 (Mando paper #53 on)
1-Intro/1st app. Baron Karza 1 2 3 5 7 9
2-10,35,37,57: 7-Man-Thing app. 8-1st app. Capt. Universe (8/79). 9-1st app. Cilicia. 35-Double size; origin Microverse; intro Death Squad; Dr. Strange app. 37-Nightcrawler app.; X-Men cameo (2 pgs.). 57-(52 pgs.) 5.00
11-34,36,38-56,58,59: 13-1st app. Jasmine. 15-Death of Microtron. 15-17-Fantastic Four app. 17-Death of Jasmine. 20-Ant-Man app. 21-Microverse series begins. 25-Origin Baron Karza. 25-29-Nick Fury app. 27-Death of Biotron. 34-Dr. Strange app. 38-First direct sale. 40-Fantastic Four app. 48-Early Guice-a begins. 59-Golden painted-c 4.00
Annual 1,2 (12/79,10/80)-Ditko-c/a 5.00
NOTE: *#38-on distributed only through comic shops. **N. Adams** c-7i. **Chaykin** a-13-18p. **Ditko** a-39p. **Giffen** a-36p, 37p(part). **Golden** a-1-12p; c-2-7p, 8-23, 24p, 38, 39, 59. **Guice** a-48-58p; c-49-58. **Gil Kane** a-38, 40-45p; c-40-45. **Layton** c-33-37. **Miller** c-31.*

MICRONAUTS (Micronauts: The New Voyages on cover)
Marvel Comics Group: Oct, 1984 - No. 20, May, 1986
V2#1-20 4.00
NOTE: ***Kelley Jones** a-1; c-1, 6. **Guice** a-4p; c-2p.*

MICRONAUTS
Image Comics: 2002 - No. 11, Sept, 2003 ($2.95)
2002 Convention Special (no cover price, B&W) previews series 3.00
1-11: 1-3-Hanson-a; Dave Johnson-c. 4-Su-a; 2 covers by Linsner & Hanson 3.00
...Vol. 1: Revolution (2003, $12.95, digest size) r/#1-5 13.00

Midget Comics #3 © STJ

Midnight Tales #8 © CC

Mighty Avengers #3 © MAR

GD VG FN VF VF/NM NM-
2.0 4.0 6.0 8.0 9.0 9.2

MICRONAUTS (Volume 2)
Devil's Due Publishing: Mar, 2004 - No. 3, May, 2004 ($2.95)
1-3-Jolley-s/Broderick-a 3.00

MICRONAUTS: KARZA
Image Comics: Feb, 2003 - No. 4, May, 2003 ($2.95)
1-4-Krueger-s/Kurth-a 3.00

MICRONAUTS SPECIAL EDITION
Marvel Comics Group: Dec, 1983 - No. 5, Apr, 1984 ($2.00, limited series, Baxter paper)
1-5: r-/original series 1-12; Guice-c(p)-all 4.00

MIDGET COMICS (Fighting Indian Stories)
St. John Publishng Co.: Feb, 1950 - No. 2, Apr, 1950 (5-3/8x7-3/8", 68 pgs.)
1-Fighting Indian Stories; Matt Baker-c 26 52 78 154 252 350
2-Tex West, Cowboy Marshal (also in #1) 14 28 42 76 108 140

MIDNIGHT (See Smash Comics #18)

MIDNIGHT
Ajax/Farrell Publ. (Four Star Comic Corp.): Apr, 1957 - No. 6, June, 1958
1-Reprints from Voodoo & Strange Fantasy with some changes
17 34 51 98 154 210
2-6 12 24 36 67 94 120

MIDNIGHTER (See The Authority)
DC Comics (WildStorm): Jan, 2007 - No. 20, Aug, 2008 ($2.99)
1-20: 1-Ennis-s/Sprouse-a/c. 6-Fabry-a. 7-Vaughan-s. 8-Gage-s. 9-Stelfreeze-a 3.00
1-4-Variant covers. 1-Michael Golden. 2-Art Adams 3-Jason Pearson. 4-Glenn Fabry 4.00
...: Anthem TPB (2008, $14.99) r/#7,10-15 15.00
...: Armageddon (12/07, $2.99) Gage-s/Coleby-a/McKone-c 3.00
...: Assassin8 TPB (2009, $14.99) r/#16-20 15.00
...: Killing Machine TPB (2008, $14.99) r/#1-6 15.00

MIDNIGHT MASS
DC Comics (Vertigo): Jun, 2002 - No. 8, Jan, 2003 ($2.50)
1-8-Rozum-s/Saiz & Palmiotti-a 3.00

MIDNIGHT MASS: HERE THERE BE MONSTERS
DC Comics (Vertigo): March, 2004 - No. 6, Aug, 2004 ($2.95, limited series)
1-6-Rozum-s/Paul Lee-a 3.00

MIDNIGHT MEN
Marvel Comics (Epic Comics/Heavy Hitters): June, 1993 - No. 4, Sept, 1993 ($2.50/$1.95, limited series)
1-($2.50)-Embossed-c; Chaykin-c/a & scripts in all 4.00
2-4 3.00

MIDNIGHT MYSTERY
American Comics Group: Jan-Feb, 1961 - No. 7, Oct, 1961
1-Sci/Fi story 8 16 24 51 96 140
2-7: 7-Gustavson-a 5 10 15 30 50 70
NOTE: *Reinman a-1, 3. Whitney a-1, 4-6; c-1-3, 5, 7.*

MIDNIGHT NATION
Image Comics (Top Cow): Oct, 2000 - No. 12, July, 2002 ($2.50/$2.95)
1-Straczynski-s/Frank-a; 2 covers 3.50
2-11: 9-Twin Towers cover 3.00
12-($2.95)Last issue 3.00
Wizard #1/2 (2001) Michael Zulli-a; two covers by Frank 3.00
Vol. 1 ('03, $29.99, TPB) r/#1-12 & Wizard #1/2; cover gallery; afterword by Straczynski 30.00

MIDNIGHT SONS UNLIMITED
Marvel Comics (Midnight Sons imprint #4 on): Apr, 1993 - No. 9, May, 1995 ($3.95, 68 pgs.)
1-9: Blaze, Darkhold (by Quesada #1), Ghost Rider, Morbius & Nightstalkers in all. 1-Painted-c. 3-Spider-Man app. 4-Siege of Darkness part 17; new Dr. Strange & new Ghost Rider app.; spot varnish-c 4.00
NOTE: *Sears a-2.*

MIDNIGHT TALES
Charlton Press: Dec, 1972 - No. 18, May, 1976
V1#1 3 6 9 16 23 30
2-10 2 4 6 10 14 18
11-18: 11-14-Newton-a(p) 2 4 6 8 11 14
12,17(Modern Comics reprint, 1977) 6.00
NOTE: *Adkins a-12i, 13i. Ditko a-12. Howard (Wood imitator) a-1-15, 17, 18; c-1-18. Don Newton a-11-14p. Staton a-1, 3-11, 13. Sutton a-3-10.*

MIGHTY, THE
DC Comics: Apr, 2009 - No. 12, Mar, 2010 ($2.99)
1-12: Tomasi & Champagne-s/Dave Johnson-c. 1-4-Snejbjerg-a. 5-12-Samnee-a 3.00
...: Volume 1 TPB (2009, $17.99) r/#1-6 18.00
...: Volume 2 TPB (2010, $17.99) r/#7-12 18.00

MIGHTY ATOM, THE (...& the Pixies #6) (Formerly The Pixies #1-5)
Magazine Enterprises: No. 6, 1949; Nov, 1957 - No. 6, Aug-Sept, 1958
6(1949-M.E.)-no month (1st Series) 7 14 21 35 43 50
1-6(2nd Series)-Pixies-r 4 8 12 18 22 25
I.W. Reprint #1(nd) 2 4 6 8 11 14

MIGHTY AVENGERS
Marvel Comics: May, 2007 - No. 36, Jun, 2010 ($3.99/$2.99)
1-($3.99) Iron Man, Ms. Marvel select new team; Bendis-s/Cho-a/c; Mole Man app. 5.00
2-6-($2.99) Ultron returns 3.00
7-15: 7-Bagley-a begins; Venom on-c. 9-11-Dr. Doom app. 3.00
12-20-Secret Invasion: 12,13-Maleev-a. 15-Romita Jr.-a. 16-Elektra. 20-Wasp funeral 3.00
21-($3.99) Dark Reign; Scarlet Witch returns; new team assembled; Pham-a 4.00
22-36: 25,26-Fantastic Four app. 35,36-Siege; Ultron returns 3.00
...: Most Wanted Files (2007, $3.99) profiles of members, accomplices & adversaries 4.00
... Vol. 1: The Ultron Initiative HC (2008, $19.99) r/#1-6; variant covers and sketch art 20.00
... Vol. 2: Venom Bomb HC (2008, $19.99) r/#7-11; B&W cover art 20.00

MIGHTY AVENGERS
Marvel Comics: Nov, 2013 - Present ($3.99)
1-9: 1-Luke Cage, White Tiger, Power Man, Spectrum & Superior Spider-Man team; Land-a. 4-Falcon app. 5-She-Hulk app. 6-8-Schiti-a. 9-Ronin unmasked 4.00

MIGHTY BEAR (Formerly Fun Comics; becomes Unsane #15)
Star Publ. No. 13,14/Ajax-Farrell (Four Star): No. 13, Jan, 1954 - No. 14, Mar, 1954; 9/57 - No. 3, 2/58
13,14-L. B. Cole-c 18 36 54 103 162 220
1-3('57-58)Four Star; becomes Mighty Ghost #4 7 14 21 35 43 50

MIGHTY COMICS (...Presents) (Formerly Flyman)
Radio Comics (Archie): No. 40, Nov, 1966 - No. 50, Oct, 1967 (All 12¢ issues)
40-Web 5 10 15 30 50 70
41-50: 41-Shield, Black Hood. 42-Black Hood. 43-Shield, Web & Black Hood. 44-Black Hood, Steel Sterling & The Shield. 45-Shield & Hangman; origin Web retold. 46-Steel Sterling, Web & Black Hood. 47-Black Hood & Mr. Justice. 48-Shield & Hangman; Wizard x-over in Shield. 49-Steel Sterling & Fox; Black Hood x-over in Steel Sterling. 50-Black Hood & Web; Inferno x-over in Web 4 8 12 28 47 65
NOTE: *Paul Reinman a-40-50.*

MIGHTY CRUSADERS, THE (Also see Adventures of the Fly, The Crusaders & Fly Man)
Mighty Comics Group (Radio Comics): Nov, 1965 - No. 7, Oct, 1966 (All 12¢)
1-Origin The Shield 7 14 21 44 82 120
2-Origin Comet 4 8 12 28 47 65
3,5-7: 3-Origin Fly-Man. 5-Intro. Ultra-Men (Fox, Web, Capt. Flag) & Terrific Three (Jaguar, Mr. Justice, Steel Sterling). 7-Steel Sterling feature; origin Fly-Girl
4 8 12 27 44 60
4-1st S.A. app. Fireball, Inferno & Fox; Firefly, Web, Bob Phantom, Blackjack, Hangman, Zambini, Kardak, Steel Sterling, Mr. Justice, Wizard, Capt. Flag, Jaguar x-over
4 8 12 28 47 65
Volume 1: Origin of a Super Team TPB (2003, $12.95) r/#1 & Fly Man #31-33 13.00
NOTE: *Reinman a-6.*

MIGHTY CRUSADERS, THE (All New Advs. of...#2)
Red Circle Prod./Archie Ent. No. 6 on: Mar, 1983 - No. 13, Sept, 1985 ($1.00, 36 pgs, Mando paper)
1-Origin Black Hood, The Fly, Fly Girl, The Shield, The Wizard, The Jaguar, Pvt. Strong & The Web. 1 2 3 4 5 7
2-10: 2-Mister Midnight begins. 4-Darkling replaces Shield. 5-Origin Jaguar, Shield begins. 7-Untold origin Jaguar. 10-Veitch-a 5.00
11-13-Lower print run 6.00
NOTE: *Buckler a-1-3, 4i, 5p, 7p, 8i, 9i; c-1-10p.*

MIGHTY CRUSADERS, THE (Also see The Shield, The Web and The Red Circle)
DC Comics: Sept, 2010 - No. 6, Feb, 2011 ($3.99, limited series)
1-6-The Shield, The Web, Fly-Girl, Inferno, War Eagle & The Comet team-up 4.00
... Special 1 (7/10, $4.99) Prequel to series; Pina-a/Lau-c 5.00

MIGHTY GHOST (Formerly Mighty Bear #1-3)
Ajax/Farrell Publ.: No. 4, June, 1958
4 7 14 21 35 43 50

MIGHTY HERCULES, THE (TV)
Gold Key: July, 1963 - No. 2, Nov, 1963
1 (10072-307) 11 22 33 77 166 255

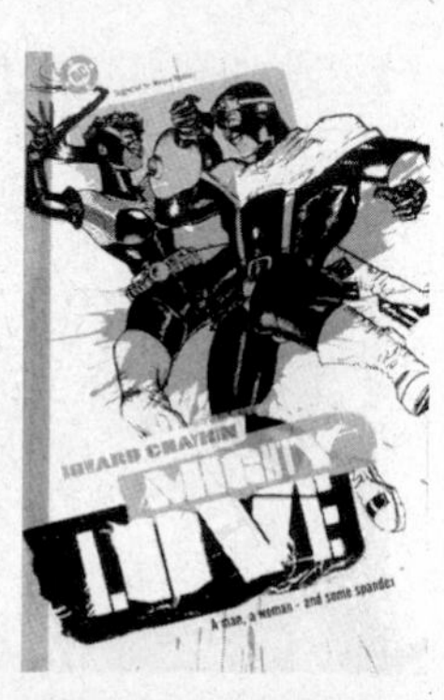

Mighty Love HC © Howard Chaykin

Mighty Marvel Western #22 © MAR

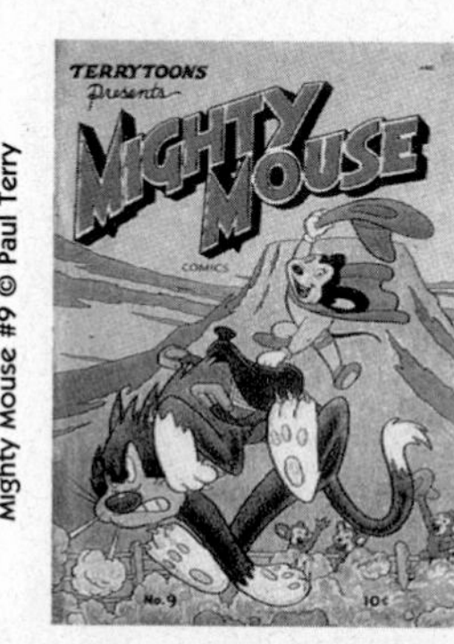

Mighty Mouse #9 © Paul Terry

GD VG FN VF VF/NM NM-
2.0 4.0 6.0 8.0 9.0 9.2

2 (10072-311) 11 22 33 73 157 240

MIGHTY HEROES, THE (TV) (Funny)
Dell Publishing Co.: Mar, 1967 - No. 4, July, 1967

1-Also has a 1957 Heckle & Jeckle-r 10 20 30 64 132 200
2-4: 4-Has two 1958 Mighty Mouse-r 7 14 21 44 82 120

MIGHTY HEROES
Spotlight Comics: 1987 (B&W, one-shot)

1-Heckle & Jeckle backup 5.00

MIGHTY HEROES
Marvel Comics: Jan, 1998 ($2.99, one-shot)

1-Origin of the Mighty Heroes 3.00

MIGHTY LOVE
DC Comics: 2003 ($24.99/$17.95, graphic novel)

HC-($24.95) Howard Chaykin-s/a; intro. Skylark and the Iron Angel 25.00
SC-($17.95) 18.00

MIGHTY MAN (From Savage Dragon titles)
Image Comics: Dec, 2004 ($7.95, one-shot)

1-Reprints seriaizedl back-up from Savage Dragon #109-118 8.00

MIGHTY MARVEL TEAM-UP THRILLERS
Marvel Comics: 1983 ($5.95, trade paperback)

1-Reprints team-up stories 3 6 9 18 28 38

MIGHTY MARVEL WESTERN, THE
Marvel Comics Group (LMC earlier issues): Oct, 1968 - No. 46, Sept, 1976 (#1-14: 68 pgs.; #15,16: 52 pgs.)

1-Begin Kid Colt, Rawhide Kid, Two-Gun Kid-r 6 12 18 40 73 105
2-5: (2-14 are 68 pgs.) 4 8 12 27 44 60
6-16: (15,16 are 52 pgs.) 3 6 9 21 33 45
17-20 2 4 6 13 18 22
21-30,32,37: 24-Kid Colt-r end. 25-Matt Slade-r begin. 32-Origin-r/Rawhide Kid #23;
Williamson-r/Kid Slade #7. 37-Williamson, Kirby-r/Two-Gun Kid 51
2 4 6 9 13 16
31,33-36,38-46: 31-Baker-r. 2 4 6 8 11 14
45-(30¢-c variant, limited distribution)(6/76) 4 8 12 27 44 60

NOTE: ***Jack Davis** a(r)-21-24. **Keller** r-1-13, 22. **Kirby** a(r)-1-3, 6, 9, 12-14, 16, 25-29, 32-38, 40, 41, 43-46; c-29. **Maneely** a(r)-22. **Severin** c-3i, 9. No Matt Slade-#43.*

MIGHTY MIDGET COMICS, THE (Miniature)
Samuel E. Lowe & Co.: No date; circa 1942-1943 (Sold 2 for 5¢, B&W and red, 36 pgs, approx. 5x4")

Bulletman #11(1943)-r/cover/Bulletman #3 16 32 48 94 147 200
Captain Marvel Adventures #11 16 32 48 94 147 200
Captain Marvel #11 (Same as above except for full color ad on back cover; this issue was glued to cover of Captain Marvel #20 and is not found in fine-mint condition)
340 680 1020 - - -
Captain Marvel Jr. #11 (Same-c as Master #27 16 32 48 94 147 200
Captain Marvel Jr. #11 (Same as above except for full color ad on back-c; this issue was glued to cover of Captain Marvel #21 and is not found in fine-mint condition)
340 680 1020 - - -
Golden Arrow #11 15 30 45 86 133 180
Golden Arrow #11 (Same as above except for full color ad on back-c; this issue was glued to cover of Captain Marvel #21 and is not found in fine-mint condition)
280 560 840 - - -
Ibis the Invincible #11(1942)-Origin; reprints cover to Ibis #1 (Predates Fawcett's Ibis the Invincible #1). 16 32 48 94 147 200
Spy Smasher #11(1942) 16 32 48 94 147 200

NOTE: *The above books came in a box called "box full of books" and was distributed with other Samuel Lowe puzzles, paper dolls, coloring books, etc. They are not titled Mighty Midget Comics. All have a war bond seal on back cover which is otherwise blank. These books came in a "Mighty Midget" flat cardboard counter display rack.*

Balbo, the Boy Magician #12 (1943)-1st book devoted entirely to character.
10 20 30 54 72 90
Bulletman #12 12 24 36 69 97 125
Commando Yank #12 (1943)-Only comic devoted entirely to character.
10 20 30 56 76 95
Dr. Voltz the Human Generator (1943)-Only comic devoted entirely to character.
10 20 30 54 72 90
Lance O'Casey #12 (1943)-1st comic devoted entirely to character (Predates Fawcett's Lance O'Casey #1). 10 20 30 54 72 90
Leatherneck the Marine (1943)-Only comic devoted entirely to character.
10 20 30 54 72 90
Minute Man #12 12 24 36 67 94 120
Mister "Q" (1943)-Only comic devoted entirely to character.
10 20 30 54 72 90
Mr. Scarlet and Pinky #12 (1943)-Only comic devoted entirely to character.
10 20 30 58 79 100
Pat Wilton and His Flying Fortress (1943)-1st comic devoted entirely to character. 10 20 30 54 72 90
The Phantom Eagle #12 (1943)-Only comic devoted entirely to character.
10 20 30 54 72 90
State Trooper Stops Crime (1943)-Only comic devoted entirely to character.
10 20 30 54 72 90
Tornado Tom (1943)-Origin, r/from Cyclone #1-3; only comic devoted entirely to character.
10 20 30 54 72 90

MIGHTY MORPHIN' POWER RANGERS: THE MOVIE (Also see Saban's Mighty Morphin' Power Rangers)
Marvel Comics: Sept, 1995 ($3.95, one-shot)

nn-Adaptation of movie 5.00

MIGHTY MOUSE (See Adventures of..., Dell Giant #43, Giant Comics Edition, March of Comics #205, 237, 247, 257, 447, 459, 471, 483, Oxydol-Dreft, Paul Terry's, & Terry-Toons Comics)

MIGHTY MOUSE (1st Series)
Timely/Marvel Comics (20th Century Fox): Fall, 1946 - No. 4, Summer, 1947

1 184 368 552 1178 2014 2850
2 71 142 213 454 777 1100
3,4 45 90 135 284 480 675

MIGHTY MOUSE (2nd Series) (Paul Terry's... #62-71)
St. John Publishing Co./Pines No. 68 (3/56) on (TV issues #72 on): Aug, 1947 - No. 67, 11/55; No. 68, 3/56 - No. 83, 6/59

5(#1) 40 80 120 246 411 575
6-10: 10-Over-sized issue 21 42 63 122 199 275
11-19 14 28 42 82 121 160
20 (11/50) - 25-(52 pg. editions) 11 22 33 64 90 115
20-25-(36 pg. editions) 10 20 30 56 76 95
26-37: 35-Flying saucer-c 9 18 27 52 69 85
38-45-(100 pgs.) 19 38 57 109 172 235
46-83: 62-64,67-Painted-c. 82-Infinity-c 9 18 27 50 65 80
Album nn (nd, 1952/53?, St. John)(100 pgs.)(Rebound issues w/new cover)
22 44 66 128 209 290
Album 1(10/52, 25¢, 100 pgs., St. John)-Gandy Goose app.
28 56 84 165 270 375
Album 2,3(11/52 & 12/52, St. John) (100 pgs.) 22 44 66 128 209 290
Fun Club Magazine 1(Fall, 1957-Pines, 25¢, 100 pgs.) (CBS TV)-Tom Terrific, Heckle & Jeckle, Dinky Duck, Gandy Goose 15 30 45 90 140 190
Fun Club Magazine 2-6(Winter, 1958-Pines) 11 22 33 62 86 110
3-D 1-(1st printing-9/53, 25¢)(St. John)-Came w/glasses; stiff covers; says World's First! on-c; 1st 3-D comic 28 56 84 165 270 375
3-D 1-(2nd printing-10/53, 25¢)-Came w/glasses; slick, glossy covers, slightly smaller
20 40 60 114 182 250
3-D 2,3(11/53, 12/53, 25¢)-(St. John)-With glasses 20 40 60 114 182 250

MIGHTY MOUSE (TV)(3rd Series)(Formerly Adventures of Mighty Mouse)
Gold Key/Dell Publ. Co. No. 166-on: No. 161, Oct, 1964 - No. 172, Oct, 1968

161(10/64)-165(9/65)-(Becomes Adventures of... No. 166 on)
4 8 12 28 47 65
166(3/66), 167(6/66)-172 3 6 9 20 31 42

MIGHTY MOUSE (TV)
Spotlight Comics: 1987 - No. 2, 1987 ($1.50, color)

1,2-New stories 4.00
...And Friends Holiday Special (11/87, $1.75) 4.00

MIGHTY MOUSE (TV)
Marvel Comics: Oct, 1990 - No. 10, July, 1991 ($1.00)(Based on Sat. cartoon)

1-10: 1-Dark Knight-c parody. 2-10: 3-Intro Bat-Bat; Byrne-c. 4,5-Crisis-c/story parodies w/Perez-c. 6-Spider-Man-c parody. 7-Origin Bat-Bat 3.00

MIGHTY MOUSE ADVENTURE MAGAZINE
Spotlight Comics: 1987 ($2.00, B&W, 52 pgs., magazine size, one-shot)

1-Deputy Dawg, Heckle & Jeckle backup stories 5.00

MIGHTY MOUSE ADVENTURES (Adventures of... #2 on)
St. John Publishing Co.: November, 1951

1 37 74 111 222 361 500

MIGHTY MOUSE ADVENTURE STORIES (Paul Terry's... on-c only)
St. John Publishing Co.: 1953 (50¢, 384 pgs.)

nn-Rebound issues 53 106 159 334 567 800

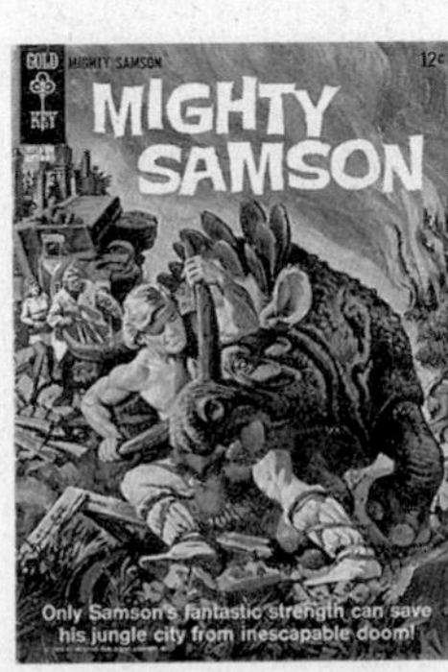

Mighty Samson #3 © GK

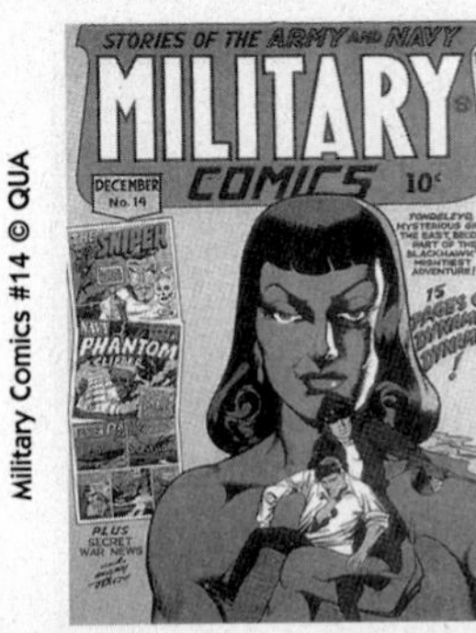

Military Comics #14 © QUA

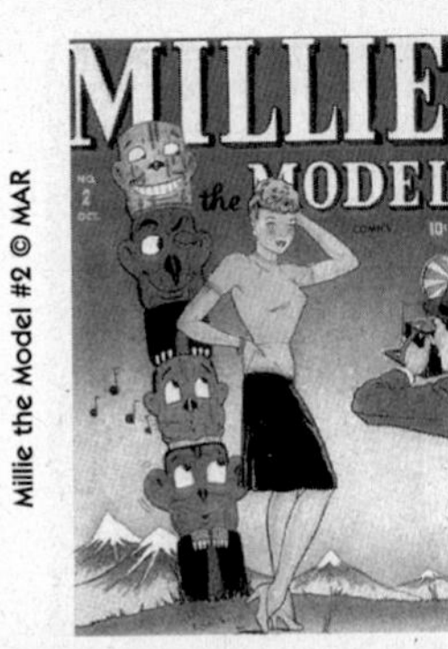

Millie the Model #2 © MAR

MIGHTY MUTANIMALS (See Teenage Mutant Ninja Turtles Adventures #19)
May, 1991 - No. 3, July, 1991 ($1.00, limited series)
Archie Comics: Apr, 1992 - No. 8, June, 1993 ($1.25)

1-3: 1-Story cont'd from TMNT Advs. #19. 6.00
1-4 (1992) 6.00
5-8: 7-1st app. Merdude 1 2 3 5 7 9

MIGHTY SAMSON (Also see Gold Key Champion)
Gold Key/Whitman #32: July, 1964 - No. 20, Nov, 1969; No. 21, Aug, 1972; No. 22, Dec, 1973 - No. 31, Mar, 1976; No. 32, Aug, 1982 (Painted-c #1-31)

1-Origin/1st app.; Thorne-a begins 7 14 21 48 89 130
2-5 4 8 12 28 47 65
6-10: 7-Tom Morrow begins, ends #20 3 6 9 20 30 40
11-20 3 6 9 16 23 30
21-31: 21,22-r 2 4 6 11 16 20
32(Whitman, 8/82)-r 2 4 6 8 10 12

MIGHTY SAMSON
Dark Horse Comics: Dec, 2010 - No. 4, Oct, 2011 ($3.50)

1-4: 1-Origin retold; Shooter & Vaughn-s/Olliffe-a/Swanland-c; r/1st app. from 1964 3.50
1-Variant-c by Olliffe 4.00

MIGHTY THOR, THE (Continues in Thor; God of Thunder)
Marvel Comics: Jun, 2011 - No. 22, Dec, 2012 ($3.99)

1-Fraction-s/Coipel-a; Silver Surfer app.; bonus concept art from the movie 4.00
1-Variant-c by Charest 6.00
1-Variant-c by Simonson 10.00
2-22: 3-6-Galactus app. 7-Fear Itself tie-in; Odin's 1st battle vs. the Serpent. 8-Tanarus. 13-17-Simonson-c. 18-21-Alan Davis-a 4.00
12.1 (6/12, $2.99) Kitson-a/Coipel-c; flashbacks from Volstagg & Sif 3.00
Annual 1 (8/12, $4.99) Silver Surfer & Galactus app.; DeMatteis-s/Elson-a 5.00

MIKE BARNETT, MAN AGAINST CRIME (TV)
Fawcett Publications: Dec, 1951 - No. 6, Oct, 1952

1 20 40 60 114 182 250
2 14 28 42 76 108 140
3,4,6 11 22 33 62 86 110
5- "Market for Morphine" cover/story 15 30 45 84 127 170

MIKE DANGER (See Mickey Spillane's...)

MIKE DEODATO'S...
Caliber Comics: 1996, ($2.95, B&W)

...FALLOUT 3000 #1, **...JONAS** (mag. size) #1,**...PRIME CUTS** (mag. size) #1, **...PROTHEUS** #1,2, **...RAMTHAR** #1,**...RAZOR NIGHTS** #1 3.00

MIKE GRELL'S SABLE (Also see Jon Sable & Sable)
First Comics: Mar, 1990 - No. 10, Dec, 1990 ($1.75)

1-10: r/Jon Sable Freelance #1-10 by Grell 3.00

MIKE MIST MINUTE MIST-ERIES (See Ms. Tree/Mike Mist in 3-D)
Eclipse Comics: April, 1981 ($1.25, B&W, one-shot)

1 3.00

MIKE SHAYNE PRIVATE EYE
Dell Publishing Co.: Nov-Jan, 1962 - No. 3, Sept-Nov, 1962

1 4 8 12 23 37 50
2,3 3 6 9 16 24 32

MILESTONE FOREVER
DC Comics: Apr, 2010 - No. 2, May, 2010 ($5.99, squarebound, limited series)

1,2-McDuffie-s/Leon & Bright-a; Icon, Blood Syndicate, Hardware and Static app. 6.00

MILITARY COMICS (Becomes Modern Comics #44 on)
Quality Comics Group: Aug, 1941 - No. 43, Oct, 1945

1-Origin/1st app. Blackhawk by C. Cuidera (Eisner scripts); Miss America, The Death Patrol by Jack Cole (also #2-7,27-30), & The Blue Tracer by Guardineer; X of the Underground, The Yankee Eagle, Q-Boat & Shot & Shell, Archie Atkins, Loops & Banks by Bud Ernest (Bob Powell)(ends #13) begin 432 864 1296 3154 5577 8000
2-Secret War News begins (by McWilliams #2-16); Cole-a; new uniform with yellow circle & hawk's head for Blackhawk 135 270 405 864 1482 2100
3-Origin/1st app. Chop Chop (9/41) 116 232 348 742 1271 1800
4 103 206 309 659 1130 1600
5-The Sniper begins; Miss America in costume #4-7 90 180 270 576 988 1400
6-9: 8-X of the Underground begins (ends #13). 9-The Phantom Clipper begins (ends #16) 71 142 213 454 777 1100
10-Classic Eisner-c 90 180 270 576 988 1400
11-Flag-c 68 136 204 435 743 1050
12-Blackhawk by Crandall begins, ends #22 71 142 213 454 777 1100
13-15: 14-Private Dogtag begins (ends #83) 58 116 174 371 636 900
16-20: 16-Blue Tracer ends. 17-P.T. Boat begins 53 106 159 334 567 800
21-31: 22-Last Crandall Blackhawk. 23-Shrunken head-c. 27-Death Patrol revived. 28-True story of Mussolini 47 94 141 296 498 700
32-43 41 82 123 256 428 600

NOTE: ***Berg** a-6. **Al Bryant** c-31-34, 38, 40-43. **J. Cole** a-1-3, 27-32. **Crandall** a-12-22; c-13-20. **Cuidera** c-2-9. **Eisner** c-1, 2(part), 9, 10. **Kotsky** c-21-29, 35, 37, 39. **McWilliams** a-2-16. **Powell** a-1-13. **Ward** Blackhawk-30, 31(15 pgs. each); c-30.*

MILK AND CHEESE (Also see Cerebus Bi-Weekly #20)
Slave Labor: 1991 - Present ($2.50, B&W)

1-Evan Dorkin story & art in all 4 8 12 23 37 50
1-2nd-6th printings 4.00
2-"Other #1" 3 6 9 16 23 30
2-reprint 3.00
3-"Third #1" 2 4 6 11 16 20
4-"Fourth #1", 5-"First Second Issue" 1 3 4 6 8 10
6,7: 6-"#666" 5.00

NOTE: *Multiple printings of all issues exist and are worth cover price unless listed here.*

MILKMAN MURDERS, THE
Dark Horse Comics: Jun, 2004 - No. 4, Aug, 2004 ($2.99, limited series)

1-4-Casey-s/Parkhouse-a 3.00

MILLENNIUM
DC Comics: Jan, 1988 - No. 8, Feb, 1988 (Weekly limited series)

1-Englehart-s/Staton c/a(p) 4.00
2-8 3.00
TPB (2008, $19.99) r/#1-8 20.00

MILLENNIUM EDITION:... (Reprints of classic DC issues, plus some WildStorm and non-DC issues with characters now published by DC)
DC Comics: Feb, 2000 - Feb, 2001 (gold foil cover stamps)

Action Comics #1, Adventure Comics #61, All Star Comics #3, All Star Comics #8, Batman #1, Detective Comics #1, Detective Comics #27, Detective Comics #38, Flash Comics #1, Military Comics #1, More Fun Comics #73, Police Comics #1, Sensation Comics #1, Superman #1, Whiz Comics #2, Wonder Woman #1 -($3.95-c) 5.00
Action Comics #252, Adventure Comics #247, Brave and the Bold #28, Brave and the Bold #85, Crisis on Infinte Earths #1, Detective #225, Detective #327, Detective #359, Detective #395, Flash #123, Gen13 #1, Green Lantern #76, House of Mystery #1, House of Secrets #92, JLA #1, Justice League #1, Mad #1, Man of Steel #1, Mysterious Suspense #1, New Gods, #1, New Teen Titans #1, Our Army at War #81, Plop! #1, Saga of the Swamp Thing #21, Shadow #1, Showcase #4, Showcase #9, Showcase #22, Superman #233, Superman (2nd) #75, Superman's Pal Jimmy Olsen #1, Watchmen #1, WildC.A.T.s #1, Wonder Woman (2nd) #1, World's Finest #71 -($2.50-c) 4.00
All-Star Western #10, Hellblazer #1, More Fun Comics #101, Preacher #1, Sandman #1, Spirit #1, Superboy #1, Superman #76, Young Romance #1-($2.95-c) 4.00
Batman: The Dark Knight Returns #1, Kingdom Come #1 -($5.95-c) 6.00
All Star Comics #3, Batman #1, Justice League #1: Chromium cover 12.00
Crisis on Infinite Earths #1 Chromium cover 20.00

MILLENNIUM FEVER
DC Comics (Vertigo): Oct, 1995 - No.4, Jan, 1996 ($2.50, limited series)

1-4: Duncan Fegredo-c/a 3.00

MILLENNIUM INDEX
Independent Comics Group: Mar, 1988 - No. 2, Mar, 1988 ($2.00)

1,2 3.00

MILLENNIUM 2.5 A.D.
ACG Comics: No. 1, 2000 ($2.95)

1-Reprints 1934 Buck Rogers daily strips #1-48 3.00

MILLIE, THE LOVABLE MONSTER
Dell Publishing Co.: Sept-Nov, 1962 - No. 6, Jan, 1973

12-523-211-Bill Woggon c/a in all 5 10 15 31 53 75
2(8-10/63) 4 8 12 28 47 65
3(8-10/64) 4 8 12 25 40 55
4(7/72), 5(10/72), 6(1/73) 3 6 9 14 19 24

NOTE: ***Woggon** a-3-6; c-3-6. 4 reprints 1; 5 reprints 2; 6 reprints 3.*

MILLIE THE MODEL (See Comedy Comics, A Date With..., Joker Comics #28, Life With..., Mad About..., Marvel Mini-Books, Misty & Modeling With...)
Marvel/Atlas/Marvel Comics(CnPC #1)(SPI/Male/VPI):1945 - No. 207, Dec, 1973

1-Origin 135 270 405 864 1482 2100
2 (10/46)-Millie becomes The Blonde Phantom to sell Blonde Phantom perfume;

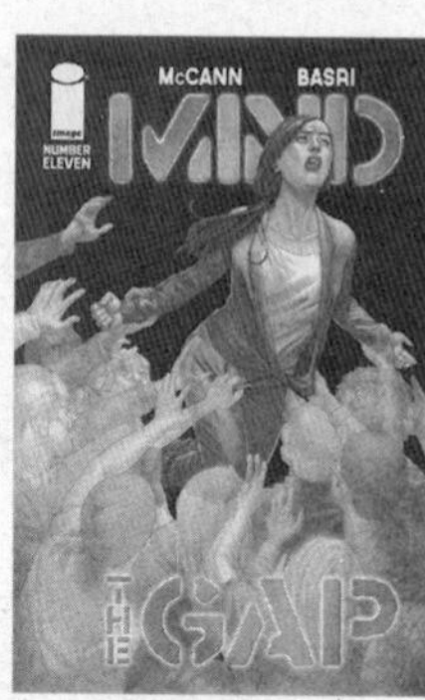

Mind the Gap #11 © Jim McCann

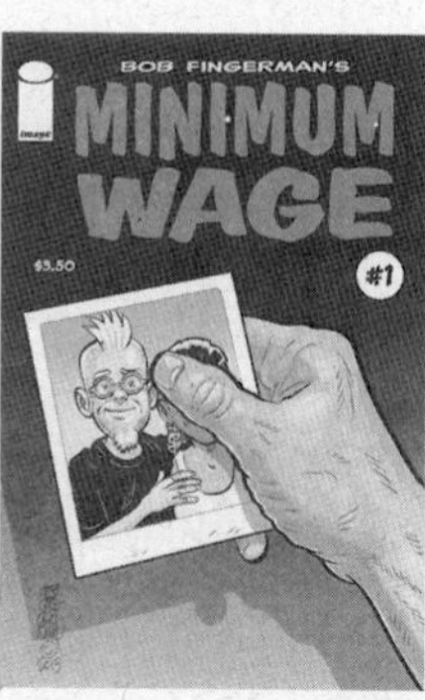

Minimum Wage (2014 series) #1 © Bob Fingerman

Miracleman (2014 series) #1 © MAR

	GD 2.0	VG 4.0	FN 6.0	VF 8.0	VF/NM 9.0	NM- 9.2
a pre-Blonde Phantom app. (see All-Select #11, Fall, 1946)	53	106	159	334	567	800
3-8,10: 4-7-Willie app. 7-Willie smokes extra strong tobacco. 8,10-Kurtzman's "Hey Look". 8-Willie & Rusty app.	41	82	123	256	428	600
9-Powerhouse Pepper by Wolverton, 4 pgs.	42	84	126	265	445	625
11-Kurtzman-a, "Giggles 'n' Grins"	26	52	78	154	252	350
12,15,17,19,20: 12-Rusty & Hedy Devine app.	22	44	66	128	209	290
13,14,16,18: 13,14,16-Kurtzman's "Hey Look". 13-Hedy Devine app. 18-Dan DeCarlo-a begins	22	44	66	132	216	300
21-30	16	32	48	94	147	200
31-40	9	18	27	59	117	175
41-60	8	16	24	51	96	140
61-99: 93-Last DeCarlo issue?	6	12	18	42	79	115
100	7	14	21	46	86	125
101-106,108-130	5	10	15	35	63	90
107-Jack Kirby app. in story	6	12	18	38	69	100
131-134,136,138-153: 141-Groovy Gears-c/s	4	8	12	28	47	65
135-(2/66) 1st app. Groovy Gears	5	10	15	35	57	80
137-2nd app. Groovy Gears	5	10	15	30	50	70
154-New Millie begins (10/67)	6	12	18	38	69	100
155-190	4	8	12	28	47	65
191,193-199,201-206	4	8	12	25	40	55
192-(52 pgs.)	4	8	12	28	47	65
200,207(Last issue)	4	8	12	28	47	65
(Beware: cut-up pages are common in all Annuals)						
Annual 1(1962)-Early Marvel annual (2nd?)	20	40	60	138	307	475
Annual 2(1963)	12	24	36	82	179	275
Annual 3-5 (1964-1966)	8	16	24	54	102	150
Annual 6-10(1967-11/71)	6	12	18	41	76	110
Queen-Size 11(9/74), 12(1975)	6	12	18	37	66	95

NOTE: ***Dan DeCarlo** a-18-93.*

MILLION DOLLAR DIGEST (Richie Rich... #23 on; also see Richie Rich...)
Harvey Publications: 11/86 - No. 7, 11/87; No. 8, 4/88 - No. 34, Nov, 1994 ($1.25/$1.75, digest size)

	GD 2.0	VG 4.0	FN 6.0	VF 8.0	VF/NM 9.0	NM- 9.2
1	1	2	3	5	6	8
2-8: 8-(68 pgs.)						6.00
9-20: 9-Begin $1.75-c. 14-May not exist	1	2	3	4	5	7
21-34	1	3	4	6	8	10

MILT GROSS FUNNIES (Also see Picture News #1)
Milt Gross, Inc. (ACG?): Aug, 1947 - No. 2, Sept, 1947

	GD 2.0	VG 4.0	FN 6.0	VF 8.0	VF/NM 9.0	NM- 9.2
1	24	48	72	142	234	325
2	17	34	51	98	154	210

MILTON THE MONSTER & FEARLESS FLY (TV)
Gold Key: May, 1966

	GD 2.0	VG 4.0	FN 6.0	VF 8.0	VF/NM 9.0	NM- 9.2
1 (10175-605)	8	16	24	54	102	150

MINDFIELD
Aspen MLT: No. 0, May, 2010 - No. 6, Sept, 2011 ($2.50/$2.99)

	NM- 9.2
0-($2.50) Krul-s/Konat-a; 3 covers	3.00
1-6-($2.99) Multiples covers on each	3.00

MIND MGMT
Dark Horse Comics: May, 2012 - Present ($3.99)

	NM- 9.2
1-Matt Kindt-s/a/c	30.00
2-6	10.00
7-20	4.00
#0 (11/12, $2.99) Prints background stories from Mind MGMT Secret Files digital site	3.00

MIND THE GAP
Image Comics: May, 2012 - Present ($2.99)

	NM- 9.2
1-16: 1-8,10-McCann-s/Esquejo-a/c. 9-McDaid-a. 11,12-Basri-a	3.00

MINIMUM CARNAGE
Marvel Comics: Dec, 2012 - Jan, 2013 ($3.99, limited series)

	NM- 9.2
...: Alpha (12/12) Venom, Carnage and Scarlet Spider app.; Medina-a/Crain-c	4.00
...: Omega (1/13) The Enigma Force in the Microverse app.	4.00

MINIMUM WAGE
Fantagraphics Books: V1#1, July, 1995 ($9.95, B&W, graphic novel, mature)
V2#1, 1995 - 1997 ($2.95, B&W, mature)

	GD 2.0	VG 4.0	FN 6.0	VF 8.0	VF/NM 9.0	NM- 9.2
V1#1-Bob Fingerman story & art	1	3	4	6	8	10
V2#1-9($2.95): Bob Fingerman story & art. 2-Kevin Nowlan back-c. 4-w/pin-ups. 5-Mignola back-c						3.00
Book Two TPB ('97, $12.95) r/V2#1-5						13.00

MINIMUM WAGE
Image Comics: Jan, 2014 - Present ($3.50, B&W&Green, mature)

	NM- 9.2
1-3-Bob Fingerman story & art; story resumes in May 2000	3.50

MINISTRY OF SPACE
Image Comics: Apr, 2001 - No. 3, Apr, 2004 ($2.95, limited series)

	NM- 9.2
1-3-Warren Ellis-s/Chris Weston-a	3.00
...Vol. 1 Omnibus (3/04, $4.95) r/1&2	5.00
TPB (12/04, $12.95) r/series; sketch & design pages; intro by Mark Millar	13.00

MINOR MIRACLES
DC Comics: 2000 ($12.95, B&W, squarebound)

	NM- 9.2
nn-Will Eisner-s/a	13.00

MINUTE MAN (See Master Comics & Mighty Midget Comics)
Fawcett Publications: Summer, 1941 - No. 3, Spring, 1942 (68 pgs.)

	GD 2.0	VG 4.0	FN 6.0	VF 8.0	VF/NM 9.0	NM- 9.2
1	213	426	639	1363	2332	3300
2-Japanese invade NYC Statue of Liberty WWII-c	155	310	465	992	1696	2400
3	123	246	369	787	1344	1900

MINX, THE
DC Comics (Vertigo): Oct, 1998 - No. 8, May, 1999 ($2.50, limited series)

	NM- 9.2
1-8-Milligan-s/Phillips-c/a	3.00

MIRACLE COMICS
Hillman Periodicals: Feb, 1940 - No. 4, Mar, 1941

	GD 2.0	VG 4.0	FN 6.0	VF 8.0	VF/NM 9.0	NM- 9.2
1-Sky Wizard Master of Space, Dash Dixon, Man of Might, Pinkie Parker, Dusty Doyle, The Kid Cop, K-7, Secret Agent, The Scorpion, & Blandu, Jungle Queen begin; Masked Angel only app. (all 1st app.)	213	426	639	1363	2332	3300
2	107	214	321	685	1168	1650
3,4: 3-Devil-c; Bill Colt, the Ghost Rider begins. 4-The Veiled Prophet & Bullet Bob (by Burnley) app.	90	180	270	576	988	1400

MIRACLEMAN
Eclipse Comics: Aug, 1985 - No. 15, Nov, 1988; No. 16, Dec, 1989 - No. 24, Aug, 1993

	GD 2.0	VG 4.0	FN 6.0	VF 8.0	VF/NM 9.0	NM- 9.2
1-r/British Marvelman series; Alan Moore scripts in #1-16	2	4	6	8	10	12
1-Gold variant (edition of 400, signed by Alan Moore, came with signed & #'d certificate of authenticity)	54	108	162	432	966	1500
1-Blue variant (edition of 600, came with signed certificate of authenticity)	34	68	102	245	548	850
2-8,10: 8-Airboy preview. 6,9,10-Origin Miracleman. 10-Snyder-c	1	2	3	5	6	8
9-Shows graphic scenes of childbirth	2	4	6	8	10	12
11-14(5/87-4/88) Totleben-a	2	4	6	11	16	20
15-($1.75-c, scarce) end of Kid Miracleman	6	12	18	41	76	110
16-Last Alan Moore-s; 1st $1.95-c (low print)	3	6	9	16	24	32
17-22: 17-"The Golden Age" begins, ends #22. Dave McKean-c begins, end #22; Neil Gaiman scripts in #17-24	2	4	6	11	16	20
23-"The Silver Age" begins; Barry W. Smith-c	3	6	9	16	23	30
24-Last issue; Smith-c	3	6	9	19	30	40
3-D #1 (12/85)	1	2	3	5	7	9
3-D #1 Blue variant (edition of 99)	3	6	9	16	23	30
3-D #1 Gold variant (edition of 199)	2	4	6	11	16	20

NOTE: *Miracleman 3-D #1 (12/85) (2D edition) Interior is the same as the 3-D version except in non 3-D format. Indicia are the same for both versions of the book with only the non 3-D art distinguishing this book from the standard 3-D version. Standard 3-D edition has house ad mentioning the non 3-D edition. Two known copies exist, one in the Michigan State University Special Collection Department. (No known sales)*

	NM- 9.2
Book One: A Dream of Flying (1988, $9.95, TPB) r/#1-5; Leach-c	25.00
Book One: A Dream of Flying-Hardcover (1988, $29.95) r/#1-5	70.00
Book Two: The Red King Syndrome (1990, $12.95, TPB) r/#6-10; Bolton-c	30.00
Book Two: The Red King Syndrome-Hardcover (1990, $30.95) r/#6-10	85.00
Book Three: Olympus (1990, $12.95, TPB) r/#11-16	130.00
Book Three: Olympus-Hardcover (1990, $30.95) r/#11-16	250.00
Book Four: The Golden Age (1992, $15.95, TPB) r/#17-22	30.00
Book Four: The Golden Age-Hardcover (1992, $33.95) r/#17-22	50.00
Book Four: The Golden Age (1993, $12.99, TPB) new McKean-c	15.00

NOTE: *Eclipse archive copies exist for #4,5,8,17,23. Each has a small Miracleman image foil-stamped on the cover.* ***Chaykin** c-3. **Gulacy** c-7. **McKean** c-17-22. **B. Smith** c-23, 24. **Starlin** c-4. **Totleben** a-11-13; c-9, 11-13. **Truman** c-6.*

MIRACLEMAN
Marvel Comics: Mar, 2014 - Present ($5.99/$4.99)

	NM- 9.2
1-($5.99) Remastered reprints of Miracleman #1 and stories from Warrior #1&2; interview with Mick Anglo; reprints of 1950s Marvelman stories; Quesada-c	6.00
2-4: 2-($4.99) R/Warrior #3-5 and Kid Marvelman debut (1955)	5.00

MIRACLEMAN: APOCRYPHA
Eclipse Comics: Nov, 1991 - No. 3, Feb, 1992 ($2.50, limited series)

Miss America Magazine V7 #24 © MAR

Miss Fury #5 © Dynamite

Mr. Anthony's Love Clinic #1 © HARV

GD 2.0 | VG 4.0 | FN 6.0 | VF 8.0 | VF/NM 9.0 | NM- 9.2

GD 2.0 | VG 4.0 | FN 6.0 | VF 8.0 | VF/NM 9.0 | NM- 9.2

1-3: 1-Stories by Neil Gaiman, Mark Buckingham, Alex Ross & others. 3-Stories by James Robinson, Kelley Jones, Matt Wagner, Neil Gaiman, Mark Buckingham & others
1 2 3 4 5 7
TPB (12/92, $15.95) r/#1-3; Buckingham-c 20.00

MIRACLEMAN FAMILY
Eclipse Comics: May, 1988 - No. 2, Sept, 1988 ($1.95, lim. series, Baxter paper)
1,2: 2-Gulacy-c 5.00

MIRACLE OF THE WHITE STALLIONS, THE (See Movie Comics)

MIRROR'S EDGE (Based on the EA video game)
DC Comics (WildStorm): Dec, 2008 - No. 6, Jun, 2009 ($3.99, limited series)
1-6: 1-Origin of Faith; Rhianna Pratchett-s/Matthew Dow Smith-a 4.00
TPB (2009, $19.99) r/#1-6 20.00

MISADVENTURES OF ADAM WEST, THE
Bluewater Comics: Jul, 2011 - Present ($3.99)
1-4: 1-Two covers; co-created by Adam West 4.00
Second series 1-3 (1/12 - No. 3, 2/12) 4.00

MISADVENTURES OF MERLIN JONES, THE (See Movie Comics & Merlin Jones as the Monkey's Uncle under Movie Comics)

MISPLACED
Image Comics: May, 2003 - No. 4, Dec, 2004 ($2.95)
1-4: 1-Three covers by Blaylock, Green and Clugston-Major; Blaylock-s/a 3.00
... @17 (12/04, $4.95) Nara from "Dead @17 " app.; Blaylock-s/a 5.00

MISS AMERICA COMICS (Miss America Magazine #2 on; also see Blonde Phantom & Marvel Mystery Comics)
Marvel Comics (20CC): 1944 (one-shot)
1-2 pgs. pin-ups 219 438 657 1402 2401 3400

MISS AMERICA COMICS 70th ANNIVERARY SPECIAL
Marvel Comics: Aug, 2009 ($3.99, one-shot)
1-Eaglesham-c; new Miss America & Whizzer story; reps. from All Winners #9-11 5.00

MISS AMERICA MAGAZINE (Formerly Miss America; Miss America #51 on)
Miss America Publ. Corp./Marvel/Atlas (MAP): V1#2, Nov, 1944 - No. 93, Nov, 1958
V1#2-Photo-c of teenage girl in Miss America costume; Miss America, Patsy Walker (intro.) comic stories plus movie reviews & stories; intro. Buzz Baxter & Hedy Wolfe; 1 pg. origin Miss America 161 322 483 1030 1765 2500
3-5-Miss America & Patsy Walker stories 74 148 222 470 810 1150
6-Patsy Walker only 43 86 129 271 461 650
V2#1(4/45)-6(9/45)-Patsy Walker continues 17 34 51 98 154 210
V3#1(10/45)-6(4/46) 15 30 45 85 130 175
V4#1(5/46),2,5(9/46) 14 28 42 80 115 150
V4#3(7/46)-Liz Taylor photo-c 36 72 108 216 351 485
V4#4 (8/46; 68 pgs.), V4#6 (10/46; 92 pgs.) 14 28 42 76 108 140
V5#1(11/46)-6(4/47), V6#1(5/47)-3(7/47) 13 26 39 74 105 135
V7#1(8/47)-23(#56, 6/49) 13 26 39 72 101 130
V7#24(#57, 7/49)-Kamen-a (becomes Best Western #58 on?) 13 26 39 74 105 135
V7#25(8/49), 27-44(3/52), VII,nn(5/52) 12 24 36 69 97 125
V7#26(9/49)-All comics 14 28 42 76 108 140
V1,nn(7/52)-V1,nn(1/53)(#46-49), V7#50(Spring '53), V1#51-V7?#54(7/53), 55-93 11 22 33 64 90 115
NOTE: *Photo-c #1, 4, V2#1, 4, 5, V3#5, V4#3, 4, 6, V7#15, 16, 24, 26, 34, 37, 38. Painted c-3.* **Powell** *a-V7#31.*

MISS BEVERLY HILLS OF HOLLYWOOD (See Adventures of Bob Hope)
National Periodical Publ.: Mar-Apr, 1949 - No. 9, July-Aug, 1950 (52 pgs.)
1 (Meets Alan Ladd) 58 116 174 371 636 900
2-William Holden photo on-c 42 84 126 265 450 635
3-5: 2-9-Part photo-c. 5-Bob Hope photo on-c 39 78 117 232 381 530
6,7,9: 6-Lucille Ball photo on-c 35 70 105 208 339 470
8-Reagan photo on-c 39 78 117 240 395 550
NOTE: *Beverly meets Alan Ladd in #1, Eve Arden #2, Betty Hutton #4, Bob Hope #5.*

MISS CAIRO JONES
Croyden Publishers: 1945
1-Bob Oksner daily newspaper-r (1st strip story); lingerie panels 20 40 60 114 182 250

MISS FURY
Adventure Comics: 1991 - No. 4, 1991 ($2.50, limited series)
1-4: 1-Origin; granddaughter of original Miss Fury 3.00
1-Limited ed. ($4.95) 5.00

MISS FURY
Dynamite Entertainment: 2013 - Present ($3.99)
1-9: 1-Multiple covers on all; Herbert-a; origin 4.00

MISS FURY COMICS (Newspaper strip reprints)
Timely Comics (NPI 1/CmPI 2/MPC 3-8): Winter, 1942-43 - No. 8, Winter, 1946 (Published twice a year)
1-Origin Miss Fury by Tarpe' Mills (68 pgs.) in costume w/paper dolls with cut-out costumes 423 846 1269 3000 5250 7500
2-(60 pgs.)-In costume w/paper dolls; hooded Nazi-c 216 432 648 1382 2366 3350
3-(60 pgs.)-In costume w/paper dolls; Hitler-c 181 362 543 1158 1979 2800
4-(52 pgs.)-Classic Nazi WWII-c with giant swastika, Tojo & Hitler photo on wall; in costume, 2 pgs. w/paper dolls 158 316 474 1011 1731 2450
5-(52 pgs.)-In costume w/paper dolls; Japanese WWII-c 118 236 354 755 1290 1825
6-(52 pgs.)-Not in costume in inside stories, w/paper dolls 103 206 309 659 1130 1600
7,8-(36 pgs.)-In costume 1 pg. each; no paper dolls 82 164 246 528 902 1275
NOTE: **Schomburg** *c-1, 5, 6.*

MISS FURY DIGITAL FIRST
Dynamite Entertainment: 2013 - No. 2, 2013 ($3.99, limited series)
1,2-Prints online stories. 1-Reis, Desjardins, Casas-a. 2-Casas-a 4.00

MISSION IMPOSSIBLE (TV) (Also see Wild!)
Dell Publ. Co.: May, 1967 - No. 4, Oct, 1968; No. 5, Oct, 1969 (All have photo-c)
1 7 14 21 49 92 135
2-5: 5-Reprints #1 5 10 15 35 63 90

MISSION IMPOSSIBLE (Movie) (1st Paramount Comics book)
Marvel Comics (Paramount Comics): May, 1996 ($2.95, one-shot)
1-Liefeld-c & back-up story 3.00

MISS LIBERTY (Becomes Liberty Comics)
Burten Publishing Co.: 1945 (MLJ reprints)
1-The Shield & Dusty, The Wizard, & Roy, the Super Boy app.; r/Shield-Wizard #13 32 64 96 188 307 425

MISS MELODY LANE OF BROADWAY (See The Adventures of Bob Hope)
National Periodical Publ.: Feb-Mar, 1950 - No. 3, June-July, 1950 (52 pgs.)
1-Movie stars photos app. on all-c. 60 120 180 385 660 935
2,3: 3-Ed Sullivan photo on-c. 39 78 117 231 378 525

MISS PEACH
Dell Publishing Co.: Oct-Dec, 1963; 1969
1-Jack Mendelsohn-a/script 7 14 21 44 82 120
...Tells You How to Grow (1969; 25¢)-Mel Lazarus-a; also given away (36 pgs.) 5 10 15 30 50 70

MISS PEPPER (See Meet Miss Pepper)

MISS SUNBEAM (See Little Miss...)

MISS VICTORY (See Captain Fearless #1,2, Holyoke One-Shot #3, Veri Best Sure Fire & Veri Best Sure Shot Comics)

MISTER AMERICA
Endeavor Comics: Apr, 1994 - No. 2, May, 1994 ($2.95, limited series)
1,2 3.00

MR. & MRS. BEANS
United Features Syndicate: No. 11, 1939
Single Series 11 34 68 102 199 325 450

MR. & MRS. J. EVIL SCIENTIST (TV)(See The Flintstones & Hanna-Barbera Band Wagon #3)
Gold Key: Nov, 1963 - No. 4, Sept, 1966 (Hanna-Barbera, all 12¢)
1 5 10 15 35 63 90
2-4 4 8 12 23 37 50

MR. ANTHONY'S LOVE CLINIC (Based on radio show)
Hillman Periodicals: Nov, 1949 - No. 5, Apr-May, 1950 (52 pgs.)
1-Photo-c on all 18 36 54 103 162 220
2 12 24 36 67 94 120
3-5 11 22 33 62 86 110

MISTER BLANK
Amaze Ink: No. 0, Jan, 1996 - No. 14, May, 2000 ($1.75/$2.95, B&W)
0-($1.75, 16 pgs.) Origin of Mr. Blank 3.00
1-14-($2.95) Chris Hicks-s/a 3.00

MR. DISTRICT ATTORNEY (Radio/TV)

Mister Miracle #25 © DC

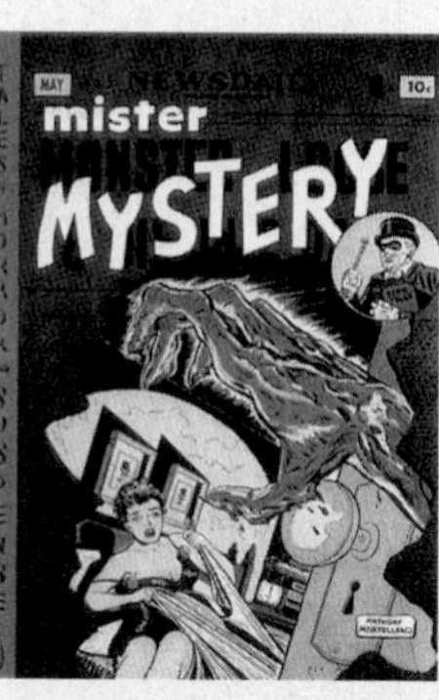
Mister Mystery #5 © Media Pub.

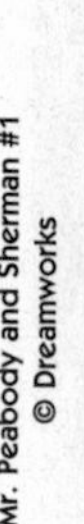
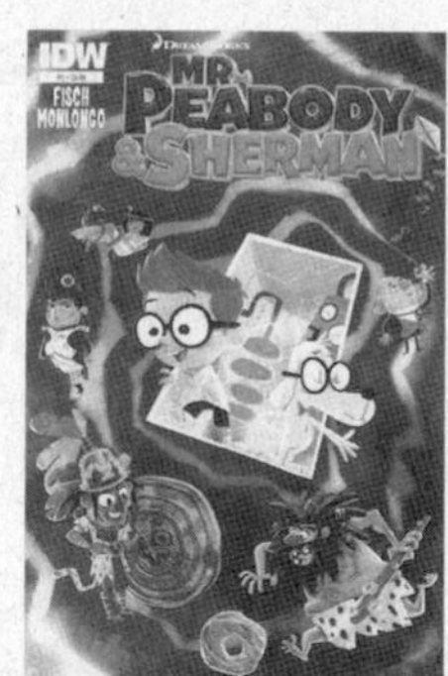
Mr. Peabody and Sherman #1 © Dreamworks

	GD 2.0	VG 4.0	FN 6.0	VF 8.0	VF/NM 9.0	NM- 9.2

National Per. Publ.: Jan-Feb, 1948 - No. 67, Jan-Feb, 1959 (1-23: 52 pgs.)

	GD	VG	FN	VF	VF/NM	NM-
1-Howard Purcell c-5-23 (most)	87	174	261	553	952	1350
2	41	82	123	256	428	600
3-5	29	58	87	170	278	385
6-10: 8-Rise & fall of Lucky Lynn	22	44	66	132	216	300
11-20	17	34	51	98	154	210
21-43: 43-Last pre-code (1-2/55)	14	28	42	76	108	140
44-67: 55-UFO story	11	22	33	62	86	110

MR. DISTRICT ATTORNEY (SeeThe Funnies #35)
Dell Publishing Co.: No. 13, 1942

	GD	VG	FN	VF	VF/NM	NM-
Four Color 13-See The Funnies #35 for 1st app.	24	48	72	168	372	575

MISTER E (Also see Books of Magic limited series)
DC Comics: Jun, 1991- No. 4, Sept, 1991($1.75, limited series)

1-4-Snyder III-c/a; follow-up to Books of Magic limited series 3.00

MISTER ED, THE TALKING HORSE (TV)
Dell Publishing Co./Gold Key: Mar-May, 1962 - No. 6, Feb, 1964 (All photo-c; photo back-c: 1-6)

	GD	VG	FN	VF	VF/NM	NM-
Four Color 1295	10	20	30	69	147	225
1(11/62) (Gold Key)-Photo-c	8	16	24	51	96	140
2-6: Photo-c	5	10	15	33	57	80

(See March of Comics #244, 260, 282, 290)

MR. GUM (From The Atomics)
Oni Press: April, 2003 ($2.99, one-shot)

1-Mike Allred-s/J. Bone-a; Madman & The Atomics app. 3.00

MR. HERO, THE NEWMATIC MAN (See Neil Gaiman's...)

MR. MAGOO (TV) (The Nearsighted..., ...& Gerald McBoing Boing 1954 issues; formerly Gerald McBoing-Boing And ...)
Dell Publishing Co.: No. 6, Nov-Jan, 1953-54; 5/54 - 3-5/62; 9-11/63 - 3-5/65

	GD	VG	FN	VF	VF/NM	NM-
6	9	18	27	58	114	170
Four Color 561(5/54),602(11/54)	9	18	27	58	114	170
Four Color 1235(#1, 12-2/62),1305(#2, 3-5/62)	7	14	21	48	89	130
3(9-11/63) - 5	6	12	18	42	79	115
Four Color 1235(12-536-505)(3-5/65)-2nd Printing	5	10	15	35	63	90

MR. MAJESTIC (See WildC.A.T.S.)
DC Comics (WildStorm): Sept, 1999 - No. 9, May, 2000 ($2.50)

1-9: 1-McGuinness-a/Casey & Holguin-s. 2-Two covers 3.00
TPB (2002, $14.95) r/#1-6 & Wildstorm Spotlight #1 15.00

MISTER MIRACLE (1st series) (See Cancelled Comic Cavalcade)
National Periodical Publications/DC Comics: 3-4/71 - V4#18, 2-3/74; V5#19, 9/77 - V6#25, 8-9/78; 1987 (Fourth World)

	GD	VG	FN	VF	VF/NM	NM-
1-1st app. Mr. Miracle (#1-3 are 15¢)	7	14	21	49	92	135
2,3: 2-Intro. Granny Goodness. 3-Last 15¢ issue	4	8	12	28	47	65
4-8: 4-Intro. Barda; Boy Commandos-r begin; all 52 pgs.	4	8	12	28	47	65
9-18: 9-Origin Mr. Miracle; Darkseid cameo. 15-Intro/1st app. Shilo Norman. 18-Barda & Scott Free wed; New Gods app. & Darkseid cameo; Last Kirby issue.	3	6	9	16	23	30
19-25 (1977-78)	2	4	6	8	10	12

Special 1(1987, $1.25, 52 pgs.) 4.00
Jack Kirby's Fourth World TPB ('01, $12.95) B&W&Grey-toned reprint of #11-18; Mark Evanier intro. 13.00
Jack Kirby's Mister Miracle TPB ('98, $12.95) B&W&Grey-toned reprint of #1-10; David Copperfield intro. 13.00
NOTE: ***Austin** a-19i. **Ditko** a-6r. **Golden** a-23-25p; c-25p. **Heath** a-24i, 25i; c-25i. **Kirby** a(p)/c-1-18. **Nasser** a-19i. **Rogers** a-19-22p; c-19, 20p, 21p, 22-24. 4-8 contain **Simon & Kirby** Boy Commandos reprints from Detective 82,76, Boy Commandos 1, 3 & Detective 64 in that order.*

MISTER MIRACLE (2nd Series) (See Justice League)
DC Comics: Jan, 1989 - No. 28, June, 1991 ($1.00/$1.25)

1-28: 13,14-Lobo app. 22-1st new Mr. Miracle w/new costume 3.00

MISTER MIRACLE (3rd Series)
DC Comics: Apr, 1996 - No. 7, Oct, 1996 ($1.95)

1-7: 2-Vs. JLA. 6-Simonson-c 3.00

MR. MIRACLE (See Capt. Fearless #1 & Holyoke One-Shot #4)

MR. MONSTER (1st Series)(Doc Stearn... #7 on; See Airboy-Mr. Monster Special, Dark Horse Presents, Super Duper Comics & Vanguard Illustrated #7)
Eclipse Comics: Jan, 1985 - No. 10, June, 1987 ($1.75, Baxter paper)

	GD	VG	FN	VF	VF/NM	NM-
1,3: 1-1st story-r from Vanguard Ill. #7(1st app.). 3-Alan Moore scripts; Wolverton-r/Weird Mysteries #5.						5.00
2-Dave Stevens-c	1	3	4	6	8	10
4-10: 6-Ditko-r/Fantastic Fears #5 plus new Giffen-a. 10- "6-D" issue						4.00

MR. MONSTER
Dark Horse Comics: Feb, 1988 - No. 8, July, 1991 ($1.75, B&W)

1-7 3.00
8-($4.95, 60 pgs.)-Origins conclusion 5.00

MR. MONSTER ATTACKS! (Doc Stearn...)
Tundra Publ.: Aug, 1992 - No. 3, Oct, 1992 ($3.95, limited series, 32 pgs.)

1-3: Michael T. Gilbert-a/scripts; Gilbert/Dorman painted-c 4.00

MR. MONSTER PRESENTS (CRACK-A-BOOM!)
Caliber Comics: 1997 - No. 3, 1997 ($2.95, B&W&Red, limited series)

1-3: Michael T. Gilbert-a/scripts: 1-Wraparound-c 3.00

MR. MONSTER'S GAL FRIDAY...KELLY!
Image Comics: Jan, 2000 - No. 3, May, 2004 ($3.50, B&W)

1-3-Michael T. Gilbert-c; story & art by various. 3-Alan Moore-s 3.50

MR. MONSTER'S SUPER-DUPER SPECIAL
Eclipse Comics: May, 1986 - No. 8, July, 1987

	GD	VG	FN	VF	VF/NM	NM-
1-(5/86)...3-D High Octane Horror #1						5.00
1-(5/86)...2-D version, 100 copies	2	4	6	9	13	16
2-(8/86)...High Octane Horror #1, 3-(9/86)...True Crime #1, 4-(11/86)...True Crime #2, 5-(1/87)...Hi-Voltage Super Science #1, 6-(3/87)...High Shock Schlock #1, 7-(5/87)...High Shock Schlock #2, 8-(7/87)...Weird Tales Of The Future #1						4.00

NOTE: ***Jack Cole** r-3, 4. **Evans** a-2r. **Kubert** a-1r. **Powell** a-5r. **Wolverton** a-2r, 7r, 8r.*

MR. MONSTER VS. GORZILLA
Image Comics: July, 1998 ($2.95, one-shot)

1-Michael T. Gilbert-a 3.00

MR. MONSTER: WORLDS WAR TWO
Atomeka Press: 2004 ($6.99, one-shot)

nn-Michael T. Gilbert-s/George Freeman-a; two covers by Horley & Dorman 7.00

MR. MUSCLES (Formerly Blue Beetle #18-21)
Charlton Comics: No. 22, Mar, 1956; No. 23, Aug, 1956

	GD	VG	FN	VF	VF/NM	NM-
22,23	9	18	27	50	65	80

MR. MXYZPTLK (VILLAINS)
DC Comics: Feb, 1998 ($1.95, one-shot)

1-Grant-s/Morgan-a/Pearson-c 3.00

MISTER MYSTERY (Tales of Horror and Suspense)
Mr. Publ. (Media Publ.) No. 1-3/SPM Publ./Stanmore (Aragon): Sept, 1951 - No. 19, Oct, 1954

	GD	VG	FN	VF	VF/NM	NM-
1-Kurtzman*esque* horror story	110	220	330	704	1202	1700
2,3-Kurtzman*esque* story. 3-Anti-Wertham edit.	65	130	195	416	708	1000
4-Bondage-c	65	130	195	416	708	1000
5,8,10	60	120	180	381	653	925
6-Classic torture-c	123	246	369	787	1344	1900
7- "The Brain Bats of Venus" by Wolverton; partially re-used in Weird Tales of the Future #7	148	296	444	947	1624	2300
9-Nostrand-a	60	120	180	381	653	925
11-Wolverton "Robot Woman" story/Weird Mysteries #2, cut up, rewritten & partially redrawn	103	206	309	659	1130	1600
12-Classic injury to eye-c	258	516	774	1651	2826	4000
13-17,19: 15- "Living Dead" junkie story. 16-Bondage-c. 17-Severed heads-c. 19-Reprints	50	100	150	315	533	750
18- "Robot Woman" by Wolverton reprinted from Weird Mysteries #2; decapitation, bondage-c	84	168	252	538	919	1300

NOTE: ***Andru** a-1, 2p, 3p. **Andru/Esposito** c-1-3. **Baily** c-10-18(most). **Mortellaro** c-5-7. Bondage c-7, 16. Some issues have graphic dismemberment scenes.*

MR. PEABODY AND SHERMAN (Based on the 2014 Dreamworks movie)
IDW Publishing: Nov, 2013 - No. 4, Jan, 2014 ($3.99)

1-4: 1-Fisch-s/Monlongo-a; 3 covers. 2-Three covers. 3,4-Two covers 4.00

MR. PUNCH
DC Comics (Vertigo): 1994 ($24.95, one-shot)

nn (Hard-c)-Gaiman scripts; McKean-c/a 40.00
nn (Soft-c) 18.00

MISTER Q (See Mighty Midget Comics & Our Flag Comics #5)

MR. RISK (Formerly All Romances; Men Against Crime #3 on)(Also see Our Flag Comics & Super-Mystery Comics)

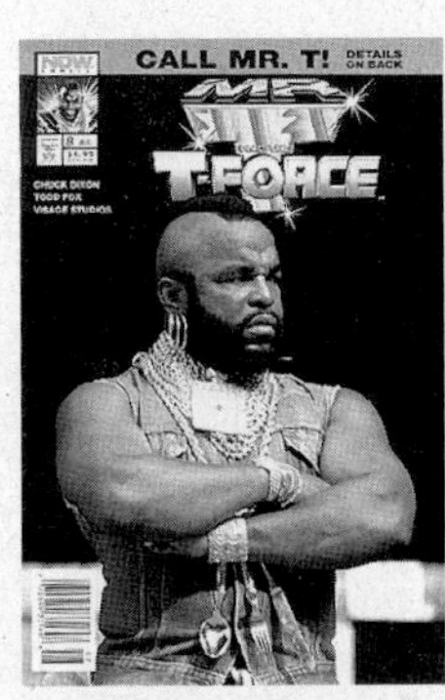

Mr. T and the T-Force #8 © NOW

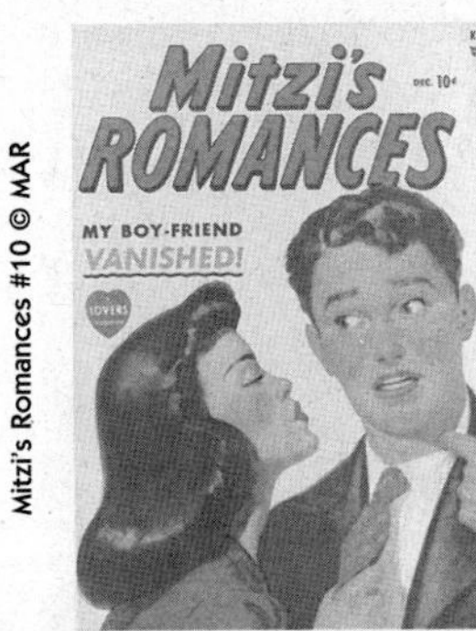

Mitzi's Romances #10 © MAR

The Mocking Dead #1 © Dynamite

	GD 2.0	VG 4.0	FN 6.0	VF 8.0	VF/NM 9.0	NM- 9.2

Ace Magazines: No. 7, Oct, 1950; No. 2, Dec, 1950

7,2 — 12 24 36 67 94 120

MR. SCARLET & PINKY (See Mighty Midget Comics)

MR. T
APComics: May, 2005 ($3.50)

1-Chris Bunting-s/Neil Edwards-a — 3.50

MR. T AND THE T-FORCE
Now Comics: June, 1993 - No. 10, May, 1994 ($1.95, color)

1-10-Newsstand editions: 1-7-polybagged with photo trading card in each. 1,2-Neal Adams-c/a(p). 3-Dave Dorman painted-c — 3.00
1-10-Direct Sale editions polybagged w/line drawn trading cards. 1-Contains gold foil trading card by Neal Adams — 3.00

MISTER TERRIFIC (DC New 52)(Leads into Earth 2 series)
DC Comics: Nov, 2011 - No. 8, Jun, 2012 ($2.99)

1-8: 1-Wallace-s/Gugliotta-a/JG Jones-c; origin re-told. 2-Intro. Brainstorm — 3.00

MISTER UNIVERSE (Professional wrestler)
Mr. Publications Media Publ. (Stanmor, Aragon): July, 1951; No. 2, Oct, 1951 - No. 5, April, 1952

1 — 23 46 69 136 223 310
2- "Jungle That Time Forgot", (24 pg. story); Andru/Esposito-c — 15 30 45 83 124 165
3-Marijuana story — 15 30 45 83 124 165
4,5-"Goes to War" cover/stories (Korean War) — 12 24 36 67 94 120

MISTER X (See Vortex)
Mr. Publications/Vortex Comics/Caliber V3#1 on: 6/84 - No. 14, 8/88 ($1.50/$2.25, direct sales, coated paper);V2#1, Apr, 1989 - V2#12, Mar, 1990 ($2.00/$2.50, B&W, newsprint) V3#1, 1996 - No. 4, 1996 ($2.95, B&W)

1-14: 11-Dave McKean story & art (6 pgs.) — 4.00
V2 #1-12: 1-11 (Second Coming, B&W): 1-Four diff.-c. 10-Photo-c — 3.00
V3 #1-4 — 3.00
Return of... ($11.95, graphic novel)-r/V1#1-4 — 12.00
Return of... ($34.95, hardcover limited edition)-r/1-4 — 35.00
Special (no date, 1990?) — 3.00

MISTER X
Dark Horse Comics: Mar, 2013 ($2.99, one-shot)

...: Hard Candy (3/13) Dean Motter-s/a — 3.00

MISTER X: CONDEMNED
Dark Horse Comics: Dec, 2008 - No. 4, Mar, 2009 ($3.50, limited series)

1-4-Dean Motter-s/a — 3.50

MISTER X: EVICTION
Dark Horse Comics: May, 2013 - No. 3, Jul, 2013 ($3.99, limited series)

1-3-Dean Motter-s/a — 4.00

MISTY
Marvel Comics (Star Comics): Dec, 1985 - No. 6, May, 1986 (Limited series)

1-6: Millie The Model's niece — 4.00

MITZI COMICS (Becomes Mitzi's Boy Friend #2-7)(See All Teen)
Timely Comics: Spring, 1948 (one-shot)

1-Kurtzman's "Hey Look" plus 3 pgs. "Giggles 'n' Grins" — 37 74 111 222 361 500

MITZI'S BOY FRIEND (Formerly Mitzi Comics; becomes Mitzi's Romances)
Marvel Comics (TCI): No. 2, June, 1948 - No. 7, April, 1949

2 — 19 38 57 109 172 235
3-7 — 15 30 45 84 127 170

MITZI'S ROMANCES (Formerly Mitzi's Boy Friend)
Timely/Marvel Comics (TCI): No. 8, June, 1949 - No. 10, Dec, 1949

8-Becomes True Life Tales #8 (10/49) on? — 15 30 45 86 133 180
9,10: 10-Painted-c — 14 28 42 80 115 150

MNEMOVORE
DC Comics (Vertigo): Jun, 2005 - No. 6, Nov, 2005 ($2.99, limited series)

1-6-Rodionoff & Fawkes-s/Huddleston-a/c — 3.00

MOBY DICK (See Feature Presentations #6, King Classics, and Classic Comics #5)
Dell Publishing Co.: No. 717, Aug, 1956

Four Color 717-Movie, Gregory Peck photo-c — 7 14 21 48 89 130

MOBY DUCK (See Donald Duck #112 & Walt Disney Showcase #2,11)
Gold Key (Disney): Oct, 1967 - No. 11, Oct, 1970; No. 12, Jan, 1974 - No. 30, Feb, 1978

1-Three Little Pigs app. — 3 6 9 20 31 42
2-5: 2-Beagle Boys app. 5-Captain Hook app. — 2 4 6 11 16 20
6-11: 6-Huey, Dewey & Louie app. — 2 4 6 9 13 16
12-30: 21,30-r — 1 3 4 6 8 10

MOCKING DEAD, THE
Dynamite Entertainment: 2013 - No. 5, 2014 ($3.99, B&W, limited series)

1-5: 1-Fred Van Lente-s/Max Dunbar-a — 4.00

MODEL FUN (With Bobby Benson)
Harle Publications: No. 2, Fall, 1954 - No. 5, July, 1955

2-Bobby Benson — 7 14 21 35 43 50
3-5-Bobby Benson — 5 10 15 23 28 32

MODELING WITH MILLIE (Formerly Life With Millie)
Atlas/Marvel Comics (Male Publ.): No. 21, Feb, 1963 - No. 54, June, 1967

21 — 8 16 24 56 108 160
22-30 — 5 10 15 34 60 85
31-53 — 5 10 15 30 50 70
54-Last issue; Gears-c & 6 pg. story; Beatles swipe imitators; FF #63 comic appears in story; "Millie the Marvel" 6 pg. story as super-hero — 5 10 15 33 57 80

MODELS, INC.
Marvel Comics: Oct, 2009 - No. 4, Jan, 2010 ($3.99, limited series)

1-4-Millie the Model, Patsy Walker, Mary Jane Watson app.; Land-c. 1-Tim Gunn app. — 4.00

MODERN COMICS (Formerly Military Comics #1-43)
Quality Comics Group: No. 44, Nov, 1945 - No. 102, Oct, 1950

44-Blackhawk continues — 52 104 156 328 557 785
45-52: 49-1st app. Fear, Lady Adventuress — 38 76 114 228 369 510
53-Torchy by Ward begins (9/46) — 42 84 126 265 445 625
54-60: 55-J. Cole-a — 32 64 96 192 314 435
61-Classic-c — 39 78 117 231 378 525
62-64,66-77,79,80: 73-J. Cole-a — 31 62 93 182 296 410
65-Classic Grim Reaper Skull-c — 53 106 159 334 567 800
78-1st app. Madame Butterfly — 34 68 102 199 325 450
81-99,101: 82,83-One pg. J. Cole-a. 83-Last 52 pg. issue 99-Blackhawks on the moon-c/story — 29 58 87 170 278 385
100 — 31 62 93 186 303 420
102-(Scarce)-J. Cole-a; Spirit by Eisner app. — 38 76 114 229 375 520

NOTE: ***Al Bryant** c-44-51, 54, 55, 66, 69. **Jack Cole** a-55, 73. **Crandall** Blackhawk-#46, 47, 50, 51, 54, 56, 58-60, 64, 67-70, 73, 74, 76-78, 80-83; c-60-65, 67, 68, 70-95. **Crandall/Cuidera** c-56-59, 96-102. **Gustavson** a-47, 49. **Ward** Blackhawk-#52, 53, 55 (15 pgs. each). Torchy in #53-102; by **Ward** only in #53-89(9/49); by **Gil Fox** #92, 93, 102.*

MODERN LOVE
E. C. Comics: June-July, 1949 - No. 8, Aug-Sept, 1950

1-Feldstein, Ingels-a — 94 188 282 602 1026 1450
2-Craig/Feldstein-c/s — 57 114 171 362 619 875
3 — 52 104 156 328 552 775
4-6 (Scarce): 4-Bra/panties panels — 63 126 189 403 689 975
7,8 — 52 104 156 328 552 775

NOTE: ***Craig** a-3. **Feldstein** a-in most issues; c-1, 2i, 3-8. **Harrison** a-4. **Iger** a-6-8. **Ingels** a-1, 2, 4-7. **Palais** a-5. **Wood** a-7. **Wood/Harrison** a-5-7. (Canadian reprints known; see Table of Contents.)*

MODERN WARFARE 2: GHOST (Based on the videogame)
DC Comics (WildStorm): Jan, 2010 - No. 6, Sept, 2010 ($3.99, limited series)

1-6: 1-Two covers; Lapham-s/West-a — 4.00
TPB (2010, $17.99) r/#1-6; cover sketches and sketch art — 18.00

MOD LOVE
Western Publishing Co.: 1967 (50¢, 36 pgs.)

1-(Low print) — 6 12 18 40 73 105

MODNIKS, THE
Gold Key: Aug, 1967 - No. 2, Aug, 1970

10206-708(#1) — 3 6 9 21 33 45
2 — 3 6 9 15 22 28

M.O.D.O.K.: REIGN DELAY
Marvel Comics: Nov, 2009 ($3.99, one-shot)

1-M.O.D.O.K. cartoony humor stories from Marvel Digital Comics; Ryan Dunlavey-s/a — 4.00

MOD SQUAD (TV)
Dell Publishing Co.: Jan, 1969 - No. 3, Oct, 1969 - No. 8, April, 1971

1-Photo-c — 6 12 18 38 69 100
2-4: 2-4-Photo-c — 4 8 12 27 44 60
5-8: 8-Photo-c; Reprints #2 — 4 8 12 23 37 50

MOD WHEELS

Molly O'Day #1 © AVON

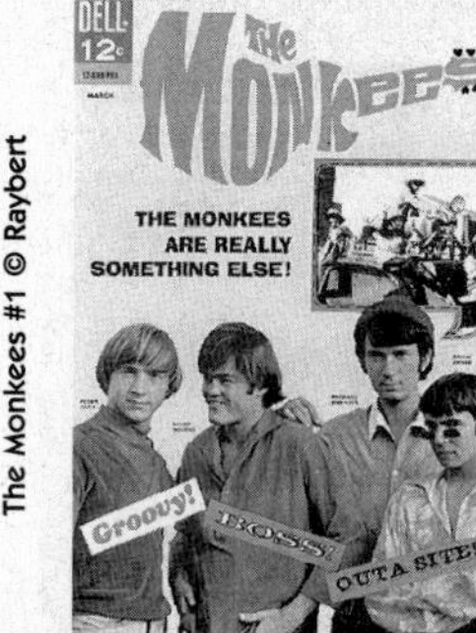

The Monkees #1 © Raybert

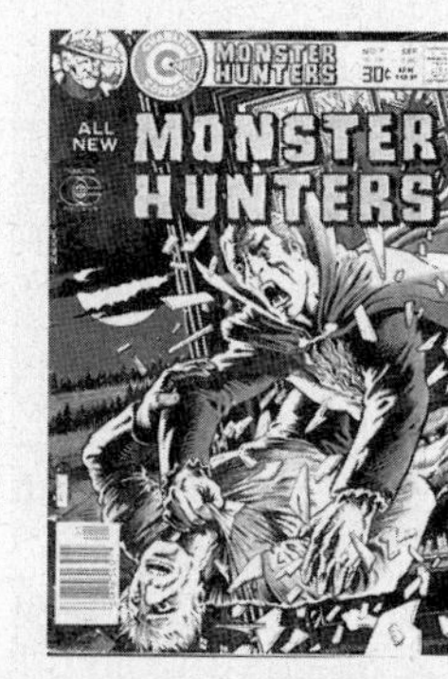

Monster Hunters #7 © CC

	GD 2.0	VG 4.0	FN 6.0	VF 8.0	VF/NM 9.0	NM- 9.2

Gold Key: Mar, 1971 - No. 19, Jan, 1976
1 4 8 12 25 40 55
2-9 3 6 9 16 23 30
10-19: 11,15-Extra 16 pgs. ads 3 6 9 14 19 24

MOE & SHMOE COMICS
O. S. Publ. Co.: Spring, 1948 - No. 2, Summer, 1948
1 9 18 27 52 69 85
2 7 14 21 35 43 50

MOEBIUS (Graphic novel)
Marvel Comics (Epic Comics): Oct, 1987 - No. 6, 1988; No. 7, 1990; No. 8, 1991 ($9.95, 8x11", mature)
1,2,4-6,8: (#2, 2nd printing, $9.95) 3 6 9 15 22 28
3,7,0: 3-(1st & 2nd printings, $12.95). 0 (1990, $12.95) 3 6 9 16 24 32
Moebius I-Signed & #'d hard-c ($45.95, Graphitti Designs, 1,500 copies printed)-r/#1-3 5 10 15 30 50 70

MOEBIUS COMICS
Caliber: May, 1996 - No. 6 ($2.95, B&W)
1-6: Moebius-c/a. 1-William Stout-a 4.00

MOEBIUS: THE MAN FROM CIGURI
Dark Horse Comics: 1996 ($7.95, digest-size)
nn-Moebius-c/a 1 2 3 5 7 9

MOLLY MANTON'S ROMANCES (Romantic Affairs #3)
Marvel Comics (SePI): Sept, 1949 - No. 2, Dec, 1949 (52 pgs.)
1-Photo-c (becomes Blaze the Wonder Collie #2 (10/49) on? & Molly Manton's Romances #2 20 40 60 117 189 260
2-Titled "Romances of..."; photo-c 14 28 42 82 121 160

MOLLY O'DAY (Super Sleuth)
Avon Periodicals: February, 1945 (1st Avon comic)
1-Molly O'Day, The Enchanted Dagger by Tuska (r/Yankee #1), Capt'n Courage, Corporal Grant app. 63 126 189 403 689 975

MOMENT OF SILENCE
Marvel Comics: Feb, 2002 ($3.50, one-shot)
1-Tributes to the heroes and victims of Sept. 11; s/a by various 3.50

MONARCHY, THE (Also see The Authority and StormWatch)
DC Comics (WildStorm): Apr, 2001 - No. 12, May, 2002 ($2.50)
1-12: 1-McCrea & Leach-a/Young-s 3.00
Bullets Over Babylon TPB (2001, $12.95) r/#1-4, Authority #21 13.00

MONKEES, THE (TV)(Also see Circus Boy, Groovy, Not Brand Echh #3, Teen-Age Talk, Teen Beam & Teen Beat)
Dell Publishing Co.: March, 1967 - No. 17, Oct, 1969
1-Photo-c 9 18 27 59 117 175
2-17: All photo-c. 17-Reprints #1 6 12 18 37 66 95

MONKEY AND THE BEAR, THE
Atlas Comics (ZPC): Sept, 1953 - No. 3, Jan, 1954
1-Howie Post-c/a in all; funny animal 11 22 33 60 83 105
2,3 8 16 24 44 57 70

MONKEYMAN AND O'BRIEN (Also see Dark Horse Presents #80, 100-5, Gen^{13}/..., Hellboy: Seed of Destruction, & San Diego Comic Con #2)
Dark Horse Comics (Legend): Jul, 1996 - No. 3, Sept, 1996 ($2.95, lim. series)
1-3: New stories; Art Adams-c/a/scripts 4.00
nn-(2/96, $2.95)-r/back-up stories from Hellboy: Seed of Destruction; Adams-c/a/scripts 4.00

MONKEYSHINES COMICS
Ace Periodicals/Publishers Specialists/Current Books/Unity Publ.: Summer, 1944 - No. 27, July, 1949
1-Funny animal 15 30 45 86 133 180
2-(Aut/44) 10 20 30 54 72 90
3-10: 3-(Win/44) 9 18 27 50 65 80
11-18,20-27: 23,24-Fago-c/a 8 16 24 40 50 60
19-Frazetta-a 9 18 27 50 65 80

MONKEY'S UNCLE, THE (See Merlin Jones As... under Movie Comics)

MONOLITH, THE
DC Comics: Apr, 2004 - No. 12, Mar, 2005 ($3.50/$2.95)
1-($3.50) Palmiotti & Gray-s/Winslade-a 3.50
2-12-($2.95): 6-8-Batman app.; Coker-a 3.00

...: Volume One HC (Image Comics, 2012, $17.99) r/#1-4; intro. by Jim Steranko 18.00

MONROES, THE (TV)
Dell Publishing Co.: Apr, 1967
1-Photo-c 3 6 9 17 26 35

MONSTER
Fiction House Magazines: 1953 - No. 2, 1953
1-Dr. Drew by Grandenetti; reprint from Rangers Comics #48; Whitman-c 55 110 165 352 601 850
2-Whitman-c 41 82 123 256 428 600

MONSTER CRIME COMICS (Also see Crime Must Stop)
Hillman Periodicals: Oct, 1952 (15¢, 52 pgs.)
1 (Scarce) 194 388 582 1242 2121 3000

MONSTER HOUSE (Companion to the 2006 movie)
IDW Publishing: June, 2006 ($7.99, one-shot)
nn-Two stories about Bones and Skull by Joshua Dysart and Simeon Wilkins 8.00

MONSTER HOWLS (Magazine)
Humor-Vision: December, 1966 (Satire) (35¢, 68 pgs.)
1-John Severin-a 5 10 15 34 60 85

MONSTER HUNTERS
Charlton Comics: Aug, 1975 - No. 9, Jan, 1977; No. 10, Oct, 1977 - No. 18, Feb, 1979
1-Howard-a; Newton-c; 1st Countess Von Bludd and Colonel Whiteshroud 3 6 9 17 26 35
2-Sutton-c/a; Ditko-a 3 6 9 14 19 24
3,4,5,7: 4-Sutton-c/a 2 4 6 9 12 15
6,8,10: 6,8,10-Ditko-a 2 4 6 10 14 18
9,11,12 1 3 4 6 8 10
13,15,18-Ditko-c/a. 18-Sutton-a 2 4 6 10 14 18
14-Special all-Ditko issue 3 6 9 16 24 32
16,17-Sutton-a 2 3 4 6 8 10
1,2 (Modern Comics reprints, 1977) 6.00
NOTE: ***Ditko** a-2, 6, 8, 10, 13-15r, 18r; c-13-15, 18.* ***Howard** a-1, 3, 17; r-13.* ***Morisi** a-1.* ***Staton** a-1, 13.* ***Sutton** a-2, 4; c-2, 4; r-16-18.* ***Zeck** a-4-9. Reprints in #12-18.*

MONSTER MADNESS (Magazine)
Marvel Comics: 1972 - No. 3, 1973 (60¢, B&W)
1-3: Stories by "Sinister" Stan Lee. 1-Frankenstein photo-c. 2-Son of Frankenstein photo-c. 3-Bride of Frankenstein photo-c 4 8 12 27 44 60

MONSTER MAN
Image Comics (Action Planet): Sept, 1997 ($2.95, B&W)
1-Mike Manley-c/s/a 3.00

MONSTER MASTERWORKS
Marvel Comics: 1989 ($12.95, TPB)
nn-Reprints 1960's monster stories; art by Kirby, Ditko, Ayers, Everett 20.00

MONSTER MATINEE
Chaos! Comics: Oct, 1997 - No. 3, Oct, 1997 ($2.50, limited series)
1-3: pin-ups 3.00

MONSTER MENACE
Marvel Comics: Dec, 1993 - No. 4, Mar, 1994 ($1.25, limited series)
1-4: Pre-code Atlas horror reprints. 6.00
NOTE: ***Ditko**-r & **Kirby**-r in all.*

MONSTER OF FRANKENSTEIN (See Frankenstein and Essential Monster of Frankenstein)

MONSTER PILE-UP
Image Comics: Aug, 2008 ($1.99)
1-New short stories of Astounding Wolf-Man, Firebreather, Perhapanauts, Proof 3.00

MONSTERS ATTACK (Magazine)
Globe Communications Corpse: Sept, 1989 - No. 5, Dec, 1990 (B&W)
1-5-Ditko, Morrow, J. Severin-a. 5-Toth, Morrow-a 1 2 3 4 5 7

MONSTERS, INC. (Based on the Disney/Pixar movie)
BOOM! Studios: Jun, 2009 - No. 4, Nov, 2009 ($2.99, limited series)
...: Laugh Factory 1-4: 1,3-Three covers. 2,4-Two covers 3.00

MONSTERS, INC. (Based on the Disney/Pixar movie)
Marvel Worldwide Inc.: Feb, 2013 - No. 2 ($2.99, limited series)
1,2-Movie adaptation 3.00
...: A Perfect Date (2013, $2.99) 3.00
...: The Humanween Party (4/13, $2.99) 3.00

Monsters on the Prowl #9 © MAR

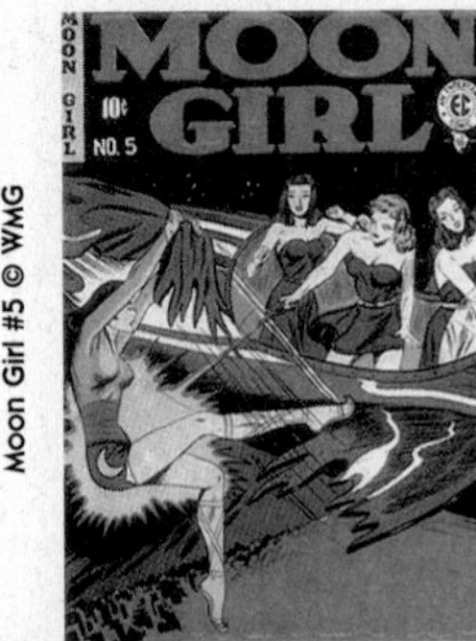

Moon Girl #5 © WMG

Moon Knight (2014 series) #2 © MAR

GD 2.0 | VG 4.0 | FN 6.0 | VF 8.0 | VF/NM 9.0 | NM- 9.2

MONSTERS ON THE PROWL (Chamber of Darkness #1-8)
Marvel Comics Group (No. 13,14: 52 pgs.): No. 9, 2/71 - No. 27, 11/73; No. 28, 6/74 - No. 30, 10/74

9-Barry Smith inks 5 10 15 30 50 70
10-12,15: 12-Last 15¢ issue 3 6 9 18 28 38
13,14-(52 pgs.) 3 6 9 21 33 45
16-(4/72)-King Kull 4th app.; Severin-c 3 6 9 21 33 45
17-30 3 6 9 16 23 30
NOTE: ***Ditko*** *r-9, 14, 16.* ***Kirby*** *r-10-17, 21, 23, 25, 27, 28, 30; c-9, 25.* ***Kirby/Ditko*** *r-14, 17-20, 22, 24, 26, 29.* ***Marie/John Severin*** *a-16(Kull). 9-13, 15 contain one new story. Woodish art by* ***Reese****-11. King Kull created by Robert E. Howard.*

MONSTERS TO LAUGH WITH (Magazine) (Becomes Monsters Unlimited #4)
Marvel Comics Group: 1964 - No. 3, 1965 (B&W)

1-Humor by Stan Lee 7 14 21 46 86 125
2,3: 3-Frankenstein photo-c 5 10 15 31 53 75

MONSTERS UNLEASHED (Magazine)
Marvel Comics Group: July, 1973 - No. 11, Apr, 1975; Summer, 1975 (B&W)

1-Soloman Kane sty; Werewolf app. 4 8 12 28 47 65
2-4: 2-The Frankenstein Monster begins, ends #10. 3-Neal Adams-c/a; The Man-Thing begins (origin-r); Son of Satan preview. 4-Werewolf app. 4 8 12 23 37 50
5-7: Werewolf in all. 5-Man-Thing. 7-Williamson-a(r) 3 6 9 17 26 35
8-11: 8-Man-Thing; N. Adams-r. 9-Man-Thing; Wendigo app. 10-Origin Tigra 3 6 9 18 28 38
Annual 1 (Summer,1975, 92 pgs.)-Kane-a 3 6 9 17 26 35
NOTE: ***Boris*** *c-2, 6.* ***Brunner*** *a-2; c-11.* ***J. Buscema*** *a-2p, 4p, 5p.* ***Colan*** *a-1, 4r.* ***Davis*** *a-3r.* ***Everett*** *a-2r.* ***G. Kane*** *a-3.* ***Krigstein*** *r-4.* ***Morrow*** *a-3; c-1.* ***Perez*** *a-8.* ***Ploog*** *a-6.* ***Reese*** *a-1, 2.* ***Tuska*** *a-3p.* ***Wildey*** *a-1r.*

MONSTERS UNLIMITED (Magazine) (Formerly Monsters To Laugh With)
Marvel Comics Group: No. 4, 1965 - No. 7, 1966 (B&W)

4-7: 4,7-Frankenstein photo-c 5 10 15 31 53 75

MONSTER WORLD
DC Comics (WildStorm): Jul, 2001 - No. 4, Oct, 2001 ($2.50, limited series)

1-4-Lobdell-s/Meglia-c/a 3.00

MONTANA KID, THE (See Kid Montana)

MONTE HALE WESTERN (Movie star; Formerly Mary Marvel #1-28; also see Fawcett Movie Comic, Motion Picture Comics, Picture News #8, Real Western Hero, Six-Gun Heroes, Western Hero & XMas Comics)
Fawcett Publ./Charlton No. 83 on: No. 29, Oct, 1948 - No. 88, Jan, 1956

29-(#1, 52 pgs.)-Photo-c begin, end #82; Monte Hale & his horse Pardner begin 26 52 78 154 252 350
30-(52 pgs.)-Big Bow and Little Arrow begin, end #34; Captain Tootsie by Beck 14 28 42 80 115 150
31-36,38-40-(52 pgs.): 34-Gabby Hayes begins, ends #80. 39-Captain Tootsie by Beck 12 24 36 67 94 120
37,41,45,49-(36 pgs.) 10 20 30 54 72 90
42-44,46-48,50-(52 pgs.): 47-Big Bow & Little Arrow app. 10 20 30 58 79 100
51,52,54-56,58,59-(52 pgs.) 9 18 27 52 69 85
53,57-(36 pgs.): 53-Slim Pickens app. 8 16 24 44 57 70
60-81: 36 pgs. #60-on. 80-Gabby Hayes ends 8 16 24 42 54 65
82-Last Fawcett issue (6/53) 9 18 27 52 69 85
83-1st Charlton issue (2/55); B&W photo back-c begin. Gabby Hayes returns, ends #86 10 20 30 58 79 100
84 (4/55) 8 16 24 44 57 70
85-86 8 16 24 42 54 65
87,88: 87-Wolverton-r, 1/2 pg. 88-Last issue 8 16 24 44 57 70
NOTE: ***Gil Kane*** *a-33?, 34? Rocky Lane -1 pg. (Carnation ad)-38, 40, 41, 43, 44, 46, 55.*

MONTY HALL OF THE U.S. MARINES (See With the Marines...)
Toby Press: Aug, 1951 - No. 11, Apr, 1953

1 13 26 39 74 105 135
2 9 18 27 47 61 75
3-5 8 16 24 42 54 65
6-11 8 16 24 40 50 60
NOTE: *Full page pin-ups (Pin-Up Pete) by* ***Jack Sparling*** *in #1-9.*

MOON, A GIRL...ROMANCE, A (Becomes Weird Fantasy #13 on; formerly Moon Girl #1-8)
E. C. Comics: No. 9, Sept-Oct, 1949 - No. 12, Mar-Apr, 1950

9-Moon Girl cameo 87 174 261 553 952 1350
10,11 73 146 219 467 796 1125
12-(Scarce) 87 174 261 553 952 1350
NOTE: ***Feldstein, Ingels*** *art in all.* ***Feldstein*** *c-9-12.* ***Wood/Harrison*** *a-10-12. Canadian reprints known; see Table of Contents.*

MOON GIRL AND THE PRINCE (#1) (Moon Girl #2-6; Moon Girl Fights Crime #7, 8; becomes A Moon, A Girl, Romance #9 on)(Also see Animal Fables #7, Int. Crime Patrol #6, Happy Houlihans & Tales From The Crypt #22)
E. C. Comics: Fall, 1947 - No. 8, Summer, 1949

1-Origin Moon Girl (see Happy Houlihans #1). Intro Santana, Queen of the Underworld 116 232 348 742 1271 1800
2-Moon Girl battles Futureman 71 142 213 454 777 1100
3,4: 3-Santana, Queen of the Underworld returns. 4-Moon Girl vs. a vampire 61 122 183 390 670 950
5-E.C.'s 1st horror story, "Zombie Terror" 135 270 405 864 1482 2100
6-8 (Scarce): 7-Origin Star (Moongirl's sidekick) 71 142 213 454 777 1100
NOTE: ***Craig*** *a-2, 5; c-1, 2.* ***Moldoff*** *a-1-8; c-3-8 (Shelly).* ***Wheelan's*** *Fat and Slat app. in #3, 4, 6. #2 & #3 are 52 pgs., #4 on, 36 pgs. Canadian reprints known; (see Table of Contents.)*

MOON KNIGHT (Also see The Hulk, Marc Spector..., Marvel Preview #21, Marvel Spotlight & Werewolf by Night #32)
Marvel Comics Group: Nov, 1980 - No. 38, Jul, 1984 (Mando paper #33 on)

1-Origin resumed in #4 2 4 6 8 10 12
2-15,25,35: 4-Intro Midnight Man. 25-Double size. 35-($1.00, 52 pgs.)-X-Men app.; F.F. cameo 5.00
16-24,26-28,31-34,36-38: 16-The Thing app. 4.00
29,30-Werewolf By Night app. 5.00
NOTE: ***Austin*** *c-27i, 31i.* ***Cowan*** *a-16; c-16, 17.* ***Kaluta*** *c-36-38; back c-35.* ***Miller*** *c-9, 12p, 13p, 15p, 27p.* ***Ploog*** *back c-35.* ***Sienkiewicz*** *a-1-15, 17-20, 22-26, 28-30, 33i, 36(4), 37; c-1-5, 7, 8, 10, 11, 14-16, 18-26, 28-30, 31p, 33, 34.*

MOON KNIGHT
Marvel Comics Group: June, 1985 - V2#6, Dec, 1985

V2#1-Double size; new costume 4.00
V2#2-6: 6-Sienkiewicz painted-c 3.00

MOON KNIGHT
Marvel Comics: Jan, 1998 - No. 4, Apr, 1998 ($2.50, limited series)

1-4-Moench-s/Edwards-c/a 3.00

MOON KNIGHT (Volume 3)
Marvel Comics: Jan, 1999 - No. 4, Feb, 1999 ($2.99, limited series)

1-4-Moench-s/Texeira-a(p) 3.00

MOON KNIGHT (Fourth series) (Leads into Vengeance of the Moon Knight)
Marvel Comics: June, 2006 - No. 30, Jul, 2009 ($2.99)

1-Finch-a/c; Huston-s 4.00
1-B&W sketch variant-c 6.00
2-19,21-26: 7-Spider-Man app. 9,10-Punisher app. 13-Suydam-c begin. 23-25-Bullseye 3.00
20-($3.99) Deodato-a; back-up r/1st app. in Werewolf By Night #32,33 4.00
Annual 1 (1/08, $3.99) Swierczynski-s/Palo-a 4.00
... Saga (2009, free) synopsis of origin and major storylines 3.00
...: Silent Knight 1 (1/09, $3.99) Milligan-s/Laurence Campbell-a/Crain-c 4.00
... Vol. 1: The Bottom HC (2006, $19.99) r/#1-6; Huston afterword; 2 covers 20.00
... Vol. 1: The Bottom SC (2007, $14.99) r/#1-6; Huston afterword 15.00
... Vol. 2: Midnight Sun HC (2008, $19.99) r/#7-13 & Annual #1 20.00
... Vol. 2: Midnight Sun SC (2008, $14.99) r/#7-13 & Annual #1 15.00

MOON KNIGHT (Fifth series)
Marvel Comics: Jul, 2011 - No. 12, Jun, 2012 ($3.99, limited series)

1-Bendis-s/Maleev-a/c; Wolverine, Spider-Man and Capt. America "app." 4.00
2-12: 2-Echo returns. 3-Bullseye-c 4.00

MOON KNIGHT (Sixth series)
Marvel Comics: May, 2014 - Present ($3.99)

1,2-Ellis-s/Shalvey-a 4.00

MOON KNIGHT: DIVIDED WE FALL
Marvel Comics: 1992 ($4.95, 52 pgs.)

nn-Denys Cowan-c/a(p) 5.00

MOON KNIGHT SPECIAL
Marvel Comics: Oct, 1992 ($2.50, 52 pgs.)

1-Shang Chi, Master of Kung Fu-c/story 4.00

MOON KNIGHT SPECIAL EDITION
Marvel Comics Group: Nov, 1983 - No. 3, Jan, 1984 ($2.00, limited series, Baxter paper)

1-3: Reprints from Hulk mag. by Sienkiewicz 4.00

MOON MULLINS (See Popular Comics, Super Book #3 & Super Comics)
Dell Publishing Co.: 1941 - 1945

Four Color 14(1941) 47 94 141 296 498 700
Large Feature Comic 29(1941) 36 72 108 216 351 485
Four Color 31(1943) 15 30 45 103 227 350

Moonshadow #1 © DeMatteis & Muth

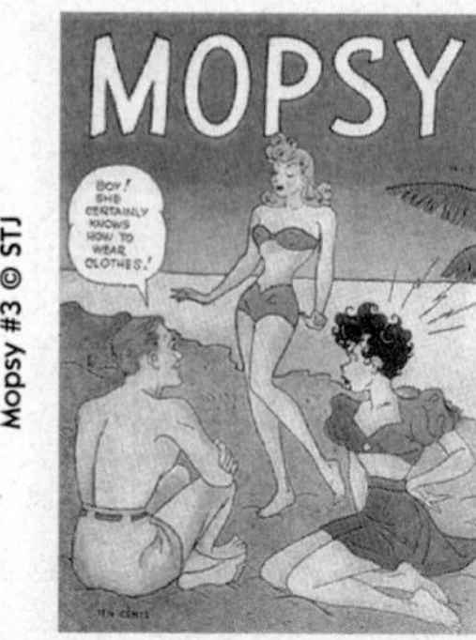

Mopsy #3 © STJ

More Fun Comics #65 © DC

	GD 2.0	VG 4.0	FN 6.0	VF 8.0	VF/NM 9.0	NM- 9.2
Four Color 81(1945)	10	20	30	64	132	200

MOON MULLINS
Michel Publ. (American Comics Group)#1-6/St. John #7,8: Dec-Jan, 1947-48 - No. 8, Mar-May, 1949 (52 pgs)

	GD 2.0	VG 4.0	FN 6.0	VF 8.0	VF/NM 9.0	NM- 9.2
1-Alternating Sunday & daily strip-r	23	46	69	136	223	310
2	14	28	42	82	121	160
3-8: 7,8-St. John Publ. 7,8-...Featuring Kayo on-c	14	28	42	80	115	150

NOTE: *Milt Gross a-2-6, 8. Frank Willard r-all.*

MOON PILOT
Dell Publishing Co.: No. 1313, Mar-May, 1962

	GD 2.0	VG 4.0	FN 6.0	VF 8.0	VF/NM 9.0	NM- 9.2
Four Color 1313-Movie, photo-c	6	12	18	40	73	105

MOONSHADOW (Also see Farewell, Moonshadow)
Marvel Comics (Epic Comics): 5/85 - #12, 2/87 ($1.50/$1.75, mature)
(1st fully painted comic book)

	GD 2.0	VG 4.0	FN 6.0	VF 8.0	VF/NM 9.0	NM- 9.2
1-Origin; J. M. DeMatteis scripts & Jon J. Muth painted-c/a.						6.00
2-12: 11-Origin						4.00
Trade paperback (1987?)-r/#1-12						14.00
Signed & #ed HC ($39.95, 1,200 copies)-r/#1-12	4	8	12	27	44	60

MOONSHADOW
DC Comics (Vertigo): Oct, 1994 - No. 12, Aug, 1995 ($2.25/$2.95)

	GD 2.0	VG 4.0	FN 6.0	VF 8.0	VF/NM 9.0	NM- 9.2
1-11: Reprints Epic series.						3.00
12 ($2.95)-w/expanded ending						4.00
The Complete Moonshadow TPB ('98, $39.95) r/#1-12 and Farewell Moonshadow; new Muth painted-c						40.00

MOON-SPINNERS, THE (See Movie Comics)

MOONSTONE MONSTERS
Moonstone: 2003 - 2005 ($2.95, B&W)

	GD 2.0	VG 4.0	FN 6.0	VF 8.0	VF/NM 9.0	NM- 9.2
...: Demons ($2.95) - Short stories by various; Frenz-c						3.00
...: Ghosts ($2.95) - Short stories by various; Frenz-c						3.00
...: Sea Creatures ($2.95) - Short stories by various; Frenz-c						3.00
...: Witches ($2.95) - Short stories by various; Frenz-c						3.00
...: Zombies ($2.95) - Short stories by various; Frenz-c						3.00
Volume 1 (2004, $16.95, TPB) r/short stories from series; Wolak-c						17.00

MOONSTONE NOIR
Moonstone: 2003 - Present ($2.95/$4.95/$5.50, B&W)

	GD 2.0	VG 4.0	FN 6.0	VF 8.0	VF/NM 9.0	NM- 9.2
...: Bulldog Drummond (2004, $4.95) - Messner-Loebs-s/Barkley-a						5.00
...: Johnny Dollar ($4.95) - Gallaher-s/Theriault-a						5.00
...: Mr. Keen, Tracer of Lost Persons 1,2 ($2.95, limited series) - Ferguson-a						3.00
...: Mysterious Traveler (2003, $5.50) - Trevor Von Eeden-a/Joe Gentile-s						5.50
...: Mysterious Traveler Returns (2004, $4.95) - Trevor Von Eeden-a/Joe Gentile-s						5.00
...: The Lone Wolf ($4.95) - Jolley-s/Croall-a						5.00

MOPSY (See Pageant of Comics & TV Teens)
St. John Publ. Co.: Feb, 1948 - No. 19, Sept, 1953

	GD 2.0	VG 4.0	FN 6.0	VF 8.0	VF/NM 9.0	NM- 9.2
1-Part-r; reprints "Some Punkins" by Neher	18	36	54	103	162	220
2	11	22	33	62	86	110
3-10(1953): 8-Lingerie panels	10	20	30	56	76	95
11-19: 19-Lingerie-c	9	18	27	52	69	85

NOTE: *#1-7, 13, 18, 19 have paper dolls.*

MORBIUS REVISITED
Marvel Comic: Aug, 1993 - No. 5, Dec, 1993 ($1.95, mini-series)

	GD 2.0	VG 4.0	FN 6.0	VF 8.0	VF/NM 9.0	NM- 9.2
1-5-Reprints Fear #27-31						3.00

MORBIUS: THE LIVING VAMPIRE (Also see Amazing Spider-Man #101,102, Fear #20, Marvel Team-Up #3, 4, Midnight Sons Unl. & Vampire Tales)
Marvel Comics (Midnight Sons imprint #16 on): Sep, 1992 - No. 32, Apr, 1995 ($1.75/$1.95)

	GD 2.0	VG 4.0	FN 6.0	VF 8.0	VF/NM 9.0	NM- 9.2
1-($2.75, 52 pgs.)-Polybagged w/poster; Ghost Rider & Johnny Blaze x-over (part 3 of Rise of the Midnight Sons)						4.00
2-11,13-24,26-32: 3,4-Vs. Spider-Man-c/s.15-Ghost Rider app. 16-Spot varnish-c. 16,17-Siege of Darkness, parts 5 &13. 18-Deathlok app. 21-Bound-in Spider-Man trading card sheet; Spider-Man app.						3.00
12-($2.25)-Outer-c is a Darkhold envelope made of black parchment w/gold ink; Midnight Massacre x-over						4.00
25-($2.50, 52 pgs.)-Gold foil logo						4.00

MORBIUS: THE LIVING VAMPIRE (Marvel NOW!)
Marvel Comics: Mar, 2013 - No. 9, Nov, 2013 ($2.99)

	GD 2.0	VG 4.0	FN 6.0	VF 8.0	VF/NM 9.0	NM- 9.2
1-9: 1-Keatinge-s/Elson-a/Dell'Otto-c. 6,7-Superior Spider-Man app.						3.00

MORE FUN COMICS (Formerly New Fun Comics #1-6)
National Periodical Publs: No. 7, Jan, 1936 - No. 127, Nov-Dec, 1947 (No. 7,9-11: paper-c)

	GD 2.0	VG 4.0	FN 6.0	VF 8.0	VF/NM 9.0	NM- 9.2
7(1/36)-Oversized, paper-c; 1 pg. Kelly-a	900	1800	2700	7200	-	-
8(2/36)-Oversized (10x12"), paper-c; 1 pg. Kelly-a; Sullivan-c	900	1800	2700	7200	-	-
9(3-4/36)(Very rare, 1st standard-sized comic book with original material)-Last multiple panel-c	1200	2400	3600	9600	-	-
10,11(7/36): 10-Last Henri Duval by Siegel & Shuster. 11-1st "Calling All Cars" by Siegel & Shuster; new classic logo begins	650	1300	1950	5200	-	-
12(8/36)-Slick-c begin	475	950	1425	3800	-	-
V2#1(9/36, #13) 1 pg. Fred Astaire photo/bio	438	876	1314	3500	-	-
2(10/36, #14)-Dr. Occult in costume (1st in color)(Superman proto-type; 1st DC appearance) continues from The Comics Magazine, ends #17	1938	3876	5814	15,500	-	-
V2#3(11/36, #15), 17(V2#5)	788	1576	2364	6300	-	-
16(V2#4)-Cover numbering begins; ties with New Comics #11 as 1st DC Christmas-c; last Superman tryout issue	813	1626	2439	6500	-	-
18-20(V2#8, 5/37)	344	688	1032	2750	-	-
21(V2#9)-24(V2#12, 9/37)	242	484	726	1452	1938	3150
25(V3#1, 10/37)-27(V3#3, 12/37): 27-Xmas-c	242	484	726	1452	1938	3150
28-30: 30-1st non-funny cover	219	438	657	1314	1754	2850
31-Has ad for Action Comics #1	246	492	738	1476	1969	3200
32-35: 32-Last Dr. Occult	219	438	657	1314	1754	2850
36-40: 36-(10/38)-The Masked Ranger & sidekick Pedro begins; Ginger Snap by Bob Kane (2 pgs.; 1st-a?). 39-Xmas-c	219	438	657	1314	1754	2850
41-50: 41-Last Masked Ranger	196	392	588	1176	1569	2550
51-The Spectre app. (in costume) in one panel ad at end of Buccaneer story	640	1280	1920	3840	5920	8000
52-(2/40)-Origin/1st app. The Spectre (in costume splash panel only), part 1 by Bernard Baily (parts 1 & 2 written by Jerry Siegel; Spectre's costume changes color from purple & blue to green & grey; last Wing Brady; Spectre-c	8400	16,800	25,200	62,000	111,000	160,000
53-Origin The Spectre (in costume at end of story), part 2; Capt. Desmo begins; Spectre-c	3250	6500	9750	22,750	52,375	82,000
54-The Spectre in costume; last King Carter; classic-Spectre-c	1800	3600	5400	13,500	25,750	38,000
55-(Scarce, 5/40)-Dr. Fate begins (1st app.); last Bulldog Martin; Spectre-c	1700	3400	5100	12,750	24,375	36,000
56-1st Dr. Fate-c (classic), origin continues. Congo Bill begins (6/40), 1st app.;	919	1838	2757	6709	11,855	17,000
57-60-All Spectre-c	486	972	1458	3550	6275	9000
61,65: 61-Classic Dr. Fate-c. 65-Classic Spectre-c	432	864	1296	3154	5577	8000
62-64,66: 63-Last Lt. Bob Neal. 64-Lance Larkin begins; all Spectre-c	343	686	1029	2400	4200	6000
67-(5/41)-Origin (1st) Dr. Fate; last Congo Bill & Biff Bronson (Congo Bill continues in Action Comics #37, 6/41)-Spectre-c	632	1264	1896	4614	8157	11,700
68-70: 68-Clip Carson begins. 70-Last Lance Larkin; all Dr. Fate-c	297	594	891	1888	3244	4600
71-Origin & 1st app. Johnny Quick by Mort Weisinger (9/41); classic sci/fi Dr. Fate-c	443	886	1329	3234	5717	8200
72-Dr. Fate's new helmet; last Sgt. Carey, Sgt. O'Malley & Captain Desmo; German submarine-c (Nazi war-c)	290	580	870	1856	3178	4500
73-Origin & 1st app. Aquaman (11/41) by Paul Norris; intro. Green Arrow & Speedy; Dr. Fate-c	1800	3600	5400	13,000	24,000	35,000
74-2nd Aquaman; 1st Percival Popp, Supercop; Dr. Fate-c	300	600	900	2010	3505	5000
75,76: 75-New origin Spectre; Nazi spy ring cover w/Hitler's photo. 76-Last Dr. Fate-c; Johnny Quick (by Meskin #76-97) begins, ends #107; last Clip Carson	258	516	774	1651	2826	4000
77-80: 77-Green Arrow-c begin	155	310	465	992	1696	2400
81-83,85,88,90: 81-Last large logo. 82-1st small logo.	103	206	309	659	1130	1600
84-Green Arrow Japanese war-c	110	220	330	704	1202	1700
86,87-Johnny Quick-c. 87-Last Radio Squad	103	206	309	659	1130	1600
89-Origin Green Arrow & Speedy Team-up	110	220	330	704	1202	1700
91-97,99: 91-1st bi-monthly issue. 93-Dover & Clover begin (1st app., 9-10/43). 97-Kubert-a	77	154	231	493	847	1200
98-Last Dr. Fate (scarce)	97	194	291	621	1061	1500
100 (11-12/44)-Johnny Quick-c	90	180	270	576	988	1400
101-Origin & 1st app. Superboy (1-2/45)(not by Siegel & Shuster); last Spectre issue; Green Arrow-c	757	1514	2271	5526	9763	14,000
102-2nd Superboy app; 1st Dover & Clover-c	145	290	435	921	1586	2250
103-3rd Superboy app; last Green Arrow-c	103	206	309	659	1130	1600
104-1st Superboy-c w/Dover & Clover	90	180	270	576	988	1400
105,106-Superboy-c	82	164	246	528	902	1275
107-Last Johnny Quick & Superboy	82	164	246	528	902	1275

More Than Mortal #1 © Liar Comics

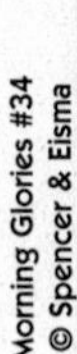
Morning Glories #34 © Spencer & Eisma

Mortie #1 © Mag. Pub.

	GD 2.0	VG 4.0	FN 6.0	VF 8.0	VF/NM 9.0	NM- 9.2

108-120: 108-Genius Jones begins; 1st c-app. (3-4/46; cont'd from Adventure Comics #102)
26 52 78 154 252 350
121-124,126: 121-123,126-Post funny animal (Jimminy & the Magic Book)-c
24 48 72 142 234 325
125-Superman c-app.w/Jimminy 82 164 246 528 902 1275
127-(Scarce)-Post-c/a 39 78 117 231 378 525
NOTE: *All issues are scarce to rare. Cover features: The Spectre-#52-55, 57-60, 62-67. Dr. Fate-#56, 61, 68-76. The Green Arrow & Speedy-#77-85, 88-97, 99, 101 (w/Dover & Clover-#98, 103). Johnny Quick-#86, 87, 100. Dover & Clover-#102, (104, 106 w/Superboy), 107, 108(w/Genius Jones), 110, 112, 114, 117, 119. Genius Jones-#109, 111, 113, 115, 116, 118, 120.* ***Baily*** *a-45, 52-on; c-52-55, 57-60, 62-67.* ***Al Capp*** *a-45(signed Koppy).* ***Ellsworth*** *c-7.* ***Creig Flessel*** *c-30, 31, 35-48(most).* ***Guardineer*** *c-47, 49, 50.* ***Kiefer*** *a-20.* ***Meskin*** *c-86, 87, 100?* ***Moldoff*** *c-51.* ***George Papp*** *c-77-85.* ***Post*** *c-121-127.* ***Vincent Sullivan*** *c-8-28, 32-34.*

MORE FUND COMICS (Benefit book for the Comic Book Legal Defense Fund)
(Also see Even More Fund Comics)
Sky Dog Press: Sept, 2003 ($10.00, B&W, trade paperback)
nn-Anthology of short stories and pin-ups by various; Hulk-c by Pérez 10.00

MORE SEYMOUR (See Seymour My Son)
Archie Publications: Oct, 1963
1-DeCarlo-a? 3 6 9 20 31 42

MORE THAN MORTAL (Also see Lady Pendragon/...)
Liar Comics: June, 1997 - No. 4, Apr, 1998 ($2.95, limited series)
Image Comics: No. 5, Dec, 1999 - No. 6, Mar, 2000 ($2.95)
1-Blue forest background-c, 1-Variant-c 4.00
1-White-c 6.00
1-2nd printing; purple sky cover 3.00
2-4: 3-Silvestri-c, 4-Two-c, one by Randy Queen 3.00
5,6: 5-1st Image Comics issue 3.00

MORE THAN MORTAL: OTHERWORLDS
Image Comics: July, 1999 - No. 4, Dec, 1999 ($2.95, limited series)
1-4-Firchow-a. 1-Two covers 3.00

MORE THAN MORTAL SAGAS
Liar Comics: Jun, 1998 - No. 3, Dec, 1998 ($2.95, limited series)
1,2-Painted art by Romano. 2-Two-c, one by Firchow 3.00
1-Variant-c by Linsner 5.00

MORE THAN MORTAL TRUTHS AND LEGENDS
Liar Comics: Aug, 1998 - No. 6, Apr, 1999 ($2.95)
1-6-Firchow-a(p) 3.00
1-Variant-c by Dan Norton 4.50

MORE TRASH FROM MAD (Annual)
E. C. Comics: 1958 - No. 12, 1969
(Note: Bonus missing = half price)
nn(1958)-8 pgs. color Mad reprint from #20 16 32 48 112 249 385
2(1959)-Market Product Labels 11 22 33 76 163 250
3(1960)-Text book covers 10 20 30 69 147 225
4(1961)-Sing Along with Mad booklet 10 20 30 69 147 225
5(1962)-Window Stickers; r/from Mad #39 8 16 24 54 102 150
6(1963)-TV Guise booklet 8 16 24 54 102 150
7(1964)-Alfred E. Neuman commemorative stamps 7 14 21 44 82 120
8(1965)-Life size poster-Alfred E. Neuman 5 10 15 35 63 90
9-12: 9,10(1966-67)-Mischief Sticker. 11(1968)-Campaign poster & bumper sticker.
12(1969)-Pocket medals 5 10 15 35 63 90
NOTE: ***Kelly Freas*** *c-1, 2, 4.* ***Mingo*** *c-3, 5-9, 12.*

MORGAN THE PIRATE (Movie)
Dell Publishing Co.: No. 1227, Sept-Nov, 1961
Four Color 1227-Photo-c 6 12 18 42 79 115

MORLOCKS
Marvel Comics: June, 2002 - No. 4, Sept, 2002 ($2.50, limited series)
1-4-Johns-s/Martinbrough-c/a 3.00

MORLOCK 2001
Atlas/Seaboard Publ.: Feb, 1975 - No. 3, July, 1975
1,2: 1-(Super-hero)-Origin & 1st app.; Milgrom-c 2 4 6 11 16 20
3-Ditko/Wrightson-a; origin The Midnight Man & The Mystery Men
3 6 9 15 22 28

MORNING GLORIES
Image Comics: Aug, 2010 - Present ($3.99/$3.50/$2.99)
1-($3.99) Nick Spencer-s/Joe Eisma-a/Rodin Esquejo-c; group cover 8.00
1-Second-Fourth printings 4.00
2-($3.50) Regular cover and white background 2nd printing 5.00
3-6-Regular covers and white background 2nd printings 4.00
7-23-($2.99) 3.00
24,25,27,28-($3.99) 4.00
26-($1.00) Start of Season Two 3.00
29-37-($3.50) 3.50
...Vol. 1 TPB (2/11, $9.99) r/#1-6 10.00

MORNINGSTAR SPECIAL
Comico: Apr, 1990 ($2.50)
1-From the Elementals; Willingham-c/a/scripts 3.00

MORTAL KOMBAT
Malibu Comics: July, 1994 - No. 6, Dec, 1994 ($2.95)
1-6: 1-Two diff. covers exist 3.00
1-Limited edition gold foil embossed-c 4.00
0 (12/94), Special Edition 1 (11/94) 3.00
Tournament Edition I12/94, $3.95), II('95)($3.95) 4.00
...: **BARAKA** ,June, 1995 ($2.95, one-shot) #1; ...**BATTLEWAVE** ,2/95 - No. 6, 7/95 , #1-6; ...**GORO, PRINCE OF PAIN** ,9/94 - No. 3, 11/94, #1-3; ...**KITANA AND MILEENA** ,8/95 , ...**KUNG LAO** ,7/95 , #1; ... **RAYDON & KANO** ,3/95 - No. 3, 5/95, #1-3: ...(all $2.95-c) 3.00
...: **U.S. SPECIAL FORCES** ,1/95 - No. 2, ($3.50), #1,2 3.50

MORTIE (Mazie's Friend; also see Flat-Top)
Magazine Publishers: Dec, 1952 - No. 4, June, 1953?
1 10 20 30 54 72 90
2-4 6 12 18 31 38 45

MORTIGAN GOTH: IMMORTALIS (See Marvel Frontier Comics Unlimited)
Marvel Comics: Sept, 1993 - No. 4, Mar, 1994 ($1.95, mini-series)
1-($2.95)-Foil-c 4.00
2-4 3.00

MORT THE DEAD TEENAGER
Marvel Comics: Nov, 1993 - No. 4, Mar, 1994 ($1.75, mini-series)
1-4 3.00

MORTY MEEKLE
Dell Publishing Co.: No. 793, May, 1957
Four Color 793 4 8 12 25 40 55

MOSES & THE TEN COMMANDMENTS (See Dell Giants)

MOSTLY WANTED
DC Comics (WildStorm): Jul, 2000 - No. 4, Nov, 2000 ($2.50, limited series)
1-4-Lobdell-s/Flores-a 3.00

MOTEL HELL (Based on the 1980 movie)
IDW Publishing: Oct, 2010 - No. 3, Dec, 2010 ($3.99, limited series)
1-3-Matt Nixon-s/Chris Moreno-a. 1,2-Bradstreet-c. 3-Moreno-c 4.00

MOTH, THE
Dark Horse Comics: Apr, 2004 - No. 4, Aug, 2004 ($2.99)
1-4-Steve Rude-c/a; Gary Martin-s 3.00
... Special (3/04, $4.95) 5.00
TPB (5/05, $12.95) r/#1-4 and Special; gallery of extras 13.00

MOTH, THE
Rude Dude Productions: May 2008 (Free Comic Book Day giveaway)
... Special Edition - Steve Rude-s/a; sketch pages 3.00

MOTHER GOOSE AND NURSERY RHYME COMICS (See Christmas With Mother Goose)
Dell Publishing Co.: No. 41, 1944 - No. 862, Nov, 1957
Four Color 41-Walt Kelly-c/a 20 40 60 135 300 465
Four Color 59, 68-Kelly c/a 16 32 48 110 243 375
Four Color 862-The Truth About..., Movie (Disney) 6 12 18 41 76 110

MOTHER TERESA OF CALCUTTA
Marvel Comics Group: 1984
1-(52 pgs.) No ads 1 3 4 6 8 10

MOTION PICTURE COMICS (See Fawcett Movie Comics)
Fawcett Publications: No. 101, 1950 - No. 114, Jan, 1953 (All-photo-c)
101- "Vanishing Westerner"; Monte Hale (1950) 15 30 45 90 140 190
102- "Code of the Silver Sage"; Rocky Lane (1/51) 15 30 45 83 124 165
103- "Covered Wagon Raid"; Rocky Lane (3/51) 15 30 45 83 124 165
104- "Vigilante Hideout"; Rocky Lane (5/51)-Book length Powell-a
15 30 45 83 124 165
105- "Red Badge of Courage"; Audie Murphy; Bob Powell-a (7/51)

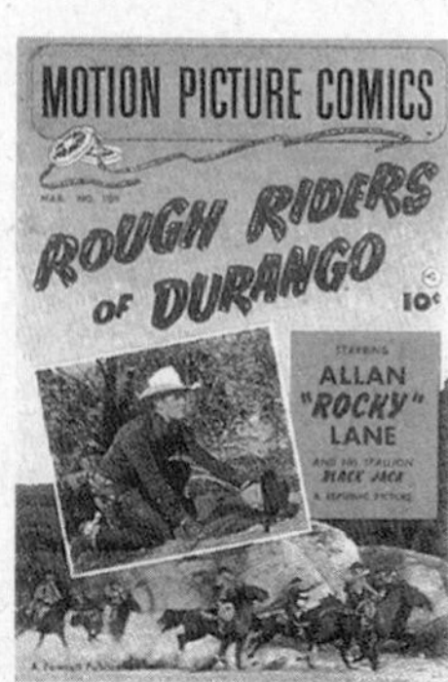

Motion Picture Comics #109 © FAW

The Movement #1 © DC

Movie Classics - Dr. Who and the Daleks © BBC

GD VG FN VF VF/NM NM-
2.0 4.0 6.0 8.0 9.0 9.2

18 36 54 105 165 225
106- "The Texas Rangers"; George Montgomery (9/51)
15 30 45 83 124 165
107- "Frisco Tornado"; Rocky Lane (11/51) 14 28 42 80 115 150
108- "Mask of the Avenger"; John Derek 12 24 36 69 97 125
109- "Rough Rider of Durango"; Rocky Lane 14 28 42 80 115 150
110- "When Worlds Collide"; George Evans-a (5/52); Williamson & Evans drew themselves in story; (also see Famous Funnies No. 72-88) 77 154 231 493 847 1200
111- "The Vanishing Outpost"; Lash LaRue 15 30 45 90 140 190
112- "Brave Warrior"; Jon Hall & Jay Silverheels 12 24 36 67 94 120
113- "Walk East on Beacon"; George Murphy; Schaffenberger-a
10 20 30 54 72 90
114- "Cripple Creek"; George Montgomery (1/53) 10 20 30 58 79 100

MOTION PICTURE FUNNIES WEEKLY (See Promotional Comics section)

MOTORHEAD (See Comic's Greatest World)
Dark Horse Comics: Aug, 1995 - No. 6, Jan, 1996 ($2.50)

1-6: Bisley-c on all. 1-Predator app. 3.00
Special 1 (3/94, $3.95, 52pgs.)-Jae Lee-c; Barb Wire, The Machine & Wolf Gang app. 4.00

MOTORMOUTH (... & Killpower #7? on)
Marvel Comics UK: June, 1992 - No. 12, May, 1993 ($1.75)

1-13: 1,2-Nick Fury app. 3-Punisher-c/story. 5,6-Nick Fury & Punisher app. 6-Cable cameo. 7-9-Cable app. 3.00

MOUNTAIN MEN (See Ben Bowie)

MOUSE MUSKETEERS (See M.G.M.'s...)

MOUSE ON THE MOON, THE (See Movie Classics)

MOVEMENT, THE
DC Comics: Jul, 2013 - No. 12 ($2.99)

1-11: 1-Gail Simone-s/Freddie Williams-a/Amanda Conner-c. 2-4-Rainmaker app. 9,10-Batgirl app. 3.00

MOVIE CARTOONS
DC Comics: Dec, 1944 (cover only ashcan)

nn-Ashcan comic, not distributed to newsstands, only for in house use. Covers were produced, but not the rest of the book. A copy sold in 2006 for $500.

MOVIE CLASSICS
Dell Publishing Co.: Apr, 1956; May-Jul, 1962 - Dec, 1969

(Before 1963, most movie adaptations were part of the 4-Color series)
(Disney movie adaptations after 1970 are in Walt Disney Showcase)

Around the World Under the Sea 12-030-612 (12/66) 3 6 9 19 30 40
Bambi 3(4/56)-Disney; r/4-Color #186 4 8 12 23 37 50
Battle of the Bulge 12-056-606 (6/66) 3 6 9 20 31 42
Beach Blanket Bingo 12-058-509 6 12 18 40 73 105
Bon Voyage 01-068-212 (12/62)-Disney; photo-c 3 6 9 21 33 45
Castilian, The 12-110-401 3 6 9 19 30 40
Cat, The 12-109-612 (12/66) 3 6 9 18 28 38
Cheyenne Autumn 12-112-506 (4-6/65) 5 10 15 31 53 75
Circus World, Samuel Bronston's 12-115-411; John Wayne app.; John Wayne photo-c
8 16 24 56 108 160
Countdown 12-150-710 (10/67)-James Caan photo-c 3 6 9 20 31 42
Creature, The 1 (12-142-302) (12-2/62-63) 8 16 24 55 105 155
Creature, The 12-142-410 (10/64) 5 10 15 30 50 70
David Ladd's Life Story 12-173-212 (10-12/62)-Photo-c
6 12 18 40 73 105
Die, Monster, Die 12-175-603 (3/66)-Photo-c 5 10 15 33 57 80
Dirty Dozen 12-180-710 (10/67) 4 8 12 27 44 60
Dr. Who & the Daleks 12-190-612 (12/66)-Peter Cushing photo-c; 1st U.S. app. of Dr. Who
10 20 30 66 138 210
Dracula 12-231-212 (10-12/62) 8 16 24 51 96 140
El Dorado 12-240-710 (10/67)-John Wayne; photo-c 10 20 30 64 132 200
Ensign Pulver 12-257-410 (8-10/64) 3 6 9 18 28 38
Frankenstein 12-283-305 (3-5/63)(see Frankenstein 8-10/64 for 2nd printing)
8 16 24 52 99 145
Great Race, The 12-299-603 (3/66)-Natallie Wood, Tony Curtis photo-c
4 8 12 27 44 60
Hallelujah Trail, The 12-307-602 (2/66) (Shows 1/66 inside); Burt Lancaster, Lee Remick photo-c 5 10 15 30 50 70
Hatari 12-340-301 (1/63)-John Wayne 7 14 21 44 82 120
Horizontal Lieutenant, The 01-348-210 (10/62) 3 6 9 18 28 38
Incredible Mr. Limpet, The 12-370-408; Don Knotts photo-c
5 10 15 30 50 70
Jack the Giant Killer 12-374-301 (1/63) 7 14 21 44 82 120
Jason & the Argonauts 12-376-310 (8-10/63)-Photo-c
8 16 24 52 99 145
Lancelot & Guinevere 12-416-310 (10/63) 5 10 15 30 50 70
Lawrence 12-426-308 (8/63)-Story of Lawrence of Arabia; movie ad on back-c; not exactly like movie 5 10 15 30 50 70
Lion of Sparta 12-439-301 (1/63) 3 6 9 21 33 45
Mad Monster Party 12-460-801 (9/67)-Based on Kurtzman's screenplay
8 16 24 51 96 140
Magic Sword, The 01-496-209 (9/62) 5 10 15 31 53 75
Masque of the Red Death 12-490-410 (8-10/64)-Vincent Price photo-c
5 10 15 35 63 90
Maya 12-495-612 (12/66)-Clint Walker & Jay North part photo-c
4 8 12 23 37 50
McHale's Navy 12-500-412 (10-12/64) 4 8 12 27 44 60
Merrill's Marauders 12-510-301 (1/63)-Photo-c 3 6 9 18 28 38
Mouse on the Moon, The 12-530-312 (10/12/63)-Photo-c
3 6 9 21 33 45
Mummy, The 12-537-211 (9-11/62) 2 versions with different back-c
8 16 24 54 102 150
Music Man, The 12-538-301 (1/63) 3 6 9 19 30 40
Naked Prey, The 12-545-612 (12/66)-Photo-c 5 10 15 31 53 75
Night of the Grizzly, The 12-558-612 (12/66)-Photo-c 3 6 9 21 33 45
None But the Brave 12-565-506 (4-6/65) 5 10 15 31 53 75
Operation Bikini 12-597-310 (10/63)-Photo-c 3 6 9 19 30 40
Operation Crossbow 12-590-512 (10-12/65) 3 6 9 19 30 40
Prince & the Pauper, The 01-654-207 (5-7/62)-Disney
3 6 9 21 33 45
Raven, The 12-680-309 (9/63)-Vincent Price photo-c 6 12 18 37 66 95
Ring of Bright Water 01-701-910 (10/69) (inside shows #12-701-909)
3 6 9 21 33 45
Runaway, The 12-707-412 (10-12/64) 3 6 9 18 28 38
Santa Claus Conquers the Martians #? (1964)-Photo-c
9 18 27 58 114 170
Santa Claus Conquers the Martians 12-725-603 (3/66, 12¢)-Reprints 1964 issue; photo-c 6 12 18 40 73 105
Another version given away with a Golden Record, SLP 170, nn, no price (3/66)-Complete with record 10 20 30 69 147 225
Six Black Horses 12-750-301 (1/63)-Photo-c 3 6 9 19 30 40
Ski Party 12-743-511 (9-11/65)-Frankie Avalon photo-c; photo inside-c; Adkins-a
4 8 12 28 47 65
Smoky 12-746-702 (2/67) 3 6 9 18 28 38
Sons of Katie Elder 12-748-511 (9-11/65); John Wayne app.; photo-c
10 20 30 64 132 200
Tales of Terror 12-793-302 (2/63)-Evans-a 5 10 15 31 53 75
Three Stooges Meet Hercules 01-828-208 (8/62)-Photo-c
8 16 24 51 96 140
Tomb of Ligeia 12-830-506 (4-6/65) 5 10 15 31 53 75
Treasure Island 01-845-211 (7-9/62)-Disney; r/4-Color #624
3 6 9 19 30 40
Twice Told Tales (Nathaniel Hawthorne) 12-840-401 (11-1/63-64); Vincent Price photo-c 5 10 15 33 57 80
Two on a Guillotine 12-850-506 (4-6/65) 3 6 9 21 33 45
Valley of Gwangi 01-880-912 (12/69) 8 16 24 52 99 145
War Gods of the Deep 12-900-509 (7-9/65) 3 6 9 19 30 40
War Wagon, The 12-533-709 (9/67); John Wayne app.
7 14 21 46 86 125
Who's Minding the Mint? 12-924-708 (8/67) 3 6 9 18 28 38
Wolfman, The 12-922-308 (6-8/63) 8 16 24 51 96 140
Wolfman, The 1(12-922-410)(8-10/64)-2nd printing; r/#12-922-308
4 8 12 22 35 48
Zulu 12-950-410 (8-10/64)-Photo-c 6 12 18 41 76 110

MOVIE COMICS (See Cinema Comics Herald & Fawcett Movie Comics)

MOVIE COMICS
National Periodical Publications/Picture Comics: April, 1939 - No. 6, Sept-Oct, 1939 (Most all photo-c)

1- "Gunga Din", "Son of Frankenstein", "The Great Man Votes", "Fisherman's Wharf", & "Scouts to the Rescue" part 1; Wheelan "Minute Movies" begin
366 732 1098 2562 4481 6400
2- "Stagecoach", "The Saint Strikes Back", "King of the Turf","Scouts to the Rescue" part 2, "Arizona Legion", Andy Devine photo-c 252 504 756 1613 2757 3900
3- "East Side of Heaven", "Mystery in the White Room", "Four Feathers", "Mexican Rose" with Gene Autry, "Spirit of Culver", "Many Secrets", "The Mikado" (1st Gene Autry photo cover) 177 354 531 1124 1937 2750

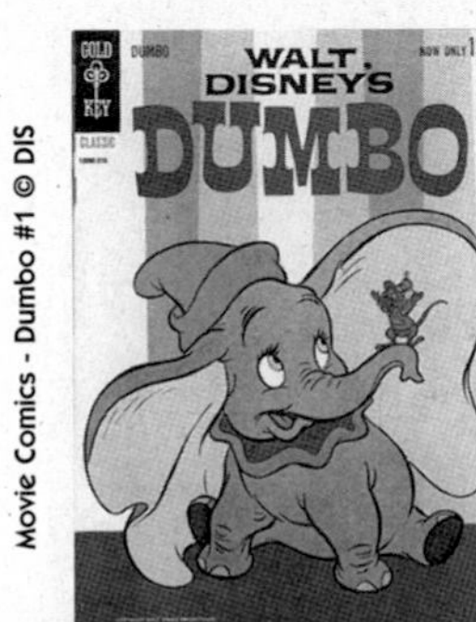

Movie Comics - Dumbo #1 © DIS

Movie Comics - Lord Jim © Columbia

Movie Comics - Merlin Jones © DIS

GD 2.0 | VG 4.0 | FN 6.0 | VF 8.0 | VF/NM 9.0 | NM- 9.2

4- "Captain Fury", Gene Autry in "Blue Montana Skies", "Streets of N.Y." with Jackie Cooper, "Oregon Trail" part 1 with Johnny Mack Brown, "Big Town Czar" with Barton MacLane, & "Star Reporter" with Warren Hull 148 296 444 947 1624 2300

5- "The Man in the Iron Mask", "Five Came Back", "Wolf Call", "The Girl & the Gambler", "The House of Fear", "The Family Next Door", "Oregon Trail" part 2 161 322 483 1030 1765 2500

6- "The Phantom Creeps", "Chumps at Oxford", & "The Oregon Trail" part 3; 2nd Robot-c 206 412 618 1318 2259 3200

NOTE: *Above books contain many original movie stills with dialogue from movie scripts. All issues are scarce.*

MOVIE COMICS

Fiction House Magazines: Dec, 1946 - No. 4, 1947

1-Big Town (by Lubbers), Johnny Danger begin; Celardo-a; Mitzi of the Movies by Fran Hopper 41 82 123 256 428 600

2-(2/47)- "White Tie & Tails" with William Bendix; Mitzi of the Movies begins; Matt Baker-a 31 62 93 186 303 420

3-(6/47)-Andy Hardy starring Mickey Rooney 31 62 93 186 303 420

4-Mitzi In Hollywood by Matt Baker; Merton of the Movies with Red Skelton; Yvonne DeCarlo & George Brent in "Slave Girl" 39 78 117 231 378 525

MOVIE COMICS

Gold Key/Whitman: Oct, 1962 - 1984

Alice in Wonderland 10144-503 (3/65)-Disney; partial reprint of 4-Color #331 3 6 9 21 33 45

Alice In Wonderland #1 (Whitman pre-pack, 3/84) 2 4 6 10 14 18

Aristocats, The 1 (30045-103)(3/71)-Disney; with pull-out poster (25¢) (No poster = half price) 6 12 18 40 73 105

Bambi 1 (10087-309)(9/63)-Disney; r/4-C #186 4 8 12 23 37 50

Bambi 2 (10087-607)(7/66)-Disney; r/4-C #186 3 6 9 19 30 40

Beneath the Planet of the Apes 30044-012 (12/70)-with pull-out poster; photo-c (No poster = half price) 8 16 24 54 102 150

Big Red 10026-211 (11/62)-Disney; photo-c 3 6 9 19 30 40

Big Red 10026-503 (3/65)-Disney; reprints 10026-211; photo-c 3 6 9 16 23 30

Blackbeard's Ghost 10222-806 (6/68)-Disney 3 6 9 18 28 38

Bullwhip Griffin 10181-706 (6/67)-Disney; Spiegle-a; photo-c 3 6 9 21 33 45

Captain Sindbad 10077-309 (9/63)-Manning-a; photo-c 5 10 15 35 63 90

Chitty Chitty Bang Bang 1 (30038-902)(2/69)-with pull-out poster; Disney; photo-c (No poster = half price) 6 12 18 37 66 95

Cinderella 10152-508 (8/65)-Disney; r/4-C #786 4 8 12 25 40 55

Darby O'Gill & the Little People 10251-001(1/70)-Disney; reprints 4-Color #1024 (Toth-a); photo-c 4 8 12 28 47 65

Dumbo 1 (10090-310)(10/63)-Disney; r/4-C #668 3 6 9 20 31 42

Emil & the Detectives 10120-502 (11/64)-Disney; photo-c & back-c photo pin-up 3 6 9 19 30 40

Escapade in Florence 1 (10043-301)(1/63)-Disney; starring Annette Funicello 7 14 21 44 82 120

Fall of the Roman Empire 10118-407 (7/64); Sophia Loren photo-c 4 8 12 23 37 50

Fantastic Voyage 10178-702 (2/67)-Wood/Adkins-a; photo-c 5 10 15 33 57 80

55 Days at Peking 10081-309 (9/63)-Photo-c 3 6 9 19 30 40

Fighting Prince of Donegal, The 10193-701 (1/67)-Disney 3 6 9 18 28 38

First Men in the Moon 10132-503 (3/65)-Fred Fredericks-a; photo-c 4 8 12 23 37 50

Gay Purr-ee 30017-301(1/63, 84 pgs.) 5 10 15 30 50 70

Gnome Mobile, The 10207-710 (10/67)-Disney; Walter Brennan photo-c & back-c photo pin-up 4 8 12 21 33 45

Goodbye, Mr. Chips 10246-006 (6/70)-Peter O'Toole photo-c 3 6 9 19 30 40

Happiest Millionaire, The 10221-804 (4/68)-Disney 3 6 9 21 33 45

Hey There, It's Yogi Bear 10122-409 (9/64)-Hanna-Barbera 6 12 18 37 66 95

Horse Without a Head, The 10109-401 (1/64)-Disney 3 6 9 18 28 38

How the West Was Won 10074-307 (7/63)-Based on the L'Amour novel; Tufts-a 4 8 12 27 44 60

In Search of the Castaways 10048-303 (3/63)-Disney; Hayley Mills photo-c 6 12 18 37 66 95

Jungle Book, The 1 (6022-801)(1/68-Whitman)-Disney; large size (10x13-1/2"); 59¢ 6 12 18 37 66 95

Jungle Book, The 1 (30033-803)(3/68, 68 pgs.)-Disney; same contents as Whitman #1 4 8 12 23 37 50

Jungle Book, The 1 (6/78, $1.00 tabloid) 3 6 9 16 23 30

Jungle Book (7/84)-r/Giant; Whitman pre-pack 2 4 6 10 14 18

Kidnapped 10080-306 (6/63)-Disney; reprints 4-Color #1101; photo-c 3 6 9 19 30 40

King Kong 30036-809(9/68-68 pgs.)-painted-c 4 8 12 25 40 55

King Kong nn-Whitman Treasury($1.00, 68 pgs.,1968), same cover as Gold Key issue 5 10 15 31 53 75

King Kong 11299(#1-786, 10x13-1/4", 68 pgs., $1.00, 1978) 3 6 9 17 26 35

Lady and the Tramp 10042-301 (1/63)-Disney; r/4-Color #629 3 6 9 20 31 42

Lady and the Tramp 1 (1967-Giant; 25¢)-Disney; reprints part of Dell #1 5 10 15 31 53 75

Lady and the Tramp 2 (10042-203)(3/72)-Disney; r/4-Color #629 3 6 9 16 23 30

Legend of Lobo, The 1 (10059-303)(3/63)-Disney; photo-c 3 6 9 16 23 30

Lt. Robin Crusoe, U.S.N. 10191-610 (10/66)-Disney; Dick Van Dyke photo-c & back-c photo pin-up 3 6 9 17 26 35

Lion, The 10035-301 (1/63)-Photo-c 3 6 9 16 24 32

Lord Jim 10156-509 (9/65)-Photo-c 3 6 9 16 24 32

Love Bug, The 10237-906 (6/69)-Disney; Buddy Hackett photo-c 4 8 12 21 33 45

Mary Poppins 10136-501 (1/65)-Disney; photo-c 5 10 15 30 50 70

Mary Poppins 30023-501 (1/65-68 pgs.)-Disney; photo-c 6 12 18 41 76 110

McLintock 10110-403 (3/64); John Wayne app.; John Wayne & Maureen O'Hara photo-c 10 20 30 66 138 210

Merlin Jones as the Monkey's Uncle 10115-510 (10/65)-Disney; Annette Funicello front/back photo-c 5 10 15 34 60 85

Miracle of the White Stallions, The 10065-306 (6/63)-Disney 3 6 9 18 28 38

Misadventures of Merlin Jones, The 10115-405 (5/64)-Disney; Annette Funicello photo front/back-c 5 10 15 34 60 85

Moon-Spinners, The 10124-410 (10/64)-Disney; Hayley Mills photo-c 6 12 18 37 66 95

Mutiny on the Bounty 1 (10040-302)(2/63)-Marlon Brando photo-c 3 6 9 21 33 45

Nikki, Wild Dog of the North 10141-412 (12/64)-Disney; reprints 4-Color #1226 3 6 9 16 23 30

Old Yeller 10168-601 (1/66)-Disney; reprints 4-Color #869; photo-c 3 6 9 16 23 30

One Hundred & One Dalmations 1 (10247-002) (2/70)-Disney; reprints Four Color #1183 3 6 9 17 26 35

Peter Pan 1 (10086-309)(9/63)-Disney; reprints Four Color #442 3 6 9 20 31 42

Peter Pan 2 (10086-909)(9/69)-Disney; reprints Four Color #442 3 6 9 16 23 30

Peter Pan 1 (3/84)-r/4-Color #442; Whitman pre-pack 2 4 6 11 16 20

P.T. 109 10123-409 (9/64)-John F. Kennedy 4 8 12 28 47 65

Rio Conchos 10143-503(3/65) 3 6 9 21 33 45

Robin Hood 10163-506 (6/65)-Disney; reprints Four Color #413 3 6 9 16 24 32

Shaggy Dog & the Absent-Minded Professor 30032-708 (8/67-Giant, 68 pgs.) Disney; reprints 4-Color #985,1199 5 10 15 30 50 70

Sleeping Beauty 1 (30042-009)(9/70)-Disney; reprints Four Color #973; with pull-out poster (No poster = half price) 6 12 18 37 66 95

Snow White & the Seven Dwarfs 1 (10091-310)(10/63)-Disney; reprints Four Color #382 3 6 9 19 30 40

Snow White & the Seven Dwarfs 10091-709 (9/67)-Disney; reprints Four Color #382 3 6 9 16 23 30

Snow White & the Seven Dwarfs 90091-204 (2/84)-Reprints Four Color #382; Whitman pre-pack 2 4 6 11 16 20

Son of Flubber 1 (10057-304)(4/63)-Disney; sequel to "The Absent-Minded Professor" 3 6 9 21 33 45

Summer Magic 10076-309 (9/63)-Disney; Hayley Mills photo-c; Manning-a 6 12 18 37 66 95

Swiss Family Robinson 10236-904 (4/69)-Disney; reprints Four Color #1156; photo-c 3 6 9 17 26 35

Sword in the Stone, The 30019-402 (2/64-Giant, 68 pgs.)-Disney (see March of Comics #258 & Wart and the Wizard 6 12 18 37 66 95

That Darn Cat 10171-602 (2/66)-Disney; Hayley Mills photo-c 6 12 18 37 66 95

Those Magnificent Men in Their Flying Machines 10162-510 (10/65); photo-c

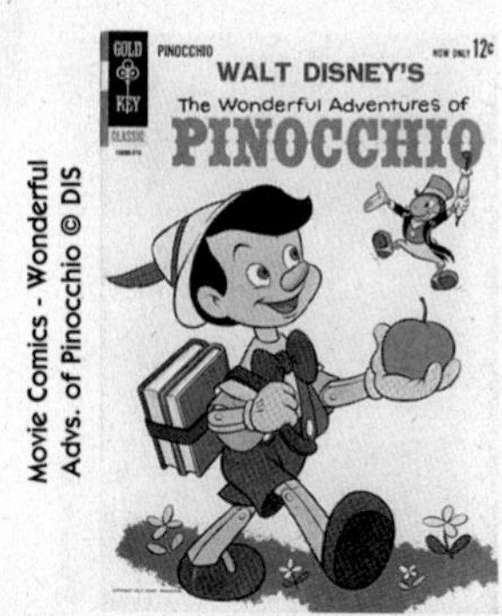

Movie Comics - Wonderful Advs. of Pinocchio © DIS

Movie Love #12 © FF

Ms. Marvel (2014 series) #1 © MAR

GD 2.0 VG 4.0 FN 6.0 VF 8.0 VF/NM 9.0 NM- 9.2

3 6 9 19 30 40
Three Stooges in Orbit 30016-211 (11/62-Giant, 32 pgs.)-All photos from movie; stiff-photo-c
8 16 24 56 108 160
Tiger Walks, A 10117-406 (6/64)-Disney; Torres?, Tufts-a; photo-c
4 8 12 23 37 50
Toby Tyler 10142-502 (2/65)-Disney; reprints Four Color #1092; photo-c
3 6 9 17 26 35
Treasure Island 1 (10200-703)(3/67)-Disney; reprints Four Color #624; photo-c
3 6 9 16 23 30
20,000 Leagues Under the Sea 1 (10095-312)(12/63)-Disney; reprints Four Color #614
3 6 9 17 26 35
Wonderful Adventures of Pinocchio, The 1 (10089-310)(10/63)-Disney; reprints Four Color #545 (see Wonderful Advs. of...) 3 6 9 20 31 42
Wonderful Adventures of Pinocchio, The 10089-109 (9/71)-Disney; reprints Four Color #545
3 6 9 16 23 30
Wonderful World of the Brothers Grimm 1 (10008-210)(10/62)
4 8 12 27 44 60
X, the Man with the X-Ray Eyes 10083-309 (9/63)-Ray Milland photo on-c
6 12 18 41 76 110
Yellow Submarine 35000-902 (2/69-Giant, 68 pgs.)-With pull-out poster;
The Beatles cartoon movie; Paul S. Newman-s 20 40 60 138 307 475
Without poster 8 16 24 56 108 160

MOVIE FABLES
DC Comics: Dec, 1944 (cover only ashcan)

nn-Ashcan comic, not distributed to newsstands, only for in house use. Covers were produced, but not the rest of the book. A copy sold in 2006 for $500.

MOVIE GEMS
DC Comics: Dec, 1944 (cover only ashcan)

nn-Ashcan comic, not distributed to newsstands, only for in house use. Covers were produced, but not the rest of the book. A copy sold in 2006 for $500.

MOVIE LOVE (Also see Personal Love)
Famous Funnies: Feb, 1950 - No. 22, Aug, 1953 (All photo-c)

1-Dick Powell, Evelyn Keyes, & Mickey Rooney photo-c
20 40 60 120 195 270
2-Myrna Loy photo-c 13 26 39 74 105 135
3-7,9: 6-Ricardo Montalban photo-c. 9-Gene Tierney, John Lund, Glenn Ford, & Rhonda Fleming photo-c. 12 24 36 69 97 125
8-Williamson/Frazetta-a, 6 pgs. 49 98 147 309 522 735
10-Frazetta-a, 6 pgs. 50 100 150 315 533 750
11,14-16: 14-Janet Leigh photo-c 12 24 36 67 94 120
12-Dean Martin & Jerry Lewis photo-c (12/51, pre-dates Advs. of Dean Martin & Jerry Lewis comic) 22 44 66 128 209 290
13-Ronald Reagan photo-c with 1 pg. biog. 29 58 87 172 281 390
17-Leslie Caron & Ralph Meeker photo-c; 1 pg. Frazetta ad
12 24 36 69 97 125
18-22: 19-John Derek photo-c. 20-Donald O'Connor & Debbie Reynolds photo-c. 21-Paul Henreid & Patricia Medina photo-c. 22-John Payne & Coleen Gray photo-c
11 22 33 64 90 115
NOTE: *Each issue has a full-length movie adaptation with photo covers.*

MOVIE MONSTERS (Magazine)
Atlas/Seaboard: Dec, 1974 - No. 4, Aug, 1975 (B&W; Film, photo & article magazine)

1-(84 pages) Planet of the Apes, King Kong, Sindbad & Harryhausen, Christopher Lee Dracula, Star Trek, Werewolf, Creature from the Black Lagoon, Hammer's Mummy, Gorgo, & Exorcist 4 8 12 23 37 50
2-(2/1975) 2001: Planet of the Apes-c; 2001: A Space Odyssey; Doc Savage; Frankenstein; Rodan; One Million Years BC; (lower print run) 4 8 12 23 37 50
3-(4/1975) Phantom of the Opera-c; Wolfman, Godzilla, Boris Karloff, Batman, Forbidden Planet, Jack the Giant Killer 4 8 12 23 37 50
4-(8/1975) Thing, Flash Gordon, Lon Chaney Jr., Lost Worlds, Loch Ness Monster, Day the Earth Stood Still, Star Trek 4 8 12 23 37 50

MOVIE THRILLERS (Movie)
Magazine Enterprises: 1949

1-Adaptation of "Rope of Sand" w/Burt Lancaster; Burt Lancaster photo-c
28 56 84 165 270 375

MOVIE TOWN ANIMAL ANTICS (Formerly Animal Antics; becomes Raccoon Kids #52 on)
National Periodical Publ.: No. 24, Jan-Feb, 1950 - No. 51, July-Aug, 1954

24-Raccoon Kids continue 12 24 36 67 94 120
25-51 10 20 30 54 72 90
NOTE: ***Sheldon Mayer** a-28-33, 35, 37-41, 43, 44, 47, 49-51.*

MOVIE TUNES COMICS (Formerly Animated...; Frankie No. 4 on)

Marvel Comics (MgPC): No. 3, Fall, 1946
3-Super Rabbit, Krazy Krow, Silly Seal & Ziggy Pig 16 32 48 94 147 200

MOWGLI JUNGLE BOOK (Rudyard Kipling's...)
Dell Publ. Co.: No. 487, Aug-Oct, 1953 - No. 620, Apr, 1955

Four Color 487 (#1) 5 10 15 35 63 90
Four Color 582 (8/54), 620 5 10 15 30 50 70

MR. (See Mister)

M. REX
Image Comics: July, 1999 - No. 2, Dec, 1999 ($2.95)

Preview ($5.00) B&W pages and sketchbook; Rouleau-a 5.00
1,2-($2.95) 1-Joe Kelly-s/Rouleau-a/Anacleto-c. 2-Rouleau-c 3.00

MS. MARVEL (Also see The Avengers #183)
Marvel Comics Group: Jan, 1977 - No. 23, Apr, 1979

1-1st app. Ms. Marvel; Scorpion app. in #1,2 6 12 18 38 69 100
2-10: 2-Origin. 5-Vision app. 6-10-(Reg. 30¢-c). 10-Last 30¢ issue
2 4 6 9 12 15
6-10-(35¢-c variants, limited dist.)(6/77) 5 10 15 30 50 70
11-15,19-23: 19-Capt. Marvel app. 20-New costume. 23-Vance Astro (leader of the Guardians) app. 1 3 4 6 8 10
16-1st brief app. Mystique 5 10 15 33 57 80
17-Brief app. Mystique 4 8 12 23 37 50
18-1st full app. Mystique; Avengers x-over 5 10 15 31 53 75
NOTE: ***Austin** c-14i, 16i, 17i, 22i. **Buscema** a-1-3p; c(p)-2, 4, 6, 7, 15. **Infantino** a-14p, 19p. **Gil Kane** c-8. **Mooney** a-4-8p, 13p, 15-18p. **Starlin** c-12.*

MS. MARVEL (Also see New Avengers)
Marvel Comics: May, 2006 - No. 50, Apr, 2010 ($2.99)

1-24: 1-Cho-c/Reed-s/De La Torre-a; Stilt-Man app. 4,5-Dr. Strange app. 6,7-Araña app. 3.00
1-Variant cover by Michael Turner 5.00
25-($3.99) Two covers by Horn and Dodson; Secret Invasion 4.00
26-49: 26-31-Secret Invasion. 34-Spider-Man app. 35-Dark Reign. 37-Carol explodes. 39,40,46,48,49-Takeda-a. 41-Carol returns. 47-Spider-Man app. 3.00
50-($3.99) Mystique and Captain Marvel app.; Takeda & Oliver-a 4.00
... Annual 1 (11/08, $3.99) Spider-Man app.; Horn-c 4.00
... Special (3/07, $2.99) Reed-s/Camuncoli-a/c 3.00
... Storyteller (1/09, $2.99) Reed-s/Camuncoli-a/c 3.00
... Vol. 1: Best of the Best HC (2006, $19.99) r/#1-5 & Giant-Size Ms. Marvel #1 20.00
... Vol. 1: Best of the Best SC (2007, $14.99) r/#1-5 & Giant-Size Ms. Marvel #1 15.00
... Vol. 2: Civil War HC (2007, $19.99) r/#6-10 & Ms. Marvel Special #1 20.00
... Vol. 2: Civil War SC (2007, $14.99) r/#6-10 & Ms. Marvel Special #1 15.00
... Vol. 3: Operation Lightning Storm HC (2007, $19.99) r/#11-17 20.00
... Vol. 4: Monster Smash HC (2008, $19.99) r/#18-24 20.00

MS. MARVEL
Marvel Comics: Apr, 2014 - Present ($2.99)

1,2: 1-Intro. Kamala Khan; G. Willow Wilson-s/Adrian Alphona-a; Pichelli-c 3.00

MS. MYSTIC
Pacific Comics: Oct, 1982 - No. 2, Feb, 1984 ($1.00/$1.50)

1,2: Neal Adams-c/a/script. 1-Origin; intro Erth, Ayre, Fyre & Watr 5.00

MS. MYSTIC
Continuity Comics: 1988 - No. 9, May, 1992 ($2.00)

1-9: 1,2-Reprint Pacific Comics issues 3.00

MS. MYSTIC
Continunity Comics: V2#1, Oct, 1993 - V2#4, Jan, 1994 ($2.50)

V2#1-4: 1-Adams-c(i)/part-i. 2-4-Embossed-c. 2-Nebres part-i. 3-Adams-c(i)/plot. 4-Adams-c(p)/plot 3.00

MS. MYSTIC DEATHWATCH 2000 (Ms. Mystic #3)
Continuity: May, 1993 - No. 3, Aug, 1993 ($2.50)

1-3-Bagged w/card; Adams plots 3.00

MS. TREE QUARTERLY / SPECIAL
DC Comics: Summer, 1990 -No. 10, 1992 ($3.95/$3.50, 84 pgs, mature)

1-10: 1-Midnight story; Batman text story, Grell-a. 2,3-Midnight stories; The Butcher text stories 4.00
NOTE: ***Cowan** c-2. **Grell** c-1, 6. **Infantino** a-8.*

MS. TREE'S THRILLING DETECTIVE ADVENTURES (Ms. Tree #4 on; also see The Best of Ms. Tree)(Baxter paper #4-9) (See Eclipse Magazine #1 for 1st app.)
Eclipse Comics/Aardvark-Vanaheim 10-18/Renegade Press 19 on:
2/83 - #9, 7/84; #10, 8/84 - #18, 5/85; #19, 6/85 - #50, 6/89

1 4.00

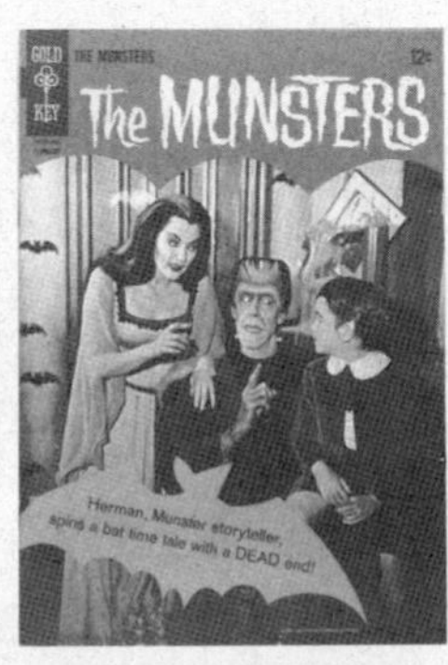

The Munsters #11 © GK

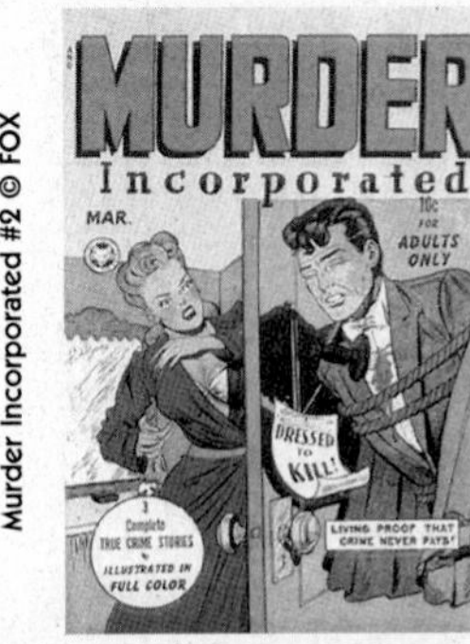

Murder Incorporated #2 © FOX

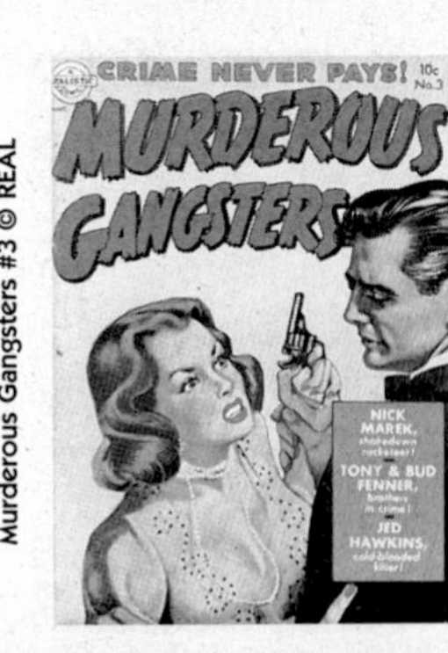

Murderous Gangsters #3 © REAL

	GD 2.0	VG 4.0	FN 6.0	VF 8.0	VF/NM 9.0	NM- 9.2
2-49: 2-Schythe begins. 9-Last Eclipse & last color issue. 10,11-two-tone						3.00
50-Contains flexi-disc ($3.95, 52 pgs.)						4.00
Ms. Tree 3-D 1 (Renegade, 8/85)-With glasses; Mike Mist app.						3.00
Summer Special 1 (8/86)						3.00
1950s Three-Dimensional Crime (7/87, no glasses)-Johnny Dynamite in 3-D						3.00

NOTE; ***Miller*** *pin-up 1-4. Johnny Dynamite-r begin #36 by* ***Morisi.***

MS. VICTORY SPECIAL(Also see Capt. Paragon & Femforce)
Americomics: Jan, 1985 (nd)

	GD	VG	FN	VF	VF/NM	NM-
1						3.00

MUCHA LUCHA (Based on Kids WB animated TV show)
DC Comics: Jun, 2003 - No. 3, Aug, 2003 ($2.25, limited series)

	GD	VG	FN	VF	VF/NM	NM-
1-3-Rikochet, Buena Girl and The Flea app.						3.00

MUDMAN
Image Comics: Nov, 2011 - Present ($3.50)

	GD	VG	FN	VF	VF/NM	NM-
1-6-Paul Grist-s/a						3.50

MUGGSY MOUSE (Also see Tick Tock Tales)
Magazine Enterprises: 1951 - No. 3, 1951; No. 4, 1954 - No. 5, 1954; 1963

	GD	VG	FN	VF	VF/NM	NM-
1(A-1 #33)	11	22	33	60	83	105
2(A-1 #36)-Racist-c	15	30	45	85	130	175
3(A-1 #39), 4(A-1 #95), 5(A-1 #99)	8	16	24	44	57	70
Super Reprint #14(1963), I.W. Reprint #1,2 (nd)	2	4	6	8	11	14

MUGGY-DOO, BOY CAT
Stanhall Publ.: July, 1953 - No. 4, Jan, 1954

	GD	VG	FN	VF	VF/NM	NM-
1-Funny animal; Irving Spector-a	9	18	27	52	69	85
2-4	6	12	18	28	34	40
Super Reprint #12('63), 16('64)	2	4	6	8	11	14

MULLKON EMPIRE (See John Jake's...)

MUMMY, THE (See Universal Presents... under Dell Giants & Movie Classics)

MUMMY, THE: THE RISE AND FALL OF XANGO'S AX (Based on the Brendan Fraser movies)
IDW Publishing: Apr, 2008 - No. 4, July, 2008 ($3.99, limited series)

	GD	VG	FN	VF	VF/NM	NM-
1-4-Prequel to '08 movie The Mummy: Tomb of the Dragon Emperor; Stephen Mooney-a						4.00

MUNDEN'S BAR ANNUAL
First Comics: Apr, 1988; 1989 ($2.95/$5.95)

	GD	VG	FN	VF	VF/NM	NM-
1-($2.95)-r/from Grimjack; Fish Police story; Ordway-c						3.00
2-($5.95)-Teenage Mutant Ninja Turtles app.						6.00

MUNSTERS, THE (TV)
Gold Key: Jan, 1965 - No. 16, Jan, 1968 (All photo-c)

	GD	VG	FN	VF	VF/NM	NM-
1 (10134-501)	16	32	48	110	243	375
2	9	18	27	59	117	175
3-5	8	16	24	51	96	140
6-16	7	14	21	44	82	120

MUNSTERS, THE (TV)
TV Comics!: Aug, 1997 - No. 4 ($2.95, B&W)

	GD	VG	FN	VF	VF/NM	NM-
1-4-All have photo-c						3.00
1,4-($7.95)-Variant-c						8.00
2-Variant-c w/Beverly Owens as Marilyn						3.00
Special Comic Con Ed. (7/97, $9.95)						10.00

MUPPET... (TV)
BOOM! Studios

	GD	VG	FN	VF	VF/NM	NM-
... King Arthur 1-4 (12/09 - No. 4, 3/10, $2.99) Benjamin & Storck-s/Alvarez-a; 2 covers						3.00
... Peter Pan 1-4 (8/09 - No. 4, 11/09, $2.99) Randolph-s/Mebberson-a; multiple covers						3.00
... Robin Hood 1-4 (4/09 - No. 4, 7/09, $2.99) Beedle-s/Villavert Jr.-a; multiple covers						3.00
... Sherlock Holmes 1-4 (8/10 - No. 4, 11/10, $2.99) Storck-s/Mebberson-a/c						3.00
... Snow White 1-4 (4/10 - No. 4, 7/10, $2.99) Snider & Storck-s/Paroline-a; 2 covers						3.00

MUPPET BABIES, THE (TV)(See Star Comics Magazine)
Marvel Comics (Star Comics)/Marvel #18 on: Aug, 1985 - No. 26, July, 1989 (Children's book)

	GD	VG	FN	VF	VF/NM	NM-
1-26						5.00

MUPPETS (The Four Seasons)
Marvel Worldwide: Sept, 2012 - No. 4, Dec, 2012 ($2.99, limited series)

	GD	VG	FN	VF	VF/NM	NM-
1-4-Roger Landridge-s/a						3.00

MUPPET SHOW, THE (TV)
BOOM! Studios: Mar, 2009 - No. 4, Jun, 2009 ($2.99, limited series)

	GD	VG	FN	VF	VF/NM	NM-
1-4-Roger Landridge-s/a; multiple covers						3.00
...: The Treasure of Peg Leg Wilson (7/09 - No. 4, 10/09) 1-4-Landridge-s/a; multiple-c						3.00

MUPPET SHOW COMIC BOOK, THE (TV)
BOOM! Studios: No. 0, Nov, 2009 - No. 11, Oct, 2010 ($2.99)

	GD	VG	FN	VF	VF/NM	NM-
0-11: 0-3-Roger Landridge-s/a; multiple covers. 0-Paroline-a; Pigs in Space						3.00

MUPPETS TAKE MANHATTAN, THE
Marvel Comics (Star Comics): Nov, 1984 - No. 3, Jan, 1985

	GD	VG	FN	VF	VF/NM	NM-
1-3-Movie adapt. r-/Marvel Super Special						4.00

MURCIELAGA, SHE-BAT
Heroic Publishing: Jan, 1993 - No. 2, 1993 (B&W)

	GD	VG	FN	VF	VF/NM	NM-
1-($1.50, 28 pgs.)						3.00
2-($2.95, 36 pgs.)-Coated-c						3.00

MURDER CAN BE FUN
Slave Labor Graphics: Feb, 1996 - No. 12 ($2.95, B&W)

	GD	VG	FN	VF	VF/NM	NM-
1-12: 1-Dorkin-c. 2-Vasquez-c.						3.00

MURDER INCORPORATED (My Private Life #16 on)
Fox Feature Syndicate: 1/48 - No. 15, 12/49; (2 No.9's); 6/50 - No. 3, 8/51

	GD	VG	FN	VF	VF/NM	NM-
1 (1st Series); 1,2 have 'For Adults Only' on-c	57	114	171	240	395	550
2-Electrocution story	41	82	123	256	428	600
3,5-7,9(4/49),10(5/49),11-15	28	56	84	165	270	375
4-Classic lingerie-c	39	78	117	240	395	550
8-Used in **SOTI**, pg. 160	31	62	93	186	303	420
9(3/49)-Possible use in **SOTI**, pg. 145; r/Blue Beetle #56('48)	28	56	84	165	270	375
5(#1, 6/50)(2nd Series)-Formerly My Desire #4; bondage-c.	22	44	66	132	216	300
2(8/50)-Morisi-a	20	40	60	117	189	260
3(8/51)-Used in **POP**, pg. 81; Rico-a; lingerie-c/panels	26	52	78	154	252	350

MURDERLAND
Image Comics: Aug, 2010 - No. 3, Nov, 2010 ($2.99)

	GD	VG	FN	VF	VF/NM	NM-
1-3-Stephen Scott-s/David Haun-a						3.00

MURDER ME DEAD
El Capitán Books: July, 2000 - No. 9, Oct, 2001 ($2.95/$4.95, B&W)

	GD	VG	FN	VF	VF/NM	NM-
1-8-David Lapham-s/a						3.00
9-($4.95)						5.00

MURDEROUS GANGSTERS
Avon Per./Realistic No. 3 on: Jul, 1951; No. 2, Dec, 1951 - No. 4, Jun, 1952

	GD	VG	FN	VF	VF/NM	NM-
1-Pretty Boy Floyd, Leggs Diamond; 1 pg. Wood-a	50	100	150	315	533	750
2-Baby-Face Nelson; 1 pg. Wood-a; classic painted-c	41	82	123	256	428	600
3-Painted-c	28	56	84	165	270	375
4- "Murder by Needle" drug story; Mort Lawrence-a; Kinstler-c	34	68	102	199	325	450

MURDER MYSTERIES (Neil Gaiman's...)
Dark Horse Comics: 2002 ($13.95, HC, one-shot)

	GD	VG	FN	VF	VF/NM	NM-
HC-Adapts Gaiman story; P. Craig Russell-script/art						14.00

MURDER TALES (Magazine)
World Famous Publications: V1#10, Nov, 1970 - V1#11, Jan, 1971 (52 pgs.)

	GD	VG	FN	VF	VF/NM	NM-
V1#10-One pg. Frazetta ad	4	8	12	28	47	65
11-Guardineer-r; bondage-c	4	8	12	25	40	55

MUSHMOUSE AND PUNKIN PUSS (TV)
Gold Key: September, 1965 (Hanna-Barbera)

	GD	VG	FN	VF	VF/NM	NM-
1 (10153-509)	7	14	21	49	92	135

MUSIC BOX (Jennifer Love Hewitt's...)
IDW Publishing: Nov, 2009 - No. 5, Apr, 2010 ($3.99, lim. series)

	GD	VG	FN	VF	VF/NM	NM-
1-5-Anthology; Scott Lobdell-s/art by various. 1-Gaydos-a. 3-Archer-a						4.00

MUSIC MAN, THE (See Movie Classics)

MUTANT CHRONICLES (Video game)
Acclaim Comics (Armada): May, 1996 - No. 4, Aug, 1996 ($2.95, lim. series)

	GD	VG	FN	VF	VF/NM	NM-
1-4: Simon Bisley-c on all, Sourcebook (#5)						3.00

MUTANT EARTH (Stan Winston's...)
Image Comics: April, 2002 - No. 4, Jan, 2003 ($2.95)

	GD	VG	FN	VF	VF/NM	NM-
1-4-Flip book w/Realm of the Claw						3.00
Trakk...His Adventures in Mutant Earth TPB (2003, $16.95) r/#1-4; Winston interview						17.00

MUTANT MISADVENTURES OF CLOAK AND DAGGER, THE
(Becomes Cloak and Dagger #14 on)

Mutant X #2 © MAR

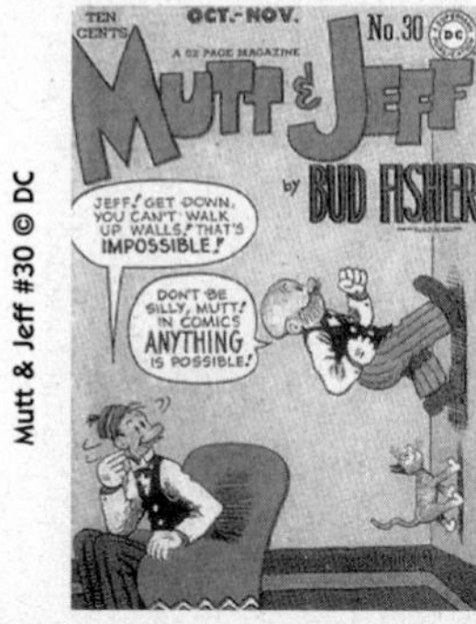

Mutt & Jeff #30 © DC

My Greatest Adventure #7 © DC

	GD	VG	FN	VF	VF/NM	NM-
	2.0	4.0	6.0	8.0	9.0	9.2

Marvel Comics: Oct, 1988 - No. 19, Aug, 1991 ($1.25/$1.50)

1-8,10-15: 1-X-Factor app. 10-Painted-c. 12-Dr. Doom app. 14-Begin new direction 3.00
9,16-19: 9-(52 pgs.) The Avengers x-over; painted-c. 16-18-Spider-Man x-over. 18-Infinity Gauntlet x-over; Thanos cameo; Ghost Rider app. 19-(52 pgs.) Origin Cloak & Dagger 4.00

NOTE: ***Austin** a-12i; c(i)-4, 12, 13; scripts-all. **Russell** a-2i. **Williamson** a-14i-16i; c-15i.*

MUTANTS & MISFITS
Silverline Comics (Solson): 1987 - No. 3, 1987 ($1.95)

1-3 3.00

MUTANTS VS. ULTRAS
Malibu Comics (Ultraverse): Nov, 1995 ($6.95, one-shot)

1-r/Exiles vs. X-Men, Night Man vs. Wolverine, Prime vs. Hulk 7.00

MUTANT, TEXAS: TALES OF SHERIFF IDA RED (Also see Jingle Belle)
Oni Press: May, 2002 - No. 4, Nov, 2002 ($2.95, B&W, limited series)

1-4-Paul Dini-s/J. Bone-c/a 3.00
TPB (2003, $11.95) r/#1-4; intro. by Joe Lansdale 12.00

MUTANT 2099
Marvel Comics (Marvel Knights): Nov, 2004 ($2.99, one-shot)

1-Kirkman-s/Pat Lee-c 3.00

MUTANT X (See X-Factor)
Marvel Comics: Nov, 1998 - No. 32, June, 2001 ($2.99/$1.99/$2.25)

1-($2.99) Alex Summers with alternate world's X-Men 4.00
2-11,13-19-($1.99): 2-Two covers. 5-Man-Spider-c/app. 3.00
12,25-($2.99): 12-Pin-up gallery by Kaluta, Romita, Byrne 4.00
20-24,26-32: 20-Begin $2.25-c. 28-31-Logan-c/app. 32-Last issue 3.00
Annual '99, '00 (5/99,'00, $3.50) '00-Doran-a(p) 4.00
Annual 2001 ($2.99) Story occurs between #31 & #32; Dracula app. 4.00

MUTANT X (Based on TV show)
Marvel Comics: May, 2002; June, 2002 ($3.50)

...: Dangerous Decisions (6/02) -Kuder-s/Immonen-a 3.50
...: Origin (5/02) -Tischman & Chaykin-s/Ferguson-a 3.50

MUTATIS
Marvel Comics (Epic Comics): 1992 - No. 3, 1992 ($2.25, mini-series)

1-3: Painted-c 3.00

MUTIES
Marvel Comics: Apr, 2002 - No. 6, Sept, 2002 ($2.50)

1-6: 1-Bollars-s/Ferguson-a. 2-Spaziante-a. 3-Haspiel-a. 4-Kanuiga-a 3.00

MUTINY (Stormy Tales of the Seven Seas)
Aragon Magazines: Oct, 1954 - No. 3, Feb, 1955

	GD	VG	FN	VF	VF/NM	NM-
1	16	32	48	94	147	200
2,3: 2-Capt. Mutiny. 3-Bondage-c	14	28	42	76	108	140

MUTINY ON THE BOUNTY (See Classics Illustrated #100 & Movie Comics)

MUTOPIA X (Also see House of M and related titles)
Marvel Comics: Sept, 2005 - No. 5, Jan, 2006 ($2.99, limited series)

1-5-Medina-a/Hine-s 3.00
House of M: Mutopia X (2006, $13.99, TPB) r/series 14.00

MUTT AND JEFF (See All-American, All-Flash #18, Cicero's Cat, Comic Cavalcade, Famous Feature Stories, The Funnies, Popular & Xmas Comics)
All American/National 1-103(6/58)/Dell 104(10/58)-115 (10-12/59)/ Harvey 116(2/60)-148: Summer, 1939 (nd) - No. 148, Nov, 1965

	GD	VG	FN	VF	VF/NM	NM-
1(nn)-Lost Wheels	174	348	522	1114	1907	2700
2(nn)-Charging Bull (Summer, 1940, nd; on sale 6/20/40)	77	154	231	493	847	1200
3(nn)-Bucking Broncos (Summer, 1941, nd)	53	106	159	334	567	800
4(Winter, '41), 5(Summer, '42)	50	100	150	315	533	750
6-10: 6-Includes Minute Man Answers the Call	30	60	90	177	289	400
11-20: 20-X-Mas-c	20	40	60	117	189	260
21-30	15	30	45	88	137	185
31-50: 32-X-Mas-c	14	28	42	78	112	145
51-75-Last Fisher issue. 53-Last 52 pgs.	11	22	33	62	86	110
76-99,101-103: 76-Last pre-code issue(1/55)	6	12	18	39	62	85
100	6	12	18	41	66	90
104-115,132-148	5	10	15	30	48	65
116-131-Richie Rich app.	5	10	15	32	51	70
...Jokes 1-3(8/60-61, Harvey)-84 pgs.; Richie Rich in all; Little Dot in #2,3; Lotta in #2	5	10	15	30	48	65
...New Jokes 1-4(10/63-11/65, Harvey)-68 pgs.; Richie Rich in #1-3; Stumbo in #1	4	8	12	24	37	50

GD VG FN VF VF/NM NM-
2.0 4.0 6.0 8.0 9.0 9.2

NOTE: *Most all issues by **Al Smith**. Issues from 1963 on have **Fisher** reprints. Clarification: early issues signed by Fisher are mostly drawn by Smith.*

MY BROTHERS' KEEPER
Spire Christian Comics (Fleming H. Revell Co.): 1973 (35/49¢, 36 pgs.)

	GD	VG	FN	VF	VF/NM	NM-
nn	2	4	6	13	18	22

MY CONFESSIONS (My Confession #7&8; formerly Western True Crime; A Spectacular Feature Magazine #11)
Fox Feature Syndicate: No. 7, Aug, 1949 - No. 10, Jan-Feb, 1950

	GD	VG	FN	VF	VF/NM	NM-
7-Wood-a (10 pgs.)	37	74	111	222	361	500
8,9: 8-Harrison/Wood-a (19 pgs.). 9-Wood-a	26	52	78	154	252	350
10	15	30	45	88	137	185

MY DATE COMICS (Teen-age)
Hillman Periodicals: July, 1947 - V1#4, Jan, 1948 (2nd Romance comic; see Young Romance)

	GD	VG	FN	VF	VF/NM	NM-
1-S&K-c/a	40	80	120	246	411	575
2-4-S&K-c/a; Dan Barry-a	28	56	84	165	270	375

MY DESIRE (Formerly Jo-Jo Comics; becomes Murder, Inc. #5 on)
Fox Feature Syndicate: No. 30, Aug, 1949 - No. 4, April, 1950

	GD	VG	FN	VF	VF/NM	NM-
30 (#1)	20	40	60	117	189	260
31 (#2, 10/49),3(2/50),4	15	30	45	88	137	185
31 (Canadian edition)	10	20	30	56	76	95
32(12/49)-Wood-a	25	50	75	150	245	340

MY DIARY (Becomes My Friend Irma #3 on?)
Marvel Comics (A Lovers Mag.): Dec, 1949 - No. 2, Mar, 1950

	GD	VG	FN	VF	VF/NM	NM-
1,2-Photo-c	17	34	51	98	154	210

MY EXPERIENCE (Formerly All Top; becomes Judy Canova #23 on)
Fox Feature Syndicate: No. 19, Sept, 1949 - No. 22, Mar, 1950

	GD	VG	FN	VF	VF/NM	NM-
19,21: 19-Wood-a. 21-Wood-a(2)	29	58	87	170	278	385
20	15	30	45	88	137	185
22-Wood-a (9 pgs.)	25	50	75	150	245	340

MY FAITH IN FRANKIE
DC Comics (Vertigo): March, 2004 - No. 4, June, 2004 ($2.95, limited series)

1-4-Mike Carey-s/Sonny Liew & Marc Hempel-a 3.00
TPB (2004, $6.95, digest-size) r/series in B&W; Dead Boy Detectives preview 7.00

MY FAVORITE MARTIAN (TV)
Gold Key: 1/64; No.2, 7/64 - No. 9, 10/66 (No. 1,3-9 have photo-c)

	GD	VG	FN	VF	VF/NM	NM-
1-Russ Manning-a	10	20	30	69	147	225
2	6	12	18	41	76	110
3-9	5	10	15	35	63	90

MY FRIEND IRMA (Radio/TV) (Formerly My Diary? and/or Western Life Romances?)
Marvel/Atlas Comics (BFP): No. 3, June, 1950 - No. 47, Dec, 1954; No. 48, Feb, 1955

	GD	VG	FN	VF	VF/NM	NM-
3-Dan DeCarlo-a in all; 52 pgs. begin, end ?	21	42	63	126	206	285
4-Kurtzman-a (10 pgs.)	20	40	60	114	182	250
5- "Egghead Doodle" by Kurtzman (4 pgs.)	15	30	45	88	137	185
6,8-10: 9-Paper dolls, 1 pg; Millie app. (5 pgs.)	14	28	42	80	115	150
7-One pg. Kurtzman-a	14	28	42	81	118	155
11-23: 23-One pg. Frazetta-a	11	22	33	62	86	110
24-48: 41,48-Stan Lee & Dan DeCarlo app.	10	20	30	56	76	95

MY GIRL PEARL
Atlas Comics: 4/55 - #4, 10/55; #5, 7/57 - #6, 9/57; #7, 8/60 - #11, ?/61

	GD	VG	FN	VF	VF/NM	NM-
1-Dan DeCarlo-c/a in #1-6	18	36	54	107	169	230
2	11	22	33	64	90	115
3-6	10	20	30	56	76	95
7-11	5	10	15	33	57	80

MY GREATEST ADVENTURE (Doom Patrol #86 on)
National Periodical Publications: Jan-Feb, 1955 - No. 85, Feb, 1964

	GD	VG	FN	VF	VF/NM	NM-
1-Before CCA	125	250	375	1000	2250	3500
2	46	92	138	340	770	1200
3-5	33	66	99	238	532	825
6-10: 6-Science fiction format begins	27	54	81	189	420	650
11-14: 12-1st S.A. issue	20	40	60	141	313	485
15-17: Kirby-a in all	22	44	66	154	340	525
18-Kirby-c/a	24	48	72	170	378	585
19,23-25	17	34	51	119	265	410
20,21,28-Kirby-a	20	40	60	141	313	485
22-Space Ranger prototype (7-8/58)(see Showcase #15 for Space Ranger debut)	18	36	54	126	281	435
26,27,29,30	13	26	39	91	201	310

My Life #8 © FOX

My Little Pony: Friendship Is Magic #5 © Hasbro

My Love Story #2 © MAR

	GD 2.0	VG 4.0	FN 6.0	VF 8.0	VF/NM 9.0	NM- 9.2
31-40	11	22	33	76	163	250
41,42,44-57,59	10	20	30	66	138	210
43-Kirby-a	10	20	30	69	147	225
58,60,61-Toth-a; Last 10¢ issue	10	20	30	67	141	215
62-76,78,79: 79-Promotes "Legion of the Strange" for next issue; renamed Doom Patrol for #80	8	16	24	56	108	160
77-Toth-a; Robotman prototype	9	18	27	57	111	165
80-(6/63)-Intro/origin Doom Patrol and begin series; origin & 1st app. Negative Man, Elasti-Girl & S.A. Robotman	50	100	150	400	900	1400
81,85-Toth-a	18	36	54	124	275	425
82-84	17	34	51	117	259	400

NOTE: ***Anderson** a-42. **Cameron** a-24. **Colan** a-77. **Meskin** a-25, 26, 32, 39, 45, 50, 56, 57, 61, 64, 70, 73, 74, 76, 79; c-76. **Moreira** a-11, 12, 15, 17, 20, 23, 25, 27, 37, 40-43, 46, 48, 55-57, 59, 60, 62-65, 67, 69, 70; c-1-4, 7-10. **Roussos** c/a-71-73. **Wildey** a-32.*

MY GREATEST ADVENTURE (Also see 2011 Weird Worlds series)
DC Comics: Dec, 2011 - No. 6, May, 2012 ($3.99, limited series)

	GD 2.0	VG 4.0	FN 6.0	VF 8.0	VF/NM 9.0	NM- 9.2
1-6-Short stories of Tanga, Robotman, and Garbage Man; Lopresti-s/a, Maguire-s/a						4.00

MY GREAT LOVE (Becomes Will Rogers Western #5)
Fox Feature Syndicate: Oct, 1949 - No. 4, Apr, 1950

	GD 2.0	VG 4.0	FN 6.0	VF 8.0	VF/NM 9.0	NM- 9.2
1	20	40	60	117	189	260
2-4	13	26	39	72	101	130

MY INTIMATE AFFAIR (Inside Crime #3)
Fox Feature Syndicate: Mar, 1950 - No. 2, May, 1950

	GD 2.0	VG 4.0	FN 6.0	VF 8.0	VF/NM 9.0	NM- 9.2
1	20	40	60	114	182	250
2	12	24	36	69	97	125

MY LIFE (Formerly Meet Corliss Archer)
Fox Feature Syndicate: No. 4, Sept, 1948 - No. 15, July, 1950

	GD 2.0	VG 4.0	FN 6.0	VF 8.0	VF/NM 9.0	NM- 9.2
4-Used in **SOTI**, pg. 39; Kamen/Feldstein-a	47	94	141	296	498	700
5-Kamen-a	29	58	87	170	278	385
6-Kamen/Feldstein-a	31	62	93	186	303	420
7-Wood-a; wash cover	25	50	75	150	245	340
8,9,11-15	15	30	45	88	137	185
10-Wood-a	22	44	66	132	216	300

MY LITTLE MARGIE (TV)
Charlton Comics: July, 1954 - No. 54, Nov, 1964

	GD 2.0	VG 4.0	FN 6.0	VF 8.0	VF/NM 9.0	NM- 9.2
1-Photo front/back-c	37	74	111	218	354	490
2-Photo front/back-c	18	36	54	107	169	230
3-7,10	12	24	36	69	97	125
8,9-Infinity-c	13	26	39	72	101	130
11-14: Part-photo-c (#13, 8/56). 14-UFO cover	10	20	30	58	79	100
15-19	10	20	30	54	72	90
20-(25¢, 100 pg. issue)	15	30	45	86	133	180
21-40: 40-Last 10¢ issue	5	10	15	30	50	70
41-53	4	8	12	27	44	60
54-(11/64) Beatles on cover; lead story spoofs the Beatle haircut craze of the 1960's; Beatles app. (scarce)	15	30	45	103	227	350

NOTE: *Doll cut-outs in 32, 33, 40, 45, 50.*

MY LITTLE MARGIE'S BOY FRIENDS (TV) (Freddy V2#12 on)
Charlton Comics: Aug, 1955 - No. 11, Apr?, 1958

	GD 2.0	VG 4.0	FN 6.0	VF 8.0	VF/NM 9.0	NM- 9.2
1-Has several Archie swipes	15	30	45	84	127	170
2	9	18	27	52	69	85
3-11	8	16	24	44	57	70

MY LITTLE MARGIE'S FASHIONS (TV)
Charlton Comics: Feb, 1959 - No. 5, Nov, 1959

	GD 2.0	VG 4.0	FN 6.0	VF 8.0	VF/NM 9.0	NM- 9.2
1	14	28	42	76	108	140
2-5	8	16	24	44	57	70

MY LITTLE PHONY: A BRONY ADVENTURE
Dynamite Entertainment: 2014 ($5.99, one-shot)

	GD 2.0	VG 4.0	FN 6.0	VF 8.0	VF/NM 9.0	NM- 9.2
1-My Little Pony fandom parody; Moreci & Seeley-a/Haeser & Baal-a; 2 covers						6.00

MY LITTLE PONY
IDW Publishing

	GD 2.0	VG 4.0	FN 6.0	VF 8.0	VF/NM 9.0	NM- 9.2
... Annual #1: Equestria Girls (10/13, $7.99) Price & Fleecs-a; multiple covers						8.00
... Art Gallery (11/13, $3.99) Pin-ups by Sara Richard & others						4.00
... Cover Gallery (8/13, $3.99) Gallery of regular and variant covers						4.00

MY LITTLE PONY: FRIENDS FOREVER
IDW Publishing: Jan, 2014 - Present ($3.99)

	GD 2.0	VG 4.0	FN 6.0	VF 8.0	VF/NM 9.0	NM- 9.2
1-3: 1-Alex De Campi-s/Carla Speed McNeil-a; multiple covers. 3-Garbowska-a						4.00

MY LITTLE PONY: FRIENDSHIP IS MAGIC
IDW Publishing: Nov, 2012 - Present ($3.99)

	GD 2.0	VG 4.0	FN 6.0	VF 8.0	VF/NM 9.0	NM- 9.2
1-Katie Cook-s/Andy Price-a; 7 covers						5.00
1-Subscription variant cover by Jill Thompson						5.00
2-17-Multiple covers on each						4.00
... #1 Hundred Penny Press (2/14, $1.00) reprints #1						3.00

MY LITTLE PONY MICRO-SERIES
IDW Publishing: Feb, 2013 - No. 10, Dec, 2013 ($3.99)

	GD 2.0	VG 4.0	FN 6.0	VF 8.0	VF/NM 9.0	NM- 9.2
1-Twilight Sparkle - Zahler-s/a						5.00
2-10: 2-Rainbow Dash. 3-Rarity. 4-Fluttershy						4.00

MY LOVE (Becomes Two Gun Western #5 (11/50) on?)
Marvel Comics (CLDS): July, 1949 - No. 4, Apr, 1950 (All photo-c)

	GD 2.0	VG 4.0	FN 6.0	VF 8.0	VF/NM 9.0	NM- 9.2
1	19	38	57	111	176	240
2,3	14	28	42	76	108	140
4-Bettie Page photo-c (see Cupid #2)	45	90	135	284	480	675

MY LOVE
Marvel Comics Group: Sept, 1969 - No. 39, Mar, 1976

	GD 2.0	VG 4.0	FN 6.0	VF 8.0	VF/NM 9.0	NM- 9.2
1	8	16	24	54	102	150
2-9: 4-6-Colan-a	5	10	15	31	53	75
10-Williamson-r/My Own Romance #71; Kirby-a	5	10	15	33	57	80
11-13,15-19	4	8	12	27	44	60
14-(52 pgs.)-Woodstock-c/sty; Morrow-c/a; Kirby/Colletta-r	6	12	18	38	69	100
20-Starlin-a	4	8	12	28	47	65
21,22,24-27,29-38: 38-Reprints	4	8	12	23	37	50
23-Steranko-r/Our Love Story #5	4	8	12	27	44	60
28-Kirby-a	4	8	12	25	40	55
39-Last issue; reprints	4	8	12	25	40	55
Special 1 (12/71)(52 pgs.)	5	10	15	34	60	85

NOTE: ***John Buscema** a-1-7, 10, 18-21, 22r(2), 24r, 25r, 29r, 34r, 36r, 37r, Spec. (r)(4); c-13, 15, 25, 27, Spec. **Colan** a-4, 5, 6, 8, 9, 16, 17, 20, 21, 22, 24r, 27r, 30r, 35r, 39r. **Colan/Everett** a-13, 15, 16, 27(r/#13). **Kirby** a-(r)-10, 14, 26, 28. **Romita** a-1-3, 19, 20, 25, 34, 38; c-1-3, 15.*

MY LOVE AFFAIR (March of Crime #7 on)
Fox Feature Syndicate: July, 1949 - No. 6, May, 1950

	GD 2.0	VG 4.0	FN 6.0	VF 8.0	VF/NM 9.0	NM- 9.2
1	20	40	60	117	189	260
2	13	26	39	72	101	130
3-6-Wood-a. 5-(3/50)-Becomes Love Stories #6	22	44	66	132	216	300

MY LOVE LIFE (Formerly Zegra)
Fox Feature Synd.: No. 6, June, 1949 - No. 13, Aug, 1950; No. 13, Sept, 1951

	GD 2.0	VG 4.0	FN 6.0	VF 8.0	VF/NM 9.0	NM- 9.2
6-Kamenish-a	20	40	60	117	189	260
7-13	13	26	39	72	101	130
13 (9/51)(Formerly My Story #12)	12	24	36	67	94	120

MY LOVE MEMOIRS (Formerly Women Outlaws; Hunted #13 on)
Fox Feature Syndicate: No. 9, Nov, 1949 - No. 12, May, 1950

	GD 2.0	VG 4.0	FN 6.0	VF 8.0	VF/NM 9.0	NM- 9.2
9,11,12-Wood-a	22	44	66	132	216	300
10	13	26	39	72	101	130

MY LOVE SECRET (Formerly Phantom Lady; Animal Crackers #31)
Fox Feature Syndicate/M. S. Distr.: No. 24, June, 1949 - No. 30, June, 1950; No. 53, 1954

	GD 2.0	VG 4.0	FN 6.0	VF 8.0	VF/NM 9.0	NM- 9.2
24-Kamen/Feldstein-a	23	46	69	136	223	310
25-Possible caricature of Wood on-c?	15	30	45	85	130	175
26,28-Wood-a	22	44	66	132	216	300
27,29,30: 30-Photo-c	14	28	42	80	115	150
53-(Reprint, M.S. Distr.) 1954? nd given; formerly Western Thrillers; becomes Crimes by Women #54; photo-c	8	16	24	44	57	70

MY LOVE STORY (Hoot Gibson Western #5 on)
Fox Feature Syndicate: Sept, 1949 - No. 4, Mar, 1950

	GD 2.0	VG 4.0	FN 6.0	VF 8.0	VF/NM 9.0	NM- 9.2
1	20	40	60	117	189	260
2	13	26	39	72	101	130
3,4-Wood-a	22	44	66	132	216	300

MY LOVE STORY
Atlas Comics (GPS): April, 1956 - No. 9, Aug, 1957

	GD 2.0	VG 4.0	FN 6.0	VF 8.0	VF/NM 9.0	NM- 9.2
1	15	30	45	84	127	170
2	10	20	30	54	72	90
3,7: Matt Baker-a. 7-Toth-a	12	24	36	69	97	125
4-6,8,9	9	18	27	50	65	80

NOTE: ***Brewster** a-3. **Colletta** a-1(2), 3, 4(2), 5; c-3.*

MYLO XYLOTO COMICS
Bongo Comics: 2013 - No. 6, 2013 ($3.99, limited series)

	GD 2.0	VG 4.0	FN 6.0	VF 8.0	VF/NM 9.0	NM- 9.2
1-6-Mark Osborne & Coldplay-s/Fuentes-a						4.00

My Own Romance #76 © MAR

My Secret Story #29 © FOX

Mysteries #7 © SUPR

MY NAME IS BRUCE
Dark Horse Comics: Sept, 2008 ($3.50, one-shot)

	GD 2.0	VG 4.0	FN 6.0	VF 8.0	VF/NM 9.0	NM- 9.2
nn-Adaptation of the Bruce Campbell movie; Cliff Richards-a/Bart Sears-c						3.50

MY NAME IS HOLOCAUST
DC Comics: May, 1995 - No. 5, Sept, 1995 ($2.50, limited series)

	GD 2.0	VG 4.0	FN 6.0	VF 8.0	VF/NM 9.0	NM- 9.2
1-5						3.00

MY ONLY LOVE
Charlton Comics: July, 1975 - No. 9, Nov, 1976

	GD 2.0	VG 4.0	FN 6.0	VF 8.0	VF/NM 9.0	NM- 9.2
1	3	6	9	14	19	24
2,4-9	2	4	6	9	13	16
3-Toth-a	2	4	6	11	16	20

MY OWN ROMANCE (Formerly My Romance; Teen-Age Romance #77 on)
Marvel/Atlas (MjPC/RCM No. 4-59/ZPC No. 60-76): No. 4, Mar, 1949 - No. 76, July, 1960

	GD 2.0	VG 4.0	FN 6.0	VF 8.0	VF/NM 9.0	NM- 9.2
4-Photo-c	18	36	54	107	169	230
5-10: 5,6,8-10-Photo-c	12	24	36	67	97	125
11-20: 14-Powell-a	11	22	33	62	86	110
21-42,55: 42-Last precode (2/55). 55-Toth-a	10	20	30	58	79	100
43-54,56-60	5	10	15	34	60	85
61-70,72,73,75,76	5	10	15	31	53	75
71-Williamson-a	5	10	15	35	63	90
74-Kirby-a	5	10	15	35	63	90

NOTE: ***Brewster** a-59. **Colletta** a-45(2), 48, 50, 55, 57(2), 59; c-58i, 59, 61. **Everett** a-25; c-58p. **Kirby** c-71, 75, 76. **Morisi** a-18. **Orlando** a-61. **Romita** a-36. **Tuska** a-10.*

MY PAL DIZZY (See Comic Books, Series I)

MY PAST (...Confessions) (Formerly Western Thrillers)
Fox Feature Syndicate: No. 7, Aug, 1949 - No. 11, Apr, 1950 (Crimes Inc. #12)

	GD 2.0	VG 4.0	FN 6.0	VF 8.0	VF/NM 9.0	NM- 9.2
7	20	40	60	117	189	260
8-10	13	26	39	72	101	130
11-Wood-a	22	44	66	132	216	300

MY PERSONAL PROBLEM
Ajax/Farrell/Steinway Comic: 11/55; No. 2, 2/56; No. 3, 9/56 - No. 4, 11/56; 10/57 - No. 3, 5/58

	GD 2.0	VG 4.0	FN 6.0	VF 8.0	VF/NM 9.0	NM- 9.2
1	9	18	27	52	69	85
2-4	7	14	21	35	43	50
1-3('57-'58)-Steinway	6	12	18	28	34	40

MY PRIVATE LIFE (Formerly Murder, Inc.; becomes Pedro #18)
Fox Feature Syndicate: No. 16, Feb, 1950 - No. 17, April, 1950

	GD 2.0	VG 4.0	FN 6.0	VF 8.0	VF/NM 9.0	NM- 9.2
16,17	15	30	45	84	127	170

MYRA NORTH (See The Comics, Crackajack Funnies & Red Ryder)
Dell Publishing Co.: No. 3, Jan, 1940

	GD 2.0	VG 4.0	FN 6.0	VF 8.0	VF/NM 9.0	NM- 9.2
Four Color 3	100	200	300	640	1095	1550

MY REAL LOVE
Standard Comics: No. 5, June, 1952 (Photo-c)

	GD 2.0	VG 4.0	FN 6.0	VF 8.0	VF/NM 9.0	NM- 9.2
5-Toth-a, 3 pgs.; Tuska, Cardy, Vern Greene-a	14	28	42	81	118	155

MY ROMANCE (Becomes My Own Romance #4 on)
Marvel Comics (RCM): Sept, 1948 - No. 3, Jan, 1949

	GD 2.0	VG 4.0	FN 6.0	VF 8.0	VF/NM 9.0	NM- 9.2
1	21	42	63	124	202	280
2,3: 2-Anti-Wertham editorial (11/48)	14	28	42	82	121	160

MY ROMANTIC ADVENTURES (Formerly Romantic Adventures)
American Comics Group: No. 68, 8/56 - No. 115, 12/60; No. 116, 7/61 - No. 138, 3/64

	GD 2.0	VG 4.0	FN 6.0	VF 8.0	VF/NM 9.0	NM- 9.2
68	8	16	24	42	54	65
69-85	7	14	21	35	43	50
86-Three pg. Williamson-a (2/58)	8	16	24	44	57	70
87-100	3	6	9	19	30	40
101-138	3	6	9	16	23	30

NOTE: ***Whitney** art in most issues.*

MY SECRET (Becomes Our Secret #4 on)
Superior Comics, Ltd.: Aug, 1949 - No. 3, Oct, 1949

	GD 2.0	VG 4.0	FN 6.0	VF 8.0	VF/NM 9.0	NM- 9.2
1	19	38	57	111	176	240
2,3	14	28	42	82	121	160

MY SECRET AFFAIR (Becomes Martin Kane #4)
Hero Book (Fox Feature Syndicate): Dec, 1949 - No. 3, April, 1950

	GD 2.0	VG 4.0	FN 6.0	VF 8.0	VF/NM 9.0	NM- 9.2
1-Harrison/Wood-a (10 pgs.)	30	60	90	177	289	400
2,3-Wood-a	24	48	72	142	234	325

MY SECRET CONFESSION
Sterling Comics: September, 1955

	GD 2.0	VG 4.0	FN 6.0	VF 8.0	VF/NM 9.0	NM- 9.2
1-Sekowsky-a	10	20	30	54	72	90

MY SECRET LIFE (Formerly Western Outlaws; Romeo Tubbs #26 on)
Fox Feature Syndicate: No. 22, July, 1949 - No. 27, July, 1950; No. 27, 9/51

	GD 2.0	VG 4.0	FN 6.0	VF 8.0	VF/NM 9.0	NM- 9.2
22	15	30	45	88	137	185
23,26-Wood-a, 6 pgs.	22	44	66	132	216	300
24,25,27	14	28	42	80	115	150
27 (9/51)	12	24	36	67	94	120

NOTE: *The title was changed to Romeo Tubbs after #25 even though #26 & 27 did come out.*

MY SECRET LIFE (Formerly Young Lovers; Sue & Sally Smith #48)
Charlton Comics: No. 19, Aug, 1957 - No. 47, Sept, 1962

	GD 2.0	VG 4.0	FN 6.0	VF 8.0	VF/NM 9.0	NM- 9.2
19	4	8	12	25	40	55
20-35	3	6	9	16	23	30
36-47: 44-Last 10¢ issue. 47-1st app. Sue & Sally Smith	3	6	9	14	20	26

MY SECRET MARRIAGE
Superior Comics, Ltd.: May, 1953 - No. 24, July, 1956 (Canadian)

	GD 2.0	VG 4.0	FN 6.0	VF 8.0	VF/NM 9.0	NM- 9.2
1	15	30	45	90	140	190
2	10	20	30	56	76	95
3-24	9	18	27	50	65	80
I.W. Reprint #9	2	4	6	8	11	14

NOTE: *Many issues contain **Kamen-ish** art.*

MY SECRET ROMANCE (Becomes A Star Presentation #3)
Hero Book (Fox Feature Syndicate): Jan, 1950 - No. 2, March, 1950

	GD 2.0	VG 4.0	FN 6.0	VF 8.0	VF/NM 9.0	NM- 9.2
1	20	40	60	114	182	250
2-Wood-a	22	44	66	132	216	300

MY SECRETS (Magazine) (Also see Gothic Romances)
Atlas/Seaboard: Feb, 1975 (B&W, 68 pgs.)

	GD 2.0	VG 4.0	FN 6.0	VF 8.0	VF/NM 9.0	NM- 9.2
Vol. 1 #1	14	28	42	96	211	325

MY SECRET STORY (Formerly Captain Kidd #25; Sabu #30 on)
Fox Feature Syndicate: No. 26, Oct, 1949 - No. 29, April, 1950

	GD 2.0	VG 4.0	FN 6.0	VF 8.0	VF/NM 9.0	NM- 9.2
26	18	36	54	103	162	220
27-29	13	26	39	72	101	130

MYSPACE DARK HORSE PRESENTS
Dark Horse Books: Sept, 2008 - Feb, 2011 ($19.95/$19.99, TPB)

	GD 2.0	VG 4.0	FN 6.0	VF 8.0	VF/NM 9.0	NM- 9.2
Vol. 1 - Short stories previously appearing on Dark Horse's MySpace.com webpage; s/a by various incl. Whedon, Bá, Bagge, Mignola, Moon, Nord, Trimpe, Warren, Way						20.00
Vol. 2 - Collects stories from online #7-12; s/a by Way, Niles, Dorkin, Hotz & others						20.00
Vol. 3 - Collects stories from online #13-19; s/a by Mignola, Cloonan & others						20.00
Vol. 4 - Collects stories from online #20-24; s/a by Whedon, Chen & others						20.00
Vol. 5 - Collects stories from online #25-30; s/a by Thompson, Aragonés & others						20.00
Vol. 6 - Collects stories from online #31-36; s/a by Sakai, Dorkin & others						20.00

MYSTERIES (...Weird & Strange)
Superior/Dynamic Publ. (Randall Publ. Ltd.): May, 1953 - No. 11, Jan, 1955

	GD 2.0	VG 4.0	FN 6.0	VF 8.0	VF/NM 9.0	NM- 9.2
1-All horror stories	45	90	135	284	480	675
2-A-Bomb blast story	30	60	90	177	289	400
3-11: 10-Kamenish-c/a reprinted from Strange Mysteries #2; cover is from a panel in Strange Mysteries #2	26	52	78	154	252	350

MYSTERIES IN SPACE (See Fireside Book Series)

MYSTERIES OF SCOTLAND YARD (Also see A-1 Comics)
Magazine Enterprises: No. 121, 1954 (one shot)

	GD 2.0	VG 4.0	FN 6.0	VF 8.0	VF/NM 9.0	NM- 9.2
A-1 121-Reprinted from Manhunt (5 stories)	15	30	45	85	130	175

MYSTERIES OF UNEXPLORED WORLDS (See Blue Bird)(Becomes Son of Vulcan V2#49 on)
Charlton Comics: Aug, 1956; No. 2, Jan, 1957 - No. 48, Sept, 1965

	GD 2.0	VG 4.0	FN 6.0	VF 8.0	VF/NM 9.0	NM- 9.2
1	37	74	111	222	361	500
2-No Ditko	16	32	48	94	147	200
3,4,8,9 Ditko-a. 3-Diko c/a (4). 4-Ditko c/a (2).	30	60	90	177	289	400
5,6,10,11: 5,6-Ditko-c/a (all). 10-Ditko-c/a(4). 11-Ditko-c/a(3); signed J. Kotdi	31	62	93	186	303	420
7-(2/58, 68 pgs.) 4 stories w/Ditko-a	34	68	102	204	332	460
12-Ditko sty (3); Baker story "The Charm Bracelet"	30	60	90	177	289	400
13-18,20	10	20	30	56	76	95
19,21-24,26-Ditko-a	23	46	69	136	223	310
25,27-30: 28-Communist A-bomb story w/Khrushchev	5	10	15	31	53	75
31-45: 43-Atomic bomb panel	4	8	12	25	40	55
46(5/65)-Son of Vulcan begins (origin/1st app.)	4	8	12	27	44	60
47,48	4	8	12	21	33	45

NOTE: ***Ditko** c-3-6, 10, 11, 19, 21-24. Covers to #19, 21-24 reprint story panels.*

Mysterious Adventures #3 © Story

Mysterious Strangers #1 © MB

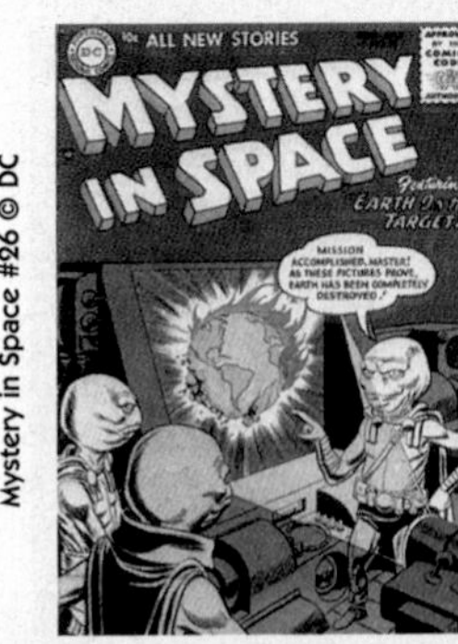

Mystery in Space #26 © DC

GD 2.0 | VG 4.0 | FN 6.0 | VF 8.0 | VF/NM 9.0 | NM- 9.2

GD 2.0 | VG 4.0 | FN 6.0 | VF 8.0 | VF/NM 9.0 | NM- 9.2

MYSTERIOUS ADVENTURES
Story Comics: Mar, 1951 - No. 24, Mar, 1955; No. 25, Aug, 1955

1-All horror stories 84 168 252 538 919 1300
2-(6/51) 45 90 135 284 480 675
3,4,6,10 42 84 126 265 445 625
5-Severed heads/bondage-c 47 94 141 296 498 700
7-Dagger in eye panel; dismemberment stories 52 104 156 328 552 775
8-Eyeball story 54 108 162 343 574 825
9-Extreme violence (8/52) 47 94 141 296 498 700
11-(12/52)-Used in **SOTI**, pg. 84 46 92 138 290 488 685
12,14: 14-E.C. Old Witch swipe 42 84 126 265 445 625
13-Classic skull-c 58 116 174 371 636 900
15-21: 18-Used in Senate Investigative report, pgs. 5,6; E.C. swipe/TFTC #35; The Coffin-Keeper & Corpse (hosts). 20-Electric chair-c; used by Wertham in the Senate hearings. 21-Bondage/beheading-c; extreme violence
52 104 156 328 552 775
22- "Cinderella" parody 43 86 129 271 461 650
23-Disbrow-a (6 pgs.); E.C. swipe "The Mystery Keeper's Tale" (host) and "Mother Ghoul's Nursery Tale" 43 86 129 267 454 640
24,25 34 68 102 199 325 450

NOTE: ***Tothish** art by **Ross Andru**-#22, 23. **Bache** a-8. **Cameron** a-5-7. **Harrison** a-12. **Hollingsworth** a-3-8, 12. **Schaffenberger** a-24, 25. **Wildey** a-15, 17.*

MYSTERIOUS ISLAND (Also see Classic Comics #34)
Dell Publishing Co.: No. 1213, July-Sept, 1961

Four Color 1213-Movie, photo-c 7 14 21 48 89 130

MYSTERIOUS ISLE
Dell Publishing Co.: Nov-Jan, 1963/64 (Jules Verne)

1-Painted-c 3 6 9 21 33 45

MYSTERIOUS RIDER, THE (See Zane Grey, 4-Color 301)

MYSTERIOUS STORIES (Formerly Horror From the Tomb #1)
Premier Magazines: No. 2, Dec-Jan, 1954-1955 - No. 7, Dec, 1955

2-Woodbridge-c; last pre-code issue 52 104 156 328 552 775
3-Woodbridge-c/a 37 74 111 222 361 500
4-7: 5-Cinderella parody. 6-Woodbridge-c 34 68 102 199 325 450

NOTE: ***Hollingsworth** a-2, 4.*

MYSTERIOUS STRANGER
DC Comics: Aug/Sept. 1952

nn-Ashcan comic, not distributed to newsstands, only for in-house use. Cover art is All Star Western #60 with interior being Sensation Comics #100. A FN/VF copy sold for $2,357.50 in 2002.

MYSTERIOUS STRANGERS
Oni Press: Jul, 2013 - Present ($3.99)

1-5: 1-Roberson-s/Kowalchuk-a 4.00

MYSTERIOUS SUSPENSE (Also see Blue Beetle #1 (1967))
Charlton Comics: Oct, 1968 (12¢)

1-Return of the Question by Ditko (c/a) 6 12 18 40 73 105

MYSTERIOUS TRAVELER (See Tales of the...)

MYSTERIOUS TRAVELER COMICS (Radio)
Trans-World Publications: Nov, 1948

1-Powell-c/a(2); Poe adaptation, "Tell Tale Heart" 63 126 189 403 689 975

MYSTERIUS
DC Comics (WildStorm): Mar, 2009 - No. 6, Aug, 2009 ($2.99, limited series)

1-6-Jeff Parker-a/Tom Fowler-a 3.00
TPB (2010, $17.99) r/#1-6 18.00

MYSTERY COMICS
William H. Wise & Co.: 1944 - No. 4, 1944 (No months given)

1-The Magnet, The Silver Knight, Brad Spencer, Wonderman, Dick Devins, King of Futuria, & Zudo the Jungle Boy begin (all 1st app.); Schomburg-c on all
145 290 435 928 1589 2250
2-Bondage-c 84 168 252 538 919 1300
3,4: 3-Lance Lewis, Space Detective begins (1st app.); Robot-c. 4-(V2#1 inside); KKK-c
77 154 231 493 847 1200

MYSTERY COMICS DIGEST
Gold Key/Whitman?: Mar, 1972 - No. 26, Oct, 1975

1-Ripley's Believe It or Not; reprint of Ripley's #1 origin Ra-Ka-Tep the Mummy; Wood-a
4 8 12 26 41 55
2-9: 2-Boris Karloff Tales of Mystery; Wood-a; 1st app. Werewolf Count Wulfstein. 3-Twilight Zone (TV); Crandall, Toth & George Evans-a; 1st app. Tragg & Simbar the Lion Lord; (2) Crandall/Frazetta-r/Twilight Zone #1 4-Ripley's Believe It or Not; 1st app. Baron Tibor, the Vampire. 5-Boris Karloff Tales of Mystery; 1st app. Dr. Spektor. 6-Twilight Zone (TV); 1st app. U.S. Marshal Reid & Sir Duane; Evans-r. 7-Ripley's Believe It or Not; origin The Lurker in the Swamp; 1st app. Duroc. 8-Boris Karloff Tales of Mystery; McWilliams-r; Orlando-r. 9-Twilight Zone (TV); Williamson, Crandall, McWilliams-a; 2nd Tragg app.;Torres, Evans, Heck/Tuska-r 3 6 9 20 30 40
10-26: 10,13-Ripley's Believe It or Not: 13-Orlando-r. 11,14-Boris Karloff Tales of Mystery. 14-1st app. Xorkon. 12,15-Twilight Zone (TV). 16,19,22,25-Ripley's Believe It or Not. 17-Boris Karloff Tales of Mystery; Williamson-r; Orlando-r. 18,21,24-Twilight Zone (TV). 20,23,26-Boris Karloff Tales of Mystery 3 6 9 16 23 30

NOTE: *Dr. Spektor app.-#5, 10-12, 21. Durak app.-#15. Duroc app.-#14 (later called Durak). King George 1st app.-#8.*

MYSTERY IN SPACE (Also see Fireside Book Series and Pulp Fiction Library: ...)
National Periodical Pub.: 4-5/51 - No. 110, 9/66; No. 111, 9/80 - No. 117, 3/81 (#1-3: 52 pgs.)

1-Frazetta-a, 8 pgs.; Knights of the Galaxy begins, ends #8
231 462 693 1906 4303 6700
2 86 172 258 688 1544 2400
3 63 126 187 504 1127 1750
4,5 50 100 150 400 900 1400
6-10: 7-Toth-a 39 78 117 289 657 1025
11-15 33 66 99 238 532 825
16-18,20-25: Interplanetary Insurance feature by Infantino in all. 21-1st app. Space Cabbie. 24-Last pre-code issue 29 58 87 209 467 725
19-Virgil Finlay-a 31 62 93 223 499 775
26-40: 26-Space Cabbie feature begins. 34-1st S.A. issue. 40-Grey-tone-c
23 46 69 161 356 550
41-52: 47-Space Cabbie feature ends 17 34 51 117 259 400
53-Adam Strange begins (8/59, 10pg. sty); robot-c 152 304 456 1254 2827 4400
54 42 84 126 311 706 1100
55-Grey tone-c 40 80 120 296 673 1050
56-60: 59-Kane/Anderson-a 23 46 69 161 356 550
61-71: 61-1st app. Adam Strange foe Ulthoon. 62-1st app. A.S. foe Mortan. 63-Origin Vandor. 66-Star Rovers begin (1st app.). 68-1st app. Dust Devils (6/61). 69-1st Mailbag. 70-2nd app. Dust Devils. 71-Last 10¢ issue 18 36 54 126 281 435
72-74,76-80 12 24 36 84 185 285
75-JLA x-over in Adam Strange (5/62)(sequel to J.L.A. #3, 2nd app. of Kanjar Ro)
21 42 63 150 350 510
81-86 10 20 30 64 132 200
87-(11/63)-Adam Strange/Hawkman double feat begins; 3rd Hawkman tryout series
15 30 45 100 220 340
88-Adam Strange & Hawkman stories 13 26 39 89 195 300
89-Adam Strange & Hawkman stories 13 26 39 86 188 290
90-Book-length Adam Strange & Hawkman story; 1st team-up (3/64); Hawkman moves to own title next month; classic-c 15 30 45 100 220 340
91-102: 91-End Infantino art on Adam Strange; double-length Adam Strange story. 92-Space Ranger begins (6/64), ends #103. 92-94,96,98-Space Ranger-c. 94,98-Adam Strange/ Space Ranger team-up. 102-Adam Strange ends (no Space Ranger)
7 14 21 44 82 120
103-Origin Ultra, the Multi-Alien; last Space Ranger 5 10 15 35 63 90
104-110: 110-(9/66)-Last 12¢ issue 5 10 15 30 50 70
V17#111(9/80)-117: 117-Newton-a(3 pgs.) 2 4 6 8 11 14

NOTE: ***Anderson** a-2, 4, 8-10, 12-17, 19, 45-48, 51, 57, 59i, 61-64, 70, 76, 87-91; c-9, 10, 15-25, 87, 89, 105-108, 110. **Aparo** a-111. **Austin** a-112i. **Bolland** a-115. **Craig** a-114, 116. **Ditko** a-111, 114-116. **Drucker** a-13, 14. **Elias** a-98, 102, 103. **Golden** a-113p. **Sid Greene** a-78, 91. **Infantino** a-1-8, 11, 14-25, 27-46, 48, 49, 51, 53-91, 103, 117; c-60-86, 88, 90, 91, 105, 107. **Gil Kane** a-14p, 15p, 18p, 19p, 26p, 29-59p(most), 100-102; c-52, 101. **Kubert** a-113; c-111-115. **Moreira** c-27, 28. **Rogers** a-111. **Sekowsky** a-52. **Simon & Kirby** a-4(2 pgs.). **Spiegle** a-111, 114. **Starlin** c-116. **Sutton** a-112. **Tuska** a-115p, 117p.*

MYSTERY IN SPACE
DC Comics: Nov, 2006 - No. 8, Jul, 2007 ($3.99, limited series)

1-8: 1-Captain Comet's rebirth; Starlin-s/Shane Davis-a; The Weird by Starlin 4.00
1-Variant cover by Neal Adams 10.00
Volume One TPB (2007, $17.99) r/#1-5 18.00
Volume Two TPB (2007, $17.99) r/#6-8 and The Weird from #1-4 18.00

MYSTERY IN SPACE
DC Comics (Vertigo): Jul, 2012 ($7.99, one-shot)

1-Short sci-fi stories by various incl. Kaluta, Allred, Baker, Diggle, Gianfelice; Sook-c 8.00

MYSTERY MEN
Marvel Comics: Aug, 2011 - No. 5, Nov, 2011 ($2.99, limited series)

1-5-Zircher-a/c; Liss-s; Pulp-era characters in 1932 3.00

MYSTERY MEN COMICS
Fox Features Syndicate: Aug, 1939 - No. 31, Feb, 1942

1-Intro. & 1st app. The Blue Beetle, The Green Mask, Rex Dexter of Mars by Briefer,

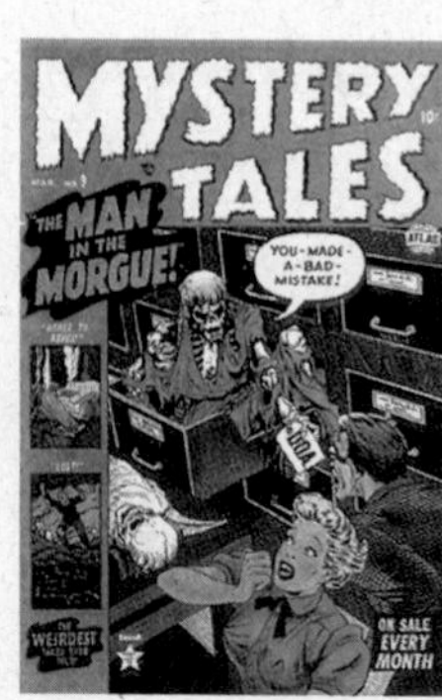
Mystery Tales #9 © MAR

Mystic #8 © MAR

Mystic Comics #6 © MAR

	GD 2.0	VG 4.0	FN 6.0	VF 8.0	VF/NM 9.0	NM- 9.2
Zanzibar by Tuska, Lt. Drake, D-13-Secret Agent by Powell, Chen Chang, Wing Turner, & Captain Denny Scott	1000	2000	3000	7600	14,050	20,500
2-Robot & sci/fi-c (2nd Robot-c w/Movie #6)	383	766	1149	2681	4691	6700
3 (10/39)-Classic Lou Fine-c	541	1082	1623	3950	6975	10,000
4,5: 4-Capt. Savage begins (11/39)	300	600	900	1980	3440	4900
6-Tuska-c	265	530	795	1694	2897	4100
7-1st Blue Beetle-c app.	300	600	900	2040	3570	5100
8-Lou Fine bondage-c	300	600	900	1920	3310	4700
9-The Moth begins; Lou Fine-c	155	310	465	992	1696	2400
10-12: All Joe Simon-c. 10-Wing Turner by Kirby; Simon bondage-c. 11-Intro. Domino	142	284	426	909	1555	2200
13-Intro. Lynx & sidekick Blackie (8/40)	77	154	231	493	847	1200
14-18	71	142	213	454	777	1100
19-Intro. & 1st app. Miss X (ends #21)	74	148	222	470	810	1150
20-31: 26-The Wraith begins	66	132	198	419	722	1025

NOTE: ***Briefer** a-1-15, 20, 24; c-9. **Cuidera** a-22. **Lou Fine** c-1-5,8,9. **Powell** a-1-15, 24. **Simon** c-10-12. **Tuska** a-1-16, 22, 24, 27; c-6. Bondage-c 1, 3, 7, 8, 10, 25, 27-29, 31. Blue Beetle c-7, 8, 10-31. D-13 Secret Agent c-6. Green Mask c-1, 3-5. Rex Dexter of Mars c-2, 9.*

MYSTERY MEN MOVIE ADAPTION
Dark Horse Comics: July, 1999 - No. 2, Aug, 1999 ($2.95, mini-series)

1,2-Fingerman-s; photo-c 3.00

MYSTERY PLAY, THE
DC Comics (Vertigo): 1994 ($19.95, one-shot)

nn-Hardcover-Morrison-s/Muth-painted art 25.00
Softcover ($9.95)-New Muth cover 10.00

MYSTERY SOCIETY
IDW Publishing: May, 2010 - No. 5, Oct, 2010 ($3.99, limited series)

1-5-Niles-s/Staples-a 4.00
... Special (3/13, $3.99) Niles-s/Ritchie-a/c 4.00

MYSTERY TALES
Atlas Comics (20CC): Mar, 1952 - No. 54, Aug, 1957

	GD 2.0	VG 4.0	FN 6.0	VF 8.0	VF/NM 9.0	NM- 9.2
1-Horror/weird stories in all	129	258	387	826	1413	2000
2-Krigstein-a	71	142	213	454	777	1100
3-10: 6-A-Bomb panel. 10-Story similar to "The Assassin" from Shock SuspenStories	61	122	183	390	670	950
11,13-21: 14-Maneely s/f story. 20-Electric chair issue. 21-Matt Fox-a; decapitation story	41	82	123	256	428	600
12,22: 12-Matt Fox-a. 22-Forte/Matt Fox-c; a(i)	43	86	129	271	461	650
23-26 (2/55)-Last precode issue	37	74	111	222	361	500
27,29-35,37,38,41-43,48,49: 43-Morisi story contains Frazetta art swipes from Untamed Love	30	60	90	177	289	400
28,36,39,40,45: 28-Jack Katz-a. 36,39-Krigstein-a. 40,45-Ditko-a (#45 is 3 pgs. only)	31	62	93	182	296	410
44,51-Williamson/Krenkel-a	32	64	96	188	307	425
46-Williamson/Krenkel-a; Crandall text illos	32	64	96	188	307	425
47-Crandall, Ditko, Powell-a	32	64	96	188	307	425
50,52,53: 50-Torres, Morrow-a	30	60	90	177	289	400
54-Crandall, Check-a	31	62	93	182	296	410

NOTE: ***Ayers** a-18, 49, 52. **Berg** a-17, 51. **Colan** a-1, 3, 18, 35, 43. **Colletta** a-18. **Drucker** a-41. **Everett** a-2, 29, 33, 35, 41; c-8-11, 14, 38, 39, 41, 43, 44, 46, 48-51, 53. **Fass** a-16. **Forte** a-21, 22, 45, 46. **Matt Fox** a-12?, 21, 22; c-22. **Heath** a-3; c-3, 15, 17, 26. **Heck** a-25. **Kinstler** a-15. **Mort Lawrence** a-26, 32, 34. **Maneely** a-1, 9, 14, 22; c-12, 23, 24, 27. **Mooney** a-3, 40. **Morisi** a-43, 49, 52. **Morrow** a-50. **Orlando** a-51. **Pakula** a-16. **Powell** a-21, 29, 37, 38, 47. **Reinman** a-1, 14, 17. **Robinson** a-7p, 42. **Romita** a-37. **Roussos** a-4, 44. **R.Q. Sale** a-45, 46, 49. **Severin** c-52. **Shores** a-17, 45. **Tuska** a-10, 12, 14. **Whitney** a-2. **Wildey** a-37.*

MYSTERY TALES
Super Comics: 1964

	GD 2.0	VG 4.0	FN 6.0	VF 8.0	VF/NM 9.0	NM- 9.2
Super Reprint #16,17('64): 16-r/Tales of Horror #2. 17-r/Eerie #14(Avon), 18-Kubert-r/Strange Terrors #4	3	6	9	14	20	25

MYSTERY TRAIL
DC Comics: Feb/Mar 1950

nn - Ashcan comic, not distributed to newsstands, only for in-house use. Cover art is Danger Trail #3 with interior being Star Spangled Comics #109. A FN/VF copy sold for $2,357.50 in 2002.

MYSTIC (3rd Series)
Marvel/Atlas Comics (CLDS 1/CSI 2-21/OMC 22-35/CSI 35-61): March, 1951 - No. 61, Aug, 1957

	GD 2.0	VG 4.0	FN 6.0	VF 8.0	VF/NM 9.0	NM- 9.2
1-Atom bomb panels; horror/weird stories in all	116	232	348	742	1271	1800
2	58	116	174	371	636	900
3-Eyes torn out	52	104	156	328	557	785
4- "The Devil Birds" by Wolverton (6 pgs.)	87	174	261	553	952	1350
5,7-10	41	82	123	256	428	600
6- "The Eye of Doom" by Wolverton (7 pgs.)	87	174	261	553	952	1350
11-20: 16-Bondage/torture c/story	36	72	108	216	351	485
21-25,27-36-Last precode (3/55). 25-E.C. swipe	30	60	90	177	289	400
26-Atomic War story; severed head story/cover	37	74	111	222	361	500
37-51,53-56,61	24	48	72	142	234	325
52-Wood-a; Crandall-a?	26	52	78	154	252	350
57-Story "Trapped in the Ant-Hill" (1957) is very similar to "The Man in the Ant Hill" in TTA #27	34	68	102	199	325	450
58,59-Krigstein-a	25	50	75	150	245	340
60-Williamson/Mayo-a (4 pgs.)	26	52	78	154	252	350

NOTE: ***Andru** a-23, 25. **Ayers** a-35, 53; c-8. **Berg** a-49. **Cameron** a-49, 51. **Check** a-31, 60. **Colan** a-3, 7, 12, 21, 37, 60. **Colletta** a-29. **Drucker** a-46, 52, 56. **Everett** a-8, 9, 17, 40, 44, 57; c-13, 18, 21, 42, 47, 49, 51-55, 57-59, 61. **Forte** a-35, 52, 58. **Fox** a-24i. **Al Hartley** a-35. **Heath** a-10; c-10, 20, 22, 23, 25, 30. **Infantino** a-12. **Kane** a-8, 24p. **Jack Katz** a-31, 33. **Mort Law.rence** a-19, 37. **Maneely** a-22, 24, 58; c-7, 15, 28, 29, 31. **Moldoff** a-29. **Morisi** a-48, 49, 52. **Morrow** a-51. **Orlando** a-57, 61. **Pakula** a-52, 57, 59. **Powell** a-52, 54-56. **Robinson** a-5. **Romita** a-11, 15. **R.Q. Sale** a-35, 53, 58. **Sekowsky** a-1, 2, 4, 5. **Severin** c-56, 60. **Tuska** a-15. **Whitney** a-33. **Wildey** a-28, 30. **Ed Win** a-17, 20. Canadian reprints known-title 'Startling.'*

MYSTIC (Also see CrossGen Chronicles)
CrossGeneration Comics: Jul, 2000 - No. 43, Jan, 2004 ($2.95)

1-43: 1-Marz-s/Peterson & Dell-a. 15-Cameos by DC & Marvel characters 3.00
...: Rite of Passage Vol. 1 TPB (5/01, $19.95) r/#1-7; Linsner-c 20.00
...: The Demon Queen Vol. 2 TPB (2002, $19.95) r/#8-14 20.00
...: Siege of Scales Vol. 3 TPB (2002, $15.95) r/#15-20 16.00
...: Out All Night Vol.4 TPB (2003, $15.95) r/#21-26 16.00
Vol. 5: Master Class (2003, $15.95) r/#27-32 16.00

MYSTIC (CrossGen characters)
Marvel Comics: Oct, 2011 - No. 4, Jan, 2012 ($2.99, limited series)

1-4-G. Willow Wilson-s/David López-a/Amanda Conner-c 3.00

MYSTICAL TALES
Atlas Comics (CCC 1/EPI 2-8): June, 1956 - No. 8, Aug, 1957

	GD 2.0	VG 4.0	FN 6.0	VF 8.0	VF/NM 9.0	NM- 9.2
1-Everett-c/a	53	106	159	334	567	800
2-4: 2-Berg-a. 3,4-Crandall-a.	29	58	87	170	278	385
5-Williamson-a (4 pgs.)	31	62	93	182	296	410
6-Torres, Krigstein-a	28	56	84	165	270	375
7-Bolle, Forte, Torres, Orlando-a	27	54	81	160	263	365
8-Krigstein, Check-a	28	56	84	165	270	375

NOTE: ***Everett** a-1; c-1-4, 6, 7. **Orlando** a-1, 2, 7. **Pakula** a-3. **Powell** a-1, 4.*

MYSTIC ARCANA
Marvel Comics: Aug, 2007 - Jan, 2008 ($2.99)

1-Magik on-c; art by Scott and Nguyen; Ian McNee and Dani Moonstar app. 3.00
(#2)...: Black Knight 1 (9/07, $2.99) Djurdjevic-c/Grummett & Hanna-a; origin retold 3.00
3-("Scarlet Witch" on cover)(10/07, $2.99) Djurdjevic-c/Santacruz-a; childhood 3.00
(#4)...: Sister Grimm 1 (1/08, $2.99) Nico Minoru from Runaways; Djurdjevic-c/Noto-a 3.00
...: The Book of Marvel Magic ('07, $3.99) Official Handbook profiles of the magic-related 4.00
HC (2007, $24.99, d.j.) r/series and ...: The Book of Marvel Magic 25.00

MYSTIC COMICS (1st Series)
Timely Comics (TPI 1-5/TCI 8-10): March, 1940 - No. 10, Aug, 1942

	GD 2.0	VG 4.0	FN 6.0	VF 8.0	VF/NM 9.0	NM- 9.2
1-Origin The Blue Blaze, The Dynamic Man, & Flexo the Rubber Robot; Zephyr Jones, 3X's & Deep Sea Demon app.; The Magician begins (all 1st app.); c-from Spider pulp V18#1, 6/39	1409	2818	4227	10,849	20,925	31,000
2-The Invisible Man & Master Mind Excello begin; Space Rangers, Zara of the Jungle, Taxi Taylor app. (scarce)	595	1190	1785	4350	7675	11,000
3-Origin Hercules, who last appears in #4	415	830	1245	2905	5103	7300
4-Origin The Thin Man & The Black Widow; Merzak the Mystic app.; last Flexo, Dynamic Man, Invisible Man & Blue Blaze (some issues have date sticker on cover; others have July w/August overprint in silver color); Roosevelt assassination-c	486	972	1458	3550	6275	9000
5-(3/41)-Origin The Black Marvel, The Blazing Skull, The Sub-Earth Man, Super Slave & The Terror; The Moon Man & Black Widow app.; 5-German war-c begin, end #10	389	778	1167	2723	4762	6800
6-(10/41)-Origin The Challenger & The Destroyer (1st app.?; also see All-Winners #2, Fall, 1941)	470	940	1410	3431	6066	8700
7-The Witness begins (12/41, origin & 1st app.); origin Davey & the Demon; last Black Widow; Hitler opens his trunk of terror-c by Simon & Kirby (classic-c)	595	1190	1785	4350	7675	11,000
8,10: 10-Father Time, World of Wonder, & Red Skeleton app.; last Challenger & Terror	371	742	1113	2600	4550	6500
9-Gary Gaunt app.; last Black Marvel, Mystic & Blazing Skull; Hitler-c	459	918	1377	3350	5925	8500

NOTE: ***Gabrielle** c-8-10. **Rico** a-9(2). **Schomburg** a-1-4; c-1-6. **Sekowsky** a-9. **Sekowsky/Klein** a-8 (Challenger). Bondage c-1, 2, 9.*

MYSTIC COMICS (2nd Series)

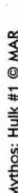

Mythos: Hulk #1 © MAR

Naked Brain #1 © Marc Hempel

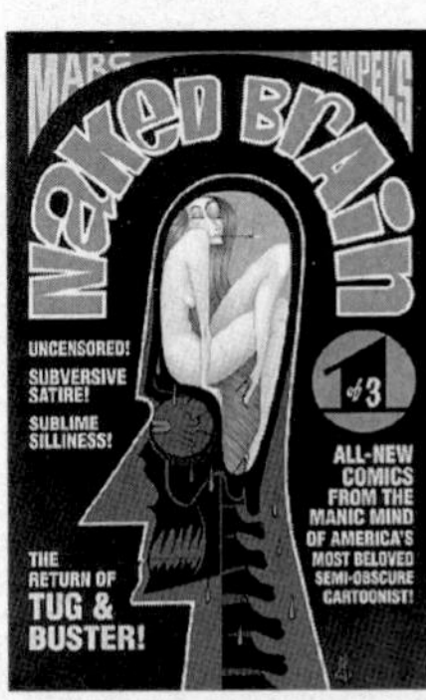

Namor, The Sub-Mariner #1 © MAR

GD 2.0 | VG 4.0 | FN 6.0 | VF 8.0 | VF/NM 9.0 | NM- 9.2

Timely Comics (ANC): Oct, 1944 - No. 3, Win, 1944-45; No. 4, Mar, 1945

1-The Angel, The Destroyer, The Human Torch, Terry Vance the Schoolboy Sleuth, & Tommy Tyme begin 284 568 852 1818 3109 4400
2-(Fall/44)-Last Human Torch & Terry Vance; bondage/hypo-c 161 322 483 1030 1765 2500
3-Last Angel (two stories) & Tommy Tyme 129 258 387 826 1413 2000
4-The Young Allies-c & app.; Schomburg-c 119 238 357 762 1306 1850

MYSTIC COMICS 70th ANNIVERARY SPECIAL
Marvel Comics: Oct, 2009 ($3.99, one-shot)

1-New story of The Vision; r/G.A. Vision app. from Marvel Myst. Comics #13 & 16 5.00

MYSTIC HANDS OF DR. STRANGE
Marvel Comics: May, 2010 ($3.99, B&W, one-shot)

1-Short stories; art by Irving, Brunner, McKeever & Marcos Martin; Parrillo-c 4.00

MYSTIQUE (See X-Men titles)
Marvel Comics: June, 2003 - No. 24, Apr, 2005 ($2.99)

1-24: 1-6-Linsner-c/Vaughan-s/Lucas-a. 7-Ryan-a begins. 8-Horn-c. 9-24-Mayhew-c 23-Wolverine & Rogue app. 3.00
... Vol. 1: Drop Dead Gorgeous TPB (2004, $14.99) r/#1-6 15.00
... Vol. 2: Tinker, Tailor, Mutant, Spy TPB (2004, $17.99) r/#7-13 18.00
... Vol. 3: Unnatural TPB (2004, $13.99) r/#14-18 14.00

MYSTIQUE & SABRETOOTH (Sabretooth and Mystique on-c)
Marvel Comics: Dec, 1996 - No. 4, Mar, 1997 ($1.95, limited series)

1-4: Characters from X-Men 3.00

MY STORY (...True Romances in Pictures #5,6; becomes My Love Life #13) (Formerly Zago)
Hero Books (Fox Features Syndicate): No. 5, May, 1949 - No. 12, Aug, 1950

5-Kamen/Feldstein-a 24 48 72 142 234 325
6-8,11,12: 12-Photo-c 15 30 45 83 124 165
9,10-Wood-a 22 44 66 132 216 300

MYTHOS
Marvel Comics: Mar, 2006 - Dec, 2007 ($3.99)

1-Retelling of X-Men #1 with painted-a by Paolo Rivera; Paul Jenkins-s 4.00
...: Captain America 1 (8/08) Retelling of origin; painted-a by Rivera; Jenkins-s 4.00
...: Fantastic Four 1 (12/07) Retelling of Fantastic Four #1; painted-a by Rivera; Jenkins-s 4.00
...: Ghost Rider 1 (3/07) Retelling of Marvel Spotlight #5; painted-a by Rivera; Jenkins-s 4.00
...: Hulk 1 (10/06) Retelling of Incredible Hulk #1; painted-a by Rivera; Jenkins-s 4.00
...: Spider-Man 1 (8/07) Retelling of Amazing Fantasy #15; painted-a by Rivera; Jenkins-s 4.00

MYTHOS: THE FINAL TOUR
DC Comics/Vertigo: Dec, 1996 - No. 3, Feb, 1997 ($5.95, limited series)

1-3: 1-Ney Rieber-s/Amaro-a. 2-Snejbjerg-a; Constantine-app. 3-Kristiansen-a; Black Orchid-app. 6.00

MYTHSTALKERS
Image Comics: Mar, 2003 - No. 8, Mar, 2004 ($2.95)

1-8-Jiro-a 3.00

MY TRUE LOVE (Formerly Western Killers #64; Frank Buck #70 on)
Fox Features Syndicate: No. 65, July, 1949 - No. 69, March, 1950

65 20 40 60 114 182 250
66,68,69: 69-Morisi-a 14 28 42 80 115 150
67-Wood-a 22 44 66 132 216 300

NAIL, THE
Dark Horse Comics: June, 2004 - No. 4, Oct, 2004 ($2.99, limited series)

1-4-Rob Zombie & Steve Niles-s/Nat Jones-a/Simon Bisley-c 3.00
TPB (2005, $12.95) r/series 13.00

NAKED BRAIN (Marc Hempel's...)
Insight Studios Group: 2002 - No. 3, 2002 ($2.95, B&W, limited series)

1-3-Marc Hempel cartoons and sketches; Tug & Buster app. 3.00

NAKED PREY, THE (See Movie Classics)

'NAM, THE (See Savage Tales #1, 2nd series & Punisher Invades...)
Marvel Comics Group: Dec, 1986 - No. 84, Sept, 1993

1-Golden a(p)/c begins, ends #13 6.00
1 (2nd printing) 3.00
2-7,9-25,27-66,70-74: 7-Golden-a (2 pgs.). 32-Death R. Kennedy. 52,53-Frank Castle (The Punisher) app. 52,53-Gold 2nd printings. 58-Silver logo. 65-Heath-c/a. 70-Lomax scripts begin 3.00
8-1st app. Fudd Verzyl, Tunnel Rat 5.00
26-2nd app. Fudd Verzyl, Tunnel Rat 4.00
67-69-Punisher 3 part story 4.00
75-($2.25, 52 pgs.) 6.00
76-84 3.00
Trade Paperback 1,2: 1-r/#1-4. 2-r/#5-8 1 2 3 5 6 8
TPB ('99, $14.95) r/#1-4; recolored 15.00

'NAM MAGAZINE, THE
Marvel Comics: Aug, 1988 - No. 10, May, 1989 ($2.00, B&W, 52pgs.)

1-10: Each issue reprints 2 issues of the comic 4.00

NAMELESS, THE
Image Comics: May, 1997 - No. 5, Sept, 1997 ($2.95, B&W)

1-5: Pruett/Hester-s/a 3.00
...: The Director's Cut TPB (2006, $15.99) r/#1-5; original proposal by Pruett 16.00

NAMES OF MAGIC, THE (Also see Books of Magic)
DC Comics (Vertigo): Feb, 2001 - No. 5, June, 2001 ($2.50, limited series)

1-5: Bolton painted-c on all; Case-a; leads into Hunter: The Age of Magic 3.00
TPB (2002, $14.95) r/#1-5 15.00

NAME OF THE GAME, THE
DC Comics: 2001 ($29.95, graphic novel)

Hardcover ($29.95) Will Eisner-s/a 30.00

NAMOR (Volume 2)
Marvel Comics: June, 2003 - No. 12, May, 2004 (25¢/$2.25/$2.99)

1-(25¢-c)Young Namor in the 1920s; Larroca-c/a 3.00
2-6-($2.25) Larroca-a 3.00
7-12-($2.99): 7-Olliffe-a begins 3.00

NAMORA (See Marvel Mystery Comics #82 & Sub-Mariner Comics)
Marvel Comics (PrPl): Fall, 1948 - No. 3, Dec, 1948

1-Sub-Mariner x-over in Namora; Namora by Everett(2), Sub-Mariner by Rico (10 pgs.) 297 594 891 1901 3251 4600
2-The Blonde Phantom & Sub-Mariner story; Everett-a 174 348 522 1114 1907 2700
3-(Scarce)-Sub-Mariner app.; Everett-a 194 388 582 1242 2121 3000

NAMORA (See Agents of Atlas)
Marvel Comics: Aug, 2010 ($3.99, one-shot)

1-Parker-s/Pichelli-a 4.00

NAMOR: THE FIRST MUTANT (Curse of the Mutants x-over with X-Men titles)
Marvel Comics: Oct, 2010 - No. 11, Aug, 2011 ($3.99/$2.99)

1-($3.99) Olivetti-a/Stuart Moore-s/Jae Lee-c; back-up retelling of origin and history 4.00
2-11-($2.99) 2-Emma Frost app. 5-Mayhew-c. 6-10-Noto-c 3.00
... Annual 1 (7/11, $3.99) Part 3 of "Escape From the Negative Zone" x-over; Fiumara-a 4.00

NAMOR, THE SUB-MARINER (See Prince Namor & Sub-Mariner)
Marvel Comics: Apr, 1990 - No. 62, May, 1995 ($1.00/$1.25/$1.50)

1-Byrne-c/a/scripts in 1-25 (scripts only #26-32) 6.00
2-5: 5-Iron Man app. 4.00
6-11,13-23,25,27-36,38-49,51-62: 16-Re-intro Iron Fist (8-cameo only). 18-Punisher cameo (1 panel); 21-23,25-Wolverine cameos. 22,23-Iron Fist app. 28-Iron Fist-c/story. 31-Dr. Doom-c/story. 33,34-Iron Fist cameo. 35-New Tiger Shark-c/story. 48-The Thing app. 3.00
12,24: 12-(52pgs.)-Re-intro. The Invaders. 24-Namor vs. Wolverine 4.00
26-Namor w/new costume; 1st Jae Lee-c/a this title (5/92) & begins 5.00
37-Aqua holografx foil-c 4.00
50-($1.75, 52 pgs.)-Newsstand ed.; w/bound-in S-M trading card sheet (both versions) 4.00
50-($2.95, 52 pgs.)-Collector edition w/foil-c 5.00
Annual 1-4 ('91-94, 68 pgs.): 1-3 pg. origin recap. 2-Return/Defenders. 3-Bagged w/card. 4-Painted-c 4.00

NOTE: *Jae Lee a-26-30p, 31-37, 38p, 39, 40; c-26-40.*

NANCY AND SLUGGO (See Comics On Parade & Sparkle Comics)
United Features Syndicate: No. 16, 1949 - No. 23, 1954

16(#1) 10 20 30 58 79 100
17-23 8 16 24 40 50 60

NANCY & SLUGGO (Nancy #146-173; formerly Sparkler Comics)
St. John/Dell #146-187/Gold Key #188 on: No. 121, Apr, 1955-No. 192, Oct, 1963

121(4/55)(St. John) 10 20 30 54 72 90
122-145(7/57)(St. John) 8 16 24 44 57 70
146(9/57)-Peanuts begins, ends #192 (Dell) 8 16 24 56 108 160
147-161 (Dell) Peanuts in all 8 16 24 51 86 120
162-165,177-180-John Stanley-a 7 14 21 44 82 120
166-176-Oona & Her Haunted House series; Stanley-a 7 14 21 49 92 135

Nascar Heroes #1 © Nascar

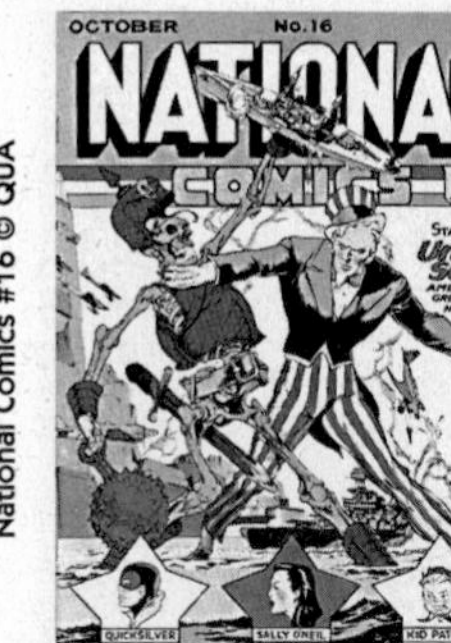

National Comics #16 © QUA

Navy Combat #6 © MAR

	GD 2.0	VG 4.0	FN 6.0	VF 8.0	VF/NM 9.0	NM- 9.2
181-187(3-5/62)(Dell)	5	10	15	35	63	90
188(10/62)-192 (Gold Key)	5	10	15	35	63	90
Four Color 1034(9-11/59)-Summer Camp	5	10	15	30	50	70

(See Dell Giant #34, 45 & Dell Giants)

NANNY AND THE PROFESSOR (TV)
Dell Publishing Co.: Aug, 1970 - No. 2, Oct, 1970 (Photo-c)

	GD 2.0	VG 4.0	FN 6.0	VF 8.0	VF/NM 9.0	NM- 9.2
1-(01-546-008)	5	10	15	30	50	70
2	4	8	12	25	40	55

NAPOLEON
Dell Publishing Co.: No. 526, Dec, 1953

	GD 2.0	VG 4.0	FN 6.0	VF 8.0	VF/NM 9.0	NM- 9.2
Four Color 526	4	8	12	25	40	55

NAPOLEON & SAMANTHA (See Walt Disney Showcase No. 10)

NAPOLEON & UNCLE ELBY (See Clifford McBride's...)
Eastern Color Printing Co.: July, 1942 (68 pgs.) (One Shot)

	GD 2.0	VG 4.0	FN 6.0	VF 8.0	VF/NM 9.0	NM- 9.2
1	43	86	129	271	461	650
1945-American Book-Strafford Press (128 pgs.) (8x10-1/2"; B&W reprints; hardcover)	15	30	45	83	124	165

NARRATIVE ILLUSTRATION, THE STORY OF THE COMICS (Also see Good Triumphs Over Evil!)
M.C. Gaines: Summer, 1942 (32 pgs., 7-1/4"x10", B&W w/color inserts)

nn-16 pgs. text with illustrations of ancient art, strips and comic covers; 4 pg. WWII War Bond promo, "The Minute Man Answers the Call" color comic drawn by Shelly and a special 8-page color comic insert of "The Story of Saul" (from Picture Stories from the Bible #10 or soon to appear in PS #10) or "Noah and His Ark" or "The Story of Ruth". Insert has special title page indicating it was part of a Sunday newspaper supplement insert series that had already run in a New England "Sunday Herald." Another version exists with insert from Picture Stories from the Bible #7.
(very rare) Estimated value... 1500.00

NOTE: ***Print, A Quarterly Journal of the Graphic Arts*** *Vol. 3 No. 2 (88 pg., square bound) features the 1st printing of Narrative Illustration, The Story of The Comics. A VG+ copy sold for $750 in 2005.*

NASCAR HEROES
Starbridge Media: 2007 - No. 3 ($3.95)

	NM- 9.2
1-3: 1-Origin of fictional racer Jimmy Dash. 3-Origin of the Daytona 500; DeStefano-s	4.00
nn-(2008, Free Comic Book Day giveaway) The Mystery of Driver Z	3.00

NASH (WCW Wrestling)
Image Comics: July, 1999 - No. 2, July, 1999 ($2.95)

	NM- 9.2
1,2-Regular and photo-c	3.00
1-($6.95) Photo-split-cover Edition	7.00

NATHANIEL DUSK
DC Comics: Feb, 1984 - No. 4, May, 1984 ($1.25, mini-series, direct sales, Baxter paper)

	NM- 9.2
1-4: 1-Intro/origin; Gene Colan-c/a in all	3.00

NATHANIEL DUSK II
DC Comics: Oct, 1985 - No. 4, Jan, 1986 ($2.00, mini-series, Baxter paper)

	NM- 9.2
1-4: Gene Colan-c/a in all	3.00

NATIONAL COMICS
Quality Comics Group: July, 1940 - No. 75, Nov, 1949

	GD 2.0	VG 4.0	FN 6.0	VF 8.0	VF/NM 9.0	NM- 9.2
1-Uncle Sam begins (1st app.); origin sidekick Buddy by Eisner; origin Wonder Boy & Kid Dixon; Merlin the Magician (ends #45); Cyclone, Kid Patrol, Sally O'Neil Policewoman, Pen Miller (by Klaus Nordling; ends #22), Prop Powers (ends #26), & Paul Bunyan (ends #22) begin	611	1222	1833	4460	7880	11,300
2	258	516	774	1651	2826	4000
3-Last Eisner Uncle Sam	187	374	561	1197	2049	2900
4-Last Cyclone	139	278	417	890	1520	2150
5-(11/40)-Quicksilver begins (1st app.; 3rd w/lightning speed?; re-intro'd by DC in 1993 as Max Mercury in Flash #76, 2nd series); origin Uncle Sam; bondage-c	161	322	483	1030	1765	2500
6,8-11: 8-Jack & Jill begins (ends #22). 9-Flag-c	132	264	396	845	1448	2050
7-Classic Lou Fine-c	300	600	900	1920	3310	4700
12	94	188	282	602	1026	1450
13-16-Lou Fine-a	97	194	291	621	1061	1500
17,19-22: 21-Classic Nazi swastika cover. 22-Last Pen Miller (moves to Crack #23)	74	148	222	470	810	1150
18-(12/41)-Shows Asians attacking Pearl Harbor; on stands one month before actual event	148	296	444	947	1624	2300
23-The Unknown & Destroyer 171 begin	76	152	228	486	831	1175
24-Japanese War-c	76	152	228	486	831	1175
25-30: 25-Nazi drug usage/hypodermic needle in story. 26-Wonder Boy ends. 27- G-2 the Unknown begins (ends #46). 29-Origin The Unknown	55	110	165	352	601	850
31-33: 33-Chic Carter begins (ends #47)	50	100	150	315	533	750
34-37,40: 35-Last Kid Patrol	43	86	129	271	461	650
38-Hitler, Tojo, Mussolini-c	74	148	222	470	810	1150
39-Hitler-c	76	152	228	486	831	1175
41,43-50: 48-Origin The Whistler	28	56	84	165	270	375
42-The Barker begins (1st app?, 5/44); The Barker covers begin	41	82	123	256	428	600
51-Sally O'Neil by Ward, 8 pgs. (12/45)	30	60	90	117	289	400
52-60	20	40	60	118	192	265
61-67: 67-Format change; Quicksilver app.	15	30	45	90	140	190
68-75: The Barker ends	15	30	45	83	124	165

NOTE: ***Cole*** *Quicksilver-13; Barker-43; c-43, 46, 47, 49-51.* ***Crandall*** *Uncle Sam-11-13 (with* ***Fine****), 25, 26; c-24-26, 30-33, 43.* ***Crandall*** *Paul Bunyan-10-13.* ***Fine*** *Uncle Sam-13 (w/****Crandall****), 17, 18; c-1-14, 16, 18, 21.* ***Gill Fox*** *c-69-74.* ***Guardineer*** *Quicksilver-27, 35.* ***Gustavson*** *Quicksilver-14-26.* ***McWilliams*** *a-23-28, 55, 57. Uncle Sam c-1-41. Barker c-42-75.*

NATIONAL COMICS (Also see All Star Comics 1999 crossover titles)
DC Comics: May, 1999 ($1.99, one-shot)

	NM- 9.2
1-Golden Age Flash and Mr. Terrific; Waid-s/Lopresti-a	3.00

NATIONAL COMICS
DC Comics: Sept, 2012 ($3.99, one-shots)

	NM- 9.2
... Eternity 1 (9/12) Re-intro of Kid Eternity; Lemire-s/Hamner-a/c	4.00
... Looker 1 (10/12) Vampire supermodel; Edginton-s/Mike S. Miller-a/March-c	4.00
... Madame X 1 (12/12) Rob Williams-s/Trevor Hairsine-a/Fiona Staples-c	4.00
... Rose & Thorn 1 (11/12) Taylor-s/Googe-a/Sook-c	4.00

NATIONAL CRUMB, THE (Magazine-Size)
Mayfair Publications: August, 1975 (52 pgs., B&W) (Satire)

	GD 2.0	VG 4.0	FN 6.0	VF 8.0	VF/NM 9.0	NM- 9.2
1-Grandenetti-c/a, Ayers-a	2	4	6	11	16	20

NATIONAL VELVET (TV)
Dell Publishing Co./Gold Key: May-July, 1961 - No. 2, Mar, 1963 (All photo-c)

	GD 2.0	VG 4.0	FN 6.0	VF 8.0	VF/NM 9.0	NM- 9.2
Four Color 1195 (#1)	6	12	18	41	76	110
Four Color 1312, 01-556-207, 12-556-210 (Dell)	4	8	12	27	44	60
1,2: 1(12/62) (Gold Key). 2(3/63)	4	8	12	27	44	60

NATION OF SNITCHES
Piranha Press (DC): 1990 ($4.95, color, 52 pgs.)

	NM- 9.2
nn	5.00

NATION X (X-Men on the Utopia island)
Marvel Comics: Feb, 2010 - No. 4, May, 2010 ($3.99, limited series)

	NM- 9.2
1-4-Short stories by various. 1,4-Allred-a. 2-Choi, Cloonan-a. 4-Doop app.	4.00
...: X-Factor (3/10, $3.99) David-s/DeLandro-a	4.00

NATURE BOY (Formerly Danny Blaze; Li'l Rascal Twins #6 on)
Charlton Comics: No. 3, March, 1956 - No. 5, Feb, 1957

	GD 2.0	VG 4.0	FN 6.0	VF 8.0	VF/NM 9.0	NM- 9.2
3-1st app./origin; Blue Beetle story (last Golden Age app.); Buscema-c/a	22	44	66	130	213	295
4,5	15	30	45	92	144	195

NOTE: ***John Buscema*** *a-3, 4p, 5; c-3.* ***Powell*** *a-4.*

NATURE OF THINGS (Disney, TV/Movie)
Dell Publishing Co.: No. 727, Sept, 1956 - No. 842, Sept, 1957

	GD 2.0	VG 4.0	FN 6.0	VF 8.0	VF/NM 9.0	NM- 9.2
Four Color 727 (#1), 842-Jesse Marsh-a	5	10	15	31	53	75

NAUSICAA OF THE VALLEY OF WIND
Viz Comics: 1988 - No. 7, 1989; 1989 - No. 4, 1990 ($2.50, B&W, 68pgs.)

	NM- 9.2
Book 1-7: 1-Contains Moebius poster	5.00
Part II, Book 1-4 ($2.95)	5.00

NAVY ACTION (Sailor Sweeney #12-14)
Atlas Comics (CDS): Aug, 1954 - No. 11, Apr, 1956; No. 15, 1/57 - No. 18, 8/57

	GD 2.0	VG 4.0	FN 6.0	VF 8.0	VF/NM 9.0	NM- 9.2
1-Powell-a	26	52	78	154	252	350
2-Lawrence-a; RQ Sale-a	15	30	45	85	130	175
3-11: 4-Last precode (2/55)	14	28	42	76	108	140
15-18	12	24	36	69	97	125

NOTE: ***Berg*** *a-7, 9.* ***Colan*** *a-8.* ***Drucker*** *a-7, 17.* ***Everett*** *a-3, 7, 16; c-16, 17.* ***Heath*** *c-1, 2, 5, 6.* ***Maneely*** *a-5, 7, 8, 18; c-9, 11.* ***Pakula*** *a-2, 3, 9.* ***Reinman*** *a-17.*

NAVY COMBAT
Atlas Comics (MPI): June, 1955 - No. 20, Oct, 1958

	GD 2.0	VG 4.0	FN 6.0	VF 8.0	VF/NM 9.0	NM- 9.2
1-Torpedo Taylor begins by Don Heck; Heath-c	25	50	75	150	245	340
2	15	30	45	84	127	170
3-10	13	26	39	74	105	135
11,13-16,18-20: 14-Torres-a	12	24	36	69	99	125
12-Crandall-a	14	28	42	76	108	140
17-Williamson-a, 4 pgs.; Torres-a	13	26	39	74	105	135

NOTE: ***Ayers*** *a-15.* ***Berg*** *a-10, 11.* ***Colan*** *a-11.* ***Drucker*** *a-7.* ***Everett*** *a-3, 20; c-8 & 9 w/****Tuska****, 10, 13-16.* ***Forte***

NecroWar #1 © Dreamwave

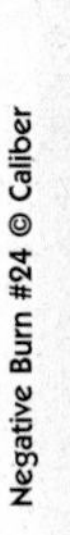

Negative Burn #24 © Caliber

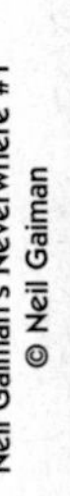

Neil Gaiman's Neverwhere #1 © Neil Gaiman

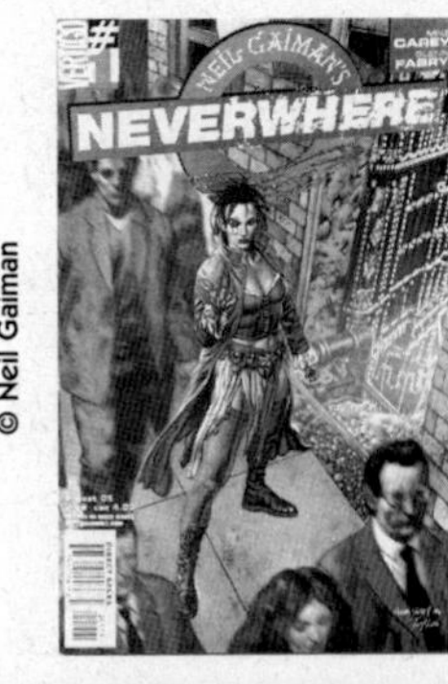

	GD 2.0	VG 4.0	FN 6.0	VF 8.0	VF/NM 9.0	NM- 9.2

a-15, 18. ***Heck*** *a-11(2), 15, 19.* ***Maneely*** *c-1, 6, 11, 17.* ***Morisi*** *a-8.* ***Pakula*** *a-7, 18.* ***Powell*** *a-20.* ***Reinman*** *a-18.*

NAVY HEROES
Almanac Publishing Co.: 1945

1-Heavy in propaganda 15 30 45 86 133 180

NAVY PATROL
Key Publications: May, 1955 - No. 4, Nov, 1955

1 9 18 27 52 69 85
2-4 7 14 21 37 46 55

NAVY TALES
Atlas Comics (CDS): Jan, 1957 - No. 4, July, 1957

1-Everett-c; Berg, Powell-a 22 44 66 132 216 300
2-Williamson/Mayo-a(5 pgs); Crandall-a 15 30 45 88 137 185
3,4-Reinman-a; Severin-c. 4-Crandall-a 14 28 42 82 121 160
NOTE: ***Colan*** *a-4.* ***Maneely*** *c-2.* ***Reinman*** *a-2-4.* ***Sinnott*** *a-4.*

NAVY TASK FORCE
Stanmor Publications/Aragon Mag. No. 4-8: Feb, 1954 - No. 8, April, 1956

1 10 20 30 58 79 100
2 8 16 24 40 50 60
3-8: 8-r/Navy Patrol #1; defeat of the Japanese Navy 7 14 21 37 46 55

NAVY WAR HEROES
Charlton Comics: Jan, 1964 - No. 7, Mar-Apr, 1965

1 4 8 12 23 37 50
2-7 3 6 9 15 22 28

NAZA (Stone Age Warrior)
Dell Publishing Co.: Nov-Jan, 1963-64 - No. 9, March, 1966

12-555-401 (#1)-Painted-c 5 10 15 31 53 75
2-9: 2-4-Painted-c 4 8 12 23 37 50

NEBBS, THE (Also see Crackajack Funnies)
Dell Publishing Co./Croydon Publishing Co.: 1941; 1945

Large Feature Comic 23(1941) 22 44 66 128 209 290
1(1945, 36 pgs.)-Reprints 13 26 39 74 105 135

NECESSARY EVIL
Desperado Publishing: Oct, 2007 - No. 9, Nov, 2008 ($3.99)

1-9: 1-Joshua Williamson-s/Marcus Harris-a/Dustin Nguyen-c 4.00

NECROMANCER
Image Comics (Top Cow): Sept, 2005 - No. 6, July 2006 ($2.99)

1-6: 1-Manapul-a/Ortega-s; three covers by Manapul, Horn & Bachalo 3.00
... Pilot Season Vol. 1 #1 (11/07, $2.99) Ortega-s/Meyers-a/Manapul-c 3.00

NECROMANCER: THE GRAPHIC NOVEL
Marvel Comics (Epic Comics): 1989 ($8.95)

nn 9.00

NECROWAR
Dreamwave Productions: July, 2003 - No. 3, Sept, 2003 ($2.95)

1-3-Furman-s/Granov-digital art 3.00

NEGATION
CrossGeneration Comics: Dec, 2001 - No. 27, Mar, 2004 ($2.95)

Prequel (12/01) 3.00
1-27: 1-(1/02) Pelletier-a/Bedard & Waid-s 3.00
... Lawbringer (11/02, $2.95) Nebres-a 3.00
Vol. 1: Bohica! (10/02, $19.95, TPB) r/ Prequel & #1-6 20.00
Vol. 2: Baptism of Fire (5/03, $15.95, TPB) r/#7-12 16.00
Vol. 3: Hounded (12/03, $15.95, TPB) r/#13-18 16.00

NEGATION WAR
CrossGeneration Comics: Apr, 2004 - No. 6 ($2.95)

1-4-Bedard-s/Pelletier-a 3.00

NEGATIVE BURN
Caliber: 1993 - No. 50, 1997 ($2.95, B&W, anthology)

1,2,4-12,14-47: Anthology by various including Bolland, Burden, Doran, Gaiman, Moebius, Moore, & Pope 4.00
3,13: 3-Bone story. 13-Strangers in Paradise story 2 4 6 8 10 12
48,49-($4.95) 5.00
50-($6.95, 96 pgs.)-Gaiman, Robinson, Bolland 7.00
...Summer Special 2005 (Image, 2005, $9.99) new short stories by various 10.00
...: The Best From 1993-1998 (Image, 1/05, $19.95) r/short stories by various 20.00
...Winter Special 2005 (Image, 2005, $9.95) new short stories by various 10.00

NEGATIVE BURN
Image Comics (Desperado): May, 2006 - No. 21 ($5.99, B&W, anthology)

1-21: 1-Art by Bolland, Powell, Luna, Smith, Hester. 2-Milk & Cheese by Dorkin 6.00

NEGRO (See All-Negro)

NEGRO HEROES (Calling All Girls, Real Heroes, & True Comics reprints)
Parents' Magazine Institute: Spring, 1947 - No. 2, Summer, 1948

1 142 284 426 909 1555 2200
2-Jackie Robinson-c/story 142 284 426 909 1555 2200

NEGRO ROMANCE (Negro Romances #4)
Fawcett Publications: June, 1950 - No. 3, Oct, 1950 (All photo-c)

1-Evans-a (scarce) 181 362 543 1158 1979 2800
2,3 (scarce) 148 296 444 947 1624 2300

NEGRO ROMANCES (Formerly Negro Romance; Romantic Secrets #5 on)
Charlton Comics: No. 4, May, 1955

4-Reprints Fawcett #2 (scarce) 116 232 348 742 1271 1800

NEIL GAIMAN AND CHARLES VESS' STARDUST
DC Comics (Vertigo): 1997 - No. 4, 1998 ($5.95/$6.95, square-bound, lim. series)

1-4: Gaiman text with Vess paintings in all 7.00
Hardcover (1998, $29.95) r/series with new sketches 35.00
Softcover (1999, $19.95) oversized; new Vess-c 20.00

NEIL GAIMAN'S LADY JUSTICE
Tekno Comix: Sept, 1995 - No. 11, May, 1996 ($1.95/$2.25)

1-11: 1-Sienkiewicz-c; pin-ups. 1-5-Brereton-c. 7-Polybagged. 11-The Big Bang Pt. 7 3.00

NEIL GAIMAN'S LADY JUSTICE
BIG Entertainment: V2#1, June, 1996 - No. 9, Feb, 1997 ($2.25)

V2#1-9: Dan Brereton-c on all. 6-8-Dan Brereton script 3.00

NEIL GAIMAN'S MIDNIGHT DAYS
DC Comics (Vertigo): 1999 ($17.95, trade paperback)

nn-Reprints Gaiman's short stories; new Swamp Thing w/ Bissette-a 18.00

NEIL GAIMAN'S MR. HERO-THE NEWMATIC MAN
Tekno Comix: Mar, 1995 - No. 17, May, 1996 ($1.95/$2.25)

1-17: 1-Intro Mr. Hero & Teknophage; bound-in game piece and trading card. 4-w/Steel edition Neil Gaiman's Teknophage #1 coupon. 13-Polybagged 3.00

NEIL GAIMAN'S MR. HERO-THE NEWMATIC MAN
BIG Entertainment: V2#1, June, 1996 ($2.25)

V2#1-Teknophage destroys Mr. Hero; includes The Big Bang Pt. 10 3.00

NEIL GAIMAN'S NEVERWHERE
DC Comics (Vertigo): Aug, 2005 - No. 9, Sept, 2006 ($2.99, limited series)

1-9-Adaptation of Gaiman novel; Carey-s/Fabry-a/c 3.00
TPB (2007, $19.99) r/series; intro. by Carey 20.00

NEIL GAIMAN'S PHAGE-SHADOWDEATH
BIG Entertainment: June, 1996 - No. 6, Nov, 1996 ($2.25, limited series)

1-6: Bryan Talbot-c & scripts in all. 1-1st app. Orlando Holmes 3.00

NEIL GAIMAN'S TEKNOPHAGE
Tekno Comix: Aug, 1995 - No. 10, Mar, 1996 ($1.95/$2.25)

1-6-Rick Veitch scripts & Bryan Talbot-c/a. 3.00
1-Steel Edition 4.00
7-10: Paul Jenkins scripts in all. 8-polybagged 3.00

NEIL GAIMAN'S WHEEL OF WORLDS
Tekno Comix: Apr, 1995 - No. 1, May, 1996 ($2.95/$3.25)

0-1st app. Lady Justice; 48 pgs.; bound-in poster 5.00
0-Regular edition 4.00
1 ($3.25, 5/96)-Bruce Jones scripts; Lady Justice & Teknophage app.; CGI photo-c 4.00

NEIL THE HORSE (See Charlton Bullseye #2)
Aardvark-Vanaheim #1-10/Renegade Press #11 on: 2/83 - No. 10, 12/84; No. 11, 4/85 - #15, 1985 (B&W)

1($1.40) 4.00
1-2nd print 3.00
2-12: 11-w/paperdolls 3.00
13-15: Double size ($3.00). 13-w/paperdolls. 15 is a flip book(2-c) 4.00

NEIL YOUNG'S GREENDALE
DC Comics (Vertigo): 2010 ($19.99, hardcover graphic novel)

Nellie the Nurse #4 © MAR

New Adventure Comics #12 © DC

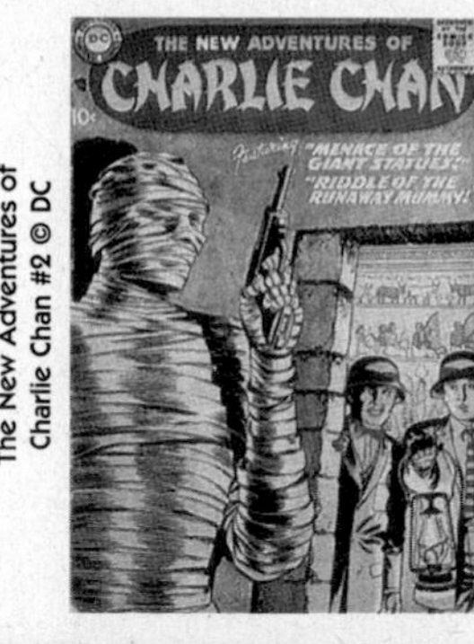

The New Adventures of Charlie Chan #2 © DC

GD 2.0 | VG 4.0 | FN 6.0 | VF 8.0 | VF/NM 9.0 | NM- 9.2

HC-Story based on the Neil Young album; Dysart-s/Chiang-a; intro. by Neil Young 20.00

NELLIE THE NURSE (Also see Gay Comics & Joker Comics)
Marvel/Atlas Comics (SPI/LMC): 1945 - No. 36, Oct, 1952; 1957

1-(1945) 53 106 159 334 567 800
2-(Spring/46) 26 52 78 154 252 350
3,4: 3-New logo (9/46) 20 40 60 120 195 270
5-Kurtzman's "Hey Look" (3); Georgie app. 21 42 63 126 206 285
6-8,10: 7,8-Georgie app. 10-Millie app. 19 38 57 111 176 240
9-Wolverton-a (1 pg.); Mille the Model app. 19 38 57 112 179 245
11,14-16,18-Kurtzman's "Hey Look" 20 40 60 114 182 250
12- "Giggles 'n' Grins" by Kurtzman 19 38 57 111 176 240
13,17,19,20: 17-Annie Oakley app. 15 30 45 88 137 185
21-30: 28-Mr. Nexdoor-r (3 pgs.) by Kurtzman/Rusty #22
14 28 42 80 115 150
31-36: 36-Post-c 13 26 39 72 101 130
1('57)-Leading Mag. (Atlas)-Everett-a, 20 pgs 14 28 42 76 108 140

NELLIE THE NURSE
Dell Publishing Co.: No. 1304, Mar-May, 1962

Four Color 1304-Stanley-a 6 12 18 41 76 110

NEMESIS (Millar & McNiven's...)
Marvel Comics (Icon): May, 2010 - No. 4, Feb, 2011 ($2.99)

1-4-Millar-s/McNiven-a 3.00
1,2-Variant covers: 1-Yu. 2-Cassaday 8.00

NEMESIS ARCHIVES (Listed with Adventures Into the Unknown)

NEMESIS: THE IMPOSTERS
DC Comics: May, 2010 - No. 4, Aug, 2010 ($2.99, limited series)

1-4-Richards-a/Luvisi-c. 1-Joker app. 2-4-Batman app. 3.00

NEMESIS THE WARLOCK (Also see Spellbinders)
Eagle Comics: Sept, 1984 - No. 7, Mar, 1985 (limited series, Baxter paper)

1-7: 2000 A.D. reprints 3.00

NEMESIS THE WARLOCK
Quality Comics/Fleetway Quality #2 on: 1989 - No. 19, 1991 ($1.95, B&W)

1-19 3.00

NEMO (The League of Extraordinary Gentlemen)
Top Shelf Productions: ($14.95, hardcover, one-shots)

...: Heart of Ice HC (2/13) Alan Moore-s/Kevin O'Neill-a 15.00
...: Roses of Berlin HC (3/14) Alan Moore-s/Kevin O'Neill-a 15.00

NEUTRO
Dell Publishing Co.: Jan, 1967

1-Jack Sparling-c/a (super hero); UFO-s 4 8 12 25 40 55

NEVADA (See Zane Grey's Four Color 412, 996 & Zane Grey's Stories of the West #1)

NEVADA (Also see Vertigo Winter's Edge #1)
DC Comics (Vertigo): May, 1998 - No. 6, Oct, 1998 ($2.50, limited series)

1-6-Gerber-s/Winslade-c/a 3.00
TPB-(1999, $14.95) r/#1-6 & Vertigo Winter's Edge preview 15.00

NEVER AGAIN (War stories; becomes Soldier & Marine V2#9)
Charlton Comics: Aug, 1955; No. 8, July, 1956 (No #2-7)

1-WWII 10 20 30 58 79 100
8-(Formerly Foxhole?) 7 14 21 35 43 50

NEVERMEN, THE (See Dark Horse Presents #148-150)
Dark Horse Comics: May, 2000 - No. 4, Aug, 2000 ($2.95, limited series)

1-4-Phil Amara-s/Guy Davis-a 3.00

NEVERMEN, THE: STREETS OF BLOOD
Dark Horse Comics: Jan, 2003 - No. 3, Apr, 2003 ($2.99, limited series)

1-3-Phil Amara-s/Guy Davis-a 3.00
TPB (7/03, $9.95) r/#1-3; Paul Jenkins intro.; Davis sketch pages 10.00

NEW ADVENTURE COMICS (Formerly New Comics; becomes Adventure Comics #32 on; V1#12 indicia says NEW COMICS #12)
National Periodical Publications: V1#12, Jan, 1937 - No. 31, Oct, 1938

V1#12-Federal Men by Siegel & Shuster continues; Jor-L mentioned;
Whitney Ellsworth-c begin, end #14 575 1150 1725 4600 – –
V2#1(2/37, #13)-(Rare) 563 1126 1689 4500 – –
V2#2 (#14) 488 976 1464 3900 – –
15(V2#3)-20(V2#8): 15-1st Adventure logo; Creig Flessel-c begin, end #31.
16-1st non-funny cover. 17-Nadir, Master of Magic begins, ends #30
392 784 1176 2156 3428 4700
21(V2#9),22(V2#10, 2/37): 22-X-Mas-c 350 700 1050 1925 3063 4200
23-25,28-31 317 634 951 1744 2772 3800
26(5/38) (scarce) has house ad for Action Comics #1 showing B&W image of cover (early published image of Superman)(prices vary widely on this book) (A CGC 5.0 sold in 2006 for $5377.50)
27(6/38) has house ad for Action Comics #1 showing B&W image of cover (scarce) (early published image of Superman) 800 1600 2400 4800 6400 8000

NEW ADVENTURES OF ABRAHAM LINCOLN, THE
Image Comics (Homage): 1998 ($19.95, one-shot)

1-Scott McCloud-s/computer art 20.00

NEW ADVENTURES OF CHARLIE CHAN, THE (TV)
National Periodical Publications: May-June, 1958 - No. 6, Mar-Apr, 1959

1 (Scarce)-John Broome-s/Sid Greene-a in all 84 168 252 538 919 1300
2 (Scarce) 53 106 159 334 567 800
3-6 (Scarce)-Greene/Giella-a 45 90 135 284 480 675

NEW ADVENTURES OF CHOLLY AND FLYTRAP, THE
Epic Comics: Dec, 1990 - No. 3, Feb, 1991 ($4.95, limited series)

1-3-Arthur Suydam-s/a/c; painted covers 5.00

NEW ADVENTURES OF HUCK FINN, THE (TV)
Gold Key: December, 1968 (Hanna-Barbera)

1- "The Curse of Thut"; part photo-c 3 6 9 21 33 45

NEW ADVENTURES OF PINOCCHIO (TV)
Dell Publishing Co.: Oct-Dec, 1962 - No. 3, Sept-Nov, 1963

12-562-212(#1) 7 14 21 48 89 130
2,3 6 12 18 38 69 100

NEW ADVENTURES OF ROBIN HOOD (See Robin Hood)

NEW ADVENTURES OF SHERLOCK HOLMES (Also see Sherlock Holmes)
Dell Publishing Co.: No. 1169, Mar-May, 1961 - No. 1245, Nov-Jan, 1961/62

Four Color 1169(#1) 12 24 36 79 170 260
Four Color 1245 10 20 30 70 150 230

NEW ADVENTURES OF SPEED RACER
Now Comics: Dec, 1993 - No. 7, 1994? ($1.95)

1-7 3.00
0-(Premiere)-3-D cover 3.00

NEW ADVENTURES OF SUPERBOY, THE (Also see Superboy)
DC Comics: Jan, 1980 - No. 54, June, 1984

1 1 2 3 5 6 8
2-6,8-10 4.00
11-49,51-54: 11-Superboy gets new power. 14-Lex Luthor app. 15-Superboy gets new parents. 28-Dial "H" For Hero begins, ends #49. 45-47-1st app. Sunburst. 48-Begin 75¢-c. 3.00
1,2,5,6,8 (Whitman variants; low print run; no issue # shown on cover)
2 4 6 9 12 15
7,50: 7-Has extra story "The Computers That Saved Metropolis" by Starlin (Radio Shack giveaway w/indicia). 50-Legion app. 5.00
NOTE: *Buckler a-9p; c-36p. Giffen a-50; c-50. 40i. Gil Kane c-32p, 33p, 35, 39, 41-49. Miller c-51. Starlin a-7. Krypto back-ups in 17, 22. Superbaby in 11, 14, 19, 24.*

NEW ADVENTURES OF THE PHANTOM BLOT, THE (See The Phantom Blot)

NEW AMERICA
Eclipse Comics: Nov, 1987 - No. 4, Feb, 1988 ($1.75, Baxter paper)

1-4: Scout limited series 3.00

NEW ARCHIES, THE (TV)
Archie Comic Publications: Oct, 1987 - No. 22, May, 1990 (75¢)

1 5.00
2-10: 3-Xmas issue 4.00
11-22: 17-22 (95¢-$1.00): 21-Xmas issue 3.00

NEW ARCHIES DIGEST (TV)(...Comics Digest Magazine #4?-10; ...Digest Magazine #11 on)
Archie Comics: May, 1988 - No. 14, July, 1991 ($1.35/$1.50, quarterly)

1 6.00
2-14: 6-Begin $1.50-c 3.50

NEW AVENGERS, THE (Also see Promotional section for military giveaway)
Marvel Comics: Jan, 2005 - No. 64, Jun, 2010 ($2.25/$2.50/$2.99/$3.99)

1-Bendis-s/Finch-a; Spider-Man app.; re-intro The Sentry; 4 covers by McNiven, Quesada & Finch; variants from #1-6 combine for one team image 5.00
1-Director's Cut ($3.99) includes alternate covers, script, villain gallery 4.00

New Avengers (2010 series) #27 © MAR

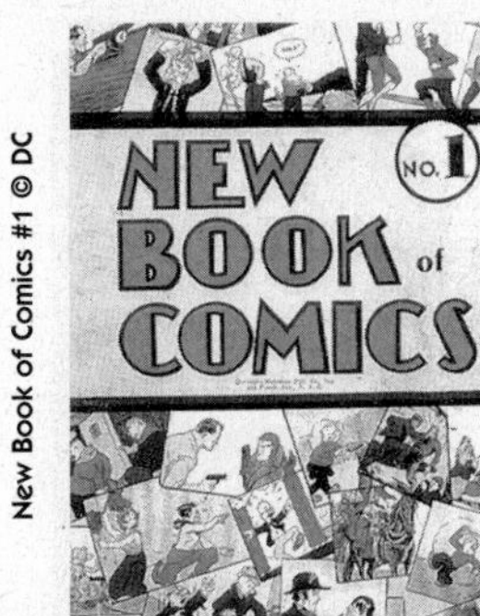

New Book of Comics #1 © DC

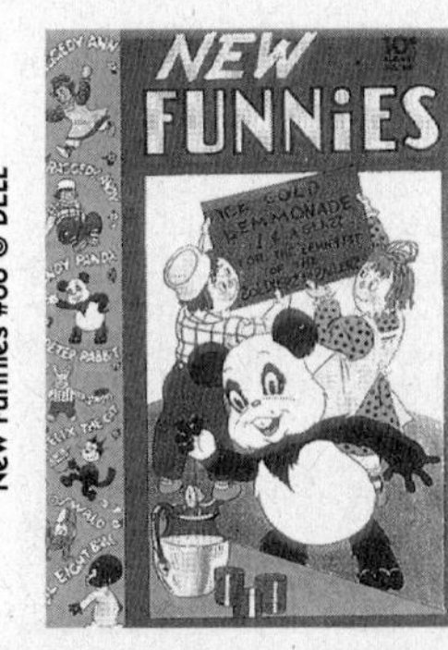

New Funnies #66 © DELL

GD 2.0 | VG 4.0 | FN 6.0 | VF 8.0 | VF/NM 9.0 | NM- 9.2

1-MGC (6/10 $1.00) r/#1 with "Marvel's Greatest Comics" cover logo 3.00
2-20: 2-6-Finch-a. 5-Wolverine app. 7-10-Origin of the Sentry; McNiven-a. 11-Debut of Ronin. 14,15-Cho-c/a. 17-20-Deodato-a 3.00
21-48: 21-26-Civil War. 21-Chaykin-a/c. 26-Maleev-a. 27-31-Yu-a; Echo & "Elektra" app. 33-37-The Hood app. 38-Gaydos-a. 39-Mack-a. 40-47-Secret Invasion 3.00
49-($3.99) Dark Reign 4.00
50-($4.99) Dark Reign; Tan, Hitch, McNiven, Yu, Horn & others-a; Tan wraparound-c 5.00
50-($4.99) Adam Kubert variant-c 6.00
51-64-($3.99) Dark Reign. 51,52-Tan & Bachalo-a. 54-Brother Voodoo becomes Sorceror Supreme. 56-Wrecking Crew app. 61-64-Siege; Steve Rogers app. 4.00
51-54-Variant covers by Bachalo 7.00
56,57-Variant covers. 56-70th Anniversary frame. 57-Super Hero Squad 6.00
Annual 1 (6/06, $3.99) Wedding of Luke Cage and Jessica Jones; Bendis-s/Coipel-a 4.00
Annual 2 (2/08, $3.99) Avengers vs. The Hood's gang; Bendis-s/Pagulayan-a 4.00
Annual 3 (2/10, $4.99) Mayhew-c/a; Dark Avengers app.; Siege preview 5.00
... Finale (6/10, $4.99) Follows Siege #4; Bendis-s/Hitch-a/c; Count Nefaria app. 5.00
...: Illuminati (5/06, $3.99) Bendis-s/Maleev-a; leads into Planet Hulk; Civil War preview 4.00
... Most Wanted Files (2006, $3.99) profile pages of Avenger villains 4.00
... Volume 1 HC (2007, $29.99) oversized r/#1-10, ... Most Wanted Files, and ... Guest Starring the Fantastic Four (militiary giveaway); new intro. by Bendis; script & sketch pages 30.00
... Volume 2 HC (2008, $29.99) oversized r/#11-20, ... Annual #1, and story from Giant-Size Spider-Woman; variant covers & sketch pages 30.00

NEW AVENGERS (The Heroic Age)
Marvel Comics: Aug, 2010 - No. 34, Jan, 2013 ($3.99)

1-Bendis-s/Immonen-a/c; Luke Cage forms new team; back-up text Avengers history 4.00
1-Variant-c by Djurdjevic 6.00
2-16: Hellstrom & Doctor Voodoo app.; back-up text Avengers history. 6-Doctor Voodoo killed. 9-13-Nick Fury flashback w/Chaykin-a. 14-16-Fear Itself. 16-Daredevil joins 4.00
16.1 (11/11, $2.99) Neal Adams-a/c; Bendis-s; Norman Osborn app. 3.00
17-23-($3.99) 17-Norman Osborn attacks; Iron Man app.; Deodato-a 4.00
24-33: 24-30-Avengers vs. X-Men tie-in. 26,27-DaVinci app. 31-Gaydos-a. 32-Pacheco-a 4.00
34-($4.99) Dr. Strange become Sorcerer Supreme again; Deodato-a; gallery of Bendis-era Avengers covers 5.00
Annual 1 (11/11, $4.99) Dell'Otto-a; Wonder Man app.; continues in Avengers Annual #1 5.00

NEW AVENGERS (Marvel NOW!)
Marvel Comics: Mar, 2013 - Present ($3.99)

1-7: 1-Hickman-s/Epting-a; Black Panther and the Illuminati. 4-Galactus app. 4.00
8-16: 8-12-Infinity tie-ins; Deodato-a. 13-Inhumanity; Bianchi-a 4.00

NEW AVENGERS: ILLUMINATI (Also see Civil War and Secret Invasion)
Marvel Comics: Feb, 2007 - No. 5, Jan, 2008 ($2.99, limited series)

1-5-Bendis & Reed-s/Cheung-a. 3-Origin of The Beyonder. 5-Secret Invasion 3.00
HC (2008, $19.99, dustjacket) r/#1-5; cover sketch art 20.00
SC (2008, $14.99) r/#1-5; cover sketch art 15.00

NEW AVENGERS: LUKE CAGE
Marvel Comics: Jun, 2010 - No. 3, Aug, 2010 ($3.99, limited series)

1-3-Arcudi-s/Canete-a; Spider-Man & Ronin app. 4.00

NEW AVENGERS: THE REUNION
Marvel Comics: May, 2009 - No. 4, Aug, 2009 ($3.99, limited series)

1-4-Mockingbird and Ronin (Hawkeye); McCann-s/López-a/Jo Chen-c 4.00

NEW AVENGERS/TRANSFORMERS
Marvel Comics: Sept, 2007 - No. 4, Dec, 2007 ($2.99, limited series)

1-4-Kirkham-a; Capt. America app. 1-Cheung-c. 2-Pearson-c 3.00
TPB (2008, $10.99) r/#1-4 11.00

NEW BOOK OF COMICS (Also see Big Book Of Fun)
National Periodical Publ.: 1937; No. 2, Spring, 1938 (100 pgs. each) (Reprints)

1(Rare)-1st regular size comic annual; 2nd DC annual; contains r/New Comics #1-4 & More Fun #9; r/Federal Men (8 pgs.), Henri Duval (1 pg.), & Dr. Occult in costume (1 pg.) by Siegel & Shuster; Moldoff, Sheldon Mayer (15 pgs.)-a
1850 3700 5550 12,000 21,000 30,000
2-Contains-r/More Fun #15 & 16; r/Dr. Occult in costume (a Superman prototype), & Calling All Cars (4 pgs.) by Siegel & Shuster 950 1900 2850 6175 11,088 16,000

NEW COMICS (New Adventure #12 on)
National Periodical Publ.: 12/35 - No. 11, 12/36 (No. 1-6: paper cover) (No. 1-5: 84 pgs.)

V1#1-Billy the Kid, Sagebrush 'n' Cactus, Jibby Jones, Needles, The Vikings, Sir Loin of Beef, Now-When I Was a Boy, & other 1-2 pg. strips; 2 pgs. Kelly art(1st)-(Gulliver's Travels); Sheldon Mayer-a(1st)(2 2pg. strips); Vincent Sullivan-c(1st)
2333 4666 7000 14,000 - -
2-1st app. Federal Men by Siegel & Shuster & begins (also see The Comics Magazine #2); Mayer, Kelly-a (Rare)(1/36) 1250 2500 3750 7600 - -
3-6: 3,4-Sheldon Mayer-a which continues in The Comics Magazine #1. 3-Vincent Sullivan-c. 4-Dickens' "A Tale of Two Cities" adaptation begins. 5-Junior Federal Men Club; Kiefer-a. 6- "She" adaptation begins 800 1600 2400 5000 - -
7-10 550 1100 1650 3400 - -
11-Ties with More Fun #16 as DC's 1st Christmas-c 600 1200 1800 3700 - -
NOTE: *#1-6 rarely occur in mint condition.* ***Whitney Ellsworth*** *c-4-11.*

NEW CRUSADERS (Rise of the Heroes)
Archie Comics (Red Circle Comics): Oct, 2012 - Present ($2.99)

1-6-The Shield and the offspring of the Mighty Crusaders 3.00

NEW DEADWARDIANS, THE
DC Comics (Vertigo): May, 2012 - No. 8, Dec, 2012 ($2.99, limited series)

1-8-Abnett-s/Culbard-a 3.00

NEW DEFENDERS (See Defenders)

NEW DNAGENTS, THE (Formerly DNAgents)
Eclipse Comics: V2#1, Oct, 1985 - V2#17, Mar, 1987 (Whole #s 25-40; Mando paper)

V2#1-17: 1-Origin recap. 7-Begin 95 cent-c. 9,10-Airboy preview 3.00
3-D 1 (1/86, $2.25) 3.00
2-D 1 (1/86)-Limited ed. (100 copies) 10.00

NEW DYNAMIX
DC Comics (WildStorm): May, 2008 - No. 5, Sept, 2008 ($2.99, limited series)

1-5-Warner-s/J.J. Kirby-a/c. 1-Variant-c by Jim Lee. 1-Convention Ed. with Lee-c 3.00

NEW ETERNALS: APOCALYPSE NOW (Also see Eternals, The)
Marvel Comics: Feb, 2000 ($3.99, one-shot)

1-Bennett & Hanna-a; Ladronn-c 4.00

NEW EXCALIBUR
Marvel Comics: Jan, 2006 - No. 24, Dec, 2007 ($2.99)

1-24: 1-Claremont-s/Ryan-a; Dazzler app. 3-Juggernaut app. 4-Lionheart app. 3.00
... Vol. 1: Defenders of the Realm TPB (2006, $17.99) r/#1-7 18.00
... Vol. 2: Last Days of Camelot TPB (2007, $19.99) r/#8-15 20.00
... Vol. 3: Battle for Eternity TPB (2007, $24.99) r/#16-24; sketch pages 25.00

NEW EXILES (Continued from Exiles #100 and Exiles - Days of Then and Now)
Marvel Comics: Mar, 2008 - No. 18, Apr, 2009 ($2.99)

1-18: 1-Claremont-s/Grummett-a; 2 covers by Land & Golden; new team 3.00
1-2nd printing with Grummett-c 3.00
Annual 1 (2/09, $3.99) Claremont-s/Grummett-a 4.00

NEWFORCE (Also see Newmen)
Image Comics (Extreme Studios): Jan, 1996-No. 4, Apr, 1996 ($2.50, lim. series)

1-4: 1-"Extreme Destroyer" Pt. 8; polybagged w/gaming card. 4-Newforce disbands 3.00

NEW FUN COMICS (More Fun #7 on; see Big Book of Fun Comics)
National Periodical Publications: Feb, 1935 - No. 6, Oct, 1935 (10x15", No. 1-4,: slick-c) (No. 1-5: 36 pgs; 40 pgs. No. 6)

V1#1 (1st DC comic); 1st app. Oswald The Rabbit; Jack Woods (cowboy) begins
7857 15,714 23,571 55,000 - -
2(3/35)-(Very Rare) 3429 6858 10,287 24,000 - -
3-5(8/35): 3-Don Drake on the Planet Soro-c/story (sci/fi, 4/35); early (maybe 1st) DC letter column. 5-Soft-c 2286 4572 6858 16,000 - -
6(10/35)-1st Dr. Occult by Siegel & Shuster (Leger & Reuths); last "New Fun" title. "New Comics" #1 begins in Dec. which is reason for title change to More Fun; Henri Duval (ends #10) by Siegel & Shuster begins; paper-c
3714 7428 11,142 26,000 - -

NEW FUNNIES (The Funnies #1-64; Walter Lantz...#109 on; New TV... #259, 260, 272, 273; TV Funnies #261-271)
Dell Publishing Co.: No. 65, July, 1942 - No. 288, Mar-Apr, 1962

65(#1)-Andy Panda in a world of real people, Raggedy Ann & Andy, Oswald the Rabbit (with Woody Woodpecker x-overs), Li'l Eight Ball & Peter Rabbit begin; Bugs Bunny and Elmer app. 75 150 225 600 1350 2100
66-70: 66-Felix the Cat begins. 67-Billy & Bonny Bee by Frank Thomas begins. 69-Kelly-a (2 pgs.); The Brownies begin (not by Kelly) 30 60 90 216 483 750
71-75: 72-Kelly illos. 75-Brownies by Kelly? 21 42 63 146 311 475
76-Andy Panda (Carl Barks & Pabian-a); Woody Woodpecker x-over in Oswald ends
50 100 150 400 900 1400
77,78: 77-Kelly-c. 78-Andy Panda in a world with real people ends
15 30 45 103 227 350
79-81 10 20 30 69 147 225
82-Brownies by Kelly begins 11 22 33 73 157 240
83-85-Brownies by Kelly in ea. 83-X-mas-c; Homer Pigeon begins. 85-Woody Woodpecker, 1 pg. strip begins 11 22 33 72 154 235
86-90: 87-Woody Woodpecker stories begin 9 18 27 57 111 165

New Gods #8 © DC

New Love #6 © Gilbert Hernandez

New Mutants #93 © MAR

GD VG FN VF VF/NM NM-
2.0 4.0 6.0 8.0 9.0 9.2

91-99 8 16 24 51 96 140
100 (6/45) 8 16 24 54 102 150
101-120: 119-X-Mas-c 7 14 21 46 86 125
121-150: 131,143-X-Mas-c 6 12 18 40 73 105
151-200: 155-X-Mas-c. 167-X-Mas-c. 182-Origin & 1st app. Knothead & Splinter. 191-X-Mas-c 5 10 15 35 63 90
201-240 5 10 15 35 57 80
241-288: 270,271-Walter Lantz c-app. 281-1st story swipes/WDC&S #100 5 10 15 30 50 70
NOTE: *Early issues written by* ***John Stanley.***

NEW GODS, THE (1st Series)(New Gods #12 on)(See Adventure #459, DC Graphic Novel #4, 1st Issue Special #13 & Super-Team Family)
National Periodical Publications/DC Comics: 2-3/71 - V2#11, 10-11/72; V3#12, 7/77 - V3#19, 7-8/78 (Fourth World)

1-Intro/1st app. Orion; 4th app. Darkseid (cameo; 3 weeks after Forever People #1) (#1-3 are 15¢ issues) 8 16 24 56 108 160
2-Darkseid-c/story (2nd full app., 4-5/71) 5 10 15 31 53 75
3-1st app. Black Racer; last 15¢ issue 4 8 12 23 37 50
4-9: (25¢, 52 pg. giants): 4-Darkseid cameo; origin Manhunter-r. 5,7,8-Young Gods feature. 7-Darkseid app. (2-3/72); origin Orion; 1st origin of all New Gods as a group. 9-1st app. Forager 4 8 12 23 37 50
10,11: 11-Last Kirby issue. 3 6 9 19 30 40
12-19: Darkseid storyline w/minor apps. 12-New costume Orion (see 1st Issue Special #13 for 1st new costume). 19-Story continued in Adventure Comics #459,460 2 4 6 8 10 12
Jack Kirby's New Gods TPB ('98, $11.95, B&W&Grey) r/#1-11 plus cover gallery of original series and "84 reprints 12.00
NOTE: *#4-9(25¢, 52 pgs.) contain Manhunter-r by* ***Simon & Kirby*** *from Adventure #73, 74, 75, 76, 77, 78 with covers in that order.* ***Adkins*** *i-12-14, 17-19.* ***Buckler*** *a(p)-15.* ***Kirby*** *c/a-1-11p.* ***Newton*** *a(p)-12-14, 16-19.* ***Starlin*** *c-17.* ***Staton*** *c-19p.*

NEW GODS (Also see DC Graphic Novel #4)
DC Comics: June, 1984 - No. 6, Nov, 1984 ($2.00, Baxter paper)

1-5: New Kirby-c; r/New Gods #1-10. 5.00
6-Reprints New Gods #11 w/48 pgs of new Kirby story & art; leads into DC Graphic Novel #4 2 4 6 8 10 12

NEW GODS (2nd Series)
DC Comics: Feb, 1989 - No. 28, Aug, 1991 ($1.50)

1-28 3.00

NEW GODS (3rd Series) (Becomes Jack Kirby's Fourth World) (Also see Showcase '94 #1 & Showcase '95 #7)
DC Comics: Oct, 1995 - No. 15, Feb, 1997 ($1.95)

1-11,13-15: 9-Giffen-a(p). 10,11-Superman app. 13-Takion, Mr. Miracle & Big Barda app. 13-15-Byrne-a(p)/scripts & Simonson-c. 15-Apokolips merged w/ New Genesis; story cont'd in Jack Kirby's Fourth World 3.00
12-(11/96, 99¢)-Byrne-a(p)/scripts & Simonson-c begin; Takion cameo; indicia reads October 1996 3.00
...Secret Files 1 (9/98, $4.95) Origin-s 5.00

NEW GUARDIANS, THE
DC Comics: Sept, 1988 - No. 12, Sept, 1989 ($1.25)

1-($2.00, 52 pgs)-Staton-c/a in #1-9 4.00
2-12 3.00

NEW HEROIC (See Heroic)

NEW INVADERS (Titled Invaders for #0 & #1) (See Avengers V3#83,84)
Marvel Comics: No. 0, Aug, 2004 - No. 9, June, 2005 ($2.99)

0-9-Roster of U.S. Agent, Sub-Mariner, Blazing Skull and others. 0-Avengers app. 3.00

NEW JUSTICE MACHINE, THE (Also see The Justice Machine)
Innovation Publishing: 1989 - No. 3, 1989 ($1.95, limited series)

1-3 3.00

NEW KIDS ON THE BLOCK, THE (Also see Richie Rich and...)
Harvey Comics: Dec, 1990 - No. 8, Dec, 1991 ($1.25)

1-8 4.00
...**Back Stage Pass** 1(12/90) - 7(11/91) **Chillin'** 1(12/90) - 7(12/91): 1-Photo-c ...**Comic Tour** '90/91 1 (12/90) - 7(12/91) **Digest** 1(1/91) - 5(1/92) **Hanging Tough** 1 (2/91) **Magic Summer Tour** 1 (Fall/90) **Magic Summer Tour** nn (Fall/90, sold at concerts) **Step By Step** 1 (Fall/90, one-shot) **Valentine Girl** 1 (Fall/90, one-shot)-Photo-c 4.00

NEW LINE CINEMA'S TALES OF HORROR (Anthology)
DC Comics (WildStorm): Nov, 2007 ($2.99, one-shot)

1-Freddy Krueger and Leatherface app.; Darick Robertson-c 3.00

NEW LOVE (See Love & Rockets)
Fantagraphics Books: Aug, 1996 - No. 6, Dec, 1997 ($2.95, B&W, lim. series)

1-6: Gilbert Hernandez-s/a 3.00

NEWMAN
Image Comics (Extreme Studios): Jan, 1996 - No. 4, Apr, 1996 ($2.50, lim. series)

1-4: 1-Extreme Destroyer Pt. 3; polybagged w/card. 4-Shadowhunt tie-in; Eddie Collins becomes new Shadowhawk 3.00

NEW MANGVERSE (Also see Marvel Mangaverse)
Marvel Comics: Mar, 2006 - No. 5, July, 2006 ($2.99, lim. series)

1-5: Cebulski-s/Ohtsuka-a; The Hand and Elektra app. 3.00
...: The Rings of Fate (2006, $7.99, digest) r/#1-5 8.00

NEWMEN (becomes The Adventures Of The...#22)
Image Comics (Extreme Studios): Apr, 1994 - No. 20, Nov, 1995; No. 21, Nov, 1996 ($1.95/$2.50)

1-21: 1-5: Matsuda-c/a. 10-Polybagged w/trading card. 11-Polybagged. 20-Has a variant-c; Babewatch! x-over. 21-(11/96)-Series relaunch; Chris Sprouse-a begins; pin-up. 16-Has a variant-c by Quesada & Palmiotti 3.00
TPB-(1996, $12.95) r/#1-4 w/pin-ups 13.00

NEW MEN OF BATTLE, THE
Catechetical Guild: 1949 (nn) (Carboard-c)

nn(V8#1-3,5,6)-192 pgs.; contains 6 issues of Topix rebound 10 20 30 54 72 90
nn(V8#7-V8#11)-160 pgs.; contains 5 iss. of Topix 9 18 27 50 65 80

NEW MUTANTS, THE (See Marvel Graphic Novel #4 for 1st app.)(Also see X-Force & Uncanny X-Men #167)
Marvel Comics Group: Mar, 1983 - No. 100, Apr, 1991

1 1 3 4 6 8 10
2-10: 3,4-Ties into X-Men #167. 10-1st app. Magma 5.00
11-15,17,19,20: 13-Kitty Pryde app. 4.00
16-1st app. Warpath (w/out costume); see Uncanny X-Men #193 1 3 4 6 8 10
18,21: 18-Intro. new Warlock. 21-Double size; origin new Warlock; newsstand version has cover price written in by Sienkiewicz 5.00
22-24,27-30: 23-25-Cloak & Dagger app. 4.00
25,26: 25-1st brief app. Legion. 26-1st full Legion app. 6.00
31-49,51-58: 35-Magneto intro'd as new headmaster. 43-Portacio-i. 58-Contains pull-out mutant registration form 4.00
50,73: 50-Double size. 73-(52 pgs.). 5.00
59-61: Fall of The Mutants series. 60-(52 pgs.) 5.00
62-72,74-85: 68-Intro Spyder. 63-X-Men & Wolverine clones app. 76-X-Factor & X-Terminator app. 85-Liefeld-c begin 4.00
86-Rob Liefeld-a begins; McFarlane-c(i) swiped from Ditko splash pg.; 1st brief app. Cable (last page teaser) 1 3 4 6 8 10
87-1st full app. Cable (3/90) 4 8 12 27 44 60
87-2nd printing; gold metallic ink-c ($1.00) 5.00
88-2nd app. Cable 1 3 4 6 8 10
92-No Liefeld-a; Liefeld-c 5.00
89,90,91,93-97,99,100: 89-3rd app. Cable. 90-New costumes. 90,91-Sabretooth app. 93,94-Cable vs. Wolverine. 95-97-X-Tinction Agenda x-over. 95-Death of new Warlock. 97-Wolverine & Cable-c, but no app. 99-1st app. of Feral (of X-Force); Byrne-c/swipe (X-Men, 1st Series #138). 100-(52 pgs.)-1st brief app. X-Force 6.00
95,100-Gold 2nd printing. 100-Silver ink 3rd printing 5.00
98-1st app. Deadpool, Gideon & Domino (2/91); 2nd Shatterstar (cameo); Liefeld-c/a 8 16 24 54 102 150
Annual 1 (1984) 1 3 4 6 8 10
Annual 2 (1986, $1.25)-1st Psylocke 4 8 12 23 37 50
Annual 3,4,6,7 ('87, '88,'90,'91, 68 pgs.): 4-Evolutionary War x-over. 6-1st new costumes by Liefeld (3 pgs.); 1st brief app. Shatterstar (of X-Force). 7-Liefeld pin-up only; X-Terminators back-up story; 2nd app. X-Force (cont'd in New Warriors Annual #1) 5.00
Annual 5 (1989, $2.00, 68 pgs.)-Atlantis Attacks; 1st Liefeld-a on New Mutants 6.00
... Classic Vol. 1 TPB (2006, $24.99) r/#1-7, Marvel Graphic Novel #4, Uncanny X-Men #167 25.00
... Classic Vol. 2 TPB (2007, $24.99) r/#8-17 25.00
... Classic Vol. 3 TPB (2008, $24.99) r/#18-25 & Annual #1 25.00
Special 1-Special Edition ('85, 68 pgs.)-Ties in w/X-Men Alpha Flight limited series; cont'd in X-Men Annual #9; Art Adams/Austin-a 6.00
Summer Special 1(Sum/90, $2.95, 84 pgs.) 5.00
NOTE: ***Art Adams*** *c-38, 39.* ***Austin*** *c-57i.* ***Byrne*** *c/a-75p.* ***Liefeld*** *a-86-91p, 93-96p, 98-100, Annual 5p, 6(3 pgs.); c-85-91p, 92, 93p, 94, 95, 96p, 97-100, Annual 5, 6p.* ***McFarlane*** *c-85-89i, 93i.* ***Portacio*** *a(i)-43.* ***Russell*** *a-48i.* ***Sienkiewicz*** *a-18-31, 35-38i; c-17-31, 35i, 37i, Annual 1.* ***Simonson*** *c-11p.* ***B. Smith*** *c-36, 40-48.* ***Williamson*** *a(i)-69, 71-73, 78-80, 82, 83; c(i)-69, 72, 73, 78i.*

NEW MUTANTS (Continues as New X-Men (Academy X))

New Mutants (2009 series) #15 © MAR

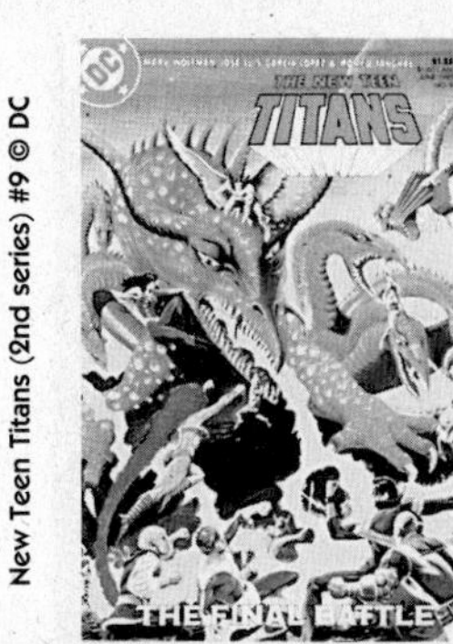

New Teen Titans (2nd series) #9 © DC

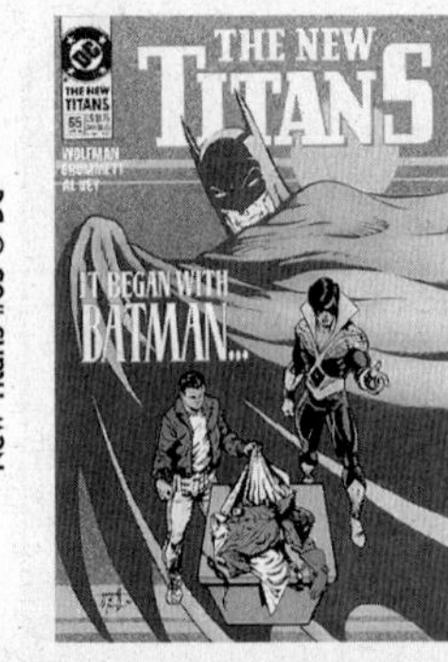

New Titans #65 © DC

Marvel Comics: July, 2003 - No. 13, June, 2004 ($2.50/$2.99)

1-7: 1-6-Josh Middleton-c. 7-Bachalo-c 3.00
8-13 ($2.99) 8-11-Bachalo-c 3.00
... Vol. 1: Back To School TPB (2005, $16.99) r/#1-6; new Middleton-c 17.00

NEW MUTANTS
Marvel Comics: July, 2009 - No. 50, Dec, 2012 ($3.99/$2.99)

1-($3.99) Neves-a; Legion app.; covers by Ross, Adam Kubert, McLeod, Benjamin 4.00
2-24-($2.99) 2-10-Adam Kubert-c. 11-Siege; Dodson-c. 12-14-Second Coming 3.00
25-($3.99) Fernandez-a; wraparound-c by Djurdjevic; Nate Grey returns 4.00
26-50: 29-32-Fear Itself tie-in. 33-Regenesis. 34-Blink returns. 42,43-Exiled x-over with Exiled #1 & Journey Into Mystery #637,638 3.00
... Saga (2009, giveaway) New Mutants character profiles and story synopsies; Neves-c 3.00

NEW MUTANTS FOREVER
Marvel Comics: Oct, 2010 - No. 5, Feb, 2011 ($3.99, limited series)

1-5-Claremont-s/Rio & McLeod-a; Red Skull app. 1-Back-up history of New Mutants 4.00

NEW MUTANTS, THE: TRUTH OR DEATH
Marvel Comics: Nov, 1997 - No. 3, Jan, 1998 ($2.50, limited series)

1-3-Raab-s/Chang-a(p) 3.00

NEW ORDER, THE
CFD Publishing: Nov, 1994 ($2.95)

1 3.00

NEW PEOPLE, THE (TV)
Dell Publishing Co.: Jan, 1970 - No. 2, May, 1970

1 3 6 9 16 24 32
2-Photo-c 3 6 9 15 21 26

NEW ROMANCES
Standard Comics: No. 5, May, 1951 - No. 21, May, 1954

5-Photo-c 17 34 51 98 154 210
6-9: 6-Barbara Bel Geddes, Richard Basehart "Fourteen Hours" photo-c. 7-Ray Milland & Joan Fontaine photo-c. 9-Photo-c from '50s movie
12 24 36 67 94 120
10,14,16,17-Toth-a 13 26 39 72 101 130
11-Toth-a; Liz Taylor, Montgomery Clift photo-c 33 66 99 194 317 440
12,13,15,18-21 11 22 33 60 83 105
NOTE: *Celardo a-9. Moreira a-6. Tuska a-7, 20. Photo c-5-16.*

NEWSBOY LEGION BY JOE SIMON AND JACK KIRBY, THE
DC Comics: 2010 ($49.99, hardcover with dustjacket)

Vol. 1 - Reprints apps. in Star Spangled Comics #7-32; new intro. by Joe Simon 50.00

NEW SHADOWHAWK, THE (Also see Shadowhawk & Shadowhunt)
Image Comics (Shadowline Ink): June, 1995 - No. 7, Mar, 1996 ($2.50)

1-7: Kurt Busiek scripts in all 3.00

NEW STATESMEN, THE
Fleetway Publications (Quality Comics): 1989 - No. 5, 1990 ($3.95, limited series, mature readers, 52pgs.)

1-5: Futuristic; squarebound; 3-Photo-c 4.00

NEWSTRALIA
Innovation Publ.: July, 1989 - No. 5, 1989 ($1.75, color)(#2 on, $2.25, B&W)

1-5: 1,2: Timothy Truman-c/a; Gustovich-i 3.00

NEW TALENT SHOWCASE (Talent Showcase #16 on)
DC Comics: Jan, 1984 - No. 19, Oct, 1985 (Direct sales only)

1-19: Features new strips & artists. 18-Williamson-c(i) 3.00

NEW TEEN TITANS, THE (See DC Comics Presents #26, Marvel and DC Present & Teen Titans; Tales of the Teen Titans #41 on)
DC Comics: Nov, 1980 - No. 40, Mar, 1984

1-Robin, Kid Flash, Wonder Girl, The Changeling (1st app.), Starfire, The Raven, Cyborg begin; partial origin 3 6 9 21 33 45
2-1st app. Deathstroke the Terminator 6 12 18 41 76 110
3-10: 3-Origin Starfire; Intro The Fearsome Five. 4-Origin continues; J.L.A. app. 6-Origin Raven. 7-Cyborg origin. 8-Origin Kid Flash retold. 9-Minor app. Deathstroke on last pg. 10-2nd app. Deathstroke the Terminator (see Marvel & DC Present for 3rd app.); origin Changeling retold 2 4 6 8 10 12
11-20: 13-Return of Madame Rouge & Capt. Zahl; Robotman revived. 14-Return of Mento; origin Doom Patrol. 15-Death of Madame Rouge & Capt. Zahl; intro. new Brotherhood of Evil. 16-1st app. Captain Carrot (free 16 pg. preview). 18-Return of Starfire. 19-Hawkman teams-up 1 2 3 4 5 7
21-40: 21-Intro Night Force in free 16 pg. insert; intro Brother Blood. 23-1st app. Vigilante (not in costume), & Blackfire. 24-Omega Men app. 25-Omega Men cameo; free 16 pg. preview Masters of the Universe. 26-1st app. Terra. 27-Free 16 pg. preview Atari Force. 29-The New Brotherhood of Evil & Speedy app. 30-Terra joins the Titans. 34-4th app. Deathstroke the Terminator. 37-Batman & The Outsiders x-over. 38-Origin Wonder Girl. 39-Last Dick Grayson as Robin; Kid Flash quits 5.00
Annual 1(11/82)-Omega Men app. 1 3 4 6 8 10
Annual V2#2(9/83)-1st app. Vigilante in costume; 1st app. Lyla
1 3 4 6 8 10
Annual 3 (See Tales of the Teen Titans Annual #3)
...: Games GN (2011, $24.99, HC) Wolfman-s/Pérez-a/c; original GN started in 1988, finished in 2011; '80s NTT roster; afterword by Pérez; Wolfman's original plot 25.00
...: Games GN (2013, $16.99, SC) same contents as HC 17.00
...: Terra Incognito TPB (2006, $19.99) r/#26,28-34 & Annual #2 20.00
...: The Judas Contract TPB (2003, $19.95) r/#39,40 plus Tales of the Teen Titans #41-44 & Annual #3 20.00
...: Who is Donna Troy? TPB (2005, $19.99) r/#38,Tales of the Teen Titans #50, New Titans #50-55 and Teen Titans/Outsiders Secret Files 2003 20.00
NOTE: *Pérez a-1-4p, 6-34p, 37-40p, Annual 1p, 2p; c-1-12, 13-17p, 18-21, 22p, 23p, 24-37, 38, 39(painted), 40, Annual 1, 2.*

NEW TEEN TITANS, THE (Becomes The New Titans #50 on)
DC Comics: Aug, 1984 - No. 49, Nov, 1988 ($1.25/$1.75; deluxe format)

1-New storyline; Pérez-c/a begins 1 3 4 6 8 10
2,3: 2-Re-intro Lilith 6.00
4-10: 5-Death of Trigon. 7-9-Origin Lilith. 8-Intro Kole. 10-Kole joins 5.00
11-49: 13,14-Crisis x-over. 20-Robin (Jason Todd) joins; original Teen Titans return. 38-Infinity, Inc. x-over. 47-Origin of all Titans; Titans (East & West) pin-up by Pérez 4.00
Annual 1-4 (9/85-'88): 1-Intro. Vanguard. 2-Byrne c/a(p); origin Brother Blood; intro new Dr. Light. 3-Intro. Danny Chase. 4-Pérez-c 4.00
...: The Terror of Trigon TPB (2003, $17.95) r/#1-5; new cover by Phil Jimenez 18.00
NOTE: *Buckler c-10. Kelley Jones a-47, Annual 4. Erik Larsen a-33. Orlando c-33p. Perez a-1-5; c-1-7, 19-23, 43. Steacy c-47.*

NEW TERRYTOONS (TV)
Dell Publishing Co./Gold Key: 6-8/60 - No. 8, 3-5/62; 10/62 - No. 54, 1/79

1(1960-Dell)-Deputy Dawg, Dinky Duck & Hashimoto-San begin (1st app. of each)
10 20 30 64 132 200
2-8(1962) 6 12 18 41 76 110
1(30010-210)(10/62-Gold Key, 84 pgs.)-Heckle & Jeckle begins
9 18 27 58 114 170
2(30010-301)-84 pgs. 7 14 21 49 92 135
3-5 4 8 12 27 44 60
6-10 4 8 12 21 33 45
11-20 3 6 9 15 22 28
21-30 2 4 6 9 13 16
31-43 1 3 4 6 8 10
44-54: Mighty Mouse-c/s in all 2 4 6 8 11 14
NOTE: *Reprints: #4-12, 38, 40, 47. (See March of Comics #379, 393, 412, 435)*

NEW TESTAMENT STORIES VISUALIZED
Standard Publishing Co.: 1946 - 1947

"New Testament Heroes–Acts of Apostles Visualized, Book I"
"New Testament Heroes–Acts of Apostles Visualized, Book II"
"Parables Jesus Told" Set.... 17 34 51 98 154 210
NOTE: *All three are contained in a cardboard case, illustrated on front and info about the set.*

NEW THUNDERBOLTS (Continues in Thunderbolts #100)
Marvel Comics: Jan, 2005 - No. 18, Apr, 2006 ($2.99)

1-18: 1-Grummett-a/Nicieza-s. 1-Captain Marvel app. 2-Namor app. 4-Wolverine app. 3.00
... Vol. 1: One Step Forward (2005, $14.99) r/#1-6 15.00
... Vol. 2: Modern Marvels (2005, $14.99) r/#7-12 15.00
... Vol. 3: Right of Power (2006, $17.99) r/#13-18 & Thunderbolts #100 18.00

NEW TITANS, THE (Formerly The New Teen Titans)
DC Comics: No. 50, Dec, 1988 - No. 130, Feb, 1996 ($1.75/$2.25)

50-Perez-c/a begins; new origin Wonder Girl 6.00
51-59: 50-55-Painted-c. 55-Nightwing (Dick Grayson) forces Danny Chase to resign; Batman app. in flashback, Wonder Girl becomes Troia 4.00
60,61: 60-A Lonely Place of Dying Part 2 continues from Batman #440; new Robin tie-in; Timothy Drake app. 61-A Lonely Place of Dying Part 4 4.00
62-70,72-99,101-124,126-130: 62-65: Deathstroke the Terminator app. 65-Tim Drake (Robin) app. 70-1st Deathstroke solo cover/sty. 72-79-Deathstroke in all: 74-Intro. Pantha. 79-Terra brought back to life; 1 panel cameo Team Titans (1st app.). Deathstroke in #80-84,86. 80-2nd full app. Team Titans. 83,84-Deathstroke kills his son, Jericho. 85-Team Titans app. 86-Deathstroke vs. Nightwing-c/story; last Deathstroke app. 87-New costume Nightwing. 90-92-Parts 2,5,8 Total Chaos (Team Titans). 115-(11/94) 3.00
71-(44 pgs.)-10th anniversary issue; Deathstroke cameo 4.00

New Warriors #25 © MAR

The New Wave #13 © ECL

New York World's Fair Comics 1939 © DC

GD 2.0 | VG 4.0 | FN 6.0 | VF 8.0 | VF/NM 9.0 | NM- 9.2

100-($3.50, 52 pgs.)-Holo-grafx foil-c 4.00
125 (3.50)-wraparound-c 4.00
#0-(10/94) Zero Hour, released between #114 & 115 3.00
Annual 5-10 ('89-'94, 68 pgs.. 7-Armaggedon 2001 x-over; 1st full app. Teen (Team) Titans (new group). 8-Deathstroke app.; Eclipso app. (minor). 10-Elseworlds story 4.00
Annual 11 (1995, $3.95)-Year One story 4.00
NOTE: ***Perez** a-50-55p, 57,60p, 58,59,61(layouts); c-50-61, 62-67i, Annual 5i; co-plots-66.*

NEW TV FUNNIES (See New Funnies)

NEW TWO-FISTED TALES, THE
Dark Horse Comics/Byron Preiss: 1993 ($4.95, limited series, 52 pgs.)
1-Kurtzman-r & new-a 5.00
NOTE: ***Eisner** c-1i. **Kurtzman** c-1p, 2.*

NEWUNIVERSAL
Marvel Comics: Feb, 2007 - No. 6, July, 2007 ($2.99)
1-6-Warren Ellis-s/Salvador Larroca-a. 1,2-Variant covers by Ribic 3.00
...: 1959 (9/08, $3.99) Aftermath of the White Event of 1953; Tony Stark app. 4.00
...: Conqueror (10/08, $3.99) The White Event of 2689 B.C.; Eric Nguyen-a 4.00
... : Everything Went White HC (2007, $19.99) r/#1-6; sketch pages 20.00
... : Everything Went White SC (2008, $14.99) r/#1-6; sketch pages 15.00

NEWUNIVERSAL: SHOCKFRONT
Marvel Comics: Jul, 2008 - Present ($2.99)
1,2-Warren Ellis-s/Steve Kurth-a 3.00

NEW WARRIORS, THE (See Thor #411,412)
Marvel Comics: July, 1990 - No. 75, 1996 ($1.00/$1.25/$1.50)
1-Williamson-i; Bagley-c/a(p) in 1-13, Annual 1 6.00
1-Gold 2nd printing (7/91) 3.00
2-5: 1,3-Guice-c(i). 2-Williamson-c/a(i). 4.00
6-24,26-49,51-75: 7-Punisher cameo (last pg.). 8,9-Punisher app. 14-Darkhawk & Namor x-over. 17-Fantastic Four & Silver Surfer x-over. 19-Gideon (of X-Force) app. 28-Intro Turbo & Cardinal. 31-Cannonball & Warpath app. 42-Nova vs. Firelord. 46-Photo-c. 47-Bound-in S-M trading card sheet. 52-12 pg. ad insert. 62-Scarlet Spider-c/app. 70-Spider-Man-c/app. 72-Avengers-c/app. 3.00
25-($2.50, 52 pgs.)-Die-cut cover 4.00
40,60: 40-($2.25)-Gold foil collector's edition 4.00
50-($2.95, 52 pgs.)-Glow in the dark-c 4.00
Annual 1-4('91-'94,68 pgs.)-1-Origins all members; 3rd app. X-Force (cont'd from New Mutants Ann. #7 & cont'd in X-Men Ann. #15); x-over before X-Force #1. 3-Bagged w/card 4.00

NEW WARRIORS, THE
Marvel Comics: Oct, 1999 - No. 10, July, 2000 ($2.99/$2.50)
0-Wizard supplement; short story and preview sketchbook 3.00
1-($2.99) 4.00
2-10: 2-Two covers. 5-Generation X app. 9-Iron Man-c 3.00

NEW WARRIORS (See Civil War #1)
Marvel Comics: Aug, 2005 - No. 6, Feb, 2006 ($2.99, limited series)
1-6-Scottie Young-a 3.00
...: Reality Check TPB (2006, $14.99) r/#1-6 15.00

NEW WARRIORS (The Initiative)
Marvel Comics: Aug, 2007 - No. 20, Mar, 2009 ($2.99)
1-19: 1-Medina-a; new team is formed. 2-Jubilee app. 14-16-Secret Invasion 3.00
20-($3.99) 4.00
...: Defiant TPB (2008, $14.99) r/#1-6 15.00

NEW WARRIORS (All-New Marvel Now)
Marvel Comics: Apr, 2014 - Present ($3.99)
1-3: 1-Nova, Speedball, Justice, Sun Girl, Scarlet Spider team; Yost-s/To-a 4.00

NEW WAVE, THE
Eclipse Comics: 6/10/86 - No. 13, 3/87 (#1-8: bi-weekly, 20pgs; #9-13: monthly)
1-13:1-Origin, concludes #5. 6-Origin Megabyte. 8,9-The Heap returns. 13-Snyder-c 3.00
...Versus the Volunteers 3-D #1,2(4/87): 1-Snyder-c 3.00

NEW WEST, THE
Black Bull Comics: Mar, 2005 - No. 2, Jun, 2005 ($4.99, limited series)
1,2-Phil Noto-a/c; Jimmy Palmiotti-s 5.00

NEW WORLD (See Comic Books, series I)

NEW WORLDS
Caliber: 1996 - No. 6 ($2.95/$3.95, 80 pgs., B&W, anthology)
1-6: 1-Mister X & other stories 4.00

NEW X-MEN (See X-Men *2nd series* #114-156)

NEW X-MEN (Academy X) (Continued from New Mutants)
Marvel Comics: July, 2004 - No. 46, Mar, 2008 ($2.99)
1-46: 1,2-Green-c/a. 16-19-House of M. 20,21-Decimation. 40-Endangered Species back-ups begin. 44-46-Messiah Complex x-over; Ramos-a 3.00
Yearbook 1 (12/05, $3.99) new story and profile pages 4.00
...: Childhood's End Vol. 1 TPB (2006, $10.99) r/#20-23 11.00
...: Childhood's End Vol. 2 TPB (2006, $10.99) r/#24-27 11.00
...: Childhood's End Vol. 3 TPB (2006, $10.99) r/#28-32 11.00
...: Childhood's End Vol. 4 TPB (2007, $10.99) r/#33-36 11.00
...: Childhood's End Vol. 5 TPB (2007, $17.99) r/#37-43 18.00
House of M: New X-Men TPB (2006, $13.99) r/#16-19 and selections from Secrets Of The House of M one-shot 14.00
... Vol. 1: Choosing Sides TPB (2004, $14.99) r/#1-6 15.00
... Vol. 2: Haunted TPB (2005, $14.99) r/#7-12 15.00
... Vol. 3: X-Posed TPB (2006, $14.99) r/#12-15 & Yearbook Special 15.00

NEW X-MEN: HELLIONS
Marvel Comics: July, 2005 - No. 4, Oct, 2005 ($2.99, limited series)
1-4-Henry-a/Weir & DeFilippis-s 3.00
TPB (2006, $9.99) r/#1-4 10.00

NEW YORK FIVE, THE
DC Comics (Vertigo): Mar, 2011 - No. 4, Jun, 2011 ($2.99, B&W, limited series)
1-4-Brian Wood-s/Ryan Kelly-a 3.00

NEW YORK GIANTS (See Thrilling True Story of the Baseball Giants)

NEW YORK STATE JOINT LEGISLATIVE COMMITTEE TO STUDY THE PUBLICATION OF COMICS, THE
N.Y. State Legislative Document: 1951, 1955
This document was referenced by Wertham for **Seduction of the Innocent.** Contains numerous repros from comics showing violence, sadism, torture, and sex. 1955 version (196p, No. 37, 2/23/55) - Sold for $180 in 1986.

NEW YORK, THE BIG CITY
Kitchen Sink Press: 1986 ($10.95, B&W); **DC Comics:** July, 2000 ($12.95, B&W)
nn-(1986, $10.95) Will Eisner-s/a 20.00
nn-(2000, $12.95) new printing 13.00

NEW YORK WORLD'S FAIR (Also see Big Book of Fun & New Book of Fun)
National Periodical Publ.: 1939, 1940 (100 pgs.; cardboard covers)
(DC's 4th & 5th annuals)
1939-Scoop Scanlon, Superman (blond haired Superman on-c), Sandman, Zatara, Slam Bradley, Ginger Snap by Bob Kane begin; 1st published app. The Sandman (see Adventure #40 for his 1st drawn story); Vincent Sullivan-c; cover background by Guardineer 1700 3400 5100 12,750 29,000 –
1940-Batman, Hourman, Johnny Thunderbolt, Red, White & Blue & Hanko (by Creig Flessel) app.; Superman, Batman & Robin-c (1st time they all appear together); early Robin app.; 1st Burnley-c/a (per Burnley) 922 1844 2766 6915 15,500 –
NOTE: *The 1939 edition was published 4/29/39 and released 4/30/39, the day the fair opened, at 25¢, and was first sold only at the fair. Since all other comics were 10¢, it didn't sell. Remaining copies were advertised beginning in the August issues of most DC comics for 25¢, but soon the price was dropped to 15¢. Everyone that sent a quarter through the mail for it received a free Superman #1 or a #2 to make up the dime difference. 15¢ stickers were placed over the 25¢ price. Four variations on the 15¢ stickers are known. The 1940 edition was published 5/11/40 and was priced at 15¢. It was a precursor to World's Best #1.*

NEW YORK: YEAR ZERO
Eclipse Comics: July, 1988 - No. 4, Oct, 1988 ($2.00, B&W, limited series)
1-4 3.00

NEXT, THE
DC Comics: Sept, 2006 - No. 6, Feb, 2007 ($2.99, limited series)
1-6-Tad Williams-s/Dietrich Smith-a; Superman app. 3.00

NEXT MEN (See John Byrne's...)

NEXT MEN: AFTERMATH (Continued from John Byrne's Next Men 2010-2011 series)
IDW Publishing: No. 40, Feb, 2012 - No. 44, Jun, 2012 ($3.99)
40-44-John Byrne-s/a/c 4.00

NEXT NEXUS, THE
First Comics: Jan, 1989 - No. 4, April, 1989 ($1.95, limited series, Baxter paper)
1-4: Mike Baron scripts & Steve Rude-c/a. 3.00
TPB (10/89, $9.95) r/series 10.00

NEXTWAVE: AGENTS OF H.A.T.E
Marvel Comics: Mar, 2006 - No. 12, Mar, 2007 ($2.99)
1-12-Warren Ellis-s/Stuart Immonen-a. 2-Fin Fang Foom app. 12-Devil Dinosaur app. 3.00
Vol. 1 - This Is What They Want HC (2006, $19.99) r/#1-6; Ellis original pitch 20.00
Vol. 1 - This Is What They Want SC (2007, $14.99) r/#1-6; Ellis original pitch 15.00
Vol. 2 - I Kick Your Face HC (2007, $19.99) r/#7-12 20.00

Nexus #4 © Capital Pub.

NFL Rush Zone #1 © NFL

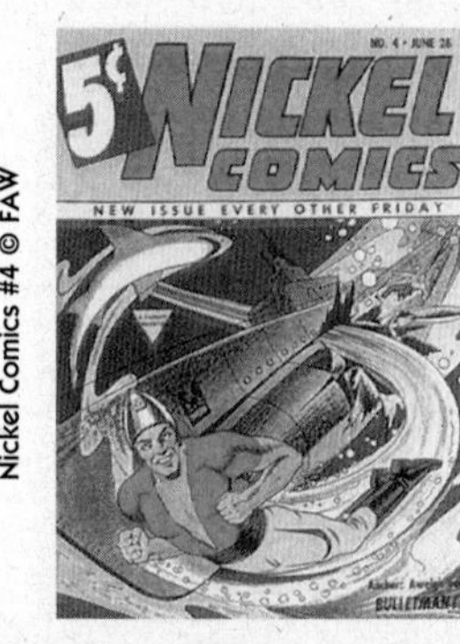

Nickel Comics #4 © FAW

	GD 2.0	VG 4.0	FN 6.0	VF 8.0	VF/NM 9.0	NM- 9.2

Vol. 2 - I Kick Your Face SC (2008, $14.99) r/#7-12 15.00

NEXUS (See First Comics Graphic Novel #4, 19 & The Next Nexus)
Capital Comics/First Comics No. 7 on: June, 1981 - No. 6, Mar, 1984; No. 7, Apr, 1985 - No. 80?, May, 1991 (Direct sales only, 36 pgs.; V2#1('83)-printed on Baxter paper)

1-B&W version; mag. size; w/double size poster 3 6 9 14 20 26
1-B&W 1981 limited edition; 500 copies printed and signed; same as above except this version has a 2-pg. poster & a pencil sketch on paperboard by Steve Rude 5 10 15 31 53 75
2-B&W, magazine size 2 4 6 11 16 20
3-B&W, magazine size; Brunner back-c; contains 33-1/3 rpm record ($2.95 price) 2 4 6 9 13 16
V2#1-Color version 4.00
2-49,51-80: 2-Nexus' origin begins. 67-Snyder-c/a 3.00
50-($3.50, 52 pgs.) 4.00
Hardcover Volume One (Dark Horse Books, 11/05, $49.95) r/#1-3 & V2 #1-4; creator bios 50.00
HC Volume Two (Dark Horse Books, 3/06, $49.95) r/V2 #5-11; creator bios 50.00
HC Volume Three (Dark Horse Books, 5/06, $49.95) r/V2 #12-18; Marz forward 50.00
HC Volume Four (Dark Horse Books, 8/06, $49.95) r/V2 #19-25; Powell forward 50.00
HC Volume Five (Dark Horse Books, 2/07, $49.95) r/V2 #26-32; Brubaker forward 50.00
HC Volume Six (Dark Horse Books, 2/07, $49.95) r/V2 #33-39; Evanier forward 50.00
HC Volume Seven (Dark Horse Books, 2/08, $49.95) r/V2 #40-46; Brunning forward 50.00
HC Volume Eight (Dark Horse Books, 1/09, $49.95) r/V2 #47-52 and The Next Nexus #1; interview with original publishers John Davis and Milton Griepp 50.00
HC Volume Nine (Dark Horse Books, 8/09, $49.95) r/V2 #53-57 & The Next Nexus #2-4 50.00
NOTE: ***Bissette*** *c-V2#29.* ***Giffen*** *c/a-V2#23.* ***Gulacy*** *c-1 (B&W), 2(B&W).* ***Mignola*** *c/a-V2#28.* ***Rude*** *c-3(B&W), V2#1-22, 24-27, 33-36, 39-42, 45-48, 50, 58-60, 75; a-1-3, V2#1-7, 8-16p, 18-22p, 24-27p, 33-36p, 39-42p, 45-48p, 50, 58, 59p, 60.* ***Paul Smith*** *a-V2#37, 38, 43, 44, 51-55p; c-V2#37, 38, 43, 44, 51-55.*

NEXUS
Rude Dude Productions: No. 99, July, 2007 - No. 102, Jun, 2009 ($2.99)

99-Mike Baron scripts & Steve Rude-c/a 3.00
100-($4.99) Part 2 of Space Opera; back-up feature: History of Nexus 5.00
101/102-(6/09, $4.95) Combined issue 5.00
..., Free Comic Book Day 2007 - Excerpts from previous issues and preview of #99 3.00
... Greatest Hits (8/07, $1.99) same content as Free Comic Book Day 2007 3.00
...: The Origin (11/07, $3.99) reprints the 7/96 one-shot 4.00

NEXUS: ALIEN JUSTICE
Dark Horse Comics: Dec, 1992 - No. 3, Feb, 1993 ($3.95, limited series)

1-3: Mike Baron scripts & Steve Rude-c/a 4.00

NEXUS: EXECUTIONER'S SONG
Dark Horse Comics: June, 1996 - No. 4, Sept, 1996 ($2.95, limited series)

1-4: Mike Baron scripts & Steve Rude-c/a 3.00

NEXUS FILES
First Comics: 1989 ($4.50, color/16pgs. B&W, one-shot, squarebound, 52 pgs.)

1-New Rude-a; info on Nexus 4.50

NEXUS: GOD CON
Dark Horse Comics: Apr, 1997 - No. 2, May, 1997 ($2.95, limited series)

1,2-Baron-s/Rude-c/a 3.00

NEXUS LEGENDS
First Comics: May, 1989 - No. 23, Mar, 1991 ($1.50, Baxter paper)\

1-23: R/1-3(Capital) & early First Comics issues w/new Rude covers #1-6,9,10 3.00

NEXUS MEETS MADMAN (...Special)
Dark Horse Comics: May, 1996 ($2.95, one-shot)

nn-Mike Baron & Mike Allred scripts, Steve Rude-c/a. 3.00

NEXUS: NIGHTMARE IN BLUE
Dark Horse Comics: July, 1997 - No. 4, Oct, 1997 ($2.95, limited series)

1-4: 1,2,4-Adam Hughes-c 3.00

NEXUS: THE LIBERATOR
Dark Horse Comics: Aug, 1992 - No. 4, Nov, 1992 ($2.95, limited series)

1-4 3.00

NEXUS: THE ORIGIN
Dark Horse Comics: July, 1996 ($3.95, one-shot)

nn-Mike Baron- scripts, Steve Rude-c/a. 4.00

NEXUS: THE WAGES OF SIN
Dark Horse Comics: Mar, 1995 - No. 4, June, 1995 ($2.95, limited series)

1-4 3.00

NFL RUSH ZONE: SEASON OF THE GUARDIANS
Action Lab Comics: Feb, 2013 - Present ($3.99)

1-4: 1-Matt Ryan & Roddy White app. 4.00
Free Comic Book Day edition (2013, giveaway) 3.00

NFL SUPERPRO
Marvel Comics: Oct, 1991 - No. 12, Sept, 1992 ($1.00)

1-12: 1-Spider-Man-c/app. 3.00
Special Edition (9/91, $2.00) Jusko painted-c 4.00
Super Bowl Edition (3/91, squarebound) Jusko painted-c 4.00

NICKEL COMICS
Dell Publishing Co.: 1938 (Pocket size - 7-1/2x5-1/2")(68 pgs.)

1- "Bobby & Chip" by Otto Messmer, Felix the Cat artist. Contains some English reprints 84 168 252 538 919 1300

NICKEL COMICS
Fawcett Publications: Feb 1940

nn - Ashcan comic, not distributed to newsstands, only for in-house use. A CGC certified 9.6 copy sold for $7,200 in 2003. In 2008, a CGC certified 8.5 sold for $2,390 and an uncertified Near Mint copy sold for $3,100.

NICKEL COMICS
Fawcett Publications: May, 1940 - No. 8, Aug, 1940 (36 pgs.; Bi-Weekly; 5¢)

	GD	VG	FN	VF	VF/NM	NM-
1-Origin/1st app. Bulletman	377	754	1131	2639	4620	6600
2	119	238	357	762	1306	1850
3	87	174	261	553	952	1350
4-The Red Gaucho begins	69	138	207	442	759	1075
5-7	68	136	204	432	746	1060
8-World's Fair-c; Bulletman moved to Master Comics #7 in October (scarce)	90	180	270	576	988	1400

NOTE: ***Beck*** *c-5-8.* ***Jack Binder*** *c-1-4. Bondage c-5. Bulletman c-1-8.*

NICK FURY, AGENT OF SHIELD (See Fury, Marvel Spotlight #31 & Shield)
Marvel Comics Group: 6/68 - No. 15, 11/69; No. 16, 11/70 - No. 18, 3/71

	GD	VG	FN	VF	VF/NM	NM-
1	13	26	39	89	195	300
2-4: 4-Origin retold	8	16	24	51	96	140
5-Classic-c	8	16	24	54	102	150
6,7: 7-Salvador Dali painting swipe	7	14	21	46	86	125
8-11,13: 9-Hate Monger begins, ends #11. 10-Smith layouts/pencil. 11-Smith-c. 13-1st app. Super-Patriot; last 12¢ issue	4	8	12	28	47	65
12-Smith-c/a	5	10	15	30	50	70
14-Begin 15¢ issues	4	8	12	25	40	55
15-1st app. & death of Bullseye-c/story(11/69); Nick Fury shot & killed; last 15¢ issue	7	14	21	48	89	130
16-18-(25¢, 52 pgs.)-r/Str. Tales #135-143	3	6	9	20	31	42

TPB (May 2000, $19.95) r/ Strange Tales #150-168 20.00
...: Who is Scorpio? TPB (11/00, $12.95) r/#1-3,5; Steranko-c 13.00
NOTE: ***Adkins*** *a-3i.* ***Craig*** *a-10i.* ***Sid Greene*** *a-12i.* ***Kirby*** *a-16-18r.* ***Springer*** *a-4, 6, 7, 8p, 9, 10p, 11; c-8, 9.* ***Steranko*** *a(p)-1-3, 5; c-1-7.*

NICK FURY AGENT OF SHIELD (Also see Strange Tales #135)
Marvel Comics: Dec, 1983 - No. 2, Jan, 1984 (2.00, 52 pgs., Baxter paper)

1,2-r/Nick Fury #1-4; new Steranko-c 1 2 3 5 6 8

NICK FURY, AGENT OF S.H.I.E.L.D.
Marvel Comics: Sept, 1989 - No. 47, May, 1993 ($1.50/$1.75)

V2#1-26,30-47: 10-Capt. America app. 13-Return of The Yellow Claw. 15-Fantastic Four app. 30,31-Deathlok app. 36-Cage app. 37-Woodgod c/story. 38-41-Flashes back to pre-Shield days after WWII. 44-Capt. America-c/s. 45-Viper-c/s. 46-Gideon x-over 3.00
27-29-Wolverine-c/stories 4.00
NOTE: ***Alan Grant*** *scripts-11.* ***Guice*** *a(p)-20-23, 25, 26; c-20-28.*

NICK FURY'S HOWLING COMMANDOS
Marvel Comics: Dec, 2005 - No. 6, May, 2006 ($2.99)

1-6: 1-Giffen-s/Francisco-a 3.00
1-Director's Cut ($3.99) r/#1 with original script and sketch design pages 4.00

NICK FURY VS. S.H.I.E.L.D.
Marvel Comics: June, 1988 - No. 6, Nov, 1988 ($3.50, 52 pgs, deluxe format)

1,2: 1-Steranko-c. 2-(Low print run) Sienkiewicz-c 6.00
3-6 5.00

NICK HALIDAY (Thrill of the Sea)
Argo: May, 1956

1-Daily & Sunday strip-r by Petree 8 16 24 44 57 70

NIGHT AND THE ENEMY (Graphic Novel)
Comico: 1988 (8-1/2x11") ($11.95, color, 80 pgs.)

1-Harlan Ellison scripts/Ken Steacy-c/a; r/Epic Illustrated & new-a (1st & 2nd printings) 12.00
1-Limited edition ($39.95) 40.00

Nightcrawler #2 © MAR

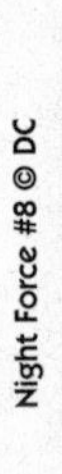
Night Force #8 © DC

Nightmare #3 © STJ

	GD	VG	FN	VF	VF/NM	NM-
	2.0	4.0	6.0	8.0	9.0	9.2

NIGHT BEFORE CHRISTMAS, THE (See March of Comics No. 152 in the Promotional Comics section)

NIGHT BEFORE CHRISTMASK, THE
Dark Horse Comics: Nov, 1994 ($9.95, one-shot)
nn-Hardcover book; The Mask; Rick Geary-c/a 10.00

NIGHTBREED (See Clive Barker's Nightbreed)

NIGHT CLUB
Image Comics: Apr, 2005 - No. 4, Dec, 2006 ($2.95/$2.99, limited series)
1-4: 1-Mike Baron-s/Mike Norton-a 3.00

NIGHTCRAWLER (X-Men)
Marvel Comics Group: Nov, 1985 - No. 4, Feb, 1986 (Mini-series from X-Men)
1-4: 1-Cockrum-c/a 5.00

NIGHTCRAWLER (Volume 2)
Marvel Comics: Feb, 2002 - No. 4, May, 2002 ($2.50, limited series)
1-4-Matt Smith-a 3.00

NIGHTCRAWLER
Marvel Comics: Nov, 2004 - No. 12, Jan, 2006 ($2.99)
1-12: 1-6-Robertson-a/Land-c. 2-Magik app. 8-Wolverine app. 10-Man-Thing app. 3.00
...: The Devil Inside TPB (2005, $14.99) r/#1-6 15.00
...: The Winding Way TPB (2006, $14.99) r/#7-12 15.00

NIGHTCRAWLER
Marvel Comics: Jun, 2014 - Present ($3.99)
1-Claremont-s/Nauck-a 4.00

NIGHTFALL: THE BLACK CHRONICLES
DC Comics (Homage): Dec, 1999 - No. 3, Feb, 2000 ($2.95, limited series)
1-3-Coker-a/Gilmore-s 3.00

NIGHT FORCE, THE (See New Teen Titans #21)
DC Comics: Aug, 1982 - No. 14, Sept, 1983 (60¢)
1 4.00
2-14: 13-Origin Baron Winter. 14-Nudity panels 3.00
NOTE: ***Colan*** *c/a-1-14p.* ***Giordano*** *c-1i, 2i, 4i, 5i, 7i, 12i.*

NIGHT FORCE
DC Comics: Dec, 1996 - No. 12, Nov, 1997 ($2.25)
1-12: 1-3-Wolfman-s/Anderson-a(p). 8-"Convergence" part 2 3.00

NIGHT FORCE
DC Comics: May, 2012 - No. 7, Nov, 2012 ($2.99, limited series)
1-7-Wolfman-s/Mandrake-a/Manco-c 3.00

NIGHT GLIDER
Topps Comics (Kirbyverse): April, 1993 ($2.95, one-shot)
1-Kirby c-1, Heck-a; polybagged w/Kirbychrome trading card 4.00

NIGHTHAWK
Marvel Comics: Sept, 1998 - No. 3, Nov, 1998 ($2.99, mini-series)
1-3-Krueger-s; Daredevil app. 3.00

NIGHTINGALE, THE
Henry H. Stansbury Once-Upon-A-Time Press, Inc.: 1948 (10¢, 7-1/4x10-1/4", 14 pgs., 1/2 B&W)
(Very Rare)-Low distribution; distributed to Westchester County & Bronx, N.Y. only; used in **Seduction of the Innocent**, pg. 312,313 as the 1st and only "good" comic book ever published. Ill. by Dong Kingman; 1,500 words of text, printed on high quality paper & no word balloons. Copyright registered 10/22/48, distributed week of 12/5/48. Only 5000 copies printed, 6 currently known to still exist. (By Hans Christian Andersen)
Estimated value........ 250.00

NIGHT MAN, THE (See Sludge #1)
Malibu Comics (Ultraverse): Oct, 1993 - No. 23, Aug, 1995 ($1.95/$2.50)
1-($2.50, 48 pgs.)-Rune flip-c/story by B. Smith (3 pgs.) 4.00
1-Ultra-Limited silver foil-c 8.00
2-15, 17: 3-Break-Thru x-over; Freex app. 4-Origin Firearm (2 pgs.) by Chaykin. 6-TNTNT app. 8-1st app. Teknight 3.00
16 ($3.50)-flip book (Ultraverse Premiere #11) 4.00
...:The Pilgrim Conundrum Saga (1/95, $3.95, 68 pgs.)-Strangers app. 4.00
18-23: 22-Loki-c/app. 3.00
Infinity ($1.50) 3.00
...Vs. Wolverine #0-Kelley Jones-c; mail in offer 1 3 4 6 8 10
NOTE: ***Zeck*** *a-16.*

NIGHT MAN, THE
Malibu Comics (Ultraverse): Sept, 1995 - No.4, Dec, 1995 ($1.50, lim. series)
1-4: Post Black September storyline 3.00

NIGHT MAN, THE /GAMBIT
Malibu Comics (Ultraverse): Mar, 1996 - No. 3, May, 1996 ($1.95, lim. series)
0-Limited Premium Edition 4.00
1-3: David Quinn scripts in all. 3-Rhiannon discovered to be The Night Man's mother 3.00

NIGHTMARE
Ziff-Davis (Approved Comics)/St. John No. 3: Summer, 1952 - No. 3, Winter, 1952, 53 (Painted-c)
1-1 pg. Kinstler-a; Tuska-a(2) 61 122 183 390 670 950
2-Kinstler-a-Poe's "Pit & the Pendulum" 42 84 126 267 451 635
3-Kinstler-a 40 80 120 244 402 560

NIGHTMARE (Weird Horrors #1-9) (Amazing Ghost Stories #14 on)
St. John Publishing Co.: No. 10, Dec, 1953 - No. 13, Aug, 1954
10-Reprints Ziff-Davis Weird Thrillers #2 w/new Kubert-c plus 2 pgs. Kinstler-a; Anderson, Colan & Toth-a 57 114 171 362 619 875
11-Krigstein-a; painted-c; Poe adapt., "Hop Frog" 42 84 126 265 445 625
12-Kubert bondage-c; adaptation of Poe's "The Black Cat"; Cannibalism story 41 82 123 256 428 600
13-Reprints Z-D Weird Thrillers #3 with new cover; Powell-a(2), Tuska-a; Baker-c 36 72 108 211 343 475

NIGHTMARE (Magazine) (Also see Psycho)
Skywald Publishing Corp.: Dec, 1970 - No. 23, Feb, 1975 (B&W, 68 pgs.)
1-Everett-a; Heck-a; Shores-a 9 18 27 62 126 190
2-5,8,9: 2,4-Decapitation story. 5-Nazi-s; Boris Karloff 4 pg. photo/text-s. 8-Features E.C. movie "Tales From the Crypt"; reprints some E.C. comics panels. 9-Wrightson-a; bondage-c; 1st Lovecraft Saggoth Chronicles/Cthulhu 6 12 18 37 66 95
6-Kaluta-a; Jeff Jones-c, photo & interview; 1st Living Gargoyle; Love Witch-s w/nudity; Boris Karloff-s 6 12 18 40 73 105
7 5 10 15 33 57 80
10-Wrightson-a (1 pg.); Princess of Earth-c/s; Edward & Mina Sartyros, the Human Gargoyles series continues from Psycho #8 6 12 18 38 69 100
11-19: 12-Excessive gore, severed heads. 13-Lovecraft-s. 15-Dracula-c/s. 17-Vampires issue; Autobiography of a Vampire series begins 4 8 12 28 47 65
20-John Byrne's 1st artwork (2 pgs.)(8/74); severed head-c; Hitler app. 8 16 24 54 102 150
21-23: 21-(1974 Summer Special)-Kaluta-a. 22-Tomb of Horror issue. 23-(1975 Winter Special) 5 10 15 31 53 75
Annual 1(1972)-Squarebound; B. Jones-a 5 10 15 31 53 75
Winter Special 1(1973)-All new material 4 8 12 28 47 65
Yearbook nn(1974)-B. Jones, Reese, Wildey-a 4 8 12 28 47 65
NOTE: ***Adkins*** *a-5.* ***Boris*** *c-2, 3, 5 (#4 is not by Boris).* ***Buckler*** *a-3, 15.* ***Byrne*** *a-20p.* ***Everett*** *a-1, 2, 4, 5, 12.* ***Jeff Jones*** *a-6, 21r(Psycho #6); c-6.* ***Katz*** *a-3, 5, 21.* ***Reese*** *a-4, 5.* ***Wildey*** *a-4, 5, 6, 21, '74 Yearbook.* ***Wrightson*** *a-9, 10.*

NIGHTMARE (Alex Nino's)
Innovation Publishing: 1989 ($1.95)
1-Alex Nino-a 3.00

NIGHTMARE
Marvel Comics: Dec, 1994 - No. 4, Mar, 1995 ($1.95, limited series)
1-4 3.00

NIGHTMARE & CASPER (See Harvey Hits #71) (Casper & Nightmare #6 on) (See Casper The Friendly Ghost #19)
Harvey Publications: Aug, 1963 - No. 5, Aug, 1964 (25¢)
1-All reprints? 7 14 21 46 86 125
2-5: All reprints? 5 10 15 30 50 70

NIGHTMARE ON ELM STREET, A (Also see Freddy Krueger's...)
DC Comics (WildStorm): Dec, 2006 - Present ($2.99)
1-8: 1-Two covers by Harris & Bradstreet; Dixon-s/West-a 3.00

NIGHTMARES (See Do You Believe in Nightmares)

NIGHTMARES
Eclipse Comics: May, 1985 - No. 2, May, 1985 ($1.75, Baxter paper)
1,2 3.00

NIGHTMARE THEATER
Chaos! Comics: Nov, 1997 - No. 4, Nov, 1997 ($2.50, mini-series)
1-4-Horror stories by various; Wrightson-a 3.00

NIGHTMARK: BLOOD & HONOR
Alpha Productions: 1994 - No. 3, 1994 ($2.50, B&W, mini-series)
1,2 3.00

NIGHTMARK MYSTERY SPECIAL

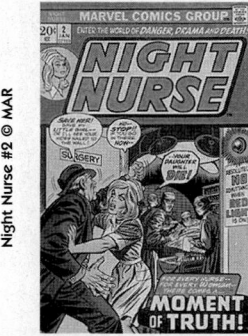

Night Nurse #2 © MAR

Nightside #1 © MAR

Nightwing (2011 series) #6 © DC

	GD 2.0	VG 4.0	FN 6.0	VF 8.0	VF/NM 9.0	NM- 9.2

Alpha Productions: Jan, 1994 ($2.50, B&W)

1 3.00

NIGHTMASK
Marvel Comics Group: Nov, 1986 - No. 12, Oct, 1987

1-12 3.00

NIGHT MASTER
Silverwolf: Feb, 1987 ($1.50, B&W)

1-Tim Vigil-c/a 3.00

NIGHTMASTER (See Shadowpact)
DC Comics: Jan, 2011 ($2.99, one-shot)

1-Wrightson-c/Beechen-s/Dwyer-a; Shadowpact app. 3.00

NIGHT MUSIC (See Eclipse Graphic Album Series, The Magic Flute)
Eclipse Comics: Dec, 1984 - No. 11, 1990 ($1.75/$3.95/$4.95, Baxter paper)

1-7: 3-Russell's Jungle Book adapt. 4,5-Pelleas And Melisande (double titled) 6-Salomé (double titled). 7-Red Dog #1 3.00
8-($3.95) Ariane and Bluebeard 4.00
9-11-($4.95) The Magic Flute; Russell adapt. 5.00

NIGHT NURSE
Marvel Comics Group: Nov, 1972 - No. 4, May, 1973

	GD 2.0	VG 4.0	FN 6.0	VF 8.0	VF/NM 9.0	NM- 9.2
1	11	22	33	76	163	250
2-4	9	18	27	57	111	165

NIGHT OF MYSTERY
Avon Periodicals: 1953 (no month) (one-shot)

	GD 2.0	VG 4.0	FN 6.0	VF 8.0	VF/NM 9.0	NM- 9.2
nn-1 pg. Kinstler-a, Hollingsworth-c	53	106	159	334	567	800

NIGHT OF THE GRIZZLY, THE (See Movie Classics)

NIGHT OF THE LIVING DEADPOOL
Marvel Comics: Mar, 2014 - No. 4, May, 2014 ($3.99, limited series)

1-4-Bunn-s/Rosanas-a; Deadpool in a zombie apocalypse 4.00

NIGHTRAVEN (See Marvel Graphic Novel)

NIGHT RIDER (Western)
Marvel Comics Group: Oct, 1974 - No. 6, Aug, 1975

	GD 2.0	VG 4.0	FN 6.0	VF 8.0	VF/NM 9.0	NM- 9.2
1: 1-6 reprint Ghost Rider #1-6 (#1-origin)	3	6	9	14	20	25
2-6	2	4	6	9	12	15

NIGHT'S CHILDREN: THE VAMPIRE
Millenium: July, 1995 - No. 2, Aug, 1995 ($2.95, B&W)

1,2: Wendy Snow-Lang story & art 3.00

NIGHTSIDE
Marvel Comics: Dec, 2001 - No. 4, Mar, 2002 ($2.99)

1-4: 1-Weinberg-s/Derenick-a; intro Sydney Taine 3.00

NIGHTS INTO DREAMS (Based on video game)
Archie Comics: Feb, 1998 -No. 6, Oct, 1998 ($1.75, limited series)

1-6 3.00

NIGHTSTALKERS (Also see Midnight Sons Unlimited)
Marvel Comics (Midnight Sons #14 on): Nov, 1992 - No. 18, Apr, 1994 ($1.75)

1-($2.75, 52 pgs.)-Polybagged w/poster; part 5 of Rise of the Midnight Sons storyline; Garney/Palmer-c/a begins; Hannibal King, Blade & Frank Drake begin 4.00
2-9,11-18: 5-Punisher app. 7-Ghost Rider app. 8,9-Morbius app. 14-Spot varnish-c. 14,15-Siege of Darkness Pts 1 & 9 3.00
10-($2.25)-Outer-c is a Darkhold envelope made of black parchment w/gold ink; Midnight Massacre part 1 4.00

NIGHT TERRORS,THE
Chanting Monks Studios: 2000 ($2.75, B&W)

1-Bernie Wrightson-c; short stories, one by Wrightson-s/a 3.00

NIGHT THRASHER (Also see The New Warriors)
Marvel Comics: Aug, 1993 - No. 21, Apr, 1995 ($1.75/$1.95)

1-($2.95, 52 pgs.)-Red holo-grafx foil-c; origin 4.00
2-21: 2-Intro Tantrum. 3-Gideon (of X-Force) app. 10-Bound-in trading card sheet; Iron Man app. 15-Hulk app. 3.00

NIGHT THRASHER: FOUR CONTROL
Marvel Comics: Oct, 1992 - No. 4, Jan, 1993 ($2.00, limited series)

1-4: 2-Intro Tantrum. 3-Gideon (of X-Force) app. 3.00

NIGHT TRIBES
DC Comics (WildStorm): July, 1999 ($4.95, one-shot)

1-Golden & Sniegoski-s/Chin-a 5.00

NIGHTVEIL (Also see Femforce)
Americomics/AC Comics: Nov, 1984 - No. 7, 1987 ($1.75)

1-7 3.00
...'s Cauldron Of Horror 1 (1989, B&W)-Kubert, Powell, Wood-r plus new Nightveil story 3.00
...'s Cauldron Of Horror 2 (1990, $2.95, B&W)-Pre-code horror-r by Kubert & Powell 3.00
...'s Cauldron Of Horror 3 (1991) 3.00
Special 1 ('88, $1.95)-Kaluta-c 3.00
One Shot ('96, $5.95)-Flip book w/ Colt 6.00

NIGHTWATCH
Marvel Comics: Apr, 1994 - No. 12, Mar, 1995 ($1.50)

1-($2.95)-Collectors edition; foil-c; Ron Lim-c/a begins; Spider-Man app. 4.00
1-12-Regular edition. 2-Bound-in S-M trading card sheet; 5,6-Venom-c & app. 7,11-Cardiac app. 3.00

NIGHTWING (Also see New Teen Titans, New Titans, Showcase '93 #11,12, Tales of the New Teen Titans & Teen Titans Spotlight)
DC Comics: Sept, 1995 - No. 4, Dec, 1995 ($2.25, limited series)

1-Dennis O'Neil story/Greg Land-a in all 5.00
2-4 4.00
...: Alfred's Return (7/95, $3.50) Giordano-a 4.00
...Ties That Bind (1997, $12.95, TPB) r/mini-series & Alfred's Return 13.00

NIGHTWING
DC Comics: Oct, 1996 - No. 153, Apr, 2009 ($1.95/$1.99/$2.25/$2.50/$2.99)

	GD 2.0	VG 4.0	FN 6.0	VF 8.0	VF/NM 9.0	NM- 9.2
1-Chuck Dixon scripts & Scott McDaniel-c/a	2	4	6	11	16	20
2,3	1	2	3	5	6	8

4-10: 6-Robin-c/app. 5.00
11-20: 13-15-Batman app. 19,20-Cataclysm pts. 2,11 4.00
21-49,51-64: 23-Green Arrow app. 26-29-Huntress-c/app. 30-Superman-c/app. 35-39-No Man's Land. 41-Land/Geraci-a begins. 46-Begin $2.25-c. 47-Texiera-c. 52-Catwoman-c/app. 54-Shrike app. 3.00
50-($3.50) Nightwing battles Torque 4.00
65-74,76-99: 65,66-Bruce Wayne: Murderer x-over pt. 3,9. 68,69: B.W.: Fugitive pt. 6,9. 70-Last Dixon-s. 71-Devin Grayson-s begin. 81-Batgirl vs. Deathstroke. 93-Blockbuster killed. 94-Copperhead app. 96-Bagged w/CD. 96-98-War Games 3.00
75-(1/03, $2.95) Intro. Tarantula 4.00
100-(2/05, $2.95) Tarantula app. 4.00
101-117: 101-Year One begins. 103-Jason Todd & Deadman app. 107-110-Hester-a. 109-Begin $2.50-c. 109,110-Villains United tie-ins. 112-Deathstroke app. 3.00
118-149,151-153: 118-One Year Later; Jason Todd as 2nd Nightwing. 120-Begin $2.99-c. 138,139-Resurrection of Ra's al Ghul x-over. 138-2nd printing. 147-Two-Face app. 3.00
150-($3.99) Batman R.I.P. x-over; Nightwing vs. Two-Face; Tan-c 4.00
#1,000,000 (11/98) teams with future Batman 3.00
Annual 1(1997, $3.95) Pulp Heroes 4.00
Annual 2 (6/07, $3.99) Dick Grayson and Barbara Gordon's shared history 4.00
...Eighty Page Giant 1 (12/00, $5.95) Intro. of Hella; Dixon-s/Haley-c 6.00
...: Big Guns (2004, $14.95, TPB) r/#47-50; Secret Files 1, Eighty Page Giant 1 15.00
...: Brothers in Blood (2007, $14.99, TPB) r/#118-124 15.00
...: A Darker Shade of Justice (2001, $19.95, TPB) r/#30-39, Secret Files #1 20.00
...: Freefall (2008, $17.99, TPB) r/#140-146 18.00
...: A Knight in Blüdhaven (1998, $14.95, TPB) r/#1-8 15.00
...: Love and Bullets (2000, $17.95, TPB) r/#1/2, 19,21,22,24-29 18.00
...: Love and War (2007, $14.99, TPB) r/#125-132 15.00
...: On the Razor's Edge (2005, $14.99, TPB) r/#52,54-60 15.00
...: Our Worlds at War (9/01, $2.95) Jae Lee-c 3.00
...: Renegade TPB (2006, $17.95) r/#112-117 18.00
...: Rough Justice (1999, $17.95, TPB) r/#9-18 18.00
Secret Files 1 (10/99, $4.95) Origin-s and pin-ups 5.00
...: The Great Leap (2009, $19.99) r/#147-153 20.00
...: The Hunt for Oracle (2003, $14.95, TPB) r/#41-46 & Birds of Prey #20,21 15.00
...: The Lost Year (2008, $14.99) r/#133-137 & Annual #2 15.00
...: The Target (2001, $5.95) McDaniel-c/a 6.00
Wizard 1/2 (Mail offer) 5.00
...: Year One (2005, $14.99) r/#101-106 15.00

NIGHTWING (DC New 52)
DC Comics: Nov, 2011 - Present ($2.99)

1-Dick Grayson in black/red costume; Higgins-s/Barrows-a/c 12.00
1-2nd printing with red background-c 10.00
2-7,10-14: 2-4-Batgirl app. 13,14-Lady Shiva app. 14-Joker cameo 4.00
8,9: 8-Night of the Owls prelude. 9-Night of the Owls x-over 5.00
15-Die-cut cover with Joker mask; Death of the Family tie-in 5.00
16-18: 16-Death of the Family tie-in. 18-Requiem; Tony Zucco returns 4.00

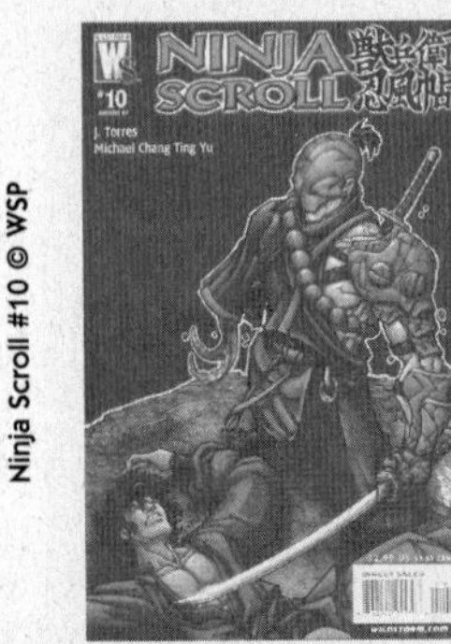

Ninja Scroll #10 © WSP

The Ninjettes #1 © Spitfire & Dynamite

The Nocturnals #2 © Dan Brereton

	GD 2.0	VG 4.0	FN 6.0	VF 8.0	VF/NM 9.0	NM- 9.2

19-24,26-29: 19-24-Prankster app. 26,27-Mad Hatter app. 28,29-Mr. Zsasz app. 3.00
25-($3.99) Zero Year flashback to Haly's Circus days; Higgins-s/Conrad & Richards-a 4.00
#0-(11/12, $2.99) Origin re-told/updated; Lady Shiva app.; DeFalco-s/Barrows-a 4.00
Annual #1 (12/13, $4.99) Batgirl Wanted! tie-in; Firefly app. 5.00

NIGHTWING (See Tangent Comics/ Nightwing)

NIGHTWING AND HUNTRESS
DC Comics: May, 1998 - No. 4, Aug, 1998 ($1.95, limited series)
1-4-Grayson-s/Land & Sienkiewicz-a 3.00
TPB (2003, $9.95) r/#1/4; cover gallery 10.00

NIGHTWINGS (See DC Science Fiction Graphic Novel)

NIKKI, WILD DOG OF THE NORTH (Disney, see Movie Comics)
Dell Publishing Co.: No. 1226, Sept, 1961
Four Color 1226-Movie, photo-c 5 10 15 31 53 75

9-11 - ARTISTS RESPOND
Dark Horse Comics: 2002 ($9.95, TPB, proceeds donated to charities)
Volume 1-Short stories about the September 11 tragedies by various Dark Horse, Chaos! and Image writers and artists; Eric Drooker-c 10.00

9-11: EMERGENCY RELIEF
Alternative Comics: 2002 ($14.95, TPB, proceeds donated to the Red Cross)
nn-Short stories by various inc. Pekar, Eisner, Hester, Oeming, Noto; Cho-c 15.00

9-11 - THE WORLD'S FINEST COMIC BOOK WRITERS AND ARTISTS TELL STORIES TO REMEMBER
DC Comics: 2002 ($9.95, TPB, proceeds donated to charities)
Volume 2-Short stories about the September 11 tragedies by various DC, MAD, and WildStorm writers and artists ; Alex Ross-c 10.00

NINE RINGS OF WU-TANG
Image Comics: July, 1999 - No. 5, July, 2000 ($2.95)
Preview (7/99, $5.00, B&W) 5.00
1-5: 1-(11/99, $2.95) Clayton Henry-a 3.00
Tower Records Variant-c 5.00
Wizard #0 Prelude 3.00
TPB (1/01, $19.95) r/#1-5, Preview & Prelude; sketchbook & cover gallery 20.00

1963
Image Comics (Shadowline Ink): Apr, 1993 - No. 6, Oct, 1993 ($1.95, lim. series)
1-6: Alan Moore scripts; Veitch, Bissette & Gibbons-a(p) 3.00
1-Gold 4.00
NOTE: ***Bissette*** *a-2-4;* ***Gibbons*** *a-1i, 2i, 6i; c-2.*

1984 (Magazine) (1994 #11 on)
Warren Publishing Co.: June, 1978 - No. 10, Jan, 1980 ($1.50, B&W with color inserts, mature content with nudity; 84 pgs. except #4 has 92 pgs.)
1-Nino-a in all; Mutant World begins by Corben 3 6 9 14 19 24
2-10: 4-Rex Havoc begins. 7-1st Ghita of Alizarr by Thorne. 9-1st Starfire 2 4 6 9 13 16
NOTE: ***Alcala*** *a-1-3,5,7i.* ***Corben*** *a-1-8; c-1,2.* ***Nebres*** *a-1-8,10.* ***Thorne*** *a-7,8,10.* ***Wood*** *a-1,2,5i.*

1994 (Formerly 1984) (Magazine)
Warren Publishing Co.: No. 11, Feb, 1980 - No. 29, Feb, 1983 (B&W with color; mature; #11-(84 pgs.); #12-16,18-21,24-(76 pgs.); #17,22,23,25-29-(68 pgs.)
11,17,18,20,22,23,29: 11,17-8 pgs. color insert. 18-Giger-c. 20-1st Diana Jacklighter Manhuntress by Maroto. 22-1st Sigmund Pavlov by Nino; 1st Ariel Hart by Hsu. 23-All Nino issue 2 4 6 8 11 14
12-16,19,21,24-28: 21-1st app. Angel by Nebres. 27-The Warhawks return 1 3 4 6 8 10
NOTE: ***Corben*** *c-26.* ***Maroto*** *a-20, 21, 24-28.* ***Nebres*** *a-11-13, 15, 16, 18, 21, 22, 25, 28.* ***Nino*** *a-11-19, 20(2), 21, 25, 26, 28; c-21.* ***Redondo*** *c-20.* ***Thorne*** *a-11-14, 17-21, 24-26, 28, 29.*

NINJA BOY
DC Comics (WildStorm): Oct, 2001 - No. 6, Mar, 2002 ($3.50/$2.95)
1-($3.50) Ale Garza-a/c 3.50
2-6-($2.95) 3.00
...: Faded Dreams TPB (2003, $14.95) r/#1-6; sketch pages 15.00

NINJA HIGH SCHOOL (1st series)
Antarctic Press: 1986 - No. 3, Aug, 1987 (B&W)
1-Ben Dunn-s/c/a; early Manga series 2 4 6 9 12 15
2,3 1 3 4 6 8 10

NINJAK (See Bloodshot #6, 7 & Deathmate)
Valiant/Acclaim Comics (Valiant) No. 16 on: Feb, 1994 - No. 26, Nov. 1995 ($2.25/$2.50)
1 ($3.50)-Chromium-c; Quesada-c/a(p) in #1-3 5.00
1-Gold 1 3 4 6 8 10
2-13: 3-Batman, Spawn & Random (from X-Factor) app. as costumes at party (cameo). 4-w/bound-in trading card. 5,6-X-O app. 4.00
0,00,14-26: 14-(4/95)-Begin $2.50-c. 0-(6/95, $2.50). 00-(6/95, $2.50) 3.00
... Black Water HC (2013, $24.99) r/#1-6, #0, #00; bonus Quesada sketch-a 25.00
Yearbook 1 (1994, $3.95) 4.00

NINJAK
Acclaim Comics (Valiant Heroes): V2#1, Mar, 1997 -No. 12, Feb, 1998 ($2.50)
V2#1-12: 1-Intro new Ninjak; 1st app. Brutakon; Kurt Busiek scripts begin; painted variant-c exists. 2-1st app. Karnivor & Zeer. 3-1st app. Gigantik, Shurikai, & Nixie. 4-Origin; 1st app. Yasuiti Motomiya; intro The Dark Dozen; Colin King cameo. 9-Copycat-c 3.00

NINJA SCROLL
DC Comics (WildStorm): Nov, 2006 - No. 12, Oct, 2007 ($2.99)
1-12: 1-J. Torres-s/Michael Chang Ting Yu-a/c. 11-Puckett-s/Meyers-a 3.00
1-3-Variant covers by Jim Lee 5.00
TPB (2007, $19.99) r/#1-3,5-7 20.00

NINJETTES (See Jennifer Blood #4)
Dynamite Entertainment: 2012 - No. 6, 2012 ($3.99, limited series)
1-6-Origin of the team; Ewing-s/Casallos-a. 6-Jennifer Blood app. 4.00

NINTENDO COMICS SYSTEM (Also see Adv. of Super Mario Brothers)
Valiant Comics: Feb, 1990 - No. 9, Oct, 1991 ($4.95, card stock-c, 68 pgs.)
1-9: 1-Featuring Game Boy, Super Mario, Clappwall. 3-Layton-c. 5-8-Super Mario Bros. 9-Dr. Mario 1st app. 1 2 3 5 6 8

NOAH (Adaptation of the 2014 movie)
Image Comics: Mar, 2014 (HC, $29.99, 8-3/4" x 11-1/2")
HC-Darren Aronofsky & Ari Handel-s/Niko Henrichon-a 30.00

NOAH'S ARK
Spire Christian Comics/Fleming H. Revell Co.: 1973,1975 (35/49¢)
nn-By Al Hartley 2 4 6 11 16 20

NOBLE CAUSES
Image Comics: July, 2001; Jan, 2002 - No. 4, May, 2002 ($2.95)
...First Impressions (7/01) Intro. the Noble family; Faerber-s 3.00
1-4: 1-(1/02) Back-up-s with Conner-a. 2-Igle back-up-a. 2-4-Two covers 3.00
...: Extended Family (5/03, $6.95) short stories by various 7.00
...: Extended Family 2 (6/04, $7.95) short stories by various 8.00
Vol. 1: In Sickness and in Health (2003, $12.95) r/#1-4 & ...First Impresssions 13.00

NOBLE CAUSES (Volume 3)
Image Comics: July, 2004 - No. 40, Mar, 2009 ($3.50)
1-24,26-40-Faerber-s. 1-Two covers. 2-Venture app. 5-Invincible app. 3.50
25-($4.99) Art by various; Randolph-c 5.00
Vol. 4: Blood and Water (2005, $14.95) r/#1-6 15.00
Vol. 5: Betrayals (2006, $14.99) r/#7-12 & The Pact V2 #2 15.00
Vol. 6: Hidden Agendas (2006, $15.99) r/#13-18 and Image Holiday Spec. 2005 story 16.00
Vol. 7: Powerless (2007, $15.99) r/#19-25; Wieringo sketch page 16.00

NOBLE CAUSES: DISTANT RELATIVES
Image Comics: Jul, 2003 - No. 4, Oct, 2003 ($2.95, B&W, limited series)
1-4-Faerber-s/Richardson & Ponce-a 3.00
Vol. 3: Distant Relatives (1/05, $12.95) r/#1-4; intro. by Joe Casey 13.00

NOBLE CAUSES: FAMILY SECRETS
Image Comics: Oct, 2002 - No. 4, Jan, 2003 ($2.95, limited series)
1-4-Faerber-s/Oeming-c. 1-Variant cover by Walker. 2,3-Valentino var-c. 4-Hester var-c 3.00
Vol. 2: Family Secrets (2004, $12.95) r/#1-4; sketch pages 13.00

NOBODY (Amado, Cho & Adlard's...)
Oni Press: Nov, 1998 - No. 4, Feb, 1999 ($2.95, B&W, mini-series)
1-4 3.00

NOCTURNALS, THE
Malibu Comics (Bravura): Jan, 1995 - No. 6, Aug, 1995 ($2.95, limited series)
1-6: Dan Brereton painted-c/a & scripts 3.00
1-Glow-in-the-Dark premium edition 5.00

NOCTURNALS, THE
Dark Horse Comics/Image Comics/Oni Press: one-shots and trade paperbacks
Black Planet TPB (Oni Press, 1998, $19.95) r/#1-6 (Malibu Comics series) 20.00
Black Planet and Other Stories HC (Olympian Publ.; 7/07, $39.95) r/Black Planet & Witching Hour contents; cover & sketch gallery with Brereton interviews 40.00
Carnival of Beasts (Image, 7/08, $6.99) short stories; Brereton-s/Brereton & others-a 7.00
Troll Bridge (Oni Press, 2000, $4.95, B&W & orange) Brereton-s/painted-c; art by Brereton,

No Honor #1 © TCOW

Northlanders #41 © Brian Wood & DC

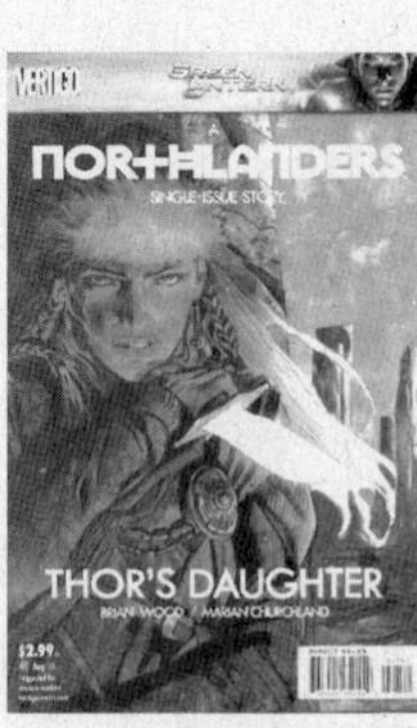

Nova #9 © MAR

GD 2.0 | VG 4.0 | FN 6.0 | VF 8.0 | VF/NM 9.0 | NM- 9.2

Chin, Art Adams, Sakai, Timm, Warren, Thompson, Purcell, Stephens and others 5.00
Unhallowed Eve TPB (Oni Press, 10/02, $9.95) r/Witching Hour & Troll Bridge one-shots 10.00
Witching Hour (Dark Horse, 5/98, $4.95) Brereton-s/a; reprints DHP stories + 8 new pgs. 5.00

NOCTURNALS: THE DARK FOREVER
Oni Press: Jul, 2001 -No. 3, Feb, 2002 ($2.95, limited series)
1-3-Brereton-s/painted-a/c 3.00
TPB (5/02, $9.95) r/#1-3; afterword & pin-ups by Alex Ross 10.00

NOCTURNE
Marvel Comics: June, 1995 - No. 4, Sept. 1995 ($1.50, limited series)
1-4 3.00

NO ESCAPE (Movie)
Marvel Comics: June, 1994 - No. 3, Aug, 1994 ($1.50)
1-3: Based on movie 3.00

NO HONOR
Image Comics (Top Cow): Feb, 2001 - No. 4, July, 2001 ($2.50)
Preview (12/00, B&W) Silvestri-c 3.00
1-4-Avery-s/Crain-a 3.00
TPB (8/03, $12.99) r/#1-4; intro. by Straczynski 13.00

NOIR
Dynamite Entertainment: 2013 - No. 5, 2014 ($3.99, limited series)
1-5: 1-Miss Fury, Black Sparrow & The Shadow app.; Gischler-s/Mutti-a 4.00

NOMAD (See Captain America #180)
Marvel Comics: Nov, 1990 - No. 4, Feb, 1991 ($1.50, limited series)
1-4: 1,4-Captain America app. 3.00

NOMAD
Marvel Comics: V2#1, May, 1992 - No. 25, May, 1994 ($1.75)
V2#1-25: 1-Has gatefold-c w/map/wanted poster. 4-Deadpool x-over. 5-Punisher vs. Nomad-c/story. 6-Punisher & Daredevil-c/story cont'd in Punisher War Journal #48. 7-Gambit-c/story. 10-Red Wolf app. 21-Man-Thing-c/story. 25-Bound-in trading card sheet 3.00

NOMAD: GIRL WITHOUT A WORLD (Rikki Barnes from Captain America V2 Heroes Reborn)
Marvel Comics: Nov, 2009 - No. 4, Feb, 2010 ($3.99, limited series)
1-4-McKeever-s. 2-Falcon app. 4-Young Avengers app. 4.00

NOMAN (See Thunder Agents)
Tower Comics: Nov, 1966 - No. 2, March, 1967 (25¢, 68 pgs.)
1-Wood/Williamson-c; Lightning begins; Dynamo cameo; Kane-a(p) & Whitney-a
8 16 24 54 102 150
2-Wood-c only; Dynamo x-over; Whitney-a 5 10 15 34 60 85

NONE BUT THE BRAVE (See Movie Classics)

NON-HUMANS
Image Comics: Oct, 2012 - No. 4, Jul, 2013 ($2.99)
1-4-Brunswick-s/Portacio-a/c 3.00

NOODNIK COMICS (See Pinky the Egghead)
Comic Media/Mystery/Biltmore: Dec, 1953; No. 2, Feb, 1954 - No. 5, Aug, 1954
3-D(1953, 25¢; Comic Media)(#1)-Came w/glasses 29 58 87 170 278 385
2-5 9 18 27 52 69 85

NORMALMAN (See Cerebus the Aardvark #55, 56)
Aardvark-Vanaheim/Renegade Press #6 on: Jan, 1984 - No. 12, Dec, 1985 ($1.70/$2.00)
1-12: 1-Jim Valentino-c/a in all. 6-12 ($2.00, B&W): 10-Cerebus cameo; Sim-a (2 pgs.) 3.00
...- Megaton Man Special 1 (Image Comics, 8/94, $2.50) 3.00
...3-D 1 (Annual, 1986, $2.25) 3.00
...Twentieth Anniversary Special (7/04, $2.95) 3.00

NORTHANGER ABBEY (Adaptation of the Jane Austen novel)
Marvel Comics: Jan, 2012 - No. 5, May, 2012 ($3.99, mini-series)
1-5-Nancy Butler-s/Janet K. Lee-a/Julian Tedesco-c 4.00

NORTH AVENUE IRREGULARS (See Walt Disney Showcase #49)

NORTH 40
DC Comics (WildStorm): Sept, 2009 - No. 6, Feb, 2010 ($2.99)
1-6-Aaron Williams-s/Fiona Staples-a 3.00
TPB (2010, $17.99) r/#1-6 18.00

NORTHLANDERS
DC Comics (Vertigo): Feb, 2008 - No. 50, Jun, 2012 ($2.99)
1-50: 1-Vikings in 980 A.D.; Wood-s/Gianfelice-a; covers by Carnivale. 35-Cloonan-a 3.00
1-3-Variant covers. 1-Adam Kubert. 2-Andy Kubert. 3-Dave Gibbons 5.00
...: Blood in the Snow TPB (2010, $14.99) r/#9,10,17-20 15.00
...: Metal and Other Stories TPB (2011, $17.99) r/#29-36 18.00
...: Sven the Returned TPB (2008, $9.99) r/#1-8; cover gallery 10.00
...: The Cross + The Hammer TPB (2009, $14.99) r/#11-16 15.00
...: The Plague Widow TPB (2010, $16.99) r/#21-28 17.00

NORTHSTAR
Marvel Comics: Apr, 1994 - No. 4, July, 1994 ($1.75, mini-series)
1-4: Character from Alpha Flight 3.00

NORTH TO ALASKA
Dell Publishing Co.: No. 1155, Dec, 1960
Four Color 1155-Movie, John Wayne photo-c 14 28 42 96 211 325

NORTHWEST MOUNTIES (Also see Approved Comics #12)
Jubilee Publications/St. John: Oct, 1948 - No. 4, July, 1949
1-Rose of the Yukon by Matt Baker; Walter Johnson-a; Lubbers-c
47 94 141 296 498 700
2-Baker-a; Lubbers-c. Ventrilo app. 39 78 117 231 378 525
3-Bondage-c, Baker-a; Sky Chief, K-9 app. 39 78 117 240 395 550
4-Baker-c/a(2 pgs.); Blue Monk & The Desperado app.
41 82 123 256 428 600

NOSFERATU WARS
Dark Horse Comics: Mar, 2014 ($3.99, one-shot)
1-Reprints serial story from Dark Horse Presents #26-29; Niles-s/Menton3-a 4.00

NO SLEEP 'TIL DAWN
Dell Publishing Co.: No. 831, Aug, 1957
Four Color 831-Movie, Karl Malden photo-c 6 12 18 37 66 95

NOSTALGIA ILLUSTRATED
Marvel Comics: Nov, 1974 - V2#8, Aug, 1975 (B&W, 76 pgs.)
V1#1 3 6 9 21 33 45
V1#2, V2#1-8 3 6 9 15 22 28

NOT BRAND ECHH (Brand Echh #1-4; See Crazy, 1973)
Marvel Comics Group (LMC): Aug, 1967 - No. 13, May, 1969
(1st Marvel parody book)
1: 1-8 are 12¢ issues 7 14 21 44 82 120
2-8: 3-Origin Thor, Hulk & Capt. America; Monkees, Alfred E. Neuman cameo. 4-X-Men app. 5-Origin/intro. Forbush Man. 7-Origin Fantastical-4 & Stuporman. 8-Beatles cameo; X-Men satire; last 12¢-c 4 8 12 25 40 55
9-13 (25¢, 68 pgs., all Giants) 9-Beatles cameo. 10-All-r; The Old Witch, Crypt Keeper & Vault Keeper cameos. 12,13-Beatles cameo 5 10 15 30 50 70
NOTE: *Colan a(p)-4, 5, 8, 9, 13. **Everett** a-1i. **Kirby** a(p)-1, 3, 5-7, 10r; c-1p. **J. Severin** a-1; c-3, 6-8, 11. **M. Severin** a-1-13; c-2, 9, 10, 12, 13. **Sutton** a-3, 4, 5i, 6i, 8, 9, 10r, 11-13; c-5. Archie satire in #9. Avengers satire in #8, 12.*

NOTHING CAN STOP THE JUGGERNAUT
Marvel Comics: 1989 ($3.95)
1-r/Amazing Spider-Man #229 & 230 5.00

NO TIME FOR SERGEANTS (TV)
Dell Publ. Co.: No. 914, July, 1958; Feb-Apr, 1965 - No. 3, Aug-Oct, 1965
Four Color 914 (Movie)-Toth-a; Andy Griffith photo-c 9 18 27 57 111 165
1(2-4/65) (TV): Photo-c 5 10 15 34 60 85
2,3 (TV): Photo-c 4 8 12 28 47 65

NOVA (The Man Called... No. 22-25)(See New Warriors)
Marvel Comics Group: Sept, 1976 - No. 25, May, 1979
1-Origin/1st app. Nova (Richard Rider) Marv Wolfman-s; John Buscema-a
5 10 15 35 63 90
2,3: 2-1st app. Condor & Powerhouse. 3-1st app. Diamondhead; Sal Buscema-p begin
2 4 6 8 10 12
4,12: 4-Thor x-over; 1st app. The Corrupter; Kirby-c. 12-Spider-Man x-over w/Amazing Spider-Man #171 2 4 6 10 14 18
5-11: 5-Nova vs. Tyrannus; Kirby-c; Marvel Bullpen app (incl. Stan Lee) 6-1st app. The Sphinx & Megaman. 7-Sphinx, Condor, Powerhouse & Diamondhead app. 8-Origin Megaman. 9-Megaman app. 10-Sphinx, Condor, Powerhouse & Diamondhead app. 11-vs. Sphinx 1 2 3 5 7 9
10,11-(35¢-c variants, limited distribution)(6,7/77) 4 8 12 28 47 65
12-(35¢-c variant, limited distribution)(8/77) 5 10 15 33 57 80
13,14-(Regular 30¢ editions)(9/77) 13-Intro Crime-Buster; Sandman app. 14-vs. Sandman
1 2 3 5 6 8
13,14-(35¢-c variants, limited distribution) 4 8 12 27 44 60
15-24: 15-Infantino-a begins. 16-18-vs. Yellow Claw; Nick Fury and SHIELD app. 19-Wally West (Kid Flash) cameo; 1st app Blackout. 20-1st Project X (Sherlock Holmes robot). 21-Richard reveals his Nova I.D to parents; vs Corrupter. 22-1st app the Comet

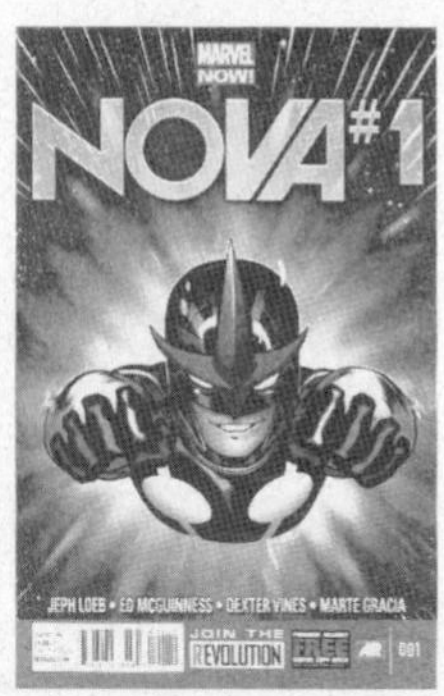
Nova (2013 series) #1 © MAR

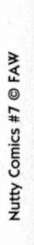

Nutty Comics #7 © FAW

NYX #5 © MAR

GD VG FN VF VF/NM NM-
2.0 4.0 6.0 8.0 9.0 9.2

GD VG FN VF VF/NM NM-
2.0 4.0 6.0 8.0 9.0 9.2

(in costume). 23-Dr. Sun app. (origin) from Tomb of Dracula; Sphinx cameo. 24-Origin Powerhouse, Diamondhead, Crime-Buster, Comet Man, Sphinx & Dr. Sun app. 1 2 3 5 6 8
25-Last issue; Powerhouse, Diamondhead, Crime-Buster, Comet Man, Sphinx & Dr. Sun app. story continues in Fantastic Four #204-214 2 4 6 8 10 12
NOTE: ***Austin** c-21i, 23i. **John Buscema** a(p)-1-3, 8, 21; c-1p, 2, 15. **Infantino** a(p)-15-20, 22-25; c-17-20, 21p, 23p, 24p. **Kirby** c-4p, 5, 7. **Nebres** c-25i. **Simonson** a-23i.*

NOVA
Marvel Comics: Jan, 1994 - June, 1995 ($1.75/$1.95) (Started as 4-part mini-series)
1-($2.95, 52 pgs.)-Collector's Edition w/gold foil-c; new Nova costume 5.00
1-($2.25, 52 pgs.)-Newsstand Edition w/o foil-c 4.00
2-18: 3-Spider-Man-c/story. 5-Stan Lee app. 5-Bound-in card sheet. 13-Firestar & Night Thrasher app.14-Darkhawk 3.00

NOVA
Marvel Comics: May, 1999 - No. 7, Nov, 1999 ($2.99/$1.99)
1-($2.99) Larsen-s/Bennett-a; wraparound-c by Larsen 4.00
2-7-($1.99): 2-Two covers; Capt. America app. 5-Spider-Man. 7-Venom 3.00

NOVA (See Secret Avengers and The Thanos Imperative)
Marvel Comics: June, 2007 - No. 36, Jun, 2010 ($2.99)
1-36: 1-Sean Chen-a/Granov-c. 2,3-Iron Man app. 3-Thunderbolts app. 14,15-Silver Surfer & Galactus app. 16-18-Secret Invasion. 21-Fantastic Four app. 23-28-War of Kings 3.00
... Annual 1 (4/08, $3.99) Origin retold; Annihilation: Conquest tie-in 4.00
...: Origin of Richard Rider (2009, $4.99) origin retold from Nova #1 & 4 ('76) 5.00
... Vol. 1: Annihilation - Conquest TPB (2007, $17.99) r/#1-7; cover sketches 18.00

NOVA (Marvel NOW!)
Marvel Comics: Apr, 2013 - Present ($3.99)
1-Loeb-s/McGuinness-a/c; Rocket Raccoon & Gamora app.; multiple variant covers 4.00
2-9: 2,3-Rocket Raccoon & Gamora app. 7-Superior Spider-Man app. 8,9-Infinity tie-in 4.00
10-($4.99) "Issue #100"; Speedball & Justice app.; cover gallery 5.00
11-15: 12-15-Beta Ray Bill app. 4.00

NOW AGE ILLUSTRATED (See Pendulum Illustrated Classics)

NOW AGE BOOKS ILLUSTRATED (See Pendulum Illustrated Classics)

NOWHERE MAN
Dynamite Entertainment: 2011 - No. 4 ($3.99)
1-4-Marc Guggenheim-s/Jeevan J. Kang-a 4.00

NOWHERE MEN
Image Comics: Nov, 2012 - Present ($2.99)
1-Stephenson-s/Bellegarde-a 25.00
1-2nd thru 5th printings 4.00
2 10.00
3-6 4.00

NTH MAN THE ULTIMATE NINJA (See Marvel Comics Presents #25)
Marvel Comics: Aug, 1989 - No. 16, Sept, 1990 ($1.00)
1-16-Ninja mercenary. 8-Dale Keown's 1st Marvel work (1/90, pencils) 3.00

NUCLEUS (Also see Cerebus)
Heiro-Graphic Publications: May, 1979 ($1.50, B&W, adult fanzine)
1-Contains "Demonhorn" by Dave Sim; early app. of Cerebus The Aardvark (4 pg. story) 5 10 15 34 60 85

NUKLA
Dell Publishing Co.: Oct-Dec, 1965 - No. 4, Sept, 1966
1-Origin & 1st app. Nukla (super hero) 4 8 12 28 47 65
2,3 3 6 9 19 30 40
4-Ditko-a, c(p) 4 8 12 23 37 50

NUMBER OF THE BEAST
DC Comics (WildStorm): June, 2008 - No. 8, Sept, 2008 ($2.99, limited series)
1-8-Beatty-s/Sprouse-a/c. 1-Variant-c by Mahnke. 6-The Authority app. 3.00
TPB (2008, $19.99) r/#1-8; character dossiers 20.00

NURSE BETSY CRANE (Formerly Teen Secret Diary) (Also see Registered Nurse for reprints)
Charlton Comics: V2#12, Aug, 1961 - V2#27, Mar, 1964 (See Soap Opera Romances)
V2#12-27 3 6 9 16 23 30

NURSE HELEN GRANT (See The Romances of...)

NURSE LINDA LARK (See Linda Lark)

NURSERY RHYMES
Ziff-Davis Publ. Co. (Approved Comics): No. 10, July-Aug, 1951 - No. 2, Winter, 1951 (Painted-c)
10 (#1), 2: 10-Howie Post-a 18 36 54 103 162 220

NURSES, THE (TV)
Gold Key: April, 1963 - No. 3, Oct, 1963 (Photo-c: #1,2)
1 4 8 12 23 37 50
2,3 3 6 9 17 26 35

NUTS! (Satire)
Premiere Comics Group: March, 1954 - No. 5, Nov, 1954
1-Hollingsworth-a 32 64 96 192 314 435
2,4,5: 5-Capt. Marvel parody 21 42 63 124 202 280
3-Drug "reefers" mentioned 21 42 63 126 206 285

NUTS (Magazine) (Satire)
Health Knowledge: Feb, 1958 - No. 2, April, 1958
1 10 20 30 54 72 90
2 7 14 21 37 46 55

NUTS & JOLTS
Dell Publishing Co.: No. 22, 1941
Large Feature Comic 22 19 38 57 109 172 235

NUTSY SQUIRREL (Formerly Hollywood Funny Folks)(See Comic Cavalcade)
National Periodical Publications: #61, 9-10/54 - #69, 1-2/56; #70, 8-9/56 - #71, 10-11/56; #72, 11/57
61-Mayer-a; Grossman-a in all 14 28 42 76 108 140
62-72: Mayer a-62,65,67-72 10 20 30 54 72 90

NUTTY COMICS
Fawcett Publications: Winter, 1946
1-Capt. Kidd story; 1 pg. Wolverton-a 14 28 42 80 115 150

NUTTY COMICS
Home Comics (Harvey Publications): 1945; No. 4, May-June, 1946 - No. 8, June-July, 1947 (No #2,3)
nn-Helpful Hank, Bozo Bear & others (funny animal) 9 18 27 50 65 80
4 7 14 21 37 46 55
5-Rags Rabbit begins(1st app.); infinity-c 8 16 24 40 50 60
6-8 6 12 18 31 38 45

NUTTY LIFE (Formerly Krazy Life #1; becomes Wotalife Comics #3 on)
Fox Features Syndicate: No. 2, Summer, 1946
2 19 38 57 109 172 235

NYOKA, THE JUNGLE GIRL (Formerly Jungle Girl; see The Further Adventures of..., Master Comics #50 & XMas Comics)
Fawcett Publications: No. 2, Winter, 1945 - No. 77, June, 1953 (Movie serial)
2 63 126 189 403 689 975
3 36 72 108 216 351 485
4,5 31 62 93 182 296 410
6-11,13,14,16-18-Krigstein-a: 17-Sam Spade ad by Lou Fine 20 40 60 118 192 265
12,15,19,20 19 38 57 111 176 240
21-30: 25-Clayton Moore photo-c? 14 28 42 78 112 145
31-40 11 22 33 64 90 115
41-50 10 20 30 58 79 100
51-60 9 18 27 52 69 85
61-77 9 18 27 47 61 75
NOTE: *Photo-c from movies 25, 30-70, 72, 75-77. Bondage c-4, 5, 7, 8, 14, 24.*

NYOKA, THE JUNGLE GIRL (Formerly Zoo Funnies; Space Adventures #23 on)
Charlton Comics: No. 14, Nov, 1955 - No. 22, Nov, 1957
14 11 22 33 64 90 115
15-22 10 20 30 54 72 90

NYX (Also see X-23 title)
Marvel Comics: Nov, 2003 - No. 7, Oct, 2005 ($2.99)
1,2: 1-Quesada-s/Middleton-a/c. intro. Kiden Nixon 3.00
3-1st app. X-23 1 3 4 6 8 10
4-6: 5,6-Teranishi-a 3.00
7-($3.99) Teranishi-a 4.00
NYX X-23 (2005, $34.99, oversized with d.j.) r/X-23 #1-6 & NYX #1-7; intro by Craig Kyle; sketch pages, development art and unused covers 35.00
...: Wannabe TPB (2006, $19.99) r/#1-7; development art and unused covers 20.00

NYX: NO WAY HOME
Marvel Comics: Oct, 2008 - No. 6, Apr, 2009 ($3.99)
1-6: 1-Andrasofszky-a/Liu-s/Urusov-c; sketch pages, character and cover design art 4.00

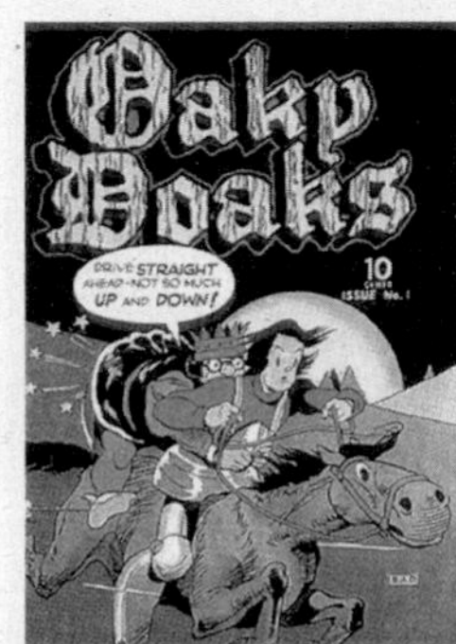

Oaky Doaks #1 © EAS

Occult Crimes Taskforce #1 © Image

Official Handbook of the Marvel Universe #2 © MAR

GD	VG	FN	VF	VF/NM	NM-
2.0	4.0	6.0	8.0	9.0	9.2

OAKLAND PRESS FUNNYBOOK, THE
The Oakland Press: 9/17/78 - 4/13/80 (16 pgs.) (Weekly)
Full color in comic book form; changes to tabloid size 4/20/80-on

Contains Tarzan by Manning, Marmaduke, Bugs Bunny, etc. (low distribution); 9/23/79 - 4/13/80 contain Buck Rogers by Gray Morrow & Jim Lawrence 3.00

OAKY DOAKS (See Famous Funnies #190)
Eastern Color Printing Co.: July, 1942 (One Shot)

1 34 68 102 199 325 450

OBERGEIST: RAGNAROK HIGHWAY
Image Comics (Top Cow/Minotaur): May, 2001 - No. 6, Nov, 2001 ($2.95, limited series)

Preview ('01, B&W, 16 pgs.) Harris painted-c 3.00
1-6-Harris-c/a/Jolley-s. 1-Three covers 3.00
... :The Directors' Cut (2002, $19.95, TPB) r/#1-6; Bruce Campbell intro. 20.00
... :The Empty Locket (3/02, $2.95, B&W) Harris & Snyder-a 3.00

OBIE
Store Comics: 1953 (6¢)

1 6 12 18 31 38 45

OBJECTIVE FIVE
Image Comics: July, 2000 - No. 6, Jan, 2001($2.95)

1-6-Lizalde-a 3.00

OBLIVION
Comico: Aug, 1995 - No. 3, May, 1996 ($2.50)

1-3: 1-Art Adams-c. 2-(1/96)-Bagged w/gaming card. 3-(5/96)-Darrow-c 3.00

OBNOXIO THE CLOWN (Character from Crazy Magazine)
Marvel Comics Group: April, 1983 (one-shot)

1-Vs. the X-Men 5.00

OCCULT CRIMES TASKFORCE
Image Comics: July, 2006 - No. 4, May, 2007 ($2.99, limited series)

1-4-Rosario Dawson & David Atchison-s/Tony Shasteen-a 3.00
... Vol. 1 TPB (2007, $14.99) r/#1-4; sketch and cover development art 15.00

OCCULTIST, THE
Dark Horse Comics: Dec, 2010 ($3.50, one-shot)

1-Richardson & Seeley-sDrujiniu-a/Morris-c 3.50

OCCULTIST, THE
Dark Horse Comics: Nov, 2011 - No. 3, Jan, 2012 ($3.50, limited series)

1-3-Seeley-s/Drujiniu-a/Morris-c. 1-Variant-c by Frison 3.50

OCCULTIST, THE
Dark Horse Comics: Oct, 2013 - No. 5, Feb, 2014 ($3.50, limited series)

1-5-Seeley-s/Norton-a/Morris-c. 1-Variant-c by Rivera 3.50

OCCULT FILES OF DR. SPEKTOR, THE
Gold Key/Whitman No. 25: Apr, 1973 - No. 24, Feb, 1977; No. 25, May, 1982 (Painted-c #1-24)

1-1st app. Lakota; Baron Tibor begins 5 10 15 33 57 80
2-5: 3-Mummy-c/s. 5-Jekyll & Hyde-c/s 3 6 9 19 30 40
6-10: 6,9-Frankenstein. 8,9-Dracula c/s. 9.-Jekyll & Hyde c/s. 9,10-Mummy-c/s
3 6 9 15 22 28
11-13,15-17,19-22,24: 11-1st app. Spektor as Werewolf. 11-13-Werewolf-c/s. 12,16-Frankenstein c/s. 17-Zombie/Voodoo-c. 19-Sea monster-c/s. 20-Mummy-s. 21-Swamp monster-c/s. 24-Dragon-c/s 2 4 6 11 16 20
14-Dr. Solar app. 3 6 9 16 24 32
18,23-Dr. Solar cameo 2 4 6 13 18 22
22-Return of the Owl c/s 2 4 6 13 18 22
25(Whitman, 5/82)-r/#1 with line drawn-c 2 4 6 9 13 16

NOTE: *Also see Dan Curtis, Golden Comics Digest 33, Gold Key Spotlight, Mystery Comics Digest 5, & Spine Tingling Tales.*

OCCUPY COMICS
Black Mask Studios: 2013 - No. 3, 2013 ($3.50)

1-3-Short stories and essays about the Occupy movement; s/a by various. 1-Allred-c 3.50

OCEAN
DC Comics (WildStorm): Dec, 2005 - No. 6, Sept, 2005 ($2.95/$2.99/$3.99, limited series)

1-5-Warren Ellis-s/Chris Sprouse-a 3.00
6-($3.99) Conclusion 4.00

ODELL'S ADVENTURES IN 3-D (See Adventures in 3-D)

ODYSSEY, THE (See Marvel Illustrated: The Odyssey)

OFFCASTES
Marvel Comics (Epic Comics/Heavy Hitters): July, 1993 - No. 3, Sept, 1993 ($1.95, limited series)

1-3: Mike Vosburg-c/a/scripts in all 3.00

OFFICIAL CRISIS ON INFINITE EARTHS INDEX, THE
Independent Comics Group (Eclipse): Mar, 1986 ($1.75)

1 5.00

OFFICIAL CRISIS ON INFINITE EARTHS CROSSOVER INDEX, THE
Independent Comics Group (Eclipse): July, 1986 ($1.75)

1-Perez-c. 5.00

OFFICIAL DOOM PATROL INDEX, THE
Independent Comics Group (Eclipse): Feb, 1986 - No. 2, Mar, 1986 ($1.50, limited series)

1,2: Byrne-c. 4.00

OFFICIAL HANDBOOK OF THE CONAN UNIVERSE (See Handbook of...)

OFFICIAL HANDBOOK OF THE MARVEL UNIVERSE, THE
Marvel Comics Group: Jan, 1983 - No. 15, May, 1984 (Limited series)

1-Lists Marvel heroes & villains (letter A) 6.00
2-15: 2 (B-C, 3-(C-D). 4-(D-G). 5-(H-J), 6-(K-L). 7-(M). 8-(N-P); Punisher-c. 9-(Q-S), 10-(S). 11-(S-U). 12-(V-Z); Wolverine-c. 13,14-Book of the Dead. 15-Weaponry catalogue 5.00

NOTE: ***Bolland** a-8. **Byrne** c/a(p)-1-14; c-15p. **Grell** a-6, 9. **Kirby** a-1, 3. **Layton** a-2, 5, 7. **Mignola** a-3, 4, 5, 6, 8, 12. **Miller** a-4-6, 8, 10. **Nebres** a-3, 4, 8. **Redondo** a-3, 4, 8, 13, 14. **Simonson** a-1, 4, 6-13. **Paul Smith** a-1-12. **Starlin** a-5, 7, 8, 10, 13, 14. **Steranko** a-8p. **Zeck**-2-14.*

OFFICIAL HANDBOOK OF THE MARVEL UNIVERSE, THE
Marvel Comics Group: Dec, 1985 - No. 20, Feb, 1988 ($1.50, maxi-series)

V2#1-Byrne-c 5.00
2-20: 2,3-Byrne-c 4.00
Trade paperback Vol. 1-10 ($6.95) 1 3 4 6 8 10

NOTE: ***Art Adams** a-7, 8, 11, 12, 14. **Bolland** a-8, 10, 13. **Buckler** a-1, 3, 5, 10. **Buscema** a-1, 5, 8, 9, 10, 13, 14. **Byrne** a-1-14; c-1-11. **Ditko** a-1, 2, 4, 6, 7, 11, 13. a-7, 11. **Mignola** a-2, 4, 9, 11, 13. **Miller** a-2, 4, 12. **Simonson** a-1, 2, 4-13, 15. **Paul Smith** a-1-5, 7-12, 14. **Starlin** a-6, 8, 9, 12, 16. **Zeck** a-1-4, 6, 7, 9-14, 16.*

OFFICIAL HANDBOOK OF THE MARVEL UNIVERSE, THE
Marvel Comics: July, 1989 - No. 8, Mid-Dec, 1990 ($1.50, lim. series, 52 pgs.)

V3#1-8: 1-McFarlane-a (2 pgs.) 4.00

OFFICIAL HANDBOOK OF THE MARVEL UNIVERSE, THE (Also see Spider-Man)
Marvel Comics: 2004 - Present ($3.99, one-shots)

...: Alternate Universes 2005 - Profile pages of 1602, MC2, 2099, Earth X, Mangaverse, Days of Future Past, Squadron Supreme, Spider-Ham's Larval Earth and others 4.00
...: Avengers 2004 - Profile pages; art by various; lists of character origins and 1st apps. 4.00
...: Avengers 2005 - Profile pages and info for New Avengers, Young Avengers & others 4.00
...: Book of the Dead 2004 - Profile pages of deceased Marvel characters; art by various; 4.00
...: Daredevil 2004 - Profile pages; art by various; lists of character origins and 1st apps. 4.00
...: Fantastic Four 2005 - Profile pages of members, friends & enemies 4.00
...: Golden Age 2005 - Profile pages; art by various; lists of character origins and 1st apps. 4.00
...: Horror 2005 - Profile pages; art by various; lists of character origins and 1st apps. 4.00
...: Hulk 2004 - Profile pages; art by various; lists of character origins and 1st apps. 4.00
...: Marvel Knights 2005 - Profile pages of characters from Marvel Knights line 4.00
...: Spider-Man 2004 - Profile pages; art by various; lists of character origins and 1st apps. 4.00
...: Spider-Man 2005 - Profile pages of Spidey's friends and foes, emphasizing the recent 4.00
...: Wolverine 2004 - Profile pages; art by various; lists of character origins and 1st apps. 4.00
...: Teams 2005 - Profile pages of Avengers, X-Men and other teams 4.00
...: Women of Marvel 2005 - Profile pages; art by various; Greg Land-c 4.00
...: X-Men 2004 - Profile pages; art by various; lists of character origins and 1st apps. 4.00
...: X-Men 2005 - Profile pages; art by various; lists of character origins and 1st apps. 4.00
...: X-Men - The Age of Apocalypse 2005 - Profile pages of characters plus Exiles 4.00

OFFICIAL HANDBOOK OF THE MARVEL UNIVERSE A-Z UPDATE
Marvel Comics: Apr, 2010 - No. 5, 2010 ($3.99, limited series)

1-5-Profile pages; Andrasofszky-c 4.00

OFFICIAL HANDBOOK OF THE ULTIMATE MARVEL UNIVERSE, THE
Marvel Comics: 2005 ($3.99, one-shots)

... 2005: The Fantastic Four and Spider-Man - Profile pages; art by various 4.00
... The Ultimates and X-Men 2005 - Profile pages; art by various; Bagley-c 4.00

OFFICIAL HAWKMAN INDEX, THE
Independent Comics Group: Nov, 1986 - No. 2, Dec, 1986 ($2.00)

1,2 4.00

OFFICIAL INDEX TO THE MARVEL UNIVERSE (Also see "Avengers, Thor...")
Marvel Comics: 2009 - No. 14, April, 2010 ($3.99)

1-14-Each issue has chronological synopsies, creator credits, character lists for 40-50 issues of apps. for Iron Man, Spider-Man and the X-Men starting with 1st apps. in issue #1 4.00

OFFICIAL JUSTICE LEAGUE OF AMERICA INDEX, THE

Official Marvel Index to the Amazing Spider-Man #1 © MAR

O.K. Comics #2 © UFS

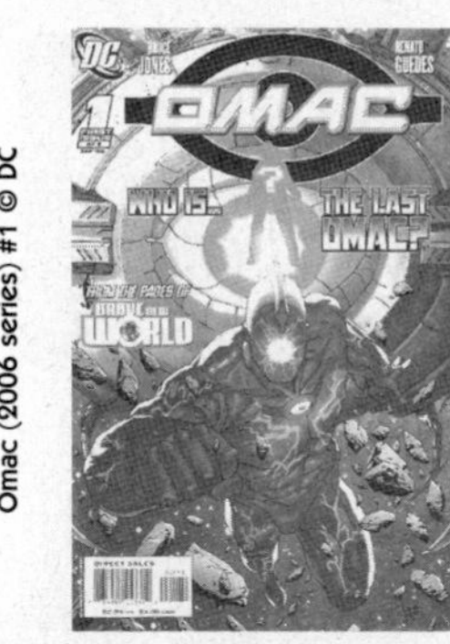

Omac (2006 series) #1 © DC

	GD	VG	FN	VF	VF/NM	NM-
	2.0	4.0	6.0	8.0	9.0	9.2

Independent Comics Group (Eclipse): April, 1986 - No. 8, Mar, 1987 ($2.00, Baxter paper)

1-8: 1,2-Perez-c. 6.00

OFFICIAL LEGION OF SUPER-HEROES INDEX, THE
Independent Comics Group (Eclipse): Dec, 1986 - No. 5, 1987 ($2.00, limited series) (No Official in Title #2 on)

1-5: 4-Mooney-c 6.00

OFFICIAL MARVEL INDEX TO MARVEL TEAM-UP
Marvel Comics Group: Jan, 1986 - No. 6, 1987 ($1.25, limited series)

1-6 4.00

OFFICIAL MARVEL INDEX TO THE AMAZING SPIDER-MAN
Marvel Comics Group: Apr, 1985 - No. 9, Dec, 1985 ($1.25, limited series)

1 ($1.00)-Byrne-c. 5.00
2-9: 5,6,8,9-Punisher-c. 4.00

OFFICIAL MARVEL INDEX TO THE AVENGERS, THE
Marvel Comics: Jun, 1987 - No. 7, Aug, 1988 ($2.95, limited series)

1-7 5.00

OFFICIAL MARVEL INDEX TO THE AVENGERS, THE
Marvel Comics: V2#1, Oct, 1994 - V2#6, 1995 ($1.95, limited series)

V2#1-#6 4.00

OFFICIAL MARVEL INDEX TO THE FANTASTIC FOUR
Marvel Comics Group: Dec, 1985 - No. 12, Jan, 1987 ($1.25, limited series)

1-12: 1-Byrne-c. 1,2-Kirby back-c (unpub. art) 4.00

OFFICIAL MARVEL INDEX TO THE X-MEN, THE
Marvel Comics: May, 1987 - No. 7, July, 1988 ($2.95, limited series)

1-7 5.00

OFFICIAL MARVEL INDEX TO THE X-MEN, THE
Marvel Comics: V2#1, Apr, 1994 - V2#5, 1994 ($1.95, limited series)

V2#1-5: 1-Covers X-Men #1-51. 2-Covers #52-122,Special #1,2,Giant-Size #1,2. 3-Byrne-c; covers #123-177, Annuals 3-7, Spec. Ed. #1. 4-Covers Uncanny X-Men #178-234, Annuals 8-12. 5-Covers #235-287, Annuals 13-15 4.00

OFFICIAL SOUPY SALES COMIC (See Soupy Sales)

OFFICIAL TEEN TITANS INDEX, THE
Indep. Comics Group (Eclipse): Aug, 1985 - No. 5, 1986 ($1.50, lim. series)

1-5 4.00

OFFICIAL TRUE CRIME CASES (Formerly Sub-Mariner #23; All-True Crime Cases #26 on)
Marvel Comics (OCI): No. 24, Fall, 1947 - No. 25, Winter, 1947-48

	GD	VG	FN	VF	VF/NM	NM-
24(#1)-Burgos-a; Syd Shores-c	24	48	72	142	234	325
25-Syd Shores-c; Kurtzman's "Hey Look"	19	38	57	111	176	240

OF SUCH IS THE KINGDOM
George A. Pflaum: 1955 (15¢, 36 pgs.)

	GD	VG	FN	VF	VF/NM	NM-
nn-Reprints from 1951 Treasure Chest	4	7	10	14	17	20

O.G. WHIZ (See Gold Key Spotlight #10)
Gold Key: 2/71 - No. 6, 5/72; No. 7, 5/78 - No. 11, 1/79 (No. 7: 52 pgs.)

	GD	VG	FN	VF	VF/NM	NM-
1-John Stanley script	5	10	15	31	53	75
2-John Stanley script	4	8	12	23	37	50
3-6(1972)	3	6	9	17	26	35
7-11(1978-79)-Part-r: 9-Tubby issue	2	4	6	9	12	15

OH, BROTHER! (Teen Comedy)
Stanhall Publ.: Jan, 1953 - No. 5, Oct, 1953

	GD	VG	FN	VF	VF/NM	NM-
1-By Bill Williams	10	20	30	58	79	100
2-5	8	16	24	40	50	60

OH MY GODDESS! (Manga)
Dark Horse Comics: Aug, 1994 - Present ($2.50-$3.99, B&W)

1-6-Kosuke Fujishima-s/a in all 3.00
... PART II 2/95 - No. 9, 9/95 ($2.50, B&W, lim.series) #1-9 3.00
... PART III 11/95 - No. 11, 9/96 ($2.95, B&W, lim. series) #1-11 3.00
... PART IV 12/96 - No. 8, 7/97 ($2.95, B&W, lim. series) #1-8 3.00
... PART V 9/97 - Np. 12, 8/98 ($2.95, B&W, lim. series)
1,2,5,8: 5-Ninja Master pt. 1 3.00
3,4,6,7,10-12-($3.95, 48 pgs.) 10-Fallen Angel. 11-Play The Game 4.00
9-($3.50) "It's Lonely At The Top" 3.50
... PART VI 10/98 - No. 5, 3/99 ($3.50/$2.95, B&W, lim. series)
1-($3.50) 3.50
2-6-($2.95)-6-Super Urd one-shot 3.00
... PART VII 5/99 - No. 8, 12/99 ($2.95, B&W, lim. series) #1-3 3.00
4-8-($3.50) 3.50
... PART VIII 1/00 - No. 6, 6/00 ($3.50, B&W, lim. series) #1-3,5,7 3.50
4-($2.95) "Hail To The Chief" begins 3.00
... PART IX 7/00 - No. 7, 1/01 ($3.50/$2.99) #1-4: 3-Queen Sayoko 3.50
5-7-($2.99) 3.00
... PART X 2/01 - No. 5, 6/01 ($3.50) #1-5 3.50
... PART XI 10/01 - No. 10, 3/02 ($3.50) #1,2,7,8 3.50
3-6,9-($2.99) Mystery Child 3.00
10-($3.99) 4.00
(Series adapts new numbering) 88-90-($3.50) Learning to Love 3.50
91-94,96-103,105,107-110: 91-94 ($2.99) Traveler. 96-98-The Phantom Racer 3.00
95,104,106-($3.50) 95-Traveler pt. 5 3.50
111,112-($3.99) 4.00

OH SUSANNA (TV)
Dell Publishing Co.: No. 1105, June-Aug, 1960 (Gale Storm)

	GD	VG	FN	VF	VF/NM	NM-
Four Color 1105-Toth-a, photo-c	9	18	27	63	129	195

OKAY COMICS
United Features Syndicate: July, 1940

	GD	VG	FN	VF	VF/NM	NM-
1-Captain & the Kids & Hawkshaw the Detective reprints	45	90	135	279	465	650

O.K. COMICS
Hit Publications: May, 1940 (ashcan)

nn-Ashcan comic, not distributed to newsstands, only for in house use. A CGC certified 8.0 copy sold in 2003 for $1,000.

O.K. COMICS
United Features Syndicate/Hit Publications: July, 1940 - No. 2, Oct, 1940

	GD	VG	FN	VF	VF/NM	NM-
1-Little Giant (w/super powers), Phantom Knight, Sunset Smith, & The Teller Twins begin	77	154	231	493	847	1200
2 (Rare)-Origin Mister Mist by Chas. Quinlan	79	158	237	502	864	1225

OKLAHOMA KID
Ajax/Farrell Publ.: June, 1957 - No. 4, 1958

	GD	VG	FN	VF	VF/NM	NM-
1	11	22	33	60	83	105
2-4	7	14	21	37	46	55

OKLAHOMAN, THE
Dell Publishing Co.: No. 820, July, 1957

	GD	VG	FN	VF	VF/NM	NM-
Four Color 820-Movie, photo-c	7	14	21	49	92	135

OKTANE
Dark Horse Comics: Aug, 1995 - Nov, 1995 ($2.50, color, limited series)

1-4-Gene Ha-a 3.00

OKTOBERFEST COMICS
Now & Then Publ.: Fall 1976 (75¢, Canadian, B&W, one-shot)

	GD	VG	FN	VF	VF/NM	NM-
1-Dave Sim-s/a; Gene Day-a; 1st app. Uncle Hans & Natter P. Bombast; The Beavers sty; 1st Cap'n Riverrat, Sim-s/Day-a	3	6	9	16	23	30

OLD GLORY COMICS
DC Comics: 1941

nn - Ashcan comic, not distributed to newsstands, only for in-house use. Cover art is Flash Comics #12 with interior being Action Comics #37 (no known sales)

OLD IRONSIDES (Disney)
Dell Publishing Co.: No. 874, Jan, 1958

	GD	VG	FN	VF	VF/NM	NM-
Four Color 874-Movie w/Johnny Tremain	6	12	18	38	69	100

OLD YELLER (Disney, see Movie Comics, and Walt Disney Showcase #25)
Dell Publishing Co.: No. 869, Jan, 1958

	GD	VG	FN	VF	VF/NM	NM-
Four Color 869-Movie, photo-c	5	10	15	33	57	80

OMAC (One Man Army; ...Corps. #4 on; also see Kamandi #59 & Warlord) (See Cancelled Comic Cavalcade)
National Periodical Publications: Sept-Oct, 1974 - No. 8, Nov-Dec, 1975

	GD	VG	FN	VF	VF/NM	NM-
1-Origin	5	10	15	33	57	80
2-8: 8-2 pg. Neal Adams ad	3	6	9	17	26	35

Jack Kirby's Omac: One Man Army Corps HC (2008, $24.99, d.j.) r/#1-8; Evanier intro. 25.00
NOTE: *Kirby a-1-8p; c-1-7p.* ***Kubert*** *c-8.*

OMAC (See DCU Brave New World)
DC Comics: Sept, 2006 - No. 8, Apr, 2007 ($2.99, limited series)

1-8: 1-Bruce Jones-s/Renato Guedes-a. 1-3-Firestorm & Cyborg app. 8-Superman app. 3.00

O.M.A.C. (DC New 52)
DC Comics: Nov, 2011 - No. 8, Jun, 2012 ($2.99)

Omega Flight #1 © MAR

The Omen #5 © Chaos!

100 Bullets #57 © Azzarello & Risso

GD VG FN VF VF/NM NM-
2.0 4.0 6.0 8.0 9.0 9.2

1-8: 1-DiDio-s/Giffen-a/c; Dubbilex and Brother Eye app. 2-Max Lord & Sarge Steel app. 5-Crossover with Frankenstein, Agent of SHADE #5. 6-Kolins-a 3.00

OMAC: ONE MAN ARMY CORPS
DC Comics: 1991 - No. 4, 1991 ($3.95, B&W, mini-series, mature, 52 pgs.)
Book One - Four: John Byrne-c/a & scripts 5.00

OMAC PROJECT, THE
DC Comics: June, 2005 - No. 6, Nov, 2005 ($2.50, limited series)
1-6-Prelude to Infinite Crisis x-over; Rucka-s/Saiz-a 3.00
...: Infinite Crisis Special 1 (5/06, $4.99) Rucka-s/Saiz-a; follows destruction of satellite 5.00
TPB (2005, $14.99) r/#1-6, Countdown to Infinite Crisis, Wonder Woman #219 15.00

O'MALLEY AND THE ALLEY CATS
Gold Key: April, 1971 - No. 9, Jan, 1974 (Disney)
1 3 6 9 16 23 30
2-9 2 4 6 9 13 16

OMEGA ELITE
Blackthorne Publishing: 1987 ($1.25)
1-Starlin-c 3.00

OMEGA FLIGHT
Marvel Comics: Jun, 2007 - No. 5, Oct, 2007 ($2.99, limited series)
1-Oeming-s/Kolins-a; Wrecking Crew app. 4.00
1-Second printing with Sasquatch variant-c 3.00
2-5: 5-Beta Ray Bill app. 3.00
...: Alpha to Omega TPB ('07, $13.99) r/#1-5, USAgent story/Civil War: Choosing Sides 14.00

OMEGA MEN, THE (See Green Lantern #141)
DC Comics: Dec, 1982 - No. 38, May, 1986 ($1.00/$1.25/$1.50; Baxter paper)
1,20: 20-2nd full Lobo story 5.00
2,4-9,11-19,21-25,28-30,32,33,36,38: 2-Origin Broot. 5,9-2nd & 3rd app. Lobo (cameo, 2 pgs. each). 7-Origin The Citadel. 19-Lobo cameo. 30-Intro new Primus 3.00
3-1st app. Lobo (5 pgs.)(6/83); Lobo-c 2 4 6 9 121 15
10-1st full Lobo story 6.00
26,27,31,34,35: 26,27-Alan Moore scripts. 31-Crisis x-over. 34,35-Teen Titans x-over 4.00
37-1st solo Lobo story (8 pg. back-up by Giffen) 5.00
Annual 1(11/84, 52 pgs.), 2(11/85) 4.00
NOTE: *Giffen c/a-1-6p. Morrow a-24r. Nino c/a-16, 21; a-Annual 1i.*

OMEGA MEN, THE
DC Comics: Dec, 2006 - No. 6, May, 2007 ($2.99, limited series)
1-6: 1-Superman, Wonder Girl, Green Lantern app.; Flint-a/Gabrych-s 3.00

OMEGA THE UNKNOWN
Marvel Comics Group: March, 1976 - No. 10, Oct, 1977
1-1st app. Omega 2 4 6 11 16 20
2,3-(Regular 25¢ editions). 2-Hulk-c/story. 3-Electro-c/story. 2 3 4 6 8 10
2,3-(30¢-c variants, limited distribution) 3 6 9 19 30 40
4-10: 8-1st brief app. 2nd Foolkiller (Greg Salinger), 1 panel only. 9,10-(Reg. 30¢ editions). 9-1st full app. 2nd Foolkiller 1 2 3 5 6 8
9,10-(35¢-c variants, limited distribution) 4 8 12 23 37 50
... Classic TPB (2005, $29.99) r/#1-10 30.00
NOTE: *Kane c(p)-3, 5, 8, 9. Mooney a-1-3, 4p, 5, 6p, 7, 8i, 9, 10.*

OMEGA: THE UNKNOWN
Marvel Comics: Dec, 2007 - No. 10, Sept, 2008 ($2.99, limited series)
1-10-Jonathan Lethem-s/Farel Dalrymple-a 3.00

OMEN
Northstar Publishing: 1989 - No. 3, 1989 ($2.00, B&W, mature)
1-Tim Vigil-c/a in all 1 2 3 5 7 9
1, (2nd printing) 3.00
2,3 6.00

OMEN, THE
Chaos! Comics: May, 1998 - No. 5, Sept, 1998 ($2.95, limited series)
1-5: 1-Six covers, ...: Vexed (10/98, $2.95) Chaos! characters appear 3.00

OMNI MEN
Blackthorne Publishing: 1987 - No. 3, 1987 ($1.25)
1-3 3.00
Graphic Novel (1989, $3.50) 4.00

ONCE UPON A TIME: SHADOW OF THE QUEEN (TV)
Marvel Comics: 2013 ($19.99, hardcover with dustjacket)
HC-Regina and the Huntsman; Bechko-s; art by Del Mundo, Lolos, Henderson, & Kaluta 20.00

GD VG FN VF VF/NM NM-
2.0 4.0 6.0 8.0 9.0 9.2

ONE, THE
Marvel Comics (Epic Comics): July, 1985 - No. 6, Feb, 1986 (Limited series, mature)
1-6: Post nuclear holocaust super-hero. 2-Intro The Other 3.00

ONE-ARM SWORDSMAN, THE
Victory Prod./Lueng's Publ. #4 on: 1987 - No. 12, 1990 ($2.75/$1.80, 52 pgs.)
1-3 ($2.75) 4.00
4-12: 4-6-$1.80-c. 7-12-$2.00-c 4.00

ONE-HIT WONDER
Image Comics: Feb, 2014 - Present ($3.50)
1,2-Sapolsky-s/Olivetti-a/c 3.50

ONE HUNDRED AND ONE DALMATIANS (Disney, see Cartoon Tales, Movie Comics, and Walt Disney Showcase #9, 51)
Dell Publishing Co.: No. 1183, Mar, 1961
Four Color 1183-Movie 9 18 27 59 117 175

101 DALMATIONS (Movie)
Disney Comics: 1991 (52 pgs., graphic novel)
nn-($4.95, direct sales)-r/movie adaptation & more 5.00
1-($2.95, newsstand edition) 3.00

101 WAYS TO END THE CLONE SAGA (See Spider-Man)
Marvel Comics: Jan, 1997 ($2.50, one-shot)
1 3.00

100 BULLETS
DC Comics (Vertigo): Aug, 1999 - No. 100, Jun, 2009 ($2.50/$2.75/$2.99)
1-Azzarello-s/Risso-a/Dave Johnson-c 3 6 9 16 23 30
2-5 6.00
6-49,51-61: 26-Series summary; art by various. 45-Preview of Losers 4.00
50-($3.50) History of the Trust 5.00
62-71: 62-Begin $2.75-c. 64-Preview of Loveless 3.00
72-99: 72-Begin $2.99-c 3.00
100-($4.99) Final issue 6.00
...#1/Crime Line Sampler Flip-Book (9/09, $1.00) r/#1 with previews of upcoming GNs 3.00
...: A Foregone Tomorrow TPB (2002, $17.95) r/#20-30 18.00
...: Decayed TPB (2006, $14.99) r/#68-75; Darwyn Cooke intro. 15.00
...: First Shot, Last Call TPB (2000, $9.95) r/#1-5, Vertigo Winter's Edge #3 10.00
...: Hang Up on the Hang Low TPB (2001, $9.95) r/#15-19; Jim Lee intro. 10.00
...: Once Upon a Crime TPB (2007, $12.99) r/#76-83 13.00
...: Samurai TPB (2003, $12.95) r/#43-49 13.00
...: Six Feet Under the Gun TPB (2003, $12.95) r/#37-42 13.00
...: Split Second Chance TPB (2001, $14.95) r/#6-14 15.00
...: Strychnine Lives TPB (2006, $14.99) r/#59-67; Manuel Ramos intro. 15.00
...: The Counterfifth Detective TPB (2003, $12.95) r/#31-36 13.00
...: The Hard Way TPB (2005, $14.99) r/#50-58 15.00
...: Wilt TPB (2009, $19.99) r/#89-100; Azzarello intro. 20.00

100 BULLETS: BROTHER LONO
DC Comics (Vertigo): Aug, 2013 - No. 8, Apr, 2014 ($3.99/$2.99, limited series)
1-($3.99) Azzarello-s/Risso-a/Dave Johnson-c 4.00
2-8-($2.99) Azzarello-s/Risso-a/Dave Johnson-c on all 3.00

100 GREATEST MARVELS OF ALL TIME
Marvel Comics: Dec, 2001 ($7.50/$3.50, limited series)
1-5-Reprints top #6-#25 stories voted by poll for Marvel's 40th ann. 7.50
6-($3.50) (#5 on-c) Reprints X-Men (2nd series) #1 4.00
7-($3.50) (#4 on-c) Reprints Giant-Size X-Men #1 4.00
8-($3.50) (#3 on-c) Reprints (Uncanny) X-Men #137 (Death of Jean Grey) 4.00
9-($3.50) (#2 on-c) Reprints Fantastic Four #1 4.00
10-($3.50) (#1 on-c) Reprints Amazing Fantasy #15 (1st app. Spider-Man) 4.00

100 PAGES OF COMICS
Dell Publishing Co.: 1937 (Stiff covers, square binding)
101(Found on back cover)-Alley Oop, Wash Tubbs, Capt. Easy, Og Son of Fire, Apple Mary, Tom Mix, Dan Dunn, Tailspin Tommy, Doctor Doom 155 310 465 992 1696 2400

100 PAGE SUPER SPECTACULAR (See DC 100 Page Super Spectacular)

100%
DC Comics (Vertigo): Aug, 2002 - No. 5, July, 2003 ($5.95, B&W, limited series)
1-5-Paul Pope-s/a 6.00
HC (2009, $39.99, dustjacket) r/#1-5; sketch pages and background info 40.00
TPB (2005, $24.99) r/#1-5; sketch pages and background info 25.00
TPB (2009, $29.99) r/#1-5; sketch pages and background info 30.00

Oni Double Feature #12 © Oni

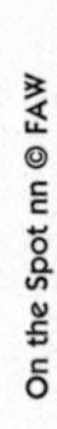

On the Spot nn © FAW

Operation Peril #15 © ACG

GD 2.0 | VG 4.0 | FN 6.0 | VF 8.0 | VF/NM 9.0 | NM- 9.2

GD 2.0 | VG 4.0 | FN 6.0 | VF 8.0 | VF/NM 9.0 | NM- 9.2

100% TRUE?
DC Comics (Paradox Press): Summer 1996 - No. 2 ($4.95, B&W)
1,2-Reprints stories from various Paradox Press books. 5.00

$1,000,000 DUCK (See Walt Disney Showcase #5)

ONE MILLION YEARS AGO (Tor #2 on)
St. John Publishing Co.: Sept, 1953
1-Origin & 1st app. Tor; Kubert-c/a; Kubert photo inside front cover 20 40 60 114 182 250

ONE MONTH TO LIVE ("Heroic Age: ..." in indicia)
Marvel Comics: Nov, 2010 - No. 5, Nov, 2010 ($2.99, weekly limited series)
1-5-Remender-s; Spider-Man and the Fantastic Four app. 3.00

ONE PLUS ONE
Oni Press: Sept, 2002 - No. 5, March, 2003 ($2.95, B&W, limited series)
1-5-Shaffer-s/Krall-a 3.00
TPB (9/03, $14.95, digest-size) r/#1-5 & story from Oni Press Color Special 2002 15.00

ONE SHOT (See Four Color...)

1001 HOURS OF FUN
Dell Publishing Co.: No. 13, 1943
Large Feature Comic 13 (nn)-Puzzles & games; by A.W. Nugent. This book was bound as #13 w/Large Feature Comics in publisher's files 31 62 93 182 296 410

ONE TRICK RIP OFF, THE (See Dark Horse Presents)

ONI (Adaption of video game)
Dark Horse Comics: Feb, 2001 - No. 3, Apr, 2001 ($2.99, limited series)
1-3-Sunny Lee-a(p) 3.00

ONI DOUBLE FEATURE (See Clerks: The Comic Book and Jay & Silent Bob)
Oni Press: Jan, 1998 - No. 13, Sept, 1999 ($2.95, B&W)
1-Jay & Silent Bob; Kevin Smith-s/Matt Wagner-a 1 3 4 6 8 10
1-2nd printing 3.00
2-11,13: 2,3-Paul Pope-s/a. 3,4-Nixey-s/a. 4,5-Sienkewicz-s/a. 6,7-Gaiman-s. 9-Bagge-c. 13-All Paul Dini-s; Jingle Belle 3.00
12-Jay & Silent Bob as Bluntman & Chronic; Smith-s/Allred-a 5.00

ONI PRESS COLOR SPECIAL
Oni Press: Jun, 2001; Jul, 2002 ($5.95, annual)
...2001-Oeming "Who Killed Madman?" cover; stories & art by various 6.00
...2002-Allred wraparound-c; stories & art by various 6.00

ONSLAUGHT: EPILOGUE
Marvel Comics: Feb, 1997 ($2.95, one-shot)
1-Hama-s/Green-a; Xavier-c; Bastion-app. 4.00

ONSLAUGHT: MARVEL
Marvel Comics: Oct, 1996 ($3.95, one-shot)
1-Conclusion to Onslaught x-over; wraparound-c 1 2 3 4 5 7

ONSLAUGHT REBORN
Marvel Comics: Jan, 2007 - No. 5, Feb, 2008 ($2.99, limited series)
1-5-Loeb-s/Liefeld-a; female Bucky app. 2-Variant-c by Joe Madureira. 3-McGuiness var-c. 4-Campbell var-c. 5-Bianchi var-c; female Bucky goes to regular Marvel Universe 3.00
1-Variant-c by Michael Turner 4.00
HC (2008, $19.99) r/#1-5; sketch pages; foreword by Liefeld 20.00

ONSLAUGHT UNLEASHED
Marvel Comics: Apr, 2011 - No. 4, Jul, 2011 ($3.99, limited series)
1-4-McKeever-s/Andrade-a/Ramos-c; Secret Avengers & Young Allies app. 4.00

ONSLAUGHT: X-MEN
Marvel Comics: Aug, 1996 ($3.95, one-shot)
1-Waid & Lobdell script; Fantastic Four & Avengers app.; Xavier as Onslaught 5.00
1-Variant-c 2 4 6 8 10 12

ON STAGE
Dell Publishing Co.: No. 1336, Apr-June, 1962
Four Color 1336-Not by Leonard Starr 5 10 15 30 50 70

ON THE DOUBLE (Movie)
Dell Publishing Co.: No. 1232, Sept-Nov, 1961
Four Color 1232 5 10 15 30 50 70

ON THE ROAD TO PERDITION (Movie)
DC Comics (Paradox Press): 2003 - Book 3, 2004 ($7.95, 8"x5 1/2", B&W, limited series)
...: Oasis, Book 1-Max Allan Collins-s/José Luis García-López-a/David Beck-c 8.00
...: Sanctuary, Book 2-Max Allan Collins-s/Steve Lieber-a/José Luis García-López-c 8.00
...: Detour, Book 3-Max Allan Collins-s/José Luis García-López-a/Steve Lieber-c/a(i) 8.00
Road to Perdition 2: On the Road (2004, $14.95) r/series; Collins intro. 15.00

ON THE ROAD WITH ANDRAE CROUCH
Spire Christian Comics (Fleming H. Revell): 1973, 1974 (39¢)
nn-1973 Edition 2 4 6 13 18 22
nn-1974 Edition 2 4 6 9 13 16

ON THE SCENE PRESENTS:...
Warren Publishing Co.: Oct, 1966 - No. 2, 1967 (B&W magazine, two #1 issues)
#1 "Super Heroes" (68 pgs.) Batman 1966 movie photo-c/s; has articles/photos/comic art from serials on Superman, Flash Gordon, Capt. America, Capt. Marvel and The Phantom 4 8 12 28 47 65
#1 "Freak Out, USA" (Fall/1966, 60 pgs.) (lower print run) articles on musicians like Zappa, Jefferson Airplane, Supremes 5 10 15 30 50 70
#2 "Freak Out, USA" (2/67, 52 pgs.) Beatles, Country Joe, Doors/Jim Morrison, Bee Gees 5 10 15 30 50 70

ON THE SPOT (Pretty Boy Floyd...)
Fawcett Publications: Fall, 1948
nn-Pretty Boy Floyd photo on-c; bondage-c 34 68 102 199 325 450

ONYX OVERLORD
Marvel Comics (Epic): Oct, 1992 - No. 4, Jan, 1993 ($2.75, mini-series)
1-4: Moebius scripts 3.00

OPEN SPACE
Marvel Comics: Mid-Dec, 1989 - No. 4, Aug, 1990 ($4.95, bi-monthly, 68 pgs.)
1-4: 1-Bill Wray-a; Freas-c 5.00
0-(1999) Wizard supplement; unpubl. early Alex Ross-a; new Ross-c 3.00

OPERATION BIKINI (See Movie Classics)

OPERATION: BROKEN WINGS, 1936
BOOM! Studios: Nov, 2011 - No. 3, Jan, 2012 ($3.99, limited series)
1-3-Hanna-s/Hairsine-a; English translation of French comic 4.00

OPERATION BUCHAREST (See The Crusaders)

OPERATION CROSSBOW (See Movie Classics)

OPERATION: KNIGHTSTRIKE (See Knightstrike)
Image Comics (Extreme Studios): May, 1995 - No.3, July, 1995 ($2.50)
1-3 3.00

OPERATION PERIL
American Comics Group (Michel Publ.): Oct-Nov, 1950 - No. 16, Apr-May, 1953 (#1-5: 52 pgs.)
1-Time Travelers, Danny Danger (by Leonard Starr) & Typhoon Tyler (by Ogden Whitney) begin 40 80 120 242 401 560
2-War-c 23 46 69 136 223 310
3-War-c; horror story 21 42 63 126 206 285
4,5-Sci/fi-c/story 23 46 69 136 223 310
6-10: 6,8,9,10-Sci/fi-c. 6-Tank vs. T-Rex-c. 7-Sabretooth-c 21 42 63 122 199 275
11,12-War-c; last Time Travelers 14 28 42 80 115 150
13-16: All war format 10 20 30 56 76 95
NOTE: ***Starr*** *a-2, 5.* ***Whitney*** *a-1, 2, 5-10, 12; c-1, 3, 5, 8, 9.*

OPERATION: STORMBREAKER
Acclaim Comics (Valiant Heroes): Aug, 1997 ($3.95, one-shot)
1-Waid/Augustyn-s, Braithwaite-a 4.00

OPTIC NERVE
Drawn and Quarterly: Apr, 1995 - Present ($2.95-$3.95, bi-annual)
1-7: Adrian Tomine-c/a/scripts in all 3.00
8-11: 8-($3.50). 9-11-($3.95) 4.00
12-($5.95) Half front-c; Amber Sweet story 6.00
32 Stories-($9.95, trade paperback)-r/Optic Nerve mini-comics 10.00
32 Stories-($29.95, hardcover)-r/Optic Nerve mini-comics; signed & numbered 30.00

ORACLE: THE CURE
DC Comics: May, 2009 - No. 3, Jul, 2009 ($2.99, limited series)
1-3-Guillem March-c; Calculator app. 3.00
TPB (2010, $17.99) r/#1-3 and Birds of Prey #126,127 18.00

ORAL ROBERTS' TRUE STORIES (Junior Partners #120 on)
TelePix Publ. (Oral Roberts' Evangelistic Assoc./Healing Waters): 1956 (no month) - No. 119, 7/59 (15¢)(No. 102: 25¢)
V1#1(1956)-(Not code approved)- "The Miracle Touch" 19 38 57 109 172 235

The Order #1 © MAR

Origin II #1 © MAR

Orion #1 © DC

GD 2.0 | VG 4.0 | FN 6.0 | VF 8.0 | VF/NM 9.0 | NM- 9.2

102-(Only issue approved by code, 10/56) "Now I See" 13 26 39 74 105 135
103-119: 115-(114 on inside) 10 20 30 54 72 90
NOTE: *Also see Happiness & Healing For You.*

ORANGE BIRD, THE
Walt Disney Educational Media Co.: No date (1980) (36 pgs.; in color; slick cover)
nn-Included with educational kit on foods, ...in Nutrition Adventures nn (1980) ...and the Nutrition Know-How Revue nn (1983) 3.00

ORB (Magazine)
Orb Publishing: 1974 - No. 6, Mar/Apr 1976 (B&W/color)
1-1st app. Northern Light & Kadaver, both series begin 5 10 15 30 50 70
2,3 (72 pgs.) 3 6 9 16 23 30
4-6 (60 pgs.): 4,5-origin Northern Light 2 4 6 10 14 18
NOTE: ***Allison** a-1-3. **Gene Day** a-1-6. **P. Hsu** a-4-6. **Steacy** s/a-3,4.*

ORBIT
Eclipse Books: 1990 - No. 3, 1990 ($4.95, 52 pgs., squarebound)
1-3: Reprints from Isaac Asimov's Science Fiction Magazine; 1-Dave Stevens-c, Bolton-a. 3-Bolton-c/a, Yeates-a 5.00

ORBITER
DC Comics (Vertigo): 2003 ($24.95, hardcover with dust jacket)
HC-Warren Ellis-s/Colleen Doran-a 25.00
SC-(2004, $17.95) Warren Ellis-s/Colleen Doran-a 18.00

ORCHID
Dark Horse Comics: Oct, 2011 - No. 12, Jan, 2013 ($1.00/$3.50)
1-Tom Morello-s/Scott Hepburn-a; covers by Carnevale & Fairey 3.00
2-12-($3.50) Carnevale-c 3.50

ORDER, THE (cont'd from Defenders V2#12)
Marvel Comics: Apr, 2002 - No. 6, Sept, 2002 ($2.25, limited series)
1-6: 1-Haley-a/Duffy & Busiek-s. 3-Avengers-c/app. 4-Jurgens-a 3.00

ORDER, THE (The Initiative following Civil War)
Marvel Comics: Sept, 2007 - No. 10, Jun, 2008 ($2.99)
1-10-California's Initiative team; Fraction-s/Kitson-a/c 3.00
... Vol. 1: The Next Right Thing TPB (2008, $14.99) r/#1-7 15.00

ORIENTAL HEROES
Jademan Comics: Aug, 1988 - No. 55, Feb, 1993 ($1.50/$1.95, 68 pgs.)
1,55 5.00
2-54 4.00

ORIGINAL ADVENTURES OF CHOLLY & FLYTRAP, THE
Image Comics: Feb, 2006 - No. 2, June, 2006 ($5.99, limited series)
1,2-Arthur Suydam-s/a; interview with Suydam and art pages 6.00

ORIGINAL ASTRO BOY, THE
Now Comics: Sept, 1987 - No. 20, Jun, 1989 ($1.50/$1.75)
1-20-All have Ken Steacy painted-c/a 4.00

ORIGINAL BLACK CAT, THE
Recollections: Oct. 6, 1988 - No. 9, 1992 ($2.00, limited series)
1-9: Elias-r; 1-Bondage-c. 2-Murphy Anderson-c 4.00

ORIGINAL DICK TRACY, THE
Gladstone Publishing: Sept, 1990 - No. 5, 1991 ($1.95, bi-monthly, 68pgs.)
1-5: 1-Vs. Pruneface. 2-& the Evil influence; begin $2.00-c 4.00
NOTE: *#1 reprints strips 7/16/43 - 9/30/43. #2 reprints strips 12/1/46 - 2/2/47. #3 reprints 8/31/46 - 11/14/46. #4 reprints 9/17/45 - 12/23/45. #5 reprints 6/10/46 - 8/28/46.*

ORIGINAL DOCTOR SOLAR, MAN OF THE ATOM, THE
Valiant: Apr, 1995 ($2.95, one-shot)
1-Reprints Doctor Solar, Man of the Atom #1,5; Bob Fugitani-r; Paul Smith-c; afterword by Seaborn Adamson 4.00

ORIGINAL E-MAN AND MICHAEL MAUSER, THE
First Comics: Oct, 1985 - No. 7, April, 1986 ($1.75/$2.00, Baxter paper)
1-6: 1-Has r-/Charlton's E-Man, Vengeance Squad. 2-Shows #4 in indicia by mistake 3.00
7-($2.00, 44 pgs.)-Staton-a 4.00

ORIGINAL GHOST RIDER, THE
Marvel Comics: July, 1992 - No. 20, Feb, 1994 ($1.75)
1-20: 1-7-r/Marvel Spotlight #5-11 by Ploog w/new-c. 3-New Phantom Rider (former Night Rider) back-ups begin by Ayers. 4-Quesada-c(p). 8-Ploog-c. 8,9-r/Ghost Rider #1,2. 10-r/Marvel Spotlight #12. 11-18,20-r/Ghost Rider #3-12. 19-r/Marvel Two-in-One #8 3.00

ORIGINAL GHOST RIDER RIDES AGAIN, THE
Marvel Comics: July, 1991 - No. 7, Jan, 1992, ($1.50, limited series, 52 pgs.)
1-7: 1-r/Ghost Rider #68(origin),69 w/covers. 2-7: R/ G.R. #70-81 w/covers 4.00

ORIGINAL MAGNUS ROBOT FIGHTER, THE
Valiant: Apr, 1995 ($2.95, one-shot)
1-Reprints Magnus, Robot Fighter 4000 #2; Russ Manning-r; Rick Leonardi-c; afterword by Seaborn Adamson 4.00

ORIGINAL NEXUS GRAPHIC NOVEL (See First Comics Graphic Novel #19)

ORIGINALS, THE
DC Comics (Vertigo): 2004 ($24.95/$17.99, B&W graphic novel)
HC (2004, $24.95) Dave Gibbons-s/a 25.00
SC (2005, $17.99) 18.00

ORIGINAL SHIELD, THE
Archie Enterprises, Inc.: Apr, 1984 - No. 4, Oct, 1984
1-4: 1,2-Origin Shield; Ayers p-1-4, Nebres c-1,2 5.00

ORIGINAL SWAMP THING SAGA, THE (See DC Special Series #2, 14, 17, 20)

ORIGINAL TUROK, SON OF STONE, THE
Valiant: Apr, 1995 - No. 2, May, 1995 ($2.95, limited series)
1,2: 1-Reprints Turok, Son of Stone #24,25,42; Alberto Gioletti-r; Rags Morales-c; afterword by Seaborn Adamson. 2-Reprints Turok, Son of Stone #24,33; Gioletti-r; McKone-c 4.00

ORIGIN OF GALACTUS (See Fantastic Four #48-50)
Marvel Comics: Feb, 1996 ($2.50, one-shot)
1-Lee & Kirby reprints w/pin-ups 4.00

ORIGIN OF THE DEFIANT UNIVERSE, THE
Defiant Comics: Feb, 1994 ($1.50, 20 pgs., one-shot)
1-David Lapham, Adam Pollina & Alan Weiss-a; Weiss-c 5.00
NOTE: *The comic was originally published as Defiant Genesis and was distributed at the 1994 Philadelphia ComicCon.*

ORIGINS OF MARVEL COMICS (Also see Fireside Book Series)
Marvel Comics: July, 2010 ($3.99, one-shot)
1-Single page origins of prominent Marvel characters; text and art by various 4.00
...: X-Men (11/10, $3.99) single page origins of X-Men and other mutants; s/a-various 4.00

ORIGIN II (Sequel to Wolverine: The Origin)
Marvel Comics: Feb, 2014 - No. 5 ($4.99/$3.99, limited series)
1-($4.99) Gillen-s/Adam Kubert-a/c; acetate overlay on cover; set in 1907 5.00
2-4-($3.99) Sabretooth app. 4.00

ORION (Manga)
Dark Horse Comics: Sept, 1992 - No. 6, July, 1993 ($2.95/$3.95, B&W, bimonthly, lim. series)
1-6:1,2,6-Squarebound): 1-Masamune Shirow-c/a/s in all 4.00

ORION (See New Gods)
DC Comics: June, 2000 - No. 25, June, 2002 ($2.50)
1-14-Simonson-s/a. 3-Back-up story w/Miller-a. 4-Gibbons-a back-up. 7-Chaykin back-up. 8-Loeb/Liefeld back-up. 10-A. Adams back-up-a 12-Jim Lee back-up-a. 13-JLA-c/app.; Byrne-a 3.00
15-($3.95) Black Racer app.; back-up story w/J.P. Leon-a 4.00
16-24-Simonson-s/a: 19-Joker: Last Laugh x-over 3.00
25-($3.95) Last issue; Mister Miracle-c/app. 4.00
The Gates of Apocalypse (2001, $12.95, TPB) r/#1-5 & various short-s 13.00

ORORO: BEFORE THE STORM (Storm from X-Men)
Marvel Comics: Aug, 2005 - No. 4, Nov, 2005 ($2.99, limited series)
1-4-Barberi-a/Sumerak-s; young Storm in Egypt 3.00
... Digest (2006, $6.99) r/#1-4 7.00

OSBORN (Green Goblin)
Marvel Comics: Jan, 2011 - No. 5, Jun, 2011 ($3.99, limited series)
1-5-Deconnick-s/Rios-a/Oliver-c 4.00

OSBORN JOURNALS (See Spider-Man titles)
Marvel Comics: Feb, 1997 ($2.95, one-shot)
1-Hotz-c/a 3.00

OSCAR COMICS (Formerly Funny Tunes; Awful...#11 & 12) (Also see Cindy Comics)
Marvel Comics: No. 24, Spring, 1947 - No. 10, Apr, 1949; No. 13, Oct, 1949
24(#1, Spring, 1947) 20 40 60 117 189 260
25(#2, Sum, 1947)-Wolverton-a plus Kurtzman's "Hey Look" 21 42 63 122 199 275
26(#3)-Same as regular #3 except #26 was printed over in black ink with #3 appearing on-c

The Other Dead #4 © Tommee's Fund

Our Army at War #2 © DC

Our Army at War #159 © DC

	GD 2.0	VG 4.0	FN 6.0	VF 8.0	VF/NM 9.0	NM- 9.2
below the over print	14	28	42	81	118	155
3-9,13: 8-Margie app.	14	28	42	81	118	155
10-Kurtzman's "Hey Look"	15	30	45	85	130	175

OSWALD THE RABBIT (Also see New Fun Comics #1)
Dell Publishing Co.: No. 21, 1943 - No. 1268, 12-2/61-62 (Walter Lantz)

	GD 2.0	VG 4.0	FN 6.0	VF 8.0	VF/NM 9.0	NM- 9.2
Four Color 21(1943)	38	76	114	282	634	985
Four Color 39(1943)	26	52	78	182	404	625
Four Color 67(1944)	15	30	45	103	227	350
Four Color 102(1946)-Kelly-a, 1 pg.	12	24	36	84	185	285
Four Color 143,183	8	16	24	56	108	160
Four Color 225,273	6	12	18	40	73	105
Four Color 315,388	5	10	15	35	63	90
Four Color 458,507,549,593	5	10	15	31	53	75
Four Color 623,697,792,894,979,1268	4	8	12	28	47	65

OSWALD THE RABBIT (See The Funnies, March of Comics #7, 38, 53, 67, 81, 95, 111, 126, 141, 156, 171, 186, New Funnies & Super Book #8, 20)

OTHER DEAD, THE
IDW Publishing: Sept, 2013 - No. 6, Feb, 2014 ($3.99)

1-6-Zombie animals; Ortega-s/Mui-a. 1-Variant-c by Dorman. 2-6-Pres. Obama app. 4.00

OTHER SIDE, THE
DC Comics (Vertigo): Dec, 2006 - No. 5, Apr, 2007 ($2.99, limited series)

1-5-Soldiers from both sides of the Vietnam War; Aaron-s/Stewart-a/c 3.00
TPB (2007, $12.99) r/#1-5; sketch pages, Stewart's travelogue to Saigon 13.00

OTHERWORLD
DC Comics (Vertigo): May, 2005 - No. 7, Nov, 2005 ($2.99)

1-7-Phil Jimenez-s/a(p) 3.00
...: Book One TPB (2006, $19.99) r/#1-7; cover gallery 20.00

OUR ARMY AT WAR (Becomes Sgt. Rock #302 on; also see Army At War)
National Periodical Publications: Aug, 1952 - No. 301, Feb, 1977

	GD 2.0	VG 4.0	FN 6.0	VF 8.0	VF/NM 9.0	NM- 9.2
1	200	400	600	1650	3725	5800
2	86	172	258	688	1544	2400
3,4: 4-Krigstein-a	64	128	192	512	1156	1800
5-7	50	100	150	400	900	1350
8-11,14-Krigstein-a	47	94	141	367	821	1275
12,15-20	42	84	126	311	706	1100
13-Krigstein-c/a; flag-c	46	92	138	368	834	1300
21-31: Last precode (2/55)	29	58	87	209	467	725
32-40	26	52	78	182	404	625
41-60: 51-1st S.A. issue. 57,60-Grey tone-c	22	44	66	154	340	525
61-70: 61-(8/57) Pre-Sgt. Rock Easy Co.-c/s. 67-Minor Sgt. Rock prototype	20	40	60	138	307	475
71-80	18	36	54	124	275	425
81-(4/59) "The Rock of Easy" - Sgt. Rock prototype. Part of lead-up trio to 1st definitive Sgt. Rock. Story features a character named "Sgt. Rocky" as a "4th grade rate" sergeant (three stripes/chevrons) who is referred to as "The Rock of Easy". Editor also promises more stories of "...Rock-like Sergeant". Andru & Esposito-a/Haney-s	286	572	858	2402	5451	8500
82-(5/59) "Hold up Easy"- 1st app. of a Sgt. Rock. Part of lead-up trio to 1st definitive Sgt. Rock. Character named Sgt. Rock appears in a supporting "motivator" role as a "4th grade rate" sergeant (three stripes/chevrons) in six panels in six page story; Haney-s/Drucker-a	96	192	288	768	1734	2700
83-(6/59) "The Rock and Wall" - 1st true appearance of Sgt. Rock. Sgt. Rock finally introduced as a Master Sergeant (three chevrons and three rockers) and is main character of story. 1st specific narration that defines the "Rock of Easy" as Sgt. Rock. 1st actual "Sgt. Rock" collaboration between creators Robert Kanigher and Joe Kubert	500	1000	1500	4250	9625	15,000
84-(7/59) "Laughter on Snakehead Hill" - 2nd appearance of Sgt. Rock. Story advances true Sgt. Rock continuity in 13-page title story featuring Sgt. Rock and Easy Co.; Kanigher-s/Novick-a/Kubert-c	54	108	162	432	966	1500
85-Origin & 1st app. Ice Cream Soldier	57	114	171	456	1028	1600
86,87-Early Sgt. Rock; Kubert-a	46	92	138	340	770	1200
88-1st Sgt. Rock-c; Kubert-c/a	57	114	171	456	1028	1600
89-"No Shot From Easy!" story; Heath-c	38	76	114	285	641	1000
90-Kubert-c/a; How Rock got his stripes	57	114	171	456	1028	1600
91-All-Sgt. Rock issue; Grandenetti-c/Kubert-a	107	214	321	856	1928	3000
92,94,96-99: 97-Regular Kubert-c begin	28	56	84	202	451	700
93-1st Zack Nolan	32	64	96	230	515	800
95,100: 95-1st app. Bulldozer	36	72	108	259	580	900
101,108,113,114: 101-1st app. Buster. 113-1st app. Wildman & Jackie Johnson	23	46	69	161	356	550
102-104,106,107,109,110,114,116-120: 104-Nurse Jane-c/s. 109-Pre Easy Co. Sgt. Rock-s. 118-Sunny injured	20	40	60	138	307	475
105-1st app. Junior	25	50	75	175	388	600
111-1st app. Wee Willie & Sunny	28	56	84	202	451	700
112-Classic Easy Co. roster-c	50	100	150	400	900	1400
115-Rock revealed as orphan; 1st x-over Mlle. Marie. 1st Sgt. Rock's battle family	27	54	81	189	420	650
121-125	15	30	45	103	227	350
126-1st app. Canary; grey tone-c	22	44	66	154	340	525
127-2nd all-Sgt. Rock issue; 1st app. Little Sure Shot	25	50	75	175	388	600
128-Training & origin Sgt. Rock; 1st Sgt. Krupp	36	72	108	266	596	925
129-139: 138-1st Sparrow. 141-1st Shaker	14	28	42	96	211	325
140-3rd all-Sgt. Rock issue	16	32	48	110	243	375
141-150: 147,148-Rock becomes a General	11	22	33	76	163	250
151-Intro. Enemy Ace by Kubert (2/65), black-c	44	88	132	326	738	1150
152-4th all-Sgt. Rock issue	14	28	42	96	211	325
153-2nd app. Enemy Ace (4/65)	20	40	60	138	307	475
154,156,157,159-161,165-167: 157-2 pg. centerfold spread pin-up as part of story. 159-1st Nurse Wendy Winston-c/s. 165-2nd Iron Major	10	20	30	64	132	200
155-3rd app. Enemy Ace (6/65)(see Showcase)	14	28	42	96	211	325
158-Origin & 1st app. Iron Major(9/65), formerly Iron Captain	11	22	33	72	154	235
162,163-Viking Prince x-over in Sgt. Rock	10	20	30	69	147	225
164-Giant G-19	15	30	45	103	227	350
168-1st Unknown Soldier app.; referenced in Star-Spangled War Stories #157; (Sgt. Rock x-over) (6/66)	15	30	45	105	233	360
169,170	8	16	24	56	108	160
171-176,178-181: 171-1st Mad Emperor	8	16	24	51	96	140
177-(80 pg. Giant G-32)	10	20	30	64	132	200
182,183,186-Neal Adams-a. 186-Origin retold	9	18	27	57	111	165
184-Wee Willie dies	9	18	27	61	123	185
185,187,188,193-195,197-199	6	12	18	41	76	110
189,191,192,196: 189-Intro. The Teen-age Underground Fighters of Unit 3. 196-Hitler cameo	6	12	18	42	79	115
190-(80 pg. Giant G-44)	8	16	24	54	102	150
200-12 pg. Rock story told in verse; Evans-a	7	14	21	44	82	120
201,202,204-207: 201-Krigstein-r/#14. 204,205-All reprints; no Sgt. Rock. 207-Last 12¢ cover	5	10	15	34	60	85
203-(80 pg. Giant G-56)-All-r, Sgt. Rock story	7	14	21	48	89	130
208-215	4	8	12	27	44	60
216,229-(80 pg. Giants G-68, G-80): 216-Has G-58 on-c by mistake	6	12	18	40	73	105
217-219: 218-1st U.S.S. Stevens	4	8	12	25	40	55
220-Classic dinosaur/Sgt. Rock-c/s	4	8	12	28	47	65
221-228,230-234: 231-Intro/death Rock's brother. 234-Last 15¢ issue	3	6	9	21	33	45
235-239,241: 52 pg. Giants	4	8	12	27	44	60
240-Neal Adams-a; 52 pg. Giant	5	10	15	31	53	75
242-Also listed as DC 100 Page Super Spectacular #9	9	18	27	58	114	170
243-246: (All 52 pgs.) 244-No Adams-a	4	8	12	25	40	55
247-250,254-268,270: 247-Joan of Arc	3	6	9	15	22	28
251-253-Return of Iron Major	3	6	9	16	24	32
269,275-(100 pgs.)	5	10	15	31	53	75
271,272,274,276-279	3	6	9	14	19	24
273-Crucifixion-c	3	6	9	16	24	32
280-(68 pgs.)-200th app. Sgt. Rock; reprints Our Army at War #81,83	4	8	12	22	35	48
281-299,301: 295-Bicentennial cover	2	4	6	13	18	22
300-Sgt. Rock-s by Kubert (2/77)	3	6	9	15	22	28

NOTE ***Alcala** a-251. **Drucker** a-27, 67, 68, 79, 82, 83, 96, 164, 177, 203, 212, 243r, 244, 269r, 275r, 280r. **Evans** a-165-175, 200, 266, 269, 270, 274, 276, 278, 280. **Glanzman** a-218, 220, 222, 223, 225, 227, 230-232, 238-241, 244, 247, 248, 256-259, 261, 265-267, 271, 282, 283, 298. **Grandenetti** c-91,120. **Grell** a-287. **Heath** a-50, 164, & most 176-281. **Kubert** a-38, 59, 67, 68 & most issues from 83-165, 171, 233, 236, 267, 275, 300; c-84, 280. **Maurer** a-233, 237, 239, 240, 45, 280, 284, 288, 290, 291, 295. **Severin** a-236, 252, 265, 267, 269r, 272. **Toth** a-235, 241, 254. **Wildey** a-283-285, 287p. **Wood** a-249.*

OUR ARMY AT WAR
DC Comics: Nov, 2010 ($3.99, one-shot)

1-Joe Kubert-c; Mike Marts-s/Victor Ibáñez-a 4.00
TPB (2011, $14.99) r/#1 and other 2010 war one-shots Weird War Tales #1, Our Fighting Forces #1, G.I. Combat #1 and Star-Spangled War Stories #1 15.00

OUR FIGHTING FORCES
National Per. Publ./DC Comics: Oct-Nov, 1954 - No. 181, Sept-Oct, 1978

	GD 2.0	VG 4.0	FN 6.0	VF 8.0	VF/NM 9.0	NM- 9.2
1-Grandenetti-c/a	125	250	375	1000	2250	3500
2	46	92	138	363	834	1300

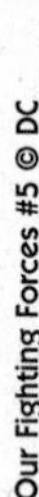
Our Fighting Forces #5 © DC

Our Gang Comics #2 © DELL

Our Secret #8 © SUPR

	GD 2.0	VG 4.0	FN 6.0	VF 8.0	VF/NM 9.0	NM- 9.2
3-Kubert-c; last precode issue (3/55)	40	80	120	296	673	1050
4,5	34	68	102	245	548	850
6-9: 7-1st S.A. issue	28	56	84	202	451	700
10-Wood-a	29	58	87	209	467	725
11-19	24	48	72	170	378	585
20-Grey tone-c (4/57)	31	62	93	225	505	785
21-30	20	40	60	135	300	465
31-40	17	34	51	117	259	400
41-Unknown Soldier tryout	20	40	60	138	307	475
42-44	16	32	48	110	243	375
45-1st app. of Gunner & Sarge, app. thru #94	50	100	150	384	867	1350
46	23	46	69	164	362	560
47	18	36	54	124	275	425
48,50	15	30	45	103	227	350
49-1st Pooch	23	46	69	161	356	550
51-Grey tone-c	22	44	66	154	340	525
52-64: 64-Last 10¢ issue	12	24	36	82	179	275
65-70	10	20	30	64	132	200
71-Classic grey tone-c; Pooch fires machine gun	17	34	51	117	259	400
72-80	8	16	24	56	108	160
81-90	7	14	21	44	82	120
91-98: 95-Devil-Dog begins, ends #98.	6	12	18	37	66	95
99-Capt. Hunter begins, ends #106	6	12	18	40	73	105
100	6	12	18	38	69	100
101-105,107-120: 116-Mlle. Marie app. 120-Last 12¢ issue	5	10	15	30	50	70
106-Hunters Hellcats begin	5	10	15	31	53	75
121,122: 121-Intro. Heller	4	8	12	27	44	60
123-The Losers (Capt. Storm, Gunner & Sarge, Johnny Cloud) begin	8	16	24	56	108	160
124-132: 132-Last 15¢ issue	4	8	12	23	37	50
133-137 (Giants). 134-Toth-a	4	8	12	27	44	60
138-145,147-150	3	6	9	16	23	30
146-Classic "Burma Sky" story; Toth-a/Goodwin-s	3	6	9	17	26	35
151-162-Kirby a(p)	3	6	9	18	28	38
163-180	3	6	9	14	19	24
181-Last issue	3	6	9	16	23	30
... (War One-Shot) 1 (11/10, $3.99) The Losers app.; B. Clay Moore-s/Chad Hardin-a						4.00

NOTE: ***N. Adams** c-147. **Drucker** a-28, 37, 39, 42-44, 49, 53, 133r. **Evans** a-149, 164-174, 177-181. **Glanzman** a-125-128, 132, 134, 138-141, 143, 144. **Heath** a-2, 16, 18, 28, 41, 44, 49, 50, 114, 135-138r; c-51. **Kirby** a-151-162p; c-152-159. **Kubert** c/a in many issues. **Maurer** a-135. **Redondo** a-166. **Severin** a-123-130, 131i, 132-150.*

OUR FIGHTING MEN IN ACTION (See Men In Action)

OUR FLAG COMICS
Ace Magazines: Aug, 1941 - No. 5, April, 1942

	GD 2.0	VG 4.0	FN 6.0	VF 8.0	VF/NM 9.0	NM- 9.2
1-Captain Victory, The Unknown Soldier (intro.) & The Three Cheers begin	258	516	774	1651	2826	4000
2-Origin The Flag (patriotic hero); 1st app?	113	226	339	723	1237	1750
3-5: 5-Intro & 1st app. Mr. Risk	87	174	261	553	952	1350

NOTE: ***Anderson** a-1, 4. **Mooney** a-1, 2; c-2.*

OUR GANG COMICS (With Tom & Jerry #39-59; becomes Tom & Jerry #60 on; based on film characters)
Dell Publishing Co.: Sept-Oct, 1942 - No. 59, June, 1949

	GD 2.0	VG 4.0	FN 6.0	VF 8.0	VF/NM 9.0	NM- 9.2
1-Our Gang & Barney Bear by Kelly, Tom & Jerry, Pete Smith, Flip & Dip, The Milky Way begin (all 1st app.)	71	142	213	568	1284	2000
2-Benny Burro begins (#2 by Kelly)	33	66	99	238	532	825
3-5	21	42	63	150	330	510
6-Bumbazine & Albert only app. by Kelly	28	56	84	205	458	710
7-No Kelly story	16	32	48	110	243	375
8-Benny Burro begins by Barks	37	74	111	274	612	950
9-Barks-a(2): Benny Burro & Happy Hound; no Kelly story	34	68	102	242	541	840
10-Benny Burro by Barks	25	50	75	175	388	600
11-1st Barney Bear & Benny Burro by Barks (5-6/44); Happy Hound by Barks	34	68	102	242	541	840
12-20	16	32	48	107	236	365
21-30: 30-X-Mas-c	11	22	33	77	166	255
31-36-Last Barks issue	9	18	27	63	129	195
37-40	7	14	21	44	82	120
41-50	6	12	18	38	69	100
51-57	5	10	15	35	63	90
58,59-No Kelly art or Our Gang stories	5	10	15	33	57	80
Our Gang Volume 1 (Fantagraphics Books, 2006, $12.95, TPB) r/Our Gang stories written and by Walt Kelly from #1-8; Leonard Maltin intro.; Jeff Smith-c						13.00
Our Gang Volume 2 (Fantagraphics Books, 2007, $12.95, TPB) r/Our Gang stories written and by Walt Kelly from #9-15; Steve Thompson intro.; Jeff Smith-c						13.00
Our Gang Volume 3 (Fantagraphics Books, 2008, $14.99, TPB) r/Our Gang stories written and by Walt Kelly from #16-23; Steve Thompson intro.; Jeff Smith-c						15.00

NOTE: ***Barks** art in part only. **Barks** did not write Barney Bear stories #30-34. (See March of Comics #3, 26). Early issues have photo back-c.*

OUR LADY OF FATIMA (Also see Fatima...)
Catechetical Guild Educational Society: 3/11/55 (15¢) (36 pgs.)

	GD 2.0	VG 4.0	FN 6.0	VF 8.0	VF/NM 9.0	NM- 9.2
395	6	12	18	28	34	40

OUR LOVE (True Secrets #3 on? or Romantic Affairs #3 on?)
Marvel Comics (SPC): Sept, 1949 - No. 2, Jan, 1950

	GD 2.0	VG 4.0	FN 6.0	VF 8.0	VF/NM 9.0	NM- 9.2
1-Photo-c	20	40	60	114	182	250
2-Photo-c	14	28	42	76	108	140

OUR LOVE STORY
Marvel Comics Group: Oct, 1969 - No. 38, Feb, 1976

	GD 2.0	VG 4.0	FN 6.0	VF 8.0	VF/NM 9.0	NM- 9.2
1	8	16	24	56	108	160
2-4,6-8,10,11	5	10	15	33	57	80
5-Steranko-a	10	20	30	70	150	230
9,12-Kirby-a	5	10	15	34	60	85
13-(10/71, 52 pgs.)	6	12	18	37	66	95
14-New story by Gary Fredrich & Tarpe' Mills	5	10	15	33	57	80
15-20,27:27-Colan/Everett-a(r?); Kirby/Colletta-r	4	8	12	25	40	55
21-26,28-37	4	8	12	23	37	50
38-Last issue	4	8	12	27	44	60

NOTE: ***J. Buscema** a-1-3, 5-7, 9, 13r, 16r, 19r(2), 21r, 22r(2), 23r, 34r, 35r; c-11, 13, 16, 22, 23, 24, 27, 35. **Colan** a-3-6, 21r(#6), 22r, 23r(#3), 24r(#4), 27; c-19. **Katz** a-17. **Maneely** a-13r. **Romita** a-13r; c-1, 2, 4-6. **Weiss** a-16, 17, 29r(#17).*

OUR MEN AT WAR
DC Comics: Aug/Sept 1952

nn - Ashcan comic, not distributed to newsstands, only for in-house use. Cover art is All Star Western #60, interior being Detective Comics #181 (a FN/VF copy sold for $1195 in 2012)

OUR MISS BROOKS
Dell Publishing Co.: No. 751, Nov, 1956

	GD 2.0	VG 4.0	FN 6.0	VF 8.0	VF/NM 9.0	NM- 9.2
Four Color 751-Photo-c	6	12	18	42	79	115

OUR SECRET (Exciting Love Stories)(Formerly My Secret)
Superior Comics Ltd.: No. 4, Nov, 1949 - No. 8, Jun, 1950

	GD 2.0	VG 4.0	FN 6.0	VF 8.0	VF/NM 9.0	NM- 9.2
4-Kamen-a; spanking scene	20	40	60	120	195	270
5,6,8	14	28	42	76	108	140
7-Contains 9 pg. story intended for unpublished Ellery Queen #5; lingerie panels	14	28	42	80	115	150

OUTBREED 999
Blackout Comics: May, 1994 - No. 6, 1994 ($2.95)

	GD 2.0	VG 4.0	FN 6.0	VF 8.0	VF/NM 9.0	NM- 9.2
1-6: 4-1st app. of Extreme Violet in 7 pg. backup story						3.00

OUTCAST, THE
Valiant: Dec, 1995 ($2.50, one-shot)

	GD 2.0	VG 4.0	FN 6.0	VF 8.0	VF/NM 9.0	NM- 9.2
1-Breyfogle-a.						3.00

OUTCASTS
DC Comics: Oct, 1987 - No. 12, Sept, 1988 ($1.75, limited series)

	GD 2.0	VG 4.0	FN 6.0	VF 8.0	VF/NM 9.0	NM- 9.2
1-12: John Wagner & Alan Grant scripts in all						3.00

OUTER LIMITS, THE (TV)
Dell Publishing Co.: Jan-Mar, 1964 - No. 18, Oct, 1969 (Most painted-c)

	GD 2.0	VG 4.0	FN 6.0	VF 8.0	VF/NM 9.0	NM- 9.2
1	10	20	30	69	147	225
2-5	6	12	18	41	76	110
6-10	5	10	15	35	63	90
11-18: 17-Reprints #1. 18-r/#2	5	10	15	31	53	75

OUTER SPACE (Formerly This Magazine Is Haunted, 2nd Series)
Charlton Comics: No. 17, May, 1958 - No. 25, Dec, 1959; Nov, 1968

	GD 2.0	VG 4.0	FN 6.0	VF 8.0	VF/NM 9.0	NM- 9.2
17-Williamson/Wood-a	14	28	42	80	115	150
18-20-Ditko-a	23	46	69	136	223	310
21-Ditko-c	20	40	60	114	182	250
22-25	14	28	42	80	115	150
V2#1(11/68)-Ditko-a, Boyette-c	5	10	15	30	50	70

OUT FOR BLOOD
Dark Horse: Sept, 1999 - No. 4, Dec, 1999 ($2.95, B&W, limited series)

	GD 2.0	VG 4.0	FN 6.0	VF 8.0	VF/NM 9.0	NM- 9.2
1-4-Kelley Jones-c; Erskine-a						3.00

OUTLANDERS (Manga)
Dark Horse Comics: Dec, 1988 - No. 33, Sept,1991 ($2.00-$2.50, B&W, 44 pgs.)

Outlaw Nation #1 © Delano & Sudzuka

Out of the Night #7 © ACG

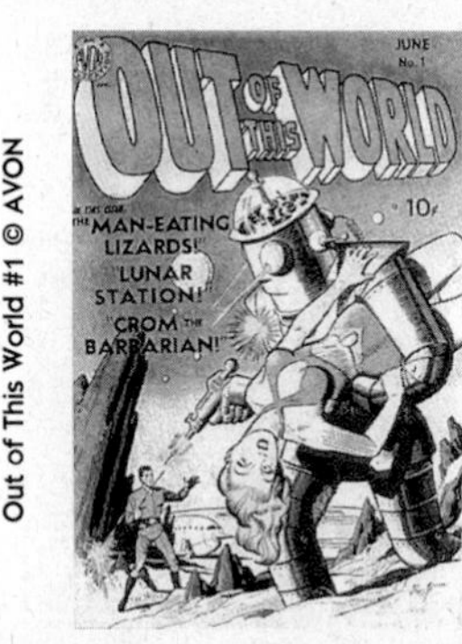
Out of This World #1 © AVON

	GD 2.0	VG 4.0	FN 6.0	VF 8.0	VF/NM 9.0	NM- 9.2

1-33: Japanese Sci-fi manga 4.00

OUTLAW (See Return of the...)

OUTLAW FIGHTERS
Atlas Comics (IPC): Aug, 1954 - No. 5, Apr, 1955

1-Tuska-a 14 28 42 80 115 150
2-5: 5-Heath-c/a, 7 pgs. 10 20 30 54 72 90
NOTE: ***Hartley** a-3. **Heath** c/a-5. **Maneely** c-2. **Pakula** a-2. **Reinman** a-2. **Tuska** a-1-3.*

OUTLAW KID, THE (1st Series; see Wild Western)
Atlas Comics (CCC No. 1-11/EPI No. 12-29): Sept, 1954 - No. 19, Sept, 1957

1-Origin; The Outlaw Kid & his horse Thunder begin; Black Rider app. 29 58 87 170 278 385
2-Black Rider app. 14 28 42 82 121 160
3-7,9: 3-Wildey-a(3) 13 26 39 72 101 130
8-Williamson/Woodbridge-a, 4 pgs. 14 28 42 76 108 140
10-Williamson-a 14 28 42 76 108 140
11-17,19: 13-Baker text illo. 15-Williamson text illo (unsigned) 10 20 30 54 72 90
18-Williamson/Mayo-a 10 20 30 58 79 100
NOTE: ***Berg** a-4, 7, 13. **Maneely** c-1-3, 5-8, 11-13, 15, 16, 18. **Pakula** a-3. **Severin** c-10, 17, 19. **Shores** a-1. **Wildey** a-1(3), 2-8, 10, 11, 12(4), 13(4), 15-19(4 each); c-4.*

OUTLAW KID, THE (2nd Series)
Marvel Comics Group: Aug, 1970 - No. 30, Oct, 1975

1-Reprints; 1-Orlando-r, Wildey-r(3) 3 6 9 19 30 40
2,3,9: 2-Reprints. 3,9-Williamson-a(r) 2 4 6 13 18 22
4-7: 7-Last 15¢ issue 2 4 6 11 16 20
8-Double size (52 pgs.); Crandall-r 3 6 9 16 24 32
10-Origin 3 6 9 19 30 40
11-20: new-a in #10-16 2 4 6 13 18 22
21-30: 27-Origin-r/#10 2 4 6 9 13 16
NOTE: ***Ayers** a-10, 27r. **Berg** a-7, 25r. **Everett** a-2(2 pgs.). **Gil Kane** c-10, 11, 15, 27r, 28. **Roussos** a-10i, 27i(r). **Severin** c-1, 9, 20, 25. **Wildey** r-1-4, 6-9, 19-22, 25, 26. **Williamson** a-28r. **Woodbridge/Williamson** a-9r.*

OUTLAW NATION
DC Comics (Vertigo): Nov, 2000 - No. 19, May, 2002 ($2.50)

1-19-Fabry painted-c/Delano-s/Sudzuka-a 3.00
TPB (Image Comics, 11/06, $15.99) B&W reprint of #1-19; Delano intro. 16.00

OUTLAW PRINCE, THE
Dark Horse Books: 2011 ($12.99, SC, 80 pgs.)

SC-Adaptation of ERB's The Outlaw of Torn; Rob Hughes-s/Thomas Yeates painted-a; origin/1st app. Norman of Torn; intro. & death of Lady Maud 13.00
Deluxe HC Limited Edition ($49.99, 112 pgs.) Bonus 2 articles (approx. 200 signed) 50.00

OUTLAWS
D. S. Publishing Co.: Feb-Mar, 1948 - No. 9, June-July, 1949

1-Violent & suggestive stories 34 68 102 204 332 460
2-Ingels-a; Baker-a 34 68 102 204 332 460
3,5,6: 3-Not Frazetta. 5-Sky Sheriff by Good app. 6-McWilliams-a 17 34 51 98 154 210
4-Orlando-a 18 36 54 103 162 220
7,8-Ingels-a in each 24 48 72 142 234 325
9-(Scarce)-Frazetta-a (7 pgs.) 48 96 144 302 514 725
NOTE: *Another #3 was printed in Canada with **Frazetta** art "Prairie Jinx," 7 pgs.*

OUTLAWS, THE (Formerly Western Crime Cases)
Star Publishing Co.: No. 10, May, 1952 - No. 13, Sep, 1953; No. 14, Apr, 1954

10-L. B. Cole-c 21 42 63 124 202 280
11-14-L. B. Cole-c. 14-Reprints Western Thrillers #4 (Fox) w/new L.B. Cole-c; Kamen, Feldstein-r 16 32 48 94 147 200

OUTLAWS
DC Comics: Sept, 1991 - No. 8, Apr, 1992 ($1.95, limited series)

1-8: Post-apocalyptic Robin Hood. 3.00

OUTLAWS OF THE WEST (Formerly Cody of the Pony Express #10)
Charlton Comics: No. 11, 7/57 - No. 81, 5/70; No. 82, 7/79 - No. 88, 4/80

11 8 16 24 44 57 70
12,13,15-17,19,20 6 12 18 27 33 38
14-(68 pgs., 2/58) 9 18 27 50 65 80
18-Ditko-a 10 20 30 56 76 95
21-30 3 6 9 16 23 30
31-50: 34-Gunmaster app. 2 4 6 13 18 22
51-63,65,67-70: 54-Kid Montana app. 2 4 6 10 14 18
64,66: 64-Captain Doom begins (1st app.). 68-Kid Montana series begins 2 4 6 13 18 22
71-79: 73-Origin & 1st app. The Sharp Shooter, last app. #74. 75-Last Capt. Doom 2 4 6 9 12 15
80,81-Ditko-a 2 4 6 13 18 22
82-88 6.00
64,79(Modern Comics-r, 1977, '78) 6.00

OUTLAWS OF THE WILD WEST
Avon Periodicals: 1952 (25¢, 132 pgs.) (4 rebound comics)

1-Wood back-c; Kubert-a (3 Jesse James-r) 36 72 108 216 351 485

OUTLAW TRAIL (See Zane Grey 4-Color 511)

OUT OF SANTA'S BAG (See March of Comics #10 in the Promotional Comics section)

OUT OF THE NIGHT (The Hooded Horseman #18 on)
Amer. Comics Group (Creston/Scope): Feb-Mar, 1952 - No. 17, Oct-Nov, 1954

1-Williamson/LeDoux-a (9 pgs.); ACG's 1st editor's page 69 138 207 442 759 1075
2-Williamson-a (5 pgs.) 48 96 144 302 514 725
3,5-10: 9-Sci/Fic story 32 64 96 188 307 425
4-Williamson-a (7 pgs.) 41 82 123 256 428 600
11-17: 13-Nostrand-a? 17-E.C. Wood swipe 24 48 72 142 234 325
NOTE: ***Landau** a-14, 16, 17. **Shelly** a-12.*

OUT OF THE SHADOWS
Standard Comics/Visual Editions: No. 5, July, 1952 - No. 14, Aug, 1954

5-Toth-p; Moreira, Tuska-a; Roussos-c 57 114 171 362 619 875
6-Toth/Celardo-a; Katz-a(2) 41 82 123 249 417 585
7,9: 7-Jack Katz-c/a(2). 9-Crandall-a(2) 37 74 111 222 361 500
8-Katz shrunken head-c 71 142 213 454 777 1100
10-Spider-c; Sekowsky-a 39 78 117 231 378 525
11-Toth-a, 2 pgs.; Katz-a; Andru-c 37 74 111 222 361 500
12-Toth/Peppe-a(2); Katz-a 41 82 123 256 428 600
13-Cannabalism story; Sekowsky-a; Roussos-c 41 82 123 256 428 600
14-Toth-a 36 72 108 216 351 485

OUT OF THE VORTEX (Comics' Greatest World:... #1-4)
Dark Horse Comics: Oct., 1993 - No. 12, Oct, 1994 ($2.00, limited series)

1-11: 1-Foil logo. 4-Dorman-c(p). 6-Hero Zero x-over 3.00
12 ($2.50) 3.00
NOTE: ***Art Adams** c-7. **Golden** c-8. **Mignola** c-2. **Simonson** c-3. **Zeck** c-10.*

OUT OF THIS WORLD
Charlton Comics: Aug, 1956 - No. 16, Dec, 1959

1 29 58 87 170 278 385
2 15 30 45 90 140 190
3-6-Ditko-c/a (3) each 34 68 102 199 325 450
7-(2/58, 15¢, 68 pgs.)-Ditko-c/a(4) 36 72 108 211 343 475
8-(5/58, 15¢, 68 pgs.)-Ditko-a(2) 32 64 96 188 307 425
9,10,12,16-Ditko-a 24 48 72 144 237 330
11-Ditko c/a (3) 29 58 87 170 278 385
13,15 14 28 42 78 112 145
14-Matt Baker-a, 7 pg. story 14 28 42 82 121 160
NOTE: ***Ditko** c-3-12, 16. **Reinman** a-10.*

OUT OF THIS WORLD
Avon Periodicals: June, 1950; Aug, 1950

1-Kubert-a(2) (one reprinted/Eerie #1, 1947) plus Crom the Barbarian by Gardner Fox & John Giunta (origin); Fawcette-c 87 174 261 553 952 1350
1-(8/50) Reprint; no month on cover 52 104 156 328 552 775

OUT OF THIS WORLD ADVENTURES
Avon Periodicals: July, 1950 - No. 2, Apr, 1951 (25¢ sci-fi pulp magazine with 32-page color comic insert)

1-Kubert-a(2); Crom the Barbarian by Fox & Giunta; text stories by Cummings, Van Vogt, del Rey, Chandler 81 162 243 518 884 1250
2-Kubert-a plus The Spider God of Akka by Gardner Fox & John Giunta pulp magazine w/comic insert; Wood-a (21 pgs.); mentioned in **SOTI,** page 120 54 108 162 343 574 825

OUT OUR WAY WITH WORRY WART
Dell Publishing Co.: No. 680, Feb, 1956

Four Color 680 4 8 12 25 40 55

OUTPOSTS
Blackthorne Publishing: June, 1987 - No. 4, 1987 ($1.25)

1-4: 1-Kaluta-c(p) 3.00

OUTSIDERS, THE
DC Comics: Nov, 1985 - No. 28, Feb, 1988

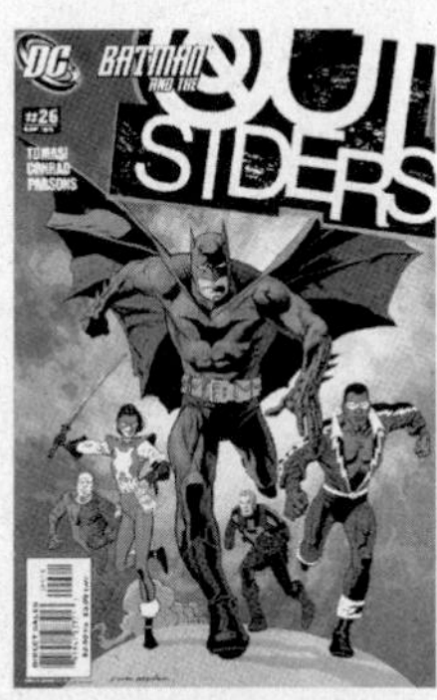
Outsiders #26 © DC

Overtaken #1 © Aspen MLT

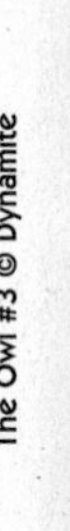

The Owl #3 © Dynamite

	GD 2.0	VG 4.0	FN 6.0	VF 8.0	VF/NM 9.0	NM- 9.2

1 4.00
2-17 3.00
18-28: 18-26-Batman returns. 21-Intro. Strike Force Kobra; 1st app. Clayface IV
22-E.C. parody; Orlando-a. 21- 25-Atomic Knight app. 27,28-Millennium tie-ins 3.00
Annual 1 (12/86, $2.50), Special 1 (7/87, $1.50) 4.00
NOTE: ***Aparo** a-1-7, 9-14, 17-22, 25, 26; c-1-7, 9-14, 17, 19-26. **Byrne** a-11. **Bolland** a-6, 18; c-16. **Ditko** a-13p. **Erik Larsen** a-24, 27 28; c-27, 28. **Morrow** a-12.*

OUTSIDERS
DC Comics: Nov, 1993 - No. 24, Nov, 1995 ($1.75/$1.95/$2.25)
1-11,0,12-24: 1-Alpha; Travis Charest-c. 1-Omega; Travis Charest-c. 5-Atomic Knight app. 8-New Batman-c/story. 11-(9/94)-Zero Hour. 0-(10/94).12-(11/94). 21-Darkseid cameo. 22-New Gods app. 3.00

OUTSIDERS (See Titans/Young Justice: Graduation Day)(Leads into Batman and the Outsiders)
DC Comics: Aug, 2003 - No. 50, Nov, 2007 ($2.50/$2.99)
1-Nightwing, Arsenal, Metamorpho app.; Winick-s/Raney-a 5.00
2-Joker and Grodd app. 4.00
3-33: 3-Joker-c. 5,6-ChrisCross-a. 8-Huntress app. 9,10-Capt. Marvel Jr. app. 24,25-X-over with Teen Titans. 26,27-Batman & old Outsiders 3.00
34-50: 34-One Year Later. 36-Begin $2.99-c. 37-Superman app. 44-Red Hood app. 3.00
Annual 1 (6/07, $3.99) McDaniel-a; Black LIghtning app. 4.00
.../Checkmate: Checkout TPB (2008, $14.99) r/#47-49 & Checkmate #13-15 15.00
... Double Feature (10/03, $4.95) r/#1,2 5.00
...: Crisis Intervention TPB (2006, $12.99) r/#29-33 13.00
...: Looking For Trouble TPB (2004, $12.95) r/#1-7 & Teen Titans/Outsiders Secret Files & Origins 2003; intro. by Winick 13.00
...: Pay As You Go TPB (2007, $14.99) r/#42-46 & Annual #1 15.00
...: Sum of All Evil TPB (2004, $14.95) r/#8-15 15.00
...: The Good Fight TPB (2006, $14.99) r/#34-41 15.00
...: Wanted TPB (2005, $14.99) r/#16-23 15.00

OUTSIDERS, THE (See Batman and the Outsiders for #1-14 and #40)
DC Comics: No. 15, Apr, 2009 - No. 39, Jun, 2011 ($2.99)
15-23,26-39: 15-Alfred assembles a new team; Garbett-a. 17-19-Deathstroke app. 3.00
24,25-($3.99) Blackest Night; Terra rises as a Black Lantern 4.00
...: The Deep TPB (2009, $14.99) r/#15-20 & Batman and the Outsiders Special #1 15.00
...: The Great Divide TPB (2011, $17.99) r/#32-40; cover gallery 18.00
...: The Hunt TPB (2010, $14.99) r/#21-25 15.00
...: The Road to Hell TPB (2010, $14.99) r/#26-31 15.00

OUTSIDERS: FIVE OF A KIND (Bridges Outsiders #49 & 50)
DC Comics: Oct, 2007 ($2.99, weekly limited series)
...Katana/Shazam! (part 2 of 5) - Barr-s/Sharpe-a 3.00
...Metamorpho/Aquaman (part 4 of 5) - Wilson-s/Middleton-a 3.00
...Nightwing/Captain Boomerang (part 1 of 5) - DeFilippis & Weir-s/Willams-a 3.00
...Thunder/Martian Manhunter (part 3 of 5) - Bedard-s/Turnbull-a; Grayven app. 3.00
...Wonder Woman/Grace (part 5 of 5) - Andreyko-s/Richards-a 3.00
TPB (2008, $14.99) r/series & Outsiders #50 15.00

OUT THERE
DC Comics(Cliffhanger): July, 2001 - No. 18, Aug, 2003 ($2.50/$2.95)
1-Humberto Ramos-c/a; Brian Augustyn-s 3.00
1-Variant-c by Carlos Meglia 4.00
2-8: 3-Variant-c by Bruce Timm 3.00
9-18: 9-Begin $2.95-c 3.00
...: The Evil Within TPB (2002, $12.95) r/#1-6; Ramos sketch pages 13.00

OVERKILL: WITCHBLADE/ ALIENS/ DARKNESS/ PREDATOR
Image Comics/Dark Horse Comics: Dec, 2000 - No. 2, 2001 ($5.95)
1,2-Jenkins-s/Lansing, Ching & Benitez-a 6.00

OVERTAKEN
Aspen MLT: Aug, 2013 ($1.00)
1-($1.00) Mastromauro-s/Lorenzana-a; multiple covers 2.00

OVER THE EDGE
Marvel Comics: Nov, 1995 - No. 10, Aug, 1996 (99¢)
1-10: 1,6,10-Daredevil-c/story. 2,7-Dr. Strange-c/story. 3-Hulk-c/story. 4,9-Ghost Rider-c/story. 5-Punisher-c/story. 8-Elektra-c/story 3.00

OWL, THE (See Crackajack Funnies #25, Popular Comics #72 and Occult Files of Dr. Spektor #22)
Gold Key: April, 1967; No. 2, April, 1968
1-Written by Jerry Siegel; '40s super hero 5 10 15 34 60 85
2 4 8 12 28 47 65

OWL, THE (See Project Superpowers)
Dynamite Entertainment: 2013 - No. 4, 2013 ($3.99, limited series)
1-4-Golden Age hero in modern times; Krul-s/H.K. Michael-a; covers by Ross & Syaf 4.00

OZ (See First Comics Graphic Novel, Marvel Treaury Of Oz & MGM's Marvelous...)

OZ
Caliber Press: 1994 - 1997 ($2.95, B&W)
0-20: 0-Released between #10 & #11 3.00
1 ($5.95)-Limited Edition; double-c 6.00
...Specials: Freedom Fighters. Lion. Scarecrow. Tin Man 3.00

OZARK IKE
Dell Publishing Co./Standard Comics B11 on: Feb, 1948; Nov, 1948 - No. 24, Dec, 1951; No. 25, Sept, 1952
Four Color 180(1948-Dell) 9 18 27 59 117 175
B11, B12, 13-15 11 22 33 60 83 105
16-25 10 20 30 54 72 90

OZ: DAEMONSTORM
Caliber Press: 1997 ($3.95, B&W, one-shot)
1 4.00

OZMA OF OZ (Dorothy Gale from Wonderful Wizard of Oz)
Marvel Comics: Jan, 2011 - No. 8, Sept, 2011 ($3.99, limited series)
1-6-Eric Shanower-s/Skottie Young-a/c 4.00
Oz Primer (5/11, $3.99) creator interviews and character profiles 4.00

OZ: ROMANCE IN RAGS
Caliber Press: 1996 ($2.95, B&W, limited series)
1-3, ..Special 3.00

OZ SQUAD
Brave New Worlds/Patchwork Press: 1992 - No. 4, 1994 ($2.50/$2.75, B&W)
1-4-Patchwork Press 3.00

OZ SQUAD
Patchwork Press: Dec, 1995 - No. 10, 1996 ($3.95/$2.95, B&W)
1-($3.95) 4.00
2-10 3.00

OZ: STRAW AND SORCERY
Caliber Press: 1997 ($2.95, B&W, limited series)
1-3 3.00

OZ-WONDERLAND WARS, THE
DC Comics: Jan, 1986 - No. 3, March, 1986 (Mini-series)(Giants)
1-3-Capt. Carrot app.; funny animals 4.00

OZZIE & BABS (TV Teens #14 on)
Fawcett Publications: Dec, 1947 - No. 13, Fall, 1949
1-Teen-age 10 20 30 58 79 100
2 7 14 21 35 43 50
3-13 6 12 18 31 38 45

OZZIE AND HARRIET (The Adventures of... on cover) (Radio)
National Periodical Publications: Oct-Nov, 1949 - No. 5, June-July, 1950
1-Photo-c 95 190 285 608 1042 1475
2 47 94 141 296 498 700
3-5 39 78 117 240 395 550

OZZY OSBOURNE (Todd McFarlane Presents)
Image Comics (Todd McFarlane Prod.): June, 1999 ($4.95, magazine-sized)
1-Bio, interview and comic story; Ormston painted-a; Ashley Wood-c 5.00

PACIFIC COMICS GRAPHIC NOVEL (See Image Graphic Novel)

PACIFIC PRESENTS (Also see Starslayer #2, 3)
Pacific Comics: Oct, 1982 - No. 2, Apr, 1983; No. 3, Mar, 1984 - No. 4, Jun, 1984
1-Chapter 3 of The Rocketeer; Stevens-c/a; Bettie Page model 2 4 6 9 12 15
2-Chapter 4 of The Rocketeer (4th app.); nudity; Stevens-c/a 2 4 6 9 12 15
3,4: 3-1st app. Vanity 3.00
NOTE: ***Conrad** a-3, 4; c-3. **Ditko** a-1-3; c-1(1/2). **Dave Stevens** a-1, 2; c-1(1/2), 2.*

PACIFIC RIM: TALES FROM YEAR ZERO
Legendary Comics: Jun, 2013 ($24.99, HC graphic novel)
HC - Prequel to the 2013 movie; Beacham-s/Alex Ross-c; art by various 25.00

PACT, THE
Image Comics: Feb, 1994 - No. 3, June, 1994 ($1.95, limited series)

Painkiller Jane #5 © Q&P

Panic #4 © WMG

Paradise X #4 © MAR

GD 2.0 VG 4.0 FN 6.0 VF 8.0 VF/NM 9.0 NM- 9.2

GD 2.0 VG 4.0 FN 6.0 VF 8.0 VF/NM 9.0 NM- 9.2

1-3: Valentino co-scripts & layouts 3.00

PACT, THE
Image Comics: Apr, 2005 - No. 4, Jan, 2006 ($2.99/$2.95)
1-4: Invincible, Shadowhawk, Firebreather & Zephyr team-up. 1-Valentino-s/a 3.00

PAGEANT OF COMICS (See Jane Arden & Mopsy)
Archer St. John: Sept, 1947 - No. 2, Oct, 1947
1,2: 1-Mopsy strip-r. 2-Jane Arden strip-r 11 22 33 60 83 105

PAINKILLER JANE
Event Comics: June, 1997 - No. 5, Nov, 1997 ($3.95/$2.95)
1-Augustyn/Waid-s/Leonardi/Palmiotti-a, variant-c 4.00
2-5: Two covers (Quesada, Leonardi) 3.00
0-(1/99, $3.95) Retells origin; two covers 4.00
Essential Painkiller Jane TPB (2007, $19.99) r/#0-5; cover gallery and pin-ups 20.00

PAINKILLER JANE
Dynamite Entertainment: 2006 - No. 3, 2006 ($2.99)
1-3-Quesada & Palmiotti-s/Moder-a. 1-Four covers by Q&P, Moder, Tan and Conner 3.00
Volume #1 TPB (2007, $9.99) r/#1-3; cover gallery and Palmiotti interview 10.00

PAINKILLER JANE
Dynamite Entertainment: No. 0, 2007 - Present ($3.50)
0-(25¢) Quesada & Palmiotti-s/Moder-a 3.00
1-5-($3.50) 1-Continued from #0; 5 covers. 4,5-Crossover with Terminator 2 #6,7 3.50
Volume #2 TPB (2007, $11.99) r/#0-3; cover gallery 12.00

PAINKILLER JANE / DARKCHYLDE
Event Comics: Oct, 1998 ($2.95, one-shot)
Preview-($6.95) DF Edition, 1-($6.95) DF Edition 7.00
1-Three covers; J.G. Jones-a 3.00

PAINKILLER JANE / HELLBOY
Event Comics: Aug, 1998 ($2.95, one-shot)
1-Leonardi & Palmiotti-a 3.00

PAINKILLER JANE: THE PRICE OF FREEDOM
Marvel Comics (ICON): Nov, 2013 - No. 4, Jan, 2014 ($3.99/$2.99, limited series)
1-($3.99) Palmiotti-s/Santacruz & Lotfi-a; covers by Amanda Conner & Dave Johnson 4.00
2-4-($2.99) Santacruz-a/Conner-c 3.00

PAINKILLER JANE VS. THE DARKNESS
Event Comics: Apr, 1997 ($2.95, one-shot)
1-Ennis-s; four variant-c (Conner, Hildebrandts, Quesada, Silvestri) 3.50

PAKKINS' LAND
Caliber Comics (Tapestry): Oct, 1996 - No. 6, July, 1997 ($2.95, B&W)
1-Gary and Rhoda Shipman-s/a 6.00
2,3 4.00
1-3-2nd printing 3.00
4-6 3.00
0-(6/97, $1.95) 3.00

PAKKINS' LAND
Alias Enterprises: Apr, 2005 - No. 2 ($2.99)
1,2-Gary Shipman-s/a 3.00

PAKKINS' LAND: FORGOTTEN DREAMS
Caliber Comics/Image Comics #4: Apr, 1998 - No. 4, Mar, 2000 ($2.95, B&W)
1-4-Gary and Rhoda Shipman-s/a 3.00

PAKKINS' LAND: QUEST FOR KINGS
Caliber Comics: Aug, 1997 - No. 6, Mar, 1998 ($2.95, B&W)
1-6: 1-Gary and Rhoda Shipman-s/a; Jeff Smith var-c 3.00

PANCHO VILLA
Avon Periodicals: 1950
nn-Kinstler-c 24 48 72 142 234 325

PANHANDLE PETE AND JENNIFER (TV) (See Gene Autry #20)
J. Charles Laue Publishing Co.: July, 1951 - No. 3, Nov, 1951
1 10 20 30 58 79 100
2,3: 2-Interior photo-cvrs 8 16 24 40 50 60

PANIC (Companion to Mad)
E. C. Comics (Tiny Tot Comics): Feb-Mar, 1954 - No. 12, Dec-Jan, 1955-56
1-Used in Senate Investigation hearings; Elder draws entire E. C. staff; Santa Claus & Mickey Spillane parody 39 78 117 312 494 675
2-Atomic bomb-c 18 36 54 144 227 310
3,4: 3-Senate Subcommittee parody; Davis draws Gaines, Feldstein & Kelly, 1 pg.; Old King Cole smokes marijuana. 4-Infinity-c; John Wayne parody 14 28 42 112 181 250
5-11: 8-Last pre-code issue (5/55). 9-Superman, Smilin' Jack & Dick Tracy app. on-c; has photo of Walter Winchell on-c. 11-Wheedies cereal box-c 13 26 39 104 167 230
12 (Low distribution; thousands were destroyed) 17 34 51 136 213 290
NOTE: *Davis a-1-12; c-12.* ***Elder*** *a-1-12.* ***Feldstein*** *c-1-3, 5.* ***Kamen*** *a-1.* ***Orlando*** *a-1-9.* ***Wolverton*** *c-4, panel-3.* ***Wood*** *a-2-9, 11, 12.*

PANIC (Magazine) (Satire)
Panic Publ.: July, 1958 - No. 6, July, 1959; V2#10, Dec, 1965 - V2#12, 1966
1 14 28 42 76 108 140
2-6 9 18 27 50 65 80
V2#10-12: Reprints earlier issues 3 6 9 17 26 35
NOTE: ***Davis*** *a-3(2 pgs.), 4, 5, 10; c-10.* ***Elder*** *a-5.* ***Powell*** *a-V2#10, 11.* ***Torres*** *a-1-5.* ***Tuska*** *a-V2#11.*

PANIC
Gemstone Publishing: March, 1997 - No. 12, Dec, 1999 ($2.50, quarterly)
1-12: E.C. reprints 4.00

PANTHA (See Vampirella-The New Monthly #16,17)

PANTHA (Also see Prophecy)
Dynamite Entertainment: 2012 - No. 6, 2013 ($3.99)
1-6: 1-Jerwa-s/Rodrix-a; covers by Sean Chen & Texiera. 2-6-Texiera-c 4.00

PANTHA: HAUNTED PASSION (Also see Vampirella Monthly #0)
Harris Comics: May, 1997 ($2.95, B&W, one-shot)
1-r/Vampirella #30,31 3.00

PANTHEON
IDW Publishing: Apr, 2010 - No. 5, Aug, 2010 ($3.99)
1-5-Andreyko-s/Molnar-a; co-created by Michael Chiklis 4.00

PAPA MIDNITE (See John Constantine - Hellblazer Special:...)

PARADE (See Hanna-Barbera...)

PARADE COMICS (See Frisky Animals on Parade)

PARADE OF PLEASURE
Derric Verschoyle Ltd., London, England: 1954 (192 pgs.) (Hardback book)
By Geoffrey Wagner. Contains section devoted to the censorship of American comic books with illustrations in color and black and white. (Also see **Seduction of the Innocent**). Distributed in USA by Library Publishers, N. Y. 125 250 375 538 644 750
with dust jacket.... 233 466 699 1002 1201 1400

PARADISE TOO!
Abstract Studios: 2000 - No. 14, 2003 ($2.95, B&W)
1-14-Terry Moore's unpublished newspaper strips and sketches 3.00
Complete Paradise Too TPB (2010, $29.95) r/#1-14 with bonus material 30.00
...: Checking For Weirdos TPB (4/03, $14.95) r/#8-12 15.00
...: Drunk Ducks! TPB (7/02, $15.95) r/#1-7 16.00

PARADISE X (Also see Earth X and Universe X)
Marvel Comics: Apr, 2002 - No. 12, Aug, 2003 ($4.50/$2.99)
0-Ross-c; Braithwaite-a 4.50
1-12-($2.99) Ross-c; Braithwaite-a. 7-Punisher on-c. 10-Kingpin on-c 3.00
...:A (10/03, $2.99) Braithwaite-a; Ross-c 3.00
...:Devils (11/02, $4.50) Sadowski-a; Ross-c 4.50
...:Ragnarok 1,2 (3/02, 4/03; $2.99) Yeates-a; Ross-c 3.00
...:X (11/03, $2.99) Braithwaite-a; Ross-c; conclusion of story 3.00
...:Xen (7/02, $4.50) Yeowell & Sienkiewicz-a; Ross-c 4.50
Earth X Vol. 4: Paradise X Book 1 (2003, $29.99, TPB) r/#0,1-5, ...: Xen; Heralds #1-3 30.00
Vol. 5: Paradise X Book 2 (2004, $29.99, TPB) r/#6-12, Ragnarok #1&2; Devils, A & X 30.00

PARADISE X: HERALDS (Also see Earth X and Universe X)
Marvel Comics: Dec, 2001 - No. 3, Feb, 2002 ($3.50)
1-3-Prelude to Paradise X series; Ross-c; Pugh-a 3.50
Special Edition (Wizard preview) Ross-c 3.00

PARADOX
Dark Visions Publ: June, 1994 - No. 2, Aug, 1994 ($2.95, B&W, mature)
1,2: 1-Linsner-c. 2-Boris-c. 3.00

PARALLAX: EMERALD NIGHT (See Final Night)
DC Comics: Nov, 1996 ($2.95, one-shot, 48 pgs.)
1-Final Night tie-in; Green Lantern (Kyle Rayner) app. 4.00

PARAMOUNT ANIMATED COMICS (See Harvey Comics Hits #60, 62)
Harvey Publications: No. 3, Jun, 1953 - No. 22, Jul, 1956

Pariah #1 © Aron Warner

Patches #1 © RH

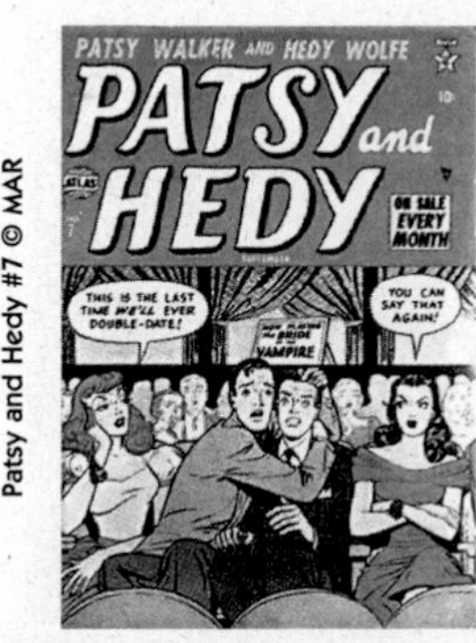

Patsy and Hedy #7 © MAR

	GD 2.0	VG 4.0	FN 6.0	VF 8.0	VF/NM 9.0	NM- 9.2
3-Baby Huey, Herman & Katnip, Buzzy the Crow begin	25	50	75	150	245	340
4-6	14	28	42	76	108	140
7-Baby Huey becomes permanent cover feature; cover title becomes Baby Huey with #9	22	44	66	132	216	300
8-10: 9-Infinity-c	12	24	36	69	97	125
11-22	10	20	30	54	72	90

PARENT TRAP, THE (Disney)
Dell Publishing Co.: No. 1210, Oct-Dec, 1961

Four Color 1210-Movie, Hayley Mills photo-c	8	16	24	52	99	145

PARIAH (Aron Warner's...)
Dark Horse Comics: Feb, 2014 - Present ($3.99)

1-Aron Warner & Philip Gelatt-s/Brett Weldele-a 4.00

PARLIAMENT OF JUSTICE
Image Comics: Mar, 2003 ($5.95, B&W, one-shot, square-bound)

1-Michael Avon Oeming-c/s; Neil Vokes-a 6.00

PARODY
Armour Publishing: Mar, 1977 - No. 3, Aug, 1977 (B&W humor magazine)

1	3	6	9	14	19	24
2,3: 2-King Kong, Happy Days. 3-Charlie's Angels, Rocky	2	4	6	10	14	18

PAROLE BREAKERS
Avon Periodicals/Realistic #2 on: Dec, 1951 - No. 3, July, 1952

1(#2 on inside)-r-c/Avon paperback #283 (painted-c)	47	94	141	296	498	700
2-Kubert-a; r-c/Avon paperback #114 (photo-c)	32	64	96	192	314	435
3-Kinstler-c	29	58	87	170	278	385

PARTRIDGE FAMILY, THE (TV)(Also see David Cassidy)
Charlton Comics: Mar, 1971 - No. 21, Dec, 1973

1-(2 versions: B&W photo-c & tinted color photo-c)	6	12	18	41	76	110
2-4,6-10	4	8	12	25	40	55
5-Partridge Family Summer Special (52 pgs.); The Shadow, Lone Ranger, Charlie McCarthy, Flash Gordon, Hopalong Cassidy, Gene Autry & others app.	7	14	21	46	86	125
11-21	3	6	9	21	33	45

PARTS OF A HOLE
Caliber Press: 1991 ($2.50, B&W)

1-Short stories & cartoons by Brian Michael Bendis 3.00

PARTS UNKNOWN
Eclipse Comics/FX: July, 1992 - No. 4, Oct, 1992 ($2.50, B&W, mature)

1-4: All contain FX gaming cards 3.00

PARTS UNKNOWN
Image Comics: May, 2000 - Sept, 2000 ($2.95, B&W)

...: Killing Attractions 1 (5/00) Beau Smith-s/Brad Gorby-a 3.00
...: Hostile Takeover 1-4 (6-9/00) 3.00

PASSION, THE
Catechetical Guild: No. 394, 1955

394	6	12	18	31	38	45

PASSOVER (See Avengelyne)
Maximum Press: Dec, 1996 ($2.99, one-shot)

1 3.00

PAT BOONE (TV)(Also see Superman's Girlfriend Lois Lane #9)
National Per. Publ.: Sept-Oct, 1959 - No. 5, May-Jun, 1960 (All have photo-c)

1	42	84	126	265	445	625
2-5: 3-Fabian, Connie Francis & Paul Anka photos on-c. 4-Previews "Journey To The Center Of The Earth". 4-Johnny Mathis & Bobby Darin photos on-c. 5-Dick Clark & Frankie Avalon photos on-c	34	68	102	199	325	450

PATCHES
Rural Home/Patches Publ. (Orbit): Mar-Apr, 1945 - No. 11, Nov, 1947

1-L. B. Cole-c	40	80	120	244	402	560
2	15	30	45	90	140	190
3,4,6,8-11: 6-Henry Aldrich story. 8-Smiley Burnette-c/s (6/47); pre-dates Smiley Burnette #1. 9-Mr. District Attorney story (radio). Leav/Keigstein-a (16 pgs.). 9-11-Leav-c. 10-Jack Carson (radio) c/story; Leav-c. 11-Red Skelton story	15	30	45	86	133	180
5-Danny Kaye-c/story; L.B. Cole-c.	20	40	60	117	189	260
7-Hopalong Cassidy-c/story	18	36	54	105	165	225

PATH, THE (Also see Negation War)
CrossGeneration Comics: Apr, 2002 - No. 23, Apr, 2004 ($2.95)

1-23: 1-Ron Marz-s/Bart Sears-a. 13-Matthew Smith-a begins 3.00
Vol. 1: Crisis of Faith (2002, $15.95, TPB) r/#1-6 16.00
Vol. 2: Blood on Snow (5/03, $15.95, TPB) r/#7-12 16.00
Vol. 3: Death and Dishonor ('03, $15.95, TPB) r/#13-18 16.00

PATHFINDER (Based on the Pathfinder roleplaying game)
Dynamite Entertainment: 2012 - No. 12, 2013 ($3.99)

1-12: 1-Jim Zub-s/Andrew Huerta-a; four covers. 2-12-Multiple covers on each 4.00
... Special 2013 ($4.99, 40 pgs.) Jim Zub-s/Kevin Stokes-a 5.00

PATHFINDER: GOBLINS! (Based on the Pathfinder roleplaying game)
Dynamite Entertainment: 2013 - No. 5, 2013 ($3.99)

1-5: Short stories by various; multiple covers on each 4.00

PATHWAYS TO FANTASY
Pacific Comics: July, 1984

1-Barry Smith-c/a; Jeff Jones-a (4 pgs.) 4.00

PATIENT ZERO
Image Comics: Mar, 2004 - No. 4, Jun, 2004 ($2.95, limited series)

1-4-Brent White-a/John McLean-Foreman-s 3.00

PATORUZU (See Adventures of...)

PATRIOTS, THE
DC Comics (WildStorm): Jan, 2000 - No. 10, Oct, 2000 ($2.50)

1-10-Choi and Peterson-s/Ryan-a 3.00

PATSY & HEDY (Teenage)(Also see Hedy Wolfe)
Atlas Comics/Marvel (GPI/Male): Feb, 1952 - No. 110, Feb, 1967

1-Patsy Walker & Hedy Wolfe; Al Jaffee-c	30	60	90	177	289	400
2	15	30	45	90	140	190
3-10: 3,7,8,9-Al Jaffee-c	14	28	42	81	118	155
11-20: 17,19,20-Al Jaffee-c	13	26	39	72	101	130
21-40	11	22	33	60	83	105
41-50	6	12	18	37	66	95
51-60	5	10	15	35	63	90
61-80,100: 88-Lingerie panel	5	10	15	33	57	80
81-87,89-99,101-110	5	10	15	31	53	75
Annual 1(1963)-Early Marvel annual	9	18	27	59	117	175

PATSY & HER PALS (Teenage)
Atlas Comics (PPI): May, 1953 - No. 29, Aug, 1957

1-Patsy Walker	22	44	66	132	216	300
2	14	28	42	80	115	150
3-10	13	26	39	72	101	130
11-29: 24-Everett-c	11	22	33	60	83	105

PATSY WALKER (See All Teen, A Date With Patsy, Girls' Life, Miss America Magazine, Patsy & Hedy, Patsy & Her Pals & Teen Comics)
Marvel/Atlas Comics (BPC): 1945 (no month) - No. 124, Dec, 1965

1-Teenage	71	142	213	454	777	1100
2	36	72	108	211	343	475
3,4,6-10	29	58	87	170	278	385
5-Injury-to-eye-c	34	68	102	199	325	450
11,12,15,16,18	18	36	54	105	165	225
13,14,17,19-22-Kurtzman's "Hey Look"	19	38	57	109	172	235
23,24	15	30	45	88	137	185
25-Rusty by Kurtzman; painted-c	19	38	57	109	172	235
26-29,31: 26-31: 52 pgs.	14	28	42	81	119	155
30(52 pgs.)-Egghead Doodle by Kurtzman (1 pg.)	15	30	45	83	124	165
32-57: Last precode (3/55)	12	24	36	69	97	125
58-80,100	6	12	18	38	69	100
81-99: 92,98-Millie x-over. 99-Linda Carter x-over	5	10	15	35	63	90
101-124	5	10	15	33	57	80
Fashion Parade 1(1966, 68 pgs.) (Beware cut-out & marked pages)	8	16	24	54	102	150

NOTE: *Painted c-25-28. Anti-Wertham editorial in #21. Georgie app. in #8, 11, 17. Millie app. in #10, 92, 98. Mitzi app. in #11. Rusty app. in #12, 25. Willie app. in #12.* **Al Jaffee** *c-44, 47, 49, 51, 57, 58.*

PATSY WALKER: HELLCAT
Marvel Comics: Sept, 2008 - No. 5, Feb, 2009 ($2.99, limited series)

1-5-Lafuente-a/Kathryn Immonen-s/Stuart Immonen-c; Hellcat joins The Initiative 3.00

PAT THE BRAT (Adventures of Pipsqueak #34 on)
Archie Publications (Radio): June, 1953; Summer, 1955 - No. 4, 5/56; No. 15, 7/56 - No. 33, 7/59

Paul the Samurai #1 © NEC

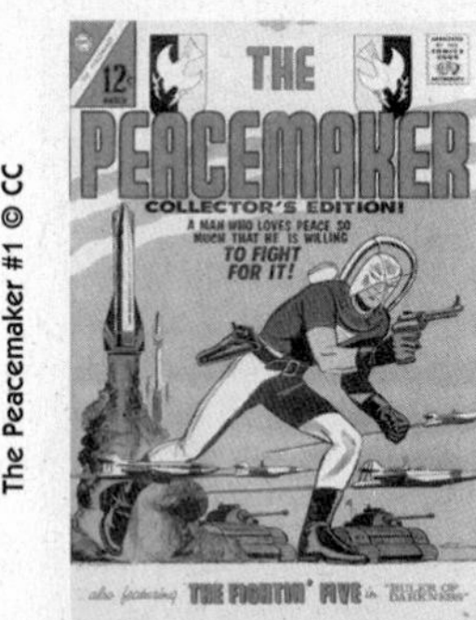

The Peacemaker #1 © CC

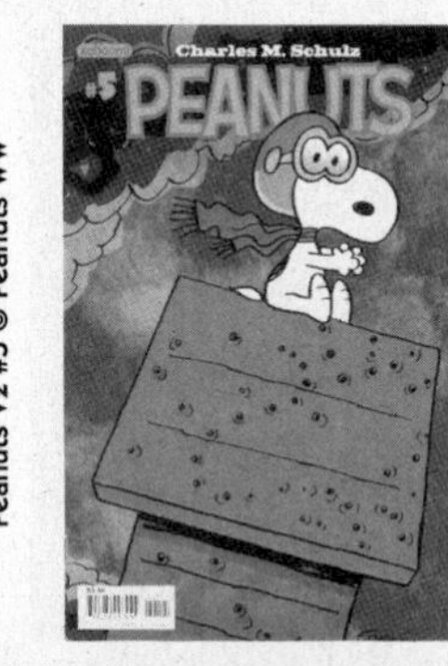

Peanuts V2 #5 © Peanuts WW

	GD 2.0	VG 4.0	FN 6.0	VF 8.0	VF/NM 9.0	NM- 9.2
nn(6/53)	14	28	42	82	121	160
1(Summer, 1955)	11	22	33	62	86	110
2-4-(5/56) (#5-14 not published). 3-Early Bolling-a	8	16	24	42	54	65
15-(7/56)-33: 18-Early Bolling-a	4	8	12	25	40	55

PAT THE BRAT COMICS DIGEST MAGAZINE
Archie Publications: October, 1980 (95¢)

	GD 2.0	VG 4.0	FN 6.0	VF 8.0	VF/NM 9.0	NM- 9.2
1-Li'l Jinx & Super Duck app.	2	4	6	9	13	16

PATTY CAKE
Permanent Press: Mar, 1995 - No. 9, Jul, 1996 ($2.95, B&W)

	GD 2.0	VG 4.0	FN 6.0	VF 8.0	VF/NM 9.0	NM- 9.2
1-9: Scott Roberts-s/a						3.00

PATTY CAKE
Caliber Press (Tapestry): Oct, 1996 - No. 3, Apr, 1997 ($2.95, B&W)

	GD 2.0	VG 4.0	FN 6.0	VF 8.0	VF/NM 9.0	NM- 9.2
1-3: Scott Roberts-s/a, ...Christmas (12/96)						3.00

PATTY CAKE & FRIENDS
Slave Labor Graphics: Nov, 1997 - Nov, 2000 ($2.95, B&W)

	GD 2.0	VG 4.0	FN 6.0	VF 8.0	VF/NM 9.0	NM- 9.2
Here There Be Monsters (10/97), 1-14: Scott Roberts-s/a						3.00
Volume 2 #1 (11/00, $4.95)						5.00

PATTY POWERS (Formerly Della Vision #3)
Atlas Comics: No. 4, Oct, 1955 - No. 7, Oct, 1956

	GD 2.0	VG 4.0	FN 6.0	VF 8.0	VF/NM 9.0	NM- 9.2
4	12	24	36	69	97	125
5-7	9	18	27	47	61	75

PAT WILTON (See Mighty Midget Comics)

PAUL
Spire Christian Comics (Fleming H. Revell Co.): 1978 (49¢)

	GD 2.0	VG 4.0	FN 6.0	VF 8.0	VF/NM 9.0	NM- 9.2
nn	2	4	6	10	14	18

PAULINE PERIL (See The Close Shaves of...)

PAUL REVERE'S RIDE (TV, Disney, see Walt Disney Showcase #34)
Dell Publishing Co.: No. 822, July, 1957

	GD 2.0	VG 4.0	FN 6.0	VF 8.0	VF/NM 9.0	NM- 9.2
Four Color 822-w/Johnny Tremain, Toth-a	7	14	21	49	92	135

PAUL TERRY (See Heckle and Jeckle)

PAUL TERRY'S ADVENTURES OF MIGHTY MOUSE (See Adventures of...)

PAUL TERRY'S COMICS (Formerly Terry-Toons Comics; becomes Adventures of Mighty Mouse No. 126 on)
St. John Publishing Co.: No. 85, Mar, 1951 - No. 125, May, 1955

	GD 2.0	VG 4.0	FN 6.0	VF 8.0	VF/NM 9.0	NM- 9.2
85,86-Same as Terry-Toons #85, & 86 with only a title change; published at same time?; Mighty Mouse, Heckle & Jeckle & Gandy Goose continue from Terry-Toons	12	24	36	67	94	120
87-99	9	18	27	50	65	80
100	10	20	30	54	72	90
101-104,107-125: 121,122,125-Painted-c	9	18	27	47	61	75
105,106-Giant Comics Edition (25¢, 100 pgs.) (9/53 & ?). 105-Little Roquefort-c/story	18	36	54	105	165	225

PAUL TERRY'S MIGHTY MOUSE (See Mighty Mouse)

PAUL TERRY'S MIGHTY MOUSE ADVENTURE STORIES (See Mighty Mouse Adventure Stories)

PAUL THE SAMURAI (See The Tick #4)
New England Comics: July, 1992 - No. 6, July, 1993 ($2.75, B&W)

	GD 2.0	VG 4.0	FN 6.0	VF 8.0	VF/NM 9.0	NM- 9.2
1-6						3.00

PAWNEE BILL
Story Comics (Youthful Magazines?): Feb, 1951 - No. 3, July, 1951

	GD 2.0	VG 4.0	FN 6.0	VF 8.0	VF/NM 9.0	NM- 9.2
1-Bat Masterson, Wyatt Earp app.	13	26	39	72	101	130
2,3: 3-Origin Golden Warrior; Cameron-a	8	16	24	42	54	65

PAY-OFF (This Is the..., ...Crime, ...Detective Stories)
D. S. Publishing Co.: July-Aug, 1948 - No. 5, Mar-Apr, 1949 (52 pgs.)

	GD 2.0	VG 4.0	FN 6.0	VF 8.0	VF/NM 9.0	NM- 9.2
1-True Crime Cases #1,2	28	56	84	165	270	375
2	17	34	51	98	154	210
3-5-Thrilling Detective Stories	15	30	45	83	124	165

PEACEMAKER, THE (Also see Fightin' Five)
Charlton Comics: V3#1, Mar, 1967 - No. 5, Nov, 1967 (All 12¢ cover price)

	GD 2.0	VG 4.0	FN 6.0	VF 8.0	VF/NM 9.0	NM- 9.2
1-Fightin' Five begins	5	10	15	31	53	75
2,3,5	3	6	9	20	31	42
4-Origin The Peacemaker	4	8	12	25	40	55
1,2(Modern Comics reprint, 1978)						6.00

PEACEMAKER (Also see Crisis On Infinite Earths & Showcase '93 #7,9,10)
DC Comics: Jan, 1988 - No. 4, Apr, 1988 ($1.25, limited series)

	GD 2.0	VG 4.0	FN 6.0	VF 8.0	VF/NM 9.0	NM- 9.2
1-4						4.00

PEANUTS (Charlie Brown) (See Fritzi Ritz, Nancy & Sluggo, Sparkle & Sparkler, Tip Top, Tip Topper & United Comics)
United Features Syndicate/Dell Publishing Co./Gold Key: 1953-54; No. 878, 2/58 - No. 13, 5-7/62; 5/63 - No. 4, 2/64

	GD 2.0	VG 4.0	FN 6.0	VF 8.0	VF/NM 9.0	NM- 9.2
1(U.F.S.)(1953-54)-Reprints United Features' Strange As It Seems, Willie, Ferdnand (scarce)	258	516	774	1651	2826	4000
Four Color 878(#1) (Dell) Schulz-s/a, with assistance from Dale Hale and Jim Sasseville thru #4	50	100	150	400	900	1400
Four Color 969,1015('59)	19	38	57	131	291	450
4(2-4/60) Schulz-s/a; one story by Anthony Pocrnich, Schulz's assistant cartoonist	12	24	36	84	185	285
5-13-Schulz-c only; s/a by Pocrnich	11	22	33	72	154	235
1(Gold Key, 5/63)	21	42	63	147	324	500
2-4	10	20	30	64	132	200

PEANUTS (Charlie Brown)
BOOM! Entertainment: No. 0, Nov, 2011 - No. 4, Apr, 2012; V2 No. 1, Aug, 2012 - Present ($1.00/$3.99)

	GD 2.0	VG 4.0	FN 6.0	VF 8.0	VF/NM 9.0	NM- 9.2
0-(11/11, $1.00) New short stories and Sunday page reprints						3.00
1-4: 1-(1/12, $3.99) New short stories and Sunday page reprints; Snoopy sled cover						4.00
1-4-Variant-c with first appearance image. 1-Charlie Brown. 2-Lucy. 3-Linus. 4-Snoopy						6.00
(Volume 2)						
1-17: 1-(8/12, "#1 of 4" on-c)						4.00
1-12-Variant-c with first appearance image. 1-Schroeder. 2-Pig-Pen. 4-Woodstock						10.00
... Free Comic Book Day Edition (5/12) Giveaway flip book with Adventure Time						3.00
Happiness is a Warm Blanket, Charlie Brown HC (Boom Entertainment, 3/2011, $19.99) adaptation of new animated special						20.00
It's Tokyo, Charlie Brown (10/12, $13.99, squarebound GN) Vicki Scott-s/a; bonus art						14.00

PEBBLES & BAMM BAMM (TV) (See Cave Kids #7, 12)
Charlton Comics: Jan, 1972 - No. 36, Dec, 1976 (Hanna-Barbera)

	GD 2.0	VG 4.0	FN 6.0	VF 8.0	VF/NM 9.0	NM- 9.2
1-From the Flintstones; "Teen Age..." on cover	4	8	12	28	47	65
2-10	3	6	9	16	24	32
11-20	2	4	6	13	18	22
21-36	2	4	6	9	13	16
nn (1973, digest, 100 pgs.) B&W one page gags	3	6	9	17	26	35

PEBBLES & BAMM BAMM (TV)
Harvey Comics: Nov, 1993 - No. 3, Mar, 1994 ($1.50) (Hanna-Barbera)

	GD 2.0	VG 4.0	FN 6.0	VF 8.0	VF/NM 9.0	NM- 9.2
V2#1-3						3.00
...Giant Size 1 (10/93, $2.25, 68 pgs.)("Summer Special" on-c)						4.00

PEBBLES FLINTSTONE (TV) (See The Flintstones #11)
Gold Key: Sept, 1963 (Hanna-Barbera)

	GD 2.0	VG 4.0	FN 6.0	VF 8.0	VF/NM 9.0	NM- 9.2
1 (10088-309)-Early Pebbles app.	8	16	24	51	96	140

PEDRO (Formerly My Private Life #17; also see Romeo Tubbs)
Fox Features Syndicate: No. 18, June, 1950 - No. 2, Aug, 1950?

	GD 2.0	VG 4.0	FN 6.0	VF 8.0	VF/NM 9.0	NM- 9.2
18(#1)-Wood-c/a(p)	23	46	69	136	223	310
2-Wood-a?	15	30	45	90	140	190

PEE-WEE PIXIES (See The Pixies)

PELLEAS AND MELISANDE (See Night Music #4, 5)

PENALTY (See Crime Must Pay the...)

PENANCE: RELENTLESS (See Civil War, Thunderbolts and related titles)
Marvel Comics: Nov, 2007 - No. 5 ($2.99)

	GD 2.0	VG 4.0	FN 6.0	VF 8.0	VF/NM 9.0	NM- 9.2
1-5-Speedball/Penance; Jenkins-s/Gulacy-a. 3-Wolverine app.						3.00
TPB (2008, $13.99) r/#1-5						14.00

PENDRAGON (Knights of... #5 on; also see Knights of...)
Marvel Comics UK, Ltd.: July, 1992 - No. 15, Sept, 1993 ($1.75)

	GD 2.0	VG 4.0	FN 6.0	VF 8.0	VF/NM 9.0	NM- 9.2
1-15: 1-4-Iron Man app. 6-8-Spider-Man app.						3.00

PENDULUM ILLUSTRATED BIOGRAPHIES
Pendulum Press: 1979 (B&W)

19-355x-George Washington/Thomas Jefferson, 19-3495-Charles Lindbergh/Amelia Earhart, 19-3509-Harry Houdini/Walt Disney, 19-3517-Davy Crockett/Daniel Boone-Redondo-a, 19-3525-Elvis Presley/Beatles, 19-3533-Benjamin Franklin/Martin Luther King Jr, 19-3541-Abraham Lincoln/Franklin D. Roosevelt, 19-3568-Marie Curie/Albert Einstein-Redondo-a, 19-3576-Thomas Edison/Alexander Graham Bell-Redondo-a, 19-3584-Vince Lombardi/Pele, 19-3592-Babe Ruth/Jackie Robinson, 19-3606-Jim Thorpe/Althea Gibson

	GD 2.0	VG 4.0	FN 6.0	VF 8.0	VF/NM 9.0	NM- 9.2
Softback						5.00
Hardback	1	2	3	4	5	7

PENDULUM ILLUSTRATED CLASSICS (Now Age Illustrated)
Pendulum Press: 1973 - 1978 (75¢, 62pp, B&W, 5-3/8x8")
(Also see Marvel Classics)

Penny #3 © AVON

Pep Comics #31 © AP

Pep Comics #48 © AP

	GD 2.0	VG 4.0	FN 6.0	VF 8.0	VF/NM 9.0	NM- 9.2

64-100x(1973)-Dracula-Redondo art, 64-131x-The Invisible Man-Nino art, 64-0968-Dr. Jekyll and Mr. Hyde-Redondo art, 64-1005-Black Beauty, 64-1010-Call of the Wild, 64-1020-Frankenstein, 64-1025-Hucklebury Finn, 64-1030-Moby Dick-Nino-a, 64-1040-Red Badge of Courage, 64-1045-The Time Machine-Nino-a, 64-1050-Tom Sawyer, 64-1055-Twenty Thousand Leagues Under the Sea, 64-1069-Treasure Island, 64-1328(1974)-Kidnapped, 64-1336-Three Musketeers-Nino art, 64-1344-A Tale of Two Cities, 64-1352-Journey to the Center of the Earth, 64-1360-The War of the Worlds-Nino-a, 64-1379-The Greatest Advs. of Sherlock Holmes-Redondo art, 64-1387-Mysterious Island, 64-1395-Hunchback of Notre Dame, 64-1409-Helen Keller-story of my life, 64-1417-Scarlet Letter, 64-1425-Gulliver's Travels, 64-2618(1977)-Around the World in Eighty Days, 64-2626-Captains Courageous, 64-2634-Connecticut Yankee, 64-2642-The Hound of the Baskervilles, 64-2650-The House of Seven Gables, 64-2669-Jane Eyre, 64-2677-The Last of the Mohicans, 64-2685-The Best of O'Henry, 64-2693-The Best of Poe-Redondo-a, 64-2707-Two Years Before the Mast, 64-2715-White Fang, 64-2723-Wuthering Heights, 64-3126(1978)-Ben Hur-Redondo art, 64-3134-A Christmas Carol, 64-3142-The Food of the Gods, 64-3150-Ivanhoe, 64-3169-The Man in the Iron Mask, 64-3177-The Prince and the Pauper, 64-3185-The Prisoner of Zenda, 64-3193-The Return of the Native, 64-3207-Robinson Crusoe, 64-3215-The Scarlet Pimpernel, 64-3223-The Sea Wolf, 64-3231-The Swiss Family Robinson, 64-3851-Billy Budd, 64-386x-Crime and Punishment, 64-3878-Don Quixote, 64-3886-Great Expectations, 64-3894-Heidi, 64-3908-The Iliad, 64-3916-Lord Jim, 64-3924-The Mutiny on Board H.M.S. Bounty, 64-3932-The Odyssey, 64-3940-Oliver Twist, 64-3959-Pride and Prejudice, 64-3967-The Turn of the Screw

	GD	VG	FN	VF	VF/NM	NM-
Softback						6.00
Hardback	1	2	3	5	6	8

NOTE: *All of the above books can be ordered from the publisher; some were reprinted as Marvel Classic Comics #1-12. In 1972 there was another brief series of 12 titles which contained Classics Ill. artwork. They were entitled* ***Now Age Books*** *Illustrated, but can be easily distinguished from later series by the small Classics Illustrated logo at the top of the front cover. The format is the same as the later series. The 48 pg. C.I. art was stretched out to make 62 pgs. After Twin Circle Publ. terminated the Classics Ill. series in 1971, they made a one year contract with Pendulum Press to print these twelve titles of C.I. art. Pendulum was unhappy with the contract, and at the end of 1972 began their own art series, utilizing the talents of the Filipino artist group. One detail which makes this rather confusing is that when they redid the art in 1973, they gave it the same identifying no. as the 1972 series. All 12 of the 1972 C.I. editions have new covers, taken from internal art panels. In spite of their recent age, all of the 1972 C.I. series are very rare. Mint copies would fetch at least $50. Here is a list of the 1972 series, with C.I. title no. counterpart:*

64-1005 (CI#60-A2) 64-1010 (CI#91) 64-1015 (CI-Jr #503) 64-1020 (CI#26)
64-1025 (CI#19-A2) 64-1030 (CI#5-A2) 64-1035 (CI#169) 64-1040 (CI#98)
64-1045 (CI#133) 64-1050 (CI#50-A2) 64-1055 (CI#47) 64-1060 (CI-Jr#535)

PENDULUM ILLUSTRATED ORIGINALS
Pendulum Press: 1979 (In color)

94-4254-Solarman: The Beginning (See Solarman) 6.00

PENDULUM'S ILLUSTRATED STORIES
Pendulum Press: 1990 - No. 72, 1990? (No cover price ($4.95), squarebound, 68 pgs.)

1-72: Reprints Pendulum Ill. Classics series 5.00

PENGUIN: PAIN & PREJUDICE (Batman)
DC Comics: Dec, 2011 - No. 5, Apr, 2012 ($2.99, limited series)

1-5-Hurwitz-s/Kudranski-a/c; Penguin's childhood and rise to power 3.00

PENGUINS OF MADAGASCAR (Based on the DreamWorks movie and TV series)
Ape Entertainment: 2010 - No. 4 ($3.95, limited series)

1-Skipper, Kowalski, Private and Rico app. 4.00

PENNY
Avon Comics: 1947 - No. 6, Sept-Oct, 1949 (Newspaper reprints)

	GD	VG	FN	VF	VF/NM	NM-
1-Photo & biography of creator	22	44	66	132	216	300
2-5	12	24	36	69	97	125
6-Perry Como photo on-c	13	26	39	74	105	135

PENNY CENTURY (See Love and Rockets)
Fantagraphics Books: Dec, 1997 - No. 7, Jul, 2000 ($2.95, B&W, mini-series)

1-7-Jaime Hernandez-s/a 3.00

PEP COMICS (See Archie Giant Series #576, 589, 601, 614, 624)
MLJ Magazines/Archie Publications No. 56 (3/46) on: Jan, 1940 - No. 411, Mar, 1987

	GD	VG	FN	VF	VF/NM	NM-
1-Intro. The Shield (1st patriotic hero) by Irving Novick; origin & 1st app. The Comet by Jack Cole, The Queen of Diamonds & Kayo Ward; The Rocket, The Press Guardian (The Falcon #1 only), Sergeant Boyle, Fu Chang, & Bentley of of Scotland Yard; Robot-c; Shield-c begin	892	1784	2676	6512	11,506	16,500
2-Origin The Rocket	277	554	831	1773	3037	4300
3	213	426	639	1363	2332	3300
4-Wizard cameo; early robot-s	174	348	522	1114	1907	2700
5-Wizard cameo in Shield story	174	348	522	1114	1907	2700
6-10: 8-Last Cole Comet; no Cole-a in #6,7	139	278	417	890	1520	2150
11-Dusty, Shield's sidekick begins (1st app.); last Press Guardian, Fu Chang	142	284	426	909	1555	2200
12-Origin & 1st app. Fireball (2/41); last Rocket & Queen of Diamonds; Danny in Wonderland begins	161	322	483	1030	1765	2500
13-15	116	232	348	742	1271	1800
16-Origin Madam Satan; blood drainage-c	184	368	552	1178	2014	2850
17-Origin/1st app. The Hangman (7/41); death of The Comet; Comet is revealed as Hangman's brother	423	846	1269	3000	5250	7500
18,19,21: 21-Last Madam Satan	110	220	330	704	1202	1700
20-Classic Nazi swastika-c; last Fireball	194	388	582	1242	2121	3000
22-Intro. & 1st app. Archie, Betty, & Jughead (12/41); (also see Jackpot)	14,000	28,000	42,000	98,000	136,500	175,000
23-Statue of Liberty-c (1/42; on sale 11/41)	568	1136	1704	4146	7323	10,500
24-Coach Kleats app. (unnamed until Archie #94); bondage/torture-c	423	846	1269	3000	5250	7500
25-1st app. Archie's jalopy; 1st skinny Mr. Weatherbee prototype	354	708	1062	2478	4339	6200
26-1st app. Veronica Lodge (4/42); "Remember Pearl Harbor!" cover caption	486	972	1458	3550	6275	9000
27,29,30: 27-Bill of Rights-c. 29-Origin Shield retold; 30-Capt. Commando begins; bondage/torture-c; 1st Miss Grundy (definitive version); see Jackpot #4	290	580	870	1856	3178	4500
28-Classic swastika/Hangman-c	300	600	900	2010	3505	5000
31-33,35: 31-MLJ offices & artists are visited in Sgt. Boyle story; 1st app. Mr. Lodge. 32-Shield dons new costume. 33-Pre-Moose tryout (see Jughead #1)	258	516	774	1651	2826	4000
34-Classic Bondage/Hypo-c	486	972	1458	3550	6275	9000
36-1st full Archie-c (2/43) w/Shield & Hangman (see Jackpot #4 where Archie's face appears in a small circle)	975	1950	2919	7100	12,550	18,000
37-40	168	336	504	1075	1838	2600
41-45: 41-Archie-c begin	129	258	387	826	1413	2000
46,47,49,50: 47-Last Hangman issue; infinity-c	110	220	330	704	1202	1700
48-Black Hood begins (5/44); ends #51,59,60; Archie fish-c	142	284	426	909	1555	2200
51-60: 52-Suzie begins; 1st Mr Weatherbee-c. 56-Last Capt. Commando. 59-Black Hood not in costume; lingerie panels; Archie dresses as his aunt; Suzie ends. 60-Katy Keene begins(3/47), ends #154	58	116	174	371	636	900
61-65-Last Shield. 62-1st app. Li'l Jinx (7/47)	47	94	141	296	498	700
66-80: 66-G-Man Club becomes Archie Club (2/48); Nevada Jones by Bill Woggon. 76-Katy Keene story. 78-1st app. Dilton	26	52	78	154	252	350
81-99	20	40	60	114	182	250
100	22	44	66	132	216	300
101-130	14	28	42	76	108	140
131(2/59)-137	6	12	18	38	69	100
138-140-Neal Adams-a (1 pg.) in each	6	12	18	41	76	110
141-149(9/61)	5	10	15	34	60	85
150-160-Super-heroes app. in each (see note). 150 (10/61?)-2nd or 3rd app. The Jaguar? 151-154,156-158-Horror/Sci/Fi-c. 157-Li'l Jinx. 159-Both 12¢ and 15¢ covers exist	7	14	21	44	82	120
161(3/63)-167,169-180: 161-3rd Josie app.; early Josie stories w/DeCarlo-a begin (see Note for others)	4	8	12	27	44	60
168,200: 168-(1/64)-Jaguar app. 200-(12/66)	4	8	12	28	47	65
181(5/65)-199: 187-Pureheart try-out story. 192-UFO-c. 198-Giantman-c(only)	3	6	9	21	33	45
201-217,219-226,228-240(4/70): 224-(12/68) 1st app. Archie's pet, Hot Dog (later becomes Jughead's pet)	3	6	9	16	23	30
218,227-Archies Band-c only	3	6	9	17	26	35
241-270(10/72)	2	4	6	13	18	22
271-297,299	2	4	6	9	12	15
298, 300: 298-Josie and the Pussycats-c. 300(4/75)	2	4	6	13	18	22
301-340(8/78)	1	3	4	6	8	10
341-382	1	2	3	4	5	7
383(4/82),393(3/84): 383-Marvelous Maureen begins (Sci/fi). 393-Thunderbunny begins	1	2	3	5	6	8
384-392,394,395,397-399,401-410						5.00
396-Early Cheryl Blossom-c	2	4	6	9	12	15
400(5/85),411: 400-Story featuring Archie staff (DeCarlo-a)	1	2	3	4	5	7

NOTE: ***Biro*** *a-2, 4, 5.* ***Jack Cole*** *a-1-5, 8.* ***Al Fagaly*** *c-55-72.* ***Fuje*** *a-39, 45, 47; c-34.* ***Meskin*** *a-2, 4, 5, 11(2).* ***Montana*** *c-30, 32, 33, 36, 73-87(most).* ***Novick*** *c-1-28, 29(w/****Schomburg****), 31i.* ***Harry Sahle*** *c-35, 39-50.* ***Schomburg*** *c-38.* ***Bob Wood*** *a-2, 4-6, 11. The Fly app. in 151, 154, 160. Flygirl app. in 153, 155, 156, 158. Jaguar app. in 150, 152, 157, 159, 168. Josie by* ***DeCarlo*** *in 161-166, 168-171, 173, 175-177, 179, 181. Katy Keene by* ***Bill Woggon*** *in 73-126. Bondage c-7, 12, 13, 15, 18, 21, 31, 32. Cover features: Shield #1-16; Shield/Hangman #17-27, 29-41; Hangman #28. Archie #36, 41-on.*

PEP COMICS FEATURING BETTY AND VERONICA
Archie Comic Publications: May, 2011 (Giveaway)

Free Comic Book Day Edition - Little Archie flashback 3.00

PEPE
Dell Publishing Co.: No. 1194, Apr, 1961

	GD	VG	FN	VF	VF/NM	NM-
Four Color 1194-Movie, photo-c	4	8	12	25	40	55

PERFECT CRIME, THE
Cross Publications: Oct, 1949 - No. 33, May, 1953 (#2-14, 52 pgs.)

Perfect Love #10 (#1) © Z-D

Personal Love #13 © FF

Peter Panzerfaust #13 © Wiebe & Jenkins

	GD 2.0	VG 4.0	FN 6.0	VF 8.0	VF/NM 9.0	NM- 9.2
1-Powell-a(2)	40	80	120	246	411	575
2 (4/50)	22	44	66	132	216	300
3-10: 7-Steve Duncan begins, ends #30. 10-Flag-c	20	40	60	117	189	260
11-Used in **SOTI**, pg. 159	22	44	66	128	209	290
12-14	19	38	57	111	176	240
15- "The Most Terrible Menace" 2 pg. drug editorial (8/51)	20	40	60	118	192	265
16,17,19-25,27-29,31-33	15	30	45	88	137	185
18-Drug cover, heroin drug propaganda story, plus 2 pg. anti-drug editorial (11/51)	36	72	108	211	343	475
26-Drug-c with hypodermic needle; drug propaganda story (7/52)	34	68	102	199	325	450
30-Strangulation cover (11/52)	34	68	102	204	332	460

NOTE: *Powell a-No. 1, 2, 4. Wildey a-1, 5. Bondage c-11.*

PERFECT LOVE
Ziff-Davis(Approved Comics)/St. John No. 9 on: #10, 8-9/51 (cover date; 5-6/51 indicia date); #2, 10-11/51 - #10, 12/53

	GD 2.0	VG 4.0	FN 6.0	VF 8.0	VF/NM 9.0	NM- 9.2
10(#1)(8-9/51)-Painted-c	24	48	72	142	234	325
2(10-11/51)	16	32	48	94	147	200
3,5-7: 3-Painted-c. 5-Photo-c	14	28	42	82	121	160
4,8 (Fall, 1952)-Kinstler-a; last Z-D issue	15	30	45	83	124	165
9,10 (10/53, 12/53, St. John): 9-Painted-c. 10-Photo-c	14	28	42	81	118	155

PERHAPANAUTS, THE
Dark Horse Comics: Nov, 2005 - No. 4, Feb, 2006 ($2.99, limited series)

	GD 2.0	VG 4.0	FN 6.0	VF 8.0	VF/NM 9.0	NM- 9.2
1-4-Todd Dezago-s/Craig Rousseau-a/c						3.00
... Annual #1 (2/08, $3.50) Two covers by Rousseau and Allred						3.50
...: Danger Down Under! 1-5 (11/12 - No. 5, 6/13, $3.50) Two covers on each						3.50
... Halloween Spooktacular 1 (10/09, $3.50) Hembeck, Rousseau and others-a						3.50
,,, - Molly's Story (2/10, $3.50) Copland-a						3.50
(2nd series) (4/08 - No. 6, $3.50) 1-6: 1-Two covers by Art Adams and Rousseau						3.50

PERHAPANAUTS: SECOND CHANCES, THE
Dark Horse Comics: Oct, 2006 - No. 4, Jan, 2007 ($2.99, limited series)

	GD 2.0	VG 4.0	FN 6.0	VF 8.0	VF/NM 9.0	NM- 9.2
1-4-Todd Dezago-s/Craig Rousseau-a/c						3.00

PERRI (Disney)
Dell Publishing Co.: No. 847, Jan, 1958

	GD 2.0	VG 4.0	FN 6.0	VF 8.0	VF/NM 9.0	NM- 9.2
Four Color 847-Movie, w/2 diff-c publ.	5	10	15	33	57	80

PERRY MASON
David McKay Publications: No. 49, 1946 - No. 50, 1946

	GD 2.0	VG 4.0	FN 6.0	VF 8.0	VF/NM 9.0	NM- 9.2
Feature Books 49, 50-Based on Gardner novels	39	78	117	240	395	550

PERRY MASON MYSTERY MAGAZINE (TV)
Dell Publishing Co.: June-Aug, 1964 - No. 2, Oct-Dec, 1964

	GD 2.0	VG 4.0	FN 6.0	VF 8.0	VF/NM 9.0	NM- 9.2
1-Raymond Burr painted-c	6	12	18	38	69	100
2-Raymond Burr photo-c	5	10	15	31	53	75

PERSONAL LOVE (Also see Movie Love)
Famous Funnies: Jan, 1950 - No. 33, June, 1955

	GD 2.0	VG 4.0	FN 6.0	VF 8.0	VF/NM 9.0	NM- 9.2
1-Photo-c	22	44	66	132	216	300
2-Kathryn Grayson & Mario Lanza photo-c	14	28	42	80	115	150
3-7,10: 7-Robert Walker & Joanne Dru photo-c. 10-Loretta Young & Joseph Cotton photo-c	13	26	39	74	105	135
8,9: 8-Esther Williams & Howard Keel photo-c. 9-Debra Paget & Louis Jourdan photo-c	14	28	42	76	108	140
11-Toth-a; Glenn Ford & Gene Tierney photo-c	15	30	45	83	124	165
12,16,17-One pg. Frazetta each. 17-Rock Hudson & Yvonne DeCarlo photo-c	14	28	42	76	108	140
13-15,18-23: 12-Jane Greer & William Lundigan photo-c. 14-Kirk Douglas photo-c. 15-Dale Robertson & Joanne Dru photo-c. 18-Gregory Peck & Susan Hayworth photo-c. 19-Anthony Quinn & Suzan Ball photo-c. 20-Robert Wagner & Kathleen Crowley photo-c. 21-Roberta Peters & Byron Palmer photo-c. 22-Dale Robertson photo-c. 23-Rhonda Fleming-c	12	24	36	69	97	125
24,27,28-Frazetta-a in each (8,8&6 pgs.). 27-Rhonda Fleming & Fernando Lamas photo-c. 28-Mitzi Gaynor photo-c	52	104	156	328	552	775
25-Frazetta-a (tribute to Bettie Page, 7 pg. story); Tyrone Power/Terry Moore photo-c from "King of the Khyber Rifles"	71	142	213	454	777	1100
26,29,30,33: 26-Constance Smith & Byron Palmer photo-c. 29-Charlton Heston & Nicol Morey photo-c. 30-Johnny Ray & Mitzi Gaynor photo-c. 33-Dana Andrews & Piper Laurie photo-c	12	24	36	69	97	125
31-Marlon Brando & Jean Simmons photo-c; last pre-code (2/55)	15	30	45	85	130	175
32-Classic Frazetta-a (8 pgs.); Kirk Douglas & Bella Darvi photo-c	69	138	207	442	759	1075

NOTE: *All have photo-c. Many feature movie stars. Everett a-5, 9, 10, 24.*

PERSONAL LOVE (Going Steady V3#3 on)
Prize Publ. (Headline): V1#1, Sept, 1957 - V3#2, Nov-Dec, 1959

	GD 2.0	VG 4.0	FN 6.0	VF 8.0	VF/NM 9.0	NM- 9.2
V1#1	12	24	36	67	94	120
2	8	16	24	44	57	70
3-6(7-8/58)	8	16	24	40	50	60
V2#1(9-10/58)-V2#6(7-8/59)	7	14	21	35	43	50
V3#1-Wood?/Orlando-a	7	14	21	37	46	55
2	6	12	18	31	38	45

PETER CANNON - THUNDERBOLT (See Crisis on Infinite Earths)(Also see Thunderbolt)
DC Comics: Sept, 1992 - No. 12, Aug, 1993 ($1.25)

	GD 2.0	VG 4.0	FN 6.0	VF 8.0	VF/NM 9.0	NM- 9.2
1-12						3.00

PETER CANNON: THUNDERBOLT
Dynamite Entertainment: 2012 - No. 13, 2013 ($3.99)

	GD 2.0	VG 4.0	FN 6.0	VF 8.0	VF/NM 9.0	NM- 9.2
1-10: 1-Darnell & Ross-s/Lau-a; back-up unpublished '80s Thunderbolt story; Pete Morisi-s/a. 1-3-Four covers on each. 4-7-Covers by Ross & Segovia						4.00

PETER COTTONTAIL
Key Publications: Jan, 1954; Feb, 1954 - No. 2, Mar, 1954 (Says 3/53 in error)

	GD 2.0	VG 4.0	FN 6.0	VF 8.0	VF/NM 9.0	NM- 9.2
1(1/54)-Not 3-D	9	18	27	52	69	85
1(2/54)-(3-D, 25¢)-Came w/glasses; written by Bruce Hamilton	21	42	63	122	199	275
2-Reprints 3-D #1 but not in 3-D	6	12	18	31	38	45

PETER GUNN (TV)
Dell Publishing Co.: No. 1087, Apr-June, 1960

	GD 2.0	VG 4.0	FN 6.0	VF 8.0	VF/NM 9.0	NM- 9.2
Four Color 1087-Photo-c	7	14	21	49	92	135

PETE ROSE: HIS INCREDIBLE BASEBALL CAREER
Masstar Creations Inc.: 1995

	GD 2.0	VG 4.0	FN 6.0	VF 8.0	VF/NM 9.0	NM- 9.2
1-John Tartaglione-a						4.00

PETER PAN (Disney) (See Hook, Movie Classics & Comics, New Adventures of... & Walt Disney Showcase #36)
Dell Publishing Co.: No. 442, Dec, 1952 - No. 926, Aug, 1958

	GD 2.0	VG 4.0	FN 6.0	VF 8.0	VF/NM 9.0	NM- 9.2
Four Color 442 (#1)-Movie	9	18	27	61	123	185
Four Color 926-Reprint of 442	4	8	12	28	47	65

PETER PAN
Disney Comics: 1991 ($5.95, graphic novel, 68 pgs.)(Celebrates video release)

	GD 2.0	VG 4.0	FN 6.0	VF 8.0	VF/NM 9.0	NM- 9.2
nn-r/Peter Pan Treasure Chest from 1953						7.00

PETER PANDA
National Periodical Publications: Aug-Sept, 1953 - No. 31, Aug-Sept, 1958

	GD 2.0	VG 4.0	FN 6.0	VF 8.0	VF/NM 9.0	NM- 9.2
1-Grossman-c/a in all	53	106	159	334	567	800
2	27	54	81	158	259	360
3,4,6-8,10	22	44	66	128	209	290
5-Classic-c (scarce)	77	154	231	493	847	1200
9-Robot-c	31	62	93	182	296	410
11-31	15	30	45	90	140	190

PETER PAN RECORDS (See Power Records)

PETER PAN TREASURE CHEST (See Dell Giants)

PETER PANZERFAUST
Image Comics (Shadowline): Feb, 2012 - Present ($3.50)

	GD 2.0	VG 4.0	FN 6.0	VF 8.0	VF/NM 9.0	NM- 9.2
1-Kurtis Wiebe-s/Tyler Jenkins-a/c; Peter Pan-type character in WWII Europe	7	14	21	46	86	125
1-Second printing	3	6	9	16	23	30
2	4	8	12	23	37	50
3	2	4	6	11	16	20
4-8	1	2	3	5	6	8
9-1st full app. Kapitan Haken	2	4	6	8	10	12
10-18						4.00

PETER PARKER (See The Spectacular Spider-Man)

PETER PARKER
Marvel Comics: May, 2010 - No. 5, Sept, 2010 ($3.99/$2.99)

	GD 2.0	VG 4.0	FN 6.0	VF 8.0	VF/NM 9.0	NM- 9.2
1-($3.99) Prints material from Marvel Digital Comics; Olliffe-a; back-up w/Hembeck-s/a						4.00
2-5-($2.99): 2-4-Olliffe-a. 3-Braithwaite-c. 5-Nauck-a; Thing app.						3.00

PETER PARKER: SPIDER-MAN
Marvel Comics: Jan, 1999 - No. 57, Aug, 2003 ($2.99/$1.99/$2.25)

	GD 2.0	VG 4.0	FN 6.0	VF 8.0	VF/NM 9.0	NM- 9.2
1-Mackie-s/Romita Jr.-a; wraparound-c	1	2	3	5	6	8
1-($6.95) DF Edition w/variant-c by the Romitas	1	3	4	6	8	10

Peter Parker: Spider-Man #45 © MAR

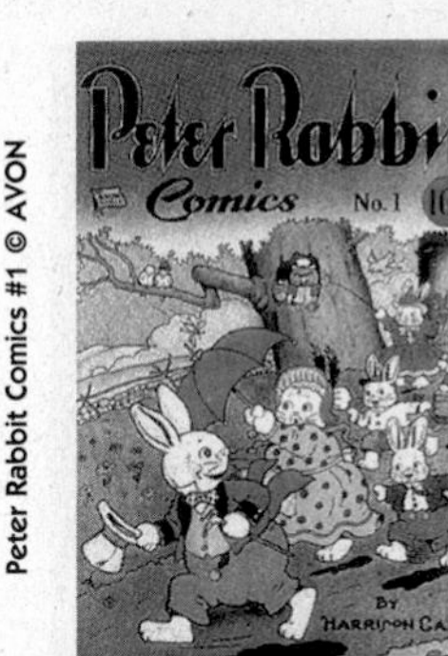

Peter Rabbit Comics #1 © AVON

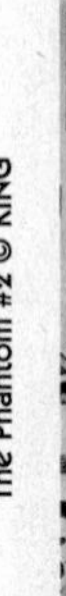
The Phantom #2 © KING

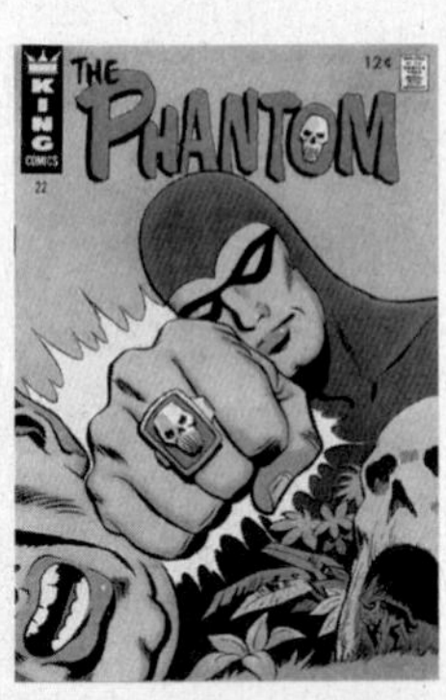

	GD 2.0	VG 4.0	FN 6.0	VF 8.0	VF/NM 9.0	NM- 9.2

2-11,13-17-($1.99): 2-Two covers; Thor app. 3-Iceman-c/app. 4-Marrow-c/app. 5-Spider-Woman app. 7,8-Blade app. 9,10-Venom app. 11-Iron Man & Thor-c/app. 3.00
12-($2.99) Sinister Six and Venom app. 4.00
18-24,26-43: 18-Begin $2.25-c. 20-Jenkins-s/Buckingham-a start. 23-Intro Typeface. 24-Maximum Security x-over. 29-Rescue of MJ. 30-Ramos-c. 42,43-Mahfood-a 3.00
25-($2.99) Two covers; Spider-Man & Green Goblin 4.00
44-47-Humberto Ramos-c/a; Green Goblin-c/app. 3.00
48,49,51-57: 48,49-Buckingham-c/a. 51,52-Herrera-a. 56,57-Kieth-a; Sandman returns 3.00
50-($3.50) Buckingham-c/a 4.00
#156.1 (10/12, $2.99, 50th Anniversary one-shot) Stern-s/De La Torre-a/Romita Jr.-c 3.00
...'99 Annual (8/99, $3.50) Man-Thing app. 4.00
...'00 Annual ($3.50) Bounty app.; Joe Bennett-a; Black Cat back-up story 4.00
...'01 Annual ($2.99) Avery-s 4.00
...: A Day in the Life TPB (5/01, $14.95) r/#20-22,26; Webspinners #10-12 15.00
...: One Small Break TPB (2002, $16.95) r/#27,28,30-34; Andrews-c 17.00
Spider-Man: Return of the Goblin TPB (2002, $8.99) r/#44-47; Ramos-c 9.00
...Vol. 4: Trials & Tribulations TPB (2003, $11.99) r/#35,37,48-50; Cho-c 12.00

PETER PAT
United Features Syndicate: No. 8, 1939

Single Series 8 36 72 108 211 343 475

PETER PAUL'S 4 IN 1 JUMBO COMIC BOOK
Capitol Stories (Charlton): No date (1953)

1-Contains 4 comics bound; Space Adventures, Space Western, Crime & Justice, Racket Squad in Action 40 80 120 246 411 575

PETER PIG
Standard Comics: No. 5, May, 1953 - No. 6, Aug, 1953

5,6 7 14 21 35 43 50

PETER PORKCHOPS (See Leading Comics #23) (Also see Capt. Carrot)
National Periodical Publications: 11-12/49 - No. 61, 9-11/59; No. 62, 10-12/60 (1-11: 52 pgs.)

1 34 68 102 199 325 450
2 15 30 45 90 140 190
3-10: 6- "Peter Rockets to Mars!" c/story 13 26 39 74 105 135
11-30 10 20 30 56 76 95
31-62 9 18 27 47 61 75

NOTE: ***Otto Feuer** a-all. **Rube Grossman**-a most issues. **Sheldon Mayer** a-30-38, 40-44, 46-52, 61.*

PETER PORKER, THE SPECTACULAR SPIDER-HAM
Star Comics (Marvel): May, 1985 - No. 17, Sept, 1987 (Also see Marvel Tails)

1-Michael Golden-c 5.00
2-17: 12-Origin/1st app. Bizarro Phil. 13-Halloween issue 4.00

NOTE: *Back-up features: 2-X-Bugs. 3-Iron Mouse. 4-Croctor Strange. 5-Thrr, Dog of Thunder.*

PETER POTAMUS (TV)
Gold Key: Jan, 1965 (Hanna-Barbera)

1-1st app. Peter Potamus & So-So, Breezly & Sneezly 8 16 24 56 108 160

PETER RABBIT (See New Funnies #65 & Space Comics)
Dell Publishing Co.: No. 1, 1942

Large Feature Comic 1 65 130 195 416 708 1000

PETER RABBIT (Adventures of...; New Advs. of... #9 on)(Also see Funny Tunes & Space Comics)
Avon Periodicals: 1947 - No. 34, Aug-Sept, 1956

1(1947)-Reprints 1943-44 Sunday strips; contains a biography & drawing of Cady 36 72 108 214 347 480
2 (4/48) 24 48 72 142 234 325
3 ('48) - 6(7/49)-Last Cady issue 21 42 63 124 202 280
7-10(1950-8/51): 9-New logo 11 22 33 62 86 110
11(11/51)-34('56)-Avon's character 9 18 27 52 69 85
...Easter Parade (1952, 25¢, 132 pgs.) 20 40 60 117 189 260
...Jumbo Book (1954-Giant Size, 25¢)-Jesse James by Kinstler (6 pgs.); space ship-c 24 48 72 140 230 320

PETER RABBIT 3-D
Eternity Comics: April, 1990 ($2.95, with glasses; sealed in plastic bag)

1-By Harrison Cady (reprints) 3.00

PETER, THE LITTLE PEST (#4 titled Petey)
Marvel Comics Group: Nov, 1969 - No. 4, May, 1970

1 6 12 18 41 76 110
2-4-r-Dexter the Demon & Melvin the Monster 5 10 15 30 50 70

PETE'S DRAGON (See Walt Disney Showcase #43)

PETE THE PANIC
Stanmor Publications: November, 1955

nn-Code approved 6 12 18 31 38 45

PETEY (See Peter, the Little Pest)

PETTICOAT JUNCTION (TV, inspired Green Acres)
Dell Publ. Co.: Oct-Dec, 1964 - No. 5, Oct-Dec, 1965 (#1-3, 5 have photo-c)

1 6 12 18 40 73 105
2-5 5 10 15 30 50 70

PETUNIA (Also see Looney Tunes and Porky Pig)
Dell Publishing Co.: No. 463, Apr, 1953

Four Color 463 4 8 12 28 47 65

PHAGE (See Neil Gaiman's Teknophage & Neil Gaiman's Phage-Shadowdeath)

PHANTACEA
McPherson Publishing Co.: Sept, 1977 - No. 6, Summer, 1980 (B&W)

1-Early Dave Sim-a (32 pgs.) 4 8 12 28 47 65
2-Dave Sim-a(10 pgs.) 3 6 9 14 19 24
3-6: 3-Flip-c w/Damnation Bridge. 4-Gene Day-a 2 4 6 10 14 18

PHANTASMO (See The Funnies #45)
Dell Publishing Co.: No. 18, 1941

Large Feature Comic 18 39 78 117 240 395 550

PHANTOM, THE
David McKay Publishing Co.: 1939 - 1949

Feature Books 20 100 200 300 640 1095 1550
Feature Books 22 71 142 213 454 777 1100
Feature Books 39 54 108 162 343 574 825
Feature Books 53,56,57 43 86 129 271 461 650

PHANTOM, THE (See Ace Comics, Defenders Of The Earth, Eat Right to Work and Win, Future Comics, Harvey Comics Hits #51,56, Harvey Hits #1, 6, 12, 15, 26, 36, 44, 48, & King Comics)

PHANTOM, THE (nn (#29)-Published overseas only) (Also see Comics Reading Libraries in the Promotional Comics section)
Gold Key(#1-17)/King(#18-28)/Charlton(#30 on): Nov, 1962 - No. 17, Jul, 1966; No. 18, Sept, 1966 - No. 28, Dec, 1967; No. 30, Feb, 1969 - No. 74, Jan, 1977

1-Origin revealed on inside-c & back-c 18 36 54 124 275 425
2-King, Queen & Jack begins, ends #11 9 18 27 61 123 185
3-5 8 16 24 55 105 155
6-10 6 12 18 42 79 115
11-17: 12-Track Hunter begins 6 12 18 37 66 95
18-Flash Gordon begins; Wood-a 5 10 15 30 50 70
19-24: 20-Flash Gordon ends (both by Gil Kane). 21-Mandrake begins. 20,24-Girl Phantom app. 4 8 12 27 44 60
25-28: 25-Jeff Jones-a(4 pgs.); 1 pg. Williamson ad. 26-Brick Bradford app. 28-Brick Bradford app. 3 6 9 21 33 45
30-33: 33-Last 12¢ issue 3 6 9 16 24 32
34-40: 36,39-Ditko-a 3 6 9 16 23 30
41-66: 46-Intro. The Piranha. 51-Grey tone-c. 62-Bolle-c 3 6 9 14 19 24
67-Origin retold; Newton-c/a; Humphrey Bogart, Lauren Bacall & Peter Lorre app. 3 6 9 16 24 32
68-73-Newton-c/a 2 4 6 13 18 22
74-Classic flag-c by Newton; Newton-a; 3 6 9 16 23 30

NOTE: ***Aparo** a-31-34, 36-38; c-31-38, 60, 61. Painted c-1-17.*

PHANTOM, THE
DC Comics: May, 1988 - No. 4, Aug, 1988 ($1.25, mini-series)

1-4: Orlando-c/a in all 4.00

PHANTOM, THE
DC Comics: Mar, 1989 - No. 13, Mar, 1990 ($1.50)

1-13: 1-Brief origin 4.00

PHANTOM, THE
Wolf Publishing: 1992 - No. 8, 1993 ($2.25)

1-8 3.00

PHANTOM, THE
Moonstone: 2003 - No. 26, Dec, 2008 ($3.50/$3.99)

1-26: 1-Cassaday-c/Raab-s/Quinn-a 4.00
... Annual #1 (2007, $6.50) Blevins-c; stroy and art by various incl. Nolan 6.50
... - Captain Action 1 (2010, $3.99) covers by Thibert, Sparacio, and Gilbert 4.00

PHANTOM BLOT, THE (#1 titled New Adventures of...)

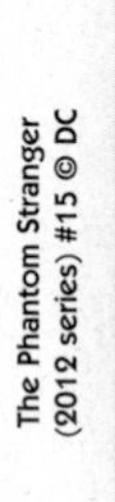

Phantom Lady #23 © FOX

The Phantom Stranger (2012 series) #15 © DC

Phantom Zone #1 © DC

	GD	VG	FN	VF	VF/NM	NM-
	2.0	4.0	6.0	8.0	9.0	9.2

Gold Key: Oct, 1964 - No. 7, Nov, 1966 (Disney)

1 (Meets The Mysterious Mr. X) 5 10 15 35 63 90
2-1st Super Goof 5 10 15 31 53 75
3-7 3 6 9 21 33 45

PHANTOM EAGLE (See Mighty Midget, Marvel Super Heroes #16 & Wow #6)

PHANTOM FORCE
Image Comics/Genesis West #0, 3-7: 12/93 - #2, 1994; #0, 3/94; #3, 5/94 - #8, 10/94 ($2.50/$3.50, limited series)

0 (3/94, $2.50)-Kirby/Jim Lee-c; Kirby-p pgs. 1,5,24-29. 4.00
1 (12/93, $2.50)-Polybagged w/trading card; Kirby/Liefeld-c; Kirby plots/pencils w/inks by Liefeld, McFarlane, Jim Lee, Silvestri, Larsen, Williams, Ordway & Miki 4.00
2 ($3.50)-Kirby-a(p); Kirby/Larson-c 5.00
3-8: 3-(5/94, $2.50)-Kirby/McFarlane-c 4-(5/94)-Kirby-c(p). 5-(6/94) 4.00

PHANTOM GUARD
Image Comics (WildStorm Productions): Oct, 1997 - No. 6, Mar, 1998 ($2.50)

1-6: 1-Two covers 3.00
1-($3.50)-Voyager Pack w/Wildcore preview 4.00

PHANTOM JACK
Image Comics: Mar, 2004 - No. 5, July, 2004 ($2.95)

1-5-Mike San Giacomo-s/Mitchell Breitweiser-a. 4-Initial printings with errors exist 3.00
The Collected Edition (Speakeasy Comics, 2005, $17.99) r/series; Bendis intro 18.00

PHANTOM LADY (1st Series) (My Love Secret #24 on) (Also see All Top, Daring Adventures, Freedom Fighters, Jungle Thrills, & Wonder Boy)
Fox Features Syndicate: No. 13, Aug, 1947 - No. 23, Apr, 1949

13(#1)-Phantom Lady by Matt Baker begins (see Police Comics #1 for 1st app.); Blue Beetle story 432 864 1296 3154 5577 8000
14-16: 14(#2)-Not Baker-c. 15-P.L. injected with experimental drug. 16-Negligee-c, panels; true crime stories begin 290 580 870 1856 3178 4500
17-Classic bondage cover; used in **SOTI**, illo "Sexual stimulation by combining 'headlights' with the sadist's dream of tying up a woman" 865 1730 2595 6315 11,158 16,000
18,19 206 412 618 1318 2259 3200
20-22 177 354 531 1133 1942 2750
23-Classic bondage-c 343 686 1029 2400 4200 6000
NOTE: ***Matt Baker** a-in all; c-13, 15-21. **Kamen** a-22, 23.*

PHANTOM LADY (2nd Series) (See Terrific Comics) (Formerly Linda)
Ajax/Farrell Publ.: V1#5, Dec-Jan, 1954/1955 - No. 4, June, 1955

V1#5(#1)-By Matt Baker 132 264 396 845 1448 2050
V1#2-Last pre-code 95 190 285 608 1042 1475
3,4-Red Rocket. 3-Heroin story 76 152 228 486 831 1175

PHANTOM LADY
Verotik Publications: 1994 ($9.95)

1-Reprints G. A. stories from Phantom Lady and All Top Comics; Adam Hughes-c 12.00

PHANTOM LADY
DC Comics: Oct, 2012 - No. 4, Jan, 2013 ($2.99, limited series)

1-4-Gray and Palmiotti-s/Staggs-a. 1-Re-intro with Doll Man; Conner-c 3.00

PHANTOM PLANET, THE
Dell Publishing Co.: No. 1234, 1961

Four Color 1234-Movie 6 12 18 40 73 105

PHANTOM STRANGER, THE (1st Series)(See Saga of Swamp Thing)
National Periodical Publications: Aug-Sept, 1952 - No. 6, June-July, 1953

1(Scarce)-1st app. 226 452 678 1446 2473 3500
2 (Scarce) 123 246 369 787 1344 1900
3-6 (Scarce) 110 220 330 704 1202 1700
Ashcan (8,9/52) Not distributed to newsstands, only for in house use (no known sales)

PHANTOM STRANGER, THE (2nd Series) (See Showcase #80) (See Showcase Presents for B&W reprints)
National Periodical Publs.: May-June, 1969 - No. 41, Feb-Mar, 1976; No. 42, Mar, 2010

1-2nd S.A. app. P. Stranger; only 12¢ issue 10 20 30 69 147 225
2,3 6 12 18 38 69 100
4-1st new look Phantom Stranger; N. Adams-a 6 12 18 41 76 110
5-7 5 10 15 31 53 75
8-14: 14-Last 15¢ issue 4 8 12 23 37 50
15-19: All 25¢ giants (52 pgs.) 4 8 12 25 40 55
20-Dark Circle begins, ends #24. 3 6 9 16 24 32
21,22 3 6 9 14 20 25
23-Spawn of Frankenstein begins by Kaluta 4 8 12 25 40 55
24,25,27-30-Last Spawn of Frankenstein 3 6 9 19 30 40

	GD	VG	FN	VF	VF/NM	NM-
	2.0	4.0	6.0	8.0	9.0	9.2

26- Book-length story featuring Phantom Stranger, Dr. 13 & Spawn of Frankenstein 3 6 9 21 33 45
31-The Black Orchid begins (6-7/74). 3 6 9 18 28 38
32,34-38: 34-Last 20¢ issue (#35 on are 25¢) 2 4 6 13 18 22
33,39-41: 33-Deadman-c/story. 39-41-Deadman app. 3 6 9 14 20 25
42-(3/10, $2.99) Blackest Night one-shot; Syaf-a; Spectre, Deadman and Blue Devil app. 3.00
NOTE: ***N. Adams** a-4; c-3-19. **Anderson** a-4, 5i. **Aparo** a-7-17, 19-26; c-20-24, 33-41. **B. Bailey** a-27-30. **DeZuniga** a-12-16, 18, 19, 21, 22, 31, 34. **Grell** a-33. **Kaluta** a-23-25; c-26. **Meskin** r-15, 16, 18, 19. **Redondo** a-32, 35, 36. **Sparling** a-20. **Starr** a-17r. **Toth** a-15r. Black Orchid by **Carrilo**-38-41. Dr. 13 solo in-13, 18, 19, 20, 21, 34. Frankenstein by **Kaluta**-23-25; by **Baily**-27-30. No Black Orchid-33, 34, 37.*

PHANTOM STRANGER (See Justice League of America #103)
DC Comics: Oct, 1987 - No. 4, Jan, 1988 (75¢, limited series)

1-4-Mignola/Russell-c/a & Eclipso app. in all. 3,4-Eclipso-c 5.00

PHANTOM STRANGER (See intro. in DC Comics - The New 52 FCBD Special Edition)
DC Comics: No. 0, Nov, 2012 - Present ($2.99)

0-18: 0-Origin retold; Spectre app.; DiDio-s/Anderson-a. 2-Pandora app. 4,5-Jae Lee-c; Justice League Dark app. 6,7-Gene Ha-a/c; The Question app. 11-Trinity War. 12-17-Forever Evil tie-in. 18-Superman app. 3.00

PHANTOM STRANGER (See Vertigo Visions-The Phantom Stranger)

PHANTOM: THE GHOST WHO WALKS
Marvel Comics: Feb, 1995 - No. 3, Apr, 1995 ($2.95, limited series)

1-3 4.00

PHANTOM: THE GHOST WHO WALKS
Moonstone: 2003 ($16.95, TPB)

nn-Three new stories by Raab, Goulart, Collins, Blanco and others; Klauba painted-c 17.00

PHANTOM 2040 (TV cartoon)
Marvel Comics: May, 1995 - No. 4, Aug, 1995 ($1.50)

1-4-Based on animated series; Ditko-a(p) in all 4.00

PHANTOM WITCH DOCTOR (Also see Durango Kid #8 & Eerie #8)
Avon Periodicals: 1952

1-Kinstler-c/a (7 pgs.) 52 104 156 328 552 775

PHANTOM ZONE, THE (See Adventure #283 & Superboy #100, 104)
DC Comics: January, 1982 - No. 4, April, 1982

1-4-Superman app. in all. 2-4: Batman, Green Lantern app. 4.00
NOTE: ***Colan** a-1-4p; c-1-4p. **Giordano** c-1-4i.*

PHAZE
Eclipse Comics: Apr, 1988 - No. 2, Oct, 1988 ($2.25)

1,2: 1-Sienkiewicz-c. 2-Gulacy painted-c 3.00

PHIL RIZZUTO (Baseball Hero)(See Sport Thrills, Accepted reprint)
Fawcett Publications: 1951 (New York Yankees)

nn-Photo-c 71 142 213 454 777 1100

PHOENIX
Atlas/Seaboard Publ.: Jan, 1975 - No. 4, Oct, 1975

1-Origin; Rovin-s/Amendola-a 2 4 6 11 16 20
2-4: 3-Origin & only app. The Dark Avenger. 4-New origin/costume The Protector (formerly Phoenix) 2 4 6 9 13 16
NOTE: ***Infantino** appears in #1, 2. **Austin** a-3i. **Thorne** c-3.*

PHOENIX
Ardden Entertainment (Atlas Comics): Mar, 2011 - No. 6, May, 2012 ($2.99)

1-6-Krueger & Deneen-s/Zachary-a; origin re-told 3.00
... Issue Zero - NY Comicon Edtion (10/10, $2.99) Dorien-a; origin prequel to #1 3.00

PHOENIX (...The Untold Story)
Marvel Comics Group: April, 1984 ($2.00, one-shot)

1-Byrne/Austin-r/X-Men #137 with original unpublished ending 2 4 6 8 10 12

PHOENIX RESURRECTION, THE
Malibu Comics (Ultraverse): 1995 - 1996 ($3.95)

Genesis #1 (12/95)-X-Men app; wraparound-c, Revelations #1 (12/95)-X-Men app; wraparound-c, Aftermath #1 (1/96)-X-Men app. 5.00
0-($1.95)-r/series 3.00
0-American Entertainment Ed. 4.00

PHOENIX WITHOUT ASHES
IDW Publishing: Aug, 2010 - No. 4, Nov, 2010 ($3.99, limited series)

1-4-Harlan Ellison-s/Alan Robinson-a 4.00

PICNIC PARTY (See Dell Giants)

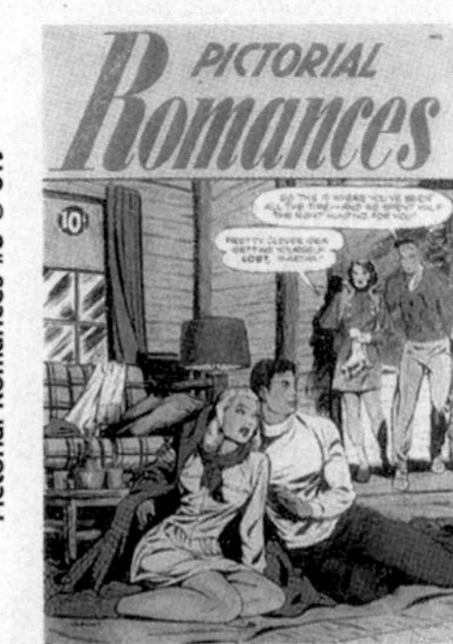

Pictorial Romances #5 © STJ

Picture Parade #1 © GIL

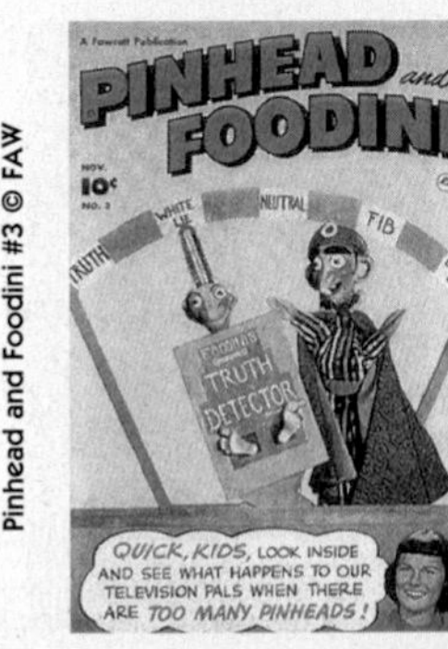

Pinhead and Foodini #3 © FAW

	GD 2.0	VG 4.0	FN 6.0	VF 8.0	VF/NM 9.0	NM- 9.2

PICTORIAL CONFESSIONS (Pictorial Romances #4 on)
St. John Publishing Co.: Sept, 1949 - No. 3, Dec, 1949

1-Baker-c/a(3) 55 110 165 352 601 850
2-Baker-a; photo-c 34 68 102 199 325 450
3-Kubert, Baker-a; part Kubert-c 36 72 108 211 343 475

PICTORIAL LOVE STORIES (Formerly Tim McCoy)
Charlton Comics: No. 22, Oct, 1949 - No. 26, July, 1950 (all photo-c)

22-26: All have "Me-Dan Cupid". 25-Fred Astaire-c 20 40 60 117 189 260

PICTORIAL LOVE STORIES
St. John Publishing Co.: October, 1952

1-Baker-c 36 72 108 216 351 485

PICTORIAL ROMANCES (Formerly Pictorial Confessions)
St. John Publ. Co.: No. 4, Jan, 1950; No. 5, Jan, 1951 - No. 24, Mar, 1954

4-Baker-a; photo-c 39 78 117 231 378 525
5,10-All Matt Baker issues. 5-Reprints all stories from #4 w/new Baker-c 37 74 111 222 361 500
6-9,12,13,15,16-Baker-c, 2-3 stories 36 72 108 211 343 475
11-Baker-c/a(3); Kubert-r/Hollywood Confessions #1 37 74 111 222 361 500
14,21-24: Baker-c/a each. 21,24-Each has signed story by Estrada 36 72 108 211 343 475
17-20(7/53, 25¢, 100 pgs.): Baker-c/a; each has two signed stories by Estrada 55 110 165 352 601 850

NOTE: ***Matt Baker*** *art in most issues.* ***Estrada*** *a-17-20(2), 21, 24.*

PICTURE CRIMES
David McKay Publ.: June, 1937

1 (a GD+ copy sold in 2012 for $478)

PICTURE NEWS
Lafayette Street Corp.: Jan, 1946 - No. 10, Jan-Feb, 1947

1-Milt Gross begins, ends No. 6; 4 pg. Kirby-a; A-Bomb-c/story 46 92 138 290 488 685
2-Atomic explosion panels; Frank Sinatra/Perry Como story 24 48 72 142 234 325
3-Atomic explosion panels; Frank Sinatra, June Allyson, Benny Goodman stories 21 42 63 126 206 285
4-Atomic explosion panels; "Caesar and Cleopatra" movie adapt. w/Claude Raines & Vivian Leigh; Jackie Robinson story 24 48 72 140 230 320
5-7: 5-Hank Greenberg story; Atomic explosion panel. 6-Joe Louis-c/story 19 38 57 109 172 235
8,10: 8-Monte Hale story (9-10/46; 1st?). 10-Dick Quick; A-Bomb story; Krigstein, Gross-a 19 38 57 112 179 245
9-A-Bomb story; "Crooked Mile" movie adaptation; Joe DiMaggio story. 21 42 63 122 199 275

PICTURE PARADE (Picture Progress #5 on)
Gilberton Company (Also see A Christmas Adventure): Sept, 1953 - V1#4, Dec, 1953 (28 pgs.)

V1#1-Andy's Atomic Adventures; A-bomb blast-c; (Teachers version distributed to schools exists) 20 40 60 114 182 250
2-Around the World with the United Nations 12 24 36 69 97 125
3-Adventures of the Lost One(The American Indian), 4-A Christmas Adventure (r-under same title in 1969) 12 24 36 69 97 125

PICTURE PROGRESS (Formerly Picture Parade)
Gilberton Corp.: V1#5, Jan, 1954 - V3#2, Oct, 1955 (28-36 pgs.)

V1#5-9,V2#1-9: 5-News in Review 1953. 6-The Birth of America. 7-The Four Seasons. 8-Paul Revere's Ride. 9-The Hawaiian Islands(5/54). V2#1-The Story of Flight(9/54). 2-Vote for Crazy River (The Meaning of Elections). 3-Louis Pasteur. 4-The Star Spangled Banner. 5-News in Review 1954. 6-Alaska: The Great Land. 7-Life in the Circus. 8-The Time of the Cave Man. 9-Summer Fun(5/55) 9 18 27 50 65 80
V3#1,2: 1-The Man Who Discovered America. 2-The Lewis & Clark Expedition 9 18 27 47 61 75

PICTURE SCOPE JUNGLE ADVENTURES (See Jungle Thrills)

PICTURE STORIES FROM AMERICAN HISTORY
National/All-American/E. C. Comics: 1945 - No. 4, Sum, 1947 (#1,2: 10¢, 56 pgs.; #3,4: 15¢, 52 pgs.)

1 30 60 90 177 289 400
2-4 24 48 72 140 230 320

PICTURE STORIES FROM SCIENCE
E.C. Comics: Spring, 1947 - No. 2, Fall, 1947

1-(15¢) 30 60 90 177 289 400
2-(10¢) 24 48 72 140 230 320

PICTURE STORIES FROM THE BIBLE (See Narrative Illustration, the Story of the Comics by M.C. Gaines)
National/All-American/E.C. Comics: 1942 - No. 4, Fall, 1943; 1944-46

1-4('42-Fall, '43)-Old Testament (DC) 24 48 72 142 234 325
Complete Old Testament Edition, (12/43-DC, 50¢, 232 pgs.);-1st printing; contains #1-4; 2nd - 8th (1/47) printings exist; later printings by E.C. some with 65¢-c 32 64 96 192 314 435
Complete Old Testament Edition (1945-publ. by Bible Pictures Ltd.)-232 pgs., hardbound, in color with dust jacket 32 64 96 192 314 435

NOTE: *Both Old and New Testaments published in England by Bible Pictures Ltd. in hardback, 1943, in color, 376 pgs. (2 vols.: O.T. 232 pgs. & N.T. 144 pgs.), and were also published by Scarf Press in 1979 (Old Test., $9.95) and in 1980 (New Test., $7.95)*

1-3(New Test.; 1944-46, DC)-52 pgs. ea. 20 40 60 114 182 250
The Complete Life of Christ Edition (1945, 25¢, 96 pgs.)-Contains #1&2 of the New Testament Edition 32 64 96 192 314 435
1,2(Old Testament-r in comic book form)(E.C., 1946; 52 pgs.) 20 40 60 114 182 250
1(DC),2(AA),3(EC)(New Testament-r in comic book form)(E.C., 1946; 52 pgs.) 20 40 60 114 182 250
Complete New Testament Edition (1945-E.C., 40¢, 144 pgs.)-Contains #1-3 1946 printing has 50¢-c 32 64 96 192 314 435

NOTE: *Another British series entitled* ***The Bible Illustrated*** *from 1947 has recently been discovered, with the same internal artwork. This eight edition series (5-OT, 3-NT) is of particular interest to Classics Ill. collectors because it exactly copied the C.I. logo format. The British publisher was Thorpe & Porter, who in 1951 began publishing the British Classics Ill. series. All editions of The Bible Ill. have new British painted covers. While this market is still new, and not all editions have as yet been found, current market value is about the same as the first U.S. editions of Picture Stories From The Bible.*

PICTURE STORIES FROM WORLD HISTORY
E.C. Comics: Spring, 1947 - No. 2, Summer, 1947 (52, 48 pgs.)

1-(15¢) 30 60 90 177 289 400
2-(10¢) 24 48 72 140 230 320

PIGS
Image Comics: Sept, 2011 - No. 8, Aug, 2012 ($2.99)

1-8: 1-Cosby & McCool-s/Tamura-a/Jock-c. 3-Conner-c. 5-Gibbons-c. 7-Ramos-c 3.00

PILGRIM, THE
IDW Publishing: 2010 - Present ($3.99, limited series)

1,2-Mike Grell-a/c; Mark Ryan-s 4.00

PILOT SEASON...
Image Comics (Top Cow): 2008 - Present ($1.00/$2.99/$3.99, one-shots)

...: Asset (9/10, $3.99) Sablik-s/Marquez-a/Frison-c 4.00
...: City of Refuge (10/11, $3.99) Foehl-s/Calero-a/c 4.00
...: Crosshair (10/10, $3.99) Katz-s/Jefferson-a/Silvestri-c 4.00
...: Declassified (10/09, $1.00) Preview of one-shots with covers, script and sketch pgs. 3.00
...: Demonic (1/10, $2.99) Kirkman-s/Benitez-a; two covers by Silvestri 3.00
...: Fleshdigger (10/11, $3.99) Denton & Keene-s; Sanchez-a; Francavilla-c 4.00
...: Forever (10/10, $3.99) Inglesby-s/Nachlik-a/Hutomo-c 4.00
...: Murdered (11/09, $2.99) Kirkman-s/Blake-a; two covers by Silvestri 3.00
...: 7 Days From Hell (10/10, $3.99) Noto-a/Hill & Levin-s/Stelfreeze-c 4.00
...: Stellar (7/10, $2.99) Kirkman-s/Chang-a/Silvestri-c 3.00
...: The Beauty (10/11, $3.99) Haun & Hurley-s/Haun-a/c 4.00
...: The Test (10/10, $3.99) Fialkov-s/Ekedal-a/Hutomo-c 4.00
...: 39 Minutes (9/10, $3.99) Harms-s/Lando-a/Albuquerque-c 4.00
...: Twilight Guardian (5/08, $3.99) Hickman-s 4.00

PINHEAD
Marvel Comics (Epic Comics): Dec, 1993 - No. 6, May, 1994 ($2.50)

1-($2.95)-Embossed foil-c by Kelley Jones; Intro Pinhead & Disciples (Snakeoil, Hangman, Fan Dancer & Dixie) 4.00
2-6 3.00

PINHEAD & FOODINI (TV)(Also see Foodini & Jingle Dingle Christmas...)
Fawcett Publications: July, 1951 - No. 4, Jan, 1952 (Early TV comic)

1-(52 pgs.)-Photo-c; based on TV puppet show 32 64 96 188 307 425
2,3-Photo-c 16 32 48 94 147 200
4 14 28 42 80 115 150

PINHEAD VS. MARSHALL LAW (Law in Hell)
Marvel Comics (Epic): Nov, 1993 - No. 2, Dec, 1993 ($2.95, lim. series)

1,2: 1-Embossed red foil-c. 2-Embossed silver foil-c 4.00

PINK DUST

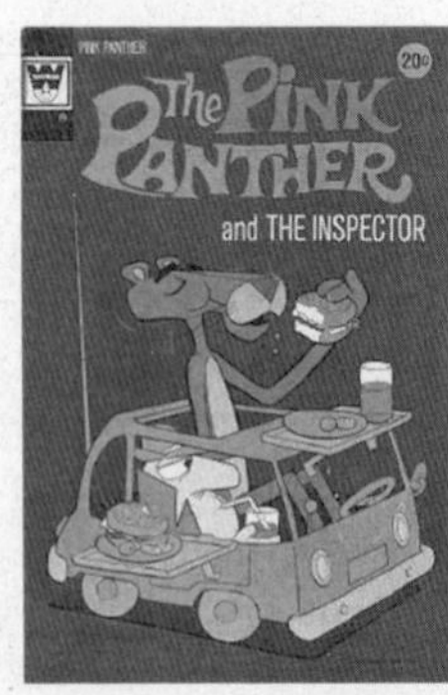

Pink Panther #13 © GK

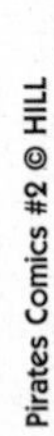

Pirates Comics #2 © HILL

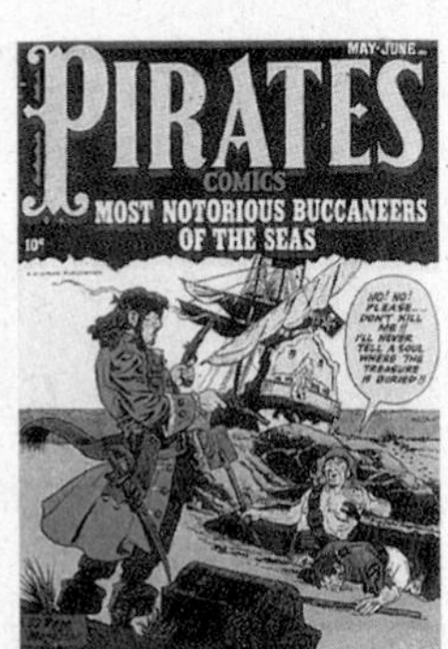

Pitt #14 © Dale Keown

Kitchen Sink Press: 1998 ($3.50, B&W, mature)

	GD 2.0	VG 4.0	FN 6.0	VF 8.0	VF/NM 9.0	NM- 9.2
1-J. O'Barr-s/a						3.50

PINK PANTHER, THE (TV)(See The Inspector & Kite Fun Book)
Gold Key #1-70/Whitman #71-87: April, 1971 - No. 87, Mar, 1984

	GD 2.0	VG 4.0	FN 6.0	VF 8.0	VF/NM 9.0	NM- 9.2
1-The Inspector begins	5	10	15	31	53	75
2-5	3	6	9	17	26	35
6-10	3	6	9	14	19	24
11-30: Warren Tufts-a #16-on	2	4	6	9	13	16
31-60	2	4	6	8	11	14
61-70	1	2	3	5	7	9
71-74,81-83: 81(2/82), 82(3/82), 83(4/82)	2	4	6	8	10	12
75(8/80)-77 (Whitman pre-pack) (scarce)	3	6	9	21	33	45
78(1/81)-80 (Whitman pre-pack) (not as scarce)	2	4	6	10	14	18
78 (1/81, 40¢-c) Cover price error variant	3	6	9	14	20	26
84-87(All #90266 on-c, no date or date code): 84(6/83), 85(8/83), 87(3/84)	3	6	9	14	20	26
Mini-comic No. 1(1976)(3-1/4x6-1/2")	1	3	4	6	8	10

NOTE: *Pink Panther began as a movie cartoon. (See Golden Comics Digest #38, 45 and March of Comics #376, 384, 390, 409, 418, 429, 441, 449, 461, 473, 486); #37, 72, 80-85 contain reprints.*

PINK PANTHER SUPER SPECIAL (TV)
Harvey Comics: Oct, 1993 ($2.25, 68 pgs.)

	GD 2.0	VG 4.0	FN 6.0	VF 8.0	VF/NM 9.0	NM- 9.2
V2#1-The Inspector & Wendy Witch stories also						4.00

PINK PANTHER, THE
Harvey Comics: Nov, 1993 - No. 9, July, 1994 ($1.50)

	GD 2.0	VG 4.0	FN 6.0	VF 8.0	VF/NM 9.0	NM- 9.2
V2#1-9						3.00

PINKY & THE BRAIN (See Animaniacs)
DC Comics: July, 1996 - No. 27, Nov, 1998 ($1.75/$1.95/$1.99)

	GD 2.0	VG 4.0	FN 6.0	VF 8.0	VF/NM 9.0	NM- 9.2
1-27, ...Christmas Special (1/96, $1.50)						3.00

PINKY LEE (See Adventures of...)

PINKY THE EGGHEAD
I.W./Super Comics: 1963 (Reprints from Noodnik)

	GD 2.0	VG 4.0	FN 6.0	VF 8.0	VF/NM 9.0	NM- 9.2
I.W. Reprint #1,2(nd)	2	4	6	8	11	14
Super Reprint #14-r/Noodnik Comics #4	2	4	6	8	11	14

PINOCCHIO (See 4-Color #92, 252, 545, 1203, Mickey Mouse Mag. V5#3, Movie Comics under Wonderful Advs. of..., New Advs. of..., Thrilling Comics #2, Walt Disney Showcase, Walt Disney's..., Wonderful Advs. of..., & World's Greatest Stories #2)
Dell Publishing Co.: No. 92, 1945 - No. 1203, Mar, 1962 (Disney)

	GD 2.0	VG 4.0	FN 6.0	VF 8.0	VF/NM 9.0	NM- 9.2
Four Color 92-The Wonderful Adventures of...; 16 pg. Donald Duck story ; entire book by Kelly	46	92	138	340	770	1200
Four Color 252 (10/49)-Origin, not by Kelly	10	20	30	66	138	210
Four Color 545 (3/54)-The Wonderful Advs. of...; part-r of 4-Color #92; Disney-movie	7	14	21	44	82	120
Four Color 1203 (3/62)	5	10	15	35	63	90

PINOCCHIO AND THE EMPEROR OF THE NIGHT
Marvel Comics: Mar, 1988 ($1.25, 52 pgs.)

	GD 2.0	VG 4.0	FN 6.0	VF 8.0	VF/NM 9.0	NM- 9.2
1-Adapts film						4.00

PINOCCHIO LEARNS ABOUT KITES (See Kite Fun Book)

PIN-UP PETE (Also see Great Lover Romances & Monty Hall...)
Toby Press: 1952

	GD 2.0	VG 4.0	FN 6.0	VF 8.0	VF/NM 9.0	NM- 9.2
1-Jack Sparling pin-ups	20	40	60	114	182	250

PIONEER MARSHAL (See Fawcett Movie Comics)

PIONEER PICTURE STORIES
Street & Smith Publications: Dec, 1941 - No. 9, Dec, 1943

	GD 2.0	VG 4.0	FN 6.0	VF 8.0	VF/NM 9.0	NM- 9.2
1-The Legless Air Ace begins; WWII-c	43	86	129	271	461	650
2 -True life story of Errol Flynn	21	42	63	122	199	275
3-5,7-9	18	36	54	103	162	220
6-Classic Japanese WWII "Remember Pearl Harbor"-c	37	74	111	222	361	500

PIONEER WEST ROMANCES (Firehair #1,2,7-11)
Fiction House Magazines: No. 3, Spring, 1950 - No. 6, Winter, 1950-51

	GD 2.0	VG 4.0	FN 6.0	VF 8.0	VF/NM 9.0	NM- 9.2
3-(52 pgs.)-Firehair continues	30	60	90	240	383	525
4-6	19	38	57	109	172	235

PIPSQUEAK (See The Adventures of...)

PIRACY
E. C. Comics: Oct-Nov, 1954 - No. 7, Oct-Nov, 1955

	GD 2.0	VG 4.0	FN 6.0	VF 8.0	VF/NM 9.0	NM- 9.2
1-Williamson/Torres-a	29	58	87	232	366	500
2-Williamson/Torres-a	19	38	57	152	239	325
3-7: 5-7-Comics Code symbol on cover	15	30	45	120	190	260

NOTE: *Crandall a-in all; c-2-4.* ***Davis*** *a-1, 2, 6.* ***Evans*** *a-3-7; c-7.* ***Ingels*** *a-3-7.* ***Krigstein*** *a-3-5, 7; c-5, 6.* ***Wood*** *a-1, 2; c-1.*

PIRACY
Gemstone Publishing: March, 1998 - No. 7, Sept, 1998 ($2.50)

	GD 2.0	VG 4.0	FN 6.0	VF 8.0	VF/NM 9.0	NM- 9.2
1-7: E.C. reprints						4.00
Annual 1 ($10.95) Collects #1-4						11.00
Annual 2 ($7.95) Collects #5-7						8.00

PIRANA (See The Phantom #46 & Thrill-O-Rama #2, 3)

PIRATE CORP$, THE (See Hectic Planet)
Eternity Comics/Slave Labor Graphics: 1987 - No. 4, 1988 ($1.95)

	GD 2.0	VG 4.0	FN 6.0	VF 8.0	VF/NM 9.0	NM- 9.2
1-4: 1,2-Color. 3,4-B&W						3.00
Special 1 ('89, B&W)-Slave Labor Publ.						3.00

PIRATE CORP$, THE (Volume 2)
Slave Labor Graphics: 1989 - No. 6, 1992 ($1.95)

	GD 2.0	VG 4.0	FN 6.0	VF 8.0	VF/NM 9.0	NM- 9.2
1-6-Dorkin-s/a						3.00

PIRATE OF THE GULF, THE (See Superior Stories #2)

PIRATES COMICS
Hillman Periodicals: Feb-Mar, 1950 - No. 4, Aug-Sept, 1950 (All 52 pgs.)

	GD 2.0	VG 4.0	FN 6.0	VF 8.0	VF/NM 9.0	NM- 9.2
1	24	48	72	142	234	325
2-Dave Berg-a	17	34	51	98	154	210
3,4-Berg-a	15	30	45	88	137	185

PIRATES OF CONEY ISLAND, THE
Image Comics: Oct, 2006 - No. 8 ($2.99)

	GD 2.0	VG 4.0	FN 6.0	VF 8.0	VF/NM 9.0	NM- 9.2
1-6-Rick Spears-s/Vasilis Lolos-a; two covers. 2-Cloonan var-c						3.00

PIRATES OF DARK WATER, THE (Hanna Barbera)
Marvel Comics: Nov, 1991 - No. 9, Aug, 1992 ($1.95)

	GD 2.0	VG 4.0	FN 6.0	VF 8.0	VF/NM 9.0	NM- 9.2
1-9: 9-Vess-c						3.00

P.I.'S: MICHAEL MAUSER AND MS. TREE, THE
First Comics: Jan, 1985 - No. 3, May, 1985 ($1.25, limited series)

	GD 2.0	VG 4.0	FN 6.0	VF 8.0	VF/NM 9.0	NM- 9.2
1-3: Staton-c/a(p)						3.00

PITT, THE (Also see The Draft & The War)
Marvel Comics: Mar, 1988 ($3.25, 52 pgs., one-shot)

	GD 2.0	VG 4.0	FN 6.0	VF 8.0	VF/NM 9.0	NM- 9.2
1-Ties into Starbrand, D.P.7						4.00

PITT (See Youngblood #4 & Gen 13 #3,#4)
Image Comics #1-9/Full Bleed #1/2,10-on: Jan, 1993 - No. 20 ($1.95, intended as a four part limited series)

	GD 2.0	VG 4.0	FN 6.0	VF 8.0	VF/NM 9.0	NM- 9.2
1/2-(12/95)-1st Full Bleed issue						4.00
1-Dale Keown-c/a. 1-1st app. The Pitt						5.00
2-13: All Dale Keown-c/a. 3 (Low distribution). 10 (1/96)-Indicia reads "January 1995"						3.00
14-20: 14-Begin $2.50-c, pullout poster						3.00
TPB-(1997, $9.95) r/#1/2, 1-4						12.00
TPB 2-(1999, $11.95) r/#5-9						12.00

PITT CREW
Full Bleed Studios: Aug, 1998 - No. 5, Dec, 1999 ($2.50)

	GD 2.0	VG 4.0	FN 6.0	VF 8.0	VF/NM 9.0	NM- 9.2
1-5: 1-Richard Pace-s/Ken Lashley-a. 2-4-Scott Lee-a						3.00

PITT IN THE BLOOD
Full Bleed Studios: Aug, 1996 ($2.50, one-shot)

	GD 2.0	VG 4.0	FN 6.0	VF 8.0	VF/NM 9.0	NM- 9.2
nn-Richard Pace-a/script						3.00

PIXIE & DIXIE & MR. JINKS (TV)(See Jinks, Pixie, and Dixie & Whitman Comic Books)
Dell Publishing Co./Gold Key: July-Sept, 1960 - Feb, 1963 (Hanna-Barbera)

	GD 2.0	VG 4.0	FN 6.0	VF 8.0	VF/NM 9.0	NM- 9.2
Four Color 1112	7	14	21	44	82	120
Four Color 1196,1264, 01-631-207 (Dell, 7/62)	5	10	15	34	60	85
1(2/63-Gold Key)	6	12	18	37	66	95

PIXIE PUZZLE ROCKET TO ADVENTURELAND
Avon Periodicals: Nov, 1952

	GD 2.0	VG 4.0	FN 6.0	VF 8.0	VF/NM 9.0	NM- 9.2
1	17	34	51	98	154	210

PIXIES, THE (Advs. of...)(The Mighty Atom and ...#6 on)(See A-1 Comics #16)
Magazine Enterprises: Winter, 1946 - No. 4, Fall?, 1947; No. 5, 1948

	GD 2.0	VG 4.0	FN 6.0	VF 8.0	VF/NM 9.0	NM- 9.2
1-Mighty Atom	10	20	30	54	72	90
2-5-Mighty Atom	6	12	18	31	38	45
I.W. Reprint #1(1958), 8-(Pee-Wee Pixies), 10-I.W. on cover, Super on inside	2	4	6	8	11	14

Planetary #14 © WSP

Planet Comics #31 © FH

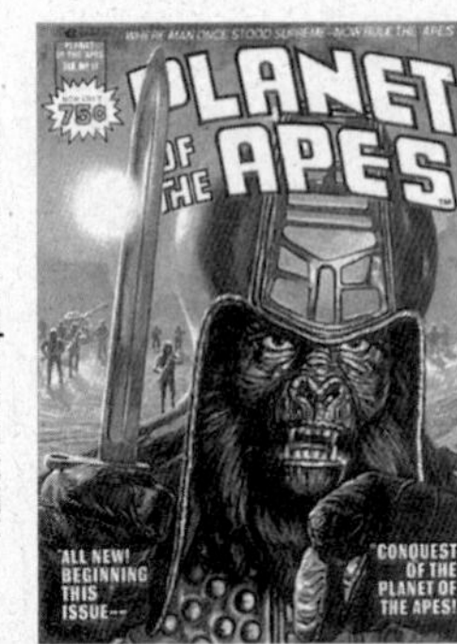

Planet of the Apes #17 © MAR

	GD 2.0	VG 4.0	FN 6.0	VF 8.0	VF/NM 9.0	NM- 9.2

PIZZAZZ
Marvel Comics: Oct, 1977 - No. 16, Jan, 1979 (slick-color kids mag. w/puzzles, games, comics)

	GD	VG	FN	VF	VF/NM	NM-
1-Star Wars photo-c/article; origin Tarzan; KISS photos/article; Iron-On bonus; 2 pg. pin-up calendars thru #8	3	6	9	19	30	40
2-Spider-Man-c; Beatles pin-up calendar	2	4	6	13	18	22
3-8: 3-Close Encounters-s; Bradbury-s. 4-Alice Cooper, Travolta; Charlie's Angels/Fonz/Hulk/Spider-Man-c. 5-Star Trek quiz. 6-Asimov-s. 7-James Bond; Spock/Darth Vader-c. 8-TV Spider-Man photo-c/article	2	4	6	11	16	20
9-14: 9-Shaun Cassidy-c. 10-Sgt. Pepper-c/s. 12-Battlestar Galactica-s; Spider-Man app. 13-TV Hulk-c/s. 14-Meatloaf-c/s	2	4	6	10	14	18
15,16: 15-Battlestar Galactica-s. 16-Movie Superman photo-c/s, Hulk.	2	4	6	11	16	20

NOTE: ***Star Wars** comics in all (1-6:Chaykin-a, 7-9: DeZuniga-a, 10-13:Simonson/Janson-a. 14-16:Cockrum-a). **Tarzan** comics, 1pg.-#1-8. 1pg. "Hey Look" by Kurtzman #12-16.*

PLANETARY (See Preview in flip book Gen13 #33)
DC Comics (WildStorm Prod.): Apr, 1999 - No. 27, Dec, 2009 ($2.50/$2.95/$2.99)

	GD	VG	FN	VF	VF/NM	NM-
1-Ellis-s/Cassaday-a/c	2	4	6	8	10	12
1-Special Edition (6/09, $1.00) r/#1 with "After Watchmen" cover frame						3.00
2-5						6.00
6-10						5.00
11-15: 12-Fourth Man revealed						4.00
16-26: 16-Begin $2.95-c. 23-Origin of The Drummer						3.00
27-($3.99) Wraparound gatefold-c						4.00
...: All Over the World and Other Stories (2000, $14.95) r/#1-6 & Preview						15.00
...: All Over the World and Other Stories-Hardcover (2000, $24.95) r/#1-6 & Preview; with dustjacket						25.00
.../Batman: Night on Earth 1 (8/03, $5.95) Ellis-s/Cassaday-a						6.00
...: Crossing Worlds (2004, $14.95) r/Batman, JLA, and The Authority x-overs						15.00
.../JLA: Terra Occulta (11/02, $5.95) Elseworlds; Ellis-s/Ordway-a						6.00
...: Leaving the 20th Century -HC (2004, $24.95) r/#13-18						25.00
...: Leaving the 20th Century -SC (2004, $14.99) r/#13-18						15.00
...: Spacetime Archaeology -HC (2010, $24.99) r/#19-27						25.00
...: Spacetime Archaeology -SC (2010, $17.99) r/#19-27						18.00
.../The Authority: Ruling the World (8/00, $5.95) Ellis-s/Phil Jimenez-a						6.00
...: The Fourth Man -Hardcover (2001, $24.95) r/#7-12						25.00
...: The Planetary Reader (8/03, $5.95) r/#13-15						6.00

PLANETARY BRIGADE (Also see Hero Squared)
Boom Studios: Feb, 2006 - No. 2, Mar, 2006 ($2.99)

	GD	VG	FN	VF	VF/NM	NM-
1-3-Giffen & DeMatteis-s/art by various; Haley-c						3.00
... Origins 1-3 (10/06-4/07, $3.99) Giffen & DeMatteis-s/Julia Bax-a						4.00

PLANET COMICS
Fiction House Magazines: 1/40 - No. 62, 9/49; No. 63, Wint, 1949-50; No. 64, Spring, 1950; No. 65, 1951(nd); No. 66-68, 1952(nd); No. 69, Wint, 1952-53; No. 70-72, 1953(nd); No. 73, Winter, 1953-54

	GD	VG	FN	VF	VF/NM	NM-
1-Origin Auro, Lord of Jupiter by Briefer (ends #61); Flint Baker & The Red Comet begin; Eisner/Fine-c	1275	2550	3825	9500	17,750	26,000
2-Lou Fine-c (Scarce)	486	972	1458	3550	6275	9000
3-Eisner-c	354	708	1062	2478	4339	6200
4-Gale Allen and the Girl Squadron begins	300	600	900	2070	3635	5200
5,6-(Scarce): 5-Eisner/Fine-c	303	606	909	2121	3711	5300
7-12: 8-Robot-c. 12-The Star Pirate begins	245	490	735	1568	2684	3800
13,14: 13-Reff Ryan begins	181	362	543	1158	1979	2800
15-(Scarce)-Mars, God of War begins (11/41); see Jumbo Comics #31 for 1st app.	371	742	1113	2600	4550	6500
16-20,22	158	316	474	1011	1731	2450
21-The Lost World & Hunt Bowman begin	165	330	495	1056	1803	2550
23-26: 26-Space Rangers begin (9/43), end #71	139	278	417	883	1517	2150
27-30	110	220	330	704	1202	1700
31-35: 33-Origin Star Pirates Wonder Boots, reprinted in #52. 35-Mysta of the Moon begins, ends #62	97	194	291	621	1061	1500
36-45: 38-1st Mysta of the Moon-c. 41-New origin of "Auro, Lord of Jupiter". 42-Last Gale Allen. 43-Futura begins	89	178	267	565	970	1375
46-60: 48-Robot-c. 53-Used in **SOTI**, pg. 32	73	146	219	467	796	1125
61-68,70: 64,70-Robot-c. 65-70-All partial-r of earlier issues. 70-r/stories from #41	54	108	162	348	594	840
69-Used in **POP**, pgs. 101,102	55	110	165	352	601	850
71-73-No series stories. 71-Space Rangers strip	43	86	129	271	461	650
I.W. Reprint 1,8,9: 1(nd)-r/#70; cover-r from Attack on Planet Mars. 8 (r/#72), 9-r/#73	8	16	24	51	96	140

NOTE: ***Anderson** a-33-38, 40-51 (Star Pirate). **Matt Baker** a-53-59 (Mysta of the Moon). **Celardo** c-12. **Bill Discount** a-71 (Space Rangers). **Elias** c-70. **Evans** a-46-49 (Auro, Lord of Jupiter), 50-64 (Lost World). **Fine** c-2, 5. **Hopper** a-31, 35 (Gale Allen), 41, 42, 48, 49 (Mysta of the Moon). **Ingels** a-24-31 (Lost World), 56-61 (Auro, Lord of Jupiter). **Lubbers** a-44-47 (Space Rangers); c-40, 41. **Moreira** a-43, 44 (Mysta of the Moon). **Renee** a-40-49 (Lost World); c-33, 35, 39. **Tuska** a-30 (Star Pirate). **M. Whitman** a-50-52 (Mysta of the Moon), 53-58 (Star Pirate); c-71-73. **Starr** a-59. **Zolnerwich** c-10. 13-25. Bondage c-53.*

PLANET COMICS
Pacific Comics: 1984 ($5.95)

	GD	VG	FN	VF	VF/NM	NM-
1-Reprints Planet Comics #1(1940)	1	2	3	5	6	8

PLANET COMICS
Blackthorne Publishing: Apr, 1988 - No. 3 ($2.00, color/B&W #3)

	GD	VG	FN	VF	VF/NM	NM-
1-New stories; Dave Stevens-c	2	4	6	11	16	20
2,3: New stories						6.00

PLANET HULK (See Incredible Hulk and Giant-Size Hulk #1 (2006))

PLANET OF THE APES (Magazine) (Also see Adventures on the... & Power Record Comics)
Marvel Comics Group: Aug, 1974 - No. 29, Feb, 1977 (B&W) (Based on movies)

	GD	VG	FN	VF	VF/NM	NM-
1-Ploog-a	4	8	12	25	40	55
2-Ploog-a	3	6	9	16	24	32
3-10	3	6	9	14	20	26
11-20	3	6	9	15	22	28
21-28 (low distribution)	3	6	9	19	30	40
29 (low distribution)	5	10	15	33	57	80

NOTE: ***Alcala** a-7-11, 17-22, 24. **Ploog** a-1-4, 6, 8, 11, 13, 14, 19. **Sutton** a-11, 12, 15, 17, 19, 20, 23, 24, 29. **Tuska** a-1-6.*

PLANET OF THE APES
Adventure Comics: Apr, 1990 - No. 24, 1992 ($2.50, B&W)

	GD	VG	FN	VF	VF/NM	NM-
1-New movie tie-in; comes w/outer-c (3 colors)						4.00
1-Limited serial numbered edition ($5.00)	1	2	3	5	6	8
1-2nd printing (no outer-c, $2.50)						3.00
2-24						3.00
Annual 1 ($3.50)						4.00
...Urchak's Folly 1-4 ($2.50, mini-series)						3.00

PLANET OF THE APES (The Human War)
Dark Horse Comics: Jun, 2001 - No. 3, Aug, 2001 ($2.99, limited series)

	GD	VG	FN	VF	VF/NM	NM-
1-3-Follows the 2001 movie; Edginton-s						3.00

PLANET OF THE APES
Dark Horse Comics: Sept, 2001 - No. 6, Feb, 2002 ($2.99, ongoing series)

	GD	VG	FN	VF	VF/NM	NM-
1-6: 1-3-Edginton-s. 1-Photo & Wagner covers. 2-Plunkett & photo-c						3.00

PLANET OF THE APES
BOOM! Studios: Apr, 2011 - No. 15, Jun, 2012 ($3.99)

	GD	VG	FN	VF	VF/NM	NM-
1-4,6-15-Takes place 1200 years before Taylor's arrival; Magno-a; three covers						4.00
5-($1.00) Three covers						3.00
Annual 1 (8/12, $4.99) Short stories by various; six covers						5.00
Giant 1 (9/13, $4.99) Gregory-s/Barreto-a						5.00
Special 1 (2/13, $4.99) Continued from #15; Diego Barreto-a						5.00
Spectacular 1 (7/13, $4.99) Gregory-s/Barreto-a						5.00

PLANET OF THE APES: CATACLYSM
BOOM! Studios: Sept, 2012 - No. 12, Aug, 2013 ($3.99)

	GD	VG	FN	VF	VF/NM	NM-
1-12-Takes place 8 years before Taylor's arrival; Couceiro-a. 1-Multiple covers						4.00

PLANET OF VAMPIRES
Seaboard Publications (Atlas): Feb, 1975 - No. 3, July, 1975

	GD	VG	FN	VF	VF/NM	NM-
1-Neal Adams-c(i); 1st Broderick-c/a(p); Hama-s	3	6	9	15	22	28
2,3: 2-Neal Adams-c. 3-Heath-c/a	2	4	6	10	14	18

PLANET TERRY
Marvel Comics (Star Comics)/Marvel: April, 1985 - No. 12, March, 1986 (Children's comic)

	GD	VG	FN	VF	VF/NM	NM-
1-12						5.00
1-Variant with "Star Chase" game on last page & inside back-c						15.00

PLASM (See Warriors of Plasm)
Defiant Comics: June, 1993

	GD	VG	FN	VF	VF/NM	NM-
0-Came bound into Diamond Previews V3#6 (6/93); price is for complete Previews with comic still attached						5.00
0-Comic only removed from Previews						3.00

PLASMER
Marvel Comics UK: Nov, 1993 - No. 4, Feb, 1994 ($1.95, limited series)

	GD	VG	FN	VF	VF/NM	NM-
1-($2.50)-Polybagged w/4 trading cards						4.00
2-4: Capt. America & Silver Surfer app.						3.00

PLASTIC FORKS
Marvel Comis (Epic Comics): 1990 - No. 5, 1990 ($4.95, 68 pgs., limited series, mature)

	GD	VG	FN	VF	VF/NM	NM-
Book 1-5: Squarebound						5.00

Plastic Man #4 © QUA

Plop! #7 © DC

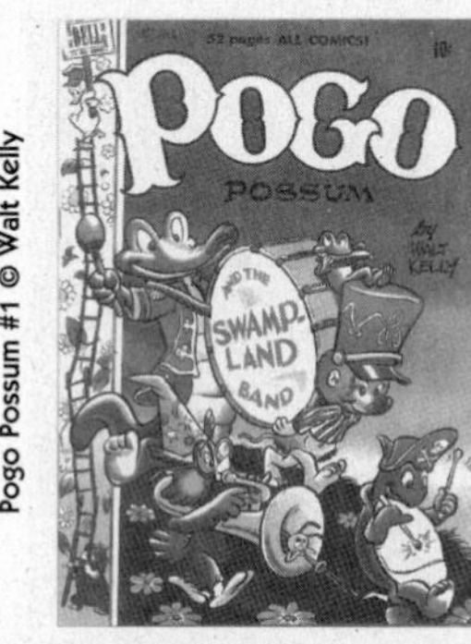

Pogo Possum #1 © Walt Kelly

PLASTIC MAN (Also see Police Comics & Smash Comics #17)
Vital Publ. No. 1,2/Quality Comics No. 3 on: Sum, 1943 - No. 64, Nov, 1956

	GD 2.0	VG 4.0	FN 6.0	VF 8.0	VF/NM 9.0	NM- 9.2
nn(#1)- "In The Game of Death"; Skull-c; Jack Cole-c/a begins; ends-#64?	423	846	1269	3088	5444	7800
nn(#2, 2/44)- "The Gay Nineties Nightmare"	181	362	543	1158	1979	2800
3 (Spr, '46)	118	236	354	749	1287	1825
4 (Sum, '46)	89	178	267	565	970	1375
5 (Aut, '46)	73	146	219	467	796	1125
6-10	60	120	180	381	653	925
11-15,17-20	53	106	159	334	567	800
16-Classic-c	61	122	183	390	670	950
21-30: 26-Last non-r issue?	41	82	123	256	428	600
31-40: 40-Used in POP, pg. 91	34	68	102	199	325	450
41-64: 53-Last precode issue. 54-Robot-c. 64-Sci-fi-c	26	52	78	152	249	345
Super Reprint 11,16,18: 11('63)-r/#16. 16-r/#18 & #21; Cole-a. 18('64)-Spirit-r by Eisner from Police #95	4	8	12	24	37	50

NOTE: *Cole r-44, 49, 56, 58, 59 at least. **Cuidera** c-32-64i.*

PLASTIC MAN (See DC Special #15 & House of Mystery #160)
National Periodical Publications/DC Comics: 11-12/66 - No. 10, 5-6/68; V4#11, 2-3/76 - No. 20, 10-11/77

	GD 2.0	VG 4.0	FN 6.0	VF 8.0	VF/NM 9.0	NM- 9.2
1-Real 1st app. Silver Age Plastic Man (House of Mystery #160 is actually tryout); Gil Kane-c/a; 12¢ issues begin	9	18	27	62	126	190
2-5: 4-Infantino-c; Mortimer-a	5	10	15	31	53	75
6-10('68): 7-G.A. Plastic Man & Woozy Winks (1st S.A. app.) app.; origin retold. 10-Sparling-a; last 12¢ issue	4	8	12	27	44	60
V4#11('76)-20: 11-20-Fradon-p. 17-Origin retold	2	4	6	8	11	14
...80-Page Giant (2003, $6.95) reprints origin and other stories in 80-Pg. Giant format						7.00
...Special 1 (8/99, $3.95)						4.00

PLASTIC MAN
DC Comics: Nov, 1988 - No. 4, Feb, 1989 ($1.00, mini-series)

	GD 2.0	VG 4.0	FN 6.0	VF 8.0	VF/NM 9.0	NM- 9.2
1-4: 1-Origin; Woozy Winks app.						4.00

PLASTIC MAN
DC Comics: Feb, 2004 - No. 20, Mar, 2006 ($2.95/$2.99)

	GD 2.0	VG 4.0	FN 6.0	VF 8.0	VF/NM 9.0	NM- 9.2
1-20-Kyle Baker-s/a in most. 1-Retells origin. 7,12-Scott Morse-s/a. 8-JLA cameo						3.00
...: On the Lam TPB (2004, $14.95) r/#1-6						15.00
...: Rubber Bandits TPB (2005, $14.99) r/#8-11,13,14						15.00

PLASTRON CAFE
Mirage Studios: Dec, 1992 - No. 4, July, 1993 ($2.25, B&W)

	GD 2.0	VG 4.0	FN 6.0	VF 8.0	VF/NM 9.0	NM- 9.2
1-4: 1-Teenage Mutant Ninja Turtles app.; Kelly Freas-c. 2-Hildebrandt painted-c. 4-Spaced & Alien Fire stories						3.00

PLAYFUL LITTLE AUDREY (TV)(Also see Little Audrey #25)
Harvey Publications: 6/57 - No. 110, 11/73; No. 111, 8/74 - No. 121, 4/76

	GD 2.0	VG 4.0	FN 6.0	VF 8.0	VF/NM 9.0	NM- 9.2
1	24	48	72	168	372	575
2	11	22	33	73	157	240
3-5	8	16	24	54	102	150
6-10	6	12	18	40	73	105
11-20	5	10	15	31	53	75
21-40	4	8	12	25	40	55
41-60	3	6	9	19	30	40
61-84: 84-Last 12¢ issue	3	6	9	15	22	28
85-99	2	4	6	11	16	20
100-52 pg. Giant	3	6	9	16	23	30
101-103: 52 pg. Giants	3	6	9	14	20	25
104-121	1	3	4	6	8	10
...In 3-D (Spring, 1988, $2.25, Blackthorne #66)						4.00

PLOP! (Also see The Best of DC #60,63 digests)
National Periodical Publications: Sept-Oct, 1973 - No. 24, Nov-Dec, 1976

	GD 2.0	VG 4.0	FN 6.0	VF 8.0	VF/NM 9.0	NM- 9.2
1-Sergio Aragonés-a begins; Wrightson-a	4	8	12	23	37	50
2-4,6-20	3	6	9	14	20	26
5-Wrightson-a	3	6	9	15	22	28
21-24 (52 pgs.). 23-No Aragonés-a	3	6	9	16	23	30

NOTE: ***Alcala** a-1-3. **Anderson** a-5. **Aragonés** a-1-22, 24. **Ditko** a-16p. **Evans** a-1. **Mayer** a-1. **Orlando** a-21, 22; c-21. **Sekowsky** a-5, 6p. **Toth** a-11. **Wolverton** r-4, 22-24(1 pg.ea.); c-1-12, 14, 17, 18. **Wood** a-14, 16i, 18-24; c-13, 15, 16, 19.*

PLUTO (See Cheerios Premiums, Four Color #537, Mickey Mouse Magazine, Walt Disney Showcase #4, 7, 13, 20, 23, 33 & Wheaties)
Dell Publ. Co.: No. 7, 1942; No. 429, 10/52 - No. 1248, 11-1/61-62 (Disney)

	GD 2.0	VG 4.0	FN 6.0	VF 8.0	VF/NM 9.0	NM- 9.2
Large Feature Comic 7(1942)-Written by Carl Barks, Jack Hannah, & Nick George (Barks' 1st comic book work)	181	362	543	1158	1979	2800
Four Color 429 (#1)	9	18	27	60	120	180
Four Color 509	6	12	18	37	66	95
Four Color 595,654,736,853	5	10	15	31	53	75
Four Color 941,1039,1143,1248	4	8	12	28	47	65

POCKET CLASSICS
Academic Inc. Publications: 1984 (B&W, 4 1/4" x 6 3/4", 68 pages)

C1(Black Beauty. C2(The Call of the Wild). C3(Dr. Jekyll and Mr. Hyde). C4(Dracula). C5(Frankenstein). C6(Huckleberry Finn). C7(Moby Dick). C8(The Red Badge of Courage). C9(The Time Machine). C10(Tom Sawyer). C11(Treasure Island). C12(20,000 Leagues Under the Sea). C13(The Great Adventures of Sherlock Holmes). C14(Gulliver's Travels). C15(The Hunchback of Notre Dame). C16(The Invisible Man). C17(Journey to the Center of the Earth). C18(Kidnapped). C19(The Mysterious Island). C20(The Scarlet Letter). C21(The Story of My Life). C22(A Tale of Two Cities). C23(The Three Musketeers). C24(The War of the Worlds). C25(Around the World in Eighty Days). C26(Captains Courageous). C27 (A Connecticut Yankee in King Arthur's Court). C28(Sherlock Holmes - The Hound of the Baskervilles). C29(The House of the Seven Gables). C30(Jane Eyre). C31(The Last of the Mohicans). C32(The Best of O. Henry). C33(The Best of Poe). C34(Two Years Before the Mast). C35(White Fang). C36(Wuthering Heights). C37(Ben Hur). C38(A Christmas Carol). C39(The Food of the Gods). C40(Ivanhoe). C41(The Man in the Iron Mask). C42(The Prince and the Pauper). C43(The Prisoner of Zenda). C44(The Return of the Native). C45(Robinson Crusoe). C46(The Scarlet Pimpernel). C47(The Sea Wolf). C48(The Swiss Family Robinson). C49(Billy Budd). C50(Crime and Punishment). C51(Don Quixote). C52(Great Expectations). C53(Heidi). C54(The Illiad). C55(Lord Jim). C56(The Mutiny on Board H.M.S. Bounty). C57(The Odyssey). C58(Oliver Twist). C59(Pride and Prejudice). C60(The Turn of the Screw) each... 8.00

Shakespeare Series:
S1(As You Like It). S2(Hamlet). S3(Julius Caesar). S4(King Lear). S5(Macbeth). S6(The Merchant of Venice). S7(A Midsummer Night's Dream). S8(Othello). S9(Romeo and Juliet). S10(The Taming of the Shrew). S11(The Tempest). S12(Twelfth Night) each... 9.00

POCKET COMICS (Also see Double Up)
Harvey Publications: Aug, 1941 - No. 4, Jan, 1942 (Pocket size; 100 pgs.) (Tied with Spitfire Comics #1 for earliest Harvey comic)

	GD 2.0	VG 4.0	FN 6.0	VF 8.0	VF/NM 9.0	NM- 9.2
1-Origin & 1st app. The Black Cat, Cadet Blakey the Spirit of '76, The Red Blazer, The Phantom, Sphinx, & The Zebra; Phantom Ranger, British Agent #99, Spin Hawkins, Satan, Lord of Evil begin (1st app. of each); Simon-c/a in #1-3	135	270	405	864	1482	2100
2 (9/41)-Black Cat on-c #2-4	110	220	330	704	1202	1700
3,4	103	206	309	659	1130	1600

POE
Cheese Comics: Sept, 1996 - No. 6, Apr, 1997 ($2.00, B&W)

	GD 2.0	VG 4.0	FN 6.0	VF 8.0	VF/NM 9.0	NM- 9.2
1-6-Jason Asala-s/a						3.00

POE
Sirius Entertainment (Dogstar Press): Oct, 1997 - No. 24 ($2.50/$2.95, B&W)

	GD 2.0	VG 4.0	FN 6.0	VF 8.0	VF/NM 9.0	NM- 9.2
1-24-Jason Asala-s/a. 20-24 ($2.95)						3.00
... Color Special (12/98, $2.95) Linsner-c						3.00

POGO PARADE (See Dell Giants)

POGO POSSUM (Also see Animal Comics & Special Delivery)
Dell Publishing Co.: No. 105, 4/46 - No. 148, 5/47; 10-12/49 - No. 16, 4-6/54

	GD 2.0	VG 4.0	FN 6.0	VF 8.0	VF/NM 9.0	NM- 9.2
Four Color 105(1946)-Kelly-c/a	49	98	147	382	854	1325
Four Color 148-Kelly-c/a	38	76	114	281	628	975
1-(10-12/49)-Kelly-c/a in all	34	68	102	245	548	850
2	22	44	66	154	340	525
3-5	15	30	45	105	233	360
6-10: 10-Infinity-c	13	26	39	91	201	310
11-16: 11-X-Mas-c	10	20	30	69	147	225

NOTE: *#1-4, 9-13: 52 pgs.; #5-8, 14-16: 36 pgs.*

POINT BLANK (See Wildcats)
DC Comics (WildStorm): Oct, 2002 - No. 5, Feb, 2003 ($2.95, limited series)

	GD 2.0	VG 4.0	FN 6.0	VF 8.0	VF/NM 9.0	NM- 9.2
1-5-Brubaker-s/Wilson-a/Bisley-c. 1-Variant-c by Wilson; Grifter and John Lynch app.						3.00
TPB (2003, $14.95), (2009, $14.99) r/#1-5; afterword by Brubaker						15.00

POINT ONE
Marvel Comics: Jan, 2012 ($5.99, one-shot)

	GD 2.0	VG 4.0	FN 6.0	VF 8.0	VF/NM 9.0	NM- 9.2
1-Short story preludes to Marvel's event storylines for 2012; s/a by various						6.00

POISON ELVES (Formerly I, Lusiphur)
Mulehide Graphics: No. 8, 1993- No. 20, 1995 (B&W, magazine/comic size, mature readers)

	GD 2.0	VG 4.0	FN 6.0	VF 8.0	VF/NM 9.0	NM- 9.2
8-Drew Hayes-c/a/scripts.	2	4	6	8	10	12
9-11: 11-1st comic size issue	2	4	6	8	10	12
12,14,16	1	2	3	5	6	8
13,15-(low print)	2	4	6	8	11	14

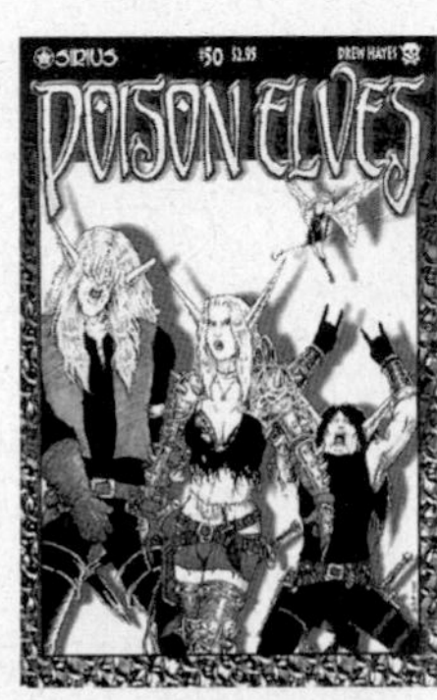

Poison Elves #50 © Drew Hayes

Polarity #3 © BOOM

Police Comics #13 © QUA

GD VG FN VF VF/NM NM-
2.0 4.0 6.0 8.0 9.0 9.2

15-2nd print 4.00
17-20 1 2 3 5 6 8
...Desert of the Third Sin-(1997, $14.95, TPB)-r/#13-18 15.00
...Patrons-($4.95, TPB)-r/#19,20 5.00
...Traumatic Dogs-(1996, $14.95,TPB)-Reprints I, Lusiphur #7, Poison Elves #8-12 15.00

POISON ELVES (See I, Lusiphur)
Sirius Entertainment: June, 1995 - No. 79, Sept, 2004 ; No. 80, Nov, 2007 ($2.50/$2.95, B&W, mature readers)

1-Linsner-c; Drew Hayes-a/scripts in all. 5.00
1-2nd print 3.00
2-25: 12-Purple Marauder-c/app. 3.00
26-45, 47-49 3.00
46,50-79: 61-Fillbäch Brothers-s/a. 74-Art by Crilley (3 pgs.) 3.00
80-($3.50) Tribute issue to Drew Hayes; sketchbook and notebook art with commentary 3.50
... Baptism By Fire-(2003, $19.95, TPB)-r/#48-59 20.00
... Color Special #1 (12/98, $2.95) 5.00
... Companion (12/02, $3.50) Back-story and character bios 3.50
... : Dark Wars TPB Vol. 1 (2005, $15.95) r/#60,62-68 16.00
... FAN Edition #1 mail-in offer; Drew Hayes-c/s/a 1 2 3 5 6 8
... Rogues-(2002, $15.95, TPB)-r/#40-47 16.00
...Salvation-(2001, $19.95, TPB)-r/#26-39 20.00
...Sanctuary-(1999, $14.95, TPB)-r/#1-12 15.00

POISON ELVES
Ape Entertainment: 2013 - Present ($2.99, B&W)

1-3: 1-Horan-s/Montos-a; Davidsen-s/Ritchie-a; 3 covers by Robertson, Montos & Moore 3.00

POISON ELVES: DOMINION
Sirius Entertainment: Sept, 2005 - No. 6, Sept, 2006 ($3.50, B&W, limited series)

1-6-Keith Davidsen-s/Scott Lewis-a 3.50

POISON ELVES: HYENA
Sirius Entertainment: Sept, 2004 - No. 4, Feb, 2005 ($2.95, B&W, limited series)

1-4-Keith Davidsen-s/Scott Lewis-a 3.00
Ventures TPB Vol. 1: The Hyena Collection (2006, $14.95) r/#1-4 & 2 short stories 15.00

POISON ELVES: LOST TALES
Sirius Entertainment: Jan, 2006 - No. 11 ($2.95, B&W, limited series)

1-11-Aaron Bordner-a; Bordner & Davidsen-s 3.00

POISON ELVES: LUSIPHUR & LIRILITH
Sirius Entertainment: 2001 - No. 4, 2001 ($2.95, B&W, limited series)

1-4-Drew Hayes-s/Jason Alexander-a 3.00
TPB (2002, $11.95) r/#1-4 12.00

POISON ELVES: PARINTACHIN
Sirius Entertainment: 2001 - No. 3, 2002 ($2.95, B&W, limited series)

1-3-Drew Hayes-c/Fillbäch Brothers-s/a 3.00
TPB (2003, $8.95) r/#1-3 9.00

POISON ELVES VENTURES
Sirius Entertainment: May, 2005 - No. 4, Apr, 2006 ($3.50, B&W, limited series)

... #1: Cassanova; ...#2: Lynn; ...#3: The Purple Marauder; #4: Jace - Bordner-a 3.50

POKÉMON (TV) (Also see Magical Pokémon Journey)
Viz Comics: Nov, 1998 - 2000 ($3.25/$3.50, B&W)

...Part 1: The Electric Tale of Pikachu
1-Toshiro Ono-s/a 2 4 6 8 10 12
1-4 (2nd through current printings) 4.00
2 6.00
3,4 5.00
TPB ($12.95) 13.00

...Part 2: Pikachu Strikes Back
1 6.00
2-4 5.00
TPB 13.00

...Part 3: Electric Pikachu Boogaloo
1 6.00
2-4 ($2.95-c) 5.00
TPB 13.00

...Part 4: Surf's Up Pikachu
1,3,4 5.00
2 ($2.95-c) 5.00
TPB 13.00

NOTE: Multiple printings exist for most issues

POKÉMON ADVENTURES
Viz Comics: Sept, 1999 - No. 4 ($5.95, B&W, magazine-size)

1-4-Includes stickers bound in 6.00

POKÉMON ADVENTURES
Viz Comics: 2000 - 2002 ($2.95/$4.95, B&W)

Part 2 (2/00-7/00) 1-6-Includes stickers bound in 5.00
Part 3 (8/00-2/01) 1-7 5.00
Part 4 (3/00-6/01) 1-4 5.00
Part 5 (7/01-10/01) 1-4 5.00
Part 6: 1-4, Part 7 1-5 5.00

POKÉMON: THE FIRST MOVIE
Viz Comics: 1999 ($3.95)

Mewtwo Strikes Back 1-4 5.00
Pikachu's Vacation 5.00

POKÉMON: THE MOVIE 2000
Viz Comics: 2000 ($3.95)

1-Official movie adaption 5.00
Pikachu's Rescue Adventure 5.00
...:The Power of One (mini-series) 1-3 5.00

POLARITY
BOOM! Studios: Apr, 2013 - No. 4 ($3.99, limited series)

1-4: 1-Bemis-s/Coelho-a; 3 covers 4.00

POLICE ACADEMY (TV)
Marvel Comics: Nov, 1989 - No. 6, Feb, 1990 ($1.00)

1-6: Based on TV cartoon; Post-c/a(p) in all 4.00

POLICE ACTION
Atlas News Co.: Jan, 1954 - No. 7, Nov, 1954

1-Violent-a by Robert Q. Sale 24 48 72 142 234 325
2 14 28 42 80 115 150
3-7: 7-Powell-a 13 26 39 74 105 135

NOTE: ***Ayers** a-4, 5. **Colan** a-1. **Forte** a-1, 2. **Mort Lawrence** a-5. **Maneely** a-3; c-1, 5. **Reinman** a-6, 7.*

POLICE ACTION
Atlas/Seaboard Publ.: Feb, 1975 - No. 3, June, 1975

1-3: 1-Lomax, N.Y.P.D., Luke Malone begin; McWilliams-a. 2-Origin Luke Malone, Manhunter; Ploog-a 2 4 6 10 14 18

NOTE: ***Ploog** art in all. **Sekowsky/McWilliams** a-1-3. **Thorne** c-3.*

POLICE AGAINST CRIME
Premiere Magazines: April, 1954 - No. 9, Aug, 1955

1-Disbrow-a; extreme violence (man's face slashed with knife); Hollingsworth-a 39 78 117 240 395 550
2-Hollingsworth-a 21 42 63 122 199 275
3-9 19 38 57 109 172 235

POLICE BADGE #479 (Formerly Spy Thrillers #1-4)
Atlas Comics (PrPl): No. 5, Sept, 1955

5-Maneely-c/a (6 pgs.); Heck-a 12 24 36 69 97 125

POLICE CASE BOOK (See Giant Comics Editions)

POLICE CASES (See Authentic... & Record Book of...)

POLICE COMICS
Quality Comics Group (Comic Magazines): Aug, 1941 - No. 127, Oct, 1953

1-Origin/1st app. Plastic Man by Jack Cole (r-in DC Special #15), The Human Bomb by Gustavson, & No. 711; intro. The Firebrand by Reed Crandall, The Mouthpiece by Guardineer, Phantom Lady, & The Sword; Chic Carter by Eisner app.; Firebrand-c 1-4 892 1784 2676 6512 11,506 16,500
2-Plastic Man smuggles opium 314 628 942 2198 3849 5500
3 239 478 717 1530 2615 3700
4 200 400 600 1280 2190 3100
5-Plastic Man-c begin; Plastic Man forced to smoke marijuana; Plastic Man covers begin, end #102 300 600 900 2070 3635 5200
6,7 174 348 522 1114 1907 2700
8-Manhunter begins (origin/1st app.) (3/42) 200 400 600 1280 2190 3100
9,10 139 278 417 883 1517 2150
11-The Spirit strip reprints begin by Eisner (origin-strip #1); 1st comic book app. The Spirit & 1st cover app. (9/42) 314 628 942 2198 3849 5500
12-Intro. Ebony 168 336 504 1075 1838 2600
13-Intro. Woozy Winks; last Firebrand 174 348 522 1114 1907 2700
14-19: 15-Last No. 711; Destiny begins 77 154 231 493 847 1200
20-The Raven x-over in Phantom Lady; features Jack Cole himself

Police Line-Up #3 © AVON

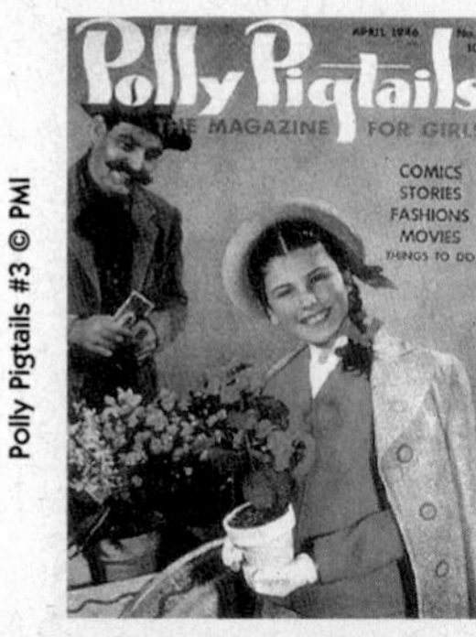

Polly Pigtails #3 © PMI

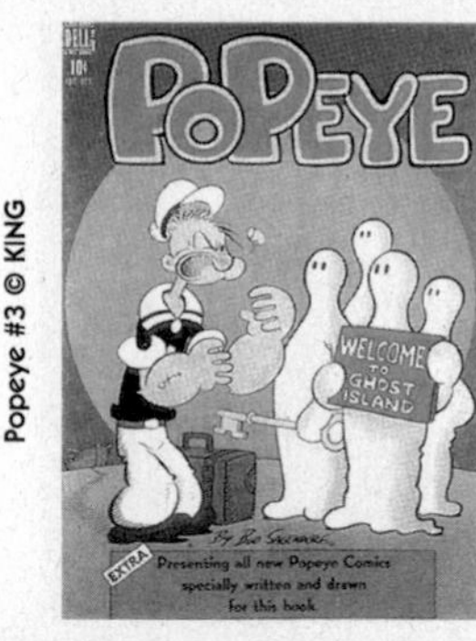

Popeye #3 © KING

	GD 2.0	VG 4.0	FN 6.0	VF 8.0	VF/NM 9.0	NM- 9.2
	77	154	231	493	847	1200
21,22: 21-Raven & Spider Widow x-over in Phantom Lady (cameo in #22)	65	130	195	416	708	1000
23-30: 23-Last Phantom Lady. 24-26-Flatfoot Burns by Kurtzman in all	58	116	174	371	636	900
31-41: 37-1st app. Candy by Sahle & begins (12/44). 41-Last Spirit-r by Eisner	50	100	150	315	533	750
42,43-Spirit-r by Eisner/Fine	41	82	123	256	428	600
44-Fine Spirit-r begin, end #88,90,92	41	82	123	256	428	600
45-50: 50-(#50 on-c, #49 on inside, 1/46)	36	72	108	214	347	480
51-60: 58-Last Human Bomb	30	60	90	177	289	400
61-88,90,92: 63-(Some issues have #65 printed on cover, but #63 on inside) Kurtzman-a, 6 pgs. 90,92-Spirit by Fine	25	50	75	150	245	340
89,91,93-No Spirit stories	23	46	69	136	223	310
94-99,101,102: Spirit by Eisner in all; 101-Last Manhunter. 102-Last Spirit & Plastic Man by Jack Cole	32	64	96	192	314	435
100	39	78	117	231	378	525
103-Content change to crime; Ken Shannon & T-Man begin (1st app. of each, 12/50)	32	64	96	188	307	425
104-112,114-127: Crandall-a most issues (not in 104,105,122,125-127). 109-Atomic bomb story. 112-Crandall-a	20	40	60	118	192	265
113-Crandall-c/a(2), 9 pgs. each	22	44	66	132	216	300

NOTE: *Most Spirit stories signed by Eisner are not by him; all are reprints.* ***Crandall*** *Firebrand-1-8. Spirit by* ***Eisner*** *1-41, 94-102; by* ***Eisner/Fine****-42, 43; by* ***Fine****-44-88, 90, 92. 103, 109.* ***Al Bryant*** *c-33, 34.* ***Cole*** *c-17-32, 35-102(most).* ***Crandall*** *c-13, 14.* ***Crandall/Cuidera*** *c-105-127.* ***Eisner*** *c-4i.* ***Gill Fox*** *c-1-3, 4p, 5-12, 15. Bondage c-103, 109, 125.*

POLICE LINE-UP
Avon Periodicals/Realistic Comics #3,4: Aug, 1951 - No. 4, July, 1952 (Painted-c #1-3)

	GD 2.0	VG 4.0	FN 6.0	VF 8.0	VF/NM 9.0	NM- 9.2
1-Wood-a, 1 pg. plus part-c; spanking panel-r/Saint #5	41	82	123	250	418	585
2-Classic story "The Religious Murder Cult", drugs, perversion; r/Saint #5; c-r/Avon paperback #329	32	64	96	188	307	425
3,4: 3-Kubert-a(r?)/part-c; Kinstler-a (inside-c only)	21	42	63	126	206	285

POLICE TRAP (Public Defender In Action #7 on)
Mainline #1-4/Charlton #5,6: 8-9/54 - No. 4, 2-3/55; No. 5, 7/55 - No. 6, 9/55

	GD 2.0	VG 4.0	FN 6.0	VF 8.0	VF/NM 9.0	NM- 9.2
1-S&K covers-all issues; Meskin-a; Kirby scripts	32	64	96	192	314	435
2-4	20	40	60	118	192	265
5,6-S&K-c/a	26	52	78	154	252	350

POLICE TRAP
Super Comics: No. 11, 1963; No. 16-18, 1964

	GD 2.0	VG 4.0	FN 6.0	VF 8.0	VF/NM 9.0	NM- 9.2
Reprint #11,16-18: 11-r/Police Trap #3. 16-r/Justice Traps the Guilty #? 17-r/Inside Crime #3 & r/Justice Traps The Guilty #83; 18-r/Inside Crime #3	2	4	6	9	13	16

POLLY & HER PALS (See Comic Monthly #1)

POLLY & THE PIRATES
Oni Press: Sept, 2005 - No. 6, June, 2006 ($2.99, B&W, limited series)

	GD 2.0	VG 4.0	FN 6.0	VF 8.0	VF/NM 9.0	NM- 9.2
1-6-Ted Naifeh-s/a; Polly is shanghaied by the pirate ship Titania						3.00
TPB (7/06, $11.95, digest) r/#1-6						12.00

POLLYANNA (Disney)
Dell Publishing Co.: No. 1129, Aug-Oct, 1960

	GD 2.0	VG 4.0	FN 6.0	VF 8.0	VF/NM 9.0	NM- 9.2
Four Color 1129-Movie, Hayley Mills photo-c	7	14	21	44	82	120

POLLY PIGTAILS (Girls' Fun & Fashion Magazine #44 on)
Parents' Magazine Institute/Polly Pigtails: Jan, 1946 - V4#43, Oct-Nov, 1949

	GD 2.0	VG 4.0	FN 6.0	VF 8.0	VF/NM 9.0	NM- 9.2
1-Infinity-c; photo-c	18	36	54	107	169	230
2-Photo-c	11	22	33	64	90	115
3-5: 3,4-Photo-c	10	20	30	58	79	100
6-10: 7-Photo-c	10	20	30	54	72	90
11-30: 22-Photo-c	9	18	27	47	61	75
31-43: 38-Natalie Wood photo-c	8	16	24	40	50	60

PONY EXPRESS (See Tales of the...)

PONYTAIL (Teen-age)
Dell Publishing Co./Charlton No. 13 on: 7-9/62 - No. 12, 10-12/65; No. 13, 11/69 - No. 20, 1/71

	GD 2.0	VG 4.0	FN 6.0	VF 8.0	VF/NM 9.0	NM- 9.2
12-641-209(#1)	4	8	12	23	37	50
2-12	3	6	9	17	26	35
13-20	3	6	9	14	19	24

POP COMICS
Modern Store Publ.: 1955 (36 pgs.; 5x7"; in color) (7¢)

	GD 2.0	VG 4.0	FN 6.0	VF 8.0	VF/NM 9.0	NM- 9.2
1-Funny animal	6	12	18	31	38	45

POPEYE (See Comic Album #7, 11, 15, Comics Reading Libraries *in the Promotional Comics section,* Eat Right to Work and Win, Giant Comic Album, King Comics, Kite Fun Book, Magic Comics, March of Comics #37,52, 66, 80, 96, 117, 134, 148, 157, 169, 194, 246, 264, 274, 294, 453, 465, 477 & Wow Comics, 1st series)

POPEYE
David McKay Publications: 1937 - 1939 (All by Segar)

	GD 2.0	VG 4.0	FN 6.0	VF 8.0	VF/NM 9.0	NM- 9.2
Feature Books nn (100 pgs.) (Very Rare)	811	1622	2433	5920	10,460	15,000
Feature Books 2 (52 pgs.)	123	246	369	787	1344	1900
Feature Books 3 (100 pgs.)-r/nn issue with new-c	100	200	300	640	1095	1550
Feature Books 5,10 (76 pgs.)	90	180	270	576	988	1400
Feature Books 14 (76 pgs.) (Scarce)	97	194	291	621	1061	1500

POPEYE (Strip reprints through 4-Color #70)
Dell #1-65/Gold Key #66-80/King #81-92/Charlton #94-138/Gold Key #139-155/Whitman #156 on: 1941 - 1947; #1, 2-4/48 - #65, 7-9/62; #66, 10/62 - #80, 5/66; #81, 8/66 - #92, 12/67; #94, 2/69 - #138, 1/77; #139, 5/78 - #171, 6/84 (no #93,160,161)

	GD 2.0	VG 4.0	FN 6.0	VF 8.0	VF/NM 9.0	NM- 9.2
Large Feature Comic 24('41)-Half by Segar	81	162	243	518	884	1250
Four Color 25('41)-by Segar	94	188	282	602	1026	1450
Large Feature Comic 10('43)	63	126	189	403	689	975
Four Color 17('43),26('43)-by Segar	40	80	120	296	673	1050
Four Color 43('44)	27	54	81	189	420	650
Four Color 70('45)-Title: ...& Wimpy	19	38	57	133	297	460
Four Color 113('46-original strips begin),127,145('47),168	12	24	36	82	179	275
1(2-4/48)(Dell)-All new stories continue	27	54	81	189	420	650
2	12	24	36	84	185	285
3-10: 5-Popeye on moon w/rocket-c	10	20	30	66	138	210
11-20	8	16	24	56	108	160
21-40,46: 46-Origin Swee' Pee	7	14	21	48	89	130
41-45,47-50	6	12	18	40	73	105
51-60	5	10	15	35	63	90
61-65 (Last Dell issue)	5	10	15	31	53	75
66(10/62),67-Both 84 pgs. (Gold Key)	6	12	18	40	73	105
68-80	4	8	12	25	40	55
81-92,94-97 (no #93): 97-Last 12¢ issue	3	6	9	20	31	42
98,99,101-107,109-138: 123-Wimpy beats Neil Armstrong to the moon. 130-1st app. Superstuff	3	6	9	14	19	24
100	3	6	9	17	26	35
108-Traces Popeye's origin from 1929	3	6	9	15	27	28
139-155: 144-50th Anniversary issue	2	4	6	8	10	12
156,157,162-167(Whitman)(no #160,161).167(3/82)	2	4	6	10	14	18
158(9/80),159(11/80)-pre-pack only	4	8	12	23	37	50
168-171:(All #90069 on-c; pre-pack) 168(6/83). 169(#168 on-c)(8/83). 170(3/84). 171(6/84)	3	6	9	16	23	30

NOTE: *Reprints-#145, 147, 149, 151, 153, 155, 157, 163-168(1/3), 170.*

POPEYE
Harvey Comics: Nov, 1993 - No. 7, Aug, 1994 ($1.50)

	GD 2.0	VG 4.0	FN 6.0	VF 8.0	VF/NM 9.0	NM- 9.2
V2#1-7						3.00
...Summer Special V2#1-(10/93, $2.25, 68 pgs.)-Sagendorf-r & others						4.00

POPEYE
IDW Publishing: Apr, 2012 - No. 12, Apr, 2013 ($3.99)

	GD 2.0	VG 4.0	FN 6.0	VF 8.0	VF/NM 9.0	NM- 9.2
1-12-New stories in classic style; Langridge-s. 1-Action #1 cover swipe. 12-Barney Google and Spark Plug app.						4.00

POPEYE (CLASSIC...)
IDW Publishing: Aug, 2012 - Present ($3.99)

	GD 2.0	VG 4.0	FN 6.0	VF 8.0	VF/NM 9.0	NM- 9.2
1-20-Reprints of Bud Sagendorf's classic stories						4.00

POPEYE SPECIAL
Ocean Comics: Summer, 1987 - No. 2, Sept, 1988 ($1.75/$2.00)

	GD 2.0	VG 4.0	FN 6.0	VF 8.0	VF/NM 9.0	NM- 9.2
1,2: 1-Origin						4.00

POPPLES (TV, movie)
Star Comics (Marvel): Dec, 1986 - No. 4, Jun, 1987

	GD 2.0	VG 4.0	FN 6.0	VF 8.0	VF/NM 9.0	NM- 9.2
1-4-Based on toys						5.00

POPPO OF THE POPCORN THEATRE
Fuller Publishing Co. (Publishers Weekly): 10/29/55 - No. 13, 1956 (weekly)

	GD 2.0	VG 4.0	FN 6.0	VF 8.0	VF/NM 9.0	NM- 9.2
1	10	20	30	54	72	90
2-5	7	14	21	37	46	55
6-13	6	12	18	31	38	45

NOTE: *By* ***Charles Biro.*** *10¢ cover, given away by supermarkets such as IGA.*

POP-POP COMICS
R. B. Leffingwell Co.: No date (Circa 1945) (52 pgs.)

	GD 2.0	VG 4.0	FN 6.0	VF 8.0	VF/NM 9.0	NM- 9.2
1-Funny animal	14	28	42	80	115	150

Popular Comics #3 © DELL

Popular Teen-Agers #10 © STAR

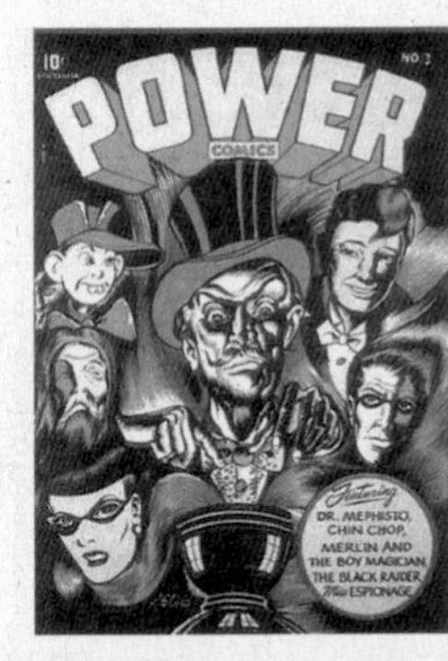
Power Comics #3 © HOKE

POPULAR COMICS
Dell Publishing Co.: Feb, 1936 - No. 145, July-Sept, 1948

	GD 2.0	VG 4.0	FN 6.0	VF 8.0	VF/NM 9.0	NM- 9.2
1-Dick Tracy (1st comic book app.), Little Orphan Annie, Terry & the Pirates, Gasoline Alley, Don Winslow (1st app.), Harold Teen, Little Joe, Skippy, Moon Mullins, Mutt & Jeff, Tailspin Tommy, Smitty, Smokey Stover, Winnie Winkle & The Gumps begin (all strip-r)	771	1542	2313	5400	-	-
2	257	514	771	1800	-	-
3	193	386	579	1350	-	-
4-6(7/36): 5-Tom Mix begins. 6-1st app. Scribbly	150	300	450	1050	-	-
7-10: 8,9-Scribbly & Reglar Fellers app.	121	242	363	850	-	-
11-20: 12-X-Mas-c	83	166	249	477	739	1000
21-27: 27-Last Terry & the Pirates, Little Orphan Annie, & Dick Tracy	63	126	189	362	556	750
28-37: 28-Gene Autry app. 31,32-Tim McCoy app. 35-Christmas-c; Tex Ritter app.	49	98	147	282	434	585
38-43: Tarzan in text only. 38-(4/39)-Gang Busters (Radio, 2nd app.) & Zane Grey's Tex Thorne begins? 43-The Masked Pilot app.; 1st non-funny-c?	47	94	141	270	415	560
44,45: 45-Hurricane Kid-c	36	72	108	207	321	435
46-Origin/1st app. Martan, the Marvel Man(12/39)	46	92	138	265	408	550
47-50	35	70	105	201	311	420
51-Origin The Voice (The Invisible Detective) strip begins (5/40)	37	74	111	213	327	440
52-Robot-c	42	84	126	242	371	500
53-59: 55-End of World story	33	66	99	190	295	400
60-Origin/1st app. Professor Supermind and Son (2/41)	34	68	102	196	303	410
61-71: 63-Smilin' Jack begins	26	52	78	150	230	310
72-The Owl & Terry & the Pirates begin (2/42); Smokey Stover reprints begin	42	84	126	242	371	500
73-75	29	58	87	167	259	350
76-78-Capt. Midnight in all (see The Funnies #57)	40	80	120	230	358	485
79-85-Last Owl	27	54	81	155	238	320
86-99: 86-Japanese WWII-c. 98-Felix the Cat, Smokey Stover-r begin	18	36	54	104	157	210
100	20	40	60	115	175	235
101-130	10	20	30	58	89	120
131-145: 142-Last Terry & the Pirates	9	18	27	52	79	105

NOTE: *Martan, the Marvel Man c-47-49, 52, 57-59. Professor Supermind c-60-63, 64(1/2), 65, 66. The Voice c-53.*

POPULAR FAIRY TALES (See March of Comics #6, 18)

POPULAR ROMANCE
Better-Standard Publications: No. 5, Dec, 1949 - No. 29, July, 1954

	GD 2.0	VG 4.0	FN 6.0	VF 8.0	VF/NM 9.0	NM- 9.2
5	15	30	45	85	130	175
6-9: 7-Palais-a; lingerie panels	12	24	36	67	94	120
10-Wood-a (2 pgs.)	14	28	42	78	112	145
11,12,14-16,18-21,28,29	10	20	30	58	79	100
13,17-Severin/Elder-a (3&8 pgs.)	11	22	33	62	86	110
22-27-Toth-a	12	24	36	69	97	125

NOTE: *All have photo-c.* ***Tuska*** *art in most issues.*

POPULAR TEEN-AGERS (Secrets of Love) (School Day Romances #1-4)
Star Publications: No. 5, Sept, 1950 - No. 23, Nov, 1954

	GD 2.0	VG 4.0	FN 6.0	VF 8.0	VF/NM 9.0	NM- 9.2
5-Toni Gay, Midge Martin & Eve Adams continue from School Day Romances; Ginger Bunn (formerly Ginger Snapp & becomes Honey Bunn #6 on) begins; all features end #8	34	68	102	199	325	450
6-8 (7/51)-Honey Bunn begins; all have L. B. Cole-c; 6-Negligee panels	27	54	81	160	263	365
9-(...Romances; 1st romance issue, 10/51)	22	44	66	132	216	300
10-(...Secrets of Love thru #23)	21	42	63	122	199	275
11,16,18,19,22,23	18	36	54	107	169	230
12,13,17,20,21-Disbrow-a	20	40	60	114	182	250
14-Harrison/Wood-a	26	52	78	154	252	350
15-Wood?, Disbrow-a	20	40	60	117	189	260
Accepted Reprint 5,6 (nd); L.B. Cole-c	9	18	27	47	61	75

NOTE: *All have* ***L. B. Cole*** *covers.*

PORKY PIG (See Bugs Bunny &..., Kite Fun Book, Looney Tunes, March of Comics #42, 57, 71, 89, 99, 113, 130, 143, 164, 175, 192, 209, 218, 367, and Super Book #6, 18, 30)

PORKY PIG (...& Bugs Bunny #40-69)
Dell Publishing Co./Gold Key No. 1-93/Whitman No. 94 on: No. 16, 1942 - No. 81, Mar-Apr, 1962; Jan, 1965 - No. 109, June, 1984

	GD 2.0	VG 4.0	FN 6.0	VF 8.0	VF/NM 9.0	NM- 9.2
Four Color 16(#1, 1942)	82	164	246	656	1478	2300
Four Color 48(1944)-Carl Barks-a	86	172	258	688	1544	2400
Four Color 78(1945)	23	46	69	161	356	550
Four Color 112(7/46)	14	28	42	96	211	325
Four Color 156,182,191('49)	10	20	30	69	147	225
Four Color 226,241('49),260,271,277,284,295	9	18	27	59	117	175
Four Color 303,311,322,330: 322-Sci/fi-c/story	7	14	21	46	86	125
Four Color 342,351,360,370,385,399,410,426	6	12	18	37	66	95
25 (11-12/52)-30	5	10	15	33	57	80
31-40	5	10	15	30	50	70
41-60	4	8	12	25	40	55
61-81(3-4/62)	3	6	9	21	33	45
1(1/65-Gold Key)(2nd Series)	5	10	15	31	53	75
2,4,5-r/4-Color 226,284 & 271 in that order	3	6	9	19	30	40
3,6-10: 3-r/Four Color #342	3	6	9	16	24	32
11-30	3	6	9	14	19	24
31-54	2	4	6	10	14	18
55-70	2	4	6	8	11	14
71-93(Gold Key)	2	3	4	6	8	10
94-96	2	4	6	8	10	12
97(9/80),98-pre-pack only (99 known not to exist)	3	6	9	21	33	45
100	2	4	6	10	14	18
101-105: 104(2/82). 105(4/82)	2	4	6	8	11	14
106-109 (All #90140 on-c, no date or date code): 106(7/83), 107(8/83), 108(2/84), 109(6/84) low print run	3	6	9	14	20	26

NOTE: *Reprints-#1-8, 9-35(2/3); 36-46(1/4-1/2), 58, 67, 69-74, 76, 78, 102-109(1/3-1/2).*

PORKY PIG'S DUCK HUNT
Saalfield Publishing Co.: 1938 (12pgs.)(large size)(heavy linen-like paper)

	GD 2.0	VG 4.0	FN 6.0	VF 8.0	VF/NM 9.0	NM- 9.2
2178-1st app. Porky Pig & Daffy Duck by Leon Schlesinger. Illustrated text story book written in verse. 1st book ever devoted to these characters. (see Looney Tunes #1 for their 1st comic book app.)	73	146	219	467	796	1125

PORTENT, THE
Image Comics: Feb, 2006 - No. 4, Aug, 2006 ($2.99)

1-4-Peter Bergting-s/a — 3.00
Vol. 1: Duende TPB (2006, 12.99) r/#1-4; pin-up art; intro. by Kaluta — 13.00

PORTIA PRINZ OF THE GLAMAZONS
Eclipse Comics: Dec, 1986 - No. 6, Oct, 1987 ($2.00, B&W, Baxter paper)

1-6 — 3.00

POSSESSED, THE
DC Comics (Cliffhanger): Sept, 2003 - No. 6, March, 2004 ($2.95, limited series)

1-6-Johns & Grimminger-s/Sharp-a — 3.00
TPB (2004, $14.95) r/#1-6; promo art and sketch pages — 15.00

POST GAZETTE (See Meet the New... in the Promotional Comics section)

POUND, THE: GHOULS NIGHT OUT
IDW Publ.: Sept, 2012 - No. 4, Dec, 2012, ($3.99, limited series)

1-4-Nilson-s/Moustafa-a — 4.00

POWDER RIVER RUSTLERS (See Fawcett Movie Comics)

POWER & GLORY (See American Flagg! & Howard Chaykin's American Flagg!
Malibu Comics (Bravura): Feb, 1994 - No. 4, May, 1994 ($2.50, limited series, mature)

1A, 1B-By Howard Chaykin; w/Bravura stamp — 3.00
1-Newsstand ed. (polybagged w/children's warning on bag), Gold ed., Silver-foil ed., Blue-foil ed.(print run of 10,000), Serigraph ed. (print run of 3,000)($2.95)-Howard Chaykin-c/a begin — 4.00
2-4-Contains Bravura stamp — 3.00
Holiday Special (Win '94, $2.95) — 3.00

POWER COMICS
Holyoke Publ. Co./Narrative Publ.: 1944 - No. 4, 1945

	GD 2.0	VG 4.0	FN 6.0	VF 8.0	VF/NM 9.0	NM- 9.2
1-L. B. Cole-c	155	310	465	992	1696	2400
2-Hitler, Hirohito-c (scarce)	174	348	522	1114	1907	2700
3-Classic L.B. Cole-c; Dr. Mephisto begins?	187	374	561	1197	2049	2900
4-L.B. Cole-c; Miss Espionage app. #3,4; Leav-a	142	284	426	909	1555	2200

POWER COMICS
Power Comics Co.: 1977 - No. 5, Dec, 1977 (B&W)

	GD 2.0	VG 4.0	FN 6.0	VF 8.0	VF/NM 9.0	NM- 9.2
1- "A Boy And His Aardvark" by Dave Sim; first Dave Sim aardvark (not Cerebus)	3	6	9	17	26	35
1-Reprint (3/77, black-c)	1	2	3	5	6	8
2-Cobalt Blue by Gustovich	1	3	4	6	8	10
3-5: 3-Nightwitch. 4-Northern Light. 5-Bluebird	1	3	4	6	8	10

POWER COMICS
Eclipse Comics (Acme Press): Mar, 1988 - No. 4, Sept, 1988 ($2.00, B&W, mini-series)

1-4: Bolland, Gibbons-r in all — 3.00

Power Girl #26 © DC

Power Man #49 © MAR

The Power of Shazam! #42 © DC

	GD 2.0	VG 4.0	FN 6.0	VF 8.0	VF/NM 9.0	NM- 9.2

POWER COMPANY, THE
DC Comics: Apr, 2002 - No. 18, Sep, 2003 ($2.50/$2.75)

1-6-Busiek-s/Grummett-a. 6-Green Arrow & Black Canary-c/app. 3.00
7-18: 7:Begin $2.75-c. 8,9-Green Arrow app. 11-Firestorm joins. 15-Batman app. 3.00
...Bork (3/02) Busiek-s/Dwyer-a; Batman & Flash (Barry Allen) app. 3.00
...Josiah Power (3/02) Busiek-s/Giffen-a; Superman app. 3.00
...Manhunter (3/02) Busiek-s/Jurgens-a; Nightwing app. 3.00
...Sapphire (3/02) Busiek-s/Bagley-a; JLA & Kobra app. 3.00
...Skyrocket (3/02) Busiek-s/Staton-a; Green Lantern (Hal Jordan) app. 3.00
...Striker Z (3/02) Busiek-s/Bachs-a; Superboy app. 3.00
...Witchfire (3/02) Busiek-s/Haley-a; Wonder Woman app. 3.00

POWER FACTOR
Wonder Color Comics #1/Pied Piper #2: May, 1987 - No. 2, 1987 ($1.95)

1,2: Super team. 2-Infantino-c 3.00

POWER FACTOR
Innovation Publishing: Oct, 1990 - No. 3, 1991 ($1.95/$2.25)

1-3: 1-R-/1st story + new-a, 2-r/2nd story + new-a. 3-Infantino-a 3.00

POWER GIRL (See All-Star #58, Infinity, Inc., JSA Classified, Showcase #97-99)
DC Comics: June, 1988 - No. 4, Sept, 1988 ($1.00, color, limited series)

1-4 4.00
TPB (2006, $14.99) r/Showcase #97-99; Secret Origins #11; JSA Classified #1-4 and pages from JSA #32,39; cover gallery 15.00

POWER GIRL
DC Comics: Jul, 2009 - No. 27, Oct, 2011 ($2.99)

1-12: 1,2-Amanda Conner-a; covers by Conner and Hughes; Ultra-Humanite app. 3-6-Covers by Conner and March 3.00
13-27: 13-23-Winick-s/Basri-a. 20,21-Crossover with Justice League: Generation Lost #18-22 23-Zatanna app. 24,25-Batman app.; Prasetya-a. 27-Cyclone app. 3.00
...: Aliens and Apes SC (2010, $17.99) r/#7-12 18.00
...: A New Beginning SC (2010, $17.99) r/#1-6; gallery of variant covers 18.00
...: Bomb Squad SC (2011, $14.99) r/#13-18 15.00

POWERHOUSE PEPPER COMICS (See Gay Comics, Joker Comics & Tessie the Typist)
Marvel Comics (20CC): No. 1, 1943; No. 2, May, 1948 - No. 5, Nov, 1948

	GD 2.0	VG 4.0	FN 6.0	VF 8.0	VF/NM 9.0	NM- 9.2
1-(60 pgs.)-Wolverton-a in all; c-2,3	223	446	669	1427	2439	3450
2	95	190	285	608	1042	1475
3,4	89	178	267	565	970	1375
5-(Scarce)	100	200	300	640	1095	1550

POWERLESS
Marvel Comics: Aug, 2004 - No. 6, Jan, 2005 ($2.99, limited series)

1-6-Peter Parker, Matt Murdock and Logan without powers; Gaydos-a 3.00
TPB (2005, $14.99) r/series; sketch page by Gaydos 15.00

POWER LINE
Marvel Comics (Epic Comics): May, 1988 - No. 8, Sept, 1989 ($1.25/$1.50)

1-8: 2-Williamson-i. 3-Dr. Zero app. 4-7-Morrow-a. 8-Williamson-i 3.00

POWER LORDS
DC Comics: Dec, 1983 - No. 3, Feb, 1984 (Limited series, Mando paper)

1-3: Based on Revell toys 4.00

POWER MAN (Formerly Hero for Hire; ...& Iron Fist #50 on; see Cage & Giant-Size...)
Marvel Comics Group: No. 17, Feb, 1974 - No. 125, Sept, 1986

	GD 2.0	VG 4.0	FN 6.0	VF 8.0	VF/NM 9.0	NM- 9.2
17-Luke Cage continues; Iron Man app.	3	6	9	19	30	40
18-20: 18-Last 20¢ issue	2	4	6	11	16	20
21-30	2	4	6	8	10	12
30-(30¢-c variant, limited distribution)(4/76)	3	6	9	19	30	40
31-46: 31-Part Neal Adams-i. 34-Last 25¢ issue. 36-r/Hero For Hire #12. 41-1st app. Thunderbolt. 45-Starlin-c.	1	3	4	6	8	10
31-34-(30¢-c variants, limited distribution)(5-8/76)	3	6	9	18	28	38
44-46-(35¢-c variants, limited distribution)(6-8/77)	4	8	12	24	37	50
47-Barry Smith-a	2	4	6	8	10	12
47-(35¢-c variant, limited distribution)(10/77)	4	8	12	23	37	60
48-50-Byrne-a(p); 48-Power Man/Iron Fist 1st meet. 50-Iron Fist joins Cage	2	4	6	11	16	20
51-56,58-65,67-77: 58-Intro El Aguila. 75-Double size. 77-Daredevil app.						6.00
57-New X-Men app. (6/79)	4	8	12	25	40	55
66-2nd app. Sabretooth (see Iron Fist #14)	5	10	15	35	63	90
78,84: 78-3rd app. Sabretooth (cameo under cloak). 84-4th app. Sabretooth	4	8	12	25	40	55
79-83,85-99,101-124: 87-Moon Knight app. 109-The Reaper app.						4.00
100-Double size; Origin K'un L'un						6.00
125-Double size; Death of Iron Fist	1	3	4	6	8	10
Annual 1(1976)-Punisher cameo in flashback	2	4	6	13	18	22

NOTE: ***Austin*** *c-102i.* ***Byrne*** *a-48-50; c-102, 104, 106, 107, 112-116.* ***Kane*** *c(p)-24, 25, 28, 48.* ***Miller*** *a-68, 76(2 pgs.); c-66-68, 70-74, 80i.* ***Mooney*** *a-38i, 53i, 55i.* ***Nebres*** *a-76p.* ***Nino*** *a-42i, 43i.* ***Perez*** *a-27.* ***B. Smith*** *a-47i.* ***Tuska*** *a(p)-17, 20, 24, 26, 28, 29, 36, 47. Painted c-75, 100.*

POWER MAN AND IRON FIST
Marvel Comics: Apr, 2011 - No. 5, Jul, 2011 ($2.99, limited series)

1-5-Van Lente-s/Alves-a; Victor Alvarez as Power Man 3.00

POWER OF PRIME
Malibu Comics (Ultraverse): July, 1995 - No. 4, Nov, 1995 ($2.50, lim. series)

1-4 3.00

POWER OF SHAZAM!, THE (See SHAZAM!)
DC Comics: 1994 (Painted graphic novel) (Prequel to new series)

	GD 2.0	VG 4.0	FN 6.0	VF 8.0	VF/NM 9.0	NM- 9.2
Hardcover-($19.95)-New origin of Shazam!; Ordway painted-c/a & script	3	6	9	14	20	25
Softcover-($7.50), Softcover-($9.95)-New-c.	2	4	6	8	10	12

POWER OF SHAZAM!, THE
DC Comics: Mar, 1995 - No. 47, Mar, 1999; No. 48, Mar, 2010 ($1.50/$1.75/$1.95/$2.50)

1-Jerry Ordway scripts begin 4.00
2-20: 4-Begin $1.75-c. 6:Re-intro of Capt. Nazi. 8-Re-intro of Spy Smasher, Bulletman & Minuteman; Swan-a (7 pgs.). 11-Re-intro of Ibis, Swan-a(2 pgs.). 14-Gil Kane-a(p). 20-Superman-c/app.; "Final Night" 3.00
21-47: 21-Plastic Man-c/app. 22-Batman-c/app. 35,36-X-over w/Starman #39,40. 38-41-Mr. Mind. 43-Bulletman app. 45-JLA-c/app. 3.00
48-(3/10, $2.99) Blackest Night one-shot; Osiris rises as a Black Lantern; Kramer-a 3.00
#1,000,000 (11/98) 853rd Century x-over; Ordway-c/s/a 3.00
Annual 1 (1996, $2.95)-Legends of the Dead Earth story; Jerry Ordway-c; Mike Manley-a 4.00

POWER OF STRONGMAN, THE (Also see Strongman)
AC Comics: 1989 ($2.95)

1-Powell G.A.-r 3.00

POWER OF THE ATOM (See Secret Origins #29)
DC Comics: Aug, 1988 - No. 18, Nov, 1989 ($1.00)

1-18: 6-Chronos returns; Byrne-p. 9-JLI app. 3.00

POWER PACHYDERMS
Marvel Comics: Sept, 1989 ($1.25, one-shot)

1-Elephant super-heroes; parody of X-Men, Elektra, & 3 Stooges 3.00

POWER PACK
Marvel Comics Group: Aug, 1984 - No. 62, Feb, 1991

1-($1.00, 52 pgs.)-Origin & 1st app. Power Pack 5.00
2-18,20-26,28,30-45,47-62 3.00
19-(52 pgs.)-Cloak & Dagger, Wolverine app. 4.00
27-Mutant massacre; Wolverine & Sabretooth app. 5.00
29,46: 29-Spider-Man & Hobgoblin app. 46-Punisher app. 4.00
Graphic Novel: Power Pack & Cloak & Dagger: Shelter From the Storm ('89, SC, $7.95) Velluto/Farmer-a 10.00
...Holiday Special 1 (2/92, $2.25, 68 pgs.) 4.00
NOTE: ***Austin*** *scripts-53.* ***Mignola*** *c-20.* ***Morrow*** *a-51.* ***Spiegle*** *a-55i.* ***Williamson*** *a(i)-43, 50, 52.*

POWER PACK (Volume 2)
Marvel Comics: Aug, 2000 - No. 4, Nov, 2000 ($2.99, limited series)

1-4-Doran & Austin-c/a 3.00

POWER PACK
Marvel Comics: June, 2005 - No. 4, Aug, 2005 ($2.99, limited series)

1-4-Sumerak-s/Gurihiru-a; back-up Franklin Richards story. 3-Fantastic Four app. 3.00
... Digest (2006, $6.99) r/#1-4 7.00

POWER PACK: DAY ONE
Marvel Comics: May, 2008 - No. 4, Aug, 2008($2.99, limited series)

1-4-Van Lente-s/Gurihiru-a; origin retold; Coover-a back-ups. 1-Fantastic Four cameo 3.00

POWERPUFF GIRLS, THE (Also see Cartoon Network Starring... #1)
DC Comics: May, 2000 - No. 70, Mar, 2006 ($1.99/$2.25)

1 5.00
2-55,57-70: 25-Pin-ups by Allred, Byrne, Baker, Mignola, Hernandez, Warren 3.00
56-($2.95) Bonus pages; Mojo Jojo-c 4.00
...Double Whammy (12/00, $3.95) r/#1,2 & a Dexter's Lab story 4.00
...Movie: The Comic (9/02, $2.95) Movie adaptation; Phil Moy & Chris Cook-a 4.00

POWERPUFF GIRLS
IDW Publishing: Sept, 2013 - Present ($3.99)

Powerpuff Girls (2013 series) #1 © CN

Powers #21 © Jinxworld

Preacher #37 © Ennis & Dillon

GD VG FN VF VF/NM NM-
2.0 4.0 6.0 8.0 9.0 9.2

1-7: 1-Five covers; Troy Little-s/a; Mojo Jojo app. 2-7-Multiple covers on each 4.00

POWER RANGERS ZEO (TV)(Saban's...)(Also see Saban's Mighty Morphin Power Rangers)
Image Comics (Extreme Studios): Aug, 1996 ($2.50)

1-Based on TV show 4.00

POWER RECORD COMICS (Named Peter Pan Record Comics for #33-47)
Marvel Comics/Power Records: 1974 - 1978 ($1.49, 7x10" comics, 20 pgs. with 45 R.P.M. record) (Clipped corners - reduce value 20%) (Comic alone - 50%; record alone - 50%) (Some copies significantly warped by shrinkwrapping - reduce value 20%) (PR22, PR23, PR38, PR43, PR44 do not exist)

PR10-Spider-Man-r/from #124,125; Man-Wolf app. PR18-Planet of the Apes-r. PR19-Escape From the Planet of the Apes-r. PR20-Beneath the Planet of the Apes-r. PR21-Battle for the Planet of the Apes-r. PR24-Spider-Man II-New-a begins. PR27-Batman "Stacked Cards"; N. Adams-a(p). PR30-Batman; N. Adams-r/Det.(7 pgs.).
With record; each... 5 10 15 33 57 80

PR11-Incredible Hulk-r/#171. PR12-Captain America-r/#168. PR13-Fantastic Four-r/#126. PR14-Frankenstein-Ploog-r/#1. PR15-Tomb of Dracula-Colan-r/#2. PR16-Man-Thing-Ploog-r/#5. PR17-Werewolf By Night-Ploog-r/Marvel Spotlight #2. PR28-Superman "Alien Creatures". PR29-Space: 1999 "Breakaway". PR31-Conan-N. Adams-a; reprinted in Conan #116. PR32-Space: 1999 "Return to the Beginning". PR33-Superman-G.A. origin, Buckler-a(p). PR34-Superman. PR35-Wonder Woman-Buckler-a(p)
With record; each... 5 10 15 30 50 70

PR11, PR24-(1981 Peter Pan records re-issues) PR11-New Abomination & Rhino-c
With record; each... 5 10 15 31 53 75

PR25-Star Trek "Passage to Moauv". PR26-Star Trek "Crier in Emptiness." PR36-Holo-Man. PR37-Robin Hood. PR39-Huckleberry Finn. PR40-Davy Crockett. PR41-Robinson Crusoe. PR42-20,000 Leagues Under the Sea. PR47-Little Women
With record; each... 4 8 12 27 44 60

PR25, PR26 (Peter Pan records re-issues with photo covers). PR45-Star Trek "Dinosaur Planet". PR46-Star Trek "The Robot Masters" 2 4 6 9 12 15

NOTE: *Peter Pan re-issues exist for #25-32 and are valued the same.*

POWERS
Image Comics: 2000 - No. 37, Feb, 2004 ($2.95)

1-Bendis-s/Oeming-a; murder of Retro Girl 2 4 6 9 12 15
2-6: 6-End of Retro Girl arc. 6.00
7-14: 7-Warren Ellis app. 12-14-Death of Olympia 4.00
15-37: 31-36-Origin of the Powers 3.00
Annual 1 (2001, $3.95) 4.00
...: Anarchy TPB (11/03, $14.95) r/#21-24; interviews, sketchbook, cover gallery 15.00
...Coloring/Activity Book (2001, $1.50, B&W, 8 x 10.5") Oeming-a 3.00
...: Forever TPB (2005, $19.95) r/#31-37; script for #31, sketchbook, cover gallery 20.00
...: Little Deaths TPB (2002, $19.95) r/#7,12-14, Ann. #1, Coloring/Activity Book; sketch pages, cover gallery 20.00
...: Roleplay TPB (2001, $13.95) r/#8-11; sketchbook, cover gallery 14.00
... Scriptbook (2001, $19.95) scripts for #1-11; Oeming sketches 20.00
...: Supergroup TPB (2003, $19.95) r/#15-20; sketchbook, cover gallery 20.00
...: The Definitive Collection Vol. 1 HC (2006, $29.99, dust jacket) r/#1-11 & Coloring/Activity Book, script for #1, sketch pages and covers, interviews, letter column highlights 30.00
...: The Definitive Collection Vol. 2 HC (2009, $29.99, dust jacket) r/#12-24 & Annual #1; cover gallery; 1st Bendis/Oeming Jinx story; interviews, letter column highlights 30.00
..: Who Killed Retro Girl TPB (2000, $21.95) r/#1-6; sketchbook, cover gallery, and promotional strips from Comic Shop News 22.00

POWERS
Marvel Comics (Icon): Jul, 2004 - No. 30, Sept, 2008 ($2.95/$3.95)

1-11,13-24-Bendis-s/Oeming-a. 14-Cover price error 3.00
12-($3.95, 64 pages) 2 covers; Bendis & Oeming interview 4.00
25-30-($3.95, 40 pages) 25-Two covers; Bendis interview 4.00
Annual 2008 (5/08, $4.95) Bendis-s/Oeming-a; interview with Brubaker, Simone, others 5.00
...: Legends TPB (2005, $17.95) r/#1-6; sketchbook, cover gallery 18.00
...: Psychotic TPB (1/06, $19.95) r/#7-12; Bendis & Oeming interview, cover gallery 20.00
...: Cosmic TPB (10/07, $19.95) r/#13-18; script and sketch pages 20.00
...: Secret Identity TPB (12/07, $19.95) r/#19-24; script pages 20.00

POWERS (Volume 3)
Marvel Comics (Icon): Nov, 2009 - No. 11, Jul, 2012 ($3.95)

1-11-Bendis-s/Oeming-a 4.00

POWERS: BUREAU (Follows Volume 3)
Marvel Comics (Icon): Feb, 2013 - Present ($3.95)

1-8-Bendis-s/Oeming-a 4.00

POWERS THAT BE (Becomes Star Seed No.7 on)
Broadway Comics: Nov, 1995 - No. 6, June, 1996 ($2.50)

1-6: 1-Intro of Fatale & Star Seed. 6-Begin $2.95-c. 3.00
Preview Editions 1-3 (9/95 - 11/95, B&W) 3.00

POW MAGAZINE (Bob Sproul's) (Satire Magazine)
Humor-Vision: Aug, 1966 - No. 3, Feb, 1967 (30¢)

1,2: 2-Jones-a 4 8 12 28 47 65
3-Wrightson-a 5 10 15 34 60 85

PREACHER
DC Comics (Vertigo): Apr, 1995 - No. 66, Oct, 2000 ($2.50, mature)

nn-Preview 10 20 30 66 138 210
1 ($2.95)-Ennis scripts, Dillon-a & Fabry-c in all; 1st app. Jesse, Tulip, & Cassidy
10 20 30 64 132 200
1-Special Edition (6/09, $1.00) r/#1 with "After Watchmen" cover frame 3.00
2-1st app. Saint of Killers. 4 8 12 27 44 60
3 3 6 9 19 30 40
4,5 3 6 9 14 20 25
6-10 2 4 6 9 12 15
11-15: 12-Polybagged w/videogame w/Ennis text. 13-Hunters storyline begins; ends #17
1 2 3 5 6 8
16-20: 19-Saint of Killers app.; begin "Crusaders", ends #24 5.00
21-25: 21-24-Saint of Killers app. 25-Origin of Cassidy. 4.00
26-49,52-64: 52-Tulip origin 3.00
50-($3.75) Pin-ups by Jim Lee, Bradstreet, Quesada and Palmiotti 4.00
51-Includes preview of 100 Bullets; Tulip origin 1 3 4 6 8 10
65,66-($3.75) 65-Almost everyone dies. 66-Final issue
1 2 3 5 6 8
Alamo (2001, $17.95, TPB) r/#59-66; Fabry-c 18.00
All Hell's a-Coming (2000, $17.95, TPB)-r/#51-58, ...:Tall in the Saddle 18.00
... Book One HC (2009, $39.99, d.j.) r/#1-12; new Ennis intro.; pin-ups from #50,66 40.00
... Book Two HC (2010, $39.99, d.j.) r/#13-26; new Stuart Moore intro. 40.00
... Book Three HC (2010, $39.99, d.j.) r/#27-33, ...Special: Saint of Killers #1-4 & ...Special: Cassidy: Blood & Whiskey #1; new Ennis intro. 40.00
... Book Four HC (2011, $39.99, d.j.) r/#34-40, ...Special: One Man's War, ...Special: The Story of You-Know-Who, & ...Special: The Good Old Boys; new Dillon intro. 40.00
...: Dead or Alive HC (2000, $29.95) Gallery of Glenn Fabry's cover paintings for every Preacher issue; commentary by Fabry & Ennis 30.00
...: Dead or Alive SC (2003, $19.95) 20.00
Dixie Fried (1998, $14.95, TPB)-r/#27-33, Special: Cassidy 15.00
Gone To Texas (1996, $14.95, TPB)-r/#1-7; Fabry-c 15.00
Proud Americans (1997, $14.95, TPB)-r/#18-26; Fabry-c 15.00
Salvation (1999, $14.95, TPB)-r/#41-50; Fabry-c 15.00
Until the End of the World (1996, $14.95, TPB)-r/#8-17; Fabry-c 15.00
War in the Sun (1999, $14.95, TPB)-r/#34-40 15.00

PREACHER SPECIAL: CASSIDY: BLOOD & WHISKEY
DC Comics (Vertigo): 1998 ($5.95, one-shot)

1-Ennis-scripts/Fabry-c/Dillon-a 6.00

PREACHER SPECIAL: ONE MAN'S WAR
DC Comics (Vertigo): Mar, 1998 ($4.95, one-shot)

1-Ennis-scripts/Fabry-c /Snejbjerg-a 5.00

PREACHER SPECIAL: SAINT OF KILLERS
DC Comics (Vertigo): Aug, 1996 - No. 4, Nov, 1996 ($2.50, lim. series, mature)

1-4: Ennis-scripts/Fabry-c. 1,2-Pugh-a. 3,4-Ezquerra-a 4.00
1-Signed & numbered 20.00

PREACHER SPECIAL: THE GOOD OLD BOYS
DC Comics (Vertigo): Aug, 1997 ($4.95, one-shot, mature)

1-Ennis-scripts/Fabry-c /Esquerra-a 5.00

PREACHER SPECIAL: THE STORY OF YOU-KNOW-WHO
DC Comics (Vertigo): Dec, 1996 ($4.95, one-shot, mature)

1-Ennis-scripts/Fabry-c/Case-a 5.00

PREACHER: TALL IN THE SADDLE
DC Comics (Vertigo): 2000 ($5.95, one-shot)

1-Ennis-scripts/Fabry-c/Dillon-a; early romance of Tulip and Jesse 6.00

PREDATOR (Also see Aliens Vs. ..., Batman vs. ..., Dark Horse Comics, & Dark Horse Presents)
Dark Horse Comics: June, 1989 - No. 4, Mar, 1990 ($2.25, limited series)

1-Based on movie; 1st app. Predator 3 6 9 16 23 30
1-2nd printing 6.00
2 1 2 3 5 6 8
3,4 6.00
Trade paperback (1990, $12.95)-r/#1-4 15.00

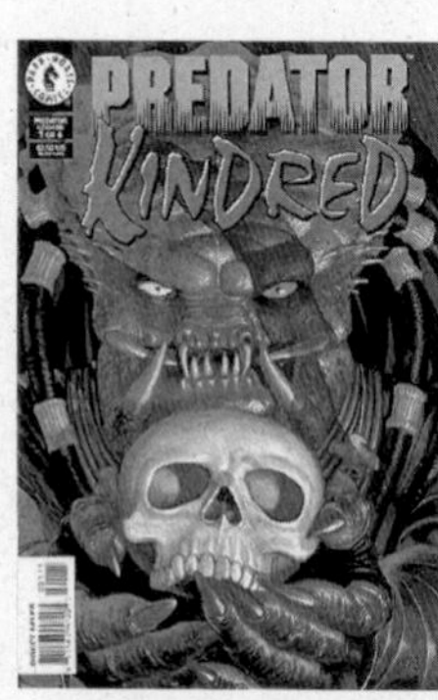
Predator: Kindred #1 © 20th Cent. Fox

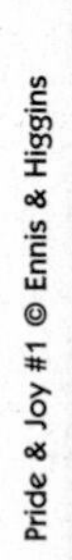
Pride & Joy #1 © Ennis & Higgins

Prime #6 © MAL

GD 2.0 | VG 4.0 | FN 6.0 | VF 8.0 | VF/NM 9.0 | NM- 9.2

... Omnibus Volume 1 (8/07, $24.95, 6" x 9") r/#1-4, ... Cold War, ... Dark River, ...Bloody Sands of Time mini-series and stories from Dark Horse Comics #1,2,4-7,10-12 — 25.00
... Omnibus Volume 2 (2/08, $24.95, 6" x 9") r/ ... Big Game, ... Race War, ...Invaders From The, Fourth Dimension mini-series and stories from Dark Horse Comics #16-18,20,21; Dark Horse Presents #46 and A Decade of Dark Horse — 25.00
... Omnibus Volume 3 (6/08, $24.95, 6" x 9") r/ ... Bad Blood, ... Kindred, ...Hell and Hot Water, ... Strange Roux mini-series and stories from Dark Horse Comics #12-14 and Dark Horse Presents #119 & 124 — 25.00

PREDATOR
Dark Horse Comics: June, 2009 - No. 4, Jan, 2010 ($3.50, limited series)

1-4-Arcudi-s/Saltares-a/Swanland-c; variant-c by Warner — 3.50

PREDATOR: (title series) **Dark Horse Comics**

--BAD BLOOD, 12/93 - No. 4, 1994 ($2.50) 1-4 — 4.00
--BIG GAME, 3/91 - No. 4, 6/91 ($2.50) 1-4: 1-3-Contain 2 Dark Horse trading cards — 4.00
--BLOODY SANDS OF TIME, 2/92 - No. 2, 2/92 ($2.50) 1,2-Dan Barry-c/a(p)/scripts — 4.00
--CAPTIVE, 4/98 ($2.95, one-shot) 1 — 4.00
--COLD WAR, 9/91 - No. 4, 12/91 ($2.50) 1-4: All have painted-c — 4.00
--DARK RIVER, 7/96 - No.4, 10/96 ($2.95)1-4: Miran Kim-c — 4.00
--HELL & HOT WATER, 4/97 - No. 3, 6/97 ($2.95) 1-3 — 4.00
--HELL COME A WALKIN', 2/98 - No. 2, 3/98 ($2.95) 1,2-In the Civil War — 4.00
--HOMEWORLD, 3/99 - No. 4, 6/99 ($2.95) 1-4 — 4.00
--INVADERS FROM THE FOURTH DIMENSION, 7/94 ($3.95, one-shot, 52 pgs.) 1 — 4.00
--JUNGLE TALES. 3/95 ($2.95t) 1-r/Dark Horse Comics — 4.00
--KINDRED, 12/96 - No. 4, 3/97 ($2.50) 1-4 — 4.00
--NEMESIS, 12/97 - No. 2, 1/98 ($2.95) 1,2-Predator in Victorian England; Taggart-c — 4.00
--PRIMAL, 7/97 - No. 2, 8/97 ($2.95) 1,2 — 4.00
--RACE WAR (See Dark Horse Presents #67), 2/93 - No. 4,10/93 ($2.50, color)
1-4,0: 1-4-Dorman painted-c #1-4, 0(4/93) — 4.00
--STRANGE ROUX, 11/96 ($2.95, one-shot) 1 — 4.00
--XENOGENESIS (Also see Aliens Xenogenesis), 8/99 - No. 4, 11/99 ($2.95)
1,2-Edginton-s — 4.00

PREDATORS (Based on the 2010 movie)
Dark Horse Comics: Jun, 2010 - No. 4, Jun, 2010 ($2.99, weekly limited series)

1-4-Prequel to the 2010 movie; stories by Andreyko and Lapham; Paul Lee-c — 3.00
... Film Adaptation (7/10, $6.99) Tobin-s/Drujiniu-s/photo-c — 7.00
...: Preserve the Game (7/10, $3.50) Sequel to the movie; Lapham-s/Jefferson-a — 3.50

PREDATOR 2
Dark Horse Comics: Feb, 1991 - No. 2, June, 1991 ($2.50, limited series)

1,2: 1-Adapts movie; both w/trading cards & photo-c — 4.00

PREDATOR VS. JUDGE DREDD
Dark Horse Comics: Oct, 1997 - No. 3 ($2.50, limited series)

1-3-Wagner-s/Alcatena-a/Bolland-c — 4.00

PREDATOR VS. MAGNUS ROBOT FIGHTER
Dark Horse/Valiant: Oct, 1992 - No. 2, 1993 ($2.95, limited series)
(1st Dark Horse/Valiant x-over)

1,2: (Reg.)-Barry Smith-c; Lee Weeks-a. 2-w/trading cards — 4.00
1 (Platinum edition, 11/92)-Barry Smith-c — 10.00

PREHISTORIC WORLD (See Classics Illustrated Special Issue)

PRELUDE TO DEADPOOL CORPS (Leads into Deadpool Corps #1)
Marvel Comics: May, 2010 - No. 5, May, 2010 ($3.99/$2.99, weekly limited series)

1-($3.99) Deadpool & Lady Deadpool vs. alternate dimension Capt. America; Liefeld-a — 4.00
2-5-($2.99) Alternate reality Deadpools team-up; Dave Johnson interlocking covers — 3.00

PRELUDE TO INFINITE CRISIS
DC Comics: 2005 ($5.99, squarebound)

nn-Reprints stories and panels with commentary leading into Infinite Crisis series — 6.00

PREMIERE (See Charlton Premiere)

PRESIDENTIAL MATERIAL
IDW Publishing: Oct, 2008 ($3.99/$7.99)

...: Barack Obama - Biography of the candidate; Mariotte-s/Morgan-a/Campbell-c — 4.00
...: John McCain - Biography of the candidate; Helfer-s/Thompson-a/Campbell-c — 4.00
Flipbook ($7.99) Both issues in flipbook format — 8.00

PRESTO KID, THE (See Red Mask)

GD 2.0 | VG 4.0 | FN 6.0 | VF 8.0 | VF/NM 9.0 | NM- 9.2

PRETTY BOY FLOYD (See On the Spot)

PRETTY DEADLY
Image Comics: Oct, 2013 - Present ($3.50)

1-5-DeConnick-s/Rios-a/c — 3.50

PREZ (See Cancelled Comic Cavalcade, Sandman #54 & Supergirl #10)
National Periodical Publications: Aug-Sept, 1973 - No. 4, Feb-Mar, 1974

	GD	VG	FN	VF	VF/NM	NM-
1-Origin; Joe Simon scripts	3	6	9	17	26	35
2-4	2	4	6	13	18	22

PRICE, THE (See Eclipse Graphic Album Series)

PRIDE & JOY
DC Comics (Vertigo): July, 1997 - No. 4, Oct, 1997 ($2.50, limited series)

1-4-Ennis-s — 3.00
TPB (2004, $14.95) r/#1-4 — 15.00

PRIDE & PREJUDICE
Marvel Comics: June, 2009 - No. 5, Oct, 2009 ($3.99, limited series)

1-5-Adaptation of the Jane Austen novel; Nancy Butler-s/Hugo Petrus-a — 4.00

PRIDE AND THE PASSION, THE
Dell Publishing Co.: No. 824, Aug, 1957

	GD	VG	FN	VF	VF/NM	NM-
Four Color 824-Movie, Frank Sinatra & Cary Grant photo-c	8	16	24	56	108	160

PRIDE OF BAGHDAD
DC Comics (Vertigo): 2006 ($19.99, hardcover with dustjacket)

HC-A pride of lions escaping from the Baghdad zoo in 2003; Vaughan-s/Henrichon-a — 20.00
SC-(2007, $12.99) — 13.00

PRIDE OF THE YANKEES, THE (See Real Heroes & Sport Comics)
Magazine Enterprises: 1949 (The Life of Lou Gehrig)

	GD	VG	FN	VF	VF/NM	NM-
nn-Photo-c; Ogden Whitney-a	84	168	252	538	919	1300

PRIEST (Also see Asylum)
Maximum Press: Aug, 1996 - No. 2, Oct, 1996 ($2.99)

1,2 — 3.00

PRIMAL FORCE
DC Comics: No. 0, Oct, 1994 - No. 14, Dec, 1995 ($1.95/$2.25)

0-14: 0- Teams Red Tornado, Golem, Jack O'Lantern, Meridian & Silver Dragon. 9-begin $2.25-c — 3.00

PRIMAL MAN (See The Crusaders)

PRIMAL RAGE
Sirius Entertainment: 1996 ($2.95)

1-Dark One-c; based of video game — 3.00

PRIME (See Break-Thru, Flood Relief & Ultraforce)
Malibu Comics (Ultraverse): June, 1993 - No. 26, Aug, 1995 ($1.95/$2.50)

1-1st app. Prime; has coupon for Ultraverse Premiere #0 — 4.00
1-With coupon missing — 2.00
1-Full cover holographic edition; 1st of kind w/Hardcase #1 & Strangers #1 — 10.00
1-Ultra 5,000 edition w/silver ink-c — 6.00
2-4,6-11,14-26: 2-Polybagged w/card & coupon for U. Premiere #0. 3,4-Prototype app. 4-Direct sale w/o card.4-($2.50)-Newsstand ed. polybagged w/card. 6-Bill & Chelsea Clinton app.115-Intro Papa Verite; Pérez-c/a. 16-Intro Turbo Charge — 3.00
5-($2.50, 48 pgs.)-Rune flip-c/story part B by Barry Smith; see Sludge #1 for 1st app. Rune; 3-pg. Night Man preview — 4.00
12-($3.50, 68 pgs.)-Flip book w/Ultraverse Premiere #3; silver foil logo — 4.00
13-($2.95, 52 pgs.)-Variant covers — 4.00
...: Gross and Disgusting 1 (10/94, $3.95)-Boris-c; "Annual" on cover, published monthly in indicia — 4.00
...Month "Ashcan" (8/94, 75¢)-Boris-c — 3.00
... Time: A Prime Collection (1994, $9.95)-r/1-4 — 10.00
...Vs. The Incredible Hulk (1995)-mail away limited edition — 10.00
...Vs. The Incredible Hulk Premium edition — 10.00
...Vs. The Incredible Hulk Super Premium edition — 15.00
NOTE: *Perez a-15; c-15, 16.*

PRIME (Also see Black September)
Malibu Comics (Ultraverse): Infinity, Sept, 1995 - V2#15, Dec, 1996 ($1.50)

Infinity, V2#1-15: Post Black September storyline. 6-8-Solitaire app. 9-Breyfogle-c/a. 10-12-Ramos-c. 15-Lord Pumpkin app. — 3.00
Infinity Signed Edition (2,000 printed) — 5.00

PRIME/CAPTAIN AMERICA
Malibu Comics: Mar, 1996 ($3.95, one-shot)

Prince Valiant FC #650 © KING

Prison Break! #1 © AVON

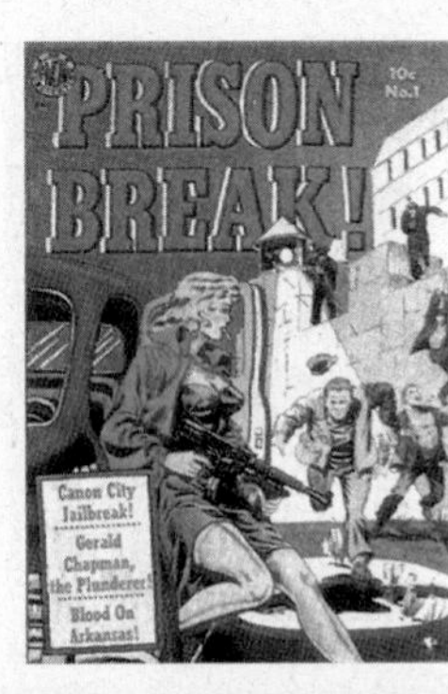

Prize Comics #6 © PRIZE

GD VG FN VF VF/NM NM-
2.0 4.0 6.0 8.0 9.0 9.2

GD VG FN VF VF/NM NM-
2.0 4.0 6.0 8.0 9.0 9.2

1-Norm Breyfogle-a 5.00

PRIME8: CREATION
Two Morrows Publishing: July, 2001 ($3.95, B&W)

1-Neal Adams-c 4.00

PRIMER (Comico...)
Comico: Oct (no month), 1982 - No. 6, Feb, 1984 (B&W)

1 (52 pgs.) 2 4 6 11 16 20
2-1st app. Grendel & Argent by Wagner 8 16 24 56 108 160
3,4 2 4 6 9 12 15
5-1st Sam Kieth art in comics ('83) & 1st The Maxx 4 8 12 23 37 50
6-Intro & 1st app. Evangeline 2 4 6 13 18 22

PRIMORTALS (Leonard Nimoy's...)

PRIMUS (TV)
Charlton Comics: Feb, 1972 - No. 7, Oct, 1972

1-Staton-a in all 2 4 6 11 16 20
2-7: 6-Drug propaganda story 2 4 6 8 11 14

PRINCE NAMOR, THE SUB-MARINER (Also see Namor ...)
Marvel Comics Group: Sept, 1984 - No. 4, Dec, 1984 (Limited-series)

1-4 5.00

PRINCE OF PERSIA: BEFORE THE SANDSTORM (Based on the 2010 movie)
Dynamite Entertainment: 2010 - No. 4, 2010 ($3.99, limited series)

1-4-Art by Fowler and various. 1-Chang-a. 2-Lopez-a. 3-Edwards-a 5.00

PRINCESS SALLY (Video game)
Archie Publications: Apr, 1995 - No. 3, June, 1995 ($1.50, limited series)

1-3: Spin-off from Sonic the Hedgehog 4.00

PRINCE VALIANT (See Ace Comics, Comics Reading Libraries *in the Promotional Comics section*, & King Comics #146, 147)
David McKay Publ./Dell: No. 26, 1941; No. 67, June, 1954 - No. 900, May, 1958

Feature Books 26 ('41)-Harold Foster-c/a; newspaper strips reprinted, pgs. 1-28,30-63; color & 68 pgs; Foster cover is only original comic book artwork by him
135 270 405 864 1482 2100
Four Color 567 (6/54)(#1)-By Bob Fuje-Movie, photo-c
9 18 27 62 126 190
Four Color 650 (9/55), 699 (4/56), 719 (8/56),-Fuje-a 7 14 21 44 82 120
Four Color 788 (4/57), 849 (1/58), 900-Fuje-a 6 12 18 41 76 110

PRINCE VALIANT
Marvel Comics: Dec, 1994 - No. 4, Mar, 1995 ($3.95, limited series)

1-4; Kaluta-c in all. 4.00

PRINCE VANDAL
Triumphant Comics: Nov, 1993 - Apr?, 1994 ($2.50)

1-6: 1,2-Triumphant Unleashed x-over 3.00

PRIORITY: WHITE HEAT
AC Comics: 1986 - No. 2, 1986 ($1.75, mini-series)

1,2-Bill Black-a 3.00

PRISCILLA'S POP
Dell Publishing Co.: No. 569, June, 1954 - No. 799, May, 1957

Four Color 569 (#1), 630 (5/55), 704 (5/56),799 4 8 12 27 44 60

PRISON BARS (See Behind...)

PRISON BREAK!
Avon Per./Realistic No. 3 on: Sept, 1951 - No. 5, Sept, 1952 (Painted c-3)

1-Wood-c & 1 pg.; has-r/Saint #7 retitled Michael Strong Private Eye
42 84 126 265 445 625
2-Wood-c; Kubert-a; Kinstler inside front-c 32 64 96 188 307 425
3-Orlando, Check-a; c-/Avon paperback #179 25 50 75 150 245 340
4,5: 4-Kinstler-c & inside f/c; Lawrence, Lazarus-a. 5-Kinstler-c; Infantino-a
22 44 66 128 209 290

PRISONER, THE (TV)
DC Comics: 1988 - No. 4, 1989 ($3.50, squarebound, mini-series)

1-4 (Books a-d) 5.00

PRISON RIOT
Avon Periodicals: 1952

1-Marijuana Murders-1 pg. text; Kinstler-c; 2 Kubert illos on text pages
30 60 90 177 289 400

PRISON TO PRAISE
Logos International: 1974 (35¢) (Religious, Christian)

nn-True Story of Merlin R. Carothers 2 4 6 13 18 22

PRIVATE BUCK
Dell Publishing Co./Rand McNally: No. 21, 1941 - No. 12, 1942 (4-1/2" x 5-1/2", 1942)

Large Feature Comic 21 (#1)(1941)(Series I), 22 (1941)(Series I), 12 (1942)(Series II)
18 36 54 105 165 225
382-Rand McNally, one panel per page; small size 10 20 30 58 79 100

PRIVATE EYE (Cover title: Rocky Jorden...#6-8)
Atlas Comics (MCI): Jan, 1951 - No. 8, March, 1952

1-Cover title: Crime Cases... #1-5 22 44 66 132 216 300
2,3-Tuska c/a(3) 14 28 42 80 115 150
4-8 12 24 36 67 94 120

NOTE: ***Henkel** a-6(3), 7; c-7. **Sinnott** a-6.*

PRIVATE EYE (See Mike Shayne...)

PRIVATE SECRETARY
Dell Publishing Co.: Dec-Feb, 1962-63 - No. 2, Mar-May, 1963

1 3 6 9 20 31 42
2 3 6 9 16 24 32

PRIVATE STRONG (See The Double Life of...)

PRIZE COMICS (...Western #69 on) (Also see Treasure Comics)
Prize Publications: March, 1940 - No. 68, Feb-Mar, 1948

1-Origin Power Nelson, The Futureman & Jupiter, Master Magician; Ted O'Neil, Secret Agent M-11, Jaxon of the Jungle, Bucky Brady & Storm Curtis begin (1st app. of each)
290 580 870 1856 3178 4500
2-The Black Owl begins (1st app.) 148 296 444 947 1624 2300
3 135 270 405 864 1482 2100
4-Classic robot-c 168 336 504 1075 1838 2600
5-Dr. Dekkar, Master of Monsters app. 119 238 357 762 1306 1850
6-Classic sci-fi-c; Dr. Dekkar app. 129 258 387 826 1413 2000
7-(Scarce)-1st app. The Green Lama (12/40); Black Owl by S&K; origin/1st app. Dr. Frost & Frankenstein; Capt. Gallant, The Great Voodini & Twist Turner begin;
271 542 813 1734 2967 4200
8,9-Black Owl & Ted O'Neil by S&K 123 246 369 787 1344 1900
10-12,14,15: 11-Origin Bulldog Denny. 14-War-c 90 180 270 576 988 1400
13-Yank & Doodle begin (8/41, origin/1st app.) 110 220 330 704 1202 1700
16-19: 16-Spike Mason begins 84 168 252 538 919 1300
20-(Rare) Frankenstein, Black Owl, Green Lama, Yank and Doodle WWII parade-c
155 310 465 992 1696 2400
21,25,27,28,31-All WWII covers 71 142 213 454 777 1100
22-24,26: 22-Statue of Liberty Japanese attack war-c. 23-Uncle Sam patriotic war-c. 24-Lincoln statue patriotic-c. 26-Liberty Bell-c 90 180 270 576 988 1400
29,30,32 53 106 159 334 567 800
33-Classic bondage/torture-c 90 180 270 576 988 1400
34-Origin Airmale, Yank & Doodle; The Black Owl joins army, Yank & Doodle's father assumes Black Owl's role 43 86 129 271 461 650
35-36,38-39: 35-Flying Fist & Bingo begin 34 68 102 199 325 450
37-Intro. Stampy, Airmale's sidekick; Hitler-c 71 142 213 454 777 1100
40-Nazi WWII-c 39 78 177 240 395 550
41-45,47-50: 45-Yank & Doodle learn Black Owl's I.D. (their father). 48-Prince Ra begins
28 56 84 165 270 375
46-Classic Zombie Horror-c/story 55 110 165 352 601 850
51-62,64,67,68: 53-Transvestism story. 55-No Frankenstein. 57-X-Mas-c. 64-Black Owl retires 20 40 60 117 189 260
63-Simon & Kirby c/a 23 46 69 136 223 310
65,66-Frankenstein-c by Briefer 22 44 66 132 216 300

NOTE: ***Briefer** a 7-on; c-65, 66. **J. Binder** a-16; c-21-29. **Guardineer** a-62. **Kiefer** c-62. **Palais** c-68. **Simon & Kirby** c-63, 75, 83.*

PRIZE COMICS WESTERN (Formerly Prize Comics #1-68)
Prize Publications (Feature): No. 69(V7#2), Apr-May, 1948 - No. 119, Nov-Dec, 1956 (No. 69-84: 52 pgs.)

69(V7#2) 14 28 42 80 115 150
70-75: 74-Kurtzman-a (8 pgs.) 12 24 36 67 94 120
76-Randolph Scott photo-c; "Canadian Pacific" movie adaptation
13 26 39 72 101 130
77-Photo-c; Severin/Elder, Mart Bailey-a; "Streets of Laredo" movie adaptation
12 24 36 67 94 120
78-Photo-c; S&K-a, 10 pgs.; Severin, Mart Bailey-a; "Bullet Code", & "Roughshod" movie adaptations 15 30 45 90 140 190
79-Photo-c; Kurtzman-a, 8 pgs.; Severin/Elder, Severin, Mart Bailey-a; "Stage To Chino" movie adaptation w/George O'Brien 15 30 45 90 140 190
80-82-Photo-c; 80,81-Severin/Elder-a(2). 82-1st app. The Preacher by Mart Bailey;

Project Superpowers #0 © SPH

Promethea #9 © ABC

Protectors #16 © MAL

	GD 2.0	VG 4.0	FN 6.0	VF 8.0	VF/NM 9.0	NM- 9.2
Severin/Elder-a(3)	13	26	39	72	101	130
83,84	10	20	30	58	79	100
85-1st app. American Eagle by John Severin & begins (V9#6, 1-2/51)	19	38	57	111	176	240
86,101-105, 109-Severin/Williamson-a	11	22	33	64	90	115
87-99,110,111-Severin/Elder-a(2-3) each	12	24	36	69	97	125
100	13	26	39	74	105	135
106-108,112	9	18	27	47	61	75
113-Williamson/Severin-a(2)/Frazetta?	12	24	36	69	97	125
114-119: Drifter series in all; by Mort Meskin #114-118	8	16	24	42	54	65

NOTE: *Fass a-81. **Severin & Elder** c-84-99. **Severin** a-72, 75, 77-79, 83-86, 96, 97, 100-105; c-92,100-109(most), 110-119. **Simon & Kirby** c-75, 83.*

PRIZE MYSTERY
Key Publications: May, 1955 - No. 3, Sept, 1955

	GD	VG	FN	VF	VF/NM	NM-
1	11	22	33	60	83	105
2,3	8	16	24	44	57	70

PRO, THE
Image Comics: July, 2002 ($5.95, squarebound, one-shot)

1-Ennis-s/Conner & Palmiotti-a; prostitute gets super-powers 8.00
1-Second printing with different cover 6.00
Hardcover Edition (10/04, $14.95) oversized reprint plus new 8 pg. story; sketch pages 15.00

PROFESSIONAL FOOTBALL (See Charlton Sport Library)

PROFESSOR COFFIN
Charlton Comics: No. 19, Oct, 1985 - No. 21, Feb, 1986

	GD	VG	FN	VF	VF/NM	NM-
19-21: Wayne Howard-a(r); low print run	1	2	3	5	6	8

PROFESSOR OM
Innovation Publishing: May, 1990 - No. 2, 1990 ($2.50, limited series)

1,2-East Meets West spin-off 3.00

PROFESSOR XAVIER AND THE X-MEN (Also see X-Men, 1st series)
Marvel Comics: Nov, 1995 - No. 18 (99¢)

1-18: Stories featuring the Original X-Men. 2-vs. The Blob. 5-Vs. the Original Brotherhood of Evil Mutants. 10-Vs. The Avengers 3.00

PROGRAMME, THE
DC Comics (WildStorm): Sept, 2007 - No. 12, Aug, 2008 ($2.99, limited series)

1-12: 1-Milligan-s/C.P. Smith-a; covers by Smith & Van Sciver 3.00
Book One TPB (2008, $17.99) r/#1-6; cover sketches 18.00
Book Two TPB (2008, $17.99) r/#7-12; cover sketches 18.00

PROJECT A-KO (Manga)
Malibu Comics: Mar, 1994 - No. 4, June, 1994 ($2.95)

1-4-Based on anime film 3.00

PROJECT A-KO 2 (Manga)
CPM Comics: May, 1995 - No. 3, Aug, 1995 ($2.95, limited series)

1-3 3.00

PROJECT A-KO VERSUS THE UNIVERSE (Manga)
CPM Comics: Oct, 1995 - No. 5, June, 1996 ($2.95, limited series, bi-monthly)

1-5 3.00

PROJECT SUPERPOWERS
Dynamite Entertainment: 2008 - No. 7, 2008 ($1.00/$3.50/$2.99)

0-($1.00) Two connecting covers by Alex Ross; re-intro of Golden Age heroes 3.00
0-($1.00) Variant cover by Michael Turner 5.00
1-($3.50) Covers by Ross and Turner; Jim Krueger-s/Carlos Paul-a 3.50
2-7-($2.99) 3.00
... Chapter One HC (2008, $29.99, dustjacket) r/#0-7; Ross sketch pages; layout art 30.00

PROJECT SUPERPOWERS: CHAPTER TWO
Dynamite Entertainment: 2009 - No. 12, 2010 ($1.00/$2.99)

... Chapter Two Prelude (2008, $1.00) Ross sketch pages and mini-series previews 3.00
0-($1.00) Three connecting covers by Alex Ross; The Inheritors assemble 3.00
1-12-($2.99) 1-Krueger & Ross-s/Salazar-a; Ross sketch pages; 2 Ross covers 3.00
... X-Mas Carol (2010, $5.99) Berkenkotter-a/Ross-c 6.00

PROJECT SUPERPOWERS: MEET THE BAD GUYS
Dynamite Entertainment: 2009 - No. 4, 2009 ($2.99)

1-4: Ross & Casey-s. 1-Bloodlust. 2-The Revolutionary. 3-Dagon. 4-Supremacy 3.00

PROMETHEA
America's Best Comics: Aug, 1999 - No. 32, Apr, 2005 ($3.50/$2.95)

1-Alan Moore-s/Williams III & Gray-a; Alex Ross painted-c 4.00
1-Variant-c by Williams III & Gray 4.00
2-31-($2.95): 7-Villarrubia photo-a. 10-"Sex, Stars & Serpents". 26-28-Tom Strong app. 27-Cover swipe of Superman vs. Spider-Man treasury ed. 3.00
32-($3.95) Final issue; pages can be cut & assembled into a 2-sided poster 6.00
32-Limited edition of 1000; variant issue printed as 2-sided poster, signed by Moore and Williams; each came with a 48 page book of Promethea covers 120.00
Book 1 Hardcover ($24.95, dust jacket) r/#1-6 25.00
Book 1 TPB ($14.95) r/#1-6 15.00
Book 2 Hardcover ($24.95, dust jacket) r/#7-12 25.00
Book 2 TPB ($14.95) r/#7-12 15.00
Book 3 Hardcover ($24.95, dust jacket) r/#13-18 25.00
Book 3 TPB ($14.95) r/#13-18 15.00
Book 4 Hardcover ($24.95, dust jacket) r/#19-25 25.00
Book 4 TPB ($14.99) r/#19-25 15.00
Book 5 Hardcover ($24.95, d.j.) r/#26-32; includes 2-sided poster image from #32 25.00
Book 5 TPB ($14.99) r/#26-32; includes 2-sided poster image from #32 15.00

PROMETHEUS (VILLAINS) (Leads into JLA #16,17)
DC Comics: Feb, 1998 ($1.95, one-shot)

1-Origin & 1st app.; Morrison-s/Pearson-c 3.00

PROPELLERMAN
Dark Horse Comics: Jan, 1993 - No. 8, Mar, 1994 ($2.95, limited series)

1-8: 2,4,8-Contain 2 trading cards 3.00

PROPHECY
Dynamite Entertainment: 2012 - No. 7, 2013 ($3.99, limited series)

1-7: 1-Marz-s/Geovani-a; Vampirella,Red Sonja, Dracula & Pantha app. 4-Ash app. 4.00

PROPHET (See Youngblood #2)
Image Comics (Extreme Studios): Oct, 1993 - No. 10, 1995 ($1.95)

1-($2.50)-Liefeld/Panosian-c/a; 1st app. Mary McCormick; Liefeld scripts in 1-4; #1-3 contain coupons for Prophet #0 4.00
1-Gold foil embossed-c edition rationed to dealers 6.00
2-10: 2-Liefeld-c(p). 3-1st app. Judas. 4-1st app. Omen; Black and White Pt. 3 by Thibert. 4-Alternate-c by Stephen Platt. 5,6-Platt-c/a. 7-(9/94, $2.50)-Platt-c/a. 8-Bloodstrike app. 10-Polybagged w/trading card; Platt-c. 3.00
0-(7/94, $2.50)-San Diego Comic Con ed. (2200 copies) 4.00

PROPHET
Image Comics (Extreme Studios): V2#1, Aug, 1995 - No. 8 ($3.50)

V2#1-8: Dixon scripts in all. 1-4-Platt-a. 1-Boris-c; F. Miller variant-c. 4-Newmen app. 5,6-Wraparound-c 3.50
Annual 1 (9/95, $2.50)-Bagged w/Youngblood gaming card; Quesada-c 3.00
Babewatch Special 1 (12/95, $2.50)-Babewatch tie-in 3.00
1995 San Diego Edition-B&W preview of V2#1. 3.00
TPB-(1996, $12.95) r/#1-7 13.00

PROPHET (Volume 3)
Awesome Comics: Mar, 2000 ($2.99)

1-Flip-c by Jim Lee and Liefeld 3.00

PROPHET
Image Comics: No. 21, Jan, 2012 - Present ($2.99/$3.99)

21-27-($2.99): 21-Two covers; Graham-s 3.00
28-43-($3.99): 29-Dalrymple-a 4.00

PROPHET/CABLE
Image Comics (Extreme): Jan, 1997 - No. 2, Mar, 1997 ($3.50, limited series)

1,2-Liefeld-c/a: 2-#1 listed on cover 4.00

PROPHET/CHAPEL: SUPER SOLDIERS
Image Comics (Extreme): May, 1996 - No. 2, June, 1996 ($2.50, limited series)

1,2: 1-Two covers exist 3.00
1-San Diego Edition; B&W-c 3.00

PROPOSITION PLAYER
DC Comics (Vertigo): Dec, 1999 - No. 6, May, 2000 ($2.50, limited series)

1-6-Willingham-s/Guinan-a/Bolton-c 3.00
TPB (2003, $14.95) r/#1-6; intro. by James McManus 15.00

PROTECTORS (Also see The Ferret)
Malibu Comics: Sept, 1992 - No. 20, May, 1994 ($1.95-$2.95)

1-20 ($2.50, direct sale)-With poster & diff-c: 1-Origin; has 3/4 outer-c. 3-Polybagged w/Skycap 3.50
1-12 ($1.95, newsstand)-Without poster 3.00

PROTECTORS, INC.
Image Comics: Nov, 2013 - Present ($2.99)

Prototype #15 © MAL

Psychoanalysis #3 © WMG

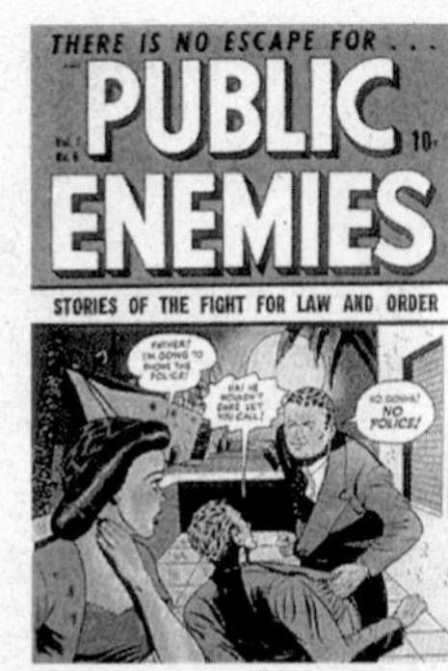

Public Enemies #6 © DS

GD 2.0 | VG 4.0 | FN 6.0 | VF 8.0 | VF/NM 9.0 | NM- 9.2

1-6-Straczynski-s/Purcell-a; multiple covers on each 3.00

PROTOCOL: ORPHANS
BOOM! Studios: Nov, 2013 - No. 4, Feb, 2014 ($3.99, limited series)
1-4-Nelson-s/Navarro-a 4.00

PROTOTYPE (Also see Flood Relief & Ultraforce)
Malibu Comics (Ultraverse): Aug, 1993 - No. 18, Feb, 1995 ($1.95/$2.50)
1-Holo-c 1 2 3 5 6 8
1-Ultra Limited silver foil-c 6.00
1,3: 3-($2.50, 48 pgs.)-Rune flip-c/story by B. Smith (3 pgs.) 4.00
2,4-12,14-18: 4-Intro Wrath. 5-Break-Thru & Strangers x-over. 6-Arena cameo. 7,8-Arena-c/story. 12-(7/94). 14 (10/94) 3.00
13 (8/94, $3.50)-Flip book (Ultraverse Premiere #6) 4.00
#0-(8/94, $2.50, 44 pgs.) 4.00
Giant Size 1 (10/94, $2.50, 44 pgs.) 4.00

PROTOTYPE (Based on the Activision video game)
DC Comics (WildStorm): Jun, 2009 - No. 6, Nov, 2009 ($3.99, limited series)
1-6-Darick Robertson-c/a 4.00
TPB (2010, $19.99) r/#1-6 20.00

PRUDENCE & CAUTION (Also see Dogs of War & Warriors of Plasm)
Defiant: May, 1994 - No. 2, June, 1994 ($3.50/$2.50)(Spanish versions exist)
1-($3.50, 52 pgs.)-Chris Claremont scripts in all 4.00
2-($2.50) 3.00

PRYDE AND WISDOM (Also see Excalibur)
Marvel Comics: Sept, 1996 - No. 3, Nov, 1996 ($1.95, limited series)
1-3: Warren Ellis scripts; Terry Dodson & Karl Story-c/a 3.00

PSI-FORCE
Marvel Comics Group: Nov, 1986 - No. 32, June, 1989 (75¢/$1.50)
1-25: 11-13-Williamson-i 3.00
26-32 3.00
Annual 1 (10/87) 4.00
... Classic Vol. 1 TPB (2008, $24.99) r/#1-9 25.00

PSI-JUDGE ANDERSON
Fleetway Publications (Quality): 1989 - No. 15, 1990 ($1.95, B&W)
1-15 4.00

PSI-LORDS
Valiant: Sept, 1994 - No. 10, June, 1995 ($2.25)
1-($3.50)-Chromium wraparound-c 5.00
1-Gold 8.00
2-10: 3-Chaos Effect Epsilon Pt. 2 3.00

PSYBA-RATS (Also see Showcase '94 #3,4)
DC Comics: Apr, 1995-No. 3, June, 1995 ($2.50, limited series)
1-3 3.00

PSYCHO (Magazine) (Also see Nightmare)
Skywald Publ. Corp.: Jan, 1971 - No. 24, Mar, 1975 (68 pgs.; B&W)
1-All reprints 8 16 24 54 102 150
2-Origin & 1st app. The Heap, series begins 6 12 18 37 68 95
3-Frankenstein series by Adkins begins 5 10 15 35 63 90
4,7,9,10: 4-7-Squarebound. 4-1st Out of Chaos/Satan-c/s 5 10 15 33 57 80
8-(Squarebound)1st app. Edward & Mina Sartyros, the Human Gargoyles 5 10 15 35 63 90
11-17: 13-Cannabalism; 3 pgs of Christopher Lee as Dracula photos 4 8 12 27 44 60
18-Injury to eye-c 5 10 15 31 53 75
19-Origin Dracula. 4 8 12 28 47 65
20-Severed Head-c 5 10 15 33 57 80
21-24: 22-1974 Fall Special; Reese, Wildey-a(r). 24-1975 Winter Special; Dave Sim scripts (1st pro work) 5 10 15 30 50 70
Annual 1 (1972)(68 pgs.) Dracula & the Heap app. 5 10 15 30 50 70
Yearbook (1974-nn)-Everett, Reese-a 4 8 12 27 44 60
NOTE: ***Boris** c-3, 5. **Buckler** a-2, 4, 5. **Gene Day** a-21, 23, 24. **Everett** a-3-6. **B. Jones** a-4. **Jeff Jones** a-6, 7, 9; c-12. **Kaluta** a-13. **Katz/Buckler** a-3. **Kim** a-24. **Morrow** a-1. **Reese** a-5. **Dave Sim** s-24. **Sutton** a-3. **Wildey** a-5.*

PSYCHO, THE
DC Comics: 1991 - No. 3, 1991 ($4.95, squarebound, limited series)
1-3-Hudnall-s/Brereton painted-a/c 5.00
TPB (Image Comics, 2006, $17.99) r/series; Brereton sketch pages; Hudnall afterword 18.00

PSYCHOANALYSIS
E. C. Comics: Mar-Apr, 1955 - No. 4, Sept-Oct, 1955
1-All Kamen-c/a; not approved by code 22 44 66 176 281 385
2-4-Kamen-c/a in all 15 30 45 120 190 260

PSYCHOANALYSIS
Gemstone Publishing: Oct, 1999 - No. 4, Jan, 2000 ($2.50)
1-4-Reprints E.C. series 4.00
Annual 1 (2000, $10.95) r/#1-4 11.00

PSYCHOBLAST
First Comics: Nov, 1987 - No. 9, July, 1988 ($1.75)
1-9 3.00

PSYCHONAUTS
Marvel Comics (Epic Comics): Oct, 1993 - No. 4, Jan, 1994 ($4.95, lim. series)
1-4: American/Japanese co-produced comic 5.00

PSYLOCKE
Marvel Comics: Jan, 2010 - No. 4, Apr, 2010 ($3.99, limited series)
1-4-Finch-c/Yost-s/Tolibao-a. 3,4-Wolverine app. 4.00

PSYLOCKE & ARCHANGEL CRIMSON DAWN
Marvel Comics: Aug, 1997 - No. 4, Nov, 1997 ($2.50, limited series)
1-4-Raab-s/Larroca-a(p) 4.00

PTOLUS: CITY BY THE SPIRE
Dabel Brothers Productions/Marvel Comics (Dabel Brothers) #2 on: June, 2006 - No. 6, Mar, 2007 ($2.99)
1-(1st printing, Dabel) Adaptation of the Monte Cook novel; Cook-s 4.00
1-(2nd printing, Marvel), 2-6 3.00
Monte Cooke's Ptolus: City By the Spire TPB (2007, $14.99) r/#1-6 15.00

P.T. 109 (See Movie Comics)

PUBLIC DEFENDER IN ACTION (Formerly Police Trap)
Charlton Comics: No. 7, Mar, 1956 - No. 12, Oct, 1957
7 11 22 33 60 83 105
8-12 8 16 24 40 50 60

PUBLIC ENEMIES
D. S. Publishing Co.: 1948 - No. 9, June-July, 1949
1-True Crime Stories 29 58 87 170 278 385
2-Used in **SOTI**, pg. 95 24 48 72 140 230 320
3-5: 5-Arrival date of 10/1/48 16 32 48 94 147 200
6,8,9 15 30 45 90 140 190
7-McWilliams-a; injury to eye panel 16 32 48 94 147 200

PUBO
Dark Horse Comics: Dec, 2002 - No. 3, Mar, 2003 ($3.50, B&W, limited series)
1-3-Leland Purvis-s/a 3.50

PUDGY PIG
Charlton Comics: Sept, 1958 - No. 2, Nov, 1958
1,2 3 6 9 17 26 35

PUFFED
Image Comics: Jul, 2003 - No. 3, Sept, 2003 ($2.95, B&W)
1-3-Layman-s/Crosland-a. 1-Two covers by Crosland & Quitely 3.00

PULP FANTASTIC (Vertigo V2K)
DC Comics (Vertigo): Feb, 2000 - No. 3, Apr, 2000 ($2.50, limited series)
1-3-Chaykin & Tischman-s/Burchett-a 3.00

PULP FICTION LIBRARY: MYSTERY IN SPACE
DC Comics: 1999 ($19.95, TPB)
nn-Reprints classic sci-fi stories from Mystery in Space, Strange Adventures, Real Fact Comics and My Greatest Adventure 20.00

PULSE, THE (Also see Alias and Deadline)
Marvel Comics: Apr, 2004 - No. 14, May, 2006 ($2.99)
1-Jessica Jones, Ben Urich, Kat Farrell app.; Bendis-s/Bagley-a 5.00
2-14: 2-5-Bendis-s/Bagley-a. 3-5-Green Goblin app. 6,7-Brent Anderson-a 9-Wolverine app. 10-House of M. 11-14-Gaydos-a 3.00
...: House of M Special (9/05, 50¢) tabloid newspaper format; Mayhew- "photos" 3.00
Vol. 1: Thin Air (2004, $13.99) r/#1-5, gallery of cover layouts and sketches 14.00
Vol. 2: Secret War (2005, $11.99) r/#6-9 12.00
Vol. 3: Fear (2006, $14.99) r/#11-14 and New Avengers Annual #1 15.00

PUMA BLUES

Punch Comics #9 © CHES

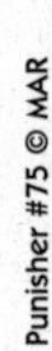

Punisher #75 © MAR

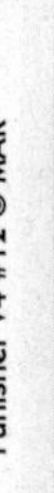

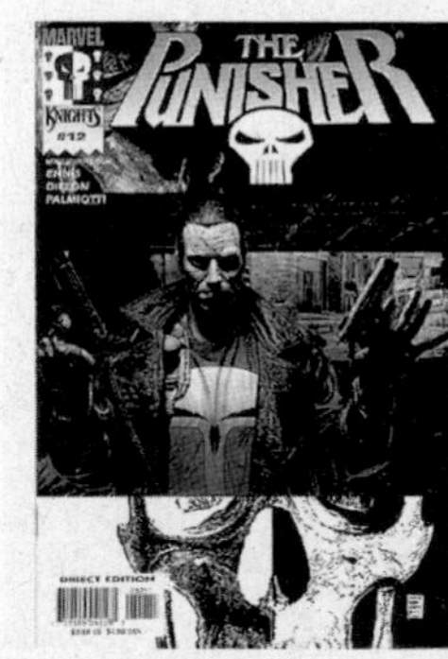

Punisher V4 #12 © MAR

	GD	VG	FN	VF	VF/NM	NM-
	2.0	4.0	6.0	8.0	9.0	9.2

Aardvark One International/Mirage Studios #21 on: 1986 - No. 26, 1990 ($1.70-$1.75, B&W)

1-19, 21-26: 1-1st & 2nd printings. 25,26-$1.75-c 3.00
20 ($2.25)-By Alan Moore, Miller, Grell, others 5.00
Trade Paperback (12/88, $14.95) 15.00

PUMPKINHEAD: THE RITES OF EXORCISM (Movie)
Dark Horse Comics: 1993 - No. 2, 1993 ($2.50, limited series)

1,2: Based on movie; painted-c by McManus 3.00

PUNCH & JUDY COMICS
Hillman Per.: 1944; No. 2, Fall, 1944 - V3#2, 12/47; V3#3, 6/51 - V3#9, 12/51

	GD	VG	FN	VF	VF/NM	NM-
V1#1-(60 pgs.)	25	50	75	150	245	340
2	14	28	42	81	118	155
3-12(7/46)	12	24	36	67	94	120
V2#1(8/49),3-9	9	18	27	52	69	85
V2#2,10-12, V3#1-Kirby-a(2) each	21	42	63	122	199	275
V3#2-Kirby-a	19	38	57	112	179	245
3-9	9	18	27	47	61	75

PUNCH COMICS
Harry 'A' Chesler: 12/41; #2, 2/42; #9, 7/44 - #19, 10/46; #20, 7/47 - #23, 1/48

	GD	VG	FN	VF	VF/NM	NM-
1-Mr. E, The Sky Chief, Hale the Magician, Kitty Kelly begin	161	322	483	1030	1765	2500
2-Captain Glory app.	100	200	300	640	1095	1550
9-Rocketman & Rocket Girl & The Master Key begin; classic-c	161	322	483	1030	1765	2500
10-Sky Chief app.; J. Cole-a; Master Key-r/Scoop #3	65	130	195	416	708	1000
11-Origin Master Key-r/Scoop #1; Sky Chief, Little Nemo app.; Jack Cole-a; Fine-*ish* art by Sultan	63	126	189	403	689	975
12-Rocket Boy & Capt. Glory app; classic Skull-c	900	1800	2700	5400	7200	9000
13-Cover has list of 4 Chesler artists' names on tombstone	84	168	252	538	919	1300
14,15,19,21: 21-Hypo needle story	61	122	183	390	670	950
16,17-Gag-c	39	78	117	240	395	550
18-Bondage-c; hypodermic panels	68	136	204	435	743	1050
20-Unique cover with bare-breasted women. Rocket Girl-c	142	284	426	909	1555	2200
22,23-Little Nemo-not by McCay. 22-Intro Baxter (teenage)(68 pgs.)	24	48	72	140	230	320

PUNCHY AND THE BLACK CROW
Charlton Comics: No. 10, Oct, 1985 - No. 12, Feb, 1986

10-12: Al Fago funny animal-r; low print run 6.00

PUNISHER (See Amazing Spider-Man #129, Blood and Glory, Born, Captain America #241, Classic Punisher, Daredevil #182-184, 257, Daredevil and the..., Ghost Rider V2#5, 6, Marc Spector #8 & 9, Marvel Preview #2, Marvel Super Action, Marvel Tales, Power Pack #46, Spectacular Spider-Man #81-83, 140, 141, 143 & new Strange Tales #13 & 14)

PUNISHER (The...)
Marvel Comics Group: Jan, 1986 - No. 5, May, 1986 (Limited series)

	GD	VG	FN	VF	VF/NM	NM-
1-Double size	4	8	12	23	37	50
2-5	2	4	6	10	14	18

Trade Paperback (1988)-r/#1-5 16.00
Circle of Blood TPB (8/01, $15.95) Zeck-c 16.00
Circle of Blood HC (2008, $19.99) two covers 20.00
NOTE: ***Zeck*** *a-1-4; c-1-5.*

PUNISHER (The...) (Volume 2)
Marvel Comics: July, 1987 - No. 104, July, 1995

	GD	VG	FN	VF	VF/NM	NM-
1	3	6	9	14	20	25

2-9: 8-Portacio/Williams-c/a begins, ends #18. 9-Scarcer, low dist. 6.00

	GD	VG	FN	VF	VF/NM	NM-
10-Daredevil app; ties in w/Daredevil #257	1	3	4	6	8	10

11-25,50: 13-18-Kingpin app. 19-Stroman-c/a. 20-Portacio-c(p). 24-1st app. Shadowmasters. 25,50:($1.50,52 pgs.). 25-Shadowmasters app. 4.00
26-49,51-74,76-85,87-89: 57-Photo-c; came w/outer-c (newsstand ed. w/o outer-c). 59-Punisher is severely cut & has skin grafts (has black skin). 60-62-Luke Cage app. 62-Punisher back to white skin. 68-Tarantula-c/story. 85-Prequel to Suicide Run Pt. 0. 87,88-Suicide Run Pt. 6 & 9 3.00
75-($2.75, 52 pgs.)-Embossed silver foil-c 4.00
86-($2.95, 52 pgs.)-Embossed & foil stamped-c; Suicide Run part 3 4.00
90-99: 90-bound-in cards. 99-Cringe app. 3.00
100,104: 100-($2.95, 68 pgs.). 104-Last issue 4.00
100-($3.95, 68 pgs.)-Foil cover 5.00
101-103: 102-Bullseye 3.50
"Ashcan" edition (75¢)-Joe Kubert-c 3.00
Annual 1-7 ('88-'94, 68 pgs.) 1-Evolutionary War x-over. 2-Atlantis Attacks x-over; Jim Lee-a(p) (back-up story, 6 pgs.); Moon Knight app. 4-Golden-c(p). 6-Bagged w/card. 4.00
...: A Man Named Frank (1994, $6.95, TPB) 7.00
...and Wolverine in African Saga nn (1989, $5.95, 52 pgs.)-Reprints Punisher War Journal #6 & 7; Jim Lee-c/a(r) 6.00
... Assassin Guild ('88, $6.95, graphic novel) 10.00
Back to School Special 1-3 (11/92-10/94, $2.95, 68 pgs.) 4.00
.../Batman: Deadly Knights (10/94, $4.95) 6.00
.../Black Widow: Spinning Doomsday's Web (1992, $9.95, graphic novel) 12.00
...Bloodlines nn (1991, $5.95, 68 pgs.) 6.00
...: Die Hard in the Big Easy nn ('92, $4.95, 52 pgs.) 6.00
...: Empty Quarter nn ('94, $6.95) 7.00
...G-Force nn (1992, $4.95, 52 pgs.)-Painted-c 6.00
...Holiday Special 1-3 (1/93-1/95,, 52 pgs.,68pgs.)-1-Foil-c 4.00
...Intruder Graphic Novel (1989, $14.95, hardcover) 20.00
...Intruder Graphic Novel (1991, $9.95, softcover) 12.00
...Invades the 'Nam: Final Invasion nn (2/94, $6.95)-J. Kubert-c & chapter break art; reprints The 'Nam #84 & unpublished #85,86 10.00
...Kingdom Gone Graphic Novel (1990, $16.95, hardcover) 20.00
...Meets Archie (8/94, $3.95, 52 pgs.)-Die cut-c; no ads; same contents as Archie Meets The Punisher 5.00
...Movie Special 1 (6/90, $5.95, squarebound, 68 pgs.) painted-c; Brent Anderson-a; contents intended for a 3 issue series which was advertised but not published 6.00
...: No Escape nn (1990, $4.95, 52 pgs.)-New-a 6.00
...Return to Big Nothing Graphic Novel (Epic, 1989, $16.95, hardcover) 25.00
...Return to Big Nothing Graphic Novel (Marvel, 1989, $12.95, softcover) 15.00
...The Prize nn (1990, $4.95, 68 pgs.)-New-a 6.00
Summer Special 1-4(8/91-7/94, 52 pgs.):1-No ads. 2-Bisley-c; Austin-a(i). 3-No ads 4.00
NOTE: ***Austin*** *c(i)-47, 48.* ***Cowan*** *c-39.* ***Golden*** *c-50, 85, 86, 100.* ***Heath*** *a-26, 27, 89, 90, 91; c-26, 27.* ***Quesada*** *c-56p, 62p.* ***Sienkiewicz*** *c-Back to School 1.* ***Stroman*** *a-76p(9 pgs.).* ***Williamson*** *a(i)-25, 60-62i, 64-70, 74, Annual 5; c(i)-62, 65-68.*

PUNISHER (Also see Double Edge)
Marvel Comics: Nov, 1995 - No. 18, Apr, 1997 ($2.95/$1.95/$1.50)

1 ($2.95)-Ostrander scripts begin; foil-c. 4.00
2-18: 7-Vs. S.H.I.E.L.D. 11-"Onslaught." 12-17-X-Cutioner-c/app. 17-Daredevil, Spider-Man-c/app. 3.00

PUNISHER (Marvel Knights)
Marvel Comics: Nov, 1998 - No. 4, Feb, 1999 ($2.99, limited series)

1-4: 1-Wrightson-a; Wrightson & Jusko-c 3.00
1-($6.95) DF Edition; Jae Lee variant-c 7.00

PUNISHER (Marvel Knights) (Volume 3)
Marvel Comics: Apr, 2000 - No. 12, Mar, 2001 ($2.99, limited series)

1-Ennis-s/Dillon & Palmiotti-a/Bradstreet-c 5.00
1-Bradstreet white variant-c 10.00
1-($6.95) DF Edition; Jurgens & Ordway variant-c 7.00
2-Two covers by Bradstreet & Dillon 3.00
3-($3.99) Bagged with Marvel Knights Genesis Edition; Daredevil app. 4.00
4-12: 9-11-The Russian app. 3.00
HC (6/02, $34.95) r/#1-12, Punisher Kills the Marvel Universe, and Marvel Knights Double Shot #1 35.00
... By Garth Ennis Omnibus (2008, $99.99) oversized r/#1-12, #1-7 & #13-37 of 2001 series, Punisher Kills the Marvel Universe, and Marvel Knights Double Shot #1; extras 100.00
.../Painkiller Jane (1/01, $3.50) Jusko-c; Ennis-s/Jusko and Dave Ross-a(p) 3.50
...: Welcome Back Frank TPB (4/01, $19.95) r/#1-12 20.00

PUNISHER (Marvel Knights) (Volume 4)
Marvel Comics: Aug, 2001 - No. 37, Feb, 2004 ($2.99)

1-Ennis-s/Dillon & Palmiotti-a/Bradstreet-c; The Russian app. 4.00
2-Two covers (Dillon & Bradstreet) Spider-Man-c/app. 3.00
3-37: 3-7-Ennis-s/Dillon-a. 9-12-Peyer-s/Gutierrez-a. 13,14-Ennis-s/Dilllon-a. 16,17-Wolverine app.; Robertson-a. 18-23,32-Dillon-a. 24-27-Mandrake-a. 27-Elektra app. 33-37-Spider-Man, Daredevil, & Wolverine app. 36,37-Hulk app. 3.00
...Army of One TPB (2/02, $15.95) r/#1-7; Bradstreet-c 16.00
Vol. 2 HC (2003, $29.95) r/#1-7,13-18; intro. by Mike Millar 30.00
Vol. 3 HC (2004, $29.95) r/#19-27; script pages for #19 30.00
Vol. 3: Business as Usual TPB (2003, $14.99) r/#13-18; Bradstreet-c 15.00
Vol. 4: Full Auto TPB (2003, $17.99) r/#20-26; Bradstreet-c 18.00
Vol. 5: Streets of Laredo TPB (2003, $17.99) r/#19,27-32 18.00
Vol. 6: Confederacy of Dunces TPB (2004, $13.99) r/#33-37 14.00

PUNISHER (Marvel MAX)(Title becomes "Punisher: Frank Castle MAX" with #66)
Marvel Comics: Mar, 2004 - No. 75, Dec, 2009 ($2.99/$3.99)

1-49,51-60: 1-Ennis-s/LaRosa-a/Bradstreet-c; flashback to his family's murder; Micro app. 6-Micro killed. 7-12,19-25-Fernandez-a. 13-18-Braithwaite-a. 31-36-Barracuda.

Punisher (2011 series) #10 © MAR

Punisher (2014 series) #1 © MAR

Punisher vs. Bullseye #3 © MAR

	GD 2.0	VG 4.0	FN 6.0	VF 8.0	VF/NM 9.0	NM- 9.2

43-49-Medina-a. 51-54-Barracuda app. 60-Last Ennis-s/Bradstreet-c 3.00
50-($3.99) Barracuda returns; Chaykin-a 4.00
61-65-Gregg Hurwitz-s/Dave Johnson-c/Laurence Campbell-a 3.00
66-73-($3.99) 66-70-Six Hours to Kill; Swierczynski-s. 71-73-Parlov-a 4.00
74,75-($4.99) 74-Parlov-a. 75-Short stories; art by Lashley, Coker, Parlov & others 5.00
Annual (11/07, $3.99) Mike Benson-s/Laurence Campbell-a 4.00
...: Bloody Valentine (4/06, $3.99) Palmiotti & Gray-s/Gulacy & Palmiotti-a; Gulacy-c 4.00
...: Force of Nature (4/08, $4.99) Swierczynski-s/Lacombe-a/Deodato-c 5.00
...: MAX MGC #1 (5/10, $1.00) reprints #1 with "Marvel's Greatest Comics" cover logo 3.00
...: MAX: Naked Kill (8/09, $3.99) Campbell-a/Bradstreet-c 4.00
...: MAX Special: Little Black Book (8/08, $3.99) Gischler-s/Palo-a/Johnson-c 4.00
...: MAX X-Mas Special (2/09, $3.99) Aaron-s/Boschi-a/Bachalo-c 4.00
...: Red X-Mas (2/05, $3.99) Palmiotti & Gray-s/Texeira & Palmiotti-a; Texeira-c 4.00
...: Silent Night (2/06, $3.99) Diggle-s/Hotz-a/Deodato-c 4.00
...: The Cell (7/05, $4.99) Ennis-s/LaRosa-a/Bradstreet-c 5.00
...: The Tyger (2/06, $4.99) Ennis-s/Severin-a/Bradstreet-c; Castle's childhood 5.00
...: Very Special Holidays TPB ('06, $12.99) r/Red X-Mas, Bloody Valentine and Silent Night 13.00
...: X-Mas Special (1/07, $3.99) Stuart Moore-s/CP Smith-a 4.00
... MAX: From First to Last HC (2006, $19.99) r/The Tyger, The Cell and The End 1-shots 20.00
... MAX Vol. 1 (2005, $29.99) oversized r/#1-12; gallery of Fernandez art from #7 shown from layout to colored pages 30.00
... MAX Vol. 2 (2006, $29.99) oversized r/#13-24; gallery of Fernandez pencil art 30.00
... MAX Vol. 3 (2007, $29.99) oversized r/#25-36; gallery of Fernandez & Parlov art 30.00
... MAX Vol. 4 (2008, $29.99) oversized r/#37-49; gallery of Fernandez & Medina art 30.00
Vol. 1: In the Beginning TPB (2004, $14.99) r/#1-6 15.00
Vol. 2: Kitchen Irish TPB (2004, $14.99) r/#7-12 15.00
Vol. 3: Mother Russia TPB (2005, $14.99) r/#13-18 15.00
Vol. 4: Up is Down and Black is White TPB (2005, $14.99) r/#19-24 15.00
Vol. 5: The Slavers TPB (2006, $15.99) r/#25-30; Fernandez pencil pages 16.00
Vol. 6: Barracuda TPB (2006, $15.99) r/#31-36; Parlov sketch page 16.00
Vol. 7: Man of Stone TPB (2007, $15.99) r/#37-42 16.00
Vol. 8: Widowmaker TPB (2007, $17.99) r/#43-49 18.00
Vol. 9: Long Cold Dark TPB (2008, $15.99) r/#50-54 16.00

PUNISHER (Frank Castle in the Marvel Universe after Secret Invasion)
(Title changes to Franken-Castle for #17-21)
Marvel Comics: Mar, 2009 - No. 21, Nov, 2010 ($3.99/$2.99)

1-($3.99) Dark Reign; Sentry app.; Remender-s/Opena-a; character history; 2 covers 4.00
2-5,710($2.99) 2-7-The Hood app. 4-Microchip returns. 5-Daredevil #183 cover swipe 3.00
6-($3.99) Huat-a/McKone-c; profile pages of resurrected villains 4.00
11-Follows Dark Reign: The List - Punisher; Franken-Castle begins; Tony Moore-a 4.00
12-16-Franken-Castle continues; Legion of Monsters app. 14-Brereton & Moore-a 3.00
Franken-Castle 17-20: 19, 20-Wolverine & Daken app. 3.00
Franken-Castle 21-($3.99) Brereton-a/c; Legion of Monsters app.; Frank gets body back 4.00
Annual 1 (11/09, $3.99) Pearson-a/c; Spider-Man app. 4.00
...: Franken-Castle - The Birth of the Monster 1 (7/10, $4.99) r/#11 & Dark Reign: The List 5.00

PUNISHER (Frank Castle in the Marvel Universe)(Continues in Punisher: War Zone [2012])
Marvel Comics: Oct, 2011 - No. 16, Nov, 2012 ($3.99/$2.99)

1-($3.99) Rucka-s/Checchetto-a/Hitch-c 4.00
1-Variant-c by Sal Buscema 6.00
1-Variant-c by Neal Adams 10.00
2-16-($2.99): 2,3-Vulture app. 10-Spider-Man & Daredevil app. 3.00
..., Moon Knight & Daredevil: The Big Shots (10/11, $3.99) Previews new series for Punisher, Moon Knight & Daredevil; creator interviews and production art 4.00

PUNISHER, THE
Marvel Comics: Apr, 2014 - Present ($3.99)

1-4-($3.99) Edmonson-s/Gerads-a; Howling Commandos app. 2-4-Electro app. 4.00

PUNISHER AND WOLVERINE: DAMAGING EVIDENCE (See Wolverine and...)

PUNISHER ARMORY, THE
Marvel Comics: 7/90 ($1.50); No. 2, 6/91; No. 3, 4/92 - 10/94($1.75/$2.00)

1-10: 1-r/weapons pgs. from War Journal. 1,2-Jim Lee-c. 3-10- All new material. 3-Jusko painted-c 4.00

PUNISHER: IN THE BLOOD (Marvel Universe Frank Castle)
Marvel Comics: Jan, 2011 - No. 5, May, 2011 ($3.99, limited series)

1-5-Remender-s/Boschi-a; Jigsaw & Microchip app. 4.00

PUNISHER KILLS THE MARVEL UNIVERSE
Marvel Comics: Nov, 1995 ($5.95, one-shot)

1-Garth Ennis script/Doug Braithwaite-a 7.00
1-2nd printing (3/00) Steve Dillon-c 6.00
1-3rd printing (2008, $4.99) original 1995 cover 5.00

PUNISHER MAGAZINE, THE
Marvel Comics: Oct, 1989 - No. 16, Nov, 1990 ($2.25, B&W, Magazine, 52 pgs.)

1-16: 1-r/Punisher #1('86). 2,3-r/Punisher 2-5. 4-16: 4-7-r/Punisher V2#1-8. 4-Chiodo-c. 8-r/Punisher #10 & Daredevil #257; Portacio & Lee-r. 14-r/Punisher War Journal #1,2 w/new Lee-c. 16-r/Punisher W. J. #3,8 4.00
NOTE: ***Chiodo** painted c-4, 7, 16.* ***Jusko** painted c-6, 8.* ***Jim Lee** r-8, 14-16; c-14.* ***Portacio/Williams** r-7-12.*

PUNISHERMAX
Marvel Comics (MAX): Jan, 2010 - No. 22, Apr, 2012 ($3.99)

1-22-Aaron-s/Dillon-a/Johnson-c. 1-5-Rise of the Kingpin. 6-11-Bullseye. 17-20-Elektra app. 21-Castle dies. 22-Afterword by Aaron 4.00
...: Butterfly (5/10, $4.99) Valerie D'Orazio-s/Laurence Campbell-a/c 5.00
...: Get Castle (3/10, $4.99) Rob Williams-s/Laurence Campbell-a/Bradstreet-c 5.00
...: Happy Ending (10/10, $3.99) Milligan-s/Ryp-a/c 4.00
...: Hot Rods of Death (11/10, $4.99) Huston-s/Martinbrough-a/Bradstreet-c 5.00
...: Tiny Ugly World (12/10, $4.99) Lapham-s/Talajic-a/Bradstreet-c 5.00

PUNISHER: NIGHTMARE
Marvel Comics: Mar, 2013 - No. 5, Mar, 2013 ($3.99, weekly limited series)

1-5-Texeira-a/c; Gimple-s 4.00

PUNISHER NOIR
Marvel Comics: Oct, 2009 - No. 4, Jan, 2010 ($3.99, limited series)

1-4-Pulp-style set in 1935; Tieri-s/Azaceta-a 4.00

PUNISHER: OFFICIAL MOVIE ADAPTATION
Marvel Comics: May, 2004 - No. 3, May, 2004 ($2.99, limited series)

1-3-Photo-c of Thomas Jane; Milligan-s/Olliffe-a 3.00

PUNISHER: ORIGIN OF MICRO CHIP, THE
Marvel Comics: July, 1993 - No. 2, Aug, 1993 ($1.75, limited series)

1,2 4.00

PUNISHER: P.O.V.
Marvel Comics: 1991 - No. 4, 1991 ($4.95, painted, limited series, 52 pgs.)

1-4: Starlin scripts & Wrightson painted-c/a in all. 2-Nick Fury app. 6.00

PUNISHER PRESENTS: BARRACUDA MAX
Marvel Comics (MAX): Apr, 2007 - No. 5, Aug, 2007 ($3.99, limited series)

1-5-Ennis-s/Parlov-a/c 4.00
SC (2007, $17.99) r/series; sketch pages 18.00

PUNISHER: THE END
Marvel Comics: June, 2004 ($4.50, one-shot)

1-Ennis-s/Corben-a/c 4.50

PUNISHER: THE GHOSTS OF INNOCENTS
Marvel Comics: Jan, 1993 - No. 2, Jan, 1993 ($5.95, 52 pgs.)

1,2-Starlin scripts 6.00

PUNISHER: THE MOVIE
Marvel Comics: 2004 ($12.99,TPB)

nn-Reprints Amazing Spider-Man #129; Official Movie Adaptation and Punisher V3 #1 13.00

PUNISHER: THE TRIAL OF THE PUNISHER
Marvel Comics: Nov, 2013 - No. 2, Dec, 2013 ($3.99, limited series)

1-Guggenheim-s/Yu-a/c. 2-Suayan-a; Matt Murdock app. 4.00

PUNISHER 2099 (See Punisher War Journal #50)
Marvel Comics: Feb, 1993 - No. 34, Nov, 1995 ($1.25/$1.50/$1.95)

1-Foil stamped-c 4.00
1-(Second printing) 3.00
2-24,26-34: 13-Spider-Man 2099 x-over; Ron Lim-c(p). 16-bound-in card sheet 3.00
25 ($2.95, 52 pgs.)-Deluxe edition; embossed foil-cover 5.00
25 ($2.25, 52 pgs.) 4.00
(Marvel Knights) #1 (11/04, $2.99) Kirkman-s/Mhan-a/Pat Lee-c 3.00

PUNISHER VS. BULLSEYE
Marvel Comics: Jan, 2006 - No. 5, May, 2006 ($2.99, limited series)

1-5-Daniel Way-s/Steve Dillon-a 3.00
TPB (2006, $13.99) r/#1-5; cover sketch pages 14.00

PUNISHER VS. DAREDEVIL
Marvel Comics: Jun, 2000 ($3.50, one-shot)

1-Reprints Daredevil #183,#184 & #257 4.00

PUNISHER WAR JOURNAL, THE
Marvel Comics: Nov, 1988 - No. 80, July, 1995 ($1.50/$1.75/$1.95)

1-Origin The Punisher; Matt Murdock cameo; Jim Lee inks begin 6.00
2-7: 2,3-Daredevil x-over; Jim Lee-c(i). 4-Jim Lee c/a begins. 6-Two part Wolverine story

Punisher War Journal #11 © MAR

Purgatori #6 © Chaos!

PvP #2 © Scott Kurtz

GD 2.0 | VG 4.0 | FN 6.0 | VF 8.0 | VF/NM 9.0 | NM- 9.2

begins. 7-Wolverine-c, story ends 4.00
8-49,51-60,62,63,65: 13-16,20-22: No Jim Lee-a. 13-Lee-c only. 13-15-Heath-i. 14,15-Spider-Man x-over. 19-Last Jim Lee-c/a.29,30-Ghost Rider app. 31-Andy & Joe Kubert art. 36-Photo-c. 47,48-Nomad/Daredevil-c/stories; see Nomad. 57,58-Daredevil & Ghost Rider-c/stories. 62,63-Suicide Run Pt. 4 & 7 3.00
50,61,64($2.95, 52 pgs.): 50-Preview of Punisher 2099 (1st app.); embossed-c. 61-Embossed foil cover; Suicide Run Pt. 1. 64-Die-cut-c; Suicide Run Pt. 10 4.00
64-($2.25, 52 pgs.)-Regular cover edition 4.00
66-74,76-80: 66-Bound-in card sheet 3.00
75 ($2.50, 52 pgs.) 4.00
NOTE: ***Golden*** *c-25-30, 40, 61, 62.* ***Jusko*** *painted c-31, 32.* ***Jim Lee*** *a-1i-3i, 4p-13p, 17p-19p; c-2i, 3i, 4p-15p, 17p, 18p, 19p. Painted c-40.*

PUNISHER WAR JOURNAL (Frank Castle back in the regular Marvel Universe)
Marvel Comics: Jan, 2007 - No. 26, Feb, 2009 ($2.99)

1-Civil War tie-in; Spider-Man app; Fraction-s/Olivetti-a 5.00
1-B&W edition (11/06) 5.00
2-5: 2,3-Civil War tie-in. 4-Deodato-a 4.00
6-11,13-24,26: 6-10-Punisher dons Captain America-*esque* outfit. 7-Two covers. 11-Winter Soldier app. 16-23-Chaykin-a. 18-23-Jigsaw app. 24-Secret Invasion 3.00
12,25-($3.99) 12-World War Hulk x-over; Fraction-s/Olivetti-a. 25-Secret Invasion 4.00
... Annual 1 (1/09, $3.99) Spurrier-s/Dell'edera-a 4.00
... Vol. 1: Civil War HC (2007, $19.99) r/#1-4 and #1 B&W edition; Olivetti sketch pages 20.00
... Vol. 1: Civil War SC (2007, $14.99) r/#1-4 and #1 B&W edition; Olivetti sketch pages 15.00
... Vol. 2: Goin' Out West HC (2007, $24.99) r/#5-11; Olivetti sketch page 25.00
... Vol. 2: Goin' Out West SC (2008, $17.99) r/#5-11; Olivetti sketch page 18.00
... Vol. 3: Hunter Hunted HC (2008, $19.99) r/#12-17 20.00

PUNISHER: WAR ZONE, THE
Marvel Comics: Mar, 1992 - No. 41, July, 1995 ($1.75/$1.95)

1-($2.25, 40 pgs.)-Die cut-c; Romita, Jr.-c/a begins 5.00
2-22,24,26,27-41: 8-Last Romita, Jr.-c/a. 19-Wolverine app. 24-Suicide Run Pt. 5. 27-Bound-in card sheet. 31-36-Joe Kubert-a 3.00
23-($2.95, 52 pgs.)-Embossed foil-c; Suicide Run part 2; Buscema-a(part) 4.00
25-($2.25, 52 pgs.)-Suicide Run part 8; painted-c 4.00
Annual 1,2 ('93, 94, $2.95, 68 pgs.)-1-Bagged w/card; John Buscema-a 4.00
...: River Of Blood TPB (2006, $15.99) r/#31-36; Joe Kubert-a 16.00
NOTE: ***Golden*** *c-23.* ***Romita, Jr.*** *c/a-1-8.*

PUNISHER: WAR ZONE
Marvel Comics: Feb, 2009 - No. 6, Mar, 2009 ($3.99, weekly limited series)

1-6-Ennis-s/Dillon-a/c; return of Ma Gnucci 4.00
1-Variant cover by John Romita, Jr. 6.00

PUNISHER: WAR ZONE (Follows Punisher 2011-2012 series)
Marvel Comics: Dec, 2012 - No. 5, Apr, 2013 ($3.99, limited series)

1-5: Rucka-s; Spider-Man and The Avengers app. 4.00

PUNISHER: YEAR ONE
Marvel Comics: Dec, 1994 - No. 4, Apr, 1995 ($2.50, limited series)

1-4 3.00

PUNK ROCK JESUS
DC Comics (Vertigo): Sept, 2012 - No. 6, Feb, 2013 ($2.99, B&W, limited series)

1-6-Sean Murphy-s/a/c; cloning of Jesus 3.00

PUNX
Acclaim (Valiant): Nov, 1995 - No. 3, Jan, 1996 ($2.50, unfinished lim. series)

1-3: Giffen story & art in all. 2-Satirizes Scott McCloud's Understanding Comics 3.00
(Manga) Special 1 (3/96, $2.50)-Giffen scripts 3.00

PUPPET COMICS
George W. Dougherty Co.: Spring, 1946 - No. 2, Summer, 1946

	GD	VG	FN	VF	VF/NM	NM-
1-Funny animal in both	17	34	51	98	154	210
2	14	28	42	76	108	140

PUPPETOONS (See George Pal's...)

PUREHEART (See Archie as...)

PURGATORI
Chaos! Comics: Prelude #-1, 5/96 ($1.50, 16 pgs.); 1996 - No. 3 Dec, 1996 ($3.50/$2.95, limited series)

Prelude #-1-Pulido story; Balent-c/a; contains sketches & interviews 3.00
0-(2/01, $2.99) Prelude to "Love Bites"; Rio-c/a 3.00
1/2 (12/00, $2.95) Al Rio-c/a 3.00
1-($3.50)-Wraparound cover; red foil embossed-c; Jim Balent-a 5.00
1-($19.95)-Premium Edition (1000 print run) 20.00
2-($3.00)-Wraparound-c 3.00

GD 2.0 | VG 4.0 | FN 6.0 | VF 8.0 | VF/NM 9.0 | NM- 9.2

2-Variant-c 5.00
...: Heartbreaker 1 (3/02, $2.99) Jolley-s 3.00
...: Love Bites 1 (3/01, $2.99) Turnbull-a/Kaminski-s 3.00
...: Mischief Night 1 (11/01, $2.99) 3.00
...: Re-Imagined 1 (7/02, $2.99) Jolley-s/Neves-a 3.00
...The Dracula Gambit-($2.95) 3.00
...The Dracula Gambit Sketchbook-($2.95) 3.00
...The Vampire's Myth 1-($19.95) Premium Ed. (10,000) 20.00
...Vs. Chastity (7/00, $2.95) Two versions (Alpha and Omega) with different endings; Rio-a 3.00
...Vs. Lady Death (1/01, $2.95) Kaminski-s 3.00
...Vs. Vampirella (4/00, $2.95) Zanier-a; Chastity app. 3.00

PURGATORI
Chaos! Comics: Oct, 1998 - No. 7, Apr, 1999 ($2.95)

1-7-Quinn-s/Rio-c/a. 2-Lady Death-c 3.00

PURGATORI: DARKEST HOUR
Chaos! Comics: Sept, 2001 - No. 2, Oct, 2001 ($2.99, limited series)

1,2 3.00

PURGATORI: EMPIRE
Chaos! Comics: May, 2000 - No. 3, July, 2000 ($2.95, limited series)

1-3-Cleavenger-c 3.00

PURGATORI: GODDESS RISING
Chaos! Comics: July, 1999 - No. 4, Oct, 1999 ($2.95, limited series)

1-4-Deodato-c/a 3.00

PURGATORI: GOD HUNTER
Chaos! Comics: Apr, 2002 - No. 2, May, 2002 ($2.99, limited series)

1,2-Molenaar-a/Jolley-s 3.00

PURGATORI: GOD KILLER
Chaos! Comics: Jun, 2002 - No. 2, July, 2002 ($2.99, limited series)

1,2-Molenaar-a/Jolley-s 3.00

PURGATORI: THE HUNTED
Chaos! Comics: Jun, 2001 - No. 2, Aug, 2001 ($2.99, limited series)

1,2 3.00

PURPLE CLAW, THE (Also see Tales of Horror)
Minoan Publishing Co./Toby Press: Jan, 1953 - No. 3, May, 1953

	GD	VG	FN	VF	VF/NM	NM-
1-Origin; horror/weird stories in all	36	72	108	216	351	485
2,3: 1-3 r-in Tales of Horror #9-11	24	48	72	144	237	330
I.W. Reprint #8-Reprints #1	3	6	9	16	23	30

PUSH (Based on the 2009 movie)
DC Comics (WildStorm): Early Jan, 2009 - No. 6, Apr, 2009 ($3.50, limited series)

1-6-Movie prequel; Bruno Redondo-a. 1-Jock-c 3.50
TPB (2009, $19.99) r/#1-6 20.00

PUSSYCAT (Magazine)
Marvel Comics Group: Oct, 1968 (B&W reprints from Men's magazines)

	GD	VG	FN	VF	VF/NM	NM-
1-(Scarce)-Ward, Everett, Wood-a; Everett-c	25	50	75	175	388	600

PUZZLE FUN COMICS (Also see Jingle Jangle)
George W. Dougherty Co.: Spring, 1946 - No. 2, Summer, 1946 (52 pgs.)

	GD	VG	FN	VF	VF/NM	NM-
1-Gustavson-a	24	48	72	142	234	325
2	15	30	45	90	140	190

NOTE: *#1 & 2('46) each contain a* ***George Carlson*** *cover plus a 6 pg. story "Alec in Fumbleland"; also many puzzles in each.*

PvP (Player vs. Player)
Image Comics: Mar, 2003 - No. 45, Mar, 2010 ($2.95/$2.99/$3.50, B&W, reads sideways)

1-34,36-Scott Kurtz-s/a in all. 1,16-Frank Cho-c. 11-Savage Dragon-c/app. 14-Invincible app. 19-Jonathan Luna-c. 25-Cho-a (2 pgs.) 3.00
35,37-45 ($3.50): 45-Brandy from Liberty Meadows app. 3.50
#0 (7/05, 50¢) Secret Origin of Skull 3.00
...: At Large TPB (7/04, $11.95) r/#1-6 12.00
... Vol. 2: Reloaded TPB (12/04, $11.95) r/#7-12 12.00
... Vol. 3: Rides Again TPB (2005, $11.99) r/#13-18 12.00
... Vol. 4: PVP Goes Bananas TPB (2007, $12.99) r/#19-24 13.00
... Vol. 5: PVP Treks On TPB (2008, $14.99) r/#25-31 15.00
...: The Dork Ages TPB (2/04, $11.95) r/#1-6 from Dork Storm Press 12.00

QUACK!
Star Reach Productions: July, 1976 - No. 6, 1977? ($1.25, B&W)

	GD	VG	FN	VF	VF/NM	NM-
1-Brunner-c/a on Duckaneer (Howard the Duck clone); Dave Stevens, Gilbert, Shaw-a	2	4	6	10	14	18

Quantum & Woody (2013 series) #2 © VAL

Queen & Country #29 © Greg Rucka

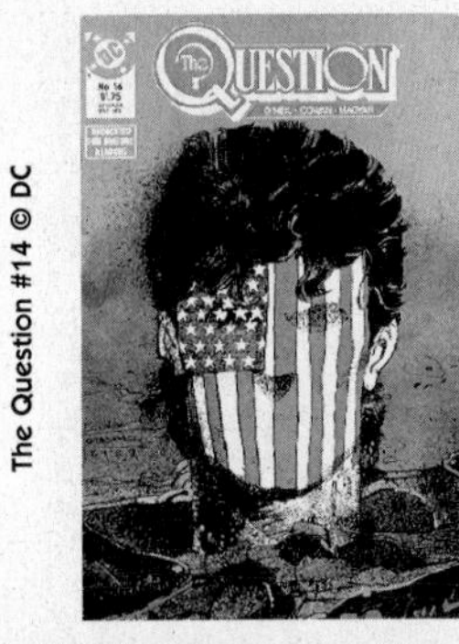

The Question #14 © DC

GD 2.0 | VG 4.0 | FN 6.0 | VF 8.0 | VF/NM 9.0 | NM- 9.2

1-2nd printing (10/76) 5.00
2-6: 2-Newton the Rabbit Wonder by Aragonés/Leialoha; Gilbert, Shaw-a; Leialoha-c. 3-The Beavers by Dave Sim begin, end #5; Gilbert, Shaw-a; Sim/Leialoha-c. 6-Brunner-a (Duckeneer); Gilbert-a 2 4 6 8 10 12

QUADRANT
Quadrant Publications: 1983 - No. 8, 1986 (B&W, nudity, adults)

1-Peter Hsu-c/a in all 2 4 6 10 14 18
2-8 2 3 4 6 8 10

QUANTUM & WOODY
Acclaim Comics: June, 1997 - No. 17, No. 32 (9/99), No. 18 - No. 21, Feb, 2000 ($2.50)

1-17: 1-1st app.; two covers. 6-Copycat-c. 9-Troublemakers app. 3.00
32-(9/99); 18-(10/99),19-21 3.00
The Director's Cut TPB ('97, $7.95) r/#1-4 plus extra pages 8.00

QUANTUM & WOODY
Valiant Entertainment: Jul, 2013 - Present ($3.99)

1-9: 1-Asmus-s/Fowler-a; covers by Ryan Sook & Marcos Martin; origin re-told 4.00
#0 -(3/14, $3.99) Story of the goat; Asmus-s/Fowler-a/c 4.00

QUANTUM LEAP (TV) (See A Nightmare on Elm Street)
Innovation Publishing: Sept, 1991 - No. 12, Jun, 1993 ($2.50, painted-c)

1-12: Based on TV show; all have painted-c. 8-Has photo gallery 4.00
Special Edition 1 (10/92)-r/#1 w/8 extra pgs. of photos & articles 4.00
Time and Space Special 1 (#13) ($2.95)-Foil logo 4.00

QUANTUM TUNNELER, THE
Revolution Studio: Oct, 2001 (no cover price, one-shot)

1-Prequel to "The One" movie; Clayton Henry-a 3.00

QUASAR (See Avengers #302, Captain America #217, Incredible Hulk #234, Marvel Team-Up #113 & Marvel Two-in-One #53)
Marvel Comics: Oct, 1989 - No. 60, Jul, 1994 ($1.00/$1.25, Direct sales #17 on)

1-Origin; formerly Marvel Boy/Marvel Man 6.00
2-15,17-24,26-49,51-60: 3-Human Torch app. 6-Venom cameo (2 pgs.). 7-Cosmic Spidey. 11-Excalibur x-over. 14-McFarlane-c. 17-Flash parody (Buried Alien). 20-Fantastic Four app. 23-Ghost Rider x-over. 26-Infinity Gauntlet x-over; Thanos-c/story. 27-Infinity Gauntlet x-over. 30-Thanos cameo in flashback; last $1.00-c. 31-Begin $1.25-c; D.P. 7 guest stars. 38-40-Infinity War x-overs. 38-Battles Warlock. 39-Thanos-c & cameo. 40-Thanos app. 42-Punisher-c/story. 53-Warlock & Moondragon app. 58-w/bound-in card sheet 3.00
16,25,50: 16-($1.50, 52 pgs.). 25-($1.50, 52 pgs.)-New costume Quasar. 50-($2.95, 52 pgs.)-Holo-grafx foil-c; Silver Surfer, Man-Thing, Ren & Stimpy app. 4.00
Special #1-3 ($1.25, newsstand)-Same as #32-34 3.00

QUEEN & COUNTRY (See Whiteout)
Oni Press: Mar, 2001 - No. 32, Aug, 2007 ($2.95/$2.99, B&W)

1-Rucka-s in all. Rolston-a/Sale-c 1 2 3 4 5 7
2-5: 2-4-Rolston-a/Sale-c. 5-Snyder-c/Hurtt-a 4.00
6-24,26-32: 6,7-Snyder-c/Hurtt-a. 13-15-Alexander-a. 16-20-McNeil-a. 21-24-Hawthorne-a 26-28-Norton-a 3.00
25-($5.99) Rolston-a 6.00
Free Comic Book Day giveaway (5/02) r/#1 with "Free Comic Book Day" banner on-c 3.00
Operation: Blackwall (10/03, $8.95, TPB) r/#13-15; John Rogers intro. 9.00
Operation: Broken Ground (2002, $11.95, TPB) r/#1-4; Ellis intro. 12.00
Operation: Crystal Ball (1/03, $14.95, TPB) r/#8-12; Judd Winick intro. 15.00
Operation: Dandelion HC (8/04, $25.00) r/#21-24; Jamie S. Rich intro. 25.00
Operation: Dandelion (8/04, $11.95, TPB) r/#21-24; Jamie S. Rich intro. 12.00
Operation: Morningstar (9/02, $8.95, TPB) r/#5-7; Stuart Moore intro. 9.00
Operation: Storm Front (3/04, $14.95, TPB) r/#16-20; Geoff Johns intro. 15.00

QUEEN & COUNTRY: DECLASSIFIED
Oni Press: Nov, 2002 - No. 3, Jan, 2003 ($2.95, B&W, limited series)

1-3-Rucka-s/Hurtt-a/Morse-c 3.00
TPB (7/03, $8.95) r/#1-3; intro. by Micah Wright 9.00

QUEEN & COUNTRY: DECLASSIFIED (Volume 2)
Oni Press: Jan, 2005 - No. 3, Feb, 2006 ($2.95/$2.99, B&W, limited series)

1-3-Rucka-s/Burchett-a/c 3.00
TPB (3/06, $8.95) r/#1-3 9.00

QUEEN & COUNTRY: DECLASSIFIED (Volume 3)
Oni Press: Jun, 2005 - No. 3, Aug, 2005 ($2.95, B&W, limited series)

1-3- "Sons & Daughters;" Johnston-s/Mitten-a/c 3.00
TPB (3/06, $8.95) r/#1-3 9.00

QUEEN OF THE WEST, DALE EVANS (TV)(See Dale Evans Comics, Roy Rogers & Western Roundup under Dell Giants)
Dell Publ. Co.: No. 479, 7/53 - No. 22, 1-3/59 (All photo-c; photo back c-4-8,15)

Four Color 479(#1, '53) 16 32 48 107 236 365
Four Color 528(#2, '54) 9 18 27 59 117 175
3,4: 3(4-6/54)-Toth-a. 4-Toth, Manning-a 7 14 21 46 86 125
5-10-Manning-a. 5-Marsh-a 6 12 18 40 73 105
11,19,21-No Manning 21-Tufts-a 5 10 15 31 53 75
12-18,20,22-Manning-a 5 10 15 34 60 85

QUEEN SONJA (See Red Sonja)
Dynamite Entertainment: 2009 - No. 35, 2013 ($2.99/$3.99)

1-10: 1-Rubi-a/Ortega-s; 3 covers; back-up r/Marvel Feature #1 4.00
11-35-($3.99) 16-Thulsa Doom returns 4.00

QUENTIN DURWARD
Dell Publishing Co.: No. 672, Jan, 1956

Four Color 672-Movie, photo-c 6 12 18 38 69 100

QUESTAR ILLUSTRATED SCIENCE FICTION CLASSICS
Golden Press: 1977 (224 pgs.) ($1.95)

11197-Stories by Asimov, Sturgeon, Silverberg & Niven; Starstream-r 3 6 9 20 30 40

QUEST FOR CAMELOT
DC Comics: July, 1998 ($4.95)

1-Movie adaption 5.00

QUEST FOR DREAMS LOST (Also see Word Warriors)
Literacy Volunteers of Chicago: July 4, 1987 ($2.00, B&W, 52 pgs.)(Proceeds donated to help fight illiteracy)

1-Teenage Mutant Ninja Turtles by Eastman/Laird, Trollords, Silent Invasion, The Realm, Wordsmith, Reacto Man, Eb'nn, Aniverse 4.00

QUESTION, THE (See Americomics, Blue Beetle (1967), Charlton Bullseye & Mysterious Suspense)

QUESTION, THE (Also see Showcase '95 #3)
DC Comics: Feb, 1987 - No. 36, Mar, 1990; No. 37, Mar, 2010 ($1.50)

1-36: Denny O'Neil scripts in all 3.00
37-(3/10, $2.99) Blackest Night one-shot; Victor Sage rises; Shiva app.; Cowan-a 3.00
Annual 1 (1988, $2.50) 4.00
Annual 2 (1989, $3.50) 4.00
...: Epitaph For a Hero TPB (2008, $19.99) r/#13-18 20.00
...: Peacemaker TPB (2010, $19.99) r/#31-36 20.00
...: Pipeline TPB (2011, $14.99) r/stories from Detective Comics #854-865; sketch-a 15.00
...: Poisoned Ground TPB (2008, $19.99) r/#7-12 20.00
...: Riddles TPB (2009, $19.99) r/#25-30 20.00
...: Welcome to Oz TPB (2009, $19.99) r/#19-24 20.00
...: Zen and Violence TPB (2007, $19.99) r/#1-6 20.00

QUESTION, THE (Also see Crime Bible and 52)
DC Comics: Jan, 2005 - No. 6, Jun, 2005 ($2.95, limited series)

1-6-Rick Veitch-s/Tommy Lee Edwards-a. 4,6-Superman app. 3.00

QUESTION QUARTERLY, THE
DC Comics: Summer, 1990 - No. 5, Spring, 1992 ($2.50/$2.95, 52pgs.)

1-5 4.00
NOTE: ***Cowan** a-1, 2, 4, 5; c-1-3, 5.* ***Mignola** a-5i.* ***Quesada** a-3-5.*

QUESTION RETURNS, THE
DC Comics: Feb, 1997 ($3.50, one-shot)

1-Brereton-c 4.00

QUESTPROBE
Marvel Comics: 8/84; No. 2, 1/85; No. 3, 11/85 (lim. series)

1-3: 1-The Hulk app. by Romita. 2-Spider-Man; Mooney-a(i). 3-Human Torch & Thing 4.00

QUICK DRAW McGRAW (TV) (Hanna-Barbera)(See Whitman Comic Books)
Dell Publishing Co./Gold Key No. 12 on: No. 1040, 12-2/59-60 - No. 11, 7-9/62; No. 12, 11/62; No. 13, 2/63; No. 14, 4/63; No. 15, 6/69 (1st show aired 9/29/59)

Four Color 1040(#1) 1st app. Quick Draw & Baba Looey, Augie Doggie & Doggie Daddy and Snooper & Blabber 11 22 33 76 163 250
2(4-6/60)-4,6: 2-Augie Doggie & Snooper & Blabber stories (8 pgs. each); pre-dates both of their #1 issues. 4-Augie Doggie & Snooper & Blabber stories. 5 10 15 35 63 90
5-1st Snagglepuss app.; last 10¢ issue 6 12 18 38 69 100
7-11 5 10 15 30 50 70
12,13-Title change to ...Fun-Type Roundup (84pgs.) 6 12 18 38 69 100
14,15: 15-Reprints 4 8 12 27 44 60

QUICK DRAW McGRAW (TV)(See Spotlight #2)

Quicksilver #10 © MAR

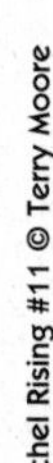
Rachel Rising #11 © Terry Moore

Radioactive Man #412 © Bongo

	GD 2.0	VG 4.0	FN 6.0	VF 8.0	VF/NM 9.0	NM- 9.2

Charlton Comics: Nov, 1970 - No. 8, Jan, 1972 (Hanna-Barbera)

1	5	10	15	30	50	70
2-8	3	6	9	18	28	38

QUICKSILVER (See Avengers)
Marvel Comics: Nov, 1997 - No. 13, Nov, 1998 ($2.99/$1.99)

1-($2.99)-Peyer-s/Casey Jones-a; wraparound-c 4.00
2-11: 2-Two covers-variant by Golden. 4-6-Inhumans app. 3.00
12-($2.99) Siege of Wundagore pt. 4 4.00
13-Magneto-c/app.; last issue 3.00

QUICK-TRIGGER WESTERN (...Action #12; Cowboy Action #5-11)
Atlas Comics (ACI #12/WPI #13-19): No. 12, May, 1956 - No. 19, Sept, 1957

12-Baker-a	16	32	48	94	147	200
13-Williamson-a, 5 pgs.	15	30	45	86	133	180
14-Everett, Crandall, Torres-a; Heath-c	15	30	45	83	124	165
15,16: 15-Torres, Crandall-a. 16-Orlando, Kirby-a	13	26	39	74	105	135
17,18: 18-Baker-a	13	26	39	72	101	130
19	10	20	30	58	79	100

NOTE: *Ayers a-17. Colan a-16. Maneely a-15, 17; c-15, 18. Morrow a-18. Powell a-14. Severin a-19; c-12, 13, 16, 17, 19. Shores a-16. Tuska a-17.*

QUINCY (See Comics Reading Libraries in the Promotional Comics section)

QUITTER, THE
DC Comics (Vertigo): 2005 ($19.99, B&W graphic novel)

HC ($19.99) Autobiography of Harvey Pekar; Pekar-s/Daen Haspiel-a 20.00
SC (2006, $12.99) 13.00

RACCOON KIDS, THE (Formerly Movietown Animal Antics)
National Periodical Publications (Arleigh No. 63,64): No. 52, Sept-Oct, 1954 - No. 62, Oct-Nov, 1956; No. 63, Sept, 1957; No. 64, Nov, 1957

52-Doodles Duck by Mayer	15	30	45	83	124	165
53-64: 53-62-Doodles Duck by Mayer	11	22	33	62	86	110

NOTE: *Otto Feuer-a most issues. Rube Grossman-a most issues.*

RACE FOR THE MOON
Harvey Publications: Mar, 1958 - No. 3, Nov, 1958

1-Powell-a(5); 1/2-pg. S&K-a; cover redrawn from Galaxy Science Fiction pulp (5/53)	18	36	54	103	162	220
2-Kirby/Williamson-c(r)/a(3); Kirby-p 7 more stys	26	52	78	154	252	350
3-Kirby/Williamson-c/a(4); Kirby-p 6 more stys	28	56	84	165	270	375

RACER-X
Now Comics: 8/88 - No. 11, 8/89; V2#1, 9/89 - V2#10, 1990 ($1.75)

0-Deluxe ($3.50) 5.00
1 (9/88) - 11, V2#1-10 4.00

RACER X (See Speed Racer)
DC Comics (WildStorm): Oct, 2000 - No. 3, Dec, 2000 ($2.95, limited series)

1-3: 1-Tommy Yune-s/Jo Chen-a; 2 covers by Yune. 2,3-Kabala app. 4.00

RACHEL RISING
Abstract Studio: 2011 - Present ($3.99, B&W)

1-Terry Moore-s/a/c; back cover by Fabio Moon; green background on cover 60.00
1-(2nd printing) Red background on cover 30.00
1-(3rd printing) Red background on cover 30.00
2 30.00
3-6 10.00
7-24 4.00

RACING PETTYS
STP Corp.: 1980 ($2.50, 68 pgs., 10 1/8" x 13 1/4")

1-Bob Kane-a. Kane bio on inside back-c. 10.00

RACK & PAIN
Dark Horse Comics: Mar, 1994 - No. 4, June, 1994 ($2.50, limited series)

1-4: Brian Pulido scripts in all. 1-Greg Capullo-c 3.00

RACK & PAIN: KILLERS
Chaos! Comics: Sept, 1996 - No. 4, Jan, 1997 ($2.95, limited series)

1-4: Reprints Dark Horse series; Jae Lee-c 3.00

RACKET SQUAD IN ACTION
Capitol Stories/Charlton Comics: May-June, 1952 - No. 29, Mar, 1958

1	31	62	93	186	303	420
2-4,6: 3,4,6-Dr. Neff, Ghost Breaker app.	16	32	48	94	147	200
5-Dr. Neff, Ghost Breaker app; headlights-c	30	60	90	177	289	400
7-10: 10-Explosion-c	15	30	45	85	130	175
11-Ditko-c/a	34	68	102	199	325	450
12-Ditko explosion-c (classic); Shuster-a(2)	54	108	162	343	574	825
13-Shuster-c(p)/a.	14	28	42	78	112	145
14-Marijuana story "Shakedown"; Giordano-c	17	34	51	98	154	210
15-28: 15,20,22,23-Giordano-c	12	24	36	69	97	125
29-(15¢, 68 pgs.)	15	30	45	83	124	165

RADIANT LOVE (Formerly Daring Love #1)
Gilmor Magazines: No. 2, Dec, 1953 - No. 6, Aug, 1954

2	15	30	45	86	133	180
3-6	12	24	36	67	94	120

RADICAL DREAMER
Blackball Comics: No. 0, May, 1994 - No. 4, Nov, 1994 ($1.99, bi-monthly)
(1st poster format comic)

0-4: 0-2-($1.99, poster format): 0-1st app. Max Wrighter. 3,4-($2.50-c) 3.00

RADICAL DREAMER
Mark's Giant Economy Size Comics: V2#1, June, 1995 - V2#6, Feb, 1996 ($2.95, B&W, limited series)

V2#1-6 3.00
Prime (5/96, $2.95) 3.00
Dreams Cannot Die!-(1996, $20.00, softcover)-Collects V1#0-4 & V2#1-6; intro by Kurt Busiek; afterward by Mark Waid 20.00
Dreams Cannot Die!-(1996, $60.00, hardcover)-Signed & limited edition; collects V1#0-4 & V2#1-6; intro by Kurt Busiek; afterward by Mark Waid 60.00

RADIOACTIVE MAN (Simpsons TV show)
Bongo Comics: 1993 - No. 6, 1994 ($1.95/$2.25, limited series)

1-($2.95)-Glow-in-the-dark-c; bound-in jumbo poster; origin Radioactive Man; (cover dated Nov. 1952) 6.00
2-6: 2-Says #88 on-c & inside & dated May 1962; cover parody of Atlas Kirby monster-c; Superior Squad app.; origin Fallout Boy. 3-($1.95)-Cover "dated" Aug 1972 #216. 4-($2.25)-Cover "dated" Oct 1980 #412; w/trading card. 5-Cover "dated" Jan 1986 #679; w/trading card. 6-(Jan 1995 #1000) 4.00
Colossal #1-($4.95) 7.00
#4 (2001, $2.50) Faux 1953 issue; Murphy Anderson-i (6 pgs.) 3.00
#100 (2000, $2.50) Comic Book Guy-c/app.; faux 1963 issue inside 3.00
#136 (2001, $2.50) Dan DeCarlo-c/a 3.00
#222 (2001, $2.50) Batton Lash-s; Radioactive Man in 1972-style 3.00
#575 (2002, $2.50) Chaykin-c; Radioactive Man in 1984-style 3.00
1963-106 (2002, $2.50) Radioactive Man in 1960s Gold Key-style; Groening-c 3.00
#7 Bongo Super Heroes Starring... (2003, $2.50) Marvel Silver Age-style Superior Squad 3.00
#8 Official Movie Adaptation (2004, $2.99) starring Rainier Wolfcastle and Milhouse 3.00
#9 (#197 on-c) (2004, $2.50) Kirby-esque New Gods spoof; Golden Age Radio Man app. 3.00

RADIO FUNNIES
DC Comics: Mar. 1939; undated variant

nn-(3/39) Ashcan comic, not distributed to newsstands, only for in-house use. Cover art is Adventure Comics #39 with interior being Detective Comics #19 (no known sales)
nn - Ashcan comic. No date. Cover art is Detective #26 with interior from Detective #17; one copy, graded at GD/VG, sold at auction for $4481.25 in Nov, 2009. Another copy graded at GD/VG sold at auction for $3346 in Feb, 2010.

RAGAMUFFINS
Eclipse Comics: Jan, 1985 ($1.75, one shot)

1-Eclipse Magazine-r, w/color; Colan-a 3.00

RAGE (Based on the id video game)
Dark Horse Comics: Jun, 2011 - No. 3, Aug, 2011 ($3.50, limited series)

1-3-Nelson-s/Mutti-a/Fabry-c. 1-Variant-c by Martiniere 3.50

RAGEMOOR
Dark Horse Comics: Mar, 2012 - No. 4, Jun, 2012 ($3.50, B&W, limited series)

1-4-Richard Corben-a/c; Jan Strnad-s 3.50

RAGGEDY ANN AND ANDY (See Dell Giants, March of Comics #23 & New Funnies)
Dell Publishing Co.: No. 5, 1942 - No. 533, 2/54; 10-12/64 - No. 4, 3/66

Four Color 5(1942)	44	88	132	326	738	1150
Four Color 23(1943)	31	62	93	223	499	775
Four Color 45(1943)	25	50	75	175	388	600
Four Color 72(1945)	20	40	60	141	313	485
1(6/46)-Billy & Bonnie Bee by Frank Thomas	28	56	84	202	451	700
2,3: 3-Egbert Elephant by Dan Noonan begins	15	30	45	100	220	340
4-Kelly-a, 16 pgs.	15	30	45	105	233	360
5,6,8-10	12	24	36	80	173	265
7-Little Black Sambo, Black Mumbo & Black Jumbo only app; Christmas-c	14	28	42	94	207	320

Rai #5 © VAL

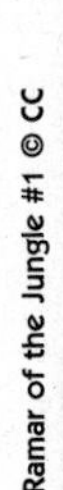
Ramar of the Jungle #1 © CC

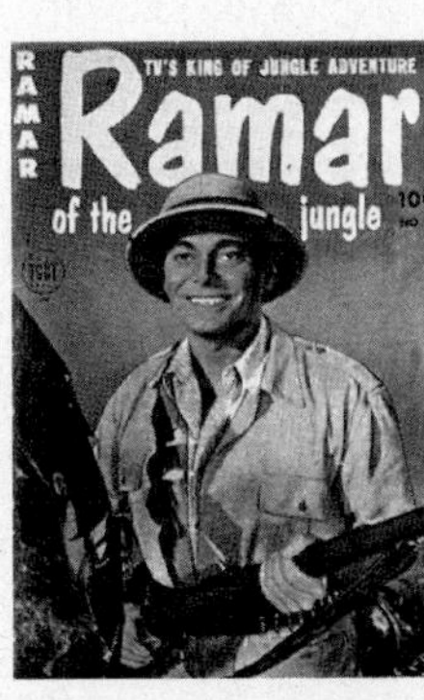

Rampaging Hulk #2 © MAR

	GD 2.0	VG 4.0	FN 6.0	VF 8.0	VF/NM 9.0	NM- 9.2
11-20	10	20	30	64	132	200
21-Alice In Wonderland cover/story	12	24	36	80	173	265
22-27,29-39(8/49), Four Color 262 (1/50): 34-"...In Candyland"	9	18	27	57	111	165
28-Kelly-c	9	18	27	59	117	175
Four Color 306,354,380,452,533	7	14	21	44	82	120
1(10-12/64-Dell)	4	8	12	23	37	50
2,3(10-12/65), 4(3/66)	3	6	9	16	23	30

NOTE: ***Kelly** art ("Animal Mother Goose")-#1-34, 36, 37; c-28. Peterkin Pottle by **John Stanley** in 32-38.*

RAGGEDY ANN AND ANDY
Gold Key: Dec, 1971 - No. 6, Sept, 1973

	GD	VG	FN	VF	VF/NM	NM-
1	3	6	9	18	28	38
2-6	3	6	9	15	21	26

RAGGEDY ANN & THE CAMEL WITH THE WRINKLED KNEES (See Dell Jr. Treasury #8)

RAGMAN (See Batman Family #20, The Brave & The Bold #196 & Cancelled Comic Cavalcade)
National Per. Publ./DC Comics No. 5: Aug-Sept, 1976 - No. 5, Jun-Jul, 1977

	GD	VG	FN	VF	VF/NM	NM-
1-Origin & 1st app.	2	4	6	13	18	22
2-5: 2-Origin ends; Kubert-c. 4-Drug use story	2	4	6	8	10	12

NOTE: ***Kubert** a-4, 5; c-1-5. **Redondo** studios a-1-4.*

RAGMAN (2nd Series)
DC Comics: Oct, 1991 - No. 8, May, 1992 ($1.50, limited series)

1-8: 1-Giffen plots/breakdowns. 3-Origin. 8-Batman-c/story 3.00

RAGMAN: CRY OF THE DEAD
DC Comics: Aug, 1993 - No. 6, Jan, 1994 ($1.75, limited series)

1-6: Joe Kubert-c 3.00

RAGMAN: SUIT OF SOULS
DC Comics: Dec, 2010 ($3.99, one-shot)

1-Gage-s/Segovia-a/Saiz-c; origin retold 4.00

RAGS RABBIT (Formerly Babe Ruth Sports #10 or Little Max #10?; also see Harvey Hits #2, Harvey Wiseguys & Tastee Freez)
Harvey Publications: No. 11, June, 1951 - No. 18, March, 1954 (Written & drawn for little folks)

	GD	VG	FN	VF	VF/NM	NM-
11-(See Nutty Comics #5 for 1st app.)	6	12	18	31	38	45
12-18	5	10	15	24	30	35

RAI (Rai and the Future Force #9-23) (See Magnus #5-8)
Valiant: Mar, 1992 - No. 0, Oct, 1992; No. 9, May, 1993 - No. 33, Jun, 1995 ($1.95/$2.25)

	GD	VG	FN	VF	VF/NM	NM-
1-Valiant's 1st original character	2	4	6	11	16	20
2-5,0: 4-Low print run. 0-(11/92)-Origin/1st app. new Rai (Rising Spirit) & 1st full app. & partial origin Bloodshot; also see Eternal Warrior #4; tells future of all characters	2	4	6	9	12	15
6-10: 6,7-Unity x-overs. 7-Death of Rai. 9-($2.50)-Gatefold-c; story cont'd from Magnus #24; Magnus, Eternal Warrior & X-O app.						6.00
11-33: 15-Manowar Armor app. 17-19-Magnus x-over. 21-1st app. The Starwatchers (cameo); trading card. 22-Death of Rai. 26-Chaos Effect Epsilon Pt. 3						4.00

NOTE: ***Layton** c-2i, 9i. **Miller** c-6. **Simonson** c-7.*

RAIDERS OF THE LOST ARK (Movie)
Marvel Comics Group: Sept, 1981 - No. 3, Nov, 1981 (Movie adaptation)

	GD	VG	FN	VF	VF/NM	NM-
1-r/Marvel Comics Super Special #18	1	2	3	5	6	8
2,3						6.00

NOTE: ***Buscema** a(p)-1-3; c(p)-1. **Simonson** a-3i; scripts-1-3.*

RAINBOW BRITE AND THE STAR STEALER
DC Comics: 1985

	GD	VG	FN	VF	VF/NM	NM-
nn-Movie adaptation	2	4	6	8	10	12

RAISE THE DEAD
Dynamite Entertainment: 2007 - No. 4, Aug, 2007 ($3.50)

1-4-Arthur Suydam-c/Leah Moore & John Reppion-s/Petrus-a; Phillips var-c on all 3.50
... Vol. 1 HC (2007, $19.99) r/#1-4; script, interview & sketch pages; cover gallery 20.00

RAISE THE DEAD 2
Dynamite Entertainment: 2010 - No. 4, 2011 ($3.99)

1-4-Leah Moore & John Reppion-s/Vilanova-a 4.00

RALPH KINER, HOME RUN KING
Fawcett Publications: 1950 (Pittsburgh Pirates)

	GD	VG	FN	VF	VF/NM	NM-
nn-Photo-c; life story	60	120	180	381	658	935

RALPH SNART ADVENTURES
Now Comics: June, 1986 - V2#9, 1987; V3#1 - #26, Feb, 1991; V4#1, 1992 - #4, 1992

1-3, V2#1-7,V3#1-23,25,26:1-($1.00, B&W)-1(B&W),V2#1(11/86), B&W), 8,9-color.
V3#1(9/88)-Color begins 3.00
V3#24-($2.50)-3-D issue, V4#1-3-Direct sale versions w/cards 3.00
V4#1-3-Newsstand versions w/random cards 3.00

	GD	VG	FN	VF	VF/NM	NM-
Book 1	1	2	3	5	6	8
3-D Special (11/92, $3.50)-Complete 12-card set w/3-D glasses						4.00

RAMAR OF THE JUNGLE (TV)
Toby Press No. 1/Charlton No. 2 on: 1954 (no month); No. 2, Sept, 1955 - No. 5, Sept, 1956

	GD	VG	FN	VF	VF/NM	NM-
1-Jon Hall photo-c; last pre-code issue	22	44	66	128	209	290
2-5: 2-Jon Hall photo-c	15	30	45	90	140	190

RAMAYAN 3392 A.D.
Virgin Comics: Sept, 2006 - No. 8, Aug, 2008 ($2.99)

1-8: 1-Alex Ross-c; re-imagining of the Indian myth of Ramayana; poster of cover inside 3.00
... Reloaded (8/07 - No. 7, 7/08, $2.99) 1-7: 1-Two covers by Kang and Oeming 3.00
... Reloaded Guidebook (4/08, $2.99) Profiles of characters and weapons 3.00

RAMM
Megaton Comics: May, 1987 - No. 2, Sept, 1987 ($1.50, B&W)

1,2-Both have 1 pg. Youngblood ad by Liefeld 3.00

RAMPAGING HULK (The Hulk #10 on; also see Marvel Treasury Edition)
Marvel Comics Group: Jan, 1977 - No. 9, June, 1978 ($1.00, B&W magazine)

	GD	VG	FN	VF	VF/NM	NM-
1-Bloodstone story w/Buscema & Nebres-a. Origin re-cap w/Simonson-a; Gargoyle, UFO story; Ken Barr-c	3	6	9	18	28	38
2-Old X-Men app; origin old w/Simonson-a & new X-Men in text w/Cockrum illos; Bloodstone story w/Brown & Nebres-a	3	6	9	15	22	28
3-9: 3-Iron Man app.; Norem-c. 4-Gallery of villains w/Giffen-a. 5,6-Hulk vs. Sub-Mariner. 7-Man-Thing story. 8-Original Avengers app. 9-Thor vs. Hulk battle; Shanna the She-Devil story w/DeZuniga-a	2	4	6	13	18	22

NOTE: ***Alcala** a-1-3i, 5i, 8i. **Buscema** a-1. **Giffen** a-4. **Nino** a-4i. **Simonson** a-1-3p. **Starlin** a-4(w/**Nino**), 7; c-4, 5, 7.*

RAMPAGING HULK
Marvel Comics: Aug, 1998 - No. 6, Jan, 1999 ($2.99/$1.99)

1-($2.99) Flashback stories of Savage Hulk; Leonardi-a 4.00
2-6-($1.99): 2-Two covers 3.00

RAMPAGING WOLVERINE
Marvel Comics: June, 2009 ($3.99, B&W, one-shot)

1-Short stories by Fialkov, Luque, Ted McKeever, Yost, Santolouco, Firth, Nelson 4.00

RANDOLPH SCOTT (Movie star)(See Crack Western #67, Prize Comics Western #76, Western Hearts #8, Western Love #1 & Western Winners #7)

RANGE BUSTERS
Fox Features Syndicate: Sept, 1950 (One shot)

	GD	VG	FN	VF	VF/NM	NM-
1 (Exist?)	20	40	60	114	182	250

RANGE BUSTERS (Formerly Cowboy Love?; Wyatt Earp, Frontier Marshall #11 on)
Charlton Comics: No. 8, May, 1955 - No. 10, Sept, 1955

	GD	VG	FN	VF	VF/NM	NM-
8	8	16	24	42	54	65
9,10	6	12	18	28	34	40

RANGELAND LOVE
Atlas Comics (CDS): Dec, 1949 - No. 2, Mar, 1950 (52 pgs.)

	GD	VG	FN	VF	VF/NM	NM-
1-Robert Taylor & Arlene Dahl photo-c	18	36	54	107	169	230
2-Photo-c	14	28	42	82	121	160

RANGER, THE (See Zane Grey, Four Color #255)

RANGE RIDER, THE (TV)(See Flying A's...)

RANGE ROMANCES
Comic Magazines (Quality Comics): Dec, 1949 - No. 5, Aug, 1950 (#5: 52 pg)

	GD	VG	FN	VF	VF/NM	NM-
1-Gustavson-c/a	25	50	75	150	245	340
2-Crandall-c/a	25	50	75	150	245	340
3-Crandall, Gustavson-a; photo-c	21	42	63	126	206	285
4-Crandall-a; photo-c	19	38	57	112	179	245
5-Gustavson-a; Crandall-a(p); photo-c	19	38	57	112	179	245

RANGERS COMICS (...of Freedom #1-7)
Fiction House Magazines: 10/41 - No. 67, 10/52; No. 68, Fall, 1952; No. 69, Winter, 1952-53 (Flying stories)

	GD	VG	FN	VF	VF/NM	NM-
1-Intro. Ranger Girl & The Rangers of Freedom; ends #7, cover app. only #5	411	822	1233	2877	5039	7200
2	116	232	348	742	1271	1800
3	81	162	243	518	884	1250
4,5	71	142	213	454	777	1100

6-10-All Japanese war covers. 8-U.S. Rangers begin

Rann-Thanagar War TPB © DC

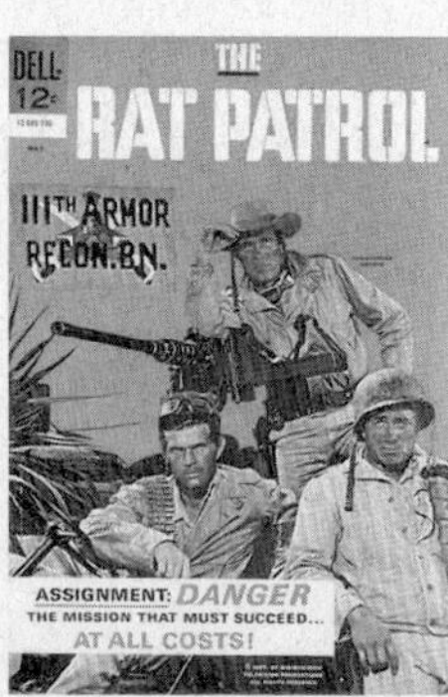

Rat Patrol #3 © DELL

Rawhide Kid #33 © MAR

	GD 2.0	VG 4.0	FN 6.0	VF 8.0	VF/NM 9.0	NM- 9.2
	58	116	174	371	636	900
11,12-Commando Rangers app.	55	110	165	352	601	850
13-Commando Ranger begins-not same as Commando Rangers; Nazi war-c	54	108	162	343	574	825
14-Classic Japanese bondage/torture WWII-c	61	122	183	390	670	950
15-20: 15,17,19-Japanese war-c. 18-Nazi war-c	47	94	141	296	498	700
21-Intro/origin Firehair (begins, 2/45)	53	106	159	334	567	800
22-25,27-30: 22-25,27-Japanese war-c. 23-Kazanda begins, ends #28. 28-Tiger Man begins (origin/1st app., 4/46), ends #46. 30-Crusoe Island begins, ends #40	39	78	117	240	395	550
26-Classic Japanese WWII good girl-c	50	100	150	315	533	750
31-40: 33-Hypodermic panels	34	68	102	199	325	450
41-46: 41-Last Werewolf Hunter	26	52	78	154	252	350
47-56- "Eisnerish" Dr. Drew by Grandenetti. 48-Last Glory Forbes. 53-Last 52 pg. issue. 55-Last Sky Rangers	24	48	72	142	234	325
57-60-Straight run of Dr. Drew by Grandenetti	18	36	54	105	165	225
61-69: 64-Suicide Smith begins. 63-Used in **POP**, pgs. 85, 99. 67-Space Rangers begin, end #69	15	30	45	90	140	190

NOTE: *Bondage, discipline covers, lingerie panels are common. Crusoe Island by* ***Larsen****-#30-36. Firehair by* ***Lubbers****-#30-49. Glory Forbes by* ***Baker****-#36-45, 47; by* ***Whitman****-#34, 35. I Confess in #41-53. Jan of the Jungle in #42-58. King of the Congo in #49-53. Tiger Man by* ***Celardo****-#30-39.* ***M. Anderson*** *a-30?* ***Baker*** *a-36-38, 42, 44.* ***John Celardo*** *a-34, 36-39.* ***Lee Elias*** *a-21-28.* ***Evans*** *a-19, 38-46, 48-52.* ***Hopper*** *a-25, 26.* ***Ingels*** *a-13-16.* ***Larsen*** *a-34.* ***Bob Lubbers*** *a-30-38, 40-44; c-40-45.* ***Moreira*** *a-41-47.* ***Tuska*** *a-16, 17, 19, 22.* ***M. Whitman*** *c-61-66.* ***Zolnerwich*** *c-1-17.*

RANGO (TV)
Dell Publishing Co.: Aug, 1967

	GD 2.0	VG 4.0	FN 6.0	VF 8.0	VF/NM 9.0	NM- 9.2
1-Photo-c of comedian Tim Conway	4	8	12	25	40	55

RANN-THANAGAR HOLY WAR (Also see Hawkman Special #1)
DC Comics: July, 2008 - No. 8, Feb, 2009 ($3.50, limited series)

	GD 2.0	VG 4.0	FN 6.0	VF 8.0	VF/NM 9.0	NM- 9.2
1-8-Adam Strange & Hawkman app.; Starlin-s/Lim-a. 1-Two covers by Starlin & Lim						3.50
Volume One TPB (2009, $19.99) r/#1-4 & Hawkman Special #1						20.00
Volume Two TPB (2009, $19.99) r/#5-8 & Adam Strange Special #1						20.00

RANN-THANAGAR WAR (See Adam Strange 2004 mini-series)(Prelude to Infinite Crisis)
DC Comics: July, 2005 - No. 6, Dec, 2005 ($2.50, limited series)

	GD 2.0	VG 4.0	FN 6.0	VF 8.0	VF/NM 9.0	NM- 9.2
1-6-Adam Strange, Hawkman and Green Lantern (Kyle Rayner) app.; Gibbons-s/Reis-a						3.00
...: Infinite Crisis Special (4/06, $4.99) Kyle Rayner becomes Ion again; Jade dies						5.00
TPB (2005, $12.99) r/#1-6; cover gallery; new Bolland-c						13.00

RAPHAEL (See Teenage Mutant Ninja Turtles)
Mirage Studios: 1985 ($1.50, 7-1/2x11", B&W w/2 color cover, one-shot)

	GD 2.0	VG 4.0	FN 6.0	VF 8.0	VF/NM 9.0	NM- 9.2
1-1st Turtles one-shot spin-off; contains 1st drawing of the Turtles as a group from 1983	4	8	12	28	47	65
1-2nd printing (11/87); new-c & 8 pgs. art	1	3	4	6	8	10

RAPHAEL BAD MOON RISING (See Teenage Mutant Ninja Turtles)
Mirage Publishing: July, 2007 - No. 4, Oct, 2007 ($3.25, B&W, limited series)

	GD 2.0	VG 4.0	FN 6.0	VF 8.0	VF/NM 9.0	NM- 9.2
1-4-Continued from Tales of the TMNT #7; Lawson-a						3.25

RAPTURE
Dark Horse Comics: May, 2009 - No. 6, Jan, 2010 ($2.99, limited series)

	GD 2.0	VG 4.0	FN 6.0	VF 8.0	VF/NM 9.0	NM- 9.2
1-6-Taki Soma & Michael Avon Oeming-s/a/c. 1-Maleev var-c. 2-Mack var-c						3.00

RASCALS IN PARADISE
Dark Horse Comics: Aug, 1994 - No. 3, Dec, 1994 ($3.95, magazine size)

	GD 2.0	VG 4.0	FN 6.0	VF 8.0	VF/NM 9.0	NM- 9.2
1-3-Jim Silke-a/story						4.00
Trade paperback-($16.95)-r/#1-3						17.00

RASL
Cartoon Books: Mar, 2008 - No. 15, Jul, 2012 ($3.50/$4.99, B&W)

	GD 2.0	VG 4.0	FN 6.0	VF 8.0	VF/NM 9.0	NM- 9.2
1-14-Jeff Smith-s/a/c						3.50
15-($4.99) Conclusion						5.00

RATCHET & CLANK (Based on the Sony videogame)
DC Comics (WildStorm thru #4): Nov, 2010 - No. 6, Apr, 2011 ($3.99/$2.99, limited series)

	GD 2.0	VG 4.0	FN 6.0	VF 8.0	VF/NM 9.0	NM- 9.2
1-4-Fixman-s/Archer-a						4.00
5,6-($2.99)						3.00
TPB (2011, $17.99) r/#1-6						18.00

RATFINK (See Frantic and Zany)
Canrom, Inc.: Oct, 1964

	GD 2.0	VG 4.0	FN 6.0	VF 8.0	VF/NM 9.0	NM- 9.2
1-Woodbridge-a	8	16	24	54	102	150

RAT PATROL, THE (TV) (Also see Wild!)
Dell Publishing Co.: Mar, 1967 - No. 5, Nov, 1967; No. 6, Oct, 1969

	GD 2.0	VG 4.0	FN 6.0	VF 8.0	VF/NM 9.0	NM- 9.2
1-Christopher George photo-c	6	12	18	40	73	105
2-6: 3-6-Photo-c	4	8	12	27	44	60

RAT QUEENS
Image Comics (Shadowline): Sept, 2013 - Present ($3.50)

	GD 2.0	VG 4.0	FN 6.0	VF 8.0	VF/NM 9.0	NM- 9.2
1-Kurtis Wiebe-s/Roc Upchurch-a/c						5.00
1-Variant-c by Fiona Staples						10.00
2-5-Two covers on each						3.50

RAVAGERS, THE (See Teen Titans and Superboy New 52 series)
DC Comics: Jul, 2012 - No. 12, Jul, 2013 ($2.99)

	GD 2.0	VG 4.0	FN 6.0	VF 8.0	VF/NM 9.0	NM- 9.2
1-12: 1-Fairchild, Beast Boy, Terra, Thunder, Lightning, Ridge team; Churchill-a						3.00
#0 (11/12, $2.99) Churchill-a; origin of Beast Boy & Terra						3.00

RAVAGE 2099 (See Marvel Comics Presents #117)
Marvel Comics: Dec, 1992 - No. 33, Aug, 1995($1.25/$1.50)

	GD 2.0	VG 4.0	FN 6.0	VF 8.0	VF/NM 9.0	NM- 9.2
1-($1.75)-Gold foil stamped-c; Stan Lee scripts						4.00
1-($1.75)-2nd printing						3.00
2-24,26-33: 5-Last Ryan-c. 6-Last Ryan-a. 14-Punisher 2099 x-over. 15-Ron Lim-c(p). 18-Bound-in card sheet						3.00
25 ($2.25, 52 pgs.)						4.00
25 ($2.95, 52 pgs.)-Silver foil embossed-c						5.00

RAVEN (See DC Special: Raven and Teen Titans titles)

RAVEN, THE (See Movie Classics)

RAVEN CHRONICLES
Caliber (New Worlds): 1995 - No. 16 ($2.95, B&W)

	GD 2.0	VG 4.0	FN 6.0	VF 8.0	VF/NM 9.0	NM- 9.2
1-16: 10-Flip book w/Wordsmith #6. 15-Flip book w/High Caliber #4						3.00

RAVENS AND RAINBOWS
Pacific Comics: Dec, 1983 (Baxter paper)(Reprints fanzine work in color)

	GD 2.0	VG 4.0	FN 6.0	VF 8.0	VF/NM 9.0	NM- 9.2
1-Jeff Jones-c/a(r); nudity scenes						3.00

RAWHIDE (TV)
Dell Publishing Co./Gold Key: Sept-Nov, 1959 - June-Aug, 1962; July, 1963 - No. 2, Jan, 1964

	GD 2.0	VG 4.0	FN 6.0	VF 8.0	VF/NM 9.0	NM- 9.2
Four Color 1028 (#1)	20	40	60	138	307	475
Four Color 1097,1160,1202,1261,1269	12	24	36	84	185	285
01-684-208 (8/62, Dell)	10	20	30	70	150	230
1(10071-307) (7/63, Gold Key)	10	20	30	70	150	230
2-(12¢)	10	20	30	64	132	200

NOTE: *All have Clint Eastwood photo-c.* ***Tufts*** *a-1028.*

RAWHIDE KID
Atlas/Marvel Comics (CnPC No. 1-16/AMI No. 17-30): Mar, 1955 - No. 16, Sept, 1957; No. 17, Aug, 1960 - No. 151, May, 1979

	GD 2.0	VG 4.0	FN 6.0	VF 8.0	VF/NM 9.0	NM- 9.2
1-Rawhide Kid, his horse Apache & sidekick Randy begin; Wyatt Earp app.; #1 was not code approved; Maneely splash pg.	129	258	387	826	1413	2000
2	45	90	135	284	480	675
3-5	36	72	108	211	343	475
6-10: 7-Williamson-a (4 pgs.)	27	54	81	158	259	360
11-16: 16-Torres-a	21	42	63	126	206	285
17-Origin by Jack Kirby; Kirby-a begins	55	110	165	352	601	850
18-21,24-30	13	26	39	89	195	300
22-Monster-c/story by Kirby/Ayers	17	34	51	117	259	400
23-Origin retold by Jack Kirby	21	42	63	147	324	500
31-35,40: 31,32-Kirby-a. 33-35-Davis-a. 34-Kirby-a. 35-Intro & death of The Raven. 40-Two-Gun Kid x-over.	10	20	30	70	150	230
36,37,39,41,42-No Kirby. 42-1st Larry Lieber issue	9	18	27	61	123	185
38-Red Raven-c/story; Kirby-c (2/64); Colan-a	12	24	36	79	170	260
43-Kirby-a (beware: pin-up often missing)	12	24	36	79	170	260
44,46: 46-Toth-a. 46-Doc Holliday-c/s	9	18	27	59	117	175
45-Origin retold, 17 pgs.	10	20	30	68	144	220
47-49,51-60	6	12	18	41	76	110
50-Kid Colt x-over; vs. Rawhide Kid	7	14	21	44	82	120
61-70: 64-Kid Colt story. 66-Two-Gun Kid story. 67-Kid Colt story. 70-Last 12¢ issue	5	10	15	33	57	80
71-78,80-83,85	3	6	9	20	31	42
79,84,86,95: 79-Williamson-a(r). 84,86: Kirby-a. 86-Origin-r; Williamson-r/Ringo Kid #13 (4 pgs.)	3	6	9	21	33	45
87-91: 90-Kid Colt app. 91-Last 15¢ issue	3	6	9	18	28	38
92,93 (52 pg.Giants). 92-Kirby-a	4	8	12	25	40	55
94,96-99	3	6	9	16	24	32
100 (6/72)-Origin retold & expanded	3	6	9	21	33	45
101-120: 115-Last new story	3	6	9	14	19	24
121-151	2	4	6	10	14	18
133,134-(30¢-c variants, limited distribution)(5,7/76)	4	8	12	28	47	65
140,141-(35¢-c variants, limited distribution)(7,9/77)	6	12	18	37	66	95
Special 1(9/71, 25¢, 68 pgs.)-All Kirby/Ayers-r	5	10	15	31	53	75

NOTE: ***Ayers*** *a-13, 14, 16, 29, 37-39, 61.* ***Colan*** *a-5, 35, 37, 38; c-145p, 148p, 149p.* ***Davis*** *a-125r.* ***Everett*** *a-*

The Ray #10 © DC

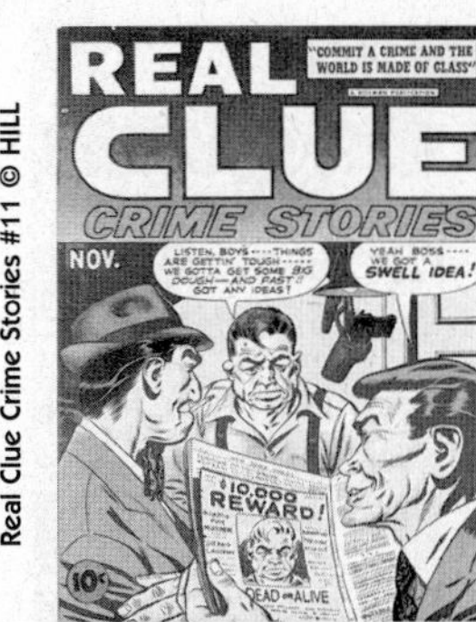

Real Clue Crime Stories #11 © HILL

Real Fact Comics #8 © DC

GD 2.0 | VG 4.0 | FN 6.0 | VF 8.0 | VF/NM 9.0 | NM- 9.2

54i, 65, 66, 88, 96i, 148i(r). ***Gulacy*** *c-147.* ***Heath*** *c-4.* ***G. Kane*** *c-101, 144.* ***Keller*** *a-5, 39, 41, 144r.* ***Kirby*** *a-17-32, 34, 42, 43, 84, 86, 92, 109r, 112r, 116r, 117r, 137r, Spec. 1; c-17-35, 37, 38, 40, 41, 43-47, 137r.* ***Maneely*** *c-1, 2, 5, 6, 14.* ***Morisi*** *a-13.* ***Morrow/Williamson*** *r-111.* ***Roussos*** *r-146i, 147i, 149-151i.* ***Severin*** *a-16; c-8, 13.* ***Sutton*** *a-61, 93.* ***Torres*** *a-99r.* ***Tuska*** *a-14.* ***Wildey*** *r-146-151(Outlaw Kid).* ***Williamson*** *r-79, 86, 95.*

RAWHIDE KID
Marvel Comics Group: Aug, 1985 - No. 4, Nov, 1985 (Mini-series)

1-4 5.00

RAWHIDE KID
Marvel Comics (MAX): Apr, 2003 - No. 5, June, 2003 ($2.99, limited series)

1-John Severin-a/Ron Zimmerman-s; Dave Johnson-c 3.00
2-5: 3-Dodson-c. 4-Darwyn Cooke-c. 5-J. Scott Campbell-c 3.00
Vol. 1: Slap Leather TPB (2003, $12.99) r/#1-5 13.00

RAWHIDE KID (The Sensational Seven)
Marvel Comics: Aug, 2010 - No. 4, Nov, 2010 ($3.99, limited series)

1-4-Chaykin-a/Zimmerman-s. 1-Cassaday-c. 2-Dave Johnson-c. 4-Suydam-c 4.00

RAY, THE (See Freedom Fighters & Smash Comics #14)
DC Comics: Feb, 1992 - No. 6, July, 1992 ($1.00, mini-series)

1-Sienkiewicz-c; Joe Quesada-a(p) in 1-5 5.00
2-6: 3-6-Quesada-c(p). 6-Quesada layouts only 3.00
...In a Blaze of Power (1994, $12.95)-r/#1-6 w/new Quesada-c 13.00

RAY, THE
DC Comics: May, 1994 - No. 28, Oct, 1996 ($1.75/$1.95/$2.25)

1-Quesada-c(p); Superboy app. 3.00
1-($2.95)-Collectors Edition w/diff. Quesada-c; embossed foil-c 4.00
2-5,0,6-24,26-28: 2-Quesada-c(p); Superboy app. 5-(9/94). 0-(10/94) 3.00
25-($3.50)-Future Flash (Bart Allen)-c/app; double size 4.00
Annual 1 ($3.95, 68 pgs.)-Superman app. 4.00

RAY, THE
DC Comics: Feb, 2012 - No. 4, May, 2012 ($2.99, limited series)

1-4: 1-Igle-a/Palmiotti & Gray-s; origin of the new Ray; intro. Lucien Gates 3.00

RAY BRADBURY COMICS
Topps Comics: Feb, 1993 - V4#1, June, 1994 ($2.95)

1-5-Polybagged w/3 trading cards each. 1-All dinosaur issue; Corben-a; Williamson/Torres/Krenkel-r/Weird Science-Fantasy #25. 3-All dinosaur issue; Steacy painted-c; Stout-a 3.00
Special Edition 1 (1994, $2.95)-The Illustrated Man 3.00
...Special: Tales of Horror #1 ($2.50), ...Trilogy of Terror V3#1 (5/94, $2.50), ...Martian Chronicles V4#1 (6/94, $2.50)-Steranko-c 3.00

NOTE: ***Kelley Jones*** *a-Trilogy of Terror V3#1.* ***Kaluta*** *a-Martian Chronicles V4#1.* ***Kurtzman/Matt Wagner*** *c-2.* ***McKean*** *c-4.* ***Mignola*** *a-4.* ***Wood*** *a-Trilogy of Terror V3#1r.*

RAZORLINE
Marvel Comics: Sept, 1993 (75¢, one-shot)

1-Clive Barker super-heroes: Ectokid, Hokum & Hex, Hyperkind & Saint Sinner 3.00

RAZOR'S EDGE, THE
DC Comics (WildStorm): Dec, 2004 - No. 5, Apr, 2005 ($2.95)

1-5-Warblade; Bisley-c/a; Ridley-s 3.00

REAL ADVENTURE COMICS (Action Adventure #2 on)
Gillmor Magazines: Apr, 1955

1 9 18 27 52 69 85

REAL ADVENTURES OF JONNY QUEST, THE
Dark Horse Comics: Sept, 1996 - No. 12, Sept, 1997 ($2.95)

1-12 3.00

REAL CLUE CRIME STORIES (Formerly Clue Comics)
Hillman Periodicals: V2#4, June, 1947 - V8#3, May, 1953

Issue	GD	VG	FN	VF	VF/NM	NM-
V2#4(#1)-S&K c/a(3); Dan Barry-a	49	98	147	309	522	735
5-7-S&K c/a(3-4). 7-Iron Lady app.	39	78	117	240	395	550
8-12	14	28	42	81	118	155
V3#1-8,10-12, V4#1-3,5-8,11,12	13	26	39	72	101	130
V3#9-Used in **SOTI**, pg. 102	15	30	45	83	124	165
V4#4-S&K-a	15	30	45	84	127	170
V4#9,10-Krigstein-a	13	26	39	74	105	135
V5#1-5,7,8,10,12	10	20	30	56	76	95
6,9,11(1/54)-Krigstein-a	11	22	33	60	83	105
V6#1-5,8,9,11	9	18	27	52	69	85
6,7,10,12-Krigstein-a. 10-Bondage-c	11	22	33	60	83	105
V7#1-3,5-11, V8#1-3: V7#6-1 pg. Frazetta ad "Prayer" - 1st app.?	10	20	30	56	76	95
4,12-Krigstein-a	11	22	33	60	83	105

NOTE: ***Barry*** *a-9, 10; c-V2#8.* ***Briefer*** *a-V6#6.* ***Fuje*** *a- V2#7(2), 8, 11.* ***Infantino*** *a-V2#8; c-V2#11.* ***Lawrence*** *a-V3#8, V5#7.* ***Powell*** *a-V4#11, 12. V5#4, 5, 7 are 68 pgs.*

REAL EXPERIENCES (Formerly Tiny Tessie)
Atlas Comics (20CC): No. 25, Jan, 1950

25-Virginia Mayo photo-c from movie "Red Light" 13 26 39 74 105 135

REAL FACT COMICS
National Periodical Publications: Mar-Apr, 1946 - No. 21, July-Aug, 1949

Issue	GD	VG	FN	VF	VF/NM	NM-
1-S&K-c/a; Harry Houdini story; Just Imagine begins (not by Finlay); Fred Ray-a	47	94	141	296	498	700
2-S&K-a; Rin-Tin-Tin & P. T. Barnum stories	28	56	84	165	270	375
3-H.G. Wells, Lon Chaney stories; early DC letter column (New Fun Comics #3 from 1935 may be the 1st)	26	52	78	154	252	350
4-Virgil Finlay-a on 'Just Imagine' begins, ends #12 (2 pgs. each); Jimmy Stewart & Jack London stories; Joe DiMaggio 1 pg. biography	29	58	87	172	281	390
5-Batman/Robin-c taken from cover of Batman #9; 5 pg. story about creation of Batman & Robin; Tom Mix story	155	310	465	992	1696	2400
6-Origin & 1st app. Tommy Tomorrow by Weisinger and Sherman (1-2/47); Flag-c; 1st writing by Harlan Ellison (letter column, non-professional); "First Man to Reach Mars" epic-c/story	84	168	252	538	919	1300
7-(No. 6 on inside)-Roussos-a; D. Fairbanks sty.	15	30	45	94	147	200
8-2nd app. Tommy Tomorrow by Finlay (5-6/47)	48	96	144	302	514	725
9-S&K-a; Glenn Miller, Indianapolis 500 stories	21	42	63	122	199	275
10-Vigilante by Meskin (based on movie serial); 4 pg. Finlay s/f story	20	40	60	118	192	265
11,12: 11-Annie Oakley, G-Men stories; Kinstler-a	14	28	42	82	121	160
13-Dale Evans and Tommy Tomorrow-c/stories	37	74	111	222	361	500
14,17,18: 14-Will Rogers story	14	28	42	80	115	150
15-Nuclear explosion part-c ("Last War on Earth" story); Clyde Beatty story	15	30	45	94	147	200
16-Tommy Tomorrow app.; 1st Planeteers?	36	72	108	211	343	475
19-Sir Arthur Conan Doyle story	15	30	45	83	124	165
20-Kubert-a, 4 pgs; Daniel Boone story	15	30	45	88	137	185
21-Kubert-a, 2 pgs; Kit Carson story	14	28	42	80	115	150

Ashcan (2/46) nn-Not distributed to newsstands, only for in house use. Covers were produced, but not the rest of the book. A copy sold in 2008 for $500.

NOTE: ***Barry*** *c-16.* ***Virgil Finlay*** *c-6, 8.* ***Meskin*** *c-10.* ***Roussos*** *a-1-4, 6.*

REAL FUNNIES
Nedor Publishing Co.: Jan, 1943 - No. 3, June, 1943

Issue	GD	VG	FN	VF	VF/NM	NM-
1-Funny animal, humor; Black Terrier app. (clone of The Black Terror)	33	66	99	194	317	440
2,3	17	34	51	98	154	210

REAL GHOSTBUSTERS, THE (Also see Slimer)
Now Comics: Aug, 1988 - No. 32, 1991 ($1.75/$1.95)

1-32: 1-Based on Ghostbusters movie. #29-32 exist? 4.00

REAL HEROES
Image Comics: Mar, 2014 - Present ($3.99)

1-Bryan Hitch-s/a 4.00

REAL HEROES COMICS
Parents' Magazine Institute: Sept, 1941 - No. 16, Oct, 1946

Issue	GD	VG	FN	VF	VF/NM	NM-
1-Roosevelt-c/story	32	64	96	188	307	425
2-J. Edgar Hoover-c/story	15	30	45	83	124	165
3-5,7-10: 4-Churchill, Roosevelt stories	14	28	42	76	108	140
6-Lou Gehrig-c/story	19	38	57	112	179	245
11-16: 13-Kiefer-a	10	20	30	54	72	90

REALISTIC ROMANCES
Realistic Comics/Avon Periodicals: July-Aug, 1951 - No. 17, Aug-Sept, 1954 (No #9-14)

Issue	GD	VG	FN	VF	VF/NM	NM-
1-Kinstler-a; c-/Avon paperback #211	36	72	108	216	351	485
2	18	36	54	107	169	230
3,4	18	36	54	103	162	220
5,8-Kinstler-a	18	36	54	105	165	225
6-c-/Diversey Prize Novels #6; Kinstler-a	18	36	54	107	169	230
7-Evans-a?; c-/Avon paperback #360	18	36	54	107	169	230
15,17: 17-Kinstler-c	17	34	51	98	154	210
16-Kinstler marijuana story-r/Romantic Love #6	18	36	54	105	165	225
I.W. Reprint #1,8,9: #1-r/Realistic Romances #4; Astarita-a. 9-r/Women To Love #1	3	6	9	14	20	25

NOTE: ***Astarita*** *a-2-4, 7, 8, 17. Photo c-1, 2. Painted c-3, 4.*

REALITY CHECK
Image Comics: Sept, 2013 - No. 4, Dec, 2013 ($2.99)

1-4-Brunswick-s/Bogdanovic-a 3.00

Realm of Kings: Son of Hulk #3 © MAR

Real Screen Comics #43 © DC

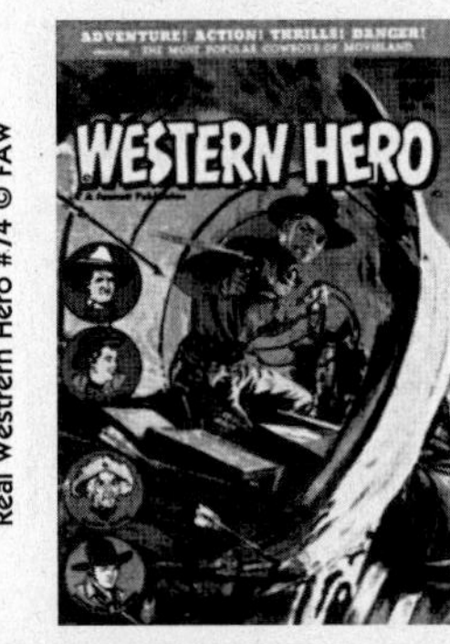

Real Western Hero #74 © FAW

REAL LIFE COMICS
Nedor/Better/Standard Publ./Pictorial Magazine No. 13: Sept, 1941 - No. 59, Sept, 1952

	GD 2.0	VG 4.0	FN 6.0	VF 8.0	VF/NM 9.0	NM- 9.2
1-Uncle Sam-c/story; Daniel Boone story	69	138	207	442	759	1075
2	34	68	102	204	332	460
3-Hitler cover	343	686	1029	2400	4200	6000
4,5: 4-Story of American flag "Old Glory"	26	52	78	154	252	350
6-10: 6-Wild Bill Hickok story	21	42	63	126	206	285
11-14,16-20: 17-Albert Einstein story	20	40	60	114	182	250
15-Japanese WWII-c by Schomburg	22	44	66	132	216	300
21-23,25,26,28-30: 29-A-Bomb story	18	36	54	103	162	220
24-Story of Baseball (Babe Ruth)	24	48	72	140	230	320
27-Schomburg A-Bomb-c; story of A-Bomb	23	46	69	136	223	310
31-33,35,36,42-44,48,49: 49-Baseball issue	15	30	45	88	137	185
34,37-41,45-47: 34-Jimmy Stewart story. 37-Story of motion pictures; Bing Crosby story. 38-Jane Froman story. 39- "1,000,000 A.D." story. 40-Bob Feller. 41-Jimmie Foxx story ("Jimmy" on-c); "Home Run" Baker story. 45-Story of Olympic games; Burl Ives & Kit Carson story. 46-Douglas Fairbanks Jr. & Sr. story. 47-George Gershwin story	16	32	48	94	147	200
50-Frazetta-a (5 pgs.)	31	62	93	182	296	410
51-Jules Verne "Journey to the Moon" by Evans; Severin/Elder-a	22	44	66	128	209	290
52-Frazetta-a (4 pgs.); Severin/Elder-a(2); Evans-a	34	68	102	199	325	450
53-57-Severin/Elder-a. 54-Bat Masterson-c/story	18	36	54	103	162	220
58-Severin/Elder-a(2)	18	36	54	105	165	225
59-1 pg. Frazetta; Severin/Elder-a	18	36	54	105	165	225

NOTE: ***Guardineer** a-40(2), 44. **Meskin** a-52. **Roussos** a-50. **Schomburg** c-1, 2, 4, 5, 7, 11, 13-21, 23, 24, 26, 28, 30-32, 34-40, 42, 44-47, 55. **Tuska** a-53. Photo-c 5, 6.*

REAL LIFE SECRETS (Real Secrets #2 on)
Ace Periodicals: Sept, 1949 (one-shot)

	GD 2.0	VG 4.0	FN 6.0	VF 8.0	VF/NM 9.0	NM- 9.2
1-Painted-c	15	30	45	86	133	180

REAL LIFE STORY OF FESS PARKER (Magazine)
Dell Publishing Co.: 1955

	GD 2.0	VG 4.0	FN 6.0	VF 8.0	VF/NM 9.0	NM- 9.2
1	8	16	24	54	102	150

REAL LIFE TALES OF SUSPENSE (See Suspense)

REAL LOVE (Formerly Hap Hazard)
Ace Periodicals (A. A. Wyn): No. 25, April, 1949 - No. 76, Nov, 1956

	GD 2.0	VG 4.0	FN 6.0	VF 8.0	VF/NM 9.0	NM- 9.2
25	15	30	45	86	133	180
26	12	24	36	67	94	120
27-L. B. Cole-a	13	26	39	74	105	135
28-35	11	22	33	60	83	105
36-66: 66-Last pre-code (2/55)	10	20	30	56	76	95
67-76	9	18	27	50	65	80

NOTE: *Photo c-50-76. Painted c-46.*

REALM, THE
Arrow Comics/WeeBee Comics #13/Caliber Press #14 on: Feb, 1986 - No. 21, 1991 (B&W)

	GD 2.0	VG 4.0	FN 6.0	VF 8.0	VF/NM 9.0	NM- 9.2
1-3,5-21						3.00
4-1st app. Deadworld (9/86)						4.00
Book 1 ($4.95, B&W)						5.00

REAL McCOYS, THE (TV)
Dell Publ. Co.: No. 1071, 1-3/60 - 5-7/1962 (All have Walter Brennan photo-c)

	GD 2.0	VG 4.0	FN 6.0	VF 8.0	VF/NM 9.0	NM- 9.2
Four Color 1071,1134-Toth-a in both	8	16	24	51	96	140
Four Color 1193,1265	7	14	21	48	89	130
01-689-207 (5-7/62)	6	12	18	42	79	115

REALM OF KINGS (Also see Guardians of the Galaxy and Nova)
Marvel Comics: Jan, 2010 ($3.99, one-shot)

	GD 2.0	VG 4.0	FN 6.0	VF 8.0	VF/NM 9.0	NM- 9.2
1-Abnett & Lanning-s/Manco & Asrar-a; Guardians of the Galaxy app.						4.00

REALM OF KINGS: IMPERIAL GUARD
Marvel Comics: Jan, 2010 - No. 5, May, 2010 ($3.99, limited series)

	GD 2.0	VG 4.0	FN 6.0	VF 8.0	VF/NM 9.0	NM- 9.2
1-5-Abnett & Lanning-s/Walker-a; Starjammers app.						4.00

REALM OF KINGS: INHUMANS
Marvel Comics: Jan, 2010 - No. 5, May, 2010 ($3.99, limited series)

	GD 2.0	VG 4.0	FN 6.0	VF 8.0	VF/NM 9.0	NM- 9.2
1-5-Abnett & Lanning-s/Raimondi-a; Mighty Avengers app.						4.00

REALM OF KINGS: SON OF HULK
Marvel Comics: Apr, 2010 - No. 4, July, 2010 ($3.99, limited series)

	GD 2.0	VG 4.0	FN 6.0	VF 8.0	VF/NM 9.0	NM- 9.2
1-4-Reed-s/Munera-a; leads into Incredible Hulk #609						4.00

REALM OF THE CLAW (Also see Mutant Earth as part of a flipbook)
Image Comics: Oct, 2003 - No. 2 ($2.95)

	GD 2.0	VG 4.0	FN 6.0	VF 8.0	VF/NM 9.0	NM- 9.2
0-(7/03, $5.95) Convention Special; cover has gold-foil title logo						6.00
1,2-Two covers by Yardin						3.00
Vol. 1 TPB (2006, $16.99) r/series; concept art & sketch pages						17.00

REAL SCREEN COMICS (#1 titled Real Screen Funnies; TV Screen Cartoons #129-138)
National Periodical Publications: Spring, 1945 - No. 128, May-June, 1959 (#1-40: 52 pgs.)

	GD 2.0	VG 4.0	FN 6.0	VF 8.0	VF/NM 9.0	NM- 9.2
1-The Fox & the Crow, Flippity & Flop, Tito & His Burrito begin	107	214	321	685	1168	1650
2	47	94	141	296	498	700
3-5	32	64	96	188	307	425
6-10 (2-3/47)	21	42	63	122	199	275
11-20 (10-11/48): 13-The Crow x-over in Flippity & Flop	16	32	48	94	147	200
21-30 (6-7/50)	14	28	42	76	108	140
31-50	11	22	33	60	83	105
51-99	10	20	30	54	72	90
100	10	20	30	56	76	95
101-128	8	16	24	44	57	70

REAL SCREEN FUNNIES
DC Comics: Spring 1945

1-Ashcan comic, not distributed to newsstands, only for in-house use. Cover art is Real Screen Funnies #1 with interior being Detective Comics #92. Only ashcan cover to be produced using the regular production first issue art and only using the color yellow. A copy sold in 2008 for $3,000. A FN/VF copy sold for $1314.50 in 2012.

REAL SECRETS (Formerly Real Life Secrets)
Ace Periodicals: No. 2, Nov, 1950 - No. 5, May, 1950

	GD 2.0	VG 4.0	FN 6.0	VF 8.0	VF/NM 9.0	NM- 9.2
2-Painted-c	12	24	36	67	94	120
3-5: 3-Photo-c	10	20	30	54	72	90

REAL SPORTS COMICS (All Sports Comics #2 on)
Hillman Periodicals: Oct-Nov, 1948 (52 pgs.)

	GD 2.0	VG 4.0	FN 6.0	VF 8.0	VF/NM 9.0	NM- 9.2
1-Powell-a (12 pgs.)	39	78	117	240	395	550

REAL WAR STORIES
Eclipse Comics: July, 1987; No. 2, Jan, 1991 ($2.00, 52 pgs.)

	GD 2.0	VG 4.0	FN 6.0	VF 8.0	VF/NM 9.0	NM- 9.2
1-Bolland-a(p), Bissette-a, Totleben-a(i); Alan Moore scripts (2nd printing exists, 2/88)						5.00
2-($4.95)						5.00

REAL WESTERN HERO (Formerly Wow #1-69; Western Hero #76 on)
Fawcett Publications: No. 70, Sept, 1948 - No. 75, Feb, 1949 (All 52 pgs.)

	GD 2.0	VG 4.0	FN 6.0	VF 8.0	VF/NM 9.0	NM- 9.2
70(#1)-Tom Mix, Monte Hale, Hopalong Cassidy, Young Falcon begin	22	44	66	132	216	300
71-75: 71-Gabby Hayes begins. 71,72-Captain Tootsie by Beck. 75-Big Bow and Little Arrow app.	15	30	45	85	130	175

NOTE: *Painted/photo c-70-73; painted c-74, 75.*

REAL WEST ROMANCES
Crestwood Publishing Co./Prize Publ.: 4-5/49 - V1#6, 3/50; V2#1, Apr-May, 1950 (All 52 pgs. & photo-c)

	GD 2.0	VG 4.0	FN 6.0	VF 8.0	VF/NM 9.0	NM- 9.2
V1#1-S&K-a(p)	26	52	78	154	252	350
2-Gail Davis and Rocky Shahan photo-c	14	28	42	80	115	150
3-Kirby-a(p) only	14	28	42	82	121	160
4-S&K-a; Whip Wilson, Reno Browne photo-c	19	38	57	111	176	240
5-Audie Murphy, Gale Storm photo-c; S&K-a	17	34	51	98	154	210
6-Produced by S&K, no S&K-a; Robert Preston & Cathy Downs photo-c	13	26	39	74	105	135
V2#1-Kirby-a(p)	13	26	39	74	105	135

NOTE: ***Meskin** a-V1#5, 6. **Severin/Elder** a-V1#3-6, V2#1. **Meskin** a-V1#6. **Leonard Starr** a-1-3. Photo-c V1#1-6, V2#1.*

REALWORLDS :...
DC Comics: 2000 ($5.95, one-shots, prestige format)

	GD 2.0	VG 4.0	FN 6.0	VF 8.0	VF/NM 9.0	NM- 9.2
Batman - Marshall Rogers-a/Golden & Sniegoski-s; Justice League of America -Dematteis-s/Barr-painted art; Superman - Vance-s/García-López & Rubenstein-a; Wonder Woman - Hanson & Neuwirth-s/Sam-a						6.00

RE-ANIMATOR IN FULL COLOR
Adventure Comics: Oct, 1991 - No. 3, 1992 ($2.95, mini-series)

	GD 2.0	VG 4.0	FN 6.0	VF 8.0	VF/NM 9.0	NM- 9.2
1-3: Adapts horror movie. 1-Dorman painted-c						3.00

REAP THE WILD WIND (See Cinema Comics Herald)

REBEL, THE (TV)(Nick Adams as Johnny Yuma)
Dell Publishing Co.: No. 1076, Feb-Apr, 1960 - No. 1262, Dec-Feb, 1961-62

	GD 2.0	VG 4.0	FN 6.0	VF 8.0	VF/NM 9.0	NM- 9.2
Four Color 1076 (#1)-Sekowsky-a, photo-c	9	18	27	57	111	165
Four Color 1138 (9-11/60), 1207 (9-11/61), 1262-Photo-c	7	14	21	49	92	135

R.E.B.E.L.S.

Red Circle Comics #4 © Enwil

Red Dragon Comics #3 © S&S

Red Hood and the Outlaws #17 © DC

	GD	VG	FN	VF	VF/NM	NM-
	2.0	4.0	6.0	8.0	9.0	9.2

DC Comics: Apr, 2009 - No. 28, Jul, 2011 ($2.99)

1-9,12-28: 1-Bedard-s/Clarke-a; Vril Dox returns; Supergirl app.; 2 covers. 15-Starfire app. 19-28-Lobo app. 3.00
10,11-($3.99) Blackest Night x-over; Vril Dox joins the Sinestro Corps 4.00
Annual 1 (12/09, $4.99) Origin on Starro the Conqueror; Despero app. 5.00
...: Sons of Brainiac TPB (2011, $14.99) r/#15-20 15.00
...: Strange Companions TPB (2010, $14.99) r/#7-9 & Annual #1 15.00
...: The Coming of Starro TPB (2010, $17.99) r/#1-6 18.00
...: The Son and the Stars TPB (2010, $17.99) r/#10-14 18.00

R.E.B.E.L.S. '94 (Becomes R.E.B.E.L.S. '95 & R.E.B.E.L.S. '96)
DC Comics: No. 0, Oct, 1994 - No. 17, Mar, 1996 ($1.95/$2.25)

0-17: 8-$2.25-c begins. 15-R.E.B.E.L.S '96 begins. 3.00

RECORD BOOK OF FAMOUS POLICE CASES
St. John Publishing Co.: 1949 (25¢, 132 pgs.)

nn-Kubert-a(3); r/Son of Sinbad; Baker-c 45 90 135 284 480 675

RED (Inspired the 2010 Bruce Willis movie)
DC Comics (Homage): Sept, 2003 - No. 3, Feb, 2004 ($2.95, limited series)

1-3-Warren Ellis-s/Cully Hamner-a/c 5.00
Red/Tokyo Storm Warning TPB (2004, $14.95) Flip book r/both series 15.00
Red: Eyes Only (2/11, $4.99) comic prequel; Hamner-s/a/c 5.00
Red: Frank (11/10, $3.99) movie prequel; Noveck-s/Masters-a/Hamner & photo-c 4.00
Red: Joe (11/10, $3.99) movie prequel; Wagner-s/Redondo-a/Hamner & photo-c 4.00
Red: Marvin (11/10, $3.99) movie prequel; Hoeber-s/Olmos-a/Hamner & photo-c 4.00
Red: Victoria (11/10, $3.99) movie prequel; Hoeber-s/Hahn-a/Hamner & photo-c 4.00
...: Better R.E.D. Than Dead TPB (2011, $14.99) r/movie prequel issues; sketch-a 15.00

RED ARROW
P. L. Publishing Co.: May-June, 1951 - No. 3, Oct, 1951

1 11 22 33 62 86 110
2,3 9 18 27 47 61 75

RED BAND COMICS
Enwil Associates: Nov, 1944, No. 2, Jan, 1945 - No. 4, May, 1945

1-Bogeyman-c/intro. (The Spirit swipe) 42 84 126 265 445 625
2-Origin Bogeyman & Santanas; c-reprint/#1 31 62 93 182 296 410
3,4-Captain Wizard app. in both (1st app.); each has identical contents/cover 29 58 87 170 278 385

REDBLADE
Dark Horse Comics: Apr, 1993 - No. 3, July, 1993 ($2.50, mini-series)

1-3: 1-Double gatefold-c 3.00

RED CIRCLE, THE (Re-introduction of characters from MLJ/Archie publications)
DC Comics: Oct, 2009 ($2.99, series of one-shots)

...Inferno 1 - Hangman app.; Straczynski-s/Greg Scott-a 5.00
...The Hangman 1 - Origin retold; Straczynski-s/Derenick & Sienkiewicz-a 5.00
...The Shield 1 - Origin retold; Straczynski-s/McDaniel-a 5.00
...The Web 1 - Straczynski-s/Robinson-a 5.00

RED CIRCLE COMICS (Also see Blazing Comics & Blue Circle Comics)
Rural Home Publications (Enwil): Jan, 1945 - No. 4, April, 1945

1-The Prankster & Red Riot begin 61 122 183 390 670 950
2-Starr-a; The Judge (costumed hero) app. 34 68 102 206 336 465
3,4-Starr-c/a. 3-The Prankster not in costume 28 56 84 165 270 375
4-(Dated 4/45)-Leftover covers to #4 were later restapled over early 1950s coverless comics; variations in the coverless comics used are endless; Woman Outlaws, Dorothy Lamour, Crime Does Not Pay, Sabu, Diary Loves, Love Confessions & Young Love V3#3 known 20 40 60 118 192 265

RED CIRCLE SORCERY (Chilling Adventures in Sorcery #1-5)
Red Circle Prod. (Archie): No. 6, Apr, 1974 - No. 11, Feb, 1975 (All 25¢ iss.)

6,8,9,11: 6-Early Chaykin-a. 7-Pino-a. 8-Only app. The Cobra 2 4 6 9 13 16
7-Bruce Jones-a with Wrightson, Kaluta, Jeff Jones 3 6 9 14 19 24
10-Wood-a(i) 2 4 6 10 14 18

NOTE: ***Chaykin** a-6, 10. **McWilliams** a-10(2 & 3 pgs.). **Mooney** a-11p. **Morrow** a-6-8, 9(text illos), 10, 11i; c-6-11. **Thorne** a-8, 10. **Toth** a-8, 9.*

RED DOG (See Night Music #7)

RED DRAGON
Comico: June, 1996 ($2.95)

1-Bisley-c 3.00

RED DRAGON COMICS (1st Series) (Formerly Trail Blazers; see Super Magician V5#7, 8)
Street & Smith Publications: No. 5, Jan, 1943 - No. 9, Jan, 1944

5-Origin Red Rover, the Crimson Crimebuster; Rex King, Man of Adventure, Captain Jack Commando, & The Minute Man begin; text origin Red Dragon; Binder-c 77 154 231 493 847 1200
6-Origin The Black Crusader & Red Dragon (3/43); 1st story app. Red Dragon & 1st cover (classic-c) 206 412 618 1318 2259 3200
7-Classic WWII-c 245 490 735 1568 2684 3800
8-The Red Knight app. 61 122 183 390 670 950
9-Origin Chuck Magnon, Immortal Man 61 122 183 390 670 950

RED DRAGON COMICS (2nd Series)(See Super Magician V2#8)
Street & Smith Publications: Nov, 1947 - No. 6, Jan, 1949; No. 7, July, 1949

1-Red Dragon begins; Elliman, Nigel app.; Edd Cartier-c/a 94 188 282 602 1026 1450
2-Cartier-c 54 108 162 343 574 825
3-1st app. Dr. Neff Ghost Breaker by Powell; Elliman, Nigel app. 43 86 129 271 461 650
4-Cartier c/a 58 116 174 371 636 900
5-7 34 68 102 199 325 450

NOTE: ***Maneely** a-5, 7. **Powell** a-2-7; c-3, 5, 7.*

RED EAGLE
David McKay Publications: No. 16, Aug, 1938

Feature Books 16 30 60 90 177 289 400

REDEYE (See Comics Reading Libraries in the Promotional Comics section)

RED FOX (Formerly Manhunt! #1-14; also see Extra Comics)
Magazine Enterprises: No. 15, 1954

15(A-1 #108)-Undercover Girl story; L.B. Cole-c/a (Red Fox); r-from Manhunt; Powell-a 19 38 57 109 172 235

RED GOOSE COMIC SELECTIONS (See Comic Selections)

RED HAWK (See A-1 Comics, Bobby Benson's ..#14-16 & Straight Arrow #2)
Magazine Enterprises: No. 90, 1953

11-(A-1 Comics #90)-Powell-c/a 13 26 39 72 101 130

RED HERRING
DC Comics (WildStorm): Oct, 2009 - No. 6, Mar, 2010 ($2.99, limited series)

1-6-Tischman-s/Bond-a 3.00

RED HOOD AND THE OUTLAWS
DC Comics: Nov, 2011 - Present ($2.99)

1-8,10-14: 1-Jason Todd, Starfire, Roy Harper team.; Lobdell-s/Rocafort-a/c. 3.00
9-Night of the Owls tie-in; Mr. Freeze vs. Talon 5.00
15-(2/13) Death of the Family tie-in; die-cut cover; Joker app. 5.00
16-18: 16,17-Death of the Family tie-in 4.00
19-24,26-29: 24,26,27-Ra's al Ghul app. 3.00
25-($3.99) Zero Year tie-in; Talia and the Red Hood Gang app.; Haun-a 4.00
#0-(11/12, $2.99) Jason Todd's origin re-told; Joker app. 3.00
Annual 1 (7/13, $4.99) Takes place between #20 & 21; Green Arrow app.; Barrionuevo-a 5.00

RED HOOD: THE LOST DAYS
DC Comics: Aug, 2010 - No. 6, Jan, 2011 ($2.99, limited series)

1-6-The Return of Jason Todd; Winick-s/Raimondi-a/Tucci-c. 6-Joker & Hush app. 3.00
TPB (2011, $14.99) r/#1-6 15.00

RED LANTERNS (DC New 52)
DC Comics: Nov, 2011 - Present ($2.99)

1-29: 1-Milligan-s/Benes-a/c; Atrocitus, Dex-Starr & Bleez app. 6-8,11-Guy Gardner app. 10-Stormwatch app. 13-15-Rise of the Third Army. 17-First Lantern app. 24-Lights Out pt. 4. 28-Flipbook with Green Lantern #28; Supergirl app. 29-Superman app. 3.00
#0-(11/12, $2.99) Origin of Atrocitus, the 1st Red Lantern; Syaf-a 3.00

RED MASK (Formerly Tim Holt; see Best Comics, Blazing Six-Guns)
Magazine Enterprises No. 42-53/Sussex No. 54 (M.E. on-c): No. 42, June-July, 1954 - No. 53, May, 1956; No. 54, Sept, 1957

42-Ghost Rider by Ayers continues, ends #50; Black Phantom continues; 3-D effect c/stories begin 21 42 63 122 199 275
43- 3-D effect-c/stories 19 38 57 109 172 235
44-52: 3-D effect stories only. 47-Last pre-code issue. 50-Last Ghost Rider. 51-The Presto Kid begins by Ayers (1st app.); Presto Kid-c begins; last 3-D effect story.
52-Origin The Presto Kid 17 34 51 98 154 210
53,54-Last Black Phantom; last Presto Kid-c 15 30 45 83 124 165
I.W. Reprint #1 (r-/#52). 2 (nd, r/#51 w/diff.-c). 3, 8 (nd; Kinstler-c); 8-r/Red Mask #52 3 6 9 16 22 28

NOTE: ***Ayers** art on Ghost Rider & Presto Kid. **Bolle** art in all (Red Mask); c-43, 44, 49. **Guardineer** a-52. Black Phantom in #42-44, 47-50, 53, 54.*

REDMASK OF THE RIO GRANDE

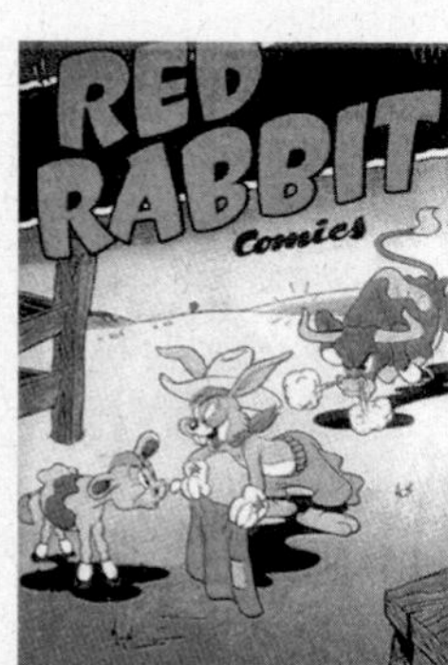

Red Rabbit Comics #2 © Dearfield

Red Ryder Comics #11 © DELL

Red Sonja (2005 series) #6 © Red Sonja Corp.

	GD 2.0	VG 4.0	FN 6.0	VF 8.0	VF/NM 9.0	NM- 9.2

AC Comics: 1990 ($2.50, 28pgs.)(Has photos of movie posters)

1-Bolle-c/a(r); photo inside-c — 3.00

RED MENACE
DC Comics (WildStorm): Jan, 2007 - No. 6, Jun, 2007 ($2.99, limited series)

1-6-Ordway-a/c; Bilson, DeMeo & Brody-s — 3.00
TPB (2007, $17.99) r/series, sketch pages & variant covers — 18.00

RED MOUNTAIN FEATURING QUANTRELL'S RAIDERS (Movie)(Also see Jesse James #28)
Avon Periodicals: 1952

nn-Alan Ladd; Kinstler-c — 30 60 90 177 289 400

RED PROPHET: THE TALES OF ALVIN MAKER
Dabel Brothers Prods./Marvel Comics (Dabel Brothers): Mar, 2006 - No. 12, Mar, 2008 ($2.99)

1-12-Adaptation of Orson Scott Card novel. 1-Miguel Montenegro-a — 3.00
... Vol. 1 HC (2007, $19.99, dustjacket) r/#1-6 — 20.00
... Vol. 1 SC (2007, $15.99) r/#1-6 — 16.00
... Vol. 2 HC (2008, $19.99, dustjacket) r/#7-12 — 20.00

"RED" RABBIT COMICS
Dearfield Comic/J. Charles Laue Publ. Co.: Jan, 1947 - No. 22, Aug-Sep, 1951

1 — 14 28 42 82 121 160
2 — 9 18 27 50 65 80
3-10 — 8 16 24 42 54 65
11-17,19-22 — 8 16 24 40 50 60
18-Flying Saucer-c (1/51) — 9 18 27 50 65 80

RED RAVEN COMICS (Human Torch #2 on)(Also see X-Men #44 & Sub-Mariner #26, 2nd series)
Timely Comics: August, 1940

1-Origin & 1st app. Red Raven; Comet Pierce & Mercury by Kirby, The Human Top & The Eternal Brain; intro. Magar, the Mystic & only app.; Kirby-c (his 1st signed work) — 1600 3200 4800 12,000 22,000 32,000

RED ROBIN (Batman: Reborn)
DC Comics: Aug, 2009 - No. 26, Oct, 2011 ($2.99)

1-26-Tim (Drake) Wayne in the Kingdom Come costume; Bachs-a. 1-Two covers — 3.00
...: Collision SC (2010, $19.99) r/#6-12 and Batgirl (2009 series) #8 — 20.00
...: The Grail SC (2010, $17.99) r/#1-5 — 18.00
...: The Hit List SC (2011, $17.99) r/#13-17 — 18.00

RED ROCKET 7
Dark Horse Comics: Aug, 1997 - No. 7, June, 1998 ($3.95, square format, limited series)

1-7-Mike Allred-c/s/a — 4.00

RED RYDER COMICS (Hi Spot #2)(Movies, radio)(See Crackajack Funnies & Super Book of Comics)
Hawley Publ. No. 1/Dell Publishing Co.(K.K.) No. 3 on: 9/40; No. 3, 8/41 - No. 5, 12/41; No. 6, 4/42 - No. 151, 4-6/57 (Beware of almost identical reprints of #1 made in the late 1980s)

1-Red Ryder, his horse Thunder, Little Beaver & his horse Papoose strip reprints begin by Fred Harman; 1st meeting of Red & Little Beaver; Harman line-drawn-c #1-85 — 245 490 735 1568 2684 3800
3-(Scarce)-Alley Oop, Capt. Easy, Dan Dunn, Freckles & His Friends, King of the Royal Mtd., Myra North strip-r begin — 50 100 150 400 900 1400
4-6: 6-1st Dell issue (4/42) — 25 50 75 175 388 600
7-10 — 21 42 63 147 324 500
11-20 — 15 30 45 103 227 350
21-32-Last Alley Oop, Dan Dunn, Capt. Easy, Freckles — 10 20 30 69 147 225
33-40 (52 pgs.): 40-Photo back-c begin, end #57 — 9 18 27 58 114 170
41 (52 pgs.)-Rocky Lane photo back-c — 9 18 27 60 120 180
42-46 (52 pgs.): 46-Last Red Ryder strip-r — 7 14 21 49 92 135
47-53 (52 pgs.): 47-New stories on Red Ryder begin. 49,52-Harmon photo back-c — 6 12 18 41 76 110
54-92: 54-73 (36 pgs.). 59-Harmon photo back-c. 73-Last King of the Royal Mtd; strip-r by Jim Gary. 74-85 (52 pgs.)-Harman line-drawn-c. 86-92 (52 pgs.)-Harman painted-c — 6 12 18 37 66 95
93-99,101-106: 94-96 (36 pgs.)-Harman painted-c. 97,98,(36 pgs.)-Harman line-drawn-c. 99,101-106 (36 pgs.)-Jim Bannon Photo-c — 5 10 15 33 57 80
100 (36 pgs.)-Bannon photo-c — 5 10 15 34 60 85
107-118 (52 pgs.)-Harman line-drawn-c — 5 10 15 31 53 75
119-129 (52 pgs.): 119-Painted-c begin, not by Harman, end #151 — 5 10 15 30 50 70
130-151 (36 pgs.): 145-Title change to Red Ryder Ranch Magazine 149-Title change to Red Ryder Ranch Comics — 4 8 12 28 47 65
Four Color 916 (7/58) — 4 8 12 28 47 65

NOTE: *Fred Harman a-1-99; c-1-98, 107-118. Don Red Barry, Allan Rocky Lane, Wild Bill Elliott & Jim Bannon starred as Red Ryder in the movies. Robert Blake starred as Little Beaver.*

RED RYDER PAINT BOOK
Whitman Publishing Co.: 1941 (8-1/2x11-1/2", 148 pgs.)

nn-Reprints 1940 daily strips — 76 152 228 479 810 1140

RED SEAL COMICS (Formerly Carnival Comics, and/or Spotlight Comics?)
Harry 'A' Chesler/Superior Publ. No. 19 on: No. 14, 10/45 - No. 18, 10/46; No. 19, 6/47 - No. 22, 12/47

14-The Black Dwarf begins (continued from Spotlight?); Little Nemo app; bondage/hypo-c; Tuska-a — 87 174 261 553 952 1350
15-Torture story; funny-c — 41 82 123 256 428 600
16-Used in **SOTI**, pg. 181, illo "Outside the forbidden pages of de Sade, you find draining a girl's blood only in children's comics;" drug club story r-later in Crime Reporter #1; Veiled Avenger & Barry Kuda app; Tuska-a; funny-c — 63 126 189 403 689 975
17,18,20: Lady Satan, Yankee Girl & Sky Chief app; 17-Tuska-a — 54 108 162 343 574 825
19-No Black Dwarf (on-c only); Zor, El Tigre app. — 53 106 159 334 567 800
21-Lady Satan & Black Dwarf app. — 33 66 99 194 317 440
22-Zor, Rocketman app. (68 pgs.) — 33 66 99 194 317 440

RED SHE-HULK (Title continues from Hulk (2008 series) #57)
Marvel Comics: No. 58, Dec, 2012 - No. 67, Sept, 2013 ($2.99)

58-67-Betty Ross character; Pagulayan-a/c. 59,60-Avengers app. 66-Man-Thing app. — 3.00

REDSKIN (Thrilling Indian Stories)(Famous Western Badmen #13 on)
Youthful Magazines: Sept, 1950 - No. 12, Oct, 1952

1-Walter Johnson-a (7 pgs.) — 18 36 54 105 165 225
2 — 12 24 36 67 94 120
3-12: 3-Daniel Boone story. 6-Geronimo story — 10 20 30 56 76 95

NOTE: ***Walter Johnson** c-3, 4. **Palais** a-11. **Wildey** a-5, 11. Bondage c-6, 12.*

RED SKULL
Marvel Comics: Sept, 2011 - No. 5, Jan, 2012 ($2.99, limited series)

1-5-Pak-s/Colak-a/Aja-c; Red Skull's childhood and origin — 3.00

RED SONJA (Also see Conan #23, Kull & The Barbarians, Marvel Feature & Savage Sword Of Conan #1)
Marvel Comics Group: 1/77 - No. 15, 5/79; V1#1, 2/83 - V2#2, 3/83; V3#1, 8/83 - V3#4, 2/84; V3#5, 1/85 - V3#13, 5/86

1-Created by Robert E. Howard — 3 6 9 17 23 35
2-10: 5-Last 30¢ issue — 2 4 6 8 10 12
4,5-(35¢-c variants, limited distribution)(7,9/77) — 3 6 9 19 30 40
11-15, V1#1,V2#2: 14-Last 35¢ issue — 1 3 4 6 8 10
V3#1-13: #1-4 ($1.00, 52 pgs.) — 5.00

NOTE: ***Brunner** c-12-14. **J. Buscema** a(p)-12, 13, 15; c-V#1. **Nebres** a-V3#3i(part). **N. Redondo** a-8i, V3#2i, 3i. **Simonson** a-V3#1. **Thorne** c/a-1-11.*

RED SONJA (Continues in Queen Sonja) (Also see Classic Red Sonja)
Dynamite Entertainment: No. 0, Apr, 2005 - No. 80, 2013 (25¢/$2.99/$3.99)

0-(4/05, 25¢) Greg Land-c/Mel Rubi-a/Oeming & Carey-s — 4.00
1-(6/05, $2.99) Five covers by Ross, Linsner, Cassaday, Turner, Rivera; Rubi-a — 5.00
2-46-Multiple covers on all. 29-Sonja dies. 34-Sonja reborn — 3.00
5-RRP Edition with Red Foil logo and Isanove-a — 12.00
50-('10, $4.99) new stories and reprints; Marcos, Chin, Desjardins-a; 4 covers — 5.00
51-79-($3.99): 51-56-Geovani-a; multiple covers on each — 4.00
80-($4.99) Red Sonja vs. Dracula; bonus interview with Gail Simone — 5.00
Annual #1 (2007, $3.50) Oeming-s/Sadowski-a; Red Sonja Comics Chronology — 4.00
Annual #2 (2009, $3.99) Gage-s/Marcos-a; wraparound Prado-c & Marcos-c — 4.00
Annual #3 (2010, $5.99) Brereton-s/c/a; Batista-a — 6.00
Annual #4 (2013, $4.99) Beatty-s/Mena-a — 5.00
... Blue (2011, $4.99) Brett-s/Geovani-a; covers by Geovani & Rubi — 5.00
... Break the Skin (2011, $4.99) Winslade-c/Van Meter-s/Salazar-a — 5.00
... Cover Showcase Vol. 1 (2007, $5.99) gallery of variant covers; Cho sketches — 6.00
... Deluge (2011, $4.99) Brereton-s/c; Bolson-a/var-c; reprint from Conan #48 ('74) — 5.00
Giant Size Red Sonja #1 (2007, $4.99) Chaykin-c; new story and reprints and pin-ups — 5.00
Giant Size Red Sonja #2 (2008, $4.99) Segovia-c; new story and reprints and pin-ups — 5.00
... Goes East ($4.99) three covers; Joe Ng-a — 5.00
...: Monster Isle ($4.99) two covers; Pablo Marcos-a/Roy Thomas-s — 5.00
... One More Day ($4.99) two covers; Liam Sharp-a — 5.00
... Raven ('12, $4.99) Antonio-a/Martin-c; bonus pin-up gallery — 5.00
...: Revenge of the Gods 1-5 (2011 - No. 5, 2011, $3.99) Sampare-a/Lieberman-s — 4.00
... Vacant Shell ($4.99) two covers; Remender-s/Renaud-a — 5.00
...: Wrath of the Gods 1-5 (2010 - No. 5, 2010, $3.99) Geovani-a — 4.00
The Adventures of Red Sonja TPB (2005, $19.99) r/Marvel Feature #1-7 — 20.00
The Adventures of Red Sonja Vol. 2 TPB (2007, $19.99) r/#1-7 of '77 Marvel series — 20.00
... Vol. 1 TPB (2006, $19.99) r/#0-6; gallery of covers and variants; creators interview — 20.00

Red Sonja: Berserker © Red Sonja LLC

Red Team #1 © Spitfire

Reggie's Wise Guy Jokes #40 © AP

	GD 2.0	VG 4.0	FN 6.0	VF 8.0	VF/NM 9.0	NM- 9.2
... Vol. 2 Arrowsmith TPB (2007, $19.99) r/#7-12; gallery of covers and variants						20.00
... Vol. 3 The Rise of Gath TPB (2007, $19.99) r/#13-18; gallery of covers and variants						20.00
... Vol. 4 Animals & More TPB (2007, $24.99) r/#19-24; gallery of covers and variants						25.00

RED SONJA (Volume 2)
Dynamite Entertainment: 2013 - Present ($3.99)

	GD	VG	FN	VF	VF/NM	NM-
1-8: 1-Gail Simone-s/Walter Geovani-a; six covers. 2-8-Three covers						4.00
...: and Cub (2014, $4.99) Nancy Collins-s/Fritz Casas-a/J.M. Linsner-c						5.00
...: Berserker (2014, $4.99) Jim Zub-s/Jonathan Lau-a/Jeffrey Cruz-c						5.00

RED SONJA: ATLANTIS RISES
Dynamite Entertainment: 2012 - No. 4, 2012 ($3.99, limited series)

1-4-Lieberman-s/Dunbar-a/Parrillo-c — 4.00

RED SONJA/CLAW: THE DEVIL'S HANDS (See Claw the Unconquered)
DC Comics (WildStorm)/Dynamite Ent.: May, 2006 - No. 4, Aug, 2006 ($2.99, limited series)

1-4-Covers by Jim Lee & Dell'Otto; Andy Smith-a 1-Alex Ross var-c. 2-Dell'Otto var-c. 3-Bermejo var-c. 4-Andy Smith var-c — 3.00
TPB (2007, $12.99) r/#1-4; cover gallery — 13.00

RED SONJA: SCAVENGER HUNT
Marvel Comics: Dec, 1995 ($2.95, one-shot)

1 — 4.00

RED SONJA: THE MOVIE
Marvel Comics Group: Nov, 1985 - No. 2, Dec, 1985 (Limited series)

1,2-Movie adapt-r/Marvel Super Spec. #38 — 4.00

RED SONJA: UNCHAINED
Dynamite Entertainment: 2013 - No. 4, 2013 ($3.99, limited series)

1-4-Follows the Red Sonja: Blue one-shot; Jadsen-a — 4.00

RED SONJA VS. THULSA DOOM
Dynamite Entertainment: 2005 - No. 4, 2006 ($3.50)

1-4-Conrad-a; Conrad & Dell'Otto covers — 3.50
..., Volume 1 TPB (2006, $14.99) r/series; cover gallery — 15.00

RED STAR, THE
Image Comics/Archangel Studios: June, 2000 - No. 9, June, 2002 ($2.95)

	NM-
1-Christian Gossett-s/a(p)	4.00
2-9: 9-Beck-c	3.00
#(7.5) Reprints Wizard #1/2 story with new pages	3.00
Annual 1 (Archangel Studios, 11/02, $3.50) "Run Makita Run"	4.00
TPB (4/01, $24.95, 9x12") oversized r/#1-4; intro. by Bendis	25.00
Nokgorka TPB (8/02, $24.95, 9x12") oversized r/#6-9; w/sketch pages	25.00
Wizard 1/2 (mail order)	10.00

RED STAR, THE (Volume 2)
CrossGen #1,2/Archangel Studios #3 on: Feb, 2003 - No. 5, July, 2004 ($2.95/$2.99)

1-5-Christian Gossett-s/a(p) — 3.00
Prison of Souls TPB (8/04, $24.95, 9x12") oversized r/#1-5; w/sketch pages — 25.00

RED STAR, THE: SWORD OF LIES
Archangel Studios: Aug, 2006 ($4.50)

1-Christian Gossett-s/a(p); origin of the Red Star team — 4.50

RED TEAM
Dynamite Entertainment: 2013 - No. 7, 2014 ($3.99)

1-7: 1-Ennis-s/Cermak-a; covers by Chaykin & Sook — 4.00

RED TORNADO (See All-American #20 & Justice League of America #64)
DC Comics: July, 1985 - No. 4, Oct, 1985 (Limited series)

1-4: Kurt Busiek scripts in all. 1-3-Superman & Batman cameos — 4.00

RED TORNADO
DC Comics: Nov, 2009 - No. 6, Apr, 2010 ($2.99, limited series)

1-6: 1-3-Benes-c. 5,6-Vixen app. — 3.00
...: Family Reunion TPB (2010, $17.99) r/#1-6 — 18.00

RED WARRIOR
Marvel/Atlas Comics (TCI): Jan, 1951 - No. 6, Dec, 1951

	GD	VG	FN	VF	VF/NM	NM-
1-Red Warrior & his horse White Wing; Tuska-a	18	36	54	103	162	220
2-Tuska-c	11	22	33	62	86	110
3-6: 4-Origin White Wing. 6-Maneely-c	9	18	27	52	69	85

RED, WHITE & BLUE COMICS
DC Comics: 1941

nn - Ashcan comic, not distributed to newsstands, only for in-house use. Cover art is All-American Comics #20 with interior being Flash Comics #17 (no known sales)

RED WING
Image Comics: Jul, 2011 - No. 4, Oct, 2011 ($3.50, limited series)

1-4-Hickman-s/Pitarra-a — 3.50

RED WOLF (See Avengers #80 & Marvel Spotlight #1)
Marvel Comics Group: May, 1972 - No. 9, Sept, 1973

	GD	VG	FN	VF	VF/NM	NM-
1-(Western hero); Gil Kane/Severin-c; Shores-a	3	6	9	17	26	35
2-9: 2-Kane-c; Shores-a. 6-Tuska-r in back-up. 7-Red Wolf as super hero begins. 9-Origin sidekick, Lobo (wolf)	2	4	6	13	18	22

REESE'S PIECES
Eclipse Comics: Oct, 1985 - No.2, Oct, 1985 ($1.75, Baxter paper)

1,2-B&W-r in color — 3.00

REFORM SCHOOL GIRL!
Realistic Comics: 1951

	GD	VG	FN	VF	VF/NM	NM-
nn-Used in **SOTI**, pg. 358, & cover ill. with caption "Comic books are supposed to be like fairy tales"; classic photo-c	649	1298	1947	4738	8369	12,000

(Prices vary widely on this book)

NOTE: *The cover and title originated from a digest-sized book published by Diversey Publishing Co. of Chicago in 1948. The original book "House of Fury", Doubleday, came out in 1941. The girl's real name which appears on the cover of the digest and comic is Marty Collins, Canadian model and ice skating star who posed for this special color photograph for the Diversey novel.*

REGENTS ILLUSTRATED CLASSICS
Prentice Hall Regents, Englewood Cliffs, NJ 07632: 1981 (Plus more recent reprintings) (48 pgs., B&W-a with 14 pgs. of teaching helps)

NOTE: *This series contains Classics Ill. art, and was produced from the same illegal source as* ***Cassette Books.*** *But when Twin Circle sued to stop the sale of the Cassette Books, they decided to permit this series to continue. This series was produced as a teaching aid. The 20 title series is divided into four levels based upon number of basic words used therein. There is also a teacher's manual for each level. All of the titles are still available from the publisher for about $5 each retail. The number to call for mail order purchases is (201)767-5937. Almost all of the issues have new covers taken from some interior art panel. Here is a list of the series by Regents ident. no. and the Classics Ill. counterpart.*

16770(Cl#24-A2)18333(Cl#3-A2)21668(Cl#13-A2)32224(Cl#21)33051(Cl#26)35788(Cl#84)37153(Cl#16)44460(Cl#19-A2)44808(Cl#18-A2)52395(Cl#4-A2)58627(Cl#5-A2)60067(Cl#30)68405(Cl#23A1)70302(Cl#29)78192(Cl#7-A2)78193(Cl#10-A2)79679(Cl#85)92046(Cl#1-A2)93062(Cl#64)93512(Cl#25)

RE: GEX
Awesome-Hyperwerks: Jul, 1998 - No. 0, Dec, 1998; ($2.50)

Preview (7/98) Wizard Con Edition — 3.00
0-(12/98) Loeb-s/Liefeld-a/Pat Lee-c, 1-(9/98) Loeb-s/Liefeld-a/c — 3.00

REGGIE (Formerly Archie's Rival...; Reggie & Me #19 on)
Archie Publications: No. 15, Sept, 1963 - No. 18, Nov, 1965

	GD	VG	FN	VF	VF/NM	NM-
15(9/63), 16(10/64), 17(8/65), 18(11/65)	5	10	15	30	50	70

NOTE: *Cover title No. 15 & 16 is Archie's Rival Reggie.*

REGGIE AND ME (Formerly Reggie)
Archie Publ.: No. 19, Aug, 1966 - No. 126, Sept, 1980 (No. 50-68: 52 pgs.)

	GD	VG	FN	VF	VF/NM	NM-
19-Evilheart app.	4	8	12	23	37	50
20-23-Evilheart app.; with Pureheart #22	3	6	9	19	30	40
24-40(3/70)	3	6	9	14	20	26
41-49(7/71)	2	4	6	11	16	20
50(9/71)-68 (1/74, 52 pgs.)	3	6	9	14	19	24
69-99	2	4	6	8	10	12
100(10/77)	2	4	6	9	12	15
101-126	1	2	3	5	7	9

REGGIE'S JOKES (See Reggie's Wise Guy Jokes)

REGGIE'S REVENGE!
Archie Comic Publications, Inc.: Spring, 1994 - No. 3 ($2.00, 52 pgs.) (Published semi-annually)

1-Bound-in pull-out poster — 5.00
2,3 — 4.00

REGGIE'S WISE GUY JOKES
Archie Publications: Aug, 1968 - No. 55, 1980 (#5-28 are Giants)

	GD	VG	FN	VF	VF/NM	NM-
1	4	8	12	27	44	60
2-4	3	6	9	14	20	26
5-16 (1/71)(68 pg. Giants)	3	6	9	16	24	32
17-28 (52 pg. Giants)	2	4	6	13	18	22
29-40(1/77)	1	3	4	6	8	10
41-55	1	2	3	5	6	8

REGISTERED NURSE
Charlton Comics: Summer, 1963

	GD	VG	FN	VF	VF/NM	NM-
1-r/Nurse Betsy Crane & Cynthia Doyle	3	6	9	16	24	32

REG'LAR FELLERS

Regular Show #4 © Cartoon Network

Ren & Stimpy Show #23 © Nick

Resident Alien #1 © Hogan & Parkhouse

GD VG FN VF VF/NM NM-
2.0 4.0 6.0 8.0 9.0 9.2

Visual Editions (Standard): No. 5, Nov, 1947 - No. 6, Mar, 1948
5,6 9 18 27 47 61 75

REG'LAR FELLERS HEROIC (See Heroic Comics)

REGULAR SHOW (Based on Cartoon Network series)
Boom Entertainment (kaBOOM!): Apr, 2013 - Present ($3.99)
1-11-Multiple covers on all 4.00

REGULAR SHOW: SKIPS (Based on Cartoon Network series)
Boom Entertainment (kaBOOM!): Nov, 2013 - No. 6 ($3.99)
1-5-Mad Rupert-s/a; multiple covers on all 4.00

REID FLEMING, WORLD'S TOUGHEST MILKMAN
Eclipse Comics/ Deep Sea Comics: 1980; 8/86; V2#1, 12/86 - V2#3, 12/88; V2#4, 11/89; V2#5, 11/90 - V2#9, 4/98 (B&W)
1-(1980, self-published) David Boswell-s/a 5.00
1-2nd, 4th & 5th printings ($2.50); (3rd print, large size, 8/86, $2.50) 3.00
V2#1 (10/86, regular size, $2.00), 1-2nd print, 3rd print ($2.00, 2/89) 3.00
2-9 , V2#2-2nd & 3rd printings, V2#4-2nd printing, V2#5 ($2.00), V2#6 (Deep Sea, r/V2#5) 7-9-New stories 3.00

REIGN IN HELL
DC Comics: Sept, 2008 - No. 8, Apr, 2009 ($3.50, limited series)
1-8-Neron, Shadowpact app.; Giffen-s; Dr. Occult back-up w/Segovia-a. 1-Two covers 3.50
TPB (2009, $19.99) r/#1-8 20.00

REIGN OF THE ZODIAC
DC Comics: Oct, 2003 - No. 8, May, 2004 ($2.75)
1-8: 1-6,8-Giffen-s/Doran-a/Harris-c. 7-Byrd-a 3.00

RELATIVE HEROES
DC Comics: Mar, 2000 - No. 6, Aug, 2000 ($2.50, limited series)
1-6-Grayson-s/Guichet & Sowd-a. 6-Superman-c/app. 3.00

RELOAD
DC Comics (Homage): May, 2003 - No. 3, Sept, 2003 ($2.95, limited series)
1-3-Warren Ellis-s/Paul Gulacy & Jimmy Palmiotti-a 3.00
.../Mek TPB (2004, $14.95, flip book) r/Reload #1-3 & Mek #1-3 15.00

RELUCTANT DRAGON, THE (Walt Disney's...)
Dell Publishing Co.: No. 13, 1940
Four Color 13-Contains 2 pgs. of photos from film; 2 pg. foreword to Fantasia by Leopold Stokowski; Donald Duck, Goofy, Baby Weems & Mickey Mouse (as the Sorcerer's Apprentice) app. 219 438 657 1402 2401 3400

REMAINS
IDW Publishing: May, 2004 - No. 5, Sept, 2004 ($3.99)
1-5-Steve Niles-s/Kieron Dwyer-a 4.00

REMARKABLE WORLDS OF PROFESSOR PHINEAS B. FUDDLE, THE
DC Comics (Paradox Press): 2000 - No. 4, 2000 ($5.95, limited series)
1-4-Boaz Yakin-s/Erez Yakin-a 6.00
TPB (2001, $19.95) r/series 20.00

REMEMBER PEARL HARBOR
Street & Smith Publications: 1942 (68 pgs.) (Illustrated story of the battle)
nn-Uncle Sam-c; Jack Binder-a 57 114 171 362 619 875

REN & STIMPY SHOW, THE (TV) (Nickelodeon cartoon characters)
Marvel Comics: Dec, 1992 - No. 44, July, 1996 ($1.75/$1.95)
1-($2.25)-Polybagged w/scratch & sniff Ren or Stimpy air fowler (equal numbers of each were made) 1 3 4 6 8 10
1-2nd & 3rd printing; different dialogue on-c 4.00
2-6: 4-Muddy Mudskipper back-up. 5-Bill Wray painted-c. 6-Spider-Man vs. Powdered Toast Man 5.00
7-17: 12-1st solo back-up story w/Tank & Brenner 4.00
18-44: 18-Powered Toast Man app. 4.00
25 ($2.95) Deluxe edition w/die cut cover 5.00
...Don't Try This at Home (3/94, $12.95, TPB)-r/#9-12 13.00
...Eenteractive Special ('95, $2.95) 4.00
...Holiday Special 1994 (2/95, $2.95, 52 pgs.) 4.00
...Mini Comic (1995) 5.00
...Pick of the Litter nn (1993, $12.95, TPB)-r/#1-4 13.00
...Radio Daze (11/95, $1.95) 4.00
...Running Joke nn (1993, $12.95, TPB)-r/#1-4 plus new-a 13.00
...Seeck Little Monkeys (1/95, $12.95)-r/#17-20 13.00
...Special 2 (7/94, $2.95, 52 pgs.), ...Special 3 (10/94, $2.95, 52 pgs.)-Choose adventure, ...Special: Around the World in a Daze ($2.95), ...Special: Four Swerks (1/95, $2.95, 52 pgs.)-FF #1 cover swipe; cover reads "Four Swerks w/5 pg. coloring book.", ...Special: Powdered Toast Man 1 (4/94, $2.95, 52 pgs.), ...Special: Powdered Toast Man's Cereal Serial (4/95, $2.95), ...Special: Sports (10/95, $2.95) 4.00
...Tastes Like Chicken nn (11/93,$12.95,TPB)-r/#5-8 13.00
...Your Pals (1994, $12.95, TPB)-r/#13-16 13.00

RENFIELD
Caliber Press: 1994 - No. 3, 1995 ($2.95, B&W, limited series)
1-3 3.00

RENO BROWNE, HOLLYWOOD'S GREATEST COWGIRL (Formerly Margie Comics; Apache Kid #53 on; also see Western Hearts, Western Life Romances & Western Love)
Marvel Comics (MPC): No. 50, April, 1950 - No. 52, Sept, 1950 (52 pgs.)
50-Reno Browne photo-c on all 29 58 87 170 278 385
51,52 24 48 72 142 234 325

REPLACEMENT GOD
Amaze Ink: June, 1995 - No. 8 ($2.95, B&W)
1-8-Zander Cannon-s/a 3.00

REPLACEMENT GOD
Image Comics: May, 1997 - No. 5 ($2.95, B&W)
1-5: 1-Flip book w/"Knute's Escapes", r/original series. 2-Flip book w/"Harris Thermidor". 3-5: 3-Flip book w/"Myth and Legend" 3.00

REPTILICUS (Becomes Reptisaurus #3 on)
Charlton Comics: Aug, 1961 - No. 2, Oct, 1961
1 (Movie) 20 40 60 138 307 475
2 10 20 30 68 144 220

REPTISAURUS (Reptilicus #1,2)
Charlton Comics: V2#3, Jan, 1962 - No. 8, Dec, 1962; Summer, 1963
V2#3-8: 3-Flying saucer-c/s. 8-Montes/Bache-c/a 5 10 15 35 63 90
Special Edition 1 (Summer, 1963) 5 10 15 34 60 85

REQUIEM FOR DRACULA
Marvel Comics: Feb, 1993 ($2.00, 52 pgs.)
nn-r/Tomb of Dracula #69,70 by Gene Colan 4.00

RESCUE (Pepper Potts in Iron Man armor)
Marvel Comics: July, 2010 ($3.99, one-shot)
1-DeConnick-s/Mutti-a/Foreman-c 4.00

RESCUERS, THE (See Walt Disney Showcase #40)

RESIDENT ALIEN
Dark Horse Comics: No. 0, Apr, 2012 - No. 3, Jul, 2012 ($3.50, limited series)
0-3-Hogan-s/Parkhouse-a: 0-Reprints chapters from Dark Horse Presents #4-6 3.50

RESIDENT ALIEN: THE SUICIDE BLONDE
Dark Horse Comics: No. 0, Aug, 2013 - No. 3, Nov, 2013 ($3.99, limited series)
0-3-Hogan-s/Parkhouse-a: 0-Reprints chapters from Dark Horse Presents #18-20 4.00

RESIDENT EVIL (Based on video game)
Image Comics (WildStorm): Mar, 1998 - No. 5 ($4.95, quarterly magazine)
1 2 4 6 8 10 12
2-5 1 2 3 5 6 8
...Code: Veronica 1-4 (2002, $14.95) English reprint of Japanese comics 15.00
...Collection One ('99, $14.95, TPB) r/#1-4 15.00

RESIDENT EVIL (Volume 2)
DC Comics (WildStorm): May, 2009 - No. 6, Feb, 2011 ($3.99)
1-6: 1,2-Liam Sharpe-a. 1-Two covers 4.00
...: Volume 2 TPB (2011, $19.99) r/#1-6 20.00

RESIDENT EVIL: FIRE AND ICE
DC Comics (WildStorm): Dec, 2000 - No. 4, May, 2001 ($2.50, limited series)
1-4-Bermejo-c 4.00
TPB (2009, $24.99) r/#1-4 plus short stories from Resident Evil magazine 25.00

RESISTANCE (Based on the video game)
DC Comics (WildStorm): Early Mar, 2009 - No. 6, Jul, 2009 ($3.99, limited series)
1-6-Ramón Pérez-a/C.P. Smith-c 4.00
TPB (2010, $19.99) r/#1-6 20.00

RESISTANCE, THE
DC Comics (WildStorm): Nov, 2002 - No. 8, June, 2003 ($2.95)
1-8-Palmiotti & Gray-s/Santacruz-a 3.00

REST (Milo Ventimiglia Presents...)
Devil's Due Publ.: No. 0, Aug, 2008 - No. 2 (99¢/$3.50)

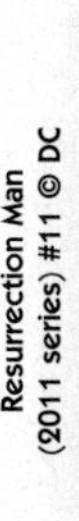

Resurrection Man (2011 series) #11 © DC

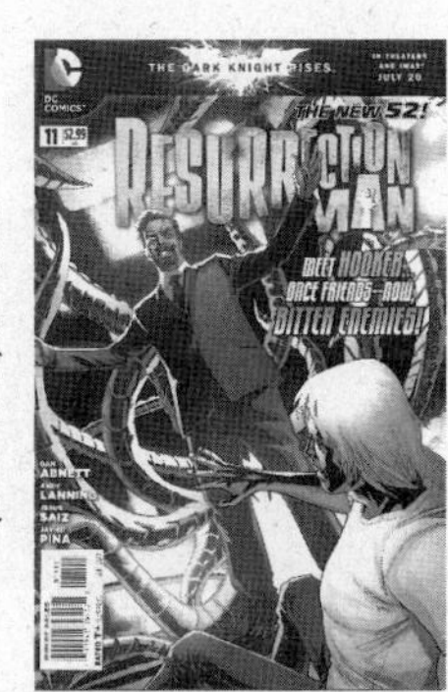

Revelations #2 © Clockstop Ent.

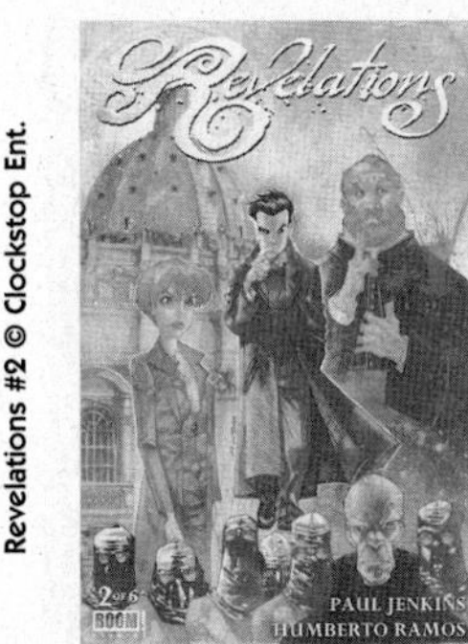

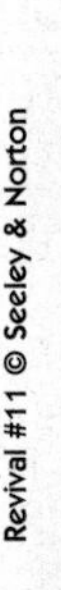

Revival #11 © Seeley & Norton

GD 2.0 | VG 4.0 | FN 6.0 | VF 8.0 | VF/NM 9.0 | NM- 9.2

GD 2.0 | VG 4.0 | FN 6.0 | VF 8.0 | VF/NM 9.0 | NM- 9.2

0-(99¢) Prelude to series; Powers-s/McManus-a 3.00

1,2-($3.50) 1-Two covers (Tim Sale art & Milo Ventimiglia photo) 3.50

RESTAURANT AT THE END OF THE UNIVERSE, THE (See Hitchhiker's Guide to the Galaxy & Life, the Universe & Everything)
DC Comics: 1994 - No. 3, 1994 ($6.95, limited series)

1-3 7.00

RESTLESS GUN (TV)
Dell Publishing Co.: No. 934, Sept, 1958 - No. 1146, Nov-Jan, 1960-61

Four Color 934 (#1)-Photo-c 9 18 27 61 123 185

Four Color 986 (5/59), 1045 (11-1/60), 1089 (3/60), 1146-Wildey-a; all photo-c 7 14 21 46 86 125

RESURRECTION MAN
DC Comics: May, 1997 - No. 27, Aug, 1999 ($2.50)

1-Lenticular disc on cover 5.00

2-5: 2-JLA app. 4.00

6-10: 6-Genesis-x-over. 7-Batman app. 10-Hitman-c/app. 3.00

11-27: 16,17-Supergirl x-over. 18-Deadman & Phantom Stranger-c/app. 21-JLA-c/app. 3.00

#1,000,000 (11/98) 853rd Century x-over 3.00

RESURRECTION MAN (DC New 52)
DC Comics: Nov, 2011 - No. 12, Oct, 2012; No. 0, Nov, 2012 ($2.99)

1-12: 1-Abnett & Lanning-s/Dagnino-a/Reis-c; Body Doubles app. 9-Suicide Squad app. 3.00

#0 (11/12) Origin of Mitch Shelley and the Body Doubles; Bachs-a/Francavilla-c 3.00

RETIEF (Keith Laumer's)
Adventure Comics (Malibu): Dec, 1989 - Vol. 2, No.6, ($2.25, B&W)

1-6,Vol. 2, #1-6,Vol. 3 (...of The CDT) #1-6 3.00

...and The Warlords #1-6, ...: Diplomatic Immunity #1 (4/91), ...: Giant Killer #1 (9/91), ...: Crime & Punishment #1 (11/91) 3.00

RETROVIRUS
Image Comics: Nov, 2012 ($12.99, hardcover GN)

HC-Gray & Palmiotti-s/Fernandez-a/Conner-c 13.00

RETURN FROM WITCH MOUNTAIN (See Walt Disney Showcase #44)

RETURNING, THE
BOOM! Studios: Mar, 2014 - No. 4 ($3.99, limited series)

1-Jason Starr-s/Andrea Mutti-a/Frazer Irving-c 4.00

RETURN OF ALISON DARE: LITTLE MISS ADVENTURES, THE (Also see Alison Dare: Little Miss Adventures)
Oni Press: Apr, 2001 - No. 3, Sept, 2001 ($2.95, B&W, limited series)

1-3-J. Torres-s/J.Bone-c/a 3.00

RETURN OF GORGO, THE (Formerly Gorgo's Revenge)
Charlton Comics: No. 2, Aug, 1963; No. 3, Fall, 1964 (12¢)

2,3-Ditko-c/a; based on M.G.M. movie 7 14 21 49 92 135

RETURN OF KONGA, THE (Konga's Revenge #2 on)
Charlton Comics: 1962

nn 7 14 21 49 92 135

RETURN OF MEGATON MAN
Kitchen Sink Press: July, 1988 - No. 3, 1988 ($2.00, limited series)

1-3: Simpson-c/a 3.00

RETURN OF THE GREMLINS (The Roald Dahl characters)
Dark Horse Comics: Mar, 2008 - No. 3, May, 2008 ($2.99, limited series)

1-3-Richardson-s/Yeagle-a. 1-Back-up reprint of intro. from 1943. 2-Back-up reprints of three Gremlin Gus 2-pagers from 1943. 3-Back-up reprints 3.00

RETURN OF THE OUTLAW
Toby Press (Minoan): Feb, 1953 - No. 11, 1955

1-Billy the Kid 10 20 30 54 72 90

2 7 14 21 35 43 50

3-11 6 12 18 31 38 45

RETURN TO JURASSIC PARK
Topps Comics: Apr, 1995 - No. 9, Feb, 1996 ($2.50/$2.95)

1-9: 3-Begin $2.95-c. 9-Artist's Jam issue 3.00

RETURN TO THE AMALGAM AGE OF COMICS: THE MARVEL COMICS COLLECTION
Marvel Comics: 1997 ($12.95, TPB)

nn-Reprints Amalgam one-shots: Challengers of the Fantastic #1, The Exciting X-Patrol #1, Iron Lantern #1, The Magnetic Men Featuring Magneto #1, Spider-Boy Team-Up #1 & Thorion of the New Asgods #1 13.00

REVEAL
Dark Horse Comics: Nov, 2002 ($6.95, squarebound)

1-Short stories of Dark Horse characters by various; Lone Wolf 2100, Buffy, Spyboy app. 7.00

REVEALING LOVE STORIES (See Fox Giants)

REVEALING ROMANCES
Ace Magazines: Sept, 1949 - No. 6, Aug, 1950

1 16 32 48 94 147 200

2 10 20 30 58 79 100

3-6 10 20 30 54 72 90

REVELATIONS
Dark Horse Comics: Aug, 2005 - No. 6, Jan, 2006 ($2.99, limited series)

1-6-Paul Jenkins-s/Humberto Ramos-a/c 3.00

1-6-(BOOM! Studios, 1/14 - No. 6, 6/14, $3.99) reprints original series 4.00

REVENGE
Image Comics: Feb, 2014 - Present ($2.99)

1,2-Jonathan Ross-s/Ian Churchill-a 3.00

REVENGE OF THE PROWLER (Also see The Prowler)
Eclipse Comics: Feb, 1988 - No. 4, June, 1988 ($1.75/$1.95)

1,3,4: 1-$1.75. 3,4-$1.95-c; Snyder III-a(p) 3.00

2 ($2.50)-Contains flexi-disc 4.00

REVIVAL
Image Comics: Jul, 2012 - Present ($2.99)

1-Tim Seeley-s/Mike Norton-a/Jenny Frison-c 10.00

1-Variant-c by Craig Thompson 15.00

1-Second-fourth printings 4.00

2-19 3.00

REVOLUTIONARY WAR
Marvel Comics: Mar, 2014 - May, 2014 ($3.99)

...: Alpha 1 (3/14) Part 1; Lanning & Cowsill-s/Elson-a; Capt. Britain & Pete Wisdom app. 4.00

...: Dark Angel 1 (3/14) Part 2; Gillen-s/Dietrich Smith-a; Mephisto app. 4.00

...: Death's Head II 1 (4/14) Part 4; Lanning & Cowsill-s/Roche-a 4.00

...: Knights of Pendragon 1 (3/14) Part 3; Williams-s/Sliney-a; Union Jack app. 4.00

...: Motormouth 1 (5/14) Part 6; Dakin-s/Cliquet-a; Killpower app. 4.00

...: Omega 1 (5/14) Part 8; conclusion; Lanning & Cowsill-s/Elson-a 4.00

...: Supersoldiers 1 (4/14) Part 5; Williams-s/Brent Anderson-a 4.00

...: Warheads 1 (5/14) Part 7; Lanning & Cowsill-s/Erskine-a 4.00

REVOLUTION ON THE PLANET OF THE APES
Mr. Comics: Dec, 2005 - No. 6, Aug, 2006 ($3.95)

1-6: 1,2-Salgood Sam-a 4.00

REX ALLEN COMICS (Movie star)(Also see Four Color #877 & Western Roundup under Dell Giants)
Dell Publ. Co.: No. 316, Feb, 1951 - No. 31, Dec-Feb, 1958-59 (All-photo-c)

Four Color 316(#1)(52 pgs.)-Rex Allen & his horse Koko begin; Marsh-a 12 24 36 80 173 265

2 (9-11/51, 36 pgs.) 8 16 24 55 105 150

3-10 6 12 18 38 69 100

11-20 5 10 15 34 60 85

21-23,25-31 5 10 15 31 53 75

24-Toth-a 5 10 15 34 60 85

NOTE: *Manning a-20, 27-30. Photo back-c F.C. #316, 2-12, 20, 21.*

REX DEXTER OF MARS (See Mystery Men Comics)
Fox Features Syndicate: Fall, 1940 (68 pgs.)

1-Rex Dexter, Patty O'Day, & Zanzibar (Tuska-a) app.; Briefer-c/a 219 438 657 1402 2401 3400

REX HART (Formerly Blaze Carson; Whip Wilson #9 on)
Timely/Marvel Comics (USA): No. 6, Aug, 1949 - No. 8, Feb, 1950 (All photo-c)

6-Rex Hart & his horse Warrior begin; Black Rider app; Captain Tootsie by Beck; Heath-a 26 52 78 154 252 350

7,8: 18 pg. Thriller in each. 7-Heath-a. 8-Blaze the Wonder Collie app. in text 18 36 54 105 165 225

REX MORGAN, M.D. (Also see Harvey Comics Library)
Argo Publ.: Dec, 1955 - No. 3, Apr?, 1956

1-r/Rex Morgan daily newspaper strips & daily panel-r of "These Women" by D'Alessio & "Timeout" by Jeff Keate 14 28 42 76 108 140

2,3 10 20 30 54 72 90

REX MUNDI (Latin for "King of the World")

Ribtickler #2 © FOX

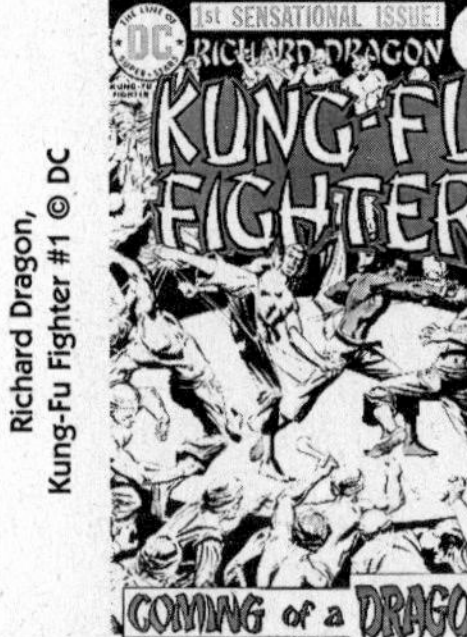

Richard Dragon, Kung-Fu Fighter #1 © DC

Richie Rich #4 © HARV

	GD 2.0	VG 4.0	FN 6.0	VF 8.0	VF/NM 9.0	NM- 9.2

Image Comics: No. 0, Aug, 2002 - No. 18, Apr, 2006 ($2.95/$2.99)

0-18-Arvid Nelson-s. 0-13-Eric Johnson-a. 14,15-Jim DiBartolo-a. 18-Ramos-c 3.00
Vol. 1: The Guardian of the Temple TPB (1/04, $14.95) r/#0-5 15.00
Book 1: The Guardian of the Temple TPB (Dark Horse, 11/06, $16.95) r/#0-5 & Brother Matthew web comic; Dysart intro. 17.00
Vol. 2: The River Underground TPB (4/05, $14.95) r/#6-11 15.00
Book 2: The River Underground (Dark Horse, 2006, $16.95) r/#6-11 17.00
Vol. 3: The Lost Kings TPB (Dark Horse, 9/06, $16.95) r/#12-17 17.00
Book Four: Crowd and Sword TPB (Dark Horse, 12/07, $16.95) r/#18 plus V2 #1-5 and story from Dark Horse Book of Monsters 17.00

REX MUNDI (Volume 2)
Dark Horse Comics: July, 2006 - No. 19, Aug, 2009 ($2.99)

1-19-Arvid Nelson-s. 1-JH Williams-c. 16-Chen-c. 18-Linsner-c 3.00
Book Five: The Valley at the End of the World TPB (11/08, $17.95) r/#6-12 18.00

REX THE WONDER DOG (See The Adventures of...)

RHUBARB, THE MILLIONAIRE CAT
Dell Publishing Co.: No. 423, Sept-Oct, 1952 - No. 563, June, 1954

	GD	VG	FN	VF	VF/NM	NM-
Four Color 423 (#1)	5	10	15	35	63	90
Four Color 466(5/53),563	5	10	15	33	57	80

RIB
Dilemma Productions: Oct, 1995 - April, 1996 ($1.95, B&W)

Ashcan, 1 3.00

RIB
Bookmark Productions: 1996 ($2.95, B&W)

1-Sakai-c; Andrew Ford-s/a 3.00

RIB
Caliber Comics: May, 1997 - No. 5, 1998 ($2.95, B&W)

1-5: 1-"Beginnings" pts. 1 & 2 3.00

RIBIT! (Red Sonja imitation)
Comico: Jan, 1989 - No. 4, April?, 1989 ($1.95, limited series)

1-4: Frank Thorne-c/a/scripts 3.00

RIBTICKLER (Also see Fox Giants)
Fox Feature Synd./Green Publ. (1957)/Norlen (1959): 1945, No. 2, 1946, No. 3, Jul-Aug, 1946 - No. 9, Jul-Aug, 1947; 1957; 1959

	GD	VG	FN	VF	VF/NM	NM-
1-Funny animal	17	34	51	98	154	210
2-(1946)	10	20	30	58	79	100
3-9: 3,5,7-Cosmo Cat app.	9	18	27	52	69	85
3,7,8 (Green Publ.-1957), 3,7,8 (Norlen Mag.-1959)	3	6	9	16	23	30

RICHARD DRAGON
DC Comics: July, 2004 - No. 12, Jun, 2005 ($2.50)

1-12: 1-Dixon-s/McDaniel-a/c; Ben Turner app. 2,3-Nightwing app. 4-6,11,12-Lady Shiva 3.00

RICHARD DRAGON, KUNG-FU FIGHTER (See The Batman Chronicles #5, Brave & the Bold, & The Question)
National Periodical Publ./DC Comics: Apr-May, 1975 - No. 18, Nov-Dec, 1977

	GD	VG	FN	VF	VF/NM	NM-
1-Intro Richard Dragon, Ben Stanley & O-Sensei; 1st app. Barney Ling; adaptation of Jim Dennis novel "Dragon's Fists" begins, ends #4	3	6	9	14	20	26
2,3: 2-Intro Carolyn Woosan; Starlin/Weiss-c/a; bondage-c. 3-Kirby-a(p); Giordano bondage-c	2	4	6	9	12	15
4-8-Wood inks. 4-Carolyn Woosan dies. 5-1st app. Lady Shiva	2	4	6	8	10	12
9-13,15-18: 9-Ben Stanley becomes Ben Turner; intro Preying Mantis. 16-1st app. Prof Ojo. 18-1st app. Ben Turner as The Bronze Tiger	1	3	4	6	8	10
14-"Spirit of Bruce Lee"	3	6	9	14	20	26

NOTE: ***Buckler** a-14. c-15, 18. **Chua** c-13. **Estrada** a-9, 13-18. **Estrada/Abel** a-10-12. **Estrada/Wood** a-4-8. **Giordano** c-1, 3-11. **Weiss** a-2(partial) c-2i.*

RICHARD THE LION-HEARTED (See Ideal a Classical Comic)

RICHIE RICH (See Harvey Collectors Comics, Harvey Hits, Little Dot, Little Lotta, Little Sad Sack, Million Dollar Digest, Mutt & Jeff, Super Richie & 3-D Dolly; also Tastee-Freez Comics in the Promotional Comics section)

RICHIE RICH (...the Poor Little Rich Boy) (See Harvey Hits #3, 9)
Harvey Publ.: Nov, 1960 - #218, Oct, 1982; #219, Oct, 1986 - #254, Jan, 1991

	GD	VG	FN	VF	VF/NM	NM-
1-(See Little Dot #1 for 1st app.)	266	532	798	2195	4948	7700
2	75	150	225	600	1350	2100
3-5	45	90	135	333	754	1175
6-10: 8-Christmas-c	27	54	81	189	420	650
11-20	16	32	48	112	249	385
21-30	11	22	33	76	163	250
31-40	9	18	27	61	123	185
41-50: 42(2/66)-X-mas-c	7	14	21	49	92	135
51-55,57-60: 59-Buck, prototype of Dollar the Dog	5	10	15	35	63	90
56-1st app. Super Richie	6	12	18	41	76	110
61-64,66-80: 71-Nixon & Robert Kennedy caricatures; outer space-c	4	8	12	28	47	65
65-Buck the Dog (Dollar prototype) on cover	6	12	18	37	66	95
81-99	3	6	9	21	33	45
100(12/70)-1st app. Irona the robot maid	4	8	12	25	40	55
101-111,117-120	3	6	9	14	20	26
112-116: All 52 pg. Giants	3	6	9	16	24	32
121-140: 137-1st app. Mr. Cheepers and Professor Keenbean	2	4	6	9	13	16
141-160: 145-Infinity-c. 155-3rd app. The Money Monster	2	4	6	8	10	12
161-180	1	3	4	6	8	10
181-199	1	2	3	5	6	8
200	1	3	4	6	8	10
201-218: 210-Stone-Age Riches app	1	2	3	4	5	7

219-254: 237-Last original material 6.00
Harvey Comics Classics Vol. 2 TPB (Dark Horse Books, 10/07, $19.95) Reprints Richie Rich's early appearances in this title, Little Dot and Richie Rich Success Stories, mostly B&W with some color stories; history and interview with Ernie Colón 20.00

RICHIE RICH
Harvey Comics: Mar, 1991 - No. 28, Nov, 1994 ($1.00, bi-monthly)

1-28: Reprints best of Richie Rich 3.00
Giant Size 1-4 (10/91-10/93, $2.25, 68 pgs.) 4.00

RICHIE RICH ADVENTURE DIGEST MAGAZINE
Harvey Comics: 1992 - No. 7, Sept, 1994 ($1.25, quarterly, digest-size)

1-7 4.00

RICHIE RICH AND...
Harvey Comics: Oct, 1987 - No. 11, May, 1990 ($1.00)

1-Professor Keenbean 4.00
2-11: 2-Casper. 3-Dollar the Dog. 4-Cadbury. 5 Mayda Munny. 6-Irona. 7-Little Dot. 8-Professor Keenbean. 9-Little Audrey. 10-Mayda Munny. 11-Cadbury 3.00

RICHIE RICH AND BILLY BELLHOPS
Harvey Publications: Oct, 1977 (52 pgs., one-shot)

	GD	VG	FN	VF	VF/NM	NM-
1	2	4	6	11	16	20

RICHIE RICH AND CADBURY
Harvey Publ.: 10/77; #2, 9/78 - #23, 7/82; #24, 7/90 - #29, 1/91 (1-10: 52pgs.)

	GD	VG	FN	VF	VF/NM	NM-
1-(52 pg. Giant)	2	4	6	11	16	20
2-10-(52 pg. Giant)	2	4	6	8	10	12

11-23 6.00
24-29: 24-Begin $1.00-c 4.00

RICHIE RICH AND CASPER
Harvey Publications: Aug, 1974 - No. 45, Sept, 1982

	GD	VG	FN	VF	VF/NM	NM-
1	3	6	9	19	30	40
2-5	2	4	6	13	18	22
6-10: 10-Xmas-c	2	4	6	9	13	16
11-20	1	3	4	6	8	10

21-45: 22-Xmas-c 6.00

RICHIE RICH AND DOLLAR THE DOG (See Richie Rich #65)
Harvey Publications: Sept, 1977 - No. 24, Aug, 1982 (#1-10: 52 pgs.)

	GD	VG	FN	VF	VF/NM	NM-
1-(52 pg. Giant)	2	4	6	11	16	20
2-10-(52 pg. Giant)	2	4	6	8	10	12

11-24 6.00

RICHIE RICH AND DOT
Harvey Publications: Oct, 1974 (one-shot)

	GD	VG	FN	VF	VF/NM	NM-
1	3	6	9	15	22	28

RICHIE RICH AND GLORIA
Harvey Publications: Sept, 1977 - No. 25, Sept, 1982 (#1-11: 52 pgs.)

	GD	VG	FN	VF	VF/NM	NM-
1-(52 pg. Giant)	2	4	6	11	16	20
2-11-(52 pg. Giant)	2	4	6	8	10	12

12-25 6.00

RICHIE RICH AND HIS GIRLFRIENDS
Harvey Publications: April, 1979 - No. 16, Dec, 1982

	GD	VG	FN	VF	VF/NM	NM-
1-(52 pg. Giant)	2	4	6	9	13	16
2-(52 pg. Giant)	1	3	4	6	8	10
3-10	1	2	3	5	6	8

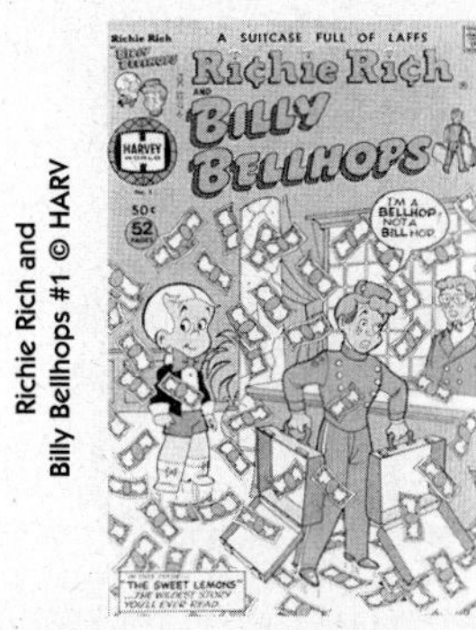

Richie Rich and Billy Bellhops #1 © HARV

Richie Rich Diamonds #19 © HARV

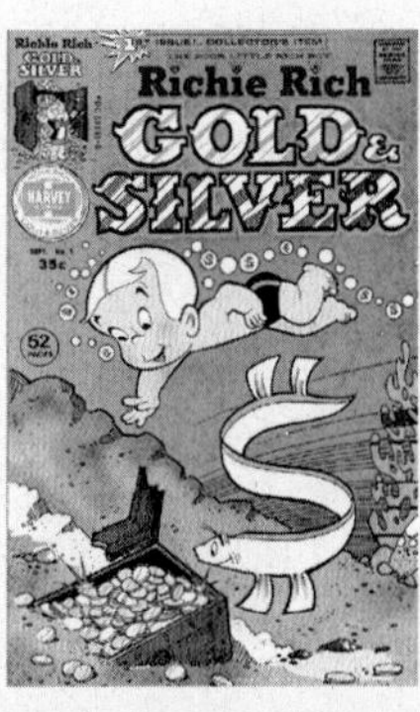

Richie Rich Gold and Silver #1 © HARV

	GD 2.0	VG 4.0	FN 6.0	VF 8.0	VF/NM 9.0	NM- 9.2
11-16						6.00

RICHIE RICH AND HIS MEAN COUSIN REGGIE
Harvey Publications: April, 1979 - No. 3, 1980 (50¢) (#1,2: 52 pgs.)

	GD 2.0	VG 4.0	FN 6.0	VF 8.0	VF/NM 9.0	NM- 9.2
1	2	4	6	9	13	16
2-3:	1	3	4	6	8	10

NOTE: *No. 4 was advertised, but never released.*

RICHIE RICH AND JACKIE JOKERS (Also see Jackie Jokers)
Harvey Publications: Nov, 1973 - No. 48, Dec, 1982

	GD 2.0	VG 4.0	FN 6.0	VF 8.0	VF/NM 9.0	NM- 9.2
1: 52 pg. Giant; contains material from unpublished Jackie Jokers #5	4	8	12	23	37	50
2,3-(52 pg. Giants). 2-R.R. & Jackie 1st meet	3	6	9	15	22	28
4,5	2	4	6	13	18	22
6-10	2	4	6	9	13	16
11-20,26: 11-1st app. Kool Katz. 26-Star Wars parody	1	3	4	6	8	10
21-25,27-40	1	2	3	4	5	7
41-48						6.00

RICHIE RICH AND PROFESSOR KEENBEAN
Harvey Comics: Sept, 1990 - No. 2, Nov, 1990 ($1.00)

	GD 2.0	VG 4.0	FN 6.0	VF 8.0	VF/NM 9.0	NM- 9.2
1,2						3.00

RICHIE RICH AND THE NEW KIDS ON THE BLOCK
Harvey Publications: Feb, 1991 - No. 3, June, 1991 ($1.25, bi-monthly)

	GD 2.0	VG 4.0	FN 6.0	VF 8.0	VF/NM 9.0	NM- 9.2
1-3: 1,2-New Richie Rich stories						4.00

RICHIE RICH AND TIMMY TIME
Harvey Publications: Sept, 1977 (50¢, 52 pgs, one-shot)

	GD 2.0	VG 4.0	FN 6.0	VF 8.0	VF/NM 9.0	NM- 9.2
1	2	4	6	11	16	20

RICHIE RICH BANK BOOK
Harvey Publications: Oct, 1972 - No. 59, Sept, 1982

	GD 2.0	VG 4.0	FN 6.0	VF 8.0	VF/NM 9.0	NM- 9.2
1	4	8	12	28	47	65
2-5: 2-2nd app. The Money Monster	3	6	9	16	23	30
6-10	2	4	6	11	16	20
11-20: 18-Super Richie app.	2	4	6	8	10	12
21-30	1	2	3	5	7	9
31-40	1	2	3	4	5	7
41-59						6.00

RICHIE RICH BEST OF THE YEARS
Harvey Publications: Oct, 1977 - No. 6, June, 1980 (128 pgs., digest-size)

	GD 2.0	VG 4.0	FN 6.0	VF 8.0	VF/NM 9.0	NM- 9.2
1(10/77)-Reprints	2	4	6	9	12	15
2-6(11/79-6/80, 95¢). #2(10/78)-Rep.. #3(6/79, 75¢)	1	2	3	5	7	9

RICHIE RICH BIG BOOK
Harvey Publications: Nov, 1992 - No. 2, May, 1993 ($1.50, 52 pgs.)

	GD 2.0	VG 4.0	FN 6.0	VF 8.0	VF/NM 9.0	NM- 9.2
1,2						4.00

RICHIE RICH BIG BUCKS
Harvey Publications: Apr, 1991 - No. 8, July, 1992 ($1.00, bi-monthly)

	GD 2.0	VG 4.0	FN 6.0	VF 8.0	VF/NM 9.0	NM- 9.2
1-8						3.00

RICHIE RICH BILLIONS
Harvey Publications: Oct, 1974 - No. 48, Oct, 1982 (#1-33: 52 pgs.)

	GD 2.0	VG 4.0	FN 6.0	VF 8.0	VF/NM 9.0	NM- 9.2
1	3	6	9	21	33	45
2-5: 2-Christmas issue	3	6	9	14	20	25
6-10	2	4	6	10	14	18
11-20	2	4	6	8	10	12
21-33	1	2	3	5	6	8
34-48: 35-Onion app.						6.00

RICHIE RICH CASH
Harvey Publications: Sept, 1974 - No. 47, Aug, 1982

	GD 2.0	VG 4.0	FN 6.0	VF 8.0	VF/NM 9.0	NM- 9.2
1-1st app. Dr. N-R-Gee	3	6	9	19	30	40
2-5	2	4	6	13	18	22
6-10	2	4	6	9	13	16
11-20	1	3	4	6	8	10
21-30	1	2	3	4	5	7
31-47: 33-Dr. Blemish app.						6.00

RICHIE RICH CASH MONEY
Harvey Comics: May, 1992 - No. 2, Aug, 1992 ($1.25)

	GD 2.0	VG 4.0	FN 6.0	VF 8.0	VF/NM 9.0	NM- 9.2
1,2						3.00

RICHIE RICH, CASPER AND WENDY - NATIONAL LEAGUE
Harvey Comics: June, 1976 (50¢)

	GD 2.0	VG 4.0	FN 6.0	VF 8.0	VF/NM 9.0	NM- 9.2
1-Newsstand version of the baseball giveaway	2	4	6	13	18	22

RICHIE RICH COLLECTORS COMICS (See Harvey Collectors Comics)

RICHIE RICH DIAMONDS
Harvey Publications: Aug, 1972 - No. 59, Aug, 1982 (#1, 23-45: 52 pgs.)

	GD 2.0	VG 4.0	FN 6.0	VF 8.0	VF/NM 9.0	NM- 9.2
1-(52 pg. Giant)	5	10	15	30	50	70
2-5	3	6	9	16	23	30
6-10	2	4	6	11	16	20
11-22	2	4	6	8	10	12
23-30-(52 pg. Giants)	2	4	6	8	11	14
31-45: 39-r/Origin Little Dot	1	2	3	5	7	9
46-50	1	2	3	4	5	7
51-59						6.00

RICHIE RICH DIGEST MAGAZINE
Harvey Publications: Oct, 1986 - No. 42, Oct, 1994 ($1.25/$1.75, digest-size)

	GD 2.0	VG 4.0	FN 6.0	VF 8.0	VF/NM 9.0	NM- 9.2
1	1	2	3	5	6	8
2-10						5.00
11-20						4.00
21-42						4.00

RICHIE RICH DIGEST STORIES (...Magazine #?-on)
Harvey Publications: Oct, 1977 - No., 17, Oct, 1982 (75¢/95¢, digest-size)

	GD 2.0	VG 4.0	FN 6.0	VF 8.0	VF/NM 9.0	NM- 9.2
1-Reprints	2	4	6	9	12	15
2-10: Reprints	1	2	3	5	7	9
11-17: Reprints						6.00

RICHIE RICH DIGEST WINNERS
Harvey Publications: Dec, 1977 - No. 16, Sept, 1982 (75¢/95¢, 132 pgs., digest-size)

	GD 2.0	VG 4.0	FN 6.0	VF 8.0	VF/NM 9.0	NM- 9.2
1	2	4	6	9	12	15
2-5	1	2	3	5	7	9
6-16						6.00

RICHIE RICH DOLLARS & CENTS
Harvey Publications: Aug, 1963 - No. 109, Aug, 1982 (#1-43: 68 pgs.; 44-60, 71-94: 52 pgs.)

	GD 2.0	VG 4.0	FN 6.0	VF 8.0	VF/NM 9.0	NM- 9.2
1: (#1-64 are all reprint issues)	16	32	48	112	249	385
2	9	18	27	60	120	180
3-5: 5-r/1st app. of R.R. from Little Dot #1	8	16	24	54	102	150
6-10	6	12	18	40	73	105
11-20	4	8	12	28	47	65
21-30: 25-r/1st app. Nurse Jenny (Little Lotta #62)	3	6	9	21	33	45
31-43: 43-Last 68 pg. issue	3	6	9	17	26	35
44-60: All 52 pgs.	3	6	9	14	19	25
61-71	1	3	4	6	8	10
72-94: All 52 pgs.	2	4	6	8	10	12
95-99,101-109						6.00
100-Anniversary issue	1	2	3	5	7	9

RICHIE RICH FORTUNES
Harvey Publications: Sept, 1971 - No. 63, July, 1982 (#1-15: 52 pgs.)

	GD 2.0	VG 4.0	FN 6.0	VF 8.0	VF/NM 9.0	NM- 9.2
1	5	10	15	34	60	85
2-5	3	6	9	19	30	40
6-10	2	4	6	13	18	22
11-15: 11-r/1st app. The Onion	2	4	6	9	12	15
16-30	1	2	3	5	7	9
31-40	1	2	3	4	5	7
41-63: 62-Onion app.						6.00

RICHIE RICH GEMS
Harvey Publications: Sept, 1974 - No. 43, Sept, 1982

	GD 2.0	VG 4.0	FN 6.0	VF 8.0	VF/NM 9.0	NM- 9.2
1	3	6	9	19	30	40
2-5	2	4	6	13	18	22
6-10	2	4	6	9	13	16
11-20	1	3	4	6	8	10
21-30	1	2	3	4	5	7
31-43: 36-Dr. Blemish, Onion app. 38-1st app. Stone-Age Riches						6.00
44-48 (Ape Entertainment, 2011-2012, $3.99) new stories w/Colon-a & reprints						4.00
... Special Collection (Ape Entertainment, 2012, $6.99) r/Valentine & Winter Specials						7.00
... Valentines Special (Ape Entertainment, 2012, $3.99) new story w/Colon-a & reprints						4.00
... Winter Special (Ape Entertainment, 2011, $3.99) new story w/Colon-a & reprints						4.00

RICHIE RICH GOLD AND SILVER
Harvey Publications: Sept, 1975 - No. 42, Oct, 1982 (#1-27: 52 pgs.)

	GD 2.0	VG 4.0	FN 6.0	VF 8.0	VF/NM 9.0	NM- 9.2
1	3	6	9	17	26	35
2-5	2	4	6	11	16	20
6-10	2	4	6	8	11	14
11-27	1	2	3	5	7	9
28-42: 34-Stone-Age Riches app.						6.00

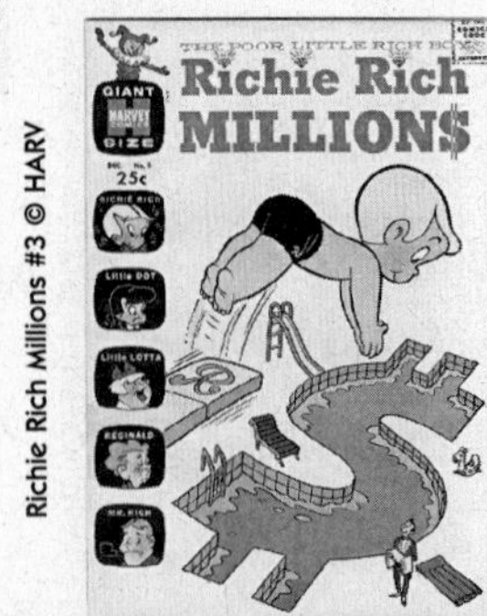

Richie Rich Millions #3 © HARV

Richie Rich Profits #1 © HARV

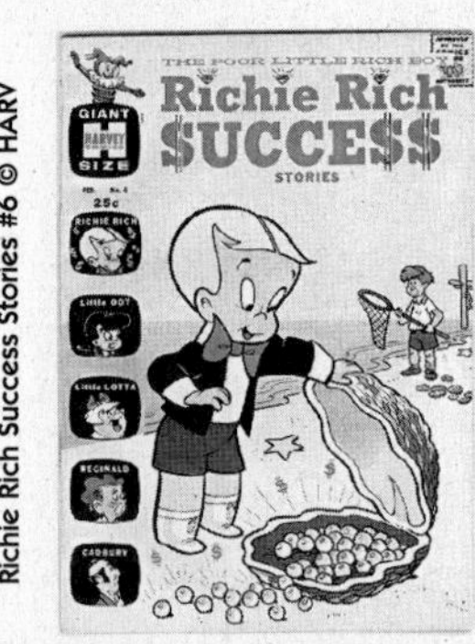

Richie Rich Success Stories #6 © HARV

	GD 2.0	VG 4.0	FN 6.0	VF 8.0	VF/NM 9.0	NM- 9.2

RICHIE RICH GOLD NUGGETS DIGEST
Harvey Publications: Dec., 1990 - No. 4, June, 1991 ($1.75, digest-size)

	GD	VG	FN	VF	VF/NM	NM-
1-4						4.00

RICHIE RICH HOLIDAY DIGEST MAGAZINE (...Digest #4)
Harvey Publications: Jan, 1980 - #3, Jan, 1982; #4, 3/88; #5, 2/89 (annual)

	GD	VG	FN	VF	VF/NM	NM-
1-X-Mas-c	1	3	4	6	8	10
2-5: 2,3: All X-Mas-c. 4-(3/88, $1.25), 5-(2/89, $1.75)	1	2	3	4	5	7

RICHIE RICH INVENTIONS
Harvey Publications: Oct, 1977 - No. 26, Oct, 1982 (#1-11: 52 pgs.)

	GD	VG	FN	VF	VF/NM	NM-
1	2	4	6	11	16	20
2-5	2	4	6	8	10	12
6-11	1	2	3	5	6	8
12-26						6.00

RICHIE RICH JACKPOTS
Harvey Publications: Oct, 1972 - No. 58, Aug, 1982 (#41-43: 52 pgs.)

	GD	VG	FN	VF	VF/NM	NM-
1-Debut of Cousin Jackpots	4	8	12	28	47	65
2-5	3	6	9	16	23	30
6-10	2	4	6	11	16	20
11-15,17-20	2	4	6	8	10	12
16-Super Richie app.	2	4	6	9	12	15
21-30	1	2	3	5	7	9
31-40,44-50: 37-Caricatures of Frank Sinatra, Dean Martin, Sammy Davis, Jr. 45-Dr. Blemish app.	1	2	3	4	5	7
41-43 (52 pgs.)	1	3	4	6	8	10
51-58						6.00

RICHIE RICH MILLION DOLLAR DIGEST (...Magazine #?-on)(See Million Dollar Digest)
Harvey Publications: Oct, 1980 - No. 10, Oct, 1982 ($1.50)

	GD	VG	FN	VF	VF/NM	NM-
1	1	3	4	6	8	10
2-10						7.00

RICHIE RICH MILLIONS
Harvey Publ.: 9/61; #2, 9/62 - #113, 10/82 (#1-48: 68 pgs.; 49-64, 85-97: 52 pgs.)

	GD	VG	FN	VF	VF/NM	NM-
1: (#1-3 are all reprint issues)	20	40	60	138	307	475
2	10	20	30	64	132	200
3-5: All other giants are new & reprints. 5-1st 15 pg. Richie Rich story	8	16	24	56	108	160
6-10	7	14	21	49	92	135
11-20	5	10	15	35	63	90
21-30	4	8	12	27	44	60
31-48: 31-1st app. The Onion. 48-Last 68 pg. Giant	3	6	9	19	30	40
49-64: 52 pg. Giants	3	6	9	14	20	25
65-67,69-73,75-84	2	4	6	8	10	12
68-1st Super Richie-c (11/74)	2	4	6	13	18	22
74-1st app. Mr. Woody; Super Richie app.	2	4	6	8	11	14
85-97: 52 pg. Giants	2	4	6	8	11	14
98,99	1	2	3	4	5	7
100	1	2	3	5	7	9
101-113						6.00

RICHIE RICH MONEY WORLD
Harvey Publications: Sept, 1972 - No. 59, Sept, 1982

	GD	VG	FN	VF	VF/NM	NM-
1-(52 pg. Giant)-1st app. Mayda Munny	5	10	15	33	57	80
2-Super Richie app.	3	6	9	17	26	35
3-5	3	6	9	16	23	30
6-10: 9,10-Richie Rich mistakenly named Little Lotta on covers	2	4	6	11	16	20
11-20: 16,20-Dr. N-R-Gee	2	4	6	8	10	12
21-30	1	2	3	5	7	9
31-50	1	2	3	4	5	7
51-59						6.00
Digest 1 (2/91, $1.75)						5.00
2-8 (12/93, $1.75)						3.00

RICHIE RICH PROFITS
Harvey Publications: Oct, 1974 - No. 47, Sept, 1982

	GD	VG	FN	VF	VF/NM	NM-
1	3	6	9	19	30	40
2-5	2	4	6	13	18	22
6-10: 10-Origin of Dr. N-R-Gee	2	4	6	9	13	16
11-20: 15-Christmas-c	1	3	4	6	8	10
21-30	1	2	3	4	5	7
31-47						6.00

RICHIE RICH RELICS
Harvey Comics: Jan, 1988 - No.4, Feb, 1989 (75¢/$1.00, reprints)

	GD	VG	FN	VF	VF/NM	NM-
1-4						3.00

RICHIE RICH RICHES
Harvey Publications: July, 1972 - No. 59, Aug, 1982 (#1, 2, 41-45: 52 pgs.)

	GD	VG	FN	VF	VF/NM	NM-
1-(52 pg. Giant)-1st app. The Money Monster	5	10	15	33	57	80
2-(52 pg. Giant)	3	6	9	19	30	40
3-5	3	6	9	16	23	30
6-10: 7-1st app. Aunt Novo	2	4	6	11	16	20
11-20: 17-Super Richie app. (3/75)	2	4	6	8	10	12
21-40	1	2	3	5	6	8
41-45: 52 pg. Giants	1	3	4	6	8	10
46-59: 56-Dr. Blemish app.						6.00

RICHIE RICH: RICH RESCUE
Ape Entertainment: 2011 - No. 4, 2011 ($3.95, limited series)

	GD	VG	FN	VF	VF/NM	NM-
1-6-New short stories by various incl. Ernie Colon; Jack Lawrence-c						4.00
FCBD Edition (2011, giveaway) Flip book with Kung Fu Panda						3.00

RICHIE RICH SUCCESS STORIES
Harvey Publications: Nov, 1964 - No. 105, Sept, 1982 (#1-38: 68 pgs., 39-55, 67-90: 52 pgs.)

	GD	VG	FN	VF	VF/NM	NM-
1	16	32	48	110	243	375
2	9	18	27	57	111	165
3-5	8	16	24	51	96	140
6-10	5	10	15	35	63	90
11-20	5	10	15	31	53	75
21-30: 27-1st Penny Van Dough (8/69)	4	8	12	23	37	50
31-38: 38-Last 68 pg. Giant	3	6	9	19	30	40
39-55-(52 pgs.): 44-Super Richie app.	3	6	9	14	20	25
56-66	2	4	6	8	10	12
67-90: 52 pgs.	2	4	6	8	11	14
91-99,101-105: 91-Onion app. 101-Dr. Blemish app.						6.00
100	1	2	3	5	7	9

RICHIE RICH SUMMER BONANZA
Harvey Comics: Oct, 1991 ($1.95, one-shot, 68 pgs.)

	GD	VG	FN	VF	VF/NM	NM-
1-Richie Rich, Little Dot, Little Lotta						4.00

RICHIE RICH TREASURE CHEST DIGEST (...Magazine #3)
Harvey Publications: Apr, 1982 - No. 3, Aug, 1982 (95¢, Digest Mag.)
(#4 advertised but not publ.)

	GD	VG	FN	VF	VF/NM	NM-
1	1	3	4	6	8	10
2,3	1	2	3	4	5	7

RICHIE RICH VACATION DIGEST
Harvey Comics: Oct, 1991; Oct, 1992; Oct, 1993 ($1.75, digest-size)

	GD	VG	FN	VF	VF/NM	NM-
1-(10/91), 1-(10/92), 1-(10/93)						4.00

RICHIE RICH VACATIONS DIGEST
Harvey Publ.: 11/77; No. 2, 10/78 - No. 7, 10/81; No. 8, 8/82; No. 9, 10/82 (Digest, 132 pgs.)

	GD	VG	FN	VF	VF/NM	NM-
1-Reprints	2	4	6	9	12	15
2-6	1	2	3	5	7	9
7-9						6.00

RICHIE RICH VAULT OF MYSTERY
Harvey Publications: Nov, 1974 - No. 47, Sept, 1982

	GD	VG	FN	VF	VF/NM	NM-
1	3	6	9	19	30	40
2-5: 5-The Condor app.	2	4	6	13	18	22
6-10	2	4	6	9	13	16
11-20	1	3	4	6	8	10
21-30	1	2	3	4	5	7
31-47						6.00

RICHIE RICH ZILLIONZ
Harvey Publ.: Oct, 1976 - No. 33, Sept, 1982 (#1-4: 68 pgs.; #5-18: 52 pgs.)

	GD	VG	FN	VF	VF/NM	NM-
1	3	6	9	17	26	35
2-4: 4-Last 68 pg. Giant	2	4	6	11	16	20
5-10	2	4	6	8	10	12
11-18: 18-Last 52 pg. Giant	1	2	3	5	6	8
19-33						6.00

RICH JOHNSTON'S... (Parody of the Avengers movie characters)
BOOM! Studios: Apr, 2012 ($3.99, series of one-shots)

	GD	VG	FN	VF	VF/NM	NM-
... Captain American Idol 1 - Rich Johnston-s/Chris Haley-a						4.00
... Iron Muslim 1 - Rich Johnston-s/Bryan Turner-a; Demon in a Bottle cover swipe						4.00
... Scienthorlogy 1 - Rich Johnston-s/Michael Netzer-a						4.00
... The Avengefuls 1 - Rich Johnston-s/Joshua Covey; two printings						4.00

The Ride #1 © Ballistic Comics

Ringo Kid #1 © MAR

Riot #4 © MAR

RICKY
Standard Comics (Visual Editions): No. 5, Sept, 1953

	GD 2.0	VG 4.0	FN 6.0	VF 8.0	VF/NM 9.0	NM- 9.2
5-Teenage humor	7	14	21	35	43	50

RICKY NELSON (TV)(See Sweethearts V2#42)
Dell Publishing Co.: No. 956, Dec, 1958 - No. 1192, June, 1961 (All photo-c)

	GD 2.0	VG 4.0	FN 6.0	VF 8.0	VF/NM 9.0	NM- 9.2
Four Color 956,998	15	30	45	100	220	340
Four Color 1115,1192: 1192-Manning-a	12	24	36	80	173	265

RIDE, THE (Also see Gun Candy flip-book)
Image Comics: June, 2004 - No. 2, July, 2004 ($2.95, B&W, anthology)

	GD 2.0	VG 4.0	FN 6.0	VF 8.0	VF/NM 9.0	NM- 9.2
1,2: Hughes-c/Wagner-s. 1-Hamner & Stelfreeze-a. 2-Jeanty & Pearson-a						3.00
... Die Valkyrie 1-3 (6/07 - No. 3, 2/08, $2.99) Stelfreeze-a/Wagner-s/Pearson-c						3.00
... Foreign Parts 1 (1/05, $2.95) Dixon-s/Haynes-a; Marz-s/Brunner-a; Pearson-c						3.00
... Halloween Special: The Key to Survival (10/07, $3.50) Tomm Coker-s/a						3.50
... Savannah 1 (4/07, $4.99) s/a by students of Savannah College of Art						5.00
... 2 For the Road 1 (10/04, $2.95) Dixon-s/Hamner & Gregory-a/Johnson-c						3.00
Vol. 1 TPB (2005, $9.99) r/#1,2, Foreign Parts, 2 For the Road; Chaykin intro.						10.00
Vol. 2 TPB (2005, $15.99) r/Gun Candy #1,2 & Die Valkyrie #1-3; sketch pages						16.00

RIDER, THE (Frontier Trail #6; also see Blazing Sixguns I.W. Reprint #10, 11)
Ajax/Farrell Publ. (Four Star Comic Corp.): Mar, 1957 - No. 5, 1958

	GD 2.0	VG 4.0	FN 6.0	VF 8.0	VF/NM 9.0	NM- 9.2
1-Swift Arrow, Lone Rider begin	13	26	39	72	101	130
2-5	8	16	24	42	54	65

RIDERS OF THE PURPLE SAGE (See Zane Grey & Four Color #372)

RIFLEMAN, THE (TV)
Dell Publ. Co./Gold Key No. 13 on: No. 1009, 7-9/59 - No. 12, 7-9/62; No. 13, 11/62 - No. 20, 10/64

	GD 2.0	VG 4.0	FN 6.0	VF 8.0	VF/NM 9.0	NM- 9.2
Four Color 1009 (#1)	18	36	54	126	281	435
2 (1-3/60)	10	20	30	65	135	200
3-Toth-a (4 pgs.); variant edition has back-c with "Something Special" comic strip	10	20	30	65	135	200
4-9: 6-Toth-a (4 pgs.)	9	18	27	59	117	175
10-Classic-c	11	22	33	76	163	250
11-20	7	14	21	46	86	125

NOTE: ***Warren Tufts*** *a-2-9. All have Chuck Connors & Johnny Crawford photo-c. Photo back c-13-15.*

RIFTWAR
Marvel Comics: July, 2009 - No. 5, Dec, 2009 ($3.99, limited series)

	GD 2.0	VG 4.0	FN 6.0	VF 8.0	VF/NM 9.0	NM- 9.2
1-5-Adaptation of Raymond E. Feist novel; Glass-s/Stegman-a						4.00

RIMA, THE JUNGLE GIRL
National Periodical Publications: Apr-May, 1974 - No. 7, Apr-May, 1975

	GD 2.0	VG 4.0	FN 6.0	VF 8.0	VF/NM 9.0	NM- 9.2
1-Origin, part 1 (#1-5: 20¢; 6,7: 25¢)	2	4	6	13	18	22
2-7: 2-4-Origin, parts 2-4. 7-Origin & only app. Space Marshal	2	3	4	6	8	10

NOTE: ***Kubert*** *c-1-7.* ***Nino*** *a-1-7.* ***Redondo*** *a-1-7.*

RING OF BRIGHT WATER (See Movie Classics)

RING OF THE NIBELUNG, THE
DC Comics: 1989 - No. 4, 1990 ($4.95, squarebound, 52 pgs., mature readers)

	GD 2.0	VG 4.0	FN 6.0	VF 8.0	VF/NM 9.0	NM- 9.2
1-4: Adapts Wagner cycle of operas, Gil Kane-c/a						5.00

RING OF THE NIBELUNG, THE
Dark Horse Comics: Feb, 2000 - Sept, 2001 ($2.95/$2.99/$5.99, limited series)

	GD 2.0	VG 4.0	FN 6.0	VF 8.0	VF/NM 9.0	NM- 9.2
Vol. 1 (The Rhinegold) 1-4: Adapts Wagner; P. Craig Russell-s/a						3.00
Vol. 2,3: Vol. 2 (The Valkyrie) 1-3: 1-(8/00). Vol. 3 (Siegfried) 1-3: 1-(12/00)						3.00
Vol. 4 (The Twilight of the Gods) 1-3: 1-(6/01)						3.00
4-(9/01, $5.99, 64 pgs.) Conclusion with sketch pages						6.00

RINGO KID, THE (2nd Series)
Marvel Comics Group: Jan, 1970 - No. 23, Nov, 1973; No. 24, Nov, 1975 - No. 30, Nov, 1976

	GD 2.0	VG 4.0	FN 6.0	VF 8.0	VF/NM 9.0	NM- 9.2
1-Williamson-a r-from #10, 1956.	3	6	9	17	26	35
2-11: 2-Severin-c. 11-Last 15¢ issue	2	4	6	11	16	20
12 (52 pg. Giant)	3	6	9	15	22	28
13-20: 13-Wildey-r. 20-Williamson-r/#1	2	4	6	9	13	16
21-30	2	4	6	8	10	12
27,28-(30¢-c variant, limited distribution)(5,7/76)	3	6	9	19	30	40

RINGO KID WESTERN, THE (1st Series) (See Wild Western & Western Trails)
Atlas Comics (HPC)/Marvel Comics: Aug, 1954 - No. 21, Sept, 1957

	GD 2.0	VG 4.0	FN 6.0	VF 8.0	VF/NM 9.0	NM- 9.2
1-Origin; The Ringo Kid begins	32	64	96	188	307	425
2-Black Rider app.; origin/1st app. Ringo's Horse Arab	17	34	51	98	154	210
3-5	14	28	42	76	108	140
6-8-Severin-a(3) each	14	28	42	80	115	150
9,11,12,14-21: 12-Orlando-a (4 pgs.)	11	22	33	62	86	110
10,13-Williamson-a (4 pgs.)	12	24	36	67	94	120

NOTE: ***Berg*** *a-8.* ***Maneely*** *a-1-5, 15, 16(text illos only), 17(4), 18, 20, 21; c-1-6, 8, 13, 15-18, 20.* ***J. Severin*** *c-10, 11.* ***Sinnott*** *a-1.* ***Wildey*** *a-16-18.*

RINSE, THE
Boom! Studios: Sept, 2011 - No. 4, Dec, 2011 ($1.00/$3.99)

	GD 2.0	VG 4.0	FN 6.0	VF 8.0	VF/NM 9.0	NM- 9.2
1-($1.00)-Phillips-s/Laming-a						3.00
2-4-($3.99)						4.00

RIN TIN TIN (See March of Comics #163,180,195)

RIN TIN TIN (TV) (...& Rusty #21 on; see Western Roundup under Dell Giants)
Dell Publishing Co./Gold Key: Nov, 1952 - No. 38, May-July, 1961; Nov, 1963 (All Photo-c)

	GD 2.0	VG 4.0	FN 6.0	VF 8.0	VF/NM 9.0	NM- 9.2
Four Color 434 (#1)	13	26	39	89	195	300
Four Color 476,523	8	16	24	51	96	140
4(3-5/54)-10	6	12	18	40	73	105
11-17,19,20	6	12	18	37	66	95
18-(4-5/57) 1st app. of Rusty and the Cavalry of Fort Apache; photo-c	7	14	21	46	86	125
21-38: 36-Toth-a (4 pgs.)	5	10	15	31	53	75
... & Rusty 1 (11/63-Gold Key)	5	10	15	33	57	80

RIO (Also see Eclipse Monthly)
Comico: June, 1987 ($8.95, 64 pgs.)

	GD 2.0	VG 4.0	FN 6.0	VF 8.0	VF/NM 9.0	NM- 9.2
1-Wildey-c/a						9.00

RIO AT BAY
Dark Horse Comics: July, 1992 - No. 2, Aug, 1992 ($2.95, limited series)

	GD 2.0	VG 4.0	FN 6.0	VF 8.0	VF/NM 9.0	NM- 9.2
1,2-Wildey-c/a						3.00

RIO BRAVO (Movie) (See 4-Color #1018)
Dell Publishing Co.: June, 1959

	GD 2.0	VG 4.0	FN 6.0	VF 8.0	VF/NM 9.0	NM- 9.2
Four Color 1018-Toth-a; John Wayne, Dean Martin, & Ricky Nelson photo-c.	20	40	60	138	307	475

RIO CONCHOS (See Movie Comics)

RIOT (Satire)
Atlas Comics (ACI No. 1-5/WPI No. 6): Apr, 1954 - No. 3, Aug, 1954; No. 4, Feb, 1956 - No. 6, June, 1956

	GD 2.0	VG 4.0	FN 6.0	VF 8.0	VF/NM 9.0	NM- 9.2
1-Russ Heath-a	39	78	117	231	378	525
2-Li'l Abner satire by Post	26	52	78	154	252	350
3-Last precode (8/54)	23	46	69	136	223	310
4-Infinity-c; Marilyn Monroe "7 Year Itch" movie satire; Mad Rip-off ads	30	60	90	177	289	400
5-Marilyn Monroe, John Wayne parody; part photo-c	31	62	93	182	296	410
6-Lorna of the Jungle satire by Everett; Dennis the Menace satire-c/story; part photo-c	23	46	69	136	223	310

NOTE: ***Berg*** *a-3.* ***Burgos*** *c-1, 2.* ***Colan*** *a-1.* ***Everett*** *a-4, 6.* ***Heath*** *a-1.* ***Maneely*** *a-1, 2, 4-6; c-3, 4, 6.* ***Post*** *a-1-4.* ***Reinman*** *a-2.* ***Severin*** *a-4-6.*

RIOT GEAR
Triumphant Comics: Sept, 1993 - No. 11, July, 1994 ($2.50, serially numbered)

	GD 2.0	VG 4.0	FN 6.0	VF 8.0	VF/NM 9.0	NM- 9.2
1-11: 1-2nd app. Riot Gear. 2-1st app. Rabin. 3,4-Triumphant Unleashed x-over. 3-1st app. Surzar. 4-Death of Captain Tich						3.00
Violent Past 1,2: 1-(2/94, $2.50)						3.00

R.I.P.
TSR, Inc.: 1990 - No. 8, 1991 ($2.95, 44 pgs.)

	GD 2.0	VG 4.0	FN 6.0	VF 8.0	VF/NM 9.0	NM- 9.2
1-8-Based on TSR game						4.00

RIPCLAW (See Cyberforce)
Image Comics (Top Cow Prod.): Apr, 1995 - No. 3, June, 1995 (Limited series)

	GD 2.0	VG 4.0	FN 6.0	VF 8.0	VF/NM 9.0	NM- 9.2
1/2-Gold, 1/2-San Diego ed., 1/2-Chicago ed.	1	3	4	6	8	10
1-3: Brandon Peterson-a(p)						3.00
Special 1 (10/95, $2.50)						3.00

RIPCLAW
Image Comics (Top Cow Prod.): V2#1, Dec, 1995 - No. 6, June, 1996 ($2.50)

	GD 2.0	VG 4.0	FN 6.0	VF 8.0	VF/NM 9.0	NM- 9.2
V2#1-6: 5-Medieval Spawn/Witchblade Preview						3.00
...: Pilot Season 1 (2007, $2.99) Jason Aaron-s/Jorge Lucas-a/Tony Moore-c						3.00

RIPCORD (TV)
Dell Publishing Co.: Mar-May, 1962

	GD 2.0	VG 4.0	FN 6.0	VF 8.0	VF/NM 9.0	NM- 9.2
Four Color 1294	6	12	18	40	73	105

R.I.P.D.
Dark Horse Comics: Oct, 1999 - No. 4, Jan, 2000 ($2.95, limited series)

	GD 2.0	VG 4.0	FN 6.0	VF 8.0	VF/NM 9.0	NM- 9.2
1-4						3.00

Rip Hunter Time Master #29 © DC

Rising Stars #6 © JMS & TCOW

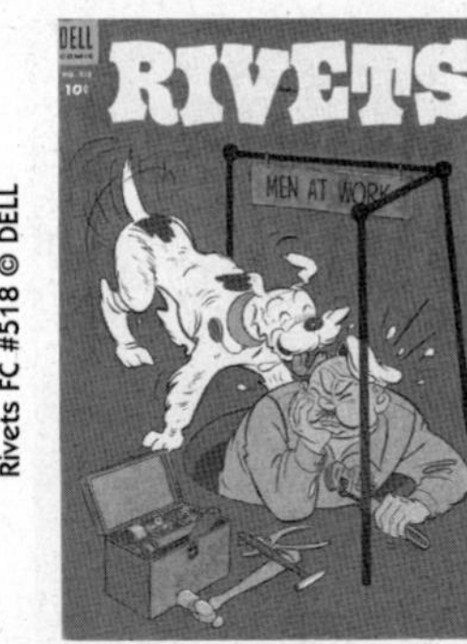

Rivets FC #518 © DELL

GD VG FN VF VF/NM NM-
2.0 4.0 6.0 8.0 9.0 9.2

TPB (2003, $12.95) r/#1-4 13.00

R.I.P.D.: CITY OF THE DAMNED
Dark Horse Comics: Nov, 2012 - No. 4, Mar, 2013 ($3.50, limited series)

1-4-Barlow-s/Parker-a/Wilkins-c 3.50

RIP HUNTER TIME MASTER (See Showcase #20, 21, 25, 26 & Time Masters)
National Periodical Publications: Mar-Apr, 1961 - No. 29, Nov-Dec, 1965

	GD 2.0	VG 4.0	FN 6.0	VF 8.0	VF/NM 9.0	NM- 9.2
1-(3-4/61)	50	100	150	400	900	1400
2	24	48	72	168	372	575
3-5: 5-Last 10¢ issue	15	30	45	103	227	350
6,7-Toth-a in each	10	20	30	66	138	210
8-15	8	16	24	54	102	150
16-19	6	12	18	41	76	110
20-Hitler-c/s	7	14	21	48	89	130
21-29: 29-Gil Kane-c	6	12	18	37	66	95

RIP IN TIME (Also see Teenage Mutant Ninja Turtles #5-7)
Fantagor Press: Aug, 1986 - No.5, 1987 ($1.50, B&W)

1-5: Corben-c/a in all 4.00

RIP KIRBY (Also see Harvey Comics Hits #57, & Street Comix)
David McKay Publications: 1948

	GD 2.0	VG 4.0	FN 6.0	VF 8.0	VF/NM 9.0	NM- 9.2
Feature Books 51,54: Raymond-c; 51-Origin	36	72	108	211	343	475

RIPLEY'S BELIEVE IT OR NOT! (See Ace Comics, All-American Comics, Mystery Comics Digest #1, 4, 7, 10, 13, 16, 19, 22, 25)

RIPLEY'S BELIEVE IT OR NOT!
Harvey Publications: Sept, 1953 - No. 4, March, 1954

	GD 2.0	VG 4.0	FN 6.0	VF 8.0	VF/NM 9.0	NM- 9.2
1-Powell-a	14	28	42	76	108	140
2-4	10	20	30	54	72	90

RIPLEY'S BELIEVE IT OR NOT! (Continuation of Ripleys'...True Ghost Stories & Ripley's...True War Stories)
Gold Key: No. 4, April, 1967 - No. 94, Feb, 1980

	GD 2.0	VG 4.0	FN 6.0	VF 8.0	VF/NM 9.0	NM- 9.2
4-Shrunken head photo-c; McWilliams-a	4	8	12	23	37	50
5-Subtitled "True War Stories"; Evans-a; 1st Jeff Jones-a in comics? (2 pgs.)	4	8	12	23	37	50
6-10: 6-McWilliams-a. 10-Evans-a(2)	3	6	9	19	30	40
11-20: 15-Evans-a	3	6	9	16	23	30
21-30	2	4	6	13	18	22
31-38,40-60	2	4	6	9	13	16
39-Crandall-a	2	4	6	10	14	18
61-73	1	3	4	6	8	10
74,77-83-(52 pgs.)	2	4	6	9	13	16
75,76,84-94	1	2	3	5	6	8
Story Digest Mag. 1(6/70)-4-3/4x6-1/2", 148pp.	5	10	15	31	53	75

NOTE: ***Evanish** art by **Luiz Dominguez** #22-25, 27, 30, 31, 40. **Jeff Jones** a-5(2 pgs.). **McWilliams** a-65, 66, 70, 89. **Orlando** a-8. **Sparling** c-68. Reprints-74, 77-84, 87 (part); 91, 93 (all). **Williamson, Wood** a-80r/#1.*

RIPLEY'S BELIEVE IT OR NOT!
Dark Horse Comics: May, 2002 - No. 3, Oct, 2002 ($2.99, B&W, unfinished limited series)

1-3-Nord-c/a. 1-Stories of Amelia Earhart & D.B. Cooper 3.00

RIPLEY'S BELIEVE IT OR NOT! TRUE GHOST STORIES (Along with Ripley's...True War Stories, the three issues together precede the 1967 series that starts its numbering with #4) (Also see Dan Curtis)
Gold Key: June, 1965 - No. 2, Oct, 1966

	GD 2.0	VG 4.0	FN 6.0	VF 8.0	VF/NM 9.0	NM- 9.2
1-Williamson, Wood & Evans-a; photo-c	7	14	21	44	82	120
2-Orlando, McWilliams-a; photo-c	4	8	12	27	44	60
Mini-Comic 1(1976-3-1/4x6-1/2")	2	4	6	8	11	14
11186(1977)-Golden Press; ($1.95, 224 pgs.)-All-r	4	8	12	23	37	50
11401(3/79)-Golden Press; ($1.00, 96 pgs.)-All-r	3	6	9	15	21	26

RIPLEY'S BELIEVE IT OR NOT! TRUE WAR STORIES (Along with Ripley's...True Ghost Stories, the three issues together precede the 1967 series that starts its numbering with #4)
Gold Key: Nov, 1965 (Aug, 1965 in indicia)

	GD 2.0	VG 4.0	FN 6.0	VF 8.0	VF/NM 9.0	NM- 9.2
1-No Williamson-a	4	8	12	27	44	60

RIPLEY'S BELIEVE IT OR NOT! TRUE WEIRD
Ripley Enterprises: June, 1966 - No. 2, Aug, 1966 (B&W Magazine)

	GD 2.0	VG 4.0	FN 6.0	VF 8.0	VF/NM 9.0	NM- 9.2
1,2-Comic stories & text	3	6	9	17	26	35

RISE OF APOCALYPSE
Marvel Comics: Oct, 1996 - No. 4, Jan, 1997 ($1.95, limited series)

1-4: Adam Pollina-c/a 3.00

RISING STARS
Image Comics (Top Cow): Mar, 1999 - No. 24, Mar, 2005 ($2.50/$2.99)

Preview-(3/99, $5.00) Straczynski-s 6.00
0-(6/00, $2.50) Gary Frank-a/c 3.00
1/2-(8/01, $2.95) Anderson-c; art & sketch pages by Zanier 3.00
1-Four covers; Keu Cha-c/a 5.00
1-($10.00) Gold Editions-four covers 10.00
1-($50.00) Holofoil-c 50.00
2-7: 5-7-Zanier & Lashley-a(p) 4.00
8-23: 8-13-Zanier & Lashley-a(p). 14-Immonen-a. 15-Flip book B&W preview of Universe. 15-23-Brent Anderson-a 3.00
24-($3.99) Series finale; Anderson-a/c 4.00
Born In Fire TPB (11/00, $19.95) r/#1-8; foreword by Neil Gaiman 20.00
Power TPB (2002, $19.95) r/#9-16 20.00
Prelude-(10/00, $2.95) Cha-a/Lashley-c 3.00
...: Visitations (2002, $8.99) r/#0, 1/2, Preview; new Anderson-c; cover gallery 9.00
Vol. 3: Fire and Ash TPB (2005, $19.99) r/#17-24; design pages & cover gallery 20.00
Vol. 4 TPB (2006, $19.99) r/Rising Stars Bright #1-3 and Voices of the Dead #1-6 20.00
Vol. 5 TPB (2007, $16.99) r/Rising Stars: Untouchable #1-5 and ...: Visitations 17.00
Wizard #0-(3/99) Wizard supplement; Straczynski-s 3.00
Wizard #1/2 5.00

RISING STARS BRIGHT
Image Comics (Top Cow): Mar, 2003 - No. 3, May, 2003 ($2.99, limited series)

1-3-Avery-s/Jurgens & Gorder-a/Beck-c 3.00

RISING STARS: UNTOUCHABLE
Image Comics (Top Cow): Mar, 2006 - No. 5, July, 2006 ($2.99, limited series)

1-5-Avery-s/Anderson-a 3.00

RISING STARS: VOICES OF THE DEAD
Image Comics (Top Cow): June, 2005 - No. 6, Dec, 2005 ($2.99, limited series)

1-6-Avery-s/Staz Johnson-a 3.00

RIVERDALE HIGH (Archie's... #7,8)
Archie Comics: Aug, 1990 - No. 8, Oct, 1991 ($1.00, bi-monthly)

1 4.00
2-8 3.00

RIVER FEUD (See Zane Grey & Four Color #484)

RIVETS
Dell Publishing Co.: No. 518, Nov, 1953

	GD 2.0	VG 4.0	FN 6.0	VF 8.0	VF/NM 9.0	NM- 9.2
Four Color 518	4	8	12	25	40	55

RIVETS (A dog)
Argo Publ.: Jan, 1956 - No. 3, May, 1956

	GD 2.0	VG 4.0	FN 6.0	VF 8.0	VF/NM 9.0	NM- 9.2
1-Reprints Sunday & daily newspaper strips	6	12	18	31	38	45
2,3	5	10	15	22	26	30

ROACHMILL
Blackthorne Publ.: Dec, 1986 - No. 6, Oct, 1987 ($1.75, B&W)

1-6 3.00

ROACHMILL
Dark Horse Comics: May, 1988 - No. 10, Dec, 1990 ($1.75, B&W)

1-10: 10-Contains trading cards 3.00

ROAD RUNNER (See Beep Beep, the...)

ROAD TO OZ (Adaptation of the L. Frank Baum book)
Marvel Comics: Nov, 2012 - No. 6, May, 2013 ($3.99, limited series)

1-6-Eric Shanower-s/Skottie Young-a/c 4.00

ROAD TO PERDITION (Inspired the 2002 Tom Hanks/Paul Newman movie) (Also see On the Road to Perdition)
DC Comics/Paradox Press: 1998, 2002 ($13.95, B&W paperback graphic novel)

nn-(1st printing) Max Allan Collins-s/Richard Piers Rayner-a 30.00
2nd & 3rd printings (2002, $13.95) 14.00
Movie photo cover edition (2002) 14.00

ROADTRIP
Oni Press: Aug, 2000 ($2.95, B&W, one-shot)

1-Reprints Judd Winick's back-up stories from Oni Double Feature #9,10 3.00

ROADWAYS
Cult Press: May, 1994 ($2.75, B&W, limited series)

1 3.00

ROARIN' RICK'S RARE BIT FIENDS
King Hell Press: July, 1994 - No. 21, Aug, 1996 ($2.95, B&W, mature)

1-21: Rick Veitch-c/a/scripts in all. 20-(5/96). 21-(8/96)-Reads Subtleman #1 on cover 3.00

Robin #106 © DC

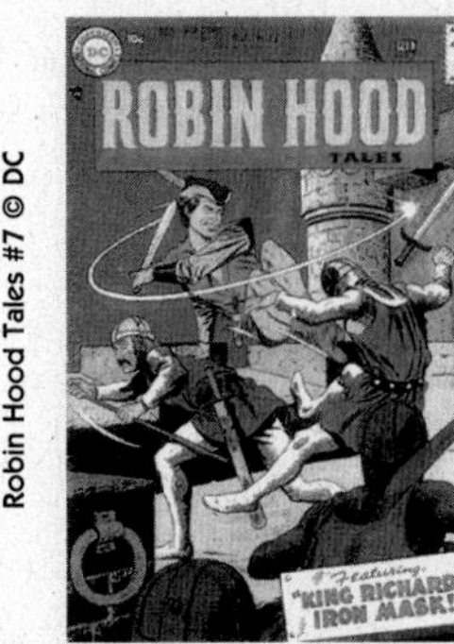

Robin Hood Tales #7 © DC

Robin III #3 © DC

	GD	VG	FN	VF	VF/NM	NM-
	2.0	4.0	6.0	8.0	9.0	9.2

Rabid Eye: The Dream Art of Rick Veitch ($14.95, B&W, TPB)-r/#1-8 & the appendix from #12 15.00
Pocket Universe (6/96, $14.95, B&W, TPB)-Reprints 15.00

ROBERT E. HOWARD'S CONAN THE BARBARIAN
Marvel Comics: 1983 ($2.50, 68 pgs., Baxter paper)
1-r/Savage Tales #2,3 by Smith, c-r/Conan #21 by Smith. 5.00

ROBERT LOUIS STEVENSON'S KIDNAPPED (See Kidnapped)

ROBIN (See Aurora, Birds of Prey, Detective Comics #38, New Teen Titans, Robin II, Robin III, Robin 3000, Star Spangled Comics #65, Teen Titans & Young Justice)

ROBIN (See Batman #457)
DC Comics: Jan, 1991 - No. 5, May, 1991 ($1.00, limited series)
1-Free poster by N. Adams; Bolland-c on all 5.00
1-2nd & 3rd printings (without poster) 3.00
2-5 4.00
2-2nd printing 3.00
Annual 1,2 (1992-93, $2.50, 68 pgs.): 1-Grant/Wagner scripts; Sam Kieth-c. 2-Intro Razorsharp; Jim Balent-c(p) 4.00

ROBIN (See Detective #668) (Also see Red Robin)
DC Comics: Nov, 1993 - No. 183, Apr, 2009 ($1.50/$1.95/$1.99/$2.25/$2.50/$2.99)
1-($2.95)-Collector's edition w/foil embossed-c; 1st app. Robin's car, The Redbird; Azrael as Batman app. 5.00
1-Newsstand ed. 3.00
0,2-49,51-66-Regular editions: 3-5-The Spoiler app. 6-The Huntress-c/story cont'd from Showcase '94 #5. 7-Knightquest: The Conclusion w/new Batman (Azrael) vs. Bruce Wayne. 8-KnightsEnd Pt. 5. 9-KnightsEnd Aftermath; Batman-c & app. 10-(9/94)-Zero Hour. 0-(10/94). 11-(11/94). 25-Green Arrow-c/app. 26-Batman app. 27-Contagion Pt. 3; Catwoman-c/app; Penguin & Azrael app. 28-Contagion Pt. 11. 29-Penguin app. 31-Wildcat-c/app. 32-Legacy Pt. 3. 33-Legacy Pt. 7. 35-Final Night. 46-Genesis. 52,53-Cataclysm pt. 7, conclusion. 55-Green Arrow app. 62-64-Flash-c/app. 3.50
14 ($2.50)-Embossed-c; Troika Pt. 4 4.00
50-($2.95)-Lady Shiva & King Snake app. 4.00
67-74,76-78: 67-72-No Man's Land 3.00
75-($2.95) 4.00
79-97: 79-Begin $2.25-c; Green Arrow app. 86-Pander Bros.-a 3.00
98,99-Bruce Wayne: Murderer x-over pt. 6, 11 3.00
100-($3.50) Last Dixon-s 4.00
101-147: 101-Young Justice x-over. 106-Kevin Lau-c. 121,122-Willingham-s/Mays-a. 125-Tim Drake quits. 126-Spoiler becomes the new Robin. 129-131-War Games. 132-Robin moves to Bludhaven, Batgirl app. 138-Begin $2.50-c. 139-McDaniel-a begins. 146-147-Teen Titans app. 3.00
148-174: 148-One Year Later; new costume. 150-Begin $2.99-c. 152,153-Boomerang app. 168,169-Resurrection of Ra's al Ghul x-over. 174 Spoiler unmasked 3.00
175-183: 175,176-Batman R.I.P. x-over. 180-Robin vs. Red Robin 3.00
#1,000,000 (11/98) 853rd Century x-over 3.00
Annual 3-5: 3-(1994, $2.95)-Elseworlds story. 4-(1995, $2.95)-Year One story. 5-(1996, $2.95)-Legends of the Dead Earth story 4.00
Annual 6 (1997, $3.95)-Pulp Heroes story. 4.00
Annual 7 (12/07, $3.99)-Pearson-c/a; prelude to Resurrection of Ra's al Ghul x-over 4.00
.../Argent 1 (2/98, $1.95) Argent (Teen Titans) app. 3.00
.../Batgirl: Fresh Blood TPB (2005, $12.99) r/#132,133 & Batgirl #58,59 13.00
...: Days of Fire and Madness (2006, $12.99, TPB) r/#140-145 13.00
...Eighty-Page Giant 1 (9/00, $5.95) Chuck Dixon-s/Diego Barreto-a 6.00
...: Flying Solo (2000, $12.95, TPB) r/#1-6, Showcase '94 #5,6 13.00
...Plus 1 (12/96, $2.95) Impulse-c/app.; Waid-s 4.00
...Plus 2 (12/97, $2.95) Fang (Scare Tactics) app. 4.00
...: Search For a Hero (2009, $19.99, TPB) r/#175-183; cover gallery 20.00
.../Spoiler Special 1 (8/08, $3.99) Follows Spoiler's return in Robin #174; Dixon-s 4.00
...: Teenage Wasteland (2007, $17.99, TPB) r/#154-162 18.00
...: The Big Leagues (2008, $12.99, TPB) r/#163-167 13.00
...: Unmasked (2004, $12.95, TPB) r/#121-125; Pearson-c 13.00
...: Violent Tendencies (2008, $17.99, TPB) r/#170-174 & Robin/Spoiler Special 1 18.00
...: Wanted (2007, $12.99, TPB) r/#148-153 13.00

ROBIN: A HERO REBORN
DC Comics: 1991 ($4.95, squarebound, trade paperback)
nn-r/Batman #455-457 & Robin #1-5; Bolland-c 1 2 3 5 6 8

ROBIN HOOD (See The Advs. of..., Brave and the Bold, Classic Comics #7, Classics Giveaways (12/44), Four Color #413, 669, King Classics, Movie Comics & Power Record Comics) (...& His Merry Men, The Illustrated Story of...)

ROBIN HOOD (Disney)
Dell Publishing Co.: No. 413, Aug, 1952; No. 669, Dec, 1955
Four Color 413-(1st Disney movie Four Color book)(8/52)-Photo-c 9 18 27 58 114 170
Four Color 669 (12/55)-Reprints #413 plus photo-c 5 10 15 34 60 85

ROBIN HOOD (Adventures of... #7, 8)
Magazine Enterprises (Sussex Pub. Co.): No. 52, Nov, 1955 - No. 6, Jun, 1957
52 (#1)-Origin Robin Hood & Sir Gallant of the Round Table 15 30 45 85 130 175
53 (#2), 3-6: 6-Richard Greene photo-c (TV) 12 24 36 67 94 120
I.W. Reprint #1,2,9: 1-r/#3. 2-r/#4. 9-r/#52 (1963) 2 4 6 9 13 16
Super Reprint #10,15: 10-r/#53. 15-r/#5 2 4 6 9 13 16
NOTE: *Bolle a-in all; c-52.* **Powell** *a-6.*

ROBIN HOOD (Not Disney)
Dell Publishing Co.: May-July, 1963 (one-shot)
1 3 6 9 16 23 30

ROBIN HOOD (Disney) (Also see Best of Walt Disney)
Western Publishing Co.: 1973 ($1.50, 8-1/2x11", 52 pgs., cardboard-c)
96151- "Robin Hood", based on movie, 96152- "The Mystery of Sherwood Forest", 96153- "In King Richard's Service", 96154- "The Wizard's Ring" each.... 3 6 9 15 22 28

ROBIN HOOD
Eclipse Comics: July, 1991 - No. 3, Dec, 1991 ($2.50, limited series)
1-3: Timothy Truman layouts 3.00

ROBIN HOOD AND HIS MERRY MEN (Formerly Danger & Adventure)
Charlton Comics: No. 28, Apr, 1956 - No. 38, Aug, 1958
28 10 20 30 54 72 90
29-37 8 16 24 42 54 65
38-Ditko-a (5 pgs.); Rocke-c 14 28 42 76 108 140

ROBIN HOOD TALES (Published by National Periodical #7 on)
Quality Comics Group (Comic Magazines): Feb, 1956 - No. 6, Nov-Dec, 1956
1-All have Baker/Cuidera-c 32 64 96 188 307 425
2-6-Matt Baker-a 30 60 90 177 289 400

ROBIN HOOD TALES (Cont'd from Quality series)(See Brave & the Bold #5)
National Periodical Publ.: No. 7, Jan-Feb, 1957 - No. 14, Mar-Apr, 1958
7-All have Andru/Esposito-c 36 72 108 211 343 475
8-14 30 60 90 177 289 400

ROBINSON CRUSOE (See King Classics & Power Record Comics)
Dell Publishing Co.: Nov-Jan, 1963-64
1 3 6 9 15 21 26

ROBIN II (The Joker's Wild)
DC Comics: Oct, 1991 - No. 4, Dec, 1991 ($1.50, mini-series)
1-(Direct sales, $1.50)-With 4 diff.-c; same hologram on each 5.00
1-(Newsstand, $1.00)-No hologram; 1 version 3.00
1-Collector's set ($10.00)-Contains all 5 versions bagged with hologram trading card inside 18.00
2-(Direct sales, $1.50)-With 3 different-c 4.00
2-4-(Newsstand, $1.00)-1 version of each 3.00
2-Collector's set ($8.00)-Contains all 4 versions bagged with hologram trading card inside 12.00
3-(Direct sale, $1.50)-With 2 different-c 4.00
3-Collector's set ($6.00)-Contains all 3 versions bagged with hologram trading card inside 10.00
4-(Direct sales, $1.50)-Only one version 4.00
4-Collector's set ($4.00)-Contains both versions bagged with Bat-Signal hologram trading card 6.00
Multi-pack (All four issues w/hologram sticker) 14.00
Deluxe Complete Set ($30.00)-Contains all 14 versions of #1-4 plus a new hologram trading card; numbered & limited to 25,000; comes with slipcase & 2 acid free backing boards 45.00

ROBIN III: CRY OF THE HUNTRESS
DC Comics: Dec, 1992 - No. 6, Mar, 1993 (Limited series)
1-6 ($2.50, collector's ed.)-Polybagged w/movement enhanced-c plus mini-poster of newsstand-c by Zeck 4.00
1-6 ($1.25, newsstand ed.): All have Zeck-c 3.00

ROBIN 3000
DC Comics (Elseworlds): 1992 - No. 2, 1992 ($4.95, mini-series, 52 pgs.)
1,2-Foil logo; Russell-c/a 6.00

ROBIN: YEAR ONE
DC Comics: 2000 - No. 4, 2001 ($4.95, square-bound, limited series)

Robocop #18 © Orion

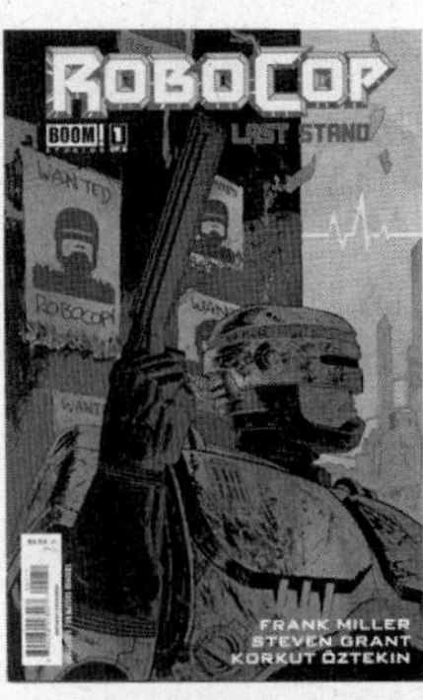

Robocop: Last Stand #1 © Orion

Robotech #9 © Harmony Gold

GD VG FN VF VF/NM NM-
2.0 4.0 6.0 8.0 9.0 9.2

GD VG FN VF VF/NM NM-
2.0 4.0 6.0 8.0 9.0 9.2

1-4: Earliest days of Robin's career; Javier Pulido-c/a. 2,4-Two-Face app. 6.00
TPB (2002, 2008, $14.95/$14.99, 2 printings) r/#1-4 15.00

ROBOCOP
Marvel Comics: Oct, 1987 ($2.00, B&W, magazine, one-shot)

1-Movie adaptation 5.00

ROBOCOP (Also see Dark Horse Comics)
Marvel Comics: Mar, 1990 - No. 23, Jan, 1992 ($1.50)

1-Based on movie 4.00
2-23 3.00
nn (7/90, $4.95, 52 pgs.)-r/B&W magazine in color; adapts 1st movie 5.00

ROBOCOP
Dynamite Entertainment: 2010 - No. 6, 2010 ($3.50, limited series)

1-6-Follows the events of the first film; Neves-a 3.50

ROBOCOP (FRANK MILLER'S...)
Avatar Press: July, 2003 - No. 9, Jan, 2006 ($3.50/$3.99, limited series)

1-9-Frank Miller-s/Juan Ryp-a. 1-Three covers by Miller, Ryp, and Barrows. 2-Two covers 4.00
Free Comic Book Day Edition (4/03) Previews Robocop & Stargate SG•1; Busch-c 3.00

ROBOCOP (Tie-ins to the 2014 movie)
BOOM! Studios: Feb, 2014 ($3.99)

...: Beta (2/14) Brisson-s/Laiso-a 4.00
...: Hominem Ex Machina (2/14) Moreci-s/Copland-a 4.00
...: Memento Mori (2/14) Barbiere-s/Vieira-a 4.00
...: To Live and Die in Detroit (2/14) Joe Harris-s/Piotr Kowalski-a 4.00

ROBOCOP: LAST STAND
BOOM! Studios: Aug, 2013 - No. 8, Mar, 2014 ($3.99, limited series)

1-8: 1-Miller & Grant-s/Oztekin-a 4.00

ROBOCOP: MORTAL COILS
Dark Horse Comics: Sept, 1993 - No. 4, Dec, 1993 ($2.50, limited series)

1-4: 1,2-Cago painted-c 3.00

ROBOCOP: PRIME SUSPECT
Dark Horse Comics: Oct, 1992 - No. 4, Jan, 1993 ($2.50, limited series)

1-4: 1,3-Nelson painted-c. 2,4-Bolton painted-c 3.00

ROBOCOP: ROAD TRIP
Dynamite Entertainment: 2012 - No. 4, 2012 ($3.99, limited series)

1-4-De Zarate-a 4.00

ROBOCOP: ROULETTE
Dark Horse Comics: Dec, 1993 - No. 4, 1994 ($2.50, limited series)

1-4: 1,3-Nelson painted-c. 2,4-Bolton painted-c 3.00

ROBOCOP 2
Marvel Comics: Aug, 1990 ($2.25, B&W, magazine, 68 pgs.)

1-Adapts movie sequel scripted by Frank Miller; Bagley-a 4.00

ROBOCOP 2
Marvel Comics: Aug, 1990; Late Aug, 1990 - #3, Late Sept, 1990 ($1.00, limited series)

nn-(8/90, $4.95, 68 pgs., color)-Same contents as B&W magazine 5.00
1: #1-3 reprint no number issue 3.00
2,3: 2-Guice-c(i) 3.00

ROBOCOP 3
Dark Horse Comics: July, 1993 - No. 3, Nov, 1993 ($2.50, limited series)

1-3: Nelson painted-c; Nguyen-a(p) 3.00

ROBOCOP VERSUS THE TERMINATOR
Dark Horse Comics: Sept, 1992 - No. 4, 1992 (Dec.) ($2.50, limited series)

1-4: Miller scripts & Simonson-c/a in all 4.00
1-Platinum Edition 8.00
NOTE: *All contain a different Robocop cardboard cut-out stand-up.*

ROBO DOJO
DC Comics (WildStorm): Apr, 2002 - No. 6, Sept, 2002 ($2.95, limited series)

1-6-Wolfman-s 3.00

ROBO-HUNTER (Also see Sam Slade...)
Eagle Comics: Apr, 1984 - No. 5, 1984 ($1.00)

1-5-2000 A.D. 4.00

R.O.B.O.T. BATTALION 2050
Eclipse Comics: Mar, 1988 ($2.00, B&W, one-shot)

1 3.00

ROBOT COMICS
Renegade Press: No. 0, June, 1987 ($2.00, B&W, one-shot)

0-Bob Burden story & art 3.00

ROBOTECH
Antarctic Press: Mar, 1997 - No. 11, Nov, 1998 ($2.95)

1-11, Annual 1 (4/98, $2.95) 4.00
...Class Reunion (12/98, $3.95, B&W) 4.00
...Escape (5/98, $2.95, B&W), ...Final Fire (12/98, $2.95, B&W) 4.00

ROBOTECH
DC Comics (WildStorm): No. 0, Feb, 2003 - No. 6, Jul, 2003 ($2.50/$2.95, limited series)

0-Tommy Yune-s; art by Jim Lee, Garza, Bermejo and others; pin-up pages by various 3.00
1-6 ($2.95)-Long Vo-a 3.00
...: From the Stars (2003, $9.95, digest-size) r/#0-6 & Sourcebook 10.00
... Sourcebook (3/03, $2.95) pin-ups and info on characters and mecha; art by various 3.00

ROBOTECH: COVERT-OPS
Antarctic Press: Aug, 1998 - No. 2, Sept, 1998 ($2.95, B&W, limited series)

1,2-Gregory Lane-s/a 4.00

ROBOTECH DEFENDERS
DC Comics: Mar, 1985 - No. 2, Apr, 1985 (Mini-series)

1,2 4.00

ROBOTECH IN 3-D (TV)
Comico: Aug, 1987 ($2.50)

1-Steacy painted-c 5.00

ROBOTECH: INVASION
DC Comics (WildStorm): Feb, 2004 - No. 5, July, 2004 ($2.95, limited series)

1-5-Faerber & Yune-s/Miyazawa & Dogan-a 3.00

ROBOTECH: LOVE AND WAR
DC Comics (WildStorm): Aug, 2003 - No. 6, Jan, 2004 ($2.95, limited series)

1-6-Long Vo & Charles Park-a/Faerber & Yune-s. 2-Variant-c by Warren 3.00

ROBOTECH MASTERS (TV)
Comico: July, 1985 - No. 23, Apr, 1988 ($1.50)

1 6.00
2-23 4.00

ROBOTECH: PRELUDE TO THE SHADOW CHRONICLES
DC Comics (WildStorm): Dec, 2005 - No. 5, Mar, 2006 ($3.50, limited series)

1-5-Yune-s/Dogan & Udon Studios-a 3.50
TPB (2010, $17.99) r/#1-5; production art 18.00

ROBOTECH: SENTINELS - RUBICON
Antarctic Press: July, 1998 ($2.95, B&W)

1 4.00

ROBOTECH SPECIAL
Comico: May, 1988 ($2.50, one-shot, 44 pgs.)

1-Steacy wraparound-c; partial photo-c 5.00

ROBOTECH THE GRAPHIC NOVEL
Comico: Aug, 1986 ($5.95, 8-1/2x11", 52 pgs.)

1-Origin SDF-1; intro T.R. Edwards, Steacy-c/a 15.00
1-Second printing (12/86) 10.00

ROBOTECH: THE MACROSS SAGA (TV)(Formerly Macross)
Comico: No. 2, Feb, 1985 - No. 36, Feb, 1989 ($1.50)

2 1 2 3 5 6 8
3-10 5.00
11-36: 12,17-Ken Steacy painted-c. 26-Begin $1.75-c. 35,36-($1.95) 4.00
Volume 1-4 TPB (WildStorm, 2003, $14.95, 5-3/4" x 8-1/4")1-Reprints #2-6 & Macross #1.
2- r/#7-12. 3-r/#13-18. 4-r/#19-24 15.00

ROBOTECH: THE NEW GENERATION
Comico: July, 1985 - No. 25, July, 1988

1 6.00
2-25 4.00

ROBOTECH: VERMILION
Antarctic Press: Mar, 1997 - No. 4, ($2.95, B&W, limited series)

1-4 4.00

ROBOTECH / VOLTRON
Dynamite Entertainment: 2013 - No. 5 ($3.99, limited series)

Rocket Comics #1 © HILL

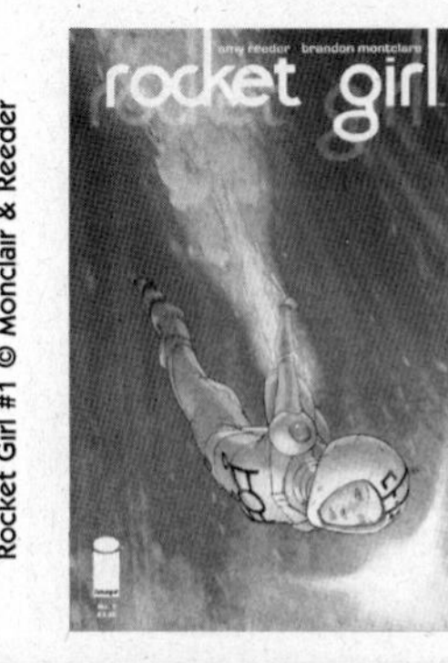

Rocket Girl #1 © Monclair & Reeder

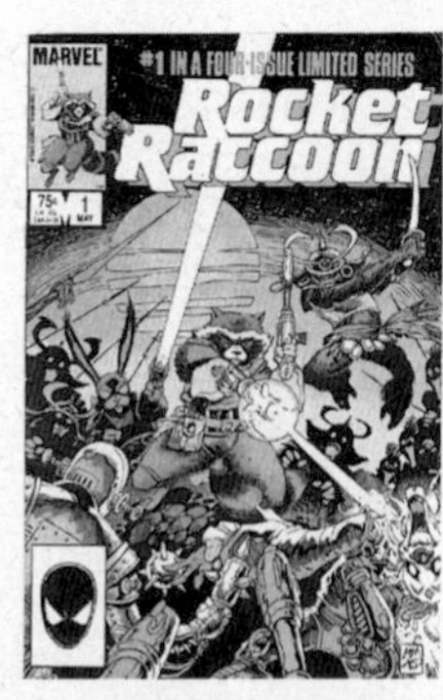

Rocket Raccoon #1 © MAR

	GD 2.0	VG 4.0	FN 6.0	VF 8.0	VF/NM 9.0	NM- 9.2

1,2-Tommy Yune-s 4.00

ROBOTECH: WINGS OF GIBRALTAR
Antarctic Press: Aug, 1998 - No. 2, Sept, 1998 ($2.95, B&W, limited series)

1,2-Lee Duhig-s/a 4.00

ROBOTIX
Marvel Comics: Feb, 1986 (75¢, one-shot)

1-Based on toy 4.00

ROBOTMEN OF THE LOST PLANET (Also see Space Thrillers)
Avon Periodicals: 1952 (Also see Strange Worlds #19)

1-McCann-a (3 pgs.); Fawcette-a 142 284 426 909 1555 2200

ROB ROY
Dell Publishing Co.: 1954 (Disney-Movie)

Four Color 544-Manning-a, photo-c 7 14 21 44 82 120

ROCK, THE (WWF Wrestling)
Chaos! Comics: June, 2001 ($2.99, one-shot)

1-Photo-c; Grant-s/Neves-a 4.00

ROCK & ROLL HIGH SCHOOL
Roger Corman's Cosmic Comics: Oct, 1995 ($2.50)

1-Bob Fingerman scripts 3.00

ROCK AND ROLLO (Formerly TV Teens)
Charlton Comics: V2#14, Oct, 1957 - No. 19, Sept, 1958

V2#14-19 6 12 18 31 38 45

ROCK COMICS
Landgraphic Publ.: Jul/Aug, 1979 ($1.25, tabloid size, 28 pgs.)

1-N. Adams-c; Thor(not Marvel's) story by Adams 3 6 9 14 20 25

ROCKET COMICS
Hillman Periodicals: Mar, 1940 - No. 3, May, 1940

1-Rocket Riley, Red Roberts the Electro Man (origin), The Phantom Ranger, The Steel Shark, The Defender, Buzzard Barnes and his Sky Devils, Lefty Larson, & The Defender, the Man with a Thousand Faces begin (1st app. of each); all have Rocket Riley-c
277 554 831 1773 3037 4350
2,3 145 290 435 928 1589 2250

ROCKET COMICS: IGNITE
Dark Horse Comics: Apr, 2003 (Free Comic Book Day giveaway)

1-Previews Dark Horse series Syn, Lone, and Go Boy 7 3.00

ROCKETEER, THE (See Eclipse Graphic Album Series, Pacific Presents & Starslayer)

ROCKETEER ADVENTURE MAGAZINE, THE
Comico/Dark Horse Comics No. 3: July, 1988 ($2.00); No. 2, July, 1989 ($2.75); No. 3, Jan, 1995 ($2.95)

1-(7/88, $2.00)-Dave Stevens-c/a in all; Kaluta back-up-a; 1st app. Jonas (character based on The Shadow) 2 4 6 8 10 12
2-(7/89, $2.75)-Stevens/Dorman painted-c 1 3 4 6 8 10
3-(1/95, $2.95)-Includes pinups by Stevens, Gulacy, Plunkett, & Mignola 5.00
Volume 2-(9/96, $9.95, magazine size TPB)-Reprints #1-3 10.00

ROCKETEER ADVENTURES
IDW Publishing: May, 2011 - No. 4, Aug, 2011 ($3.99, limited series)

1-4-Anthology of new stories by various; covers by Alex Ross and Dave Stevens 4.00

ROCKETEER ADVENTURES VOLUME 2
IDW Publishing: Mar, 2012 - No. 4, Jun, 2012 ($3.99, limited series)

1-4-Anthology by various; covers by Darwyn Cooke and Stevens. 1-Sakai-a. 4-Simonson & Byrne-a 4.00

ROCKETEER: CARGO OF DOOM
IDW Publishing: Aug, 2012 - No. 4, Nov, 2012 ($3.99, limited series)

1-4-Waid-s/Samnee-a/c; variant-c by Stevens on all 4.00

ROCKETEER: HOLLYWOOD HORROR
IDW Publishing: Feb, 2013 - No. 4, May, 2013 ($3.99, limited series)

1-4-Langridge-s/Bone-a/Simonson-c; variant-c on all 4.00

ROCKETEER JETPACK TREASURY EDITION
IDW Publishing: Nov, 2011 ($9.99, oversized 13" x 9-3/4" format)

1-Recolored r/Starslayer #1-3, Pacific Presents #1,2 & Rocketeer Special Edition 10.00

ROCKETEER SPECIAL EDITION, THE
Eclipse Comics: Nov, 1984 ($1.50, Baxter paper)(Chapter 5 of Rocketeer serial)

1-Stevens-c/a; Kaluta back-c; pin-ups inside 2 4 6 10 14 18

	GD 2.0	VG 4.0	FN 6.0	VF 8.0	VF/NM 9.0	NM- 9.2

NOTE: *Originally intended to be published in Pacific Presents.*

ROCKETEER, THE: THE COMPLETE ADVENTURES
IDW Publishing: Oct, 2009 ($29.99/$75.00, hardcover)

HC-Reprints of Dave Stevens' Rocketeer stories in Starslayer #1-3, Pacific Presents #1,2, Rocketeer Special Edition and Rocketeer Adventure Magazine #1-3; all re-colored 30.00
... Deluxe Edition ($75.00, 8"x12" slipcased HC) larger size reprints of HC content plus 100 bonus pages of sketch art, layouts, design work; intro. by Thomas Jane 110.00
... Deluxe Edition 2nd printing ($75.00, oversized slipcased HC) 75.00

ROCKETEER, THE: THE OFFICIAL MOVIE ADAPTATION
W. D. Publications (Disney): 1991

nn-($5.95, 68 pgs.)-Squarebound deluxe edition 6.00
nn-($2.95, 68 pgs.)-Stapled regular edition 4.00
3-D Comic Book (1991, $7.98, 52 pgs.) 8.00

ROCKETEER/THE SPIRIT: PULP FRICTION
IDW Publishing: Jul, 2013 - No. 4, Dec, 2013 ($3.99, limited series)

1-4: 1-Waid-s/Paul Smith-a; covers by Smith & Darwyn Cooke. 2-Wallace-a. 3,4-Bone-a 4.00

ROCKET GIRL
Image Comics: Oct, 2013 - Present ($3.50)

1-4-Brandon Montclare-a/Amy Reeder-a/c 3.50

ROCKET KELLY (See The Bouncer, Green Mask #10); becomes Li'l Pan #6)
Fox Feature Syndicate: 1944; Fall, 1945 - No. 5, Oct-Nov, 1946

nn (1944), 1 (Fall, 1945) 39 78 117 240 395 550
2-The Puppeteer app. (costumed hero) 27 54 81 158 259 360
3-5: 5-(#5 on cover, #4 inside) 24 48 72 140 230 320

ROCKETMAN (Strange Fantasy #2 on) (See Hello Pal & Scoop Comics)
Ajax/Farrell Publications: June, 1952 (Strange Stories of the Future)

1-Rocketman & Cosmo 42 84 126 265 445 625

ROCKET RACCOON (Also see Marvel Preview #7 and Incredible Hulk #271)
Marvel Comics: May, 1985 - No. 4, Aug, 1985 (color, limited series)

1-Mignola-a/Mantlo-s in all 4 8 12 27 44 60
2-4 2 4 6 11 16 20
...: Tales From Half-World 1 (10/13, $7.99) r/#1-4; new cover by McNiven 8.00

ROCKET SHIP X
Fox Features Syndicate: September, 1951; 1952

1 64 128 192 406 696 985
1952 (nn, nd, no publ.)-Edited 1951-c (exist?) 39 78 117 231 378 525

ROCKET TO ADVENTURE LAND (See Pixie Puzzle...)

ROCKET TO THE MOON
Avon Periodicals: 1951

nn-Orlando-c/a; adapts Otis Adelbert Kline's "Maza of the Moon"
142 284 426 909 1555 2200

ROCK FANTASY COMICS
Rock Fantasy Comics: Dec, 1989 - No. 16?, 1991 ($2.25/$3.00, B&W)(No cover price)

1-Pink Floyd part 1 5.00
1-2nd printing ($3.00-c) 3.00
2,3: 2-Rolling Stones #1. 3-Led Zeppelin #1 4.00
2,3: 2nd printings ($3.00-c, 1/90 & 2/90) 3.00
4-Stevie Nicks Not published
5-Monstrosities of Rock #1; photo back-c 4.00
5-2nd printing ($3.00, 3/90 indicia, 2/90-c) 3.00
6-9,11-15,17,18: 6-Guns n' Roses #1 (1st & 2nd printings, 3/90)-Begin $3.00-c. 7-Sex Pistols #1. 8-Alice Cooper; not published. 9-Van Halen #1; photo back-c. 11-Jimi Hendrix #1; wraparound-c 3.00
10-Kiss #1; photo back-c 2 4 6 8 10 12
16-($5.00, 68 pgs.)-The Great Gig in the Sky(Floyd) 5.00

ROCK HAPPENING (See Bunny and Harvey Pop Comics:...)

ROCK N' ROLL COMICS
DC Comics: Dec./Jan 1956 (ashcan)

nn-Ashcan comic, not distributed to newsstands, only for in house use (no known sales)

ROCK N' ROLL COMICS
Revolutionary Comics: Jun, 1989 - No. 65 ($1.50/$1.95/$2.50, B&W/col. #15 on)

1-Guns N' Roses 1 3 4 6 8 10
1-2nd thru 7th printings. 7th printing (full color w/new-c/a) 3.00
2-Metallica 1 3 4 6 8 10
2-2nd thru 6th printings (6th in color) 3.00
3-Bon Jovi (no reprints) 1 2 3 5 6 8

Rocky and Bullwinkle #1 © Ward Prop.

Rocky Lane Western #5 © FAW

Rogue (2004 series) #7 © MAR

	GD 2.0	VG 4.0	FN 6.0	VF 8.0	VF/NM 9.0	NM- 9.2

4-8,10-65: 4-Motley Crue(2nd printing only, 1st destroyed). 5-Def Leppard (2 printings). 6-Rolling Stones(4 printings). 7-The Who (3 printings). 8-Skid Row; not published. 10-Warrant/Whitesnake(2 printings; 1st has 2 diff.-c). 11-Aerosmith (2 printings?). 12-New Kids on the Block(2 printings). 12-3rd printing; rewritten & titled NKOTB Hate Book. 13-Led Zeppelin. 14-Sex Pistols. 15-Poison; 1st color issue. 16-Van Halen. 17-Madonna. 18-Alice Cooper. 19-Public Enemy/2 Live Crew. 20-Queensryche/Tesla. 21-Prince? 22-AC/DC; begin $2.50-c. 23-Living Colour. 26-Michael Jackson. 29-Ozzy. 45,46-Grateful Dead. 49-Rush. 50,51-Bob Dylan. 56-David Bowie — 5.00
9-Kiss — 2 4 6 8 10 12
9-2nd & 3rd printings — 3.00

NOTE: *Most issues were reprinted except #3. Later reprints are in color. #8 was not released.*

ROCKO'S MODERN LIFE (TV)
Marvel Comics: June, 1994 - No. 7, Dec, 1994 ($1.95) (Nickelodeon cartoon)
1-7 — 3.00

ROCKY AND BULLWINKLE (TV)
IDW Publishing: Mar, 2014 - Present ($3.99)
1-Evanier-s/Langridge-a; bonus Dudley Do-Right short story.; two covers — 4.00

ROCKY AND HIS FIENDISH FRIENDS (TV)(Bullwinkle)
Gold Key: Oct, 1962 - No. 5, Sept, 1963 (Jay Ward)

	GD	VG	FN	VF	VF/NM	NM-
1 (25¢, 80 pgs.)	13	26	39	86	188	290
2,3 (25¢, 80 pgs.)	9	18	27	62	126	190
4,5 (Regular size, 12¢)	7	14	21	46	86	125

ROCKY AND HIS FRIENDS (See Kite Fun Book & March of Comics #216 in the Promotional Comics section)

ROCKY AND HIS FRIENDS (TV)
Dell Publishing Co.: No. 1128, 8-10/60 - No.1311,1962 (Jay Ward)

	GD	VG	FN	VF	VF/NM	NM-
Four Color 1128 (#1) (8-10/60)	25	50	75	175	388	600
Four Color 1152 (12-2/61), 1166, 1208, 1275, 1311('62)	16	32	48	107	236	365

ROCKY HORROR PICTURE SHOW THE COMIC BOOK, THE
Caliber Press: Jul, 1990 - No. 3, Jan, 1991 ($2.95, mini-series, 52 pgs.)

	GD	VG	FN	VF	VF/NM	NM-
1-3: 1-Adapts cult film plus photos, etc., 1-2nd printing	1	2	3	5	6	8
...Collection ($4.95)	2	4	6	8	10	12

ROCKY JONES SPACE RANGER (See Space Adventures #15-18)

ROCKY JORDEN PRIVATE EYE (See Private Eye)

ROCKY LANE WESTERN (Allan Rocky Lane starred in Republic movies & TV for a short time as Allan Lane, Red Ryder & Rocky Lane) (See Black Jack Fawcett Movie Comics, Motion Picture Comics & Six-Gun Heroes)
Fawcett Publications/Charlton No. 56 on: May, 1949 - No. 87, Nov, 1959

	GD	VG	FN	VF	VF/NM	NM-
1 (36 pgs.)-Rocky, his stallion Black Jack, & Slim Pickens begin; photo-c begin, end #57; photo back-c	55	110	165	352	601	850
2 (36 pgs.)-Last photo back-c	22	44	66	132	216	300
3-5 (52 pgs.): 4-Captain Tootsie by Beck	17	34	51	98	154	210
6,10 (36 pgs.): 10-Complete western novelette "Badman's Reward"	14	28	42	76	108	140
7-9 (52 pgs.)	14	28	42	82	121	160
11-13,15-17,19,20 (52 pgs.): 15-Black Jack's Hitching Post begins, ends #25. 20-Last Slim Pickens	12	24	36	67	94	120
14,18 (36 pgs.)	10	20	30	58	79	100
21,23,24 (52 pgs.): 21-Dee Dickens begins, ends #55,57,65-68	10	20	30	58	79	100
22,25-28,30 (36 pgs. begin)	10	20	30	54	72	90
29-Classic complete novel "The Land of Missing Men" with hidden land of ancient temple ruins (r-in #65)	14	28	42	76	108	140
31-40	9	18	27	52	69	85
41-54	9	18	27	47	61	75
55-Last Fawcett issue (1/54)	9	18	27	52	69	85
56-1st Charlton issue (2/54)-Photo-c	14	28	42	82	121	160
57,60-Photo-c	10	20	30	54	72	90
58,59,61-64,66-78,80-86: 59-61-Young Falcon app. 64-Slim Pickens app. 66-68: Reprints #30,31,32	8	16	24	44	57	70
65-r/#29, "The Land of Missing Men"	9	18	27	50	65	80
79-Giant Edition (68 pgs.)	10	20	30	58	79	100
87-Last issue	9	18	27	52	69	85

NOTE: *Complete novels in #10, 14, 18, 22, 25, 30-32, 36, 38, 39, 49. Captain Tootsie in #4, 12, 20. Big Bow and Little Arrow in #11, 28, 63. Black Jack's Hitching Post in #15-25, 64, 73.*

ROCKY LANE WESTERN
AC Comics: 1989 ($2.50, B&W, one-shot?)
1-Photo-c; Giordano reprints — 4.00

Annual 1 (1991, $2.95, B&W, 44 pgs.)-photo front/back & inside-c; reprints — 4.00

ROD CAMERON WESTERN (Movie star)
Fawcett Publications: Feb, 1950 - No. 20, Apr, 1953

	GD	VG	FN	VF	VF/NM	NM-
1-Rod Cameron, his horse War Paint, & Sam The Sheriff begin; photo front/back-c begin	30	60	90	177	289	400
2	15	30	45	86	133	180
3-Novel length story "The Mystery of the Seven Cities of Cibola"	14	28	42	82	121	160
4-10: 9-Last photo back-c	12	24	36	69	97	125
11-19	10	20	30	58	79	100
20-Last issue & photo-c	11	22	33	62	86	110

NOTE: *Novel length stories in No. 1-8, 12-14.*

RODEO RYAN (See A-1 Comics #8)

ROGAN GOSH
DC Comics (Vertigo): 1994 ($6.95, one-shot)
nn-Peter Milligan scripts — 7.00

ROGER DODGER (Also in Exciting Comics #57 on)
Standard Comics: No. 5, Aug, 1952
5-Teen-age — 7 14 21 35 43 50

ROGER RABBIT (Also see Marvel Graphic Novel)
Disney Comics: June, 1990 - No. 18, Nov, 1991 ($1.50)
1-18-All new stories — 3.00
In 3-D 1 (1992, $2.50)-Sold at Wal-Mart?; w/glasses — 4.00

ROGER RABBIT'S TOONTOWN
Disney Comics: Aug, 1991 - No. 5, Dec, 1991 ($1.50)
1-5 — 3.00

ROGER ZELAZNY'S AMBER: THE GUNS OF AVALON
DC Comics: 1996 - No. 3, 1996 ($6.95, limited series)
1-3: Based on novel — 7.00

ROG 2000
Pacific Comics: June, 1982 ($2.95, 44 pgs., B&W, one-shot, magazine)

	GD	VG	FN	VF	VF/NM	NM-
nn-Byrne-c/a (r)	2	4	6	8	10	12
2nd printing (7/82)	1	2	3	4	5	7

ROG 2000
Fantagraphics Books: 1987 - No. 2, 1987 ($2.00, limited series)
1,2-Byrne-r — 3.00

ROGUE (From X-Men)
Marvel Comics: Jan, 1995 - No. 4, Apr, 1995 ($2.95, limited series)
1-4: 1-Gold foil logo — 4.00
TPB-($12.95) r/#1-4 — 13.00

ROGUE (Volume 2)
Marvel Comics: Sept, 2001 - No. 4, Dec, 2001 ($2.50, limited series)
1-4-Julie Bell painted-c/Lopresti-a; Rogue's early days with X-Men — 3.00

ROGUE (From X-Men)
Marvel Comics: Sept, 2004 - No. 12, Aug, 2005 ($2.99)
1-12: 1-Richards-a. 4-Gambit app. 11-Sunfire dies, Rogue absorbs his powers — 3.00
...: Going Rogue TPB (2005, $14.99) r/#1-6 — 15.00
...: Forget-Me-Not TPB (2006, $14.99) r/#7-12 — 15.00

ROGUE ANGEL: TELLER OF TALL TALES (Based on the Alex Archer novels)
IDW Publishing: Feb, 2008 - No. 5, Jun, 2008 ($3.99)
1-5-Annja Creed adventures; Barbara-Kesel-s/Renae De Liz-a — 4.00

ROGUES GALLERY
DC Comics: 1996 ($3.50, one-shot)
1-Pinups of DC villains by various artists — 4.00

ROGUE TROOPER
IDW Publishing: Feb, 2014 - Present ($3.99)
1-Ruckley-s/Ponticelli-a/Fabry-c — 4.00

ROGUES, THE (VILLAINS) (See The Flash)
DC Comics: Feb, 1998 ($1.95, one-shot)
1-Augustyn-s/Pearson-c — 3.00

ROKKIN
DC Comics (WildStorm): Sept, 2006 - No. 6, Feb, 2007 ($2.99, limited series)
1-6-Hartnell-s/Bradshaw-a — 3.00

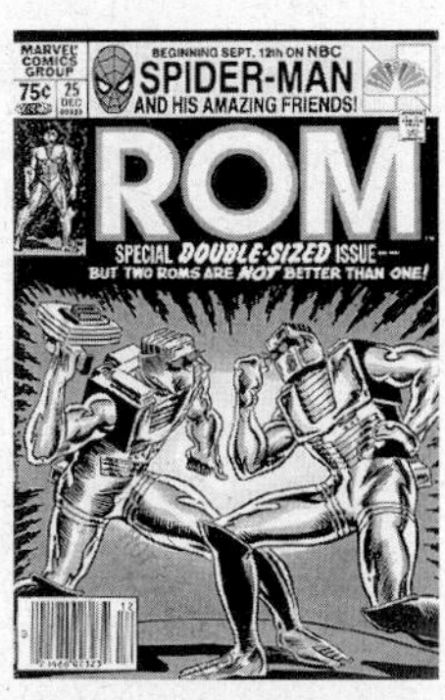

Rom #25 © Parker Bros.

Romantic Confessions #9 © HILL

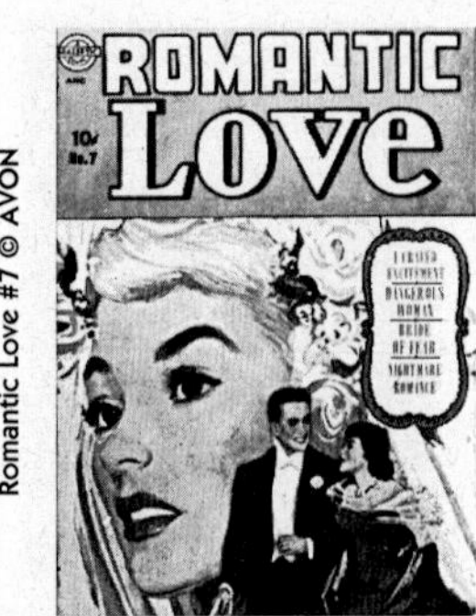

Romantic Love #7 © AVON

GD 2.0 | VG 4.0 | FN 6.0 | VF 8.0 | VF/NM 9.0 | NM- 9.2

ROLLING STONES: VOODOO LOUNGE
Marvel Comics: 1995 ($6.95, Prestige format, one-shot)
nn-Dave McKean-script/design/art 7.00

ROLY POLY COMIC BOOK
Green Publishing Co.: 1945 - No. 15, 1946 (MLJ reprints)
1-(No number on cover or indicia, "1945 issue" on cover) Red Rube & Steel Sterling begin; Sahle-c 34 68 102 206 336 465
6-The Blue Circle & The Steel Fist app. 21 42 63 126 206 285
10-Origin Red Rube retold; Steel Sterling story (Zip #41) 28 56 84 165 270 375
11,12: The Black Hood app. in both 21 42 63 126 206 285
14-Classic decapitation-c; the Black Hood app. 194 388 582 1242 2121 3000
15-The Blue Circle & The Steel Fist app.; cover exact swipe from Fox Blue Beetle #1 34 68 102 206 336 465

ROM (Based on the Parker Brothers toy)
Marvel Comics Group: Dec, 1979 - No. 75, Feb, 1986
1-Origin/1st app. 3 6 9 19 30 40
2-16,19-23,28-30: 5-Dr. Strange. 13-Saga of the Space Knights begins. 19-X-Men cameo. 23-Powerman & Iron Fist app. 1 2 3 5 6 8
17,18-X-Men app. 2 4 6 9 12 15
24-27: 24-F.F. cameo; Skrulls, Nova & The New Champions app. 25-Double size. 26,27-Galactus app. 1 2 3 5 7 9
31-49,51-60: 31,32-Brotherhood of Evil Mutants app. 32-X-Men cameo. 34,35-Sub-Mariner app. 41,42-Dr. Strange app. 56,57-Alpha Flight app. 58,59-Ant-Man app. 6.00
50-Skrulls app. (52 pgs.) Pin-ups by Konkle, Austin 1 2 3 4 5 7
61-74: 65-West Coast Avengers & Beta Ray Bill app. 65,66-X-Men app. 6.00
75-Last issue 2 4 6 9 12 15
Annual 1-4: (1982-85, 52 pgs.) 6.00
NOTE: **Austin** *c-3i, 18i, 61i.* **Byrne** *a-74i; c-56, 57, 74.* **Ditko** *a-59-75p, Annual 4.* **Golden** *c-7-12, 19.* **Guice** *a-61i; c-55, 58, 60p, 70p.* **Layton** *a-59i, 72i; c-15, 59i, 69.* **Miller** *c-2p?, 3p, 17p, 18p.* **Russell** *a(i)-64, 65, 67, 69, 71, 75; c-64, 65i, 66, 71i, 75.* **Severin** *c-41p.* **Sienkiewicz** *a-53i; c-46, 47, 52-54, 68, 71p, Annual 2.* **Simonson** *c-18.* **P. Smith** *c-59p.* **Starlin** *c-67.* **Zeck** *c-50.*

ROMANCE (See True Stories of...)

ROMANCE AND CONFESSION STORIES (See Giant Comics Edition)
St. John Publishing Co.: No date (1949) (25¢, 100 pgs.)
1-Baker-c/a; remaindered St. John love comics 65 130 195 416 708 1000

ROMANCE DIARY
Marvel Comics (CDS)(CLDS): Dec, 1949 - No. 2, Mar, 1950
1,2-Photo-c 18 36 54 103 162 220

ROMANCE OF FLYING, THE
David McKay Publications: 1942
Feature Books 33 (nn)-WW II photos 15 30 45 88 137 185

ROMANCES OF MOLLY MANTON (See Molly Manton)

ROMANCES OF NURSE HELEN GRANT, THE
Atlas Comics (VPI): Aug, 1957
1 11 22 33 62 86 110

ROMANCES OF THE WEST (Becomes Romantic Affairs #3?)
Marvel Comics (SPC): Nov, 1949 - No. 2, Mar, 1950 (52 pgs.)
1-Movie photo-c of Yvonne DeCarlo & Howard Duff (Calamity Jane & Sam Bass) 24 48 72 142 234 325
2-Photo-c 15 30 45 88 137 185

ROMANCE STORIES OF TRUE LOVE (Formerly True Love Problems & Advice Illustrated)
Harvey Publications: No. 45, 5/57 - No. 50, 3/58; No. 51, 9/58 - No. 52, 11/58
45-51: 45,46,48-50-Powell-a 6 12 18 31 38 45
52-Matt Baker-a 9 18 27 47 61 75

ROMANCE TALES (Formerly Western Winners #6?)
Marvel Comics (CDS): No. 7, Oct, 1949 - No. 9, April, 1950 (7-9: photo-c)
7 15 30 45 90 140 190
8,9: 8-Everett-a 12 24 36 67 94 120

ROMANCE TRAIL
National Periodical Publications: July-Aug, 1949 - No. 6, May-June, 1950 (All photo-c & 52 pgs.)
1-Kinstler, Toth-a; Jimmy Wakely photo-c 57 114 171 362 619 875
2-Kinstler-a; Jim Bannon photo-c 32 64 96 188 307 425
3-Tex Williams photo-c; Kinstler, Toth-a 34 68 102 199 325 450
4-Jim Bannon as Red Ryder photo-c; Toth-a 24 48 72 144 237 330
5,6: Photo-c on both. 5-Kinstler-a 22 44 66 132 216 300

ROMAN HOLIDAYS, THE (TV)
Gold Key: Feb, 1973 - No. 4, Nov, 1973 (Hanna-Barbera)
1 4 8 12 27 44 60
2-4 3 6 9 17 26 35

ROMANTIC ADVENTURES (My... #49-67, covers only)
American Comics Group (B&I Publ. Co.): Mar-Apr, 1949 - No. 67, July, 1956 (Becomes My... #68 on)
1 20 40 60 120 195 270
2 13 26 39 74 105 135
3-10 11 22 33 60 83 105
11-20 (4/52) 10 20 30 54 72 90
21-45,51,52: 52-Last Pre-code (2/55) 9 18 27 50 65 80
46-49-3-D effect-c/stories (TrueVision) 14 28 42 82 121 160
50-Classic cover/story "Love of A Lunatic" 14 28 42 80 115 150
53-67 8 16 24 44 57 70
NOTE: *#1-23, 52 pgs.* **Shelly** *a-40. Whitney c/art in many issues.*

ROMANTIC AFFAIRS (Formerly Molly Manton's Romances #2 and/or Romances of the West #2 and/or Our Love #2?)
Marvel Comics (SPC): No. 3, Mar, 1950
3-Photo-c from Molly Manton's Romances #2 12 24 36 67 94 120

ROMANTIC CONFESSIONS
Hillman Periodicals: Oct, 1949 - V3#1, Apr-May, 1953
V1#1-McWilliams-a 20 40 60 114 182 250
2-Briefer-a; negligee panels 12 24 36 69 97 125
3-12 11 22 33 60 83 105
V2#1,2,4-8,10-12: 2-McWilliams-a 10 20 30 56 76 95
3-Krigstein-a 11 22 33 62 86 110
9-One pg. Frazetta ad 10 20 30 56 76 95
V3#1 10 20 30 54 72 90

ROMANTIC HEARTS
Story Comics/Master/Merit Pubs.: Mar, 1951 - No. 10, Oct, 1952; July, 1953 - No. 12, July, 1955
1(3/51) (1st Series) 16 32 48 94 147 200
2 10 20 30 58 79 100
3-10: Cameron-a 10 20 30 54 72 90
1(7/53) (2nd Series)-Some say #11 on-c 12 24 36 67 94 120
2 9 18 27 52 69 85
3-12 9 18 27 47 61 75

ROMANTIC LOVE
Avon Periodicals/Realistic (No #14-19): 9-10/49 - #3, 1-2/50; #4, 2-3/51 - #13, 10/52; #20, 3-4/54 - #23, 9-10/54
1-c-/Avon paperback #252 37 74 111 222 361 500
2-5: 3-c-/paperback Novel Library #12. 4-c-/paperback Diversey Prize Novel #5. 5-c-/paperback Novel Library #34 22 44 66 132 216 300
6- "Thrill Crazy" marijuana story; c-/Avon paperback #207; Kinstler-a 32 64 96 192 314 435
7,8: 8-Astarita-a(2) 21 42 63 126 206 285
9-12: 9-c-/paperback Novel Library #41; Kinstler-a. 10-c-/Avon paperback #212. 11-c-/paperback Novel Library #17; Kinstler-a. 12-c-/paperback Novel Library #13 23 46 69 136 223 310
13,21-23: 22,23-Kinstler-c 21 42 63 126 206 285
20-Kinstler-c/a 22 44 66 132 216 300
nn(1-3/53)(Realistic-r) 15 30 45 85 130 175
NOTE: **Astarita** *a-7, 10, 11, 21. Painted c-1-3, 5, 7-11, 13. Photo c-4, 6.*

ROMANTIC LOVE
Quality Comics Group: 1963-1964
I.W. Reprint #2,3,8,11: 2-r/Romantic Love #2 2 4 6 11 16 20

ROMANTIC MARRIAGE (Cinderella Love #25 on)
Ziff-Davis/St. John No. 18 on (#1-8: 52 pgs.): #1-3 (1950, no months); #4, 5-6/51 - #17, 9/52; #18, 9/53 - #24, 9/54
1-Photo-c; Cary Grant/Betsy Drake photo back-c. 23 46 69 136 223 310
2-Painted-c; Anderson-a (also #15) 15 30 45 88 137 185
3-9: 3,4,8,9-Painted-c; 5-7-Photo-c 15 30 45 83 124 165
10-Unusual format; front-c is a painted-c; back-c is a photo-c complete with logo, price, etc. 23 46 69 136 223 310
11-17 13-Photo-c. 15-Signed story by Anderson. 17-(9/52)-Last Z-D issue 14 28 42 80 115 150
18-22,24: 20-Photo-c 14 28 42 80 115 150
23-Baker-c; all stories are reprinted from #15 16 32 48 94 147 200

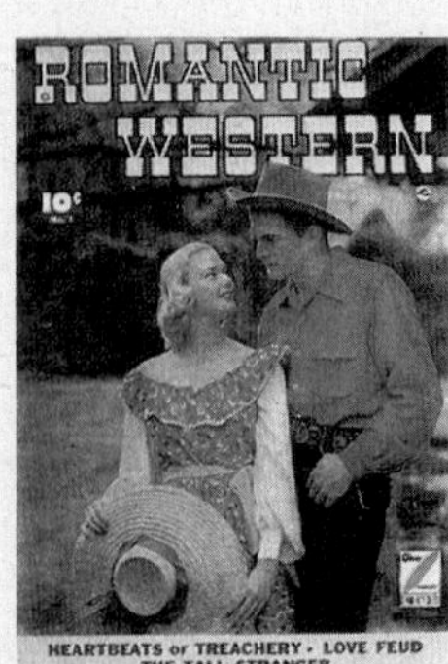

Romantic Western #1 © FAW

Ronin #4 © Frank Miller

Route 666 #21 © CRO

ROMANTIC PICTURE NOVELETTES
Magazine Enterprises: 1946

	GD 2.0	VG 4.0	FN 6.0	VF 8.0	VF/NM 9.0	NM- 9.2
1-Mary Worth-r; Creig Flessel-c	17	34	51	98	154	210

ROMANTIC SECRETS (Becomes Time For Love)
Fawcett/Charlton Comics No. 5 (10/55) on: Sept, 1949 - No. 39, 4/53; No. 5, 10/55 - No. 52, 11/64 (#1-39: photo-c)

	GD 2.0	VG 4.0	FN 6.0	VF 8.0	VF/NM 9.0	NM- 9.2
1-(52 pg. issues begin, end #?)	18	36	54	103	162	220
2,3	11	22	33	62	86	110
4,9-Evans-a	12	24	36	67	94	120
5-8,10(9/50)	9	18	27	52	69	85
11-23	9	18	27	47	61	75
24-Evans-a	9	18	27	52	69	85
25-39('53)	8	16	24	44	57	70
5 (Charlton, 2nd Series)(10/55, formerly Negro Romances #4)	10	20	30	58	79	100
6-10	8	16	24	44	57	70
11-20	4	8	12	22	35	48
21-35	3	6	9	19	30	40
36-52('64)	3	6	9	16	23	30

NOTE: **Bailey** a-20. **Powell** a(1st series)-5, 7, 10, 12, 16, 17, 20, 26, 29, 33, 34, 36, 37. **Sekowsky** a-26. **Swayze** a(1st series)-16, 18, 19, 23, 26-28, 31, 32, 39.

ROMANTIC STORY (Cowboy Love #28 on)
Fawcett/Charlton Comics No. 23 on: 11/49 - #22, Sum, 1953; #23, 5/54 - #27, 12/54; #28, 8/55 - #130, 11/73

	GD 2.0	VG 4.0	FN 6.0	VF 8.0	VF/NM 9.0	NM- 9.2
1-Photo-c begin, end #24; 52 pgs. begins	18	36	54	103	162	220
2	11	22	33	62	86	110
3-5	10	20	30	54	72	90
6-14	9	18	27	50	65	80
15-Evans-a	10	20	30	54	72	90
16-22(Sum, '53; last Fawcett issue). 21-Toth-a?	8	16	24	42	54	65
23-39: 26,29-Wood swipes	7	14	21	37	46	55
40-(100 pgs.)	11	22	33	64	90	115
41-50	3	6	9	20	31	42
51-80: 57-Hypo needle story	3	6	9	16	23	30
81-99	2	4	6	10	14	18
100	2	4	6	13	28	22
101-130: 120-Bobby Sherman pin-up	2	4	6	9	12	15

NOTE: **Jim Aparo** a-94. **Powell** a-7, 8, 16, 20, 30. **Marcus Swayze** a-2, 12, 20, 32.

ROMANTIC THRILLS (See Fox Giants)

ROMANTIC WESTERN
Fawcett Publications: Winter, 1949 - No. 3, June, 1950 (All Photo-c)

	GD 2.0	VG 4.0	FN 6.0	VF 8.0	VF/NM 9.0	NM- 9.2
1	22	44	66	128	209	290
2-(Spr/50)-Williamson, McWilliams-a	20	40	60	114	182	250
3	15	30	45	85	130	175

ROMEO TUBBS (...That Lovable Teenager; formerly My Secret Life)
Fox Feature Syndicate/Green Publ. Co. No. 27: No. 26, 5/50 - No. 28, 7/50; No. 1, 1950; No. 27, 12/52

	GD 2.0	VG 4.0	FN 6.0	VF 8.0	VF/NM 9.0	NM- 9.2
26-Teen-age	12	24	36	67	94	120
28 (7/50)	11	22	33	60	83	105
27 (12/52)-Contains Pedro on inside; Wood-a (exist?)	15	30	45	85	130	175

RONALD McDONALD (TV)
Charlton Press: Sept, 1970 - No. 4, March, 1971

	GD 2.0	VG 4.0	FN 6.0	VF 8.0	VF/NM 9.0	NM- 9.2
1-Bill Yates-a in all	7	14	21	48	89	130
2-4: 2 & 3 both dated Jan, 1971	5	10	15	30	50	70
V2#1-4-Special reprint for McDonald systems; new cover art on each; "Not for resale" on cover	5	10	15	34	60	85

RONIN
DC Comics: July, 1983 - No. 6, Aug, 1984 ($2.50, limited series, 52 pgs.)

	GD 2.0	VG 4.0	FN 6.0	VF 8.0	VF/NM 9.0	NM- 9.2
1-5-Frank Miller-c/a/scripts in all	2	3	4	6	8	10
6-Scarcer; has fold-out poster.	2	4	6	8	10	12
Trade paperback (1987, $12.95)-Reprints #1-6						18.00

RONNA
Knight Press: Apr, 1997 ($2.95, B&W, one-shot)

	GD 2.0	VG 4.0	FN 6.0	VF 8.0	VF/NM 9.0	NM- 9.2
1-Beau Smith-s						3.00

ROOK (See Eerie Magazine & Warren Presents: The Rook)
Warren Publications: Oct, 1979 - No. 14, April, 1982 (B&W magazine)

	GD 2.0	VG 4.0	FN 6.0	VF 8.0	VF/NM 9.0	NM- 9.2
1-Nino-a/Corben-c; with 8 pg. color insert	3	6	9	16	23	30
2-4,6,7: 2-Voltar by Alcala begins. 3,4-Toth-a	2	4	6	9	13	16
5,8-14: 11-Zorro-s. 12-14-Eagle by Severin	2	4	6	9	13	16

ROOK
Harris Comics: No. 0, Jun, 1995 - No. 4, 1995 ($2.95)

	GD 2.0	VG 4.0	FN 6.0	VF 8.0	VF/NM 9.0	NM- 9.2
0-4: 0-short stories (3) w/preview. 4-Brereton-c.						3.00

ROOKIE COP (Formerly Crime and Justice?)
Charlton Comics: No. 27, Nov, 1955 - No. 33, Aug, 1957

	GD 2.0	VG 4.0	FN 6.0	VF 8.0	VF/NM 9.0	NM- 9.2
27	9	18	27	47	61	75
28-33	6	12	18	31	38	45

ROOM 222 (TV)
Dell Publishing Co.: Jan, 1970; No. 2, May, 1970 - No. 4, Jan, 1971

	GD 2.0	VG 4.0	FN 6.0	VF 8.0	VF/NM 9.0	NM- 9.2
1	5	10	15	31	53	75
2-4-Photo-c. 3-Marijuana story. 4 r/#1	3	6	9	21	34	45

ROOTIE KAZOOTIE (TV)(See 3-D-ell)
Dell Publishing Co.: No. 415, Aug, 1952 - No. 6, Oct-Dec, 1954

	GD 2.0	VG 4.0	FN 6.0	VF 8.0	VF/NM 9.0	NM- 9.2
Four Color 415 (#1)	9	18	27	57	111	165
Four Color 459,502(#2,3), 4(4-6/54)-6	6	12	18	41	76	110

ROOTS OF THE SWAMP THING
DC Comics: July, 1986 - No.5, Nov, 1986 ($2.00, Baxter paper, 52 pgs.)

	GD 2.0	VG 4.0	FN 6.0	VF 8.0	VF/NM 9.0	NM- 9.2
1-5: r/Swamp Thing #1-10 by Wrightson & House of Mystery-r. 1-new Wrightson-c (2-5 reprinted covers).						5.00

ROSE (See Bone)
Cartoon Books: Nov, 2000 - No. 3, Feb, 2002 ($5.95, lim. series, square-bound)

	GD 2.0	VG 4.0	FN 6.0	VF 8.0	VF/NM 9.0	NM- 9.2
1-3-Prequel to Bone; Jeff Smith-s/Charles Vess painted-a/c						6.00
HC (2001, $29.95) r/#1-3; new Vess cover painting						30.00
SC (2002, $19.95) r/#1-3; new Vess cover painting						20.00
1-($6.00)-Blood & Glory Edition						6.00

ROSE AND THORN
DC Comics: Feb, 2004 - No. 6, July, 2004 ($2.95, limited series)

	GD 2.0	VG 4.0	FN 6.0	VF 8.0	VF/NM 9.0	NM- 9.2
1-6-Simone-s/Melo-a/Hughes-c						3.00

ROSWELL: LITTLE GREEN MAN (See Simpsons Comics #19-22)
Bongo Comics: 1996 - No. 6 ($2.95, quarterly)

	GD 2.0	VG 4.0	FN 6.0	VF 8.0	VF/NM 9.0	NM- 9.2
1-6						4.00
...Walks Among Us ('97, $12.95, TPB) r/ #1-3 & Simpsons flip books						13.00

ROUND TABLE OF AMERICA: PERSONALITY CRISIS (See Big Bang Comics)
Image Comics: Aug, 2005 ($3.50, one-shot)

	GD 2.0	VG 4.0	FN 6.0	VF 8.0	VF/NM 9.0	NM- 9.2
1-Carlos Rodriguez-a/Pedro Angosto-s						3.50

ROUNDUP (...Western Crime Stories)
D. S. Publishing Co.: July-Aug, 1948 - No. 5, Mar-Apr, 1949 (All 52 pgs.)

	GD 2.0	VG 4.0	FN 6.0	VF 8.0	VF/NM 9.0	NM- 9.2
1-Kiefer-a	19	38	57	111	176	240
2-5: 2-Marijuana drug mention story	15	30	45	83	124	165

ROUTE 666
CrossGeneration Comics: July, 2002 - No. 22, Jun, 2004 ($2.95)

	GD 2.0	VG 4.0	FN 6.0	VF 8.0	VF/NM 9.0	NM- 9.2
1-22-Bedard-s/Moline-a in most. 5-Richards-a. 15-McCrea-a						3.00
...: Highway to Horror (4/03, $15.95, TPB) r/#1-6						16.00
Vol. 2: Three-Ring Circus (2003, $15.95) r/#7-12						16.00

ROYAL ROY
Marvel Comics (Star Comics): May, 1985 - No.6, Mar, 1986 (Children's book)

	GD 2.0	VG 4.0	FN 6.0	VF 8.0	VF/NM 9.0	NM- 9.2
1-6						4.00

ROYALS, THE: MASTERS OF WAR
DC Comics (Vertigo): Apr, 2014 - No. 6 ($2.99, limited series)

	GD 2.0	VG 4.0	FN 6.0	VF 8.0	VF/NM 9.0	NM- 9.2
1,2-Rob Williams-s/Simon Coleby-a/c; super-powered Royal families during WWII						3.00

ROY CAMPANELLA, BASEBALL HERO
Fawcett Publications: 1950 (Brooklyn Dodgers)

	GD 2.0	VG 4.0	FN 6.0	VF 8.0	VF/NM 9.0	NM- 9.2
nn-Photo-c; life story	61	122	183	390	670	950

ROY ROGERS (See March of Comics #17, 35, 47, 62, 68, 73, 77, 86, 91, 100, 105, 116, 121, 131, 136, 146, 151, 161, 167, 176, 191, 206, 221, 236, 250)

ROY ROGERS AND TRIGGER
Gold Key: Apr, 1967

	GD 2.0	VG 4.0	FN 6.0	VF 8.0	VF/NM 9.0	NM- 9.2
1-Photo-c; reprints	4	8	12	27	44	60

ROY ROGERS ANNUAL
Wilson Publ. Co., Toronto/Dell: 1947 ("Giant Edition" on-c)(132 pgs., 50¢)

nn-Five known copies. Front and back cover art are from Roy Rogers #2. Stories reprinted from Roy Rogers #2, Four Color #137 and Four Color #153. (A copy in VG/FN was sold in 1986 for $400, in 1996 for $1200 & in 2000 for $1500; a FN+ sold for $1,650;

Roy Rogers Comics #15 © Roy Rogers

Rulah Jungle Goddess #18 © FOX

Runaways #25 © MAR

a GD sold for $448 in 2008 and a FN sold for $717 in 2009.)

ROY ROGERS COMICS (See Western Roundup under Dell Giants)
Dell Publishing Co.: No. 38, 4/44 - No. 177, 12/47 (#38-166: 52 pgs.)

	GD 2.0	VG 4.0	FN 6.0	VF 8.0	VF/NM 9.0	NM- 9.2
Four Color 38 (1944)-49 pg. story; photo front/back-c on all 4-Color issues (1st western comic with photo-c)	152	306	456	1216	2733	4250
Four Color 63 (1945)-Color photos on all four-c	37	74	111	274	612	950
Four Color 86,95 (1945)	27	54	81	189	420	650
Four Color 109 (1946)	20	40	60	138	307	475
Four Color 117,124,137,144	16	32	48	110	243	375
Four Color 153,160,166: 166-48 pg. story	15	30	45	100	220	340
Four Color 177 (36 pgs.)-32 pg. story	14	28	42	94	207	320
HC (Dark Horse Books, 8/08, $49.95) r/Four Color #38,63,86,95,109; Roy Rogers Jr intro.						50.00

ROY ROGERS COMICS (...& Trigger #92(8/55)-on)(Roy starred in Republic movies, radio & TV) (Singing cowboy) (Also see Dale Evans, It Really Happened #8, Queen of the West Dale Evans, & Roy Rogers' Trigger)
Dell Publishing Co.: Jan, 1948 - No. 145, Sept-Oct, 1961 (#1-19: 36 pgs.)

	GD 2.0	VG 4.0	FN 6.0	VF 8.0	VF/NM 9.0	NM- 9.2
1-Roy, his horse Trigger, & Chuck Wagon Charley's Tales begin; photo-c begin, end #145	56	112	168	448	1012	1575
2	20	40	60	135	300	465
3-5	14	28	42	96	211	325
6-10	12	24	36	80	173	265
11-19: 19-Chuckwagon Charley's Tales ends	10	20	30	68	144	220
20 (52 pgs.)-Trigger feature begins, ends #46	10	20	30	69	147	225
21-30 (52 pgs.)	9	18	27	60	120	180
31-46 (52 pgs.): 37-X-Mas-c	8	16	24	51	96	140
47-56 (36 pgs.): 47-Chuck Wagon Charley's Tales returns, ends #133. 49-X-mas-c. 55-Last photo back-c	6	12	18	40	73	105
57 (52 pgs.)-Heroin drug propaganda story	6	12	18	41	76	110
58-70 (52 pgs.): 58-Heroin drug use/dealing story. 61-X-Mas-c	6	12	18	40	73	105
71-80 (52 pgs.): 73-X-Mas-c	5	10	15	35	63	90
81-91 (36 pgs. #81-on): 85-X-Mas-c	5	10	15	34	60	85
92-99,101-110,112-118: 92-Title changed to Roy Rogers and Trigger (8/55)	5	10	15	33	57	80
100-Trigger feature returns, ends #131	6	12	18	37	66	95
111,119-124-Toth-a	6	12	18	38	69	100
125-131: 125-Toth-a (1 pg.)	5	10	15	31	53	75
132-144-Manning-a. 132-1st Dale Evans-sty by Russ Manning. 138,144-Dale Evans featured	5	10	15	34	60	85
145-Last issue	6	12	18	40	73	105

NOTE: ***Buscema** a-74-108(2 stories each). **Manning** a-123, 124, 132-144. **Marsh** a-110. Photo back-c No. 1-9, 11-35, 38-55.*

ROY ROGERS' TRIGGER
Dell Publishing Co.: No. 329, May, 1951 - No. 17, June-Aug, 1955

	GD 2.0	VG 4.0	FN 6.0	VF 8.0	VF/NM 9.0	NM- 9.2
Four Color 329 (#1)-Painted-c	12	24	36	84	185	285
2 (9-11/51)-Photo-c	9	18	27	63	129	195
3-5: 3-Painted-c begin, end #17, most by S. Savitt	6	12	18	37	66	95
6-17: Title merges with Roy Rogers after #17	5	10	15	31	53	75

ROY ROGERS WESTERN CLASSICS
AC Comics: 1989 -No. 4 ($2.95/$3.95, 44pgs.) (24 pgs. color, 16 pgs. B&W)

	GD 2.0	VG 4.0	FN 6.0	VF 8.0	VF/NM 9.0	NM- 9.2
1-4: 1-Dale Evans-r by Manning, Trigger-r by Buscema; photo covers & interior photos by Roy & Dale. 2-Buscema-r (3); photo-c & B&W photos inside. 3-Dale Evans-r by Manning; Trigger-r by Buscema plus other Buscema-r; photo-c						4.00

RUDOLPH, THE RED-NOSED REINDEER
National Per. Publ.: 1950 - No. 13, Winter, 1962-63 (Issues are not numbered)

	GD 2.0	VG 4.0	FN 6.0	VF 8.0	VF/NM 9.0	NM- 9.2
1950 issue (#1); Grossman-c/a in all	24	48	72	140	230	320
1951-53 issues (3 total)	15	30	45	83	124	165
1954/55, 55/56, 56/57	14	28	42	78	112	145
1957/58, 58/59, 59/60, 60/61, 61/62	7	14	21	48	89	130
1962/63 (rare)(84 pgs.)(shows "Annual" in indicia)	10	20	30	70	150	230

NOTE: *13 total issues published. Has games & puzzles also.*

RUDOLPH, THE RED-NOSED REINDEER (Also see Limited Collectors' Edition C-20, C-24, C-33, C-42, C-50; and All-New Collectors' Edition C-53 & C-60)
National Per. Publ.: Christmas 1972 (Treasury-size)

	GD 2.0	VG 4.0	FN 6.0	VF 8.0	VF/NM 9.0	NM- 9.2
nn-Precursor to Limited Collectors' Edition title (scarce) (implied to be Lim. Coll .Ed. C-20)	19	38	57	131	291	450

RUFF AND REDDY (TV)
Dell Publ. Co.: No. 937, 9/58 - No. 12, 1-3/62 (Hanna-Barbera)(#9 on: 15¢)

	GD 2.0	VG 4.0	FN 6.0	VF 8.0	VF/NM 9.0	NM- 9.2
Four Color 937(#1)(1st Hanna-Barbera comic book)	10	20	30	67	141	215
Four Color 981,1038	7	14	21	44	82	120
4(1-3/60)-12: 8-Last 10¢ issue	6	12	18	38	69	100

RUGGED ACTION (Strange Stories of Suspense #5 on)
Atlas Comics (CSI): Dec, 1954 - No. 4, June, 1955

	GD 2.0	VG 4.0	FN 6.0	VF 8.0	VF/NM 9.0	NM- 9.2
1-Brodsky-c	15	30	45	83	124	165
2-4: 2-Last precode (2/55)	11	22	33	62	86	110

NOTE: ***Ayers** a-2, 3. **Maneely** c-2, 3. **Severin** a-2.*

RUINS
Marvel Comics (Alterniverse): July, 1995 - No. 2, Sept, 1995 ($5.00, painted, limited series)

	GD 2.0	VG 4.0	FN 6.0	VF 8.0	VF/NM 9.0	NM- 9.2
1,2: Phil Sheldon from Marvels; Warren Ellis scripts; acetate-c						6.00
Reprint (2009, $4.99) r/#1,2; cover gallery						5.00

RULAH JUNGLE GODDESS (Formerly Zoot; I Loved #28 on) (Also see All Top Comics & Terrors of the Jungle)
Fox Features Syndicate: No. 17, Aug, 1948 - No. 27, June, 1949

	GD 2.0	VG 4.0	FN 6.0	VF 8.0	VF/NM 9.0	NM- 9.2
17	139	278	417	890	1520	2150
18-Classic girl-fight interior splash	86	172	258	546	936	1325
19,20	77	154	231	493	847	1200
21-Used in **SOTI**, pg. 388,389	81	162	243	518	884	1250
22-Used in **SOTI**, pg. 22,23	81	162	243	518	884	1250
23-27	58	116	174	371	636	900

NOTE: ***Kamen** c-17-19, 21, 22.*

RUNAWAY, THE (See Movie Classics)

RUNAWAYS
Marvel Comics: July, 2003 - No. 18, Nov, 2004 ($2.95/$2.25/$2.99)

	GD 2.0	VG 4.0	FN 6.0	VF 8.0	VF/NM 9.0	NM- 9.2
1-($2.95) Vaughan-s/Alphona-a/Jo Chen-c						4.00
2-9-($2.50)						3.00
10-18-($2.99) 11,12-Miyazawa-a; Cloak and Dagger app. 16-The mole revealed						3.00
Hardcover (2005, $34.99) oversized r/#1-18; proposal & sketch pages; Vaughan intro.						35.00
Marvel Age Runaways Vol. 1: Pride and Joy (2004, $7.99, digest size) r/#1-6						8.00
...Vol. 2: Teenage Wasteland (2004, $7.99, digest size) r/#7-12						8.00
...Vol. 3: The Good Die Young (2004, $7.99, digest size) r/#13-18						8.00

RUNAWAYS (Also see X-Men/Runaways 2006 FCBD Edition in the Promotional Section)
Marvel Comics: Apr, 2005 - No. 30, Aug, 2008 ($2.99)

	GD 2.0	VG 4.0	FN 6.0	VF 8.0	VF/NM 9.0	NM- 9.2
1-24: 1-6-Vaughan-s/Alphona-a/Jo Chen-c. 7,8-Miyazawa-a/Bachalo-c. 11-Spider-Man app. 12-New Avengers app. 18-Gert killed						3.00
25-30-Joss Whedon-s/Michael Ryan-a. 25-Punisher app.						3.00
...: Dead End Kids HC (2008, $19.99) r/#25-30						20.00
... Saga (2007, $3.99) re-caps the 2 series thru #24; 4 new pages w/Ramos-a; Ramos-c						4.00
Hardcover (2006, $24.99) oversized r/#1-12 & X-Men/Runaways; script & sketch pages						25.00
Hardcover Vol. 3 (2007, $24.99) oversized r/#13-24; sketch pages						25.00
...Vol. 4: True Believers (2006, $7.99, digest size) r/#1-6						8.00
...Vol. 5: Escape To New York (2006, $7.99, digest size) r/#7-12						8.00
...Vol. 6: Parental Guidance (2006, $7.99, digest size) r/#13-18						8.00

RUNAWAYS (3rd series)
Marvel Comics: Oct, 2008 - No. 14, Nov, 2009 ($2.99/$3.99)

	GD 2.0	VG 4.0	FN 6.0	VF 8.0	VF/NM 9.0	NM- 9.2
1-9,11-14: 1-6-Terry Moore-s/Humberto Ramos-a/c. 7-9-Miyazawa-a						3.00
10-($3.99) Wolverine & the X-Men app.; Yost & Asmus-s; Pichelli & Rios-a; Lafuente-c						4.00

RUN BABY RUN
Logos International: 1974 (39¢, Christian religious)

	GD 2.0	VG 4.0	FN 6.0	VF 8.0	VF/NM 9.0	NM- 9.2
nn-By Tony Tallarico from Nicky Cruz's book	2	4	6	11	16	20

RUN, BUDDY, RUN (TV)
Gold Key: June, 1967 (Photo-c)

	GD 2.0	VG 4.0	FN 6.0	VF 8.0	VF/NM 9.0	NM- 9.2
1 (10204-706)	3	6	9	17	26	35

RUNE (See Curse of Rune, Sludge & all other Ultraverse titles for previews)
Malibu Comics (Ultraverse): 1994 - No. 9, Apr, 1995 ($1.95)

	GD 2.0	VG 4.0	FN 6.0	VF 8.0	VF/NM 9.0	NM- 9.2
0-Obtained by sending coupons from 11 comics; came w/Solution #0, poster, temporary tattoo, card	1	2	3	5	6	8
1,2,4-9: 1-Barry Windsor-Smith-c/a/stories begin, ends #6. 5-1st app. of Gemini. 6-Prime & Mantra app.						3.00
1-(1/94)-"Ashcan" edition flip book w/Wrath #1						3.00
1-Ultra 5000 Limited silver foil edition						6.00
3-(3/94, $3.50, 68 pgs.)-Flip book w/Ultraverse Premiere #1						4.00
Giant Size 1 ($2.50, 44 pgs.)-B.Smith story & art.						4.00

RUNE (2nd Series)(Formerly Curse of Rune)(See Ultraverse Unlimited #1)
Malibu Comics (Ultraverse): Infinity, Sept, 1995 - V2#7, Apr, 1996 ($1.50)

	GD 2.0	VG 4.0	FN 6.0	VF 8.0	VF/NM 9.0	NM- 9.2
Infinity, V2#1-7: Infinity-Black September tie-in; black-c & painted-c exist. 1,3-7-Marvel's Adam Warlock app; regular & painted-c exist. 2-Flip book w/ "Phoenix Resurrection" Pt. 6						3.00
...Vs. Venom 1 (12/95, $3.95)						4.00

Ruse #4 © MAR

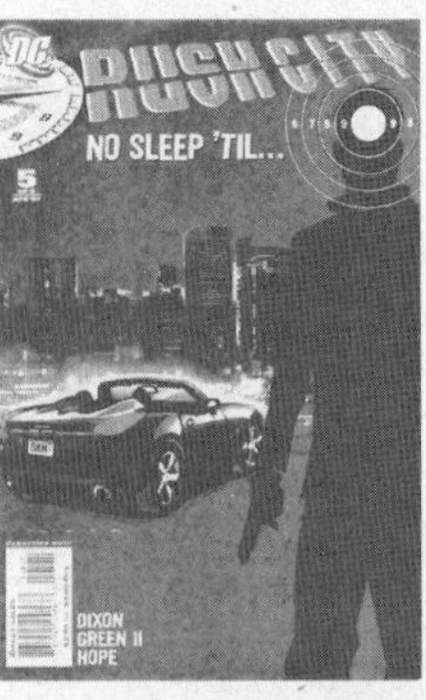

Rush City #5 © DC

Sabrina the Teenage Witch #9 © AP

	GD 2.0	VG 4.0	FN 6.0	VF 8.0	VF/NM 9.0	NM- 9.2

RUNE: HEARTS OF DARKNESS
Malibu Comics (Ultraverse): Sept, 1996 - No. 3, Nov, 1996 ($1.50, lim. series)

1-3: Moench scripts & Kyle Hotz-c/a; flip books w/6 pg. Rune story by the Pander Bros. 3.00

RUNE/SILVER SURFER
Marvel Comics/Malibu Comics (Ultraverse): Apr, 1995 ($5.95/$2.95, one-shot)

1 ($5.95, direct market)-BWS-c 6.00
1 ($2.95, newstand)-BWS-c 3.00
1-Collector's limited edition 6.00

RUSE (Also see Archard's Agents)
CrossGeneration Comics: Nov, 2001 - No. 26, Jan, 2004 ($2.95)

1-Waid-s/Guice & Perkins-a 5.00
2-26: 6-Jeff Johnson-a. 11,15-Paul Ryan-a. 12-Last Waid-s 3.00
Enter the Detective Vol. 1 TPB (2002, $15.95) r/#1-6; Guice-c 16.00
...: The Silent Partner Vol. 2 (3/03, $15.95, TPB) r/#7-12 16.00
...: Criminal Intent Vol. 3 ('03, $15.95, TPB) r/#13-18 16.00
Traveler 1,2 ($9.95): Digest-size editions of the TPBs 10.00

RUSE
Marvel Comics: May, 2011 - No. 4 ($2.99, limited series)

1-4-Waid-s/Guice-c. 1,3,4-Pierfederici-a 3.00

RUSH CITY
DC Comics: Sept, 2006 - No. 6, May, 2007 ($2.99, limited series)

1-6: 1-Dixon-s/Green-a/Jock-c. 2,3-Black Canary app. 3.00

RUSTLERS, THE (See Zane Grey Four Color 532)

RUSTY, BOY DETECTIVE
Good Comics/Lev Gleason: Mar-April, 1955 - No. 5, Nov, 1955

	GD	VG	FN	VF	VF/NM	NM-
1-Bob Wood, Carl Hubbell-a begins	9	18	27	47	61	75
2-5	6	12	18	31	38	45

RUSTY COMICS (Formerly Kid Movie Comics; Rusty and Her Family #21, 22; The Kelleys #23 on; see Millie The Model)
Marvel Comics (HPC): No. 12, Apr, 1947 - No. 22, Sept, 1949

	GD	VG	FN	VF	VF/NM	NM-
12-Mitzi app.	25	50	75	150	245	340
13	15	30	45	86	133	180
14-Wolverton's Powerhouse Pepper (4 pgs.) plus Kurtzman's "Hey Look"	24	48	72	140	230	320
15-17-Kurtzman's "Hey Look"	18	36	54	103	162	220
18,19	15	30	45	83	124	165
20-Kurtzman-a (5 pgs.)	18	36	54	107	169	230
21,22-Kurtzman-a (17 & 22 pgs.)	22	44	66	132	216	300

RUSTY DUGAN (See Holyoke One-Shot #2)

RUSTY RILEY
Dell Publishing Co.: No. 418, Aug, 1952 - No. 554, April, 1954 (Frank Godwin strip reprints)

	GD	VG	FN	VF	VF/NM	NM-
Four Color 418 (...a Boy, a Horse, and a Dog #1)	5	10	15	31	53	75
Four Color 451(2/53), 486 ('53), 554	4	8	12	25	40	55

RUULE
Beckett Comics: Dec, 2003 - No. 5, Apr, 2004 ($2.99)

1-5-David Mack-c/Mike Hawthorne-a 3.00

RUULE: KISS & TELL
Beckett Comics: Jun, 2004 - No. 8 ($1.99)

1-8: 1-Amano-s/c; Rousseau-a. 4-Maleev-c 3.00
TPB (2005, $19.99) r/#1-8 20.00

RYDER OF THE STORM
Radical Comics: Oct, 2010 - No. 3, Apr, 2011 ($4.99, limited series)

1-3-David Hine-s/Wayne Nichols-a 5.00

SAARI ("The Jungle Goddess")
P. L. Publishing Co.: November, 1951

	GD	VG	FN	VF	VF/NM	NM-
1	50	100	150	315	533	750

SABAN POWERHOUSE (TV)
Acclaim Books: 1997 ($4.50, digest size)

1,2-Power Rangers, BeetleBorgs, and others 4.50

SABAN PRESENTS POWER RANGERS TURBO VS. BEETLEBORGS METALLIX (TV)
Acclaim Books: 1997 ($4.50, digest size, one-shot)

nn 4.50

SABAN'S MIGHTY MORPHIN POWER RANGERS
Hamilton Comics: Dec, 1994 - No. 6, May, 1995 ($1.95, limited series)

1-6: 1-w/bound-in Power Ranger Barcode Card 4.00

SABAN'S MIGHTY MORPHIN POWER RANGERS (TV)
Marvel Comics: 1995 - No. 8, 1996 ($1.75)

1-8 4.00

SABLE (Formerly Jon Sable, Freelance; also see Mike Grell's...)
First Comics: Mar, 1988 - No. 27, May, 1990 ($1.75/$1.95)

1-27: 10-Begin $1.95-c 3.00

SABLE & FORTUNE (Also see Silver Sable and the Wild Pack)
Marvel Comics: Mar, 2006 - No. 4, June, 2006 ($2.99, limited series)

1-4-John Burns-a/Brendan Cahill-s 3.00

SABRE (See Eclipse Graphic Album Series)
Eclipse Comics: Aug, 1982 - No. 14, Aug, 1985 (Baxter paper #4 on)

1-14: 1-Sabre & Morrigan Tales begin. 4-6-Incredible Seven origin 3.00

SABRETOOTH (See Iron Fist, Power Man, X-Factor #10 & X-Men)
Marvel Comics: Aug, 1993 - No. 4, Nov, 1993 ($2.95, lim. series, coated paper)

1-4: 1-Die-cut-c. 3-Wolverine app. 5.00
...Special 1 "In the Red Zone" (1995, $4.95) Chromium wraparound-c 6.00
V2 #1 (1/98, $5.95, one-shot) Wildchild app. 6.00
Trade paperback (12/94, $12.95) r/#1-4 13.00

SABRETOOTH
Marvel Comics: Dec, 2004 - No. 4, Feb, 2005 ($2.99, limited series)

1-4-Sears-a. 3,4-Wendigo app. 3.00
...: Open Season TPB (2005, $9.99) r/#1-4 10.00

SABRETOOTH AND MYSTIQUE (See Mystique and Sabretooth)

SABRETOOTH CLASSIC
Marvel Comics: May, 1994 - No. 15, July, 1995 ($1.50)

1-15: 1-3-r/Power Man & Iron Fist #66,78,84. 4-r/Spec. S-M #116. 9-Uncanny X-Men #212, 10-r/Uncanny X-Men #213. 11-r/ Daredevil #238. 12-r/Classic X-Men #10 3.00

SABRETOOTH: MARY SHELLEY OVERDRIVE
Marvel Comics: Aug, 2002 - No. 4, Nov, 2002 ($2.99, limited series)

1-4-Jolley-s; Harris-c 3.00

SABRINA (Volume 2) (Based on animated series)
Archie Publications: Jan, 2000 - No. 104, Sept, 2009 ($1.79/$1.99/$2.19/$2.25/$2.50)

1-Teen-age Witch magically reverted to 12 years old 5.00
2-10: 4-Begin $1.99-c 4.00
11-104: 38-Sabrina aged back to 16 years old. 39-Begin $2.19-c. 58-Manga-style begins; Tania Del Rio-a. 67-Josie and the Pussycats app. 101-Young Salem; begin $2.50-c 3.00

SABRINA'S CHRISTMAS MAGIC (See Archie Giant Series Magazine #196, 207, 220, 231, 243, 455, 467, 479, 491, 503, 515)

SABRINA'S HALLOWEEN SPOOOKTACULAR
Archie Publications: 1993 - 1995 ($2.00, 52 pgs.)

	GD	VG	FN	VF	VF/NM	NM-
1-Neon orange ink-c; bound-in poster	1	2	3	5	6	8
2,3-Titled "Sabrina's Holiday Spectacular"						5.00

SABRINA, THE TEEN-AGE WITCH (TV)(See Archie Giant Series, Archie's Madhouse 22, Archie's TV..., Chilling Advs. In Sorcery, Little Archie #59)
Archie Publications: April, 1971 - No. 77, Jan, 1983 (52 pg.Giants No. 1-17)

	GD	VG	FN	VF	VF/NM	NM-
1-52 pgs. begin, end #17	13	26	39	89	195	300
2-Archie's group x-over	8	16	24	54	102	150
3-5: 3,4-Archie's Group x-over	5	10	15	35	63	90
6-10	5	10	15	31	53	75
11-17(2/74)	4	8	12	25	40	55
18-30	3	6	9	18	28	38
31-40(8/77)	3	6	9	14	20	26
41-60(6/80)	2	4	6	10	14	18
61-70	2	4	6	8	11	14
71-76-low print run	2	4	6	11	16	20
77-Last issue; low print run	3	6	9	14	20	26

SABRINA, THE TEEN-AGE WITCH
Archie Publications: 1996 ($1.50, 32 pgs., one-shot)

1-Updated origin 6.00

SABRINA, THE TEEN-AGE WITCH (Continues in Sabrina, Vol. 2)
Archie Publications: May, 1997 - No. 32, Dec, 1999 ($1.50/$1.75/$1.79)

	GD	VG	FN	VF	VF/NM	NM-
1-Photo-c with Melissa Joan Hart	1	3	4	6	8	10
2-10: 9-Begin $1.75-c						6.00
11-20						5.00

Saddle Justice #8 © WMG

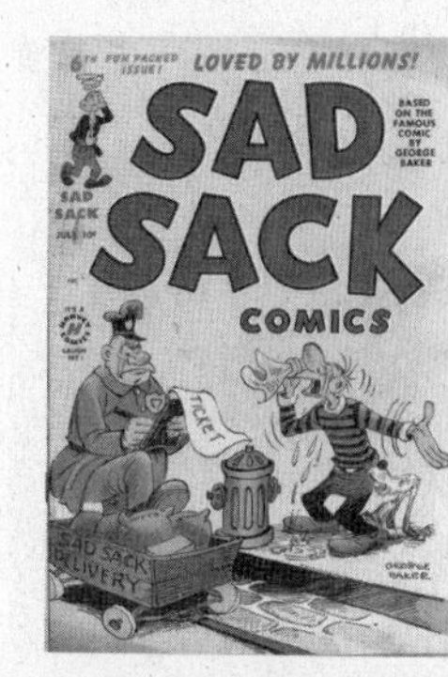

Sad Sack Comics #6 © HARV

Sad Sack and the Sarge #61 © HARV

	GD 2.0	VG 4.0	FN 6.0	VF 8.0	VF/NM 9.0	NM- 9.2
21-32: 24-Begin $1.79-c. 28-Sonic the Hedgehog-c/app.						4.00

SABU, "ELEPHANT BOY" (Movie; formerly My Secret Story)
Fox Features Syndicate: No. 30, June, 1950 - No. 2, Aug, 1950

	GD 2.0	VG 4.0	FN 6.0	VF 8.0	VF/NM 9.0	NM- 9.2
30(#1)-Wood-a; photo-c from movie	26	52	78	154	252	350
2-Photo-c from movie; Kamen-a	19	38	57	111	176	240

SACHS & VIOLENS
Marvel Comics (Epic Comics): Nov, 1993 - No. 4, July, 1994 ($2.25, limited series, mature)

	GD 2.0	VG 4.0	FN 6.0	VF 8.0	VF/NM 9.0	NM- 9.2
1-($2.75)-Embossed-c w/bound-in trading card						3.00
1-($3.50)-Platinum edition (1 for each 10 ordered)						4.00
2-4: Perez-c/a; bound-in trading card: 2-(5/94)						3.00
TPB (DC, 2006, $14.99) r/series; intro. by Peter David; creator bios.						15.00

SACRAMENTS, THE
Catechetical Guild Educational Society: Oct, 1955 (35¢)

	GD 2.0	VG 4.0	FN 6.0	VF 8.0	VF/NM 9.0	NM- 9.2
30304	6	12	18	31	38	45

SACRED AND THE PROFANE, THE (See Eclipse Graphic Album Series #9 & Epic Illustrated #20)

SADDLE JUSTICE (Happy Houlihans #1,2) (Saddle Romances #9 on)
E. C. Comics: No. 3, Spring, 1948 - No. 8, Sept-Oct, 1949

	GD 2.0	VG 4.0	FN 6.0	VF 8.0	VF/NM 9.0	NM- 9.2
3-The 1st E.C. by Bill Gaines to break away from M. C. Gaines' old Educational Comics format. Craig, Feldstein, H. C. Kiefer, & Stan Asch-a; mentioned in Love and Death	60	120	180	381	653	925
4-1st Graham Ingels-a for E.C.	52	104	156	328	552	775
5-8-Ingels-a in all	48	96	144	302	514	725

NOTE: ***Craig** and **Feldstein** art in most issues. Canadian reprints known; see Table of Contents. **Craig** c-3, 4. **Ingels** c-5-8. #4 contains a biography of **Craig**.*

SADDLE ROMANCES (Saddle Justice #3-8; Weird Science #12 on)
E. C. Comics: No. 9, Nov-Dec, 1949 - No. 11, Mar-Apr, 1950

	GD 2.0	VG 4.0	FN 6.0	VF 8.0	VF/NM 9.0	NM- 9.2
9,11: 9-Ingels-c/a. 11-Ingels-a; Feldstein-c	52	104	156	328	552	775
10-Wally Wood's 1st work at E. C.; Ingels-a; Feldstein-c	53	106	159	334	567	800

NOTE: *Canadian reprints known; see Table of Contents. **Wood/Harrison** a-10, 11.*

SADHU
Virgin Comics: July, 2006 - No. 8, June, 2007 ($2.99)

	GD 2.0	VG 4.0	FN 6.0	VF 8.0	VF/NM 9.0	NM- 9.2
1-8: 1,2-Gotham Chopra-s/Jeevan Kang-a						3.00
...: The Silent Ones (8/07 - No. 5, 2/08, $2.99) 1-5						3.00
...: Wheel of Destiny (4/08 - No. 5, $2.99) 1,2						3.00

SADIE SACK (See Harvey Hits #93)

SAD SACK AND THE SARGE
Harvey Publications: Sept, 1957 - No. 155, June, 1982

	GD 2.0	VG 4.0	FN 6.0	VF 8.0	VF/NM 9.0	NM- 9.2
1	12	24	36	79	170	260
2	7	14	21	46	86	125
3-10	5	10	15	35	63	90
11-20	5	10	15	30	50	70
21-30	3	6	9	19	30	40
31-50	3	6	9	14	20	25
51-70	2	4	6	9	13	16
71-90,97-99	1	3	4	6	8	10
91-96: All 52 pg. Giants	2	4	6	9	13	16
100	2	4	6	8	10	12
101-120	1	2	3	4	5	7
121-155						5.00

NOTE: ***George Baker** covers on numerous issues.*

SAD SACK COMICS (See Harvey Collector's Comics #16, Little Sad Sack, Tastee Freez Comics #4 & True Comics #55 for 1st app.)
Harvey Publications/Lorne-Harvey Publications (Recollections) #288 On: Sept, 1949 - No. 287, Oct, 1982; No. 288, 1992 - No. 291, 1993

	GD 2.0	VG 4.0	FN 6.0	VF 8.0	VF/NM 9.0	NM- 9.2
1-Infinity-c; Little Dot begins (1st app.); civilian issues begin, end #21; based on comic strip (first app. in True Comics #55)	118	236	354	944	2122	3300
2-Flying Fool by Powell	29	58	87	209	467	725
3	17	34	51	117	259	400
4-10	12	24	36	79	170	260
11-21	8	16	24	54	102	150
22-("Back In The Army Again" on covers #22-36); "The Specialist" story about Sad Sack's return to Army	9	18	27	59	117	175
23-30	5	10	15	34	60	85
31-50	4	8	12	28	47	65
51-80,100: 62-"The Specialist" reprinted	3	6	9	21	33	45
81-99	3	6	9	16	23	30
101-140	3	6	9	14	19	24
141-170,200	2	4	6	11	16	20
171-199	2	4	6	9	13	16
201-207: 207-Last 12¢ issue	2	4	6	8	11	14
208-222	1	3	4	6	8	10
223-228 (25¢ Giants, 52 pgs.)	2	4	6	8	11	14
229-250	1	3	4	6	8	10
251-285						6.00
286,287-Limited distribution	1	2	3	5	7	9
288,289 ($2.75, 1992): 289-50th anniversary issue						6.00
290,291 ($1.00, 1993, B&W)						3.00
3-D 1 (1/54, 25¢)-Came with 2 pairs of glasses; titled "Harvey 3-D Hits"	14	28	42	93	204	315
...At Home for the Holidays 1 (1993, no-c price)-Publ. by Lorne-Harvey' X-Mas issue						4.00

NOTE: *The Sad Sack Comics comic book was a spin-off from a Sunday Newspaper strip launched through John Wheeler's Bell Syndicate. The previous Sunday page and the first 21 comics depicted the Sad Sack in civvies. Unpopularity caused the Sunday page to be discontinued in the early '50s. Meanwhile Sad Sack returned to the Army, by popular demand, in issue No. 22, remaining there ever since. Incidentally, relatively few of the first 21 issues were ever collected and remain scarce due to this. **George Baker** covers on numerous issues.*

SAD SACK FUN AROUND THE WORLD
Harvey Publications: 1974 (no month)

	GD 2.0	VG 4.0	FN 6.0	VF 8.0	VF/NM 9.0	NM- 9.2
1-About Great Britain	2	4	6	11	16	20

SAD SACK GOES HOME
Harvey Publications: 1951 (16 pgs. in color, no cover price)

	GD 2.0	VG 4.0	FN 6.0	VF 8.0	VF/NM 9.0	NM- 9.2
nn-By George Baker	5	10	15	31	53	75

SAD SACK LAUGH SPECIAL
Harvey Publications: Winter, 1958-59 - No. 93, Feb, 1977 (#1-9: 84 pgs.; #10-60: 68 pgs.; #61-76: 52 pgs.)

	GD 2.0	VG 4.0	FN 6.0	VF 8.0	VF/NM 9.0	NM- 9.2
1-Giant 25¢ issues begin	9	18	27	60	120	180
2	5	10	15	35	63	90
3-10	5	10	15	30	50	70
11-30	4	8	12	25	40	55
31-60: 31-Hi-Fi Tweeter app. 60-Last 68 pg. Giant	3	6	9	16	23	30
61-76-(All 52 pg. issues)	2	4	6	10	14	18
77-93	1	2	3	5	6	8

SAD SACK NAVY, GOBS 'N' GALS
Harvey Publications: Aug, 1972 - No. 8, Oct, 1973

	GD 2.0	VG 4.0	FN 6.0	VF 8.0	VF/NM 9.0	NM- 9.2
1: 52 pg. Giant	3	6	9	16	23	30
2-8	2	4	6	9	12	15

SAD SACK'S ARMY LIFE (See Harvey Hits #8, 17, 22, 28, 32, 39, 43, 47, 51, 55, 58, 61, 64, 67, 70)

SAD SACK'S ARMY LIFE (...Parade #1-57, ...Today #58 on)
Harvey Publications: Oct, 1963 - No. 60, Nov, 1975; No. 61, May, 1976

	GD 2.0	VG 4.0	FN 6.0	VF 8.0	VF/NM 9.0	NM- 9.2
1-(68 pg. issues begin)	7	14	21	44	82	120
2-10	4	8	12	27	44	60
11-20	3	6	9	19	30	40
21-34: Last 68 pg. issue	3	6	9	16	23	30
35-51: All 52 pgs.	2	4	6	10	14	18
52-61	1	3	4	6	8	10

SAD SACK'S FUNNY FRIENDS (See Harvey Hits #75)
Harvey Publications: Dec, 1955 - No. 75, Oct, 1969

	GD 2.0	VG 4.0	FN 6.0	VF 8.0	VF/NM 9.0	NM- 9.2
1	9	18	27	60	120	180
2-10	5	10	15	35	63	90
11-20	4	8	12	23	37	50
21-30	3	6	9	17	26	35
31-50	3	6	9	14	20	25
51-75	2	4	6	9	13	16

SAD SACK'S MUTTSY (See Harvey Hits #74, 77, 80, 82, 84, 87, 89, 92, 96, 99, 102, 105, 108, 111, 113, 115, 117, 119, 121)

SAD SACK USA (...Vacation #8)
Harvey Publications: Nov, 1972 - No. 7, Nov, 1973; No. 8, Oct, 1974

	GD 2.0	VG 4.0	FN 6.0	VF 8.0	VF/NM 9.0	NM- 9.2
1	3	6	9	14	20	25
2-8	2	4	6	8	10	12

SAD SACK WITH SARGE & SADIE
Harvey Publications: Sept, 1972 - No. 8, Nov, 1973

	GD 2.0	VG 4.0	FN 6.0	VF 8.0	VF/NM 9.0	NM- 9.2
1-(52 pg. Giant)	3	6	9	14	20	25
2-8	2	4	6	8	10	12

SAD SAD SACK WORLD
Harvey Publ.: Oct, 1964 - No. 46, Dec, 1973 (#1-31: 68 pgs.; #32-38: 52 pgs.)

	GD 2.0	VG 4.0	FN 6.0	VF 8.0	VF/NM 9.0	NM- 9.2
1	6	12	18	41	76	110
2-10	4	8	12	25	40	55
11-20	3	6	9	19	30	40

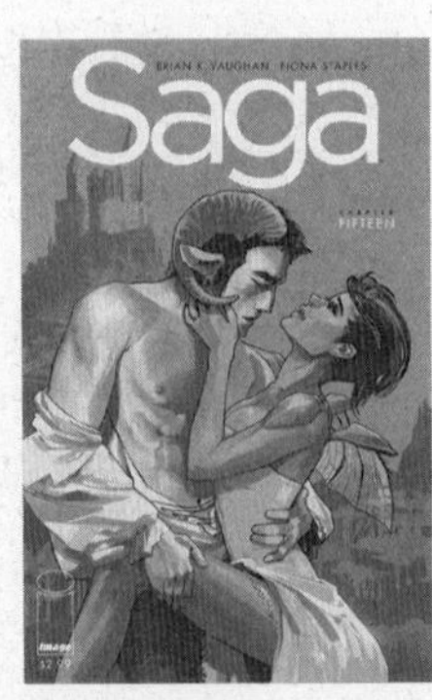

Saga #15 © BKV & Fiona Staples

The Saint #9 © AVON

Sam and Twitch #6 © TMP

	GD 2.0	VG 4.0	FN 6.0	VF 8.0	VF/NM 9.0	NM- 9.2
21-31: 31-Last 68 pg. issue	3	6	9	16	23	30
32-39-(All 52 pgs)	2	4	6	10	14	18
40-46	1	3	4	6	8	10

SAFEST PLACE IN THE WORLD, THE
Dark Horse Comics: 1993 ($2.50, one-shot)

1-Steve Ditko-c/a/scripts 4.00

SAFETY-BELT MAN
Sirius Entertainment: June, 1994 - No. 6, 1995 ($2.50, B&W)

1-6: 1-Horan-s/Dark One-a/Sprouse-c. 2,3-Warren-c. 4-Linsner back-up story. 5,6-Crilley-a 3.00

SAFETY-BELT MAN ALL HELL
Sirius Entertainment: June, 1996 - No. 6, Mar, 1997 ($2.95, color)

1-6-Horan-s/Fillbach Bros.-a 3.00

SAGA
Image Comics: Mar, 2012 - Present ($2.99)

	GD	VG	FN	VF	VF/NM	NM-
1-Brian K. Vaughan-s/Fiona Staples-a/c	4	8	12	27	44	90
1-Second printing						15.00
2-5						20.00
6-12						6.00
13-18						4.00

SAGA OF BIG RED, THE
Omaha World-Herald: Sept, 1976 ($1.25) (In color)

nn-by Win Mumma; story of the Nebraska Cornhuskers (sports) 6.00

SAGA OF CRYSTAR, CRYSTAL WARRIOR, THE
Marvel Comics: May, 1983 - No. 11, Feb, 1985 (Remco toy tie-in)

1,6: 1-(Baxter paper). 6-Nightcrawler app; Golden-c 5.00
2-5,7-11: 3-Dr. Strange app. 3-11-Golden-c (painted-4,5). 11-Alpha Flight app. 4.00

SAGA OF RA'S AL GHUL, THE
DC Comics: Jan, 1988 - No. 4, Apr, 1988 ($2.50, limited series)

1-4-r/N. Adams Batman 6.00

SAGA OF SABAN'S MIGHTY MORPHIN POWER RANGERS (Also see Saban's Mighty Morphin Power Rangers)
Hamilton Comics: 1995 - No. 4, 1995 ($1.95, limited series)

1-4 4.00

SAGA OF SEVEN SUNS, THE : VEILED ALLIANCES
DC Comics (WildStorm): 2004 ($24.95, hardcover graphic novel with dustjacket)

HC-Kevin J. Anderson-s/Robert Teranishi-a 25.00
SC-(2004, $17.95) 18.00

SAGA OF THE ORIGINAL HUMAN TORCH
Marvel Comics: Apr, 1990 - No. 4, July, 1990 ($1.50, limited series)

1-4: 1-Origin; Buckler-c/a(p). 3-Hitler-c 4.00

SAGA OF THE SUB-MARINER, THE
Marvel Comics: Nov, 1988 - No. 12, Oct, 1989 ($1.25/$1.50 #5 on, maxi-series)

1-12: 9-Original X-Men app. 4.00

SAGA OF THE SWAMP THING, THE (See Swamp Thing)

SAILOR MOON (Manga)
Mixx Entertainment Inc.: 1998 - Present ($2.95)

	GD	VG	FN	VF	VF/NM	NM-
1	3	6	9	14	20	25
1-(San Diego edition)	3	6	9	16	23	30
2-5	2	4	6	9	12	15
6-10	1	3	4	6	8	10
11-25	1	2	3	4	5	7
26-35						5.00
... Rini's Moon Stick 1						15.00

SAILOR ON THE SEA OF FATE (See First Comics Graphic Novel #11)

SAILOR SWEENEY (Navy Action #1-11, 15 on)
Atlas Comics (CDS): No. 12, July, 1956 - No. 14, Nov, 1956

	GD	VG	FN	VF	VF/NM	NM-
12-14: 12-Shores-a. 13,14-Severin-c	11	22	33	60	83	105

SAINT, THE (Also see Movie Comics(DC) #2 & Silver Streak #18)
Avon Periodicals: Aug, 1947 - No. 12, Mar, 1952

	GD	VG	FN	VF	VF/NM	NM-
1-Kamen bondage-c/a	97	194	291	621	1061	1500
2	45	90	135	284	480	675
3-5: 4-Lingerie panels	40	80	120	246	411	575
6-Miss Fury app. by Tarpe Mills (14 pgs.)	65	130	195	416	708	1000
7-c-/Avon paperback #118	34	68	102	199	325	450
8,9(12/50): Saint strip-r in #8-12; 9-Kinstler-c	30	60	90	177	289	400
10-Wood-a, 1 pg; c-/Avon paperback #289	30	60	90	177	289	400
11	24	48	72	142	234	325
12-c-/Avon paperback #123	26	52	78	154	252	350

NOTE: *Lucky Dale, Girl Detective in #1,2,4,6.* **Hollingsworth** *a-4, 6. Painted-c 7, 8, 10-12.*

SAINT ANGEL
Image Comics: Mar, 2000 - No. 4, Mar, 2001 ($2.95/$3.95)

0-Altstaetter & Napton-s/Altstaetter-a 3.00
1-4-($3.95) Flip book w/Deity. 1-(6/00). 2-(10/00) 4.00

ST. GEORGE
Marvel Comics (Epic Comics): June, 1988 - No.8, Oct, 1989 ($1.25,/$1.50)

1-8: Sienkiewicz-c. 3-begin $1.50-c 3.00

SAINT GERMAINE
Caliber Comics: 1997 - No. 8, 1998 ($2.95)

1-8: 1,5-Alternate covers 3.00

ST. SWITHIN'S DAY
Trident Comics: Apr, 1990 ($2.50, one-shot)

1-Grant Morrison scripts 3.00

ST. SWITHIN'S DAY
Oni Press: Mar, 1998 ($2.95, B&W, one-shot)

1-Grant Morrison-s/Paul Grist-a 3.00

SALOMÉ (See Night Music #6)

SALVATION RUN
DC Comics: Jan, 2008 - No. 7, Jul, 2008 ($2.99/$3.50, limited series)

1-6-DC villains banished to an alien planet; Willingham-s/Chen-a/c. 1-Var-c by Corroney 3.00
7-($3.50) Luthor cover by Chen 3.50
7-($3.50) Variant Joker cover by Neal Adams 5.00

SAM AND MAX, FREELANCE POLICE SPECIAL
Fishwrap Prod./Comico: 1987 ($1.75, B&W); Jan, 1989 ($2.75, 44 pgs.)

1 ($1.75, B&W, Fishwrap) 4.00
2 ($2.75, color, Comico) 4.00

SAM AND TWITCH (See Spawn and Case Files:...)
Image Comics (Todd McFarlane Prod.): Aug, 1999 - No. 26, Feb, 2004 ($2.50)

1-26: 1-19-Bendis-s. 1-14-Medina-a. 15-19-Maleev-a. 20-24-McFarlane-s/Maleev-a 3.00
Book One: Udaku (2000, $21.95, TPB) B&W reprint of #1-8 22.00
...: The Brian Michael Bendis Collection Vol. 1 (2/06, $24.95) r/#1-9 in color; sketch pages 25.00
...: The Brian Michael Bendis Collection Vol. 2 (6/07, $24.95) r/#10-19; cover gallery 25.00

SAM AND TWITCH: THE WRITER
Image Comics (Todd McFarlane Prod.): May, 2010 - No. 4, Jun, 2010 ($2.99)

1-4-Blengino-s/Erbetta-a/c 3.00

SAM HILL PRIVATE EYE
Close-Up (Archie): 1950 - No. 7, 1951

	GD	VG	FN	VF	VF/NM	NM-
1	18	36	54	107	169	230
2	11	22	33	64	90	115
3-7	10	20	30	56	76	95

SAMSON (1st Series) (Captain Aero #7 on; see Big 3 Comics)
Fox Features Syndicate: Fall, 1940 - No. 6, Sept, 1941 (See Fantastic Comics)

	GD	VG	FN	VF	VF/NM	NM-
1-Samson begins, ends #6; Powell-a, signed 'Rensie;' Wing Turner by Tuska app; Fine-c?	194	388	582	1242	2121	3000
2-Dr. Fung by Powell; Fine-c?	80	160	240	508	874	1240
3-Navy Jones app.; Joe Simon-c	60	120	180	381	653	925
4-Yarko the Great, Master Magician begins	53	106	159	334	567	800
5,6: 6-Origin The Topper	43	86	129	271	461	650

SAMSON (2nd Series) (Formerly Fantastic Comics #10, 11)
Ajax/Farrell Publications (Four Star): No. 12, April, 1955 - No. 14, Aug, 1955

	GD	VG	FN	VF	VF/NM	NM-
12-Wonder Boy	30	60	90	177	289	400
13,14: 13-Wonder Boy, Rocket Man	26	52	78	154	252	350

SAMSON (See Mighty Samson)

SAMSON & DELILAH (See A Spectacular Feature Magazine)

SAMUEL BRONSTON'S CIRCUS WORLD (See Circus World under Movie Classics)

SAMURAI (Also see Eclipse Graphic Album Series #14)
Aircel Publications: 1985 - No. 23, 1987 ($1.70, B&W)

1, 14-16-Dale Keown-a 4.00
1-(reprinted),2-12,17-23: 2 (reprinted issue exists) 3.00

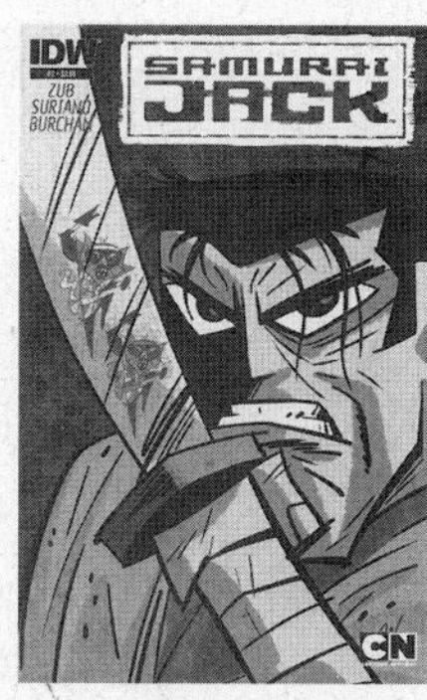

Samurai Jack #2 © CN

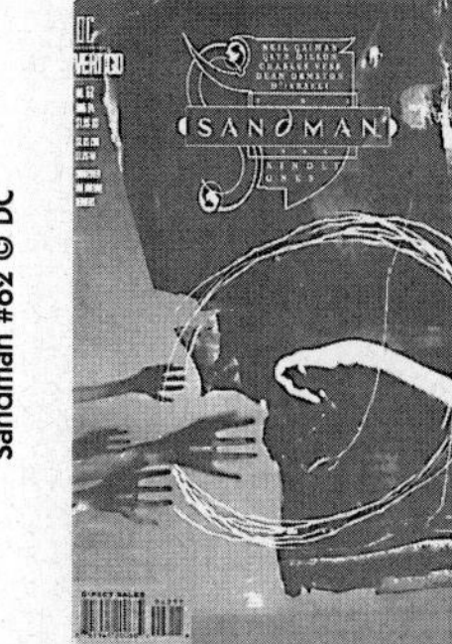

Sandman #62 © DC

Sandman Mystery Theater #50 © DC

GD VG FN VF VF/NM NM-
2.0 4.0 6.0 8.0 9.0 9.2

13-Dale Keown's 1st published artwork (1987) 6.00

SAMURAI
Warp Graphics: May, 1997 ($2.95, B&W)
1 3.00

SAMURAI CAT
Marvel Comics (Epic Comics): June, 1991 - No. 3, Sept, 1991 ($2.25, limited series)
1-3: 3-Darth Vader-c/story parody 3.00

SAMURAI: HEAVEN & EARTH
Dark Horse Comics: Dec, 2004 - No. 5, Dec, 2005 ($2.99)
1-5-Luke Ross-a/Ron Marz-s 3.00
TPB (4/06, $14.95) r/#1-5; sketch pages and cover and pin-up gallery 15.00

SAMURAI: HEAVEN & EARTH (Volume 2)
Dark Horse Comics: Nov, 2006 - No. 5, June, 2007 ($2.99)
1-5-Luke Ross-a/Ron Marz-s 3.00
TPB (10/07, $14.95) r/#1-5; sketch pages and cover and pin-up gallery 15.00

SAMURAI JACK (TV)
IDW Publishing: Oct, 2013 - Present ($3.99)
1-6: 1-5-Jim Zub-s/Andy Suriano-a; multiple covers on each 4.00
... Special - Director's Cut (2/14, $7.99) Reprints '02 DC issue; commentary by Bill Wray 8.00

SAMURAI JACK SPECIAL (TV)
DC Comics: Sept, 2002 ($3.95, one-shot)
1-Adaptation of pilot episode with origin story; Tartakovsky-s/Naylor & Wray-a 4.00

SAMURAI: LEGEND
Marvel Comics (Soleil): 2008 - No. 4, 2009 ($5.99)
1-4-Genet-a/DiGiorgio-s; English version of French comic; preview of other titles 6.00

SAMUREE
Continuity Comics: May, 1987 - No. 9, Jan, 1991
1-9 3.00

SAMUREE
Continuity Comics: V2#1, May, 1993 - V2#4, Jan,1994 ($2.50)
V2#1-4-Embossed-c: 2,4-Adams plot, Nebres-i. 3-Nino-c(i) 3.00

SAMUREE
Acclaim Comics (Windjammer): Oct, 1995 - No. 2, Nov,1995 ($2.50, lim. series)
1,2 3.00

SAN DIEGO COMIC CON COMICS
Dark Horse Comics: 1992 - No.4, 1995 (B&W, promo comic for the San Diego Comic Con)
1-(1992)-Includes various characters published from Dark Horse including Concrete, The Mask, RoboCop and others; 1st app. of Sprint from John Byrne's Next Men; art by Quesada, Byrne, Rude, Burden, Moebius & others; pin-ups by Rude, Dorkin, Allred & others; Chadwick-c 2 4 6 8 10 12
2-(1993)-Intro of Legend imprint; 1st app. of John Byrne's Danger Unlimited, Mike Mignola's Hellboy (also see John Byrne's Next Men #21), Art Adams' Monkeyman & O'Brien; contains stories featuring Concrete, Sin City, Martha Washington & others; Grendel, Madman, & Big Guy pin-ups; Don Martin-c 5 10 15 33 57 80
3-(1994)-Contains stories featuring Barb Wire, The Mask, The Dirty Pair, & Grendel by Matt Wagner; contains pin-ups of Ghost, Predator & Rascals In Paradise; The Mask-c 1 2 3 5 6 8
4-(1995)-Contains Sin City story by Miller (3pg.), Star Wars, The Mask, Tarzan, Foot Soldiers; Sin City & Star Wars flip-c 1 2 3 5 6 8

SANDMAN, THE (1st Series) (Also see Adventure Comics #40, New York World's Fair & World's Finest #3)
National Periodical Publ.: Winter, 1974; No. 2, Apr-May, 1975 - No. 6, Dec-Jan, 1975-76
1-1st app. Bronze Age Sandman by Simon & Kirby (last S&K collaboration) 6 12 18 41 76 110
2-6: 6-Kirby/Wood-c/a 3 6 9 21 33 45
The Sandman By Joe Simon & Jack Kirby HC (2009, $39.99, d.j.) r/Sandman app. from World's Finest #6,7, Adventure Comics #72-102 and Sandman #1; Morrow intro. 40.00
NOTE: *Kirby a-1p, 4-6p; c-1-5, 6p.*

SANDMAN (2nd Series) (See Books of Magic, Vertigo Jam & Vertigo Preview)
DC Comics (Vertigo imprint #47 on): Jan, 1989 - No. 75, Mar, 1996 ($1.50-$2.50, mature)
1 ($2.00, 52 pgs.)-1st app. Modern Age Sandman (Morpheus); Neil Gaiman scripts begin; Sam Kieth-a(p) in #1-5; Wesley Dodds (G.A. Sandman) cameo. 5 10 15 31 53 75
2-Cain & Abel app. (from HOM & HOS) 3 6 9 14 19 24
3-5: 3-John Constantine app. 2 4 6 10 14 18
6,7 2 4 6 8 11 14

GD VG FN VF VF/NM NM-
2.0 4.0 6.0 8.0 9.0 9.2

8-Death-c/story (1st app.)-Regular ed. has Jeanette Kahn publishorial & American Cancer Society ad w/no indicia on inside front-c 3 6 9 19 30 40
8-Limited ed. (600+ copies?); has Karen Berger editorial and next issue teaser on inside covers (has indicia) 10 20 30 64 132 200
9-14: 10-Has explaination about #8 mixup; has bound-in Shocker movie poster. 14-(52 pgs.)-Bound-in Nightbreed fold-out 2 4 6 8 10 12
15-20: 16-Photo-c. 17,18-Kelley Jones-a. 19-Vess-a 1 2 3 5 6 8
18-Error version w/1st 3 panels on pg. 1 in blue ink 4 8 12 23 37 50
19-Error version w/pages 18 & 20 facing each other 3 6 9 17 26 35
21,23-27: Seasons of Mist storyline. 22-World Without End preview. 24-Kelley Jones/Russell-a 6.00
22-1st Daniel (Later becomes new Sandman) 2 4 6 8 10 12
28-30 5.00
31-49,51-74: 36-(52 pgs.). 41,44-48-Metallic ink on-c. 48-Cerebus appears as a doll. 54-Re-intro Prez; Death app.; Belushi, Nixon & Wildcat cameos. 57-Metallic ink on c. 65-w/bound-in trading card. 69-Death of Sandman. 70-73-Zulli-a. 74-Jon J. Muth-a. 4.00
50-($2.95, 52 pgs.)-Black-c w/metallic ink by McKean; Russell-a; McFarlane pin-up 5.00
50-($2.95)-Signed & limited (5,000) Treasury Edition with sketch of Neil Gaiman 2 4 6 9 12 15
50-Platinum 20.00
75-($3.95)-Vess-a. 5.00
Special 1 (1991, $3.50, 68 pgs.)-Glow-in-the-dark-c 5.00
Absolute Sandman Special Edition #1 (2006, 50¢) sampling from HC; recolored r/#1 3.00
Absolute Sandman Volume One (2006, $99.00, slipcased hardcover) recolored r/#1-20; Gaiman's original proposal; script and pencils from #19; character sketch gallery 100.00
Absolute Sandman Volume Two (2007, $99.00, slipcased hardcover) recolored r/#21-39; r/A Gallery of Dreams one-shot; bonus stories, scripts and pencil art 100.00
Absolute Sandman Volume Three (2008, $99.00, slipcased hardcover) recolored r/#40-56; & Special #1; bonus galleries, scripts and pencil art; Jill Thompson intro. 100.00
Absolute Sandman Volume Four (2008, $99.00, slipcased hardcover) recolored r/#57-75; scripts & sketch pages for #57 & 75; gallery of Dreaming memorabilia; Berger intro. 100.00
...: A Gallery of Dreams ($2.95)-Intro by N. Gaiman 4.00
...: Preludes & Nocturnes ($29.95, HC)-r/#1-8. 30.00
...: The Doll's House (1990, $29.95, HC)-r/#8-16. 30.00
...: Dream Country ($29.95, HC)-r/#17-20. 30.00
...: Season of Mists ($29.95, Leatherbound HC)-r/#21-28. 50.00
...: A Game of You ($29.95, HC)-r/32-37, ...: Fables and Reflections ($29.95, HC)-r/Vertigo Preview #1, Sandman Special #1, #29-31, #38-40 & #50. ...: Brief Lives ($29.95, HC)-r/#41-49. ...: World's End ($29.95, HC)-r/#51-56 30.00
...: The Kindly Ones (1996, $34.95, HC)-r/#57-69 & Vertigo Jam #1 35.00
...: The Wake ($29.95, HC)-r/#70-75. 30.00
NOTE: *A new set of hardcover printings with new covers was introduced in 1998-99. Multiple printings exist of softcover collections. Recolored (from the Absolute HC) softcover editions were released in 2010.* ***Bachalo*** *a-12;* ***Kelley Jones*** *a-17, 18, 22, 23, 26, 27.* ***Vess*** *a-19, 75.*

SANDMAN: ENDLESS NIGHTS
DC Comics (Vertigo): 2003 ($24.95, hardcover, with dust jacket)
HC-Neil Gaiman stories of Morpheus and the Endless illustrated by Fabry, Manara, Prado, Quitely, Russell, Sienkiewicz, and Storey; McKean-c 25.00
...Special (11/03, $2.95) Previews hardcover; Dream story w/Prado-a; McKean-c 4.00
SC (2004, $17.95) 18.00

SANDMAN MIDNIGHT THEATRE
DC Comics (Vertigo): Sept, 1995 ($6.95, squarebound, one-shot)
nn-Modern Age Sandman (Morpheus) meets G.A. Sandman; Gaiman & Wagner story; McKean-c; Kristiansen-a 7.00

SANDMAN MYSTERY THEATRE (Also see Sandman (2nd Series) #1)
DC Comics (Vertigo): Apr, 1993 - No. 70, Feb, 1999 ($1.95/$2.25/$2.50)
1-G.A. Sandman advs. begin; Matt Wagner scripts begin 5.00
2-49: 5-Neon ink logo. 29-32-Hourman app. 38-Ted Knight (G.A. Starman) app. 42-Jim Corrigan (Spectre) app. 45-48-Blackhawk app. 3.00
50-($3.50, 48 pgs.) w/bonus story of S.A. Sandman, Torres-a 4.00
51-70 3.00
Annual 1 (10/94, $3.95, 68 pgs.)-Alex Ross, Bolton & others-a 5.00
...: Dr. Death and the Night of the Butcher (2007, $19.99) r/#21-28 20.00
...: The Blackhawk and The Return of the Scarlet Ghost (2010, $19.99) r/#45-52 20.00
...: The Face and the Brute (2004, $19.95) r/#5-12 20.00
...: The Hourman and The Python (2008, $19.99) r/#29-36 20.00
...: The Mist and The Phantom of the Fair (2009, $19.99) r/#37-44 20.00
...: The Scorpion (2006, $12.99) r/#17-20 13.00
...: The Tarantula (1995, $14.95) r/#1-4 15.00
...: The Vamp (2005, $12.99) r/#13-16 13.00

SANDMAN MYSTERY THEATRE (2nd Series)
DC Comics (Vertigo): Feb, 2007 - No. 5, Jun, 2007 ($2.99, limited series)

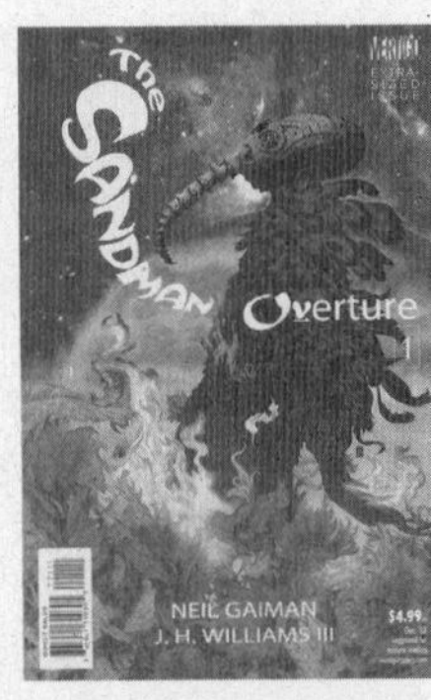

Sandman: Overture #1 © DC

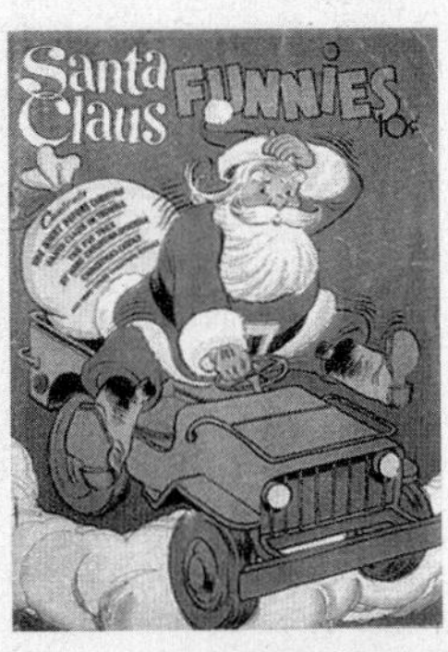

Santa Claus Funnies nn © DELL

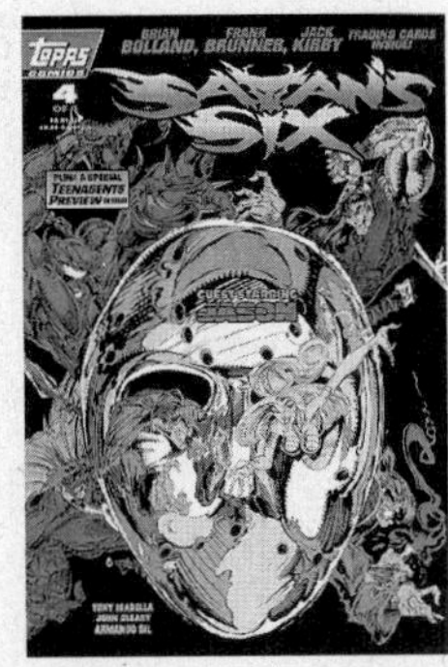

Satan's Six #4 © Jack Kirby

	GD 2.0	VG 4.0	FN 6.0	VF 8.0	VF/NM 9.0	NM- 9.2
1-5-Wesley Dodds and Dian in 1997; Rieber-s/Nguyen-a						3.00

SANDMAN: OVERTURE
DC Comics (Vertigo): Dec, 2013 - No. 6 ($4.99, limited series)

1,2-Prelude to Sandman #1 ('89); Gaiman-s/JH Williams III-a/c; variant-c by McKean						5.00
... Special Edition 1 (1/14, $5.99) B&W version of #1 with creator interviews; bonus info						6.00

SANDMAN PRESENTS...
DC Comics (Vertigo)

Taller Tales TPB (2003, $19.95) r/S.P: The Thessaliad #1-4; Merv Pumpkinhead, Agent...; The Dreaming #55; S.P. Everything You Always...; new McKean-c; intro by Willingham						20.00

SANDMAN PRESENTS: BAST
DC Comics (Vertigo): Mar, 2003 - No. 3, May, 2003 ($2.95, limited series)

1-3-Kiernan-s/Bennett-a/McKean-c						3.00

SANDMAN PRESENTS: DEADBOY DETECTIVES (See Sandman #21-28)
DC Comics (Vertigo): Aug, 2001 - No. 4, Nov, 2001 ($2.50, limited series)

1-4;Talbot-a/McKean-c/Brubaker-s						3.00
TPB (2008, $12.99) r/#1-4						13.00

SANDMAN PRESENTS: EVERYTHING YOU ALWAYS WANTED TO KNOW ABOUT DREAMS...BUT WERE AFRAID TO ASK
DC Comics (Vertigo): Jul, 2001 ($3.95, one-shot)

1-Short stories by Willingham; art by various; McKean-c						4.00

SANDMAN PRESENTS: LOVE STREET
DC Comics (Vertigo): Jul, 1999 - No. 3, Sept, 1999 ($2.95, limited series)

1-3: Teenage Hellblazer in 1968 London; Zulli-a						3.00

SANDMAN PRESENTS: LUCIFER
DC Comics (Vertigo): Mar, 1999 - No. 3, May, 1999 ($2.95, limited series)

1-3: Scott Hampton painted-c/a						3.00

SANDMAN PRESENTS: PETREFAX
DC Comics (Vertigo): Mar, 2000 - No. 4, Jun, 2000 ($2.95, limited series)

1-4-Carey-s/Leialoha-a						3.00

SANDMAN PRESENTS: THE CORINTHIAN
DC Comics (Vertigo): Dec, 2001 - No. 3, Feb, 2002 ($2.95, limited series)

1-3-Macan-s/Zezelj-a/McKean-c						3.00

SANDMAN PRESENTS, THE: THE FURIES
DC Comics (Vertigo): 2002 ($24.95, one-shot)

Hardcover-Mike Carey-s/John Bolton-painted art; Lyta Hall's reunion with Daniel						30.00
Softcover-(2003, $17.95)						18.00

SANDMAN PRESENTS, THE: THESSALY: WITCH FOR HIRE
DC Comics (Vertigo): Apr, 2004 - No. 4, July, 2004 ($2.95, limited series)

1-4-Willingham-s/McManus-a/McPherson-c						3.00
TPB-(2005, $12.99) r/#1-4						13.00

SANDMAN PRESENTS, THE: THE THESSALIAD
DC Comics (Vertigo): Mar, 2002 - No. 4, Jun, 2002 ($2.95, limited series)

1-4-Willingham-s/McManus-a/McKean-c						3.00

SANDMAN, THE: THE DREAM HUNTERS
DC Comics (Vertigo): Oct, 1999 ($29.95/$19.95, one-shot graphic novel)

Hardcover-Neil Gaiman-s/Yoshitaka Amano-painted art						30.00
Softcover-(2000, $19.95) new Amano-c						20.00

SANDMAN, THE: THE DREAM HUNTERS
DC Comics (Vertigo): Jan, 2009 - No. 4, Apr, 2009 ($2.99, limited series)

1-4-Adaptation of the Gaiman/Amano GN by P. Craig Russell-s/a; 2 covers on each						3.00
HC (2009, $24.99) afterwords by Gaiman, Russell, Berger; cover gallery & sketch art						25.00
SC (2010, $19.99) afterwords by Gaiman, Russell, Berger; cover gallery & sketch art						20.00

SANDS OF THE SOUTH PACIFIC
Toby Press: Jan, 1953

1	21	42	63	122	199	275

SANTA AND HIS REINDEER (See March of Comics #166)

SANTA AND THE ANGEL (See Dell Junior Treasury #7)
Dell Publishing Co.: Dec, 1949 (Combined w/Santa at the Zoo) (Gollub-a condensed from FC#128)

Four Color 259	5	10	15	33	57	80

SANTA AT THE ZOO (See Santa And The Angel)

SANTA CLAUS AROUND THE WORLD (See March of Comics #241 in Promotional Comics section)

SANTA CLAUS CONQUERS THE MARTIANS (See Movie Classics)

SANTA CLAUS FUNNIES (Also see Dell Giants)
Dell Publishing Co.: Dec?, 1942 - No. 1274, Dec, 1961

	GD 2.0	VG 4.0	FN 6.0	VF 8.0	VF/NM 9.0	NM- 9.2
nn(#1)(1942)-Kelly-a	32	64	96	230	515	800
2(12/43)-Kelly-a	21	42	63	147	324	500
Four Color 61(1944)-Kelly-a	20	40	60	141	313	485
Four Color 91(1945)-Kelly-a	15	30	45	105	233	360
Four Color 128('46),175('47)-Kelly-a	12	24	36	84	185	285
Four Color 205,254-Kelly-a	11	22	33	76	163	250
Four Color 302,361,525,607,666,756,867	6	12	18	41	76	110
Four Color 958,1063,1154,1274	6	12	18	37	66	95

NOTE: *Most issues contain only one Kelly story.*

SANTA CLAUS PARADE
Ziff-Davis (Approved Comics)/St. John Publishing Co.: 1951; No. 2, Dec, 1952; No. 3, Jan, 1955 (25¢)

nn(1951-Ziff-Davis)-116 pgs. (Xmas Special 1,2)	33	66	99	194	317	440
2(12/52-Ziff-Davis)-100 pgs.; Dave Berg-a	25	50	75	150	245	340
V1#3(1/55-St. John)-100 pgs.; reprints-c/#1	20	40	60	114	182	250

SANTA CLAUS' WORKSHOP (See March of Comics #50,168 in Promotional Comics section)

SANTA IS COMING (See March of Comics #197 in Promotional Comics section)

SANTA IS HERE (See March of Comics #49 in Promotional Comics section)

SANTA'S BUSY CORNER (See March of Comics #31 in Promotional Comics section)

SANTA'S CANDY KITCHEN (See March of Comics #14 in Promotional Comics section)

SANTA'S CHRISTMAS BOOK (See March of Comics #123 in Promotional Comics section)

SANTA'S CHRISTMAS COMICS
Standard Comics (Best Books): Dec, 1952 (100 pgs.)

nn-Supermouse, Dizzy Duck, Happy Rabbit, etc.	20	40	60	117	189	260

SANTA'S CHRISTMAS LIST (See March of Comics #255 in Promotional Comics section)

SANTA'S HELPERS (See March of Comics #64, 106, 198 in Promotional Comics section)

SANTA'S LITTLE HELPERS (See March of Comics #270 in Promotional Comics section)

SANTA'S SHOW (See March of Comics #311 in Promotional Comics section)

SANTA'S SLEIGH (See March of Comics #298 in Promotional Comics section)

SANTA'S SURPRISE (See March of Comics #13 in Promotional Comics section)

SANTA'S TINKER TOTS
Charlton Comics: 1958

1-Based on "The Tinker Tots Keep Christmas"	4	8	12	28	47	65

SANTA'S TOYLAND (See March of Comics #242 in Promotional Comics section)

SANTA'S TOYS (See March of Comics #12 in Promotional Comics section)

SANTA'S VISIT (See March of Comics #283 in Promotional Comics section)

SANTA THE BARBARIAN
Maximum Press: Dec, 1996 ($2.99, one-shot)

1-Fraga/Mhan-s/a						3.00

SANTIAGO (Movie)
Dell Publishing Co.: Sept, 1956 (Alan Ladd photo-c)

Four Color 723-Kinstler-a	8	16	24	54	102	150

SARGE SNORKEL (Beetle Bailey)
Charlton Comics: Oct, 1973 - No. 17, Dec, 1976

1	2	4	6	11	16	20
2-10	2	4	6	8	10	12
11-17	1	2	3	5	7	9

SARGE STEEL (Becomes Secret Agent #9 on; also see Judomaster)
Charlton Comics: Dec, 1964 - No. 8, Mar-Apr, 1966 (All 12¢ issues)

1-Origin & 1st app.	4	8	12	23	37	50
2-5,7,8	3	6	9	16	23	30
6-2nd app. Judomaster	3	6	9	19	30	40

SATAN'S SIX
Topps Comics (Kirbyverse): Apr, 1993 - No. 4, July, 1993 ($2.95, lim. series)

1-4: 1-Polybagged w/Kirbychrome trading card; Kirby/McFarlane-c plus 8 pgs. Kirby-a(p); has coupon for Kirbychrome ed. of Secret City Saga #0. 2-4-Polybagged w/3 cards. 4-Teenagents preview						4.00

NOTE: *Ditko a-1. Miller a-1.*

SATAN'S SIX: HELLSPAWN
Topps Comics (Kirbyverse): June, 1994 - No. 3, July, 1994 ($2.50, limited series)

1-3: 1-(6/94)-Indicia incorrectly shows "Vol 1 #2". 2-(6/94)						3.00

Satellite Sam #1 © MCM & Chaykin

Savage Dragon #59 © Erik Larsen

Savage Hawkman #11 © DC

GD VG FN VF VF/NM NM-
2.0 4.0 6.0 8.0 9.0 9.2

SATELLITE SAM
Image Comics: Jul, 2013 - Present ($3.50, B&W, mature)
1-7-Matt Fraction-s/Howard Chaykin-a/c 3.50

SAUCER COUNTRY
DC Comics (Vertigo): May, 2012 - No. 14, Jun, 2013 ($2.99)
1-14: 1-Cornell-s/Kelly-a. 6-Broxton-a. 11-Colak-a 3.00

SAURIANS: UNNATURAL SELECTION (See Sigil)
CrossGeneration Comics: Feb, 2002 - No. 2, Mar, 2002 ($2.95, limited series)
1,2-Waid-s/DiVito-a 3.00

SAVAGE
Image Comics (Shadowline): Oct, 2008 - No. 4, Jan, 2009 ($3.50, limited series)
1-4-Mayhew-c/a; Niles and Frank-s 3.50

SAVAGE AXE OF ARES
Marvel Comics: June, 2010 ($3.99, B&W, one-shot)
1-B&W short stories by Hurwitz, Palo, McKeever, Swierczynski, Manco and others 4.00

SAVAGE COMBAT TALES
Atlas/Seaboard Publ.: Feb, 1975 - No. 3, July, 1975
1,3: 1-Sgt. Stryker's Death Squad begins (origin); Goodwin-s 2 4 6 9 13 16
2-Toth-a; only app. War Hawk; Goodwin-s 2 4 6 10 14 18
NOTE: *Buckler c-3. McWilliams a-1-3; c-1. Sparling a-1, 3.*

SAVAGE DRAGON, THE (See Megaton #3 & 4)
Image Comics (Highbrow Entertainment): July, 1992 - No. 3, Dec, 1992 ($1.95, lim. series)
1-Erik Larsen-c/a/scripts & bound-in poster in all; 4 cover color variations w/4 different posters; 1st Highbrow Entertainment title 5.00
2-Intro SuperPatriot-c/story (10/92) 4.00
3-Contains coupon for Image Comics #0 4.00
3-With coupon missing 2.00
...Vs. Savage Megaton Man 1 (3/93, $1.95)-Larsen & Simpson-c/a. 4.00
TPB-('93, $9.95) r/#1-3 10.00

SAVAGE DRAGON, THE
Image Comics (Highbrow Entertainment): June, 1993 - Present ($1.95/$2.50/$2.99/$3.50)
1-Erik Larsen-c/a/scripts 5.00
2-($2.95, 52 pgs.)-Teenage Mutant Ninja Turtles-c/story; flip book features Vanguard #0 (See Megaton for 1st app.); 1st app. Supreme 4.00
3-30: 3-7: Erik Larsen-c/a/scripts. 3-Mighty Man back-up story w/Austin-a(i). 4-Flip book w/Ricochet. 5-Mighty Man flip-c & back-up plus poster. 6-Jae Lee poster. 7-Vanguard poster. 8-Deadly Duo poster by Larsen. 13A (10/94)-Jim Lee-c/a; 1st app. Max Cash (Condition Red). 13B (6/95)-Larsen story. 15-Dragon poster by Larsen. 22-TMNT-c/a; Bisley pin-up. 27-"Wondercon Exclusive" new-c. 28-Maxx-c/app. 29-Wildstar-c/app. 30-Spawn app. 3.50
25 ($3.95)-variant-c exists. 4.00
31-49,51-71: 31-God vs. The Devil; alternate version exists w/o expletives (has "God Is Good" inside Image logo) 33-Birth of Dragon/Rapture's baby. 34,35-Hellboy-c/app. 51-Origin of She-Dragon. 70-Ann Stevens killed 3.50
50-($5.95, 100 pgs.) Kaboom and Mighty Man app.; Matsuda back-c; pin-ups by McFarlane, Simonson, Capullo and others 6.00
72-74: 72-Begin $2.95-c 3.50
75-($5.95) 6.00
76-99,101-106,108-114,116-124,126-127,129-131,133-136,138: 76-New direction starts. 83,84-Madman-c/app. 84-Atomics app. 97-Dragon returns home; Mighty Man app. 134-Bomb Queen app. 3.50
100-($8.95) Larsen-s/a; inked by various incl. Sienkiewicz, Timm, Austin, Simonson, Royer; plus pin-ups by Timm, Silvestri, Miller, Cho, Art Adams, Pacheco 9.00
107-($3.95) Firebreather, Invincible, Major Damage-c/app.; flip book w/Major Damage 4.00
115-($7.95, 100 pgs.) Wraparound-c; Freak Force app.; Larsen & Englert-a 8.00
125-($4.99, 64 pgs.) new story, The Fly, & various Mr. Glum reprints 5.00
128-Wesley and the villains from Wanted app.; J.G. Jones-c 4.00
132-($6.99, 80 pgs.) new story with Larsen-a; back-up story with Fosco-a 7.00
137-(8/08) Madman and Amazing Joy Buzzards-c/app. 5.00
137-(8/08) Variant cover with Barack Obama endorsed by Savage Dragon; yellow bkgrd 6 12 18 38 69 100
137-(8/08) 2nd printing of variant cover with Barack Obama and red background 1 3 4 6 8 10
137-3rd & 4th printings: 3rd-Blue background. 4th-Purple background 6.00
139-144,146-149,151-174,176-183: 139-Start $3.50-c; Invincible app. 140,141-Witchblade, Spawn app. 148-Also a FCBD edition.155-160-Dragon War. 160-163-Flip book 3.50
145-Obama-c/app. 1 2 3 5 6 8
150-($5.99, 100 pgs.) back up r/Daredevil's origin from Daredevil #18 (1943) 6.00
175-($3.99, 48 pgs.) Darklord app.; Vanguard back-c and back-up story 4.00
184-194-($3.99) 184,186-188-The Claw app. 190-Regular & digest-size versions 4.00
#0-(7/06, $1.95) reprints origin story from 2005 Image Comics Hardcover 3.50
...Archives Vol. 1 (12/06, $19.99) B&W rep. 1st mini-series #1-3 & #1-21 20.00
...Archives Vol. 2 (2007, $19.99) B&W rep. #22-50; roster pages of Dragon's fellow cops 20.00
...Companion (7/02, $2.95) guide to issues #1-100, character backgrounds 3.50
...Endgame (2/04, $15.95, TPB) r/#47-52 16.00
The Fallen (11/97, $12.95, TPB) r/#7-11, ...Possessed (9/98, $12.95, TPB) r/#12-16, ...Revenge (1998, $12.95, TPB) r/#17-21 13.00
...Gang War (4/00, $16.95, TPB) r/#22-26 17.00
.../Hellboy (10/02, $5.95) r/#34 & #35; Mignola-c 6.00
Image Firsts: Savage Dragon #1 (4/10, $1.00) reprints #1 3.00
...Team-Ups (10/98, $19.95, TPB) r/team-ups 20.00
...: Terminated HC (2/03, $28.95) r/#34-40 & #1/2 29.00
...: This Savage World HC (2002, $24.95) r/#76-81; intro. by Larsen 25.00
...: This Savage World SC (2003, $15.95) r/#76-81; intro. by Larsen 16.00
...: Worlds at War SC (2004, $16.95) r/#41-46; intro. by Larsen; sketch pages 17.00

SAVAGE DRAGON ARCHIVES (Also see Dragon Archives, The)

SAVAGE DRAGONBERT: FULL FRONTAL NERDITY
Image Comics: Oct, 2002 ($5.95, B&W, one-shot)
1-Reprints of the Savage Dragon/Dilbert spoof strips 6.00

SAVAGE DRAGON/DESTROYER DUCK, THE
Image Comics/ Highbrow Entertainment: Nov, 1996 ($3.95, one-shot)
1 4.00

SAVAGE DRAGON: GOD WAR
Image Comics: July, 2004 - No. 4, Oct, 2005 ($2.95, limited series)
1-4-Kirkman-s/Englert-a 3.50

SAVAGE DRAGON/MARSHALL LAW
Image Comics: July, 1997 - No. 2, Aug, 1997 ($2.95, B&W, limited series)
1,2-Pat Mills-s, Kevin O'Neill-a 3.50

SAVAGE DRAGON: SEX & VIOLENCE
Image Comics: Aug, 1997 - No. 2, Sept, 1997 ($2.50, limited series)
1,2-T&M Bierbaum-s, Mays, Lupka, Adam Hughes-a 3.50

SAVAGE DRAGON/TEENAGE MUTANT NINJA TURTLES CROSSOVER
Mirage Studios: Sept, 1993 ($2.75, one-shot)
1-Erik Larsen-c(i) only 4.00

SAVAGE DRAGON: THE RED HORIZON
Image Comics/ Highbrow Entertainment: Feb, 1997 - No. 3 ($2.50, lim. series)
1-3 3.50

SAVAGE FISTS OF KUNG FU
Marvel Comics Group: 1975 (Marvel Treasury)
1-Iron Fist, Shang Chi, Sons of Tiger; Adams, Starlin-a 3 6 9 17 26 35

SAVAGE HAWKMAN, THE (DC New 52)
DC Comics: Nov, 2011 - No. 20, Jun, 2013 ($2.99)
1-20: 1-Tony Daniel-s/Philip Tan-a/c; Carter Hall bonds with the Nth metal 3.00
#0-(11/12, $2.99) Origin story of Katar Hol on Thanagar; Bennett-a/c 3.00

SAVAGE HULK, THE (Also see Incredible Hulk)
Marvel Comics: Jan, 1996 ($6.95, one-shot)
1-Bisley-c; David, Lobdell, Wagner, Loeb, Gibbons, Messner-Loebs scripts; McKone, Kieth, Ramos & Sale-a. 7.00

SAVAGE RAIDS OF GERONIMO (See Geronimo #4)

SAVAGE RANGE (See Luke Short, Four Color 807)

SAVAGE RED SONJA: QUEEN OF THE FROZEN WASTES
Dynamite Entertainment: 2006 - No. 4, 2006 ($3.50, limited series)
1-4: 1-Three covers by Cho, Texeira & Homs; Cho & Murray-s/Homs-a 3.50
TPB (2007, $14.99) r/series; cover gallery and sketch pages 15.00

SAVAGE RETURN OF DRACULA
Marvel Comics: 1992 ($2.00, 52 pgs.)
1-r/Tomb of Dracula #1,2 by Gene Colan 4.00

SAVAGE SHE-HULK, THE (See The Avengers, Marvel Graphic Novel #18 & The Sensational She-Hulk)
Marvel Comics Group: Feb, 1980 - No. 25, Feb, 1982
1-Origin & 1st app. She-Hulk 3 6 9 14 20 25
2-5,25: 25-(52 pgs.) 1 2 3 5 6 8
6-24: 6-She-Hulk vs. Iron Man. 8-Vs. Man-Thing 5.00

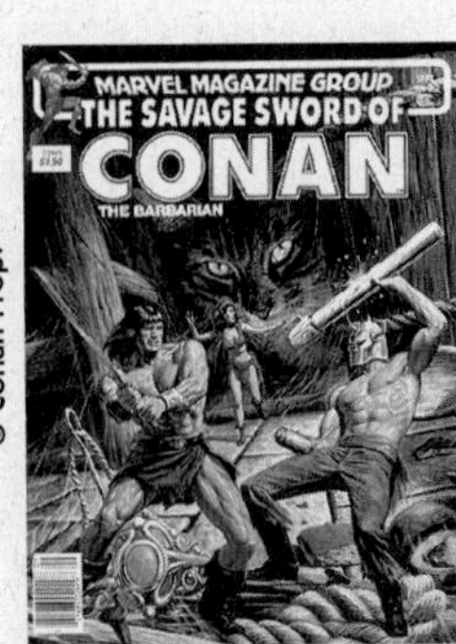

Savage Sword of Conan #92 © Conan Prop.

Savage Wolverine #3 © MAR

Scarab #7 © DC

GD VG FN VF VF/NM NM-
2.0 4.0 6.0 8.0 9.0 9.2

NOTE: ***Austin** a-25i; c-23i-25i. **J. Buscema** a-1p; c-1, 2p. **Golden** c-8-11.*

SAVAGE SHE-HULK (Titled All New Savage She Hulk for #3,4)
Marvel Comics: Jun, 2009 - No. 4, Sept, 2009 ($3.99, limited series)

1-4-Lyra, daughter of the Hulk; She-Hulk & Dark Avengers app. 2-Campbell-c 4.00

SAVAGE SKULLKICKERS (See Skullkickers #20)

SAVAGE SWORD (ROBERT E. HOWARD'S...)
Dark Horse Comics: Dec, 2010 - Present ($7.99, squarebound)

1-7-Short stories by various incl. Roy Thomas, Barry-Windsor-Smith; Conan app. 8.00

SAVAGE SWORD OF CONAN (The... #41 on; ...The Barbarian #175 on)
Marvel Comics Group: Aug, 1974 - No. 235, July, 1995 ($1.00/$1.25/$2.25, B&W magazine, mature)

	GD 2.0	VG 4.0	FN 6.0	VF 8.0	VF/NM 9.0	NM- 9.2
1-Smith-r; J. Buscema/N. Adams/Krenkel-a; origin Blackmark by Gil Kane (part 1, ends #3); Blackmark's 1st app. in magazine form-r/from paperback) & Red Sonja (3rd app.)	9	18	27	62	126	190
2-Neal Adams-c; Chaykin/N. Adams-a	5	10	15	34	60	85
3-Severin/B. Smith-a; N. Adams-a	4	8	12	27	44	60
4-Neal Adams/Kane-a(r)	3	6	9	21	33	45
5-10: 5-Jeff Jones frontispiece (r)	3	6	9	17	26	35
11-20	2	4	6	13	18	22
21-30	2	4	6	10	14	18
31-50: 34-3 pg. preview of Conan newspaper strip. 35-Cover similar to Savage Tales #1. 45-Red Sonja returns; begin $1.25-c	2	4	6	8	11	14
51-99: 63-Toth frontispiece. 65-Kane-a w/Chaykin/Miller/Simonson/Sherman finishes. 70-Article on movie. 83-Red Sonja-r by Neal Adams from #1	1	2	3	5	7	9
100	1	3	4	6	8	10
101-176: 163-Begin $2.25-c. 169-King Kull story. 171-Soloman Kane by Williamson (i). 172-Red Sonja story						6.00
177-199: 179,187,192-Red Sonja app. 190-193-4 part King Kull story. 196-King Kull story						5.00
200-220: 200-New Buscema-a; Robert E. Howard app. with Conan in story. 202-King Kull story. 204-60th anniversary (1932-92). 211-Rafael Kayanan's 1st Conan-a. 214-Sequel to Red Nails by Howard						6.00
221-230	2	4	6	8	10	12
231-234	2	4	6	11	16	20
235-Last issue	4	8	12	27	44	60
Special 1(1975, B&W)-B. Smith-r/Conan #10,13	3	6	9	16	24	32
Volume 1 TPB (Dark Horse Books, 12/07, $17.95, B&W) r/#1-10 and selected stories from Savage Tales #1-5 with covers						18.00
Volume 2 TPB (Dark Horse Books, 3/08, $17.95, B&W) r/#11-24						18.00
Volume 3 TPB (Dark Horse Books, 5/08, $19.95, B&W) r/#25-36 and selected pin-ups						20.00
Volume 4 TPB (Dark Horse Books, 9/08, $19.95, B&W) r/#37-48 and selected pin-ups						20.00
Volume 5 TPB (Dark Horse Books, 2/09, $19.95, B&W) r/#49-60 and selected pin-ups						20.00

NOTE: ***N. Adams** a-14p, 60, 83p(r). **Alcala** a-2, 4, 7, 12, 15-20, 23, 24, 28, 59, 67, 69, 75, 76i, 80i, 82i, 83i, 89, 180i, 184i, 187i, 189i, 216p. **Austin** a-78i. **Boris** painted c-1, 4, 5, 7, 9, 10, 12, 15. **Brunner** a-30; c-8, 30. **Buscema** a-1-5, 7, 10-12, 15-24, 26-28, 31, 32, 36-43, 45, 47-58p, 60-67p, 70, 71-74p, 76-81p, 87-96p, 98, 99-101p, 190-204p; painted c-40. **Chaykin** c-31. **Chiodo** painted c-71, 76, 79, 81, 84, 85, 178. **Conrad** c-215, 217. **Corben** a-4, 16, 29. **Finlay** a-16. **Golden** a-98, 101; c-98, 101, 105, 106, 117, 124, 150. **Kaluta** a-11, 18; c-3, 91, 93. **Gil Kane** a-2, 3, 8, 13r, 29, 47, 64, 65, 67, 85p, 86p. **Rafael Kayanan** a-211-213, 215, 217. **Krenkel** a-9, 11, 14, 16, 24. **Morrow** a-7. **Nebres** a-93i, 101i, 107, 114. **Newton** a-6. **Nino** c/a-6. **Redondo** painted c-48-50, 52, 56, 57, 85i, 90, 96i. **Marie & John Severin** a-Special 1. **Simonson** a-7, 8, 12, 15-17. **Barry Smith** a-7, 16, 24, 82r, Special 1r. **Starlin** c-26. **Toth** a-64. **Williamson** a(i)-162, 171, 186. No. 8, 10 & 16 contain a Robert E. Howard Conan adaptation.*

SAVAGE TALES (...Featuring Conan #4 on)(Magazine)
Marvel Comics Group: May, 1971; No. 2, 10/73; No. 3, 2/74 - No. 12, Summer, 1975 (B&W)

	GD 2.0	VG 4.0	FN 6.0	VF 8.0	VF/NM 9.0	NM- 9.2
1-Origin/1st app. The Man-Thing by Morrow; Conan the Barbarian by Barry Smith (1st Conan x-over outside his own title); Femizons by Romita-r/in #3; Ka-Zar story by Buscema	15	30	45	103	227	350
2-B. Smith, Brunner, Morrow, Williamson-a; Wrightson King Kull reprint/ Creatures on the Loose #10	5	10	15	35	63	90
3-B. Smith, Brunner, Steranko, Williamson-a	5	10	15	30	50	70
4,5-N. Adams-c; last Conan (Smith-r/#4) plus Kane/N. Adams-a. 5-Brak the Barbarian begins, ends #8	4	8	12	27	44	60
6-Ka-Zar begins; Williamson-r; N. Adams-c	3	6	9	19	30	40
7-N. Adams-i	3	6	9	15	22	28
8,9,11: 8-Shanna, the She-Devil app. thru #10; Williamson-r	3	6	9	14	20	26
10-Neal Adams-a(i), Williamson-r	3	6	9	15	22	28
...Featuring Ka-Zar Annual 1 (Summer, '75, B&W)(#12 on inside)-Ka-Zar origin by Gil Kane; B. Smith-r/Astonishing Tales	3	6	9	16	24	32

NOTE: ***Boris** c-7, 10. **Buscema** a-5r, 6p, 8p; c-2. **Colan** a-1p. **Fabian** c-8. **Golden** a-1, 4; c-1. **Heath** a-10p, 11p. **Kaluta** c-9. **Maneely** r-2, 4(The Crusader in both). **Morrow** a-1, 2, Annual 1. **Reese** a-2. **Severin** a-1-7. **Starlin** a-5. Robert E. Howard adaptations-1-4.*

SAVAGE TALES (Volume 2)
Marvel Comics Group: Oct, 1985 - No. 8, Dec, 1986 ($1.50, B&W, magazine, mature)

1-1st app. The Nam; Golden, Morrow-a (indicia incorrectly lists this as Volume 1) 6.00
2-8: 2,7-Morrow-a. 4-2nd Nam story; Golden-a 4.00

SAVAGE TALES
Dynamite Entertainment: 2007 - No. 10 ($4.99)

1-10: 1-Anthology; Red Sonja app.; three covers 5.00

SAVAGE WOLVERINE
Marvel Comics: Mar, 2013 - Present ($3.99)

1-5-Frank Cho-s/a/c; Shanna & Amadeus Cho app. 4.00
1-Variant-c by Skottie Young 8.00
6-16: 6-8-Wells-s/Madureira-a/c; Elektra, Kingpin & Spider-Man app. 9-11-Jock-s/a. 14-16-Isanove-s/a 4.00

SAVANT GARDE (Also see WildC.A.T.S...)
Image Comics/WildStorm Productions: Mar, 1997 - No. 7, Sept, 1997 ($2.50)

1-7 3.00

SAVED BY THE BELL (TV)
Harvey Comics: Mar, 1992 - No. 5, May, 1993 ($1.25, limited series)

1-5, Holiday Special (3/92), Special 1 (9/92, $1.50)-photo-c, Summer Break 1 (10/92) 3.00

SAW: REBIRTH (Based on 2004 movie Saw)
IDW Publ.: Oct, 2005 ($3.99, one-shot)

1-Guedes-a 4.00

SCALPED
DC Comics (Vertigo): Mar, 2007 - No. 60, Oct, 2012 ($2.99, limited series)

1-60: 1-Aaron-s/Guera-a/Jock-c. 12-Leon-a. 50-Bonus pin-ups by various 3.00
1-Special Edition (7/10, $1.00) r/#1 with "What's Next?" cover frame 3.00
...: Casino Blood TPB (2008, $14.99) r/#6-11; intro. by Garth Ennis 15.00
...: Dead Mothers TPB (2008, $17.99) r/#12-18 18.00
...: High Lonesome TPB (2009, $14.99) r/#25-29; intro. by Jason Starr 15.00
...: Indian Country TPB (2007, $9.99) r/#1-5; intro. by Brian K. Vaughan 10.00
...: Rez Blues (2011, $17.99) r/#35-42 18.00
...: The Gnawing (2010, $14.99) r/#30-34; intro. by Matt Fraction 15.00
...: The Gravel in Your Guts (2009, $14.99) r/#19-24; intro. by Ed Brubaker 15.00

SCAMP (Walt Disney)(See Walt Disney's Comics & Stories #204)
Dell Publ. Co./Gold Key: No. 703, 5/56 - No. 1204, 8-10/61; 11/67 - No. 45, 1/79

	GD 2.0	VG 4.0	FN 6.0	VF 8.0	VF/NM 9.0	NM- 9.2
Four Color 703(#1)	8	16	24	51	96	140
Four Color 777,806('57),833	6	12	18	37	66	95
5(3-5/58)-10(6-8/59)	5	10	15	31	53	75
11-16(12-2/60-61), Four Color 1204(1961)	4	8	12	27	44	60
1(12/67-Gold Key)-Reprints begin	4	8	12	25	40	55
2(3/69)-10	2	4	6	13	18	22
11-20	2	4	6	8	11	14
21-45	1	2	3	4	5	7

NOTE: *New stories-#20(in part), 22-25, 27, 29-31, 34, 36-40, 42-45. New covers-#11, 12, 14, 15, 17-25, 27, 29-31, 34, 36-38.*

SCARAB
DC Comics (Vertigo): Nov, 1993 - No. 8, June, 1994 ($1.95, limited series)

1-8-Glenn Fabry painted-c: 1-Silver ink-c. 2-Phantom Stranger app. 3.00

SCARECROW OF ROMNEY MARSH, THE (See W. Disney Showcase #53)
Gold Key: April, 1964 - No. 3, Oct, 1965 (Disney TV Show)

	GD 2.0	VG 4.0	FN 6.0	VF 8.0	VF/NM 9.0	NM- 9.2
10112-404 (#1)	5	10	15	35	63	90
2,3	4	8	12	27	44	60

SCARECROW (VILLAINS) (See Batman)
DC Comics: Feb, 1998 ($1.95, one-shot)

1-Fegredo-a/Milligan-s/Pearson-c 3.00

SCARE TACTICS
DC Comics: Dec, 1996 - No. 12, Mar, 1998 ($2.25)

1-12: 1-1st app. 3.00

SCAR FACE (See The Crusaders)

SCARFACE: SCARRED FOR LIFE (Based on the 1983 movie)
IDW Publishing: Dec, 2006 - No. 5, Apr, 2007 ($3.99, limited series)

1-5-Tony Montana survives his shooting; Layman-s/Crosland-a 4.00
Scarface: Devil in Disguise (7/07 - No. 4, 10/07, $3.99) Alberto Dose-a 4.00

SCARLET
Marvel Comics (ICON): July, 2010 - Present ($3.95)

1-7-Bendis-s/Maleev-a. 1-Second printing exists 4.00

Scarlet #5 © Jinxworld

Science Comics #5 © FOX

Sci-Spy #1 © Moench & Gulacy

	GD 2.0	VG 4.0	FN 6.0	VF 8.0	VF/NM 9.0	NM- 9.2

1,2-Variant covers. 1-Deodato & Lafuente. 2-Oeming & Mack. 3,4-Oeming. 5-Bendis 6.00

SCARLET O'NEIL (See Harvey Comics Hits #59 & Invisible...)

SCARLET SPIDER
Marvel Comics: Nov, 1995 - No. 2, Jan, 1996 ($1.95, limited series)

1,2: Replaces Spider-Man title 3.00

SCARLET SPIDER
Marvel Comics: Mar, 2012 - No. 25, Feb, 2014 ($3.99/$2.99)

1-Kaine following "Spider Island"; Yost-s/Stegman-a; 2 covers by Stegman 4.00
2-12, 12.1, 13-24-($2.99) 10,11-Carnage & Venom app. 17-19-Wolverine app. 3.00
25-($3.99) Last issue; Yost-s/Baldeon-a 4.00

SCARLET SPIDER UNLIMITED
Marvel Comics: Nov, 1995 ($3.95, one-shot)

1-Replaces Spider-Man Unlimited title 4.00

SCARLET WITCH (See Avengers #16, Vision &... & X-Men #4)
Marvel Comics: Jan, 1994 - No. 4, Apr, 1994 ($1.75, limited series)

1-4 3.00

SCARY GODMOTHER (Hardcover story books)
Sirius: 1997 - Present ($19.95, HC with dust jackets, one-shots)

Volume 1 (9/97) Jill Thompson-s/a; first app. of Scary Godmother 20.00
Vol. 2 - The Revenge of Jimmy (9/98, $19.95) 20.00
Vol. 3 - The Mystery Date (10/99, $19.95) 20.00
Vol. 4 - The Boo Flu (9/02, $19.95) 20.00

SCARY GODMOTHER
Sirius: 2001 - No. 6, 2002 ($2.95, B&W, limited series)

1-6-Jill Thompson-s/a 3.00
...: Activity Book (12/00, $2.95, B&W) Jill Thompson-s/a 3.00
...: Bloody Valentine Special (2/98, $3.95, B&W) Jill Thompson-s/a; pin-ups by Ross, Mignola, Russell 4.00
...: Ghoul's Out For Summer (2002,$14.95, B&W) r/#1-6 15.00
...: Holiday Spooktakular (11/98, $2.95, B&W) Jill Thompson-s/a; pin-ups by Brereton, LaBan, Dorkin, Fingerman 3.00

SCARY GODMOTHER: WILD ABOUT HARRY
Sirius: 2000 - No. 3 ($2.95, B&W, limited series)

1-3-Jill Thompson-s/a 3.00
TPB (2001, $9.95) r/series 10.00

SCARY TALES
Charlton Comics: 8/75 - #9, 1/77; #10, 9/77 - #20, 6/79; #21, 8/80 - #46, 10/84

	GD	VG	FN	VF	VF/NM	NM-
1-Origin/1st app. Countess Von Bludd, not in #2	3	6	9	21	33	45
2,4,6,9,10: 4,9-Sutton-c/a. 4-Man-Thing copy	2	4	6	11	16	20
3-Sutton painted-c; Ditko-a	3	6	9	14	20	25
5,11-Ditko-c/a.	3	6	9	16	23	30
7,8-Ditko-a	2	4	6	13	18	22
12,15,16,19,21,39-Ditko-a	2	4	6	11	16	20
13,17,20	2	4	6	9	12	15
14,18,30,32-Ditko-c/a	3	6	9	14	20	25
22-29,33-37,39,40: 37,38,40-New-a. 39-All Ditko reprints and cover	2	4	6	8	10	12
31,38: 31-Newton-c/a. 38-Mr. Jigsaw app.	2	4	6	8	10	12
41-45-New-a. 41-Ditko-a(3). 42-45-(Low print)	2	4	6	9	12	15
46-Reprints (Low print)	2	4	6	11	16	20
1(Modern Comics reprint, 1977)	1	3	4	6	8	10

NOTE: ***Adkins*** *a-31i; c-31i.* ***Ditko*** *a-3, 5, 7, 8(2), 11, 12, 14-16r, 18(3)r, 19r, 21r, 30r, 32, 39r, 41(3); c-5, 11, 14, 18, 30, 32.* ***Newton*** *a-31p; c-31p.* ***Powell*** *a-18r.* ***Staton*** *a-1(2 pgs.), 4, 20r; c-1, 20.* ***Sutton*** *a-4, 9; c-4, 9.* ***Zeck*** *a-9.*

SCATTERBRAIN
Dark Horse Comics: Jun, 1998 - No. 4, Sept, 1998 ($2.95, limited series)

1-4-Humor anthology by Aragonés, Dorkin, Stevens and others 3.00

SCAVENGERS
Quality Comics: Feb, 1988 - No. 14, 1989 ($1.25/$1.50)

1-14: 9-13-Guice-c 3.00

SCAVENGERS
Triumphant Comics: 1993(nd, July) - No. 11, May, 1994 ($2.50, serially numbered)

1-9,0,10,11: 5,6-Triumphant Unleashed x-over. 9-(3/94). 0-Retail ed. (3/94, $2.50, 36 pgs.). 0-Giveaway edition (3/94, 20 pgs.). 0-Coupon redemption edition. 10-(4/94) 3.00

SCENE OF THE CRIME (Also see Vertigo: Winter's Edge #2)
DC Comics (Vertigo): May, 1999 - No. 4, Aug, 1999 ($2.50, limited series)

1-4-Brubaker-s/Lark-a 3.00
...: A Little Piece of Goodnight TPB ('00, $12.95) r/#1-4; Winter's Edge #2 13.00

SCHOOL DAY ROMANCES (...of Teen-Agers #4; Popular Teen-Agers #5 on)
Star Publications: Nov-Dec, 1949 - No. 4, May-June, 1950 (Teenage)

	GD	VG	FN	VF	VF/NM	NM-
1-Toni Gayle (later Toni Gay), Ginger Snapp, Midge Martin & Eve Adams begin	30	60	90	177	289	400
2,3: 3-Jane Powell photo on-c & true life story	21	42	63	122	199	275
4-Ronald Reagan photo on-c; L.B. Cole-c	33	66	99	194	317	440

NOTE: *All have* ***L. B. Cole*** *covers.*

SCHWINN BICYCLE BOOK (...Bike Thrills, 1959)
Schwinn Bicycle Co.: 1949; 1952; 1959 (10¢)

	GD	VG	FN	VF	VF/NM	NM-
1949	6	12	18	28	34	40
1952-Believe It or Not facts; comic format; 36 pgs.	5	10	14	20	24	28
1959	3	6	8	11	13	15

SCIENCE COMICS (1st Series)
Fox Features Syndicate: Feb, 1940 - No. 8, Sept, 1940

	GD	VG	FN	VF	VF/NM	NM-
1-Origin Dynamo (1st app., called Electro in #1), The Eagle (1st app.), & Navy Jones; Marga, The Panther Woman (1st app.), Cosmic Carson & Perisphere Payne, Dr. Doom begin; bondage/hypo-c; Electro-c	524	1048	1572	3825	6763	9700
2-Classic Lou Fine Dynamo-c	300	600	900	1920	3310	4700
3-Classic Lou Fine Dynamo-c	245	490	735	1568	2684	3800
4-Kirby-a; Cosmic Carson-c by Joe Simon	213	426	639	1363	2332	3300
5-8: 5,8-Eagle-c. 6,7-Dynamo-c	116	232	348	742	1271	1800

NOTE: *Cosmic Carson by* ***Tuska****-#1-3; by* ***Kirby****-#4.* ***Lou Fine*** *c-1-3 only.*

SCIENCE COMICS (2nd Series)
Humor Publications (Ace Magazines?): Jan, 1946 - No. 5, 1946

	GD	VG	FN	VF	VF/NM	NM-
1-Palais-c/a in #1-3; A-Bomb-c	21	42	63	124	202	280
2	13	26	39	74	105	135
3-Feldstein-a (6 pgs.); Palais-c	17	34	51	98	154	210
4,5: 4-Palais-c	10	20	30	56	76	95

SCIENCE COMICS
Ziff-Davis Publ. Co.: May, 1947 (8 pgs. in color)

	GD	VG	FN	VF	VF/NM	NM-
nn-Could be ordered by mail for 10¢; like the nn Amazing Adventures (1950) & Boy Cowboy (1950); used to test the market	43	86	129	271	461	650

SCIENCE COMICS (True Science Illustrated)
Export Publication Ent., Toronto, Canada: Mar, 1951 (Distr. in U.S. by Kable News Co.)

	GD	VG	FN	VF	VF/NM	NM-
1-Science Adventure stories plus some true science features; man on moon story	14	28	42	82	121	160

SCIENCE DOG SPECIAL (Also see Invincible)
Image Comics: Aug, 2010; No. 2, May, 2011 ($3.50)

1,2: 1-Kirkman-s/Walker-a/c; leads into Invincible #75 3.50

SCIENCE FICTION SPACE ADVENTURES (See Space Adventures)

SCION (Also see CrossGen Chronicles)
CrossGeneration Comics: July, 2000 - No. 43, Apr, 2004 ($2.95)

1-43: 1-Marz-s/Cheung-a 3.00
...: Conflict of Conscience Vol. 1 TPB (5/01, $19.95) r/#1-7; Adam Hughes-c 20.00
...: Blood For Blood Vol. 2 TPB (2002, $19.95) r/#8-14 & CrossGen Chronicles #2 20.00
...: Divided Loyalties Vol. 3 TPB (2002, $15.95) r/#15-21 16.00
...: Sanctuary Vol. 4 TPB (2003, $15.95) r/#22-27 16.00
Vol. 5: The Far Kingdom (2003, $15.95) r/#28-33 16.00
Vol. 6: The Royal Wedding (2004, $15.95) r/#34-39 16.00
Traveler Vol. 1-3 ($9.95) Digest-sized reprints of TPBs 10.00

SCI-SPY
DC Comics (Vertigo): Apr, 2002 - No. 6, Sept, 2002 ($2.50, limited series)

1-6-Moench-s/Gulacy-c/a 3.00

SCI-TECH
DC Comics (WildStorm): Sept, 1999 - No. 4, Dec, 1999 ($2.50, limited series)

1-4-Benes-a/Choi & Peterson-s 3.00

SCOOBY DOO (TV)(...Where are you? #1-16,26; ...Mystery Comics #17-25, 27 on)
(See March Of Comics #356, 368, 382, 391 in the Promotional Comics section)
Gold Key: Mar, 1970 - No. 30, Feb, 1975 (Hanna-Barbera)

	GD	VG	FN	VF	VF/NM	NM-
1	37	74	111	274	612	950
2-5	11	22	33	76	163	250
6-10	9	18	27	61	123	185
11-20: 11-Tufts-a	6	12	18	41	76	110
21-30	5	10	15	35	63	90

SCOOBY DOO (TV)
Charlton Comics: Apr, 1975 - No. 11, Dec, 1976 (Hanna-Barbera)

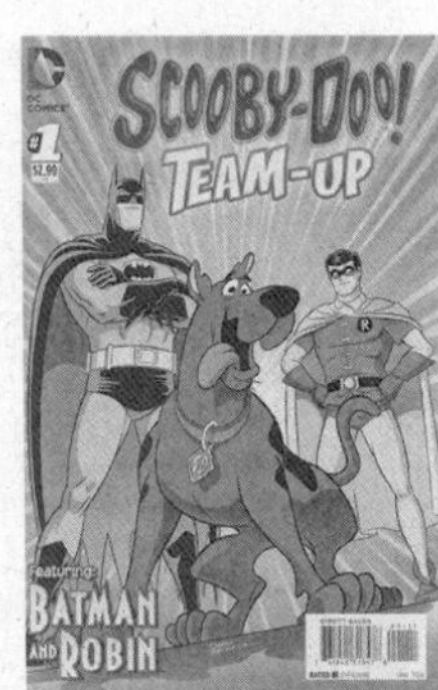

Scooby-Doo Team-Up #1 © H-B

Scoop Comics #3 © CHES

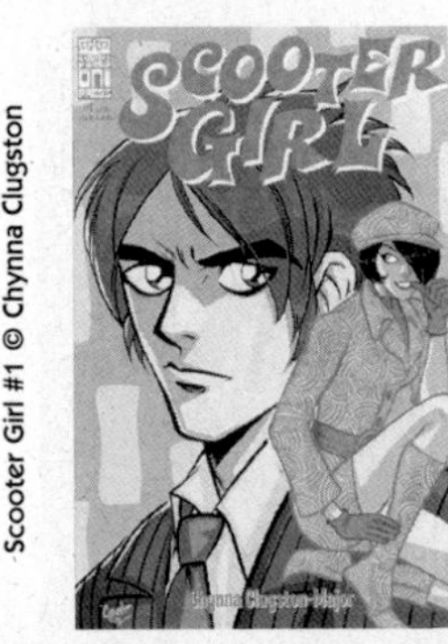

Scooter Girl #1 © Chynna Clugston

GD 2.0 | VG 4.0 | FN 6.0 | VF 8.0 | VF/NM 9.0 | NM- 9.2

GD 2.0 | VG 4.0 | FN 6.0 | VF 8.0 | VF/NM 9.0 | NM- 9.2

1 7 14 21 46 86 125
2-5 5 10 15 31 53 75
6-11 4 8 12 27 44 60
nn-(1976, digest, 68 pgs., B&W) 4 8 12 27 44 60

SCOOBY-DOO (TV)(Newsstand sales only) (See Dynamutt & Laff-A-Lympics)
Marvel Comics Group: Oct, 1977 - No. 9, Feb, 1979 (Hanna-Barbera)

1-Dyno-Mutt begins 4 8 12 27 44 60
1-(35¢-c variant, limited distribution)(10/77) 9 18 27 60 120 180
2-5 3 6 9 17 26 35
6-9 3 6 9 19 30 40

SCOOBY-DOO (TV)
Harvey Comics: Sept, 1992 - No. 3, May, 1993 ($1.25)

V2#1,2 2 4 6 8 10 12
Big Book 1,2 (11/92, 4/93, $1.95, 52 pgs.) 1 2 3 5 7 9
Giant Size 1,2 (10/92, 3/93, $2.25, 68 pgs.) 1 2 3 5 7 9

SCOOBY DOO (TV)
Archie Comics: Oct, 1995 -No. 21, June, 1997 ($1.50)

1 2 4 6 9 12 15
2-21: 12-Cover by Scooby Doo creative designer Iwao Takamoto 6.00

SCOOBY DOO (TV)
DC Comics: Aug, 1997 - No. 159, Oct, 2010 ($1.75/$1.95/$1.99/$2.25/$2.50/$2.99)

1 1 2 3 5 6 8
2-10: 5-Begin-$1.95-c 5.00
11-45: 14-Begin $1.99-c 4.00
46-89,91-157: 63-Begin $2.25-c. 75-With 2 Garbage Pail Kids stickers. 100-Wray-c 3.00
90,158,159: 90-($2.95) Bonus stories. 158,159-($2.99-c) 4.00
...Spooky Spectacular 1 (10/99, $3.95) Comic Convention story 4.00
...Spooky Spectacular 2000 (10/00, $3.95) 4.00
...Spooky Summer Special 2001 (8/01, $3.95) Staton-a 4.00
...Super Scarefest (8/02, $3.95) r/#20,25,30-32 4.00

SCOOBY-DOO-TEAM-UP (TV)
DC Comics: Jan, 2014 - Present ($2.99)

1,2: 1-Batman & Robin app.; Man-Bat app. 2-Ace the Bat-Hound app. 3-Bat-Mite app. 3.00

SCOOBY DOO: WHERE ARE YOU? (TV)
DC Comics: Nov, 2010 - Present ($2.99)

1-43: 32-KISS spoof 3.00

SCOOP COMICS (Becomes Yankee Comics #4-7, a digest sized cartoon book; then after #8 it becomes Snap #9)
Harry 'A' Chesler (Holyoke): November, 1941 - No. 3, Mar, 1943; No. 8, 1944

1-Intro. Rocketman & Rocketgirl & begins; origin The Master Key & begins; Dan Hastings begins; Charles Sultan-c/a 155 310 465 992 1696 2400
2-Rocket Boy begins; injury to eye story (reprinted in Spotlight #3); classic-c 206 412 618 1318 2259 3200
3-Injury to eye story-r from #2; Rocket Boy 81 162 243 518 884 1250
8-Formerly Yankee Comics; becomes Snap 54 108 162 343 574 825

SCOOTER (See Swing With...)

SCOOTER COMICS
Rucker Publ. Ltd. (Canadian): Apr, 1946

1-Teen-age/funny animal 14 28 42 80 115 150

SCOOTER GIRL
Oni Press: May, 2003 - No. 6, Feb, 2004 ($2.99, B&W, limited series)

1-6-Chynna Clugston-Major-s/a 3.00
TPB (5/04, $14.95, digest size) r/series; sketch pages 15.00

SCORPION
Atlas/Seaboard Publ.: Feb, 1975 - No. 3, July, 1975

1-Intro.; bondage-c by Chaykin 3 6 9 14 19 24
2-Chaykin-a w/Wrightson, Kaluta, Simonson assists(p) 3 6 9 14 19 24
3-Jim Craig-c/a 2 4 6 11 16 20
NOTE: ***Chaykin** a-1, 2; c-1. **Colon** c-2. **Craig** c/a-3.*

SCORPION KING, THE (Movie)
Dark Horse Comics: March, 2002 - No. 2, Apr, 2002 ($2.99, limited series)

1,2-Photo-c of the Rock; Richards-a 3.00

SCORPIO ROSE
Eclipse Comics: Jan, 1983 - No. 2, Oct, 1983 ($1.25, Baxter paper)

1,2: Dr. Orient back-up story begins. 2-origin. 4.00

SCOTLAND YARD (Inspector Farnsworth of)(Texas Rangers in Action #5 on?)
Charlton Comics Group: June, 1955 - No. 4, Mar, 1956

1-Tothish-a 14 28 42 80 115 150
2-4: 2-Tothish-a 10 20 30 54 72 90

SCOTT PILGRIM, ... (Inspired the 2010 movie)
Oni Press: Jul, 2004 - Vol. 6, Jul, 2010 ($11.99, B&W, 7-1/2" x 5", multiple printings exist)

Scott Pilgrim's Precious Little Life (Vol. 1) Bryan Lee O'Malley-s/a in all 12.00
Scott Pilgrim Vs. The World (Vol. 2), S.P. & The Infinite Sadness (Vol. 3), S.P. Gets it Together (Vol. 4), S.P. Vs. The Universe (Vol. 5), Scott Pilgrim's Finest Hour (Vol. 6) each 12.00
Free Scott Pilgrim #1 (Free Comic Book Day Edition, 2006) 15.00
Full-Colour Odds & Ends 2008 12.00

SCOURGE, THE
Aspen MLT: No. 0, Aug, 2010 - No. 6, Dec, 2011 ($2.50/$2.99)

0-($2.50) Lobdell-s/Battle-a; multiple covers 3.00
1-6-($2.99) Lobdell-s/Battle-a; multiple covers 3.00

SCOURGE OF THE GODS
Marvel Comics (Soleil): 2009 - No. 3, 2009 ($5.99, limited series)

1-3-Mangin-s/Gajic-a; English version of French comic 6.00
...: The Fall 1-3 (2009 - No. 3, 2009) 6.00

SCOUT (See Eclipse Graphic Album #16, New America & Swords of Texas)
(Becomes Scout: War Shaman)
Eclipse Comics: Dec, 1985 - No. 24, Oct, 1987($1.75/$1.25, Baxter paper)

1-15,17,18,20-24: 19-Airboy preview. 10-Bissette-a. 11-Monday, the Eliminator begins. 15-Swords of Texas 3.00
16,19: 16-Scout 3-D Special ($2.50), 16-Scout 2-D Limited Edition, 19-contains flexidisk ($2.50) 4.00
...Handbook 1 (8/87, $1.75, B&W) 3.00
Mount Fire (1989, $14.95, TPB) r/#8-14 15.00

SCOUT: WAR SHAMAN (Formerly Scout)
Eclipse Comics: Mar, 1988 - No. 16, Dec, 1989 ($1.95)

1-16 3.00

SCRATCH
DC Comics: Aug, 2004 - No. 5, Dec, 2004 ($2.50, limited series)

1-5-Sam Kieth-s/a/c; Batman app. 3.00

SCREAM (...Comics) (Andy Comics #20 on)
Humor Publications/Current Books(Ace Magazines): Autumn, 1944 - No. 19, Apr, 1948

1-Teenage humor 17 34 51 98 154 210
2 11 22 33 60 83 105
3-16: 11-Racist humor (Indians). 16-Intro. Lily-Belle 9 18 27 52 69 85
17,19 9 18 27 47 61 75
18-Hypo needle story 9 18 27 52 69 85

SCREAM (Magazine)
Skywald Publ. Corp.: Aug, 1973 - No. 11, Feb, 1975 (68 pgs., B&W) (Painted-c on all)

1-Nosferatu-c/1st app. (series thru #11); Morrow-a. Cthulhu/Necronomicon-s 7 14 21 49 92 135
2,3: 2-(10/73) Lady Satan 1st app. & series begins; Edgar Allan Poe adaptations begin (thru #11); Phantom of the Opera-s. 3-(12/73) Origin Lady Satan 5 10 15 33 57 80
4-1st Cannibal Werewolf and 1st Lunatic Mummy 4 8 12 28 50 70
5,7,8: 5,7-Frankenstein app. 8-Buckler-a; Werewolf-s; Slither-Slime Man-s 4 8 12 28 50 70
6, 9,10: 6-(6/74) Saga of The Victims/ I Am Horror, classic GGA Hewetson series begins (thru #11); Frankenstein 2073-s. 9-Severed head-c; Marcos-a. 9,10-Werewolf-s. 10-Dracula-c/s 5 10 15 31 53 75
11- (1975 Winter Special) "Mr. Poe and the Raven" story 5 10 15 33 57 80
NOTE: ***Buckler** a-8. **Hewetson** s-1-11. **Marcos** a-9. **Miralles** c-2. **Morrow** a-1. **Poe** s-2-11. **Segrelles** a-7; c-1.*

SCREEN CARTOONS
DC Comics: Dec, 1944 (cover only ashcan)

nn-Ashcan comic, not distributed to newsstands, only for in house use. Covers were produced, but not the rest of the book. A copy sold in 2006 for $400 and in 2008 for $500.

SCREEN COMICS
DC Comics: Dec, 1944 (cover only ashcan)

nn-Ashcan comic, not distributed to newsstands, only for in house use. Covers were produced, but not the rest of the book. A copy sold in 2006 for $400, in 2008 for $500 and in 2013 for $500.

SCREEN FABLES
DC Comics: Dec, 1944 (cover only ashcan)

nn-Ashcan comic, not distributed to newsstands, only for in house use. Covers were produced,

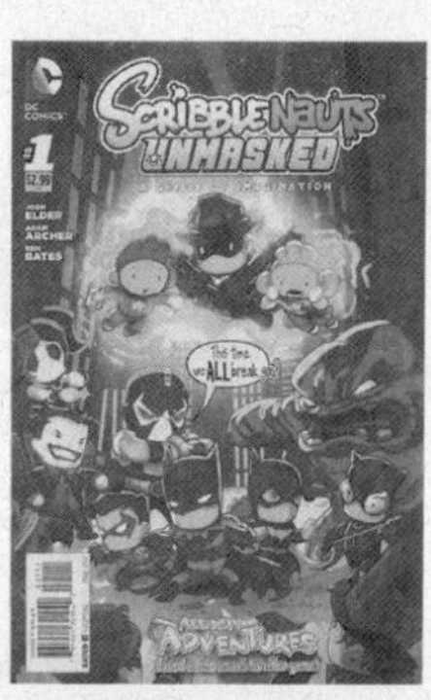

Scribblenauts Unmasked #1 © DC

Sea Devils #28 © DC

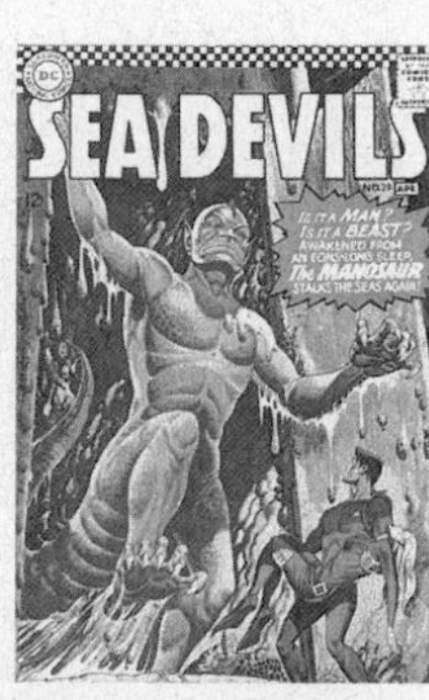

Secret Agent #1 © GK

	GD 2.0	VG 4.0	FN 6.0	VF 8.0	VF/NM 9.0	NM- 9.2

but not the rest of the book. A copy sold in 2006 for $400 and in 2008 for $500.

SCREEN FUNNIES
DC Comics: Dec, 1944 (cover only ashcan)

nn-Ashcan comic, not distributed to newsstands, only for in house use. Covers were produced, but not the rest of the book. A copy sold in 2006 for $400 and in 2008 for $500.

SCREEN GEMS
DC Comics: Dec, 1944 (cover only ashcan)

nn-Ashcan comic, not distributed to newsstands, only for in house use. Covers were produced, but not the rest of the book. A copy sold in 2010 for $891 and a VF copy sold for $775.

SCREWBALL SQUIRREL
Dark Horse Comics: July, 1995 - No. 3, Sept, 1995 ($2.50, limited series)

1-3: Characters created by Tex Avery						3.00

SCRIBBLENAUTS UNMASKED: A CRISIS OF IMAGINATION (Based on the video game)
DC Comics: Mar, 2014 - Present ($2.99)

1-3: 1-The Bat Family, the Joker and Phantom Stranger app. 3-The Anti-Monitor app.						3.00

SCRIBBLY (See All-American Comics, Buzzy, The Funnies, Leave It To Binky & Popular Comics)
National Periodical Publ.: 8-9/48 - No. 13, 8-9/50; No. 14, 10-11/51 - No. 15, 12-1/51-52

1-Sheldon Mayer-c/a in all; 52 pgs. begin	87	174	261	553	952	1350
2	55	110	165	352	601	850
3-5	45	90	135	284	480	675
6-10	36	72	108	216	351	485
11-15: 13-Last 52 pgs.	31	62	93	184	300	415

SCUD: TALES FROM THE VENDING MACHINE
Fireman Press: 1998 - No. 5 ($2.50, B&W)

1-5: 1-Kaniuga-a. 2-Ruben Martinez-a						3.00

SCUD: THE DISPOSABLE ASSASSIN
Fireman Press: Feb, 1994 - No. 20, 1997 ($2.95, B&W)
Image Comics: No. 21, Feb, 2008 - No. 24, May, 2008 ($3.50, B&W)

1						6.00
1-2nd printing in color						3.00
2,3						4.00
4-20						3.00
21-24: 21-(2/08, $3.50) Ashley Wood-c. 22-Mahfood-c						3.50
Heavy 3PO ($12.95, TPB) r/#1-4						13.00
Programmed For Damage ($14.95, TPB) r/#5-9						15.00
Solid Gold Bomb ($17.95, TPB) r/#10-15						18.00

SEA DEVILS (See Limited Collectors' Edition #39,45, & Showcase #27-29)
National Periodical Publications: Sept-Oct, 1961 - No. 35, May-June, 1967

1-(9-10/61)	55	110	165	440	983	1525
2-Last 10¢ issue; grey-tone-c	27	54	81	194	435	675
3-Begin 12¢ issues thru #35; grey-tone-c	18	36	54	124	275	425
4,5-Grey-tone-c	15	30	45	105	233	360
6-10	10	20	30	69	147	225
11,12,14-20: 12-Grey-tone-c	8	16	24	54	102	150
13-Kubert, Colan-a; Joe Kubert app. in story	8	16	24	55	105	155
21-35: 22-Intro. International Sea Devils; origin & 1st app. Capt. X & Man Fish. 33,35-Grey-tone-c	6	12	18	40	73	105

NOTE: ***Heath*** *a-Showcase 27-29, 1-10; c-Showcase 27-29, 1-10, 14-16.* ***Moldoff*** *a-16i.*

SEA DEVILS (See Tangent Comics/ Sea Devils)

SEADRAGON (Also see the Epsilion Wave)
Elite Comics: May, 1986 - No. 8, 1987 ($1.75)

1-8: 1-1st & 2nd printings exist						3.00

SEAGUY
DC Comics (Vertigo): July, 2004 - No. 3, Sept, 2004 ($2.95, limited series)

1-3-Grant Morrison-s/Cameron Stewart-a/c						3.00
TPB (2005, $9.95) r/#1-3						10.00

SEAGUY: THE SLAVES OF MICKEY EYE
DC Comics (Vertigo): Jun, 2009 - No. 3, Aug, 2009 ($3.99, limited series)

1-3-Grant Morrison-s/Cameron Stewart-a/c						4.00

SEA HOUND, THE (Captain Silver's Log Of The...)
Avon Periodicals: 1945 (no month) - No. 2, Sept-Oct, 1945

nn (#1)-29 pg. novel length sty-"The Esmeralda's Treasure"	18	36	54	105	165	225
2	13	26	39	74	105	135

SEA HOUND, THE (Radio)
Capt. Silver Syndicate: No. 3, July, 1949 - No. 4, Sept, 1949

3,4	10	20	30	54	72	90

SEA HUNT (TV)
Dell Publishing Co.: No. 928, 8/58 - No. 1041, 10-12/59; No. 4, 1-3/60 - No. 13, 4-6/62 (All have Lloyd Bridges photo-c)

Four Color 928(#1)	10	20	30	64	132	200
Four Color 994(#2), 4-13: Manning-a #4-6,8-11,13	7	14	21	46	86	125
Four Color 1041(#3)-Toth-a	7	14	21	46	86	125

SEA OF RED
Image Comics: Mar, 2005 - No. 13, Nov, 2006 ($2.95/$2.99/$3.50)

1-12-Vampirates at sea; Remender & Dwyer-s/Dwyer & Sam-a						3.00
13-($3.50)						3.50
Vol. 1: No Grave But The Sea (9/05, $8.95) r/#1-4						9.00
Vol. 2: No Quarter (2006, $11.99) r/#5-8						12.00
Vol. 3: The Deadlights (2006, $14.99) r/#9-13						15.00

SEAQUEST (TV)
Nemesis Comics: Mar, 1994 ($2.25)

1-Has 2 diff-c stocks (slick & cardboard); Alcala-i						3.00

SEARCH FOR LOVE
American Comics Group: Feb-Mar, 1950 - No. 2, Apr-May, 1950 (52 pgs.)

1	14	28	42	76	108	140
2	9	18	27	52	69	85

SEARCHERS, THE (Movie)
Dell Publishing Co.: No. 709, 1956

Four Color 709-John Wayne photo-c	20	40	60	138	307	475

SEARCHERS, THE
Caliber Comics: 1996 - No. 4, 1996 ($2.95, B&W)

1-4						3.00

SEARCHERS, THE : APOSTLE OF MERCY
Caliber Comics: 1997 - No. 2, 1997 ($2.95/$3.95, B&W)

1-($2.95)						3.00
2-($3.95)						4.00

SEARS (See Merry Christmas From...)

SEASON'S GREETINGS
Hallmark (King Features): 1935 (6-1/4x5-1/4", 24 pgs. in color)

nn-Cover features Mickey Mouse, Popeye, Jiggs & Skippy. "The Night Before Christmas" told one panel per page, each panel by a famous artist featuring their character. Art by Alex Raymond, Gottfredson, Swinnerton, Segar, Chic Young, Milt Gross, Sullivan (Messmer), Herriman, McManus, Percy Crosby & others (22 artists in all)
Estimated value... 950.00

SEBASTIAN O
DC Comics (Vertigo): May, 1993 - No. 3, July, 1993 ($1.95, limited series)

1-3-Grant Morrison scripts; Steve Yeowell-a						3.00
TPB (2004, $9.95) r/#1-3; intro. chronology by Morrison						10.00

SECOND LIFE OF DOCTOR MIRAGE, THE (See Shadowman #16)
Valiant: Nov, 1993 - No. 18, May, 1995 ($2.50)

1-18: 1-With bound-in poster. 5-Shadowman x-over. 7-Bound-in trading card						3.00
1-Gold ink logo edition; no price on-c						6.00

SECRET AGENT (Formerly Sarge Steel)
Charlton Comics: V2#9, Oct, 1966; V2#10, Oct, 1967

V2#9-Sarge Steel part-r begins	3	6	9	16	24	32
10-Tiffany Sinn, CIA app. (from Career Girl Romances #39); Aparo-a	3	6	9	14	19	24

SECRET AGENT (TV) (See Four Color #1231)
Gold Key: Nov, 1966; No. 2, Jan, 1968

1-John Drake photo-c	7	14	21	49	92	135
2-Photo-c	5	10	15	35	63	90

SECRET AGENT X-9 (See Flash Gordon #4 by King)
David McKay Publ.: 1934 (Book 1: 84 pgs.; Book 2: 124 pgs.) (8x7-1/2")

Book 1-Contains reprints of the first 13 weeks of the strip by Alex Raymond; complete except for 2 dailies	43	86	129	271	461	650
Book 2-Contains reprints immediately following contents of Book 1, for 20 weeks by Alex Raymond; complete except for two dailies. Note: Raymond mis-dated the last five strips from 6/34, and while the dating sequence is confusing, the continuity is correct	39	78	117	234	385	535

SECRET AGENT X-9 (See Magic Comics)

Secret Avengers #3 © MAR

Secret Defenders #19 © MAR

Secret Invasion #4 © MAR

	GD 2.0	VG 4.0	FN 6.0	VF 8.0	VF/NM 9.0	NM- 9.2
Dell Publishing Co.: Dec, 1937 (Not by Raymond)						
Feature Books 8	47	94	141	296	498	700

SECRET AGENT Z-2 (See Holyoke One-Shot No. 7)

SECRET AVENGERS (The Heroic Age)
Marvel Comics: Jul, 2010 - No. 37, Mar, 2013 ($3.99)

1-Bendis-s/Deodato-a/Djurdjevic-c; Steve Rogers assembles covert squad 4.00
1-Variant-c by Yardin 6.00
2-12: 2-Two covers. 2-4-Deodato-a. 5-Nick Fury app.; Aja-a 4.00
12.1 ($2.99) Spencer-s/Eaton-a/Deodato-c 3.00
13-21: 13-15-Fear Itself tie-in; Granov-c. 15-Aftermath of Bucky's demise. 16-21-Ellis-s 4.00
21.2-($2.99) Remender-s/Zircher-a; intro. new Masters of Evil 3.00
22-37: 22-25-Remender-s/Hardman-a/Art Adams-c. 23-Venom joins. 26-28-A vs. X 4.00

SECRET AVENGERS (Marvel NOW!)
Marvel Comics: Apr, 2013 - No. 16, Apr, 2014 ($3.99)

1-16: 1-5-Spencer-s/Luke Ross-a/Coker-c; Agent Coulson app. 5,7-Hulk app. 7,9-Guice-a 9,16-Winter Soldier app. 4.00

SECRET AVENGERS (All-New Marvel NOW!)
Marvel Comics: May, 2014 - Present ($3.99)

1,2-Ales Kot-s/Michael Walsh-a; M.O.D.O.K. app. 4.00

SECRET CITY SAGA (See Jack Kirby's Secret City Saga)

SECRET DEFENDERS (Also see The Defenders & Fantastic Four #374)
Marvel Comics: Mar, 1993 - No. 25, Mar, 1995 ($1.75/$1.95)

1-($2.50)-Red foil stamped-c; Dr. Strange, Nomad, Wolverine, Spider Woman & Darkhawk begin 4.00
2-11,13-24: 9-New team w/Silver Surfer, Thunderstrike, Dr. Strange & War Machine. 13-Thanos replaces Dr. Strange as leader; leads into Cosmic Powers limited series; 14-Dr. Druid. 15-Bound in card sheet. 18-Giant Man & Iron Fist app. 3.00
12,25: 12-($2.50)-Prismatic foil-c. 25 ($2.50, 52 pgs.) 4.00

SECRET DIARY OF EERIE ADVENTURES
Avon Periodicals: 1953 (25¢ giant, 100 pgs., one-shot)

	GD 2.0	VG 4.0	FN 6.0	VF 8.0	VF/NM 9.0	NM- 9.2
nn-(Rare)-Kubert-a; Hollingsworth-c; Sid Check back-c	258	516	774	1651	2826	4000

SECRET FILES & ORIGINS GUIDE TO THE DC UNIVERSE
DC Comics: Mar, 2000; Feb, 2002 ($6.95/$4.95)

2000 (3/00, $6.95)-Overview of DC characters; profile pages by various 7.00
2001-2002 (2/02, $4.95) Olivetti-c 5.00

SECRET FILES PRESIDENT LUTHOR
DC Comics: Mar, 2001 ($4.95, one-shot)

1-Short stories & profile pages by various; Harris-c 5.00

SECRET HEARTS
National Periodical Publications (Beverly)(Arleigh No. 50-113):
9-10/49 - No. 6, 7-8/50; No. 7, 12-1/51-52 - No. 153, 7/71

	GD 2.0	VG 4.0	FN 6.0	VF 8.0	VF/NM 9.0	NM- 9.2
1-Kinstler-a; photo-c begin, end #6	58	116	174	371	636	900
2-Toth-a (1 pg.); Kinstler-a	32	64	96	188	307	425
3,6 (1950)	28	56	84	165	270	375
4,5-Toth-a	28	56	84	168	274	380
7(12-1/51-52) (Rare)	41	82	123	256	428	600
8-10 (1952)	21	42	63	125	199	275
11-20	16	32	48	94	147	200
21-26: 26-Last precode (2-3/55)	15	30	45	83	124	165
27-40	7	14	21	44	82	120
41-50	5	10	15	35	63	90
51-60	5	10	15	31	53	75
61-75,100: 75-Last 10¢ issue	5	10	15	30	50	70
76-99,101-109	4	8	12	23	37	50
110- "Reach for Happiness" serial begins, ends #138	4	8	12	25	40	55
111-119,121-126	3	6	9	17	26	35
120,134-Neal Adams-c	4	8	12	25	40	55
127 (4/68)-Beatles cameo	4	8	12	25	40	55
128-133,135-142: 141,142- "20 Miles to Heartbreak", Chapter 2 & 3 (see Young Love for Chapters 1 & 4); Toth, Colletta-a	3	6	9	16	24	32
143-148,150-152: 144-Morrow-a	3	6	9	14	20	26
149,153: 149-Toth-a. 153-Kirby-i	3	6	9	15	22	28

SECRET HISTORY OF THE AUTHORITY: HAWKSMOOR
DC Comics (WildStorm): May, 2008 - No. 6, Oct, 2008 ($2.99, limited series)

1-6-Costa-s/Staples-a/Hamner-c 3.00
TPB (2009, $19.99) r/#1-6 20.00

SECRET INVASION (Also see Mighty Avengers, New Avengers, and Skrulls!)
Marvel Comics: June, 2008 - No. 8, Jan, 2009 ($3.99, limited series)

1-Skrull invasion; Bendis-s/Yu-a/Dell'Otto-c 4.00
1-Variant cover with blank area for sketches 4.00
1-McNiven variant-c 12.00
1-Yu variant-c 30.00
1-2nd printing with old Avengers variant-c by Yu 4.00
1 Director's Cut (2008, $4.99) r/#1 with script; concept and promo art; cover gallery 5.00
2-8-Dell'Otto-c. 8-Wasp killed 4.00
2-4-McNiven variant-c. 2-Avengers. 3-Nick Fury. 4-Tony Stark, Spider-Woman, Black Widow 6.00
2-8-Yu variant-c. 2-Hawkeye & Mockingbird. 3-Spider-Woman. 4-Nick Fury 10.00
5-Rubi variant-c 5.00
6-Cho Spider-Woman variant-c 8.00
...:Aftermath: Beta Ray Bill - The Green of Eden (6/09, $3.99) Brereton-a 4.00
...: Chronicles 1,2 (4/09,6/09, $5.99) reprints from New Avengers & Illuminati issues 6.00
... Dark Reign (2/09, $3.99) villain meeting after #8; previews new series; Maleev-a/c 4.00
... Dark Reign (2/09, $3.99) Variant Green Goblin cover by Bryan Hitch 8.00
... Requiem (2009, $3.99) Hank Pym becomes The Wasp; r/TTA #44 & Avengers #215 4.00
... Saga (2008, giveaway) history of the Skrulls told through reprint panels and text 3.00
...: The Infiltration TPB (2008, $19.99) r/FF #2; New Avengers #31,32,38,39; New Avengers: Illuminati #1,5; Mighty Avengers #7; and Avengers: The Initiative Annual #1 20.00
...: War of Kings (2/09, $3.99) Black Bolt and the Inhumans; Pelletier & Dazo-a 4.00
...: Who Do You Trust? (8/08, $3.99) short tie-in stories by various; Jimenez-c 4.00

SECRET INVASION: AMAZING SPIDER-MAN
Marvel Comics: Oct, 2008 - No. 3, Dec, 2008 ($2.99, limited series)

1-3-Jackpot battles a Super-Skrull; Santucci-a. 2-Menace app. 3.00

SECRET INVASION: FANTASTIC FOUR
Marvel Comics: July, 2008 - No. 3, Sept, 2008 ($2.99, limited series)

1-3-Skrulls and Lyja invade; Kitson-a/Davis-c 3.00
1-Variant Skrull cover by McKone 5.00

SECRET INVASION: FRONT LINE
Marvel Comics: Sept, 2008 - No. 5, Jan, 2009 ($2.99, limited series)

1-5-Ben Urich covering the Skrull invasion; Reed-s/Castiello-a 3.00

SECRET INVASION: INHUMANS
Marvel Comics: Oct, 2008 - No. 4, Jan, 2009 ($2.99, limited series)

1-4-Raney-a/Sejic-c/Pokasky-s; search for Black Bolt 3.00

SECRET INVASION: RUNAWAYS/YOUNG AVENGERS (Follows Runaways #30)
Marvel Comics: Aug, 2008 - No. 3, Nov, 2008 ($2.99, limited series)

1-3-Miyazawa-a/Ryan-c 3.00

SECRET INVASION: THOR
Marvel Comics: Oct, 2008 - No. 3, Dec, 2008 ($2.99, limited series)

1-3-Fraction-s/Braithwaite-a; Skrulls invade Asgard; Beta Ray Bill app. 3.00
1-2nd printing with Beta Ray Bill cover 3.00

SECRET INVASION: X-MEN
Marvel Comics: Oct, 2008 - No. 4, Jan, 2009 ($2.99, limited series)

1-4-Carey-s/Nord-a/Dodson-c; Skrulls invade San Francisco 3.00
1-2nd printing with variant Nord-c 3.00

SECRET ISLAND OF OZ, THE (See First Comics Graphic Novel)

SECRET LOVE (See Fox Giants & Sinister House of...)

SECRET LOVE
Ajax-Farrell/Four Star Comic Corp. No. 2 on: 12/55 - No. 3, 8/56; 4/57 - No. 5, 2/58; No. 6, 6/58

	GD 2.0	VG 4.0	FN 6.0	VF 8.0	VF/NM 9.0	NM- 9.2
1(12/55-Ajax, 1st series)	11	22	33	62	86	110
2,3	8	16	24	44	57	70
1(4/57-Ajax, 2nd series)	9	18	27	52	69	85
2-6: 5-Bakerish-a	8	16	24	40	50	60

SECRET LOVES
Comic Magazines/Quality Comics Group: Nov, 1949 - No. 6, Sept, 1950

	GD 2.0	VG 4.0	FN 6.0	VF 8.0	VF/NM 9.0	NM- 9.2
1-Ward-c	28	56	84	165	270	375
2-Ward-c	22	44	66	132	216	300
3-Crandall-a	15	30	45	86	133	180
4,6	14	28	42	76	108	140
5-Suggestive art "Boom Town Babe"; photo-c	15	30	45	90	140	190

SECRET LOVE STORIES (See Fox Giants)

SECRET MISSIONS (Admiral Zacharia's...)
St. John Publishing Co.: February, 1950

Secret Mysteries #16 © Ribage

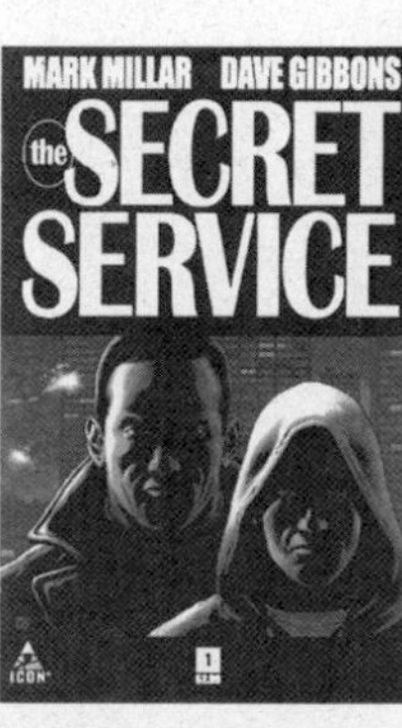

Secret Service #1 © Millarworld

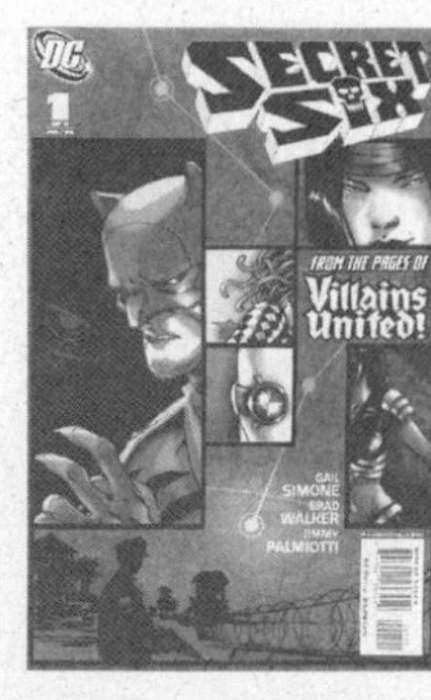

Secret Six (2006 series) #1 © DC

GD VG FN VF VF/NM NM-
2.0 4.0 6.0 8.0 9.0 9.2

1-Joe Kubert-c; stories of U.S. foreign agents 20 40 60 117 189 260

SECRET MYSTERIES (Formerly Crime Mysteries & Crime Smashers)
Ribage/Merit Publications No. 17 on: No. 16, Nov, 1954 - No. 19, July, 1955

16-Horror, Palais-a; Myron Fass-c 36 72 108 211 343 475
17-19-Horror. 17-Fass-c; mis-dated 3/54? 26 52 78 154 252 350

SECRET ORIGINS (1st Series) (See 80 Page Giant #8)
National Periodical Publications: Aug-Oct, 1961 (Annual) (Reprints)

1-Origin Adam Strange (Showcase #17), Green Lantern (Green Lantern #1), Challengers (partial-r/Showcase #6, 6 pgs. Kirby-a), J'onn J'onzz (Det. #225), The Flash (Showcase #4), Green Arrow (1 pg. text), Superman-Batman team (World's Finest #94), Wonder Woman (Wonder Woman #105) 41 82 123 303 689 1075
Replica Edition (1998, $4.95) r/entire book and house ads 5.00
Even More Secret Origins (2003, $6.95) reprints origins of Hawkman, Eclipso, Kid Flash, Blackhawks, Green Lantern's oath, and Jimmy Olsen-Robin team in 80 pg. Giant style 7.00

SECRET ORIGINS (2nd Series)
National Periodical Publications: Feb-Mar, 1973 - No. 6, Jan-Feb, 1974; No. 7, Oct-Nov, 1974 (All 20¢ issues) (All origin reprints)

1-Superman(r/1 pg. origin/Action #1, 1st time since G.A.), Batman(Detective #33), Ghost(Flash #88), The Flash(Showcase #4) 5 10 15 31 53 75
2-7: 2-Green Lantern & The Atom(Showcase #22 & 34), Supergirl(Action #252). 3-Wonder Woman (W.W. #1), Wildcat (Sensation #1). 4-Vigilante (Action #42) by Meskin, Kid Eternity(Hit #25). 5-The Spectre by Baily (More Fun #52,53). 6-Blackhawk(Military #1) & Legion of Super-Heroes(Superboy #147). 7-Robin (Detective #38), Aquaman (More Fun #73) 3 6 9 19 30 40

NOTE: ***Infantino** a-1. **Kane** a-2. **Kubert** a-1.*

SECRET ORIGINS (3rd Series)
DC Comics: 4/86 - No. 50, 8/90 (All origins)(52 pgs. #6 on)(#27 on: $1.50)

1-Origin Superman 1 2 3 5 6 8
2-6: 2-Blue Beetle. 3-Shazam. 4-Firestorm. 5-Crimson Avenger. 6-Halo/G.A. Batman 4.00
7-9,11,12,14-20,22-26: 7-Green Lantern (Guy Gardner)/G.A. Sandman. 8-Shadow Lass/Doll Man. 9-G.A. Flash/Skyman.11-G.A. Hawkman/Power Girl. 12-Challengers of Unknown/ G.A. Fury (2nd modern app.). 14-Suicide Squad; Legends spin-off. 15-Spectre/Deadman. 16-G.A. Hourman/Warlord. 17-Adam Strange story by Carmine Infantino; Dr. Occult. 18-G.A. Gr. Lantern/The Creeper. 19-Uncle Sam/The Guardian. 20-Batgirl/G.A. Dr. Mid-Nite. 22-Manhunters. 23-Floronic Man/Guardians of the Universe. 24-Blue Devil/Dr. Fate. 25-LSH/Atom. 26-Black Lightning/Miss America 4.00
10-Phantom Stranger w/Alan Moore scripts; Legends spin-off 4.00
13-Origin Nightwing; Johnny Thunder app. 4.00
21-Jonah Hex/Black Condor 4.00
27-30,36-38,40-49: 27-Zatara/Zatanna. 28-Midnight/Nightshade. 29-Power of the Atom/Mr. America; new 3 pg. Red Tornado story by Mayer (last app. of Scribbly, 8/88). 30-Plastic Man/Elongated Man. 36-Poison Ivy by Neil Gaiman & Mark Buckingham/Green Lantern. 37-Legion Of Substitute Heroes/Doctor Light. 38-Green Arrow/Speedy; Grell scripts. 40-All Ape issue. 41-Rogues Gallery of Flash. 42-Phantom Girl/GrimGhost. 43-Original Hawk & Dove/Cave Carson/Chris KL-99. 44-Batman app.; story based on Det. #40. 45-Blackhawk/ El Diablo. 46-JLA/LSH/New Titans. 47-LSH. 48-Ambush Bug/Stanley & His Monster/Rex the Wonder Dog/Trigger Twins. 49-Newsboy Legion/Silent Knight/Bouncing Boy 3.00
31-35,39: 31-JSA. 32-JLA. 33-35-JLI. 39-Animal Man-c/story continued in Animal Man #10; Grant Morrison scripts; Batman app. 3.00
50-($3.95, 100 pgs.)-Batman & Robin in text, Flash of Two Worlds, Johnny Thunder, Dolphin, Black Canary & Space Museum 5.00
Annual 1 (8/87)-Capt. Comet/Doom Patrol 4.00
Annual 2 ('88, $2.00)-Origin Flash II & Flash III 4.00
Annual 3 ('89, $2.95, 84 pgs.)-Teen Titans; 1st app. new Flamebird who replaces original Bat-Girl 4.00
Special 1 (10/89, $2.00)-Batman villains: Penguin, Riddler, & Two-Face; Bolland-c; Sam Kieth-a; Neil Gaiman scripts(2) 5.00

NOTE: ***Art Adams** a-33i(part). **M. Anderson** 8, 19, 21, 25i; c-19(part). **Aparo** c/a-10. **Bissette** c-23. **Bolland** c-7. **Byrne** c/a-Annual 1. **Colan** c/a-5p. **Forte** a-37. **Giffen** a-18p, 44p, 48. **Infantino** a-17, 50p. **Kaluta** c-39. **Gil Kane** a-2, 28; c-2p. **Kirby** c-19(part). **Erik Larsen** a-13. **Mayer** a-29. **Morrow** a-21. **Orlando** a-10. **Perez** a-50i, Annual 3i; c- Annual 3. **Rogers** a-6p. **Russell** a-27i. **Simonson** c-22. **Staton** a-36, 50p. **Steacy** a-35. **Tuska** a-4p, 9p.*

SECRET ORIGINS 80 PAGE GIANT (Young Justice)
DC Comics: Dec, 1998 ($4.95, one-shot)

1-Origin-s of Young Justice members; Ramos-a (Impulse) 5.00

SECRET ORIGINS FEATURING THE JLA
DC Comics: 1999 ($14.95, TPB)

1-Reprints recent origin-s of JLA members; Cassaday-c 15.00

SECRET ORIGINS OF SUPER-HEROES (See DC Special Series #10, 19)

SECRET ORIGINS OF SUPER-VILLAINS 80 PAGE GIANT
DC Comics: Dec, 1999 ($4.95, one-shot)

GD VG FN VF VF/NM NM-
2.0 4.0 6.0 8.0 9.0 9.2

1-Origin-s of Sinestro, Amazo and others; Gibbons-c 5.00

SECRET ORIGINS OF THE WORLD'S GREATEST SUPER-HEROES
DC Comics: 1989 ($4.95, 148 pgs.)

nn-Reprints Superman, JLA origins; new Batman origin-s; Bolland-c 1 2 3 4 5 7

SECRET ROMANCE
Charlton Comics: Oct, 1968 - No. 41, Nov, 1976; No. 42, Mar, 1979 - No. 48, Feb, 1980

1-Begin 12¢ issues, ends #? 3 6 9 17 26 35
2-10: 9-Reese-a 2 4 6 11 16 20
11-16,18,19,21-30 2 4 6 9 13 16
17,20: 17-Susan Dey poster. 20-David Cassidy pin-up 2 4 6 11 16 20
31-48 2 4 6 8 10 12

NOTE: *Beyond the Stars app.-No. 9, 11, 12, 14.*

SECRET ROMANCES (Exciting Love Stories)
Superior Publications Ltd.: Apr, 1951 - No. 27, July, 1955

1 18 36 54 105 165 225
2 13 26 39 74 105 135
3-10 11 22 33 60 83 105
11-13,15-18,20-27 10 20 30 54 72 90
14,19-Lingerie panels 10 20 30 56 76 95

SECRET SERVICE (See Kent Blake of the...)

SECRET SERVICE
Marvel Comics (Icon): Jun, 2012 - No. 6, Jun, 2013 ($2.99/$4.99, limited series)

1-5-Mark Millar-s/Dave Gibbons-a/c 3.00
6-($4.99) 5.00

SECRET SIX (See Action Comics Weekly)
National Periodical Publications: Apr-May, 1968 - No. 7, Apr-May, 1969 (12¢)

1-Origin/1st app. 5 10 15 35 63 90
2-7 3 6 9 21 33 45

SECRET SIX (See Tangent Comics/ Secret Six)

SECRET SIX (See Villains United)
DC Comics: Jul, 2006 - No. 6, Jan, 2007 ($2.99, limited series)

1-6-Gail Simone-s/Brad Walker-a. 4-Doom Patrol app. 3.00
...: Six Degrees of Devastation TPB (2007, $14.99) r/#1-6 15.00

SECRET SIX
DC Comics: Nov, 2008 - No. 36, Oct, 2011 ($2.99)

1-36: 1-Gail Simone-s/Nicola Scott-a. 2-Batman app. 8-Rodriguez-a. 11-13-Wonder Woman & Artemis app. 16-Black Alice app. 17,18-Blackest Night 3.00
...: Cats in the Cradle TPB (2011, $14.99) r/#19-24 15.00
...: Danse Macabre TPB (2010, $14.99) r/#15-18 & Suicide Squad #67 (Blackest Night) 15.00
...: Depths TPB (2010, $14.99) r/#8-14 15.00
...: The Reptile Brain TPB (2011, $14.99) r/#25-29 15.00
...: Unhinged TPB (2009, $14.99) r/#1-7; intro. by Paul Cornell 15.00

SECRET SKULL
IDW Publ.: Aug, 2004 - No. 4, Nov, 2004 ($3.99)

1-4-Steve Niles-s/Chuck BB-a 4.00

SECRET SOCIETY OF SUPER-VILLAINS
National Per. Publ./DC Comics: May-June, 1976 - No. 15, June-July, 1978

1-Origin; JLA cameo & Capt. Cold app. 3 6 9 14 19 24
2-5,15: 2-Re-intro/origin Capt. Comet; Green Lantern x-over. 5-Green Lantern, Hawkman x-over; Darkseid app. 15-G.A. Atom, Dr. Midnite, & JSA app. 2 4 6 8 11 14
6-14: 9,10-Creeper x-over. 11-Capt. Comet; Orlando-i 2 3 4 6 8 10

SECRET SOCIETY OF SUPER-VILLAINS SPECIAL (See DC Special Series #6)

SECRETS OF HAUNTED HOUSE
National Periodical Publications/DC Comics: 4-5/75 - #5, 12-1/75-76; #6, 6-7/77 - #14, 10-11/78; #15, 8/79 - #46, 3/82

1 5 10 15 34 60 85
2-4 3 6 9 19 30 40
5-Wrightson-c 4 8 12 23 37 50
6-14 2 4 6 11 16 20
15-30 2 4 6 8 11 14
31,44: 31-(12/80) Mr. E series begins (1st app.), ends #41. 44-Wrightson-c 2 4 6 9 13 16
32-(1/81) Origin of Mr. E 2 4 6 8 11 14
33-43,45,46: 34,35-Frankenstein Monster app. 1 3 4 6 8 10

NOTE: ***Aparo** c-7. **Aragones** a-1. **B. Bailey** a-8. **Bissette** a-46. **Buckler** c-32-40p. **Ditko** a-9, 12, 41, 45. **Golden***

Secrets of Haunted House #30 © DC

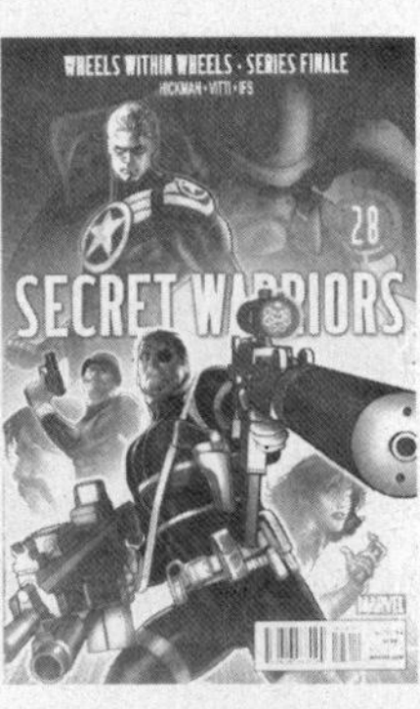

Secret Warriors #28 © MAR

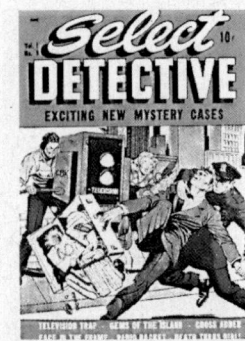

Select Detective #3 © D.S. Pub.

	GD	VG	FN	VF	VF/NM	NM-
	2.0	4.0	6.0	8.0	9.0	9.2

a-10. ***Howard*** *a-13i.* ***Kaluta*** *c-8, 10, 11, 14, 16, 29.* ***Kubert*** *c-41, 42.* ***Sheldon Mayer*** *a-43p.* ***McWilliams*** *a-35.* ***Nasser*** *a-24.* ***Newton*** *a-30p.* ***Nino*** *a-1, 13, 19.* ***Orlando*** *c-13, 30, 43, 45i.* ***N. Redondo*** *a-4, 5, 29.* ***Rogers*** *c-26.* ***Spiegle*** *a-31-41.* ***Wrightson*** *c-5, 44.*

SECRETS OF HAUNTED HOUSE SPECIAL (See DC Special Series #12)

SECRETS OF LIFE (Movie)
Dell Publishing Co.: 1956 (Disney)

Four Color 749-Photo-c 5 10 15 30 50 70

SECRETS OF LOVE (See Popular Teen-Agers...)

SECRETS OF LOVE AND MARRIAGE
Charlton Comics: V2#1, Aug, 1956 - V2#25, June, 1961

V2#1-Matt Baker-c? 5 10 15 31 53 75
V2#2-6 3 6 9 21 33 45
V2#7-9-(All 68 pgs.) 5 10 15 33 57 80
10-25 3 6 9 18 28 38

SECRETS OF MAGIC (See Wisco)

SECRETS OF SINISTER HOUSE (Sinister House of Secret Love #1-4)
National Periodical Publ.: No. 5, June-July, 1972 - No. 18, June-July, 1974

5-(52 pgs.). 65 10 15 35 63 90
6-9: 7-Redondo-a 4 8 12 23 37 50
10-Neal Adams-a(i) 4 8 12 25 40 55
11-18: 15-Redondo-a. 17-Barry-a; early Chaykin 1 pg. strip
3 6 9 16 23 30

NOTE: ***Alcala*** *a-6, 13, 14.* ***Glanzman*** *a-7.* ***Kaluta*** *c-6, 7.* ***Nino*** *a-8, 11-13. Ambrose Bierce adapt.-#14.*

SECRETS OF THE LEGION OF SUPER-HEROES
DC Comics: Jan, 1981 - No. 3, Mar, 1981 (Limited series)

1-3: 1-Origin of the Legion. 2-Retells origins of Brainiac 5, Shrinking Violet, Sun-Boy, Bouncing Boy, Ultra-Boy, Matter-Eater Lad, Mon-El, Karate Kid & Dream Girl 5.00

SECRETS OF TRUE LOVE
St. John Publishing Co.: Feb, 1958

1 8 16 24 44 57 70

SECRETS OF YOUNG BRIDES
Charlton Comics: No. 5, Sept, 1957 - No. 44, Oct, 1964; July, 1975 - No. 9, Nov, 1976

5 5 10 15 30 50 70
6-10: 8-Negligee panel 3 6 9 21 33 45
11-20 3 6 9 19 30 40
21-30: Last 10¢ issue? 3 6 9 17 26 35
31-44(10/64) 3 6 9 14 19 24
1-(2nd series) (7/75) 3 6 9 14 20 26
2-9 2 4 6 8 11 14

SECRET SQUIRREL (TV)(See Kite Fun Book)
Gold Key: Oct, 1966 (12¢) (Hanna-Barbera)

1-1st Secret Squirrel and Morocco Mole, Squiddly Diddly, Winsome Witch
9 18 27 61 123 185

SECRET STORY ROMANCES (Becomes True Tales of Love)
Atlas Comics (TCI): Nov, 1953 - No. 21, Mar, 1956

1-Everett-a; Jay Scott Pike-c 19 38 57 111 176 240
2 12 24 36 67 94 120
3-11: 11-Last pre-code (2/55) 11 22 33 60 83 105
12-21 10 20 30 54 72 90

NOTE: ***Colletta*** *a-10, 14, 15, 17, 21; c-10, 14, 17.*

SECRET VOICE, THE (See Great American Comics Presents...)

SECRET WAR
Marvel Comics: Apr, 2004 - No. 5, Dec, 2005 ($3.99, limited series)

1-Bendis-s/Dell'Otto painted-a/c; 5.00
1-2nd printing with gold logo on white cover and full-color Spider-Man 4.00
1-3rd printing with white cover and B&W sketched Spider-Man 4.00
2-5: 2-Wolverine-c. 3-Capt. America-c. 4-Black Widow-c. 5-Daredevil-c 4.00
2-2nd printing with white cover and B&W sketched Wolverine 4.00
... : From the Files of Nick Fury (2005, $3.99) Fury's journal entries; profiles of characters 4.00
HC (2005, $29.99, dust jacket) r/#1-5 & ...From the Files of Nick Fury; additional art 30.00
SC (2006, $24.99) r/#1-5 & ...From the Files of Nick Fury; additional art 25.00

SECRET WARRIORS (Also see 2009 Dark Reign titles)
Marvel Comics: Apr, 2009 - No. 28, Sept, 2011 ($3.99/$2.99)

1-Bendis & Hickman-s/Caselli-a/Cheung-c; Nick Fury app.; Hydra dossier; sketch pages 4.00
2-24,26-28-($2.99) 8-Dark Avengers app. 17-19-Howling Commandos return 3.00
25-($3.99) Baron Strucker app.; Vitti-a 4.00

SECRET WARS II (Also see Marvel Super Heroes...)
Marvel Comics Group: July, 1985 - No. 9, Mar, 1986 (Maxi-series)

1,9: 9-(52 pgs.) X-Men app., Spider-Man app. 6.00
2-8: 2,8-X-Men app. 5-1st app. Boom Boom. 5,8-Spider-Man app. 4.00

SECRET WEAPONS
Valiant: Sept, 1993 - No. 21, May, 1995 ($2.25)

1-10,12-21: 3-Reese-a(i). 5-Ninjak app. 9-Bound-in trading card. 12-Bloodshot app. 3.00
11-(Sept. on envelope, Aug on-c, $2.50)-Enclosed in manilla envelope; Bloodshot app; intro new team. 3.00

SECTAURS
Marvel Comics: June, 1985 - No. 8, Sept, 1986 (75¢) (Based on Coleco Toys)

1-8, 1-Giveaway; same-c with "Coleco 1985 Toy Fair Collectors' Edition" 4.00

SECTION ZERO
Image Comics (Gorilla): June, 2000 - No. 3, Sept, 2000 ($2.50)

1-3-Kesel-s/Grummett-a 3.00

SEDUCTION OF THE INNOCENT (Also see New York State Joint Legislative Committee to Study...)
Rinehart & Co., Inc., N. Y.: 1953, 1954 (400 pgs.) (Hardback, $4.00)(Written by Fredric Wertham, M.D.)(Also printed in Canada by Clarke, Irwin & Co. Ltd.)

(1st Version)-with bibliographical note intact (pages 399 & 400)(several copies got out before the comic publishers forced the removal of this page)
183 366 549 787 944 1100
Dust jacket only 39 78 117 240 395 550
(1st Version)-without bibliographical note 92 184 276 396 473 550
Dust jacket only 21 42 63 122 199 275
(2nd Version)-Published in England by Rinehart, 1954, 399 pgs. has bibliographical page; "Second print" listed on inside flap of the dust jacket; publication page has no "R" colophon; unlike 1st version 16 32 48 94 147 200
1972 r-/of 2nd version; 400 pgs. w/bibliography page; Kennikat Press
5 10 15 31 53 75
2004 r/with new intro. by Wertham scholar James E. Reibman, 424 pgs; 6" x 9"; limited to 220 copies 6 12 18 38 69 100

NOTE: *Material from this book appeared in the November, 1953 (Vol.70, pp50-53,214) issue of the* ***Ladies' Home Journal*** *under the title "What Parents Don't Know About Comic Books". With the release of this book, Dr. Wertham reveals seven years of research attempting to link juvenile delinquency to comic books. Many illustrations showing excessive violence, sex, sadism, and torture are shown. This book was used at the Kefauver Senate hearings which led to the Comics Code Authority. Because of the influence this book had on the comic industry and the collector's interest in it, we feel this listing is justified. Modern printings exist in limited editions. Also see* ***Parade of Pleasure.***

SEDUCTION OF THE INNOCENT! (Also see Halloween Horror)
Eclipse Comics: Nov, 1985 - 3-D#2, Apr, 1986 ($1.75)

1-6: Double listed under cover title from #7 on 4.00
3-D 1 (10/85, $2.25, 36 pgs.)-contains unpublished Advs. Into Darkness #15 (pre-code); Dave Stevens-c 1 2 3 5 6 8
2-D 1 (100 copy limited signed & #ed edition)(B&W) 1 3 4 6 8 10
3-D 2 (4/86)-Baker, Toth, Wrightson-c 5.00
2-D 2 (100 copy limited signed & #ed edition)(B&W) 1 3 4 6 8 10

NOTE: ***Anderson*** *r-2, 3.* ***Crandall*** *c/a(r)-1.* ***Meskin*** *c/a(r)-3, 3-D 1.* ***Moreira*** *r-2.* ***Toth*** *a-1-6r; c-4r.* ***Tuska*** *r-6.*

SEEKER
Sky Comics: Apr, 1994 ($2.50, one-shot)

1 3.00

SEEKERS INTO THE MYSTERY
DC Comics (Vertigo): Jan, 1996 - No. 15, Apr, 1997 ($2.50)

1-14: J.M. DeMatteis scripts in all. 1-4-Glenn Barr-a. 5,10-Muth-c/a. 6-9-Zulli-c/a. 11-14-Bolton-c; Jill Thompson-a 3.00
15-($2.95)-Muth-c/a 3.00

SEEKER 3000 (See Marvel Premiere #41)
Marvel Comics: Jun, 1998 - No. 4, Sept, 1998 ($2.99/$2.50, limited series)

1-($2.99)-Set 25 years after 1st app.; wraparound-c 4.00
2-4-($2.50) 3.00
...Premiere 1 (6/98, $1.50) Reprints 1st app. from Marvel Premiere #41; wraparound-c 3.00

SELECT DETECTIVE (Exciting New Mystery Cases)
D. S. Publishing Co.: Aug-Sept, 1948 - No. 3, Dec-Jan, 1948-49

1-Matt Baker-a 32 64 96 188 307 425
2-Baker, McWilliams-a 21 42 63 122 199 275
3 16 32 48 94 147 200

SEMPER FI (Tales of the Marine Corp)
Marvel Comics: Dec, 1988- No.9, Aug, 1989 (75¢)

1-9: Severin-c/a 4.00

SENSATIONAL POLICE CASES (Becomes Captain Steve Savage, 2nd Series)

Sensational Spider-Man #6 © MAR

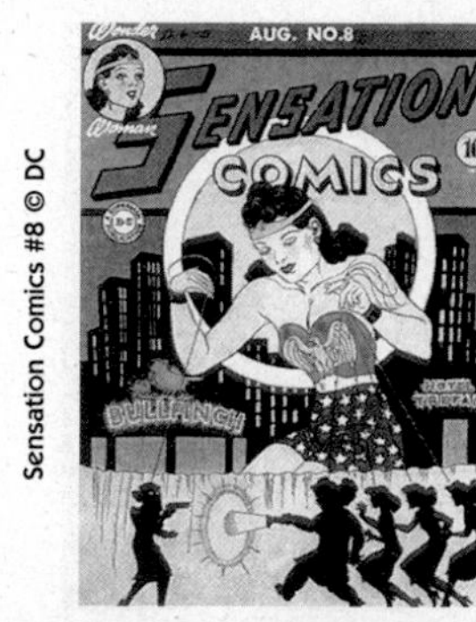

Sensation Comics #8 © DC

The Sentry #2 © MAR

GD 2.0 VG 4.0 FN 6.0 VF 8.0 VF/NM 9.0 NM- 9.2

Avon Periodicals: 1952; No. 2, 1954 - No. 4, July-Aug, 1954

nn-(1952, 25¢, 100 pgs.)-Kubert-a?; Check, Larsen, Lawrence & McCann-a; Kinstler-c
45 90 135 284 480 675
2-4: 2-Kirbyish-a (3-4/54). 4-Reprint/Saint #5 17 34 51 98 154 210
I.W. Reprint #5-(1963?, nd)-Reprints Prison Break #5(1952-Realistic); Infantino-a 3 6 9 16 23 30

SENSATIONAL SHE-HULK, THE (She-Hulk #21-23) (See Savage She-Hulk)
Marvel Comics: V2#1, 5/89 - No. 60, Feb, 1994 ($1.50/$1.75, deluxe format)

V2#1-Byrne-c/a(p)/scripts begin, end #8 1 2 3 5 6 8
2,3,5-8: 3-Spider-Man app. 3.00
4,14-17,21-23: 4-Reintro G.A. Blonde Phantom. 14-17-Howard the Duck app. 21-23-Return of the Blonde Phantom. 22-All Winners Squad app. 3.00
9-13,18-20,24-49,51-60: 25-Thor app. 26-Excalibur app.; Guice-c. 29-Wolverine app. (3 pgs.). 30-Hobgoblin-c & cameo. 31-Byrne-c/a/scripts begin again. 35-Last $1.50-c. 37-Wolverine/Punisher/Spidey-c, but no app. 39-Thing app. 56-War Zone app.; Hulk cameo. 57-Vs. Hulk-c/story. 58-Electro-c/story. 59-Jack O'Lantern app. 3.00
50-($2.95, 52 pgs.)-Embossed green foil-c; Byrne app.; last Byrne-c/a; Austin, Chaykin, Simonson-a; Miller-a(2 pgs.) 4.00

NOTE: ***Dale Keown** a(p)-13, 15-22.*

SENSATIONAL SHE-HULK IN CEREMONY, THE
Marvel Comics: 1989 - No. 2, 1989 ($3.95, squarebound, 52 pgs.)

nn-Part 1, nn-Part 2 5.00

SENSATIONAL SPIDER-MAN
Marvel Comics: Apr, 1989 ($5.95, squarebound, 80 pgs.)

1-r/Amazing Spider-Man Annual #14,15 by Miller & Annual #8 by Kirby & Ditko 6.00

SENSATIONAL SPIDER-MAN, THE
Marvel Comics: Jan, 1996 - No. 33, Nov, 1998 ($1.95/$1.99)

0 ($4.95)-Lenticular-c; Jurgens-a/scripts 5.00
1 5.00
1-($2.95) variant-c; polybagged w/cassette 1 2 3 5 6 8
2-5: 2-Kaine & Rhino app. 3-Giant-Man app. 4.00
6-18: 9-Onslaught tie-in; revealed that Peter & Mary Jane's unborn baby is a girl. 11-Revelations. 13-15-Ka-Zar app. 14,15-Hulk app. 3.00
19-24: Living Pharoah app. 22,23-Dr. Strange app. 3.00
25-($2.99) Spiderhunt pt. 1; Normie Osborne kidnapped 4.00
25-Variant-c 1 2 3 5 6 8
26-33: 26-Nauck-a. 27-Double-c with "The Sensational Hornet #1"; Vulture app. 28-Hornet vs. Vulture. 29,30-Black Cat-c/app. 33-Last issue; Gathering of Five concludes 3.00
33.1, 33.2 (10/12, $2.99) DeFalco-s/Barberi-a/Bianchi-c 3.00
#(-1) Flashback(7/97) Dezago-s/Wieringo-a 3.00
'96 Annual ($2.95) 4.00

SENSATIONAL SPIDER-MAN, THE (Previously Marvel Knights Spider-Man #1-22)
Marvel Comics: No. 23, Apr, 2006 - No. 41, Dec, 2007 ($2.99)

23-40: 23-25-Aguirre-Sacasa-s/Medina-a. 23-Wraparound-c. 24,34,37-Black Cat app. 26-New costume. 28-Unmasked; Dr. Octopus app.; Crain-a. 35-Black costume resumes 3.00
41-($3.99) One More Day pt. 3; Straczynski-s/Quesada-a/c 4.00
... Annual 1 (2007, $3.99) Flashbacks of Peter & MJ's relationship; Larroca-a/Fraction-s 4.00
... Feral HC (2006, $19.99, dustjacket) r/#23-27; sketch pages 20.00
Civil War: Peter Parker, Spider-Man TPB (2007, $17.99) r/#28-34; Crain cover concepts 18.00

SENSATION COMICS (Sensation Mystery #110 on)
National Per. Publ./All-American: Jan, 1942 - No. 109, May-June, 1952

1-Origin Mr. Terrific(1st app.), Wildcat(1st app.), The Gay Ghost, & Little Boy Blue; Wonder Woman (cont'd from All Star #8), The Black Pirate begin; intro. Justice & Fair Play Club
3200 6400 9600 22,400 43,200 64,000

1-Reprint, Oversize 13-1/2x10". WARNING: This comic is an exact duplicate reprint of the original except for its size. DC published it in 1974 with a second cover titling it as a Famous First Edition. There have been many reported cases of the outer cover being removed and the interior sold as the original edition. The reprint with the new outer cover removed is practically worthless. See Famous First Edition for value.

2-Etta Candy begins 486 972 1458 3550 6275 9000
3-W. Woman gets secretary's job 300 600 900 2010 3505 5000
4-1st app. Stretch Skinner in Wildcat 226 452 678 1446 2473 3500
5-Intro. Justin, Black Pirate's son 184 368 552 1178 2014 2850
6-Origin/1st app. Wonder Woman's magic lasso 194 388 582 1242 2121 3000
7-10 148 296 444 947 1624 2300
11,12,14-20 110 220 330 704 1202 1700
13-Hitler, Tojo, Mussolini-c (as bowling pins) 187 374 561 1197 2049 2900
21-30 86 172 258 546 936 1325
31-33 66 132 198 419 722 1025
34-Sargon, the Sorcerer begins (10/44), ends #36; begins again #52
69 138 207 442 759 1075
35-40: 38-X-Mas-c 63 126 189 403 689 975
41-50: 43-The Whip app. 61 122 183 390 670 950
51-60: 51-Last Black Pirate. 56,57-Sargon by Kubert
58 116 174 371 636 900
61-67,69-80: 63-Last Mr. Terrific. 66-Wildcat by Kubert
53 106 159 334 567 800
68-Origin & 1st app. Huntress (8/47) 58 116 174 371 636 900
81-Used in **SOTI**, pg. 33,34; Krigstein-a 57 114 171 362 619 875
82-93: 83-Last Sargon. 86-The Atom app. 90-Last Wildcat. 91-Streak begins by Alex Toth. 92-Toth-a (2 pgs.) 53 106 159 334 567 800
94-1st all girl issue 90 180 270 576 988 1400
95-99,101-106: 95-Unmasking of Wonder Woman-c/story. 99-1st app. Astra, Girl of the Future, ends #106. 103-Robot-c. 105-Last 52 pgs. 106-Wonder Woman ends
74 148 222 470 810 1150
100-(11-12/50) 84 168 252 538 919 1300
107-(Scarce, 1-2/52)-1st mystery issue; Johnny Peril by Toth(p), 8 pgs. & begins; continues from Danger Trail #5 (3-4/51)(see Comic Cavalcade #15 for 1st app.)
84 168 252 538 919 1300
108-(Scarce)-Johnny Peril by Toth(p) 71 142 213 454 777 1100
109-(Scarce)-Johnny Peril by Toth(p) 84 168 252 538 919 1300

NOTE: ***Krigstein** a-(Wildcat)-81, 83, 84. **Moldoff** Black Pirate-1-25; Black Pirate not in 34-36, 43-48. **Oskner** c(i)-89-91, 94-106. Wonder Woman by **H. G. Peter**, all issues except #8, 17-19, 21; c-4-7, 9-18, 20-88, 92, 93. **Toth** a-91, 98; c-107. Wonder Woman c-1-106.*

SENSATION COMICS (Also see All Star Comics 1999 crossover titles)
DC Comics: May, 1999 ($1.99, one-shot)

1-Golden Age Wonder Woman and Hawkgirl; Robinson-s 3.00

SENSATION MYSTERY (Formerly Sensation Comics #1-109)
National Periodical Publ.: No. 110, July-Aug, 1952 - No. 116, July-Aug, 1953

110-Johnny Peril continues 54 108 162 343 574 825
111-116-Johnny Peril in all. 116-M. Anderson-a 54 108 162 343 574 825

NOTE: ***M. Anderson** c-110. **Colan** a-114p. **Giunta** a-112. **G. Kane** c(p)-108, 109, 111-115.*

SENSE & SENSABILITY
Marvel Comics: July, 2010 - No. 5, Nov, 2010 ($3.99, limited series)

1-5-Adaptation of the Jane Austen novel; Nancy Butler-s/Sonny Liew-a/c 4.00

SENSUOUS STREAKER
Marvel Publ.: 1974 (B&W magazine, 68pgs.)

1 4 8 12 27 44 60

SENTENCES: THE LIFE OF M.F. GRIMM
DC Comics (Vertigo): 2007 ($19.99, B&W graphic novel)

HC-Autobiography of Percy Carey (M.F. Grimm); Ronald Wimberly-a 20.00
SC (2008, $14.99) 15.00

SENTINEL
Marvel Comics: June, 2003 - No. 12, April, 2004 ($2.99/$2.50)

1-Sean McKeever-s/Udon Studios-a 3.00
2-12 3.00
Marvel Age Sentinel Vol. 1: Salvage (2004, $7.99, digest size) r/#1-6 8.00
Vol. 2: No Hero (2004, $7.99, digest size) r/#7-12; sketch pages 8.00

SENTINEL (2nd series)
Marvel Comics: Jan, 2006 - No. 5, May, 2006 ($2.99, limited series)

1-5-Sean McKeever-s/Joe Vriens-a 3.00
Vol. 3: Past Imperfect (2006, $7.99, digest size) r/#1-5 8.00

SENTINELS OF JUSTICE, THE (See Americomics & Captain Paragon &...)

SENTINEL SQUAD O*N*E
Marvel Comics: Mar, 2006 - No. 5, July, 2006 ($2.99, limited series)

1-5-Lopresti-a/Layman-s 3.00
Decimation: Sentinel Squad O*N*E (2006, $13.99, TPB) r/series; sketch pg. by Caliafore 14.00

SENTRY (Also see New Avengers and Siege)
Marvel Comics: Sept, 2000 - No. 5, Jan, 2001 ($2.99, limited series)

1-5-Paul Jenkins-s/Jae Lee-a. 3-Spider-Man-c/app. 4-X-Men, FF app. 3.00
.../Fantastic Four (2/01, $2.99) Continues story from #5; Winslade-a 3.00
.../Hulk (2/01, $2.99) Sienkiewicz-c/a 3.00
.../Spider-Man (2/01, $2.99) back story of the Sentry; Leonardi-a 3.00
.../The Void (2/01, $2.99) Conclusion of story; Jae Lee-a 3.00
.../X-Men (2/01, $2.99) Sentry and Archangel; Texeira-a 3.00
TPB (10/01, $24.95) r/#1-5 & all one-shots; Stan Lee interview 25.00
TPB (2nd edition, 2005, $24.99) 25.00

SENTRY (Follows return in New Avengers #10)
Marvel Comics: Nov, 2005 - No. 8, Jun, 2006 ($2.99, limited series)

Serenity: Float Out #1 © Universal

Sgt. Fury #4 © MAR

Sgt. Rock #329 © DC

GD 2.0 VG 4.0 FN 6.0 VF 8.0 VF/NM 9.0 NM- 9.2
GD 2.0 VG 4.0 FN 6.0 VF 8.0 VF/NM 9.0 NM- 9.2

	GD 2.0	VG 4.0	FN 6.0	VF 8.0	VF/NM 9.0	NM- 9.2
1-8-Paul Jenkins-s/John Romita Jr.-a. 1-New Avengers app. 3-Hulk app.						3.00
1-(Rough Cut) (12/05, $3.99) Romita sketch art and Jenkins script; cover sketches						4.00
...: Fallen Sun (7/10, $3.99) Siege epilogue; Jenkins-s/Raney-a/Yu-c						4.00
...: Reborn TPB (2006, $21.99) r/#1-8						22.00

SENTRY SPECIAL
Innovation Publishing: 1991 ($2.75, one-shot)(Hero Alliance spin-off)

1-Lost in Space preview (3 pgs.)						3.00

SERAPHIM
Innovation Publishing: May, 1990 ($2.50, mature readers)

1						3.00

SERENITY (Based on 2005 movie Serenity and 2003 TV series Firefly)
Dark Horse Comics: July, 2005 - No. 3, Sept, 2005 ($2.99, limited series)

1-3: Whedon & Matthews-s/Conrad-a. Three covers for each issue by various						4.00
...: Float Out (6/10, $3.50) Story of Wash; Patton Oswalt-s; covers by Jo Chen & Stockton						3.50
...: One For One (9/10, $1.00) reprints #1, Cassaday-c with red cover frame						3.00
...: Those Left Behind HC (11/07, $19.95, dustjacket) r/series; intro. by Nathan Fillion; pre-production art for the movie; Hughes-c						20.00
...: Those Left Behind TPB (1/06, $9.95) r/series; intro. by Nathan Fillion; Hughes-c						10.00

SERENITY BETTER DAYS (Firefly)
Dark Horse Comics: Mar, 2008 - No. 3, May, 2008 ($2.99, limited series)

1-3: Whedon & Matthews-s/Conrad-a; Adam Hughes-c						3.00

SERENITY: FIREFLY CLASS 03-K64 - LEAVES ON THE WIND (Follows movie)
Dark Horse Comics: Jan, 2014 - No. 6 ($3.50, limited series)

1-3: Zack Whedon-s/Georges Jeanty-a; covers by Dos Santos & Jeanty						3.50

SERGEANT BARNEY BARKER (Becomes G. I. Tales #4 on)
Atlas Comics (MCI): Aug, 1956 - No. 3, Dec, 1956

	GD 2.0	VG 4.0	FN 6.0	VF 8.0	VF/NM 9.0	NM- 9.2
1-Severin-c/a(4)	19	38	57	109	172	235
2,3: 2-Severin-c/a(4). 3-Severin-c/a(5)	14	28	42	78	112	145

SERGEANT BILKO (Phil Silvers Starring as...) (TV)
National Periodical Publications: May-June, 1957 - No. 18, Mar-Apr, 1960

	GD 2.0	VG 4.0	FN 6.0	VF 8.0	VF/NM 9.0	NM- 9.2
1-All have Bob Oskner-c	58	116	174	371	636	900
2	31	62	93	186	303	420
3-5	26	52	78	154	252	350
6-18: 11,12,15,17-Photo-c	21	42	63	124	202	280

SGT. BILKO'S PVT. DOBERMAN (TV)
National Periodical Publications: June-July, 1958 - No. 11, Feb-Mar, 1960

	GD 2.0	VG 4.0	FN 6.0	VF 8.0	VF/NM 9.0	NM- 9.2
1-Bob Oskner c-1-4,7,11	21	42	63	147	324	500
2	12	24	36	79	170	260
3-5: 5-Photo-c	19	18	27	60	120	180
6-11: 6,9-Photo-c	7	14	21	44	82	120

SGT. DICK CARTER OF THE U.S. BORDER PATROL (See Holyoke One-Shot)

SGT. FURY (& His Howling Commandos)(See Fury & Special Marvel Edition)
Marvel Comics Group (BPC earlier issues): May, 1963 - No. 167, Dec, 1981

	GD 2.0	VG 4.0	FN 6.0	VF 8.0	VF/NM 9.0	NM- 9.2
1-1st app. Sgt. Nick Fury (becomes agent of Shield in Strange Tales #135); Kirby/Ayers-c/a; 1st Dum-Dum Dugan & the Howlers	333	666	1000	2831	6416	10,000
2-Kirby-a	56	112	168	448	999	1550
3-5: 3-Reed Richards x-over. 4-Death of Junior Juniper. 5-1st Baron Strucker app.; Kirby-a	29	58	87	209	467	725
6-10: 8-Baron Zemo, 1st Percival Pinkerton app. 9-Hitler-c & app. 10-1st app. Capt. Savage (the Skipper)(9/64)	15	30	45	103	227	350
11,12,14-20: 14-1st Blitz Squad. 18-Death of Pamela Hawley	9	18	27	60	120	180
13-Captain America & Bucky app.(12/64); 2nd solo Capt. America x-over outside The Avengers; Kirby-a	38	76	114	285	641	1000
13-2nd printing (1994)	2	4	6	8	10	12
21-24,26,28-30	6	12	18	40	73	105
25,27: 25-Red Skull app. 27-1st app. Eric Koenig; origin Fury's eye patch	6	12	18	41	76	110
31-33,35-50: 35-Eric Koenig joins Howlers. 43-Bob Hope, Glen Miller app. 44-Flashback on Howlers' 1st mission	4	8	12	27	44	60
34-Origin Howling Commandos	4	8	12	28	47	65
51-60	4	8	12	23	37	50
61-67: 64-Capt. Savage & Raiders x-over; peace symbol-c. 67-Last 12¢ issue; flag-c	3	6	9	19	30	40
68-80: 76-Fury's Father app. in WWI story	3	6	9	16	24	32
81-91: 91-Last 15¢ issue	3	6	9	14	20	26
92-(52 pgs.)	3	6	9	16	24	32
93-99: 98-Deadly Dozen x-over	3	6	9	14	19	24
100-Capt. America, Fantastic 4 cameos; Stan Lee, Martin Goodman & others app.	3	6	9	16	24	32
101-120: 101-Origin retold	2	4	6	10	14	18
121-130: 121-123-r/#19-21	2	4	6	8	11	14
131-167: 167-Reprints (from 1963)	2	4	6	8	10	12
133,134-(30¢-c variants, limited dist.)(5,7/76)	3	6	9	15	22	28
141,142-(35¢-c variants, limited dist.)(7,9/77)	3	6	9	21	33	45
Annual 1(1965, 25¢, 72 pgs.)-r/#4,5 & new-a	13	26	39	89	195	300
Special 2(1966)	6	12	18	40	73	105
Special 3(1967) All new material	5	10	15	30	50	70
Special 4(1968)	3	6	9	21	33	45
Special 5-7(1969-11/71)	3	6	9	17	26	35

NOTE: ***Ayers*** *a-8, Annual 1.* ***Ditko*** *a-15i.* ***Gil Kane*** *c-37, 96.* ***Kirby*** *a-1-7, 13p, 167p(r). Special 5; c-1-8, 10-20, 25, 167p.* ***Severin*** *a-44-46, 48, 162, 164; inks-49-79, Special 4, 6; c-4i, 5, 6, 44, 46, 110, 149i, 155i, 162-166.* ***Sutton*** *a-57p. Reprints in #80, 82, 85, 87, 89, 91, 93, 95, 99, 101, 103, 105, 107, 109, 111, 121-123, 145-155, 167.*

SGT. FURY AND HIS HOWLING COMMANDOS
Marvel Comics: July, 2009 ($3.99, one-shot)

1-John Paul Leon-a/c; WWII tale set in 1942; Baron Strucker app.						4.00

SGT. FURY AND HIS HOWLING DEFENDERS (See The Defenders #147)

SERGEANT PRESTON OF THE YUKON (TV)
Dell Publishing Co.: No. 344, Aug, 1951 - No. 29, Nov-Jan, 1958-59

	GD 2.0	VG 4.0	FN 6.0	VF 8.0	VF/NM 9.0	NM- 9.2
Four Color 344(#1)-Sergeant Preston & his dog Yukon King begin; painted-c begin, end #18	10	20	30	69	147	225
Four Color 373,397,419('52)	7	14	21	46	86	125
5(11-1/52-53)-10(2-4/54): 6-Bondage-c.	5	10	15	35	63	90
11,12,14-17	5	10	15	33	57	80
13-Origin Sgt. Preston	5	10	15	35	63	90
18-Origin Yukon King; last painted-c	5	10	15	35	63	90
19-29: All photo-c	6	12	18	41	76	110

SGT. ROCK (Formerly Our Army at War; see Brave & the Bold #52 & Showcase #45)
National Periodical Publications/DC Comics: No. 302, Mar, 1977 - No. 422, July, 1988

	GD 2.0	VG 4.0	FN 6.0	VF 8.0	VF/NM 9.0	NM- 9.2
302	4	8	12	28	47	65
303-310	3	6	9	16	23	30
311-320: 318-Reprints	2	4	6	10	16	20
321-350	2	4	6	8	11	14
329-Whitman variant	3	6	9	14	19	24
351-399,401-421: 412-Mlle Marie & Haunted Tank	1	2	3	5	7	9
400-(6/85) Anniversary issue	2	4	6	8	11	14
422-1st Joe, Adam, Andy Kubert-a team; last issue	2	4	6	10	14	18
Annual 2-4: 2(1982)-Formerly Sgt. Rock's Prize Battle Tales #1. 3(1983). 4(1984)	2	4	6	8	10	12

NOTE: ***Estrada*** *a-322, 327, 331, 336, 337, 341, 342i.* ***Glanzman*** *a-384, 421.* ***Kubert*** *a-302, 303, 305r, 306, 328, 351, 356, 368, 373, 422; c-317, 318r, 319-323, 325-333-on, Annual 2, 3.* ***Severin*** *a-347.* ***Spiegle*** *a-382, Annual 2, 3.* ***Thorne*** *a-384.* ***Toth*** *a-385r.* ***Wildey*** *a-307, 311, 313, 314.*

SGT. ROCK: BETWEEN HELL AND A HARD PLACE
DC Comics (Vertigo): 2003 ($24.95, hardcover one-shot)

HC-Joe Kubert-a/c; Brian Azzarello-s						25.00
SC (2004, $17.95)						18.00

SGT. ROCK'S COMBAT TALES
DC Comics: 2005 ($9.99, digest)

Vol. 1-Reprints early app. in Our Army at War, G.I. Combat, Star Spangled War Stories						10.00

SGT. ROCK SPECIAL (Sgt. Rock #14 on; see DC Special Series #3)
DC Comics: Oct, 1988 - No. 21, Feb, 1992; No. 1, 1992; No. 2, 1994 ($2.00, quarterly/monthly, 52 pgs)

	GD 2.0	VG 4.0	FN 6.0	VF 8.0	VF/NM 9.0	NM- 9.2
1-Reprint begin	2	4	6	8	11	14
2-21: All-r; 5-r/early Sgt. Rock/Our Army at War #81. 7-Tomahawk-r by Thorne. 9-Enemy Ace-r by Kubert. 10-All Rock issue. 11-r/1st Haunted Tank story. 12-All Kubert issue; begins monthly. 13-Dinosaur story by Heath(r). 14-Enemy Ace-r (22 pgs.) by Adams/Kubert. 15-Enemy Ace (22 pgs.) by Kubert. 16-Iron Major-c/story. 16,17-Enemy Ace-r. 19-r/Batman/Sgt. Rock team-up/B&B #108 by Aparo	1	2	3	5	6	8
1 (1992, $2.95, 68 pgs.)-Simonson-c; unpubbed Kubert-a; Glanzman, Russell, Pratt, & Wagner-a						6.00
2 (1994, $2.95) Brereton painted-c						4.00

NOTE: ***Neal Adams*** *r-1, 8, 14p.* ***Chaykin*** *a-2; r-3, 9(2pgs.); c-3.* ***Drucker*** *r-6.* ***Glanzman*** *r-20.* ***Golden*** *a-1.* ***Heath*** *a-2; r-5, 9-13, 16, 19, 21.* ***Krigstein*** *r-4, 8.* ***Kubert*** *r-1-17, 20, 21; c-1p, 2, 8, 14-21.* ***Miller*** *r-6p.* ***Severin*** *r-3, 6, 10.* ***Simonson*** *r-2, 4; c-4.* ***Thorne*** *r-7.* ***Toth*** *r-2, 8, 11.* ***Wood*** *r-4.*

SGT. ROCK SPECTACULAR (See DC Special Series #13)

SGT. ROCK'S PRIZE BATTLE TALES (Becomes Sgt. Rock Annual #2 on; see DC Special Series #18 & 80 Page Giant #7)
National Periodical Publications: Winter, 1964 (Giant - 80 pgs., one-shot)

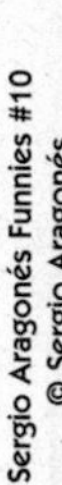

Sergio Aragonés Funnies #10 © Sergio Aragonés

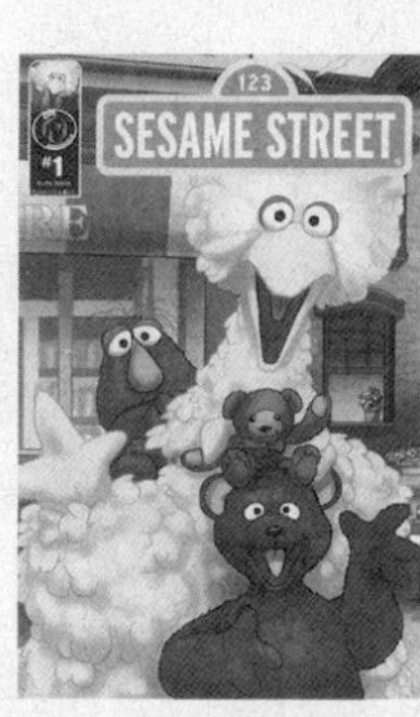

Sesame Street #1 © Sesame Workshop

Seven Soldiers: Bulleteer #4 © DC

	GD 2.0	VG 4.0	FN 6.0	VF 8.0	VF/NM 9.0	NM- 9.2
1-Kubert, Heath-r; new Kubert-c	33	66	99	238	532	825

... Replica Edition (2000, $5.95) Reprints entire issue 6.00

SGT. ROCK: THE LOST BATTALION
DC Comics: Jan, 2009 - No. 6, Jun, 2009 ($2.99, limited series)
1-6-Billy Tucci-s/a. 1-Tucci & Sparacio-c 3.00
HC (2009, $24.99, d.j.) r/#1-6; production art; cover art gallery 25.00
SC (2010, $17.99) r/#1-6; production art; cover art gallery 18.00

SGT. ROCK: THE PROPHECY
DC Comics: Mar, 2006 - No. 6, Aug, 2006 ($2.99, limited series)
1-6-Joe Kubert-s/a/c. 1-Variant covers by Andy and Adam Kubert 3.00
TPB (2007, $17.99) r/#1-6 18.00

SGT. STRYKER'S DEATH SQUAD (See Savage Combat Tales)

SERGIO ARAGONÉS' ACTIONS SPEAK
Dark Horse Comics: Jan, 2001 - No. 6, Jun, 2001 ($2.99, B&W, limited series)
1-6-Aragonés-c/a; wordless one-page cartoons 3.00

SERGIO ARAGONÉS' BLAIR WHICH?
Dark Horse Comics: Dec, 1999 ($2.95, B&W, one-shot)
nn-Aragonés-c/a; Evanier-s. Parody of "Blair Witch Project" movie 3.00

SERGIO ARAGONÉS' BOOGEYMAN
Dark Horse Comics: June, 1998 - No. 4, Sept, 1998 ($2.95, B&W, lim. series)
1-4-Aragonés-c/a 3.00

SERGIO ARAGONÉS DESTROYS DC
DC Comics: June, 1996 ($3.50, one-shot)
1-DC Superhero parody book; Aragonés-c/a; Evanier scripts 4.00

SERGIO ARAGONÉS' DIA DE LOS MUERTOS
Dark Horse Comics: Oct, 1998 ($2.95, one-shot)
1-Aragonés-c/a; Evanier scripts 3.00

SERGIO ARAGONÉS FUNNIES
Bongo Comics: 2011 - Present ($3.50)
1-12-Color and B&W humor strips by Aragonés 3.50

SERGIO ARAGONÉS' GROO & RUFFERTO
Dark Horse Comics: Dec, 1998 - No. 4, Mar, 1999 ($2.95, lim. series)
1-3-Aragonés-c/a 3.00

SERGIO ARAGONÉS' GROO: DEATH AND TAXES
Dark Horse Comics: Dec, 2001 - No. 4, Apr, 2002 ($2.99, lim. series)
1-4-Aragonés-c/a; Evanier-s 3.00

SERGIO ARAGONÉS' GROO: HELL ON EARTH
Dark Horse Comics: Nov, 2007 - No. 4, Apr, 2008 ($2.99, lim. series)
1-4-Aragonés-c/a; Evanier-s 3.00

SERGIO ARAGONÉS' GROO: MIGHTIER THAN THE SWORD
Dark Horse Comics: Jan, 2000 - No. 4, Apr, 2000 ($2.95, lim. series)
1-4-Aragonés-c/a; Evanier-s 3.00

SERGIO ARAGONÉS' GROO: THE HOGS OF HORDER
Dark Horse Comics: Oct, 2009 - No. 4, Mar, 2010 ($3.99, lim. series)
1-4-Aragonés-c/a; Evanier-s 4.00

SERGIO ARAGONÉS' GROO THE WANDERER (See Groo...)

SERGIO ARAGONÉS' GROO: 25TH ANNIVERSARY SPECIAL
Dark Horse Comics: Aug, 2007 ($5.99, one-shot)
nn-Aragonés-c/a; Evanier scripts; wraparound cover 6.00

SERGIO ARAGONÉS' LOUDER THAN WORDS
Dark Horse Comics: July, 1997 - No. 6, Dec, 1997 ($2.95, B&W, limited series)
1-6-Aragonés-c/a 3.00

SERGIO ARAGONÉS MASSACRES MARVEL
Marvel Comics: June, 1996 ($3.50, one-shot)
1-Marvel Superhero parody book; Aragonés-c/a; Evanier scripts 4.00

SERGIO ARAGONÉS STOMPS STAR WARS
Marvel Comics: Jan, 2000 ($2.95, one-shot)
1-Star Wars parody; Aragonés-c/a; Evanier scripts 3.00

SESAME STREET
Ape Entertainment: 2013 ($3.99)
1-Short stories by various; multiple covers 4.00
Free Comic Book Day edition (2013) Flip book with Strawberry Shortcake 3.00

GD 2.0	VG 4.0	FN 6.0	VF 8.0	VF/NM 9.0	NM- 9.2

SEVEN
Intrinsic Comics: July, 2007 ($3.00)
1-Jim Shooter-s/Paul Creddick-a 3.00

SEVEN BLOCK
Marvel Comics (Epic Comics): 1990 ($4.50, one-shot, 52 pgs.)
1-Dixon-s/Zaffino-a 6.00
nn-(IDW Publ., 2004, $5.99) reprints #1 6.00

SEVEN BROTHERS (John Woo's...)
Virgin Comics: Oct, 2006 - No. 5, Feb, 2007 ($2.99)
1-5-Garth Ennis-s/Jeevan Kang-a. 1-Two covers by Amano & Horn. 2-Kang var-c 3.00
TPB (6/07, $14.99) r/#1-5; cover gallery, deleted scenes and concept art 15.00
Volume 2 (9/07 - No. 5, 2/08) 1-Edison George-a. 4,5-David Mack-c 3.00

SEVEN DEAD MEN (See Complete Mystery #1)

SEVEN DWARFS (Also see Snow White)
Dell Publishing Co.: No. 227, 1949 (Disney-Movie)

	GD	VG	FN	VF	VF/NM	NM-
Four Color 227	9	18	27	58	114	170

SEVEN MILES A SECOND
DC Comics (Vertigo Verité): 1996 ($7.95, one-shot)
nn-Wojnarowicz-s/Romberg-a 8.00

SEVEN SAMUROID, THE (See Image Graphic Novel)

SEVEN SEAS COMICS
Universal Phoenix Features/Leader No. 6: Apr, 1946 - No. 6, 1947(no month)

	GD	VG	FN	VF	VF/NM	NM-
1-South Sea Girl by Matt Baker, Capt. Cutlass begin; Tugboat Tessie by Baker app.	94	188	282	602	1026	1450
2-Swashbuckler-c	71	142	213	454	777	1100
3,5,6: 3-Six pg. Feldstein-a	90	180	270	576	988	1400
4-Classic Baker-c	161	322	483	1030	1765	2500

NOTE: *Baker a-1-6; c-3-6.*

SEVEN SOLDIERS OF VICTORY (Book-ends for seven related mini-series)
DC Comics: No. 0, Apr, 2005; No. 1; Dec, 2006 ($2.95/$3.99)
0-Grant Morrison-s/J.H. Williams-a 3.00
1-($3.99) Series conclusion; Grant Morrison-s/J.H. Williams-a 4.00
... Volume One (2006, $14.99) r/#0, Shining Knight #1,2; Zatanna #1,2; Guardian #1,2; and Klarion the Witch Boy #1; intro. by Morrison; character design sketches 15.00
... Volume Two (2006, $14.99) r/Shining Knight #3,4; Zatanna #3; Guardian #3,4; and Klarion the Witch Boy #2,3 15.00
... Volume Three ('06, $14.99) r/Zatanna #4; Mister Miracle #1,2; Bulleteer #1,2; Frankenstein #1 and Klarion the Witch Boy #4; 15.00
... Volume Four ('07, $14.99) r/Mister Miracle #3,4; Bulleteer #3,4; Frankenstein #2-4 and Seven Soldiers of Victory #1; script pages 15.00

SEVEN SOLDIERS: BULLETEER
DC Comics: Jan, 2006 - No. 4, May, 2006 ($2.99, limited series)
1-4-Grant Morrison-s/Yanick Paquette-a/c 3.00

SEVEN SOLDIERS: FRANKENSTEIN
DC Comics: Jan, 2006 - No. 4, May, 2006 ($2.99, limited series)
1-4-Grant Morrison-s/Doug Mahnke-a/c 3.00

SEVEN SOLDIERS: GUARDIAN
DC Comics: May, 2005 - No. 4, Nov, 2005 ($2.99, limited series)
1-4-Grant Morrison-s/Cameron Stewart-a; Newsboy Army app. 3.00

SEVEN SOLDIERS: KLARION THE WITCH BOY
DC Comics: June, 2005 - No. 4, Dec, 2005 ($2.99, limited series)
1-4-Grant Morrison-s/Frazer Irving-a 3.00

SEVEN SOLDIERS: MISTER MIRACLE
DC Comics: Nov, 2005 - No. 4, May, 2006 ($2.99, limited series)
1-4: 1-Grant Morrison-s/Pasqual Ferry-a/c. 3,4-Freddie Williams II-a/c 3.00

SEVEN SOLDIERS: SHINING KNIGHT
DC Comics: May, 2005 - No. 4, Oct, 2005 ($2.99, limited series)
1-4-Grant Morrison-s/Simone Bianchi-a 3.00

SEVEN SOLDIERS: ZATANNA
DC Comics: June, 2005 - No. 4, Dec, 2005 ($2.99, limited series)
1-4-Grant Morrison-s/Ryan Sook-a 3.00

1776 (See Charlton Classic Library)

7TH VOYAGE OF SINBAD, THE (Movie)
Dell Publishing Co.: Sept, 1958 (photo-c)

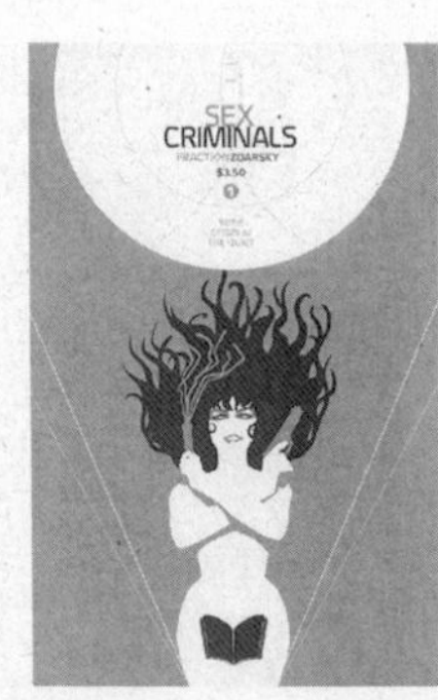

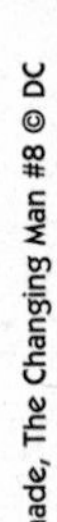
Sex Criminals #1 © Milkfed & Zdarsky

Shade, The Changing Man #8 © DC

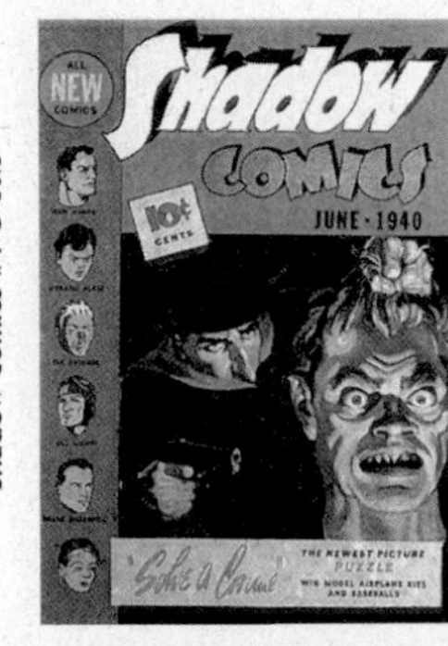

Shadow Comics #4 © S&S

	GD 2.0	VG 4.0	FN 6.0	VF 8.0	VF/NM 9.0	NM- 9.2
Four Color 944-Buscema-a	10	20	30	70	150	230

77 SUNSET STRIP (TV)
Dell Publ. Co./Gold Key: No. 1066, Jan-Mar, 1960 - No. 2, Feb, 1963 (All photo-c)

	GD	VG	FN	VF	VF/NM	NM-
Four Color 1066-Toth-a	9	18	27	60	120	180
Four Color 1106,1159-Toth-a	7	14	21	49	92	135
Four Color 1211,1263,1291, 01-742-209(7-9/62)-Manning-a in all	7	14	21	46	86	125
1,2: Manning-a. 1(11/62-G.K.)	7	14	21	46	86	125

77TH BENGAL LANCERS, THE (TV)
Dell Publishing Co.: May, 1957

	GD	VG	FN	VF	VF/NM	NM-
Four Color 791-Photo-c	6	12	18	40	73	105

SEVERED
Image Comics: Aug, 2011 - No. 7, Feb, 2012 ($2.99)

1-7-Scott Snyder & Scott Tuft-s/Attila Futaki-a/c 3.00

SEX
Image Comics: Mar, 2013 - Present ($2.99)

1-12-Joe Casey-s/Piotr Kowalski-a/c 3.00

SEX CRIMINALS
Image Comics: Sept, 2013 - Present ($2.99)

1-Matt Fraction-s/Chip Zdarsky-a/c 12.00
1-Variant-c by Shimizu 8.00
2 8.00
3-5 5.00

SEYMOUR, MY SON (See More Seymour)
Archie Publications (Radio Comics): Sept, 1963

	GD	VG	FN	VF	VF/NM	NM-
1-DeCarlo-c/a	4	8	12	23	37	50

SHADE, THE (See Starman)
DC Comics: Apr, 1997 - No. 4, July, 1997 ($2.25, limited series)

1-4-Robinson-s/Harris-c: 1-Gene Ha-a. 2-Williams/Gray-a 3-Blevins-a. 4-Zulli-a 3.00

SHADE, THE (From Starman)
DC Comics: Dec, 2011 - No. 12, Nov, 2012 ($2.99, limited series)

1-12: 1-Robinson-s/Hamner-a/Harris-c; Deathstroke app. 4-Cooke-a. 8-Thompson-a 12-Origin of the Shade; Gene Ha-a 3.00
1-12-Variant covers. 1-3-Hamner. 4-Darwyn Cooke. 5-7-Pulido. 11-Irving 4.00

SHADE, THE CHANGING MAN (See Cancelled Comic Cavalcade)
National Per. Publ./DC Comics: June-July, 1977 - No. 8, Aug-Sept, 1978

	GD	VG	FN	VF	VF/NM	NM-
1-1st app. Shade; Ditko-c/a in all	2	4	6	11	16	20
2-8	2	3	4	6	8	10

SHADE, THE CHANGING MAN (2nd series) (Also see Suicide Squad #16)
DC Comics (Vertigo imprint #33 on): July, 1990 - No. 70, Apr, 1996 ($1.50-$2.25, mature)

1-($2.50, 52 pgs.)-Peter Milligan scripts in all 4.00
2-41,45-49,51-59: 6-Preview of World Without End. 17-Begin $1.75-c. 33-Metallic ink on-c. 41-Begin $1.95-c 3.00
42-44-John Constantine app. 3.50
50-($2.95, 52 pgs.) 4.00
60-70: 60-begin $2.25-c 3.00
...: Edge of Vision TPB (2009, $19.99) r/#7-13 20.00
...: Scream Time TPB (2010, $19.99) r/#14-19 20.00
...: The American Scream TPB (2003, 2009, $17.95/$17.99) r/#1-6 18.00
NOTE: *Bachalo a-1-9, 11-13, 15-21, 23-26, 33-39, 42-45, 47, 49, 50; c-30, 33-41.*

SHADO: SONG OF THE DRAGON (See Green Arrow #63-66)
DC Comics: 1992 - No. 4, 1992 ($4.95, limited series, 52 pgs.)

Book One - Four: Grell scripts; Morrow-a(i) 6.00

SHADOW, THE (See Batman #253, 259 & Marvel Graphic Novel #35)

SHADOW, THE (Pulp, radio)
Archie Comics (Radio Comics): Aug, 1964 - No. 8, Sept, 1965 (All 12¢)

	GD	VG	FN	VF	VF/NM	NM-
1-Jerrry Siegel scripts in all; Shadow-c.	8	16	24	55	105	155
2-8: 2-App. in super-hero costume on-c only; Reinman-a(backup). 3-Superhero begins; Reinman-a (book-length novel). 3,4,6,7-The Fly 1 pg. strips. 4-8-Reinman-a. 5-8-Siegel scripts. 7-Shield app.	5	10	15	33	57	80

SHADOW, THE
National Periodical Publications: Oct-Nov, 1973 - No. 12, Aug-Sept, 1975

	GD	VG	FN	VF	VF/NM	NM-
1-Kaluta-a begins	6	12	18	37	66	95
2	3	6	9	21	33	45
3-Kaluta/Wrightson-a	4	8	12	23	37	50
4,6-Kaluta-a ends. 4-Chaykin, Wrightson part-i	3	6	9	18	28	38
5,7-12: 11-The Avenger (pulp character) x-over	2	4	6	13	18	22

NOTE: *Craig a-10. Cruz a-10-12. Kaluta a-1, 2, 3p, 4, 6; c-1-4, 6, 10-12. Kubert c-9. Robbins a-5, 7-9; c-5, 7, 8.*

SHADOW, THE
DC Comics: May, 1986 - No. 4, Aug, 1986 (limited series)

1-4: Howard Chaykin art in all 4.00
Blood & Judgement ($12.95)-r/1-4 13.00

SHADOW, THE
DC Comics: Aug, 1987 - No. 19, Jan, 1989 ($1.50)

1-19: Andrew Helfer scripts in all. 4.00
Annual 1,2 (12/87, '88,)-2-The Shadow dies; origin retold (story inspired by the movie "Citizen Kane"). 5.00
NOTE: *Kyle Baker a-7i, 8-19, Annual 2. Chaykin c-Annual 1. Helfer scripts in all. Orlando a-Annual 1. Rogers c/a-7. Sienkiewicz c/a-1-6.*

SHADOW, THE (Movie)
Dark Horse Comics: June, 1994 - No. 2, July, 1994 ($2.50, limited series)

1,2-Adaptation from Universal Pictures film 4.00
NOTE: *Kaluta c/a-1, 2.*

SHADOW, THE
Dynamite Entertainment: 2012 - Present ($3.99)

1-23: 1-Ennis-s/Campbell-a; multiple covers on all. 7-10-Gischler-s 4.00
Annual 1 (2012, $4.99) Sniegoski-s/Calero-a/Alex Ross-c 5.00
Annual 2013 ($4.99) Parks-s/Evely-a/Worley-c 5.00
Special 1 (2012, $4.99) Beatty-s/Cliquet-a/Alex Ross-c 5.00

SHADOW AND DOC SAVAGE, THE
Dark Horse Comics: July, 1995 - No. 2, Aug, 1995 ($2.95, limited series)

1,2 4.00

SHADOW AND THE MYSTERIOUS 3, THE
Dark Horse Comics: Sept, 1994 ($2.95, one-shot)

1-Kaluta co-scripts. 4.00
NOTE: *Stevens c-1.*

SHADOW CABINET (See Heroes)
DC Comics (Milestone): No. 0, Jan, 1994 - No. 17, Oct, 1995 ($1.75/$2.50)

0-(1/94, $2.50, 52 pgs.)-Silver ink-c; Simonson-c 4.00
1-17: 1-(6/94) Byrne-c 3.00

SHADOW COMICS (Pulp, radio)
Street & Smith Publications: Mar, 1940 - V9#5, Aug-Sept, 1949
NOTE: *The Shadow first appeared on radio in 1929 and was featured in pulps beginning in April, 1931, written by Walter Gibson. The early covers of this series were reprinted from the pulp covers.*

	GD	VG	FN	VF	VF/NM	NM-
V1#1-Shadow, Doc Savage, Bill Barnes, Nick Carter (radio), Frank Merriwell, Iron Munro, the Astonishing Man begin	503	1006	1509	3672	6486	9300
2-The Avenger begins, ends #6; Capt. Fury only app.	219	438	657	1402	2401	3400
3(nn-5/40)-Norgil the Magician app.; cover is exact swipe of Shadow pulp from 1/33	158	316	474	1011	1731	2450
4,5: 4-The Three Musketeers begins, ends #8. 5-Doc Savage ends	116	232	348	742	1271	1800
6,8,9: 9-Norgil the Magician app.	97	194	291	621	1061	1500
7-Origin/1st app. The Hooded Wasp & Wasplet (11/40); series ends V3#8; Hooded Wasp/Wasplet app. on-c thru #9	102	204	306	648	1112	1575
10-Origin The Iron Ghost, ends #11; The Dead End Kids begins, ends #14	95	190	285	603	1039	1475
11-Origin Hooded Wasp & Wasplet retold	95	190	285	603	1039	1475
12-Dead End Kids app.	89	178	267	565	970	1375
V2#1(11/41, Vol.II#2 in indicia) Dead End Kids -s	87	174	261	553	952	1350
2-(Rare, 1/42, Vol.II#3 in indicia) Nazi WWII explosion-c	168	336	504	1075	1838	2600
3-Origin & 1st app. Supersnipe (3/42); series begins; Little Nemo story (Vol.II#4 in indicia)	139	278	417	883	1517	2150
4,5: 4,8-Little Nemo story	77	154	231	493	847	1200
6-9: 6-Blackstone the Magician story	74	148	222	470	810	1150
10,12: 10-Supersnipe app.' Skull-c	73	146	219	467	796	1125
11-Classic Devil Kyoti World War 2 sunburst-c	94	188	282	602	1026	1450
V3#1,2,5,7-12: 10-Doc Savage begins, not in V5#5, V6#10-12, V8#4	71	142	213	454	777	1100
3-1st Monstrodamus-c/sty	94	188	282	602	1026	1450
4-2nd Monstrodamus; classic-c of giant salamander getting shot in the head	100	200	300	640	1095	1550
6-Classic underwater-c	103	206	309	659	1130	1600
V4#1,3-12	50	100	150	315	533	750

Shadowhawk V2 #5 © Jim Valentino

Shadowland: Power Man #1 © MAR

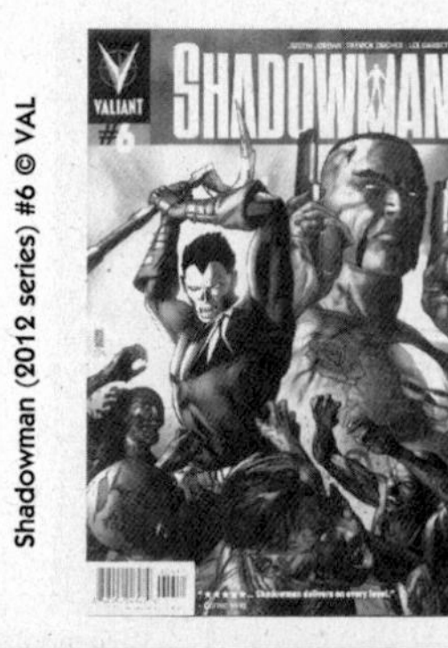

Shadowman (2012 series) #6 © VAL

	GD 2.0	VG 4.0	FN 6.0	VF 8.0	VF/NM 9.0	NM- 9.2
2-Severed head-c	77	154	231	493	847	1200
V5#1-12	43	86	129	271	461	650
V6#1-11: 9-Intro. Shadow, Jr. (12/46)	40	80	120	246	411	575
12-Powell-c/a; atom bomb panels	43	86	129	271	461	650
V7#1,2,5,7-9,12: 2,5-Shadow, Jr. app.; Powell-a	40	80	120	246	411	575
3,6,11-Powell-c/a	45	90	135	284	480	675
4-Powell-c/a; Atom bomb panels	47	94	141	296	498	700
10(1/48)-Flying Saucer-c/story (2nd of this theme; see The Spirit 9/28/47); Powell-c/a	65	130	195	416	708	1000
V8#1,2,4-12-Powell-a.	45	90	135	284	480	675
3-Powell Spider-c/a	47	94	141	296	498	700
V9#1,5-Powell-a	43	86	129	271	461	650
2-4-Powell-c/a	45	90	135	284	480	675

NOTE: *__Binder__ c-V3#1. __Powell__ art in most issues beginning V6#12. Painted c-1-6.*

SHADOWDRAGON
DC Comics: 1995 ($3.50, annual)

Annual 1-Year One story 4.00

SHADOW EMPIRES: FAITH CONQUERS
Dark Horse Comics: Aug, 1994 - No. 4, Nov, 1994 ($2.95, limited series)

1-4 3.00

SHADOW/GREEN HORNET: DARK NIGHTS (Pulp characters)
Dynamite Entertainment: 2013 - No. 5, 2013 ($3.99)

1-5-Lamont Cranston & Britt Reid team-up in 1939; Uslan-s; multiple covers on each 4.00

SHADOWHAWK (See Images of Shadowhawk, New Shadowhawk, Shadowhawk II, Shadowhawk III & Youngblood #2)
Image Comics (Shadowline Ink): Aug, 1992 - No. 4, Mar, 1993; No. 12, Aug, 1994 - No. 18, May, 1995 ($1.95/$2.50)

1-($2.50)-Embossed silver foil stamped-c; Valentino/Liefeld-c; Valentino-c/a/scripts in all; has coupon for Image #0; 1st Shadowline Ink title 5.00
1-With coupon missing 2.00
1-($1.95)-Newsstand version w/o foil stamp 3.00
2-13,0,1418: 2-Shadowhawk poster w/McFarlane-i; brief Spawn app.; wraparound-c w/silver ink highlights. 3-($2.50)-Glow-in-the-dark-c. 4-Savage Dragon-c/story; Valentino/Larsen-c. 5-11-(See Shadowhawk II and III). 12-Cont'd from Shadowhawk III; pull-out poster by Texeira.13-w/ShadowBone poster; WildC.A.T.s app. 0 (10/94)-Liefeld c/a/story; ShadowBart poster. 14-(10/94, $2.50)-The Others app. 16-Supreme app. 17-Spawn app.; story cont'd from Badrock & Co. #6. 18-Shadowhawk dies; Savage Dragon & Brigade app. 3.00
Special 1(12/94, $3.50, 52 pgs.)-Silver Age Shadowhawk flip book 4.00
Gallery (4/94, $1.95) 3.00
Out of the Shadows ($19.95)-r/Youngblood #2, Shadowhawk #1-4, Image Zero #0, Operation: Urban Storm (Never published) 20.00
.../Vampirella (2/95, $4.95)-Pt.2 of x-over (See Vampirella/Shadowhawk for Pt. 1) 5.00

NOTE: *Shadowhawk was originally a four issue limited series. The story continued in Shadowhawk II, Shadowhawk III & then became Shadowhawk again with issue #12.*

SHADOWHAWK II (Follows Shadowhawk #4)
Image Comics (Shadowline Ink): V2#1, May, 1993 - V2#3, Aug, 1993 ($3.50/$1.95/$2.95, limited series)

V2#1 ($3.50)-Cont'd from Shadowhawk #4; die-cut mirricard-c 4.00
2 ($1.95)-Foil embossed logo; reveals identity; gold-c variant exists 4.00
3 ($2.95)-Pop-up-c w/Pact ashcan insert 4.00

SHADOWHAWK III (Follows Shadowhawk II #3)
Image Comics (Shadowline Ink): V3#1, Nov, 1993 - V3#4, Mar, 1994 ($1.95, limited series);

V3#1-4: 1-Cont'd from Shadowhawk II; intro Valentine; gold foil & red foil stamped-c variations. 2-(52 pgs.)-Shadowhawk contracts HIV virus; U.S. Male by M. Anderson (p) in free 16 pg.insert. 4-Continues in Shadowhawk #12 4.00

SHADOWHAWK (Volume 2) (Also see New Man #4)
Image Comics: May, 2005 - No. 15, Sept, 2006 ($2.99/$3.50)

1-4-Eddie Collins as Shadowhawk; Rodríguez-a; Valentino-co-plotter 3.50
5-15-($3.50) 5-Cover swipe of Superman Vs. Spider-Man treasury edition 3.50
...One Shot #1 (7/06, $1.99) r/Return of Shadowhawk 3.00
Return of Shadowhawk (12/04, $2.99) Valentino-s/a/c; Eddie Collins origin retold 3.00

SHADOWHAWK (Volume 3)
Image Comics: May, 2010 - No. 5, Dec, 2010 ($3.50)

1-5-Rodríguez-a. 1-Back-up with Valentino-a/Niles-s 3.50

SHADOWHAWKS OF LEGEND
Image Comics (Shadowline Ink): Nov, 1995 ($4.95, one-shot)

nn-Stories of past Shadowhawks by Kurt Busiek, Beau Smith & Alan Moore 5.00

SHADOW, THE: HELL'S HEAT WAVE (Movie, pulp, radio)
Dark Horse Comics: Apr, 1995 - No. 3, June, 1995 ($2.95, limited series)

1-3: Kaluta story 4.00

SHADOW HUNTER (Jenna Jameson's...)
Virgin Comics: No. 0, Dec, 2007 - No. 3 ($2.99)

0-Preview issue; creator interviews; gallery of covers for upcoming issues; Greg Horn-c 3.00
1-3: 1-Two covers by Horn & Land; Jameson & Christina Z-s/Singh-a. 2-Three covers 3.00

SHADOWHUNT SPECIAL
Image Comics (Extreme Studios): Apr, 1996 ($2.50)

1-Retells origin of past Shadowhawks; Valentino script; Chapel app. 3.00

SHADOW, THE: IN THE COILS OF THE LEVIATHAN (Movie, pulp, radio)
Dark Horse Comics: Oct, 1993 - No. 4, Apr, 1994 ($2.95, limited series)

1-4-Kaluta-c & co-scripter 4.00
Trade paperback (10/94, $13.95)-r/1-4 14.00

SHADOWLAND (Also see Daredevil #508-512 & Black Panther: The Man Without Fear #513)
Marvel Comics: Sept, 2010 - No. 5, Jan, 2011 ($3.99, limited series)

1-5: 1-Diggle-s/Tan-a; Bullseye killed; Cassaday-c. 2-Ghost Rider app. 4.00
1-Variant-c by Tan 6.00
...: After the Fall 1 (2/11, $3.99) Finch-c; Black Panther app. 4.00
...: Bullseye 1 (10/10, $3.99) Chen-a; Bullseye's funeral 4.00
...: Elektra 1 (11/10, $3.99) Wells-s/Rios-a/Takeda-c 4.00
...: Ghost Rider 1 (11/10, $3.99) Williams-s/Crain-a/c 4.00
...: Spider-Man 1 (12/10, $3.99) Shang-Chi & Mr. Negative app.; Siqueira-a 4.00

SHADOWLAND: BLOOD IN THE STREETS (Leads into Heroes For Hire)
Marvel Comics: Oct, 2010 - No. 4, Jan, 2011 ($3.99, limited series)

1-4-Johnston-s/Alves-a; Misty Knight, Silver Sable, Paladin, Shroud app. 4.00

SHADOWLAND: DAUGHTERS OF THE SHADOW
Marvel Comics: Oct, 2010 - No. 3, Dec, 2010 ($3.99, limited series)

1-3-Henderson-s/Rodriguez-a; Colleen Wing app. 3-Preview of Black Panther #513 4.00

SHADOWLAND: MOON KNIGHT
Marvel Comics: Oct, 2010 - No. 3, Dec, 2010 ($3.99, limited series)

1-3-Hurwitz-s/Dazo-a 4.00

SHADOWLAND: POWER MAN
Marvel Comics: Oct, 2010 - No. 4, Jan, 2011 ($3.99, limited series)

1-4-Van Lente-s/Asrar-a. 1-New Power Man debut; Iron Fist app. 4.00

SHADOWLINE SAGA: CRITICAL MASS, A
Marvel Comics (Epic): Jan, 1990 - No. 7, July, 1990 ($4.95, lim. series, 68 pgs)

1-6: Dr. Zero, Powerline, St. George 5.00
7 ($5.95, 84 pgs.)-Morrow-a, Williamson-c(i) 6.00

SHADOWMAN (See X-O Manowar #4)
Valiant/Acclaim Comics (Valiant): May, 1992 - No. 43, Dec, 1995 ($2.50)

	GD 2.0	VG 4.0	FN 6.0	VF 8.0	VF/NM 9.0	NM- 9.2
1-Partial origin	2	4	6	10	14	18

2-5: 3-1st app. Sousa the Soul Eater 5.00
6-43: 8-1st app. Master Darque. 16-1st app. Dr. Mirage (8/93). 15-Minor Turok app. 17,18-Archer & Armstrong x-over. 19-Aerosmith-c/story. 23-Dr. Mirage x-over. 24-(4/94). 25-Bound-in trading card. 29-Chaos Effect. 43-Shadowman jumps to his death 4.00
0-($2.50, 4/94)-Regular edition 6.00
0-($3.50)-Wraparound chromium-c edition 5.00
0-Gold 20.00
Yearbook 1 (12/94, $3.95) 5.00

SHADOWMAN (Volume 2)
Acclaim Comics (Valiant Heroes): Mar, 1997 - No. 20 ($2.50, mature)

1-20: 1-1st app. Zero; Garth Ennis scripts begin, end #4. 2-Zero becomes new Shadowman. 4-Origin; Jack Boniface (original Shadowman) rises from the grave. 5-Jamie Delano scripts begin. 9-Copycat-c 3.00
1-Variant painted cover 3.00
#0 Gold 5.00

SHADOWMAN (Volume 3)
Acclaim Comics: July, 1999 - No. 5, Nov, 1999 ($3.95/$2.50)

1-($3.95)-Abnett & Lanning-s/Broome & Benjamin-a 4.00
2-5-($2.50): 3,4-Flip book with Unity 2000 3.00

SHADOWMAN
Valiant Entertainment: Nov, 2012 - Present ($3.99)

1-16: 1-6-Jordan-s/Zircher-a. 1-Two covers by Zircher (regular & pullbox) 4.00
1-Variant-c by Dave Johnson 8.00
1-Variant-c by Bill Sienkiewicz 16.00
2-4-Pullbox variants 6.00
5-16-Pullbox variants 4.00

Shadowpact #1 © DC

Shahrazad #1 © Tom Hutchinson

Shanna, The She-Devil #1 © MAR

GD 2.0 | VG 4.0 | FN 6.0 | VF 8.0 | VF/NM 9.0 | NM- 9.2

11-Variant-c with detachable Halloween mask 4.00
13X-(10/13, bagged with Bleeding Cool Magazine #7) prelude to #13; Milligan-s 3.00
#0-(5/13, $3.99) Origin of Master Darque 4.00

SHADOWMASTERS
Marvel Comics: Oct, 1989 - No.4, Jan, 1990 ($3.95, squarebound, 52 pgs.)
1-4: Heath-a(i). 1-Jim Lee-c; story cont'd from Punisher 4.00

SHADOW NOW, THE (Pulp character)
Dynamite Entertainment: 2013 - No. 6, 2014 ($3.99, limited series)
1-6: 1-David Liss-s/ColtonWorley-a; The Shadow in present day New York 4.00

SHADOW OF THE BATMAN
DC Comics: Dec, 1985 - No. 5, Apr, 1986 ($1.75, limited series)
1-Detective-r (all have wraparound-c) 1 2 3 5 6 8
2,3,5: 3-Penguin-c & cameo. 5-Clayface app. 6.00
4-Joker-c/story 1 2 3 4 5 7
NOTE: ***Austin*** *a(new)-2i, 3i; r-2-4i.* ***Rogers*** *a(new)-1, 2p, 3p, 4, 5; r-1-5p; c-1-5.* ***Simonson*** *a-1r.*

SHADOW ON THE TRAIL (See Zane Grey & Four Color #604)

SHADOWPACT (See Day of Vengeance)
DC Comics: Jul, 2006 - No. 25, Jul, 2008 ($2.99)
1-25: 1-Bill Willingham-s; Detective Chimp, Ragman, Blue Devil, Nightshade, Enchantress and Nightmaster app. 1-Superman app. 13-Zauriel app.; S. Hampton-a 3.00
...: Cursed TPB (2007, $14.99) r/#4,9-13 15.00
...: Darkness and Light TPB (2008, $14.99) r/#14-19 15.00
...: The Burning Age TPB (2008, $17.99) r/#20-25 18.00
...: The Pentacle Plot TPB (2007, $14.99) r/#1-3,5-8 15.00

SHADOW PLAY (Tales of the Supernatural)
Whitman Publications: June, 1982
1-Painted-c 1 2 3 5 6 8

SHADOWPLAY
IDW Publ.: Sept, 2005 - No. 4, Dec, 2005 ($3.99)
1-4-Benson-s/Templesmith-a; Christina Z-s/Wood-a; 2 covers by Templesmith & Wood 4.00
TPB (3/06, $17.99) r/series; flip book format 18.00

SHADOW REAVERS
Black Bull Ent.: Oct, 2001 - No. 5, Mar, 2002 ($2.99)
1-5-Nelson-a; two covers for each issue 3.00
Limited Preview Edition (5/01, no cover price) 3.00

SHADOW RIDERS
Marvel Comics UK, Ltd.: June, 1993 - No. 4, Sept, 1993 ($1.75, limited series)
1-($2.50)-Embossed-c; Cable-c/story 4.00
2-4-Cable app. 2-Ghost Rider app. 3.00

SHADOWS
Image Comics: Feb, 2003 - No. 4, Nov, 2003 ($2.95)
1-4-Jade Dodge-s/Matt Camp-a/c 3.00

SHADOWS & LIGHT
Marvel Comics: Feb, 1998 - No. 3, July, 1998 ($2.99, B&W, quarterly)
1-3: 1-B&W anthology of Marvel characters; Black Widow art by Gene Ha, Hulk by Wrightson, Iron Man by Ditko & Daredevil by Stelfreeze; Stelfreeze painted-c. 2-Weeks, Sharp, Starlin, Thompson-a. 3-Buscema, Grindberg, Giffen, Layton-a 3.00

SHADOW'S FALL
DC Comics (Vertigo): Nov, 1994 - No. 6, Apr, 1995 ($2.95, limited series)
1-6: Van Fleet-c/a in all. 3.00

SHADOWS FROM BEYOND (Formerly Unusual Tales)
Charlton Comics: V2#50, October, 1966
V2#50-Ditko-c 4 8 12 25 40 55

SHADOW STATE
Broadway Comics: Dec, 1995 - No. 5, Apr, 1996 ($2.50)
1-5: 1,2-Fatale back-up story; Cockrum-a(p) 3.00
Preview Edition 1,2 (10-11/95, $2.50, B&W) 3.00

SHADOW STRIKES!, THE (Pulp, radio)
DC Comics: Sept, 1989 - No.31, May, 1992 ($1.75)
1-4,7-31: 31-Mignola-c 4.00
5,6-Doc Savage x-over 5.00
Annual 1 (1989, $3.50, 68 pgs.)-Spiegle a; Kaluta-c 5.00

SHADOW WALK
Legendary Comics: Nov, 2013 ($24.99, graphic novel)
HC - Mark Waid-s/Shane Davis-a 25.00

GD 2.0 | VG 4.0 | FN 6.0 | VF 8.0 | VF/NM 9.0 | NM- 9.2

SHADOW WAR OF HAWKMAN
DC Comics: May, 1985 - No. 4, Aug, 1985 (limited series)
1-4 4.00

SHADOW, THE: YEAR ONE
Dynamite Entertainment: 2012 - Present ($3.99)
1-8: 1-Matt Wagner-s/Wilfredo Torres-a; multiple covers 4.00

SHAGGY DOG (See Movie Comics & Walt Disney Showcase #46)(Disney-Movie)
Dell Publ. Co.: No. 985, Apr-Jun, 1959
Four Color 985 6 12 18 42 79 115

SHAGGY DOG & THE ABSENT-MINDED PROFESSOR (See Movie Comics & Walt Disney Showcase #46)(Disney-Movie)
Dell Publ. Co.: No. 1199, Aug, 1967
Four Color 1199-Movie, photo-c 6 12 18 42 79 115

SHAHRAZAD
Big Dog Ink: No. 0, Apr, 2013 - Present ($1.99/$3.50)
0-($1.99) Hutchison-s/Krome-a; multiple covers 3.00
1-3 ($3.99) Hutchison & Castor-s/Krome-a; multiple covers on each 4.00

SHALOMAN (Jewish-themed stories and history)
Al Wiesner/ Mark 1 Comics: 1988 - 2012 (B&W)
V1#1-Al Wiesner-s/a in all 5.00
2-9 3.00
V2 #1(The New Adventures)-4,6-10, V3 (The Legend of...) #1-12 3.00
V2 #5 (Color)-Shows Vol 2, No. 4 in indicia 3.00
V4 (The Saga of ...) #1(2004), 2-8: 8-Chanukah & The Holocaust 3.00
...: The Sequel (2010) "11-9" , ...: The Sequel 2 (2011) Genesis #2 Jews in Space 3.00
...: The Sequel 3 (2012) Purim and the X-Suit 3.00
The Saga of Shaloman (20th Anniversary Edition) TPB (10/08, $15.99) r/V4 #1-8 16.00

SHAMAN'S TEARS (Also see Maggie the Cat)
Image Comics (Creative Fire Studio): 5/93 - No. 2, 8/93; No. 3, 11/94 - No. 0, 1/96 ($2.50/$1.95)
0-2: 0-(DEC-c, 1/96)-Last Issue. 1-(5/93)-Embossed red foil-c; Grell-c/a & scripts in all. 2-Cover unfolds into poster (8/93-c, 7/93 inside) 4.00
3-12: 3-Begin $1.95-c. 5-Re-intro Jon Sable. 12-Re-intro Maggie the Cat (1 pg.) 3.00

SHAME ITSELF
Marvel Comics: Jan, 2012 ($3.99, one-shot)
1-Spoof of "Fear Itself" x-over event; short stories by various incl. Cenac & Kupperman 4.00

SHANG-CHI: MASTER OF KUNG-FU ("Master of Kung Fu" on cover for #1&2)
Marvel Comics: Nov, 2002 - No. 6, Apr, 2003 ($2.99, limited series)
1-6-Moench-s/Gulacy-c/a 3.00
...One-Shot 1 (11/09, $3.99, B&W) Deadpool app. 4.00
...: Vol. 1: The Hellfire Apocalypse TPB (2003, $14.99) r/#1-6 15.00

SHANGRI-LA
Image Comics: Jan, 2004 ($7.95, B&W, square-bound graphic novel)
1-Marc Bryant-s/Shepherd Hendrix-a 8.00

SHANNA, THE SHE-DEVIL (See Savage Tales #8)
Marvel Comics Group: Dec, 1972 - No. 5, Aug, 1973 (All are 20¢ issues)
1-1st app. Shanna; Steranko-c; Tuska-a(p) 4 8 12 25 40 55
2-Steranko-c; heroin drug story 3 6 9 21 33 45
3-5 3 6 9 14 20 25

SHANNA, THE SHE-DEVIL
Marvel Comics: Apr, 2005 - No. 7, Oct, 2005 ($3.50, limited series)
1-7-Reintro of Shanna; Frank Cho-s/a/c in all 3.50
HC (2005, $24.99, dust jacket) r/#1-7 25.00
SC (2006, $16.99) r/#1-7 17.00

SHANNA, THE SHE-DEVIL: SURVIVAL OF THE FITTEST
Marvel Comics: Oct, 2007 - No. 4, Jan, 2008 ($2.99, limited series)
1-4-Khari Evans-a/c; Gray & Palmiotti-s 3.00
SC (2008, $10.99) r/#1-4 11.00

SHAOLIN COWBOY
Burlyman Entertainment: Dec, 2004 - No. 7, May, 2007 ($3.50)
1-7-Geof Darrow-s/a. 3-Moebius-c 3.50

SHAOLIN COWBOY
Dark Horse Comics: Oct, 2013 - No. 4, Feb, 2014 ($3.99)
1-4-Geof Darrow-s/a. 1-Variant-c by Simonson 4.00

Shatter #1 © FC

Shazam! #33 © DC

Sheena, Queen of the Jungle #18 © FH

GD 2.0 VG 4.0 FN 6.0 VF 8.0 VF/NM 9.0 NM- 9.2

SHARK FIGHTERS, THE (Movie)
Dell Publishing Co.: Jan, 1957
Four Color 762-Buscema-a; photo-c 7 14 21 44 82 120

SHARK-MAN
Thrill House/Image Comics: Jul, 2006; Jul, 2007; Jan, 2008 - No. 3, Jun, 2008 ($3.99/$3.50)
1,2: 1-(Thrill House, 7/06, $3.99)-Steve Pugh-s/a. 2-(Image Comics, 7/07) 4.00
1-3: 1-(Image, 1/08, $3.50) reprints Thrill House #1 3.50

SHARKY
Image Comics: Feb, 1998 - No. 4, 1998 ($2.50, bi-monthly)
1-4: 1-Mask app.; Elliot-s/a. Horley painted-c. 3-Three covers by Horley, Bisley, & Horley/Elliot. 4-Two covers (swipe of Avengers #4 and wraparound) 3.00
1-($2.95) "$1,000,000" variant 3.00
2-($2.50) Savage Dragon variant-c 3.00

SHARP COMICS (Slightly large size)
H. C. Blackerby: Winter, 1945-46 - V1#2, Spring, 1946 (52 pgs.)
V1#1-Origin Dick Royce Planetarian 43 86 129 271 461 650
2-Origin The Pioneer; Michael Morgan, Dick Royce, Sir Gallagher, Planetarian, Steve Hagen, Weeny and Pop app. 39 78 117 240 395 550

SHARPY FOX (See Comic Capers & Funny Frolics)
I. W. Enterprises/Super Comics: 1958; 1963
1,2-I.W. Reprint (1958): 2-r/Kiddie Kapers #1 2 4 6 8 11 14
14-Super Reprint (1963) 2 4 6 8 10 12

SHATTER (See Jon Sable #25-30)
First Comics: June, 1985; Dec, 1985 - No. 14, Apr, 1988. ($1.75, Baxter paper/deluxe paper)
1 (6/85)-1st computer generated-a in a comic book (1st printing) 4.00
1-(2nd print.); 1(12/85)-14: computer generated-a & lettering in all 3.00
Special 1 (1988) 3.00

SHATTERED IMAGE
Image Comics (WildStorm Productions): Aug, 1996 - No. 4, Dec, 1996 ($2.50, lim. series)
1-4: 1st Image company-wide x-over; Kurt Busiek scripts in all. 1-Tony Daniel-c/a(p). 2-Alex Ross-c/swipe (Kingdom Come) by Ryan Benjamin & Travis Charest 3.00

SHAUN OF THE DEAD (Movie)
IDW Publishing: June, 2005 - No. 4, Sept, 2005 ($3.99, limited series)
1-4-Adaptation of 2004 movie; Zach Howard-a 4.00
TPB (12/05, $17.99) r/series; sketch pages and cover gallery 18.00

SHAZAM (See Billy Batson and the Magic of Shazam!, Giant Comics to Color, Limited Collectors' Edition, Power Of Shazam! and Trials of Shazam!)

SHAZAM! (TV)(See World's Finest #253 for story from unpublished #36)
National Periodical Publ./DC Comics: Feb, 1973 - No. 35, May-June, 1978
1-1st revival of original Captain Marvel since G.A. (origin retold), by C.C. Beck; Mary Marvel & Captain Marvel Jr. app.; Superman-c 6 12 18 37 66 95
2-5: 2-Infinity photo-c.; re-intro Mr. Mind & Tawny. 3-Capt. Marvel-r. (10/46). 4-Origin retold; Capt. Marvel-r. (1949). 5-Capt. Marvel Jr. origin retold; Capt. Marvel-r. (1948, 7 pgs.) 3 6 9 17 26 35
6,7,9-11: 6-photo-c; Capt. Marvel-r (1950, 6 pgs.). 9-Mr. Mind app. 10-Last C.C. Beck issue. 11-Schaffenberger-a begins. 3 6 9 14 20 26
8 (100 pgs.) 8-r/Capt. Marvel Jr. by Raboy; origin/C.M. #80; origin Mary Marvel/C.M.A. #18; origin Mr. Tawny/C.M.A. #79 5 10 15 35 63 90
12-17-(All 100 pgs.). 15-vs. Lex Luthor & Mr. Mind 5 10 15 30 50 70
18-24,26-30: 21-24-All reprints. 26-Sivana app. (10/76). 27-Kid Eternity teams up w/Capt. Marvel. 28-1st S.A. app. of Black Adam. 30-1st DC app. 3 Lt. Marvels 2 4 6 11 16 20
25-1st app. Isis 3 6 9 14 19 24
31-35: 31-1st DC app. Minuteman. 34-Origin Capt. Nazi & Capt. Marvel Jr. retold 3 6 9 14 19 24
...: The Greatest Stories Ever Told TPB (2008, $24.99) reprints; Alex Ross-c 25.00
NOTE: *Reprints in #1-8, 10, 12-17, 21-24.* ***Beck*** *a-1-10, 12-17r, 21-24r; c-1, 3-9.* ***Nasser*** *c-35p.* ***Newton*** *a-35p.* ***Raboy*** *a-5r, 8r, 17r.* ***Schaffenberger*** *a-11, 14-20, 25, 26, 27p, 28, 29-31p, 33i, 35i; c-20, 22, 23, 25, 26i, 27i, 28-33.*

SHAZAM!
DC Comics: March, 2011 ($2.99, one-shot)
1-Richards-a/Chiang-c; Blaze app.; story continues in Titans #32 3.00

SHAZAM! AND THE SHAZAM FAMILY! ANNUAL
DC Comics: 2002 ($5.95, squarebound, one-shot)
1-Reprints Golden Age stories including 1st Mary Marvel and 1st Black Adam 6.00

SHAZAM!: POWER OF HOPE
DC Comics: Nov, 2000 ($9.95, treasury size, one-shot)
nn-Painted art by Alex Ross; story by Alex Ross and Paul Dini 10.00

SHAZAM!: THE MONSTER SOCIETY OF EVIL
DC Comics: 2007 - No. 4, 2007 ($5.99, square-bound, limited series)
1-4: Jeff Smith-s/a/c in all. 1-Retelling of origin. 2-Mary Marvel & Dr. Sivana app. 6.00
HC (2007, $29.99, over-sized with dust jacket that unfolds to a poster) r/#1-4; Alex Ross intro.; Smith afterword; sketch pages, script pages and production notes 30.00
SC (2009, $19.99) r/#1-4; Alex Ross intro. 20.00

SHAZAM: THE NEW BEGINNING
DC Comics: Apr, 1987 - No. 4, July, 1987 (Legends spin-off) (Limited series)
1-4: 1-New origin & 1st modern app. Captain Marvel; Marvel Family cameo. 2-4-Sivana & Black Adam app. 4.00

SHEA THEATRE COMICS
Shea Theatre: No date (1940's) (32 pgs.)
nn-Contains Rocket Comics; MLJ cover in one color 12 24 36 67 94 120

SHE-BAT (See Murcielaga, She-Bat & Valeria the She-Bat)

SHE-DRAGON (See Savage Dragon #117)
Image Comics: July, 2006 ($5.99, one-shot)
nn- She-Dragon in Dimension-X; origin retold; Franchesco-a/Larsen-s; sketch pages 6.00

SHEENA (Movie)
Marvel Comics: Dec, 1984 - No. 2, Feb, 1985 (limited series)
1,2-r/Marvel Comics Super Special #34; Tanya Roberts movie 4.00

SHEENA, QUEEN OF THE JUNGLE (See Jerry Iger's Classic..., Jumbo Comics, & 3-D Sheena)
Fiction House Magazines: Spr, 1942; No. 2, Wint, 1942-43; No. 3, Spr, 1943; No. 4, Fall, 1948; No. 5, Sum, 1949; No. 6, Spr, 1950; No. 7-10, 1950(nd); No. 11, Spr, 1951 - No. 18, Wint, 1952-53 (#1-3: 68 pgs.; #4-7: 52 pgs.)
1-Sheena begins 290 580 870 1856 3178 4500
2 (Winter, 1942-43) 139 278 417 890 1520 2150
3 (Spring, 1943) Classic Giant Ape-c 123 246 369 787 1344 1900
4,5 (Fall, 1948, Sum, 1949): 4-New logo; cover swipe from Jumbo #20 55 110 165 352 601 850
6,7 (Spring, 1950, 1950) 46 92 138 288 487 685
8-10(1950 - Win/50, 36 pgs.) 41 82 123 260 435 610
11-17: 15-Cover swipe from Jumbo #43 38 76 114 228 369 510
18-Used in **POP**, pg. 98 40 80 120 246 411 575
I.W. Reprint #9-r/#18; c-r/White Princess #3 4 8 12 28 44 60
NOTE: ***Baker*** *c-5-10?* ***Whitman*** *c-11-18(most).*

SHEENA, QUEEN OF THE JUNGLE
Devil's Due Publishing: Mar, 2007; Jun, 2007 - No. 5, Jan, 2008 (99¢/$3.50)
1-5: 1-Rodi-s/Merhoff-a; 5 covers 3.50
... 99¢ Special (3/07) Revival of the character; Rodi-s/Cummings-a; sketch pages; history 3.00
...: Dark Rising (10/08 - No. 3, 12/08) 1-3 3.50
... Trail of the Mapinguari (4/08, $5.50) Two covers 5.50

SHEENA 3-D SPECIAL (Also see Blackthorne 3-D Series #1)
Eclipse Comics: Jan, 1985 ($2.00)
1-Dave Stevens-c 1 3 4 6 8 10

SHE-HULK (Also see The Savage She-Hulk & The Sensational She-Hulk)
Marvel Comics: May, 2004 - No. 12, Apr, 2005 ($2.99)
1-4-Bobillo-a/Slott-s/Granov-c. 1-Avengers app. 4-Spider-Man-c/app. 3.00
5-12: Mayhew-c. 9-12-Pelletier-a. 10-Origin of Titania 3.00
Vol. 1: Single Green Female TPB (2004, $14.99) r/#1-6 15.00
Vol. 2: Superhuman Law TPB (2005, $14.99) r/#7-12 15.00

SHE-HULK (2nd series)
Marvel Comics: Dec, 2005 - No. 38, Apr, 2009 ($2.99)
1,2,4-7,9-24: 1-Bobillo-a/Slott-s/Horn-c. 1-New Avengers app. 2-Hawkeye-c/app. 9-Jen marries John Jameson. 12-Thanos app. 16-Wolverine app. 3.00
3-($3.99) 100th She-Hulk issue; new story w/art by various incl. Bobillo, Conner, Mayhew & Powell; r/Savage She-Hulk #1 and r/Sensational She-Hulk #1 4.00
8-Civil War 15.00
8-2nd printing with variant Bobillo-c 3.00
25-($3.99) Intro. the Behemoth; Juggernaut cameo; Handbook bio pages of She-Hulk 4.00
26-37: 27-Iron Man app. 30-Hercules app. 31-X-Factor app. 32,33-Secret Invasion 3.00
38-($3.99) Thundra, Valkyrie and Invisible Woman app. 4.00
...: Cosmic Collision 1 (2/09, $3.99) Lady Liberators app.; David-s/Asrar-a/Sejic-c 4.00
... Sensational 1 (5/10, $4.99) 30th Anniversary celebration; Stan Lee app.; Frank-c 5.00
Vol. 3: Time Trials (2006, $14.99) r/#1-5; Bobillo sketch page 15.00
Vol. 4: Laws of Attraction (2007, $19.99) r/#6-12; Paul Smith sketch page 20.00
Vol. 5: Planet Without a Hulk (2007, $19.99) r/#14-21; Slott's original series pitch 20.00
...: Jaded HC (2008, $19.99) r/#22-27; cover gallery 20.00

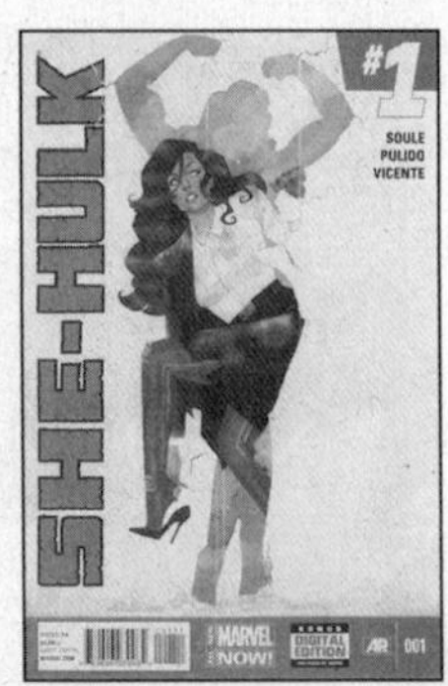

She-Hulk (3rd series) #1 © MAR

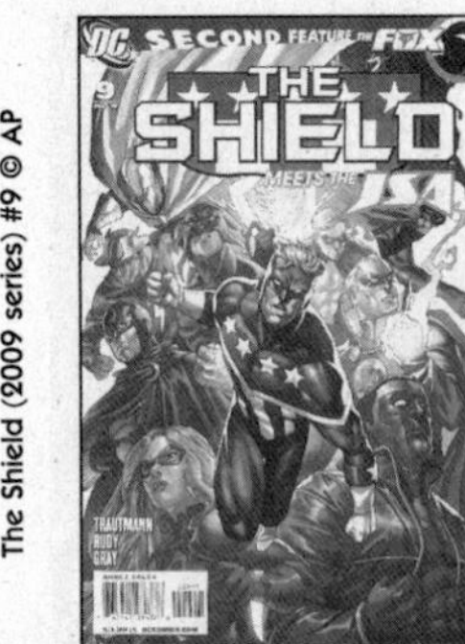

The Shield (2009 series) #9 © AP

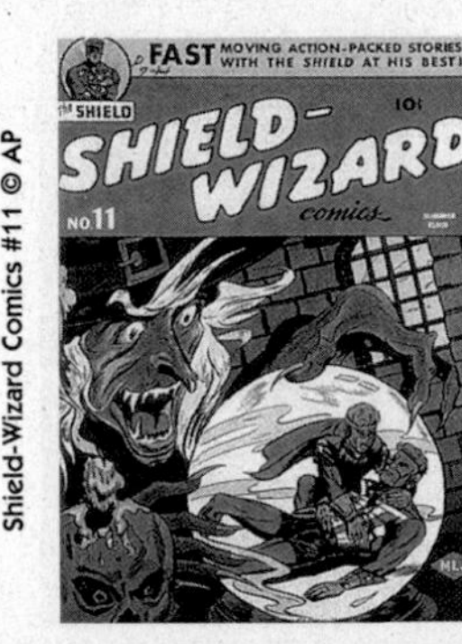

Shield-Wizard Comics #11 © AP

GD VG FN VF VF/NM NM-
2.0 4.0 6.0 8.0 9.0 9.2

SHE-HULK (3rd series)
Marvel Comics: Apr, 2014 - Present ($2.99)
1-3-Soule-s/Pulido-a/Wada-c. 1-Tony Stark app. 2-Hellcat app. 3.00

SHE-HULKS
Marvel Comics: Jan, 2011 - No. 4, Apr, 2011 ($3.99/$2.99, limited series)
1-($3.99) She-Hulk & Lyra team-up; Stegman-a/McGuinness-c; character profile pages 4.00
2-4-($2.99) McGuinness-c 3.00

SHELTERED
Image Comics: Jul, 2013 - Present ($2.99)
1-7-Brisson-s/Christmas-a 3.00

SHERIFF BOB DIXON'S CHUCK WAGON (TV) (See Wild Bill Hickok #22)
Avon Periodicals: Nov, 1950
1-Kinstler-c/a(3) 15 30 45 83 124 165

SHERIFF OF TOMBSTONE
Charlton Comics: Nov, 1958 - No. 17, Sept, 1961
V1#1-Giordano-c; Severin-a 6 12 18 41 66 90
2 4 8 12 22 34 45
3-10 3 6 9 17 25 32
11-17 3 6 9 14 20 25

SHERLOCK HOLMES (See Classic Comics #33, Marvel Preview, New Adventures of..., & Spectacular Stories)

SHERLOCK HOLMES (All New Baffling Adventures of...)(Young Eagle #3 on?)
Charlton Comics: Oct, 1955 - No. 2, Mar, 1956
1-Dr. Neff, Ghost Breaker app. 40 80 120 243 402 560
2 35 70 105 208 339 470

SHERLOCK HOLMES (Also see The Joker)
National Periodical Publications: Sept-Oct, 1975
1-Cruz-a; Simonson-c 3 6 9 16 23 30

SHERLOCK HOLMES
Dynamite Entertainment: 2009 - No. 5, 2009 ($3.50, limited series)
1-5-Cassaday-c/Moore & Reppion-s/Aaron Campbell-a 3.50

SHERLOCK HOLMES: MORIARTY LIVES
Dynamite Entertainment: 2014 - Present ($3.99, limited series)
1-3-Liss-s/Indro-a/Francavilla-c 4.00

SHERLOCK HOLMES: THE LIVERPOOL DEMON
Dynamite Entertainment: 2012 - No. 5, 2013 ($3.99, limited series)
1-5-Moore & Reppion-s/Triano-a/Francavilla-c 4.00

SHERLOCK HOLMES: YEAR ONE
Dynamite Entertainment: 2011 - No. 6, 2011 ($3.99, limited series)
1-6-Beatty-s; multiple covers on each 4.00

SHERRY THE SHOWGIRL (Showgirls #4)
Atlas Comics: July, 1956 - No. 3, Dec, 1956; No. 5, Apr, 1957 - No. 7, Aug, 1957
1-Dan DeCarlo-c/a in all 22 44 66 128 209 290
2 15 30 45 83 124 165
3,5-7 14 28 42 80 115 150

SHE'S JOSIE (See Josie)

SHEVA'S WAR
DC Comics (Helix): Oct, 1998 - No. 5, Feb, 1999 ($2.95, mini-series)
1-5-Christopher Moeller-s/painted-a/c 3.00

SHI (one-shots and TPBs)
Crusade Comics
...: Akai (2001, $2.99)-Intro. Victoria Cross; Tucci-a/c; J.C. Vaughn-s 3.00
...: Akai Victoria Cross Ed. ($5.95, edition of 2000) variant Tucci-c 6.00
...: C.G.I. (2001, $4.99) preview of unpublished series 5.00
.../ Cyblade: The Battle for the Independents (9/95, $2.95) Tucci-c; Hellboy, Bone app. 3.00
.../ Cyblade: The Battle for the Independents (9/95, $2.95) Silvestri variant-c . 3.00
.../ Daredevil: Honor Thy Mother (1/97, $2.95) Flip book 3.00
...: Judgment Night (200, $3.99) Wolverine app.; Battlebook card and pages; Tucci-a 4.00
...: Kaidan (10/96, $2.95) Two covers; Tucci-c; Jae Lee wraparound-c 3.00
...: Masquerade (3/98, $3.50) Painted art by Lago, Texeira, and others 3.50
...: Nightstalkers (9/97, $3.50) Painted art by Val Mayerik 3.50
...: Rekishi (1/97, $2.95) Character bios and story summaries of Shi: The Way of the Warrior told in Detective Joe Labianca's point of view; Christopher Golden script; Tucci-c; J.G. Jones-a; flip book w/Shi: East Wind Rain preview 3.00
...: The Art of War Tourbook (1998, $4.95) Blank cover for sketches; early Tucci-a inside 5.00
.../ Vampirella (10/97, $2.95) Ellis-s/Lau-a 3.00
... Vs. Tomoe (8/96, $3.95) Tucci-a/scripts; wraparound foil-c 4.00
... Vs. Tomoe (6/96, $5.00. B&W)-Preview Ed.; sold at San Diego Comic Con 5.00
The Definitive Shi Vol. 1 (2006-2007, $24.99, TPB) B&W r/Way of the Warrior, Tomoe, Rekishi, and Senryaku series; cover gallery with sketches; Tucci & Sparacio-c 25.00

SHI: BLACK, WHITE AND RED
Crusade Comics: Mar, 1998 - No. 2, May, 1998 ($2.95, B&W&Red, mini-series)
1,2-J.G. Jones-painted art 3.00
...- Year of the Dragon Collected Edition (2000, $5.95) r/#1&2 6.00

SHIDIMA
Image Comics: Jan, 2001 - No. 7, Nov, 2002 ($2.95, limited series)
1-7-Prequel to Warlands 3.00
#0-(10/01, $2.25) Short story and sketch pages 3.00

SHI: EAST WIND RAIN
Crusade Comics: Nov, 1997 - No. 2, Feb, 1998 ($3.50, limited series)
1,2-Shi at WW2 Pearl Harbor 3.50

S.H.I.E.L.D. (Nick Fury & His Agents of...) (Also see Nick Fury)
Marvel Comics Group: Feb, 1973 - No. 5, Oct, 1973 (All 20¢ issues)
1-All contain reprint stories from Strange Tales #146-155; new Steranko-c
3 6 9 16 23 30
2-New Steranko flag-c 2 4 6 11 16 20
3-5: 3-Kirby/Steranko-c(r). 4-Steranko-c(r) 2 4 6 9 12 15
NOTE: ***Buscema** a-3p(r). **Kirby** layouts 1-5; c-3 (w/**Steranko**). **Steranko** a-3r, 4r(2).*

S.H.I.E.L.D.
Marvel Comics: Jun, 2010 - No. 6, Apr, 2011; Aug, 2011 - No. 4, Feb, 2012 ($3.99/$2.99)
1-($3.99) Leonardo DaVinci app.; Weaver-a/Hickman-s/Parel-c; 4 printings 4.00
1-Variant-c by Weaver 6.00
1-Director's Cut (9/10, $4.99) r/#1 with character sketch-a and bios; design-a 5.00
2-6-($2.99) 2-Three printings. 3-Galactus app. 3.00
Infinity (6/11, $4.99) DaVinci, Nostradamus, Newton & Tesla app.; Parel-c 5.00
1 (2nd series) (8/11, $3.99) Weaver-a/Hickman-s/Parel-c; profile pgs of main characters 4.00
2-4-($2.99) 3.00
... Origins (1/14, $7.99) r/Battle Scars #6, Secret Avengers #1, Strange Tales #135 8.00

SHIELD, THE (Becomes Shield-Steel Sterling #3; #1 titled Lancelot Strong; also see Advs. of the Fly, Double Life of Private Strong, Fly Man, Mighty Comics, The Mighty Crusaders, The Original... & Pep Comics #1)
Archie Enterprises, Inc.: June, 1983 - No. 2, Aug, 1983
1,2: Steel Sterling app. 2-Kanigher-s 5.00
America's 1st Patriotic Comic Book Hero, The Shield (2002, $12.95, TPB) r/Pep Comics #1-5, Shield-Wizard Comics #1; foreward by Robert M. Overstreet 13.00

SHIELD, THE (Archie Ent. character) (Continued from The Red Circle)
DC Comics: Nov, 2009 - No. 10, Aug, 2010 ($3.99)
1-10: 1-Magog app.; Inferno back-up feature thru #6; Green Arrow app. 2,3-Grodd app. 7-10-The Fox back-up feature; Oeming-a 4.00
...: Kicking Down the Door TPB ('10, $19.99) r/#1-6, Red Circle: The Web & RC: The Shield 20.00

SHIELD, THE: SPOTLIGHT (TV)
IDW Publishing: Jan, 2004 - No. 5, May, 2004 ($3.99)
1-5-Jeff Marriote-s/Jean Diaz-a/Tommy Lee Edwards-c 4.00
TPB (7/04, $19.99) r/#1-5; Michael Chiklis photo-c 20.00

SHIELD-STEEL STERLING (Formerly The Shield)
Archie Enterprises, Inc.: No. 3, Dec, 1983 (Becomes Steel Sterling No. 4)
3-Nino-a; Steel Sterling by Kanigher & Barreto 5.00

SHIELD WIZARD COMICS (Also see Pep Comics & Top-Notch Comics)
MLJ Magazines: Summer, 1940 - No. 13, Spring, 1944
1-(V1#5 on inside)-Origin The Shield by Irving Novick & The Wizard by Ed Ashe, Jr; Flag-c
514 1028 1542 3750 6625 9500
2-(Winter/40)-Origin The Shield retold; Wizard's sidekick, Roy the Super Boy begins (see Top-Notch #8 for 1st app.) 274 548 822 1754 3002 4250
3,4 181 362 543 1158 1979 2800
5-Dusty, the Boy Detective begins; Nazi bondage-c 161 322 483 1030 1765 2500
6,7: 6-Roy the Super Boy app. 7-Shield dons new costume (Summer, 1942); S & K-c?
155 310 465 992 1696 2400
8-Nazi bondage-c; Hitler photo on-c 194 388 582 1242 2121 3000
9-Japanese WWII bondage-c 135 270 405 864 1482 2100
10-Nazi swastica-c 142 284 426 909 1555 2200
11,12 113 226 339 723 1237 1750
13-Japanese WWII bondage/torture-c (scarce) 148 296 444 947 1624 2300
NOTE: ***Bob Montana** c-13. **Novick** c-1,3-6,8-11. **Harry Sahle** c-12.*

Shi: The Way of the Warrior #2 © Billy Tucci

Ship of Fools #2 © Michael Oeming

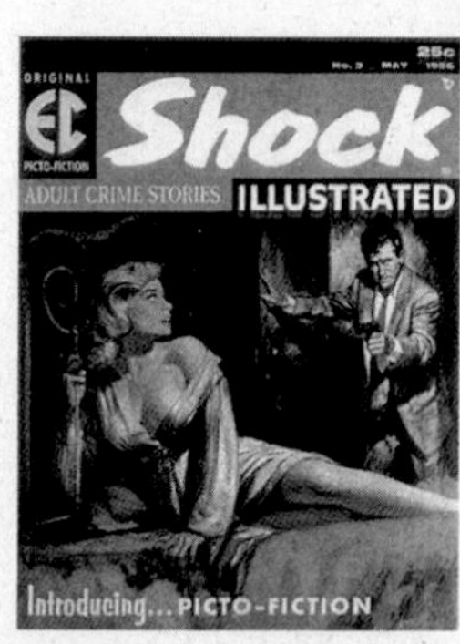

Shock Illustrated #3 © WMG

	GD 2.0	VG 4.0	FN 6.0	VF 8.0	VF/NM 9.0	NM- 9.2

SHI: FAN EDITIONS
Crusade Comics: 1997

1-3-Two covers polybagged in FAN #19-21 3.00
1-3-Gold editions 4.00

SHI: HEAVEN AND EARTH
Crusade Comics: June, 1997 - No. 4, Apr, 1998 ($2.95)

1-4 3.00
4-($4.95) Pencil-c variant 5.00
Rising Sun Edition-signed by Tucci in FanClub Starter Pack 4.00
"Tora No Shi" variant-c 3.00

SHI: JU-NEN
Dark Horse Comics: July, 2004 - No. 4, May, 2005 ($2.99, mini-series)

1-4-Tucci-a/Tucci & Vaughn-s; origin retold 3.00
TPB (2/06, $12.95) r/#1-4; Tucci and Sparacio-c 13.00

SHINING KNIGHT (See Adventure Comics #66)

SHINKU
Image Comics: Jun, 2011 - No. 5, Oct, 2012 ($2.99)

1-5-Marz-s/Moder-a 3.00

SHINOBI (Based on Sega video game)
Dark Horse Comics: Aug, 2002 ($2.99, one-shot)

1-Medina-a/c 3.00

SHIP AHOY
Spotlight Publishers: Nov, 1944 (52 pgs.)

1-L. B. Cole-c 20 40 60 114 182 250

SHIP OF FOOLS
Image Comics: Aug, 1997 - No. 3 ($2.95, B&W)

0-3-Glass-s/Oeming-a 3.00

SHI: POISONED PARADISE
Avatar Press: July, 2002 - No. 2, Aug, 2002 ($3.50, limited series)

1,2-Vaughn and Tucci-s/Waller-a; 1-Four covers 3.50

SHIPWRECKED! (Disney-Movie)
Disney Comics: 1990 ($5.95, graphic novel, 68 pgs.)

nn-adaptation; Spiegle-a 6.00

SHI: SEMPO
Avatar Press: Aug, 2003 - No. 2, ($3.50, B&W, limited series)

1,2-Vaughn and Tucci-s/Alves-a; 1-Four covers 3.50

SHI: SENRYAKU
Crusade Comics: Aug, 1995 - No. 3, Nov, 1995 ($2.95, limited series)

1-3: 1-Tucci-c; Quesada, Darrow, Sim, Lee, Smith-a. 2-Tucci-c; Silvestri, Balent, Perez, Mack-a. 3-Jusko-c; Hughes, Ramos, Bell, Moore-a 3.00
1-variant-c (no logo) 4.00
Hardcover ($24.95)-r/#1-3; Frazetta-c. 25.00
Trade Paperback ($13.95)-r/#1-3; Frazetta-c. 14.00

SHI: THE ILLUSTRATED WARRIOR
Crusade Comics: 2002 - No. 7, 2003 ($2.99, B&W)

1-7-Story text with Tucci full page art 3.00

SHI: THE SERIES
Crusade Comics: Aug, 1997 - No. 13 ($2.95, color #1-10, B&W #11)

1-10 3.00
11-13: 11-B&W. 12-Color; Lau-a 3.00
#0 Convention Edition 5.00

SHI: THE WAY OF THE WARRIOR
Crusade Comics: Mar, 1994 - No. 12, Apr, 1997 ($2.50/$2.95)

1/2 4.00
1 2 4 6 8 10 12
1-Commemorative ed., B&W, new-c; given out at 1994 San Diego Comic Con 2 4 6 10 14 18
1-Fan appreciation edition -r/#1 3.00
1-Fan appreciation edition (variant) 6.00
1- 10th Anniversary Edition (2004, $2.99) 3.00
2 5.00
2-Commemorative edition (3,000) 2 4 6 9 13 16
2-Fan appreciation edition -r/#2 3.00
3 4.00
4-7: 4-Silvestri poster. 7-Tomoe app. 3.00
5,6: 5-Silvestri variant-c. 6-Tomoe #1 variant-c 3.50
5-Gold edition 12.00
6,8-12: 6-Fan appreciation edition 3.00
8-Combo Gold edition 6.00
8-Signed Edition-(5000) 4.00
Trade paperback (1995, $12.95)-r/#1-4 15.00
Trade paperback (1995, $14.95)-r/#1-4 revised; Julie Bell-c 15.00

SHI: YEAR OF THE DRAGON
Crusade Comics: 2000 - No. 3, 2000 ($2.99, limited series)

1-3: 1-Two covers; Tucci-a/c; flashback to teen-aged Ana 3.00

SHMOO (See Al Capp's... & Washable Jones &...)

SHOCK (Magazine)
Stanley Publ.: May, 1969 - V3#4, Sept, 1971 (B&W reprints from horror comics, including some pre-code) (No V2#1,3)

V1#1-Cover-r/Weird Tales of the Future #7 by Bernard Baily; r/Weird Chills #1 7 14 21 48 89 130
2-Wolverton-r/Weird Mysteries 5; r-Weird Mysteries #7 used in **SOTI**; cover reprints cover to Weird Chills #1 5 10 15 35 63 90
3,5,6 4 8 12 28 47 65
4-Harrison/Williamson-r/Forbid. Worlds #6 5 10 15 30 50 70
V2#2(5/70), V1#8(7/70), V2#4(9/70)-6(1/71), V3#1-4: V2#4-Cover swipe from Weird Mysteries #6 4 8 12 27 44 60

NOTE: ***Disbrow** r-V2#4; **Bondage** c-V1#4, V2#6, V3#1.*

SHOCK DETECTIVE CASES (Formerly Crime Fighting Detective)
(Becomes Spook Detective Cases No. 22)
Star Publications: No. 20, Sept, 1952 - No. 21, Nov, 1952

20,21-L.B. Cole-c; based on true crime cases 24 48 72 142 234 325

NOTE: ***Palais** a-20. No. 21-Fox-r.*

SHOCK ILLUSTRATED (...Adult Crime Stories; Magazine format)
E. C. Comics: Sept-Oct, 1955 - No. 3, Spring, 1956 (Adult Entertainment on-c #1,2)(All 25¢)

1-All by Kamen; drugs, prostitution, wife swapping 20 40 60 117 189 260
2-Williamson-a redrawn from Crime SuspenStories #13 plus Ingels, Crandall, Evans & part Torres-i; painted-c 20 40 60 117 189 260
3-Only 100 known copies bound & given away at E.C. office; Crandall, Evans-a; painted-c; shows May, 1956 on-c 135 270 405 864 1482 2100

SHOCKING MYSTERY CASES (Formerly Thrilling Crime Cases)
Star Publications: No. 50, Sept, 1952 - No. 60, Oct, 1954 (All crime reprints?)

50-Disbrow "Frankenstein" story 48 96 144 302 514 725
51-Disbrow-a 32 64 96 188 307 425
52-60: 56-Drug use story 30 60 90 177 289 400

NOTE: ***L. B. Cole** covers on all; a-60(2 pgs.). **Hollingsworth** a-52. **Morisi** a-55.*

SHOCKING TALES DIGEST MAGAZINE
Harvey Publications: Oct, 1981 (95¢)

1-1957-58-r; Powell, Kirby, Nostrand-a 2 4 6 9 13 16

SHOCK ROCKETS
Image Comics (Gorilla): Apr, 2000 - No. 6, Oct, 2000 ($2.50)

1-6-Busiek-s/Immonen & Grawbadger-a. 6-Flip book w/Superstar preview 3.00
...: We Have Ignition TPB (Dark Horse, 8/04, $14.95, 6" x 9") r/#1-6 15.00

SHOCK SUSPENSTORIES (Also see EC Archives • Shock SuspenStories)
E. C. Comics: Feb-Mar, 1952 - No. 18, Dec-Jan, 1954-55

1-Classic Feldstein electrocution-c 103 206 309 824 1312 1800
2 50 100 150 400 638 875
3,4: 3-Classic decapitation splash. 4-Used in **SOTI**, pg. 387,388 40 80 120 320 510 700
5-Hanging-c 51 102 153 408 654 900
6-Classic hooded vigilante bondage-c 71 142 213 568 909 1250
7-Classic face melting-c 60 120 180 480 765 1050
8-Williamson-a 40 80 120 320 510 700
9-11: 9-Injury to eye panel. 10-Junkie story 33 66 99 264 420 575
12- "The Monkey" classic junkie cover/story; anti-drug propaganda issue 44 88 132 352 564 775
13-Frazetta's only solo story for E.C., 7 pgs, draws himself as main male character 47 94 141 376 601 825
14-Used in Senate Investigation hearings 29 58 87 232 482 500
15-Used in 1954 Reader's Digest article, "For the Kiddies to Read" 26 52 78 208 329 450
16-18: 16- "Red Dupe" editorial; rape story 24 48 72 192 309 425

NOTE: ***Ray Bradbury** adaptations-1, 7, 9. **Craig** a-11; c-11. **Crandall** a-9-13, 15-18. **Davis** a-1-5. **Evans** a-7, 8, 14-18; c-16-18. **Feldstein** c-1, 7-9, 12. **Ingels** a-1, 2, 6. **Kamen** a-in all; c-10, 13, 15. **Krigstein** a-14, 18. **Orlando** a-1, 3-7, 9, 10, 12, 16, 17. **Wood** a-2-15; c-2-6, 14.*

Shorty Shiner #1 © C. Biro

Showcase #29 © DC

Showcase #73 © DC

	GD 2.0	VG 4.0	FN 6.0	VF 8.0	VF/NM 9.0	NM- 9.2
SHOCK SUSPENSTORIES (Also see EC Archives • Shock SuspenStories)						
Russ Cochran/Gemstone Publishing: Sept, 1992 - No. 18, Dec, 1996 ($1.50/$2.00/$2.50, quarterly)						
1-18: 1-3: Reprints with original-c. 17-r/HOF #17						4.00
SHOGUN WARRIORS						
Marvel Comics Group: Feb, 1979 - No. 20, Sept, 1980 (Based on Mattel toys of the classic Japanese animation characters) (1-3: 35¢; 4-19: 40¢; 20: 50¢)						
1-Raydeen, Combatra, & Dangard Ace begin; Trimpe-a	2	4	6	10	14	18
2-20: 2-Lord Maurkon & Elementals of Evil app.; Rok-Korr app. 6-Shogun vs. Shogun. 7,8-Cerberus. 9-Starchild. 11-Austin-c. 12-Simonson-c. 14-16-Doctor Demonicus. 17-Juggernaut. 19,20-FF x-over	2	3	4	6	8	10
SHOOK UP (Magazine) (Satire)						
Dodsworth Publ. Co.: Nov, 1958						
V1#1	4	8	12	28	44	60
SHORT RIBS						
Dell Publishing Co.: No. 1333, Apr - June, 1962						
Four Color 1333	5	10	15	33	57	80
SHORTSTOP SQUAD (Baseball)						
Ultimate Sports Ent. Inc.: 1999 ($3.95, one-shot)						
1-Ripken Jr., Larkin, Jeter, Rodriguez app.; Edwards-c/a						4.00
SHORT STORY COMICS (See Hello Pal,...)						
SHORTY SHINER (The Five-Foot Fighter in the Ten Gallon Hat)						
Dandy Magazine (Charles Biro): June, 1956 - No. 3, Oct, 1956						
1	7	14	21	37	46	55
2,3	5	10	15	24	30	35
SHOTGUN SLADE (TV)						
Dell Publishing Co.: No. 1111, July-Sept, 1960						
Four Color 1111-Photo-c	6	12	18	37	66	95
SHOWCASE (See Cancelled Comic Cavalcade & New Talent...)						
National Per. Publ./DC Comics: 3-4/56 - No. 93, 9/70; No. 94, 8-9/77 - No. 104, 9/78						
1-Fire Fighters; w/Fireman Farrell	283	566	849	2335	5268	8200
2-Kings of the Wild; Kubert-a (animal stories)	100	200	300	800	1800	2800
3-The Frogmen by Russ Heath; Heath greytone-c (early DC example, 7-8/56)	100	200	300	800	1800	2800
4-Origin/1st app. The Flash (1st DC Silver Age hero, Sept-Oct, 1956); Kanigher-s; Infantino & Kubert-c/a; 1st app. Iris West and The Turtle; r/in Secret Origins #1 ('61 & '73); Flash shown reading G.A. Flash Comics #13; back-up story w/Broome-s/Infantino & Kubert-a	2000	4000	6000	23,000	46,500	70,000
5-Manhunters; Meskin-a	89	178	267	712	1606	2500
6-Origin/1st app. Challengers of the Unknown by Kirby, partly r/in Secret Origins #1 & Challengers #64,65 (1st S.A. hero team & 1st original concept S.A. series)(1-2/57)	303	606	909	2500	5650	8800
7-Challengers of the Unknown by Kirby (2nd app.) reprinted in Challengers of the Unknown #75	145	290	435	1196	2698	4200
8-The Flash (5-6/57, 2nd app.); origin & 1st app. Captain Cold	840	1680	2520	7600	13,300	19,000
9-Lois Lane (Pre-#1, 7-8/57) (1st Showcase character to win own series) Superman app. on-c	660	1320	1980	5280	9640	14,000
10-Lois Lane; Jor-El cameo; Superman app. on-c	220	440	660	1815	4108	6400
11-Challengers of the Unknown by Kirby (3rd)	139	278	417	1112	2506	3900
12-Challengers of the Unknown by Kirby (4th)	139	278	417	1112	2506	3900
13-The Flash (3rd app.); origin Mr. Element	317	634	951	2615	5908	9200
14-The Flash (4th app.); origin Dr. Alchemy, former Mr. Element (rare in NM)	338	676	1014	2805	6303	9800
15-Space Ranger (7-8/58, 1st app., also see My Greatest Aventure #22)	155	310	465	1279	2890	4500
16-Space Ranger (9-10/58, 2nd app.)	79	158	237	632	1416	2200
17-(11-12/58)-Adventures on Other Worlds; origin/1st app. Adam Strange by Gardner Fox & Mike Sekowsky	221	442	663	1823	4112	6400
18-Adventures on Other Worlds (2nd A. Strange)	89	178	267	712	1606	2500
19-Adam Strange; 1st Adam Strange logo	100	200	300	800	1800	2800
20-Rip Hunter; origin & 1st app. (5-6/59); Moreira-a	89	178	267	712	1606	2500
21-Rip Hunter (7-8/59, 2nd app.); Sekowsky-c/a	46	92	138	359	805	1250
22-Origin & 1st app. Silver Age Green Lantern by Gil Kane and John Broome (9-10/59); reprinted in Secret Origins #2	750	1500	3000	9000	20,500	32,000
23-Green Lantern (11-12/59, 2nd app.); nuclear explosion-c	190	380	570	1568	3534	5500
24-Green Lantern (1-2/60, 3rd app.)	159	318	477	1312	2956	4600
25,26-Rip Hunter by Kubert. 25-Grey tone-c	38	76	114	285	641	1000
27-Sea Devils (7-8/60, 1st app.); Heath-c/a; Grey tone-c	77	154	231	616	1383	2150
28-Sea Devils (9-10/60, 2nd app.); Heath-c/a; Grey tone-c	38	78	117	282	634	985
29-Sea Devils; Heath-c/a; grey tone c-27-29	41	82	123	303	682	1060
30-Origin Silver Age Aquaman (1-2/61) (see Adventure #260 for 1st S.A. origin)	75	150	225	600	1350	2100
31-33-Aquaman	38	76	114	285	641	1000
34-Origin & 1st app. Silver Age Atom by Gil Kane & Murphy Anderson (9-10/61); reprinted in Secret Origins #2	111	222	333	888	1994	3100
35-The Atom by Gil Kane (2nd); last 10¢ issue	50	100	150	400	900	1400
36-The Atom by Gil Kane (1-2/62, 3rd app.)	40	80	120	296	673	1050
37-Metal Men (3-4/62, 1st app.)	57	114	171	456	1028	1600
38-Metal Men (5-6/62, 2nd app.)	30	60	90	219	490	760
39-Metal Men (7-8/62, 3rd app.)	23	46	69	164	362	560
40-Metal Men (9-10/62, 4th app.)	21	42	63	147	324	500
41,42-Tommy Tomorrow (parts 1 & 2). 42-Origin	13	26	39	91	201	310
43-Dr. No (James Bond); Nodel-a; originally published as British Classics Illustrated #158A & as #6 in a European Detective series, all with diff. painted-c. This Showcase #43 version is actually censored, deleting all racial skin color and dialogue thought to be racially demeaning (1st DC S.A. movie adaptation)(based on Ian Fleming novel & movie)	46	92	138	340	770	1200
44-Tommy Tomorrow	10	20	30	66	138	210
45-Sgt. Rock (7-8/63); pre-dates B&B #52; origin retold; Heath-c	33	66	99	238	532	825
46,47-Tommy Tomorrow	9	18	27	61	123	185
48,49-Cave Carson (3rd tryout series; see B&B)	8	16	24	54	102	150
50,51-I Spy (Danger Trail-r by Infantino), King Farady story (#50 has new 4 pg. story)	7	14	21	48	89	130
52-Cave Carson	7	14	21	49	92	135
53,54-G.I. Joe (11-12/64, 1-2/65); Heath-a	10	20	30	66	138	210
55-Dr. Fate & Hourman (3-4/65); origin of each in text; 1st solo app. G.A. Green Lantern in Silver Age (pre-dates Gr. Lantern #40); 1st S.A. app. Solomon Grundy	22	44	66	154	340	525
56-Dr. Fate & Hourman	12	24	36	84	185	285
57-Enemy Ace by Kubert (7-8/65, 4th app. after Our Army at War #155)	19	38	57	131	291	450
58-Enemy Ace by Kubert (5th app.)	16	32	48	107	236	365
59-Teen Titans (11-12/65, 3rd app.)	15	30	45	100	220	340
60-1st S. A. app. The Spectre; Anderson-a (1-2/66); origin in text	24	48	72	168	372	575
61-The Spectre by Anderson (2nd app.)	12	24	36	82	179	275
62-Origin & 1st app. Inferior Five (5-6/66)	8	16	24	56	108	160
63,65-Inferior Five. 63-Hulk parody. 65-X-Men parody (11-12/66)	6	12	18	37	66	95
64-The Spectre by Anderson (5th app.)	12	24	36	80	173	265
66,67-B'wana Beast	5	10	15	35	63	90
68-Maniaks (1st app., spoof of The Monkees)	5	10	15	35	63	90
69,71-Maniaks. 71-Woody Allen-c/app.	5	10	15	34	60	85
70-Binky (9-10/67)-Tryout issue; 1950's Leave It To Binky reprints with art changes	6	12	18	37	66	95
72-Top Gun (Johnny Thunder-r)-Toth-a	5	10	15	31	53	75
73-Origin/1st app. Creeper; Ditko-c/a (3-4/68)	10	20	30	69	147	225
74-Intro/1st app. Anthro; Post-c/a (5/68)	7	14	21	49	92	135
75-Origin/1st app. Hawk & the Dove; Ditko-c/a	10	20	30	64	132	200
76-1st app. Bat Lash (8/68)	7	14	21	49	92	135
77-1st app. Angel & The Ape (9/68)	6	12	18	41	76	110
78-1st app. Jonny Double (11/68)	5	10	15	30	50	70
79-1st app. Dolphin (12/68); Aqualad origin-r	6	12	18	37	66	95
80-1st S.A. app. Phantom Stranger (1/69); Neal Adams-c	10	20	30	64	132	200
81-Windy & Willy; r/Many Loves of Dobie Gillis #26 with art changes	5	10	15	34	60	85
82-1st app. Nightmaster (5/69) by Grandenetti & Giordano; Kubert-c	6	12	18	41	76	110
83,84-Nightmaster by Wrightson w/Jones/Kaluta ink assist in each; Kubert-c. 83-Last 12¢ issue 84-Origin retold; begin 15¢	6	12	18	41	76	110
85-87-Firehair; Kubert-a	3	6	9	16	23	30
88-90-Jason's Quest: 90-Manhunter 2070 app.	3	6	9	14	20	25
91-93-Manhunter 2070: 92-Origin. 93-(9/70) Last 15¢ issue	3	6	9	14	20	25
94-Intro/origin new Doom Patrol & Robotman(8-9/77)	2	4	6	11	16	20
95,96-The Doom Patrol. 95-Origin Celsius	2	3	4	6	8	10

Showcase '94 #2 © DC

Showcase '96 #12 © DC

Showcase Presents LSH V1 © DC

	GD 2.0	VG 4.0	FN 6.0	VF 8.0	VF/NM 9.0	NM- 9.2
97-99-Power Girl; origin-97,98; JSA cameos	2	4	6	8	10	12
100-(52 pgs.)-Most Showcase characters featured	2	4	6	11	16	20
101-103-Hawkman; Adam Strange x-over	2	3	4	6	8	10
104-(52 pgs.)-O.S.S. Spies at War	2	3	4	6	8	10

NOTE: ***Anderson*** *a-22-24i, 34-36i, 55, 56, 60, 61, 64, 101-103i; c-50i, 51i, 55, 56, 60, 61, 64.* ***Aparo*** *c-94-96.* ***Boring*** *c-10.* ***Estrada*** *a-104.* ***Fraden*** *c(p)-30, 31, 33.* ***Heath*** *c-3, 27-29.* ***Infantino*** *c/a(p)-4, 8, 13, 14; c-50p, 51p.* ***Gil Kane*** *a-22-24p, 34-36p; c-17-19, 22-24p(w/**Giella**), 31.* ***Kane/Anderson*** *c-34-36.* ***Kirby*** *c-11, 12.* ***Kirby/Stein*** *c-6, 7.* ***Kubert*** *a-2, 4i, 25, 26, 45, 53, 54, 72; c-25, 26, 53, 54, 57, 58, 82-87, 101-104; c-2, 4i.* ***Moreira*** *c-5.* ***Orlando*** *a-62p, 63p, 97i; c-62, 63, 97i.* ***Sekowsky*** *a-65p.* ***Sparling*** *a-78.* ***Staton*** *a-94, 95-99p, 100; c-97-100p.*

SHOWCASE '93
DC Comics: Jan, 1993 - No. 12, Dec, 1993 ($1.95, limited series, 52 pgs.)

1-12: 1-Begin 4 part Catwoman story & 6 part Blue Devil story; begin Cyborg story; Art Adams/Austin-c. 3-Flash by Charest (p). 6-Azrael in Bat-costume (2 pgs.). 7,8-Knightfall parts 13 & 14. 6-10-Deathstroke app. (6,10-cameo). 9,10-Austin-i. 10-Azrael as Batman in new costume app.; Gulacy-c. 11-Perez-c. 12-Creeper app.; Alan Grant scripts 4.00

NOTE: ***Chaykin*** *c-9.* ***Fabry*** *c-8.* ***Giffen*** *a-12.* ***Golden*** *c-3.* ***Zeck*** *c-6.*

SHOWCASE '94
DC Comics: Jan, 1994 - No. 12, Dec, 1994 ($1.95, limited series, 52 pgs.)

1-12: 1,2-Joker & Gunfire stories. 1-New Gods. 4-Riddler story. 5-Huntress-c/story w/app. new Batman. 6-Huntress-c/story w/app. Robin; Atom story. 7-Penguin story by Peter David, P. Craig Russell, & Michael T. Gilbert; Penguin-c by Jae Lee. 8,9-Scarface origin story by Alan Grant, John Wagner,& Teddy Kristiansen; Prelude to Zero Hour. 10-Zero Hour tie-in story. 11-Man-Bat. 4.00

NOTE: ***Alan Grant*** *scripts-3, 4.* ***Kelley Jones*** *c-12.* ***Mignola*** *c-3.* ***Nebres*** *a(i)-2.* ***Quesada*** *c-10.* ***Russell*** *a-7p.* ***Simonson*** *c-5.*

SHOWCASE '95
DC Comics: Jan, 1995 - No. 12, Dec, 1995 ($2.50/$2.95, limited series)

1-4-Supergirl story. 3-Eradicator-c.; The Question story. 4-Thorn c/story 4.00
5-12: 5-Thorn-c/story; begin $2.95-c. 8-Spectre story. 12-The Shade story by James Robinson & Wade Von Grawbadger; Maitresse story by Claremont & Alan Davis 4.00

SHOWCASE '96
DC Comics: Jan, 1996 - No. 12, Dec, 1996 ($2.95, limited series)

1-12: 1-Steve Geppi cameo. 3-Black Canary & Lois Lane-c/story; Deadman story by Jamie Delano & Wade Von Grawbadger, Gary Frank-c. 4-Firebrand & Guardian-c/story; The Shade & Dr. Fate "Times Past" story by James Robinson & Matt Smith begins, ends #5. 6-Superboy-c/app.; Atom app.; Capt. Marvel (Mary Marvel)-c/app. 8-Supergirl by David & Dodson. 11-Scare Tactics app. 11,12-Legion of Super-Heroes vs. Brainiac. 12-Jesse Quick app. 4.00

SHOWCASE PRESENTS... (B&W archive reprints of DC Silver Age stories)
DC Comics: 2005 - Present ($9.99/$16.99/$17.99/$19.99, B&W, over 500 pgs., squarebound)

Adam Strange Vol. 1 (2007, $16.99) r/Showcase #17-19 & Mystery in Space #53-84 17.00
Ambush Bug (2009, $16.99) r/first app. in DC Comics Presents #52 other early app. 17.00
Aquaman Vol. 1 (2007, $16.99) r/Aquaman #1-6 & other early app. 17.00
Aquaman Vol. 2 (2008, $16.99) r/Aquaman #7-23 & other early app. 17.00
Aquaman Vol. 3 (2009, $16.99) r/Aquaman #24-39 & other early app. 17.00
The Atom Vol. 1 (2007, $16.99) r/Showcase #34-36 & The Atom #1-17 17.00
The Atom Vol. 2 (2008, $16.99) r/The Atom #18-38 17.00
Batgirl Vol. 1 (2007, $16.99) r/early apps. from Detective #359 (1967) thru 1975 17.00
Bat Lash Vol. 1 (2009, $9.99) r/#1-7, Showcase #76, DC Special Series #16, and Jonah Hex #49,51,52 10.00
Batman Vol. 1 (2006, $16.99) r/"new look" from Detective #327-342, Batman #164-174 17.00
Batman Vol. 2 (2007, $16.99) r/"new look" from Detective #343-358, Batman #175-188 17.00
Batman Vol. 3 (2008, $16.99) r/"new look" from Detective #359-375, Batman #189, 190-192,194-197,199-202 17.00
Batman and the Outsiders Vol. 1 (2007, $16.99) r/#1-19, Annual #1; Brave and the Bold #200; and New Teen Titans #37 17.00
Blackhawk Vol. 1 (2008, $16.99) r/#108-127 17.00
Booster Gold Vol. 1 (2008, $16.99) r/#1-25 & Action Comics #594 17.00
The Brave and the Bold Batman Team-ups Vol. 1 (2007, $16.99) r/#59,64,67-71,74-87 17.00
The Brave and the Bold Batman Team-ups Vol. 2 (2007, $16.99) r/#88-108 17.00
The Brave and the Bold Batman Team-ups Vol. 3 (2008, $16.99) r/#109-134 17.00
Challengers of the Unknown Vol. 1 (2006, $16.99) r/#1-17 & Showcase #6,7,11,12 17.00
Challengers of the Unknown Vol. 2 (2008, $16.99) r/#18-37 17.00
DC Comics Presents: The Superman Team-ups Vol. 1 (2009, $17.99) r/#1-26 18.00
Dial H For Hero ('10, $9.99) r/early apps. in House of Mystery #156-173 10.00
Doc Savage ('11, $19.99) r/Doc Savage #1-8 (1975-77 Marvel B&W magazine) 20.00
The Doom Patrol Vol. 1 (2009, $16.99) r/#86-101 and My Greatest Adventure #80-85 17.00
The Doom Patrol Vol. 2 (2010, $19.99) r/#102-121 20.00
The Elongated Man Vol. 1 ('06, $16.99) r/early apps. in Flash & Detective ('60-'68) 17.00
Eclipso Vol. 1 (2009, $9.99) r/stories from House of Secrets #61-80 10.00
Enemy Ace Vol. 1 (2008, $16.99) r/Our Army at War #151 & other early app. 17.00
The Flash Vol. 1 (2007, $16.99) r/Flash Comics #104 (last G.A. issue), Showcase #4,8,13,14 & The Flash #105-119 17.00
The Flash Vol. 2 (2008, $16.99) r/The Flash #120-140 17.00
The Flash Vol. 3 (2009, $16.99) r/The Flash #141-161 17.00
The Flash, The Trial of ... (2011, $19.99) r/The Flash #323-327,329-336,340-350 20.00
The Great Disaster Featuring The Atomic Knights and Hercules Vol. 1 (2007, $16.99) 17.00
Green Arrow Vol. 1 (2006, $16.99) r/Adventure #250-269, Brave and the Bold #50,71,85; Justice League of America #4; World's Finest #95-134,136,138,140 17.00
Green Lantern Vol. 1 (2005, $9.99) r/Showcase #22-24 & Green Lantern #1-17 20.00
Green Lantern Vol. 1 (2010, $19.99) r/Showcase #22-24 & Green Lantern #1-17 20.00
Green Lantern Vol. 2 (2007, $16.99) r/Green Lantern #18-38 17.00
Green Lantern Vol. 3 (2008, $16.99) r/Green Lantern #39-59 17.00
Green Lantern Vol. 4 (2009, $16.99) r/Green Lantern #60-75 17.00
Green Lantern Vol. 5 (2011, $19.99) r/Green Lantern #76-87,89 and back up stories from Flash #217-246 20.00
Haunted Tank Vol. 1 ('06, $16.99) r/G.I. Combat #87-119, Brave & The Bold #52 and Our Army at War #155; Russ Heath-c 17.00
Haunted Tank Vol. 2 ('08, $16.99) r/G.I. Combat #120-156 17.00
Hawkman Vol. 1 ('07, $16.99) r/Brave & The Bold #34-36,42-44, Mystery in Space #87-90, Hawkman #1-11, and The Atom #7 17.00
Hawkman Vol. 2 ('08, $16.99) r/Brave & The Bold #70, Hawkman #12-27, The Atom #31, & The Atom and Hawkman #39-45 17.00
The House of Mystery Vol. 1 ('06, $16.99) r/House of Mystery #174-194 ('68-'71) 17.00
The House of Mystery Vol. 2 ('07, $16.99) r/House of Mystery #195-211 ('71-'73) 17.00
The House of Mystery Vol. 3 ('09, $16.99) r/House of Mystery #212-226 ('73-'74) 17.00
The House of Secrets Vol. 1 ('08, $16.99) r/House of Secrets #81-98 ('69-'72) 17.00
The House of Secrets Vol. 2 ('09, $17.99) r/House of Secrets #99-119 ('72-'74) 18.00
Jonah Hex Vol. 1 (2005, $16.99) r/All Star Western #10-12, Weird Western Tales #13,14, 16-33; plus the complete adventures of Outlaw from All Star Western #2-8 17.00
Justice League of America Vol. 1 ('05, $16.99) r/Brave & the Bold #28-30, J.L. of A. #1-16 and Mystery in Space #75 17.00
Justice League of America Vol. 2 ('07, $16.99) r/Justice League of America #17-36 17.00
Justice League of America Vol. 3 ('07, $16.99) r/Justice League of America #37-60 17.00
Justice League of America Vol. 4 ('09, $16.99) r/Justice League of America #61-83 17.00
Justice League of America Vol. 5 ('11, $19.99) r/Justice League of America #84-106 20.00
Legion of Super-Heroes Vol. 1 ('07, $16.99) r/Adventure #247 & early app. thru 1964 17.00
Legion of Super-Heroes Vol. 2 ('08, $16.99) r/app. in Adventure & Superboy 1964-66 17.00
Legion of Super-Heroes Vol. 3 ('09, $16.99) r/Adventure #349-368 & S.P. Jimmy Olsen #106 17.00
Legion of Super-Heroes Vol. 4 ('10, $19.99) r/app. in Adv., Action & Superboy 1968-72 20.00
Martian Manhunter Vol. 1 (2007, $16.99) r/Detective #225-304 & Batman #78 (prototype) 17.00
Martian Manhunter Vol. 2 ('09, $16.99) r/Detective #305-326 & House of Myst. #143-173 17.00
Metal Men Vol. 1 (2007, $16.99) r/#1-16; Brave & Bold #55, Showcase #37-40 17.00
Metamorpho Vol. 1 ('05, $16.99) r/Brave&Bold #57,58,66,68; Metamorpho #1-17;JLA #42 17.00
Our Army at War Vol. 1 ('10, $19.99) r/#1-20 20.00
Phantom Stranger Vol. 1 (2006, $16.99) r/#1-21 (2nd series) & Showcase #80 17.00
Phantom Stranger Vol. 2 (2008, $16.99) r/#22-41 and various 1970-1978 appearances 17.00
Robin The Boy Wonder Vol. 1 (2007, $16.99) r/back-ups from Batman, Detective, WF 17.00
Secrets of Sinister House ('10, $17.99) r/#5-18 and Sinister House of Secret Love #1-4 18.00
Sgt. Rock Vol. 1 ('07, $16.99) r/G.I. Combat #68, Our Army at War #81-117 17.00
Sgt. Rock Vol. 2 ('08, $16.99) r/Our Army at War #118-148 17.00
Sgt. Rock Vol. 3 ('10, $19.99) r/Our Army at War #149-163,165-172,174-176,178-180 20.00
Shazam! Vol. 1 ('06, $16.99) r/#1-33 17.00
Strange Adventures Vol. 1 ('08, $16.99) r/#54-73 17.00
Supergirl Vol. 1 ('07, $16.99) r/prototype from Superman #123 (8/58); 1st app. Action #252 (5/59) and early appearances thru Nov. 1961 17.00
Supergirl Vol. 2 ('08, $16.99) r/appearances in Action Comics #283-321 (1961-1965) 17.00
Superman Vol. 1 ('05, $9.99) r/Action #241-257 & Superman #122-134 (1958-59) 20.00
Superman Vol. 1 ('10, $19.99) r/Action #241-257 & Superman #122-134 (1958-59) 20.00
Superman Vol. 2 ('06, $16.99) r/Action #258-275 & Superman #134-145 (1959-61) 17.00
Superman Vol. 3 ('07, $16.99) r/Action #279-292 & Superman #146-156 & Annual #3,4 17.00
Superman Vol. 4 ('08, $16.99) r/Action #293-309 & Superman #157-166 (1962-64) 17.00
Superman Family Vol. 1 ('06, $16.99) Superman's Pal, Jimmy Olsen #1-22; Showcase #9 and Superman #22 17.00
Superman Family Vol. 2 ('08, $16.99) Superman's Pal, Jimmy Olsen #23-34; Showcase #10 and Superman's Girl Friend, Lois Lane #1-7 17.00
Superman Family Vol. 3 ('09, $16.99) Superman's Pal, Jimmy Olsen #35-44 and Superman's Girl Friend, Lois Lane #8-16 17.00
Teen Titans Vol. 1 ('06, $16.99) r/#1-18; Brave & the Bold #54,60; Showcase #59 17.00
Teen Titans Vol. 2 ('07, $16.99) r/#19-37, World's Finest #205 and Brave & Bold #83,94 17.00
The Unknown Soldier Vol. 1 ('06, $16.99) r/Star Spangled War Stories #158-188 17.00
The War That Time Forgot Vol. 1 ('07, $16.99) r/S.S.W.S. #90,92,94-125,127,128 17.00
Warlord Vol. 1 ('09, $16.99) r/#1-28 and debut in 1st Issue Special #1 17.00
The Witching Hour Vol. 1 ('11, $19.99) r/#1-19 20.00
Wonder Woman Vol. 1 ('07, $16.99) r/#98-117 17.00
Wonder Woman Vol. 2 ('08, $16.99) r/#118-137 17.00

The Shroud #1 © MAR

Sick #5 © Feature Pub.

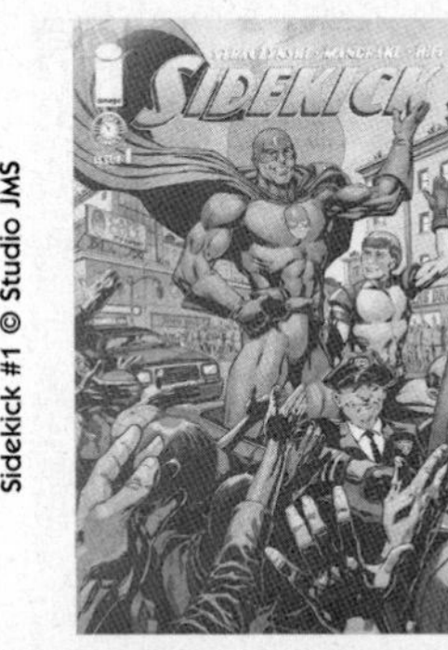

Sidekick #1 © Studio JMS

GD VG FN VF VF/NM NM-
2.0 4.0 6.0 8.0 9.0 9.2

GD VG FN VF VF/NM NM-
2.0 4.0 6.0 8.0 9.0 9.2

World's Finest Vol. 1 ('07, $16.99) r/#71-111 & Superman #76 17.00
World's Finest Vol. 2 ('08, $16.99) r/#112-145 17.00
World's Finest Vol. 3 ('10, $17.99) r/#146-160,162-169,171-173 ('64-'68) 18.00

SHOWGIRLS (Formerly Sherry the Showgirl #3)
Atlas Comics (MPC No. 2): No. 4, 2/57; June, 1957 - No. 2, Aug, 1957

4-(2/57) Dan DeCarlo-c/a begins 14 28 42 80 115 150
1-(6/57) Millie, Sherry, Chili, Pearl & Hazel begin 15 30 45 86 133 180
2 13 26 39 74 105 135

SHREK (Movie)
Dark Horse Comics: Sept, 2003 - No. 3, Dec, 2003 ($2.99, limited series)

1-3-Takes place after 1st movie; Evanier-s/Bachs-a; CGI cover 4.00

SHREK (Movie)
Ape Entertainment: 2010 - No. 4, 2011 ($3.95, limited series)

1-3-Short stories by various 4.00

SHROUD, THE (See Super-Villain Team-Up #5)
Marvel Comics: Mar, 1994 - No. 4, June, 1994 ($1.75, mini-series)

1-4: 1,2,4-Spider-Man & Scorpion app. 3.00

SHROUD OF MYSTERY
Whitman Publications: June, 1982

1 1 2 3 4 5 7

SHRUGGED
Aspen MLT, Inc.: No. 0, June, 2006 - No. 8, Feb, 2009 ($2.50/$2.99)

0-($2.50) Turner & Mastromauro-s/Gunnell-a; intro. story and character profiles 3.00
1-8-($2.99) 1-Six covers. 2-Three covers 3.00
... : Beginnings (5/06, $1.99) Prequel intro. to Ange and Dev; Gunnell-a; development art 3.00
Volume 2 (3/13, $1.00) 1-Marks & Gunnell-a; multiple covers 3.00
V2 #2-4-($3.99) Mastromauro-s/Marks-a 4.00

SHUTTER
Image Comics: Apr, 2014 - Present ($3.50)

1-Keatinge-s/Del Duca-a 3.00

SHUT UP AND DIE
Image Comics/Halloween: 1998 - No. 3, 1998 ($2.95,B&W, bi-monthly)

1-3: Hudnall-s 3.00

SICK (Sick Special #131) (Magazine) (Satire)
Feature Publ./Headline Publ./Crestwood Publ. Co./Hewfred Publ./ Pyramid Comm./Charlton Publ. No. 109 (4/76) on: Aug, 1960 - No. 134, Fall, 1980

V1#1-Jack Paar photo on-c; Torres-a; Untouchables-s; Ben Hur movie photo-s 14 28 42 96 211 325
2-Torres-a; Elvis app.; Lenny Bruce app. 9 18 27 61 123 185
3-5-Torres-a in all. 3-Khruschev-c; Hitler-s. 4-Newhart-s; Castro-s; John Wayne. 5-JFK/Castro-c; Elvis pin-up; Hitler. 8 16 24 55 105 155
6-Photo-s of Ricky Nelson & Marilyn Monroe; JFK 9 18 27 57 111 165
V2#1,2,4-8 (#7,8,10-14): 1-(#7) Hitler-s; Brando photo-s. 2-(#8) Dick Clark-s. 4-(#10) Untouchables-c; Candid Camera-s. 5-(#11) Nixon-c; Lone Ranger-s; JFK-s. 6-(#12) Beatnik-c/s. 8-(#14) Liz Taylor pin-up, JFK-s; Dobie Gillis-s; Sinatra & Dean Martin photo-s 8 16 24 51 96 140
3-(#9) Marilyn Monroe/JFK-c; Kingston Trio-s 8 16 24 55 105 155
V3#1-7(#15-21): 1-(#15) JFK app.; Liz Tayor/Richard Burton-s. 2-(#16) Ben Casey/ Frankenstein-c/s; Hitler photo-s. 5-(#19) Nixon back-c/s; Sinatra photo-s. 6-(#20) 1st Huckleberry Fink-c 5 10 15 33 57 80
8-(#22) Cassius Clay vs. Liston-s; 1st Civil War Blackouts-/Pvt. Bo Reargard w/ Jack Davis-a 5 10 15 35 63 90
V4#1-5 (#23-27): Civil War Blackouts-/Pvt. Bo Reargard w/ Jack Davis-a in all. 1-(#23) Smokey Bear-c; Tarzan-s. 2-(#24) Goldwater & Paar-s; Castro-s. 3-(#25) Frankenstein-c; Cleopatra/Liz Taylor-s; Steve Reeves photo-s. 4-(#26) James Bond-s; Hitler-s. 5-(#27) Taylor/Burton pin-up; Sinatra, Martin, Andress, Ekberg photo-s 4 8 12 27 44 60
28,31,36,39: 31-Pink Panther movie photo-s; Burke's Law-s. 39-Westerns; Elizabeth Montgomery photo-s; Beat mag-s 4 8 12 23 37 50
29,34,37,38: 29-Beatles-c by Jack Davis. 34-Two pg. Beatles-s & photo pin-up. 37-Playboy parody issue. 38-Addams Family-s 4 8 12 27 44 60
30,32,35,40: 30-Beatles photo pin-up; James Bond photo-s. 32-Ian Fleming-s; LBJ-s; Tarzan-s. 35-Beatles cameo; Three Stooges parody. 40-Tarzan-s; Crosby/Hope-s; Beatles parody 4 8 12 28 47 65
33-Ringo Starr photo-c & spoof on "A Hard Day's Night"; inside-c has Beatles photos 5 10 15 35 63 90
41,50,51,53,54,60: 41-Sports Illustrated parody-c/s. 50-Mod issue; flip-c w/1967 calendar w/Bob Taylor-a. 51-Get Smart-s. 53-Beatles cameo; nudity panels. 54-Monkees-c. 60-TV Daniel Boone-s 3 6 9 19 30 40
42-Fighting American-c revised from Simon/Kirby-c; "Good girl" art by Sparling; profile on Bob Powell; superhero parodies 5 10 15 33 57 80
43-49,52,55-59: 43-Sneaker set begins by Sparling. 45-Has #44 on-c & #45 on inside; TV Westerns-s; Beatles cameo. 46-Hell's Angels-s; NY Mets-s. 47-UFO/Space-c. 49-Men's Adventure mag. parody issue; nudity. 52-LBJ-s. 55-Underground culture special. 56-Alfred E. Neuman-c; inventors issue. 58-Hippie issue-c/s. 59-Hippie-s 3 6 9 16 24 32
61-64,66-69,71,73,75-80: 63-Tiny Tim-c & poster; Monkees-s. 64-Flip-c. 66-Flip-c; Mod Squad-s. 69-Beatles cameo; Peter Sellers photo-s. 71-Flip-c; Clint Eastwood-s. 76-Nixon-s; Marcus Welby-s. 78-Ma Barker-s; Courtship of Eddie's Father-s; Abbie Hoffman-s 3 6 9 15 22 28
65,70,74: 65-Cassius Clay/Brando/J. Wayne-c; Johnny Carson-s. 70-(9/69) John & Yoko-c, 1/2 pg. story. 74-Clay, Agnew, Namath & others as superheroes-c/s; Easy Rider-s; Ghost and Mrs. Muir-s 3 6 9 16 24 32
72-(84 pgs.) Xmas issue w/2 pg. slick color poster; Tarzan-s; 2 pg. Superman & superheroes-s 3 6 9 21 33 45
81-85,87-95,98,99: 81-(2/71) Woody Allen photo-s. 85 Monster Mag. parody-s; Nixon-s w/Ringo & John cameo. 88-Klute photo-s; Nixon paper dolls page. 92-Lily Tomlin; Archie Bunker pin-up. 93-Woody Allen 2 4 6 13 18 22
86,96,97,100: 86-John & Yoko, Tiny Tim-c; Love Story movie photo-s. 96-Kung Fu-c; Mummy-s, Dracula & Frankenstein app. 97-Superman-s; 1974 Calendar; Charlie Brown & Snoopy pin-up. 100-Serpico-s; Cosell-s; Jacques Cousteau-s 3 6 9 14 19 24
101-103,105-114,116,119,120: 101-Three Musketeers-s; Dick Tracy-s. 102-Young Frankenstein-s. 103-Kojak-s; Evel Knievel-s. 105-Towering Inferno-s; Peanuts/Snoopy-s. 106-Cher-c/s. 10 7-Jaws-c/s. 108-Pink Panther-c/s; Archie-s. 109-Adam & Eve-s(nudity). 110-Welcome Back Kotter-s. 111-Sonny & Cher-s. 112-King Kong-c/s. 120-Star Trek-s 2 4 6 9 13 16
104,115,117,118: 104-Muhammad Ali-c/s. 115-Charlie's Angels-s. 117-Bionic Woman & Six Million $ Man-c/s; Cher D'Flower begins by Sparling (nudity). 118-Star Wars-s; Popeye-s 2 4 6 11 16 20
121-125,128-130: 122-Darth Vader-s. 123-Jaws II-s. 128-Superman-c/movie parody. 130-Alien movie-s 2 4 6 10 14 18
126,127: 126-(68 pgs.) Battlestar Galactica-c/s; Star Wars-s; Wonder Woman-s. 127-Mork & Mindy-s; Lord of the Rings-s 2 4 6 13 18 22
131-(1980 Special) Star Wars/Star Trek/Flash Gordon wraparound-c/s; Superman parody; Battlestar Galactica-s 3 6 9 14 19 24
132,133: 132-1980 Election-c/s; Apocalypse Now-s. 133-Star Trek-s; Chips-s; Superheroes page 2 4 6 13 18 22
134 (scarce)(68 pg. Giant)-Star Wars-c; Alien-s; WKRP-s; Mork & Mindy-s; Taxi-s; MASH-s 4 8 12 19 30 40
Annual 1- Birthday Annual (1966)-3 pg. Huckleberry Fink fold out 4 8 12 23 37 50
Annual 2- 7th Annual Yearbook (1967)-Davis-c, 2 pg. glossy poster insert 4 8 12 23 37 50
Annual 3 (1968) "Big Sick Laff-in" on-c (84 pgs.)-w/psychedelic posters; Frankenstein poster 3 6 9 17 26 35
Annual 1969 "Great Big Fat Annual Sick", 1969 "9th Year Annual Sick", 1970, 1971 3 6 9 16 24 32
Annual 12,13-(1972,1973, 84 pgs.) 13-Monster-c 3 6 9 16 24 32
Annual 14,15-(1974,1975, 84 pgs.) 14-Hitler photo-s 3 6 9 16 24 32
Annual 2-4 (1980) 2 4 6 9 13 16
Special 1 (1980) Buck Rogers-c/s; MASH-s 3 6 9 14 19 24
Special 2 (1980) Wraparound Star Wars:Empire Strikes Back-c; Charlie's Angels/Farrah-s; Rocky-s; plus reprints 3 6 9 14 19 24
Yearbook 15(1975, 84 pgs.) Paul Revere-c 3 6 9 16 23 30

NOTE: ***Davis** a-42, 87; c-22, 23, 25, 29, 31, 32. **Powell** a-7, 31, 57. **Simon** a-1-3, 10, 41, 42, 87, 99; c-1, 47, 57, 59, 69, 91, 95-97, 99, 100, 102, 107, 112. **Torres** a-1-3, 29, 31, 47, 49. **Tuska** a-14, 41-43. Civil War Blackouts-23, 24. #42 has biography of Bob Powell.*

SIDEKICK (Paul Jenkins'...)
Image Comics (Desperado): June, 2006 - No. 5, May, 2007 ($3.50, limited series)

1-5-Paul Jenkins-s/Chris Moreno-a 3.50
... Super Summer Sidekick Spectacular 1 (7/07, $2.99) 3.50
... Super Summer Sidekick Spectacular 2 (9/07, $3.50) 3.50

SIDEKICK
Image Comics (Joe's Comics): Aug, 2013 - Present ($2.99)

1-6: 1-Straczynski-a/Mandrake-a; intro. The Cowl and Flyboy; 6 covers. 4-6-Two covers 3.00

SIDEKICKS
Fanboy Ent., Inc.: Jun, 2000 - No. 3, Apr, 2001 ($2.75, B&W, lim. series)

1-3-J.Torres-s/Takesi Miyazawa-a. 3-Variant-c by Wieringo 3.00
...: Super Fun Summer Special (Oni Press, 7/03, $2.99) art by various incl. Wieringo 3.00

Sigil (2011 series) #1 © MAR

Silent War #1 © MAR

Silly Tunes #4 © MAR

	GD 2.0	VG 4.0	FN 6.0	VF 8.0	VF/NM 9.0	NM- 9.2

...: The Substitute (Oni Press, 7/02, $2.95) 3.00
...: The Transfer Student TPB (Oni Press, 6/02, $8.95, 9" x 6") r/#1-3 9.00
...: The Transfer Student TPB 2nd Ed. (10/03, $11.95, 9" x 6") r/#1-3; The Substitute 12.00

SIDESHOW
Avon Periodicals: 1949 (one-shot)

	GD	VG	FN	VF	VF/NM	NM-
1-(Rare)-Similar to Bachelor's Diary	81	162	243	518	884	1250

SIEGE
Marvel Comics: Mar, 2010 - No. 4, Jun, 2010 ($3.99, limited series)

1-4-Asgard is invaded; Bendis-s/Coipel-a. 4-End of The Sentry 4.00
1-4-Variant covers by Dell'Otto 8.00
...: Captain America (6/10, $2.99) Gage-s/Dallocchio-a/Djurdjevic-c; both Caps app. 4.00
...: Loki (6/10, $2.99) Gillen-s/McKelvie-a/Djurdjevic-c; Hela & Mephisto app. 4.00
...: Secret Warriors (6/10, $2.99) Hickman-s/Vitti-a/Djurdjevic-c; Phobos attacks 4.00
...: Spider-Man (6/10, $2.99) Reed-s/Santucci-a/Djurdjevic-c; Venom & Ms. Marvel app. 4.00
...: Storming Asgard - Heroes & Villains (3/10, $3.99) Dossiers on participants; Land-c 4.00
...: The Cabal (2/10, $3.99) series prelude; Bendis-s/Lark-a; covers by Finch & Davis 4.00
...: Young Avengers (6/10, $2.99) McKeever-s/Asrar-a/Djurdjevic-c; Wrecking Crew app. 4.00

SIEGE: EMBEDDED
Marvel Comics: Mar, 2010 - No. 4, Jul, 2010 ($3.99, limited series)

1-4-Reed-s/Samnee-a/Granov-c; Ben Urich & Volstagg cover the invasion 4.00

SIEGEL AND SHUSTER: DATELINE 1930s
Eclipse Comics: Nov, 1984 - No. 2, Sept, 1985 ($1.50/$1.75, Baxter paper #1)

1,2: 1-Unpublished samples of strips from the '30s; includes 'Interplanetary Police'; Shuster-c. 2 ($1.75, B&W)-unpublished strips; Shuster-c 4.00

SIF (See Thor titles)
Marvel Comics: Jun, 2010 ($3.99, one shot)

1-Deconnick-s/Stegman-a/Foreman-c; Beta Ray Bill app. 4.00

SIGIL (Also see CrossGen Chronicles)
CrossGeneration Comics: Jul, 2000 - No. 43, Jan, 2004 ($2.95)

1-43: 1-Barbara Kesel-s/Ben & Ray Lai-a. 12-Waid-s begin. 21-Chuck Dixon-s begin 3.00
...: Mark of Power TPB (5/01, $19.95) r/#1-7; Moeller painted-c 20.00
...: The Marked Man Vol. 2 TPB (2002, $19.95) r/#8-14 20.00
...: The Lizard God Vol. 3 TPB (2002, $15.95) r/#15-20 16.00
Vol. 4: Hostage Planet (4/03, $15.95) r/#21-26 16.00
Vol. 5: Death Match (2003, $15.95) r/#27-32 16.00

SIGIL
Marvel Comics: May, 2011 - No. 4, Aug, 2011 ($2.99)

1-4-Carey-s/Kirk-a 3.00
1-Variant-c by McGuinness 5.00

SIGMA
Image Comics (WildStorm): March, 1996 - No. 3, June, 1996 ($2.50, limited series)

1-3: 1-"Fire From Heaven" prelude #2; Coker-a. 2-"Fire From Heaven" pt. 6. 3-"Fire From Heaven" pt. 14. 3.00

SILENT DRAGON
DC Comics (WildStorm): Sept, 2005 - No. 6, Feb, 2006 ($2.99, limited series)

1-6-Tokyo 2066 A.D.; Leinil Yu-a/c; Andy Diggle-s 3.00
TPB (2006, $19.99) r/series; sketch page 20.00

SILENT HILL: DEAD/ALIVE
IDW Publishing: Dec, 2005 - No. 5, Apr, 2006 ($3.99, limited series)

1-5-Stakal-a/Ciencin-s. 1-Four covers. 2-5-Two covers 4.00

SILENT HILL: DYING INSIDE
IDW Publishing: Feb, 2004 - No. 5, June, 2004 ($3.99, limited series)

1-5-Based on the Konami computer game. 1-Templesmith-a; Ashley Wood-c 4.00
...: Paint It Black (2/05, $7.49) Ciencin-s/Thomas-a 7.50
...: The Grinning Man 5/05, $7.49) Ciencin-s/Stakal-a 7.50
TPB (8/04, $19.99) r/#1-5; Ashley Wood-c 20.00

SILENT HILL: PAST LIFE
IDW Publishing: Oct, 2010 - No. 4, Jan, 2011 ($3.99, limited series)

1-4-Waltz-s; two covers on each 4.00

SILENT HILL: SINNER'S REWARD
IDW Publishing: Feb, 2008 - No. 4, Apr, 2008 ($3.99, limited series)

1-4-Waltz-s/Stamb-a 4.00

SILENT INVASION, THE
Rengade Press: Apr, 1986 - No.12, Mar, 1988 ($1.70/$2.00, B&W)

1-12-UFO sightings of the '50's 3.00

Book 1- reprints ($7.95) 8.00

SILENT MOBIUS
Viz Select Comics: 1991 - No. 5, 1992 ($4.95, color, squarebound, 44 pgs.)

1-5: Japanese stories translated to English 5.00

SILENT SCREAMERS (Based on the Aztech Toys figures)
Image Comics: Oct, 2000 ($4.95)

Nosferatu Issue - Alex Ross front & back-c 5.00

SILENT WAR
Marvel Comics: Mar, 2007 - No. 6, Aug, 2007 ($2.99, limited series)

1-6-Inhumans, Black Bolt and Fantastic Four app.; Hine-s/Irving-a/Watson-c 3.00
TPB (2007, $14.99) r/series 15.00

SILKE
Dark Horse Comics: Jan, 2001 - No. 4, Sept, 2001 ($2.95)

1-4-Tony Daniel-s/a 3.00

SILKEN GHOST
CrossGen Comics: June, 2003 - No. 5, Oct, 2003 ($2.95, limited series)

1-5-Dixon-s/Rosado-a 3.00
Traveler Vol. 1 (2003, $9.95) digest-sized reprint #1-5 10.00

SILLY PILLY (See Frank Luther's...)

SILLY SYMPHONIES (See Dell Giants)

SILLY TUNES
Timely Comics: Fall, 1945 - No. 7, June, 1947

	GD	VG	FN	VF	VF/NM	NM-
1-Silly Seal, Ziggy Pig begin	27	54	81	158	259	360
2-(2/46)	15	30	45	86	133	180
3-7: 6-New logo	14	28	42	80	115	150

SILVER (See Lone Ranger's Famous Horse...)

SILVER AGE
DC Comics: July, 2000 ($3.95, limited series)

1-Waid-s/Dodson-a; "Silver Age" style x-over; JLA & villains switch bodies 4.00
...: Challengers of the Unknown ($2.50) Joe Kubert-c; vs. Chronos 3.00
...: Dial H For Hero ($2.50) Jim Mooney-c; vs. Martian Manhunter 3.00
...: Doom Patrol ($2.50) Ramona Fradon-c/Peyer-s 3.00
...: Flash ($2.50) Carmine Infantino-c; Kid Flash and Elongated Man app. 3.00
...: Green Lantern ($2.50) Gil Kane-c/Busiek-s/Anderson-a; vs. Sinestro 3.00
...: Justice League of America ($2.50) Ty Templeton-c 3.00
...: Showcase ($2.50) Dick Giordano-c/a; Batgirl, Adam Strange app. 3.00
... Secret Files ($4.95) Intro. Agamemno; short stories & profile pages 5.00
...: Teen Titans ($2.50) Nick Cardy-c; vs. Penguin, Mr. Element, Black Manta 3.00
...: The Brave and the Bold ($2.50) Jim Aparo-c; Batman & Metal Men 3.00
... 80-Page Giant ($5.95) Conclusion of x-over; "lost" Silver Age stories 6.00

SILVERBACK
Comico: 1989 - No. 3, 1990 ($2.50, color, limited series, mature readers)

1-3: Character from Grendel: Matt Wagner-a 3.00

SILVERBLADE
DC Comics: Sept, 1987 - No. 12, Sept, 1988

1-12: Colan-c/a in all 4.00

SILVERHAWKS
Star Comics/Marvel Comics #6: Aug, 1987 - No. 6, June, 1988 ($1.00)

1-6 4.00

SILVERHEELS
Pacific Comics: Dec, 1983 - No. 3, May, 1984 ($1.50)

1-3 4.00

SILVER KID WESTERN
Key/Stanmor Publications: Oct, 1954 - No. 5, July, 1955

	GD	VG	FN	VF	VF/NM	NM-
1	10	20	30	54	72	90
2	6	12	18	31	38	45
3-5	6	12	18	28	34	40
I.W. Reprint #1,2-Severin-c: 1-r/#? 2-r/#1	2	4	6	8	11	14

SILVER SABLE AND THE WILD PACK (See Amazing Spider-Man #265 and Sable & Fortune)
Marvel Comics: June, 1992 - No. 35, Apr, 1995 ($1.25/$1.50

1-($2.00)-Embossed & foil stamped-c; Spider-Man app. 4.00
2-24,26-35: 4,5-Dr. Doom-c/story. 6,7-Deathlok-c/story. 9-Origin Silver Sable. 10-Punisher-c/s. 15-Capt. America-c/s. 16,17-Intruders app. 18,19-Venom-c/s. 19-Siege of Darkness x-over. 23-Daredevil (in new costume) & Deadpool app. 24-Bound-in card sheet. Li'l Sylvie backup story 3.00

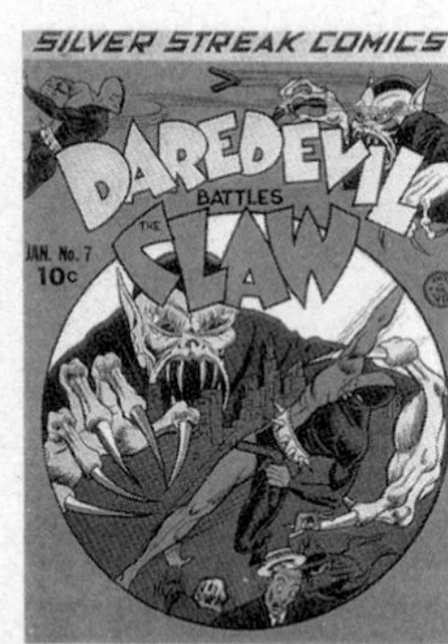

Silver Streak Comics #7 © LEV

Silver Surfer #4 © MAR

Silver Surfer #139 © MAR

GD 2.0 | VG 4.0 | FN 6.0 | VF 8.0 | VF/NM 9.0 | NM- 9.2

25-($2.00, 52 pgs.)-Li'l Sylvie backup story 4.00

SILVER STAR (Also see Jack Kirby's...)
Pacific Comics: Feb, 1983 - No. 6, Jan, 1984 ($1.00)

1-6: 1-1st app. Last of the Viking Heroes. 1-5-Kirby-c/a. 2-Ditko-a 5.00
...: Graphite Edition TPB (TwoMorrows Publ., 3/06, $19.95) r/series in B&W including Kirby's original pencils; sketch pages; original screenplay 20.00
Jack Kirby's Silver Star, Volume 1 HC (Image Comics, 2007, $34.99) r/series in color; sketch pages; original screenplay 35.00

SILVER STREAK COMICS (Crime Does Not Pay #22 on)
Your Guide Publs. No. 1-7/New Friday Publs. No. 8-17/Comic House Publ./ Newsbook Publ.: Dec, 1939 - No. 21, May, 1942; No. 23, 1946; No # 22 (Silver logo-#1-5)

1-(Scarce)-Intro the Claw by Cole (r-in Daredevil #21), Red Reeves Boy Magician (ends #2), Captain Fearless (ends #2), The Wasp (ends #2), Mister Midnight (ends #2) begin; Spirit Man only app. Calling The Duke begins (ends #2). Barry Lane only app. Silver Metallic-c begin, end #5; Claw-c 1,2,6-8 1000 2000 3000 7600 13,800 20,000
2-The Claw ends (by Cole); makes pact w/Hitler; Simon-c/a (The Claw); ad for Marvel Mystery Comics #2 (12/39). Lance Hale begins (receives super powers). Solar Patrol app. 421 842 1263 2947 5174 7400
3-1st app. & origin Silver Streak (2nd with Lightning speed); Dickie Dean the Boy Inventor, Lance Hale, Ace Powers (ends #6), Bill Wayne The Texas Terror (ends #6) & The Planet Patrol (ends #6) begin. Detective Snoop, Sergeant Drake only app. 366 732 1098 2562 4481 6400
4-Sky Wolf begins (ends #6); Silver Streak by Jack Cole (new costume); 1st app. Jackie, Lance Hale's sidekick. Lance Hale gains immortality 168 336 504 1075 1838 2600
5-Cole c/a(2); back-c ad for Claw app. in #6 200 400 600 1280 2190 3100
6-(Scarce, 9/40)-Origin & 1st app. Daredevil (blue & yellow costume) by Jack Binder; The Claw returns as the Green Claw; classic Cole Claw-c 1500 3000 4500 11,200 20,600 30,000
7-Claw vs. Daredevil serial begins c/sty, ends #11. Daredevil new costume-blue & red by Jack Cole & 3 other Cole stories (38 pgs.). Origin Whiz, S. S.'s Falcon 2nd app. Daredevil & 1st Daredevil-c (by Cole). Cloud Curtis, Presto Martin begins. Dynamo Hill & Zongar The Miracleman only app. 811 1622 2433 5920 10,460 15,000
8-Claw vs. Daredevil by Cole c/sty; last Cole Silver streak. Dan Dearborn begins (ends) #12. Secret Agent X-101 begins, ends #9 459 918 1377 3350 5925 8500
9-Claw vs. Daredevil by Cole. Silver Streak-c by Bob Wood 239 478 717 1530 2615 3700
10-Origin & 1st app. Captain Battle (5/41) by Binder; Claw vs. Daredevil by Cole; Silver Streak/robot-c by Bob Wood 194 388 582 1242 2121 3000
11-Intro. Mercury by Bob Wood, Silver Streak's sidekick; conclusion Claw vs. Daredevil by Rico; in 'Presto Martin,' 2nd pg., newspaper says 'Roussos does it again' 155 310 465 992 1696 2400
12-Daredevil-c by Rico; Lance Hale finds lost valley w/cave men, battles dinosaurs, sabre-toothed cats; his last app. 129 258 387 826 1413 2000
13-15: 13-Origin Thun-Dohr. Bingham Boys app. 116 232 348 742 1271 1800
16-Hitler-c 148 296 444 947 1624 2300
17-Last Daredevil issue. 113 226 339 723 1598 1750
18-The Saint begins (2/42, 1st app.) by Leslie Charteris (see Movie Comics #2 by DC); The Saint-c 110 220 330 704 1202 1700
19-21 (1942): 19,20-Ned of the Navy app.; Wolverton's Scoop Scuttle in 20,21. 20-Last Captain Battle, Dickie Dean & Cloud Curtis; Red Reed, Alonzo Appleseed only app. 21-Hitler app. in strip on cover 57 114 171 362 619 875
23(1946(An Atomic Comic)-Reprints; bondage-c 68 136 204 435 743 1050
nn(11/46)(Newsbook Publ.)-R-/S.S. story from #4-7 plus 2 Captain Fearless stories, all in color; bondage/torture-c (scarce) 97 194 291 621 1061 1500

NOTE: ***Jack Binder*** *a-8-12, 15; c-3, 4, 13-15, 17.* ***Dick Briefer*** *a-9-20.* ***Jack Cole*** *a-(Claw)-#2, 3, 6-10. (Daredevil)-#6-10, (Dickie Dean)-#3-10, (Pirate Prince)-#7, (Silver Streak)-#4-8, nn; c-5 (Silver Streak), 6 (Claw), 7, 8 (Daredevil).* ***Bill Everett*** *Red Reed begins #20.* ***Fred Guardineer*** *a-#8-12.* ***Don Rico*** *a-11-17 (Daredevil), 15, 19 (Silver Streak); c-11, 12, 16.* ***Joe Simon*** *a-2 (Solar Patrol), 3 (Silver Streak); c-2.* ***Basil Wolverton*** *a-20.* ***Bob Wood*** *a-8-15 (Presto Martin), 9 (Silver Streak); c-9, 10. Captain Battle c-11, 13-15, 17. Claw c-#1, 2, 6-8. Daredevil c-7, 8, 12. Dickie Dean c-19. Ned of the Navy c-20 (war). The Saint c-18. Silver Streak c-5, 10, 16, 23.*

SILVER STREAK COMICS (Homage with Golden Age size and Golden Age art styles)
Image Comics: No. 24, Dec, 2009 ($3.99, one-shot)

24-New Daredevil, Claw, Silver Streak & Captain Battle stories; Larsen, Grist, Gilbert-a 5.00

SILVER SURFER (See Fantastic Four, Fantasy Masterpieces V2#1, Fireside Book Series, Marvel Graphic Novel, Marvel Presents #8, Marvel's Greatest Comics & Tales To Astonish #92)

SILVER SURFER, THE (Also see Essential Silver Surfer)
Marvel Comics Group: Aug, 1968 - No. 18, Sept, 1970; June, 1982

1-More detailed origin by John Buscema (p); The Watcher back-up stories begin (origin), end #7; (No. 1-7: 25¢, 68 pgs.) 50 100 150 400 900 1400
2-1st app. Badoon 19 38 57 131 291 450
3-1st app. Mephisto 18 36 54 126 281 435
4-Lower distribution; Thor & Loki app. 42 84 126 311 706 1100

GD 2.0 | VG 4.0 | FN 6.0 | VF 8.0 | VF/NM 9.0 | NM- 9.2

5-7-Last giant size. 5-The Stranger app.; Fantastic Four app. 6-Brunner inks. 7-(8/69)-Early cameo Frankenstein's monster (see X-Men #40) 12 24 36 84 185 285
8-10: 8-18-(15¢ issues) 10 20 30 68 144 220
11-13,15-18: 15-Silver Surfer vs. Human Torch; Fantastic Four app. 17-Nick Fury app. 18-Vs. The Inhumans; Kirby-a; Trimpe-c 10 20 30 64 132 200
14-Spider-Man x-over 15 30 45 100 220 340
... Omnibus Vol. 1 Hardcover (2007, $74.99, dustjacket) r/#1-18 re-colored with original letter pages, Fantastic Four Annual #5 & Not Brand Echh #13; Lee and Buscema bios 75.00
V2#1 (6/82, 52 pgs.)-Byrne-c/a 2 4 6 9 12 15

NOTE: ***Adkins*** *a-8-15i.* ***Brunner*** *a-6i.* ***J. Buscema*** *a-1-17p.* ***Colan*** *a-1-3p.* ***Reinman*** *a-1-4i. #1-14 were reprinted in Fantasy Masterpieces V2#1-14.*

SILVER SURFER (Volume 3) (See Marvel Graphic Novel #38)
Marvel Comics Group: V3#1, July, 1987 - No. 146, Nov, 1998

1-Double size ($1.25) 2 4 6 8 10 12
2-10 6.00
11-17,25,31: 15-Ron Lim-c/a begins (9/88). 25,31 ($1.50, 52 pgs.) 25-Skrulls app. 5.00
18-24,26-30,32,33,39-43: 32,39-No Ron Lim-c/a. 39-Alan Grant scripts 4.00
34-Thanos returns (cameo); Starlin scripts begin 6.00
35-38: 35-1st full Thanos app. in Silver Surfer (3/90); reintro Drax the Destroyer on last pg. (cameo). 36-Recaps history of Thanos; Capt. Marvel & Warlock app. in recap. 37-1st full app. Drax the Destroyer; Drax-c. 38-Silver Surfer battles Thanos 1 2 3 5 6 8
44,45,49-Thanos stories (c-44,45) 6.00
46-48: 46-Return of Adam Warlock (2/91); re-intro Gamora & Pip the Troll. 47-Warlock battles Drax. 48-Last Starlin scripts (also #50) 6.00
50-($1.50, 52 pgs.)-Embossed & silver foil-c; Silver Surfer has brief battle w/Thanos; story cont'd in Infinity Gauntlet #1 2 4 6 9 12 15
50-2nd & 3rd printings 5.00
51-59: 51-53: Infinity Gauntlet x-over . 54-57: Infinity Gauntlet x-overs. 54-Rhino app. 55,56-Thanos-c & app. 57-Thanos-c & cameo. 58,59-Infinity Gauntlet x-overs; 58-Lim-c only. 59-Thanos battles Silver Surfer-c/story; Thanos joins 5.00
60-74,76-81,-83-99,101-124,126-139: 63-Capt. Marvel app. 67-69-Infinity War x-overs. 76-78-Jack of Hearts-c/s. 83-85-Infinity Crusade x-over; 83,84-Thanos cameo. 85-Storm, Wonder Man x-over. 86-Thor-c/s. 87-Dr. Strange & Warlock app. 88-Thanos-c/s. 95-FF app. 96-Hulk & FF app. 97-Terrax & Nova app. 101-Bound in card sheet. 106-Doc Doom app. 121-Quasar & Beta Ray Bill app. 123-w/card insert; begin Garney-a. 126-Dr. Strange-c/app. 128-Spider-Man & Daredevil-c/app. 138-Thing-c 3.00
75,82: 75-($2.50, 52 pgs.)-Embossed foil-c; Lim-c/a. 82-(52 pgs.) 4.00
100 ($2.25, 52 pgs.)-Wraparound-c 4.00
100 ($3.95, 52 pgs.)-Enhanced-c 5.00
125 ($2.95)-Wraparound-c; Vs. Hulk-c/app. 4.00
140-146: 140-142,144,145-Muth-c/a. 143,146-Cowan-a. 146-Last issue 3.00
#(-1) Flashback (7/97) 3.00
Annual 1 (1988, $1.75)-Evolutionary War app.; 1st Ron Lim-a on Silver Surfer (20 pg. back-up story & pin-ups) 5.00
Annual 2-7 ('89-'94, 68 pgs.): 2-Atlantis Attacks. 4-3 pg. origin story; Silver Surfer battles Guardians of the Galaxy. 5-Return of the Defenders, part 3; Lim-c/a (3 pgs. of pin-ups only). 6-Polybagged w/trading card; 1st app. Legacy; card is by Lim/Austin 4.00
Annual '97 ($2.99), .../Thor Annual '98 ($2.99) 4.00
Ashcan (1995, 75¢) reprints part of V1#3; Lim-c 3.00
...Dangerous Artifacts-(1996, $3.95)-Ron Marz scripts; Galactus-c/app. 5.00
Graphic Novel (1988, HC, $14.95) Judgment Day; Lee-s/Buscema-a 20.00
The Enslavers Graphic Novel (1990, $16.95) 20.00
Homecoming Graphic Novel (1991, $12.95, softcover) Starlin-s 15.00
Inner Demons TPB (4/98, $3.50)r/#123,125,126 5.00
...: Rebirth of Thanos TPB (2006, $24.99) r/#34-38, Thanos Quest #1,2; Logan's Run #6 25.00
...: The First Coming of Galactus nn (11/92, $5.95, 68 pgs.)-Reprints Fantastic Four #48-50 with new Lim-c 6.00
Wizard 1/2 2 4 6 9 12 15

NOTE: ***Austin*** *c(i)-7, 8, 71, 73, 74, 76, 79.* ***Cowan*** *a-143,146.* ***Cully Hamner*** *a-83p.* ***Ron Lim*** *a(p)-15-31, 33-38, 40-55, (56, 57-part-p), 60-65, 73-82, Annual 2, 4; c(p)-15-31, 32-38, 40-84, 86-92, Annual 2, 4-6.* ***Muth*** *c/a-140-142,144,145.* ***M. Rogers*** *a-1-10, 12, 19, 21; c-1-9, 11, 12, 21.*

SILVER SURFER (Volume 4)
Marvel Comics: Sept, 2003 - No. 14, Dec, 2004 ($2.25/$2.99)

1-6: 1-Milx-a; Jusko-c. 2-Jae Lee-c 3.00
7-14-($2.99) 3.00
...Vol. 1: Communion (2004, $14.99) r/#1-6 15.00

SILVER SURFER (Volume 5)
Marvel Comics: Apr, 2011 - No. 5, Aug, 2011 ($2.99, limited series)

1-5-Pagulayan-c. 1-Segovia-a. 4,5-Fantastic Four app. 3.00

SILVER SURFER
Marvel Comics: May, 2014 - Present ($3.99)

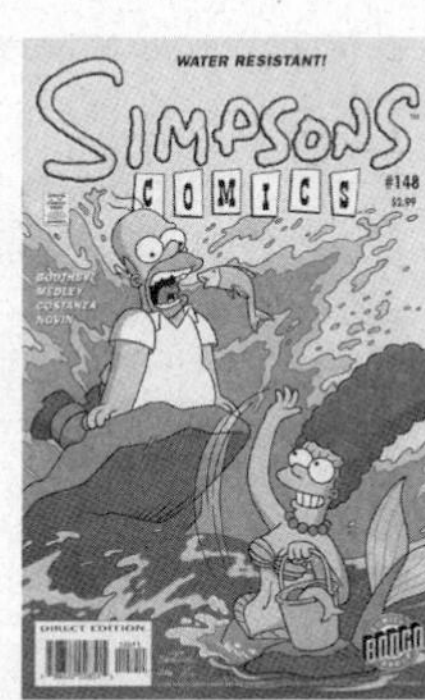

Simpsons Comics #148 © Bongo

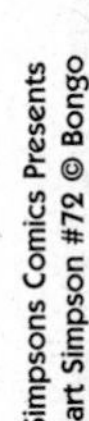

Simpsons Comics Presents Bart Simpson #72 © Bongo

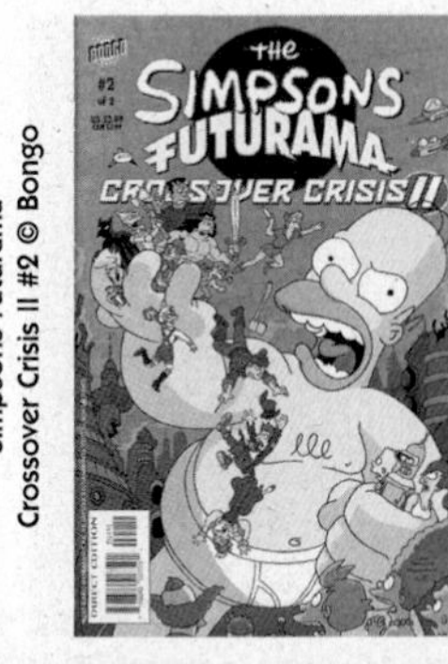

Simpsons Futurama Crossover Crisis II #2 © Bongo

	GD 2.0	VG 4.0	FN 6.0	VF 8.0	VF/NM 9.0	NM- 9.2

1-Dan Slott-s/Michael Allred-a/c 4.00

SILVER SURFER, THE
Marvel Comics (Epic): Dec, 1988 - No. 2, Jan, 1989 ($1.00, lim. series)

1,2: By Stan Lee scripts & Moebius-c/a 5.00
HC (1988, $19.95, dust jacket) r/#1,2; "Making Of" text section and sketch pages 30.00
... By Stan Lee & Moebius (3/13, $7.99) r/#1&2; bonus production diary from Moebius 8.00
...: Parable ('98, $5.99) r/#1&2 6.00

SILVER SURFER: IN THY NAME
Marvel Comics: Jan, 2008 - No. 4, Apr, 2008 ($2.99, limited series)

1-4-Spurrier-s/Huat-a. 1-Turner-c. 2-Dell'Otto-c. 3-Paul Pope-c. 4-Galactus app. 3.00

SILVER SURFER: LOFTIER THAN MORTALS
Marvel Comics: Oct, 1999 - No. 2, Oct, 1999 ($2.50, limited series)

1,2-Remix of Fantastic Four #57-60; Velluto-a 3.00

SILVER SURFER: REQUIEM
Marvel Comics: July, 2007 - No. 4, Oct, 2007 ($3.99, limited series)

1-4-Straczynski-s/Ribic-a. 1-Origin retold; Fantastic Four app. 4.00
HC (2007, $19.99) r/#1-4, Ribic cover sketches 20.00

SILVER SURFER/SUPERMAN
Marvel Comics: 1996 ($5.95,one-shot)

1-Perez-s/Lim-c/a(p) 6.00

SILVER SURFER VS. DRACULA
Marvel Comics: Feb, 1994 ($1.75, one-shot)

1-r/Tomb of Dracula #50; Everett Vampire-r/Venus #19; Howard the Duck back-up by Brunner; Lim-c(p) 4.00

SILVER SURFER/WARLOCK: RESURRECTION
Marvel Comics: Mar, 1993 - No. 4, June, 1993 ($2.50, limited series)

1-4: Starlin-c/a & scripts 4.00

SILVER SURFER/WEAPON ZERO
Marvel Comics: Apr, 1997 ($2.95, one-shot)

1-"Devil's Reign" pt. 8 3.00

SILVERTIP (Max Brand)
Dell Publishing Co.: No. 491, Aug, 1953 - No. 898, May, 1958

	GD	VG	FN	VF	VF/NM	NM-
Four Color 491 (#1); all painted-c	7	14	21	46	86	125
Four Color 572,608,637,667,731,789,898-Kinstler-a	5	10	15	30	50	70
Four Color 835	5	10	15	30	50	70

SIMON DARK
DC Comics: Dec, 2007 - No. 18, May, 2009 ($2.99)

1-Intro. Simon Dark; Steve Niles-s/Scott Hampton-a/c 4.00
1-Second printing with full face variant cover 3.00
2-18 3.00
...: Ashes TPB (2009, $17.99) r/#7-12 18.00
...: The Game of Life TPB (2009, $17.99) r/#13-18 18.00
...: What Simon Does TPB (2008, $14.99) r/#1-6 18.00

SIMPSONS COMICS (See Bartman, Futurama, Itchy & Scratchy & Radioactive Man)
Bongo Comics Group: 1993 - Present ($1.95/$2.50/$2.99)

	GD	VG	FN	VF	VF/NM	NM-
1-($2.25)-FF#1-c swipe; pull-out poster; flip book	2	4	6	11	16	20
2-5: 2-Patty & Selma flip-c/sty. 3-Krusty, Agent of K.L.O.W.N. flip-c/story. 4-Infinity-c; flip-c of Busman #1; w/trading card. 5-Wraparound-c w/trading card	1	2	3	5	6	8

6-40: All Flip books. 6-w/Chief Wiggum's "Crime Comics". 7-w/"McBain Comics". 8-w/"Edna, Queen of the Congo". 9-w/"Barney Gumble". 10-w/"Apu". 11-w/"Homer". 12-w/"White Knuckled War Stories". 13-w/"Jimbo Jones' Wedgie Comics". 14-w/"Grampa". 15-w/"Itchy & Scratchy". 16-w/"Bongo Grab Bag". 17-w/"Headlight Comics". 18-w/"Milhouse". 19,20-w/"Roswell." 21,22-w/"Roswell". 23-w/"Hellfire Comics". 24-w/"Lil' Homey". 36-39-Flip book w/Radioactive Man 5.00
41-49,51-99: 43-Flip book w/Poochie. 52-Dini-s. 77-Dixon-s. 85-Begin $2.99-c 4.00

	GD	VG	FN	VF	VF/NM	NM-
50-($5.95) Wraparound-c; 80 pgs.; square-bound	1	2	3	5	6	8
100-($6.99) 100 pgs.; square-bound; clip issue of past highlights	1	2	3	5	6	8

101-182,184-199,201-210: 102-Barks Ducks homage. 117-Hank Scorpio app. 122-Archie spoof. 132-Movie poster enclosed. 132-133-Two-parter. 144-Flying Hellfish flashback. 150-w/Poster. 163-Aragonés-s/a 3.00
183-Archie Comics #1 cover swipe; Archie homage with Stan Goldberg-a 3.00
200-(2013, $4.99) Wraparound-c; short stories incl. Dorkin-s/a; Matt Groening cameo 5.00
... A Go-Go (1999, $11.95)-r/#32-35; ...Big Bonanza (1998, $11.95)-r/#28-31, ...Extravaganza (1994, $10.00)-r/#1-4; infinity-c, ...On Parade (1998, $11.95)-r/#24-27, ...Simpsorama (1996, $10.95)-r/#11-14 12.00

Simpsons Classics 1-30 (2004-Present, $3.99, magazine-size, quarterly) reprints 4.00
Simpsons Comics Barn Burner ('04, $14.95) r/#57-61,63 15.00
Simpsons Comics Beach Blanket Bongo ('07, $14.95) r/#71-75,77 15.00
Simpsons Comics Belly Buster ('04, $14.95) r/#49,51,53-56 15.00
Simpsons Comics Hit the Road! ('08, $15.95) r/#85,86,88,89,90 16.00
Simpsons Comics Jam-Packed Jamboree ('06, $14.95) r/#64-69 15.00
Simpsons Comics Madness ('03, $14.95) r/#43-48 15.00
Simpsons Comics Royale ('01, $14.95) r/various Bongo issues 15.00
Simpsons Comics Treasure Trove 1-4 ('08-'09, $3.99, 6" x 8") r/various Bongo issues 4.00
Simpsons Summer Shindig ('07-'13, $4.99) 1-7-Anthology. 1-Batman/Ripken insert 5.00
Simpsons Winter Wing Ding ('06-'13, $4.99) 1-8-Holiday anthology. 1-Dini-s 5.00

SIMPSONS COMICS AND STORIES
Welsh Publishing Group: 1993 ($2.95, one-shot)

	GD	VG	FN	VF	VF/NM	NM-
1-(Direct Sale)-Polybagged w/Bartman poster	3	6	9	14	20	25
1-(Newsstand Edition)-Without poster						6.00

SIMPSONS COMICS PRESENTS BART SIMPSON
Bongo Comics Group: 2000 - Present ($2.50/$2.99)

1-89: 7-9-Dan DeCarlo-layouts. 13-Begin $2.99-c. 17,37-Bartman app. 50-Aragonés-s/a 3.00
The Big Book of Bart Simpson TPB (2002, $12.95) r/#1-4 15.00
The Big Bad Book of Bart Simpson TPB (2003, $12.95) r/#5-8 15.00
The Big Bratty Book of Bart Simpson TPB (2004, $12.95) r/#9-12 15.00
The Big Beefy Book of Bart Simpson TPB (2005, $13.95) r/#13-16 15.00
The Big Bouncy Book of Bart Simpson TPB (2006, $13.95) r/#17-20 15.00
The Big Beastly Book of Bart Simpson TPB (2007, $14.95) r/#21-24 15.00
The Big Brilliant Book of Bart Simpson TPB (2008, $14.95) r/#25-28 15.00

SIMPSONS FUTURAMA CROSSOVER CRISIS II (TV) (Also see Futurama/Simpsons Infinitely Secret Crossover Crisis)
Bongo Comics: 2005 - No. 2, 2005 ($3.00, limited series)

1,2-The Professor brings the Simpsons' Springfield crew to the 31st century 3.00

SIMPSONS ILLUSTRATED (TV)
Bongo Comics: 2012 - Present ($3.99, quarterly)

1-10-Reprints 4.00

SIMPSONS ONE-SHOT WONDERS (TV)
Bongo Comics: 2012 - 2013 ($2.99)

...: Bart Simpson's Pal Milhouse 1 - Short stories; centerfold with decal 3.00
...: Li'l Homer 1 - Short stories of Homer's childhood; centerfold with cut-outs 3.00
...: Lisa 1 - Short stories by Matsumoto and others; sticker page centerfold 3.00
...: Maggie 1 - Short stories by Aragonés and others; paperdoll centerfold; Aragonés-c 3.00
...: Mr. Burns 1 - Short stories incl. Richie Rich spoof; Fruit Bat Man mask 3.00
...: Professor Frink 1 - Short stories; 3-D glasses insert; 3-D story and back-c 3.00
...: Ralph Wiggums Comics 1 - Short stories by Aragonés and others 3.00

SIMPSONS SUPER SPECTACULAR (TV)
Bongo Comics: 2006 - Present ($2.99)

1-16: 2-Bartman, Stretch Dude and The Cupcake Kid team up; back-up story Brereton-a. 5-Fradon-a on Metamorpho spoof. 8-Spirit spoof. 9,10,14-16-Radioactive Man app. 3.00

SINBAD, JR (TV Cartoon)
Dell Publishing Co.: Sept-Nov, 1965 - No. 3, May, 1966

	GD	VG	FN	VF	VF/NM	NM-
1	4	8	12	23	37	50
2,3	3	6	9	17	26	35

SIN BOLDLY
Image Comics: Dec, 2013 ($3.50, B&W, one-shot)

1-J.M. Linsner-s/a/c; short stories with Sinful Suzi and Obsidian Stone 3.50

SIN CITY (See Dark Horse Presents, A Decade of Dark Horse, & San Diego Comic Con Comics #2,4)
Dark Horse Comics (Legend)
TPB ($15.00) Reprints early DHP stories 15.00
Booze, Broads & Bullets TPB ($15.00) 15.00
Frank Miller's Sin City: One For One (8/10, $1.00) reprints debut story from DHP #51 3.00

SIN CITY (FRANK MILLER'S...) (Reissued TPBs to coincide with the April 2005 movie)
Dark Horse Books: Feb, 2005 ($17.00/$19.00, 6" x 9" format with new Miller covers)

Volume 1: The Hard Goodbye ($17.00) reprints stories from Dark Horse Presents #51-62 and DHP Fifth Anniv. Special; covers and publicity pieces 17.00
Volume 2: A Dame to Kill For ($17.00) r/Sin City: A Dame to Kill For #1-6 17.00
Volume 3: The Big Fat Kill ($17.00) r/Sin City: The Big Fat Kill #1-5; pin-up gallery 17.00
Volume 4: That Yellow Bastard ($19.00) r/Sin City: That Yellow Bastard #1-6; pin-up gallery by Mike Allred, Kyle Baker, Jeff Smith and Bruce Timm; cover gallery 19.00
Volume 5: Family Values ($12.00) r/Sin City: Family Values GN 12.00
Volume 6: Booze, Broads & Bullets ($15.00) r/Sin City: The Babe Wore Red and Other Stories;

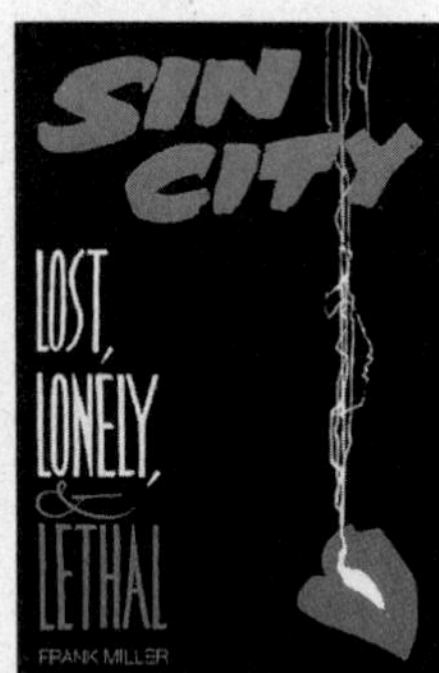

Sin City: Lost, Lonely & Lethal © Frank Miller

Single Series #14 © UFS

Siren Special #1 © MAL

	GD	VG	FN	VF	VF/NM	NM-
	2.0	4.0	6.0	8.0	9.0	9.2

Silent Night; story from A Decade of Dark Horse; Lost Lonely & Lethal; Sex & Violence; and Just Another Saturday Night 15.00
Volume 7: Hell and Back ($28.00) r/Sin City: Hell and Back #1-9; pin-up gallery 28.00

SIN CITY: A DAME TO KILL FOR
Dark Horse Comics (Legend): Nov, 1993 - No. 6, May, 1994 ($2.95, B&W, limited series)

1-6: Frank Miller-c/a & story in all. 1-1st app. Dwight. 6.00
Limited Edition Hardcover 85.00
Hardcover 25.00
TPB ($15.00) 15.00

SIN CITY: FAMILY VALUES
Dark Horse Comics (Legend): Oct, 1997 ($10.00, B&W, squarebound, one-shot)

nn-Miller-c/a & story 10.00
Limited Edition Hardcover 75.00

SIN CITY: HELL AND BACK
Dark Horse (Maverick): Jul, 1999 - No. 9 ($2.95/$4.95, B&W, limited series)

1-8-Miller-c/a & story. 7-Color 4.00
9-($4.95) 6.00

SIN CITY: JUST ANOTHER SATURDAY NIGHT
Dark Horse Comics (Legend): Aug, 1997 (Wizard 1/2 offer, B&W, one-shot)

1/2-Miller-c/a & story 1 2 3 5 6 8
nn (10/98, $2.50) r/#1/2 4.00

SIN CITY: LOST, LONELY & LETHAL
Dark Horse Comics (Legend): Dec, 1996 ($2.95, B&W and blue, one-shot)

nn-Miller-c/s/a; w/pin-ups 5.00

SIN CITY: SEX AND VIOLENCE
Dark Horse Comics (Legend): Mar, 1997 ($2.95, B&W and blue, one-shot)

nn-Miller-c/a & story 5.00

SIN CITY: SILENT NIGHT
Dark Horse Comics (Legend): Dec, 1995 ($2.95, B&W, one-shot)

1-Miller-c/a & story; Marv app. 6.00

SIN CITY: THAT YELLOW BASTARD (Second Ed. TPB listed under Sin City (Frank Miller's...)
Dark Horse Comics (Legend): Feb, 1996 - No. 6, July, 1996 ($2.95/$3.50, B&W and yellow, limited series)

1-5: Miller-c/a & story in all. 1-1st app. Hartigan. 6.00
6-($3.50) Error & corrected 6.00
Limited Edition Hardcover 25.00
TPB ($15.00) 15.00

SIN CITY: THE BABE WORE RED AND OTHER STORIES
Dark Horse Comics (Legend): Nov, 1994 ($2.95, B&W and red, one-shot)

1-r/serial run in Previews as well as other stories; Miller-c/a & scripts; Dwight app. 6.00

SIN CITY: THE BIG FAT KILL (Second Edition TPB listed under Sin City (Frank Miller's...)
Dark Horse Comics (Legend): Nov, 1994 - No. 5, Mar, 1995 ($2.95, B&W, limited series)

1-5-Miller story & art in all; Dwight app. 6.00
Hardcover 25.00
TPB ($15.00) 15.00

SIN CITY: THE FRANK MILLER LIBRARY
Dark Horse Books: Set 1, Nov, 2005; Set 2, Mar, 2006 ($150, slipcased hardcover, 8" x 12")

Set 1 - Individual hardcovers for Volume 1: The Hard Goodbye, Volume 2: A Dame to Kill For, Volume 3: The Big Fat Kill, Volume 4: That Yellow Bastard; new red foil stamped covers; slipcase box is black with red foil graphics 150.00
Set 2 - Individual hardcovers for Volume 5: Family Values, Volume 6: Booze, Broads & Bullets, Volume 7: Hell and Back, new red foil stamped covers; The Art of Sin City red hardcover; slipcase box is black with red foil graphics 150.00

SINDBAD (See Capt. Sindbad under Movie Comics, and Fantastic Voyages of Sindbad)

SINGING GUNS (See Fawcett Movie Comics)

SINGLE SERIES (Comics on Parade #30 on)(Also see John Hix...)
United Features Syndicate: 1938 - No. 28, 1942 (All 68 pgs.)

Note: See Individual Alphabetical Listings for prices

1-Captain and the Kids (#1)
2-Broncho Bill (1939) (#1)
3-Ella Cinders (1939)
4-Li'l Abner (1939) (#1)
5-Fritzi Ritz (#1)
6-Jim Hardy by Dick Moores (#1)
7-Frankie Doodle
8-Peter Pat (On sale 7/14/39)
9-Strange As It Seems
10-Little Mary Mixup
11-Mr. and Mrs. Beans
12-Joe Jinks
13-Looy Dot Dope
14-Billy Make Believe
15-How It Began (1939)
16-Illustrated Gags (1940)-Has ad for Captain and the Kids #1 reprint listed below
17-Danny Dingle
18-Li'l Abner (#2 on-c)
19-Broncho Bill (#2 on-c)
20-Tarzan by Hal Foster
21-Ella Cinders (#2 on-c; on sale 3/19/40)
22-Iron Vic
23-Tailspin Tommy by Hal Forrest (#1)
24-Alice in Wonderland (#1)
25-Abbie and Slats
26-Little Mary Mixup (#2 on-c, 1940)
27-Jim Hardy by Dick Moores (1942)
28-Ella Cinders & Abbie and Slats (1942)
1-Captain and the Kids (1939 reprint)-2nd Edition
1-Fritzi Ritz (1939 reprint)-2nd ed.

NOTE: *Some issues given away at the 1939-40 New York World's Fair (#6).*

SINISTER DEXTER
IDW Publishing: Dec, 2013 - No. 7, ($3.99)

1-4: 1-Dan Abnett-s/Andy Clarke-a; two covers by Clarke and Fuso 4.00

SINISTER HOUSE OF SECRET LOVE, THE (Becomes Secrets of Sinister House No. 5 on)
National Periodical Publ.: Oct-Nov, 1971 - No. 4, Apr-May, 1972

1 (All 52 pgs.) -Grey-tone-c 13 26 39 91 201 310
2,4: 2-Jeff Jones-c 7 14 21 48 89 130
3-Toth-a; Grey-tone-c 8 16 24 51 96 140

SINS OF YOUTH... (Also see Young Justice: Sins of Youth)
DC Comics: May 2000 ($4.95/$2.50, limited crossover series)

Secret Files 1 ($4.95) Short stories and profile pages; Nauck-c 5.00
...Aquaboy/Lagoon Man; Batboy and Robin; JLA Jr.; Kid Flash/Impulse; Starwoman and the JSA, Superman, Jr./Superboy, Sr.; The Secret/ Deadboy, Wonder Girls ($2.50-c) Old and young heroes switch ages 3.00

SIR CHARLES BARKLEY AND THE REFEREE MURDERS
Hamilton Comics: 1993 ($9.95, 8-1/2" x 11", 52 pgs.)

nn-Photo-c; Sports fantasy comic book fiction (uses real names of NBA superstars). Script by Alan Dean Foster, art by Joe Staton. Comes with bound-in sheet of 35 gummed "Moods of Charles Barkley" stamps. Photo/story on Barkley 2 4 6 9 12 15
Special Edition of 100 copies for charity signed on an affixed book plate by Barkley, Foster & Staton 175.00
Ashcan edition given away to dealers, distributors & promoters (low distribution). Four pages in color, balance of story in b&w 2 4 6 9 12 15

SIR EDWARD GREY, WITCHFINDER: IN THE SERVICE OF ANGELS (From Hellboy)
Dark Horse Comics: July, 2009 - No. 5, Nov, 2009 ($2.99, limited series)

1-5-Mignola-s/c; Stenbeck-a 3.00

SIREN (Also see Eliminator & Ultraforce)
Malibu Comics (Ultraverse): Sept, 1995 - No. 3, Dec, 1995 ($1.50)

Infinity, 1-3: Infinity-Black-c & painted-c exists. 1-Regular-c & painted-c; War Machine app. 2-Flip book w/Phoenix Resurrection Pt. 3 3.00
Special 1-(2/96, $1.95, 28 pgs.)-Origin Siren; Marvel Comic's Juggernaut-c/app. 3.00

SIREN: SHAPES
Image Comics: May, 1998 - No. 3, Nov, 1998 ($2.95, B&W, limited series)

1-3-J. Torres -s 3.00

SIR LANCELOT (TV)
Dell Publishing Co.: No. 606, Dec, 1954 - No. 775, Mar, 1957

Four Color 606 (not TV) 6 12 18 41 76 110
Four Color 775(...and Brian)-Buscema-a; photo-c 8 16 24 56 108 160

SIR WALTER RALEIGH (Movie)
Dell Publishing Co.: May, 1955 (Based on movie "The Virgin Queen")

Four Color 644-Photo-c 6 12 18 40 73 105

SISTERHOOD OF STEEL (See Eclipse Graphic Adventure Novel #13)
Marvel Comics (Epic Comics): Dec, 1984 -No. 8, Feb, 1986 ($1.50, Baxter paper, mature)

1-8 4.00

SITUATION, THE (TV's Jersey Shore)
Wizard World: July, 2012 (no cover price)

1-Jenkins-s/Caldwell-a; two covers by Horn & Caldwell 3.00

6 BLACK HORSES (See Movie Classics)

SIX FROM SIRIUS
Marvel Comics (Epic Comics): July, 1984 - No. 4, Oct, 1984 ($1.50, limited series, mature)

1-4: Moench scripts; Gulacy-c/a in all 4.00

SIX FROM SIRIUS II
Marvel Comics (Epic Comics): Feb, 1986 - No. 4, May, 1986 ($1.50, limited series, mature)

1-4: Moench scripts; Gulacy-c/a in all 4.00

SIX-GUN GORILLA

Six-Gun Gorilla #1 © BOOM

Six Million Dollar Man Season Six #1 © Dynamite

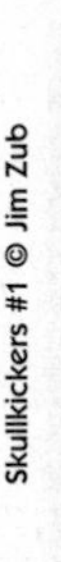
Skullkickers #1 © Jim Zub

BOOM! Studios: Jun, 2013 - No. 6, Nov, 2013 ($3.99, limited series)

	GD 2.0	VG 4.0	FN 6.0	VF 8.0	VF/NM 9.0	NM- 9.2
1-6: 1-Spurrier-s/Stokely-a						4.00

SIX-GUN HEROES
Fawcett Publications: March, 1950 - No. 23, Nov, 1953 (Photo-c #1-23)

	GD 2.0	VG 4.0	FN 6.0	VF 8.0	VF/NM 9.0	NM- 9.2
1-Rocky Lane, Hopalong Cassidy, Smiley Burnette begin (same date as Smiley Burnette #1)	31	62	93	186	303	420
2	16	32	48	94	147	200
3-5: 5-Lash LaRue begins	14	28	42	76	108	140
6-15	11	22	33	62	86	110
16-22: 17-Last Smiley Burnette. 18-Monte Hale begins	10	20	30	54	72	90
23-Last Fawcett issue	10	20	30	58	79	100

NOTE: *Hopalong Cassidy photo c-1-3. Monte Hale photo c-18. Rocky Lane photo c-4, 5, 7, 9, 11, 13, 15, 17, 20, 21, 23. Lash LaRue photo c-6, 8, 10, 12, 14, 16, 19, 22.*

SIX-GUN HEROES (Cont'd from Fawcett; Gunmasters #84 on) (See Blue Bird)
Charlton Comics: No. 24, Jan, 1954 - No. 83, Mar-Apr, 1965 (All Vol. 4)

	GD 2.0	VG 4.0	FN 6.0	VF 8.0	VF/NM 9.0	NM- 9.2
24-Lash LaRue, Hopalong Cassidy, Rocky Lane & Tex Ritter begin; photo-c	14	28	42	80	115	150
25	10	20	30	54	72	90
26-30: 26-Rod Cameron story. 28-Tom Mix begins?	9	18	27	47	61	75
31-40: 38-40-Jingles & Wild Bill Hickok (TV)	8	16	24	42	54	65
41-46,48,50: 41-43-Wild Bill Hickok (TV)	8	16	24	40	50	60
47-Williamson-a, 2 pgs; Torres-a	8	16	24	42	54	65
49-Williamson-a (5 pgs.)	9	18	27	50	65	80
51-56,58-60: 58-Gunmaster app.	3	6	9	19	30	40
57-Origin & 1st app. Gunmaster	4	8	12	25	40	55
61,63-70	3	6	9	16	23	30
62-Origin Gunmaster	3	6	9	19	30	40
71-75,77,78,80-83	2	4	6	13	18	22
76,79: 76-Gunmaster begins. 79-1st app. & origin of Bullet, the Gun-Boy	3	6	9	14	19	24

SIXGUN RANCH (See Luke Short & Four Color #580)

SIX GUNS
Marvel Comics: Jan, 2012 - No. 5, Apr, 2012 ($2.99, limited series)

	GD 2.0	VG 4.0	FN 6.0	VF 8.0	VF/NM 9.0	NM- 9.2
1-5-Diggle-s/Gianfelice-a; Tarantula and Tex Dawson app.						3.00

SIX-GUN WESTERN
Atlas Comics (CDS): Jan, 1957 - No. 4, July, 1957

	GD 2.0	VG 4.0	FN 6.0	VF 8.0	VF/NM 9.0	NM- 9.2
1-Crandall-a; two Williamson text illos	19	38	57	111	176	240
2,3-Williamson-a in both	14	28	42	82	121	160
4-Woodbridge-a	11	22	33	60	83	105

NOTE: ***Ayers** a-2, 3. **Maneely** a-1; c-2, 3. **Orlando** a-2. **Pakula** a-2. **Powell** a-3. **Romita** a-1, 4. **Severin** c-1, 4. **Shores** a-2.*

SIX MILLION DOLLAR MAN, THE (TV) (Also see The Bionic Man)
Charlton Comics: 6/76 - No. 4, 12/76; No. 5, 10/77; No. 6, 2/78 - No. 9, 6/78

	GD 2.0	VG 4.0	FN 6.0	VF 8.0	VF/NM 9.0	NM- 9.2
1-Staton-c/a; Lee Majors photo on-c	3	6	9	17	26	35
2-Neal Adams-c; Staton-a	3	6	9	14	20	25
3-9	2	4	6	13	18	22

SIX MILLION DOLLAR MAN, THE (TV)(Magazine)
Charlton Comics: July, 1976 - No. 7, Nov, 1977 (B&W)

	GD 2.0	VG 4.0	FN 6.0	VF 8.0	VF/NM 9.0	NM- 9.2
1-Neal Adams-c/a	3	6	9	21	33	45
2-Neal Adams-c	3	6	9	16	23	30
3-N. Adams part inks; Chaykin-a	3	6	9	14	19	24
4-7	2	4	6	11	16	20

SIX MILLION DOLLAR MAN, THE: SEASON 6 (TV)
Dynamite Entertainment: 2014 - Present ($3.99)

	GD 2.0	VG 4.0	FN 6.0	VF 8.0	VF/NM 9.0	NM- 9.2
1-Jim Kuhoric-s/Juan Antonio Ramirez-a; covers by Alex Ross & Ken Haeser & photo-c						4.00

SIX STRING SAMURAI
Awesome-Hyperwerks: Sept, 1998 ($2.95)

	GD 2.0	VG 4.0	FN 6.0	VF 8.0	VF/NM 9.0	NM- 9.2
1-Stinsman & Fraga-a						3.00

67 SECONDS
Marvel Comics (Epic Comics): 1992 ($15.95, 54 pgs., graphic novel)

	GD 2.0	VG 4.0	FN 6.0	VF 8.0	VF/NM 9.0	NM- 9.2
nn-James Robinson scripts; Steve Yeowell-c/a	2	4	6	11	14	18

SKAAR: KING OF THE SAVAGE LAND
Marvel Comics: Jun, 2011 - No. 5 ($2.99, limited series)

	GD 2.0	VG 4.0	FN 6.0	VF 8.0	VF/NM 9.0	NM- 9.2
1-5-Shanna & Ka-Zar app.; Ching-a. 1-Komarck-c. 2-McGuinness-c						3.00

SKAAR: SON OF HULK (Title continues in Son of Hulk #13)(Also see World War Hulk x-over)
Marvel Comics: Aug, 2008 - No. 12, Aug, 2009 ($2.99)

	GD 2.0	VG 4.0	FN 6.0	VF 8.0	VF/NM 9.0	NM- 9.2
1-Garney-a/Pak-s; 2 covers by Pagulayan and Julie Bell; origin						4.00
1-Second printing - 2 covers by Garney and Hulk movie image						3.00
1-Third printing - Garney sketch variant-c						3.00
2-12: 2-6-Back-up story with Guice-a. 7-12-Silver Surfer app.						3.00
Planet Skaar Prologue 1 (7/09, $3.99) Panosian-a; Fantastic Four & She-Hulk app.						4.00
... Presents - Savage World of Sakaar (11/08, $3.99) Pak-s/art by various; Garney-c						4.00

SKATEMAN
Pacific Comics: Nov, 1983 (Baxter paper, one-shot)

	GD 2.0	VG 4.0	FN 6.0	VF 8.0	VF/NM 9.0	NM- 9.2
1-Adams-c/a						4.00

SKELETON HAND (...In Secrets of the Supernatural)
American Comics Gr. (B&M Dist. Co.): Sept-Oct, 1952 - No. 6, Jul-Aug, 1953

	GD 2.0	VG 4.0	FN 6.0	VF 8.0	VF/NM 9.0	NM- 9.2
1	50	100	150	315	533	750
2	36	72	108	216	351	485
3-6	29	58	87	170	278	385

SKELETON KEY
Amaze Ink: July, 1995 - No. 30, Jan, 1998 ($1.25/$1.50/$1.75, B&W)

	GD 2.0	VG 4.0	FN 6.0	VF 8.0	VF/NM 9.0	NM- 9.2
1-30						3.00
Special #1 (2/98, $4.95) Unpublished short stories						5.00
Sugar Kat Special (10/98, $2.95) Halloween stories						3.00
Beyond The Threshold TPB (6/96. $11.95)-r/#1-6						12.00
Cats and Dogs TPB ($12.95)-r/#25-30						13.00
The Celestial Calendar TPB ($19.95)-r/#7-18						20.00
Telling Tales TPB ($12.95)-r/#19-24						13.00

SKELETON KEY (Volume 2)
Amaze Ink: 1999 - No. 4, 1999 ($2.95, B&W)

	GD 2.0	VG 4.0	FN 6.0	VF 8.0	VF/NM 9.0	NM- 9.2
1-4-Andrew Watson-s/a						3.00

SKELETON WARRIORS
Marvel Comics: Apr, 1995 - No. 4, July, 1995 ($1.50)

	GD 2.0	VG 4.0	FN 6.0	VF 8.0	VF/NM 9.0	NM- 9.2
1-4: Based on animated series.						3.00

SKIN GRAFT: THE ADVENTURES OF A TATTOOED MAN
DC Comics (Vertigo): July, 1993 - No. 4, Oct, 1993 ($2.50, lim. series, mature)

	GD 2.0	VG 4.0	FN 6.0	VF 8.0	VF/NM 9.0	NM- 9.2
1-4						3.00

SKINWALKER
Oni Press: May, 2002 - No. 4, Sept, 2002 ($2.95, limited series)

	GD 2.0	VG 4.0	FN 6.0	VF 8.0	VF/NM 9.0	NM- 9.2
1-4-Hurtt & Dela Cruz-a; Talon-c						3.00
1-(5/05) Free Comic Book Day Edition						3.00

SKI PARTY (See Movie Classics)

SKREEMER
DC Comics: May, 1989 - No. 6, Oct, 1989 ($2.00, limited series, mature)

	GD 2.0	VG 4.0	FN 6.0	VF 8.0	VF/NM 9.0	NM- 9.2
1-6: Contains graphic violence; Milligan-s						3.00
TPB (2002, $19.95) r/#1-6						20.00

SKRULL KILL KREW
Marvel Comics: Sept, 1995 - No. 5, Dec, 1995 ($2.95, limited series)

	GD 2.0	VG 4.0	FN 6.0	VF 8.0	VF/NM 9.0	NM- 9.2
1-5: Grant Morrison & Mark Millar scripts; Steve Yeowell-a. 2,3-Cap America app.						5.00
TPB (2006, $16.99) r/#1-5						17.00

SKRULL KILL KREW
Marvel Comics: Jun, 2009 - No. 5, Dec, 2009 ($3.99, limited series)

	GD 2.0	VG 4.0	FN 6.0	VF 8.0	VF/NM 9.0	NM- 9.2
1-5-Felber-s/Robinson-a						4.00

SKRULLS! (Tie-in to Secret Invasion crossover)
Marvel Comics: 2008 ($4.99, one-shot)

	GD 2.0	VG 4.0	FN 6.0	VF 8.0	VF/NM 9.0	NM- 9.2
1-Skrull history, profiles of Skrulls, their allies & foes; checklist of appearances; Horn-c						5.00

SKRULLS VS. POWER PACK (Tie-in to Secret Invasion crossover)
Marvel Comics: Sept, 2008 - No. 4 ($2.99, limited series)

	GD 2.0	VG 4.0	FN 6.0	VF 8.0	VF/NM 9.0	NM- 9.2
1-4-Van Lente-s/Hamscher-a; Franklin Richards app.						3.00

SKUL, THE
Virtual Comics (Byron Preiss Multimedia): Oct, 1996 - No. 3, Dec, 1996 ($2.50, lim. series)

	GD 2.0	VG 4.0	FN 6.0	VF 8.0	VF/NM 9.0	NM- 9.2
1-3: Ron Lim & Jimmy Palmiotti-a						3.00

SKULL & BONES
DC Comics: 1992 - No. 3, 1992 ($4.95, limited series, 52 pgs.)

	GD 2.0	VG 4.0	FN 6.0	VF 8.0	VF/NM 9.0	NM- 9.2
Book 1-3: 1-1st app.						5.00

SKULLKICKERS
Image Comics: Sept, 2010 - Present ($2.99)

	GD 2.0	VG 4.0	FN 6.0	VF 8.0	VF/NM 9.0	NM- 9.2
1-Jim Zubkavich-s/Edwin Huang-a; two covers						4.00
1-(2nd & 3rd printings), 2-18						3.00

Skull, The Slayer #3 © MAR

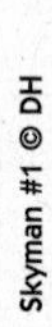

Skyman #1 © DH

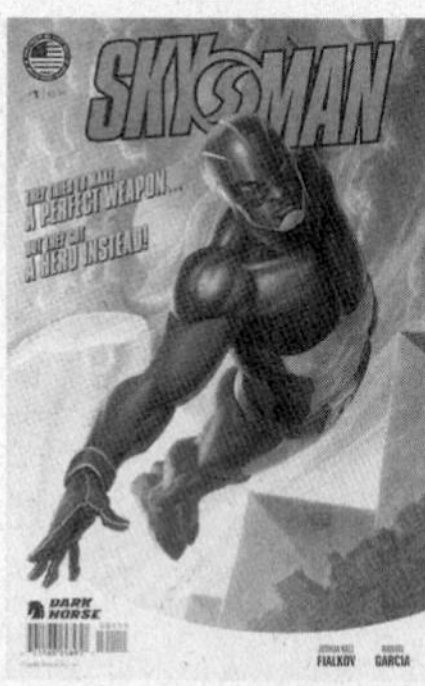

Slam-Bang Comics #2 © FAW

GD VG FN VF VF/NM NM-
2.0 4.0 6.0 8.0 9.0 9.2

24,25: 24-($3.50) "Before Watchmen" cover swipe 3.50
All-New Secret Skullkickers 1 (6/13, $3.50) issue #22; cover swipe of X-Men #125 ('79) 3.50
Dark Skullkickers Dark 1 (7/13, $3.50) issue #23; cover swipe of Green Lantern #85 ('71) 3.50
Savage Skullkickers 1 (3/13, $3.50) issue #20; cover swipe of Savage Wolverine #1 3.50
The Mighty Skullkickers 1 (4/13, $3.50) issue #21; cover swipe of Thor #337 3.50
Uncanny Skullkickers 1 (2/13, $3.50) issue #19 3.50

SKULL, THE SLAYER
Marvel Comics Group: Aug, 1975 - No. 8, Nov, 1976 (20¢/25¢)

1-Origin & 1st app.; Gil Kane-c 2 4 6 13 18 22
2-8: 2-Gil Kane-c. 5,6-(Regular 25¢-c). 8-Kirby-c 2 4 6 8 10 12
5,6-(30¢-c variants, limited distribution)(5,7/76) 3 6 9 17 26 35

SKY BLAZERS (CBS Radio)
Hawley Publications: Sept, 1940 - No. 2, Nov, 1940

1-Sky Pirates, Ace Archer, Flying Aces begin 71 142 213 454 777 1100
2-WWII air battle grey-tone-c 40 80 120 246 411 575

SKY DOLL
Marvel Comics (Soleil): 2008 - No. 3, 2008 ($5.99, mature)

1-3-Barbucci & Canepa-s/a; English version of French comic; preview of other titles 6.00
...: Doll's Factory 1,2 (2009 - No. 2, 2009, $5.99) Barbucci & Canepa-s/a 6.00
...: Lacrima Christi 1,2 (9/10 - No. 2, 10/10, $5.99) Barbucci & Canepa and others-s/a 6.00
...: Space Ship 1,2 (7/10 - No. 2, 8/10, $5.99) Barbucci & Canepa and others-s/a 6.00

SKYE RUNNER
DC Comics (WildStorm): June, 2006 - No. 6, Mar, 2007 ($2.99)

1-6: 1-Three covers; Warner-s/Garza-a. 2-Three covers, incl. Campbell 3.00

SKYMAN (See Big Shot Comics & Sparky Watts)
Columbia Comics Gr.: Fall?, 1941 - No. 2, Fall?, 1942; No. 3, 1948 - No. 4, 1948

1-Origin Skyman, The Face, Sparky Watts app.; Whitney-c/a; 3rd story-r from Big Shot #1; Whitney c-1-4 126 252 378 806 1378 1950
2 (1942)-Yankee Doodle 66 132 198 419 722 1025
3,4 (1948) 40 80 120 246 411 575

SKYMAN (Also see Captain Midnight 2013 series #4)
Dark Horse Comics: Jan, 2014 - Present ($2.99)

1-3: 1-Fialkov-s/Garcia-a; origin of a new Skyman. 3-Captain Midnight app. 3.00

SKYPILOT
Ziff-Davis Publ. Co.: No. 10, 1950(nd) - No. 11, Apr-May, 1951

10,11-Frank Borth-a; Saunders painted-c 15 30 45 86 133 180

SKY RANGER (See Johnny Law...)

SKYROCKET
Harry 'A' Chesler: 1944

nn-Alias the Dragon, Dr. Vampire, Skyrocket & The Desperado app.; WWII Japan zero-c 40 80 120 246 411 575

SKY SHERIFF (Breeze Lawson...) (Also see Exposed & Outlaws)
D. S. Publishing Co.: Summer, 1948

1-Edmond Good-c/a 14 28 42 80 115 150

SKY WOLF (Also see Airboy)
Eclipse Comics: Mar, 1988 - No. 3, Oct, 1988 ($1.25/$1.50/$1.95, lim. series)

1-3 3.00

SLAINE, THE BERSERKER (Slaine the King #21 on)
Quality: July, 1987 - No. 28, 1989 ($1.25/$1.50)

1-28 3.00

SLAINE, THE HORNED GOD
Fleetway: 1998 - No. 3 ($6.99)

1-3-Reprints series from 2000 A.D.; Bisley-a 7.00

SLAM BANG COMICS (Western Desperado #8)
Fawcett Publications: Mar, 1940 - No. 7, Sept, 1940 (Combined with Master Comics #7)

1-Diamond Jack, Mark Swift & The Time Retarder, Lee Granger, Jungle King begin & continue in Master 239 478 717 1530 2615 3700
2 97 194 291 621 1061 1500
3-Classic monster-c (scarce) 256 516 774 1651 2826 4000
4-7: 6-Intro Zoro, the Mystery Man (also in #7) 77 154 231 493 847 1200
Ashcan (1940) Not distributed to newsstands, only for in house use. A copy sold in 2006 for $4,500.

SLAPSTICK
Marvel Comics: Nov, 1992 - No. 4, Feb, 1993 ($1.25, limited series)

1-4: Fry/Austin-c/a. 4-Ghost Rider, D.D., F.F. app. 3.00

GD VG FN VF VF/NM NM-
2.0 4.0 6.0 8.0 9.0 9.2

SLAPSTICK COMICS
Comic Magazines Distributors: nd (1946?) (36 pgs.)

nn-Firetop feature; Post-a(2) 28 56 84 165 270 375

SLASH-D DOUBLECROSS
St. John Publishing Co.: 1950 (Pocket-size, 132 pgs.)

nn-Western comics 21 42 63 124 202 280

SLAUGHTERMAN
Comico: Feb, 1983 - No. 2, 1983 ($1.50, B&W)

1,2 4.00

SLAVE GIRL COMICS (See Malu... & White Princess of the Jungle #2)
Avon Periodicals/Eternity Comics (1989): Feb, 1949 - No. 2, Apr, 1949 (52 pgs.); Mar, 1989 (B&W, 44 pgs)

1-Larsen-c/a 107 214 321 685 1168 1650
2-Larsen-a 74 148 222 470 810 1150
1-(3/89, $2.25, B&W, 44 pgs.)-r/#1 5.00

SLAVE LABOR STORIES
SLG Publishing: May, 2003 (Giveaway, B&W)

1-Free Comic Book Day Edition; short stories by various; Dorkin Milk & Cheese-c 3.00

SLEDGE HAMMER (TV)
Marvel Comics: Feb, 1988 - No. 2, Mar,1988 ($1.00, limited series)

1,2 3.00

SLEDGEHAMMER 44
Dark Horse Comics: Mar, 2013 - No. 2, Apr, 2013 ($3.50, limited series)

1,2-Mignola & Arcudi-s/Latour-a; Mignola-c 3.50

SLEDGEHAMMER 44: THE LIGHTNING WAR
Dark Horse Comics: Nov, 2013 - No. 3, Jan, 2014 ($3.50, limited series)

1-3-Mignola & Arcudi-s/Laurence Campbell-a. 1-Mignola-c. 2,3-Campbell-c 3.50

SLEEPER
DC Comics (WildStorm): Mar, 2003 - No. 12, Mar, 2004 ($2.95)

1-12-Brubaker-s/Phillips-c/a. 3-Back-up preview of The Authority: High Stakes pt. 2 3.00
...: All False Moves TPB (2004, $17.95) r/#7-12 18.00
...: Out in the Cold TPB (2004, $17.95) r/#1-6 18.00

SLEEPER: SEASON TWO
DC Comics (WildStorm): Aug, 2004 - No. 12, July, 2005 ($2.95/$2.99)

1-12-Brubaker-s/Phillips-c/a. 3.00
TPB (2009, $24.99) r/#1-12 25.00
...: A Crooked Line TPB (2005, $17.99) r/#1-6 18.00
...: The Long Way Home TPB (2005, $14.99) r/#7-12 15.00

SLEEPING BEAUTY (See Dell Giants & Movie Comics)
Dell Publishing Co.: No. 973, May, 1959 - No. 984, June, 1959 (Disney)

Four Color 973 (...and the Prince) 10 20 30 64 132 200
Four Color 984 (...Fairy Godmother's) 8 16 24 54 102 150

SLEEPWALKER
Marvel Comics: June, 1991 - No. 33, Feb, 1994 ($1.00/$1.25)

1-1st app. Sleepwalker 4.00
2-33: 4-Williamson-i. 5-Spider-Man-c/stor. 7-Infinity Gauntlet x-over. 8-Vs. Deathlok-c/story. 11-Ghost Rider-c/story. 12-Quesada-c/a(p) 14-Intro Spectra. 15-F.F.-c/story. 17-Darkhawk & Spider-Man x-over. 18-Infinity War x-over; Quesada/Williamson-c. 21,22-Hobgoblin app. 19-($2.00)-Die-cut Sleepwalker mask-c 3.00
25-($2.95, 52 pgs.)-Holo-grafx foil-c; origin 4.00
Holiday Special 1 (1/93, $2.00, 52 pgs.)-Quesada-c(p) 4.00

SLEEPWALKING
Hall of Heroes: Jan, 1996 ($2.50, B&W)

1-Kelley Jones-c 3.00

SLEEPY HOLLOW (Movie Adaption)
DC Comics (Vertigo): 2000 ($7.95, one-shot)

1-Kelley Jones-a/Seagle-s 8.00

SLEEZE BROTHERS, THE
Marvel Comics (Epic Comics): Aug, 1989 - No. 6, Jan, 1990 ($1.75, mature)

1-6: 4-6 (9/89 - 11/89 indicia dates) 3.00
nn-(1991, $3.95, 52 pgs.) 4.00

SLICK CHICK COMICS
Leader Enterprises: 1947(nd) - No. 3, 1947(nd)

1-Teenage humor 16 32 48 94 147 200

Sludge #7 © MAL

Smallville Season 11 #14 © DC

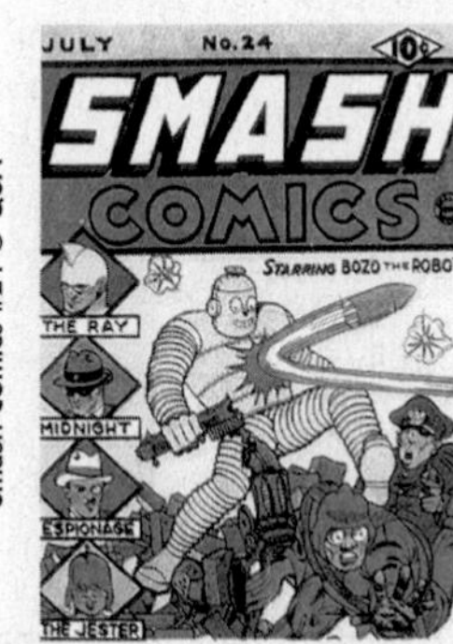

Smash Comics #24 © QUA

	GD	VG	FN	VF	VF/NM	NM-
	2.0	4.0	6.0	8.0	9.0	9.2

GD VG FN VF VF/NM NM- 2.0 4.0 6.0 8.0 9.0 9.2

2,3 12 24 36 67 94 120

SLIDERS (TV)
Acclaim Comics (Armada): June, 1996 - No. 2, July, 1996 ($2.50, lim. series)

1,2: D.G. Chichester scripts; Dick Giordano-a. 3.00

SLIDERS: DARKEST HOUR (TV)
Acclaim Comics (Armada): Oct, 1996 - No. 3, Dec, 1996 ($2.50, limited series)

1-3 3.00

SLIDERS SPECIAL
Acclaim Comics (Armada): Nov, 1996 - No 3, Mar, 1997 ($3.95, limited series)

1-3: 1-Narcotica-Jerry O'Connell-s. 2-Blood and Splendor. 3-Deadly Secrets 4.00

SLIDERS: ULTIMATUM (TV)
Acclaim Comics (Armada): Sept, 1996 - No. 2, Sept, 1996 ($2.50, lim. series)

1,2 3.00

SLIMER! (TV cartoon) (Also see the Real Ghostbusters)
Now Comics: 1989 - No. 19, Feb?, 1991 ($1.75)

1-19: Based on animated cartoon 4.00

SLIM MORGAN (See Wisco)

SLINGERS (See Spider-Man: Identity Crisis issues)
Marvel Comics: Dec, 1998 - No. 12, Nov, 1999 ($2.99/$1.99)

0-(Wizard #88 supplement) Prelude story 3.00
1-($2.99) Four editions w/different covers for each hero, 16 pages common to all, the other pages from each hero's perspective 4.00
2-12: 2-Two-c. 12-Saltares-a 3.00

SLITHISS ATTACKS! (Also see Very Weird Tales)
Oceanspray Comics Group: Dec, 2001 – No. 4, Aug, 2004 ($3.00/$4.00)

1-($3.00) Origin and 1st app. of the monster Slithiss; 1st app. Overconfident Man 15.00
2-($4.00) 2nd app. Overconfident Man; "Chris Lamo" Newport, OR murder parody 12.00
3-($3.00) Rutland Vermont Halloween x-over; 3rd app. Overconfident Man 12.00
4-($3.00) 4th app. Overconfident Man 10.00
Special Edition 1($20.00) reprints #1-2 without letter column 20.00
Special Edition 1($20.00) second printing 20.00
NOTE: *Created in prevention classes taught by Jon McClure at the Oceanspray Family Center in Newport, OR and paid for by the Housing Authority of Lincoln County, all books are b&w with color covers. Bob Overstreet and other comics' professionals wrote letters of encouragement that were published in issues #2-4. Issues #1-2 penciled and inked by various artists; #3-4 penciled by James Gilmer. All comics feature characters created by students, signed and numbered by Jon McClure. Issue #1 had a 200 issue print run, while issues #2-4 have print runs of 100 each. Special Edition #1 had a print run of 26 issues, while the second printing had a 10 issue print run. Ties in with live action movie Face Eater released in 2007 and card game FaceEater released in 2010.*

SLUDGE
Malibu Comics (Ultraverse): Oct, 1993 - No. 12, Dec, 1994 ($2.50/$1.95)

1-($2.50, 48 pgs.)-Intro/1st app. Sludge; Rune flip-c/story Pt. 1 (1st app., 3 pgs.) by Barry Smith; The Night Man app. (3 pg. preview); The Mighty Magnor 1 pg strip begins by Aragonés (cont. in other titles) 4.00
1-Ultra 5000 Limited silver foil 8.00
2-11: 3-Break-Thru x-over. 4-2 pg. Mantra origin. 8-Bloodstorm app. 3.00
12 ($3.50)-Ultraverse Premiere #8 flip book; Alex Ross poster 4.00
...:Red Xmas (12/94, $2.50, 44 pgs.) 4.00

SLUGGER (Little Wise Guys Starring...)(Also see Daredevil Comics)
Lev Gleason Publications: April, 1956

1-Biro-c 7 14 21 37 46 55

SMALLVILLE (Based on TV series)
DC Comics: May, 2003 - No. 11, Jan, 2005 ($3.50/$3.95, bi-monthly)

1-6-Photo-c. 1-Plunkett-a; interviews with cast; season 1 episode guide begins 4.00
7-11-($3.95) 7-Chloe Chronicles begin; season 2 episode guide begins 4.00
Vol. 1 TPB (2004, $9.95) r/#1-4 & Smallville: The Comic; photo-c 10.00

SMALLVILLE SEASON 11 (Based on TV series)
DC Comics: Jul, 2012 - No. 19, Jan, 2014 ($3.99, printings of previously released digital comics)

1-19: 1-Two covers by Gary Frank & Cat Staggs; Pere Perez-a. 5-8-Batman app. 13-15-Legion app. 15-Doomsday app. 16-19-Diana of Themyscira app. 4.00
... Special 1 (7/13, $4.99) Batman, Nightwing and Martian Manhunter app. 5.00
... Special 2 (9/13, $4.99) Lana Lang and John Corben app. 5.00
... Special 3 (12/13, $4.99) Spotlight on Luthor and Tess; Lobel-a 5.00
... Special 4 (3/14, $4.99) Superboy, Jay Garrick, Blue Beetle, Wonder Twins app. 5.00

SMALLVILLE: ALIEN (Based on TV series)
DC Comics: Feb, 2014 - No. 4, May, 2014 ($3.99, printings of previously released digital comics)

1-4: 1-The Monitor lands on Earth; Staggs-a. 2-4-Batman app. 4.00

SMALLVILLE: THE COMIC (Based on TV series)
DC Comics: Nov, 2002 ($3.95, 64 pages, one-shot)

1-Photo-c; art by Martinez and Leon; interviews with cast; season 2 preview 5.00

SMASH COMICS (Becomes Lady Luck #86 on)
Quality Comics Group: Aug, 1939 - No. 85, Oct, 1949

1-Origin Hugh Hazard & His Iron Man, Bozo the Robot, Espionage, Starring Black X by Eisner, & Hooded Justice (Invisible Justice #2 on); Chic Carter & Wings Wendall begin; 1st Robot on the cover of a comic book (Bozo) 331 662 993 2317 4059 5800
2-The Lone Star Rider app; Invisible Hood gains power of invisibility; bondage/torture-c 135 270 405 864 1482 2100
3-Captain Cook & Eisner's John Law begin 76 152 228 486 831 1175
4,5: 4-Flash Fulton begins 73 146 219 467 796 1125
6-12: 12-One pg. Fine-a 69 138 207 442 759 1075
13-Magno begins (8/40); last Eisner issue; The Ray app. in full page ad; The Purple Trio begins 71 142 213 454 777 1100
14-Intro. The Ray (9/40) by Lou Fine & others 300 600 900 2010 3505 5000
15-1st Ray-c, 2nd app. 148 296 444 947 1624 2300
16-The Scarlet Seal begins 129 258 387 826 1413 2000
17-Wun Cloo becomes plastic super-hero by Jack Cole (9-months before Plastic Man); Ray-c 135 270 405 864 1482 2100
18-Midnight by Jack Cole begins (origin & 1st app., 1/41) 171 342 513 1094 1872 2650
19-22: Last Ray by Fine; The Jester begins-#22. 19,21-Ray-c 90 180 270 576 988 1400
23,24: 23-Ray-c. 24-The Sword app.; last Chic Carter; Wings Wendall dons new costume #24,25 68 136 204 435 743 1050
25-Origin/1st app. Wildfire; Rookie Rankin begins; Ray-c 76 152 228 486 831 1175
26-30: 28-Midnight-c begin, end #85 64 128 192 406 696 985
31,32,34: The Ray by Rudy Palais; also #33 54 108 162 346 591 835
33-Origin The Marksman 62 124 186 394 680 965
35-37 49 98 147 309 522 735
38-The Yankee Eagle begins; last Midnight by Jack Cole; classic-c by Cole 102 204 306 653 1114 1575
39,40-Last Ray issue 50 100 150 315 533 750
41,44-50 41 82 123 250 418 585
42-Lady Luck begins by Klaus Nordling 135 270 405 864 1482 2100
43-Lady Luck-c (1st & only in Smash) 77 154 231 493 847 1200
51-60 30 60 90 177 289 400
61-70 23 46 69 136 223 310
71-85: 79-Midnight battles the Men from Mars-c/s 21 42 63 122 199 275
NOTE: ***Al Bryant** c-54, 63-68. **Cole** a-17-38, 68, 69, 72, 73, 78, 80, 83, 85; c-38, 60-62, 69-84. **Crandall** a-(Ray)-23-29, 35-38; c-36, 39, 40, 42-44, 46. **Fine** a(Ray)-14, 15, 16(w/**Tuska**), 17-22. **Fox** c-24-35. **Fuje** Ray-30. **Gil Fox** a-6-7, 9, 11-13. **Guardineer** a-(The Marksman)-39-?, 49, 52. **Gustavson** a-4-7, 9, 11-13 (The Jester)-22-46; (Magno)-13-21; (Midnight)-39(Cole inks), 49, 52, 63-65. **Kotzky** a-(Espionage)-33-38; c-45, 47-53. **Nordling** a-49, 52, 63-65. **Powell** a-11, 12, (Abdul the Arab)-13-24.Black X c-2, 6, 9, 11, 13, 16. Bozo the Robot c-1, 3, 5, 8, 10, 12, 14, 18, 20, 22, 24, 26. Midnight c-28-85. The Ray c-15, 17, 19, 21, 23, 25, 27. Wings Wendall c-4, 7.*

SMASH COMICS (Also see All Star Comics 1999 crossover titles)
DC Comics: May, 1999 ($1.99, one-shot)

1-Golden Age Doctor Mid-nite and Hourman 3.00

SMASH HIT SPORTS COMICS
Essankay Publications: V2#1, Jan, 1949

V2#1-L.B. Cole-c/a 29 58 87 170 278 385

SMAX (Also see Top Ten)
America's Best Comics: Oct, 2003 - No. 5, May, 2004 ($2.95, limited series)

1-5-Alan Moore-s/Zander Cannon-a 3.00
... Collected Edition (2004, $19.95, HC with dustjacket) r/#1-5 20.00
... Collected Edition SC (2005, $12.99) r/#1-5 13.00

SMILE COMICS (Also see Gay Comics, Tickle, & Whee)
Modern Store Publ.: 1955 (52 pgs.; 5x7-1/4") (7¢)

1 7 14 21 35 43 50

SMILEY BURNETTE WESTERN (Also see Patches #8 & Six-Gun Heroes)
Fawcett Publ.: March, 1950 - No. 4, Oct, 1950 (All photo front & back-c)

1-Red Eagle begins 25 50 75 150 245 340
2-4 16 32 48 94 147 200

SMILEY (THE PSYCHOTIC BUTTON) (See Evil Ernie)
Chaos! Comics: July, 1998 - May, 1999 ($2.95, one-shots)

1-Ivan Reis-a 3.00
... Holiday Special (1/99), ...'s Spring Break (4/99), ...Wrestling Special (5/99) 3.00

SMILIN' JACK (See Famous Feature Stories and Popular Comics) (Also see Super Book of Comics #1&2 and Super-Book of Comics #7&19 in the Promotional Comics section)

Smokey the Bear FC #708 © DELL

Snake Woman #10 © Virgin

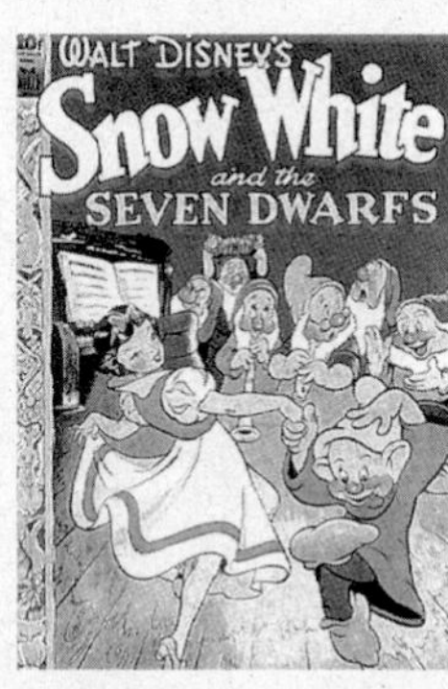

Snow White FC #49 © DIS

Dell Publishing Co.: No. 5, 1940 - No. 8, Oct-Dec, 1949

	GD 2.0	VG 4.0	FN 6.0	VF 8.0	VF/NM 9.0	NM- 9.2
Four Color 5	77	154	231	493	847	1200
Four Color 10 (1940)	65	130	195	416	708	1000
Large Feature Comic 12,14,25 (1941)	61	122	183	390	670	950
Four Color 4 (1942)	35	70	105	252	564	875
Four Color 14 (1943)	27	54	81	194	435	675
Four Color 36,58 (1943-44)	20	40	60	138	307	475
Four Color 80 (1945)	13	26	39	86	188	290
Four Color 149 (1947)	9	18	27	61	123	185
1 (1-3/48)	10	20	30	64	132	200
2	6	12	18	38	69	100
3-8 (10-12/49)	5	10	15	33	57	80

SMILING SPOOK SPUNKY (See Spunky)

SMITTY (See Popular Comics, Super Book #2, 4 & Super Comics)
Dell Publishing Co.: No. 11, 1940 - No. 7, Aug-Oct, 1949; No. 909, Apr, 1958

	GD 2.0	VG 4.0	FN 6.0	VF 8.0	VF/NM 9.0	NM- 9.2
Four Color 11 (1940)	48	96	144	302	514	725
Large Feature Comic 26 (1941)	39	78	117	231	378	525
Four Color 6 (1942)	19	38	57	131	291	450
Four Color 32 (1943)	14	28	42	94	207	320
Four Color 65 (1945)	11	22	33	76	163	250
Four Color 99 (1946)	9	18	27	62	126	190
Four Color 138 (1947)	8	16	24	56	108	160
1 (2-4/48)	8	16	24	55	105	150
2-(5-7/48)	5	10	15	30	50	70
3,4: 3-(8-10/48), 4-(11-1/48-49)	4	8	12	27	44	60
5-7, Four Color 909 (4/58)	4	8	12	23	37	50

SMOKEY BEAR (TV) (See March Of Comics #234, 362, 372, 383, 407)
Gold Key: Feb, 1970 - No. 13, Mar, 1973

	GD 2.0	VG 4.0	FN 6.0	VF 8.0	VF/NM 9.0	NM- 9.2
1	3	6	9	18	28	38
2-5	2	4	6	10	14	18
6-13	2	4	6	8	10	12

SMOKEY STOVER (See Popular Comics, Super Book #5,17,29 & Super Comics)
Dell Publishing Co.: No. 7, 1942 - No. 827, Aug, 1957

	GD 2.0	VG 4.0	FN 6.0	VF 8.0	VF/NM 9.0	NM- 9.2
Four Color 7 (1942)-Reprints	24	48	72	170	378	585
Four Color 35 (1943)	14	28	42	96	211	325
Four Color 64 (1944)	11	22	33	76	163	250
Four Color 229 (1949)	6	12	18	38	69	100
Four Color 730,827	5	10	15	31	53	75

SMOKEY THE BEAR (See Forest Fire for 1st app.)
Dell Publ. Co.: No. 653, 10/55 - No. 1214, 8/61 (See March of Comics #234)

	GD 2.0	VG 4.0	FN 6.0	VF 8.0	VF/NM 9.0	NM- 9.2
Four Color 653 (#1)	9	18	27	62	126	190
Four Color 708,754,818,932	6	12	18	37	66	95
Four Color 1016,1119,1214	4	8	12	28	47	65

SMOKY (See Movie Classics)

SMURFS (TV)
Marvel Comics: 1982 (Dec) - No. 3, 1983

	GD 2.0	VG 4.0	FN 6.0	VF 8.0	VF/NM 9.0	NM- 9.2
1-3	2	4	6	11	16	20
...Treasury Edition 1 (64 pgs.)-r/#1-3	3	6	9	17	26	35

SNAFU (Magazine)
Atlas Comics (RCM): Nov, 1955 - V2#2, Mar, 1956 (B&W)

	GD 2.0	VG 4.0	FN 6.0	VF 8.0	VF/NM 9.0	NM- 9.2
V1#1-Heath/Severin-a; Everett, Maneely-a	16	32	48	94	147	200
V2#1,2-Severin-a	14	28	42	76	108	140

SNAGGLEPUSS (TV)(See Hanna-Barbera Band Wagon, Quick Draw McGraw #5 & Spotlight #4)
Gold Key: Oct, 1962 - No. 4, Sept, 1963 (Hanna-Barbera)

	GD 2.0	VG 4.0	FN 6.0	VF 8.0	VF/NM 9.0	NM- 9.2
1	7	14	21	49	92	135
2-4	6	12	18	37	66	95

SNAKE EYES (G.I. Joe)
Devil's Due Publ.: Aug, 2005 - No. 6, Jan, 2006 ($2.95)

	GD 2.0	VG 4.0	FN 6.0	VF 8.0	VF/NM 9.0	NM- 9.2
1-6-Santalucia-a						3.00
...: Declassified TPB (4/06, $18.95) r/series; source guide						19.00

SNAKE EYES (... and Storm Shadow #13-on)(Cont. from G.I. Joe: Snake Eyes, Volume 2 #7)
IDW Publishing: No. 8, Dec, 2011 - Present ($3.99)

	GD 2.0	VG 4.0	FN 6.0	VF 8.0	VF/NM 9.0	NM- 9.2
8-21: 13-Title change to Snake Eyes and Storm Shadow						4.00

SNAKE PLISSKEN CHRONICLES, (John Carpenter's...)
Hurricane Entertainment: June, 2003 - No. 4 ($2.99)

	GD 2.0	VG 4.0	FN 6.0	VF 8.0	VF/NM 9.0	NM- 9.2
Preview Issue (8/02, no cover price) B&W preview; John Carpenter interview						3.00
1-4: 1-Three covers; Rodriguez-a						3.00

SNAKES AND LADDERS
Eddie Campbell Comics: 2001 ($5.95, B&W, one-shot)

	GD 2.0	VG 4.0	FN 6.0	VF 8.0	VF/NM 9.0	NM- 9.2
nn-Alan Moore-s/Eddie Campbell-a						6.00

SNAKES ON A PLANE (Adaptation of the 2006 movie)
Virgin Comics: Oct, 2006 - No. 2, Nov, 2006 ($2.99, limited series)

	GD 2.0	VG 4.0	FN 6.0	VF 8.0	VF/NM 9.0	NM- 9.2
1,2: 1-Dixon-s/Purcell-a. JG Jones and photo-c. 2-Klebs, Jr.-a; Moore & photo-c						3.00

SNAKE WOMAN (Shekhar Kapur's...)
Virgin Comics: July, 2006 - No. 10, Apr, 2007 ($2.99)

	GD 2.0	VG 4.0	FN 6.0	VF 8.0	VF/NM 9.0	NM- 9.2
1-10: 1-6-Michael Gaydos-a/Zeb Wells-s. 1-Two covers by Gaydos & Singh						3.00
#0 (5/07, 99¢) origin of the Snake Goddess; background info; Gaydos-a/c						3.00
... Curse of the 68 (3/08 - No. 4, 5/08, $2.99) 1-4: 1-Ingale-a. 2-Manu-a						3.00
... Tale of the Snake Charmer 1-6 (6/07-12/07, $2.99) Vivek Shinde-a						3.00
... Vol. 1 TPB (6/07, $14.99) r/#1-5; Gaydos sketch pages; creator commentary						15.00
... Vol. 2 TPB (9/07, $14.99) r/#6-10; Cebulski intro.						15.00

SNAP (Formerly Scoop #8; becomes Jest #10,11 & Komik Pages #10)
Harry 'A' Chesler: No. 9, 1944

	GD 2.0	VG 4.0	FN 6.0	VF 8.0	VF/NM 9.0	NM- 9.2
9-Manhunter, The Voice; WWII gag-c	30	60	90	177	289	400

SNAPPY COMICS
Cima Publ. Co. (Prize Publ.): 1945

	GD 2.0	VG 4.0	FN 6.0	VF 8.0	VF/NM 9.0	NM- 9.2
1-Airmale app.; 9 pg. Sorcerer's Apprentice adapt; Kiefer-a	33	66	99	194	317	440

SNAPSHOT
Image Comics: Feb, 2013 - No. 4, May, 2013 ($2.99, B&W, limited series)

	GD 2.0	VG 4.0	FN 6.0	VF 8.0	VF/NM 9.0	NM- 9.2
1-4-Andy Diggle-s/Jock-a/c						3.00

SNARKED
Boom Entertainment (Kaboom!): No. 0, Aug, 2011 - No. 12, Sept, 2012 ($1.00/$3.99)

	GD 2.0	VG 4.0	FN 6.0	VF 8.0	VF/NM 9.0	NM- 9.2
0-($1.00) Roger Langridge-s/a; sketch gallery, bonus content and games						3.00
1-12: 1-($3.99) Covers by Langridge & Samnee						4.00

SNARKY PARKER (See Life With...)

SNIFFY THE PUP
Standard Publ. (Animated Cartoons): No. 5, Nov, 1949 - No. 18, Sept, 1953

	GD 2.0	VG 4.0	FN 6.0	VF 8.0	VF/NM 9.0	NM- 9.2
5-Two Frazetta text illos	13	26	39	72	101	130
6-10	8	16	24	42	54	65
11-18	7	14	21	37	46	55

SNOOPER AND BLABBER DETECTIVES (TV) (See Whitman Comic Books)
Gold Key: Nov, 1962 - No. 3, May, 1963 (Hanna-Barbera)

	GD 2.0	VG 4.0	FN 6.0	VF 8.0	VF/NM 9.0	NM- 9.2
1	6	12	18	41	76	110
2,3	5	10	15	33	57	80

SNOW WHITE (See Christmas With... (in Promotional Comics section), Mickey Mouse Magazine, Movie Comics & Seven Dwarfs)
Dell Publishing Co.: No. 49, July, 1944 - No. 382, Mar, 1952 (Disney-Movie)

	GD 2.0	VG 4.0	FN 6.0	VF 8.0	VF/NM 9.0	NM- 9.2
Four Color 49 (...& the Seven Dwarfs)	46	92	138	340	770	1200
Four Color 382 (1952)-origin; partial reprint of Four Color 49	9	18	27	59	117	175

SNOW WHITE
Marvel Comics: Jan, 1995 ($1.95, one-shot)

	GD 2.0	VG 4.0	FN 6.0	VF 8.0	VF/NM 9.0	NM- 9.2
1-r/1937 Sunday newspaper pages						3.00

SNOW WHITE AND THE SEVEN DWARFS
Whitman Publications: April, 1982 (60¢)

	GD 2.0	VG 4.0	FN 6.0	VF 8.0	VF/NM 9.0	NM- 9.2
nn-r/Four Color 49	1	3	4	6	8	10

SNOW WHITE AND THE SEVEN DWARFS GOLDEN ANNIVERSARY
Gladstone: Fall, 1987 ($2.95, magazine size, 52 pgs.)

	GD 2.0	VG 4.0	FN 6.0	VF 8.0	VF/NM 9.0	NM- 9.2
1-Contains poster	2	4	6	9	13	16

SOAP OPERA LOVE
Charlton Comics: Feb, 1983 - No. 3, June, 1983

	GD 2.0	VG 4.0	FN 6.0	VF 8.0	VF/NM 9.0	NM- 9.2
1-3-Low print run	3	6	9	19	30	40

SOAP OPERA ROMANCES
Charlton Comics: July, 1982 - No. 5, March, 1983

	GD 2.0	VG 4.0	FN 6.0	VF 8.0	VF/NM 9.0	NM- 9.2
1-5-Nurse Betsy Crane-r; low print run	3	6	9	19	30	40

SOCK MONKEY
Dark Horse Comics: Sept, 1998 - No. 2, Oct, 1998 ($2.95/$2.99, B&W)

	GD 2.0	VG 4.0	FN 6.0	VF 8.0	VF/NM 9.0	NM- 9.2
1,2-Tony Millionaire-s/a						4.00

Vol. 2 -(Tony Millionaire's Sock Monkey) July, 1999 - No. 2, Aug, 1999

Sojourn #4 © CRO

Solar #12 © VAL

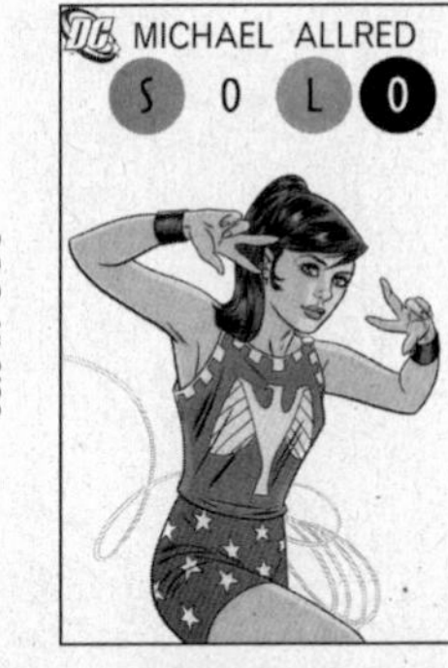

Solo #7 © DC

1,2 3.00

Vol. 3 -(Tony Millionaire's Sock Monkey) Nov, 2000 - No. 2, Dec, 2000

1,2 3.00

Vol. 4 -(Tony Millionaire's Sock Monkey) May, 2003 - No. 2, Aug, 2003

1,2 3.00

...The Inches Incident (Sept, 2006 - No. 4, Apr, 2007) 1-4-Tony Millionaire-s/a 3.00

SOJOURN
White Cliffs Publ. Co.: Sept, 1977 - No. 2, 1978 ($1.50, B&W & color, tabloid size)

1,2: 1-Tor by Kubert, Eagle by Severin, E. V. Race, Private Investigator by Doug Wildey, T. C. Mars by Aragonés begin plus other strips 2 4 6 8 10 12

NOTE: Most copies came folded. Unfolded copies are worth 50% more.

SOJOURN
CrossGeneration Comics: July, 2001 - No. 34, May, 2004 ($2.95)

Prequel -Ron Marz-s/Greg Land-c/a; preview pages 3.00
1-Ron Marz-s/Greg Land-c/a in most 6.00
2,3 5.00
4-24: 7-Immonen-a. 12-Brigman-a. 17-Lopresti-a. 21-Luke Ross-a 3.00
25-34: 25-$1.00-c. 34-Cariello-a 3.00
...: From the Ashes TPB (2001, $19.95) r/#1-6; Land painted-c 20.00
...: The Dragon's Tale TPB (2002, $15.95) r/#7-12; Jusko painted-c 16.00
...: The Warrior's Tale TPB (2003, $15.95) r/#13-18 16.00
Vol. 4: The Thief's Tale (2003, $15.95) r/#19-24 16.00
Vol. 5: The Sorcerer's Tale (Checker Book Publ.,2007, $17.95) r/#25-30 18.00
Vol. 6: The Berzerker's Tale (Checker Book Publ.,2007, $17.95) r/#31-34, Prequel 18.00
Traveler Vol.1,2 ($9.95) digest-sized reprints of TPBs 10.00

SOLAR (...Man of the Atom) (Also see Doctor Solar)
Valiant/Acclaim Comics (Valiant): Sept, 1991 - No. 60, Apr, 1996 ($1.75-$2.50, 44 pgs.)

1-Layton-a(i) on Solar; Barry Windsor-Smith-c/a 2 4 6 9 12 15
2-9: 2-Layton-a(i) on Solar, B. Smith-a. 3-1st app. Harada (11/91). 7-vs. X-O Armor 1 2 3 5 6 8
10-(6/92, $3.95)-1st app. Eternal Warrior (6 pgs.); black embossed-c; origin & 1st app. Geoff McHenry (Geomancer) 3 6 9 15 22 28
10-($3.95)-2nd printing 6.00
11-15: 11-1st full app. Eternal Warrior. 12,13-Unity x-overs. 14-1st app. Fred Bender (becomes Dr. Eclipse). 15-2nd Dr. Eclipse 5.00
16-60: 17-X-O Manowar app. 23-Solar splits. 29-1st Valiant Vision book. 33-Valiant Vision; bound-in trading card. 38-Chaos Effect Epsilon Pt.1. 46-52-Dan Jurgens-a(p)/scripts w/Giordano-i. 53,54-Jurgens scripts only. 60-Giffen scripts; Jeff Johnson-a(p) 4.00
0-($9.95, trade paperback)-r/Alpha and Omega origin story; polybagged w/poster 12.00
...:Second Death (1994, $9.95)-r/issues #1-4. 10.00

NOTE: *#1-10 all have free 8 pg. insert "Alpha and Omega" which is a 10 chapter Solar origin story. All 10 centerfolds can pieced together to show climax of story.* ***Ditko*** *a-11p, 14p.* ***Giordano*** *a-46, 47, 48, 49, 50, 51, 52i.* ***Johnson*** *a-60p.* ***Jurgens*** *a-46, 47, 48, 49, 50 , 51, 52p.* ***Layton*** *a-1-3i; c-2i, 11i, 17i, 25i.* ***Miller*** *c-12.* ***Quesada*** *c-17p, 20-23p, 29p.* ***Simonson*** *c-13.* ***B. Smith*** *a-1-10; c-1, 3, 5, 7, 19i.* ***Thibert*** *c-22i, 23i.*

SOLAR LORD
Image Comics: Mar, 1999 - No. 7, Sept, 1999 ($2.50)

1-7-Khoo Fuk Lung-s/a 3.00

SOLARMAN (See Pendulum Ill. Originals)
Marvel Comics: Jan, 1989 - No. 2, May, 1990 ($1.00, limited series)

1,2 3.00

SOLAR, MAN OF THE ATOM (Man of the Atom on cover)
Acclaim Comics (Valiant Heroes): Vol. 2, May, 1997 ($3.95, one-shot, 46 pgs)
(1st Valiant Heroes Special Event)

Vol. 2-Reintro Solar; Ninjak cameo; Warren Ellis scripts; Darick Robertson-a 4.00

SOLAR, MAN OF THE ATOM: HELL ON EARTH
Acclaim Comics (Valiant Heroes): Jan, 1998 - No. 4 ($2.50, limited series)

1-4-Priest-s/ Zircher-a(p) 3.00

SOLAR, MAN OF THE ATOM: REVELATIONS
Acclaim Comics (Valiant Heroes): Nov, 1997 ($3.95, one-shot, 46 pgs.)

1-Krueger-s/ Zircher-a(p) 4.00

SOLDIER & MARINE COMICS (Fightin' Army #16 on)
Charlton Comics (Toby Press of Conn. V1#11): No. 11, Dec, 1954 - No. 15, Aug, 1955; V2#9, Dec, 1956

V1#11 (12/54)-Bob Powell-a 10 20 30 58 79 100
V1#12(2/55)-15: 12-Photo-c. 14-Photo-c; Colan-a 8 16 24 40 50 60
V2#9(Formerly Never Again; Jerry Drummer V2#10 on) 7 14 21 37 46 55

SOLDIER COMICS
Fawcett Publications: Jan, 1952 - No. 11, Sept, 1953

1 14 28 42 76 108 140
2 8 16 24 44 57 70
3-5 8 16 24 42 54 65
6-11: 8-Illo. in **POP** 8 16 24 40 50 60

SOLDIERS OF FORTUNE
American Comics Group (Creston Publ. Corp.): Mar-Apr, 1951 - No. 13, Feb-Mar, 1953

1-Capt. Crossbones by Shelly, Ace Carter, Lance Larson begin 23 46 69 136 223 310
2 14 28 42 81 118 155
3-10: 6-Bondage-c 12 24 36 69 97 125
11-13 (War format) 9 18 27 47 61 75

NOTE: ***Shelly*** *a-1-3, 5.* ***Whitney*** *a-6, 8-11, 13; c-1-3, 5, 6.*

SOLDIERS OF FREEDOM
Americomics: 1987 - No. 2, 1987 ($1.75)

1,2 3.00

SOLDIER X (Continued from Cable)
Marvel Comics: Sept, 2002 - No. 12, Aug, 2003 ($2.99/$2.25)

1,10,11,12-($2.99) 1-Kordey-a/Macan-s. 10-Bollers-s/Ranson-a 3.00
2-9-($2.25) 3.00

SOLDIER ZERO (From Stan Lee)
BOOM! Studios: Oct, 2010 - No. 12, Sept, 2011 ($3.99)

1-12: 1-4-Cornell-s/Pina-a 4.00

SOLITAIRE (Also See Prime V2#6-8)
Malibu Comics (Ultraverse): Nov, 1993 - No. 12, Dec, 1994 ($1.95)

1-($2.50)-Collector's edition bagged w/playing card 4.00
1-12: 1-Regular edition w/o playing card. 2,4-Break-Thru x-over. 3-2 pg. origin The Night Man. 4-Gatefold-c. 5-Two pg. origin the Strangers 3.00

SOLO
Marvel Comics: Sept, 1994 - No. 4, Dec, 1994 ($1.75, limited series)

1-4: Spider-Man app. 3.00

SOLO (Movie)
Dark Horse Comics: July, 1996 - No. 2, Aug, 1996 ($2.50, limited series)

1,2: Adaptation of film; photo-c 3.00

SOLO (Anthology showcasing individual artists)
DC Comics: Dec, 2004 - No. 12, Oct, 2006 ($4.95/$4.99)

1-11: 1-Tim Sale-a; stories by Sale and various. 2-Richard Corben-a; stories by Corben and Arcudi. 3-Paul Pope. 4-Howard Chaykin. 5-Darwyn Cooke. 6-Jordi Bernet. 7-Michael Allred; Teen Titans & Doom Patrol app. 8-Teddy Kristiansen. 9-Scott Hampton. 10-Damion Scott. 11-Sergio Aragonés. 12-Brendan McCarthy 5.00

SOLO AVENGERS (Becomes Avenger Spotlight #21 on)
Marvel Comics: Dec, 1987 - No. 20, July, 1989 (75¢/$1.00)

1-Jim Lee-a on back-up story 6.00
2-20: 11-Intro Bobcat 4.00

SOLOMON AND SHEBA (Movie)
Dell Publishing Co.: No. 1070, Jan-Mar, 1960

Four Color 1070-Sekowsky-a; photo-c 8 16 24 51 96 140

SOLOMON GRUNDY
DC Comics: May, 2009 - No. 7, Nov, 2009 ($2.99)

1-7-Scott Kolins-s/a. 2-Bizarro app. 7-Blackest Night prelude 3.00
TPB (2010, $19.99) r/#1-7 20.00

SOLOMON KANE (Based on the Robert E. Howard character. Also see Blackthorne 3-D Series #60 & Marvel Premiere)
Marvel Comics: Sept, 1985 - No. 6, July, 1986 (Limited series)

1-Double size 5.00
2-6: 3-6-Williamson-a(i) 4.00

SOLOMON KANE
Dark Horse Comics: Sept, 2008 - No. 5, Feb, 2009 ($2.99)

1-5: 1-Two covers by Cassaday and Joe Kubert; Guevara-a 3.00
...: Death's Black Riders 1-4 (1/10 - No. 4, 6/10, $3.50) Robertson-c 3.50
...: Red Shadows 1-4 (4/11 - No. 4, 7/11, $3.50) Bruce Jones-s/Rahsan Ekedal-a; two covers by Davis & Manchess on each 3.50

SOLUS
CG Entertainment, Inc.: Apr, 2003 - No. 8, Jan, 2004 ($2.95)

1-8: 1-4,6,7-George Pérez-a/c; Barbara Kesel-s. 5-Ryan-a. 8-Kirk-a 3.00
Vol. 1: Genesis (1/04, $15.95) r/#1-6 16.00

Sonic the Hedgehog #6 © SEGA

Son of Satan #2 © MAR

Sons of Anarchy #5 © 20th Cent. Fox

GD VG FN VF VF/NM NM-
2.0 4.0 6.0 8.0 9.0 9.2

SOLUTION, THE
Malibu Comics (Ultraverse): Sept, 1993 - No. 17, Feb, 1995 ($1.95)
1,3-15: 1-Intro Meathook, Deathdance, Black Tiger, Tech. 4-Break-Thru x-over; gatefold-c. 5-2 pg. origin The Strangers. 11-Brereton-c 3.00
1-($2.50)-Newsstand ed. polybagged w/trading card 4.00
1-Ultra 5000 Limited silver foil 8.00
0-Obtained w/Rune #0 by sending coupons from 11 comics 5.00
2-($2.50, 48 pgs.)-Rune flip-c/story by B. Smith; The Mighty Magnor 1 pg. strip by Aragonés 4.00
16 ($3.50)-Flip-c Ultraverse Premiere #10 4.00
17 ($2.50) 3.00

SOMERSET HOLMES (See Eclipse Graphic Novel Series)
Pacific Comics/ Eclipse Comics No. 5, 6: Sept, 1983 - No. 6, Dec, 1984 ($1.50, Baxter paper)
1-6: 1-Brent Anderson-c/a. Cliff Hanger by Williamson in all 4.00

SONG OF THE SOUTH (See Brer Rabbit)

SONIC & KNUCKLES
Archie Comics: Aug, 1995 ($2.00)
1 1 3 4 6 8 10

SONIC DISRUPTORS
DC Comics: Dec, 1987 - No. 7, July, 1988 ($1.75, unfinished limited series)
1-7 3.00

SONIC'S FRIENDLY NEMESIS KNUCKLES
Archie Publications: July, 1996 - No. 3, Sept, 1996 ($1.50, limited series)
1-3 6.00

SONIC SUPER SPECIAL
Archie Publications: 1997 - No. 15, Feb, 2001 ($2.00/$2.25/$2.29, 48 pgs)
1-3 5.00
4-6,8-15: 10-Sabrina-c/app. 15-Sin City spoof 4.00
7-(w/Image) Spawn, Maxx, Savage Dragon-c/app.; Valentino-a 4.00

SONIC SUPER SPECIAL DIGEST
Archie Publications: Dec, 2012 - Present ($3.99)
1-11 4.00

SONIC THE HEDGEHOG (TV, video game)
Archie Comics: No. 0, Feb, 1993 - No. 3, May, 1993 ($1.25, mini-series)
0(2/93),1: Shaw-a(p) & covers on all 4 8 12 23 37 50
2,3 3 6 9 16 23 30
Beginnings TPB (2003, $10.95) r/#0-3 11.00
...: The Beginning TPB (2006, $10.95) r/#0-3 11.00

SONIC THE HEDGEHOG (TV, video game)
Archie Comics: July, 1993 - Present ($1.25-$2.99)
1 4 8 12 27 44 60
2,3 3 6 9 16 23 30
4-10: 8-Neon ink-c. 2 4 6 11 16 20
11-20 2 4 6 9 13 16
21-30 ($1.50): 25-Silver ink-c 2 4 6 8 10 12
31-50 1 2 3 5 6 8
51-93 4.00
94-212: 117-Begin $2.19-c. 152-Begin $2.25-c. 157-Shadow app. 198-Begin $2.50 3.00
213-249,251-259: 213-Begin $2.99-c. 248-258-Two covers 3.00
250-($3.99) Wraparound-c; part 9 of Worlds Collide x-over with Mega Man 4.00
Free Comic Book Day Edition 1 (2007)- Leads into Sonic the Hedgehog #175 3.00
Free Comic Book Day Edition 2009 - Reprints Sonic the Hedgehog #1 from July 1993 3.00
Free Comic Book Day Edition 2010 - 2012: 2010-New story 3.00
Sonic and Mega Man: World's Collide Prelude, FCBD Edition (6-7/13) 3.00
Triple Trouble Special (10/95, $2.00, 48 pgs.) 1 3 4 6 8 10

SONIC UNIVERSE (Sonic the Hedgehog)
Archie Publications: Apr, 2009 - Present ($2.50/$2.99)
1-15 3.00
16-62: 16-Begin $2.99-c. 51-62-Two covers. 51-54-Worlds Collide 3.00

SONIC VS. KNUCKLES "BATTLE ROYAL" SPECIAL
Archie Publications: 1997 ($2.00, one-shot)
1 1 2 3 5 6 8

SONIC X (Sonic the Hedgehog)
Archie Publications: Nov, 2005 - No. 40, Feb, 2009 ($2.25)
1-Sam Speed app. 4.00
2-40 3.00

SON OF AMBUSH BUG (See Ambush Bug)
DC Comics: July, 1986 - No. 6, Dec, 1986 (75¢)
1-6: Giffen-c/a in all. 5-Bissette-a. 4.00

SON OF BLACK BEAUTY (Also see Black Beauty)
Dell Publishing Co.: No. 510, Oct, 1953 - No. 566, June, 1954
Four Color 510, 566 4 8 12 27 44 60

SON OF FLUBBER (See Movie Comics)

SON OF HULK (Continues from Skaar: Son of Hulk #12) (See Realm of Kings)
Marvel Comics: No. 13, Sept, 2009 - No. 17, Jan, 2010 ($2.99)
13-17: 13,15-17-Galactus app. 3.00

SON OF M (Also see House of M series)
Marvel Comics: Feb, 2006 - No. 6, July, 2006 ($2.99, limited series)
1-6: 1-Powerless Quicksilver; Martinez-a. 2-Quicksilver regains powers; Inhumans app. 3.00
Decimation: Son of M (2006, $13.99, TPB) r/series; Martinez sketch pages 14.00

SON OF MERLIN
Image Comics (Top Cow): Feb, 2013 - No. 5, Jun, 2013 ($1.00/$2.99, limited series)
1-5: 1-($1.00-c); Napton-s/Zid-a; covers by Zid & Sejic. 2-($2.99) 3.00

SON OF MUTANT WORLD
Fantagor Press: 1990 - No. 5, 1990? ($2.00, bi-monthly)
1-5: 1-3: Corben-c/a. 4,5 ($1.75, B&W) 3.00

SON OF ORIGINS OF MARVEL COMICS (See Fireside Book Series)

SON OF SATAN (Also see Ghost Rider #1 & Marvel Spotlight #12)
Marvel Comics Group: Dec, 1975 - No. 8, Feb, 1977 (25¢)
1-Mooney-a; Kane-c(p), Starlin splash(p) 3 6 9 18 27 40
2,6-8: 2-Origin The Possessor. 8-Heath-a 2 4 6 10 14 18
3-5-(Regular 25¢ editions)(4-8/76): 5-Russell-p 2 4 6 10 14 18
3-5-(30¢-c variants, limited distribution) 4 8 12 20 30 40

SON OF SINBAD (Also see Abbott & Costello & Daring Adventures)
St. John Publishing Co.: Feb, 1950
1-Kubert-c/a 51 102 153 318 539 760

SON OF SUPERMAN (Elseworlds)
DC Comics: 1999 ($14.95, prestige format, one-shot)
nn-Chaykin & Tischman-s/Williams III & Gray-a 15.00

SON OF TOMAHAWK (See Tomahawk)

SON OF VULCAN (Formerly Mysteries of Unexplored Worlds #1-48; Thunderbolt V3#51 on)
Charlton Comics: V2#49, Nov, 1965 - V2#50, Jan, 1966
V2#49,50: 50-Roy Thomas scripts (1st pro work) 3 6 9 17 26 35

SONS OF ANARCHY (Based on the TV series)
BOOM! Studios: Sept, 2013 - Present ($3.99, originally a 6-issue limited series)
1-8: 1-6-Christopher Golden-s/Damian Couceiro-a; multiple covers on each 4.00

SONS OF KATIE ELDER (See Movie Classics)

SORCERY (See Chilling Adventures in... & Red Circle...)

SORORITY SECRETS
Toby Press: July, 1954
1 12 24 36 67 94 120

SOULFIRE (MICHAEL TURNER PRESENTS:...)
Aspen MLT, Inc.: No. 0, 2004 - No. 10, Jul, 2009 ($2.50/$2.99)
0-($2.50) Turner-a/c; Loeb-s; intro. to characters & development sketches 3.00
1-($2.99) Two covers 3.00
1-Diamond Previews Exclusive 5.00
2-9: 2,3-Two covers. 4-Four covers 3.00
10-($3.99) Benitez-a 4.00
...: The Collected Edition Vol. 1 (5/05, $6.99) r/#1,2; cover gallery 7.00
Hardcover Volume 1 (12/05, $24.99) r/#0-5 & preview from Wizard Mag.; Johns intro. 25.00

SOULFIRE (MICHAEL TURNER PRESENTS:...) (Volume 2)
Aspen MLT, Inc.: No. 0, Oct, 2009 - No. 9, Jan, 2011 ($2.50/$2.99)
0-($2.50) Marcus To-a 3.00
1-9-($2.99) 1-Five covers. 9-Covers by To and Linsner 3.00

SOULFIRE (MICHAEL TURNER'S...) (Volume 3)
Aspen MLT, Inc.: No. 0, Apr, 2011 - No. 8, May, 2012 ($1.99/$2.99)
0-($1.99) Krul-s/Fabok-a; 4 covers 3.00
1-8-($2.99) 1-Four covers 3.00

Soulfire V4 #7 © Aspen MLT

Sovereign Seven #36 © C. Claremont

Space Adventures #3 © CC

	GD 2.0	VG 4.0	FN 6.0	VF 8.0	VF/NM 9.0	NM- 9.2
... Despair (7/12, $3.99) Schwartz-s/Marks-a; 3 covers						4.00
... Faith (7/12, $3.99) McMurray-s/Oum-a; 3 covers						4.00
... Hope (7/12, $3.99) Krul-s/Varese-a; 3 covers						4.00
... Power (7/12, $3.99) Wohl-s/Randolph-a; 3 covers						4.00
... Primer (6/12, $1.00) Reprints and story summaries						3.00

SOULFIRE (MICHAEL TURNER'S...) (Volume 4)
Aspen MLT, Inc.: Aug, 2012 - No. 8, Oct, 2013 ($3.99)

1-8-Krul-s/DeBalfo-a; multiple covers on each — 4.00

SOULFIRE (MICHAEL TURNER'S...) (Volume 5)
Aspen MLT, Inc.: Nov, 2013 - Present ($1.00/$3.99)

1-($1.00) Krul-s/Marion-a; multiple covers — 3.00
2,3-($3.99) Multiple covers on each — 4.00

SOULFIRE: CHAOS REIGN
Aspen MLT, Inc.: No. 0, June, 2006 - No. 3, Jan, 2007 ($2.50/$2.99)

0-($2.50) Three covers; Marcus To-a; J.T. Krul-s — 3.00
1-3-($2.99) 1-Three covers — 3.00
...: Beginnings (7/06, $1.99) Marcus To-a; J.T. Krul-s — 3.00
...: Beginnings 1 (7/07, $1.99) Francisco Herrera-a; J.T. Krul-s — 3.00

SOULFIRE: DYING OF THE LIGHT
Aspen MLT, Inc.: No. 0, 2004 - No. 5, Feb, 2006 ($2.50/$2.99)

0-($2.50) Three covers; Gunnell-a; Krul-s; back-story to the Soulfire universe — 3.00
1-5-($2.99) 1-Five covers — 3.00
... Vol. 1 TPB (2007, $14.99) r/#0-5; Gunnell sketch pages, cover gallery — 15.00

SOULFIRE: NEW WORLD ORDER
Aspen MLT, Inc.: No. 0, Jul, 2007; May, 2009 - No. 5, Dec, 2009 ($2.50/$2.99)

0 (7/07, $2.50) Two covers; Herrera-a/Krul-s — 3.00
1-5-($2.99) 1-Four covers — 3.00

SOULFIRE: SHADOW MAGIC
Aspen MLT, Inc.: No. 0, Nov, 2008 - No. 5, May, 2009 ($2.50/$2.99)

0-($2.50) Two covers; Sana Takeda-a — 3.00
1-5-($2.99) 1-Two covers — 3.00

SOUL SAGA
Image Comics (Top Cow): Feb, 2000 - No. 5, Apr, 2001 ($2.50)

1-5: 1-Madureira-c; Platt & Batt-a — 3.00

SOULSEARCHERS AND COMPANY
Claypool Comics: June, 1995 - No. 82, Jan, 2007 ($2.50, B&W)

1-10: Peter David scripts — 5.00
11-25 — 3.00
26-82 — 3.00

SOULWIND
Image Comics: Mar, 1997 - No. 8 ($2.95, B&W, limited series)

1-8: 5-"The Day I Tried To Live" pt. 1 — 3.00
Book Five; The August Ones (Oni Press, 3/01, $8.50) — 8.50
...The Kid From Planet Earth (1997, $9.95, TPB) — 10.00
...The Kid From Planet Earth (Oni Press, 1/00, $8.50, TPB) — 8.50
...The Day I Tried to Live (Oni Press, 4/00, $8.50, TPB) — 8.50
The Complete Soulwind TPB ($29.95, 11/03, 8" x 5 1/2") r/Oni Books #1-5 — 30.00

SOUPY SALES COMIC BOOK (TV)(The Official...)
Archie Publications: 1965

	GD	VG	FN	VF	VF/NM	NM-
1	8	16	24	52	99	145

SOUTHERN KNIGHTS, THE (See Crusaders #1)
Guild Publ/Fictioneer Books: No. 2, 1983 - No. 41, 1993 (B&W)

	GD	VG	FN	VF	VF/NM	NM-
2-Magazine size	1	2	3	5	6	8
3-35, 37-41						3.00
36-($3.50-c)						4.00
Dread Halloween Special 1, Primer Special 1 (Spring, 1989, $2.25)						3.00
Graphic Novels #1-4						4.00

SOVEREIGN SEVEN (Also see Showcase '95 #12)
DC Comics: July, 1995 - No. 36, July, 1998 ($1.95) (1st creator-owned mainstream DC comic)

1-1st app. Sovereign Seven (Reflex, Indigo, Cascade, Finale, Cruiser, Network & Rampart); 1st app. Maitresse; Darkseid app.; Chris Claremont-s & Dwayne Turner-c/a begins — 4.00
1-Gold — 8.00
1-Platinum — 40.00
2-25: 2-Wolverine cameo. 4-Neil Gaiman cameo. 5,8-Batman app. 7-Ramirez cameo (from the movie Highlander). 9-Humphrey Bogart cameo from Casablanca. 10-Impulse app; Manoli Wetherell & Neal Conan cameo from Uncanny X-Men #226. 11-Robin app. 16-Final Night. 24-Superman app. 25-Power Girl app. — 3.00
26-36: 26-Begin $2.25-c. 28-Impulse-c/app. — 3.00
Annual 1 (1995, $3.95)-Year One story; Big Barda & Lobo app.; Jeff Johnson-c/a — 4.00
Annual 2 (1996, $2.95)-Legends of the Dead Earth; Leonardi-c/a — 4.00
...Plus 1(2/97, $2.95)-Legion-c/app. — 4.00
TPB-($12.95) r/#1-5, Annual #1 & Showcase '95 #12 — 13.00

SPACE: ABOVE AND BEYOND (TV)
Topps Comics: Jan, 1996 - No. 3, Mar, 1996 ($2.95, limited series)

1-3: Adaptation of pilot episode; Steacy-c. — 3.00

SPACE: ABOVE AND BEYOND--THE GAUNTLET (TV)
Topps Comics: May, 1996 -No. 2, June, 1996 ($2.95, limited series)

1,2 — 3.00

SPACE ACE (Also see Manhunt!)
Magazine Enterprises: No. 5, 1952

	GD	VG	FN	VF	VF/NM	NM-
5(A-1 #61)-Guardineer-a	60	120	180	381	653	925

SPACE ACE: DEFENDER OF THE UNIVERSE (Based on the Don Bluth video game)
CrossGen Comics: Oct, 2003 - No. 6 ($2.95, limited series)

1,2-Kirkman-s/Borges-a — 3.00

SPACE ACTION
Ace Magazines (Junior Books): June, 1952 - No. 3, Oct, 1952

	GD	VG	FN	VF	VF/NM	NM-
1-Cameron-a in all (1 story)	82	164	246	528	902	1275
2,3	55	110	165	352	601	850

SPACE ADVENTURES (War At Sea #22 on)
Capitol Stories/Charlton Comics: 7/52 - No. 21, 8/56; No. 23, 5/58 - No. 59, 11/64; V3#60, 10/67; V1#2, 7/68 - V1#8, 7/69; No. 9, 5/78 - No. 13, 3/79

	GD	VG	FN	VF	VF/NM	NM-
1-Fago/Morales world on fire-c	60	120	180	381	653	925
2	30	60	90	177	289	400
3-5: 4,6-Flying saucer-c/stories	24	48	72	142	234	325
6-9: 7-Sex change story "Transformation". 8-Robot-c. 9-A-Bomb panel	22	44	66	132	216	300
10,11-Ditko-c/a. 10-Robot-c. 11-Two Ditko stories	57	114	171	362	619	875
12-Ditko-c (classic)	123	246	369	787	1344	1900
13-(Fox-r, 10-11/54); Blue Beetle-c/story	16	32	48	94	147	200
14,15,17,18: 14-Blue Beetle-c/story; Fox-r (12-1/54-55, last pre-code). 15,17,18-Rocky Jones-c/s.(TV); 15-Part photo-c	20	40	60	118	192	265
16-Krigstein-a; Rocky Jones-c/story (TV)	22	44	66	128	209	290
19	15	30	45	88	137	185
20-Reprints Fawcett's "Destination Moon"	22	44	66	132	216	300
21-(8/56) (no #22)(Becomes War At Sea)	15	30	45	88	137	185
23-(5/58; formerly Nyoka, The Jungle Girl)-Reprints Fawcett's "Destination Moon"	20	40	60	118	192	265
24,25,31,32-Ditko-a. 24-Severin-a(signed "LePoer")	20	40	60	118	192	265
26,27-Ditko-a(4) each. 26,28-Flying saucer-c	21	42	63	126	206	285
28-30	11	22	33	64	90	115
33-Origin/1st app. Capt. Atom by Ditko (3/60)	52	104	156	328	552	775
34-40,42-All Captain Atom by Ditko	21	42	63	124	202	280
41,43,45-59: 43-Alan Shephard strory, 2nd man in space. 45-Mercury Man app.	5	10	15	30	50	70
44-1st app. Mercury Man	5	10	15	31	53	75
V3#60(#1, 10/67)-Presents UFO origin & 1st app. Paul Mann & The Saucers From the Future	5	10	15	30	50	70
2,5,6,8 (1968-69)-Ditko-a: 2-Aparo-c/a	3	6	9	19	30	40
3,4,7: 4-Aparo-c/a	3	6	9	16	23	30
9-13(1978-79)-Capt. Atom-r/Space Adventures by Ditko; 9-Reprints origin/1st app. Capt. Atom from #33						6.00

NOTE: ***Aparo** a-V3#60. c-V3#8. **Ditko** c-12, 31-42. **Giordano** c-3, 4, 7-9, 18p. **Krigstein** c-15. **Shuster** a-11. Issues 13 & 14 have Blue Beetle logos; #15-18 have Rocky Jones logos.*

SPACE BUSTERS
Ziff-Davis Publ. Co.: Spring, 1952 - No. 2, Fall, 1952

	GD	VG	FN	VF	VF/NM	NM-
1-Krigstein-a(3); Painted-c by Norman Saunders	86	172	258	546	936	1325
2-Kinstler-a(2 pgs.); Saunders painted-c	66	132	198	419	722	1025

NOTE: ***Anderson** a-2. Bondage c-2.*

SPACE CADET (See Tom Corbett,...)

SPACE CIRCUS
Dark Horse Comics: July, 2000 - No. 4, Oct, 2000 ($2.95, limited series)

1-4-Aragonés-a/Evanier-s — 3.00

SPACE COMICS (Formerly Funny Tunes)
Avon Periodicals: No. 4, Mar-Apr, 1954 - No. 5, May-June, 1954

4,5-Space Mouse, Peter Rabbit, Super Pup (formerly Spotty the Pup), & Merry Mouse

Spaced #12 © ECL

Spaceman #5 © MAR

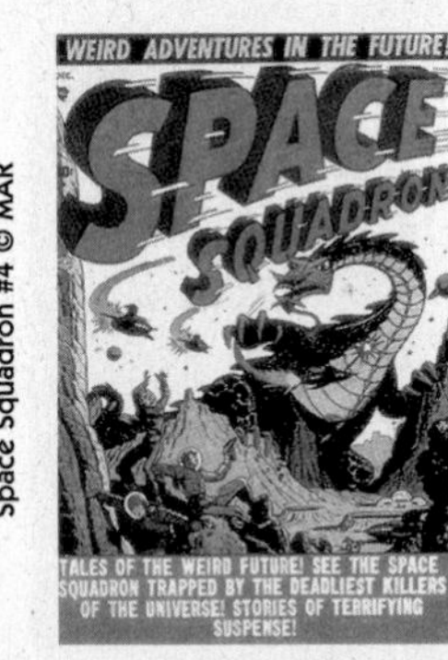

Space Squadron #4 © MAR

GD VG FN VF VF/NM NM-
2.0 4.0 6.0 8.0 9.0 9.2

continue from Funny Tunes 8 16 24 44 57 70
I.W. Reprint #8 (nd)-Space Mouse-r 2 4 6 8 11 14

SPACED
Anthony Smith Publ. #1,2/Unbridled Ambition/Eclipse Comics #10 on: 1982 - No. 13, 1988 ($1.25/$1.50, B&W, quarterly)
1-($1.25-c) 4.00
2-13, Special Edition (1983, Mimeo) 3.00

SPACE DETECTIVE
Avon Periodicals: July, 1951 - No. 4, July, 1952
1-Rod Hathway, Space Detective begins, ends #4; Wood-c/a(3)-23 pgs.; "Opium Smugglers of Venus" drug story; Lucky Dale-r/Saint #4 135 270 405 864 1482 2100
2-Tales from the Shadow Squad story; Wood/Orlando-c; Wood inside layouts; "Slave Ship of Saturn" story 103 206 309 659 1130 1600
3,4: 3-Kinstler-c. 4-Kinstlerish-a by McCann 48 96 144 302 514 725
I.W. Reprint #1(Reprints #2), 8(Reprints cover #1 & part Famous Funnies #191) 4 8 12 23 37 50

SPACE EXPLORER (See March of Comics #202)

SPACE FAMILY ROBINSON (TV)(...Lost in Space #15-37, ...Lost in Space On Space Station One #38 on)(See Gold Key Champion)
Gold Key: Dec, 1962 - No. 36, Oct, 1969; No. 37, 10/73 - No. 54, 11/78; No. 55, 3/81 - No. 59, 5/82 (All painted covers)
1-(Low distribution); Spiegle-a in all 25 50 75 175 388 600
2(3/63)-Family becomes lost in space 11 22 33 73 157 240
3-5 7 14 21 46 86 125
6-10: 6-Captain Venture back-up stories begin 6 12 18 37 66 95
11-20: 14-(10/65). 15-Title change (1/66) 4 8 12 28 47 65
21-36: 28-Last 12¢ issue. 36-Captain Venture ends 3 6 9 21 33 45
37-48: 37-Origin retold 2 4 6 10 14 18
49-59: Reprints #49,50,55-59 2 4 6 8 10 12
NOTE: *The TV show first aired on 9/15/65. Title changed after TV show debuted.*

SPACE FAMILY ROBINSON (See March of Comics #320, 328, 352, 404, 414)

SPACE GHOST (TV) (Also see Golden Comics Digest #2 & Hanna-Barbera Super TV Heroes #3-7)
Gold Key: March, 1967 (Hanna-Barbera) (TV debut was 9/10/66)
1 (10199-703)-Spiegle-a 25 50 75 175 388 600

SPACE GHOST (TV cartoon)
Comico: Mar, 1987 ($3.50, deluxe format, one-shot) (Hanna-Barbera)
1-Steve Rude-c/a 2 4 6 9 12 15

SPACE GHOST (TV cartoon)
DC Comics: Jan, 2005 - No. 6, June, 2005 ($2.95/$2.99, limited series)
1-6-Alex Ross-c/Ariel Olivetti-a/Joe Kelly-s; origin of Space Ghost 3.00
TPB (2005, $14.99) r/series; cover gallery 15.00

SPACE GIANTS, THE (TV cartoon)
FBN Publications: 1979 ($1.00, B&W, one-shots)
1-Based on Japanese TV series 2 4 6 9 12 15

SPACEHAWK
Dark Horse Comics: 1989 - No. 3, 1990 ($2.00, B&W)
1-3-Wolverton-c/a(r) plus new stories by others. 4.00

SPACE JAM
DC Comics: 1996 ($5.95, one-shot, movie adaption)
1-Wraparound photo cover of Michael Jordan 1 2 3 5 6 8

SPACE KAT-ETS (...in 3-D)
Power Publishing Co.: Dec, 1953 (25¢, came w/glasses)
1 30 60 90 177 289 400

SPACEKNIGHTS
Marvel Comics: Oct, 2000 - No. 5, Feb, 2001 ($2.99, limited series)
1-5-Starlin-s/Batista-a 3.00

SPACEKNIGHTS
Marvel Comics: Dec, 2012 - No. 3, Feb, 2013 ($3.99, limited series)
1-3-Reprints the 2000-2001 series & Annihilation: Conquest Prologue 4.00

SPACEMAN (Speed Carter...)
Atlas Comics (CnPC): Sept, 1953 - No. 6, July, 1954
1-Grey tone-c 90 180 270 576 988 1400
2 48 96 144 302 514 725
3-6: 4-A-Bomb explosion-c 42 84 126 265 445 625
NOTE: ***Everett** c-1, 3. **Heath** a-1. **Maneely** a-1(3), 2(4), 3(3), 4-6; c-5, 6. **Romita** a-1. **Sekowsky** c-4.*
***Sekowsky/Abel** a-4(3). **Tuska** a-5(3).*

GD VG FN VF VF/NM NM-
2.0 4.0 6.0 8.0 9.0 9.2

SPACE MAN
Dell Publ. Co.: No. 1253, 1-3/62 - No. 8, 3-5/64; No. 9, 7/72 - No. 10, 10/72
Four Color 1253 (#1)(1-3/62)(15¢-c) 7 14 21 44 82 120
2,3: 2-(15¢-c). 3-(12¢-c) 4 8 12 27 44 60
4-8-(12¢-c) 3 6 9 21 33 45
9,10-(15¢-c): 9-Reprints #1253. 10-Reprints #2 2 4 6 9 12 15

SPACEMAN (From the Atomics)
Oni Press: July, 2002 ($2.95, one-shot)
1-Mike Allred-s/a; Lawrence Marvit additional art 3.00

SPACEMAN
DC Comics (Vertigo): Dec, 2011 - No. 9, Oct, 2012 ($1.00/$2.99, limited series)
1-($1.00) Azzarello-s/Risso-a/Johnson-c 4.00
2-9-($2.99) 3.00

SPACE MOUSE (Also see Funny Tunes & Space Comics)
Avon Periodicals: April, 1953 - No. 5, Apr-May, 1954
1 12 24 36 67 94 120
2 8 16 24 42 54 65
3-5 7 14 21 37 46 55

SPACE MOUSE (Walter Lantz...#1; see Comic Album #17)
Dell Publishing Co./Gold Key: No. 1132, Aug-Oct, 1960 - No. 5, Nov, 1963 (Walter Lantz)
Four Color 1132,1244, 1(11/62)(G.K.) 4 8 12 28 47 65
2-5 4 8 12 23 37 50

SPACE MYSTERIES
I.W. Enterprises: 1964 (Reprints)
1-r/Journey Into Unknown Worlds #4 w/new-c 3 6 9 15 22 28
8,9: 9-r/Planet Comics #73 3 6 9 15 22 28

SPACE: 1999 (TV) (Also see Power Record Comics)
Charlton Comics: Nov, 1975 - No. 7, Nov, 1976
1-Origin Moonbase Alpha; Staton-c/a 3 6 9 16 23 30
2,7: 2-Staton-a 2 4 6 13 18 22
3-6: All Byrne-a; c-3,5,6 3 6 9 16 23 30
nn (Charlton Press, digest, 100 pgs., B&W, no cover price) new stories & art 4 8 12 27 44 60

SPACE: 1999 (TV)(Magazine)
Charlton Comics: Nov, 1975 - No. 8, Nov, 1976 (B&W) (#7 shows #6 inside)
1-Origin Moonbase Alpha; Morrow-c/a 3 6 9 15 22 28
2-8: 2,3-Morrow-c/a. 4-6-Morrow-c. 5,8-Morrow-a 2 4 6 11 16 20

SPACE PATROL (TV)
Ziff-Davis Publishing Co. (Approved Comics): Summer, 1952 - No. 2, Oct-Nov, 1952 (Painted-c by Norman Saunders)
1-Krigstein-a 95 190 285 603 1039 1475
2-Krigstein-a(3) 67 134 201 426 731 1035

SPACE PIRATES (See Archie Giant Series #533)

SPACE: PUNISHER
Marvel Comics: Sept, 2012 - No. 4, Dec, 2012 ($3.99, limited series)
1-4-Outer space sci-fi pulp version of the Punisher; Tieri-s/Texeira-a/c 4.00

SPACE RANGER (See Mystery in Space #92, Showcase #15 & Tales of the Unexpected)

SPACE SQUADRON (In the Days of the Rockets)(Becomes Space Worlds #6)
Marvel/Atlas Comics (ACI): June, 1951 - No. 5, Feb, 1952
1-Space team; Brodsky c-1,5 81 162 243 518 884 1250
2: Tuska c-2-4 60 120 180 381 653 925
3-5: 3-Capt. Jet Dixon by Tuska(3). 4-Weird advs. begin 53 106 159 334 567 800

SPACE THRILLERS
Avon Periodicals: 1954 (25¢ Giant)
nn-(Scarce)-Robotmen of the Lost Planet; contains 3 rebound comics of The Saint & Strange Worlds. Contents could vary 139 278 417 890 1520 2150

SPACE TRIP TO THE MOON (See Space Adventures #23)

SPACE USAGI
Mirage Studios: June, 1992 - No. 3, 1992 ($2.00, B&W, mini-series) V2#1, Nov, 1993 - V2#3, Jan, 1994 ($2.75)
1-3: Stan Sakai-c/a/scripts, V2#1-3 3.00

SPACE USAGI
Dark Horse Comics: Jan, 1996 - No. 3, Mar, 1996 ($2.95, B&W, limited series)

Sparkler Comics #15 © UFS

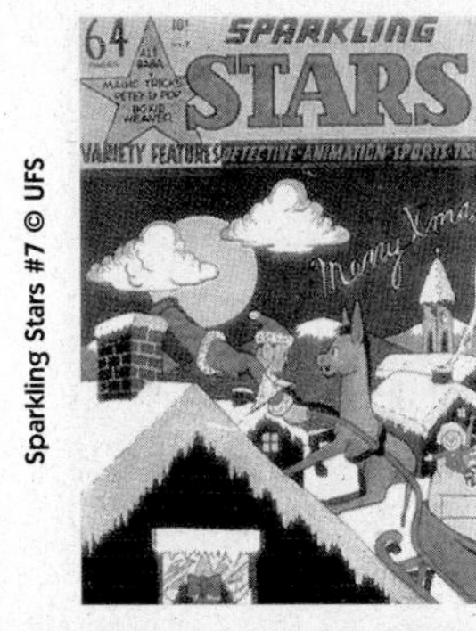

Sparkling Stars #7 © UFS

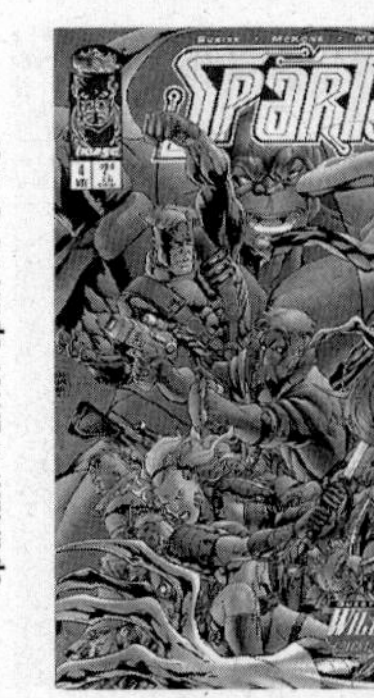

Spartan: Warrior Spirit #4 © WSP

GD VG FN VF VF/NM NM-
2.0 4.0 6.0 8.0 9.0 9.2

1-3: Stan Sakai-c/a/scripts 3.00

SPACE WAR (Fightin' Five #28 on)
Charlton Comics: Oct, 1959 - No. 27, Mar, 1964; No. 28, Mar, 1978 - No. 34, 3/79
V1#1-Giordano-c begin, end #3 11 22 33 76 163 250
2,3 7 14 21 46 86 125
4-6,8,10-Ditko-c/a 11 22 33 76 163 250
7,9,11-15 (3/62): Last 10¢ issue 5 10 15 35 63 90
16 (6/52)-27 (3/64): 18,19-Robot-c 5 10 15 31 53 75
28 (3/78),29-31,33,34-Ditko-c/a(r): 30-Staton, Sutton/Wood-a. 31-Ditko-c/a(3); same-c as Strange Suspense Stories #2 (1968); atom blast-c
1 3 4 6 8 10
32-r/Charlton Premiere V2#2; Sutton-a 6.00

SPACE WARPED
Boom Entertainment (Kaboom!): Jun, 2011 - No. 6, Dec, 2011 ($3.99, limited series)
1-6-Star Wars spoof; Bourhis-s/Spiessert-a 4.00

SPACE WESTERN (Formerly Cowboy Western Comics; becomes Cowboy Western Comics #46 on)
Charlton Comics (Capitol Stories): No. 40, Oct, 1952 - No. 45, Aug, 1953
40-Intro Spurs Jackson & His Space Vigilantes; flying saucer story
55 110 165 352 601 850
41,43,44: 41-Flying saucer-c. 44-Cowboys battle Nazis on Mars
41 82 123 256 428 600
42-Atom bomb explosion-c 43 86 129 271 456 640
45-"The Valley That Time Forgot", a pre-Turok story with dinosaurs & a bow-hunting Indian; Hitler app. 43 86 129 271 461 650

SPACE WORLDS (Formerly Space Squadron #1-5)
Atlas Comics (Male): No. 6, April, 1952
6-Sol Brodsky-c 50 100 150 315 533 750

SPANKY & ALFALFA & THE LITTLE RASCALS (See The Little Rascals)

SPARKIE, RADIO PIXIE (Radio)(Becomes Big Jon & Sparkie #4)
Ziff-Davis Publ. Co.: Winter, 1951 - No. 3, July-Aug, 1952 (Painted-c)(Sparkie #2,3; #1?)
1-Based on children's radio program 27 54 81 158 259 360
2,3: 3-Big Jon and Sparkie on-c only 18 36 54 105 165 225

SPARKLE COMICS
United Features Synd.: Oct-Nov, 1948 - No. 33, Dec-Jan, 1953-54
1-Li'l Abner, Nancy, Captain & the Kids, Ella Cinders (#1-3: 52 pgs.)
15 30 45 83 124 165
2 9 18 27 50 65 80
3-10 8 16 24 40 50 60
11-20 7 14 21 35 43 50
21-32 6 12 18 28 34 40
33-(2-3/54) 2 pgs. early Peanuts by Schulz 10 20 30 54 72 90

SPARKLE PLENTY (See Harvey Comics Library #2 & Dick Tracy)
Dell Publishing Co.: 1949
Four Color 215 - Dick Tracy reprint by Gould 10 20 30 66 138 210

SPARKLER COMICS (1st series)
United Feature Comic Group: July, 1940 - No. 2, 1940
1-Jim Hardy 39 78 117 231 378 525
2-Frankie Doodle 28 56 84 165 270 375

SPARKLER COMICS (2nd series)(Nancy & Sluggo #121 on)(Cover title becomes Nancy and Sluggo #101? on)
United Features Syndicate: July, 1941 - No. 120, Jan, 1955
1-Origin 1st app. Sparkman; Tarzan (by Hogarth in all issues), Captain & the Kids, Ella Cinders, Danny Dingle, Dynamite Dunn, Nancy, Abbie & Slats, Broncho Bill, Frankie Doodle, begin; Spark Man c-1-9,11,12; Hap Hopper c-10,13
161 322 483 1030 1765 2500
2 55 110 165 352 601 850
3,4 42 84 126 265 445 625
5-9: 9-Spark Man's new costume 37 74 111 222 361 500
10-Spark Man's secret ID revealed 37 74 111 222 361 500
11,12-Spark Man war-c. 12-Spark Man's new costume (color change)
34 68 102 199 325 450
13-Hap Hopper war-c 30 60 90 177 289 400
14-Tarzan-c by Hogarth 41 82 123 256 428 600
15,17: 15-Capt & Kids-c. 17-Nancy & Sluggo-c 22 44 66 132 216 300
16,18-Spark Man war-c 37 74 111 222 361 500
19-1st Race Riley and the Commandos-c/s 34 68 102 199 325 450
20-Nancy war-c 26 52 78 154 252 350
21,25,28,31,34,37,39-Tarzan-c by Hogarth 42 84 126 267 451 635
22-24,26,27,29,30: 22-Race Riley & the Commandos strips begin, ends #44
21 42 63 122 199 275
32,33,35,36,38,40 13 26 39 74 105 135
41,43,45,46,48,49 10 20 30 58 79 100
42,44,47,50-Tarzan-c (42,47,50 by Hogarth) 22 44 66 132 216 300
51,52,54-68,70: 57-Li'l Abner begins (not in #58); Fearless Fosdick app. in #58
10 20 30 56 76 95
53-Tarzan-c by Hogarth 22 44 66 132 216 300
69-Wolverton-*esque* Horror-c 12 24 36 67 94 120
71-80 9 18 27 47 61 75
81,82,84-86: 86 Last Tarzan; lingerie panels 8 16 24 40 50 60
83-Tarzan-c; Li'l Abner ends 12 24 36 67 94 120
87-96,98-99 7 14 21 37 46 55
97-Origin Casey Ruggles by Warren Tufts 8 16 24 42 54 65
100 8 16 24 42 54 65
101-107,109-112,114-119 6 12 18 31 38 45
108,113-Toth-a 7 14 21 37 46 55
120-(10-11/54) 2 pgs. early Peanuts by Schulz 10 20 30 54 72 90

SPARKLING LOVE
Avon Periodicals/Realistic (1953): June, 1950; 1953
1(Avon)-Kubert-a; photo-c 30 60 90 177 289 400
nn(1953)-Reprint; Kubert-a 13 26 39 74 105 135

SPARKLING STARS
Holyoke Publishing Co.: June, 1944 - No. 33, March, 1948
1-Hell's Angels, FBI, Boxie Weaver, Petey & Pop, & Ali Baba begin
20 40 60 114 182 250
2-Speed Spaulding story 12 24 36 69 97 125
3-Actual FBI case photos & war photos 10 20 30 54 72 90
4-10: 7-X-Mas-c 9 18 27 50 65 80
11-19: 13-Origin/1st app. Jungo the Man-Beast-c/s 8 16 24 44 57 70
20-Intro Fangs the Wolf Boy 9 18 27 50 65 80
21-33: 29-Bondage-c. 31-Sid Greene-a 8 16 24 42 54 65

SPARK MAN (See Sparkler Comics)
Frances M. McQueeny: 1945 (36 pgs., one-shot)
1-Origin Spark Man r/Sparkler #1-3; female torture story; cover redrawn from Sparkler #1
32 64 96 188 307 425

SPARKS (William Katt Presents...)
Catastrophic Comics: June, 2008 - Present ($2.99)
1,2: 1-Folino-s/Ringuet-a; origin of Sparks 3.00

SPARKY WATTS (Also see Big Shot Comics & Columbia Comics)
Columbia Comic Corp.: Nov?, 1942 - No. 10, 1949
1(1942)-Skyman & The Face app; Hitler-c 87 174 261 553 952 1350
2(1943) 32 64 96 192 314 435
3(1944) 22 44 66 132 216 300
4(1944)-Origin 20 40 60 114 182 250
5(1947)-Skyman app.; Boody Rogers-c/a 16 32 48 94 147 200
6,7,9,10: 6(1947). 9-Haunted House-c. 10(1949) 12 24 36 67 94 120
8(1948)-Surrealistic-c 14 28 42 80 115 150
NOTE: *Boody Rogers c-1-8.*

SPARTACUS (Movie)
Dell Publishing Co.: No. 1139, Nov, 1960 (Kirk Douglas photo-c)
Four Color 1139-Buscema-a 10 20 30 69 147 225

SPARTACUS (Television series)
Devil's Due Publishing: Oct, 2009 - No. 2 ($3.99)
1,2: 1-DeKnight-s. 2-Palmiotti-s 4.00

SPARTAN: WARRIOR SPIRIT (Also see WildC.A.T.S: Covert Action Teams)
Image Comics (WildStorm Productions): July, 1995 - No. 4, Nov, 1995 ($2.50, lim. series)
1-4: Kurt Busiek scripts; Mike McKone-c/a 3.00

SPARTA: USA
DC Comics (WildStorm): May, 2010 - No. 6, Oct, 2010 ($2.99, limited series)
1-6: 1-Lapham-s/Timmons-a; covers by Timmons and Lapham 3.00

SPAWN (Also see Curse of the Spawn and Sam & Twitch)
Image Comics (Todd McFarlane Prods.): May, 1992 - Present ($1.95/$2.50/$2.99)
1-1st app. Spawn; McFarlane-c/a begins; McFarlane/Steacy-c; 1st Todd McFarlane Productions title. 3 6 9 14 20 25
1-Black & white edition 7 14 21 48 89 130
2,3: 2-1st app. Violator; McFarlane/Steacy-c 2 4 6 9 12 15

Spawn #48 © TMP

Spawn: The Dark Ages #1 © TMP

Special Marvel Edition #7 © MAR

	GD 2.0	VG 4.0	FN 6.0	VF 8.0	VF/NM 9.0	NM- 9.2

4-Contains coupon for Image Comics #0 2 4 6 8 10 12
4-With coupon missing 3.00
4-Newsstand edition w/o poster or coupon 3.00
5-Cerebus cameo (1 pg.) as stuffed animal; Spawn mobile poster #1
1 3 4 6 8 10
6-8,10: 7-Spawn Mobile poster #2. 8-Alan Moore scripts; Miller poster. 10-Cerebus app.; Dave Sim scripts; 1 pg. cameo app. by Superman 6.00
9-Neil Gaiman scripts; Jim Lee poster; 1st Angela. 3 6 9 14 20 25
11-17,19,20,22-30: 11-Miller script; Darrow poster. 12-Bloodwulf poster by Liefeld. 14,15-Violator app. 16,17-Grant Morrison scripts; Capullo-c/a(p). 23,24-McFarlane-a/stories. 25-(10/94). 19-(10/94). 20-(11/94) 5.00
18-Grant Morrison script, Capullo-c/a(p); low distr. 1 3 4 6 8 10
21-low distribution 1 3 4 6 8 10
31-49: 31-1st app. The Redeemer; new costume (brief). 32-1st full app. new costume. 38-40,42,44,46,48-Tony Daniel-c/a(p). 38-1st app. Cy-Gor. 40,41-Cy-Gor & Curse app. 4.00
50-($3.95, 48 pgs.) 6.00
51-66: 52-Savage Dragon app. 56-w/ Darkchylde preview. 57-Cy-Gor-c/app. 64-Polybagged w/McFarlane Toys catalog. 65-Photo-c of movie Spawn and McFarlane 4.00
67-96: 81-Billy Kincaid returns 4.00
97-Angela-c/app. 1 2 3 5 6 8
98,99-Angela app. 5.00
100-($4.95) Angela dies; 6 total covers; the 3 variants by McFarlane, Miller, and Mignola
2 4 6 8 10 12
100-($4.95) 3 variant covers by Ross, Capullo, and Wood
1 2 3 5 6 8
101-149-($2.50) 3.00
150-($4.95) 4 covers by McFarlane, Capullo, Tan, Jim Lee 5.00
151-184: 151-($2.95) Wraparound-c by Tan. 167-Clown app. 179-Mayhew-a 3.00
185-199,201-219: 185-McFarlane & Holguin-s/Portacio-a begins. 193-Sam & Twitch app. 210-215-Michael Golden-c 3.00
200-(1/11, $3.99) 7 covers by McFarlane, Capullo, Finch, Jim Lee, Liefeld, Silvestri, Wood 4.00
220-(6/12, $3.99) 20th Anniversary issue; McFarlane-s/Kudranski-a; bonus interview, timeline and cover gallery 4.00
220: 20th Anniversary Collector's Special-(6/12, $4.99) B&W version of #220 w/bonuses 5.00
221-242: 221-231-Cover swipes of classic covers. 221-Amazing Fantasy #15. 225-Election special with 2 covers (Obama & Romney). 228-Action #1 c-swipe. 231-Spider-Man #1 ('90) c-swipe. 234-Haunt app. 3.00
Annual 1-Blood & Shadows ('99, $4.95) Ashley Wood-c/a; Jenkins-s 5.00
...: Architects of Fear (2/11, $6.99, squarebound GN) Briclot-a 7.00
...: Armegeddon Complete Collection TPB ('07, $29.95) r/#150-163 30.00
...: Armegeddon, Part 1 TPB (10/06, $14.99) r/#150-155 15.00
...: Armegeddon, Part 2 TPB (2/07, $15.95) r/#156-164 16.00
...Bible-(8/96, $1.95)-Character bios 4.00
Book 1 TPB($9.95) r/#1-5; Book 2-r/#6-9,11; Book 3 -r/#12-15, Book 4- r/#16-20; Book 5-r/#21-25; Book 6- r/#26-30; Book 7-r/#31-34; Book 8-r/#35-38; Book 9-r/#39-42; Book 10-r/#43-47 11.00
Book 11 TPB ($10.95) r/#48-50; Book 12-r/#51-54 11.00
... Collection Vol. 1 (10/05, $19.95) r/#1-8,11,12; intro. by Frank Miller 20.00
... Collection Vol. 2 HC (7/07, $49.95) r/#13-33 50.00
... Collection Vol. 2 SC (9/06, $29.95) r/#13-33 30.00
... Collection Vol. 3 (3/07, $29.95) r/#34-54 30.00
... Collection Vol. 4 (9/07, $29.95) r/#55-75 30.00
... Collection Vol. 5 ('08, $29.95) r/#76-95 30.00
... Collection Vol. 6 (8/08, $29.95) r/#96-116; cover gallery 30.00
Image Firsts: Spawn #1 (4/10, $1.00) reprints #1 3.00
... Godslayer Vol. 1 (9/06, $6.99) Anacleto-c/a; Holguin-s; sketch pages 7.00
...: Neonoir TPB (11/08, $14.95) r/#170-175 15.00
...: New Flesh TPB ('07, $14.95) r/#166-169 15.00
...Simony (5/04, $7.95) English translation of French Spawn story; Briclot-a 8.00
NOTE: *Capullo a-16p-18p; c-16p-18p. Daniel a-38-40, 42, 44, 46. McFarlane a-1-15; c-1-15p. Thibert a-16i(part). Posters come with issues 1, 4, 7-9, 11, 12. #25 was released before #19 & 20.*

SPAWN-BATMAN (Also see Batman/Spawn: War Devil under Batman: One-Shots)
Image Comics (Todd McFarlane Productions): 1994 ($3.95, one-shot)
1-Miller scripts; McFarlane-c/a 2 4 6 8 10 12

SPAWN: BLOOD FEUD
Image Comics (Todd McFarlane Prods.): June, 1995 - No. 4, Sept, 1995 ($2.25, lim. series)
1-4-Alan Moore scripts, Tony Daniel-a 4.00

SPAWN FAN EDITION
Image Comics (Todd McFarlane Productions): Aug, 1996 - No. 3, Oct, 1996 (Giveaway, 12 pgs.) (Polybagged w/Overstreet's FAN)
1-3: Beau Smith scripts; Brad Gorby-a(p). 1-1st app. Nordik, the Norse Hellspawn. 2-1st app. McFallon. 3-1st app. Mercy 1 2 3 5 6 8
1-3-(Gold): All retailer incentives 16.00
1-3-Variant-c 1 2 3 5 6 8
2-(Platinum)-Retailer incentive 25.00

SPAWN GODSLAYER
Image Comics (Todd McFarlane Prods.): May, 2007 - No. 8, Apr, 2008 ($2.99)
1-8: 1-Holguin-s/Tan-a/Anacleto-c 3.00

SPAWN: THE DARK AGES
Image Comics (Todd McFarlane Productions): Mar, 1999 - No. 28, Oct, 2001 ($2.50)
1-Fabry-c; Holguin-s/Sharp-a; variant-c by McFarlane 3.00
2-28 3.00

SPAWN THE IMPALER
Image Comics (Todd McFarlane Prods.): Oct, 1996 - No. 3, Dec, 1996 ($2.95, limited series)
1-3-Mike Grell scripts, painted-a 4.00

SPAWN: THE UNDEAD
Image Comics (Todd McFarlane Prod.): Jun, 1999 - No. 9, Feb, 2000 ($1.95/$2.25)
1-9-Dwayne Turner-c/a; Jenkins-s. 7-9-($2.25-c) 3.00
TPB (6/08, $24.99) r/#1-9 25.00

SPAWN/WILDC.A.T.S
Image Comics (WildStorm): Jan, 1996 - No. 4, Apr, 1996 ($2.50, lim. series)
1-4: Alan Moore scripts in all. 4.00

SPEAKER FOR THE DEAD (ORSON SCOTT CARD'S...) (Ender's Game)
Marvel Comics: Mar, 2011 - No. 5, Jul, 2011 ($3.99, limited series)
1-3-Johnston-s/Mhan-a/Camuncoli-c 4.00

SPECIAL AGENT (Steve Saunders...)(Also see True Comics #68)
Parents' Magazine Institute (Commended Comics No. 2): Dec, 1947 - No. 8, Sept, 1949 (Based on true FBI cases)
1-J. Edgar Hoover photo on-c 14 28 42 76 108 140
2 8 16 24 44 57 70
3-8 8 16 24 40 50 60

SPECIAL COLLECTORS' EDITION (See Savage Fists of Kung-Fu)

SPECIAL COMICS (Becomes Hangman #2 on)
MLJ Magazines: Winter, 1941-42
1-Origin The Boy Buddies (Shield & Wizard x-over); death of The Comet retold (see Pep #17); origin The Hangman retold; Hangman-c 366 732 1098 2562 4481 6400

SPECIAL EDITION (See Gorgo and Reptisaurus)

SPECIAL EDITION COMICS (See Promotional Section)

SPECIAL EDITION COMICS
Fawcett Publications: 1940 (August) (68 pgs., one-shot)
1-1st book devoted entirely to Captain Marvel; C.C. Beck-c/a; only app. of Captain Marvel with belt buckle; Capt. Marvel appears with button-down flap; 1st story (came out before Captain Marvel #1) 811 1622 2433 5920 10,460 15,000
NOTE: *Prices vary widely on this book. Since this book is all Captain Marvel stories, it is actually a pre-Captain Marvel #1. There is speculation that this book almost became **Captain Marvel** #1. After **Special Edition** was published, there was an editor change at Fawcett. The new editor commissioned Kirby to do a nn **Captain Marvel** book early in 1941. This book was followed by a 2nd book several months later. This 2nd book was advertised as a #3 (making Special Edition the #1, & the nn issue the #2). However, the 2nd book did come out as a #2.*

SPECIAL EDITION: SPIDER-MAN VS. THE HULK (See listing under The Amazing Spider-Man)

SPECIAL EDITION X-MEN
Marvel Comics Group: Feb, 1983 ($2.00, one-shot, Baxter paper)
1-r/Giant-Size X-Men #1 plus one new story 2 4 6 9 12 15

SPECIAL FORCES
Image Comics: Oct, 2007 - No. 4, Mar, 2009 ($2.99)
1-4-Iraq war combat; Kyle Baker-s/a/c 3.00

SPECIAL MARVEL EDITION (Master of Kung Fu #17 on)
Marvel Comics Group: Jan, 1971 - No. 16, Feb, 1974 (#1-3: 25¢, 68 pgs.; #4: 52 pgs.; #5-16: 20¢, regular ed.)
1-Thor-r by Kirby; 68 pgs. 4 8 12 25 40 55
2-4: Thor-r by Kirby; 2,3-68 pg. Giant. 4-(52 pgs.) 3 6 9 16 23 30
5-14: Sgt. Fury-r; 11-r/Sgt. Fury #13 (Capt. America) 2 4 6 9 12 15
15-Master of Kung Fu (Shang-Chi) begins (1st app., 12/73); Starlin-a; origin/1st app. Nayland Smith & Dr. Petrie 22 44 66 128 209 290
16-1st app. Midnight; Starlin-a (2nd Shang-Chi) 6 12 18 41 76 110
NOTE: *Kirby c-10-14.*

SPECIAL MISSIONS (See G.I. Joe...)

SPECIAL WAR SERIES (Attack V4#3 on?)
Charlton Comics: Aug, 1965 - No. 4, Nov, 1965

Spectacular Spider-Man #18 © MAR

Spectacular Spider-Man #238 © MAR

Spectacular Spider-Man (2003 series) #5 © MAR

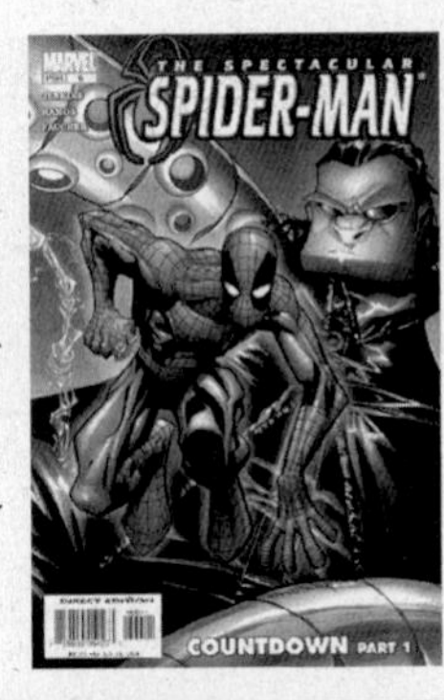

	GD 2.0	VG 4.0	FN 6.0	VF 8.0	VF/NM 9.0	NM- 9.2
V4#1-D-Day (also see D-Day listing)	4	8	12	25	40	55
2-Attack!	3	6	9	16	23	30
3-War & Attack (also see War & Attack)	3	6	9	14	20	25
4-Judomaster (intro/1st app.; see Sarge Steel)	7	14	21	48	89	130

SPECIES (Movie)
Dark Horse Comics: June, 1995 - No. 4, Sept, 1995 ($2.50, limited series)

1-4: Adaptation of film 3.00

SPECIES: HUMAN RACE (Movie)
Dark Horse Comics: Nov, 1996 - No. 4, Feb, 1997 ($2.95, limited series)

1-4 3.00

SPECTACULAR ADVENTURES (See Adventures)

SPECTACULAR FEATURE MAGAZINE, A (Formerly My Confessions)
(Spectacular Features Magazine #12)
Fox Feature Syndicate: No. 11, April, 1950

	GD	VG	FN	VF	VF/NM	NM-
11 (#1)-Samson and Delilah	27	54	81	160	263	365

SPECTACULAR FEATURES MAGAZINE (Formerly A Spectacular Feature Magazine)
Fox Feature Syndicate: No. 12, June, 1950 - No. 3, Aug, 1950

	GD	VG	FN	VF	VF/NM	NM-
12 (#2)-Iwo Jima; photo flag-c	27	54	81	158	259	360
3-True Crime Cases From Police Files	22	44	66	128	209	290

SPECTACULAR SCARLET SPIDER
Marvel Comics: Nov, 1995 - No. 2, Dec, 1995 ($1.95, limited series)

1,2: Replaces Spectacular Spider-Man 3.00

SPECTACULAR SPIDER-GIRL
Marvel Comics: Jul, 2010 - No. 4, Oct, 2010 ($3.99, limited series)

1-4-Frenz-a; Frank Castle and the Hobgoblin app. 4.00

SPECTACULAR SPIDER-MAN, THE (See Marvel Special Edition and Marvel Treasury Edition)

SPECTACULAR SPIDER-MAN, THE (Magazine)
Marvel Comics Group: July, 1968 - No. 2, Nov, 1968 (35¢)

	GD	VG	FN	VF	VF/NM	NM-
1-(B&W)-Romita/Mooney 52 pg. story plus updated origin story with Everett-a(i)	10	20	30	69	147	225
1-Variation w/single c-price of 40¢	10	20	30	69	147	225
2-(Color)-Green Goblin-c & 58 pg. story; Romita painted-c (story reprinted in King Size Spider-Man #9); Romita/Mooney-a	9	18	27	61	123	185

SPECTACULAR SPIDER-MAN, THE (Peter Parker...#54-132, 134)
Marvel Comics Group: Dec, 1976 - No. 263, Nov, 1998

	GD	VG	FN	VF	VF/NM	NM-
1-Origin recap in text; return of Tarantula	5	10	15	35	63	90
2-Kraven the Hunter app.	3	6	9	17	26	35
3-5: 3-Intro Lightmaster. 4-Vulture app.	3	6	9	14	20	25
6-8-Morbius app.; 6-r/Marvel Team-Up #3 w/Morbius	3	6	9	15	22	28
7,8-(35¢-c variants, limited distribution)(6,7/77)	5	10	15	31	53	75
9-20: 9,10-White Tiger app. 11-Last 30¢-c. 17,18-Angel & Iceman app. (from Champions); Ghost Rider cameo. 18-Gil Kane-c	2	4	6	8	11	14
9-11-(35¢-c variants, limited distribution)(8-10/77)	3	6	9	19	30	40
21,24-26: 21-Scorpion app. 26-Daredevil app.	2	3	4	6	8	10
22,23-Moon Knight app.	2	4	6	8	10	12
27-Miller's 1st art on Daredevil (2/79); also see Captain America #235	5	10	15	34	60	85
28-Miller Daredevil (p)	4	8	12	25	40	55
29-55,57,59: 33-Origin Iguana. 38-Morbius app.	1	2	3	4	5	7
56-2nd app. Jack O'Lantern (Macendale) & 1st Spidey/Jack O'Lantern battle (7/81)	1	2	3	5	6	8
58-Byrne-a(p)	1	2	3	5	6	8
60-Double size; origin retold with new facts revealed	1	2	3	5	6	8
61-63,65-68,71-74: 65-Kraven the Hunter app.						6.00
64-1st app. Cloak & Dagger (3/82)	3	6	9	16	23	30
69,70-Cloak & Dagger app.	1	2	3	5	7	9
75-Double size	1	2	3	4	5	7
76-80: 78,79-Punisher cameo						6.00
81,82-Punisher, Cloak & Dagger app.	1	2	3	5	6	8
83-Origin Punisher retold (10/83)	2	4	6	8	10	12
84,86-89,91-99: 94-96-Cloak & Dagger app. 98-Intro The Spot						6.00
85-Hobgoblin (Ned Leeds) app. (12/83); gains powers of original Green Goblin (see Amazing Spider-Man #238)	2	4	6	8	10	12
90-Spider-Man's new black costume, last panel (ties w/Amazing Spider-Man #252 & Marvel Team-Up #141 for 1st app.)	2	4	6	10	14	18
100-(3/85)-Double size	1	2	3	4	5	7
101-115,117,118,120-129: 107-110-Death of Jean DeWolff. 111-Secret Wars II tie-in. 128-Black Cat new costume						5.00
116,119-Sabretooth-c/story	2	3	4	6	8	10
130-132: 130-Hobgoblin app. 131-Six part Kraven tie-in. 132-Kraven tie-in	2	3	4	6	8	10
133-140: 138-1st full app. Tombstone (origin #139). 140-Punisher cameo						5.00
141-143-Punisher app.	1	2	3	4	5	7
144-146,148-157: 151-Tombstone returns						4.00
147-1st brief app. new Hobgoblin (Macendale), 1 page; continued in Web of Spider-Man #48	2	4	6	8	11	14
158-Spider-Man gets new powers (1st Cosmic Spidey, cont'd in Web of Spider-Man #59)	1	2	3	5	6	8
159-Cosmic Spider-Man app.	1	2	3	4	5	7
160-170: 161-163-Hobgoblin app. 168-170-Avengers x-over. 169-1st app. The Outlaws						3.00
171-188,190-199: 180,181,183,184-Green Goblin app. 197-199-Original X-Men-c/story						3.00
189-($2.95, 52 pgs.)-Silver hologram on-c; battles Green Goblin; origin Spidey retold; Vess poster w/Spidey & Hobgoblin						6.00
189-(2nd printing)-Gold hologram on-c						4.00
195-(Deluxe ed.)-Polybagged w/"Dirt" magazine #2 & Beastie Boys/Smithereens music cassette						4.00
200-($2.95)-Holo-grafx foil-c; Green Goblin-c/story						5.00
201-219,221,222,224,226-228,230-247: 212-w/card sheet. 203-Maximum Carnage x-over. 204-Begin 4 part death of Tombstone story. 207,208-The Shroud-c/story. 208-Siege of Darkness x-over (#207 is a tie-in). 209-Black Cat back-up. 215,216-Scorpion app. 217-Power & Responsibility Pt. 4. 231-Return of Kaine; Spider-Man corpse discovered. 232-New Doc Octopus app. 233-Carnage-c/app. 235-Dragon Man cameo. 236-Dragon Man-c/app; Lizard app.; Peter Parker regains powers. 238,239-Lizard app. 239-w/card insert. 240-Revelations storyline begins. 241-Flashback						3.00
213-Collectors ed. polybagged w/16 pg. preview & animation cel; foil-c; 1st meeting Spidey & Typhoid Mary						4.00
213-Version polybagged w/Gamepro #7; no-c date, price						3.00
217,219 ($2.95)-Deluxe edition foil-c: flip book						4.00
220 ($2.25, 52 pgs.)-Flip book, Mary Jane reveals pregnancy						4.00
223,229: ($2.50) 229-Spidey quits						4.00
223,225: ($2.95)-223-Die Cut-c. 225-Newsstand ed.						4.00
225,229: ($3.95) 225-Direct Market Holodisk-c (Green Goblin). 229-Acetate-c, Spidey quits						5.00
240-Variant-c						4.00
248,249,251-254,256: 249-Return of Norman Osborn 256-1st app. Prodigy						3.00
250-($3.25) Double gatefold-c						4.00
255-($2.99) Spiderhunt pt. 4						4.00
257-262: 257-Double cover with "Spectacular Prodigy #1"; battles Jack O'Lantern. 258-Spidey is cleared. 259,260-Green Goblin & Hobgoblin app. 262-Byrne-s						3.00
263-Final issue; Byrne-c; Aunt May returns						5.00
#(-1) Flashback (7/97)						3.00
# 1000 (6/11, $4.99) Punisher app.; Nauck & Ryan-a/Rivera-c; r/ASM #129						5.00
Annual 1 (1979)-Doc Octopus-c & 46 pg. story	2	4	6	8	11	14
Annual 2 (1980)-Origin/1st app. Rapier	1	2	3	5	6	8
Annual 3-5: ('81-'83) 3-Last Man-Wolf						5.00
Annual 6-14: 8 ('88,$ 1.75)-Evolutionary War x-over; Daydreamer returns Gwen Stacy "clone" back to real self (not Gwen Stacy). 9 ('89, $2.00, 68 pgs.)-Atlantis Attacks. 10 ('90, $2.00, 68 pgs.)-McFarlane-a. 11 ('91, $2.00, 68 pgs.)-Iron Man app. 12 ('92, $2.25, 68 pgs.)-Venom solo story cont'd from Amazing Spider-Man Annual #26. 13 ('93, $2.95, 68 pgs.)-Polybagged w/trading card; John Romita, Sr. back-up-a						4.00
Special 1 (1995, $3.95)-Flip book						4.00

NOTE: ***Austin*** *c-21i, Annual 11i.* ***Buckler*** *a-103, 107-111, 116, 117, 119, 122, Annual 1, Annual 10; c-103, 107-111, 113, 116-119, 122, Annual 1.* ***Buscema*** *a-121.* ***Byrne*** *c(p)-17, 43, 58, 101, 102.* ***Giffen*** *a-120p.* ***Hembeck*** *c/a-86p.* ***Larsen*** *c-Annual 11p.* ***Miller*** *c-46p, 48p, 50, 51p, 52p, 54p, 55, 56p, 57, 60.* ***Mooney*** *a-7i, 11i, 21p, 23p, 25p, 26p, 29-34p, 36p, 37p, 39i, 41, 42i, 49p, 50i, 51i, 53p, 54-57i, 59-66i, 68i, 71i, 73-79i, 81-83i, 85i, 87-99i, 102i, 125p, Annual 1i, 2p.* ***Nasser*** *c-37p.* ***Perez*** *c-10.* ***Simonson*** *c-54i.* ***Zeck*** *a-22, 118, 131, 132; c-131, 132.*

SPECTACULAR SPIDER-MAN (2nd series)
Marvel Comics: Sept, 2003 - No. 27, June, 2005 ($2.25/$2.99)

	NM-
1-Jenkins-s/Ramos-a/c; Venom-c/app.	4.00
2-26: 2-5-Venom app. 6-9-Dr. Octopus app. 11-13-The Lizard app. 14-Rivera painted-a. 15,16-Capt. America app. 17,18-Ramos-a. 20-Spider-Man gets organic webshooters 21,22-Caldwell-a. 23-26-Sarah & Gabriel app.; Land-c	3.00
27-($2.99) Last issue; Uncle Ben app. in flashback; Buckingham-a	4.00
... Vol. 1: The Hunger TPB (2003, $11.99) r/#1-5	12.00
... Vol. 2: Countdown TPB (2004, $11.99) r/#6-10	12.00
... Vol. 3: Here There Be Monsters TPB (2004, $9.99) r/#11-14	10.00
... Vol. 4: Disassembled TPB (2004, $14.99) r/#15-20	15.00
... Vol. 5: Sins Remembered (2005, $9.99) r/#23-26	10.00
... Vol. 6: The Final Curtain (2005, $14.99) r/#21,22,27 & Peter Parker: Spider-Man #39-41	15.00

SPECTACULAR STORIES MAGAZINE (Formerly A Star Presentation)
Fox Feature Syndicate (Hero Books): No. 4, July, 1950; No. 3, Sept, 1950

The Spectre (3rd series) #62 © DC

Speed Comics #6 © HARV

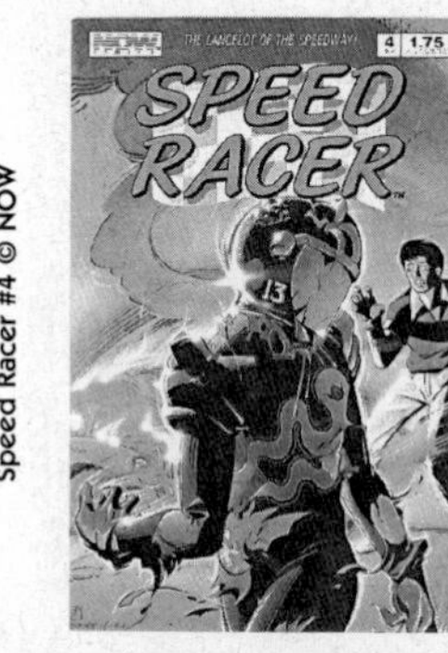

Speed Racer #4 © NOW

	GD 2.0	VG 4.0	FN 6.0	VF 8.0	VF/NM 9.0	NM- 9.2
4-Sherlock Holmes (true crime stories)	36	72	108	216	351	485
3-The St. Valentine's Day Massacre (true crime)	24	48	72	142	234	325

SPECTRE, THE (1st Series) (See Adventure Comics #431-440, More Fun & Showcase)
National Periodical Publ.: Nov-Dec, 1967 - No. 10, May-June, 1969 (All 12¢)

1-(11-12/67)-Anderson-c/a	12	24	36	84	185	285
2-5-Neal Adams-c/a; 3-Wildcat x-over	9	18	27	57	111	165
6-8,10: 6-8-Anderson inks. 7-Hourman app.	6	12	18	41	76	110
9-Wrightson-a	7	14	21	44	82	120

SPECTRE, THE (2nd Series) (See Saga of the Swamp Thing #58, Showcase '95 #8 & Wrath of the...)
DC Comics: Apr, 1987 - No. 31, Oct, 1989 ($1.00, new format)

1-Colan-a begins 5.00
2-32: 9-Nudity panels. 10-Batman cameo. 10,11-Millennium tie-ins 3.00
Annual 1 (1988, $2.00)-Deadman app. 4.00
NOTE: *Art Adams c-Annual 1. Colan a-1-6. Kaluta c-1-3. Mignola c-7-9. Morrow a-9-15. Sears c/a-22. Vess c-13-15.*

SPECTRE, THE (3rd Series) (Also see Brave and the Bold #72, 75, 116, 180, 199 & Showcase '95 #8)
DC Comics: Dec, 1992 - No. 62, Feb, 1998 ($1.75/$1.95/$2.25/$2.50)

1-($1.95)-Glow-in-the-dark-c; Mandrake-a begins 5.00
2,3 4.00
4-7,9-12,14-20: 10-Kaluta-c. 11-Hildebrandt painted-c. 16-Aparo/K. Jones-a. 19-Snyder III-c. 20-Sienkiewicz-c 3.00
8,13-($2.50)-Glow-in-the-dark-c 4.00
21-62: 22-(9/94)-Superman-c & app. 23-(11/94). 43-Kent Williams-c. 44-Kaluta-c. 47-Final Night x-over. 49-Begin Bolton-c. 51-Batman-c/app. 52-Gianni-c. 54-Corben-c. 60-Harris-c 3.00
#0 (10/94) Released between #22 & #23 3.00
Annual 1 (1995, $3.95)-Year One story 4.00
NOTE: *Bisley c-27. Fabry c-2. Kelley Jones c-31. Vess c-5.*

SPECTRE, THE (4th Series) (Hal Jordan; also see Day of Judgment #5 and Legends of the DC Universe #33-36)
DC Comics: Mar, 2001 - No. 27, May, 2003 ($2.50/$2.75)

1-DeMatteis-s/Ryan Sook-c/a 4.00
2-27: 3,4-Superman & Batman-c/app. 5-Two-Face-c/app. 20-Begin $2.75-c. 21-Sinestro returns. 24-JLA app. 3.00

SPECTRE, THE (See Crisis Aftermath: The Spectre)

SPEEDBALL (See Amazing Spider-Man Annual #12, Marvel Super-Heroes & The New Warriors)
Marvel Comics: Sept, 1988(10/88-inside) - No. 11, July, 1989 (75¢)

1-11: Ditko/Guice-a-1-4, c-1; Ditko a-1-10; c-1-11p 4.00

SPEED BUGGY (TV)(Also see Fun-In #12, 15)
Charlton Comics: July, 1975 - No. 9, Nov, 1976 (Hanna-Barbera)

1	3	6	9	15	22	28
2-9	2	4	6	10	14	18

SPEED CARTER SPACEMAN (See Spaceman)

SPEED COMICS (New Speed)(Also see Double Up)
Brookwood Publ./Speed Publ./Harvey Publications No. 14 on:
10/39 - #11, 8/40; #12, 3/41 - #44, 1-2/47 (#14-16: pocket size, 100 pgs.)

1-Origin & 1st app. Shock Gibson; Ted Parrish, the Man with 1000 Faces begins; Powell-a; becomes Champion #2 on?; has earliest? full page panel in comics	366	732	1098	2562	4481	6400
2-Powell-a	126	252	378	806	1378	1950
3	74	148	222	470	810	1150
4,5: 4-Powell-a? 5-Dinosaur-c	65	130	193	416	708	1000
6-11: 7-Mars Mason begins, ends #11	61	122	183	390	670	950
12 (3/41; shows #11 in indicia)-The Wasp begins; Major Colt app. (Capt. Colt #12)	65	130	195	416	708	1000
13-Intro. Captain Freedom & Young Defenders; Girl Commandos, Pat Parker (costumed heroine), War Nurse begins; Major Colt app.	77	154	231	493	847	1200
14-16 (100 pg. pocket size, 1941): 14-2nd Harvey comic (See Pocket); Shock Gibson dons new costume; Nazi war-c. 15-Pat Parker dons costume, last in costume #23; no Girl Commandos	181	362	543	1158	1979	2800
17-Black Cat begins (4/42, early app.; see Pocket #1); origin Black Cat-r/Pocket #1; not in #40,41; S&K-c	155	310	465	992	1696	2400
18-20-S&K-c. 20-Japanese war-c	135	270	405	864	1482	2100
21-Hitler, Tojo-c; Kirby-c	194	388	582	1242	2121	3000
22-Kirby-c	123	246	369	787	1344	1900
23-Origin Girl Commandos; Kirby-c	123	246	369	787	1344	1900
24-Pat Parker team-up with Girl Commandos; Hitler, Tojo, & Mussolini-c	181	362	543	1158	1979	2800
25,27,29,30	116	232	348	742	1271	1800
26-Flag-c	129	258	387	826	1413	2000
28-Classic Nazi monster WWII-c	161	322	483	1030	1765	2500
31-Schomburg Hitler & Tojo-c	206	412	618	1318	2259	3200
32-35-Schomburg-c. 32,34-Nazi war-c. 33,35-Japanese war-c	123	246	369	787	1344	1900
36-Schomburg Japanese war-c	84	168	252	538	919	1300
37,39-42,44: 37-Japanese war-c	41	82	123	256	428	600
38-Iwo-Jima Flag-c	45	90	135	284	480	675
43-Robot-c	45	90	135	284	480	675

NOTE: *Al Avison c-14-16, 30, 43. Briefer a-6, 7. Jon Henri (Kirbyesque) c-17-20. Kubert a-37, 38, 42-44. Kirby/Caseneuve c-21-23. Cecelia Munson a-7-11(Mars Mason). Palais c-37, 39-42. Powell a-1, 2, 4-7, 28, 31, 44. Schomburg c-31-36. Tuska a-3, 6, 7. Bondage c-18, 35. Captain Freedom c-16-24, 25(part), 26-44(w/Black Cat #27, 29, 31, 32-40). Shock Gibson c-1-15.*

SPEED DEMON (Also see Marvel Versus DC #3 & DC Versus Marvel #4)
Marvel Comics (Amalgam): Apr, 1996 ($1.95, one-shot)

1 3.00

SPEED DEMONS (Formerly Frank Merriwell at Yale #1-4?; Submarine Attack #11 on)
Charlton Comics: No. 5, Feb, 1957 - No. 10, 1958

5-10	7	14	21	35	43	50

SPEED FORCE (See The Flash 2nd Series #143-Cobalt Blue)
DC Comics: Nov, 1997 ($3.95, one-shot)

1-Flash & Kid Flash vs. Cobalt Blue; Waid-s/Aparo & Sienkiewicz-a; Flash family stories and pin-ups by various 4.00

SPEED RACER (Also see The New Adventures of...)
Now Comics: July, 1987 - No. 38, Nov, 1990 ($1.75)

1 4.00
2-38, 1-2nd printing 3.00
Special 1 (1988, $2.00) 4.00
Special 2 (1988, $3.50) 4.00

SPEED RACER (Also see Racer X)
DC Comics (WildStorm): Oct, 1999 - No. 3, Dec, 1999 ($2.50, limited series)

1-3-Tommy Yune-s/a; origin of Racer X; debut of the Mach 5 3.00
...: Born To Race (2000, $9.95, TPB) r/series & conceptual art 10.00
...: The Original Manga Vol. 1 ('00, $9.95, TPB) r/1950s B&W manga 10.00

SPEED RACER: CHRONICLES OF THE RACER
IDW Publishing: 2007 - No. 4, Apr, 2008 ($3.99)

1-4-Multiple covers for each 4.00

SPEED RACER FEATURING NINJA HIGH SCHOOL
Now Comics: Aug, 1993 - No. 2, 1993 ($2.50, mini-series)

1,2: 1-Polybagged w/card. 2-Exists? 3.00

SPEED RACER: RETURN OF THE GRX
Now Comics: Mar, 1994 - No. 2, Apr, 1994 ($1.95, limited series)

1,2 3.00

SPEED SMITH-THE HOT ROD KING (Also see Hot Rod King)
Ziff-Davis Publishing Co.: Spring, 1952

1-Saunders painted-c	24	48	72	142	234	325

SPEEDY GONZALES
Dell Publishing Co.: No. 1084, Mar, 1960

Four Color 1084	5	10	15	34	60	85

SPEEDY RABBIT (See Television Puppet Show)
Realistic/I. W. Enterprises/Super Comics: nd (1953); 1963

nn (1953)-Realistic Reprint?	2	4	6	11	16	20
I.W. Reprint #1 (2 versions w/diff. c/stories exist)-Peter Cottontail #?						
Super Reprint #14(1963)	2	4	6	8	11	14

SPELLBINDERS
Quality: Dec, 1986 - No. 12, Jan, 1988 ($1.25)

1-12: Nemesis the Warlock, Amadeus Wolf 3.00

SPELLBINDERS
Marvel Comics: May, 2005 - No. 6, Oct, 2005 ($2.99, limited series)

1-6-Carey-s/Perkins-a 3.00
...: Signs and Wonders TPB (2006, $7.99, digest) r/#1-6 8.00

SPELLBOUND (See The Crusaders)

SPELLBOUND (Tales to Hold You... #1, Stories to Hold You...)
Atlas Comics (ACI 1-15/Male 16-23/BPC 24-34): Mar, 1952 - #23, June, 1954; #24, Oct,

Spellbound #1 © MAR

The Spider #12 © Argosy

Spider-Girl #60 © MAR

	GD 2.0	VG 4.0	FN 6.0	VF 8.0	VF/NM 9.0	NM- 9.2
1955 - #34, June, 1957						
1-Horror/weird stories in all	97	194	291	621	1061	1500
2-Edgar A. Poe app.	50	100	150	315	533	750
3-5: 3-Whitney-a; cannibalism story	43	86	129	271	461	650
6-Krigstein-a	43	86	129	271	461	650
7-10: 8-Ayers-a	39	78	117	240	395	550
11-16,18-20: 14-Ed Win-a	36	72	108	211	343	475
17-Krigstein-a	41	82	123	256	428	600
21-23: 23-Last precode (6/54)	28	56	84	165	270	375
24-28,30,31,34: 25-Orlando-a	26	52	78	154	252	350
29-Ditko-a (4 pgs.)	28	56	84	165	270	375
32,33-Torres-a	26	52	78	154	252	350

NOTE: ***Brodsky** a-5; c-1, 5-7, 10, 11, 13, 15, 25-27, 32. **Colan** a-17. **Everett** a-2, 5, 7, 10, 16, 28, 31; c-2, 8, 9, 14, 17-19, 28, 30. **Forgione/Abel** a-29. **Forte/Fox** a-16. **Al Hartley** a-2. **Heath** a-2, 4, 8, 9, 12, 14, 16; c-3, 4, 12, 16, 20, 21. **Infantino** a-15. **Keller** a-5. **Kida** a-2, 14. **Maneely** a-7, 14, 27; c-24, 29, 31. **Mooney** a-5, 13, 18. **Mac Pakula** a-22, 32. **Post** a-8. **Powell** a-19, 20, 32. **Robinson** a-1. **Romita** a-24, 26, 27. **R.Q. Sale** a-29. **Sekowsky** a-5. **Severin** c-29. **Sinnott** a-8, 16, 17.*

SPELLBOUND
Marvel Comics: Jan, 1988 - Apr, 1988 ($1.50, bi-weekly, Baxter paper)

1-5 3.00
6 ($2.25, 52 pgs.) 4.00

SPELLJAMMER (Also see TSR Worlds Comics Annual)
DC Comics: Sept, 1990 - No. 15, Nov, 1991 ($1.75)

1-15: Based on TSR game. 11-Heck-a. 3.00

SPENCER SPOOK (Formerly Giggle Comics)
American Comics Group: No. 100, Mar-Apr, 1955 - No. 101, May-June, 1955

	GD 2.0	VG 4.0	FN 6.0	VF 8.0	VF/NM 9.0	NM- 9.2
100,101	8	16	24	40	50	60

SPIDER, THE
Eclipse Books: 1991 - Book 3, 1991 ($4.95, 52 pgs., limited series)

Book 1-3-Truman-c/a 5.00

SPIDER, THE
Dynamite Entertainment: 2012 - No. 18, 2014 ($3.99)

1-18: 1-Revival of the pulp character; Liss-s/Worley-a; 4 covers. 2-18-Multiple covers 4.00
Annual 1 (2013, $4.99) Denton-s/Vitorino-a/c 5.00

SPIDER-BOY (Also see Marvel Versus DC #3)
Marvel Comics (Amalgam): Apr, 1996 ($1.95)

1-Mike Wieringo-c/a; Karl Kesel story; 1st app. of Bizarnage, Insect Queen, Challengers of the Fantastic, Sue Storm: Agent of S.H.I.E.L. D., & King Lizard 3.00

SPIDER-BOY TEAM-UP
Marvel Comics (Amalgam): June, 1997 ($1.95, one-shot)

1-Karl Kesel & Roger Stern-s/Jo Ladronn-a(p) 3.00

SPIDER-GIRL (See What If... #105)
Marvel Comics: Oct, 1998 - No. 100, Sept, 2006 ($1.99/$2.25/$2.99)

	GD 2.0	VG 4.0	FN 6.0	VF 8.0	VF/NM 9.0	NM- 9.2
0-($2.99)-r/1st app. Peter Parker's daughter from What If #105; previews regular series, Avengers-Next and J2	1	2	3	4	5	7
1-DeFalco-s/Olliffe & Williamson-s	1	2	3	5	6	8

2-Two covers 4.00
3-16,18-20: 3-Fantastic Five-c/app. 10,11-Spider-Girl time-travels to meet teenaged Spider-Man 3.00
17-($2.99) Peter Parker suits up 4.00
21-24,26-49,51-59: 21-Begin $2.25-c. 31-Avengers app. 3.00
25-($2.99) Spider-Girl vs. the Savage Six 4.00
50-($3.50) 4.00
59-99-($2.99) 59-Avengers app.; Ben Parker born. 75-May in Black costume. 82-84-Venom bonds with Normie Osborn. 93-Venom-c. 95-Tony Stark app. 3.00
100-($3.99) Last issue; story plus Rogues Gallery, profile pages; r/#27,53 4.00
1999 Annual ($3.99) 4.00
...: The End! (10/10, $3.99) Frenz & Buscema-a; Mayhem app. 4.00
Wizard #1/2 (1999) 3.00
... A Fresh Start (1/99,$5.99, TPB) r/#1&2 6.00
... Presents The Buzz and Darkdevil (2007, $7.99, digest) r/mini-series 8.00
TPB (10/01, $19.95) r/#0-8; new Olliffe-c 20.00
Marvel Age Spider-Girl Vol. 1: Legacy (2004, $7.99, digest size) r/#0-5 8.00
Marvel Age Spider-Girl Vol. 2: Like Father, Like Daughter (2004, $7.99, digest) r/#6-11 8.00
Spider-Girl Vol. 3: Avenging Allies (2005, $7.99, digest) r/#12-16 & 1999 Annual 8.00
Spider-Girl Vol. 4: Turning Point (2005, $7.99, digest) r/#17-21 & #1/2 8.00
Spider-Girl Vol. 5: Endgame (2006, $7.99, digest) r/#22-27 8.00
Spider-Girl Vol. 6: Too Many Spiders! (2006, $7.99, digest) r/#28-33 8.00
Spider-Girl Vol. 7: Betrayed (2006, $7.99, digest) r/#34-38 & #51 8.00
Spider-Girl Vol. 8: Duty Calls (2007, $7.99, digest) r/#39-44 8.00
Spider-Girl Vol. 9: Secret Lives (2007, $7.99, digest) r/#45-50 8.00

SPIDER-GIRL (Araña Corazon from Arana Heart of the Spider)
Marvel Comics: Jan, 2011 - No. 8, Sept, 2011 ($3.99/$2.99)

1-($3.99) Tobin-s/Henry-a/Kitson-c; back-up w/Haspiel-a; Fantastic Four app. 4.00
1-Variant-c by Del Mundo 5.00
2-8-($2.99) 2,3-Red Hulk app. 4,5-Ana Kravenoff app. 6-Hobgoblin app. 8-Powers return 3.00

SPIDER-HAM 25TH ANNIVERSARY SPECIAL
Marvel Comics: Aug, 2010 ($3.99, one-shot)

1-Jusko-c/DeFalco-s/Chabot-a; Peter Porker vs. the Swinester Six 4.00

SPIDER ISLAND... (one-shots) (See Amazing Spider-Man #666-673)
Marvel Comics

...: Deadly Foes 1 (10/11, $4.99) Hobgoblin & Jackal stories; Caselli-c 5.00
...: Emergence of Evil - Jackal & Hobgoblin 1 (10/11, $4.99) Hobgoblin & Jackal reprints 5.00
...: Heroes For Hire 1 (12/11, $2.99) Misty Knight & Paladin; Hotz-a/Yardin-c 3.00
...: I Love New York City 1 (11/11, $3.99) Short stories by various; Punisher app. 4.00
...: Spider-Woman 1 (11/11, $2.99) Van Lente-s/Camuncoli-a; Alicia Masters app. 3.00
... Spotlight 1 ('11, $3.99) Creator interviews and story previews 4.00
...: The Avengers 1 (11/11, $2.99) McKone-a/Yu-c; Frog-Man app. 3.00

SPIDER ISLAND: CLOAK & DAGGER (See Amazing Spider-Man #666-673)
Marvel Comics: Oct, 2011 - No. 3 ($2.99, limited series)

1,2-Spencer-s/Rios-a/Choi-c; Mr. Negative app. 3.00

SPIDER ISLAND: DEADLY HANDS OF KUNG FU (See Amazing Spider-Man #666-673)
Marvel Comics: Oct, 2011 - No. 3, Dec, 2011 ($2.99, limited series)

1-3-Johnston-s/Fiumara-a; Madame Web & Iron Fist app. 3.00

SPIDER ISLAND: THE AMAZING SPIDER-GIRL (Continued from Spider-Girl #8)
Marvel Comics: Oct, 2011 - No. 3, Dec, 2011 ($2.99, limited series)

1-3-Hobgoblin & Kingpin app.; Tobin-s/Larraz-a 3.00

SPIDER-MAN (See Amazing..., Friendly Neighborhood..., Giant-Size..., Marvel Age..., Marvel Knights..., Marvel Tales, Marvel Team-Up, Spectacular..., Spidey Super Stories, Ultimate Marvel Team-Up, Ultimate..., Venom, & Web Of...)

SPIDER-MAN (Peter Parker Spider-Man on cover but not indicia #75-on)
Marvel Comics: Aug, 1990 - No. 98, Nov, 1998 ($1.75/$1.95/ $1.99)

	GD 2.0	VG 4.0	FN 6.0	VF 8.0	VF/NM 9.0	NM- 9.2
1-Silver edition, direct sale only (unbagged)	1	3	4	6	8	10
1-Silver bagged edition; direct sale, no price on comic, but $2.00 on plastic bag (125,000 print run)	3	6	9	14	20	25
1-Regular edition w/Spidey face in UPC area (unbagged); green-c	1	2	3	5	6	8
1-Regular bagged edition w/Spidey face in UPC area; green cover (125,000)						12.00
1-Newsstand bagged w/UPC code						8.00
1-Gold edition, 2nd printing (unbagged) with Spider-Man in box (400,000-450,000)	3	6	9	14	20	25
1-Gold 2nd printing w/UPC code; (less than 10,000 print run) intended for Wal-Mart; much scarcer than originally believed	8	16	24	54	102	150
1-Platinum ed. mailed to retailers only (10,000 print run); has new McFarlane-a & editorial material instead of ads; stiff-c, no cover price	8	16	24	54	102	150

2-10: 2-McFarlane-c/a/scripts continue. 6,7-Ghost Rider & Hobgoblin app. 8-Wolverine cameo; Wolverine storyline begins 6.00
11-25: 12-Wolverine storyline ends. 13-Spidey's black costume returns; Morbius app. 14-Morbius app. 15-Erik Larsen-c/a; Beast c/s. 16-X-Force-c/story w/Liefeld assists; continues in X-Force #4; reads sideways; last McFarlane issue. 17-Thanos-c/story; Leonardi/Williamson-c/a. 18-Ghost Rider-c/story. 18-23-Sinister Six storyline w/Erik Larsen-c/a/scripts. 19-Hulk & Hobgoblin-c & app. 20-22-Deathlok app. 22,23-Ghost Rider, Hulk, Hobgoblin app. 23-Wrap-around gatefold-c. 24-Infinity War x-over w/Demogoblin & Hobgoblin-c/story. 24-Demogoblin dons new costume & battles Hobgoblin-c/story 4.00
26-($3.50, 52 pgs.)-Silver hologram on-c w/gatefold poster by Ron Lim; origin retold 5.00
26-2nd printing; gold hologram on-c 4.00
27-45: 32-34-Punisher-c/story. 37-Maximum Carnage x-over. 39,40-Electro-c/s (cameo #38). 41-43-Iron Fist-c/stories w/Jae Lee-c/a. 42-Intro Platoon. 44-Hobgoblin app. 3.50
46-49,51-53, 55, 56,58-74,76-81: 46-Begin $1.95-c; bound-in card sheet. 51-Power & Responsibility Pt. 3. 52,53-Venom app. 60-Kaine revealed. 61-Origin Kaine. 65-Mysterio app. 66-Kaine-c/app.; Peter Parker app. 67-Carnage-c/app. 68,69-Hobgoblin-c/app. 72-Onslaught x-over; Spidey vs. Sentinels. 74-Daredevil-c/app. 77-80-Morbius-c/app. 3.00
46-($2.95)-Polybagged; silver ink-c w/16 pg. preview of cartoon series & animation style print; bound-in trading card sheet 4.00
50-($2.50)-Newsstand edition 4.00
50-($3.95)-Collectors edition w/holographic-c 5.00
51-($2.95)-Deluxe edition foil-c; flip book 4.00
54-($2.75, 52 pgs.)-Flip book 4.00
57-($2.50) 4.00
57-($2.95)-Die cut-c 5.00

Spider-Man #48 © MAR

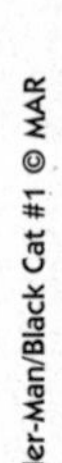

Spider-Man/Black Cat #1 © MAR

Spider-Man: Blue #4 © MAR

	GD 2.0	VG 4.0	FN 6.0	VF 8.0	VF/NM 9.0	NM- 9.2

65-($2.95)-Variant-c; polybagged w/cassette 4.00
75-($2.95)-Wraparound-c; Green Goblin returns; death of Ben Reilly (who was the clone) 4.00
82-97: 84-Juggernaut app. 91-Double cover with "Dusk #1"; battles the Shocker. 93-Ghost Rider app. 3.00
98-Double cover; final issue 4.00
#(-1) Flashback (7/97) 3.00
Annual '97 ($2.99), '98 ($2.99)-Devil Dinosaur-c/app. 4.00
NOTE: ***Erik Larsen** c/a-15, 18-23. **M. Rogers/Keith Williams** c/a-27, 28.*

SPIDER-MAN (one-shots, hardcovers and TPBs)
...& Arana Special: The Hunter Revealed (5/06, $3.99) Del Rio-s; art by Del Rio & various 4.00
...and Batman ('95, $5.95) DeMatteis-s; Joker, Carnage app. 8.00
...and Daredevil ('84, $2.00) 1-r/Spectacular Spider-Man #26-28 by Miller 6.00
...and The Human Torch in...Bahia de Los Muertos! 1 (5/09, $3.99) Beland-s/Juan Doe-a; Diablo app.; printed in two versions (English and Spanish language) 4.00
...: Back in Black HC (2007, $34.99, dustjacket) oversized r/Amaz. S-M #539-543, Friendly Neighborhood S-M #17-23 & Annual #1; cover pencils and sketch pages 35.00
...: Back in Black SC (2008, $24.99) same contents as HC 25.00
...: Back in Black Handbook (2007, $3.99) Official Handbook format; Lopresti-c 10.00
...: Back in Quack (11/10, $3.99) Howard the Duck, Beverly and Man-Thing app. 4.00
...: Birth of Venom TPB (2007, $29.99) r/Secret Wars #8, AS-M #252-259,298-300,315-317, AS-M Annual #25, Fantastic Four #274 and Web of Spider-Man #1 30.00
...: Brand New Day HC (2008, $24.99, dustjacket) r/Amaz. S-M #546-551, Spider-Man: Swing Shift and story from Venom Super-Special 25.00
...: Carnage nn (6/93, $6.95, TPB)-r/Amazing S-M #344,345,359-363; spot varnish-c 10.00
.../Daredevil (10/02, $2.99) Vatche Mavlian-c/a; Brett Matthews-s 3.00
...: Dead Man's Hand 1 (4/97, $2.99) 3.00
...: Death of the Stacys HC (2007, $19.99, dustjacket) r/Amazing Spider-Man #88-92 and #121,122; intro. by Gerry Conway; afterword by Romita; cover gallery incl. reprints 20.00
.../Dr. Strange: "The Way to Dusty Death" nn (1992, $6.95, 68 pgs.) 8.00
...: Election Day HC (2009, $29.99) r/#584-588; includes Barack Obama app from #583 30.00
.../Elektra '98-($2.99) vs. The Silencer 3.00
... Family (2005, $4.99, 100 pgs.) new story and reprints; Spider-Ham app. 5.00
... Fear Itself (3/09, $3.99) Spider-Man and Man-Thing; Stuart Moore-s/Joe Suitor-a 4.00
... Fear Itself Graphic Novel (2/92, $12.95) 18.00
Free Comic Book Day 2012 (Spider-Man: Season One) #1 (Giveaway) Previews the GN 3.00
Giant-Sized Spider-Man (12/98, $3.99) r/team-ups 4.00
...: Grim Hunt - The Kraven Saga (5/10, free) prelude to Grim Hunt arc; Kraven history 3.00
Holiday Special 1995 ($2.95) 4.00
...: Hot Shots nn (1/96, $2.95) fold out posters by various, inc. Vess and Ross 4.00
Identity Crisis (9/98, $19.95, TPB) 20.00
...: Kraven's Last Hunt HC (2006, $19.99) r/Amaz. S-M #293,294; Web of S-M #31,32 and Spect. S-M #131-132; intro. by DeMatteis; Zeck-a; cover pencils and interior pencils 20.00
...: Legacy of Evil 1 (6/96, $3.95) Kurt Busiek script & Mark Texeira-c/a 4.00
...Legends Vol. 1: Todd McFarlane ('03, $19.95, TPB)-r/Amaz. S-M #298-305 20.00
...Legends Vol. 2: Todd McFarlane ('03, $19.99, TPB)-r/Amaz. S-M #306-314, & Spec. Spider-Man Annual #10 20.00
...Legends Vol. 3: Todd McFarlane ('04, $24.99, TPB)-r/Amaz. S-M #315-323,325,328 25.00
...Legends Vol. 4: Spider-Man & Wolverine ('03, $13.95, TPB) r/Spider-Man & Wolverine #1-4 and Spider-Man/Daredevil #1 14.00
.../Marrow (2/01, $2.99) Garza-a 3.00
.../Mary Jane: ... You Just Hit the Jackpot TPB (2009, $24.99) early apps. & key stories 25.00
...: One More Day HC (2008. $24.99, dustjacket) r/Amaz. S-M #544-545, Friendly N.S-M #24, Sensational S-M #41 and Marvel Spotlight: Spider-Man-One More Day 25.00
...: Origin of the Hunter (6/10, $3.99) r/Kraven apps. in ASM #15 & 34; new Mayhew-a 4.00
..., Peter Parker: Back in Black HC (2007, $34.99) oversized r/Sensational Spider-Man #35-40 & Annual #1, Spider-Man Family #1,2; Marvel Spotlight: Spider-Man and Spider-Man Back in Black Handbook; cover sketches 35.00
..., Punisher, Sabretooth: Designer Genes (1993, $8.95) 10.00
...Return of the Goblin TPB (See Peter Parker: Spider-Man)
...Revelations ('97, $14.99, TPB) r/end of Clone Saga plus 14 new pages by Romita Jr. 15.00
...: Saga of the Sandman TPB (2007, $19.99) r/1st app. Amazing S-M #4 and other app. 20.00
...: Season One HC (2012, $24.99) Origin and early days; Bunn-s/Neil Edwards-a 25.00
...: Son of the Goblin (2004, $15.99, TPB) r/AS-M#136-137,312 & Spec. S-M #189,200 16.00
... Special: Black and Blue and Read All Over 1 (11/06, $3.99) new story and r/ASM #12 4.00
Special Edition 1 (12/92-c, 11/92 inside)-The Trial of Venom; ordered thru mail with $5.00 donation or more to UNICEF; embossed metallic ink; came bagged w/bound-in poster; Daredevil app. 2 4 6 9 12 15
Super Special (7/95, $3.95)-Planet of the Symbiotes 4.00
The Best of Spider-Man Vol. 2 (2003, $29.99, HC with dust jacket) r/AS-M V2 #37-45, Peter Parker: S-M #44-47, and S-M's Tangled Web #10,11; Pearson-c 30.00
The Best of Spider-Man Vol. 3 (2004, $29.99, HC with d.j.) r/AS-M V2 #46-58, 500 30.00
The Best of Spider-Man Vol. 4 (2005, $29.99, HC with d.j.) r/#501-514; sketch pages 30.00
The Best of Spider-Man Vol. 5 (2006, $29.99, HC with d.j.) r/#515-524; sketch pages 30.00
The Complete Frank Miller Spider-Man (2002, $29.95, HC) r/Miller-s/a 30.00

	GD 2.0	VG 4.0	FN 6.0	VF 8.0	VF/NM 9.0	NM- 9.2

The Death of Captain Stacy ($3.50) r/AS-M#88-90 5.00
The Death of Gwen Stacy ($14.95) r/AS-M#96-98,121,122 15.00
...: The Movie ($12.95) adaptation by Stan Lee-s/Alan Davis-a; plus r/Ultimate Spider-Man #8, Peter Parker #35, Tangled Web #10; photo-c 13.00
...: The Official Movie Adaptation ($5.95) Stan Lee-s/Alan Davis-a 6.00
...: The Other HC (2006, $29.99, dust jacket) r/Amazing S-M #525-528, Friendly Neighborhood S-M #1-4 and Marvel Knights S-M #19-22; gallery of variant covers 30.00
...: The Other SC (2006, $24.99) r/crossover; gallery of variant covers 25.00
...: The Other Sketchbook (2005, $2.99) sketch page preview of 2005-6 x-over 3.00
Torment TPB (5/01$15.95) r/#1-5, Spec. S-M #10 16.00
... Vs. Doctor Octopus ($17.95) reprints early battles; Sean Chen-c 18.00
... Vs. Punisher (7/00, $2.99) Michael Lopez-c/a 3.00
...Vs. Silver Sable (2006, $15.99, TPB)-r/Amazing Spider-Man #265,279-281 & Peter Parker, The Spectacular Spider-Man #128,129 16.00
...Vs. The Black Cat (2005, $14.99, TPB)-r/Amaz. S-M #194,195,204,205,226,227 15.00
...Vs. Vampires (12/10, $3.99) Blade app.; Castro-a/Grevioux-s 4.00
...Vs. Venom (1990, $8.95, TPB)-r/Amaz. S-M #300,315-317 w/new McFarlane-c 12.00
...Visionaries (10/01, $19.95, TPB)-r/Amaz. S-M #298-305; McFarlane-a 20.00
...Visionaries: John Romita (8/01, $19.95, TPB)-r/Amaz. S-M #39-42, 50,68,69,108,109; new Romita-c 20.00
...Visionaries: Kurt Busiek (2006, $19.99, TPB)-r/Untold Tales of Spider-Man #1-8 20.00
...Visionaries: Roger Stern (2007, $24.99, TPB)-r/Amazing Spider-Man #206 & Spectacular Spider-Man #43-52,54; Stern interview 25.00
Wizard 1/2 ($10.00) Leonardi-a; Green Goblin app. 10.00

SPIDER-MAN ADVENTURES
Marvel Comics: Dec, 1994 - No. 15, Mar, 1996 ($1.50)
1-15 ($1.50)-Based on animated series 3.00
1-($2.95)-Foil embossed-c 4.00

SPIDER-MAN AND HIS AMAZING FRIENDS (See Marvel Action Universe)
Marvel Comics Group: Dec, 1981 (one-shot)
1-Adapted from NBC TV cartoon show; Green Goblin-c/story; 1st Spidey, Firestar, Iceman team-up; Spiegle-p 2 4 6 8 10 12

SPIDER-MAN AND POWER PACK
Marvel Comics: Jan, 2007 - No. 4, Apr, 2007 ($2.99, limited series)
1-4-Sumerak-s/Gurihiru-a; Sandman app. 3,4-Venom app. 3.00
...: Big City Heroes (2007, $6.99, digest) r/#1-4 7.00

SPIDER-MAN AND THE FANTASTIC FOUR
Marvel Comics: Jun, 2007 - No. 4, Sept, 2007 ($2.99, limited series)
1-4-Mike Wieringo-a/c; Jeff Parker-s. 1,4-Impossible Man app. 3.00
...: Silver Rage TPB (2007, $10.99) r/#1-4; series outline and cover sketches 11.00

SPIDER-MAN AND THE SECRET WARS
Marvel Comics: Feb, 2010 - No. 4, May, 2010 ($2.99, limited series)
1-4-Tobin-s/Scherberger-a. 3-Black costume app. 3.00

SPIDER-MAN AND THE INCREDIBLE HULK (See listing under Amazing...)

SPIDER-MAN AND THE UNCANNY X-MEN
Marvel Comics: Mar, 1996 ($16.95, trade paperback)
nn-r/Uncanny X-Men #27, Uncanny X-men #35, Amazing Spider-Man #92, Marvel Team-Up Annual #1, Marvel Team-Up #150, & Spectacular Spider-Man #197-199 17.00

SPIDER-MAN & WOLVERINE (See Spider-Man Legends Vol. 4 for TPB reprint)
Marvel Comics: Aug, 2003 - No. 4, Nov, 2003 ($2.99, limited series)
1-4-Matthews-s/Mavlian-a 3.00

SPIDER-MAN AND X-FACTOR
Marvel Comics: May, 1994 - No. 3, July, 1994 ($1.95, limited series)
1-3 3.00

SPIDER-MAN /BADROCK
Maximum Press: Mar, 1997 ($2.99, mini-series)
1A, 1B(#2)-Jurgens-s 3.00

SPIDER-MAN/BLACK CAT: THE EVIL THAT MEN DO (Also see Marvel Must Haves)
Marvel Comics: Aug, 2002 - No. 6, Mar, 2006 ($2.99, limited series)
1-6-Kevin Smith-s/Terry Dodson-c/a 3.00
HC (2006, $19.99, dust jacket) r/#1-6; script to #6 with sketches 20.00

SPIDER-MAN: BLUE
Marvel Comics: July, 2002 - No. 6, Apr, 2003 ($3.50, limited series)
1-6: Jeph Loeb-s/Tim Sale-a/c; flashback to early MJ and Gwen Stacy 3.50
HC (2003, $21.99, with dust jacket) over-sized r/#1-6; intro. by John Romita 22.00
SC (2004, $14.99) r/#1-6; cover gallery 15.00

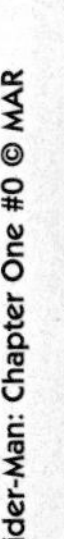

Spider-Man Family #1 © MAR

Spider-Man Loves Mary Jane #5 © MAR

GD 2.0 | VG 4.0 | FN 6.0 | VF 8.0 | VF/NM 9.0 | NM- 9.2

SPIDER-MAN: BRAND NEW DAY (See Amazing Spider-Man Vol. 2)

SPIDER-MAN: BREAKOUT (See New Avengers #1)
Marvel Comics: June, 2005 - No. 5, Oct, 2005 ($2.99, limited series)
1-5-Bedard-s/Garcia-a. 1-U-Foes app. 5-New Avengers app. 3.00
TPB (2006, $13.99) r/#1-5 14.00

SPIDER-MAN: CHAPTER ONE
Marvel Comics: Dec, 1998 - No. 12, Oct, 1999 ($2.50, limited series)
1-Retelling/updating of origin; John Byrne-s/c/a 3.00
1-($6.95) DF Edition w/variant-c by Jae Lee 7.00
2-11: 2-Two covers (one is swipe of ASM #1); Fantastic Four app. 9-Daredevil. 11-Giant-Man-c/app. 3.00
12-($3.50) Battles the Sandman 4.00
0-(5/99) Origins of Vulture, Lizard and Sandman 3.00

SPIDER-MAN CLASSICS
Marvel Comics: Apr, 1993 - No. 16, July, 1994 ($1.25)
1-14,16: 1-r/Amaz. Fantasy #15 & Strange Tales #115. 2-16-r/Amaz. Spider-Man #1-15. 6-Austin-c(i) 3.00
15-($2.95)-Polybagged w/16 pg. insert & animation style print; r/Amazing Spider-Man #14 (1st Green Goblin) 4.00

SPIDER-MAN COLLECTOR'S PREVIEW
Marvel Comics: Dec, 1994 ($1.50, 100 pgs., one-shot)
1-wraparound-c; no comics 4.00

SPIDER-MAN COMICS MAGAZINE
Marvel Comics Group: Jan, 1987 - No. 13, 1988 ($1.50, digest-size)
1-13-Reprints 6.00

SPIDER-MAN: DEATH AND DESTINY
Marvel Comics: Aug, 2000 - No. 3, Oct, 2000 ($2.99, limited series)
1-3-Aftermath of the death of Capt. Stacy 3.00

SPIDER-MAN/ DOCTOR OCTOPUS: OUT OF REACH
Marvel Comics: Jan, 2004 - No. 5, May, 2004 ($2.99, limited series)
1-5: 1-Keron Grant-a/Colin Mitchell-s 3.00
Marvel Age... TPB (2004, $5.99, digest size) r/#1-5 6.00

SPIDER-MAN/ DOCTOR OCTOPUS: YEAR ONE
Marvel Comics: Aug, 2004 - No. 5, Dec, 2004 ($2.99, limited series)
1-5-Kaare Andrews-a/Zeb Wells-s 3.00

SPIDER-MAN FAIRY TALES
Marvel Comics: July, 2007 - No. 4, Oct, 2007 ($2.99, limited series)
1-4: 1-Cebulski-s/Tercio-a. 2-Henrichon-a. 3-Kobayashi-a. 4-Dragotta-p/Allred-i 3.00
TPB (2007, $10.99) r/#1-4 11.00

SPIDER-MAN FAMILY (Also see Amazing Spider-Man Family)
Marvel Comics: Apr, 2007 - No. 9, Aug, 2008 ($4.99, anthology)
1-9-New tales and reprints. 1-Black costume, Sandman, Black Cat app. 4-Agents of Atlas app., Kirk-a; Puppet Master by Eliopoulos. 8-Iron Man app. 9-Hulk app. 5.00
... Featuring Spider-Clan 1 (1/07, $4.99) new Spider-Clan story; reprints w/Spider-Man 2099 and Amazing Spider-Man #252 (black costume) 5.00
... Featuring Spider-Man's Amazing Friends 1 (10/06, $4.99) new story with Iceman and Firestar; Mini Marvels w/Giarrusso-a; reprints w/Spider-Man 2099 5.00
...: Back In Black (2007, $7.99, digest) r/new content from #1-3 8.00
...: Untold Team-Ups (2008, $9.99, digest) r/new content from #4-6 10.00

SPIDER-MAN/FANTASTIC FOUR (Spider-Man and the Fantastic Four on cover)
Marvel Comics: Sept, 2010 - No. 4, Dec, 2010 ($3.99, limited series)
1-4-Gage-s/Alberti-a; Dr. Doom app. 4.00

SPIDER-MAN: FEVER
Marvel Comics: Jun, 2010 - No. 3, Aug, 2010 ($3.99, limited series)
1-3-Brendan McCarthy-s/a; Dr. Strange app. 4.00

SPIDER-MAN: FRIENDS AND ENEMIES
Marvel Comics: Jan, 1995 - No. 4, Apr, 1995 ($1.95, limited series)
1-4-Darkhawk, Nova & Speedball app. 3.00

SPIDER-MAN: FUNERAL FOR AN OCTOPUS
Marvel Comics: Mar, 1995 - No. 3, May, 1995 ($1.50, limited series)
1-3 3.00

SPIDER-MAN/ GEN 13
Marvel Comics: Nov, 1996 ($4.95, one-shot)
nn-Peter David-s/Stuart Immonen-a 5.00

SPIDER-MAN: GET KRAVEN
Marvel Comics: Aug, 2002 - No. 6, Jan, 2003 ($2.99/$2.25, limited series)
1-($2.99) McCrea-a/Quesada-c; back-up story w/Rio-a 4.00
2-6-($2.25) 2-Sub-Mariner app. 3.00

SPIDER-MAN: HOBGOBLIN LIVES
Marvel Comics: Jan, 1997 - No. 3, Mar, 1997 ($2.50, limited series)
1-3-Wraparound-c 3.00
TPB (1/98, $14.99) r/#1-3 plus timeline 15.00

SPIDER-MAN: HOUSE OF M (Also see House of M and related x-overs)
Marvel Comics: Aug, 2005 - No. 5, Dec, 2005 ($2.99, limited series)
1-5-Waid & Peyer-s/Larroca-a; rich and famous Peter Parker in mutant-ruled world 3.00
House of M: Spider-Man TPB (2006, $13.99) r/series 14.00

SPIDER-MAN/ HUMAN TORCH
Marvel Comics: Mar, 2005 - No. 5, July, 2005 ($2.99, limited series)
1-5-Ty Templeton-a/Dan Slott-s; team-ups from early days to the present 3.00
...: I'm With Stupid (2006, $7.99, digest) r/#1-5 8.00

SPIDER-MAN: INDIA
Marvel Comics: Jan, 2005 - No. 4, Apr, 2005 ($2.99, limited series)
1-4-Pavitr Prabhakar gains spider powers; Kang-a/Seetharaman-s 3.00

SPIDER-MAN: LEGEND OF THE SPIDER-CLAN (See Marvel Mangaverse for TPB)
Marvel Comics: Dec, 2002 - No. 5, Apr, 2003 ($2.25, limited series)
1-5-Marvel Mangaverse Spider-Man; Kaare Andrews-s/Skottie Young-c/a 3.00

SPIDER-MAN: LIFELINE
Marvel Comics: Apr, 2001 - No. 3, June, 2001 ($2.99, limited series)
1-3-Nicieza-s/Rude-c/a; The Lizard app. 3.00

SPIDER-MAN LOVES MARY JANE (Also see Mary Jane limited series)
Marvel Comics: Feb, 2006 - No. 20, Sept, 2007 ($2.99)
1-20-Mary Jane & Peter in high school; McKeever-s/Miyazawa-a/c. 5-Gwen Stacy app. 16-18,20-Firestar app. 17-Felecia Hardy app. 3.00
... Vol. 1: Super Crush (2006, $7.99, digest) r/#1-5; cover concepts page 8.00
... Vol. 2: The New Girl (2006, $7.99, digest) r/#6-10; sketch pages 8.00
... Vol. 3: My Secret Life (2007, $7.99, digest) r/#11-15; sketch pages 8.00
... Vol. 4: Still Friends (2007, $7.99, digest) r/#16-20 8.00
Hardcover Vol. 1 (2007, $24.99) oversized reprints of #1-5, Mary Jane #1-4 and Mary Jane: Homecoming #1-4; series proposals, sketch pages and covers; coloring process 25.00
Hardcover Vol. 2 (2008, $39.99) oversized reprints of #6-20, sketch & layout pages 40.00

SPIDER-MAN LOVES MARY JANE SEASON 2
Marvel Comics: Oct, 2008 - No. 5, Feb, 2009 ($2.99, limited series)
1-5-Terry Moore-s/c; Craig Rousseau-a 3.00
1-Variant-c by Alphona 8.00

SPIDER-MAN: MADE MEN
Marvel Comics: Aug, 1998 ($5.99, one-shot)
1-Spider-Man & Daredevil vs. Kingpin 6.00

SPIDER-MAN MAGAZINE
Marvel Comics: 1994 - No. 3, 1994 ($1.95, magazine)
1-3: 1-Contains 4 S-M promo cards & 4 X-Men Ultra Fleer cards; Spider-Man story by Romita, Sr.; X-Men story; puzzles & games. 2-Doc Octopus & X-Men stories 4.00

SPIDER-MAN: MAXIMUM CLONAGE
Marvel Comics: 1995 ($4.95)
Alpha #1-Acetate-c, Omega #1-Chromium-c. 6.00

SPIDER-MAN MEGAZINE
Marvel Comics: Oct, 1994 - No. 6, Mar, 1995 ($2.95, 100 pgs.)
1-6: 1-r/ASM #16,224,225, Marvel Team-Up #1 5.00

SPIDER-MAN NOIR
Marvel Comics: Dec, 2008 - No. 4, May, 2009 ($3.99, limited series)
1-4-Pulp-style Spider-Man in 1933; DiGiandomenico-a; covers by Zircher & Calero 4.00
...: Eyes Without a Face 1-4 (2/10 - No. 4, 5/10) DiGiandomenico-a; Zircher & Calero-c 4.00

SPIDER-MAN: POWER OF TERROR
Marvel Comics: Jan, 1995 - No. 4, Apr, 1995 ($1.95, limited series)
1-4-Silvermane & Deathlok app. 3.00

SPIDER-MAN/PUNISHER: FAMILY PLOT
Marvel Comics: Feb, 1996 - No. 2, Mar, 1996 ($2.95, limited series)
1,2 3.00

SPIDER-MAN: QUALITY OF LIFE

Spider-Man/ Red Sonja #5 © MAR

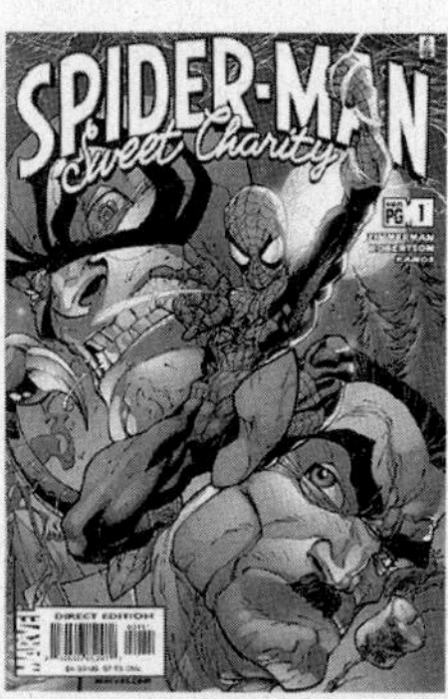

Spider-Man: Sweet Charity #1 © MAR

Spider-Man Unlimited #2 © MAR

GD VG FN VF VF/NM NM-
2.0 4.0 6.0 8.0 9.0 9.2

Marvel Comics: Jul, 2002 - No. 4, Oct, 2002 ($2.99, limited series)

1-4-All CGI art by Scott Sava; Rucka-s; Lizard app. 3.00
TPB (2002, $12.99) r/#1-4; a "Making of..." section detailing the CGI process 13.00

SPIDER-MAN: REDEMPTION
Marvel Comics: Sept, 1996 - No. 4, Dec, 1996 ($1.50, limited series)

1-4: DeMatteis scripts; Zeck-a 3.00

SPIDER-MAN/ RED SONJA
Marvel Comics: Oct, 2007 - No. 5, Feb, 2008 ($2.99, limited series)

1-5-Rubi-a/Oeming-s/Turner-c; Venom & Kulan Gath app. 3.00
HC (2008, $19.99, dustjacket) r/#1-5 and Marvel Team-Up #79; sketch pages 20.00

SPIDER-MAN: REIGN
Marvel Comics: Feb, 2007 - No. 4, May, 2007 ($3.99, limited series)

1-Kaare Andrews-s/a; red costume on cover 4.00
1-Variant cover with black costume 10.00
2-4 4.00
HC (2007, $19.99, dustjacket) r/#1-4; sketch pages and cover variant gallery 20.00
HC 2nd printing (2007, $19.99, dustjacket) with variant black cover 20.00
SC (2008, $14.99) r/#1-4; sketch pages and cover variant gallery 15.00

SPIDER-MAN: REVENGE OF THE GREEN GOBLIN
Marvel Comics: Oct, 2000 - No. 3, Dec, 2000 ($2.99, limited series)

1-3-Frenz & Olliffe-a; continues in AS-M #25 & PP:S-M #25 3.00

SPIDER-MAN SAGA
Marvel Comics: Nov, 1991 - No. 4, Feb, 1992 ($2.95, limited series)

1-4: Gives history of Spider-Man: text & illustrations 3.00

SPIDER-MAN 1602
Marvel Comics: Dec, 2009 - No. 5, Apr, 2010 ($3.99, limited series)

1-5- Peter Parquagh from Marvel 1602; Parker-s/Rosanas-a 4.00

SPIDER-MAN: SWEET CHARITY
Marvel Comics: Aug, 2002 ($4.95, one-shot)

1-The Scorpion-c/app.; Campbell-c/Zimmerman-s/Robertson-a 5.00

SPIDER-MAN'S TANGLED WEB (Titled **"Tangled Web"** in indicia for #1-4)
Marvel Comics: Jun, 2001 - No. 22, Mar, 2003 ($2.99)

1-3: "The Thousand" on-c; Ennis-s/McCrea-a/Fabry-c 4.00
4-"Severance Package" on-c; Rucka-s/Risso-a; Kingpin-c/app. 5.00
5,6-Flowers for Rhino; Milligan-s/Fegredo-a 3.00
7-10,12,15-20,22: 7-9-Gentlemen's Agreement; Bruce Jones-s/Lee Weeks-a. 10-Andrews-s/a. 12-Fegredo-a. 15-Paul Pope-s/a. 18-Ted McKeever-s/a. 19-Mahfood-a. 20-Haspiel-a 3.00
11,13,21-($3.50) 11-Darwyn Cooke-s/a. 13-Phillips-a. 21-Christmas-s by Cooke & Bone 4.00
14-Azzarello & Scott Levy (WWE's Raven)-s about Crusher Hogan 4.00
TPB (10/01, $15.95) r/#1-6 16.00
Volume 2 TPB (4/02, $14.95) r/#7-11 15.00
Volume 3 TPB (2002, $15.99) r/#12-17; Jason Pearson-c 16.00
Volume 4 TPB (2003, $15.99) r/#18-22; Frank Cho-c 16.00

SPIDER-MAN TEAM-UP
Marvel Comics: Dec, 1995 - No. 7, June, 1996 ($2.95)

1-7: 1-w/ X-Men. 2-w/Silver Surfer. 3-w/Fantastic Four. 4-w/Avengers. 5-Gambit & Howard the Duck-c/app. 7-Thunderbolts-c/app. 4.00
... Special 1 (5/05, $2.99) Fantastic Four app.; Todd Dezago-s/Shane Davis-a 4.00

SPIDER-MAN: THE ARACHNIS PROJECT
Marvel Comics: Aug, 1994 - No. 6, Jan, 1995 ($1.75, limited series)

1-6-Venom, Styx, Stone & Jury app. 3.00

SPIDER-MAN: THE CLONE JOURNAL
Marvel Comics: Mar, 1995 ($2.95, one-shot)

1 4.00

SPIDER-MAN: THE CLONE SAGA
Marvel Comics: Nov, 2009 - No. 6, Apr, 2010 ($3.99, limited series)

1-6-Retelling of the saga with different ending; DeFalco & Mackie-s/Nauck-a 4.00

SPIDER-MAN: THE FINAL ADVENTURE
Marvel Comics: Nov, 1995 - No. 4, Feb, 1996 ($2.95, limited series)

1-4: 1-Nicieza scripts; foil-c 3.00

SPIDER-MAN: THE JACKAL FILES
Marvel Comics: Aug, 1995 ($1.95, one-shot)

1 3.00

SPIDER-MAN: THE LOST YEARS

GD VG FN VF VF/NM NM-
2.0 4.0 6.0 8.0 9.0 9.2

Marvel Comics: Aug, 1995-No. 3, Oct, 1995; No. 0, 1996 ($2.95/$3.95,lim. series)

0-(1/96, $3.95)-Reprints. 4.00
1-3-DeMatteis scripts, Romita, Jr.-c/a 3.00
NOTE: ***Romita*** *c-0i.* ***Romita, Jr.*** *a-0r, 1-3p. c-0-3p.* ***Sharp*** *a-0r.*

SPIDER-MAN: THE MANGA
Marvel Comics: Dec, 1997 - No. 31, June, 1999 ($3.99/$2.99, B&W, bi-weekly)

1-($3.99)-English translation of Japanese Spider-Man 4.00
2-31-($2.99) 3.00

SPIDER-MAN: THE MUTANT AGENDA
Marvel Comics: No. 0, Feb, 1994; No. 1, Mar, 1994 - No. 3, May, 1994 ($1.75, limited series)

0-(2/94, $1.25, 52 pgs.)-Crosses over w/newspaper strip; has empty pages to paste in newspaper strips; gives origin of Spidey 4.00
1-3: Beast & Hobgoblin app. 1-X-Men app. 3.00

SPIDER-MAN: THE MYSTERIO MANIFESTO (Listed as "Spider-Man and Mysterio" in indicia)
Marvel Comics: Jan, 2001 - No. 3, Mar, 2001 ($2.99, limited series)

1-3-Daredevil-c/app.; Weeks & McLeod-a 3.00

SPIDER-MAN: THE PARKER YEARS
Marvel Comics: Nov, 1995 ($2.50, one-shot)

1 3.00

SPIDER-MAN 2: THE MOVIE
Marvel Comics: Aug, 2004 ($3.50/$12.99, one-shot)

1-($3.50) Movie adaptation; Johnson, Lim & Olliffe-a 4.00
TPB-($12.99) Movie adaptation; r/Amazing Spider-Man #50, Ultimate Spider-Man #14,15 13.00

SPIDER-MAN 2099 (See Amazing Spider-Man #365)
Marvel Comics: Nov, 1992 - No. 46, Aug, 1996 ($1.25/$1.50/$1.95)

1-(stiff-c)-Red foil stamped-c; begins origin of Miguel O'Hara (Spider-Man 2099); Leonardi/Williamson-c/a begins 1 2 3 5 6 8
1-2nd printing, 2-12,14-24,26-34,39,40: 2-Origin continued, ends #3. 4-Doom 2099 app. 19-Bound-in trading cards. 3.00
13-Extra 16 pg. insert on Midnight Sons 4.00
25-($2.25, 52 pgs.)-Newsstand edition 4.00
25-($2.95, 52 pgs.)-Deluxe edition w/embossed foil-c 5.00
35-38-Venom app. 35-Variant-c. 36-Two-c; Jae Lee-a. 37,38-Two-c 5.00
41-46: 46-The Vulture app; Mike McKone-a(p) 3.00
Annual 1 (1994, $2.95, 68 pgs.) 4.00
Special 1 (1995, $3.95) 4.00
NOTE: ***Chaykin*** *c-37.* ***Ron Lim*** *a(p)-18; c(p)-13, 16, 18.* ***Kelley Jones*** *c/a-9.* ***Leonardi/Williamson*** *a-1-8, 10-13, 15-17, 19, 20, 22-25; c-1-13, 15, 17-19, 20, 22-25, 35.*

SPIDER-MAN 2099 MEETS SPIDER-MAN
Marvel Comics: 1995 ($5.95, one-shot)

nn-Peter David script; Leonardi/Williamson-c/a. 6.00

SPIDER-MAN UNIVERSE
Marvel Comics: Mar, 2000 - No. 7, Oct, 2000 ($4.95/$3.99, reprints)

1-5-Reprints recent issues from the various Spider-Man titles 5.00
6,7-($3.99) 4.00

SPIDER-MAN UNLIMITED
Marvel Comics: May, 1993 - No. 22, Nov, 1998 ($3.95, #1-12 were quarterly, 68 pgs.)

1-Begin Maximum Carnage storyline, ends; Carnage-c/story 5.00
2-12: 2-Venom & Carnage-c/story; Lim-c/a(p) in #2-6. 10-Vulture app. 4.00
13-22: 13-Begin $2.99-c; Scorpion-c/app. 15-Daniel-c; Puma-c/app. 19-Lizard-c/app. 20-Hannibal King and Lilith app. 21,22-Deodato-a 3.00

SPIDER-MAN UNLIMITED (Based on the TV animated series)
Marvel Comics: Dec, 1999 - No. 5, Apr, 2000 ($2.99/$1.99)

1-($2.99) Venom and Carnage app. 4.00
2-5: 2-($1.99) Green Goblin app. 3.00

SPIDER-MAN UNLIMITED (3rd series)
Marvel Comics: Mar, 2004 - No. 15, July, 2006 ($2.99)

1-16: 1-Short stories by various incl. Miyazawa & Chen-a. 2-Mays-a. 6-Allred-c. 14-Finch-c/a; Black Cat app. 3.00

SPIDER-MAN UNMASKED
Marvel Comics: Nov, 1996 ($5.95, one-shot)

nn-Art w/text 6.00

SPIDER-MAN: VENOM AGENDA
Marvel Comics: Jan, 1998 ($2.99, one-shot)

1-Hama-s/Lyle-c/a 3.00

Spider-Man: Web of Doom #2 © MAR

Spider-Woman V2 #4 © MAR

Spike vs. Dracula #2 © 20th Cent. Fox

	GD 2.0	VG 4.0	FN 6.0	VF 8.0	VF/NM 9.0	NM- 9.2

SPIDER-MAN VS. DRACULA
Marvel Comics: Jan, 1994 ($1.75, 52 pgs., one-shot)

1-r/Giant-Size Spider-Man #1 plus new Matt Fox-a 4.00

SPIDER-MAN VS. WOLVERINE
Marvel Comics Group: Feb, 1987; V2#1, 1990 (68 pgs.)

1-Williamson-c/a(i); intro Charlemagne; death of Ned Leeds (old Hobgoblin) 2 4 6 13 18 22
V2#1 (1990, $4.95)-Reprints #1 (2/87) 6.00

SPIDER-MAN: WEB OF DOOM
Marvel Comics: Aug, 1994 - No. 3, Oct, 1994 ($1.75, limited series)

1-3 3.00

SPIDER-MAN: WITH GREAT POWER...
Marvel Comics: Mar, 2008 - No. 5, Sept, 2008 ($3.99, limited series)

1-5-Origin and early days re-told; Lapham-s/Harris-a/c 4.00

SPIDER-MAN: WITH GREAT POWER COMES GREAT RESPONSIBILITY
Marvel Comics: Jun, 2011 - No. 7, Dec, 2011 ($3.99, limited series)

1-7: Reprints of noteworthy Spider-Man stories. 1-R/Ultimate Spider-Man #33,97, and Ultimate Comics Spider-Man #1. 4-R/ Amazing Spider-Man #1,11,20 4.00

SPIDER-MAN: YEAR IN REVIEW
Marvel Comics: Feb, 2000 ($2.99)

1-Text recaps of 1999 issues 3.00

SPIDER-MEN
Marvel Comics: Aug, 2012 - No. 5, Nov, 2012 ($3.99, limited series)

1-5-Peter Parker goes to Ultimate Universe; teams with Miles Morales; Pichelli-a 4.00

SPIDER REIGN OF THE VAMPIRE KING, THE (Also see The Spider)
Eclipse Books: 1992 - No. 3, 1992 ($4.95, limited series, coated stock, 52 pgs.)

Book One - Three: Truman scripts & painted-c 5.00

SPIDER'S WEB, THE (See G-8 and His Battle Aces)

SPIDER-WOMAN (Also see The Avengers #240, Marvel Spotlight #32, Marvel Super Heroes Secret Wars #7, Marvel Two-In-One #29 and New Avengers)
Marvel Comics Group: April, 1978 - No. 50, June, 1983 (New logo #47 on)

1-New complete origin & mask added 3 6 9 14 20 25
2-5,7-18: 2-Excalibur app. 3,11,12-Brother Grimm app. 13,15-The Shroud-c/s. 16-Sienkiewicz-c 1 2 3 4 5 7
6,19,20,28,29,32: 6-Morgan LeFay app. 6,19,32-Werewolf by Night-c/s. 20,28,29-Spider-Man app. 32-Universal Monsters photo/Miller-c 1 2 3 5 6 8
21-27,30,31,33-36 6.00
37,38-X-Men x-over: 37-1st app. Siryn of X-Force; origin retold 2 4 6 8 10 12
39-49: 46-Kingpin app. 49-Tigra-c/story 5.00
50-(52 pgs.)-Death of Spider-Woman; photo-c 2 4 6 9 13 16
NOTE: *Austin* a-37i. *Byrne* c-26p. *Infantino* a-1-19. *Layton* c-19. *Miller* c-32p.

SPIDER-WOMAN
Marvel Comics: Nov, 1993 - No. 4, Feb, 1994 ($1.75, mini-series)

V2#1-4: 1,2-Origin; U.S. Agent app. 3.00

SPIDER-WOMAN
Marvel Comics: July, 1999 - No. 18, Dec, 2000 ($2.99/$1.99/$2.25)

1-($2.99) Byrne-s/Sears-a 4.00
2-18: 2-11-($1.99). 2-Two covers. 12-Begin $2.25-c. 15-Capt. America-c/app. 3.00

SPIDER-WOMAN (Printed version of the motion comic for computers)
Marvel Comics: Nov, 2009 - No. 7, May, 2010 ($3.99/$2.99)

1-($3.99) Bendis-s/Maleev-a; covers by Maleev & Alex Ross; Jessica joins S.W.O.R.D. 4.00
2-6-($2.99) 2-4-Madame Hydra app. 6-Thunderbolts app. 3.00
7-($3.99) New Avengers app. 4.00

SPIDER-WOMAN: ORIGIN (Also see New Avengers)
Marvel Comics: Feb, 2006 - No. 5, June, 2006 ($2.99, limited series)

1-5-Bendis & Reed-s/Jonathan & Joshua Luna-a/c 3.00
1-Variant cover by Olivier Coipel 3.00
HC (2006, $19.99) r/series 20.00
SC (2007, $13.99) r/series 14.00

SPIDEY SUPER STORIES (Spider-Man) (Also see Fireside Books)
Marvel/Children's TV Workshop: Oct, 1974 - No. 57, Mar, 1982 (35¢, no ads)

1-Origin (stories simplified for younger readers) 5 10 15 30 50 70
2-Kraven 3 6 9 17 26 35
3-10,15: 6-Iceman. 15-Storm-c/sty 3 6 9 14 20 26
11-14,16-20: 19,20-Kirby-c 3 6 9 14 19 24
21-30 2 4 6 13 18 22
31-53: 31-Moondragon-c/app.; Dr. Doom app. 33-Hulk. 34-Sub-Mariner. 38-F.F. 39-Thanos-c/story. 44-Vision. 45-Silver Surfer & Dr. Doom app. 2 4 6 11 16 20
54-57: 56-Battles Jack O'Lantern-c/sty (exactly one year after 1st app. in Machine Man #19) 3 6 9 14 20 26

SPIKE AND TYKE (See M.G.M.'s...)

SPIKE... (Also see Buffy the Vampire Slayer and related titles)
IDW Publ.: Aug, 2005; Jan, 2006; Apr, 2006 ($7.49, squarebound, one-shots)

...: Lost & Found (4/06, $7.49) Scott Tipton-s/Fernando Goni-a 8.00
...: Old Times (8/05, $7.49) Peter David-s/Fernando Goni-a; Cecily/Halfrek app. 8.00
...: Old Wounds (1/06, $7.49) Tipton-s/Goni-a; flashback to Black Dahlia murder case 8.00
TPB (7/06, $19.99) r/one-shots 20.00

SPIKE (Buffy the Vampire Slayer)
IDW Publ.: Oct, 2010 - No. 8, May, 2011 ($3.99, limited series)

1-8-Lynch-s; multiple covers on each. 1,2-Urru-a. 5-7-Willow app. 4.00
... 100 Page Spectacular (6/11, $7.99) reprints of four IDW Spike stories; Frison-c 8.00

SPIKE (A Dark Place) (From Buffy the Vampire Slayer)
Dark Horse Comics: Aug, 2012 - No. 5, Dec, 2012 ($2.99, limited series)

1-5-Paul Lee-a; 2 covers by Frison & Morris on each 3.00

SPIKE: AFTER THE FALL (Also see Angel: After the Fall) (Follows the last Angel TV episode)
IDW Publ.: July, 2008 - No. 4, Oct, 2008 ($3.99, limited series)

1-4-Lynch-s/Urru-a; multiple covers on each 4.00

SPIKE: ASYLUM (Buffy the Vampire Slayer)
IDW Publ.: Sept, 2006 - No. 5, Jan, 2007 ($3.99, limited series)

1-5-Lynch-s/Urru-a; multiple covers on each 4.00

SPIKE: SHADOW PUPPETS (Buffy the Vampire Slayer)
IDW Publ.: June, 2007 - No. 4, Sept, 2007 ($3.99, limited series)

1-4-Lynch-s/Urru-a; multiple covers on each 4.00

SPIKE: THE DEVIL YOU KNOW (Buffy the Vampire Slayer)
IDW Publ.: Jun, 2010 - No. 4, Sept, 2010 ($3.99, limited series)

1-4-Bill Williams-s/Chris Cross-a/Urru-c 4.00

SPIKE VS. DRACULA (Buffy the Vampire Slayer)
IDW Publ.: Feb, 2006 - No. 5, Mar, 2006 ($3.99, limited series)

1-5: 1-Peter David-s/Joe Corroney-a; Dru and Bela Lugosi app. 4.00

SPIN & MARTY (TV) (Walt Disney's)(See Walt Disney Showcase #32)
Dell Publishing Co. (Mickey Mouse Club): No. 714, June, 1956 - No. 1082, Mar-May, 1960 (All photo-c)

Four Color 714 (#1) 10 20 30 69 147 225
Four Color 767,808 (#2,3) 8 16 24 54 102 150
Four Color 826 (#4)-Annette Funicello photo-c 18 36 54 124 275 425
5(3-5/58) - 9(6-8/59) 7 14 21 44 82 120
Four Color 1026,1082 7 14 21 44 82 120

SPIN ANGELS
Marvel Comics (Soleil): 2009 - No. 4, 2009 ($5.99)

1-4-English version of French comics; Jean-Luc Sala-s/Pierre-Mony Chan-a 6.00

SPINE-TINGLING TALES (Doctor Spektor Presents...)
Gold Key: May, 1975 - No. 4, Jan, 1976 (All 25¢ issues)

1-1st Tragg-r/Mystery Comics Digest #3 2 4 6 9 13 16
2-4: 2-Origin Ra-Ka-Tep-r/Mystery Comics Digest #1; Dr. Spektor #12. 3-All Durak-r issue; 4-Baron Tibor's 1st app.-r/Mystery Comics Digest #4; painted-c 1 2 3 5 7 9

SPINWORLD
Amaze Ink (Slave Labor Graphics): July, 1997 - No. 4, Jan, 1998 ($2.95/$3.95, B&W, mini-series)

1-3-Brent Anderson-a(p) 3.00
4-($3.95) 4.00

SPIRAL PATH, THE
Eclipse Comics: July, 1986 - No. 2 ($1.75, Baxter paper, limited series)

1,2 3.00

SPIRAL ZONE
DC Comics: Feb, 1988 - No. 4, May, 1988 ($1.00, mini-series)

1-4-Based on Tonka toys 3.00

SPIRIT, THE (Newspaper comics - see Promotional Comics section)

The Spirit #22 © Will Eisner Studios

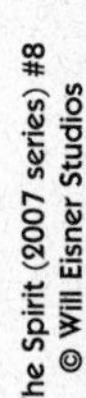
The Spirit (2007 series) #8 © Will Eisner Studios

Spitfire #133 © MH

	GD 2.0	VG 4.0	FN 6.0	VF 8.0	VF/NM 9.0	NM- 9.2

SPIRIT, THE (1st Series)(Also see Police Comics #11 and The Best of the Spirit TPB)
Quality Comics Group (Vital): 1944 - No. 22, Aug, 1950

	GD	VG	FN	VF	VF/NM	NM-
nn(#1)- "Wanted Dead or Alive"	135	270	405	864	1482	2100
nn(#2)- "Crime Doesn't Pay"	53	106	159	334	567	800
nn(#3)- "Murder Runs Wild"	46	96	138	290	488	685
4,5: 4-Flatfoot Burns begins, ends #22. 5-Wertham app.	39	78	117	234	385	535
6-10	34	68	102	204	332	460
11-Crandall-c	32	64	96	192	314	435
12-17-Eisner-c. 19-Honeybun app.	42	84	126	267	451	635
18,19-Strip-r by Eisner; Eisner-c	58	116	174	371	636	900
20,21-Eisner good girl covers; strip-r by Eisner	71	142	213	454	777	1100
22-Used by N.Y. Legis. Comm; classic Eisner-c	258	516	774	1651	2826	4000
Super Reprint #11-r/Quality Spirit #19 by Eisner	3	6	9	18	27	35
Super Reprint #12-r/Spirit #17 by Fine; Sol Brodsky-c	3	6	9	18	27	35

SPIRIT, THE (2nd Series)
Fiction House Magazines: Spring, 1952 - No. 5, 1954

	GD	VG	FN	VF	VF/NM	NM-
1-Not Eisner	47	94	141	296	498	700
2-Eisner-c/a(2)	45	90	135	284	480	675
3-Eisner/Grandenetti-c	40	80	120	246	411	575
4-Eisner/Grandenetti-c; Eisner-a	41	82	123	250	418	585
5-Eisner-c/a(4)	43	86	129	271	461	650

SPIRIT, THE
Harvey Publications: Oct, 1966 - No. 2, Mar, 1967 (Giant Size, 25¢, 68 pgs.)

	GD	VG	FN	VF	VF/NM	NM-
1-Eisner-r plus 9 new pgs.(origin Denny Colt, Take 3, plus 2 filler pgs.) (#3 was advertised, but never published)	8	16	24	54	102	150
2-Eisner-r plus 9 new pgs.(origin of the Octopus)	7	14	21	44	82	120

SPIRIT, THE (Underground)
Kitchen Sink Enterprises (Krupp Comics): Jan, 1973 - No. 2, Sept, 1973 (Black & White)

	GD	VG	FN	VF	VF/NM	NM-
1-New Eisner-c & 4 pgs. new Eisner-a plus-r (titled Crime Convention)	4	8	12	23	37	50
2-New Eisner-c & 4 pgs. new Eisner-a plus-r (titled Meets P'Gell)	4	8	12	25	40	55

SPIRIT, THE (Magazine)
Warren Publ. Co./Krupp Comic Works No. 17 on: 4/74 - No. 16, 10/76; No. 17, Winter, 1977 - No. 41, 6/83 (B&W w/color) (#6-14,16 are squarebound)

	GD	VG	FN	VF	VF/NM	NM-
1-Eisner-r begin; 8 pg. color insert	6	12	18	41	76	110
2-5: 2-Powder Pouf-s; UFO-s. 4-Silk Satin-s	4	8	12	27	44	60
6-9,11-15: 7-All Ebony issue. 8-Female Foes issue. 8,12-Sand Seref-s. 9-P'Gell & Octopus-s. 12-X-Mas issue	4	8	12	25	40	55
10-Giant Summer Special ($1.50)-Origin	4	8	12	27	44	60
16-Giant Summer Special ($1.50)-Olga Bustle-c/s	4	8	12	25	40	55
17,18(8/78): 17-Lady Luck-r	3	6	9	17	26	35
19-21-New Eisner-a. 20,21-Wood-r (#21-r/A DP on the Moon by Wood). 20-Outer Space-r	3	6	9	17	26	35
22-41: 22,23-Wood-r (#22-r/Mission the Moon by Wood). 28-r/last story (10/5/52). 30-(7/81)-Special Spirit Jam issue w/Caniff, Corben, Bolland, Byrne, Miller, Kurtzman, Rogers, Sienkiewicz-a & 40 others. 36-Begin Spirit Section-r; r/1st story (6/2/40) in color; new Eisner-c/a(18 pgs.)($2.95). 37-r/2nd story in color plus 18 pgs. new Eisner-a. 38-41: r/3rd - 6th stories in color. 41-Lady Luck Mr. Mystic in color	3	6	9	15	22	28
Special 1(1975)-All Eisner-a (mail only, 1500 printed, full color)	13	26	39	89	195	300

NOTE: *Covers pencilled/inked by* ***Eisner*** *only #1-9,12-16; painted by Eisner & Ken Kelly #10 & 11; painted by Eisner #17-up; one color story reprinted in #1-10.* ***Austin*** *a-30i.* ***Byrne*** *a-30p.* ***Miller*** *a-30p.*

SPIRIT, THE
Kitchen Sink Enterprises: Oct, 1983 - No. 87, Jan, 1992 ($2.00, Baxter paper)

1-60: 1-Origin-r/12/23/45 Spirit Section. 2-r/ 1/20/46-2/10/46. 3-r/2/17/46-3/10/46. 4-r/3/17/46-4/7/46. 11-Last color issue. 54-r/section 2/19/50 — 4.00
61-87: 85-87-Reprint the Outer Space Spirit stories by Wood. 86-r/A DP on the Moon by Wood from 1952 — 4.00

SPIRIT, THE (Also see Batman/The Spirit in Batman one-shots)
DC Comics: Feb, 2007 - No. 32, Oct, 2009 ($2.99)

1-32: 1-6,8-12-Darwyn Cooke-s/a/c. 2-P'Gell app. 3-Origin re-told. 7-Short stories by Baker, Bernet, Palmiotti, Simonson & Sprouse; Cooke-c. 13-Short stories by various — 3.00
... Femme Fatales TPB (2008, $19.99) r/1940s stories focusing on the Spirit's female adversaries like Silk Satin, P'gell, Powder Pouf and Silken Floss; Michael Uslan intro. — 20.00
... Special 1 (2008, $2.99) r/stories from '47, '49, '50 newspaper strips; the Octopus app. — 3.00

SPIRIT, THE (First Wave)
DC Comics: Jun, 2010 - No. 17, Oct, 2011 ($3.99/$2.99)(B&W back-up stories by various)

1-10: 1-Schultz-s/Moritat-a; covers by Ladronn and Schultz; back-up by O'Neil & Sienkiewicz. 2-Back-up by Ellison & Baker. 7-Corben-a back-up. 8-Ploog-a back-up — 4.00
11-17-($2.99) 11-16-Hine-s/Moritat-a; no back-up story. 17-B&W; Bolland, Russell-a — 3.00
...: Angel Smerti TPB (2011, $17.99) r/#1-7 — 18.00

SPIRIT JAM
Kitchen Sink Press: Aug, 1998 ($5.95, B&W, oversized, square-bound)

nn-Reprints Spirit (Magazine) #30 by Eisner & 50 others; and "Cerebus Vs. The Spirit" from Cerebus Jam #1 — 6.00

SPIRIT, THE: THE NEW ADVENTURES
Kitchen Sink Press: 1997 - No. 8, Nov, 1998 ($3.50, anthology)

1-Moore-s/Gibbons-c/a — 4.00
2-8: 2-Gaiman-s/Eisner-c. 3-Moore-s/Bolland-c/Moebius back-c. 4-Allred-s/a; Busiek-s/Anderson-a. 5-Chadwick-s/c/a(p); Nyberg-i. 6-S.Hampton & Mandrake-a — 3.50
Will Eisner's The Spirit Archives Volume 27 (Dark Horse, 2009, $49.95) r/#1-8 — 50.00

SPIRIT: THE ORIGIN YEARS
Kitchen Sink Press: May, 1992 - No. 10, Dec, 1993 ($2.95, B&W)

1-10: 1-r/sections 6/2/40(origin)-6/23/40 (all 1940s) — 3.00

SPIRITMAN (Also see Three Comics)
No publisher listed: No date (1944) (10¢)
(Triangle Sales Co. ad on back cover)

	GD	VG	FN	VF	VF/NM	NM-
1-Three 16pg. Spirit sections bound together, (1944, 10¢, 52 pgs.)	24	48	72	142	234	325
2-Two Spirit sections (3/26/44, 4/2/44) bound together; by Lou Fine	21	42	63	122	199	275

SPIRIT OF THE BORDER (See Zane Grey & Four Color #197)

SPIRIT OF THE TAO
Image Comics (Top Cow): Jun, 1998 - No. 15, May, 2000 ($2.50)

Preview — 5.00
1-14: 1-D-Tron-s/Tan & D-Tron-a — 3.00
15-($4.95) — 5.00

SPIRIT WORLD (Magazine)
Hampshire Distributors Ltd.: Fall, 1971 (B&W)

	GD	VG	FN	VF	VF/NM	NM-
1-New Kirby-a; Neal Adams-c; poster inside (1/2 price without poster)	6	12	18	40	73	105

SPITFIRE (Female undercover agent)
Malverne Herald (Elliot)(J. R. Mahon): No. 132, 1944 (Aug) - No. 133, 1945

	GD	VG	FN	VF	VF/NM	NM-
132,133: Both have Classics Gift Box ads on b/c with checklist to #20. 132-British spitfire WWII-c. 133-Female agent/Nazi WWII-c	28	56	84	165	270	375

SPITFIRE (WW2 speedster from MI:13)
Marvel Comics: Oct, 2010 ($3.99, one-shot)

1-Cornell-s/Casagrande-a; Blade app. — 4.00

SPITFIRE AND THE TROUBLESHOOTERS
Marvel Comics: Oct, 1986 - No. 9, June, 1987 (Codename: Spitfire #10 on)

1-3,5-9 — 3.00
4-McFarlane-a — 4.00

SPITFIRE COMICS (Also see Double Up) (Tied with Pocket Comics #1 for earliest Harvey)
Harvey Publications: Aug, 1941 - No. 2, Oct, 1941 (Pocket size; 100 pgs.)

	GD	VG	FN	VF	VF/NM	NM-
1-Origin The Clown, The Fly-Man, The Spitfire & The Magician From Bagdad; British spitfire, Nazi bomber WWII-c	82	164	246	528	902	1275
2-(Rare) Fly-Man-c	76	152	228	486	831	1175

SPLITTING IMAGE
Image Comics: Mar, 1993 - No. 2, 1993 ($1.95)

1,2-Simpson-c/a; parody comic — 3.00

SPONGEBOB COMICS (TV's Spongebob Squarepants)
United Plankton Pictures: 2011 - Present ($2.99)

1-31-Short stories by various. 1-Kochalka back-c. 3-Aquaman homage w/Fradon-a — 3.00
Annual-Size Super-Giant Swimtacular 1 (2013, $4.99) art by Fradon, Ordway, Kochalka — 5.00
SpongeBob Freestyle Funnies 1 (2013, Free Comic Book Day giveaway) Short stories — 3.00

SPOOF
Marvel Comics Group: Oct, 1970; No. 2, Nov, 1972 - No. 5, May, 1973

	GD	VG	FN	VF	VF/NM	NM-
1-Infinity-c; Dark Shadows-c & parody	4	8	12	23	37	50
2-5: 2-All in the Family. 3-Beatles, Osmond's, Jackson 5, David Cassidy, Nixon & Agnew-c. 5-Rod Serling, Woody Allen, Ted Kennedy-c	3	6	9	16	24	32

SPOOK (Formerly Shock Detective Cases)
Star Publications: No. 22, Jan, 1953 - No. 30, Oct, 1954

Spooky #1 © HARV

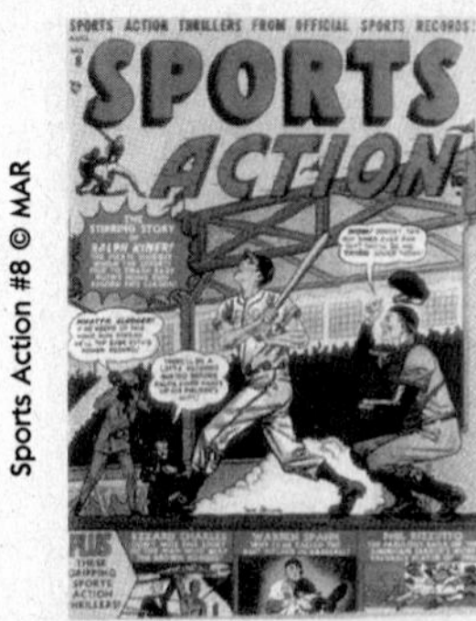

Sports Action #8 © MAR

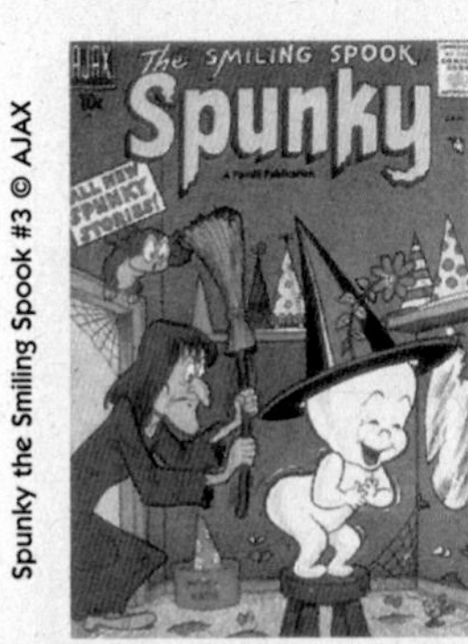

Spunky the Smiling Spook #3 © AJAX

	GD 2.0	VG 4.0	FN 6.0	VF 8.0	VF/NM 9.0	NM- 9.2
22-Sgt. Spook-r; acid in face story; hanging-c	41	82	123	256	428	600
23,25,27: 25-Jungle Lil-r. 27-Two Sgt. Spook-r	32	64	96	188	307	425
24-Used in **SOTI**, pgs. 182,183-r/Inside Crime #2; Transvestism story	34	68	102	199	325	450
26,28-30: 26-Disbrow-a. 28,29-Rulah app. 29-Jo-Jo app. 30-Disbrow-c/a(2); only Star-c	32	64	96	188	307	425

NOTE: *L. B. Cole covers-all issues except #30; a-28(1 pg.).* ***Disbrow*** *a-26(2), 28, 29(2), 30(2); No. 30 r/Blue Bolt Weird Tales #114.*

SPOOK COMICS
Baily Publications/Star: 1946

	GD 2.0	VG 4.0	FN 6.0	VF 8.0	VF/NM 9.0	NM- 9.2
1-Mr. Lucifer story	34	68	102	204	332	460

SPOOKY (The Tuff Little Ghost; see Casper The Friendly Ghost)
Harvey Publications: 11/55 - 139, 11/73; No. 140, 7/74 - No. 155, 3/77; No. 156, 12/77 - No. 158, 4/78; No. 159, 9/78; No. 160, 10/79; No. 161, 9/80

	GD 2.0	VG 4.0	FN 6.0	VF 8.0	VF/NM 9.0	NM- 9.2
1-Nightmare begins (see Casper #19)	50	100	150	400	900	1400
2	20	40	60	138	307	475
3-10(1956-57)	11	22	33	76	163	250
11-20(1957-58)	7	14	21	44	82	120
21-40(1958-59)	5	10	15	33	57	80
41-60	4	8	12	27	44	60
61-80,100	3	6	9	19	30	40
81-99	3	6	9	16	24	32
101-120	2	4	6	11	16	20
121-126,133-140	2	4	6	8	11	14
127-132: All 52 pg. Giants	2	4	6	11	16	20
141-161	1	2	3	5	7	9

SPOOKY
Harvey Comics: Nov, 1991 - No. 4, Sept, 1992 ($1.00/$1.25)

	NM- 9.2
1	4.00
2-4: 3-Begin $1.25-c	3.00
...Digest 1-3 (10/92, 6/93, 10/93, $1.75, 100 pgs.)-Casper, Wendy, etc.	4.00

SPOOKY HAUNTED HOUSE
Harvey Publications: Oct, 1972 - No. 15, Feb, 1975

	GD 2.0	VG 4.0	FN 6.0	VF 8.0	VF/NM 9.0	NM- 9.2
1	3	6	9	17	26	35
2-5	2	4	6	10	14	18
6-10	2	4	6	8	10	12
11-15	1	2	3	5	7	9

SPOOKY MYSTERIES
Your Guide Publ. Co.: No date (1946) (10¢)

	GD 2.0	VG 4.0	FN 6.0	VF 8.0	VF/NM 9.0	NM- 9.2
1-Mr. Spooky, Super Snooper, Pinky, Girl Detective app.	21	42	63	124	202	280

SPOOKY SPOOKTOWN
Harvey Publ.: 9/61; No. 2, 9/62 - No. 52, 12/73; No. 53, 10/74 - No. 66, 12/76

	GD 2.0	VG 4.0	FN 6.0	VF 8.0	VF/NM 9.0	NM- 9.2
1-Casper, Spooky; 68 pgs. begin	14	28	42	94	207	320
2	8	16	24	54	102	150
3-5	6	12	18	38	69	100
6-10	5	10	15	31	53	75
11-20	4	8	12	23	37	50
21-39: 39-Last 68 pg. issue	3	6	9	19	30	40
40-45: All 52 pgs.	2	4	6	11	16	20
46-66: 61-Hot Stuff/Spooky team-up story	1	2	3	5	7	9

SPORT COMICS (Becomes True Sport Picture Stories #5 on)
Street & Smith Publications: Oct, 1940 (No mo.) - No. 4, Nov, 1941

	GD 2.0	VG 4.0	FN 6.0	VF 8.0	VF/NM 9.0	NM- 9.2
1-Life story of Lou Gehrig	55	110	165	352	601	850
2	31	62	93	182	296	410
3,4: 4-Story of Notre Dame coach Frank Leahy	26	52	78	154	252	350

SPORT LIBRARY (See Charlton Sport Library)

SPORTS ACTION (Formerly Sport Stars)
Marvel/Atlas Comics (ACI No. 2,3/SAI No. 4-14): No. 2, Feb, 1950 - No. 14, Sept, 1952

	GD 2.0	VG 4.0	FN 6.0	VF 8.0	VF/NM 9.0	NM- 9.2
2-Powell painted-c; George Gipp life story	43	86	129	269	455	640
1-(nd,no price, no publ., 52pgs, #1 on-c; has same-c as #2; blank inside-c (giveaway?)	22	44	66	132	216	300
3-Everett-a	24	48	72	142	234	325
4-11,14: Weiss-a	22	44	66	128	209	290
12,13: 12-Everett-c. 13-Krigstein-a	23	46	69	136	223	310

NOTE: *Title may have changed after No. 3, to Crime Must Lose No. 4 on, due to publisher change.* ***Sol Brodsky*** *c-4-7, 13, 14.* ***Maneely*** *c-3, 8-11.*

SPORT STARS
Parents' Magazine Institute (Sport Stars): Feb-Mar, 1946 - No. 4, Aug-Sept, 1946 (Half comic, half photo magazine)

	GD 2.0	VG 4.0	FN 6.0	VF 8.0	VF/NM 9.0	NM- 9.2
1-"How Tarzan Got That Way" story of Johnny Weissmuller	40	80	120	243	402	560
2-Baseball greats	26	52	78	154	252	350
3,4	23	46	69	136	223	310

SPORT STARS (Becomes Sports Action #2 on)
Marvel Comics (ACI): Nov, 1949 (52 pgs.)

	GD 2.0	VG 4.0	FN 6.0	VF 8.0	VF/NM 9.0	NM- 9.2
1-Knute Rockne; painted-c	45	90	135	284	480	675

SPORT THRILLS (Formerly Dick Cole; becomes Jungle Thrills #16)
Star Publications: No. 11, Nov, 1950 - No. 15, Nov, 1951

	GD 2.0	VG 4.0	FN 6.0	VF 8.0	VF/NM 9.0	NM- 9.2
11-Dick Cole begins; Ted Williams & Ty Cobb life stories	28	56	84	165	270	375
12-Joe DiMaggio, Phil Rizzuto stories & photos on-c; L.B. Cole-c/a	22	44	66	132	216	300
13-15-All L. B. Cole-c. 13-Jackie Robinson, Pee Wee Reese stories & photo on-c. 14-Johnny Weissmuler life story	22	44	66	132	216	300
Accepted Reprint #11 (#15 on-c, nd); L.B. Cole-c	10	20	30	54	72	90
Accepted Reprint #12 (nd); L.B. Cole-c; Joe DiMaggio & Phil Rizzuto life stories-r/#12	10	20	30	54	72	90

SPOTLIGHT (TV) (newsstand sales only)
Marvel Comics Group: Sept, 1978 - No. 4, Mar, 1979 (Hanna-Barbera)

	GD 2.0	VG 4.0	FN 6.0	VF 8.0	VF/NM 9.0	NM- 9.2
1-Huckleberry Hound, Yogi Bear; Shaw-a	3	6	9	19	30	40
2,4: 2-Quick Draw McGraw, Augie Doggie, Snooper & Blabber. 4-Magilla Gorilla, Snagglepuss	3	6	9	16	23	30
3-The Jetsons; Yakky Doodle	3	6	9	19	30	40

SPOTLIGHT COMICS
Country Press Inc.: Sept, 1940

nn-Ashcan, not distributed to newsstands, only for in house use. A NM copy sold in 2009 for $1015.

SPOTLIGHT COMICS (Becomes Red Seal Comics #14 on?)
Harry 'A' Chesler (Our Army, Inc.): Nov, 1944, No. 2, Jan, 1945 - No. 3, 1945

	GD 2.0	VG 4.0	FN 6.0	VF 8.0	VF/NM 9.0	NM- 9.2
1-The Black Dwarf (cont'd in Red Seal?), The Veiled Avenger, & Barry Kuda begin; Tuska-c	123	246	369	787	1344	1900
2	63	126	189	403	689	975
3-Injury to eye story (reprinted from Scoop #3)	66	132	198	419	722	1025

SPOTTY THE PUP (Becomes Super Pup #4, see Television Puppet Show)
Avon Periodicals/Realistic Comics: No. 2, Oct-Nov, 1953 - No. 3, Dec-Jan, 1953-54 (Also see Funny Tunes)

	GD 2.0	VG 4.0	FN 6.0	VF 8.0	VF/NM 9.0	NM- 9.2
2,3	8	16	24	40	50	60
nn (1953, Realistic-r)	5	10	15	22	26	30

SPUNKY (...Junior Cowboy)(...Comics #2 on)
Standard Comics: April, 1949 - No. 7, Nov, 1951

	GD 2.0	VG 4.0	FN 6.0	VF 8.0	VF/NM 9.0	NM- 9.2
1-Text illos by Frazetta	13	26	39	72	101	130
2-Text illos by Frazetta	9	18	27	52	69	85
3-7	7	14	21	37	46	55

SPUNKY THE SMILING SPOOK
Ajax/Farrell (World Famous Comics/Four Star Comic Corp.): Aug, 1957 - No. 4, May, 1958

	GD 2.0	VG 4.0	FN 6.0	VF 8.0	VF/NM 9.0	NM- 9.2
1-Reprints from Frisky Fables	10	20	30	56	76	95
2-4	7	14	21	35	43	50

SPY AND COUNTERSPY (Becomes Spy Hunters #3 on)
American Comics Group: Aug-Sept, 1949 - No. 2, Oct-Nov, 1949 (52 pgs.)

	GD 2.0	VG 4.0	FN 6.0	VF 8.0	VF/NM 9.0	NM- 9.2
1-Origin, 1st app. Jonathan Kent, Counterspy	27	54	81	160	263	365
2	17	34	51	98	154	210

SPYBOY
Dark Horse Comics: Oct, 1999 - No. 17, May, 2001 ($2.50/$2.95/$2.99)

	NM- 9.2
1-17: 1-6-Peter David-s/Pop Mhan-a. 7,8-Meglia-a. 9-17-Mhan-a	3.00
13.1-13.3 (4/03-8/03, $2.99), 13.2,13.3-Mhan-a	3.00
... Special (5/02, $4.99) David-s/Mhan-a	5.00

SPYBOY: FINAL EXAM
Dark Horse Comics: May, 2004 - No. 4, Aug, 2004 ($2.99, limited series)

	NM- 9.2
1-4-Peter David-s/Pop Mhan-a/c	3.00
TPB (2005, $12.95) r/series	13.00

SPYBOY/ YOUNG JUSTICE
Dark Horse Comics: Feb, 2002 - No. 3, Apr, 2002 ($2.99, limited series)

	NM- 9.2
1-3: 1-Peter David-s/Todd Nauck-a/Pop Mhan-c. 2-Mhan-a	3.00

SPY CASES (Formerly The Kellys)

Spy-Hunters #5 © ACG

Squeeks #2 © LEV

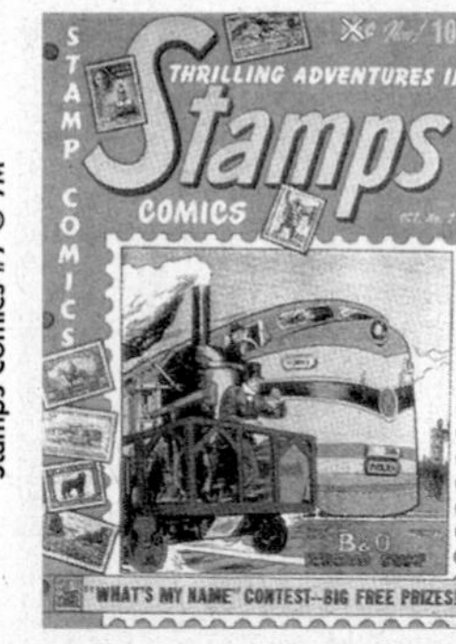

Stamps Comics #7 © YM

Marvel/Atlas Comics (Hercules Publ.): No. 26, Sept, 1950 - No. 19, Oct, 1953

	GD 2.0	VG 4.0	FN 6.0	VF 8.0	VF/NM 9.0	NM- 9.2
26 (#1)	27	54	81	158	259	360
27(#2),28(#3, 2/51): 27-Everett-a; bondage-c	15	30	45	86	133	180
4(4/51) - 7,9,10: 4-Heath-a	14	28	42	81	118	155
8-A-Bomb-c/story	15	30	45	86	133	180
11-19: 10-14-War format	13	26	39	74	105	135

NOTE: *Sol Brodsky c-1-5, 8, 9, 11-14, 17, 18. Maneely a-8; c-7, 10. Tuska a-7.*

SPY FIGHTERS
Marvel/Atlas Comics (CSI): March, 1951 - No. 15, July, 1953
(Cases from official records)

	GD 2.0	VG 4.0	FN 6.0	VF 8.0	VF/NM 9.0	NM- 9.2
1-Clark Mason begins; Tuska-a; Brodsky-c	27	54	81	158	259	360
2-Tuska-a	15	30	45	85	130	175
3-13: 3-5-Brodsky-c. 7-Heath-c	14	28	42	81	118	155
14,15-Pakula-a(3), Ed Win-a. 15-Brodsky-c	14	28	42	82	121	160

SPY-HUNTERS (Formerly Spy & Counterspy)
American Comics Group: No. 3, Dec-Jan, 1949-50 - No. 24, June-July, 1953 (#3-14: 52 pgs.)

	GD 2.0	VG 4.0	FN 6.0	VF 8.0	VF/NM 9.0	NM- 9.2
3-Jonathan Kent continues, ends #10	23	46	69	136	223	310
4-10: 4,8,10-Starr-a	14	28	42	80	115	150
11-15,17-22,24: 18-War-c begin. 21-War-c/stories begin	10	20	30	56	76	95
16-Williamson-a (9 pgs.)	15	30	45	88	137	185
23-Graphic torture, injury to eye panel	20	40	60	114	182	250

NOTE: *Drucker a-12. Whitney a-many issues; c-7, 8, 10-12, 15, 16.*

SPYMAN (Top Secret Adventures on cover)
Harvey Publications (Illustrated Humor): Sept, 1966 - No. 3, Feb, 1967 (12¢)

	GD 2.0	VG 4.0	FN 6.0	VF 8.0	VF/NM 9.0	NM- 9.2
1-Origin and 1st app. of Spyman. Steranko-a(p)-1st pro work; 1 pg. Neal Adams ad; Tuska-c/a, Crandall-a(i)	6	12	18	38	69	100
2-Simon-c; Steranko-a(p)	4	8	12	27	44	60
3-Simon-c	4	8	12	25	40	55

SPY SMASHER (See Mighty Midget, Whiz & Xmas Comics) (Also see Crime Smasher)
Fawcett Publications: Fall, 1941 - No. 11, Feb, 1943

	GD 2.0	VG 4.0	FN 6.0	VF 8.0	VF/NM 9.0	NM- 9.2
1-Spy Smasher begins; silver metallic-c	331	662	993	2317	4059	5800
2-Raboy-c	152	304	456	965	1658	2350
3,4: 3-Bondage-c. 4-Irvin Steinberg-c	102	204	306	648	1112	1575
5-7: Raboy-a; 6-Raboy-c/a. 7-Part photo-c (movie) Japanese dragon-c	87	174	261	553	952	1350
8,11: War-c	73	146	219	468	802	1135
9-Hitler, Tojo, Mussolini-c.	123	246	369	787	1344	1900
10-Hitler-c	116	232	348	742	1271	1800

SPY THRILLERS (Police Badge No. 479 #5)
Atlas Comics (PrPI): Nov, 1954 - No. 4, May, 1955

	GD 2.0	VG 4.0	FN 6.0	VF 8.0	VF/NM 9.0	NM- 9.2
1-Brodsky c-1,2	22	44	66	132	216	300
2-Last precode (1/55)	14	28	42	82	121	160
3,4	12	24	36	69	97	125

SQUADRON SUPREME (Also see Marvel Graphic Novel - ...: Death of a Universe)
Marvel Comics Group: Aug, 1985 - No. 12, Aug, 1986 (Maxi-series)

	NM- 9.2
1-Double size	5.00
2-12	4.00
TPB ($24.99) r/#1-12; Alex Ross painted-c; printing inks contain some of the cremated remains of late writer Mark Gruenwald	50.00
TPB-2nd printing ($24.99): Inks contain no ashes	25.00
...Death of a Universe TPB (2006, $24.99) r/Marvel Graphic Novel, Thor #280, Avengers #5,6; Avengers/Squadron Supreme Annual and Squadron Supreme: New World Order	25.00

SQUADRON SUPREME (Also see Supreme Power)
Marvel Comics: May, 2006 - No. 7, Nov, 2006 ($2.99)

	NM- 9.2
1-7-Straczynski-s/Frank-a/c	3.00
Saga of Squadron Supreme (2006, $3.99) summary of Supreme Power #1-18; plus Hyperion and Nighthawk limited series; wraparound-c; preview of Squadron Supreme #1	4.00
... Vol. 1: The Pre-War Years (2006, $20.99, dustjacket) r/#1-5 & Saga of S.S.	21.00

SQUADRON SUPREME
Marvel Comics: Sept, 2008 - No. 12, Aug, 2009 ($2.99)

	NM- 9.2
1-12: 1-Set 5 years after Ultimate Power; Nick Fury app.; Chaykin-s/Turini-a/Land-c	3.00

SQUADRON SUPREME: HYPERION VS. NIGHTHAWK
Marvel Comics: Mar, 2007 - No. 4, June, 2007 ($2.99, limited series)

	NM- 9.2
1-4-Hyperion and Nighthawk in Darfur; Gulacy-a/c; Guggenheim-s	3.00
TPB (2007, $10.99) r/#1-4	11.00

SQUADRON SUPREME: NEW WORLD ORDER
Marvel Comics: Sept, 1998 ($5.99, one-shot)

	NM- 9.2
1-Wraparound-c; Kaminski-s	6.00

SQUALOR
First Comics: Dec, 1989 - Aug, 1990 ($2.75, limited series)

	NM- 9.2
1-4: Sutton-a	3.00

SQUEE (Also see Johnny The Homicidal Maniac)
Slave Labor Graphics: Apr, 1997 - No. 4, May, 1998 ($2.95, B&W)

	NM- 9.2
1-4: Jhonen Vasquez-s/a in all	3.00

SQUEEKS (Also see Boy Comics)
Lev Gleason Publications: Oct, 1953 - No. 5, June, 1954

	GD 2.0	VG 4.0	FN 6.0	VF 8.0	VF/NM 9.0	NM- 9.2
1-Funny animal; Biro-c; Crimebuster's pet monkey "Squeeks" begins	10	20	30	54	72	90
2-Biro-c	6	12	18	31	38	45
3-5: 3-Biro-c	6	12	18	28	34	40

S.R. BISSETTE'S SPIDERBABY COMIX
SpiderBaby Grafix: Aug, 1996 - No. 2 ($3.95, B&W, magazine size)

	NM- 9.2
Preview-(8/96, $3.95)-Graphic violence & nudity; Laurel & Hardy app.	4.00
1,2	4.00

S.R. BISSETTE'S TYRANT
SpiderBaby Grafix: Sept, 1994 - No. 4 ($2.95, B&W)

	NM- 9.2
1-4	4.00

STALKER (Also see All Star Comics 1999 and crossover issues)
National Periodical Publications: June-July, 1975 - No. 4, Dec-Jan, 1975-76

	GD 2.0	VG 4.0	FN 6.0	VF 8.0	VF/NM 9.0	NM- 9.2
1-Origin & 1st app; Ditko/Wood-c/a	2	4	6	10	14	18
2-4-Ditko/Wood-c/a	2	3	4	6	8	10

STALKERS
Marvel Comics (Epic Comics): Apr, 1990 - No. 12, Mar, 1991 ($1.50)

	NM- 9.2
1-12: 1-Chadwick-c	3.00

STAMP COMICS (Stamps... on-c; Thrilling Adventures In...#8)
Youthful Magazines/Stamp Comics, Inc.: Oct, 1951 - No. 7, Oct, 1952

	GD 2.0	VG 4.0	FN 6.0	VF 8.0	VF/NM 9.0	NM- 9.2
1-(15¢) ('Stamps' on indicia No. 1-3,5,7)	26	52	78	152	249	345
2	15	30	45	86	133	180
3-6: 3,4-Kiefer, Wildey-a	14	28	42	81	118	155
7-Roy Krenkel (4 pgs.)	17	34	51	98	154	210

NOTE: *Promotes stamp collecting; gives stories behind various commemorative stamps. No. 2, 10¢ printed over 15¢ c-price. Kiefer a-1-7. Kirkel a-1-6. Napoli a-2-7. Palais a-2-4, 7.*

STAND, THE ... (Based on the Stephen King novel)
Marvel Comics: 2008 - Present ($3.99, limited series)

	NM- 9.2
...: American Nightmares 1-5 (5/09 - No. 5, 10/09, $3.99) Aguirre-Sacasa-s/Perkins-a	4.00
...: Captain Trips 1-5 (12/08 - No. 5, 3/09, $3.99) Aguirre-Sacasa-s/Perkins-a	4.00
...: Hardcases 1-5 (8/10 - No. 5, 1/11, $3.99) Aguirre-Sacasa-s/Perkins-a	4.00
...: No Man's Land 1-5 (4/11 - No. 5, 8/11, $3.99) Aguirre-Sacasa-s/Perkins-a	4.00
...: Soul Survivors 1-5 (12/09 - No. 5, 5/10, $3.99) Aguirre-Sacasa-s/Perkins-a	4.00
...: The Night Has Come 1-6 (10/11 - No. 6, 3/12, $3.99) Aguirre-Sacasa-s/Perkins-a	4.00

STAN LEE MEETS...
Marvel Comics: Nov, 2006 - Jan, 2007 ($3.99, series of one-shots)

	NM- 9.2
Doctor Doom 1 (12/06) Lee-s/Larroca-a/c; Loeb-s/McGuinness-a; r/Fantastic Four #87	4.00
Doctor Strange 1 (11/06) Lee-s/Davis-a/c; Bendis-s/Bagley-a; r/Marvel Premiere #3	4.00
Silver Surfer 1 (1/07) Lee-s/Wieringo-a/c; Jenkins-s/Buckingham-a; r/S.S. #14	4.00
Spider-Man 1 (11/06) Lee-s/Coipel-a/c; Whedon-s/Gaydos-a; Hembeck-s/a; r/AS-M #87	4.00
The Thing 1 (12/06) Lee-s/Weeks-a/c; Thomas-s/Kolins-a; r/FF #79; FF #51 cover swipe	4.00
HC (2007, $24.99, dustjacket) r/one-shots; interviews and features	25.00

STAN LEE'S MIGHTY 7
Archie Comics (Stan Lee Comics): May, 2012 - No. 3, Sept, 2012 ($2.99, limited series)

	NM- 9.2
1-3-Co-written by Stan Lee; Alex Saviuk-a; multiple covers on each	3.00

STANLEY & HIS MONSTER (Formerly The Fox & the Crow)
National Periodical Publ.: No. 109, Apr-May, 1968 - No. 112, Oct-Nov, 1968

	GD 2.0	VG 4.0	FN 6.0	VF 8.0	VF/NM 9.0	NM- 9.2
109-112	3	6	9	21	33	45

STANLEY & HIS MONSTER
DC Comics: Feb, 1993 - No. 4, May, 1993 ($1.50, limited series)

	NM- 9.2
1-4	3.00

STAN SHAW'S BEAUTY & THE BEAST
Dark Horse Comics: Nov, 1993 ($4.95, one-shot)

	NM- 9.2
1	5.00

STAR
Image Comics (Highbrow Entertainment): June, 1995 - No. 4, Oct, 1995 ($2.50, lim. series)

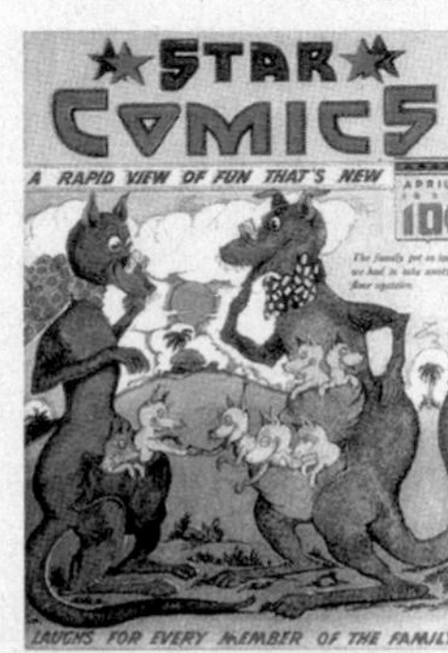

Star Comics #2 © CEN

Starfire #1 © DC

Starlight #1 © Millar & Parlov

	GD 2.0	VG 4.0	FN 6.0	VF 8.0	VF/NM 9.0	NM- 9.2

1-4 3.00

STARBLAST
Marvel Comics: Jan, 1994 - No. 4, Apr, 1994 ($1.75, limited series)

1-($2.00, 52 pgs.)-Nova, Quasar, Black Bolt; painted-c 4.00
2-4 3.00

STAR BLAZERS
Comico: Apr, 1987 - No. 4, July, 1987 ($1.75, limited series)

1-4 3.00

STAR BLAZERS
Comico: 1989 ($1.95/$2.50, limited series)

1-5- Steacy wraparound painted-c on all 3.00

STAR BLAZERS (The Magazine of Space Battleship Yamato)
Argo Press: No. 0, Aug, 1995 - No. 3, Dec, 1995 ($2.95)

0-3 3.00

STARBORN (From Stan Lee)
BOOM! Studios: Dec, 2010 - No. 12, Nov, 2011 ($3.99)

1-12: 1-9,11-Roberson-s/Randolph-a. 1-7-Three covers on each. 10-Scalera-a 4.00

STAR BRAND
Marvel Comics (New Universe): Oct, 1986 - No. 19, May, 1989 (75¢/$1.25)

1-15: 14-begin $1.25-c 3.00
16-19-Byrne story & art; low print run 5.00
Annual 1 (10/87) 4.00
... Classic Vol. 1 TPB (2006, $19.99) r/#1-7 20.00

STARCHILD
Tailspin Press: 1992 - No. 12 ($2.25/$2.50, B&W)

1,2-('92),0(4/93),3-12: 0-Illos by Chadwick, Eisner, Sim, M. Wagner. 3-(7/93). 4-(11/93). 6-(2/94) 3.00

STARCHILD: MYTHOPOLIS
Image Comics: No. 0, July, 1997 - No. 4, Apr, 1998 ($2.95, B&W, limited series)

0-4-James Owen-s/a 3.00

STAR COMICS
Ultem Publ. (Harry `A' Chesler)/Centaur Publications: Feb, 1937 - V2#7 (No. 23), Aug, 1939 (#1-6: large size)

V1#1-Dan Hastings (s/f) begins 314 628 942 2198 3849 5500
2 174 348 522 1114 1907 2700
3-Classic Black Americana cover (rare) 326 652 978 2282 3991 5700
4-6 (#6, 9/37): 4,5-Little Nemo-c/stories 161 322 483 1030 1765 2500
7-9: 8-Severed head centerspread; Impy & Little Nemo by Winsor McCay Jr, Popeye app. by Bob Wood; Mickey Mouse & Popeye app. as toys in Santa's bag on-c; X-Mas-c 116 232 348 742 1271 1800
10 (1st Centaur; 3/38)-Impy by Winsor McCay Jr; Don Marlow by Guardineer begins 142 284 426 909 1555 2200
11-1st Jack Cole comic-a, 1 pg. (4/38) 168 336 504 1075 1838 2600
12-15: 12-Riders of the Golden West begins; Little Nemo app. 15-Speed Silvers by Gustavson & The Last Pirate by Burgos begins 87 174 261 553 952 1350
16 (12/38)-The Phantom Rider & his horse Thunder begins, ends V2#6 97 194 291 621 1061 1500
V2#1(#17, 2/39)-Phantom Rider-c (only non-funny-c) 110 220 330 704 1202 1700
2-7(#18-23): 2-Diana Deane by Tarpe Mills app. 3-Drama of Hollywood by Mills begins. 7-Jungle Queen app. 71 142 213 454 777 1100

NOTE: ***Biro** c-6, 9, 10. **Burgos** a-15, 16, V2#1-7. **Ken Ernst** a-10, 12, 14. **Filchock** c-15, 18, 22. **Gill Fox** c-14, 19. **Guardineer** a-6, 8-14. **Gustavson** a-13-16, V2#1-7. **Winsor McCay** c-4, 5. **Tarpe Mills** a-15, V2#1-7. **Schwab** c-20, 23. **Bob Wood** a-10, 12, 13; c-7, 8.*

STAR COMICS MAGAZINE
Marvel Comics (Star Comics): Dec, 1986 - No. 13, 1988 ($1.50, digest-size)

1,9-Spider-Man-c/s 2 4 6 8 11 14
2-8-Heathcliff, Ewoks, Top Dog, Madballs-r in #1-13 1 2 3 5 7 9
10-13 2 4 6 8 10 12

S.T.A.R. CORPS
DC Comics: Nov, 1993 - No. 6, Apr, 1994 ($1.50, limited series)

1-6: 1,2-Austin-c(i). 1-Superman app. 3.00

STARCRAFT (Based on the video game)
DC Comics (WildStorm): July, 2009 - No. 7, Jan, 2010 ($2.99)

1-7-Furman-s; two covers on each 3.00
HC (2010, $19.99, dustjacket) r/#1-7 20.00
SC (2011, $14.99) r/#1-7 15.00

STAR CROSSED
DC Comics (Helix): June, 1997 - No. 3, Aug, 1997 ($2.50, limited series)

1-3-Matt Howarth-s/a 3.00

STARDUST (See Neil Gaiman and Charles Vess' Stardust)

STARDUST KID, THE
Image Comics/Boom! Studios #4-on: May, 2005 - No. 4 ($3.50)

1-4-J.M. DeMatteis-s/Mike Ploog-a 3.50

STAR FEATURE COMICS
I. W. Enterprises: 1963

Reprint #9-Stunt-Man Stetson-r/Feat. Comics #141 2 4 6 10 13 16

STARFIRE (Not the Teen Titans character)
National Periodical Publ./DC Comics: Aug-Sept, 1976 - No. 8, Oct-Nov, 1977

1-Origin (CCA stamp fell off cover art; so it was approved by code) 2 4 6 8 11 14
2-8 1 2 3 5 6 8

STARGATE
Dynamite Entertainment

...: Daniel Jackson 1-4 (2010 - No. 4, 2010, $3.99) Watson-a/Murray-s 4.00
...: Vala Mal Doran 1-5 (2010 - No. 5, 2010, $3.99) Razek-a/Jerwa-s 4.00

STAR HUNTERS (See DC Super Stars #16)
National Periodical Publ./DC Comics: Oct-Nov, 1977 - No. 7, Oct-Nov, 1978

1,7: 1-Newton-a(p). 7-44 pgs. 2 4 6 8 10 12
2-6 1 2 3 4 5 7

NOTE: ***Buckler** a-4-7p; c-1-7p. **Layton** a-1-5i; c-1-6i. **Nasser** a-3p. **Sutton** a-6i.*

STARJAMMERS (See X-Men Spotlight on Starjammers)

STARJAMMERS (Also see Uncanny X-Men)
Marvel Comics: Oct, 1995 - No. 4, Jan, 1996 ($2.95, limited series)

1-4: Foil-c; Ellis scripts 4.00

STARJAMMERS
Marvel Comics: Sept, 2004 - No. 6, Jan, 2005 ($2.99, limited series)

1-6-Kevin J. Anderson-s. 1-Garza-a. 2-6-Lucas-a 3.00

STARK TERROR
Stanley Publications: Dec, 1970 - No. 5, Aug, 1971 (B&W, magazine, 52 pgs.) (1950s Horror reprints, including pre-code)

1-Bondage, torture-c 7 14 21 44 82 120
2-4 (Gillmor/Aragon-r) 4 8 12 27 44 65
5 (ACG-r) 4 8 12 25 38 55

STARLET O'HARA IN HOLLYWOOD (Teen-age) (Also see Cookie)
Standard Comics: Dec, 1948 - No. 4, Sept, 1949

1-Owen Fitzgerald-a in all 28 56 84 165 270 375
2 15 30 45 88 137 185
3,4 14 28 42 80 115 150

STARLIGHT
Image Comics: Mar, 2014 - Present ($2.99)

1,2-Mark Millar-s/Goran Parlov-a. 1-Covers by Cassaday & Parlov. 2-Sienkiewicz var-c 3.00

STAR-LORD THE SPECIAL EDITION (Also see Marvel Comics Super Special #10, Marvel Premiere & Preview & Marvel Spotlight V2#6,7)
Marvel Comics Group: Feb, 1982 (one-shot, direct sales) (1st Baxter paper comic)

1-Byrne/Austin-a; Austin-c; 8 pgs. of new-a by Golden (p); Dr. Who story by Dave Gibbons; 1st deluxe format comic 2 4 6 9 12 15

STARLORD
Marvel Comics: Dec, 1996 - No. 3, Feb, 1997 ($2.50, limited series)

1-3-Timothy Zahn-s 3.00

STAR-LORD (Guardians of the Galaxy)
Marvel Comics: Aug, 2013; 2014 ($7.99, series of reprints)

...: Annihilation - Conquest 1 (2014) r/Annihilation: Conquest - Starlord #1-4; design art 8.00
...: Tears For Heaven 1 (2014) r/Marvel Preview #18, Marvel Spotlight #6,7, and Marvel Premiere #61; bonus art; new cover by Pichelli 8.00
...: The Hollow Crown 1 (8/13) r/Marvel Preview #4,11 and Star-Lord Special Edition 8.00

STARLORD MEGAZINE
Marvel Comics: Nov, 1996 ($2.95, one-shot)

1-Reprints w/preview of new series 3.00

STARMAN (1st Series) (Also see Justice League & War of the Gods)

Starman (2nd series) #42 © DC

Star Ranger #2 © CEN

Stars and S.T.R.I.P.E. #12 © DC

GD 2.0 VG 4.0 FN 6.0 VF 8.0 VF/NM 9.0 NM- 9.2

DC Comics: Oct, 1988 - No. 45, Apr, 1992 ($1.00)

1-Origin 5.00
2-25,29-45: 4-Intro The Power Elite. 9,10,34-Batman app. 14-Superman app. 17-Power Girl app. 38-War of the Gods x-over. 42-45-Eclipso-c/stories 3.00
26-1st app. David Knight (G.A.Starman's son). 5.00
27,28: 27-Starman (David Knight) app. 28-Starman disguised as Superman; leads into Superman #50 4.00

STARMAN (2nd Series) (Also see The Golden Age, Showcase 95 #12, Showcase 96 #4,5)
DC Comics: No. 0, Oct, 1994 - No. 80, Aug, 2001; No. 81, Mar, 2010 ($1.95/$2.25/$2.50)

0,1: 0-James Robinson scripts, Tony Harris-c/a(p) & Wade Von Grawbadger-a(i) begins; Sins of the Father storyline begins, ends #3; 1st app. new Starman (Jack Knight); reintro of the G.A. Mist & G.A. Shade; 1st app. Nash; David Knight dies 1 3 4 6 8 10
2-7: 2-Reintro Charity from Forbidden Tales of Dark Mansion. 3-Reintro/2nd app. "Blue" Starman (1st app. in 1st Issue Special #12); Will Payton app. (both cameos). 5-David Knight app. 6-The Shade "Times Past" story; Kristiansen-a. 7-The Black Pirate cameo 5.00
8-17: 8-Begin $2.25-c. 10-1st app. new Mist (Nash). 11-JSA "Times Past" story; Matt Smith-a. 12-16-Sins of the Child. 17-The Black Pirate app. 4.00
18-37: 18-G.A. Starman "Times Past" story; Watkiss-a. 19-David Knight app. 20-23-G.A. Sandman app. 24-26-Demon Quest; all 3 covers make-up triptych. 33-36-Batman-c/app. 37-David Knight and deceased JSA members app. 3.00
38-49,51-56: 38-Nash vs. Justice League Europe. 39,40-Crossover w/ Power of Shazam! #35,36; Bulletman app. 42-Demon-c/app. 43-JLA-c/app. 44-Phantom Lady-c/app. 46-Gene Ha-a. 51-Jor-El app. 52,53-Adam Strange-c/app. 3.00
50-($3.95) Gold foil logo on-c; Star Boy (LSH) app. 4.00
57-79: 57-62-Painted covers by Harris and Alex Ross. 72-Death of Ted Knight 3.00
80-($3.95) Final issue; cover by Harris & Robinson 4.00
81-(3/10, $2.99) Blackest Night one-shot; The Shade vs. David Knight; Harris-c 3.00
#1,000,000 (11/98) 853rd Century x-over; Snejbjerg-a 3.00
Annual 1 (1996, $3.50)-Legends of the Dead Earth story; Prince Gavyn & G.A. Starman stories; J.H. Williams III, Bret Blevins, Craig Hamilton-c/a(p) 4.00
Annual 2 (1997, $3.95)-Pulp Heroes story; 4.00
...80 Page Giant (1/99, $4.95) Harris-c 5.00
...Secret Files 1 (4/98, $4.95)-Origin stories and profile pages 5.00
...The Mist (6/98, $1.95) Girlfrenzy; Mary Marvel app. 3.00
A Starry Knight-($17.95, TPB) r/#47-53 18.00
Grand Guignol-(2004, $19.95, TPB)-r/#61-73 20.00
Infernal Devices-($17.95, TPB) r/#29-35,37,38 18.00
Night and Day-($14.95, TPB)-r/#7-10,12-16 15.00
Sins of the Father-($12.95, TPB)-r/#0-5 13.00
Sons of the Father-($14.99, TPB)-r/#75-80 15.00
Stars My Destination-(2003, $14.95, TPB)-r/#55-60 15.00
Times Past-($17.95, TPB)-r/stories of other Starmen 18.00
The Starman Omnibus Vol. One (2008, $49.99, HC with dj) r/#0,1-16; Robinson intro. 50.00
The Starman Omnibus Vol. Two (2009, $49.99, HC with dj) r/#17-29, Annual #1, Showcase '95 #12, Showcase '96 #4,5; Harris intro.; merchandise gallery 50.00
The Starman Omnibus Vol. Three (2009, $49.99, HC with dj) r/#30-38, Annual #2, Starman Secret Files #1 and The Shade #1-4 50.00
The Starman Omnibus Vol. Four (2010, $49.99, HC with dj) r/#39-46, 80 Page Giant #1, Power of Shazam! #35,36; Starman: The Mist #1 and Batman/Hellboy/Starman #1,2 50.00
The Starman Omnibus Vol. Five (2010, $49.99, HC with dj) r/#47-60, #1,000,000; Stars and S.T.R.I.P.E. #0; All Star Comics 80 Page Giant #1; JSA: All Stars #4 50.00
The Starman Omnibus Vol. Six (2011, $49.99, HC with dj) r/#61-81, Johns intro. 50.00

STARMAN/CONGORILLA (See Justice League: Cry For Justice)
DC Comics: Mar, 2011 ($2.99, one-shot)

1-Animal Man and Rex the Wonder Dog app.; Robinson-s/Booth-a/Ha-c 3.00

STARMASTERS
Marvel Comics: Dec, 1995 - No. 3, Feb, 1996 ($1.95, limited series)

1-3-Continues in Cosmic Powers Unlimited #4 3.00

STAR PRESENTATION, A (Formerly My Secret Romance #1,2; Spectacular Stories #4 on) (Also see This Is Suspense)
Fox Features Syndicate (Hero Books): No. 3, May, 1950

3-Dr. Jekyll & Mr. Hyde by Wood & Harrison (reprinted in Startling Terror Tales #10); "The Repulsing Dwarf" by Wood; Wood-c 64 128 192 406 696 985

STAR QUEST COMIX (Warren Presents... on cover)
Warren Publications: Oct, 1978 ($1.50, B&W magazine, 84 pgs., square-bound)

1-Corben, Maroto, Neary-a; Ken Kelly-c; Star Wars 2 4 6 9 12 15

STAR RAIDERS (See DC Graphic Novel #1)

STAR RANGER (Cowboy Comics #13 on)
Chesler Publ./Centaur Publ.: Feb, 1937 - No. 12, May, 1938 (Large size: No. 1-6)

1-(1st Western comic)-Ace & Deuce, Air Plunder; Creig Flessel-a 265 530 795 1694 2897 4100
2 116 232 348 742 1271 1800
3-6 107 214 321 685 1168 1650
7-9: 8(12/37)-Christmas-c; Air Patrol, Gold coast app.; Guardineer centerfold 84 168 252 538 919 1300
V2#10 (1st Centaur; 3/38) 110 220 330 704 1202 1700
11,12 84 168 252 538 919 1300

NOTE: ***J. Cole*** *a-10, 12; c-12.* ***Ken Ernst*** *a-11.* ***Gill Fox*** *a-8(illo), 9, 10.* ***Guardineer*** *a-1, 3, 6, 7, 8(illos), 9, 10, 12.* ***Gustavson*** *a-8-10, 12.* ***Fred Schwab*** *c-2-11.* ***Bob Wood*** *a-8-10.*

STAR RANGER FUNNIES (Formerly Cowboy Comics)
Centaur Publications: V1#15, Oct, 1938 - V2#5, Oct, 1939

V1#15-Lyin Lou, Ermine, Wild West Junior, The Law of Caribou County by Eisner, Cowboy Jake, The Plugged Dummy, Spurs by Gustavson, Red Coat, Two Buckaroos & Trouble Hunters begin 107 214 321 685 1168 1650
V2#1 (1/39) 84 168 252 538 919 1300
2-5: 2-Night Hawk by Gustavson. 4-Kit Carson app. 73 146 219 467 796 1125

NOTE: ***Jack Cole*** *a-V2#1, 3; c-V2#1.* ***Filchock*** *c-V2#2, 3.* ***Guardineer*** *a-V2#3.* ***Gustavson*** *a-V2#2.* ***Pinajian*** *c/a-V2#5.*

STAR REACH (Mature content)
Star Reach Publ.: Apr, 1974 - No. 18, Oct, 1979 (B&W, #12-15 w/color)

1-(75¢, 52 pgs.) Art by Starlin, Simonson. Chaykin-c/a; origin Death. Cody Starbuck-sty 3 6 9 17 26 35
1-2nd, 3th, and 4th printings ($1.00-$1.50-c) 6.00
2-11: 2-Adams, Giordano-a; 1st Stephanie Starr-c/s. 3-1st Linda Lovecraft. 4-1st Sherlock Duck. 5-1st Gideon Faust by Chaykin. 6-Elric-c. 7-BWS-c. 9-14-Sacred & Profane-c/s by Steacy. 11-Samurai 2 4 6 8 11 14
2-2nd printing 4.00
12-15 (44 pgs.): 12-Zelazny-s. Nasser-a, Brunner-c 2 4 6 9 13 16
16-18-Magazine size: 17-Poe's Raven-c/s 2 4 6 9 13 16

NOTE: ***Adams*** *c-2.* ***Bonivert*** *a-17.* ***Brunner*** *a-3,5; c-3,10,12.* ***Chaykin*** *a-1,4,5; c-1(1st ed),4,5; back-c-1(2nd,3rd,4th ed).* ***Gene Day*** *a-6,8,9,11,15.* ***Friedrich*** *s-2,3,8,10.* ***Gasbarri*** *a-7.* ***Gilbert*** *a-9,12.* ***Giordano*** *a-2.* ***Gould*** *a-6.* ***Hirota/Mukaide*** *s/a-7.* ***Jones*** *c-6.* ***Konz*** *a-17.* ***Leialoha*** *a-3,4,6-i, 13,15; c-13,15.* ***Lyda*** *a-6,12-15.* ***Marrs*** *a-2-5,7,10,14,15,16,18; c-18; back-c-2.* ***Mukaide*** *a-18.* ***Nasser*** *a-12.* ***Nino*** *a-6;* ***Russell*** *a-8,10; c-8.* ***Dave Sim*** *s-7; lettering-9.* ***Simonson*** *a-1.* ***Skeates*** *a-1,2.* ***Starlin*** *a-1(x2), 2(x2); back-c-1(1st ed); c-1(2nd,3rd,4th ed).* ***Barry Smith*** *c-7.* ***Staton*** *a-5,6,7.* ***Steacy*** *a-8-14; c-9,11,14,16.* ***Vosburg*** *a-2-5,7,10.* ***Workman*** *a-2-5,8.* *Nudity panels in most. Wraparound-c: 3-5,7-11,13-16,18.*

STAR REACH CLASSICS
Eclipse Comics: Mar, 1984 - No. 6, Aug, 1984 ($1.50, Baxter paper)

1-6: 1-Neal Adams-r/Star Reach #1; Sim & Starlin-a 3.00

STARR FLAGG, UNDERCOVER GIRL (See Undercover...)

STARRIORS
Marvel Comics: Aug, 1984 - Feb, 1985 (Limited series) (Based on Tomy toys)

1-4 4.00

STARR THE SLAYER
Marvel Comics (MAX): Nov, 2009 - No. 4, Feb, 2010 ($3.99, limited series)

1-4- Richard Corben-c/a; Daniel Way-s 4.00

STARS AND S.T.R.I.P.E. (Also see JSA)
DC Comics: July, 1999 - No. 14, Sept, 2000 ($2.95/$2.50)

0-($2.95) Moder and Weston-a; Starman app. 3.00
1-Johns and Robinson-s/Moder-a; origin new Star Spangled Kid 3.00
2-14: 4-Marvel Family app. 9-Seven Soldiers of Victory-c/app. 3.00
JSA Presents: Stars and S.T.R.I.P.E. Vol. 1 TPB (2007, $17.99) r/#1-8; Johns intro. 18.00
JSA Presents: Stars and S.T.R.I.P.E. Vol. 2 TPB (2008, $17.99) r/#0,9-14 18.00

STARS AND STRIPES COMICS
Centaur Publications: No. 2, May, 1941 - No. 6, Dec, 1941

2(#1)-The Shark, The Iron Skull, A-Man, The Amazing Man, Mighty Man, Minimidget begin; The Voice & Dash Dartwell, the Human Meteor, Reef Kinkaid app.; Gustavson Flag-c 242 484 726 1549 2650 3750
3-Origin Dr. Synthe; The Black Panther app. 135 270 405 864 1482 2100
4-Origin/1st app. The Stars and Stripes; injury to eye-c 113 226 339 723 1237 1750
5(#5 on cover & inside) 81 162 243 518 884 1250
5(#6)-(#5 on cover, #6 on inside) 81 162 243 518 884 1250

NOTE: ***Gustavson*** *c/a-3.* ***Myron Strauss*** *c-4, 5(#5), 5(#6).*

STAR SEED (Formerly Powers That Be)
Broadway Comics: No. 7, 1996 - No. 9 ($2.95)

7-9 3.00

Star Slammers (2014 series) #1 © Walt Simonson

Star Spangled Comics #11 © DC

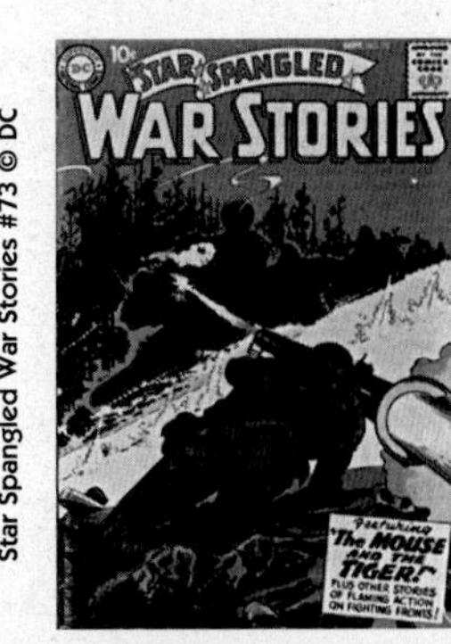

Star Spangled War Stories #73 © DC

GD VG FN VF VF/NM NM-
2.0 4.0 6.0 8.0 9.0 9.2

GD VG FN VF VF/NM NM-
2.0 4.0 6.0 8.0 9.0 9.2

STARSHIP TROOPERS
Dark Horse Comics: 1997 - No. 2, 1997 ($2.95, limited series)
1,2-Movie adaptation 3.00

STARSHIP TROOPERS: BRUTE CREATIONS
Dark Horse Comics: 1997 ($2.95, one-shot)
1 3.00

STARSHIP TROOPERS: DOMINANT SPECIES
Dark Horse Comics: Aug, 1998 - No. 4, Nov, 1998 ($2.95, limited series)
1-4-Strnad-s/Bolton-c 3.00

STARSHIP TROOPERS: INSECT TOUCH
Dark Horse Comics: 1997 - No. 3, 1997 ($2.95, limited series)
1-3 3.00

STAR SLAMMERS (See Marvel Graphic Novel #6)
Malibu Comics (Bravura): May, 1994 - No. 4, Aug, 1994 ($2.50, unfinished limited series)
1-4: W. Simonson-a/stories; contain Bravura stamps 3.00

STAR SLAMMERS
IDW Publishing: Mar, 2014 - Present ($3.99)
1-Recolored reprint of 1994 series; Walt Simonson-s/a; 2 covers by Simonson 4.00

STAR SLAMMERS SPECIAL
Dark Horse Comics (Legend): June, 1996 ($2.95, one-shot)
nn-Simonson-c/a/scripts; concludes Bravura limited series. 3.00

STARSLAYER
Pacific Comics/First Comics No. 7 on: Feb, 1982 - No. 6, Apr, 1983; No. 7, Aug, 1983 - No. 34, Nov, 1985
1-Origin & 1st app.; 1 pg. Rocketeer brief app. which continues in #2
2 4 6 9 12 15
2-Origin/1st full app. the Rocketeer (4/82) by Dave Stevens (Chapter 1 of Rocketeer saga; see Pacific Presents #1,2) 3 6 9 14 20 25
3-Chapter 2 of Rocketeer saga by Stevens 2 4 6 10 14 18
4,6,7: 7-Grell-a ends 4.00
5-2nd app. Groo the Wanderer by Aragonés 2 4 6 8 10 12
8,9,11-34: 18-Starslayer meets Grimjack. 20-The Black Flame begins (9/84, 1st app.), ends #33. 27-Book length Black Flame story 3.00
10-1st app. Grimjack (11/83, ends #17) 5.00
NOTE: ***Grell** a-1-7; c-1-8. **Stevens** back c-2, 3. **Sutton** a-17p, 20-22p, 24-27p, 29-33p.*

STARSLAYER (The Director's Cut)
Acclaim Comics (Windjammer): June, 1994 - No. 8, Dec, 1995 ($2.50)
1-8: Mike Grell-c/a/scripts 3.00

STAR SPANGLED COMICS (Star Spangled War Stories #131 on)
National Periodical Publications: Oct, 1941 - No. 130, July, 1952
1-Origin/1st app. Tarantula; Captain X of the R.A.F., Star Spangled Kid (see Action #40), Armstrong of the Army begin; Robot-c 519 1038 1557 3789 6695 9600
2 174 348 520 1114 1907 2700
3-5 108 216 324 691 1183 1675
6-Last Armstrong/Army; Penniless Palmer begins 66 132 198 419 722 1025
7-(4/42)-Origin/1st app. The Guardian by S&K, & Robotman (by Paul Cassidy & created by Siegel);The Newsboy Legion (1st app.), Robotman & TNT begin; last Captain X
768 1536 2304 5606 9903 14,200
8-Origin TNT & Dan the Dyna-Mite 248 496 744 1587 2719 3850
9,10 168 336 504 1075 1838 2600
11-17 123 246 369 787 1344 1900
18-Origin Star Spangled Kid 155 310 465 992 1696 2400
19-Last Tarantula 123 246 369 787 1344 1900
20-Liberty Belle begins (5/43) 148 296 444 947 1624 2300
21-29-Last S&K issue; 23-Last TNT. 25-Robotman by Jimmy Thompson begins.
29-Intro Robbie the Robotdog 103 206 309 659 1130 1600
30-40: 31-S&K-c 61 122 183 390 670 950
41-51: 41,49-Kirby-c. 51-Robot-c by Kirby 55 110 165 352 601 850
52-64: 53 by S&K. 64-Last Newsboy Legion & The Guardian
50 100 150 315 533 750
65-Robin begins with c/app. (2/47); Batman cameo in 1 panel; Robin-c begins, end #95
200 400 600 1280 2190 3100
66-Batman cameo in Robin story 89 178 267 565 970 1375
67,68,70-80: 68-Last Liberty Belle? 72-Burnley Robin-c
69 138 207 442 759 1075
69-Origin/1st app. Tomahawk by F. Ray; atom bomb story & splash (6/47); black-c (rare in high grade) 213 426 639 1363 2332 3300
81-Origin Merry, Girl of 1000 Gimmicks in Star Spangled Kid story
60 120 180 381 653 925
82,85: 82-Last Robotman? 85-Last Star Spangled Kid?
54 108 162 343 574 825
83-Tomahawk enters the lost valley, a land of dinosaurs; Capt. Compass begins, ends #130
57 114 171 362 619 875
84,87 (Rare): 87-Batman cameo in Robin 86 172 258 546 936 1325
86-Batman cameo in Robin story 60 120 180 384 660 935
88(1/49)-94: Batman-c/stories in all. 91-Federal Men begin, end #93. 94-Manhunters Around the World begin, end #121 65 130 195 416 708 1000
95-Batman story; last Robin-c 57 114 171 362 619 875
96,98-Batman cameo in Robin stories. 96-1st Tomahawk-c (also #97-121)
40 80 120 246 411 575
97,99 36 72 108 211 343 475
100 (1/50)-Pre-Bat-Hound tryout in Robin story (pre-dates Batman #92).
42 84 123 265 445 625
101-109,118,119,121: 121-Last Tomahawk-c 32 64 96 192 314 435
110,111,120-Batman cameo in Robin stories. 120-Last 52 pg. issue
34 68 102 199 325 450
112-Batman & Robin story 36 72 108 216 351 485
113-Frazetta-a (10 pgs.) 41 82 123 256 428 600
114-Retells Robin's origin (3/51); Batman & Robin story
43 86 129 271 461 650
115,117-Batman app. in Robin stories 36 72 108 211 343 475
116-Flag-c 36 72 108 211 343 475
122-(11/51)-Ghost Breaker-c/stories begin (origin/1st app.), ends #130 (Ghost Breaker covers #122-130) 50 100 150 315 533 750
123-126,128,129 34 68 102 204 322 460
127-Batman app. 36 72 108 216 351 485
130-Batman cameo in Robin story 39 78 117 231 378 525
NOTE: *Most all issues after #29 signed by Simon & Kirby are not by them. **Bill Ely** c-122-130. **Mortimer** c-65-74(most), 76-95(most). **Fred Ray** c-96-106, 109, 110, 112, 113, 115-120. **S&K** c-7-31, 33, 34, 36, 37, 39, 40, 48, 49, 50-54, 56-58. **Hal Sherman** c-1-6. **Dick Sprang** c-75.*

STAR SPANGLED COMICS (Also see All Star Comics 1999 crossover titles)
DC Comics: May, 1999 ($1.99, one-shot)
1-Golden Age Sandman and the Star Spangled Kid 3.00

STAR SPANGLED KID (See Action #40, Leading Comics & Star Spangled Comics)

STAR SPANGLED WAR STORIES
DC Comics: Aug/Sept 1952
nn - Ashcan comic, not distributed to newsstands, only for in-house use. Cover art is Western Comics #28 with interior being Western Comics #13 (a VG- copy sold for $2151 in 2012)

STAR SPANGLED WAR STORIES (Formerly Star Spangled Comics #1-130; Becomes The Unknown Soldier #205 on) (See Showcase)
National Periodical Publications: No. 131, 8/52 - No. 133, 10/52; No. 3, 11/52 - No. 204, 2-3/77
131(#1) 174 348 522 1114 1907 2700
132 100 200 300 640 1095 1550
133-Used in **POP**, pg. 94 87 174 261 553 952 1350
3-6: 4-Devil Dog Dugan app. 6-Evans-a 60 120 180 381 653 925
7-10 29 58 87 209 467 725
11-20 26 52 78 182 404 625
21-30: 30-Last precode (2/55) 22 44 66 154 340 525
31-33,35-40 18 36 54 124 275 425
34-Krigstein-a 18 36 54 126 281 435
41-44,46-50: 50-1st S.A. issue 16 32 48 112 249 385
45-1st DC grey tone war-c (5/56) 39 78 117 289 657 1025
51,52,54-63,65,66, 68-83 14 28 42 96 211 325
53-"Rock Sergeant," 3rd Sgt. Rock prototype; inspired "P.I. & The Sand Fleas" in G.I. Combat #56 (1/57) 24 48 72 168 372 575
64-Pre-Sgt. Rock Easy Co. story (12/57) 18 36 54 124 275 425
67-Two Easy Co. stories without Sgt. Rock 18 36 54 126 281 435
84-Origin Mlle. Marie 27 54 81 189 420 650
85-89-Mlle. Marie in all 17 34 51 117 259 400
90-1st app. "War That Time Forgot" series; dinosaur issue-c/story (4-5/60) (also see Weird War Tales #94 & #99) 61 122 183 488 1094 1700
91,93-No dinosaur stories 16 32 48 110 243 375
92-2nd dinosaur-c/s 25 50 75 175 388 600
94 (12/60)- "Ghost Ace" story; Baron Von Richter as The Enemy Ace (predates Our Army at War #151) 28 56 84 202 451 700
95-99: Dinosaur-c/s 19 38 57 131 291 450
100-Dinosaur-c/story. 21 42 63 147 324 500
101-115: All dinosaur issues 15 30 45 105 233 360
116-125,127-133,135-137: 120-1st app. Caveboy and Dino. 137-Last dinosaur story; Heath Birdman-#129,131 13 26 39 89 195 300

Startling Comics #16 © Nedor

Startling Terror Tales #13 © STAR

Star Trek #49 © Paramount

	GD 2.0	VG 4.0	FN 6.0	VF 8.0	VF/NM 9.0	NM- 9.2
126-No dinosaur story	11	22	33	73	157	240
134-Dinosaur story; Neal Adams-a	15	30	45	103	227	350
138-New Enemy Ace-c/stories begin by Joe Kubert (4-5/68), end #150 (also see Our Army at War #151 and Showcase #57)	16	32	48	110	243	375
139-Origin Enemy Ace (7/68)	10	20	30	69	147	225
140-143,145: 145-Last 12¢ issue (6-7/69)	8	16	24	54	102	150
144-Neal Adams/Kubert-a	9	18	27	58	114	170
146-Enemy Ace-c/app.	6	12	18	41	76	110
147,148-New Enemy Ace stories	7	14	21	48	89	130
149,150-Last new Enemy Ace by Kubert. Viking Prince by Kubert	7	14	21	44	82	120
151-1st solo app. Unknown Soldier (6-7/70); Enemy Ace-r begin (from Our Army at War, Showcase & SSWS); end #161	17	34	51	117	259	400
152-Reprints 2nd Enemy Ace app.	6	12	18	38	69	100
153,155-Enemy Ace reprints; early Unknown Soldier stories	5	10	15	34	60	85
154-Origin Unknown Soldier	12	24	36	84	185	285
156-1st Battle Album; Unknown Soldier story; Kubert-c/a	5	10	15	31	53	75
157-Sgt. Rock x-over in Unknown Soldier story.	4	8	12	28	47	65
158-163-(52 pgs.): New Unknown Soldier stories; Kubert-c/a. 161-Last Enemy Ace-r	4	8	12	25	40	55
164-183,200: 181-183-Enemy Ace vs. Balloon Buster serial app; Frank Thorne-a. 200-Enemy Ace back-up	3	6	9	15	22	28
184-199,201-204	2	4	6	13	18	22

NOTE: ***Anderson** a-28. **Chaykin** a-167. **Drucker** a-59, 61, 64, 66, 67, 73-84. **Estrada** a-149. **John Giunta** a-72. **Glanzman** a-167, 171, 172, 174. **Heath** a-42,122, 132, 133; c-67, 122, 132-134. **Kaluta** a-197i; c-167. **G. Kane** a-169. **Kubert** a-6-163(most later issues), 200. **Maurer** a-160, 165. **Severin** a-65, 162. **S&K** c-7-31, 33, 34, 37, 40. **Simonson** a-170, 172, 174, 180. **Sutton** a-168. **Thorne** a-183. **Toth** a-164. **Wildey** a-161. Suicide Squad in 110, 116-118, 120, 121, 127.*

STAR SPANGLED WAR STORIES (Featuring Mademoiselle Marie)
DC Comics: Nov, 2010 ($3.99, one-shot)

1-Mademoiselle Marie in 1944 France; Tucci-s/Justiniano-a/Bolland-c 4.00

STARSTREAM (Adventures in Science Fiction)(See Questar illustrated)
Whitman/Western Publishing Co.: 1976 (79¢, 68 pgs, cardboard-c)

1-4: 1-Bolle-a. 2-4-McWilliams & Bolle-a 2 4 6 10 14 18

STARSTRUCK
Marvel Comics (Epic Comics): Feb, 1985 - No. 6, Feb, 1986 ($1.50, mature)

1-6: Kaluta-a 6.00

STARSTRUCK
Dark Horse Comics: Aug, 1990 - No. 4, Nov?, 1990 ($2.95, B&W, 52pgs.)

1-3: Kaluta-r/Epic series plus new-c/a in all 4.00
4 (68 pgs.)-contains 2 trading cards 5.00
Reprint 1-13 (IDW, 8/09 - No. 13, Sept, 2010, $3.99) newly colored; Galactic Girl Guides 4.00

STAR STUDDED
Cambridge House/Superior Publishers: 1945 (25¢, 132 pgs.); 1945 (196 pgs.)

	GD	VG	FN	VF	VF/NM	NM-
nn-Captain Combat by Giunta, Ghost Woman, Commandette, & Red Rogue app.; Infantino-a	39	78	117	234	385	535
nn-The Cadet, Edison Bell, Hoot Gibson, Jungle Lil (196 pgs.); copies vary; Blue Beetle in some	41	82	123	250	418	585

STARTLING COMICS
Better Publications (Nedor): June, 1940 - No. 53, Sept, 1948

	GD	VG	FN	VF	VF/NM	NM-
1-Origin Captain Future-Man Of Tomorrow, Mystico (By Sansone), The Wonder Man; The Masked Rider & his horse Pinto begins; Masked Rider formerly in pulps; drug use story	326	652	978	2282	3991	5700
2 -Don Davis, Espionage Ace begins	123	246	369	787	1344	1900
3	103	206	309	659	1130	1600
4	74	148	222	470	810	1150
5,6,9	63	126	189	403	689	975
7,8-Nazi WWII-c	71	142	213	454	777	1100
10-The Fighting Yank begins (9/41, origin/1st app.); Nazi WWII-c	503	1006	1509	3672	6486	9300
11-2nd app. Fighting Yank; Nazi WWII-c	174	348	522	1114	1907	2700
12-Hitler, Tojo, Mussolini-c	213	426	639	1363	2332	3300
13-15	84	168	252	538	919	1300
16-Origin The Four Comrades; not in #32,35	87	174	261	553	952	1350
17-Last Masked Rider & Mystico	65	130	195	416	708	1000
18-Pyroman begins (12/42, origin)(also see America's Best Comics #3 for 1st app., 11/42)	119	238	357	762	1306	1850
19-Nazi WWII-c	90	180	270	576	988	1400
20-Classic hooded Nazi giant snake bondage/torture-c (scarce); The Oracle begins (3/43); not in issues 26,28,33,34	103	206	309	659	1130	1600
21-Origin The Ape, Oracle's enemy; Schomburg hypo-c	97	194	291	621	1061	1500
22-34: All have Schomburg WWII-c. 34-Origin The Scarab & only app.	90	180	270	576	988	1400
35-Hypodermic syringe attacks Fighting Yank in drug story; Schomburg WWII-c	84	168	252	538	919	1300
36-43: 36-Last Four Comrades. 38-Bondage/torture-c. 40-Last Capt. Future & Oracle. 41-Front Page Peggy begins; A-Bomb-c. 43-Last Pyroman	55	110	165	352	601	850
44,45: 44-Lance Lewis, Space Detective begins; Ingels-c; sci/fi-c begin. 45-Tygra begins (intro/origin, 5/47); Ingels-c/a (splash pg. & inside f/c B&W ad)	90	180	270	576	988	1400
46-Classic Ingels-c; Ingels-a	129	258	387	826	1413	2000
47,48,50-53: 50,51-Sea-Eagle app.	90	180	270	576	988	1400
49-Classic Schomburg Robot-c; last Fighting Yank	622	1244	1866	4541	8021	11,500

NOTE: ***Ingels** a-44, 45; c-44, 45, 46(wash). **Schomburg (Xela)** c-21-43; 47-53 (airbrush). **Tuska** c-45? Bondage c-16, 21, 37, 46-49. Captain Future c-1-9, 13, 14. Fighting Yank c-10-12, 15-17, 21, 22, 24, 26, 28, 30, 32, 34, 36, 38, 40, 42. Pyroman c-18-20, 23, 25, 27, 29, 31, 33, 35, 37, 39, 41, 43.*

STARTLING STORIES: BANNER
Marvel Comics: July, 2001 - No. 4, Oct, 2001 ($2.99, limited series)

1-4-Hulk story by Azzarello; Corben-c/a 3.00
TPB (11/01, $12.95) r/1-4 13.00

STARTLING STORIES: FANTASTIC FOUR - UNSTABLE MOLECULES (See Fantastic Four - ...)

STARTLING STORIES: THE MEGALOMANIACAL SPIDER-MAN
Marvel Comics: Jun, 2002 ($2.99, one-shot)

1-Spider-Man spoof; Peter Bagge-s/a 3.00

STARTLING STORIES: THE THING
Marvel Comics: 2003 ($3.50, one-shot)

1-Zimmerman-s/Kramer-a; Inhumans and the Hulk app. 3.50

STARTLING STORIES: THE THING - NIGHT FALLS ON YANCY STREET
Marvel Comics: Jun, 2003 - No. 4, Sept, 2003 ($3.50, limited series)

1-4-Dorkin-s/Haspiel-a. 2,3-Frightful Four app. 3.50

STARTLING TERROR TALES
Star Publications: No. 10, May, 1952 - No. 14, Feb, 1953; No. 4, Apr, 1953 - No. 11, 1954

	GD	VG	FN	VF	VF/NM	NM-
10-(1st Series)-Wood/Harrison-a (r/A Star Presentation #3) Disbrow/Cole-c; becomes 4 different titles after #10; becomes Confessions of Love #11 on, The Horrors #11 on, Terrifying Tales #11 on, Terrors of the Jungle #11 on & continues w/Startling Terror #11	82	164	246	528	902	1275
11-(8/52)-L. B. Cole Spider-c; r-Fox's "A Feature Presentation" #5 (blue-c)	226	452	678	1446	2473	3500
11-Black-c (variant; believed to be a pressrun change) (Unique)	232	464	696	1485	2543	3600
12,14	36	72	108	216	351	485
13-Jo-Jo-r; Disbrow-a	37	74	111	222	361	500
4-9,11(1953-54) (2nd Series): 11-New logo	34	68	102	199	325	450
10-Disbrow-a	39	78	117	231	378	525

NOTE: ***L. B. Cole** covers-all issues. **Palais** a-V2#8r, V2#11r.*

STAR TREK (TV) (See Dan Curtis Giveaways, Dynabrite Comics & Power Record Comics)
Gold Key: 7/67; No. 2, 6/68; No. 3, 12/68; No. 4, 6/69 - No. 61, 3/79

	GD	VG	FN	VF	VF/NM	NM-
1-Photo-c begin, end #9; photo back-c is on all copies, no variant exists with an ad on the back-c	59	118	177	472	1061	1650
2-Regular version has an ad on back-c	23	46	69	161	356	550
2 (rare variation w/photo back-c)	35	70	105	252	564	875
3-5-All have back-c ads	15	30	45	103	227	350
3 (rare variation w/photo back-c)	25	50	75	175	388	600
6-9	10	20	30	70	150	230
10-20	6	12	18	37	66	95
21-30	5	10	15	31	53	80
31-40	4	8	12	27	44	60
41-61: 52-Drug propaganda story	3	6	9	21	33	45
...the Enterprise Logs nn (8/76)-Golden Press, ($1.95, 224 pgs.)-r/#1-8 plus 7 pgs. by McWilliams (#11185)-Photo-c	5	10	15	34	60	85
...the Enterprise Logs Vol. 2 ('76)-r/#9-17 (#11187)-Photo-c	5	10	15	31	53	75
...the Enterprise Logs Vol. 3 ('77)-r/#18-26 (#11188); McWilliams-a (4 pgs.)-Photo-c	5	10	15	31	53	75
Star Trek Vol. 4 (Winter '77)-Reprints #27,28,30-34,36,38 (#11189) plus 3 pgs. new art	5	10	15	31	53	75

... : The Key Collection (Checker Book Publ. Group, 2004, $22.95) r/#1-8 23.00
... : The Key Collection Volume 2 (Checker, 2004, $22.95) r/#9-16 23.00

STAR TREK
McCOY, FINALLY GETS THE LAST WORD

Star Trek (1984 series) #28 © Paramount

Star Trek (2011 series) #27 © CBS Studios

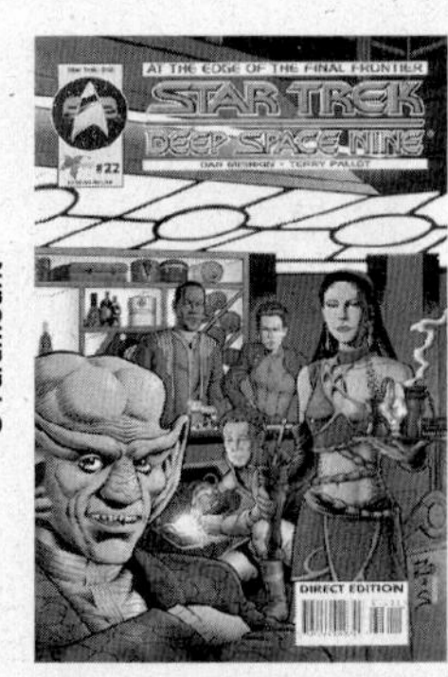

AT THE EDGE OF THE FINAL FRONTIER
STAR TREK
DEEP SPACE NINE
#22
DIRECT EDITION

Star Trek: Deep Space Nine #22 © Paramount

GD 2.0 | VG 4.0 | FN 6.0 | VF 8.0 | VF/NM 9.0 | NM- 9.2

... : The Key Collection Volume 3 (Checker, 2005, $22.95) r/#17-24 23.00
... : The Key Collection Volume 4 (Checker, 2005, $22.95) r/#25-33 23.00
... : The Key Collection Volume 5 (Checker, 2006, $22.95) r/#34,36,38,39,40-43 23.00
NOTE: ***McWilliams** a-38, 40-44, 46-61. #29 reprints #1; #35 reprints #4; #37 reprints #5; #45 reprints #7. The tabloids all have photo covers and blank inside covers. Painted covers #10-44, 46-59.*

STAR TREK
Marvel Comics Group: April, 1980 - No. 18, Feb, 1982

1: 1-3-r/Marvel Super Special; movie adapt. 2 4 6 11 16 20
2-16: 5-Miller-c 1 3 4 6 8 10
17-Low print run 2 4 6 8 11 14
18-Last issue; low print run 2 4 6 11 16 20
NOTE: ***Austin** c-18i. **Buscema** a-13. **Gil Kane** a-15. **Nasser** c/a-7. **Simonson** c-17.*

STAR TREK (Also see Who's Who In Star Trek)
DC Comics: Feb, 1984 - No. 56, Nov, 1988 (75¢, Mando paper)

1-Sutton-a(p) begins 2 4 6 8 10 12
2-5 6.00
6-10: 7-Origin Saavik 5.00
11-20: 19-Walter Koenig story 4.00
21-32 4.00
33-($1.25, 52 pgs.)-20th anniversary issue 5.00
34-49: 37-Painted-c 4.00
50-($1.50, 52 pgs.) 5.00
51-56 4.00
Annual 1-3: 1(1985). 2(1986). 3(1988, $1.50) 5.00
...: To Boldly Go TPB (Titan Books, 7/05, $19.95) r/#1-6; Koenig foreward; cast interviews 20.00
...: The Trial of James T. Kirk TPB (Titan Books, 6/06, $19.95) r/#7-12; cast interviews 20.00
...: The Return of the Worthy TPB (Titan Books, 12/06, $19.95) r/#13-18; cast interviews 20.00
NOTE: ***Morrow** a-28, 35, 36, 56. **Orlando** c-8i. **Perez** c-1-3. **Spiegle** a-19. **Starlin** c-24, 25. **Sutton** a-1-6p, 8-18p, 20-27p, 29p, 31-34p, 39-52p, 55p; c-4-6p, 8-22p, 46p.*

STAR TREK
DC Comics: Oct, 1989 - No. 80, Jan, 1996 ($1.50/$1.75/$1.95/$2.50)

1-Capt. Kirk and crew 6.00
2,3 4.00
4-23,25-30: 10-12-The Trial of James T. Kirk. 21-Begin $1.75-c 3.00
24-($2.95, 68 pgs.)-40 pg. epic w/pin-ups 4.00
31-49,51-60 3.00
50-($3.50, 68 pgs.)-Painted-c 4.00
61-74,76-80 3.00
75 ($3.95) 4.00
Annual 1-6('90-'95, 68 pgs.): 1-Morrow-a. 3-Painted-c 4.00
Special 1-3 ('9-'95, 68 pgs.)-1-Sutton-a. 4.00
...: The Ashes of Eden (1995, $14.95, 100 pgs.)-Shatner story 18.00
...Generations (1994, $3.95, 68 pgs.)-Movie adaptation 4.00
...Generations (1994, $5.95, 68 pgs.)-Squarebound 6.00

STAR TREK...(TV)
DC Comics (WildStorm): one-shots

All of Me (4/00, $5.95, prestige format) Lopresti-a 6.00
Enemy Unseen TPB (2001, $17.95) r/Perchance to Dream, Embrace the Wolf, The Killing Shadows; Struzan-c 18.00
Enter the Wolves (2001, $5.95) Crispin & Weinstein-s; Mota-a/c 6.00
New Frontier - Double Time (11/00, $5.95)-Captain Calhoun's USS Excalibur; Peter David-s; Stelfreeze-c 6.00
Other Realities TPB (2001, $14.95) r/All of Me, New Frontier - Double Time, and DS9-N-Vector; Van Fleet-c 15.00
Special (2001, $6.95) Stories from all 4 series by various; Van Fleet-c 7.00

STAR TREK (Further adventures of the crew from the 2009 movie)
IDW Publishing: Sept, 2011 - Present ($3.99)

1-31: 1,2-Gary Mitchell app.; Molnar-a. 11,12-Tribbles. 15,16-Mirror Universe. 21-Follows the 2013 movie; Klingons & Section 31 app. 4.00
Annual (12/13, $7.99) "Strange New Worlds" on cover; photonovel by John Byrne 8.00
... #1: Hundred Penny Press (8/13, $1.00) reprints #1 3.00
... Space Spanning Treasury Edition (4/13, $9.99, 13" x 8.5") Reprints #9,10,13 10.00

STAR TREK: ALIEN SPOTLIGHT
IDW Publishing: Sept, 2007 - Feb, 2008 ($3.99, series of one-shots)

... Andorians (11/07) Storrie-s/O'Grady-a; Counselor Troi app.; two art & one photo-c 4.00
... Borg (1/08) Harris-s/Murphy-a; Janeway & Next Gen crew app.; two art & one photo-c 4.00
... Cardassians (12/09) Padilla-a; Garak & Kira app. 4.00
... The Gorn (9/07) Messina-a; Chekov app.; two art & one photo-c 4.00
... Orions (12/07) Casagrande-a; Capt. Pike app.; two art & one photo-c 4.00
... Q (8/09) Casagrande-a; takes place after Star Trek 8 movie; two art & one photo-c 4.00
... Romulans (2/08) John Byrne-s/a; Kirk era; two art & one photo-c 4.00
... Romulans (5/09) Wagner Reis-a; David Williams-c 4.00
... Tribbles (3/09) Hawthorne-a; first encounter with Klingons; one art & one photo-c 4.00
... Vulcans (10/07) Spock's early Enterprise days with Capt. Pike; two art & one photo-c 4.00

STAR TREK: ASSIGNMENT EARTH
IDW Publishing: May, 2008 - No. 5, Sept, 2008 ($3.99, limited series)

1-5-Further adventures of Gary Seven and Roberta; John Byrne-s/a/c. 5-Nixon app. 4.00

STAR TREK: BURDEN OF KNOWLEDGE
IDW Publishing: Jun, 2010 - No. 4, Sept, 2010 ($3.99, limited series)

1-4-Original series Kirk and crew; Manfredi-a 4.00

STAR TREK: CAPTAIN'S LOG
IDW Publishing: one-shots

...: Harriman (4/10, $3.99) Captain of the Enterprise-B following Kirk's "demise"; Currie-a 4.00
...: Jellico (10/10, $3.99) Woodward-a 4.00
...: Pike (9/10, $3.99) Events that put Pike in the chair; Woodward-a 4.00
...: Sulu (1/10, $3.99) Manfredi-a 4.00

STAR TREK: COUNTDOWN (Prequel to the 2009 movie)
IDW Publishing: Jan, 2009 - No. 4, Apr, 2009 ($3.99, limited series)

1-4: 1-Ambassador Spock on Romulus; intro. Nero; Messina-a 4.00
Hundred Penny Press: Star Trek: Countdown #1 (4/11, $1.00) r/#1 w/new cover frame 3.00

STAR TREK: COUNTDOWN TO DARKNESS (Prequel to the 2013 movie)
IDW Publishing: Jan, 2013 - No. 4, Apr, 2013 ($3.99, limited series)

1-4-Captain April app.; Messina-a; regular & photo covers on each 4.00

STAR TREK: CREW
IDW Publishing: Mar, 2009 - No. 5, Jul, 2009 ($3.99, limited series)

1-5: John Byrne-s/a; Captain Pike era 4.00

STAR TREK: DEBT OF HONOR
DC Comics: 1992 ($24.95/$14.95, graphic novel)

Hardcover ($24.95) Claremont-s/Hughes-a(p) 25.00
Softcover ($14.95) 15.00

STAR TREK: DEEP SPACE NINE (TV)
Malibu Comics: Aug, 1993 - No. 32, Jan, 1996 ($2.50)

1-Direct Sale Edition w/line drawn-c 5.00
1-Newsstand Edition with photo-c 4.00
0-(1/95, $2.95)-Terok Nor 4.00
2-30: 2-Polybagged w/trading card. 9-4 pg. prelude to Hearts & Minds 4.00
31-($3.95) 5.00
32-($3.50) 5.00
Annual 1 (1/95, $3.95, 68 pgs.) 5.00
Special 1 (1995, $3.50) 5.00
Ultimate Annual 1 (12/95, $5.95) 6.00
...:Lightstorm (12/94, $3.50) 5.00

STAR TREK: DEEP SPACE NINE (TV)
Marvel Comics (Paramount Comics): Nov, 1996 - No. 15, Mar, 1998 ($1.95/$1.99)

1-15: 12,13-"Telepathy War" pt. 2,3 4.00

STAR TREK: DEEP SPACE NINE: FOOL'S GOLD
IDW Publishing: Dec, 2009 - No. 4, Mar, 2010 ($3.99)

1-4-Mantovani-a 4.00

STAR TREK: DEEP SPACE NINE -- N-VECTOR (TV)
DC Comics (WildStorm): Aug, 2000 - No. 4, Nov, 2000 ($2.50, limited series)

1-4-Cypress-a 3.00

STAR TREK DEEP SPACE NINE-THE CELEBRITY SERIES
Malibu Comics: May, 1995 ($2.95)

1-Blood and Honor; Mark Lenard script 4.00
1-Rules of Diplomacy; Aron Eisenberg script 4.00

STAR TREK: DEEP SPACE NINE HEARTS AND MINDS
Malibu Comics: June, 1994 - No. 4, Sept, 1994 ($2.50, limited series)

1-4 4.00
1-Holographic-c 5.00

STAR TREK: DEEP SPACE NINE, THE MAQUIS
Malibu Comics: Feb, 1995 - No. 3, Apr, 1995 ($2.50, limited series)

1-3-Newsstand-c, 1-Photo-c 4.00

STAR TREK: DEEP SPACE NINE/THE NEXT GENERATION
Malibu Comics: Oct, 1994 - No. 2, Nov, 1994 ($2.50, limited series)

1,2: Parts 2 & 4 of x-over with Star Trek: TNG/DS9 from DC Comics 4.00

Star Trek: Khan #1 © CBS Studios

Star Trek: Starfleet Academy #18 © Paramount

Star Trek: The Next Generation #24 © Paramount

GD 2.0 | VG 4.0 | FN 6.0 | VF 8.0 | VF/NM 9.0 | NM- 9.2

STAR TREK: DEEP SPACE NINE WORF SPECIAL
Malibu Comics: Dec, 1995 ($3.95, one-shot)
1-Includes pinups 5.00

STAR TREK: DIVIDED WE FALL
DC Comics (WildStorm): July, 2001 - No. 4, Oct, 2001 ($2.95, limited series)
1-4: Ordover & Mack-s; Lenara Kahn, Verad and Odan app. 3.00

STAR TREK EARLY VOYAGES (TV)
Marvel Comics (Paramount Comics): Feb, 1997 - No. 17, Jun, 1998 ($2.95/$1.95/$1.99)
1-($2.95) 5.00
2-17 4.00

STAR TREK: ENTERPRISE EXPERIMENT
IDW Publishing: Apr, 2008 - No. 5, Aug, 2008 ($3.99, limited series)
1-5-Year Four story; D.C. Fontana & Derek Chester-s; Purcell-a 4.00

STAR TREK: FIRST CONTACT (Movie)
Marvel Comics (Paramount Comics): Nov, 1996 ($5.95, one-shot)
nn-Movie adaption 6.00

STAR TREK: INFESTATION (Crossover with G.I. Joe, Transformers & Ghostbusters)
IDW Publishing: Feb, 2011 - No. 2, Feb, 2011 ($3.99, limited series)
1,2-Zombies in the Kirk era; Maloney & Erskine-a; two covers on each 4.00

STAR TREK: KHAN
IDW Publishing: Oct, 2013 - No. 5, Feb, 2014 ($3.99, limited series)
1-5-Follows the 2013 movie; Khan's origin; Messina & Balboni-a 4.00

STAR TREK: KHAN RULING IN HELL
IDW Publishing: Oct, 2010 - No. 4, Jan, 2011 ($3.99, limited series)
1-4-Khan and the Botany Bay crew after banishment on Ceti Alpha V; Mantovani-a 4.00

STAR TREK: KLINGONS: BLOOD WILL TELL
IDW Publishing: Apr, 2007 - No. 5 ($3.99, limited series)
1-5-Star Trek TOS episodes from the Klingon viewpoint; Messina-a. 2-Tribbles 4.00
1-($4.99) Klingon Language Variant; comic with Kliingon text; English script 5.00

STAR TREK/ LEGION OF SUPER-HEROES
IDW Publishing: Oct, 2011 - No. 6, Mar, 2012 ($3.99, limited series)
1-6-Jeff Moy-a/Jimenez-c 1-Giffen var-c. 2-Lightle var-c. 3-Grell var-c. 5-Allred var-c 4.00

STAR TREK: LEONARD McCOY, FRONTIER DOCTOR
IDW Publishing: Apr, 2010 - No. 4, Jul, 2010 ($3.99, limited series)
1-4-Dr. McCoy right before Star Trek: TMP; John Byrne-s/a 4.00

STAR TREK: MIRROR IMAGES
IDW Publishing: June, 2008 - No. 5, Nov, 2008 ($3.99, limited series)
1-5-Further adventures in the Mirror Universe. 3-Mirror-Picard app. 4.00

STAR TREK: MIRROR MIRROR
Marvel Comics (Paramount Comics): Feb, 1997 ($3.95, one-shot)
1-DeFalco-s 4.00

STAR TREK: MISSION'S END
IDW Publishing: Mar, 2009 - No. 5, July, 2009 ($3.99, limited series)
1-5-Kirk, Spock, Bones crew, their last mission on the pre-movie Enterprise 4.00

STAR TREK MOVIE ADAPTATION
IDW Publishing: Feb, 2010 - No. 6, Aug, 2010 ($3.99, limited series)
1-6-Adaptation of 2009 movie; Messina-a; regular & photo-c on each 4.00

STAR TREK MOVIE SPECIAL
DC Comics: 1984 (June) - No. 2, 1987 ($1.50); No. 1, 1989 ($2.00, 52 pgs)
nn-(#1)-Adapts Star Trek III; Sutton-p (68 pgs.) 5.00
2-Adapts Star Trek IV; Sutton-a; Chaykin-c. (68 pgs.) 5.00
1 (1989)-Adapts Star Trek V; painted-c 5.00

STAR TREK: NERO
IDW Publishing: Aug, 2009 - No. 4, Nov, 2009 ($3.99, limited series)
1-4-Nero's ship after the attack on the Kelvin to the arrival of Spock 4.00

STAR TREK: NEW FRONTIER
IDW Publishing: Mar, 2008 - No. 5, July, 2008 ($3.99, limited series)
1-5-Capt. Calhoun & Adm. Shelby app.; Peter David-s 4.00

STAR TREK 100 PAGE...
IDW Publishing: Nov, 2011 - Present ($7.99)
...Spectacular #1 (11/11) Reprints stories of the original crew; s/a by Byrne and others 8.00
...Spectacular 2012 (2/12) Reprints; Khan, Q, Capt. Pike, the Gorn app. 8.00

GD 2.0 | VG 4.0 | FN 6.0 | VF 8.0 | VF/NM 9.0 | NM- 9.2

...Spectacular Summer 2012 (8/12) Reprints of TNG and Voyager stories 8.00
...Spectacular Winter 2012 (8/12) Reprints; Capt. Harriman, Mirror Universe 8.00

STAR TREK: OPERATION ASSIMILATION
Marvel Comics (Paramount Comics): Dec, 1996 ($2.95, one-shot)
1 4.00

STAR TREK: ROMULANS SCHISMS
IDW Publishing: Sept, 2009 - No. 3, Nov, 2009 ($3.99, limited series)
1-3-John Byrne-s/a/c 4.00

STAR TREK: ROMULANS THE HOLLOW CROWN
IDW Publishing: Sept, 2008 - No. 2, Oct, 2008 ($3.99, limited series)
1,2-John Byrne-s/a/c 4.00

STAR TREK VI: THE UNDISCOVERED COUNTRY (Movie)
DC Comics: 1992
1-($2.95, regular edition, 68 pgs.)-Adaptation of film 5.00
nn-($5.95, prestige edition)-Has photos of movie not included in regular edition; painted-c by Palmer; photo back-c 1 2 3 5 6 8

STAR TREK: SPOCK: REFLECTIONS
IDW Publishing: July, 2009 - No. 4, Oct, 2009 ($3.99, limited series)
1-4-Flashbacks of Spock's childhood and career; Messina & Manfredi-a 4.00

STAR TREK: STARFLEET ACADEMY
Marvel Comics (Paramount Comics): Dec, 1996 - No. 19, Jun, 1998 ($1.95/$1.99)
1-19: Begin new series. 12-"Telepathy War" pt. 1. 18-English & Klingon editions 4.00

STAR TREK: TELEPATHY WAR
Marvel Comics (Paramount Comics): Nov, 1997 ($2.99, 48 pgs., one-shot)
1-"Telepathy War" x-over pt. 6 4.00

STAR TREK - THE MODALA IMPERATIVE
DC Comics: Late July, 1991 - No. 4, Late Sept, 1991 ($1.75, limited series)
1-4 4.00
TPB ($19.95) r/series and ST:TNG - The Modala Imperative 20.00

STAR TREK: THE NEXT GENERATION (TV)
DC Comics: Feb, 1988 - No. 6, July, 1988 (limited series)
1 ($1.50, 52 pgs.)-Sienkiewicz painted-c 1 2 3 5 7 9
2-6 ($1.00) 5.00

STAR TREK: THE NEXT GENERATION (TV)
DC Comics: Oct, 1989 -No. 80, 1995 ($1.50/$1.75/$1.95)
1-Capt. Picard and crew from TV show 2 4 6 8 10 12
2,3 6.00
4-10 5.00
11-23,25-49,51-60 4.00
24,50: 24-($2.50, 52 pgs.). 50-($3.50, 68 pgs.)-Painted-c 6.00
61-74,76-80 4.00
75-($3.95, 50 pgs.) 5.00
Annual 1-6 ('90-'95, 68 pgs.) 5.00
Special 1 -3('93-'95, 68 pgs.)-1-Contains 3 stories 5.00
...-The Series Finale (1994, $3.95, 68 pgs.) 5.00

STAR TREK: THE NEXT GENERATION (TV)
DC Comics (WildStorm): one-shots
Embrace the Wolf (6/00, $5.95, prestige format) Golden & Sniegoski-s 6.00
Forgiveness (2001, $24.95, HC) David Brin-s/Scott Hampton painted-a; dust jacket-c 30.00
Forgiveness (2002, $17.95, SC) 18.00
The Gorn Crisis (1/01, $29.95, HC) Kordey painted-a/dust jacket-c 30.00
The Gorn Crisis (1/01, $17.95, SC) Kordey painted-a 18.00

STAR TREK: THE NEXT GENERATION/DEEP SPACE NINE (TV)
DC Comics: Dec, 1994 - No. 2, Jan, 1995 ($2.50, limited series)
1,2-Parts 1 & 3 of x-over with Star Trek: DS9/TNG from Malibu Comics 4.00

STAR TREK: THE NEXT GENERATION / DOCTOR WHO: ASSIMILATION^2
IDW Publishing: May, 2012 - No. 8, Dec, 2012 ($3.99, limited series)
1-8-The Borg and Cybermen team-up; Tipton-s/Woodward-a; multiple covers on each 4.00

STAR TREK: THE NEXT GENERATION: GHOSTS
IDW Publishing: Nov, 2009 - No. 5, Mar, 2010 ($3.99)
1-5-Cannon-s/Aranda-a 4.00

STAR TREK: THE NEXT GENERATION - ILL WIND
DC Comics: Nov, 1995 - No. 4, Feb, 1996 ($2.50, limited series)
1-4: Hugh Fleming painted-c on all 4.00

Star Trek Untold Voyages #5 © Paramount

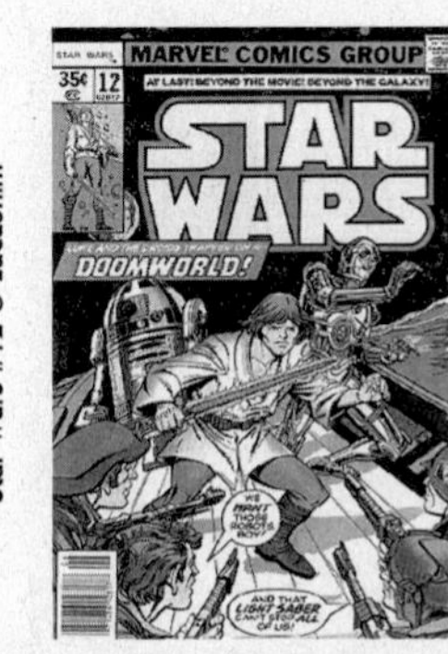

Star Wars #12 © Lucasfilm

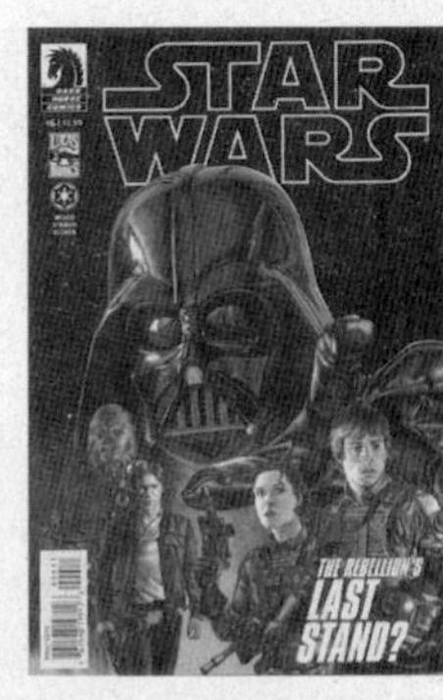

Star Wars (2013 series) #6 © Lucasfilm

GD 2.0 | VG 4.0 | FN 6.0 | VF 8.0 | VF/NM 9.0 | NM- 9.2

STAR TREK: THE NEXT GENERATION: INTELLIGENCE GATHERING
IDW Publishing: Jan, 2008 - No. 5, May, 2008 ($3.99)
1-5-Messina-a/Scott & David Tipton-s; two covers on each 4.00

STAR TREK: THE NEXT GENERATION - PERCHANCE TO DREAM
DC Comics/WildStorm: Feb, 2000 - No. 4, May, 2000 ($2.50, limited series)
1-4-Bradstreet-c 3.00

STAR TREK: THE NEXT GENERATION - RIKER
Marvel Comics (Paramount Comics): July, 1998 ($3.50, one-shot)
1-Riker joins the Maquis 4.00

STAR TREK: THE NEXT GENERATION - SHADOWHEART
DC Comics: Dec, 1994 - No. 4, Mar, 1995 ($1.95, limited series)
1-4 4.00

STAR TREK: THE NEXT GENERATION - THE KILLING SHADOWS
DC Comics/WildStorm: Nov, 2000 - No. 4, Feb, 2001 ($2.50, limited series)
1-4-Scott Ciencin-s; Sela app. 3.00

STAR TREK: THE NEXT GENERATION: THE LAST GENERATION
IDW Publishing: Nov, 2008 - No. 5, Mar, 2009 ($3.99, limited series)
1-5-Purcell-a; alternate timeline with Klingon war; Sulu app. 4.00

STAR TREK: THE NEXT GENERATION - THE MODALA IMPERATIVE
DC Comics: Early Sept, 1991 - No. 4, Late Oct, 1991 ($1.75, limited series)
1-4 4.00

STAR TREK: THE NEXT GENERATION: THE SPACE BETWEEN
IDW Publishing: Jan, 2007 - No. 6, June, 2007 ($3.99)
1-6-Single issue stories from various seasons; photo & art covers 4.00

STAR TREK: THE WRATH OF KHAN
IDW Publishing: Jun, 2009 - No. 3, Jul, 2009 ($3.99, limited series)
1-3-Movie adaptation; Chee Yang Ong-a 4.00

STAR TREK: TNG: HIVE
IDW Publishing: Sept, 2012 - No. 4, Feb, 2013 ($3.99, limited series)
1-4-Brannon Braga-s/Joe Corroney-a; Next Generation crew vs. the Borg 4.00

STAR TREK UNLIMITED
Marvel Comics (Paramount Comics): Nov, 1996 - No. 10, July, 1998 ($2.95/$2.99)
1,2-Stories from original series and Next Generation 5.00
3-10: 3-Begin $2.99-c. 6-"Telepathy War" pt. 4. 7-Q & Trelane swap Kirk & Picard 4.00

STAR TREK UNTOLD VOYAGES
Marvel Comics (Paramount Comics): May, 1998 - No. 5, July, 1998 ($2.50)
1-5-Kirk's crew after the 1st movie 4.00

STAR TREK: VOYAGER
Marvel Comics (Paramount Comics): Nov, 1996 - No. 15, Mar, 1998 ($1.95/$1.99)
1-15: 13-"Telepathy War" pt. 5. 14-Seven of Nine joins crew 4.00

STAR TREK: VOYAGER
DC Comics/WildStorm: one-shots and trade paperbacks
- Elite Force (7/00, $5.95) The Borg app.; Abnett & Lanning-s 6.00
... Encounters With the Unknown TPB (2001, $19.95) reprints 20.00
- False Colors (1/00, $5.95) Photo-c and Jim Lee-c; Jeff Moy-a 6.00

STAR TREK: VOYAGER-- THE PLANET KILLER
DC Comics/WildStorm: Mar, 2001 - No. 3, May, 2001 ($2.95, limited series)
1-3-Voyager vs. the Planet Killer from the ST:TOS episode; Teranishi-a 3.00

STAR TREK: VOYAGER SPLASHDOWN
Marvel Comics (Paramount Comics): Apr, 1998 - No. 4, July, 1998 ($2.50, limited series)
1-4-Voyager crashes on a water planet 4.00

STAR TREK/ X-MEN
Marvel Comics (Paramount Comics): Dec, 1996 ($4.99, one-shot)
1-Kirk's crew & X-Men; art by Silvestri, Tan, Winn & Finch; Lobdell-s 6.00

STAR TREK/ X-MEN: 2ND CONTACT
Marvel Comics (Paramount Comics): May, 1998 ($4.99, 64 pgs., one-shot)
1-Next Gen. crew & X-Men battle Kang, Sentinels & Borg following First Contact movie 6.00
1-Painted wraparound variant cover 6.00

STAR TREK: YEAR FOUR (Also see Star Trek: Enterprise Experiment)
IDW Publishing: July, 2007 - No. 5, Nov, 2007 ($3.99, limited series)
1-5: 1-Original series crew; Tischman-s/Conley-a; three covers on each 4.00

STAR WARS (Movie) (See Classic..., Contemporary Motivators, Dark Horse Comics, The Droids, The Ewoks, Marvel Movie Showcase, Marvel Special Ed.)
Marvel Comics Group: July, 1977 - No. 107, Sept, 1986
1-(Regular 30¢ edition)-Price in square w/UPC code; #1-6 adapt first movie; first issue on sale before movie debuted 7 14 21 46 86 125
1-(35¢-c; limited distribution - 1500 copies?)- Price in square w/UPC code (Prices vary widely on this book. In 2005 a CGC certified 9.4 sold for $6,500, a CGC certified 9.2 sold for $3,403, and a CGC certified 6.0 sold for $610) 190 380 570 1568 3534 5500
NOTE: *The rare 35¢ edition has the cover price in a square box, and the UPC box in the lower left hand corner has the UPC code lines running through it.*
1-9: Reprints; has "reprint" in upper lefthand corner of cover or on inside or price and number inside a diamond with no date or UPC on cover; 30¢ and 35¢ issues published 4.00
2-4-(30¢ issues). 4-Battle with Darth Vader 4 8 12 27 44 60
2-4-(35¢ with UPC code; not reprints) 25 50 75 175 388 600
5,6: 5-Begin 35¢-c on all editions. 6-Stevens-a(i). 3 6 9 16 24 32
7-20 2 4 6 10 14 18
21-70: 39-44-The Empire Strikes Back-r by Al Williamson in all. 50-Giant. 68-Reintro Boba Fett. 2 4 6 8 10 12
71-80 2 4 6 8 11 14
81-90: 81-Boba Fett app. 2 4 6 9 13 16
91,93-99: 98-Williamson-a. 2 4 6 11 16 20
92,100-106: 92,100-($1.00, 52 pgs.). 3 6 9 14 20 26
107(low dist.); Portacio-a(i) 6 12 18 39 62 85
Annual 1 (12/79, 52 pgs.)-Simonson-c 2 4 6 8 11 14
Annual 2 (11/82, 52 pgs.), 3(12/83, 52 pgs.) 2 4 6 8 10 12
... A Long Time Ago...Vol. 1 TPB (Dark Horse Comics, 6/02, $29.95) r/#1-14 30.00
... A Long Time Ago...Vol. 2 TPB (Dark Horse Comics, 7/02, $29.95) r/#15-28 30.00
... A Long Time Ago...Vol. 3 TPB (Dark Horse Comics, 11/02, $29.95) r/#39-53 30.00
... A Long Time Ago...Vol. 4 TPB (Dark Horse Comics, 1/03, $29.95) r/#54-67 & Ann. 2 30.00
... A Long Time Ago...Vol. 5 TPB (Dark Horse Comics, 3/03, $29.95) r/#68-81 & Ann. 3 30.00
... A Long Time Ago...Vol. 6 TPB (Dark Horse Comics, 5/03, $29.95) r/#82-93 30.00
... A Long Time Ago...Vol. 7 TPB (Dark Horse Comics, 6/03, $29.95) r/#96-107 30.00
***Austin** a-11-15i, 21i, 38; c-12-15i, 21i. **Byrne** c-13p. **Chaykin** a-1-10p; c-1. **Golden** c/a-38. **Miller** c-47p; pin-up-43. **Nebres** c/a-Annual 2i. **Portacio** a-107i. **Sienkiewicz** c-92i, 98. **Simonson** a-16p, 49p, 51-63p, 65p, 66p; c-16, 49-51, 52p, 53-62, Annual 1. **Steacy** painted a-105i, 106i; c-105. **Williamson** a-39-44p, 50p, 98; c-39, 40, 41-44p. Painted c-81, 87, 92, 95, 98, 100, 105.*

STAR WARS (Monthly series) (Becomes Star Wars Republic #46-on)
Dark Horse Comics: Dec, 1998 - No. 45, Aug, 2005 ($2.50/$2.95/$2.99)
1-Prelude To Rebellion; Strnad-s 1 2 3 5 6 8
2-45: 2-6-Prelude To Rebellion; Strnad-s. 4-Brereton-c. 7-12-Outlander. 13,17-18-($2.95). 13-18-Emissaries to Malastare; Truman-s. 14-16-($2.50) Schultz-c. 19-22-Twilight; Duursema-a. 23-26-Infinity's End. 42-45-Rite of Passage 3.00
5,6 (Holochrome-c variants) 6.00
#0 Another Universe.com Ed.($10.00) r/serialized pages from Pizzazz Magazine; new Dorman painted-c 10.00
... A Valentine Story (2/03, $3.50) Leia & Han Solo on Hoth; Winick-s/Chadwick-a/c 3.50
...: Rite of Passage (2004, $12.95) r/#42-45 13.00
...: The Stark Hyperspace War (903, $12.95) r/#36-39 13.00

STAR WARS (Monthly series)
Dark Horse Comics: Jan, 2013 - Present ($2.99)
1-Takes place after Episode IV; Brian Wood-s/Carlos D'Anda-a/Alex Ross-c 8.00
2-Ross-c 5.00
3-16: 3,4-Ross-c. 5-7-Migliari-c 3.00

STAR WARS
Dark Horse Comics (Free Comic Book Day giveaways)
...: and Captain Midnight (5/13) flip book with new Captain Midnight story & Avatar 3.00
...: Clone Wars #0 (5/09) flip book with short stories of Usagi Yojimbo, Emily the Strange 3.00
...: Clone Wars Adventures (7/04) based on Cartoon Network series; Fillbach Bros. -a 3.00
...: FCBD 2005 Special (5/05) Anakin & Obi-Wan during Clone Wars 3.00
...: FCBD 2006 Special (5/06) Clone Wars story; flip book with Conan FCBD Special 3.00
...: Tales - A Jedi's Weapon (5/02, 16 pgs.) Anakin Skywalker Episode 2 photo-c 3.00
Free Comic Book Day and Star Wars: The Clone Wars (5/11) flip book with Avatar: The Last Airbender 3.00

STAR WARS, THE
Dark Horse Comics: Sept, 2013 - No. 8 ($3.99)
1-7-Adaptation of George Lucas' original rough-draft screenplay; Mayhew-a/Runge-c 4.00
#0-(1/14, $3.99) Design work of characters, settings, vehicles 4.00

STAR WARS: AGENT OF THE EMPIRE - HARD TARGETS
Dark Horse Comics: Oct, 2012 - No. 5, Feb, 2013 ($2.99, limited series)
1-5: 1-Ostrander-s/Fabbri-a; Boba Fett app. 3.00

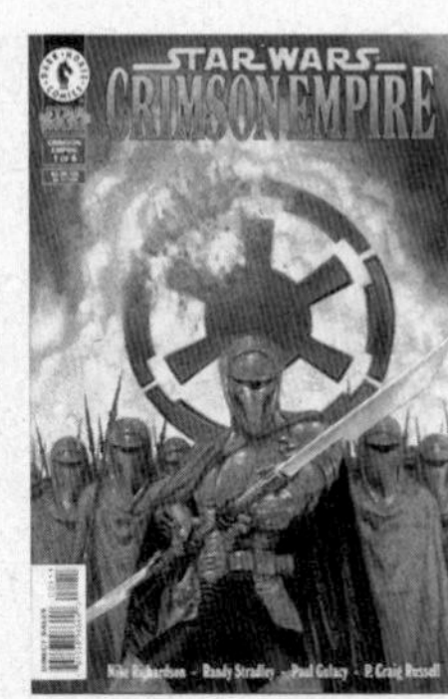

Star Wars: Crimson Empire #1 © Lucasfilm

Star Wars: Dark Times #2 © Lucasfilm

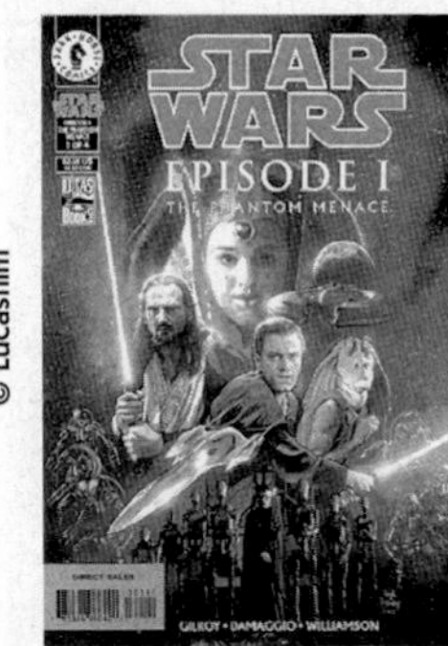

Star Wars: Episode 1 TPM #1 © Lucasfilm

	GD 2.0	VG 4.0	FN 6.0	VF 8.0	VF/NM 9.0	NM- 9.2

STAR WARS: AGENT OF THE EMPIRE - IRON ECLIPSE
Dark Horse Comics: Dec, 2011 - No. 5, Apr, 2012 ($3.50, limited series)
1-5: 1-Ostrander-s/Roux-a; Han Solo & Chewbacca app. 3.50

STAR WARS: A NEW HOPE - THE SPECIAL EDITION
Dark Horse Comics: Jan, 1997 - No. 4, Apr, 1997 ($2.95, limited series)
1-4-Dorman-c 4.00

STAR WARS: BLOOD TIES - BOBA FETT IS DEAD
Dark Horse Comics: Apr, 2012 - No. 4, Jul, 2012 ($3.50, limited series)
1-4-Scalf painted-a/c 3.50

STAR WARS: BLOOD TIES: JANGO AND BOBA FETT
Dark Horse Comics: Aug, 2010 - No. 4, Nov, 2010 ($3.50, limited series)
1-4-Scalf painted-a/c 3.50

STAR WARS: BOBA FETT
Dark Horse Comics: Dec, 1995 - No. 3, Aug, 1997 ($3.95) (Originally intended as a one-shot)
1-Kennedy-c/a 6.00
2,3 5.00
Death, Lies, & Treachery TPB (1/98, $12.95) r/#1-3 13.00
... - Agent of Doom (11/00, $2.99) Ostrander-s/Cam Kennedy-a 3.00
... - Overkill (3/06, $2.99) Hughes-c/Andrews-s/Velasco-a 3.00
Twin Engines of Destruction (1/97, $2.95) 4.00

STAR WARS: BOBA FETT: ENEMY OF THE EMPIRE
Dark Horse Comics: Jan, 1999 - No. 4, Apr, 1999 ($2.95, limited series)
1-4-Recalls 1st meeting of Fett and Vader 4.00

STAR WARS: CHEWBACCA
Dark Horse Comics: Jan, 2000 - No. 4, Apr, 2000 ($2.95, limited series)
1-4-Macan-s/art by various incl. Anderson, Kordey, Gibbons; Phillips-c 3.00

STAR WARS: CLONE WARS ADVENTURES
Dark Horse Comics: 2004 - No. 10, 2007 ($6.95, digest-sized)
1-10-Short stories inspired by Clone Wars animated series 7.00

STAR WARS: CRIMSON EMPIRE
Dark Horse Comics: Dec, 1997 - No. 6, May, 1998 ($2.95, limited series)
1-Richardson-s/Gulacy-a 1 2 3 4 5 7
2-6 5.00

STAR WARS: CRIMSON EMPIRE II: COUNCIL OF BLOOD
Dark Horse Comics: Nov, 1998 - No. 6, Apr, 1999 ($2.95, limited series)
1-6-Richardson & Stradley-s/Gulacy-a 4.00

STAR WARS: CRIMSON EMPIRE III: EMPIRE LOST
Dark Horse Comics: Oct, 2011 - No. 6, Apr, 2012 ($3.50, limited series)
1-6: 1-Richardson-s/Gulacy-a/Dorman-c 3.50

STAR WARS: DARK EMPIRE
Dark Horse Comics: Dec, 1991 - No. 6, Oct, 1992 ($2.95, limited series)
Preview-(99¢) 4.00
1-All have Dorman painted-c 1 3 4 6 8 10
1-3-2nd printing 4.00
2-Low print run 2 4 6 8 10 12
3 6.00
4-6 4.00
Gold Embossed Set (#1-6)-With gold embossed foil logo (price is for set) 90.00
Platinum Embossed Set (#1-6) 120.00
Trade paperback (4/93, 16.95) 17.00
Dark Empire 1 - TPB 3rd printing (2003, $16.95) 17.00
Ltd. Ed. Hardcover ($99.95) Signed & numbered 100.00

STAR WARS: DARK EMPIRE II
Dark Horse Comics: Dec, 1994 - No. 6, May, 1995 ($2.95, limited series)
1-Dave Dorman painted-c 5.00
2-6: Dorman-c in all. 4.00
Platinum Embossed Set (#1-6) 35.00
Trade paperback ($17.95) 18.00
TPB Second Edition (9/06, $19.95) r/#1-6 and Star Wars: Empire's End #1,2 20.00

STAR WARS: DARK FORCE RISING
Dark Horse Comics: May, 1997 - No. 6, Oct, 1997 ($2.95, limited series)
1-6 4.00
TPB (2/98, $17.95) r/#1-6 18.00

STAR WARS: DARK TIMES (Continued from Star Wars Republic #84)(Continues in Star Wars: Rebellion #15)
Dark Horse Comics: Oct, 2006 - No. 17, Jun, 2010 ($2.99)
1-17-Nineteen years before Episode IV; Doug Wheatley-a. 11-Celeste Morne awakens 13-17-Blue Harvest 3.00
#0-(7/09, $2.99) Prologue to Blue Harvest 3.00
... Volume 1: The Path To Nowhere (1/08, $17.95, TPB) r/#1-5 18.00

STAR WARS: DARK TIMES - A SPARK REMAINS
Dark Horse Comics: Jul, 2013 - No. 5, Dec, 2013 ($3.50, limited series)
1-5-Stradley-s/Wheatley-a; Darth Vader app. 3.50

STAR WARS: DARK TIMES - FIRE CARRIER
Dark Horse Comics: Feb, 2013 - No. 5, Jun, 2013 ($2.99, limited series)
1-5-Stradley-s/Guzman-a; Darth Vader app. 3.00

STAR WARS: DARK TIMES - OUT OF THE WILDERNESS
Dark Horse Comics: Aug, 2011 - No. 5, Apr, 2012 ($2.99, limited series)
1-5-Doug Wheatley-a 3.00

STAR WARS: DARTH MAUL
Dark Horse Comics: Sept, 2000 - No. 4, Dec, 2000 ($2.95, limited series)
1-4-Photo-c and Struzan painted-c; takes place 6 months before Ep. 1 3.00

STAR WARS: DARTH MAUL - DEATH SENTENCE
Dark Horse Comics: Jul, 2012 - No. 4, Oct, 2012 ($2.99, limited series)
1-4-Tom Taylor-s/Bruno Redondo-a/Dave Dorman-c 3.00

STAR WARS: DARTH VADER AND THE CRY OF SHADOWS
Dark Horse Comics: Dec, 2013 - No. 5, ($3.50, limited series)
1-4-Siedell-s/Guzman-a/Massaferra-c 3.50

STAR WARS: DARTH VADER AND THE GHOST PRISON
Dark Horse Comics: May, 2012 - No. 5, Sept, 2012 ($3.50, limited series)
1-5-Blackman-s/Alessio-a/Wilkins-c. 1-Variant-c by Sanda 3.50

STAR WARS: DARTH VADER AND THE LOST COMMAND
Dark Horse Comics: Jan, 2011 - No. 5, May, 2011 ($3.50, limited series)
1-5-Blackman-s/Leonardi-a/Sanda-c. 1-Variant-c by Wheatley 3.50

STAR WARS: DARTH VADER AND THE NINTH ASSASSIN
Dark Horse Comics: Apr, 2013 - No. 5, Aug, 2013 ($3.50, limited series)
1-5-Siedell-s. 1,2,4-Thompson-a. 3,5-Fernandez-a 3.50

STAR WARS: DAWN OF THE JEDI
Dark Horse Comics: No. 0, Feb, 2012 - Present ($3.50)
0-Guide to the worlds, characters, sites, vehicles; Migliari-c 3.50
... - Force Storm (2/12 - No. 5, 6/12, $3.50) 1-5-Ostrander-s/Duursema-a/c 3.50
... - Force War (11/13 - No. 5, 3/14, $3.50) 1-5-Ostrander-s/Duursema-a/c 3.50
... - Prisoner of Bogan (11/12 - No. 5, 5/13, $2.99) 1-5-Ostrander-s/Duursema-a/c 3.00

STAR WARS: DROIDS (See Dark Horse Comics #17-19)
Dark Horse Comics: Apr, 1994 - #6, Sept, 1994; V2#1, Apr, 1995 - V2#8, Dec, 1995 ($2.50, limited series)
1-($2.95)-Embossed-c 5.00
2-6 , Special 1 (1/95, $2.50), V2#1-8 4.00
Star Wars Omnibus: Droids One TPB (6/08, $24.95) r/#1-6, Special 1, V2#1-8, Star Wars: The Protocol Offensive and "Artoo's Day Out" story from Star Wars Galaxy Magazine #1 25.00

STAR WARS: EMPIRE
Dark Horse Comics: Sept, 2002 - No. 40, Feb, 2006 ($2.99)
1-40: 1-Benjamin-a; takes place weeks before SW: A New Hope. 7,28-Boba Fett-c. 14-Vader after the destruction of the Death Star. 15-Death of Biggs; Wheatley-a 3.00
... Volume 1 (2003, $12.95, TPB) r/#1-4 13.00
... Volume 2 (2004, $17.95, TPB) r/#8-12,15 18.00
... Volume 3: The Imperial Perspective (2004, $17.95, TPB) r/#13,14,16-19 18.00
... Volume 4: The Heart of the Rebellion (2005, $17.95, TPB) r/#5,6,20-22 & Star Wars: A Valentine Story 18.00
... Volume 5 (2006, $14.95, TPB) r/#23-27 15.00
... Volume 6: In the Shadows of Their Fathers (10/06, $17.95, TPB) r/#29-34 18.00
... Volume 7: The Wrong Side of the War (1/07, $17.95, TPB) r/#34-40 18.00

STAR WARS: EMPIRE'S END
Dark Horse Comics: Oct, 1995 - No. 2, Nov, 1995 ($2.95, limited series)
1,2-Dorman-c 4.00

STAR WARS: EPISODE 1 THE PHANTOM MENACE
Dark Horse Comics: May, 1999 - No. 4 ($2.95, movie adaptation)
1-4-Regular and photo-c; Damaggio & Williamson-a 4.00
TPB ($12.95) r/#1-4 13.00
...Anakin Skywalker-Photo-c & Bradstreet-c, ...Obi-Wan Kenobi-Photo-c & Egeland-c,

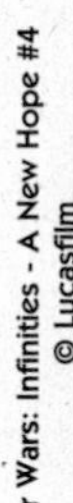
Star Wars: Infinities - A New Hope #4 © Lucasfilm

STAR WARS
LEGACY
THE FUTURE OF STAR WARS BEGINS NOW!

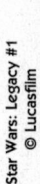

Star Wars: Legacy #1 © Lucasfilm

Star Wars: Rebellion #1 © Lucasfilm

	GD 2.0	VG 4.0	FN 6.0	VF 8.0	VF/NM 9.0	NM- 9.2

...Queen Amidala-Photo-c & Bradstreet-c, ...Qui-Gon Jinn-Photo-c & Bradstreet-c 4.00
Gold foil covers; Wizard 1/2 10.00

STAR WARS: EPISODE II - ATTACK OF THE CLONES
Dark Horse Comics: Apr, 2002 - No. 4, May, 2002 ($3.99, movie adaptation)

1-4-Regular and photo-c; Duursema-a 4.00
TPB ($17.95) r/#1-4; Struzan-c 18.00

STAR WARS: EPISODE III - REVENGE OF THE SITH
Dark Horse Comics: May, 2005 - No. 4, May, 2005 ($2.99, movie adaptation)

1-4-Wheatley-a/Dorman-c 3.00
TPB ($12.95) r/#1-4; Dorman-c 13.00

STAR WARS: GENERAL GRIEVOUS
Dark Horse Comics: Mar, 2005 - No. 4, June, 2005 ($2.99, limited series)

1-4-Leonardi-a/Dixon-s 3.00
TPB (2005, $12.95) r/#1-4 13.00

STAR WARS HANDBOOK
Dark Horse Comics: July, 1998 - Mar, 2000 ($2.95, one-shots)

...X-Wing Rogue Squadron (7/98)-Guidebook to characters and spacecraft 4.00
...Crimson Empire (7/99) Dorman-c 4.00
...Dark Empire (3/00) Dorman-c 4.00

STAR WARS: HEIR TO THE EMPIRE
Dark Horse Comics: Oct, 1995 - No.6, Apr, 1996 ($2.95, limited series)

1-6: Adaptation of Zahn novel 4.00

STAR WARS: INFINITIES - A NEW HOPE
Dark Horse Comics: May, 2001 - No. 4, Oct, 2001 ($2.99, limited series)

1-4: "What If..." the Death Star wasn't destroyed in Episode 4 3.00
TPB (2002, $12.95) r/ #1-4 13.00

STAR WARS: INFINITIES - THE EMPIRE STRIKES BACK
Dark Horse Comics: July, 2002 - No. 4, Oct, 2002 ($2.99, limited series)

1-4: "What If..." Luke died on the ice planet Hoth; Bachalo-c 3.00
TPB (2/03, $12.95) r/ #1-4 13.00

STAR WARS: INFINITIES - RETURN OF THE JEDI
Dark Horse Comics: Nov, 2003 - No. 4, Mar, 2004 ($2.99, limited series)

1-4:"What If..." ; Benjamin-a 3.00

STAR WARS: INVASION
Dark Horse Comics: July, 2009 - No. 5, Nov, 2009 ($2.99)

1-5-Jo Chen-c 3.00
#0-(10/09, $3.50) Dorman-c; Han Solo and Chewbacca app. 3.50
... - Rescues 1-6 (5/10 - No. 6, 12/10) Chen-c 3.00
... - Revelations 1-5 (7/11 - No. 5, 11/11, $3.50) Luke Skywalker app.; Scalf-c 3.50

STAR WARS: JABBA THE HUTT
Dark Horse Comics: Apr, 1995 ($2.50, one-shots)

nn, ...The Betrayal, ...The Dynasty Trap, ...The Hunger of Princess Nampi 4.00

STAR WARS: JANGO FETT - OPEN SEASONS
Dark Horse Comics: Apr, 2002 - No. 4, July, 2002 ($2.99, limited series)

1-4: 1-Bachs & Fernandez-a 3.00

STAR WARS: JEDI
Dark Horse Comics: Feb, 2003 - Jun, 2004 ($4.99, one-shots)

... - Aayla Secura (8/03) Ostrander-s/Duursema-a 5.00
... - Count Dooku (11/03) Duursema-a 5.00
... - Mace Windu (2/03) Duursema-a 5.00
... - Shaak Ti (5/03) Ostrander-s/Duursema-a 5.00
... - Yoda (6/04) Barlow-s/Hoon-a 5.00

STAR WARS: JEDI ACADEMY - LEVIATHAN
Dark Horse Comics: Oct, 1998 - No. 4, Jan, 1999 ($2.95, limited series)

1-4: 1-Lago-c. 2-4-Chadwick-c 4.00

STAR WARS: JEDI COUNCIL: ACTS OF WAR
Dark Horse Comics: Jun, 2000 - No. 4, Sept, 2000 ($2.95, limited series)

1-4-Stradley-s; set one year before Episode 1 3.00

STAR WARS: JEDI QUEST
Dark Horse Comics: Sept, 2001 - No. 4, Dec, 2001 ($2.99, limited series)

1-4-Anakin's Jedi training; Windham-s/Mhan-a 3.00

STAR WARS: JEDI - THE DARK SIDE
Dark Horse Comics: May, 2011 - No. 5, Sept, 2011 ($2.99, limited series)

1-5: 1-Qui-Gon Jinn 21 years befor Episode 1; Asrar-a 3.00

STAR WARS: JEDI VS. SITH
Dark Horse Comics: Apr, 2001 - No. 6, Sept, 2001 ($2.99, limited series)

1-6: Macan-s/Bachs-a/Robinson-c 3.00

STAR WARS: KNIGHT ERRANT
Dark Horse Comics: Oct, 2010 - No. 5, Feb, 2011 ($2.99)

1-5: 1-John Jackson Miller-s/Federico Dallocchio-a 3.00
... - Deluge 1-5 (8/11 - No. 5 12/11, $3.50) 1-Miller-s/Rodriguez-a/Quinones-c 3.50
... - Escape 1-5 (6/12 - No. 5 10/12, $3.50) 1-Miller-s/Castiello-a/Carré-c 3.50

STAR WARS: KNIGHTS OF THE OLD REPUBLIC
Dark Horse Comics: Jan, 2006 - No. 50, Feb, 2010 ($2.99)

1-50-Takes place 3,964 years before Episode IV. 1-6-Brian Ching-a/Travis Charest-c 3.00
... Handbook (11/07, $2.99) profiles of characters, ships, locales 3.00
.../Rebellion #0 (3/06, 25¢) flip book preview of both series 3.00
... - War 1-5 (1/12 - No. 5, 5/12, $3.50) J.J. Miller-s/Mutti-a 3.50
... Vol. 1 Commencement TPB (11/06, $18.95) r/#0-6 19.00
... Vol. 2 Flashpoint TPB (5/07, $18.95) r/#17-12 19.00
... Vol. 3 Days of Fear, Nights of Anger TPB (1/08, $18.95) r/#13-18 19.00

STAR WARS: LEGACY
Dark Horse Comics: No. 0, June, 2006 - No. 50, Aug, 2010 ($2.99)
Volume 2, Mar, 2013 - Present ($2.99)

0-(25¢) Dossier of characters, settings, ships and weapons; Duursema-c 3.00
0 1/2-(1/08, $2.99) Updated dossier of characters, settings, ships, and history 3.00
1-50: 1-Takes place 130 years after Episode IV; Hughes-c/Duursema-a. 4-Duursema-c 7,39-Luke Skywalker on-c. 16-Obi-Wan Kenobi app. 50-Wraparound-c 3.00
...: Broken Vol. 1 TPB (4/07, $17.95) r/#1-3,5,6 18.00
...: One for One (9/10, $1.00) reprints #1 with red cover frame 3.00
... Volume Two 1 (3/13 - Present, $2.99) 1-13: 1-Bechko-s/Hardman-a/Wilkins-c 3.00
... War 1-6 (12/10 - No. 6, 5/11, $3.50) 1-Ostrander-s/Duursema-a; Darth Krayt app. 3.50

STAR WARS: LOST TRIBE OF THE SITH - SPIRAL
Dark Horse Comics: Aug, 2012 - No. 5, Dec, 2012 ($2.99, limited series)

1-5-J.J. Miller-s/Mutti-a/Renaud-c 3.00

STAR WARS: MARA JADE
Dark Horse Comics: Aug, 1998 - No. 6, Jan, 1999 ($2.95, limited series)

1-6-Ezquerra-a 4.00

STAR WARS: OBSESSION (Clone Wars)
Dark Horse Comics: Nov, 2004 - No. 5, Apr, 2005 ($2.99, limited series)

1-5-Blackman-s/Ching-a/c; Anakin & Obi-Wan 5 months before Episode III 3.00
...: Clone Wars Vol. 7 (2005, $17.95) r/#1-5 and 2005 Free Comic Book Day edition 18.00

STAR WARS: PURGE
Dark Horse Comics: Dec, 2005 ($2.99, one-shot)

nn-Vader vs. remaining Jedi one month after Episode III; Hughes-c/Wheatley-a 5.00
... - Seconds To Die (11/09, $3.50) Vader app.; Charest-c/Ostrander-s 3.50
... - The Hidden Blade (4/10, $3.50) Vader app.; Scalf-c/a; Blackman-s 3.50
... - The Tyrant's Fist 1,2 (12/12 - No, 2, 1/13, $3.50) Vader app.; Freed-s/Dan Scott-c 3.50

STAR WARS: QUI-GON & OBI-WAN - LAST STAND ON ORD MANTELL
Dark Horse Comics: Dec, 2000 - No. 3, Mar, 2001 ($2.99, limited series)

1-3: 1-Three covers (photo, Tony Daniel, Bachs) Windham-s 3.00

STAR WARS: QUI-GON & OBI-WAN - THE AURORIENT EXPRESS
Dark Horse Comics: Feb, 2002 - No. 2, Mar, 2002 ($2.99, limited series)

1,2-Six years prior to Phantom Menace; Marangon-a 3.00

STAR WARS: REBELLION (Also see Star Wars: Knights of the Old Republic flip book)
Dark Horse Comics: Apr, 2006 - Present ($2.99)

1-16-Takes place 9 months after Episode IV; Luke Skywalker app. 1-Badeaux-a/c 3.00
Vol. 1 TPB (2/07, $14.95) r/#0 (flip book) & #1-5 15.00

STAR WARS: REPUBLIC (Formerly Star Wars monthly series)
Dark Horse Comics: No. 46, Sept, 2002 - No. 83, Feb, 2006 ($2.99)

46-83-Events of the Clone Wars 3.00
...: Clone Wars Vol. 1 (2003, $14.95) r/#46-50 15.00
...: Clone Wars Vol. 2 (2003, $14.95) r/#51-53 & Star Wars: Jedi - Shaak Ti 15.00
...: Clone Wars Vol. 3 (2004, $14.95) r/#55-59 15.00
...: Clone Wars Vol. 4 (2004, $16.95) r/#54, 63 & Star Wars: Jedi - Aayla Secura & Dooku 17.00
...: Clone Wars Vol. 5 (2004, $17.95) r/#60-62, 64 & Star Wars: Jedi - Yoda 18.00
...: Clone Wars Vol. 6 (2005, $17.95) r/#65-71 18.00
(Clone Wars Vol. 7 - see Star Wars: Obsession)
...: Clone Wars Vol. 8 (2006, $17.95) r/#72-78 18.00
...: Clone Wars Vol. 9 (2006, $17.95) r/#79-83 & Star Wars: Purge 18.00
...: Honor and Duty TPB (5/06, $12.95) r/#46-48,78 13.00

Star Wars: Tag & Bink Are Dead #1 © Lucasfilm

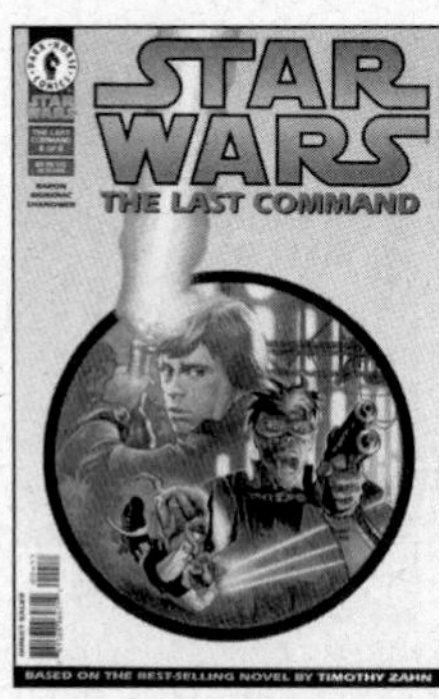

Star Wars: The Last Command #4 © Lucasfilm

Static Shock: Rebirth of the Cool #1 © Milestone

GD VG FN VF VF/NM NM-
2.0 4.0 6.0 8.0 9.0 9.2

STAR WARS: RETURN OF THE JEDI (Movie)
Marvel Comics Group: Oct, 1983 - No. 4, Jan, 1984 (limited series)
1-Williamson-p in all; r/Marvel Super Special #27 2 4 6 11 16 20
2-4-Continues r/Marvel Super Special #27 2 4 6 9 12 15
Oversized issue (1983, $2.95, 10-3/4x8-1/4", 68 pgs., cardboard-c)-r/#1-4 2 4 6 10 13 16

STAR WARS: RIVER OF CHAOS
Dark Horse Comics: June, 1995 - No. 4, Sept, 1995 ($2.95, limited series)
1-4: Louise Simonson scripts 4.00

STAR WARS: SHADOWS OF THE EMPIRE
Dark Horse Comics: May, 1996 - No. 6, Oct, 1996 ($2.95, limited series)
1-6: Story details events between The Empire Strikes Back & Return of the Jedi; Russell-a(i). 4.00

STAR WARS: SHADOWS OF THE EMPIRE - EVOLUTION
Dark Horse Comics: Feb, 1998 - No. 5, June, 1998 ($2.95, limited series)
1-5: Perry-s/Fegredo-c. 4.00

STAR WARS: SHADOW STALKER
Dark Horse Comics: Sept, 1997 ($2.95, one-shot)
nn-Windham-a. 4.00

STAR WARS: SPLINTER OF THE MIND'S EYE
Dark Horse Comics: Dec, 1995 - No. 4, June, 1996 ($2.50, limited series)
1-4: Adaption of Alan Dean Foster novel 4.00

STAR WARS: STARFIGHTER
Dark Horse Comics: Jan, 2002 - No. 3, March, 2002 ($2.99, limited series)
1-3-Williams & Gray-c 3.00

STAR WARS: TAG & BINK ARE DEAD
Dark Horse Comics: Oct, 2001 - No. 2, Nov, 2001($2.99, limited series)
1,2-Rubio-s 3.00
Star Wars: Tag & Bink Were Here TPB (11/06, $14.95) r/both SW: Tag & Bink series 15.00

STAR WARS: TAG & BINK II
Dark Horse Comics: Mar, 2006 - No. 2, Apr, 2006($2.99, limited series)
1-Tag & Bink invade Return of the Jedi; Rubio-s. 2-Tag & Bink as Jedi younglings during Ep II 3.00

STAR WARS TALES
Dark Horse Comics: Sept, 1999 - No. 24, Jun, 2005 ($4.95/$5.95/$5.99, anthology)
1-4-Short stories by various 6.00
5-24 ($5.95/$5.99-c) Art and photo-c on each 6.00
Volume 1-6 ($19.95) 1-(1/02) r/#1-4. 2-('02) r/#5-8. 3-(1/03) r/#9-12. 4-(1/04) r/#13-16 5-(1/05) r/#17-20; introduction pages from #1-20. 6-(1/06) r/#21-24 20.00

STAR WARS: TALES FROM MOS EISLEY
Dark Horse Comics: Mar, 1996 ($2.95, one-shot)
nn-Bret Blevins-a. 4.00

STAR WARS: TALES OF THE JEDI (See Dark Horse Comics #7)
Dark Horse Comics: Oct, 1993 - No. 5, Feb, 1994 ($2.50, limited series)
1-5: All have Dave Dorman painted-c. 3-r/Dark Horse Comics #7-9 w/new coloring & some panels redrawn 5.00
1-5-Gold foil embossed logo; limited # printed-7500 (set) 50.00
Star Wars Omnibus: Tales of the Jedi Volume One TPB (11/07, $24.95) r/#1-5, ... - The Golden Age of the Sith #0-5 and ... - The Fall of the Sith Empire #1-5 25.00

STAR WARS: TALES OF THE JEDI-DARK LORDS OF THE SITH
Dark Horse Comics: Oct, 1994 - No. 6, Mar, 1995 ($2.50, limited series)
1-6: 1-Polybagged w/trading card 4.00

STAR WARS: TALES OF THE JEDI-REDEMPTION
Dark Horse Comics: July, 1998 - No. 5, Nov, 1998 ($2.95, limited series)
1-5: 1-Kevin J. Anderson-s/Kordey-c 4.00

STAR WARS: TALES OF THE JEDI-THE FALL OF THE SITH EMPIRE
Dark Horse Comics: June, 1997 - No. 5, Oct, 1997 ($2.95, limited series)
1-5 4.00

STAR WARS: TALES OF THE JEDI-THE FREEDON NADD UPRISING
Dark Horse Comics: Aug, 1994 - No. 2, Nov, 1994 ($2.50, limited series)
1,2 4.00

STAR WARS: TALES OF THE JEDI-THE GOLDEN AGE OF THE SITH
Dark Horse Comics: July, 1996 - No. 5, Feb, 1997 (99¢/$2.95, limited series)
0-(99¢)-Anderson-s 3.00
1-5-Anderson-s 4.00

STAR WARS: TALES OF THE JEDI-THE SITH WAR
Dark Horse Comics: Aug, 1995 - No. 6, Jan, 1996 ($2.50, limited series)
1-6: Anderson scripts 4.00

STAR WARS: THE BOUNTY HUNTERS
Dark Horse Comics: July, 1999 - Oct, 1999 ($2.95, one-shots)
...Aurra Sing (7/99), ...Kenix Kil (10/99), ...Scoundrel's Wages (8/99) Lando Calrissian app. 4.00

STAR WARS: THE CLONE WARS (Based on the Cartoon Network series)
Dark Horse Comics: Sept, 2008 - No. 12, Jan, 2010 ($2.99)
1-12: 1-6-Gilroy-s/Hepburn-a/Filoni-c 3.00

STAR WARS: THE FORCE UNLEASHED (Based on the LucasArts video game)
Dark Horse Comics: Aug, 2008 ($15.95, one-shot graphic novel)
GN-Intro. Starkiller, Vader's apprentice; takes place 2 years before Battle of Yavin 16.00

STAR WARS: THE JABBA TAPE
Dark Horse Comics: Dec, 1998 ($2.95, one-shot)
nn-Wagner-s/Plunkett-a 4.00

STAR WARS: THE LAST COMMAND
Dark Horse Comics: Nov, 1997 - No. 6, July, 1998 ($2.95, limited series)
1-6: Based on the Timothy Zaun novel 4.00

STAR WARS: THE OLD REPUBLIC (Based on the video game)
Dark Horse Comics: July, 2010 - No. 6, Dec, 2010 ($2.99, limited series)
1-3 (Threat of Peace)-Chestny-s/Sanchez-a. 1-Two covers 3.00
4-6 (Blood of the Empire)-Freed-s/Dave Ross-a 3.00

STAR WARS: THE OLD REPUBLIC - THE LOST SUNS (Based on the video game)
Dark Horse Comics: Jun, 2011 - No. 5, Oct, 2011 ($3.50, limited series)
1-5-Freed-s/Carré-c/Freeman-a 3.50

STAR WARS: THE PROTOCOL OFFENSIVE
Dark Horse Comics: Sept, 1997 ($4.95, one-shot)
nn-Anthony Daniels & Ryder Windham-s 5.00

STAR WARS: UNDERWORLD - THE YAVIN VASSILIKA
Dark Horse Comics: Dec, 2000 - No. 5, June, 2001 ($2.99, limited series)
1-5-(Photo and Robinson covers) 3.00

STAR WARS: UNION
Dark Horse Comics: Nov, 1999 - No. 4, Feb, 2000 ($2.95, limited series)
1-4-Wedding of Luke and Mara Jade; Teranishi-a/Stackpole-s 4.00

STAR WARS: VADER'S QUEST
Dark Horse Comics: Feb, 1999 - No. 4, May, 1999 ($2.95, limited series)
1-4-Follows destruction of 1st Death Star; Gibbons-a 4.00

STAR WARS: VISIONARIES
Dark Horse Comics: Apr, 2005 ($17.95, TPB)
nn-Short stories from the concept artists for Revenge of the Sith movie 18.00

STAR WARS: X-WING ROGUE SQUADRON (Star Wars: X-Wing Rogue Squadron-The Phantom Affair #5-8 appears on cover only)
Dark Horse Comics: July, 1995 - No. 35, Nov, 1998 ($2.95)
1/2 8.00
1-24,26-35: 1-4-Baron scripts. 5-20-Stackpole scripts 4.00
25-($3.95) 5.00
The Phantom Affair TPB ($12.95) r/#5-8 13.00

STAR WARS: X-WING ROGUE SQUADRON: ROGUE LEADER
Dark Horse Comics: Sept, 2005 - No. 3, Nov, 2005 ($2.99)
1-3-Takes place one week after the Batttle of Endor 3.00

S.T.A.T.
Majestic Entertainment: Dec, 1993 ($2.25)
1 3.00

STATIC (See Charlton Action: Featuring "Static")

STATIC (See Heroes)
DC Comics (Milestone): June, 1993 - No. 45, Mar, 1997 ($1.50/$1.75/$2.50)
1-($2.95)-Collector's Edition; polybagged w/poster & trading card & backing board (direct sales only) 4.00
1-Platinum Edition with red background cover 6.00
1-13,15-24,26-45: 2-Origin. 8-Shadow War; Simonson silver ink-c. 27-Kent Williams-c 3.00
14-($2.50, 52 pgs.)-Worlds Collide Pt. 14 4.00

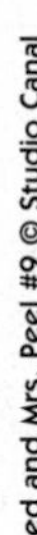
Steed and Mrs. Peel #9 © Studio Canal

Steel #51 © DC

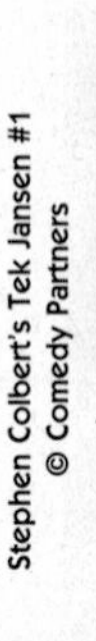
Stephen Colbert's Tek Jansen #1 © Comedy Partners

GD 2.0 | VG 4.0 | FN 6.0 | VF 8.0 | VF/NM 9.0 | NM- 9.2

25 ($3.95) 4.00
...: Trial by Fire (2000, $9.95) r/#1-4; Leon-c 10.00

STATIC SHOCK (DC New 52)
DC Comics: Nov, 2011 - No. 8, Jun, 2012 ($2.99)
1-8: 1-McDaniel & Rozum-s/McDaniel-a/c. 6-Hardware & Technique app. 8-Origin retold 3.00

STATIC SHOCK!: REBIRTH OF THE COOL (TV)
DC Comics: Jan, 2001 - No. 4, Sept, 2001 ($2.50, limited series)
1-4: McDuffie-s/Leon-c/a 3.00

STATIC SHOCK SPECIAL
DC Comics: Aug, 2011 ($2.99, one-shot)
1-Cowan-a/Williams III-c; pin-ups by various; tribute to Dwayne McDuffie 3.00

STATIC-X
Chaos! Comics: Aug, 2002 ($5.99)
1-Polybagged with music CD; metal band as super-heroes; Pulido-s 6.00

STEALTH (Pilot Season: ...)
Image Comics (Top Cow): May, 2010 ($2.99)
1-Kirkman-s/Mitchell-a/Silvestri-c 3.00

STEAMPUNK
DC/WildStorm (Cliffhanger): Apr, 2000 - No. 12, Aug, 2002 ($2.50/$3.50)
Catechism (1/00) Prologue -Kelly-s/Bachalo-a 3.00
1-4,6-11: 4-Four covers by Bachalo, Madureira, Ramos, Campbell 3.00
5,12-($3.50) 4.00
...: Drama Obscura ('03, $14.95) r/#6-12 15.00
...: Manimatron ('01, $14.95) r/#1-5, Catechism, Idiosincratica 15.00

STEED AND MRS. PEEL (TV)(Also see The Avengers)
Eclipse Books/ ACME Press: 1990 - No. 3, 1991 ($4.95, limited series)
Books One - Three: Grant Morrison scripts/Ian Gibson-a 5.00
1-6: 1-(BOOM! Studios, 1/12 - No. 6, 6/12, $3.99) r/Books One - Three 4.00

STEED AND MRS. PEEL (TV)(The Avengers)
BOOM! Studios: No. 0, Aug, 2012 - No. 11, Jul, 2013 ($3.99)
0-11: 0-Mark Waid-s/Steve Bryant-a; eight covers. 1-3-Sliney-a; five covers 4.00

STEEL (Also see JLA)
DC Comics: Feb, 1994 - No. 52, July, 1998 ($1.50/$1.95/$2.50)
1-8,0,9-52: 1-From Reign of the Supermen storyline. 6,7-Worlds Collide Pt. 5 &12. 8-(9/94). 0-(10/94). 9-(11/94). 46-Superboy-c/app. 50-Millennium Giants x-over 3.00
1-(3/11, $2.99, one-shot) Benes-a/Garner-c; Reign of Doomsday x-over 4.00
Annual 1 (1994, $2.95)-Elseworlds story 4.00
Annual 2 (1995, $3.95)-Year One story 4.00
...Forging of a Hero TPB (1997, $19.95) reprints early app. 20.00

STEEL: THE OFFICIAL COMIC ADAPTION OF THE WARNER BROS. MOTION PICTURE
DC Comics: 1997 ($4.95, Prestige format, one-shot)
nn-Movie adaption; Bogdanove & Giordano-a 5.00

STEELGRIP STARKEY
Marvel Comics (Epic): June, 1986 - No. 6, July, 1987 ($1.50, lim. series, Baxter paper)
1-6 3.00

STEEL STERLING (Formerly Shield-Steel Sterling; see Blue Ribbon, Jackpot, Mighty Comics, Mighty Crusaders, Roly Poly & Zip Comics)
Archie Enterprises, Inc.: No. 4, Jan, 1984 - No. 7, July, 1984
4-7: 4-6-Kanigher-s; Barreto-a. 5,6-Infantino-a. 6-McWilliams-a 5.00

STEEL, THE INDESTRUCTIBLE MAN (See All-Star Squadron #8 and J.L. of A. Annual #2)
DC Comics: Mar, 1978 - No. 5, Oct-Nov, 1978
1 2 4 6 8 11 14
2-5: 5-44 pgs. 1 2 3 4 6 8

STEELTOWN ROCKERS
Marvel Comics: Apr, 1987 - No. 6, Sept, 1990 ($1.00, limited series)
1-6: Small town teens form rock band 3.00

STEPHEN COLBERT'S TEK JANSEN (From the animated shorts on The Colbert Report)
Oni Press: July, 2007 - No. 5, Jan, 2009 ($3.99, limited series)
1-Chantier-a/Layman & Peyer-s; back-up story by Massey-s/Rodriguez-a; Chantier-c 4.00
1-Variant-c by John Cassaday 6.00
1-Second printing with flip book of Cassaday & Chantier covers 4.00
2-5: 2-(6/08) Flip book with covers by Rodriguez & Wagner. 3-Flip-c by Darwyn Cooke 4.00

STEPHEN KING'S N. THE COMIC SERIES
Marvel Comics: May, 2010 - No. 4, Aug, 2010 ($3.99, limited series)
1-4-Guggenheim-s/Maleev-a/c 4.00

STEVE AUSTIN (See Stone Cold Steve Austin)

STEVE CANYON (See Harvey Comics Hits #52)
Dell Publishing Co.: No. 519, 11/53 - No. No. 1033, 9/59 (All Milton Caniff-a except #519, 939, 1033)
Four Color 519 (1, '53) 7 14 21 49 92 135
Four Color 578 (8/54), 641 (7/55), 737 (10/56), 804 (5/57), 939 (10/58), 1033 (9/59) (photo-c) 5 10 15 31 53 75

STEVE CANYON
Grosset & Dunlap: 1959 (6-3/4x9", 96 pgs., B&W, no text, hardcover)
100100-Reprints 2 stories from strip (1953, 1957) 6 12 18 31 38 45
100100 (softcover edition) 5 10 15 24 30 35

STEVE CANYON COMICS
Harvey Publ.: Feb, 1948 - No. 6, Dec, 1948 (Strip reprints, No. 4,5: 52pgs.)
1-Origin; has biography of Milton Caniff; Powell-a, 2 pgs.; Caniff-a 20 40 60 117 189 260
2-Caniff, Powell-a in #2-6 14 28 42 80 115 150
3-6: 6-Intro Madame Lynx-c/story 14 28 42 76 108 140

STEVE CANYON IN 3-D
Kitchen Sink Press: June, 1986 ($2.25, one-shot)
1-Contains unpublished story from 1954 5.00

STEVE DITKO'S STRANGE AVENGING TALES
Fantagraphics Books: Feb, 1997 ($2.95, B&W)
1-Ditko-c/s/a 5.00

STEVE DONOVAN, WESTERN MARSHAL (TV)
Dell Publishing Co.: No. 675, Feb, 1956 - No. 880, Feb, 1958 (All photo-c)
Four Color 675-Kinstler-a 7 14 21 46 86 125
Four Color 768-Kinstler-a 6 12 18 37 66 95
Four Color 880 5 10 15 30 50 70

STEVE ROGERS: SUPER-SOLDIER (Captain America - The Heroic Age)
Marvel Comics: Sept, 2010 - No. 4, Dec, 2010 ($3.99, limited series)
1-4-Brubaker-s/Eaglesham-a/Pacheco-c. 1-Back-up rep. of origin from CA #1 ('41) 4.00
Annual 1 (6/11, $3.99) Continued from Uncanny X-Men Annual #3; Roberson-a 4.00

STEVE ROPER
Famous Funnies: Apr, 1948 - No. 5, Dec, 1948
1-Contains 1944 daily newspaper-r 12 24 36 69 97 125
2 9 18 27 47 61 75
3-5 8 16 24 40 50 60

STEVE SAUNDERS SPECIAL AGENT (See Special Agent)

STEVE SAVAGE (See Captain...)

STEVE ZODIAC & THE FIRE BALL XL-5 (TV)
Gold Key: Jan, 1964
10108-401 (#1) 7 14 21 44 82 120

STEVIE (Mazie's boy friend)(Also see Flat-Top, Mazie & Mortie)
Mazie (Magazine Publ.): Nov, 1952 - No. 6, Apr, 1954
1-Teenage humor; Stevie, Mortie & Mazie begin 9 18 27 50 65 80
2-6 6 12 18 31 38 45

STEVIE MAZIE'S BOY FRIEND (See Harvey Hits #5)

STEWART THE RAT (See Eclipse Graphic Album Series)

ST. GEORGE (See listing under Saint...)

STIG'S INFERNO
Vortex/Eclipse: 1985 - No. 7, Mar, 1987 ($1.95, B&W)
1-7 ($1.95) 3.00
Graphic Album (1988, $6.95, B&W, 100 pgs.) 7.00

STING OF THE GREEN HORNET (See The Green Hornet)
Now Comics: June, 1992 - No. 4, 1992 ($2.50, limited series)
1-4: Butler-c/a 3.00
1-4 ($2.75)-Collectors Ed.; polybagged w/poster 4.00

STOKER'S DRACULA (Reprints unfinished Dracula story from 1974-75 with new ending)
Marvel Comics: 2004 - No. 4, May, 2005 ($3.99, B&W)
1-4: 1-Reprints from Dracula Lives! #5-8; Roy Thomas-s/Dick Giordano-a. 2-R/#10,11 & Legion of Monsters #1. 3,4-New story/artwork to finish story. 4-Giordano afterword 4.00

Stone #1 © Haberlin & Portacio

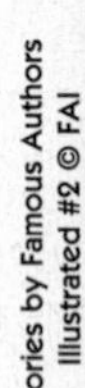
Stories by Famous Authors Illustrated #2 © FAI

Stormwatch (2011 series) #12 © DC

GD 2.0 | VG 4.0 | FN 6.0 | VF 8.0 | VF/NM 9.0 | NM- 9.2

HC (2005, $24.99) r/#1-4; foreward by Thomas; Giordano afterword; bonus art & covers 25.00

STONE
Avalon Studios: Aug, 1998 - No. 4, Apr, 1999 ($2.50, limited series)

1-4-Portacio-a/Haberlin-s 3.00
1-Alternate-c 5.00
2-($14.95) DF Stonechrome Edition 15.00

STONE (Volume 2)
Avalon Studios: Aug, 1999 - No. 4, May, 2000 ($2.50)

1-4-Portacio-a/Haberlin-s 3.00
1-Chrome-c 5.00

STONE COLD STEVE AUSTIN (WWF Wrestling)
Chaos! Comics: Oct, 1999 - No. 4, Feb, 2000 ($2.95)

1-4-Reg. & photo-c; Steven Grant-s 3.00
1-Premium Ed. ($10.00) 10.00
Preview ($5.00) 5.00

STONE PROTECTORS
Harvey Pubications: May, 1994 - No. 3, Sept, 1994

nn (1993, giveaway)(limited distribution, scarce) 6.00
1-3-Ace Novelty action figures 4.00

STONEY BURKE (TV Western)
Dell Publishing Co.: June-Aug, 1963 - No. 2, Sept-Nov, 1963

1,2-Jack Lord photo-c on both 3 6 9 16 24 32

STONY CRAIG
Pentagon Publishing Co.: 1946 (No #)

nn-Reprints Bell Syndicate's "Sgt. Stony Craig" newspaper strips 8 16 24 40 50 60

STORIES BY FAMOUS AUTHORS ILLUSTRATED (Fast Fiction #1-5)
Seaboard Publ./Famous Authors Ill.: No. 6, Aug, 1950 - No. 13, Mar, 1951

1-Scarlet Pimpernel-Baroness Orczy 27 54 81 160 263 365
2-Capt. Blood-Raphael Sabatini 26 52 78 154 252 350
3-She, by Haggard 30 60 90 177 289 400
4-The 39 Steps-John Buchan 18 36 54 107 169 230
5-Beau Geste-P. C. Wren 18 36 54 107 169 230
NOTE: *The above five issues are exact reprints of Fast Fiction #1-5 except for the title change and new Kiefer covers on #1 and 2. Kiefer c(r)-3-5. The above 5 issues were released before Famous Authors #6.*
6-Macbeth, by Shakespeare; Kiefer art (8/50); used in **SOTI**, pg. 22,143; Kiefer-c; 36 pgs. 24 48 72 142 234 325
7-The Window; Kiefer-c/a; 52 pgs. 18 36 54 107 169 230
8-Hamlet, by Shakespeare; Kiefer-c/a; 36 pgs. 21 42 63 126 206 285
9,10: 9-Nicholas Nickleby, by Dickens; G. Schrotter-a; 52 pgs. 10-Romeo & Juliet, by Shakespeare; Kiefer-c/a; 36 pgs. 18 36 54 107 169 230
11-13: 11-Ben-Hur; Schrotter-a; 52 pgs. 12-La Svengali; Schrotter-a; 36 pgs. 13-Scaramouche; Kiefer-c/a; 36 pgs. 18 36 54 103 162 220
NOTE: *Artwork was prepared/advertised for #14, The Red Badge Of Courage. Gilberton bought out Famous Authors, Ltd. and used that story as C.I. #98. Famous Authors, Ltd. then published the Classics Junior series. The Famous Authors titles were published as part of the regular Classics Ill. Series in Brazil starting in 1952.*

STORIES FROM THE TWILIGHT ZONE
Skylark Pub: Mar, 1979, 68 pgs. (B&W comic digest, 5-1/4x7-5/8")

15405-2: Pfevfer-a, 56 pgs, new comics 3 6 9 17 26 35

STORIES OF ROMANCE (Formerly Meet Miss Bliss)
Atlas Comics (LMC): No. 5, Mar, 1956 - No. 13, Aug, 1957

5-Baker-a? 13 26 39 74 105 135
6-10,12,13 9 18 27 52 69 85
11-Baker, Romita-a; Colletta-c/a 12 24 36 69 97 125
NOTE: ***Ann Brewster** a-13. **Colletta** a-9(2), 11; c-5, 11.*

STORM
Marvel Comics: Feb, 1996 - No. 4, May, 1996 ($2.95, limited series)

1-4-Foil-c; Dodson-a(p); Ellis-s: 2-4-Callisto app. 4.00

STORM
Marvel Comics: Apr, 2006 - No. 6, Sept, 2006 ($2.99, limited series)

1-6: Ororo and T'Challa meet as teens; Eric Jerome Dickey-s 3.00
HC (2007, $19.99, dustjacket) r/#1-6 20.00
SC (2008, $14.99) r/#1-6 15.00

STORMBREAKER: THE SAGA OF BETA RAY BILL (Also see Thor)
Marvel Comics: Mar, 2005 - No. 6, Aug, 2005 ($2.99, limited series)

1-6-Oeming & Berman-s/DiVito-a; Galactus app. 6-Spider-Man app. 3.00
TPB (2006, $16.99) r/#1-6 17.00

STORMING PARADISE
DC Comics (WildStorm): Sept, 2008 - No. 6, Aug, 2009 ($2.99, limited series)

1-6-WWII invasion of Japan; Dixon-s/Guice-a/c 3.00
TPB (2009, $19.99) r/#1-6 20.00

STORM SHADOW (G.I. Joe character)
Devil's Due Publishing: May, 2007 - No. 7, Nov, 2007 ($3.50)

1-7-Larry Hama-s 3.50

STORMWATCH (Also see The Authority)
Image Comics (WildStorm Prod.): May, 1993 - No. 50, Jul, 1997 ($1.95/$2.50)

1-8,0,9-36: 1-Intro StormWatch (Battalion, Diva, Winter, Fuji, & Hellstrike); 1st app. Weatherman; Jim Lee-c & part scripts; Lee plots in all. 1-Gold edition.1-3-Includes coupon for limited edition StormWatch trading card #00 by Lee. 3-1st brief app. Backlash. 0-($2.50)-Polybagged w/card; 1st full app. Backlash. 9-(4/94, $2.50)-Intro Defile. 10-(6/94),11,12-Both (8/94). 13,14-(9/94). 15-(10/94). 21-Reads #1 on-c. 22-Direct Market; Wildstorm Rising Pt. 9, bound-in card. 23-Spartan joins team. 25-(6/94, June 1995 on-c, $2.50). 35-Fire From Heaven Pt. 5. 36-Fire From Heaven Pt. 12 3.00
10-Alternate Portacio-c, see Deathblow #5 3.00
22-($1.95)-Newsstand, Wildstorm Rising Pt. 9 3.00
37-(7/96, $3.50, 38 pgs.)-Weatherman forms new team; 1st app. Jenny Sparks, Jack Hawksmoor & Rose Tattoo; Warren Ellis scripts begin; Justice League #1-c/swipe 4.00
38-49: 44-Three covers. 3.00
50-($4.50) 4.50
Special 1 ,2(1/94, 5/95, $3.50, 52 pgs.) 4.00
Sourcebook 1 (1/94, $2.50) 3.00
Forces of Nature ('99, $14.95, TPB) r/V1 #37-42 15.00
Lightning Strikes ('00, $14.95, TPB) r/V1 #43-47 15.00

STORMWATCH (Also see The Authority)
Image Comics (WildStorm): Oct, 1997 - No. 11, Sept, 1998 ($2.50)

1-Ellis-s/Jimenez-a(p); two covers by Bennett 3.00
1-($3.50)-Voyager Pack bagged w/Gen 13 preview 4.00
2-4: 4-1st app. Midnighter and Apollo 3.00
5-11: 7,8-Freefall app. 9-Gen13 & DV8 app. 3.00
A Finer World ('99, $14.95, TPB) r/V2 #4-9 15.00
Change or Die ('99, $14.95, TPB) r/V1 #48-50 & V2 #1-3 15.00
Final Orbit ('01, $9.95, TPB) r/V2 #10,11 & WildC.A.T.S./Aliens; Hitch-c 10.00

STORMWATCH (DC New 52)
DC Comics: Nov, 2011 - No. 30, Jun, 2014 ($2.99)

1-Cornell-s/Sepulveda-a; Martian Manhunter app.; blue bkgrd cover 4.00
1-(2nd printing, cover has red bkgrd), 2-8: 7,8-Jenkins-s. 12-Martian Manhunter leaves 3.00
13-30: 13,14-Etrigan returns. 18-Team re-booted; Starlin-s/c. 20-Lobo origin 3.00
#0-(11/12, $2.99) Flashback to Demon Knights; Milligan-s/Conrad-a 3.00

STORMWATCHER
Eclipse Comics (Acme Press): Apr, 1989 - No. 4, Dec, 1989 ($2.00, B&W)

1-4 3.00

STORMWATCH: P.H.D. (Post Human Division)
DC Comics (WildStorm): Jan, 2007 - No. 24, Jan, 2010 ($2.99)

1-24: 1-Two covers by Mahnke & Hairsine; Gage-s/Mahnke-a. 2-Var-c by Dell'Otto 3.00
...: Armageddon 1 (2/08, $2.99) Gage-s/Fernández-a/McKone-c 3.00
TPB (2007, $17.99) r/#1-4,6,7 & story from Worldstorm #1 18.00
... Book Two TPB (2008, $17.99) r/#5,8-12; sketch pages and concept art 18.00
... Book Three TPB (2009, $17.99) r/#13-19 18.00

STORMWATCH: TEAM ACHILLES
DC Comics (WildStorm): Sept, 2002 - No. 23, Aug, 2004 ($2.95)

1-8: 1-Two covers by Portacio; Portacio-a/Wright-s. 5,6-The Authority app. 3.00
9-23: 9-Back-up preview of The Authority: High Stakes pt. 1 3.00
TPB (2003, $14.95) r/Wizard Preview and #1-6; Portacio art pages 15.00
Book 2 (2004, $14.95) r/#7-11 & short story from Eye of the Storm Annual 15.00

STORMY (Disney) (Movie)
Dell Publishing Co.: No. 537, Feb, 1954

Four Color 537 (...the Thoroughbred)-on top 2/3 of each page; Pluto story on bottom 1/3 5 10 15 30 50 70

STORY OF JESUS (See Classics Illustrated Special Issue)

STORY OF MANKIND, THE (Movie)
Dell Publishing Co.: No. 851, Jan, 1958

Four Color 851-Vincent Price/Hedy Lamarr photo-c 6 12 18 41 76 110

STORY OF MARTHA WAYNE, THE
Argo Publ.: April, 1956

Straight Arrow #10 © ME

The Strain: The Fall #1 © G. del Toro

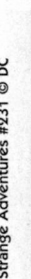

Strange Adventures #231 © DC

	GD 2.0	VG 4.0	FN 6.0	VF 8.0	VF/NM 9.0	NM- 9.2
1-Newspaper strip-r	6	12	18	29	36	42

STORY OF RUTH, THE
Dell Publishing Co.: No. 1144, Nov-Jan, 1961 (Movie)

	GD 2.0	VG 4.0	FN 6.0	VF 8.0	VF/NM 9.0	NM- 9.2
Four Color 1144-Photo-c	7	14	21	49	92	135

STORY OF THE COMMANDOS, THE (Combined Operations)
Long Island Independent: 1943 (15¢, B&W, 68 pgs.) (Distr. by Gilberton)

	GD 2.0	VG 4.0	FN 6.0	VF 8.0	VF/NM 9.0	NM- 9.2
nn-All text (no comics); photos & illustrations; ad for Classic Comics on back cover (Rare)	39	78	117	231	378	525

STORY OF THE GLOOMY BUNNY, THE (See March of Comics #9)

STRAIGHT ARROW (Radio)(See Best of the West & Great Western)
Magazine Enterprises: Feb-Mar, 1950 - No. 55, Mar, 1956 (All 36 pgs.)

	GD 2.0	VG 4.0	FN 6.0	VF 8.0	VF/NM 9.0	NM- 9.2
1-Straight Arrow (alias Steve Adams) & his palomino Fury begin; 1st mention of Sundown Valley & the Secret Cave	47	94	141	296	498	700
2-Red Hawk begins (1st app?) by Powell (origin), ends #55	23	46	69	136	223	310
3-Frazetta-c	31	62	93	182	296	410
4,5: 4-Secret Cave-c	21	42	63	122	199	275
6-10	17	34	51	100	158	215
11-Classic story "The Valley of Time", with an ancient civilization made of gold	22	44	66	128	209	290
12-19	14	28	42	82	121	160
20-Origin Straight Arrow's Shield	16	32	48	92	144	195
21-Origin Fury	19	38	57	109	172	235
22-Frazetta-c	25	50	75	147	241	335
23,25-30: 25-Secret Cave-c. 28-Red Hawk meets The Vikings	11	22	33	62	86	110
24-Classic story "The Dragons of Doom!" with prehistoric pteradactyls	14	28	42	82	121	160
31-38: 36-Red Hawk drug story by Powell	10	20	30	54	72	90
39-Classic story "The Canyon Beast", with a dinosaur egg hatching a Tyranosaurus Rex	14	28	42	76	108	140
40-Classic story "Secret of The Spanish Specters", with Conquistadors' lost treasure	11	22	33	64	90	115
41,42,44-54: 45-Secret Cave-c	9	18	27	50	65	80
43-Intro & 1st app. Blaze, S. Arrow's Warrior dog	10	20	30	58	79	100
55-Last issue	11	22	33	62	86	110

NOTE: ***Fred Meagher** a 1-55; c-1, 2, 4-21, 23-55. **Powell** a 2-55. **Whitney** a-1. Many issues advertise the radio premiums associated with Straight Arrow.*

STRAIGHT ARROW'S FURY (Also see A-1 Comics)
Magazine Enterprises: No. 119, 1954 (one-shot)

	GD 2.0	VG 4.0	FN 6.0	VF 8.0	VF/NM 9.0	NM- 9.2
A-1 119-Origin; Fred Meagher-c/a	15	30	45	85	130	175

STRAIN, THE (Adaptation of novels by Guillermo del Toro and Chuck Hogan)
Dark Horse Comics: Dec, 2011 - No. 11, Feb, 2013 ($1.00/$3.50)

	GD 2.0	VG 4.0	FN 6.0	VF 8.0	VF/NM 9.0	NM- 9.2
1-($1.00) Lapham, Hogan & del Toro-s/Huddleston-a/c; variant-c by Morris						3.50
2-11-($3.50) Lapham-s/Huddleston-a/c						3.50

STRAIN, THE: THE FALL (Guillermo del Toro and Chuck Hogan)
Dark Horse Comics: Jul, 2013 - Present ($3.99)

	GD 2.0	VG 4.0	FN 6.0	VF 8.0	VF/NM 9.0	NM- 9.2
1-9-Lapham, Hogan & del Toro-s/Huddleston-a/Gist-c						4.00

STRANGE (Tales You'll Never Forget)
Ajax-Farrell Publ. (Four Star Comic Corp.): March, 1957 - No. 6, May, 1958

	GD 2.0	VG 4.0	FN 6.0	VF 8.0	VF/NM 9.0	NM- 9.2
1	24	48	72	142	234	325
2-Censored r/Haunted Thrills	15	30	45	83	124	165
3-6	12	24	36	69	97	125

STRANGE (Dr. Strange)
Marvel Comics (Marvel Knghts): Nov, 2004 - No. 6, July, 2005 ($3.50)

	GD 2.0	VG 4.0	FN 6.0	VF 8.0	VF/NM 9.0	NM- 9.2
1-6-Straczynski & Barnes-s/Peterson-a; Dr. Strange's origin retold						3.50
...: Beginnings and Endings TPB (2006, $17.99) r/#1-6						18.00

STRANGE (Dr. Strange)
Marvel Comics: Jan, 2010 - No. 4, Apr, 2010 ($3.99, limited series)

	GD 2.0	VG 4.0	FN 6.0	VF 8.0	VF/NM 9.0	NM- 9.2
1-4-Waid-s/Rios-a/Coker-c						4.00

STRANGE ADVENTURES
DC Comics: July/Aug 1950

nn - Ashcan comic, not distributed to newsstands, only for in-house use. Cover art is All Star Comics #47 with interior being Detective Comics #140. A second example has the interior of Detective Comics #146. A third example has an unidentified issue of Detective Comics as the interior. This is the only ashcan with multiple interiors. A FN+ copy sold for $1,000 in 2007.

STRANGE ADVENTURES
National Periodical Publ.: Aug-Sept, 1950 - No. 244, Oct-Nov, 1973 (No. 1-12: 52 pgs.)

	GD 2.0	VG 4.0	FN 6.0	VF 8.0	VF/NM 9.0	NM- 9.2
1-Adaptation of "Destination Moon"; preview of movie w/photo-c from movie (also see Fawcett Movie Comic #2); adapt. of Edmond Hamilton's "Chris KL-99" in #1-3; Darwin Jones begins	159	318	477	1312	2956	4600
2	73	146	219	584	1317	2050
3,4	53	106	159	424	937	1450
5-8,10: 7-Origin Kris KL-99	46	92	138	359	805	1250
9-(6/51)-Origin/1st app. Captain Comet (c/story)	102	204	306	816	2241	2850
11-20: 12,13,17,18-Toth-a. 14-Robot-c	31	62	93	223	504	785
21-30: 28-Atomic explosion panel. 30-Robot-c	28	56	84	202	451	700
31,34-38	27	54	81	189	420	650
32,33-Krigstein-a	28	56	84	190	425	660
39-Ill. in **SOTI** "Treating police contemptuously" (top right)	30	60	90	216	483	750
40-49-Last Capt. Comet; not in 45,47,48	27	54	81	184	410	635
50-53-Last precode issue (2/55)	22	44	66	154	340	525
54-70	17	34	51	117	259	400
71-99: 80-Grey-tone-c	14	28	42	94	207	320
100	15	30	45	100	220	340
101-110: 104-Space Museum begins by Sekowsky	11	22	33	76	163	250
111-116,118,119: 114-Star Hawkins begins, ends #185; Heath-a in Wood E.C. style	11	22	33	73	157	240
117-(6/60)-Origin/1st app. Atomic Knights.	46	92	138	340	770	1200
120-2nd app. Atomic Knights	21	42	63	147	324	500
121,122,125,127,128,130,131,133,134: 134-Last 10¢ issue	10	20	30	66	138	210
123,126-3rd & 4th app. Atomic Knights	12	24	36	84	185	285
124-Intro/origin Faceless Creature	12	24	36	80	173	265
129,132,135,138,141,147-Atomic Knights app.	11	22	33	72	154	235
136,137,139,140,143,145,146,148,149,151,152,154,155,157-159: 136-Robot cover. 159-Star Rovers app.; Gil Kane/Anderson-a.	8	16	24	56	108	160
142-2nd app. Faceless Creature	9	18	27	61	123	185
144-Only Atomic Knights-c (by M. Anderson)	11	22	33	76	163	250
150,153,156,160: Atomic Knights in each. 150-Greytone-c. 153-(6/63)-3rd app. Faceless Creature; atomic explosion-c. 160-Last Atomic Knights	9	18	27	59	117	175
161-179: 161-Last Space Museum. 163-Star Rovers app. 170-Infinity-c. 177-Intro/origin Immortal Man	7	14	21	44	82	120
180-Origin/1st app. Animal Man	19	38	57	131	291	450
181-183,185-189: 187-Intro/origin The Enchantress	6	12	18	37	66	95
184-2nd app. Animal Man by Gil Kane	10	20	30	64	132	200
190-1st app. Animal Man in costume	11	22	33	76	163	250
191-194,196-200,202-204	5	10	15	34	60	85
195-1st full app. Animal Man	7	14	21	44	82	120
201-Last Animal Man; 2nd full app.	6	12	18	37	66	95
205-(10/67)-Intro/origin Deadman by Infantino & begin series, ends #216	20	40	60	138	307	475
206-Neal Adams-a begins	11	22	33	73	157	240
207-210	9	18	27	61	123	185
211-216: 211-Space Museum-r. 216-(1-2/69)-Deadman story finally concludes in Brave & the Bold #86 (10-11/69); secret message panel by Neal Adams (pg. 13); tribute to Steranko	8	16	24	56	108	160
217-r/origin & 1st app. Adam Strange from Showcase #17, begin-r; Atomic Knights-r begin	3	6	9	16	23	30
218-221,223-225: 218-Last 12¢ issue. 225-Last 15¢ issue	3	6	9	14	20	26
222-New Adam Strange story; Kane/Anderson-a	3	6	9	20	31	42
226,227,230-236-(68-52 pgs.): 226, 227-New Adam Strange text story w/illos by Anderson (8,6 pgs.) 231-Last Atomic Knights-r. 235-JLA-c/s	3	6	9	14	20	26
228,229 (68 pgs.)	3	6	9	16	24	32
237-243	2	4	6	10	14	18
244-Last issue	2	4	6	11	16	20

NOTE: ***Neal Adams** a-206-216; c-207-218, 228, 235. **Anderson** a-8-52, 94, 96, 99, 115, 117, 119-163, 217r, 218r, 222, 223-225r, 226, 229r, 242i(r); c-18, 19, 21, 23, 24, 27, 30, 32-44(most); c/r-157i, 190i, 217-224, 228-231, 233, 235-239, 241-243. **Ditko** a-188, 189. **Drucker** a-42, 43, 45. **Elias** a-212. **Finlay** a-2, 3, 6, 7, 210r, 229r. **Giunta** a-237r. **Heath** a-116. **Infantino** a-10-101, 106-151, 154, 157-163, 180, 190, 218-221r, 223-244p(r); c-50; c(r)-190p, 197, 199-211, 218-221, 223-244. **Kaluta** c-238, 240. **Gil Kane** a-8-116, 124, 125, 130, 138, 146-157, 173-186, 204r, 222r, 227-231r; c(p)-11-17, 25, 154, 157. **Kubert** a-55(2 pgs.), 226; c-219, 220, 225-227, 232, 234. **Moreira** c-26, 28, 29, 71. **Morrow** c-230. **Mortimer** c-8. **Powell** a-4. **Sekowsky** a-71p, 97-162p, 217p(r), 218p(r); c-206, 217-219r. **Simon & Kirby** a-2r (2 pgs) **Sparling** a-201. **Toth** a-8, 12, 13, 17-19. **Wood** a-154i. Atomic Knights in #117, 120, 123, 126, 129, 132, 135, 138, 141, 144, 147, 150, 153, 156, 160. Atomic Knights reprints by **Anderson** in 217-221, 223-231. Chris KL99 in 1-3, 5, 7, 9, 11, 15. Capt. Comet covers-9-14, 17-19, 24, 26, 27, 32-44.*

STRANGE ADVENTURES
DC Comics (Vertigo): Nov, 1999 - No. 4, Feb, 2000 ($2.50, limited series)

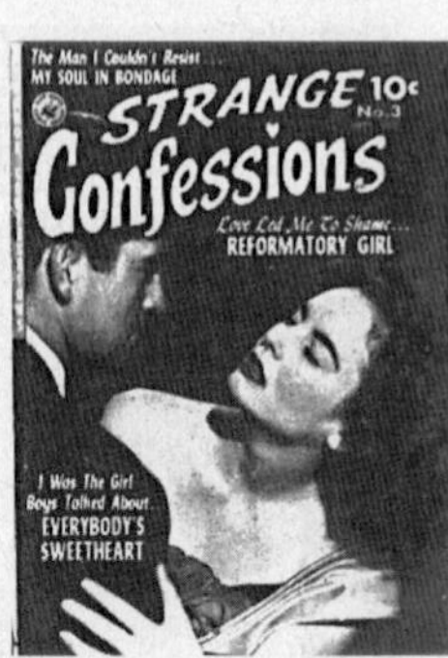

Strange Confessions #3 © Z-D

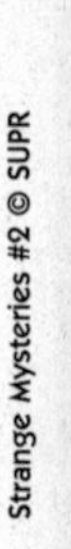
Strange Mysteries #2 © SUPR

The Strangers #14 © MAL

GD 2.0 | VG 4.0 | FN 6.0 | VF 8.0 | VF/NM 9.0 | NM- 9.2

1-4: 1-Bolland-c; art by Bolland, Gibbons, Quitely 3.00

STRANGE ADVENTURES
DC Comics: May, 2009 - No. 8, Dec, 2009 ($3.99, limited series)
1-8: 1-Starlin-s in all; Adam Strange, Capt. Comet, Bizarro & Prince Gavyn app. 4.00
TPB (2010, $19.99) r/#1-8; cover gallery 20.00

STRANGE ADVENTURES
DC Comics (Vertigo): Jul, 2011 ($7.99, one-shot)
1-Short story anthology; s/a by Azzarello, Risso, Milligan and others; Paul Pope-c 8.00

STRANGE ADVENTURES MAGAZINE
CJH Publications: Dec, 1936 (10¢)
1-Flash Gordon, The Master of Mars, text stories w/some full pg. panels of art by Fred Meagher (a FN+ copy sold for $1075 in 2012)

STRANGE AS IT SEEMS (See Famous Funnies-A Carnival of Comics, Feature Funnies #1, The John Hix Scrap Book & Peanuts)

STRANGE AS IT SEEMS
United Features Syndicate: 1939
Single Series 9, 1, 2 34 68 102 204 332 460

STRANGE ATTRACTORS
RetroGraphix: 1993 - No. 15, Feb, 1997 ($2.50, B&W)
1-15: 1-(5/93), 2-(8/93), 3-(11/93), 4-(2/94) 3.00
Volume One-($14.95, trade paperback)-r/#1-7 15.00

STRANGE ATTRACTORS: MOON FEVER
Caliber Comics: Feb, 1997 - No. 3, June, 1997 ($2.95, B&W, mini-series)
1-3 3.00

STRANGE COMBAT TALES
Marvel Comics (Epic Comics): Oct, 1993 - No. 4, Jan, 1994 ($2.50, limited series)
1-4 3.00

STRANGE CONFESSIONS
Ziff-Davis Publ. Co.: Jan-Mar (Spring on-c), 1952 - No. 4, Fall, 1952 (All have photo-c)
1(Scarce)-Kinstler-a 61 122 183 390 670 950
2(Scarce, 7-8/52) 42 84 126 265 445 625
3(Scarce, 9-10/52)-#3 on-c, #2 on inside; Reformatory girl story; photo-c 41 82 123 256 428 600
4(Scarce) 40 80 120 246 411 575

STRANGE DAYS
Eclipse Comics: Oct, 1984 - No. 3, Apr, 1985 ($1.75, Baxter paper)
1-3: Freakwave, Johnny Nemo, & Paradax from Vanguard Illustrated; nudity, violence & strong language 4.00

STRANGE DAYS (Movie)
Marvel Comics: Dec, 1995 ($5.95, squarebound, one-shot)
1-Adaptation of film 6.00

STRANGE FANTASY (Eerie Tales of Suspense!)(Formerly Rocketman #1)
Ajax-Farrell: Aug, 1952 - No. 14, Oct-Nov, 1954
2(#1, 8/52)-Jungle Princess story; Kamenish-a; reprinted from Ellery Queen #1 55 110 165 352 601 850
2(10/52)-No Black Cat or Rulah; Bakerish, Kamenish-a; hypo/meathook-c 48 96 144 302 514 725
3-Rulah story, called Pulah 41 82 123 260 435 610
4-Rocket Man app. (2/53) 40 80 120 246 411 575
5,6,8,10,12,14 34 68 102 199 325 450
7-Madam Satan/Slave story 41 82 123 250 418 585
9(w/Black Cat), 9(w/Boy's Ranch; S&K-a), 9(w/War)(A rebinding of Harvey interiors; not publ. by Ajax) 37 74 111 222 361 500
9-Regular issue; Steve Ditko's 3rd published work (tied with Captain 3D) 53 106 159 334 567 800
11-Jungle story 40 80 120 246 411 575
13-Bondage-c; Rulah (Kolah) story 40 80 120 246 411 575

STRANGE GALAXY
Eerie Publications: V1#8, Feb, 1971 - No. 11, Aug, 1971 (B&W, magazine)
V1#8-Reprints-c/Fantastic V19#3 (2/70) (a pulp) 3 6 9 21 33 45
9-11 3 6 9 17 26 35

STRANGE GIRL
Image Comics: June, 2005 - No. 18, Sept, 2007 ($2.95/$2.99/$3.50)
1-12: 1-Rick Remender-s/Eric Nguyen-a 3.50
13-18-($3.50) 3.50
... Vol. 1: Girl Afraid TPB (2005, $12.99) r/#1-4; sketch pages and pin-ups 13.00

STRANGE JOURNEY
America's Best (Steinway Publ.) (Ajax/Farrell): Sept, 1957 - No. 4, Jun, 1958 (Farrell reprints)
1-The Phantom Express 20 40 60 117 189 260
2-4: 2-Flying saucer-c. 3-Titanic-c 15 30 45 85 130 175

STRANGE LOVE (See Fox Giants)

STRANGE MYSTERIES
Superior/Dynamic Publications: Sept, 1951 - No. 21, Jan, 1955
1-Kamenish-a & horror stories begin 74 148 222 470 810 1150
2 41 82 123 256 428 600
3-5 39 78 117 240 395 550
6-8 36 72 108 216 351 485
9-Bondage 3-D effect-c 41 82 123 250 418 585
10-Used in **SOTI**, pg. 181 37 74 111 222 369 500
11-18 28 56 84 165 270 375
19-r/Journey Into Fear #1; cover is a splash from one story; Baker-r(2) 29 58 87 170 278 385
20,21-Reprints; 20-r/#1 with new-c (The Devil) 21 42 63 126 206 285

STRANGE MYSTERIES
I. W. Enterprises/Super Comics: 1963 - 1964
I.W. Reprint #9; Rulah-r/Spook #28; Disbrow-a 3 6 9 19 30 40
Super Reprint #10-12,15-17(1963-64): 10,11-r/Strange #2,1. 12-r/Tales of Horror #5 (3/53) less-c. 15-r/Dark Mysteries #23. 16-r/The Dead Who Walk. 17-r/Dark Mysteries #22 3 6 9 19 30 40
Super Reprint #18-r/Witchcraft #1; Kubert-a 3 6 9 19 30 40

STRANGE PLANETS
I. W. Enterprises/Super Comics: 1958; 1963-64
I.W. Reprint #1(nd)-Reprints E. C. Incredible S/F #30 plus-c/Strange Worlds #3 5 10 15 34 60 85
I.W. Reprint #9-Orlando/Wood-r/Strange Worlds #4; cover-r from Flying Saucers #1 6 12 18 41 76 110
Super Reprint #10-Wood-r (22 pg.) from Space Detective #1; cover-r/Attack on Planet Mars 6 12 18 41 76 110
Super Reprint #11-Wood-r (25 pg.) from An Earthman on Venus 7 14 21 46 86 125
Super Reprint #12-Orlando-r/Rocket to the Moon 6 12 18 41 76 110
Super Reprint #15-Reprints Journey Into Unknown Worlds #8; Heath, Colan-r 4 8 12 27 44 60
Super Reprint #16-Reprints Avon's Strange Worlds #6; Kinstler, Check-a 4 8 12 28 47 65
Super Reprint #18-r/Great Exploits #1 (Daring Adventures #6); Space Busters, Explorer Joe, The Son of Robin Hood; Krigstein-a 4 8 12 23 37 50

STRANGERS
Image Comics: Mar, 2003 - No. 6, Sept, 2003 ($2.95)
1-6-Randy & Jean-Marc Lofficier-s; two covers. 2-Nexus back-up story 3.00

STRANGERS, THE
Malibu Comics (Ultraverse): June, 1993 - No. 24, May, 1995 ($1.95/$2.50)
1-4,6-12,14-20: 1-1st app. The Strangers; has coupon for Ultraverse Premiere #0; 1st app. the Night Man (not in costume). 2-Polybagged w/trading card. 7-Break-Thru x-over. 8-2 pg. origin Solution. 12-Silver foil logo; wraparound-c. 17-Rafferty app. 3.00
1-With coupon missing 2.00
1-Full cover holographic edition, 1st of kind w/Hardcase #1 & Prime #1 1 2 3 5 6 8
1-Ultra 5000 limited silver foil 6.00
4-($2.50)-Variant Newsstand edition bagged w/card 4.00
5-($2.50, 52 pgs.)-Rune flip-c/story by B. Smith (3 pgs.); The Mighty Magnor 1 pg. strip by Aragones; 3-pg. Night Man preview 4.00
13-($3.50, 68 pgs.)-Mantra app.; flip book w/Ultraverse Premiere #4 4.00
21-24 ($2.50) 3.00
...:The Pilgrim Conundrum Saga (1/95, $3.95, 68pgs.) 4.00

STRANGERS IN PARADISE
Antarctic Press: Nov, 1993 - No. 3, Feb, 1994 ($2.75, B&W, limited series)
1 8 16 24 54 102 150
1-2nd/3rd prints 1 3 4 6 8 10
2 (2300 printed) 4 8 12 27 44 60
3 3 6 9 16 23 30
Trade paperback (Antarctic Press, $6.95)-Red -c (5000 print run) 10.00
Trade paperback (Abstract Studios, $6.95)-Red-c (2000 print run) 15.00
Trade paperback (Abstract Studios, $6.95, 1st-4th printing)-Blue- 7.00
Hardcover ('98, $29.95) includes first draft pages 30.00

Strangers in Paradise #86 © Terry Moore

Strange Suspense Stories #62 © DC

Strange Tales #19 © MAR

	GD 2.0	VG 4.0	FN 6.0	VF 8.0	VF/NM 9.0	NM- 9.2
Gold Reprint Series ($2.75) 1-3-r/#1-3						3.00

STRANGERS IN PARADISE
Abstract Studios: Sept, 1994 - No. 14, July, 1996 ($2.75, B&W)

	GD 2.0	VG 4.0	FN 6.0	VF 8.0	VF/NM 9.0	NM- 9.2
1	2	4	6	9	13	16
1,3- 2nd printings						4.00
2,3: 2-Color dream sequence	1	2	3	5	6	8
4-10						4.00
4-6-2nd printings						3.00
11-14: 14-The Letters of Molly & Poo						4.00
Gold Reprint Series ($2.75) 1-13-r/#1-13						3.00
I Dream Of You ($16.95, TPB) r/#1-9						17.00
It's a Good Life ($8.95, TPB) r/#10-13						9.00

STRANGERS IN PARADISE (Volume Three)
Homage Comics #1-8/Abstract Studios #9-on: Oct, 1996 - No. 90, May, 2007 ($2.75-$2.99, color #1-5, B&W #6-on)

	GD 2.0	VG 4.0	FN 6.0	VF 8.0	VF/NM 9.0	NM- 9.2
1-Terry Moore-c/s/a in all; dream seq. by Jim Lee-a						5.00
1-Jim Lee variant-c	1	2	3	6	7	8
2-5						4.00
6-16: 6-Return to B&W. 13-15-High school flashback. 16-Xena Warrior Princess parody; two covers						3.00
17-89: 33-Color issue. 46-Molly Lane. 49-Molly & Poo. 86-David dies						3.00
90-Last issue; 3 covers of Katchoo, Francine and David forming a triptych						3.00
...Lyrics and Poems (2/99)						3.00
...Source Book (2003, $2.95) Background on characters & story arcs, checklists						3.00
Brave New World ('02, $8.95, TPB) r/#44,45,47,48						9.00
Child of Rage ($15.95, TPB) r/#31-38						16.00
David's Story (6/04, $8.95, TPB) r/#61-63						9.00
Ever After ('07, $15.95, TPB) r/#83-90						16.00
Flower to Flame ('03, $15.95, TPB) r/#55-60						16.00
Heart in Hand ('03, $12.95, TPB) r/#50-54						13.00
High School ('98, $8.95, TPB) r/#13-16						9.00
Immortal Enemies ('98, $14.95, TPB) r/#6-12						15.00
Love & Lies (2006, $14.95, TPB)r/#77-82						15.00
Love Me Tender ($12.95, TPB) r/#1-5 in B&W w/ color Lee seq.						13.00
Molly & Poo (2005, $8.95, TPB)r/#46,49,73						9.00
My Other Life ($14.95, TPB) r/#25-30						15.00
Pocket Book 1-5 ($17.95, 5 1/2" x 8", TPB) 1-r/Vol.1 & 2. 2-r/#1-17 in B&W. 3-r/#18-24,26-32,34-38. 4-r/#41-45,47,48,50-60. 5-r/#46,49,61-76						18.00
Sanctuary ($15.95, TPB) r/#17-24						16.00
Tattoo ($14.95, TPB) r/#70-76; sketch pages and fan tattoo photos						15.00
Tomorrow Now (11/04, $14.95, TPB) r/#64-69						15.00
Tropic of Desire ($12.95, TPB) r/#39-43						15.00
The Complete... : Volume 3 Part 1 HC ($49.95) r/#1-12						50.00
The Complete... : Volume 3 Part 2 HC ($49.95) r/#13-15,17-25						50.00
The Complete... : Volume 3 Part 3 HC ('01, $49.95) r/#26-38						50.00
The Complete... : Volume 3 Part 4 HC ('02, $39.95) r/#39-46,49						40.00
The Complete... : Volume 3 Part 5 HC ('03, $49.95) r/#47,48,50-57						50.00
The Complete... : Volume 3 Part 6 HC ('04, $49.95) r/#58-69						50.00
The Complete... : Volume 3 Part 7 HC ('06, $49.95) r/#70-80						50.00

STRANGE SPORTS STORIES (See Brave & the Bold #45-49, DC Special, and DC Super Stars #10)
National Periodical Publications: Sept-Oct, 1973 - No. 6, July-Aug, 1974

	GD 2.0	VG 4.0	FN 6.0	VF 8.0	VF/NM 9.0	NM- 9.2
1-Devil-c	3	6	9	16	23	30
2-6: 2-Swan/Anderson-a	2	4	6	9	13	16

STRANGE STORIES FROM ANOTHER WORLD (Unknown World #1)
Fawcett Publications: No. 2, Aug, 1952 - No. 5, Feb, 1953

	GD 2.0	VG 4.0	FN 6.0	VF 8.0	VF/NM 9.0	NM- 9.2
2-Saunders painted-c	50	100	150	315	533	750
3-5-Saunders painted-c	39	78	117	240	395	550

STRANGE STORIES OF SUSPENSE (Rugged Action #1-4)
Atlas Comics (CSI): No. 5, Oct, 1955 - No. 16, Aug, 1957

	GD 2.0	VG 4.0	FN 6.0	VF 8.0	VF/NM 9.0	NM- 9.2
5(#1)	43	86	129	271	461	650
6,9	29	58	87	170	278	385
7-E. C. swipe cover/Vault of Horror #32	30	60	90	177	289	400
8-Morrow/Williamson-a; Pakula-a	31	62	93	182	296	410
10-Crandall, Torres, Meskin-a	30	60	90	177	289	400
11-13: 12-Torres, Pakula-a. 13-E.C. art swipes	25	50	75	150	245	340
14-16: 14-Williamson/Mayo-a. 15-Krigstein-a. 16-Fox, Powell-a	27	54	81	160	263	365

NOTE: ***Everett** a-6, 7, 13; c-8, 9, 11-14. **Forte** a-12, 16. **Heath** a-5. **Maneely** c-5. **Morisi** a-11. **Morrow** a-13. **Powell** a-8. **Sale** a-11. **Severin** c-7. **Wildey** a-14.*

STRANGE STORY (Also see Front Page)
Harvey Publications: June-July, 1946 (52 pgs.)

	GD 2.0	VG 4.0	FN 6.0	VF 8.0	VF/NM 9.0	NM- 9.2
1-The Man in Black Called Fate by Powell	36	72	108	216	351	485

STRANGE SUSPENSE STORIES (Lawbreakers Suspense Stories #10-15; This Is Suspense #23-26; Captain Atom V1#78 on)
Fawcett Publications/Charlton Comics No. 16 on: 6/52 - No. 5, 2/53; No. 16, 1/54 - No. 22, 11/54; No. 27, 10/55 - No. 77, 10/65; V3#1, 10/67 - V1#9, 9/69

	GD 2.0	VG 4.0	FN 6.0	VF 8.0	VF/NM 9.0	NM- 9.2
1-(Fawcett)-Powell, Sekowsky-a	90	180	270	576	988	1400
2-George Evans horror story	50	100	150	315	533	750
3-5 (2/53)-George Evans horror stories	41	82	123	256	428	600
16(1-2/54)-Formerly Lawbreakers S.S.	32	64	96	188	307	425
17	25	50	75	150	245	340
18-E.C. swipe/HOF 7; Ditko-c/a(2)	43	86	129	271	461	650
19-Ditko electric chair-c; Ditko-a	65	130	195	416	708	1000
20-Ditko-c/a(2)	41	82	123	256	428	600
21-Shuster-a; a woman dangling over an alligator pit while a madman smashes her fingers with a hammer	37	74	111	222	361	500
22(11/54)-Ditko-c, Shuster-a; last pre-code issue; becomes This Is Suspense	37	74	111	222	361	500
27(10/55)-(Formerly This Is Suspense #26)	15	30	45	86	133	180
28-30,38	12	24	36	69	97	125
31-33,35,37,40-Ditko-c/a(2-3 each)	21	42	63	126	206	285
34-Story of ruthless business man, Wm. B. Gaines; Ditko-c/a	47	94	141	296	498	700
36-(15¢, 68 pgs.); Ditko-a(4)	26	52	78	154	252	350
39,41,52,53-Ditko-a	19	38	57	111	176	240
42-44,46,49,54-60	5	10	15	34	60	85
45,47,48,50,51-Ditko-c/a	12	24	36	80	173	265
61-74	4	8	12	28	47	65
75(6/65)-Reprints origin/1st app. Captain Atom by Ditko from Space Advs. #33; r/Severin-a/Space Advs. #24 (75-77: 12¢ issues)	10	20	30	66	138	210
76,77-Captain Atom-r by Ditko/Space Advs.	6	12	18	37	66	95
V3#1(10/67): 12¢ issues begin	3	6	9	19	30	40
V1#2-Ditko-c/a; atom bomb-c	3	6	9	19	30	40
V1#3-9: 3-8-All 12¢ issues. 9-15¢ issue	2	4	6	13	18	22

NOTE: ***Alascia** a-19. **Aparo** a-60, V3#1, 2, 4; c-V1#4, 8, 9. **Baily** a-1-3; c-2, 5. **Evans** c-3, 4. **Giordano** c-16, 17p, 24p, 25p. **Montes/Bache** c-66. **Powell** a-4. **Shuster** a-19, 21. **Marcus Swayze** a-27.*

STRANGE TALENT OF LUTHER STRODE, THE (Also see The Legend of Luther Strode)
Image Comics: Oct, 2011 - No. 6, Mar, 2012 ($2.99, limited series)

	GD 2.0	VG 4.0	FN 6.0	VF 8.0	VF/NM 9.0	NM- 9.2
1-6: Justin Jordan-s/Tradd Moore-a						3.00

STRANGE TALES (...Featuring Warlock #178-181; Doctor Strange #169 on)
Atlas (CCPC #1-67/ZPC #68-79/VPI #80-85)/Marvel #86(7/61) on:
June, 1951 - No. 168, May, 1968; No. 169, Sept, 1973 - No. 188, Nov, 1976

	GD 2.0	VG 4.0	FN 6.0	VF 8.0	VF/NM 9.0	NM- 9.2
1-Horror/weird stories begin	411	822	1233	2877	5039	7200
2	148	296	444	947	1624	2300
3,5: 3-Atom bomb panels	116	232	348	742	1271	1800
4-Cosmic eyeball story "The Evil Eye"	119	238	357	762	1306	1850
6-9: 6-Heath-c/a. 7-Colan-a	90	180	270	576	988	1400
10-Krigstein-a	92	184	276	589	1007	1425
11-14,16-20	65	130	195	416	708	1000
15-Krigstein-a	66	132	198	419	722	1025
21,23-27,29-34: 27-Atom bomb panels. 33-Davis-a. 34-Last pre-code issue (2/55)	55	110	165	352	601	850
22-Krigstein, Forte/Fox-a	57	114	171	362	619	875
28-Jack Katz story used in Senate Investigation report, pgs. 7 & 169	58	116	174	371	636	900
35-41,43,44: 37-Vampire story by Colan	30	60	90	216	483	750
42,45,59,61-Krigstein-a; #61 (2/58)	31	62	93	223	499	775
46-57,60: 51-(10/56) 1st S.A. issue. 53,56-Crandall-a. 60-(8/57)	27	54	81	194	435	675
58,64-Williamson-a in each, with Mayo-#58	28	56	84	202	451	700
62,63,65,66: 62-Torres-a. 66-Crandall-a	27	54	81	194	435	675
67-Prototype ish. (Quicksilver)	31	62	93	223	499	775
68,71,72,74,77,80: Ditko/Kirby-a in #67-80	30	60	90	216	483	750
69,70,73,75,76,78,79: 69-Prototype ish. (Prof. X). 70-Prototype ish. (Giant Man). 73-Prototype ish. (Ant-Man). 75-Prototype ish. (Iron Man). 76-Prototype ish. (Human Torch). 78-Prototype ish. (Ant-Man). 79-Prototype ish. (Dr. Strange) (12/60)	33	66	99	238	532	825
81-83,85-88,90,91-Ditko/Kirby-a in all: 86-Robot-c. 90-(11/61)-Atom bomb blast panel	28	56	84	202	451	700
84-Prototype ish. (Magneto)(5/61); has powers like Magneto of X-Men, but two years earlier; Ditko/Kirby-a	32	64	96	230	515	800
89-1st app. Fin Fang Foom (10/61) by Kirby	86	172	258	688	1544	2400

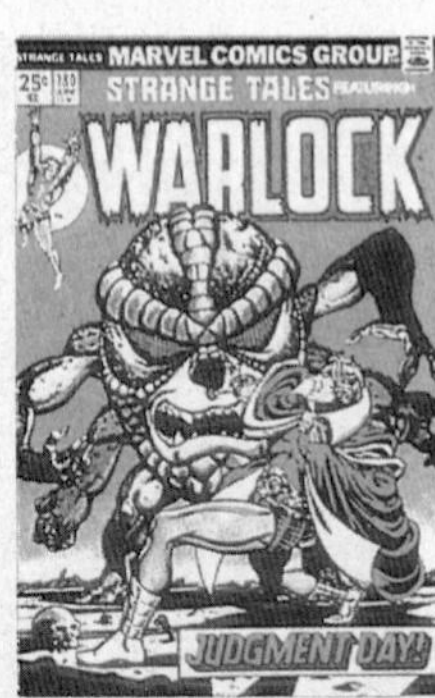

Strange Tales #180 © MAR

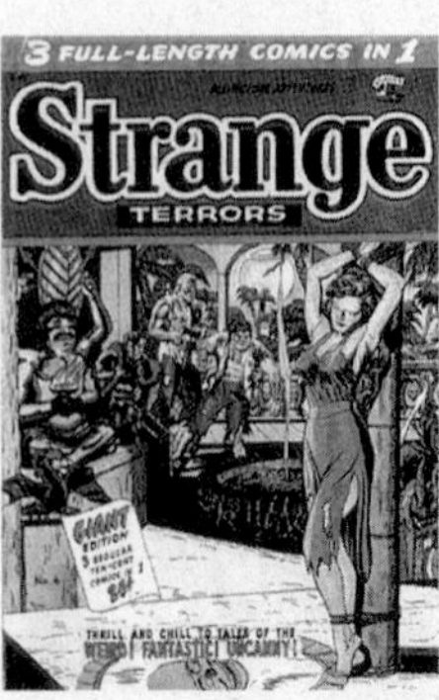

Strange Terrors #6 © STJ

Strange Worlds #7 © AVON

	GD 2.0	VG 4.0	FN 6.0	VF 8.0	VF/NM 9.0	NM- 9.2
92-Prototype ish. (Ancient One & Ant-Man); last 10¢ issue	27	54	81	189	420	650
93,95,96,98-100: Kirby-a	25	50	75	175	388	600
94-Creature similar to The Thing; Kirby-a	27	54	81	194	435	675
97-1st app. Aunt May & Uncle Ben by Ditko (6/62), before Amazing Fantasy #15; (see Tales Of Suspense #7); Kirby-a	71	142	213	568	1284	2000
101-Human Torch begins by Kirby (10/62); origin recap Fantastic Four & Human Torch; Human Torch-c begin	141	282	423	1142	2571	4000
102-1st app. Wizard; robot-c	41	82	123	303	689	1075
103-105: 104-1st app. Trapster. 105-2nd Wizard	36	72	108	266	596	925
106,108,109: 106-Fantastic Four guests (3/63)	28	56	84	202	451	700
107-(4/63)-Human Torch/Sub-Mariner battle; 4th S.A. Sub-Mariner app. & 1st x-over outside of Fantastic Four	44	88	132	326	738	1150
110-(7/63)-Intro Doctor Strange, Ancient One & Wong by Ditko	350	700	1400	3000	6000	9000
111-2nd Dr. Strange	41	82	123	303	689	1075
112,113	21	42	63	147	324	500
114-Acrobat disguised as Captain America, 1st app. since the G.A.; intro. & 1st app. Victoria Bentley; 3rd Dr. Strange app. & begin series (11/63)	41	82	123	303	689	1075
115-Origin Dr. Strange; Human Torch vs. Sandman (Spidey villain; 2nd app. & brief origin); early Spider-Man x-over, 12/63	49	98	147	382	854	1325
116-(1/64)-Human Torch battles The Thing; 1st Thing x-over	18	36	54	124	275	425
117,118,120: 120-1st Iceman x-over (from X-Men)	14	28	42	96	211	325
119-Spider-Man x-over (2 panel cameo)	16	32	48	110	243	375
121,122,124,126-134: Thing/Torch team-up in 121-134. 126-Intro Clea. 128-Quicksilver & Scarlet Witch app. (1/65). 130-The Beatles cameo. 134-Last Human Torch; The Watcher-c/story; Wood-a(i)	11	22	33	76	163	250
123-1st app. The Beetle (see Amazing Spider-Man #21 for next app.); 1st Thor x-over (8/64); Loki app.	13	26	39	89	195	300
125-Torch & Thing battle Sub-Mariner (10/64)	14	28	42	96	211	325
135-Col. (formerly Sgt.) Nick Fury becomes Nick Fury Agent of Shield (origin/1st app.) by Kirby (8/65); series begins	34	68	102	245	548	850
136-140: 138-Intro Eternity	8	16	24	51	96	140
141-147,149: 145-Begins alternating-c features w/Nick Fury (odd #'s) & Dr. Strange (even #'s). 146-Last Ditko Dr. Strange who is in consecutive stories since #113; only full Ditko Dr. Strange-c this title. 147-Dr. Strange (by Everett #147-152) continues thru #168, then Dr. Strange #169	6	12	18	40	73	105
148-Origin Ancient One	8	16	24	51	96	140
150(11/66)-John Buscema's 1st work at Marvel	6	12	18	42	79	115
151-Kirby/Steranko-c/a; 1st Marvel work by Steranko	9	18	27	58	114	170
152,153-Kirby/Steranko-a	7	14	21	44	82	120
154-158-Steranko-a/script	7	14	21	44	82	120
159-Origin Nick Fury retold; Intro Val; Captain America-c/story; Steranko-a	8	16	24	54	102	150
160-162-Steranko-a/scripts; Capt. America app.	7	14	21	44	82	120
163-166,168-Steranko-a(p). 168-Last Nick Fury (gets own book next month) & last Dr. Strange who also gets own book	6	12	18	42	79	115
167-Steranko pen/script; classic flag-c	8	16	24	54	102	150
169-1st app. Brother Voodoo(origin in #169,170) & begin series, ends #173.	3	6	9	19	30	40
170-174: 174-Origin Golem	3	6	9	14	20	25
175-177: 177-Brunner-c	2	4	6	13	18	22
178-(2/75)-Warlock by Starlin begins; origin Warlock & Him retold; 1st app. Magus; Starlin-c/a/scripts in #178-181 (all before Warlock #9)	4	8	12	23	37	50
179,181-All Warlock. 179-Intro/1st app. Pip the Troll. 181-(8/75)-Warlock story continued in Warlock #9	3	6	9	17	26	35
180-(6/75) Intro. Gamora (Guardians of the Galaxy); Warlock by Starlin	7	14	21	46	86	125
182-188: 185,186-(Regular 25¢ editions)	2	4	6	8	10	12
185,186-(30¢-c variants, limited distribution)(5,7/76)	2	4	6	11	16	25
Annual 1(1962)-Reprints from Strange Tales #73,76,78, Tales of Suspense #7,9, Tales to Astonish #1,6,7, & Journey Into Mystery #53,55,59; (1st Marvel annual?)	54	108	162	432	966	1500
Annual 2(7/63)-Reprints from Strange Tales #67, Strange Worlds (Atlas) #1-3, World of Fantasy #16; new Human Torch vs. Spider-Man story by Kirby/Ditko (1st Spidey x-over; 4th app.); Kirby-c	86	172	258	688	1544	2400

NOTE: ***Briefer*** *a-17.* ***Burgos*** *a-123p.* ***J. Buscema*** *a-174p.* ***Colan*** *a-7, 11, 20, 37, 53, 169-173p, 188p.* ***Davis*** *c-71.* ***Ditko*** *a-46, 50, 67-122, 123-125p, 126-146, 175r, 182-188r; c-51, 93, 115, 121, 146.* ***Everett*** *a-4, 21, 40-42, 73, 147-152, 164i; c-8, 10, 11, 13, 15, 24, 45, 49-54, 56, 58, 60, 61, 63, 148, 150, 152, 158i.* ***Forte*** *a-27, 43, 50, 53, 54, 60.* ***Heath*** *a-2, 6; c-6, 18-20.* ***Kamen*** *a-45.* ***G. Kane*** *c-170-173, 182p.* ***Kirby*** *Human Torch-101-105, 108, 109, 114, 120; Nick Fury-135p, 141-143p; (Layouts)-135-153; other* ***Kirby*** *a-67-100p; c-68-70, 72-74, 76-92, 94, 95, 101-114, 116-123, 125-130, 132-135, 136p, 138-145, 147, 149, 151p.* ***Kirby/Ayers*** *c-101-106, 108-110.* ***Kirby/Ditko*** *a-80, 88, 121; c-75, 93, 97, 100, 139.* ***Lawrence*** *a-29.* ***Leiber/ Fox*** *a-110-113.* ***Maneely*** *a-3, 7, 37, 42; c-33, 40.* ***Moldoff*** *a-20.* ***Mooney*** *a-174i.* ***Morisi*** *a-53, 56.* ***Morrow*** *a-54.* ***Orlando*** *a-41, 44, 46, 49, 52.* ***Powell*** *a-42, 44, 49, 54, 130-134p; c-131p.* ***Reinman*** *a-11, 50, 74, 88, 91, 95, 104, 106, 112i, 124-127i.* ***Robinson*** *a-17.* ***Romita*** *c-169.* ***Roussos*** *c-201i.* ***R.Q. Sale*** *a-56; c-16.* ***Sekowski*** *a-3, 11.* ***Severin*** *a(i)-136-138; c-137.* ***Starlin*** *a-178, 179, 180p, 181p; c-178-180, 181p.* ***Steranko*** *a-151-161, 162-168p; c-151i, 153, 155, 157, 159, 161, 163, 165, 167.* ***Torres*** *a-53, 62.* ***Tuska*** *a-14, 166p.* ***Whitney*** *a-149.* ***Wildey*** *a-42, 56.* ***Woodbridge*** *a-59. Fantastic Four cameos #101-134. Jack Katz app.-26.*

STRANGE TALES
Marvel Comics Group: Apr, 1987 - No. 19, Oct, 1988

	GD 2.0	VG 4.0	FN 6.0	VF 8.0	VF/NM 9.0	NM- 9.2
V2#1-19						4.00

STRANGE TALES
Marvel Comics: Nov, 1994 ($6.95, one-shot)

	GD 2.0	VG 4.0	FN 6.0	VF 8.0	VF/NM 9.0	NM- 9.2
V3#1-acetate-c	1	2	3	5	6	8

STRANGE TALES (Anthology; continues stories from Man-Thing #8 and Werewolf By Night #6)
Marvel Comics: Sept, 1998 - No. 2, Oct, 1998 ($4.99)

	GD 2.0	VG 4.0	FN 6.0	VF 8.0	VF/NM 9.0	NM- 9.2
1,2: 1-Silver Surfer app. 2-Two covers						5.00

STRANGE TALES (Humor anthology)
Marvel Comics: Nov, 2009 - No. 3, Jan, 2010 ($4.99, limited series)

	GD 2.0	VG 4.0	FN 6.0	VF 8.0	VF/NM 9.0	NM- 9.2
1-3: 1-Paul Pope, Kochalka, Bagge and others-s/a. 2-Bagge-c/a. 3-Sakai-c/a						5.00

STRANGE TALES II (Humor anthology)
Marvel Comics: Dec, 2010 - No. 3, Feb, 2011 ($4.99, limited series)

	GD 2.0	VG 4.0	FN 6.0	VF 8.0	VF/NM 9.0	NM- 9.2
1-3: 2-Jaime Hernandez-c. 3-Terry Moore-s/a; Pekar-s/Templeton-a						5.00

STRANGE TALES: DARK CORNERS
Marvel Comics: May, 1998 ($3.99, one-shot)

	GD 2.0	VG 4.0	FN 6.0	VF 8.0	VF/NM 9.0	NM- 9.2
1-Anthology; stories by Baron & Maleev, McGregor & Dringenberg, DeMatteis & Badger; Estes painted-c						4.00

STRANGE TALES OF THE UNUSUAL
Atlas Comics (ACI No. 1-4/WPI No. 5-11): Dec, 1955 - No. 11, Aug, 1957

	GD 2.0	VG 4.0	FN 6.0	VF 8.0	VF/NM 9.0	NM- 9.2
1-Powell-a	48	96	144	302	514	725
2	32	64	96	188	307	425
3-Williamson-a (4 pgs.)	32	64	96	192	314	435
4,6,8,11	24	48	72	142	234	325
5-Crandall, Ditko-a	29	58	87	170	278	385
7,9: 7-Kirby, Orlando-a. 9-Krigstein-a	26	52	78	154	252	350
10-Torres, Morrow-a	24	48	72	142	234	325

NOTE: ***Baily*** *a-6.* ***Brodsky*** *c-2-4.* ***Everett*** *a-2, 6; c-6, 9, 11.* ***Heck*** *a-1.* ***Maneely*** *c-1.* ***Orlando*** *a-7.* ***Pakula*** *a-10.* ***Romita*** *a-1.* ***R.Q. Sale*** *a-3.* ***Wildey*** *a-3.*

STRANGE TERRORS
St. John Publishing Co.: June, 1952 - No. 7, Mar, 1953

	GD 2.0	VG 4.0	FN 6.0	VF 8.0	VF/NM 9.0	NM- 9.2
1-Bondage-c; Zombies spelled Zoombies on-c; Fine-*esque* -a	68	136	204	435	743	1050
2	39	78	117	231	378	525
3-Kubert-a; painted-c	45	90	135	284	480	675
4-Kubert-a (reprinted in Mystery Tales #18); Ekgren painted-c; Fine-*esque* -a; Jerry Iger caricature	65	130	195	416	708	1000
5-Kubert-a; painted-c	45	90	135	284	480	675
6-Giant (25¢, 100 pgs.)(1/53); bondage-c	60	120	180	381	653	925
7-Giant (25¢, 100 pgs.); Kubert-c/a	60	120	180	381	653	925

NOTE: ***Cameron*** *a-6, 7.* ***Morisi*** *a-6.*

STRANGE WORLD OF YOUR DREAMS
Prize Publications: Aug, 1952 - No. 4, Jan-Feb, 1953

	GD 2.0	VG 4.0	FN 6.0	VF 8.0	VF/NM 9.0	NM- 9.2
1-Simon & Kirby-a	64	128	192	406	696	985
2,3-Simon & Kirby-c/a. 2-Meskin-a	50	100	150	315	533	750
4-S&K-c; Meskin-a	41	82	123	256	428	600

STRANGE WORLDS (#18 continued from Avon's Eerie #1-17)
Avon Periodicals: 11/50 - No. 9, 11/52; No. 18, 10-11/54 - No. 22, 9-10/55 (No #11-17)

	GD 2.0	VG 4.0	FN 6.0	VF 8.0	VF/NM 9.0	NM- 9.2
1-Kenton of the Star Patrol by Kubert (r/Eerie #1 from 1947); Crom the Barbarian by John Giunta	155	310	465	992	1696	2400
2-Wood-a; Crom the Barbarian by Giunta; Dara of the Vikings app.; used in **SOTI**, pg. 112; injury to eye panel	139	278	417	890	1520	2150
3-Wood/Orlando-a (Kenton), Wood/Williamson/Frazetta/Krenkel/Orlando-a (7 pgs.); Malu Slave Girl Princess app.; Kinstler-c	258	516	774	1651	2826	4000
4-Wood-c/a (Kenton); Orlando-a; origin The Enchanted Daggar; Sultan-a; classic cover	168	336	504	1075	1838	2600
5-Orlando/Wood-a (Kenton); Wood-c	87	174	261	553	952	1350
6-Kinstler-a(2); Orlando/Wood-c; Check-a	53	106	159	334	567	800
7-Fawcette & Becker/Alascia-a	45	90	135	284	480	675
8-Kubert, Kinstler, Hollingsworth & Lazarus-a; Lazarus Robot-c	45	90	135	284	480	675

Stray Bullets #25 © David Lapham

Street Sharks #1 © Streetwise

Strikeback #3 © MAL

	GD 2.0	VG 4.0	FN 6.0	VF 8.0	VF/NM 9.0	NM- 9.2
9-Kinstler, Fawcette, Alascia, Kubert-a	42	84	126	265	445	625
18-(Formerly Eerie #17)-Reprints "Attack on Planet Mars" by Kubert	34	68	102	199	325	450
19-r/Avon's "Robotmen of the Lost Planet"; last pre-code issue; Robot-c	34	68	102	199	325	450
20-War-c/story; Wood-c(r)/U.S. Paratroops #1	11	22	33	62	86	110
21,22-War-c/stories. 22-New logo	10	20	30	54	72	90
I.W. Reprint #5-Kinstler-a(r)/Avon's #9	4	8	12	24	37	50

STRANGE WORLDS
Marvel Comics (MPI No. 1,2/Male No. 3,5): Dec, 1958 - No. 5, Aug, 1959

	GD	VG	FN	VF	VF/NM	NM-
1-Kirby & Ditko-a; flying saucer issue	100	200	300	640	1095	1550
2-Ditko-c/a	55	110	165	352	601	850
3-Kirby-a(2)	47	94	141	296	498	700
4-Williamson-a	45	90	135	284	480	675
5-Ditko-a	40	80	120	246	411	575

NOTE: *Buscema a-3, 4. Ditko a-1-5; c-2.. Heck a-2. Kirby a-1, 3. Kirby/Brodsky c-1, 3-5.*

STRAWBERRY SHORTCAKE
Marvel Comics (Star Comics): Jun, 1985 - No. 6, Feb, 1986 (Children's comic)

	GD	VG	FN	VF	VF/NM	NM-
1-6: Howie Post-a	2	4	6	8	10	12

STRAWBERRY SHORTCAKE
Ape Entertainment: 2011 - No. 4, 2011 ($3.95, limited series)

	NM-
1-4: 1-Scratch 'n' sniff cover	4.00
Volume 2 (2012, $3.99) 1,2	4.00

STRAY
DC Comics (Homage Comics): 2001 ($5.95, prestige format, one-shot)

	NM-
1-Pollina-c/a; Lobdell & Palmiotti-s	6.00

STRAY BULLETS
El Capitan Books/Image Comics: 1995 - Present ($2.95/$3.50, B&W, mature readers)

	GD	VG	FN	VF	VF/NM	NM-
1-David Lapham-c/a/scripts	2	4	6	8	10	12
2,3						6.00
4-8						4.00
9-21,31,32-($2.95)						3.50
22-30,33-41-($3.50) 22-Includes preview to Murder Me Dead. 40-(10/05). 41-(3/14)						3.50
Free Comic Book Day giveaway (5/02) Reprints #2 with "Free Comic Book Day" banner on-c; flip book with The Matrix (printing of internet comic)						3.00
Innocence of Nihilism Volume 1 HC ($29.95, hardcover) r/#1-7						30.00
Somewhere Out West Volume 2 HC ($34.95, hardcover) r/#8-14						35.00
Other People Volume 3 HC ($34.95, hardcover) r/#15-22						35.00
Volume 1-3 TPB ($11.95, softcover) 1-r/#1-4. 2-r/#5-8. 3-r/ #9-12						12.00
Volume 4-7 TPB ($14.95) 4- r/#13-16. 5- r/#17-20. 6- r/#21-24. 7-r/#25-28						15.00

NOTE: *Multiple printings of most issues exist & are worth cover price.*

STRAY BULLETS: KILLERS
Image Comics(El Capitan Books): Mar, 2014 - Present ($3.50, B&W, mature readers)

	NM-
1-David Lapham-c/a/scripts; set in 1978	3.50

STRAY TOASTERS
Marvel Comics (Epic Comics): Jan, 1988 - No. 4, April, 1989 ($3.50, squarebound, limited series)

	NM-
1-4: Sienkiewicz-c/a/scripts	4.00

STREET COMIX
Street Enterprises/King Features: 1973 (50¢, B&W, 36 pgs.)(20,000 print run)

	GD	VG	FN	VF	VF/NM	NM-
1-Rip Kirby	2	4	6	8	11	14
2-Flash Gordon	2	4	6	10	14	18

STREETFIGHTER
Ocean Comics: Aug, 1986 - No. 4, Spr, 1987 ($1.75, limited series)

	NM-
1-4: 2-Origin begins	3.00

STREET FIGHTER
Malibu Comics: Sept, 1993 - No. 3, Nov, 1993 ($2.95)

	NM-
1-3: 3-Includes poster; Ferret x-over	3.00

STREET FIGHTER
Image Comics: Sept, 2003 - No. 14, Feb, 2005 ($2.95)

	NM-
1-Back-up story w/Madureira-a; covers by Madureira and Tsang	3.00
2-6,8-14: 2-Two covers by Campbell and Warren; back-up story w/Warren-a	3.00
7-($4.50) Larocca-c	4.50
... Vol. 1 (3/04, $9.99, digest-size) r/main stories from #1-6	10.00

STREET FIGHTER: THE BATTLE FOR SHADALOO
DC Comics/CAP Co. Ltd.: 1995 ($3.95, one-shot)

	NM-
1-Polybagged w/trading card & Tattoo	4.00

STREET FIGHTER II
Tokuma Comics (Viz): Apr, 1994 - No. 8, Nov, 1994 ($2.95, limited series)

	NM-
1-8	3.00

STREET FIGHTER II
UDON Comics: No. 0, Oct, 2005 - No. 6, Nov, 2006 ($1.99/$3.95/$2.95)

	NM-
0-(10/05, $1.99) prelude to series; Alvin Lee-a	3.00
1-($3.95) Two covers by Alvin Lee & Ed McGuinness	4.00
2-6-($2.95)	3.00

STREET FIGHTER LEGENDS
UDON Comics: Aug, 2006 ($3.95)

	NM-
1-Spotlight on Sakura; two covers	4.00

STREETS
DC Comics: 1993 - No. 3, 1993 ($4.95, limited series, 52 pgs.)

	NM-
Book 1-3-Estes painted-c	5.00

STREET SHARKS
Archie Publications: Jan, 1996 - No. 3, Mar, 1996 ($1.50, limited series)

	NM-
1-3	3.00

STREET SHARKS
Archie Publications: May, 1996 - No. 6 ($1.50, published 8 times a year)

	NM-
1-6	3.00

STRICTLY PRIVATE (You're in the Army Now)
Eastern Color Printing Co.: July, 1942 (#1 on sale 6/15/42)

	GD	VG	FN	VF	VF/NM	NM-
1,2: Private Peter Plink. 2-Says 128 pgs. on-c	28	56	84	165	270	375

STRIKE!
Eclipse Comics: Aug, 1987 - No. 6, Jan, 1988 ($1.75)

	NM-
1-6, ...Vs. Sgt. Strike Special 1 (5/88, $1.95)	3.00

STRIKEBACK! (The Hunt For Nikita)
Malibu Comics (Bravura): Oct, 1994 - No. 3, Jan, 1995 ($2.95, unfinished limited series)

	NM-
1-3: Jonathon Peterson script, Kevin Maguire-c/a	3.00
1-Gold foil embossed-c	5.00

STRIKEBACK!
Image Comics (WildStorm Productions): Jan, 1996 - No. 5, May, 1996 ($2.50, lim. series)

	NM-
1-5: Reprints original Bravura series w/additional story & art by Kevin Maguire & Jonathon Peterson; new Maguire-c in all. 4,5-New story & art	3.00

STRIKEFORCE: AMERICA
Comico: Dec, 1995 ($2.95)

	NM-
V2#1-Polybagged w/gaming card; S. Clark-a(p)	3.00

STRIKEFORCE: MORITURI
Marvel Comics Group: Dec, 1986 - No. 31, July, 1989

	NM-
1,13: 13-Double size	4.00
2-12,14-31: 14-Williamson-i. 25-Heath-c	3.00
... – We Who Are About To Die 1 (3/12, $0.99) r/#1 with profile pages and cover gallery	3.00

STRIKEFORCE MORITURI: ELECTRIC UNDERTOW
Marvel Comics: Dec, 1989 - No. 5, Mar, 1990 ($3.95, 52 pgs., limited series)

	NM-
1-5 Squarebound	4.00

STRONG GUY REBORN (See X-Factor)
Marvel Comics: Sept, 1997 ($2.99, one-shot)

	NM-
1-Dezago-s/Andy Smith, Art Thibert-a	3.00

STRONG MAN (Also see Complimentary Comics & Power of...)
Magazine Enterprises: Mar-Apr, 1955 - No. 4, Sept-Oct, 1955

	GD	VG	FN	VF	VF/NM	NM-
1(A-1 #130)-Powell-c/a	23	46	69	136	223	310
2-4: (A-1 #132,134,139)-Powell-a. 2-Powell-c	18	36	54	105	165	225

STRONTIUM DOG
Eagle Comics: Dec, 1985 - No. 4, Mar, 1986 ($1.25, limited series)

	NM-
1-4, Special 1: 4-Moore script. Special 1 (1986)-Moore script	4.00

STRYFE'S STRIKE FILE
Marvel Comics: Jan, 1993 ($1.75, one-shot, no ads)

	NM-
1-Stroman, Capullo, Andy Kubert, Brandon Peterson-a; silver metallic ink-c; X-Men tie-in to X-Cutioner's Song	4.00
1-Gold metallic ink 2nd printing	3.00

STRYKEFORCE
Image Comics (Top Cow): May, 2004 - No. 5, Oct, 2004 ($2.99)

	NM-
1-5-Faerber-s/Kirkham-a. 4,5-Preview of HumanKind	3.00

Stupid, Stupid Rat Tails #1 © Jeff Smith

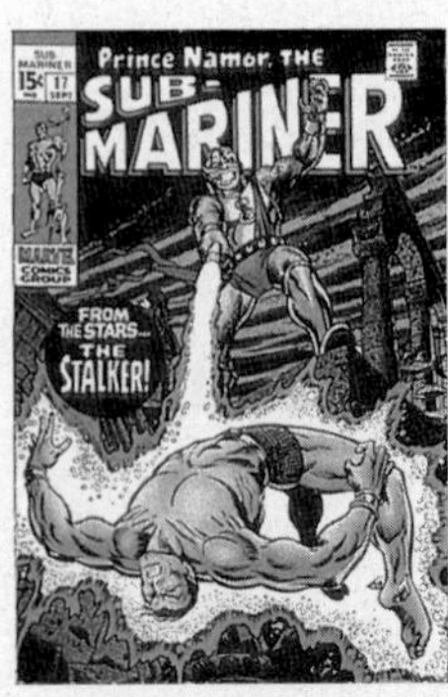

Sub-Mariner #17 © MAR

Sub-Mariner Comics #7 © MAR

GD 2.0 VG 4.0 FN 6.0 VF 8.0 VF/NM 9.0 NM- 9.2

Vol. 1 TPB (2005, $16.99) r/#1-5 & Codename: Strykeforce #0-3; sketch pages 17.00

STUMBO THE GIANT (See Harvey Hits #49,54,57,60,63,66,69,72,78,88 & Hot Stuff #2)

STUMBO TINYTOWN
Harvey Publications: Oct, 1963 - No. 13, Nov, 1966 (All 25¢ giants)
1-Stumbo, Hot Stuff & others begin 13 26 39 86 188 290
2 8 16 24 52 99 145
3-5 6 12 18 38 69 100
6-13 5 10 15 33 57 80

STUNT DAWGS
Harvey Comics: Mar, 1993 ($1.25, one-shot)
1 3.00

STUNTMAN COMICS (Also see Thrills Of Tomorrow)
Harvey Publ.: Apr-May, 1946 - No. 2, June-July, 1946; No. 3, Oct-Nov, 1946
1-Origin Stuntman by S&K reprinted in Black Cat #9; S&K-c
116 232 348 742 1271 1800
2-S&K-c/a; The Duke of Broadway story 68 136 204 435 743 1050
3-Small size (5-1/2x8-1/2"; B&W; 32 pgs.); distributed to mail subscribers only; S&K-a; Kid Adonis by S&K reprinted in Green Hornet #37
116 232 348 742 1271 1800
(Also see All-New #15, Boy Explorers #2, Flash Gordon #5 & Thrills of Tomorrow)

STUPID COMICS (Also see 40 oz. Collected)
Oni Press/Image Comics: July, 2000; Sept, 2002 - Present ($2.95, B&W)
1-(Oni Press, 7/00) Jim Mahfood 1 page satire strips reprinted from JAVA magazine 3.00
1-3-(Image Comics, 9/02; 10/03) Jim Mahfood 1 page and 2 page satire strips 3.00
TPB (4/06, $12.99) r/#1(Oni) and #1-3(Image); Phoenix New Times strips 13.00

STUPID HEROES
Mirage Studios: Sept, 1993 - No. 3, Dec, 1994 ($2.75, unfinished limited series)
1-3-Laird-c/a & scripts; 2 trading cards bound in 3.00

STUPID, STUPID RAT TAILS (See Bone)
Cartoon Books: Dec, 1999 - No. 3, Feb, 2000 ($2.95, limited series)
1-3-Jeff Smith-a/Tom Sniegoski-s 3.00

SUBHUMAN
Dark Horse Comics: Nov, 1998 - No. 4, Feb, 1999 ($2.95, limited series)
1-4-Mark Schultz-c 3.00

SUBMARINE ATTACK (Formerly Speed Demons)
Charlton Comics: No. 11, May, 1958 - No. 54, Feb-Mar, 1966
11 4 8 12 27 44 60
12-20: 16-Atomic bomb panels 3 6 9 19 30 40
21-30 3 6 9 17 26 35
31-54: 43-Cuban missile crisis story. 47-Atomic bomb panels
3 6 9 15 22 28
NOTE: *Glanzman c/a-25. Montes/Bache a-38, 40, 41.*

SUB-MARINER (See All-Select, All-Winners, Blonde Phantom, Daring, The Defenders, Fantastic Four #4, Human Torch, The Invaders, Iron Man &..., Marvel Mystery, Marvel Spotlight #27, Men's Adventures, Motion Picture Funnies Weekly, Namora, Namor, The..., Prince Namor, The Sub-Mariner, Saga Of The..., Tales to Astonish #70 & 2nd series, USA & Young Men)

SUB-MARINER, THE (2nd Series)(Sub-Mariner #31 on)
Marvel Comics Group: May, 1968 - No. 72, Sept, 1974 (No. 43: 52 pgs.)
1-Origin Sub-Mariner; story continued from Iron Man & Sub-Mariner #1
21 42 63 147 324 500
2-Triton app. 9 18 27 62 126 190
3-5: 5-1st Tiger Shark (9/68) 7 14 21 46 86 125
6,7,9,10: 6-Tiger Shark-c & 2nd app., cont'd from #5. 7-Photo-c. (1968). 9-1st app. Serpent Crown (origin in #10 & 12) 5 10 15 33 57 80
8-Sub-Mariner vs. Thing 9 18 27 59 117 175
8-2nd printing (1994) 2 4 6 8 10 12
11-13,15: 15-Last 12¢ issue 4 8 12 28 47 65
14-Sub-Mariner vs. G.A. Toro, who assumes identity of G. A. Human Torch; death of Toro (1st modern app. & only app. Toro, 6/69) 6 12 18 37 66 95
16-20: 19-1st Sting Ray (11/69); Stan Lee, Romita, Heck, Thomas, Everett & Kirby cameos. 20-Dr. Doom app. 3 6 9 21 33 45
21,23-33,37-39,41,42: 25-Origin Atlantis. 30-Capt. Marvel x-over. 37-Death of Lady Dorma. 38-Origin retold. 42-Last 15¢ issue. 3 6 9 16 24 32
22,40: 22-Dr. Strange x-over. 40-Spider-Man x-over 3 6 9 17 26 35
34-Prelude (w/#35) to 1st Defenders story; Hulk & Silver Surfer x-over
8 16 24 54 102 150
35-Namor/Hulk/Silver Surfer team-up to battle The Avengers-c/story (3/71); hints at teaming up again 6 12 18 41 76 110
36-Wrightson-a(i) 3 6 9 19 30 40
43-King Size Special (52 pgs.) 3 6 9 20 31 42
44,45-Sub-Mariner vs. Human Torch 3 6 9 18 28 38
46-49,56,62,64-72: 47,48-Dr. Doom app. 49-Cosmic Cube story. 62-1st Tales of Atlantis, ends #66. 64-Hitler cameo. 67-New costume; F.F. x-over. 69-Spider-Man x-over (6 panels)
2 4 6 9 13 16
50-1st app. Nita, Namor's niece (later Namorita in New Warriors)
2 4 6 11 16 20
51-55,57,58,60,61,63-Everett issues: 57-Venus app. (1st since 4/52); anti-Vietnam War panels. 61-Last artwork by Everett; 1st 4 pgs. completed by Mortimer; pgs. 5-20 by Mooney
2 4 6 10 14 18
59-1st battle with Thor; Everett-a 3 6 9 20 31 42
Special 1 (1/71)-r/Tales to Astonish #70-73 3 6 9 20 31 42
Special 2 (1/72)-(52 pgs.)-r/T.T.A. #74-76; Everett-a 3 6 9 16 24 32
NOTE: *Bolle a-67i. Buscema a(p)-1-8, 20, 24. Colan a(p)-10, 11, 40, 43, 46-49, Special 1, 2; c(p)-10, 11, 40. Craig a-17i, 19-23i. Everett a-45r, 50-55, 57, 58, 59-61(plot), 63(plot); c-47, 48i, 55, 57, 58-59i, 61, Spec. 2. G. Kane c(p)-42-52, 58, 66, 70, 71. Mooney a-24i, 25i, 32-35i, 39i, 42i, 44i, 45i, 60i, 61i, 65p, 66p, 68i. Severin c/a-38i. Starlin c-59p. Tuska a-41p, 42p, 69-71p. Wrightson a-36i. #53, 54-r/stories Sub-Mariner Comics #41 & 39.*

SUB-MARINER (The Initiative, follows Civil War series)
Marvel Comics: Aug, 2007 - No. 6, Jan, 2008 ($2.99, limited series)
1-6: 1-Turner-c/Briones-a/Cherniss & Johnson-s; Iron Man app. 3-Yu-c; Venom app. 3.00
...: Revolution TPB (208, $14.99) r/#1-6 15.00

SUB-MARINER COMICS (1st Series) (The Sub-Mariner #1, 2, 33-42)(Official True Crime Cases #24 on; Amazing Mysteries #32 on; Best Love #33 on)
Timely/Marvel Comics (TCI 1-7/SePI 8/MPI 9-32/Atlas Comics (CCC 33-42)): Spring, 1941 - No. 23, Sum, 1947; No. 24, Wint, 1947 - No. 31, 4/49; No. 32, 7/49; No. 33, 4/54 - No. 42, 10/55
1-The Sub-Mariner by Everett & The Angel begin
2700 5400 8100 20,000 46,000 72,000
2-Everett-a 649 1298 1947 4738 8369 12,000
3-Churchill assassination-c; 40 pg. S-M story 568 1136 1704 4146 7323 10,500
4-Everett-a, 40 pgs.; 1 pg. Wolverton-a 423 846 1269 3000 5250 7500
5-Gabrielle/Klein-c 354 708 1062 2478 4339 6200
6-8,10: 7,10-Japanese WWII-c 331 662 993 2317 4059 5800
9-Classic Japanese WWII flag-c (Spr. 1943); Wolverton-a, 3 pgs.
343 686 1029 2400 4200 6000
11-Classic Schomburg-c 371 742 1113 2600 4550 6500
12-15 290 580 870 1856 3178 4500
16-20: 17-Japanese WWII-c 232 464 696 1485 2543 3600
21-Last Angel; Everett-a 142 284 426 909 1555 2200
22-Young Allies app. 142 284 426 909 1555 2200
23-The Human Torch, Namora x-over (Sum/47); 2nd app. Namora after Marvel Mystery #82 174 348 522 1114 1907 2700
24-Namora x-over (3rd app.) 174 348 522 1114 1907 2700
25-The Blonde Phantom begins (Spr/48), ends No. 31; Kurtzman-a; Namora x-over; last quarterly issue 161 322 483 1030 1765 2500
26,27: 26-Namora c/app. 148 296 444 947 1624 2300
28-Namora cover; Everett-a 168 336 504 1075 1838 2600
29-31 (4/49): 29-The Human Torch app. 31-Capt. America app.
155 310 465 992 1696 2400
32 (7/49, Scarce)-Origin Sub-Mariner 300 600 900 2070 3635 5200
33 (4/54)-Origin Sub-Mariner; The Human Torch app.; Namora x-over in Sub-Mariner #33-42
123 246 369 787 1344 1900
34,35-Human Torch in ea. 34-Namora bondage-c 98 196 294 627 1076 1525
36,37,39-41: 36,39-41-Namora app. 97 194 291 621 1061 1500
38-Origin Sub-Mariner's wings; Namora app.; last pre-code (2/55)
102 204 306 653 1114 1575
42-Last issue 107 214 321 685 1168 1650
NOTE: *Angel by Gustavson-#1, 8. Brodsky c-34-36, 42. Everett a-1-4, 22-24, 26-42; c-32, 33, 40. Maneely a-38; c-37, 39-41. Rico c-27-31. Schomburg c-1-4, 6, 8-18, 20. Sekowsky c-24. 25, 26(w/Rico). Shores c-21-23, 38. Bondage c-13, 22, 24, 25, 34.*

SUB-MARINER COMICS 70th ANNIVERARY SPECIAL
Marvel Comics: June, 2009 ($3.99, one-shot)
1-New WWII story, Breitweiser-a; Williamson-a; r/debut app. from Marvel Comics #1 5.00

SUB-MARINER: THE DEPTHS
Marvel Comics: Nov, 2008 - No. 5, May, 2009 ($3.99, limited series)
1-5-Peter Milligan-s/Esad Ribic-a/c 4.00

SUBSPECIES
Eternity Comics: May, 1991 - No. 4, Aug, 1991 ($2.50, limited series)
1-4: New stories based on horror movie 3.00

SUBTLE VIOLENTS
CFD Productions: 1991 ($2.50, B&W, mature)
1-Linsner-c & story 1 3 4 8 10 12

Sugar & Spike #12 © DC

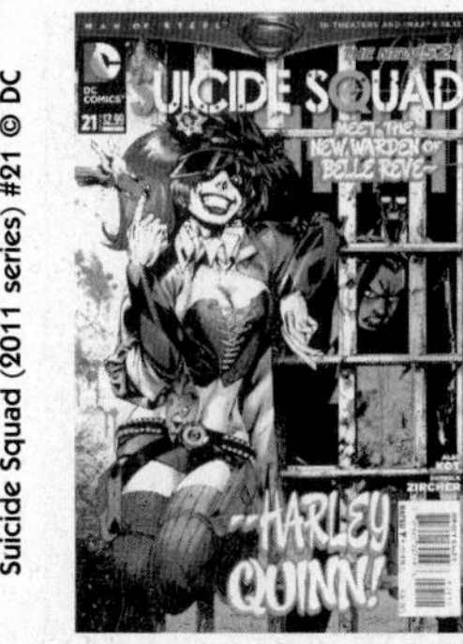

Suicide Squad (2011 series) #21 © DC

Sunfire & Big Hero Six #1 © MAR

	GD 2.0	VG 4.0	FN 6.0	VF 8.0	VF/NM 9.0	NM- 9.2
San Diego Limited Edition	4	8	12	23	37	50

SUE & SALLY SMITH (Formerly My Secret Life)
Charlton Comics: V2#48, Nov, 1962 - No. 54, Nov, 1963 (Flying Nurses)

	GD 2.0	VG 4.0	FN 6.0	VF 8.0	VF/NM 9.0	NM- 9.2
V2#48-2nd app.	3	6	9	16	24	32
49-54	2	4	6	13	18	22

SUGAR & SPIKE (Also see The Best of DC & DC Silver Age Classics)
National Periodical Publications: Apr-May, 1956 - No. 98, Oct-Nov, 1971

	GD 2.0	VG 4.0	FN 6.0	VF 8.0	VF/NM 9.0	NM- 9.2
1 (Scarce)	371	742	1113	2600	4550	6500
2	135	270	405	864	1482	2100
3-5: 3-Letter column begins	81	162	243	518	884	1250
6-10	50	100	150	315	533	750
11-20	39	78	117	231	378	525
21-29: 26-Christmas-c	26	52	78	154	252	350
30-Scribbly & Scribbly, Jr. x-over	27	54	81	158	259	360
31-40	20	40	60	117	189	260
41-60	8	16	24	54	102	150
61-80: 69-1st app. Tornado-Tot-c/story. 72-Origin & 1st app. Bernie the Brain	6	12	18	42	79	115
81-84,86-93,95: 84-Bernie the Brain apps. as Superman in 1 panel (9/69)	5	10	15	34	60	85
85 (68 pgs.)-r/#72	6	12	18	37	66	95
94-1st app. Raymond, African-American child	6	12	18	37	66	95
96 (68 pgs.)	6	12	18	40	73	105
97,98 (52 pgs.)	6	12	18	37	66	95
No. 1 Replica Edition (2002, $2.95) reprint of #1						4.00

NOTE: *All written and drawn by* ***Sheldon Mayer.*** *Issues with Paper Doll pages cut or missing are common.*

SUGAR BOWL COMICS (Teen-age)
Famous Funnies: May, 1948 - No. 5, Jan, 1949

	GD 2.0	VG 4.0	FN 6.0	VF 8.0	VF/NM 9.0	NM- 9.2
1-Toth-c/a	15	30	45	83	124	165
2,4,5	9	18	27	50	65	80
3-Toth-a	10	20	30	56	76	95

SUGARFOOT (TV)
Dell Publishing Co.: No. 907, May, 1958 - No. 1209, Oct-Dec, 1961

	GD 2.0	VG 4.0	FN 6.0	VF 8.0	VF/NM 9.0	NM- 9.2
Four Color 907 (#1)-Toth-a, photo-c	10	20	30	67	141	215
Four Color 992 (5-7/59), Toth-a, photo-c	9	18	27	63	129	195
Four Color 1059 (11-1/60), 1098 (5-7/60), 1147 (11-1/61), 1209-all photo-c. 1059,1098,1147-all have variant edition, back-c comic strip	7	14	21	49	92	135

SUGARSHOCK (Also see MySpace Dark Horse Presents)
Dark Horse Comics: Oct, 2009 ($3.50, one-shot)

	GD 2.0	VG 4.0	FN 6.0	VF 8.0	VF/NM 9.0	NM- 9.2
1-Joss Whedon-s/Fabio Moon-a/c; story from online comic; Moon sketch pgs.						3.50

SUICIDE RISK
BOOM! Studios: May, 2013 - Present ($3.99)

	GD 2.0	VG 4.0	FN 6.0	VF 8.0	VF/NM 9.0	NM- 9.2
1-12: 1-Carey-s/Casagrande-a. 5-Joëlle Jones-a. 10-Coelho-a						4.00

SUICIDE SQUAD (See Brave & the Bold, Doom Patrol & Suicide Squad Spec., Legends #3 & note under Star Spangled War stories)
DC Comics: May, 1987 - No. 66, June, 1992; No. 67, Mar, 2010 (Direct sales only #32 on)

	GD 2.0	VG 4.0	FN 6.0	VF 8.0	VF/NM 9.0	NM- 9.2
1-Chaykin-c						6.00
2-66: 9-Millennium x-over. 10-Batman-c/story. 13-JLI app. (Batman). 16-Re-intro Shade The Changing Man. 23-1st Oracle. 27-34,36,37-Snyder-a. 40-43-"The Phoenix Gambit" Batman storyline. 40-Free Batman/Suicide Squad poster						3.00
67-(3/10, $2.99) Blackest Night one-shot; Fiddler rises as a Black Lantern; Califiore-a						3.00
Annual 1 (1988, $1.50)-Manhunter x-over						4.00
...: Trial By Fire TPB (2011, $19.99) r/#1-8 & Secret Origins #14						20.00

SUICIDE SQUAD (2nd series)
DC Comics: Nov, 2001 - No. 12, Oct, 2002 ($2.50)

	GD 2.0	VG 4.0	FN 6.0	VF 8.0	VF/NM 9.0	NM- 9.2
1-12-Giffen-s/Medina-a; Sgt. Rock app. 4-Heath-a. 10-J. Severin-a. 12-JSA app.						3.00

SUICIDE SQUAD (3rd series)
DC Comics: Nov, 2007 - No. 8, Jun, 2008 ($2.99, limited series)

	GD 2.0	VG 4.0	FN 6.0	VF 8.0	VF/NM 9.0	NM- 9.2
1-8-Ostrander-s/Pina-a/Snyder III-c						3.00
...: From the Ashes TPB (2008, $19.99) r/#1-8						20.00

SUICIDE SQUAD (DC New 52)
DC Comics: Nov, 2011 - No. 30, Jun, 2014 ($2.99)

	GD 2.0	VG 4.0	FN 6.0	VF 8.0	VF/NM 9.0	NM- 9.2
1-13,16-29: 1-Harley Quinn, Deadshot, King Shark, El Diablo, Voltaic, Black Spider team up 19-Unknown Soldier joins. 24-29-Forever Evil tie-in. 24-Omac returns						3.00
14,15-Death of the Family tie-in; Joker app.						4.00
14-Variant die-cut Joker mask-c; Death of the Family tie-in						5.00
#0 (11/12, $2.99) Amanda Waller pre-Suicide Squad; Dagnino-a						3.00
...: Amanda Waller (5/14, $4.99) Jim Zub-s/Coelho-a						5.00

SUMMER FUN (See Dell Giants)

SUMMER FUN (Formerly Li'l Genius; Holiday Surprise #55)
Charlton Comics: No. 54, Oct, 1966 (Giant)

	GD 2.0	VG 4.0	FN 6.0	VF 8.0	VF/NM 9.0	NM- 9.2
54	3	6	9	21	33	45

SUMMER FUN (Walt Disney's...)
Disney Comics: Summer, 1991 ($2.95, annual, 68 pgs.)

	GD 2.0	VG 4.0	FN 6.0	VF 8.0	VF/NM 9.0	NM- 9.2
1-D. Duck, M. Mouse, Brer Rabbit, Chip 'n' Dale & Pluto, Li'l Bad Wolf, Super Goof, Scamp stories						4.00

SUMMER LOVE (Formerly Brides in Love?)
Charlton Comics: V2#46, Oct, 1965; V2#47, Oct, 1966; V2#48, Nov, 1968

	GD 2.0	VG 4.0	FN 6.0	VF 8.0	VF/NM 9.0	NM- 9.2
V2#46-Beatles-c & 8 pg. story	11	22	33	76	163	250
47-(68 pgs.) Beatles-c & 12 pg. story	9	18	27	61	123	185
48	3	6	9	15	22	28

SUMMER MAGIC (See Movie Comics)

SUNDANCE (See Hotel Deparee...)

SUNDANCE KID (Also see Blazing Six-Guns)
Skywald Publications: June, 1971 - No. 3, Sept, 1971 (52 pgs.)(Pre-code reprints & new-s)

	GD 2.0	VG 4.0	FN 6.0	VF 8.0	VF/NM 9.0	NM- 9.2
1-Durango Kid; Two Kirby Bullseye-r	3	6	9	16	23	30
2,3: 2-Swift Arrow, Durango Kid, Bullseye by S&K; Meskin plus 1 pg. origin. 3-Durango Kid, Billy the Kid, Red Hawk-r	2	4	6	11	16	20

SUNDAY PIX (Christian religious)
David C. Cook Pub/USA Weekly Newsprint Color Comics: V1#1, Mar,1949 - V16#26, July 19, 1964 (7x10", 12 pgs., mail subscription only)

	GD 2.0	VG 4.0	FN 6.0	VF 8.0	VF/NM 9.0	NM- 9.2
V1#1	8	16	24	42	54	65
V1#2-up	6	12	18	27	33	38
V2#1-52 (1950)	5	10	15	23	28	32
V3-V6 (1951-1953)	4	9	13	18	22	26
V7-V11#1-7,23-52 (1954-1959)	2	4	6	13	18	22
V11#8-22 (2/22-5/31/59) H.G. Wells First Men in the Moon serial	3	6	9	14	19	24
V12#1-19,21-52; V13-V15#1,2,9-52; V16#1-26(7/19/64)	2	4	6	10	14	18
V12#20 (5/15/60) 2 page interview with Peanuts' Charles Schulz	4	8	12	23	37	50
V15#3-8 (2/24/63) John Glenn, Christian astronaut	3	6	9	16	23	30

SUN DEVILS
DC Comics: July, 1984 - No. 12, June, 1985 ($1.25, maxi series)

	GD 2.0	VG 4.0	FN 6.0	VF 8.0	VF/NM 9.0	NM- 9.2
1-12: 6-Death of Sun Devil						4.00

SUNDIATA: A LEGEND OF AFRICA
NBM Publishing Inc.: 2002 ($15.95, hardcover with dustjacket)

	GD 2.0	VG 4.0	FN 6.0	VF 8.0	VF/NM 9.0	NM- 9.2
nn-Will Eisner-s/a; adaptation of an African folk tale						16.00

SUN FUN KOMIKS
Sun Publications: 1939 (15¢, B&W & red)

	GD 2.0	VG 4.0	FN 6.0	VF 8.0	VF/NM 9.0	NM- 9.2
1-Satire on comics (rare); 1st Hitler app. in comics?	459	918	1377	3350	5925	8500

NOTE: *Hitler, Stalin and Mussolini featured gag in 1-page story written in Hebrew and English. Nazi swastika and Nazi flag app. in a different 1-page "Gussie the Gob" story.*

SUNFIRE & BIG HERO SIX (See Alpha Flight)
Marvel Comics: Sept, 1998 - No. 3, Nov, 1998 ($2.50, limited series)

	GD 2.0	VG 4.0	FN 6.0	VF 8.0	VF/NM 9.0	NM- 9.2
1-3-Lobdell-s						3.00

SUN GIRL (See The Human Torch & Marvel Mystery Comics #88)
Marvel Comics (CCC): Aug, 1948 - No. 3, Dec, 1948

	GD 2.0	VG 4.0	FN 6.0	VF 8.0	VF/NM 9.0	NM- 9.2
1-Sun Girl begins; Miss America app.	206	412	618	1318	2259	3200
2,3: 2-The Blonde Phantom begins	142	284	426	909	1555	2200

SUNNY, AMERICA'S SWEETHEART (Formerly Cosmo Cat #1-10)
Fox Features Syndicate: No. 11, Dec, 1947 - No. 14, June, 1948

	GD 2.0	VG 4.0	FN 6.0	VF 8.0	VF/NM 9.0	NM- 9.2
11-Feldstein-c/a	129	258	387	826	1413	2000
12-14: 12,13-Feldstein-a; 13,14-Lingerie panels. 13-L.B. Cole-a	90	180	270	576	988	1400
I.W. Reprint #8-Feldstein-a; r/Fox issue	10	20	30	73	129	185

SUN-RUNNERS (Also see Tales of the...)
Pacific Comics/Eclipse Comics/Amazing Comics: 2/84 - No. 3, 5/84; No. 4, 11/84 - No. 7, 1986 (Baxter paper)

	GD 2.0	VG 4.0	FN 6.0	VF 8.0	VF/NM 9.0	NM- 9.2
1-7: P. Smith-a in #2-4						4.00
Christmas Special 1 (1987, $1.95)-By Amazing						4.00

SUNSET CARSON (Also see Cowboy Western)

Superboy #53 © DC

Superboy #228 © DC

Superboy (3rd series) #6 © DC

GD VG FN VF VF/NM NM-
2.0 4.0 6.0 8.0 9.0 9.2

Charlton Comics: Feb, 1951 - No. 4, 1951 (No month) (Photo-c on each)
1-Photo/retouched-c (Scarce, all issues) 58 116 174 371 636 900
2-Kit Carson story; adapts "Kansas Raiders" w/Brian Donlevy, Audie Murphy & Margaret Chapman 41 82 123 256 428 600
3,4 34 68 102 199 325 450

SUNSET PASS (See Zane Grey & 4-Color #230)

SUPER ANIMALS PRESENTS PIDGY & THE MAGIC GLASSES
Star Publications: Dec, 1953 (25¢, came w/glasses)
1-(3-D Comics)-L. B. Cole-c 40 80 120 246 411 575

SUPER BAD JAMES DYNOMITE
5-D Comics: Dec, 2005 - No. 5, Feb, 2007 ($3.99)
1-5-Created by the Wayans brothers 4.00

SUPERBOY
DC Comics: Jan, 1942
nn-Ashcan comic, not distributed to newsstands, only for in house use. Covers were produced, but not the rest of the book. A CGC certified 9.2 copy sold in 2003 for $6,600.

SUPERBOY (See Adventure, Aurora, DC Comics Presents, DC 100 Page Super Spectacular #15, DC Super Stars, 80 Page Giant #10, More Fun Comics, The New Advs. of... & Superman Family #191, Young Justice)

SUPERBOY (1st Series)(...& the Legion of Super-Heroes with #231)
(Becomes The Legion of Super-Heroes No. 259 on)
National Periodical Publ./DC Comics: Mar-Apr, 1949 - No. 258, Dec, 1979 (#1-16: 52 pgs.)
1-Superman cover; intro in More Fun #101 (1-2/45) 946 1892 2838 6906 12,203 17,500
2-Used in **SOTI**, pg. 35-36,226 252 504 756 1613 2757 3900
3 194 388 582 1242 2121 3000
4,5: 5-1st pre-Supergirl tryout (c/story, 11-12/49) 135 270 405 864 1482 2100
6-9: 8-1st Superbaby 119 238 357 762 1306 1850
10-1st app. Lana Lang 129 258 387 826 1413 2000
11-15: 11-2nd Lana Lang app.; 1st Lana cover 89 178 267 565 970 1375
16-20: 20-2nd Jor-El cover 61 122 183 390 670 950
21-26,28-30: 21-Lana Lang app. 53 106 159 334 567 800
27-Low distribution 54 108 162 343 574 825
31-38: 38-Last pre-code issue (1/55) 45 90 135 284 480 675
39-48,50 (7/56) 41 82 123 256 428 600
49 (6/56)-1st app. Metallo (Jor-El's robot) 53 106 159 334 567 800
51-60: 51-Krypto app. 52-1st S.A. issue. 56-Krypto-c 34 68 102 199 325 450
61-67 28 56 84 165 270 375
68-Origin/1st app. original Bizarro (10-11/58) 116 232 348 742 1271 1800
69-77,79: 76-1st Supermonkey 24 48 72 142 234 325
78-Origin Mr. Mxyzptlk & Superboy's costume 32 64 96 188 307 425
80-1st meeting Superboy/Supergirl (4/60) 31 62 93 182 296 410
81,83-85,87,88: 83-Origin/1st app. Kryptonite Kid 13 26 39 86 188 290
82-1st Bizarro Krypto 13 26 39 91 201 310
86-(1/61)-4th Legion app; Intro Pete Ross 22 44 66 154 340 525
89-(6/61)-1st app. Mon -El; 2nd Phantom Zone 29 58 87 209 467 725
90-92: 90-Pete Ross learns Superboy's I.D. 92-Last 10¢ issue 11 22 33 76 163 250
93-10th Legion app.(12/61); Chameleon Boy app. 12 24 36 79 170 260
94-97,99: 94-1st app. Superboy Revenge Squad 10 20 30 68 144 220
98-(7/62) Legion app; origin & 1st app. Ultra Boy; Pete Ross joins Legion 13 26 39 89 195 300
100-(10/62)-Ultra Boy app; 1st app. Phantom Zone villains, Dr. Xadu & Erndine. 2 pg. map of Krypton; origin Superboy retold; r-cover of Superman #1 17 34 51 117 259 400
101-120: 104-Origin Phantom Zone. 115-Atomic bomb-c. 117-Legion app. 9 18 27 57 111 165
121-128: 124-(10/65)-1st app. Insect Queen (Lana Lang). 125-Legion cameo. 126-Origin Krypto the Super Dog retold with new facts 7 14 21 49 92 135
129-(80-pg. Giant G-22)-Reprints origin Mon-El 9 18 27 57 111 165
130-137,139,140: 131-Legion statues cameo in Dog Legionnaires story. 132-1st app. Supremo. 133-Superboy meets Robin 6 12 18 41 76 110
138 (80-pg. Giant G-35) 7 14 21 46 86 125
141-146,148-155,157: 145-Superboy's parents regain their youth. 148-Legion app. 157-Last 12¢ issue 5 10 15 35 63 90
147(6/68)-Giant G-47; 1st origin of L.S.H. (Saturn Girl, Lightning Lad, Cosmic Boy); origin Legion of Super-Pets-r/Adv. #293 6 12 18 41 76 110
147 Replica Edition (2003, $6.95) reprints entire issue; cover recreation by Ordway 7.00
156-(Giant G-59) 6 12 18 38 69 100
158-164,166-171,175: 171-1st app. Aquaboy 3 6 9 18 28 38
165,174 (Giant G-71,G-83): 165-r/1st app. Krypto the Superdog from Adventure Comics #210 5 10 15 34 60 85
172,173,176-Legion app.: 172-1st app. & origin Yango (The Super Ape). 176-Partial photo-c; last 15¢ issue 3 6 9 19 30 40
177-184,186,187 (All 52 pgs.): 182-All new origin of the classic World's Finest team (Superman & Batman) as teenagers (2/72, 22pgs). 184-Origin Dial H for Hero-r 3 6 9 20 31 42
185-Also listed as DC 100 Pg. Super Spectacular #12; Legion-c/story; Teen Titans, Kid Eternity(r/Hit #46), Star Spangled Kid-r(S.S. #55) 7 14 21 46 86 125
188-190,192,194,196: 188-Origin Karkan. 196-Last Superboy solo story 3 6 9 14 19 24
191,193,195: 191-Origin Sunboy retold; Legion app. 193-Chameleon Boy & Shrinking Violet get new costumes. 195-1st app. Erg-1/Wildfire; Phantom Girl gets new costume 3 6 9 14 20 26
197-Legion series begins; Lightning Lad's new costume 3 6 9 19 30 40
198,199: 198-Element Lad & Princess Projectra get new costumes 3 6 9 14 20 26
200-Bouncing Boy & Duo Damsel marry; J'onn J'onzz cameo 3 6 9 16 23 30
201,204,206,207,209: 201-Re-intro Erg-1 as Wildfire. 204-Supergirl resigns from Legion. 206-Ferro Lad & Invisible Kid app. 209-Karate Kid gets new costume 2 4 6 11 16 20
202,205-(100 pgs.): 202-Light Lass gets new costume; Mike Grell's 1st comic work-i (5-6/74) 4 8 12 28 47 65
203-Invisible Kid killed by Validus 3 6 9 15 22 28
208,210: 208-(68 pgs.). 208-Legion of Super-Villains app. 210-Origin Karate Kid 3 6 9 14 20 26
211-220: 212-Matter-Eater Lad resigns. 216-1st app. Tyroc, who joins the Legion in #218 2 4 6 9 13 16
221-230,246-249: 226-Intro. Dawnstar. 228-Death of Chemical King 2 4 6 8 10 12
231-245: (Giants). 240-Origin Dawnstar. 242-(52 pgs.). 243-Legion of Substitute Heroes app. 243-245-(44 pgs.). 2 4 6 9 13 16
244,245-(Whitman variants; low print run, no issue# shown on cover) 3 6 9 14 20 26
246-248-(Whitman variants; low ...) 2 4 6 11 16 20
250-258: 253-Intro Blok. 257-Return of Bouncing Boy & Duo Damsel by Ditko 2 3 4 6 8 10
251-258-(Whitman variants; low print run) 2 4 6 10 14 18
Annual 1 (Sum/64, 84 pgs.)-Origin Krypto-r 15 30 45 103 227 350
Spectacular 1 (1980, Giant)-1st comic distributed only through comic stores; mostly-r 2 4 6 8 10 12
...: The Greatest Team-Up Stories Ever Told TPB (2010, $19.99) r/team-ups with Robin, Supergirl, young versions of Aquaman, Green Arrow, Bruce Wayne; Davis-c 20.00
NOTE: ***Neal Adams** c-143, 145, 146, 148-155, 157-161, 163, 164, 166-168, 172, 173, 175, 176, 178. **M. Anderson** a-178,179, 245i. **Ditko** a-257p. **Grell** a-202i, 203-219, 220-224p, 235p; c-207-232, 235, 236p, 237, 239p, 240p, 243p, 246, 258. **Nasser** a(p)-222, 225, 226, 230, 231, 233, 236. **Simonson** a-237p. **Starlin** a(p)-239, 250, 251; c-238. **Staton** a-227p, 243-249p, 252-258p; c-247-251p. **Swan/Moldoff** c-109. **Tuska** a-172, 173, 176, 183, 235p. **Wood** inks-153-155, 157-161. Legion app.-172, 173, 176, 177, 183, 184, 188, 190, 191, 193, 195, 197-258.*

SUPERBOY (TV)(2nd Series)(The Adventures of...#19 on)
DC Comics: Feb, 1990 - No. 22, Dec, 1991 ($1.00/$1.25)
1-Photo-c from TV show; Mooney-a(p) 4.00
2-22: Mooney-a in 2-8,18-20; 8-Bizarro-c/story; Arthur Adams-a(i). 9-12,14-17-Swan-a 3.00
...Special 1 (1992, $1.75) Swan-a 4.00

SUPERBOY (3rd Series)
DC Comics: Feb, 1994 - No. 100, Jul, 2002 ($1.50/$1.95/$1.99/$2.25)
1-Metropolis Kid from Reign of the Supermen 4.00
2-8,0,9-24,26-76: 6,7-Worlds Collide Pts. 3 & 8. 8-(9/94)-Zero Hour x-over. 0-(10/94). 9-(11/94)-King Shark app. 21-Legion app. 28-Supergirl-c/app. 33-Final Night. 38-41-"Meltdown". 45-Legion-c/app. 47-Green Lantern-c/app. 50-Last Boy on Earth begins. 60-Crosses Hypertime. 68-Demon-c/app. 3.00
25-($2.95)-New Gods & Female Furies app.; w/pin-ups 4.00
77-99: 77-Begin $2.25-c. 79-Superboy's powers return. 80,81-Titans app. 83-New costume. 85-Batgirl app. 90,91-Our Worlds at War x-over 3.00
100-($3.50) Sienkiewicz-c; Grummett & McCrea-a; Superman cameo 4.00
#1,000,000 (11/98) 853rd Century x-over 3.00
Annual 1 (1994, $2.95, 68 pgs.)-Elseworlds story, Pt. 2 of The Super Seven (see Adventures Of Superman Annual #6) 4.00
Annual 2 (1995, $3.95)-Year One story 4.00
Annual 3 (1996, $2.95)-Legends of the Dead Earth 4.00
Annual 4 (1997, $3.95)-Pulp Heroes story 4.00
...Plus 1 (Jan, 1997, $2.95) w/Capt. Marvel Jr. 4.00
...Plus 2 (Fall, 1997, $2.95) w/Slither (Scare Tactics) 4.00

Superboy (2011 series) #16 © DC

Super Comics #74 © DELL

Super Dinosaur #20 © Kirkman & Howard

	GD 2.0	VG 4.0	FN 6.0	VF 8.0	VF/NM 9.0	NM- 9.2

.../Risk Double-Shot 1 (Feb, 1998, $1.95) w/Risk (Teen Titans) 3.00

SUPERBOY (4th Series)
DC Comics: Jan, 2011 - No. 11, Early Oct, 2011 ($2.99)

1-11: 1-Lemire-s/Gallo-a/Albuquerque-c; Parasite & Poison Ivy app. 2,3-Noto-c 3.00
1-5: 1-Variant-c by Cassaday. 2-March-var-c. 3-Nguyen var-c. 4-Lau var-c. 5-Manapul 4.00

SUPERBOY (DC New 52)
DC Comics: Nov, 2011 - Present ($2.99)

1-29: 1-New origin; Lobdell-s/Silva-a/Canete-c; Caitlin Fairchild app. 6-Supergirl app. 8-Grunge, Beast Boy & Terra app. 9-"The Culling" x-over cont. from Teen Titans Annual #1; Teen Titans and the Legion app. 14-17-H'El on Earth tie-in; Batman app. 3.00
#0-(11/12, $2.99) Origin of Kryptonian clones; Silva-a 3.00
Annual 1 (3/13, $4.99) H'El on Earth tie-in between Superboy #16 & Superman #16 5.00

SUPERBOY AND THE LEGION OF SUPER-HEROES
DC Comics: 2011 ($14.99, TPB)

SC-Reprints stories from Adventure Comics #515-520 15.00

SUPERBOY & THE RAVERS
DC Comics: Sept, 1996 - No. 19, March, 1998 ($1.95)

1-19: 4-Adam Strange app. 7-Impulse-c/app. 9-Superman-c/app. 3.00

SUPERBOY COMICS
DC Comics: Jan. 1942

nn - Ashcan comic, not distributed to newsstands, only for in-house use. Cover art is Detective Comics #57 with interior being Action Comics #38. A CGC certified 9.2 copy sold for $6,600 in 2003 and for $15,750 in 2008.

SUPERBOY/ROBIN: WORLD'S FINEST THREE
DC Comics: 1996 - No. 2, 1996 ($4.95, squarebound, limited series)

1,2: Superboy & Robin vs. Metallo & Poison Ivy; Karl Kesel & Chuck Dixon scripts; Tom Grummett-c(p)/a(p) 5.00

SUPERBOY'S LEGION (Elseworlds)
DC Comics: 2001 - No. 2, 2001 ($5.95, squarebound, limited series)

1,2-31st century Superboy forms Legion; Farmer-s/i; Davis-a(p)/c 6.00

SUPERBOY: THE BOY OF STEEL
DC Comics: 2010 ($19.99, hardcover with dustjacket)

HC-Reprints stories from Adventure Comics #0-3,5,6 & Superman Secret Files 2009 20.00
SC-(2011, $14,99) Same contents as HC 15.00

SUPER BRAT (Li'l Genius #6 on)
Toby Press: Jan, 1954 - No. 4, July, 1954

1 9 18 27 52 69 85
2-4: 4-Li'l Teevy by Mel Lazarus 6 12 18 31 38 45
I.W. Reprint #1,2,3,7,8('58): 1-r/#1 2 4 6 8 11 14
I.W. (Super) Reprint #10('63) 2 4 6 8 10 12

SUPERCAR (TV)
Gold Key: Nov, 1962 - No. 4, Aug, 1963 (All painted-c)

1 10 20 30 69 147 225
2,3 6 12 18 41 76 110
4-Last issue 7 14 21 46 86 125

SUPER CAT (Formerly Frisky Animals; also see Animal Crackers)
Star Publications #56-58/Ajax/Farrell Publ. (Four Star Comic Corp.):
No. 56, Nov, 1953 - No. 58, May, 1954; Aug, 1957 - No. 4, May, 1958

56-58-L.B. Cole-c on all 19 38 57 112 179 245
1(1957-Ajax)- "The Adventures of..." c-only 10 20 30 54 72 90
2-4 7 14 21 35 43 50

SUPER CIRCUS (TV)
Cross Publishing Co.: Jan, 1951 - No. 5, Sept, 1951 (Mary Hartline)

1-(52 pgs.)-Cast photos on-c 16 32 48 94 147 200
2-Cast photos on-c 11 22 33 60 83 105
3-5 9 18 27 52 69 85

SUPER CIRCUS (TV)
Dell Publ. Co.: No. 542, Mar, 1954 - No. 694, Mar, 1956 (Mary Hartline)

Four Color 542: Mary Hartline photo-c 6 12 18 41 76 110
Four Color 592,694: Mary Hartline photo-c 6 12 18 37 66 95

SUPER COMICS
Dell Publishing Co.: May, 1938 - No. 121, Feb-Mar, 1949

1-Terry & The Pirates, The Gumps, Dick Tracy, Little Orphan Annie, Little Joe, Gasoline Alley, Smilin' Jack, Smokey Stover, Smitty, Tiny Tim, Moon Mullins, Harold Teen, Winnie Winkle begin 226 452 678 1446 2473 3500
2 82 164 246 528 902 1275
3 73 146 219 467 796 1125
4,5: 4-Dick Tracy-c; also #8-10,17,26(part),31 57 114 171 362 619 875
6-10 47 94 141 296 498 700
11-20: 20-Smilin' Jack-c (also #29,32) 39 78 117 240 395 550
21-29: 21-Magic Morro begins (origin & 1st app., 2/40). 22,27-Ken Ernst-c (also #25?); Magic Morro c-22,25,27,34 34 68 102 199 325 450
30- "Sea Hawk" movie adaptation-c/story with Errol Flynn 35 70 105 208 339 470
31-40: 34-Ken Ernst-c 28 56 84 165 270 375
41-50: 41-Intro Lightning Jim. 43-Terry & The Pirates ends 23 46 69 138 227 315
51-60 19 38 57 109 172 235
61-70: 62-Flag-c. 65-Brenda Starr-r begin? 67-X-Mas-c 17 34 51 98 154 210
71-80 14 28 42 80 115 150
81-99 13 26 39 74 105 135
100 14 28 42 78 112 145
101-115-Last Dick Tracy (moves to own title) 10 20 30 56 76 95
116-121: 116,118-All Smokey Stover. 117-All Gasoline Alley. 119-121-Terry & The Pirates app. in all 9 18 27 50 65 80

SUPER COPS, THE
Red Circle Productions (Archie): July, 1974 (one-shot)

1-Morrow-c/a; art by Pino, Hack, Thorne 2 4 6 8 11 14

SUPER COPS
Now Comics: Sept, 1990 - No. 4, Dec?, 1990 ($1.75)

1-($2.75, 52 pgs.)-Dave Dorman painted-c (both printings) 4.00
2-4 3.00

SUPER CRACKED (See Cracked)

SUPERCROOKS
Marvel Comics (Icon): May, 2012 - No. 4, Aug, 2012 ($2.99/$4.99)

1-3-($2.99) Millar-s/Yu-a. 1-Covers by Yu & Gibbons. 2-Covers by Yu & Hitch 3.00
4-($4.99) Bonus preview of Jupiter's Children (later re-titled Jupiter's Legacy) 5.00

SUPER DC GIANT (25-50¢, all 68-52 pg. Giants)
National Per. Publ.: No. 13, 9-10/70 - No. 26, 7-8/71; V3#27, Summer, 1976 (No #1-12)

S-13-Binky 10 20 30 64 132 200
S-14-Top Guns of the West; Kubert-c; Trigger Twins, Johnny Thunder, Wyoming Kid-r; Moreira-r (9-10/70) 5 10 15 33 57 80
S-15-Western Comics; Kubert-c; Pow Wow Smith, Vigilante, Buffalo Bill-r; new Gil Kane-a (9-10/70) 5 10 15 33 57 80
S-16-Best of the Brave & the Bold; Batman-r & Metamorpho origin-r from Brave & the Bold; Spectre pin-up. 4 8 12 27 44 60
S-17-Love 1970 (scarce) 23 46 69 161 356 550
S-18-Three Mouseketeers; Dizzy Dog, Doodles Duck, Bo Bunny-r; Sheldon Mayer-a 9 18 27 57 111 165
S-19-Jerry Lewis; Neal Adams pin-up 9 18 27 59 117 175
S-20-House of Mystery; N. Adams-c; Kirby-r(3) 7 14 21 44 82 120
S-21-Love 1971 (scarce) 27 54 81 194 435 675
S-22-Top Guns of the West; Kubert-c 4 8 12 25 40 55
S-23-The Unexpected 4 8 12 28 47 65
S-24-Supergirl 4 8 12 25 40 55
S-25-Challengers of the Unknown; all Kirby/Wood-r 4 8 12 22 35 48
S-26-Aquaman (1971)-r/S.A. Aquaman origin story from Showcase #30 4 8 12 22 35 48
27-Strange Flying Saucers Adventures (Sum, 1976) 3 6 9 18 28 38
NOTE: *Sid Greene r-27p(2), Heath r-27. G. Kane a-14r(2), 15, 27r(p). Kubert r-16.*

SUPER DINOSAUR
Image Comics: Apr, 2011 - Present ($2.99)

1-22: 1-Robert Kirkman-s/Jason Howard-a; origin story and character profiles 3.00
... Origin Special #1 FCBD Edition (5/11, giveaway) r/#1 3.00

SUPER-DOOPER COMICS
Able Mfg. Co./Harvey: 1946 - No. 7, May, 1946; No. 8, 1946 (10¢, 32 pgs., paper-c)

1-The Clock, Gangbuster app. (scarce) 58 116 174 371 636 900
2 16 32 48 94 147 200
3-6 15 30 45 85 130 175
7,8-Shock Gibson. 7-Where's Theres A Will by Ed Wheelan, Steve Case Crime Rover, Penny & Ullysses Jr. 8-Sam Hill app. 16 32 48 94 147 200

SUPER DUCK COMICS (The Cockeyed Wonder) (See Jolly Jingles)
MLJ Mag. No. 1-4(9/45)/Close-Up No. 5 on (Archie): Fall, 1944 - No. 94, Dec, 1960 (Also see Laugh #24)(#1-5 are quarterly)

Super Friends #18 © DC

Supergirl #6 © DC

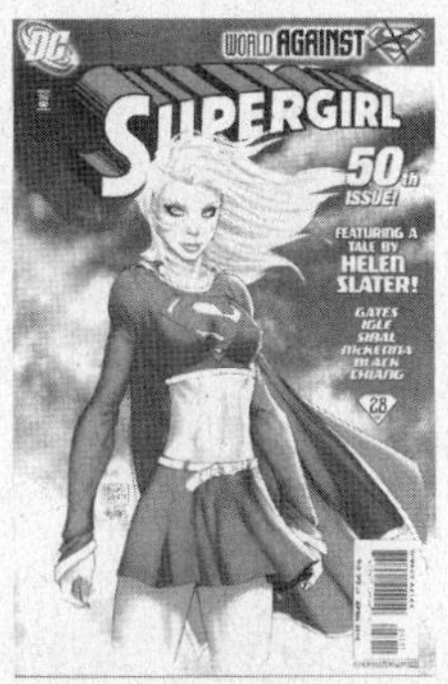

Supergirl (2005 series) #50 © DC

	GD 2.0	VG 4.0	FN 6.0	VF 8.0	VF/NM 9.0	NM- 9.2
1-Origin; Hitler & Hirohito-c	113	226	339	723	1237	1750
2-Bill Vigoda-c	32	64	96	192	314	435
3-5: 4-20-Al Fagaly-c (most)	21	42	63	126	206	285
6-10	15	30	45	86	133	180
11-20(6/48)	12	24	36	67	94	120
21,23-40 (10/51)	10	20	30	58	79	100
22-Used in **SOTI**, pg. 35,307,308	12	24	36	69	97	125
41-60 (2/55)	9	18	27	50	65	80
61-94	8	16	24	40	50	60

SUPER DUPER (Formerly Pocket Comics #1-4?)
Harvey Publications: No. 5, 1941 - No. 11, 1941

	GD 2.0	VG 4.0	FN 6.0	VF 8.0	VF/NM 9.0	NM- 9.2
5-Captain Freedom & Shock Gibson app.	39	78	117	234	385	535
8,11	24	48	72	142	234	325

SUPER DUPER COMICS (Formerly Latest Comics?)
F. E. Howard Publ.: No. 3, May-June, 1947

	GD 2.0	VG 4.0	FN 6.0	VF 8.0	VF/NM 9.0	NM- 9.2
3-1st app. Mr. Monster	26	52	78	154	252	350

SUPER FRIENDS (TV) (Also see Best of DC & Limited Collectors' Edition)
National Periodical Publications/DC Comics: Nov, 1976 - No. 47, Aug, 1981 (#14 is 44 pgs.)

	GD 2.0	VG 4.0	FN 6.0	VF 8.0	VF/NM 9.0	NM- 9.2
1-Superman, Batman, Robin, Wonder Woman, Aquaman, Atom, Wendy, Marvin & Wonder Dog begin (1st Super Friends)	5	10	15	30	50	70
2-Penquin-c/sty	3	6	9	16	23	30
3-5	3	6	9	14	20	26
6-10,14: 7-1st app. Wonder Twins & The Seraph. 8-1st app. Jack O'Lantern. 9-1st app. Icemaiden. 14-Origin Wonder Twins	2	4	6	13	18	22
11-13,15-30: 13-1st app. Dr. Mist. 25-1st app. Fire as Green Fury. 28-Bizarro app.	2	4	6	9	13	16
13-16,20-23,25,32-(Whitman variants; low print run, no issue# on cover)	2	4	6	11	16	20
31,47: 31-Black Orchid app. 47-Origin Fire & Green Fury	2	4	6	10	14	18
32-46: 36,43-Plastic Man app.	2	4	6	8	11	14
TBP (2001, $14.95) r/#1,6-9,14,21,27 & Limited Collectors' Edition C-41; Alex Ross-c						15.00
...: Truth, Justice and Peace TPB (2003, $14.95) r/#10,12,13,25,28,29,31,36,37						15.00

NOTE: ***Estrada*** *a-1p, 2p.* ***Orlando*** *a-1p.* ***Staton*** *a-43, 45.*

SUPER FRIENDS (All ages stories with puzzles and games)(Based on Mattel toy line)
DC Comics: May, 2008 - No. 29, Sept, 2010 ($2.25/$2.99)

	NM- 9.2
1-29-Superman, Batman, Wonder Woman, Aquaman, Flash & Green Lantern. 29-Begin $2.99-c; Bat-Mite & Mr. Mxyzptlk app.	3.00
...: Calling All Super Friends TPB (2009, $12.99) r/#8-14; puzzles and games	13.00
...: For Justice TPB (2009, $12.99) r/#1-7; puzzles and games	13.00
...: Head of the Class TPB (2010, $12.99) r/#15-21; puzzles and games	13.00
...: Mystery in Space TPB (2011, $12.99) r/#22-28; puzzles and games	13.00

SUPER FUN
Gillmor Magazines: Jan, 1956 (By A.W. Nugent)

	GD 2.0	VG 4.0	FN 6.0	VF 8.0	VF/NM 9.0	NM- 9.2
1-Comics, puzzles, cut-outs by A.W. Nugent	8	16	24	40	50	60

SUPER FUNNIES (...Western Funnies #3,4)
Superior Comics Publishers Ltd. (Canada): Dec, 1953 - No. 4, Sept, 1954

	GD 2.0	VG 4.0	FN 6.0	VF 8.0	VF/NM 9.0	NM- 9.2
1-(3-D, 10¢)-...Presents Dopey Duck; make your own 3-D glasses cut-out inside front-c; did not come w/glasses	39	78	117	231	378	525
2-Horror & crime satire	15	30	45	86	133	180
3-Phantom Ranger-c/s; Geronimo, Billy the Kid app.	10	20	30	56	76	95
4-Phantom Ranger-c/story	10	20	30	56	76	95

SUPERGIRL
DC Comics: Feb. 1944

nn - Ashcan comic, not distributed to newsstands, only for in-house use. Cover art is Boy Commandos #1 with interior being Action Comics #80. A copy sold for $15,750 in 2008.

SUPERGIRL (See Action, Adventure #281, Brave & the Bold, Crisis on Infinite Earths #7, Daring New Advs. of..., Super DC Giant, Superman Family, & Super-Team Family)

SUPERGIRL
National Periodical Publ.: Nov, 1972 - No. 9, Dec-Jan, 1973-74; No. 10, Sept-Oct, 1974 (1st solo title)(20¢)

	GD 2.0	VG 4.0	FN 6.0	VF 8.0	VF/NM 9.0	NM- 9.2
1-Zatanna back-up stories begin, end #5	7	14	21	46	86	125
2-4,6,7,9	4	8	12	25	40	55
5,8,10: 5-Zatanna origin-r. 8-JLA x-over; Batman cameo. 10-Prez	4	8	12	27	44	60

NOTE: *Zatanna in #1-5, 7(Guest); Prez app. in #10. #1-10 are 20¢ issues.*

SUPERGIRL (Formerly Daring New Adventures of...)
DC Comics: No. 14, Dec, 1983 - No. 23, Sept, 1984

	NM- 9.2
14-23: 16-Ambush Bug app. 20-JLA & New Teen Titans app.	4.00
...Movie Special (1985)-Adapts movie; Morrow-a; photo back-c	4.00

SUPERGIRL
DC Comics: Feb, 1994 - No. 4, May, 1994 ($1.50, limited series)

	NM- 9.2
1-4: Guice-a(i)	3.00

SUPERGIRL (See Showcase '96 #8)
DC Comics: Sept, 1996 - No. 80, May, 2003 ($1.95/$1.99/$2.25/$2.50)

	GD 2.0	VG 4.0	FN 6.0	VF 8.0	VF/NM 9.0	NM- 9.2
1-Peter David scripts & Gary Frank-c/a	1	2	3	5	6	8
1-2nd printing						3.00
2,4-9: 4-Gorilla Grodd-c/app. 6-Superman-c/app. 9-Last Frank-a						4.00
3-Final Night, Gorilla Grodd app.						5.00
10-19: 14-Genesis x-over. 16-Power Girl app.						3.50
20-35: 20-Millennium Giants x-over; Superman app. 23-Steel-c/app. 24-Resurrection Man x-over. 25-Comet ID revealed; begin $1.99-c						3.00
36-46: 36,37-Young Justice x-over						3.00
47-49,51-74: 47-Begin $2.25-c. 51-Adopts costume from animated series. 54-Green Lantern app. 59-61-Our Worlds at War x-over. 62-Two-Face-c/app. 66,67-Demon-c/app. 68-74-Mary Marvel app. 70-Nauck-a. 73-Begin $2.50-c						3.00
50-($3.95) Supergirl's final battle with the Carnivore						4.00
75-80: 75-Re-intro. Kara Zor-El; cover swipe of Action Comics #252 by Haynes; Benes-a. 78-Spectre app. 80-Last issue; Romita-c						3.00
#1,000,000 (11/98) 853rd Century x-over						3.00
Annual 1 (1996, $2.95)-Legends of the Dead Earth						4.00
Annual 2 (1997, $3.95)-Pulp Heroes; LSH app.; Chiodo-c						4.00
...: Many Happy Returns TPB (2003, $14.95) r/#75-80; intro. by Peter David						15.00
...Plus (2/97, $2.95) Capt.(Mary) Marvel-c/app.; David-s/Frank-a						4.00
.../Prysm Double-Shot 1 (Feb, 1998, $1.95) w/Prysm (Teen Titans)						3.00
...: Wings (2001, $5.95) Elseworlds; DeMatteis-s/Tolagson-a						6.00
TPB-('98, $14.95) r/Showcase '96 #8 & Supergirl #1-9						15.00

SUPERGIRL (See Superman/Batman #8 & #19)
DC Comics: No. 0, Oct, 2005 - No. 67, Oct, 2011 ($2.99)

	NM- 9.2
0-Reprints Superman/Batman #19 with white variant of that cover	3.00
1-Loeb-s/Churchill-a; two covers by Churchill & Turner; Power Girl app.	5.00
1-2nd printing with B&W sketch variant of Turner-c	3.00
1-3rd printing with variant-c homage to Action Comics #252 by Churchill	3.00
2-4: 2-Teen Titans app. 3-Outsiders app.; covers by Turner & Churchill	3.00
5-($3.99) Supergirl vs. Supergirl; Churchill & Turner-c	4.00
6-49: 6-9-One Year Later; Power Girl app. 11-Intro. Powerboy. 12-Terra debut; Conner-a 20-Amazons Attack x-over. 21,22-Karate Kid app. 28-31-Resurrection Man app. 35,36-New Krypton x-over; Argo City story re-told; Superwoman app. 35-Ross-c. 36-Zor-El dies	3.00
50-($4.99) Lana Lang Insect Queen app.; Superwoman returns; back-up story co-written by Helen Slater with Chiang-a; Turner-c	5.00
50-Variant cover by Middleton	6.00
51-67: 51-52-New Krypton. 52-Brainiac 5 app. 53-57-Bizarro-Girl app. 55-63-Reeder-c	3.00
58-DC 75th Anniversary variant cover by Conner	6.00
Annual 1 (11/09, $3.99) Origin of Superwoman	4.00
Annual 2 (12/10, $4.99) Silver Age Legion of Super-Heroes app.; Reeder-c	5.00
...: Beyond Good and Evil TPB (2008, $17.99) r/#23-27 and Action Comics #850	18.00
...: Bizarrogirl TPB (2011, $19.99) r/#53-59 & Annual #2	20.00
...: Candor TPB (2007, $14.99) r/#6-9; and pages from JSA Classified #2, Superman #223, Superman/Batman #27 and JLA #122,123	15.00
...: Death & The Family TPB (2010, $17.99) r/#48-50 & Annual #1	18.00
...: Friends & Fugitives TPB (2010, $17.99) r/#43,45-47; Action Comics #881,882	18.00
...: Identity TPB (2007, $19.99) r/#10-16 and story from DCU Infinite Holiday Special	20.00
...: Power TPB (2006, $14.99) r/#1-5 and Superman/Batman #19; variant-c gallery	15.00
...: Way of the World TPB (2009, $17.99) r/#28-33	18.00
...: Who is Superwoman TPB (2009, $17.99) r/#34,37-42	18.00

SUPERGIRL (DC New 52)
DC Comics: Nov, 2011 - Present ($2.99)

	NM- 9.2
1-New origin; Green & Johnson-s/Asrar-a/c; Superman app.	4.00
2-29: 2,3-Superman app. 8-Pérez-a. 14-17-H'El on Earth tie-in. 17-Wonder Woman app. 19,20-Power Girl app. 19-Power Girl gets classic costume. 23,24-Cyborg Superman app. 26-28-Lobo app. 28-Kara joins Red Lanterns	3.00
#0-(11/12, $2.99) Kara's escape from Krypton	3.00

SUPERGIRL AND THE LEGION OF SUPER-HEROES (Continues from Legion of Super-Heroes #15, Apr, 2006)(Continues as Legion of Super-Heroes #37)
DC Comics: No. 16, May, 2006 - No. 36, Jan, 2008 ($2.99)

	NM- 9.2
16-Supergirl appears in the 31st century	4.00
16-2nd printing	3.00
17-36: 23-Mon-El cameo. 24,25-Mon-El returns	3.00
...: Adult Education TPB (2007, $14.99) r/#20-25 & LSH #6,9,13-15	15.00
...: Dominator War TPB (2007, $14.99) r/#26-30	15.00

Superior Spider-Man #9 © MAR

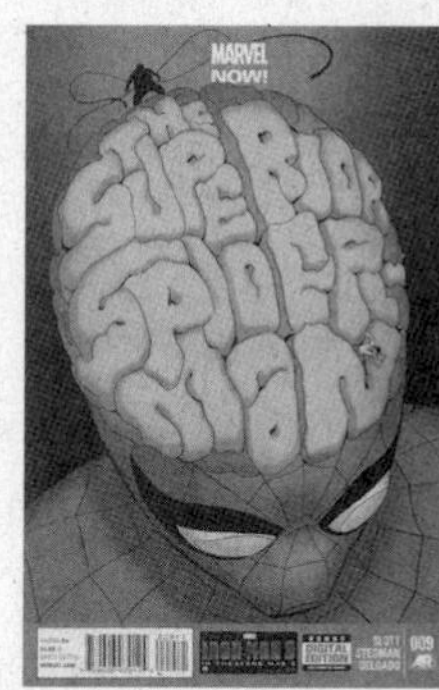

Super Magician Comics #3 © CN

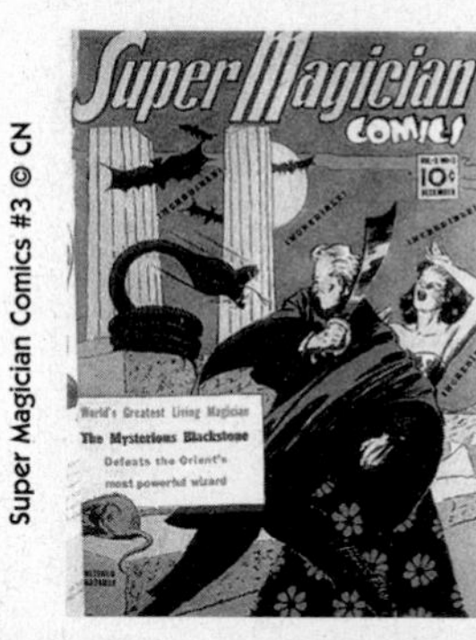

Superman #18 © DC

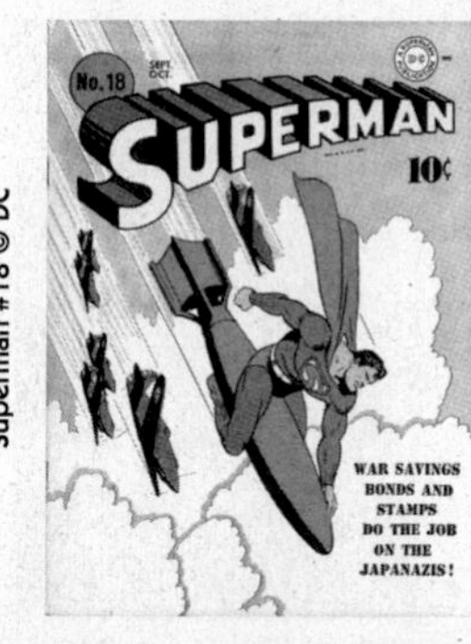

	GD 2.0	VG 4.0	FN 6.0	VF 8.0	VF/NM 9.0	NM- 9.2

...: Strange Visitor From Another Century TPB (2006, $14.99) r/#16-19 & LSH #11,12,15 15.00
...: The Quest For Cosmic Boy TPB (2008, $14.99) r/#31-36 15.00

SUPERGIRL: COSMIC ADVENTURES IN THE 8TH GRADE (Cartoony all-ages title)
DC Comics: Feb, 2008 - No. 6, Jul, 2009 ($2.50, limited series)

1-6: 1-Supergirl lands on Earth; Eric Jones-a. 5,6-Comet & Streaky app. 3.00
TPB (2009, $12.99) r/#1-6; sketch art 13.00

SUPERGIRL/LEX LUTHOR SPECIAL (Supergirl and Team Luthor on-c)
DC Comics: 1993 ($2.50, 68 pgs., one-shot)

1-Pin-ups by Byrne & Thibert 4.00

SUPERGOD (Warren Ellis'...)
Avatar Press: Oct, 2009 - No. 5, Nov, 2010 ($3.99, limited series)

1-5-Warren Ellis-s/Garrie Gastony-a; multiple covers on each 4.00

SUPER GOOF (Walt Disney) (See Dynabrite & The Phantom Blot)
Gold Key No. 1-57/Whitman No. 58 on: Oct, 1965 - No. 74, July, 1984

	GD	VG	FN	VF	VF/NM	NM-
1	4	8	12	27	44	60
2-5	3	6	9	16	23	30
6-10	3	6	9	14	19	24
11-20	2	4	6	8	11	14
21-30	1	3	4	6	8	10
31-50	1	2	3	4	5	7
51-57						6.00
58,59 (Whitman)	1	2	3	5	6	8
60(8/80), 62(11/80) 3-pack only (scarce)	4	8	12	27	44	60
61(9-10/80) 3-pack only (rare)	4	8	12	28	47	65
63-66('81)	1	2	3	5	6	8
63 (1/81, 40¢-c) Cover price error variant (scarce)	2	4	6	10	14	18
67-69: 67(2/82), 68(2-3/82), 69(3/82)						6.00
70-74 (#90180 on-c; pre-pack, nd, nd code): 70(5/83), 71(8/83), 72(5/84), 73(6/84), 74(7/84)	3	6	9	15	22	28

NOTE: *Reprints in #16, 24, 28, 29, 37, 38, 43, 45, 46, 54(1/2), 56-58, 65(1/2), 72(r-#2).*

SUPER GREEN BERET (Tod Holton...)
Lightning Comics (Milson Publ. Co.): Apr, 1967 - No. 2, Jun, 1967

	GD	VG	FN	VF	VF/NM	NM-
1-(25¢, 68 pgs)	5	10	15	30	50	70
2-(25¢, 68 pgs)	3	6	9	21	33	45

SUPER HEROES (See Giant-Size... & Marvel...)

SUPER HEROES
Dell Publishing Co.: Jan, 1967 - No. 4, June, 1967

	GD	VG	FN	VF	VF/NM	NM-
1-Origin & 1st app. Fab 4	4	8	12	23	37	50
2-4	3	6	9	16	24	32

SUPER-HEROES BATTLE SUPER-GORILLAS (See DC Special #16)
National Periodical Publications: Winter, 1976 (52 pgs., all reprints, one-shot)

	GD	VG	FN	VF	VF/NM	NM-
1-Superman, Batman, Flash stories; Infantino-a(p)	2	4	6	11	16	20

SUPER HEROES VERSUS SUPER VILLAINS
Archie Publications (Radio Comics): July, 1966 (no month given)(68 pgs.)

	GD	VG	FN	VF	VF/NM	NM-
1-Flyman, Black Hood, Web, Shield-r; Reinman-a	6	12	18	37	66	95

SUPER HERO SQUAD (See Marvel Super Hero Squad)

SUPERHERO WOMEN, THE - FEATURING THE FABULOUS FEMALES OF MARVEL COMICS (See Fireside Book Series)

SUPERICHIE (Formerly Super Richie)
Harvey Publications: No. 5, Oct, 1976 - No. 18, Jan, 1979 (52 pgs. giants)

	GD	VG	FN	VF	VF/NM	NM-
5-Origin/1st app. new costumes for Rippy & Crashman	2	4	6	9	13	16
6-18	2	4	6	8	10	12

SUPERIOR
Marvel Comics (ICON): Dec, 2010 - No. 7, Mar, 2012 ($2.99/$4.99)

1-6-Mark Millar-s/Leinil Yu-a. 1-1st & 2nd printings 3.00
7-($4.99) Bonus preview of Supercrooks #1 5.00
... World Record Special 1 (12/11, $2.99, B&W) Comic created in less than 12 hours 3.00

SUPERIOR CARNAGE
Marvel Comics: Sept, 2013 - No. 5, Jan, 2014 ($3.99)

1-5: 1-Shinick-s/Segovia-a; covers by Crain & Checchetto. 2-5-Superior Spider-Man app. 4.00
Annual 1 (4/14, $4.99) Bunn-s/Jacinto & Henderson-a; follows #5; Kasady in prison 5.00

SUPERIOR FOES OF SPIDER-MAN (Superior Spider-Man)
Marvel Comics: Sept, 2013 - Present ($3.99)

1-11: 1-Boomerang, Shocker, Overdrive, Speed Demon & Beetle team; Spencer-s 4.00

SUPERIOR SPIDER-MAN (Follows Amazing Spider-Man #700)
Marvel Comics: Mar, 2013 - No. 31, Jun, 2014 ($3.99)

1-Doc Ock as Spider-Man; new Sinister Six app.; Slott-s/Stegman-a 8.00
1-Variant baby-c by Skottie Young 10.00
2-6: 4,5-Camuncoli-a. 4-Green Goblin cameo. 6-Ramos-a 5.00
6AU (5/13, $3.99) Alternate timeline Age of Ultron tie-in; Gage-s/Soy-a 4.00
7-24: 7,8-Ramos-a; Avengers app. 9-Peter's memories removed. 14-New costume. 17-19-Spider-Man 2099 app. 20-Black Cat app. 22-24-Venom app. 4.00
25-($4.99) Superior Venom vs. the Avengers; Ramos-a 5.00
26-30: 27-Goblin Nation begins. 29-Spider-Man 2099 app. 4.00
31-($5.99) Goblin Nation finale; covers by Camuncoli & Campbell; Silver Surfer bonus 6.00
Annual 1 (1/14, $4.99) Blackout app.; Gage-s/Rodriguez-a 5.00
Annual 2 (5/14, $4.99) Leads into Superior Spider-Man #30; Gage-s/Rodriguez-a 5.00

SUPERIOR SPIDER-MAN TEAM UP
Marvel Comics: Sept, 2013 - No. 12, Jun, 2014 ($3.99)

1-10: 1-Avengers app. 8-Namor app. 9,10-Daredevil & The Punisher app. 4.00
... Special 1 (12/13, $4.99) Hulk & the original X-Men app.; Dialynas-a/Lozano-c 5.00

SUPERIOR STORIES
Nesbit Publishers, Inc.: May-June, 1955 - No. 4, Nov-Dec, 1955

	GD	VG	FN	VF	VF/NM	NM-
1-The Invisible Man by H.G. Wells	23	46	69	136	223	310
2-4: 2-The Pirate of the Gulf by J.H. Ingrahams. 3-Wreck of the Grosvenor by William Clark Russell. 4-The Texas Rangers by O'Henry	11	22	33	62	86	110

NOTE: ***Morisi** c/a in all. Kiwanis stories in #3 & 4. #4 has photo of Gene Autry on-c.*

SUPER MAGIC (Super Magician Comics #2 on)
Street & Smith Publications: May, 1941

	GD	VG	FN	VF	VF/NM	NM-
V1#1-Blackstone the Magician-c/story; origin/1st app. Rex King (Black Fury); Charles Sultan-c; Blackstone-c begin	194	388	582	1242	2121	3000

SUPER MAGICIAN COMICS (Super Magic #1)
Street & Smith Publications: No. 2, Sept, 1941 - V5#8, Feb-Mar, 1947

	GD	VG	FN	VF	VF/NM	NM-
V1#2-Blackstone the Magician continues; Rex King, Man of Adventure app.	71	142	213	454	777	1100
3-Tao-Anwar, Boy Magician begins	45	90	135	284	480	675
4-7,9-12: 4-Origin Transo. 11-Supersnipe app.	41	82	123	256	428	600
8-Abbott & Costello story (1st app?, 11/42)	42	84	126	265	445	625
V2#1-The Shadow app.	41	82	123	260	435	610
2-12: 5-Origin Tigerman. 8-Red Dragon begins	24	48	72	142	234	325
V3#1-12: 5-Origin Mr. Twilight	24	48	72	140	230	320
V4#1-4,6-12: 11-Nigel Elliman Ace of Magic begins (3/46)	20	40	60	114	182	250
5-KKK-c/sty	20	40	60	118	192	265
V5#1-6	20	40	60	114	182	250
7,8-Red Dragon by Edd Cartier-c/a	39	78	117	240	395	550

NOTE: ***Jack Binder** c-1-14(most). Red Dragon c-V5#7, 8.*

SUPERMAN (See Action Comics, Advs. of..., All-New Coll. Ed., All-Star Comics, Best of DC, Brave & the Bold, Cosmic Odyssey, DC Comics Presents, Heroes Against Hunger, JLA, The Kents, Krypton Chronicles, Limited Coll. Ed., Man of Steel, Phantom Zone, Power Record Comics, Special Edition, Steel, Super Friends, Superman: The Man of Steel, Superman: The Man of Tomorrow, Taylor's Christmas Tabloid, Three-Dimension Advs., World Of Krypton, World Of Metropolis, World Of Smallville & World's Finest)

SUPERMAN (Becomes Adventures of...#424 on)
National Periodical Publ./DC Comics: Summer, 1939 - No. 423, Sept, 1986
(#1-5 are quarterly)

	GD	VG	FN	VF	VF/NM	NM-
1(nn)-1st four Action stories reprinted; origin Superman by Siegel & Shuster; has a new 2 pg. origin plus 4 pgs. omitted in Action story; see The Comics Magazine #1 & More Fun #14-17 for Superman prototype app.; cover r/splash page from Action #10; 1st pin-up Superman on back-c - 1st pin-up in comics	40,000	80,000	140,000	350,000	575,000	800,000

1-Reprint, Oversize 13-1/2x10". **WARNING**: This comic is an exact duplicate reprint of the original except for its size. DC published it in 1978 with a second cover titling it as a Famous First Edition. There have been many reported cases of the outer cover being removed and the interior sold as the original edition. The reprint with the new outer cover removed is practically worthless. See Famous First Edition for value.

	GD	VG	FN	VF	VF/NM	NM-
2-All daily strip-r; full pg. ad for N.Y. World's Fair	2250	4500	6750	17,000	35,500	54,000
3-2nd story-r from Action #5; 3rd story-r from Action #6	1250	2500	3750	9500	19,250	29,000
4-2nd mention of Daily Planet (Spr/40); also see Action #23; 2nd & 3rd app. Luthor (red-headed; also see Action #23)	784	1568	2352	5723	10,112	14,500
5-4th Luthor app. (grey hair)	649	1298	1947	4738	8369	12,000
6,7: 6-1st splash pg. in a Superman comic. 7-1st Perry White? (11-12/40)	443	886	1329	3234	5717	8200
8-10: 10-5th app. Luthor (1st bald Luthor, 5-6/41)	411	822	1233	2877	5039	7200
11-13,15: 13-Jimmy Olsen & Luthor app.	309	618	927	2163	3782	5400
14-Patriotic Shield-c classic by Fred Ray	676	1352	2028	4935	8718	12,500
16,19,20: 16-1st Lois Lane-c this title (5-6/42); 2nd Lois-c after Action #29	290	580	870	1856	3178	4500

Superman #96 © DC

Superman #423 © DC

Superman Annual #7 © DC

	GD 2.0	VG 4.0	FN 6.0	VF 8.0	VF/NM 9.0	NM- 9.2
17-Hitler, Hirohito-c	568	1136	1704	4146	7323	10,500
18-Classic WWII-c	300	600	900	2070	3635	5200
21,22,25: 25-Clark Kent's only military service; Fred Ray's only super-hero story	187	374	561	1197	2049	2900
23-Classic periscope-c	300	600	900	1920	3310	4700
24-Classic Jack Burnley flag-c	389	778	1167	2723	4762	6800
26-Classic war-c	300	600	900	2070	3635	5200
27-29: 27,29-Lois Lane-c. 28-Lois Lane Girl Reporter series begins, ends #40,42	161	322	483	1030	1765	2500
28-Overseas edition for Armed Forces; same as reg. #28	161	322	483	1030	1765	2500
30-Origin & 1st app. Mr. Mxyztplk (9-10/44)(pronounced "Mix-it-plk") in comic books; name later became Mxyzptlk ("Mix-yez-pit-l-ick"); the character was inspired by a combination of the name of Al Capp's Joe Blyfstyk (the little man with the black cloud over his head) & the devilish antics of Bugs Bunny; he first app. in newspapers 3/7/44; Superman flies for the first time	297	594	891	1901	3251	4600
31-40: 33-(3-4/45)-3rd app. Mxyztplk. 35,36-Lois Lane-c. 38-Atomic bomb story (1-2/46); delayed because of gov't censorship; Superman shown reading Batman #32 on cover. 40-Mxyztplk-c	129	258	387	826	1413	2000
41-50: 42-Lois Lane-c. 45-Lois Lane as Superwoman (see Action #60 for 1st app.). 46-(5-6/47)-1st app. Superboy this title? 48-1st time Superman travels thru time	110	220	330	704	1202	1700
51,52: 51-Lois Lane-c	102	204	306	653	1114	1575
53-Third telling of Superman origin; 10th anniversary issue ('48); classic origin-c by Boring	331	662	993	2317	4059	5800
54,56-60: 57-Lois Lane as Superwoman-c. 58-Intro Tiny Trix. 59-Early use of heat vision (possibly first time)	102	204	306	653	1114	1575
55-Used in **SOTI**, pg. 33	103	206	309	659	1130	1600
61-Origin Superman retold; origin Green Kryptonite (1st Kryptonite story); Superman returns to Krypton for 1st time & sees his parents for 1st time since infancy, discovers he's not an Earth man	174	348	522	1114	1907	2700
62-70: 62-Orson Welles-c/story. 65-1st Krypton Foes: Mala, Kizo, & U-Ban. 66-2nd Superbaby story. 67-Perry Como-c/story. 68-1st Luthor-c this title (see Action Comics)	100	200	300	640	1095	1550
71-75: 74-2nd Luthor-c this title. 75-Some have #74 on-c	97	194	291	621	1061	1500
76-Batman x-over; Superman & Batman learn each other's I.D. for the 1st time (5-6/52) (also see World's Finest #71)	258	516	774	1651	2826	4000
77-81: 78-Last 52 pg. issue. 81-Used in **POP**, pg. 88. 81-"Superwoman From Space" story	84	168	252	538	919	1300
82-87,89,90: 89-1st Curt Swan-c in title	77	154	231	493	847	1200
88-Prankster, Toyman & Luthor team-up	81	162	243	518	884	1250
91-95: 95-Last precode issue (2/55)	69	138	207	442	759	1075
96-99: 96-Mr. Mxyztplk-c/story	63	126	189	403	689	975
100 (9-10/55)-Shows cover to #1 on-c	252	504	756	1613	2757	3900
101-105,107-110: 109-1st S.A. issue	52	104	156	328	639	950
106 (7/56)-Retells origin	53	106	159	334	630	925
111-120	47	94	141	296	592	850
121,122,124-127,129: 127-Origin/1st app. Titano. 129-Intro/origin Lori Lemaris, The Mermaid	41	82	123	256	503	750
123-Pre-Supergirl tryout-c/story (8/58).	80	160	240	560	1530	2500
128-(4/59)-Red Kryptonite used. Bruce Wayne x-over who protects Superman's i.d. (3rd story)	42	84	126	265	520	775
130-(7/59)-2nd app, Krypto, the Superdog with Superman (see Sup.'s Pal Jimmy Olsen #29) (all other previous app. w/Superboy)	43	86	129	271	528	785
131-139: 135-2nd Lori Lemaris app. 139-Lori Lemaris app.;	34	68	102	199	375	550
140-1st Blue Kryptonite & Bizarro Supergirl; origin Bizarro Jr. #1	34	68	102	206	375	550
141-145,148: 142-2nd Batman x-over	29	58	87	170	341	475
146-(7/61)-Superman's life story; back-up hints at Earth II. Classic-c	39	78	117	235	480	725
147(8/61)-7th Legion app; 1st app. Legion of Super-Villains; 1st app. Adult Legion; swipes-c to Adv. #247	36	72	108	216	408	600
149(11/61)-8th Legion app. (cameo); "The Death of Superman" imaginary story; last 10¢ issue	34	68	102	199	387	575
150,151,153,154,157,159,160: 157-Gold Kryptonite used (see Adv. #299); Mon -El app.; Lightning Lad cameo (11/62)	13	26	39	89	195	300
152,155,156,158,162: 152(4/62)-15th Legion app. 155-(8/62)-Legion app; Lightning Man & Cosmic Man, & Adult Legion app. 156,162-Legion app. 158-1st app. Flamebird & Nightwing & Nor-Kan of Kandor (12/62)	13	26	39	91	201	310
161-1st told death of Ma and Pa Kent	13	26	39	89	195	300
161-2nd printing (1987, $1.25)-New DC logo; sold thru So Much Fun Toy Stores (cover title: Superman Classic)						4.00

	GD 2.0	VG 4.0	FN 6.0	VF 8.0	VF/NM 9.0	NM- 9.2
163-166,168-180: 166-XMas-c. 168-All Luthor issue; JFK tribute/memorial. 169-Bizarro Invasion of Earth-c/story; last Sally Selwyn. 170-Pres. Kennedy story is finally published after delay from #168 due to assassination. 172,173-Legion cameos. 174-Super-Mxyzptlk; Bizarro app. 176-Legion of Super-Pets	10	20	30	69	147	225
167-New origin Brainiac, text reference of Brainiac 5 descending from adopted human son Brainiac II; intro Tharla (later Luthor's wife)	12	24	36	84	185	285
181,182,184-186,188-192,194-196,198,200: 181-1st 2465 story/series. 182-1st S.A. app. of The Toyman (1/66). 189-Origin/destruction of Krypton II.	8	16	24	56	108	160
183 (Giant G-18)	11	22	33	73	157	240
187,193,197 (Giants G-23,G-31,G-36)	9	18	27	59	117	175
199-1st Superman/Flash race (8/67): also see Flash #175 & World's Finest #198,199 (r-in Limited Coll. Ed. C-48)	28	56	84	202	451	700
201,203-206,208-211,213-216: 213-Brainiac-5 app. 216-Last 12¢ issue	6	12	18	37	66	95
202 (80-pg. Giant G-42)-All Bizarro issue	6	12	18	41	76	110
207,212,217 (Giants G-48,G-54,G-60): 207-30th anniversary Superman (6/68)	6	12	18	41	76	110
218-221,223-226,228-231	5	10	15	33	57	80
222,239(Giants, G-66,G-84)	6	12	18	38	69	100
227,232(Giants, G-72,G-78)-All Krypton issues	6	12	18	38	69	100
233-2nd app. Morgan Edge; Clark Kent switches from newspaper reporter to TV newscaster; all Kryptonite on Earth destroyed; classic Neal Adams-c; 1st Fabulous World of Krypton story; Superman pin-up by Swan	9	18	27	61	123	185
234-238	5	10	15	31	53	75
240-Kaluta-a; last 15¢ issue	4	8	12	27	44	60
241-244 (All 52 pgs.): 241-New Wonder Woman app. 243-G.A.-r/#38	4	8	12	28	47	65
245-Also listed as DC 100 Pg. Super Spectacular #7; Air Wave, Kid Eternity, Hawkman-r; Atom-r/Atom #3	9	18	27	60	120	180
246-248,250,251,253 (All 52 pgs.): 246-G.A.-r/#40. 248-World of Krypton story. 251-G.A.-r/#45. 253-Finlay-a, 2 pgs., G.A.-r/#1	4	8	12	28	47	65
249,254-Neal Adams-a. 249-(52 pgs.); 1st app. Terra-Man (Swan-a) & origin-s by Dick Dillin (p) & Neal Adams (inks)	5	10	15	35	63	90
252-Also listed as DC 100 Pg. Super Spectacular #13; Ray(r/Smash #17), Black Condor, (r/Crack #18), Hawkman(r/Flash #24); Starman-r/Adv. #67; Dr. Fate & Spectre-r/More Fun #57; N. Adams-c	10	20	30	66	138	210
255-271,273-277,279-283: 263-Photo-c. 264-1st app. Steve Lombard. 276-Intro Capt. Thunder. 279-Batman, Batgirl app. 282-Luthor battlesuit	3	6	9	14	19	24
272,278,284-All 100 pgs. G.A.-r in all. 272-r/2nd app. Mr. Mxyztplk from Action #80	5	10	15	30	50	70
285-299: 289-Partial photo-c. 292-Origin Lex Luthor retold	2	4	6	9	13	16
300-(6/76) Superman in the year 2001	3	6	9	19	30	40
301-316,318-350: 301,320-Solomon Grundy app. 323-Intro. Atomic Skull. 327-329-(44 pgs.). 327-Kobra app. 330-More facts revealed about I.D. 331,332-1st/2nd app. Master Jailer. 335-Mxyzptlk marries Ms. Bgbznz. 336-Rose & Thorn app. 338-(8/79) 40th Anniv. issue; the bottled city of Kandor enlarged. 344-Frankenstein & Dracula app.	1	3	4	6	8	10
317-Neal Adams kryptonite cover	2	4	6	9	13	16
321-323,325-327,329-332,335-345,348,350 (Whitman variants; low print run; no issue # on cover)	2	4	6	9	13	16
351-399: 353-Brief origin. 354,355,357-Superman 2020 stories (354-Debut of Superman III). 356-World of Krypton story (also #360,367,375). 366-Fan letter by Todd McFarlane. 369-Christmas-c. 372-Superman 2021 story. 376-Free 16 pg. preview Daring New Advs. of Supergirl. 377-Free 16 pg. preview Masters of the Universe	1	2	3	4	5	7
400 (10/84, $1.50, 68 pgs.)-Many top artists featured; Chaykin painted cover, Miller back-c; Steranko-s/a (10 pages)	1	3	4	6	8	10
401-422: 405-Super-Batman story. 408-Nuclear Holocaust-c/story. 411-Special Julius Schwartz tribute issue. 414,415-Crisis x-over. 422-Horror-c						6.00
409-(7/85) Variant-c with Superman/Superhombre logo	(no reported sales)					
423-Alan Moore scripts; Curt Swan-a/George Pérez-a(i); "Whatever Happened to the Man of Tomorrow?" story, cont'd in Action #583	2	4	6	8	10	12
Annual 1(10/60, 84 pgs.)-Reprints 1st Supergirl story/Action #252; r/Lois Lane #1; Krypto-r (1st Silver Age DC annual)	80	160	240	640	1445	2250
Annual 2(Win, 1960-61)-Super-villain issue; Brainiac, Titano, Metallo, Bizarro origin-r	35	70	105	252	564	875
Annual 3(Sum, 1961)-Strange Lives of Superman	23	46	69	164	362	560
Annual 4(Win, 1961-62)-11th Legion app; 1st Legion origins (text & pictures); advs. in time, space & on alien worlds	20	40	60	135	300	465
Annual 5(Sum, 1962)-All Krypton issue	16	32	48	112	249	385
Annual 6(Win, 1962-63)-Legion-r/Adv. #247	14	28	42	97	214	330
Annual 7(Sum, 1963)-Silver Anniversary Issue; origin-r/Superman-Batman team/Adv. #275;						

Superman (2nd series) #7 © DC

Superman (2nd series) #201 © DC

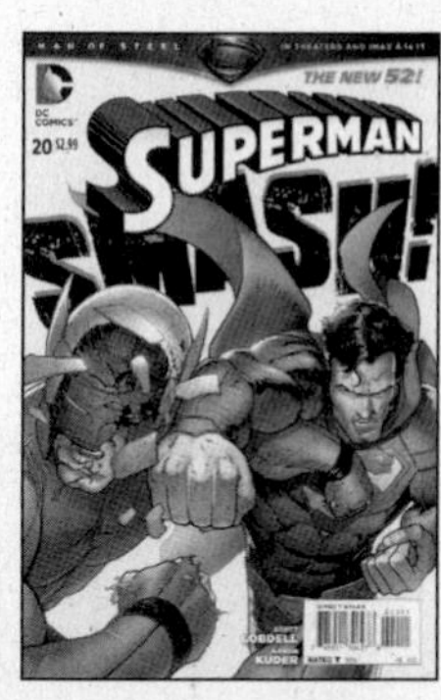

Superman (2011 series) #20 © DC

GD VG FN VF VF/NM NM-
2.0 4.0 6.0 8.0 9.0 9.2

cover gallery of famous issues 11 22 33 76 163 250
Annual 8(Win, 1963-64)-All origins issue 10 20 30 69 147 225
Annual 9(8/64)-Was advertised but came out as 80 Page Giant #1 instead
Annual 9(1983)-Toth/Austin-a 1 2 3 4 5 7
Annuals 10-12: 10(1984, $1.25)-M. Anderson-i. 11(1985)-Moore-s. 12(1986)-Bolland-c 6.00
Special 1-3('83-'85): 1-G. Kane-c/a; contains German-r 6.00
The Amazing World of Superman "Official Metropolis Edition" (1973, $2.00, treasury-size)-
Origin retold; Wood-r(i) from Superboy #153,161; poster incl. (half price if poster missing)
4 8 12 27 44 60
11195 (2/79, $1.95, 224 pgs.)-Golden Press 4 8 12 23 37 50
NOTE: **N. Adams** *a-249i, 254p; c-204-206, 210, 212-215, 219, 231i, 233-237, 240-243, 249-252, 254, 263, 307, 308, 313, 314, 317.* **Adkins** *a-323i.* **Austin** *c-368i.* **Wayne Boring** *art-late 1940's to early 1960's.* **Buckler** *a(p)-352, 363, 364, 369; c(p)-324-327, 356, 363, 368, 369, 373, 376, 378.* **Burnley** *a-252r; c-19-25, 30, 33, 34, 35p, 38p, 39p, 45p.* **Fine** *a-252r.* **Kaluta** *a-400.* **Gil Kane** *a-272r, 367, 372, 375, Special 2; c-374p, 375p, 377, 381, 382, 384-390, 392, Annual 9, Special 2.* **Joe Kubert** *c-216.* **Morrow** *a-238.* **Mortimer** *a-250r.* **Perez** *c-364p.* **Fred Ray** *a-25; c-6, 8-18.* **Starlin** *c-355.* **Staton** *a-354i, 355i.* **Swan/Moldoff** *c-149.* **Williamson** *a(i)-408-410, 412-416; c-408i, 409i.* **Wrightson** *a-400, 416.*

SUPERMAN (2nd Series) (Title continues numbering from Adventures of Superman #649)
DC Comics: Jan, 1987 - No. 226, Apr, 2006; No. 650, May, 2006 - No. 714, Oct, 2011

0-(10/94) Zero Hour; released between #93 & #94 3.00
1-Byrne-c/a begins; intro new Metallo 1 2 3 5 6 8
2-8,10: 3-Legends x-over; Darkseid-c & app. 7-Origin/1st app. Rampage. 8-Legion app. 4.00
9-Joker-c 5.00
11-15,17-20,22-49,51,52,54-56,58-67: 11-1st new Mr. Mxyzptlk. 12-Lori Lemaris revived. 13-1st app. new Toyman. 13,14-Millennium x-over. 20-Doom Patrol app.; Supergirl cameo. 31-Mr. Mxyzptlk app. 37-Newsboy Legion app. 41-Lobo app. 44-Batman storyline, part 1. 45-Free extra 8 pgs. 54-Newsboy Legion story. 63-Aquaman x-over. 67-Last $1.00-c 3.00
16,21: 16-1st app. new Supergirl (4/88). 21-Supergirl-c/story; 1st app. Matrix who becomes new Supergirl 4.00
50-($1.50, 52 pgs.)-Clark Kent proposes to Lois 5.00
50-2nd printing 4.00
53-Clark reveals i.d. to Lois (Cont'd from Action #662) 4.00
53-2nd printing 3.00
57-($1.75, 52 pgs.) 4.00
68-72: 65,66,68-Deathstroke-c/stories. 70-Superman & Robin team-up 3.00
73-Doomsday cameo 6.00
74-Doomsday Pt. 2 (Cont'd from Justice League #69); Superman battles Doomsday
1 2 3 5 6 8
73,74-2nd printings 3.00
75-($2.50)-Collector's Ed.; Doomsday Pt. 6; Superman dies; polybagged w/poster of funeral, obituary from Daily Planet, postage stamp & armband premiums (direct sales only)
2 4 6 11 16 20
75-Direct sales copy (no upc code, 1st print) 1 3 4 6 8 10
75-Direct sales copy (no upc code, 2nd-4th prints) 4.00
75-Newsstand copy w/upc code 1 3 4 6 8 10
75-Platinum Edition; given away to retailers 5 10 15 35 63 90
76,77-Funeral For a Friend parts 4 & 8 4.00
78-($1.95)-Collector's Edition with die-cut outer-c & mini poster; Doomsday cameo 4.00
78-($1.50)-Newsstand Edition w/poster and different-c; Doomsday-c & cameo 3.00
79-81,83-89: 83-Funeral for a Friend epilogue; new Batman (Azrael) cameo. 87,88-Bizarro-c/story 3.00
82-($3.50)-Collector's Edition w/all chromium-c; real Superman revealed; Green Lantern x-over from G.L. #46; no ads 6.00
82-($2.00, 44 pgs.)-Regular Edition w/different-c 4.00
90-99: 93-(9/94)-Zero Hour. 94-(11/94). 95-Atom app. 96-Brainiac returns 3.00
100-Death of Clark Kent foil-c 4.00
100-Newsstand 3.00
101-122: 101-Begin $1.95-c; Black Adam app. 105-Green Lantern app. 110-Plastic Man-c/app. 114-Brainiac app; Dwyer-c. 115-Lois leaves Metropolis. 116-(10/96)-1st app. Teen Titans by Jurgens & Perez in 8 pg. preview. 117-Final Night. 118-Wonder Woman app. 119-Legion app. 122-New powers 3.00
123-Collector's Edition w/glow in the dark-c, new costume 6.00
123-Standard ed., new costume 4.00
124-149: 128-Cyborg-c/app. 131-Birth of Lena Luthor. 132-Superman Red/Superman Blue. 134-Millennium Giants. 136,137-Superman 2999. 139-Starlin-a. 140-Grindberg-a 3.00
150-($2.95) Standard Ed.; Brainiac 2.0 app.; Jurgens-s 4.00
150-($3.95) Collector's Ed. w/holo-foil enhanced variant-c 5.00
151-158: 151-Loeb-s begins; Daily Planet reopens 3.00
159-174: 159-$2.25-c begin. 161-Joker-c/app. 162-Aquaman-c/app. 163-Young Justice app. 165-JLA app.; Ramos; Madureira, Liefeld, A. Adams, Wieringo, Churchill-a. 166-Collector's and reg. editions. 167-Return to Krypton. 168-Batman-c/app.(cont'd in Detective #756). 171-173-Our Worlds at War. 173-Sienkiewicz-a (2 pgs.). 174-Adopts black & red "S" logo 3.00
175-($3.50) Joker: Last Laugh x-over; Doomsday-c/app. 4.00
176-189,191-199: 176,180-Churchill-a. 180-Dracula app. 181-Bizarro-c/app. 184-Return to Krypton II. 189-Van Fleet-c. 192,193,195,197-199-New Supergirl app. 3.00
190-($2.25) Regular edition 3.00
190-($3.95) Double-Feature Issue; included reprint of Superman: The 10¢ Adventure 4.00
200-($3.50) Gene Ha-c/art by various; preview art by Yu & Bermejo 4.00
201-Mr Majestic-c/app.; cover swipe of Action #1 3.00
202,203-Godfall parts 3,6; Turner-c; Caldwell-a(p). 203-Jim Lee sketch pages 3.00
204-Jim Lee-c/a begins; Azzarello-s 3.00
204-Diamond Retailer Summit edition with sketch-c 5 10 15 31 53 75
205-214: 205-Two covers by Jim Lee and Michael Turner. 208-JLA app. 211-Battles Wonder Woman 3.00
215-($2.99) Conclusion to Azzarello/Lee arc 4.00
216-218,220-226: 216-Captain Marvel app. 221-Bizarro & Zoom app. 226-Earth-2 Superman story; Chaykin,Sale, Benes, Ordway-a 3.00
219-Omac/Sacrifice pt. 1; JLA app. 4.00
219-2nd printing with red background variant-c 3.00
(Title continues numbering from Adventures of Superman #649)
650-(5/06) One Year Later; Clark powerless after Infinite Crisis 4.00
651-665,667-669,671-674.676-680: 652-Begin $2.99-c. 654-658,662-664,667-Pacheco-a. 665-Origin of Jimmy Olsen. 671-673-Insect Queen. 676-680-Ross-c 3.00
666, 670,675-($3.99) 666-Simonson-a. 670-The Third Kryptonian. 675-Ross-c 4.00
681-699: 681-683-New Krypton x-over; Ross-c. 685-Mon-El freed from Phantom Zone. 694-Mon-El new costume. 698,699-Last Stand of New Krypton x-over 3.00
700-(8/10, $4.99) Cover by Gary Frank; Robinson-s; Straczynski-s begin 5.00
700-Variant-c by Risso 8.00
701-714: 701-"Grounded" begins; Straczynski-s/Cassaday-c. 704,706-Wilson-s 3.00
701-DC 75th Variant-c by Cassaday (Superman #1 swipe) 8.00
#1,000,000 (11/98) 853rd Century x-over; Gene Ha-c 3.00
Annual 1,2: 1 (1987)-No Byrne-a. 2 (1988)-Byrne-a; Newsboy Legion; Guardian returns 4.00
Annual 3-6 ('91-'94 68 pgs.): 1-Armageddon 2001 x-over; Batman app.; Austin-c(i) & part inks. 4-Eclipso app. 6-Elseworlds sty 4.00
Annual 3-2nd & 3rd printings; 3rd has silver ink 4.00
Annual 7 (1995, $3.95, 69 pgs.)-Year One story 4.00
Annual 8 (1996, $2.95)-Legends of the Dead Earth story 4.00
Annual 9 (1997, $3.95)-Pulp Heroes story 4.00
Annual 10 (1998, $2.95)-Ghosts; Wrightson-c 4.00
Annual 11 (1999, $2.95)-JLApe; Art Adams-c 4.00
Annual 12 (2000, $3.50)-Planet DC 4.00
Annual 13 (1/08, $3.99) Finale of Camelot Falls 4.00
Annual 14 (10/09, $3.99) Origin of Mon-El re-told; Pina-a/Guedes-c 4.00
...: 80 Page Giant (2/99, $4.95) Jurgens-c 6.00
...: 80 Page Giant 1 (5/10, $5.99) Lopresti-c; short stories by various 6.00
...: 80 Page Giant 2 (6/99, $4.95) Harris-c 6.00
...: 80 Page Giant 3 (11/00, $5.95) Nowlan-c; art by various 6.00
...: 80 Page Giant 2011 (4/11, $5.99) Nguyen-c; art by various; Bizarros app. 6.00
Special 1 (1992, $3.50, 68 pgs.)-Simonson-c/a 6.00

SUPERMAN (DC New 52)
DC Comics: Nov, 2011 - Present ($2.99)

1-Pérez-s/c; Merino-a 2 4 6 9 12 15
1-Variant-c by Jim Lee 15.00
2-23: 3-6-Nicola Scott-a. 6-Supergirl app. 13-Clark quits job. 14-17-H'El on Earth x-over with Superboy & Supergirl. 17-H'El on Earth conclusion. 19,20-Orion app. 3.00
23.1, 23.2, 23.3, 23.4 (11/13, $2.99, regular covers) 3.00
23.1 (11/13, $3.99, 3-D cover) "Bizarro #1" on cover; Fisch-s/Kuder-c/Jeff Johnson-a 5.00
23.2 (11/13, $3.99, 3-D cover) "Brainiac #1" on cover; origin; Bedard-s/Alixe-a 5.00
23.3 (11/13, $3.99, 3-D cover) "H'El #1" on cover; Jor-El app.; Lobdell-s/Jurgens-a 5.00
23.4 (11/13, $3.99, 3-D cover) "Parasite #1" on cover; origin; Kuder-s/a 5.00
24-29: 25-Krypton Returns pt. 4. 26,27-Parasite app. 28,29-Starfire app. 3.00
#0-(11/12, $2.99) Jor-El & Lara flashback on Krypton; Rocafort-a/c 3.00
Annual 1 (10/12, $4.99) Alixe-a/Rocafort-c; Helspont app. 5.00
Annual 2 (9/13, $4.99) Jurgens-a/Andy Kubert-c; Brainiac app. 5.00

SUPERMAN (Hardcovers and Trade Paperbacks)
... and the Legion of Super-Heroes HC (2008, $24.99) r/Action Comics #858-863, covers and variants; intro. by Giffen; Gary Frank design sketch pages 25.00
... and the Legion of Super-Heroes SC (2009, $14.99) same contents as HC 15.00
...: Back in Action TPB (2007, $14.99) r/Action Comics #841-843 and DC Comics Presents #4,17,24; commentary by Busiek 15.00
.../Batman: Saga of the Super Sons TPB (2007, $19.99) r/Super Sons stories from '70s World's Finest #215,216,221,222,224,228,230,231,233,242,263 & Elseworlds 80-Page Giant 20.00
...: Brainiac HC (2009, $19.99, dustjacket) r/Action Comics #866-870 & Superman: New Krypton Special #1 20.00
...: Brainiac SC (2010, $12.99) r/Action #866-870 & Superman: New Krypton Spec. #1 13.00
...: Camelot Falls HC (2007, $19.99, dustjacket) r/Superman #654-658 20.00
...: Camelot Falls SC (2008, $12.99) r/Superman #654-658 13.00

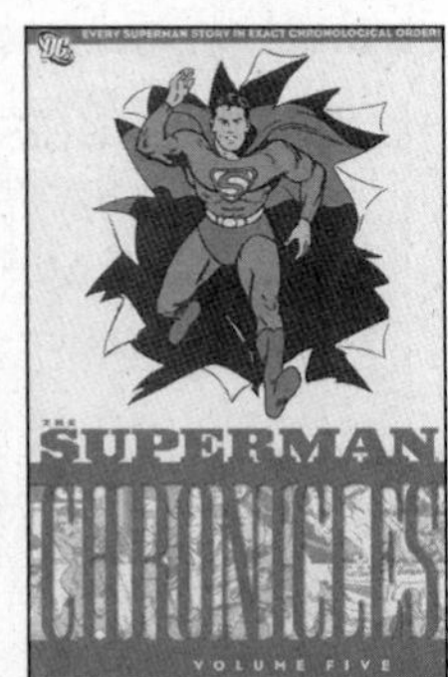

Superman: Chronicles Vol. 5 © DC

Superman: Tales From the Phantom Zone © DC

Superman: Unconventional Warfare © DC

GD VG FN VF VF/NM NM-
2.0 4.0 6.0 8.0 9.0 9.2

...: Camelot Falls Vol. 2 HC (2008, $19.99, dj) r/Superman #662-664,667 & Ann. #13 20.00
...: Camelot Falls Vol. 2 The Weight of the World SC (2008, $12.99) r/Superman #662-664,667 & Ann. #13 13.00
...: Chronicles Vol. 1 ('06, $14.99, TPB) r/early Superman app. in Action Comics #1-13, New York World's Fair 1939 and Superman #1 15.00
...: Chronicles Vol. 2 ('07, $14.99, TPB) r/early Superman app. in Action Comics #14-20 and Superman #2,3 15.00
...: Chronicles Vol. 3 ('07, $14.99, TPB) r/early Superman app. in Action Comics #21-25, Superman #3,4 and New York World's Fair 1940 15.00
...: Chronicles Vol. 4 ('08, $14.99, TPB) r/early Superman app. in Action Comics #26-31, Superman #6,7 15.00
...: Chronicles Vol. 5 ('08, $14.99, TPB) r/early Superman app. in Action Comics #32-36, Superman #8,9 and World's Best Comics #1 15.00
...: Chronicles Vol. 6 ('09, $14.99, TPB) r/early Superman app. in Action Comics #37-40, Superman #10,11 and World's Finest Comics #2,3 15.00
...: Chronicles Vol. 7 ('09, $14.99, TPB) r/early Superman app. in Action Comics #41-43, Superman #12,13 and World's Finest Comics #4 15.00
...: Chronicles Vol. 8 ('10, $14.99, TPB) r/early Superman app. in Action Comics #44-47, and Superman #14,15 15.00
...: Chronicles Vol. 9 ('11, $17.99, TPB) r/early Superman app. in Action Comics #48-52, and Superman #16,17 and World's Finest Comics #6 18.00
...: Codename: Patriot HC ('10, $24.99, d.j.) r/partial New Krypton storyline 25.00
...: Codename: Patriot SC ('11, $14.99) r/partial New Krypton storyline 15.00
...: Critical Condition ('03, $14.95, TPB) r/2000 Kryptonite poisoning storyline 15.00
.../ Doomsday: The Collection Edition (2006, $19.99) r/Superman/Doomsday: Hunter/Prey #1-3, Doomsday Ann. #1, Superman: The Doomsday Wars #1-3, Advs. of Superman #594 and Superman #175; intro. by Dan Jurgens 20.00
...: Daily Planet (2006, $19.99, TPB)-Reprints stories of Daily Planet staff 20.00
... Earth One HC (2010, $19.99)-Updated re-imagining of Superman's debut in Metropolis; Straczynski-s/Shane Davis-a; sketch pages by Davis 20.00
... Earth One Volume Two HC (2012, $22.99)-Straczynski-s/Davis-a; sketch pages 23.00
...: Emperor Joker TPB (2007, $14.99) reprints 2000 x-over from Superman titles 15.00
...: Endgame (2000, $14.95, TPB)-Reprints Y2K and Brainiac story line 15.00
...: Ending Battle (2009, $14.99, TPB) r/crossover of Superman titles from 2002 15.00
...: Eradication! The Origin of the Eradicator (1996, $12.95, TPB) 13.00
...: Escape From Bizarro World HC (2008, $24.99, dustjacket) r/Action #855-857; early apps. in Superman #140, DC Comics Presents #71 and Man of Steel #5; Vaughan intro. 25.00
...: Escape From Bizarro World SC (2009, $14.99) same contents as hardcover 15.00
...: Exile (1998, $14.95, TPB)-Reprints space exile following execution of Kryptonian criminals; 1st Eradicator 15.00
...: For Tomorrow Volume 1 HC (2005, $24.99, dustjacket) r/#204-209; intro by Azzarello; new cover and sketch section by Lee 25.00
...: For Tomorrow Volume 1 SC (2005, $14.99) r/#204-209; foil-stamped S emblem-c 15.00
...: For Tomorrow Volume 2 HC (2005, $24.99, dustjacket) r/#210-215; afterword and sketch section by Lee; new Lee-c with foil-stamped S emblem 25.00
...: For Tomorrow Volume 2 SC (2005, $14.99) r/#210-215; foil-stamped S emblem-c 15.00
...: Godfall HC (2004, $19.95, dustjacket) r/Action #812-813, Advs. of Superman #625-626, Superman #202-203; Caldwell sketch pages; Turner cover gallery; new Turner-c 20.00
...: Godfall SC (2004, $9.99) r/Action #812-813, Advs. of Superman #625-626, Superman #202-203; Caldwell sketch pages; Turner cover gallery; new Turner-c 10.00
...: Infinite Crisis TPB (2006, $12.99) r/Infinite Crisis #5, I.C. Secret Files and Origins 2006, Action Comics #836, Superman #226 and Advs. of Superman #649 13.00
... In the Forties ('05, $19.99, TPB) Intro. by Bob Hughes 20.00
... In the Fifties ('02, $19.95, TPB) Intro. by Mark Waid 20.00
... In the Sixties ('01, $19.95, TPB) Intro. by Mark Waid 20.00
... In the Seventies ('00, $19.95, TPB) Intro. by Christopher Reeve 20.00
... In the Eighties ('06, $19.99, TPB) Intro. by Jerry Ordway 20.00
... In the Name of Gog ('05, $17.99, TPB) r/Action Comics #820-825 18.00
... Kryptonite HC ('08, $24.99) r/Superman Confidential #1-5,11; Darwyn Cooke intro. 25.00
...: Last Son HC (2008, $19.99) r/Action Comics #844-846,851 and Annual #11; sketch pages and variant covers; Marc McClure intro. 20.00
... Mon-El HC ('10, $24.99) r/Superman #684-690, Action #874 & Annual #1, Superman: Secret Files 2009 #1 25.00
... Mon-El SC ('11, $17.99) r/Superman #684-690, Action #874 & Annual #1, Superman: Secret Files 2009 #1 18.00
... Mon-El - Man of Valor HC ('10, $24.99) r/Superman #692-697 & Annual #14, Adventure #11, Superman: Secret Files 2009 #1 25.00
... : New Krypton Vol. 1 HC ('09, $24.99, d.j.) r/Superman #681, Action #871 & one-shots 25.00
... : New Krypton Vol. 1 SC ('10, $17.99) r/Superman #681, Action #871 & one-shots 18.00
... : New Krypton Vol. 2 HC ('09, $24.99, d.j.) r/Superman #682,683, Action #872,873 & Supergirl #35,36; gallery of covers and variants 25.00
... : New Krypton Vol. 2 SC ('10, $17.99) same contents as HC 18.00
... : New Krypton Vol. 3 HC ('10, $24.99, d.j.) r/Superman: World of New Krypton #1-5 & Action Comics Annual #10; gallery of covers and variants 25.00
... : New Krypton Vol. 3 SC ('11, $17.99) same contents as HC 18.00
... : New Krypton Vol. 4 HC ('10, $24.99, d.j.) r/Superman: World of New Krypton #6-12; gallery of covers and variants; sketch and design art 25.00
... : New Krypton Vol. 4 SC ('11, $17.99) same contents as HC 18.00
... : Nightwing and Flamebird HC ('10, $24.99, d.j.) r/Action #875-879 & Annual #12 25.00
... : Nightwing and Flamebird SC ('10, $17.99) r/Action #875-879 & Annual #12 18.00
... : Nightwing and Flamebird Vol. 2 HC ('10, $24.99, d.j.) r/Action #883-889, Superman #696 & Adventure Comics #8-10 25.00
... No Limits ('00, $14.95, TPB) Reprints early 2000 stories 15.00
...: Our Worlds at War Book 1 ('02, $19.95, TPB) r/1st half of x-over 20.00
...: Our Worlds at War Book 2 ('02, $19.95, TPB) r/2nd half of x-over 20.00
...: Our Worlds at War - The Complete Collection ('06, $24.99, TPB) r/entire x-over 25.00
...: Past and Future (2008, $19.99, TPB) r/time travel stories 1947-1983 20.00
...: President Lex TPB (2003, $17.95) r/Luthor's run for the White House; Harris-c 18.00
...: Redemption TPB (2007, $12.99) r/Superman #659,666 & Action Comics #848,849 13.00
...: Return to Krypton (2004, $17.95, TPB) r/2001-2002 x-over 18.00
...: Sacrifice (2005, $14.99, TPB) prelude x-over to Infinite Crisis; r/Superman #218-220, Advs. of Superman #642,643; Action #829, Wonder Woman #219,220 15.00
...: Shadows Linger (2008, $14.99, TPB) r/Superman #671-675 15.00
... : Strange Attractors (2006, $14.99, TPB) r/Action Comics #827,828,830-835 15.00
... : Tales From the Phantom Zone ('09, $19.99, TPB) r/Phantom Zone stories 1961-68 20.00
...: That Healing Touch TPB (2005, $14.99) r/Advs. of Superman #633-638 & Superman Secret Files 2004 15.00
...: The Adventures of Nightwing and Flamebird TPB (2009, $19.99)-reprints appearances in Superman Family #173,183-194 20.00
...: The Black Ring Volume One HC (2011, $19.99, d.j.) r/Action Comics #890-895 20.00
The Bottle City of Kandor TPB (2007, $14.99)-Reprints 1st app. in Action #242 and other stories; Nightwing and Flamebird app. 15.00
The Coming of Atlas HC (2009, $19.99, dustjacket)-r/Superman #677-680 & Atlas' debut from First Issue Special #1 (1975); intro by James Robinson 20.00
The Coming of Atlas SC (2010, $14.99) same contents as HC 15.00
The Death of Clark Kent (1997, $19.95, TPB)-Reprints Man of Steel #43 (1 page), Superman #99 (1 page),#100-102, Action #709 (1 page), #710,711, Advs. of Superman #523-525, Superman:The Man of Tomorrow #1 20.00
The Death of Superman (1993, $4.95, TPB)-Reprints Man of Steel #17-19, Superman #73-75, Advs. of Superman #496,497, Action #683,684, & Justice League #69
2 4 6 9 12 15
The Death of Superman, 2nd & 3rd printings 1 3 4 6 8 10
The Death of Superman Platinum Edition 25.00
...: The Greatest Stories Ever Told ('04, $19.95, TPB) Ross-c, Uslan intro. 20.00
...: The Greatest Stories Ever Told Vol. 2 ('06, $19.99, TPB) Ross-c, Greenberger intro. 20.00
...: The Journey ('06, $14.99, TPB) r/Action Comics #831 & Superman #217,221-225 15.00
...: The Man of Steel Vol. 2 ('03, $19.95, TPB) r/Superman #1-3, Action #584-586, Advs. of Superman #424-426 & Who's Who Update '87 20.00
...: The Man of Steel Vol. 3 ('04, $19.95, TPB) r/Superman #4-6, Action #587-589, Advs. of Superman #427-429; intro. by Ordway; new Ordway-c 20.00
...: The Man of Steel Vol. 4 ('05, $19.99, TPB) r/Superman #7,8; Action #590,591; Advs. of Superman #430,431; Legion of Super-Heroes #37,38; new Ordway-c 20.00
...: The Man of Steel Vol. 5 ('06, $19.99, TPB) r/Superman #9-11, Action #592-593, Advs. of Superman #432-435; intro. by Mike Carlin; new Ordway-c 20.00
...: The Man of Steel Vol. 6 ('08, $19.99, TPB) r/Superman #12 & Ann. #1, Action #594-595 & Ann. #1, Advs. of Superman Ann.#1; Booster Gold #23; new Ordway-c 20.00
The Third Kryptonian ('08, $14.99, TPB) r/Action #847, Superman #668-670 & Ann. #13 15.00
The Trial of Superman ('97, $14.95, TPB) reprints story arc 15.00
The World of Krypton ('08, $14.99, TPB) r/World of Krypton Vol. 2 #1-4 and various tales of Krypton and its history; Kupperberg intro. 15.00
The Wrath of Gog ('05, $14.99, TPB) reprints Action Comics #812-819 15.00
...: They Saved Luthor's Brain ('00, $14.95) r/ "death" and return of Luthor 15.00
...: 3-2-1 Action! ('08, $14.99) Jimmy Olsen super-powered stories; Steve Rude-c 15.00
...: 'Til Death Do Us Part ('01, $17.95) reprints; Mahnke-c 18.00
...: Time and Time Again (1994, $7.50, TPB)-Reprints 10.00
...: Transformed ('98, $12.95, TPB) r/post Final Night powerless Superman to Electric Superman 13.00
...: Unconventional Warfare (2005, $14.95, TPB) r/Adventures of Superman #625-632 and pages from Superman Secret Files 2004 15.00
...: Up, Up and Away! (2006, $14.99, TPB) r/Superman #650-653 and Action #837-840 15.00
... Vs. Brainiac (2008, $19.99, TPB) reprints 1st meeting in Action #242 and other duels 20.00
... Vs. Lex Luthor (2006, $19.99, TPB) reprints 1st meeting in Action #23 and 11 other classic duels 1940-2001 20.00
... Vs. The Flash (2005, $19.99, TPB) reprints their races from Superman #199, Flash #175, World's Finest #198, DC Comics Presents #1&2, Advs. of Superman #463 & DC First: Flash/Superman; new Alex Ross-c 20.00
... Vs. The Revenge Squad (1999, $12.95, TPB) 13.00
...: Whatever Happened to the Man of Tomorrow? TPB (1/97, $5.99) r/Superman #423 &

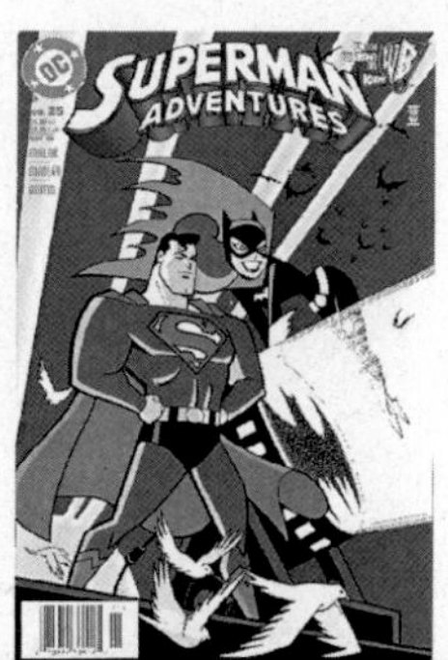

Superman Adventures #25 © DC

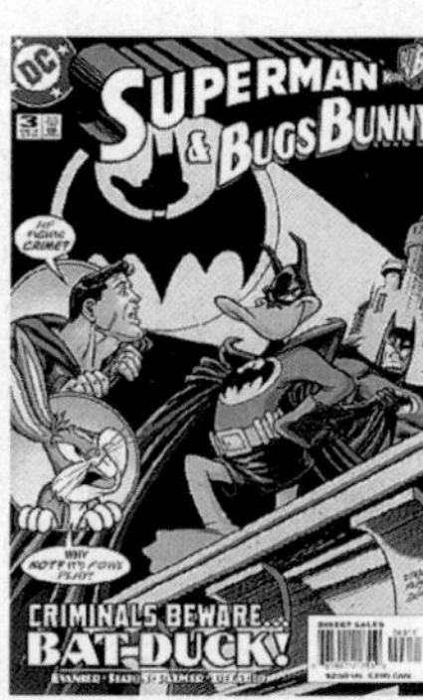

Superman & Bugs Bunny #3 © DC & WB

Superman / Batman #9 © DC

	GD 2.0	VG 4.0	FN 6.0	VF 8.0	VF/NM 9.0	NM- 9.2

Action Comics #583, intro. by Paul Kupperberg 8.00
...: Whatever Happened to the Man of Tomorrow? Deluxe Edition HC (2009, $24.99, d.j.) r/Superman #423, Action #583, DC Comics Presents #85, Superman Ann #11 25.00
...: Whatever Happened to the Man of Tomorrow? SC (2010, $14.99) r/same as HC 15.00
NOTE: ***Austin*** *a(i)-1-3.* ***Byrne*** *a-1-16p, 17, 19-21p, 22; c-1-17, 20-22; scripts-1-22.* ***Guice*** *c/a-64.* ***Kirby*** *c-37p.* ***Joe Quesada*** *c-Annual 4.* ***Russell*** *c/a-23i.* ***Simonson*** *c-69i. #19-21 2nd printings sold in multi-packs.*

SUPERMAN (one-shots)
Daily News Magazine Presents DC Comics' Superman nn-(1987, 8 pgs.)-Supplement to New York Daily News; Perez-c/a 5.00
...: A Nation Divided (1999, $4.95)-Elseworlds Civil War story 5.00
... & Savage Dragon: Chicago (2002, $5.95) Larsen-a; Ross-c 6.00
... & Savage Dragon: Metropolis (11/99, $4.95) Bogdanove-a 5.00
...: At Earth's End (1995, $4.95)-Elseworlds story 5.00
...Beyond #0 (10/11, $3.99) The Batman Beyond future; Frenz-a/Nguyen-c 4.00
...: Blood of My Ancestors (2003, $6.95)-Gil Kane & John Buscema-a 7.00
...: Distant Fires (1998, $5.95)-Elseworlds; Chaykin-s 6.00
...: Emperor Joker (10/00, $3.50)-Follows Action #769 4.00
...: End of the Century (2/00, $24.95, HC)-Immonen-s/a 25.00
...: End of the Century (2003, $17.95, SC)-Immonen-s/a 18.00
... For Earth (1991, $4.95, 52 pgs, printed on recycled paper)-Ordway wraparound-c 6.00
...IV Movie Special (1987, $2.00)-Movie adaptation; Heck-a 4.00
...Gallery, The 1 (1993, $2.95)-Poster-a 3.00
..., Inc. (1999, $6.95)-Elseworlds Clark as a sports hero; Garcia-Lopez-a 7.00
...: Infinite City HC (2005, $24.99, dustjacket) Mike Kennedy-s/Carlos Meglia-a 25.00
...: Infinite City SC (2006, $17.99) Mike Kennedy-s/Carlos Meglia-a 18.00
...: Kal (1995, $5.95)-Elseworlds story 6.00
...: Lex 2000 (1/01, $3.50) Election night for the Luthor Presidency 4.00
...: Lois Lane 1 (4/14, $4.99) Marguerite Bennett-s; Rocafort-c 5.00
...: Monster (1999, $5.95)-Elseworlds story; Anthony Williams-a 6.00
... Movie Special-(9/83)-Adaptation of Superman III; other versions exist with store logos on bottom 1/3 of-c 4.00
...: New Krypton Special 1-(12/08, $3.99) Funeral of Pa Kent; newly enlarged Kandor 4.00
...: Our Worlds at War Secret Files 1-(8/01, $5.95)-Stories & profile pages 6.00
... Plus 1(2/97, $2.95)-Legion of Super-Heroes-c/app. 4.00
...'s Metropolis-(1996, $5.95, prestige format)-Elseworlds; McKeever-c/a 6.00
...: Speeding Bullets-(1993, $4.95, 52 pgs.)-Elseworlds 6.00
.../Spider-Man-(1995, $3.95)-r/DC and Marvel Presents... 4.00
... 10-Cent Adventure 1 (3/02, 10¢) McDaniel-a; intro. Cir-El Supergirl 3.00
...: The Earth Stealers 1-(1988, $2.95, 52 pgs, prestige format) Byrne script; painted-c 6.00
...: The Earth Stealers 1-2nd printing 4.00
...: The Legacy of Superman #1 (3/93, $2.50, 68 pgs.)-Art Adams-c; Simonson-a 6.00
...: The Last God of Krypton ('99,$4.95) Hildebrandt Bros.-a/Simonson-s 5.00
...: The Last Son of Krypton FCBD Special Edition (7/13) r/Action #844; Jim Lee-c 3.00
...: The Odyssey ('99, $4.95) Clark Kent's post-Smallville journey 5.00
...: 3-D (12/98, $3.95)-with glasses 4.00
.../Thundercats (1/04, $5.95) Winick-s/Garza-a; two covers by Garza & McGuinness 6.00
.../Through the Ages (2006, $3.99) r/Action #1, Superman ('87) #7; origins and pin-ups 4.00
.../Toyman-(1996, $1.95) 3.00
...: True Brit (2004, $24.95, HC w/dust jacket) Elseworlds; Kal-El's rocket lands in England; co-written by John Cleese and Kim Howard Johnson; John Byrne-a 25.00
...: True Brit (2005, $17.99, TPB) Elseworlds; Kal-El's rocket lands in England 18.00
...: Under A Yellow Sun (1994, $5.95, 68 pgs.)-A Novel by Clark Kent; embossed-c 6.00
... Vs. Darkseid: Apokolips Now! 1 (3/03, $2.95) McKone-a; Kara (Supergirl #75) app. 4.00
...: War of the Worlds (1999, $5.95)-Battles Martians 6.00
...: Where is thy Sting? (2001, $6.95)-McCormack-Sharp-c/a 7.00
...: Y2K (2/00, $4.95)-1st Brainiac 13 app.; Guice-c/a 5.00

SUPERMAN ADVENTURES, THE (Based on animated series)
DC Comics: Oct, 1996 - No. 66, Apr, 2002 ($1.75/$1.95/$1.99)
1-Rick Burchett-c/a begins; Paul Dini script; Lex Luthor app.; silver ink, wraparound-c 4.00
2-20,22: 2-McCloud scripts begin; Metallo-c/app. 3-Brainiac-c/app. 6-Mxyzptlk-c/app. 3.00
21-($3.95) 1st animated Supergirl 5.00
23-66: 23-Begin $1.99-c; Livewire app. 25-Batgirl-c/app. 28-Manley-a. 54-Retells Superman #233 "Kryptonite Nevermore" 58-Ross-c 3.00
Annual 1 (1997, $3.95)-Zatanna and Bruce Wayne app. 4.00
Special 1 (2/98, $2.95) Superman vs. Lobo 4.00
TPB (1998, $7.95) r/#1-6 8.00
... Vol 1: Up, Up and Away (2004, $6.95, digest) r/#16,19,22-24; Amancio-a 7.00
... Vol 2: The Never-Ending Battle (2004, $6.95) r/#25-29 7.00
... Vol 3: Last Son of Krypton (2006, $6.99) r/#30-34 7.00
... Vol 4: The Man of Steel (2006, $6.99) r/#35-39 7.00

SUPERMAN ALIENS 2: GOD WAR (Also see Superman Vs. Aliens)
DC Comics/Dark Horse Comics: May, 2002 - No. 4, Nov, 2002 ($2.99, limited series)
1-4-Bogdanove & Nowlan-a; Darkseid & New Gods app. 3.00

	GD 2.0	VG 4.0	FN 6.0	VF 8.0	VF/NM 9.0	NM- 9.2

TPB (6/03, $12.95) r/#1-4 13.00

SUPERMAN & BATMAN: GENERATIONS (Elseworlds)
DC Comics: 1999 - No. 4, 1999 ($4.95, limited series)
1-4-Superman & Batman team-up from 1939 to the future; Byrne-c/s/a 5.00
TPB (2000, $14.95) r/series 15.00

SUPERMAN & BATMAN: GENERATIONS II (Elseworlds)
DC Comics: 2001 - No. 4, 2001 ($5.95, limited series)
1-4-Superman, Batman & others team-up from 1942-future; Byrne-c/s/a 6.00
TPB (2003, $19.95) r/series 20.00

SUPERMAN & BATMAN: GENERATIONS III (Elseworlds)
DC Comics: Mar, 2003 - No. 12, Feb, 2004 ($2.95, limited series)
1-12-Superman & Batman through the centuries; Byrne-c/s/a 3.00

SUPERMAN & BATMAN VS. ALIENS AND PREDATOR
DC Comics: 2007 - No. 2, 2007 ($5.99, squarebound, limited series)
1,2-Schultz-s/Olivetti-a 6.00
TPB (2007, $12.99) r/#1,2; pencil breakdown pages 13.00

SUPERMAN AND BATMAN VS. VAMPIRES AND WEREWOLVES
DC Comics: Early Dec, 2008 - No. 6, Late Feb, 2009 ($2.99, limited series)
1-6-Van Hook-s/Mandrake-a/c. 1-Wonder Woman app. 5-Demon-c/app. 3.00
TPB (2009, $14.99) r/#1-6; intro. by John Landis 15.00

SUPERMAN & BATMAN: WORLD'S FUNNEST (Elseworlds)
DC Comics: 2000 ($6.95, square-bound, one-shot)
nn-Mr. Mxyzptlk and Bat-Mite destroy each DC Universe; Dorkin-s; art by various incl. Ross, Timm, Miller, Allred, Moldoff, Gibbons, Cho, Jimenez 7.00

SUPERMAN & BUGS BUNNY
DC Comics: Jul, 2000 - No. 4, Oct, 2000 ($2.50, limited series)
1-4-JLA & Looney Tunes characters meet 3.00

SUPERMAN/BATMAN
DC Comics: Oct, 2003 - No. 87, Oct, 2011 ($2.95/$2.99)
1-Two covers (Superman or Batman in foreground) Loeb-s/McGuinness-a; Metallo app. 5.00
1-2nd printing (Batman cover) 3.00
1-3rd printing; new McGuinness cover 3.00
1-Diamond/Alliance Retailer Summit Edition-variant 7 14 21 44 82 120
1-(6/06, Free Comic Book Day giveaway) reprints #1 3.00
2-6: 2,5-Future Superman app. 6-Luthor in battlesuit 3.00
7-Pat Lee-c/a; Superboy & Robin app. 3.00
8-Michael Turner-c/a; intro. new Kara Zor-El 5.00
8-Second printing with sketch cover 3.00
8-Third printing with new Turner cover 3.00
9-13-Michael Turner-c/a; Wonder Woman app. 10,13-Variant-c by Jim Lee 3.00
14-25: 14-18-Pacheco-a; Lightning Lord, Saturn Queen & Cosmic King app. 19-Supergirl app.; leads into Supergirl #1. 21-25-Bizarro app. 25-Superman & Batman covers; 2nd printing with white bkgrd cover 3.00
26-($3.99) Sam Loeb tribute issue; 2 covers by Turner; story & art by 26 various; back-up by Loeb & Sale 5.00
27-49: 27-Flashback to Earth-2 Power Girl & Huntress; Maguire-a. 34-36-Metal Men app. 3.00
50-($3.99) Thomas Wayne meets Jor-El; Justice League app. 4.00
51-74: 51,52-Mr. Mxyzptlk app. 66,67-Blackest Night; Man-Bat and Bizarro app. 3.00
75-($4.99) Quitely-c; Legion of Super-Heroes app.; Ordway-a; 2-pg. features by various 5.00
76-87: 76-Aftermath of Batman's "death". 77-Supergirl/Damian team-up 3.00
Annual #1 (12/06, $3.99) Re-imaging of 1st meeting from World's Finest #71 4.00
Annual #2 (5/08, $3.99) Kolins-a; re-imaging of Superman as Supernova story 4.00
Annual #3 (3/09, $3.99) Composite Superman-c by Wrightson; Batista-a 4.00
Annual #4 (8/10, $4.99) Batman Beyond; Levitz-s/Guedes-a/Lau-c 8.00
Annual #5 (6/11, $4.99) Reign of Doomsday x-over, Cyborg Superman app.; Sepulveda-a 5.00
...Absolute Power HC (2005, $19.99) r/#14-18 20.00
...Absolute Power SC (2006, $12.99) r/#14-18 13.00
...Big Noise SC (2010, $14.99) r/#64,68-71 15.00
...Enemies Among Us SC (2009, $12.99) r/#28-33 13.00
...Finest Worlds SC (2010, $14.99) r/#50-56 15.00
...Night and Day HC (2010, $19.99) r/#60-63,65-67 20.00
...Public Enemies HC (2004, $19.95) r/#1-6 & Secret Files 2003; sketch art pages 20.00
...Public Enemies SC (2005, $12.99) r/#1-6 & Secret Files 2003; sketch art pages 15.00
...Public Enemies SC (2009, $14.99) r/#1-6 & Secret Files 2003; sketch art pages 15.00
...Secret Files 2003 (11/03, $4.95) Reis-a; pin-ups by various; Loeb/Sale short-s 5.00
... : Supergirl HC (2004, $19.95) r/#8-13; intro by Loeb, cover gallery, sketch pages 20.00
... : Supergirl SC (2005, $12.99) r/#8-13; intro by Loeb, cover gallery, sketch pages 13.00
... : The Search For Kryptonite HC (2008, $19.99) r/#44-49; Davis sketch pages 20.00
... : The Search For Kryptonite SC (2009, $12.99) r/#44-49; Davis sketch pages 13.00

Superman Confidential #1 © DC

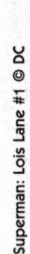

Superman: Lois Lane #1 © DC

Superman: Peace on Earth © DC

	GD	VG	FN	VF	VF/NM	NM-
	2.0	4.0	6.0	8.0	9.0	9.2

... : Torment HC (2008, $19.99) r/#37-42; cover gallery, Nguyen sketch pages 20.00
... : Vengeance HC (2006, $19.99) r/#20-25; sketch pages 20.00
... : Vengeance SC (2008, $12.99) r/#20-25; sketch pages 13.00
... : Worship SC (2011, $17.99) r/#72-75 & Annual #4 18.00

SUPERMAN/BATMAN: ALTERNATE HISTORIES
DC Comics: 1996 ($14.95, trade paperback)

nn-Reprints Detective Comics Annual #7, Action Comics Annual #6, Steel Annual #1, Legends of the Dark Knight Annual #4 15.00

SUPERMAN: BIRTHRIGHT
DC Comics: Sept, 2003 - No. 12, Sept, 2004 ($2.95, limited series)

1-12-Waid-s/Leinil Yu-a; retelling of origin and early Superman years 3.00
HC (2004, $29.95, dustjacket) r/series; cover gallery; Waid proposal with Yu concept art 30.00
SC (2005, $19.99) r/series; cover gallery; Waid proposal with Yu concept art 20.00

SUPERMAN COMICS
DC Comics: 1939

nn - Ashcan comic, not distributed to newsstands, only for in-house use. Cover art is Action Comics #7 with interior being Action Comics #8. A CGC certified 9.0 copy sold for $37,375 in 2005 and for $90,000 in 2007.

SUPERMAN CONFIDENTIAL (See Superman Hardcovers and TPBs listings for reprint)
DC Comics: Jan, 2007 - No. 14, Jun, 2008 ($2.99)

1-14: 1-5,9-Darwyn Cooke-s/Tim Sale-a/c; origin of Kryptonite re-told. 8-10-New Gods and Darkside app. 3.00
...: Kryptonite TPB (2009, $14.99) r/#1-5,11; intro. by Darwyn Cooke; Tim Sale sketch-a 15.00

SUPERMAN: DAY OF DOOM
DC Comics: Jan, 2003 - No. 4, Feb, 2003 ($2.95, weekly limited series)

1-4-Jurgens-s/Jurgens & Sienkiewicz-a 3.00
TPB (2003, $9.95) r/#1-4 10.00

SUPERMAN/DOOMSDAY: HUNTER/PREY
DC Comics: 1994 - No. 3, 1994 ($4.95, limited series, 52 pgs.)

1-3 6.00

SUPERMAN FAMILY, THE (Formerly Superman's Pal Jimmy Olsen)
National Per. Publ./DC Comics: No. 164, Apr-May, 1974 - No. 222, Sept, 1982

	GD	VG	FN	VF	VF/NM	NM-
164-(100 pgs.) Jimmy Olsen, Supergirl, Lois Lane begin	4	8	12	28	47	65
165-169 (100 pgs.)	3	6	9	18	28	38
170-176 (68 pgs.)	3	6	9	14	19	24
177-190 (52 pgs.): 177-181-52 pgs. 182-Marshall Rogers-a; $1.00 issues begin; Krypto begins, ends #192. 183-Nightwing-Flamebird begins, ends #194. 189-Brainiac 5, Mon -El app.	2	4	6	9	13	16
191-193,195-199: 191-Superboy begins, ends #198	2	3	4	6	8	10
194,200: 194-Rogers-a. 200-Book length sty	2	4	6	8	10	12
201-210,212-222	1	2	3	5	6	8
211-Earth II Batman & Catwoman marry	2	4	6	8	11	14

NOTE: ***N. Adams*** *c-182-185.* ***Anderson*** *a-186i.* ***Buckler*** *c(p)-190, 191, 209, 210, 215, 217, 220.* ***Jones*** *a-191-193.* ***Gil Kane*** *c(p)-221, 222.* ***Mortimer*** *a(p)-191-193, 199, 201-222.* ***Orlando*** *a(i)-186, 187.* ***Rogers*** *a-182, 194.* ***Staton*** *a-191-194, 196p.* ***Tuska*** *a(p)-203, 207-209.*

SUPERMAN FAMILY ADVENTURES
DC Comics: Jul, 2012 - No. 12, Jun, 2013 ($2.99)

1-12-Young-reader stories, games and DC Nation character profiles; Baltazar-a 3.00

SUPERMAN/FANTASTIC FOUR
DC Comics/Marvel Comics: 1999 ($9.95, tabloid size, one-shot)

1-Battle Galactus and the Cyborg; wraparound-c by Alex Ross and Dan Jurgens; Jurgens-s/a; Thibert-a 10.00

SUPERMAN FOR ALL SEASONS
DC Comics: 1998 - No, 4, 1998 ($4.95, limited series, prestige format)

1-Loeb-s/Sale-a/c; Superman's first year in Metropolis 6.00
2-4 5.00
Hardcover (1999, $24.95) r/#1-4 25.00

SUPERMAN FOR EARTH (See Superman one-shots)

SUPERMAN FOREVER
DC Comics: Jun, 1998 ($5.95, one-shot)

1-($5.95)-Collector's Edition with a 7-image lenticular-c by Alex Ross; Superman returns to normal; s/a by various 7.00
1-($4.95) Standard Edition with single image Ross-c 5.00

SUPERMAN/GEN13
DC Comics (WildStorm): Jun, 2000 - No. 3, Aug, 2000 ($2.50, limited series)

1-3-Hughes-s/ Bermejo-a; Campbell variant-c for each 3.00
TPB (2001, $9.95) new Bermejo-c; cover gallery 10.00

SUPERMAN: KING OF THE WORLD
DC Comics: June, 1999 ($3.95/$4.95, one-shot)

1-($3.95) Regular Ed. 4.00
1-($4.95) Collectors' Ed. with gold foil enhanced-c 5.00

SUPERMAN: LAST SON OF EARTH
DC Comics: 2000 - No. 2, 2000 ($5.95, limited series, prestige format)

1,2-Elseworlds; baby Clark rockets to Krypton; Gerber-s/Wheatley-a 6.00

SUPERMAN: LAST STAND OF NEW KRYPTON
DC Comics: May, 2010 - No. 3, Late June, 2010 ($3.99, limited series)

1-3-Robinson & Gates-s/Woods-a. 2-Pérez-c. 3-Sook-c 4.00
HC (2010, $24.99, DJ) r/#1,2, Adventure Comics #8,9, Supergirl #51 & Superman #698 25.00
Vol. 2 HC (2010, $19.99, DJ) r/#3, Adventure #10,11, Supergirl #52 & Superman #699 20.00

SUPERMAN: LAST STAND ON KRYPTON
DC Comics: 2003 ($6.95, one-shot, prestige format)

1-Sequel to Superman: Last Son of Earth; Gerber-s/Wheatley-a 7.00

SUPERMAN: LOIS LANE (Girlfrenzy)
DC Comics: Jun, 1998 ($1.95, one shot)

1-Connor & Palmiotti-a 3.00

SUPERMAN/MADMAN HULLABALOO!
Dark Horse Comics: June, 1997 - No. 3, Aug, 1997 ($2.95, limited series)

1-3-Mike Allred-c/s/a 3.00
TPB (1997, $8.95) 9.00

SUPERMAN: METROPOLIS
DC Comics: Apr, 2003 - No. 12, Mar, 2004 ($2.95, limited series)

1-12-Focus on Jimmy Olsen; Austen-s. 1-6-Zezelj-a. 7-12-Kristiansen-a. 8,9-Creeper app. 3.00

SUPERMAN METROPOLIS SECRET FILES
DC Comics: Jun, 2000 ($4.95, one shot)

1-Short stories, pin-ups and profile pages; Hitch and Neary-c 5.00

SUPERMAN: PEACE ON EARTH
DC Comics: Jan, 1999 ($9.95, Treasury-sized, one-shot)

1-Alex Ross painted-c/a; Paul Dini-s 12.00

SUPERMAN: RED SON
DC Comics: 2003 - No. 3, 2003 ($5.95, limited series, prestige format)

1-Elseworlds; Superman's rocket lands in Russia; Mark Millar-s/Dave Johnson-c/a 10.00
2,3 6.00
TPB (2004, $17.95) r/#1-3; intro. by Tom DeSanto; sketch pages 18.00
... - The Deluxe Edition HC (2009, $24.99, d.j.) r/#1-3; sketch art by various 25.00

SUPERMAN RED/ SUPERMAN BLUE
DC Comics: Feb, 1998 ($4.95, one shot)

1-Polybagged w/3-D glasses and reprint of Superman 3-D (1955); Jurgens-plot/3-D cover; script and art by various 5.00
1-($3.95)-Standard Ed.; comic only, non 3-D cover 4.00

SUPERMAN RETURNS... (2006 movie)
DC Comics: Aug, 2006 ($3.99, movie tie-in stories by Singer, Dougherty and Harris)

Prequel 1 - Krypton to Earth; Olivetti-a/Hughes-c; retells Jor-El's story 6.00
Prequel 2 - Ma Kent; Kerschl-a/Hughes-c; Ma Kent during Clark childhood and absence 4.00
Prequel 3 - Lex Luthor; Leonardi-a/Hughes-c; Luthor's 5 years in prison 4.00
Prequel 4 - Lois Lane; Dias-a/Hughes-c; Lois during Superman's absence 4.00
The Movie and Other Tales of the Man of Steel (2006, $12.99, TPB) adaptation; origin from Amazing World of Superman; Action #810, Superman #185; Advs. of Superman #575 13.00
The Official Movie Adaptation (2006, $6.99) Pasko-s/Haley-a; photo-c 7.00
...: The Prequels TPB (2006, $12.99) r/the 4 prequels 13.00

SUPERMAN: SAVE THE PLANET
DC Comics: Oct, 1998 ($2.95, one-shot)

1-($2.95) Regular Ed.; Luthor buys the Daily Planet 3.00
1-($3.95) Collector's Ed. with acetate cover 4.00

SUPERMAN SCRAPBOOK (Has blank pages; contains no comics)

SUPERMAN: SECRET FILES
DC Comics: Jan, 1998; May 1999 ($4.95)

1,2: 1-Retold origin story, "lost" pages & pin-ups 5.00
... & Origins 2004 (8/04) pin-ups by Lee, Turner and others 5.00
... & Origins 2005 (1/06) short stories and pin-ups by various 5.00
... 2009 (10/09, $4.99) short stories and pin-ups about New Krypton x-over 5.00

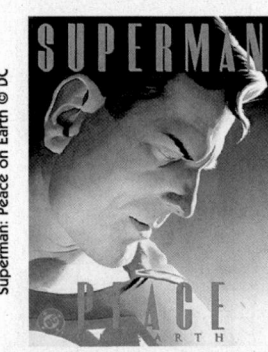

Superman's Girlfriend Lois Lane #97 © DC

Superman's Pal Jimmy Olsen #135 © DC

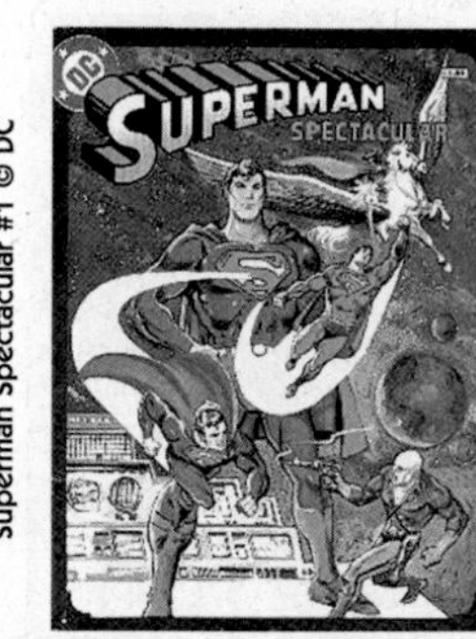

Superman Spectacular #1 © DC

SUPERMAN: SECRET IDENTITY
DC Comics: 2004 - No. 4, 2004 ($5.95, squarebound, limited series)

Issue	GD 2.0	VG 4.0	FN 6.0	VF 8.0	VF/NM 9.0	NM- 9.2
1-4-Busiek-s/Immonen-a/c						6.00

SUPERMAN: SECRET ORIGIN
DC Comics: Nov, 2009 - No. 6, Oct, 2010 ($3.99, limited series)

Issue	GD 2.0	VG 4.0	FN 6.0	VF 8.0	VF/NM 9.0	NM- 9.2
1-6-Geoff Johns-s/Gary Frank-a/c; origin mythos re-told. 2-Legion app. 5-Metallo app.						4.00
1-6-Variant covers by Frank						6.00
HC (2011, $29.99) r/#1-6; intro. by David Goyer; variant covers						30.00

SUPERMAN'S GIRLFRIEND LOIS LANE (See Action Comics #1, 80 Page Giant #3, 14, Lois Lane, Showcase #9, 10, Superman #28 & Superman Family)

SUPERMAN'S GIRLFRIEND LOIS LANE (See Showcase #9,10)
National Periodical Publ.: Mar-Apr, 1958 - No. 136, Jan-Feb, 1974; No. 137, Sept-Oct, 1974

Issue	GD 2.0	VG 4.0	FN 6.0	VF 8.0	VF/NM 9.0	NM- 9.2
1-(3-4/58)	350	700	1050	2975	6738	10,500
2	89	178	267	712	1606	2500
3	61	122	183	488	1094	1700
4,5	45	90	135	333	754	1175
6,7	36	72	108	259	580	900
8-10: 9-Pat Boone-c/story	30	60	90	216	483	750
11-13,15-19: 12-(10/59)-Aquaman app. 17-(5/60) 2nd app. Brainiac.	18	36	54	128	284	440
14-Supergirl x-over; Batman app. on-c only	20	40	60	135	300	465
20-Supergirl-c/sty	19	38	57	131	291	450
21-28: 23-1st app. Lena Thorul, Lex Luthor's sister; 1st Lois as Elastic Lass. 27-Bizarro-c/story	14	28	42	96	211	325
29-Aquaman, Batman, Green Arrow cover app. and cameo; last 10¢ issue	15	30	45	103	227	350
30-32,34-46,48,49	9	18	27	59	117	175
33(5/62)-Mon -El app.	9	18	27	61	123	185
47-Legion app.	9	18	27	61	123	185
50(7/64)-Triplicate Girl, Phantom Girl & Shrinking Violet app.	9	18	27	61	123	185
51-55,57-67,69: 59-Jor -El app.; Batman back-up sty	7	14	21	44	82	120
56-Saturn Girl app.	7	14	21	46	86	125
68-(Giant G-26)	8	16	24	54	102	150
70-Penguin & Catwoman app. (1st S.A. Catwoman, 11/66; also see Detective #369 for 3rd app.); Batman & Robin cameo	23	46	69	161	356	550
71-Batman & Robin cameo (3 panels); Catwoman story cont'd from #70 (2nd app.); see Detective #369 for 3rd app	10	20	30	69	147	225
72,73,75,76,78	5	10	15	34	60	85
74-1st Bizarro Flash (5/67); JLA cameo	5	10	15	35	63	90
77-(Giant G-39)	6	12	18	42	79	115
79-Neal Adams-c or c(i) begin, end #95,108	5	10	15	35	63	90
80-85,87,88,90-92: 92-Last 12¢ issue	4	8	12	28	47	65
86,95 (Giants G-51,G-63)-Both have Neal Adams-c	6	12	18	37	66	95
89,93: 89-Batman x-over; all N. Adams-c. 93-Wonder Woman-c/story	5	10	15	30	50	70
94,96-99,101-103,107-110	4	8	12	23	37	50
100	4	8	12	25	40	55
104-(Giant G-75)	5	10	15	34	60	85
105-Origin/1st app. The Rose & the Thorn.	5	10	15	34	60	85
106-"I Am Curious (Black)" story; Lois changes her skin color to black	7	14	21	48	89	130
111-Justice League-c/s; Morrow-a; last 15¢ issue	4	8	12	25	40	55
112,114-123 (52 pgs.): 122-G.A. Lois Lane-r/Superman #30. 123-G.A. Batman-r/Batman #35 (w/Catwoman)	4	8	12	23	37	50
113-(Giant G-87) Kubert-a (previously unpublished G.A. story)(scarce in NM)	6	12	18	37	66	95
124-135: 130-Last Rose & the Thorn. 132-New Zatanna story	3	6	9	16	23	30
136,137: 136-Wonder Woman x-over	3	6	9	17	26	35
Annual 1(Sum, 1962)-r/L. Lane #12; Aquaman app.	18	36	54	124	275	425
Annual 2(Sum, 1963)	12	24	36	84	185	285

NOTE: ***Buckler** a-117-121p. **Curt Swan or Kurt Schaffenberger** a-1-81(most); c(p)-1-15.*

SUPERMAN/SHAZAM: FIRST THUNDER
DC Comics: Nov, 2005 - No. 4, Feb, 2006 ($3.50, limited series)

Issue	GD 2.0	VG 4.0	FN 6.0	VF 8.0	VF/NM 9.0	NM- 9.2
1-4-Retells first meeting; Winick-s/Middleton-a. Dr. Sivana app.						3.50

SUPERMAN: SILVER BANSHEE
DC Comics: Dec, 1998 - No. 2, Jan, 1999 ($2.25, mini-series)

Issue	GD 2.0	VG 4.0	FN 6.0	VF 8.0	VF/NM 9.0	NM- 9.2
1,2-Brereton-s/c; Chin-a						3.00

SUPERMAN'S NEMESIS: LEX LUTHOR
DC Comics: Mar, 1999 - No. 4, Jun, 1999 ($2.50, mini-series)

Issue	GD 2.0	VG 4.0	FN 6.0	VF 8.0	VF/NM 9.0	NM- 9.2
1-4-Semeiks-a						3.00

SUPERMAN'S PAL JIMMY OLSEN (Superman Family #164 on)
(See Action Comics #6 for 1st app. & 80 Page Giant)
National Periodical Publ.: Sept-Oct, 1954 - No. 163, Feb-Mar, 1974 (Fourth World #133-148)

Issue	GD 2.0	VG 4.0	FN 6.0	VF 8.0	VF/NM 9.0	NM- 9.2
1	500	1000	1750	5000	10,250	15,500
2	155	310	465	1279	2890	4500
3-Last pre-code issue	93	186	279	744	1672	2600
4,5	59	118	177	472	1061	1650
6-10	41	82	123	303	689	1075
11-20: 15-1st S.A. issue	30	60	90	216	483	750
21-28,30	20	40	60	138	307	475
29-(6/58) 1st app. Krypto with Superman	21	42	63	147	324	500
31-Origin & 1st app. Elastic Lad (Jimmy Olsen)	18	36	54	124	275	425
32-40: 33-One pg. biography of Jack Larson (TV Jimmy Olsen). 36-Intro Lucy Lane. 37-2nd app. Elastic Lad & 1st cover app.	13	26	39	89	195	300
41-50: 41-1st J.O. Robot. 48-Intro/origin Superman Emergency Squad	10	20	30	66	138	210
51-56: 56-Last 10¢ issue	8	16	24	54	102	150
57-62,64-70: 57-Olsen marries Supergirl. 62-Mon-El & Elastic Lad app. but not as Legionnaires. 70-Element Boy (Lad) app.	6	12	18	40	73	105
63(9/62)-Legion of Super-Villains app.	6	12	18	41	76	110
71,74,75,78,80-84,86,89,90: 86-Jimmy Olsen Robot becomes Congorilla	5	10	15	33	57	80
72,73,76,77,79,85,87,88: 72(10/63)-Legion app; Elastic Lad (Olsen) joins. 73-Ultra Boy app. 76,85-Legion app. 76-Legion app. 77-Olsen with Colossal Boy's powers & costume; origin Titano retold. 79-(9/64)-Titled The Red-headed Beatle of 1000 B.C. 85-Legion app. 87-Legion of Super-Villains app. 88-Star Boy app.	5	10	15	34	60	85
91-94,96-98	4	8	12	28	47	65
95 (Giant G-25)	6	12	18	40	73	105
99-Olsen w/powers & costumes of Lightning Lad, Sun Boy & Element Lad	5	10	15	30	50	70
100-Legion cameo	5	10	15	31	53	75
101-103,105-112,114-120: 106-Legion app. 110-Infinity-c. 117-Batman & Legion cameo. 120-Last 12¢ issue	4	8	12	23	37	50
104 (Giant G-38)	5	10	15	34	60	85
113,122,131,140 (Giants G-50,G-62,G-74,G-86)	5	10	15	31	53	75
121,123-130,132	3	6	9	21	33	45
133-(10/70)-Jack Kirby story & art begins; re-intro Newsboy Legion; 1st app. Morgan Edge	5	10	15	35	63	90
134-1st app. Darkseid (1 panel, 12/70)	21	42	63	147	324	500
135-2nd app. Darkseid (1 pg. cameo; see New Gods & Forever People); G.A. Guardian app.	6	12	18	38	69	100
136-139: 136-Origin new Guardian. 138-Partial photo-c. 139-Last 15¢ issue	4	8	12	23	37	50
141-150: (25¢,52 pgs.). 141-Photo-c; Newsboy Legion-r by S&K begin; full pg. self-portrait of Jack Kirby; Don Rickles cameo. 149,150-G.A. Plastic Man-r in both; 150-Newsboy Legion app.	3	6	9	21	33	45
151-163	3	6	9	16	23	30
... Special 1 (12/08, $4.99) New Krypton tie-in; The Guardian and Dubbilex app.						5.00
... Special 2 (10/09, $4.99) New Krypton tie-in; Mon-El app.; Chang-a						5.00
Superman: The Amazing Transformations of Jimmy Olsen TPB (2007, $14.99) reprints Olsen's transformations into Wolf-Man, Elastic Lad, Turtle Boy and others; new Bolland-c						15.00

NOTE: *Issues #141-148 contain **Simon & Kirby** Newsboy Legion reprints from Star Spangled #7, 8, 9, 10, 11, 12, 13, 14 in that order. **N. Adams** c-109-112, 115, 117, 118, 120, 121, 132, 134-136, 147, 148. **Kirby** a-133-139p, 141-148p; c-133, 137, 139, 142, 145p. **Kirby/N. Adams** c-137, 138, 141-144, 146. **Curt Swan** c-1-14(most)., 140.*

SUPERMAN SPECTACULAR (Also see DC Special Series #5)
DC Comics: 1982 (Magazine size, 52 pgs., square binding)

Issue	GD 2.0	VG 4.0	FN 6.0	VF 8.0	VF/NM 9.0	NM- 9.2
1-Saga of Superman Red/ Superman Blue; Luthor and Terra-Man app.; Gonzales & Colletta-a	1	3	4	6	8	10

SUPERMAN: STRENGTH
DC Comics: 2005 - No. 3, 2005 ($5.95, limited series)

Issue	GD 2.0	VG 4.0	FN 6.0	VF 8.0	VF/NM 9.0	NM- 9.2
1-3: Alex Ross-c/Scott McCloud-s/Aluir Amancio-a						6.00

SUPERMAN / SUPERGIRL: MAELSTROM
DC Comics: Early Jan, 2009 - No. 5, Mar, 2009 ($2.99, limited series)

Issue	GD 2.0	VG 4.0	FN 6.0	VF 8.0	VF/NM 9.0	NM- 9.2
1-5: Palmiotti & Gray-s/Noto-c/a; Darkseid app.						3.00
TPB (2009, $12.99) r/#1-5						13.00

SUPERMAN / SUPERHOMBRE
DC Comics: Apr, 1945

nn - Ashcan comic, not distributed to newsstands, only for in-house use (no known sales)

SUPERMAN / TARZAN: SONS OF THE JUNGLE

Superman: The Man of Steel #37 © DC

Superman: The Secret Years #2 © DC

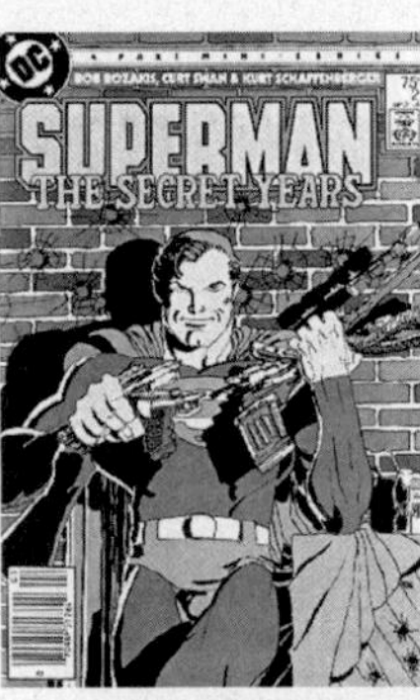

Superman / Wonder Woman #1 © DC

	GD 2.0	VG 4.0	FN 6.0	VF 8.0	VF/NM 9.0	NM- 9.2

Dark Horse Comics: Oct, 2001 - No. 3, May, 2002 ($2.99, limited series)
1-3-Elseworlds; Kal-El lands in the jungle; Dixon-s/Meglia-a/Ramos-c 3.00

SUPERMAN: THE DARK SIDE
DC Comics: 1998 - No. 3, 1998 ($4.95, squarebound, mini-series)
1-3: Elseworlds; Kal-El lands on Apokolips 5.00

SUPERMAN: THE DOOMSDAY WARS
DC Comics: 1998 - No. 3, 1999 ($4.95, squarebound, mini-series)
1-3: Superman & JLA vs. Doomsday; Jurgens-s/a(p) 5.00

SUPERMAN: THE KANSAS SIGHTING
DC Comics: 2003 - No. 2, 2003 ($6.95, squarebound, mini-series)
1,2-DeMatteis-s/Tolagson-a 7.00

SUPERMAN: THE LAST FAMILY OF KRYPTON
DC Comics: Oct, 2010 - No. 3, Dec, 2010 ($4.99, limited series)
1-3-Elseworlds; the El family lands on Earth; Bates-s/Arlem-a/Massafera-c 5.00

SUPERMAN: THE MAN OF STEEL (Also see Man of Steel, The)
DC Comics: July, 1991 - No. 134, Mar, 2003 ($1.00/$1.25/$1.50/$1.95/$2.25)

	GD	VG	FN	VF	VF/NM	NM-
0-(10/94) Zero Hour; released between #37 & #38						3.00
1-($1.75, 52 pgs.)-Painted-c						5.00
2-16: 3-War of the Gods x-over. 5-Reads sideways. 10-Last $1.00-c. 14-Superman & Robin team-up						3.00
17-1st brief app. Doomsday	4	8	12	23	37	50
17,18: 17-2nd printing. 18-2nd thru 5th printings	2	4	6	9	12	15
18-1st full app. Doomsday	3	6	9	16	23	30
19-Doomsday battle issue (c/story)	1	3	4	6	8	10
20-22: 20,21-Funeral for a Friend. 22-($1.95)-Collector's Edition w/die-cut outer-c & bound-in poster; Steel-c/story						5.00
22-($1.50)-Newsstand Ed. w/poster & different-c						4.00
23-49,51-99: 30-Regular edition. 32-Bizarro-c/story. 35,36-Worlds Collide Pt. 1 & 10. 37-(9/94)-Zero Hour x-over. 38-(11/94). 48-Aquaman app. 54-Spectre-c/app; Lex Luthor app. 56-Mxyzptlk-c/app. 57-G.A. Flash app. 58-Supergirl app. 59-Parasite-c/app.; Steel app. 60-Reintro Bottled City of Kandor. 62-Final Night. 64-New Gods app. 67-New powers. 75-"Death" of Mxyzptlk. 78,79-Millennium Giants. 80-Golden Age style. 92-JLA app. 98-Metal Men app.						3.00
30-($2.50)-Collector's Edition; polybagged with Superman & Lobo vinyl clings that stick to wraparound-c; Lobo-c/story						4.00
50 ($2.95)-The Trial of Superman						4.00
100-($2.99) New Fortress of Solitude revealed						3.00
100-($3.99) Special edition with fold out cardboard-c						4.00
101,102-101-Batman app.						3.00
103-133: 103-Begin $2.25. 105-Batman-c/app. 111-Return to Krypton. 115-117-Our Worlds at War. 117-Maxima killed. 121-Royal Flush Gang app. 128-Return to Krypton II.						3.00
134-($2.75) Last issue; Steel app.; Bogdanove-c						3.00
#1,000,000 (11/98) 853rd Century x-over; Gene Ha-c						3.00
Annual 1-5 ('92-'96,68 pgs.): 1-Eclipso app.; Joe Quesada-c(p). 2-Intro Edge. 3 -Elseworlds; Mignola-c; Batman app. 4-Year One story. 5-Legends of the Dead Earth story						4.00
Annual 6 (1997, $3.95)-Pulp Heroes story						4.00
...Gallery (1995, $3.50) Pin-ups by various						4.00

SUPERMAN: THE MAN OF TOMORROW
DC Comics: 1995 - No. 15, Fall, 1999 ($1.95-$2.95, quarterly)
1-15: 1-Lex Luthor app. 3-Lex Luthor-c/app; Joker app. 4-Shazam! app. 5-Wedding of Lex Luthor. 10-Maxima-c/app. 13-JLA-c/app. 3.00
#1,000,000 (11/98) 853rd Century x-over; Gene Ha-c 3.00

SUPERMAN: THE SECRET YEARS
DC Comics: Feb, 1985 - No. 4, May, 1985 (limited series)
1-4-Miller-c on all 4.00

SUPERMAN: THE WEDDING ALBUM
DC Comics: Dec, 1996 ($4.95, 96 pgs, one-shot)
1-Standard Edition-Story & art by past and present Superman creators; gatefold back-c. Byrne-c 5.00
1-Collector's Edition-Embossed cardstock variant-c w/ metallic silver ink and matte and gloss varnishes 8.00
Retailer Rep. Program Edition (#'d to 250, signed by Bob Rozakis on back-c) 50.00
TPB ('97, $14.95) r/Wedding and honeymoon stories 15.00

SUPERMAN 3-D (See Three-Dimension Adventures)

SUPERMAN-TIM (See Promotional Comics section)

SUPERMAN UNCHAINED (DC New 52)
DC Comics: Aug, 2013 - Present ($4.99/$3.99)
1-($4.99) Snyder-s/Jim Lee-a/c; back-up with Nguyen-a; bonus creator interviews 5.00
1-Director's Cut (9/13, $5.99) Lee's pencil art and Scott Snyder's scripts; cover gallery 6.00
2-6-($3.99) 2,6-Batman app. 4.00

SUPERMAN VILLAINS SECRET FILES
DC Comics: Jun, 1998 ($4.95, one shot)
1-Origin stories, "lost" pages & pin-ups 5.00

SUPERMAN VS. ALIENS (Also see Superman Aliens 2: God War)
DC Comics/Dark Horse Comics: July, 1995 - No. 3, Sept, 1995 ($4.95, limited series)
1-3: Jurgens/Nowlan-a 5.00

SUPERMAN VS. MUHAMMAD ALI (See All-New Collectors' Edition C-56 for original 1978 printing)
DC Comics: 2010
... Deluxe Edition (2010, $19.99, HC w/dustjacket) recolored reprint in comic size; new intro. by Neal Adams; afterword by Jenette Kahn; sketch pages, key to cover celebs 20.00
... Facsimile Edition (2010, $39.99, HC no dustjacket) recolored reprint in original Treasury size; new intro. by Neal Adams; key to cover celebs 40.00

SUPERMAN VS. PREDATOR
DC Comics/Dark Horse Comics: 2000 - No. 3, 2000 ($4.95, limited series)
1-3-Micheline-s/Maleev-a 5.00
TPB (2001, $14.95) r/series 15.00

SUPERMAN VS. THE AMAZING SPIDER-MAN (Also see Marvel Treasury Edition No. 28)
National Periodical Publications/Marvel Comics Group: 1976
($2.00, Treasury sized, 100 pgs.)

	GD	VG	FN	VF	VF/NM	NM-
1-Superman and Spider-Man battle Lex Luthor and Dr. Octopus; Andru/Giordano-a; 1st Marvel/DC x-over.	7	14	21	46	86	125
1-2nd printing; 5000 numbered copies signed by Stan Lee & Carmine Infantino on front cover & sold through mail	12	24	36	79	170	260
nn-(1995, $5.95)-r/#1						6.00

SUPERMAN VS. THE TERMINATOR: DEATH TO THE FUTURE
Dark Horse/DC Comics: Dec, 1999 - No. 4, Mar, 2000 ($2.95, limited series)
1-4-Grant-s/Pugh-a/c: Steel and Supergirl app. 3.00

SUPERMAN: WAR OF THE SUPERMEN
DC Comics: No. 0, Jun, 2010 - No. 4, Jul, 2010 ($2.99, limited series)
0-Free Comic Book Day issue; Barrows-c 3.00
1-4: 1-New Krypton destroyed 3.00
HC (2011, $19.99) r/#0-4 & Superman #700 20.00

SUPERMAN/WONDER WOMAN (DC New 52)
DC Comics: Dec, 2013 - Present ($3.99)
1-Soule-s/Daniel-a; wraparound gatefold-c; Doomsday app. 4.00
2-6-Zod app. 4-6-Faora app. 4.00

SUPERMAN/WONDER WOMAN: WHOM GODS DESTROY
DC Comics: 1997 ($4.95, prestige format, limited series)
1-4-Elseworlds; Claremont-s 5.00

SUPERMAN WORKBOOK
National Periodical Publ./Juvenile Group Foundation: 1945 (B&W, reprints, 68 pgs)

	GD	VG	FN	VF	VF/NM	NM-
nn-Cover-r/Superman #14	219	438	657	1402	2401	3400

SUPERMAN: WORLD OF NEW KRYPTON
DC Comics: May, 2009 - No. 12,Apr, 2010 ($2.99, limited series)
1-12: Robinson & Rucka-s/Woods-a; Frank-c and variant for each. 4-Green Lantern app. 3.00

SUPER MARIO BROS. (Also see Adventures of the..., Blip, Gameboy, and Nintendo Comics System)
Valiant Comics: 1990 - No. 5?, 1991 ($1.95, slick-c) V2#1, 1991 - No. 5, 1991

	GD	VG	FN	VF	VF/NM	NM-
1-Wildman-a	2	4	6	10	14	18
2-5, V2#1-5-($1.50)	1	2	3	5	6	8
Special Edition 1 (1990, $1.95)-Wildman-a	1	2	3	5	6	8

SUPER MARKET COMICS
Fawcett Publications: No date (1950s)
nn - Ashcan comic, not distributed to newsstands, only for in-house use (no known sales)

SUPER MARKET VARIETIES
Fawcett Publications: No date (1950s)
nn - Ashcan comic, not distributed to newsstands, only for in-house use (no known sales)

SUPERMEN OF AMERICA
DC Comics: Mar, 1999 ($3.95/$4.95, one-shot)
1-($3.95) Regular Ed.; Immonen-s/art by various 4.00
1-($4.95) Collectors' Ed. with membership kit 5.00

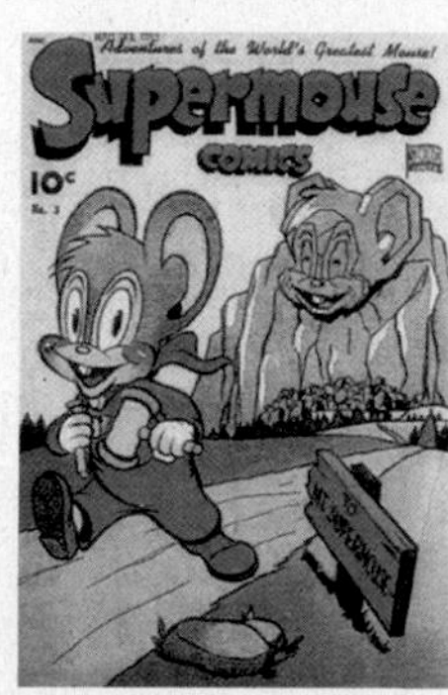

Supermouse Comics #3 © STD

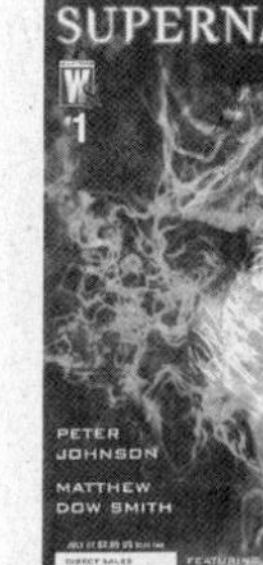

Supernatural: Origins #1 © WB

Superpatriot #1 © Image

	GD 2.0	VG 4.0	FN 6.0	VF 8.0	VF/NM 9.0	NM- 9.2

SUPERMEN OF AMERICA (Mini-series)
DC Comics: Mar, 2000 - No. 6, Aug, 2000 ($2.50)

1-6-Nicieza-s/Braithwaite-a 3.00

SUPERMOUSE (...the Big Cheese; see Coo Coo Comics)
Standard Comics/Pines No. 35 on (Literary Ent.): Dec, 1948 - No. 34, Sept, 1955; No. 35, Apr, 1956 - No. 45, Fall, 1958

	GD	VG	FN	VF	VF/NM	NM-
1-Frazetta text illos (3)	28	56	84	165	270	375
2-Frazetta text illos	15	30	45	84	127	170
3,5,6-Text illos by Frazetta in all	13	26	39	74	105	135
4-Two pg. text illos by Frazetta	14	28	42	78	112	145
7-10	9	18	27	47	61	75
11-20: 13-Racist humor (Indians)	7	14	21	37	46	55
21-45	6	12	18	31	38	45
1-Summer Holiday issue (Summer, 1957, 25¢, 100 pgs.)-Pines	14	28	42	80	115	150
2-Giant Summer issue (Summer, 1958, 25¢, 100 pgs.)-Pines; has games, puzzles & stories	10	20	30	58	79	100

SUPER-MYSTERY COMICS
Ace Magazines (Periodical House): July, 1940 - V8#6, July, 1949

	GD	VG	FN	VF	VF/NM	NM-
V1#1-Magno, the Magnetic Man & Vulcan begins (1st app.); Q-13, Corp. Flint, & Sky Smith begin	331	662	993	2317	4059	5800
2	110	220	330	704	1202	1700
3-The Black Spider begins (1st app.)	87	174	261	553	952	1350
4-Origin Davy	63	126	189	403	689	975
5-Intro. The Clown & begin series (12/40)	68	136	204	435	743	1050
6(2/41)	55	110	165	352	601	850
V2#1(4/41)-Origin Buckskin	54	108	162	343	574	825
2-6(2/42): 6-Vulcan begins again	52	104	156	328	557	785
V3#1(4/42),2: 1-Black Ace begins	47	94	141	296	498	700
3-Intro. The Lancer; Dr. Nemesis & The Sword begin; Kurtzman-c/a(2) (Mr. Risk & Paul Revere Jr.); Robot-c	61	122	183	390	670	950
4-Kurtzman-c/a; classic-c	100	200	300	640	1095	1550
5-Kurtzman-a(2); L.B. Cole-a; Mr. Risk app.	60	120	180	381	653	925
6(10/43)-Mr. Risk app.; Kurtzman's Paul Revere Jr.; L.B. Cole-a	54	108	162	343	574	825
V4#1(1/44)-L.B. Cole-a	47	94	141	296	498	700
2-6(4/45): 2,5,6-Mr. Risk app.	34	68	102	206	336	465
V5#1(7/45)-6	34	68	102	206	336	465
V6#1,2,4,5,6: 4-Last Magno. Mr. Risk app. in #2,4-6. 6-New logo	29	58	87	172	281	390
3-Torture c-story	45	90	135	284	480	675
V7#1-6, V8#1-4,6	27	54	81	158	259	360
V8#5-Meskin, Tuska, Sid Greene-a	27	54	81	160	263	365

NOTE: ***Sid Greene** a-V7#4. **Mooney** c-V1#5, 6, V2#1-6. **Palais** a-V5#3, 4; c-V4#6-V5#4, V6#2, V8#4. Bondage c-V2#5, 6, V3#2, 5. Magno c-V1#1-V3#6, V4#2-V5#5, V6#2. The Sword c-V4#1, 6(w/Magno).*

SUPERNATURAL (Volume 4) (Based on the CW television series)
DC Comics: Dec, 2011 - No. 6, May, 2012 ($2.99, limited series)

1-6: 1-Sam in Scotland; Brian Wood-s/Grant Bond-a 3.00

SUPERNATURAL: BEGINNING'S END (Based on the CW television series)
DC Comics (WildStorm): Mar, 2010 - No. 6, Aug, 2010 ($2.99, limited series)

1-6-Prequel to the series; Dabb & Loflin-s/Olmos-a. 1-Olmos and photo-c 3.00
TPB (2010, $14.99) r/#1-6; character sketch pages 15.00

SUPERNATURAL FREAK MACHINE: A CAL MCDONALD MYSTERY
IDW Publishing: Mar, 2005 - No. 3 ($3.99)

1-3-Steve Niles-s/Kelley Jones-a 4.00

SUPERNATURAL LAW (Formerly Wolff & Byrd, Counselors of the Macabre)
Exhibit A Press: No. 24, Oct, 1999 - Present ($2.50/$2.95/$3.50, B&W)

24-35-Batton Lash-s/a. 29-Marie Severin-c. 33-Cerebus spoof 3.00
36-40-($2.95). 37-Frank Cho pin-up and story panels 3.00
(#41) ...First Amendment Issue (2005, $3.50) anti-censorship story; CBLDF info 3.50
(#42) With a Silver Bullet (2006, $3.50) new stories and pin-ups 3.50
(#43) At the Box Office (2006, $3.50) new stories and pin-ups 3.50
(#44) Wolff & Byrd: The Movie (2007, $3.50) new stories and pin-ups 3.50
45-($3.50) Toxic Avenger and Lloyd Kaufman app. 3.50
#1 (2005, $2.95) r/Wolff & Byrd with redrawn and re-toned art; relettered 3.00

SUPERNATURAL LAW SECRETARY MAVIS
Exhibit A Press: 2001 - No. 5 ($2.95/$3.50, B&W)

1-3: 3-DeCarlo-c 3.00
4,5-($3.50) Jaime Hernandez-c 3.50

SUPERNATURAL: ORIGINS (Based on the CW television series)
DC Comics (WildStorm): July, 2007 - No. 6, Dec, 2007 ($2.99, limited series)

1-6: 1-Bradstreet-c; Johnson-s/Smith-a; back-up w/Johns-s/Hester-a 3.00
TPB (2008, $14.99) r/#1-6; sketch pages 15.00

SUPERNATURAL: RISING SON (Based on the CW television series)
DC Comics (WildStorm): Jun, 2008 - No. 6, Nov, 2008 ($2.99, limited series)

1-6-Johnson & Dessertine-s/Olmos-a. 1-Oliver-c 3.00
1-Variant-c by Nguyen 6.00
TPB (2009, $14.99) r/#1-6 15.00

SUPERNATURALS
Marvel Comics: Dec, 1998 - No. 4, Dec, 1998 ($3.99, weekly limited series)

1-4-Pulido-s/Balent-c; bound-in Halloween masks 4.00
1-4-With bound-in Ghost Rider mask (1 in 10) 4.00

SUPERNATURAL THRILLERS
Marvel Comics Group: Dec, 1972 - No. 6, Nov, 1973; No. 7, Jun, 1974 - No. 15, Oct, 1975

	GD	VG	FN	VF	VF/NM	NM-
1-It!; Sturgeon adap. (see Astonishing Tales #21)	3	6	9	21	33	45
2-4,6: 2-The Invisible Man; H.G. Wells adapt. 3-The Valley of the Worm; R.E. Howard adapt. 4-Dr. Jekyll & Mr. Hyde; R.L. Stevenson adapt.. 6-The Headless Horseman; last 20¢ issue	3	6	9	14	20	25
5-1st app. The Living Mummy	6	12	18	40	73	105
7-15: 7-The Living Mummy begins	3	6	9	17	26	35

NOTE: ***Brunner** c-11. **Buckler** a-5p. **Ditko** a-8r, 9r. **G. Kane** a-3p; c-3, 9p, 15p. **Mayerik** a-2p, 7, 8, 9p, 10p, 11. **McWilliams** a-14i. **Mortimer** a-4. **Steranko** c-1, 2. **Sutton** a-15. **Tuska** a-6p.*

SUPERPATRIOT (Also see Freak Force & Savage Dragon #2)
Image Comics (Highbrow Entertainment): July, 1993 - No. 4, Dec, 1993 ($1.95, lim. series)

1-4: Dave Johnson-c/a; Larsen scripts; Giffen plots 3.00

SUPERPATRIOT: AMERICA'S FIGHTING FORCE
Image Comics: July, 2002 - No. 4, Oct, 2002 ($2.95, limited series)

1-4-Cory Walker-a/c; Savage Dragon app. 3.00

SUPERPATRIOT: LIBERTY & JUSTICE
Image Comics (Highbrow Entertainment): July, 1995 - No. 4, Oct, 1995 ($2.50, lim. series)

1-4: Dave Johnson-c/a. 1-1st app. Liberty & Justice 3.00
TPB (2002, $12.95) r/#1-4; new cover by Dave Johnson; sketch pages 13.00

SUPERPATRIOT: WAR ON TERROR
Image Comics: July, 2004 - No. 4, May, 2007 ($2.95/$2.99, limited series)

1-4-Kirkman-s/Su-a 3.00

SUPER POWERS (1st Series)
DC Comics: July, 1984 - No. 5, Nov, 1984

1-5: 1-Joker/Penguin-c/story; Batman app.; all Kirby-c. 5-Kirby c/a 6.00

SUPER POWERS (2nd Series)
DC Comics: Sept, 1985 - No. 6, Feb, 1986

1-6: Kirby-c/a; Capt. Marvel & Firestorm join; Batman cameo; Darkseid storyline in all. 4-Batman cameo. 5,6-Batman app. 5.00

SUPER POWERS (3rd Series)
DC Comics: Sept, 1986 - No. 4, Dec, 1986

1-4: 1-Cyborg joins; 1st app. Samurai from Super Friends TV show. 1-4-Batman cameos; Darkseid storyline in #1-4 4.00

SUPER PUP (Formerly Spotty The Pup) (See Space Comics)
Avon Periodicals: No. 4, Mar-Apr, 1954 - No. 5, 1954

	GD	VG	FN	VF	VF/NM	NM-
4,5: 4-Atom bomb-c. 5-Robot-c	8	16	24	42	54	65

SUPER RABBIT (See All Surprise, Animated Movie Tunes, Comedy Comics, Comic Capers, Ideal Comics, It's A Duck's Life, Movie Tunes & Wisco)
Timely Comics (CmPI): Fall, 1944 - No. 14, Nov, 1948

	GD	VG	FN	VF	VF/NM	NM-
1-Hitler & Hirohito-c; war effort paper recycling PSA by S&K; Ziggy Pig & Silly Seal begin	226	452	678	1446	2473	3500
2	43	86	129	271	461	650
3-5	30	60	90	177	289	400
6-Origin	31	62	93	182	296	410
7-10: 9-Infinity-c	20	40	60	114	182	250
11-Kurtzman's "Hey Look"	20	40	60	117	189	260
12-14	20	40	60	114	182	250
I.W. Reprint #1,2('58),7,10('63): 1-r/#13. 2-r/#10.	2	4	6	10	14	18

SUPER RICHIE (Superichie #5 on) (See Richie Rich Millions #68)
Harvey Publications: Sept, 1975 - No. 4, Mar, 1976 (All 52 pg. Giants)

	GD	VG	FN	VF	VF/NM	NM-
1	3	6	9	16	23	30
2-4	2	4	6	11	16	20

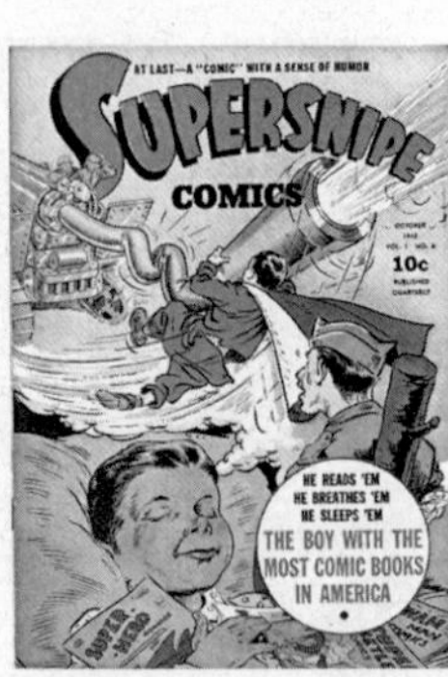

Supersnipe Comics #6 © S&S

Super-Villain Team-Up #6 © MAR

Superworld Comics #1 © Gernsback

	GD	VG	FN	VF	VF/NM	NM-
	2.0	4.0	6.0	8.0	9.0	9.2

GD VG FN VF VF/NM NM-
2.0 4.0 6.0 8.0 9.0 9.2

SUPER SLUGGERS (Baseball)
Ultimate Sports Ent. Inc.: 1999 ($3.95, one-shot)

1-Bonds, Piazza, Caminiti, Griffey Jr. app.; Martinbrough-c/a 4.00

SUPERSNIPE COMICS (Formerly Army & Navy #1-5)
Street & Smith Publications: V1#6, Oct, 1942 - V5#1, Aug-Sept, 1949
(See Shadow Comics V2#3)

V1#6-Rex King - Man of Adventure (costumed hero, see Super Magic/Magician) by Jack Binder begins; Supersnipe by George Marcoux continues from Army & Navy #5; Bill Ward-a 71 142 213 454 777 1100
7,10-12: 10,11-Little Nemo app. 40 80 120 246 411 575
8-Hitler, Tojo, Mussolini in Hell with Devil-c 168 336 504 1075 1838 2600
9-Doc Savage x-over in Supersnipe; Hitler-c 161 322 483 1030 1765 2500
V2 #1: Both V2#1(2/44) & V2#2(4/44) have V2#1 on outside-c; Huck Finn by Clare Dwiggins begins, ends V3#5 (rare) 57 114 171 362 619 875
V2#2 (4/44) has V2#1 on outside-c; classic shark-c 37 74 111 222 361 500
3-12 22 44 66 132 216 300
V3#1-12: 8-Bobby Crusoe by Dwiggins begins, ends V3#12. 9-X-Mas-c 20 40 60 114 182 250
V4#1-12, V5#1: V4#10-X-Mas-c 16 32 48 94 147 200
NOTE: ***George Marcoux** c-V1#6-V3#4. Doc Savage app. in some issues.*

SUPER SOLDIER (See Marvel Versus DC #3)
DC Comics (Amalgam): Apr, 1996 ($1.95, one-shot)

1-Mark Waid script & Dave Gibbons-c/a. 3.00

SUPER SOLDIER: MAN OF WAR
DC Comics (Amalgam): June, 1997 ($1.95, one-shot)

1-Waid & Gibbons-s/Gibbons & Palmiotti-c/a. 3.00

SUPER SOLDIERS
Marvel Comics UK: Apr, 1993 - No. 8, Nov, 1993 ($1.75)

1-($2.50)-Embossed silver foil logo 4.00
2-8: 5-Capt. America app. 6-Origin; Nick Fury app.; neon ink-c 3.00

SUPERSPOOK (Formerly Frisky Animals on Parade)
Ajax/Farrell Publications: No. 4, June, 1958

4 8 16 24 44 57 70

SUPER SPY (See Wham Comics)
Centaur Publications: Oct, 1940 - No. 2, Nov, 1940 (Reprints)

1-Origin The Sparkler 87 174 261 553 952 1350
2-The Inner Circle, Dean Denton, Tim Blain, The Drew Ghost, The Night Hawk by Gustavson, & S.S. Swanson by Glanz app. 54 108 162 343 574 825

SUPERSTAR: AS SEEN ON TV
Image Comics (Gorilla): 2001 ($5.95)

1-Busiek-s/Immonen-a 6.00

SUPER STAR HOLIDAY SPECIAL (See DC Special Series #21)

SUPER-TEAM FAMILY
National Periodical Publ./DC Comics: Oct-Nov, 1975 - No. 15, Mar-Apr, 1978

1-Reprints by Neal Adams & Kane/Wood; 68 pgs. begin, ends #4. New Gods app. 3 6 9 16 23 30
2,3: New stories 3 6 9 14 20 25
4-7: Reprints. 4-G.A. JSA-r & Superman/Batman/Robin-r from World's Finest. 5-52 pgs. begin 2 4 6 10 14 18
8-14: 8-10-New Challengers of the Unknown stories. 9-Kirby-a. 11-14: New stories 3 6 9 14 19 24
15-New Gods app. New stories 3 6 9 14 20 26
NOTE: ***Neal Adams** r-1-3. **Brunner** c-3. **Buckler** c-8p. **Tuska** a-7r. **Wood** a-1i(r), 3.*

SUPER TV HEROES (See Hanna-Barbera...)

SUPER-VILLAIN CLASSICS
Marvel Comics Group: May, 1983

1-Galactus -The Origin; Kirby-a 6.00

SUPER-VILLAIN TEAM-UP (See Fantastic Four #6 & Giant-Size...)
Marvel Comics Group: 8/75 - No. 14, 10/77; No. 15, 11/78; No. 16, 5/79; No. 17, 6/80

1-Continued from Giant-Size Super-Villain Team-Up #2; Sub-Mariner & Dr. Doom begin, end #10 4 8 12 28 47 65
2-5: 5-1st app. The Shroud 3 6 9 14 19 24
5-(30¢-c variant, limited distribution)(4/76) 4 8 12 22 35 48
6,7-(25¢ editions) 6-(6/76)-F.F., Shroud app. 7-Origin Shroud 2 4 6 8 11 14
6,7-(30¢-c, limited distribution)(6,8/76) 3 6 9 19 30 40
8-17: 9-Avengers app. 11-15-Dr. Doom & Red Skull app. 2 4 6 8 11 14
12-14-(35¢-c variants, limited distribution)(6,8,10/77) 4 8 12 23 37 50
NOTE: ***Buckler** c-4p, 5p, 7p. **Buscema** c-1. **Byrne/Austin** c-14. **Evans** a-1p, 3p. **Everett** a-1p. **Giffen** a-8p, 13p; c-13p. **Kane** c-2p, 9p. **Mooney** a-4i. **Starlin** c-6. **Tuska** r-1p, 15p. **Wood** r-15p.*

SUPER-VILLAIN TEAM-UP/ MODOK'S 11
Marvel Comics: Sept, 2007 - No. 5, Jan, 2008 ($2.99, limited series)

1-5: 1-MODOK's origin re-told; Portela-a/Powell-c; Purple Man & Mentallo app. 3.00
... TPB (2008, $13.99) r/#1-5 14.00

SUPER WESTERN COMICS (Also see Buffalo Bill)
Youthful Magazines: Aug, 1950 (One shot)

1-Buffalo Bill begins; Wyatt Earp, Calamity Jane & Sam Slade app; Powell-c/a 15 30 45 83 124 165

SUPER WESTERN FUNNIES (See Super Funnies)

SUPERWOMAN
DC Comics: Jan 1942

nn - Ashcan comic, not distributed to newsstands, only for in-house use. Cover art is More Fun Comics #73 with interior being Action Comics #38 (no known sales)

SUPERWORLD COMICS
Hugo Gernsback (Komos Publ.): Apr, 1940 - No. 3, Aug, 1940 (68 pgs.)

1-Origin & 1st app. Hip Knox, Super Hypnotist; Mitey Powers & Buzz Allen, the Invisible Avenger, Little Nemo begin; cover by Frank R. Paul (all have sci/fi-c) (Scarce) 865 1730 2595 6315 12,158 18,000
2-Marvo 1-2 Go+, the Super Boy of the Year 2680 (1st app.); Paul-c (Scarce) 459 918 1377 3350 6425 9500
3 (Scarce) 383 766 1149 2681 5091 7500

SUPER ZOMBIES
Dynamite Entertainment: 2009 - No. 5, 2009 ($3.50)

1-5- Mel Rubi-a; Guggenheim & Gonzales-s; two covers for each by Rubi & Neves 3.50

SUPREME (Becomes ...The New Adventures #43-48)(See Youngblood #3)
(Also see Bloodwulf Special, Legend of Supreme, & Trencher #3)
Image Comics (Extreme Studios)/ Awesome Entertainment #49 on:
V2#1, Nov, 1992 - V2#42, Sept, 1996; V3#49 - No. 56, Feb, 1998

V2#1-Liefeld-a(i) & scripts; embossed foil logo 4.00
1-Gold Edition 1 2 3 5 6 8
2-(3/93)-Liefeld co-plots & inks; 1st app. Grizlock 3.00
3-42: 3-Intro Bloodstrike; 1st app. Khrome. 5-1st app. Thor. 6-1st brief app. The Starguard. 7-1st full app. The Starguard. 10-Black and White Pt 1 (1st app.) by Art Thibert (2 pgs. ea. installment). 25-(5/94)-Platt-c. 11-Coupon #4 for Extreme Prejudice #0; Black and White Pt. 7 by Thibert. 12-(4/94)-Platt-c. 13,14-(6/94). 15 (7/94). 16 (7/94)-Stormwatch app. 18-Kid Supreme Sneak Preview; Pitt app.19,20-Polybagged w/trading card. 20-1st app. Woden & Loki (as a dog); Overtkill app. 21-1st app. Loki (in true form). 21-23-Poly-bagged trading card. 32-Lady Supreme cameo. 33-Origin & 1st full app. of Lady Supreme (Probe from the Starguard); Babewatch! tie-in. 37-Intro Loki; Fraga-c. 40-Retells Supreme's past advs. 41-Alan Moore scripts begin; Supreme revised; intro The Supremacy; Jerry Ordway-c (Joe Bennett variant-c exists). 42-New origin w/Rick Veitch-a; intro Radar, The Hound Supreme & The League of Infinity 3.00
28-Variant-c by Quesada & Palmiotti 3.00
(#43-48-**See Supreme: The New Adventures**)
V3#49,51: 49-Begin $2.99-c 3.00
50-($3.95)-Double sized, 2 covers, pin-up gallery 4.00
52a,52b-($3.50) 4.00
53-56: 53-Sprouse-a begins. 56-McGuinness-c 3.00
Annual 1-(1995, $2.95) 4.00
...: Supreme Sacrifice (3/06, $3.99) Flip book with Suprema; Kirkman-s/Malin-a 4.00
...: The Return TPB (Checker Book Publ., 2003, $24.95) r/#53-56 & Supreme; The Return #1-6; Ross-c; additional sketch pages by Ross 25.00
...: The Story of the Year TPB (Checker Book Publ., 2002, $26.95) r/#41-52; Ross-c 27.00
NOTE: ***Rob Liefeld** a(i)-1, 2; co-plots-2-4; scripts-1, 5, 6. **Ordway** c-41. **Platt** c-12, 25. **Thibert** c(i)-7-9.*

SUPREME
Image Comics: No. 63, Apr, 2012 - Present ($2.99)

63-66: 63-Moore-s; two covers by Larsen & Hamscher 3.00
67,68-($3.99) 67-Onmi-Man app. 4.00

SUPREME: GLORY DAYS
Image Comics (Extreme Studios): Oct, 1994 - No. 2, Dec, 1994 ($2.95/$2.50, limited series)

1,2: 2-Diehard, Roman, Superpatriot, & Glory app. 3.00

SUPREME POWER (Also see Squadron Supreme 2006 series)
Marvel Comics (MAX): Oct, 2003 - No. 18, Oct, 2005 ($2.99)

1-($2.99) Straczynski-s/Frank-a; Frank-c 3.00
1-($4.99) Special Edition with variant Quesada-c; includes r/early Squadron Supreme apps. 5.00

Supreme Power #3 © MAR

Suspense Comics #5 © Continental

Swamp Thing #13 © DC

GD 2.0 | VG 4.0 | FN 6.0 | VF 8.0 | VF/NM 9.0 | NM- 9.2

2-18: 4-Intro. Nighthawk. 6-The Blur debuts. 10-Princess Zarda returns. 17-Hyperion revealed as alien. 18-Continues in mini-series 3.00
... MGC #1 (7/11, $1.00) r/#1 with "Marvel's Greatest Comics" banner on cover 3.00
Vol. 1: Contact TPB (2004, $14.99) r/#1-6 15.00
Vol. 2: Powers & Principalities TPB (2004, $14.99) r/#7-12 15.00
Vol. 3: High Command TPB (2005, $14.99) r/#13-18 15.00
Vol. 1 HC (2005, $29.99, 7 1/2" x 11" with dustjacket) r/#1-12; Avengers #85 & 86, Straczynski intro., Frank cover sketches and character design pages 30.00
Vol. 2 HC (2006, $29.99, 7 1/2" x 11" with dustjacket) r/#13-18; ...: Hyperion #1-5; character design pages 30.00

SUPREME POWER
Marvel Comics (MAX): Aug, 2011 - No. 4, Nov, 2011 ($3.99, limited series)
1-4-Higgins-s/Garcia-a/Fiumara-c; Doctor Spectrum app. 4.00

SUPREME POWER: HYPERION
Marvel Comics (MAX): Nov, 2005 - No. 5, Mar, 2006 ($2.99, limited series)
1-5: 1-Straczynski-s/Jurgens-a/Dodson-c 3.00
TPB (2006, $14.99) r/#1-5 15.00

SUPREME POWER: NIGHTHAWK
Marvel Comics (MAX): Nov, 2005 - No. 6, Apr, 2006 ($2.99, limited series)
1-6-Daniel Way-s/Steve Dillon-a; origin of Whiteface 3.00
TPB (2006, $16.99) r/#1-6; cover concept art 17.00

SUPREME: THE NEW ADVENTURES (Formerly Supreme)
Maximum Press: V3#43, Oct, 1996 - V3#48, May, 1997 ($2.50)
V3#43-48: 43-Alan Moore scripts begin; Joe Bennett-a; Rick Veitch-a (8 pgs.); Dan Jurgens-a (1 pg.); intro Citadel Supreme & Suprematons; 1st Allied Supermen of America 3.00

SUPREME: THE RETURN
Awesome Entertainment: May, 1999 - No. 6, June, 2000 ($2.99)
1-6: Alan Moore-s. 1,2-Sprouse & Gordon-a/c. 2,4-Liefeld-c. 6-Kirby app. 3.00

SUPURBIA (GRACE RANDOLPH'S...)
BOOM! Studios: Mar, 2012 - No. 4, Jun, 2012 ($3.99, limited series)
1-4-Grace Randolph-s/Dauterman-a. 1-Garza-c 4.00

SUPURBIA (GRACE RANDOLPH'S...)(Volume 2)
BOOM! Studios: Nov, 2012 - No. 12, Oct, 2013 ($3.99, limited series)
1-12-Grace Randolph-s/Dauterman-a; multiple covers on #1-5 4.00

SURE-FIRE COMICS (Lightning Comics #4 on)
Ace Magazines: June, 1940 - No. 4, Oct, 1940 (Two No. 3's)
V1#1-Origin Flash Lightning & begins; X-The Phantom Fed, Ace McCoy, Buck Steele, Marvo the Magician, The Raven, Whiz Wilson (Time Traveler) begin (all 1st app.); Flash Lightning c-1-4 187 374 561 1197 2049 2900
2 86 172 258 546 936 1325
3(9/40), 3(#4)(10/40)-nn on-c, #3 on inside 65 130 195 416 708 1000

SURF 'N' WHEELS
Charlton Comics: Nov, 1969 - No. 6, Sept, 1970
1 3 6 9 19 30 40
2-6 3 6 9 14 19 24

SURGE
Eclipse Comics: July, 1984 - No. 4, Jan, 1985 ($1.50, lim. series, Baxter paper)
1-4 Ties into DNAgents series 3.00

SURVIVE (Follows Cataclysm: The Ultimates Last Stand)
Marvel Comics: May, 2014 ($3.99, one-shot)
1-Bendis-s/Quinones-a; the new Ultimates team is formed 4.00

SURPRISE ADVENTURES (Formerly Tormented)
Sterling Comic Group: No. 3, Mar, 1955 - No. 5, July, 1955
3-5: 3,5-Sekowsky-a 10 20 30 54 72 90

SUSIE Q. SMITH
Dell Publishing Co.: No. 323, Mar, 1951 - No. 553, Apr, 1954
Four Color 323 (#1) 5 10 15 31 53 75
Four Color 377, 453 (2/53), 553 4 8 12 27 44 60

SUSPENSE (Radio/TV issues #1-11; Real Life Tales of... #1-4) (Amazing Detective Cases #3 on?)
Marvel/Atlas Comics (CnPC No. 1-10/BFP No. 11-29): Dec, 1949 - No. 29, Apr, 1953 (#1-8, 17-23: 52 pgs.)
1-Powell-a; Peter Lorre, Sidney Greenstreet photo-c from Hammett's "The Verdict" 71 142 213 454 777 1100
2-Crime stories; Dennis O'Keefe & Gale Storm photo-c from Universal movie "Abandoned" 39 78 117 231 378 525
3-Change to horror 45 90 135 284 480 675
4,7-10: 7-Dracula-sty 37 74 111 222 361 500
5-Krigstein, Tuska, Everett-a 39 78 117 231 378 525
6-Tuska, Everett, Morisi-a 38 76 114 228 369 510
11-13,15-17,19,20 31 62 93 182 296 410
14-Clasic Heath Hypo-c; A-Bomb panels 41 82 123 256 428 600
18,22-Krigstein-a 31 62 93 186 303 420
21,23,24,26-29: 24-Tuska-a 27 54 81 158 259 360
25-Electric chair-c/story 36 72 108 216 351 485
NOTE: ***Ayers** a-20. **Briefer** a-5, 7, 27. **Brodsky** c-4, 6-9, 11, 16, 17, 25. **Colan** a-8(2), 9. **Everett** a-5, 6(2), 19, 23, 28; c-21-23, 26. **Fuje** a-29. **Heath** a-5, 6, 8, 10, 12, 14; c-14, 19, 24. **Maneely** a-12, 23, 24, 28, 29; c-5, 6p, 10, 13, 15, 18. **Mooney** a-24, 28. **Morisi** a-6, 12. **Palais** a-10. **Rico** a-7-9. **Robinson** a-29. **Romita** a-20(2), 25. **Sekowsky** a-11, 13, 14. **Sinnott** a-23, 25. **Tuska** a-5, 6(2), 12; c-12. **Whitney** a-15, 16, 22. **Ed Win** a-27.*

SUSPENSE COMICS
Continental Magazines: Dec, 1943 - No. 12, Sept, 1946
1-The Grey Mask begins; bondage/torture-c; L. B. Cole-a (7 pgs.) 486 972 1458 3550 6275 9000
2-Intro. The Mask; Rico, Giunta, L. B. Cole-a (7 pgs.) 277 554 831 1760 3030 4300
3-L.B. Cole-a; classic Schomburg-c (Scarce) 5500 11,000 16,500 33,000 49,000 65,000
4-L. B. Cole-c begin 258 516 774 1651 2826 4000
5,6 216 432 648 1382 2366 3350
7,9,10,12: 9-L.B. Cole eyeball-c 165 330 495 1056 1803 2550
8-Classic L. B. Cole spider-c 423 846 1269 3067 5384 7700
11-Classic Devil-c 331 662 993 2317 4059 5800
NOTE: ***L. B. Cole** c-4-12. **Fuje** a-8. **Larsen** a-11. **Palais** a-10, 11. Bondage c-1, 3, 4.*

SUSPENSE DETECTIVE
Fawcett Publications: June, 1952 - No. 5, Mar, 1953
1-Evans-a (11 pgs); Baily-c/a 45 90 135 284 480 675
2-Evans-a (10 pgs.) 27 54 81 160 263 365
3-5 23 46 69 136 223 310
NOTE: ***Baily** a-4, 5; c-1-3. **Sekowsky** a-2, 4, 5; c-5.*

SUSPENSE STORIES (See Strange Suspense Stories)

SUSSEX VAMPIRE, THE (Sherlock Holmes)
Caliber Comics: 1996 ($2.95, 32 pgs., B&W, one-shot)
nn-Adapts Sir Arthur Conan Doyle's story; Warren Ellis scripts 3.00

SUZIE COMICS (Formerly Laugh Comix; see Laugh Comics, Liberty Comics #10, Pep Comics & Top-Notch Comics #28)
Close-Up No. 49,50/MLJ Mag./Archie No. 51 on: No. 49, Spring, 1945 - No. 100, Aug, 1954
49-Ginger begins 37 74 111 222 361 500
50-55: 54-Transvestism story. 55-Woggon-a 20 40 60 117 189 260
56-Katy Keene begins by Woggon 21 42 63 122 199 275
57-65 15 30 45 86 133 180
66-80 14 28 42 81 118 155
81-87,89-99 13 26 39 72 101 130
88,100: 88-Used in **POP**, pgs. 76,77; Bill Woggon draws himself in story. 100-Last Katy Keene 14 28 42 81 118 155
NOTE: ***Al Fagaly** c-49-67. Katy Keene app. in 53-82, 85-100.*

SWAMP FOX, THE (TV, Disney)(See Walt Disney Presents #2)
Dell Publishing Co.: No. 1179, Dec, 1960
Four Color 1179-Leslie Nielsen photo-c 7 14 21 48 89 130

SWAMP THING (See Brave & the Bold, Challengers of the Unknown #82, DC Comics Presents #8 & 85, DC Special Series #2, 14, 17, 20, House of Secrets #92, Limited Collectors' Edition C-59, & Roots of the...)

SWAMP THING
National Per. Publ./DC Comics: Oct-Nov, 1972 - No. 24, Aug-Sept, 1976
1-Wrightson-c/a begins; origin 15 30 45 103 227 350
2-1st brief app. Patchwork Man (1 panel) 8 16 24 51 96 140
3-1st full app. Patchwork Man (see House of Secrets #140) 6 12 18 40 73 105
4-6, 5 10 15 34 60 85
7-Batman-c/story 6 12 18 37 66 95
8-10: 10-Last Wrightson issue 5 10 15 31 53 75
11-20: 11-19-Redondo-a. 13-Origin retold (1 pg.) 3 6 9 18 28 38
21-24: 23,24-Swamp Thing reverts back to Dr. Holland. 23-New logo 3 6 9 18 28 38
Secret of the Swamp Thing (2005, $9.99, digest) r/#1-10 10.00
NOTE: ***J. Jones** a-9i(assist). **Kaluta** a-9i. **Redondo** c-12-19, 21. **Wrightson** issues (#1-10) reprinted in DC Special Series #2, 14, 17, 20 & Roots of the Swamp Thing.*

SWAMP THING (Saga Of The... #1-38,42-45) (See Essential Vertigo:...)
DC Comics (Vertigo imprint #129 on): May, 1982 - No. 171, Oct, 1996
(Direct sales #65 on)

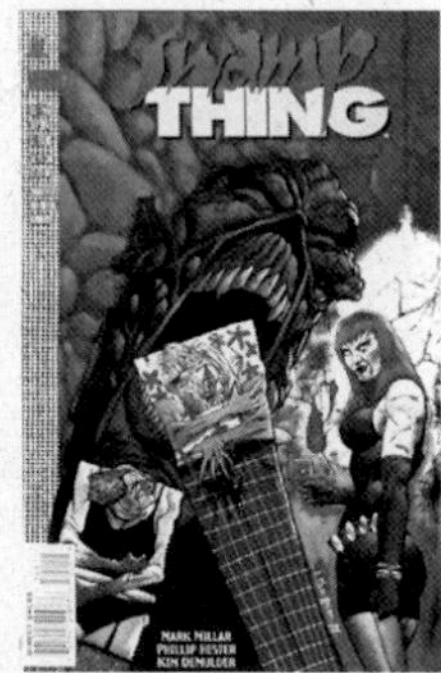

Swamp Thing #146 © DC

Swamp Thing (2011 series) #13 © DC

Sweetheart Diary #2 © FAW

	GD 2.0	VG 4.0	FN 6.0	VF 8.0	VF/NM 9.0	NM- 9.2
1-Origin retold; Phantom Stranger series begins; ends #13; Yeates-c/a begins	1	2	3	5	6	8
2-15: 2-Photo-c from movie. 13-Last Yeates-a						4.00
16-19: Bissette-a.						5.00
20-1st Alan Moore issue	3	6	9	16	24	32
21-New origin	3	6	9	14	19	24
21 Special Editon (5/09, $1.00) reprint with "After Watchmen" cover frame						3.00
22,23	2	4	6	9	12	15
24-JLA x-over; last Yeates-c.	2	4	6	9	13	16
25-John Constantine 1-panel cameo	3	6	9	19	30	40
26-30	1	2	3	5	6	8
31-33,35,36: 33-r/1st app. from House of Secrets #92						6.00
34	1	2	3	5	7	9
37-1st app. John Constantine (Hellblazer) (6/85)	7	14	21	44	82	120
38-40: John Constantine app.	2	4	6	8	10	12
41-52,54-64: 44-Batman cameo. 44-51-John Constantine app. 46-Crisis x-over; Batman cameo. 49-Spectre app. 50-($1.25, 52 pgs.)-Deadman, Dr. Fate, Demon. 52-Arkham Asylum-c/story; Joker-c/cameo. 58-Spectre preview. 64-Last Moore issue						4.00
53-($1.25, 52 pgs.)-Arkham Asylum; Batman-c/story						5.00
65-83,85-99,101-124,126-149,151-153: 65-Direct sales only begins. 66-Batman & Arkham Asylum story. 70,76-John Constantine x-over; 76-X-over w/Hellblazer #9. 79-Superman-c/story. 85-Jonah Hex app. 102-Preview of World Without End. 116-Photo-c. 129-Metallic ink on-c. 140-Millar scripts begin, end #171						3.00
84-Sandman (Morpheus) cameo.						4.00
100,125,150: 100 ($2.50, 52 pgs.). 125-($2.95, 52 pgs.)-20th anniversary issue. 150 (52 pgs.)-Anniversary issue						4.00
154-171: 154-$2.25-c begins. 165-Curt Swan-a(p). 166,169,171-John Constantine & Phantom Stranger app. 168-Arcane returns						3.00
Annual 1,3-6('82-91): 1-Movie Adaptation; painted-c. 3-New format; Bolland-c. 4-Batman-c/story. 5-Batman cameo; re-intro Brother Power (Geek),1st app. since 1968						4.00
Annual 2 (1985)-Moore scripts; Bissette-a(p); Deadman, Spectre app.						7.00
Annual 7(1993, $3.95)-Children's Crusade						4.00
...A Murder of Crows (2001, $19.95)-r/#43-50; Moore-s						20.00
...: Earth To Earth (2002, $17.95)-r/#51-56; Batman app.						18.00
...: Infernal Triangles (2006, $19.99, TPB) r/#77-81 & Annual #3; cover gallery						20.00
...Love and Death (1990, $17.95)-r/#28-34 & Annual #2; Totleben painted-c						18.00
...: Regenesis (2004, $17.95, TPB) r/#65-70; Veitch-s						18.00
...: Reunion (2003, $19.95, TPB) r/#57-64; Moore-s						20.00
...: Roots (1998, $7.95) Jon J Muth-s/painted-a/c						8.00
Saga of the Swamp Thing ('87, '89)-r/#21-27 (1st & 2nd print)						15.00
Saga of the Swamp Thing Book One HC (2009, $24.99, d.j.) r/#20-27; Wein intro.						25.00
Saga of the Swamp Thing Book Two HC (2009, $24.99, d.j.) r/#28-34 & Annual #2						25.00
Saga of the Swamp Thing Book Three HC (2010, $24.99, d.j.) r/#35-42; Bissette intro.						25.00
Saga of the Swamp Thing Book Four HC (2010, $24.99, d.j.) r/#43-50; Gaiman foreword						25.00
Saga of the Swamp Thing Book Five HC (2011, $24.99, d.j.) r/#51-56; Bissette intro.						25.00
...: Spontaneous Generation (2005, $19.99) r/#71-76						20.00
...: The Curse (2000, $19.95, TPB) r/#35-42; Bisley-c						20.00

NOTE: ***Bissette** a(p)-16-19, 21-27, 29, 30, 34-36, 39-42, 44, 46, 50, 64; c-17i, 24-32p, 35-37p, 40p, 44p, 46-50p, 51-58, 61, 62, 63p. **Kaluta** c/a-74. **Spiegle** a-1-3, 6. **Sutton** a-98p. **Totleben** a(i)-10, 16-27, 29, 31, 34-40, 42, 44, 46, 48, 50, 53, 55i; c-25-32i, 33, 35-40i, 42i, 44i, 46-50i, 53, 55i, 59p, 64, 65, 68, 73, 76, 80, 82, 84, 89, 91-100, Annual 4, 5. **Vess** painted c-121, 129-139, Annual 7. **Williamson** 86i. **Wrightson** a-18i(r), 33r. John Constantine appears in #37-40, 44-51, 65-67, 70-77, 80-90, 99, 114, 115, 130, 134-138.*

SWAMP THING

DC Comics (Vertigo): May, 2000 - No. 20, Dec, 2001 ($2.50)

	GD 2.0	VG 4.0	FN 6.0	VF 8.0	VF/NM 9.0	NM- 9.2
1-3-Tefé Holland's return; Vaughan-s/Petersen-a; Hale painted-c.						4.00
4-20: 7-9-Bisley-c. 10-John Constantine-c/app. 10-12-Fabry-c. 13-15-Mack-c 18-Swamp Thing app.						3.00
Preview-16 pg. flip book w/Lucifer Preview						3.00

SWAMP THING

DC Comics (Vertigo): May, 2004 - No. 29, Sept, 2006 ($2.95/$2.99)

	GD 2.0	VG 4.0	FN 6.0	VF 8.0	VF/NM 9.0	NM- 9.2
1-29: 1-Diggle-s/Breccia-a; Constantine app. 2-6-Sargon app. 7,8,20-Corben-c/a. 21-29-Eric Powell-c						3.00
...: Bad Seed (2004, $9.95) r/#1-6						10.00
...: Healing the Breach (2006, $17.99) r/#15-20						18.00
...: Love in Vain (2005, $14.99) r/#9-14						15.00

SWAMP THING (DC New 52)

DC Comics: Nov, 2011 - Present ($2.99)

	GD 2.0	VG 4.0	FN 6.0	VF 8.0	VF/NM 9.0	NM- 9.2
1-Snyder-s/Paquette-a; Superman app.						8.00
1-(2nd & 3rd printing)						3.00
2-18: 2-Abigail Arcane returns. 7-Holland transforms. 10-Francavilla-a; Anton Arcane returns. 12-X-over with Animal Man #12. 13-Poison Ivy & Deadman app.; leads into Annual #1						3.00
19-23: 19-Soule-s/Kano-a begin. 19,20-Superman app. 22,23-Constantine app.						3.00
23.1 (11/13, $2.99, regular cover)						3.00
23.1 (11/13, $3.99, 3-D cover) "Arcane #1" on cover; Soule-s/Saiz-a/c; origin of Arcane						5.00
24-30: 24-Leads into Annual #2. 26-Woodrue's origin; Animal Man app.						3.00
#0-(11/12, $2.99) Kano-a; Arcane app.; Swamp Thing origin re-told						3.00
Annual #1 (12/12, $4.99) Flashback to 1st meeting of Alec & Abby; Cloonan-a						5.00
Annual #2 (12/13, $4.99) Soule-s/Pina-a						5.00

SWAT MALONE (America's Home Run King)

Swat Malone Enterprises: Sept, 1955

	GD 2.0	VG 4.0	FN 6.0	VF 8.0	VF/NM 9.0	NM- 9.2
V1#1-Hy Fleishman-a	11	22	33	62	86	110

SWEATSHOP

DC Comics: Jun, 2003 - No. 6, Nov, 2003 ($2.95)

	GD 2.0	VG 4.0	FN 6.0	VF 8.0	VF/NM 9.0	NM- 9.2
1-6-Peter Bagge-s/a; Destefano-a						3.00

SWEENEY (Formerly Buz Sawyer)

Standard Comics: No. 4, June, 1949 - No. 5, Sept, 1949

	GD 2.0	VG 4.0	FN 6.0	VF 8.0	VF/NM 9.0	NM- 9.2
4,5: 5-Crane-a	9	18	27	47	61	75

SWEE'PEA (Also see Popeye #46)

Dell Publishing Co.: No. 219, Mar, 1949

	GD 2.0	VG 4.0	FN 6.0	VF 8.0	VF/NM 9.0	NM- 9.2
Four Color 219	8	16	24	51	96	140

SWEET CHILDE

Advantage Graphics Press: 1995 - No. 2, 1995 ($2.95, B&W, mature)

	GD 2.0	VG 4.0	FN 6.0	VF 8.0	VF/NM 9.0	NM- 9.2
1,2						3.00

SWEETHEART DIARY (Cynthia Doyle #66-on)

Fawcett Publications/Charlton Comics No. 32 on: Wint, 1949; #2, Spr, 1950; #3, 6/50 - #5, 10/50; #6, 1951(nd); #7, 9/51 - #14, 1/53; #32, 10/55; #33, 4/56 - #65, 8/62 (#1-14: photo-c)

	GD 2.0	VG 4.0	FN 6.0	VF 8.0	VF/NM 9.0	NM- 9.2
1	20	40	60	114	182	250
2	12	24	36	69	97	125
3,4-Wood-a	15	30	45	86	133	180
5-10: 8-Bailey-a	10	20	30	56	76	95
11-14: 13-Swayze-a. 14-Last Fawcett issue	9	18	27	47	61	75
32 (10/55; 1st Charlton issue)(Formerly Cowboy Love #31)	9	18	27	52	69	85
33-40: 34-Swayze-a	7	14	21	35	43	50
41-(68 pgs.)	8	16	24	40	50	60
42-60	3	6	9	19	30	40
61-65	3	6	9	17	26	35

SWEETHEARTS (Formerly Captain Midnight)

Fawcett Publications/Charlton No. 122 on: #68, 10/48 - #121, 5/53; #122, 3/54; V2#23, 5/54 - #137, 12/73

	GD 2.0	VG 4.0	FN 6.0	VF 8.0	VF/NM 9.0	NM- 9.2
68-Photo-c begin	18	36	54	103	162	220
69,70	11	22	33	62	86	110
71-80	9	18	27	52	69	85
81-84,86-93,95-99,105	9	18	27	47	61	75
85,94,103,110,117-George Evans-a	10	20	30	54	72	90
100	9	18	27	52	69	85
101,107-Powell-a	9	18	27	50	65	80
102,104,106,108,109,112-116,118	8	16	24	44	57	70
111-1 pg. Ronald Reagan biography	10	20	30	56	76	95
119-Marilyn Monroe & Richard Widmark photo-c (1/54?); also appears in story; part Wood-a	69	138	207	442	759	1075
120-Atom Bomb story	12	24	36	67	94	120
121-Liz Taylor/Fernanado Lamas photo-c	34	68	102	204	332	460
122-(1st Charlton? 3/54)-Marijuana story	13	26	39	72	101	130
V2#23 (5/54)-28: 28-Last precode issue (2/55)	8	16	24	42	54	65
29-39,41,43,45,47-50	4	8	12	25	40	55
40-Photo-c; Tommy Sands story	4	8	12	27	44	60
42-Ricky Nelson photo-c/story	7	14	21	49	92	135
44-Pat Boone photo-c/story	4	8	12	27	44	60
46-Jimmy Rodgers photo-c/story	4	8	12	27	44	60
51-60	3	6	9	21	33	45
61-80,100	3	6	9	18	28	38
81-99	3	6	9	16	24	32
101-110	2	4	6	13	18	22
111-120,122-124,126-137	2	4	6	10	14	18
121,125-David Cassidy pin-ups	2	4	6	13	18	22

NOTE: *Photo c-68-121(Fawcett), 40, 42, 46(Charlton). **Swayze** a(Fawcett)-70-118(most).*

SWEETHEART SCANDALS (See Fox Giants)

SWEETIE PIE

Dell Publishing Co.: No. 1185, May-July, 1961 - No. 1241, Nov-Jan, 1961/62

	GD 2.0	VG 4.0	FN 6.0	VF 8.0	VF/NM 9.0	NM- 9.2
Four Color 1185 (#1)	5	10	15	30	50	70
Four Color 1241	4	8	12	25	40	55

Sweet Sixteen #5 © PMI

Swing With Scooter #3 © DC

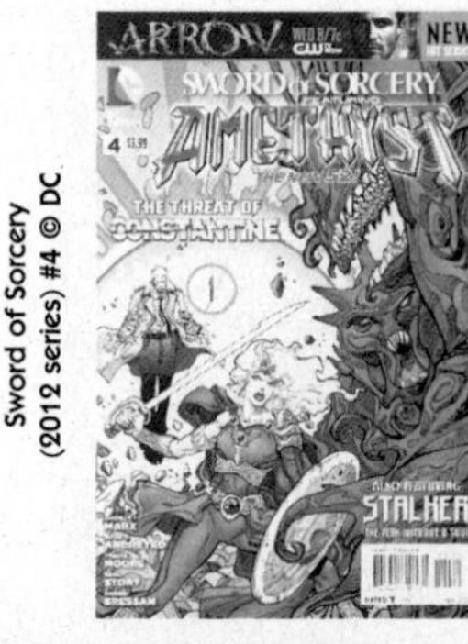

Sword of Sorcery (2012 series) #4 © DC

GD VG FN VF VF/NM NM-
2.0 4.0 6.0 8.0 9.0 9.2

SWEETIE PIE
Ajax-Farrell/Pines (Literary Ent.): Dec, 1955 - No. 15, Fall, 1957

1-By Nadine Seltzer 10 20 30 54 72 90
2 (5/56; last Ajax?) 7 14 21 35 43 50
3-15 6 12 18 28 34 40

SWEET LOVE
Home Comics (Harvey): Sept, 1949 - No. 5, May, 1950 (All photo-c)

1 10 20 30 58 79 100
2 7 14 21 37 46 55
3,4: 3-Powell-a 6 12 18 31 38 45
5-Kamen, Powell-a 9 18 27 47 61 75

SWEET ROMANCE
Charlton Comics: Oct, 1968

1 3 6 9 14 20 25

SWEET SIXTEEN (...Comics and Stories for Girls)
Parents' Magazine Institute: Aug-Sept, 1946 - No. 13, Jan, 1948 (All have movie stars photos on covers)

1-Van Johnson's life story; Dorothy Dare, Queen of Hollywood Stunt Artists begins (in all issues); part photo-c 25 50 75 150 245 340
2-Jane Powell, Roddy McDowall "Holiday in Mexico" photo on-c; Alan Ladd story 17 34 51 98 154 210
3,5,6,8-11: 5-Ann Francis photo on-c; Gregory Peck story. 6-Dick Haymes story. 8-Shirley Jones photo on-c. 10-Jean Simmons photo on-c; James Stewart story 14 28 42 80 115 150
4-Elizabeth Taylor photo on-c 32 64 96 188 307 425
7-Ronald Reagan's life story 25 50 75 150 245 340
12-Bob Cummings, Vic Damone story 14 28 42 82 121 160
13-Robert Mitchum's life story 15 30 45 83 124 165

SWEET XVI
Marvel Comics: May, 1991 - No. 5, Sept, 1991 ($1.00)

1-5: Barbara Slate story & art 4.00

SWEET TOOTH
DC Comics (Vertigo): Nov, 2009 - No. 40, Feb, 2013 ($1.00/$2.99)

1-($1.00) Jeff Lemire-s/a 3.00
2-39-($2.99) 18,33-Printed sideways. 26-28-Kindt-a 3.00
40-($4.99) Final issue; two covers by Lemire and Truman 5.00
...: Animal Armies TPB (2011, $14.99) r/#12-17 15.00
...: In Captivity TPB (2010, $12.99) r/#6-11 13.00
...: Out of the Deep Woods TPB (2010, $9.99) r/#1-5 10.00

SWIFT ARROW (Also see Lone Rider & The Rider)
Ajax/Farrell Publications: Feb-Mar, 1954 - No. 5, Oct-Nov, 1954; Apr, 1957 - No. 3, Sept, 1957

1(1954) (1st Series) 16 32 48 92 144 195
2 10 20 30 56 76 95
3-5: 5-Lone Rider story 9 18 27 50 65 80
1 (2nd Series) (Swift Arrow's Gunfighters #4) 9 18 27 50 65 80
2,3: 2-Lone Rider begins 8 16 24 40 50 60

SWIFT ARROW'S GUNFIGHTERS (Formerly Swift Arrow)
Ajax/Farrell Publ. (Four Star Comic Corp.): No. 4, Nov, 1957

4 8 16 24 40 50 60

SWING WITH SCOOTER
National Periodical Publ.: June-July, 1966 - No. 35, Aug-Sept, 1971; No. 36, Oct-Nov, 1972

1 8 16 24 56 108 160
2,6-10: 9-Alfred E. Newman swipe in last panel 5 10 15 33 57 80
3-5: 3-Batman cameo on-c. 4-Batman cameo inside. 5-JLA cameo 5 10 15 34 60 85
11-13,15-19: 18-Wildcat of JSA 1pg. text. 19-Last 12¢-c 3 6 9 20 31 42
14-Alfred E. Neuman cameo 3 6 9 21 33 45
20 (68 pgs.) 5 10 15 30 50 70
21-23,25-31 3 6 9 17 26 35
24-Frankenstein-c. 3 6 9 21 33 45
32-34 (68 pgs.). 32-Batman cameo. 33-Interview with David Cassidy. 34-Interview with Rick Ely (The Rebels) 4 8 12 28 47 65
35-(52 pgs.). 1 pg. app. Clark Kent and 4 full pgs. of Superman 6 12 18 42 79 115
36-Bat-signal refererence to Batman 3 6 9 21 33 45

NOTE: ***Aragonés*** *a-13 (1pg.), 18(1pg.), 30(2pgs.)* ***Orlando*** *a-1-11; c-1-11, 13. #20, 33, 34: 68 pgs.; #35: 52 pgs.*

SWISS FAMILY ROBINSON (Walt Disney's..; see King Classics & Movie Comics)
Dell Publishing Co.: No. 1156, Dec, 1960

Four Color 1156-Movie-photo-c 6 12 18 42 79 115

S.W.O.R.D. (Sentient World Observation and Response Department)
Marvel Comics: Jan, 2010 - No. 5, May, 2010 ($3.99/$2.99)

1-($3.99) Cassaday-c/Gillen-s/Sanders-a; Commander Brand & Henry Gyrich app. 4.00
2-5-($2.99): 2,3-Cassaday-c. 4,5-Del Mundo-c 3.00

SWORD, THE
Image Comics: Oct, 2007 - No. 24, May, 2010 ($2.99/$4.99)

1-Luna Brothers-s/a 4.00
1-(2nd printing) 3.00
2-23: 12-Zakros killed 3.00
24-($4.99) Final issue 5.00
..., Vol. 1: Fire (TPB, 2008, $14.99) r/#1-6 15.00
..., Vol. 2: Water (TPB, 2008, $14.99) r/#7-12 15.00
..., Vol. 3: Earth (TPB, 2009, $14.99) r/#13-18 15.00
..., Vol. 4: Water (TPB, 2010, $14.99) r/#19-24 15.00

SWORD & THE DRAGON, THE
Dell Publishing Co.: No. 1118, June, 1960

Four Color 1118-Movie, photo-c 7 14 21 44 82 120

SWORD & THE ROSE, THE (Disney)
Dell Publishing Co.: No. 505, Oct, 1953 - No. 682, Feb, 1956

Four Color 505-Movie, photo-c 7 14 21 49 92 135
Four Color 682-When Knighthood Was in Flower-Movie, reprint of #505; Renamed the Sword & the Rose for the novel; photo-c 6 12 18 40 73 105

SWORD IN THE STONE, THE (See March of Comics #258 & Movie Comics & Wart and the Wizard)

SWORD OF DAMOCLES
Image Comics (WildStorm Productions): Mar, 1996 - No. 2, Apr, 1996 ($2.50, limited series)

1,2: Warren Ellis scripts. 1-Prelude to "Fire From Heaven" x-over; 1st app. Sword 3.00

SWORD OF DRACULA
Image Comics: Oct, 2003 - No. 6, Sept, 2004 ($2.95, B&W, limited series)

1-6-Tony Harris-c. 1,2-Greg Scott-a 3.00
TPB (IDW, 2/05, $14.99) r/series 15.00

SWORD OF RED SONJA: DOOM OF THE GODS
Dynamite Entertainment: 2007 - No. 4, 2007 ($3.50, limited series)

1-4-Lui Antonio-a; multiple covers on each 3.50

SWORD OF SORCERY
National Periodical Publications: Feb-Mar, 1973 - No. 5, Nov-Dec, 1973 (20¢)

1-Leiber Fafhrd & The Grey Mouser; Chaykin/Neal Adams (Crusty Bunkers) art; Kaluta-c 3 6 9 16 23 30
2,3: 2-Wrightson-c(i); Adams-a(i). 3-Wrightson-i(5 pgs.) 2 4 6 9 13 16
4,5: 5-Starlin-a(p); Conan cameo 2 4 6 8 10 12

NOTE: ***Chaykin*** *a-1-4p; c-2p, 3-5.* ***Kaluta*** *a-3i.* ***Simonson*** *a-3i, 4i, 5p; c-5.*

SWORD OF SORCERY (DC New 52)
DC Comics: No. 0, Nov, 2012 - No. 8, Jun, 2013 ($3.99)

0-8: 0-Origin of Amethyst retold; Lopresti-a; Beowulf back-up; Saiz-a. 4-Stalker back-up 4.00

SWORD OF THE ATOM
DC Comics: Sept, 1983 - No. 4, Dec, 1983 (Limited series)

1-4: Gil Kane-c/a in all 4.00
Special 1-3('84, '85, '88): 1,2-Kane-c/a each 4.00
TPB (2007, $19.99) r/#1-4 and Special #1-3 20.00

SWORDS OF TEXAS (See Scout #15)
Eclipse Comics: Oct, 1987 - No. 4, Jan, 1988 ($1.75, color, Baxter paper)

1-4: Scout app. 3.00

SWORDS OF THE SWASHBUCKLERS (See Marvel Graphic Novel)
Marvel Comics (Epic Comics): May, 1985 - No. 12, Jun, 1987 ($1.50; mature)

1-12-Butch Guice-c/a (Cont'd from Marvel G.N.) 3.00

SWORN TO PROTECT
Marvel Comics: Sept, 1995 ($1.95) (Based on card game)

nn-Overpower Game Guide; Jubilee story 3.00

SYN
Dark Horse Comics: Aug, 2003 - No. 5, Feb, 2004 ($2.99, limited series)

1-5-Giffen-s/Titus-a 3.00

SYPHONS
Now Comics: V2#1, May, 1994 - V2#3, 1994 ($2.50, limited series)

Taffy Comics #6 © Orbit

Takio #4 © Jinxworld

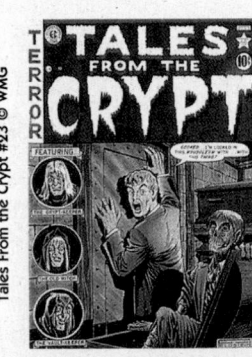

Tales From the Crypt #23 © WMG

	GD	VG	FN	VF	VF/NM	NM-
	2.0	4.0	6.0	8.0	9.0	9.2

V2#1-3: 1-Stardancer, Knightfire, Raze & Brigade begin 3.00
TPB (9/04, $15.95) B&W reprints #1-3; intro. by Tony Caputo 16.00

SYSTEM, THE
DC Comics (Vertigo Verite): May, 1996 - No. 3, July, 1996 ($2.95, lim. series)

1-3: Kuper-c/a 3.00
TPB (1997, $12.95) r/#1-3 13.00

TAFFY COMICS (Also see Dotty Dripple)
Rural Home/Orbit Publ.: Mar-Apr, 1945 - No. 12, 1948

1-L.B. Cole-c; origin & 1st app. of Wiggles The Wonderworm plus 7 chapter WWII funny animal adventures	61	122	183	390	670	950
2-L.B. Cole-c with funny animal Hitler; Wiggles-c/stories in #1-4	41	82	123	256	428	600
3,4,6-12: 6-Perry Como-c/story. 7-Duke Ellington, 2 pgs. 8-Glenn Ford-c/story. 9-Lon McCallister part photo-c & story. 10-Mort Leav-c. 11-Mickey Rooney-c/story	15	30	45	85	130	175
5-L.B. Cole-c; Van Johnson-c/story	21	42	63	126	206	285

TAILGUNNER JO
DC Comics: Sept, 1988 - No. 6, Jan, 1989 ($1.25)

1-6 3.00

TAILS
Archie Publications: Dec, 1995 - No. 3, Feb, 1996 ($1.50, limited series)

1-3: Based on Sonic, the Hedgehog video game 6.00

TAILS OF THE PET AVENGERS (Also see Lockjaw and the Pet Avengers)
Marvel Comics: Apr, 2010 ($3.99, one-shot)

1-Lockjaw, Frog Thor, Zabu, Lockheed and Redwing in short solo stories by various 4.00
...: The Dogs of Summer (9/10, $3.99) Eliopolous-s; see Avengers vs. the Pet Avengers 4.00

TAILSPIN
Spotlight Publishers: November, 1944

nn-Firebird app.; L.B. Cole-c	31	62	93	186	303	420

TAILSPIN TOMMY (Also see Popular Comics)
United Features Syndicate/Service Publ. Co.: 1940; 1946

Single Series 23(1940)	40	80	120	246	411	575
1-Best Seller (nd, 1946)-Service Publ. Co.	16	32	48	94	147	200

TAKE A CHANCE (C.E. Murphy's...)
Dabel Brothers Prods.: Dec, 2008 - No. 5, Apr, 2009 ($3.99)

1-4-C.E. Murphy-s/Ardian Syaf-a/c 4.00

TAKIO
Marvel Comics (Icon): 2011; May, 2012 - Present ($3.95/$9.95)

HC (2011, $9.95) Bendis-s/Oeming-a/c; Oeming sketch pages 10.00
1-4: 1-(5/12, $3.95) Bendis-s/Oeming-a/c 4.00

TAKION
DC Comics: June, 1996 - No. 7, Dec, 1996 ($1.75)

1-7: Lopresti-c/a(p). 1-Origin; Green Lantern app. 6-Final Night x-over 3.00

TALENT SHOWCASE (See New Talent Showcase)

TALE OF ONE BAD RAT, THE
Dark Horse Comics: Oct, 1994 - No. 4, Jan, 1995 ($2.95, limited series)

1-4: Bryan Talbot-c/a/scripts 3.00
HC ($69.95, signed and numbered) R/#1-4 70.00

TALES CALCULATED TO DRIVE YOU BATS
Archie Publications: Nov, 1961 - No. 7, Nov, 1962; 1966 (Satire)

1-Only 10¢ issue; has cut-out Werewolf mask (price includes mask)	12	24	36	84	185	285
2-Begin 12¢ issues	8	16	24	51	96	140
3-6: 3-UFO cover	6	12	18	41	76	110
7-Storyline change	6	12	18	40	73	105
1(1966, 25¢, 44 pg. Giant)-r/#1; UFO cover	6	12	18	38	69	100

TALES CALCULATED TO DRIVE YOU MAD
E.C. Publications: Summer, 1997 - No. 8, Winter, 1999 ($3.99/$4.99, satire)

1-6-Full color reprints of Mad: 1-(#1-3), 2-(#4-6), 3-(#7-9), 4-(#10-12) 5-(#13-15), 6-(#16-18) 6.00
7,8-($4.99-c): 7-(#19-21), 8-(#22,23) 6.00

TALES FROM RIVERDALE DIGEST
Archie Publ.: June, 2005 - No. 39, Oct, 2010 ($2.39/$2.49/$2.69, digest-size)

1-39: 1-Sabrina and Josie & the Pussycats app. 11-Begin $2.49-c. 34-Begin $2.69 3.00

TALES FROM THE AGE OF APOCALYPSE
Marvel Comics: 1996 ($5.95, prestige format, one-shots)

1, ...: Sinister Bloodlines (1997, $5.95) 6.00

TALES FROM THE BOG
Aberration Press: Nov, 1995 - No. 7, Nov, 1997 ($2.95/$3.95, B&W)

1-7 4.00
Alternate #1 (Director's Cut) (1998, $2.95) 3.00

TALES FROM THE BULLY PULPIT
Image Comics: Aug, 2004 ($6.95, square-bound)

1-Teddy Roosevelt and Edison's ghost with a time machine; Cereno-s/MacDonald-a 7.00

TALES FROM THE CLERKS (See Jay and Silent Bob, Clerks and Oni Double Feature)
Graphitti Designs, Inc.: 2006 ($29.95, TPB)

nn-Reprints all the Kevin Smith Clerks and Jay and Silent Bob stories; new Clerks II story with Mahfood-a; cover gallery, sketch pages, Mallrats credits covers; Smith intro. 30.00

TALES FROM THE CRYPT (Formerly The Crypt Of Terror; see Three Dimensional...) (Also see EC Archives • Tales From the Crypt)
E.C. Comics: No. 20, Oct-Nov, 1950 - No. 46, Feb-Mar, 1955

20-See Crime Patrol #15 for 1st Crypt Keeper	120	240	360	960	1530	2100
21-Kurtzman-r/Haunt of Fear #15(#1)	101	202	303	808	1292	1775
22-Moon Girl costume at costume party, one panel	79	158	237	632	1004	1375
23-25: 24-E. A. Poe adaptation	64	128	192	512	819	1125
26-30: 26-Wood's 2nd EC-c	51	102	153	408	654	900
31-Williamson-a(1st at E.C.); B&W and color illos. in **POP**; Kamen draws himself, Gaines & Feldstein; Ingels, Craig & Davis draw themselves in his story	53	106	159	424	675	925
32,35-39: 38-Censored-c	46	92	138	368	584	800
33-Origin The Crypt Keeper	66	132	198	528	839	1150
34-Used in **POP**, pg. 83; lingerie panels	47	94	141	376	601	825
40-Used in Senate hearings & in Hartford Courant anti-comics editorials-1954	46	92	138	368	589	810
41-45: 45-2 pgs. showing E.C. staff	45	90	135	360	573	785
46-Low distribution; pre-advertised cover for unpublished 4th horror title "Crypt of Terror" used on this book	51	102	153	408	654	900

NOTE: ***Ray Bradbury** adaptations-34, 36. **Craig** a-20, 22-24; c-20. **Crandall** a-38, 44. **Davis** a-24-46; c-29-46. **Elder** a-37, 38. **Evans** a-32-34, 36, 40, 41, 43, 46. **Feldstein** a-20-23; c-21-25, 28. Ingels a-in all. **Kamen** a-20, 22, 25, 27-31, 33-36, 39, 41-45. **Krigstein** a-40, 42, 45. **Kurtzman** a-21. **Orlando** a-27-30, 35, 37, 39, 41-45. **Wood** a-21, 24, 25; c-26, 27. Canadian reprints known; see Table of Contents.*

TALES FROM THE CRYPT (Magazine)
Eerie Publications: No. 10, July, 1968 (35¢, B&W)

10-Contains Farrell reprints from 1950s	5	10	15	35	63	90

TALES FROM THE CRYPT
Gladstone Publishing: July, 1990 - No. 6, May, 1991 ($1.95/$2.00, 68 pgs.)

1-r/TFTC #33 & Crime S.S. #17; Davis-c(r) 5.00
2-6: 2,3,5,6-Davis-c(r). 4-Begin $2.00-c; Craig-c(r) 5.00

TALES FROM THE CRYPT
Extra-Large Comics (Russ Cochran)/Gemstone Publishing: Jul, 1991 - No. 6 ($3.95, 10 1/4 x13 1/4", 68 pgs.)

1-Davis-c(r); Craig back-c(r); E.C. reprints 5.00
2-6 ($2.00, comic sized) 5.00

TALES FROM THE CRYPT
Russ Cochran: Sept, 1991 - No. 7, July, 1992 ($2.00, 64 pgs.)

1-7 5.00

TALES FROM THE CRYPT (Also see EC Archives • Tales From the Crypt)
Russ Cochran/Gemstone: Sept, 1992 - No. 30, Dec, 1999 ($1.50, quarterly)

1-4-r/Crypt of Terror #17-19, TFTC #20 w/original-c 4.00
5-30: 5-15 ($2.00)-r/TFTC #21-23 w/original-c. 16-30 ($2.50) 4.00
Annual 1-6('93-'99) 1-r/#1-5. 2- r/#6-10. 3- r/#11-15. 4- r/#16-20. 5-r/#21-25. 6- r/#26-30 14.00

TALES FROM THE CRYPT
Papercutz: July, 2007 - Present ($3.95)

1-6: 1-New stories in the same vein as the originals; Cryptkeeper app. Kyle Baker-c 4.00

TALES FROM THE GREAT BOOK
Famous Funnies: Feb, 1955 - No. 4, Jan, 1956 (Religious themes)

1-Story of Samson; John Lehti-a in all	9	18	27	50	65	80
2-4: 2-Joshua. 3-Joash the Boy King. 4-David	7	14	21	35	43	50

TALES FROM THE HEART OF AFRICA (The Temporary Natives)
Marvel Comics (Epic Comics): Aug, 1990 ($3.95, 52 pgs.)

1 4.00

Tales of Horror #10 © Minoan

Tales of Suspense #20 © MAR

Tales of Suspense #39 © MAR

TALES FROM THE TOMB (Also see Dell Giants)
Dell Publishing Co.: Oct, 1962 (25¢ giant)

	GD 2.0	VG 4.0	FN 6.0	VF 8.0	VF/NM 9.0	NM- 9.2
1(02-810-210)-All stories written by John Stanley	13	26	39	86	188	290

TALES FROM THE TOMB (Magazine)
Eerie Publications: V1#6, July, 1969 - V7#3, 1975 (52 pgs.)

	GD 2.0	VG 4.0	FN 6.0	VF 8.0	VF/NM 9.0	NM- 9.2
V1#6	8	16	24	51	96	140
V1#7,8	6	12	18	38	69	100
V2#1-6: 4-LSD story-r/Weird V3#5. 6-Rulah-r	5	10	15	34	60	85
V3#1-Rulah-r	5	10	15	34	60	85
2-6('71),V4#1-5('72),V5#1-6('73),V6#1-6('74),V7#1-3('75)	5	10	15	31	53	75

TALES OF ASGARD
Marvel Comics Group: Oct, 1968 (25¢, 68 pgs.); Feb, 1984 ($1.25, 52 pgs.)

	GD 2.0	VG 4.0	FN 6.0	VF 8.0	VF/NM 9.0	NM- 9.2
1-Reprints Tales of Asgard (Thor) back-up stories from Journey into Mystery #97-106; new Kirby-c; Kirby-a	5	10	15	35	63	90
V2#1 (2/84)-Thor-r; Simonson-c						5.00

TALES OF ARMY OF DARKNESS
Dynamite Entertainment: 2006 ($5.95, one-shot)

	GD 2.0	VG 4.0	FN 6.0	VF 8.0	VF/NM 9.0	NM- 9.2
1-Short stories by Kuhoric, Kirkman, Bradshaw, Sablik, Ottley, Acs, O'Hare and others						6.00

TALES OF EVIL
Atlas/Seaboard Publ.: Feb, 1975 - No. 3, July, 1975 (All 25¢ issues)

	GD 2.0	VG 4.0	FN 6.0	VF 8.0	VF/NM 9.0	NM- 9.2
1-3: 1-Werewolf w/Sekowsky-a. 2-Intro. The Bog Beast; Sparling-a. 3-Origin The Man-Monster; Buckler-a(p)	2	4	6	11	16	20

NOTE: ***Grandenetti** a-1, 2. **Lieber** c-1. **Sekowsky** a-1. **Sutton** a-2. **Thorne** c-2.*

TALES OF GHOST CASTLE
National Periodical Publications: May-June, 1975 - No. 3, Sept-Oct, 1975 (All 25¢ issues)

	GD 2.0	VG 4.0	FN 6.0	VF 8.0	VF/NM 9.0	NM- 9.2
1-Redondo-a; 1st app. Lucien the Librarian from Sandman (1989 series)	3	6	9	17	26	35
2,3: 2-Nino-a. 3-Redondo-a.	2	4	6	10	14	18

TALES OF G.I. JOE
Marvel Comics: Jan, 1988 - No. 15, Mar, 1989

	GD 2.0	VG 4.0	FN 6.0	VF 8.0	VF/NM 9.0	NM- 9.2
1 ($2.25, 52 pgs.)						4.00
2-15 ($1.50): 1-15-r/G.I. Joe #1-15						3.00

TALES OF HONOR (Based on the David Weber novels)
Image Comics (Top Cow): Mar, 2014 - Present ($2.99)

	GD 2.0	VG 4.0	FN 6.0	VF 8.0	VF/NM 9.0	NM- 9.2
1-Matt Hawkins-s/Jung-Geun Yoon-a						3.00

TALES OF HORROR
Toby Press/Minoan Publ. Corp.: June, 1952 - No. 13, Oct, 1954

	GD 2.0	VG 4.0	FN 6.0	VF 8.0	VF/NM 9.0	NM- 9.2
1	43	86	129	271	461	650
2-Torture scenes	36	72	108	211	343	475
3-11,13: 9-11-Reprints Purple Claw #1-3	24	48	72	144	237	330
12-Myron Fass-c/a; torture scenes	26	52	78	154	252	350

NOTE: ***Andru** a-5. **Baily** a-5. **Myron Fass** a-2, 3, 12; c-1-3, 12. **Hollingsworth** a-2. **Sparling** a-6, 9; c-9.*

TALES OF JUSTICE
Atlas Comics(MjMC No. 53-66/Male No. 67): No. 53, May, 1955 - No. 67, Aug, 1957

	GD 2.0	VG 4.0	FN 6.0	VF 8.0	VF/NM 9.0	NM- 9.2
53	15	30	45	86	133	180
54-57: 54-Powell-a	11	22	33	64	90	115
58,59-Krigstein-a	13	26	39	72	101	130
60-63,65: 60-Powell-a	10	20	30	58	79	100
64,66,67: 64,67-Crandall-a. 66-Torres, Orlando-a	11	22	33	60	83	105

NOTE: ***Everett** a-53, 60. **Orlando** a-65, 66. **Severin** a-64; c-58, 60, 65. **Wildey** a-64, 67.*

TALES OF LEONARDO BLIND SIGHT (See Tales of the TMNT Vol. 2 #5)
Mirage Publishing: June, 2006 - No. 4, Sept, 2006 ($3.25, B&W, limited series)

	GD 2.0	VG 4.0	FN 6.0	VF 8.0	VF/NM 9.0	NM- 9.2
1-4-Jim Lawson-s/a						3.25

TALES OF SUSPENSE (Becomes Captain America #100 on)
Atlas (WPI No. 1,2/Male No. 3-12/VPI No. 13-18)/Marvel No. 19 on:
Jan, 1959 - No. 99, Mar, 1968

	GD 2.0	VG 4.0	FN 6.0	VF 8.0	VF/NM 9.0	NM- 9.2
1-Williamson-a (5 pgs.); Heck-c; #1-4 have sci/fi-c	207	414	621	1708	3854	6000
2,3: 2-Ditko robot-c. 3-Flying saucer-c/story	71	142	213	568	1284	2000
4-Williamson-a (4 pgs.); Kirby/Everett-c/a	57	114	171	456	1028	1600
5-Kirby monster-c begin	50	100	150	400	900	1400
6,8,10	44	88	132	326	738	1150
7-Prototype ish. (Lava Man); 1 panel app. Aunt May (see Str. Tales #97)	45	90	135	333	754	1175
9-Prototype ish. (Iron Man)	45	90	135	333	754	1175
11,12,15,17-19: 12-Crandall-a.	36	72	108	259	580	900
13-Elektro-c/story	36	72	108	266	596	925
14-Intro/1st app. Colossus-c/sty	42	84	126	311	706	1100
16-1st Metallo-c/story (4/61, Iron Man prototype)	38	76	114	281	628	975
20-Colossus-c/story (2nd app.)	37	74	111	274	612	950
21-25: 25-Last 10¢ issue	31	62	93	223	499	775
26,27,29,30,33,34,36-38: 33-(9/62)-Hulk 1st x-over cameo (picture on wall)	30	60	90	216	483	750
28-Prototype ish. (Stone Men)	31	62	93	223	499	775
31-Prototype ish. (Dr. Doom)	33	66	99	238	532	825
32-Prototype ish. (Dr. Strange)(8/62)-Sazzik The Sorcerer app.; "The Man and the Beehive" story, 1 month before TTA #35 (2nd Antman), came out after "The Man in the Ant Hill" in TTA #27 (1/62) (1st Antman)-Characters from both stories were tested to see which got best fan response	40	80	120	296	673	1050
35-Prototype issue (The Watcher)	32	64	96	230	515	800
39 (3/63)-Origin/1st app. Iron Man & begin series; 1st Iron Man story has Kirby layouts	1100	2200	3300	9000	21,000	38,000
40-2nd app. Iron Man (in new armor)	193	386	579	1592	3596	5600
41-3rd app. Iron Man; Dr. Strange (villain) app.	114	228	342	912	2056	3200
42-45: 45-Intro. & 1st app. Happy & Pepper	79	158	237	632	1416	2200
46,47: 46-1st app. Crimson Dynamo	54	108	162	432	966	1500
48-New Iron Man armor by Ditko	61	122	183	488	1094	1700
49-1st X-Men x-over (same date as X-Men #3, 1/64); also 1st Avengers x-over (w/o Captain America); 1st Tales of the Watcher back-up story & begins (2nd app. Watcher; see F.F. #13)	79	158	237	632	1416	2200
50-1st app. Mandarin	50	100	150	384	867	1350
51-1st Scarecrow	29	58	87	209	467	725
52-1st app. The Black Widow (4/64)	61	122	183	488	1094	1700
53-Origin The Watcher; 2nd Black Widow app.	30	60	90	216	483	750
54,55-2nd & 3rd Mandarin app.	23	46	69	161	356	550
56-1st app. Unicorn	24	48	72	168	372	575
57-Origin/1st app. Hawkeye (9/64)	71	142	213	568	1284	2000
58-Captain America battles Iron Man (10/64)-Classic-c; 2nd Kraven app. (Cap's 1st app. in this title)	50	100	150	384	867	1350
59-Iron Man plus Captain America double feature begins (11/64); 1st S.A. Captain America solo story; intro Jarvis, Avenger's butler; classic-c	40	80	120	296	673	1050
60-2nd app. Hawkeye (#64 is 3rd app.)	25	50	75	175	388	600
61,62,64: 62-Origin Mandarin (2/65)	15	30	45	100	220	340
63-1st Silver Age origin Captain America (3/65)	29	58	87	209	467	725
65-G.A. Red Skull in WWII stories(also in #66);-1st Silver-Age Red Skull (5/65).	25	50	75	175	388	600
66-Origin Red Skull	17	34	51	117	259	400
67-70: 69-1st app. Titanium Man. 70-Begin alternating-c features w/Capt. America (even #'s) & Iron Man (odd #'s)	9	18	27	61	123	185
71-74,77,78: 78-Col. Nick Fury app.	7	14	21	46	86	125
75-1st app. Agent 13 later named Sharon Carter; intro Batroc	13	26	39	89	195	300
76-2nd app. Batroc & 1st cover app.	8	16	24	51	96	140
79-Begin 3 part Iron Man Sub-Mariner battle story; Sub-Mariner-c & cameo; 1st app. Cosmic Cube; 1st modern Red Skull	9	18	27	57	111	165
80-Iron Man battles Sub-Mariner story cont'd in Tales to Astonish #82; classic Red Skull-c	9	18	27	57	111	165
81-93,95,96,98: 82-Intro the Adaptoid by Kirby (also in #83,84). 88-Mole Man app. in Iron Man story. 92-1st Nick Fury x-over (cameo, as Agent of S.H.I.E.L.D., 8/67). 95-Capt. America's i.d. revealed. 98-1st brief app. new Zemo (son?); #99 is 1st full app.	6	12	18	40	73	105
94-Intro Modok	7	14	21	44	2	120
97-1st Whiplash	8	16	24	54	102	150
99-Captain America story cont'd in Captain America #100; Iron Man story cont'd in Iron Man & Sub-Mariner #1	7	14	21	49	92	135

Onmibus (See Iron Man Omnibus for reprints of #39-83)

NOTE: ***Abel** a-73-81i(as Gary Michaels), **J. Buscema** a-1; c-3. **Colan** a-39, 73-99p; c(p)-73, 75, 77, 79, 81, 83, 85-87, 89, 91, 93, 95, 97, 99. **Crandall** a-12. **Davis** a-38. **Ditko** a-1-15, 17-44, 46, 47-49p; c-2, 10i, 13i, 23i. **Kirby/Ditko** a-7; c-10, 13, 22, 28, 34. **Everett** a-8. **Forte** a-5, 9. **Giacoia** a-82. **Heath** a-2, 10. **Gil Kane** a-88p, 89-91; c-88, 89-91p. **Kirby** a(p)-2-4, 6-35, 40, 41, 43, 59-75, 77-86, 92-99; layouts-69-75, 77; c(p)4-28(most), 29-56, 58-72, 74, 76, 78, 80, 82, 84, 86, 92, 94, 96, 98. **Leiber/Fox** a-42, 43, 45, 51. **Reinman** a-13, 26, 44i, 49i, 52i, 53i. **Tuska** a-58, 70-74. **Wood** c/a-71i.*

TALES OF SUSPENSE
Marvel Comics: V2#1, Jan, 1995 ($6.95, one-shot)

	GD 2.0	VG 4.0	FN 6.0	VF 8.0	VF/NM 9.0	NM- 9.2
V2#1-James Robinson script; acetate-c.	1	2	3	5	6	8

TALES OF SUSPENSE: CAPTAIN AMERICA & IRON MAN #1 COMMEMORATIVE EDITION
Marvel Comics: 2004 ($3.99, one-shot)

	GD 2.0	VG 4.0	FN 6.0	VF 8.0	VF/NM 9.0	NM- 9.2
nn-Reprints Captain America (2004) #1 and Iron Man (2004) #1						5.00

TALES OF SWORD & SORCERY (See Dagar)

TALES OF TELLOS (See Tellos)

Tales of the Darkness #3 © TCOW

Tales of the L.S.H. #325 © DC

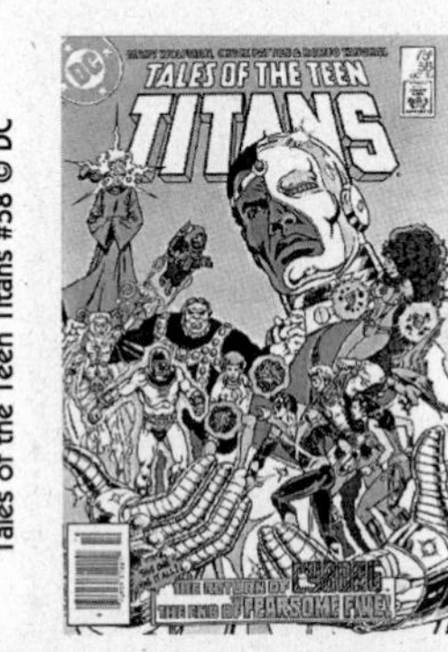
Tales of the Teen Titans #58 © DC

Image Comics: Oct, 2004 - No. 3, ($3.50, anthology)

	GD 2.0	VG 4.0	FN 6.0	VF 8.0	VF/NM 9.0	NM- 9.2
1-3: 1-Dezago-s; art by Yates & Rousseau; Wieringo-c. 3-Porter-a						3.50

TALES OF TERROR
Toby Press Publications: 1952 (no month)

	GD 2.0	VG 4.0	FN 6.0	VF 8.0	VF/NM 9.0	NM- 9.2
1-Fawcette-c; Ravielli-a	30	60	90	177	289	400

NOTE: *This title was cancelled due to similarity to the E.C. title.*

TALES OF TERROR (See Movie Classics)

TALES OF TERROR (Magazine)
Eerie Publications: Summer, 1964

	GD 2.0	VG 4.0	FN 6.0	VF 8.0	VF/NM 9.0	NM- 9.2
1	6	12	18	40	73	105

TALES OF TERROR
Eclipse Comics: July, 1985 - No. 13, July, 1987 ($2.00, Baxter paper, mature)

	GD 2.0	VG 4.0	FN 6.0	VF 8.0	VF/NM 9.0	NM- 9.2
1-13: 5-1st Lee Weeks-a. 7-Sam Kieth-a. 10-Snyder-a. 12-Vampire story						4.00

TALES OF TERROR (IDW's...)
IDW Publishing: Sept, 2004 ($16.99, hardcover)

	GD 2.0	VG 4.0	FN 6.0	VF 8.0	VF/NM 9.0	NM- 9.2
1-Anthology of short graphic stories and text stories; incl. 30 Days of Night						17.00

TALES OF TERROR ANNUAL
E.C. Comics: 1951 - No. 3, 1953 (25¢, 132 pgs., 16 stories each)

	GD 2.0	VG 4.0	FN 6.0	VF 8.0	VF/NM 9.0	NM- 9.2
nn(1951)(Scarce)-Feldstein infinity-c	1000	2000	3000	8000	-	-
2(1952)-Feldstein-c	277	554	831	1773	3037	4300
3(1953)-Feldstein bondage/torture-c	226	452	678	1446	2473	3500

NOTE: *No. 1 contains three horror and one science fiction comic which came out in 1950. No. 2 contains a horror, crime, and science fiction book which generally had cover dates in 1951, and No. 3 had horror, crime, and shock books that generally appeared in 1952. All E.C. annuals contain four complete books that did not sell on the stands which were rebound in the annual format, minus the covers, and sold from the E.C. office and on the stands in key cities. The contents of each annual may vary in the same year. Crypt Keeper, Vault Keeper, Old Witch app. on all-c.*

TALES OF TERROR ILLUSTRATED (See Terror Illustrated)

TALES OF TEXAS JOHN SLAUGHTER (See Walt Disney Presents, 4-Color #997)

TALES OF THE BEANWORLD
Beanworld Press/Eclipse Comics: Feb, 1985 - No. 19, 1991; No. 20, 1993 - No. 21, 1993 ($1.50/$2.00, B&W)

	GD 2.0	VG 4.0	FN 6.0	VF 8.0	VF/NM 9.0	NM- 9.2
1-21						3.00

TALES OF THE BIZARRO WORLD
DC Comics: 2000 ($14.95, TPB)

	GD 2.0	VG 4.0	FN 6.0	VF 8.0	VF/NM 9.0	NM- 9.2
nn-Reprints early Bizarro stories; new Jaime Hernandez-c						15.00

TALES OF THE DARKNESS
Image Comics (Top Cow): Apr, 1998 - No. 4, Dec, 1998 ($2.95)

	GD 2.0	VG 4.0	FN 6.0	VF 8.0	VF/NM 9.0	NM- 9.2
1-4: 1,2-Portacio-c/a(p). 3,4-Lansing & Nocon-a(p)						3.00
1-American Entertainment Ed.						3.00
#1/2 (1/01, $2.95)						3.00

TALES OF THE DRAGON GUARD (English version of French comic title)
Marvel Comics (Soleil): Apr, 2010 - No. 3, Jun, 2010 ($5.99, limited series)

	GD 2.0	VG 4.0	FN 6.0	VF 8.0	VF/NM 9.0	NM- 9.2
1-3: 1-Ange-s/Varanda-a. 2-Briones-a. 3-Guinebaud-a						6.00
...: Into the Veil 1-3 (11/10 - No. 3, 1/11) 1-Briones-a. 2-Paty-a. 3-Sieurac-a						6.00

TALES OF THE GREEN BERET
Dell Publishing Co.: Jan, 1967 - No. 5, Oct, 1969

	GD 2.0	VG 4.0	FN 6.0	VF 8.0	VF/NM 9.0	NM- 9.2
1-Glanzman-a in 1-4 & 5r	3	6	9	19	30	40
2-5: 5-Reprints #1	3	6	9	16	23	30

TALES OF THE GREEN HORNET
Now Comics: Sept, 1990 - No. 2, 1990; V2#1, Jan, 1992 - No.4, Apr, 1992; V3#1, Sept, 1992 - No. 3, Nov, 1992

	GD 2.0	VG 4.0	FN 6.0	VF 8.0	VF/NM 9.0	NM- 9.2
1,2						3.00
V2#1-4 ($1.95)						3.00
V3#1 ($2.75)-Polybagged w/hologram trading card						4.00
V3#2,3 ($2.50)						3.00

TALES OF THE GREEN LANTERN CORPS (See Green Lantern #107)
DC Comics: May, 1981 - No. 3, July, 1981 (Limited series)

	GD 2.0	VG 4.0	FN 6.0	VF 8.0	VF/NM 9.0	NM- 9.2
1-Origin of G.L. & the Guardians	2	4	6	9	12	15
2	1	3	4	6	8	10
3	1	2	3	5	6	8
Annual 1 (1/85)-Gil Kane-c/a	1	2	3	5	6	8
TPB (2009, $19.99) r/#1-3 & stories from G.L. #148-151-154,161,162,164-167 ('82-'83)						20.00
Volume 2 TPB (2010, $19.99) r/Annual #1 and stories from G.L. ('83-'85)						20.00
Volume 3 TPB (2010, $19.99) r/Green Lantern #201-206 ('86)						20.00

TALES OF THE INVISIBLE SCARLET O'NEIL (See Harvey Comics Hits #59)

TALES OF THE KILLERS (Magazine)
World Famous Periodicals: V1#10, Dec, 1970 - V1#11, Feb, 1971 (B&W, 52 pg)

	GD 2.0	VG 4.0	FN 6.0	VF 8.0	VF/NM 9.0	NM- 9.2
V1#10-One pg. Frazetta; r/Crime Does Not Pay	5	10	15	30	50	70
11-similar-c to Crime Does Not Pay #47; contains r/Crime Does Not Pay	4	8	12	27	44	60

TALES OF THE LEGION (Formerly Legion of Super-Heroes)
DC Comics: No. 314, Aug, 1984 - No. 354, Dec, 1987

	GD 2.0	VG 4.0	FN 6.0	VF 8.0	VF/NM 9.0	NM- 9.2
314-354: 326-r-begin						4.00
Annual 4,5 (1986, 1987)-Formerly LSH Annual						5.00

TALES OF THE MARINES (Formerly Devil-Dog Dugan #1-3)
Atlas Comics (OPI): No. 4, Feb, 1957 (Marines At War #5 on)

	GD 2.0	VG 4.0	FN 6.0	VF 8.0	VF/NM 9.0	NM- 9.2
4-Powell-a; Severin-c	13	26	39	74	105	135

TALES OF THE MARVELS
Marvel Comics: 1995/1996 (all acetate, painted-c)

	GD 2.0	VG 4.0	FN 6.0	VF 8.0	VF/NM 9.0	NM- 9.2
...Blockbuster 1 (1995, $5.95, one-shot), ...Inner Demons 1 (1996, $5.95, one shot), ...Wonder Years 1,2 (1995, $4.95, limited series)						6.00

TALES OF THE MARVEL UNIVERSE
Marvel Comics: Feb, 1997 ($2.95, one-shot)

	GD 2.0	VG 4.0	FN 6.0	VF 8.0	VF/NM 9.0	NM- 9.2
1-Anthology; wraparound-c; Thunderbolts, Ka-Zar app.						4.00

TALES OF THE MYSTERIOUS TRAVELER (See Mysterious...)
Charlton Comics: Aug, 1956 - No. 13, June, 1959; V2#14, Oct, 1985 - No. 15, Dec, 1985

	GD 2.0	VG 4.0	FN 6.0	VF 8.0	VF/NM 9.0	NM- 9.2
1-No Ditko-a; Giordano/Alascia-c	50	100	150	315	533	750
2-Ditko-a(1)	41	82	123	256	428	600
3-Ditko-c/a(1)	42	84	126	265	445	625
4-7-Ditko-c/a(3-4 stories each)	48	96	144	302	514	725
8,9-Ditko-a(1-3 each). 8-Rocke-c	41	82	123	250	418	585
10,11-Ditko-c/a(3-4 each)	44	88	132	277	469	660
12	18	36	54	105	165	225
13-Baker-a (r?)	19	38	57	111	176	240
V2#14,15 (1985)-Ditko-c/a-low print run	2	3	4	6	8	10

TALES OF THE NEW GODS
DC Comics: 2008 ($19.99, TPB)

	GD 2.0	VG 4.0	FN 6.0	VF 8.0	VF/NM 9.0	NM- 9.2
SC-Reprints from Jack Kirby's Fourth World, Orion and Mister Miracle Special						20.00

TALES OF THE NEW TEEN TITANS
DC Comics: June, 1982 - No. 4, Sept, 1982 (Limited series)

	GD 2.0	VG 4.0	FN 6.0	VF 8.0	VF/NM 9.0	NM- 9.2
1-4						5.00

TALES OF THE PONY EXPRESS (TV)
Dell Publishing Co.: No. 829, Aug, 1957 - No. 942, Oct, 1958

	GD 2.0	VG 4.0	FN 6.0	VF 8.0	VF/NM 9.0	NM- 9.2
Four Color 829 (#1) -Painted-c	5	10	15	30	50	70
Four Color 942-Title -Pony Express	5	10	15	30	50	70

TALES OF THE REALM
CrossGen Comics/MVCreations #4-on: Oct, 2003 - No. 5, May, 2004 ($2.95, limited series)

	GD 2.0	VG 4.0	FN 6.0	VF 8.0	VF/NM 9.0	NM- 9.2
1-5-Robert Kirkman-s/Matt Tyree-a						3.00
Volume 1 HC (8/04, $39.95, dust jacket) r/#1-5; sketch pages and concept art						40.00

TALES OF THE SINESTRO CORPS (See Green Lantern and Green Lantern Corps x-over)
DC Comics: Nov, 2007 - Jan, 2008 ($2.99/$3.99, one-shots)

	GD 2.0	VG 4.0	FN 6.0	VF 8.0	VF/NM 9.0	NM- 9.2
...: Cyborg-Superman (12/07, $2.99) Burnett-s/Blaine-a/VanSciver-c; JLA app.						3.00
...: Ion (1/08, $2.99) Marz-s/Lacombe-a/Benes-c; Sodam Yat app.						3.00
...: Parallax (11/07, $2.99) Marz-s/Melo-a; Kyle Rayner vs. Parallax						3.00
...: Superman-Prime (12/07, $3.99) Johns-s/VanSciver-c; origin re-told w/Ordway-a						4.00

TALES OF THE TEENAGE MUTANT NINJA TURTLES (See Teenage Mutant...)
Mirage Studios: May, 1987 - No. 7, Aug (Apr-c), 1989 (B&W, $1.50)

	GD 2.0	VG 4.0	FN 6.0	VF 8.0	VF/NM 9.0	NM- 9.2
1-7: 2-Title merges w/Teenage Mutant Ninja...						6.00

TALES OF THE TEEN TITANS (Formerly The New Teen Titans)
DC Comics: No. 41, Apr, 1984 - No. 91, July, 1988 (75¢)

	GD 2.0	VG 4.0	FN 6.0	VF 8.0	VF/NM 9.0	NM- 9.2
41,45-49: 46-Aqualad & Aquagirl join						4.00
42,43: The Judas Contract parts 1&2 with Deathstroke the Terminator; concludes with part 4 in Annual #3.						6.00
44-Dick Grayson becomes Nightwing (3rd to be Nightwing) & joins Titans; Judas Contract part 3; Jericho (Deathstroke's son) joins; origin Deathstroke	4	8	12	25	40	55
50-Double size; app. Betty Kane (Bat-Girl) out of costume						6.00
51,52,56-91: 52-1st brief app. Azrael (not same as newer character). 56-Intro Jinx. 57-Neutron app. 59-r/DC Comics Presents #26. 60-91-r/New Teen Titans Baxter series. 68-B. Smith-c. 70-Origin Kole						3.00
53-55: 53-1st full app. Azrael; Deathstroke cameo. 54,55-Deathstroke-c/stories						4.00

Tales of the Unexpected #30 © DC

Tales of the Mysterious Traveler #3 © CC

Tales to Astonish #10 © MAR

	GD 2.0	VG 4.0	FN 6.0	VF 8.0	VF/NM 9.0	NM- 9.2

Annual 3(1984, $1.25)-Part 4 of The Judas Contract; Deathstroke-c/story; Death of Terra; indicia says Teen Titans Annual; previous annuals listed as New Teen Titans Annual #1,2 — 1 2 3 5 6 8
Annual 4-(1986, $1.25) — 4.00

TALES OF THE TEXAS RANGERS (See Jace Pearson...)

TALES OF THE THING (Fantastic Four)
Marvel Comics: May, 2005 - No. 3, July, 2005 ($2.50, limited series)
1-3-Dr. Strange app; Randy Green-c — 3.00

TALES OF THE TMNT (Also see Teenage Mutant Ninja Turtles)
Mirage Studios: Jan, 2004 - Present ($2.95/$3.25, B&W)
1-7: 1-Brizuela-a — 3.25
8-70: 8-Begin $3.25-c. 47-Origin of the Super Turtles — 3.25

TALES OF THE UNEXPECTED (Becomes The Unexpected #105 on)(See Adventure #75, Super DC Giant)
National Periodical Publications: Feb-Mar, 1956 - No. 104, Dec-Jan, 1967-68

	GD	VG	FN	VF	VF/NM	NM-
1	111	222	333	888	1994	3100
2	44	88	132	326	738	1150
3-5	32	64	96	230	515	800
6-10: 6-1st Silver Age issue	26	52	78	182	404	625
11,14,19,20	19	38	57	131	291	450
12,13,16,18,21-24: All have Kirby-a. 16-Characters named 'Thor' (with a magic hammer) and Loki by Kirby (8/57, characters do not look like Marvel's Thor & Loki)	22	44	66	154	340	525
15,17-Grey tone-c; Kirby-a	25	50	75	175	388	600
25-30	16	32	48	110	243	375
31-39	14	28	42	96	211	325
40-Space Ranger begins (8/59, 3rd ap.), ends #82	107	214	321	856	1928	3000
41,42-Space Ranger stories	38	76	114	285	641	1000
43-1st Space Ranger-c this title; grey tone-c	68	136	204	544	1222	1900
44-46	28	56	84	202	451	700
47-50	24	48	72	168	372	575
51-60: 54-Dinosaur-c/story	20	40	60	138	307	475
61-67: 67-Last 10¢ issue	16	32	48	110	243	375
68-82: 82-Last Space Ranger	10	20	30	66	138	210
83-90,92-99	6	12	18	40	73	105
91,100: 91-1st Automan (also in #94,97)	6	12	18	41	76	110
101-104	6	12	18	37	66	95

NOTE: ***Neal Adams*** *c-104.* ***Anderson*** *a-50.* ***Brown*** *a-50-82(Space Ranger); c-19, 40, & many Space Ranger-c.* ***Cameron*** *a-24, 27, 29; c-24.* ***Heath*** *a-49.* ***Bob Kane*** *a-24, 48.* ***Kirby*** *a-12, 13, 15-18, 21-24; c-13, 18, 22.* ***Meskin*** *a-15, 18, 26, 27, 35, 66.* ***Moreira*** *a-16, 20, 29, 38, 44, 62, 71; c-38.* ***Roussos*** *c-10.* ***Wildey*** *a-31.*

TALES OF THE UNEXPECTED (See Crisis Aftermath: The Spectre)
DC Comics: Dec, 2006 - No. 8, Jul, 2007 ($3.99, limited series)
1-8-The Spectre, Lapham-s/Battle-a; Dr. 13, Azzarello-s/Chiang-a. 4-Wrightson-c — 4.00
1-Variant Spectre cover by Neal Adams — 5.00
The Spectre: Tales of the Unexpected TPB (2007, $14.99) r/#4-8 — 15.00

TALES OF THE VAMPIRES (Also see Buffy the Vampire Slayer and related titles)
Dark Horse Comics: 2003 - No. 5, Apr, 2004 ($2.99, limited series)
1-Short stories by Joss Whedon and others. 1-Totleben-c. 3-Powell-c. 4-Edlund-c — 3.00
TPB (11/04, $15.95) r/#1-5; afterword by Marv Wolfman — 16.00

TALES OF THE WEST (See 3-D...)

TALES OF THE WITCHBLADE
Image Comics (Top Cow Productions): Nov, 1996 - No. 9 ($2.95)

	GD	VG	FN	VF	VF/NM	NM-
1/2	1	2	3	5	7	9
1/2 Gold	2	4	6	9	12	15
1-Daniel-c/a(p)	1	3	4	6	8	10
1-Variant-c by Turner	2	4	6	9	12	15
1-Platinum Edition	3	6	9	16	23	30
2,3						6.00
4-6: 6-Green-c						5.00
7-9: 9-Lara Croft-c						4.00
7-Variant-c by Turner	1	2	3	5	6	8
Witchblade: Distinctions (4/01, $14.95, TPB) r/#1-6; Green-c						15.00

TALES OF THE WITCHBLADE COLLECTED EDITION
Image Comics (Top Cow): May, 1998 - No. 2 ($4.95/$5.95, square-bound)
1,2: 1-r/#1,2. 2-($5.95) r/#3,4 — 6.00

TALES OF THE WIZARD OF OZ (See Wizard of OZ, 4-Color #1308)

TALES OF THE ZOMBIE (Magazine)
Marvel Comics Group: Aug, 1973 - No. 10, Mar, 1975 (75¢, B&W)

	GD	VG	FN	VF	VF/NM	NM-
V1#1-Reprint/Menace #5; origin	5	10	15	33	57	80
2,3: 2-Everett biog. & memorial	4	8	12	25	40	55
V2#1(#4)-Photos & text of James Bond movie "Live & Let Die"	3	6	9	20	31	42
5-10: 8-Kaluta-a	3	6	9	18	28	38
Annual 1(Summer,'75)(#11)-B&W; Everett, Buscema-a	3	6	9	20	31	42

NOTE: Brother Voodoo app. 2, 5, 6, 10. ***Alcala*** *a-7-9.* ***Boris*** *c-1-4.* ***Colan*** *a-2r, 6.* ***Heath*** *a-5r.* ***Reese*** *a-2.* ***Tuska*** *a-2r.*

TALES OF THUNDER
Deluxe Comics: Mar, 1985
1-Dynamo, Iron Maiden, Menthor app.; Giffen-a — 4.00

TALES OF VOODOO
Eerie Publications: V1#11, Nov, 1968 - V7#6, Nov, 1974 (Magazine)

	GD	VG	FN	VF	VF/NM	NM-
V1#11	7	14	21	48	89	130
V2#1(3/69)-V2#4(9/69)	5	10	15	33	57	80
V3#1-6('70): 4- "Claws of the Cat" redrawn from Climax #1	4	8	12	28	47	65
V4#1-6('71), V5#1-7('72), V6#1-6('73), V7#1-6('74)	4	8	12	28	47	65
Annual 1	5	10	15	30	50	70

NOTE: *Bondage-c-V1#10, V2#4, V3#4.*

TALES OF WELLS FARGO (TV)(See Western Roundup under Dell Giants)
Dell Publishing Co.: No. 876, Feb, 1958 - No. 1215, Oct-Dec, 1961

	GD	VG	FN	VF	VF/NM	NM-
Four Color 876 (#1)-Photo-c	8	16	24	51	96	140
Four Color 968 (2/59), 1023, 1075 (3/60), 1113 (7-9/60)-All photo-c. 1075,1113-Both have variant edition, back-c comic strip	7	14	21	48	89	130
Four Color 1167 (3-5/61), 1215-Photo-c	7	14	21	44	82	120

TALESPIN (Also see Cartoon Tales & Disney's Talespin Limited Series)
Disney Comics: June, 1991 - No. 7, Dec, 1991 ($1.50)
1-7 — 3.00

TALES TO ASTONISH (Becomes The Incredible Hulk #102 on)
Atlas (MAP No. 1/ZPC No. 2-14/VPI No. 15-21/Marvel No. 22 on: Jan, 1959 - No. 101, Mar, 1968

	GD	VG	FN	VF	VF/NM	NM-
1-Jack Davis-a; monster-c.	207	414	621	1708	3854	6000
2-Ditko flying saucer-c (Martians); #2-4 have sci/fi-c.	79	158	237	632	1416	2200
3,4	57	114	171	456	1028	1600
5-Prototype issue (Stone Men); Williamson-a (4 pgs.); Kirby monster-c begin	54	108	162	432	966	1500
6-Prototype issue (Stone Men)	45	90	135	333	754	1175
7-Prototype issue (Toad Men)	45	90	135	333	754	1175
8-10	44	88	132	326	738	1150
11,12,14,17-20	36	72	108	259	580	900
13-(11/60) 1st app. Groot (Guardians of the Galaxy) by Kirby-cvr/sty; swipes story from Menace #8	300	600	900	1800	2400	3000
15-Prototype issue (Electro)	38	76	114	281	628	975
16-Prototype issue (Stone Men) named "Thorr"	37	74	111	274	612	950
21-(7/61)-Hulk prototype	37	74	111	274	612	950
22-26,28-31,33,34	30	60	90	216	483	750
27-1st Ant-Man app. (1/62); last 10¢ issue (see Strange Tales #73,78 & Tales of Suspense #32)	700	1400	2450	8000	20,000	32,000
32-Sandman prototype	31	62	93	223	499	775
35-(9/62)-2nd app. Ant-Man, 1st in costume; begin series & Ant-Man-c	259	518	777	2137	4819	7500
36-3rd app. Ant-Man	82	164	246	656	1478	2300
37,39,40	47	94	141	363	819	1275
38-1st app. Egghead	50	100	150	400	900	1400
41-43	40	80	120	296	673	1050
44-Origin & 1st app. The Wasp (6/63)	57	114	171	456	1028	1600
45-47	27	54	81	189	420	650
48-Origin & 1st app. The Porcupine	27	54	81	194	435	675
49-Ant-Man becomes Giant Man (11/63)	32	64	96	230	515	800
50,51,53-56,58: 50-Origin/1st app. Human Top (alias Whirlwind). 58-Origin Colossus	17	34	51	117	259	400
52-Origin/1st app. Black Knight (2/64)	21	42	63	147	324	500
57-Early Spider-Man app. (7/64)	36	72	108	266	596	925
59-Giant Man vs. Hulk feature story (9/64); Hulk's 1st app. this title; 1st mention that anger triggers his transformation	32	64	96	230	515	800
60-Giant Man & Hulk double feature begins	24	48	72	168	372	575
61,64-69: 61-All Ditko issue; 1st app. of Glenn Talbot; 1st mailbag. 65-New Giant Man costume. 68-New Human Top costume. 69-Last Giant Man	12	24	36	82	179	275

62-1st app./origin The Leader; new Wasp costume; Hulk pin-up page missing from many

Tales to Astonish #93 © MAR

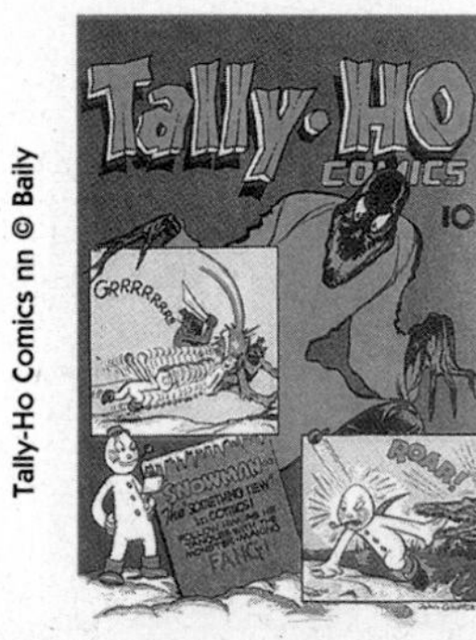

Tally-Ho Comics nn © Baily

Talon #9 © DC

	GD 2.0	VG 4.0	FN 6.0	VF 8.0	VF/NM 9.0	NM- 9.2
copies	15	30	45	103	227	350
63-Origin Leader continues	13	26	39	89	195	300
70-Sub-Mariner & Incredible Hulk begins (8/65)	13	26	39	91	201	310
71-81: 72-Begin alternating-c features w/Sub-Mariner (even #'s) & Hulk (odd #'s). 79-Hulk vs. Hercules-c/story. 81-1st app. Boomerang	7	14	21	44	82	120
82-Iron Man battles Sub-Mariner (1st Iron Man x-over outside The Avengers & TOS); story cont'd from Tales of Suspense #80	8	16	24	52	99	145
83-89,94-99: 97-X-Men cameo (brief)	6	12	18	37	66	95
90-1st app. The Abomination	7	14	21	49	92	135
91-The Abomination debut continues & 1st cover	7	14	21	49	92	135
92-1st Silver Surfer x-over (outside of Fantastic Four, 6/67); 1 panel cameo only	7	14	21	48	89	130
93-Hulk battles Silver Surfer-c/story (1st full x-over)	18	36	54	124	275	425
100-Hulk battles Sub-Mariner full-length story	7	14	21	48	89	130
101-Hulk story cont'd in Incredible Hulk #102; Sub-Mariner story continued in Iron Man & Sub-Mariner #1	8	16	24	51	96	140

NOTE: ***Ayers** c(i)-9-12, 16, 18, 19. **Berg** a-1. **Burgos** a-62-64p. **Buscema** a-85-87p. **Colan** a(p)-70-76, 78-82, 84, 85, 101; c(p)-71-76, 78, 80, 82, 84, 86, 88, 90. **Ditko** a-1, 3-48, 50i, 60-67p; c-2, 7i, 8i, 14i, 17i. **Everett** a-78, 79i, 80-84, 85-90i, 94i, 95, 96; c(i)-79-81, 83, 86, 88. **Forte** a-6. **Kane** a-76, 88-91; c-89, 91. **Kirby** a(p)-1, 5-34-40, 44, 49-51, 68-70, 82, 83; layouts-71-84; c(p)-1, 3-48, 50-70, 72, 73, 75, 77, 78, 79, 81, 85, 90. **Kirby/Ditko** a-7, 8, 12, 13, 50; c-7, 8, 10, 13. **Leiber/Fox** a-47, 48, 50, 51. **Powell** a-65-69p, 73, 74. **Reinman** a-6, 36, 45, 46, 54i, 56-60i.*

TALES TO ASTONISH (2nd Series)
Marvel Comics Group: Dec, 1979 - No. 14, Jan, 1981

V1#1-Reprints Sub-Mariner #1 by Buscema 2 4 6 10 14 18
2-14: Reprints Sub-Mariner #2-14 1 3 4 6 8 10

TALES TO ASTONISH
Marvel Comics: V3#1, Oct, 1994 ($6.95, one-shot)

V3#1-Peter David scripts; acetate, painted-c 7.00

TALES TO HOLD YOU SPELLBOUND (See Spellbound)

TALES TO OFFEND
Dark Horse Comics: July, 1997 ($2.95, one-shot)

1-Frank Miller-s/a, EC-style cover 4.00

TALES TOO TERRIBLE TO TELL (Becomes Terrology #10, 11)
New England Comics: Wint, 1989-90 - No. 11, Nov-Dec.1993 ($2.95/$3.50, B&W with card-stock covers)

1-($2.95) Reprints of non-EC pre-code horror; EC-style cover by Bissette 5.00
1-($3.50, 5-6/93) Second printing with alternate cover not by Bissette 4.00
2-8-($3.50) Story reprints, history of the pre-code titles and creators; cover galleries (B&W) inside & on back-c (color) 4.00
9-11-($2.95) 10,11-"Terrology" on cover 4.00

TALEWEAVER
DC Comics (WildStorm): Nov, 2001 - No. 6, Apr, 2002 ($3.50, limited series)

1-6-Philip Tan-a/Leonard Banaag-s. 2-Variant-c by Anacleto 3.50

TALKING KOMICS
Belda Record & Publ. Co.: 1947 (20 pgs, slick-c)

Each comic contained a record that followed the story - much like the Golden Record sets. Known titles: Chirpy Cricket, Lonesome Octopus, Sleepy Santa, Grumpy Shark, Flying Turtle, Happy Grasshopper
with records... 3 6 9 17 26 35

TALLY-HO COMICS
Swappers Quarterly (Baily Publ. Co.): Dec, 1944

nn-Frazetta's 1st work as Giunta's assistant; Man in Black horror story; violence; Giunta-c 53 106 159 334 567 800

TALULLAH (See Comic Books Series I)

TALON (From Batman Court of Owls crossover)
DC Comics: No. 0, Nov, 2012 - No. 17, May, 2014 ($2.99)

0-17: 0-Origin of Calvin Rose; March-a. 7-11-Bane app. 3.00

TAMMY, TELL ME TRUE
Dell Publishing Co.: No. 1233, 1961

Four Color 1233-Movie 6 12 18 37 66 95

TANGENT COMICS
.../ THE ATOM, DC Comics: Dec, 1997 ($2.95, one-shot)
1-Dan Jurgens-s/Jurgens & Paul Ryan-a 3.00
.../ THE BATMAN, DC Comics: Sept, 1998 ($1.95, one-shot)
1-Dan Jurgens-s/Klaus Janson-a 3.00
.../ DOOM PATROL, DC Comics: Dec, 1997 ($2.95, one-shot)
1- Dan Jurgens-s/Sean Chen & Kevin Conrad-a 3.00
.../ THE FLASH, DC Comics: Dec, 1997 ($2.95, one-shot)
1-Todd Dezago-s/Gary Frank & Cam Smith-a 3.00
.../ GREEN LANTERN, DC Comics: Dec, '97 ($2.95, one-shot)
1-James Robinson-s/J.H. Williams III & Mick Gray-a 3.00
.../ JLA, DC Comics: Sept, 1998 ($1.95, one-shot)
1-Dan Jurgens-s/Banks & Rapmund-a 3.00
.../ THE JOKER, DC Comics: Dec, 1997 ($2.95, one-shot)
1-Karl Kesel-s/Matt Haley & Tom Simmons-a 3.00
.../ THE JOKER'S WILD, DC Comics: Sept, 1998 ($1.95, one-shot)
1-Kesel & Simmons-s/Phillips & Rodriguez-a 3.00
.../ METAL MEN, DC Comics: Dec, 1997 ($2.95, one-shot)
1-Ron Marz-s/Mike McKone & Mark McKenna-a 3.00
.../ NIGHTWING, DC Comics: Dec, 1997 ($2.95, one-shot)
1-John Ostrander-s/Jan Duursema-a 3.00
.../ NIGHTWING: NIGHTFORCE, DC Comics: Sept, 1998 ($1.95, one-shot)
1-John Ostrander-s/Jan Duursema-a 3.00
.../ POWERGIRL, DC Comics: Sept, 1998 ($1.95, one-shot)
1-Marz-s/Abell & Vines-a 3.00
.../ SEA DEVILS, DC Comics: Dec, 1997 ($2.95, one-shot)
1-Kurt Busiek-s/Vince Giarrano & Tom Palmer-a 3.00
.../ SECRET SIX, DC Comics: Dec, 1997 ($2.95, one-shot)
1-Chuck Dixon-s/Tom Grummett & Lary Stucker-a 3.00
.../ THE SUPERMAN, DC Comics: Sept, 1998 ($1.95, one-shot)
1-Millar-s/Guice-a 3.00
.../ TALES OF THE GREEN LANTERN, DC Comics: Sept, 1998 ($1.95, one-shot)
1-Story & art by various 3.00
.../ THE TRIALS OF THE FLASH, DC Comics: Sept, 1998 ($1.95, one-shot)
1-Dezago-s/Pelletier & Lanning-a 3.00
.../ WONDER WOMAN DC Comics: Sept, 1998 ($1.95, one-shot),
1-Peter David-s/Unzueta & Mendoza-a 3.00
... Volume One TPB (2007, $19.99) r/The Atom, Metal Men, Green Lantern, The Flash, Sea Devils one-shots; intro and new cover by Jurgens 20.00
... Volume Two TPB (2008, $19.99) r/Batman, Doom Patrol, Joker, Nightwing and Secret Six one-shots; new cover by Jurgens 20.00
... Volume Three TPB (2008, $19.99) r/The Superman, Wonder Woman, Nightwing: Nightforce, The Joker's Wild, The Trials of the Flash, Tales of the Green Lantern, Powergirl, and JLA one-shots; new cover by Jurgens 20.00

TANGENT: SUPERMAN'S REIGN
DC Comics: May, 2008 - No. 12, Apr, 2009 ($2.99, limited series)

1-12-Jurgens-s; Flash & Green Lantern app.; back-up histories of Tangent heroes 3.00
Volume 1 TPB (2009, $19.99) r/#1-6 & Justice League of America #16 20.00
Volume 2 TPB (2009, $19.99) r/#7-12 20.00

TANGLED WEB (See Spider-Man's Tangled Web)

TANK GIRL
Dark Horse Comics: May, 1991 - No. 4, Aug, 1991 ($2.25, B&W, mini-series)

1-Contains Dark Horse trading cards 6.00
2-4 4.00
...: Dark Nuggets (Image Comics, 12/09, $3.99) Martin-s/Dayglo-a 4.00
...: Dirty Helmets (Image Comics, 4/10, $3.99) Martin-s/Dayglo-a 4.00
...: Hairy Heroes (Image Comics, 8/10, $3.99) Martin-s/Dayglo-a 4.00

TANK GIRL: APOCALYPSE
DC Comics: Nov, 1995 - No. 4, Feb, 1996 ($2.25, limited series)

1-4 4.00

TANK GIRL: MOVIE ADAPTATION
DC Comics: 1995 ($5.95, 68 pgs., one-shot)

nn-Peter Milligan scripts 6.00

TANK GIRL: THE GIFTING
IDW Publishing: May, 2007 - No. 4, Aug, 2007 ($3.99, limited series)

1-4: 1-Ashley Wood-a/c; Alan Martin-s; 3 covers 4.00

TANK GIRL: THE ODYSSEY
DC Comics: May, 1995 - No.4, Oct, 1995 ($2.25, limited series)

1-4: Peter Milligan scripts; Hewlett-a 4.00

TANK GIRL: THE ROYAL ESCAPE
IDW Publishing: Mar, 2010 - No. 4, Jun, 2010 ($3.99, limited series)

1-4: Alan Martin-s/Rufus Dayglo-a/c 4.00

Target Comics V6 #3 © NOVP

Tarot: Witch of the Black Rose #83 © Jim Balent

Tarzan #27 © ERB

GD VG FN VF VF/NM NM-
2.0 4.0 6.0 8.0 9.0 9.2

GD VG FN VF VF/NM NM-
2.0 4.0 6.0 8.0 9.0 9.2

TANK GIRL 2
Dark Horse Comics: June, 1993 - No. 4, Sept, 1993 ($2.50, lim. series, mature)
1-4: Jamie Hewlett & Alan Martin-s/a 4.00
TPB (2/95, $17.95) r/#1-4 18.00

TAPPAN'S BURRO (See Zane Grey & 4-Color #449)

TAPPING THE VEIN (Clive Barker's...)
Eclipse Comics: 1989 - No. 5, 1992 ($6.95, squarebound, mature, 68 pgs.)
Book 1-5: 1-Russell-a, Bolton-c. 2-Bolton-a. 4-Die-cut-c 7.00
TPB (2002, $24.95, Checker Book Publ. Group) r/#1-5 25.00

TARANTULA (See Weird Suspense)

TARGET: AIRBOY
Eclipse Comics: Mar, 1988 ($1.95)
1 3.00

TARGET COMICS (...Western Romances #106 on)
Funnies, Inc./Novelty Publications/Star Publ.: Feb, 1940 - V10#3 (#105), Aug-Sept, 1949
V1#1-Origin & 1st app. Manowar, The White Streak by Burgos, & Bulls-Eye Bill by Everett; City Editor (ends #5), High Grass Twins by Jack Cole (ends #4), T-Men by Joe Simon (ends #9), Rip Rory (ends #4), Fantastic Feature Films by Tarpe Mills (ends #39), & Calling 2-R (ends #14) begin; marijuana use story
459 918 1377 3350 5925 8500
2-Everett-c/a 232 464 696 1485 2543 3600
3,4-Everett, Jack Cole-a 139 278 417 890 1520 2150
5-Origin The White Streak in text; Space Hawk by Wolverton begins (6/40) (see Blue Bolt & Circus) 443 886 1329 3234 5717 8200
6-The Chameleon by Everett begins (7/40, 1st app.); White Streak origin cont'd. in text; early mention of comic collecting in letter column; 1st letter column in comics? (7/40)
236 472 708 1510 2580 3650
7-Wolverton Spacehawk-c/story (Scarce) 1100 2200 3300 8000 15,000 22,000
8-Classic sci-fi cover 271 542 813 1734 2967 4200
9,12: 12-(1/41) 145 290 435 928 1589 2250
10-Intro/1st app. The Target (11/40); Simon-c; Spacehawk-s; text piece by Wolverton
277 554 831 1760 3030 4300
11-Origin The Target & The Targeteers 187 374 561 1197 2049 2900
V2#1-Target by Bob Wood; Uncle Sam flag-c 95 190 285 608 1042 1475
2-Ten part Treasure Island serial begins; Harold Delay-a; reprinted in Catholic Comics V3#1-10 (see Key Comics #5) 68 136 204 435 743 1050
3-5: 4-Kit Carter, The Cadet begins 61 122 183 390 670 950
6-9: Red Seal with White Streak in #6-10 58 116 174 371 636 900
10-Classic-c 108 216 324 691 1183 1675
11,12: 12-10-part Last of the Mohicans serial begins; Delay-a
57 114 171 362 619 875
V3#1-3,5-7,9,10: 10-Last Wolverton issue 47 94 141 296 498 700
4-V for Victory-c 65 130 195 416 708 1000
8-Hitler, Tojo, Flag-c; 6-part Gulliver Travels serial begins; Delay-a.
87 174 261 553 952 1350
11,12 20 40 60 114 182 250
V4#1-4,7-12: 8-X-Mas-c 14 28 42 82 121 160
5-Classic Statue of Liberty-c 18 36 54 105 165 225
6-Targetoons by Wolverton 17 34 51 98 154 210
V5#1-8 13 26 39 74 105 135
V6#1-4,6-10 13 26 39 72 101 130
5-Classic Tojo hanging/Buy War Bonds WWII-c 58 116 174 371 636 900
V7#1-12 11 22 33 62 86 110
V8#1,3-5,8,9,11,12 10 20 30 56 76 95
2,6,7-Krigstein-a 11 22 33 62 86 110
10-L.B. Cole-c 25 50 75 150 245 340
V9#1,4,6,8,10-L.B. Cole-c 25 50 75 150 245 340
2,3,5,7,9,11, V10#1 10 20 30 56 76 95
12-Classic L.B. Cole-c 37 74 111 222 361 500
V10#2,3-L.B. Cole-c 25 50 75 150 245 340
NOTE: ***Certa** c-V8#9, 11, 12, V9#5, 9, 11, V10#1. **Jack Cole** a-1-8. **Everett** a-1-9; c(signed Blake)-1, 2. **Al Fago** c-V6#8. **Sid Greene** c-V2#9, 12, V3#3. **Walter Johnson** c-V5#6, V6#4. **Tarpe Mills** a-1-4, 6, 8, 11, V3#1. **Rico** a-V7#4, 10, V8#5, 6, V9#3; c-V7#6, 8, 10, V8#2, 4, 6, 7. **Simon** a-1, 2. **Bob Wood** c-V2#2, 3, 5, 6.*

TARGET: THE CORRUPTORS (TV)
Dell Publishing Co.: No. 1306, Mar-May, 1962 - No. 3, Oct-Dec, 1962
(All have photo-c)
Four Color 1306(#1), #2,3 5 10 15 33 57 80

TARGET WESTERN ROMANCES (Formerly Target Comics; becomes Flaming Western Romances #3)
Star Publications: No. 106, Oct-Nov, 1949 - No. 107, Dec-Jan, 1949-50
106(#1)-Silhouette nudity panel; L.B. Cole-c 25 50 75 150 245 340
107(#2)-L.B. Cole-c; lingerie panels 22 44 66 132 216 300

TARGITT
Atlas/Seaboard Publ.: March, 1975 - No. 3, July, 1975
1-3: 1-Origin; Nostrand-a in all. 2-1st in costume. 3-Becomes Man-Stalker
2 4 6 10 14 18

TAROT: WITCH OF THE BLACK ROSE
Broadsword Comics: Mar, 2000 - Present ($2.95, mature)
1-Jim Balent-s/c/a; at least two covers on all issues 4 8 12 23 37 50
1-Second printing (10/00) 5.00
2 2 4 6 11 16 20
3-20 1 2 3 5 6 8
21-40 5.00
41-85: 84-The Krampus app. 3.00

TARZAN (See Aurora, Comics on Parade, Crackajack, DC 100-Page Super Spec., Edgar Rice Burroughs'..., Famous Feature Stories #1, Golden Comics Digest #4, 9, Jeep Comics #1-29, Jungle Tales of..., Limited Collectors' Edition, Popular, Sparkler, Sport Stars #1, Tip Top & Top Comics)

TARZAN
Dell Publishing Co./United Features Synd.: No. 5, 1939 - No. 161, Aug, 1947
Large Feature Comic 5('39)-(Scarce)-By Hal Foster; reprints 1st dailies from 1929
213 426 639 1363 2332 3300
Single Series 20('40)-By Hal Foster 142 284 426 909 1555 2200
Four Color 134(2/47)-Marsh-c/a 53 106 159 413 932 1450
Four Color 161(8/47)-Marsh-c/a 43 86 129 318 722 1125

TARZAN (...of the Apes #138 on)
Dell Publishing Co./Gold Key No. 132 on: 1-2/48 - No. 131, 7-8/62; No. 132, 11/62 - No. 206, 2/72
1-Jesse Marsh-a begins 96 192 288 768 1734 2700
2 42 84 126 311 706 1100
3-5 30 60 90 216 483 750
6-10: 6-1st Tantor the Elephant. 7-1st Valley of the Monsters
25 50 75 175 388 600
11-15: 11-Two Against the Jungle begins, ends #24. 13-Lex Barker photo-c begin
19 38 57 131 291 450
16-20 15 30 45 105 233 360
21-24,26-30 13 26 39 86 188 290
25-1st "Brothers of the Spear" episode; series ends #156,160,161,196-206
14 28 42 96 211 325
31-40 10 20 30 66 138 210
41-54: Last Barker photo-c 8 16 24 56 108 160
55-60: 56-Eight pg. Boy story 7 14 21 49 92 135
61,62,64-70 6 12 18 41 76 110
63-Two Tarzan stories, 1 by Manning 6 12 18 42 79 115
71-79 6 12 18 37 66 95
80-99: 80-Gordon Scott photo-c begin 5 10 15 34 60 85
100 6 12 18 37 66 95
101-109 5 10 15 33 57 80
110 (Scarce)-Last photo-c 6 12 18 37 66 95
111-120 5 10 15 31 53 75
121-131: Last Dell issue 5 10 15 30 50 70
132-1st Gold Key issue 5 10 15 31 53 75
133-138,140-154 4 8 12 25 40 55
139-(12/63)-1st app. Korak (Boy); leaves Tarzan & gets own book (1/64)
6 12 18 38 69 100
155-Origin Tarzan; text article on Tarzana, CA 5 10 15 30 50 70
156-161: 157-Banlu, Dog of the Arande begins, ends #159, 195. 169-Leopard Girl app.
3 6 9 21 33 45
162,165,168,171 (TV)-Ron Ely photo covers 4 8 12 22 35 48
163,164,166,167,169,170: 169-Leopard Girl app. 3 6 9 20 31 42
172-199,201-206: 178-Tarzan origin-r/#155; Leopard Girl app., also in #179, 190-193
3 6 9 18 28 38
200 3 6 9 21 33 45
Story Digest 1-(6/70, G.K., 148pp.)(scarce) 6 12 18 41 76 110
NOTE: *#162, 165, 168, 171 are TV issues. #1-153 all have **Marsh** art on Tarzan. #154-161, 163, 164, 166, 167, 172-177 all have **Manning** art on Tarzan. #178, 202 have **Manning** Tarzan reprints. No "Brothers of the Spear" in #1-24, 157-159, 162-195. #39-126, 128-156 all have **Russ Manning** art on "Brothers of the Spear". #196-201, 203-205 all have **Manning** B.O.T.S. reprints; #25-38, 127 all have Jesse **Marsh** art on B.O.T.S. #206 has a Marsh B.O.T.S. reprint. **Gollub** c-8-12. **Marsh** c-1-7. **Doug Wildey** a-162, 179-187. Many issues have front and back photo covers.*

TARZAN (Continuation of Gold Key series)
National Periodical Publications: No. 207, Apr, 1972 - No. 258, Feb, 1977
207-Origin Tarzan by Joe Kubert, part 1; John Carter begins (origin); 52 pg. issues thru #209 5 10 15 35 63 90

Tarzan (1977 series) #27 © ERB

Tarzan Family #62 © ERB

Team One: StormWatch #1 © WSP

GD 2.0 VG 4.0 FN 6.0 VF 8.0 VF/NM 9.0 NM- 9.2

208,209-(52 pgs.): 208-210-Parts 2-4 of origin. 209-Last John Carter
3 6 9 21 33 45
210-220: 210-Kubert-a. 211-Hogarth, Kubert-a. 212-214: Adaptations from "Jungle Tales of Tarzan". 213-Beyond the Farthest Star begins, ends #218. 215-218,224,225-All by Kubert. 215-part Foster-r. 219-223: Adapts "The Return of Tarzan" by Kubert
3 6 9 14 20 25
221-229: 221-223-Continues adaptation of "The Return of Tarzan". 226-Manning-a
2 4 6 10 14 18
230-DC 100 Page Super Spectacular; Kubert, Kaluta-a(p); Korak begins, ends #234; Carson of Venus app. 4 8 12 25 40 55
231-235-New Kubert-a.: 231-234-(All 100 pgs.)-Adapts "Tarzan and the Lion Man"; Rex, the Wonder Dog r-#232, 233. 235-(100 pgs.)-Last Kubert issue.
4 8 12 23 37 50
236,237,239-258: 240-243 adapts "Tarzan & the Castaways". 250-256 adapts "Tarzan the Untamed." 252,253-r/#213 2 4 6 8 10 12
238-(68 pgs.) 2 4 6 13 18 22
Digest 1-(Fall, 1972, 50¢, 164 pgs.)(DC)-Digest size; Kubert-c; Manning-a
4 8 12 25 40 55
Edgar Rice Burroughs' Tarzan The Joe Kubert Years - Volume One HC (Dark Horse Books, 10/05, $49.95, dust jacket) recolored r/#207-214; intro. by Joe Kubert 50.00
Edgar Rice Burroughs' Tarzan The Joe Kubert Years - Volume Two HC (Dark Horse Books, 2/06, $49.95, dust jacket) recolored r/#215-224; intro. by Joe Kubert 50.00
Edgar Rice Burroughs' Tarzan The Joe Kubert Years - Volume Three HC (Dark Horse Books, 6/06, $49.95, dust jacket) recolored r/#225,227-235; Kubert intro. and sketch pages 50.00
NOTE: ***Anderson*** *a-207, 209, 217, 218.* ***Chaykin*** *a-216.* ***Finlay*** *a(r)-212.* ***Foster*** *strip-r #207-209, 211, 212, 221.* ***Heath*** *a-230i.* ***G. Kane*** *a(r)-232p, 233p.* ***Kubert*** *a-207-225, 227-235, 257r, 258r; c-207-249, 253.* ***Lopez*** *a-250-255p; c-250p, 251, 252, 254.* ***Manning*** *strip-r 230-235, 238.* ***Morrow*** *a-208.* ***Nino*** *a-231-234.* ***Sparling*** *a-230, 231.* ***Starr*** *a-233r.*

TARZAN (Lord of the Jungle)
Marvel Comics Group: June, 1977 - No. 29, Oct, 1979

1-New adaptions of Burroughs stories; Buscema-a 2 4 6 11 16 20
1-(35¢-c variant, limited distribution)(6/77) 5 10 15 31 53 75
2-29: 2-Origin by John Buscema. 9-Young Tarzan. 12-14-Jungle Tales of Tarzan. 25-29-New stories 1 2 3 5 6 8
2-5-(35¢-c variants, limited distribution)(7-10/77) 3 6 9 19 30 40
Annual 1-3: 1-(1977). 2-(1978). 3-(1979) 1 3 4 6 8 10
NOTE: ***N. Adams*** *c-11i, 12i.* ***Alcala*** *a-9i, 10i; c-8i, 9i.* ***Buckler*** *c-25-27p, Annual 3p.* ***John Buscema*** *a-1-3, 4-18p, Annual 1; c-1-7, 8p, 9p, 10, 11p, 12p, 13, 14-19p, 21p, 22, 23p, 24p, 28p, Annual 1.* ***Mooney*** *a-22i.* ***Nebres*** *a-22i.* ***Russell*** *a-29i.*

TARZAN
Dark Horse Comics: July, 1996 - No. 20, Mar, 1998 ($2.95)

1-20: 1-6-Suydam-c 3.00

TARZAN / CARSON OF VENUS
Dark Horse Comics: May, 1998 - No. 4, Aug, 1998 ($2.95, limited series)

1-4-Darko Macan-s/Igor Korday-a 3.00

TARZAN FAMILY, THE (Formerly Korak, Son of Tarzan)
National Periodical Publications: No. 60, Nov-Dec, 1975 - No. 66, Nov-Dec, 1976

60-62-(68 pgs.): 60-Korak begins; Kaluta-r 2 4 6 11 16 20
63-66 (52 pgs.) 2 4 6 9 12 15
NOTE: *Carson of Venus-r 60-65. New John Carter-62-64, 65r, 66r. New Korak-60-66. Pellucidar feature-66. Foster strip r-60(9/4/32-10/16/32), 62(6/29/32-7/31/32), 63(10/11/31-12/13/31).* ***Kaluta*** *Carson of Venus-60-65.* ***Kubert*** *a-61, 64; c-60-64.* ***Manning*** *strip-r 60-62, 64.* ***Morrow*** *a-66r.*

TARZAN/JOHN CARTER: WARLORDS OF MARS
Dark Horse Comics: Jan, 1996 - No. 4, June, 1996 ($2.50, limited series)

1-4: Bruce Jones scripts in all. 1,2,4-Bret Blevins-c/a. 2-(4/96)-Indicia reads #3 3.00

TARZAN KING OF THE JUNGLE (See Dell Giant #37, 51)

TARZAN, LORD OF THE JUNGLE
Gold Key: Sept, 1965 (Giant) (25¢, soft paper-c)

1-Marsh-r 7 14 21 48 89 130

TARZAN: LOVE, LIES AND THE LOST CITY (See Tarzan the Warrior)
Malibu Comics: Aug. 10, 1992 - No. 3, Sept, 1992 ($2.50, limited series)

1-($3.95, 68 pgs.)-Flip book format; Simonson & Wagner scripts 4.00
2,3-No Simonson or Wagner scripts 3.00

TARZAN MARCH OF COMICS (See March of Comics #82, 98, 114, 125, 144, 155, 172, 185, 204, 223, 240, 252, 262, 272, 286, 300, 332, 342, 354, 366)

TARZAN OF THE APES
Metropolitan Newspaper Service: 1934? (Hardcover, 4x12", 68 pgs.)

1-Strip reprints 25 50 75 150 245 340

TARZAN OF THE APES
Marvel Comics Group: July, 1984 - No. 2, Aug, 1984 (Movie adaptation)

1,2: Origin-r/Marvel Super Spec. 4.00

TARZAN'S JUNGLE ANNUAL (See Dell Giants)

TARZAN'S JUNGLE WORLD (See Dell Giant #25)

TARZAN: THE BECKONING
Malibu Comics: 1992 - No. 7, 1993 ($2.50, limited series)

1-7 3.00

TARZAN: THE LOST ADVENTURE (See Edgar Rice Burroughs' ...)

TARZAN-THE RIVERS OF BLOOD
Dark Horse Comics: Nov, 1999 - No. 8 ($2.95, limited series)

1-4: Korday-c/a 3.00

TARZAN THE SAVAGE HEART
Dark Horse Comics: Apr, 1999 - No. 4, July, 1999 ($2.95, limited series)

1-4: Grell-c/a 3.00

TARZAN THE WARRIOR (Also see Tarzan: Love, Lies and the Lost City)
Malibu Comics: Mar, 19, 1992 - No. 5, 1992 ($2.50, limited series)

1-5: 1-Bisley painted pack-c (flip book format-c) 3.00
1-2nd printing w/o flip-c by Bisley 3.00

TARZAN VS. PREDATOR AT THE EARTH'S CORE
Dark Horse Comics: Jan, 1996 - No. 4, June, 1996 ($2.50, limited series)

1-4: Lee Weeks-c/a; Walt Simonson scripts 3.00

TASKMASTER
Marvel Comics: Apr, 2002 - No. 4, July, 2002 ($2.99, limited series)

1-4-Udon Studio-s/a. 1-Iron Man app. 3.00

TASKMASTER
Marvel Comics: Nov, 2010 - No. 4, ($3.99, limited series)

1-4-Van Lente-s/Palo-a; Hydra & A.I.M. app. 4.00

TASMANIAN DEVIL & HIS TASTY FRIENDS
Gold Key: Nov, 1962 (12¢)

1-Bugs Bunny, Elmer Fudd, Sylvester, Yosemite Sam, Road Runner & Wile E. Coyote x-over
14 28 42 96 211 325

TATTERED BANNERS
DC Comics (Vertigo): Nov, 1998 - No. 4, Feb, 1999 ($2.95, limited series)

1-4-Grant & Giffen-s/McMahon-a 3.00

TATTERED MAN
Image Comics: May 2011 ($4.99, one-shot)

1-Justin Gray & Jimmy Palmiotti-s/Norberto Fernandez-a; covers by Fernandez & Conner 5.00

TEAM AMERICA (See Captain America #269)
Marvel Comics Group: June, 1982 - No. 12, May, 1983

1,12: 1-Origin; Ideal Toy motorcycle characters. 12-Double size 5.00
2-11: 9-Iron Man app. 11-Ghost Rider app. 4.00
NOTE: *There are 16 pg. variants known for most issues, possibly all. The only ad is on the inside front cover.*

TEAM HELIX
Marvel Comics: Jan, 1993 - No. 4, Apr, 1993 ($1.75, limited series)

1-4: Teen Super Group. 1,2-Wolverine app. 3.00

TEAM ONE: STORMWATCH (Also see StormWatch)
Image Comics (WildStorm Productions): June, 1995 - No. 2, Aug, 1995 ($2.50, lim. series)

1,2: Steven T. Seagle scripts 3.00

TEAM ONE: WILDC.A.T.S (Also see WildC.A.T.S)
Image Comics (WildStorm Productions): July, 1995 - No. 2, Aug, 1995 ($2.50, lim. series)

1,2: James Robinson scripts 3.00

TEAM 7
Image Comics (WildStorm): Oct, 1994 - No.4, Feb, 1995 ($2.50, limited series)

1-4: Dixon scripts in all, 1-Portacio variant-c 3.00

TEAM 7 (DC New 52)
DC Comics: No. 0, Nov, 2012 - No. 8, Jul, 2013 ($2.99)

0-8: 0-Merino-a/Lashley-c; Slade Wilson, John Lynch, Grifter and others assemble team. 3,4-Eclipso returns. 7-Pandora & Majestic app. 3.00

TEAM 7-DEAD RECKONING
Image Comics (WildStorm): Jan, 1996 - No. 4, Apr, 1996 ($2.50, limited series)

1-4: Dixon scripts in all 3.00

TEAM 7-OBJECTIVE HELL
Image Comics (WildStorm): May, 1995 - No. 3, July, 1995 ($1.95/$2.50, limited series)

Teena #22 © STD

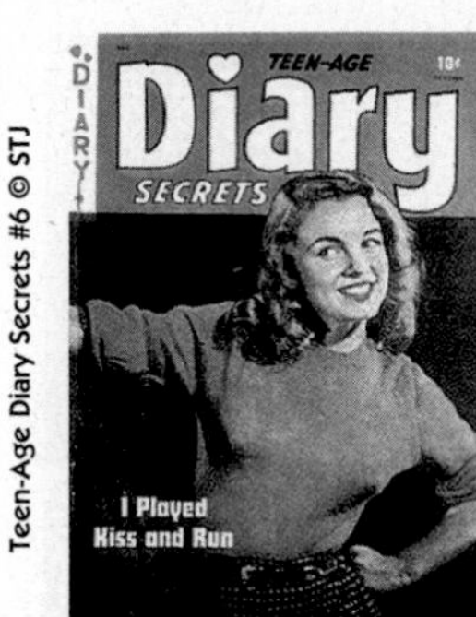

Teen-Age Diary Secrets #6 © STJ

Teenage Mutant Ninja Turtles #16 © MS

	GD 2.0	VG 4.0	FN 6.0	VF 8.0	VF/NM 9.0	NM- 9.2
1-($1.95)-Newstand; Dixon scripts in all; Barry Smith-c						3.00
1-3: 1-($2.50)-Direct Market; Barry Smith-c, bound-in card						3.00

TEAM SUPERMAN
DC Comics: July, 1999 ($2.95, one-shot)

	GD	VG	FN	VF	VF/NM	NM-
1-Jeanty-a/Stelfreeze-c						3.00
...Secret Files 1 (5/98, $4.95)Origin-s and pin-ups of Superboy, Supergirl and Steel						5.00

TEAM TITANS (See Deathstroke & New Titans Annual #7)
DC Comics: Sept, 1992 - No. 24, Sept, 1994 ($1.75/$1.95)

	GD	VG	FN	VF	VF/NM	NM-
1-Five different #1s exist w/origins in 1st half & the same 2nd story in each: Kilowat, Mirage, Nightrider w/Netzer/Pérez-a, Redwing, & Terra w/part Pérez-p; Total Chaos Pt. 3						4.00
2-24: 2-Total Chaos Pt 6. 11-Metallik app. 24-Zero Hour x-over						3.00
Annual 1,2 ('93, '94, $3.50, 68 pgs.): 2-Elseworlds tory						4.00

TEAM X/TEAM 7
Marvel Comics: Nov, 1996 ($4.95, one-shot)

	GD	VG	FN	VF	VF/NM	NM-
1						5.00

TEAM X 2000
Marvel Comics: Feb, 1999 ($3.50, one-shot)

	GD	VG	FN	VF	VF/NM	NM-
1-Kevin Lau-a; Bishop vs. Shi'ar Empire						4.00

TEAM YANKEE
First Comics: Jan, 1989 - No. 6, Feb, 1989 ($1.95, weekly limited series)

	GD	VG	FN	VF	VF/NM	NM-
1-6						3.00

TEAM YOUNGBLOOD (Also see Youngblood)
Image Comics (Extreme Studios): Sept, 1993 - No. 22, Sept, 1995 ($1.95/$2.50)

	GD	VG	FN	VF	VF/NM	NM-
1-22: 1-9-Liefeld scripts in all: 1,2,4-6,8-Thibert-c(i). 1-1st app. Dutch & Masada. 3-Spawn cameo. 5-1st app. Lynx. 7,8-Coupons 1 & 4 for Extreme Prejudice #0; Black and White Pt. 4 & 8 by Thibert. 8-Coupon #4 for E. P. #0. 9-Liefeld wraparound-c &(p)/a(p) on Pt. I. 16,17-Bagged w/trading card. 21-Angela & Glory-app.						3.00

TEAM ZERO
DC Comics (WildStorm Productions): Feb, 2006 - No. 6, Jul, 2006 ($2.99, limited series)

	GD	VG	FN	VF	VF/NM	NM-
1-6-Dixon-s/Mahnke-a						3.00
TPB (2008, $17.99) r/#1-6						18.00

TECH JACKET
Image Comics: Nov, 2002 - No. 6, Apr, 2003 ($2.95)

	GD	VG	FN	VF	VF/NM	NM-
1-6-Kirkman-s/Su-a						3.00
Vol. 1: Lost and Found TPB (7/03, $12.95, 7-3/4" x 5-1/4") B&W r/#1-6; Valentino intro.						13.00

TEDDY ROOSEVELT & HIS ROUGH RIDERS (See Real Heroes #1)
Avon Periodicals: 1950

	GD	VG	FN	VF	VF/NM	NM-
1-Kinstler-c; Palais-a; Flag-c	18	36	54	107	169	230

TEDDY ROOSEVELT ROUGH RIDER (See Battlefield #22 & Classics Illustrated Special Issue)

TED MCKEEVER'S METROPOL (See Transit)
Marvel Comics (Epic Comics): Mar, 1991 - No. 12, Mar, 1992 ($2.95, limited series)

	GD	VG	FN	VF	VF/NM	NM-
V1#1-12: Ted McKeever-c/a/scripts						4.00

TED MCKEEVER'S METROPOL A.D.
Marvel Comics (Epic Comics): Oct, 1992 - No. 3, Dec, 1992 ($3.50, limited series)

	GD	VG	FN	VF	VF/NM	NM-
V2#1-3: Ted McKeever-c/a/scripts						4.00

TEENA
Magazine Enterprises/Standard Comics No. 20 on: No. 11, 1948 - No. 15, 1948; No. 20, Aug, 1949 - No. 22, Oct, 1950

	GD	VG	FN	VF	VF/NM	NM-
A-1 #11-Teen-age; Ogden Whitney-c	10	20	30	58	79	100
A-1 #12, 15	9	18	27	50	65	80
20-22 (Standard)	7	14	21	37	46	55

TEEN-AGE BRIDES (True Bride's Experiences #8 on)
Harvey/Home Comics: Aug, 1953 - No. 7, Aug, 1954

	GD	VG	FN	VF	VF/NM	NM-
1-Powell-a	11	22	33	62	86	110
2-Powell-a	8	16	24	44	57	70
3-7: 3,6-Powell-a	8	16	24	40	50	60

TEEN-AGE CONFESSIONS (See Teen Confessions)

TEEN-AGE CONFIDENTIAL CONFESSIONS
Charlton Comics: July, 1960 - No. 22, 1964

	GD	VG	FN	VF	VF/NM	NM-
1	4	8	12	23	37	50
2-10	3	6	9	16	23	30
11-22	2	4	6	13	18	22

TEEN-AGE DIARY SECRETS (Formerly Blue Ribbon Comics; becomes Diary Secrets #10 on)
St. John Publishing Co.: No. 4, 9/49; nn (#5), 9/49 - No. 7, 11/49; No. 8, 2/50; No. 9, 8/50

	GD	VG	FN	VF	VF/NM	NM-
4(9/49)-Oversized; part mag., part comic	48	96	144	302	514	725
nn(#5)(no indicia)-Oversized, all comics; contains sty "I Gave Boys the Green Light."	47	94	141	296	498	700
6,8: (Reg. size) -Photo-c; Baker-a(2-3) in each	53	106	159	334	567	800
7,9-Digest size (Pocket Comics); Baker-a(5); both have same contents; diff.-c	68	136	204	435	743	1050

TEEN-AGE DOPE SLAVES (See Harvey Comics Library #1)

TEENAGE HOTRODDERS (Top Eliminator #25 on; see Blue Bird)
Charlton Comics: Apr, 1963 - No. 24, July, 1967

	GD	VG	FN	VF	VF/NM	NM-
1	5	10	15	33	57	80
2-10	3	6	9	19	30	40
11-24	3	6	9	16	24	32

TEEN-AGE LOVE (See Fox Giants)

TEEN-AGE LOVE (Formerly Intimate)
Charlton Comics: V2#4, July, 1958 - No. 96, Dec, 1973

	GD	VG	FN	VF	VF/NM	NM-
V2#4	4	8	12	27	44	60
5-9	3	6	9	19	30	40
10(9/59)-20	3	6	9	16	24	32
21-35	3	6	9	15	22	28
36-70	2	4	6	13	18	22
71-79,81,82,85-87,90-96: 61&62-Jonnie Love begins (origin)	2	4	6	10	14	18
80,84,88-David Cassidy pin-ups	3	6	9	14	19	24
83,89: 83-Bobby Sherman pin-up. 89-Danny Bonaduce pin-up	2	4	6	13	18	22

TEENAGE MUTANT NINJA TURTLES (Also see Anything Goes, Donatello, First Comics Graphic Novel, Gobbledygook, Grimjack #26, Leonardo, Michaelangelo, Raphael & Tales Of The...)
Mirage Studios: 1984 - No. 62, Aug, 1993 ($1.50/$1.75, B&W; all 44-52 pgs.)

	GD	VG	FN	VF	VF/NM	NM-
1-1st printing (3000 copies)-Origin and 1st app. of the Turtles and Splinter. Only printing to have ad for Gobbledygook #1 & 2; Shredder app. (#1-4: 7-1/2x11")	350	700	1050	1750	2625	3500
1-2nd printing (6/84)(15,000 copies)	17	34	51	117	259	400
1-3rd printing (2/85)(36,000 copies)	10	20	30	64	132	200
1-4th printing, new-c (50,000 copies)	3	6	9	14	20	25
1-5th printing, new-c (8/88-c, 11/88 inside)	2	4	6	11	16	20
1-Counterfeit. **Note**: Most counterfeit copies have a half inch wide white streak or scratch marks across the center of back cover. Black part of cover is a bluish black instead of a deep black. Inside paper is very white & inside cover is bright white (no value)						
2-1st printing (1984; 15,000 copies)	11	22	33	76	163	250
2-2nd printing	3	6	9	14	20	25
2-3rd printing; new Corben-c/a (2/85)	2	4	6	9	12	15
2-Counterfeit with glossy cover stock (no value).						
3-1st printing (1985, 44 pgs.)	8	16	24	56	108	160
3-Variant, 500 copies, cover printed at different plant, has 'Laird's Photo' in white rather than light blue	25	50	75	175	388	600
3-2nd printing; contains new back-up story	2	4	6	8	10	12
4-1st printing (1985, 44 pgs.)	6	12	18	38	69	100
4-2nd printing (5/87) all have manufacturing error	8	16	24	54	102	150
5-Fugitoid begins, ends #7; 1st full color-c (1985)	4	8	12	28	47	65
5-2nd printing (11/87)	1	3	4	6	8	10
6-1st printing (1986)	3	6	9	17	26	35
6-2nd printing (4/88-c, 5/88 inside)						5.00
7-4 pg. Eastman/Corben color insert; 1st color TMNT (1986, $1.75-c); Bade Biker back-up story	2	4	6	13	18	22
7-2nd printing (1/89) w/o color insert						5.00
8-Cerebus-c/story with Dave Sim-a (1986)	2	4	6	10	14	18
9,10: 9-(9/86)-Rip In Time by Corben	2	4	6	8	10	12
11-15	1	3	4	6	8	10
16-18: 18-Mark Bode'-a	1	2	3	5	6	8
18-2nd printing ($2.25, color, 44 pgs.)-New-c						5.00
19-34: 19-Begin $1.75-c. 24-26-Veitch-c/a.						6.00
32-2nd printing ($2.75, 52 pgs., full color)						5.00
35-49,51: 35-Begin $2.00-c.						5.00
50-Features pin-ups by Larsen, McFarlane, Simonson, etc.	1	2	3	5	6	8
52-62: 52-Begin $2.25-c						5.00
nn (1990, $5.95, B&W)-Movie adaptation						6.00
Book 1,2($1.50, B&W): 2-Corben-c						6.00
...Christmas Special 1 (12/90, $1.75, B&W, 52 pgs.)-Cover title: Michaelangelo Christmas Special; r/Michaelangelo one-shot plus new Raphael story	1	3	4	6	8	10

Teenage Mutant Ninja Turtles (2011 series) #16 © MS

Teenage Mutant Ninja Turtles Adventures #4 © MS

Teen-Age Romances #2 © STJ

GD VG FN VF VF/NM NM-
2.0 4.0 6.0 8.0 9.0 9.2

... Color Special (11/09, $3.25) full color reprint of #1
1 3 4 6 8 10
...Special (The Maltese Turtle) nn (1/93, $2.95, color, 44 pgs.) 6.00
...Special: "Times" Pipeline nn (9/92, $2.95, color, 44 pgs.)-Mark Bode-c/a 6.00
Hardcover ($100)-r/#1-10 plus one-shots w/dust jackets - limited to 1000 w/letter of authenticity 120.00
Softcover ($40)-r/#1-10 45.00

TEENAGE MUTANT NINJA TURTLES
Mirage Studios: V2#1, Oct, 1993 - V2#13, Oct, 1995 ($2.75)

V2#1-Wraparound-c 1 2 3 5 6 8
2-13 4.00

TEENAGE MUTANT NINJA TURTLES
Image Comics (Highbrow Ent.): June, 1996 - No. 23, Oct, 1999 ($1.95-$2.95)

1-Erik Larsen-c(i) 1 2 3 5 6 8
2-23: 2-8-Erik Larsen-c(i) on all. 10-Savage Dragon-c/app. 4.00

TEENAGE MUTANT NINJA TURTLES
Mirage Publishing: V4#1, Dec, 2001 - No. 28 ($2.95, B&W)

V4#1-9,11-28-Laird-s/a(i)/Lawson-a(p). 3.00
10-($3.95) Splinter dies 4.00

TEENAGE MUTANT NINJA TURTLES
Dreamwave Productions: June 2003 - No. 7 ($2.95, color)

1-7-Animated style; Peter David-s/Lesean-a 3.00
Vol. 1 TPB (2003, $9.95) r/#1-4; cover gallery and sketch pages 10.00

TEENAGE MUTANT NINJA TURTLES
IDW Publishing: Aug, 2011 - Present ($3.99)

1-Kevin Eastman-s & layouts; four covers by Duncan (each turtle); origin flashback
1 2 3 5 6 8
1-Variant-c by Eastman 2 4 6 11 16 20
1-Halloween Edition (10/12, no cover price) Reprints #1 4.00
2-32-Multiple variant covers on each 4.00
Annual 2012 (10/12, $8.99) Eastman-s/a; wraparound-c 9.00
... Kevin Eastman Cover Gallery (12/13, $3.99) Collection of recent Eastman covers 4.00
... Microseries 1-8 (11/11 - No. 8, 9/12) 1-Raphael. 2-Michelangelo. 3-Donatello. 4-Leonardo. 5-Splinter. 6-Casey Jones. 7-April. 8-Fugitoid 4.00
...100 Page Spectacular (4/12, $7.99) r/TMNT Adventures (1988) mini-series #1-3 8.00
... Villains Microseries 1-8 (4/13 - No. 8, 11/13, $3.99) 1-Krang. 2-Baxter. 8-Shredder 4.00

TEENAGE MUTANT NINJA TURTLES (Adventures)
Archie Publications: Jan, 1996 - No. 3, Mar, 1996 ($1.50, limited series)

1 1 3 4 6 8 10
2,3 4.00

TEENAGE MUTANT NINJA TURTLES ADVENTURES (TV)
Archie Comics: Oct, 1988 - No. 3, Dec, 1988; Mar, 1989 - No. 72, Oct, 1995 ($1.00-$1.75)

1-Adapts TV cartoon; not by Eastman/Laird 2 4 6 9 1 15
2,3 (Mini-series) 6.00
1 (2nd on-going series) 2 4 6 8 10 12
1-2nd printing 5.00
2-18,20-30: 5-Begins original stories not based on TV. 14-Simpson-a(p). 22-Colan-c/a 5.00
2-11: 2nd printings 4.00
19,20,51-54: 19-1st Mighty Mutanimals (also in #20, 51-54
2 4 6 9 12 15
31-49 5.00
50-Poster by Eastman/Laird 1 2 3 5 7 9
55-60 1 2 3 4 5 7
61-70: 62-w/poster 2 3 4 6 8 10
71 2 4 6 8 10 12
72- Last issue 2 4 6 9 13 16
nn (1990, $2.50)-Movie adaptation 5.00
nn (Spring, 1991, $2.50, 68 pgs.)-(Meet Archie) 5.00
nn (Sum, 1991, $2.50, 68 pgs.)-(Movie II)-Adapts movie sequel 5.00
...Meet the Conservation Corps 1 (1992, $2.50, 68 pgs.) 4.00
...III The Movie: The Turtles are Back...In Time (1993, $2.50, 68 pgs.) 5.00
Special 1,4,5 (Sum/92, Spr/93, Sum/93, 68 pgs.)-1-Bill Wray-c 4.00
Giant Size Special 6 (Fall/93, $1.95, 52 pgs.) 4.00
Special 7-10 (Win/93-Fall//94, 52 pgs.): 9-Jeff Smith-c 4.00
NOTE: *There are 2nd printings of #1-11 w/B&W inside covers. Originals are color.*

TEENAGE MUTANT NINJA TURTLES CLASSICS DIGEST (TV)
Archie Comics: Aug, 1993 - No. 8, Mar, 1995? ($1.75)

1-8: Reprints TMNT Advs. 4.00

TEENAGE MUTANT NINJA TURTLES COLOR CLASSICS
IDW Publishing: May, 2012 - Present ($3.99)

1-11-Colored reprints of the original 1984 B&W series 4.00
...: Donatello Micro-Series One-Shot (3/13, $3.99) r/Donatello, TMNT #1 (1986) 4.00
...: Leonardo Micro-Series One-Shot (4/13, $3.99) r/Leonardo, TMNT #1 4.00
...: Michaelangelo Micro-Series One-Shot (12/12, $3.99) r/Michaelangelo, TMNT #1 4.00
...: Raphael Micro-Series One-Shot (8/12, $3.99) r/Raphael #1 (1985) 4.00
... Volume 2 (11/13 - Present, $3.99) 1-5: 1-Reprints TMNT #12 (1987) 4.00

TEENAGE MUTANT NINJA TURTLES/FLAMING CARROT CROSSOVER
Mirage Publishing: Nov, 1993 - No. 4, Feb, 1994 ($2.75, limited series)

1-4: Bob Burden story 4.00

TEENAGE MUTANT NINJA TURTLES NEW ANIMATED ADVENTURES
IDW Publishing: Jul, 2013 - Present ($3.99)

1-8-Multiple covers on each 4.00
... Free Comic Book Day (5/13) Burnham-s/Brizuela-a 3.00

TEENAGE MUTANT NINJA TURTLES PRESENTS: APRIL O'NEIL
Archie Comics: Mar, 1993 - No. 3, June, 1993 ($1.25, limited series)

1-3 4.00

TEENAGE MUTANT NINJA TURTLES PRESENTS: DONATELLO AND LEATHERHEAD
Archie Comics: July, 1993 - No. 3, Sept, 1993 ($1.25, limited series)

1-3 4.00

TEENAGE MUTANT NINJA TURTLES PRESENTS: MERDUDE
Archie Comics: Oct, 1993 - No. 3, Dec, 1993 ($1.25, limited series)

1-3-See Mighty Mutanimals #7 for 1st app. Merdude 4.00

TEENAGE MUTANT NINJA TURTLES/SAVAGE DRAGON CROSSOVER
Mirage Studios: Aug, 1995 ($2.75, one-shot)

1 4.00

TEENAGE MUTANT NINJA TURTLES: THE SECRET HISTORY OF THE FOOT CLAN
IDW Publishing: Dec, 2012 - No. 4, Mar, 2013 ($3.99, limited series)

1-4-Santolouco-a/Santolouco & Burnham-s 4.00

TEENAGE MUTANT NINJA TURTLES UTROM EMPIRE
IDW Publishing: Jan, 2014 - Present ($3.99, limited series)

1,2-PAul Allor-s/Andy Kuhn-a 4.00

TEEN-AGE ROMANCE (Formerly My Own Romance)
Marvel Comics (ZPC): No. 77, Sept, 1960 - No. 86, Mar, 1962

77-83 5 10 15 33 57 80
84-86-Kirby-c. 84-Kirby-a(2 pgs.). 85,86-(3 pgs.) 6 12 18 37 66 95

TEEN-AGE ROMANCES
St. John Publ. Co. (Approved Comics): Jan, 1949 - No. 45, Dec, 1955 (#3,7,10-18,21 are 1/2 inch taller than other issues)

1-Baker-c/a(1) 84 168 252 538 919 1300
2,3: 2-Baker-c/a. 3-Baker-c/a(3) 50 100 150 315 533 750
4,5,7,8-Photo-c; Baker-a(2-3) each 36 72 108 211 343 475
6-Photo-c; part magazine; Baker-a (10/49) 39 78 117 231 378 525
9-Baker-c/a; Kubert-a 50 100 150 315 533 750
10-12,20-Baker-c/a(2-3) each 43 86 129 271 461 650
13-19,21,22-Complete issues by Baker 48 96 144 302 514 725
23-25-Baker-c/a(2-3) each 42 84 126 265 445 625
26,27,33,34,36,37,39,40,42: Baker-c/a. 33,40-Signed story by Estrada. 42-r/Cinderella Love #9; last pre-code (3/55) 37 74 111 222 361 500
28-30-No Baker-a 15 30 45 85 130 175
31,32-Baker-c. 31-Estrada-s 32 64 96 188 307 425
35-Baker-c/a (16 pgs.) 37 74 111 222 361 500
38-Baker-c/a; suggestive-c 47 94 141 296 498 700
41-Baker-c; Infantino-a(r); all stories are Ziff-Davis-r 32 64 96 188 307 425
43-45-Baker-c/a 36 72 108 211 343 475

TEEN-AGE TALK
I.W. Enterprises: 1964

Reprint #1 2 4 6 10 14 18
Reprint #5,8,9: 5-r/Hector #? 9-Punch Comics #?; L.B. Cole-c reprint from School Day Romances #1 2 4 6 9 13 16

TEEN-AGE TEMPTATIONS (Going Steady #10 on)(See True Love Pictorial)
St. John Publishing Co.: Oct, 1952 - No. 9, Aug, 1954

1-Baker-c/a; has story "Reform School Girl" by Estrada
97 194 291 621 1061 1500
2,4-Baker-c 47 94 141 296 498 700
3,5-7,9-Baker-c/a 53 106 159 334 567 800

Teen Love Stories #2 © WAR

Teen Titans #26 © DC

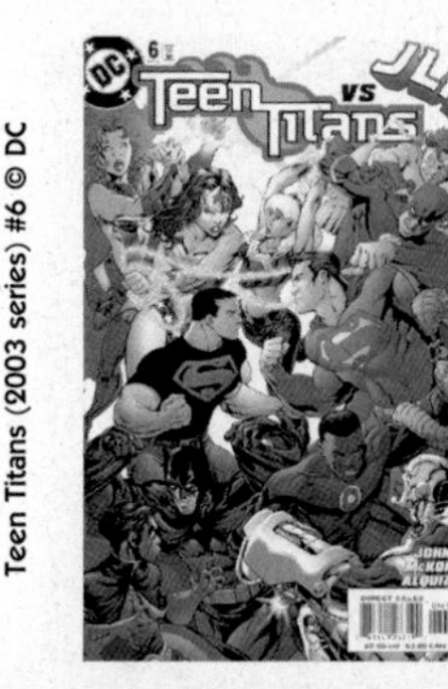

Teen Titans (2003 series) #6 © DC

	GD 2.0	VG 4.0	FN 6.0	VF 8.0	VF/NM 9.0	NM- 9.2
8-Teenagers smoke reefer; Baker-c/a	65	130	195	416	708	1000

NOTE: *Estrada a-1, 3-5.*

TEEN BEAM (Formerly Teen Beat #1)
National Periodical Publications: No. 2, Jan-Feb, 1968

	GD	VG	FN	VF	VF/NM	NM-
2-Superman cameo; Herman's Hermits, Yardbirds, Simon & Garfunkel, Lovin Spoonful, Young Rascals app.; Orlando, Drucker-a(r); Monkees photo-c;	15	30	45	105	233	360

TEEN BEAT (Becomes Teen Beam #2)
National Periodical Publications: Nov-Dec, 1967

	GD	VG	FN	VF	VF/NM	NM-
1-Photos & text only; Monkees photo-c; Beatles, Herman's Hermits, Animals, Supremes, Byrds app.	17	34	51	117	259	400

TEEN COMICS (Formerly All Teen; Journey Into Unknown Worlds #36 on)
Marvel Comics (WFP): No. 21, Apr, 1947 - No. 35, May, 1950

	GD	VG	FN	VF	VF/NM	NM-
21-Kurtzman's "Hey Look"; Patsy Walker, Cindy (1st app.?), Georgie, Margie app.; Syd Shores-a begins, end #23	20	40	60	120	195	270
22,23,25,27,29,31-35: 22-(6/47)-Becomes Hedy Devine #22 (8/47) on?	15	30	45	90	140	190
24,26,28,30-Kurtzman's "Hey Look". 30-Has anti-Wertham editorial	16	32	48	94	147	200

TEEN CONFESSIONS
Charlton Comics: Aug, 1959 - No. 97, Nov, 1976

	GD	VG	FN	VF	VF/NM	NM-
1	7	14	21	44	82	120
2	4	8	12	27	44	60
3-10	3	6	9	21	33	45
11-30	3	6	9	17	26	35
31-Beatles-c	10	20	30	66	138	210
32-36,38-55	3	6	9	15	21	26
37 (1/66)-Beatles Fan Club story; Beatles-c	10	20	30	66	138	210
56-58,60-76,78-97: 89,90-Newton-c	2	4	6	10	14	18
59-Kaluta's 1st pro work? (12/69)	3	6	9	19	30	40
77-Partridge Family poster	3	6	9	14	20	24

TEENIE WEENIES, THE (America's Favorite Kiddie Comic)
Ziff-Davis Publishing Co.: No. 10, 1950 - No. 11, Apr-May, 1951 (Newspaper reprints)

	GD	VG	FN	VF	VF/NM	NM-
10,11-Painted-c	20	40	60	114	182	250

TEEN-IN (Tippy Teen)
Tower Comics: Summer, 1968 - No. 4, Fall, 1969

	GD	VG	FN	VF	VF/NM	NM-
nn(#1, Summer, 1968)(25¢) Has 3 full pg. B&W photos of Sonny & Cher, Donovan and Herman's Hermits; interviews and photos of Eric Clapton, Jim Morrison and others	9	18	27	62	126	190
nn(#2, Spring, 1969),3,4	6	12	18	37	66	95

TEEN LIFE (Formerly Young Life)
New Age/Quality Comics Group: No. 3, Winter, 1945 - No. 5, Fall, 1945 (Teenage magazine)

	GD	VG	FN	VF	VF/NM	NM-
3-June Allyson photo on-c & story	14	28	42	76	108	140
4-Duke Ellington photo on-c & story	11	22	33	64	90	115
5-Van Johnson, Woody Herman & Jackie Robinson articles; Van Johnson & Woody Herman photos on-c	14	28	42	78	112	145

TEEN LOVE STORIES (Magazine)
Warren Publ. Co.: Sept, 1969 - No. 3, Jan, 1970 (68 pgs., photo covers, B&W)

	GD	VG	FN	VF	VF/NM	NM-
1-Photos & articles plus 36-42 pgs. new comic stories in all; Frazetta-a	8	16	24	51	96	140
2,3: 2-Anti-marijuana story	5	10	15	34	60	85

TEEN ROMANCES
Super Comics: 1964

	GD	VG	FN	VF	VF/NM	NM-
10,11,15-17-Reprints	2	4	6	8	11	14

TEEN SECRET DIARY (Nurse Betsy Crane #12 on)
Charlton Comics: Oct, 1959 - No. 11, June, 1961

	GD	VG	FN	VF	VF/NM	NM-
1	5	10	15	30	50	70
2	3	6	9	20	31	42
3-11	3	6	9	17	26	35

TEEN TALK (See Teen)

TEEN TITANS (See Brave & the Bold #54,60, DC Super-Stars #1, Marvel & DC Present, New Teen Titans, New Titans, Official...Index and Showcase #59)
National Periodical Publications/DC Comics: 1-2/66 - No. 43, 1-2/73; No. 44, 11/76 - No. 53, 2/78

	GD	VG	FN	VF	VF/NM	NM-
1-(1-2/66)-Titans join Peace Corps; Batman, Flash, Aquaman, Wonder Woman cameos	33	66	99	238	532	825
2	14	28	42	96	211	325
3-5: 4-Speedy app.	9	18	27	62	126	190
6-10: 6-Doom Patrol app.; Beast Boy x-over; readers polled on him joining Titans	7	14	21	49	92	135
11-18: 11-Speedy app. 13-X-Mas-c	6	12	18	40	73	105
19-Wood-i; Speedy begins as regular	6	12	18	41	76	110
20-22: All Neal Adams-a. 21-Hawk & Dove app.; last 12¢ issue. 22-Origin Wonder Girl	8	16	24	56	108	160
23-Wonder Girl dons new costume	5	10	15	33	57	80
24-31: 25-Flash, Aquaman, Batman, Green Arrow, Green Lantern, Superman, & Hawk & Dove guests; 1st app. Lilith who joins T.T. West in #50. 29-Hawk & Dove & Ocean Master app. 30-Aquagirl app. 31-Hawk & Dove app.	5	10	15	30	50	70
32-34,40-43: 34-Last 15¢ issue	3	6	9	19	30	40
35-39-(52 pgs.): 36,37-Superboy-r. 38-Green Arrow/Speedy-r; Aquaman/Aqualad story. 39-Hawk & Dove-r.	4	8	12	22	35	48
44-(11/76) Dr. Light app.; Mal becomes the Guardian	3	6	9	14	20	26
45,47,49,51,52	3	6	9	14	19	24
46,48: 46-Joker's daughter begins (see Batman Family). 48-Intro Bumblebee; Joker's daughter becomes Harlequin	3	6	9	16	24	32
50-1st revival original Bat-Girl; intro. Teen Titans West	3	6	9	21	33	45
53-Origin retold	3	6	9	15	22	28
... Lost Annual 1 (3/08, $4.99) Sixties-era story by Bob Haney; Jay Stephens & Mike Allred-a; President Kennedy app.; Nick Cardy-c and sketch pages						5.00

NOTE: ***Aparo** a-36. **Buckler** c-46-53. **Cardy** c-1-16. **Kane** a(p)-19, 22-24, 39r. **Tuska** a(p)-31, 36, 38, 39. DC Super-Stars #1 (3/76) was released before #44.*

TEEN TITANS (Also see Titans Beat in the Promotional Comics section)
DC Comics: Oct, 1996 - No. 24, Sept, 1998 ($1.95)

	NM-
1-Dan Jurgens-c/a(p)/scripts & George Pérez-c/a(i) begin; Atom forms new team (Risk, Argent, Prysm, & Joto); 1st app. Loren Jupiter & Omen; no indicia. 1-3-Origin.	4.00
2-24: 4,5-Robin, Nightwing, Supergirl, Capt. Marvel Jr. app. 12-"Then and Now" begins w/original Teen Titans-c/app. 15-Death of Joto. 17-Capt. Marvel Jr. and Fringe join. 19-Millennium Giants x-over. 23,24-Superman app.	3.00
Annual 1 (1997, $3.95)-Pulp Heroes story	4.00

TEEN TITANS (Also see Titans/Young Justice: Graduation Day)
DC Comics: Sept, 2003 - No. 100, Late Oct, 2011 ($2.50/$2.99/$3.99)

	NM-
1-McKone-c/a;Johns-s	5.00
1-Variant-c by Michael Turner	6.00
1-2nd and 3rd printings	3.00
2-Deathstroke app.	5.00
2-2nd printing	3.00
3-15: 4-Impulse becomes Kid Flash. 5-Raven returns. 6-JLA app.	4.00
16-33: 16-Titans go to 31st Century; Legion and Fatal Five app. 17-19-Future Titans app. 21-23-Dr. Light. 24,25-Outsiders #24,25 x-over. 27,28-Liefeld-a. 32,33-Infinite Crisis	3.00
34-49,51-71: 34-One Year Later begins; two covers by Daniel and Benes. 36-Begin $2.99-c. 40-Jericho returns. 42-Kid Devil origin; Snejbjerg-a. 43-Titans East. 48,49-Amazons Attack x-over; Supergirl app. 51-54-Future Titans app.	3.00
50-($3.99) Art by Pérez (4 pgs.), McKone (6 pgs.), Nauck and Green; future Titans app.	4.00
72-88: 72-Begin $3.99-c; Ravager back-up features. 77,78-Blackest Night. 83-87-Coven of Three back-up; Naifeh-a. 88-Nicola Scott-a begins	4.00
89-99-($2.99) 89-Robin (Damian) joins. 93-Solstice app. 98 Superboy-Prime returns	3.00
100-($4.99) Nicola Scott-a; pin-ups by various	5.00
Annual 1 (4/06, $4.99) Infinite Crisis x-over; Benes-c	5.00
Annual 2009 (6/09, $4.99) Deathtrap x-over prelude; McKeever-s	5.00
... And Outsiders Secret Files and Origins 2005 (10/05, $4.99) Daniel-c	5.00
...: Cold Case (2/11, $4.99) Captain Cold and the Rogues app.; Sean Murphy-a	6.00
.../Legion Special (11/04, $3.50) (cont'd from #16) Reis-a; leads into 2005 Legion of Super-Heroes series; LSH preview by Waid & Kitson	4.00
#1/2 (Wizard mail offer) origin of Ravager; Reis-a	8.00
.../Outsiders Secret Files 2003 (12/03, $5.95) Reis & Jimenez-a; pin-ups by various	6.00
...: A Kid's Game TPB (2004, $9.95) r/#1-7; Turner-c from #1; McKone sketch pages	10.00
...: Beast Boys and Girls TPB (2005, $9.99) r/#13-15 and Beast Boy #1-4	10.00
...: Changing of the Guard TPB (2009, $14.99) r/#62-69	15.00
...: Child's Play TPB (2010, $14.99) r/#71-78	15.00
...: Deathtrap TPB (2009, $14.99) r/#70, Annual #1, Titans #12,13, Vigilante #4-6	15.00
...: Family Lost TPB (2004, $9.95) r/#8-12 & #1/2	10.00
...: Life and Death TPB (2006, $14.99) r/#29-33 and pages from Infinite Crisis x-over	15.00
...: On the Clock TPB (2008, $14.99) r/#55-61	15.00
.../ Outsiders: The Death and Return of Donna Troy (2006, $14.99) r/Titans/Young Justice: Graduation Day #1-3, Teen Titans/Outsiders Secret Files 2003 and DC Special: The Return of Donna Troy #1-4; cover gallery	15.00
.../ Outsiders: The Insiders (2006, $14.99) r/Teen Titans/ #24-26 & Outsiders #24,25,28	15.00
...: Ravager - Fresh Hell TPB (2010, $14.99) r/#71-76,79-82 & Faces of Evil: Deathstroke	15.00
... Spotlight: Cyborg TPB (2009, $19.99) r/DC Special: Cyborg #1-6	20.00

Teen Titans Go! (2014 series) #1 © DC

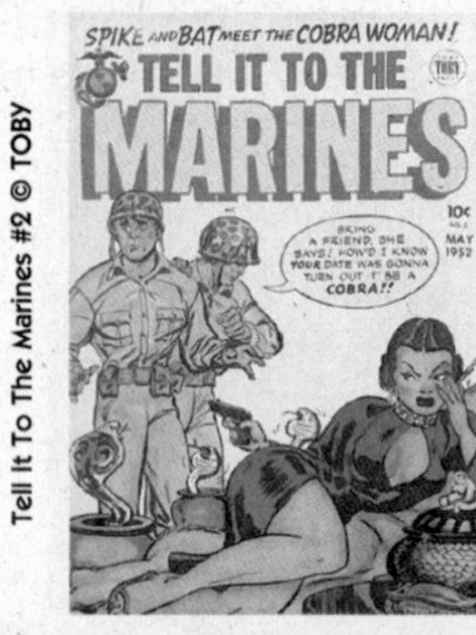

Tell It To The Marines #2 © TOBY

Ten Grand #1 © Studio JMS

	GD 2.0	VG 4.0	FN 6.0	VF 8.0	VF/NM 9.0	NM- 9.2

... Spotlight: Raven TPB (2008, $14.99) r/DC Special: Raven #1-5 15.00
...: The Future is Now (2005, $9.99) r/#15-23 & Teen Titans/Legion Special 10.00
...: The Hunt For Raven (2011, $17.99) r/#79-87 18.00
...: Titans Around the World TPB (2007, $14.99) r/#34-41 15.00
...: Titans of Tomorrow TPB (2008, $14.99) r/#50-54 15.00

TEEN TITANS (DC New 52)
DC Comics: Nov, 2011 - No. 30, Jun, 2014 ($2.99)

1-14,17-23: 1-Lobdell-s/Booth-a/c; Red Robin assembles a team; Kid Flash, Wonder Girl app. 5-Superboy app. 9-The Culling conclusion. 13,14-Wonder Girl origin; Garza-a 3.00
15,16-"Death of the Family" tie-in. 15-Die-cut Joker mask cover. 16-Red Hood app. 5.00
23.1, 23.2 (11/13, $2.99, regular covers) 3.00
23.1 (11/13, $3.99, 3-D cover) "Trigon #1" on cover; origin; Wolfman-s/Cafu-a 5.00
23.2 (11/13, $3.99, 3-D cover) "Deathstroke #1" on cover; flashback; Deathblow app. 5.00
24-29: 24-Leads into Annual #2. 25,26-Origin of Kid Flash 3.00
#0 (11/12, $2.99) Origin of Red Robin; Kirkham-a 3.00
Annual 1 (7/12, $4.99) The Culling x-over part 1; Legion Lost members app. 5.00
Annual 2 (12/13, $4.99) Future Teen Titans; Lobdell-s/Kitson-a 5.00

TEEN TITANS GO! (Based on Cartoon Network series)
DC Comics: Jan, 2004 - No. 55, Jul, 2008 ($2.25)

1-12,14-55: 1,2-Nauck-a/Bullock-c/J. Torres-s. 8-Mad Mod app. 14-Speedy-c. 28-Doom Patrol app. 31-Nightwing app. 36-Wonder Girl. 38-Mad Mod app.; Clugston-a 3.00
1-(9/04, Free Comic Book Day giveaway) r/#1; 2 bound-in Wacky Packages stickers 4.00
13-($2.95) Bonus pages with Shazam! reprint 4.00
Jam Packed Action (2005, $7.99, digest) adaptations of two TV episodes 8.00
... Vol 1: Truth, Justice, Pizza! (2004, $6.95, digest-size) r/#1-5 7.00
... Vol 2: Heroes on Patrol (2005, $6.99, digest-size) r/#6-10 7.00
... Vol 3: Bring It On! (2005, $6.99, digest-size) r/#11-15 7.00
... Vol 4: Ready For Action! (2006, $6.99, digest-size) r/#16-20 7.00
... Vol 5: On The Move! (2006, $6.99, digest-size) r/#21-25 7.00
... Titans Together TPB (2007, $12.99) r/#26-32 13.00

TEEN TITANS GO! (Based on the 2013 Cartoon Network series)
DC Comics: Feb, 2014 - Present ($2.99)

1,2-Fisch-s. 2-Brotherhood of Evil app. 3.00

TEEN TITANS SPOTLIGHT
DC Comics: Aug, 1986 - No. 21, Apr, 1988

1-21: 7-Guice's 1st work at DC. 14-Nightwing; Batman app. 15-Austin-c(i). 18,19-Millennium x-over. 21-($1.00-c)-Original Teen Titans; Spiegle-a 4.00
*Note: **Guice** a-7p, 8p; c-7,8. **Orlando** c/a-11p. **Perez** c-1, 17i, 19. **Sienkiewicz** c-10*

TEEN TITANS YEAR ONE
DC Comics: Mar, 2008 - No. 6, Aug, 2008 ($2.99, limited series)

1-6-The original five form a team; Wolfram-s/Kerschl-a 3.00
TPB (2008, $14.99) r/#1-6; bonus pin-up 15.00

TEEN WOLF: BITE ME (Based on the MTV series)
Image Comics (Top Cow): Sept, 2011 - No. 3, Nov, 2011 ($3.99, limited series)

1-3: 1-Tischman-s/Mooney-a/c 4.00

TEEPEE TIM (...Heap Funny Indian Boy)(Formerly Ha Ha Comics)(Also see "Cookie")
American Comics Group: No. 100, Feb-Mar, 1955 - No. 102, June-July, 1955

100-102 7 14 21 35 43 50

TEGRA JUNGLE EMPRESS (Zegra Jungle Empress #2 on)
Fox Features Syndicate: August, 1948

1-Blue Beetle, Rocket Kelly app.; used in **SOTI**, pg. 31 76 152 228 486 831 1175

TEK JANSEN (See Stephen Colbert's...)

TEKNO COMIX HANDBOOK
Tekno Comix: May, 1996 ($3.95, one-shot)

1-Guide to the Tekno Universe 4.00

TEKNOPHAGE (See Neil Gaiman's...)

TEKNOPHAGE VERSUS ZEERUS
BIG Entertainment: July, 1996 ($3.25, one-shot)

1-Paul Jenkins script 3.25

TEKWORLD (William Shatner's... on-c only)
Epic Comics (Marvel): Sept, 1992 - Aug, 1994 ($1.75)

1-Based on Shatner's novel, TekWar, set in L.A. in the year 2120 4.00
2-24 3.00

TELARA CHRONICLES (Based on the videogame Rift: Planes of Telara)
DC Comics (WildStorm): Jan, 2010; Nov, 2010 - No. 4, Feb, 2011 ($3.99, limited series)

0-(1/10, free) Preview of series 3.00
1-4-Pop Mhan-a/Drew Johnson-c 4.00
TPB (2011, $17.99) r/#0-4; background info on Telara 18.00

TELEVISION (See TV)

TELEVISION COMICS (Early TV comic)
Standard Comics (Animated Cartoons): No. 5, Feb, 1950 - No. 8, Nov, 1950

5-1st app. Willy Nilly 10 20 30 54 72 90
6-8: #6 on inside has #2 on cover 8 16 24 42 54 65

TELEVISION PUPPET SHOW (Early TV comic) (See Spotty the Pup)
Avon Periodicals: 1950 - No. 2, Nov, 1950

1-1st app. Speedy Rabbit, Spotty The Pup 21 42 63 122 199 275
2 15 30 45 85 130 175

TELEVISION TEENS MOPSY (See TV Teens)

TELL IT TO THE MARINES
Toby Press Publications: Mar, 1952 - No. 15, July, 1955

1-Lover O'Leary and His Liberty Belles (with pin-ups), ends #6; Spike & Bat begin, end #6 26 52 78 154 252 350
2-Madame Cobra-c/story 17 34 51 98 154 210
3-5 14 28 42 80 115 150
6-12,14,15: 7-9,14,15-Photo-c 11 22 33 60 83 105
13-John Wayne photo-c 16 32 48 94 147 200
I.W. Reprint #9-r/#1 above 2 4 6 11 16 20
Super Reprint #16(1964)-r/#4 above 2 4 6 8 11 14

TELLOS
Image Comics: May, 1999 - No. 10, Nov, 2000 ($2.50)

1-Dezago-s/Wieringo-a 3.00
1-Variant-c ($7.95) 8.00
2-10: 4-Four covers 3.00
...: Maiden Voyage (3/01, $5.95) Didier Crispeels-a/c 6.00
...: Sons & Moons (2002, $5.95) Nick Cardy-c 6.00
...: The Last Heist (2001, $5.95) Rousseau-a/c 6.00
Prelude ($5.00, AnotherUniverse.com) 5.00
Prologue ($3.95, Dynamic Forces) 4.00
...Collected Edition 1 (12/99, $8.95) r/#1-3 9.00
... Colossal, Vol. 1 TPB (2008, $17.99) r/#1-10, Prelude, Prologue, Scatterjack-s from Section Zero #1, cover gallery, Wieringo sketch pages; Dezago afterword 18.00
...: Kindred Spirits (2/01, $17.95) r/#6-10, Section Zero #1 (Scatterjack-s) 18.00
...: Reluctant Heroes (2/01, $17.95) r/#1-5, Prelude, Prologue; sketchbook 18.00

TEMPEST (See Aquaman, 3rd Series)
DC Comics: Nov, 1996 - No. 4, Feb, 1997 ($1.75, limited series)

1-4: Formerly Aqualad; Phil Jimenez-c/a/scripts in all 3.00

TEMPUS FUGITIVE
DC Comics: 1990 - No. 4, 1991 ($4.95, squarebound, 52 pgs.)

Book 1,2: Ken Steacy painted-c/a & scripts 6.00
Book 3,4-($5.95-c) 6.00
TPB (Dark Horse Comics, 1/97, $17.95) 18.00

TEN COMMANDMENTS (See Moses & the... and Classics Illustrated Special)

TENDER LOVE STORIES
Skywald Publ. Corp.: Feb, 1971 - No. 4, July, 1971 (Pre-code reprints and new stories)

1 (All 25¢, 52 pgs.) 6 12 18 40 73 105
2-4 5 10 15 30 50 70

TENDER ROMANCE (Ideal Romance #3 on)
Key Publications (Gilmour Magazines): Dec, 1953 - No. 2, Feb, 1954

1-Headlight & lingerie panels; B. Baily-c 22 44 66 132 216 300
2-Bernard Baily-c 14 28 42 80 115 150

TEN GRAND
Image Comics (Joe's Comics): May, 2013 - Present ($2.99)

1-8: 1-4-Straczynski-s/Templesmith-a. 1-Multiple variant covers. 2-Two covers 3.00

TENSE SUSPENSE
Fago Publications: Dec, 1958 - No. 2, Feb, 1959

1 11 22 33 62 86 110
2 8 16 24 44 57 70

TEN STORY LOVE (Formerly a pulp magazine with same title)
Ace Periodicals: V29#3, June-July, 1951 - V36#5(#209), Sept, 1956 (#3-6: 52 pgs.)

V29#3(#177)-Part comic, part text; painted-c 17 34 51 98 154 210
4-6(1/52) 11 22 33 62 86 110

Terminal City #2 © Dean Motter

The Terminator: Hunters and Killers #3 © Studio Canal

The Terminator: 2029 #2 © Studio Canal

	GD 2.0	VG 4.0	FN 6.0	VF 8.0	VF/NM 9.0	NM- 9.2
V30#1(3/52)-6(1/53)	11	22	33	60	83	105
V31#1(2/53),V32#2(4/53)-6(12/53)	10	20	30	58	79	100
V33#1(1/54)-3(5#54, #195), V34#4(7/54, #196)-6(10/54, #198)	10	20	30	56	76	95
V35#1(12/54, #199)-3(4/55, #201)-Last precode	10	20	30	54	72	90
V35#4-6(9/55, #201-204), V36#1(11/55, #205)-3, 5(9/56, #209)	9	18	27	52	69	85
V36#4-L.B. Cole-a	11	22	33	60	83	105

TENTH, THE
Image Comics: Jan, 1997 - No. 4, June, 1997 ($2.50, limited series)

1-4-Tony Daniel-c/a, Beau Smith-s 5.00
Abuse of Humanity TPB ($10.95) r/#1-4 12.00
Abuse of Humanity TPB (10/98, $11.95) r/#1-4 & 0(8/97) 12.00

TENTH, THE
Image Comics: Sept, 1997 - No. 14, Jan, 1999 ($2.50)

0-(8/97, $5.00) American Ent. Ed. 6.00
1-Tony Daniel-c/a, Beau Smith-s 6.00
2-9: 3,7-Variant-c 4.00
10-14 3.00
...Configuration (8/98) Re-cap and pin-ups 3.00
...Collected Edition 1 ('98, $4.95, square-bound) r/#1,2 5.00
...Special (4/00, $2.95) r/#0 and Wizard #1/2 3.00
Wizard #1/2-Daniel-s/Steve Scott-a 10.00

TENTH, THE (Volume 3) (The Black Embrace)
Image Comics: Mar, 1999 - No. 4, June, 1999 ($2.95)

1-4-Daniel-c/a 3.00
TPB (1/00, $12.95) r/#1-4 13.00

TENTH, THE (Volume 4) (Evil's Child)
Image Comics: Sept, 1999 - No. 4, Mar, 2000 ($2.95, limited series)

1-4-Daniel-c/a 3.00

TENTH, THE (Darkk Dawn)
Image Comics: July, 2005 ($4.99, one-shot)

1-Kirkham-a/Bonny-s 5.00

TENTH, THE : RESURRECTED
Dark Horse Comics: July, 2001 - No. 4, Feb, 2002 ($2.99, limited series)

1-4: 1-Two covers; Daniel-s/c; Romano-a 3.00

10th MUSE
Image Comics (TidalWave Studios): Nov, 2000 - No. 9, Jan, 2002 ($2.95)

1-Character based on wrestling's Rena Mero; regular & photo covers 3.00
2-9: 2-Photo and 2 Lashley covers; flip book Dollz preview. 5-Savage Dragon app.; 2 covers by Lashley and Larsen. 6-Tellos x-over 3.00

TEN WHO DARED (Disney)
Dell Publishing Co.: No. 1178, Dec, 1960

	GD 2.0	VG 4.0	FN 6.0	VF 8.0	VF/NM 9.0	NM- 9.2
Four Color 1178-Movie, painted-c; cast member photo on back-c	6	12	18	41	76	110

TERMINAL CITY
DC Comics (Vertigo): July, 1996 - No. 9, Mar, 1997 ($2.50, limited series)

1-9: Dean Motter scripts, 7,8-Matt Wagner-c 3.00
TPB ('97, $19.95) r/series 20.00

TERMINAL CITY: AERIAL GRAFFITI
DC Comics (Vertigo): Nov, 1997 - No. 5, Mar, 1998 ($2.50, limited series)

1-5: Dean Motter-s/Lark-a/Chiarello-c 3.00

TERMINATOR, THE (See Robocop vs. ... & Rust #12 for 1st app.)
Now Comics: Sept, 1988 - No. 17, 1989 ($1.75, Baxter paper)

	GD 2.0	VG 4.0	FN 6.0	VF 8.0	VF/NM 9.0	NM- 9.2
1-Based on movie	1	3	4	6	8	10
2-5						6.00
6-11,13-17						4.00
12-($2.95, 52 pgs.)-Intro. John Connor						5.00
Trade paperback (1989, $9.95)						15.00

TERMINATOR, THE
Dark Horse Comics: Aug, 1990 - No. 4, Nov, 1990 ($2.50, limited series)

1-Set 39 years later than the movie 5.00
2-4 4.00

TERMINATOR, THE
Dark Horse Comics: 1998 - No. 4, Dec, 1998 ($2.95, limited series)

1-4-Alan Grant-s/Steve Pugh-a/c 4.00
...Special (1998, $2.95) Darrow-c/Grant-s 4.00

TERMINATOR, THE: ALL MY FUTURES PAST
Now Comics: V3#1, Aug, 1990 - V3#2, Sept, 1990 ($1.75, limited series)

V3#1,2 4.00

TERMINATOR, THE: ENDGAME
Dark Horse Comics: Sept, 1992 - No. 3, Nov, 1992 ($2.50, limited series)

1-3: Guice-a(p); painted-c 4.00

TERMINATOR, THE: ENEMY OF MY ENEMY
Dark Horse Comics: Feb, 2014 - No. 6 ($3.99, limited series)

1,2-Jolley-s/Igle-a; set in 1985 4.00

TERMINATOR, THE: HUNTERS AND KILLERS
Dark Horse Comics: Mar, 1992 - No. 3, May, 1992 ($2.50, limited series)

1-3 4.00

TERMINATOR, THE: 1984
Dark Horse Comics: Sept, 2010 - No. 3, Nov, 2010 ($3.50, limited series)

1-3: Takes place during and after the 1st movie; Zack Whedon-s/Andy MacDonald-a 3.50

TERMINATOR, THE: ONE SHOT
Dark Horse Comics: July, 1991 ($5.95, 56 pgs.)

nn-Matt Wagner-a; contains stiff pop-up inside 6.00

TERMINATOR: REVOLUTION (Follows Terminator 2: Infinity series)
Dynamite Entertainment: 2008 - No. 5, 2009 ($3.50, limited series)

1-5-Furman-s/Antonio-a. 1-3-Two covers 3.50

TERMINATOR / ROBOCOP: KILL HUMAN
Dynamite Entertainment: 2011 - No. 4, 2011 ($3.99, limited series)

1-4: 1-Covers by Simonson, Lau & Feister. 2-4-Three covers on each 4.00

TERMINATOR: SALVATION MOVIE PREQUEL
IDW Publishing: Jan, 2009 - No. 4, Apr, 2009 ($3.99, limited series)

1-4: Alan Robinson-a/Dara Naraghi-s 4.00
0-Salvation Movie Preview (4/09) Mariotte-s/Figueroa-a 4.00

TERMINATOR SALVATION: THE FINAL BATTLE
Dark Horse Comics: Dec, 2013 - No. 12 ($3.99, limited series)

1-4: 1-Straczynski-s/Woods-a 4.00

TERMINATOR, THE: SECONDARY OBJECTIVES
Dark Horse Comics: July, 1991 - No. 4, Oct, 1991 ($2.50, limited series)

1-4: Gulacy-c/a(p) in all 4.00

TERMINATOR, THE: THE BURNING EARTH
Now Comics: V2#1, Mar, 1990 - V2#5, July, 1990 ($1.75, limited series)

	GD 2.0	VG 4.0	FN 6.0	VF 8.0	VF/NM 9.0	NM- 9.2
V2#1: Alex Ross painted art (1st published work)	2	4	6	9	12	15
2-5: Ross-c/a in all	1	3	4	6	8	10
Trade paperback (1990, $9.95)-Reprints V2#1-5						18.00
Trade paperback (ibooks, 2003, $17.95)-Digitally remastered reprint						18.00

TERMINATOR, THE: THE DARK YEARS
Dark Horse Comics: Aug, 1999 - No. 4, Dec, 1999 ($2.95, limited series)

1-4-Alan Grant-s/Mel Rubi-a; Jae Lee-c 4.00

TERMINATOR, THE: THE ENEMY FROM WITHIN
Dark Horse Comics: Nov, 1991 - No. 4, Feb, 1992 ($2.50, limited series)

1-4: All have Simon Bisley painted-c 4.00

TERMINATOR, THE: 2029
Dark Horse Comics: Mar, 2010 - No. 3, May, 2010 ($3.50, limited series)

1-3: Kyle Reese before his time-jump to 1984; Zack Whedon-s/Andy MacDonald-a 3.50

TERMINATOR 2: CYBERNETIC DAWN
Malibu: Nov, 1995 - No.4, Feb, 1996; No. 0. Apr, 1996 ($2.50, lim. series)

0 (4/96, $2.95)-Erskine-c/a; flip book w/Terminator 2: Nuclear Twilight 4.00
1-4: Continuation of film. 4.00

TERMINATOR 2: INFINITY
Dynamite Entertainment: 2007 - No. 7 ($3.50)

1-7: 1-Furman-s/Raynor-a; 3 covers. 6,7-Painkiller Jane x-over 3.50

TERMINATOR 2: JUDGEMENT DAY
Marvel Comics: Early Sept, 1991 - No. 3, Early Oct, 1991 ($1.00, lim. series)

1-3: Based on movie sequel; 1-3-Same as nn issues 4.00
nn (1991, $4.95, squarebound, 68 pgs.)-Photo-c 6.00
nn (1991, $2.25, B&W, magazine, 68 pgs.) 4.00

Terrific Comics #5 © Continental

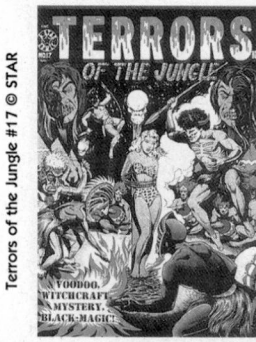

Terrors of the Jungle #17 © STAR

Terry and the Pirates #21 © NYNS

	GD 2.0	VG 4.0	FN 6.0	VF 8.0	VF/NM 9.0	NM- 9.2

GD VG FN VF VF/NM NM- 2.0 4.0 6.0 8.0 9.0 9.2

TERMINATOR 2: NUCLEAR TWILIGHT
Malibu: Nov, 1995 - No.4, Feb, 1996; No. 0, Apr, 1996 ($2.50, lim. series)

0 (4/96, $2.95)-Erskine-c/a; flip book w/Terminator 2: Cybernetic Dawn 4.00
1-4:Continuation of film. 4.00

TERMINATOR 3: RISE OF THE MACHINES (... BEFORE THE RISE on cover)
Beckett Comics: July, 2003 - No. 6, Jan, 2004 ($5.95, limited series)

1-6: 1,2-Leads into movie; 2 covers on each. 3-6-Movie adaptation 6.00

TERM LIFE
Image Comics (Shadowline): Jan, 2011 ($16.99, graphic novel)

SC-Lieberman-s/Thornborrow-a/DeStefano-l 17.00

TERRA (See Supergirl {2005 series} #12)
DC Comics: Jan, 2009 - No. 4, Feb, 2009 ($2.99, limited series)

1-4-Conner-a/c. 1,2,4-Power Girl app. 2-4-Geo-Force app. 3.00
TPB (2009, $14.99) r/#1-4 & Supergirl #12 15.00

TERRAFORMERS
Wonder Color Comics: April, 1987 - No. 2, 1987 ($1.95, limited series)

1,2-Kelley Jones-a 3.00

TERRANAUTS
Fantasy General Comics: Aug, 1986 - No. 2, 1986 ($1.75, limited series)

1,2 3.00

TERRA OBSCURA (See Tom Strong)
America's Best Comics: Aug, 2003 - No. 6, Feb, 2004 ($2.95)

1-6-Alan Moore & Peter Hogan-s/Paquette-a 3.00
TPB (2004, $14.95) r/#1-6 15.00

TERRA OBSCURA VOLUME 2 (See Tom Strong)
America's Best Comics: Oct, 2004 - No. 6, May, 2005 ($2.95)

1-6-Alan Moore & Peter Hogan-s/Paquette-a; Tom Strange app. 3.00
TPB (2005, $14.99) r/#1-6 15.00

TERRARISTS
Marvel Comics (Epic): Nov, 1993 - No. 4, Feb, 1994 ($2.50, limited series)

1-4-Bound-in trading cards in all 3.00

TERRIFIC COMICS (Also see Suspense Comics)
Continental Magazines: Jan, 1944 - No. 6, Nov, 1944

	GD	VG	FN	VF	VF/NM	NM-
1-Kid Terrific; opium story	326	652	978	2282	3991	5700
2-1st app. The Boomerang by L.B. Cole & Ed Wheelan's "Comics" McCormick, called the world's #1 comic book fan begins	245	490	735	1568	2684	3800
3-Diana becomes Boomerang's costumed aide; L.B. Cole-c	232	464	696	1485	2543	3600
4-Classic war-c (Scarce)	423	846	1269	3088	5444	7800
5-The Reckoner begins; Boomerang & Diana by L.B. Cole; Classic Schomburg bondage & hooded vigilante-c (Scarce)	1250	2500	3750	7500	14,500	26,000
6-L.B. Cole-c/a	210	420	630	1334	2292	3250

NOTE: ***L.B. Cole** a-1, 2(2), 3-6. **Fuje** a-5, 6. **Rico** a-2; c-1. **Schomburg** c-2, 5.*

TERRIFIC COMICS (Formerly Horrific; Wonder Boy #17 on)
Mystery Publ.(Comic Media)/(Ajax/Farrell): No. 14, Dec, 1954; No. 16, Mar, 1955 (No #15)

	GD	VG	FN	VF	VF/NM	NM-
14-Art swipe/Advs. into the Unknown #37; injury-to-eye-c; pg. 2, panel 5 swiped from Phantom Stranger #4; surrealistic Palais-a; Human Cross story; classic-c	86	172	258	546	936	1325
16-Wonder Boy-c/story (last pre-code)	29	58	87	170	278	385

TERRIFYING TALES (Formerly Startling Terror Tales #10)
Star Publications: No. 11, Jan, 1953 - No. 15, Apr, 1954

	GD	VG	FN	VF	VF/NM	NM-
11-Used in **POP**, pgs. 99,100; all Jo-Jo-r	53	106	159	334	567	800
12-Reprints Jo-Jo #19 entirely; L.B. Cole splash	50	100	150	315	533	750
13-All Rulah-r; classic devil-c	58	116	174	371	636	900
14-All Rulah reprints	47	94	141	296	498	700
15-Rulah, Zago-r; used in **SOTI**-r/Rulah #22	47	94	141	296	498	700

NOTE: *All issues have **L.B. Cole** covers; bondage covers-No. 12-14.*

TERROR ILLUSTRATED (Adult Tales of...)
E.C. Comics: Nov-Dec, 1955 - No. 2, Spring (April on-c), 1956 (Magazine, 25¢)

	GD	VG	FN	VF	VF/NM	NM-
1-Adult Entertainment on-c	24	48	72	142	234	325
2-Charles Sultan-a	17	34	51	98	154	210

NOTE: ***Craig, Evans, Ingels, Orlando** art in each. **Crandall** c-1, 2.*

TERROR INC. (See A Shadowline Saga #3)
Marvel Comics: July, 1992 - No. 13, July, 1993 ($1.75)

1-8,11-13: 6,7-Punisher-c/story. 13-Ghost Rider app. 3.00
9,10-Wolverine-c/story 4.00

TERROR INC.
Marvel Comics (MAX): Oct, 2007 - No. 5, Apr, 2008 ($3.99, limited series)

1-5: 1-Lapham-s/Zircher-a; origin of Mr. Terror retold 4.00

TERROR INC. - APOCALYPSE SOON
Marvel Comics (MAX): July, 2009 - No. 4, Sept, 2009 ($3.99, limited series)

1-4: 1-Lapham-s/Turnbull-a 4.00

TERRORS OF DRACULA (Magazine)
Modern Day Periodical/Eerie Publ.: Vol. 1 #3, May, 1979 - Vol. 3 #2, Sept, 1981 (B&W)

	GD	VG	FN	VF	VF/NM	NM-
Vol. 1 #3 (5/79, 1st issue)	4	8	12	25	40	55
#4(8/79), #5(11/79)	3	6	9	19	30	40
Vol. 2 #1-3: 1-(2/80). 2-(5/80). 3-(8/80)	3	6	9	16	24	32
Vol. 3 #1 (5/81), #2 (9/81)	3	6	9	18	28	38

TERRORS OF THE JUNGLE (Formerly Jungle Thrills)
Star Publications: No. 17, 5/52 - No. 21, 2/53; No. 4, 4/53 - No. 10, 9/54

	GD	VG	FN	VF	VF/NM	NM-
17-Reprints Rulah #21, used in **SOTI**; L.B. Cole bondage-c	53	106	159	334	567	800
18-Jo-Jo-r	39	78	117	240	395	550
19,20(1952)-Jo-Jo-r; Disbrow-a	39	78	117	231	378	525
21-Jungle Jo, Tangi-r; used in **POP**, pg. 100 & color illos.	40	80	120	246	411	575
4-10: All Disbrow-a. 5-Jo-Jo-r. 8-Rulah, Jo-Jo-r. 9-Jo-Jo-r; Disbrow-a; Tangi by Orlando10-Rulah-r	40	80	120	246	411	575

NOTE: ***L.B. Cole** c-all; bondage c-17, 19, 21, 5, 7.*

TERROR TALES (See Beware Terror Tales)

TERROR TALES (Magazine)
Eerie Publications: V1#7, 1969 - V6#6, Dec, 1974; V7#1, Apr, 1976 - V10, 1979? (V1-V6: 52 pgs.; V7 on: 68 pgs.)

	GD	VG	FN	VF	VF/NM	NM-
V1#7	7	14	21	49	92	135
V1#8-11('69): 9-Bondage-c	5	10	15	33	57	80
V2#1-6('70), V3#1-6('71), V4#1-7('72), V5#1-6('73), V6#1-6('74), V7#1,4('76) (no V7#2), V8#1-3('77)	5	10	15	30	50	70
V7#3-(7/76) LSD story-r/Weird V3#5	5	10	15	30	50	70
V9#2-4, V10#1(1/79)	5	10	15	31	53	75

TERROR TITANS
DC Comics: Dec, 2008 - No. 6, May, 2009 ($2.99, limited series)

1-6: 1-Ravager and Clock King at the Dark Side Club; Bennett-a. 3-Static app. 3.00
TPB (2009, $17.99) r/#1-6 18.00

TERRY AND THE PIRATES (See Famous Feature Stories, Merry Christmas From Sears Toyland, Popular Comics, Super Book #3,5,9,16,28, & Super Comics)

TERRY AND THE PIRATES
Dell Publishing Co.: 1939 - 1953 (By Milton Caniff)

	GD	VG	FN	VF	VF/NM	NM-
Large Feature Comic 2(1939)	94	188	282	602	1026	1450
Large Feature Comic 6(1938)-r/1936 dailies	76	152	228	486	831	1175
Four Color 9(1940)	71	142	213	454	777	1100
Large Feature Comic 27('41), 6('42)	61	122	183	390	670	950
Four Color 44('43)	30	60	90	216	483	750
Four Color 101('45)	19	38	57	131	291	450
Family Album(1942)	20	40	60	117	189	260

TERRY AND THE PIRATES (Formerly Boy Explorers; Long John Silver & the Pirates #30 on) (Daily strip-r) (Two #26's)
Harvey Publications/Charlton No. 26-28: No. 3, 4/47 - No. 26, 4/51; No. 26, 6/55 - No. 28, 10/55

	GD	VG	FN	VF	VF/NM	NM-
3(#1)-Boy Explorers by S&K; Terry & the Pirates begin by Caniff; 1st app. The Dragon Lady	39	78	117	234	385	535
4-S&K Boy Explorers	22	44	66	132	216	300
5-11: 11-Man in Black app. by Powell	13	26	39	72	101	130
12-20: 16-Girl threatened with red hot poker	10	20	30	56	76	95
21-26(4/51)-Last Caniff issue & last pre-code issue	10	20	30	54	72	90
26-28('55)(Formerly This Is Suspense)-No Caniff-a	9	18	27	47	61	75

NOTE: ***Powell** a (Tommy Tween)-5-10, 12, 14; 15-17(1/2 to 2 pgs. each).*

TERRY BEARS COMICS (TerryToons, The... #4)
St. John Publishing Co.: June, 1952 - No. 3, Mar, 1953

	GD	VG	FN	VF	VF/NM	NM-
1-By Paul Terry	10	20	30	58	79	100
2,3	8	16	24	40	50	60

TERRY-TOONS ALBUM (See Giant Comics Edition)

TERRY-TOONS COMICS (1st Series) (Becomes Paul Terry's Comics #85 on; later issues titled "Paul Terry's...")
Timely/Marvel No. 1-59 (8/47)(Becomes Best Western No. 58 on?, Marvel)/

Terry-Toons Comics #44 © Paul Terry

Tessie the Typist #7 © MAR

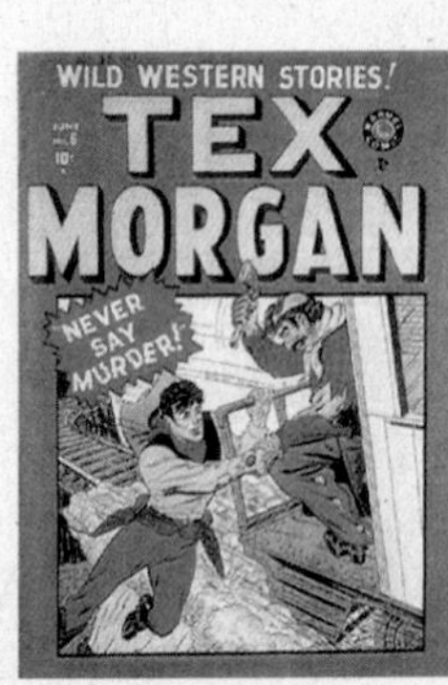

Tex Morgan #6 © MAR

GD VG FN VF VF/NM NM-
2.0 4.0 6.0 8.0 9.0 9.2

St. John No. 60 (9/47) on: Oct, 1942 - No. 86, May, 1951

1 (Scarce)-Features characters that 1st app. on movie screen; Gandy Goose & Sourpuss begin; war-c; Gandy Goose c-1-37 239 478 717 1530 2615 3700
2 81 162 243 518 884 1250
3-5 55 110 165 352 601 850
6,8-10: 9,10-World War II gag-c 41 82 123 256 428 600
7-Hitler, Hirohito, Mussolini-c 129 258 387 826 1413 2000
11-20 30 60 90 177 289 400
21-37 21 42 63 122 199 275
38-Mighty Mouse begins (1st app., 11/45); Mighty Mouse-c begin, end #86; Gandy, Sourpuss welcome Mighty Mouse on-c 190 380 570 1216 2083 2950
39-2nd app. Mighty Mouse 60 120 180 381 653 925
40-49: 43-Infinity-c 34 68 102 199 325 450
50-1st app. Heckle & Jeckle (11/46) 55 110 165 352 601 850
51-60: 55-Infinity-c. 60-(9/47)-Atomic explosion panel; 1st St. John issue 19 38 57 111 176 240
61-86: 85,86-Same book as Paul Terry's Comics #85,86 with only a title change; published at same time? 15 30 45 86 133 180

TERRY-TOONS COMICS (2nd Series)
St. John Publishing Co./Pines: June, 1952 - No. 9, Nov, 1953; 1957; 1958

1-Gandy Goose & Sourpuss begin by Paul Terry 18 36 54 105 165 225
2 10 20 30 56 76 95
3-9 9 18 27 52 69 85
Giant Summer Fun Book 101,102-(Sum, 1957, Sum, 1958, 25¢, Pines)(TV) CBS Television Presents...; Tom Terrific, Mighty Mouse, Heckle & Jeckle Gandy Goose app. 14 28 42 80 115 150

TERRYTOONS, THE TERRY BEARS (Formerly Terry Bears Comics)
Pines Comics: No. 4, Summer, 1958 (CBS Television Presents...)

4 8 16 24 40 50 60

TESSIE THE TYPIST (Tiny Tessie #24; see Comedy Comics, Gay Comics & Joker Comics)
Timely/Marvel Comics (20CC): Summer, 1944 - No. 23, Aug, 1949

1-Doc Rockblock & others by Wolverton 110 220 330 704 1202 1700
2-Wolverton's Powerhouse Pepper 47 94 141 296 498 700
3-(3/45)-No Wolverton 26 52 78 154 252 350
4,5,7,8-Wolverton-a. 4-(Fall/45) 37 74 111 222 361 500
6-Kurtzman's "Hey Look", 2 pgs. Wolverton-a 37 74 111 222 361 500
9-Wolverton's Powerhouse Pepper (8 pgs.) & 1 pg. Kurtzman's "Hey Look" 39 78 117 236 388 540
10-Wolverton's Powerhouse Pepper (4 pgs.) 37 74 111 222 361 500
11-Wolverton's Powerhouse Pepper (8 pgs.) 39 78 117 236 388 540
12-Wolverton's Powerhouse Pepper (4 pgs.) & 1 pg. Kurtzman's "Hey Look" 37 74 111 222 361 500
13-Wolverton's Powerhouse Pepper (4 pgs.) 37 74 111 222 361 500
14,15: 14-Wolverton's Dr. Whackyhack (1 pg.); 1-1/2 pgs. Kurtzman's "Hey Look". 15-Kurtzman's "Hey Look" (3 pgs.) & 3 pgs. Giggles 'n' Grins 28 56 84 165 270 375
16-18-Kurtzman's "Hey Look" (?, 2 & 1 pg.) 21 42 63 122 199 275
19-Annie Oakley story (8 pgs.) 15 30 45 90 140 190
20-23: 20-Anti-Wertham editorial (2/49) 15 30 45 86 133 180
NOTE: *Lana app.-21. Millie The Model app.-13, 15, 17, 21. Rusty app.-10, 11, 13, 15, 17.*

TESTAMENT
DC Comics (Vertigo): Feb, 2006 - No. 22, Mar, 2008 ($2.99)

1-22: 1-5-Rushkoff-s/Sharp-a. 6,7-Gross & Erskine-a 3.00
...: Akedah TPB (2006, $9.99) r/#1-5; Rushkoff intro. 10.00
...: Babel TPB (2007, $12.99) r/#11-16 13.00
...: Exodus TPB (2008, $14.99) r/#17-22 15.00
...: West of Eden TPB (2007, $12.99) r/#6-10; Rushkoff commentary 13.00

TEXAN, THE (Fightin' Marines #15 on; Fightin' Texan #16 on)
St. John Publishing Co.: Aug, 1948 - No. 15, Oct, 1951

1-Buckskin Belle 17 34 51 98 154 210
2 11 22 33 60 83 105
3,10: 10-Oversized issue 11 22 33 60 83 105
4,5,7,15-Baker-c/a 22 44 66 132 216 300
6,9-Baker-c 18 36 54 105 165 225
8,11,13,14-Baker-c/a(2-3) each 26 52 78 154 252 350
12-All Matt Baker-c/a; Peyote story 32 64 96 188 307 425
NOTE: ***Matt Baker** c-4-9, 11-15. **Larsen** a-4-6, 8-10, 15. **Tuska** a-1, 2, 7-9.*

TEXAN, THE (TV)
Dell Publishing Co.: No. 1027, Sept-Nov, 1959 - No. 1096, May-July, 1960

Four Color 1027 (#1)-Photo-c 7 14 21 48 89 130
Four Color 1096-Rory Calhoun photo-c 7 14 21 44 82 120

TEXAS CHAINSAW MASSACRE
DC Comics (WildStorm): Jan, 2007 - No. 6, Jun, 2007 ($2.99, limited series)

1-6: 1-Two covers by Bermejo & Bradstreet; Abnett & Lanning-s 3.00
...: About a Boy #1 (9/07, $2.99) Abnett & Lanning-s/Gomez-a/Robertson-c 3.00
...: Book Two TPB (2009, $14.99) r/one shots & New Line Cinema's Tales of Horror story 15.00
...: By Himself #1 (10/07, $2.99) Abnett & Lanning-s/Craig-a/Robertson-c 3.00
...: Cut! #1 (8/07, $2.99) Pfeiffer-s/Raffaele-a/Robertson-c 3.00
...: Raising Cain 1-3 (7/08 - No. 3, 9/08, $3.50) Bruce Jones-s/Chris Gugliotti-a 3.50

TEXAS JOHN SLAUGHTER (See Walt Disney Presents, 4-Color #997, 1181 & #2)

TEXAS KID (See Two-Gun Western, Wild Western)
Marvel/Atlas Comics (LMC): Jan, 1951 - No. 10, July, 1952

1-Origin; Texas Kid (alias Lance Temple) & his horse Thunder begin; Tuska-a 25 50 75 150 245 340
2 14 28 42 80 115 150
3-10 11 22 33 60 83 105
NOTE: ***Maneely** a-1-4; c-1, 3, 5-10.*

TEXAS RANGERS, THE (See Jace Pearson of... and Superior Stories #4)

TEXAS RANGERS IN ACTION (Formerly Captain Gallant or Scotland Yard?)
Charlton Comics: No. 5, Jul, 1956 - No. 79, Aug, 1970 (See Blue Bird Comics)

5 8 16 24 44 57 70
6,7,9,10 6 12 18 28 34 40
8-Ditko-a (signed) 10 20 30 54 72 90
11-(68 pg. Giant) Williamson-a (5&8 pgs.); Torres/Williamson-a (5 pgs.) 10 20 30 54 72 90
12-(68 pg. Giant, 6/58) 6 12 18 28 34 40
13-Williamson-a (5 pgs); Torres, Morisi-a 8 16 24 42 54 65
14-20 5 10 15 23 28 32
21-30 3 6 9 15 22 28
31-59: 32-Both 10¢-c & 15¢-c exist 2 4 6 13 18 22
60-Riley's Rangers begin 3 6 9 14 19 24
61-65,68-70 2 4 6 8 11 14
66,67: 66-1st app. The Man Called Loco. 67-Origin 2 4 6 9 13 16
71-79: 77-(4/70) Ditko-c & a (8 pgs.) 1 3 4 6 8 10
76 (Modern Comics-r, 1977) 6.00

TEXAS SLIM (See A-1 Comics)

TEX DAWSON, GUN-SLINGER (Gunslinger #2 on)
Marvel Comics Group: Jan, 1973 (20¢)(Also see Western Kid, 1st series)

1-Steranko-c; Williamson-r (4 pgs.); Tex Dawson-r by Romita(3) from 1955; Tuska-r 3 6 9 17 26 35

TEX FARNUM (See Wisco)

TEX FARRELL (...Pride of the Wild West)
D. S. Publishing Co.: Mar-Apr, 1948

1-Tex Farrell & his horse Lightning; Shelly-c 15 30 45 88 137 185

TEX GRANGER (Formerly Calling All Boys; see True Comics)
Parents' Magazine Inst./Commended: No. 18, Jun, 1948 - No. 24, Sept, 1949

18-Tex Granger & his horse Bullet begin 12 24 36 67 94 120
19 10 20 30 54 72 90
20-24: 22-Wild Bill Hickok story. 23-Vs. Billy the Kid; Tim Holt app. 8 16 24 44 57 70

TEX MORGAN (See Blaze Carson and Wild Western)
Marvel Comics (CCC): Aug, 1948 - No. 9, Feb, 1950

1-Tex Morgan, his horse Lightning & sidekick Lobo begin 28 56 84 165 270 375
2 18 36 54 105 165 225
3-6: 3,4-Arizona Annie app. 5-Blaze Carson app. 14 28 42 76 108 140
7-9: All photo-c. 7-Captain Tootsie by Beck. 8-18 pg. story "The Terror of Rimrock Valley"; Diablo app. 18 36 54 105 165 225
NOTE: *Tex Taylor app. 2-6, 7, 9. **Brodsky** c-6. **Syd Shores** c-2, 5.*

TEX RITTER WESTERN (Movie star; singing cowboy; see Six-Gun Heroes and Western Hero)
Fawcett No. 1-20 (1/54)/Charlton No. 21 on: Oct, 1950 - No. 46, May, 1959 (Photo-c: 1-21)

1-Tex Ritter, his stallion White Flash & dog Fury begin; photo front/back-c begin 43 86 129 271 461 650
2 21 42 63 124 202 280
3-5: 5-Last photo back-c 16 32 48 94 147 200
6-10 14 28 42 80 115 150
11-19 10 20 30 58 79 100
20-Last Fawcett issue (1/54) 11 22 33 62 86 110

Tex Taylor #7 © MAR

Thanos Rising #2 © MAR

The Thing (2006 series) #1 © MAR

GD VG FN VF VF/NM NM-
2.0 4.0 6.0 8.0 9.0 9.2

21-1st Charlton issue; photo-c (3/54) 14 28 42 80 115 150
22-B&W photo back-c begin, end #32 9 18 27 52 69 85
23-30: 23-25-Young Falcon app. 9 18 27 47 61 75
31-38,40-45 8 16 24 42 54 65
39-Williamson-a; Whitman-c (1/58) 9 18 27 47 61 75
46-Last issue 8 16 24 44 57 70

TEX TAYLOR (...The Fighting Cowboy on-c #1, 2)(See Blaze Carson, Kid Colt, Tex Morgan, Wild West, Wild Western, & Wisco)
Marvel Comics (HPC): Sept, 1948 - No. 9, March, 1950

1-Tex Taylor & his horse Fury begin; Blaze Carson app.
29 58 87 170 278 385
2-Blaze Carson app. 15 30 45 88 137 185
3-Arizona Annie app. 14 28 42 82 121 160
4-6: All photo-c; Blaze Carson app. 4-Anti-Wertham editorial
15 30 45 92 144 195
7-9: 7-Photo-c;18 pg. Movie-Length Thriller "Trapped in Time's Lost Land!" with sabretoothed tigers, dinosaurs; Diablo app. 8-Photo-c; 18 pg. Movie-Length Thriller "The Mystery of Devil-Tree Plateau!" with dwarf horses, dwarf people & a lost miniature Inca type village; Diablo app. 9-Photo-c; 18 pg. Movie-Length Thriller "Guns Along the Border!" Captain Tootsie by Schreiber; Nimo the Mountain Lion app.; Heth-a
19 38 57 109 172 235
NOTE: *Syd Shores c-1-3.*

THANE OF BAGARTH (Also see Hercules, 1967 series)
Charlton Comics: No. 24, Oct, 1985 - No. 25, Dec, 1985

24,25-Low print run 6.00

THANOS
Marvel Comics: Dec, 2003 - No. 12, Sept, 2004 ($2.99)

1-12: 1-6-Starlin-s/a(p)/Milgrom-i; Galactus app. 7-12-Giffen-s/Lim-a 4.00
...: The Final Threat (11/12, $4.99) r/Avengers Ann. #7 & Marvel Two-In-One Ann. #2 5.00
Vol. 4: Epiphany TPB (2004, $14.99) r/#1-6 15.00
Vol. 5: Samaritan TPB (2004, $14.99) r/#7-12 15.00

THANOS IMPERATIVE, THE
Marvel Comics: Aug, 2010 - No. 6, Jan, 2011 ($3.99, limited series)

1-6-Abnett & Lanning-s/Sepulveda-a; Vision and Silver Surfer app. 4.00
...: Devastation (3/11, $3.99) Sepulveda-a; leads into The Annihilators #1 4.00
...: Ignition (7/10, $3.99) Walker-a; prequel to series 4.00
Thanos Sourcebook (8/10, $3.99) profiles/history of Thanos and Nova Corps members 4.00

THANOS QUEST, THE (See Capt. Marvel #25, Infinity Gauntlet, Iron Man #55, Logan's Run, Marvel Feature #12, Marvel Universe: The End, Silver Surfer #34 & Warlock #9)
Marvel Comics: 1990 - No. 2, 1990 ($4.95, squarebound, 52 pgs.)

1,2-Both have Starlin scripts & covers (both printings) 2 4 6 11 16 20
1-(3/2000, $3.99) r/material from #1&2 5.00
1-(11/12, $7,99) r/#1&2, new cover by Andy Park 8.00

THANOS RISING
Marvel Comics: Jun, 2013 - No. 5, Oct, 2013 ($3.99, limited series)

1-5: 1-Thanos birth and childhood; Aaron-s/Bianchi-a/c 4.00

THAT DARN CAT (See Movie Comics & Walt Disney Showcase #19)

THAT'S MY POP! GOES NUTS FOR FAIR
Bystander Press: 1939 (76 pgs., B&W)

nn-by Milt Gross 34 68 102 199 325 450

THAT WILKIN BOY (Meet Bingo...)
Archie Publications: Jan, 1969 - No. 52, Oct, 1982

1-1st app. Bingo's Band, Samantha & Tough Teddy 4 8 12 27 44 60
2-5 3 6 9 16 23 30
6-11 2 4 6 13 18 22
12-26-Giants. 12-No # on-c 3 6 9 14 20 26
27-40(1/77) 2 4 6 8 10 12
41-49 1 2 3 4 5 7
50-52 (low print) 2 4 6 8 10 12

THB
Horse Press: Oct, 1994 - 2002 ($5.50/$2.50/$2.95, B&W)

1 ($5.50) Paul Pope-s/a in all 3 6 9 14 20 25
1 (2nd Printing)-r/#1 w/new material 4.00
2 ($2.50) 1 3 4 6 8 10
3-5 6.00
69 (1995, no price, low distribution, 12 pgs.)-story reprinted in #1 (2nd Printing) 3.00
Giant THB-($4.95) 5.00
Giant THB 1 V2-(2003, $6.95) 7.00

GD VG FN VF VF/NM NM-
2.0 4.0 6.0 8.0 9.0 9.2

...M3/THB: Mars' Mightiest Mek #1 (2000, $3.95) 4.00
...6A: Mek-Power #1, 6B: Mek-Power #2, 6C: Mek-Power #3 (2000, $3.95) 4.00
... 6D: Mek-Power #4 (2002, $4.95) 5.00

T.H.E. CAT (TV)
Dell Publishing Co.: Mar, 1967 - No. 4, Oct, 1967 (All have photo-c)

1 3 6 9 21 33 45
2-4 3 6 9 16 24 32

THERE'S A NEW WORLD COMING
Spire Christian Comics/Fleming H. Revell Co.: 1973 (35/49¢)

nn 2 4 6 10 14 18

THEY ALL KISSED THE BRIDE (See Cinema Comics Herald)

THIEF OF BAGHDAD
Dell Publishing Co.: No. 1229, Oct-Dec, 1961 (one-shot)

Four Color 1229-Movie, Crandall/Evans-a, photo-c 6 12 18 40 73 105

THIEF OF THIEVES
Image Comics: Feb, 2012 - Present ($2.99)

1-Kirkman & Spencer-s/Martinbrough-a/c 50.00
1-Second printing 8.00
2 25.00
3,4 15.00
5-19: 8-13-Asmus-s 3.00

THIMK (Magazine) (Satire)
Counterpoint: May, 1958 - No. 6, May, 1959

1 10 20 30 58 79 100
2-6 8 16 24 40 50 60

THING!, THE (Blue Beetle #18 on)
Song Hits No. 1,2/Capitol Stories/Charlton: Feb, 1952 - No. 17, Nov, 1954

1-Weird/horror stories in all; shrunken head-c 103 206 309 659 1130 1600
2,3 65 130 195 416 708 1000
4,6,8,10 58 116 174 371 636 900
5-Severed head-c; headlights 65 130 195 416 708 1000
7-Injury to eye-c & inside panel 77 154 231 493 842 1200
9-Used in **SOTI**, pg. 388 & illo "Stomping on the face is a form of brutality which modern children learn early" 90 180 270 576 988 1400
11-Necronomicon story; Hansel & Gretel parody; Injury-to-eye panel; Check-a
71 142 213 454 777 1100
12-1st published Ditko-c; "Cinderella" parody; lingerie panels. Ditko-a
116 232 348 742 1271 1800
13,15-Ditko-c/a(3 & 5) 103 206 309 659 1130 1600
14-Extreme violence/torture; Rumpelstiltskin story; Ditko-c/a(4)
107 214 321 685 1168 1650
16-Injury to eye panel 36 72 108 214 347 480
17-Ditko-c; classic parody "Through the Looking Glass"; Powell-r/Beware Terror Tales #1 & recolored 87 174 261 553 952 1350
NOTE: *Excessive violence, severed heads, injury to eye are common No. 5 on.* ***Al Fago*** *c-4.* ***Forgione*** *c-1i, 2, 6, 8, 9. All* ***Ditko*** *issues #14, 15.* ***Giordano*** *a-6.*

THING, THE (See Fantastic Four, Marvel Fanfare, Marvel Feature #11,12, Marvel Two-In-One and Startling Stories:...- Night Falls on Yancy Street)
Marvel Comics Group: July, 1983 - No. 36, June, 1986

1-Life story of Ben Grimm; Byrne scripts begin 3 6 9 16 23 30
2-5: 5-Spider-Man, She-Hulk app. 6.00
6-10 5.00
11-36 4.00
NOTE: ***Byrne*** *a-2i, 7; c-1, 7, 36i; scripts-1-13, 19-22.* ***Sienkiewicz*** *c-13i.*

THING, THE (Fantastic Four)
Marvel Comics: Jan, 2006 - No. 8, Aug, 2006 ($2.99)

1-8: 1-DiVito-a/Slott-s. 4-Lockjaw app. 6-Spider-Man app. 8-Super-Hero poker game 3.00
...: Idol of Millions TPB (2006, $20.99) r/#1-8; Divito sketch page 21.00

THING & SHE-HULK: THE LONG NIGHT (Fantastic Four)
Marvel Comics: May, 2002 ($2.99, one-shot)

1-Hitch-c/a(pg. 1-25); Reis-a(pg. 26-39); Dezago-s 3.00

THING, THE (From Another World)
Dark Horse Comics: 1991 - No. 2, 1992 ($2.95, mini-series, stiff-c)

1,2-Based on Universal movie; painted-c/a 5.00

THING, THE: FREAKSHOW (Fantastic Four)
Marvel Comics: Aug, 2002 - No. 4, Nov, 2002 ($2.99, limited series)

1-4-Geoff Johns-s/Scott Kolins-a 3.00

30 Days of Night Annual 2004 © Niles & Templesmith

This is War #7 © STD

This Magazine is Haunted #13 © FAW

GD 2.0 | VG 4.0 | FN 6.0 | VF 8.0 | VF/NM 9.0 | NM- 9.2

TPB (2005, $17.99) r/#1-4 & Thing & She-Hulk: The Long Night one-shot 18.00

THING FROM ANOTHER WORLD: CLIMATE OF FEAR, THE
Dark Horse Comics: July, 1992 - No. 4, Dec, 1992 ($2.50, mini-series)

1-4: Painted-c 4.00

THING FROM ANOTHER WORLD: ETERNAL VOWS
Dark Horse Comics: Dec, 1993 - No. 4, 1994 ($2.50, mini-series)

1-4-Gulacy-c/a 4.00

THIRTEEN (...Going on 18)
Dell Publishing Co.: 11-1/61-62 - No. 25, 12/67; No. 26, 7/69 - No. 29, 1/71

	GD	VG	FN	VF	VF/NM	NM-
1	5	10	15	35	63	90
2-10	4	8	12	28	47	65
11-25	4	8	12	23	37	50
26-29-r	3	6	9	17	26	35

NOTE: ***John Stanley** script-No. 3-29; art?*

13: ASSASSIN
TSR, Inc.: 1990 - No. 8, 1991 ($2.95, 44 pgs.)

1-8: Agent 13; Alcala-a(i); Springer back-up-a 4.00

13th SON, THE
Dark Horse Comics: Nov, 2005 - No. 4, Feb, 2006 ($2.99, limited series)

1-4-Kelley Jones-s/a/c 3.00

30 DAYS OF NIGHT
Idea + Design Works: June, 2002 - No. 3, Oct, 2002 ($3.99, limited series)

1-Vampires in Alaska; Steve Niles-s/Ben Templesmith-a/Ashley Wood-c 50.00
1-2nd printing 10.00
2 15.00
3 10.00
Annual 2004 (1/04, $4.99) Niles-s/art by Templesmith and others 5.00
Annual 2005 (12/05, $7.49) Niles-s/art by Nat Jones 7.50
... 5th Anniversary (10/07 - No. 3, $2.99) reprints original series 3.00
... Sourcebook (10/07, $7.49) Illustrated guide to the 30 Days world 7.50
... Three Tales TPB (7/06, $19.99) r/Annual 2005, ...: Dead Space #1-3, and short story from Tales of Terror (IDW's...) 20.00
Hundred Penny Press: 30 Days of Night #1 (5/11, $1.00) r/#1 3.00
TPB (2003, $17.99) r/#1-3, foreward by Clive Barker; script for #1 18.00
The Complete 30 Days of Night (2004, $75.00, oversized hardcover with slipcase) r/#1-3; prequel; script pages for #1-3; original cover and promotional materials 75.00

30 DAYS OF NIGHT
IDW Publishing: July, 2004 (Free Comic Book Day edition)

Previews CSI: Bad Rap; The Shield: Spotlight; 24: One Shot; and 30 Days of Night 3.00

30 DAYS OF NIGHT (Ongoing series)
IDW Publishing: Oct, 2011 - No. 12, Nov, 2012 ($3.99)

1-12: 1-4-Niles-s/Kieth-a; covers by Kieth and Furno. 5-12-Niles-s 4.00

30 DAYS OF NIGHT: BEYOND BARROW
IDW Publishing: Sept, 2007 - No. 3, Dec, 2007 ($3.99, limited series)

1-3-Niles-s/Sienkiewicz-a/c 4.00

30 DAYS OF NIGHT: BLOODSUCKER TALES
IDW Publishing: Oct, 2004 - No. 8, May, 2005 ($3.99, limited series)

1-8-Niles-s/Chamberlain-a; Fraction-s/Templesmith-a/c 4.00
HC (8/05, $49.99) r/#1-8; cover gallery 50.00
SC (8/05, $24.99) r/#1-8; cover gallery 25.00

30 DAYS OF NIGHT: DEAD SPACE
IDW Publishing: Jan, 2006 - No. 3, Mar, 2006 ($3.99, limited series)

1-3-Niles and Wickline-s/Milx-a/c 4.00

30 DAYS OF NIGHT: EBEN & STELLA
IDW Publishing: May, 2007 - No. 3, July, 2007 ($3.99, limited series)

1-3-Niles and DeConnick-s/Randall-a/c 4.00

30 DAYS OF NIGHT: NIGHT, AGAIN
IDW Publishing: May, 2011 - No. 4, Aug, 2011 ($3.99, limited series)

1-4-Lansdale-s/Kieth-a/c 4.00

30 DAYS OF NIGHT: RED SNOW
IDW Publishing: Aug, 2007 - No. 3, Oct, 2007 ($3.99, limited series)

1-3-Ben Templesmith-s/a/c 4.00

30 DAYS OF NIGHT: RETURN TO BARROW
IDW Publishing: Mar, 2004 - No. 6, Aug, 2004 ($3.99, limited series)

1-6-Steve Niles-s/Ben Templesmith-a/c 4.00
TPB (2004, $19.99) r/#1-6; cover gallery 20.00

30 DAYS OF NIGHT: SPREADING THE DISEASE
IDW Publishing: Dec, 2006 - No. 5, Apr, 2007 ($3.99, limited series)

1-5: 1-Wickline-s/Sanchez-a. 3-5-Sandoval-a 4.00

30 DAYS OF NIGHT: 30 DAYS 'TIL DEATH
IDW Publishing: Dec, 2008 - No. 4, Mar, 2009 ($3.99, limited series)

1-4-David Lapham-s/a; covers by Lapham and Templesmith 4.00

THIRTY SECONDS OVER TOKYO (See American Library)

THIS IS SUSPENSE! (Formerly Strange Suspense Stories; Strange Suspense Stories #27 on)
Charlton Comics: No. 23, Feb, 1955 - No. 26, Aug, 1955

	GD	VG	FN	VF	VF/NM	NM-
23-Wood-a(r)/A Star Presentation #3 "Dr. Jekyll & Mr. Hyde"; last pre-code issue	24	48	72	140	230	320
24-Censored Fawcett-r; Evans-a (r/Suspense Detective #1)	14	28	42	80	115	150
25,26: 26-Marcus Swayze-a	10	20	30	56	76	95

THIS IS THE PAYOFF (See Pay-Off)

THIS IS WAR
Standard Comics: No. 5, July, 1952 - No. 9, May, 1953

	GD	VG	FN	VF	VF/NM	NM-
5-Toth-a	15	30	45	85	130	175
6,9-Toth-a	12	24	36	69	97	125
7,8: 8-Ross Andru-c	10	20	30	54	72	90

THIS IS YOUR LIFE, DONALD DUCK (See Donald Duck..., Four Color #1109)

THIS MAGAZINE IS CRAZY (Crazy #? on)
Charlton Publ. (Humor Magazines): V3#2, July, 1957 - V4#8, Feb, 1959 (25¢, magazine, 68 pgs.)

	GD	VG	FN	VF	VF/NM	NM-
V3#2-V4#7: V4#5-Russian Sputnik-c parody	10	20	30	58	79	100
V4#8-Davis-a (8 pgs.)	11	22	33	62	86	110

THIS MAGAZINE IS HAUNTED (Danger and Adventure #22 on)
Fawcett Publications/Charlton No. 15(2/54) on: Oct, 1951 - No. 14, 12/53; No. 15, 2/54 - V3#21, Nov, 1954

	GD	VG	FN	VF	VF/NM	NM-
1-Evans-a; Dr. Death as host begins	71	142	213	454	777	1100
2,5-Evans-a	46	92	138	290	488	685
3,4: 3-Vampire-c/story	39	78	117	231	378	525
6-9,11,12	32	64	96	188	307	425
10-Severed head-c	55	110	165	352	601	850
13-Severed head-c/story	54	108	162	343	574	825
14-Classic burning skull-c	37	74	111	222	361	500
15,20: 15-Dick Giordano-c. 20-Cover is swiped from panel in The Thing #16	24	48	72	142	234	325
16,19-Ditko-c. 19-Injury-to-eye panel; story-r/#1	43	86	129	271	461	650
17-Ditko-c/a(4); blood drainage story	53	106	159	334	567	800
18-Ditko-c/a(1 story); E.C. swipe/Haunt of Fear #5; injury-to-eye panel; reprints "Caretaker of the Dead" from Beware Terror Tales & recolored	45	90	135	284	480	675
21-Ditko-c, Evans-r/This Magazine Is Haunted #1	39	78	117	240	395	550

NOTE: ***Baily** a-1, 3, 4, 21r/#1. **Moldoff** c/a-1-13. **Powell** a-3-5, 11, 12, 17. **Shuster** a-18-20. Issues 19-21 have reprints which have been recolored from This Magazine is Haunted #1.*

THIS MAGAZINE IS HAUNTED (2nd Series) (Formerly Zaza the Mystic; Outer Space #17 on)
Charlton Comics: V2#12, July, 1957 - V2#16, May, 1958

	GD	VG	FN	VF	VF/NM	NM-
V2#12-14-Ditko-c/a in all	42	84	126	265	445	625
15-No Ditko-c/a	15	30	45	88	137	185
16-Ditko-a(4).	32	64	96	188	307	425

THIS MAGAZINE IS WILD (See Wild)

THIS WAS YOUR LIFE (Religious)
Jack T. Chick Publ.: 1964 (3 1/2 x 5 1/2", 40 pgs., B&W and red)

	GD	VG	FN	VF	VF/NM	NM-
nn, Another version (5x2 3/4", 26 pgs.)	2	4	6	10	14	18

THOR (See Avengers #1, Giant-Size..., Marvel Collectors Item Classics, Marvel Graphic Novel #33, Marvel Preview, Marvel Spectacular, Marvel Treasury Edition, Special Marvel Edition & Tales of Asgard)

THOR (Journey Into Mystery #1-125, 503-on)(The Mighty Thor #413-490)
Marvel Comics Group: No. 126, Mar, 1966 - No. 502, Sept, 1996

	GD	VG	FN	VF	VF/NM	NM-
126-Thor continues (#125-130 Thor vs. Hercules)	30	60	90	216	483	750
127-130: 127-1st app. Pluto	10	20	30	66	138	210
131-133,135,137-140: 132-1st app. Ego. 137 – 1st Ulik the Troll	9	18	27	57	111	165
134-Intro High Evolutionary and Man-Beast	9	18	27	57	123	185
136-(1/67) Re-intro. Sif	9	18	27	59	117	175

141-150: 142-Thor vs. Super-Skrull. 143,144-Thor vs. the Enchanters. 146-Inhumans begin

Thor #333 © MAR

Thor #479 © MAR

Thor V2 #5 © MAR

	GD 2.0	VG 4.0	FN 6.0	VF 8.0	VF/NM 9.0	NM- 9.2

(early app.), end #151 (see Fantastic Four #45 for 1st app.). 146,147-Origin The Inhumans. 148-1st app. Wrecker. 148,149-Origin Black Bolt in each. 149-Origin Medusa, Crystal, Maximus, Gorgon, Karnak 7 14 21 49 92 135
151-157,159: 151,152-Destroyer and Ulik app. 154-1st Mangog. 155-157-Thor vs Mangog. 159-Origin Dr. Blake (Thor) concl. 6 12 18 42 79 115
158-Origin-r/#83; origin Dr. Blake 9 18 27 57 111 165
160-162-Galactus app. 7 14 21 44 82 120
163,164-2nd & 3th brief app. Warlock (Him) 5 10 15 35 63 90
165-1st full app. Warlock (Him) (6/69, see Fantastic Four #67); last 12¢ issue; Kirby-a 17 34 51 117 259 400
166-2nd full app. Warlock (Him); battles Thor; see Marvel Premiere #1 8 16 24 56 108 160
167,170-179: 178-1st Buscema-a. 179-Last Kirby issue 5 10 15 34 60 85
168,169-Origin Galactus; Kirby-a 8 16 24 51 96 140
180,181-Neal Adams-a 6 12 18 37 66 95
182,183-Thor vs. Doctor Doom; Buscema-a begins 5 10 15 34 60 85
184-192: 187-Thor vs Odin. 192-Last 15¢ issue 4 8 12 27 44 60
193-(25¢, 52 pgs.); Silver Surfer x-over; last Stan Lee story as regular writer 10 20 30 69 147 225
194-199 4 8 12 23 37 50
200-Special Ragnarok issue by Stan Lee 4 8 12 28 47 65
201-206,208-224: 221-Thor vs. Hercules 3 6 9 14 20 25
207-Rutland, Vermont Halloween x-over; leads into Avengers/Defenders war 3 6 9 19 30 40
225-Intro. Firelord 5 10 15 31 53 75
226-Galactus app. 3 6 9 14 20 25
227-231 2 4 6 10 14 18
232,233: 232-Firelord app. 233-Numerous guest stars; Asgard invades Earth 3 6 9 14 20 25
234-245: 240-1st Egyptian gods. 242-245-Thor vs. Time-Twisters 2 4 6 10 14 18
246-250-(Regular 25¢ editions)(4-8/76): 246-247-Firelord app. 249-250-Thor vs. Mangog 2 4 6 10 14 18
246-250-(30¢-c variants, limited distribution) 4 8 12 23 37 50
251-280: 261-272-Simonson-a. 252-253-Thor vs. Ulik. 255-Re-intro Stone Men of Saturn. 264-265-Thor vs. Loki. 271-Iron Man x-over. 274-Death of Balder the Brave. 276-Thor vs. Red Norvell Thor. 280-Thor vs. Hyperion 1 3 4 6 8 10
260-264-(35¢-c variants, limited distribution)(6-10/77) 4 8 12 23 37 50
281-299: 283,284-Celestials app. 285-286-Eternals app. 287-288-Thor vs. the Forgotten one. 291,292-Asgard vs Olympus. 294-Origin Asgard & Odin 1 2 3 5 6 8
300-(12/80)-End of Asgard; origin of Odin & The Destroyer; double-size 2 4 6 8 10 12
301-Numerous pantheons (skyfathers) app. 1 2 3 5 6 8
302-304 5.00
305-306: 305-Airwalker app. 306-Firelord 1 2 3 5 6 8
307-331,334-336: 310-Thor vs. Mephisto. 314-Moondragon and Drax app. 315,316-Bi-Beast & Man-Beast app. 316-Iron Man x-over. 325-Mephisto app. 331-1st Crusader 5.00
332,333-Dracula app. 1 2 3 5 6 8
337-Simonson-c/a begins, ends #382; Beta Ray Bill becomes new Thor 3 6 9 14 20 25
338-Beta Ray Bill vs. Thor 1 3 4 6 8 10
339,340: 339-Beta Ray Bill gains Thor's powers. 340-Donald Blake returns as Thor 6.00
341-343,345-373,375-381,383,386: 341-Clark Kent & Lois Lane cameo. 345-349-Malekith the Accursed app. 350-352-Avengers app. 353-'Death' of Odin. 356-Hercules app. 363-Secret Wars II crossover. 364-366-Thor as a frog. 367-Malekith app. 373-X-Factor tie-in. 383-Secret Wars flashback 4.00
344-(6/84) 1st app. of Malekith the Accursed (Ruler of the Dark Elves)(villain in the 2013 movie Thor: The Dark World); Simonson-c/a 3 6 9 14 20 25
374-Mutant Massacre; X-Factor app. 5.00
382-($1.25)-Anniversary issue; last Simonson-a 6.00
384-Intro. Thor of the 26th century (Dargo Ktor) 6.00
385-Thor vs. Hulk by Stan Lee and Erik Larsen 5.00
387,388,390-399: Thor vs. the Celestials. 390-Avengers app.; Captain America lifts Mjolnir. 391-Spider-Man x-over; 1st Eric Masterson. 393-395-Daredevil app. 395-Intro. Earth Force. 396-399-Black Knight app. 4.00
389- 'Alone against the Celestials' climax 5.00
400-($1.75, 68 pgs.)-Origin Loki 6.00
401-410: 404,405-Annihilus app. 409-410-Dr. Doom app. 4.00
411-Intro New Warriors (appear in costume in last panel); Juggernaut-c/story 2 4 6 8 10 12
412-1st full app. New Warriors (Marvel Boy, Kid Nova, Namorita, Night Thrasher, Firestar & Speedball) 2 4 6 8 10 12
413-426: 413-Dr. Strange app. 419-425-Black Galaxy saga; origin Celestials 4.00
427-428-Excalibur app. 428-Ghost Rider app. 5.00
429-431: 429-Thor vs Juggernaut; Ghost Rider app. 430-Ghost Rider app. 3.00
432-(52 pgs.) Thor's 350th issue (vs. Loki) reprints origin and 1st app. from Journey into Mystery #83 4.00
433-449,451-467: 433-Intro. Eric Masterson as Thor. 434,435-Annihilus app. 437-Quasar app.; Tales of Asgard back-up stories begin. 438-441-Thor War; Beta Ray Bill app. 443-Dr. Strange & Silver Surfer x-over; last $1.00-c. 445,446-Operation Galactic Storm. 445-Thor vs. Gladiator. 448-Spider-Man app. 451,452-Bloodaxe app. 457-Original Thor returns. 458-Thor vs. Thor. 459-Intro Thunderstrike. 460-Starlin scripts begin. 461-Thor vs. Beta Ray Bill. 463-467-Infinity Crusade x-over. 466-Drax app. 3.00
450-($2.50, 68 pgs.)-Flip-book format; r/story JIM #85 (1st Loki) plus-c plus a gallery of past-c; gatefold-c 4.00
468,469-Blood and Thunder x-over. 468-Thor vs. Silver Surfer. 469-Infinity Watch app. 5.00
470,471-Blood and Thunder x-over. 470-Thanos and the Infinity Watch app. 471-Blood and Thunder story conclusion; Infinity Watch and Silver Surfer app. 6.00
472-474: 472-Intro the Godlings. 474-Begin $1.50-c; bound-in trading cards 3.00
475 ($2.00, 52 pgs.)-Regular edition; High Evolutionary and Man-Beast app. 4.00
475 ($2.50, 52 pgs.)-Collectors edition w/foil embossed-c 5.00
476-481: 476-Destroyer app. 477-Thunderstrike app. 478-Return of Red Norvell Thor. 479-Detailed Origin of Thor 3.00
482 ($2.95, 84 pgs.)-400th Thor issue 5.00
483,486,487,488: 486-Kurse app. 4.00
484,485,490: 484-War Machine app. 485-Thing app. 490-Absorbing Man app.; Buscema-a 5.00
489-Hulk app. 6.00
491-Warren Ellis scripts begins, ends #494; Worldengine pt.1; Deodato-c/a begins 6.00
492-494: Worldengine pt. 2-4. 492-Reintro The Enchantress; Beta Ray Bill dies 5.00
495-499: 495-Messner-Loebs scripts begin; Isherwood-c/a. 496-Captain America app. 3.00
500 ($2.50)-Double-size; wraparound-c; Deodato-c/a; Dr. Strange app. 5.00
501-Reintro Red Norvell 4.00
502-(9/96) Onslaught tie-in; Red Norvell, Jane Foster & Hela app. 5.00
NOTE: *Numbering continues with Journey Into Mystery #503 (11/96)*
600-up (See Thor 2007 series)
Special 2(9/66)-(See Journey Into Mystery for 1st annual) Destroyer app. 9 18 27 59 117 175
Special 2 (2nd printing, 1994) 2 4 6 8 10 12
King Size Special 3 (1/71) 4 8 12 23 37 50
Special 4 (12/71)-r/Thor #131,132 & JIM #113 3 6 9 19 30 40
Annual 5 (11/76)-Asgard vs Olympus; Hercules app. 2 4 6 11 16 20
Annual 6 (10/77)-Guardians of the Galaxy app. 4 8 12 23 37 50
Annual 7,8: 7 (1978)-Eternals app. 8 (1979)-Thor vs. Zeus-c/story 2 4 6 8 10 12
Annual 9-13: 9 ('81)-Dormammu app. 10 ('82)-1st Demogorge-the God Eater. 11 ('83)-Origin of Thor expanded. 12 ('84)-Intro Vidar (Thor's brother). 13 ('85)-Mephisto app. 6.00
Annual 14-19 ('86-'94, 68 pgs.): 14-Atlantis Attacks. 15 ('90)-Terminus factor Pt. 3. 16-3 pg. origin; Guardians of the Galaxy x-over. 17 ('92)-Citizen Kang Pt. 2. 18-Polybagged w/card; intro the Flame. 19 ('94) vs. Pluto 4.00
...Alone Against the Celestials nn (6/92, $5.95)-r/Thor #387-389 6.00
...Legends Vol. 2: Walter Simonson Book 2 TPB (2003, $24.99) r/#349-355,357-359 25.00
...Legends Vol. 3: Walter Simonson Book 3 TPB (2004, $24.99) r/#360-369 25.00
...: The Eternals Saga TPB (2006, $24.99) r/#283-291 & Annual #7; profile pages 25.00
...: The Eternals Saga Vol. 2 TPB ('07, $24.99) r/#292-301; Thomas & Gruenwald essays 25.00
... Visionaries: Mike Deodato Jr. TPB (2004, $19.99) r/#491-494,498-500 20.00
... Visionaries: Walter Simonson (Vol. 1) TPB (5/01, $24.95) r/#337-348 25.00
... Visionaries: Walter Simonson Vol. 4 TPB (2007, $24.99) r/#371-373 & Balder the Brave #1-4 25.00
... Visionaries: Walter Simonson Vol. 5 TPB (2008, $24.95) r/#375-382 25.00
...: Worldengine (8/96, $9.95)-r/#491-494; Deodato-c/a; story & new intermission by Warren Ellis 10.00

NOTE: ***Neal Adams** a-180,181; c-179-181. **Austin** a-342i, 346i; c-312i. **Buscema** a(p)-178, 182-213, 215-226, 231-238, 241-253, 254r, 256-259, 272-278, 283-285, 370, Annual 6, 8, 11i; c(p)-175, 178, 182-196, 198-200, 202-204, 206, 211, 212, 215, 219, 221, 226, 256, 259, 261, 262, 272-278, 283, 289, 370, Annual 6. **Everett** a(i)-143, 170-175; c(i)-171, 172, 174, 176, 241. **Gil Kane** a-318p; c(p)-201, 205, 207-210, 216, 220, 222, 223, 231, 233-240, 242, 243, 318. **Kirby** a(p)-126-177, 179, 194r, 254r; c(p)-126-169, 171-174, 176, 177, 249-253, 255, 257, 258, Annual 5, Special 2-4. **Mooney** a(i)-201, 204, 214-216, 218, 322i, 324i, 325i, 327i. **Sienkiewicz** c-332, 333, 335. **Simonson** a-260-271p, 337-354, 357-367, 380, Annual 7p; c-260, 263-271, 337-355, 357-369, 371, 373-382, Annual 7. **Starlin** c-213.*

THOR (Volume 2)
Marvel Comics: July, 1998 - No. 85, Dec, 2004 ($2.99/$1.99/$2.25)

1-($2.99)-Follows Heroes Return; Jurgens-s/Romita Jr. & Janson-a; wraparound-c; battles the Destroyer 6.00
1-Variant-c 1 2 3 5 6 8
1-Rough Cut-($2.99) Features original script and pencil pages 3.00
1-Sketch cover 25.00
2-($1.99) Two covers; Avengers app. 4.00

Thor V2 #85 © MAR

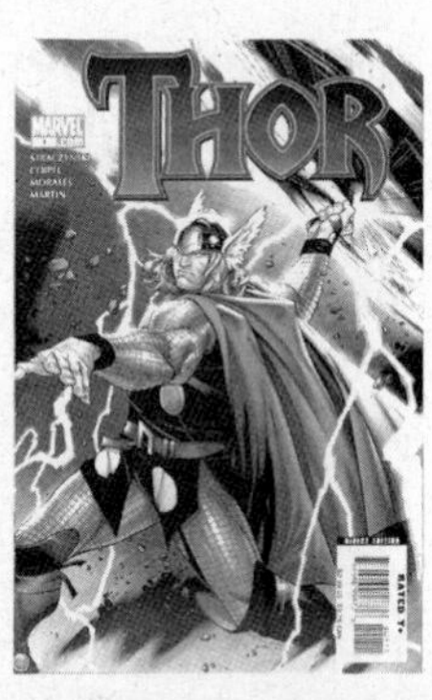

Thor (2007 series) #1 © MAR

Thor: God of Thunder #14 © MAR

GD 2.0 | VG 4.0 | FN 6.0 | VF 8.0 | VF/NM 9.0 | NM- 9.2

3-11,13-23: 3-Assumes Jake Olson ID. 4-Namor-c/app. 8-Spider-Man-c/app.
14-Iron Man c/app. 17-Juggernaut-c 3.00
12-($2.99) Wraparound-c; Hercules appears 4.00
12-($10.00) Variant-c by Jusko 10.00
24,26-31,33,34: 24-Begin $2.25-c. 26-Mignola-c/Larsen-a. 29-Andy Kubert-a.
30-Maximum Security x-over; Beta Ray Bill-c/app. 33-Intro. Thor Girl 3.00
25-($2.99) Regular edition 4.00
25-($3.99) Gold foil enhanced cover 5.00
32-($3.50, 100 pgs.) new story plus reprints w/Kirby-a; Simonson-a 5.00
35-($2.99) Thor battles The Gladiator; Andy Kubert-a 4.00
36-49,51-61: 37-Starlin-a. 38,39-BWS-c. 38-42-Immonen-a. 40-Odin killed. 41-Orbik-c.
44-'Nuff Said silent issue. 51-Spider-Man app. 57-Art by various. 58-Davis-a; x-over with Iron Man #64. 60-Brereton-c 3.00
50-($4.95) Raney-c/a; back-ups w/Nuckols-a & Armenta-s/Bennett-a 5.00
62-84: 62-Begin $2.99-c. 64-Loki-c/app. 80-Oeming-s begins; Avengers app. 3.00
85-Last issue; Thor dies; Oeming-s/DiVito-a/Epting-c 4.00
...1999 Annual ($3.50) Jurgens-s/a(p) 4.00
...2000 Annual ($3.50) Jurgens-s/Ordway-a(p); back-up stories 4.00
...2001 Annual ($3.50) Jurgens-s/Grummett-a(p); Lightle-c 4.00
...Across All Worlds (9/01, $19.95, TPB) r/#28-35 20.00
Avengers Disassembled: Thor TPB (2004, $16.99) r/#80-85; afterword by Oeming 17.00
...Resurrection ($5.99, TPB) r/#1,2 6.00
...: The Dark Gods (7/00, $15.95, TPB) r/#9-13 16.00
...Vol. 1: The Death of Odin (7/02, $12.99, TPB) r/#39-44 13.00
...Vol. 2: Lord of Asgard (9/02, $15.99, TPB) r/#45-50 16.00
...Vol. 3: Gods on Earth (2003, $21.99, TPB) r/#51-58, Avengers #63, Iron Man #64,
Marvel Double-Shot #1; Beck-c 22.00
...Vol. 4: Spiral (2003, $19.99, TPB) r/#59-67; Brereton-c 20.00
...Vol. 5: The Reigning (2004, $17.99, TPB) r/#68-74 18.00
...Vol. 6: Gods and Men (2004, $13.99, TPB) r/#75-79 14.00

THOR (Also see Fantastic Four #538)(Resumes original numbering with #600)
Marvel Comics: Sept, 2007 - No. 12, Mar, 2009; No. 600, Apr, 2009 - No. 621, May, 2011 ($2.99/$3.99) (Continues numbering as Journey Into Mystery #622) (Also see Mighty Thor #1)

1-Straczynski-s/Coipel-a/c 4.00
1-Variant-c by Michael Turner 5.00
1-Zombie variant-c by Suydam 5.00
1-Non-zombie variant-c by Suydam 5.00
1-"Marvel's Greatest Comics" edition (5/10, $1.00) r/#1 3.00
2-12: 2-Two covers by Dell'Otto and Coipel. 3-Iron Man app.; McGuinness var-c. 4-Bermejo var-c. 5-Campbell var-c. 6-Art Adams var-c. 7,8-Djurdjevic-a/c; Coipel var-c 3.00
2-Second printing with wraparound-c 3.00
7-"Marvel's Greatest Comics" edition (6/11, $1.00) r/#7 3.00

(After #12 [Mar, 2009] numbering reverted back to original Journey Into Mystery/Thor numbering with #600, Apr, 2009)

600 (4/09, $4.99) Two wraparound-c by Coipel & Djurdjevic; Coipel, Djurdjevic & Aja-a; r/Tales of Asgard from Journey Into Mystery #106,107,112,113,115; Kirby-a 5.00
601-603,611-621-($3.99) 601-603-Djurdjevic-a. 602-Sif returns. 617-Loki returns 4.00
604-610-($2.99) Tan-a. 607-609-Siege x-over. 610-Braithwaite-a; Ragnarok app. 3.00
620.1 (5/11, $2.99) Brooks-a; Grey Gargoyle app. 3.00
Annual 1 (11/09, $3.99) Suayan, Grindberg, Gaudiano-a; Djurdjevic-c 4.00
...: Ages of Thunder (6/08, $3.99) Fraction-s/Zircher-a/Djurdjevic-c 4.00
... & Hercules: Encyclopædia Mythologica (2009, $4.99) profile pages of the Pantheons 5.00
... Asgard's Avenger 1 (6/11, $4.99) profile pages of Thor characters 5.00
... Crown of Fools 1 (12/13, $3.99) Di Vito & Simonson-a 4.00
... Giant-Size Finale 1 (1/01, $3.99) Dr. Doom app.; r/origin from JIM #83 4.00
... God-Size Special (2/09, $3.99) story of Skurge the Executioner re-told; art by Brereton, Braithwaite, Allred and Sepulveda; plus reprint of Thor #362 (1985) 4.00
... Goes Hollywood 1 ('11, $3.99) Collection of movie-themed variant Thor covers 4.00
...: Man of War (1/09, $3.99) Fraction-s/Mann & Zircher-a/Djurdjevic-c 4.00
...: Reign of Blood (8/08, $3.99) Fraction-s/Evans & Zircher-a/Djurdjevic-c 4.00
...: Spotlight (5/11, $3.99) movie photo-c; movie preview; creator interviews 4.00
...: The Rage of Thor (10/10, $3.99) Milligan-s/Suayan-c/a 4.00
...: The Trial of Thor (8/09, $3.99) Milligan-s/Nord-c/a 4.00
...: Truth of History (12/08, $3.99) Thor and crew in ancient Egypt; Alan Davis-s/a/c 4.00
...: Whosoever Wields This Hammer 1 (6/11, $4.99) recolored r/J.I.M. #83,84,88 5.00
...: Wolves of the North (2/11, $3.99) Carey-s/Perkins-a 4.00
... By J. Michael Straczynski Vol. 1 HC (2008, $19.99) r/#1-6; variant cover gallery 20.00

THOR ADAPTATION (MARVEL'S...)
Marvel Comics: Mar, 2012 - No. 2, Apr, 2012 ($2.99, limited series)

1,2-Adaptation of 2012 movie; Gage-s/Medina-a; photo-c 3.00

THOR AND THE WARRIORS FOUR
Marvel Comics: Jun, 2010 - No. 4, Sept, 2010 ($2.99, limited series)

1-4-Thor and Power Pack team-up; Gurihiru-a; back-up with Coover-s/a 3.00

THOR: BLOOD OATH
Marvel Comics: Nov, 2005 - No. 6, Feb, 2006 ($2.99, limited series)

1-6-Oeming-s/Kolins-a/c 3.00
HC (2006, $19.99, dust jacket) r/series; afterword by Oeming 20.00
SC (2006, $14.99) r/series; afterword by Oeming 15.00

THOR CORPS
Marvel Comics: Sept, 1993 - No. 4, Jan, 1994 ($1.75, limited series)

1-4: 1-Invaders cameo. 2-Invaders app. 3-Spider-Man 2099, Rawhide Kid, Two-Gun Kid & Kid Colt app. 4-Painted-c 3.00

THOR: FIRST THUNDER
Marvel Comics: Nov, 2010 - No. 5, Mar, 2011 ($3.99, limited series)

1-5: 1-Huat-a; new retelling of origin; reprint of debut in JIM #83 4.00

THOR: FOR ASGARD
Marvel Comics: Nov, 2010 - No. 6, Apr, 2011 ($3.99, limited series)

1-6-Bianchi-a/c. 1-Frost Giants app. 4.00

THOR: GOD OF THUNDER (Marvel NOW!)
Marvel Comics: Jan, 2013 - Present ($3.99)

1-20: 1-5-Aaron-s/Ribic-a. 6-Guice-a. 13-17-Malekith app. 19,20-Galactus app. 4.00

THOR: GODSTORM
Marvel Comics: Nov, 2001 - No. 3, Jan, 2002 ($3.50, limited series)

1-3-Steve Rude-c/a; Busiek-s; Avengers app. 4.00

THOR: HEAVEN & EARTH
Marvel Comics: Sept, 2011 - No. 4, Nov, 2011 ($2.99, limited series)

1-4: 1-Jenkins-s/Olivetti-a/c; Loki app. 2-Texeira-a/c. 3-Alixe-a. 4-Medina-a 3.00

THORION OF THE NEW ASGODS
Marvel Comics (Amalgam): June, 1997 ($1.95, one-shot)

1-Keith Giffen-s/John Romita Jr.-c/a 3.00

THOR: SON OF ASGARD
Marvel Comics: May, 2004 - No. 12, Mar, 2005 ($2.99, limited series)

1-12: Teenaged Thor, Sif, and Balder; Tocchini-a. 1-6-Granov-c. 7-12-Jo Chen-c 3.00
... Vol. 1: The Warriors Teen (2004, $7.99, digest) r/#1-6 8.00
... Vol. 2: Worthy (2005, $7.99, digest) r/#7-12 8.00

THOR: TALES OF ASGARD BY STAN LEE & JACK KIRBY
Marvel Comics: 2009 - No. 6, 2009 ($3.99, limited series)

1-6-Reprints back-up stories from Journey Into Mystery #97-120; new covers by Coipel 4.00

THOR: THE DEVIANTS SAGA
Marvel Comics: Jan, 2012 - No. 5, ($3.99, limited series)

1-5-Rodi-s/Segovia-a; Ereshkigal app. 4.00

THOR: THE DARK WORLD PRELUDE (MARVEL'S...)
Marvel Comics: Aug, 2013 - No. 2, Aug, 2013 ($2.99, limited series)

1,2-Prelude to 2013 movie; Eaton-a; photo-c 3.00

THOR: THE LEGEND
Marvel Comics: Sept, 1996 ($3.95, one-shot)

nn-Tribute issue 4.00

THOR THE MIGHTY AVENGER
Marvel Comics: Sept, 2010 - No. 8, Mar, 2011 ($2.99, limited series)

1-8-Re-imagining of Thor's origin; Langridge-s/Samnee-a. 1-Mr. Hyde app. 3.00
Free Comic Book Day 2011 (giveaway) Captain America app. 3.00

THOR: VIKINGS
Marvel Comics (MAX): Sept, 2003 - No. 5, Jan, 2004 ($3.50, limited series)

1-5-Garth Ennis-s/Glenn Fabry-a/c 3.50
TPB (2004, $13.99) r/series 14.00

THOSE MAGNIFICENT MEN IN THEIR FLYING MACHINES (See Movie Comics)

THRAX
Event Comics: Nov, 1996 ($2.95, one-shot)

1 3.00

THREE
Image Comics: Oct, 2013 - No. 5, Feb, 2014 ($2.99)

1-5-Spartans 100 years after the Battle of Thermopylae; Ryan Kelly-a/Kieron Gillen-s 3.00

THREE CABALLEROS (Walt Disney's...)
Dell Publishing Co.: No. 71, 1945

3-D Circus #1 © FH

3-D Dolly #1 © HARV

3 Geeks #10 © 3 Finger Prints

	GD 2.0	VG 4.0	FN 6.0	VF 8.0	VF/NM 9.0	NM- 9.2

Four Color 71-by Walt Kelly, c/a 56 112 168 450 1013 1575

THREE CHIPMUNKS, THE (TV) (Also see Alvin)
Dell Publishing Co.: No. 1042, Oct-Dec, 1959

Four Color 1042 (#1)-(Alvin, Simon & Theodore) 8 16 24 56 108 160

THREE COMICS (Also see Spiritman)
The Penny King Co.: 1944 (10¢, 52 pgs.) (2 different covers exist)

1,3,4-Lady Luck, Mr. Mystic, The Spirit app. (3 Spirit sections bound together); Lou Fine-a
27 54 81 160 263 365

NOTE: *No. 1 contains Spirit Sections 4/9/44 - 4/23/44, and No. 4 is also from 4/44.*

3-D (NOTE: The prices of all the 3-D comics listed include glasses. Deduct 40-50 percent if glasses are missing, and reduce slightly if glasses are loose.)

3-D ACTION
Atlas Comics (ACI): Jan, 1954 (Oversized, 15¢)(2 pairs of glasses included)

1-Battle Brady; Sol Brodsky-c 40 80 120 246 411 575

3-D ADVENTURE COMICS
Stats, Etc.: Aug, 1986 (one shot)

1-Promo material 4.00

3-D ALIEN TERROR
Eclipse Comics: June, 1986 ($2.50)

1-Old Witch, Crypt-Keeper, Vault Keeper cameo; Morrow, John Pound-a, Yeates-c 6.00
...in 2-D: 100 copies signed, numbered(B&W) 1 3 4 8 10 12

3-D ANIMAL FUN (See Animal Fun)

THREE DAYS IN EUROPE
Oni Press: Nov, 2002 - No. 5, Apr, 2003 ($2.95, B&W, limited series)

1-5-Johnston-s/Hawthorne-a 3.00
TPB (11/03, $14.95, digest-sized) r/#1-5 15.00

3-D BATMAN (Also see Batman 3-D)
National Periodical Publications: 1953 (Reprinted in 1966)

1953-(25¢)-Reprints Batman #42 & 48 (Penguin-c/story); Tommy Tomorrow story; came with pair of 3-D Bat glasses 103 206 309 659 1130 1600
1966-Reprints 1953 issue; new cover by Infantino/Anderson; has inside-c photos of Batman & Robin from TV show (50¢) 19 38 57 131 291 450

3-D CIRCUS
Fiction House Magazines (Real Adventures Publ.): 1953 (25¢, w/glasses)

1 28 56 84 165 270 375

3-D COMICS (See Mighty Mouse, Tor and Western Fighters)

3-D DOLLY
Harvey Publications: December, 1953 (25¢, came with 2 pairs of glasses)

1-Richie Rich story redrawn from his 1st app. in Little Dot #1; shows cover in 3-D on inside
47 94 141 296 498 700

3-D-ELL
Dell Publishing Co.: No. 1, 1953; No. 3, 1953 (3-D comics) (25¢, came w/glasses)

1-Rootie Kazootie (#2 does not exist) 30 60 90 177 289 400
3-Flukey Luke 28 56 84 165 270 375

3-D EXOTIC BEAUTIES
The 3-D Zone: Nov, 1990 ($2.95, 28 pgs.)

1-L.B. Cole-c 1 2 3 5 7 9

3-D FEATURES PRESENTS JET PUP
Dimensions Publications: Oct-Dec (Winter on-c), 1953 (25¢, came w/glasses)

1-Irving Spector-a(2) 30 60 90 177 289 400

3-D FUNNY MOVIES
Comic Media: 1953 (25¢, came w/glasses)

1-Bugsey Bear & Paddy Pelican 34 68 102 199 325 450

THREE-DIMENSION ADVENTURES (Superman)
National Periodical Publications: 1953 (25¢, large size, came w/glasses)

nn-Origin Superman (new art) 103 206 309 659 1130 1600

THREE DIMENSIONAL ALIEN WORLDS (See Alien Worlds)
Pacific Comics: July, 1984 (1st Ray Zone 3-D book)(one-shot)

1-Bolton-a(p); Stevens-a(i); Art Adams 1st published-a(p) 6.00

THREE DIMENSIONAL DNAGENTS (See New DNAgents)

THREE DIMENSIONAL E. C. CLASSICS (Three Dimensional Tales From the Crypt No. 2)
E. C. Comics: Spring, 1954 (Prices include glasses; came with 2 pair)

1-Stories by Wood (Mad #3), Krigstein (W.S. #7), Evans (F.C. #13), & Ingels (CSS #5); Kurtzman-c (rare in high grade due to unstable paper)
100 200 300 640 1095 1550

NOTE: *Stories redrawn to 3-D format. Original stories not necessarily by artists listed. CSS: Crime SuspenStories; F.C.: Frontline Combat; W.S.: Weird Science.*

THREE DIMENSIONAL TALES FROM THE CRYPT (Formerly Three Dimensional E. C. Classics)(Cover title: ...From the Crypt of Terror)
E. C. Comics: No. 2, Spring, 1954 (Prices include glasses; came with 2 pair)

2-Davis (TFTC #25), Elder (VOH #14), Craig (TFTC #24), & Orlando (TFTC #22) stories; Feldstein-c (rare in high grade) 98 196 294 627 1076 1525

NOTE: *Stories redrawn to 3-D format. Original stories not necessarily by artists listed. TFTC: Tales From the Crypt; VOH: Vault of Horror.*

3-D LOVE
Steriographic Publ. (Mikeross Publ.): Dec, 1953 (25¢, came w/glasses)

1 34 68 102 199 325 450

3-D NOODNICK (See Noodnick)

3-D ROMANCE
Steriographic Publ. (Mikeross Publ.): Jan, 1954 (25¢, came w/glasses)

1 34 68 102 199 325 450

3-D SHEENA, JUNGLE QUEEN (Also see Sheena 3-D)
Fiction House Magazines: 1953 (25¢, came w/glasses)

1-Maurice Whitman-c 68 136 204 432 746 1060

3-D SUBSTANCE
The 3-D Zone: July, 1990 ($2.95, 28 pgs.)

1-Ditko-c/a(r) 5.00

3-D TALES OF THE WEST
Atlas Comics (CPS): Jan, 1954 (Oversized) (15¢, came with 2 pair of glasses)

1 (3-D)-Sol Brodsky-c 39 78 117 240 395 550

3-D THREE STOOGES (Also see Three Stooges)
Eclipse Comics: Sept, 1986 - No. 2, Nov, 1986; No. 3, Oct, 1987; No. 4, 1989 ($2.50)

1-4: 3-Maurer-r. 4-r-/"Three Missing Links" 5.00
1-3 (2-D) 5.00

3-D WHACK (See Whack)

3-D ZONE, THE
The 3-D Zone (Renegade Press)/Ray Zone: Feb, 1987 - No. 20, 1989 ($2.50)

1,3,4,7-9,11,12,14,15,17,19,20: 1-r/A Star Presentation. 3-Picture Scope Jungle Advs. 4-Electric Fear. 7-Hollywood 3-D Jayne Mansfield photo-c. 8-High Seas 3-D, 9-Redmask-r. 11-Danse Macabre; Matt Fox c/a(r). 12-3-D Presidents. 14-Tyranostar. 15-3-Dementia Comics; Kurtzman-c, Kubert, Maurer-a. 17-Thrilling Love. 19-Cracked Classics. 20-Commander Battle and His Atomic Submarine 1 2 3 5 6 8
2,5,6,10,13,18: 2-Wolverton-r. 5-Krazy Kat-r. 6-Ratfink. 10-Jet 3-D; Powell & Williamson-r. 13-Flash Gordon. 18-Spacehawk; Wolverton-r 1 2 3 5 7 9
16-Space Vixens; Dave Stevens-c/a 3 6 9 19 30 40

NOTE: ***Davis** r-19. **Ditko** r-19. **Elder** r-19. **Everett** r-19. **Feldstein** r-17. **Frazetta** r-17. **Heath** r-19. **Kamen** r-17. **Severin** r-19. **Ward** r-17,19. **Wolverton** r-2,18,19. **Wood** r-1,17. Photo c-12*

3 GEEKS, THE (Also see Geeksville)
3 Finger Prints: 1996 - No. 11, Jun, 1999 (B&W)

1,2 -Rich Koslowski-s/a in all 1 2 3 5 6 8
1-(2nd printing) 3.00
3-7, 9-11 3.00
8-(48 pgs.) 4.00
10-Variant-c 3.50
...48 Page Super-Sized Summer Spectacular (7/04, $4.95) 5.00
...Full Circle (7/03, $4.95) Origin story of the 3 Geeks; "Buck Rodinski" app. 5.00
How to Pick Up Girls If You're a Comic Book Geek (color)(7/97) 4.00
When the Hammer Fallls TPB (2001, $14.95) r/#8-11 15.00

3 GEEKS: SLAB MADNESS!
3 Finger Prints: Sept, 2008 - No. 3, Mar, 2009 ($2.99, B&W, limited series)

1-3-Rich Koslowski-s/a; intro. The Cee-Gee-Cee 3.00

3 GUNS
BOOM! Studios: Aug, 2013 - No. 6, Jan, 2014 ($3.99)

1-6-Steven Grant-s/Emilio Laiso-a 4.00

300 (Adapted for 2007 movie)
Dark Horse Comics: May, 1998 - No. 5, Sept, 1998 ($2.95/$3.95, limited series)

1-Frank Miller-s/c/a; Spartans vs. Persians war 2 4 6 11 16 20
1-Second printing 5.00
2-4 2 4 6 8 10 12
5-($3.95-c) 2 4 6 8 10 12

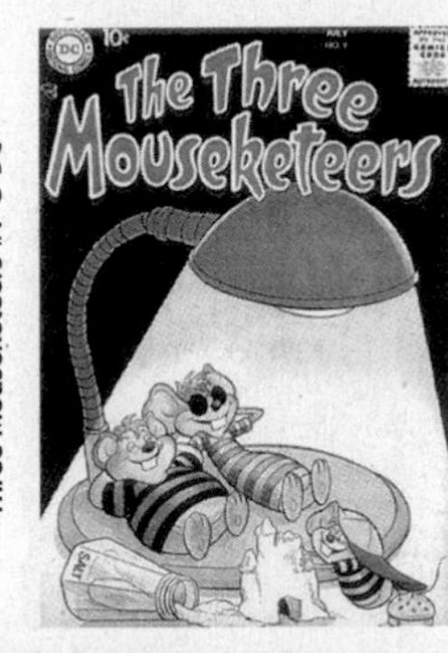

Three Mouseketeers #9 © DC

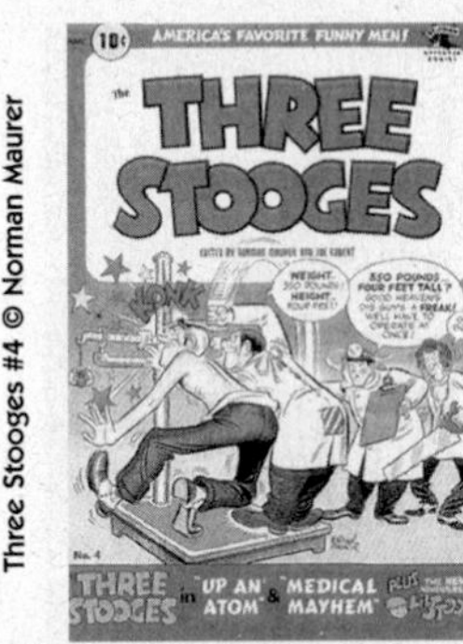

Three Stooges #4 © Norman Maurer

Thrilling Comics #11 © BP

GD 2.0 | VG 4.0 | FN 6.0 | VF 8.0 | VF/NM 9.0 | NM- 9.2

HC ($30.00) -oversized reprint of series 30.00

3 LITTLE KITTENS
BroadSword Comics: Aug, 2002 - No. 3, Dec, 2002 ($2.95, limited series)

1-3-Jim Balent-s/a; two covers 3.00

3 LITTLE PIGS (Disney)(...and the Wonderful Magic Lamp)
Dell Publishing Co.: No. 218, Mar, 1949

Four Color 218 (#1) 9 18 27 61 123 185

3 LITTLE PIGS, THE (See Walt Disney Showcase #15 & 21)
Gold Key: May, 1964; No. 2, Sept, 1968 (Walt Disney)

1-Reprints Four Color #218 3 6 9 19 30 40
2 3 6 9 15 21 26

THREE MOUSEKETEERS, THE (1st Series)(See Funny Stuff #1)
National Per. Publ.: 3-4/56 - No. 24, 9-10/59; No. 25, 8-9/60 - No. 26, 10-12/60

1 22 44 66 154 340 525
2 10 20 30 69 147 225
3-5,7,9,10 8 16 24 54 102 150
6,8-Grey tone-c 10 20 30 64 132 200
11-26: 24-Cover says 11/59, inside says 9-10/59 7 14 21 46 86 125
NOTE: ***Rube Grossman** a-1-26. **Sheldon Mayer** a-1-8; c-1-7.*

THREE MOUSEKETEERS, THE (2nd Series) (See Super DC Giant)
National Periodical Publications: May-June, 1970 - No. 7, May-June, 1971 (#5-7: 68 pgs.)

1-Mayer-r in all 6 12 18 40 73 105
2-4: 4-Doodles Duck begins (1st app.) 4 8 12 25 40 55
5-7:(68 pgs.). 5-Dodo & the Frog, Bo Bunny begin 5 10 15 31 53 75

THREE MUSKETEERS, THE (Also see Disney's The Three Musketeers)
Gemstone Publishing: 2004 ($3.95, squarebound, one-shot)

nn-Adaptation of the 2004 DVD movie; Petrossi-c/a 4.00

THREE NURSES (Confidential Diary #12-17; Career Girl Romances #24 on)
Charlton Comics: V3#18, May, 1963 - V3#23, Mar, 1964

V3#18-23 3 6 9 17 26 35

THREE RASCALS
I. W. Enterprises: 1958; 1963

I.W. Reprint #1,2,10: 1-(Says Super Comics on inside)-(M.E.'s Clubhouse Rascals) DeCarlo-a. #2-(1958). 10-(1963)-r/#1 2 4 6 8 11 14

THREE RING COMICS
Spotlight Publishers: March, 1945

1-Funny animal 18 36 54 103 162 220

THREE RING COMICS (Also see Captain Wizard & Meteor Comics)
Century Publications: April, 1946

1-Prankster-c; Captain Wizard, Impossible Man, Race Wilkins, King O'Leary, & Dr. Mercy app. 37 74 111 222 361 500

THREE ROCKETEERS (See Blast-Off)

THREE STOOGES (See Comic Album #18, Top Comics, The Little Stooges, March of Comics #232, 248, 268, 280, 292, 304, 316, 336, 373, Movie Classics & Comics & 3-D Three Stooges)

THREE STOOGES
Jubilee No. 1/St. John No. 1 (9/53) on: Feb, 1949 - No. 2, May, 1949; Sept, 1953 - No. 7, Oct, 1954

1-(Scarce, 1949)-Kubert-a; infinity-c 129 258 387 826 1413 2000
2-(Scarce)-Kubert, Maurer-a 87 174 261 553 952 1350
1(9/53)-Hollywood Stunt Girl by Kubert (7 pgs.) 74 148 222 470 810 1150
2(3-D, 10/53, 25¢)-Came w/glasses; Stunt Girl story by Kubert 41 82 123 256 428 600
3(3-D, 10/53, 25¢)-Came w/glasses; has 3-D-c 39 78 117 240 395 550
4(3/54)-7(10/54): 4-1st app. Li'l Stooge? 39 78 117 240 395 550
NOTE: *All issues have **Kubert-Maurer** art & **Maurer** covers. 6, 7-Partial photo-c.*

THREE STOOGES
Dell Publishing Co./Gold Key No. 10 (10/62) on: No. 1043, Oct-Dec, 1959 - No. 55, June, 1972

Four Color 1043 (#1) 21 42 63 147 324 500
Four Color 1078,1127,1170,1187 10 20 30 70 150 230
6(9-11/61) - 10: 6-Professor Putter begins; ends #16 9 18 27 58 114 170
11-14,16,18-20 7 14 21 48 89 130
15-Go Around the World in a Daze (movie scenes) 8 16 24 51 96 140
17-The Little Monsters begin (5/64)(1st app.?) 8 16 24 51 96 140
21,23-30 6 12 18 38 69 100
22-Movie scenes from "The Outlaws Is Coming" 6 12 18 41 76 110
31-55 5 10 15 31 53 75
NOTE: *All Four Colors, 6-50, 52-55 have photo-c.*

THREE STOOGES IN 3-D, THE
Eternity Comics: 1991 ($3.95, high quality paper, w/glasses)

1-Reprints Three Stooges by Gold Key; photo-c 5.00

3 WORLDS OF GULLIVER
Dell Publishing Co.: No. 1158, July, 1961 (2 issues exist with diff. covers)

Four Color 1158-Movie, photo-c 6 12 18 40 73 105

THRESHOLD
DC Comics: Mar, 2013 - No. 8 ($3.99)

1-8-Anthology. 1-5-Back-up Larfleeze stories. 5,6-Brainiac app. 4.00

THRILL COMICS (See Flash Comics, Fawcett)

THRILLER
DC Comics: Nov, 1983 - No. 12, Nov, 1984 ($1.25, Baxter paper)

1-12: 1-Intro Seven Seconds; Von Eeden-c/a begins. 2-Origin. 5,6-Elvis satire 4.00

THRILLING ADVENTURES IN STAMPS COMICS (Formerly Stamp Comics)
Stamp Comics, Inc. (Very Rare): V1#8, Jan, 1953 (25¢, 100 pgs.)

V1#8-Harrison, Wildey, Kiefer, Napoli-a 75 150 225 476 818 1160

THRILLING ADVENTURE STORIES (See Tigerman)
Atlas/Seaboard Publ.: Feb, 1975 - No. 2, Aug, 1975 (B&W, 68 pgs.)

1-Tigerman, Kromag the Killer begin; Heath, Thorne-a; Doc Savage movie photos of Ron Ely 3 6 9 17 26 35
2-Heath, Toth, Severin, Simonson-a; Adams-c 4 8 12 23 37 50

THRILLING COMICS
Better Publ./Nedor/Standard Comics: Feb, 1940 - No. 80, April, 1951

1-Origin & 1st app. Dr. Strange (37 pgs.), ends #?; Nickie Norton of the Secret Service begins 331 662 993 2317 4059 5800
2-The Rio Kid, The Woman in Red, Pinocchio begins 148 296 444 947 1624 2300
3-The Ghost & Lone Eagle begin 103 206 309 659 1130 1600
4-6,8,9: 5-Dr. Strange changed to Doc Strange 84 168 252 538 919 1300
7-Classic-c 129 258 387 826 1413 2000
10-1st WWII-c (Nazi)(11/40) 97 194 291 621 1061 1500
11-18,20 81 162 243 518 884 1250
19-Origin & 1st app. The American Crusader (8/41), ends #39,41 90 180 270 576 988 1400
21-30: 24-Intro. Mike, Doc Strange's sidekick (1/42). 27-Robot-c. 29-Last Rio Kid 71 142 213 454 777 1100
31-40: 36-Commando Cubs begin (7/43, 1st app.) 68 136 204 435 743 1050
41-Classic Hitler & Mussolini WWII-c 290 580 870 1856 3178 4500
42,43,46-51: 51(12/45)-Last WWII-c (Japanese) 58 116 174 371 636 900
44-Hitler WWII-c by Schomburg 245 490 735 1568 2684 3800
45-Hitler pict. on-c 74 148 222 470 810 1150
52-Classic Schomburg hooded bondage-c; the Ghost ends 69 138 207 442 759 1075
53,54: 53-The Phantom Detective begins. The Cavalier app. in both; no Commando Cubs in either 43 86 129 271 461 650
55-The Lone Eagle ends 40 80 120 246 411 575
56 (10/46)-Princess Pantha begins (not on-c), 1st app. 53 106 159 334 567 800
57-Doc Strange-c; 2nd Princess Pantha 47 94 141 296 498 700
58-66: All Princess Pantha jungle-c, w/Doc Strange #59, his last-c. 61-Ingels-a; The Lone Eagle app. 65-Last Phantom Detective & Commando Cubs. 66-Frazetta text illo 43 86 129 271 461 650
67,70,71-Last jungle-c; Frazetta-a(5-7 pgs.) in each 52 104 156 328 552 775
68,69-Frazetta-a(2), 8 & 6 pgs.; 9 & 7 pgs. 54 108 162 343 574 825
72,73: 72-Buck Ranger, Cowboy Detective c/stys begin (western theme), end #80; Frazetta-a(5-7 ps.) in each 40 80 120 244 402 560
74-Last Princess Pantha; Tara app. 28 56 84 165 270 375
75-78: 75-All western format begins 14 28 42 82 121 160
79-Krigstein-a 15 30 45 84 127 170
80-Severin & Elder, Celardo, Moreira-a 15 30 45 84 127 170
NOTE: *Bondage c-5, 9, 13, 20, 22, 27-30, 38, 41, 52, 54, 70. **Kinstler** a-45. **Leo Morey** a-7. **Schomburg** (sometimes signed as **Xela**) c-7, 9-19, 36-80 (airbrush 62-71). **Tuska** a-62, 63. Woman in Red not in #19, 23, 31-33, 39-45. No. 45 exists as a Canadian reprint but numbered #48. No. 72 exists as a Canadian reprint with no **Frazetta** story. American Crusader c-20-24. Buck Ranger c-72-80. Commando Cubs c-37, 39, 41, 43, 45, 47, 49, 51. Doc Strange c-1-19, 25-36, 38, 40, 42, 44, 46, 48, 50, 52-57, 59. Princess Pantha c-58, 60-71.*

THRILLING COMICS (Also see All Star Comics 1999 crossover titles)
DC Comics: May, 1999 ($1.99, one-shot)

Thrilling Romances #10 © STD

Thrillkiller #1 © DC

Thun'da #5 © Dynamite

GD VG FN VF VF/NM NM-
2.0 4.0 6.0 8.0 9.0 9.2

1-Golden Age Hawkman and Wildcat; Russ Heath-a 3.00

THRILLING CRIME CASES (Formerly 4Most; becomes Shocking Mystery Cases #50 on)
Star Publications: No. 41, June-July, 1950 - No. 49, July, 1952

41 31 62 93 186 303 420
42-45: 42-L. B. Cole-c/a (1); Chameleon story (Fox-r)
27 54 81 158 259 360
46-48: 47-Used in **POP**, pg. 84 26 52 78 154 252 350
49-(7/52)-Classic L. B. Cole-c 68 136 204 435 743 1050
NOTE: ***L. B. Cole*** *c-all; a-43p, 45p, 46p, 49(2 pgs.).* ***Disbrow*** *a-48.* ***Hollingsworth*** *a-48.*

THRILLING ROMANCES
Standard Comics: No. 5, Dec, 1949 - No. 26, June, 1954

5 18 36 54 103 162 220
6,8 12 24 36 67 94 120
7-Severin/Elder-a (7 pgs.) 14 28 42 78 112 145
9,10-Severin/Elder-a; photo-c 13 26 39 74 105 135
11,14-21,26: 14-Gene Tierney & Danny Kaye photo-c from movie "On the Riviera". 15-Tony Martin/Janet Leigh photo-c 11 22 33 62 86 110
12-Wood-a (2 pgs.); Tyrone Power/ Susan Hayward photo-c
14 28 42 80 115 150
13-Severin-a 12 24 36 67 94 120
22-25-Toth-a 13 26 39 74 105 135
NOTE: *All photo-c.* ***Celardo*** *a-9, 16.* ***Colletta*** *a-23, 24(2).* ***Toth*** *text illos-19.* ***Tuska*** *a-9.*

THRILLING SCIENCE TALES
AC Comics: 1989 - No. 2 ($3.50, 2/3 color, 52 pgs.)

1,2: 1-r/Bob Colt #6(saucer); Frazetta, Guardineer (Space Ace), Wood, Krenkel, Orlando, Williamson-r; Kaluta-c. 2-Capt. Video-r by Evans, Capt. Science-r by Wood, Star Pirate-r by Whitman & Mysta of the Moon-r by Moreira 4.00

THRILLING TRUE STORY OF THE BASEBALL...
Fawcett Publications: 1952 (Photo-c, each)

...Giants-photo-c; has Willie Mays rookie photo-biography; Willie Mays, Eddie Stanky & others photos on-c 68 136 204 432 746 1060
...Yankees-photo-c; Yogi Berra, Joe DiMaggio, Mickey Mantle & others photos on-c
66 132 198 419 722 1025

THRILLING WONDER TALES
AC Comics : 1991 ($2.95, B&W)

1-Includes a Bob Powell Thun'da story 3.00

THRILLKILLER
DC Comics : Jan, 1997 - No. 3, Mar, 1997($2.50, limited series)

1-3-Elseworlds Robin & Batgirl; Chaykin-s/Brereton-c/a 3.00
...'62 ('98, $4.95, one-shot) Sequel; Chaykin-s/Brereton-c/a 5.00
TPB-(See Batman: Thrillkiller)

THRILLOGY
Pacific Comics: Jan, 1984 (One-shot, color)

1-Conrad-c/a 4.00

THRILL-O-RAMA
Harvey Publications (Fun Films): Oct, 1965 - No. 3, Dec, 1966

1-Fate (Man in Black) by Powell app.; Doug Wildey-a(2); Simon-c
5 10 15 31 53 75
2-Pirana begins (see Phantom #46); Williamson 2 pgs.; Fate (Man in Black) app.; Tuska/Simon-c 3 6 9 21 33 45
3-Fate (Man in Black) app.; Sparling-c 3 6 9 18 28 38

THRILLS OF TOMORROW (Formerly Tomb of Terror)
Harvey Publications: No. 17, Oct, 1954 - No. 20, April, 1955

17-Powell-a (horror); r/Witches Tales #7 15 30 45 88 137 185
18-Powell-a (horror); r/Tomb of Terror #1 14 28 42 82 121 160
19,20-Stuntman-c/stories by S&K (r/from Stuntman #1 & 2); 19 has origin & is last pre-code (2/55) 31 62 93 182 296 410
NOTE: ***Kirby*** *c-19, 20.* ***Palais*** *a-17.* ***Simon*** *c-18?*

THROBBING LOVE (See Fox Giants)

THROUGH GATES OF SPLENDOR
Spire Christian Comics (Flemming H. Revell Co.): 1973, 1974 (36 pages) (39-49 cents)

nn-1973 Edition 3 6 9 14 19 24
nn-1974 Edition 2 4 6 9 13 16

THULSA DOOM (Robert E. Howard character)
Dynamite Entertainment: 2009 - No. 4, 2009 ($3.50, limited series)

1-4-Alex Ross-c/Lui Antonio-a 3.50

THUMPER (Disney)
Dell Publishing Co.: No, 19, 1942 - No. 243, Sept, 1949

Four Color 19-Walt Disney's...Meets the Seven Dwarfs; reprinted in Silly Symphonies
41 82 123 303 689 1075
Four Color 243-...Follows His Nose 10 20 30 66 138 210

THUN'DA (...King of the Congo)
Magazine Enterprises: 1952 - No. 6, 1953

1(A-1 #47)-Origin; Frazetta c/a; only comic done entirely by Frazetta; all Thun'da stories, no Cave Girl 187 374 561 1197 2049 2900
2(A-1 #56)-Powell-c/a begins, ends #6; Intro/1st app. Cave Girl in filler strip (also app. in 3-6)
28 56 84 165 270 375
3(A-1 #73), 4(A-1 #78) 20 40 60 114 182 250
5(A-1 #83), 6(A-1 #86) 19 38 57 111 176 240

THUN'DA
Dynamite Entertainment: 2012 - No. 5, 2012 ($3.99, limited series)

1-5-Napton-s/Richards-a/Jae Lee-c. 1-4-Bonus reprints of Thun'da #1 (1952) Frazetta-a 4.00

THUN'DA TALES (See Frank Frazetta's...)

THUNDER AGENTS (See Dynamo, Noman & Tales Of Thunder)
Tower Comics: 11/65 - No. 17, 12/67; No. 18, 9/68, No. 19, 11/68, No. 20, 11/69 (No. 1-16: 68 pgs.; No. 17 on: 52 pgs.)(All are 25¢)

1-Origin & 1st app. Dynamo, Noman, Menthor, & The Thunder Squad; 1st app. The Iron Maiden 17 34 51 119 265 410
2-Death of Egghead; A-bomb blast panel 9 18 27 61 123 185
3-5: 4-Guy Gilbert becomes Lightning who joins Thunder Squad; Iron Maiden app.
7 14 21 49 92 135
6-10: 7-Death of Menthor. 8-Origin & 1st app. The Raven
6 12 18 38 69 100
11-15: 13-Undersea Agent app.; no Raven story 5 10 15 35 63 90
16-19 5 10 15 34 60 85
20-Special Collectors Edition; all reprints 4 8 12 27 44 60
...Archives Vol. 1 (DC Comics, 2003, $49.95, HC) r/#1-4, restored and recolored 50.00
...Archives Vol. 2 (DC Comics, 2003, $49.95, HC) r/#5-7, Dynamo #1 50.00
...Archives Vol. 3 (DC Comics, 2003, $49.95, HC) r/#8-10, Dynamo #2 50.00
...Archives Vol. 4 (DC Comics, 2004, $49.95, HC) r/#11, Noman #1,2 & Dynamo #3 50.00
NOTE: ***Crandall*** *a-1, 4p, 5p, 18, 20r; c-18.* ***Ditko*** *a-6, 7p, 12p, 13?, 14p, 16, 18.* ***Giunta*** *a-6.* ***Kane*** *a-1, 5p, 6p?, 14, 16p; c-14, 15.* ***Reinman*** *a-13.* ***Sekowsky*** *a-6.* ***Tuska*** *a-1p, 7, 8, 10, 13-17, 19.* ***Whitney*** *a-9p, 10, 13, 15, 17, 18; c-17.* ***Wood*** *a-1-11, 15(w/****Ditko****-12, 18), (inks-#9, 13, 14, 16, 17), 19i, 20r; c-1-8, 9i, 10-13(#10 w/****Williamson****(p)), 16.*

T.H.U.N.D.E.R. AGENTS (See Blue Ribbon Comics, Hall of Fame Featuring the..., JCP Features & Wally Wood's...)
JC Comics (Archie Publications): May, 1983 - No. 2, Jan, 1984

1,2: 1-New Manna/Blyberg-c/a. 2-Blyberg-c 6.00

T.H.U.N.D.E.R. AGENTS
DC Comics: Jan, 2011 - No. 10, Oct, 2011 ($3.99/$2.99)

1-3-($3.99): 1-Spencer-s/Cafu-a/Quitely-c. 3-Chaykin-a (5 pgs.) 4.00
4-10-($2.99): 4-Pérez-a (5 pgs.). 7-10-Grell & Dragotta-a 3.00
1-Variant-c by Darwyn Cooke 8.00

T.H.U.N.D.E.R. AGENTS
DC Comics: Jan, 2012 - No. 6, Jun, 2012 ($2.99, limited series)

1-6-Spencer-s/Craig-a. 1-Andy Kubert-c. 3-Craig & Simonson-a 3.00

T.H.U.N.D.E.R. AGENTS
IDW Publishing: Aug, 2013 - Present ($3.99)

1-6-Hester-s/Di Vito-a. 1-Four interlocking covers by Di Vito 4.00

THUNDER BIRDS (See Cinema Comics Herald)

THUNDERBOLT (See The Atomic...)

THUNDERBOLT (Peter Cannon...; see Crisis on Infinite Earths, Peter Cannon, Captain Atom and Judomaster)
Charlton Comics: Jan, 1966; No. 51, Mar-Apr, 1966 - No. 60, Nov, 1967

1-Origin & 1st app. Thunderbolt 4 8 12 27 44 60
51-(Formerly Son of Vulcan #50) 3 6 9 19 30 40
52-Judomaster story 3 6 9 16 23 30
53-Captain Atom story, 2 pgs. 3 6 9 16 23 30
54-59: 54-Sentinels begin. 59-Last Thunderbolt & Sentinels (back-up story)
3 6 9 14 19 24
60-Prankster only app. 3 6 9 15 21 26
57,58 ('77)-Modern Comics-r 6.00
NOTE: ***Aparo*** *a-60.* ***Morisi*** *a-1, 51-56, 58; c-1, 51-56, 58, 59.*

THUNDERBOLT JAXON (Revival of 1940s British comics character)
DC Comics (WildStorm): Apr, 2006 - No. 5, Sept, 2006 ($2.99, limited series)

Thunderbolts #2 © MAR

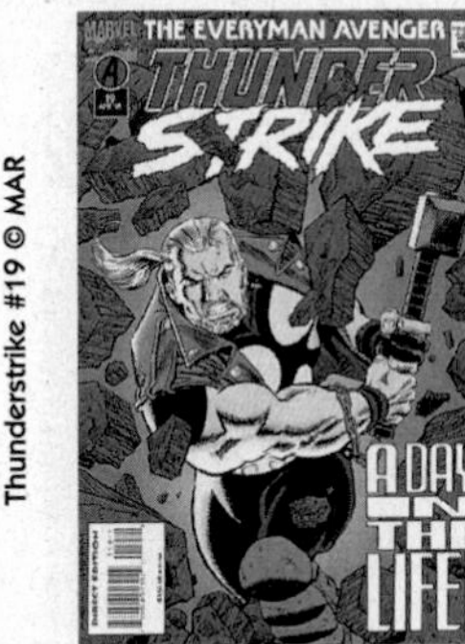

Thunderstrike #19 © MAR

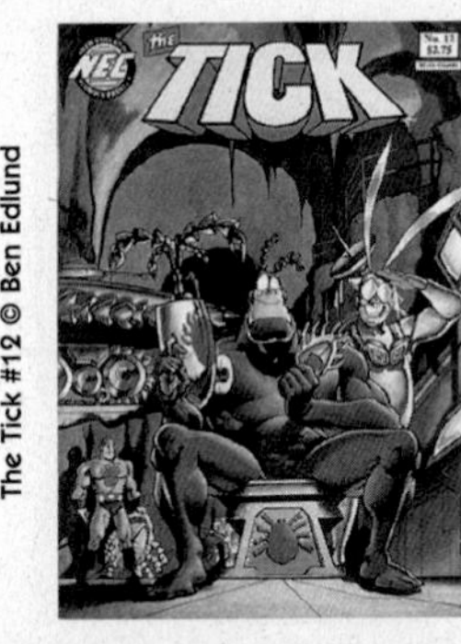

The Tick #12 © Ben Edlund

GD 2.0 | VG 4.0 | FN 6.0 | VF 8.0 | VF/NM 9.0 | NM- 9.2

1-5-Dave Gibbons-s/John Higgins-a 3.00
TPB (2007, $19.99) r/#1-5; intro. by Gibbons; cover gallery 20.00

THUNDERBOLTS (Title re-named Dark Avengers with #175)(Also see New Thunderbolts and Incredible Hulk #449)
Marvel Comics: Apr, 1997 - No. 81, Sept, 2003; No. 100, May, 2006 - No. 174, Jul, 2012 ($1.95-$2.99)

1-($2.99)-Busiek-s/Bagley-c/a 1 2 3 5 7 9
1-2nd printing; new cover colors 3.00
2-4: 2-Two covers. 4-Intro. Jolt 6.00
5-11: 9-Avengers app. 3.50
12-($2.99)-Avengers and Fantastic Four-c/app. 4.00
13-24: 14-Thunderbolts return to Earth. 21-Hawkeye app. 3.00
25-($2.99) Wraparound-c 4.00
26-38: 26-Manco-a 3.00
39-($2.99) 100 Page Monster; Iron Man reprints 4.00
40-49: 40-Begin $2.25-c; Sandman-c/app. 44-Avengers app. 47-Captain Marvel app. 49-Zircher-a 3.00
50-($2.99) Last Bagley-a; Captain America becomes leader 4.00
51-74,76,77,80,81: 51,52-Zircher-a; Dr. Doom app. 80,81-Spider-Man app. 3.00
75-($3.50) Hawkeye leaves the team; Garcia-a 4.00
78,79-($2.99-c) Velasco-a begins 3.00
(See New Thunderbolts for #82-99)
100 (5/06, $3.99) resumes from New Thunderbolts #18; back-up origin stories 4.00
101-109: 103-105-Civil War x-over 3.00
110-New team begins including Bullseye, Venom and Norman Osborn; Ellis-s/Deodato-a 5.00
111-136,138-149: 111-121-Ellis-s/Deodato-a. 112-Stan Lee cameo. 123-125-Secret Invasion x-over. 128-Dark Reign begins. 130,131-X-over with Deadpool #8,9. 141-143-Siege 3.00
137-(12/09, $3.99) Iron Fist and Luke Cage app. 4.00
150-(1/11, $4.99) Thunderbolts vs. Avengers; r/#1; storyline synopses of #1-150 5.00
151-158,160-163, 163.1, 164-174-($2.99) 151-153-Land-c. 155-Satana joins. 158-162-Fear Itself tie-in. 163-165-Thunderbolts in WWII; Invaders app. 3.00
159-($4.99) Fear Itelf tie-in; Juggernaut app.; short stories of escape from The Raft 5.00
Annual '97 ($2.99)-Wraparound-c 4.00
Annual 2000 ($3.50) Breyfogle-a 4.00
...: Breaking Point (1/08, $2.99, one-shot) Gage-s/Denham-a/Djurdjevic-c 3.00
... By Warren Ellis Vol. 1 HC (2007, $24.99, dustjacket) r/#150-154, ...: Desperate Measures and stories from Civil War: Choosing Sides and The Initiative 25.00
... By Warren Ellis Vol. 1: Faith in Monsters SC (2008, $19.99) same contents as HC 20.00
Civil War: Thunderbolts TPB (2007, $13.99) r/#101-105 14.00
...: Desperate Measures (9/07, $2.99, one-shot) Jenkins-s/Steve Lieber-a 3.00
...: Distant Rumblings (#-1) (7/97, $1.95) Busiek-s 5.00
First Strikes (1997, $4.99,TPB) r/#1,2 5.00
...: From the Marvel Vault (6/11, $3.99) Jack Monroe app.; Nicieza-s/Aucoin-a 4.00
...: Guardian Protocols (2007, $10.99) r/#106-109 11.00
...: International Incident (4/08, $2.99, one-shot) Gage-s/Oliver-a/Djurdjevic-c 3.00
...: Life Sentences (7/01, $3.50) Adlard-a 4.00
...: Marvel's Most Wanted TPB ('98, $16.99) r/origin stories of original Masters of Evil 17.00
...: Reason in Madness (7/08, $2.99, one-shot) Gage-s/Oliver-a/Djurdjevic-c 3.00
Wizard #0 (bagged with Wizard #89) 3.00

THUNDERBOLTS (Marvel NOW!)
Marvel Comics: Feb, 2013 - Present ($2.99)

1-24: 1-Punisher, Red Hulk, Elektra, Venom & Deadpool team; Dillon-a. 7-11-Noto-a. 14-18-Infinity tie-ins; Soule-s/Palo-a. 20-Ghost Rider joins 3.00
Annual 1 (2/14, $4.99) Dr. Strange & Elsa Bloodstone app.; Lolli-a 5.00

THUNDERBOLTS PRESENTS: ZEMO - BORN BETTER
Marvel Comics: Apr, 2007 - No. 4, July, 2007 ($2.99, limited series)

1-4-History of Baron Zemo; Nicieza-s/Grummett-a/c 3.00
TPB (2007, $10.99) r/#1-4 11.00

THUNDERBUNNY (See Blue Ribbon Comics #13, Charlton Bullseye & Pep Comics #393)
Red Circle Comics: Jan, 1984 (Direct sale only)
WaRP Graphics: Second series No. 1, 1985 - No. 6, 1985
Apple Comics: No. 7, 1986 - No. 12, 1987

1-Humor/parody; origin Thunderbunny; 2 page pin-up by Anderson 5.00
(2nd series) 1,2-Magazine size 4.00
3-12-Comic size 4.00

THUNDERCATS (TV)
Marvel Comics (Star Comics)/Marvel #22 on: Dec, 1985 - No. 24, June, 1988 (75¢)

1-Mooney-c/a begins 2 4 6 10 14 18
2-20: 2-(65¢ & 75¢ cover exists). 12-Begin $1.00-c. 18-20-Williamson-i 1 2 3 5 7 9
21-24: 23-Williamson-c(i) 1 3 4 6 8 10

THUNDERCATS (TV)
DC Comics (WildStorm): No. 0, Oct, 2002 - No. 5, Feb, 2003 ($2.50/$2.95, limited series)

0-($2.50) J. Scott Campbell-c/a 3.00
1-5-($2.95) 1-McGuinness-a/c; variant cover by Art Adams; rebirth of Mumm-Ra 3.00
.../ Battle of the Planets (7/03, $4.95) Kaare Andrews-s/a; 2 covers by Campbell & Ross 5.00
...: Origins-Heroes & Villains (2/04, $3.50) short stories by various 3.50
...Reclaiming Thundera TPB (2003, $12.95) r/#0-5 13.00
... Sourcebook (1/03, $2.95) pin-ups and info on characters; art by various; A. Adams-c 3.00

THUNDERCATS: DOGS OF WAR
DC Comics (WildStorm): Aug, 2003 - No. 5, Dec, 2003 ($2.95, limited series)

1-5: 1-Two covers by Booth & Pearson; Booth-a/Layman-s. 2-4-Two covers 3.00
TPB (2004, $14.95) r/#1-5 15.00

THUNDERCATS: ENEMY'S PRIDE
DC Comics (WildStorm): Aug, 2004 - No. 5 ($2.95, limited series)

1-5-Vriens-a/Layman-s 3.00
TPB (2005, $14.99) r/#1-5 15.00

THUNDERCATS: HAMMERHAND'S REVENGE
DC Comics (WildStorm): Dec, 2003 - No. 5, Apr, 2004 ($2.95, limited series)

1-5-Avery-s/D'Anda-a. 2-Variant-c by Warren 3.00
TPB (2004, $14.95) r/#1-5 15.00

THUNDERCATS: THE RETURN
DC Comics (WildStorm): Apr, 2003 - No. 5, Aug, 2003 ($2.95, limited series)

1-5: 1-Two covers by Benes & Cassaday; Gilmore-s 3.00
TPB (2004, $12.95) r/series 13.00

THUNDER MOUNTAIN (See Zane Grey, Four Color #246)

THUNDERSTRIKE (See Thor #459)
Marvel Comics: June, 1993 - No. 24, July, 1995 ($1.25)

1-($2.95, 52 pgs.)-Holo-grafx lightning patterned foil-c; Bloodaxe returns 4.00
2-24: 2-Juggernaut-c/s. 4-Capt. America app. 4-6-Spider-Man app. 8-bound-in trading card sheet. 18-Bloodaxe app. 24-Death of Thunderstrike 3.00
Marvel Double Feature...Thunderstrike/Code Blue #13 ($2.50)-Same as Thunderstrike #13 w/Code Blue flip book 4.00

THUNDERSTRIKE
Marvel Comics: Jan, 2011 - No. 5, Jun, 2011 ($3.99, limited series)

1-5-DeFalco-s/Frenz-a. 1-Back-up origin retold; Nauck-a 4.00

TICK, THE (Also see The Chroma-Tick)
New England Comics Press: Jun, 1988 - No. 12, May, 1993 ($1.75/$1.95/$2.25; B&W, over-sized)

Special Edition 1-1st comic book app. serially numbered & limited to 5,000 copies 5 10 15 31 53 75
Special Edition 1-(5/96, $5.95)-Double-c; foil-c; serially numbered (5,001 thru 14,000) & limited to 9,000 copies 1 2 3 5 6 8
Special Edition 2-Serially numbered and limited to 3000 copies 4 8 12 28 47 65
Special Edition 2-(8/96, $5.95)-Double-c; foil-c; serially numbered (5,001 thru 14,000) & limited to 9,000 copies 1 2 3 5 6 8
1-Regular Edition 1st printing; reprints Special Ed. 1 w/minor changes 4 8 12 24 37 50
1-2nd printing 6.00
1-3rd-5th printing 4.00
2-Reprints Special Ed. 2 w/minor changes 2 4 6 13 18 22
2-8-All reprints 4.00
3-5 ($1.95): 4-1st app. Paul the Samurai 1 3 4 6 8 10
6,8 ($2.25) 6.00
7-1st app. Man-Eating Cow 1 2 3 5 6 8
8-Variant with no logo, price, issue number or company logos. 2 4 6 11 16 20
9-12 ($2.75) 5.00
12-Special Edition; card-stock, virgin foil-c; numbered edition 2 4 6 13 18 22
100: The Tick Meets Invincible (6/12, $6.99) Invincible travels to Tick's universe 7.00
101: The Tick Meets Madman (11/12, $6.99) Bonus publishing history of the Tick 7.00
Pseudo-Tick #13 (11/00, $3.50) Continues story from #12 (1993) 5.00
Promo Sampler-(1990)-Tick-c/story 1 2 3 5 6 8

TICK, THE (One shots)
... Big Back to School Special 1-(10/98, $3.50, B&W) Tick & Arthur undercover in H.S. 4.00
... Big Cruise Ship Vacation Special 1-(9/00, $3.50, B&W) 4.00
... Big Father's Day Special 1-(6/00, $3.50, B&W) 4.00
... Big Halloween Special 1-(10/99, $3.50, B&W) 4.00

The Tick and Arthur #1 © Ben Edlund

Tigra #3 © MAR

Time Breakers #3 © Pollack & Weston

GD 2.0 | VG 4.0 | FN 6.0 | VF 8.0 | VF/NM 9.0 | NM- 9.2

... Big Halloween Special 2000 (10/00, $3.50) 4.00
... Big Halloween Special 2001 (9/01, $3.95) 4.00
... Big Mother's Day Special 1-(4/00, $3.50, B&W) 4.00
... Big Red-N-Green Christmas Spectacle 1-(12/01, $3.95) 4.00
... Big Romantic Adventure 1-(2/98, $2.95, B&W) Candy box-c with candy map on back 4.00
... Big Summer Annual 1-(7/99, $3.50, B&W) Chainsaw Vigilante vs. Barry 4.00
... Big Summer Fun Special 1-(8/98, $3.50, B&W) Tick and Arthur at summer camp 4.00
... Big Tax Time Terror 1-(4/00, $3.50, B&W) 4.00
... Big Year 2000 Spectacle 1-(3/00, $3.50, B&W) 4.00
... Incredible Internet Comic 1-(7/01, $3.95, color) r/New England Comics website story 4.00
FCBD Special Edition (5/10) - reprints debut from 1988; Ben Edlund-s/a 3.00
Free Comic Book Day 2013 (6/13) - New stories; McClelland-s/Redhead-a 3.00
Introducing the Tick 1-(4/02, $3.95, color) summary of Tick's life and adventures 4.00
The Tick's Back #0 -(8/97, $2.95, B&W) 4.00
The Tick's Comic Con Extravaganza -(6/07, $3.95, color) Wang-c 4.00
The Tick's 20th Anniversary Special Edition #1 (5/07, $5.95) short stories by various; history of the character; creator profiles; 2 covers by Suydam & Bisley 6.00

--MASSIVE SUMMER DOUBLE SPECTACLE
1,2-(7,8/00, $3.50, B&W) 4.00

TICK & ARTIE
1-(6/02, $3.50, color) prints strips from Internet comic 4.00
2-(10/02, $3.95) 4.00

TICK AND ARTHUR, THE
New England Comics: Feb, 1999 - No. 6 ($3.50, B&W)
1-6-Sean Wang-s/a 4.00

TICK BIG BLUE DESTINY, THE
New England Comics: Oct, 1997 - No. 9 ($2.95)
1-4: 1-"Keen" Ed. 2-Two covers 4.00
1-($4.95) "Wicked Keen" Ed. w/die cut-c 5.00
5-($3.50) 4.00
6-Luny Bin Trilogy Preview #0 (7/98, $1.50) 4.00
7-9: 7-Luny Bin Trilogy begins 4.00

TICK BIG BLUE YULE LOG SPECIAL, THE
New England Comics: Dec, 1997; 1999 ($2.95, B&W)
1-"Jolly" and "Traditional" covers; flip book w/"Arthur Teaches the Tick About Hanukkah" 4.00
...1999 ($3.50) 4.00
Tick Big Yule Log Special 2001-(12/00, $3.50, B&W) 4.00

TICK, THE : CIRCUS MAXIMUS
New England Comics: Mar, 2000 - No. 4, Jun, 2000 ($3.50, B&W)
1-4-Encyclopedia of characters from Tick comics 4.00
Giant No. 1 (8/03, $14.95) r/#1-4, Redux 15.00
Redux No. 1 (4/01, $3.50) 4.00

TICK, THE - COLOR
New England Comics: Jan, 2001 - Present ($3.95)
1-6: 1-Marc Sandroni-a 4.00

TICK, THE : DAYS OF DRAMA
New England Comics: July, 2005 - No. 6, June, 2006 ($4.95/$3.95, limited series)
1-($4.95) Dave Garcia-a; has a mini-comic attached to cover 5.00
2-6-($3.95) 4.00

TICK, THE - HEROES OF THE CITY
New England Comics: Feb, 1999 - No. 6 ($3.50, B&W)
1-6-Short stories by various 4.00

TICK KARMA TORNADO (The...)
New England Comics Press: Oct, 1993 - No. 9, Mar, 1995 ($2.75, B&W)
1-($3.25) 5.00
2-9: 2-$2.75-c begins 4.00

TICK NEW SERIES (The...)
New England Comics: Dec, 2009 - No. 8 ($4.95)
1-8 5.00

TICK'S BIG XMAS TRILOGY, THE
New England Comics: Dec, 2002 - No. 3, Dec, 2002 ($3.95, limited series)
1-3 4.00

TICK'S GOLDEN AGE COMIC, THE
New England Comics: May, 2002 - No. 3, Feb, 2003 ($4.95, Golden Age size)
1-3-Facsimile 1940s-style Tick issue; 2 covers 5.00
Giant Edition TPB (9/03, $12.95) r/#1-3 13.00

GD 2.0 | VG 4.0 | FN 6.0 | VF 8.0 | VF/NM 9.0 | NM- 9.2

TICK'S GIANT CIRCUS OF THE MIGHTY, THE
New England Comics: Summer, 1992 - No. 3, Fall, 1993 ($2.75, B&W, magazine size)
1-(A-O). 2-(P-Z). 3-1993 Update 5.00

TICKLE COMICS (Also see Gay, Smile, & Whee Comics)
Modern Store Publ.: 1955 (7¢, 5x7-1/4", 52 pgs)
1 6 12 18 31 38 45

TICK TOCK TALES
Magazine Enterprises: Jan, 1946 - V3#33, Jan-Feb, 1951
1-Koko & Kola begin 19 38 57 111 176 240
2 12 24 36 67 94 120
3-10 11 22 33 60 83 105
11-33: 19-Flag-c. 23-Muggsy Mouse, The Pixies & Tom-Tom the Jungle Boy app. 24-X-mas-c. 25-The Pixies & Tom-Tom app. 10 20 30 54 72 90

TIGER (Also see Comics Reading Libraries in the Promotional Comics section)
Charlton Press (King Features): Mar, 1970 - No. 6, Jan, 1971 (15¢)
1 3 6 9 14 19 24
2-6: 3-Ad for life-size inflatable doll 2 4 6 8 11 14

TIGER BOY (See Unearthly Spectaculars)

TIGER GIRL
Gold Key: Sept, 1968 (15¢)
1(10227-809)-Sparling-c/a; Jerry Siegel scripts; advertising on back-c 4 8 12 25 40 55
1-Variant edition with pin-up on back cover 5 10 15 31 53 75

TIGERMAN (Also see Thrilling Adventure Stories)
Seaboard Periodicals (Atlas): Apr, 1975 - No. 3, Sept, 1975 (All 25¢ issues)
1-3: 1-Origin; Colan-c. 2,3-Ditko-p in each 2 4 6 11 16 20

TIGER WALKS, A (See Movie Comics)

TIGRA (The Avengers)
Marvel Comics: May, 2002 - No. 4, Aug, 2002 ($2.99, limited series)
1-4-Christina Z-s/Deodato-c/a 3.00

TIGRESS, THE
Hero Graphics: Aug, 1992 - No. 6?, June, 1993 ($3.95/$2.95/$3.95, B&W)
1,6: 1-Tigress vs. Flare. 6-44 pgs. 4.00
2-5: 2-$2.95-c begins 3.00

TILLIE THE TOILER (See Comic Monthly)
Dell Publishing Co.: No. 15, 1941 - No. 237, July, 1949
Four Color 15(1941) 50 100 150 315 533 750
Large Feature Comic 30(1941) 36 72 108 211 343 475
Four Color 8(1942) 21 42 63 147 324 500
Four Color 22(1943) 15 30 45 105 233 360
Four Color 55(1944), 89(1945) 12 24 36 79 170 260
Four Color 106('45),132('46): 132-New stories begin 9 18 27 60 120 180
Four Color 150,176,184 8 16 24 56 108 160
Four Color 195,213,237 7 14 21 46 86 125

TIMBER WOLF (See Action Comics #372, & Legion of Super-Heroes)
DC Comics: Nov, 1992 - No. 5, Mar, 1993 ($1.25, limited series)
1-5 3.00

TIME BANDITS
Marvel Comics Group: Feb, 1982 (one-shot, Giant)
1-Movie adaptation 4.00

TIME BEAVERS (See First Comics Graphic Novel #2)

TIME BOMB
Radical Comics: Jul, 2010 - No. 3, Dec, 2010 ($4.99, limited series)
1-3-Palmiotti & Gray-s/Gulacy-a/c 5.00

TIME BREAKERS
DC Comics (Helix): Jan, 1997 - No. 5, May, 1997 ($2.25, limited series)
1-5-Pollack-s 3.00

TIMECOP (Movie)
Dark Horse Comics: Sept, 1994 - No. 2, Nov, 1994 ($2.50, limited series)
1,2-Adaptation of film 3.00

TIME FOR LOVE (Formerly Romantic Secrets)
Charlton Comics: V2#53, Oct, 1966; Oct, 1967 - No. 47, May, 1976
V2#53(10/66) Herman-s Hermits app. 3 6 9 19 30 40
1-(10/67) 3 6 9 21 33 45

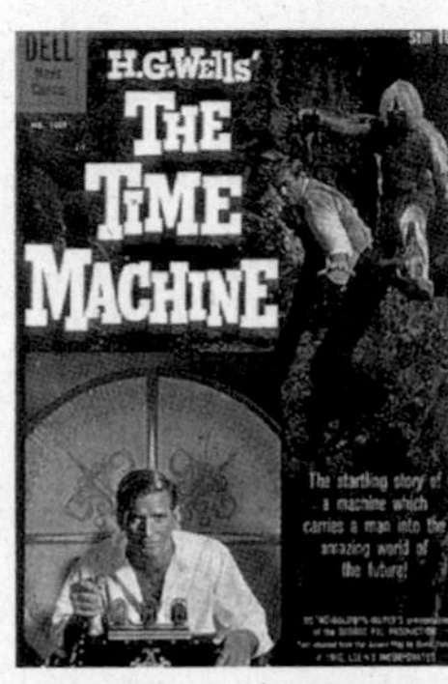

The Time Machine FC #1085 © Lowe's

Time Twisters #12 © IPC

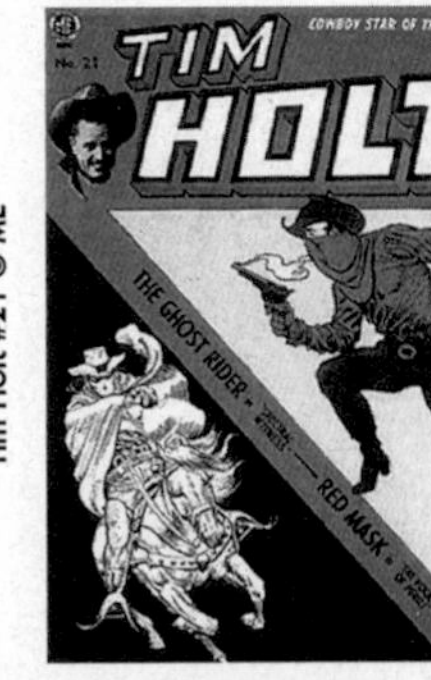

Tim Holt #21 © ME

GD 2.0 | VG 4.0 | FN 6.0 | VF 8.0 | VF/NM 9.0 | NM- 9.2

2-(12/67) -10 3 6 9 15 21 26
11,12,14-20 2 4 6 11 16 20
13-(11/69) Ditko-a (7 pgs.) 3 6 9 16 23 30
21-27 2 4 6 9 13 16
28,29,31: 28-Shirley Jones poster. 29-Bobby Sherman pin-up. 31-Bobby Sherman pin-up
2 4 6 11 16 20
30-(10/72)-David Cassidy full page poster 3 6 9 16 24 32
32-47 2 4 6 8 11 14

TIMELESS TOPIX (See Topix)

TIMELY PRESENTS: ALL WINNERS
Marvel Comics: Dec, 1999 ($3.99)
1-Reprints All Winners Comics #19 (Fall 1946); new Lago-c 5.00

TIMELY PRESENTS: HUMAN TORCH
Marvel Comics: Feb, 1999 ($3.99)
1-Reprints Human Torch Comics #5 (Fall 1941); new Lago-c 5.00

TIME MACHINE, THE
Dell Publishing Co.: No. 1085, Mar, 1960 (H.G. Wells)
Four Color 1085-Movie, Alex Toth-a; Rod Taylor photo-c
12 24 36 80 173 265

TIME MASTERS
DC Comics: Feb, 1990 - No. 8, Sept, 1990 ($1.75, mini-series)
1-8: New Rip Hunter series. 5-Cave Carson, Viking Prince app. 6-Dr. Fate app. 3.00
TPB (2008, $19.99) r/#1-8 and Secret Origins #43; intro. by Geoff Johns 20.00

TIME MASTERS: VANISHING POINT (Tie-in to Batman: The Return of Bruce Wayne)
DC Comics: Sept, 2010 - No. 6, Feb, 2011 ($3.99, limited series)
1-6-Jurgens-s/a/c; Rip Hunter, Superman, Green Lantern & Booster Gold app. 4.00
TPB (2011, $14.99) r/#1-6 15.00

TIMESLIP COLLECTION
Marvel Comics: Nov, 1998 ($2.99, one-shot)
1-Pin-ups reprinted from Marvel Vision magazine 3.00

TIMESLIP SPECIAL (The Coming of the Avengers)
Marvel Comics: Oct, 1998 ($5.99, one-shot)
1-Alternate world Avengers vs. Odin 6.00

TIMESTORM 2009/2099
Marvel Comics: June, 2009 - No. 4, Oct, 2009 ($3.99, limited series)
1-4-Punisher 2099 transports Spider-Man to 2099; Wolverine app.; Battle-a 4.00
...: Spider-Man One Shot (8/09, $3.99) Reed-s/Craig-a/Renaud-c 4.00
...: X-Men One Shot (8/09, $3.99) Reed-s/Irving-a/Renaud-c 4.00

TIME TO RUN (Based on 1973 Billy Graham movie)
Spire Christian Comics (Fleming H. Revell Co.): 1975 (39¢)
nn-By Al Hartley 2 4 6 13 18 22

TIME TUNNEL, THE (TV)
Gold Key: Feb, 1967 - No. 2, July, 1967 (12¢)
1-Photo back-c on both issues 6 12 18 40 73 105
2 5 10 15 31 53 75

TIME TWISTERS
Quality Comics: Sept, 1987 - No. 21, 1989 ($1.25/$1.50)
1-21: Alan Moore scripts in 1-4, 6-9, 14 (2 pg.). 14-Bolland-a (2 pg.). 15,16-Guice-c 4.00

TIME 2: THE EPIPHANY (See First Comics Graphic Novel #9)

TIMEWALKER (Also see Archer & Armstrong)
Valiant: Jan, 1994 - No. 15, Oct, 1995 ($2.50)
1-15,0(3/96): 2-"JAN" on-c, February, 1995 in indicia. 3.00
Yearbook 1 (5/95, $2.95) 3.00

TIME WARP (See The Unexpected #210)
DC Comics, Inc.: Oct-Nov, 1979 - No. 5, June-July, 1980 ($1.00, 68 pgs.)
1 2 4 6 11 16 20
2-5 2 4 6 8 11 14
NOTE: ***Aparo*** a-1. ***Buckler*** a-1p. ***Chaykin*** a-2. ***Ditko*** a-1-4. ***Kaluta*** c-1-5. ***G. Kane*** a-2. ***Nasser*** a-4. ***Newton*** a-1-5p. ***Orlando*** a-2. ***Sutton*** a-1-3.

TIME WARP
DC Comics (Vertigo): May, 2013 ($7.99, one-shot)
1-Short story anthology by various incl. Lindelof, Simone; covers by Risso & Jae Lee 8.00

TIME WARRIORS: THE BEGINNING
Fantasy General Comics: 1986 (Aug) - No. 2, 1986? ($1.50)
1,2-Alpha Track/Skellon Empire 3.00

TIM HOLT (Movie star) (Becomes Red Mask #42 on; also see Crack Western #72, & Great Western)
Magazine Enterprises: 1948 - No. 41, April-May, 1954 (All 36 pgs.)
1-(A-1 #14)-Line drawn-c w/Tim Holt photo on-c; Tim Holt, His horse Lightning & sidekick Chito begin 50 100 150 315 533 750
2-(A-1 #17)(9-10/48)-Photo-c begin, end #18 26 52 78 154 252 350
3-(A-1 #19)-Photo back-c 20 40 60 117 189 260
4(1-2/49),5: 5-Photo front/back-c 15 30 45 85 130 175
6-(5/49)-1st app. The Calico Kid (alias Rex Fury), his horse Ebony & Sidekick Sing-Song (begin series); photo back-c 22 44 66 132 216 300
7-10: 7-Calico Kid by Ayers. 8-Calico Kid by Guardineer (r-in/Great Western #10). 9-Map of Tim's Home Range 14 28 42 82 121 160
11-The Calico Kid becomes The Ghost Rider (origin & 1st app.) by Dick Ayers (r-in/Great Western I.W. #8); his horse Spectre & sidekick Sing-Song begin series
45 90 135 284 480 675
12-16,18-Last photo-c 13 26 39 74 105 135
17-Frazetta Ghost Rider-c 40 80 120 246 411 575
19,22,24: 19-Last Tim Holt-c; Bolle line-drawn-c begin; Tim Holt photo on covers #19-28, 30-41. 22-interior photo-c 11 22 33 62 86 110
20-Tim Holt becomes Redmask (origin); begin series; Redmask-c #20-on
15 30 45 86 133 180
21-Frazetta Ghost Rider/Redmask-c 36 72 108 216 351 485
23-Frazetta Redmask-c 28 56 84 165 270 375
25-1st app. Black Phantom 18 36 54 105 165 225
26-30: 28-Wild Bill Hickok, Bat Masterson team up with Redmask. 29-B&W photo-c
10 20 30 58 79 100
31-33-Ghost Rider ends 10 20 30 54 72 90
34-Tales of the Ghost Rider begins (horror)-Classic "The Flower Women" & "Hard Boiled Harry!" 14 28 42 82 121 160
35-Last Tales of the Ghost Rider 11 22 33 62 86 110
36-The Ghost Rider returns, ends #41; liquid hallucinogenic drug story
13 26 39 74 105 135
37-Ghost Rider classic "To Touch Is to Die!", about Inca treasure
13 26 39 74 105 135
38-The Black Phantom begins (not in #39); classic Ghost Rider "The Phantom Guns of Feather Gap!" 13 26 39 74 105 135
39-41: All 3-D effect c/stories 14 28 42 81 118 155
NOTE: ***Dick Ayers*** a-7, 9-41. ***Bolle*** a-1-41; c-19, 20, 22, 24-28, 30-41.

TIM McCOY (Formerly Zoo Funnies; Pictorial Love Stories #22 on)
Charlton Comics: No. 16, Oct, 1948 - No. 21, Aug, 1949 (Western Movie Stories)
16-John Wayne, Montgomery Clift app. in "Red River"; photo back-c
34 68 102 199 325 450
17-21: 17-Allan "Rocky" Lane guest stars. 18-Rod Cameron guest stars. 19-Whip Wilson, Andy Clyde guest star; Jesse James story. 20-Jimmy Wakely guest stars. 21-Johnny Mack Brown guest stars 24 48 72 142 234 325

TIMMY
Dell Publishing Co.: No. 715, Aug, 1956 - No. 1022, Aug-Oct, 1959
Four Color 715 (#1) 5 10 15 30 50 70
Four Color 823 (8/57), 923 (8/58), 1022 4 8 12 27 44 60

TIMMY THE TIMID GHOST (Formerly Win-A-Prize?; see Blue Bird)
Charlton Comics: No. 3, 2/56 - No. 44, 10/64; No. 45, 9/66; 10/67 - No. 23, 7/71; V4#24, 9/85 - No. 26, 1/86
3(1956) (1st Series) 13 26 39 72 101 130
4,5 8 16 24 42 54 65
6-10 3 6 9 19 30 40
11,12(4/58,10/58)-(100 pgs.) 6 12 18 37 66 95
13-20 3 6 9 17 26 35
21-45(1966): 27-Nazi story 3 6 9 14 19 24
1(10/67, 2nd series) 3 6 9 15 22 28
2-10 2 4 6 10 14 18
11-23: 23 (7/71) 1 3 4 8 10 12
24-26 (1985-86): Fago-r (low print run) 6.00

TIM TYLER (See Harvey Comics Hits #54)

TIM TYLER (Also see Comics Reading Libraries in the Promotional Comics section)
Better Publications: 1942
1 15 30 45 85 130 175

TIM TYLER COWBOY
Standard Comics (King Features Synd.): No. 11, Nov, 1948 - No. 18, Aug, 1950
11-By Lyman Young 9 18 27 50 65 80

Tiny Titans #25 © DC

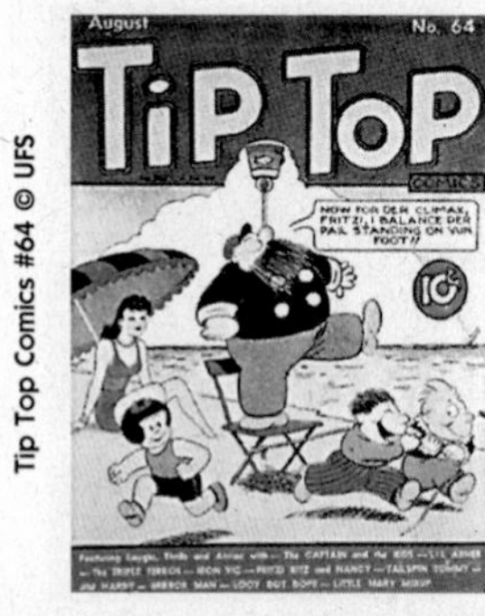

Tip Top Comics #64 © UFS

Titans #2 © DC

	GD 2.0	VG 4.0	FN 6.0	VF 8.0	VF/NM 9.0	NM- 9.2
12-18: 13-15-Full length western adventures	7	14	21	35	43	50

TINKER BELL (Disney, TV)(See Walt Disney Showcase #37)
Dell Publishing Co.: No. 896, Mar, 1958 - No. 982, Apr-June, 1959

	GD	VG	FN	VF	VF/NM	NM-
Four Color 896 (#1)-The Adventures of...	8	16	24	54	102	150
Four Color 982-The New Advs. of...	8	16	24	51	96	140

TINY FOLKS FUNNIES
Dell Publishing Co.: No. 60, 1944

	GD	VG	FN	VF	VF/NM	NM-
Four Color 60	13	26	39	89	195	300

TINY TESSIE (Tessie #1-23; Real Experiences #25)
Marvel Comics (20CC): No. 24, Oct, 1949 (52 pgs.)

	GD	VG	FN	VF	VF/NM	NM-
24	15	30	45	84	127	170

TINY TIM (Also see Super Comics)
Dell Publishing Co.: No. 4, 1941 - No. 235, July, 1949

	GD	VG	FN	VF	VF/NM	NM-
Large Feature Comic 4('41)	42	84	126	265	445	625
Four Color 20(1941)	39	78	117	231	378	525
Four Color 42(1943)	15	30	45	100	220	340
Four Color 235	5	10	15	35	63	90

TINY TITANS (Teen Titans)
DC Comics: Apr, 2008 - No. 50, May, 2012 ($2.25/$2.50/$2.99)

	GD	VG	FN	VF	VF/NM	NM-
1-29-All ages stories of Teen Titans in Elementary school; Baltazar & Franco-s/a						3.00
1-(6/08, Free Comic Book Day giveaway) r/#1; Baltazar & Franco-s/a						3.00
30-50: 30-Begin $2.99-c. 37-Marvel Family app. 44-Doom Patrol app.						3.00
...: Adventures in Awesomeness TPB (2009, $12.99) r/#7-12; pin-ups						13.00
...: Field Trippin' TPB (2011, $12.99) r/#26-32; pin-ups						13.00
...: Sidekickin' It TPB (2010, $12.99) r/#13-18; pin-ups						13.00
...: The First Rule of Pet Club... TPB (2010, $12.99) r/#19-25; pin-ups						13.00
...: Welcome To The Treehouse TPB (2009, $12.99) r/#1-6; pin-ups						13.00

TINY TITANS / LITTLE ARCHIE (Teen Titans) (Digest-size reprint in World of Archie Double Digest Magazine #5)
DC Comics: Dec, 2010 - No. 3, Feb, 2011 ($2.99)

	GD	VG	FN	VF	VF/NM	NM-
1-3-Character crossover; Baltazar & Franco-s/a. 2-Josie and the Pussycats app.						3.00

TINY TOT COMICS
E. C. Comics: Mar, 1946 - No. 10, Nov-Dec, 1947 (For younger readers)

	GD	VG	FN	VF	VF/NM	NM-
1(nn)-52 pg. issues begin, end #4	41	82	123	256	428	600
2 (5/46)	24	48	72	142	234	325
3-10: 10-Christmas-c	22	44	66	132	216	300

TINY TOT FUNNIES (Formerly Family Funnies; becomes Junior Funnies)
Harvey Publ. (King Features Synd.): No. 9, June, 1951

	GD	VG	FN	VF	VF/NM	NM-
9-Flash Gordon, Mandrake, Dagwood, Daisy, etc.	8	16	24	42	54	65

TINY TOTS COMICS
Dell Publishing Co.: 1943 (Not reprints)

	GD	VG	FN	VF	VF/NM	NM-
1-Kelly-a(2); fairy tales	39	78	117	240	395	550

TIPPY & CAP STUBBS (See Popular Comics)
Dell Publishing Co.: No. 210, Jan, 1949 - No. 242, Aug, 1949

	GD	VG	FN	VF	VF/NM	NM-
Four Color 210 (#1)	5	10	15	35	63	90
Four Color 242	4	8	12	28	47	65

TIPPY'S FRIENDS GO-GO & ANIMAL
Tower Comics: July, 1966 - No. 15, Oct, 1969 (25¢)

	GD	VG	FN	VF	VF/NM	NM-
1	9	18	27	61	123	185
2-5,7,9-15: 12-15 titled "Tippy's Friend Go-Go"	5	10	15	35	63	90
6-The Monkees photo-c	8	16	24	54	102	150
8-Beatles app. on front/back-c	10	20	30	66	138	210

TIPPY TEEN (See Vicki)
Tower Comics: Nov, 1965 - No. 25, Oct, 1969 (25¢)

	GD	VG	FN	VF	VF/NM	NM-
1	10	20	30	68	144	220
2-4,6-10	6	12	18	40	73	105
5-1 pg. Beatles pin-up	7	14	21	44	82	120
11-20: 16-Twiggy photo-c	6	12	18	37	66	95
21-25	5	10	15	34	60	85
Special Collectors' Editions nn-(1969, 25¢)	6	12	18	37	66	95

TIPPY TERRY
Super/I. W. Enterprises: 1963

	GD	VG	FN	VF	VF/NM	NM-
Super Reprint #14('63)-r/Little Groucho #1	2	4	6	8	10	12
I.W. Reprint #1 (nd)-r/Little Groucho #1	2	4	6	8	10	12

TIP TOP COMICS
United Features #1-188/St. John #189-210/Dell Publishing Co. #211 on:
4/36 - No. 210, 1957; No. 211, 11-1/57-58 - No. 225, 5-7/61

	GD	VG	FN	VF	VF/NM	NM-
1-Tarzan by Hal Foster, Li'l Abner, Broncho Bill, Fritzi Ritz, Ella Cinders, Capt. & The Kids begin; strip-r (1st comic book app. of each)	800	1600	2400	4800	8400	12,000
2-Tarzan-c	181	362	543	1158	1979	2800
3-Tarzan-c	165	330	495	1056	1803	2550
4	94	188	282	597	1024	1450
5-8,10: 7-Photo & biography of Edgar Rice Burroughs. 8-Christmas-c	66	132	198	419	722	1025
9-Tarzan-c	86	172	258	546	936	1325
11,13,16,18-Tarzan-c: 11-Has Tarzan pin-up	65	130	195	416	708	1000
12,14,15,17,19,20: 20-Christmas-c	49	98	147	309	522	735
21,24,27,30-(10/38)-Tarzan-c	53	106	159	334	567	800
22,23,25,26,28,29	39	78	117	229	375	520
31,35,38,40	36	72	108	211	343	475
32,36-Tarzan-c: 32-1st published Jack Davis-a (cartoon). 36-Kurtzman panel (1st published comic work)	54	108	162	343	574	825
33,34,37,39-Tarzan-c	50	100	150	315	533	750
41-Reprints 1st Tarzan Sunday; Tarzan-c	54	108	162	343	574	825
42,44,46,48,49	30	60	90	177	289	400
43,45,47,50,52-Tarzan-c. 43-Mort Walker panel	39	78	117	240	395	550
51,53	29	58	87	170	278	385
54-Origin Mirror Man & Triple Terror, also featured on cover	37	74	111	218	354	490
55,56,58: Last Tarzan by Foster	24	48	72	142	234	325
57,59-62-Tarzan by Hogarth	31	62	93	182	296	410
63-80: 65,67-70,72-74,77,78-No Tarzan	15	30	45	88	137	185
81-90	14	28	42	80	115	150
91-99	13	26	39	72	101	130
100	14	28	42	76	108	140
101-140: 110-Gordo story. 111-Li'l Abner app. 118, 132-No Tarzan. 137-Sadie Hawkins Day story	10	20	30	54	72	90
141-170: 145,151-Gordo stories. 153-Fritzi Ritz lingerie panels. 157-Last Li'l Abner; lingerie panels	8	16	24	44	57	70
171,172,174-183: 171-Tarzan reprints by B. Lubbers begin; end #188	9	18	27	47	61	75
173-Peanuts by Schulz	20	40	60	114	182	250
184-Peanuts app.	14	28	42	80	115	150
185-188-Peanuts stories with Charlie Brown & Snoopy on the covers	75	150	225	450	675	900
189,191-225-Peanuts apps.(4 pg. to 8 pg stories) in most						
Issues with Peanuts	10	20	30	58	79	100
Issues without Peanuts	8	16	24	40	50	60
190-Peanuts with Charlie Brown & Snoopy partial-c (comic strip at bottom of cover)	20	40	60	114	182	250
Bound Volumes (Very Rare) sold at 1939 World's Fair; bound by publisher in pictorial comic boards (also see Comics on Parade)						
Bound issues 1-12 (Rare)	343	686	1029	2400	4200	6000
Bound issues 13-24	181	362	543	1158	1979	2800
Bound issues 25-36	155	310	465	992	1696	2400

NOTE: *Tarzan by **Foster**-#1-40, 44-50; by **Rex Maxon**-#41-43; by **Burne Hogarth**-#57, 59, 62.*

TIP TOPPER COMICS
United Features Syndicate: Oct-Nov, 1949 - No. 28, 1954

	GD	VG	FN	VF	VF/NM	NM-
1-Li'l Abner, Abbie & Slats	14	28	42	76	108	140
2	9	18	27	47	61	75
3-5: 5-Fearless Fosdick app.	8	16	24	42	54	65
6-10: 6-Fearless Fosdick app.	7	14	21	37	46	55
11-16	6	12	18	31	38	45
17(6-7/52) (2nd app. of Peanuts by Schulz in comics?) (see United Comics #22 for 5-6/52 app.)	20	40	60	114	182	250
18-26: 18-24,26-Early Peanuts (2 pgs.). 25-Early Peanuts (3 pgs.) 26-Twin Earths	14	28	42	80	115	150
27,28-Twin Earths	8	16	24	42	54	65

NOTE: *Many lingerie panels in Fritzi Ritz stories.*

TITAN A.E.
Dark Horse Comics: May, 2000 - No. 3, July, 2000 ($2.95, limited series)

	GD	VG	FN	VF	VF/NM	NM-
1-3-Movie prequel; Al Rio-a						3.00

TITANS (Also see Teen Titans, New Teen Titans and New Titans)
DC Comics: Mar, 1999 - No. 50, Apr, 2003 ($2.50/$2.75)

	GD	VG	FN	VF	VF/NM	NM-
1-Titans re-form; Grayson-s; 2 covers						4.00
2-11,13-24,26-50: 2-Superman-c/app. 9,10,21,22-Deathstroke app. 24-Titans from "Kingdom Come" app. 32-36-Asamiya-c. 44-Begin $2.75-c						3.00

Titans East Special #1 © DC

T-Man #17 © QUA

Tomahawk #1 © DC

	GD 2.0	VG 4.0	FN 6.0	VF 8.0	VF/NM 9.0	NM- 9.2
12-($3.50, 48 pages)						4.00
25-($3.95) Titans from "Kingdom Come" app.; Wolfman & Faerber-s; art by Pérez, Cardy, Grumment, Jimenez, Dodson, Pelletier						4.00
Annual 1 ('00, $3.50) Planet DC; intro Bushido						4.00
... East Special 1 (1/08, $3.99) Winick-s/Churchill-a; continues in Titans #1 (2008)						4.00
...Secret Files 1,2 (3/99, 10/00; $4.95) Profile pages & short stories						5.00

TITANS (Also see Teen Titans)
DC Comics: Jun, 2008 - No. 38, Oct, 2011 ($3.50/$2.99)

	GD 2.0	VG 4.0	FN 6.0	VF 8.0	VF/NM 9.0	NM- 9.2
1-($3.50) Titans re-form again; Winick-s/Churchill-a; covers by Churchill & Van Sciver						4.00
2-38: 2-4-Trigon returns. 6-10-Jericho app. 24-Deathstroke & Luthor app.						3.00
Annual 1 (9/11, $4.99) Justice League app.; Jericho returns; Richards-a						5.00
...: Villains For Hire Special 1 (7/10, $4.99) Deathstroke's team; Atom (Ryan Choi) killed						5.00
...: Fractured TPB (2010, $17.99) r/#14,16-22						18.00
...: Lockdown TPB (2009, $14.99) r/#7-11						15.00
...: Old Friends HC (2008, $24.99) r/#1-6 & Titans East Special						25.00
...: Villains For Hire TPB (2011, $14.99) r/#24-27 & Villains For Hire Special 1						15.00

TITANS/ LEGION OF SUPER-HEROES: UNIVERSE ABLAZE
DC Comics: 2000 - No. 4, 2000 ($4.95, prestige format, limited series)

	GD 2.0	VG 4.0	FN 6.0	VF 8.0	VF/NM 9.0	NM- 9.2
1-4-Jurgens-s/a; P. Jimenez-a; teams battle Universo						5.00

TITAN SPECIAL
Dark Horse Comics: June, 1994 ($3.95, one-shot)

	GD 2.0	VG 4.0	FN 6.0	VF 8.0	VF/NM 9.0	NM- 9.2
1-($3.95, 52 pgs.)						4.00

TITANS: SCISSORS, PAPER, STONE
DC Comics: 1997 ($4.95, one-shot)

	GD 2.0	VG 4.0	FN 6.0	VF 8.0	VF/NM 9.0	NM- 9.2
1-Manga style Elseworlds; Adam Warren-s/a(p)						5.00

TITANS SELL-OUT SPECIAL
DC Comics: Nov, 1992 ($3.50, 52 pgs., one-shot)

	GD 2.0	VG 4.0	FN 6.0	VF 8.0	VF/NM 9.0	NM- 9.2
1-Fold-out Nightwing poster; 1st Teeny Titans						4.00

TITANS/ YOUNG JUSTICE: GRADUATION DAY
DC Comics: Early July, 2003 - No. 3, Aug, 2003 ($2.50, limited series)

	GD 2.0	VG 4.0	FN 6.0	VF 8.0	VF/NM 9.0	NM- 9.2
1,2-Winick-s/Garza-a; leads into Teen Titans and The Outsiders series. 2-Lilith dies						3.00
3-Death of Donna Troy (Wonder Girl)						3.00
TPB (2003, $6.95) r/#1-3; plus previews of Teen Titans and The Outsiders series						7.00

T-MAN (Also see Police Comics #103)
Quality Comics Group: Sept, 1951 - No. 38, Dec, 1956

	GD 2.0	VG 4.0	FN 6.0	VF 8.0	VF/NM 9.0	NM- 9.2
1-Pete Trask, T-Man begins; Jack Cole-a	45	90	135	284	480	675
2-Crandall-c	25	50	75	150	245	340
3,7,8: All Crandall-c	23	46	69	136	223	310
4,5-Crandall-c/a each	24	48	72	144	237	330
6-"The Man Who Could Be Hitler" c/story; Crandall-c.	32	64	96	188	307	425
9,10-Crandall-c	20	40	60	120	195	270
11-Used in **POP**, pg. 95 & color illo.	18	36	54	103	162	220
12,13,15-19,22-26: 23-H-Bomb panel. 24-Last pre-code issue (4/55). 25-Not Crandall-a	15	30	45	83	124	165
14-Hitler-c	23	46	69	136	223	310
20-H-Bomb explosion-c/story	18	36	54	107	169	230
21- "The Return of Mussolini" c/story	18	36	54	105	165	225
27-33,35-38	14	28	42	80	115	150
34-Hitler-c	21	42	63	122	199	275

NOTE: *Anti-communist stories common.* ***Crandall*** *c-2-10p.* ***Cuidera*** *c(i)-1-38. Bondage c-15.*

TMNT... (Also see Teenage Mutant Ninja Turtles and related titles)
Mirage Publishing: March 2007 ($3.25/$4.95, B&W, one-shots)

	GD 2.0	VG 4.0	FN 6.0	VF 8.0	VF/NM 9.0	NM- 9.2
...: Raphael Movie Prequel 1; ...: Michelangelo Movie Prequel 2; ...: Donatello Movie Prequel 3; ...: April Movie Prequel 4; ...: Leonardo Movie Prequel 5; back-story for movie						3.25
...: The Official Movie Adaptation ($4.95) adapts 2007 movie; Munroe-c						5.00

TMNT MUTANT UNIVERSE SOURCEBOOK
Archie Comics: 1992 - No. 3, 1992? ($1.95, 52 pgs.)(Lists characters from A-Z)

	GD 2.0	VG 4.0	FN 6.0	VF 8.0	VF/NM 9.0	NM- 9.2
1-3: 3-New characters; fold-out poster						5.00

TNT COMICS
Charles Publishing Co.: Feb, 1946 (36 pgs.)

	GD 2.0	VG 4.0	FN 6.0	VF 8.0	VF/NM 9.0	NM- 9.2
1-Yellowjacket app.	33	66	99	194	317	440

TOBY TYLER (Disney, see Movie Comics)
Dell Publishing Co.: No. 1092, Apr-June, 1960

	GD 2.0	VG 4.0	FN 6.0	VF 8.0	VF/NM 9.0	NM- 9.2
Four Color 1092-Movie, photo-c	6	12	18	37	66	95

TODAY'S BRIDES
Ajax/Farrell Publishing Co.: Nov, 1955; No. 2, Feb, 1956; No. 3, Sept, 1956; No. 4, Nov, 1956

	GD 2.0	VG 4.0	FN 6.0	VF 8.0	VF/NM 9.0	NM- 9.2
1	10	20	30	58	79	100
2-4	8	16	24	42	54	65

TODAY'S ROMANCE
Standard Comics: No. 5, March, 1952 - No. 8, Sept, 1952 (All photo-c?)

	GD 2.0	VG 4.0	FN 6.0	VF 8.0	VF/NM 9.0	NM- 9.2
5-Photo-c	13	26	39	72	101	130
6-Photo-c; Toth-a	13	26	39	74	105	135
7,8	10	20	30	56	76	95

TODD, THE UGLIEST KID ON EARTH
Image Comics: Jan, 2013 - No. 8, Jan, 2014 ($2.99)

	GD 2.0	VG 4.0	FN 6.0	VF 8.0	VF/NM 9.0	NM- 9.2
1-8-Perker-a/Kristensen-s						3.00

TOE TAGS FEATURING GEORGE A. ROMERO
DC Comics: Dec, 2004 - No. 6, May, 2005 ($2.95/$2.99)

	GD 2.0	VG 4.0	FN 6.0	VF 8.0	VF/NM 9.0	NM- 9.2
1-6-Zombie story by George Romero; Wrightson-c/Castillo-a						3.00

TOKA (Jungle King)
Dell Publishing Co.: Aug-Oct, 1964 - No. 10, Jan, 1967 (Painted-c #1,2)

	GD 2.0	VG 4.0	FN 6.0	VF 8.0	VF/NM 9.0	NM- 9.2
1	4	8	12	28	47	65
2	3	6	9	17	26	35
3-10	3	6	9	15	22	28

TOKYO STORM WARNING (See Red/Tokyo Storm Warning for TPB)
DC Comics (Cliffhanger): Aug, 2003 - No. 3, Dec, 2003 ($2.95, limited series)

	GD 2.0	VG 4.0	FN 6.0	VF 8.0	VF/NM 9.0	NM- 9.2
1-3-Warren Ellis-s/James Raiz-a						3.00

TOMAHAWK (Son of... on-c of #131-140; see Star Spangled Comics #69 & World's Finest Comics #65)
National Periodical Publications: Sept-Oct, 1950 - No. 140, May-June, 1972

	GD 2.0	VG 4.0	FN 6.0	VF 8.0	VF/NM 9.0	NM- 9.2
1-Tomahawk & boy sidekick Dan Hunter begin by Fred Ray	181	362	543	1158	1979	2800
2-Frazetta/Williamson-a (4 pgs.)	66	132	198	419	722	1025
3-5	41	82	123	256	428	600
6-10: 7-Last 52 pg. issue	36	72	108	211	343	475
11-20	24	48	72	142	234	325
21-27,30: 30-Last precode (2/55)	21	42	63	126	206	285
28-1st app. Lord Shilling (arch-foe)	22	44	66	132	216	300
29-Frazetta-r/Jimmy Wakely #3 (3 pgs.)	26	52	78	154	252	350
31-40	18	36	54	107	169	230
41-50	9	18	27	61	123	185
51-56,58-60	8	16	24	55	105	155
57-Frazetta-r/Jimmy Wakely #6 (3 pgs.)	9	18	27	61	123	185
61-77: 77-Last 10¢ issue	8	16	24	51	96	140
78-85: 81-1st app. Miss Liberty. 83-Origin Tomahawk's Rangers	6	12	18	42	79	115
86-99: 96-Origin/1st app. The Hood, alias Lady Shilling	5	10	15	34	60	85
100	5	10	15	35	63	90
101-110: 107-Origin/1st app. Thunder-Man	4	8	12	28	47	65
111-115,120,122: 122-Last 12¢ issue	4	8	12	27	44	60
116-1st Neal Adams cover	6	12	18	38	69	100
117-119,121,123-130-Neal Adams-c	5	10	15	30	50	70
131-Frazetta-r/Jimmy Wakely #7 (3 pgs.); origin Firehair retold	3	6	9	21	33	45
132-135: 135-Last 15¢ issue	3	6	9	16	24	32
136-138,140 (52 pg. Giants)	3	6	9	19	30	40
139-Frazetta-r/Star Spangled #113	3	6	9	21	33	45

NOTE: ***Fred Ray*** *c-1, 2, 8, 11, 30, 34, 35, 40-43, 45, 46, 82. Firehair by* ***Kubert****-131-134, 136.* ***Maurer*** *a-138.* ***Severin*** *a-135.* ***Starr*** *a-5.* ***Thorne*** *a-137, 140.*

TOM AND JERRY (See Comic Album #4, 8, 12, Dell Giant #21, Dell Giants, Golden Comics Digest #1, 5, 8, 13, 15, 18, 22, 25, 28, 35, Kite fun Book & March of Comics #21, 46, 61, 70, 88, 103, 119, 128, 145, 154, 173, 190, 207, 224, 281, 295, 305, 321,333, 345, 361, 365, 388, 400, 444, 451, 463, 480)

TOM AND JERRY (...Comics, early issues) (M.G.M.)
(Formerly Our Gang No. 1-59) (See Dell Giants for annuals)
Dell Publishing Co./Gold Key No. 213-327/Whitman No. 328 on: No. 193, 6/48; No. 60, 7/49 - No. 212, 7-9/62; No. 213, 11/62 - No. 291, 2/75; No. 292, 3/77 - No. 342, 5/82 - No. 344, 6/84

	GD 2.0	VG 4.0	FN 6.0	VF 8.0	VF/NM 9.0	NM- 9.2
Four Color 193 (#1)-Titled "M.G.M. Presents..."	22	44	66	154	340	525
60-Barney Bear, Benny Burro cont. from Our Gang; Droopy begins	10	20	30	69	147	225
61	9	18	27	57	111	165
62-70: 66-X-Mas-c	7	14	21	48	89	130
71-80: 77,90-X-Mas-c. 79-Spike & Tyke begin	6	12	18	38	69	100
81-99	5	10	15	35	63	90
100	6	12	18	37	66	95

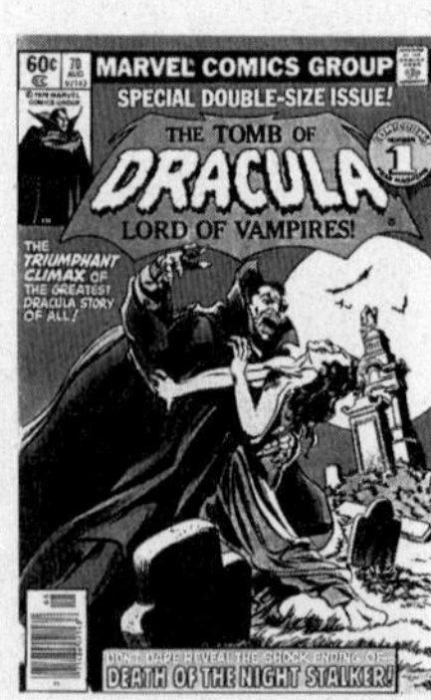

Tomb of Dracula #70 © MAR

Tomb of Terror #14 © HARV

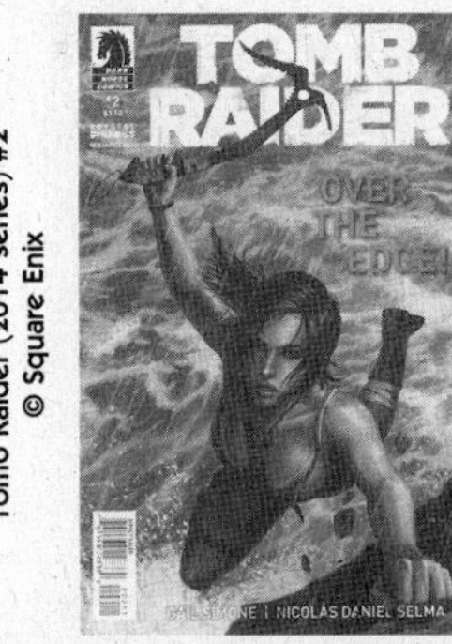

Tomb Raider (2014 series) #2 © Square Enix

GD VG FN VF VF/NM NM-
2.0 4.0 6.0 8.0 9.0 9.2

101-120 5 10 15 31 53 75
121-140: 126-X-Mas-c 4 8 12 28 47 65
141-160 4 8 12 25 40 55
161-200 4 8 12 23 37 50
201-212(7-9/62)(Last Dell issue) 3 6 9 21 33 45
213,214-(84 pgs.)-Titled "...Funhouse" 5 10 15 35 63 90
215-240: 215-Titled "...Funhouse" 3 6 9 16 24 32
241-270 2 4 6 11 16 20
271-300: 286- "Tom & Jerry" 2 4 6 8 11 14
301-327 (Gold Key) 1 3 4 6 8 10
328,329 (Whitman) 2 4 6 8 11 14
330(8/80),331(10/80), 332-(3-pack only) 4 8 12 23 37 50
333-341: 339(2/82), 340(2-3/82), 341(4/82) 2 4 6 8 10 12
342-344 (All #90058, no date, date code, 3-pack): 342(6/83), 343(8/83), 344(6/84)
3 6 9 16 23 30
Mouse From T.R.A.P. 1(7/66)-Giant, G. K. 4 8 12 28 47 65
Summer Fun 1(7/67, 68 pgs.)(Gold Key)-Reprints Barks' Droopy from Summer Fun #1
4 8 12 28 47 65

NOTE: *#60-87, 98-121, 268, 277, 289, 302 are 52 pgs.. Reprints-#225, 241, 245, 247, 252, 254, 266, 268, 270, 292-327, 329-342, 344.*

TOM & JERRY
Harvey Comics: Sept, 1991 - No. 18, Aug, 1994 ($1.25)

1-18: 1-Tom & Jerry, Barney Bear-r by Carl Barks 3.00
50th Anniversary Special 1 (10/91, $2.50, 68 pgs.)-Benny the Lonesome Burro-r by Barks (story/a)/Our Gang #9 4.00

TOMB OF DARKNESS (Formerly Beware)
Marvel Comics Group: No. 9, July, 1974 - No. 23, Nov, 1976

9 3 6 9 19 30 40
10-23: 11,16,18-21-Kirby-a. 15,19-Ditko-r. 17-Woodbridge-r/Astonishing #62; Powell-r. 20-Everett Venus-r/Venus #19. 23-Everett-r 3 6 9 14 20 25
20,21-(30¢-c variants, limited distribution)(5,7/76) 4 8 12 27 44 60

TOMB OF DRACULA (See Giant-Size Dracula, Dracula Lives, Nightstalkers, Power Record Comics & Requiem for Dracula)
Marvel Comics Group: Apr, 1972 - No. 70, Aug, 1979

1-1st app. Dracula & Frank Drake; Colan-p in all; Neal Adams-c
15 30 45 105 233 360
2 8 16 24 51 96 140
3-6: 3-Intro. Dr. Rachel Van Helsing & Inspector Chelm. 6-Neal Adams-c
6 12 18 40 73 105
7-9 5 10 15 35 63 90
10-1st app. Blade the Vampire Slayer (who app. in 1998, 2002 and 2004 movies)
20 40 60 138 307 475
11,14-16,20: 5 10 15 30 50 70
12-2nd app. Blade; Brunner-c(p) 8 16 24 54 102 150
13-Origin Blade 9 18 27 61 123 185
17,19: 17-Blade bitten by Dracula. 19-Blade discovers he is immune to vampire's bite. 1st mention of Blade having vampire blood in him 6 12 18 38 69 100
18-Two-part x-over cont'd in Werewolf by Night #15 5 10 15 35 63 90
21,24-Blade app. 5 10 15 30 50 70
22,23,26,27,29 3 6 9 19 30 40
25-1st app. & origin Hannibal King 4 8 12 27 44 60
25-2nd printing (1994) 2 4 6 8 10 12
28-Blade app. on-c & inside as an illusion 4 8 12 27 44 60
30,41,42,44,45-Blade app. 45-Intro. Deacon Frost, the vampire who bit Blade's mother
4 8 12 25 40 55
31-40 3 6 9 17 26 35
43-Blade-c by Wrightson 4 8 12 28 47 65
43-45-(30¢-c variants, limited distribution) 6 12 18 38 69 100
46,47-(Regular 25¢ editions)(4-8/76) 3 6 9 14 20 25
46,47-(30¢-c variants, limited distribution) 4 8 12 25 40 55
48,49,51-57,59,60: 57,59,60-(30¢-c) 3 6 9 14 20 25
50-Silver Surfer app. 4 8 12 23 37 50
57,59,60-(35¢-c variants)(6-9/77) 4 8 12 23 37 50
58-All Blade issue (Regular 30¢ edition) 4 8 12 28 47 65
58-(35¢-c variant)(7/77) 7 14 21 48 89 130
61-69 3 6 9 14 20 25
70-Double size 4 8 12 23 37 50

NOTE: ***N. Adams** c-1, 6. **Colan** a-1-70p; c(p)-8, 38-42, 44-56, 58-70. **Wrightson** c-43.*

TOMB OF DRACULA, THE (Magazine)
Marvel Comics Group: Oct, 1979 - No. 6, Aug, 1980 (B&W)

1,3: 1-Colan-a; features on movies "Dracula" and "Love at First Bite" w/photos. 3-Good girl cover-a; Miller-a (2 pg. sketch) 2 4 6 11 16 20

GD VG FN VF VF/NM NM-
2.0 4.0 6.0 8.0 9.0 9.2

2,6: 2-Ditko-a (36 pgs.); Nosferatu movie feature. 6-Lilith story w/Sienkiewicz-a
2 4 6 8 11 14
4,5: Stephen King interview 2 4 6 13 18 22

NOTE: ***Buscema** a-4p, 5p. **Chaykin** c-5, 6. **Colan** a(p)-1, 3-6. **Miller** a-3. **Romita** a-2p.*

TOMB OF DRACULA
Marvel Comics (Epic Comics): 1991 - No. 4, 1992 ($4.95, 52 pgs., squarebound, mini-series)

Book 1-4: Colan/Williamson-a; Colan painted-c 5.00

TOMB OF DRACULA
Marvel Comics: Dec, 2004 - No. 4, Mar, 2005 ($2.99, limited series)

1-4-Blade app.; Tolagson-a/Sienkiewicz-c 3.00

TOMB OF DRACULA PRESENTS: THRONE OF BLOOD
Marvel Comics: Jun, 2011 ($3.99, one-shot)

1-Story of Raizo Kodo in 1585 Japan; Parlov-a; Hitch-c 4.00

TOMB OF LEGEIA (See Movie Classics)

TOMB OF TERROR (Thrills of Tomorrow #17 on)
Harvey Publications: June, 1952 - No. 16, July, 1954

1 50 100 150 315 533 750
2 34 68 102 199 325 450
3-Bondage-c; atomic disaster story 34 68 102 204 332 460
4-12: 4-Heart ripped out. 8-12-Nostrand-a 32 64 96 188 307 425
13-Special S/F issue (1/54) 41 82 123 256 428 600
14-Classic S/F-c; Check-a 61 122 183 390 670 950
15-S/F issue; c-shows face exploding 142 284 426 909 1555 2200
16-Special S/F issue; horror-c; Nostrand-a 39 78 117 240 395 550

NOTE: ***Edd Cartier** a-13? **Elias** c-2, 5-16. **Kremer** a-1, 7; c-1. **Nostrand** a-8-12, 15r 16. **Palais** a-2, 3, 5-7. **Powell** a-1, 3, 5, 9-16. **Sparling** a-12, 13, 15.*

TOMB OF TERROR
Marvel Comics: Dec, 2010 ($3.99, B&W, one-shot)

1-Short stories of Man-Thing, Son of Satan, Werewolf By Night & The Living Mummy 4.00

TOMB RAIDER
Dark Horse Comics: Feb, 2014 - Present ($3.50)

1,2-Gail Simone-s/Nicolás Daniel Selma-a 3.50

TOMB RAIDER (one-shots)
Image Comics (Top Cow Prod.)

...: Arabian Nights (8/04, $5.99) Avery-s/Tan-a/c 6.00
... Cover Gallery 2006 (4/06, $2.99) artist galleries and series gallery; pin-ups 3.00
.../The Darkness Special 1 (2001, TopCowStore.com)-Wohl-s/Tan-a 3.00
Epiphany 1 (8/03, $4.99)-Jurgens-s/Banks-a/Haley-c; preview of Witchblade Animated 5.00
Takeover 1 (1/04, $2.99)-Benefiel-a/Daniel-c 3.00
... Vs. The Wolf-Men: Monster War 2005 (7/05, $2.99) 2nd part of Monster War x-over 3.00
.../Witchblade/Magdalena/Vampirella #1 (8/05, $2.99, B&W) three covers; Chin-a 3.00

TOMB RAIDER: JOURNEYS
Image Comics (Top Cow Prod.): Jan, 2002 - No. 12, May, 2003 ($2.50/$2.99)

1-12: 1-Avery-s/Drew Johnson-a. 1-Two covers by Johnson & Hughes 3.00

TOMB RAIDER: THE GREATEST TREASURE OF ALL
Image Comics (Top Cow Prod.): 2002; Oct, 2005 ($6.99)

Prelude (2002, 16 pgs., no cover price) Jusko-c/a 3.00
1-(10/05, $6.99) Jusko-a/Jurgens-s; sketch pages, reference photos, art in progress 7.00

TOMB RAIDER: THE SERIES (Also see Witchblade/Tomb Raider)
Image Comics (Top Cow Prod.): Dec, 1999 - No. 50, Mar, 2005 ($2.50/$2.99)

1-Jurgens-s/Park-a; 3 covers by Park, Finch, Turner 5.00
2-24,26-29,31-50: 21-Black-c w/foil. 31-Mhan-a. 37-Flip book preview of Stryke Force 3.00
25-Michael Turner-c/a; Witchblade app.; Endgame x-over with Witchblade #60 & Evo #1 4.00
30-($4.99) Tony Daniel-a 5.00
#0 (6/01, $2.50) Avery-s/Ching-a/c 3.00
#1/2 (10/01, $2.95) Early days of Lara Croft; Jurgens-s/Lopez-a 3.00
...: Chasing Shangri-La (2002, $12.95, TPB) r/#11-15 13.00
Free Comic Book Day giveaway - (5/02) r/#1 with "Free Comic Book Day" banner on-c 3.00
... Gallery (12/00, $2.95) Pin-ups & previous covers by various 3.00
... Magazine (6/01, $4.95) Hughes-c; r/#1,2; Jurgens interview 5.00
...: Mystic Artifacts (2001, $14.95, TPB) r/#5-10 15.00
...: Saga of the Medusa Mask (9/00, $9.95, TPB) r/#1-4; new Park-c 10.00
... Vol. 1 Compendium (11/06, $59.99) r/#1-50; variant covers and pin-up art 60.00

TOMB RAIDER/WITCHBLADE SPECIAL (Also see Witchblade/Tomb Raider)
Top Cow Prod.: Dec, 1997 (mail-in offer, one-shot)

1-Turner-s/a(p); green background cover 1 3 4 6 8 10
1-Variant-c with orange sun background 1 3 4 6 8 10

Tom Mix Western #20 © FAW

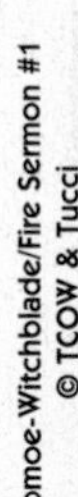

Tomoe-Witchblade/Fire Sermon #1 © TCOW & Tucci

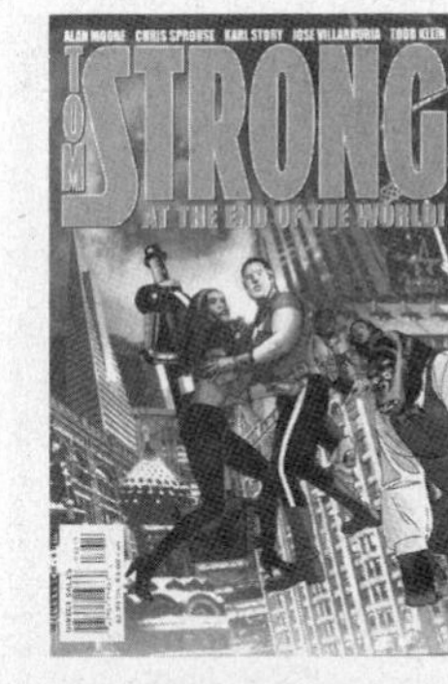

Tom Strong #36 © ABC

	GD 2.0	VG 4.0	FN 6.0	VF 8.0	VF/NM 9.0	NM- 9.2
1-Variant-c with black sides	1	3	4	6	8	10
1-Revisited (12/98, $2.95) reprints #1, Turner-c						3.00
...: Trouble Seekers TPB (2002, $7.95) rep. T.R./W & W/T.R. & W/T.R. 1/2; new Turner-c						8.00

TOMBSTONE TERRITORY
Dell Publishing Co.: No. 1123, Aug, 1960

Four Color 1123	7	14	21	49	92	135

TOM CAT (Formerly Bo; Atom The Cat #9 on)
Charlton Comics: No. 4, Apr, 1956 - No. 8, July, 1957

4-Al Fago-c/a	8	16	24	44	57	70
5-8	6	12	18	31	38	45

TOM CORBETT, SPACE CADET (TV)
Dell Publishing Co.: No. 378, Jan-Feb, 1952 - No. 11, Sept-Nov, 1954 (All painted covers)

Four Color 378 (#1)-McWilliams-a	15	30	45	103	227	350
Four Color 400,421-McWilliams-a	9	18	27	61	123	185
4(11-1/53) - 11	7	14	21	46	86	125

TOM CORBETT SPACE CADET (See March of Comics #102)

TOM CORBETT SPACE CADET (TV)
Prize Publications: V2#1, May-June, 1955 - V2#3, Sept-Oct, 1955

V2#1-Robot-c	34	68	102	199	325	450
2,3-Meskin-c	24	48	72	144	237	330

TOM, DICK & HARRIET (See Gold Key Spotlight)

TOM LANDRY AND THE DALLAS COWBOYS
Spire Christian Comics/Fleming H. Revell Co.: 1973 (35/49¢)

nn-35¢ edition	3	6	9	16	23	30
nn-49¢ edition	2	4	6	10	16	20

TOM MIX WESTERN (Movie, radio star) (Also see The Comics, Crackajack Funnies, Master Comics, 100 Pages Of Comics, Popular Comics, Real Western Hero, Six Gun Heroes, Western Hero & XMas Comics)
Fawcett Publications: Jan, 1948 - No. 61, May, 1953 (1-17: 52 pgs.)

1 (Photo-c, 52 pgs.)-Tom Mix & his horse Tony begin; Tumbleweed Jr. begins, ends #52,54,55	53	106	159	334	567	800
2 (Photo-c)	25	50	75	150	245	340
3-5 (Painted/photo-c): 5-Billy the Kid & Oscar app.	19	38	57	111	176	240
6-8: 6,7 (Painted/photo-c). 8-Kinstler tempera-c	16	32	48	94	147	200
9,10 (Paint/photo-c) 9-Used in **SOTI**, pgs. 323-325	15	30	45	90	140	190
11-Kinstler oil-c	14	28	42	82	121	160
12 (Painted/photo-c)	14	28	42	78	112	145
13-17 (Painted-c, 52 pgs.)	14	28	42	78	112	145
18,22 (Painted-c, 36 pgs.)	12	24	36	69	97	125
19 (Photo-c, 52 pgs.)	13	26	39	74	105	135
20,21,23 (Painted-c, 52 pgs.)	12	24	36	69	97	125
24,25,27-29 (52 pgs.): 24-Photo-c begin, end #61. 29-Slim Pickens app.	11	22	33	60	83	105
26,30 (36 pgs.)	10	20	30	56	76	95
31-33,35-37,39,40,42 (52 pgs.): 39-Red Eagle app.	10	20	30	56	76	95
34,38 (36 pgs. begin)	9	18	27	52	69	85
41,43-60: 57-(9/52)-Dope smuggling story	8	16	24	40	50	60
61-Last issue	9	18	27	47	61	75

NOTE: Photo-c from 1930s Tom Mix movies (he died in 1940). Many issues contain ads for Tom Mix, Rocky Lane, Space Patrol and other premiums. Captain Tootsie by ***C.C. Beck*** *in #6-11, 20.*

TOM MIX WESTERN
AC Comics: 1988 - No. 2, 1989? ($2.95, B&W w/16 pgs. color, 44 pgs.)

1-Tom Mix-r/Master #124,128,131,102 plus Billy the Kid-r by Severin; photo front/back/inside-c						4.00
2-($2.50, B&W)-Gabby Hayes-r; photo covers						4.00
...Holiday Album 1 (1990, $3.50, B&W, one-shot, 44 pgs.)-Contains photos & 1950s Tom Mix-r; photo inside-c						4.00

TOMMY OF THE BIG TOP (Thrilling Circus Adventures)
King Features Synd./Standard Comics: No. 10, Sep, 1948 - No. 12, Mar, 1949

10-By John Lehti	10	20	30	58	79	100
11,12	8	16	24	40	50	60

TOMMYSAURUS REX
Image Comics: Aug, 2004 ($11.95, B&W, graphic novel)

Vol. 1 - Doug TenNapel-s/a						12.00

TOMMY TOMORROW (See Action Comics #127, Real Fact #6, Showcase #41,42,44,46,47 & World's Finest #102)

TOMOE (Also see Shi: The Way Of the Warrior #6)
Crusade Comics: July, 1995 - No. 3, June, 1996($2.95)

	GD 2.0	VG 4.0	FN 6.0	VF 8.0	VF/NM 9.0	NM- 9.2
0-3: 2-B&W Dogs o' War preview. 3-B&W Demon Gun preview						3.00
0 (3/96, $2.95)-variant-c.						3.00
0-Commemorative edition (5,000)	2	4	6	8	10	12
1-Commemorative edition (5,000)	2	4	6	9	12	15
1-($2.95)-FAN Appreciation edition						3.00
TPB (1997, $14.95) r/#0-3						15.00

TOMOE: UNFORGETTABLE FIRE
Crusade Comics: June, 1997 ($2.95, one-shot)

1-Prequel to Shi: The Series						3.00

TOMOE-WITCHBLADE/FIRE SERMON
Crusade Comics: Sept, 1996 ($3.95, one-shot)

1-Tucci-c						5.00
1-($9.95)-Avalon Ed. w/gold foil-c						10.00

TOMOE-WITCHBLADE/MANGA SHI PREVIEW EDITION
Crusade Comics: July, 1996 ($5.00, B&W)

nn-San Diego Preview Edition						5.00

TOMORROW KNIGHTS
Marvel Comics (Epic Comics): June, 1990 - No. 6, Mar, 1991 ($1.50)

1-($1.95, 52 pgs.)						4.00
2-6						3.00

TOMORROW STORIES
America's Best Comics: Oct, 1999 - No. 12, Aug, 2002 ($3.50/$2.95)

1-Two covers by Ross and Nowlan; Moore-s						4.00
2-12-($2.95)						3.00
... Special (1/06, $6.99) Nowlan-c; Moore-s; Greyshirt tribute to Will Eisner						7.00
... Special 2 (5/06, $6.99) Gene Ha-c; Moore-s; Promethea app.						7.00
Book 1 Hardcover (2002, $24.95) r/#1-6						25.00
Book 1 TPB (2003, $17.95) r/#1-6						18.00
Book 2 Hardcover (2004, $24.95) r/#7-12						25.00
Book 2 TPB (2005, $17.99) r/#7-12						18.00

TOM SAWYER (See Adventures of... & Famous Stories)

TOM SKINNER-UP FROM HARLEM (See Up From Harlem)

TOM STRONG (Also see Many Worlds of Tesla Strong)
America's Best Comics: June, 1999 - No. 36, May, 2006 ($3.50/$2.95/$2.99)

1-Two covers by Ross and Sprouse; Moore-s/Sprouse-a						4.00
1-Special Edition (9/09, $1.00) reprint with "After Watchmen" cover frame						3.00
2-36: 4-Art Adams-a (8 pgs.) 13-Fawcett homage w/art by Sprouse, Baker, Heath 20-Origin of Tom Stone. 22-Ordway-a. 31,32-Moorcock-s						3.00
...: Book One HC ('00, $24.95) r/#1-7, cover gallery and sketchbook						25.00
...: Book One TPB ('01, $14.95) r/#1-7, cover gallery and sketchbook						15.00
...: Book Two HC ('02, $24.95) r/#8-14, sketchbook						25.00
...: Book Two TPB ('03, $14.95) r/#8-14, sketchbook						15.00
...: Book Three HC ('04, $24.95) r/#15-19, sketchbook						25.00
...: Book Three TPB ('04, $17.95) r/#15-19, sketchbook						18.00
...: Book Four HC ('04, $24.95) r/#20-25, sketch pages						25.00
...: Book Four TPB ('05, $17.99) r/#20-25, sketch pages						18.00
...: Book Five HC ('05, $24.99) r/#26-30, sketch pages						25.00
...: Book Five TPB ('06, $17.99) r/#26-30, sketch pages						18.00
...: Book Six HC ('06, $24.99) r/#31-36						25.00
...: Book Six TPB ('08, $17.99) r/#31-36						18.00
...: The Deluxe Edition Book One (2009, $39.99, d.j.) r/#1-12; Moore intro.; sketch-a						40.00
...: The Deluxe Edition Book Two (2010, $39.99, d.j.) r/#13-24; sketch-a						40.00

TOM STRONG AND THE PLANET OF PERIL
DC Comics (Vertigo): Sept, 2013 - No. 6, Feb, 2014 ($2.99, limited series)

1-6-Hogan-s/Sprouse-a/c. 2-Travel to Terra Obscura						3.00

TOM STRONG AND THE ROBOTS OF DOOM
DC Comics (WildStorm): Aug, 2010 - No. 6, Jan, 2011 ($3.99, limited series)

1-6-Hogan-s/Sprouse-a. 1-Covers by Sprouse & Williams						4.00
TPB (2011, $17.99) r/#1-6						18.00

TOM STRONG'S TERRIFIC TALES
America's Best Comics: Jan, 2002 - No. 12 ($3.50/$2.95)

1-Short stories; Moore-s; art by Adams, Rivoche, Hernandez, Weiss						3.50
2-12-($2.95) 2-Adams, Ordway, Weiss-a; Adams-c. 4-Rivoche-a. 5-Pearson, Aragonés-a 11-Timm-a						3.00
...: Book One HC ('04, $24.95) r/#1-6, cover gallery and sketch pages						25.00
...: Book One SC ('05, $17.99) r/#1-6, cover gallery and sketch pages						18.00
...: Book Two HC ('05, $24.95) r/#7-12, covers						25.00

Too Much Coffee Man Special #1 © Shannon Wheeler

Top Cat #21 © H-B

Top Comics #2 Porky Pig © WB

	GD 2.0	VG 4.0	FN 6.0	VF 8.0	VF/NM 9.0	NM- 9.2

TOM TERRIFIC! (TV)(See Mighty Mouse Fun Club Magazine #1)
Pines Comics (Paul Terry): Summer, 1957 - No. 6, Fall, 1958
(See Terry Toons Giant Summer Fun Book)

1-1st app.?; CBS Television Presents...	21	42	63	126	206	285
2-6-(scarce)	16	32	48	94	147	200

TOM THUMB
Dell Publishing Co.: No. 972, Jan, 1959

Four Color 972-Movie, George Pal	8	16	24	51	96	140

TOM-TOM, THE JUNGLE BOY (See A-1 Comics & Tick Tock Tales)
Magazine Enterprises: 1947 - No. 3, 1947; Nov, 1957 - No. 3, Mar, 1958

1-Funny animal	12	24	36	67	94	120
2,3(1947): 3-Christmas issue	9	18	27	50	65	80
Tom-Tom & Itchi the Monk 1(11/57) - 3(3/58)	5	10	15	24	30	35
I.W. Reprint No. 1,2,8,10: 1,2,8-r/Koko & Kola #?	2	4	6	8	10	12

TONGUE LASH
Dark Horse Comics: Aug, 1996 - No. 2, Sept, 1996 ($2.95, lim. series, mature)

1,2: Taylor-c/a 3.00

TONGUE LASH II
Dark Horse Comics: Feb, 1999 - No. 2, Mar, 1999 ($2.95, lim. series, mature)

1,2: Taylor-c/a 3.00

TONKA (Disney)
Dell Publishing Co.: No. 966, Jan, 1959

Four Color 966-Movie (Starring Sal Mineo)-photo-c	8	16	24	51	96	140

TONTO (See The Lone Ranger's Companion...)

TONY TRENT (The Face #1,2)
Big Shot/Columbia Comics Group: No. 3, 1948 - No. 4, 1949

3,4: 3-The Face app. by Mart Bailey	18	36	54	105	165	225

TOODLES, THE (The Toodle Twins with #1)
Ziff-Davis (Approved Comics)/Argo: No. 10, July-Aug, 1951; Mar, 1956 (Newspaper-r)

10-Painted-c, some newspaper-r by The Baers	14	28	42	76	108	140
...Twins 1(Argo, 3/56)-Reprints by The Baers	8	16	24	42	54	65

TOO MUCH COFFEE MAN
Adhesive Comics: July, 1993 - No. 10, Dec, 2000 ($2.50, B&W)

1-Shannon Wheeler story & art	2	4	6	9	12	15
2,3	1	2	3	5	7	9
4,5						6.00
6-10						4.00
Full Color Special-nn($2.95),2-(7/97, $3.95)						4.00

TOO MUCH COFFEE MAN SPECIAL
Dark Horse Comics: July, 1997 ($2.95, B&W)

nn-Reprints Dark Horse Presents #92-95 4.00

TOO MUCH HOPELESS SAVAGES
Oni Press: June, 2003 - No. 4, Apr, 2004 ($2.99, B&W, limited series)

1-4-Van Meter-s/Norrie-a 3.00
TPB (8/04, $11.95, digest-size) r/series 12.00

TOOTS AND CASPER
Dell Publishing Co.: No. 5, 1942

Large Feature Comic 5	21	42	63	122	199	275

TOP ADVENTURE COMICS
I. W. Enterprises: 1964 (Reprints)

1-r/High Adv. (Explorer Joe #2); Krigstein-r	2	4	6	11	16	20
2-Black Dwarf-r/Red Seal #22; Kinstler-c	2	4	6	13	18	22

TOP CAT (TV) (Hanna-Barbera)(See Kite Fun Book)
Dell Publishing Co./Gold Key No. 4 on: 12-2/61-62 - No. 3, 6-8/62; No. 4, 10/62 - No. 31, 9/70

1 (TV show debuted 9/27/61)	13	26	39	86	188	290
2-Augie Doggie back-ups in #1-4	7	14	21	48	89	130
3-5: 3-Last 15¢ issue. 4-Begin 12¢ issues; Yakky Doodle app. in 1 pg. strip. 5-Touché Turtle app.	6	12	18	37	66	95
6-10	5	10	15	30	50	70
11-20	4	8	12	23	37	50
21-31-Reprints	3	6	9	18	28	38

TOP CAT (TV) (Hanna-Barbera)(See TV Stars #4)
Charlton Comics: Nov, 1970 - No. 20, Nov, 1973

1	5	10	15	35	63	90
2-10	3	6	9	19	30	40
11-20	3	6	9	16	24	32

NOTE: *#8 (1/72) went on sale late in 1972 between #14 and #15 with the 1/73 issues.*

TOP COMICS
K. K. Publications/Gold Key: July, 1967 (All reprints)

nn-The Gnome-Mobile (Disney-movie)	2	4	6	13	18	22
1-Beagle Boys (#7), Beep Beep the Road Runner (#5), Bugs Bunny, Chip 'n' Dale, Daffy Duck (#50), Flipper, Huey, Dewey & Louie, Junior Woodchucks, Lassie, The Little Monsters (#71), Moby Duck, Porky Pig (has Gold Key label - says Top Comics on inside), Scamp, Super Goof, Tom & Jerry, Top Cat (#21), Tweety & Sylvester (#7), Walt Disney C&S (#322), Woody Woodpecker known issues; each character given own book	2	4	6	9	13	16
1-Donald Duck (not Barks), Mickey Mouse	2	4	6	13	18	22
1-Flintstones	3	6	9	21	33	45
1-Huckleberry Hound, Yogi Bear (#30)	3	6	9	14	19	24
1-The Jetsons	4	8	12	28	47	65
1-Tarzan of the Apes (#169)	3	6	9	15	22	28
1-Three Stooges (#35)	3	6	9	17	26	35
1-Uncle Scrooge (#70)	3	6	9	16	23	30
1-Zorro (r/G.K. Zorro #7 w/Toth-a; says 2nd printing)	3	6	9	14	19	24
2-Bugs Bunny, Daffy Duck, Mickey Mouse (#114), Porky Pig, Super Goof, Tom & Jerry, Tweety & Sylvester, Walt Disney's C&S (r/#325), Woody Woodpecker	2	4	6	9	12	15
2-Donald Duck (not Barks), Three Stooges, Uncle Scrooge (#71)-Barks-c, Yogi Bear (#30), Zorro (r/#8; Toth-a)	2	4	6	11	16	20
2-Snow White & 7 Dwarfs(6/67)(1944-r)	2	4	6	10	14	18
3-Donald Duck	2	4	6	11	16	20
3-Uncle Scrooge (#72)	2	4	6	13	18	22
3,4-The Flintstones	3	6	9	21	33	45
3,4: 3-Mickey Mouse (r/#115), Tom & Jerry, Woody Woodpecker, Yogi Bear. 4-Mickey Mouse, Woody Woodpecker	2	4	6	9	12	15

NOTE: *Each book in this series is identical to its counterpart except for cover, and came out at same time. The number in parentheses is the original issue it contains.*

TOP COW (Company one-shots)
Image Comics (Top Cow Productions)

... Book of Revelations (7/03, $3.99)-Pin-ups and info; art by various; Gossett-c 4.00
... Convention Sketchbook 2004 (4/04, $3.00, B&W) art by various 3.00
... Holiday Special Vol. 1 (12/10, $12.99) Flip book with Jingle Belle 13.00
... Preview Book 2005 (3/05, 99¢) Preview pages of Tomb Raider, Darkness, Rising Stars 3.00
... Productions, Inc./Ballistic Studios Swimsuit Special (5/95, $2.95) 3.00
...'s Best of: Dave Finch Vol. 1 TPB (8/06, $19.99) r/issues of Cyberforce, Aphrodite IX, Ascension and The Darkness; art & cover gallery 20.00
...'s Best of: Michael Turner Vol. 1 TPB (12/05, $24.99) r/Witchblade #1,10,12,18,19,25 & Witchblade/Tomb Raider chapters 1&3; Tomb Raider #25; art & cover gallery 25.00
... Secrets: Special Winter Lingerie Edition 1 (1/96, $2.95) Pin-ups 3.00
... 2001 Preview (no cover price) Preview pages of Tomb Raider; Jusko-a; flip cover & pages of Inferno 3.00

TOP COW CLASSICS IN BLACK AND WHITE
Image Comics (Top Cow): Feb, 2000 - Present ($2.95, B&W reprints)

...: Aphrodite IX #1(9/00) B&W reprint 3.00
...: Ascension #1(4/00) B&W reprint plus time-line of series 3.00
...: Battle of the Planets #1(1/03) B&W reprint plus script and cover gallery 3.00
...: Darkness #1(3/00) B&W reprint plus time-line of series 3.00
...: Fathom #1(5/00) B&W reprint 3.00
...: Magdalena #1(10/02) B&W reprint plus time-line of series 3.00
...: Midnight Nation #1(9/00) B&W preview 3.00
...: Rising Stars #1(7/00) B&W reprint plus cover gallery 3.00
...: Tomb Raider #1(12/00) B&W reprint plus back-story 3.00
...: Witchblade #1(2/00) B&W reprint plus back-story 3.00
...: Witchblade #25(5/01) B&W reprint plus interview with Wohl & Haberlin 3.00

TOP DETECTIVE COMICS
I. W. Enterprises: 1964 (Reprints)

9-r/Young King Cole #14; Dr. Drew (not Grandenetti)	2	4	6	10	14	18

TOP DOG (See Star Comics Magazine, 75¢)
Star Comics (Marvel): Apr, 1985 - No. 14, June, 1987 (Children's book)

1-14: 10-Peter Parker & J. Jonah Jameson cameo 5.00

TOP ELIMINATOR (Teenage Hotrodders #1-24; Drag 'n' Wheels #30 on)
Charlton Comics: No. 25, Sept, 1967 - No. 29, July, 1968

25-29	3	6	9	16	23	30

TOP FLIGHT COMICS: Four Star Publ.: 1947 (Advertised, not published)

Topix #9 © CG

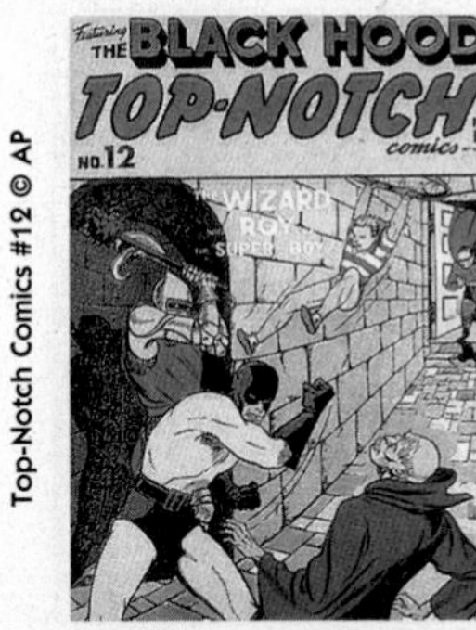

Top-Notch Comics #12 © AP

Top Spot Comics #1 © Top Spot

TOP FLIGHT COMICS
St. John Publishing Co.: July, 1949

	GD 2.0	VG 4.0	FN 6.0	VF 8.0	VF/NM 9.0	NM- 9.2
1(7/49, St. John)-Hector the Inspector; funny animal	10	20	30	56	76	95

TOP GUN (See Luke Short, 4-Color #927 & Showcase #72)

TOP GUNS OF THE WEST (See Super DC Giant)

TOPIX (...Comics) (Timeless Topix-early issues) (Also see Men of Battle, Men of Courage & Treasure Chest)(V1-V5#1,V7 on-paper-c)
Catechetical Guild Educational Society: 11/42 - V10#15, 1/28/52
(Weekly - later issues)

	GD 2.0	VG 4.0	FN 6.0	VF 8.0	VF/NM 9.0	NM- 9.2
V1#1(8 pgs.,8x11")	24	48	72	140	230	320
2,3(8 pgs.,8x11")	14	28	42	80	115	150
4-8(16 pgs.,8x11")	11	22	33	64	90	115
V2#1-10(16 pgs.,8x11"): V2#8-Pope Pius XII	10	20	30	56	76	95
V3#1-10(16 pgs.,8x11"): V3#1-(9/44)	10	20	30	54	72	90
V4#1-10: V4#1-(9/45)	9	18	27	47	61	75
V5#1(10/46,52 pgs.,2(11/46),no #3),4(1/47)-9(6/47),10(7/47), no #13,4(10/47), 14(11/47),15(12/47)	8	16	24	40	50	60
11(8/47),12(9/47)-Life of Christ editions	10	20	30	54	72	90
V6#4(1/48),5(2/48),7(3/48),8(4/48),9(5/48),10(6/48),11(7/48)-14 (no #1-3,6)	7	14	21	35	43	50
V7#1(9/1/48)-20(6/15/49), 36 pgs.	6	12	18	29	36	42
V8#1(9/19/49)-3,5-11,13-30(5/15/50)	6	12	18	28	34	40
4-Dagwood Splits the Atom(10/10/49)-Magazine format	8	16	24	42	54	65
12-Ingels-a	10	20	30	54	72	90
V9#1(9/25/50)-11,13-30(5/14/51)	6	12	18	27	33	38
12-Special 36 pg. Xmas issue, text illos format	6	12	18	28	34	40
V10#1(10/1/51)-15: 14-Hollingsworth-a	6	12	18	27	33	38

TOP JUNGLE COMICS
I. W. Enterprises: 1964 (Reprint)

	GD 2.0	VG 4.0	FN 6.0	VF 8.0	VF/NM 9.0	NM- 9.2
1(nd)-Reprints White Princess of the Jungle #3, minus cover; Kintsler-a	3	6	9	16	23	30

TOP LOVE STORIES (Formerly Gasoline Alley #2)
Star Publications: No. 3, 5/51 - No. 19, 3/54

	GD 2.0	VG 4.0	FN 6.0	VF 8.0	VF/NM 9.0	NM- 9.2
3(#1)	22	44	66	132	216	300
4,5,7-9: 8-Wood story	19	38	57	111	176	240
6-Wood-a	24	48	72	140	230	320
10-16,18,19-Disbrow-a	19	38	57	111	176	240
17-Wood art (Fox-r)	20	40	60	114	182	250

NOTE: *All have **L. B. Cole** covers.*

TOP-NOTCH COMICS (...Laugh #28-45; Laugh Comix #46 on)
MLJ Magazines: Dec, 1939 - No. 45, June, 1944

	GD 2.0	VG 4.0	FN 6.0	VF 8.0	VF/NM 9.0	NM- 9.2
1-Origin/1st app. The Wizard; Kardak the Mystic Magician, Swift of the Secret Service (ends #3), Air Patrol, The Westpointer, Manhunters (by J. Cole), Mystic (ends #2) & Scott Rand (ends #3) begin; Wizard covers begin, end #8	530	1060	1590	3869	6835	9800
2-(1/40)-Dick Storm (ends #8), Stacy Knight M.D. (ends #4) begin; Jack Cole-a; 1st app. Nazis swastika on-c	255	510	765	1632	2791	3950
3-Bob Phantom, Scott Rand on Mars begin; J. Cole-a	177	354	531	1133	1942	2750
4-Origin/1st app. Streak Chandler on Mars; Moore of the Mounted only app.; J. Cole-a	155	310	465	992	1696	2400
5-Flag-c; origin/1st app. Galahad; Shanghai Sheridan begins (ends #8); Shield cameo; Novick-a; classic-c	177	354	531	1133	1942	2750
6-Meskin-a	118	236	354	755	1290	1825
7-The Shield x-over in Wizard; The Wizard dons new costume	148	296	444	947	1624	2300
8-Origin/1st app. The Firefly & Roy, the Super Boy (9/40, 2nd costumed boy hero after Robin?; also see Toro in Human Torch #1 (Fall/40)	155	310	465	992	1696	2400
9-Origin & 1st app. The Black Hood; 1st Black Hood-c & logo (10/40); Fran Frazier begins (Scarce)	649	1298	1947	4738	8369	12,000
10-2nd app. Black Hood	219	438	657	1402	2401	3400
11-3rd Black Hood	135	270	405	864	1482	2100
12-15	116	232	348	742	1271	1800
16-18,20	103	206	309	659	1130	1600
19-Classic bondage-c	110	220	330	704	1202	1700
21-30: 23-26-Roy app. 24-No Wizard. 25-Last Bob Phantom. 27-Last Firefly; Nazi war-c. 28-Suzie, Pokey Oakey begin. 29-Last Kardak	71	142	213	454	777	1100
31-44: 33-Dotty & Ditto by Woggon begins (2/43, 1st app.). 44-Black Hood series ends	42	84	126	267	451	635
45-Last issue	47	94	141	296	498	700

NOTE: ***J. Binder** a-1-3. **Meskin** a-2, 3, 6, 15. **Bob Montana** a-30; c-28-31. **Harry Sahle** c-42-45. **Woggon** a-33-40, 42. Bondage c-17, 19. Black Hood also appeared on radio in 1944.Black Hood app. on c-9-34, 41-44. Roy the Super Boy app. on c-8, 9, 11-27. The Wizard app. on c-1-8, 11-13, 15-22, 24, 25, 27. Pokey Oakey app. on c-28-43. Suzie app. on c-44-on.*

TOPPER & NEIL (TV)
Dell Publishing Co.: No. 859, Nov, 1957

	GD 2.0	VG 4.0	FN 6.0	VF 8.0	VF/NM 9.0	NM- 9.2
Four Color 859	5	10	15	30	50	70

TOPPS COMICS: Four Star Publications: 1947 (Advertised, not published)

TOPS
July, 1949 - No. 2, Sept, 1949 (25¢, 10-1/4x13-1/4", 68 pgs.)
Tops Magazine, Inc. (Lev Gleason): (Large size-magazine format; for the adult reader)

	GD 2.0	VG 4.0	FN 6.0	VF 8.0	VF/NM 9.0	NM- 9.2
1 (Rare)-Story by Dashiell Hammett; Crandall/Lubbers, Tuska, Dan Barry, Fuje-a; Biro painted-c	226	452	678	1446	2473	3500
2 (Rare)-Crandall/Lubbers, Biro, Kida, Fuje, Guardineer-a	194	388	582	1242	2121	3000

TOPS COMICS
Consolidated Book Publishers: 1944 (10¢, 132 pgs.)

	GD 2.0	VG 4.0	FN 6.0	VF 8.0	VF/NM 9.0	NM- 9.2
2000-(Color-c, inside in red shade & some in full color)-Ace Kelly by Rick Yager, Black Orchid, Don on the Farm, Dinky Dinkerton (Rare)	37	74	111	222	361	500

NOTE: *This book is printed in such a way that when the staple is removed, the strips on the left side of the book correspond with the same strips on the right side. Therefore, if strips are removed from the book, each strip can be folded into a complete comic section of its own.*

TOPS COMICS (See Tops in Humor)
Consolidated Book (Lev Gleason): 1944 (7-1/4x5", 32 pgs.)

	GD 2.0	VG 4.0	FN 6.0	VF 8.0	VF/NM 9.0	NM- 9.2
2001-The Jack of Spades (costumed hero)	21	42	63	122	199	275
2002-Rip Raider	14	28	42	80	115	150
2003-Red Birch (gag cartoons)	9	18	27	47	61	75
2004-Gag cartoons	17	34	51	98	154	210

TOP SECRET
Hillman Publ.: Jan, 1952

	GD 2.0	VG 4.0	FN 6.0	VF 8.0	VF/NM 9.0	NM- 9.2
1	21	42	63	122	199	275

TOP SECRET ADVENTURES (See Spyman)

TOP SECRETS (...of the F.B.I.)
Street & Smith Publications: Nov, 1947 - No. 10, July-Aug, 1949

	GD 2.0	VG 4.0	FN 6.0	VF 8.0	VF/NM 9.0	NM- 9.2
1-Powell-c/a	36	72	108	211	343	475
2-Powell-c/a	25	50	75	147	241	335
3-6,8,10-Powell-a	22	44	66	132	216	300
9-Powell-c/a	23	46	69	136	223	310
7-Used in **SOTI**, pg. 90 & illo. "How to hurt people"; used by N.Y. Legis. Comm.; Powell-c/a	34	68	102	206	336	465

NOTE: ***Powell** c-1-3, 5-10.*

TOPS IN ADVENTURE
Ziff-Davis Publishing Co.: Fall, 1952 (25¢, 132 pgs.)

	GD 2.0	VG 4.0	FN 6.0	VF 8.0	VF/NM 9.0	NM- 9.2
1-Crusader from Mars, The Hawk, Football Thrills, He-Man; Powell-a; painted-c	49	98	147	309	522	735

TOPS IN HUMOR (See Tops Comics?)
Consolidated Book Publ. (Lev Gleason)/Wise Publs.: 1944 (7-1/4x5", #2 digest size)

	GD 2.0	VG 4.0	FN 6.0	VF 8.0	VF/NM 9.0	NM- 9.2
2001(#1)-Origin The Jack of Spades, Ace Kelly by Rick Yager, Black Orchid (female crime fighter) app.	20	40	60	114	182	250
2-Wise Publs.; WWII serviceman humor	14	28	42	76	108	140

TOP SPOT COMICS
Top Spot Publ. Co.: 1945

	GD 2.0	VG 4.0	FN 6.0	VF 8.0	VF/NM 9.0	NM- 9.2
1-The Menace, Duke of Darkness app.	37	74	111	222	361	500

TOPSY-TURVY (Teenage)
R. B. Leffingwell Publ.: Apr, 1945

	GD 2.0	VG 4.0	FN 6.0	VF 8.0	VF/NM 9.0	NM- 9.2
1-1st app. Cookie	20	40	60	114	182	250

TOP TEN
America's Best Comics: Sept, 1999 - No. 12, Oct, 2001 ($3.50/$2.95)

	NM- 9.2
1-Two covers by Ross and Ha/Cannon; Alan Moore-s/Gene Ha-a	3.50
2-11-($2.95)	3.00
12-($3.50)	3.50
Hardcover ('00, $24.95) Dust jacket with Gene Ha-a; r/#1-7	25.00
Softcover ('00, $14.95) new Gene Ha-c; r/#1-7	15.00
Book 2 HC ('02, $24.95) Dust jacket with Gene Ha-a; r/#8-12	25.00
Book 2 SC ('03, $14.95) new Gene Ha-c; r/#8-12	15.00
...: The Forty-Niners HC (2005, $24.99, dust jacket) prequel set in 1949; Moore-s/Ha-a	25.00

Torchy #3 © QUA

Total Justice #3 © DC

Tower of Shadows #4 © MAR

GD 2.0 | VG 4.0 | FN 6.0 | VF 8.0 | VF/NM 9.0 | NM- 9.2

TOP TEN: BEYOND THE FARTHEST PRECINCT
America's Best Comics: Oct, 2005 - No. 5, Feb, 2006 ($2.99, limited series)
1-5-Jerry Ordway-a/Paul DiFilippo-s 3.00
TPB (2006, $14.99) r/series; cover sketch pages 15.00

TOP TEN SEASON TWO
America's Best Comics: Dec, 2008 - No. 4, Mar, 2009 ($2.99, limited series)
1-4-Cannon-s/Ha-a 3.00
... Special (5/09, $2.99) Cannon-s/Daxiong-a/Ha-c 3.00

TOR (Prehistoric Life on Earth) (Formerly One Million Years Ago)
St. John Publ. Co.: No. 2, Oct, 1953; No. 3, May, 1954 - No. 5, Oct, 1954
3-D 2(10/53)-Kubert-c/a 14 28 42 76 108 140
3-D 2(10/53)-Oversized, otherwise same contents 12 24 36 67 94 120
3-D 2(11/53)-Kubert-c/a; has 3-D cover 12 24 36 67 94 120
3-5-Kubert-c/a: 3-Danny Dreams by Toth; Kubert 1 pg. story (w/self portrait)
14 28 42 76 108 140
NOTE: *The two October 3-D's have same contents and* **Powell** *art; the October & November issues are titled 3-D Comics. All 3-D issues are 25¢ and came with 3-D glasses.*

TOR (See Sojourn)
National Periodical Publications: May-June, 1975 - No. 6, Mar-Apr, 1976
1-New origin by Kubert 2 4 6 9 13 16
2-6: 2-Origin-r/St. John #1 1 2 3 5 6 8
NOTE: ***Kubert*** *a-1, 2-6r; c-1-6.* ***Toth*** *a(p)-3r.*

TOR (3-D)
Eclipse Comics: July, 1986 - No. 2, Aug, 1987 ($2.50)
1,2: 1-r/One Million Years Ago. 2-r/Tor 3-D #2 5.00
...2-D: 1,2-Limited signed & numbered editions 1 3 4 6 8 10

TOR
Marvel Comics (Epic Comics/Heavy Hitters): June, 1993 - No. 4, 1993 ($5.95, lim. series)
1-4: Joe Kubert-c/a/scripts 6.00

TOR (Joe Kubert's...)
DC Comics: Jul, 2008 - No. 6, Dec, 2008 ($2.99, limited series)
1-6-New story; Joe Kubert-c/a/scripts 3.00
...: A Prehistoric Odyssey HC (2009, $24.99, DJ) r/#1-6; Roy Thomas intro.; sketch-a 25.00
...: A Prehistoric Odyssey SC (2010, $14.99) r/#1-6; Roy Thomas intro.; sketch-a 15.00

TOR BY JOE KUBERT
DC Comics: 2001 - 2003 ($49.95, hardcovers with dust jacket)
Volume 1 (2001) r/One Million Years Ago #1 & 3-D Comics #1&2 in flat color; script pages, sketch pages, proposals for TV and newspapers strips; intro. by Roy Thomas 50.00
Volume 2 (2002) r/Tor (St. John) #3-5; Danny Dreams; portfolio section 50.00
Volume 3 (2003) r/Tor (DC '75) #1; (Marvel '93) #1-4; portfolio section 50.00

TORCH, THE
Marvel Comics (with Dynamite Ent.): Nov, 2009 - No. 8, Jul, 2010 ($3.99, limited series)
1-8-Thinker resurrects the Golden Age Human Torch; Toro app; Alex Ross-c on all; Berkenkotter-a. 3-5-Namor app. 4.00

TORCH OF LIBERTY SPECIAL
Dark Horse Comics (Legend): Jan, 1995 ($2.50, one-shot)
1-Byrne scripts 3.00

TORCHWOOD (Based on the BBC TV series)
Titan Comics: Sept, 2010 - No. 6, Jan, 2011 ($3.99)
1-6: 1-Barrowman-s/Edwards-a; Churchill & photo-c. 2-Art by Yeowell & Grist 4.00

TORCHY (...Blonde Bombshell) (See Dollman, Military, & Modern)
Quality Comics Group: Nov, 1949 - No. 6, Sept, 1950
1-Bill Ward-c, Gil Fox-a 187 374 561 1197 2049 2900
2,3-Fox-c/a 79 158 237 502 864 1225
4-Fox-c/a(3), Ward-a (9 pgs.) 95 190 285 608 1042 1475
5,6-Ward-c/a, 9 pgs; Fox-a(3) each 110 220 330 704 1202 1700
Super Reprint #16(1964)-r/#4 with new-c 7 14 21 49 92 135

TO RIVERDALE AND BACK AGAIN (Archie Comics Presents...)
Archie Comics: 1990 ($2.50, 68 pgs.)
nn-Byrne-c, Colan-a(p); adapts NBC TV movie 5.00

TORMENTED, THE (Becomes Surprise Adventures #3 on)
Sterling Comics: July, 1954 - No. 2, Sept, 1954
1,2: Weird/Horror stories 32 64 96 188 307 425

TORNADO TOM (See Mighty Midget Comics)

TORSO (See Jinx: Torso)

TOTAL ECLIPSE
Eclipse Comics: May, 1988 - No. 5, Apr, 1989 ($3.95, 52 pgs., deluxe size)
Book 1-5: 3-Intro/1st app. new Black Terror. 4-Many copies have upside down pages and are mis-cut 5.00

TOTAL ECLIPSE
Image Comics: July, 1998 (one-shot)
1-McFarlane-c; Eclipse Comics character pin-ups by Image artists 3.00

TOTAL ECLIPSE: THE SERAPHIM OBJECTIVE
Eclipse Comics: Nov, 1988 ($1.95, one-shot, Baxter paper)
1-Airboy, Valkyrie, The Heap app. 3.00

TOTAL JUSTICE
DC Comics: Oct, 1996 - No. 3, Nov, 1996 ($2.25, bi-weekly limited series) (Based on toyline)
1-3 3.00

TOTAL RECALL (Movie)
DC Comics: 1990 ($2.95, 68 pgs., movie adaptation, one-shot)
1-Arnold Schwarzenegger photo-c 4.00

TOTAL RECALL (Continuation of movie)
Dynamite Entertainment: 2011 - No. 4, 2011 ($3.99, limited series)
1-4-Quaid and Melina on Mars following the movie; Razek-a/Robertson-c 4.00

TOTAL WAR (M.A.R.S. Patrol #3 on)
Gold Key: July, 1965 - No. 2, Oct, 1965 (Painted-c)
1-Wood-a in both issues 6 12 18 38 69 100
2 5 10 15 31 53 75

TOTEMS (Vertigo V2K)
DC Comics (Vertigo): Feb, 2000 ($5.95, one-shot)
1-Swamp Thing, Animal Man, Zatanna, Shade app.; Fegredo-c 6.00

TO THE HEART OF THE STORM
Kitchen Sink Press: 1991 (B&W, graphic novel)
Softcover-Will Eisner-s/a/c 20.00
Hardcover ($24.95) 30.00
TPB-(DC Comics, 9/00, $14.95) reprints 1991 edition 15.00

TO THE LAST MAN (See Zane Grey Four Color #616)

TOUCH OF SILVER, A
Image Comics: Jan, 1997 - No. 6, Nov, 1997 ($2.95, B&W, bi-monthly)
1-6-Valentino-s/a; photo-c: 5-color pgs. w/Round Table 3.00
TPB ($12.95) r/#1-6 13.00

TOUGH KID SQUAD COMICS
Timely Comics (TCI): Mar, 1942
1-(Scarce)-Origin & 1st app.The Human Top & The Tough Kid Squad; The Flying Flame app.
919 1838 2757 6709 12,355 18,000

TOWER OF SHADOWS (Creatures on the Loose #10 on)
Marvel Comics Group: Sept, 1969 - No. 9, Jan, 1971
1-Romita-c, classic Steranko-a; Craig-a(p) 8 16 24 51 96 140
2,3: 2-Neal Adams-a. 3-Barry Smith, Tuska-a 5 10 15 30 50 70
4,6: 4-Marie Severin-c. 6-Wood-a 4 8 12 27 44 60
5-B. Smith-a(p), Wood-a; Wood draws himself (1st pg., 1st panel)
4 8 12 28 47 65
7-9: 7-B. Smith-a(p), Wood-a. 8-Wood-a; Wrightson-c. 9-Wrightson-c; Roy Thomas app. 5 10 15 30 50 70
Special 1(12/71, 52 pgs.)-Neal Adams-a; Romita-c 4 8 12 27 44 60
NOTE: ***J. Buscema*** *a-1p, 2p, Special 1r.* ***Colan*** *a-3p, 6p, Special 1.* ***J. Craig*** *a(r)-1p.* ***Ditko*** *a-6, 8, 9r, Special 1.* ***Everett*** *a-9(i)r; c-5i.* ***Kirby*** *a-9(p)r.* ***Severin*** *c-5p, 6.* ***Steranko*** *a-1p.* ***Tuska*** *a-3.* ***Wood*** *a-5-8. Issues 1-9 contain new stories with some pre-Marvel age reprints in 6-9.* ***H. P. Lovecraft*** *adaptation-9.*

TOXIC AVENGER (Movie)
Marvel Comics: Apr, 1991 - No. 11, Feb, 1992 ($1.50)
1-11: Based on movie character. 3,10-Photo-c 3.00

TOXIC CRUSADERS (TV)
Marvel Comics: May, 1992 - No. 8, Dec, 1992 ($1.25)
1-8: 1-3,8-Sam Kieth-c; based on USA Network cartoon 3.00

TOXIC GUMBO
DC Comics (Vertigo): 1998 ($5.95, one-shot, mature)
1-McKeever-a/Lydia Lunch-s 6.00

TOXIN (Son of Carnage)
Marvel Comics: June, 2005 - No. 6, Nov, 2005 ($2.99, limited series)

Toyland Comics #3 © FH

Transformers #63 © Hasbro

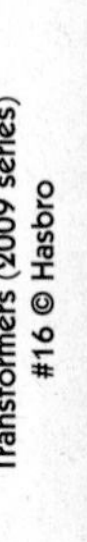
Transformers (2009 series) #16 © Hasbro

	GD 2.0	VG 4.0	FN 6.0	VF 8.0	VF/NM 9.0	NM- 9.2

1-6-Milligan-s/Robertson-a; Spider-Man app. 3.00
...: The Devil You Know TPB (2006, $17.99) r/#1-6 18.00

TOYBOY
Continuity Comics: Oct, 1986 - No. 7, Mar, 1989 ($2.00, Baxter paper)

1-7 3.00

*NOTE: **N. Adams** a-1; c-1, 2,5. **Golden** a-7p; c-6,7. **Nebres** a(i)-1,2.*

TOYLAND COMICS
Fiction House Magazines: Jan, 1947 - No. 2, Mar, 1947; No. 3, July, 1947

	GD	VG	FN	VF	VF/NM	NM-
1-Wizard of the Moon begins	30	60	90	177	289	400
2,3-Bob Lubbers-c. 3-Tuska-a	17	34	51	100	158	215

NOTE: *All above contain strips by **Al Walker.***

TOY STORY (Disney/Pixar movies)
BOOM! Entertainment (BOOM! KIDS): No. 0, Nov, 2009 - No. 7, Sept, 2010 ($2.99)

0-7: 0,1-Three covers. 2-7-Two covers 3.00
Free Comic Book Day Edition (5/10, giveaway) r/#0 The Return of Buzz Lightyear 3.00
...: The Return of Buzz Lightyear (10/10, Halloween giveaway, 8-1/2" x 5-1/4") 3.00

TOY STORY (Disney/Pixar movies)
Marvel Comics: May, 2012 - No. 4, 2012 ($2.99, limited series)

1-4: 1-Master Woody. 2-A Scary Night. 3-To The Attic. 4-Water Rescue 3.00

TOY STORY: MYSTERIOUS STRANGER (Disney/Pixar movies)
BOOM! Entertainment (BOOM! KIDS): May, 2009 - No. 4, July, 2009 ($2.99)

1-4-Jolley-s/Moreno-a. 1-Three covers. 2-4-Two covers 3.00

TOY STORY: TALES FROM THE TOY CHEST (Disney/Pixar movies)
BOOM! Entertainment (BOOM! KIDS): July, 2010 - No. 4, Oct, 2010 ($2.99)

1-4-Snider-s/Luthi-a. 1-Two covers. 2-4-One cover 3.00

TOY TOWN COMICS
Toytown/Orbit Publ./B. Antin/Swapper Quarterly: 1945 - No. 7, May, 1947

	GD	VG	FN	VF	VF/NM	NM-
1-Mertie Mouse; L. B. Cole-c/a; funny animal	39	78	117	240	395	550
2-L. B. Cole-a	22	44	66	132	216	300
3-7-L. B. Cole-a. 5-Wiggles the Wonderworm-c	20	40	60	114	182	250

TRACKER
Image Comics (Top Cow): Nov, 2009 - No. 5, Sept, 2010 ($2.99/$3.99)

1,2-Lincoln-s/Tsai-a. 1-Two covers 3.00
3-5-($3.99) 4.00

TRAGG AND THE SKY GODS (See Gold Key Spotlight, Mystery Comics Digest #3,9 & Spine Tingling Tales)
Gold Key/Whitman No. 9: June, 1975 - No. 8, Feb, 1977; No. 9, May, 1982 (Painted-c #3-8)

	GD	VG	FN	VF	VF/NM	NM-
1-Origin	3	6	9	14	19	24
2-8: 4-Sabre-Fang app. 8-Ostellon app.	2	4	6	8	11	14
9-(Whitman, 5/82) r/#1	1	2	3	5	7	9

NOTE: ***Santos** a-1, 2, 9r; c-3-7. **Spiegel** a-3-8.*

TRAILBLAZER
Image Comics: June 2011 ($5.99, one shot, graphic novel)

nn-Gray & Palmiotti-s/Daly-a; covers by Johnson and Conner 6.00

TRAIL BLAZERS (Red Dragon #5 on)
Street & Smith Publications: 1941; No. 2, Apr, 1942 - No. 4, Oct, 1942
(True stories of American heroes)

	GD	VG	FN	VF	VF/NM	NM-
1-Life story of Jack Dempsey & Wright Brothers	37	74	111	222	361	500
2-Brooklyn Dodgers-c/story; Ben Franklin story	22	44	66	132	216	300
3,4: 3-Fred Allen, Red Barber, Yankees stories	20	40	60	117	189	260

TRAIL COLT (Also see Extra Comics, Manhunt! & Undercover Girl)
Magazine Enterprises: 1949 - No. 2, 1949

	GD	VG	FN	VF	VF/NM	NM-
nn(A-1 #24)-7 pg. Frazetta-a r-in Manhunt #13; Undercover Girl app.; The Red Fox by L. B. Cole; Ingels-c; Whitney-a (Scarce)	39	78	117	240	395	550
2(A-1 #26)-Undercover Girl; Ingels-c; L. B. Cole-a (6 pgs.)	31	62	93	182	296	410

TRANSFORMERS, THE (TV)(See G.I. Joe and...)
(Continues in Transformers: Regeneration)
Marvel Comics Group: Sept, 1984 - No. 80, July, 1991 (75¢/$1.00)

	GD	VG	FN	VF	VF/NM	NM-
1-Based on Hasbro Toys	3	6	9	21	33	45
2-5: 2-Golden-c. 3-(1/85) Spider-Man (black costume)-c/app. 4-Texeira-c; brief app. of Dinobots	2	4	6	11	16	20
2-10: 2nd & 3rd prints						4.00
6-10: 6-1st Josie Beller. 8-Dinobots 1st full app. 9-Circuit Breaker 1st full app. 10-Intro Constructicons	2	4	6	8	11	14
11-49: 11-1st app. Jetfire. 14-Jetfire becomes an Autobot; 1st app. of Grapple, Hoist, Smokescreen, Skids, and Tracks. 17-1st app. of Blaster, Powerglide, Cosmos, Seaspray, Warpath, Beachcomber, Preceptor, Straxus, Kickback, Bombshell, Shrapnel, Dirge, and Ramjet. 19-1st Omega Supreme. 21-1st app. of Aerialbots; 1st Slingshot; Circuit Breaker app. 22-Retells origin of Circuit Breaker, 1st Stunticons. 23-Battle at Statue of Liberty. 24-1st app. Protectobots, Combaticons; Optimus Prime killed. 25-1st Predacons. 26-Intro The Mechanic, Prime's Funeral. 27-1st Trypticon app.; Grimlock named new Autobot leader. 28-The Mechanic app. 29-Intro Scraplets, 1st app. of Triple Changers	1	2	3	5	6	8
50-60: 53-Jim Lee-c. 54-Intro Micromasters. 60-Brief 1st app. of Primus	2	4	6	8	10	12
61-70: 61-Origin of Cybertron and the Transformers, Unicron app.; app. of Primus, creator of the Transformers. 62-66 Matrix Quest 5-part series. 67-Jim Lee-c	2	4	6	10	14	18
71-77: 75-($1.50, 52 pgs.) (Low print run)	3	6	9	17	26	35
78,79 (Low print run)	4	8	12	23	37	50
80-Last issue	4	8	12	28	47	65

*NOTE: Second and third printings of most early issues (1-9?) exist and are worth less than originals. Was originally planned as a four issue mini-series. **Wrightson** a-64i(4 pgs.).*

TRANSFORMERS
IDW Publishing: No. 0, Oct, 2005 (99¢, one-shot)

0-Prelude to Transformers: Infiltration series; Furman-s/Su-a; 4 covers 3.00

TRANSFORMERS
IDW Publishing: Nov, 2009 - No. 31, Dec, 2011 ($3.99)

1-31: Multple covers on each, 21-Chaos arc begins 4.00
...: Continuum (11/09, $3.99) Plot synopses of recent Transformers storylines 4.00
...: Death of Optimus Prime (12/11, $3.99) Roche-a 4.00
Hundred Penny Press: Transformers Classics #1 (6/11, $1.00) r/#1 (1984 Marvel series) 3.00
Hundred Penny Press (3/14, $1.00) r/#1 (1984 Marvel series) 3.00

TRANSFORMERS (Free Comic Book Day Editions)
Dreamwave Productions/IDW Publishing

... Animated (IDW, 5/08) Free Comic Book Day Edition; from the Cartoon Network series 3.00
... Armada (Dreamwave Prods., 5/03) Free Comic Book Day Edition 3.00
.../Beast Wars Special (IDW, 2006) Free Comic Book Day Edition; flip book 3.00
.../G.I. Joe (IDW, 2009) Free Comic Book Day Edition; flip book 3.00
... Movie Prequel (IDW, 5/07) Free Comic Book Day Edition; Figueroa-c 3.00

TRANSFORMERS: ALL HAIL MEGATRON
IDW Publishing: Jul, 2008 - No. 16, Oct, 2009 ($3.99, limited series)

1-16: 1-8,10-12-McCarthy-s/Guidi-a; 2 covers 4.00

TRANSFORMERS: ALLIANCE (Prequel to 2009 Transformers 2 movie)
IDW Publishing: Dec, 2008 - No. 4, Mar, 2009 ($3.99, limited series)

1-4-Milne-a; 2 covers 4.00

TRANSFORMERS ANIMATED: THE ARRIVAL
IDW Publishing: Sept, 2008 - No. 5, Dec, 2008 ($3.99, limited series)

1-5-Brizuela-a; 2 covers 4.00

TRANSFORMERS ARMADA (Continues as Transformers Energon with #19)
Dreamwave Productions: July, 2002 - No. 18, Dec, 2003 ($2.95)

1-Sarracini-s/Raiz-a; wraparound gatefold-c 5.00
2-18 4.00
Vol. 1 TPB (2003, $13.95) r/#1-5 14.00
Vol. 2 TPB (2003, $15.95) r/#6-11 16.00

TRANSFORMERS ARMADA: MORE THAN MEETS THE EYE
Dreamwave Productions: Mar, 2004 - No. 3, May, 2004 ($4.95, limited series)

1-3-Pin-ups with tech info; art by Pat Lee & various 5.00

TRANSFORMERS, BEAST WARS: THE ASCENDING
IDW Publishing: Aug, 2007 - No. 4, Nov, 2007 ($3.99, limited series)

1-4-Furman-s/Figueroa-a; multiple covers on all 4.00

TRANSFORMERS, BEAST WARS: THE GATHERING
IDW Publishing: Feb, 2006 - No. 4, May, 2006 ($2.99, limited series)

1-4-Furman-s/Figueroa-a; multiple covers on all 4.00
TPB (8/06, $17.99) r/series; sketch pages & gallery of covers and variants 18.00

TRANSFORMERS: BUMBLEBEE
IDW Publishing: Dec, 2009 - No. 4, Mar, 2010 ($3.99, limited series)

1-4: Zander Cannon-s; multiple covers on all 4.00

TRANSFORMERS COMICS MAGAZINE (Digest)
Marvel Comics: Jan, 1987 - No. 10, July, 1988

	GD	VG	FN	VF	VF/NM	NM-
1,2-Spider-Man-c/s	2	4	6	9	12	15
3-10	2	4	6	8	10	12

Transformers: Generation One #1 © Hasbro

Transformers: More Than Meets the Eye #26 © Hasbro

Transformers: Regeneration One #92 © Hasbro

GD 2.0 | VG 4.0 | FN 6.0 | VF 8.0 | VF/NM 9.0 | NM- 9.2

TRANSFORMERS: DARK CYBERTRON
IDW Publishing: Nov, 2013 ($3.99)
1-Part 1 of a 12-part crossover with Transformers: More Than Meets the Eye #23-27 and Transformers: Robots in Disguise #23-27; multiple covers 4.00
1-Deluxe Edition ($7.99, squarebound) r/#1 with bonus script and B&W art pages 8.00
... Finale (3/14, $3.99) Three covers 4.00

TRANSFORMERS: DARK OF THE MOON MOVIE ADAPTATION (2011 movie)
IDW Publishing: Jun, 2011 - No. 4, Jun, 2011 ($3.99, weekly limited series)
1-4-Barber-s/Jimenez-a 4.00

TRANSFORMERS: DEFIANCE (Prequel to 2009 Transformers 2 movie)
IDW Publishing: Jan, 2009 - No. 4, Apr, 2009 ($3.99, limited series)
1-4-Mowry-s; 2 covers 4.00

TRANSFORMERS: DEVASTATION
IDW Publishing: Sept, 2007 - No. 6, Feb, 2008 ($3.99, limited series)
1-6-Furman-s/Su-a; multiple covers on all 4.00

TRANSFORMERS: DRIFT
IDW Publishing: Sept, 2010 - No. 4, Oct, 2010 ($3.99, limited series)
1-4-McCarthy-s/Milne-a; multiple covers on all 4.00

TRANSFORMERS ENERGON (Continued from Transformers Armada #18)
Dreamwave Productions: No. 19, Jan, 2004 - No. 30, Dec, 2004 ($2.95)
19-30-Furman-s 4.00

TRANSFORMERS: ESCALATION
IDW Publishing: Nov, 2006 - No. 6, Apr, 2007 ($3.99, limited series)
1-6-Furman-s/Su-a; multiple covers 4.00

TRANSFORMERS: EVOLUTIONS - HEARTS OF STEEL
IDW Publishing: June, 2006 - No. 4, Sept, 2006 ($2.99, limited series)
1-4-Bumblebee meets John Henry in 1880s railroad times 4.00

TRANSFORMERS: FOUNDATION (Prequel to 2011 Transformers: Dark of the Moon movie)
IDW Publishing: Feb, 2011 - No. 4, May, 2011 ($3.99, limited series)
1-4-Barber-s/Griffith-a; 2 covers 4.00

TRANSFORMERS: GENERATION 1
Dreamwave Productions: Apr, 2002 - No. 6, Oct, 2002 ($2.95)
Preview- 6 pg. story; robot sketch pages; Pat Lee-a 3.00
1-Pat Lee-a; 2 wraparound covers by Lee 5.00
2-6: 2-Optimus Prime reactivated; 2 covers by Pat Lee 4.00
...Vol. 1 HC (2003, $49.95) r/#1-6; black hardcover with red foil lettering and art 50.00
...Vol. 1 TPB (2002, $17.95) r/#1-6 plus six page preview; 8 pg. preview of future issues 18.00

TRANSFORMERS: GENERATION 1 (Volume 2)
Dreamwave Productions: Apr, 2003 - No. 6, Sept, 2003 ($2.95)
1-6: 1-Pat Lee-a; 2 wraparound gatefold covers by Lee 4.00
1-($5.95) Chrome wraparound variant-c 6.00
...Vol. 2 TPB (IDW Publ., 3/06, $19.99) r/#1-6 plus cover gallery 20.00

TRANSFORMERS: GENERATION 1 (Volume 3)
Dreamwave Productions: No. 0, Dec, 2003 - Present ($2.95)
0-10: 0-Pat Lee-a. 1-Figueroa-a; wrapaound-c 4.00

TRANSFORMERS: GENERATION 2
Marvel Comics: Nov, 1993 - No. 12, Oct, 1994 ($1.75)
1-($2.95, 68 pgs.)-Collector's ed. w/bi-fold metallic-c 1 3 4 6 8 10
1-11: 1-Newsstand edition (68 pgs.). 2-G.I. Joe app., Snake-Eyes, Scarlett, Cobra Commander app. 5-Red Alert killed, Optimus Prime gives Grimlock leadership of Autobots. 6-G.I. Joe app. 1 2 3 4 5 7
12-($2.25, 52 pgs.) 1 3 4 6 8 10

TRANSFORMERS: GENERATIONS
IDW Publishing: Mar, 2006 - No. 12, Mar, 2007 ($1.99/$2.49/$3.99)
1,2: 1-R/Transformers #7 (1985); preview of Transformers, Beast Wars. 2-R/#13 4.00
3-10-($2.49) 3-R/Transformers #14 (1986). 4-6-Reprint #16-18. 7-R/#24 4.00
11,12-($3.99) 4.00
Volume 1 (12/06, $19.99) r/#1-6; cover gallery 20.00

TRANSFORMERS/G.I. JOE
Dreamwave Productions: Aug, 2003 - No. 6, Mar, 2004 ($2.95/$5.25)
1-Art & gatefold wraparound-c by Jae Lee; Ney Rieber-s; variant-c by Pat Lee 4.00
1-($5.95) Holofoil wraparound-c by Norton 6.00
2-6-Jae Lee-a/c 4.00
TPB (8/04, $17.95) r/#1-6; cover gallery and sketch pages 18.00

TRANSFORMERS/G.I. JOE: DIVIDED FRONT
Dreamwave Productions: Oct, 2004 ($2.95)
1-Art & gatefold wraparound-c by Pat Lee 4.00

TRANSFORMERS: HEADMASTERS
Marvel Comics Group: July, 1987 - No. 4, Jan, 1988 ($1.00, limited series)
1-Springer, Akin, Garvey-a 1 2 3 5 6 8
2-4-Springer-c on all 6.00

TRANSFORMERS: HEART OF DARKNESS
IDW Publishing: Mar, 2011 - No. 4, Jun, 2011 ($3.99, limited series)
1-4-Abnett & Lanning-s/Farinas-a 4.00

TRANSFORMERS: INFESTATION (Crossover with Star Trek, Ghostbusters & G.I. Joe)
IDW Publishing: Feb, 2011 - No. 2, Feb, 2011 ($3.99, limited series)
1,2-Abnett & Lanning-s/Roche-a; covers by Roche & Snyder III 4.00

TRANSFORMERS: INFILTRATION
IDW Publishing: Jan, 2006 - No. 6, June, 2006 ($2.99, limited series)
1-6-Furman-s/Su-a; multiple covers on all 4.00
... Cover Gallery (8/06, $5.99) 6.00

TRANSFORMERS: IRONHIDE
IDW Publishing: May, 2010 - No. 4, Aug, 2010 ($3.99, limited series)
1-4: Mike Costa-s; multiple covers on all 4.00

TRANSFORMERS: LAST STAND OF THE WRECKERS
IDW Publishing: Jan, 2010 - No. 5, May, 2010 ($3.99, limited series)
1-5-Nick Roche-s/a; two covers 4.00

TRANSFORMERS: MAXIMUM DINOBOTS
IDW Publishing: Dec, 2008 - No. 5, Apr, 2009 ($3.99, limited series)
1-5-Furman-s/Roche-a; 2 covers for each 4.00

TRANSFORMERS: MEGATRON ORIGIN
IDW Publishing: May, 2007 - No. 4, Sept, 2008 ($3.99, limited series)
1-4-Alex Milne-a; 2 covers 4.00

TRANSFORMERS: MICROMASTERS
Dreamwave Productions: June, 2004 - No. 4 ($2.95, limited series)
1-4-Ruffolo-a; Pat Lee-c 4.00

TRANSFORMERS: MONSTROSITY
IDW Publishing: Jun, 2013 - No. 4, Sept, 2013 ($3.99)
1-4: 1-Three covers; Ramondelli-a 4.00

TRANSFORMERS: MORE THAN MEETS THE EYE
Dreamwave Productions: Apr, 2003 - No. 8, Nov, 2003 ($5.25)
1-8-Pin-ups with tech info on Autobots and Decepticons; art by Pat Lee & various 5.25
Vol. 1,2 (2004, $24.95, TPB) 1-r/#1-4. 2-r/#5-8 25.00

TRANSFORMERS: MORE THAN MEETS THE EYE
IDW Publishing: Jan, 2012 - Present ($3.99)
1-27: 1-Five covers; Roche-a. 2-Three covers; Milne-a. 23-27-Dark Cybertron x-over 4.00
Annual 2012 (8/12, $7.99) Salgado & Cabaltierra-a; three covers 8.00

TRANSFORMERS: MOVIE ADAPTATION (For the 2007 live action movie)
IDW Publishing: June, 2007 - No. 4, June, 2007 ($3.99, weekly limited series)
1-4: Wraparound covers on each; Milne-a 4.00

TRANSFORMERS: MOVIE PREQUEL (For the 2007 live action movie)
IDW Publishing: Feb, 2007 - No. 4, May, 2007 ($3.99, limited series)
1-4: 1-Origin of the Transformers on Cybertron; multiple covers on each 4.00
Special (6/08, $3.99) 2 covers 4.00
TPB (6/07, $19.99) r/series; gallery of covers and variants 20.00

TRANSFORMERS: NEFARIOUS (Sequel to Transformers: Revenge of the Fallen movie)
IDW Publishing: Mar, 2010 - No. 6, Aug, 2010 ($3.99, limited series)
1-6: Furman-s; multiple covers on all 4.00

TRANSFORMERS: PRIME
IDW Publishing: Jan, 2011 - No. 4, Jan, 2011 ($3.99, weekly limited series)
1-4: 1-Mike Johnson-s/E.J. Su-a 4.00

TRANSFORMERS PRIME: BEAST HUNTERS
IDW Publishing: May, 2013 - No. 8, Dec, 2013($3.99, limited series)
1-8-Agustin Padilla-a 4.00

TRANSFORMERS PRIME: RAGE OF THE DINOBOTS
IDW Publishing: Nov, 2012 - No. 4, Feb, 2013 ($3.99, limited series)

Transfusion #2 © IDW

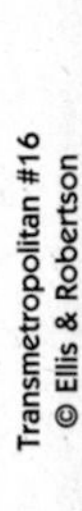

	GD 2.0	VG 4.0	FN 6.0	VF 8.0	VF/NM 9.0	NM- 9.2

1-4: 1-Mike Johnson-s/Agustin Padilla-a 4.00

TRANSFORMERS: REGENERATION ONE (Continues story from Transformers #80 (1991))
IDW Publishing: No. 80.5, May, 2012 - Present ($3.99)

80.5 (5/12, Free Comic Book Day giveaway) Furman-s/Wildman-a 3.00
81-99 ($3.99) 81-92-Furman-s/Wildman-a; multiple covers on all 4.00
#0 (9/13, $3.99) Hot Rod in the timestream; various artists; 4 covers 4.00
... 100-Page Spectacular (7/12, $7.99) Reprints Transformers #76-80 (1991) 8.00

TRANSFORMERS: REVENGE OF THE FALLEN OFFICIAL MOVIE ADAPTATION
(For the 2009 live action movie sequel)
IDW Publishing: May, 2009 - No. 4, June, 2009 ($3.99, weekly limited series)

1-4: Furman-s; 2 covers on each 4.00

TRANSFORMERS: RISING STORM (Prequel to 2011 Transformers: Dark of the Moon movie)
IDW Publishing: Feb, 2011 - No. 4, May, 2011 ($3.99, limited series)

1-3-Barber-s/Magno-a; 2 covers 4.00

TRANSFORMERS: ROBOTS IN DISGUISE
IDW Publishing: Jan, 2012 - Present ($3.99)

1-27: 1-Five covers; Griffith-a. 2-27-Three covers. 23-27-Dark Cybertron x-over 4.00

TRANSFORMERS: SAGA OF THE ALLSPARK (From the 2007 live action movie)
IDW Publishing: Jul, 2008 - No. 4, Oct, 2008 ($3.99, limited series)

1-4-Launch of the Allspark into outer space; Furman-s/Roche-c 4.00

TRANSFORMERS: SECTOR 7 (From the 2007 live action movie)
IDW Publishing: Sept, 2010 - No. 5, Jan, 2011 ($3.99, limited series)

1-5-Barber-s 4.00

TRANSFORMERS: SPOTLIGHT
IDW Publishing: Sept, 2006 - Present ($3.99, multiple covers on each)

... Arcee (2/08); ... Blaster (1/08); ... Blurr (11/08); ... Bumblebee (3/13); ... Cliffjumper (6/09); ... Cyclonus (6/08); ...Doubledealer (8/08); ...Drift (4/09); ...Galvatron (7/07);...Grimlock (3/08); ...Hardhead (7/08); ... Hoist (5/13); ... Hot Rod (11/06); ... Jazz (3/09); ... Kup (4/07); ... Megatron (2/13); ... Metroplex (7/09); ... Mirage (3/08); ... Nightbeat (10/06); ... Orion Pax (12/12); ... Prowl (4/10);... Ramjet (11/07); ... Shockwave (9/06); ... Sideswipe (9/08); ... Sixshot (12/06); ... Soundwave (3/07); Thundercracker (1/13); ... Trailcutter (4/13); ... Ultra Magnus (1/07) 4.00
... Optimus Prime: 3-D (11/08, $5.99, with glasses) Furman-s/Figueroa-a 6.00

TRANSFORMERS: STORMBRINGER
IDW Publishing: Jul, 2006 - No. 4, Oct, 2006 ($2.99, limited series)

1-4-Furman-s/Figueroa-a; multiple covers on all 4.00
TPB (2/07, $17.99) r/series; cover gallery and sketch pages 18.00

TRANSFORMERS SUMMER SPECIAL
Dreamwave Productions: May, 2004 ($4.95)

1-Pat Lee-a; Figueroa-a 5.00

TRANSFORMERS: TALES OF THE FALLEN
IDW Publishing: Aug, 2009 - No. 6 ($3.99, limited series)

1-6: 2,4-Furman-s mulitple covers on all 4.00

TRANSFORMERS: TARGET 2006
IDW Publishing: Apr, 2007 - No. 5, Aug, 2007 ($3.99, limited series)

1-5-Reprints from 1980s series; multiple covers on all 4.00

TRANSFORMERS: THE ANIMATED MOVIE
IDW Publishing: Oct, 2006 - No. 4, Jan, 2007 ($3.99, limited series)

1-4-Adapts animated movie; Don Figueroa-a 4.00

TRANSFORMERS, THE MOVIE
Marvel Comics Group: Dec, 1986 - No. 3, Feb, 1987 (75¢, limited series)

1-3-Adapts animated movie 1 3 4 6 8 10

TRANSFORMERS: THE REIGN OF STARSCREAM
IDW Publishing: Apr, 2008 - No. 5, Aug, 2008 ($3.99, limited series)

1-5-Continuation of the 2007 movie; Milne-a; multiple covers 4.00

TRANSFORMERS: THE WAR WITHIN
Dreamwave Productions: Oct, 2002 - No. 6, Mar, 2003 ($2.95)

1-6-Furman-s/Figueroa-a. 1-Wraparound gatefold-c 4.00
TPB (2003, $15.95) r/#1-6; plus cover gallery 16.00

TRANSFORMERS UNIVERSE
Marvel Comics Group: Dec, 1986 - No. 4, Mar, 1987 ($1.25, limited series)

1-4-A guide to all characters 1 2 3 5 6 8
TPB-r/#1-4 15.00

TRANSFORMERS WAR WITHIN: THE AGE OF WRATH
Dreamwave Productions: Sept, 2004 - No. 6 ($2.95, limited series)

1-3-Furman-s/Ng-a 4.00

TRANSFORMERS WAR WITHIN: THE DARK AGES
Dreamwave Productions: Oct, 2003 - No. 6 ($2.95)

1-6: 1-Furman-s/Wildman-a; two covers by Pat Lee & Figueroa 4.00
TPB (2004, $17.95) r/#1-6; plus cover gallery and design sketches 18.00

TRANSFUSION
IDW Publishing: Oct, 2012 - No. 3, Feb, 2013 ($3.99, limited series)

1-3-Vampires vs. Robots; Niles-s/Menton3-a 4.00

TRANSIT
Vortex Publ.: March, 1987 - No. 5, Nov, 1987 (B&W)

1-5-Ted McKeever-s/a 1 2 3 5 6 8

TRANSMETROPOLITAN
DC Comics (Helix/Vertigo): Sept, 1997 - No. 60, Nov, 2002 ($2.50)

1-Warren Ellis-s/Darick Robertson-a(p) 4 8 12 27 44 60
1-Special Edition (5/09, $1.00) r/#1 with "After Watchmen" cover frame 3.00
2,3 1 3 4 6 8 10
4-8 5.00
9-60: 15-Jae Lee-c. 25-27-Jim Lee-c. 37-39-Bradstreet-c 3.00
Back on the Street ('97, $7.95) r/#1-3 10.00
Back on the Street ('09, $14.99) r/#1-6; intro. by Garth Ennis 15.00
Dirge ('03/'10, $14.95/$14.95) r/#43-48 15.00
Filth of the City ('01, $5.95) Spider's columns with pin-up art by various 6.00
Gouge Away ('02/'09, $14.95/$14.99) r/#31-36 15.00
I Hate It Here ('00, $5.95) Spider's columns with pin-up art by various 6.00
Lonely City ('01/'09, $14.95/$14.99) r/#25-30; intro. by Patrick Stewart 15.00
Lust For Life ('98, $14.95) r/#4-12 20.00
Lust For Life ('09, $14.99) r/#7-12 15.00
One More Time ('04, $14.95) r/#55-60 15.00
One More Time ('11, $19.99) r/#55-60 & Filth of the City & I Hate It Here one-shots 20.00
Spider's Thrash ('02/'10, $14.95/$14.99) r/#37-42; intro. by Darren Aronofsky 15.00
Tales of Human Waste ('04, $9.95) r/Filth of the City, I Hate It Here & story from Vertigo Winter's Edge 2 10.00
The Cure ('03/'11, $14.95/$14.99) r/#49-54 15.00
The New Scum ('00, $12.95) r/#19-24 & Vertigo: Winter's Edge #3 15.00
The New Scum ('09, $14.99) r/#19-24 & Vertigo: Winter's Edge #3 15.00
Year of the Bastard ('99, $12.95)('09, $12.99) r/#13-18 13.00

TRANSMUTATION OF IKE GARUDA, THE
Marvel Comics (Epic Comics): July, 1991 - No. 2, 1991 ($3.95, 52 pgs.)

1,2 4.00

TRAPPED!
Periodical House Magazines (Ace): Oct, 1954 - No. 4, April, 1955

1 (All reprints) 10 20 30 54 72 90
2-4: 4-r/Men Against Crime #4 in its entirety 7 14 21 35 43 50
NOTE: *Colan a-1, 4.* ***Sekowsky*** *a-1.*

TRASH
Trash Publ. Co.: Mar, 1978 - No. 4, Oct, 1978 (B&W, magazine, 52 pgs.)

1,2: 1-Star Wars parody. 2-UFO-c 2 4 6 10 14 18
3-Parodies of KISS, the Beatles, and monsters 3 6 9 14 19 24
4-(84 pgs.)-Parodies of Happy Days, Rocky movies 3 6 9 14 20 26

TRAVELER, THE (Developed by Stan Lee)
BOOM! Studios: Nov, 2010 - No. 12, Oct, 2011 ($3.99)

1-12-Waid-s/Hardin-a; three covers on each 4.00

TRAVELS OF JAIMIE McPHEETERS, THE (TV)
Gold Key: Dec, 1963

1-Kurt Russell photo on-c plus photo back-c 4 8 12 25 40 55

TREASURE CHEST (Catholic Guild; also see Topix)
George A. Pflaum: 3/12/46 - V27#8, July, 1972 (Educational comics)
(Not published during Summer)

V1#1 30 60 90 177 289 400
2-6 (5/21/46): 5-Dr. Styx app. by Baily 14 28 42 80 115 150
V2#1-20 (9/3/46-5/27/47) 11 22 33 60 83 105
V3#1-5,7-20 (1st slick cover) 10 20 30 54 72 90
V3#6-Jules Verne's "Voyage to the Moon" 12 24 36 67 94 120
V4#1-20 (9/9/48-5/31/49) 9 18 27 47 61 75
V5#1-20 (9/6/49-5/31/50) 8 16 24 44 57 70
V6#1-20 (9/14/50-5/31/51) 8 16 24 42 54 65

Treasure Comics #7 © Prize

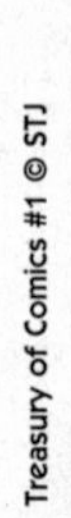
Treasury of Comics #1 © STJ

Treehouse of Horror #6 © Bongo

	GD 2.0	VG 4.0	FN 6.0	VF 8.0	VF/NM 9.0	NM- 9.2
V7#1-20 (9/13/51-6/5/52)	8	16	24	40	50	60
V8#1-20 (9/11/52-6/4/53)	7	14	21	37	46	55
V9#1-20 ('53-'54), V10#1-20 ('54-'55)	7	14	21	35	43	50
V11('55-'56), V12('56-'57)	6	12	18	29	36	42
V13#1,3-5,7,9-20-V17#1 ('57-'63)	6	12	18	27	33	38
V13#2,6,8-Ingels-a	5	10	15	35	63	90
V17#2- "This Godless Communism" series begins(not in odd #'d issues); cover shows hammer & sickle over Statue of Liberty; 8 pg. Crandall-a of family life under communism (9/28/61)	16	32	48	112	249	385
V17#3,5,7,9,11,13,15,17,19	3	6	9	16	24	32
V17#4,6,14- "This Godless Communism" stories	12	24	36	84	185	285
V17#8-Shows red octopus encompassing Earth, firing squad; 8 pgs. Crandall-a (12/21/61)	15	30	45	105	233	360
V17#10- "This Godless Communism" - how Stalin came to power, part I; Crandall-a	13	26	39	91	201	310
V17#12-Stalin in WWII, forced labor, death by exhaustion; Crandall-a	13	26	39	91	201	310
V17#16-Kruschev takes over; de-Stalinization	13	26	39	91	201	310
V17#18-Kruschev's control; murder of revolters, brainwash, space race by Crandall	13	26	39	91	201	310
V17#20-End of series; Kruschev-people are puppets, firing squads hammer & sickle over Statue of Liberty, snake around communist manifesto by Crandall	16	32	48	112	249	385
V18#1,3,4,6-10,12-20, V19#11-20, V20#1-20(1964-65)	3	6	9	16	23	30
V18#2-Kruschev on-c (9/27/62)	3	6	9	19	30	40
V18#5- "What About Red China?" - describes how communists took over China	9	18	27	58	99	140
V18#11-Crandall draws himself & 13 other artists on cover (1/31/63)	3	6	9	20	30	40
V19#1-10- "Red Victim" anti-communist series in all	8	16	24	51	96	140
V21, V22 #1-16,18-20,V23-V25(1965-70)-(two V24#5's 11/7/68 & 11/21/68) (no V24#6):	3	6	9	14	19	24
V22#17-Flying saucer wraparound-c	3	6	9	16	24	32
V26, V27#1-8 (V26,27-68 pgs.)	3	6	9	15	22	28
Summer Edition V1#1-6('66), V2#1-6('67)	3	6	9	16	23	30

NOTE: ***Anderson*** *a-V18#13.* ***Borth*** *a-V7#10-19 (serial), V8#8-17 (serial), V9#1-10 (serial), V13#2, 6, 11, V14-V25 (except V22#1-3, 11-13), Summer Ed. V1#3-6.* ***Crandall*** *a-V16#7, 9, 12, 14, 16-18, 20; V17#1, 2, 4-6, 10, 12, 14, 16-18, 20; V18#1, 2, 3(2 pg.), 7, 9-20; V19#4, 11, 13, 16, 19, 20; V20#1, 2, 4, 6, 8-10, 12, 14-16, 18, 20; V21#1-5, 8-11, 13, 16-18; V22#3, 7, 9-11, 14; V23#3, 6, 9, 16, 18; V24#7, 8, 10, 13, 16; V25#8, 16; V27#1-7r, 8r(2 pg.), Summer Ed. V1#3-5, V2#3; c-V16#7, V18#2(part), 7, 11, V19#4, 19, 20, V20#15, V21#5, 9, V22#3, 7, 9, 11, V23#9, 16, V24#13, 16, V25#8, Summer Ed. V1#2 (back c-V1#2-5).* ***Powell*** *a-V10#11. V19#11, 15, V10#13, V13#6, 8 all have wraparound covers.*

TREASURE CHEST OF THE WORLD'S BEST COMICS
Superior, Toronto, Canada: 1945 (500 pgs., hard-c)

	GD 2.0	VG 4.0	FN 6.0	VF 8.0	VF/NM 9.0	NM- 9.2
Contains Blue Beetle, Captain Combat, John Wayne, Dynamic Man, Nemo, Li'l Abner; contents can vary - represents random binding of extra books; Captain America on-c	116	232	348	742	1271	1800

TREASURE COMICS
Prize Publications? (no publisher listed): No date (1943) (50¢, 324 pgs., cardboard-c)

	GD 2.0	VG 4.0	FN 6.0	VF 8.0	VF/NM 9.0	NM- 9.2
1-(Rare)-Contains rebound Prize Comics #7-11 from 1942 (blank inside-c)	300	600	900	2010	3505	5000

TREASURE COMICS
Prize Publ. (American Boys' Comics): June-July, 1945 - No. 12, Fall, 1947

	GD 2.0	VG 4.0	FN 6.0	VF 8.0	VF/NM 9.0	NM- 9.2
1-Paul Bunyan & Marco Polo begin; Highwayman & Carrot Topp only app.; Kiefer-a	52	104	156	328	557	785
2-Arabian Knight, Gorilla King, Dr. Styx begin	31	62	93	186	303	420
3,4,9,12: 9-Kiefer-a	25	50	75	150	245	340
5-Marco Polo-c; Krigstein-a	32	64	96	190	310	430
6,11-Krigstein-a; 11-Krigstein-c	31	62	93	186	303	420
7,8-Frazetta-a (5 pgs. each). 7-Capt. Kidd Jr. app.	41	82	123	260	435	610
10-Simon & Kirby-c/a	38	76	114	228	369	510

NOTE: ***Barry*** *a-9-11; c-12.* ***Kiefer*** *a-3, 5, 7; c-2, 6, 7.* ***Roussos*** *a-11.*

TREASURE ISLAND (See Classics Illustrated #64, Doc Savage Comics #1, King Classics, Movie Classics & Movie Comics)
Dell Publishing Co.: No. 624, Apr, 1955 (Disney)

	GD 2.0	VG 4.0	FN 6.0	VF 8.0	VF/NM 9.0	NM- 9.2
Four Color 624-Movie, photo-c	7	14	21	46	86	125

TREASURY OF COMICS
St. John Publishing Co.: 1947; No. 2, July, 1947 - No. 4, Sept, 1947; No. 5, Jan, 1948

	GD 2.0	VG 4.0	FN 6.0	VF 8.0	VF/NM 9.0	NM- 9.2
nn(#1)-Abbie an' Slats (nn on-c, #1 on inside)	14	28	42	80	115	150
2-Jim Hardy Comics; featuring Windy & Paddles	11	22	33	62	86	110
3-Bill Bumlin	10	20	30	54	72	90
4-Abbie an' Slats	11	22	33	62	86	110
5-Jim Hardy Comics #1	11	22	33	62	86	110

TREASURY OF COMICS
St. John Publishing Co.: Mar, 1948 - No. 5, 1948 (Reg. size); 1948-1950 (Over 500 pgs., $1.00)

	GD 2.0	VG 4.0	FN 6.0	VF 8.0	VF/NM 9.0	NM- 9.2
1	19	38	57	111	176	240
2(#2 on-c, #1 on inside)	12	24	36	67	94	120
3-5	10	20	30	56	76	95
1-(1948, 500 pgs., hard-c)-Abbie & Slats, Abbott & Costello, Casper, Little Annie Rooney, Little Audrey, Jim Hardy, Ella Cinders (16 books bound together) (Rare)	168	336	504	1075	1838	2600
1(1949, 500 pgs.)-Same format as above	135	270	405	864	1482	2100
1(1950, 500 pgs.)-Same format as above; different-c; (also see Little Audrey Yearbook) (Rare)	135	270	405	864	1482	2100

TREASURY OF DOGS, A (See Dell Giants)

TREASURY OF HORSES, A (See Dell Giants)

TREEHOUSE OF HORROR (Bart Simpson's...)
Bongo Comics: 1995 - Present ($2.95/$2.50/$3.50/$4.50/$4.99, annual)

	GD 2.0	VG 4.0	FN 6.0	VF 8.0	VF/NM 9.0	NM- 9.2
1-(1995, $2.95)-Groening-c; Allred, Robinson & Smith stories						6.00
2-(1996, $2.50)-Stories by Dini & Bagge; infinity-c by Groening						5.00
3-(1997, $2.50)-Dorkin-s/Groening-c						5.00
4-(1998, $2.50)-Lash & Dixon-s/Groening-c						5.00
5-(1999, $3.50)-Thompson-s; Shaw & Aragonés-s/a; TenNapel-s/a						5.00
6-(2000, $4.50)-Mahfood-s/a; DeCarlo-a; Morse-s/a; Kuper-s/a						5.00
7-(2001, $4.50)-Hamill-s/Morrison-a; Ennis-s/McCrea-a; Sakai-s/a; Nixey-s/a; Brereton back-c						5.00
8-(2002, $3.50)-Templeton, Shaw, Barta, Simone, Thompson-s/a						5.00
9-(2003, $4.99)-Lord of the Rings-Brereton-a; Dini, Naifeh, Millidge, Boothby, Noto-s/a						5.00
10-(2004, $4.99)-Monsters of Rock w/Alice Cooper, Gene Simmons, Rob Zombie and Pat Boone; art by Rodriguez, Morrison, Morse, Templeton						5.00
11-(2005, $4.99)-EC style w/art by John Severin, Angelo Torres & Al Williamson and flip book with Dracula by Wolfman/Colan and Squish Thing by Wein/Wrightson						5.00
12-(2006, $4.99)-Terry Moore, Kyle Baker, Eric Powell-s/a						5.00
13-(2007, $4.99)-Oswalt, Posehn, Lennon-s; Guerra, Austin, Barta, Rodriguez-a						5.00
14-(2008, $4.99)-s/a by Niles & Fabry; Boothby & Matsumoto; Gilbert Hernandez						5.00
15-(2009, $4.99)-s/a by Jeffrey Brown, Tim Hensley, Ben Jones and others						5.00
16-(2010, $4.99)-s/a by Kelley Jones, Evan Dorkin and others; Mars Attacks homage						5.00
17-(2011, $4.99)-s/a by Gene Ha, Jane Wiedlin and others; Nosferatu homage						5.00
18-(2012, $4.99)-s/a by Jim Valentino, Phil Noto and others; Rosemary's Baby spoof						5.00
19-(2013, $4.99)-s/a by Len Wein, Dan Brereton and others; Cthulhu spoof						5.00

TREKKER (See Dark Horse Presents #6)
Dark Horse Comics: May, 1987 - No. 6, Mar,1988 ($1.50, B&W)

	GD 2.0	VG 4.0	FN 6.0	VF 8.0	VF/NM 9.0	NM- 9.2
1-6: Sci/Fi stories						3.00
Color Special 1 (1989, $2.95, 52 pgs.)						4.00
Collection ($5.95, B&W)						6.00
Special 1 (6/99, $2.95, color)						3.00

TRENCHCOAT BRIGADE, THE
DC Comics (Vertigo): Mar, 1999 - No. 4, Jun, 1999 ($2.50, limited series)

	GD 2.0	VG 4.0	FN 6.0	VF 8.0	VF/NM 9.0	NM- 9.2
1-4: Hellblazer, Phantom Stranger, Mister E, Dr. Occult app.						3.00

TRENCHER (See Blackball Comics)
Image Comics: May, 1993 - No. 4, Oct, 1993 ($1.95, unfinished limited series)

	GD 2.0	VG 4.0	FN 6.0	VF 8.0	VF/NM 9.0	NM- 9.2
1-4: Keith Giffen-c/a/scripts. 3-Supreme-c/story						3.00

TRIALS OF SHAZAM!
DC Comics: Oct, 2006 - No. 12, May, 2008 ($2.99)

	GD 2.0	VG 4.0	FN 6.0	VF 8.0	VF/NM 9.0	NM- 9.2
1-12: 1-8-Winick-s/Porter-a. 9-11-Cascioli-a. 10-Shadowpact app. 12-JLA app.						3.00
... Volume 1 TPB (2007, $14.99) r/#1-6 and story from DCU Brave New World #1						15.00
... Volume 2 TPB (2008, $14.99) r/#7-12						15.00

TRIB COMIC BOOK, THE
Winnipeg Tribune: Sept. 24, 1977 - Vol. 4, #36, 1980 (8-1/2"x11", 24 pgs., weekly) (155 total issues)

	GD 2.0	VG 4.0	FN 6.0	VF 8.0	VF/NM 9.0	NM- 9.2
V1# 1-Color pages (Sunday strips)-Spiderman, Asterix, Disney's Scamp, Wizard of Id, Doonesbury, Inside Woody Allen, Mary Worth, & others (similar to Spirit sections)	2	4	6	10	14	18
V1#2-15, V2#1-52, V3#1-52, V4#1-33	1	3	4	6	8	10
V4#34-36 (not distributed)	2	4	6	11	16	20

NOTE: *All issues have Spider-Man. Later issues contain Star Trek and Star Wars. 20 strips in ea. The first newspaper to put Sunday pages into a comic book format.*

TRIBE (See WildC.A.T.S #4)
Image Comics/Axis Comics No. 2 on: Apr, 1993; No. 2, Sept, 1993 - No. 3, 1994

Trigger #3 © Hall & Watkiss

Trinity of Evil: Pandora #5 © DC

Tron #1 © DIS

	GD 2.0	VG 4.0	FN 6.0	VF 8.0	VF/NM 9.0	NM- 9.2

($2.50/$1.95)
1-By Johnson & Stroman; gold foil & embossed on black-c 4.00
1-($2.50)-Ivory Edition; gold foil & embossed on white-c; available only through the creators 4.00
2,3: 2-1st Axis Comics issue. 3-Savage Dragon app. 3.00

TRIBUTE TO STEVEN HUGHES, A
Chaos! Comics: Sept, 2000 ($6.95)
1-Lady Death & Evil Ernie pin-ups by various artists; testimonials 7.00

TRICK 'R TREAT
DC Comics (WildStorm): 2009 ($19.95,SC)
nn-Short Halloween-themed story anthology; Andreyko-s; art by Huddleston & others 20.00

TRIGGER (See Roy Rogers'...)

TRIGGER
DC Comics (Vertigo): Feb, 2005 - No. 8, Sept, 2005 ($2.95/$2.99)
1-8-Jason Hall-s/John Watkiss-a/c 3.00

TRIGGER TWINS
National Periodical Publications: Mar-Apr, 1973 (20¢, one-shot)
1-Trigger Twins & Pow Wow Smith-r/All-Star Western #94,103 & Western Comics #81; Infantino-r(p) 2 4 6 13 18 22

TRILLIUM
DC Comics (Vertigo): Oct, 2013 - No. 8, Jun, 2014 ($2.99)
1-8-Jeff Lemire-s/a. 1-Flip-book 3.00

TRINITY (See DC Universe: Trinity)

TRINITY
DC Comics: Aug, 2008 - No. 52, July, 2009 ($2.99, weekly series)
1-52-Superman, Batman & Wonder Woman star; Busiek-s/Bagley-a. 52-Wraparound-c 3.00
Vol. 1 TPB (2009, $29.99) r/#1-17 30.00
Vol. 2 TPB (2009, $29.99) r/#18-35 30.00
Vol. 3 TPB (2009, $29.99) r/#36-52 30.00

TRINITY ANGELS
Acclaim Comics (Valiant Heroes): July, 1997 - No. 12, June, 1998 ($2.50)
1-12-Maguire-s/a(p):4-Copycat-c 3.00

TRINITY: BLOOD ON THE SANDS
Image Comics (Top Cow): July, 2009 ($2.99, one-shot)
1-Witchblade, The Darkness and Angelus in the 14th century Arabian desert 3.00

TRINITY OF SIN: PANDORA (DC New 52)
DC Comics: Aug, 2013 - Present ($2.99)
1-9: 1-Fawkes-s; origin re-told. 1-3-Trinity War tie-ins. 4-9-Forever Evil tie-ins 3.00

TRIO (Continues in Triple Helix #1)
IDW Publishing: May, 2012 - No. 4, Aug, 2012 ($3.99, limited series)
1-4-John Byrne-s/a/c 4.00

TRIPLE GIANT COMICS (See Archie All-Star Specials under Archie Comics)

TRIPLE HELIX (Also see Trio)
IDW Publishing: Oct, 2013 - No. 4, Jan, 2014 ($3.99, limited series)
1-4-John Byrne-s/a/c; The Trio app. 4.00

TRIPLE THREAT
Special Action/Holyoke/Gerona Publ.: Winter, 1945
1-Duke of Darkness, King O'Leary 34 68 102 199 325 450

TRISH OUT OF WATER
Aspen MLT: Oct, 2013 - No. 5, Mar, 2014 ($1.00/$3.99)
1-($1.00) Vince Hernandez-s/Giuseppe Cafaro-a; multiple covers 3.00
2-5-($3.99) Multiple covers on each 4.00

TRIUMPH (Also see JLA #28-30, Justice League Task Force & Zero Hour)
DC Comics: June, 1995 - No. 4, Sept, 1995 ($1.75, limited series)
1-4: 3-Hourman, JLA app. 3.00

TRIUMPHANT UNLEASHED
Triumphant Comics: No. 0, Nov, 1993 - No. 1, Nov, 1993 ($2.50, lim. series)
0-Serially numbered, 0-Red logo, 0-White logo (no cover price; giveaway), 1-Cover is negative & reverse of #0-c 3.00

TROJAN WAR (Adaptation of Trojan war histories from ancient Greek and Roman sources)
Marvel Comics: July, 2009 - No. 5, Nov, 2009 ($3.99, limited series)
1-5-Roy Thomas-s/Miguel Sepulveda-a/Dennis Calero-c 4.00

TROLL (Also see Brigade)
Image Comics (Extreme Studios): Dec, 1993 ($2.50, one-shot, 44 pgs.)
1-1st app. Troll; Liefeld scripts; Matsuda-c/a(p) 4.00
Halloween Special (1994, $2.95)-Maxx app. 4.00
...Once A Hero (8/94, $2.50) 4.00

TROLLORDS
Tru Studios/Comico V2#1 on: 2/86 - No. 15, 1988; V2#1, 11/88 - V2#4, 1989 (1-15: $1.50, B&W)
1-First printing 5.00
1-Second printing, 2-15: 6-Christmas issue; silver logo 3.00
V2#1-4 ($1.75, color, Comico) 3.00
Special 1 ($1.75, 2/87, color)-Jerry's Big Fun Bk. 3.00

TROLLORDS
Apple Comics: July, 1989 - No. 6, 1990 ($2.25, B&W, limited series)
1-6: 1-"The Big Batman Movie Parody" 3.00

TROLL PATROL
Harvey Comics: Jan, 1993 ($1.95, 52 pgs.)
1 4.00

TROLL II (Also see Brigade)
Image Comics (Extreme Studios): July, 1994 ($3.95, one-shot)
1 4.00

TRON (Based on the video game and film)
Slave Labor Graphics: Apr, 2006 - No. 6 ($3.50/$3.95)
1-4: 1-DeMartinis-a/Walker & Jones-s 4.00
5,6-($3.95) 4.00

TRON: BETRAYAL
Marvel Comics: Nov, 2010 - No. 2, Dec, 2010 ($3.99, limited series)
1,2-Prequel to Tron Legacy movie; Larroca-c 4.00

TRON: ORIGINAL MOVIE ADAPTATION
Marvel Comics: Jan, 2011 - No. 2, Feb, 2011 ($3.99, limited series)
1,2-Peter David-s/Mirco Pierfederici-a/Greg Land-c 4.00

TROUBLE
Marvel Comics (Epic): Sept, 2003 - No. 5, Jan, 2004 ($2.99, limited series)
1-5-Photo-c; Richard and Ben meet Mary and May; Millar-s/Dodson-a 3.00
1-2nd printing with variant Frank Cho-c 5.00

TROUBLED SOULS
Fleetway: 1990 ($9.95, trade paperback)
nn-Garth Ennis scripts & John McCrea painted-c/a. 10.00

TROUBLEMAKERS
Acclaim Comics (Valiant Heroes): Apr, 1997 - No. 19, June, 1998 ($2.50)
1-19: Fabian Nicieza scripts in all. 1-1st app. XL, Rebound & Blur; 2 covers. 8-Copycat-c. 12-Shooting of Parker 3.00

TROUBLE SHOOTERS, THE (TV)
Dell Publishing Co.: No. 1108, Jun-Aug, 1960
Four Color 1108-Keenan Wynn photo-c 5 10 15 33 57 80

TROUBLE WITH GIRLS, THE
Malibu Comics (Eternity Comics) #7-14/Comico V2#1-4/Eternity V2#5 on: 8/87 - #14, 1988; V2#1, 2/89 - V2#23, 1991? ($1.95, B&W/color)
1-14 ($1.95, B&W, Eternity)-Gerard Jones scripts & Tim Hamilton-c/a in all. 3.00
V2#1-23-Jones scripts, Hamilton-c/a. 3.00
Annual 1 (1988, $2.95) 4.00
Christmas Special 1 (12/91, $2.95, B&W, Eternity)-Jones scripts, Hamilton-c/a 4.00
Graphic Novel 1,2 (7/88, B&W)-r/#1-3 & #4-6 8.00

TROUBLE WITH GIRLS, THE: NIGHT OF THE LIZARD
Marvel Comics (Epic Comics/Heavy Hitters): 1993 - No. 4, 1993 ($2.50/$1.95, lim. series)
1-Embossed-c; Gerard Jones scripts & Bret Blevins-c/a in all 4.00
2-4: 2-Begin $1.95-c. 3.00

TROUT
Oni Press: Oct, 2001 - No. 2, Feb, 2002 ($2.95, B&W, limited series)
1,2-Troy Nixey-s/a 3.00

TRUE ADVENTURES (Formerly True Western)(Men's Adventures #4 on)
Marvel Comics (CCC): No. 3, May, 1950 (52 pgs.)
3-Powell, Sekowsky-a; Brodsky-c 20 40 60 114 182 250

True Aviation Picture Stories #4 © PMI

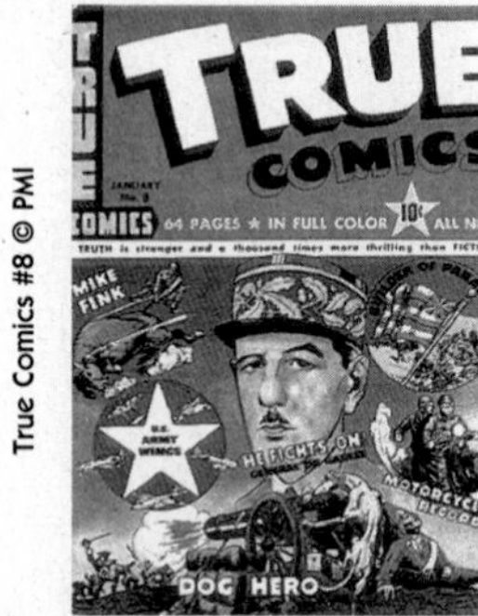

True Comics #8 © PMI

True Crime Comics #5 © Mag. Village

	GD	VG	FN	VF	VF/NM	NM-
	2.0	4.0	6.0	8.0	9.0	9.2

TRUE ANIMAL PICTURE STORIES
True Comics Press: Winter, 1947 - No. 2, Spring-Summer, 1947
1,2 11 22 33 60 83 105

TRUE AVIATION PICTURE STORIES (Becomes Aviation Adventures & Model Building #16 on)
Parents' Mag. Institute: 1942; No. 2, Jan-Feb, 1943 - No. 15, Sept-Oct, 1946
1-(#1 & 2 titled ...Aviation Comics Digest)(not digest size)
16 32 48 94 147 200
2 11 22 33 60 83 105
3-14: 3-10-Plane photos on-c. 11,13-Photo-c 10 20 30 54 72 90
15-(Titled "True Aviation Adventures & Model Building")
9 18 27 50 65 80

TRUE BELIEVERS
Marvel Comics: Sept, 2008 - No. 5, Jan, 2009 ($2.99, limited series)
1-5-Cary Bates-s/Paul Gulacy-a. 1,2-Reed Richards app. 3-Luke Cage app. 3.00

TRUE BLOOD (Based on the HBO vampire series)
IDW Publishing: Aug, 2010 - No. 6, Dec, 2010 ($3.99)
1-Messina-a; 4 covers by Messina, Campbell, Currie and Corroney 5.00
2-6-Multiple covers on each 4.00
...: Legacy Edition (1/11, $4.99) r/#1, cover gallery; full script 5.00

TRUE BLOOD (2nd series)(Based on the HBO vampire series)
IDW Publishing: May, 2012 - No. 14, Jun, 2013 ($3.99)
1-14-Gaydos-a in most; 2 covers (photo & Bradstreet-c) on each. 5-Manfredi-a 4.00

TRUE BLOOD: TAINTED LOVE (Based on the HBO vampire series)
IDW Publishing: Feb, 2011 - No. 6, Jul, 2011 ($3.99, limited series)
1-4: 1,2,4,5-Corroney-a; multiple covers. 3-Molnar-a 4.00
... Legacy Edition 1 (7/11, $4.99) r/#1 with full script and cover gallery 5.00

TRUE BLOOD: THE FRENCH QUARTER (Based on the HBO vampire series)
IDW Publishing: Aug, 2011 - No. 6, Jan, 2012 ($3.99, limited series)
1-6-Huehner & Tischman-s; multiple covers. 3-Molnar-a 4.00

TRUE BLOOD: THE GREAT REVELATION (Prequel to the 2008 HBO vampire series)
HBO/Top Cow: July, 2008 (no cover price, one shot continued on HBO website)
1-David Wohl-s/Jason Badower-a/c 4.00

TRUE BRIDE'S EXPERIENCES (Formerly Teen-Age Brides)
(True Bride-To-Be Romances No. 17 on)
True Love (Harvey Publications): No. 8, Oct, 1954 - No. 16, Feb, 1956
8-"I Married a Farmer" 9 18 27 50 65 80
9,10: 10-Last pre-code (2/55) 7 14 21 37 46 55
11-15 6 12 18 31 38 45
16-Last issue 7 14 21 37 46 55
NOTE: *Powell a-8-10, 12, 13.*

TRUE BRIDE-TO-BE ROMANCES (Formerly True Bride's Experiences)
Home Comics/True Love (Harvey): No. 17, Apr, 1956 - No. 30, Nov, 1958
17-S&K-c, Powell-a 10 20 30 56 76 95
18-20,22,25-28,30 6 12 18 31 38 45
21,23,24,29-Powell-a. 29-Baker-a (1 pg.) 7 14 21 35 43 50

TRUE COMICS (Also see Outstanding American War Heroes)
True Comics/Parents' Magazine Press: April, 1941 - No. 84, Aug, 1950
1-Marathon run story; life story Winston Churchill 32 64 96 188 307 425
2-Red Cross story; Everett-a 15 30 45 86 133 180
3-Baseball Hall of Fame story; Chiang Kai-Shek-c/s 17 34 51 100 158 215
4,5: 4-Story of American flag "Old Glory". 5-Life story of Joe Louis
14 28 42 80 115 150
6-Baseball World Series story 15 30 45 90 140 190
7-10: 7-Buffalo Bill story. 10,11-Teddy Roosevelt 11 22 33 62 86 110
11-14,16,18-20: 11-Thomas Edison, Douglas MacArthur stories. 13-Harry Houdini story. 14-Charlie McCarthy story. 18-Story of America begins, ends #26. 19-Eisenhower-c/s
10 20 30 54 72 90
15-Flag-c; Bob Feller story 10 20 30 58 79 100
17-Brooklyn Dodgers story 11 22 33 64 90 115
21-30: 24-Marco Polo story. 28-Origin of Uncle Sam. 29-Beethoven story. 30-Cooper Brothers baseball story 9 18 27 47 61 75
31-Red Grange "Galloping Ghost" story 8 16 24 40 50 60
32-46: 33-Origin/1st app. Steve Saunders, Special Agent of the FBI, series begins. 35-Mark Twain story. 38-General Bradley-c/s. 39-FDR story. 44-Truman story. 46-George Gershwin story 7 14 21 37 46 55
47-Atomic bomb issue (c/story, 3/46) 10 20 30 56 76 95
48-54,56-65: 49-1st app. Secret Warriors. 53-Bobby Riggs story. 58-Jim Jeffries (boxer) story; Harry Houdini story. 59-Bob Hope story; pirates-c/s. 60-Speedway Speed Demon-c/story.
7 14 21 35 43 50
55-(12/46)-1st app. Sad Sack by Baker (1/2 pg.) 16 32 48 94 147 200
66-Will Rogers-c/story 7 14 21 37 46 55
67-1st oversized issue (12/47); Steve Saunders, Special Agent begins
8 16 24 42 54 65
68-70,74-77,79: 68-70,74-77-Features Steve Sanders True FBI advs. 68-Oversized; Admiral Byrd-c/s. 69-Jack Benny story. 74-Amos 'n' Andy story
6 12 18 31 38 45
71-Joe DiMaggio-c/story. 9 18 27 47 61 75
72-Jackie Robinson story; True FBI advs. 8 16 24 40 50 60
73-Walt Disney's life story 9 18 27 47 61 75
78-Stan Musial-c/story; True FBI advs. 8 16 24 40 50 60
80-84 (Scarce)-All distr. to subscribers through mail only; paper-c. 80-Rocket trip to the moon story. 81-Red Grange story. 84-Wyatt Earp app. (1st app. in comics?); Rube Marquard story
18 36 54 103 162 220
(Prices vary widely on issues 80-84)
NOTE: ***Bob Kane** a-7. **Palais** a-80. **Powell** c/a-80. #80-84 have soft covers and combined with Tex Granger, Jack Armstrong, and Calling All Kids. #68-78 featured true FBI adventures.*

TRUE COMICS AND ADVENTURE STORIES
Parents' Magazine Institute: 1965 (Giant) (25¢)
1,2: 1-Fighting Hero of Viet Nam; LBJ on-c 3 6 9 17 26 35

TRUE COMPLETE MYSTERY (Formerly Complete Mystery)
Marvel Comics (PrPl): No. 5, Apr, 1949 - No. 8, Oct, 1949
5-Criminal career of Rico Mancini 27 54 81 160 263 365
6-8: 6-8-Photo-c 20 40 60 118 192 265

TRUE CONFIDENCES
Fawcett Publications: 1949 (Fall) - No. 4, June, 1950 (All photo-c)
1-Has ad for Fawcett Love Adventures #1, but publ. as Love Memoirs #1 as Marvel published the title first; Swayze-a 18 36 54 105 165 225
2-4: 3-Swayze-a. 4-Powell-a 12 24 36 67 94 120

TRUE CRIME CASES (...From Official Police Files)
St. John Publishing Co.: 1944 (25¢, 100 pg. Giant)
nn-Matt Baker-c 55 110 165 352 601 850

TRUE CRIME COMICS (Also see Complete Book of...)
Magazine Village: No. 2, May, 1947; No. 3, July-Aug, 1948 - No. 6, June-July, 1949; V2#1, Aug-Sept, 1949 (52 pgs.)
2-Jack Cole-c/a; used in **SOTI**, pgs. 81,82 plus illo. "A sample of the injury-to-eye motif" & illo. "Dragging living people to death"; used in **POP**, pg. 105; "Murder, Morphine and Me" classic drug propaganda story used by N.Y. Legis. Comm.
206 412 618 1318 2259 3200
3-Classic Cole-c/a; drug story with hypo, opium den & with drawing addict
142 284 426 909 1555 2200
4-Jack Cole-c/a; c-taken from a story panel in #3 (r-(2) **SOTI** & **POP** stories/#2?) 107 214 321 685 1168 1650
5-Jack Cole-c, Marijuana racket story (Canadian ed. w/cover similar to #3 exists w/out drug story) 74 148 222 470 810 1150
6-Not a reprint, original story (Canadian ed. reprints #4 w/different coloring on-c)
61 122 183 390 670 950
V2#1-Used in **SOTI**, pgs. 81,82 & illo. "Dragging living people to death"; Toth, Wood (3 pgs.), Roussos-a; Cole-r from #2 97 194 291 621 1061 1500
NOTE: *V2#1 was reprinted in Canada as V2#9 (12/49); same-c & contents minus Wood-a.*

TRUE FAITH
Fleetway: 1990 ($9.95, graphic novel)
nn-Garth Ennis scripts 2 4 6 12 16 20
Reprinted by DC/Vertigo ('97, $12.95) 13.00

TRUE GHOST STORIES (See Ripley's...)

TRUE LIFE ROMANCES (...Romance on cover)
Ajax/Farrell Publications: Dec, 1955 - No. 3, Aug, 1956
1 12 24 36 67 94 120
2 8 16 24 44 57 70
3-Disbrow-a 9 18 27 50 65 80

TRUE LIFE SECRETS
Romantic Love Stories/Charlton: Mar-April, 1951 - No. 28, Sept, 1955; No. 29, Jan, 1956
1-Photo-c begin, end #3? 17 34 51 98 154 210
2 11 22 33 60 83 105
3-11,13-19: 10 20 30 54 72 90
12-"I Was An Escort Girl" story 12 24 36 69 97 125
20-22,24-29: 25-Last precode (3/55) 9 18 27 47 61 75
23-Classic-c 16 32 48 94 147 200

True Love Pictorial #2 © STJ

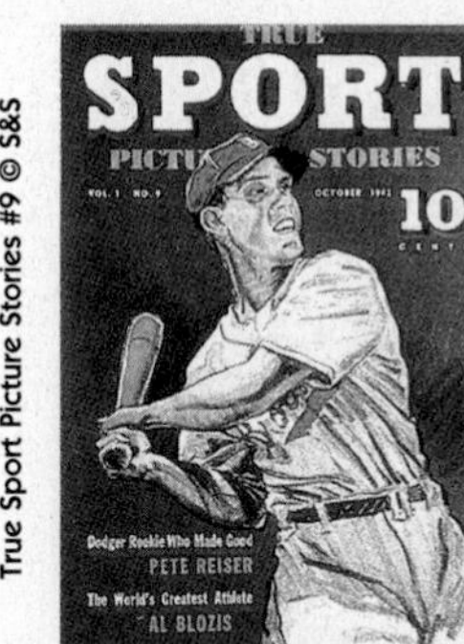

True Sport Picture Stories #9 © S&S

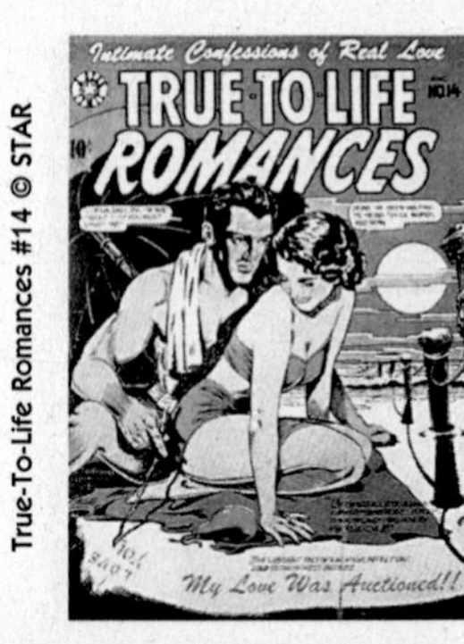

True-To-Life Romances #14 © STAR

GD VG FN VF VF/NM NM-
2.0 4.0 6.0 8.0 9.0 9.2

GD VG FN VF VF/NM NM-
2.0 4.0 6.0 8.0 9.0 9.2

TRUE LIFE TALES (Formerly Mitzi's Romances #8?)
Marvel Comics (CCC): No. 8, Oct, 1949 - No. 2, Jan, 1950 (52 pgs.)
8(#1, 10/49), 2-Both have photo-c 14 28 42 76 108 140

TRUE LIVES OF THE FABULOUS KILLJOYS
Dark Horse Comics: Jun, 2013 - No. 6, Jan, 2014 ($3.99)
1-6-Gerald Way & Shaun Simon-s/Becky Cloonan-a; covers by Cloonan & Bá 4.00

TRUE LOVE
Eclipse Comics: Jan, 1986 - No. 2, Jan, 1986 ($2.00, Baxter paper)
1-Love stories reprinted from pre-code Standard Comics; Toth-a(p); Dave Stevens-c
1 2 3 5 6 8
2-Toth-a; Mayo-a 4.00

TRUE LOVE CONFESSIONS
Premier Magazines: May, 1954 - No. 11, Jan, 1956
1-Marijuana story 15 30 45 90 140 190
2 10 20 30 56 76 95
3-11 9 18 27 52 69 85

TRUE LOVE PICTORIAL
St. John Publishing Co.: Dec, 1952 - No. 11, Aug, 1954
1-Only photo-c 26 52 78 154 252 350
2-Baker-c/a 43 86 129 271 461 650
3-5(All 25¢, 100 pgs.): 4-Signed story by Estrada. 5-(4/53)-Formerly Teen-Age Temptations; Kubert-a in #3; Baker-c/a in #3-5 65 130 195 416 708 1000
6,7: Baker-c/a; signed stories by Estrada 41 82 123 256 428 600
8,10,11-Baker-c/a 41 82 123 256 428 600
9-Baker-c 37 74 111 222 361 500

TRUE LOVE PROBLEMS AND ADVICE ILLUSTRATED (Becomes Romance Stories of True Love No. 45 on)
McCombs/Harvey Publ./Home Comics: June, 1949 - No. 6, Apr, 1950; No. 7, Jan, 1951 - No. 44, Mar, 1957
V1#1 15 30 45 86 133 180
2-Elias-c 10 20 30 54 72 90
3-10: 3,4,7-9-Elias-c 8 16 24 42 54 65
11-13,15-23,25-31: 31-Last pre-code (1/55) 7 14 21 35 43 50
14,24-Rape scene 7 14 21 37 46 55
32-37,39-44 6 12 18 29 36 42
38-S&K-c 9 18 27 52 69 85
NOTE: *Powell a-1, 2, 7-14, 17-25, 28, 29, 33, 40, 41. #3 has True Love... on inside.*

TRUE MOVIE AND TELEVISION (Part teenage magazine)
Toby Press: Aug, 1950 - No. 3, Nov, 1950; No. 4, Mar, 1951 (52 pgs.)(1-3: 10¢)
1-Elizabeth Taylor photo-c; Gene Autry, Shirley Temple app.
63 126 189 403 689 975
2-(9/50)-Janet Leigh/Liz Taylor/Ava Gardner & others photo-c; Frazetta John Wayne illo from J.Wayne Adv. Comics #2 (4/50) 47 94 141 296 498 700
3-June Allyson photo-c; Montgomery Cliff, Esther Williams, Andrews Sisters app; Li'l Abner featured; Sadie Hawkins' Day 32 64 96 192 314 435
4-Jane Powell photo-c (15¢) 20 40 60 120 195 270
NOTE: *16 pgs. in color, rest movie material in black & white.*

TRUE SECRETS (Formerly Our Love?)
Marvel (IPS)/Atlas Comics (MPI) #4 on: No. 3, Mar, 1950; No. 4, Feb, 1951 - No. 40, Sept, 1956
3 (52 pgs.)(IPS one-shot) 18 36 54 103 162 220
4,5,7-10 12 24 36 67 94 120
6,22-Everett-a 14 28 42 78 112 145
11-20 11 22 33 60 83 105
21,23-28: 24-Colletta-c. 28-Last pre-code (2/55) 10 20 30 56 76 95
29-40: 34,36-Colletta-a 9 18 27 52 69 85

TRUE SPORT PICTURE STORIES (Formerly Sport Comics)
Street & Smith Publications: V1#5, Feb, 1942 - V5#2, July-Aug, 1949
V1#5-Joe DiMaggio-c/story 37 74 111 218 354 490
6-12 (1942-43): 12-Jack Dempsey story 21 42 63 122 199 275
V2#1-12 (1943-45): 7-Stan Musial-c/story; photo story of the New York Yankees
20 40 60 115 185 255
V3#1-12 (1946-47): 7-Joe DiMaggio, Stan Musial, Bob Feller & others back from the armed service story. 8-Billy Conn vs. Joe Louis-c/story
19 38 57 111 176 240
V4#1-12 (1947-49), V5#1,2: v4#8-Joe Louis on-c 18 36 54 105 165 225
NOTE: *Powell a-V3#10, V4#1-4, 6-8, 10-12; V5#1, 2; c-V3#10-12, V4#2-7, 9-12. Ravielli c-V5#2.*

TRUE STORIES OF ROMANCE
Fawcett Publications: Jan, 1950 - No. 3, May, 1950 (All photo-c)
1 15 30 45 84 127 170
2,3: 3-Marcus Swayze-a 11 22 33 62 86 110

TRUE STORY OF JESSE JAMES, THE (See Jesse James, Four Color 757)

TRUE SWEETHEART SECRETS
Fawcett Publs.: 5/50; No. 2, 7/50; No. 3, 1951(nd); No. 4, 9/51 - No. 11, 1/53 (All photo-c)
1-Photo-c; Debbie Reynolds? 17 34 51 98 154 210
2-Wood-a (11 pgs.) 20 40 60 114 182 250
3-11: 4,5-Powell-a. 8-Marcus Swayze-a. 11-Evans-a
13 26 39 72 101 130

TRUE TALES OF LOVE (Formerly Secret Story Romances)
Atlas Comics (TCI): No. 22, April, 1956 - No. 31, Sept, 1957
22 12 24 36 67 94 120
23-24,26-31-Colletta-a in most: 9 18 27 52 69 85
25-Everett-a; Colletta-a 10 20 30 56 76 95

TRUE TALES OF ROMANCE
Fawcett Publications: No. 4, June, 1950
4-Photo-c 11 22 33 62 86 110

TRUE 3-D
Harvey Publications: Dec, 1953 - No. 2, Feb, 1954 (25¢)(Both came with 2 pair of glasses)
1-Nostrand, Powell-a 5 10 15 35 55 75
2-Powell-a 6 12 18 37 59 80
NOTE: *Many copies of #1 surfaced in 1984.*

TRUE-TO-LIFE ROMANCES (Formerly Guns Against Gangsters)
Star Publ.: #8, 11-12/49; #9, 1-2/50; #3, 4/50 - #5, 9/50; #6, 1/51 - #23, 10/54
8(#1, 1949) 26 52 78 154 252 350
9(#2),4-10 19 38 57 111 176 240
3-Janet Leigh/Glenn Ford photo on-c plus true life story of each
20 40 60 117 189 260
11,22,23 17 34 51 98 154 210
12-14,17-21-Disbrow-a 18 36 54 105 165 225
15,16-Wood & Disbrow-a in each 20 40 60 117 189 260
NOTE: *Kamen a-13. Kamen/Feldstein a-14. All have L.B. Cole covers.*

TRUE WAR EXPERIENCES
Harvey Publications: Aug, 1952 - No. 4, Dec, 1952
1-Korean War 8 16 24 56 93 130
2-4 5 10 15 32 51 70

TRUE WAR ROMANCES (Becomes Exotic Romances #22 on)
Quality Comics Group: Sept, 1952 - No. 21, June, 1955
1-Photo-c 15 30 45 86 133 180
2-(10/52) 10 20 30 54 72 90
3-10: 3-(12/52). 8,9-Whitney-a 9 18 27 50 65 80
11-21: 20-Last precode (4/55). 14-Whitney-a 8 16 24 44 57 70

TRUE WAR STORIES (See Ripley's...)

TRUE WESTERN (True Adventures #3)
Marvel Comics (MMC): Dec, 1949 - No. 2, March, 1950
1-Photo-c; Billy The Kid story 16 32 48 94 147 200
2-Alan Ladd photo-c 19 38 57 112 179 245

TRUMP
HMH Publishing Co.: Jan, 1957 - No. 2, Mar, 1957 (50¢, magazine)
1-Harvey Kurtzman satire 26 52 78 154 252 350
2-Harvey Kurtzman satire 20 40 60 118 192 265
NOTE: *Davis, Elder, Heath, Jaffee art-#1,2; Wood a-1. Article by Mel Brooks in #2.*

TRUMPETS WEST (See Luke Short, Four Color #875)

TRUTH ABOUT CRIME (See Fox Giants)

TRUTH ABOUT MOTHER GOOSE (See Mother Goose, Four Color #862)

TRUTH BEHIND THE TRIAL OF CARDINAL MINDSZENTY, THE (See Cardinal Mindszenty in the Promotional Comics section))

TRUTHFUL LOVE (Formerly Youthful Love)
Youthful Magazines: No. 2, July, 1950
2-Ingrid Bergman's true life story 14 28 42 76 108 140

TRUTH RED, WHITE & BLACK
Marvel Comics: Jan, 2003 - No. 6 ($3.50, limited series)
1-Kyle Baker-a/Robert Morales-s; the testing of Captain America's super-soldier serum 3.50
2-7: 3-Isaiah Bradley 1st dons the Captain America costume 3.50
TPB (2004, $17.99) r/series 18.00

Tsunami Girl #2 © Mark Paniccia

Tug & Buster #1 © Marc Hempel

Turok: Dinosaur Hunter #1 © RH

	GD 2.0	VG 4.0	FN 6.0	VF 8.0	VF/NM 9.0	NM- 9.2

TRY-OUT WINNER BOOK
Marvel Comics: Mar, 1988

1-Spider-Man vs. Doc Octopus 5.00

TSR WORLD (...Annual on cover only)
DC Comics: 1990 ($3.95, 84 pgs.)

1-Advanced D&D, ForgottenRealms, Dragonlance & 1st app. Spelljammer 4.00

TSUNAMI GIRL
Image Comics: 1999 - No. 3, 1999 ($2.95)

1-3-Sorayama-c/Paniccia-s/a 3.00

TUBBY (See Marge's...)

TUFF GHOSTS STARRING SPOOKY
Harvey Publications: July, 1962 - No. 39, Nov, 1970; No. 40, Sept, 1971 - No. 43, Oct, 1972

	GD	VG	FN	VF	VF/NM	NM-
1-12¢ issues begin	10	20	30	69	147	225
2-5	6	12	18	38	69	100
6-10	5	10	15	30	50	70
11-20	4	8	12	23	37	50
21-30: 29-Hot Stuff/Spooky team-up story	3	6	9	16	23	30
31-39,43	2	4	6	13	18	22
40-42: 52 pg. Giants	3	6	9	14	20	25

TUFFY
Standard Comics: No. 5, July, 1949 - No. 9, Oct, 1950

	GD	VG	FN	VF	VF/NM	NM-
5-All by Sid Hoff	8	16	24	42	54	65
6-9	6	12	18	29	36	42

TUFFY TURTLE
I. W. Enterprises: No date

	GD	VG	FN	VF	VF/NM	NM-
1-Reprint	2	4	6	8	11	14

TUG & BUSTER
Art & Soul Comics: Nov, 1995 - No. 7, Feb, 1998 ($2.95, B&W, bi-monthly)

1-7: Marc Hempel-c/a/scripts 3.00
1-(Image Comics, 8/98, $2.95, B&W) 3.00

TURF
Image Comics: Apr, 2010 - No. 2 ($2.99, limited series)

1,2-Jonathan Ross-s/Tommy Lee Edwards-a 3.00

TUROK
Acclaim Comics: Mar, 1998 - No. 4, Jun, 1998 ($2.50)

1-4-Nicieza-s/Kayanan-a 3.00
..., Child of Blood 1 (1/98, $3.95) Nicieza-s/Kayanan-a 4.00
... Evolution 1 (8/02, $2.50) Nicieza-s/Kayanan-a 3.00
..., Redpath 1 (10/97, $3.95) Nicieza-s/Kayanan-a 4.00
... / Shadowman 1 (2/99, $3.95) Priest-s/Broome & Jimenez-a 4.00
...: Spring Break in the Lost Land 1 (7/97, $3.95) Nicieza-s/Kayanan-a 4.00
...: Tales of the Lost Land 1 (4/98, $3.95) 4.00
...: The Empty Souls 1 (4/97, $3.95) Nicieza-s/Kayanan-a; variant-c 4.00

TUROK, DINOSAUR HUNTER (See Magnus Robot Fighter #12 & Archer & Armstrong #2)
Valiant/Acclaim Comics: June, 1993 - No. 47, Aug, 1996 ($2.50)

1-($3.50)-Chromium & foil-c 4.00
1-Gold foil-c variant 10.00
0, 2-47: 4-Andar app. 5-Death of Andar. 7-9-Truman/Glanzman-a. 11-Bound-in trading card. 16-Chaos Effect 3.00
Yearbook 1 (1994, $3.95, 52 pgs.) 4.00

TUROK: DINOSAUR HUNTER
Dynamite Entertainment: 2014 - Present ($3.99)

1-3-New version; Greg Pak-s/Mirko Colak-a; Sears-c 4.00
1-3-Variant-c by Jae Lee 4.00

TUROK, SON OF STONE (See Dan Curtis, Golden Comics Digest #31, Space Western #45 & March of Comics #378, 399, 408)
Dell Publ. Co. #1-29(9/62)/Gold Key #30(12/62)-85(7/73)/Gold Key or Whitman #86(9/73)-125(1/80)/Whitman #126(3/81) on: No. 596, 12/54 - No. 29, 9/62; No. 30, 12/62 - No. 91, 7/74; No. 92, 9/74 - No. 125, 1/80; No. 126, 3/81 - No. 130, 4/82

	GD	VG	FN	VF	VF/NM	NM-
Four Color 596 (12/54)(#1)-1st app./origin Turok & Andar; dinosaur-c. Created by Matthew H. Murphy; written by Alberto Giolitti	63	126	189	504	1127	1750
Four Color 656 (10/55)(#2)-1st mention of Lanok	31	62	93	223	499	775
3(3-5/56)-5: 3-Cave men	20	40	60	141	313	485
6-10: 8-Dinosaur of the deep; Turok enters Lost Valley; series begins. 9-Paul S. Newman-s (most issues thru end)	14	28	42	97	214	330
11-20: 17-Prehistoric Pygmies	11	22	33	76	163	250
21-29	9	18	27	58	114	170
30-1st Gold Key. 30-33-Painted back-c.	9	18	27	59	117	175
31-Drug use story	9	18	27	58	114	170
32-40	7	14	21	46	86	125
41-50	6	12	18	37	66	95
51-57,59,60	5	10	15	34	60	85
58-Flying Saucer c/story	5	10	15	35	63	90
61-70: 62-12¢ & 15¢ covers. 63,68-Line drawn-c	5	10	15	30	50	70
71-84: 84-Origin & 1st app. Hutec	4	8	12	27	44	60
85-99: 93-r-c/#19 w/changes. 94-r-c/#28 w/changes. 97-r-c/#31 w/changes. 98-r/#58 w/o spaceship & spacemen on-c. 99-r-c/#52 w/changes.	3	6	9	21	33	45
100	4	8	12	27	44	60
101-129: 114,115-(52 pgs.). 129(2/82)	4	8	12	22	35	48
130(4/82)-Last issue	5	10	15	34	60	85
Giant 1(30031-611) (11/66)-Slick-c; r/#10-12 & 16 plus cover to #11	9	18	27	63	126	190
Giant 1-Same as above but with paper-c	10	20	30	67	141	210

NOTE: *Most painted-c; line-drawn #63 & 130.* ***Alberto Gioletti*** *a-24-27, 30-119, 123; painted-c No. 30-129.* ***Sparling*** *a-117, 120-130. Reprints-#36, 54, 57, 75, 112, 114(1/3), 115(1/3), 118, 121, 125, 127(1/3), 128, 129(1/3), 130(1/3), Giant 1. Cover r-93, 94, 97-99, 126(all different from original covers.*

TUROK, SON OF STONE
Dark Horse Comics: Oct, 2010 - No. 4, Oct, 2011 ($3.50)

1-4: 1-Shooter-s/Francisco-a/Swanland-c; back-up reprint of debut in Four Color 596 3.50
1-Variant-c by Francisco 3.50

TUROK THE HUNTED
Valiant/Acclaim Comics: Mar, 1995 - No. 2, Apr, 1995 ($2.50, limited series)

1,2-Mike Deodato-a(p); price omitted on #1 3.00

TUROK THE HUNTED
Acclaim Comics (Valiant): Feb, 1996 - No. 2, Mar, 1996 ($2.50, limited series)

1,2-Mike Grell story 3.00

TUROK, TIMEWALKER
Acclaim Comics (Valiant): Aug, 1997 - No. 2, Sept, 1997 ($2.50, limited series)

1,2-Nicieza story 3.00

TUROK 2 (Magazine)
Acclaim Comics: Oct, 1998 ($4.99, magazine size)

...Seeds of Evil-Nicieza-s/Broome & Benjamin-a; origin back-up story 5.00
#2 Adon's Curse -Mack painted-c/Broome & Benjamin-a; origin pt. 2 5.00

TUROK 3: SHADOW OF OBLIVION
Acclaim Comics: Sept, 2000 ($4.95, one-shot)

1-Includes pin-up gallery 5.00

TURTLE SOUP
Mirage Studios: Sept, 1987 ($2.00, 76 pgs., B&W, one-shot)

	GD	VG	FN	VF	VF/NM	NM-
1-Featuring Teenage Mutant Ninja Turtles	1	2	3	5	6	8

TURTLE SOUP
Mirage Studios: Nov, 1991 - No. 4, 1992 ($2.50, limited series, coated paper)

1-4: Features the Teenage Mutant Ninja Turtles 4.00

TV CASPER & COMPANY
Harvey Publications: Aug, 1963 - No. 46, April, 1974 (25¢ Giants)

	GD	VG	FN	VF	VF/NM	NM-
1- 68 pg. Giants begin; Casper, Little Audrey, Baby Huey, Herman & Catnip, Buzzy the Crow begin	10	20	30	66	138	210
2-5	6	12	18	37	66	95
6-10	4	8	12	28	47	65
11-20	4	8	12	23	37	50
21-31: 31-Last 68 pg. issue	3	6	9	17	26	35
32-46: All 52 pgs.	3	6	9	16	23	30

NOTE: *Many issues contain reprints.*

TV FUNDAY FUNNIES (See Famous TV...)

TV FUNNIES (See New Funnies)

TV FUNTIME (See Little Audrey)

TV LAUGHOUT (See Archie's...)

TV SCREEN CARTOONS (Formerly Real Screen)
National Periodical Publ.: No. 129, July-Aug, 1959 - No. 138, Jan-Feb, 1961

	GD	VG	FN	VF	VF/NM	NM-
129-138 (Scarce) Fox and the Crow	6	12	18	37	66	95

TV STARS (TV) (Newsstand sales only)
Marvel Comics Group: Aug, 1978 - No. 4, Feb, 1979 (Hanna-Barbera)

	GD	VG	FN	VF	VF/NM	NM-
1-Great Grape Ape app.	3	6	9	17	26	35

Tweety and Sylvester #19 © WB

2099 Unlimited #7 © MAR

2020 Visions #2 © Jamie Delano

	GD 2.0	VG 4.0	FN 6.0	VF 8.0	VF/NM 9.0	NM- 9.2
2,4: 4-Top Cat app.	3	6	9	15	22	28
3-Toth-c/a; Dave Stevens inks	3	6	9	16	24	32

TV TEENS (Formerly Ozzie & Babs; Rock and Rollo #14 on)
Charlton Comics: V1#14, Feb, 1954 - V2#13, July, 1956

	GD 2.0	VG 4.0	FN 6.0	VF 8.0	VF/NM 9.0	NM- 9.2
V1#14 (#1)-Ozzie & Babs	10	20	30	54	72	90
15 (#2)	6	12	18	33	41	48
V2#3(6/54) - 6-Don Winslow	6	12	18	31	38	45
7-13-Mopsy. 8(7/55). 9-Paper dolls	6	12	18	29	36	42

TWEETY AND SYLVESTER (1st Series) (TV) (Also see Looney Tunes and Merrie Melodies)
Dell Publishing Co.: No. 406, June, 1952 - No. 37, June-Aug, 1962

	GD 2.0	VG 4.0	FN 6.0	VF 8.0	VF/NM 9.0	NM- 9.2
Four Color 406 (#1)	11	22	33	73	157	240
Four Color 489,524	7	14	21	44	82	120
4 (3-5/54) - 20	5	10	15	34	60	85
21-37	5	10	15	30	50	70

(See March of Comics #421, 433, 445, 457, 469, 481)

TWEETY AND SYLVESTER (2nd Series)(See Kite Fun Book)
Gold Key No. 1-102/Whitman No. 103 on: Nov, 1963; No. 2, Nov, 1965 - No. 121, Jun, 1984

	GD 2.0	VG 4.0	FN 6.0	VF 8.0	VF/NM 9.0	NM- 9.2
1	5	10	15	33	57	80
2-10	3	6	9	17	26	35
11-30	2	4	6	13	18	22
31-50	2	4	6	9	12	15
51-70	1	3	4	6	8	10
71-102	1	2	3	5	6	8
103,104 (Whitman)	1	3	4	6	8	10
105(9/80),106(10/80),107(12/80) 3-pack only	4	8	12	23	37	50
108-116: 113(2/82),114(2-3/82),115(3/82),116(4/82)	2	4	6	8	10	12
117-121 (All # 90094 on-c; nd, nd code): 117(6/83). 118(7/83). 119(2/84)-r(1/3). 120(5/84). 121(6/84)	3	6	9	16	23	30
Digest nn (Charlton/Xerox Pub., 1974) (low print run)	3	6	9	16	23	30
Mini Comic No. 1(1976, 3-1/4x6-1/2")	1	3	4	6	8	10

TWELVE, THE (Golden Age Timely heroes)
Marvel Comics: No. 0; 2008; No. 1, Mar, 2008 - No. 12, Jun, 2012 ($2.99, limited series)

	NM- 9.2
0-Rockman, Laughing Mask & Phantom Reporter intro. stories (1940s); series preview	4.00
1/2 (2008, $3.99) r/early app. of Fiery Mask, Mister E and Rockman; Weston-c	5.00
1-12-Straczynski-s/Weston-a; Timely heroes re-surface in the present	4.00
... Must Have 1 (4/12, $3.99) r/#7,8	4.00
...: Spearhead 1 (5/10, $3.99) Weston-s/a; Phantom Reporter in WW2; Invaders app.	5.00

12 O'CLOCK HIGH (TV)
Dell Publishing Co.: Jan-Mar, 1965 - No. 2, Apr-June, 1965 (Photo-c)

	GD 2.0	VG 4.0	FN 6.0	VF 8.0	VF/NM 9.0	NM- 9.2
1- Sinnott-a	5	10	15	34	60	85
2	4	8	12	28	47	65

TWELVE REASONS TO DIE
Black Mask Studios: 2013 - Present ($3.50)

1-6: 1-Five covers; created by Ghostface Killah — 3.50

2099 A.D.
Marvel Comics: May, 1995 ($3.95, one-shot)

1-Acetate-c by Quesada & Palmiotti — 4.00

2099 APOCALYPSE
Marvel Comics: Dec, 1995 ($4.95, one-shot)

1-Chromium wraparound-c; Ellis script — 5.00

2099 GENESIS
Marvel Comics: Jan, 1996 ($4.95, one-shot)

1-Chromium wraparound-c; Ellis script — 5.00

2099 MANIFEST DESTINY
Marvel Comics: Mar, 1998 ($5.99, one-shot)

1-Origin of Fantastic Four 2099; intro Moon Knight 2099 — 6.00

2099 UNLIMITED
Marvel Comics: Sept, 1993 - No. 10, 1996 ($3.95, 68 pgs.)

1-10: 1-1st app. Hulk 2099 & begins. 1-3-Spider-Man 2099 app. 9-Joe Kubert-c; Len Wein & Nancy Collins scripts — 4.00

2099 WORLD OF DOOM SPECIAL
Marvel Comics: May, 1995 ($2.25, one-shot)

1-Doom's "Contract w/America" — 3.00

2099 WORLD OF TOMORROW
Marvel Comics: Sept, 1996 - No. 8, Apr, 1997 ($2.50) (Replaces 2099 titles)

1-8: 1-Wraparound-c. 2-w/bound-in card. 4,5-Phalanx — 3.00

21
Image Comics (Top Cow Productions): Feb, 1996 - No. 3, Apr, 1996 ($2.50)

	NM- 9.2
1-3: Len Wein scripts	3.00
1-Variant-c	3.00

21 DOWN
DC Comics (WildStorm): Nov, 2002 - No. 12, Nov, 2003 ($2.95)

	NM- 9.2
1-12: 1-Palmiotti & Gray-s/Saiz-a/Jusko-c	3.00
...: The Conduit (2003, $19.95, TPB) r/#1-7; intro. by Garth Ennis	20.00

24 (Based on TV series)
IDW Publishing: July, 2004 - July, 2005 ($6.99/$7.49, square-bound, one-shots)

	NM- 9.2
...: Midnight Sun (7/05, $7.49) J.C. Vaughn & Mark Haynes-s; Renato Guedes-a	7.50
...: One Shot (7/04, $6.99)-Jack Bauer's first day on the job at CTU; Vaughn & Haynes-s; Guedes-a	7.50
...: Stories (1/05, $7.49) Manny Clark-a; Vaughn & Haynes-s	7.50

24: NIGHTFALL (Based on TV series)
IDW Publishing: Nov, 2006 - No. 6 ($3.99, limited series)

1-5-Two years before Season One; Vaughn & Haynes-s; Diaz-a; two covers — 4.00

28 DAYS LATER (Based on the 2002 movie)
Boom! Studios: July, 2009 - No. 24, Jun, 2011 ($3.99)

1-24: 1-Covers by Bradstreet and Phillips — 4.00

2020 VISIONS
DC Comics (Vertigo): May, 1997 - No. 12, Apr, 1998 ($2.25, limited series)

1-12-Delano-s: 1-3-Quitely-a. 4-"la tormenta"-Pleece-a — 3.00

20,000 LEAGUES UNDER THE SEA (Movie)(See King Classics, Movie Comics & Power Record Comics)
Dell Publishing Co.: No. 614, Feb, 1955 (Disney)

	GD 2.0	VG 4.0	FN 6.0	VF 8.0	VF/NM 9.0	NM- 9.2
Four Color 614-Movie, painted-c	8	16	24	51	96	140

TWICE TOLD TALES (See Movie Classics)

TWILIGHT
DC Comics: 1990 - No. 3, 1991 ($4.95, 52 pgs, lim. series, squarebound, mature)

1-3: Tommy Tomorrow app; Chaykin scripts, Garcia-Lopez-c/a — 5.00

TWILIGHT EXPERIMENT
DC Comics (WildStorm): Apr, 2004 - No. 6, Sept, 2005 ($2.95, limited series)

	NM- 9.2
1-6-Gray & Palmiotti-s/Santacruz-a	3.00
TPB (2011, $17.99) r/#1-6	18.00

TWILIGHT GUARDIAN (Also see Pilot Season: Twilight Guardian)
Image Comics (Top Cow): Jan, 2011 - No. 4, Apr, 2011 ($3.99, limited series)

1-4-Hickman-s/Kotean-a — 4.00

TWILIGHT MAN
First Publishing: June, 1989 - No. 4, Sept, 1989 ($2.75, limited series)

1-4 — 3.00

TWILIGHT ZONE, THE (TV) (See Dan Curtis & Stories From...)
Dell Publishing Co./Gold Key/Whitman No. 92: No. 1173, 3-5/61 - No. 91, 4/79; No. 92, 5/82

	GD 2.0	VG 4.0	FN 6.0	VF 8.0	VF/NM 9.0	NM- 9.2
Four Color 1173 (#1)-Crandall-c/a	18	36	54	128	284	440
Four Color 1288-Crandall/Evans-c/a	10	20	30	69	147	225
01-860-207 (5-7/62-Dell, 15¢)	8	16	24	54	102	150
12-860-210 on-c; 01-860-210 on inside(8-10/62-Dell)-Evans-c/a (3 stories); art by Frazetta & Crandall	8	16	24	54	102	150
1(11/62-Gold Key)-Crandall/Frazetta-a (10 & 11 pgs.); Evans-a	12	24	36	83	182	280
2	7	14	21	49	92	135
3-11: 3(11 pgs.),4(10 pgs.),9-Toth-a	6	12	18	37	66	95
12-15: 12-Williamson-a. 13,15-Crandall-a. 14-Orlando/Crandall/Torres-a	5	10	15	31	53	75
16-20	4	8	12	25	40	55
21-25: 21-Crandall-a(r). 25-Evans/Crandall-a(r); Toth-r/#4; last 12¢ issue	3	6	9	19	30	40
26,27: 26-Flying Saucer-c/story; Crandall, Evans-a(r). 27-Evans-r(2)	3	6	9	18	28	38
28-32: 32-Evans-a(r)	3	6	9	16	24	32
33-51: 43-Celardo-a. 51-Williamson-a	2	4	6	13	18	22
52-70	2	4	6	10	14	18
71-82,86-91: 71-Reprint	2	4	6	8	11	14
83-(52 pgs.)	3	6	9	14	20	25
84-(52 pgs.) Frank Miller's 1st comic book work	8	16	24	54	102	150
85-Frank Miller-a (2nd)	4	8	12	27	44	60

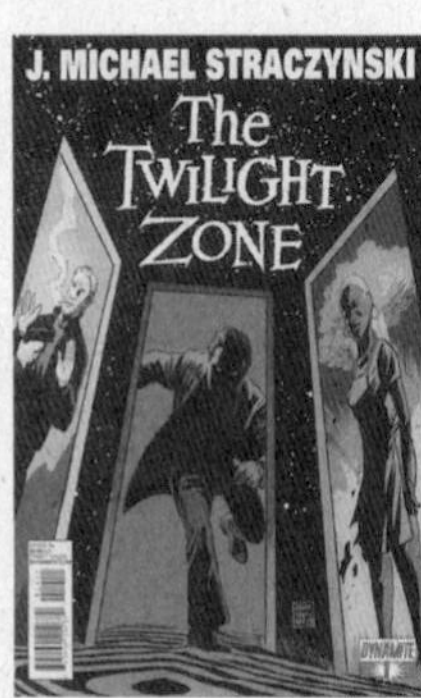

The Twilight Zone (2014 series) #1 © CBS

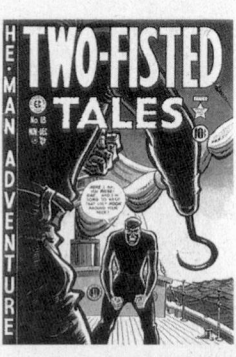

Two-Fisted Tales #18 © WMG

Two-Gun Kid #12 © MAR

	GD 2.0	VG 4.0	FN 6.0	VF 8.0	VF/NM 9.0	NM- 9.2
92-(Whitman, 5/82) Last issue; r/#1.	2	4	6	9	13	16
Mini Comic #1(1976, 3-1/4x6-1/2")	2	4	6	8	10	12

NOTE: *Bolle a-13(w/McWilliams), 50, 55, 57, 59, 77, 78, 80, 83, 84. McWilliams a-59, 78, 80, 82, 84. Miller a-84, 85. Orlando a-15, 19, 20, 22, 23. Sekowsky a-3. Simonson a-50, 54, 55, 83r. Weiss a-39, 79r(#39). (See Mystery Comics Digest 3, 6, 9, 12, 15, 18, 21, 24). Reprints-26(1/3), 71, 73, 79, 83, 84, 86, 92. Painted c-1-91.*

TWILIGHT ZONE, THE (TV)
Now Comics: Nov, 1990 ($2.95); Oct, 1991; V2#1, Nov, 1991 - No. 11, Oct, 1992 ($1.95); V3#1, 1993 - No. 4, 1993 ($2.50)

	GD 2.0	VG 4.0	FN 6.0	VF 8.0	VF/NM 9.0	NM- 9.2
1-(11/90, $2.95, 52 pgs.)-Direct sale edition; Neal Adams-a, Sienkiewicz-c; Harlan Ellison scripts						5.00
1-(11/90, $1.75)-Newsstand ed. w/N. Adams-c						4.00
1-Prestige Format (10/91, $4.95)-Reprints above with extra Harlan Ellison short story						5.00
1-Collector's Edition (10/91, $2.50)-Non-code approved and polybagged; reprints 11/90 issue; gold logo, 1-Reprint ($2.50)-r/direct sale 11/90 version, 1-Reprint ($2.50)-r/newsstand 11/90 version each...						4.00
V2#1-Direct sale & newsstand ed. w/different-c						3.00
V2#2-8,10-11						3.00
V2#9-($2.95)-3-D Special; polybagged w/glasses & hologram on-c						4.00
V2#9-($4.95)-Prestige Edition; contains 2 extra stories & a different hologram on-c; polybagged w/glasses						5.00
V3#1-4, Anniversary Special 1 (1992, $2.50)						3.00
Annual 1 (4/93, $2.50)-No ads						4.00
...Science Fiction Special (3/93, $3.50)						4.00

TWILIGHT ZONE, THE (TV)
Dynamite Entertainment: 2014 - Present ($3.99)

	GD 2.0	VG 4.0	FN 6.0	VF 8.0	VF/NM 9.0	NM- 9.2
1-4-Straczynski-s/Vilanova-a/Francavilla-c						4.00

TWINKLE COMICS
Spotlight Publishers: May, 1945

	GD 2.0	VG 4.0	FN 6.0	VF 8.0	VF/NM 9.0	NM- 9.2
1	24	48	72	144	237	330

TWIST, THE
Dell Publishing Co.: July-Sept, 1962

	GD 2.0	VG 4.0	FN 6.0	VF 8.0	VF/NM 9.0	NM- 9.2
01-864-209-Painted-c	4	8	12	23	37	50

TWISTED TALES (See Eclipse Graphic Album Series #15)
Pacific Comics/Independent Comics Group (Eclipse) #9,10: 11/82 - No. 8, 5/84; No. 9, 11/84; No. 10, 12/84 (Baxter paper)

	GD 2.0	VG 4.0	FN 6.0	VF 8.0	VF/NM 9.0	NM- 9.2
1-9: 1-B. Jones/Corben-c; Alcala-a; nudity/violence in al. 2-Wrightson-c; Ploog-a						5.00
10-Wrightson painted art; Morrow-a	1	2	3	4	5	7

NOTE: *Bolton painted c-4, 6, 7; a-7. Conrad a-1, 3, 5; c-1i, 3, 5. Guice a-8. Wildey a-3.*

TWO BIT THE WACKY WOODPECKER (See Wacky...)
Toby Press: 1951 - No. 3, May, 1953

	GD 2.0	VG 4.0	FN 6.0	VF 8.0	VF/NM 9.0	NM- 9.2
1	10	20	30	58	79	100
2,3	7	14	21	35	43	50

TWO FACE: YEAR ONE
DC Comics: 2008 - No. 2, 2008 ($5.99, squarebound, limited series)

	GD 2.0	VG 4.0	FN 6.0	VF 8.0	VF/NM 9.0	NM- 9.2
1,2-Origin re-told; Sable-s/Saiz & Haun-a						6.00

TWO-FISTED TALES (Formerly Haunt of Fear #15-17)
(Also see EC Archives • Two-Fisted Tales)
E. C. Comics: No. 18, Nov-Dec, 1950 - No. 41, Feb-Mar, 1955

	GD 2.0	VG 4.0	FN 6.0	VF 8.0	VF/NM 9.0	NM- 9.2
18(#1)-Kurtzman-c	100	200	300	800	1275	1750
19-Kurtzman-c	70	140	210	560	893	1225
20-Kurtzman-c	47	94	141	376	601	825
21,22-Kurtzman-c	39	78	117	312	494	675
23-25-Kurtzman-c	30	60	90	240	383	525
26-29,31-Kurtzman-c. 31-Civil War issue	23	46	69	184	292	400
30-Classic Davis-c	24	48	72	192	309	425
32-35: 33- "Atom Bomb" by Wood. 35-Civil War issue	23	46	69	184	292	400
36-41	17	34	51	136	218	300
Two-Fisted Annual (1952, 25¢, 132 pgs.)	110	220	330	825	1263	1700
Two-Fisted Annual (1953, 25¢, 132 pgs.)	81	162	243	608	929	1250

NOTE: *Berg a-29. Colan a-30,39p. Craig a-18, 19, 32. Crandall a-35, 36. Davis a-20-36, 40; c-30, 34, 35, 41, Annual 2. Estrada a-30. Evans a-34, 40, 41; c-40. Feldstein a-18. Krigstein a-41. Kubert a-32, 33. Kurtzman a-18-25; c-18-29, 31, Annual 1. Severin a-26, 28, 29, 31, 34-41 (No. 37-39 are all-Severin issues); c-36-39. Severin/Elder a-19-29, 31, 33, 36. Wood a-18-28, 30-35, 41; c-32, 33. Special issues: #26 (ChanJin Reservoir), 31 (Civil War), 35 (Civil War). Canadian reprints known; see Table of Contents. #25-Davis biog. #27-Wood biog. #28-Kurtzman biog.*

TWO-FISTED TALES
Russ Cochran/Gemstone Publishing: Oct, 1992 - No. 24, May, 1998 ($1.50/$2.00/$2.50)

	GD 2.0	VG 4.0	FN 6.0	VF 8.0	VF/NM 9.0	NM- 9.2
1-24: 1-4r/Two-Fisted Tales #18-21 w/original-c						4.00

TWO-GUN KID (Also see All Western Winners, Best Western, Black Rider, Blaze Carson, Kid Colt, Western Winners, Wild West, & Wild Western)
Marvel/Atlas (MCI No. 1-10/HPC No. 11-59/Marvel No. 60 on): 3/48(No mo.) - No. 10, 11/49; No. 11, 12/53 - No. 59, 4/61; No. 60, 11/62 - No. 92, 3/68; No. 93, 7/70 - No. 136, 4/77

	GD 2.0	VG 4.0	FN 6.0	VF 8.0	VF/NM 9.0	NM- 9.2
1-Two-Gun Kid & his horse Cyclone begin; The Sheriff begins	129	258	387	826	1413	2000
2	52	104	156	328	552	775
3,4: 3-Annie Oakley app.	39	78	117	240	395	550
5-Pre-Black Rider app. (Wint. 48/49); Anti-Wertham editorial (1st?)	40	80	120	246	411	575
6-10(11/49): 8-Blaze Carson app. 9-Black Rider app.	32	64	96	188	307	425
11(12/53)-Black Rider app.; 1st to have Atlas globe on-c; explains how Kid Colt became an outlaw	25	50	75	150	245	340
12-Black Rider app.	22	44	66	132	216	300
13-20: 14-Opium story	19	38	57	109	172	235
21-24,26-29	17	34	51	98	154	210
25,30: 25-Williamson-a (5 pgs.). 30-Williamson/Torres-a (4 pgs.)	18	36	54	103	162	220
31-33,35,37-40	9	18	27	58	114	170
34-Crandall-a	9	18	27	59	117	175
36,41,42,48-Origin in all	9	18	27	61	123	185
43,44,47	8	16	24	54	102	150
45,46-Davis-a	8	16	24	56	108	160
49,50,52,53-Severin-a(2/3) in each	8	16	24	51	96	140
51-Williamson-a (5 pgs.)	8	16	24	56	108	160
54,55,57,59-Severin-a(3) in each. 59-Kirby-a; last 10¢ issue (4/61)	8	16	24	51	96	140
56	7	14	21	48	89	130
58,60-New origin. 58-Kirby/Ayers-c/a "The Monster of Hidden Valley" cover/story (Kirby monster-c)	11	22	33	76	163	250
60-Edition w/handwritten issue number on cover	12	24	36	82	179	275
61,62-Kirby-a	7	14	21	48	89	130
63-74: 64-Intro. Boom-Boom	5	10	15	35	63	90
75-77-Kirby-a (reprint). 77-Black Panther-esque villain	6	12	18	37	66	95
78-89	4	8	12	27	44	60
90,95-Kirby-a	4	8	12	28	47	65
91,92: 92-Last new story; last 12¢ issue	4	8	12	25	40	55
93,94,96-99	3	6	9	16	23	30
100-Last 15¢-c	3	6	9	16	24	32
101-Origin retold/#58; Kirby-a	3	6	9	16	24	32
102-120-reprints	2	4	6	11	16	20
121-136-reprints. 129-131-(Regular 25¢ editions)	2	4	6	11	16	20
129-131-(30¢-c variants, limited distribution)(4-8/76)	4	8	12	27	44	60

NOTE: *Ayers a-13, 24, 26, 27, 63, 66. Davis c-45-47. Drucker a-23. Everett a-82, 91. Fuje a-13. Heath a-3(2), 4(3), 5(2), 7; c-13, 21, 23, 53. Keller a-16, 19, 28, 42. Kirby a-54, 55, 57-62, 75-77, 90, 95, 101, 119, 120, 129; c-10, 52, 54-65, 67-72, 74-76, 116. Maneely a-20; c-11, 12, 16, 19, 20, 24-28, 30, 35, 41, 42, 49. Powell a-38, 102, 104. Severin a-9, 29, 51, 55, 57, 99r(3); c-9, 39, 51. Shores c-1-8, 11. Trimpe c-99. Tuska a-11, 12. Whitney a-87, 89-92, 98-113, 124, 129; c-87, 89, 91, 113. Wildey a-21. Williamson a-110r. Kid Colt in #13, 14, 16-21.*

TWO GUN KID: SUNSET RIDERS
Marvel Comics: Nov, 1995 - No. 2, Dec, 1995 ($6.95, squarebound, lim. series)

	GD 2.0	VG 4.0	FN 6.0	VF 8.0	VF/NM 9.0	NM- 9.2
1,2: Fabian Nicieza scripts in all. 1-Painted-c.						7.00

TWO GUN WESTERN (1st Series) (Formerly Casey Crime Photographer #1-4? or My Love #1-4?)
Marvel/Atlas Comics (MPC): No. 5, Nov, 1950 - No. 14, June, 1952

	GD 2.0	VG 4.0	FN 6.0	VF 8.0	VF/NM 9.0	NM- 9.2
5-The Apache Kid (Intro & origin) & his horse Nightwind begin by Buscema	27	54	81	160	263	365
6-10: 8-Kid Colt, The Texas Kid & his horse Thunder begin?	20	40	60	114	182	250
11-14: 13-Black Rider app.	14	28	42	82	121	160

NOTE: *Maneely a-6, 7, 9; c-6, 11-13. Morrow a-9. Romita a-8. Wildey a-8.*

2-GUN WESTERN (2nd Series) (Formerly Billy Buckskin #1-3; Two-Gun Western #5 on)
Atlas Comics (MgPC): No. 4, May, 1956

	GD 2.0	VG 4.0	FN 6.0	VF 8.0	VF/NM 9.0	NM- 9.2
4-Colan, Ditko, Severin, Sinnott-a; Maneely-c	15	30	45	90	140	190

TWO-GUN WESTERN (Formerly 2-Gun Western)
Atlas Comics (MgPC): No. 5, July, 1956 - No. 12, Sept, 1957

	GD 2.0	VG 4.0	FN 6.0	VF 8.0	VF/NM 9.0	NM- 9.2
5-Return of the Gun-Hawk-c/story; Black Rider app.	15	30	45	86	133	180
6,7	12	24	36	69	97	125
8,10,12-Crandall-a	13	26	39	74	105	135
9,11-Williamson-a in both (5 pgs. each)	14	28	42	78	112	145

NOTE: *Ayers a-9. Colan a-5. Everett c-12. Forgione a-5, 6. Kirby a-12. Maneely a-6, 8, 12; c-5, 6, 8, 11. Morrow a-9, 10. Powell a-7, 11. Severin c-10. Sinnott a-5. Wildey a-9.*

TWO MINUTE WARNING

2001: A Space Odyssey #2 © MAR

Uber #3 © Avatar

Ultimate Extinction #1 © MAR

	GD 2.0	VG 4.0	FN 6.0	VF 8.0	VF/NM 9.0	NM- 9.2

Ultimate Sports Ent.: 2000 - No. 2 ($3.95, cardstock covers)

1,2-NFL players & Teddy Roosevelt battle evil 4.00

TWO MOUSEKETEERS, THE (See 4-Color #475, 603, 642 under M.G.M.'s...;

TWO ON A GUILLOTINE (See Movie Classics)

TWO-STEP
DC Comics (Cliffhanger): Dec, 2003 - No. 3, Jul, 2004 ($2.95, limited series)

1-3-Warren Ellis-s/Amanda Conner-a 3.00
TPB (2010, $19.99) r/#1-3; sketch pages; script for #1 with B&W art 20.00

2000 A.D. MONTHLY/PRESENTS (Showcase #25 on)
Eagle Comics/Quality Comics No. 5 on: 4/85 - #6, 9/85; 4/86 - #54, 1991 ($1.25-$1.50, Mando paper)

1-6,1-25:1-4 r/British series featuring Judge Dredd; Alan Moore scripts begin.
1-25 ($1.25)-Reprints from British 2000 AD 4.00
26,27/28, 29/30, 31-54: 27/28, 29/30,31-Guice-c 3.00

2001, A SPACE ODYSSEY (Movie) (See adaptation in Treasury edition)
Marvel Comics Group: Dec, 1976 - No. 10, Sept, 1977 (30¢)

	GD	VG	FN	VF	VF/NM	NM-
1-Kirby-c/a in all	3	6	9	17	26	35
2-7,9,10	2	4	6	9	12	15
7,9,10-(35¢-c variants, limited distribution)(6-9/77)	4	8	12	23	37	50
8-Origin/1st app. Machine Man (called Mr. Machine)	5	10	15	31	53	75
8-(35¢-c variant, limited distribution)(6,8/77)	11	22	33	76	163	250
...Treasury 1 ('76, 84 pgs.)-All new Kirby-a	3	6	9	16	23	30

2001 NIGHTS
Viz Premiere Comics: 1990 - No. 10, 1991 ($3.75, B&W, lim. series, mature readers, 84 pgs.)

1-10: Japanese sci-fi. 1-Wraparound-c 5.00

2010 (Movie)
Marvel Comics Group: Apr, 1985 - No. 2, May, 1985

1,2-r/Marvel Super Special movie adaptation. 4.00

TYPHOID (Also see Daredevil)
Marvel Comics: Nov, 1995 - No. 4, Feb, 1996 ($3.95, squarebound, lim. series)

1-4: Van Fleet-c/a 4.00

ÜBER
Avatar Press: No. 0, Mar, 2013 - Present ($3.99)

0-10-Kieron Gillen-s/Caanan White-a 4.00
... Special 1 (3/14, $5.99) Andrade-a 6.00

UFO & ALIEN COMIX
Warren Publishing Co.: Jan, 1978 (B&W magazine, 84 pgs., one-shot)

	GD	VG	FN	VF	VF/NM	NM-
nn-Toth-a, J. Severin-a(r); Pie-s	2	4	6	10	14	18

UFO & OUTER SPACE (Formerly UFO Flying Saucers)
Gold Key: No. 14, June, 1978 - No. 25, Feb, 1980 (All painted covers)

	GD	VG	FN	VF	VF/NM	NM-
14-Reprints UFO Flying Saucers #3	1	3	4	6	8	10
15,16-Reprints	1	3	4	6	8	10
17-25: 17-20-New material. 23-McWilliams-a. 24-(3 pg.-r). 25-Reprints UFO Flying Saucers #2 w/cover	1	3	4	6	8	10

UFO ENCOUNTERS
Western Publishing Co.: May, 1978 ($1.95, 228 pgs.)

	GD	VG	FN	VF	VF/NM	NM-
11192-Reprints UFO Flying Saucers	4	8	12	27	44	60
11404-Vol.1 (128 pgs.)-See UFO Mysteries for Vol. 2	4	8	12	23	37	50

UFO FLYING SAUCERS (UFO & Outer Space #14 on)
Gold Key: Oct, 1968 - No. 13, Jan, 1977 (No. 2 on, 36 pgs.)

	GD	VG	FN	VF	VF/NM	NM-
1(30035-810) (68 pgs.)	5	10	15	33	57	80
2(11/70), 3(11/72), 4(11/74)	3	6	9	17	26	35
5(2/75)-13: Bolle-a #4 on	2	4	6	13	18	22

UFO MYSTERIES
Western Publishing Co.: 1978 ($1.00, reprints, 96 pgs.)

	GD	VG	FN	VF	VF/NM	NM-
11400-(Vol.2)-Cont'd from UFO Encounters, pgs. 129-224	4	8	12	23	37	50

ULTIMAN GIANT ANNUAL (See Big Bang Comics)
Image Comics: Nov, 2001 ($4.95, B&W, one-shot)

1-Homage to DC 1960's annuals 5.00

ULTIMATE... (Collects 4-issue alternate titles from X-Men Age of Apocalypse crossovers)
Marvel Comics: May, 1995 ($8.95, trade paperbacks, gold foil covers)

Amazing X-Men, Astonishing X-Men, Factor-X, Gambit & the X-Ternals, Generation Next, X-Calibre, X-Man 9.00
Weapon X 10.00

ULTIMATE ADVENTURES
Marvel Comics: Nov, 2002 - No. 6, Dec, 2003 ($2.25)

1-6: 1-Intro. Hawk-Owl; Zimmerman-s/Fegredo-a. 3-Ultimates app. 3.00
One Tin Soldier TPB (2005, $12.99) r/#1-6 13.00

ULTIMATE ANNUALS
Marvel Comics: 2006; 2007 ($13.99, SC)

Vol. 1 (2006, $13.99) r/Ult. FF Ann. #1, Ult. X-Men Ann. #1, Ult S-M #1, Ultimates Ann #1 14.00
Vol. 2 (2007, $13.99) r/Ult. FF Ann. #2, Ult. X-Men Ann. #2, Ult S-M #2, Ultimates Ann #2 14.00

ULTIMATE ARMOR WARS (Follows Ultimatum x-over)
Marvel Comics: Nov, 2009 - No. 4, Apr, 2010 ($3.99, limited series)

1-4-Warren Ellis-s/Steve Kurth-a/Brandon Peterson-c. 1-Variant-c by Kurth 4.00

ULTIMATE AVENGERS (Follows Ultimatum x-over)
Marvel Comics: Oct, 2009 - No. 18 ($3.99)

1-6-Mark Millar-s/Carlos Pacheco-a/c; Red Skull app. 4.00
1-Variant Red Skull-c by Leinil Yu 8.00
7-12-(Ultimate Avengers 2 #1-6 on cover) Yu-a; Punisher joins. 10-Origin Ghost Rider 4.00
7-Variant Ghost Rider-c by Silvestri 8.00
13-18-(Ultimate Avengers 3 #1-6 on cover) Dillon-a; Blade and a new Daredevil app. 4.00

ULTIMATE AVENGERS VS. NEW ULTIMATES (Death of Spider-Man tie-in)
Marvel Comics: Apr, 2011 - No. 6, Sept, 2011 ($3.99, limited series)

1-6: 1-Millar-s/Yu-a/c; variant covers by Cho & Hitch. 3-6-Punisher app. 4.00

ULTIMATE CAPTAIN AMERICA
Marvel Comics: Mar, 2011 - No. 4, Jun, 2011 ($3.99)

1-4: 1-Aaron-s/Garney-a; 2 covers by Garney & McGuinness 4.00
Annual 1 (12/08, $3.99, one-shot) Origin of the Black Panther; Djurdjevic-a 4.00

ULTIMATE CIVIL WAR: SPIDER-HAM (See Civil War and related titles)
Marvel Comics: March, 2007 ($2.99, one-shot)

1-Spoof of Civil War series featuring Spider-Ham; art by various incl. Olivetti, Severin 3.00

ULTIMATE COMICS IRON MAN
Marvel Comics: Dec, 2012 - No. 4, Mar, 2013 ($3.99, limited series)

1-4-Edmonson-s/Buffagni-a/Stockton-c 4.00

ULTIMATE COMICS SPIDER-MAN (See Ultimate Spider-Man 2011 series)

ULTIMATE COMICS ULTIMATES (See Ultimates 2011 series)

ULTIMATE COMICS WOLVERINE
Marvel Comics: May, 2013 - No. 4, Jul, 2013 ($3.99, limited series)

1-4: 1-Bunn-s/Messina-a/Art Adams-c; Wolverine app. in flashback 4.00

ULTIMATE COMICS X-MEN (See Ultimate X-Men 2011 series)

ULTIMATE DAREDEVIL AND ELEKTRA
Marvel Comics: Jan, 2003 - No. 4, Mar, 2003 ($2.25, limited series)

1-4-Rucka-s/Larroca-c/a; 1st meeting of Elektra and Matt Murdock 3.00
... Vol.1 TPB (2003, $11.99) r/#1-4, Daredevil Vol. 2 #9; Larroca sketch pages 12.00

ULTIMATE DOOM (Follows Ultimate Mystery mini-series)
Marvel Comics: Feb, 2011 - No. 4, May, 2011 ($3.99, limited series)

1-4-Bendis-s/Sandoval-a; Fantastic Four, Spider-Man, Jessica Drew & Nick Fury app. 4.00

ULTIMATE ELEKTRA
Marvel Comics: Oct, 2004 - No. 5, Feb, 2005 ($2.25, limited series)

1-5-Carey-s/Larroca-c/a. 2-Bullseye app. 3.00
... : Devil's Due TPB (2005, $11.99) r/#1-5 12.00

ULTIMATE ENEMY (Follows Ultimatum x-over)(Leads into Ultimate Mystery)
Marvel Comics: Mar, 2010 - No. 4, July, 2010 ($3.99, limited series)

1-4-Bendis-s/Sandoval-a 1-Covers by McGuinness and Pearson 4.00

ULTIMATE EXTINCTION (See Ultimate Nightmare and Ultimate Secret limited series)
Marvel Comics: Mar, 2006 - No. 5, July, 2006 ($2.99, limited series)

1-5-The coming of Gah Lak Tus; Ellis-s/Peterson-a 3.00
TPB (2006, $12.99) r/#1-5 13.00

ULTIMATE FALLOUT (Follows Death of Spider-Man in Ultimate Spider-Man #160)
Marvel Comics: Sept, 2011 - No. 6, Oct, 2011 ($3.99, weekly limited series)

1-3,5,6: 1-Bendis-s/Bagley-a/c. 2,6-Hitch-c. 3,5-Andy Kubert-c 4.00

	GD	VG	FN	VF	VF/NM	NM-
4-Debut of Miles Morales as the new Spider-Man; polybagged	2	4	6	11	16	20

ULTIMATE FANTASTIC FOUR (Continues in Ultimatum mini-series)
Marvel Comics: Feb, 2004 - No. 60, Apr, 2009 ($2.25/$2.50/$2.99)

Ultimate Fantastic Four #7 © MAR

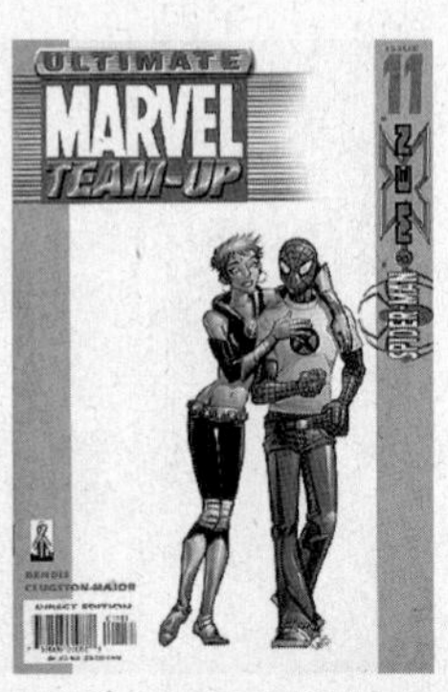

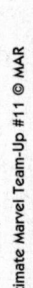

Ultimate Marvel Team-Up #11 © MAR

Ultimates 2 #12 © MAR

	GD 2.0	VG 4.0	FN 6.0	VF 8.0	VF/NM 9.0	NM- 9.2

1-Bendis & Millar-s/Adam Kubert-a/Hitch-c 5.00
2-20: 2-Adam Kubert-a/c; intro. Moleman 7-Ellis-s/Immonen-a begin; Dr. Doom app. 13-18-Kubert-a. 19,20-Jae Lee-a. 20-Begin $2.50-c 3.50
21-Marvel Zombies; begin Greg Land-c/a; Mark Millar-s; variant-c by Land 5.00
22-29,33-59: 24-26-Namor app. 28-President Thor. 33-38-Ferry-a. 42-46-Silver Surfer 3.00
30-32-Marvel Zombies; Millar-s/Land-a; Dr. Doom app. 5.00
30-32-Zombie variant-c by Suydam 6.00
50-White variant-c by Kirkham 5.00
60-($3.99) Ultimatum crossover; Kirkham-a 4.00
Annual 1 (10/05, $3.99) The Inhumans app.; Jae Lee-a/Mark Millar-s/Greg Land-c 4.00
Annual 2 (10/06, $3.99) Mole Man app.; Immonen & Irving-a/Carey-s 4.00
... MGC #1 (6/11, $1.00) r/#1 with "Marvel's Greatest Comics" logo on cover 3.00
.../Ult. X-Men Annual 1 (11/08, $3.99) Continued from Ult. X-Men/Ult. F.F. Annual #1 4.00
.../X-Men 1 (3/06, $2.99) Carey-s/Ferry-a; continued from Ult. X-Men/Fantastic Four #1 3.00
... Vol. 1: The Fantastic (2004, $12.99, TPB) r/#1-6; cover gallery 13.00
... Vol. 2: Doom (2004, $12.99, TPB) r/#7-12 13.00
... Vol. 3: N-Zone (2005, $12.99, TPB) r/#13-18 13.00
... Vol. 4: Inhuman (2005, $12.99, TPB) r/#19,20 & Annual #1 13.00
... Vol. 5: Crossover (2006, $12.99, TPB) r/#21-26 13.00
... Vol. 6: Frightful (2006, $14.99, TPB) r/#27-32; gallery of cover sketches & variants 15.00
... Vol. 7: God War (2007, $16.99, TPB) r/#33-38 17.00
... Vol. 8: Devils (2007, $12.99, TPB) r/#39-41 & Annual #2 13.00
... Vol. 9: Silver Surfer (2007, $13.99, TPB) r/#42-46 14.00
Volume 1 HC (2005, $29.99, 7x11", dust jacket) r/#1-12; introduction, proposals and scripts by Millar and Bendis; character design pages by Hitch 30.00
Volume 2 HC (2006, $29.99, 7x11", dust jacket) r/#13-20; Jae Lee sketch page 30.00
Volume 3 HC (2007, $29.99, 7x11", dust jacket) r/#21-32; Greg Land sketch pages 30.00
Volume 4 HC (2007, $29.99, 7x11", dust jacket) r/#33-41, Annual #2, Ultimate FF/X-Men and Ultimate X-Men/FF; character design pages 30.00
Volume 5 HC (2008, $34.99, 7x11", dust jacket) r/#42-53 35.00

ULTIMATE GALACTUS TRILOGY
Marvel Comics: 2007 ($34.99, hardcover, dustjacket)

HC-Oversized reprint of Ultimate Nightmare #1-5, Ultimate Secret #1-4, Ultimate Vision #0, and Ultimate Extinction #1-5; sketch pages and cover gallery 35.00

ULTIMATE HAWKEYE (Ultimate Comics)
Marvel Comics: Oct, 2011 - No. 4, Jan, 2012 ($3.99, limited series)

1-4: 1-Hickman-s/Sandoval-a/Andrews-c; polybagged. 2-4-Hulk app. 4.00
1-Variant-c by Neal Adams 6.00
1-Variant-c by Adam Kubert 8.00

ULTIMATE HULK
Marvel Comics: Dec, 2008 ($3.99, one-shot)

Annual 1 (12/08, $3.99) Zarda battles Hulk; McGuinness & Djurdjevic-a/Loeb-s 4.00

ULTIMATE HUMAN
Marvel Comics: Mar, 2008 - No. 4, Jun, 2008 ($2.99, limited series)

1-4-Iron Man vs. The Hulk; The Leader app.; Ellis-s/Nord-a 3.00
HC (2008, $19.99) r/#1-4 20.00

ULTIMATE IRON MAN
Marvel Comics: May, 2005 - No. 5, Feb, 2006 ($2.99, limited series)

1-Origin of Iron Man; Orson Scott Card-s/Andy Kubert-a; two covers 4.00
1-2nd & 3rd printings; each with B&W variant-c 3.00
2-5-Kubert-c 3.00
Volume 1 HC (2006, $19.99, dust jacket) r/#1-5; rough cut of script for #1, cover sketches 20.00
Volume 1 SC (2006, $14.99) r/#1-5; rough cut of script for #1, cover sketches 15.00

ULTIMATE IRON MAN II
Marvel Comics: Feb, 2008 - No. 5, July, 2008 ($2.99, limited series)

1-5-Early days of the Iron Man prototype; Orson Scott Card-s/Pasqual Ferry-a/c 3.00

ULTIMATE MARVEL FLIP MAGAZINE
Marvel Comics: July, 2005 - No. 26, Aug, 2007 ($3.99/$4.99)

1-11-Reprints Ultimate Fantastic Four and Ultimate X-Men in flip format 4.00
12-26-($4.99) 5.00

ULTIMATE MARVEL MAGAZINE
Marvel Comics: Feb, 2001 - No. 11, 2002 ($3.99, magazine size)

1-11: Reprints of recent stories from the Ultimate titles plus Marvel news and features. 1-Reprints Ultimate Spider-Man #1&2. 11-Lord of the Rings-c 4.00

ULTIMATE MARVEL SAMPLER
Marvel Comics: 2007 (no cover price, limited series)

1-Previews of 2008 Ultimate Marvel story arcs; Finch-c 3.00

ULTIMATE MARVEL TEAM-UP (Spider-Man Team-up)
Marvel Comics: Apr, 2001 - No. 16, July, 2002 ($2.99/$2.25)

1-Spider-Man & Wolverine; Bendis-s in all; Matt Wagner-a/c 5.00
2,3-Hulk; Hester-a 3.50
4,5,9-16: 4,5-Iron Man; Allred-a. 9-Fantastic Four; Mahfood-a. 10-Man-Thing; Totleben-a. 11-X-Men; Clugston-Major-a. 12,13-Dr. Strange; McKeever-a.14-Black Widow; Terry Moore-a. 15,16-Shang-Chi; Mays-a 3.00
6-8-Punisher; Sienkiewicz-a. 7,8-Daredevil app. 4.00
TPB (11/01, $14.95) r/#1-5 15.00
... Ultimate Collection TPB ('06, $29.99) r/#1-16 & Ult. Spider-Man Spec.; sketch pages 30.00
HC (8/02, $39.99) r/#1-16 & Ult. Spider-Man Special; Bendis afterword 40.00
...: Vol. 2 TPB (2003, $11.99) r/#9-13; Mahfood-c 12.00
...: Vol. 3 TPB (2003, $12.99) r/#14-16 & Ultimate Spider-Man Super Special; Moore-c 13.00

ULTIMATE MYSTERY (Follows Ultimate Enemy)(Leads into Ultimate Doom)
Marvel Comics: Sept, 2010 - No. 4, Dec, 2010 ($3.99, limited series)

1-4-Bendis-s/Sandoval-a; Rick Jones returns; Captain Marvel app. 1-3-Campbell-c 4.00

ULTIMATE NEW ULTIMATES (Follows Ultimatum x-over)
Marvel Comics: May, 2010 - No. 5, Mar, 2011 ($3.99)

1-5: 1-Jeph Loeb-s/Frank Cho-a; 6-page wraparound-c by Cho; Defenders app. 4.00
1-Villains variant-c by Yu 8.00

ULTIMATE NIGHTMARE (Leads into Ultimate Secret limited series)
Marvel Comics: Oct, 2004 - No. 5, Feb, 2005 ($2.25, limited series)

1-5: Ellis-s; Ultimates, X-Men, Nick Fury app. 1,2,4,5-Hairsine-a/c. 3-Epting-a 3.00
Ultimate Galactus Book 1: Nightmare TPB (2005, $12.99) r/Ultimate Nightmare #1-5 13.00

ULTIMATE ORIGINS
Marvel Comics: Aug, 2008 - No. 5, Dec, 2008 ($2.99, limited series)

1-5-Bendis-s/Guice-a. 1-Nick Fury origin in the 1940s. 2-Capt. America origin 3.00

ULTIMATE POWER
Marvel Comics: Dec, 2006 - No. 9, Feb, 2008 ($2.99, limited series)

1-9: 1-Ultimate FF meets the Squadron Supreme; Bendis-s; Land-a/c. 2-Spider-Man, X-Men and the Ultimates app. 6-Doom app. 3.00
1-Variant sketch-c 5.00
1-Director's Cut (2007, $3.99) r/#1 and B&W pencil and ink pages; covers to #2,3 4.00
HC (2008, $34.99) oversized r/series; profile pages; B&W sketch art 35.00

ULTIMATES, THE (Avengers of the Ultimate line)
Marvel Comics: Mar, 2002 - No. 13, Apr, 2004 ($2.25)

1-Intro. Capt. America; Millar-s/Hitch-a & wraparound-c 6.00
2-Intro. Giant-Man and the Wasp 4.00
3-12: 3-1st Capt. America in new costume. 4-Intro. Thor. 5-Ultimates vs. The Hulk. 8-Intro. Hawkeye 3.00
13-($3.50) 4.00
... MGC #1 (5/11, $1.00) r/#1 with "Marvel's Greatest Comics" logo on cover 3.00
... Saga (2007, $3.99) Re-caps 1st 2 Ultimates series; new framing art by Charest; prelude to Ultimates 3 series; Brooks-c 4.00
... Volume 1 HC (2004, $29.99) oversized r/series; commentary pages with Millar & Hitch; cover gallery and character design pages; intro. by Joss Whedon 30.00
... Volume 1: Super-Human TPB (8/02, $12.99) r/#1-6 13.00
... Volume 2: Homeland Security TPB (2004, $17.99) r/#7-13 18.00

ULTIMATES (Ultimate Comics) (Continues in Hunger)
Marvel Comics: Oct, 2011 - No. 30, Nov, 2013 ($3.99)

1-30: 1-Hickman-s/Ribic-a/Andrews-c; polybagged. 4-Reed Richards returns 4.00
1-Variant-c by Esad Ribic 6.00
#18.1 (2/13, $2.99) Eaglesham-a; Stark gets the Iron Patriot armor 3.00
Ultimate Comics Ultimates Must Have 1 (2/12, $4.99) r/#1-3 5.00

ULTIMATES 2
Marvel Comics: Feb, 2005 - No. 13, Feb, 2007 ($2.99/$3.99)

1-Millar-s/Hitch-a; Giant-Man becomes Ant-Man 4.00
2-11: 6-Intro. The Defenders. 7-Hawkeye shot. 8-Intro The Liberators 3.00
12,13-($3.99) Wraparound-c; X-Men, Fantastic Four, Spider-Man app. 4.00
13-Variant white cover featuring The Wasp 15.00
Annual 1 (10/05, $3.99) Millar-s/Dillon-a/Hitch-c; Defenders app. 4.00
Annual 2 (10/06, $3.99) Deodato-a; flashback to WWII with Sook-a; Falcon app. 4.00
HC (2007, $34.99) oversized r/series; commentary pages with Millar & Hitch; cover gallery, sketch and script pages; intro. by Jonathan Ross 35.00
... Volume 1: Gods & Monsters TPB (2005, $15.99) r/#1-6 16.00
... Volume 2: Grand Theft America TPB (2007, $19.99) r/#7-13; cover gallery w/sketches 20.00

ULTIMATES 3
Marvel Comics: Feb, 2008 - No. 5, Nov, 2008 ($2.99)

1-Loeb-s/Madureira-a; two gatefold wraparound covers by Madureira; Scarlet Witch shot 4.00

Ultimate Spider-Man #60 © MAR

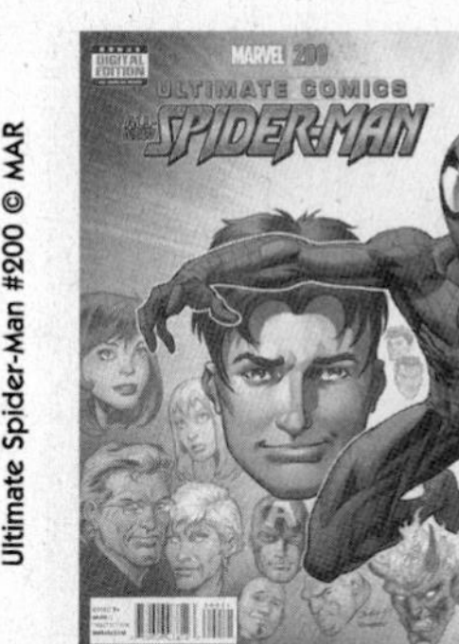

Ultimate Spider-Man #200 © MAR

Ultimate Vision #1 © MAR

GD VG FN VF VF/NM NM-
2.0 4.0 6.0 8.0 9.0 9.2

1,2-Second printings: 1-Wraparound cover by Madureira. 2-Madureira-c 3.00
2-5: 2-Spider-Man app. 3-Wolverine app. 5-Two gatefold wraparound-c (Heroes & Ultron) 3.00
2-Variant Thor cover by Turner 8.00
3-Variant Scarlet Witch cover by Cho 8.00
4-Variant Valkyrie cover by Finch 4.00

ULTIMATE SECRET (See Ultimate Nightmare limited series)
Marvel Comics: May, 2005 - No. 4, Dec, 2005 ($2.99, limited series)

1-4-Ellis-s; Captain Marvel app. 1,2-McNiven-a. 2,3-Ultimates & FF app. 3.00
Ultimate Galactus Book 2: Secret TPB (2006, $12.99) r/#1-4 13.00

ULTIMATE SECRETS
Marvel Comics: 2008 ($3.99, one-shot)

1-Handbook-styled profiles of secondary teams and characters from Ultimate universe 4.00

ULTIMATE SIX (Reprinted in Ultimate Spider-Man Vol. 5 hardcover)
Marvel Comics: Nov, 2003 - No. 7, June, 2004 ($2.25) (See Ultimate Spider-Man for TPB)

1-The Ultimates & Spider-Man team-up; Bendis-s/Quesada & Hairsine-a; Cassaday-c 5.00
2-7-Hairsine-a; Cassaday-c 3.00

ULTIMATE SPIDER-MAN
Marvel Comics: Oct, 2000 - No. 133, June, 2009 ($2.99/$2.25/$2.99/$3.99)

1-Bendis-s/Bagley & Thibert-a; cardstock-c; introduces revised origin and cast separate from regular Spider-continuity 6 12 18 41 76 110
1-Variant white-c (Retailer incentive) 9 18 27 59 117 175
1-DF Edition 5 10 15 34 60 85
1-Kay Bee Toys variant edition 2 4 6 9 12 15
2-Cover with Spider-Man on car 3 6 9 18 27 35
2-Cover with Spider-Man swinging past building 3 6 9 18 27 35
3,4: 4-Uncle Ben killed 2 4 6 10 14 18
5-7: 6,7-Green Goblin app. 2 4 6 9 12 15
8-13: 13-Reveals secret to MJ 1 3 4 6 8 10
14-21: 14-Intro. Gwen Stacy & Dr. Octopus 5.00
22-($3.50) Green Goblin returns 6.00
23-32 4.00
33-1st Ultimate Venom-c; intro. Eddie Brock 5.00
34-38-Ultimate Venom 4.00
39-49,51-59: 39-Nick Fury app. 43,44-X-Men app. 46-Prelude to Ultimate Six; Sandman app. 51-53-Elektra app. 54-59-Doctor Octopus app. 3.00
50-($2.99) Intro. Black Cat 4.00
60-Intro. Ultimate Carnage on cover 4.00
61-Intro Ben Reilly; Punisher app. 3.00
62-Gwen Stacy killed by Carnage 4.00
63-92: 63,64-Carnage app. 66,67-Wolverine app. 68,69-Johnny Storm app. 78-Begin $2.50-c. 79-Debut Moon Knight. 81-85-Black Cat app. 90-Vulture app. 91-94-Deadpool 3.00
93-99: 93-Begin $2.99-c. 95-Morbius & Blade app. 97-99-Clone Saga 3.00
100-($3.99) Wraparound-c; Clone Saga; re-cap of previous issues 4.00
101-103-Clone Saga continues; Fantastic Four app. 102-Spider-Woman origin 3.00
104-($3.99) Clone Saga concludes; Fantastic Four and Dr. Octopus app. 4.00
105-132: 106-110-Daredevil app. 111-Last Bagley art; Immonen-a (6 pgs.) 112-Immonen-a; Norman Osborn app. 118-Liz Allen ignites. 123,128-Venom app. 129-132-Ultimatum 3.00
133-($3.99) Ultimatum crossover; Spider-Woman app. 4.00
(Issues #150-up, see second series)
Annual 1 (10/05, $3.99) Kitty Pryde app.; Bendis-s/Brooks-a/Bagley-c 4.00
Annual 2 (10/06, $3.99) Punisher, Moon Knight and Daredevil app.; Bendis-s/Brooks-a 4.00
Annual 3 (12/08, $3.99) Mysterio app.; Bendis-s/Lafuente-a 4.00
Collected Edition (1/01, $3.99) r/#1-3 4.00
Free Comic Book Day giveaway (5/02) - r/#1 with "Free Comic Book Day" banner on-c 3.00
... MGC #1 (5/11, $1.00) r/#1 with "Marvel's Greatest Comics" logo on cover 3.00
...Special (7/02, $3.50) art by Bagley and various incl. Romita, Sr., Brereton, Cho, Mack, Sienkiewicz, Phillips, Pearson, Oeming, Mahfood, Russell 4.00
Ultimate Spider-Man 100 Project (2007, $10.00, SC, charity book for the HERO Initiative) collection of 100 variant covers by Romita Sr. & Jr., Cho, Bagley, Quesada and more 10.00
...: Venom HC (2007, $19.99) r/#33-39 20.00
...(Vol. 1): Power and Responsibility TPB (4/01, $14.95) r/#1-7 15.00
...(Vol. 2): Learning Curve TPB (12/01, $14.95) r/#8-13 15.00
...(Vol. 3): Double Trouble TPB (6/02, $17.95) r/#14-21 18.00
Vol. 4: Legacy TPB (2002, $14.99) r/#22-27 15.00
Vol. 5: Public Scrutiny TPB (2003, $11.99) r/#28-32 12.00
Vol. 6: Venom TPB (2003, $15.99) r/#33-39 16.00
Vol. 7: Irresponsible TPB (2003, $12.99) r/#40-45 13.00
Vol. 8: Cats & Kings TPB (2004, $17.99) r/#47-53 18.00
Vol. 9: Ultimate Six TPB (2004, $17.99) r/#46 & Ultimate Six #1-7 18.00
Vol. 10: Hollywood TPB (2004, $12.99) r/#54-59 13.00
Vol. 11: Carnage TPB (2004, $12.99) r/#60-65 13.00
Vol. 12: Superstars TPB (2005, $12.99) r/#66-71 13.00

GD VG FN VF VF/NM NM-
2.0 4.0 6.0 8.0 9.0 9.2

Vol. 13: Hobgoblin TPB (2005, $15.99) r/#72-78 16.00
Vol. 14: Warriors TPB (2005, $17.99) r/#79-85 18.00
Vol. 15: Silver Sable TPB (2006, $15.99) r/#86-90 & Annual #1 16.00
Vol. 16: Deadpool TPB (2006, $19.99) r/#91-96 & Annual #2 20.00
Vol. 17: Clone Saga TPB (2007, $24.99) r/#97-105 25.00
Vol. 18: Ultimate Knights TPB (2007, $13.99) r/#106-111 14.00
Vol. 19: Death of a Goblin TPB (2008, $14.99) r/#112-117 15.00
Hardcover (3/02, $34.95, 7x11", dust jacket) r/#1-13 & Amazing Fantasy #15; sketch pages and Bill Jemas' initial plot and character outlines 35.00
Volume 2 HC (2003, $29.99, 7x11", dust jacket) r/#14-27; pin-ups & sketch pages 30.00
Volume 3 HC (2003, $29.99, 7x11", dust jacket) r/#28-39 & #1/2; script pages 30.00
Volume 4 HC (2004, $29.99, 7x11", dust jacket) r/#40-45, 47-53; sketch pages 30.00
Volume 5 HC (2004, $29.99, 7x11", dust jacket) r/#46,54-59, Ultimate Six #1-7 30.00
Volume 6 HC (2005, $29.99, 7x11", dust jacket) r/#60-71; sketch page 30.00
Volume 7 HC (2006, $29.99, 7x11", dust jacket) r/#72-85; sketch & profile pages 30.00
Volume 8 HC (2007, $29.99, 7x11", dust jacket) r/#86-96 & Annual #1&2; sketch page 30.00
Volume 9 HC (2008, $39.99, 7x11", dust jacket) r/#97-111; sketch pages 40.00
Volume 10 HC (2009, $39.99, 7x11", dust jacket) r/#112-122; sketch pages 40.00
Wizard #1/2 1 3 4 6 8 10

ULTIMATE SPIDER-MAN (2nd series)(Follows Ultimatum x-over)
Marvel Comics: Oct, 2009 - No. 15, Dec, 2010; No. 150, Jan, 2011 - No. 160, Aug, 2011 ($3.99)

1-15: 1-Bendis-s/Lafuente-a/c; new Mysterio. 1-Variant-c by Djurdjevic. 7,8-Miyazawa-a. 9-Spider-Woman app. 4.00
150-(1/11, $5.99) Resumes original numbering; wraparound-c by Lafuente; Bendis-s with art by Lafuente, Pichelli, Joëlle Jones, McKelvie & Young; r/Ult. S-M Special #1 6.00
150-Variant wraparound-c by Bagley 10.00
151-159: 151-154-Black Cat & Mysterio app. 157-Spider-Man shot by Punisher 4.00
153-159-Variant covers. 153-155-Pichelli. 157-McGuinness. 158-McNiven. 159-Cho 8.00
160-Black Polybagged; Bagley cover inside; Death of Spider-Man part 5 4.00
160-Red Polybagged variant; Kaluta cover inside; Death of Spider-Man part 5 20.00

ULTIMATE SPIDER-MAN (3rd series, with Miles Morales)(See Ultimate Fallout #4 for debut)
Marvel Comics: Nov, 2011 - No. 28, Dec, 2013 ($3.99)

1-Polybagged, with Kaare Andrews-c; Bendis-s/Pichelli-a; origin 5.00
1-Variant Pichelli-c with unmasked Spider-Man 4 8 12 27 44 60
1-Variant Pichelli-c with Spider-Man & city bkgrd 5 10 15 35 63 90
2-28: 4,5-Spider-Woman app. 5-Nick Fury & Ultimates app. 6-Samnee-a. 19-22-Venom War; Pichelli-a. 23-Cloak and Dagger app. 28-Leads into Cataclysm 4.00
#16.1 (12/12, $2.99) Marquez-a; Venom returns 3.00
200-(6/14, $4.99) Art by Marquez and others; 2 interlocking covers by Bagley & Marquez 5.00
Ultimate Comics Spider-Man Must Have 1 (2/12, $4.99) r/#1-3 5.00

ULTIMATE SPIDER-MAN (Based on the animated series)(Titled Marvel Universe... for #1)
Marvel Comics: Jun, 2012 - Present ($2.99)

1-24: 1-Agent Coulson app. 13-Iron Man app. 15-Hulk app. 16,19-Venom app. 3.00

ULTIMATE TALES FLIP MAGAZINE
Marvel Comics: July, 2005 - No. 26, Aug, 2007 ($3.99/$4.99)

1-11-Each reprints 2 issues of Ultimate Spider-Man in flip format 4.00
12-26-($4.99) 5.00

ULTIMATE THOR
Marvel Comics: Dec, 2010 - No. 4, Apr, 2011 ($3.99, limited series)

1-4: 1-Hickman-s/Pacheco-a; two covers by Pacheco & Choi; origin story 4.00

ULTIMATE VISION
Marvel Comics: No. 0, Jan, 2007 - No. 5, Jan, 2008 ($2.99, limited series)

0-Reprints back-up serial from Ultimate Extinction and related series; pin-ups 3.00
1-5: 1-(2/07) Carey-s/Peterson-a/c 3.00
TPB (2007, $14.99) r/#0-5; design pages and cover gallery 15.00

ULTIMATE WAR
Marvel Comics: Feb, 2003 - No. 4, Apr, 2003 ($2.25, limited series)

1-4-Millar-s/Bachalo-c/a; The Ultimates vs. Ultimate X-Men 3.00
Ultimate X-Men Vol. 5: Ultimate War TPB (2003, $10.99) r/#1-4 11.00

ULTIMATE WOLVERINE VS. HULK
Marvel Comics: Feb, 2006 - No. 6, July, 2009 ($2.99, limited series)

1,2-Leinil Yu-a/c; Damon Lindelof-s. 2-(4/06) 4.00
1,2-(2009) New printings 3.00
3-6: 3-(5/09) Intro. She-Hulk. 4-Origin She-Hulk 3.00

ULTIMATE X (Follows Ultimatum x-over)
Marvel Comics: Apr, 2010 - No. 5, Aug, 2011 ($3.99)

1-5: 1-Jeph Loeb-s/Art Adams-a; two covers by Adams. 5-Hulk app. 4.00

Ultimate X-Men #34 © MAR

Ultimatum #1 © MAR

Ultraforce (2nd series) #15 © MAL

GD VG FN VF VF/NM NM-
2.0 4.0 6.0 8.0 9.0 9.2

ULTIMATE X-MEN
Marvel Comics: Feb, 2001 - No. 100, Apr, 2009 ($2.99/$2.25/$2.50)

1-Millar-s/Adam Kubert & Thibert-a; cardstock-c; introduces revised origin and cast separate from regular X-Men continuity 2 4 6 9 12 15
1-DF Edition 2 4 6 9 12 15
1-DF Sketch Cover Edition 3 6 9 14 20 25
1-Free Comic Book Day Edition (7/03) r/#1 with "Free Comic Book Day" banner on-c 3.00
2 2 4 6 9 12 15
3-6 1 3 4 6 8 10
7-10 6.00
11-24,26-33: 13-Intro. Gambit. 18,19-Bachalo-a. 23,24-Andrews-a 4.00
25-($3.50) leads into the Ultimate War mini-series; Kubert-a 5.00
34-Spider-Man-c/app.; Bendis-s begin; Finch-a 5.00
35-74: 35-Spider-Man app. 36,37-Daredevil-c/app. 40-Intro. Angel. 42-Intro. Dazzler. 44-Beast dies. 46-Intro. Mr. Sinister. 50-53-Kubert-a; Gambit app. 54-57,59-63-Immonen-a. 60-Begin $2.50-c. 61-Variant Coipel-c. 66-Kirkman-s begin. 69-Begin $2.99-c 3.00
61-Retailer Edition with variant Coipel B&W sketch-c 10.00
75-($3.99) Turner-c; intro. Cable; back-up story with Emma Frost's students 4.00
76-99: 76-Intro. Bishop. 91-Fantastic Four app. 92-96-Phoenix app. 96-Spider-Man app. 99-Ultimatum x-over 3.00
100-($3.99) Ultimatum x-over; Brooks-a 4.00
Annual 1 (10/05, $3.99) Vaughan-s/Raney-a; Gambit & Rogue in Vegas 4.00
Annual 2 (10/06, $3.99) Kirkman-s/Larroca-a; Nightcrawler & Dazzler 4.00
.../Fantastic Four 1 (2/06, $2.99) Carey-s/Ferry-a; concluded in Ult. Fantastic Four/X-Men 3.00
... MGC #1 (6/11, $1.00) r/#1 with "Marvel's Greatest Comics" logo on cover 3.00
.../Ult. Fantastic Four Ann. 1 (11/08, $3.99) Continues in Ult. F.F./Ult. X-Men Annual #1 4.00
.../Fantastic Four TPB (2006, $12.99) reprints Ult X-Men/Ult. FF x-over and Official Handbook of the Ultimate Marvel Universe #1-2 13.00
... Ultimate Collection Vol. 1 (2006, $24.99) r/#1-12 & #1/2; unused Bendis script for #1 25.00
... Ultimate Collection Vol. 2 (2007, $24.99) r/#13-25; Kubert cover sketch pages 25.00
...: (Vol. 1) The Tomorrow People TPB (7/01, $14.95) r/#1-6 15.00
...: (Vol. 2) Return to Weapon X TPB (4/02, $14.95) r/#7-12 15.00
Vol. 3: World Tour TPB (2002, $17.99) r/#13-20 18.00
Vol. 4: Hellfire and Brimstone TPB (2003, $12.99) r/#21-25 13.00
Vol. 5 (See Ultimate War)
Vol. 6: Return of the King TPB (2003, $16.99) r/#26-33 17.00
Vol. 7: Blockbuster TPB (2004, $12.99) r/#34-39 13.00
Vol. 8: New Mutants TPB (2004, $12.99) r/#40-45 13.00
Vol. 9: The Tempest TPB (2004, $10.99) r/#46-49 11.00
Vol. 10: Cry Wolf TPB (2005, $8.99) r/#50-53 9.00
Vol. 11: The Most Dangerous Game TPB (2005, $9.99) r/#54-57 10.00
Vol. 12: Hard Lessons TPB (2005, $12.99) r/#58-60 & Annual #1 13.00
Vol. 13: Magnetic North TPB (2006, $12.99) r/#61-65 13.00
Vol. 14: Phoenix? TPB (2006, $14.99) r/#66-71 15.00
Vol. 15: Magical TPB (2007, $11.99) r/#72-74 & Annual #2 12.00
Vol. 16: Cable TPB (2007, $14.99) r/#75-80; sketch pages 15.00
Vol. 17: Sentinels TPB (2008, $17.99) r/#81-88 18.00
Volume 1 HC (8/02, $34.99, 7x11", dust jacket) r/#1-12 & Giant-Size X-Men #1; sketch pages and Millar and Bendis' initial plot and character outlines 35.00
Volume 2 HC (2003, $29.99, 7x11", dust jacket) r/#13-25; script for #20 30.00
Volume 3 HC (2003, $29.99, 7x11", dust jacket) r/#26-33 & Ultimate War #1-4 30.00
Volume 4 HC (2005, $29.99, 7x11", dust jacket) r/#34-45 30.00
Volume 5 HC (2006, $29.99, 7x11", dust jacket) r/#46-57; Vaughan intro.; sketch pages 30.00
Volume 6 HC (2006, $29.99, 7x11", dust jacket) r/#58-65, Annual #1 & Wizard #1/2 30.00
Volume 7 HC (2007, $29.99, 7x11", dust jacket) r/#66-74, Annual #2 30.00
Wizard #1/2 2 4 6 9 12 15

ULTIMATE X-MEN (Ultimate Comics X-Men) (See Cataclysm)
Marvel Comics: Nov, 2011 - No. 33, Dec, 2013 ($3.99)

1-Spencer-s/Medina-a/Andrews-c; polybagged 4.00
1-Variant-c by Mark Bagley 6.00
2-33: 2-Rogue returns. 6-Prof. X returns. 21-Iron Patriot app. 4.00
#18.1 (1/13, $2.99) Andrade-a/Pichelli-c 3.00
Ultimate Comics X-Men Must Have 1 (2/12, $4.99) r/#1-3 5.00

ULTIMATUM
Marvel Comics: Jan, 2009 - No. 5, July, 2009 ($3.99, limited series)

1-5-Loeb-s/Finch-a; cover by Finch & ; Ultimate heroes vs. Magneto 4.00
1-5-Variant covers by McGuinness 8.00
5-Double gatefold variant-c by Finch 4.00
March on Ultimatum Saga ('08, giveaway) text and art panel history of Ultimate universe 3.00
...: Fantastic Four Requiem 1 (9/09,$3.99) Pokaski-s/Atkins-a; Dr. Strange app. 4.00
...: Spider-Man Requiem 1,2 (8/09, 9/09,$3.99) Bendis-s/Bagley & Immonen-a 4.00
...: X-Men Requiem 1 (9/09,$3.99) Coleite-s/Oliver-a/Brooks-c 4.00
NOTE: *Numerous variant covers and 2nd & 3rd printings exist.*

ULTRA
Image Comics: Aug, 2004 - No. 8, Mar, 2005 ($2.95, limited series)

1-8: 1-Intro. Ultra/Pearl Penalosa; Luna Brothers-s/a 3.00
Vol. 1: Seven Days TPB (4/05, $17.95) r/#1-8; sketch pages 18.00

ULTRAFORCE (1st Series) (Also see Avengers/Ultraforce #1)
Malibu Comics (Ultraverse): Aug, 1994 - No. 10, Aug, 1995 ($1.95/$2.50)

0 (9/94, $2.50)-Perez-c/a. 4.00
1-($2.50, 44 pgs.)-Bound-in trading card; team consisting of Prime, Prototype, Hardcase, Pixx, Ghoul, Contrary & Topaz; Gerard Jones scripts begin, ends #6; Pérez-c/a begins 4.00
1-Ultra 5000 Limited Silver Foil Edition 1 2 3 5 6 8
1-Holographic-c, no price 1 2 3 6 8 10
2-5: Perez-c/a in all. 2 (10/94, $1.95)-Prime quits, Strangers cameo. 3-Origin of Topaz; Prime rejoins. 5-Pixx dies. 3.00
2 ($2.50)-Florescent logo; limited edition stamp on-c 4.00
6-10: 6-Begin $2.50-c, Perez-c/a. 7-Ghoul story, Steve Erwin-a. 8-Marvel's Black Knight enters the Ultraverse (last seen in Avengers #375); Perez-c/a. 9,10-Black Knight app.; Perez-c. 10-Leads into Ultraforce/Avengers Prelude 3.00
Malibu "Ashcan ": Ultraforce #0A (6/94) 3.00
.../Avengers Prelude 1 (8/95, $2.50)-Perez-c. 3.00
.../Avengers 1 (8/95, $3.95)-Warren Ellis script; Perez-c/a; foil-c 4.00

ULTRAFORCE (2nd Series)(Also see Black September)
Malibu Comics (Ultraverse): Infinity, Sept, 1995 - V2#15, Dec, 1996 ($1.50)

Infinity, V2#1-15: Infinity-Team consists of Marvel's Black Knight, Ghoul, Topaz, Prime & redesigned Prototype; Warren Ellis scripts begin, ends #3; variant-c exists. 1-1st app.Cromwell, Lament & Wreckage. 2-Contains free encore presentation of Ultraforce #1; flip book "Phoenix Resurrection" Pt. 7. 7-Darick Robertson, Jeff Johnson & others-a. 8,9-Intro. Future Ultraforce (Prime, Hellblade, Angel of Destruction, Painkiller & Whipslash); Gary Erskine-c/a. 9-Foxfire app. 10-Len Wein scripts & Deodato Studios-c/a begin. 10-Lament back-up story. 11-Ghoul back-up story by Pander Bros. 12-Ultraforce vs. Maxis (cont'd in Ultraverse Unlimited #2); Exiles & Iron Clad app. 13-Prime leaves; Hardcase returns 3.00
Infinity (2000 signed) 4.00
.../Spider-Man ($3.95)-Marv Wolfman script; Green Goblin app; 2 covers exist. 4.00

ULTRAGIRL
Marvel Comics: Nov, 1996 - No. 3 Mar, 1997($1.50, limited series)

1-3: 1-1st app. 3.00

ULTRA KLUTZ
Onward Comics: 1981; 6/86 - #27, 1/89, #28, 4/90 - #31, 1990? ($1.50/$1.75/$2.00, B&W)

1 (1981)-Re-released after 2nd #1 3.00
1-30: 1-(6/86). 27-Photo back-c 3.00
31-($2.95, 52 pgs.) 4.00

ULTRAMAN
Nemesis Comics: Mar, 1994 - No. 4, Sept, 1994 ($1.75/$1.95)

1-($2.25)-Collector's edition; foil-c; special 3/4 wraparound-c 4.00
1-($1.75)-Newsstand edition 3.00
2-4: 3-$1.95-c begins 3.00
#(-1) (3/93) 3.00

ULTRAMAN TIGA
Dark Horse Comics: Aug, 2003 - No. 10, June, 2004 ($3.99)

1-10-Khoo Fuk Lung-a/Tony Wong-s 4.00

ULTRAVERSE DOUBLE FEATURE
Malibu Comics (Ultraverse): Jan, 1995 ($3.95, one-shot, 68 pgs.)

1-Flip-c featuring Prime & Solitaire. 4.00

ULTRAVERSE ORIGINS
Malibu Comics (Ultraverse): Jan, 1994 (99¢, one-shot)

1-Gatefold-c; 2 pg. origins all characters 3.00
1-Newsstand edition; different-c, no gatefold 3.00

ULTRAVERSE PREMIERE
Malibu Comics (Ultraverse): 1994 (one-shot)

0-Ordered thru mail w/coupons 5.00

ULTRAVERSE UNLIMITED
Malibu Comics (Ultraverse): June, 1996; No. 2, Sept, 1996 ($2.50)

1,2: 1-Adam Warlock returns to the Marvel Universe; Rune-c/app. 2-Black Knight, Reaper & Sierra Blaze return to the Marvel Universe 3.00

ULTRAVERSE YEAR ONE
Malibu Comics (Ultraverse): 1994 ($4.95, one-shot)

nn-In-depth synopsis of the first year's titles & stories. 5.00

Umbral #1 © Johnston & Mitten

Uncanny Avengers #13 © MAR

Uncle Charlie's Fables #4 © LEV

GD 2.0 | VG 4.0 | FN 6.0 | VF 8.0 | VF/NM 9.0 | NM- 9.2

ULTRAVERSE YEAR TWO
Malibu Comics (Ultraverse): Aug, 1995 ($4.95, one-shot)

nn-In-depth synopsis of second year's titles & stories 5.00

ULTRAVERSE YEAR ZERO: THE DEATH OF THE SQUAD
Malibu Comics (Ultraverse): Apr, 1995 - No. 4, July, 1995 ($2.95, lim. series)

1-4: 3-Codename: Firearm back-up story. 3.00

ULTRON (See Age of Ultron series)
Marvel Comics: Jun, 2013 ($3.99, one-shot)

1AU-Victor Mancha from the Runaways (son of Ultron); K. Immonen-s/Pinna-a 4.00

UMBRAL
Image Comics: Nov, 2013 - Present ($2.99)

1-5-Johnston-s/Mitten-a 3.00

UMBRELLA ACADEMY (Zero Killer & Pantheon City on back-c)
Dark Horse Comics: Apr, 2007

1-Free Comic Book Day Edition - previews of the upcoming series; James Jean-c 5.00

UMBRELLA ACADEMY: APOCALYPSE SUITE
Dark Horse Comics: Sept, 2007 - No. 6, Feb, 2008 ($2.99, limited series)

1-Origin of the Umbrella Academy; Gerald Way-s/Gabriel Bá-a/James Jean-c 5.00
1-White variant-c by Bá 25.00
1-Variant-c by Gerald Way 20.00
1-2nd printing with variant-c by Bá 3.00
2-6 3.00
...: One for One (9/10, $1.00) r/#1 with red cover frame 3.00
Vol.1: Apocalypse Suite TPB (7/08, $17.95) r/#1-6, FCBD story and web shorts; design art; Grant Morrison intro.; cover gallery 18.00

UMBRELLA ACADEMY: DALLAS
Dark Horse Comics: Nov, 2008 - No. 6, May, 2009 ($2.99, limited series)

1-6-Gerald Way-s/Gabriel Bá-a/c 3.00
1-Wraparound variant-c by Jim Lee 5.00

UNBIRTHDAY PARTY WITH ALICE IN WONDERLAND (See Alice In Wonderland, Four Color #341)

UNBOUND
Image Comics (Desperado): Jan, 1998 ($2.95, B&W)

1-Pruett-s/Peters-a 3.00

UNCANNY
Dynamite Entertainment: 2013 - No. 6, 2014 ($3.99)

1-6-Andy Diggle-s/Aaron Campbell-a 4.00

UNCANNY AVENGERS (Marvel NOW!)
Marvel Comics: Dec, 2012 - Present ($3.99)

1-18: 1-Capt. America, Thor, Scarlet Witch, Wolverine, Havok & Rogue team; Remender-s/Cassaday-a; Red Skull app. 5-Coipel-a. 6-11-Acuña-a. 14-Rogue & Scarlet Witch die 4.00
8AU-(7/13, $3.99) Age of Ultron tie-in; Adam Kubert-a 4.00

UNCANNY ORIGINS
Marvel Comics: Sept, 1996 - No. 14, Oct, 1997 (99¢)

1-14: 1-Cyclops. 2-Quicksilver. 3-Archangel. 4-Firelord. 5-Hulk. 6-Beast. 7-Venom. 8-Nightcrawler. 9-Storm. 10-Black Cat. 11-Black Knight. 12-Dr. Strange. 13-Daredevil. 14-Iron Fist 3.00

UNCANNY SKULLKICKERS (See Skullkickers #19)

UNCANNY TALES
Atlas Comics (PrPI/PPI): June, 1952 - No. 56, Sept, 1957

1-Heath-a; horror/weird stories begin 110 220 330 704 1202 1700
2 57 114 171 362 619 875
3-5 52 104 156 328 552 775
6-Wolvertonish-a by Matt Fox 53 106 159 334 567 800
7-10: 8-Atom bomb story; Tothish-a (by Sekowsky?). 9-Crandall-a
43 86 129 271 461 650
11-20: 17-Atom bomb panels; anti-communist story; Hitler story. 19-Krenkel-a. 20-Robert Q. Sale-c 36 72 108 211 343 475
21-25,27: 25-Nostrand-a? 32 64 96 188 307 425
26-Spider-Man prototype c/story 43 86 129 271 461 650
28-Last precode issue (1/55); Kubert-a; #1-28 contain 2-3 sci/fi stories each
33 66 99 194 317 440
29-41,43-49,51 22 44 66 132 216 300
42,54,56-Krigstein-a 23 46 69 136 223 310
50,53,55-Torres-a 22 44 66 132 216 300
52-Oldest Iron Man prototype (2/57) 34 68 102 199 325 450

NOTE: ***Andru** a-15, 27. **Ayers** a-14, 22, 28, 37. **Bailey** a-51. **Briefer** a-19, 20. **Brodsky** c-1, 3, 4, 6, 8, 12-16, 19. **Brodsky/Everett** c-9. **Cameron** a-47. **Colan** a-11, 16, 17, 49, 52. **Drucker** a-37, 42, 45. **Everett** a-2, 9, 12, 32, 36, 39, 48; c-7, 11, 17, 39, 41, 50, 52, 53. **Fass** a-9, 10, 15, 24. **Forte** a-18, 27, 33-35, 52, 53. **Heath** a-13, 14; c-5, 10, 18. **Keller** a-3. **Lawrence** a-14, 17, 19, 23, 27, 28, 35. **Maneely** a-4, 8, 10, 16, 29, 35; c-2, 22, 26, 33, 38. **Moldoff** a-23. **Morisi** a-48, 52. **Morrow** a-46, 51. **Orlando** a-49, 50, 53. **Powell** a-12, 18, 34, 36, 38, 43, 50, 56. **Robinson** a-3, 13. **Reinman** a-12, 36. **Romita** a-10. **Roussos** a-8. **Sale** a-34, 47, 53; c-20. **Sekowsky** a-25. **Sinnott** a-14, 15, 38, 52. **Torres** a-53. **Tothish**-a by **Andru**-27. **Wildey** a-22, 48.*

UNCANNY TALES
Marvel Comics Group: Dec, 1973 - No. 12, Oct, 1975

1-Crandall-r/Uncanny Tales #9('50s) 4 8 12 25 40 55
2-12: 7,12-Kirby-a 3 6 9 17 26 35
NOTE: *Ditko reprints-#4, 6-8, 10-12.*

UNCANNY X-FORCE
Marvel Comics: Dec, 2010 - No. 35, Feb, 2013 ($3.99)

1-17: 1-Wolverine, Psylocke, Archangel, Fantomex & Deadpool team; Opeña-a; Ribic-c 4.00
1-Variant-c by Clayton Crain 10.00
5.1 (5/11, $2.99) Albuquerque-a/Bianchi-c; Lady Deathstrike app. 3.00
18-Polybagged; Dark Angel Saga conclusion 4.00
19-35: 19-Grampa-c. 20-Yu-c 4.00
19.1 (3/12, $2.99) Remender-s/Tan-a; other-dimension X-Men vs. Apocalypse 3.00
...: The Apocalypse Solution 1 (5/11, $4.99) r/#1-3 5.00

UNCANNY X-FORCE (Marvel NOW!)
Marvel Comics: Mar, 2013 - No. 17, Mar, 2014 ($3.99)

1-17: 1-Storm, Psylocke, Spiral, Fantomex & Puck team; Bishop app.; Garney-a 4.00

UNCANNY X-MEN, THE (See **X-Men, The**, 1st series, #142-on)

UNCANNY X-MEN (2nd series) (X-Men Regenesis)
Marvel Comics: Dec, 2010 - No. 20, Dec, 2012 ($3.99)

1-10: 1-3-Gillen-s/Pacheco-a/c; Mr. Sinister app. 4-Peterson-a. 5-8-Land-a 4.00
1-Variant-c by Keown 6.00
11-20: 11-19-Avengers vs. X-Men x-over 4.00

UNCANNY X-MEN (3rd series) (Marvel NOW!)
Marvel Comics: Apr, 2013 - Present ($3.99)

1-20: 1-Cyclops, Emma Frost, Magneto, Magik team; Bendis-s/Bachalo-a. 2,3-Avengers app. 5-7,10,11-Irving-a. 8,9,12,13,16,17,19,20-Bachalo-a. 12,13-Battle of the Atom 4.00

UNCANNY X-MEN AND THE NEW TEEN TITANS (See Marvel and DC Present...)

UNCANNY X-MEN: FIRST CLASS
Marvel Comics: Sept, 2009 - No. 8, Apr, 2010 ($2.99)

1-8: 1-The X-Men #94 (1975) team; Cruz-a; Inhumans app. 3.00
... Giant-Size Special (8/09, $3.99) short stories by various; Scottie Young-c 4.00

UNCENSORED MOUSE, THE
Eternity Comics: Apr, 1989 - No. 2, Apr, 1989 ($1.95, B&W)(Came sealed in plastic bag)
(Both contain racial stereotyping & violence)

1,2-Early Gottfredson strip-r in each 2 4 6 11 16 20
NOTE: *Both issues contain unauthorized reprints. Series was cancelled. **Win Smith** r-1, 2.*

UNCHARTED (Based on the video game)
DC Comics: Jan, 2012 - No. 6, Jun, 2012 ($2.99, limited series)

1-6-Williamson-s/Sandoval-a. 1-3-Harris-c 3.00

UNCLE CHARLIE'S FABLES (Also see Adventures in Wonderland)
Lev Gleason Publ.: Jan, 1952 - No. 5, Sept, 1952 (All have Biro painted-c)

1-Peter Pester by Hy Mankin begins, ends #5. Michael the Misfit by Kida, Janice & the Lazy Giant by Maurer, Lawrence the Fortune Teller app.; has photo of Biro
15 30 45 88 137 185
2-Fuje-a; Biro photo 10 20 30 54 72 90
3-5: 5-Two Who Built a Dream, The Blacksmith & The Gypsies by Maurer, The Sleepy King by Hubbel; has photo of Biro 9 18 27 47 61 75
NOTE: ***Kida** a-1. Hubbell a-5. **Hy Mankin** a-1-5. **Norman Maurer** a-1, 5. **Dick Rockwell** a-5.*

UNCLE DONALD & HIS NEPHEWS DUDE RANCH (See Dell Giant #52)

UNCLE DONALD & HIS NEPHEWS FAMILY FUN (See Dell Giant #38)

UNCLE JOE'S FUNNIES
Centaur Publications: 1938 (B&W)

1-Games, puzzles & magic tricks, some interior art; Bill Everett-c
97 194 291 621 1061 1500

UNCLE MILTY (TV)
Victoria Publications/True Cross: Dec, 1950 - No. 4, July, 1951 (52 pgs.)(Early TV comic)

1-Milton Berle photo on-c of #1,2 54 108 162 343 574 825
2 35 70 105 208 339 470
3,4 29 58 87 172 281 390

UNCLE REMUS & HIS TALES OF BRER RABBIT (See Brer Rabbit, 4-Color #129, 208, 693)

Uncle Sam #1 © DC

Uncle Scrooge #13 © DIS

Uncle Scrooge #404 © DIS

	GD 2.0	VG 4.0	FN 6.0	VF 8.0	VF/NM 9.0	NM- 9.2

UNCLE SAM
DC Comics (Vertigo): 1997 - No. 2, 1997 ($4.95, limited series)

1,2-Alex Ross painted c/a. Story by Ross and Steve Darnell 5.00
Hardcover (1998, $17.95) 18.00
Softcover (2000, $9.95) 10.00

UNCLE SAM AND THE FREEDOM FIGHTERS
DC Comics: Sept, 2006 - No. 8, Apr, 2007 ($2.99, limited series)

1-8-Acuña-a/c; Gray & Palmiotti-s. 3-Intro. Black Condor 3.00
TPB (2007, $14.99) r/#1-8 and story from DCU Brave New World #1 15.00

UNCLE SAM AND THE FREEDOM FIGHTERS
DC Comics: Nov, 2007 - No. 8, Jun, 2008 ($2.99, limited series)

1-8-Gray & Palmiotti-s/Arlem-a/Johnson-c 3.00
...: Brave New World TPB (2008, $14.99) r/#1-8 15.00

UNCLE SAM QUARTERLY (Blackhawk #9 on)(See Freedom Fighters)
Quality Comics Group: Autumn, 1941 - No. 8, Autumn, 1943 (see National Comics)

1-Origin Uncle Sam; Fine/Eisner-c, chapter headings, 2 pgs. by Eisner;
(2 versions: dark cover, no price; light cover with price sticker); Jack Cole-a
377 754 1131 2639 4620 6600
2-Cameos by The Ray, Black Condor, Quicksilver, The Red Bee, Alias the Spider, Hercules
& Neon the Unknown; Eisner, Fine-c/a 135 270 405 864 1482 2100
3-Tuska-c/a; Eisner-a(2) 97 194 291 621 1061 1500
4 90 180 270 576 988 1400
5,7-Hitler, Mussolini & Tojo-c 129 258 387 826 1413 2000
6,8 68 136 204 435 743 1050
NOTE: ***Kotzky** (or **Tuska**) a-3-8.*

UNCLE SCROOGE (Disney) (Becomes Walt Disney's... #210 on) (See Cartoon Tales, Dell Giants #33, 55, Disney Comic Album, Donald and Scrooge, Dynabrite, Four Color #178, Gladstone Comic Album, Walt Disney's Comics & Stories #98, Walt Disney's ...)
Dell #1-39/Gold Key #40-173/Whitman #174-209: No. 386, 3/52 - No. 39, 8-10/62; No. 40, 12/62 - No. 209, 7/84

Four Color 386(#1)-in "Only a Poor Old Man" by Carl Barks; r-in Uncle Scrooge & Donald Duck #1('65) & The Best of Walt Disney Comics ('74). The 2nd cover app. of Uncle Scrooge (see Dell Giant Vacation Parade #2 (7/51) for 1st-c) 179 358 537 1477 3339 5200
1-(1986)-Reprints F.C. #386; given away with lithograph "Dam Disaster at Money Lake" & as a subscription offer giveaway to Gladstone subscribers
3 6 9 15 20 24
Four Color 456(#2)-in "Back to the Klondike" by Carl Barks; r-in Best of U.S. & D.D. #1('66) & Gladstone C.A. #4 88 176 264 704 1577 2450
Four Color 495(#3)-r-in #105 59 118 177 472 1061 1650
4(12-2/53-54)-r-in Gladstone Comic Album #11 43 86 129 318 722 1125
5-r-in Gladstone Special #2 & Walt Disney Digest #1
36 72 108 266 596 925
6-r-in U.S. #106,165,233 & Best of U.S. & D.D. #1('66)
31 62 93 223 499 775
7-The Seven Cities of Cibola by Barks; r-in #217 & Best of D.D. & U.S. #2 ('67)
28 56 84 202 451 700
8-10: 8-r-in #111,222. 9-r-in #104,214. 10-r-in #67 25 50 75 175 388 600
11-20: 11-r-in #237. 17-r-in #215. 19-r-in Gladstone C.A. #1. 20-r-in #213
20 40 60 141 313 485
21-30: 24-X-Mas-c. 26-r-in #211 16 32 48 112 249 385
31-35,37-40: 34-r-in #228. 40-X-Mas-c 13 26 39 89 195 300
36-1st app. Magica De Spell; Number one dime 1st identified by name
15 30 45 100 220 340
41-60: 48-Magica De Spell-c/story (3/64). 49-Sci/fi-c. 51-Beagle Boys-c/story (8/64) 11 22 33 73 157 240
61-63,65,66,68-71:71-Last Barks issue w/original story (#71-he only storyboarded the script)
10 20 30 66 138 210
64-(7/66) Barks Vietnam War story "Treasure of Marco Polo" banned for reprints by Disney from 1977-1989 because of its Third World revolutionary war theme. It later appeared in the hardcover Carl Barks Library set (4/89) and Walt Disney's Uncle Scrooge Adventures #42 (1/97) 15 30 45 100 220 340
67,72,73: 67,72,73-Barks-r 9 18 27 60 120 180
74-84: 74-Barks-r(1pg.). 75-81,83-Not by Barks. 82,84-Barks-r begin
7 14 21 44 82 120
85-100 6 12 18 38 69 100
101-110 5 10 15 33 57 80
111-120 4 8 12 27 44 60
121-141,143-152,154-157 3 6 9 21 33 45
142-Reprints Four Color #456 with-c 4 8 12 22 35 48
153,158,162-164,166,168-170,178,180: No Barks 3 6 9 15 22 28
159-160,165,167 3 6 9 16 23 30
161(r/#14), 171(r/#11), 177(r/#16),183(r/#6)-Barks-r 3 6 9 16 23 30
172(1/80),173(2/80)-Gold Key. Barks-a 3 6 9 17 26 35
174(3/80),175(4/80),176(5/80)-Whitman. Barks-a 4 8 12 22 35 48
177(6/80),178(7/80) 4 8 12 23 37 50
179(9/80)(r/#9)-(Very low distribution) 36 72 108 266 596 925
180(11/80),181(12/80, r/4-Color #495), pre-pack? 8 16 24 51 96 140
182-195: 182-(50¢-c). 184,185,187,188-Barks-a. 182,186,191-194-No Barks. 189(r/#5), 190(r/#4), 195(r/4-Color #386) 3 6 9 16 23 30
182(1/81, 40¢-c) Cover price error variant 4 8 12 22 35 48
196(4/82),197(5/82): 196(r/#13) 3 6 9 17 26 35
198-209 (All #90038 on-c; pre-pack; no date or date code): 198(4/83), 199(5/83), 200(6/83), 201(6/83), 202(7/83), 203(7/83), 204(8/83), 205(8/83), 206(4/84), 207(5/83), 208(6/84), 209(7/84). 198-202,204-206: No Barks. 203(r/#12), 207(r/#93,92), 208(r/U.S. #18), 209(r/U.S. #21)-Barks-r 3 6 9 21 33 45
Uncle Scrooge & Money(G.K.)-Barks-r/from WDC&S #130 (3/67)
5 10 15 31 53 75
Mini Comic #1(1976)(3-1/4x6-1/2")-r/U.S. #115; Barks-c
2 4 6 8 10 12
NOTE: ***Barks** c-Four Color 386, 456, 495, #4-37, 39, 40, 43-71.*

UNCLE SCROOGE (See Walt Disney's Uncle Scrooge for previous issues)
Boom Entertainment (BOOM! Kids): No. 384, Oct, 2009 - No. 404, Jun, 2011 ($2.99/$3.99)

384-399: 384-Magica de Spell app.; 2 covers. 392-399-Duck Tales 3.00
400-(2/11, $3.99) "Carl Barks" apps. as Scrooge story-teller; Rosa wraparound-c 4.00
400-$6.99) Deluxe Edition with Barks painted cover of Four Color #386 cover image 7.00
401-404: 401-($3.99)-Rosa-s/a 4.00
...: The Mysterious Stone Ray and Cash Flow (5/11, $6.99) reprints; Barks-s/a; Rosa-s/a 7.00

UNCLE SCROOGE AND DONALD DUCK
Gold Key: June, 1965 (25¢, paper cover)

1-Reprint of Four Color #386(#1) & lead story from Four Color #29
7 14 21 46 86 125

UNCLE SCROOGE COMICS DIGEST
Gladstone Publishing: Dec, 1986 - No. 5, Aug, 1987 ($1.25, Digest-size)

1,3 1 2 3 5 6 8
2,4 6.00
5 (low print run) 1 2 3 5 7 9

UNCLE SCROOGE GOES TO DISNEYLAND (See Dell Giants)
Gladstone Publishing Ltd.: Aug, 1985 ($2.50)

1-Reprints Dell Giant w/new-c by Mel Crawford, based on old cover
2 4 6 8 10 12
...Comics Digest 1 ($1.50, digest size) 2 4 6 8 11 14

UNCLE SCROOGE IN COLOR
Gladstone Publishing: 1987 ($29.95, Hardcover, 9-1/4"X12-1/4", 96 pgs.)

nn-Reprints "Christmas on Bear Mountain" from Four Color 178 by Barks; Uncle Scrooge's Christmas Carol (published as Donald Duck & the Christmas Carol, A Little Golden Book), reproduced from the original art as adapted by Norman McGary from pencils by Barks; and Uncle Scrooge the Lemonade King, reproduced from the original art, plus Barks' original pencils 4 8 12 23 37 50
nn-Slipcase edition of 750, signed by Barks, issued at $79.95 300.00

UNCLE SCROOGE THE LEMONADE KING
Whitman Publishing Co.: 1960 (A Top Top Tales Book, 6-3/8"x7-5/8", 32 pgs.)

2465-Storybook pencilled by Carl Barks, finished art adapted by Norman McGary
32 64 96 230 515 800

UNCLE WIGGILY (See March of Comics #19) (Also see Animal Comics)
Dell Publishing Co.: No. 179, Dec, 1947 - No. 543, Mar, 1954

Four Color 179 (#1)-Walt Kelly-c 13 26 39 89 195 300
Four Color 221 (3/49)-Part Kelly-c 8 16 24 56 108 160
Four Color 276 (5/50), 320 (#1, 3/51) 7 14 21 46 86 125
Four Color 349 (9-10/51), 391 (4-5/52) 6 12 18 38 69 100
Four Color 428 (10/52), 503 (10/53), 543 5 10 15 33 57 80

UNDEAD, THE
Chaos! Comics (Black Label): Feb, 2002 ($4.99, B&W)

1-Pulido-s/Denham-a 5.00

UNDERCOVER GIRL (Starr Flagg) (See Extra Comics, Manhunt! & Trail Colt)
Magazine Enterprises: No. 5, 1952 - No. 7, 1954

5(#1)(A-1 #62)-Fallon of the F.B.I. in all 28 56 84 165 270 375
6(A-1 #98), 7(A-1 #118)-All have Starr Flagg 26 52 78 154 252 350
NOTE: ***Powell** c-6, 7. **Whitney** a-5-7.*

UNDERDOG (TV)(See Kite Fun Book, March of Comics #426, 438, 467, 479)
Charlton Comics/Gold Key: July, 1970 - No. 10, Jan, 1972; Mar, 1975 - No. 23, Feb, 1979

Undertaker #5 © Chaos!

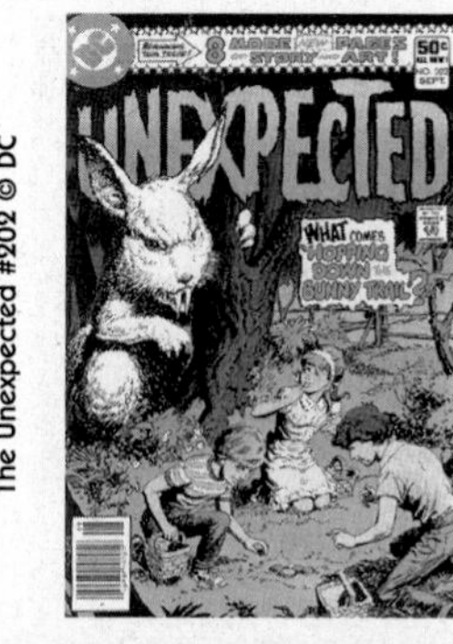

The Unexpected #202 © DC

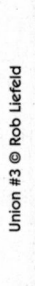

Union #3 © Rob Liefeld

	GD 2.0	VG 4.0	FN 6.0	VF 8.0	VF/NM 9.0	NM- 9.2
1 (1st series, Charlton)-1st app. Underdog	9	18	27	62	126	190
2-10	5	10	15	35	63	90
1 (2nd series, Gold Key)	6	12	18	40	73	105
2-10	4	8	12	23	37	50
11-20: 13-1st app. Shack of Solitude	3	6	9	18	28	38
21-23	3	6	9	19	30	40

UNDERDOG
Spotlight Comics: 1987 - No. 3?, 1987 ($1.50)

1-3 4.00

UNDERDOG (Volume 2)
Harvey Comics: Nov, 1993 - No. 5, July, 1994 ($2.25)

1-5 4.00
Summer Special (10/93, $2.25, 68 pgs.) 4.00

UNDERSEA AGENT
Tower Comics: Jan, 1966 - No. 6, Mar, 1967 (25¢, 68 pgs.)

1-Davy Jones, Undersea Agent begins 8 16 24 51 96 140
2-6: 2-Jones gains magnetic powers. 5-Origin & 1st app. of Merman.
6-Kane/Wood-c(r) 5 10 15 34 60 85
NOTE: *Gil Kane a-3-6; c-4, 5.* ***Moldoff*** *a-2i.*

UNDERSEA FIGHTING COMMANDOS (See Fighting Undersea…)
I.W. Enterprises: 1964

I.W. Reprint #1,2('64): 1-r/#? 2-r/#1; Severin-c 2 4 6 9 13 16

UNDERTAKER (World Wrestling Federation)(Also see WWE Undertaker)
Chaos! Comics: Feb, 1999 - No. 10, Jan, 2000 ($2.50/$2.95)

Preview (2/99) 3.00
1-10: Reg. and photo covers for each. 1-(4/99) 3.00
1-($6.95) DF Ed.; Brereton painted-c 7.00
...Halloween Special (10/99, $2.95) Reg. & photo-c 3.00
Wizard #0 3.00

UNDERWATER CITY, THE
Dell Publishing Co.: No. 1328, 1961

Four Color 1328-Movie, Evans-a 6 12 18 41 76 110

UNDERWORLD (...True Crime Stories)
D. S. Publishing Co.: Feb-Mar, 1948 - No. 9, June-July, 1949 (52 pgs.)

1-Moldoff (Shelly)-c; excessive violence 50 100 150 315 533 750
2-Moldoff (Shelly)-c; Ma Barker story used in **SOTI**, pg. 95; female electrocution panel;
lingerie art 44 88 132 277 469 660
3-McWilliams-c/a; extreme violence, mutilation 41 82 123 250 418 585
4-Used in Love and Death by Legman; Ingels-a 37 74 111 222 361 500
5-Ingels-a 24 48 72 142 234 325
6-9: 8-Ravielli-a. 9-R.Q. Sale-a 20 40 60 114 182 250

UNDERWORLD
DC Comics: Dec, 1987 - No. 4, Mar, 1988 ($1.00, limited series, mature)

1-4 3.00

UNDERWORLD (Movie)
IDW Publishing: Sept, 2003; Dec, 2005 ($6.99)

1-Movie adaptation; photo-c 7.00
... Evolution (12/05, $7.49) adaptation of movie sequel; Vazquez-a 7.50
TPB (7/04, $19.99) r/#1 and Underworld:Red in Tooth and Claw #1-3 20.00

UNDERWORLD
Marvel Comics: Apr, 2006 - No. 5, Aug, 2006 ($2.99, limited series)

1-5: Staz Johnson-a. 2-Spider-Man app. 3,4-Punisher app. 3.00

UNDERWORLD CRIME
Fawcett Publications: June, 1952 - No. 9, Oct, 1953

1 34 68 102 199 325 450
2 21 42 63 122 199 275
3-6,8,9 (8,9-exist?) 19 38 57 112 179 245
7-(6/53)-Red hot poker/bondage/torture-c 65 130 195 416 708 1000

UNDERWORLD: RED IN TOOTH AND CLAW (Movie)
IDW Publishing: Feb, 2004 - No. 3, Apr, 2004 ($3.99, limited series)

1-3-The early days of the Vampire and Lycan war; Postic & Marinkovich-a 4.00

UNDERWORLD: RISE OF THE LYCANS (Movie)
IDW Publishing: Nov, 2008 - No. 2, Nov, 2008 ($3.99, limited series)

1,2-Grevioux-s/Huerta-a 4.00

UNDERWORLD STORY, THE (Movie)
Avon Periodicals: 1950

nn-(Scarce)-Ravielli-c 30 60 90 177 289 400

UNDERWORLD UNLEASHED
DC Comics: Nov, 1995 - No. 3, Jan, 1996 ($2.95, limited series)

1-3: Mark Waid scripts & Howard Porter-c/a(p) 3.50
...: Abyss: Hell's Sentinel 1-($2.95)-Alan Scott, Phantom Stranger, Zatanna app. 3.00
...: Apokolips-Dark Uprising 1 ($1.95) 3.00
...: Batman-Devil's Asylum 1-($2.95)-Batman app. 3.00
...: Patterns of Fear-($2.95) 3.00
TPB (1998, $17.95) r/#1-3 & Abyss-Hell's Sentinel 18.00

UNEARTHLY SPECTACULARS
Harvey Publications: Oct, 1965 - No. 3, Mar, 1967

1-(12¢)-Tiger Boy; Simon-c 4 8 12 25 40 55
2-(25¢ giants)-Jack Q. Frost, Tiger Boy & Three Rocketeers app.; Williamson, Wood, Kane-a;
r-1 story/Thrill-O-Rama #2 4 8 12 28 47 65
3-(25¢ giants)-Jack Q. Frost app.; Williamson/Crandall-a; r-from Alarming Advs. #1,1962
4 8 12 28 47 65
NOTE: ***Crandall*** *a-3r.* ***G. Kane*** *a-2.* ***Orlando*** *a-3.* ***Simon, Sparling, Wood*** *c-2.* ***Simon/Kirby*** *a-3r.* ***Torres*** *a-1?.* ***Wildey*** *a-1(3).* ***Williamson*** *a-2, 3r.* ***Wood*** *a-2(2).*

UNEXPECTED, THE (Formerly Tales of the…)
National Per. Publ./DC Comics: No. 105, Feb-Mar, 1968 - No. 222, May, 1982

105-Begin 12¢ cover price 6 12 18 40 73 105
106-113: 113-Last 12¢ issue (6-7/69) 5 10 15 30 50 70
114,115,117,118,120-125 4 8 12 22 35 48
116 (36 pgs.)-Wrightson-a 4 8 12 23 37 50
119-Wrightson-a, 8pgs.(36 pgs.) 5 10 15 31 53 75
126,127,129-136-(52 pgs.) 4 8 12 22 35 48
128(52 pgs.)-Wrightson-a 5 10 15 31 53 75
137-156 3 6 9 15 22 28
157-162-(100 pgs.) 4 8 12 28 47 65
163-188: 187,188-(44 pgs.) 2 4 6 11 16 20
189,190,192-195 ($1.00, 68 pgs.): 189 on are combined with House of Secrets
& The Witching Hour 2 4 6 13 18 22
191-Rogers-a(p) ($1.00, 68 pgs.) 3 6 9 14 19 24
196-222: 200-Return of Johhny Peril by Tuska. 205-213-Johnny Peril app.
210-Time Warp story. 222-Giffen-a 2 4 6 8 10 12
NOTE: ***Neal Adams*** *c-110, 112-115, 118, 121, 124.* ***J. Craig*** *a-195.* ***Ditko*** *a-189, 221p, 222p; c-222.* ***Drucker*** *a-107r, 132r.* ***Giffen*** *a-219, 222.* ***Kaluta*** *c-203, 212.* ***Kirby*** *a-127r, 162.* ***Kubert*** *c-204, 214-216, 219-221.* ***Mayer*** *a-217p, 220, 221p.* ***Moldoff*** *a-136r.* ***Moreira*** *a-133.* ***Mortimer*** *a-212p.* ***Newton*** *a-204p.* ***Orlando*** *a-202; c-191.* ***Perez*** *a-217p.* ***Redondo*** *a-155, 166, 195.* ***Reese*** *a-145.* ***Sparling*** *a-107, 205-209p, 212p.* ***Spiegle*** *a-217.* ***Starlin*** *c-198.* ***Toth*** *a-126r, 127r.* ***Tuska*** *a-127, 132, 134, 136, 139, 152, 180, 200p.* ***Wildey*** *a-128r, 193.* ***Wood*** *a-122i, 133i, 137i, 138i.* ***Wrightson*** *a-161r(2 pgs.). Johnny Peril in #106-114, 116, 117, 200, 205-213.*

UNEXPECTED, THE
DC Comics: Dec, 2011 ($7.99, one-shot)

1-Short horror stories by various incl. Gibbons, Thompson, Lapham, Fialkov; 2 covers 8.00

UNEXPECTED ANNUAL, THE (See DC Special Series #4)

UNHOLY UNION
Image Comics (Top Cow): July, 2007 ($3.99, one-shot)

1-Witchblade & The Darkness meet Hulk, Ghost Rider & Doctor Strange; Silvestri-c 4.00

UNIDENTIFIED FLYING ODDBALL (See Walt Disney Showcase #52)

UNION
Image Comics (WildStorm Productions): June, 1993 - No. 0, July, 1994 ($1.95, lim. series)

0-(7/94, $2.50) 3.00
0-Alternate Portacio-c (See Deathblow #5) 5.00
1-($2.50)-Embossed foil-c; Texeira-c/a in all 4.00
1-($1.95)-Newsstand edition w/o foil-c 3.00
2-4: 4-(7/94) 3.00

UNION
Image Comics (WildStorm Prod.): Feb, 1995 - No. 9, Dec, 1995 ($2.50)

1-3,5-9: 3-Savage Dragon app. 6-Fairchild from Gen 13 app. 3.00
4-($1.95, Newsstand)-WildStorm Rising Pt. 3 3.00
4-($2.50, Direct Market)-WildStorm Rising Pt. 3, bound-in card 3.00

UNION: FINAL VENGEANCE
Image Comics (WildStorm Productions): Oct, 1997 ($2.50)

1-Golden-c/Heisler-s 3.00

UNION JACK
Marvel Comics: Dec, 1998 - No. 3, Feb, 1999 ($2.99, limited series)

1-3-Raab-s/Cassaday-s/a 3.00

UNION JACK
Marvel Comics: Nov, 2006 - No. 4, Feb, 2007 ($2.99, limited series)

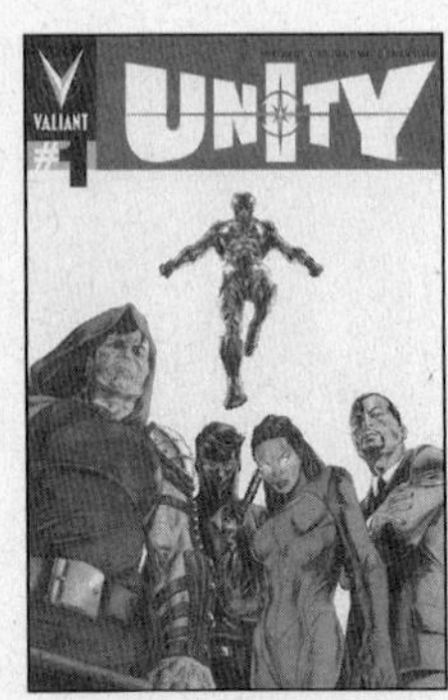

Unity (2013 series) #1 © VAL

Universe X #9 © MAR

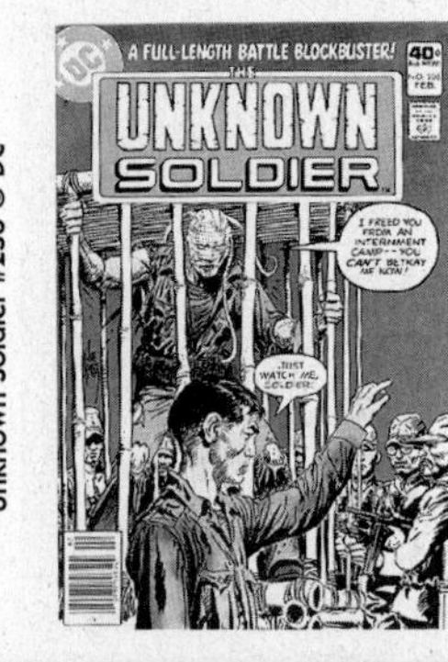

Unknown Soldier #236 © DC

	GD	VG	FN	VF	VF/NM	NM-
	2.0	4.0	6.0	8.0	9.0	9.2

1-4-Gage-s/Perkins-c/a 3.00
...: London Falling TPB (2007, $10.99) r/#1-4; Perkins sketch page 11.00

UNITED COMICS (Formerly Fritzi Ritz #7; has Fritzi Ritz logo)
United Features Syndicate: Aug, 1940; No. 8, 1950 - No. 26, Jan-Feb, 1953

1(68 pgs.)-Fritzi Ritz & Phil Fumble 26 52 78 154 252 350
8-Fritzi Ritz, Abbie & Slats 9 18 27 50 65 80
9-21: 20-Strange As It Seems; Russell Patterson Cheesecake-a
8 16 24 42 54 65
22-(5-6/52) 2 pgs. early Peanuts by Schulz (1st in comics?)
30 60 90 177 289 400
23-26: 23-(7-8/52). 24-(9-10/52). 25-(11-12/52). 26-(1-2/53). All have 2 pgs. early Peanuts by Schulz 18 36 54 105 165 225
NOTE: *Abbie & Slats reprinted from Tip Top.*

UNITED NATIONS, THE (See Classics Illustrated Special Issue)

UNITED STATES AIR FORCE PRESENTS: THE HIDDEN CREW
U.S. Air Force: 1964 (36 pgs.)

nn-Schaffenberger-a 2 4 6 11 16 20

UNITED STATES FIGHTING AIR FORCE (Also see U.S. Fighting Air Force)
Superior Comics Ltd.: Sept, 1952 - No. 29, Oct, 1956

1 15 30 45 84 127 170
2 9 18 27 52 69 85
3-10 9 18 27 47 61 75
11-29 8 16 24 42 54 65

UNITED STATES MARINES
William H. Wise/Life's Romances Publ. Co./Magazine Ent. #5-8/Toby Press #7-11: 1943 - No. 4, 1944; No. 5, 1952 - No. 8, 1952; No. 7 - No. 11, 1953

nn-Mart Bailey-c/a; Marines in the Pacific theater 28 56 84 165 270 375
2-Bailey-a; Tojo classic-c 84 168 252 538 919 1300
3-Classic WWII Tojo-c 71 142 213 454 777 1100
4-WWII photos; Tony DiPreta-a; grey-tone-c 17 34 51 98 154 210
5(A-1 #55)-Bailey-a, 6(A-1 #60), 7(A-1 #68), 8(A-1 #72)
12 24 36 67 94 120
7-11 (Toby) 11 22 33 60 83 105
NOTE: *Powell a-5-7.*

UNITY
Valiant: No. 0, Aug, 1992 - No. 1, 1992 (Free comics w/limited dist., 20 pgs.)

0 (Blue)-Prequel to Unity x-overs in all Valiant titles; B. Smith-c/a. (Free to everyone that bought all 8 titles that month.) 5.00
0 (Red)-Same as above, but w/red logo (5,000) 4 8 12 23 37 50
1-Epilogue to Unity x-overs; B. Smith-c/a. (1 copy available for every 8 Valiant books ordered by dealers.) 5.00
1 (Gold), 1-(Platinum)-Promotional copy. 2 4 6 8 10 12
... : The Lost Chapter 1 (Yearbook) (2/95, $3.95)-"1994" in indicia 4.00

UNITY
Valiant Entertainment: Nov, 2013 - Present ($3.99)

1-6: Multiple covers on each. 1-Kindt-s/Braithwaite-a. 5,6-Cafu-a 4.00

UNITY 2000 (See preludes in Shadowman #3,4 flipbooks)
Acclaim Comics: Nov, 1999 - No. 3, Jan, 2000 ($2.50, unfinished limited series planned for 6 issues)

Preview -B&W plot preview and cover art; paper cover 3.00
1-3-Starlin-a/Shooter-s 3.00

UNIVERSAL MONSTERS
Dark Horse Comics: 1993 ($4.95/$5.95, 52 pgs.)(All adapt original movies)

Creature From the Black Lagoon nn-($4.95)-Art Adams/Austin-c/a, Dracula nn-($4.95), Frankenstein nn-($3.95)-Painted-c/a, The Mummy nn-($4.95)-Painted-c
1 2 3 4 5 7
...: Cavalcade of Horror TPB (1/06, $19.95) r/one-shots; Eric Powell intro. & cover 20.00

UNIVERSAL PRESENTS DRACULA-THE MUMMY& OTHER STORIES
Dell Publishing Co.: Sept-Nov, 1963 (one-shot, 84 pgs.) (Also see Dell Giants)

02-530-311-r/Dracula 12-231-212, The Mummy 12-437-211 & part of Ghost Stories No. 1
15 30 45 100 220 340

UNIVERSAL SOLDIER (Movie)
Now Comics: Sept, 1992 - No. 3, Nov, 1992 (Limited series, polybagged, mature)

1-3 ($2.50, Direct Sales) 1-Movie adapatation; hologram on-c (all direct sales editions have painted-c) 4.00
1-3 ($1.95, Newsstand)-Rewritten & redrawn code approved version; all newsstand editions have photo-c 3.00

	GD	VG	FN	VF	VF/NM	NM-
	2.0	4.0	6.0	8.0	9.0	9.2

UNIVERSAL WAR ONE
Marvel Comics (Soleil): 2008 - No. 3, 2008 ($5.99, limited series)

1-3-Denis Bajram-s/a; English version of French comic. 1-Bajram interview 6.00
...: Revelations 1-3 (2009 - No. 3, 2009, $5.99) Bajram-s/a 6.00

UNIVERSE
Image Comics (Top Cow): Sept, 2001 - No. 8, July, 2002 ($2.50)

1-7-Jenkins-s 3.00
8-($4.95) extra short-s by Jenkins; pin-up pages 5.00

UNIVERSE X (See Earth X)
Marvel Comics: Sept, 2000 - No. 12, Sept, 2001 ($3.99/$3.50, limited series)

0-Ross-c/Braithwaite-a/Ross & Krueger-s 4.00
1-12: 5-Funeral of Captain America 4.00
... Beasts (6/00, $3.99) Yeates-a/Ross-c 4.00
... Cap (Capt. America) (2/01, $3.99) Yeates & Totleben-a/Ross-c; Cap dies 4.00
... 4 (Fantastic 4) (10/00, $3.99) Brent Anderson-a/Ross-c 4.00
... Iron Men (9/01, $3.99) Anderson-a/Ross-c; leads into #12 4.00
... Omnibus (6/01, $3.99) Ross B&W sketchbook and character bios 4.00
Sketchbook- Wizard supplement; B&W character sketches and bios 3.00
...Spidey (1/01, $3.99) Romita Sr. flashback-a/Guice-a/Ross-c 4.00
...X (11/01, $3.99) Series conclusion; Braithwaith-a/Ross wraparound-c 4.00
Volume 1 TPB (1/02, $24.95) r/#0-7 & Spidey, 4, & Cap; new Ross-c 25.00
Volume 2 TPB (6/02, $24.95) r/#8-12 &X, Beasts, Iron Men and Omnibus 25.00

UNKNOWN, THE
BOOM! Studios: May, 2009 - No. 4, Aug, 2009 ($3.99)

1-4-Mark Waid-s/Minck Oosterveer-a; two covers on each 4.00
...: The Devil Made Flesh 1-4 (9/09 - No. 4, 12/09, $3.99) Waid-s/Oosterveer-a 4.00

UNKNOWN MAN, THE (Movie)
Avon Periodicals: 1951

nn-Kinstler-c 29 58 87 172 281 390

UNKNOWN SOLDIER (Formerly Star-Spangled War Stories)
National Periodical Publications/DC Comics: No. 205, Apr-May, 1977 - No. 268, Oct, 1982 (See Our Army at War #168 for 1st app.)

205 3 6 9 17 26 35
206-210,220,221,251: 220,221 (44pgs.). 251-Enemy Ace begins
3 6 9 14 19 24
211-218,222-247,250,252-264 2 4 6 11 16 20
219-Miller-a (44 pgs.) 3 6 9 16 23 30
248,249,265-267: 248,249-Origin. 265-267-Enemy Ace vs. Balloon Buster.
2 4 6 11 16 20
268-Death of Unknown Soldier 3 6 9 19 30 40
NOTE: ***Chaykin** a-234. **Evans** a-265-267; c-235. **Kubert** c-Most. **Miller** a-219p. **Severin** a-251-253, 260, 261, 265-267. **Simonson** a-254-256. **Spiegle** a-258, 259, 262-264.*

UNKNOWN SOLDIER, THE (Also see Brave &the Bold #146)
DC Comics: Winter, 1988-'89 - No. 12, Dec, 1989 ($1.50, maxi-series, mature)

1-12: 8-Begin $1.75-c 5.00

UNKNOWN SOLDIER
DC Comics (Vertigo): Apr, 1997 - No 4, July, 1997 ($2.50, mini-series)

1-Ennis-s/Plunkett-a/Bradstreet-c in all 6.00
2-4 4.00
TPB (1998, $12.95) r/#1-4 13.00

UNKNOWN SOLDIER
DC Comics (Vertigo): Dec, 2008 - No. 25, Dec, 2010 ($2.99)

1-25: 1-Dysart-s/Ponticelli-a; intro. Lwanga Moses; two covers by Kordey and Corben. 2-20,22-25-Ponticelli-a. 21-Veitch-a 3.00
...: Beautiful World TPB (2011, $14.99) r/#21-25; Dysart afterword; sketch/design art 15.00
...: Dry Season TPB (2010, $14.99) r/#15-20; war history 15.00
...: Easy Kill TPB (2010, $17.99) r/#7-14; war history 18.00
...: Haunted House TPB (2009, $9.99) r/#1-6; glossary 10.00

UNKNOWN WORLD (Strange Stories From Another World #2 on)
Fawcett Publications: June, 1952

1-Norman Saunders painted-c 50 100 150 315 533 750

UNKNOWN WORLDS (See Journey Into...)

UNKNOWN WORLDS
American Comics Group/Best Synd. Features: Aug, 1960 - No. 57, Aug, 1967

1-Schaffenberger-c 17 34 51 117 259 400
2-Dinosaur-c/story 10 20 30 64 132 200
3-5 8 16 24 56 108 160

Unknown Worlds #35 © ACG

Untold Tales of Spider-Man #6 © MAR

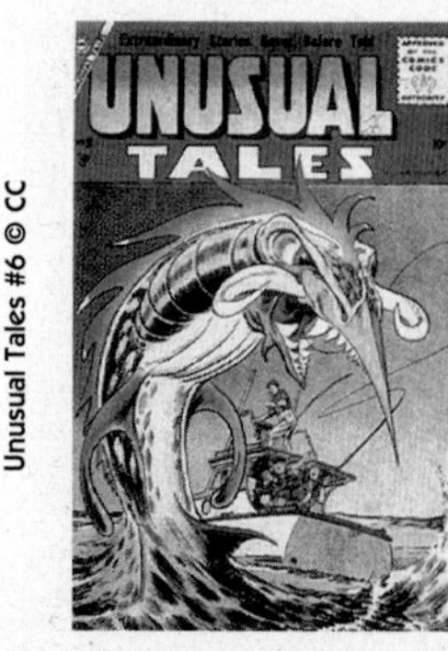

Unusual Tales #6 © CC

	GD 2.0	VG 4.0	FN 6.0	VF 8.0	VF/NM 9.0	NM- 9.2
6-11: 9-Dinosaur-c/story. 11-Last 10¢ issue	7	14	21	46	86	125
12-19: 12-Begin 12¢ issues?; ends #57	6	12	18	37	66	95
20-Herbie cameo (12-1/62-63)	6	12	18	38	69	100
21-35: 27-Devil on-c. 31-Herbie one pagers thru #39	5	10	15	30	50	70
36- "The People vs. Hendricks" by Craig; most popular ACG story ever	5	10	15	31	53	75
37-46	4	8	12	27	44	60
47-Williamson-a r-from Adventures Into the Unknown #96, 3 pgs.; Craig-a	4	8	12	28	47	65
48-57: 53-Frankenstein app.	4	8	12	25	40	55

NOTE: ***Ditko** a-49, 50p, 54. **Forte** a-3, 6, 11. **Landau** a-56(2). **Reinman** a-3, 9, 13, 20, 22, 23, 36, 38, 54. **Whitney** c/a-most issues. John Force, Magic Agent app.-35, 36, 48, 50, 52, 54, 56.*

UNKNOWN WORLDS OF FRANK BRUNNER
Eclipse Comics: Aug, 1985 - No. 2, Aug, 1985 ($1.75)

	GD	VG	FN	VF	VF/NM	NM-
1,2-B&W-r in color						4.00

UNKNOWN WORLDS OF SCIENCE FICTION
Marvel Comics: Jan, 1975 - No. 6, Nov, 1975; 1976 ($1.00, B&W Magazine)

	GD	VG	FN	VF	VF/NM	NM-
1-Williamson/Krenkel/Torres/Frazetta-r/Witzend #1, Neal Adams-r/Phase 1; Brunner & Kaluta-r; Freas/Romita-c	3	6	9	16	23	30
2-6: 5-Kaluta text illos	3	6	9	14	19	24
Special 1(1976,100 pgs.)-Newton painted-c	3	6	9	15	22	28

NOTE: ***Brunner** a-2; c-4, 6. **Buscema** a-Special 1p. **Chaykin** a-5. **Colan** a(p)-1, 3, 5, 6. **Corben** a-4. **Kaluta** a-2, Special 1(ext illos); c-2. **Morrow** a-3, 5. **Nino** a-3, 6, Special 1. **Perez** a-2, 3. Ray Bradbury interview in #1.*

UNLIMITED ACCESS (Also see Marvel Vs. DC))
Marvel Comics: Dec, 1997 - No. 4, Mar, 1998 ($2.99/$1.99, limited series)

	GD	VG	FN	VF	VF/NM	NM-
1-Spider-Man, Wonder Woman, Green Lantern & Hulk app.						4.00
2,3-($1.99): 2-X-Men, Legion of Super-Heroes app. 3-Original Avengers vs. original Justice League						3.00
4-($2.99) Amalgam Legion vs. Darkseid & Magneto						4.00

UN-MEN, THE
DC Comics (Vertigo): Oct, 2007 - No. 13, Oct, 2008 ($2.99)

	GD	VG	FN	VF	VF/NM	NM-
1-13-Whalen-s/Hawthorne-a/Hanuka-c						3.00
...: Children of Paradox TPB (2008, $19.99) r/#6-13						20.00
...: Get Your Freak On! TPB (2008, $9.99) r/#1-5; cover gallery						10.00

UNSANE (Formerly Mighty Bear #13, 14? or The Outlaws #10-14?)(Satire)
Star Publications: No. 15, June, 1954

	GD	VG	FN	VF	VF/NM	NM-
15-Disbrow-a(2); L. B. Cole-c	34	68	102	199	325	450

UNSEEN, THE
Visual Editions/Standard Comics: No. 5, 1952 - No. 15, July, 1954

	GD	VG	FN	VF	VF/NM	NM-
5-Horror stories in all; Toth-a	45	90	135	284	480	675
6,7,9,10-Jack Katz-a	37	74	111	222	361	500
8,11,13,14	32	64	96	188	307	425
12,15-Toth-a. 12-Tuska-a	37	74	11	222	361	500

NOTE: ***Nick Cardy** c-12. **Fawcette** a-13, 14. **Sekowsky** a-7, 8(2), 10, 13, 15.*

UNTAMED
Marvel Comics (Epic Comics/Heavy Hitters): June, 1993 - No. 3, Aug, 1993 ($1.95, lim. series)

	GD	VG	FN	VF	VF/NM	NM-
1-($2.50)-Embossed-c						4.00
2,3						3.00

UNTAMED LOVE (Also see Frank Frazetta's Untamed Love)
Quality Comics Group (Comic Magazines): Jan, 1950 - No. 5, Sept, 1950

	GD	VG	FN	VF	VF/NM	NM-
1-Ward-c, Gustavson-a	30	60	90	177	289	400
2,4: 2-5-Photo-c	19	38	57	111	176	240
3,5-Gustavson-a	20	40	60	114	182	250

UNTOLD LEGEND OF CAPTAIN MARVEL, THE
Marvel Comics: Apr, 1997 - No. 3, June, 1997 ($2.50, limited series)

	GD	VG	FN	VF	VF/NM	NM-
1-3						4.00

UNTOLD LEGEND OF THE BATMAN, THE (Also see Promotional section)
DC Comics: July, 1980 - No. 3, Sept, 1980 (Limited series)

	GD	VG	FN	VF	VF/NM	NM-
1-Origin; Joker-c; Byrne's 1st work at DC	1	2	3	5	6	8
2,3						5.00

NOTE: ***Aparo** a-1i, 2, 3. **Byrne** a-1p.*

UNTOLD ORIGIN OF THE FEMFORCE, THE (Also see Femforce)
AC Comics: 1989 ($4.95, 68 pgs.)

	GD	VG	FN	VF	VF/NM	NM-
1-Origin Femforce; Bill Black-a(i) & scripts						6.00

UNTOLD TALES OF BLACKEST NIGHT (Also see Blackest Night crossover titles)
DC Comics: Dec, 2010 ($4.99, one-shot)

	GD	VG	FN	VF	VF/NM	NM-
1-Short stories by various incl. Johns, Benes, Booth; 2 covers by Kirkham & Van Sciver						5.00

UNTOLD TALES OF CHASTITY
Chaos! Comics: Nov, 2000 ($2.95, one-shot)

	GD	VG	FN	VF	VF/NM	NM-
1-Origin; Steven Grant-s/Peter Vale-c/a						3.00
1-Premium Edition with glow in the dark cover						10.00

UNTOLD TALES OF LADY DEATH
Chaos! Comics: Nov, 2000 ($2.95, one-shot)

	GD	VG	FN	VF	VF/NM	NM-
1-Origin of Lady Death; Cremator app.; Kaminski-s						3.00
1-Premium Edition with glow in the dark cover by Steven Hughes						10.00

UNTOLD TALES OF PUNISHER MAX
Marvel Comics: Aug, 2012 - No. 5, Dec, 2012 ($4.99/$3.99, limited series)

	GD	VG	FN	VF	VF/NM	NM-
1-($4.99) Anthology; Starr-s/Boschi-a/c						5.00
2-5-($3.99) 2-Andrews-c. 3-Ribic-c. 5-Skottie Young-s/Del Mundo-c						4.00

UNTOLD TALES OF PURGATORI
Chaos! Comics: Nov, 2000 ($2.95, one-shot)

	GD	VG	FN	VF	VF/NM	NM-
1-Purgatori in 57 B.C.; Rio-a/Grant-s						3.00
1-Premium Edition with glow in the dark cover						10.00

UNTOLD TALES OF SPIDER-MAN (Also see Amazing Fantasy #16-18)
Marvel Comics: Sept, 1995 - No. 25, Sept, 1997 (99¢)

	GD	VG	FN	VF	VF/NM	NM-
1-Kurt Busiek scripts begin; Pat Olliffe-c/a in all (except #9).						4.00
2-22, -1(7/97), 23-25: 2-1st app. Batwing. 4-1st app. The Spacemen (Gantry, Orbit, Satellite & Vacuum). 8-1st app. The Headsman; The Enforcers (The Big Man, Montana, The Ox & Fancy Dan) app. 9-Ron Frenz-a. 10-1st app. Commanda. 16-Reintro Mary Jane Watson. 21-X-Men-c/app. 25-Green Goblin						3.00
...'96-(1996, $1.95, 46 pgs.)-Kurt Busiek scripts; Mike Allred-c/a; Kurt Busiek & Pat Olliffe app. in back-up story; contains pin-ups						4.00
...'97-(1997, $1.95)-Wraparound-c						4.00
...: Strange Encounters ('98, $5.99) Dr. Strange app.						6.00

UNTOLD TALES OF THE NEW UNIVERSE (Based on Marvel's 1986 New Universe titles)
Marvel Comics: May, 2006 ($2.99, series of one-shots)

	GD	VG	FN	VF	VF/NM	NM-
...: D. P. 7 - Takes place between issues #4 & 5 of D. P. 7 series; Bright-a/Cebulski-s						3.00
...: Justice - Peter David-s/Carmine Di Giandomenico-a						3.00
...: Nightmask - Takes place between issues #4 & 5 of Nightmask series; The Gnome app.						3.00
...: Psi-Force - Tony Bedard-s/Russ Braun-a						3.00
...: Star Brand - Romita & Romita Jr.-c/Pulido-a						3.00
TPB (2006, $15.99) r/one-shots & stories from Amaz. Fantasy #18,19 & New Avengers #16						16.00

UNTOUCHABLES, THE (TV)
Dell Publishing Co.: No. 1237, 10-12/61 - No. 4, 8-10/62 (All have Robert Stack photo-c)

	GD	VG	FN	VF	VF/NM	NM-
Four Color 1237(#1)	17	34	51	114	252	390
Four Color 1286	12	24	36	80	173	265
01-879-207, 12-879-210(01879-210 on inside)	8	16	24	54	102	150

UNTOUCHABLES
Caliber Comics: Aug, 1997 - No. 4 ($2.95, B&W)

	GD	VG	FN	VF	VF/NM	NM-
1-4: 1-Pruett-s; variant covers by Kaluta & Showman						3.00

UNUSUAL TALES (Blue Beetle & Shadows From Beyond #50 on)
Charlton Comics: Nov, 1955 - No. 49, Mar-Apr, 1965

	GD	VG	FN	VF	VF/NM	NM-
1	32	64	96	192	314	435
2	17	34	51	98	154	210
3-5	14	28	42	82	121	160
6-Ditko-c only	20	40	60	114	182	250
7,8-Ditko-c/a. 8-Robot-c	30	60	90	177	289	400
9-Ditko-c/a (20 pgs.)	32	64	96	192	314	435
10-Ditko-c/a(4)	34	68	102	199	325	450
11-(3/58, 68 pgs.)-Ditko-a(4)	32	64	96	192	314	435
12,14-Ditko-a	20	40	60	114	182	250
13,16-20	6	12	18	41	76	110
15-Ditko-c/a	25	50	75	150	245	340
21,24,28	5	10	15	35	63	90
22,23,25-27,29-Ditko-a	19	18	27	59	117	175
30-49	5	10	15	30	50	70

NOTE: ***Colan** a-11. **Ditko** c-22, 23, 25-27, 31(part).*

UNWRITTEN, THE
DC Comics (Vertigo): July, 2009 - Present ($1.00/$2.99)

	GD	VG	FN	VF	VF/NM	NM-
1-($1.00) Intro. Tommy Taylor; Mike Carey-s/Peter Gross-a; two covers (white & black)						3.00
2-16,18-31,(31.5), 32, (32.5), 33, (33.5), 34, (34.5), (35.5), 36-49-($2.99): 31.5-Art by Gross, Kaluta, Geary & Talbot. 37-Series re-cap						3.00
17-($3.99) Story printed sideways; Pick-a-Story format						4.00
35-($4.99)						5.00
50-(8/13, $4.99) Fables characters app.; Carey & Willingham-s; Gross & Buckingham-a						5.00

USA Comics #11 © MAR

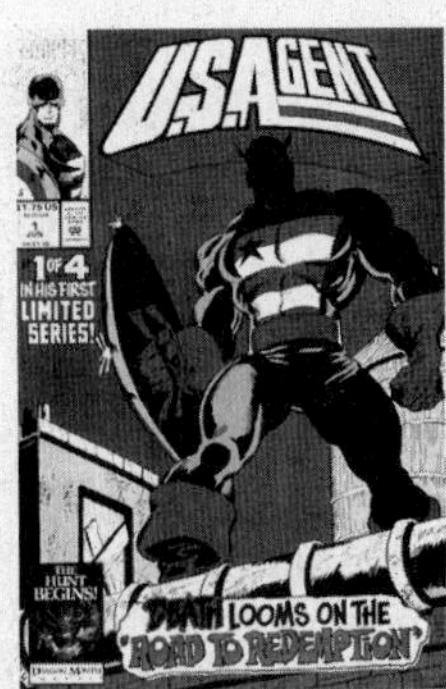

Usagi Yojimbo #25 © Stan Sakai

GD VG FN VF VF/NM NM-
2.0 4.0 6.0 8.0 9.0 9.2

51-54-Fables characters app. 3.00
...: Dead Man's Knock TPB (2011, $14.99) r/#13-18; intro. by novelist Steven Hall 15.00
...: Inside Man TPB (2010, $12.99) r/#6-12; intro. by Paul Cornell 13.00
...: Tommy Taylor and the Bogus Identity TPB (2010, $9.99) r/#1-5; sketch art; prose 10.00

UNWRITTEN, THE: APOCALYPSE
DC Comics (Vertigo): Mar, 2014 - Present ($3.99)

1-3-Mike Carey-s/Peter Gross-a 4.00

UP FROM HARLEM (Tom Skinner...)
Spire Christian Comics (Fleming H. Revell Co.): 1973 (35/49¢)

nn-(35¢ cover) 3 6 9 14 19 24
nn-(49¢ cover) 2 4 6 9 13 16

UP-TO-DATE COMICS
King Features Syndicate: No date (1938) (36 pgs.; B&W cover) (10¢)

nn-Popeye & Henry cover; The Phantom, Jungle Jim & Flash Gordon by Raymond, The Katzenjammer Kids, Curley Harper & others. Note: Variations in content exist. 28 56 84 165 270 375

UP YOUR NOSE AND OUT YOUR EAR (Satire)
Klevart Enterprises: Apr, 1972 - No. 2, June, 1972 (52 pgs., magazine)

V1#1,2 2 4 6 11 16 20

URTH 4 (Also see Earth 4)
Continuity Comics: May, 1989 - No. 4, Dec, 1990 ($2.00, deluxe format)

1-4: Ms. Mystic characters. 2-Neal Adams-c(i) 3.00

URZA-MISHRA WAR ON THE WORLD OF MAGIC THE GATHERING
Acclaim Comics (Armada): 1996 - No. 2, 1996 ($5.95, limited series)

1,2 6.00

U.S. (See Uncle Sam)

USA COMICS
Timely Comics (USA): Aug, 1941 - No. 17, Fall, 1945

1-Origin Major Liberty (called Mr. Liberty #1), Rockman by Wolverton; 1st app. The Whizzer by Avison; The Defender with sidekick Rusty & Jack Frost begin; The Young Avenger only app.; S&K-c plus 1 pg. art 1000 2000 3000 7000 12,500 20,000
2-Origin Captain Terror & The Vagabond; last Wolverton Rockman; Hitler-c 432 864 1296 3154 5577 8000
3-No Whizzer 331 662 993 2317 4059 5800
4-Last Rockman, Major Liberty, Defender, Jack Frost, & Capt. Terror; Corporal Dix app. 314 628 942 2198 3849 5500
5-Origin American Avenger & Roko the Amazing; The Blue Blade, The Black Widow & Victory Boys, Gypo the Gypsy Giant & Hills of Horror only app.; Sergeant Dix begins; no Whizzer; Hitler, Mussolini & Tojo-c 423 846 1269 3000 5250 7500
6-Captain America (ends #17), The Destroyer, Jap Buster Johnson, Jeep Jones begin; Terror Squad only app. 541 1082 1623 3950 6975 10,000
7-Captain Daring, Disk-Eyes the Detective by Wolverton app.; origin & only app. Marvel Boy (3/43); Secret Stamp begins; no Whizzer, Sergeant Dix; classic Schomburg-c 676 1352 2028 4935 8718 12,500
8,10: 10-The Thunderbird only app. 432 864 1296 3154 5577 8000
9-Last Secret Stamp; Hitler-c; classic-c 514 1028 1542 3450 6625 9500
11-13: 11-No Jeep Jones. 13-No Whizzer; Jeep Jones ends; Schomburg Japanese WWII-c 314 628 942 2198 3849 5500
14-17: 15-No Destroyer; Jap Buster Johnson ends 174 348 522 1114 1907 2700

NOTE: ***Brodsky** c-14. **Gabrielle** c-4. **Schomburg** c-6, 7, 10, 12, 13, 15-17. **Shores** a-1, 4; c-9, 11. **Ed Win** a-4. Cover features: 1-The Defender; 2, 3-Captain Terror; 4-Major Liberty; 5-Victory Boys; 6-17-Captain America & Bucky.*

USA COMICS 70TH ANNIVERSARY SPECIAL
Marvel Comics: Sept, 2009 ($3.99, one-shot)

1-New story of The Destroyer; Arcudi-s/Ellis-a; r/All Winners #3; two covers 5.00

U.S. AGENT (See Jeff Jordan...)

U.S. AGENT (See Captain America #354)
Marvel Comics: June, 1993 - No. 4, Sept, 1993 ($1.75, limited series)

1-4 3.00

U.S. AGENT
Marvel Comics: Aug, 2001 - No. 3, Oct, 2001 ($2.99, limited series)

1-3: Ordway-s/a(p)/c. 2,3-Captain America app. 3.00

USAGI YOJIMBO (See Albedo, Doomsday Squad #3 & Space Usagi)
Fantagraphics Books: July, 1987 - No. 38 ($2.00/$2.25, B&W)

1 2 4 6 9 12 15
1,8,10-2nd printings 3.00
2-9 4.00
10,11: 10-Leonardo app. (TMNT). 11-Aragonés-a 6.00
12-29 3.00
30-38: 30-Begin $2.25-c 3.00
Color Special 1 (11/89, $2.95, 68 pgs.)-new & r 4.00
Color Special 2 (10/91, $3.50) 4.00
Color Special #3 (10/92, $3.50)-Jeff Smith's Bone promo on inside-c 4.00
Summer Special 1 (1986, B&W, $2.75)-r/early Albedo issues 4.00

USAGI YOJIMBO
Mirage Studios: V2#1, Mar, 1993 - No. 16, 1994 ($2.75)

V2#1-16: 1-Teenage Mutant Ninja Turtles app. 3.00

USAGI YOJIMBO
Dark Horse Comics: V3#1, Apr, 1996 - Present ($2.95/$2.99/$3.50, B&W)

V3#1-99,101-116: Stan Sakai-c/a 3.00
100-(1/07, $3.50) Stan Sakai roast by various incl. Aragonés, Wagner, Miller, Geary 3.50
117-144-($3.50) 136-Variant-c. 141-"200th issue" 3.50
...: One For One (8/10, $1.00) Reprints #1 3.00
Color Special #4 (7/97, $2.95) "Green Persimmon" 3.00
Daisho TPB ('98, $14.95) r/Mirage series #7-14 15.00
Demon Mask TPB ('01, $15.95) 16.00
Glimpses of Death TPB (7/06, $15.95) r/#76-82 16.00
Grasscutter TPB ('99, $16.95) r/#13-22 17.00
Gray Shadows TPB ('00, $14.95) r/#23-30 15.00
Seasons TPB ('99, $14.95) r/#7-12 15.00
Shades of Death TPB ('97, $14.95) r/Mirage series #1-6 15.00
The Brink of Life and Death TPB ('98, $14.95) r/Mirage series #13,15,16 & Dark Horse series #1-6 15.00
The Shrouded Moon TPB (1/03, $15.95) r/#46-52 16.00

U.S. AIR FORCE COMICS (Army Attack #38 on)
Charlton Comics: Oct, 1958 - No. 37, Mar-Apr, 1965

1 6 12 18 41 76 110
2 4 8 12 25 40 55
3-10 3 6 9 21 33 45
11-20 3 6 9 19 30 40
21-37 3 6 9 16 23 30

NOTE: ***Glanzman** c/a-9, 10, 12. **Montes/Bache** a-33.*

USA IS READY
Dell Publishing Co.: 1941 (68 pgs., one-shot)

1-War propaganda 43 86 129 271 461 650

U.S. BORDER PATROL COMICS (Sgt. Dick Carter of the...) (See Holyoke One Shot)

USER
DC Comics (Vertigo): 2001 - No. 3, 2001 ($5.95, limited series)

1-3-Devin Grayson-s; Sean Phillips & John Bolton-a 6.00

U.S. FIGHTING AIR FORCE (Also see United States Fighting Air Force)
I. W. Enterprises: No date (1960s?)

1,9(nd): 1-r/United States Fighting...#?. 9-r/#1 2 4 6 8 11 14

U.S. FIGHTING MEN
Super Comics: 1963 - 1964 (Reprints)

10-r/With the U.S. Paratroops #4(Avon) 2 4 6 9 13 16
11,12,15-18: 11-r/Monty Hall #10. 12,16,17,18-r/U.S. Fighting Air Force #10,3,?&? 15-r/Man Comics #11 2 4 6 9 13 16

U.S. JONES (Also see Wonderworld Comics #28)
Fox Features Syndicate: Nov, 1941 - No. 2, Jan, 1942

1-U.S. Jones & The Topper begin; Nazi-c 148 296 444 947 1624 2300
2-Nazi-c 103 206 309 659 1130 1600

U.S. MARINES
Charlton Comics: Fall, 1964 (12¢, one-shot)

1-1st app. Capt. Dude; Glanzman-a 4 8 12 27 44 60

U.S. MARINES IN ACTION
Avon Periodicals: Aug, 1952 - No. 3, Dec, 1952

1-Louis Ravielli-c/a 12 24 36 67 94 120
2,3: 3-Kinstler-c 9 18 27 50 65 80

U.S. 1
Marvel Comics Group: May, 1983 - No. 12, Oct, 1984 (7,8: painted-c)

1-12: 2-Sienkiewicz-c. 3-12-Michael Golden-c 4.00

U.S. PARATROOPS (See With the...)

U.S. PARATROOPS

U.S. War Machine #12 © MAR

Valeria the She Bat #1 © Neal Adams

Vampirella #12 © WP

	GD	VG	FN	VF	VF/NM	NM-
	2.0	4.0	6.0	8.0	9.0	9.2

I. W. Enterprises: 1964?
1,8: 1-r/With the U.S. Paratroops #1; Wood-c. 8-r/With the U.S. Paratroops #6; Kinstler-c 2 4 6 9 13 16

U.S. TANK COMMANDOS
Avon Periodicals: June, 1952 - No. 4, Mar, 1953
1-Kinstler-c 12 24 36 69 97 125
2-4: Kinstler-c 9 18 27 50 65 80
I.W. Reprint #1,8: 1-r/#1. 8-r/#3 2 4 6 9 13 16
NOTE: *Kinstler a-I.W. #1; c-1-4, I.W. #1, 8.*

U.S. WAR MACHINE (Also see Iron Man and War Machine)
Marvel Comics (MAX): Nov, 2001 - No. 12, Jan, 2002 ($1.50, B&W, weekly limited series)
1-12-Chuck Austen-s/a/c 3.00
TPB (12/01, $14.95) r/#1-12 15.00

U.S. WAR MACHINE 2.0
Marvel Comics (MAX): Sept, 2003 - No. 3, Sept, 2003 ($2.99, weekly, limited series)
1-3-Austen-s/Christian Moore-CGI art 3.00

"V" (TV)
DC Comics: Feb, 1985 - No. 18, July, 1986
1-Based on TV movie & series (Sci/Fi) 5.00
2-18: 17,18-Denys Cowan-c/a 4.00

VACATION COMICS (Also see A-1 Comics)
Magazine Enterprises: No. 16, 1948 (one-shot)
A-1 16-The Pixies, Tom Tom, Flying Fredd & Koko & Kola 8 16 24 40 50 60

VACATION DIGEST
Harvey Comics: Sept, 1987 ($1.25, digest size)
1 1 2 3 5 6 8

VACATION IN DISNEYLAND (Also see Dell Giants)
Dell Publishing Co./Gold Key (1965): Aug-Oct, 1959; May, 1965 (Walt Disney)
Four Color 1025-Barks-a 14 28 42 93 204 315
1(30024-508)(G.K., 5/65, 25¢)-r/Dell Giant #30 & cover to #1 ('58); celebrates Disneyland's 10th anniversary 5 10 15 31 53 75

VACATION PARADE (See Dell Giants)

VALEN THE OUTCAST
BOOM! Studios: Dec, 2011 - No. 8, Jul, 2012 ($1.00/$3.99)
1-($1.00) Nelson-s/Scalera-a; eight covers 3.00
2-8-($3.99) 2-4-Six covers on each. 5-8-Five covers on each 4.00

VALERIA THE SHE BAT
Continuity Comics: May, 1993 - No. 5, Nov, 1993
1-Premium; acetate-c; N. Adams-a/scripts; given as gift to retailers 1 2 3 5 6 8
5 (11/93)-Embossed-c; N. Adams-a/scripts 3.00
NOTE: *Due to lack of continuity, #2-4 do not exist.*

VALERIA THE SHE BAT
Acclaim Comics (Windjammer): Sept, 1995 - No.2, Oct, 1995 ($2.50, limited series)
1,2 3.00

VALIANT...
Valiant Entertainment: May, 2012 - Present (giveaways)
... Comics FCBD 2012 Special 1 (5/12) Previews X-O Manowar, Harbinger and other Valiant 2012 titles; creator interviews 3.00
... FCBD 2013 Special #1 (5/13) Previews Harbinger Wars, X-O Manowar and others 3.00
... Masters: 2013 Showcase Edition #1 (5/13) Samples of hardcover volume offerings 3.00

VALKYRIE (See Airboy)
Eclipse Comics: May, 1987 - No. 3, July, 1987 ($1.75, limited series)
1-3: 2-Holly becomes new Black Angel 3.00

VALKYRIE
Marvel Comics: Jan, 1997; Nov, 2010 ($2.95/$3.99, one-shots)
1-(1/97, $2.95) w/pin-ups 3.00
1-(11/10, $3.99) Origin re-told; Winslade-a/Glass-s; Anacleto-c 4.00

VALKYRIE!
Eclipse Comics: July, 1988 - No. 3, Sept, 1988 ($1.95, limited series)
1-3 3.00

VALLEY OF THE DINOSAURS (TV)
Charlton Comics: Apr, 1975 - No. 11, Dec, 1976 (Hanna-Barbara)
1-W. Howard-i 3 6 9 14 19 24
2,4-11: 2-W. Howard-i 2 4 6 8 11 14
3-Byrne text illos (early work, 7/75) 2 4 6 10 14 18

VALLEY OF THE DINOSAURS (Volume 2)
Harvey Comics: Oct, 1993 ($1.50, giant-sized)
1-Reprints 5.00

VALLEY OF GWANGI (See Movie Classics)

VALOR
E. C. Comics: Mar-Apr, 1955 - No. 5, Nov-Dec, 1955
1-Williamson/Torres-a; Wood-c/a 29 58 87 232 366 500
2-Williamson-c/a; Wood-a 23 46 69 184 292 400
3,4: 3-Williamson, Crandall-a. 4-Wood-c 17 34 51 136 218 300
5-Wood-c/a; Williamson/Evans-a 16 32 48 128 202 275
NOTE: ***Crandall** a-3, 4. **Ingels** a-1, 2, 4, 5. **Krigstein** a-1-5. **Orlando** a-3, 4; c-3. **Wood** a-1, 2, 5; c-1, 4, 5.*

VALOR
Gemstone Publishing: Oct, 1998 - No. 5, Feb, 1999 ($2.50)
1-5-Reprints 4.00

VALOR (Also see Legion of Super-Heroes & Legionnaires)
DC Comics: Nov, 1992 - No. 23, Sept, 1994 ($1.25/$1.50)
1-22: 1-Eclipso The Darkness Within aftermath. 2-Vs. Supergirl. 4-Vs. Lobo. 12-Lobo cameo. 14-Legionnaires, JLA app. 17-Austin-c(i); death of Valor. 18-22-Build-up to Zero Hour 3.00
23-Zero Hour tie-in 3.00

VALOR THUNDERSTAR AND HIS FIREFLIES
Now Comics: Dec, 1986 ($1.50)
1-Ordway-c(p) 3.00

VAMPI (Vampirella's...)
Harris Publications (Anarchy Studios): Aug, 2000 - No. 25, Feb, 2003 ($2.95/$2.99)
Limited Edition Preview Book (5/00) Preview pages & sketchbook 3.00
1-(8/00, $2.95) Lau-a(p)/Conway-s 5.00
1-Platinum Edition 20.00
2-25: 17-Barberi-a 4.00
2-25-Deluxe Edition variants ($9.95): 4-Finch-c. 5-Wieringo-c. 6-Cha-c 10.00
...Digital 1 (11/01, $2.95) CGI art; Haberlin-s 4.00
...Digital Preview (Anarchy Studios, 7/01, $2.95) preview of CGI art 4.00
Switchblade Kiss HC (2001, $24.95) r/#1-6 25.00
Vicious Preview Ed. (Apr, 2003, $1.99) Flip book w/ Xin: Journey of the Monkey King Preview Ed. 4.00
Wizard #1/2 (mail order, $9.95) includes sketch pages 10.00

VAMPIRE BITES
Brainstorm Comics: May, 1995 - No. 2, Sept, 1996 ($2.95, B&W)
1,2:1-Color pin-up 3.00

VAMPIRE DIARIES, THE (Based on the CW television series)
DC Comics: Mar, 2014 - Present ($3.99, printings of online comics)
1-4: 1,3-Doran-s/Shasteen-a 3.00

VAMPIRE LESTAT, THE
Innovation Publishing: Jan, 1990 - No. 12, 1991 ($2.50, painted limited series)
1-Adapts novel; Bolton painted-c on all 2 4 6 10 14 18
1-2nd printing (has UPC code, 1st prints don't) 3.00
1-3rd & 4th printings 3.00
2-1st printing 1 2 3 5 6 8
2-2nd & 3rd printings 3.00
3-5 5.00
3-6,9-2nd printings 3.00
6-12 4.00

VAMPIRELLA (Magazine)(See Warren Presents)(Also see Heidi Saha)
Warren Publishing Co./Harris Publications #113: Sept, 1969 - No. 112, Feb, 1983; No. 113, Jan, 1988? (B&W)
1-Intro. Vampirella in original costume & wings; Frazetta-c/intro. page; Adams-a; Crandall-a 44 88 132 326 738 1150
2-1st app. Vampirella's cousin Evily-c/s; 1st/only app. Draculina, Vampirella's blonde twin sister 11 22 33 76 163 250
3 (Low distribution) 25 50 75 175 388 600
4,6 8 16 24 54 102 150
5,7,9: 5,7-Frazetta-c. 9-Barry Smith-a; Boris/Wood-c 9 18 27 57 111 165
8-Vampirella begins by Tom Sutton as serious strip (early issues-gag line) 9 18 27 59 117 175
10-No Vampi story; Brunner, Adams, Wood-a 6 12 18 40 73 105
11-Origin & 1st app. Pendragon; Frazetta-c 7 14 21 46 86 125

Vampirella #28 © WP

Vampirella (2001 series) #3 © Harris

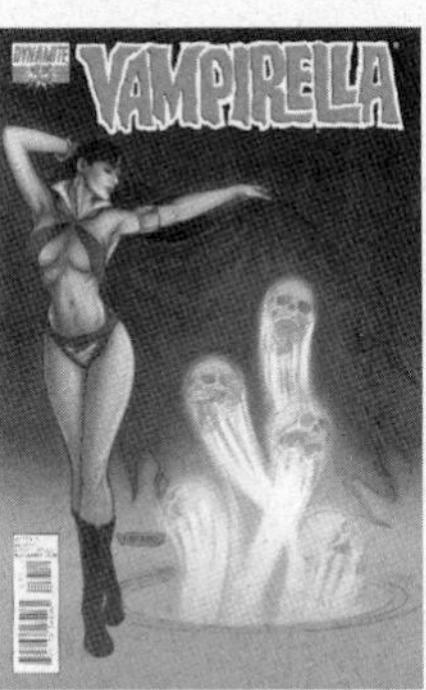

Vampirella (2010 series) #35 © Dynamite

	GD 2.0	VG 4.0	FN 6.0	VF 8.0	VF/NM 9.0	NM- 9.2
12-Vampi by Gonzales begins	7	14	21	46	86	125
13-15: 14-1st Maroto-a; Ploog-a	6	12	18	42	79	115
16,22,25: 16-1st full Dracula-c/app. 22-Color insert preview of Maroto's Dracula. 25-Vampi on cocaine-s	6	12	18	41	76	110
17,18,20,21,23,24: 17-Tomb of the Gods begins by Maroto, ends #22. 18-22-Dracula-s	6	12	18	38	69	100
19 (1973 Annual) Creation of Vampi text bio	7	14	21	44	82	120
26,28,34,35,39,40: All have 8 pg. color inserts. 28-Board game inside covers. 34,35-1st Fleur the Witch Woman. 39,40-Color Dracula-s. 40-Wrightson bio	5	10	15	33	57	80
27 (1974 Annual) New color Vampi-s; mostly-r	6	12	18	37	66	95
29,38,45: 38-2nd Vampi as Cleopatra/Blood Red Queen of Hearts; 1st Mayo-a.	5	10	15	31	53	75
30-32: 30-Intro. Pantha; Corben-a(color). 31-Origin Luana, the Beast Girl. 32-Jones-a	5	10	15	33	57	80
33-Wrightson-a; Pantha ends	5	10	15	33	57	80
36,37: 36-1st Vampi as Cleopatra/Blood Red Queen of Hearts; issue has 8 pg. color insert. 37-(1975 Annual)	5	10	15	34	60	85
41-44,47,48: 41-Dracula-s	4	8	12	28	47	65
46-(10/75) Origin-r from Annual 1	5	10	15	30	50	70
49-1st Blind Priestess; The Blood Red Queen of Hearts storyline begins; Poe-s	4	8	12	28	47	65
50-Spirit cameo by Eisner; 40 pg. Vampi-s; Pantha & Fleur app.; Jones-a	4	8	12	28	47	65
51-53,56,57,59-62,65,66,68,75,79,80,82-86,88,89: 60-62,65,66-The Blood Red Queen of Hearts app. 60-1st Blind Priestess-c	4	8	12	23	37	50
54,55,63,81,87: 54-Vampi-s (42 pgs.); 8 pg. color Corben-a. 55-All Gonzales-a(r). 63-10 pgs. Wrightson-a	4	8	12	23	37	50
58,70,72: 58-(92 pgs.) 70-Rook app.	4	8	12	27	44	60
64,73: 64-(100 pg. Giant) All Mayo-a; 70 pg. Vampi-s. 73-69 pg. Vampi-s; Mayo-a	4	8	12	28	47	65
67,69,71,74,76-78-All Barbara Leigh photo-c	4	8	12	27	44	60
90-99: 90-Toth-a. 91-All-r; Gonzales-a. 93-Cassandra St. Knight begins, ends #103; new Pantha series begins, ends #108	4	8	12	23	37	50
100 (96 pg. r-special)-Origin reprinted from Ann. 1; mostly reprints; Vampirella appears topless in new 21 pg. story	6	12	18	41	76	110
101-104,106,107: All lower print run. 101,102-The Blood Red Queen of Hearts app. 107-All Maroto reprint-a issue	5	10	15	34	60	85
105,108-110: 108-Torpedo series by Toth begins; Vampi nudity splash page. 110-(100 pg. Summer Spectacular)	5	10	15	34	60	85
111,112: Low print run. 111-Giant Collector's Edition ($2.50) 112-(84 pgs.) last Warren issue	7	14	21	46	86	125
113 (1988)-1st Harris Issue; very low print run	23	46	69	161	356	550
Annual 1(1972)-New definitive origin of Vampirella by Gonzales; reprints by Neal Adams (from #1), Wood (from #9)	19	38	57	131	291	450
Special 1 (1977) Softcover (color, large-square bound)-Only available thru mail order	14	28	42	94	207	320
Special 1 (1977) Hardcover (color, large-square bound)-Only available through mail order (scarce)(500 produced, signed & #'d)	30	60	90	212	476	740
#1 1969 Commemorative Edition (2001, $4.95) reprints entire #1						5.00
...Crimson Chronicles Vol. 1 (2004, $19.95, TPB) reprints stories from #1-10						20.00
...Crimson Chronicles Vol. 2 (2005, $19.95, TPB) reprints stories from #11-18						20.00
...Crimson Chronicles Vol. 3 (2005, $19.95, TPB) reprints stories from #19-28						20.00
...Crimson Chronicles Vol. 4 (2006, $19.95, TPB) reprints stories from #29-41						20.00

NOTE: ***Ackerman*** *s-1-3.* ***Neal Adams*** *a-1, 10p, 19p(r/#10), 44(1 pg.), Annual 1.* ***Alcala*** *a-78, 90, 93i.* ***Bodé/Todd*** *c-3.* ***Bodé/Jones*** *c-4.* ***Boris/Wood*** *c-9.* ***Brunner*** *a-10, 12(1 pg.).* ***Corben*** *a-30, 31, 33, 36, 54; c-30, 31, 33, 54.* ***Crandall*** *a-1, 19(r/#1).* ***Frazetta*** *c-1, 5, 7, 11, 31.* ***Heath*** *a-58, 61, 67, 76-78, 83.* ***Infantino*** *a-57-62.* ***Jones*** *a-5, 9, 12, 27, 32 (color), 33(2 pg.), 34, 50i, 83r.* ***Ken Kelly*** *c-6, 38, 39, 40(back-c), 46, 70, 95.* ***Nebres*** *a-84, 88-90, 92-96.* ***Nino*** *a-59i, 61i, 67, 76, 85, 90.* ***Ploog*** *a-14.* ***Barry Smith*** *a-9.* ***Starlin*** *a-78.* ***Sutton*** *a-1-5, 7-11, Annual 1.* ***Toth*** *a-90i, 108, 110.* ***Wood*** *a-9, 10, 12, 19(r/#12), 27r, Annual 1; c-9(partial).* ***Wrightson*** *a-33(w/****Jones****), 40(Bio cameo) 63r. All reprint issues-19, 74, 83, 91, 105, 107, 109, 111. Annuals from 1973 on are included in regular numbering. Later annuals are same format as regular issues. Color inserts (8 pgs.) in 22, 25-28, 30-35, 39, 40, 45, 46, 49, 54, 55, 67, 72. 16 pg color insert in #36.*

VAMPIRELLA (Also see Cain/... & Vengeance of...)
Harris Publications: Nov, 1992 - No. 5, Nov, 1993 ($2.95)

	GD 2.0	VG 4.0	FN 6.0	VF 8.0	VF/NM 9.0	NM- 9.2
0-Bagged						6.00
0-Gold	3	6	9	16	23	30
1-Jim Balent inks in #1-3; Adam Hughes c-1-3	2	4	6	11	16	20
1-2nd printing						5.00
1-(11/97) Commemorative Edition						4.00
2	2	4	6	9	12	15
3-5: 4-Snyder III-c. 5-Brereton painted-c	1	2	3	5	6	8
Trade paperback nn (10/93, $5.95)-r/#1-4; Jusko-c	1	3	4	6	8	10

NOTE: *Issues 1-5 contain certificates for free* ***Dave Stevens*** *Vampirella poster.*

VAMPIRELLA (THE NEW MONTHLY)
Harris Publications: Nov, 1997 - No. 26, Apr, 2000 ($2.95)

	GD 2.0	VG 4.0	FN 6.0	VF 8.0	VF/NM 9.0	NM- 9.2
1-3-"Ascending Evil" -Morrison & Millar-s/Conner & Palmiotti-a. 1-Three covers by Quesada/Palmiotti, Conner, and Conner/Palmiotti						5.00
1-3-($9.95) Jae Lee variant covers						10.00
1-($24.95) Platinum Ed.w/Quesada-c						25.00
4-6-"Holy War"-Small & Stull-a, 4-Linsner variant-c						4.00
7-9-"Queen's Gambit"-Shi app. 7-Two covers. 8-Pantha-c/app.						4.00
7-($9.95) Conner variant-c						10.00
10-12-"Hell on Earth"; Small-a/Coney-s. 12-New costume						4.00
10-Jae Lee variant-c	1	3	4	6	8	10
13-15-"World's End" Zircher-p; Pantha back-up, Texeira-a						4.00
16,17: 16-Pantha-c;Texeira-a; Vampi back-up story. 17-(Pantha #2)						4.00
18-20-"Rebirth": Jae Lee-c on all. 18-Loeb-s/Sale-a. 19-Alan Davis-a. 20-Bruce Timm-a						4.00
18-20-($9.95) Variant covers: 18-Sale. 19-Davis. 20-Timm						12.00
21-26: 21,22-Dangerous Games; Small-a. 23-Lady Death-c/app.; Cleavenger-a. 24,25-Lau-a. 26-Lady Death & Pantha-c/app.; Cleavenger-a.						4.00
0-(1/99) also variant-c with Pantha #0; same contents						4.00
TPB ($7.50) r/#1-3 "Ascending Evil"						8.00
Ascending Evil Ashcan (8/97, $1.00)						3.00
...: Grant Morrison/Mark Millar Collection TPB (2006, $24.95) r/#1-6; interviews						25.00
Hell on Earth Ashcan (7/98, $1.00)						3.00
... Presents: Tales of Pantha TPB (2006, $19.95) r/stories from #13-17 & one-shots						20.00
The End Ashcan (3/00, $6.00)						6.00
...30th Anniversary Celebration Preview (7/99) B&W preview of #18-20						10.00

VAMPIRELLA
Harris Publications: June, 2001 - No. 22, Aug, 2003 ($2.95/$2.99)

	GD 2.0	VG 4.0	FN 6.0	VF 8.0	VF/NM 9.0	NM- 9.2
1-Four covers (Mayhew w/foil logo, Campbell, Anacleto, Jae Lee) Mayhew-a; Mark Millar-s						5.00
2-22: 2-Two covers (Mayhew & Chiodo). 3-Timm var-c. 4-Horn var-c. 7-10-Dawn Brown-a; Pantha back-up w/Texeira-a. 15-22-Conner-c						4.00
Giant-Size Ashcan (5/01, $5.95) B&W preview art and Mayhew interview						6.00
...: Halloween Trick & Treat (10/04, $4.95) stories & art by various; three covers						5.00
... : Nowheresville Preview Edition (3/01, $2.95)- previews Mayhew art and photo models						4.00
...Nowheresville TPB (1/02, $12.95) r/#1-3 with cover gallery						13.00
... Summer Special #1 (2005, $5.95) Batman Begins photo-c and 2 variant-c						6.00
...: 2006 Halloween Special (2006, $2.95) Conner-c; Hester-s/Segovia-a; 4 covers						4.00

VAMPIRELLA
Dynamite Entertainment: 2010 - No. 38, 2014 ($3.99)

	GD 2.0	VG 4.0	FN 6.0	VF 8.0	VF/NM 9.0	NM- 9.2
1-Four covers (Campbell, Madureira, J. Djurdjevic, Alex Ross swipe of Frazetta's #1)						4.00
1-Variant-c of blood-soaked Vampirella by Alex Ross						8.00
2-37: 2-6-Trautmann-s/Wagner Reis-a; four covers. 7-Geovani-a						4.00
38-($4.99, 40 pgs.) Pantha and Dracula app.						5.00
Annual 1 (2011, $4.99) Jerwa-s/Casalos-a; reprint with Alan Davis-a						5.00
Annual 2 (2012, $4.99) Rahner-s/Kyriazis-a; reprint with Pantha app.; Linsner-c						5.00
Annual 2013 ($4.99) Rahner-s/Valiente-a/Bolson-c						5.00
...: NuBlood (2013, $4.99) Spoof of True Blood; Rahner-s/Razek-a/c; back-up w/Timm-a						5.00
... Vs. Fluffy (2012, $4.99) Spoof of Buffy the Vampire Slayer; Bradshaw-c						5.00

VAMPIRELLA & PANTHA SHOWCASE
Harris Publications: Jan, 1997 ($1.50, one-shot)

	GD 2.0	VG 4.0	FN 6.0	VF 8.0	VF/NM 9.0	NM- 9.2
1-Millar-s/Texeira-c/a; flip book w/"Blood Lust"; Robinson-s/Jusko-c/a						4.00

VAMPIRELLA & THE BLOOD RED QUEEN OF HEARTS
Harris Publications: Sept, 1996 ($9.95, 96 pgs., B&W, squarebound, one-shot)

	GD 2.0	VG 4.0	FN 6.0	VF 8.0	VF/NM 9.0	NM- 9.2
nn-r/Vampirella #49,60-62,65,66,101,102; John Bolton-c; Michael Bair back-c	1	3	4	6	8	10

VAMPIRELLA AND THE SCARLET LEGION
Dynamite Entertainment: 2011 - No. 5 ($3.99)

	GD 2.0	VG 4.0	FN 6.0	VF 8.0	VF/NM 9.0	NM- 9.2
1-5: 1-Three covers (Campbell, Chen and Tucci); Malaga-a						4.00

VAMPIRELLA: BLOODLUST
Harris Publications: July, 1997 - No. 2, Aug, 1997 ($4.95, limited series)

	GD 2.0	VG 4.0	FN 6.0	VF 8.0	VF/NM 9.0	NM- 9.2
1,2-Robinson-s/Jusko-painted c/a						5.00

VAMPIRELLA CLASSIC
Harris Publications: Feb, 1995 - No. 5, Nov, 1995 ($2.95, limited series)

	GD 2.0	VG 4.0	FN 6.0	VF 8.0	VF/NM 9.0	NM- 9.2
1-5: Reprints Archie Goodwin stories.						4.00

VAMPIRELLA COMICS MAGAZINE
Harris Publications: Oct, 2003 - No. 9 ($3.95/$9.95, magazine-sized)

	GD 2.0	VG 4.0	FN 6.0	VF 8.0	VF/NM 9.0	NM- 9.2
1-9-($3.95) 1-Texiera-c; b&w and color stories, Alan Moore interview; reviews. 2-KISS interview. 4-Chiodo-c. 6-Brereton-c						4.00
1-9-($9.95) 1-Three covers (Model Photo cover, Palmiotti-c, Wheatley Frankenstein-c)						10.00

Vampirella Lives #2 © Harris

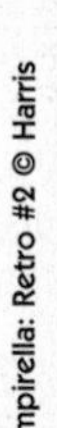
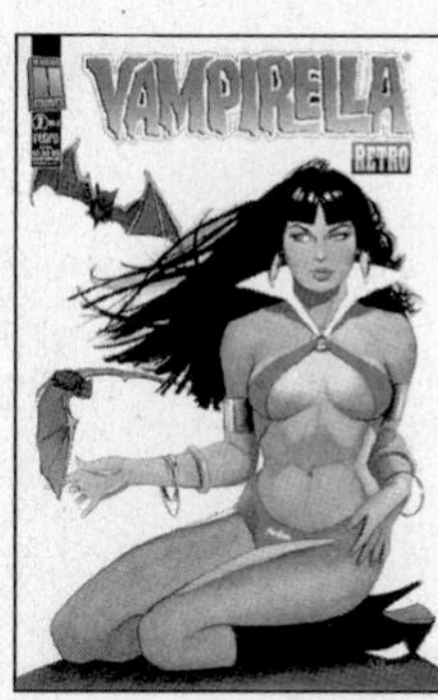
Vampirella: Retro #2 © Harris

Vampirella Strikes (2013 series) #6 © Dynamite

	GD	VG	FN	VF	VF/NM	NM-
	2.0	4.0	6.0	8.0	9.0	9.2

VAMPIRELLA: CROSSOVER GALLERY
Harris Publications: Sept, 1997 ($2.95, one-shot)

1-Wraparound-c by Campbell, pinups by Jae Lee, Mack, Allred, Art Adams, Quesada & Palmiotti and others 4.00

VAMPIRELLA: DEATH & DESTRUCTION
Harris Publications: July, 1996 - No. 3, Sept, 1996 ($2.95, limited series)

1-3: Amanda Conner-a(p) in all. 1-Tucci-c. 2-Hughes-c. 3-Jusko-c 4.00
1-($9.95)-Limited Edition; Beachum-c 10.00

VAMPIRELLA/DRACULA & PANTHA SHOWCASE
Harris Publications: Aug, 1997 ($1.50, one-shot)

1-Ellis, Robinson, and Moore-s; flip book w/"Pantha" 4.00

VAMPIRELLA/DRACULA: THE CENTENNIAL
Harris Publications: Oct, 1997 ($5.95, one-shot)

1-Ellis, Robinson, and Moore-s; Beachum, Frank/Smith, and Mack/Mays-a Bolton-painted-c 6.00

VAMPIRELLA: INTIMATE VISIONS
Harris Publications: 2006 ($3.95, one-shots)

..., Amanda Conner 1 - r/Vampirella Monthly #1 with commentary; interview; 2 covers 4.00
..., Joe Jusko 1 - r/Vampirella; Blood Lust #1 with commentary; interview; 2 covers 4.00

VAMPIRELLA: JULIE STRAIN SPECIAL
Harris Publications: Sept, 2000 ($3.95, one-shot)

1-Photo-c w/yellow background; interview and photo gallery 4.00
1-Limited Edition ($9.95); cover photo w/black background 10.00

VAMPIRELLA/LADY DEATH (Also see Lady Death/Vampirella)
Harris Publications: Feb, 1999 ($3.50, one-shot)

1-Small-a/Nelson painted-c 4.00
1-Valentine Edition ($9.95); pencil-c by Small 10.00

VAMPIRELLA: LEGENDARY TALES
Harris Publications: May, 2000 - No. 2, June, 2000 ($2.95, B&W)

1,2-Reprints from magazine; Cleavenger painted-c 4.00
1,2-($9.95) Variant painted-c by Mike Mayhew 10.00

VAMPIRELLA LIVES
Harris Publications: Dec, 1996 - No. 3, Feb, 1997 ($3.50/$2.95, limited series)

1-Die cut-c; Quesada & Palmiotti-c, Ellis-s/Conner-a 5.00
1-Deluxe Ed.-photo-c 5.00
2,3-($2.95)-Two editions (1 photo-c): 3-J. Scott Campbell-c 4.00

VAMPIRELLA: MORNING IN AMERICA
Harris Publications/Dark Horse Comics: 1991 - No. 4, 1992 ($3.95, B&W, lim. series, 52 pgs.)

1,2-All have Kaluta painted-c 1 2 3 5 6 8
3,4 1 3 4 6 8 10

VAMPIRELLA OF DRAKULON
Harris Publications: Jan, 1996 - No. 5, Sept, 1996 ($2.95)

0-5: All reprints. 0-Jim Silke-c. 3-Polybagged w/card. 4-Texeira-c 4.00

VAMPIRELLA/PAINKILLER JANE
Harris Publications: May, 1998 ($3.50, one-shot)

1-Waid & Augustyn-s/Leonardi & Palmiotti-a 4.00
1-($9.95) Variant-c 10.00

VAMPIRELLA PIN-UP SPECIAL
Harris Publications: Oct, 1995 ($2.95, one-shot)

1-Hughes-c, pin-ups by various 5.00
1-Variant-c 5.00

VAMPIRELLA QUARTERLY
Harris Publications: Spring, 2007 - Summer, 2008 ($4.95/$4.99, quarterly)

Spring, 2007 - Summer, 2008-New stories and re-colored reprints; five or six covers 5.00

VAMPIRELLA: RETRO
Harris Publications: Mar, 1998 - No. 3, May, 1998 ($2.50, B&W, limited series)

1-3: Reprints; Silke painted covers 4.00

VAMPIRELLA: REVELATIONS
Harris Publications: No. 0, Oct, 2005 - No. 3, Feb, 2006 ($2.99, limited series)

0-3-Vampirella's origin retold, Lilith app.; Carey-s/Lilly-a; two covers on each 4.00
... Book 1 TPB (2006, $12.95) r/series; Carey interview, script for #1, Lilly sketch pages 13.00

VAMPIRELLA: SAD WINGS OF DESTINY
Harris Publications: Sept, 1996 ($3.95, one-shot)

1-Jusko-c 5.00

VAMPIRELLA: SECOND COMING
Harris Publications: 2009 - No. 4 ($1.99, limited series)

1-4: 1-Hester-s/Sampere-a; multiple covers on each. 3,4-Rio-a 4.00

VAMPIRELLA/SHADOWHAWK: CREATURES OF THE NIGHT (Also see Shadowhawk)
Harris Publications: 1995 ($4.95, one-shot)

1 5.00

VAMPIRELLA/SHI (See Shi/Vampirella)
Harris Publications: Oct, 1997 ($2.95, one-shot)

1-Ellis-s 4.00
1-Chromium-c 6.00

VAMPIRELLA: SILVER ANNIVERSARY COLLECTION
Harris Publications: Jan, 1997 - No. 4 Apr, 1997 ($2.50, limited series)

1-4: Two editions: Bad Girl by Beachum, Good Girl by Silke 4.00

VAMPIRELLA: SOUTHERN GOTHIC
Dynamite Entertainment: 2013 - No. 5, 2014 ($3.99)

1-5-Nate Cosby-s/José Luis-a; regular & photo-c on each 4.00

VAMPIRELLA'S SUMMER NIGHTS
Harris Publications: 1992 (one-shot)

1-Art Adams infinity cover; centerfold by Stelfreeze 2 4 6 9 12 15

VAMPIRELLA STRIKES
Harris Publications: Sept, 1995 - No. 8, Dec, 1996 ($2.95, limited series)

1-8: 1-Photo-c. 2-Deodato-c; polybagged w/card. 5-Eudaemon-c/app; wraparound-c; alternate-c exists. 6-(6/96)-Mark Millar script; Texeira-c; alternate-c exists. 7-Flip book 4.00
1-Newsstand Edition; diff. photo-c., 1-Limited Ed.; diff. photo-c 4.00
Annual 1-(12/96, $2.95) Delano-s; two covers 4.00

VAMPIRELLA STRIKES
Dynamite Entertainment: 2013 - No. 6, 2013 ($3.99)

1-6: 1-Five covers (Turner, Finch, Manara, Desjardins & photo); Desjardins-a 4.00

VAMPIRELLA THE RED ROOM
Dynamite Entertainment: 2012 - No. 4, 2012 ($3.99)

1-4-Three covers on each; Brereton-s/Diaz-a 4.00

VAMPIRELLA: 25TH ANNIVERSARY SPECIAL
Harris Publications: Oct, 1996 ($5.95, squarebound, one-shot)

nn-Reintro The Blood Red Queen of Hearts; James Robinson, Grant Morrison & Warren Ellis scripts; Mark Texeira, Michael Bair & Amanda Conner-a(p); Frank Frazetta-c 7.00
nn-($6.95)-Silver Edition 8.00

VAMPIRELLA VS. DRACULA
Dynamite Entertainment: 2012 - No. 6, 2012 ($3.99, limited series)

1-6-Harris-s/Rodriguez-a/Linsner-c 4.00

VAMPIRELLA VS. HEMORRHAGE
Harris Publications: Apr, 1997 ($3.50)

1 4.00

VAMPIRELLA VS. PANTHA
Harris Publications: Mar, 1997 ($3.50)

1-Two covers; Millar-s/Texeira-c/a 4.00

VAMPIRELLA/WETWORKS (See Wetworks/Vampirella)
Harris Publications: June, 1997 ($2.95, one-shot)

1 4.00
1-($9.95) Alternate Edition; cardstock-c 10.00

VAMPIRELLA/WITCHBLADE
Harris Publications: 2003; Oct, 2004; Oct, 2005 ($2.99, one-shots)

1-Brian Wood-s/Steve Pugh-a; 3 covers by Texeira, Conner and Pugh 4.00
...: The Feast (10/05, $2.99) Joyce Chin-a; covers by Chin, Conner, Rodriguez 4.00
...: Union of the Damned (10/04, $2.99, one-shot) Sharp-a; three covers 4.00
Trilogy TPB (2006, $12.95) r/one-shots; art gallery and gallery of multiple covers 13.00

VAMPIRE, PA
Moonstone: 2010 - No. 3, Oct, 2010 ($3.99)

1-3: 1-Intro. Vampire Hunter Dean; J.C. Vaughn-s/Brendon & Brian Fraim-a; three covers. 3-Zombie Proof back-up; Spencer-a 4.00

VAMPIRE'S CHRISTMAS, THE (Also see Dark Ivory)
Image Comics: Oct, 2003 ($5.95, over-sized graphic novel)

nn-Linsner-s/a; Dubisch-painted-a 6.00

Vampire Tales #7 © MAR

Vandroid #2 © Vandroid Ltd.

Vault of Horror #17 © WMG

GD 2.0 | VG 4.0 | FN 6.0 | VF 8.0 | VF/NM 9.0 | NM- 9.2

VAMPIRES: THE MARVEL UNDEAD
Marvel Comics: Dec, 2011 ($3.99, one-shot)
1-Handbook-style profiles of vampire characters in the Marvel Universe; Seeley-c 4.00

VAMPIRE TALES
Marvel Comics Group: Aug, 1973 - No. 11, June, 1975 (75¢, B&W, magazine)
1-Morbius, the Living Vampire begins by Pablo Marcos (1st solo Morbius series & 5th Morbius app.) 6 12 18 41 76 110
2-Intro. Satana; Steranko-r 5 10 15 30 50 70
3,5,6: 3-Satana app. 5-Origin Morbius. 6-1st Lilith app. in this title (see Giant-Size Chillers #1 for debut) 4 8 12 27 44 60
4,7 3 6 9 21 33 45
8-1st solo Blade story (see Tomb of Dracula) 5 10 15 30 50 70
9-Blade app. 4 8 12 27 44 60
10,11 3 6 9 21 33 45
Annual 1(10/75)-Heath-r/#9 3 6 9 21 33 45
NOTE: ***Alcala** a-6, 8, 9i. **Boris** c-4, 6. **Chaykin** a-7. **Everett** a-1r. **Gulacy** a-7p. **Heath** a-9. **Infantino** a-3r. **Gil Kane** a-4, 5r.*

VAMPIRE VERSES, THE
CFD Productions: Aug, 1995 - No. 4, 1995 ($2.95, B&W, mature)
1-4 3.00

VAMPI VICIOUS
Harris Publications (Anarchy Studios): Aug, 2003 - No. 3, Nov, 2003 ($2.99)
1-3: 1-McKeever-s/Dogan-a; 3 covers by Dogan, Lau & Noto. 3-Kau-a 4.00

VAMPI VICIOUS CIRCLE
Harris Publications (Anarchy Studios): Jun, 2004 - No. 3, Sept, 2004 ($2.99/$9.95)
1-3: B. Clay Moore-s 4.00
1-3-($9.95) Limited Edition w/variant-c. 1-Noto-c. 2-Norton-c. 3-Lucas-c 10.00

VAMPI VICIOUS RAMPAGE
Harris Publications (Anarchy Studios): Feb, 2005 - No. 2, Apr, 2005 ($2.99)
1,2: Raab-s/Lau-a; two covers on each 4.00

VAMPI VS. XIN
Harris Publications (Anarchy Studios): Oct, 2004 - No. 2, Jan, 2005 ($2.99)
1,2-Faerber-s/Lau-a; two covers 4.00

VAMPS
DC Comics (Vertigo): Aug, 1994 - No. 6, Jan, 1995 ($1.95, lim. series, mature)
1-6-Bolland-c 3.00
Trade paperback ($9.95)-r/#1-6 10.00

VAMPS: HOLLYWOOD & VEIN
DC Comics (Vertigo): Feb, 1996 - No. 6, July, 1996 ($2.25, lim. series, mature)
1-6: Winslade-c 3.00

VAMPS: PUMPKIN TIME
DC Comics (Vertigo): Dec, 1998 - No. 3, Feb, 1999 ($2.50, lim. series, mature)
1-3: Quitely-c 3.00

VANDROID
Dark Horse Comics: Feb, 2014 - No. 5 ($3.99, limited series)
1-Tommy Lee Edwards & Noah Smith-s/Dan McDaid-a/Edwards-c 4.00

VANGUARD (...Outpost: Earth) (See Megaton)
Megaton Comics: 1987 ($1.50)
1-Erik Larsen-c(p) 4.00

VANGUARD (See Savage Dragon #2)
Image Comics (Highbrow Entertainment): Oct, 1993 - No. 6, 1994 ($1.95)
1-6: 1-Wraparound gatefold-c; Erik Larsen back-up-a; Supreme x-over. 3-(12/93)-Indicia says December 1994. 4-Berzerker back-up. 5-Angel Medina-a(p) 3.00

VANGUARD (See Savage Dragon #2)
Image Comics: Aug, 1996 - No. 4, Feb, 1997 ($2.95, B&W, limited series)
1-4 3.00

VANGUARD: ETHEREAL WARRIORS
Image Comics: Aug, 2000 ($5.95, B&W)
1-Fosco & Larsen-a 6.00

VANGUARD ILLUSTRATED
Pacific Comics: Nov, 1983 - No. 11, Oct, 1984 (Baxter paper)(Direct sales only)
1,3-6,8-11: 1-Nudity scenes 3.00
2-1st app. Stargrazers (see Legends of the Stargrazers; Dave Stevens-c 1 2 3 5 6 8
7-1st app. Mr. Monster (r-in Mr. Monster #1); nudity scenes 5.00
NOTE: ***Evans** a-7. **Kaluta** c-5, 7p. **Perez** a-6; c-6. **Rude** a-1-4; c-4. **Williamson** c-3.*

VANGUARD: STRANGE VISITORS
Image Comics: Oct, 1996 - No.4, Feb, 1997 ($2.95, B&W, limited series)
1-4: 3-Supreme-c/app. 3.00

VAN HELSING: FROM BENEATH THE RUE MORGUE (Based on the 2004 movie)
Dark Horse Comics: Apr, 2004 ($2.99, one-shot)
1-Hugh Jackman photo-c; Dysart-s/Alexander-a 3.00

VANITY (See Pacific Presents #3)
Pacific Comics: Jun, 1984 - No. 2, Aug, 1984 ($1.50, direct sales)
1,2: Origin 3.00

VARIETY COMICS (The Spice of Comics)
Rural Home Publ./Croyden Publ. Co.: 1944 - No. 2, 1945; No. 3, 1946
1-Origin Captain Valiant 22 44 66 132 216 300
2-Captain Valiant 15 30 45 83 124 165
3(1946-Croyden)-Captain Valiant 14 28 42 76 108 140

VARIETY COMICS (See Fox Giants)

VARSITY
Parents' Magazine Institute: 1945
1 9 18 27 52 69 85

VAULT OF EVIL
Marvel Comics Group: Feb, 1973 - No. 23, Nov, 1975
1 (1950s reprints begin) 4 8 12 23 37 50
2-23: 3,4-Brunner-c. 11-Kirby-a 3 6 9 16 23 30
NOTE: ***Ditko** a-14r, 15r, 20-22r. **Drucker** a-10r(Mystic #52), 13r(Uncanny Tales #42). **Everett** a-11r(Menace #2), 13r(Menace #4); c-10. **Heath** a-5r. **Gil Kane** c-1, 6. **Kirby** a-11. **Krigstein** a-20r(Uncanny Tales #54). **Reinman** r-1. **Tuska** a-6r.*

VAULT OF HORROR (Formerly War Against Crime #1-11) (Also see EC Archives)
E. C. Comics: No. 12, Apr-May, 1950 - No. 40, Dec-Jan, 1954-55
12 (Scarce)-ties w/Crypt Of Terror as 1st horror comic 503 1006 1509 4024 6412 8800
13-Morphine story 104 208 312 832 1329 1825
14 90 180 270 720 1148 1575
15- "Terror in the Swamp" is same story w/minor changes as "The Thing in the Swamp" from Haunt of Fear #15 79 158 237 632 1004 1375
16 62 124 186 496 791 1085
17-Classic werewolf-c 71 142 213 568 909 1250
18,19 49 98 147 392 626 860
20-25: 22-Frankenstein-c & adaptation. 23-Used in **POP**, pg. 84; Davis-a(2); Ingels bio. 24-Craig bio. 42 84 126 336 536 735
26-B&W & color illos in **POP** 42 84 126 336 536 735
27-29,31-34,36: 31-Ray Bradbury biog. 32-Censored-c. 36- "Pipe Dream" classic opium addict story by Krigstein; "Twin Bill" cited in articles by T.E. Murphy, Wertham 36 72 108 288 462 635
30-Dismemberment-c 48 96 144 384 610 835
35-X-Mas-c 48 96 144 384 610 835
37-1st app. Drusilla, a Vampirella look alike; Williamson-a 38 76 114 304 482 660
38-39: 39-Bondage-c 36 72 108 288 457 625
40-Low distribution 42 84 126 336 536 735
NOTE: ***Craig** art in all but No. 13 & 33; c-12-40. **Crandall** a-33, 34, 39. **Davis** a-17-38. **Evans** a-27, 28, 30, 32, 33. **Feldstein** a-12-16. **Ingels** a-13-20, 22-40. **Kamen** a-15-22, 25, 29, 35. **Krigstein** a-36, 38-40. **Kurtzman** a-12, 13. **Orlando** a-24, 31, 40. **Wood** a-12-14. #22, 29 & 31 have Ray Bradbury adaptations. #16 & 17 have H. P. Lovecraft adaptations.*

VAULT OF HORROR, THE
Gladstone Publ.: Aug, 1990 - No. 6, June, 1991 ($1.95, 68 pgs.)(#4 on: $2.00)
1-Craig-c(r); all contain EC reprints 5.00
2-6: 2,4-6-Craig-c(r). 3-Ingels-c(r) 5.00

VAULT OF HORROR
Russ Cochran/Gemstone Publishing: Sept, 1991 - No. 5, May, 1992 ($2.00); Oct, 1992 - No. 29, Oct, 1999 ($1.50/$2.00/$2.50)
1-29: E.C reprints. 1-4r/VOH #12-15 w/original-c 4.00

V...–COMICS (Morse code for "V" - 3 dots, 1 dash)
Fox Features Syndicate: Jan, 1942 - No. 2, Mar-Apr, 1942
1-Origin V-Man & the Boys; The Banshee & The Black Fury, The Queen of Evil, & V-Agents begin; Nazi-c 148 296 444 947 1624 2300
2-Nazi bondage/torture-c 116 232 348 742 1271 1800

VECTOR

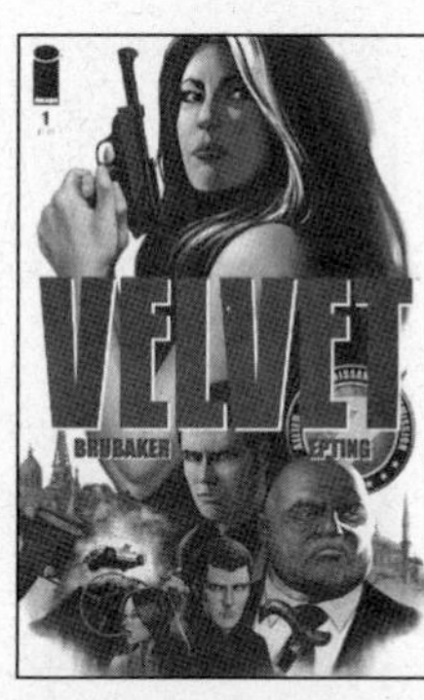

Velvet #1 © Basement Gang & Epting

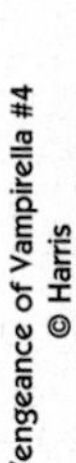

Vengeance of Vampirella #4 © Harris

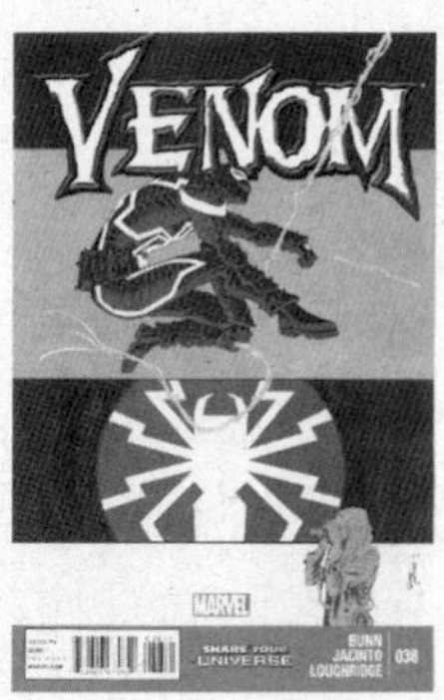

Venom #38 © MAR

	GD	VG	FN	VF	VF/NM	NM-
	2.0	4.0	6.0	8.0	9.0	9.2

Now Comics: 1986 - No. 4, 1986? ($1.50, 1st color comic by Now Comics)

1-4: Computer-generated art 3.00

VEIL

Dark Horse Comics: Mar, 2014 - Present ($3.50)

1,2-Greg Rucka-s/Toni Fejzula-a/c 3.50

VEILS

DC Comics (Vertigo): 1999 ($24.95, one-shot)

Hardcover-($24.95) Painted art and photography; McGreal-s 25.00
Softcover ($14.95) 15.00

VELOCITY (Also see Cyberforce)

Image Comics (Top Cow Productions): Nov, 1995 - No. 3, Jan, 1996 ($2.50, limited series)

1-3: Kurt Busiek scripts in all. 2-Savage Dragon-c/app. 3.00
...: Pilot Season 1 (10/07, $2.99) Casey-s/Maguire-a 3.00
Vol. 2 #1-4 (6/10 - No. 4, 4/11, $3.99) Rocafort-a/Marz-s; multiple covers 4.00

VELVET

Image Comics: Oct, 2013 - Present ($3.50)

1-4-Brubaker-s/Epting-a/c 3.50

VENGEANCE

Marvel Comics: Sept, 2011 - No. 6, Feb, 2012 ($3.99, limited series)

1-6-Casey-s/Dragotta-a. 1-Magneto and Red Skull app. 4-Loki cover 4.00

VENGEANCE OF THE MOON KNIGHT

Marvel Comics: Nov, 2009 - No. 10, Sept, 2010 ($3.99/$2.99)

1,9: 1-($3.99) Hurwitz-s/Opeña-a; covers by Yu, Ross & Finch; back-up r/Moon Knight #1 ('80) 9-Spider-Man & Sandman app.; Campbell-c 4.00
2-8,10: 2-Sentry app. 5-Spider-Man app. 7,8-Deadpool app. 10-Secret Avengers app. 3.00

VENGEANCE OF VAMPIRELLA (Becomes Vampirella: Death & Destruction)

Harris Comics: Apr, 1994 - No. 25, Apr, 1996 ($2.95)

1-($3.50)-Quesada/Palmiotti "bloodfoil" wraparound-c 1 2 3 5 6 8
1-2nd printing; blue foil-c 4.00
1-Gold 20.00
2-8: 8-Polybagged w/trading card 5.00
9-25: 10-w/coupon for Hyde -25 poster. 11,19-Polybagged w/ trading card. 25-Quesada & Palmiotti red foil-c 4.00
...: Bloodshed (1995, $6.95) 7.00

VENGEANCE OF VAMPIRELLA: THE MYSTERY WALK

Harris Comics: Nov, 1995 ($2.95, one-shot)

0 4.00

VENGEANCE SQUAD

Charlton Comics: July, 1975 - No. 6, May, 1976 (#1-3 are 25¢ issues)

1-Mike Mauser, Private Eye begins by Staton 2 4 6 9 13 16
2-6: Morisi-a in all 1 2 3 5 7 9
5,6 (Modern Comics-r, 1977) 6.00

VENOM

Marvel Comics: June, 2003 - No. 18, Nov, 2004 ($2.25)

1-7-Herrera-a/Way-s. 6,7-Wolverine app. 3.00
8-18-($2.99): 8-10-Wolverine-c/app.; Kieth-c. 11-Fantastic Four app. 3.00
... Vol. 1: Shiver (2004, $13.99, TPB) r/#1-5 14.00
... Vol. 2: Run (2004, $19.99, TPB) r/#6-13 20.00
... Vol. 3: Twist (2004, $13.99, TPB) r/#14-18 14.00

VENOM (See Amazing Spider-Man #654 & 654.1)(Also see Secret Avengers)

Marvel Comics: May, 2011 - Present ($3.99/$2.99)

1-Flash Thompson with the symbiote; Remender-s/Tony Moore-a/Quesada-c 4.00
2-12-($2.99) 2-Cover swipe of ASM #300; Kraven app. 3-Deodato-c. 6-8-Spider Island 3.00
13-($3.99) Circle of Four; Red Hulk, X-23, and Ghost Rider app. 4.00
13.1, 13.2, 13.3, 13.4, 14-($2.99) Circle of Four parts 2-6 3.00
15-27, 27.1, 28-42: 15-Secret Avengers app. 16,17-Toxin app. 26,27-Minimum Carnage. 38-1st app. Mania. 42-Mephisto app. 3.00
...: Flashpoint 1 (2011, $4.99) r/Amazing Spider-Man #654, 654.1 and Venom #1 5.00

VENOM: Marvel Comics (Also see Amazing Spider-Man #298-300)

... ALONG CAME A SPIDER, 1/96 - No. 4, 4/96 ($2.95)-Spider-Man & Carnage app. 4.00

... CARNAGE UNLEASHED, 4/95 - No. 4, 7/95 ($2.95) 4.00

... DARK ORIGIN, 10/08 - No. 5, 2/09 ($2.99) 1-5-Medina-a 3.00

... /DEADPOOL: WHAT IF?, 4/11 ($2.99) Remender-s/Moll-a/Young-c; Galactus app. 3.00

... DEATHTRAP: THE VAULT, 3/93 ($6.95) r/Avengers: Deathtrap: The Vault 7.00

... FUNERAL PYRE, 8/93- No. 3, 10/93 ($2.95)-#1-Holo-grafx foil-c; Punisher app. in all 4.00

VENOM: LETHAL PROTECTOR

Marvel Comics: Feb, 1993 - No. 6, July, 1993 ($2.95, limited series)

1-Red holo-grafx foil-c; Bagley-c/a in all 6.00
1-Gold variant sold to retailers 3 6 9 19 30 40
1-Black-c (at least 134 copies have been authenticated by CGC since 2000) 11 22 33 76 163 250

NOTE: Counterfeit copies of the black-c exist and are valueless

2-6: Spider-Man app. in all 4.00

... LICENSE TO KILL, 6/97 - No. 3, 8/97 ($1.95) 3.00

... NIGHTS OF VENGEANCE, 8/94 - No. 4, 11/94 ($2.95), #1-Red foil-c 4.00

... ON TRIAL, 3/97 - No. 3, 5/97 ($1.95) 3.00

... SEED OF DARKNESS, 7/97 ($1.95) #(-1) Flashback 3.00

... SEPARATION ANXIETY, 12/94- No. 4, 3/95 ($2.95) #1-Embossed-c 4.00

... SIGN OF THE BOSS, 3/97 - No. 2, 10/97 ($1.99) 3.00

... SINNER TAKES ALL, 8/95 - No. 5, 10/95 ($2.95) 4.00

... SUPER SPECIAL, 8/95($3.95) #1-Flip book 4.00

... THE ENEMY WITHIN, 2/94 - No. 3, 4/94 ($2.95)-Demogoblin & Morbius app.
1-Glow-in-the-dark-c 4.00

... THE FINALE, 11/97 - No. 3, 1/98 ($1.99) 3.00

... THE HUNGER, 8/96- No. 4, 11/96 ($1.95) 3.00

... THE HUNTED, 5/96-No. 3, 7/96 ($2.95) 4.00

... THE MACE, 5/94 - No. 3, 7/94 ($2.95)-#1-Embossed-c 4.00

... THE MADNESS, 11/93- No. 3, 1/94 ($2.95)-Kelley Jones-c/a(p).
1-Embossed-c; Juggernaut app. 4.00

... TOOTH AND CLAW, 12/96 - No. 3, 2/97 ($1.95)-Wolverine-c/app. 3.00

... VS. CARNAGE, 9/04 - No. 4, 12/04 ($2.99)-Milligan-s/Crain-a; Spider-Man app. 3.00
TPB (2004, $9.99) r/#1-4 10.00

VENTURE

AC Comics (Americomics): Aug, 1986 - No. 3, 1986? ($1.75)

1-3: 1-3-Bolt. 1-Astron. 2-Femforce. 3-Fazers 3.00

VENTURE

Image Comics: Jan, 2003 - No. 4, Sept, 2003 ($2.95)

1-4-Faerber-s/Igle-a 3.00

VENUS (See Agents of Atlas, Marvel Spotlight #2 & Weird Wonder Tales)

Marvel/Atlas Comics (CMC 1-9/LCC 10-19): Aug, 1948 - No. 19, Apr, 1952 (Also see Marvel Mystery #91)

1-Venus & Hedy Devine begin; 1st app. Venus; Kurtzman's "Hey Look" 187 374 561 1197 2049 2900
2 103 206 309 659 1130 1600
3,5 68 136 204 435 743 1050
4-Kurtzman's "Hey Look" 69 138 207 442 759 1075
6-9: 6-Loki app. 7,8-Painted-c. 9-Begin 52 pgs.; book-length feature "Whom the Gods Destroy!" 58 116 174 371 636 900
10-S/F-horror issues begin (7/50) 87 174 261 553 952 1350
11-S/F end of the world (11/50) 103 206 309 659 1130 1600
12-Colan-a 57 114 171 362 619 875
13-16-Venus by Everett, 2-3 stories each; covers-#13,15,16; 14-Everett part cover (Venus). 110 220 330 704 1202 1700
17-19-Classic Everett horror & skull covers; Venus app. 17-Bondage-c (scarce) 258 516 774 1651 2826 4000

NOTE: *Berg s/f story-13. Everett c-13, 14(part; Venus only), 15-19. Heath s/f story-11. Maneely s/f story 10(3pg.), 16. Morisi a-19. Syd Shores c-6.*

VERI BEST SURE FIRE COMICS

Holyoke Publishing Co.: No date (circa 1945) (Reprints Holyoke one-shots)

1-Captain Aero, Alias X, Miss Victory, Commandos of the Devil Dogs, Red Cross, Hammerhead Hawley, Capt. Aero's Sky Scouts, Flagman app.; same-c as Veri Best Sure Shot #1 42 84 126 265 445 625

VERI BEST SURE SHOT COMICS

Holyoke Publishing Co.: No date (circa 1945) (Reprints Holyoke one-shots)

1-Capt. Aero, Miss Victory by Quinlan, Alias X, The Red Cross, Flagman, Commandos of the Devil Dogs, Hammerhead Hawley, Capt. Aero's Sky Scouts; same-c as Veri Best Sure Fire #1 42 84 126 265 445 625

VERMILLION

DC Comics (Helix): Oct, 1996 - No. 12, Sept, 1997 ($2.25/$2.50)

1-12: 1-4: Lucius Shepard scripts. 4,12-Kaluta-c 3.00

Veronica #49 © AP

Vertigo Pop! Tokyo #1 © Vankin & Fisher

Vertigo Visions: Doctor 13 #1 © DC

	GD	VG	FN	VF	VF/NM	NM-
	2.0	4.0	6.0	8.0	9.0	9.2

GD VG FN VF VF/NM NM- 2.0 4.0 6.0 8.0 9.0 9.2

VERONICA (Also see Archie's Girls, Betty &...)
Archie Comics: Apr, 1989 - No. 210, Feb, 2012

1-(75¢-c) 1 2 3 5 6 8
2-10: 2-(75¢-c) 5.00
11-38 4.00
39-Love Showdown pt. 4, Cheryl Blossom 6.00
40-70: 34-Neon ink-c 3.00
71-201,203-206: 134-Begin $2.19-c. 152,155-Cheryl Blossom app. 163-Begin $2.25-c 3.00
202-Intro. Kevin Keller, 1st openly gay Archie character; cover has blue background 8.00
202-Second printing; cover has black background 5.00
207-210-Kevin Keller mini-series 3.00

VERONICA'S PASSPORT DIGEST MAGAZINE (Becomes Veronica's Digest Magazine #3 on)
Archie Comics: Nov, 1992 - No. 6 ($1.50/$1.79, digest size)

1 5.00
2-6 3.00

VERONICA'S SUMMER SPECIAL (See Archie Giant Series Magazine #615, 625)

VERTICAL
DC Comics (Vertigo): 2003 ($4.95, 3-1/4" wide pages, one-shot)

1-Seagle-s/Allred & Bond-a; odd format 1/2 width pages with some 20" long spreads 5.00

VERTIGO DOUBLE SHOT
DC Comics (Vertigo): 2008 ($2.99)

1-Reprints House of Mystery (2008) #1 and Young Liars #1 in flip-book format 3.00

VERTIGO ESSENTIALS
DC Comics (Vertigo): Dec, 2013 - Feb, 2014 ($1.00, Flip book reprints with DC & Vertigo Essential Graphics novels catalog)

...: American Vampire 1 (2/14) Reprints #1; flip-c by Ryan Sook 3.00
...: Fables 1 (1/14) Reprints #1; flip-c by Ryan Sook 3.00
...: 100 Bullets 1 (2/14) Reprints #1; flip-c by Ryan Sook 3.00
...: The Sandman #1 (12/13, $1.00) Reprints Sandman #1 (1989) with flipbook 3.00
...: V For Vendetta 1 (12/13) Reprints first chapter; flip-c by Ryan Sook 3.00
...: Y: The Last Man 1 (1/14) Reprints #1; flip-c by Ryan Sook 3.00

VERTIGO: FIRST BLOOD
DC Comics (Vertigo): Feb, 2012 ($7.99, squarebound)

TPB-Reprints first issues of American Vampire, I Zombie, The Unwritten & Sweet Tooth 8.00

VERTIGO: FIRST CUT
DC Comics (Vertigo): 2008 ($4.99, TPB)

TPB-Reprints first issues of DMZ, Army@Love, Jack of Fables, Exterminators, Scalped, Crossing Midnight, and Loveless; preview of Air 5.00

VERTIGO: FIRST OFFENSES
DC Comics (Vertigo): 2005 ($4.99, TPB)

TPB-Reprints first issues of The Invisibles, Preacher, Fables, Sandman Mystery Theater, and Lucifer 5.00

VERTIGO: FIRST TASTE
DC Comics (Vertigo): 2005 ($4.99, TPB)

TPB-Reprints first issues of Y: The Last Man, 100 Bullets, Transmetropolitan, Books of Magick: Life During Wartime, Death: The High Cost of Living, and Saga of the Swamp Thing #21 (Alan Moore's first story on that title) 5.00

VERTIGO GALLERY, THE: DREAMS AND NIGHTMARES
DC Comics (Vertigo): 1995 ($3.50, one-shot)

1-Pin-ups of Vertigo characters by Sienkiewicz, Toth, Van Fleet & others; McKean-c 4.00

VERTIGO JAM
DC Comics (Vertigo): Aug, 1993 ($3.95, one-shot, 68 pgs.)(Painted-c by Fabry)

1-Sandman by Neil Gaiman, Hellblazer, Animal Man, Doom Patrol, Swamp Thing, Kid Eternity & Shade the Changing Man 5.00

VERTIGO POP! BANGKOK
DC Comics (Vertigo): July, 2003 - No. 4, Oct, 2003 ($2.95, limited series)

1-4-Camuncoli-c/a; Jonathan Vankin-s 3.00

VERTIGO POP! LONDON
DC Comics (Vertigo): Jan, 2003 - No. 4, Apr, 2003 ($2.95, limited series)

1-4-Philip Bond-c/a; Peter Milligan-s 3.00

VERTIGO POP! TOKYO
DC Comics (Vertigo): Sept, 2002 - No. 4, Dec, 2002 ($2.95, limited series)

1-4-Seth Fisher-c/a; Jonathan Vankin-s 3.00
Tokyo Days, Bangkok Nights TPB (2009, $19.99) r/#1-4 & Vertogo Pop! Bangkok #1-4 20.00

VERTIGO PREVIEW
DC Comics (Vertigo): 1992 (75¢, one-shot, 36 pgs.)

1-Vertigo previews; Sandman story by Neil Gaiman 3.00

VERTIGO RAVE
DC Comics (Vertigo): Fall, 1994 (99¢, one-shot)

1-Vertigo previews 3.00

VERTIGO RESURRECTED: ...
DC Comics (Vertigo): Dec, 2010 - Present ($7.99, squarebound, reprints)

The Extremist 1 (1/11, 12/13) r/The Extremist #1-4 8.00
Finals 1 (5/11) r/Finals #1-4; Jill Thompson-a 8.00
Hellblazer 1 (2/11) r/Hellblazer #57,58,245,246 8.00
Hellblazer - Bad Blood 1 (6/11) r/Hellblazer Special: Bad Blood #1-4 8.00
Jonny Double 1 (10/11) r/Jonny Double #1-4; Azzarello-s/Risso-a 8.00
My Faith in Frankie 1 (1/12) r/My Faith in Frankie #1-4; Carey-s 8.00
Sandman Presents - Petrefax 1 (8/11) r/Sandman Presents: Petrefax #1-4 8.00
Sgt. Rock: Between Hell and a Hard Place 1,2 (1/12, 2/12) r/the 2003 HC 8.00
Shoot 1 (12/10) r/short stories by various incl. Quitely, Sale, Bolland, Risso, Jim Lee 8.00
The Eaters 1 (12/11) r/Vertigo Visions - The Eaters and other short stories 8.00
Winter's Edge 1 (2/11) r/Vertigo's Winter Edge #1-3; Bermejo-c 8.00

VERTIGO SECRET FILES
DC Comics (Vertigo): Aug, 2000 ($4.95)

...: Hellblazer 1 (8/00, $4.95) Background info and story summaries 5.00
...: Swamp Thing 1 (11/00, $4.95) Backstories and origins; Hale-c 5.00

VERTIGO VERITE: THE UNSEEN HAND
DC Comics (Vertigo): Sept, 1996 - No. 4, Dec, 1996 ($2.50, limited series)

1-4: Terry LaBan scripts in all 3.00

VERTIGO VISIONS
DC Comics (Vertigo): June, 1993 - Present (one-shots)

Dr. Occult 1 (7/94, $3.95) 4.00
Dr. Thirteen 1 (9/98, $5.95) Howarth-s 6.00
Prez 1 (7/95, $3.95) 4.00
The Geek 1 (6/93, $3.95) 4.00
The Eaters ($4.95, 1995)-Milligan story. 5.00
The Phantom Stranger 1 (10/93, $3.50) 4.00
Tomahawk 1 (7/98, $4.95) Pollack-s 5.00

VERTIGO WINTER'S EDGE
DC Comics (Vertigo): 1998, 1999 ($7.95/$6.95, square-bound, annual)

1-Winter stories by Vertigo creators; Desire story by Gaiman/Bolton; Bolland wraparound-c 8.00
2,3-($6.95)-Winter stories: 2-Allred-c. 3-Bond-c; Desire by Gaiman/Zulli 7.00

VERTIGO X ANNIVERSARY PREVIEW
DC Comics (Vertigo): 2003 (99¢, one-shot, 48 pgs.)

1-Previews of upcoming titles and interviews; Endless Nights, Shade, The Originals 4.00

VERY BEST OF DENNIS THE MENACE, THE
Fawcett Publ.: July, 1979 - No. 2, Apr, 1980 (95¢/$1.00, digest-size, 132 pgs.)

1,2-Reprints 2 4 6 8 10 12

VERY BEST OF DENNIS THE MENACE, THE
Marvel Comics Group: Apr, 1982 - No. 3, Aug, 1982 ($1.25, digest-size)

1-3: Reprints 2 3 4 6 8 10
1,2-Mistakenly printed with DC logo on cover 2 4 6 9 12 15

NOTE: ***Hank Ketcham** c-all. A few thousand of #1 & 2 were printed with DC emblem.*

VERY VICKY
Meet Danny Ocean: 1993? - No. 8, 1995 ($2.50, B&W)

1-8, ...: Calling All Hillbillies (1995, $2.50) 3.00

VERY WEIRD TALES (Also see Slithiss Attacks!)
Oceanspray Comics Group: Aug, 2002 - No. 2, Oct, 2002 ($4.00)

1-Mutant revenge, methamphetamine, corporate greed horror stories 1 3 4 6 8 10
2-Weird fantasy and horror stories 1 2 3 5 6 8

NOTE: *Created in prevention classes taught by Jon McClure at the Oceanspray Family Center in Newport, Oregon, and paid for by the Housing Authority of Lincoln County. All books are b&w with color covers. Issues #1-2 penciled and inked by various artists. All comics feature characters created by students and are signed and numbered by Jon McClure. Issues #1-2 have print runs of 100 each.*

VEXT
DC Comics: Mar, 1999 - No. 6, Aug, 1999 ($2.50, limited series)

1-6-Giffen-s. 1-Superman app. 3.00

V FOR VENDETTA
DC Comics: Sept, 1988 - No. 10, May, 1989 ($2.00, maxi-series)

Vic Flint #1 © STJ

Victories V2 #1 © Mike Oeming

Vigilante #17 © DC

	GD 2.0	VG 4.0	FN 6.0	VF 8.0	VF/NM 9.0	NM- 9.2
1-Alan Moore scripts in all; David Lloyd-a	3	6	9	17	26	35
2-10	1	2	3	5	6	8
HC (1990) Limited edition						60.00
HC (2005, $29.99, dustjacket) r/series; foreward by Lloyd; promo art and sketches						30.00
Trade paperback (1990, $14.95)						20.00

VIBE (See Justice League of America's Vibe)

VIC BRIDGES FAZERS SKETCHBOOK AND FACT FILE
AC Comics: Nov, 1986 ($1.75)

1 — 3.00

VICE
Image Comics (Top Cow): Nov, 2005 - No. 5 ($2.99)

1-5-Coleite-s/Kirkham-a. 1-Three covers — 3.00
1-Code Red Edition; variant Benitez-c — 3.00

VIC FLINT(Crime Buster...)(See Authentic Police Cases #10-14 & Fugitives From Justice #2)
St. John Publ. Co.: Aug, 1948 - No. 5, Apr, 1949 (Newspaper reprints; NEA Service)

1	15	30	45	85	130	175
2	11	22	33	60	83	105
3-5	10	20	30	54	72	90

VIC FLINT (Crime Buster...)
Argo Publ.: Feb, 1956 - No. 2, May, 1956 (Newspaper reprints)

1,2	9	18	27	47	61	75

VIC JORDAN (Also see Big Shot Comics #32)
Civil Service Publ.: April, 1945

1-1944 daily newspaper-r	14	28	42	82	121	160

VICKI (Humor)
Atlas/Seaboard Publ.: Feb, 1975 - No. 4, Aug, 1975 (No. 1,2: 68 pgs.)

1,2-(68 pgs.)-Reprints Tippy Teen; Good Girl art	5	10	15	30	50	70
3,4 (Low print)	5	10	15	31	53	75

VICKI VALENTINE (...Summer Special #1)
Renegade Press: July, 1985 - No. 4, July, 1986 ($1.70, B&W)

1-4: Woggon, Rausch-a; all have paper dolls. 2-Christmas issue — 3.00

VICKY
Ace Magazine: Oct, 1948 - No. 5, June, 1949

nn(10/48)-Teenage humor	9	18	27	50	65	80
4(12/48), nn(2/49), 4(4/49), 5(6/49): 5-Dotty app.	8	16	24	44	57	70

VICTORIAN UNDEAD
DC Comics (WildStorm): Jan, 2010 - No. 6, Jun, 2010 ($2.99)

1-6-Sherlock Holmes vs. Zombies; Edginton-s/Fabbri-a. 1-Two covers (Moore, Coleby) — 3.00
...: Sherlock Holmes vs. Jekyll and Hyde (12/10, $4.99) Domingues-a/Van Sciver-c — 5.00
...: Sherlock Holmes vs. Zombies TPB (2010, $17.99) r/#1-6; character design sketch art — 18.00
... Volume 2 (1/11 - No. 5, 5/11) 1-3-($3.99) "Sherlock Holmes vs. Dracula" on-c; Fabbri-a — 4.00
... Volume 2 - 4,5-($2.99) "Sherlock Holmes vs. Dracula" on-c; Fabbri-a — 3.00

VICTORIES, THE
Dark Horse Comics: Aug, 2012 - No. 5, Dec, 2012 ($3.99 limited series)

1-5-Michael Avon Oeming-s/a/c — 4.00
...Volume 2: Transhuman 1-10 (6/13 - No. 10, 3/14) Oeming-s/a/c — 4.00

VIC TORRY & HIS FLYING SAUCER (Also see Mr. Monster's...#5)
Fawcett Publications: 1950 (one-shot)

nn-Book-length saucer story by Powell; photo/painted-c	69	138	207	442	759	1075

VICTORY
Topps Comics: June, 1994 ($2.50, unfinished limited series)

1-Kurt Busiek script; Giffen-c/a; Rob Liefeld variant-c exists — 3.00

VICTORY
Image Comics: May, 2003 - No. 4, Feb, 2004 ($2.95, limited series)

1-4: 1-Two covers; Francisco-a. 4-Two covers — 3.00

VICTORY (Volume 2)
Image Comics: Aug, 2004 - No. 4, Jan, 2005 ($2.95, limited series)

1-4: 1-Three covers; Francisco-a — 3.00

VICTORY COMICS
Hillman Periodicals: Aug, 1941 - No. 4, Dec, 1941 (#1 by Funnies, Inc.)

1-The Conqueror by Bill Everett, The Crusader, & Bomber Burns begin; Conqueror's origin in text; Everett-c	309	618	927	2163	3782	5400
2-Everett-c/a	142	284	426	909	1555	2200
3,4	103	206	309	659	1130	1600

VIC VERITY MAGAZINE
Vic Verity Publ: 1945; No. 2, Jan?, 1947 - No. 7, Sept, 1946 (A comic book)

1-C. C. Beck-c/a	37	74	111	222	361	500
2-Beck-c	22	44	66	132	216	300
3-7: 6-Beck-a. 7-Beck-c	21	42	63	122	199	275

VIDEO JACK
Marvel Comics (Epic Comics): Nov, 1987 - No. 6, Nov, 1988 ($1.25)

1-5 — 3.00
6-Neal Adams, Keith Giffen, Wrightson, others-a — 5.00

VIETNAM JOURNAL
Apple Comics: Nov, 1987 - No. 16, Apr, 1991 ($1.75/$1.95, B&W)

1-16: Don Lomax-c/a/scripts in all, 1-2nd print — 4.00
...: Indian Country Vol. 1 (1990, $12.95)-r/#1-4 plus one new story — 13.00

VIETNAM JOURNAL: VALLEY OF DEATH
Apple Comics: June, 1994 - No. 2, Aug, 1994 ($2.75, B&W, limited series)

1,2: By Don Lomax — 4.00

VIGILANTE, THE (Also see New Teen Titans #23 & Annual V2#2)
DC Comics: Oct, 1983 - No. 50, Feb, 1988 ($1.25, Baxter paper)

1-Origin — 6.00
2-16,19-49: 3-Cyborg app. 4-1st app. The Exterminator; Newton-a(p). 6,7-Origin. 20,21-Nightwing app. 35-Origin Mad Bomber. 47-Batman-c/s — 4.00
17,18-Alan Moore scripts — 5.00
50-Ken Steacy painted-c — 5.00
Annual nn, 2 ('85, '86) — 5.00

VIGILANTE
DC Comics: Nov, 2005 - No. 6, Apr, 2006 ($2.99, limited series)

1-6-Bruce Jones-s. 1,2,4-6-Ben Oliver-a — 3.00

VIGILANTE
DC Comics: Feb, 2009 - No. 12, Jan, 2010 ($2.99)

1-12: 1-Wolfman-s/Leonardi-a. 3-Nightwing app. 5-X-over with Titans and Teen Titans — 3.00

VIGILANTE: CITY LIGHTS, PRAIRIE JUSTICE (Also see Action Comics #42, Justice League of America #78, Leading Comics & World's Finest #244)
DC Comics: Nov, 1995 - No. 4, Feb, 1996 ($2.50, limited series)

1-4: James Robinson scripts/Tony Salmons-a/Mark Chiarello-c — 3.00
TPB (2009, $19.99) r/#1-4 — 20.00

VIGILANTES, THE
Dell Publishing Co.: No. 839, Sept, 1957

Four Color 839-Movie	6	12	18	41	76	110

VIGILANTE 8: SECOND OFFENSE
Chaos! Comics: Dec, 1999 ($2.95, one-shot)

1-Based on video game — 3.00

VIKING PRINCE, THE
DC Comics: 2010 ($39.99, hardcover with dustjacket)

HC-Recolored reprints of apps. in Brave and the Bold #1-5, 7-24 & team-up with Sgt. Rock in Our Army at War #162,163; new intro. by Joe Kubert — 40.00

VIKINGS, THE (Movie)
Dell Publishing Co.: No. 910, May, 1958

Four Color 910-Buscema-a, Kirk Douglas photo-c	7	14	21	48	89	130

VILLAINS AND VIGILANTES
Eclipse Comics: Dec, 1986 - No. 4, May, 1987 ($1.50/$1.75, limited series, Baxter paper)

1-4: Based on role-playing game. 2-4 ($1.75-c) — 3.00

VILLAINS FOR HIRE
Marvel Comics: No. 0.1, Jan, 2012; No. 1, Feb, 2012 - No. 4, May, 2012 ($2.99)

0.1-Misty Knight, Silver Sable, Black Panther app.; Arlem-a — 3.00
1-4-Abnett & Lanning-s/Arlem-a; Misty Knight app. — 3.00

VILLAINS UNITED (Leads into Infinite Crisis)
DC Comics: July, 2005 - No. 6, Dec, 2005 ($2.95/$2.50, limited series)

1-6-Simone-s/JG Jones-c. 1-The Secret Six and the "Society" form — 3.00
...: Infinite Crisis Special 1 (6/06, $4.99) Simone-s/Eaglesham-a — 5.00
TPB (2005, $12.99) r/#1-6; background info on villains — 13.00

VILLAINY OF DOCTOR DOOM, THE
Marvel Comics: 1999 ($17.95, TPB)

nn-Reprints early battle with the Fantastic Four — 18.00

Vimanarama #1 © Morrison & Bond

The Vision #2 © MAR

Vooda #20 © AJAX

	GD	VG	FN	VF	VF/NM	NM-
	2.0	4.0	6.0	8.0	9.0	9.2

VIMANARAMA
DC Comics (Vertigo): Apr, 2005 - No. 3, June, 2005 ($2.95, limited series)
1-3-Grant Morrison-s/Philip Bond-a 3.00
TPB (2005, $12.99) r/#1-3 13.00

VINTAGE MAGNUS (...Robot Fighter)
Valiant: Jan, 1992 - No. 4, Apr, 1992 ($2.25, limited series)
1-4: 1-Layton-c; r/origin from Magnus R.F. #22 3.00

VINYL UNDERGROUND
DC Comics (Vertigo): Dec, 2007 - No. 12, Nov, 2008 ($2.99)
1-12: 1-Spencer-s/Gane & Stewart-a/Phillips-c 3.00
...: Pretty Dead Things TPB ('08, $17.99) r/#6-12 18.00
...: Watching the Detectives TPB ('08, $9.99) r/#1-5; David Laphan intro. 10.00

VIOLATOR (Also see Spawn #2)
Image Comics (Todd McFarlane Prods.): May, 1994 - No. 3, Aug, 1994 ($1.95, lim. series)
1-Alan Moore scripts in all 5.00
2,3: Bart Sears-c(p)/a(p) 4.00

VIOLATOR VS. BADROCK
Image Comics (Extreme Studios): May, 1995 - No. 4, Aug, 1995 ($2.50, limited series)
1-4: Alan Moore scripts in all. 1-1st app Celestine; variant-c (3?) 3.00

VIOLENT MESSIAHS (...: Lamenting Pain on cover for #9-12, numbered as #1-4)
Image Comics: June, 2000 - No. 12 ($2.95)
1-Two covers by Travis Smith and Medina 4.00
1-Tower Records variant edition 5.00
2-8: 5-Flip book sketchbook 3.00
9-12-Lamenting Pain; 2 covers on each 3.00
...: Genesis (12/01, $5.95) r/'97 B&W issue, Wizard 1/2 prologue 6.00
...: The Book of Job TPB (7/02, $24.95) r/#1-8; Foreward by Gossett 25.00

VIP (TV)
TV Comics: 2000 ($2.95, unfinished series)
1-Based on the Pamela Lee (Anderson) TV show; photo-c 3.00

VIPER (TV)
DC Comics: Aug, 1994 - No. 4, Nov, 1994 ($1.95, limited series)
1-4-Adaptation of television show 3.00

VIRGINIAN, THE (TV)
Gold Key: June, 1963
1(10060-306)-Part photo-c of James Drury plus photo back-c
4 8 12 27 44 60

VIRTUA FIGHTER (Video Game)
Marvel Comics: Aug, 1995 (2.95, one-shot)
1-Sega Saturn game 3.00

VIRUS
Dark Horse Comics: 1993 - No. 4, 1993 ($2.50, limited series)
1-4: Ploog-c 3.00

VISION, THE
Marvel Comics: Nov, 1994 - No. 4, Feb, 1995 ($1.75, limited series)
1-4 3.00

VISION, THE (AVENGERS ICONS: ...)
Marvel Comics: Oct, 2002 - No. 4, Jan, 2003 ($2.99, limited series)
1-4-Geoff Johns-s/Ivan Reis-a 3.00
...: Yesterday and Tomorrow TPB (2005, $14.99) r/#1-4 & Avengers #57 (1st app.) 15.00

VISION AND THE SCARLET WITCH, THE (See Marvel Fanfare)
Marvel Comics Group: Nov, 1982 - No. 4, Feb, 1983 (Limited series)
1-4: 2-Nuklo & Future Man app. 4.00

VISION AND THE SCARLET WITCH, THE
Marvel Comics Group: Oct, 1985 - No. 12, Sept, 1986 (Maxi-series)
V2#1-12: 1-Origin; 1st app. in Avengers #57. 2-West Coast Avengers x-over 4.00

VISIONS
Vision Publications: 1979 - No. 5, 1983 (B&W, fanzine)
1-Flaming Carrot begins (1st app?); N. Adams-c 5 10 15 35 63 90
2-N. Adams, Rogers-a; Gulacy back-c; signed & numbered to 2000
5 10 15 30 50 70
3-Williamson-c(p); Steranko back-c 3 6 9 21 33 45
4-Flaming Carrot-c & info. 4 8 12 23 37 50
5-1 pg. Flaming Carrot 3 6 9 17 26 35

NOTE: ***Eisner** a-4. **Miller** a-4. **Starlin** a-3. **Williamson** a-5. After #4, Visions became an annual publication of The Atlanta Fantasy Fair.*

VISITOR, THE
Valiant/Acclaim Comics (Valiant): Apr, 1995 - No. 13, Nov, 1995 ($2.50)
1-13: 8-Harbinger revealed. 13-Visitor revealed to be Sting from Harbinger 3.00

VISITOR VS. THE VALIANT UNIVERSE, THE
Valiant: Feb, 1995 - No. 2, Mar, 1995 ($2.95, limited series)
1,2 3.00

VIXEN: RETURN OF THE LION (From Justice League of America)
DC Comics: Dec, 2008 - No. 5, Apr, 2009 ($2.99, limited series)
1-5-G. Willow Wilson-s/Cafu-a; Justice League app. 3.00
TPB (2009, $17.99) r/#1-5 18.00

VOGUE (Also see Youngblood)
Image Comics (Extreme Studios): Oct, 1995 - No.3, Jan, 1996 ($2.50, limited series)
1-3: 1-Liefeld-c, 1-Variant-c 3.00

VOID INDIGO (Also see Marvel Graphic Novel)
Marvel Comics (Epic Comics): 11/84 - No. 2, 3/85 ($1.50, direct sales, unfinished series, mature)
1,2: Cont'd from Marvel G.N.; graphic sex & violence 3.00

VOLCANIC REVOLVER
Oni Press: Dec, 1998 - No. 3, Mar, 1999 ($2.95, B&W, limited series)
1-3: Scott Morse-s/a 3.00
TPB (12/99, $9.95, digest size) r/#1-3 and Oni Double Feature #7 prologue 10.00

VOLTRON (TV)
Modern Publishing: 1985 - No. 3, 1985 (75¢, limited series)
1-3: Ayers-a in all 1 3 4 6 8 10

VOLTRON (Volume 1)
Dynamite Entertainment: 2011 - No. 12, 2013 ($3.99)
1-12: 1-Padilla-a; covers by Alex Ross, Sean Chen & Wagner Reis. 2-5-Two covers 4.00

VOLTRON: A LEGEND FORGED (TV)
Devils Due Publishing: Jul, 2008 - No. 5, Apr, 2009 ($3.50)
1-5-Blaylock-s/Bear-a; 4 covers 3.50

VOLTRON: DEFENDER OF THE UNIVERSE (TV)
Image Comics: No. 0, May, 2003 - No. 5, Sept, 2003 ($2.50)
0-Jolley-s/Brooks-a; character pin-ups with background info 3.00
1-5-($2.95) 1-Three covers by Norton, Brooks and Andrews; Norton-a 3.00
...: Revelations TPB (2004, $11.95, digest-sized) r/#1-5; cover gallery 12.00

VOLTRON: DEFENDER OF THE UNIVERSE (TV)
Image Comics: Jan, 2004 - No. 11, Dec, 2004 ($2.95)
1-11: 1-Jolley-s; wraparound-c 3.00

VOLTRON: YEAR ONE
Dynamite Entertainment: 2012 - No. 6, 2012 ($3.99, limited series)
1-6: 1-Two covers; Brandon Thomas-s/Craig Cermak-a 4.00

VOODA (Jungle Princess) (Formerly Voodoo) (See Crown Comics)
Ajax-Farrell (Four Star Publications): No. 20, April, 1955 - No. 22, Aug, 1955
20-Baker-c/a (r/Seven Seas #6) 42 84 126 265 445 625
21,22-Baker-a plus Kamen/Baker story, Kimbo Boy of Jungle, & Baker-c(p) in all. 22-Censored Jo-Jo-r (name Powaa) 39 78 117 240 395 550
NOTE: *#20-22 each contain one heavily censored-r of South Sea Girl by **Baker** from Seven Seas Comics with name changed to Vooda. #20-r/Seven Seas #6; #21-r/#4; #22-r/#3.*

VOODOO (Weird Fantastic Tales) (Vooda #20 on)
Ajax-Farrell (Four Star Publ.): May, 1952 - No. 19, Jan-Feb, 1955
1-South Sea Girl-r by Baker 68 136 204 435 743 1050
2-Rulah story-r plus South Sea Girl from Seven Seas #2 by Baker (name changed from Alani to El'nee) 55 110 165 352 601 850
3-Bakerish-a; man stabbed in face 43 86 129 271 461 650
4,8-Baker-r. 8-Severed head panels 43 86 129 271 461 650
5-Nazi death camp story (flaying alive) 41 82 123 256 428 600
6,7,9,10: 6-Severed head panels 39 78 117 240 395 550
11-18: 14-Zombies take over America. 15-Opium drug story-r/Ellery Queen #3. 16-Post nuclear world story.17-Electric chair panels
39 78 117 231 378 525
19-Bondage-c; Baker-r(2)/Seven Seas #5 w/minor changes & #1, heavily modified; last pre-code; contents & covers change to jungle theme
41 82 123 256 428 600
Annual 1(1952, 25¢, 100 pgs.)-Baker-a (scarce) 155 310 465 992 1696 2400

Voodoo (2011 series) #3 © DC

Wagon Train #8 © DELL

The Walking Dead #40 © Robert Kirkman

GD 2.0 | VG 4.0 | FN 6.0 | VF 8.0 | VF/NM 9.0 | NM- 9.2

VOODOO
Image Comics (WildStorm): Nov, 1997 - No. 4, Mar, 1998 ($2.50, lim. series)
1-4: Alan Moore-s in all; Hughes-c. 2-4-Rio-a 3.00
1-Platinum Ed 10.00
Dancing on the Dark TPB ('99, $9.95) r/#1-4 10.00
...-Zealot: Skin Trade (8/95, $4.95) 5.00

VOODOO (DC New 52) (Also see Grifter)
DC Comics: Nov, 2011 - No. 12, Oct, 2012; No. 0, Nov, 2012 ($2.99)
1-12: 1-Marz-s/Basri-a/c. 3-Green Lantern (Kyle) app. 3.00
#0 (11/12, $2.99) Origin of Voodoo; Basri-a/c 3.00

VOODOO (See Tales of...)

VOODOO CHILD (Weston Cage & Nicolas Cage's...)
Virgin Comics: July, 2007 - No. 6, Dec, 2007 ($2.99)
1-6: 1-Mike Carey-s/Dean Hyrapiet-a; covers by Hyrapiet & Templesmith 3.00
Vol. 1 TPB (1/08, $14.99) r/#1-6; variant covers; intro by Weston Cage & Nicolas Cage 15.00

VOODOOM
Oni Press: June, 2000 ($4.95, B&W)
1-Scott Morse-s/Jim Mahfood-a 5.00

VORTEX
Vortex Publs.: Nov, 1982 - No. 15, 1988 (No month) ($1.50/$1.75, B&W)
1 ($1.95)-Peter Hsu-a; Ken Steacy-c; nudity 1 2 3 5 7 9
2,12: 2-1st app. Mister X (on-c only). 12-Sam Kieth-a 6.00
3-11,13-15 3.00

VORTEX
Comico: 1991 - No. 2? ($2.50, limited series)
1,2: Heroes from The Elementals 3.00

VOYAGE TO THE BOTTOM OF THE SEA (Movie, TV)
Dell Publishing Co./Gold Key: No. 1230, Sept-Nov, 1961; Dec, 1964 - #16, Apr, 1970 (Painted-c)
Four Color 1230 (1961) 9 18 27 62 126 190
10133-412(#1, 12/64)(Gold Key) 7 14 21 44 82 120
2(7/65) - 5: Photo back-c, 1-5 5 10 15 31 53 75
6-14 4 8 12 27 44 60
15,16-Reprints 3 6 9 17 26 35

VOYAGE TO THE DEEP
Dell Publishing Co.: Sept-Nov, 1962 - No. 4, Nov-Jan, 1964 (Painted-c)
1 5 10 15 31 53 75
2-4 4 8 12 23 37 50

WACKO
Ideal Publ. Corp.: Sept, 1980 - No. 3, Oct, 1981 (84 pgs., B&W, magazine)
1-3 2 4 6 8 11 14

WACKY ADVENTURES OF CRACKY (Also see Gold Key Spotlight)
Gold Key: Dec, 1972 - No. 12, Sept, 1975
1 3 6 9 14 20 26
2 2 4 6 10 14 18
3-12 2 4 6 8 10 12
(See March of Comics #405, 424, 436, 448)

WACKY DUCK (...Comics #3-6; formerly Dopey Duck; Justice Comics #7 on) (See Film Funnies)
Marvel Comics (NPP): No. 3, Fall, 1946 - No. 6, Summer, 1947; Aug, 1948 - No. 2, Oct, 1948
3 27 54 81 158 259 360
4-Infinity-c 22 44 66 132 216 300
5,6(1947)-Becomes Justice comics 20 40 60 114 182 250
1(1948) 20 40 60 114 182 250
2(1948) 15 30 45 85 130 175
I.W. Reprint #1,2,7('58): 1-r/Wacky Duck #6 2 4 6 10 14 18
Super Reprint #10(I.W. on-c, Super-inside) 2 4 6 9 13 16

WACKY QUACKY (See Wisco)

WACKY RACES (TV)
Gold Key: Aug, 1969 - No. 7, Apr, 1972 (Hanna-Barbera)
1 5 10 15 31 53 75
2-7 3 6 9 21 33 45

WACKY SQUIRREL (Also see Dark Horse Presents)
Dark Horse Comics: Oct, 1987 - No. 4, 1988 ($1.75, B&W)
1-4: 4-Superman parody 3.00
Halloween Adventure Special 1 (1987, $2.00) 3.00
Summer Fun Special 1 (1988, $2.00) 3.00

WACKY WITCH (Also see Gold Key Spotlight)
Gold Key: March, 1971 - No. 21, Dec, 1975
1 4 8 12 23 37 50
2 3 6 9 14 20 26
3-10 2 4 6 10 14 18
11-21 2 4 6 8 10 12
(See March of Comics #374, 398, 410, 422, 434, 446, 458, 470, 482)

WACKY WOODPECKER (See Two Bit the...)
I. W. Enterprises/Super Comics: 1958; 1963
I.W. Reprint #1,2,7 (nd-reprints Two Bit...): 7-r/Two-Bit, the Wacky Woodpecker #1.
2 4 6 9 13 16
Super Reprint #10('63): 10-r/Two-Bit, The Wacky Woodpecker #?
2 4 6 8 11 14

WAGON TRAIN (1st Series) (TV) (See Western Roundup under Dell Giants)
Dell Publishing Co.: No. 895, Mar, 1958 - No. 13, Apr-June, 1962 (All photo-c)
Four Color 895 (#1) 9 18 27 61 123 185
Four Color 971(#2),1019(#3) 6 12 18 40 73 105
4(1-3/60),6-13 5 10 15 34 60 85
5-Toth-a 6 12 18 37 66 95

WAGON TRAIN (2nd Series)(TV)
Gold Key: Jan, 1964 - No. 4, Oct, 1964 (All front & back photo-c)
1-Tufts-a in all 5 10 15 30 50 70
2-4 4 8 12 23 37 50

WAITING PLACE, THE
Slave Labor Graphics: Apr, 1997 - No. 6, Sept, 1997 ($2.95)
1-6-Sean McKeever-s 3.00
Vol. 2 - 1(11/99), 2-11 3.00
12-($4.95) 5.00

WAITING ROOM WILLIE (See Sad Case of...)

WAKE, THE
DC Comics (Vertigo): Jul, 2013 - No. 10 ($2.99)
1-Scott Snyder-s/Sean Murphy-a/c 5.00
1-Variant-c by Andy Kubert 8.00
1-Director's Cut (10/13, $4.99) B&W version, behind-the-scenes production content 5.00
2-7: 6-Story jumps 200 years ahead; Leeward app. 3.00
... Part One TPB (2/14, $9.99) r/#1-5 10.00

WAKE THE DEAD
IDW Publ.: Sept, 2003 - No. 5, Mar, 2004 ($3.99, limited series)
1-5-Steve Niles-s/Chee-a 4.00
TPB (6/04, $19.99) r/series; intro. by Michael Dougherty; embossed die cut cover 20.00

WALK IN (Dave Stewart's ...)
Virgin Comics: Dec, 2006 - No. 6, May, 2007 ($2.99)
1-6: 1-5-Parker-s/Padlekar-a. 6-Parker-a 3.00

WALKING DEAD, THE (Inspired the 2010 AMC television series)
Image Comics: Oct, 2003 - Present ($2.95/$2.99, B&W)
1-Robert Kirkman-s in all/Tony Moore-a 36 72 108 259 580 900
1 Special Edition (5/08, $3.99) r/#1; Kirkman afterword; original script and proposal
3 6 9 21 33 45
2-Tony Moore-a through #6 13 26 39 89 195 300
3 8 16 24 55 108 160
4 6 12 18 41 76 110
5,6: 6-Shane killed 5 10 15 35 63 90
7-Charlie Adlard-a begins; 1st app. Tyreese 5 10 15 33 57 80
8-10 3 6 9 21 33 45
11-18,20: 13-Prison arc begins 3 6 9 16 23 30
19-1st app. Michonne 10 20 30 69 147 225
21-26,28-47,49,50: 25-Adlard covers begin. 28-Rick loses his hand. 46-Tyreese killed.
2 4 6 9 12 15
27-1st app of The Governor 7 14 21 49 92 135
48-Lori, Herschel, others killed 4 8 12 25 40 55
50-Variant wraparound superhero-style cover by Erik Larsen
5 10 15 33 57 80
51,52,54-60: 58-Morgan returns 2 4 6 8 10 12
53-1st app. Abraham & Rosita 3 6 9 19 30 40
61-Preview of Chew; 1st app. Gabriel 3 6 9 21 33 45
62,64-74: 66-Dale dies. 70-1st Douglas Monroe 1 3 4 6 8 10

The Walking Dead #106 © Robert Kirkman

Walt Disney Comics Digest #44 © DIS

Walt Disney Giant #6 © DIS

GD VG FN VF VF/NM NM-
2.0 4.0 6.0 8.0 9.0 9.2

63-Flip book with B&W reprint of Chew #1 3 6 9 14 20 25
75-(7/10, $3.99) Orange background-c; back-up alien/sci-fi "fantasy" in color; TV series preview with cast photos 2 4 6 8 10 12
75-Variant-c homage to issue #1 3 6 9 14 20 25
76-91: 85-Flip book w/Witch Doctor #0. 86-Flip book w/Elephantmen
1 2 3 5 6 8
92-Intro. Paul Monroe (Jesus) 3 6 9 17 26 35
93-96 6.00
97-99,101-114: 97-"Something to Fear" pt. 1. 98-Abraham killed. 107-Intro Ezekiel 4.00
100-(7/12, $3.99) 1st app. Negan; Glen killed; multiple covers by Adlard, Silvestri, Quitely, McFarlane, Phillips, Hitch, & Ottley 4.00
100-Wraparound-c by Adlard 5.00
106-Variant wraparound-c by Adlard for his 100th issue 5.00
115-"All Out War" begins; 10 connecting covers by Adlard 4.00
116-125-"All Out War" 4.00
... FCBD 2013 Special (5/13, giveaway) reprints bonus stories from Michonne Special and The Governor Special; new Tyreese background story 3.00
Image Firsts: The Walking Dead #1 (3/10, $1.00) reprints #1
2 4 6 9 12 15
...: Michonne Special (10/12, $2.99) Reprints debut from #19 and story from Playboy 5.00
...: Michonne Special - 2nd printing (3/13, $2.99) 3.00
... #1 Tenth Anniversary Special (10/13, $5.99) reprints #1 with color; Kirkman's original series proposal; Kirkman interview 6.00
...: The Governor Special (2/13, $2.99) Reprints debut from #27 and story from CBLDF Liberty Annual 2012 3.00
...: Tyreese Special (10/13, $2.99) Reprints debut from #7 and story from FCBD 2013 3.00
... Book 1 HC (2006, $29.99) r/#1-12; sketch pages, cover gallery; Kirkman afterword 45.00
... Book 2 HC (2006, $29.99) r/#13-24; sketch pages, cover gallery 40.00
... Book 3 HC (2007, $29.99) r/#25-36; sketch pages, cover gallery 35.00
... Book 4 HC (2008, $29.99) r/#37-48; sketch pages, cover gallery 35.00
... Book 5 HC (2010, $29.99) r/#49-60; sketch pages, cover gallery 35.00
... Book 6 HC (2010, $34.99) r/#61-72; sketch pages, cover gallery 35.00
... Book 7 HC (2011, $34.99) r/#73-84; sketch pages, cover gallery 35.00
... Book 8 HC (2012, $34.99) r/#85-96; sketch pages, cover gallery 35.00
... Book 9 HC (2013, $34.99) r/#97-108; sketch pages, cover gallery 35.00
...Vol. 1: Days Gone Bye (5/04, $9.95, TPB) r/#1-4 20.00
...Vol. 2: Miles Behind Us (10/04, $12.95, TPB) r/#7-12 18.00
...Vol. 3: Safety Behind Bars (2005, $12.95, TPB) r/#13-18 18.00
...Vol. 4: The Heart's Desire (2005, $12.99, TPB) r/#19-24 18.00
...Vol. 5: The Best Defense (2006, $12.99, TPB) r/#25-30 18.00
...Vol. 6: This Sorrowful Life (2007, $12.99, TPB) r/#31-36 15.00
...Vol. 7: The Calm Before (2007, $12.99, TPB) r/#37-42 15.00
...Vol. 8: Made to Suffer (2008, $14.99, TPB) r/#43-48 15.00
...Vol. 9: Here We Remain (2009, $14.99, TPB) r/#49-54 15.00
...Vol. 10: The Road Ahead (2009, $14.99, TPB) r/#55-60 15.00
...Vol. 11: Fear the Hunters (2010, $14.99, TPB) r/#61-66 15.00
...Vol. 12: Life Among Them (2010, $14.99, TPB) r/#67-72 15.00
...Vol. 13: Too Far Gone (2010, $14.99, TPB) r/#73-78 15.00
...Vol. 14: No Way Out (2011, $14.99, TPB) r/#79-84 15.00
...Vol. 15: We Find Ourselves (2011, $14.99, TPB) r/#85-90 15.00
...Vol. 16: A Larger World (2012, $14.99, TPB) r/#91-96 15.00
...Vol. 17: Something to Fear (2012, $14.99, TPB) r/#97-102 15.00
...Vol. 18: What Comes After (2013, $14.99, TPB) r/#103-108 15.00
...Vol. 19: March To War (2013, $14.99, TPB) r/#109-114 15.00
...Vol. 20: All Out War Part 1 (2014, $14.99, TPB) r/#115-120 15.00

WALKING DEAD SURVIVORS' GUIDE, THE
Image Comics: Apr, 2011 - No. 4 ($2.99, B&W)

1-4-Alphabetical listings of character profiles, first (and last) apps. and current status 6.00

WALKING DEAD WEEKLY, THE (Reprints)
Image Comics: Jan, 2011 - No. 52, Dec, 2011 ($2.99, B&W, weekly)

1-Reprints issues with original letter columns; new Kirkman afterword
3 6 9 21 33 45
1-Arizona Comic Con variant-c 3 6 9 16 23 30
2-7 1 3 4 6 8 10
8-18,20-26,28-52 5.00
19-r/1st Michonne 4 8 12 23 37 50
27-r/1st app. The Governor 3 6 9 14 20 25

WALL·E (Based on the Disney/Pixar movie)
BOOM! Studios: No. 0, Nov, 2009 - No. 7, Jun, 2010 ($2.99)

0-7: 0-Prequel; J. Torres-s 3.00

WALLY (Teen-age)
Gold Key: Dec, 1962 - No. 4, Sept, 1963

GD VG FN VF VF/NM NM-
2.0 4.0 6.0 8.0 9.0 9.2

1 3 6 9 20 31 42
2-4 3 6 9 16 24 32

WALLY THE WIZARD
Marvel Comics (Star Comics): Apr, 1985 - No. 12, Mar, 1986 (Children's comic)

1-12: Bob Bolling a-1,3; c-1,9,11,12 5.00
1-Variant with "Star Chase" game on last page and inside back-c
2 4 6 9 12 15

WALLY WOOD'S T.H.U.N.D.E.R. AGENTS (See Thunder Agents)
Deluxe Comics: Nov, 1984 - No. 5, Oct, 1986 ($2.00, 52 pgs.)

1-5: 5-Jerry Ordway-c/a in Wood style 6.00

NOTE: ***Anderson** a-2i, 3i. **Buckler** a-4. **Ditko** a-3, 4. **Giffen** a-1p-4p. **Perez** a-1p, 2, 4; c-1-4.*

WALT DISNEY CHRISTMAS PARADE (Also see Christmas Parade)
Whitman Publ. Co. (Golden Press): Wint, 1977 ($1.95, cardboard-c, 224 pgs.)

11191-Barks-r/Christmas in Disneyland #1, Dell Christmas Parade #9 & Dell Giant #53
4 8 12 25 40 55

WALT DISNEY COMICS DIGEST
Gold Key: June, 1968 - No. 57, Feb, 1976 (50¢, digest size)

1-Reprints Uncle Scrooge #5; 192 pgs. 6 12 18 42 79 115
2-4-Barks-r 5 10 15 31 53 75
5-Daisy Duck by Barks (8 pgs.); last published story by Barks (art only) plus 21 pg. Scrooge-r by Barks 7 14 21 44 82 120
6-13-All Barks-r 3 6 9 21 33 45
14,15 3 6 9 16 23 30
16-Reprints Donald Duck #26 by Barks 3 6 9 20 31 42
17-20-Barks-r 3 6 9 17 26 35
21-31,33,35-37-Barks-r; 24-Toth Zorro 3 6 9 16 23 30
32,41,45,47-49 2 4 6 11 16 20
34,38,39: 34-Reprints 4-Color #318. 38-Reprints Christmas in Disneyland #1. 39-Two Barks-r/WDC&S #272, 4-Color #1073 plus Toth Zorro-r
3 6 9 16 23 30
40-Mickey Mouse-r by Gottfredson 2 4 6 13 18 22
42,43-Barks-r 2 4 6 13 18 22
44-(Has Gold Key emblem, 50¢)-Reprints 1st story of 4-Color #29,256,275,282
5 10 15 30 50 70
44-Republished in 1976 by Whitman; not identical to original; a bit smaller, blank back-c, 69¢
3 6 9 16 23 30
46,50,52-Barks-r. 52-Barks-r/WDC&S #161,132 2 4 6 11 16 20
51-Reprints 4-Color #71 3 6 9 16 23 30
53-55: 53-Reprints Dell Giant #30. 54-Reprints Donald Duck Beach Party #2. 55-Reprints Dell Giant #49 2 4 6 10 14 18
56-r/Uncle Scrooge #32 (Barks) 2 4 6 13 18 22
57-r/Mickey Mouse Almanac('57) & two Barks stories 2 4 6 11 16 20

NOTE: ***Toth** a-52r. #1-10, 196 pgs.; #11-41, 164 pgs.; #42 on, 132 pgs. Old issues were being reprinted & distributed by Whitman in 1976.*

WALT DISNEY GIANT (Disney)
Bruce Hamilton Co. (Gladstone): Sept, 1995 - No. 7, Sept, 1996 ($2.25, bi-monthly, 48 pgs.)

1-7: 1-Scrooge McDuck in the Yukon; Rosa-c/a/scripts plus r/F.C. #218. 2-Uncle Scrooge-r by Barks plus 17 pg. text story. 3-Donald the Mighty Duck; Rosa-c; Barks & Rosa-r. 4-Mickey and Goofy; new-a (story actually stars Goofy. Mickey Mouse by Caesar Ferioli; Donald Duck by Giorgio Cavazzano (1st in U.S.). 6-Uncle Scrooge & the Jr. Woodchucks; new-a and Barks-r. 7-Uncle Scrooge-r by Barks plus new-a 4.00

NOTE: *Series was initially solicited as Uncle Walt's Collectory. Issue #8 was advertised, but later cancelled.*

WALT DISNEY PAINT BOOK SERIES
Whitman Publ. Co.: No dates; circa 1975 (Beware! Has 1930s copyright dates) (79¢-c, 52 pgs. B&W, treasury-sized) (Coloring books, text stories & comics-r)

#2052 (Whitman #886-r) Mickey Mouse & Donald Duck Gag Book
3 6 9 20 31 42
#2053 (Whitman #677-r) 3 6 9 20 31 42
#2054 (Whitman #670-r) Donald-c 4 8 12 22 35 48
#2055 (Whitman #627-r) Mickey-c 3 6 9 20 31 42
#2056 (Whitman #660-r) Buckey Bug-c 3 6 9 18 28 38
#2057 (Whitman #887-r) Mickey & Donald-c 3 6 9 20 31 42

WALT DISNEY PRESENTS (TV)(Disney)
Dell Publishing Co.: No. 997, 6-8/59 - No. 6, 12-2/1960-61; No. 1181, 4-5/61 (All photo-c)

Four Color 997 (#1) 6 12 18 41 76 110
2(12-2/60)-The Swamp Fox(origin), Elfego Baca, Texas John Slaughter (Disney TV show) begin 5 10 15 30 50 70
3-6: 5-Swamp Fox by Warren Tufts 4 8 12 28 47 65
Four Color 1181-Texas John Slaughter 5 10 15 34 60 85

WALT DISNEY'S CHRISTMAS PARADE (Also see Christmas Parade)

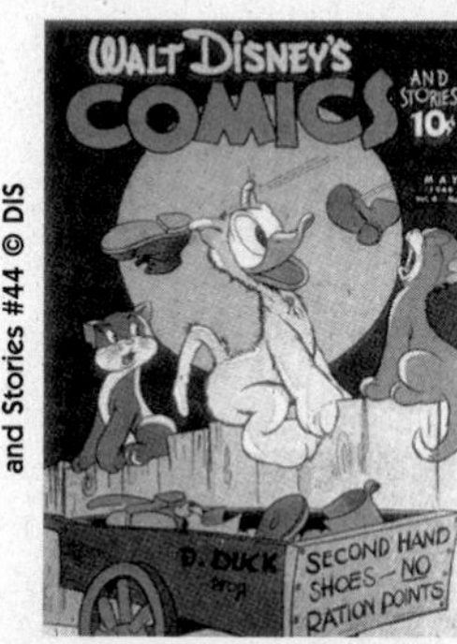

Walt Disney's Comics and Stories #44 © DIS

Walt Disney's Comics and Stories #100 © DIS

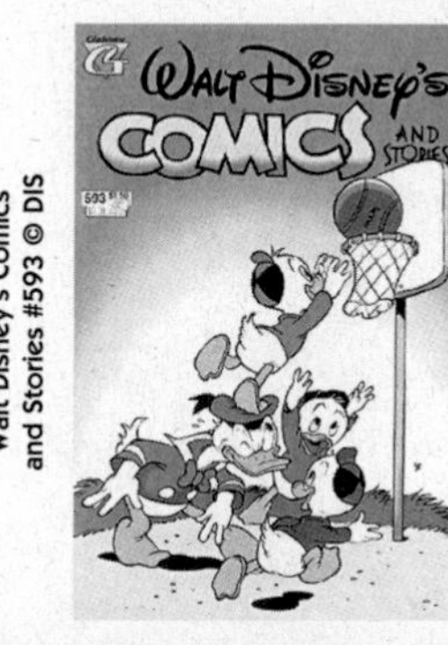

Walt Disney's Comics and Stories #593 © DIS

	GD 2.0	VG 4.0	FN 6.0	VF 8.0	VF/NM 9.0	NM- 9.2

Gladstone: Winter, 1988; No. 2, Winter, 1989 ($2.95, 100 pgs.)

1-Barks-r/painted-c	2	4	6	8	10	12
2-Barks-r	1	2	3	5	7	9

WALT DISNEY'S CHRISTMAS PARADE

Gemstone Publishing: Dec, 2003; 2004, 2005, 2006,2008 ($8.95/$9.50, prestige format)

1-4: 1-Reprints and 3 new European holiday stories. 2-All reprints. 3-Reprints and 2 new stories, 4-Reprints and 5 new stories — 9.00

5-($9.50) R/Uncle Scrooge #47 and European stories — 9.50

WALT DISNEY'S COMICS AND STORIES (Cont. of Mickey Mouse Magazine) (#1-30 contain Donald Duck newspaper reprints) (Titled "Comics And Stories" #264 to #?; titled "Walt Disney's Comics And Stories" #511 on)

Dell Publishing Co./Gold Key #264-473/Whitman #474-510/Gladstone #511-547/ Disney Comics #548-585/Gladstone #586-633/Gemstone Publishing #634-698/ Boom! Kids #699-on: 10/40 - #263, 8/62; #264, 10/62 - #510, 7/84; #511, 10/86 - #633, 2/99; #634, 7/03 - #698, 11/08; #699, 10/09 - #720, 6/11

NOTE: The whole number can always be found at the bottom of the title page in the lower left-hand or right hand panel.

	GD	VG	FN	VF	VF/NM	NM-
1(V1#1-c; V2#1-indicia)-Donald Duck strip-r by Al Taliaferro & Gottfredson's Mickey Mouse begin	2250	4500	6750	15,750	30,875	46,000
2	892	1784	2676	6512	11,756	17,000
3	389	778	1167	2723	5262	7800
4-X-Mas-c; 1st Huey, Dewey & Louie-c this title (See Mickey Mouse Magazine V4#2 for 1st-c ever)	300	600	900	1920	3860	5800
4-Special promotional, complimentary issue; cover same except one corner was blanked out & boxed in to identify the giveaway (not a paste-over). This special pressing was probably sent out to former subscribers to Mickey Mouse Mag. whose subscriptions had expired. (Very rare-5 known copies)	423	846	1269	3000	6000	9000
5-Goofy-c	245	490	735	1568	2884	4200
6-10: 8-Only Clarabelle Cow-c. 9-Taliaferro-c (1st)	206	412	618	1318	2459	3600
11-14: 11-Huey, Dewey & Louie-c/app.	155	310	465	992	1846	2700
15-17: 15-The 3 Little Kittens (17 pgs.). 16-The 3 Little Pigs (29 pgs.); X-Mas-c. 17-The Ugly Duckling (4 pgs.)	135	270	405	864	1582	2300
18-21	119	238	357	762	1431	2100
22-30: 22-Flag-c. 24-The Flying Gauchito (1st original comic book story done for WDC&S). 27-Jose Carioca by Carl Buettner (2nd original story in WDC&S)	100	200	300	635	1193	1750
31-New Donald Duck stories by Carl Barks begin (See F.C. #9 for 1st Barks Donald Duck)	400	800	1200	2800	5100	7400
32-Barks-a	232	464	696	1485	2543	3600
33-Barks-a; Gremlins app. (Vivie Risto-s/a); infinity-c	161	322	483	1030	1765	2500
34-Gremlins by Walt Kelly begin, end #41; Barks-a	129	258	387	826	1413	2000
35,36-Barks-a	123	246	369	787	1344	1900
37-Donald Duck by Jack Hannah	71	142	213	454	827	1200
38-40-Barks-a. 39-X-Mas-c. 40,41-Gremlins by Kelly	81	162	243	518	909	1300
41-50-Barks-a. 43-Seven Dwarfs-c app. (4/44). 45-50-Nazis in Gottfredson's Mickey Mouse Stories	68	136	204	435	780	1125
51-60-Barks-a. 51-X-Mas-c. 52-Li'l Bad Wolf begins, ends #203 (not in #55). 58-Kelly flag-c	32	64	96	230	515	800
61-70: Barks-a. 61-Dumbo story. 63,64-Pinocchio stories. 63-Cover swipe from New Funnies #94. 64-X-Mas-c. 65-Pluto story. 66-Infinity-c. 67,68-Mickey Mouse Sunday-r by Bill Wright	28	56	84	202	451	700
71-80: Barks-a. 75-77-Brer Rabbit stories, no Mickey Mouse. 76-X-Mas-c	25	50	75	175	388	600
81-87,89,90: Barks-a. 82-Goofy-c. 82-84-Bongo stories. 86-90-Goofy & Agnes app. 89-Chip 'n' Dale story	20	40	60	138	307	475
88-1st app. Gladstone Gander by Barks (1/48)	24	48	72	168	372	575
91-97,99: Barks-a. 95-1st WDC&S Barks-c. 96-No Mickey Mouse; Little Toot begins, ends #97. 99-X-Mas-c	18	36	54	126	281	435
98-1st Uncle Scrooge app. in WDC&S (11/48)	29	58	87	209	467	725
100-(1/49)-Barks-a	21	42	63	147	324	500
101-110-Barks-a. 107-Taliaferro-c; Donald acquires super powers	16	32	48	107	236	365
111,114,117-All Barks-a	13	26	39	89	195	300
112-Drug (ether) issue (Donald Duck)	12	24	36	84	185	285
113,115,116,118-123: No Barks. 116-Dumbo x-over. 121-Grandma Duck begins, ends #168; not in #135,142,146,155	10	20	30	64	132	200
124,126-130-All Barks-a. 124-X-Mas-c	10	20	30	70	150	230
125-1st app. Junior Woodchucks (2/51); Barks-a	15	30	45	105	233	360
131,133,135-137,139-All Barks-a	10	20	30	67	141	215
132-Barks-a(2) (D. Duck & Grandma Duck)	10	20	30	69	147	225
134-Intro. & 1st app. The Beagle Boys (11/51)	18	36	54	122	271	420
138-Classic Scrooge money story	14	28	42	96	211	325
140-(5/52)-1st app. Gyro Gearloose by Barks; 2nd Barks Uncle Scrooge-c; 3rd Uncle Scrooge cover app.	18	36	54	122	271	420
141-150-All Barks-a. 143-Little Hiawatha begins, ends #151,159	9	18	27	58	114	170
151-170-All Barks-a	8	16	24	51	96	140
171-199-All Barks-a	7	14	21	46	86	125
200	7	14	21	49	92	135
201-240: All Barks-a. 204-Chip 'n' Dale & Scamp begin	6	12	18	40	73	105
241-283: Barks-a. 241-Dumbo x-over. 247-Gyro Gearloose begins, ends #274. 256-Ludwig Von Drake begins, ends #274	5	10	15	35	63	90
284,285,287,290,295,296,309-311-Not by Barks	3	6	9	19	30	40
286,288,291-294,297,298,308-All Barks stories; 293-Grandma Duck's Farm Friends. 297-Gyro Gearloose. 298-Daisy Duck's Diary-r	4	8	12	23	37	50
289-Annette-c & back-c & story; Barks-s	4	8	12	27	44	60
299-307-All contain early Barks-r (#43-117). 305-Gyro Gearloose	4	8	12	25	40	55
312-Last Barks issue with original story	4	8	12	25	40	55
313-315,317-327,329-334,336-341	3	6	9	15	22	28
316-Last issue published during life of Walt Disney	3	6	9	15	22	28
328,335,342-350-Barks-r	3	6	9	15	22	28
351-360-With posters inside; Barks reprints (2 versions of each with & without posters)	4	8	12	25	40	55
351-360-Without posters...	3	6	9	14	19	24
361-400-Barks-r	3	6	9	14	20	26
401-429-Barks-r	3	6	9	14	19	24
430,433,437,438,441,444,445,466-No Barks	2	4	6	8	11	14
431,432,434-436,439,440,442,443-Barks-r	2	4	6	10	14	18
446-465,467-473-Barks-r	2	4	6	9	13	16
474(3/80),475-478 (Whitman)	3	6	9	14	19	24
479(8/80),481(10/80)-484(1/81) pre-pack only	5	10	15	30	50	70
480 (8-12/80)-(Very low distribution)	10	20	30	66	138	210
484 (1/81, 50¢-c) Cover price error variant (scarce)	6	12	18	38	69	100
485-499: 494-r/WDC&S #98	2	4	6	11	16	20
500-510 (All #90011 on-c; pre-packs): 500(4/83), 501(5/83), 502&503(7/83), 504-506(all 8/83), 507(4/84), 508(5/84), 509(6/84), 510(7/84). 506-No Barks	2	4	6	13	18	22
511-Donald Duck by Daan Jippes (1st in U.S.; in all through #518); Gyro Gearloose Barks-r begins (in most through #547); Wuzzles by Disney Studio (1st by Gladstone)	3	6	9	16	24	32
512,513	2	4	6	10	14	18
514-516,520	2	4	6	8	10	12
517-519,521,522,525,527,529,530,532-546: 518-Infinity-c. 522-r/1st app. Huey, Dewey & Louie from D. Duck Sunday. 535-546-Barks-r. 537-1st Donald Duck by William Van Horn in WDC&S. 541-545-52 pgs. 546,547-68 pgs. 546-Kelly-r. 547-Rosa-a						6.00
523,524,526,528,531,547: Rosa-s/a in all. 523-1st Rosa 10 pager	2	4	6	9	12	15
548-($1.50, 6/90)-1st Disney issue; new-a; no M. Mouse	1	2	3	4	5	7
549,551-570,572,573,577-579,581,584 ($1.50): 549-Barks-r begin, ends #585, not in #555, 556, & 564. 551-r/1 story from F.C. #29. 556,578-r/Mickey Mouse Cheerios Premium by Dick Moores. 562,563,568-570, 572, 581-Gottfredson strip-r. 570-Valentine issue; has Mickey/Minnie centerfold. 584-Taliaferro strip-r						4.00
550 ($2.25, 52 pgs.)-Donald Duck by Barks; previously printed only in The Netherlands (1st time in U.S.); r/Chip 'n Dale & Scamp from #204						5.00
571-($2.95, 68 pgs)-r/Donald Duck's Atom Bomb by Barks from 1947 Cheerios premium						6.00
574-576,580,582,583 ($2.95, 68 pgs.): 574-r/1st Pinocchio Sunday strip (1939-40). 575-Gottfredson-r, Pinocchio-r/WDC&S #64. 580-r/Donald Duck's 1st app. from Silly Symphony strip 12/16/34 by Taliaferro; Gottfredson strip-r begin; not in #584 & 600. 582,583-r/Mickey Mouse on Sky Island from WDC&S #1,2						5.00
585 ($2.50, 52 pgs.)-r/#140; Barks-r/WDC&S #140						5.00
586,587: 586-Gladstone issues begin again; begin $1.50-c; Gottfredson-r begins (not in #600). 587-Donald Duck by William Van Horn begins						4.00
588-597: 588,591-599-Donald Duck by William Van Horn						3.00
598,599 ($1.95, 36 pgs.): 598-r/1st drawings of Mickey Mouse by Ub Iwerks						3.00
600 ($2.95, 48 pgs.)-L.B. Cole-c(r)/WDC&S #1; Barks-r/WDC&S #32 plus Rosa, Jippes, Van Horn-r and new Rosa centerspread						4.00
601-611 ($5.95, 64 pgs., squarebound, bi-monthly): 601-Barks-c, r/Mickey Mouse V1#1, Rosa-a/scripts. 602-Rosa-c. 604-Taliaferro strip-r/1st Silly Symphony Sundays from 1932. 604,605-Jippes-a. 605-Walt Kelly-c; Gottfredson "Mickey Mouse Outwits the Phantom Blot" r/F.C. #16						6.00
612-633 ($6.95): 633-(2/99) Last Gladstone issue						7.00

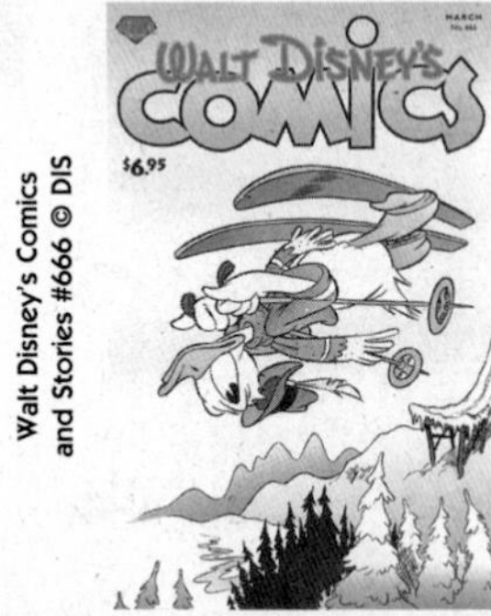

Walt Disney's Comics and Stories #666 © DIS

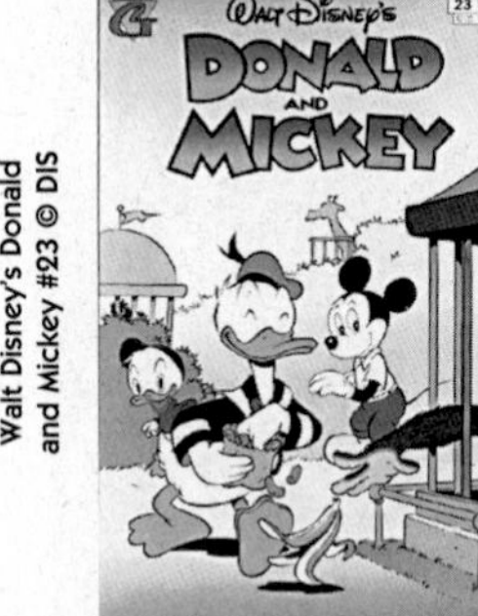

Walt Disney's Donald and Mickey #23 © DIS

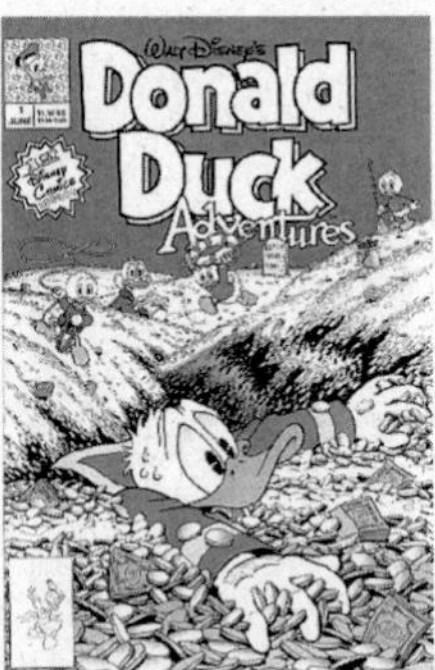

Walt Disney's Donald Duck Adventures #1 © DIS

GD VG FN VF VF/NM NM-
2.0 4.0 6.0 8.0 9.0 9.2

634-675: 634-(7/03) First Gemstone issue; William Van Horn-c. 666-Mickey's Inferno 7.00
676-681: 676-Begin $7.50-c. 677-Bucky Bug's 75th Anniversary 7.50
682-698-($7.99) 8.00
699-714: 699-(9/09, $2.99) First BOOM! Kids issue. 700-Back-up story w/Van Horn-a 3.00
715-720: 715-(1/11, $3.99) 70th Anniverary issue; cover swipe of #1 by Van Horn; Jippes, Rosa-a. 716-Barks reprints 4.00

NOTE: *(#1-38, 68 pgs.; #39-42, 60 pgs.; #43-57, 61-134, 143-168, 446, 447, 52 pgs.; #58-60, 135-142, 169-540, 36 pgs.)*

NOTE: ***Barks** art in all issues #31 on, except where noted; c-95, 96, 104, 108, 109, 130-172, 174-178, 183, 198-200, 204, 206-209, 212-216, 218, 220, 226, 228-233, 235-238, 240-243, 247, 250, 253, 256, 260, 261, 276-283, 288-292, 295-298, 301, 303, 304, 306, 307, 309, 310, 313-316, 319, 321, 322, 324, 326, 328, 329, 331, 332, 334, 341, 342, 350, 351, 527r, 530r, 540(never before published), 546r, 557-586r(most), 596p, 601p. **Kelly** a-24p, 34-41, 43; r-522-524, 546, 547, 582, 583; covers(most)-34-118, 531r, 537r, 541r-543r, 562r, 571r, 605r. Walt Disney's Comics & Stories featured Mickey Mouse serials which were in practically every issue from #1 through #394 and #511 to date. The titles of the serials, along with the issues they are in, are listed in previous editions of this price guide. **Floyd Gottfredson** Mickey Mouse serials in issues #1-14, 18-66, 69-74, 78-100, 128, 562, 563, 568-572, 582, 583, 586-599 , 601-603 , 605-present , plus "Service with a Smile" in #13; "Mickey Mouse in a Warplant" (3 pgs.), and "Pluto Catches a Nazi Spy" (4 pgs.) in #62; "Mystery Next Door", #93; "Sunken Treasure", #94; "Aunt Marissa", #95 (r in #575); "Gangland", #98 (r in #562); "Thanksgiving Dinner", #99 (r in #567); and "The Talking Dog", #100 (r in #563); "Morty's Escapade," #128. "The Brave Little Tailor", #580; "Introducing Mickey Mouse Movies ", #581; Circus Roustabout, #585; "Rumplewatt the Giant", #604. Mickey Mouse by **Paul Murry** #152-547 except 155-57 (**Dick Moore**), 327-29 (**Tony Strobl**), 348-50 (**Jack Manning**), 533 (**Bill Wright**). **Don Rosa** story/a-523, 524, 526, 528, 531, 547, 601-present. **Al Taliaferro** Silly Symphonies in #5-"Three Little Pigs"; #13-"Birds of a Feather"; #14-"The Boarding School Mystery"; #15-"Cookieland" and "Three Little Kittens"; #16-"The Practical Pig"; #17-"The Ugly Duckling"; "The Wise Little Hen" in #580; and "Ambrose the Robber Kitten"; #19-"Penguin Isle"; and "Bucky Bug" in #20-23, 25, 26, 28 (one continuous story from 1932-34; first 2 pgs. not Taliaferro). **Gottfredson** strip r-562, 563, 568-572, 581, 585, 586, 590. **Taliaferro** strip r-584, 580. **Van Horn** a-537, 545, 561, 574, 587, 588, 591-present.*

WALT DISNEY'S COMICS DIGEST
Gladstone: Dec, 1986 - No. 7, Sept, 1987

1 1 2 3 5 6 8
2-7 6.00

WALT DISNEY'S COMICS PENNY PINCHER
Gladstone: May, 1997 - No. 4, Aug, 1997 (99¢, limited series)

1-4 3.00

WALT DISNEY'S DONALD AND MICKEY (Formerly Walt Disney's Mickey and Donald)
Gladstone (Bruce Hamilton Co.): No. 19, Sept, 1993 - No. 30, 1995 ($1.50, 36 & 68 pgs.)

19,21-24,26-30: New & reprints. 19,21,23,24-Barks-r. 19,26-Murry-r. 22-Barks "Omelet" story r/WDC&S #146. 27-Mickey Mouse story by Caesar Ferioli (1st U.S work). 29-Rosa-c; Mickey Mouse story actually starring Goofy (does not include Mickey except on title page.) 4.00
20,25-($2.95, 68 pgs.): 20-Barks, Gottfredson-r 5.00
NOTE: *Donald Duck stories were all reprints.*

WALT DISNEY'S DONALD DUCK
Gemstone Publishing: 2006

... Free Comic Book Day (5/06) r/WDC&S #531; Rosa-s/a; P&S. Block-s/a; Van Horn-s/a 3.00

WALT DISNEY'S DONALD DUCK ADVENTURES (D.D. Adv. #1-3)
Gladstone: 11/87-No. 20, 4/90 (1st Series); No. 21,8/93-No. 48, 2/98(3rd Series)

1 1 2 3 5 6 8
2-r/F.C. #308 4.00
3,4,6,7,9-11,13,15-18: 3-r/F.C. #223. 4-r/F.C. #62. 9-r/F.C. #159, "Ghost of the Grotto". 11-r/F.C. #159, "Adventure Down Under." 16-r/F.C. #291; Rosa-c. 18-r/FC #318; Rosa-c 4.00
5,8: 5-Don Rosa-c/a. 8-Rosa-a 5.00
12($1.50, 52pgs)-Rosa-c/s/a; "Return to Plain Awful" story; sequel to Four Color #223 (square egg story); Barks centerfold poster 6.00
14-r/F.C. #29, "Mummy's Ring" 4.00
19($1.95, 68 pgs.)-Barks-r/F.C. #199 (1 pg.) 4.00
20($1.95, 68 pgs.)-Barks-r/F.C. #189 & cover-r; William Van Horn-a 4.00
21,22: 21-r/D.D. #46. 22-r/F.C. #282 3.00
23-25,27,29,31,32-($1.50, 36 pgs.): 21,23,29-Rosa-c. 23-Intro/1st app. Andold Wild Duck by Marco Rota. 24-Van Horn-a. 27-1st Pat Block-a, "Mystery of Widow's Gap." 31,32-Block-c 3.00
26,28($2.95, 68 pgs.): 26-Barks-r/F.C. #108, "Terror of the River". 28-Barks-r/F.C. #199, "Sheriff of Bullet Valley" 4.00
30($2.95, 68 pgs.)-r/F.C. #367, Barks' "Christmas for Shacktown" 4.00
33($1.95, 68 pgs.)-r/F.C. #408, Barks' "The Golden Helmet;"Van Horn-c 4.00
34-43: 34-Resume $1.50-c. 34,35,37-Block-a/scripts. 38-Van Horn-c/a 3.00
44-48-($1.95-c) 3.00
NOTE: ***Barks** a-1-22r, 26r, 28r, 33r, 36r; c-3r, 8r, 10r, 14r, 20r. **Block** a-27, 30, 34, 35, 37; c-27, 30-32, 34, 35, 37; c-27, 30, 31, 32, 34, 35, 37. **Rosa** a-5, 8, 12, 43; c-13, 16, 18, 21, 23, 43.*

WALT DISNEY'S DONALD DUCK ADVENTURES (2nd Series)
Disney Comics: June, 1990 - No. 38, July, 1993 ($1.50)

1-Rosa-a & scripts 5.00
2-21,23,25,27-33,35,36,38: 2-Barks-r/WDC&S #35; William Van Horn-a begins, ends #20. 9-Barks-r/F.C. #178. 9,11,14,17-No Van Horn-a. 11-Mad #1 cover parody. 14-Barks-r. 17-Barks-r. 21-r/FC #203 by Barks. 29-r/MOC #20 by Barks 3.00
22,24,26,34,37: 22-Rosa-a (10 pgs.) & scripts. 24-Rosa-a & scripts. 26-r/March of Comics #41 by Barks. 34-Rosa-c/a. 37-Rosa-a; Barks-r 4.00
NOTE: ***Barks** r-2, 4, 9(F.C. #178), 14(D.D. #45), 17, 21, 26, 27, 29 , 35, 36(D.D #60)-38. **Taliaferro** a-34r, 36r.*

GD VG FN VF VF/NM NM-
2.0 4.0 6.0 8.0 9.0 9.2

WALT DISNEY'S DONALD DUCK ADVENTURES
Gemstone Publishing: May, 2003 (giveaway promoting 2003 return of Disney Comics)

...Free Comic Book Day Edition - cover logo on red background; reprints "Maharajah Donald" & "The Peaceful Hills" from March of Comics #4; Barks-s/a; Kelly original-c on back-c 3.00
...San Diego Comic-Con 2003 Edition - cover logo on gold background 3.00
...ANA World's Fair of Money Baltimore Edition - cover logo on green background 3.00
...WizardWorld Chicago 2003 Edition - cover logo on blue background 3.00

WALT DISNEY'S DONALD DUCK ADVENTURES (Take-Along Comic)
Gemstone Publishing: July, 2003 - No. 21, Nov, 2006 ($7.95, 5" x 7-1/2")

1-21-Mickey Mouse & Uncle Scrooge app. 9-Christmas-c 8.00
... , The Barks/Rosa Collection Vol. 2 (3/08, $8.99) reprints Donald Duck's Atom Bomb, Super Snooper & The Trouble With Dimes by Barks; The Duck Who Fell to Earth, Super Snooper Strikes Again & The Money Pit by Rosa 9.00
... , The Barks/Rosa Collection Vol. 3 (9/08, $8.99) r/FC #408 "The Golden Helmet" by Barks & DDA #43 "The Lost Charts of Columbus" by Rosa; cover gallery and bonus art 9.00

WALT DISNEY'S DONALD DUCK AND FRIENDS (Continues as Donald Duck and Friends)
Gemstone Publishing: No. 308, Oct, 2003 - No. 346, Dec, 2006 ($2.95)

308-346: 308-Numbering resumes from Gladstone Donald Duck series; Halloween-c. 332-Halloween-c; r/#26 by Carl Barks 3.00

WALT DISNEY'S DONALD DUCK AND MICKEY MOUSE (Formerly Walt Disney's Donald and Mickey)
Gladstone (Bruce Hamilton Company): Sept, 1995 - No. 7, Sept, 1996 ($1.50, 32 pgs.)

1-7: 1-Barks-r and new Mickey Mouse stories in all. 5,6-Mickey Mouse stories by Caesar Ferioli. 7-New Donald Duck and Mickey Mouse x-over story; Barks-r/WDC&S #51 3.00
NOTE: *Issue #8 was advertised, but cancelled.*

WALT DISNEY'S DONALD DUCK AND UNCLE SCROOGE
Gemstone Publishing: Nov, 2005 ($6.95, square-bound one-shot)

nn-New story by John Lustig and Pat Block and r/Uncle Scrooge #59 7.00

WALT DISNEY'S DONALD DUCK FAMILY
Gemstone Publishing: Jun, 2008 ($8.99, square-bound)

... The Daan Jippes Collection Vol. 1 - R/Barks-s re-drawn by Jippes for Dutch comics 9.00

WALT DISNEY'S DONALD DUCK IN THE CASE OF THE MISSING MUMMY
Gemstone Publishing: Oct, 2007 ($8.99, square-bound one-shot)

nn-New story by Shelley and Pat Block and r/Donald Duck FC #29 9.00

WALT DISNEY'S GYRO GEARLOOSE
Gemstone Publishing: May, 2008

... Free Comic Book Day (5/08) short stories by Barks, Rosa, Van Horn, Gerstein 3.00

WALT DISNEY SHOWCASE
Gold Key: Oct, 1970 - No. 54, Jan, 1980 (No. 44-48: 68pgs., 49-54: 52pgs.)

Issue	GD 2.0	VG 4.0	FN 6.0	VF 8.0	VF/NM 9.0	NM- 9.2
1-Boatniks (Movie)-Photo-c	3	6	9	17	26	35
2-Moby Duck	3	6	9	14	19	24
3,4,7: 3-Bongo & Lumpjaw-r. 4,7-Pluto-r	2	4	6	10	14	18
5-$1,000,000 Duck (Movie)-Photo-c	3	6	9	15	22	28
6-Bedknobs & Broomsticks (Movie)	3	6	9	15	22	28
8-Daisy & Donald	2	4	6	11	16	20
9- 101 Dalmatians (cartoon feat.); r/F.C. #1183	3	6	9	16	24	32
10-Napoleon & Samantha (Movie)-Photo-c	3	6	9	15	22	28
11-Moby Duck-r	2	4	6	10	14	18
12-Dumbo-r/Four Color #668	2	4	6	11	16	20
13-Pluto-r	2	4	6	10	14	18
14-World's Greatest Athlete (Movie)-Photo-c	3	6	9	15	22	28
15- 3 Little Pigs-r	2	4	6	11	16	20
16-Aristocats (cartoon feature); r/Aristocats #1	3	6	9	15	22	28
17-Mary Poppins; r/M.P. #10136-501-Photo-c	3	6	9	15	22	28
18-Gyro Gearloose; Barks-r/F.C. #1047,1184	3	6	9	17	26	35
19-That Darn Cat; r/That Darn Cat #10171-602-Hayley Mills photo-c	3	6	9	15	22	28
20,23-Pluto-r	2	4	6	11	16	20
21-Li'l Bad Wolf & The Three Little Pigs	2	4	6	10	14	18
22-Unbirthday Party with Alice in Wonderland; r/Four Color #341	3	6	9	14	19	24
24-26: 24-Herbie Rides Again (Movie); sequel to "The Love Bug"; photo-c. 25-Old Yeller (Movie); r/F.C. #869; Photo-c. 26-Lt. Robin Crusoe USN (Movie); r/Lt. Robin Crusoe USN #10191-601; photo-c	2	4	6	11	16	20

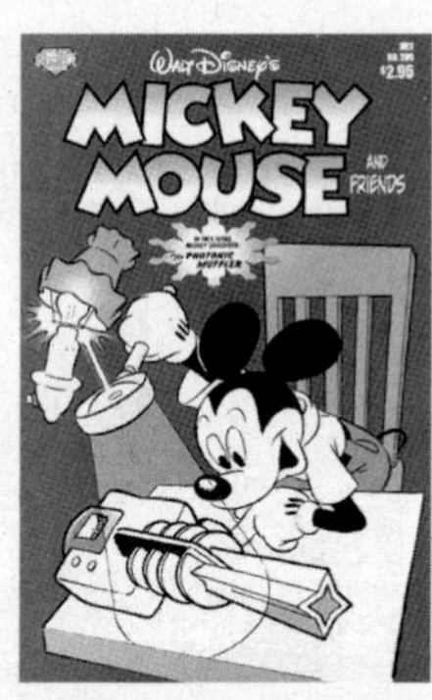

Walt Disney's Mickey Mouse and Friends #290 © DIS

Walt Disney's Mickey Mouse Meets Blotman © DIS

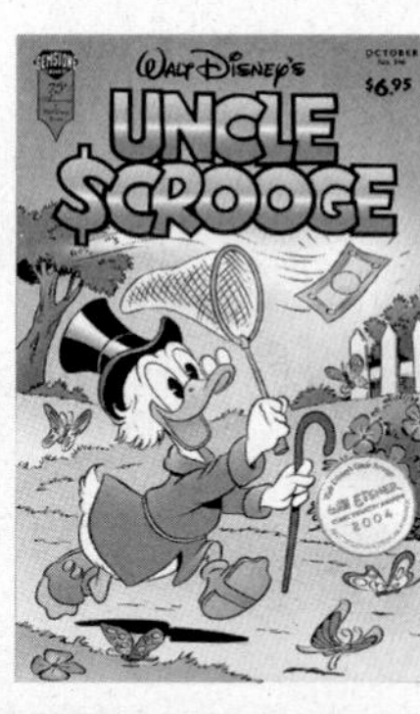

Walt Disney's Uncle Scrooge #346 © DIS

	GD 2.0	VG 4.0	FN 6.0	VF 8.0	VF/NM 9.0	NM- 9.2

27-Island at the Top of the World (Movie)-Photo-c 3 6 9 14 19 24
28-Brer Rabbit, Bucky Bug-r/WDC&S #58 2 4 6 11 16 20
29-Escape to Witch Mountain (Movie)-Photo-c 3 6 9 14 19 24
30-Magica De Spell; Barks-r/Uncle Scrooge #36 & WDC&S #258
3 6 9 20 31 42
31-Bambi (cartoon feature); r/Four Color #186 2 4 6 13 18 22
32-Spin & Marty-r/F.C. #1026; Mickey Mouse Club (TV)-Photo-c
3 6 9 14 19 24
33-40: 33-Pluto-r/F.C. #1143. 34-Paul Revere's Ride with Johnny Tremain (TV); r/F.C. #822. 35-Goofy-r/F.C. #952. 36-Peter Pan-r/F.C. #442. 37-Tinker Bell & Jiminy Cricket-r/F.C. #982,989. 38,39-Mickey & the Sleuth, Parts 1 & 2. 40-The Rescuers (cartoon feature)
2 4 6 9 13 16
41-Herbie Goes to Monte Carlo (Movie); sequel to "Herbie Rides Again"; photo-c
2 4 6 10 14 18
42-Mickey & the Sleuth 2 4 6 9 13 16
43-Pete's Dragon (Movie)-Photo-c 2 4 6 13 18 22
44-Return From Witch Mountain (new) & In Search of the Castaways-r (Movies)-Photo-c; 68 pg. giants begin 3 6 9 14 19 24
45-The Jungle Book (Movie); r/#30033-803 3 6 9 16 24 32
46-48: 46-The Cat From Outer Space (Movie)(new), & The Shaggy Dog (Movie)-r/F.C. #985; photo-c. 47-Mickey Mouse Surprise Party-r. 48-The Wonderful Advs. of Pinocchio-r/F.C. #1203; last 68 pg. issue 2 4 6 10 14 18
49-54: 49-North Avenue Irregulars (Movie); Zorro-r/Zorro #11; 52 pgs. begin; photo-c. 50-Bedknobs & Broomsticks-r/#6; Mooncussers-r/World of Adv. #1; photo-c. 51-101 Dalmatians-r. 52-Unidentified Flying Oddball (Movie); r/Picnic Party #8; photo-c. 53-The Scarecrow-r (TV). 54-The Black Hole (Movie)-Photo-c (predates Black Hole #1)
2 4 6 9 13 16

WALT DISNEY'S MAGAZINE (TV)(Formerly Walt Disney's Mickey Mouse Club Magazine) (50¢, bi-monthly)
Western Publishing Co.: V2#4, June, 1957 - V4#6, Oct, 1959

V2#4-Stories & articles on the Mouseketeers, Zorro, & Goofy and other Disney characters & people 6 12 18 38 69 100
V2#5, V2#6(10/57) 5 10 15 35 63 90
V3#1(12/57), V3#3-5 5 10 15 33 57 80
V3#2-Annette Funicello photo-c 9 18 27 63 129 195
V3#6(10/58)-TV Zorro photo-c 7 14 21 44 82 120
V4#1(12/58) - V4#2-4,6(10/59) 5 10 15 33 57 80
V4#5-Annette Funicello photo-c, w/ 2-photo articles 9 18 27 63 129 195
NOTE: *V2#4-V3#6 were 11-1/2x8-1/2", 48 pgs.; V4#1 on were 10x8", 52 pgs. (Peak circulation of 400,000).*

WALT DISNEY'S MERRY CHRISTMAS (See Dell Giant #39)

WALT DISNEY'S MICKEY AND DONALD (M & D #1,2)(Becomes Walt Disney's Donald & Mickey #19 on)
Gladstone: Mar, 1988 - No. 18, May, 1990 (95¢)

1-Don Rosa-a; r/1949 Firestone giveaway 6.00
2-8: 3-Infinity-c. 4-8-Barks-r 4.00
9-15: 9-r/1948 Firestone giveaway; X-Mas-c 3.00
16($1.50, 52 pgs.)-r/FC #157 5.00
17-(68 pgs.) Barks M.M.-r/FC #79 plus Barks D.D.-r; Rosa-a; x-mas-c 6.00
18($1.95, 68 pgs.)-Gottfredson-r/WDC&S #13,72-74; Kelly-c(r); Barks-r 5.00
NOTE: ***Barks** reprints in 1-15, 17, 18. **Kelly** c-13r, 14 (r/Walt Disney's C&S #58), 18r.*

WALT DISNEY'S MICKEY MOUSE
Gemstone Publishing: May, 2007

... Free Comic Book Day (5/07) Floyd Gottfredson-s/a 3.00

WALT DISNEY'S MICKEY MOUSE ADVENTURES (Take-Along Comic)
Gemstone Publishing: Aug, 2004 - No. 12 ($7.95, 5" x 7-1/2")

1-12-Goofy, Donald Duck & Uncle Scrooge app. 8.00

WALT DISNEY'S MICKEY MOUSE AND BLOTMAN IN BLOTMAN RETURNS
Gemstone Publishing: Dec, 2006 ($5.99, squarebound, one-shot)

nn-Wraparound-c by Noel Van Horn; Super Goof back-up story 6.00

WALT DISNEY'S MICKEY MOUSE AND FRIENDS (See Mickey Mouse and Friends for #296)
Gemstone Publishing: No. 257, Oct, 2003 - No. 295, Dec, 2006 ($2.95)

257-295: 257-Numbering resumes from Gladstone Mickey Mouse series; Halloween-c. 285-Return of the Phantom Blot 3.00

WALT DISNEY'S MICKEY MOUSE AND UNCLE SCROOGE
Gemstone Publishing: June, 2004 (Free Comic Book Day giveaway)

nn-Flip book with r/Uncle Scrooge #15 and r/Mickey Mouse Four Color #79 (only Barks drawn Mickey Mouse story) 3.00

WALT DISNEY'S MICKEY MOUSE CLUB MAGAZINE (TV)(Becomes Walt Disney's Magazine)
Western Publishing Co.: Winter, 1956 - V2#3, Apr, 1957 (11-1/2x8-1/2", quarterly, 48 pgs.)

V1#1 12 24 36 83 182 280
2-4 8 16 24 51 96 140
V2#1,2 6 12 18 41 76 110
3-Annette photo-c 11 22 33 76 163 250
Annual(1956)-Two different issues; ($1.50-Whitman); 120 pgs., cardboard covers, 11-3/4x8-3/4"; reprints 12 24 36 83 182 280
Annual(1957)-Same as above 10 20 30 69 147 225

WALT DISNEY'S MICKEY MOUSE MEETS BLOTMAN
Gemstone Publishing: Aug, 2005 ($5.99, squarebound, one-shot)

nn-Wraparound-c by Noel Van Horn; Super Goof back-up story 6.00

WALT DISNEY'S PINOCCHIO SPECIAL
Gladstone: Spring, 1990 ($1.00)

1-50th anniversary edition; Kelly-r/F.C. #92 3.00

WALT DISNEY'S SPRING FEVER
Gemstone Publishing: Apr, 2007; Apr, 2008 ($9.50, squarebound)

1,2: 1-New stories and reprints incl. "Mystery of the Swamp" by Carl Barks 9.50

WALT DISNEY'S THE ADVENTUROUS UNCLE SCROOGE MCDUCK
Gladstone: Jan, 1998 - No. 2, Mar, 1998 ($1.95)

1,2: 1-Barks-a(r). 2-Rosa-a(r) 3.00

WALT DISNEY'S THE JUNGLE BOOK
W.D. Publications (Disney Comics): 1990 ($5.95, graphic novel, 68 pgs.)

nn-Movie adaptation; movie rereleased in 1990 6.00
nn-($2.95, 68 pgs.)-Comic edition; wraparound-c 4.00

WALT DISNEY'S UNCLE SCROOGE (Formerly Uncle Scrooge #1-209)
Gladstone #210-242/Disney Comics #243-280/Gladstone #281-318/Gemstone #319 on: No. 210, 10/86 - No. 242, 4/90; No. 243, 6/90 - No. 318, 2/99; No. 319, 7/03 - No. 383, 11/08

210-1st Gladstone issue; r/WDC&S #134 (1st Beagle Boys)
2 4 6 9 13 16
211-218: 216-New story ("Go Slowly Sands of Time") plotted and partly scripted by Barks. 217-r/U.S. #7, "Seven Cities of Cibola" 2 4 6 9 12 15
219-"Son Of The Sun" by Rosa (his 1st pro work) 3 6 9 14 20 25
220-Don Rosa-a/scripts 1 2 3 5 6 8
221-223,225,228-234,236-240 4.00
224,226,227,235: 224-Rosa-c/a. 226,227-Rosa-a. 235-Rosa-a/scripts 5.00
241-($1.95, 68 pgs.)-Rosa finishes over Barks-r 6.00
242-($1.95, 68 pgs.)-Barks-r; Rosa-a(1 pg.) 6.00
243-249,251-260,264-275,277-280,282-284-($1.50): 243-1st by Disney Comics. 274-All Barks issue. 275-Contains centerspread by Rosa. 279-All Barks issue; Rosa-c. 283-r/WDC&S #98 3.00
250-($2.25, 52 pgs.)-Barks-r; wraparound-c 4.00
261-263,276-Don Rosa-c/a 5.00
281-Gladstone issues start again; Rosa-c 6.00
285-The Life and Times of Scrooge McDuck Pt. 1; Rosa-c/a/scripts
1 3 4 6 8 10
286-293: The Life and Times of Scrooge McDuck Pt. 2-8; Rosa-c/a/scripts. 293-($1.95, 36 pgs.)-The Life and Times of Scrooge McDuck Pt. 9 6.00
294-299, 301-308-($1.50, 32 pgs.): 294-296-The Life and Times of Scrooge McDuck Pt. 10-12. 296-Christmas-c. 297-The Life and Times of Uncle Scrooge Pt. 0; Rosa-c/a/scripts 3.00
300-($2.25, 48 pgs.)-Rosa-c; Barks-r/WDC&S #104 and U.S. #216; r/U.S. #220; includes new centerfold. 4.00
309-($6.95) Low print run 3 6 9 14 20 25
310-($6.95) Low print run 4 8 12 27 44 60
311-320-($6.95) 318-(2/99) Last Gladstone issue. 319-(7/03) First Gemstone issue; The Dutchman's Secret by Don Rosa 2 4 6 8 10 12
321-360 7.00
361-366: 361-Begin $7.50-c 7.50
367-383-($7.99) 8.00
... Adventures, The Barks/Rosa Collection Vol. 1 (Gemstone, 7/07, $8.50) reprints Pygmy Indians appearances in U.S. #18 by Barks and WDC&S #633 by Rosa 8.50
Walt Disney's The Life and Times of Scrooge McDuck by Don Rosa TPB (Gemstone, 2005, $16.99) Reprints #285-296, with foreword, commentaries & sketch pages by Rosa 17.00
Walt Disney's The Life and Times of Scrooge McDuck Companion by Don Rosa TPB (Gemstone, 2006, $16.99) additional chapters, with foreword & commentaries 17.00
NOTE: ***Barks** r-210-218, 220-223, 224(2pg.), 225-234, 236-242, 245, 246, 250-253, 255, 256, 258, 261(2 pg.), 265, 267, 268, 270(2), 272-284, 299-present; c(r)-210, 212, 221, 228, 229, 232, 233, 284. scripts-287, 293. **Rosa** a-219, 220, 224, 226, 227, 235, 261-263, 268, 275-277, 285-297; c-219, 224, 231, 261-263, 276, 278-281, 285-296; scripts-219, 220, 224, 235, 261-263, 268, 276, 285-296.*

WALT DISNEY'S UNCLE SCROOGE
Gemstone Publishing

nn-(5/05, FCBD) Reprints Uncle Scrooge's debut in Four Color Comics #386; Barks-s/a 3.00

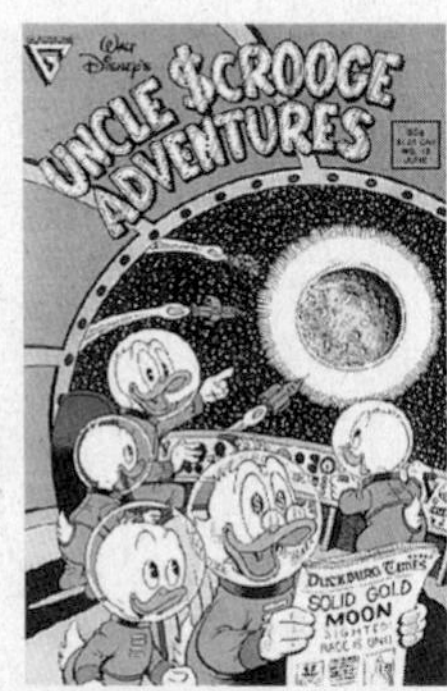

Walt Disney's Uncle Scrooge Adventures #13 © DIS

Wambi, Jungle Boy #2 © FH

Wanted #3 © Millar & Jones

GD 2.0 | VG 4.0 | FN 6.0 | VF 8.0 | VF/NM 9.0 | NM- 9.2

WALT DISNEY'S UNCLE SCROOGE ADVENTURES (U. Scrooge Advs. #1-3)
Gladstone Publishing: Nov, 1987 - No. 21, May, 1990; No. 22, Sept, 1993 - No. 54, Feb, 1998

1-Barks-r begin, ends #26 2 4 6 8 10 12
2-4 4.00
5,9,14: 5-Rosa-c/a; no Barks-r. 9,14-Rosa-a 5.00
6-8,10-13,15-19: 10-r/U.S. #18(all Barks) 3.00
20,21 ($1.95, 68 pgs.) 20-Rosa-c/a. 21-Rosa-a 5.00
22 ($1.50)-Rosa-c; r/U.S. #26 5.00
23-($2.95, 68 pgs.)-Vs. The Phantom Blot-r/P.B. #3; Barks-r 4.00
24-26,29,31,32,34-36: 24,25,29,31,32-Rosa-c. 25-r/U.S. #21 3.00
27-Guardians of the Lost Library - Rosa-c/a/story; origin of Junior Woodchuck Guidebook 4.00
28-($2.95, 68 pgs.)-r/U.S. #13 w/restored missing panels 4.00
30-($2.95, 68 pgs.)-r/U.S. #12; Rosa-c 4.00
33-($2.95, 64 pgs.)-New Barks story 4.00
37-54 3.00

NOTE: ***Barks** r-1-4, 6-8, 10-13, 15-21, 23, 22, 24; c(r)-15, 16, 17, 21. **Rosa** a-5, 9, 14, 20, 21, 27, 51; c-5, 13, 14, 17(finishes), 20, 22, 24, 25, 27, 28, 51; scripts-5, 9, 14, 27.*

WALT DISNEY'S UNCLE SCROOGE AND DONALD DUCK
Gladstone: Jan, 1998 - No. 2, Mar, 1998 ($1.95)

1,2: 1-Rosa-a(r) 3.00

WALT DISNEY'S UNCLE SCROOGE ADVENTURES IN COLOR
Gladstone Publ.: Dec, 1995 - Present ($8.95/$9.95, squarebound, 56 issue limited series) (Polybagged w/card) (Series chronologically reprints all the stories written & drawn by Carl Barks)

1-56: 1-(12/95)-r/FC #386. 15-(12/96)-r/US #15. 16-(12/96)-r/US #16. 18-(1/97)-r/US #18 10.00

WALT DISNEY'S VACATION PARADE
Gemstone Publishing: 2004 - No. 5, July, 2008 ($8.95/$9.95, squarebound, annual)

1-3: 1-Reprints stories from Dell Giant Comics Vacation Parade 1 (July 1950) 10.00
4,5-($9.95): 4-(5/07). 5-(7/08) 10.00

WALT DISNEY'S WHEATIES PREMIUMS (See Wheaties in the Promotional section)

WALT DISNEY'S WORLD OF THE DRAGONLORDS
Gemstone Publishing: 2005 ($12.99, squarebound, graphic novel)

SC-Uncle Scrooge, Donald & nephews app.; Byron Erickson-s/Giorgio Cavazzano-a 13.00

WALT DISNEY TREASURES - DISNEY COMICS: 75 YEARS OF INNOVATION
Gemstone Publishing: 2006 ($12.99, TPB)

SC-Reprints from 1930-2004, including debut of Mickey Mouse newspaper strip 13.00

WALT DISNEY TREASURES - UNCLE SCROOGE: A LITTLE SOMETHING SPECIAL
Gemstone Publishing: 2008 ($16.99, TPB)

SC-Uncle Scrooge classics from 1954-2006, including "The Seven Cities of Cibola" 17.00

WALTER LANTZ ANDY PANDA (Also see Andy Panda)
Gold Key: Aug, 1973 - No. 23, Jan, 1978 (Walter Lantz)

1-Reprints 3 6 9 14 19 24
2-10-All reprints 2 4 6 9 12 15
11-23: 15,17-19,22-Reprints 1 2 3 5 7 9

WALT KELLY'S...
Eclipse Comics: Dec, 1987; Apr, 1988 ($1.75/$2.50, Baxter paper)

...Christmas Classics 1 (12/87)-Kelly-r/Peter Wheat & Santa Claus Funnies, ...Springtime Tales 1 (4/88, $2.50)-Kelly-r 4.00

WALTONS, THE (See Kite Fun Book)

WALT SCOTT (See Little People)

WALT SCOTT'S CHRISTMAS STORIES (See Little People, 4-Color #959, 1062)

WAMBI, JUNGLE BOY (See Jungle Comics)
Fiction House Magazines: Spr, 1942; No. 2, Win, 1942-43; No. 3, Spr, 1943; No. 4, Fall, 1948; No. 5, Sum, 1949; No. 6, Spr, 1950; No. 7-10, 1950(nd); No. 11, Spr, 1951 - No. 18, Win, 1952-53 (#1-3: 68 pgs.)

1-Wambi, the Jungle Boy begins 95 190 285 603 1039 1475
2 (1942)-Kiefer-c 40 80 120 246 411 575
3 (1943)-Kiefer-c/a 34 68 102 199 325 450
4 (1948)-Origin in text 26 52 78 154 252 350
5 (Fall, 1949, 36 pgs.)-Kiefer-c/a 20 40 60 114 182 250
6-10: 7-(52 pgs.)-New logo 15 30 45 88 137 185
11-18 14 28 42 76 108 140
I.W. Reprint #8('64)-r/#12 with new-c 3 6 9 14 20 25

NOTE: ***Alex Blum** c-8. **Kiefer** c-1-5. **Whitman** c-11-18.*

WANDERERS (See Adventure Comics #375, 376)
DC Comics: June, 1988 - No. 13, Apr, 1989 ($1.25) (Legion of Super-Heroes spin off)

1-13: 1,2-Steacy-c. 3-Legion app. 3.00

GD 2.0 | VG 4.0 | FN 6.0 | VF 8.0 | VF/NM 9.0 | NM- 9.2

WANDERING STAR
Pen & Ink Comics/Sirius Entertainment No. 12 on: 1993 - No. 21, Mar, 1997 ($2.50/$2.75, B&W)

1-1st printing; Teri Sue Wood c/a/scripts in all 1 2 3 5 6 8
1-2nd and 3rd printings 3.00
2-1st printing. 4.00
2-21: 2-2nd printing. 12-(1/96)-1st Sirius issue 3.00
Trade paperback ($11.95)-r/1-7; 1st printing of 1000, signed and #'d 18.00
Trade paperback-2nd printing, 2000 signed 15.00
TPB Volume 2,3 (11/98, 12/98, $14.95) 2-r/#8-14, 3-r/#15-21 15.00

WANTED
Image Comics (Top Cow): Dec, 2003 - No. 6, Feb, 2004 ($2.99)

1-Three covers; Mark Millar-s/J.G. Jones-a; intro Wesley Gibson 4.00
1-4-Death Row Edition; r/#1-4 with extra sketch pages and deleted panels 3.00
2-6: 2-Cameos of DC villains. 6-Giordano-a in flashback scenes 3.00
...Dossier (5/04, $2.99) Pin-ups and character info; art by Jones, Romita Jr. & others 3.00
Image Firsts: Wanted #1 (9/10, $1.00) reprints #1 3.00
... Movie Edition Vol. 1 TPB (2008, $19.99) r/#1-6 & Dossier; movie photo-c; sketch pages & cover gallery; interviews with movie cast and director 20.00
HC (2005, $29.99) r/#1-6 & Dossier; intro by Vaughan, sketch pages & cover gallery 30.00

WANTED COMICS
Toytown Publications/Patches/Orbit Publ.: No. 9, Sept-Oct, 1947 - No. 53, April, 1953 (#9-33: 52 pgs.)

9-True crime cases; radio's Mr. D. A. app. 30 60 90 177 289 400
10,11: 10-Giunta-a; radio's Mr. D. A. app. 19 38 57 111 176 240
12-Used in **SOTI**, pg. 277 20 40 60 118 192 265
13-Heroin drug propaganda story 19 38 57 111 176 240
14-Marijuana drug mention story (2 pgs.) 17 34 51 98 154 210
15-17,19,20 15 30 45 84 127 170
18-Marijuana story, "Satan's Cigarettes"; r-in #45 & retitled 31 62 93 186 303 420
21,22: 21-Krigstein-a. 22-Extreme violence 15 30 45 85 130 175
23,25-32,34,36-38,40-44,46-48,53 14 28 42 80 115 150
24-Krigstein-a; "The Dope King", marijuana mention story 18 36 54 105 165 225
33-Spider web-c 17 34 51 98 154 210
35-Used in **SOTI**, pg. 160 18 36 54 103 162 220
39-Drug propaganda story "The Horror Weed" 22 44 66 132 216 300
45-Marijuana story from #18 15 30 45 84 127 170
49-Has unstable pink-c that fades easily; rare in mint condition 18 36 54 105 165 225
50-Has unstable pink-c like #49; surrealist-c by Buscema; horror stories 19 38 57 111 176 240
51- "Holiday of Horror" junkie story; drug-c 21 42 63 122 199 275
52-Classic "Cult of Killers" opium use story 22 44 66 132 216 300

NOTE: ***Buscema** c-50, 51. **Lawrence** and **Leav** c/a most issues. **Syd Shores** c/a-48; c-37. Issues 9-46 have wanted criminals with their descriptions & drawn picture on cover.*

WANTED: DEAD OR ALIVE (TV)
Dell Publishing Co.: No. 1102, May-July, 1960 - No. 1164, Mar-May, 1961

Four Color 1102 (#1)-Steve McQueen photo-c 10 20 30 69 147 225
Four Color 1164-Steve McQueen photo-c 8 16 24 54 102 150

WANTED, THE WORLD'S MOST DANGEROUS VILLAINS (See DC Special)
National Periodical Publ.: July-Aug, 1972 - No. 9, Aug-Sept, 1973 (All reprints & 20¢ issues)

1-Batman, Green Lantern (story r-from G.L. #1), & Green Arrow 3 6 9 21 33 45
2-Batman/Joker/Penguin-c/story r-from Batman #25; plus Flash story (r-from Flash #121) 3 6 9 16 24 32
3-9: 3-Dr. Fate(r/More Fun #65), Hawkman(r/Flash #100), & Vigilante(r/Action #69). 4-Green Lantern(r/All-American #61) & Kid Eternity(r/Kid Eternity #15). 5-Dollman/Green Lantern. 6-Burnley Starman; Wildcat/Sargon. 7-Johnny Quick(r/More Fun #76), Hawkman(r/Flash #90), Hourman by Baily(r/Adv. #72). 8-Dr. Fate/Flash(r/Flash #114). 9-S&K Sandman/Superman 3 6 9 14 20 26

NOTE: ***B. Bailey** a-7r. **Infantino** a-2r. **Kane** r-1, 5. **Kubert** r-3i, 6, 7. **Meskin** r-3, 7. **Reinman** r-4, 6.*

WAR (See Fightin' Marines #122)
Charlton Comics: Jul, 1975 - No. 9, Nov, 1976; No. 10, Sept, 1978 - No. 47, 1984

1-Boyette painted-c 3 6 9 14 19 24
2-10: 3-Sutton painted-c 2 4 6 8 10 12
11-20 1 2 3 5 6 8
21-40 1 2 3 4 5 7

War Against Crime #9 © WMG

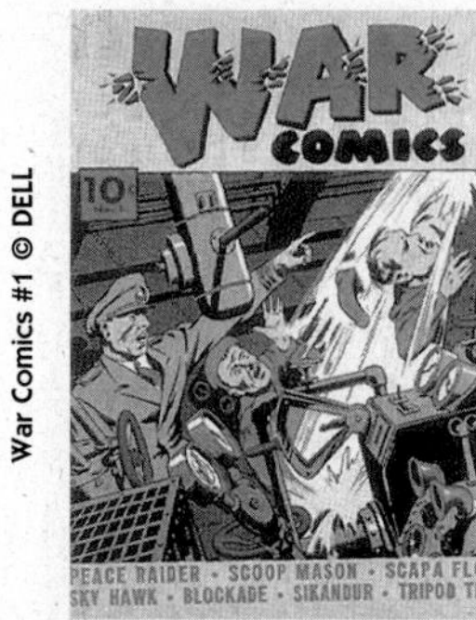

War Comics #1 © DELL

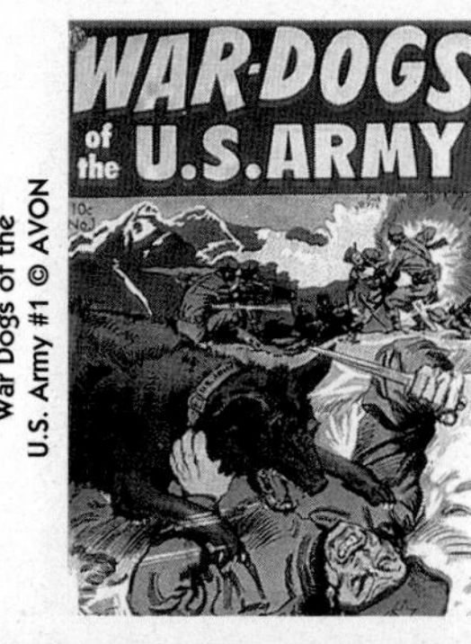

War Dogs of the U.S. Army #1 © AVON

	GD 2.0	VG 4.0	FN 6.0	VF 8.0	VF/NM 9.0	NM- 9.2
41,42,44-47 (lower print run): 47-Reprints	1	2	3	5	6	8
43 (2/84) (lower print run) Ditko-a (7 pgs.)	2	4	6	8	10	12
7,9 (Modern Comics-r, 1977)						6.00

WAR, THE (See The Draft & The Pitt)
Marvel Comics: 1989 - No. 4, 1990 ($3.50, squarebound, 52 pgs.)

	GD 2.0	VG 4.0	FN 6.0	VF 8.0	VF/NM 9.0	NM- 9.2
1-4: Characters from New Universe						4.00

WAR ACTION (Korean War)
Atlas Comics (CPS): April, 1952 - No. 14, June, 1953

	GD 2.0	VG 4.0	FN 6.0	VF 8.0	VF/NM 9.0	NM- 9.2
1	24	48	72	140	230	320
2-Hartley-a	14	28	42	82	121	160
3-10,14: 7-Pakula-a. 14-Colan-a	13	26	39	72	101	130
11-13-Krigstein-a. 11-Romita-a	14	28	42	76	108	140

NOTE: *Berg c-11. Brodsky a-2; c-1-4. Heath a-1; c-7, 14. Keller a-6. Maneely a-1; c-12. Sale a-7. Tuska a-2, 8.*

WAR ADVENTURES
Atlas Comics (HPC): Jan, 1952 - No. 13, Feb, 1953

	GD 2.0	VG 4.0	FN 6.0	VF 8.0	VF/NM 9.0	NM- 9.2
1-Tuska-a	24	48	72	140	230	320
2	14	28	42	82	121	160
3-7,9-13: 3-Pakula-a. 7-Maneely-c. 9-Romita-a	13	26	39	72	101	130
8-Krigstein-a	14	28	42	76	108	140

NOTE: *Brodsky c-1-3, 6, 8, 11, 12. Heath a-2, 5, 7, 10; c-4, 5, 9, 13. Reinman a-13. Robinson a-3; c-10.*

WAR ADVENTURES ON THE BATTLEFIELD (See Battlefield)

WAR AGAINST CRIME! (Becomes Vault of Horror #12 on)
E. C. Comics: Spring, 1948 - No. 11, Feb-Mar, 1950

	GD 2.0	VG 4.0	FN 6.0	VF 8.0	VF/NM 9.0	NM- 9.2
1-Real Stories From Police Records on-c #1-9	97	194	291	621	1061	1500
2,3	53	106	159	334	567	800
4-9	47	94	141	296	498	700
10-1st Vault Keeper app. & 1st Vault of Horror	206	412	618	1318	2259	3200
11-2nd Vault Keeper app.; 1st EC horror-c	142	284	426	909	1555	2200

NOTE: *All have Johnny Craig covers. Feldstein a-4, 7-9. Harrison/Wood a-11. Ingels a-1, 2, 8. Palais a-8. Changes to horror with #10.*

WAR AGAINST CRIME
Gemstone Publishing: Apr, 2000 - No. 11, Feb, 2001 ($2.50)

	GD 2.0	VG 4.0	FN 6.0	VF 8.0	VF/NM 9.0	NM- 9.2
1-11: E.C. reprints						4.00

WAR AND ATTACK (Also see Special War Series #3)
Charlton Comics: Fall, 1964; V2#54, June, 1966 - V2#63, Dec, 1967

	GD 2.0	VG 4.0	FN 6.0	VF 8.0	VF/NM 9.0	NM- 9.2
1-Wood-a (25 pgs.)	5	10	15	34	60	85
V2#54(6/66)-#63 (Formerly Fightin' Air Force)	3	6	9	15	22	28

NOTE: *Montes/Bache a-55, 56, 60, 63.*

WAR AT SEA (Formerly Space Adventures)
Charlton Comics: No. 22, Nov, 1957 - No. 42, June, 1961

	GD 2.0	VG 4.0	FN 6.0	VF 8.0	VF/NM 9.0	NM- 9.2
22	8	16	24	42	54	65
23-30: 26-Pearl Harbor, FDR app.	6	12	18	29	36	42
31-42: 42-Cuba's Fidel Castro story	3	6	9	18	28	38

WAR BATTLES
Harvey Publications: Feb, 1952 - No. 9, Dec, 1953

	GD 2.0	VG 4.0	FN 6.0	VF 8.0	VF/NM 9.0	NM- 9.2
1-Powell-a; Elias-c	9	18	27	63	107	150
2-Powell-a	5	10	15	34	55	75
3,4,7-9: 3,7-Powell-a	5	10	15	32	51	70
5-Flamethrower cover	14	28	42	82	121	160
6-Nostrand-a	6	12	18	39	62	85

WAR BIRDS
Fiction House Magazines: 1952(nd) - No. 3, Winter, 1952-53

	GD 2.0	VG 4.0	FN 6.0	VF 8.0	VF/NM 9.0	NM- 9.2
1	19	38	57	111	176	240
2,3	12	24	36	69	97	125

WARBLADE: ENDANGERED SPECIES (Also see WildC.A.T.S: Covert Action Teams)
Image Comics (WildStorm Productions): Jan, 1995 - No. 4, Apr, 1995 ($2.50, limited series)

	GD 2.0	VG 4.0	FN 6.0	VF 8.0	VF/NM 9.0	NM- 9.2
1-4: 1-Gatefold wraparound-c						3.00

WAR COMBAT (Becomes Combat Casey #6 on)
Atlas Comics (LBI No. 1/SAI No. 2-5): March, 1952 - No. 5, Nov, 1952

	GD 2.0	VG 4.0	FN 6.0	VF 8.0	VF/NM 9.0	NM- 9.2
1	22	44	66	132	216	300
2	14	28	42	80	115	150
3-5	13	26	39	72	101	130

NOTE: *Berg a-2, 4, 5. Brodsky c-1, 2, 4, 5. Henkel a-5. Maneely a-1, 4; c-3. Reinman a-2.*

WAR COMICS (War Stories #5 on)(See Key Ring Comics)
Dell Publishing Co.: May, 1940 (No month given) - No. 4, Sept, 1941

	GD 2.0	VG 4.0	FN 6.0	VF 8.0	VF/NM 9.0	NM- 9.2
1-Sikandur the Robot Master, Sky Hawk, Scoop Mason, War Correspondent begin; McWilliams-c; 1st war comic	90	180	270	576	988	1400
2-Origin Greg Gilday (5/41)	39	78	117	240	395	550
3-Joan becomes Greg Gilday's aide	30	60	90	177	289	400
4-Origin Night Devils	31	62	93	182	296	410

WAR COMICS
Marvel/Atlas (USA No. 1-41/JPI No. 42-49): Dec, 1950 - No. 49, Sept, 1957

	GD 2.0	VG 4.0	FN 6.0	VF 8.0	VF/NM 9.0	NM- 9.2
1	34	68	102	199	325	450
2	18	36	54	105	165	225
3-10	15	30	45	88	137	185
11-Flame thrower w/burning bodies on-c	26	52	78	154	252	350
12-20: 16-Romita-a	14	28	42	82	121	160
21,23-32: 26-Valley Forge story. 32-Last pre-code issue (2/55)	14	28	42	76	108	140
22-Krigstein-a	14	28	42	80	115	150
33-37,39-42,44,45,47,48: 40-Romita-a	13	26	39	72	101	130
38-Kubert/Moskowitz-a	14	28	42	76	108	140
43,49-Torres-a. 43-Severin/Elder E.C. swipe from Two-Fisted Tales #31	14	28	42	76	108	140
46-Crandall-a	14	28	42	76	108	140

NOTE: *Ayers a-17. Berg a-13. Colan a-4, 36, 48, 49; c-17. Drucker a-37, 43, 48. Everett a-17. Heath a-6-9, 16, 19, 25, 36; c-11, 16, 19, 23, 25, 26, 29-32, 36. G. Kane a-19. Lawrence a-36. Maneely a-7, 9, 13, 14, 20, 23; c-6, 27, 37. Orlando a-42, 48. Pakula a-26, 40. Ravielli a-27. Reinman a-11, 16, 26. Robinson a-15; c-13. Severin a-26, 27; c-48. Shores a-13. Sinnott a-37.*

WAR DANCER (Also see Charlemagne, Doctor Chaos #2 & Warriors of Plasm)
Defiant: Feb, 1994 - No. 6, July, 1994 ($2.50)

	GD 2.0	VG 4.0	FN 6.0	VF 8.0	VF/NM 9.0	NM- 9.2
1-3,5,6: 1-Intro War Dancer; Weiss-c/a begins. 1-3-Weiss-a(p). 6-Pre-Schism issue						3.00
4-($3.25, 52 pgs.)-Charlemagne app.						4.00

WAR DOGS OF THE U.S. ARMY
Avon Periodicals: 1952

	GD 2.0	VG 4.0	FN 6.0	VF 8.0	VF/NM 9.0	NM- 9.2
1-Kinstler-c/a	15	30	45	88	137	185

WAREHOUSE 13 (Based on the Syfy TV series)
Dynamite Entertainment: 2011 - No. 5, 2012 ($3.99)

	GD 2.0	VG 4.0	FN 6.0	VF 8.0	VF/NM 9.0	NM- 9.2
1-5: 1-Raab & Hughes-s/Morse-a						4.00

WARFRONT
Harvey Publications: 9/51 - #35, 11/58; #36, 10/65; #39, 2/67

	GD 2.0	VG 4.0	FN 6.0	VF 8.0	VF/NM 9.0	NM- 9.2
1-Korean War	9	18	27	59	117	175
2	5	10	15	34	60	85
3-10	5	10	15	30	50	70
11,12,14,16-20	4	8	12	27	44	60
13,15,22-Nostrand-a	5	10	15	34	60	85
21,23-27,31-33,35	4	8	12	27	44	60
28-30,34-Kirby-c	5	10	15	35	63	90
36-(12/66)-Dynamite Joe begins, ends #39; Williamson-a	5	10	15	30	50	70
37-Wood-a (17 pgs.)	5	10	15	30	50	70
38,39-Wood-a, 2-3 pgs.; Lone Tiger app.	4	8	12	27	44	60

NOTE: *Powell a-1-6, 9-11, 14, 17, 20, 23, 25-28, 30, 31, 34, 36. Powell/Nostrand a-12, 13, 15. Simon c-36?, 38.*

WAR FURY
Comic Media/Harwell (Allen Hardy Assoc.): Sept, 1952 - No. 4, Mar, 1953

	GD 2.0	VG 4.0	FN 6.0	VF 8.0	VF/NM 9.0	NM- 9.2
1-Heck-c/a in all; Palais-a; bullet hole in forehead-c; all issues are very violent; soldier using flame thrower on enemy	58	116	174	371	636	900
2-4: 4-Morisi-a	26	52	78	154	252	350

WAR GODS OF THE DEEP (See Movie Classics)

WARHAWKS
TSR, Inc.: 1990 - No. 10, 1991 ($2.95, 44 pgs.)

	GD 2.0	VG 4.0	FN 6.0	VF 8.0	VF/NM 9.0	NM- 9.2
1-10-Based on TSR game, Spiegle a-1-6						4.00

WARHEADS
Marvel Comics UK: June, 1992 - No. 14, Aug, 1993 ($1.75)

	GD 2.0	VG 4.0	FN 6.0	VF 8.0	VF/NM 9.0	NM- 9.2
1-Wolverine-c/story; indicia says #2 by mistake						4.00
2-14: 2-Nick Fury app. 3-Iron Man-c/story. 4,5-X-Force. 5-Liger vs. Cable. 6,7-Death's Head II app. (#6 is cameo)						3.00

WAR HEROES (See Marine War Heroes)

WAR HEROES
Dell Publishing Co.: 7-9/42 (no month); No. 2, 10-12/42 - No. 10, 10-12/44 (Quarterly)

	GD 2.0	VG 4.0	FN 6.0	VF 8.0	VF/NM 9.0	NM- 9.2
1-General Douglas MacArthur-c	27	54	81	160	263	365
2-James Doolittle and other officers-c	15	30	45	86	133	180
3,5: 3-Pro-Russian back-c; grey-tone-c. 5-General Patton-c	14	28	42	76	108	140
4-Disney's Gremlins app.; grey-tone-c	18	36	54	107	169	230
6-10: 6-Tothish-a by Discount. 6,9-Grey-tone-c	10	20	30	56	76	95

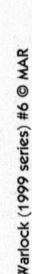

War is Hell #9 © MAR

Warlock (1999 series) #6 © MAR

Warlord #47 © DC

	GD 2.0	VG 4.0	FN 6.0	VF 8.0	VF/NM 9.0	NM- 9.2

NOTE: *No. 1 was to be released in July, but was delayed. Painted c-4, 6-9.*

WAR HEROES
Ace Magazines: May, 1952 - No. 8, Apr, 1953

	GD	VG	FN	VF	VF/NM	NM-
1	14	28	42	80	115	150
2-Lou Cameron-a	10	20	30	54	72	90
3-8: 6,7-Cameron-a	9	18	27	47	61	75

WAR HEROES (Also see Blue Bird Comics)
Charlton Comics: Feb, 1963 - No. 27, Nov, 1967

	GD	VG	FN	VF	VF/NM	NM-
1,2: 2-John F. Kennedy story	4	8	12	25	40	55
3-10	3	6	9	17	26	35
11-26: 22-True story about plot to kill Hitler	3	6	9	14	20	26
27-1st Devils Brigade by Glanzman	3	6	9	17	26	35

NOTE: ***Montes/Bache** a-3-7, 21, 25, 27; c-3-7.*

WAR HEROES
Image Comics: July, 2008 - No. 6 ($2.99, limited series)

1-3-Soldiers given super powers; Mark Millar-s/Tony Harris-a/c; four covers 3.00

WAR IS HELL
Marvel Comics Group: Jan, 1973 - No. 15, Oct, 1975

	GD	VG	FN	VF	VF/NM	NM-
1-Williamson-a(r), 5 pgs.; Ayers-a	3	6	9	16	24	32
2-8-Reprints. 6-(11/73). 7-(6/74). 7,8-Kirby-a	2	4	6	10	14	18
9-Intro Death	5	10	15	30	50	70
10-15-Death app.	3	6	9	16	24	32

NOTE: ***Bolle** a-3r. **Powell** a-1. **Woodbridge** a-1. Sgt. Fury reprints-7, 8.*

WAR IS HELL: THE FIRST FLIGHT OF THE PHANTOM EAGLE
Marvel Comics (MAX): May, 2008 - No. 5, Sept, 2008 ($3.99, limited series)

1-5-World War I fighter pilots; Ennis-s/Chaykin-a/Cassaday-c 4.00

WARLANDS
Image Comics: Aug, 1999 - No. 12, Feb, 2001 ($2.50)

1-9,11,12-Pat Lee-a(p)/Adrian Tsang-s 3.00
10-($2.95) Flip book w/Shidima preview 4.00
... Chronicles 1,2 (2/00, 7/00; $7.95) 1-r/#1-3. 2-r/#4-6 8.00
...Darklyte TPB (8/01, $14.95) r/#0,1/2,1-6 w/cover gallery; new Lee-c 15.00
...Epilogue: Three Stories (3/01, $5.95) includes r/Wizard #1/2 & AE #0 6.00
Another Universe #0 3.00
Wizard #1/2 5.00

WARLANDS: THE AGE OF ICE (Volume 2)
Image Comics: July, 2001 - No. 9, Nov, 2002 ($2.95)

#0-(2/02, $2.25) 3.00
#1/2 (4/02, $2.25) 3.00
1-9: 2-Flip book preview of Banished Knights 3.00
TPB (2003, $15.95) r/#1-9 16.00

WARLANDS: DARK TIDE RISING (Volume 3)
Image Comics: Dec, 2002 - No. 6, May, 2003 ($2.95)

1-6: 1-Wraparound gatefold-c 3.00

WARLOCK (The Power of...)(Also see Avengers Annual #7, Fantastic Four #66, 67, Incredible Hulk #178, Infinity Crusade, Infinity Gauntlet, Infinity War, Marvel Premiere #1, Marvel Two-In-One Annual #2, Silver Surfer V3#46, Strange Tales #178-181 & Thor #165)
Marvel Comics Group: Aug, 1972 - No. 8, Oct, 1973; No. 9, Oct, 1975 - No. 15, Nov, 1976

	GD	VG	FN	VF	VF/NM	NM-
1-Origin by Kane	8	16	24	51	96	140
2,3	4	8	12	27	44	60
4-8: 4-Death of Eddie Roberts	3	6	9	17	26	35
9-Starlin's 2nd Thanos saga begins, ends #15; new costume Warlock; Thanos cameo only; story cont'd from Strange Tales #178-181; Starlin-c/a in #9-15	4	8	12	27	44	60
10-Origin Thanos & Gamora; recaps events from Capt. Marvel #25-34. Thanos vs.The Magus-c/story	4	8	12	28	47	65
11-Thanos app.; Warlock dies	3	6	9	20	31	42
12-14: (Regular 25¢ edition) 14-Origin Star Thief; last 25¢ issue	3	6	9	17	26	35
12-14-(30¢-c, limited distribution)	5	10	15	30	50	70
15-Thanos-c/story	3	6	9	19	30	40

NOTE: ***Buscema** a-2p; c-8p. **G. Kane** a-1p, 3-5p; c-1p, 2, 3, 4p, 5p, 7p. **Starlin** a-9-14p, 15; c-9, 10, 11p, 12p, 13-15. **Sutton** a-1-8i.*

WARLOCK (...Special Edition on-c)
Marvel Comics Group: Dec, 1982 - No. 6, May, 1983 ($2.00, slick paper, 52 pgs.)

1-Warlock-r/Strange Tales #178-180. 6.00
2-6: 2-r/Str. Tales #180,181 & Warlock #9. 3-r/Warlock #10-12(Thanos origin recap). 4-r/Warlock #12-15. 5-r/Warlock #15, Marvel Team-Up #55 & Avengers Ann. #7. 6-r/2nd half Avengers Annual #7 & Marvel Two-in-One Annual #2 5.00
Special Edition #1(12/83) 5.00

NOTE: ***Byrne** a-5r. **Starlin** a-1-6r; c-1-6(new). Direct sale only.*

WARLOCK
Marvel Comics: V2#1, May, 1992 - No. 6, Oct, 1992 ($2.50, limited series)

V2#1-6: 1-Reprints 1982 reprint series w/Thanos 4.00

WARLOCK
Marvel Comics: Nov, 1998 - No. 4, Feb, 1999 ($2.99, limited series)

1-4-Warlock vs. Drax 3.00

WARLOCK (M-Tech)
Marvel Comics: Oct, 1999 - No. 9, June, 2000 ($1.99/$2.50)

1-5: 1-Quesada-c. 2-Two covers 3.00
6-9: 6-Begin $2.50-c. 8-Avengers app. 3.00

WARLOCK
Marvel Comics: Nov, 2004 - No. 4, Feb, 2005 ($2.99, limited series)

1-4-Adlard-a/Williams-c 3.00

WARLOCK AND THE INFINITY WATCH (Also see Infinity Gauntlet)
Marvel Comics: Feb, 1992 - No. 42, July, 1995 ($1.75) (Sequel to Infinity Gauntlet)

1-Starlin-scripts begin; brief origin recap; sequel to Infinity Gauntlet 5.00
2,3: 2-Reintro Moondragon 4.00
4-24,26: 7-Reintro The Magus; Moondragon app.; Thanos cameo on last 2 pgs. 8,9-Thanos battles Gamora-c/story. 8-Magus & Moondragon app. 10-Thanos-c/story; Magus app. 13-Hulk x-over. 21-Drax vs. Thor 4.00
25-($2.95, 52 pgs.)-Die-cut & embossed double-c; Thor & Thanos app. 5.00
28-42: 28-$1.95-c begins; bound-in card sheet 3.00

NOTE: ***Austin** c/a-1-4i, 7i. **Leonardi** a(p)-3, 4. **Medina** c/a(p)-1, 2, 5; 6, 9, 10, 14, 15, 20. **Williams** a(i)-8, 12, 13, 16-19.*

WARLOCK CHRONICLES
Marvel Comics: June, 1993 - No. 8, Feb, 1994 ($2.00, limited series)

1-($2.95)-Holo-grafx foil & embossed-c; origin retold; Starlin scripts begin; Keith Williams-a(i) in all 5.00
2-8: 3-Thanos & Mephisto-c/story. 4-Vs. Magus-c/s. 8-Contains free 16 pg. Razorline insert 4.00

WARLOCK 5
Aircel Pub.: 11/86 - No. 22, 5/89; V2#1, June, 1989 - V2#5, 1989 ($1.70, B&W)

1-5,7-11-Gordon Derry-s/Denis Beauvais-a thru #11. 5-Green Cyborg on-c. 5-Misnumbered as #6 (no #6); Blue Girl on-c. 3.00
12-22-Barry Blair-s/a. 18-$1.95-c begins 4.00
V2#1-5 ($2.00, B&W)-All issues by Barry Blair 3.00
Compilation 1,2: 1-r/#1-5 (1988, $5.95); 2-r/#6-9 6.00

WARLORD (See 1st Issue Special #8) (B&W reprints in Showcase Presents: Warlord)
National Periodical Publications/DC Comics #123 on: 1-2/76; No.2, 3-4/76; No.3, 10-11/76 - No. 133, Win, 1988-89

	GD	VG	FN	VF	VF/NM	NM-
1-Story cont'd. from 1st Issue Special #8	4	8	12	23	37	50
2-Intro. Machiste	3	6	9	14	20	25
3-5	2	4	6	9	12	15
6-10: 6-Intro Mariah. 7-Origin Machiste. 9-Dons new costume	1	3	4	6	8	10
11-20: 11-Origin-r. 12-Intro Aton. 15-Tara returns; Warlord has son						6.00
21-36,40,41: 27-New facts about origin. 28-1st app. Wizard World. 32-Intro Shakira. 40-Warlord gets new costume						5.00
22-Whitman variant edition	2	4	6	13	18	22
37-39: 37,38-Origin Omac by Starlin. 38-Intro Jennifer Morgan, Warlord's daughter. 39-Omac ends.						6.00
42-48: 42-47-Omac back-up series. 48-(52 pgs.)-1st app. Arak; contains free 14 pg. Arak Son of Thunder; Claw The Unconquered app.						5.00
49-62,64-99,101-132: 49-Claw The Unconquered app. 50-Death of Aton. 51-Reprints #1. 55-Arion Lord of Atlantis begins, ends #62. 91-Origin w/new facts. 114,115-Legends x-over. 125-Death of Tara. 131-1st DC work by Rob Liefeld (9/88)						4.00
63-The Barren Earth begins; free 16pg. Masters of the Universe preview						5.00
100-($1.25, 52 pgs.)						5.00
133-($1.50, 52 pgs.)						5.00
Annual 1-6 ('82-'87): 1-Grell-c,/a(p). 6-New Gods app.						5.00
The Savage Empire TPB (1991, $19.95) r/#1-10,12 & First Issue Special #8; Grell intro.						25.00

NOTE: ***Grell** a-1-15, 16-50p, 51r, 52p, 59p, Annual 1p; c-1-70, 100-104, 112, 116, 117, Annual 1, 5. **Wayne Howard** a-64i. **Starlin** a-37-39p.*

WARLORD
DC Comics: Jan, 1992 - No. 6, June, 1992 ($1.75, limited series)

1-6: Grell-c & scripts in all 3.00

WARLORD

Warlord of Mars #32 © Dynamite

War Machine #8 © MAR

Warren Presents #1 © WP

	GD 2.0	VG 4.0	FN 6.0	VF 8.0	VF/NM 9.0	NM- 9.2

DC Comics: Apr, 2006 - No. 10, Jan, 2007 ($2.99)

1-10: 1-Bruce Jones-s/Bart Sears-a. 10-Winslade-a 3.00

WARLORD
DC Comics: Jun, 2009 - No. 16, Sept, 2010 ($2.99)

1-16: 1-Grell-s/Prado-a/Grell-c. 7-9,11,12,15,16-Grell-s/a/c. 10-Hardin-a 3.00
...: The Saga SC (2010, $17.99) r/#1-6; cover gallery 18.00

WARLORD OF MARS
Dynamite Entertainment: 2010 - Present ($1.00/$3.99)

1-($1.00) John Carter on Earth; Sadowski-a; covers by Ross, Campbell, Jusko. Parrillo 3.00
2-34-($3.99) Multiple covers on each. 3-Carter arrives on Mars. 4-Dejah Thoris intro. 4.00
... Annual 1 (2012, $4.99) Sadowski-a/Parrillo-c 5.00

WARLORD OF MARS: DEJAH THORIS
Dynamite Entertainment: 2011 - No. 37, 2014 ($3.99/$4.99)

1-36: 1-Five covers; Nelson-s/Rafael-a. 2-5-Four covers. 6-31-Multiple covers on all 4.00
37-($4.99) Napton-s/Carita-a; Neves & Anacleto-c 5.00

WARLORD OF MARS: FALL OF BARSOOM
Dynamite Entertainment: 2011 - No. 5, 2012 ($3.99, limited series)

1-5-Napton-s/Castro-a/Jusko-c 4.00

WARLORDS (See DC Graphic Novel #2)

WAR MACHINE (Also see Iron Man #281,282 & Marvel Comics Presents #152)
Marvel Comics: Apr, 1994 - No. 25, Apr, 1996 ($1.50)

"Ashcan" edition (nd, 75¢, B&W, 16 pgs.) 3.00
1-($2.00, 52 pgs.)-Newsstand edition; Cable app. 4.00
1-($2.95, 52 pgs.)-Collectors ed.; embossed foil-c 5.00
2-14, 16-25: 2-Bound-in trading card sheet; Cable app. 2,3-Deathlok app. 8-red logo 3.00
8-($2.95)-Polybagged w/16 pg. Marvel Action Hour preview & acetate print; yellow logo 4.00
15 ($2.50)-Flip book 4.00

WAR MACHINE (Also see Dark Reign and Secret Invasion crossovers)
Marvel Comics: Feb, 2009 - No. 12, Feb, 2010 ($2.99)

1-12: 1-5-Pak-s/Manco-a/c; cyborg Jim Rhodes. 10-12-Dark Reign 3.00
1-Variant Titanium Man cover by Deodato 6.00

WAR MAN
Marvel Comics (Epic Comics): Nov, 1993 - No. 2, Dec, 1993 ($2.50, lim. series)

1,2 3.00

WAR OF KINGS
Marvel Comics: May, 2009 - No. 6, Oct, 2009 ($3.99, limited series)

1-6-Pelletier-a/Abnett & Lanning-s; Inhumans vs. the Shi'Ar 4.00
... Saga (2009, giveaway) synopsies of stories involving Kree, Shi'Ar, Inhumans, etc. 3.00
...: Savage World of Skaar 1 (8/09, $3.99) Gorgon & Starbolt land on Sakaar 4.00
...: Who Will Rule? 1 (11/09, $3.99) Pelletier-a; profile pages 4.00

WAR OF KINGS: ASCENSION
Marvel Comics: June, 2009 - No. 4, Sept, 2009 ($3.99, limited series)

1-4-Alves-a/Abnett & Lanning-s; Darkhawk app. 4.00

WAR OF KINGS: DARKHAWK (Leads into War Of Kings: Ascension limited series)
Marvel Comics: Apr, 2009 - No. 2, May, 2009 ($3.99, limited series)

1,2-Cebulski-s/Tolibao & Dazo-a/Peterson-c; r/Darkhawk #1,2 (1991) origin 4.00

WAR OF KINGS: WARRIORS
Marvel Comics: Sept, 2009 - No. 2, Oct, 2009 ($3.99, limited series)

1,2-Prequel to x-over; Gage-s/Asrar & Magno-a 4.00

WAR OF THE GODS
DC Comics: Sept, 1991 - No. 4, Dec, 1991 ($1.75, limited series)

1-4: Perez layouts, scripts & covers. 1-Contains free mini posters (Robin, Deathstroke). 2-4-Direct sale versions include 4 pin-ups printed on cover stock plus different-c 4.00

WAR OF THE GREEN LANTERNS: AFTERMATH
DC Comics: Sept, 2011 - No. 2, Oct, 2011 ($3.99, limited series)

1,2: 1-Bedard-s/Sepulveda & Kirkham-a. 2-Getty & Smith-a 4.00

WAR OF THE UNDEAD
IDW Publishing: Jan, 2007 - No. 3, Apr, 2007 ($3.99, limited series)

1-3-Bryan Johnson-s/Walter Flanagan-a 4.00

WAR OF THE WORLDS, THE
Caliber: 1996 - No. 5 ($2.95, B&W, 32 pgs.)(Based on H. G. Wells novel)

1-5: 1-Randy Zimmerman scripts begin 3.00

WARP
First Comics: Mar, 1983 - No. 19, Feb, 1985 ($1.00/$1.25, Mando paper)

1-Sargon-Mistress of War app.; Brunner-c/a thru #9 4.00
2-19: 2-Faceless Ones begin. 10-New Warp advs., & Outrider begin 3.00
Special 1-3: 1(7/83, 36 pgs.)-Origin Chaos-Prince of Madness; origin of Warp Universe begins, ends #3. 2(1/84)-Lord Cumulus vs. Sargon Mistress of War ($1.00). 3(6/84)-Chaos-Prince of Madness 3.00

WARPATH (Indians on the...)
Key Publications/Stanmor: Nov, 1954 - No. 3, Apr, 1955

	GD 2.0	VG 4.0	FN 6.0	VF 8.0	VF/NM 9.0	NM- 9.2
1	11	22	33	62	86	110
2,3	8	16	24	40	50	60

WARPED
Empire Entertainment (Solson): Jun, 1990 - No. 2, Oct-Nov, 1990 (B&W mag)

1,2 3.00

WARP GRAPHICS ANNUAL
WaRP Graphics: Dec, 1985; 1988 ($2.50)

1-Elfquest, Blood of the Innocent, Thunderbunny & Myth Adventures 5.00
1 (1988) 4.00

WARREN PRESENTS
Warren Publications: Jan, 1979 - No. 14, Nov, 1981(B&W magazine)

	GD 2.0	VG 4.0	FN 6.0	VF 8.0	VF/NM 9.0	NM- 9.2
1-Eerie, Creepy, & Vampirella-r; Ring of the Warlords; Merlin-s; Dax-s; Sanjulian-c	3	6	9	15	21	26
2-6(10/79): 2-The Rook. 3-Alien Invasions Comix. 4-Movie Aliens. 5-Dracula '79. 6-Strange Stories of Vampires Comix	2	4	6	9	13	16
8(10/80)-r/1st app. Pantha from Vamp. #30	2	4	6	11	16	20
9(11/80) Empire Encounters Comix	2	4	6	10	14	18
13(10/81),14(11/81):13-Sword and Sorcery Comix	3	6	9	14	19	24
(#7,10,11,12 may not exist, or may be a Special below)						
Special-Alien Collectors Edition (1979)	3	6	9	14	19	24
Special-Close Encounters of the Third Kind (1978)	2	4	6	9	13	16
Special-Lord of the Rings (6/79)	3	6	9	18	28	38
Special-Meteor (1/80)	2	4	6	9	13	16
Special-Moonraker/James Bond (10/79)	2	4	6	9	13	16
Special-Star Wars (1977)	3	6	9	18	28	38

WAR REPORT
Ajax/Farrell Publications (Excellent Publ.): Sept, 1952 - No. 5, May, 1953

	GD 2.0	VG 4.0	FN 6.0	VF 8.0	VF/NM 9.0	NM- 9.2
1	15	30	45	86	133	180
2-Flame thrower w/burning bodies on-c	19	38	57	111	176	240
3,5	10	20	30	54	72	90
4-Used in **POP**, pg. 94	10	20	30	58	79	100

WARRIOR (Wrestling star)
Ultimate Creations: May, 1996 - No. 4, 1997 ($2.95)

1-4: Warrior scripts; Callahan-c/a. 3-Wraparound-c. 4-Warrior #3 in indicia; pin-ups 3.00
1-Variant-c. 5.00
X-Mas (11/96, $3.50) listed as "No. 3" in indicia; pin-ups by various; Quesada-c 4.00

WARRIOR COMICS
H.C. Blackerby: 1945 (1930s DC reprints)

	GD 2.0	VG 4.0	FN 6.0	VF 8.0	VF/NM 9.0	NM- 9.2
1-Wing Brady, The Iron Man, Mark Markon	21	42	63	126	206	285

WARRIOR OF WAVERLY STREET, THE
Dark Horse Comics: Nov, 1996 - No. 2, Dec, 1996 ($2.95, mini-series)

1,2-Darrow-c 3.00

WARRIORS
CFD Productions: 1993 (B&W, one-shot)

	GD 2.0	VG 4.0	FN 6.0	VF 8.0	VF/NM 9.0	NM- 9.2
1-Linsner, Dark One-a	2	4	6	10	14	18

WARRIORS, THE: OFFICIAL MOVIE ADAPTATION (Based on the 1979 movie)
Dabel Brothers Publishing/Dynamite Ent.: Feb, 2009 - No. 5, 2010 ($3.99, limited series)

1-5: 1-Three covers plus wraparound photo-c; Dibari-a. 3-Eric Powell-c 4.00
...: Jailbreak 1 (7/09, $3.99) Apon & Herman-a 4.00

WARRIORS OF MARS (Also see Warlord of Mars titles)
Dynamite Entertainment: 2012 - No. 5, 2012 ($3.99, limited series)

1-5-Gullivar Jones visits Barsoom; Jusko-c 4.00

WARRIORS OF PLASM (Also see Plasm)
Defiant: Aug, 1993 - No. 13, Aug, 1995 ($2.95/$2.50)

1-4: Shooter-scripts; Lapham-c/a: 1-1st app. Glory. 4-Bound-in fold-out poster 4.00
5-7,10-13: 5-Begin $2.50-c. 13-Schism issue 3.00
8,9-($2.75, 44 pgs.) 4.00
The Collected Edition (2/94, $9.95)-r/Plasm #0, WOP #1-4 & Splatterball 10.00

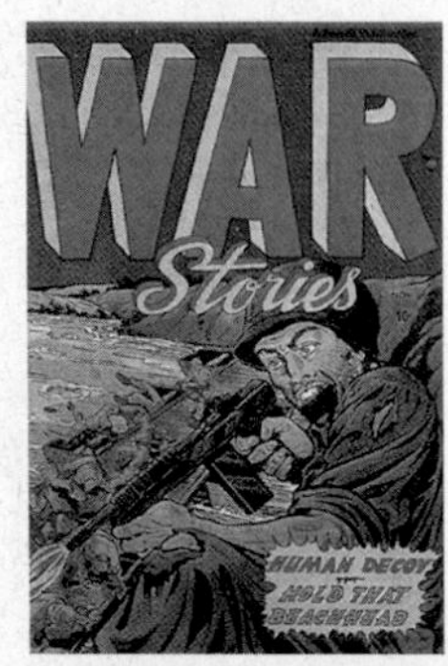

War Stories #2 © AJAX

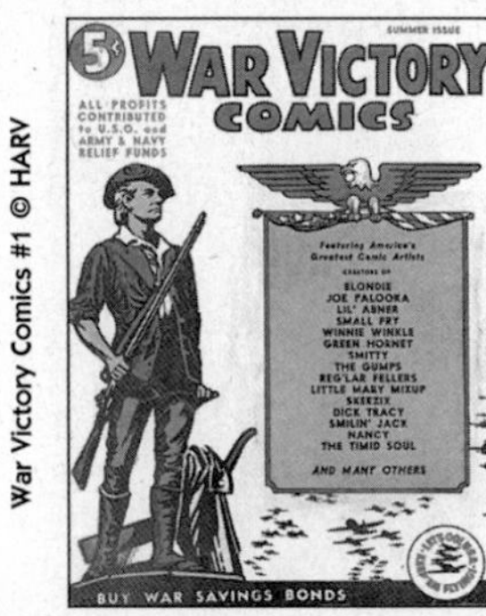

War Victory Comics #1 © HARV

Watchmen #3 © DC

	GD 2.0	VG 4.0	FN 6.0	VF 8.0	VF/NM 9.0	NM- 9.2

WARRIORS THREE (Fandral, Volstagg, and Hogun from Thor)
Marvel Comics: Jan, 2011 - No. 4, Apr, 2011 ($3.99, limited series)
1-4-Bill Willingham-s/Neil Edwards-a. 2,4-Conner-c 4.00

WAR ROMANCES (See True...)

WAR SHIPS
Dell Publishing Co.: 1942 (36 pgs.)(Similar to Large Feature Comics)
nn-Cover by McWilliams; contains photos & drawings of U.S. war ships
18 36 54 107 169 230

WAR STORIES (Formerly War Comics)
Dell Publ. Co.: No. 5, 1942(nd); No. 6, Aug-Oct, 1942 - No. 8, Feb-Apr, 1943
5-Origin The Whistler 30 60 90 177 289 400
6-8: 6-8-Night Devils app. 8-Painted-c 22 44 66 132 216 300

WAR STORIES (Korea)
Ajax/Farrell Publications (Excellent Publ.): Sept, 1952 - No. 5, May, 1953
1 15 30 45 86 133 180
2 10 20 30 54 72 90
3-5 9 18 27 52 69 85

WAR STORIES (See Star Spangled...)

WAR STORY
DC Comics (Vertigo): Nov, 2001 - Apr, 2003 ($4.95, series of World War II one-shots)
...: Archangel (4/03) Ennis-s/Erskine-a 5.00
...: Condors (3/03) Ennis-s/Ezquerra-a 5.00
...: D-Day Dodgers (12/01) Ennis-s/Higgins-a 5.00
...: J For Jenny (2/03) Ennis-s/Lloyd-a 5.00
...: Johann's Tiger (11/01) Ennis-s/Weston-a 5.00
...: Nightingale (2/02) Ennis-s/Lloyd-a 5.00
...: Screaming Eagles (1/02) Ennis-s/Gibbons-a 5.00
...: The Reivers (1/03) Ennis-s/Kennedy-a 5.00
Vol. 1 (2004, $19.95) r/Johann's Tiger, D-Day Dodgers, Screaming Eagles, Nightingale 20.00
Vol. 2 (2006, $19.99) r/J For Jenny, The Reivers, Condors, Archangel; Ennis afterword 20.00

WARSTRIKE
Malibu Comics (Ultraverse): May, 1994 - No. 7, Nov, 1995 ($1.95)
1-7: 1-Simonson-c 3.00
1-Ultra 5000 Limited silver foil 6.00
Giant Size 1 (12/94, $2.50, 44pgs.)-Prelude to Godwheel 4.00

WART AND THE WIZARD (See The Sword & the Stone under Movie Comics)
Gold Key: Feb, 1964 (Walt Disney)(Characters from Sword in the Stone movie)
1 (10102-402) 4 8 12 27 44 60

WAR THAT TIME FORGOT, THE
DC Comics: Jul, 2008 - No. 12, Jun, 2009 ($2.99, limited series)
1-12: 1-Bruce Jones-s/Al Barrionuevo-a/Neal Adams-c; Enemy Ace app. 3.00
... Vol. 1 TPB (2009, $17.99) r/#1-6 18.00
... Vol. 2 TPB (2009, $17.99) r/#7-12 18.00

WARTIME ROMANCES
St. John Publishing Co.: July, 1951 - No. 18, Nov, 1953
1-All Baker-c/a 58 116 174 371 636 900
2-All Baker-c/a 40 80 120 246 411 575
3,4-All Baker-c/a 39 78 117 240 395 550
5-8-Baker-c/a(2-3) each 39 78 117 231 378 525
9,11,12,16,18: Baker-c/a each. 9-Two signed stories by Estrada
34 68 102 199 325 450
10,13-15,17-Baker-c only 29 58 87 170 278 385

WAR VICTORY ADVENTURES (#1 titled War Victory Comics)
U.S. Treasury Dept./War Victory/Harvey Publ.: Sum, 1942 - No. 3, Wint, 1943-44 (5¢/10¢)
1-(5¢)(Promotion of Savings Bonds)-Featuring America's greatest comic art by top syndicated cartoonists; Blondie, Joe Palooka, Green Hornet, Dick Tracy, Superman, Gumps, etc.; (36 pgs.); all profits were contributed to U.S.O. & Army/Navy relief funds
50 100 150 315 533 750
2-(10¢) Battle of Stalingrad story; Powell-a (8/43); flag & WWII Japanese-c
58 116 174 371 636 900
3-(10¢) Capt. Red Cross-c & text only; WWII Nazi-c; Powell-a
47 94 141 296 498 700

WAR WAGON, THE (See Movie Classics)

WAR WINGS
Charlton Comics: Oct, 1968
1 3 6 9 14 20 26

WARWORLD!
Dark Horse Comics: Feb, 1989 ($1.75, B&W, one-shot)
1-Gary Davis sci/fi art in Moebius style 3.00

WASHABLE JONES AND THE SHMOO (Also see Al Capp's Shmoo)
Toby Press: June, 1953
1- "Super-Shmoo" 19 38 57 111 176 240

WASH TUBBS (See The Comics, Crackajack Funnies)
Dell Publishing Co.: No. 11, 1942 - No. 53, 1944
Four Color 11 (#1) 24 48 72 168 372 575
Four Color 28 (1943) 16 32 48 110 243 375
Four Color 53 12 24 36 82 179 275

WASTELAND
DC Comics: Dec, 1987 - No. 18, May, 1989 ($1.75-$2.00 #13 on, mature)
1-5(4/88), 5(5/88), 6(5/88)-18: 13,15-Orlando-a 3.00
NOTE: ***Orlando** a-12, 13, 15. **Truman** a-10; c-13.*

WATCHMEN (Also see 2012-2013 Before Watchmen prequel titles)
DC Comics: Sept, 1986 - No. 12, Oct, 1987 (maxi-series)
1-Alan Moore scripts & Dave Gibbons-c/a in all 4 8 12 23 34 50
1-(2009, $1.50) Second printing 3.00
2-12 2 4 6 10 14 18
Hardcover Collection-Slip-cased-r/#1-12 w/new material; produced by Graphitti Designs 100.00
HC (2008, $39.99) recolored r/#1-12; design & promotional art; Moore & Gibbons intros 40.00
Trade paperback (1987, $14.95)-r/#1-12 25.00

WATER BIRDS AND THE OLYMPIC ELK (Disney)
Dell Publishing Co.: No. 700, Apr, 1956
Four Color 700-Movie 5 10 15 31 53 75

WATERWORLD: CHILDREN OF LEVIATHAN
Acclaim Comics: Aug, 1997 - No. 4, Nov, 1997 ($2.50, mini-series)
1-4 3.00

WAY OF THE RAT
CrossGeneration Comics: Jun, 2002 - No. 24, June, 2004 ($2.95)
1-24: 1-Dixon-s/ Jeff Johnson-a. 5-Whigham-a. 9,14-Luke Ross-a 3.00
Free Comic Book Day Special (6/03) reprints #1 w/features, interviews, CrossGen info 3.00
...: The Walls of Zhumar Vol. 1 (1/03, $15.95) r/#1-6 16.00
Vol. 2: The Dragon's Wake (2003, $15.95) r/#7-12 16.00

WEAPON X
Marvel Comics: Apr, 1994 ($12.95, one-shot)
nn-r/Marvel Comics Presents #72-84 13.00

WEAPON X
Marvel Comics: Mar, 1995 - No. 4, June, 1995 ($1.95)
1-Age of Apocalypse 4.00
2-4 3.00

WEAPON X
Marvel Comics: Nov, 2002 - No. 28, Nov, 2004 ($2.25/$2.99)
1-7: 1-Sabretooth-c/app.; Tieri-s/Jeanty-a 3.00
8-28: 8-Begin $2.99-c. 14-Invaders app. 15-Chamber joins. 16-18,21-25-Wolverine app. 3.00
Vol. 1: The Draft TPB (2003, $21.99) r/#1-5, #1/2 & The Draft one-shots 22.00
Vol. 2: The Underground TPB (2003, $19.99) r/#6-13 20.00
Wizard #1/2 (2002) 5.00

WEAPON X: DAYS OF FUTURE NOW
Marvel Comics: Sept, 2005 - No. 5, Jan, 2006 ($2.99, limited series)
1-5-Tieri-s/Sears-a; Chamber, Sauron & Fantomex app. 3.00
TPB (2006, $13.99) r/#1-5 14.00

WEAPON X: FIRST CLASS
Marvel Comics: Jan, 2009 - No. 3, Mar, 2009 ($3.99, limited series)
1-3:1-Sabretooth-c/app. 2-Deadpool-c/app. 4.00

WEAPON X NOIR
Marvel Comics: May, 2010 ($3.99, one-shot)
1-Dennis Calero-s/a; C.P. Smith-c 4.00

WEAPON X: THE DRAFT (Leads into 2002 Weapon X series)
Marvel Comics: Oct, 2002 ($2.25, one-shots)
...Kane 1- JH Williams-c/Raimondi-a 3.00
...Marrow 1- JH Williams-c/Badeaux-a 3.00
...Sauron 1- JH Williams-c/Kerschl-a; Emma Frost app. 3.00
...Wild Child 1- JH Williams-c/Van Sciver-a; Aurora (Alpha Flight) app. 3.00

Weapon Zero #9 © TCOW

Web of Evil #10 © CM

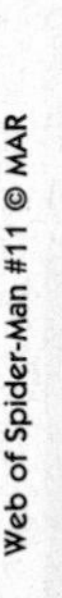
Web of Spider-Man #11 © MAR

	GD 2.0	VG 4.0	FN 6.0	VF 8.0	VF/NM 9.0	NM- 9.2

...Zero 1- JH Williams-c/Plunkett-a; Wolverine app. 3.00

WEAPON ZERO
Image Comics (Top Cow Productions): No. T-4(#1), June, 1995 - No. T-0(#5), Dec, 1995 ($2.50, limited series)

T-4(#1): Walt Simonson scripts in all. 5.00
T-3(#2) - T-1(#4) 4.00
T-0(#5) 3.00

WEAPON ZERO
Image Comics (Top Cow Productions): V2#1, Mar, 1996 - No. 15, Dec, 1997 ($2.50)

V2#1-Walt Simonson scripts. 4.00
2-14: 8-Begin Top Cow. 10-Devil's Reign 3.00
15-($3.50) Benitez-a 4.00

WEAPON ZERO/SILVER SURFER
Image Comics/Marvel Comics: Jan, 1997($2.95, one-shot)

1-Devil's Reign Pt. 1 3.00

WEASELGUY: ROAD TRIP
Image Comics: Sept, 1999 - No. 2 ($3.50, limited series)

1,2-Steve Buccellato-s/a 3.50
1-Variant-c by Bachalo 5.00

WEASELGUY/WITCHBLADE
Hyperwerks: July, 1998 ($2.95, one-shot)

1-Steve Buccellato-s/a; covers by Matsuda and Altstaetter 3.00

WEASEL PATROL SPECIAL, THE (Also see Fusion #17)
Eclipse Comics: Apr, 1989 ($2.00, B&W, one-shot)

1-Funny animal 3.00

WEAVEWORLD
Marvel Comics (Epic): Dec, 1991 - No. 3, 1992 ($4.95, lim. series, 68 pgs.)

1-3: Clive Barker adaptation 5.00

WEB, THE (Also see Mighty Comics & Mighty Crusaders)
DC Comics (Impact Comics): Sept, 1991 - No. 14, Oct, 1992 ($1.00)

1-14: 5-The Fly x-over 9-Trading card inside 5.00
Annual 1 (1992, $2.50, 68 pgs.)-With Trading card 5.00
NOTE: ***Gil Kane** c-5, 9, 10, 12-14. **Bill Wray** a(i)-1-9, 10(part).*

WEB, THE (Continued from The Red Circle)
DC Comics: Nov, 2009 - No. 10, Aug, 2010 ($3.99)

1-10: 1-Roger Robinson-a; The Hangman back-up feature. 3-Batgirl app. 5-Caldwell-a 4.00

WEB OF EVIL
Comic Magazines/Quality Comics Group: Nov, 1952 - No. 21, Dec, 1954

	GD	VG	FN	VF	VF/NM	NM-
1-Used in **SOTI**, pg. 388. Jack Cole-a; morphine use story	68	136	204	435	743	1050
2-4,6,7: 2,3-Jack Cole-a. 4,6,7-Jack Cole-c/a	45	90	135	284	480	675
5-Electrocution-c/story; Jack Cole-c/a	58	116	174	371	636	900
8-11-Jack Cole-a	41	82	123	256	428	600
12,13,15,16,19-21	30	60	90	177	289	400
14-Part Crandall-c; Old Witch swipe	32	64	96	188	307	425
17-Opium drug propaganda story	31	62	93	186	303	420
18-Acid-in-face story	32	64	96	188	307	425

NOTE: ***Jack Cole** a(2 each)-2, 6, 8, 9. **Cuidera** c-1-21i. **Ravielli** a-13.*

WEB OF HORROR
Major Magazines: Dec, 1969 - No. 3, Apr, 1970 (Magazine)

	GD	VG	FN	VF	VF/NM	NM-
1-Jeff Jones painted-c; Wrightson-a, Kaluta-a	8	16	24	51	96	140
2-Jones painted-c; Wrightson-a(2), Kaluta-a	7	14	21	44	82	120
3-Wrightson-c/a (1st published-c); Brunner, Kaluta, Bruce Jones-a	8	16	24	56	108	160

WEB OF MYSTERY
Ace Magazines (A. A. Wyn): Feb, 1951 - No. 29, Sept, 1955

	GD	VG	FN	VF	VF/NM	NM-
1	61	122	183	390	670	950
2-Bakerish-a	36	72	108	211	343	475
3-10: 4-Colan-a	32	64	96	188	307	425
11-18,20-26: 12-John Chilly's 1st cover art. 13-Surrealistic-c. 20-r/The Beyond #1	28	56	84	165	270	375
19-Reprints Challenge of the Unknown #6 used in N.Y. Legislative Committee	28	56	84	165	270	375
27-Bakerish-a(r/The Beyond #2); last pre-code ish	24	48	72	142	234	325
28,29: 28-All-r	20	40	60	115	185	250

NOTE: *This series was to appear as "Creepy Stories", but title was changed before publication. **Cameron** a-6, 8, 11-13, 17-20, 22, 24, 25, 27; c-8, 13, 17. **Palais** a-28r. **Sekowsky** a-1-3, 7, 8, 11, 14, 21, 29. **Tothish** a-by **Bill** Discount #16. 29-all-r, 19-28-partial-r.*

WEB OF SCARLET SPIDER
Marvel Comics: Oct, 1995 - No. 4, Jan, 1996 ($1.95, limited series)

1-4: Replaces "Web of Spider-Man" 3.00

WEB OF SPIDER-MAN (Replaces Marvel Team-Up)
Marvel Comics Group: Apr, 1985 - No. 129, Sept, 1995

	GD	VG	FN	VF	VF/NM	NM-
1-Painted-c (5th app. black costume?)	2	4	6	10	14	18
2,3						6.00
4-8: 7-Hulk x-over; Wolverine splash						5.00
9-13: 10-Dominic Fortune guest stars; painted-c						4.00
14-17,19-28: 19-Intro Humbug & Solo						4.00
18-1st app. Venom (behind the scenes, 9/86)	1	2	3	5	6	8
29-Wolverine, new Hobgoblin (Macendale) app.	1	2	3	5	6	8
30-Origin recap The Rose & Hobgoblin I (entire book is flashback story); Punisher & Wolverine cameo						5.00
31,32-Six part Kraven storyline begins	1	3	4	6	8	10
33-37,39-47,49: 36-1st app. Tombstone						3.00
38-Hobgoblin app.; begin $1.00-c						4.00
48-Origin Hobgoblin II(Demogoblin) cont'd from Spectacular Spider-Man #147; Kingpin app.	1	2	3	5	7	9
50-($1.50, 52 pgs.)						4.00
51-58						3.00
59-Cosmic Spidey cont'd from Spect. Spider-Man						4.00
60-89,91-99,101-106: 66,67-Green Goblin (Norman Osborn) app. as a super-hero. 69,70-Hulk x-over. 74-76-Austin-c(i). 76-Fantastic Four x-over. 78-Cloak & Dagger app. 81-Origin/1st app. Bloodshed. 84-Begin 6 part Rose & Hobgoblin II storyline; last $1.00-c. 86-Demon leaves Hobgoblin; 1st Demogoblin. 93-Gives brief history of Hobgoblin. 93,94-Hobgoblin (Macendale) Reborn-c/story, parts 1,2; MoonKnight app. 94-Venom cameo. 95-Begin 4 part x-over w/Spirits of Venom w/Ghost Rider/Blaze/Spidey vs. Venom & Demogoblin (cont'd in Ghost Rider/Blaze #5,6). 96-Spirits of Venom part 3; painted-c. 101,103-Maximum Carnage x-over. 103-Venom & Carnage app. 104-106-Nightwatch back-up stories						3.00
90-($2.95, 52 pgs.)-Polybagged w/silver hologram-c, gatefold poster showing Spider-Man & Spider-Man 2099 (Williamson-i)						6.00
90-2nd printing; gold hologram-c						4.00
100-($2.95, 52 pgs.)-Holo-grafx foil-c; intro new Spider-Armor						4.00
107-111: 107-Intro Sandstorm; Sand & Quicksand app.						3.00
112-116, 118, 119, 121-124, 126-128: 112-Begin $1.50-c; bound-in trading card sheet. 113-Regular Ed.; Gambit & Black Cat app. 118-1st solo clone story; Venom app.						3.00
113-($2.95)-Collector's ed. polybagged w/foil-c; 16 pg. preview of Spider-Man cartoon & animation cel						4.00
117-($1.50)-Flip book; Power & Responsibility Pt.1						3.00
117-($2.95)-Collector's edition; foil-c; flip book						4.00
119-($6.45)-Direct market edition; polybagged w/ Marvel Milestone Amazing Spider-Man #150 & coupon for Amazing Spider-Man #396, Spider-Man #53, & Spectacular Spider-Man #219.						7.00
120 ($2.25)-Flip book w/ preview of the Ultimate Spider-Man						4.00
125 ($3.95)-Holodisk-c; Gwen Stacy clone						5.00
125,129: 125 ($2.95)-Newsstand. 129-Last issue						4.00
#129.1, #129.2 (both 10/12, $2.99) Brooklyn Avengers app.; Damion Scott-a						3.00
Annual 1 (1985)						5.00
Annual 2 (1986)-New Mutants; Art Adams-a	1	2	3	5	6	8
Annual 3-10 ('87-'94, 68 pgs.): 4-Evolutionary War x-over. 5-Atlantis Attacks; Captain Universe by Ditko (p) & Silver Sable stories; F.F. app. 6-Punisher back-up plus Capt. Universe by Ditko; G. Kane-a. 7-Origins of Hobgoblin I, Hobgoblin II, Green Goblin I & II & Venom; Larsen/Austin-c. 9-Bagged w/card						4.00
Super Special 1 (1995, $3.95)-flip book						4.00

NOTE: ***Art Adams** a-Annual 2. **Byrne** c-3-6. **Chaykin** c-10. **Mignola** a-Annual 2. **Vess** c-1, 8, Annual 1, 2. **Zeck** a-6i, 31, 32; c-31, 32.*

WEB OF SPIDER-MAN (Anthology)
Marvel Comics: Dec, 2009 - No. 12, Nov, 2010 ($3.99)

1-12: 1-Spider-Girl app. thru #7; Ben Reilly app. 2-6-Origins of villains retold. 7-Kraven origin; Paper Doll app.; Mahfood-a. 9-11-Jackpot back-up; Takeda-a. 11,12-Black Cat app. 4.00

WEBSPINNERS: TALES OF SPIDER-MAN
Marvel Comics: Jan, 1999 - No. 18, Jun, 2000 ($2.99/$2.50)

1-DeMatteis-s/Zulli-a; back-up story w/Romita Sr. art 4.00
1-($6.95) DF Edition 7.00
2,3: 2-Two covers 3.00
4-11,13-18: 4,5-Giffen-a; Silver Surfer-c/app. 7-9-Kelly-s/Sears and Smith-a. 10,11-Jenkins-s/Sean Phillips-a 3.00
12-($3.50) J.G. Jones-c/a; Jenkins-s 4.00

WEDDING BELLS

Wedding of Dracula #1 © MAR

Weird Chills #3 © Key Pub.

Weird Fantasy #8 © WMG

GD 2.0 VG 4.0 FN 6.0 VF 8.0 VF/NM 9.0 NM- 9.2

Quality Comics Group: Feb, 1954 - No. 19, Nov, 1956
1-Whitney-a 18 36 54 103 162 220
2 11 22 33 64 90 115
3-9: 8-Last precode (4/55) 10 20 30 54 72 90
10-Ward-a (9 pgs.) 15 30 45 85 130 175
11-14,17 9 18 27 50 65 80
15-Baker-c 14 28 42 82 121 160
16-Baker-c/a 16 32 48 94 147 200
18,19-Baker-a each 13 26 39 72 101 130

WEDDING OF DRACULA
Marvel Comics: Jan, 1993 ($2.00, 52 pgs.)
1-Reprints Tomb of Dracula #30,45,46 4.00

WEDNESDAY COMICS (Newspaper-style, twice folded pages on 20" x 14" newsprint)
DC Comics: Sept, 2009 - No. 12, Nov, 2009 ($3.99, weekly limited series)
1-12-Superman, Batman, Kamandi, Hawkman, Deadman, Green Lantern, Flash, Teen Titans, Metamorpho, Adam Strange, Supergirl, Metal Men, Wonder Woman, The Demon with Catwoman, Sgt. Rock; s-a/ by various incl. Ryan Sook, Joe Kubert, Gaiman, Allred, Risso, Kyle Baker, Paul Pope, Conner, Simonson, Garcia-Lopez, Stelfreeze, Bermejo 4.00

WEEKENDER, THE (Illustrated...)
Rucker Pub. Co.: V1#1, Sept, 1945? - V1#4, Nov, 1945; V2#1, Jan, 1946 - V2#3, Aug, 1946 (52 pgs.)
V1#1-4: 1-Same-c as Zip Comics #45, inside-c and back-c blank; Steel Sterling, Senor Banana, Red Rube and Ginger. 2-Capt. Victory on-c. 3-Super hero-c; Mr. E, Dan Hastings, Sky Chief and the Echo. 4-Same-c as Punch Comics #10 (9/44); r/Hale the Magician (7 pgs.) & r/Mr. E (8 pgs.-Lou Fine? or Gustavson?) plus 3 humor strips & many B&W photos & r/newspaper articles plus cheesecake photos of Hollywood stars
22 44 66 132 216 300
V2#1-Same-c as Dynamic Comics #11; 36 pgs. comics, 16 in newspaper format with photos; partial Dynamic Comics reprints; 4 pgs. of cels from the Disney film Pinocchio; Little Nemo story by Winsor McCay, Jr.; Jack Cole-a 30 60 90 177 289 400
V2#2,3: 2-Same-c as Dynamic Comics #9 by Raboy; Dan Hastings (Tuska), Rocket Boy, The Echo, Lucky Coyne. 3-Humor-c by Boddington?; Dynamic Man, Ima Slooth, Master Key, Dynamic Boy, Captain Glory 22 44 66 132 216 300

WEIRD
Eerie Publications: V1#10, 1/66 - V8#6, 12/74; V9#1, 1/75 - V14#3, Nov, 1981 (Magazine) (V1-V8: 52 pgs.; V9 on: 68 pgs.)
V1#10(#1)-Intro. Morris the Caretaker of Weird (ends V2#10); Burgos-a
8 16 24 54 102 150
11,12 5 10 15 35 63 90
V2#1-4(10/67), V3#1(1/68), V2#6(4/68)-V2#7,9,10(12/68)
5 10 15 35 63 90
V2#8-r/Ditko's 1st story/Fantastic Fears #5 6 12 18 40 73 105
V3#1(2/69)-V3#4 5 10 15 33 57 80
V3#5(12/69)-Rulah reprint; "Rulah" changed to "Pulah", LSD story reprinted in Horror Tales V4#4, Tales From the Tomb V2#4, & 20 5 10 15 33 57 80
V4#1-6('70), V5#1-6('71), V6#1-7('72), V7#1-7('73), V8#1-3, V8#4(8/74), V8#4(10/74), (V8#5 does not exist), V8#6('74), V9#1-4(1/75-'76), V10#1-3('77), V11#1-4('78), V12#1(2/79)-V14#3(11/81) 5 10 15 31 53 75
NOTE: *There are two V8#4 issues (8/74 & 10/74). V9#4 (12/76) has a cover swipe from Horror Tales V5#1 (2/73). There are two V13#3 issues (6/80 & 9/80).*

WEIRD
DC Comics (Paradox Press): Sum, 1997 - No. 4 ($2.99, B&W, magazine)
1-4: 4-Mike Tyson-c 3.00

WEIRD, THE
DC Comics: Apr, 1988 - No. 4, July, 1988 ($1.50, limited series)
1-4: Wrightson-c/a in all 5.00

WEIRD ADVENTURES
P. L. Publishing Co. (Canada): May-June, 1951 - No. 3, Sept-Oct, 1951
1- "The She-Wolf Killer" by Matt Baker (6 pgs.) 64 128 192 393 689 985
2-Bondage/hypodermic panel 48 96 144 301 511 720
3-Male bondage/torture-c; severed head story 41 82 123 264 442 620

WEIRD ADVENTURES
Ziff-Davis Publishing Co.: No. 10, July-Aug, 1951
10-Painted-c 41 82 123 250 418 585

WEIRD CHILLS
Key Publications: July, 1954 - No. 3, Nov, 1954
1-Wolverton-r/Weird Mysteries No. 4; blood transfusion-c by Baily
129 258 387 826 1413 2000
2-Extremely violent injury to eye-c by Baily; Hitler story
142 284 426 909 1555 2200
3-Bondage E.C. swipe-c by Baily 54 108 162 343 574 825

WEIRD COMICS
Fox Features Syndicate: Apr, 1940 - No. 20, Jan, 1942
1-The Birdman, Thor, God of Thunder (ends #5), The Sorceress of Zoom, Blast Bennett, Typhon, Voodoo Man, & Dr. Mortal begin; George Tuska bondage-c
567 1134 1701 4139 7320 10,500
2-Lou Fine-c 271 542 813 1734 2967 4200
3,4: 3-Simon-c. 4-Torture-c 158 316 474 1011 1731 2450
5-Intro. Dart & sidekick Ace (8/40) (ends #20); bondage/hypo-c
161 322 483 1030 1765 2500
6,7-Dynamite Thor app. in each. 6-Super hero covers begin
98 196 294 627 1076 1525
8-Dynamo, the Eagle (11/40, early app.; see Science #1) & sidekick Buddy & Marga, the Panther Woman begin 97 194 291 621 1061 1500
9,10: 10-Navy Jones app. 79 158 237 502 864 1225
11-19: 16-Flag-c. 17-Origin The Black Rider. 61 122 183 390 670 950
20-Origin The Rapier; Swoop Curtis app; Churchill & Hitler-c
194 388 582 1242 2121 3000
NOTE *Cover features: Sorceress of Zoom-4; Dr. Mortal-5; Dart & Ace-6-13, 15; Eagle-14, 16-20.*

WEIRD FANTASY (Formerly A Moon, A Girl, Romance; becomes Weird Science-Fantasy #23 on)
E. C. Comics: No. 13, May-June, 1950 - No. 22, Nov-Dec, 1953
13(#1) (1950) 217 434 651 1736 2768 3800
14-Necronomicon story; Cosmic Ray Bomb explosion-c/story by Feldstein; Feldstein & Gaines star 109 218 327 872 1386 1900
15,16: 16-Used in **SOTI**, pg. 144 80 160 240 640 1020 1400
17 (1951) 59 118 177 472 749 1025
6-10: 6-Robot-c 50 100 150 400 638 875
11-13 (1952): 11-Feldstein bio. 12-E.C. artists cameo; Orlando bio. 13-Anti-Wertham "Cosmic Correspondence" 41 82 123 328 527 725
14-Frazetta/Williamson(1st team-up at E.C.)/Krenkel-a (7 pgs.); Orlando draws E.C. staff
51 102 153 408 654 900
15-Williamson/Evans-a(3), 4,3,&7 pgs. 43 86 129 344 547 750
16-19-Williamson/Krenkel-a in all. 17-Feldstein dinosaur-c; classic sci-fi story "The Aliens". 18-Williamson/Feldstein-c; classic anti-prejudice story "Judgment Day". 19-Williamson bio.
40 80 120 320 510 700
20-Frazetta/Williamson-a (7 pgs.); contains house ad for original, uncensored cover to Vault of Horror #32 (meat cleaver in forehead) 44 88 132 352 564 775
21-Frazetta/Williamson-c & Williamson/Krenkel-a 60 120 180 480 765 1050
22-Bradbury adaptation 33 66 99 264 420 575
NOTE: ***Crandall** a-22. **Elder** a-17. **Feldstein** a-13(#1)-8; c-13(#1)-18 (#18 w/**Williamson**), 20. **Harrison/Wood** a-13. **Kamen** a-13(#1)-16, 18-22. **Krigstein** a-22. **Kurtzman** a-13(#1)-17(#5), 6. **Orlando** a-9-22 (2 stories in #16); c-19, 22. **Severin/Elder** a-18-21. **Wood** a-13(#1)-14, 17(2 stories ea. in #10-13). Ray Bradbury adaptations in #13,17-22. Canadian reprints exist; see Table of Contents.*

WEIRD FANTASY
Russ Cochran/Gemstone Publ.: Oct, 1992 - No. 22, Jan, 1998 ($1.50/$2.00/$2.50)
1-22: 1,2: 1,2-r/Weird Fantasy #13,14; Feldstein-c. 3-5-r/Weird Fantasy #15-17 4.00

WEIRD HORRORS (Nightmare #10 on)
St. John Publishing Co.: June, 1952 - No. 9, Oct, 1953
1-Tuska-a 68 136 204 435 743 1050
2,3: 3-Hashish story 37 78 117 240 395 550
4,5 36 72 108 211 343 475
6-Ekgren-c; atomic bomb story 68 136 204 435 743 1050
7-Ekgren-c; Kubert, Cameron-a 68 136 204 435 743 1050
8,9-Kubert-c/a 43 86 129 271 461 650
NOTE: ***Cameron** a-7, 9. **Finesque** a-1-5. **Forgione** a-6. **Morisi** a-3. Bondage c-8.*

WEIRD MYSTERIES
Gillmor Publications: Oct, 1952 - No. 12, Sept, 1954
1-Partial Wolverton-c swiped from splash page "Flight to the Future" in Weird Tales of the Future #2; "Eternity" has an Ingels swipe 129 258 387 826 1413 2000
2- "Robot Woman" by Wolverton; Bernard Baily-c reprinted in Mister Mystery #18; acid in face panel 181 362 543 1158 1979 2800
3,6: Both have decapitation-c 87 174 261 553 952 1350
4- "The Man Who Never Smiled" (3 pgs.) by Wolverton; Classic B. Baily skull-c
271 542 813 1734 2967 4200
5-Wolverton story "Swamp Monster" (6 pgs.). Classic exposed brain-c
343 686 1029 2400 4200 6000
7-Used in **SOTI**, illo "Indeed", illo "Sex and blood" 123 246 369 787 1344 1900
8-Wolverton-c panel-r/#5; used in a '54 Readers Digest anti-comics article by T. E. Murphy entitled "For the Kiddies to Read" 73 146 219 467 796 1125
9-Excessive violence, gore & torture 66 132 198 419 722 1025

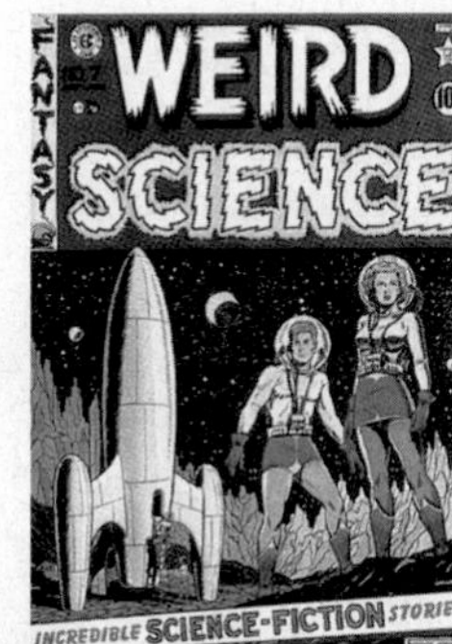

Weird Science #7 © WMG

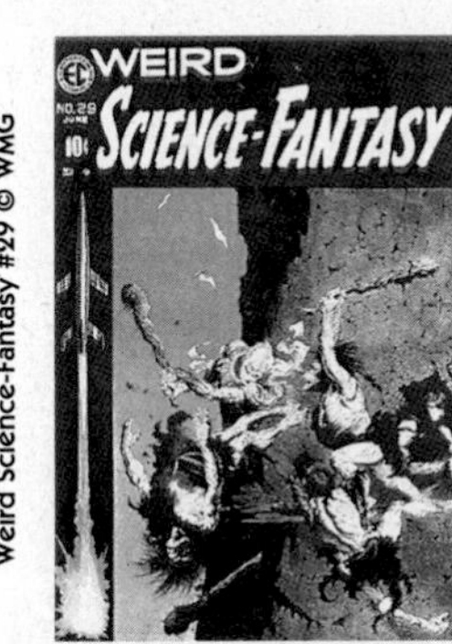

Weird Science-Fantasy #29 © WMG

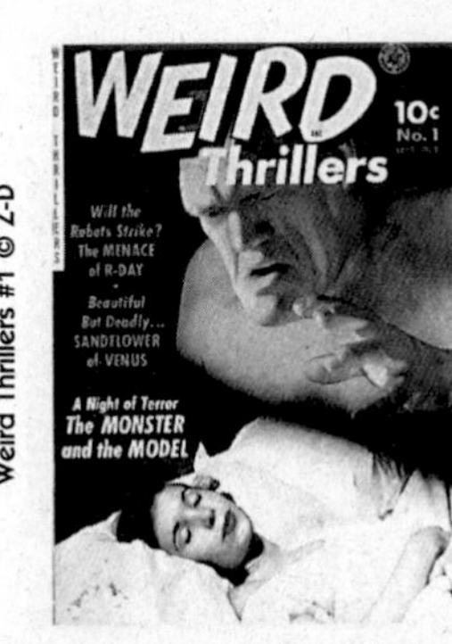

Weird Thrillers #1 © Z-D

GD 2.0 | VG 4.0 | FN 6.0 | VF 8.0 | VF/NM 9.0 | NM- 9.2

10-Silhouetted nudity panel 60 120 180 381 653 925
11,12: 12-r/Mr. Mystery #8(2), Weird Mysteries #3 & Weird Tales of the Future #6
58 116 174 371 636 900
NOTE: ***Baily*** *c-2-12. Anti-Wertham column in #5. #1-12 all have 'The Ghoul Teacher' (host).*

WEIRD MYSTERIES (Magazine)
Pastime Publications: Mar-Apr, 1959 (35¢, B&W, 68 pgs.)
1-Torres-a; E. C. swipe from Tales From the Crypt #46 by Tuska "The Ragman"
12 24 36 69 97 125

WEIRD MYSTERY TALES (See DC 100 Page Super Spectacular)

WEIRD MYSTERY TALES (See Cancelled Comic Cavalcade)
National Periodical Publications: July-Aug, 1972 - No. 24, Nov, 1975
1-Kirby-a; Wrightson splash pg. 5 10 15 33 57 80
2-Titanic-c/s 3 6 9 20 31 42
3,21: 21-Wrightson-c 3 6 9 17 26 35
4-10 3 6 9 14 19 24
11-20,22-24 2 4 6 11 16 20
NOTE: ***Alcala*** *a-5, 10, 13, 14.* ***Aparo*** *c-4.* ***Bailey*** *a-8.* ***Bolle*** *a-8?.* ***Howard*** *a-4.* ***Kaluta*** *a-4, 24; c-1.* ***G. Kane*** *a-10.* ***Kirby*** *a-1, 2p, 3p.* ***Nino*** *a-5, 6, 9, 13, 16, 21.* ***Redondo*** *a-9, 17.* ***Sparling*** *c-6.* ***Starlin*** *a-3?, 4.* ***Wood*** *a-23.*

WEIRD ROMANCE (Seduction of the Innocent #9)
Eclipse Comics: Feb, 1988 ($2.00, B&W)
1-Pre-code horror-r; Lou Cameron-r(2) 4.00

WEIRD SCIENCE (Formerly Saddle Romances) (Becomes Weird Science-Fantasy #23 on)
(Also see EC Archives • Weird Science)
E. C. Comics: No. 12, May-June, 1950 - No. 22, Nov-Dec, 1953
12(#1) (1950)-"Lost in the Microcosm" classic-c/story by Kurtzman; "Dream of Doom" stars Gaines & E.C. artists 217 434 651 1736 2768 3800
13-Flying saucers over Washington-c/story, 2 years before supposed UFO sighting
106 212 318 848 1349 1850
14-Robot, End of the World-c/story by Feldstein 97 194 291 776 1238 1700
15-War of Worlds-c/story (1950) 87 174 261 696 1111 1525
5-Atomic explosion-c 64 128 192 512 819 1125
6-8,10 56 112 168 448 712 975
9-Wood's 1st EC-c 63 126 189 504 802 1100
11-14 (1952) 11-Kamen bio. 12-Wood bio 41 82 123 328 527 725
15-18-Williamson/Krenkel-a in each; 15-Williamson-a. 17-Used in **POP**, pgs. 81,82. 18-Bill Gaines doll app. in story 43 86 129 344 547 750
19,20-Williamson/Frazetta-a (7 pgs. each). 19-Used in **SOTI**, illo "A young girl on her wedding night stabs her sleeping husband to death with a hatpin..." 19-Bradbury bio.
53 106 159 504 715 925
21-Williamson/Frazetta-a (6 pgs.); Wood draws E.C. staff; Gaines & Feldstein app. in story
53 106 159 504 715 925
22-Williamson/Frazetta/Krenkel-a (8 pgs.); Wood draws himself in his story (last pg. & panel) 53 106 159 504 715 925
NOTE: ***Elder*** *a-14, 19.* ***Evans*** *a-22.* ***Feldstein*** *a-12(#1)-8; c-12(#1)-8, 11.* ***Ingels*** *a-15.* ***Kamen*** *a-12(#1)-13, 15-18, 20, 21.* ***Kurtzman*** *a-12(#1)-7.* ***Orlando*** *a-10-22.* ***Wood*** *a-12(#1), 13(#2), 5-22 (#9, 10, 12, 13 all have 2* ***Wood*** *stories); c-9, 10, 12-22. Canadian reprints exist; see Table of Contents. Ray Bradbury adaptations in #17-22.*

WEIRD SCIENCE
Gladstone Publishing: Sept, 1990 - No. 4, Mar, 1991 ($1.95/$2.00, 68 pgs.)
1-4: Wood-c(r); all reprints in each 5.00

WEIRD SCIENCE (Also see EC Archives • Weird Science)
Russ Cochran/Gemstone Publishing: Sept, 1992 - No. 22, Dec, 1997 ($1.50/$2.00/$2.50)
1-22: 1,2: r/Weird Science #12,13 w/original-c. ,4-r/#14,15. 5-7-w/original-c 4.00

WEIRD SCIENCE-FANTASY (Formerly Weird Science & Weird Fantasy)
(Becomes Incredible Science Fiction #30)
E. C. Comics: No. 23 Mar, 1954 - No. 29, May-June, 1955 (#23,24: 15¢)
23-Williamson, Wood-a; Bradbury adaptation 39 78 117 312 494 675
24-Williamson & Wood-a; Harlan Ellison's 1st professional story, "Upheaval!", later adapted into a short story as "Mealtime", and then into a TV episode of Voyage to the Bottom of the Sea as "The Price of Doom" 39 78 117 312 494 675
25-Williamson dinosaur-c; Williamson/Torres/Krenkel-a plus Wood-a; Bradbury adaptation and fan letter; cover price back to 10¢ 42 84 126 336 536 735
26-Flying Saucer Report; Wood, Crandall-a; A-bomb panels
40 80 120 320 510 700
27-Adam Link/I Robot series begins 39 78 117 312 494 675
28-Williamson/Krenkel/Torres-a; Wood-a 39 78 117 312 499 685
29-Classic Frazetta-c; Williamson/Krenkel & Wood-a; Adam Link/I Robot series concludes; last pre-code issue; new logo 137 274 411 1096 1748 2400
NOTE: ***Crandall*** *a-26, 27, 29.* ***Evans*** *a-26.* ***Feldstein*** *c-24, 26, 28.* ***Kamen*** *a-27, 28.* ***Krigstein*** *a-23-25.* ***Orlando*** *a-in all.* ***Wood*** *a-in all; c-23, 27. The cover to #29 was originally intended for Famous Funnies #217 (Buck Rogers), but was rejected for being "too violent."*

WEIRD SCIENCE-FANTASY
Russ Cochran/Gemstone Publishing: Nov, 1992 - No. 7, May , 1994 ($1.50/$2.00/$2.50)
1-7: 1,2: r/Weird Science-Fantasy #23,24. 3-7 r/#25-29 4.00

WEIRD SCIENCE-FANTASY ANNUAL
E. C. Comics: 1952, 1953 (Sold thru the E. C. office & on the stands in some major cities) (25¢, 132 pgs.)
1952-Feldstein-c 284 568 852 1818 3109 4400
1953-Feldstein-c 168 336 504 1260 1930 2600
NOTE: *The 1952 annual contains books cover-dated in 1951 & 1952, and the 1953 annual from 1952 & 1953. Contents of each annual may vary in same year.*

WEIRD SECRET ORIGINS
DC Comics: Oct, 2004 ($5.95, square-bound, one-shot)
nn-Reprints origins of Dr. Fate, Spectre, Congorilla, Metamorpho, Animal Man & others 6.00

WEIRD SUSPENSE
Atlas/Seaboard Publ.: Feb, 1975 - No. 3, July, 1975
1-3: 1-Tarantula begins. 3-Freidrich-s 2 4 6 10 14 18
NOTE: ***Boyette*** *a-1-3.* ***Buckler*** *c-1, 3.*

WEIRD SUSPENSTORIES
Superior Comics (Canada): Oct, 1951 - No. 3, Dec, 1951; No. 3, no date (EC reprints)
1-3,3(no date)-(Rare): 3(nd) reprints cover of Crime SuspenStories #3
800 1600 2400 - - -

WEIRD TALES ILLUSTRATED
Millennium Publications: 1992 - No. 2, 1992 ($2.95, high quality paper)
1,2-Bolton painted-c. 1-Adapts E.A. Poe & Harlan Ellison stories. 2-E.A. Poe & H.P. Lovecraft adaptations 4.00
1-($4.95, 52 pgs.)-Deluxe edition w/Tim Vigil-a not in regular #1; stiff-c; Bolton painted-c 6.00

WEIRD TALES OF THE FUTURE
S.P.M. Publ. No. 1-4/Aragon Publ. No. 5-8: Mar, 1952 - No. 8, July-Aug, 1953
1-Andru-a(2); Wolverton partial-c 116 232 348 742 1271 1800
2,3-Wolverton-c/a(3) each. 2- "Jumpin Jupiter" satire by Wolverton begins, ends #5
226 452 678 1446 2473 3500
4- "Jumpin Jupiter" satire, partial Wolverton-c 152 306 456 973 1662 2350
5-Wolverton-c/a(2); "Jumpin Jupiter" satire 226 452 678 1446 2473 3500
6-Bernard Baily-c 63 126 189 403 689 975
7- "The Mind Movers" from the art to Wolverton's "Brain Bats of Venus" from Mr. Mystery #7 which was cut apart, pasted up, partially redrawn, and rewritten by Harry Kantor, the editor; Baily-c 155 310 465 992 1696 2400
8-Reprints Weird Mysteries #1(10/52) minus cover; gory cover showing heart ripped out, by B. Baily 129 258 387 826 1413 2000

WEIRD TALES OF THE MACABRE (Magazine)
Atlas/Seaboard Publ.: Jan, 1975 - No. 2, Mar, 1975 (75¢, B&W)
1-Jeff Jones painted-c; Boyette-a 4 8 12 28 47 65
2-Boris Vallejo painted-c; Severin-a 5 10 15 32 53 75

WEIRD TERROR (Also see Horrific)
Allen Hardy Associates (Comic Media): Sept, 1952 - No. 13, Sept, 1954
1- "Portrait of Death", adapted from Lovecraft's "Pickman's Model"; lingerie panels, Hitler story 65 130 195 416 708 1000
2,3: 2-Text on Marquis DeSade, Torture, Demonology, & St. Elmo's Fire. 3-Extreme violence, whipping, torture; article on sin eating, dowsing
53 106 159 334 567 800
4-Dismemberment, decapitation, article on human flesh for sale, Devil, whipping
53 106 159 334 567 800
5-Article on body snatching, mutilation; cannibalism story
47 94 141 296 498 700
6-Dismemberment, decapitation, man hit by lightning
50 100 150 315 533 750
7-Body burning in fireplace-c 50 100 150 315 533 750
8,11: 8-Decapitation story; Ambrose Bierce adapt. 11-End of the world story w/atomic blast panels; Tothish-a by Bill Discount 47 94 141 296 498 700
9,10,13: 13-Severed head panels 40 80 120 246 411 575
12-Discount-a 40 80 120 246 411 575
NOTE: ***Don Heck*** *a-most issues; c-1-13.* ***Landau*** *a-6.* ***Morisi*** *a-2-5, 7, 9, 12.* ***Palais*** *a-1, 5, 6, 8(2), 10, 12.* ***Powell*** *a-10.* ***Ravielli*** *a-11.*

WEIRD THRILLERS
Ziff-Davis Publ. Co. (Approved Comics): Sept-Oct, 1951 - No. 5, Oct-Nov, 1952
(#2-5: painted-c)
1-Rondo Hatton photo-c 98 196 294 627 1076 1525
2-Toth, Anderson, Colan-a 68 136 204 438 749 1060
3-Two Powell, Tuska-a; classic-c; Everett-a 97 194 291 621 1061 1500
4-Kubert, Tuska-a 64 128 192 406 696 985

Weird War Tales #104 © DC

Weird Wonder Tales #17 © MAR

Welcome Back, Kotter #2 © Wolper

	GD 2.0	VG 4.0	FN 6.0	VF 8.0	VF/NM 9.0	NM- 9.2
5-Powell-a	58	116	174	371	636	900

NOTE: ***M. Anderson*** *a-2, 3.* ***Roussos*** *a-4. #2, 3 reprinted in Nightmare #10 & 13; #4, 5 reprinted in Amazing Ghost Stories #16 & #15.*

WEIRD VAMPIRE TALES (Comic magazine)
Modern Day Periodical Pub.: V3 #1, Apr, 1979 - V5 #3, Mar, 1982 (B&W)

	GD 2.0	VG 4.0	FN 6.0	VF 8.0	VF/NM 9.0	NM- 9.2
V3 #1 (4/79) First issue, no V1 or V2	4	8	12	25	40	55
V3 #2-4	3	6	9	19	30	40
V4 #2 (4/80), V4 #3 (7/80) (no V4 #1)	3	6	9	17	26	35
V5 #1 (1/81), V5 #2 (two issues, 4/81 & 8/81)	3	6	9	17	26	35
V5 #3 (3/82) Last issue; low print	3	6	9	21	33	45

WEIRD WAR TALES
National Periodical Publ./DC Comics: Sept-Oct, 1971 - No. 124, June, 1983 (#1-5: 52 pgs.)

	GD 2.0	VG 4.0	FN 6.0	VF 8.0	VF/NM 9.0	NM- 9.2
1-Kubert-a in #1-4,7; c-1-7	21	42	63	147	324	500
2,3-Drucker-a: 2-Crandall-a. 3-Heath-a	10	20	30	64	132	200
4,5: 5-Toth-a; Heath-a	8	16	24	54	102	150
6,7,9,10: 6,10-Toth-a. 7-Heath-a	6	12	18	37	66	95
8-Neal Adams-c/a(i)	6	12	18	41	76	110
11-20	4	8	12	22	35	48
21-35	3	6	9	16	24	32
36-(68 pgs.)-Crandall & Kubert-r/#2; Heath-r/#3; Kubert-c	3	6	9	18	28	38
37-50: 38,39-Kubert-c	2	4	6	10	14	18
51-63: 58-Hitler-c/app. 60-Hindenburg-c/s	2	4	6	9	13	16
64-Frank Miller-a (1st DC work)	5	10	15	31	53	75
65-67,69-89,91,92: 89-Nazi Apes-c/s.	2	4	6	8	10	12
68-Frank Miller-a (2nd DC work)	3	6	9	21	33	45
90-Hitler app.	2	4	6	8	11	14
93-Intro/origin Creature Commandos	2	4	6	8	11	14
94-Return of War that Time Forgot; dinosaur-c/s	2	4	6	10	14	18
95,96,98,102-123: 98-Sphinx-c. 102-Creature Commandos battle Hitler. 110-Origin/1st app. Medusa. 123-1st app. Captain Spaceman	2	4	6	8	10	12
97,99,100,101,124: 99-War that Time Forgot. 100-Creature Commandos in War that Time Forgot. 101-Intro/origin G.I. Robot	2	4	6	8	11	14

NOTE: ***Chaykin*** *a-76, 82.* ***Ditko*** *a-95, 99, 104-106.* ***Evans*** *c-73, 74, 83, 85.* ***Kane*** *c-116, 118.* ***Kubert*** *c-55, 58, 60, 62, 72, 75-81, 87, 88, 90-96, 100, 103, 104, 106, 107.* ***Newton*** *a-122.* ***Starlin*** *c-89.* ***Sutton*** *a-91, 92, 103.* ***Creature Commandos*** *-93, 97, 100, 102, 105, 108-112, 114, 116-119, 121, 124.* ***G.I. Robot*** *- 101, 108, 111, 113, 116-118, 120, 122.* ***War That Time Forgot*** *- 94, 99, 100, 103, 106, 109, 120.*

WEIRD WAR TALES
DC Comics (Vertigo): June, 1997 - No. 4, Sept, 1997 ($2.50)

	NM- 9.2
1-4-Anthology by various	3.00

WEIRD WAR TALES
DC Comics (Vertigo): April, 2000 ($4.95, one-shot)

	NM- 9.2
1-Anthology by various; last Biukovic-a	5.00

WEIRD WAR TALES
DC Comics: Nov, 2010 ($3.99, one-shot)

	NM- 9.2
1-Anthology by various incl. Cooke, Strnad, Pugh; Cooke-c	4.00

WEIRD WESTERN TALES (Formerly All-Star Western)
National Per. Publ./DC Comics: No. 12, June-July, 1972 - No. 70, Aug, 1980

	GD 2.0	VG 4.0	FN 6.0	VF 8.0	VF/NM 9.0	NM- 9.2
12-(52 pgs.)-3rd app. Jonah Hex; Bat Lash, Pow Wow Smith reprints; El Diablo by Neal Adams/Wrightson	12	24	36	82	179	275
13-Jonah Hex-c & 4th app.; Neal Adams-a	8	16	24	56	108	160
14-Toth-a	6	12	18	41	76	110
15-Adams-c/a; no Jonah Hex	4	8	12	28	47	65
16,17,19,20	4	8	12	28	47	65
18,29: 18-1st all Jonah Hex issue (7-8/73) & begins. 29-Origin Jonah Hex	6	12	18	37	66	95
21-28,30: Jonah Hex in all	4	8	12	23	37	50
31-38: Jonah Hex in all. 38-Last Jonah Hex	3	6	9	18	28	38
39-Origin/1st app. Scalphunter & begins	2	4	6	13	18	22
40-47,50-69: 64-Bat Lash-c/story	2	4	6	8	10	12
48,49: (44 pgs.)-1st & 2nd app. Cinnamon	2	4	6	8	11	14
70-Last issue	2	4	6	9	13	16

NOTE: ***Alcala*** *a-16, 17.* ***Evans*** *inks-39-48; c-39i, 40, 47.* ***G. Kane*** *a-15, 20.* ***Kubert*** *c-12, 33.* ***Starlin*** *c-44, 45.* ***Wildey*** *a-26. 48 & 49 are 44 pgs..*

WEIRD WESTERN TALES (Blackest Night crossover)
DC Comics: No. 71, March, 2010 ($2.99, one-shot)

	NM- 9.2
71-Jonah Hex, Scalphunter, Super-Chief, Firehair and Bat Lash rise as Black Lanterns	3.00

WEIRD WESTERN TALES
DC Comics (Vertigo): Apr, 2001 - No. 4, Jul, 2001 ($2.50, limited series)

	NM- 9.2
1-4-Anthology by various	3.00

WEIRD WONDER TALES
Marvel Comics Group: Dec, 1973 - No. 22, May, 1977

	GD 2.0	VG 4.0	FN 6.0	VF 8.0	VF/NM 9.0	NM- 9.2
1-Wolverton-r/Mystic #6 (Eye of Doom)	4	8	12	23	37	50
2-10	3	6	9	16	23	30
11-22: 16-18-Venus-r by Everett from Venus #19,18 & 17. 19-22-r/Dr. Droom (re-named Dr. Druid) by Kirby. 22-New art by Byrne	3	6	9	15	22	28
15-17-(30¢-c variants, limited distribution)(4-8/76)	4	8	12	23	37	50

NOTE: *All 1950s & early 1960s reprints.* ***Check*** *r-1.* ***Colan*** *r-17.* ***Ditko*** *r-4, 5, 10-13, 19-21.* ***Drucker*** *r-12, 20.* ***Everett*** *r-3(Spellbound #16), 6(Astonishing #10), 9(Adv. Into Mystery #5).* ***Heath*** *a-13r.* ***Heck*** *a-1or, 14r.* ***Gil Kane*** *c-1, 2, 10.* ***Kirby*** *r-4, 6, 10, 11, 13, 15-22; c-17, 19, 20.* ***Krigstein*** *r-19.* ***Kubert*** *r-22.* ***Maneely*** *r-8.* ***Mooney*** *r-7p.* ***Powell*** *r-3, 7.* ***Torres*** *r-7.* ***Wildey*** *r-2, 7.*

WEIRD WORLD OF JACK STAFF (See Jack Staff)
Image Comics: Feb, 2010 - Present ($3.50)

	NM- 9.2
1-6-Paul Grist-s/a. 2-Ian Churchill-c	3.50

WEIRD WORLDS (See Adventures Into...)

WEIRD WORLDS (Magazine)
Eerie Publications: V1#10(12/70), V2#1(2/71) - No. 4, Aug, 1971 (52 pgs.)

	GD 2.0	VG 4.0	FN 6.0	VF 8.0	VF/NM 9.0	NM- 9.2
V1#10-Sci-fi/horror	5	10	15	33	57	80
V2#1-4	5	10	15	30	50	70

WEIRD WORLDS (Also see Ironwolf: Fires of the Revolution)
National Periodical Publications: Aug-Sept, 1972 - No. 9, Jan-Feb, 1974; No. 10, Oct-Nov, 1974 (All 20¢ issues)

	GD 2.0	VG 4.0	FN 6.0	VF 8.0	VF/NM 9.0	NM- 9.2
1-Edgar Rice Burrough's John Carter Warlord of Mars & David Innes begin (1st DC app.); Kubert-c	3	6	9	15	22	28
2-4: 2-Infantino/Orlando-c. 3-Murphy Anderson-c. 4-Kaluta-a	2	4	6	10	14	18
5-7: .5-Kaluta-c. 7-Last John Carter.	2	4	6	8	11	14
8-10: 8-Iron Wolf begins by Chaykin (1st app.)	2	4	6	8	11	14

NOTE: ***Neal Adams*** *a-2i, 3i. John Carter by* ***Andersonin*** *#1-3.* ***Chaykin*** *c-7, 8.* ***Kaluta*** *a-4; c-4-6, 10.* ***Orlando*** *a-4i; c-2, 3, 4i.* ***Wrightson*** *a-2i, 4i.*

WEIRD WORLDS
DC Comics: Mar, 2011 - No. 6, Aug, 2011 ($3.99, limited series)

	NM- 9.2
1-6-Short stories of Lobo, Garbage Man and Tanga; Ordway-a; Maguire-s/a; Lopresti-s/a	4.00

WELCOME BACK, KOTTER (TV) (See Limited Collectors' Edition #57 for unpublished #11)
National Periodical Publ./DC Comics: Nov, 1976 - No. 10, Mar-Apr, 1978

	GD 2.0	VG 4.0	FN 6.0	VF 8.0	VF/NM 9.0	NM- 9.2
1-Sparling-a(p)	3	6	9	16	23	30
2-10: 3-Estrada-a	2	4	6	10	14	18

WELCOME SANTA (See March of Comics #63,183)

WELCOME TO HOLSOM
Gospel Publishing House: 2005 - Present (no cover price)

	NM- 9.2
1-12-Craig Schutt-s/Steven Butler-a	3.00

WELCOME TO THE LITTLE SHOP OF HORRORS
Roger Corman's Cosmic Comics: May, 1995 -No. 3, July, 1995 ($2.50, limited series)

	NM- 9.2
1-3	3.00

WELCOME TO TRANQUILITY
DC Comics (WildStorm): Feb, 2007 - No. 12, Jan, 2008 ($2.99)

	NM- 9.2
1-12: 1-Simone-s/Googe-a; two covers by Googe and Campbell. 8-Pearson-a	3.00
...: Armageddon 1 (1/08, $2.99) Gage-s/Googe-a	3.00
...: One Foot in the Grave 1-6 (7/10 - No. 6, 2/11, $3.99) Simone-s/Domingues-a	4.00
...: One Foot in the Grave TPB (2011, $17.99) r/mini-series #1-6	18.00
... Book One TPB (2008, $19.99) r/#1-6 and variant cover gallery	20.00
... Book Two TPB (2008, $19.99) r/#7-12; sketch pages	20.00

WELLS FARGO (See Tales of...)

WENDY AND THE NEW KIDS ON THE BLOCK
Harvey Comics: Mar, 1991 - No. 3, July, 1991 ($1.25)

	NM- 9.2
1-3	5.00

WENDY DIGEST
Harvey Comics: Oct, 1990 - No. 5, Mar, 1992 ($1.75, digest size)

	NM- 9.2
1-5	4.00

WENDY PARKER COMICS
Atlas Comics (OMC): July, 1953 - No. 8, July, 1954

	GD 2.0	VG 4.0	FN 6.0	VF 8.0	VF/NM 9.0	NM- 9.2
1	13	26	39	74	105	135
2	10	20	30	54	72	90
3-8	9	18	27	47	61	75

WENDY, THE GOOD LITTLE WITCH (TV)
Harvey Publ.: 8/60 - #82, 11/73; #83, 8/74 - #93, 4/76; #94, 9/90 - #97, 12/90

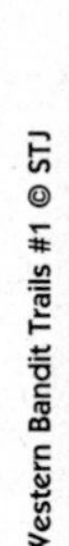
Werewolf By Night V2 #4 © MAR

Western Bandit Trails #1 © STJ

Western Comics #3 © DC

	GD 2.0	VG 4.0	FN 6.0	VF 8.0	VF/NM 9.0	NM- 9.2
1-Wendy & Casper the Friendly Ghost begin	29	58	87	209	467	725
2	12	24	36	84	185	285
3-5	9	18	27	62	126	190
6-10	7	14	21	44	82	120
11-20	5	10	15	34	60	85
21-30	4	8	12	27	44	60
31-50	3	6	9	17	26	35
51-64,66-69	2	4	6	13	18	22
65 (2/71)-Wendy origin.	3	6	9	16	24	32
70-74: All 52 pg. Giants	3	6	9	16	23	30
75-93	2	4	6	9	13	16
94-97 (1990, $1.00-c): 94-Has #194 on-c						5.00

(See Casper the Friendly Ghost #20 & Harvey Hits #7, 16, 21, 23, 27, 30, 33)

WENDY THE GOOD LITTLE WITCH (2nd Series)
Harvey Comics: Apr, 1991 - No. 15, Aug, 1994 ($1.00/$1.25 #7-11/$1.50 #12-15)

	GD	VG	FN	VF	VF/NM	NM-
1-15-Reprints Wendy & Casper stories. 12-Bunny app.						3.00

WENDY WITCH WORLD
Harvey Publications: 10/61; No. 2, 9/62 - No. 52, 12/73; No. 53, 9/74

	GD	VG	FN	VF	VF/NM	NM-
1-(25¢, 68 pg. Giants begin)	12	24	36	83	182	280
2-5	7	14	21	44	82	120
6-10	5	10	15	33	57	80
11-20	4	8	12	27	44	60
21-30	3	6	9	21	33	45
31-39: 39-Last 68 pg. issue	3	6	9	16	24	32
40-45: 52 pg. issues	2	4	6	13	18	22
46-53	2	4	6	9	13	16

WEREWOLF (Super Hero) (Also see Dracula & Frankenstein)
Dell Publishing Co.: Dec, 1966 - No. 3, April, 1967

	GD	VG	FN	VF	VF/NM	NM-
1-1st app.	4	8	12	23	37	50
2,3	3	6	9	16	23	30

WEREWOLF BY NIGHT (See Giant-Size..., Marvel Spotlight #2-4 & Power Record Comics)
Marvel Comics Group: Sept, 1972 - No. 43, Mar, 1977

	GD	VG	FN	VF	VF/NM	NM-
1-Ploog-a cont'd. from Marvel Spotlight #4	11	22	33	76	163	250
2	6	12	18	40	73	105
3-5	5	10	15	31	53	75
6-10	4	8	12	25	40	55
11-14,16-20	3	6	9	18	28	38
15-New origin Werewolf; Dracula-c/story cont'd from Tomb of Dracula #18; classic Ploog-c	4	8	12	28	47	65
21-31	3	6	9	14	20	26
32-Origin & 1st app. Moon Knight (8/75)	17	34	51	117	259	400
33-2nd app. Moon Knight	6	12	18	40	73	105
34,36,38-43	3	6	9	14	19	24
35-Starlin/Wrightson-c	3	6	9	16	23	30
37-Moon Knight app; part Wrightson-c	4	8	12	23	37	50
38,39-(30¢-c variants, limited distribution)(5,7/76)	4	8	12	23	37	50

NOTE: ***Bolle** a-6i. **G. Kane** a-11p, 12p; c-21, 22, 24-30, 34p. **Mooney** a-7i. **Ploog** 1-4p, 5, 6p, 7p, 13-16p; c-5-8, 13-16. **Reinman** a-8i. **Sutton** a(i)-9, 11, 16, 35.*

WEREWOLF BY NIGHT (Vol. 2, continues in Strange Tales #1 (9/98))
Marvel Comics Group: Feb, 1998 - No. 6, July, 1998 ($2.99)

	GD	VG	FN	VF	VF/NM	NM-
1-6-Manco-a: 2-Two covers. 6-Ghost Rider-c/app.						3.00

WEREWOLVES & VAMPIRES (Magazine)
Charlton Comics: 1962 (One Shot)

	GD	VG	FN	VF	VF/NM	NM-
1	9	18	27	58	114	170

WEREWOLVES ON THE MOON: VERSUS VAMPIRES
Dark Horse Comics: June, 2009 - No. 3 ($3.50, limited series)

	GD	VG	FN	VF	VF/NM	NM-
1,2-Dave Land-s & Fillbach Brothers-s/a						3.50

WEST COAST AVENGERS
Marvel Comics Group: Sept, 1984 - No. 4, Dec, 1984 (lim. series, Mando paper)

	GD	VG	FN	VF	VF/NM	NM-
1-Origin & 1st app. W.C. Avengers (Hawkeye, Iron Man, Mockingbird & Tigra)	1	2	3	5	6	8
2-4						5.00

WEST COAST AVENGERS (Becomes Avengers West Coast #48 on)
Marvel Comics Group: Oct, 1985 - No. 47, Aug, 1989

	GD	VG	FN	VF	VF/NM	NM-
V2#1						5.00
2-41						4.00
42-47: 42-Byrne-a(p)/scripts begin. 46-Byrne-c; 1st app. Great Lakes Avengers						4.00
Annual 1-3 (1986-1988): 3-Evolutionary War app.						5.00
Annual 4 (1989, $2.00)-Atlantis Attacks; Byrne/Austin-a						5.00

WESTERN ACTION
I. W. Enterprises: No. 7, 1964

	GD	VG	FN	VF	VF/NM	NM-
7-Reprints Cow Puncher #? by Avon	2	4	6	8	11	14

WESTERN ACTION
Atlas/Seaboard Publ.: Feb, 1975

	GD	VG	FN	VF	VF/NM	NM-
1-Kid Cody by Wildey & The Comanche Kid stories; intro. The Renegade	2	4	6	11	16	20

WESTERN ACTION THRILLERS
Dell Publishers: Apr, 1937 (10¢, square binding; 100 pgs.)

	GD	VG	FN	VF	VF/NM	NM-
1-Buffalo Bill, The Texas Kid, Laramie Joe, Two-Gun Thompson, & Wild West Bill app.	87	174	261	553	952	1350

WESTERN ADVENTURES COMICS (Western Love Trails #7 on)
Ace Magazines: Oct, 1948 - No. 6, Aug, 1949

	GD	VG	FN	VF	VF/NM	NM-
nn(#1)-Sheriff Sal, The Cross-Draw Kid, Sam Bass begin	21	42	63	122	199	275
nn(#2)(12/48)	13	26	39	74	105	135
nn(#3)(2/49)-Used in **SOTI**, pgs. 30,31	14	28	42	76	108	140
4-6	11	22	33	62	86	110

WESTERN BANDITS
Avon Periodicals: 1952 (Painted-c)

	GD	VG	FN	VF	VF/NM	NM-
1-Butch Cassidy, The Daltons by Larsen; Kinstler-a; c-part-r/paperback Avon Western Novel #1	17	34	51	98	154	210

WESTERN BANDIT TRAILS (See Approved Comics)
St. John Publishing Co.: Jan, 1949 - No. 3, July, 1949

	GD	VG	FN	VF	VF/NM	NM-
1-Tuska-a; Baker-c; Blue Monk, Ventrilo app.	30	60	90	177	289	400
2-Baker-c	24	48	72	140	230	320
3-Baker-c/a; Tuska-a	28	56	84	165	270	375

WESTERN COMICS (See Super DC Giant #15)
National Per. Publ: Jan-Feb, 1948 - No. 85, Jan-Feb, 1961 (1-27: 52pgs.)

	GD	VG	FN	VF	VF/NM	NM-
1-Wyoming Kid & his horse Racer, The Vigilante in "Jesse James Rides Again" (Meskin-a), Cowboy Marshal, Rodeo Rick begin	74	148	222	470	810	1150
2	36	72	108	211	343	475
3,4-Last Vigilante	32	64	96	188	307	425
5-Nighthawk & his horse Nightwind begin (not in #6); Captain Tootsie by Beck	27	54	81	158	259	360
6,7,9,10	21	42	63	122	199	275
8-Origin Wyoming Kid; 2 pg. pin-ups of rodeo queens	34	68	102	199	325	450
11-20	18	36	54	103	162	220
21-40: 24-Starr-a. 27-Last 52 pgs. 28-Flag-c	14	28	42	82	121	160
41,42,44-49: 49-Last precode issue (2/55)	14	28	42	80	115	150
43-Pow Wow Smith begins, ends #85	14	28	42	81	118	155
50-60	12	24	36	67	94	120
61-85-Last Wyoming Kid. 77-Origin Matt Savage Trail Boss. 82-1st app. Fleetfoot, Pow Wow's girlfriend	10	20	30	56	76	95

NOTE: ***G. Kane, Infantino** art in most. **Meskin** a-1-4. **Moreira** a-28-39. **Post** a-3-5.*

WESTERN CRIME BUSTERS
Trojan Magazines: Sept, 1950 - No. 10, Mar-Apr, 1952

	GD	VG	FN	VF	VF/NM	NM-
1-Six-Gun Smith, Wilma West, K-Bar-Kate, & Fighting Bob Dale begin; headlight-a	36	72	108	216	351	485
2	19	38	57	111	176	240
3-5: 3-Myron Fass-c	18	36	54	105	165	225
6-Wood-a	32	64	96	188	307	425
7-Six-Gun Smith by Wood	32	64	96	188	307	425
8	18	36	54	105	165	225
9-Tex Gordon & Wilma West by Wood; Lariat Lucy app.	32	64	96	188	307	425
10-Wood-a	29	58	87	172	281	390

WESTERN CRIME CASES (Formerly Indian Warriors #7,8; becomes The Outlaws #10 on)
Star Publications: No. 9, Dec, 1951

	GD	VG	FN	VF	VF/NM	NM-
9-White Rider & Super Horse; L. B. Cole-c	21	42	63	122	199	275

WESTERNER, THE (Wild Bill Pecos)
"Wanted" Comic Group/Toytown/Patches: No. 14, June, 1948 - No. 41, Dec, 1951 (#14-31: 52 pgs.)

	GD	VG	FN	VF	VF/NM	NM-
14	15	30	45	85	130	175
15-17,19-21: 19-Meskin-a	9	18	27	52	69	85
18,22-25-Krigstein-a	11	22	33	60	83	105
26(4/50)-Origin & 1st app. Calamity Kate, series ends #32; Krigstein-a						

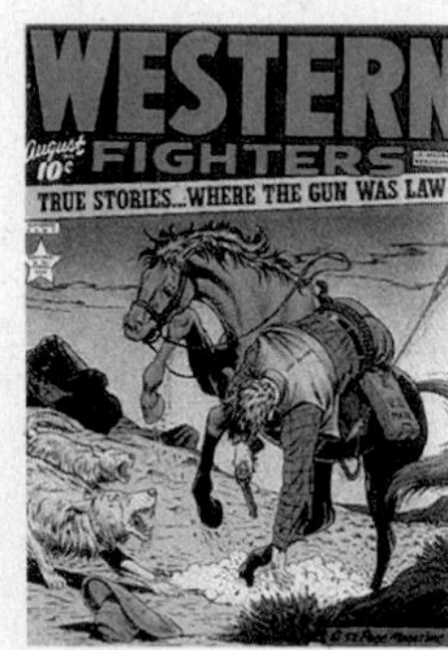

Western Fighters #7 © HILL

Western Hearts #5 © STD

Western Love #2 © PRIZE

	GD	VG	FN	VF	VF/NM	NM-
	2.0	4.0	6.0	8.0	9.0	9.2
	14	28	42	78	112	145
27-Krigstein-a(2)	13	26	39	74	105	135
28-41: 33-Quest app. 37-Lobo, the Wolf Boy begins	8	16	24	40	50	60

NOTE: ***Mort Lawrence** a-20-27, 29, 37, 39; c-19, 22-24, 26, 27. **Leav** c-14-18, 20, 31. **Syd Shores** a-39; c-34, 35, 37-41.*

WESTERNER, THE
Super Comics: 1964

	GD	VG	FN	VF	VF/NM	NM-
Super Reprint 15-17: 15-r/Oklahoma Kid #? 16-r/Crack West. #65; Severin-c; Crandall-r. 17-r/Blazing Western #2; Severin-c	2	4	6	8	11	14

WESTERN FIGHTERS
Hillman Periodicals/Star Publ.: Apr-May, 1948 - V4#7, Mar-Apr, 1953
(#1-V3#2: 52 pgs.)

	GD	VG	FN	VF	VF/NM	NM-
V1#1-Simon & Kirby-c	36	72	108	216	351	485
2-Not Kirby-a	14	28	42	80	115	150
3-Fuje-c	12	24	36	67	94	120
4-Krigstein, Ingels, Fuje-a	13	26	39	74	105	135
5,6,8,9,12	10	20	30	54	72	90
7,10-Krigstein-a	11	22	33	62	86	110
11-Williamson/Frazetta-a	30	60	90	177	289	400
V2#1-Krigstein-a	11	22	33	62	86	110
2-12: 4-Berg-a	8	16	24	44	57	70
V3#1-11,V4#1,4-7	8	16	24	42	54	65
12,V4#2,3-Krigstein-a	11	22	33	62	86	110
3-D 1(12/53, 25¢, Star Publ.)-Came w/glasses; L. B. Cole-c	36	72	108	211	343	475

NOTE: ***Kinstlerish** a-V2#6, 8, 9, 12; V3#2, 5-7, 11, 12; V4#1(plus cover). **McWilliams** a-11. **Powell** a-V2#2. **Reinman** a-1-12, V4#3. **Rowich** c-5, 6i. **Starr** a-5.*

WESTERN FRONTIER
P. L. Publishers: Apr-May, 1951 - No. 7, 1952

	GD	VG	FN	VF	VF/NM	NM-
1	14	28	42	76	108	140
2	8	16	24	44	57	70
3-7	7	14	21	37	46	55

WESTERN GUNFIGHTERS (1st Series) (Apache Kid #11-19)
Atlas Comics (CPS): No. 20, June, 1956 - No. 27, Aug, 1957

	GD	VG	FN	VF	VF/NM	NM-
20	14	28	42	78	112	145
21-Crandall-a	14	28	42	78	112	145
22-Wood & Powell-a	18	36	54	107	169	230
23,24: 23-Williamson-a. 24-Toth-a	14	28	42	78	112	145
25-27	10	20	30	56	76	95

NOTE: ***Berg** a-20. **Colan** a-20, 26, 27. **Crandall** a-21. **Heath** a-25. **Maneely** a-24, 25; c-22, 23, 25. **Morisi** a-24. **Morrow** a-26. **Pakula** a-23. **Severin** c-20, 27. **Torres** a-26. **Woodbridge** a-27.*

WESTERN GUNFIGHTERS (2nd Series)
Marvel Comics Group: Aug, 1970 - No. 33, Nov, 1975 (#1-6: 25¢, 68 pgs.)

	GD	VG	FN	VF	VF/NM	NM-
1-Ghost Rider begins; Fort Rango, Renegades & Gunhawk app.	5	10	15	34	60	85
2,3,5,6: 2-Origin Nightwind (Apache Kid's horse)	3	6	9	21	33	45
4-Barry Smith-a	4	8	12	23	37	50
7-(52 pgs) Origin Ghost Rider retold	3	6	9	19	30	40
8-13: 10-Origin Black Rider. 12-Origin Matt Slade	3	6	9	14	20	25
14-Steranko-c	3	6	9	16	24	32
15-20	2	4	6	10	14	18
21-33	2	4	6	9	13	16

NOTE: ***Baker** r-2, 3. **Colan** r-2. **Drucker** r-3. **Everett** a-6i. **G. Kane** c-29, 31. **Kirby** a-1p(r), 5, 10-12; c-19, 21. **Kubert** r-2. **Maneely** r-2, 10. **Morrow** r-29. **Severin** c-10. **Shores** a-3, 4. **Barry Smith** a-4. **Steranko** c-14. **Sutton** a-1, 2i, 5, 4. **Torres** r-26('57). **Wildey** r-8, 9. **Williamson** r-2, 18. **Woodbridge** r-27('57). Renegades in #4, 5; Ghost Rider in #1-7.*

WESTERN HEARTS
Standard Comics: Dec, 1949 - No. 10, Mar, 1952 (All photo-c)

	GD	VG	FN	VF	VF/NM	NM-
1-Severin-a; Whip Wilson & Reno Browne photo-c	23	46	69	136	223	310
2-Beverly Tyler & Jerome Courtland photo-c from movie "Palomino"; Williamson/Frazetta-a (2 pgs.)	23	46	69	136	223	310
3-Rex Allen photo-c	14	28	42	80	115	150
4-7,10: 4-Severin & Elder, Al Carreno-a. 5-Ray Milland & Hedy Lamarr photo-c from movie "Copper Canyon". 6-Fred MacMurray & Irene Dunn photo-c from movie "Never a Dull Moment". 7-Jock Mahoney photo-c. 10-Bill Williams & Jane Nigh photo-c	14	28	42	78	112	145
8-Randolph Scott & Janis Carter photo-c from "Santa Fe"; Severin & Elder-a	14	28	42	80	115	150
9-Whip Wilson & Reno Browne photo-c; Severin & Elder-a	15	30	45	83	124	165

WESTERN HERO (Wow Comics #1-69; Real Western Hero #70-75)
Fawcett Publications: No. 76, Mar, 1949 - No. 112, Mar, 1952

	GD	VG	FN	VF	VF/NM	NM-
76(#1, 52 pgs.)-Tom Mix, Hopalong Cassidy, Monte Hale, Gabby Hayes, Young Falcon (ends #78,80), & Big Bow and Little Arrow (ends #102,105) begin; painted-c begin	16	32	48	94	147	200
77 (52 pgs.)	11	22	33	64	90	115
78,80-82 (52 pgs.): 81-Capt. Tootsie by Beck	11	22	33	60	83	105
79,83 (36 pgs.): 83-Last painted-c	10	20	30	54	72	90
84-86,88-90 (52 pgs.): 84-Photo-c begin, end #112. 86-Last Hopalong Cassidy	10	20	30	53	76	95
87,91,95,99 (36 pgs.): 87-Bill Boyd begins, ends #95	9	18	27	50	65	80
92-94,96-98,101 (52 pgs.): 96-Tex Ritter begins. 101-Red Eagle app.	9	18	27	52	69	85
100 (52 pgs.)	10	20	30	56	76	95
102-111: 102-Begin 36 pg. issues	9	18	27	50	65	80
112-Last issue	9	18	27	52	69	85

NOTE: *1/2 to 1 pg. Rocky Lane (Carnation) in 80-83, 86, 88, 97. Photo covers feature Hopalong Cassidy #84, 86, 89; Tom Mix #85, 87, 90, 92, 94, 97; Monte Hale #88, 91, 93, 95, 98, 100, 104, 107, 110; Tex Ritter #96, 99, 101, 105, 108, 111; Gabby Hayes #103.*

WESTERN KID (1st Series)
Atlas Comics (CPC): Dec, 1954 - No. 17, Aug, 1957

	GD	VG	FN	VF	VF/NM	NM-
1-Origin; The Western Kid (Tex Dawson), his stallion Whirlwind & dog Lightning begin	19	38	57	111	176	240
2 (2/55)-Last pre-code	11	22	33	64	90	115
3-8	10	20	30	56	76	95
9,10-Williamson-a in both (4 pgs. each)	10	20	30	58	79	100
11-17	9	18	27	47	61	75

NOTE: ***Ayers** a-6, 7. **Heck** a-3. **Maneely** c-2-7, 10, 13-15. **Romita** a-1-17; c-1, 12. **Severin** c-11, 16, 17.*

WESTERN KID, THE (2nd Series)
Marvel Comics Group: Dec, 1971 - No. 5, Aug, 1972 (All 20¢ issues)

	GD	VG	FN	VF	VF/NM	NM-
1-Reprints; Romita-c/a(3)	3	6	9	17	26	35
2,4,5: 2-Romita-a; Severin-c. 4-Everett-r	2	4	6	13	18	22
3-Williamson-a	3	6	9	14	20	26

WESTERN KILLERS
Fox Features Syndicate: nn, July?, 1948; No. 60, Sept, 1948 - No. 64, May, 1949; No. 6, July, 1949

	GD	VG	FN	VF	VF/NM	NM-
nn(#59?)(nd, F&J Trading Co.)-Range Busters; formerly Blue Beetle #57?	24	48	72	140	230	320
60 (#1, 9/48)-Extreme violence; lingerie panel	26	52	78	152	249	345
61-Jack Cole, Starr-a	21	42	63	122	199	275
62-64, 6 (#6-exist?)	19	38	57	111	176	240

WESTERN LIFE ROMANCES (My Friend Irma #3 on?)
Marvel Comics (IPP): Dec, 1949 - No. 2, Mar, 1950 (52 pgs.)

	GD	VG	FN	VF	VF/NM	NM-
1-Whip Wilson & Reno Browne photo-c	20	40	60	114	182	250
2-Audie Murphy & Gale Storm photo-c	16	32	48	94	147	200

WESTERN LOVE
Prize Publ.: July-Aug, 1949 - No. 5, Mar-Apr, 1950 (All photo-c & 52 pgs.)

	GD	VG	FN	VF	VF/NM	NM-
1-S&K-a; Randolph Scott photo-c from movie "Canadian Pacific" (see Prize Comics #76)	31	62	93	182	296	410
2,5-S&K-a: 2-Whip Wilson & Reno Browne photo-c. 5-Dale Robertson photo-c	23	46	69	136	223	310
3,4: 3-Pat Williams photo-c	15	30	45	85	130	175

NOTE: ***Meskin & Severin/Elder** a-2-5.*

WESTERN LOVE TRAILS (Formerly Western Adventures)
Ace Magazines (A. A. Wyn): No. 7, Nov, 1949 - No. 9, Mar, 1950

	GD	VG	FN	VF	VF/NM	NM-
7	12	24	36	67	94	120
8,9	10	20	30	54	72	90

WESTERN MARSHAL (See Steve Donovan...)
Dell Publishing Co.: No. 534, 2-4/54 - No. 640, 7/55 (Based on Ernest Haycox's "Trailtown")

	GD	VG	FN	VF	VF/NM	NM-
Four Color 534 (#1)-Kinstler-a	5	10	15	35	63	90
Four Color 591 (10/54), 613 (2/55), 640-All Kinstler-a	5	10	15	33	57	80

WESTERN OUTLAWS (Junior Comics #9-16; My Secret Life #22 on)
Fox Features Syndicate: No. 17, Sept, 1948 - No. 21, May, 1949

	GD	VG	FN	VF	VF/NM	NM-
17-Kamen-a; Iger shop-a in all; 1 pg. "Death and the Devil Pills" r-in Ghostly Weird #122	32	64	96	188	307	425
18-21	19	38	57	111	176	240

WESTERN OUTLAWS
Atlas Comics (ACI No. 1-14/WPI No. 15-21): Feb, 1954 - No. 21, Aug, 1957

	GD	VG	FN	VF	VF/NM	NM-
1-Heath, Powell-a; Maneely hanging-c	22	44	66	132	216	300
2	13	26	39	74	105	135

Western Picture Stories #1 © CM

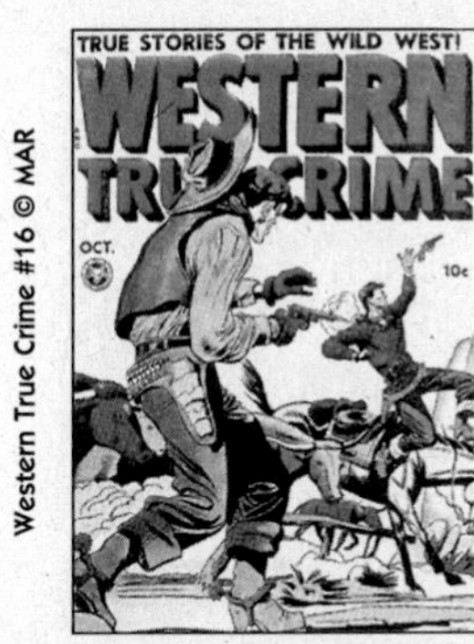

Western True Crime #16 © MAR

Wetworks #1 © WSP

	GD 2.0	VG 4.0	FN 6.0	VF 8.0	VF/NM 9.0	NM- 9.2
3-10: 7-Violent-a by R.Q. Sale	10	20	30	58	79	100
11,14-Williamson-a in both (6 pgs. each)	11	22	33	64	90	115
12,18,20,21: Severin covers	10	20	30	54	72	90
13,15: 13-Baker-a. 15-Torres-a	10	20	30	58	79	100
16-Williamson text illo	10	20	30	54	72	90
17,19-Crandall-a. 17-Williamson text illo	10	20	30	58	79	100

NOTE: ***Ayers** a-7, 10, 18, 20. **Bolle** a-21. **Colan** a-5, 10, 11, 17. **Drucker** a-11. **Everett** a-9, 10. **Heath** a-1; c-3, 4, 8, 16. **Kubert** a-9p. **Maneely** a-13, 16, 17, 19; c-1, 5, 7, 9, 10, 12, 13. **Morisi** a-18. **Powell** a-3, 16. **Romita** a-7, 13. **Severin** a-8, 16, 19; c-17, 18, 20, 21. **Tuska** a-6, 15.*

WESTERN OUTLAWS & SHERIFFS (Formerly Best Western)
Marvel/Atlas Comics (IPC): No. 60, Dec, 1949 - No. 73, June, 1952

	GD	VG	FN	VF	VF/NM	NM-
60 (52 pgs.) Photo-c	21	42	63	126	206	285
61-65: 61-Photo-c	17	34	51	98	154	210
66-Story contains 5 hangings	18	36	54	103	162	220
67-Cannibalism story	18	36	54	103	162	220
68-72	14	28	42	78	112	145
73-Black Rider story; Everett-c	15	30	45	84	127	170

NOTE: ***Maneely** a-62, 67; c-62, 69-73. **Robinson** a-68. **Sinnott** a-70. **Tuska** a-69-71.*

WESTERN PICTURE STORIES (1st Western comic)
Comics Magazine Company: Feb, 1937 - No. 4, June, 1937

	GD	VG	FN	VF	VF/NM	NM-
1-Will Eisner-a	219	438	657	1402	2401	3400
2-Will Eisner-a	113	226	339	723	1237	1750
3,4: 3-Eisner-a. 4-Caveman Cowboy story	97	194	291	621	1061	1500

WESTERN PICTURE STORIES (See Giant Comics Edition #6, 11)

WESTERN ROMANCES (See Target...)

WESTERN ROUGH RIDERS
Gillmor Magazines No. 1,4 (Stanmor Publ.): Nov, 1954 - No. 4, May, 1955

	GD	VG	FN	VF	VF/NM	NM-
1	9	18	27	52	69	85
2-4	7	14	21	37	46	55

WESTERN ROUNDUP (See Dell Giants & Fox Giants)

WESTERN SERENADE
DC Comics: May/June, 1949

nn - Ashcan comic, not distributed to newsstands, only for in-house use (no known sales)

WESTERN TALES (Formerly Witches...)
Harvey Publications: No. 31, Oct, 1955 - No. 33, July-Sept, 1956

	GD	VG	FN	VF	VF/NM	NM-
31,32-All S&K-a; Davy Crockett app. in each	15	30	45	86	133	180
33-S&K-a; Jim Bowie app.	15	30	45	84	127	170

NOTE: *#32 & 33 contain Boy's Ranch reprints. **Kirby** c-31.*

WESTERN TALES OF BLACK RIDER (Formerly Black Rider; Gunsmoke Western #32 on)
Atlas Comics (CPS): No. 28, May, 1955 - No. 31, Nov, 1955

	GD	VG	FN	VF	VF/NM	NM-
28 (#1): The Spider (a villain) dies	20	40	60	114	182	250
29-31	15	30	45	83	124	165

NOTE: ***Lawrence** a-30. **Maneely** c-28-30. **Severin** a-28. **Shores** c-31.*

WESTERN TEAM-UP
Marvel Comics Group: Nov, 1973 (20¢)

	GD	VG	FN	VF	VF/NM	NM-
1-Origin & 1st app. The Dakota Kid; Rawhide Kid-r; Gunsmoke Kid-r by Jack Davis	3	6	9	21	33	45

WESTERN THRILLERS (My Past Confessions #7 on)
Fox Features Syndicate/M.S. Distr. No. 52: Aug, 1948 - No. 6, June, 1949; No. 52, 1954?

	GD	VG	FN	VF	VF/NM	NM-
1- "Velvet Rose" (Kamenish-a); "Two-Gun Sal", "Striker Sisters" (all women outlaws issue); Brodsky-c	53	106	159	334	567	800
2	24	48	72	142	234	325
3-6: 4,5-Bakerish-a; 5-Butch Cassidy app.	20	40	60	114	182	250
52-(Reprint, M.S. Dist.)-1954? No date given (becomes My Love Secret #53)	9	18	27	50	65	80

WESTERN THRILLERS (Cowboy Action #5 on)
Atlas Comics (ACI): Nov, 1954 - No. 4, Feb, 1955 (All-r/Western Outlaws & Sheriffs)

	GD	VG	FN	VF	VF/NM	NM-
1	15	30	45	90	140	190
2-4	10	20	30	54	72	90

NOTE: ***Heath** c-3. **Maneely** a-1; c-2. **Powell** a-4. **Robinson** a-4. **Romita** c-4. **Tuska** a-2.*

WESTERN TRAILS (Ringo Kid Starring in...)
Atlas Comics (SAI): May, 1957 - No. 2, July, 1957

	GD	VG	FN	VF	VF/NM	NM-
1-Ringo Kid app.; Severin-c	14	28	42	78	112	145
2-Severin-c	9	18	27	52	69	85

NOTE: ***Bolle** a-1, 2. **Maneely** a-1, 2. **Severin** c-1, 2.*

WESTERN TRUE CRIME (Becomes My Confessions)
Fox Features Syndicate: No. 15, Aug, 1948 - No. 6, June, 1949

	GD	VG	FN	VF	VF/NM	NM-
15(#1)-Kamen-a; formerly Zoot #14 (5/48)?	32	64	96	188	307	425
16(#2)-Kamenish-a; headlight panels, violence	23	46	69	136	223	310
3-Kamen-a	25	50	75	147	241	335
4-6: 4-Johnny Craig-a	15	30	45	90	140	190

WESTERN WINNERS (Formerly All-Western Winners; becomes Black Rider #8 on & Romance Tales #7 on?)
Marvel Comics (CDS): No. 5, June, 1949 - No. 7, Dec, 1949

	GD	VG	FN	VF	VF/NM	NM-
5-Two-Gun Kid, Kid Colt, Black Rider; Shores-c	31	62	93	182	296	410
6-Two-Gun Kid, Black Rider, Heath Kid Colt story; Captain Tootsie by C.C. Beck	26	52	78	152	249	345
7-Randolph Scott Photo-c w/true stories about the West	26	52	78	152	249	345

WEST OF THE PECOS (See Zane Grey, 4-Color #222)

WESTWARD HO, THE WAGONS (Disney)(Also see Classic Comics #14)
Dell Publishing Co.: No. 738, Sept, 1956 (Movie)

	GD	VG	FN	VF	VF/NM	NM-
Four Color 738-Fess Parker photo-c	8	16	24	54	102	150

WE3
DC Comics (Vertigo): Oct, 2004 - No. 3, May, 2005 ($2.95, limited series)

	NM-
1-3-Domestic animal cyborgs: Grant Morrison-s/Frank Quitely-a	3.00
TPB (2005, $12.99) r/series	13.00

WETWORKS (See WildC.A.T.S: Covert Action Teams #2)
Image Comics (WildStorm): June, 1994 - No. 43, Aug, 1998 ($1.95/$2.50)

	NM-
1-"July" on-c; gatefold wraparound-c; Portacio/Williams-c/a	4.00
1-Chicago Comicon edition	6.00
1-(2/98, $4.95) "3-D Edition" w/glasses	5.00
2-4	3.00
2-Alternate Portacio-c, see Deathblow #5	6.00
5-7,9-24: 5-($2.50). 13-Portacio-c. 16,17-Fire From Heaven Pts. 4 & 11	3.00
8 ($1.95)-Newstand, Wildstorm Rising Pt. 7	3.00
8 ($2.50)-Direct Market, Wildstorm Rising Pt. 7	3.00
25-($3.95)	4.00
26-43: 32-Variant-c by Pat Lee & Charest. 39,40-Stormwatch app. 42-Gen 13 app.	3.00
Sourcebook 1 (10/94, $2.50)-Text & illustrations (no comics)	3.00
Voyager Pack (8/97, $3.50)- #32 w/Phantom Guard preview	4.00

WETWORKS
DC Comics (WildStorm): Nov, 2006 - No. 15, Jan, 2008 ($2.99)

	NM-
1-15: 1-Carey-s/Portacio-a; two covers by Portacio and Van Sciver. 2-Golden var-c 3-Pearson var-c. 4-Powell var-c	3.00
...: Armageddon 1 (1/08, $2.99) Gage-s/Badeaux-a	3.00
... Book One (2007, $14.99) r/#1-5 and stories from Eye of the storm Annual and Coup D'Etat Afterword	15.00
... Book Two (2008, $14.99) r/#6-9,13-15	15.00
...: Mutations 1 (11/10, $3.99) Grevioux & Long-s/Gopez-a	4.00

WETWORKS/VAMPIRELLA (See Vampirella/Wetworks)
Image Comics (WildStorm Productions): July, 1997 ($2.95, one-shot)

	NM-
1-Gil Kane-c	4.00

WHACK (Satire)
St. John Publishing Co. (Jubilee Publ.): Oct, 1953 - No. 3, May, 1954

	GD	VG	FN	VF	VF/NM	NM-
1-(3-D, 25¢)-Kubert-a; Maurer-c; came w/glasses	24	48	72	142	234	325
2,3-Kubert-a in each. 2-Bing Crosby on-c; Mighty Mouse & Steve Canyon parodies. 3-Li'l Orphan Annie parody; Maurer-c	15	30	45	84	127	170

WHACKY (See Wacky)

WHA...HUH?
Marvel Comics: 2005 ($3.99, one-shot)

	NM-
1-Humor spoofs of Marvel characters; Mahfood-a/c; Bendis, Stan Lee and others-s	4.00

WHAM COMICS (See Super Spy)
Centaur Publications: Nov, 1940 - No. 2, Dec, 1940

	GD	VG	FN	VF	VF/NM	NM-
1-The Sparkler, The Phantom Rider, Craig Carter and his Magic Ring, Detecto, Copper Slug, Speed Silvers by Gustavson, Speed Centaur & Jon Linton (s/f) begin	177	354	531	1133	1942	2750
2-Origin Blue Fire & Solarman; The Buzzard app.	123	246	369	787	1344	1900

WHAM-O GIANT COMICS
Wham-O Mfg. Co. : April, 1967 (98¢, newspaper size, one-shot)(Six issue subscription was advertised)

	GD	VG	FN	VF	VF/NM	NM-
1-Radian & Goody Bumpkin by Wood; 1 pg. Stanley-a; Fine, Tufts-a; flying saucer reports; wraparound-c	9	18	27	59	117	175

WHATEVER HAPPENED TO BARON VON SHOCK?

What If...? #65 © MAR

What If... Jessica Jones #1 © MAR

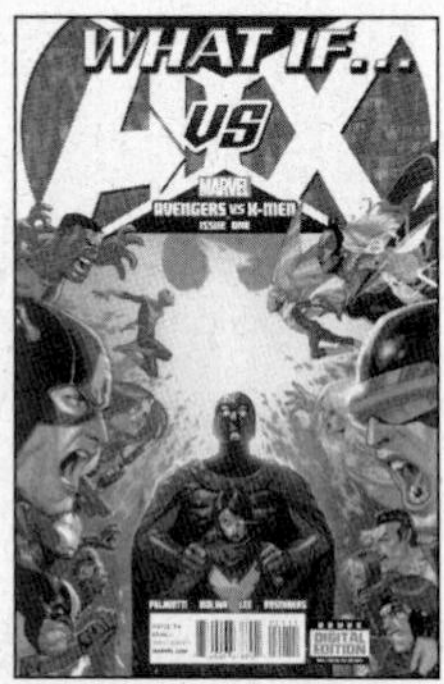

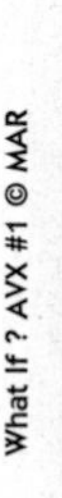
What If ? AVX #1 © MAR

GD 2.0 VG 4.0 FN 6.0 VF 8.0 VF/NM 9.0 NM- 9.2

Image Comics: May, 2010 - Present ($3.99)

1-4-Rob Zombie-s/Donny Hadiwidjaja-a 4.00

WHAT IF? (1st Series) (What If? Featuring... #13 & #?-33) (Also see Hero Initiative)
Marvel Comics Group: Feb, 1977 - No. 47, Oct, 1984; June, 1988 (All 52 pgs.)

1-Brief origin Spider-Man, Fantastic Four 3 6 9 19 30 40
2-Origin The Hulk retold 2 4 6 10 14 18
3-5: 3-Avengers. 4-Invaders. 5-Capt. America 2 4 6 8 11 14
6-10,13,17: 7-Betty Brant as Spider-Girl. 8-Daredevil; Spidey parody. 9-Origins Venus, Marvel Boy, Human Robot, 3-D Man. 13-Conan app.; John Buscema-c/a(p). 17-Ghost Rider & Son of Satan app. 2 3 4 6 8 10
11,12,14-16: 11-Marvel Bullpen as F.F. 1 2 3 5 6 8
18-26,29: 18-Dr. Strange. 19-Spider-Man. 22-Origin Dr. Doom retold 1 2 3 4 5 7
27-X-Men app.; Miller-c 3 6 9 14 20 26
28-Daredevil by Miller; Ghost Rider app. 2 4 6 10 16 20
30-"What If...Spider-Man's Clone Had Lived?" 2 4 6 8 10 12
31-Begin $1.00-c; featuring Wolverine & the Hulk; X-Men app.; death of Hulk, Wolverine & Magneto 3 6 9 15 22 28
32-34,36-47: 32,36-Byrne-a. 34-Marvel crew each draw themselves. 37-Old X-Men & Silver Surfer app. 39-Thor battles Conan 5.00
35-What if Elektra had lived?; Miller/Austin-a. 2 4 6 8 10 12
Special 1 ($1.50, 6/88)-Iron Man, F.F., Thor app. 5.00
... Classic Vol. 1 TPB (2004, $24.99) r/#1-6; checklist 25.00
... Classic Vol. 2 TPB (2005, $24.99) r/#7-12 25.00
... Classic Vol. 3 TPB (2006, $24.99) r/#14,15,17-20 25.00
... Classic Vol. 4 TPB (2007, $24.99) r/#21-26; checklist of all What If? series/issues 25.00

NOTE: ***Austin*** *a-27p, 32i, 34, 35i; c-35i, 36i.* ***J. Buscema*** *a-13p, 15p; c-10, 13p, 23p.* ***Byrne*** *a-32i, 36; c-36p.* ***Colan*** *a-21p; c-17p, 18p, 21p.* ***Ditko*** *a-35, Special 1.* ***Golden*** *c-29, 40-42.* ***Guice*** *a-40p.* ***Gil Kane*** *a-3p, 24p; c(p)-2-4, 7, 8.* ***Kirby*** *a-11p; c-9p, 11p.* ***Layton*** *a-32i, 33i; c-30, 32p, 33i, 34.* ***Mignola*** *c-39i.* ***Miller*** *a-28p, 32i, 34(1), 35p; c-27, 28p.* ***Mooney*** *a-8i, 30i.* ***Perez*** *a-15p.* ***Robbins*** *a-4p.* ***Sienkiewicz*** *c-43-46.* ***Simonson*** *a-15p, 32i.* ***Starlin*** *a-32i.* ***Stevens*** *a-8, 16i(part).* ***Sutton*** *a-2i, 18p, 28.* ***Tuska*** *a-5p.* ***Weiss*** *a-37p.*

WHAT IF...? (2nd Series)
Marvel Comics: V2#1, July, 1989 - No. 114, Nov, 1998 ($1.25/$1.50)

V2#1-...The Avengers Had Lost the Evolutionary War 5.00
2-5: 2-Daredevil, Punisher app. 4.00
6-X-Men app. 5.00
7-Wolverine app.; Liefeld-c/a(1st on Wolvie?) 6.00
8,10,11,13-15,17-30: 10-Punisher app. 11-Fantastic Four app.; McFarlane-c(i).13-Prof. X; Jim Lee-c. 14-Capt. Marvel; Lim/Austin-c.15-F.F.; Capullo-c/a(p). 17-Spider-Man/Kraven. 18-F.F. 19-Vision. 20,21-Spider-Man. 22-Silver Surfer by Lim/Austin-c/a 23-X-Men. 24-Wolverine; Punisher app. 25-(52 pgs.)-Wolverine app. 26-Punisher app. 27-Namor/F.F. 28,29-Capt. America. 29-Swipes cover to Avengers #4. 30-(52 pgs.)-F.F. 4.00
9,12-X-Men 5.00
16-Wolverine battles Conan; Red Sonja app.; X-Men cameo 5.00
31-40,42-49: 31-Cosmic Spider-Man & Venom app.; Hobgoblin cameo. 32,33-Phoenix; X-Men app. 35-Fantastic Five (w/Spidey). 36-Avengers vs. Guardians of the Galaxy. 37-Wolverine; Thibert-c(i). 38-Thor; Rogers-p(part). 40-Storm; X-Men app. 42-Spider-Man. 43-Wolverine. 44-Venom/Punisher. 45-Ghost Rider. 46-Cable. 47-Magneto. 49-Infinity Gauntlet w/Silver Surfer & Thanos 3.00
41,50: 41-(52 pgs.)-Avengers vs. Galactus. 50-(52 pgs.)-Foil embossed-c; "What If Hulk Had Killed Wolverine" 4.00
51-(7/93) "What If the Punisher Became Captain America" (see it happen in 2007's Punisher War Journal #6-10) 6.00
52-99,101-104: 52-Dr. Doom. 54-Death's Head. 57-Punisher as Shield. 58-"What if Punisher Had Killed Spider-Man" w/cover similar to Amazing S-M #129. 59-...Wolverine led Alpha Flight. 60-X-Men Wedding Album. 61-Bound-in card sheet. 61,86,88-Spider-Man. 74,77,81,84,85-X-Men. 76-Last app. Watcher in title. 78-Bisley-c. 80-Hulk. 87-Sabretooth. 89-Fantastic Four. 90-Cyclops & Havok. 91-The Hulk. 93-Wolverine. 94-Juggernaut. 95-Ghost Rider 3.00
100-($2.99, double-sized) Gambit and Rogue, Fantastic Four 4.00
105-Spider-Girl (Peter Parker's daughter) debut; Sienkiewicz-a; (Betty Brant also app. as a Spider-Girl in What If? (1st series) #7) 3 6 9 14 20 25
106-114: 106-Gambit. 108-Avengers. 111-Wolverine. 114-Secret Wars 3.00
#(-1) Flashback (7/97) 3.00

WHAT IF...? (one-shots)
Marvel Comics: Feb, 2005 ($2.99)

... Aunt May Had Died Instead of Uncle Ben? - Brubaker-s/DiVito-a/Brase-c 3.00
... Dr. Doom Had Become The Thing? - Karl Kesel-s/Paul Smith-a/c 3.00
... General Ross Had Become The Hulk? - Peter David-s/Pat Olliffe-a/Gary Frank-c 3.00
... Jessica Jones Had Joined The Avengers? - Bendis-s/Gaydos-a/McNiven-c 3.00
... Karen Page Had Lived? - Bendis-s/Lark-a/c 3.00
... Magneto and Professor X Had Formed The X-Men Together? - Claremont-s/Raney-a 3.00
What If...: Why Not? TPB (2005, $16.99) r/one-shots 17.00

WHAT IF... (one-shots)
Marvel Comics: Feb, 2006 ($2.99)

... : Captain America - Fought in the Civil War?; Bedard-s/Di Giandomenico-a 3.00
... : Daredevil - The Devil Who Dares; Daredevil in feudal Japan; Veitch-s/Edwards-a 3.00
... : Fantastic Four - Were Cosmonauts?; Marshall Rogers-a/c; Mike Carey-s 3.00
... : Submariner - Grew Up on Land?; Pak-s/Lopez-a 3.00
... : Thor - Was the Herald of Galactus?; Kirkman-s/Oeming-a/c 3.00
... : Wolverine - In the Prohibition Era; Way-s/Proctor-a/Harris-c 3.00
What If: Mirror Mirror TPB (2006, $16.99) r/one-shots; design pages and Rogers sketches 17.00

WHAT IF ?... (one-shots altering recent Marvel "event" series)
Marvel Comics: Jan, 2007 - Feb, 2007 ($3.99)

... Avengers Disassembled; Parker-s/Lopresti-a/c 4.00
... Spider-Man The Other; Peter David-s/Khoi Pham-a; Venom app. 4.00
... Wolverine Enemy of the State; Robinson-s/DiGiandomenico-a/Alexander-c 4.00
... X-Men Age of Apocalypse; Remeder-s/Wilkins-a/Djurdjevic-c 4.00
... X-Men Deadly Genesis; Hine-s/Yardin-a/c 4.00
What If?: Event Horizon TPB (2007, $16.99) r/one-shots; design pages and cover sketches 17.00

WHAT IF ?... (one-shots altering recent Marvel "event" series)
Marvel Comics: Dec, 2007 - Feb, 2008 ($3.99)

... Annihilation; Nova, Iron Man and Captain America app. 4.00
... Civil War; 2 covers by Silvestri & Djurdjevic 4.00
... Planet Hulk; Pagulayan-c; Kirk, Sandoval & Hembeck-a 4.00
... Spider-Man vs. Wolverine; Romita Jr.-c; Henry-a; Nick Fury app. 4.00
... X-Men - Rise and Fall of the Shi'ar Empire; Coipel-c 4.00
What If?: Civil War TPB (2008, $16.99) r/one-shots; design pages and cover sketches 17.00

WHAT IF ?... (one-shots altering recent Marvel "event" series)
Marvel Comics: Feb, 2009 ($3.99) (Serialized back-up Runaways story in each issue)

... Fallen Son; if Iron Man had died instead of Capt. America; McGuinness-c 4.00
... House of M; if the Scarlet Witch had said "No more powers" instead; Cheung-c 4.00
... Newer Fantastic Four; team of Spider-Man, Hulk, Iron Man and Wolverine 4.00
... Secret Wars; if Doctor Doom had kept the Beyonder's power; origin re-told 4.00
... Spider-Man Back in Black; if Mary Jane had been shot instead of Aunt May 4.00

WHAT IF ?... (one-shots)
Marvel Comics: Feb, 2010 ($3.99)

... Astonishing X-Men; if Ord resurrected Jean Grey; Campbell-c 4.00
... Daredevil vs. Elektra; Kayanan-a; Klaus Janson-c swipe of Daredevil #168 4.00
... Secret Invasion; if the Skrulls succeeded; Yu-c 4.00
... Spider-Man: House of M; if Gwen Stacy survived the House of M; Dodson-c 4.00
... World War Hulk; if the heroes lost the war; Romita Jr.-c 4.00

WHAT IF ?... (one-shots) (4 part Deadpool back-up story in all but #200)
Marvel Comics: Feb, 2011 ($3.99)

... #200 ($4.99) Siege on cover; if Osborn won the Siege of Asgard; Stan Lee back-up 5.00
... Dark Reign; if Norman Osborn was killed; Tanaka-a/Deodato-c 4.00
... Iron Man: Demon in an Armor; if Tony Stark became Dr. Doom; Nolan-a 4.00
... Spider-Man; if Spider-Man killed Kraven; Jimenez-c 4.00
... Wolverine: Father; if Wolverine raised Daken; Tocchini-a; Yu-a 4.00

WHAT IF ? AGE OF ULTRON
Marvel Comics: Jun, 2014 - No. 5 ($3.99, weekly limited series)

1,2: 1-Hank Pym's story. 2-Wolverine, Hulk, Spider-Man, Ghost Rider app. 4.00

WHAT IF ? AVX (Avengers vs. X-Men)
Marvel Comics: Sept, 2013 - No. 4, Sept, 2013 ($3.99, weekly limited series)

1-4-Palmiotti-s/Molina-a; Hope merges with the Phoenix force 4.00

'WHAT'S NEW? - THE COLLECTED ADVENTURES OF PHIL & DIXIE'
Palliard Press: Oct, 1991 - No. 2, 1991 ($5.95, mostly color, sq.-bound, 52 pgs.)

1,2-By Phil Foglio 6.00

WHAT THE- -?!
Marvel Comics: Aug, 1988 - No. 26, 1993 ($1.25/$1.50/$2.50, semi-annual #5 on)

1-All contain parodies 4.00
2-24: 3-X-Men parody; Todd McFarlane-a. 5-Punisher/Wolverine parody; Jim Lee-a. 6-Punisher, Wolverine, Alpha Flight. 9-Wolverine. 16-EC back-c parody. 17-Wolverine/Punisher parody. 18-Star Trek parody w/Wolverine. 19-Punisher, Wolverine, Ghost Rider. 21-Weapon X parody. 22-Punisher/Wolverine parody 3.00
25-Summer Special 1 (1993, $2.50)-X-Men parody 4.00
26-Fall Special ($2.50, 68 pgs.)-Spider-Ham 2099-c/story; origin Silver Surfer; Hulk & Doomsday parody; indica reads "Winter Special." 4.00

NOTE: ***Austin*** *a-6i.* ***Byrne*** *a-2, 6, 10; c-2, 6-8, 10, 12, 13.* ***Golden*** *a-22.* ***Dale Keown*** *a-8p(8 pgs.).* ***McFarlane*** *a-3.* ***Rogers*** *c-15i, 16p.* ***Severin*** *a-2.* ***Staton*** *a-21p.* ***Williamson*** *a-2i.*

WHEE COMICS (Also see Gay, Smile & Tickle Comics)

Where Monsters Dwell #2 © MAR

White Princess of the Jungle #2 © AVON

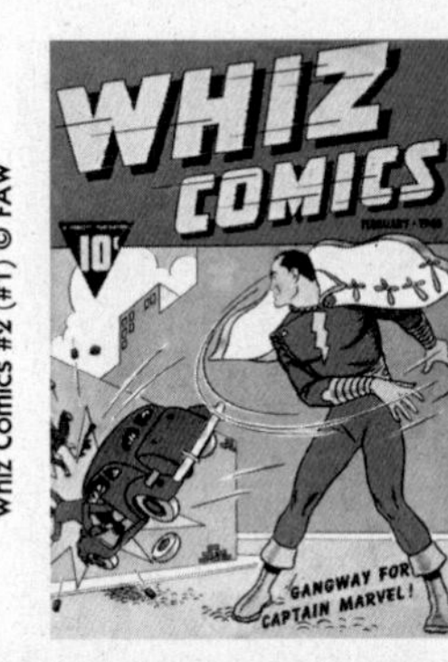

Whiz Comics #2 (#1) © FAW

	GD 2.0	VG 4.0	FN 6.0	VF 8.0	VF/NM 9.0	NM- 9.2

Modern Store Publications: 1955 (7¢, 5x7-1/4", 52 pgs.)

1-Funny animal	6	12	18	31	38	45

WHEEDIES (See Panic #11 -EC Comics)

WHEELIE AND THE CHOPPER BUNCH (TV)
Charlton Comics: July, 1975 - No. 7, July, 1976 (Hanna-Barbera)

1-3: 1-Byrne text illo (see Nightmare for 1st art); Staton-a. 2-Byrne-a. 2,3-Mike Zeck text illos. 3-Staton-a; Byrne-c/a	3	6	9	17	26	35
4-7-Staton-a	2	4	6	12	16	20

WHEN KNIGHTHOOD WAS IN FLOWER (See The Sword & the Rose, 4-Color #505, 682)

WHEN SCHOOL IS OUT (See Wisco in Promotional Comics section)

WHERE CREATURES ROAM
Marvel Comics Group: July, 1970 - No. 8, Sept, 1971

1-Kirby/Ayers-c/a(r)	5	10	15	30	50	70
2-8: 2-5,7,8-Kirby-c/a(r). 6-Kirby-a(r)	3	6	9	21	33	45

NOTE: *Ditko r-1-6, 7. Heck r-2, 5. All contain pre super-hero reprints.*

WHERE IN THE WORLD IS CARMEN SANDIEGO (TV)
DC Comics: June, 1996 - No. 4, Dec, 1996 ($1.75)

1-4: Adaptation of TV show 3.00

WHERE MONSTERS DWELL
Marvel Comics Group: Jan, 1970 - No. 38, Oct, 1975

1-Kirby/Ditko-r; all contain pre super-hero-r	5	10	15	31	53	75
2-5,7-10: 4-Crandall-a(r)	3	6	9	21	33	45
6-(11/70) Reprints Groot's 1st app. in Tales to Astonish #13	4	8	12	23	37	50
11,13-20: 11-Last 15¢ issue. 18,20-Starlin-c	3	6	9	18	28	38
12-Giant issue (52 pgs.)	4	8	12	23	37	50
21-Reprints 1st Fin Fang Foom app.	3	6	9	17	26	35
22-37	3	6	9	16	23	30
38-Williamson-r/World of Suspense #3	3	6	9	16	24	32

NOTE: *Colan r-12. Ditko a(r)-4, 6, 8, 10, 12, 17-19, 23-25, 37. Kirby r-1-3, 5-16, 18-27, 30-32, 34-36, 38; c-12? Reinman a-3r, 4r, 12r. Severin c-15.*

WHERE'S HUDDLES? (TV) (See Fun-In #9)
Gold Key: Jan, 1971 - No. 3, Dec, 1971 (Hanna-Barbera)

1	3	6	9	18	28	38
2,3: 3-r/most #1	2	4	6	11	16	20

WHIP WILSON (Movie star) (Formerly Rex Hart; Gunhawk #12 on; see Western Hearts, Western Life Romances, Western Love)
Marvel Comics: No. 9, April, 1950 - No. 11, Sept, 1950 (#9,10: 52 pgs.)

9-Photo-c; Whip Wilson & his horse Bullet begin; origin Bullet; issue #23 listed on splash page; cover changed to #9	49	98	147	309	522	735
10,11: Both have photo-c. 11-36 pgs.	28	56	84	168	274	380
I.W. Reprint #1(1964)-Kinstler-c; r-Marvel #11	3	6	9	15	22	28

WHIRLWIND COMICS (Also see Cyclone Comics)
Nita Publication: June, 1940 - No. 3, Sept, 1940

1-Origin & 1st app. Cyclone; Cyclone-c	300	600	900	1920	3310	4700
2,3: Cyclone-c	129	258	387	826	1413	2000

WHIRLYBIRDS (TV)
Dell Publishing Co.: No. 1124, Aug, 1960 - No. 1216, Oct-Dec, 1961

Four Color 1124 (#1)-Photo-c	7	14	21	48	89	130
Four Color 1216-Photo-c	7	14	21	44	82	120

WHISKEY DICKEL, INTERNATIONAL COWGIRL
Image Comics: Aug, 2003 ($12.95, softcover, B&W)

nn-Mark Ricketts-s/Mike Hawthorne-a; pin-up by various incl. Oeming, Thompson, Mack 13.00

WHISPER (Female Ninja)
Capital Comics: Dec, 1983 - No. 2, 1984 ($1.75, Baxter paper)

1,2: 1-Origin; Golden-c, Special (11/85, $2.50) 4.00

WHISPER (Vol. 2)
First Comics: Jun, 1986 - No. 37, June, 1990 ($1.25/$1.75/$1.95)

1-37 3.00

WHISPER
Boom! Studios: Nov, 2006 ($3.99)

1-Grant-s/Dzialowski-a 4.00

WHISPERS
Image Comics: Jan, 2012 - No. 6, Oct, 2013 ($2.99)

1-6-Joshua Luna-s/a 3.00

WHITE CHIEF OF THE PAWNEE INDIANS
Avon Periodicals: 1951

nn-Kit West app.; Kinstler-c	17	34	51	98	154	210

WHITE EAGLE INDIAN CHIEF (See Indian Chief)

WHITE FANG
Disney Comics: 1990 ($5.95, 68 pgs.)

nn-Graphic novel adapting new Disney movie 6.00

WHITE INDIAN
Magazine Enterprises: No. 11, July, 1953 - No. 15, 1954

11(A-1 94), 12(A-1 101), 13(A-1 104)-Frazetta-r(Dan Brand) in all from Durango Kid. 11-Powell-c	20	40	60	114	182	250
14(A-1 117), 15(A-1 135)-Check-a; Torres-a-#15	14	28	42	76	108	140

NOTE: *#11 contains reprints from Durango Kid #1-4; #12 from #5, 9, 10, 11; #13 from #7, 12, 13, 16. #14 & 15 contain all new stories.*

WHITEOUT (Also see Queen & Country)
Oni Press: July, 1998 - No. 4, Nov, 1998 ($2.95, B&W, limited series)

1-4: 1-Matt Wagner-c. 2-Mignola-c. 3-Gibbons-c 3.00
TPB (5/99, $10.95) r/#1-4; Miller-c 11.00

WHITEOUT: MELT
Oni Press: Sept, 1999 - No. 4, Feb, 2000 ($2.95, B&W, limited series)

1-4-Greg Rucka-s/Steve Lieber-a 3.00
Whiteout: Melt, The Definitive Edition TPB (9/07, $13.95) r/#1-4; Rucka afterword 14.00

WHITE PRINCESS OF THE JUNGLE (Also see Jungle Adventures & Top Jungle Comics)
Avon Periodicals: July, 1951 - No. 5, Nov, 1952

1-Origin of White Princess (Taanda) & Capt'n Courage (r); Kinstler-c	60	120	180	381	653	925
2-Reprints origin of Malu, Slave Girl Princess from Avon's Slave Girl Comics #1 w/Malu changed to Zora; Kinstler-c/a(2)	41	82	123	256	428	600
3-Origin Blue Gorilla; Kinstler-c/a	39	78	117	231	378	525
4-Jack Barnum, White Hunter app.; r/Sheena #9	34	68	102	199	325	450
5-Blue Gorilla by McCann?; Kinstler inside-c; Fawcette/Alascia-a(3)	36	72	108	211	343	475

WHITE RIDER AND SUPER HORSE (Formerly Humdinger V2#2; Indian Warriors #7 on; also see Blue Bolt #1, 4Most & Western Crime Cases)
Novelty-Star Publications/Accepted Publ.: No. 4, 9/50 - No. 6, 3/51

4-6-Adapts "The Last of the Mohicans". 4(#1)-(9/50)-Says #11 on inside	16	32	48	92	144	195
Accepted Reprint #5(r/#5),6 (nd); L.B. Cole-c	9	18	27	50	65	80

NOTE: *All have L. B. Cole covers.*

WHITE SUITS, THE
Dark Horse Comics: Feb, 2014 - No. 4 ($3.99, limited series)

1-Barbiere-s/Cypress-a 4.00

WHITE TIGER
Marvel Comics: Jan, 2007 - No. 6, Nov, 2007 ($2.99, limited series)

1-6: 1-David Mack-c; Pierce & Liebe-s/Briones-a; Spider-Man & Black Widow app. 3.00
...: A Hero's Compulsion SC (2007,$14.99) r/#1-6; re-cap art and profile page 15.00

WHITE WILDERNESS (Disney)
Dell Publishing Co.: No. 943, Oct, 1958

Four Color 943-Movie	6	12	18	37	66	95

WHITMAN COMIC BOOK, A
Whitman Publishing Co.: Sept., 1962 (136 pgs.; 7-3/4x5-3/4; hardcover) (B&W)

1-3,5,7: 1-Yogi Bear. 2-Huckleberry Hound. 3-Mr. Jinks and Pixie & Dixie. 5-Augie Doggie & Loopy de Loop. 7-Bugs Bunny-r from #47,51,53,54 & 55	6	12	18	38	69	100
4,6: 4-The Flintstones. 6-Snooper & Blabber Fearless Detectives/Quick Draw McGraw of the Wild West	6	12	18	41	76	110
8-Donald Duck-reprints most of WDC&S #209-213. Includes 5 Barks stories, 1 complete Mickey Mouse serial by Paul Murry & 1 Mickey Mouse serial missing the 1st episode	7	14	21	46	86	125

NOTE: *Hanna-Barbera #1-6(TV), reprints of British tabloid comics. Dell reprints-#7,8.*

WHIZ COMICS (Formerly Flash & Thrill Comics #1)(See 5 Cent Comics)
Fawcett Publications: No. 2, Feb, 1940 - No. 155, June, 1953

1-(nn on cover, #2 inside)-Origin & 1st newsstand app. Captain Marvel (formerly Captain Thunder) by C. C. Beck (created by Bill Parker), Spy Smasher, Golden Arrow, Ibis the Invincible, Dan Dare, Scoop Smith, Sivana, & Lance O'Casey begin	10,000	20,000	30,000	70,000	110,000	150,000

(The only Mint copy sold in 1995 for $176,000 cash)

Whodunnit? #3 © ECL

The Wicked #5 © Avalon Studios

Wilbur Comics #6 © AP

GD 2.0 | VG 4.0 | FN 6.0 | VF 8.0 | VF/NM 9.0 | NM- 9.2

1-Reprint, oversize 13-1/2x10". **WARNING**: This comic is an exact duplicate reprint (except for dropping "Gangway for Captain Marvel" from-c) of the original except for its size. DC published it in 1974 with a second cover titling it as a Famous First Edition. There have been many reported cases of the outer cover being removed and the interior sold as the original edition. The reprint with the new outer cover removed is practically worthless. See Famous First Edition for value.

	GD	VG	FN	VF	VF/NM	NM-
2-(3/40, nn on cover, #3 inside); cover to Flash #1 redrawn, pg. 12, panel 4; Spy Smasher reveals I.D. to Eve	595	1190	1785	4344	7672	11,000
3-(4/40, #3 on-c, #4 inside)-1st app. Beautia	400	800	1200	2800	4900	7000
4-(5/40, #4 on cover, #5 inside)-Brief origin Capt. Marvel retold	343	686	1029	2400	4200	6000
5-Captain Marvel wears button-down flap on splash page only	300	600	900	2010	3505	5000
6-10: 7-Dr. Voodoo begins (by Raboy-#9-22)	213	426	639	1363	2332	3300
11-14: 12-Capt. Marvel does not wear cape	145	290	435	928	1589	2250
15-Origin Sivana; Dr. Voodoo by Raboy	152	304	456	973	1662	2350
16-18-Spy Smasher battles Captain Marvel	161	322	483	1030	1765	2500
19-Classic shark-c	155	310	465	992	1696	2400
20	100	200	300	640	1095	1550
21-(9/41)-Origin & 1st cover app. Lt. Marvels, the 1st team in Fawcett comics. In this issue, Capt. Death similar to Ditko's later Dr. Strange	103	206	309	659	1130	1600
22-24: 23-Only Dr. Voodoo by Tuska	84	168	252	538	919	1300
25-(12/41)-Captain Nazi jumps from Master Comics #21 to take on Capt. Marvel solo after being beaten by Capt. Marvel/Bulletman team, causing the creation of Capt. Marvel Jr.; 1st app./origin of Capt. Marvel Jr. (part II of trilogy origin by CC. Beck & Mac Raboy); Captain Marvel sends Jr. back to Master #22 to aid Bulletman against Capt. Nazi; origin Old Shazam in text	514	1028	1542	3750	6625	9500
26-30	60	120	180	381	658	935
31,32: 32-1st app. The Trolls; Hitler/Mussolini satire by Beck	53	106	159	334	567	800
33-Spy Smasher, Captain Marvel x-over on cover and inside	60	120	180	381	658	935
34,36-40: 37-The Trolls app. by Swayze	41	82	123	249	417	585
35-Captain Marvel & Spy Smasher-c	49	98	147	309	522	735
41-50: 42-Classic time travel-c. 43-Spy Smasher, Ibis, Golden Arrow x-over in Capt. Marvel. 44-Flag-c. 47-Origin recap (1 pg.)	36	72	108	216	351	485
51-60: 52-Capt. Marvel x-over in Ibis. 57-Spy Smasher, Golden Arrow, Ibis cameo	29	58	87	172	281	390
61-70	27	54	81	160	263	365
71,77-80	26	52	78	152	249	345
72-76-Two Captain Marvel stories in each; 76-Spy Smasher becomes Crime Smasher	26	52	78	154	252	350
81-85,87-99: 91-Infinity-c	26	52	78	152	249	345
86-Captain Marvel battles Sivana Family; robot-c	30	60	90	177	289	400
100-(8/48)-Anniversary issue	34	68	102	199	325	450
101-106: 102-Commando Yank app. 106-Bulletman app.	28	56	84	165	270	375
107-149: 107-Capitol Building photo-c. 108-Brooklyn Bridge photo-c. 112-Photo-c. 139-Infinity-c. 140-Flag-c. 142-Used in **POP**, pg. 89	28	56	84	165	270	375
150-152-(Low dist.)	36	72	108	211	343	475
153-155-(Scarce):154,155-1st/2nd Dr. Death stories	43	86	129	271	461	650

NOTE: ***C.C. Beck*** *Captain Marvel-No. 25(part).* ***Krigstein*** *Golden Arrow-No. 75, 78, 91, 95, 96, 98-100.* ***Mac Raboy*** *Dr. Voodoo-No. 9-22. Captain Marvel-No. 25(part).* ***M.Swayze*** *a-37, 38, 59; c-38.* ***Schaffenberger*** *c-138-155(most).* ***Wolverton*** *1/2 pg. "Culture Corner"-No. 65-67, 68(2 1/2 pgs), 70-85, 87-96, 98-100, 102-109, 112-121, 123, 125, 126, 128-131, 133, 134, 136, 142, 143, 146.*

WHIZ KIDS (Also see Big Bang Comics)
Image Comics: Apr, 2003 ($4.95, B&W, one-shot)

1-Galahad, Cyclone, Thunder Girl and Moray app.; Jeff Austin-a 5.00

WHOA, NELLIE (Also see Love & Rockets)
Fantagraphics Books: July, 1996 - No. 3, Sept, 1996 ($2.95, B&W, lim. series)

1-3: Jamie Hernandez-c/a/scripts 3.00

WHODUNIT
D.S. Publishing Co.: Aug-Sept, 1948 - No. 3, Dec-Jan, 1948-49 (#1,2: 52 pgs.)

	GD	VG	FN	VF	VF/NM	NM-
1-Baker-a (7 pgs.)	26	52	78	154	252	350
2,3-Detective mysteries	14	28	42	80	115	150

WHODUNNIT?
Eclipse Comics: June, 1986 - No. 3, Apr, 1987 ($2.00, limited series)

1-3: Spiegle-a. 2-Gulacy-c 3.00

WHO FRAMED ROGER RABBIT (See Marvel Graphic Novel)

WHO IS NEXT?
Standard Comics: No. 5, Jan, 1953

	GD	VG	FN	VF	VF/NM	NM-
5-Toth, Sekowsky, Andru-a; crime stories	26	52	78	154	252	350

WHO IS THE CROOKED MAN?
Crusade: Sept, 1996 ($3.50, B&W, 40 pgs.)

1-Intro The Martyr, Scarlet 7 & Garrison 4.00

WHO'S MINDING THE MINT? (See Movie Classics)

WHO'S WHO IN STAR TREK
DC Comics: Mar, 1987 - #2, Apr, 1987 ($1.50, limited series)

1,2 6.00

NOTE: ***Byrne*** *a-1, 2.* ***Chaykin*** *c-1, 2.* ***Morrow*** *a-1, 2.* ***McFarlane*** *a-2.* ***Perez*** *a-1, 2.* ***Sutton*** *a-1, 2.*

WHO'S WHO IN THE LEGION OF SUPER-HEROES
DC Comics: Apr, 1987 - No. 7, Nov, 1988 ($1.25, limited series)

1-7 4.00

WHO'S WHO: THE DEFINITIVE DIRECTORY OF THE DC UNIVERSE
DC Comics: Mar, 1985 - No. 26, Apr, 1987 (Maxi-series, no ads)

1-DC heroes from A-Z 4.00
2-26: All have 1-2 pgs-a by most DC artists 4.00

NOTE: ***Art Adams*** *a-4, 11, 18, 20.* ***Anderson*** *a-1-5, 7-12, 14, 15, 19, 21, 23-25.* ***Aparo*** *a-2, 3, 9, 10, 12, 13, 14, 15, 17, 18, 21, 23.* ***Byrne*** *a-4, 7, 14, 16, 18i, 19, 22i, 24; c-22.* ***Cowan*** *a-3-5, 8, 10-13, 16-18, 22-25.* ***Ditko*** *a-19-22.* ***Evans*** *a-20.* ***Giffen*** *a-1, 3,-6, 8, 13, 15, 17, 18, 23.* ***Grell*** *a-6, 9, 14, 20, 23, 25, 26.* ***Infantino*** *a-1-10, 12, 15, 17-22, 24, 25.* ***Kaluta*** *a-14, 21.* ***Gil Kane*** *a-1-11, 13, 14, 16, 19, 21-23, 25.* ***Kirby*** *a-2-6, 8-18, 20, 22, 25.* ***Kubert*** *a-2, 3, 7-11, 19, 20, 25.* ***Erik Larsen*** *a-24.* ***McFarlane*** *a-10-12, 17, 19, 25, 26.* ***Morrow*** *a-4, 7, 25, 26.* ***Orlando*** *a-1, 4, 10, 11, 21i.* ***Perez*** *a-1-5, 8-19, 22-26; c-1-4, 13-18.* ***Rogers*** *a-1, 2, 5-7, 11, 12, 15, 24.* ***Starlin*** *a-13, 14, 16.* ***Stevens*** *a-4, 7, 18.*

WHO'S WHO UPDATE '87
DC Comics: Aug, 1987 - No. 5, Dec, 1987 ($1.25, limited series)

1-5: Contains art by most DC artists 4.00

NOTE: ***Giffen*** *a-1.* ***McFarlane*** *a-1-4; c-4.* ***Perez*** *a-1-4.*

WHO'S WHO UPDATE '88
DC Comics: Aug, 1988 - No. 4, Nov, 1988 ($1.25, limited series)

1-4: Contains art by most DC artists 4.00

NOTE: ***Giffen*** *a-1.* ***Erik Larsen*** *a-1.*

WICKED, THE
Avalon Studios: Dec, 1999 - No. 7, Aug, 2000 ($2.95)

Preview-(7/99, $5.00, B&W) 5.00
1-7-Anacleto-c/Martinez-a 3.00
...: Medusa's Tale (11/00, $3.95, one shot) story plus pin-up gallery 4.00
...: Vol. 1: Omnibus (2003, $19.95) r/#0-8; Drew-c 20.00

WIDOWMAKER
Marvel Comics: Feb, 2011 - No. 4, Apr, 2011 ($3.99, limited series)

1-4-Black Widow, Hawkeye & Mockingbird app. 1,2-Jae Lee-c. 3,4-Noto-c 4.00

WIDOW WARRIORS
Dynamite Entertainment: 2010 - No. 4, 2010 ($3.99, limited series)

1-4-Pat Lee-a/c 4.00

WILBUR COMICS (Teen-age) (Also see Laugh Comics, Laugh Comix, Liberty Comics #10 & Zip Comics)
MLJ Magazines/Archie Publ. No. 8, Spring, 1946 on: Sum', 1944 - No. 87, 11/59; No. 88, 9/63; No. 89, 10/64; No. 90, 10/65 (No. 1-46: 52 pgs.) (#1-11 are quarterly)

	GD	VG	FN	VF	VF/NM	NM-
1	61	122	183	390	670	950
2(Fall, 1944)	34	68	102	204	332	460
3,4(Wint, '44-45; Spr, '45)	24	48	72	142	234	325
5-1st app. Katy Keene (Sum, '45) & begin series; Wilbur story same as Archie story in Archie #1 except Wilbur replaces Archie	129	258	387	826	1413	2000
6-10: 10-(Fall, 1946)	27	54	81	160	263	365
11-20	16	32	48	94	147	200
21-30: 30-(4/50)	12	24	36	69	97	125
31-50	10	20	30	54	72	90
51-70	9	18	27	47	61	75
71-90: 88-Last 10¢ issue (9/63)	4	8	12	27	44	60

NOTE: *Katy Keene in No. 5-56, 58-61, 63-69.* ***Al Fagaly*** *c-6-9, 12-24 at least.* ***Vigoda*** *c-2.*

WILD
Atlas Comics (IPC): Feb, 1954 - No. 5, Aug, 1954

	GD	VG	FN	VF	VF/NM	NM-
1	30	60	90	177	289	400
2	18	36	54	107	169	230
3-5	16	32	48	94	147	200

NOTE: ***Berg*** *a-5; c-4.* ***Burgos*** *c-3.* ***Colan*** *a-4.* ***Everett*** *a-1-3.* ***Heath*** *a-2, 3, 5.* ***Maneely*** *a-1-3, 5; c-1, 5.* ***Post*** *a-2, 5.* ***Ed Win*** *a-1, 3.*

WILD! (This Magazine Is...) (Satire)
Dell Publishing Co.: Jan, 1968 - No. 3, 1968 (35¢, magazine, 52 pgs.)

	GD	VG	FN	VF	VF/NM	NM-
1-3: Hogan's Heroes, The Rat Patrol & Mission Impossible TV spoofs	3	6	9	16	23	30

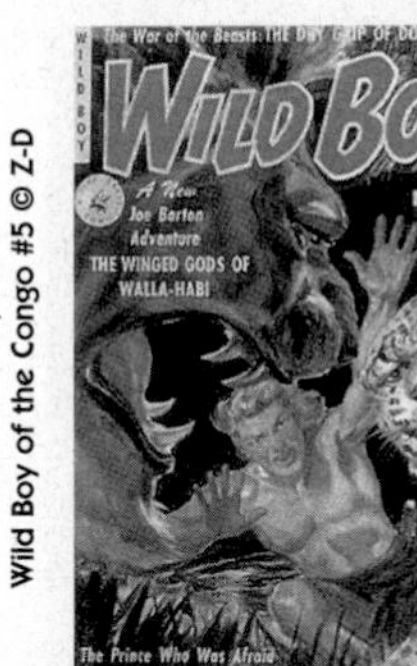
Wild Boy of the Congo #5 © Z-D

WildC.A.T.S #27 © WSP

Wildcats V4 #1 © WSP

WILD ANIMALS
Pacific Comics: Dec, 1982 ($1.00, one-shot, direct sales)

	GD 2.0	VG 4.0	FN 6.0	VF 8.0	VF/NM 9.0	NM- 9.2
1-Funny animal; Sergio Aragonés-a; Shaw-c/a						4.00

WILD BILL ELLIOTT (Also see Western Roundup under Dell Giants)
Dell Publishing Co.: No. 278, 5/50 - No. 643, 7/55 (No #11,12) (All photo-c)

	GD 2.0	VG 4.0	FN 6.0	VF 8.0	VF/NM 9.0	NM- 9.2
Four Color 278 (#1, 52pgs.)-Titled "Bill Elliott"; Bill & his horse Stormy begin; photo front/back-c begin	11	22	33	73	157	240
2 (11/50), 3 (52 pgs.)	7	14	21	44	82	120
4-10 (10-12/52)	5	10	15	35	63	90
Four Color 472 (6/53), 520(12/53)-Last photo back-c	5	10	15	33	57	80
13 (4-6/54) - 17 (4-6/55)	5	10	15	30	50	70
Four Color 643 (7/55)	5	10	15	30	50	70

WILD BILL HICKOK (Also see Blazing Sixguns)
Avon Periodicals: Sept-Oct, 1949 - No. 28, May-June, 1956

	GD 2.0	VG 4.0	FN 6.0	VF 8.0	VF/NM 9.0	NM- 9.2
1-Ingels-c	25	50	75	150	245	340
2-Painted-c; Kit West app.	14	28	42	82	121	160
3-5-Painted-c (4-Cover by Howard Winfield)	11	22	33	62	86	110
6-10,12: 8-10-Painted-c. 12-Kinsler-c?	11	22	33	60	83	105
11,13,14-Kinstler-c/a (#11-c & inside-f/c art only)	11	22	33	64	90	115
15,17,18,20: 18-Kit West story. 20-Kit West by Larsen	10	20	30	54	72	90
16-Kamen-a; r-3 stories/King of the Badmen of Deadwood	10	20	30	56	76	95
19-Meskin-a	10	20	30	54	72	90
21-Reprints 2 stories/Chief Crazy Horse	9	18	27	52	69	85
22-McCann-a?; r/Sheriff Bob Dixon's...	9	18	27	52	69	85
23-27: 23-Kinstler-c. 24-27-Kinstler-c/a(r) (24,25-r?)	9	18	27	52	69	85
28-Kinstler-c/a (new); r-/Last of the Comanches	10	20	30	54	72	90
I.W. Reprint #1-r/#2; Kinstler-c	2	4	6	9	13	16
Super Reprint #10-12: 10-r/#18. 11-r/#?. 12-r/#8	2	4	6	9	13	16

NOTE: #23, 25 contain numerous editing deletions in both art and script due to code. ***Kinstler*** *c-6, 7, 11-14, 17, 18, 20-22, 24-28.* ***Howard Larsen*** *a-1, 2, 4, 5, 6(3), 7-9, 11, 12, 17, 18, 20-24, 26.* ***Meskin*** *a-7.* ***Reinman*** *a-6, 17.*

WILD BILL HICKOK AND JINGLES (TV)(Formerly Cowboy Western) (Also see Blue Bird)
Charlton Comics: No. 68, Aug, 1958 - No. 75, Dec, 1959

	GD 2.0	VG 4.0	FN 6.0	VF 8.0	VF/NM 9.0	NM- 9.2
68,69-Williamson-a (all are 10¢ issues)	11	22	33	60	83	105
70-Two pgs. Williamson-a	8	16	24	42	54	65
71-75 (#76, exist?)	6	12	18	28	34	40

WILD BILL PECOS WESTERN (Also see The Westerner)
AC Comics: 1989 ($3.50, 1/2 color, 1/2 B&W, 52 pgs.)

	GD 2.0	VG 4.0	FN 6.0	VF 8.0	VF/NM 9.0	NM- 9.2
1-Syd Shores-c/a(r)/Westerner; photo back-c						4.00

WILD BOY OF THE CONGO (Also see Approved Comics)
Ziff-Davis No. 10-12,4-8/St. John No. 9,11 on: No. 10, 2-3/51 - No. 12, 8-9/51; No. 4, 10-11/51 - No. 9, 10/53; No. 11-#15,6/55 (No #10, 1953)

	GD 2.0	VG 4.0	FN 6.0	VF 8.0	VF/NM 9.0	NM- 9.2
10(#1)(2-3/51)-Origin; bondage-c by Saunders (painted); used in **SOTI**, pg. 189; painted-c begin thru #9 (except #7)	28	56	84	165	270	375
11(4-5/51),12(8-9/51)-Norman Saunders painted-c	15	30	45	86	133	180
4(10-11/51)-Saunders painted bondage-c	15	30	45	86	133	180
5(Winter,'51)-Saunders painted-c	14	28	42	82	121	160
6,8,9(10/53): Painted-c. 6-Saunders-c	14	28	42	82	121	160
7(8-9/52)-Kinstler-a	15	30	45	86	133	180
11-13-Baker-c. 11-r/#7 w/new Baker-c; Kinstler-a (2 pgs.)	17	34	51	98	154	210
14(4/55)-Baker-c; r-#12('51)	17	34	51	98	154	210
15(6/55)	13	26	39	74	105	135

WILDCAT (See Sensation Comics #1)

WILDC.A.T.S ADVENTURES (TV cartoon)
Image Comics (WildStorm): Sept, 1994 - No. 10, June, 1995 ($1.95/$2.50)

	NM- 9.2
1-10	3.00
Sourcebook 1 (1/95, $2.95)	3.00

WILDC.A.T.S: COVERT ACTION TEAMS (Also see Alan Moore's... for TPB reprints)
Image Comics (WildStorm Productions): Aug, 1992 - No. 4, Mar, 1993; No. 5, Nov, 1993 - No. 50, June, 1998 ($1.95/$2.50)

	NM- 9.2
1-1st app; Jim Lee/Williams-c/a & Lee scripts begin; contains 2 trading cards (Two diff versions of cards inside); 1st WildStorm Productions title	5.00
1-All gold foil signed edition	20.00
1-All gold foil unsigned edition	10.00
1-Newsstand edition w/o cards	3.00
1-"3-D Special"(8/97, $4.95) w/3-D glasses; variant-c by Jim Lee.	5.00
2-($2.50)-Prism foil stamped-c; contains coupon for Image Comics #0 & 4 pg. preview to Portacio's Wetworks (back-up)	5.00
2-With coupon missing	2.00
2-Direct sale misprint w/o foil-c	5.00
2-Newsstand ed., no prism or coupon	3.00
3-Lee/Liefeld-c (1/93-c, 12/92 inside)	4.00
4-($2.50)-Polybagged w/Topps trading card; 1st app. Tribe by Johnson & Stroman; Youngblood cameo	4.00
4-Variant w/red card	6.00
5-7-Jim Lee/Williams-c/a; Lee script	3.00
8-X-Men's Jean Grey & Scott Summers cameo	4.00
9-12: 10-1st app. Huntsman & Soldier; Claremont scripts begin, ends #13. 11-1st app. Savant, Tapestry & Mr. Majestic.	3.00
11-Alternate Portacio-c, see Deathblow #5	5.00
13-19,21-24: 15-James Robinson scripts begin, ends #20. 15,16-Black Razor story. 21-Alan Moore scripts begin, end #34; intro Tao & Ladytron; new WildC.A.T.S team forms (Mr. Majestic, Savant, Condition Red (Max Cash), Tao & Ladytron). 22-Maguire-a	3.00
20-($2.50)-Direct Market, WildStorm Rising Pt. 2 w/bound-in card	4.00
20-($1.95)-Newsstand, WildStorm Rising Part 2	3.00
25-($4.95)-Alan Moore script; wraparound foil-c.	5.00
26-49: 29-(5/96)-Fire From Heaven Pt 7; reads Apr on-c. 30-(6/96)-Fire From Heaven Pt. 13; Spartan revealed to have transplanted personality of John Colt (from Team One: WildC.A.T.S). 31-(9/96)-Grifter rejoins team; Ladytron dies	3.00
40-($3.50)Voyager Pack bagged w/Divine Right preview	5.00
50-($3.50) Stories by Robinson/Lee, Choi & Peterson/Benes, and Moore/Charest; Charest sketchbook; Lee wraparound-c	4.00
50-Chromium cover	6.00
Annual 1 (2/98, $2.95) Robinson-s	4.00
Compendium (1993, $9.95)-r/#1-4; bagged w/#0	15.00
Sourcebook 1 (9/93, $2.50)-Foil embossed-c	3.00
Sourcebook 1-($1.95)-Newsstand ed. w/o foil embossed-c	3.00
Sourcebook 2 (11/94, $2.50)-wraparound-c	3.00
Special 1 (11/93, $3.50, 52 pgs.)-1st Travis Charest WildC.A.T.S-a	4.00
...A Gathering of Eagles (5/97, $9.95, TPB) r/#10-12	10.00
.../ Cyberforce: Killer Instinct TPB (2004, $14.95) r/#5-7 & Cyberforce V2 #1-3	15.00
...Gang War ('98, $16.95, TPB) r/#28-34	17.00
...Homecoming (8/98, $19.95, TPB) r/#21-27	20.00
James Robinson's Complete Wildc.a.t.s TPB (2009, $24.99) r/#15-20,50; Annual 1, WildStorm Rising #1, Team One Wildc.a.t.s #1,2; cover and pin-up gallery	25.00

WILDCATS (3rd series)
DC Comics (WildStorm): Mar, 1999 - No. 28, Dec, 2001 ($2.50)

	NM- 9.2
1-Charest-a; six covers by Lee, Adams, Bisley, Campbell, Madureira and Ramos; Lobdell-s	4.00
1-($6.95) DF Edition; variant cover by Ramos	7.00
2-28: 2-Voodoo cover. 3-Bachalo variant-c. 5-Hitch-a/variant-c. 7-Meglia-a. 8-Phillips-a begins. 17-J.G. Jones-c. 18,19-Jim Lee-c. 20,21-Dillon-a	3.00
Annual 2000 (12/00, $3.50) Bermejo-a; Devil's Night x-over	4.00
...: Battery Park ('03, $17.95, TPB) r/#20-28; Phillips-c	18.00
... Ladytron (10/00, $5.95) Origin; Casey-s/Canete-a	6.00
... Mosaic (2/00, $3.95) Tuska-a (10 pg. back-up story)	4.00
...: Serial Boxes ('01, $14.95, TPB) r/#14-19; Phillips-c	15.00
...: Street Smart ('00, $24.95, HC) r/#1-6; Charest-c	25.00
...: Street Smart ('02, $14.95, SC) r/#1-6; Charest-c	15.00
...: Vicious Circles ('00, $14.95, TPB) r/#8-13; Phillips-c	15.00

WILDCATS (Volume 4)
DC Comics (WildStorm): Dec, 2006 ($2.99)

	NM- 9.2
1-Grant Morrison-s/Jim Lee-a; Jim Lee-c	3.00
1-Variant-c by Todd McFarlane/Jim Lee	6.00
...: Armageddon 1 (2/08, $2.99) Gage-s/Caldwell-a	3.00

WILDCATS (Volume 5) (World's End on cover for #1,2)
DC Comics (WildStorm): Sept, 2008 - No. 30, Feb, 2011 ($2.99)

	NM- 9.2
1-30: 1-Christos Gage-s/Neil Googe-a. 5-Woods-a	3.00
...: Family Secrets TPB (2010, $17.99) r/#8-12	18.00
...: World's End TPB (2009, $17.99) r/#1-7	18.00

WILDC.A.T.S/ ALIENS
Image Comics/Dark Horse: Aug, 1998 ($4.95, one-shot)

	GD 2.0	VG 4.0	FN 6.0	VF 8.0	VF/NM 9.0	NM- 9.2
1-Ellis-s/Sprouse-a/c; Aliens invade Skywatch; Stormwatch app.; death of Winter; destruction of Skywatch	1	2	3	5	6	8
1-Variant-c by Gil Kane	1	3	4	6	8	10

WILDCATS: NEMESIS
DC Comics (WildStorm): Nov, 2005 - No. 9, July, 2006 ($2.99, limited series)

	NM- 9.2
1-9: 1-Robbie Morrison-s/Talent Caldwell & Horacio Domingues-a/Caldwell-c	3.00

Wild Dog #3 © DC

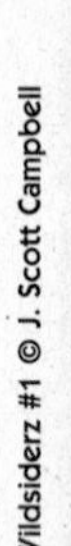
Wildsiderz #1 © J. Scott Campbell

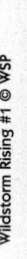

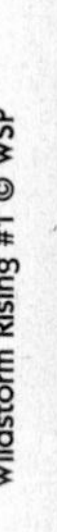
Wildstorm Rising #1 © WSP

GD	VG	FN	VF	VF/NM	NM-
2.0	4.0	6.0	8.0	9.0	9.2

GD VG FN VF VF/NM NM-
2.0 4.0 6.0 8.0 9.0 9.2

TPB (2006, $19.99) r/#1-9; cover gallery 20.00

WILDC.A.T.S: SAVANT GARDE FAN EDITION
Image Comics/WildStorm Productions: Feb, 1997 - No. 3, Apr, 1997 (Giveaway, 8 pgs.) (Polybagged w/Overstreet's FAN)

1-3: Barbara Kesel-s/Christian Uche-a(p) 3.00
1-3-(Gold): All retailer incentives 10.00

WILDC.A.T.S TRILOGY
Image Comics (WildStorm Productions): June, 1993 - No. 3, Dec, 1993 ($1.95, lim. series)

1-($2.50)-1st app. Gen 13 (Fairchild, Burnout, Grunge, Freefall) Multi-color foil-c; Jae Lee-c/a in all 5.00
1-($1.95)-Newsstand ed. w/o foil-c 3.00
2,3-($1.95)-Jae Lee-c/a 3.00

WILDCATS VERSION 3.0
DC Comics (WildStorm): Oct, 2002 - No. 24, Oct, 2004 ($2.95)

1-24: 1-Casey-s/Nguyen-a; two covers by Nguyen and Rian Hughes and Nguyen. 8-Back-up preview of The Authority: High Stakes pt. 3 3.00
...: Brand Building TPB (2003, $14.95) r/#1-6 15.00
...: Full Disclosure TPB (2004, $14.95) r/#7-12 15.00
...: Year One TPB (2010, $24.99) r/#1-12 25.00
...: Year Two TPB (2011, $24.99) r/#13-24 25.00

WILDC.A.T.S/ X-MEN: THE GOLDEN AGE (See also X-Men/WildC.A.T.S.: The Dark Age)
Image Comics (WildStorm Productions): Feb, 1997 ($4.50, one-shot)

1-Lobdell-s/Charest-a; Two covers (Charest, Jim Lee) 5.00
1-"3-D" Edition ($6.50) w/glasses 7.00

WILDC.A.T.S/ X-MEN: THE MODERN AGE
Image Comics (WildStorm Productions): Aug, 1997 ($4.50, one-shot)

1-Robinson-s/Hughes-a; Two covers (Hughes, Paul Smith) 5.00
1-"3-D" Edition ($6.50) w/glasses 7.00

WILDC.A.T.S/ X-MEN: THE SILVER AGE
Image Comics (WildStorm Productions): June, 1997 ($4.50, one-shot)

1-Lobdell-s/Jim Lee-a; Two covers(Neal Adams, Jim Lee) 5.00
1-"3-D" Edition ($6.50) w/glasses 7.00

WILDCORE
Image Comics (WildStorm Prods.): Nov, 1997 - No. 10, Dec, 1998 ($2.50)

1-10: 1-Two covers (Booth/McWeeney, Charest) 3.00
1-($3.50)-Voyager Pack w/DV8 preview 4.00
1-Chromium-c 5.00

WILD DOG
DC Comics: Sept, 1987 - No. 4, Dec, 1987 (75¢, limited series)

1-4 3.00
Special 1 (1989, $2.50, 52 pgs.) 4.00

WILDERNESS TREK (See Zane Grey, Four Color 333)

WILDFIRE (See Zane Grey, FourColor 433)

WILDFLOWER
Sirius Entertainment/Neko Press: 1996 - Present (B&W)

1-5-('96, $2.50) Billy Martinez-s/a 3.00
... Beginnings TPB (Neko Press, 2003, $14.99) r/#1-5 15.00
... Dark Euphoria 1 (2004, $2.99) Kiethan Jones-a/c; Martinez-s 3.00
... Dark Euphoria 1,2 (2004, $3.99) w/alternate-c by Martinez 4.00
... Tribal Screams 1-4 (12/00 - 2/03, $2.99) 3.00
... Tribal Screams 1 ($4.99) w/alternate-c by Dark One 5.00
... Y2K (16 pgs, edition of 2000) each contains an original Martinez sketch 10.00

WILD FRONTIER (Cheyenne Kid #8 on)
Charlton Comics: Oct, 1955 - No. 7, Apr, 1957

	GD	VG	FN	VF	VF/NM	NM-
1-Davy Crockett	10	20	30	54	72	90
2-6-Davy Crockett in all	7	14	21	37	46	55
7-Origin & 1st app. Cheyenne Kid	9	18	27	47	61	75

WILD GIRL
DC Comics (WildStorm): Jan, 2005 - No. 6, Jun, 2005 ($2.95/$2.99)

1-6-Leah Moore & John Reppion-s/Shawn McManus-a/c 3.00

WILDGUARD: CASTING CALL
Image Comics: Sept, 2003 - No. 6, Feb, 2004 ($2.95)

1-6: 1-Nauck-s/a; two covers by Nauck and McGuinness. 2-Wieringo var-c. 6-Noto var-c 3.00
... Vol. 1: Casting Call (1/05, $17.95, TPB) r/#1-6; cover gallery; Todd Nauck bio 18.00
Wildguard: Fire Power 1 (12/04, $3.50) Nauck-a; two covers 3.50
Wildguard: Fool's Gold (7/05 - No. 2, 7/05, $3.50) 1,2-Todd Nauck-s/a 3.50
Wildguard: Insider (5/08 - No. 3, 7/08, $3.50) 1-3-Todd Nauck-s/a 3.50

WILDSIDERZ
DC Comics (WildStorm): No. 0, Aug, 2005 - No. 2, Jan, 2006 ($1.99/$3.50)

0-(8/05, $1.99) Series preview & character profiles; J. Scott Campbell-a 3.00
1,2: 1-(10/05, $3.50) J. Scott Campbell-s/a; Andy Hartnell-s 3.50

WILDSTAR (Also see The Dragon & The Savage Dragon)
Image Comics (Highbrow Entertainment): Sept, 1995 - No. 3, Jan, 1996 ($2.50, lim. series)

1-3: Al Gordon scripts; Jerry Ordway-c/a 3.00

WILDSTAR: SKY ZERO
Image Comics (Highbrow Entertainment): Mar, 1993 - No. 4, Nov, 1993 ($1.95, lim. series)

1-4: 1-($2.50)-Embossed-c w/silver ink; Ordway-c/a in all 3.00
1-($1.95)-Newsstand ed. w/silver ink-c, not embossed 3.00
1-Gold variant 6.00

WILD STARS
Collector's Edition/Little Rocket Productions: Summer, 1984 - Present (B&W)

Vol. 1 #1 (Summer 1984, $1.50) 5.00
Vol. 2 #1 (Winter 1988, $1.95) Foil-c; die-cut front & back-c 5.00
Vol. 3: #1-6-Brunner-c; Tierney-s. 1,2-Brewer-a. 3-6-Simons-a 3.00
7-($5.95) Simons-a 6.00
TPB (2004, $17.95) r/Vol. 1-3 18.00

WILDSTORM
Image Comics/DC Comics (WildStorm Publishing): 1994 - Present (one-shots, TPBs)

... After the Fall TPB (2009, $19.99) r/back-up stories from Wildcats V5 #1-11, The Authority V5 #1-11; Gen 13 V4 #21-28, and Stormwatch: PHD #13-20 20.00
...Annual 2000 (12/00, $3.50) Devil's Night x-over; Moy-a 4.00
...: Armageddon TPB (2008, $17.99) r/Armageddon one-shots in Midnighter, Welcome To Tranquility, Wetworks, Gen13, Stormwatch PHD, and Wildcats titles 18.00
...Chamber of Horrors (10/95, $3.50)-Bisley-c 4.00
...Fine Arts: Spotlight on Gen13 (2/08, $3.50) art and covers with commentary 3.50
...Fine Arts: Spotlight on Jim Lee (2/07, $3.50) art and covers by Lee with commentary 3.50
...Fine Arts: Spotlight on J. Scott Campbell (5/07, $3.50) art and covers with commentary 3.50
...Fine Arts: Spotlight on The Authority (1/08, $3.50) art and covers with commentary 3.50
...Fine Arts: Spotlight on WildCATs (3/08, $3.50) art and covers with commentary 3.50
...Fine Arts: The Gallery Collection (12/98, $19.95) Lee-c 20.00
...Halloween 1 (10/97, $2.50) Warner-c 3.00
...Rarities 1(12/94, $4.95, 52 pgs.)-r/Gen 13 1/2 & other stories 5.00
...Summer Special 1 (2001, $5.95) Short stories by various; Hughes-c 6.00
...Swimsuit Special 1 (12/94, $2.95), ...Swimsuit Special 2 (1995, $2.50) 3.00
...Swimsuit Special '97 #1 (7/97, $2.50) 3.00
...Thunderbook 1 (10/00, $6.95) Short stories by various incl. Hughes, Moy 7.00
...Ultimate Sports 1 (8/97, $2.50) 3.00
...Universe Sourcebook (5/95, $2.50) 3.00
...Universe 2008 Convention Exclusive ('08, no cover price) preview of World's End x-over 3.00

WILDSTORM!
Image Comics (WildStorm Publishing): Aug, 1995 - No. 4, Nov, 1995 ($2.50, B&W/color, anthology)

1-4: 1-Simonson-a 3.00

WILDSTORM PRESENTS: ...
DC Comics (WildStorm): Jan, 2011 - Present ($7.99, squarebound, reprints)

1-(1/11) r/short stories by various incl. Pearson, Conner, Corben, Jeanty, Mahnke 8.00
Planetary: Lost Worlds (2/11) r/Planetary/Authority & Planetary/JLA: Terra Occulta 8.00

WILDSTORM REVELATIONS
DC Comics (WildStorm): Mar, 2008 - No. 6, May, 2008 ($2.99, limited series)

1-6-Beatty & Gage-s/Craig-a. 2-The Authority app. 3.00
TPB (2008, $17.99) r/#1-6; cover sketches 18.00

WILDSTORM RISING
Image Comics (WildStorm Publishing): May, 1995 - No.2, June, 1995 ($1.95/$2.50)

1-($2.50)-Direct Market, WildStorm Rising Pt. 1 w/bound-in card 3.00
1-($1.95)-Newstand, WildStorm Rising Pt. 1 3.00
2-($2.50)-Direct Market, WildStorm Rising Pt. 10 w/bound-in card; continues in WildC.A.T.S #21. 3.00
2-($1.95)-Newstand, WildStorm Rising Pt. 10 3.00
Trade paperback (1996, $19.95)-Collects x-over; B. Smith-c 20.00

WILDSTORM SPOTLIGHT
Image Comics (WildStorm Publishing): Feb, 1997 - No. 4 ($2.50)

1-4: 1-Alan Moore-s 3.00

WILDSTORM UNIVERSE '97

Wild West #1 © MAR

Wild Western #4 © MAR

Will to Power #6 © DH

GD 2.0 | VG 4.0 | FN 6.0 | VF 8.0 | VF/NM 9.0 | NM- 9.2

Image Comics (WildStorm Publishing): Dec, 1996 - No. 3 ($2.50, limited series)
1-3: 1-Wraparound-c. 3-Gary Frank-c 3.00

WILDTHING
Marvel Comics UK: Apr, 1993 - No. 7, Oct, 1993 ($1.75)
1-($2.50)-Embossed-c; Venom & Carnage cameo 4.00
2-7: 2-Spider-Man & Venom. 6-Mysterio app. 3.00

WILD THING (Wolverine's daughter in the M2 universe)
Marvel Comics: Oct, 1999 - No. 5, Feb, 2000 ($1.99)
1-5: 1-Lim-a in all. 2-Two covers 3.00
Wizard #0 supplement; battles the Hulk 3.00
Spider-Girl Presents Wild Thing. Crash Course (2007, $7.99, digest) r/#0-5 8.00

WILDTIMES
DC Comics (WildStorm Productions): Aug, 1999 ($2.50, one-shots)
...Deathblow #1 -set in 1899; Edwards-a; Jonah Hex app., ...DV8 #1 -set in 1944; Altieri-s/p; Sgt. Rock app., ...Gen13 #1 -set in 1969; Casey-s/Johnson-a; Teen Titans app., ...Grifter #1 -set in 1923; Paul Smith-a, ...Wetworks #1 -Waid-s/Lopresti-a; Superman app. 3.00
...WildC.A.T.s #0 -Wizard supplement; Charest-c 3.00

WILD WEST (Wild Western #3 on)
Marvel Comics (WFP): Spring, 1948 - No. 2, July, 1948
1-Two-Gun Kid, Arizona Annie, & Tex Taylor begin; Shores-c 34 68 102 199 325 450
2-Captain Tootsie by Beck; Shores-c 22 44 66 132 216 300

WILD WEST (Black Fury #1-57)
Charlton Comics: V2#58, Nov, 1966
V2#58 2 4 6 11 16 20

WILD WEST C.O.W.-BOYS OF MOO MESA (TV)
Archie Comics: Dec, 1992 - No. 3, Feb, 1993 (limited series)
V2#1, Mar, 1993 - No. 3, July, 1993 ($1.25)
1-3,V2#1-3 3.00

WILD WESTERN (Formerly Wild West #1,2)
Marvel/Atlas (WFP): No. 3, 9/48 - No. 57, 9/57 (3-11: 52 pgs, 12-on: 36 pgs)
3(#1)-Tex Morgan begins; Two-Gun Kid, Tex Taylor, & Arizona Annie continue from Wild West 27 54 81 158 259 360
4-Last Arizona Annie; Captain Tootsie by Beck; Kid Colt app. 20 40 60 114 182 250
5-2nd app. Black Rider (1/49); Blaze Carson, Captain Tootsie (by Beck) app. 23 46 69 136 223 310
6-8: 6-Blaze Carson app; anti-Wertham editorial 15 30 45 88 137 185
9-Photo-c; Black Rider app., also in #11-19 19 38 57 109 172 235
10-Charles Starrett photo-c 22 44 66 128 209 290
11-(Last 52 pg. issue) The Prairie Kid app. 15 30 45 85 130 175
12-14,16-19: All Black Rider-c/stories. 12-14-The Prairie Kid & his horse Fury app. 15 30 45 83 124 165
15-Red Larabee, Gunhawk (origin), his horse Blaze, & Apache Kid begin, end #22; Black Rider-c/story 15 30 45 84 127 170
20-30: 20-Kid Colt-c begin. 24-Has 2 Kid Colt stories. 26-1st app. The Ringo Kid? (2/53); 4 pg. story. 30-Katz-a 12 24 36 69 97 125
31-40 10 20 30 54 72 90
41-47,49-51,53,57 9 18 27 47 61 75
48-Williamson/Torres-a (4 pgs); Drucker-a 10 20 30 56 76 95
52-Crandall-a 10 20 30 56 76 95
54,55-Williamson-a in both (5 & 4 pgs.), #54 with Mayo plus 2 text illos 10 20 30 56 76 95
56-Baker-a? 9 18 27 47 61 75
NOTE: *Annie Oakley in #46, 47. Apache Kid in #15-22, 39. Arizona Kid in #21, 23. Arrowhead in #34-39. Black Rider in #5, 9-19, 33-44. Fighting Texan in #17. Kid Colt in #4-6, 9-11, 20-47, 52, 54-56. Outlaw Kid in #43. Red Hawkins in #13, 14. Ringo Kid in #26, 39, 41, 43, 44, 46, 47, 50, 52-56. Tex Morgan in #3, 4, 6, 9, 11. Tex Taylor in #3-6, 9, 11. Texas Kid in #23-25. Two-Gun Kid in #3-6, 9, 11, 12, 33-39, 41. Wyatt Earp in #47.* ***Ayers** a-41, 42, 53, 54.* ***Berg** a-26; c-24.* ***Colan** a-49.* ***Forte** a-28, 30.* ***Al Hartley** a-16.* ***Heath** a-4, 5, 8; c-34, 44.* ***Keller** a-24, 26(2), 29-40, 44-46, 48, 52.* ***Maneely** a-10, 12, 15, 16, 28, 35, 38, 40-45; c-18-22, 33, 35, 36, 38-42, 45, 53, 54, 56, 57.* ***Morisi** a-23, 52.* ***Pakula** a-42, 52.* ***Powell** a-51.* ***Romita** a-24(2).* ***Severin** a-46, 47; c-48.* ***Shores** a-3, 5, 30, 31, 33, 35, 36, 38, 41; c-3-5.* ***Sinnott** a-34-39.* ***Wildey** a-43. Bondage c-19.*

WILD WESTERN ACTION (Also see The Bravados)
Skywald Publ. Corp.: Mar, 1971 - No. 3, June, 1971 (25¢, reprints, 52 pgs.)
1-Durango Kid, Straight Arrow-r; with all references to "Straight" in story relettered to "Swift"; Bravados begin; Shores-a (new) 3 6 9 16 24 32
2,3: 2-Billy Nevada, Durango Kid. 3-Red Mask, Durango Kid 2 4 6 13 18 22

WILD WESTERN ROUNDUP
Red Top/Decker Publications/I. W. Enterprises: Oct, 1957; 1960-'61
1(1957)-Kid Cowboy-r 5 10 15 22 26 30
I.W. Reprint #1('60-61)-r/#1 by Red Top 2 4 6 8 11 14

WILD WEST RODEO
Star Publications: 1953 (15¢)
1-A comic book coloring book with regular full color cover & B&W inside 9 18 27 47 61 75

WILD WILD WEST, THE (TV)
Gold Key: June, 1966 - No. 7, Oct, 1969 (All have Robert Conrad photo-c)
1-McWilliams-a 10 20 30 67 141 215
1-Variant edition with photo back-c (scarce) 11 22 33 73 157 240
2-Robert Conrad photo-c; McWilliams-a 8 16 24 51 96 140
2-Variant edition with Conrad photo back-c (scarce) 8 16 24 56 108 160
3-7 6 12 18 42 79 115
3-Variant edition with photo back-c (scarce) 8 16 24 51 96 140

WILD, WILD WEST, THE (TV)
Millennium Publications: Oct, 1990 - No. 4, Jan?, 1991 ($2.95, limited series)
1-4-Based on TV show 3.00

WILKIN BOY (See That...)

WILL EISNER READER
Kitchen Sink Press: 1991 ($9.95, B&W, 8 1/2" x 11", TPB)
nn-Reprints stories from Will Eisner's Quarterly; Eisner-s/a/c 15.00
nn-(DC Comics, 10/00, $9.95) 10.00

WILL EISNER'S JOHN LAW: ANGELS AND ASHES, DEVILS AND DUST
IDW Publ.: Apr, 2006 - No. 4 ($3.99, B&W, limited series)
1-New stories with Will Eisner's characters; Gary Chaloner-s/a 4.00

WILLIE COMICS (Formerly Ideal #1-4; Crime Cases #24 on; Li'l Willie #20 & 21) (See Gay Comics, Laugh, Millie The Model & Wisco)
Marvel Comics (MgPC): #5, Fall, 1946 - #19, 4/49; #22, 1/50 - #23, 5/50 (No #20 & 21)
5(#1)-George, Margie, Nellie the Nurse & Willie begin 30 60 90 177 289 400
6,8,9 16 32 48 94 147 200
7(1),10,11-Kurtzman's "Hey Look" 17 34 51 98 154 210
12,14-18,22,23 15 30 45 86 133 180
13,19-Kurtzman's "Hey Look" (#19-last by Kurtzman?) 15 30 45 88 137 185
NOTE: *Cindy app. in #17. Jeanie app. in #17. Little Lizzie app. in #22.*

WILLIE MAYS (See The Amazing...)

WILLIE THE PENGUIN
Standard Comics: Apr, 1951 - No. 6, Apr, 1952
1-Funny animal 10 20 30 54 72 90
2-6 6 12 18 31 38 45

WILLIE THE WISE-GUY (Also see Cartoon Kids)
Atlas Comics (NPP): Sept, 1957
1-Kida, Maneely-a 11 22 33 60 83 105

WILLOW
Marvel Comics: Aug, 1988 - No. 3, Oct, 1988 ($1.00)
1-3-R/Marvel Graphic Novel #36 (movie adaptation) 4.00

WILLOW (From Buffy the Vampire Slayer)
Dark Horse Comics: Nov, 2012 - No. 5, Mar, 2013 ($2.99, limited series)
1-5-Jeff Parker-s/Brian Ching-a; covers by David Mack & Megan Lara; Aluwyn app. 3.00

WILL ROGERS WESTERN (Formerly My Great Love #1-4; see Blazing & True Comics #66)
Fox Features Syndicate: No. 5, June, 1950 - No. 2, Aug, 1950
5(#1) 31 62 93 186 303 420
2: Photo-c 26 52 78 154 252 350

WILL TO POWER (Also see Comic's Greatest World)
Dark Horse Comics: June, 1994 - No. 12, Aug, 1994 ($1.00, weekly limited series, 20 pgs.)
1-12: 12-Vortex kills Titan. 3.00
NOTE: ***Mignola** c-10-12.* ***Sears** c-1-3.*

WILL-YUM!
Dell Publishing Co.: No. 676, Feb, 1956 - No. 902, May, 1958
Four Color 676 (#1), 765 (1/57), 902 4 8 12 27 44 60

WIN A PRIZE COMICS (Timmy The Timid Ghost #3 on?)
Charlton Comics: Feb, 1955 - No. 2, Apr, 1955

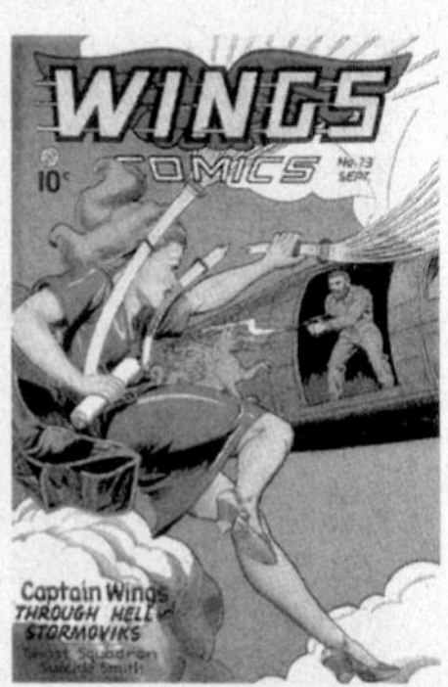

Wings Comics #73 © FH

The Winter Men #1 © Lewis & Leon

Witchblade #6 © TCOW

	GD 2.0	VG 4.0	FN 6.0	VF 8.0	VF/NM 9.0	NM- 9.2
V1#1-S&K-a; Poe adapt; E.C. War swipe	67	134	201	426	731	1035
2-S&K-a	48	96	144	302	514	725

WINDY & WILLY (Also see Showcase #81)
National Periodical Publications: May-June, 1969 - No. 4, Nov-Dec, 1969

	GD	VG	FN	VF	VF/NM	NM-
1- r/Dobie Gillis with some art changes begin	5	10	15	31	53	75
2-4	3	6	9	21	33	45

WINGS COMICS
Fiction House Mag.: 9/40 - No. 109, 9/49; No. 110, Wint, 1949-50; No. 111, Spring, 1950; No. 112, 1950(nd); No. 113 - No. 115, 1950(nd); No. 116, 1952(nd); No. 117, Fall, 1952 - No. 122, Wint, 1953-54; No. 123 - No. 124, 1954(nd)

	GD	VG	FN	VF	VF/NM	NM-
1-Skull Squad, Clipper Kirk, Suicide Smith, Jane Martin, War Nurse, Phantom Falcons, Greasemonkey Griffin, Parachute Patrol & Powder Burns begin	290	580	870	1856	3178	4500
2	113	226	339	723	1237	1750
3-5	77	154	231	493	847	1200
6-10: 8-Indicia shows #7 (#8 on cover)	61	122	183	390	670	950
11-15	55	110	165	352	601	850
16-Origin & 1st app. Captain Wings & begin series	60	120	180	381	653	925
17-20: 20-(4/42) 1st Japanese WWII-c	48	96	144	302	514	725
21-25,27-30	45	90	135	284	480	675
26-1st Good Girl WWII-c for this title	54	108	162	343	574	825
31-40: 35-Classic Nazi WWII-c	40	80	120	244	402	560
41-50	34	68	102	204	332	460
51-60: 60-Last Skull Squad	31	62	93	186	303	420
61-67: 66-Ghost Patrol begins (becomes Ghost Squadron #71 on), ends #112?	29	58	87	170	278	385
68,69: 68-Clipper Kirk becomes The Phantom Falcon-origin, Part 1; part 2 in #69	29	58	87	170	278	385
70-72: 70-1st app. The Phantom Falcon in costume, origin-Part 3; Capt. Wings battles Col. Kamikaze in all	27	54	81	162	266	370
73-88,92,93,95-99: 80-Phantom Falcon by Larsen. 99-King of the Congo begins?	27	54	81	162	266	370
89-91,94-Classic Good Girl covers	53	106	159	334	567	800
100-(12/48)	28	56	84	168	274	380
101-124: 111-Last Jane Martin. 112-Flying Saucer-c/story (1950). 115-Used in **POP**, pg. 89. 121-Atomic Explosion-c. 122-Korean War	20	40	60	120	195	270

NOTE: *World War II covers (Nazi or Japanese) on #1-17, 19-67. Bondage covers are common. Captain Wings battles Sky Hag-#75, 76; ...Mr. Atlantis-#85-92; ...Mr. Pupin(Red Agent)-#98-103. Capt. Wings by* ***Elias****-#52-64, 68, 69; by* ***Lubbers****-#29-32, 70-111; by* ***Renee****-#33-46.* ***Evans*** *a-85-106, 108-111(Jane Martin); text illos-72-84.* ***Larsen*** *a-52, 59, 64, 73-77. Jane Martin by* ***Fran Hopper****-#68-84; Suicide Smith by* ***John Celardo****-#72, 74, 76, 80-104; by* ***Hollingsworth****-#68-70, 105-109, 111; Ghost Squadron by* ***Astarita****-#67-79; by* ***Maurice Whitman****-#80-111. King of the Congo by* ***Moreira****-#99, 100. Skull Squad by* ***M. Baker****-#52-60; Clipper Kirk by* ***Baker****-#60, 61; by* ***Colan****-#53; by* ***Ingels****-(some issues?). Phantom Falcon by* ***Larsen****-#73-84.* ***Elias*** *c-58-72.* ***Fawcette*** *c-3-12, 16, 17, 19, 22-33.* ***Lubbers*** *c-74-109.* ***Tuska*** *a-5.* ***Whitman*** *c-110-124.* ***Zolnerwich*** *c-15, 21.*

WINGS OF THE EAGLES, THE
Dell Publishing Co.: No. 790, Apr, 1957 (10¢ & 15¢ editions exist)

	GD	VG	FN	VF	VF/NM	NM-
Four Color 790-Movie; John Wayne photo-c; Toth-a	12	24	36	79	170	260

WINKY DINK (Adventures of...)
Pines Comics: No. 75, Mar, 1957 (one-shot)

	GD	VG	FN	VF	VF/NM	NM-
75-Marv Levy-c/a	6	12	18	31	38	45

WINKY DINK (TV)
Dell Publishing Co.: No. 663, Nov, 1955

	GD	VG	FN	VF	VF/NM	NM-
Four Color 663 (#1)	7	14	21	48	89	130

WINNIE-THE-POOH (Also see Dynabrite Comics)
Gold Key No. 1-17/Whitman No. 18 on: January, 1977 - No. 33, July, 1984
(Walt Disney) (Winnie-The-Pooh began as Edward Bear in 1926 by Milne)

	GD	VG	FN	VF	VF/NM	NM-
1-New art	4	8	12	23	37	50
2-5: 5-New material	2	4	6	13	18	22
6-17: 12-up-New material	2	4	6	9	13	16
18,19(Whitman)	2	4	6	13	18	22
20,21('80) pre-pack only	4	8	12	27	44	60
22('80) (scarcer) pre-pack only	5	10	15	33	57	80
23-28: 27(2/82), 28(4/82)	3	6	9	14	19	24
29-33 (#90299 on-c, no date or date code; pre-pack): 29(4/82), 30(5/83), 31(8/83), 32(4/84), 33(7/84)	3	6	9	19	30	40

WINNIE WINKLE (See Popular Comics & Super Comics)
Dell Publishing Co.: 1941 - No. 7, Sept-Nov, 1949

	GD	VG	FN	VF	VF/NM	NM-
Large Feature Comic 2 (1941)	30	60	90	177	289	400
Four Color 94 (1945)	11	22	33	73	157	240
Four Color 174	8	16	24	51	96	140
1(3-5/48)-Contains daily & Sunday newspaper-r from 1939-1941	7	14	21	46	86	125
2 (6-8/48)	5	10	15	33	57	80
3-7	4	8	12	27	44	60

WINTER MEN, THE
DC Comics (WildStorm): Oct, 2005 - No. 5, Nov, 2006 ($2.99, limited series)

1-5-Brett Lewis-s/John Paul Leon-a 3.00
... Winter Special (2/09, $3.99) Lewis-s/Leon-a 4.00
TPB (2010, $19.99) r/#1-5 & Winter Special; original proposal, development & sketch-a 20.00

WINTER SOLDIER (See Captain America 2005 series)
Marvel Comics: Apr, 2012 - No. 19, Aug, 2013 ($2.99)

1-19: 1-Black Widow app.; Brubaker-s/Guice-a/Bermejo-c. 3-5-Dr. Doom app. 3.00

WINTER SOLDIER: THE BITTER MARCH
Marvel Comics: Apr, 2014 - No. 5 ($3.99, limited series)

1,2: 1-Remender-s/Boschi-a/Robinson-c; set in 1966; Nick Fury app. 4.00

WINTER SOLDIER: WINTER KILLS
Marvel Comics: Feb, 2007 ($3.99, one-shot)

1-Flashback to Christmas Eve 1944; Toro & Sub-Mariner app.; Brubaker-s/Weeks-a 5.00

WINTERWORLD
Eclipse Comics: Sept, 1987 - No. 3, Mar, 1988 ($1.75, limited series)

1-3 3.00

WISDOM
Marvel Comics (MAX): Jan, 2007 - No. 6, July, 2007 ($3.99, limited series)

1-6: 1-Hairsine-a/c; Cornell-s. 3-6-Manuel Garcia-a 4.00
...: Rudiments of Wisdom TPB (2007, $21.99) r/#1-6; series pitch and sketch page 22.00

WISE GUYS (See Harvey...)

WISE LITTLE HEN, THE
David McKay Publ./Whitman: 1934 ,1935(48 pgs.); 1937 (Story book)

	GD	VG	FN	VF	VF/NM	NM-
nn-(1934 edition w/dust jacket)(48 pgs. with color, 8-3/4x9-3/4") -Debut of Donald Duck (see Advs. of Mickey Mouse); Donald app. on cover with Wise Little Hen & Practical Pig; painted cover; same artist as the B&W's from Silly Symphony Cartoon, The Wise Little Hen (1934) (McKay)						
Book w/dust jacket	245	490	735	1568	2684	3800
Dust jacket only	58	116	174	371	636	900
nn-(1935 edition w/dust jacket), same as 1934 ed.	142	284	426	909	1555	2200
888 (1937)(9-1/2x13", 12 pgs.)(Whitman) Donald Duck app.	36	72	108	211	343	475

WISE SON: THE WHITE WOLF
DC Comics (Milestone): Nov, 1996 - No. 4, Feb, 1997 ($2.50, limited series)

1-4: Ho Che Anderson-c/a 3.00

WIT AND WISDOM OF WATERGATE (Humor magazine)
Marvel Comics: 1973, 76 pgs., squarebound

	GD	VG	FN	VF	VF/NM	NM-
1-Low print run	5	10	15	31	53	75

WITCHBLADE (Also see Cyblade/Shi, Tales Of The..., & Top Cow Classics)
Image Comics (Top Cow Productions): Nov, 1995 - Present ($2.50/$2.99)

	GD	VG	FN	VF	VF/NM	NM-
0	1	2	3	5	6	8
1/2-Mike Turner/Marc Silvestri-c.	3	6	9	19	30	40
1/2 Gold Ed., 1/2 Chromium-c	3	6	9	19	30	40
1/2-(Vol. 2, 11/02, $2.99) Wohl-s/Ching-a/c						3.00
1-Mike Turner-a(p)	4	8	12	19	30	40
1,2-American Ent. Encore Ed.	1	2	3	4	5	7
2,3	2	4	6	11	16	20
4,5	2	4	6	8	10	12
6-9: 8-Wraparound-c. 9-Tony Daniel-a(p)	1	2	3	5	6	8
9-Sunset variant-c	2	4	6	8	10	12
9-DF variant-c	2	4	6	9	12	15
10-Flip book w/Darkness #0, 1st app. the Darkness	1	3	4	6	8	10
10-Variant-c	2	4	6	8	10	12
10-Gold logo	3	6	9	14	20	25
10-($3.95) Dynamic Forces alternate-c	1	2	3	5	6	8
11-15						5.00
16-19: 18,19-"Family Ties" Darkness x-over pt. 1,4						4.00
18-Face to face variant-c, 18-American Ent. Ed., 19-AE Gold Ed.	1	2	3	5	6	8
20-25: 24-Pearson, Green-a. 25-($2.95) Turner-a(p)						4.00
25 (Prism variant)						25.00
25 (Special)						10.00
26-39: 26-Green-a begins						3.00

Witchblade #137 © TCOW

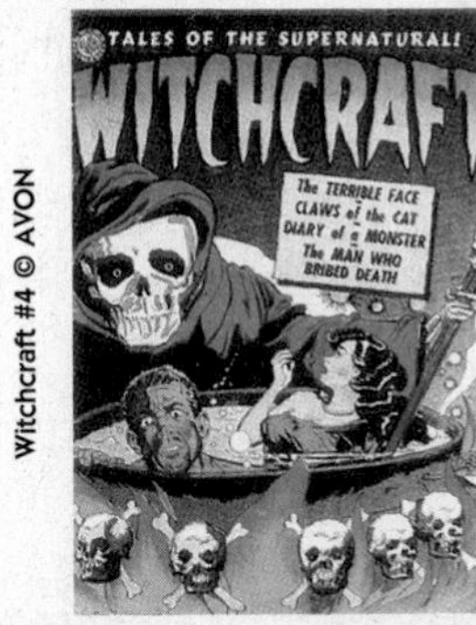

Witchcraft #4 © AVON

Witches Tales #15 © HARV

	GD	VG	FN	VF	VF/NM	NM-
	2.0	4.0	6.0	8.0	9.0	9.2

27 (Variant) 6.00
40-49,51-53: 40-Begin Jenkins & Veitch-s/Keu Cha-a. 47-Zulli-c/a 3.00
40-Pittsburgh Convention Preview edition; B&W preview of #40 3.00
49-Gold logo 5.00
50-($4.95) Darkness app.; Ching-a; B&W preview of Universe 5.00
54-59: 54-Black outer-c with gold foil logo; Wohl-s/Manapul-a 3.00
60-74,76-91,93-99: 60-($2.99) Endgame x-over with Tomb Raider #25 & Evo #1. 64,65-Magdalena app. 71-Kirk-a. 77,81-85-Land-c. 80-Four covers. 87-Bachalo-a 3.00
75-($4.99) Manapul-a 5.00
92-($4.99) Origin of the Witchblade; art by various incl. Bachalo, Perez, Linsner, Cooke 5.00
100-($4.99) Five covers incl. Turner, Silvestri, Linsner; art by various; Jake dies 5.00
101-124,126-143: 103-Danielle Baptiste gets the Witchblade; Linsner variant-c. 116-124,140,141-Sejic-a. 126-128-War of the Witchblades. 134-136-Aphrodite IV app. 139-Gaydos-a. 143-Matt Dow Smith-a 3.00
125-($3.99) War of the Witchblades begins; 3 covers; Sejic-a 4.00
144-($4.99) Origin retold; wraparound-c; Sejic-a; back-up w/Sablik-s; pin-up gallery 5.00
145-149-($3.99) Sejic-a/c. 149-Angelus app. 4.00
150-($4.99) Four covers; last Marz-s; Sejic-a; cover gallery & series timeline 5.00
151-173-($2.99) Altered reality after Artifacts #13; Seeley-s; multiple covers 3.00
... and Tomb Raider (4/05, $2.99) Jae Lee-c; art by Lee and Texiera 3.00
...: Animated (8/03, $2.99) Magdalena & Darkness app.; Dini-s/Bone, Bullock, Cooke-a/c 3.00
... Annual 2009 (4/09, $3.99) Basaldua-a 4.00
... Annual #1 (12/10, $4.99) the Witchblade in Stalingrad 1942, Shasteen-a; Haley-a 5.00
...: Art of the Witchblade (7/06, $2.99) pin-ups by various incl. Turner, Land, Linsner 3.00
...: Bearers of the Blade (7/06, $2.99) pin-up/profiles of bearers of the Witchblade 3.00
...: Blood Oath (8/04, $4.99) Sara teams with Phenix & Sibilla; Roux-a 5.00
...: Blood Relations TPB (2003, $12.99) r/#54-58 13.00
... Compendium Vol. 1 (2006, $59.99) r/#1-50; gallery of variant covers and art 60.00
... Compendium Vol. 2 (2007, $59.99) r/#51-100; gallery of variant covers and art 60.00
... Cover Gallery Vol. 1 (12/05, $2.99) intro. by Stan Lee 3.00
.../Darkchylde (7/00, $2.50) Green-s/a(p) 3.00
.../Dark Minds (6/04, $9.99) new story plus r/Dark Minds/Witchblade #1 10.00
.../Darkness: Family Ties Collected Edition (10/98, $9.95) r/#18,19 and Darkness #9,10 10.00
.../Darkness Special (12/99, $3.95) Green-c/a 4.00
... Day of the Outlaws (4/13, $3.99) Fialkov-s/Blake-a; Witchblade in 1878 Colorado 4.00
... Demon 1 (2003, $6.99) Mark Millar-s/Jae Lee-c/a 7.00
.../Devi (4/08, $3.99) Basaldua-a/Land-c; continues in Devi/Witchblade 4.00
...: Distinctions (See Tales of the Witchblade)
...: Due Process (8/10, $3.99) Alina Urusov-a/c; Phil Smith-s 4.00
.../Elektra (3/97, $2.95) Devil's Reign Pt. 6 4.00
... Gallery (11/00, $2.95) Profile pages and pin-ups by various; Turner-c 3.00
Image Firsts: Witchblade #1 (4/10, $1.00) reprints #1 3.00
Infinity (5/99, $3.50) Lobdell-s/Pollina-c/a 4.00
.../Lady Death (11/01, $4.95) Manapul-c/a 5.00
...: Prevailing TPB (2000, $14.95) r/#20-25; new Turner-c 15.00
...: Revelations TPB (2000, $24.95) r/#9-17; new Turner-c 25.00
.../The Punisher (6/07, $3.99) Marz-s/Melo-a/Linsner-c 4.00
.../Tomb Raider #1/2 (7/00, $2.95) Covers by Turner and Cha 4.00
... Unbalanced Pieces FCBD Edition (5/12, giveaway) Christopher-c 3.00
...: Vol. 1 TPB (1/08, $4.99) r/#80-85; Marz intro.; cover gallery 5.00
...: Vol. 2 TPB (2/08, $14.99) r/#86-92; cover gallery 15.00
...: Vol. 3 TPB (3/08, $14.99) r/#93-100; Edginton intro.; cover gallery 15.00
... vs. Frankenstein: Monster War 2005 (8/05, $2.99) pt. 3 of x-over 3.00
...: Witch Hunt Vol. 1 TPB (2/06, $14.99) r/#80-85; Marz intro.; Choi afterward; cover gallery 15.00
Wizard #500 10.00
.../Wolverine (6/04, $2.99) Basaldua-c/a; Claremont-s 3.00

WITCHBLADE/ALIENS/THE DARKNESS/PREDATOR
Dark Horse Comics/Top Cow Productions: Nov, 2000 ($2.99)

1-3-Mel Rubi-a 4.00

WITCHBLADE COLLECTED EDITION
Image Comics (Top Cow Productions): July, 1996 - No. 8 ($4.95/$6.95, squarebound, limited series)

1-7-($4.95): Two issues reprinted in each 5.00
8-($6.95) r/#15-17 7.00
...Slipcase (10/96, $10.95)-Packaged w/ Coll. Ed. #1-4 11.00

WITCHBLADE: DEMON REBORN
Dynamite Entertainment: 2012 - No. 4, 2012 ($3.99, limited series)

1-4-Ande Parks-s/Jose Luis-a; covers by Calero & Jae Lee 4.00

WITCHBLADE: DESTINY'S CHILD
Image Comics (Top Cow): Jun, 2000 - No. 3, Sept, 2000 ($2.95, limited series)

1-3: 1-Boller-a/Keu Cha-c 3.00

WITCHBLADE: MANGA (Takeru Manga)
Image Comics (Top Cow): Feb, 2007 - No. 12, Mar, 2008 ($2.99/$3.99)

1-4-Colored reprints of Japanese Witchblade manga. 1-Three covers. 2-Two covers 3.00
5-12-($3.99) 4.00

WITCHBLADE: OBAKEMONO
Image Comics (Top Cow Productions): 2002 ($9.95, one-shot graphic novel)

1-Fiona Avery-s/Billy Tan-a; forward by Straczynski 10.00

WITCHBLADE/ RED SONJA
Dynamite Ent./Top Cow: 2012 - No. 5, 2012 ($3.99, limited series)

1-5-Doug Wagner-s/Cezar Razek-a/Alé Garza-c 4.00

WITCHBLADE: SHADES OF GRAY
Dynamite Ent./Top Cow: 2007 - No. 4, 2007 ($3.50, lim. series)

1,2: 1-Sara Pezzini meets Dorian Gray; Segovia-a; multiple covers 3.50

WITCHBLADE/ TOMB RAIDER SPECIAL (Also see Tomb Raider/...)
Image Comics (Top Cow Productions): Dec, 1998 ($2.95)

1-Based on video game character; Turner-a(p) 4.00
1-Silvestri variant-c 6.00
1-Turner bikini variant-c 10.00
1-Prism-c 12.00
Wizard 1/2 -Turner-s 10.00

WITCHCRAFT (See Strange Mysteries, Super Reprint #18)
Avon Periodicals: Mar-Apr, 1952 - No. 6, Mar, 1953

	GD 2.0	VG 4.0	FN 6.0	VF 8.0	VF/NM 9.0	NM- 9.2
1-Kubert-a; 1 pg. Check-a	81	162	243	518	884	1250
2-Kubert & Check-a; classic skull-c	65	130	195	416	708	1000
3,6: 3-Lawrence-a; Kinstler inside-c	45	90	135	284	480	675
4-People cooked alive c/story	61	122	183	390	670	950
5-Kelly Freas painted-c	68	136	204	435	743	1050

NOTE: ***Hollingsworth** a-4-6; c-4, 6. **McCann** a-3?*

WITCHCRAFT
DC Comics (Vertigo): June, 1994 - No. 3, Aug, 1994 ($2.95, limited series)

1-3: James Robinson scripts & Kaluta-c in all 4.00
1-Platinum Edition 15.00
Trade paperback-(1996, $14.95)-r/#1-3; Kaluta-c 15.00

WITCHCRAFT: LA TERREUR
DC Comics (Vertigo): Apr, 1998 - No. 3, Jun, 1998 ($2.50, limited series)

1-3: Robinson-s/Zulli & Locke-a; interlocking cover images 3.00

WITCH DOCTOR (See Walking Dead #85 flip book for preview)
Image Comics: Jun, 2011 - No. 4, Nov, 2011 ($2.99, limited series)

1-4-Seifert-s/Ketner-a/c 3.00
...: Mal Practice 1-6 (11/12 - No. 6, 4/13, $2.99) Seifert-s/Ketner-a/c 3.00
...: The Resuscitation (12/11, $2.99) Seifert-s/Ketner-a/c 3.00

WITCHER, THE
Dark Horse Comics: Mar, 2014 - No. 5 ($3.99, limited series)

1-Tobin-s/Querio-a 4.00

WITCHES
Marvel Comics: Aug, 2004 - No. 4, Sept, 2004 ($2.99, limited series)

1-4: 1,2-Deodato, Jr-a; Dr. Strange app. 3,4-Conrad-a 3.00
... Vol. 1: The Gathering (2004, $9.99) r/series 10.00

WITCHES TALES (Witches Western Tales #29,30)
Witches Tales/Harvey Publications: Jan, 1951 - No. 28, Dec, 1954 (date misprinted as 4/55)

	GD 2.0	VG 4.0	FN 6.0	VF 8.0	VF/NM 9.0	NM- 9.2
1-Powell-a (1 pg.)	61	122	183	390	670	950
2-Eye injury panel	37	74	111	222	361	500
3-7,9,10	30	60	90	177	289	400
8-Eye injury panels	32	64	96	192	314	435
11-13,15,16: 12-Acid in face story	28	56	84	165	270	375
14,17-Powell/Nostrand-a. 17-Atomic disaster story	29	58	87	170	278	385
18-Nostrand-a; E.C. swipe/Shock S.S.	29	58	87	170	278	385
19-Nostrand-a; E.C. swipe/ "Glutton"; Devil-c	34	68	102	199	325	450
20-24-Nostrand-a. 21-E.C. swipe; rape story. 23-Wood E.C. swipes/Two-Fisted Tales #34	29	58	87	170	278	385
25-Nostrand-a; E.C. swipe/Mad Barber; decapitation-c	65	130	195	416	708	1000
26-28: 27-r/#6 with diff.-c. 28-r/#8 with diff.-c	20	40	60	118	192	265

NOTE: ***Check** a-24. **Elias** c-8, 10, 16-27. **Kremer** a-18; c-25. **Nostrand** a-17-25; 14, 17(w/**Powell**). **Palais** a-1, 2, 4(2), 5(2), 7-9, 12, 14, 15, 17. **Powell** a-3-7, 10, 11, 19-27. Bondage-c 1, 3, 5, 6, 8, 9.*

WITCHES TALES (Magazine)
Eerie Publications: V1#7, July, 1969 - V7#1, Feb, 1975 (B&W, 52 pgs.)

Witching Hour #83 © DC

Witness #1 © MAR

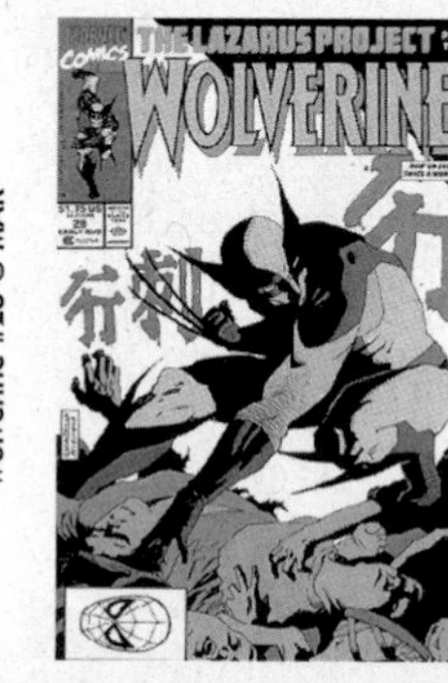

Wolverine #28 © MAR

	GD 2.0	VG 4.0	FN 6.0	VF 8.0	VF/NM 9.0	NM- 9.2
V1#7(7/69)	7	14	21	46	86	125
V1#8(9/69), 9(11/69)	6	12	18	37	66	95
V2#1-6('70), V3#1-6('71)	5	10	15	31	53	75
V4#1-6('72), V5#1-6('73), V6#1-6('74), V7#1	4	8	12	28	47	65

NOTE: *Ajax/Farrell reprints in early issues.*

WITCHES' WESTERN TALES (Formerly Witches Tales)(Western Tales #31 on)
Harvey Publications: No. 29, Feb, 1955 - No. 30, Apr, 1955

	GD 2.0	VG 4.0	FN 6.0	VF 8.0	VF/NM 9.0	NM- 9.2
29,30-Featuring Clay Duncan & Boys' Ranch; S&K-r/from Boys' Ranch including-c. 29-Last pre-code	15	30	45	86	133	180

WITCHFINDER, THE
Image Comics (Liar): Sept, 1999 - No. 3, Jan, 2000 ($2.95)

	GD 2.0	VG 4.0	FN 6.0	VF 8.0	VF/NM 9.0	NM- 9.2
1-3-Romano-a/Sharon & Matthew Scott-plot						3.00

WITCHFINDER: LOST AND GONE FOREVER
Dark Horse Comics: Feb, 2011 - No. 5, Jun, 2011 ($3.50, limited series)

	GD 2.0	VG 4.0	FN 6.0	VF 8.0	VF/NM 9.0	NM- 9.2
1-5-John Severin-a; Mignola & Arcudi-s. 1-Two covers by Mignola & Severin						3.50

WITCH HUNTER
Malibu Comics (Ultraverse): Apr, 1996 ($2.50, one-shot)

	GD 2.0	VG 4.0	FN 6.0	VF 8.0	VF/NM 9.0	NM- 9.2
1						3.00

WITCHING, THE
DC Comics (Vertigo): Aug, 2004 - No. 10, May, 2005 ($2.95/$2.99)

	GD 2.0	VG 4.0	FN 6.0	VF 8.0	VF/NM 9.0	NM- 9.2
1-10-Vankin-s/Gallagher-a/McPherson-c. 1,2-Lucifer app.						3.00

WITCHING HOUR ("The ..." in later issues)
National Periodical Publ./DC Comics: Feb-Mar, 1969 - No. 85, Oct, 1978

	GD 2.0	VG 4.0	FN 6.0	VF 8.0	VF/NM 9.0	NM- 9.2
1-Toth-a, plus Neal Adams-a (2 pgs.)	12	24	36	84	185	285
2,6: 6-Toth-a	6	12	18	42	79	115
3,5-Wrightson-a; Toth-p. 3-Last 12¢ issue	7	14	21	46	86	125
4,12-Toth-a	5	10	15	31	53	75
7-11-Adams-c; Toth-a in all. 8-Adams-a	6	12	18	41	76	110
13-Neal Adams-c/a, 2pgs.	6	12	18	42	79	115
14-Williamson/Garzon, Jones-a; N. Adams-c	7	14	21	44	82	120
15	3	6	9	19	30	40
16-21-(52 pg. Giants)	4	8	12	23	37	50
22-37,39,40	3	6	9	14	19	24
38-(100 pgs.)	5	10	15	31	53	75
41-60	2	4	6	10	14	18
61-83,85	2	4	6	8	11	14
84-(44 pgs.)	2	4	6	9	13	16

NOTE: *Combined with The Unexpected with #189.* ***Neal Adams*** *c-7-11, 13, 14.* ***Alcala*** *a-24, 27, 33, 41, 43.* ***Anderson*** *a-9, 38.* ***Cardy*** *c-4, 5.* ***Kaluta*** *a-7.* ***Kane*** *a-12p.* ***Morrow*** *a-10, 13, 15, 16.* ***Nino*** *a-31, 40, 45, 47.* ***Redondo*** *a-20, 23, 24, 34, 65; c-53.* ***Reese*** *a-23.* ***Sparling*** *a-1.* ***Toth*** *a-1, 3-12, 38r.* ***Tuska*** *a-11, 12.* ***Wood*** *a-15.*

WITCHING HOUR, THE
DC Comics (Vertigo): 1999 - No. 3, 2000 ($5.95, limited series)

	GD 2.0	VG 4.0	FN 6.0	VF 8.0	VF/NM 9.0	NM- 9.2
1-3-Bachalo & Thibert-c/a; Loeb & Bachalo-s						6.00
Hardcover (2000, $29.95) r/#1-3; embossed cover						30.00
Softcover (2003, $19.95), (2009, $19.99) r/#1-3						20.00

WITCHING HOUR, THE
DC Comics (Vertigo): Dec, 2013 ($7.99, one-shot)

	GD 2.0	VG 4.0	FN 6.0	VF 8.0	VF/NM 9.0	NM- 9.2
1-Short story anthology by various incl. DeConnick, Doyle, Buckingham; Frison-c						8.00

WITHIN OUR REACH
Star Reach Productions: 1991 ($7.95, 84 pgs.)

	GD 2.0	VG 4.0	FN 6.0	VF 8.0	VF/NM 9.0	NM- 9.2
nn-Spider-Man, Concrete by Chadwick, Gift of the Magi by Russell; Christmas stories; Chadwick-c; Spidey back-c						8.00

WITH THE MARINES ON THE BATTLEFRONTS OF THE WORLD
Toby Press: 1953 (no month) - No. 2, Mar, 1954 (Photo covers)

	GD 2.0	VG 4.0	FN 6.0	VF 8.0	VF/NM 9.0	NM- 9.2
1-John Wayne story	30	60	90	177	289	400
2-Monty Hall in #1,2	11	22	33	60	83	105

WITH THE U.S. PARATROOPS BEHIND ENEMY LINES (Also see U.S. Paratroops...; #2-6 titled U.S. Paratroops...)
Avon Periodicals: 1951 - No. 6, Dec, 1952

	GD 2.0	VG 4.0	FN 6.0	VF 8.0	VF/NM 9.0	NM- 9.2
1-Wood-c & inside f/c	19	38	57	111	176	240
2-Kinstler-c & inside f/c only	12	24	36	67	94	120
3-6: 6-Kinstler-c & inside f/c only	11	22	33	60	83	105

NOTE: ***Kinstler*** *c-2, 4-6.*

WITNESS, THE (Also see Amazing Mysteries, Captain America #71, Ideal #4, Marvel Mystery #92 & Mystic #7)
Marvel Comics (MjMe): Sept, 1948

	GD 2.0	VG 4.0	FN 6.0	VF 8.0	VF/NM 9.0	NM- 9.2
1(Scarce)-Rico-c?	290	580	870	1856	3178	4500

WITTY COMICS
Irwin H. Rubin Publ./Chicago Nite Life News No. 2: 1945 - No. 2, 1945

	GD 2.0	VG 4.0	FN 6.0	VF 8.0	VF/NM 9.0	NM- 9.2
1-The Pioneer, Junior Patrol; Japanese war-c	34	68	102	199	325	450
2-The Pioneer, Junior Patrol	16	32	48	94	147	200

WIZARD OF FOURTH STREET, THE
Dark Horse Comics: Dec, 1987 - No. 2, 1988 ($1.75, B&W, limited series)

	GD 2.0	VG 4.0	FN 6.0	VF 8.0	VF/NM 9.0	NM- 9.2
1,2: Adapts novel by S/F author Simon Hawke						3.00

WIZARD OF OZ (See Classics Illustrated Jr. 535, Dell Jr. Treasury No. 5, First Comics Graphic Novel, Marvelous..., & Marvel Treasury of Oz)
Dell Publishing Co.: No. 1308, Mar-May, 1962 (TV)

	GD 2.0	VG 4.0	FN 6.0	VF 8.0	VF/NM 9.0	NM- 9.2
Four Color 1308	10	20	30	66	138	210

WIZARDS OF MICKEY (Mickey Mouse)
BOOM! Studios: Jan, 2010 - No. 8, Aug, 2010 ($2.99)

	GD 2.0	VG 4.0	FN 6.0	VF 8.0	VF/NM 9.0	NM- 9.2
1-8: 1,2-Ambrosio-s; 3 covers on each. 3-8-Two covers						3.00

WIZARD'S TALE, THE
Image Comics (Homage Comics): 1997 ($19.95, squarebound, one-shot)

	GD 2.0	VG 4.0	FN 6.0	VF 8.0	VF/NM 9.0	NM- 9.2
nn-Kurt Busiek-s/David Wenzel-painted-a/c						20.00

WOLF & RED
Dark Horse Comics: Apr, 1995 - No. 3, June, 1995 ($2.50, limited series)

	GD 2.0	VG 4.0	FN 6.0	VF 8.0	VF/NM 9.0	NM- 9.2
1-3: Characters created by Tex Avery						3.00

WOLFF & BYRD, COUNSELORS OF THE MACABRE (Becomes Supernatural Law with issue #24)
Exhibit A Press: May, 1994 - No. 23, Aug, 1999 ($2.50, B&W)

	GD 2.0	VG 4.0	FN 6.0	VF 8.0	VF/NM 9.0	NM- 9.2
1-23-Batton Lash-s/a						3.00

WOLF GAL (See Al Capp's...)

WOLFMAN, THE (See Movie Classics)

WOLFPACK
Marvel Comics: Feb, 1988 ($7.95); Aug, 1988 - No. 12, July, 1989 (Lim. series)

	GD 2.0	VG 4.0	FN 6.0	VF 8.0	VF/NM 9.0	NM- 9.2
1-1st app./origin (Marvel Graphic Novel #31)	1	3	4	6	8	10
1-12						4.00

WOLVERINE (See Alpha Flight, Daredevil #196, 249, Ghost Rider; Wolverine; Punisher, Havok &..., Incredible Hulk #180, Incredible Hulk &..., Kitty Pryde And..., Marvel Comics Presents, New Avengers, Power Pack, Punisher and..., Rampaging ..., Spider-Man vs... & X-Men #94)

WOLVERINE (See Incredible Hulk #180 for 1st app.)
Marvel Comics Group: Sept, 1982 - No. 4, Dec, 1982 (limited series)

	GD 2.0	VG 4.0	FN 6.0	VF 8.0	VF/NM 9.0	NM- 9.2
1-Frank Miller-c/a(p) in all; Claremont-s	5	10	15	33	57	80
2-4	4	8	12	25	40	55
... By Claremont & Miller HC (2006, $19.99) r/#1-4 & Uncanny X-Men #172-173						20.00
TPB 1(7/87, $4.95)-Reprints #1-4 with new Miller-c	2	4	6	11	16	20
TPB nn (2nd printing, $9.95)-r/#1-4	2	4	6	8	10	12

WOLVERINE
Marvel Comics: Nov, 1988 - No. 189, June, 2003 ($1.50/$1.75/$1.95/$1.99/$2.25)

	GD 2.0	VG 4.0	FN 6.0	VF 8.0	VF/NM 9.0	NM- 9.2
1	4	8	12	23	37	50
2	3	6	9	14	20	25
3-5: 4-BWS back-c	2	4	6	9	13	16
6-9: 6-McFarlane back-c. 7,8-Hulk app.	1	3	4	6	8	10
10-1st battle with Sabretooth (before Wolverine had his claws)	3	6	9	19	30	40
11-16: 11-New costume	1	2	3	5	6	8
17-20: 17-Byrne-c/a(p) begins, ends #23	1	2	3	4	5	7
21-30: 24,25,27-Jim Lee-c. 26-Begin $1.75-c						5.00
31-40,44,47						4.00
41-Sabretooth claims to be Wolverine's father; Cable cameo	1	2	3	5	6	8
41-Gold 2nd printing ($1.75)	1	2	3	5	6	8
42-Sabretooth, Cable & Nick Fury app.; Sabretooth proven not to be Wolverine's father	1	3	4	6	8	10
42-Gold ink 2nd printing ($1.75)						4.00
43-Sabretooth cameo (2 panels); saga ends						5.00
45,46-Sabretooth-c/stories						5.00
48,49,51-Sabretooth app. 48-Begin 3 part Weapon X sequel. 51-Sabretooth-c & app.						5.00
50-(64 pgs.)-Die cut-c; Wolverine back to old yellow costume; Forge, Cyclops, Jubilee, Jean Grey & Nick Fury app.	1	2	3	5	6	8
52-74,76-80: 54-Shatterstar (from X-Force) app. 55-Gambit, Jubilee, Sunfire-c/story. 55-57,73-Gambit app. 57-Mariko Yashida dies (Late 7/92). 58,59-Terror, Inc. x-over. 60-64-Sabretooth storyline (60,62,64-c)						4.00
75-($3.95, 68 pgs.)-Wolverine hologram on-c						6.00

Wolverine #125 © MAR

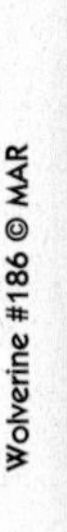
Wolverine #186 © MAR

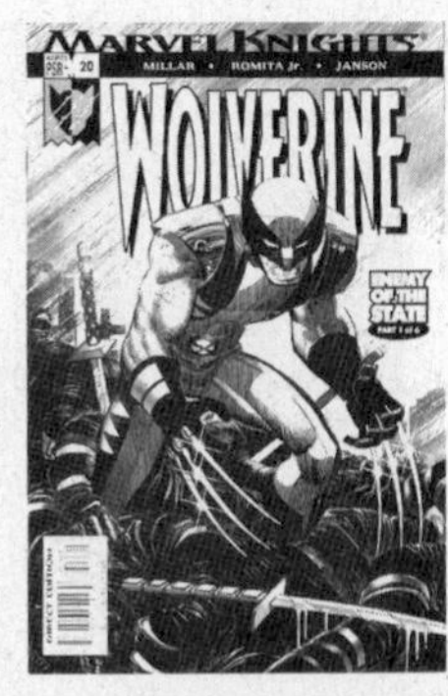

Wolverine (2003 series) #20 © MAR

GD VG FN VF VF/NM NM-
2.0 4.0 6.0 8.0 9.0 9.2

81-84,86: 81-bound-in card sheet 4.00
85-($2.50)-Newsstand edition 4.00
85-($3.50)-Collectors edition 5.00
87-90 ($1.95)-Deluxe edition 4.00
87-90 ($1.50)-Regular edition 3.00
91-99,101-114: 91-Return from "Age of Apocalypse," 93-Juggernaut app. 94-Gen X app. 101-104-Elektra app. 104-Origin of Onslaught. 105-Onslaught x-over. 110-Shaman-c/app. 114-Alternate-c 3.00
100 ($3.95)-Hologram-c; Wolverine loses humanity 1 3 4 6 8 10
100 ($2.95)-Regular-c. 5.00
102.5 (1996 Wizard mail-away)-Deadpool app.; Vallejo-c/Buckingham-a 75.00
115-124: 115- Operation Zero Tolerance 3.00
125-($2.99) Wraparound-c; Viper secret 4.00
125-($6.95) Jae Lee variant-c 8.00
126-144: 126,127-Sabretooth-c/app. 128-Sabretooth & Shadowcat app.; Platt-a. 129-Wendigo-c/app. 131-Initial printing contained lettering error. 133-Begin Larsen-s/ Matsuda-a. 138-Galactus-c/app. 139-Cable app.; Yu-a. 142,143-Alpha Flight app. 3.00
145-($2.99) 25th Anniversary issue; Hulk and Sabretooth app. 4.00
145-($3.99) Foil enhanced cover (also see Promotional section for Nabisco mail-in ed.) 5.00
146-149: 147-Apocalypse: The Twelve; Angel-c/app. 149-Nova-c/app. 3.00
150-($2.99) Steve Skroce-s/a 4.00
151-174,176-182,184-189: 151-Begin $2.25-c. 154,155-Liefeld-s/a. 156-Churchill-a. 159-Chen-a begins. 160-Sabretooth app. 163-Texeira-a(p). 167-BWS-c. 172,173-Alpha Flight app. 176-Colossus app. 185,186-Punisher app. 3.00
175,183-($3.50) 175-Sabretooth app. 4.00
#(-1) Flashback (7/97) Logan meets Col. Fury; Nord-a 3.00
Annual nn (1990, $4.50, squarebound, 52 pgs.)-The Jungle Adventure; Simonson scripts; Mignola-c/a 6.00
Annual 2 (12/90, $4.95, squarebound, 52 pgs.)-Bloodlust 6.00
Annual nn (#3, 8/91, $5.95, 68 pgs.)-Rahne of Terror; Cable & The New Mutants app.; Andy Kubert-c/a (2nd print exists) 6.00
Annual '95 (1995, $3.95) 4.00
Annual '96 (1996, $2.95)- Wraparound-c; Silver Samurai, Yukio, and Red Ronin app. 4.00
Annual '97 ($2.99) - Wraparound-c 4.00
Annual 1999, 2000 ($3.50) : 1999-Deadpool app. 4.00
Annual 2001 ($2.99) - Tieri-s; JH Williams-c 4.00
...Battles The Incredible Hulk nn (1989, $4.95, squarebound, 52 pg.) r/Incr. Hulk #180,181 1 2 3 5 6 8
Best of Wolverine Vol. 1 HC (2004, $29.99) oversized reprints of Hulk #181, mini-series #1-4, Capt. America Ann, #8, Uncanny X-Men #205 & Marvel Comics Presents #72-84 30.00
...Black Rio (11/98, $5.99)-Casey-s/Oscar Jimenez-a 6.00
...Blood Debt TPB (7/01, $12.95)-r/#150-153; Skroce-c 13.00
...Blood Hungry nn (1993, $6.95, 68 pgs.)-Kieth-r/Marvel Comics Presents #85-92 w/ new Kieth-c 7.00
...: Bloody Choices nn (1993, $7.95, 68 pgs.)-r/Graphic Novel; Nick Fury app. 8.00
... Cable Guts and Glory (10/99, $5.99) Platt-a 6.00
... Classic Vol. 1 TPB (2005, $12.99) r/#1-5 15.00
... Classic Vol. 2 TPB (2005, $12.99) r/#6-10 15.00
... Classic Vol. 3 TPB (2006, $14.99) r/#11-16; The Gehenna Stone Affair 15.00
... Classic Vol. 4 TPB (2006, $14.99) r/#17-23 15.00
... Classic Vol. 5 TPB (2007, $14.99) r/#24-30 15.00
.../Deadpool: Weapon X TPB (7/02, $21.99)-r/#162-166 & Deadpool #57-60 22.00
... Doombringer (11/97, $5.99)-Silver Samurai-c/app. 6.00
... Evilution (9/94, $5.95) 6.00
...: Global Jeopardy 1 (12/93, $2.95, one-shot)-Embossed-c; Sub-Mariner, Zabu, Ka-Zar, Shanna & Wolverine app.; produced in cooperation with World Wildlife Fund 5.00
...:Inner Fury nn (1992, $5.95, 52 pgs.)-Sienkiewicz-c/a 6.00
...: Judgment Night (2000, $3.99) Shi app.; Battlebook 4.00
...: Killing (9/93)-Kent Williams-a 6.00
...: Knight of Terra (1995, $6.95)-Ostrander script 7.00
... Legends Vol. 2: Meltdown (2003, $19.99) r/Havok & Wolverine: Meltdown #1-4 20.00
... Legends Vol. 3 (2003, $12.99) r/#181-186 13.00
... Legends Vol. 4,5: 4-(See Wolverine: Xisle). 5-(See Wolverine: Snikt!)
... Legends Vol. 6: Marc Silvestri Book 1 (2004, $19.99) r/#31-34, 41-42, 48-50 20.00
.../ Nick Fury: The Scorpio Connection Hardcover (1989, $16.95) 25.00
.../ Nick Fury: The Scorpio Connection Softcover(1990, $12.95) 15.00
...: Not Dead Yet (12/98, $14.95, TPB)-r/#119-122 15.00
...: Save The Tiger 1 (7/92, $2.95, 84 pgs.)-Reprints Wolverine stories from Marvel Comics Presents #1-10 w/new Kieth-c 4.00
...Scorpio Rising ($5.95, prestige format, one-shot) 6.00
.../Shi: Dark Night of Judgment (Crusade Comics, 2000, $2.99) Tucci-a 4.00
...Triumphs And Tragedies-(1995, $16.95, trade paperback)-r/Uncanny X-Men #109,172,173, Wolverine limited series #4, & Wolverine #41,42,75 17.00
...Typhoid's Kiss (6/94, $6.95)-r/Wolverine stories from Marvel Comics Presents #109-116 7.00

GD VG FN VF VF/NM NM-
2.0 4.0 6.0 8.0 9.0 9.2

...Vs. Spider-Man 1 (3/95, $2.50) -r/Marvel Comics Presents #48-50 5.00
.../Witchblade 1 (3/97, $2.95) Devil's Reign Pt. 5 4.00
Wizard #1/2 (1997) Joe Phillips-a(p) 10.00
NOTE: ***Austin*** *c-3i.* ***Bolton*** *c(back)-5.* ***Buscema*** *a-1-16,25,27p; c-1-10.* ***Byrne*** *a-17-22p, 23; c-1(back), 17-22, 23p.* ***Colan*** *a-24.* ***Andy Kubert*** *c/a-51.* ***Jim Lee*** *c-24, 25, 27.* ***Silvestri*** *a(p)-31-43, 45, 46, 48-50, 52, 53, 55-57; c-31-42p, 43, 45p, 46p, 48, 49p, 50p, 52p, 53p, 55-57p.* ***Stroman*** *a-44p; c-60p.* ***Williamson*** *a-1i, 3-8i; c(i)-1, 3-6.*

WOLVERINE (Volume 3) (Titled Dark Wolverine from #75-90)(See Daken: Dark Wolverine)
Marvel Comics: July, 2003 - No. 90, Oct, 2010 ($2.25/$2.50/$2.99)

1-Rucka-s/Robertson-a 5.00
2-19: 6-Nightcrawler app. 13-16-Sabretooth app. 3.00
20-Millar-s/Romita, Jr.-a begin, Elektra app. 4.00
20-B&W variant-c 5.00
21-39: 21-Elektra-c/app. 23,24-Daredevil app. 26-28-Land-c. 29-Quesada-c; begin $2.50-c. 33-35-House of M. 36,37-Decimation. 36-Quesada-c. 39-Winter Soldier app. 3.00
40,43-48: 40-Begin $2.99-c; Winter Soldier app.; Texeira-a. 43-46-Civil War; Ramos-a. 45-Sub-Mariner app. 3.00
41,49-($3.99) 41-C.P. Smith-a/Stuart Moore-s 4.00
42-Civil War 5.00
50-($3.99) Sabretooth app.; Bianchi-a/c & Loeb-s begin; wraparound-c; McGuinness-a 4.00
50-($3.99) Variant Edition; uncolored art and cover; Bianchi pencil art page 4.00
51-55-(Regular and variant uncolored editions) Bianchi-a/Loeb-s; Sabretooth app. 3.00
55-EC-style variant-c by Greg Land 5.00
56-($3.99) Howard Chaykin-a/c 4.00
57-65: 57-61-Suydam Zombie-c; Chaykin-a. 62-65-Mystique app. 3.00
66-Old Man Logan begins; Millar-s/McNiven-a; McNiven wraparound-c 5.00
66-Variant-c by Michael Turner 1 2 3 4 5 7
66-Variant sketch-c by Michael Turner 30.00
66-2nd printing with McNiven variant-c of Logan and Hulk gang member 3.00
66-(5/10, $1.00) Reprint with "Marvel's Greatest Comics" on cover 3.00
67-74: 67-72-Old Man Logan (concludes in Wolverine: Old Man Logan Giant-Sized Special). 67-Intro. Ashley, Spider-Man's granddaughter.72-Red Skull app. 73,74-Andy Kubert-a 4.00
75-($3.99) Dark Reign, Daken as Wolverine on Osborn's team; Camuncoli-a 5.00
76-90: 76-86-Multiple covers for each. 76-Dark Reign; Yu-c. 82-84-Siege. 88,89-Franken-Castle x-over; Punisher app. 3.00
#900 (7/10, $4.99) Short stories by various incl. Finch, Rivera, Segovia, McGuinness 5.00
Annual 1 (12/07, $3.99) Hurwitz-s/Frusin-a 4.00
Annual 2 (11/08, $3.99) Swierczynski-s/Deodato-a/c 4.00
...: Blood & Sorrow TPB (2007, $13.99) r/#41,49, stories from Giant-Size Wolverine #1 and X-Men Unlimited #12 14.00
...: Chop Shop 1 (1/09, $2.99) Benson-s/Boschi-a/Hanuka-c 3.00
Civil War: Wolverine TPB (2007, $17.99) r/#42-48; gallery of B&W cover inks 18.00
... Dangerous Games 1 (8/08, $3.99) Spurrier-s/Oliver-a; Remender-s/Opena-a 4.00
...Enemy of the State HC Vol. 1 (2005, $19.99) r/#20-25; Ennis intro.; variant covers 20.00
...Enemy of the State HC Vol. 2 (2005, $19.99) r/#26-32 20.00
...Enemy of the State SC Vol. 1 (2005, $14.99) r/#20-25; Ennis intro.; variant covers 15.00
...Enemy of the State SC Vol. 2 (2006, $16.99) r/#26-32 17.00
...Enemy of the State - The Complete Edition (2006, $34.99) r/#20-32; Ennis intro.; sketch pages, variant covers and pin-up art 35.00
...: Evolution SC (2008, $14.99) r/#50-55 15.00
...: Flies to a Spider (2/09, $3.99) Bradstreet-c/Hurwitz-s/Opena-a 4.00
...: Killing Made Simple (10/08, $3.99) Yost-s/Turnbull-a 4.00
...: Enemy of the State MGC #20 (7/11, $1.00) r/#20 with "Marvel's Greatest Comics" logo 3.00
...: Japan's Most Wanted HC (2014, $34.99) printing of material that debuted online 35.00
...: Mr. X (5/10, $3.99) Tieri-s/Diaz-a/Mattina-c 4.00
...: Old Man Logan Giant-Sized Special (11/09, $4.99) Continued from #72; cover gallery 5.00
...Origins & Endings HC (2006, $19.99) r/#36-40 20.00
...Origins & Endings SC (2006, $13.99) r/#36-40 14.00
...: Origin of an X-Man Free Comic Book Day 2009 (5/09) Gurihiru-a/McGuinness-c 3.00
...: Revolver (8/09, $3.99) Gischler-s/Pastoras-a 4.00
... Saga (2009, giveaway) history of the character in text and comic panels 3.00
...: Saudade (2008, $4.99) English adaptation of Wolverine story from French comic 5.00
...: Savage (4/10, $3.99) J. Scott Campbell-c; The Lizard app. 4.00
...Special: Firebreak (2/08, $3.99) Carey-s/Kolins-a; Lolos-a 4.00
...: Switchback 1 (3/09, $3.99) short stories; art by Pastoras & Doe 4.00
...: The Amazing Immortal Man & Other Bloody Tales (7/08, $3.99) Lapham short stories 4.00
...: The Anniversary (6/09, $3.99) Mariko flashback short stories; art by various 4.00
...: The Death of Wolverine HC (2008, $19.99) r/#56-61 20.00
...: The Road to Hell (11/10, $3.99) Previews new Wolverine titles and Generation Hope 4.00
...: Under the Boardwalk (2/10, $3.99) Coker-a 4.00
...Vol. 1: The Brotherhood (2003, $12.99) r/#1-6 13.00
...Vol. 2: Coyote Crossing (2004, $11.99) r/#7-11 12.00
... Weapon X Files (2009, $4.99) Handbook-style pages of Wolverine characters 5.00
...: Wendigo! 1 (3/10, $3.99) Gulacy-a; back-up with Thor 4.00

Wolverine (2013 series) #7 © MAR

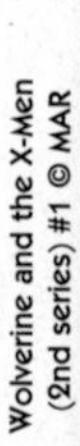
Wolverine and the X-Men (2nd series) #1 © MAR

Wolverine: Noir #3 © MAR

GD 2.0	VG 4.0	FN 6.0	VF 8.0	VF/NM 9.0	NM- 9.2

WOLVERINE (Volume 4) (Also see Savage Wolverine)
Marvel Comics: Nov, 2010 - No. 20, Feb, 2012; No. 300, Mar, 2012 - No. 317, Feb, 2013 ($3.99/$4.99)

1-5-Jae Lee-c/Guedes-a; Wolverine Goes to Hell. 1-Back-up with Silver Samurai 4.00
5.1-(4/11, $2.99) Aaron-s/Palo-a/Rivera-c 3.00
6-20: 6-Jae Lee-c/Acuña-a; X-Men & Magneto app. 20-Kingpin & Sabretooth app. 4.00
300-(3/12, $4.99) Adam Kubert-c; Sabretooth & new Silver Samurai app. 5.00
301-308,310-317: 301-304-Aaron-s. 302-Art Adams-c. 310-313-Bianchi-a/c 4.00
309-($4.99) Elixir with X-Force; Albuquerque-a; Ribic-c 5.00
#1000 (4/11, $4.99) Short stories by various incl. Palmiotti, Green, Luke Ross; Segovia-c 5.00
Annual 1 (10/12, $4.99) Alan Davis-s/a/c; the Clan Destine app. (see Daredevil Ann. #1) 5.00
...: Debt of Death 1 (11/11, $3.99) Lapham-s/Aja-a/c; Nick Fury app. 4.00
.../Deadpool: The Decoy 1 (9/11, $3.99) prints online story from Marvel.com; Young-c 4.00

WOLVERINE (5th series)
Marvel Comics: May, 2013 - No. 13, Mar, 2014 ($3.99)

1-13: 1-4-Cornell-s/Alan Davis-a/c; Nick Fury II app. 5-7-Pierfederici-a. 8-13-Killable 4.00
... In the Flesh (9/13, $3.99) Cosentino-s/Talajic-a 4.00

WOLVERINE (6th series)
Marvel Comics: Apr, 2014 - Present ($3.99)

1-3: 1-Cornell-s/Stegman-a. 2-Superior Spider-Man app. 4.00

WOLVERINE & BLACK CAT: CLAWS 2 (See Claws for 1st series)
Marvel Comics: Aug, 2011 - No. 3, Nov, 2011 ($3.99, limited series)

1-3-Linsner-a/c; Palmiotti & Gray-s; Killraven app. 4.00

WOLVERINE AND JUBILEE
Marvel Comics: Mar, 2011 - No. 4, Jun, 2011 ($2.99, limited series)

1-4: 1-Vampire Jubilee; Kathryn Immonen-s/Phil Noto-a; Coipel-c 3.00

WOLVERINE AND POWER PACK
Marvel Comics: Jan, 2009 - No. 4, Apr, 2009 ($2.99, limited series)

1-4-Sumerak-s. 1,2-GuriHiru-a. 1-Sauron app. 3-Meet Wolverine as a child; Koblish-a 3.00

WOLVERINE AND THE PUNISHER: DAMAGING EVIDENCE
Marvel Comics: Oct, 1993 - No. 3, Dec, 1993 ($2.00, limited series)

1-3: 2,3-Indicia says "The Punisher and Wolverine..." 4.00

WOLVERINE & THE X-MEN (Regenesis)(See X-Men: Schism)
Marvel Comics: Dec, 2011 - No. 42, Apr, 2014 ($3.99)

1-8: 1-3-Aaron-s/Bachalo-a/c. 3-Sabretooth app. 4-Bradshaw-a; Deathlok app. 4.00
9-27: 9-16,18-Avengers vs. X-Men tie-in. 17-Allred-a 4.00
27AU (6/13, $3.99) Age of Ultron tie-in; continues in Age of Ultron #6 4.00
28-41: 30-35-Hellfire Saga. 36,37-Battle of the Atom 4.00
42-($4.99) Cover swipe of X-Men #141 (1981) Graduation Day 5.00
Annual 1 (1/14, $4.99) Aaron-s/Bradshaw-a; Gladiator app. 5.00

WOLVERINE & THE X-MEN (2nd series)
Marvel Comics: May, 2014 - Present ($3.99)

1,2: 1-Latour-s/Asrar-a; Fantomex app. 4.00

WOLVERINE AND THE X-MEN: ALPHA & OMEGA
Marvel Comics: Dec, 2011 - No. 5, Jul, 2012 ($3.99, limited series)

1-5-Brooks-c/Boschi & Brooks-a; Quentin Quire vs. Wolverine 4.00

WOLVERINE/CAPTAIN AMERICA
Marvel Comics: Apr, 2004 - No. 4, Apr, 2004 ($2.99, limited series)

1-4-Derenick-a/c 3.00

WOLVERINE: DAYS OF FUTURE PAST
Marvel Comics: Dec, 1997 - No. 3, Feb, 1998 ($2.50, limited series)

1-3: J.F. Moore-s/Bennett-a 4.00

WOLVERINE/DOOP (Also see X-Force and X-Statix)(Reprinted in X-Statix Vol. 2)
Marvel Comics: July, 2003 - No. 2, July, 2003 ($2.99, limited series)

1,2-Peter Milligan-s/Darwyn Cooke & J. Bone-a 3.00

WOLVERINE: FIRST CLASS
Marvel Comics: May, 2008 - No. 21, Jan, 2010 ($2.99)

1-21: 1-Wolverine and Kitty Pryde's first mission; DiVito-a. 2,9-Sabretooth app. 3.00

WOLVERINE/GAMBIT: VICTIMS
Marvel Comics: Sept, 1995 - No. 4, Dec, 1995 ($2.95, limited series)

1-4: Jeph Loeb scripts & Tim Sale-a; foil-c 5.00

WOLVERINE/HERCULES: MYTHS, MONSTERS & MUTANTS
Marvel Comics: May, 2011 - No. 4, Aug, 2011 ($2.99, limited series)

1-4-Tieri-s/Santacruz-a/Jusko-c 3.00

WOLVERINE/HULK
Marvel Comics: Apr, 2002 - No. 4, July, 2002 ($3.50, limited series)

1-4-Sam Kieth-s/a/c 4.00
Wolverine Legends Vol. 1: Wolverine/Hulk (2003, $9.99, TPB) r/#1-4 10.00

WOLVERINE: MANIFEST DESTINY
Marvel Comics: Dec, 2008 - No. 4, Mar, 2009 ($2.99, limited series)

1-4-Aaron-s/Segovia-a 3.00

WOLVERINE MAX
Marvel Comics: Dec, 2012 - No. 15, Mar, 2014 ($3.99)

1-15: 1-5-Starr-s/Boschi-a/Jock-c; Victor Creed app. 4.00

WOLVERINE: NETSUKE
Marvel Comics: Nov, 2002 - No. 4, Feb, 2003 ($3.99, limited series)

1-4-George Pratt-s/painted-a 4.00

WOLVERINE: NOIR (1930s Pulp-style)
Marvel Comics: Apr, 2009 - No. 4, Sept, 2009 ($3.99, limited series)

1-4-C.P. Smith-a/Stuart Moore; covers by Smith & Calero; alternate Logan as detective 4.00

WOLVERINE: ORIGINS
Marvel Comics: June, 2006 - No. 50, Sept, 2010 ($2.99)

1-15: 1-Daniel Way-s/Steve Dillon-a/Quesada-c 3.00
1-10-Variant covers. 1-Turner. 2-Quesada & Hitch. 3-Bianchi. 4-Dell'Otto. 7-Deodato 4.00
16-($3.99) Captain America WW2 app.; preview of Wolverine #56; r/X-Men #268 4.00
16-Variant-c by McGuinness 4.00
17-24: 17-20-Capt. America & Bucky app. 21-24-Deadpool app.; Bianchi-c 3.00
25-($3.99) Deadpool app.; Bianchi-c; r/Deadpool's 1st app. in New Mutants #98 4.00
26-49: 26-Origin of Dakan; Way-s/Segovia-a/Land-c. 28-Hulk & Wendigo app. 3.00
50-($3.99) Last issue; Nick Fury app. 4.00
Annual 1 (9/07, $3.99) Way-s/Andrews-a; flashback to 1932 4.00
... Vol. 1 - Born in Blood HC (2006, $19.99, dustjacket) r/#1-5; variant covers 20.00
... Vol. 1 - Born in Blood SC (2007, $13.99) r/#1-5; variant covers 14.00
... Vol. 2 - Savior HC (2007, $19.99, dustjacket) r/#6-10; variant covers 20.00
... Vol. 2 - Savior SC (2007, $13.99) r/#6-10; variant covers 14.00
... Vol. 3 - Swift & Terrible HC (2007, $19.99, dustjacket) r/#11-15 20.00
... Vol. 3 - Swift & Terrible SC (2007, $13.99) r/#11-15 14.00
... Vol. 4 - Our War HC (2008, $19.99, dustjacket) r/#16-20 & Annual #1 20.00
... Vol. 4 - Our War SC (2008, $14.99) r/#16-20 & Annual #1 15.00

WOLVERINE/PUNISHER
Marvel Comics: May, 2004 - No. 5, Sept, 2004 ($2.99, limited series)

1-5: Milligan-s/Weeks-a 3.00
... Vol. 1 TPB (2004, $13.99) r/series 14.00

WOLVERINE, PUNISHER & GHOST RIDER: OFFICIAL INDEX TO THE MARVEL UNIVERSE
Marvel Comics: Oct, 2011 - No. 8, May, 2012 ($3.99)

1-8-Each issue has chronological synopsies, creator credits, character lists for 30-40 issues of their own titles and headlining mini-series 4.00

WOLVERINE/PUNISHER REVELATIONS (Marvel Knights)
Marvel Comics: Jun, 1999 - No. 4, Sept, 1999 ($2.95, limited series)

1-4: Pat Lee-a(p) 4.00
...: Revelation (4/00, $14.95, TPB) r/#1-4 15.00

WOLVERINE SAGA
Marvel Comics: Sept, 1989 - No. 4, Mid-Dec, 1989 ($3.95, lim. series, 52 pgs.)

1-Gives history; Liefeld/Austin-c (front & back) 6.00
2-4: 2-Romita, Jr./Austin-c. 4-Kaluta-c 6.00

WOLVERINE: SNIKT!
Marvel Comics: July, 2003 - No. 5, Nov, 2003 ($2.99, limited series)

1-5-Manga-style; Tsutomu Nihei-s/a 3.00
Wolverine Legends Vol. 5: Snikt! TPB (2003, $13.99) r/#1-5 14.00

WOLVERINE: SOULTAKER
Marvel Comics: May, 2005 - No. 5, Aug, 2005 ($2.99, limited series)

1-5-Yoshida-s/Nagasawa-a/Terada-c; Yukio app. 3.00
TPB (2005, $13.99) r/#1-5 14.00

WOLVERINE: THE BEST THERE IS
Marvel Comics: Feb, 2011 - No. 12, Jan, 2012 ($3.99)

1-12: 1,2-Huston-s/Ryp-a; covers by Hitch and Djurdjevic. 3-12-Hitch-c 4.00
... - Contagion 1 (6/11, $4.99) r/#1-3, cover gallery 5.00

WOLVERINE: THE END
Marvel Comics: Jan, 2004 - No. 6, Dec, 2004 ($2.99, limited series)

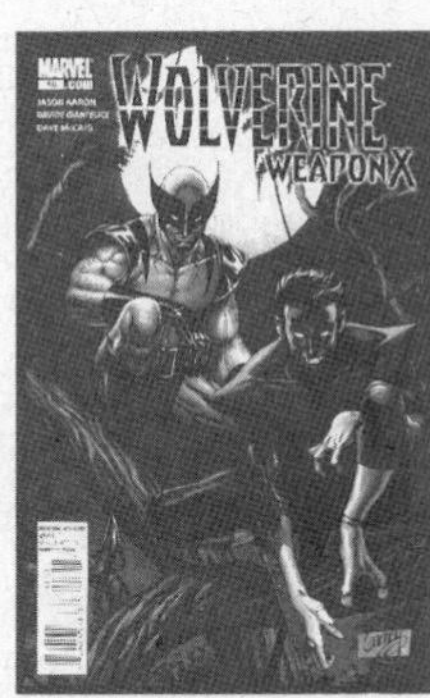
Wolverine Weapon X #16 © MAR

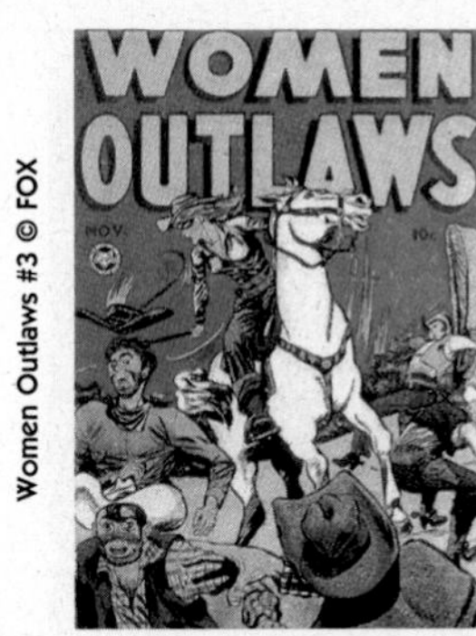

Women Outlaws #3 © FOX

Wonder Comics #11 © BP

GD 2.0 VG 4.0 FN 6.0 VF 8.0 VF/NM 9.0 NM- 9.2

1-5-Jenkins-s/Castellini-a 3.00
1-Wizard World Texas variant-c 20.00
TPB (2005, $14.99) r/#1-5 15.00

WOLVERINE: THE ORIGIN
Marvel Comics: Nov, 2001 - No. 6, July, 2002 ($3.50, limited series)

1-Origin of Logan; Jenkins-s/Andy Kubert-a; Quesada-c 35.00
1-DF edition 25.00
2 10.00
3-6 6.00
HC (3/02, $34.95, 11" x 7-1/2") r/#1-6; dust jacket; sketch pages and treatments 35.00
HC (2006, $19.99) r/#1-6; dust jacket; sketch pages and treatments 20.00
SC (2002, $14.95) r/#1-6; afterwords by Jemas and Quesada 15.00

WOLVERINE WEAPON X
Marvel Comics: June, 2009 - No. 16, Oct, 2010 ($3.99)

1-16: 1-5,11-Aaron-s/Garney-a. 1-Four covers. 2,3-Two covers. 11-15-Deathlok app. 4.00

WOLVERINE: XISLE
Marvel Comics: June, 2003 - No. 5, June, 2003 ($2.50, weekly limited series)

1-5-Bruce Jones-s/Jorge Lucas-a 3.00
Wolverine Legends Vol. 4 TPB (2003, $13.99) r/ #1-5 14.00

WOMANTHOLOGY: SPACE
IDW Publishing: Sept, 2012 - Present ($3.99)

1-5-Anthology of short stories by women creators 4.00

WOMEN IN LOVE (A Feature Presentation #5)
Fox Features Synd./Hero Books: Aug, 1949 - No. 4, Feb, 1950

1 39 78 117 231 378 525
2-Kamen/Feldstein-c 32 64 96 188 307 425
3 21 42 63 126 206 285
4-Wood-a 26 52 78 154 252 350

WOMEN IN LOVE (Thrilling Romances for Adults)
Ziff-Davis Publishing Co.: Winter, 1952 (25¢, 100 pgs.)

nn-(Scarce)-Kinstler-a; painted-c 68 136 204 435 743 1050

WOMEN OF MARVEL
Marvel Comics: 2006, 2007 ($24.99, TPB)

SC-Reprints 1st apps. of Dazzler, Ms. Marvel, Shanna, The Cat plus notable stories of other female Marvel characters; Mayhew-c 25.00
Vol. 2 (2007) More stories of female Marvel characters; Mayhew-c; cover process art 25.00

WOMEN OF MARVEL
Marvel Comics: Jan, 2011 - No. 2, Feb, 2011 ($3.99, limited series)

1,2-Short stories of female Marvel characters. 1-Pichelli-c. 2-Land-c 4.00

WOMEN OUTLAWS (My Love Memories #9 on)(Also see Red Circle)
Fox Features Syndicate: July, 1948 - No. 8, Sept, 1949

1-Used in **SOTI**, illo "Giving children an image of American womanhood"; negligee panels
81 162 243 518 884 1250
2,3: 3-Kamenish-a 60 120 180 381 653 925
4-8 47 94 141 296 498 700
nn(nd)-Contains Cody of the Pony Express; same cover as #7
22 44 66 132 216 300

WOMEN TO LOVE
Realistic: No date (1953)

nn-(Scarce)-Reprints Complete Romance #1; c-/Avon paperback #165
40 80 120 246 411 575

WONDER BOY (Formerly Terrific Comics) (See Blue Bolt, Bomber Comics & Samson)
Ajax/Farrell Publ.: No. 17, May, 1955 - No. 18, July, 1955 (Code approved)

17-Phantom Lady app. Bakerish-c/a 47 94 141 296 498 700
18-Phantom Lady app. 39 78 117 240 395 550
NOTE: *Phantom Lady not by Matt Baker.*

WONDER COMICS (Wonderworld #3 on)
Fox Features Syndicate: May, 1939 - No. 2, June, 1939 (68 pgs.)

1-(Scarce)-Wonder Man only app. by Will Eisner; Dr. Fung (by Powell), K-5 begins; Bob Kane-a; Eisner-c 1900 3800 5700 14,000 25,000 36,000
2-(Scarce)-Yarko the Great, Master Magician (see Samson) by Eisner begins; 'Spark' Stevens by Bob Kane, Patty O'Day, Tex Mason app. Lou Fine's 1st-c; Fine-a (2 pgs.); Yarko-c (Wonder Man-c #1) 568 1136 1704 4146 7323 10,500

WONDER COMICS
Great/Nedor/Better Publications: May, 1944 - No. 20, Oct, 1948

1-The Grim Reaper & Spectro, the Mind Reader begin; Hitler/Hirohito bondage-c
290 580 870 1856 3178 4500
2-Origin The Grim Reaper; Super Sleuths begin, end #8,17; Schomburg Nazi WWII-c
123 246 369 787 1344 1900
3-5: All Schomburg Nazi WWII-c. 3-Indicia reads "Vol. 1, #2"
116 232 348 742 1271 1800
6-10: 6-Flag-c. 8-Last Spectro. 9-Wonderman begins
68 136 204 435 743 1050
11-14: 11-Dick Devens, King of Futuria begins, ends #14. 11,12-Ingels-c & splash pg.
14-Bondage-c 87 174 261 553 952 1350
15-Tara begins (origin), ends #20 123 246 369 787 1344 1900
16,18: 16-Spectro app.; last Grim Reaper. 18-The Silver Knight begins
71 142 213 454 777 1100
17-Wonderman with Frazetta panels; Jill Trent with all Frazetta inks
74 148 222 470 810 1150
19-Frazetta panels 74 148 222 470 810 1150
20-Most of Silver Knight by Frazetta 87 174 261 553 952 1350
NOTE: ***Ingels** c-11, 12. **Roussos** a-19. **Schomburg (Xela)** c-1-10; (airbrush)-13-20. Bondage c-12, 13, 15. Cover features: Grim Reaper #1-8; Wonder Man #9-15; Tara #16-20.*

WONDER DUCK (See Wisco)
Marvel Comics (CDS): Sept, 1949 - No. 3, Mar, 1950

1-Funny animal 20 40 60 114 182 250
2,3 14 28 42 80 115 150

WONDERFUL ADVENTURES OF PINOCCHIO, THE (See Movie Comics & Walt Disney Showcase #48)
Whitman Publishing Co.: April, 1982 (Walt Disney)

nn-(#3 Continuation of Movie Comics?); r/FC #92 6.00

WONDERFUL WIZARD OF OZ (Adaptation of the original 1900 L. Frank Baum book)
(Also see the sequels Marvelous Land of Oz, Ozma of Oz, and Dorothy & The Wizard in Oz)
Marvel Comics: Feb, 2009 - No. 8, Sept, 2009 ($3.99, limited series)

1-8-Eric Shanower-a/Skottie Young-a/c 4.00
1-Variant Good Witch & Dorothy wraparound cover by J. Scott Campbell 8.00
1-Variant Scarecrow & Dorothy cover by Eric Shanower 10.00
1-(4/10, $1.00) Reprint with "Marvel's Greatest Comics" on cover 3.00
... Sketchbook (2008, giveaway) Young character design sketches; Shanower intro. 3.00
HC (2009, $29.99, dustjacket) r/#1-8; Shanower intro.; cover gallery; sketch art 30.00

WONDERFUL WORLD FOR BOYS AND GIRLS
DC Comics: May, 1964

nn - Ashcan comic, not distributed to newsstands, only for in-house use (no known sales)

WONDERFUL WORLD OF DISNEY, THE (Walt Disney)
Whitman Publishing Co.: 1978 (Digest, 116 pgs.)

1-Barks-a (reprints) 3 6 9 16 23 30
2 (no date) 2 4 6 11 16 20

WONDERFUL WORLD OF THE BROTHERS GRIMM (See Movie Comics)

WONDER GIRL (Cassandra Sandsmark from Teen Titans)
DC Comics: Nov, 2007 - No. 6, Apr, 2008 ($2.99, limited series)

1-6-Torres-s/Greene-a; Hercules app. 2-6-Female Furies app. 5,6-Wonder Woman app. 3.00
Teen Titans Spotlight: Wonder Girl TPB (2008, $17.99) r/#1-6 18.00
1-(3/11, $2.99, one-shot) Nicola Scott-c; intro. Solstice 3.00

WONDERLAND COMICS
Feature Publications/Prize: Summer, 1945 - No. 9, Feb-Mar, 1947

1-Alex in Wonderland begins; Howard Post-c 26 52 78 154 252 350
2-Howard Post-c/a(2) 15 30 45 85 130 175
3-9: 3,4-Post-c 14 28 42 80 115 150

WONDER MAN (See The Avengers #9, 151)
Marvel Comics Group: Mar, 1986 ($1.25, one-shot, 52 pgs.)

1 5.00

WONDER MAN
Marvel Comics Group: Sept, 1991 - No. 29, Jan, 1994 ($1.00)

1-29: 1-Free fold out poster by Johnson/Austin. 1-3-Johnson/Austin-c/a. 2-Avengers West Coast x-over. 4 Austin-c(i) 3.00
Annual 1 (1992, $2.25)-Immonen-a (10 pgs.) 4.00
Annual 2 (1993, $2.95)-Bagged w/trading card 4.00

WONDER MAN
Marvel Comics: Feb, 2007 - No. 5, June, 2007 ($2.99, limited series)

1-5: 1-Peter David-s/Andrew Currie-a; Beast app. 4-Nauck-a 3.00
...: My Fair Super Hero TPB (2007, $13.99) r/#1-5; Currie sketch page 14.00

WONDERS OF ALADDIN, THE
Dell Publishing Co.: No. 1255, Feb-Apr, 1962

Wonder Woman #3 © DC

Wonder Woman #159 © DC

Wonder Woman (2nd series) #88 © DC

	GD 2.0	VG 4.0	FN 6.0	VF 8.0	VF/NM 9.0	NM- 9.2
Four Color 1255-Movie	6	12	18	37	66	95

WONDER WOMAN (See Adventure Comics #459, All-Star Comics, Brave & the Bold, DC Comics Presents, JLA, Justice League of America, Legend of..., Power Record Comics, Sensation Comics, Super Friends and World's Finest Comics #244)

WONDER WOMAN
DC Comics: Jan 1942

1-Ashcan comic, not distributed to newsstands, only for in-house use. Cover art is Sensation Comics #1 with interior being Sensation Comics #2. A CGC certified 8.5 copy sold for $17,250 in 2002.

WONDER WOMAN
National Periodical Publications/All-American Publ./DC Comics:
Summer, 1942 - No. 329, Feb, 1986

	GD 2.0	VG 4.0	FN 6.0	VF 8.0	VF/NM 9.0	NM- 9.2
1-Origin Wonder Woman retold (more detailed than All Star #8); H. G. Peter-c/a begins	3000	6000	9000	22,500	41,250	60,000

1-Reprint, Oversize 13-1/2x10". **WARNING:** This comic is an exact reprint of the original except for its size. DC published it in 1974 with a second cover titling it as a Famous First Edition. There have been many reported cases of the outer cover being removed and the interior sold as the original edition. The reprint with the new outer cover removed is practically worthless. See Famous First Edition for value.

	GD 2.0	VG 4.0	FN 6.0	VF 8.0	VF/NM 9.0	NM- 9.2
2-Origin/1st app. Mars; Duke of Deception app.	443	886	1329	3234	5717	8200
3	297	594	891	1901	3251	4600
4,5: 5-1st Dr. Psycho app.	239	478	717	1530	2615	3700
6-1st Cheetah app.	290	580	870	1856	3178	4500
7-Wonder Woman for President-c/sty	300	600	900	1920	3310	4700
8,9	181	362	543	1158	1979	2800
10-Invasion from Saturn classic sci-fi-c/s	187	374	561	1197	2049	2900
11-20	116	232	348	742	1271	1800
21-30: 23-Story from Wonder Woman's childhood	100	200	300	640	1095	1550
31-33,35-40: 38-Last H.G. Peter-c	87	174	261	553	952	1350
34-Robot-c	90	180	270	576	988	1400
41-44,46-48	77	154	231	493	847	1200
45-Origin retold	148	296	444	947	1624	2300
49-Used in **SOTI**, pgs. 234,236; last 52 pg. issue	79	158	237	502	864	1225
50-(44 pgs.)-Used in **POP**, pg. 97	79	158	237	502	864	1225
51-60: 60-New logo	71	142	213	454	777	1100
61-72: 62-Origin of W.W. i.d. 64-Story about 3-D movies. 70-1st Angle Man app. 72-Last pre-code (2/55)	66	132	198	419	722	1025
73-90: 80-Origin The Invisible Plane. 89-Flying saucer-c/story	57	114	171	362	619	875
91-94,96,97,99: 97-Last H. G. Peter-a	48	96	144	302	514	725
95-A-Bomb-c	52	104	156	328	552	775
98-(5/58) 1st Silver Age Wonder Woman; new origin & new art team (Andru & Esposito) begin; Kanigher-s; 1st meets Steve Trevor	53	106	159	334	567	800
99-New origin continues; origin Diana Prince i.d.	50	100	150	315	533	750
100-(8/58)	54	108	162	343	574	825
101-104,106,108-110	41	82	123	256	428	600
105-(Scarce, 4/59)-Wonder Woman's origin (part 3); she appears as a girl (no costume yet) (called Wonder Girl - see DC Super-Stars #1)	194	388	582	1242	2121	3000
107-1st advs. of Wonder Girl; 1st Merboy; tells how Wonder Woman won her costume	47	94	141	298	504	710
111-120	34	68	102	199	325	450
121-126: 121-1st app. Wonder Woman Family. 122-1st app. Wonder Tot. 124-Wonder Woman Family app. 126-Last 10¢ issue	27	54	81	160	263	365
127-130: 128-Origin The Invisible Plane retold. 129-3rd app. Wonder Woman Family (#133 is 4th app.)	12	24	36	83	182	280
131-150: 132-Flying saucer-c	10	20	30	69	147	225
151-155,157,158,160-170 (1967): 151-Wonder Girl solo issue	8	16	24	54	102	150
156-(8/65)-Early mention of a comic book shop & comic collecting; mentions DCs selling for $100 a copy	9	18	27	57	111	165
159-Origin retold (1/66); 1st S.A. origin?	10	20	30	64	132	200
171-176	6	12	18	41	76	110
177-W. Woman/Supergirl battle	8	16	24	54	102	150
178-1st new Wonder Woman on-c only; appears in old costume w/powers inside	8	16	24	56	108	160
179-Classic-c; wears no costume to issue #203	8	16	24	54	102	150
180-195: 180-Death of Steve Trevor. 182-Last 12¢ issue. 195-Wood inks	5	10	15	33	57	80
196 (52 pgs.)-Origin-r/All Star #8 (6 out of 9 pgs.)	5	10	15	34	60	85
197,198 (52 pgs.)-Reprints	5	10	15	34	60	85
199-Jeff Jones painted-c; 52 pgs.	8	16	24	54	102	150
200 (5-6/72)-Jeff Jones-c; 52 pgs.	8	16	24	55	105	155
201,202-Catwoman app. 202-Fafhrd & The Grey Mouser debut.	4	8	12	25	40	55
203,205-210,212: 212-The Cavalier app.	3	6	9	18	28	38
204-Return to old costume; death of I Ching	4	8	12	25	40	55
211,214-(100 pgs.)	7	14	21	44	82	120
213,215,216,218-220: 220-N. Adams assist	3	6	9	16	24	32
217: (68 pgs.)	3	6	9	21	33	45
221,222,224-227,229,230,233-236,238-240: 227-Judy Garland tribute	2	4	6	10	14	18
223,228,231,232,237,241,248: 223-Steve Trevor revived as Steve Howard & learns W.W.'s I.D. 228-Both Wonder Women team up & new World War II stories begin, end #243. 231,232: JSA app. 237-Origin retold. 240-G.A. Flash app. 241-Intro Bouncer; Spectre app. 248-Steve Trevor Howard dies (44 pgs.)	2	4	6	11	16	20
242-246,252-266,269,270: 243-Both W. Women team-up again. 269-Last Wood a(i) for DC? (7/80)	2	3	4	6	8	10
247,249-251,271: 247,249 (44 pgs.). 249-Hawkgirl app. 250-Origin/1st app. Orana, the new Wonder Woman. 251-Orana dies. 271-Huntress & 3rd Life of Steve Trevor begin	2	4	6	8	10	12
250-252,255-262,264-(Whitman variants, low print run, no issue # on cover)	2	4	6	11	16	20
267,268-Re-intro Animal Man (5/80 & 6/80)	2	4	6	8	10	12
272-280,284-286,289,290,294-299,301-325						6.00
281-283: Joker-c/stories in Huntress back-ups	2	3	4	6	8	10
287,288,291-293: 287-New Teen Titans x-over. 288-New costume & logo. 291-293-Three part epic with Super-Heroines	1	2	3	4	5	7
300-($1.50, 76 pgs.)-Anniv. issue; Giffen-a; New Teen Titans, Bronze Age Sandman, JLA & G.A. Wonder Woman app.; 1st app. Lyta Trevor who becomes Fury in All-Star Squadron #25; G.A. Wonder Woman & Steve Trevor revealed as married	1	2	3	5	7	9
326-328	1	2	3	4	5	7
329 (Double size)-S.A. W.W. & Steve Trevor wed	2	4	6	9	13	16
...: Chronicles Vol. 1 TPB (2010, $17.99) reprints debut in All Star Comics #8, apps. in Sensation Comics #1-9 and Wonder Woman #1						18.00
Diana Prince: Wonder Woman Vol. 1 TPB (2008, $19.99) r/#178-183						20.00
Diana Prince: Wonder Woman Vol. 2 TPB (2008, $19.99) r/#185-189, Brave and the Bold #87, and Superman's Girl Friend, Lois Lane #93						20.00
Diana Prince: Wonder Woman Vol. 3 TPB ('08, $19.99) r/#190-198, World's Finest #204						20.00
Diana Prince: Wonder Woman Vol. 4 TPB ('09, $19.99) r/#199-204, Brave & Bold #105						20.00
...: The Greatest Stories Ever Told TPB (2007, $19.99) intro. by Lynda Carter; Ross-c						20.00

NOTE: ***Andru/Esposito** c-66-160(most). **Buckler** a-300. **Colan** a-288-305p; c-288-290p. **Giffen** a-300p. **Grell** c-217. **Kaluta** c-297. **Gil Kane** c-294p, 303-305, 307, 312, 314. **Miller** c-298p. **Morrow** c-233. **Nasser** a-232p; c-231p, 232p. **Bob Oskner** c(i)-39-65(most). **Perez** c-283p, 284p. **Spiegle** a-312. **Staton** a(p)-241, 271-287, 289, 290, 294-299; c(p)-241, 245, 246. Huntress back-up stories 271-287, 289, 290, 294-299, 301-321.*

WONDER WOMAN
DC Comics: Feb, 1987 - No. 226, Apr, 2006 (75¢/$1.00/$1.25/$1.95/$1.99/$2.25/$2.50)

	GD 2.0	VG 4.0	FN 6.0	VF 8.0	VF/NM 9.0	NM- 9.2
0-(10/94) Zero Hour; released between #90 & #91						5.00
1-New origin; Perez-c/a begins	2	4	6	10	14	18
2-5						6.00
6-20: 9-Origin Cheetah. 12,13-Millennium x-over. 18,26-Free 16 pg. story						5.00
21-49: 24-Last Perez-a; scripts continue thru #62						4.00
50-($1.50, 52 pgs.)-New Titans, Justice League						5.00
51-62: Perez scripts. 60-Vs. Lobo; last Perez-c. 62-Last $1.00-c						4.00
63-New direction & Bolland-c begin; Deathstroke story continued from W. W. Special #1						5.00
64-84						4.00
85-1st Deodato-a; ends #100	3	5	7	10	12	14
86-88: 88-Superman-c & app.						6.00
89-97: 90-(9/94)-1st Artemis. 91-(11/94). 93-Hawkman app. 96-Joker-c						5.00
98,99						4.00
100 ($2.95, Newsstand)-Death of Artemis; Bolland-c ends.						4.00
100 ($3.95, Direct Market)-Death of Artemis; foil-c.						6.00
101-119, 121-125: 101-Begin $1.95-c; Byrne-c/a/scripts begin. 101-104-Darkseid app. 105-Phantom Stranger cameo. 106-108-Phantom Stranger & Demon app. 107,108-Arion app. 111-1st app. new Wonder Girl. 111,112-Vs. Doomsday. 112-Superman app. 113-Wonder Girl-c/app; Sugar & Spike app.						3.00
120 ($2.95)-Perez-c						4.00
126-149: 128-Hippolyta becomes new W.W. 130-133-Flash (Jay Garrick) & JSA app. 136-Diana returns to W.W. role; last Byrne issue. 137-Priest-s. 139-Luke-s/Paquette-a begin; Hughes-c thru #146						3.00
150-($2.95) Hughes-c/Clark-a; Zauriel app.						4.00
151-158-Hughes-c. 153-Superboy app.						3.00
159-163: 159-Begin $2.25-c. 160,161-Clayface app. 162,163-Aquaman app.						3.00
164-171: Phil Jimenez-s/a begin; Hughes-c; Batman app. 168,169-Pérez co-plot 169-Wraparound-c.170-Lois Lane-c/app.						3.00
172-Our Worlds at War; Hippolyta killed						4.00
173,174: 173-Our Worlds at War; Darkseid app. 174-Every DC heroine app.						3.00
175-($3.50) Joker: Last Laugh; JLA app.; Jim Lee-c						4.00

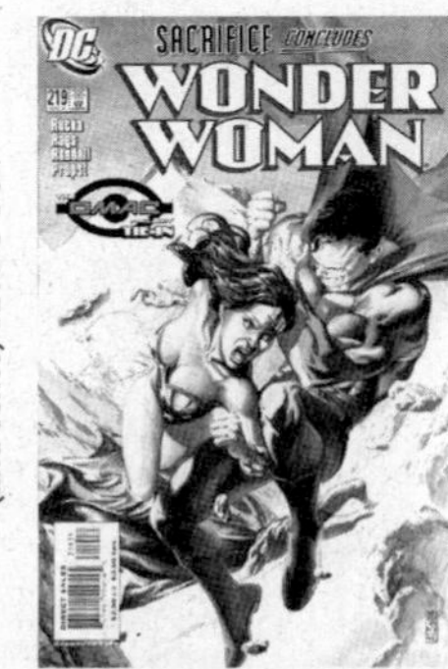

Wonder Woman (2nd series) #219 © DC

Wonder Woman (2011 series) #17 © DC

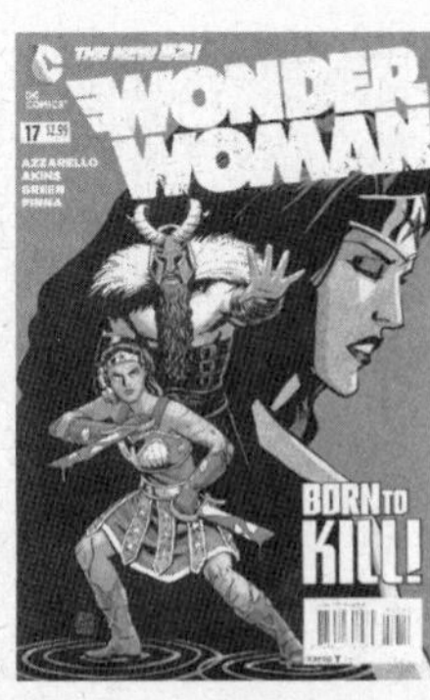

Wonderworld Comics #3 © FOX

	GD 2.0	VG 4.0	FN 6.0	VF 8.0	VF/NM 9.0	NM- 9.2

176-199: 177-Paradise Island returns. 179-Jimenez-c. 184,185-Hippolyta-c/app.; Hughes-c 186-Cheetah app. 189-Simonson-s/Ordway-a begin. 190-Diana's new look. 195-Rucka-s/Drew Johnson-a begin. 197-Flash-c/app. 198,199-Noto-c 3.00
200-($3.95) back-up stories in 1940s and 1960s styles; pin-ups by various 4.00
201-218,220-225: 203,204-Batman-c/app. 204-Matt Wagner-c. 212-JLA app. 214-Flash app. 215-Morales-a begins. 218-Begin $2.50-c. 220-Batman app. 3.00
219-Omac tie-in/Sacrifice pt. 4; Wonder Woman kills Max Lord; Superman app. 4.00
219-(2nd printing) Altered cover with red background 3.00
226-Last issue; flashbacks to meetings with Superman; Rucka-s/Richards-a 4.00
#1,000,000 (11/98) 853rd Century x-over; Deodato-c 3.00
Annual 1,2: 1 ('88, $1.50)-Art Adams-a. 2 ('89, $2.00, 68 pgs.)-All women artists issue; Perez-c(i)/a. 4.00
Annual 3 (1992, $2.50, 68 pgs.)-Quesada-c(p) 4.00
Annual 4 (1995, $3.50)-Year One 4.00
Annual 5 (1996, $2.95)-Legends of the Dead Earth story; Byrne scripts; Cockrum-a 4.00
Annual 6 (1997, $3.95)-Pulp Heroes 4.00
Annual 7,8 ('98,'99, $2.95)-7-Ghosts; Wrightson-c. 8-JLApe, A.Adams-c 4.00
...: Beauty and the Beasts TPB (2005, $19.95) r/#15-19 & Action Comics #600 20.00
...: Bitter Rivals TPB (2004, $13.95) r/#200-205; Jones-c 14.00
...: Challenge of the Gods TPB ('04, $19.95) r/#8-14; Pérez-s/a 20.00
...: Destiny Calling TPB (2006, $19.99) r/#20-24 & Annual #1; Pérez-c & pin-up gallery 20.00
...Donna Troy (6/98, $1.95) Girlfrenzy; Jimenez-a 3.00
...: Down To Earth TPB (2004, $14.95) r/#195-200; Greg Land-c 15.00
... 80-Page Giant 1 (2002, $4.95) reprints in format of 1960s' 80-Page Giants 5.00
...: Eyes of the Gorgon TPB ('05, $19.95) r/#206-213 20.00
Gallery (1996, $3.50)-Bolland-c; pin-ups by various 4.00
...: Gods and Mortals TPB ('04, $19.95) r/#1-7; Pérez-a 20.00
...: Gods of Gotham TPB ('01, $5.95) r/#164-167; Jimenez-s/a 6.00
...: Land of the Dead TPB ('06, $12.99) r/#214-217 & Flash #219 13.00
Lifelines TPB ('98, $9.95) r/#106-112; Byrne-c/a 10.00
...: Mission's End TPB ('06, $19.99) r/#218-226; cover gallery 20.00
...: Our Worlds at War (10/01, $2.95) History of the Amazons; Jae Lee-c 3.00
...: Paradise Found TPB ('03, $14.95) r/#171-177, Secret Files #3; Jimenez-s/a 15.00
...: Paradise Lost TPB ('02, $14.95) r/#164-170; Jimenez-s/a 15.00
Plus 1 (1/97, $2.95)-Jesse Quick-c/app. 4.00
Second Genesis TPB (1997, $9.95)-r/#101-105 10.00
Secret Files 1-3 (3/98, 7/99, 5/02; $4.95) 5.00
Special 1 (1992, $1.75, 52 pgs.)-Deathstroke-c/story continued in Wonder Woman #63 5.00
...: The Blue Amazon (2003, $6.95) Elseworlds; McKeever-a 7.00
The Challenge Of Artemis TPB (1996, $9.95)-r/#94-100; Deodato-c/a 10.00
...: The Once and Future Story (1998, $4.95) Trina Robbins-s/Doran & Guice-a 5.00

NOTE: ***Art Adams** a-Annual 1. **Byrne** c/a 101-107. **Bolton** a-Annual 1. **Deodato** a-85-100. **Perez** a-Annual 1; c-Annual 1(i). **Quesada** c(p)-Annual 3.*

WONDER WOMAN (Also see Amazons Attack mini-series)
DC Comics: Aug, 2006 - No. 44, Jul, 2010; No. 600, Aug, 2010 - No. 614, Oct, 2011 ($2.99)

1-Donna Troy as Wonder Woman after Infinite Crisis; Heinberg-s/Dodson-a/c 3.00
1-Variant-c by Adam Kubert 4.00
2-44: 2-4-Giganta & Hercules app. 6-Jodi Picoult-s begins. 8-Hippolyta returns. 9-12-Amazons Attack tie-in; JLA app. 14-17-Simone-s/Dodson-a/c. 20-23-Stalker app. 26-33-Rise of the Olympian. 40,41-Power Girl app. 3.00
14-DC Nation Convention giveaway edition 6.00
(Title re-numbered after #44, July 2010 to cumilative numbering of #600)
600-(8/10, $4.99) Short stories and pin-ups by various incl. Pérez, Conner, Kramer, Jim Lee; intro. by Lynda Carter; debut of new costume; cover by Pérez 5.00
600-Variant cover by Adam Hughes 8.00
600-2nd printing with new costume cover by Don Kramer 5.00
601-614: 601-606-Kramer-a; two covers by Kramer and Garner. 608-Borges-a 3.00
... Annual 1 (11/07, $3.99) Story cont'd from #4; Heinberg-s/Dodson-a/c; back-up Frank-a 4.00
...: Contagion SC (2010, $14.99) r/#40-44 15.00
...: Ends of the Earth HC (2009, $24.99) r/#20-25 25.00
...: Ends of the Earth SC (2010, $14.99) r/#20-25 15.00
...: Love and Murder HC (2007, $19.99) r/#6-10 20.00
...: Odyssey Volume One HC (2011, $22.99) r/#600-606; afterwords by Jim Lee & JMS 23.00
...: Rise of the Olympian HC (2009, $24.99) r/#26-33 & pages from DC Universe #0 25.00
...: Rise of the Olympian SC (2009, $14.99) r/#26-33 & pages from DC Universe #0 15.00
...: The Circle HC (2008, $24.99) r/#14-19; Mercedes Lackey intro.;Dodson sketch pages 25.00
...: The Circle SC (2009, $14.99) r/#14-19; Mercedes Lackey intro.;Dodson sketch pages 15.00
...: Warkiller SC (2010, $14.99) r/#34-39 15.00
...: Who is Wonder Woman? HC (2007, $19.99) r/#1-4 & Annual #1; Vaughan intro. 20.00
...: Who is Wonder Woman? SC (2009, $14.99) r/#1-4 & Annual #1; Vaughan intro. 15.00

WONDER WOMAN (DC New 52)
DC Comics: Nov, 2011 - Present ($2.99)

1-Azzarello-s/Chiang-a/c 6.00
2-23: 2-4-Azzarello-s/Chiang-a/c. 5,6,9,10,13,14,17-Akins-a. 14-19,21-23-Orion app. 3.00
23.1, 23.2 (11/13, $2.99, regular covers) 3.00
23.1 (11/13, $3.99, 3-D cover) "Cheetah #1" on cover; origin; Ostrander-s/Ibanez-a 5.00
23.2 (11/13, $3.99, 3-D cover) "First Born #1" on cover; origin; Azzarello-s/Aco-a 5.00
24-29: 25-Orion app. 29-Diana becomes God of War. 3.00
#0 (11/12, $2.99) 12 year-old Princess Diana's training; Azzarello-s/Chiang-a/c 3.00

WONDER WOMAN: AMAZONIA
DC Comics: 1997 ($7.95, Graphic Album format, one shot)

1-Elseworlds; Messner-Loebs-s/Winslade-a 8.00

WONDER WOMAN SPECTACULAR (See DC Special Series #9)

WONDER WOMAN: SPIRIT OF TRUTH
DC Comics: Nov, 2001 ($9.95, treasury size, one-shot)

nn-Painted art by Alex Ross; story by Alex Ross and Paul Dini 10.00

WONDER WOMAN: THE HIKETEIA
DC Comics: 2002 ($24.95, hardcover, one-shot)

nn-Wonder Woman battles Batman; Greg Rucka-s/J.G. Jones-a 25.00
Softcover (2003, $17.95) 18.00

WONDERWORLD COMICS (Formerly Wonder Comics)
Fox Features Syndicate: No. 3, July, 1939 - No. 33, Jan, 1942

	GD 2.0	VG 4.0	FN 6.0	VF 8.0	VF/NM 9.0	NM- 9.2
3-Intro The Flame by Fine; Dr. Fung (Powell-a), K-51 (Powell-a?), & Yarko the Great, Master Magician (Eisner-a) continues; Eisner/Fine-c	784	1568	2352	5723	10,112	14,500
4-Lou Fine-c	360	720	1080	2520	4410	6300
5,6,9,10: Lou Fine-c	219	438	657	1402	2401	3400
7-Classic Lou Fine-c	432	864	1296	3154	5577	8000
8-Classic Lou Fine-c	331	662	339	2317	4059	5800
11-Origin The Flame	181	362	543	1158	1979	2800
12-15:13-Dr. Fung ends; last Fine-c(p)	142	284	426	909	1555	2200
16-20	94	188	282	602	1026	1450
21-Origin The Black Lion & Cub	87	174	261	553	952	1350
22-27: 22,25-Dr. Fung app.	69	138	207	442	759	1075
28-Origin & 1st app. U.S. Jones (8/41); Lu-Nar, the Moon Man begins	100	200	300	640	1095	1550
29,31,33	58	116	174	371	636	900
30-Intro & Origin Flame Girl	95	190	285	608	1042	1475
32-Hitler-c	129	258	387	826	1413	2000

NOTE: *Spies at War by **Eisner** in #13, 17. Yarko by **Eisner** in #3-11. **Eisner** text illos-3. **Lou Fine** a-3-11; c-3-13, 15(i); text illos-4. **Nordling** a-4-14. **Powell** a-3-12. **Tuska** a-5-9. Bondage-c 14, 15, 28, 31, 32. Cover features: The Flame-#3, 5-31; U.S. Jones-#32, 33.*

WONDERWORLDS
Innovation Publishing: 1992 ($3.50, squarebound, 100 pgs.)

1-Rebound super-hero comics, contents may vary; Hero Alliance, Terraformers, etc. 5.00

WOODSY OWL (See March of Comics #395)
Gold Key: Nov, 1973 - No. 10, Feb, 1976 (Some Whitman printings exist)

	GD 2.0	VG 4.0	FN 6.0	VF 8.0	VF/NM 9.0	NM- 9.2
1	2	4	6	13	18	22
1-Whitman variant	3	6	9	14	20	25
2-10	2	4	6	8	10	12

WOODY WOODPECKER (Walter Lantz... #73 on?)(See Dell Giants for annuals)
(Also see The Funnies, Jolly Jingles, Kite Fun Book, New Funnies)
Dell Publishing Co./Gold Key No. 73-187/Whitman No. 188 on:
No. 169, 10/47 - No. 72, 5-7/62; No. 73, 10/62 - No. 201, 3/84 (nn 192)

	GD 2.0	VG 4.0	FN 6.0	VF 8.0	VF/NM 9.0	NM- 9.2
Four Color 169(#1)-Drug turns Woody into a Mr. Hyde	17	34	51	117	259	400
Four Color 188	10	20	30	68	144	220
Four Color 202,232,249,264,288	8	16	24	54	102	150
Four Color 305,336,350	6	12	18	38	69	100
Four Color 364,374,390,405,416,431('52)	5	10	15	34	60	85
16 (12-1/52-53) - 30('55)	4	8	12	27	44	60
31-50	3	6	9	21	33	45
51-72 (Last Dell)	3	6	9	17	26	35
73-75 (Giants, 84 pgs., Gold Key)	5	10	15	30	50	70
76-80	3	6	9	15	22	28
81-103: 103-Last 12¢ issue	3	6	9	14	19	24
104-120	2	4	6	11	16	20
121-140	2	4	6	9	12	15
141-160	1	3	4	6	8	10
161-187	1	2	3	5	7	9
188,189 (Whitman)	2	4	6	9	13	16
190(9/80),191(11/80)-pre-pack only	4	8	12	27	44	60

(No #192)

World Around Us #11 © GIL

World of Archie #5 © AP

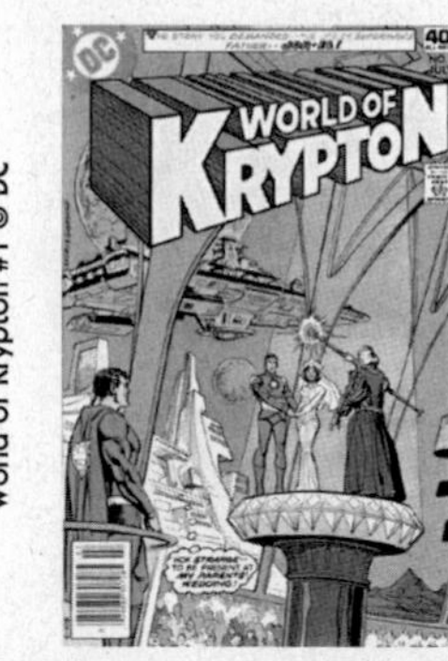

World of Krypton #1 © DC

GD 2.0 | VG 4.0 | FN 6.0 | VF 8.0 | VF/NM 9.0 | NM- 9.2

193-197: 196(2/82), 197(4/82) 2 4 6 11 16 20
198-201 (All #90062 on-c, no date or date code, pre-pack): 198(6/83), 199(7/83), 200(8/83), 201(3/84) 3 6 9 16 23 30
Christmas Parade 1(11/68-Giant)(G.K.) 4 8 12 25 40 55
Summer Fun 1(6/66-G.K.)(84 pgs.) 4 8 12 28 47 65
nn (1971, 60¢, 100 pgs. digest) B&W one page gags 3 6 9 16 24 32
NOTE: *15¢ Canadian editions of the 12¢ issues exist. Reprints-No. 92, 102, 103, 105, 106, 124, 125, 152, 153, 157, 162, 165, 194(1/3)-200(1/3).*

WOODY WOODPECKER (See Comic Album #5,9,13, Dell Giant #24, 40, 54, Dell Giants, The Funnies, Golden Comics Digest #1, 3, 5, 8, 15, 16, 20, 24, 32, 37, 44, March of Comics #16, 34, 85, 93, 109, 124, 139, 158, 177, 184, 203, 222, 239, 249, 261, 420, 454, 466, 478, New Funnies & Super Book #12, 24)

WOODY WOODPECKER
Harvey Comics: Sept, 1991 - No. 15, Aug, 1994 ($1.25)

1-15: 1-r/W.W. #53 4.00
50th Anniversary Special 1 (10/91, $2.50, 68 pgs.) 5.00

WOODY WOODPECKER AND FRIENDS
Harvey Comics: Dec, 1991 - No. 4, 1992 ($1.25)

1-4 4.00

WORD WARRIORS (Also see Quest for Dreams Lost)
Literacy Volunteers of Chicago: 1987 ($1.50, B&W)(Proceeds donated to help literacy)

1-Jon Sable by Grell, Ms. Tree, Streetwolf; Chaykin-c 3.00

WORLD AROUND US, THE (Illustrated Story of...)
Gilberton Publishers (Classics Illustrated): Sep, 1958 -No. 36, Oct, 1961 (25¢)

1-Dogs; Evans-a 9 18 27 52 69 85
2-4: 2-Indians; Check-a. 3-Horses; L. B. Cole-c. 4-Railroads; L. B. Cole-a (5 pgs.) 9 18 27 47 61 75
5-Space; Ingels-a 10 20 30 56 76 95
6-The F.B.I.; Disbrow, Evans, Ingels-a 10 20 30 56 76 95
7-Pirates; Disbrow, Ingels, Kinstler-a 9 18 27 52 69 85
8-Flight; Evans, Ingels, Crandall-a 9 18 27 52 69 85
9-Army; Disbrow, Ingels, Orlando-a 9 18 27 47 61 75
10-13: 10-Navy; Disbrow, Kinstler-a. 11-Marine Corps. 12-Coast Guard; Ingels-a (9 pgs.). 13-Air Force; L.B. Cole-c 9 18 27 47 61 75
14-French Revolution; Crandall, Evans, Kinstler-a 10 20 30 56 76 95
15-Prehistoric Animals; Al Williamson-a, 6 & 10 pgs. plus Morrow-a 10 20 30 58 79 100
16-18: 16-Crusades; Kinstler-a. 17-Festivals; Evans, Crandall-a. 18-Great Scientists; Crandall, Evans, Torres, Williamson, Morrow-a 9 18 27 52 69 85
19-Jungle; Crandall, Williamson, Morrow-a 10 20 30 58 79 100
20-Communications; Crandall, Evans, Torres-a 10 20 30 56 76 95
21-American Presidents; Crandall/Evans, Morrow-a 10 20 30 56 76 95
22-Boating; Morrow-a 8 16 24 44 57 70
23-Great Explorers; Crandall, Evans-a 9 18 27 52 69 85
24-Ghosts; Morrow, Evans-a 10 20 30 56 76 95
25-Magic; Evans, Morrow-a 10 20 30 56 76 95
26-The Civil War 11 22 33 62 86 110
27-Mountains (High Advs.); Crandall/Evans, Morrow, Torres-a 9 18 27 52 69 85
28-Whaling; Crandall, Evans, Morrow, Torres, Wildey-a; L.B. Cole-c 9 18 27 52 69 85
29-Vikings; Crandall, Evans, Torres, Morrow-a 10 20 30 58 79 100
30-Undersea Adventure; Crandall/Evans, Kirby, Morrow, Torres-a 10 20 30 56 76 95
31-Hunting; Crandall/Evans, Ingels, Kinstler, Kirby-a 9 18 27 52 69 85
32,33: 32-For Gold & Glory; Morrow, Kirby, Crandall, Evans-a. 33-Famous Teens; Torres, Crandall, Evans-a 9 18 27 52 69 85
34-36: 34-Fishing; Crandall/Evans-a. 35-Spies; Kirby, Morrow?, Evans-a. 36-Fight for Life (Medicine); Kirby-a 9 18 27 52 69 85
NOTE: See Classics Illustrated Special Edition. Another *World Around Us* issue entitled *The Sea* had been prepared in 1962 but was never published in the U.S. It was published in the British/European *World Around Us* series. Those series then continued with seven additional WAU titles not in the U.S. series.

WORLD BELOW, THE
Dark Horse Comics: Mar, 1999 - No. 4, Jun, 1999 ($2.50, limited series)

1-4-Paul Chadwick-s/c/a 3.00
TPB (1/07, $12.95) r/#1-4; intro. by Chadwick; gallery of sketches and covers 13.00

WORLD BELOW, THE: DEEPER AND STRANGER
Dark Horse Comics: Dec, 1999 - No. 4, Mar, 2000 ($2.95, B&W)

1-4-Paul Chadwick-s/c/a 3.00

WORLD FAMOUS HEROES MAGAZINE
Comic Corp. of America (Centaur): Oct, 1941 - No. 4, Apr, 1942 (comic book)

1-Gustavson-c; Lubbers, Glanzman-a; Davy Crockett, Paul Revere, Lewis & Clark, John Paul Jones stories; Flag-c 116 232 348 742 1271 1800
2-Lou Gehrig life story; Lubbers-a 53 106 159 334 567 800
3,4-Lubbers-a. 4-Wild Bill Hickok story; 2 pg. Marlene Dietrich story 50 100 150 315 533 750

WORLD FAMOUS STORIES
Croyden Publishers: 1945

1-Ali Baba, Hansel & Gretel, Rip Van Winkle, Mid-Summer Night's Dream 14 28 42 76 108 140

WORLD IS HIS PARISH, THE
George A. Pflaum: 1953 (15¢)

nn-The story of Pope Pius XII 6 12 18 31 38 45

WORLD OF ADVENTURE (Walt Disney's...)(TV)
Gold Key: Apr, 1963 - No. 3, Oct, 1963 (12¢)

1-Disney TV characters; Savage Sam, Johnny Shiloh, Capt. Nemo, The Mooncussers 3 6 9 20 31 42
2,3 3 6 9 15 21 26

WORLD OF ARCHIE, THE (See Archie Giant Series Mag. #148, 151, 156, 160, 165, 171, 177, 182, 188, 193, 200, 208, 213, 225, 232, 237, 244, 249, 456, 461, 468, 473, 480, 485, 492, 497, 504, 509, 516, 521, 532, 543, 554, 565, 574, 587, 599, 612, 627)

WORLD OF ARCHIE
Archie Comics: Aug, 1992 - No. 22 ($1.25/$1.50)

1 4.00
2-15: 9-Neon ink-c 3.00
16-22 3.00

WORLD OF ARCHIE DOUBLE DIGEST MAGAZINE
Archie Comics: Dec, 2010 - Present ($3.99/$4.99)

1-29,31-37: 5-Reprints Tiny Titans/Little Archie #1-3 with sketch pages. 17-Archie babies 4.00
30-($5.99) Double Double Digest 6.00
38-Begin $4.99-c 5.00
World of Archie Digest, Free Comic Book Day Edition (6-7/13, giveaway) Reprints 3.00

WORLD OF FANTASY
Atlas Comics (CPC No. 1-15/ZPC No. 16-19): May, 1956 - No. 19, Aug, 1959

1 65 130 195 416 708 1000
2-Williamson-a (4 pgs.) 39 78 117 231 378 525
3-Sid Check, Roussos-a 36 72 108 211 343 475
4-7 30 60 90 177 289 400
8-Matt Fox, Orlando, Berg-a 32 64 96 188 307 425
9-Krigstein-a 30 60 90 177 289 400
10-15: 10-Colan-a. 11-Torres-a 26 52 78 154 252 350
16-Williamson-a (4 pgs.); Ditko, Kirby-a 39 78 117 231 378 525
17-19-Ditko, Kirby-a 39 78 117 231 378 525
NOTE: ***Ayers** a-3. **B. Baily** a-4. **Berg** a-5, 6, 8. **Brodsky** c-3. **Check** a-3. **Ditko** a-17, 19. **Everett** a-2; c-4-7, 9, 12, 13. **Forte** a-4, 8. **Infantino** a-14. **Kirby** c-15, 17-19. **Krigstein** a-9. **Maneely** c-2, 14. **Mooney** a-14. **Morrow** a-7. **Orlando** a-8, 13, 14. **Pakula** a-9. **Powell** a-4, 6. **Reinman** a-8, 10. **R.Q. Sale** a-3, 7, 9, 10. **Severin** c-1.*

WORLD OF GIANT COMICS, THE (See Archie All-Star Specials under Archie Comics)

WORLD OF GINGER FOX, THE (Also see Ginger Fox)
Comico: Nov, 1986 ($6.95, 8 1/2 x 11", 68 pgs., mature)

Graphic Novel ($6.95) 10.00
Hardcover ($27.95) 30.00

WORLD OF JUGHEAD, THE (See Archie Giant Series Mag. #9, 14, 19, 24, 30, 136, 143, 149, 152, 157, 161, 166, 172, 178, 183, 189, 194, 202, 209, 215, 227, 233, 239, 245, 251, 457, 463, 469, 475, 481, 487, 493, 499, 505, 511, 517, 523, 531, 542, 553, 564, 577, 590, 602)

WORLD OF KRYPTON, THE (World of...#3) (See Superman #248)
DC Comics, Inc.: 7/79 - No. 3, 9/79; 12/87 - No. 4, 3/88 (Both are lim. series)

1-3 (1979, 40¢; 1st comic book mini-series): 1-Jor-El marries Lara. 3-Baby Superman sent to Earth; Krypton explodes; Mon-el app. 1 2 3 5 6 8
1-4 (75¢)-Byrne scripts; Byrne/Simonson-c 4.00

WORLD OF METROPOLIS, THE
DC Comics: Aug, 1988 - No. 4, July, 1988 ($1.00, limited series)

1-4: Byrne scripts 4.00

WORLD OF MYSTERY
Atlas Comics (GPI): June, 1956 - No. 7, July, 1957

1-Torres, Orlando-a; Powell-a? 52 104 156 328 552 775
2-Woodish-a 22 44 66 132 216 300
3-Torres, Davis, Ditko-a 26 52 78 154 252 350
4-Pakula, Powell-a 26 52 78 154 252 350
5,7: 5-Orlando-a 22 44 66 128 209 290
6-Williamson/Mayo-a (4 pgs.); Ditko-a; Colan-a; Crandall text illo

World of Suspense #7 © MAR

Worlds' Finest #15 © DC

World's Finest Comics #18 © DC

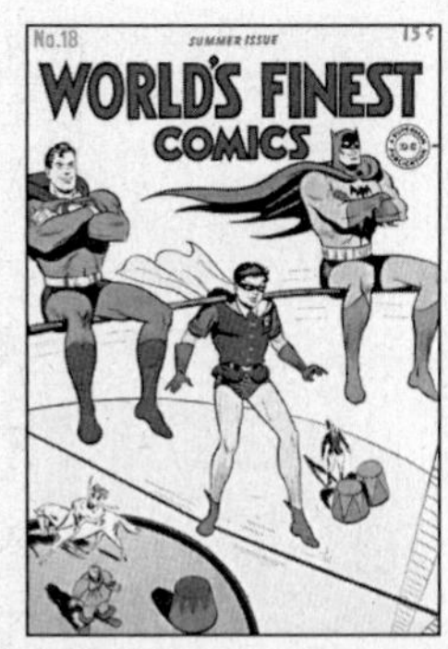

GD VG FN VF VF/NM NM-
2.0 4.0 6.0 8.0 9.0 9.2

26 52 78 154 252 350

NOTE: *Ayers a-4. Brodsky c-2, 5, 6. Colan a-6, 7. Everett c-1, 3. Pakula a-4, 6. Romita a-2. Severin c-7.*

WORLD OF SMALLVILLE
DC Comics: Apr, 1988 - No. 4, July, 1988 (75¢, limited series)

1-4: Byrne scripts 4.00

WORLD OF SUSPENSE
Atlas News Co.: Apr, 1956 - No. 8, July, 1957

1 45 90 135 284 480 675
2-Ditko-a (4 pgs.) 26 52 78 154 252 350
3,7-Williamson-a in both (4 pgs.); #7-with Mayo 25 50 75 150 245 340
4-6,8 22 44 66 128 209 290

NOTE: *Berg a-6. Cameron a-2. Ditko a-2. Drucker a-1. Everett a-1, 5; c-6. Heck a-5. Maneely a-1; c-1-3. Orlando a-5. Powell a-6. Reinman a-4. Roussos a-6. Shores a-1.*

WORLD OF WARCRAFT (Based on the Blizzard Entertainment video game)
DC Comics (WildStorm): Jan, 2008 - No. 25, Jan, 2010 ($2.99)

1-Walt Simonson-s/Lullabi-a; cover by Samwise Didier 8.00
1-Variant cover by Jim Lee 12.00
1,2-Second printing with Jim Lee sketch cover 5.00
2-Two covers by Jim Lee and Samwise Didier 5.00
3-24: 3-14-Two covers on each 3.00
25-($3.99) Walt & Louise Simonson-s 4.00
... Special 1 (2/10, $3.99) Costa-s/Mhan-a/c 4.00
... Book One HC (2008, $19.99, dustjacket) r/#1-7; intro. by Chris Metzen of Blizzard 20.00
... Book One SC (2009, $14.99) r/#1-7; intro. by Chris Metzen of Blizzard 15.00
... Book Two HC (2009, $19.99, dustjacket) r/#8-14 20.00
... Book Two SC (2010, $14.99) r/#8-14 15.00
... Book Three HC (2010, $19.99, dustjacket) r/#15-21 20.00
... Book Three SC (2011, $17.99) r/#15-21 18.00

WORLD OF WARCRAFT: ASHBRINGER
DC Comics (WildStorm): Nov, 2008 - No. 4, Feb, 2009 ($3.99)

1-4-Neilson-s/Lullabi & Washington-a; 2 covers by Robinson & Lullabi 4.00
TPB (2010, $14.99) r/#1-4 15.00

WORLD OF WARCRAFT: CURSE OF THE WORGEN
DC Comics (WildStorm #1,2): Jan, 2011 - No. 5, May, 2011 ($3.99/$2.99)

1,2-($3.99) Neilson & Waugh-s/Lullabi & Washington-a; Polidora-c 4.00
3-5-($2.99) 3.00

WORLD OF WHEELS (Formerly Dragstrip Hotrodders)
Charlton Comics: No. 17, Oct, 1967 - No. 32, June, 1970

17-20-Features Ken King 3 6 9 17 26 35
21-32-Features Ken King 3 6 9 15 22 28
Modern Comics Reprint 23(1978) 6.00

WORLD OF WOOD
Eclipse Comics: 1986 - No. 4, 1987; No. 5, 2/89 ($1.75, limited series)

1,2: 1-Dave Stevens-c. 2-Wood/Stevens-c 1 3 4 6 8 10
3-5: 5-($2.00, B&W)-r/Avon's Flying Saucers 5.00

WORLD'S BEST COMICS
DC Comics: Feb 1940

nn - Ashcan comic, not distributed to newsstands, only for in-house use. Cover art is Action Comics #29 with interior being Action Comics #24. One copy sold for $21,000 in 2000.

WORLD'S BEST COMICS (World's Finest Comics #2 on)
National Per. Publications (100 pgs.): Spring, 1941 (Cardboard-c)(DC's 6th annual format comic)

1-The Batman, Superman, Crimson Avenger, Johnny Thunder, The King, Young Dr. Davis, Zatara, Lando, Man of Magic, & Red, White & Blue begin; Superman, Batman & Robin covers begin (inside-c is blank); Fred Ray-c; 15¢ cover price
1475 2950 4425 10,400 17,700 25,000

WORLD'S BEST COMICS: GOLDEN AGE SAMPLER
DC Comics: 2003 (99¢, one-shot, samples from DC Archive editions)

1-Golden Age reprints from Superman #6, Batman #5, Sensation #11, Police #11 3.00

WORLD'S BEST COMICS: SILVER AGE SAMPLER
DC Comics: 2004 (99¢, one-shot, samples from DC Archive editions)

1-Silver Age reprints from Justice League #4, Adventure #247, Our Army at War #81 3.00

WORLDS BEYOND (Stories of Weird Adventure)(Worlds of Fear #2 on)
Fawcett Publications: Nov, 1951

1-Powell, Bailey-a; Moldoff-c 55 110 165 352 601 850

WORLDS COLLIDE
DC Comics: July, 1994 ($2.50, one-shot)

1-($2.50, 52 pgs.)-Milestone & Superman titles x-over 4.00
1-($3.95, 52 pgs.)-Polybagged w/vinyl clings 5.00

WORLD'S FAIR COMICS (See New York...)

WORLD'S FINEST (Also see Legends of The World's Finest)
DC Comics: 1990 - No. 3, 1990 ($3.95, squarebound, limited series, 52 pgs.)

1-3: Batman & Superman team-up against The Joker and Lex Luthor; Dave Gibbons scripts & Steve Rude-c/a. 2,3-Joker/Luthor painted-c by Steve Rude 5.00
TPB-(1992, $19.95) r/#1-3; Gibbons intro. 20.00
...: The Deluxe Edition HC (2008, $29.99) r/#1-3; Gibbons intro. from 1992; Gibbons story outline and sketches; Rude sketch pages and notes 30.00

WORLD'S FINEST
DC Comics: Dec, 2009 - No. 4, Mar, 2010 ($2.99, limited series)

1-4: Gates-s/two covers by Noto on each. 3-Supergirl/Batgirl team up. 4-Noto-a 3.00
TPB (2010, $14.99) r/#1-4, Action Comics #865 & DC Comics Presents #31 15.00

WORLDS' FINEST (Also see Earth 2 series)
DC Comics: Jul, 2012 - Present ($2.99)

1-21: 1-Huntress and Power Girl; Levitz-s/art by Pérez & Maguire. 6,7-Damian app. 19-Huntress meets Batman. 20,21-X-over with Batman/Superman #8,9 3.00
1-Variant-c by Maguire 5.00
#0-(11/12, $2.99) Flashback to Robin's and Supergirl's training 3.00
Annual 1 (3/14, $4.99) Earth 2 flashback; Wonder Woman & Fury app. 5.00

WORLD'S FINEST COMICS (Formerly World's Best Comics #1)
National Periodical Publ./DC Comics: No. 2, Sum, 1941 - No. 323, Jan, 1986 (#1-17 have cardboard covers) (#2-9 have 100 pgs.)

2 (100 pgs.)-Superman, Batman & Robin covers continue from World's Best; (cover price 15¢ #2-70) 423 846 1269 3000 5250 7500
3-The Sandman begins; last Johnny Thunder; origin & 1st app. The Scarecrow
320 640 960 2240 3920 5600
4-Hop Harrigan app.; last Young Dr. Davis 245 490 735 1568 2684 3800
5-Intro. TNT & Dan the Dyna-Mite; last King & Crimson Avenger
245 490 735 1568 2684 3800
6-Star Spangled Kid begins (Sum/42); Aquaman app.; S&K Sandman with Sandy in new costume begins, ends #7 181 362 543 1158 1979 2800
7-Green Arrow begins (Fall/42); last Lando & Red, White & Blue; S&K art
190 380 570 1216 2083 2950
8-Boy Commandos begin (by Simon(p) #12); last The King; includes "Minute Man Answers the Call" promo 171 342 513 1086 1868 2650
9-Batman cameo in Star Spangled Kid; S&K-a; last 100 pg. issue; Hitler, Mussolini, Tojo-c 226 452 678 1446 2473 3500
10-S&K-a; 76 pg. issues begin 161 322 483 1030 1765 2500
11-17: 17-Last cardboard cover issue 142 284 426 909 1555 2200
18-20: 18-Paper covers begin; last Star Spangled Kid. 19-Joker story. 20-Last quarterly issue
135 270 405 864 1482 2100
21-30: 21-Begin bi-monthly. 30-Johnny Everyman app.
90 180 270 576 988 1400
31-40: 33-35-Tomahawk app. 35-Penguin app. 89 178 267 565 970 1375
41-43,45-50: 41-Boy Commandos end. 42-The Wyoming Kid begins (9-10/49), ends #63. 43-Full Steam Foley begins, ends #48. 48-Last square binding. 49-Tom Sparks, Boy Inventor begins; robot-c 81 162 243 518 884 1250
44-Used in SOTI, ref. to Batman & Robin being gay, and a cop being shot in the face
90 180 270 576 988 1400
51-60: 51-Zatara ends. 54-Last 76 pg. issue. 59-Manhunters Around the World begins (7-8/52), ends #62 77 154 231 493 847 1200
61-64: 61-Joker story. 63-Capt. Compass app. 76 152 228 486 831 1175
65-Origin Superman; Tomahawk begins (7-8/53), ends #101
103 206 309 659 1130 1600
66-70-(15¢ issues, scarce)-Last 15¢, 68pg. issue 81 162 243 518 884 1250
71-(10¢ issue, scarce)-Superman & Batman begin as team (7-8/54); were in separate stories until now; Superman & Batman exchange identities; 10¢ issues begin
177 354 531 1133 1942 2750
72,73-(10¢ issue, scarce) 111 222 333 710 1218 1725
74-Last pre-code issue 79 158 237 502 864 1225
75-(1st code approved, 3-4/55) 77 154 231 493 847 1200
76-80: 77-Superman loses powers & Batman obtains them
60 120 180 381 653 925
81-90: 84-1st S.A. issue. 88-1st Joker/Luthor team-up. 89-2nd Batmen of All Nations (aka Club of Heroes). 90-Batwoman's 1st app. in World's Finest (10/57, 3rd app. anywhere) plus-c app. 29 58 87 209 467 725
91-93,95-99: 96-99-Kirby Green Arrow. 99-Robot-c 22 44 66 154 340 525
94-Origin Superman/Batman team retold 52 104 156 408 917 1425
100 (3/59) 33 66 99 238 532 825

World's Finest Comics #166 © DC

World's Finest Comics #211 © DC

World War Hulk #2 © MAR

	GD 2.0	VG 4.0	FN 6.0	VF 8.0	VF/NM 9.0	NM- 9.2
101-110: 102-Tommy Tomorrow begins, ends #124	14	28	42	96	211	325
111-121: 111-1st app. The Clock King. 113-Intro. Miss Arrowette in Green Arrow; 1st Bat-Mite/Mr. Mxyzptlk team-up (11/60). 117-Batwoman-c. 121-Last 10¢ issue	12	24	36	79	170	260
122-128: 123-2nd Bat-Mite/Mr. Mxyzptlk team-up (2/62). 125-Aquaman begins (5/62), ends #139 (Aquaman #1 is dated 1-2/62)	10	20	30	64	132	200
129-Joker/Luthor team-up-c/story	11	22	33	73	157	240
130-142: 135-Last Dick Sprang story. 140-Last Green Arrow. 142-Origin The Composite Superman (villain); Legion app.	8	16	24	51	96	140
143-150: 143-1st Mailbag. 144-Clayface/Brainiac team-up. 148-Clayface/Luthor team-up; last Clayface until Action #443	6	12	18	42	79	115
151-153,155,157-160: 157-2nd Super Sons story; last app. Kathy Kane (Bat-Woman) until Batman Family #10; 1st Bat-Mite Jr.	5	10	15	35	63	90
154-1st Super Sons story; last Bat-Woman in costume until Batman Family #10.	6	12	18	38	69	100
156-1st Bizarro Batman; Joker-c/story	9	18	27	58	114	170
161,170 (80-Pg. Giants G-28,G-40)	6	12	18	40	73	105
162-165,167,168,171,172: 168,172-Adult Legion app.	5	10	15	31	53	75
166-Joker-c/story	5	10	15	35	63	90
169-3rd app. new Batgirl(9/67)(cover and 1 panel cameo); 3rd Bat-Mite/Mr. Mxyzptlk team-up	5	10	15	35	63	90
173-('68)-1st S.A. app. Two-Face as Batman becomes Two-Face in story	8	16	24	54	102	150
174-Adams-c	5	10	15	33	57	80
175,176-Neal Adams-c/a; both reprint J'onn J'onzz origin/Detective #225,226	5	10	15	35	63	90
177-Joker/Luthor team-up-c/story	5	10	15	35	63	90
178-(9/68) Intro. of Super Nova (revived in "52" weekly series); Adams-c	6	12	18	37	66	95
179-(80 Page Giant G-52) -Adams-c; r/#94	6	12	18	37	66	95
180,182,183,185,186: Adams-c on all. 182-Silent Knight-r/Brave & Bold #6. 185-Last 12¢ issue. 186-Johnny Quick-r	4	8	12	27	44	60
181,184,187: 187-Green Arrow origin-r by Kirby (Adv. #256)	4	8	12	23	37	50
188,197:(Giants G-64,G-76; 64 pages)	5	10	15	34	60	85
189-196: 190-193-Robin-r	3	6	9	20	31	42
198,199-3rd Superman/Flash race (see Flash #175 & Superman #199). 199-Adams-c	9	18	27	57	111	165
200-Adams-c	4	8	12	25	40	55
201-203: 203-Last 15¢ issue.	3	6	9	18	38	38
204,205-(52 pgs.) Adams-c: 204-Wonder Woman app. 205-Shining Knight-r (6 pgs.) by Frazetta/Adv. #153; Teen Titans x-over	3	6	9	21	33	45
206 (Giant G-88, 64 pgs.)	5	10	15	30	50	70
207,212-(52 pgs.)	3	6	9	20	31	42
208-211(25¢-c) Adams-c: 208-(52 pgs.) Origin Robotman-r/Det. #138. 209-211-(52 pgs.)	3	6	9	21	33	45
213,214,216-222,229: 217-Metamorpho begins, ends #220; Batman/Superman team-ups resume. 229-r/origin Superman-Batman team	2	4	6	13	18	22
215-(12/72-1/73) Intro. Batman Jr. & Superman Jr. (see Superman/Batman: Saga of the Super Sons TPB for all the Super Sons stories)	3	6	9	18	28	38
223-228-(100 pgs.). 223-N. Adams-r. 223-Deadman origin. 226-N. Adams, S&K, Toth-r; Manhunter part origin-r/Det. #225,226. 227-Deadman app.	5	10	15	30	50	70
230-(68 pgs.)	3	6	9	17	26	35
231-243: 231, 233, 238, 242-Super Sons	2	4	6	9	13	16
244-246-Adams-c: 244-$1.00, 84 pg. issues begin; Green Arrow, Black Canary, Wonder Woman, Vigilante begin; 246-Death of Stuff in Vigilante; origin Vigilante retold	3	6	9	14	20	26
247-252 (84 pgs.): 248-Last Vigilante. 249-The Creeper begins by Ditko, 84 pgs. 250-The Creeper origin retold by Ditko. 252-Last 84 pg. issue	2	4	6	13	18	22
253-257,259-265: 253-Capt. Marvel begins; 68 pgs. begin, end #265. 255-Last Creeper. 256-Hawkman begins. 257-Black Lightning begins. 263-Super Sons. 264-Clay Face app.	2	4	6	8	11	14
258-Adams-c	2	4	6	10	14	18
266-270,272-282-(52 pgs.). 267-Challengers of the Unknown app.; 3 Lt. Marvels return. 268-Capt. Marvel Jr. origin retold. 274-Zatanna begins. 279, 280-Capt. Marvel Jr. & Kid Eternity learn they are brothers	1	3	4	6	8	10
271-(52pgs.) Origin Superman/Batman team retold	2	4	6	8	10	12
283-299: 284-Legion app.	1	2	3	4	5	7
300-($1.25, 52pgs.)-Justice League of America, New Teen Titans & The Outsiders app.; Perez-a (4 pgs.)	1	2	3	5	7	9
301-322: 304-Origin Null and Void. 309,319-Free 16 pg. story in each (309-Flash Force 2000, 319-Mask preview)						5.00
323-Last issue						6.00

NOTE: ***Neal Adams** a-230ir; c-174-176, 178-180, 182, 183, 185, 186, 199-205, 208-211, 244-246, 258. **Austin** a-244-246i. **Burnley** a-8, 10; c-7-9, 11-14, 15p?, 16-18p, 20-31p. **Colan** a-274p, 297, 299. **Ditko** a-249-255. **Giffen** a-322; c-284p, 322. **G. Kane** a-38, 174r, 282, 283; c-281, 282, 289. **Kirby** a-187. **Kubert** Zatara-40-44. **Miller** c-285p. **Mooney** c-134. **Morrow** a-245-248. **Mortimer** c-16-21, 26-71. **Nasser** a(p)-244-246, 259, 260. **Newton** a-253-281p. **Orlando** a-224r. **Perez** a-300i; c-271, 276, 277p, 278p. **Fred Ray** c-1-5. **Fred Ray/Robinson** c-13-16. **Robinson** a-5, 6, 9-11, 13?, 14-16; c-6. **Rogers** a-259p. **Roussos** a-212r. **Simonson** c-291. **Spiegle** a-275-278, 284. **Staton** a-262p, 273p. **Swan/Moldoff** c-126. **Swan/Mortimer** c-79-82. **Toth** a-228r. **Tuska** a-230r, 250p, 252p, 254p, 257p, 283p, 284p, 308p. Boy Commandos by **Infantino** #39-41.*

WORLD'S FINEST COMICS DIGEST (See DC Special Series #23)

WORLD'S FINEST: OUR WORLDS AT WAR
DC Comics: Oct, 2001 ($2.95, one-shot)

1-Concludes the Our Worlds at War x-over; Jae Lee-c; art by various — 3.00

WORLD'S GREATEST ATHLETE (See Walt Disney Showcase #14)

WORLD'S GREATEST SONGS
Atlas Comics (Male): Sept, 1954

	GD	VG	FN	VF	VF/NM	NM-
1-(Scarce)-Heath & Harry Anderson-a; Eddie Fisher life story plus-c; gives lyrics to Frank Sinatra song "Young at Heart"	41	82	123	256	428	600

WORLD'S GREATEST STORIES
Jubilee Publications: Jan, 1949 - No. 2, May, 1949

	GD	VG	FN	VF	VF/NM	NM-
1-Alice in Wonderland; Lewis Carroll adapt.	32	64	96	188	307	425
2-Pinocchio	30	60	90	177	289	400

WORLDS OF ASPEN
Aspen MLT, Inc.: 2006 - Present (Free Comic Book Day giveaways)

...: FCBD 2006, 2007, #3, #4 Editions; Fathom, Soulfire, Shrugged short stories; Turner-c — 3.00
... 2010 (5/10) Previews Fathom, Mindfield, Soulfire, Executive Assistant: Iris and Dellec — 3.00
... 2011 (5/11) Previews Fathom, Soulfire, Charismagic, Lady Mechanika & others — 3.00
... 2012 (5/12) Previews Fathom, Homecoming, Idolized, Shrugged & others — 3.00
... 2013 (5/13) Flip book; previews Fathom, Zoo Hunters & others — 3.00

WORLDS OF FEAR (Stories of Weird Adventure)(Formerly Worlds Beyond #1)
Fawcett Publications: V1#2, Jan, 1952 - V2#10, June, 1953

	GD	VG	FN	VF	VF/NM	NM-
V1#2	50	100	150	315	533	750
3-Evans-a	42	84	126	265	445	625
4-6(9/52)	39	78	117	240	395	550
V2#7,8	39	78	117	231	378	525
9-Classic drowning-c (4/53)	39	78	117	240	395	550
10-Saunders painted-c; man with no eyes surrounded by eyeballs-c plus eyes ripped out story	135	270	405	864	1482	2100

NOTE: ***Moldoff** c-2-8. **Powell** a-2, 4, 5. **Sekowsky** a-4, 5.*

WORLDSTORM
DC Comics (WildStorm): Nov, 2006 (Dec on cover) - No. 2, May, 2007 ($2.99)

1,2-Previews and pin-ups for re-launched WildStorm titles.1-Art Adams-c — 3.00

WORLDS UNKNOWN
Marvel Comics Group: May, 1973 - No. 8, Aug, 1974

	GD	VG	FN	VF	VF/NM	NM-
1-r/from Astonishing #54; Torres, Reese-a	3	6	9	16	23	30
2-8	2	4	6	11	16	20

NOTE: ***Adkins/Mooney** a-5. **Buscema** c/a-4p. **W. Howard** c/a-3i. **Kane** a(p)-1,2; c(p)-5, 6, 8. **Sutton** a-2. **Tuska** a(p)-7, 8; c-7p. No. 7, 8 has Golden Voyage of Sinbad movie adaptation.*

WORLD WAR HULK (See Incredible Hulk #106)
Marvel Comics: Aug, 2007 - No. 5, Jan, 2008 ($3.99, limited series)

1-Hulk returns to Earth; Iron Man and Avengers app.; Romita Jr.-a/Pak-s/Finch-c — 4.00
1-Variant cover by Romita Jr. — 6.00
2-5: 2-Hulk battles The Avengers and FF; Finch-c. 3,4-Dr. Strange app. 5-Sentry app. — 4.00
2-5-Variant cover by Romita Jr. — 6.00
...: Aftersmash 1 (1/08, $3.99) Sandoval-a/Land-c; Hercules, Iron Man app. — 4.00
...: Gamma Files (2007, $3.99) profile pages of Hulk characters — 4.00
...Prologue: World Breaker 1 (7/07, one-shot) Rio, Weeks, Phillips, Miyazawa-a — 4.00
TPB (2008, $19.99) r/#1-5 — 20.00

WORLD WAR HULK AFTERSMASH: DAMAGE CONTROL
Marvel Comics: Mar, 2008 - No. 3, May, 2008 ($2.99, limited series)

1-3-The clean-up; McDuffie-s. 2-Romita- Jr.-c. 3-Romita Sr.-c — 3.00

WORLD WAR HULK AFTERSMASH: WARBOUND
Marvel Comics: Feb, 2008 - No. 5, Jun, 2008 ($2.99, limited series)

1-5-Kirk & Sandoval-a/Cheung-c — 3.00

WORLD WAR HULK: FRONT LINE (See Incredible Hulk #106)
Marvel Comics: Aug, 2007 - No. 6, Dec, 2007 ($2.99, limited series)

1-6-Ben Urich & Sally Floyd report World War Hulk; Jenkins-s/Bachs-a — 3.00

Worst From Mad #12 © EC Pub.

Wow Comics #10 © FAW

The Wraith #1 © IDW

	GD 2.0	VG 4.0	FN 6.0	VF 8.0	VF/NM 9.0	NM- 9.2

TPB (2008, $16.99) r/#1-5 & WWH Prologue: World Breaker 17.00

WORLD WAR HULK: GAMMA CORPS
Marvel Comics: Sept, 2007 - No. 4, Jan, 2008 ($2.99, limited series)

1-4-Tieri-s/Ferreira-a/Roux-c 3.00
TPB (2008, $10.99) r/#1-4 11.00

WORLD WAR HULKS
Marvel Comics: Jun, 2010; Sept, 2010 ($3.99, one-shot & limited series)

1-Short stories by various; Deadpool app.; Romita Jr.-c 4.00
...: Spider-Man vs. Thor 1,2 (9/10 - No. 2, 9/10) Gillen-s/Molina-a 4.00
...: Wolverine vs. Captain America 1,2 (9/10 - No. 2, 9/10) "Capt America vs Wolv." on-c 4.00

WORLD WAR HULK: X-MEN (See New Avengers: Illuminati and Incredible Hulk #92)
Marvel Comics: Aug, 2007 - No. 3, Oct, 2007 ($2.99, limited series)

1-3-Gage-s/DiVito-a/McGuinness-c; Hulk invades the Xavier Institute 3.00
TPB (2008, $24.99) r/#1-3, Avengers: The Initiative #4-5, Irredeemable Ant-Man #10, Iron Man #19-20, and Ghost Rider #12-13 25.00

WORLD WAR STORIES
Dell Publishing Co.: Apr-June, 1965 - No. 3, Dec, 1965

1-Glanzman-a in all 4 8 12 25 40 55
2,3 3 6 9 16 24 32

WORLD WAR II (See Classics Illustrated Special Issue)

WORLD WAR II: 1946
Antarctic Press: Oct, 1998 - No. 2 ($3.95, B&W)

1,2-Nomura-s/a 4.00

WORLD WAR III
Ace Periodicals: Mar, 1953 - No. 2, May, 1953

1-(Scarce)-Atomic bomb blast-c; Cameron-a 148 296 444 947 1624 2300
2-Used in **POP**, pg. 78 & B&W & color illos; Cameron-a
72 146 219 467 796 1125

WORLDWATCH
Wild and Wooly Press: June, 2004 - No. 3, Dec, 2004 ($2.95)

1-3-Austen-s/Derenick-a. 1-B&W. 2,3-Color 3.00

WORLD WITHOUT END
DC Comics: 1990 - No. 6, 1991 ($2.50, limited series, mature, stiff-c)

1-6: Horror/fantasy; all painted-c/a 3.00

WORLD WRESTLING FEDERATION BATTLEMANIA
Valiant: 1991 - No. 5?, 1991 ($2.50, magazine size, 68 pgs.)

1-5: 5-Includes 2 free pull-out posters 4.00

WORST FROM MAD, THE (Annual)
E. C. Comics: 1958 - No. 12, 1969 (Each annual cover is reprinted from the cover of the Mad issues being reprinted)(Value is 1/2 if bonus is missing)

nn(1958)-Bonus; record labels & travel stickers; 1st Mad annual; r/Mad #29-34
43 86 129 271 461 650
2(1959)-Bonus is small 33 1/3 rpm record entitled "Meet the Staff of Mad"; r/Mad #35-40
42 84 126 265 445 625
3(1960)-Has 20x30" campaign poster "Alfred E. Neuman for President"; r/Mad #41-46
15 30 45 103 227 350
4(1961)-Sunday comics section; r/Mad #47-54 14 28 42 97 214 330
5(1962)-Has 33-1/3 record; r/Mad #55-62 20 40 60 138 307 475
6(1963)-Has 33-1/3 record; r/Mad #63-70 20 40 60 138 307 475
7(1964)-Mad protest signs; r/Mad #71-76 9 18 27 61 123 185
8(1965)-Build a Mad Zeppelin 10 20 30 66 138 210
9(1966)-33-1/3 rpm record; Beatles on-c 14 28 42 94 207 320
10(1967)-Mad bumper sticker 6 12 18 40 73 105
11(1968)-Mad cover window stickers 6 12 18 37 66 95
12(1969)-Mad picture postcards; Orlando-a 6 12 18 37 66 95
NOTE: *Covers:* ***Bob Clarke-#8. Mingo-****#7, 9-12.*

WOTALIFE COMICS (Formerly Nutty Life #2; Phantom Lady #13 on)
Fox Features Syndicate/Norlen Mag.: No. 3, Aug-Sept, 1946 - No. 12, July, 1947; 1959

3-Cosmo Cat, Li'l Pan, others begin 13 26 39 74 105 135
4-12-Cosmo Cat, Li'l Pan in all 10 20 30 56 76 95
1(1959-Norlen)-Atomic Rabbit, Atomic Mouse; reprints cover to #6; reprints entire book?
8 16 24 40 50 60

WOTALIFE COMICS
Green Publications: 1959 - No. 5, 1959

1-Funny animal; Li'l Pan & Tamale app. 7 14 21 35 43 50
2-5 5 10 15 22 26 30

WOW COMICS ("Wow, What A Magazine!" on cover of first issue)
Henle Publishing Co.: July, 1936 - No. 4, Nov, 1936 (52 pgs., magazine size)

1-Buck Jones in "The Phantom Rider" (1st app. in comics), Fu Manchu; Capt. Scott Dalton begins; Will Eisner-a (1st in comics); Baily-a(1); Briefer-c
343 686 1029 2400 4200 6000
2-Ken Maynard, Fu Manchu, Popeye by Segar plus article on Popeye; Eisner-a
258 516 774 1651 2826 4000
3-Eisner-c/a(3); Popeye by Segar, Fu Manchu, Hiram Hick by Bob Kane, Space Limited app.; Jimmy Dempsey talks about Popeye's punch; Bob Ripley Believe it or Not begins; Briefer-a
245 490 735 1568 2684 3800
4-Flash Gordon by Raymond, Mandrake, Popeye by Segar, Tillie The Toiler, Fu Manchu, Hiram Hick by Bob Kane; Eisner-a(3); Briefer-c/a
290 580 870 1856 3178 4500

WOW COMICS (Real Western Hero #70 on)(See XMas Comics)
Fawcett Publ.: Winter, 1940-41; No. 2, Summer, 1941 - No. 69, Fall, 1948

nn(#1)-Origin Mr. Scarlet by S&K; Atom Blake, Boy Wizard, Jim Dolan, & Rick O'Shay begin; Diamond Jack, The White Rajah, & Shipwreck Roberts, only app.; 1st mention of Gotham City in comics; the cover was printed on unstable paper stock and is rarely found in fine or mint condition; blank inside-c; bondage-c by Beck
1350 2700 4050 10,400 18,700 27,000
2 (Scarce)-The Hunchback begins 174 348 522 1114 1907 2700
3 (Fall, 1941) 103 206 309 659 1130 1600
4-Origin & 1st app. Pinky 105 210 315 667 1146 1625
5 61 122 183 390 670 950
6-Origin & 1st app. The Phantom Eagle (7/15/42); Commando Yank begins
61 122 183 390 670 950
7,8 54 108 162 343 574 825
9-(1/6/43)-Capt. Marvel, Capt. Marvel Jr., Shazam app.; Scarlet & Pinky x-over; Mary Marvel-c/stories begin 194 388 582 1242 2121 3000
10-Swayze-c/a on Mary Marvel 66 132 198 419 722 1025
11-17,19,20: 15-Flag-c 52 104 156 328 552 775
18-1st app. Uncle Marvel (10/43); infinity-c 53 106 159 334 567 800
21-30: 23-Robot-c. 28-Pinky x-over in Mary Marvel 36 72 108 211 343 475
31-40: 32-68-Phantom Eagle by Swayze 24 48 72 142 234 325
41-50 22 44 66 132 216 300
51-58: Last Mary Marvel 21 42 63 124 202 280
59-69: 59-Ozzie (teenage) begins. 62-Flying Saucer gag-c (1/48). 65-69-Tom Mix stories (cont'd in Real Western Hero) 19 38 57 112 179 245
NOTE: *Cover features: Mr. Scarlet-#1-5; Commando Yank-#6, 7, (w/Mr. Scarlet #8); Mary Marvel-#9-56, (w/Commando Yank-#46-50), (w/Mr. Scarlet & Commando Yank-#51), (w/Mr. Scarlet & Pinky #53), (w/Phantom Eagle #54, 56), (w/Commando Yank & Phantom Eagle #58); Ozzie-#59-69.*

WRAITH (Prequel to the novel NOS4A2)
IDW Publishing: Nov, 2013 (incorrect Nov, 2012 in indicia) - Present ($3.99)

1-5: Joe Hill-s/C.P. Wilson III-a. 5-(incorrect #4 in indicia) 4.00

WRAITHBORN
DC Comics (WildStorm): Nov, 2005 - No. 6, July, 2006 ($2.99, limited series)

1-6-Marcia Chen & Joe Benitez-s/a 3.00
TPB (2007, $19.99) r/series; sketch pages and unused cover sketches 20.00

WRATH (Also see Prototype #4)
Malibu Comics: Jan, 1994 - No. 9, Nov, 1995 ($1.95)

1-9: 2-Mantra x-over. 3-Intro/1st app. Slayer. 4,5-Freex app. 8-Mantra & Warstrike app. 9-Prime app. 3.00
1-Ultra 5000 Limited silver foil 6.00
Giant Size 1 (2.50, 44 pgs.) 4.00

WRATH OF THE SPECTRE, THE
DC Comics: May, 1988 - No. 4, Aug, 1988 ($2.50, limited series)

1-3: Aparo-r/Adventure #431-440 5.00
4-Three scripts intended for Adventure #441-on, but not drawn by Aparo until 1988
1 2 3 5 6 8
TPB (2005, $19.99) r/series; Peter Sanderson intro. 20.00

WRECK OF GROSVENOR (See Superior Stories #3)

WRETCH, THE
Caliber: 1996 ($2.95, B&W)

1-Phillip Hester-a/scripts 3.00

WRETCH, THE
Amaze Ink: 1997 - No. 4, 1998 ($2.95, B&W)

1-4-Phillip Hester-a/scripts 3.00
... Vol. 1: Everyday Doomsday (4/03, $13.95) 14.00

WRINGLE WRANGLE (Disney)

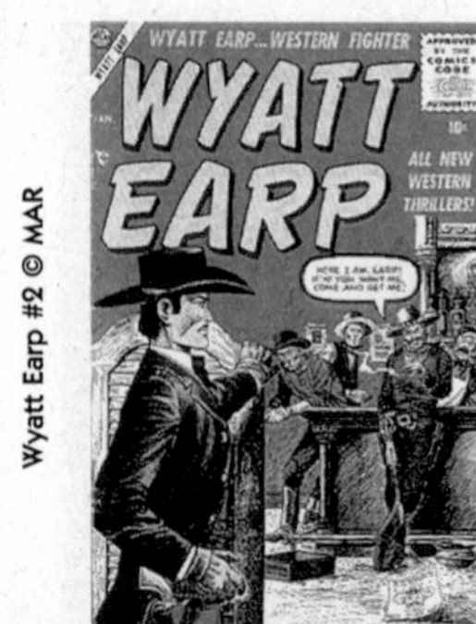

Wyatt Earp #2 © MAR

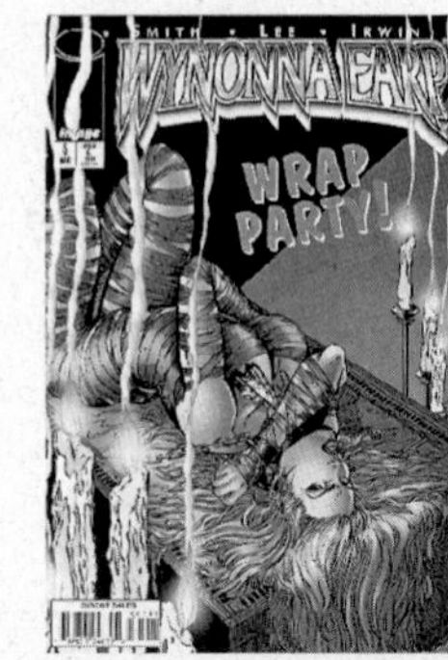

Wynonna Earp #5 © Beau Smith

X (2013 series) #7 © DH

GD VG FN VF VF/NM NM-
2.0 4.0 6.0 8.0 9.0 9.2

Dell Publishing Co.: No. 821, July, 1957

Four Color 821-Based on movie "Westward Ho, the Wagons"; Marsh-a; Fess Parker photo-c 7 14 21 46 86 125

WULF
Ardden Entertainment: Mar, 2011 - No. 6, Sept, 2012 ($2.99)

1-6-Steve Niles-s/Nat Jones-a/c; Lomax app. 3-6-Iron Jaw app. 3.00

WULF THE BARBARIAN
Atlas/Seaboard Publ.: Feb, 1975 - No. 4, Sept, 1975

1,2: 1-Origin; Janson-a. 2-Intro. Berithe the Swordswoman; Janson-a w/Neal Adams, Wood, Reese-a assists 2 4 6 11 16 20
3,4: 3-Skeates-s. 4-Friedrich-s 2 4 6 9 13 16

WWE HEROES (WWE Wrestling) (#7 titled WWE Undertaker)
Titan Comics: Apr, 2010 - No. 8 ($3.99)

1-6: 1-Two covers by Andy Smith and Liam Sharp. 5-Covers by Smith and Mayhew 4.00
7,8-"Undertaker" on cover; Rey Mysterio app. 4.00

WWE SUPERSTARS (WWE Wrestling)
Papercutz (Super Genius): Dec, 2013 - Present ($2.99/$3.99)

1-($2.99)-Mick Foley-s; John Cena, Randy Orton & CM Punk app. 3.00
2-($3.99) Mick Foley-s 4.00

WYATT EARP
Atlas Comics/Marvel No. 23 on (IPC): Nov, 1955 - #29, June, 1960; #30, Oct, 1972 - #34, June, 1973

1 21 42 63 122 199 275
2-Williamson-a (4 pgs.) 14 28 42 76 108 140
3-6,8-11: 3-Black Bart app. 8-Wild Bill Hickok app. 11 22 33 60 83 105
7,12-Williamson-a, 4 pgs. ea.; #12 with Mayo 11 22 33 64 90 115
13-20: 17-1st app. Wyatt's deputy, Grizzly Grant 10 20 30 54 72 90
21-Davis-c 9 18 27 50 65 80
22-24,26-29: 22-Ringo Kid app. 23-Kid From Texas app. 29-Last 10¢ issue 8 16 24 42 54 65
25-Davis-a 8 16 24 44 57 70
30-Williamson-r (1972) 2 4 6 13 18 22
31-34-Reprints. 32-Torres-a(r) 2 4 6 9 13 16

NOTE: ***Ayers*** *a-8, 10(2), 16(4), 17, 20(4), 26(5), 29(3).* ***Berg*** *a-9.* ***Everett*** *c-6.* ***Kirby*** *c-25, 29.* ***Maneely*** *a-1; c-1-4, 8, 12, 17, 20.* ***Maurer*** *a-2(2), 3(4), 4(4), 8(4).* ***Severin*** *a-4, 9(4), 10; c-2, 9, 10, 14.* ***Wildey*** *a-5, 17, 24, 28.*

WYATT EARP (TV) (Hugh O'Brian Famous Marshal)
Dell Publishing Co.: No. 860, Nov, 1957 - No. 13, Dec-Feb, 1960-61 (Hugh O'Brian photo-c)

Four Color 860 (#1)-Manning-a 9 18 27 57 111 165
Four Color 890,921(6/58)-All Manning-a 6 12 18 41 76 110
4 (9-11/58) - 12-Manning-a. 4-Variant edition exists with back-c comic strip; Russ Manning-a. 5-Photo back-c 5 10 15 33 57 80
13-Toth-a 5 10 15 34 60 85

WYATT EARP FRONTIER MARSHAL (Formerly Range Busters) (Also see Blue Bird)
Charlton Comics: No. 12, Jan, 1956 - No. 72, Dec, 1967

12 9 18 27 47 61 75
13-19 6 12 18 31 38 45
20-(68 pgs.)-Williamson-a(4), 8,5,5,& 7 pgs. 10 20 30 54 72 90
21-(100 pgs.) Mastroserio, Maneely, Severin-a (signed LePoer) 5 10 15 30 50 70
22-30 3 6 9 16 23 30
31-50 2 4 6 12 16 20
51-72 (1967) 2 4 6 9 11 14

WYNONNA EARP
Image Comics (WildStorm Productions): Dec, 1996 - No. 5, Apr, 1997 ($2.50)

1-5-Beau Smith-s/Chin-a 3.00

WYNONNA EARP: HOME ON THE STRANGE
IDW Publishing: Dec, 2003 - No. 3, Feb, 2004 ($3.99)

1-3-Beau Smith-s/Ferreira-a 4.00

WYNONNA EARP: THE YETI WARS
IDW Publishing: May, 2011 - No. 4, Aug, 2011 ($3.99)

1-4-Beau Smith-s/Enrique Villagran-a 4.00

WYRMS
Marvel Comics (Dabel Brothers): Feb, 2007 - No. 6, Jan, 2008 ($2.99)

1-6-Orson Scott Card & Jake Black-s. 1-3-Batista-a 3.00
TPB (2008, $14.99) r/#1-6 15.00

X (Comics' Greatest World: X #1 only) (Also see Comics' Greatest World & Dark Horse Comics #8)
Dark Horse Comics: Feb, 1994 - No. 25, Apr, 1996 ($2.00/$2.50)

1-25: 3-Pit Bulls x-over. 8-Ghost-c & app. 18-Miller-c.; Predator app. 19-22-Miller-c. 3.00
Hero Illustrated Special #1,2 (1994, $1.00, 20 pgs.) 3.00
One Shot to the Head (1994, $2.50, 36 pgs.)-Miller-c. 3.00

NOTE: ***Miller*** *c-18-22.* ***Quesada*** *c-6.* ***Russell*** *a-6.*

X (Comics' Greatest World)
Dark Horse Comics: No. 0, Apr, 2013 - Present ($2.99)

0-12: 0-Swierczynski-s/Eric Nguyen-a 3.00
One For One (1/14, $1.00) r/#1 3.00

XANADU COLOR SPECIAL
Eclipse Comics: Dec, 1988 ($2.00, one-shot)

1-Continued from Thoughts & Images 3.00

XAVIER INSTITUTE ALUMNI YEARBOOK (See X-Men titles)
Marvel Comics: Dec, 1996 ($5.95, square-bound, one-shot)

1-Text w/art by various 6.00

X-BABIES
Marvel Comics: Dec, 2009 - No. 4, Mar, 2010 ($3.99, limited series)

1-4-Schigiel-s/Chabot-a; Skottie Young-c 4.00
...: Murderama (8/98, $2.95) J.J. Kirby-a 4.00
...: Reborn (1/00, $3.50) J.J. Kirby-a 4.00

X-CALIBRE
Marvel Comics: Mar, 1995 - No. 4, July, 1995 ($1.95, limited series)

1-4-Age of Apocalypse 3.00

X-CAMPUS
Marvel Comics: July, 2010 - No. 4, Nov, 2010 ($4.99, limited series)

1-4-Alternate version of X-Men; stories by European creators; Nauck-c 5.00

X-CLUB
Marvel Comics: Feb, 2012 - No. 5, Jun, 2012 ($2.99, limited series)

1-5-X-Men scientist team; Dr. Nemesis & Danger app. 1-Bradshaw-c. 2-5-Esquejo-c 3.00

XENA (TV)
Dynamite Entertainment: 2006 - 2007 ($3.50)

1-4-Three covers on each; Neves-a/Layman-s 3.50
Vol. 2 #1-4-(Dark Xena) Four covers; Salonga-a/Layman-s 3.50
Annual 1 (2007, $4.95) Three covers; Salonga-a/Champagne-s 5.00
... Vol. 2: Dark Xena TPB (2007, $14.99) r/Vol. 2 #1-4; variant cover gallery 15.00

XENA / ARMY OF DARKNESS: WHAT...AGAIN?!
Dynamite Entertainment: 2008 - No. 4, 2009 ($3.50, limited series)

1-4-Xena, Gabrielle, & Autolycus team up with Ash; Montenegro-a; two covers on each 3.50

XENA: WARRIOR PRINCESS (TV)
Topps Comics: Aug, 1997 - No. 0, Oct, 1997 ($2.95)

1-Two stories by various; J. Scott Campbell-c 1 3 4 6 8 10
1,2-Photo-c 1 3 4 6 8 10
2-Stevens-c 1 3 4 6 8 10
0-(10/97)-Lopresti-c, 0-(10/97)-Photo-c 1 2 3 5 6 8
...First Appearance Collection ('97, $9.95) r/Hercules the Legendary Journeys #3-5 and 5-page story from TV Guide 10.00

XENA: WARRIOR PRINCESS (TV)
Dark Horse Comics: Sept, 1999 - No. 14, Oct, 2000 ($2.95/$2.99)

1-14: 1-Mignola-c and photo-c. 2,3-Bradstreet-c & photo-c 3.50

XENA: WARRIOR PRINCESS AND THE ORIGINAL OLYMPICS (TV)
Topps Comics: Jun, 1998 - No. 3, Aug, 1998 ($2.95, limited series)

1-3-Regular and Photo-c; Lim-a/T&M Bierbaum-s 3.50

XENA: WARRIOR PRINCESS-BLOODLINES (TV)
Topps Comics: May, 1998 - No. 2, June, 1998 ($2.95, limited series)

1,2-Lopresti-s/c/a. 2-Reg. and photo-c 3.50
1-Bath photo-c, 1-American Ent. Ed. 4.50

XENA: WARRIOR PRINCESS / JOXER: WARRIOR PRINCE (TV)
Topps Comics: Nov, 1997 - No. 3, Jan, 1998 ($2.95, limited series)

1-3-Regular and Photo-c; Lim-a/T&M Bierbaum-s 3.50

XENA: WARRIOR PRINCESS-THE DRAGON'S TEETH (TV)
Topps Comics: Dec, 1997 - No. 3, Feb, 1998 ($2.95, limited series)

1-3-Regular and Photo-c; Teranishi-a/Thomas-s 3.50

XENA: WARRIOR PRINCESS-THE ORPHEUS TRILOGY (TV)

X-Factor #48 © MAR

X-Factor V2 #3 © MAR

The X-Files #16 © 20th Cent. Fox

	GD 2.0	VG 4.0	FN 6.0	VF 8.0	VF/NM 9.0	NM- 9.2

Topps Comics: Mar, 1998 - No. 3, May, 1998 ($2.95, limited series)

1-3-Regular and Photo-c; Teranishi-a/T&M Bierbaum-s 3.50

XENA: WARRIOR PRINCESS VS. CALLISTO (TV)
Topps Comics: Feb, 1998 - No. 3, Apr, 1998 ($2.95, limited series)

1-3-Regular and Photo-c; Morgan-a/Thomas-s 3.50

XENOBROOD
DC Comics: No. 0, Oct, 1994 - No. 6, Apr, 1995 ($1.50, limited series)

0-6: 0-Indicia says "Xenobroods" 3.00

XENON
Eclipse Comics: Dec, 1987 - No. 23, Nov. 1, 1988 ($1.50, B&W, bi-weekly)

1-23 3.00

XENOZOIC TALES (Also see Cadillacs & Dinosaurs, Death Rattle #8)
Kitchen Sink Press: Feb, 1986 - No. 14, Oct, 1996

1-Mark Schultz-s/a in all 2 4 6 9 12 15
1(2nd printing)(1/89) 4.00
2-14 6.00
Volume 1 ($14.95) r/#1-6 & Death Rattle #8 15.00
Volume 2 (5/03, $14.95, TPB) B&W r/#7-14; intro by Frank Cho 15.00

XENYA
Sanctuary Press: Apr, 1994 - No. 3 ($2.95)

1-3: 1-Hildebrandt-c; intro Xenya 3.00

XERO
DC Comics: May, 1997 - No. 12, Apr, 1998 ($1.75)

1-7 3.00
8-12 3.00

X-FACTOR (Also see The Avengers #263, Fantastic Four #286 and Mutant X)
Marvel Comics Group: Feb, 1986 - No. 149, Sept, 1998

1-($1.25, 52 pgs)-Story recaps 1st app. from Avengers #263; story cont'd from F.F. #286; return of original X-Men (now X-Factor); Guice/Layton-a; Baby Nathan app. (2nd after X-Men #201) 1 3 4 6 8 10
2-4 6.00
5-1st brief app. Apocalypse (1 page) 3 6 9 14 20 25
6-1st full app. Apocalypse 5 10 15 35 63 90
7-10: 10-Sabretooth app. (11/86, 3 pgs.) cont'd in X-Men #212; 1st app. in an X-Men comic book 5.00
11-22: 13-Baby Nathan app. in flashback. 14-Cyclops vs. The Master Mold. 15-Intro wingless Angel 4.00
23-1st brief app. Archangel (2 pages) 1 3 4 6 8 10
24-1st full app. Archangel (now in Uncanny X-Men); Fall Of The Mutants begins; origin Apocalypse 3 6 9 19 30 40
25,26: Fall Of The Mutants; 26-New outfits 6.00
27-37,39,41-49,51-59,63-70,72-83,87-91,93-99,101: 35-Origin Cyclops. 51-53-Sabretooth app. 52-Liefeld-c(p). 54-Intro Crimson; Silvestri-c/a(p). 63-Portacio/Thibert-c/a(p) begins, ends #69. 65-68-Lee co-plots. 65-The Apocalypse Files begins, ends #68. 66,67-Baby Nathan app. 67-Inhumans app. 68-Baby Nathan is sent into future to save his life. 69,70-X-Men(w/Wolverine) x-over. 77-Cannonball (of X-Force) app. 87-Quesada-c/a(p) in monthly comic begins,ends #92. 88-1st app. Random 3.00
38,50,60-62,71,75: 38,50-(52 pgs.): 50-Liefeld/McFarlane-c. 60-X-Tinction Agenda x-over; New Mutants (w/Cable) x-over in #60-62; Wolverine in #62. 61,62-X-Tinction Agenda. 62-Jim Lee-c. 71-New team begins (Havok, Polaris, Strong Guy, Wolfsbane & Madrox); Stroman-c/a begins. 75-(52 pgs.) 4.00
40-Rob Liefeld-c/a (4/89, 1st at Marvel?) 5.00
60,71-2nd printings. 60-Gold ink 2nd printing. 71-2nd printing ($1.25) 3.00
84-86 -Jae Lee a(p); 85,86-Jae Lee-c. Polybagged with trading card in each; X-Cutioner's Song x-overs. 4.00
92-($3.50, 68 pgs.)-Wraparound-c by Quesada w/Havok hologram on-c; begin X-Men 30th anniversary issues; Quesada-a. 6.00
92-2nd printing 4.00
100-($2.95, 52 pgs.)-Embossed foil-c; Multiple Man dies. 6.00
100-($1.75, 52 pgs.)-Regular edition 4.00
102-105,107: 102-bound-in card sheet 3.00
106-($2.00)-Newsstand edition 3.00
106-($2.95)-Collectors edition 4.00
108-124,126-148: 112-Return from Age of Apocalypse. 115-card insert. 119-123-Sabretooth app. 123-Hound app. 124-w/Onslaught Update. 126-Onslaught x-over; Beast vs. Dark Beast. 128-w/card insert; return of Multiple Man. 130-Assassination of Grayson Creed. 146,148-Moder-a 3.00
125-($2.95)-"Onslaught"; Post app.; return of Havok 4.00
149-Last issue 4.00
#(-1) Flashback (7/97) Matsuda-a 3.00
Annual 1-9: 1-(10/86-'94, 68 pgs.) 3-Evolutionary War x-over. 4-Atlantis Attacks; Byrne/Simonson-a;Byrne-c. 5-Fantastic Four, New Mutants x-over; Keown 2 pg. pin-up. 6-New Warriors app.; 5th app. X-Force cont'd from X-Men Annual #15. 7-1st Quesada-a(p) on X-Factor plus-c(p). 8-Bagged w/trading card. 9-Austin-a(i) 4.00
...Prisoner of Love (1990, $4.95, 52 pgs.)-Starlin scripts; Guice-a 5.00
... Visionaries: Peter David Vol. 1 TPB (2005, $15.99) r/#71-75 16.00
... Visionaries: Peter David Vol. 2 TPB (2007, $15.99) r/#76-78 & Incr. Hulk #390-392 16.00
... Visionaries: Peter David Vol. 3 TPB (2007, $15.99) r/#79-83 & Annual #7 16.00

NOTE: ***Art Adams** a-41p, 42p. **Buckler** a-50p. **Liefeld** a-40; c-40, 50i, 52p. **McFarlane** c-50i. **Mignola** c-70. **Brandon Peterson** a-78p(part). **Whilce Portacio** c/a(p)-63-69. **Quesada** a(p)-87-92, Annual 7. c(p)-78, 79, 82, Annual 7. **Simonson** c/a-10, 11, 13-15, 17-19, 21, 23-31, 33, 34, 36-39; c-12, 16. **Paul Smith** a-44-48; c-43. **Stroman** a(p)-71-75, 77, 78(part), 80, 81; c(p)-71-77, 80, 81, 84. **Zeck** c-2.*

X-FACTOR (Volume 2)
Marvel Comics: June, 2002 - No. 4, Oct, 2002 ($2.50)

1-4: Jensen-s/Ranson-a. 1-Phillips-c. 2,3-Edwards-c 3.00

X-FACTOR (Volume 3)
Marvel Comics: Jan, 2006 - No. 262, Nov, 2013 ($2.99)

1-24: 1-Peter David-s/Ryan Sook-a. 8,9-Civil War. 21-24-Endangered Species back-up 3.00
25-49: 25-27-Messiah Complex x-over; Finch-c. 26-2nd printing with new Eaton-c 3.00
50-(12/09, $3.99) Madrox in the future; DeLandro-a/Yardin-c 4.00
200-(2/10, $4.99) Resumes original series numbering; 3 covers; Fantastic Four app. 5.00
201-224,224.1, 225-262 ($2.99) 201,202-Dr. Doom & Fant. Four app. 211,212-Thor app. 230-Wolverine app.; Havok & Polaris return 3.00
... Special: Layla Miller (10/08, $3.99) David-s/DeLandro-a 4.00
...: The Quick and the Dead (7/08, $2.99) Raimondi-a; Quicksilver regains powers 3.00
...: The Longest Night HC (2006, $19.99, dust jacket) r/#1-6; sketch pages by Sook 20.00
...: The Longest Night SC (2007, $14.99) r/#1-6; sketch pages by Sook 15.00
...: Life and Death Matters HC (2007, $19.99, dust jacket) r/#7-12 20.00
...: Life and Death Matters SC (2007, $14.99) r/#7-12 15.00
...: The Many Lives of Madrox SC (2007, $14.99) r/#13-17 15.00
...: Heart of Ice HC (2007, $19.99, dust jacket) r/#18-24 20.00
...: Heart of Ice SC (2008, $17.99, dust jacket) r/#18-24 18.00

X-FACTOR FOREVER
Marvel Comics: May, 2010 - No. 5, Sept, 2010 ($3.99, limited series)

1-5-Louise Simonson-s/Dan Panosian-a; back-up origin of Apocalypse 4.00

X-51 (Machine Man)
Marvel Comics: Sept, 1999 - No. 12, Jul, 2000 ($1.99/$2.50)

1-7: 1-Joe Bennett-a. 2-Two covers 3.00
8-12: 8-Begin $2.50-c 3.00
Wizard #0 3.00

X-FILES, THE (TV)
Topps Comics: Jan, 1995 - No. 41, July, 1998 ($2.50)

-2(9/96)-Black-c; r/X-Files Magazine #1&2 5.00
-1(9/96)-Silver-c; r/Hero Illustrated Giveaway 5.00
0-($3.95)-Adapts pilot episode 4.00
0-"Mulder" variant-c 1 2 3 5 6 8
0-"Scully" variant-c 1 2 3 5 6 8
1/2-W/certificate 1 2 3 5 6 8
1-New stories based on the TV show; direct market & newsstand editions; Miran Kim-c on all 3 6 9 14 20 25
2 1 2 3 6 8 10
3,4 6.00
5-10: 6-Begin $2.95-c 5.00
11-41: 21-W/bound-in card. 40,41-Reg. & photo-c 4.00
Annual 1,2 ($3.95) 4.00
Afterflight TPB ($5.95) Art by Thompson, Saviuk, Kim 6.00
Classics #1: Hundred Penny Press Edition (12/13 $1.00) r/#1 3.00
Collection 1 TPB ($19.95)-r/#1-6. 20.00
Collection 2 TPB ($19.95)-r/#7-12, Annual #1. 20.00
...Fight the Future ('98, $5.95) Movie adaptation 6.00
Hero Illustrated Giveaway (3/95) 1 2 3 5 6 8
Special Edition 1-5 ($3.95/$4.95)-r/#1-3, 4-6, 7-9, 10-12, 13, Annual 1 5.00
Star Wars Galaxy Magazine Giveaway (B&W) 1 3 4 6 8 10
Trade paperback ($19.95) 20.00
Volume 1 TPB (Checker Books, 2005, $19.95) r/#13-17, #0, Season One: Squeeze 20.00
Volume 2 TPB (Checker Books, 2005, $19.95) r/#18-24, #1/2, Comics Digest #1 20.00
Volume 3 TPB (Checker Books, 2006, $19.95) r/#23-26, Fire, Ice, Hero Ill. Giveaway 20.00

X-FILES, THE (TV)
DC Comics (WildStorm): No. 0, Sept, 2008 - No. 6, Jun, 2009 ($3.99/$3.50)

0-($3.99) Spotnitz-s/Denham-a; photo-c 4.00

The X-Files: Conspiracy #1 © 20th Cent. Fox

X-Force #38 © MAR

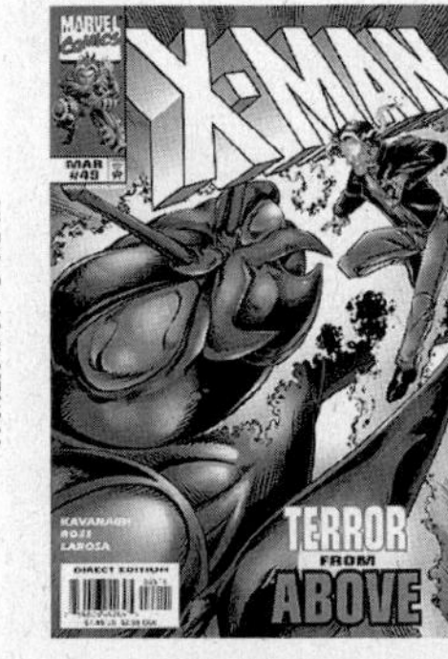

X-Man #49 © MAR

	GD	VG	FN	VF	VF/NM	NM-
	2.0	4.0	6.0	8.0	9.0	9.2

1-6-($3.50) 1-Spotnitz-s/Denham-a; 2 covers. 4-Wolfman-s 3.50
TPB (2009, $19.99) r/#0-6 20.00

X-FILES COMICS DIGEST, THE
Topps Comics: Dec, 1995 - No. 3 ($3.50, quarterly, digest-size)

1-3: 1,2: New X-Files stories w/Ray Bradbury Comics-r. 1-Reg. & photo-c 4.00
NOTE: *Adlard a-1, 2. Jack Davis a-2r. Russell a-1r.*

X-FILES, THE: CONSPIRACY
IDW Publishing: Jan, 2014 - No. 2, Mar, 2014 ($3.99, limited series)

1,2-Bookends for 6-part Lone Gunmen series; Crilley-s/Stanisci-a; Kim & Corroney-c 4.00
X-Files/Ghostbusters: Conspiracy (1/14, $3.99) Part 2; Navarro-a 4.00
X-Files/Teenage Mutant Ninja Turtles: Conspiracy (2/14, $3.99) Part 3; Walsh-a 4.00
X-Files/Transformers: Conspiracy (2/14, $3.99) Part 4; Verma-a 4.00
X-Files/The Crow: Conspiracy (3/14, $3.99) Part 5; Malhotra-a 4.00

X-FILES, THE: GROUND ZERO (TV)
Topps Comics: Nov, 1997 - No. 4, March, 1998 ($2.95, limited series)

1-4-Adaptation of the Kevin J. Anderson novel 4.00

X-FILES, THE: SEASON ONE (TV)
Topps Comics: July, 1997 - July, 1998 ($4.95, adaptations of TV episodes)

1,2,Squeeze, Conduit, Ice, Space, Fire, Beyond the Sea, Shadows 5.00

X-FILES, THE: SEASON 10 (TV)
IDW Publishing: Jun, 2013 - Present ($3.99)

1-10: 1-5-Co-written by Chris Carter; multiple covers on each. 6,7-Flukeman returns 4.00

X-FILES, THE / 30 DAYS OF NIGHT
DC Comics (WildStorm)/IDW: Sept, 2010 - No. 6, Feb, 2011 ($3.99, limited series)

1-6-Steve Niles & Adam Jones-s/Tom Mandrake-a. 1-Three covers 4.00
TPB (2011, $17.99) r/#1-6; cover gallery 18.00

X-FORCE (Becomes X-Statix) (Also see The New Mutants #100)
Marvel Comics: Aug, 1991 - No. 129, Aug, 2002 ($1.00-$2.25)

1-($1.50, 52 pgs.)-Polybagged with 1 of 5 diff. Marvel Universe trading cards inside (1 each); 6th app. of X-Force; Liefeld-c/a begins 5.00
1-1st printing with Cable trading card inside 6.00
1-2nd printing; metallic ink-c (no bag or card) 4.00
2-4: 2-Deadpool-c/story. 3-New Brotherhood of Evil Mutants app. 4-Spider-Man x-over; cont'd from Spider-Man #16; reads sideways 4.00
5-11: 6-Last $1.00-c. 7,9-Weapon X back-ups. 8-Intro The Wild Pack (Cable, Kane, Domino, Hammer, G.W. Bridge, & Grizzly); Liefeld-c/a (4); Mignola-a. 10-Weapon X full-length story (part 3). 11-1st Weapon Prime; Deadpool-c/story 4.00
12-15,19-24,26-33: 15-Cable leaves X-Force 3.00
16-18-Polybagged w/trading card in each; X-Cutioner's Song x-overs 4.00
25-($3.50, 52 pgs.)-Wraparound-c w/Cable hologram on-c; Cable returns 5.00
34-37,39-45: 34-bound-in card sheet 3.00
38,40-43: 38-($2.00)-Newsstand edition. 40-43 ($1.95)-Deluxe edition 3.00
38-($2.95)-Collectors edition (prismatic) 5.00
44-49,51-67: 44-Return from Age of Apocalypse. 45-Sabretooth app. 49-Sebastian Shaw app. 52-Blob app., Onslaught cameo. 55-Vs. S.H.I.E.L.D. 56-Deadpool app. 57-Mr. Sinister & X-Man-c/app. 57,58-Onslaught x-over. 59-W/card insert; return of Longshot. 60-Dr. Strange 3.00
50 ($3.95)-Gatefold wrap-around foil-c 4.00
50 ($3.95)-Liefeld variant-c 5.00
68-74: 68-Operation Zero Tolerance 3.00
75,100-($2.99): 75-Cannonball-c/app. 4.00
76-99,101,102: 81-Pollina poster. 95-Magneto-c. 102-Ellis-s/Portacio-a 3.00
103-115: 103-Begin $2.25-c; Portacio-a thru #106. 115-Death of old team 3.00
116-New team debuts; Allred-c/a; Milligan-s; no Comics Code stamp on-c 4.00
117-129: 117-Intro. Mr. Sensitive. 120-Wolverine-c/app. 123-'Nuff Said issue. 124-Darwyn Cooke-a/c. 128-Death of U-Go Girl. 129-Fegredo-a 3.00
#(-1) Flashback (7/97) story of John Proudstar; Pollina-a 3.00
Annual 1-3 ('92-'94, 68 pgs.) 1-1st Greg Capullo-a(p) on X-Force. 2-Polybagged w/trading card; intro X-Treme & Neurtap 4.00
...And Cable '95 (12/95, $3.95)-Impossible Man app. 4.00
...And Cable '96, ...'97 ('96, 7/97) -'96-Wraparound-c 4.00
...And Spider-Man: Sabotage nn (11/92, $6.95)-Reprints X-Force #3,4 & Spider-Man #16 7.00
.../ Champions '98 ($3.50) 4.00
Annual 99 ($3.50) 4.00
...: Famous, Mutant & Mortal HC (2003, $29.99) oversized r/#116-129; foreward by Milligan; gallery of covers and pin-ups; script for #123 30.00
...New Beginnings TPB (10/01, $14.95) r/#116-120 15.00
...Rough Cut ($2.99) Pencil pages and script for #102 3.00
...Youngblood (8/96, $4.95)-Platt-c 5.00
NOTE: *Capullo a(p)-15-25, Annual 1; c(p)-14-27. Rob Liefeld a-1-7, 9p; c-1-9, 11p; plots-1-12. Mignola a-8p.*

X-FORCE
Marvel Comics: Oct, 2004 - No. 6, Mar, 2005 ($2.99, limited series)

1-6-Liefeld-c/a; Nicieza-s. 5,6-Wolverine & The Thing app. 3.00
X-Force & Cable Vol. 1: The Legend Returns (2005, $14.99) r/#1-6 15.00

X-FORCE (Also see Uncanny X-Force)
Marvel Comics: Apr, 2008 - No. 28, Sept, 2010 ($2.99)

1-Crain-a; Wolverine & X-23 app.; two covers (regular and bloody) by Crain on #1-5 4.00
2-21,23-28: 2,3-Bastion app. 4-6-Archangel app. 7-10-Choi-a. 9-11-Ghost Rider app. 26-28-Second Coming x-over; Granov-c. 26-Nightcrawler killed 3.00
22-($3.99) Necrosha x-over; Crain-a 4.00
...: Angels and Demons MGC #1 (5/11, $1.00) r/#1 with "Marvel's Greatest Comics" on-c 3.00
...Annual 1 (2/10, $3.99) Kirkman-s/Pearson-a/c; Deadpool back-up w/Barberi-a 4.00
.../Cable: Messiah War 1 (5/09, $3.99) Choi-a; covers by Andrews and Choi 4.00
... Special: Ain't No Dog (8/08, $3.99) Huston-s/Palo-a; Dell'Edera-a; Hitch-c 4.00

X-FORCE
Marvel Comics: Apr, 2014 - Present ($3.99)

1,2: 1-Team of Cable, Fantomex, Psylocke & Marrow; Rock-He Kim-a 4.00

X-FORCE MEGAZINE
Marvel Comics: Nov, 1996 ($3.95, one-shot)

1-Reprints 4.00

X-FORCE: SEX AND VIOLENCE
Marvel Comics: Sept, 2010 - No. 3, Nov, 2010 ($3.99, limited series)

1-3-Dell'Otto-a/Kyle & Yost-s; Domino & Wolverine vs. The Hand & The Assassins Guild 4.00

X-FORCE: SHATTERSTAR
Marvel Comics: Apr, 2005 - No. 4, July, 2005 ($2.99, limited series)

1-4-Liefeld-c/s; Michaels-a 3.00
TPB (2005, $15.99) r/#1-4 & New Mutants #99,100 16.00

X-INFERNUS
Marvel Comics: Feb, 2009 - No. 4, May, 2009 ($3.99, limited series)

1-4-Illyana Rasputin in Limbo; Cebulski-s/Camuncoli-a/Finch-c 4.00

XIN: JOURNEY OF THE MONKEY KING
Anarchy Studios: May, 2003 - No. 3, July, 2003 ($2.99)

Preview Edition (Apr, 2003, $1.99) Flip book w/ Vampi Vicious Preview Edition 3.00
1-3-Kevin Lau-a. 1-Three covers by Lau, Park and Nauck. 2-Three covers 3.00

XIN: LEGEND OF THE MONKEY KING
Anarchy Studios: Nov, 2002 - No. 3, Jan, 2003 ($2.99)

Preview Edition (Summer 2002, Diamond Dateline supplement) 3.00
1-3-Kevin Lau-a. 1-Two covers by Lau & Madureira. 2-Two covers by Lau & Oeming 3.00
TPB (10/03, $12.95) r/#1-3; cover gallery and sketch pages 13.00

X-MAN (Also see X-Men Omega & X-Men Prime)
Marvel Comics: Mar, 1995 - No. 75, May, 2001 ($1.95/$1.99/$2.25)

1-Age of Apocalypse 5.00
1-2nd print 3.00
2-4,25: 25-($2.99)-Wraparound-c 4.00
5-24, 26-28: 5-Post Age of Apocalypse stories begin. 5-7-Madelyne Pryor app. 10-Professor X app. 12-vs. Excalibur. 13-Marauders, Cable app. 14-Vs. Cable; Onslaught app. 15-17-Vs. Holocaust. 17-w/Onslaught Update. 18-Onslaught x-over; X-Force-c/app; Marauders app. 19-Onslaught x-over. 20-Abomination-c/app.; w/card insert. 23-Bishop app. 24-Spider-Man, Morbius-c/app. 27-Re-appearance of Aurora(Alpha Flight) 3.00
29-49,51-62: 29-Operation Zero Tolerance. 37,38-Spider-Man-c/app. 56-Spider-Man app. 3.00
50-($2.99) Crossover with Generation X #50 4.00
63-74: 63-Ellis & Grant-s/Olivetti-a begins. 64-Begin $2.25-c 3.00
75 ($2.99) Final issue; Alcatena-a 4.00
#(-1) Flashback (7/97) 3.00
...'96, ...'97-($2.95)-Wraparound-c; '96-Age of Apocalypse 4.00
...: All Saints' Day ('97, $5.99) Dodson-a 6.00
.../Hulk '98 ($2.99) Wraparound-c; Thanos app. 4.00

XMAS COMICS
Fawcett Publications: 12?/1941 - No. 2, 12?/1942; (50¢, 324 pgs.)
No. 7, 12?/1947 (25¢, 132 pgs.)(#3-6 do not exist)

	GD 2.0	VG 4.0	FN 6.0	VF 8.0	VF/NM 9.0	NM- 9.2
1-Contains Whiz #21, Capt. Marvel #3, Bulletman #2, Wow #3, & Master #18; front & back-c by Raboy. Not rebound, remaindered comics; printed at same time as originals	432	864	1296	3154	5577	8000
2-Capt. Marvel, Bulletman, Spy Smasher	194	388	582	1242	2121	3000
7-Funny animals (Hoppy, Billy the Kid & Oscar)	74	148	222	470	810	1150

XMAS COMICS
Fawcett Publications: No. 4, Dec, 1949 - No. 7, Dec, 1952 (50¢, 196 pgs.)

X-Men #7 © MAR

Uncanny X-Men #173 © MAR

Uncanny X-Men #257 © MAR

GD VG FN VF VF/NM NM-
2.0 4.0 6.0 8.0 9.0 9.2

4-Contains Whiz, Master, Tom Mix, Captain Marvel, Nyoka, Capt. Video, Bob Colt, Monte Hale, Hot Rod Comics, & Battle Stories. Not rebound, remaindered comics; printed at the same time as originals. Stocking on cover is made of green or red felt 103 206 309 659 1130 1600
5-7-Same as above. 5- Red felt on-c. 7-Bill Boyd app.; stocking on cover is made of green felt (novelty cover) 81 162 243 518 884 1250

X-MEN, THE (See Adventures of Cyclops and Phoenix, Amazing Adventures, Archangel, Brotherhood, Capt. America #172, Classic X-Men, Exiles, Further Adventures of Cyclops & Phoenix, Gambit, Giant-Size..., Heroes For Hope..., Kitty Pryde & Wolverine, Marvel & DC Present, Marvel Collector's Edition:..., Marvel Fanfare, Marvel Graphic Novel, Marvel Super Heroes, Marvel Team-Up, Marvel Triple Action, The Marvel X-Men Collection, New Mutants, Nightcrawler, Official Marvel Index To..., Rogue, Special Edition..., Ultimate..., Uncanny..., Wolverine, X-Factor, X-Force, X-Terminators)

X-MEN, THE (1st series)(Becomes Uncanny X-Men at #142)(The X-Men #1-93; X-Men #94-141) (The Uncanny X-Men on-c only #114-141)
Marvel Comics Group: Sept, 1963 - No. 66, Mar, 1970; No. 67, Dec, 1970 - No. 141, Jan, 1981; Uncanny X-Men No. 142, Feb, 1981 - No. 544, Dec, 2011

1-Origin/1st app. X-Men (Angel, Beast, Cyclops, Iceman & Marvel Girl); 1st app. Magneto & Professor X 1000 2000 3000 10,000 23,000 42,000
2-1st app. The Vanisher 148 296 444 1221 2761 4300
3-1st app. The Blob (1/64) 89 178 267 712 1606 2500
4-1st Quicksilver & Scarlet Witch & Brotherhood of the Evil Mutants (3/64); 1st app. Toad; 2nd app. Magneto 114 228 342 912 2056 3200
5-Magneto & Evil Mutants-c/story 63 126 189 504 1127 1750
6,7: 6-Sub-Mariner app. 7-Magneto app. 50 100 150 390 870 1350
8,9,11: 8-1st Unus the Untouchable. 9-Early Avengers app. (1/65); 1st Lucifer. 11-1st app. The Stranger. 42 84 126 311 706 1100
10-1st S.A. app. Ka-Zar & Zabu the sabertooth (3/65) 43 86 129 318 722 1125
12-Origin Prof. X; Origin/1st app. Juggernaut 46 92 138 368 834 1300
13-Juggernaut and Human Torch app. 30 60 90 216 483 750
14,15: 14-1st app. Sentinels. 15-Origin Beast 31 62 93 223 499 775
16-20: 19-1st app. The Mimic (4/66) 19 38 57 131 291 450
21-27,29,30: 27-Re-enter The Mimic (r-in #75); Spider-Man cameo 13 26 39 89 195 300
28-1st app. The Banshee (1/67)(r-in #76) 19 38 57 131 291 450
28-2nd printing (1994) 2 4 6 8 10 12
31-34,36,37,39: 34-Adkins-c/a. 39-New costumes 10 20 30 69 147 225
35-Spider-Man x-over (8/67)(r-in #83); 1st app. Changeling 23 46 69 161 356 550
38,40: 38-Origins of the X-Men series begins, ends #57. 40-(1/68) 1st app. Frankenstein's monster at Marvel 11 22 33 73 157 240
41-49: 42-Death of Prof. X (Changeling disguised as). 44-1st S.A. app. G.A. Red Raven. 49-Steranko-c; 1st Polaris 10 20 30 64 132 200
50,51-Steranko-c/a 10 20 30 68 144 220
52 9 18 27 61 123 185
53-Barry Smith-c/a (his 1st comic book work) 10 20 30 66 138 210
54,55-B. Smith-c. 54-1st app. Alex Summers who later becomes Havok. 55-Summers discovers he has mutant powers 10 20 30 67 141 215
56,57,59-63,65-Neal Adams-a(p). 56-Intro Havok w/o costume. 60-1st Sauron. 65-Return of Professor X. 11 22 33 73 157 240
58-1st app. Havok in costume; N. Adams-a(p) 13 26 39 86 188 290
62,63-2nd printings (1994) 2 4 6 8 10 12
64-1st app. Sunfire 10 20 30 69 147 225
66-Last new story w/original X-Men; battles Hulk 11 22 33 76 163 250
67-70: 67-Reprints begin, end #93. 67-70: (52 pgs.) 9 18 27 58 114 170
71-93: 71-Last 15¢ issue. 72: (52 pgs.). 73-86-r/#25-38 w/new-c. 83-Spider-Man-c/story. 87-93-r/#39-45 with covers 8 16 24 51 96 140
94 (8/75)-New X-Men begin (see Giant-Size X-Men for 1st app.); Colossus, Nightcrawler, Thunderbird, Storm, Wolverine, & Banshee join; Angel, Marvel Girl & Iceman resign 67 134 201 536 931 1325
95-Death of Thunderbird 15 30 45 103 227 350
96,97 10 20 30 64 132 200
98,99-(Regular 25¢ edition)(4,6/76) 9 18 27 63 129 195
98,99-(30¢-c variants, limited distribution) 17 34 51 114 252 390
100-Old vs. New X-Men; part origin Phoenix; last 25¢ issue (8/76) 10 20 30 70 150 230
100-(30¢-c variant, limited distribution) 19 38 57 133 297 460
101-Phoenix origin concludes 12 24 36 82 179 275
102-104: 102-Origin Storm. 104-1st brief app. Starjammers; Magneto-c/story 7 14 21 49 92 135
105-107-(Regular 30¢ editions). 106-(8/77)Old vs. New X-Men. 107-1st full app. Starjammers; last 30¢ issue 7 14 21 46 86 125
105-107-(35¢-c variants, limited distribution) 11 22 33 76 163 250
108-Byrne-a begins (see Marvel Team-Up #53) 7 14 21 49 92 135
109-1st app. Weapon Alpha (becomes Vindicator) 7 14 21 46 86 125
110,111: 110-Phoenix joins 6 12 18 38 69 100
112-116 6 12 18 38 69 100
117-119: 117-Origin Professor X 5 10 15 34 60 85
120-1st app. Alpha Flight, story line begins (4/79); 1st app. Vindicator (formerly Weapon Alpha); last 35¢ issue 7 14 21 46 86 125
121-1st full Alpha Flight story 6 12 18 42 79 115
122-128: 123-Spider-Man x-over. 124-Colossus becomes Proletarian 5 10 15 31 53 75
129-Intro Kitty Pryde (1/80); last Banshee; Dark Phoenix saga begins; intro. Emma Frost (White Queen) 7 14 21 49 92 135
130-1st app. The Dazzler by Byrne (2/80) 5 10 15 33 57 80
131-135: 131-Dazzler app.; 1st White Queen-c. 133-1st Wolverine solo-c. 134-Phoenix becomes Dark Phoenix 5 10 15 31 53 75
136,138: 138-History of the X-Men recounted; Dazzler app.; Cyclops leaves 4 8 12 28 47 65
137-Giant; death of Phoenix 6 12 18 37 66 95
139-Alpha Flight app.; Kitty Pryde joins; new costume for Wolverine 5 10 15 31 53 75
140-Alpha Flight app. 5 10 15 31 53 75
141-Intro Future X-Men & The New Brotherhood of Evil Mutants; 1st app. Rachel (Phoenix II); Death of alt. future Franklin Richards 7 14 21 46 86 125

X-MEN: Titled THE UNCANNY X-MEN No. 142, Feb, 1981 - No. 544, Dec, 2011

142-Rachel app.; deaths of alt. future Wolverine, Storm & Colossus 6 12 18 37 66 95
143-Last Byrne issue 4 8 12 23 37 50
144-150: 144-Man-Thing app. 145-Old X-Men app. 148-Spider-Woman, Dazzler app. 150-Double size 2 4 6 9 13 16
151-157,159-161,163,164: 161-Origin Magneto. 163-Origin Binary. 164-1st app. Binary as Carol Danvers 2 4 6 8 10 12
158-1st app. Rogue in X-Men (6/82, see Avengers Annual #10) 3 6 9 16 23 30
162-Wolverine solo story 2 4 6 10 14 18
165-Paul Smith-c/a begins, ends #175 2 4 6 8 11 14
166-170: 166-Double size; Paul Smith-a. 167-New Mutants app. (3/83); same date as New Mutants #1; 1st meeting w/X-Men; ties into N.M. #3,4; Starjammers app.; contains skin "Tattooz" decals. 168-1st brief app. Madelyne Pryor (last page) in X-Men (see Avengers Annual #10) 2 3 4 6 8 10
171-Rogue joins X-Men; Simonson-c/a 2 4 6 13 18 22
172-174: 172,173-Two part Wolverine solo story. 173-Two cover variations, blue & black. 174-Phoenix cameo 1 3 4 6 8 10
175-(52 pgs.)-Anniversary issue; Phoenix returns 2 4 6 8 10 12
176-185,187-192,194-199: 181-Sunfire app. 182-Rogue solo story. 184-1st app. Forge (8/84). 190,191-Spider-Man & Avengers x-over. 195-Power Pack x-over 1 2 3 5 7 9
186,193: 186-Double-size; Barry Smith/Austin-a. 193-Double size; 100th app. New X-Men; 1st app. Warpath in costume (see New Mutants #16) 1 3 4 6 8 10
200-(12/85, $1.25, 52 pgs.) 2 4 6 8 10 12
201-(1/86)-1st app. Cable? (as baby Nathan; see X-Factor #1); 1st Whilce Portacio-c/a(i) on X-Men (guest artist) 3 6 9 17 26 35
202-204,206-209: 204-Nightcrawler solo story; 2nd Portacio-a(i) on X-Men. 207-Wolverine/Phoenix story 1 2 3 5 7 9
205-Wolverine solo story by Barry Smith 2 4 6 9 13 16
210,211-Mutant Massacre begins 3 6 9 14 19 24
212,213-Wolverine vs. Sabretooth (Mutant Mass.) 3 6 9 15 22 28
214-221,223,224: 219-Havok joins (7/87); brief app. Sabretooth. 221-1st app. Mr. Sinister 1 2 3 5 6 8
222-Wolverine battles Sabretooth-c/story 3 6 9 14 20 26
225-242: 225-227: Fall Of The Mutants. 226-Double size. 240-Sabretooth app. 242-Double size, X-Factor app., Inferno tie-in 1 2 3 5 6 8
243,245-247: 245-Rob Liefeld-a(p) 1 2 3 5 6 8
244-1st app. Jubilee 3 6 9 19 30 40
248-1st Jim Lee art on X-Men (1989) 3 6 9 14 20 25
248-2nd printing (1992, $1.25) 6.00
249-252: 252-Lee-c 1 2 3 4 5 7
253-255: 253-All new X-Men begin. 254-Lee-c 1 2 3 4 5 7
256,257-Jim Lee-c/a begins 1 2 3 5 7 9
258-Wolverine solo story; Lee-c/a 1 2 3 5 7 9
259-Silvestri-c/a; no Lee-a 1 2 3 4 5 7
260-265-No Lee-a. 260,261,264-Lee-c 1 2 3 4 5 7
266-(8/90) 1st full app. Gambit (see Annual #14)-No Lee-a 5 10 15 31 53 75
267-Jim Lee-c/a resumes; 2nd full Gambit app. 2 4 6 9 13 16
268-Capt. America, Black Widow & Wolverine team-up; Lee-c/a

Uncanny X-Men #308 © MAR

Uncanny X-Men #450 © MAR

Uncanny X-Men #505 © MAR

	GD 2.0	VG 4.0	FN 6.0	VF 8.0	VF/NM 9.0	NM- 9.2
	2	4	6	11	16	20
268,270: 268-2nd printing. 270-Gold 2nd printing						6.00
269,273,274: 269-Lee-a. 273-New Mutants (Cable) & X-Factor x-over; Golden, Byrne & Lee part pencils	1	2	3	4	5	7
270-X-Tinction Agenda begins	1	2	3	5	6	8
271,272-X-Tinction Agenda	1	2	3	5	6	8
275-(52 pgs.)-Tri-fold-c by Jim Lee (p); Prof. X	1	2	3	5	6	8
275-Gold 2nd printing						5.00
276-280: 277-Last Lee-c/a. 280-X-Factor x-over						6.00
281-(10/91)-New team begins (Storm, Archangel, Colossus, Iceman & Marvel Girl); Whilce Portacio-c/a begins; Byrne scripts begin; wraparound-c (white logo)	1	2	3	5	6	8
281-2nd printing with red metallic ink logo w/o UPC box ($1.00-c); does not say 2nd printing inside						4.00
282-1st brief app. Bishop (cover & 1 page)	2	4	6	13	18	22
282-Gold ink 2nd printing ($1.00-c)	1	2	3	5	6	8
283-1st full app. Bishop (12/91)	2	4	6	8	10	12
284-299: 284-Last $1.00-c. 286,287-Lee plots. 287-Bishop joins team. 288-Lee/Portacio plots. 290-Last Portacio-c/a. 294-Peterson-a(p) begins (#292 is 1st Peterson-c). 294-296 ($1.50)-Bagged w/trading card in each; X-Cutioner's Song x-overs; Peterson/Austin-c/a on all						4.00
297,303,307-Gold Edition	3	6	9	21	33	45
300-($3.95, 68 pgs.)-Holo-grafx foil-c; Magneto app.						6.00
301-303,305-309,311						3.00
304-($3.95, 68 pgs.)-Wraparound-c with Magneto hologram on-c; 30th anniversary issue; Jae Lee-a (4 pgs.)						6.00
310-($1.95)-Bound-in trading card sheet						3.00
312-$1.50-c begins; bound-in card sheet; 1st Madureira						4.00
313-321						3.00
316,317-($2.95)-Foil enhanced editions						4.00
318-321-($1.95)-Deluxe editions						3.00
322-Onslaught						5.00
323,324,326-346: 323-Return from Age of Apocalypse. 328-Sabretooth-c. 329,330-Dr. Strange app. 331-White Queen-c/app. 334-Juggernaut app.; w/Onslaught Update. 335-Onslaught, Avengers, Apocalypse, & X-Man app. 336-Onslaught. 338-Archangel's wings return to normal. 339-Havok vs. Cyclops; Spider-Man app. 341-Gladiator-c/app. 342-Deathbird cameo; two covers. 343,344-Phalanx						3.00
325-($3.95)-Anniversary issue; gatefold-c						5.00
342-Variant-c	1	3	4	6	8	10
347-349:347-Begin $1.99-c. 349-"Operation Zero Tolerance"						3.00
350-($3.99, 48 pgs.) Prismatic etched foil gatefold wraparound-c; Trial of Gambit; Seagle-s begin	1	2	3	5	6	8
351-359: 353-Bachalo-a begins. 354-Regular-c. 355-Alpha Flight-c/app. 356-Original X-Men-c						3.00
354-Dark Phoenix variant-c						5.00
360-($2.99) 35th Anniv. issue; Pacheco-c						4.00
360-($3.99) Etched Holo-foil enhanced-c						5.00
360-($6.95) DF Edition with Jae Lee variant-c						7.00
361-374: 361-Gambit returns; Skroce-a. 362-Hunt for Xavier pt. 1; Bachelo-a. 364-Yu-a. 366-Magneto-c. 369-Juggernaut-c						3.00
375-($2.99) Autopsy of Wolverine						4.00
376-379: 376,377-Apocalypse: The Twelve						3.00
380-($2.99) Polybagged with X-Men Revolution Genesis Edition preview						4.00
381,382,384-389,391-393: 381-Begin $2.25-c; Claremont-s. 387-Maximum Security						3.00
383-($2.99)						4.00
390-Colossus dies to cure the Legacy Virus						4.00
394-New look X-Men begins; Casey-s/Churchill-c/a						4.00
395-399-Poptopia. 398-Phillips & Wood-a						3.00
400-($3.50) Art by Ashley Wood, Eddie Campbell, Hamner, Phillips, Pulido and Matt Smith; wraparound-c by Wood						5.00
401-415: 401-'Nuff Said issue; Garney-a. 404,405,407-409,413-415-Phillips-a						3.00
416-421: 416-Asamiya-a begins. 421-Garney-a						3.00
422-($3.50) Alpha Flight app.; Garney-a						4.00
423-(25¢-c) Holy War pt. 1; Garney-a/Philip Tan-c						3.00
424-449,452-454: 425,426,429,430-Tan-a. 428-Birth of Nightcrawler. 437-Larroca-a begins. 444-New team, new costumes; Claremont-s/Davis-a begins. 448,449-Coipel-a						3.00
450,451,455-459-X-23 app.; Davis-a						3.00
460-471: 460-Begin $2.50-c; Raney-a. 462-465-House of M. 464-468-Bachalo-a						3.00
472-499: 472-Begin $2.99-c; Bachalo-a. 475-Wraparound-c. 492-494-Messiah Complex						3.00
500-($3.99) X-Men new HQ in San Francisco; Magneto app.; Land & Dodson-a; wraparound covers by Alex Ross and Greg Land						6.00
500-Classic X-Men Dynamic Forces variant-c by Ross						8.00
500-X-Men variant-c by Michael Turner						40.00
500-X-Women variant-c by Dodson	5	10	15	31	53	75
501-511,515-521,523-525: 501-Brubaker & Fraction-s/Land-a. 523-525-Second Coming						3.00

	GD 2.0	VG 4.0	FN 6.0	VF 8.0	VF/NM 9.0	NM- 9.2
512-514,522-($3.99). 513,514-Utopia x-over. 522-Kitty Pryde returns to Earth; Portacio-a						4.00
526-543-($3.99) 526-The Heroic Age; aftermath of Second Coming. 530-534-Land-a 540-543-Fear Itself tie-in, Juggernaut attacks; Land-a. 542-Colossus becomes the Juggernaut						4.00
534.1 (6/11, $2.99) Pacheco-a/c						3.00
544-(12/11, $3.99) Final issue; Land-a/c; Mr. Sinister app.						4.00
#(-1) Flashback (7/97) Ladronn-c/Hitch & Neary-a						3.00
Special 1(12/70)-Kirby-c/a; origin The Stranger	10	20	30	64	132	200
Special 2(11/71, 52 pgs.)	7	14	21	49	92	135
Annual 3(1979, 52 pgs.)-New story; Miller/Austin-c; Wolverine still in old yellow costume	5	10	15	30	48	65
Annual 4(1980, 52 pgs.)-Dr. Strange guest stars	3	6	9	14	20	25
Annual 5(1981, 52 pgs.)	2	4	6	8	10	12
Annual 6-8('82-'84 52 pgs.)-6-Dracula app.	1	2	3	5	6	8
Annual 9,10('85, '86)-9-New Mutants x-over cont'd from New Mutants Special Ed. #1; Art Adams-a. 10-Art Adams-a	2	4	6	8	10	12
Annual 11-13:('87-'89, 68 pgs.): 12-Evolutionary War; A.Adams-a(p). 13-Atlantis Attacks						5.00
Annual 14(1990, $2.00, 68 pgs.)-1st app. Gambit (minor app., 5 pgs.); Fantastic Four, New Mutants (Cable) & X-Factor x-over; Art Adams-c/a(p)	3	6	9	17	26	35
Annual 15 (1991, $2.00, 68 pgs.)-4 pg. origin; New Mutants x-over; 4 pg. Wolverine solo back-up story; 4th app. X-Force cont'd from New Warriors Annual #1						5.00
Annual 16-18 ('92-'94, 68 pgs.)-16-Jae Lee-c/a(p). 17-Bagged w/card						4.00
Annual '95-(11/95, $3.95)-Wraparound-c						4.00
Annual '96,'97-Wraparound-c						4.00
.../Fantastic Four Annual '98 ($2.99) Casey-s						4.00
Annual '99 ($3.50) Jubilee app.						4.00
Annual 2000 ($3.50) Cable app.; Ribic-a						4.00
Annual 2001 ($3.50, printed wide-ways) Ashley Wood-c/a; Casey-s						4.00
Annual (Vol. 2) #1 (8/06, $3.99) Storm & Black Panther wedding prelude						4.00
Annual (Vol. 2) #2 (3/09, $3.99) Dark Reign; flashback to Sub-Mariner/Emma Frost						4.00
Annual (Vol. 2) #3 (5/11, $3.99) Escape From the Negative Zone; Bradshaw-a						4.00
....At The State Fair of Texas (1983, 36 pgs., one-shot); Supplement to the Dallas Times Herald	2	4	6	9	12	15
...: The Dark Phoenix Saga TPB 1st printing (1984, $12.95)						40.00
...: The Dark Phoenix Saga TPB 2nd-5th printings						25.00
...: The Dark Phoenix Saga TPB 6th-10th printings						20.00
... Days of Future Past TPB (2004, $19.99) r/#138-143 & Annual #4						20.00
... Eve of Destruction TPB (2005, $14.99) r/#391-393 & X-Men #111-113; Churchill-c						15.00
...:Dream's End (2004, $17.99)-r/Death of Colossus story arc from Uncanny X-Men #388-390, Cable #87, Bishop #16 and X-Men #108,110; debut pages from Giant-Size X-Men #1						18.00
... From The Ashes TPB (1990, $14.95) r/#168-176						15.00
... Future History - The Messiah War Sourcebook (2009, $3.99) Cable's files on X-Men						4.00
...: God Loves, Man Kills ($6.95)-r/Marvel Graphic Novel #5						7.00
...: God Loves, Man Kills - Special Edition (2003, $4.99)-reprint with new Hughes-c						5.00
...: God Loves, Man Kills HC (2007, $19.99) reprint with Claremont & Anderson interviews; original artist Neal Adams' six sketch pages and interview						20.00
...: Hope (5/10, $2.99) Collects Cable and Hope back-ups; Dillon-a						3.00
House of M: Uncanny X-Men TPB (2006, $13.99) r/#462-465 and selections from Secrets Of The House of M one-shot						14.00
...In The Days of Future Past TPB (1989, $3.95, 52 pgs.)						10.00
...Old Soldiers TPB (2004, $19.99) r/#213,215 & Ann. #11; New Mutants Ann. #2&3						20.00
...Poptopia TPB (10/01, $15.95) r/#394-399						16.00
...: Rise & Fall of the Shi'Ar Empire HC (2007, $34.99, dustjacket) r/#475-486; bonus art						35.00
...: Rise & Fall of the Shi'Ar Empire SC (2008, $29.99) r/#475-486; bonus art						30.00
...: Season One HC (2012, $24.99) Origin re-told; Hopeless-s/McKelvie-a						25.00
...: Sword of the Braddocks (5/09, $3.99) Psylocke vs. Slaymaster; Claremont-s						4.00
...: The Complete Onslaught Epic Book 1 TPB (2007, $29.99) r/X-Men #53-54, Uncanny X-Men #334-335, Fantastic Four #414-415, Avengers #400-401, Onslaught: X-Men, Cable #34 and Incredible Hulk #444						30.00
...: The Complete Onslaught Epic Book 2 TPB ('08, $29.99) r/Excalibur #100, Wolverine #104, X-Factor #125-126, Amazing Spider-Man #415, Green Goblin #12, Spider-Man #72, Punisher #11, X-Man #18 & X-Force #57						30.00
...: The Extremists TPB (2007, $13.99) r/#487-491						14.00
...: The Heroic Age (9/10, $3.99) Beast, Steve Rogers and Princess Powerful app.						4.00
Uncanny X-Men Omnibus Vol. 1 HC (2006, $99.99, dust jacket) r/Giant-Size X-Men #1, (Uncanny) X-Men #94-131 & Annual #3; cover gallery, promo and sketch art						140.00
Vignettes TPB (9/01, $17.95) r/Claremont & Bolton Classic X-Men #1-13						18.00
Vignettes Vol. 2 TPB (2005, $17.99) r/Claremont & Bolton Classic X-Men #14-25						18.00
... Vol. 1: Hope TPB (2003, $12.99) r/#410-415; Harris-c						13.00
... Vol. 2: Dominant Species TPB (2003, $11.99) r/#416-420; Asamiya-c						12.00
... Vol. 3: Holy War TPB (2003, $17.99) r/#421-427						18.00
... Vol. 4: The Draco TPB (2004, $15.99) r/#428-434						16.00
... Vol. 5: She Lies with Angels TPB (2004, $11.99) r/#437-441						12.00

X-Men (2nd series) #71 © MAR

X-Men (2nd series) #115 © MAR

X-Men (2nd series) #152 © MAR

GD 2.0 | VG 4.0 | FN 6.0 | VF 8.0 | VF/NM 9.0 | NM- 9.2

... Vol. 6: Bright New Mourning TPB (2004, $14.99) r/#435,436,442,443 & (New) X-Men #155,156; Larroca sketch covers 15.00
...Vs. Apocalypse Vol. 1: The Twelve TPB (2008, $29.99) r/#376-377, Cable #73-76, X-Men #96,97 and Wolverine #145-147 30.00
... - The New Age Vol. 1: The End of History (2004, $12.99) r/#444-449 13.00
... - The New Age Vol. 2: The Cruelest Cut (2005, $11.99) r/#450-454 12.00
... - The New Age Vol. 3: On Ice (2006, $15.99) r/#455-461 16.00
... - The New Age Vol. 4: End of Greys (2006, $14.99) r/#466-471 15.00
... - The New Age Vol. 5: First Foursaken (2006, $11.99) r/#472-474 & Annual #1 12.00

NOTE: **Art Adams** *a-Annual 9, 10p, 12p, 14p; c-218p.* **Neal Adams** *a-56-63p, 65p; c-56-63.* **Adkins** *a-34, 35p; c-31, 34, 35.* **Austin** *a-108i, 109i, 111-117i, 119-143i, 186i, 204i, 228i, 294-297i, Annual 3i, 7i, 9i, 13; c-109-111i, 114-122i, 123, 124-141i, 142, 143, 196i, 204i, 228i, 294-297i, Annual 3i.* **J. Buscema** *c-42, 43, 45.* **Buscema/Tuska** *a-45.* **Byrne** *a(p)-108, 109, 111-143, 273; c(p)-113-116, 127, 129, 131-141.* **Capullo** *c-14.* **Ditko** *r-86, 89-91, 93.* **Everett** *c-73.* **Golden** *a-273, Annual 7p.* **Guice** *a-216p, 217p.* **G. Kane** *c(p)-33, 74-76, 79, 80, 94, 95.* **Kirby** *a(p)-1-17 (#12-17, 67r-layouts); c(p)-1-17, 25, 30 (18, 26-parts).* **Layton** *a-105i; c-112i, 113i.* **Jim Lee** *a(p)-248, 256-258, 267-277; c(p)-252, 254, 256-261, 264, 267, 270, 275-277, 286.* **Perez** *a-Annual 3p; c(p)-112, 128, Annual 3.* **Peterson** *a(p)-294-300, 304(part); c(p)-294-299.* **Whilce Portacio** *a(p)-281-286, 289, 290; a(i)-267; c-281-285p, 289p, 290; c(i)-267.* **Romita, Jr.** *a-300; c-300.* **Roussos** *a-84i.* **Simonson** *a-171p; c-171, 217.* **B. Smith** *a-53, 186p, 198p, 205, 214; c-53-55, 186p, 198, 205, 212, 214, 216.* **Paul Smith** *a(p)-165-170, 172-175, 278; c-165-170, 172-175, 278.* **Sparling** *a-78p.* **Steranko** *a-50p, 51p; c-49-51.* **Sutton** *a-106i.* **Art Thibert** *a(i)-281-286; c(i)-281, 282, 284, 285.* **Toth** *a-12p, 67p(r).* **Tuska** *a-40-42i, 43-46p, 88i(r); c-39-41, 77p, 78p.* **Williamson** *a-202i, 203i, 211i; c-202i, 203i, 206i.* **Wood** *c-14i.*

UNCANNY X-MEN AND THE NEW TEEN TITANS (See Marvel and DC Present...)

X-MEN (2nd Series)(Titled New X-Men with #114) (Titled X-Men Legacy with #210)
Marvel Comics: Oct, 1991 - No. 275, Dec, 2012 ($1.00-$2.99)

1 a-d (four different covers, $1.50, 52 pgs.)-Jim Lee-c/a begins, ends #11; new team begins (Cyclops, Beast, Wolverine, Gambit, Psylocke & Rogue); new Uncanny X-Men & Magneto app.; 6.00
1 e ($3.95)-Double gate-fold-c consisting of all four covers from 1a-d by Jim Lee; contains all pin-ups from #1a-d plus inside-c foldout poster; no ads; printed on coated stock 1 2 3 5 6 8
1-20th Anniversary Edition-(12/11, $3.99) r/#1 with double gatefold-c; Jim Lee pin-ups 5.00
2-7: 4-Wolverine back to old yellow costume (same date as Wolverine #50); last $1.00-c. 5-Byrne scripts. 6-Sabretooth-c/story 5.00
8-10: 8-Gambit vs. Bishop-c/story; last Lee-a; Ghost Rider cameo cont'd in Ghost Rider #26. 9-Wolverine vs. Ghost Rider; cont'd/G.R. #26. 10-Return of Longshot 5.00
11-13,17-24,26-29,31: 12,13-Art Thibert-c/a. 28,29-Sabretooth app. 4.00
11-Silver ink 2nd printing; came with X-Men board game 2 4 6 9 12 15
14-16-($1.50)-Polybagged with trading card in each; X-Cutioner's Song x-overs; 14-Andy Kubert-c/a begins 5.00
25-($3.50, 52 pgs.)-Wraparound-c with Gambit hologram on-c; Professor X erases Magneto's mind 2 4 6 9 12 15
25-30th anniversary issue w/B&W-c with Magneto in color & Magneto hologram & no price on-c 3 6 9 19 30 40
25-Gold 50.00
30-($1.95)-Wedding issue w/bound-in trading card sheet 5.00
32-37: 32-Begin $1.50-c; bound-in card sheet. 33-Gambit & Sabretooth-c/story 4.00
36,37-($2.95)-Collectors editions (foil-c) 5.00
38-44,46-49,51-53, 55-65: 42,43- Paul Smith-a. 46,49,53-56-Onslaught app. 51-Waid scripts begin, end #56. 54-(Reg. edition)-Onslaught revealed as Professor X. 55,56-Onslaught x-over; Avengers, FF & Sentinels app. 56-Dr. Doom app. 57-Xavier taken into custody; Byrne-c/swipe (X-Men,1st Series #138). 59-Hercules-c/app. 61-Juggernaut-c/app. 62-Re-intro. Shang Chi; two covers. 63-Kingpin cameo. 64- Kingpin app. 4.00
45-($3.95)-Annual issue; gatefold-c 6.00
50-($2.95)-Vs. Onslaught, wraparound-c. 6.00
50-($3.95)-Vs. Onslaught, wraparound foil-c. 6.00
50-($2.95)-Variant gold-c. 3 6 9 21 33 45
50-($2.95)-Variant silver-c. 2 4 6 9 12 15
54-(Limited edition)-Embossed variant-c; Onslaught revealed as Professor X 3 6 9 17 26 35
66-69,71-74,76-79: 66-Operation Zero Tolerance. 76-Origin of Maggott 3.00
70-($2.99, 48 pgs.)-Joe Kelly-s begin, new members join 4.00
75-($2.99, 48 pgs.) vs. N'Garai; wraparound-c 4.00
80-($3.99) 35th Anniv. issue; holo-foil-c 5.00
80-($2.99) Regular-c 4.00
80-($6.95) Dynamic Forces Ed.; Quesada-c 7.00
81-93,95: 82-Hunt for Xavier pt. 2. 85-Davis-a. 86-Origin of Joseph. 87-Magneto War ends. 88-Juggernaut app. 3.00
94-($2.99) Contains preview of X-Men: Hidden Years 4.00
96-99: 96,97-Apocalypse: The Twelve 3.00
100-($2.99) Art Adams-c; begin Claremont-s/Yu-a 4.00
100-DF alternate-c 1 3 4 6 8 10
101-105,107,108,110-114: 101-Begin $2.25-c. 107-Maximum Security x-over; Bishop-c/app. 108-Moira MacTaggart dies; Senator Kelly shot. 111-Magneto-c. 112,113-Eve of Destruction 3.00
106-($2.99) X-Men battle Domina 4.00
109-($3.50, 100 pgs.) new and reprinted Christmas-themed stories 5.00
114-(7/01) Title change to "New X-Men," Morrison-s/Quitely-c/a begins 4.00
114-(8/10, $1.00) "Marvel's Greatest Comics" reprint 3.00
115-Two covers (Quitely & BWS) 4.00
116-125,127,129-149: 116-Emma Frost joins. 117,118-Van Sciver-a. 121,122,135-Quitely-a. 127-Leon & Sienkiewicz-a. 132,139-141-Jimenez-a. 136-138-Quitely-a. 142-Sabretooth app.; Bachalo-c/a thru #145. 146-Magneto returns; Jimenez-a 3.00
126-($3.25) Quitely-a; defeat of Cassanova 4.00
128-1st app. Fantomex; Kordey-a 2 4 6 9 12 15
150-($3.50) Jean Grey dies again; last Jimenez-a 4.00
151-156: 151-154-Silvestri-c/a 3.00
157-169: 157-X-Men Reload begins 3.00
170-184: 171- Begin $2.50-c. 175,176-Crossover with Black Panther #8,9. 181-184-Apocalypse returns 3.00
185-199,201-229,231-249,251-261: 185-Begin $2.99-c. 188-190,192-194,197-199-Bachalo-a. 195,196,201-203-Ramos-a. 201-204-Endangered Species back-up. 205-207-Messiah Complex x-over. 208-Romita Jr.-a. 210-Starts X-Men: Legacy. 228,229-Acuña-a. 235-237-Second Coming x-over. 238-The Heroic Age. 245-Age of X begins 3.00
200-($3.99) Two wraparound covers by Bachalo & Finch; Bachalo & Ramos-a 4.00
230-($3.99) Acuña-a; Rogue vs. Emplate 4.00
250-($4.99) Suayan-c/Pham-a; back-up r/New Mutants #27 5.00
261.1-(3/12, $2.99) The N'Garai app.; Brooks-c 3.00
262-275-Brooks-c. 266-270-Avengers vs. X-Men tie-in 3.00
#(-1) Flashback (7/97); origin of Magneto 3.00
Annual 1-3 ('92-'94, $2.25-$2.95, 68 pgs.) 1-Lee-c & layouts; #2-Bagged w/card 4.00
Special '95 ($3.95) 4.00
... '96,...'97-Wraparound-c 4.00
.../ Dr. Doom '98 Annual ($2.99) Lopresti-a 4.00
... Annual '99 ($3.50) Adam Kubert-c 4.00
Annual 2000 ($3.50) Art Adams-c/Claremont-s/Eaton-a 4.00
...2001 Annual ($3.50) Morrison-s/Yu-a; issue printed sideways 4.00
...2007 Annual #1 (3/07, $3.99) Casey-s/Brooks-a; Cable and Mystique app. 4.00
...Legacy Annual 1 (11/09, $3.99) Acuña-a; Emplate returns 4.00
Animation Special Graphic Novel (12/90, $10.95) adapts animated series 12.00
Ashcan #1 (1994, 75¢) Introduces new team members 3.00
... Archives Sketchbook (12/00, $2.99) Early B&W character design sketches by various incl. Lee, Davis, Yu, Pacheco, BWS, Art Adams, Liefeld 3.00
...: Bizarre Love Triangle TPB (2005, $9.99)-r/X-Men #171-174 10.00
.../ Black Panther TPB (2006, $11.99)-r/X-Men #175,176 & Black Panther (2005) #8,9 12.00
...: Blinded By the Light (2007, $14.99)-r/X-Men #200-204 15.00
...: Blind Science (7/10, $3.99) Second Coming x-over; Parel-c 4.00
...: Blood of Apocalypse (2006, $17.99)-r/X-Men #182-187 18.00
...: Day of the Atom (2005, $19.99)-r/X-Men #157-165 20.00
Decimation: X-Men - The Day After TPB (2006, $15.99) r/#177-181 & Decimation: House of M - The Day After 16.00
...: Declassified (10/00, $3.50) Profile pin-ups by various; Jae Lee-c 4.00
...: Earth's Mutant Heroes (7/11, $4.99) Handbook-style profiles of mutants 5.00
...: Endangered Species (8/07, $3.99) prologue to 17-part back-up series in X-Men titles 4.00
...: Endangered Species HC (2008, $24.99, d.j.) over-sized r/prologue and 17-part series 25.00
...: Evolutions 1 (12/11, $3.99) Collection of variant covers from May 2011 Marvel titles 4.00
...: Fatal Attractions ('94, $17.95)-r/x-Factor #92, X-Force #25, Uncanny X-Men #304, X-Men #25, Wolverine #75, & Excalibur #71 18.00
...: Golgotha (2005, $12.99)-r/X-Men #166-170 13.00
... Millennial Visions (8/00, $3.99) Various artists interpret future X-Men 4.00
... Millennial Visions 2 (1/02, $3.50) Various artists interpret future X-Men 4.00
...: Mutant Genesis (2006, $19.99)-r/X-Men #1-7; sketch pages and extra art 20.00
New X-Men: E is for Extinction TPB (11/01, $12.95) r/#114-117 13.00
New X-Men: Imperial TPB (7/02, $19.99) r/#118-126; Quitely-c 20.00
New X-Men: New Worlds TPB (2002, $14.99) r/#127-133; Quitely-c 15.00
New X-Men: Riot at Xavier's TPB (2003, $11.99) r/#134-138; Quitely-c 12.00
New X-Men: Vol. 5: Assault on Weapon Plus TPB (2003, $14.99) r/#139-145 15.00
New X-Men: Vol. 6: Planet X TPB (2004, $12.99) r/#146-150 13.00
New X-Men: Vol. 7: Here Comes Tomorrow TPB (2004, $10.99) r/#151-154 11.00
New X-Men: Volume 1 HC (2002, $29.99) oversized r/#114-126 & 2001 Annual 30.00
New X-Men: Volume 2 HC (2003, $29.99) oversized r/#127-141; sketch & script pages 30.00
New X-Men: Volume 3 HC (2004, $29.99) oversized r/#142-154; sketch & script pages 30.00
New X-Men Omnibus HC (2006, $99.99) oversized r/#114-154 & Annual 2001; Morrison's original pitch; sketch & script pages; variant covers & promo art; Carey intro. 140.00
...: Odd Men Out (2008, $3.99) Two unpublished stories with Dave Cockrum-a 4.00
... Original Sin 1 (12/08, $3.99) Wolverine and Daken; Deodato & Eaton-a 4.00
... Origin: Colossus (7/08, $3.99) Yost-s/Hairsine-a; Piotr Rasputin before joining X-Men 4.00
... Phoenix Force Handbook (9/10, $4.99) bios of those related to the Phoenix; Raney-c 5.00
...: Pixies and Demons Director's Cut (2008, $3.99) r/FCBD 2008 story with script 4.00

X-Men (2010 series) #4 © MAR

X-Men (2013 series) #10 © MAR

X-Men Classic #74 © MAR

GD VG FN VF VF/NM NM-
2.0 4.0 6.0 8.0 9.0 9.2

... Pizza Hut Mini-comics-(See Marvel Collector's Edition: X-Men in Promotional Comics section)
... Premium Edition #1 (1993)-Cover says "Toys 'R' Us Limited Edition X-Men" 3.00
...: Rarities (1995, $5.95)-Reprints 6.00
...: Return of Magik Must Have (2008, $3.99) r/X-Men Unlimited #14, New X-Men #37 and X-Men: Divided We Stand #2; Coipel-c 4.00
...: Road Trippin' ('99, $24.95, TPB) r/X-Men road trips 25.00
...: Supernovas ('07, $34.99, oversized HC w/d.j.) r/X-Men 188-199 & Annual #1 35.00
...: Supernovas ('08, $29.99, SC) r/X-Men 188-199 & Annual #1 30.00
...: The Coming of Bishop ('95, $12.95)-r/Uncanny X-Men #282-285, 287,288 13.00
...: The Magneto War (3/99, $2.99) Davis-a 4.00
...: The Rise of Apocalypse ('98, $16.99)-r/Rise Of Apocalypse #1-4, X-Factor #5,6 17.00
... Visionaries: Chris Claremont ('98, $24.95)-r/Claremont-s; art by Byrne, BWS, Jim Lee 25.00
... Visionaries: Jim Lee ('02, $29.99)-r/Jim Lee-a from various issues between Uncanny X-Men #248 & 286; r/Classic X-Men #39 and X-Men Annual #1 30.00
... Visionaries: Joe Madureira (7/00, $17.95)-r/Uncanny X-Men #325,326,329,330,341-343; new Madureira-c 18.00
... Vs. Hulk (3/09, $3.99) Claremont-s/Raapack-a; r/X-Men #66 4.00
...: Zero Tolerance ('00, $24.95, TPB) r/crossover series 25.00

NOTE: ***Jim Lee*** *a-1-11p; c-1-6p, 7, 8, 9p, 10, 11p.* ***Art Thibert*** *a-6-9i, 12, 13; c-6i, 12, 13.*

X-MEN (3rd series)
Marvel Comics: Sept, 2010 - No. 41, Apr, 2013 ($3.99)

1-41: 1-6-"Curse of the Mutants" x-over; Medina-a. 7-10-Spider-Man app.; Bachalo-a. 12-Continued from X-Men Giant-Size #1. 16-19-FF & Skull the Slayer app. 20-23-War Machine app. 16-Deadpool app. 28-FF & Spider-Man app. 38,39-Domino & Daredevil team-up 4.00
15.1 ($2.99) Pearson-c/Conrad-a; Ghost Rider app. 3.00
...: Curse of the Mutants - Blade 1 (10/10, $3.99) Tim Green-a 4.00
...: Curse of the Mutants - Smoke and Blood 1 (11/10, $3.99) Crain-c 4.00
...: Curse of the Mutants Spotlight 1 (1/11, $3.99) creator profiles and interviews 4.00
...: Curse of the Mutants - Storm and Gambit 1 (11/10, $3.99) Bachalo-a; 2 covers 4.00
...: Curse of the Mutants - X-Men vs. Vampires 1,2 (11/10 - No. 2, 12/10, $3.99) Bradshaw-c 4.00
... Giant-Size 1 (7/11, $4.99) Medina & Talajic-a; cover swipe of Giant-Size X-Men #1 5.00
...: Regenesis 1 (12/11, $3.99) Splits X-Men into 2 teams; Tan-a/Bachalo-c 4.00
... Spotlight 1 (7/11, $3.99) Character profiles and creator interviews 4.00
...: With Great Power 1 (2011, $4.99) r/#7-9 5.00

X-MEN (4th series)
Marvel Comics: Jul, 2013 - Present ($3.99)

1-12: 1-All-female team; Brian Wood-s/Olivier Coipel-a. 5,6-Battle of the Atom 4.00

X-MEN (Free Comic Book Day giveaways)
Marvel Comics: 2006; May, 2008

FCBD 2008 Edition #1-(5/08) Features Pixie; Carey-s/Land-a/c 3.00
.../Runaways: FCBD 2006 Edition; new x-over story; Mighty Avengers preview; Chen-c 3.00

X-MEN ADVENTURES (TV)
Marvel Comics: Nov, 1992 - No. 15, Jan, 1994 ($1.25)(Based on animated series)

1,15: 1-Wolverine, Cyclops, Jubilee, Rogue, Gambit. 15-($1.75, 52 pgs.) 4.00
2-14: 3-Magneto-c/story. 6-Sabretooth-c/story. 7-Cable-c/story. 10-Archangel guest star. 11-Cable-c/story. 3.00

X-MEN ADVENTURES II (TV)
Marvel Comics: Feb, 1994 - No. 13, Feb, 1995 ($1.25/$1.50)(Based on 2nd TV season)

1-13: 4-Bound-in trading card sheet. 5-Alpha Flight app. 3.00
...Captive Hearts/Slave Island (TPB, $4.95)-r/X-Men Adventures #5-8 5.00
...The Irresistible Force, The Muir Island Saga (5.95, 10/94, TPB) r/X-Men Advs. #9-12 6.00

X-MEN ADVENTURES III (TV)(See Adventures of the X-Men)
Marvel Comics: Mar, 1995 - No. 13, Mar, 1996 ($1.50) (Based on 3rd TV season)

1-13 3.00

X-MEN: AGE OF APOCALYPSE
Marvel Comics: May, 2005 - No. 6, June, 2005 ($2.99, weekly limited series)

1-6-Bachalo-c/a; Yoshida-s; follows events in the "Age of Apocalypse" storyline 3.00
... One Shot (5/05, $3.99) prequel to series; Hitch wraparound-c; pin-ups by various 4.00
X-Men: The New Age of Apocalypse TPB (2005, $20.99) r/#1-6 & one-shot 21.00

X-MEN ALPHA
Marvel Comics: 1994 ($3.95, one-shot)

nn-Age of Apocalypse; wraparound chromium-c 1 3 4 6 8 10
nn ($49.95)-Gold logo 50.00

X-MEN/ALPHA FLIGHT
Marvel Comics Group: Dec, 1985 - No. 2, Dec, 1985 ($1.50, limited series)

1,2: 1-Intro The Berserkers; Paul Smith-a 5.00

X-MEN/ALPHA FLIGHT
Marvel Comics Group: May, 1998 - No. 2, June, 1998 ($2.99, limited series)

1,2-Flashback to early meeting; Raab-s/Cassaday-s/a 3.00

X-MEN AND POWER PACK
Marvel Comics: Dec, 2005 - No. 4, Mar, 2006 ($2.99, limited series)

1-4-Sumerak-s/Gurihiru-a. 1-Wolverine & Sabretooth app. 3.00
...: The Power of X (2006, $6.99, digest size) r/#1-4 7.00

X-MEN AND THE MICRONAUTS, THE
Marvel Comics Group: Jan, 1984 - No. 4, Apr, 1984 (Limited series)

1-4: Guice-c/a(p) in all 5.00

X-MEN: APOCALYPSE/DRACULA
Marvel Comics: Apr, 2006 - No. 4, July, 2006 ($2.99, limited series)

1-4-Tieri-s/Henry-a/Jae Lee-c 3.00
TPB (2006, $10.99) r/series; cover gallery 11.00

X-MEN ARCHIVES
Marvel Comics: Jan, 1995 - No. 4, Apr, 1995 ($2.25, limited series)

1-4: Reprints Legion stories from New Mutants. 4-Magneto app. 3.00

X-MEN ARCHIVES FEATURING CAPTAIN BRITAIN
Marvel Comics: July, 1995 - No. 7, 1996 ($2.95, limited series)

1-7: Reprints early Capt. Britain stories 3.00

X-MEN: BATTLE OF THE ATOM
Marvel Comics: Nov, 2013 - No. 2, Dec, 2013 ($3.99, bookends for X-Men title crossover)

1,2: 1-Bendis-s/Cho-a/Art Adams-c; bonus pin-ups of the various X-teams 4.00

X-MEN BLACK SUN (See Black Sun:...)

X-MEN BOOKS OF ASKANI
Marvel Comics: 1995 ($2.95, one-shot)

1-Painted pin-ups w/text 3.00

X-MEN: CHILDREN OF THE ATOM
Marvel Comics: Nov, 1999 - No. 6 ($2.99, limited series)

1-6-Casey-s; X-Men before issue #1. 1-3-Rude-c/a. 4-Paul Smith-a/Rude-c. 5,6-Essad Ribic-c/a 3.00
TPB (11/01, $16.95) r/series; sketch pages; Casey intro. 17.00

X-MEN CHRONICLES
Marvel Comics: Mar, 1995 - No. 2, June, 1995 ($3.95, limited series)

1,2: Age of Apocalypse x-over. 1-wraparound-c 5.00

X-MEN: CLANDESTINE
Marvel Comics: Oct, 1996 - No. 2, Nov, 1996 ($2.95, limited series, 48 pgs.)

1,2: Alan Davis-c(p)/a(p)/scripts & Mark Farmer-c(i)/a(i) in all; wraparound-c 4.00

X-MEN CLASSIC (Formerly Classic X-Men)
Marvel Comics: No. 46, Apr, 1990 - No. 110, Aug, 1995 ($1.25/$1.50)

46-110: Reprints from X-Men. 54-(52 pgs.). 57,60-63,65-Russell-c(i); 62-r/X-Men #158(Rogue). 66-r/#162(Wolverine). 69-Begins-r of Paul Smith issues (#165 on). 70,79,90,97(52 pgs.). 70-r/X-Men #166. 90-r/#186. 100-($1.50). 104-r/X-Men #200 4.00

X-MEN CLASSICS
Marvel Comics Group: Dec, 1983 - No. 3, Feb, 1984 ($2.00, Baxter paper)

1-3: X-Men-r by Neal Adams 6.00

NOTE: ***Zeck*** *c-1-3.*

X-MEN: COLOSSUS BLOODLIINE
Marvel Comics: Nov, 2005 - No. 5, Mar, 2006 ($2.99, limited series)

1-5-Colossus returns to Russia; David Hine-s/Jorge Lucas-a; Bachalo-c 3.00
TPB (2006, $13.99) r/#1-5 14.00

X-MEN: DEADLY GENESIS (See Uncanny X-Men #475)
Marvel Comics: Jan, 2006 - No. 6, July, 2006 ($3.99/$3.50, limited series)

1-($3.99) Silvestri-c swipe of Giant-Size X-Men #1; Hairsine-a/Brubaker-s 4.00
2-6-($3.50) 2-Silvestri-c; Banshee killed. 4-Intro Kid Vulcan 3.50
HC (2006, $24.99, dust jacket) r/#1-6 25.00
SC (2006, $19.99) r/#1-6 20.00

X-MEN: DIE BY THE SWORD
Marvel Comics: Dec, 2007 - No. 5, Feb, 2008 ($2.99, limited series)

1-5-Excalibur and The Exiles app.; Claremont-s/Santacruz-a 3.00
TPB (2008, $13.99) r/#1-5; handbook pages of Merlyn, Roma and Saturne 14.00

X-MEN: DIVIDED WE STAND
Marvel Comics: June, 2008 - No. 2, July, 2008 ($3.99, limited series)

1,2-Short stories by various; Peterson-c 4.00

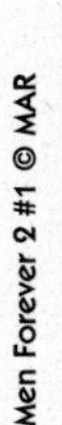
X-Men Fairy Tales #1 © MAR

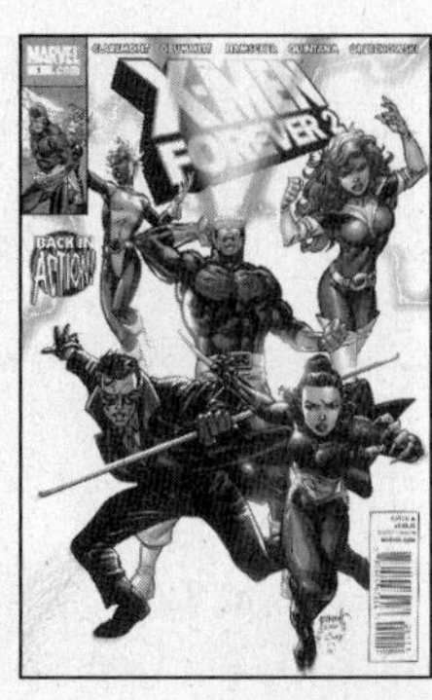
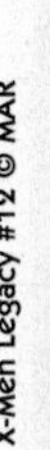
X-Men Forever 2 #1 © MAR

X-Men Legacy #12 © MAR

GD 2.0 | VG 4.0 | FN 6.0 | VF 8.0 | VF/NM 9.0 | NM- 9.2

X-MEN: EARTHFALL
Marvel Comics: Sept, 1996 ($2.95, one-shot)
1-r/Uncanny X-Men #232-234; wraparound-c 4.00

X-MEN: EMPEROR VULCAN
Marvel Comics: Nov, 2007 - No. 5, Mar, 2008 ($2.99, limited series)
1-5: 1-Starjammers app.; Yost-s/Diaz-a/Tan-c 3.00
TPB (2008, $13.99) r/#1-5 14.00

X-MEN: EVOLUTION (Based on the animated series)
Marvel Comics: Feb, 2002 - No. 9, Sept, 2002 ($2.25)
1-9: 1-8-Grayson-s/Udon-a. 9-Farber-s/J.J.Kirby-a 3.00
TPB (7/02, $8.99) r/#1-4 9.00
Vol. 2 TPB (2003, $11.99) r/#5-9; Asamiya-c 12.00

X-MEN FAIRY TALES
Marvel Comics: July, 2006 - No. 4, Oct, 2006 ($2.99, limited series)
1-4-Re-imagining of classic stories; Cebulski-s. 2-Baker-a. 3-Sienkiewicz-a. 4-Kobayashi-a 3.00
TPB (2006, $10.99) r/#1-4 11.00

X-MEN/ FANTASTIC FOUR
Marvel Comics: Feb, 2005 - No. 5, June, 2005 ($3.50, limited series)
1-5-Pat Lee-a/c; Yoshida-s; the Brood app. 3.50
HC (2005, $19.99, 7 1/2" x 11", dustjacket) oversized r/#1-5; cover gallery 20.00

X-MEN FIRST CLASS
Marvel Comics: Nov, 2006 - No. 8, Jun, 2007 ($2.99, limited series)
1-8-Xavier's first class of X-Men; Cruz-a/Parker-s. 5-Thor app. 7-Scarlet Witch app. 3.00
... Special 1 (7/07, $3.99) Nowlan-c; Nowlan, Paul Smith, Coover, Dragotta & Allred-a 4.00
... - Tomorrow's Brightest HC (2007, $24.99, d.j) r/#1-8; cover & character design art 25.00
... - Tomorrow's Brightest SC (2007, $19.99) r/#1-8; cover & character design art 20.00

X-MEN FIRST CLASS (2nd series)
Marvel Comics: Aug, 2007 - No. 16, Nov, 2008 ($2.99)
1-16: 1-Cruz-a/Parker-s; Fantastic Four app. 8-Man-Thing app. 10-Romita Jr.-c 3.00
... Giant-Size Special 1 (12/08, $3.99) 5 new short stories; Haspiel-a; r/X-Men #40 4.00
... - Mutant Mayhem TPB (2008, $13.99) r/#1-5 & X-Men First Class Special 14.00

X-MEN FIRST CLASS FINALS
Marvel Comics: Apr, 2009 - No. 4, July, 2009 ($3.99, limited series)
1-4-Cruz-a/Parker-s. 1-3-Coover-a 4.00

X-MEN FIRSTS
Marvel Comics: Feb, 1996 ($4.95, one-shot)
1-r/Avengers Annual #10, Uncanny X-Men #266, #221; Incredible Hulk #181 5.00

X-MEN FOREVER
Marvel Comics: Jan, 2001 - No. 6, June, 2001 ($3.50, limited series)
1-6-Jean Grey, Iceman, Mystique, Toad, Juggernaut app.; Maguire-a 4.00

X-MEN FOREVER
Marvel Comics: Aug, 2009 - No. 24, July, 2010 ($3.99)
1-24: 1-Claremont-s/Grummett-a/c. 7-Nick Fury app. 4.00
... Alpha 1 (2009, $4.99) r/X-Men (1991) #1-3; 8 page preview of X-Men Forever #1 5.00
... Annual 1 (6/10, $4.99) Wolverine & Jean Grey romance; Sana Takeda-a/c 5.00
... Giant-Size 1 (7/10, $3.99) Grell-a/c; Lilandra & Gladiator app.; r/(Uncanny)X-Men #108 4.00

X-MEN FOREVER 2
Marvel Comics: Aug, 2010 - No. 16, Mar, 2011 ($3.99)
1-16: 1-Claremont-s/Grummett-a/c. 2,3-Spider-Man app. 9,10-Grell-a 4.00

X-MEN: GOLD
Marvel Comics: Jan, 2014 ($5.99, one-shot)
1-50th Anniversary anthology; short stories by various incl. Stan Lee, Simonson, Claremont, Thomas, Olliffe, Wein, Molina, McLeod, Larroca; Coipel-c 6.00

X-MEN: HELLBOUND
Marvel Comics: July, 2010 - No. 3, Sept, 2010 ($3.99, limited series)
1-3-Second Coming x-over; Tolibao-a/Djurdjevic-c; Majik rescued from Limbo 4.00

X-MEN: HELLFIRE CLUB
Marvel Comics: Jan, 2000 - No. 4, Apr, 2000 ($2.50, limited series)
1-4-Origin of the Hellfire Club 3.00

X-MEN: HIDDEN YEARS
Marvel Comics: Dec, 1999 - No. 22, Sept. 2001 ($3.50/$2.50)
1-New adventures from pre-#94 era; Byrne-s/a(p) 4.00
2-4,6-11,13-22-($2.50): 2-Two covers. 3-Ka-Zar app. 8,9-FF-c/app. 3.00
5-($2.75) 3.00
12-($3.50) Magneto-c/app. 4.00

GD 2.0 | VG 4.0 | FN 6.0 | VF 8.0 | VF/NM 9.0 | NM- 9.2

X-MEN: KING BREAKER
Marvel Comics: Feb, 2009 - No. 4, May, 2009 ($3.99, limited series)
1-4-Emperor Vulcan and a Shi'ar invasion; Havok, Rachel Grey and Polaris app. 4.00

X-MEN: KITTY PRYDE - SHADOW & FLAME
Marvel Comics: Aug, 2005 - No. 5, Dec, 2005 ($2.99, limited series)
1-5-Akira Yoshida-s/Paul Smith-a/c; Kitty & Lockheed go to Japan 3.00
TPB (2006, $14.99) r/#1-5 15.00

X-MEN LEGACY (See X-Men 2nd series)

X-MEN LEGACY (Marvel NOW!)
Marvel Comics: Jan, 2013 - No. 24, Apr, 2014; No. 300, May, 2014 ($2.99)
1-24: 1-Legion (Professor X's son); Spurrier-s/Huat-a. 2-X-Men app. 5,6-Molina-a 3.00
300-(5/14, $4.99) Spurrier, Carey & Gage-s/Huat, Kurth & Sandoval-a; Mann-c 5.00

X-MEN: LIBERATORS
Marvel Comics: Nov, 1998 - No. 4, Feb, 1999 ($2.99, limited series)
1-4-Wolverine, Nightcrawler & Colossus; P. Jimenez 4.00

X-MEN LOST TALES
Marvel Comics: 1997 ($2.99)
1,2-r/Classic X-Men back-up stories 4.00

X-MEN: MAGNETO TESTAMENT
Marvel Comics: Nov, 2008 - No. 5, Mar, 2009 ($3.99, limited series)
1-5-Max Eisenhardt in 1930s Nazi-occupied Poland; Pak-s/DiGiandomenico-a. 5-Back-up story of artist Dina Babbitt with Neal Adams-a 4.00

X-MEN: MANIFEST DESTINY
Marvel Comics: Nov, 2008 - No. 5, Mar, 2009 ($3.99, limited series)
1-5-Short stories of X-Men re-location to San Francisco; s/a by various 4.00
... Nightcrawler 1 (5/09, $3.99) Molina & Syaf-a; Mephisto app. 4.00

X-MEN: MESSIAH COMPLEX
Marvel Comics: Dec, 2007 ($3.99)
1-Part 1 of x-over with X-Men, Uncanny X-Men, X-Factor and New X-Men; 2 covers 4.00
... - Mutant Files (2007, $3.99) Handbook pages of x-over participants; Kolins-c 4.00
HC (2008, $39.99, oversized) r/#1, Uncanny X-Men #492-494, X-Men #205-207, New X-Men #44-46 and X-Factor #25-27 40.00

X-MEN NOIR
Marvel Comics: Nov, 2008 - No. 4, May, 2009 ($3.99, limited series)
1-4-Pulp-style story set in 1930s NY; Van Lente-s/Calero-a 4.00
...: Mark of Cain (2/10 - No. 4, 5/10, $3.99) an Lente-s/Calero-a 4.00

X-MEN OMEGA
Marvel Comics: June, 1995 ($3.95, one-shot)
nn-Age of Apocalypse finale 1 3 4 6 8 10
nn-($49.95)-Gold edition 50.00

X-MEN: ORIGINS
Marvel Comics: Oct, 2008 - Present ($3.99, series of one-shots)
...: Beast (11/08) High school years; Carey-s; painted-a/c by Woodward 4.00
...: Cyclops (3/10) Magneto app.; Delperdang-a/Granov-c 4.00
...: Deadpool (9/10) Fernandez-a/Swierczynski-s 4.00
...: Emma Frost (7/10) Moline-a; r/excerpt from 1st app. in Uncanny X-Men #129 4.00
...: Gambit (8/09) Mr. Sinister, Sabretooth and the Marauders app.; Yardin-a 4.00
...: Iceman (1/10) Noto-a 4.00
...: Jean Grey (10/08) Childhood & early X-days; McKeever-s; Mayhew painted-a/c 4.00
...: Nightcrawler (5/10) Cary Nord-a; r/excerpt from 1st app. in Giant-Size X-Men #1 4.00
...: Sabretooth (4/09) Childhood and early meetings with Wolverine; Panosian-a/c 4.00
...: Wolverine (6/09) Pre-X-Men days and first meeting with Xavier; Texeira-a/c 4.00

X-MEN: PHOENIX
Marvel Comics: Dec, 1999 - No. 3, Mar, 2000 ($2.50, limited series)
1-3: 1-Apocalypse app. 4.00

X-MEN: PHOENIX - ENDSONG
Marvel Comics: Mar, 2005 - No. 5, June, 2005 ($2.99, limited series)
1-5-The Phoenix Force returns to Earth; Greg Land-c/a; Greg Pak-s 3.00
HC (2005, $19.99, dust jacket) r/#1-5; Land sketch pages 20.00
SC (2006, $14.99) 15.00

X-MEN: PHOENIX - LEGACY OF FIRE
Marvel Comics: July, 2003 - No. 3, Sep, 2003 ($2.99, limited series)
1-3-Manga-style; Ryan Kinnard-s/a/c; intro page art by Adam Warren 3.00

X-Men: Search For Cyclops #1 © MAR

X-Men: The Manga #6 © MAR

X-Men Unlimited #3 © MAR

	GD	VG	FN	VF	VF/NM	NM-
	2.0	4.0	6.0	8.0	9.0	9.2

GD VG FN VF VF/NM NM-
2.0 4.0 6.0 8.0 9.0 9.2

X-MEN: PHOENIX - WARSONG
Marvel Comics: Nov, 2006 - No. 5, Mar, 2007 ($2.99, limited series)

1-5-Tyler Kirkham-a/Greg Pak-s/Marc Silvestri-c 3.00
HC (2007, $19.99, dustjacket) r/#1-5; variant cover gallery and Handbook pages 20.00
SC (2007, $14.99) r/#1-5; variant cover gallery and Handbook pages 15.00

X-MEN: PIXIE STRIKES BACK
Marvel Comics: Apr, 2010 - No. 4, July, 2010 ($3.99, limited series)

1-4-Kathryn Immonen-s/Sara Pichelli-a/Stuart Immonen-c 4.00

X-MEN: PRELUDE TO SCHISM
Marvel Comics: Jul, 2011 - No. 4, Aug, 2011 ($2.99, limited series)

1-4-Jenkins-s/Camuncoli-c. 1-De La Torre-a. 2-Magneto childhood. 3-Conrad-a 3.00

X-MEN PRIME
Marvel Comics: July, 1995 ($4.95, one-shot)

nn-Post Age of Apocalyse begins 1 3 4 6 8 10

X-MEN RARITIES
Marvel Comics: 1995 ($5.95, one-shot)

nn-Reprints hard-to-find stories 6.00

X-MEN ROAD TO ONSLAUGHT
Marvel Comics: Oct, 1996 ($2.50, one-shot)

nn-Retells Onslaught Saga 3.00

X-MEN: RONIN
Marvel Comics: May, 2003 - No. 5, July, 2003 ($2.99, limited series)

1-5-Manga-style X-Men; Torres-s/Nakatsuka-a 3.00

X-MEN: SCHISM
Marvel Comics: Sept, 2011 - No. 5, Dec, 2011 ($4.99/$3.99, limited series)

1-($4.99) Aaron-s/Pacheco-a/c 5.00
2-5-($3.99) 2-Cho-a/c. 3-Acuña-a/c. 4-Alan Davis-a/c. 5-Adam Kubert-a 4.00

X-MEN: SEARCH FOR CYCLOPS
Marvel Comics: Oct, 2000 - No. 4, Mar, 2001 ($2.99, limited series)

1-4-Two covers (Raney, Pollina); Raney-a 4.00

X-MEN: SECOND COMING
Marvel Comics: May, 2010 - No. 2, Sept, 2010 ($3.99)

1-Cable & Hope return to the present; Bastion app.; Finch-a; covers by Granov & Finch 4.00
2-Conclusion to x-over; covers by Granov & Finch 4.00
...: Prepare (4/10, free) previews x-over; short story w/Immonen-a; cover sketch art 3.00

X-MEN / SPIDER-MAN ("X-Men and Spider-Man" on cover)
Marvel Comics: Jan, 2009 - No. 4, Apr, 2009 ($3.99, limited series)

1-4: 1-Team-up from pre-blue Beast days; Kraven app.; Gage-s/Alberti-a 4.00

X-MEN SPOTLIGHT ON... STARJAMMERS (Also see X-Men #104)
Marvel Comics: 1990 - No. 2, 1990 ($4.50, 52 pgs.)

1,2: Features Starjammers 5.00

X-MEN SURVIVAL GUIDE TO THE MANSION
Marvel Comics: Aug, 1993 ($6.95, spiralbound)

1 7.00

X-MEN: THE COMPLETE AGE OF APOCALYPSE EPIC
Marvel Comics: 2005 - Vol. 4, 2006 ($29.99, TPB)

Book 1-4: Chronological reprintings of the crossover 30.00

X-MEN: THE EARLY YEARS
Marvel Comics: May, 1994 - No. 17, Sept, 1995 ($1.50/$2.50)

1-16: r/X-Men #1-8 w/new-c 3.00
17-$2.50-c; r/X-Men #17,18 4.00

X-MEN: THE END
Marvel Comics: Oct, 2004 - No. 6, Feb, 2005 ($2.99, limited series)

1-6-Claremont-s/Chen-a/Land-c 3.00
... Book One: Dreamers and Demons TPB (2005, $14.99) r/#1-6 15.00

X-MEN: THE END - HEROES AND MARTYRS (Volume 2)
Marvel Comics: May, 2005 - No. 6, Oct, 2005 ($2.99, limited series)

1-6-Claremont-s/Chen-a/Land-c; continued from X-Men: The End 3.00
... Vol. 2 TPB (2006, $14.99) r/#1-6 15.00

X-MEN: THE END (MEN & X-MEN) (Volume 3)
Marvel Comics: Mar, 2006 - No. 6, Aug, 2006 ($2.99, limited series)

1-6-Claremont-s/Chen-a. 1-Land-c. 2-6-Gene Ha-c 3.00
... Vol. 3 TPB (2006, $14.99) r/#1-6 15.00

X-MEN: THE MANGA
Marvel Comics: Mar, 1998 - No. 26, June, 1999 ($2.99, B&W)

1-26-English version of Japanese X-Men comics: 23,24-Randy Green-c 4.00

X-MEN: THE MOVIE
Marvel Comics: Aug, 2000; Sept, 2000

Adaptation (9/00, $5.95) Macchio-s/Williams & Lanning-a 6.00
Adaptation TPB (9/00, $14.95) Movie adaptation and key reprints of main characters; four photo covers (movie X, Magneto, Rogue, Wolverine) 15.00
Prequel: Magneto (8/00, $5.95) Texeira & Palmiotti-a; art & photo covers 6.00
Prequel: Rogue (8/00, $5.95) Evans & Nikolakakis-a; art & photo covers 6.00
Prequel: Wolverine (8/00, $5.95) Waller & McKenna-a; art & photo covers 6.00
TPB X-Men: Beginnings (8/00, $14.95) reprints 3 prequels w/photo-c 15.00

X-MEN 2: THE MOVIE
Marvel Comics: 2003

Adaptation (6/03, $3.50) Movie adaptation; photo-c; Austen-s/Zircher-a 4.00
Adaptation TPB (2003, $12.99) Movie adaptation & r/Prequels Nightcrawler & Wolverine 13.00
Prequel: Nightcrawler (5/03, $3.50) Kerschl-a; photo cover 4.00
Prequel: Wolverine (5/03, $3.50) Mandrake-a; photo cover; Sabretooth app. 4.00

X-MEN: THE 198 (See House of M)
Marvel Comics: Mar, 2006 - No. 5, July, 2006 ($2.99, limited series)

1-5-Hine-s/Muniz-a 3.00
... Files (2006, $3.99) profiles of the 198 mutants who kept their powers after House of M 4.00
Decimation: The 198 (2006, $15.99, TPB) r/#1-5 & X-Men: The 198 Files 16.00

X-MEN: THE TIMES AND LIFE OF LUCAS BISHOP
Marvel Comics: Apr, 2009 - No. 3, June, 2009 ($3.99, limited series)

1-3-Swierczynski-s/Stroman-a. 1-Bishop's birth and childhood 4.00

X-MEN: THE ULTRA COLLECTION
Marvel Comics: Dec, 1994 - No. 5, Apr, 1995 ($2.95, limited series)

1-5: Pin-ups; no scripts 3.00

X-MEN: THE WEDDING ALBUM
Marvel Comics: 1994 ($2.95, magazine size, one-shot)

1-Wedding of Scott Summers & Jean Grey 4.00

X-MEN: TO SERVE AND PROTECT
Marvel Comics: Jan, 2011 - No. 4, Apr, 2011 ($3.99, limited series)

1-4-Short story anthology by various.1-Bradshaw-c. 2-Camuncoli-c 4.00

X-MEN TRUE FRIENDS
Marvel Comics: Sept, 1999 - No. 3, Nov, 1999 ($2.99, limited series)

1-3-Claremont-s/Leonardi-a 4.00

X-MEN 2099 (Also see 2099: World of Tomorrow)
Marvel Comics: Oct, 1993 - No. 35, Aug, 1996 ($1.25/$1.50/$1.95)

1-($1.75)-Foil-c; Ron Lim/Adam Kubert-a begins 4.00
1-2nd printing ($1.75) 3.00
1-Gold edition (15,000 made); sold thru Diamond for $19.40 20.00
2-24,26-35: 3-Death of Tina; Lim-c/a(p) in #1-8. 8-Bound-in trading card sheet. 35-Nostromo (from X-Nation) app; storyline cont'd in 2099: World of Tomorrow 3.00
25-($2.50)-Double sized 4.00
Special 1 ($3.95) 4.00
...: Oasis ($5.95, one-shot) -Hildebrandt Bros.-c/a 6.00

X-MEN ULTRA III PREVIEW
Marvel Comics: 1995 ($2.95)

nn-Kubert-a 3.00

X-MEN UNIVERSE
Marvel Comics: Dec, 1999 - No. 15, Feb, 2001 ($4.99/$3.99)

1-8-Reprints stories from recent X-Men titles 5.00
9-15-($3.99) 4.00

X-MEN UNIVERSE: PAST, PRESENT AND FUTURE
Marvel Comics: Feb, 1999 ($2.99, one-shot)

1-Previews 1999 X-Men events; background info 3.00

X-MEN UNLIMITED
Marvel Comics: 1993 - No. 50, Sept, 2003 ($3.95/$2.99, 68 pgs.)

1-Chris Bachalo-c/a; Quesada-a. 6.00
2-11: 2-Origin of Magneto script. 3-Sabretooth-c/story. 10-Dark Beast vs. Beast; Mark Waid script. 11-Magneto & Rogue 5.00
12-33: 12-Begin $2.99-c; Onslaught x-over; Juggernaut-c/app. 19-Caliafore-a. 20-Generation X app. 27-Origin Thunderbird. 29-Maximum Security x-over; Bishop-c/app. 30-Mahfood-a.

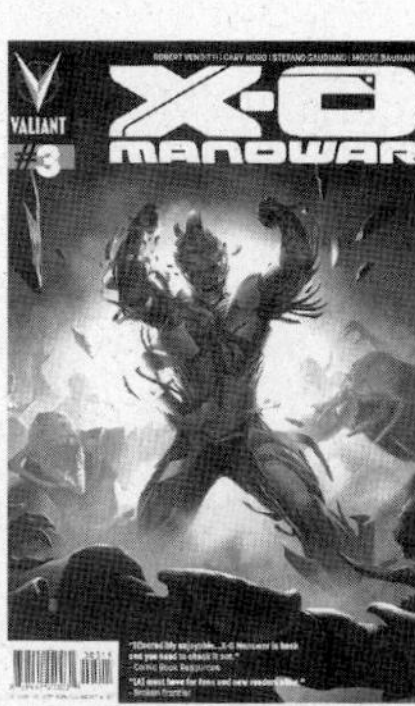

X-O Manowar (2012 series) #3 © VAL

Xombi #9 © Milestone

X-Statix #15 © MAR

GD 2.0 VG 4.0 FN 6.0 VF 8.0 VF/NM 9.0 NM- 9.2

31-Stelfreeze-c/a. 32-Dazzler; Thompson-c/a 33-Kaluta-c 4.00
34-37,39,40-42-($3.50) 34-Von Eeden-a. 35-Finch, Conner, Maguire-a. 36-Chiodo-c/a; Larroca, Totleben-a. 39-Bachalo-c; Pearson-a. 41-Bachalo-c; X-Statix app. 4.00
38-($2.25) Kitty Pryde; Robertson-a 3.00
43-50-($2.50) 43-Sienkiewicz-c/a; Paul Smith-a. 45-Noto-c. 46-Bisley-a. 47-Warren-s/Mays-a. 48-Wolverine story w/Isanove painted-a 3.00
X-Men Legends Vol. 4: Hated and Feared TPB (2003, $19.99) r/stories by various 20.00
NOTE: *Bachalo c/a-1. Quesada a-1. Waid scripts-10*

X-MEN UNLIMITED
Marvel Comics: Apr, 2004 - No. 14, Jun, 2006 ($2.99)
1-14: 1-6-Pat Lee-c; short stories by various. 2-District X preview; Granov-a 3.00

X-MEN VS. AGENTS OF ATLAS
Marvel Comics: Dec, 2009 - No. 2, Jan, 2010 ($3.99, limited series)
1,2-Pagulayan-a. 1-McGuinness-c. 2-Granov-c 4.00

X-MEN VS. DRACULA
Marvel Comics: Dec, 1993 ($1.75)
1-r/X-Men Annual #6; Austin-c(i) 4.00

X-MEN VS. THE AVENGERS, THE
Marvel Comics Group: Apr, 1987 - No. 4, July, 1987 ($1.50, limited series, Baxter paper)
1-Silvestri-a/c 1 2 3 5 6 8
2-4: 2,3-Silvestri-a/c. 4-Pollard-a/c 5.00

X-MEN VS. THE BROOD, THE
Marvel Comics Group: Sept, 1996 - No. 2, Oct, 1996 ($2.95, limited series)
1,2-Wraparound-c; Ostrander-s/Hitch-a(p) 4.00
TPB('97, $16.99) reprints X-Men/Brood: Day of Wrath #1,2 & Uncanny X-Men #232-234 17.00

X-MEN VISIONARIES
Marvel Comics: 1995,1996,2000 (trade paperbacks)
nn-($8.95) Reprints X-Men stories; Adam & Andy Kubert-a 9.00
...2: The Neal Adams Collection (1996) r/X-Men #56-63,65 30.00
...2: The Neal Adams Col. (2nd printing, 2000, $24.95) new Adams-c 25.00

X-MEN/WILDC.A.T.S.: THE DARK AGE (See also WildC.A.T.S./X-Men...)
Marvel Comics: 1998 ($4.50, one-shot)
1-Two covers (Broome & Golden); Ellis-s 5.00

X-MEN: WORLDS APART
Marvel Comics: Dec, 2008 - No. 4, Mar, 2009 ($3.99, limited series)
1-4-Storm and the Black Panther vs. the Shadow King. 1-Campbell-c 4.00

X-NATION 2099
Marvel Comics: Mar, 1996 - No. 6, Aug, 1996 ($1.95)
1-($3.95)-Humberto Ramos-a(p); wraparound, foil-c 5.00
2-6: 2,3-Ramos-a. 4-Exodus-c/app. 6-Reed Richards app 3.00

X NECROSIA
Marvel Comics: Dec, 2009 ($3.99)
1-Beginning of X-Force/X-Men/New Mutants x-over; Crain-a; Selene returns 4.00
...: The Gathering (2/10, $3.99) Wither, Blink, Senyaka. Mortis & Eliphas short stories 4.00

X-O MANOWAR (1st Series)
Valiant/Acclaim Comics (Valiant) No. 43 on: Feb, 1992 - No. 68, Sept, 1996 ($1.95/$2.25/$2.50, high quality)
0-(8/93, $3.50)-Wraparound embossed chromium-c by Quesada; Solar app.; origin Aric (X-O Manowar) 5.00
0-Gold variant 2 4 6 11 16 20
1-Intro/1st app. & partial origin of Aric (X-O Manowar); Barry Smith/Layton-a 2 4 6 9 12 15
2-4: 2-B. Smith/Layton-c. 3-Layton-c(i). 4-1st app. Shadowman 1 3 4 6 8 10
5-15: 5-B. Smith-c. 6-Begin $2.25-c; Ditko-a(p). 7,8-Unity x-overs. 7-Miller-c. 8-Simonson-c. 12-1st app. Randy Calder. 14,15-Turok-c/stories 4.00
15-Hot pink logo variant; came with Ultra Pro Rigid Comic Sleeves box; no price on-c 1 2 3 5 6 8
16-24,26-43: 20-Serial number contest insert. 27-29-Turok x-over. 28-Bound-in trading card. 30-1st app. new "good skin"; Solar app. 33-Chaos Effect Delta Pt. 3. 42-Shadowman app.; includes X-O Manowar Birthquake! Prequel 3.00
25-($3.50)-Has 16 pg. Armorines #0 bound-in w/origin 4.00
44-68: 44-Begin $2.50-c. 50-X, 50-O, 51, 52, 63-Bart Sears-c/a/scripts. 68-Revealed that Aric's past stories were premonitions of his future 3.00
...: Birth HC (2008, $24.95) recolored reprints #0-6; script and breakdowns for #0; cover gallery; new "The Rise of Lydia" story by Layton and Leeke 25.00
Trade paperback nn (1993, $9.95)-Polybagged with copy of X-O Database #1 inside 15.00

Yearbook 1 (4/95, $2.95) 4.00
NOTE: *Layton a-1i, 2i(part); c-1, 2i, 3i, 6i, 21i. Reese a-4i(part); c-26i.*

X-O MANOWAR (2nd Series)(Also see Iron Man/X-O Manowar: Heavy Metal)
Acclaim Comics (Valiant Heroes): V2#1, Oct, 1996 - No. 21, Jun, 1998 ($2.50)
V2#1-21: 1-Mark Waid & Brian Augustyn scripts begin; 1st app. Donavon Wylie; Rand Banion dies; painted variant-c exists. 2-Donavon Wylie becomes new X-O Manowar. 7-9-Augustyn-s. 10-Copycat-c 3.00

X-O MANOWAR (3rd series)
Valiant Entertainment: May, 2012 - Present ($3.99)
1-Robert Venditti-s/Cary Nord-a/Esad Ribic-c; origin re-told 4.00
1-Pullbox variant-c by Nord 5.00
1-Variant-c by David Aja 10.00
1-QR Voice variant-c by Jelena Kevic-Djurdjevic 20.00
2-23: 2-Origin continues. 2,3-Kevic-Djurdjevic-c. 5-8-Ninjak app.; Garbett-a. 9,10-Hairsine-a 11-14-Planet Death; Nord-a. 19-21-Unity tie-in 4.00
2-5,8-14-Pullbox variant covers. 2-Lozzi. 3-Suayan. 4-Kramer. 5-Tan. 14-Eight-bit art 5.00

X-O MANOWAR FAN EDITION
Acclaim Comics (Valiant Heroes): Feb, 1997 (Overstreet's FAN giveaway)
1-Reintro the Armorines & the Hard Corps; 1st app. Citadel; Augustyn scripts; McKone-c/a 4.00

X-O MANOWAR/IRON MAN: IN HEAVY METAL (See Iron Man/X-O Manowar: Heavy Metal)
Acclaim Comics (Valiant Heroes): Sept, 1996 ($2.50, one-shot)
(1st Marvel/Valiant x-over)
1-Pt 1 of X-O Manowar/Iron Man x-over; Arnim Zola app.; Nicieza scripts; Andy Smith-a 5.00

XOMBI
DC Comics (Milestone): Jan, 1994 - No. 21, Feb, 1996 ($1.75/$2.50)
0-($1.95)-Shadow War x-over; Simonson silver ink varnish-c 3.00
1-21: 1-John Byrne-c 3.00
1-Platinum 8.00

XOMBI
DC Comics: May, 2011 - No. 6, Oct, 2011 ($2.99)
1-6-Rozum-s/Irving-a/c 3.00

X-PATROL
Marvel Comics (Amalgam): Apr, 1996 ($1.95, one-shot)
1-Cruz-a(p) 3.00

XSE
Marvel Comics: Nov, 1996 - No. 4, Feb, 1997 ($1.95, limited series)
1-4: 1-Bishop & Shard app. 3.00
1-Variant-c 4.00

X-STATIX
Marvel Comics: Sept, 2002 - No. 26, Oct, 2004 ($2.99/$2.25)
1-($2.99) Allred-a/c; intro. Venus Dee Milo; back-up w/Cooke-a 4.00
2-9-($2.25) 4-Quitely-c. 5-Pope-c/a 3.00
10-26: 10-Begin $2.99-c; Bond-a; U-Go Girl flashback. 13,14-Spider-Man app. 21-25-Avengers app. 26-Team dies 3.00
... Vol. 1: Good Omens TPB (2003, $11.99) r/#1-5 12.00
... Vol. 2: Good Guys & Bad Guys TPB (2003, $15.99) r/#6-10 & Wolverine/Doop #1&2 16.00
... Vol. 3: Back From the Dead TPB (2004, $19.99) r/#11-18 20.00
... Vol. 4: X-Statix Vs. the Avengers TPB (2004, $19.99) r/#19-26; pin-ups 20.00

X-STATIX PRESENTS: DEAD GIRL
Marvel Comics: Mar, 2006 - No. 5, July, 2006 ($2.99, limited series)
1-5-Dr. Strange, Dead Girl, Miss America, Tike app. Milligan-s/Dragotta & Allred-a 3.00
TPB (2006, $13.99) r/series 14.00

X-TERMINATION (Crossover with Astonishing X-Men and X-Treme X-Men)
Marvel Comics: May, 2013 - No. 2, Jun, 2013 ($3.99)
1,2-Lapham-s/David Lopez-a 4.00

X-TERMINATORS
Marvel Comics: Oct, 1988 - No. 4, Jan, 1989 ($1.00, limited series)
1-1st app.; X-Men/X-Factor tie-in; Williamson-i 5.00
2-4 4.00

X, THE MAN WITH THE X-RAY EYES (See Movie Comics)

X-TREME X-MEN (Also see Mekanix)
Marvel Comics: July, 2001 - No. 46, Jun, 2004 ($2.99/$3.50)
1-Claremont-s/Larroca-c/a 4.00
2-24: 2-Two covers (Larroca & Pacheco); Psylocke killed 3.00
25-35, 40-46: 25-30-God Loves, Man Kills II; Stryker app.; Kordey-a 3.00

X-Treme X-Men #7 © MAR

X-Venture #2 © Victory Mag.

Yankee Comics #2 © CHES

36-39-($3.50) 3.50
Annual 2001 ($4.95) issue opens longways 5.00
... Vol. 1: Destiny TPB (2002, $19.95) r/#1-9 20.00
... Vol. 2: Invasion TPB (2003, $19.99) r/#10-18 20.00
... Vol. 3: Schism TPB (2003, $16.99) r/#19-23; X-Treme X-Posé #1&2 17.00
... Vol. 4: Mekanix TPB (2003, $16.99) r/Mekanix #1-6 17.00
... Vol. 5: God Loves Man Kills TPB (2003, $19.99) r/#25-30 20.00
... Vol. 6: Intifada TPB (2004, $16.99) r/#24,31-35 17.00
... Vol. 7: Storm the Arena TPB (2004, $16.99) r/#36-39 17.00
... Vol. 8: Prisoner of Fire TPB (2004, $19.99) r/#40-46 and Annual 2001 20.00

X-TREME X-MEN
Marvel Comics: Sept, 2012 - No. 13, Jun, 2013 ($2.99)

1-13: 1-Pak-s/Segovia-a; Dazzler with alternate reality Wolverine, Nightcrawler, Emma 3.00
7.1-(2/12) Cyclops & The Brood app. 3.00

X-TREME X-MEN: SAVAGE LAND
Marvel Comics: Nov, 2001 - No. 4, Feb, 2002 ($2.99, limited series)

1-4-Claremont-s/Sharpe-c/a; Beast app. 3.00

X-TREME X-POSE
Marvel Comics: Jan, 2003 - No. 2, Feb, 2003 ($2.99, limited series)

1,2-Claremont-s/Ranson-a/Migliari-c 3.00

X-23 (See debut in NYX #3)(See NYX X-23 HC for reprint)
Marvel Comics: Mar, 2005 - No. 6, July, 2005 ($2.99, limited series)

1-Origin of the Wolverine clone girl; Tan-a 4.00
1-Variant Billy Tan-c with red background 5.00
2-6-Origin continues 3.00
2-Variant B&W sketch-c 5.00
One shot 1 (5/10, $3.99) Urasov-c/Lui-s; Wolverine & Jubilee app. 4.00
...: Innocence Lost MGC 1 (5/11, $1.00) r/#1 with "Marvel's Greatest Comics" cover logo 3.00
...: Innocence Lost TPB (2006, $15.99) r/#1-6 16.00

X-23
Marvel Comics: Nov, 2010 - No. 21, May, 2012 ($3.99/$2.99)

1-Marjorie Liu-s/Will Conrad-a; three covers by Luo, Djurdjevic & Dell'Otto; origin retold 4.00
2-21-($2.99) 2-Covers by Luo and Mayhew. 3,10-12,17-19-Takeda-a. 8,9-Daken app. 13-16-Spider-Man app.; Noto-a. 20-Jubilee app.; Noto-a. 21-Silent issue; Noto-a 3.00

X-23: TARGET X
Marvel Comics: Feb, 2007 - No. 6, July, 2007 ($2.99, limited series)

1-6-Kyle & Yost-s/Choi & Oback-a. 6-Gallery of variant covers and sketches 3.00
TPB (2007, $15.99) r/#1-6; gallery of variant covers and sketches 16.00

X-UNIVERSE
Marvel Comics: May, 1995 - No. 2, June, 1995 ($3.50, limited series)

1,2: Age of Apocalypse 5.00

X-VENTURE (Super Heroes)
Victory Magazines Corp.: July, 1947 - No. 2, Nov, 1947

1-Atom Wizard, Mystery Shadow, Lester Trumble begin
113 226 339 723 1237 1750
2 55 110 165 352 601 850

X-WOMEN
Marvel Comics: 2010 ($4.99, one-shot)

1-Milo Manara-a/Chris Claremont-s; a female X-Men adventure; Quesada afterword 5.00

XYR (See Eclipse Graphic Album Series #21)

YAK YAK
Dell Publishing Co.: No. 1186, May-July, 1961 - No. 1348, Apr-June, 1962

Four Color 1186 (#1)- Jack Davis-c/a; 2 versions, one minus 3 pgs.
8 16 24 51 96 140
Four Color 1348 (#2)-Davis c/a 7 14 21 46 86 125

YAKKY DOODLE & CHOPPER (TV) (See Dell Giant #44)
Gold Key: Dec, 1962 (Hanna-Barbera)

1 6 12 18 42 79 115

YANG (See House of Yang)
Charlton Comics: Nov, 1973 - No. 13, May, 1976; V14#15, Sept, 1985 - No. 17, Jan, 1986 (No V14#14, series resumes with #15)

1-Origin; Sattler-a begins; slavery-s 2 4 6 11 16 20
2-13(1976) 1 2 3 6 9 10
15-17(1986): 15-Reprints #1 (Low print run) 6.00
3,10,11(Modern Comics-r, 1977) 6.00

YANKEE COMICS
Harry 'A' Chesler: Sept, 1941 - No. 7, 1942?

1-Origin The Echo, The Enchanted Dagger, Yankee Doodle Jones, The Firebrand, & The Scarlet Sentry; Black Satan app.; Yankee Doodle Jones app. on all covers
200 400 600 1280 2190 3100
2-Origin Johnny Rebel; Major Victory app.; Barry Kuda begins
84 168 252 538 919 1300
3,4: 4-(3/42) 61 122 183 390 670 950
4 (nd, 1940s; 7-1/4x5", 68 pgs, distr. to the service)-Foxy Grandpa, Tom, Dick & Harry, Impy, Ace & Deuce, Dot & Dash, Ima Slooth by Jack Cole (Remington Morse publ.)
17 34 51 98 154 210
5-7 (nd; 10¢, 7-1/4x5", 68 pgs.)(Remington Morse publ.)-urges readers to send their copies to servicemen. 15 30 45 83 124 165

YANKEE DOODLE THE SPIRIT OF LIBERTY
Spire Publications: 1984 (no price, 36 pgs)

nn-Al Hartley-s/c/a 2 4 6 9 13 16

YANKS IN BATTLE
Quality Comics Group: Sept, 1956 - No. 4, Dec, 1956; 1963

1-Cuidera-c(i) 11 22 33 62 86 110
2-4: Cuidera-c(i) 8 16 24 40 50 60
I.W. Reprint #3(1963)-r/#?; exist? 2 4 6 9 12 15

YARDBIRDS, THE (G. I. Joe's Sidekicks)
Ziff-Davis Publishing Co.: Summer, 1952

1-By Bob Oskner 11 22 33 60 83 105

YARNS OF YELLOWSTONE
World Color Press: 1972 (50¢, 36 pgs.)

nn-Illustrated by Bill Chapman 2 4 6 9 12 15

YEAH!
DC Comics (Homage): Oct, 1999 - No. 9, Jun, 2000 ($2.95)

1-Bagge-s/Hernandez-a 3.00
2-9: 2-Editorial page contains adult language 3.00

YELLOW CLAW (Also see Giant Size Master of Kung Fu)
Atlas Comics (MjMC): Oct, 1956 - No. 4, Apr, 1957

1-Origin by Joe Maneely 123 246 369 787 1344 1900
2-Kirby-a 97 194 291 621 1061 1500
3,4-Kirby-a; 4-Kirby/Severin-a 94 188 282 602 1026 1450
NOTE: *Everett c-3. **Maneely** c-1. **Reinman** a-2i, 3. **Severin** c-2, 4.*

YELLOWJACKET COMICS (Jack in the Box #11 on)(See TNT Comics)
E. Levy/Frank Comunale/Charlton: Sept, 1944 - No. 10, June, 1946

1-Intro & origin Yellowjacket; Diana, the Huntress begins; E.A. Poe's "The Black Cat" adaptation 68 136 204 435 743 1050
2-Yellowjacket-c begin, end #10 43 86 129 271 461 650
3,5 42 84 126 265 445 625
4-E.A. Poe's "Fall of the House Of Usher" adaptation; Palais-a
42 84 126 265 445 625
6 41 82 123 256 428 600
7-Classic skull-c; Toth-a (1 pg. gag feature) 65 130 195 416 708 1000
8-10: 1,3,4,6-10-Have stories narrated by old witch in "Tales of Terror" (1st horror series?)
40 80 120 246 411 575

YELLOWSTONE KELLY (Movie)
Dell Publishing Co.: No. 1056, Nov-Jan, 1959/60

Four Color 1056-Clint Walker photo-c 5 10 15 34 60 85

YELLOW SUBMARINE (See Movie Comics)

YEAR ONE: BATMAN/RA'S AL GHUL
DC Comics: 2005 - No. 2, 2005 ($5.99, squarebound, limited series)

1-Devin Grayson-s/Paul Gulacy-a 6.00
TPB (2006, $9.99) r/#1,2 10.00

YEAR ONE: BATMAN SCARECROW
DC Comics: 2005 - No. 2, 2005 ($5.99, squarebound, limited series)

1-Scarecrow's origin; Bruce Jones-s/Sean Murphy-a 6.00

YOGI BEAR (See Dell Giant #41, Golden Comics Digest, Kite Fun Book, March of Comics #253, 265, 279, 291, 309, 319, 337, 344, Movie Comics under "Hey There It's..." & Whitman Comic Books)

YOGI BEAR (TV) (Hanna-Barbera) (See Four Color #990)
Dell Publishing Co./Gold Key No. 10 on: No. 1067, 12-2/59-60 - No. 9, 7-9/62; No. 10, 10/62 - No. 42, 10/70

Four Color 1067 (#1)-TV show debuted 1/30/61 11 22 33 73 157 240
Four Color 1104,1162 (5-7/61) 7 14 21 48 89 130

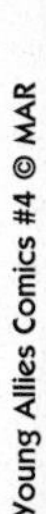

Young Allies Comics #4 © MAR

Young Avengers #10 © MAR

Youngblood V2 #14 © Rob Liefeld

	GD 2.0	VG 4.0	FN 6.0	VF 8.0	VF/NM 9.0	NM- 9.2

4(8-9/61) - 6(12-1/61-62) 5 10 15 33 57 80
Four Color 1271(11/61) 5 10 15 35 63 90
Four Color 1349(1/62)-Photo-c 7 14 21 49 92 135
7(2-3/62) - 9(7-9/62)-Last Dell 5 10 15 33 57 80
10(10/62-G.K.), 11(1/63)-titled "Yogi Bear Jellystone Jollies" (80 pgs.); 11-X-Mas-c
6 12 18 41 76 110
12(4/63), 14-20 4 8 12 28 47 65
13(7/63, 68 pgs.)-Surprise Party 6 12 18 40 73 105
21-30 3 6 9 19 30 40
31-42 3 6 9 16 24 32

YOGI BEAR (TV)
Charlton Comics: Nov, 1970 - No. 35, Jan, 1976 (Hanna-Barbera)

1 5 10 15 30 50 70
2-6,8-10 3 6 9 16 24 32
7-Summer Fun (Giant, 52 pgs.) 4 8 12 27 44 60
11-20 3 6 9 15 22 28
21-35: 28-31-partial-r 2 4 6 11 16 20
Digest (nn, 1972, 75¢-c, B&W, 100 pgs.) (scarce) 3 6 9 18 28 38

YOGI BEAR (TV)(See The Flintstones, 3rd series & Spotlight #1)
Marvel Comics Group: Nov, 1977 - No. 9, Mar, 1979 (Hanna-Barbera)

1,7-9: 1-Flintstones begin (Newsstand sales only) 3 6 9 16 23 30
2-6 2 4 6 11 16 20

YOGI BEAR (TV)
Harvey Comics: Sept, 1992 - No. 6, Mar, 1994 ($1.25/$1.50) (Hanna-Barbera)

V2#1-6 3.00
...Big Book V2#1,2 ($1.95, 52 pgs): 1-(11/92). 2-(3/93) 4.00
...Giant Size V2#1,2 ($2.25, 68 pgs.): 1-(10/92). 2-(4/93) 4.00

YOGI BEAR (TV)
Archie Publ.: May, 1997

1 3.00

YOGI BEAR'S EASTER PARADE (See The Funtastic World of Hanna-Barbera #2)

YOGI BERRA (Baseball hero)
Fawcett Publications: 1951 (Yankee catcher)

nn-Photo-c (scarce) 74 148 222 470 810 1150

YOSEMITE SAM (...& Bugs Bunny) (TV)
Gold Key/Whitman: Dec, 1970 - No. 81, Feb, 1984

1 5 10 15 30 50 70
2-10 3 6 9 16 23 30
11-20 2 4 6 11 16 20
21-30 2 4 6 9 13 16
31-50 2 4 6 8 10 12
51-65 (Gold Key) 1 2 3 5 7 9
66,67 (Whitman) 2 4 6 8 10 12
68(9/80), 69(10/80), 70(12/80) 3-pack only 4 8 12 23 37 50
71-78: 76(2/82), 77(3/82), 78(4/82) 2 4 6 9 13 16
79-81 (All #90263 on-c, no date or date code; 3-pack): 79(7/83). 80(8/83). 81(2/84)-(1/3-r)
3 6 9 16 23 30
(See March of Comics #363, 380, 392)

YOSSEL
DC Comics: 2003/2011 ($14.99, B&W graphic novel)

SC-Joe Kubert-s/a/c; Nazi-occupied Poland during World War II 15.00

YOUNG ALLIES
Marvel Comics: Aug, 2010 - No. 6, Jan, 2011 ($3.99/$2.99)

1-($3.99) Wraparound-c; Nomad, Araña, Firestar, Gravity, Toro team-up; origin pages 4.00
2-6-($2.99) 2-Lafuente-c/McKeever-s/Baldeon-a. 6-Miyazawa-c; Emma Frost app. 3.00

YOUNG ALLIES COMICS (All-Winners #21; see Kid Komics #2)
Timely Comics (USA 1-7/NPI 8,9/YAI 10-20): Sum, 1941 - No. 20, Oct, 1946

1-Origin/1st app. The Young Allies (Bucky, Toro, others); 1st meeting of Captain America & Human Torch; Red Skull-c & app.; S&K-c/splash; Hitler-c; Note: the cover was altered after its preview in Human Torch #5. Stalin was shown with Hitler but was removed due to Russia becoming an ally 1300 2600 3900 9100 16,250 26,000
2-(Winter, 1941)-Captain America & Human Torch app.; Simon & Kirby-c
423 846 1269 3000 5250 7500
3-Remember Pearl Harbor issue (Spring, 1942); Stan Lee scripts; Vs. Japanese-c/full-length story; Captain America & Human Torch app.; Father Time story by Alderman
371 742 1113 2600 4550 6500
4-The Vagabond & Red Skull, Capt. America, Human Torch app. Classic Red Skull-c
514 1028 1542 3750 6625 9500
5-Captain America & Human Torch app. 245 490 735 1568 2684 3800
6,7: 6-Japanese/Nazi war-c 174 348 522 1114 1907 2700
8-Classic Schomburg WWII Japanese bondage-c 194 388 582 1242 2121 3000
9-Hitler, Tojo, Mussolini-c. 271 542 813 1734 2967 4200
10-Classic Schomburg Hooded Villain bondage-c; origin Tommy Tyme & Clock of Ages; ends #19 174 348 522 1114 1907 2700
11-16: 12-Classic decapitation story; Japanese war-c. 16-Last Schomburg WWII-c
142 284 426 909 1555 2200
17-20 107 214 321 685 1168 1650
NOTE: ***Brodsky** c-15. **Ferstadt** a-3. **Gabriele** a-3; c-3, 4. **S&K** c-1, 2. **Schomburg** c-5-13, 16-19. **Shores** c-20.*

YOUNG ALLIES 70TH ANNIVERSARY SPECIAL
Marvel Comics: Aug, 2009 ($3.99, one-shot)

1-Bucky & Young Allies app.; Stern-s/Rivera-a; Terry Vance rep. from Marvel Myst. #14 5.00

YOUNG ALL-STARS
DC Comics: June, 1987 - No. 31, Nov, 1989 ($1.00, deluxe format)

1-31: 1-1st app. Iron Munro & The Flying Fox. 8,9-Millennium tie-ins 4.00
Annual 1 (1988, $2.00) 4.00

YOUNG AVENGERS
Marvel Comics: Apr, 2005 - No. 12, Aug, 2006 ($2.99)

1-Intro. Iron Lad, Patriot, Hulkling, Asgardian; Heinberg-s/Cheung-a 5.00
1-Director's Cut (2005, $3.99) r/#1 plus character sketches; original script 4.00
2-12: 3-6-Kang app. 7-DiVito-a. 9-Skrulls app. 3.00
... Special 1 (2/06, $3.99) origins of the heroes; art by various incl. Neal Adams, Jae Lee, Bill Sienkiewicz, Gene Ha, Michael Gaydos and Pasqual Ferry 4.00
... Vol. 1: Sidekicks HC (2005, $19.99, dustjacket) r/#1-6; character design sketches 20.00
... Vol. 1: Sidekicks TPB (2006, $14.99) r/#1-6; character design sketches 15.00
... Vol. 2: Family Matters HC (2006, $22.99, dustjacket) r/#7-12 & YA Special #1 23.00
... Vol. 2: Family Matters SC (2007, $17.99) r/#7-12 & YA Special #1 18.00
HC (2008, $29.99, d.j.) oversized reprint of #1-12 and Special #1; script & sketch pages 30.00

YOUNG AVENGERS (Marvel NOW!)
Marvel Comics: Mar, 2013 - No. 15, Mar, 2014 ($2.99)

1-15: 1-Loki assembles team; Marvel Boy, Miss America app.; Gillen-s/McKelvie-a/c. 11-Loki ages back to adult. 14,15-Multiple artists 3.00
1-Variant-c by Bryan Lee O'Malley 6.00
1-Variant-c by Skottie Young 6.00

YOUNG AVENGERS PRESENTS
Marvel Comics: Mar, 2008 - No. 6, Aug, 2008 ($2.99, limited series)

1-6: 1-Patriot; Bucky app. 2-Hulkling; Captain Marvel app. 3-Wiccan & Speed. 4-Vision. 5-Stature. 6-Hawkeye; Clint Barton app.; Alan Davis-a 3.00

YOUNGBLOOD (See Brigade #4, Megaton Explosion & Team Youngblood)
Image Comics (Extreme Studios): Apr, 1992 - No. 4, Feb, 1993 ($2.50, lim. series); No. 6, June, 1994 (No #5) - No. 10, Dec, 1994 ($1.95/$2.50)

1-Liefeld-c/a/scripts in all; flip book format with 2 trading cards; 1st Image/Extreme Studios title. 5.00
1,2-2nd printing 3.00
2-(JUN-c, July 1992 indicia)-1st app. Shadowhawk in solo back-up story; 2 trading cards inside; flip book format; 1st app. Prophet, Kirby, Berzerkers, Darkthorn 4.00
3,0,4,5: 3-(OCT-c, August 1992 indicia)-Contains 2 trading cards inside (flip book); 1st app. Supreme in back-up story; 1st app. Showdown. 0-(12/92, $1.95)-Contains 2 trading cards; 2 cover variations exist, green or beige logo; w/Image #0 coupon. 4-(2/93)-Glow-in-the-dark cover w/2 trading cards; 2nd app. Dale Keown's The Pitt; Bloodstrike app. 5-Flip book w/Brigade #4 3.00
6-($3.50, 52 pgs.)-Wraparound-c 4.00
7-10: 7, 8-Liefeld-c(p)/a(p)/story. 8,9-(9/94) 9-Valentino story & art 3.00
Battlezone 1 (May-c, 4/93 inside, $1.95)-Arsenal book; Liefeld-c(p) 3.00
Battlezone 2 (7/94, $2.95)-Wraparound-c 4.00
Image Firsts: Youngblood #1 (3/10, $1.00) reprints #1 3.00
...Super Special (Winter '97, $2.99) Sprouse -a 4.00
Yearbook 1 (7/93, $2.50)-Fold out panel; 1st app. Tyrax & Kanan 4.00
Vol. 1 HC (2008, $34.99) oversized r/#1-5, recolored and remastered; sketch art and cover gallery; Mark Millar intro. 35.00
TPB (1996, $16.95)-r/Team Youngblood #8-10 & Youngblood #6-8,10 17.00

YOUNGBLOOD
Image Comics (Extreme Studios)/Maximum Press No. 14: V2#1, Sept, 1995 - No. 14, Dec, 1996 ($2.50)

V2#1-10,14: Roger Cruz-a in all. 4-Extreme Destroyer Pt. 4 w/gaming card. 5-Variant-c exists. 6-Angela & Glory. 7-Shadowhunt Pt. 3; Shadowhawk app. 8,10-Thor (from Supreme) app. 10-(7/96). 14-(12/96)-1st Maximum Press issue 3.00

YOUNGBLOOD (Volume 3)
Awesome/ Awesome-Hyperwerks #2: Feb, 1998 - No. 2, Aug, 1998 ($2.50)

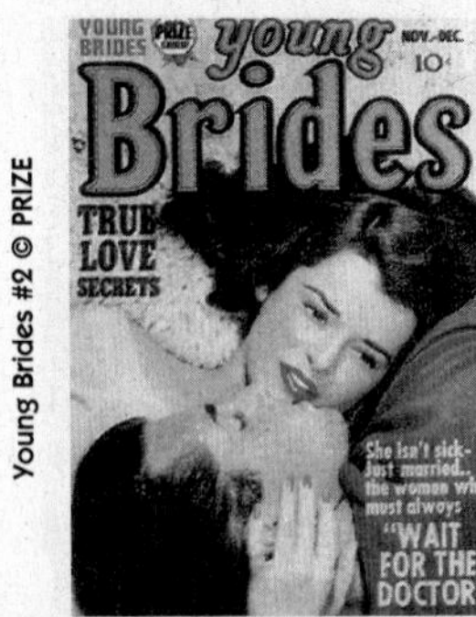

Young Brides #2 © PRIZE

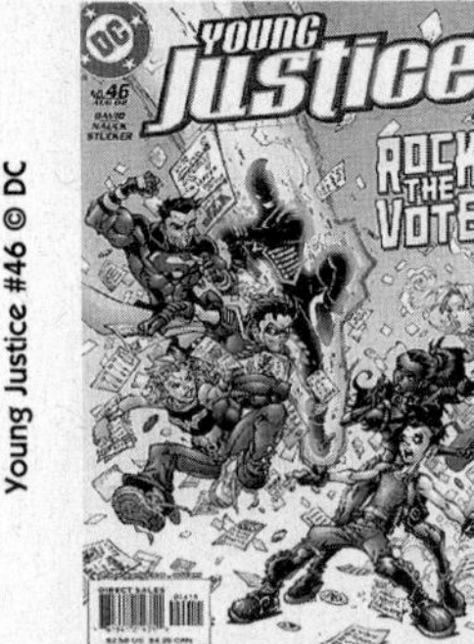

Young Justice #46 © DC

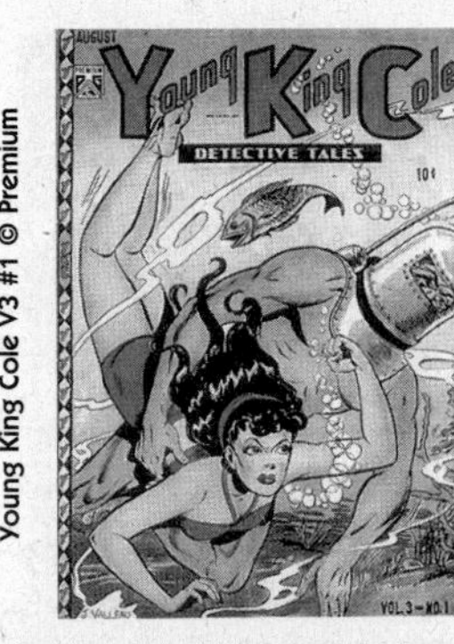

Young King Cole V3 #1 © Premium

	GD 2.0	VG 4.0	FN 6.0	VF 8.0	VF/NM 9.0	NM- 9.2

1-Alan Moore-s/Skroce & Stucker-a; 12 diff. covers 3.00
2-(8/98) Skroce & Liefeld covers 3.00
...Imperial 1 (Arcade Comics, 6/04, $2.99) Kirkman-sMychaels-a 3.00

YOUNGBLOOD (Volume 4)
Image Comics: Jan, 2008 - No. 9, Sept, 2009; No. 71, May, 2012 - Present ($2.99/$3.99)

1-7-Casey-s/Donovan-a; two covers by Donovan & Liefeld on each 3.00
8-Obama flip cover by Liefeld; Obama app. in story 3.00
9-(9/09, $3.99) Obama flip cover by Liefeld; Free Agent rejoins; Obama app. in story 4.00
71-74: 71-(5/12, $2.99) Liefeld & Malin-a; three covers 3.00
75-(1/13, $4.99) Five covers; Malin-a 5.00
76-78-($3.99) Malin-a 4.00

YOUNGBLOOD: STRIKEFILE
Image Comics (Extreme Studios): Apr, 1993 - No. 11, Feb, 1995 ($1.95/$2.50/$2.95)

1-10: 1-($1.95)-Flip book w/Jae Lee-c/a & Liefeld-c/a in #1-3; 1st app. The Allies,Giger, & Glory. 3-Thibert-i asisst. 4-Liefeld-c(p); no Lee-a. 5-Liefeld-c(p). 8-Platt-c 3.00
NOTE: *Youngblood: Strikefile began as a four issue limited series.*

YOUNGBLOOD/X-FORCE
Image Comics (Extreme Studios): July, 1996 ($4.95, one-shot)

1-Cruz-a(p); two covers exist 5.00

YOUNG BRIDES (True Love Secrets)
Feature/Prize Publ.: Sept-Oct, 1952 - No. 30, Nov-Dec, 1956 (Photo-c: 1-6)

	GD	VG	FN	VF	VF/NM	NM-
V1#1-Simon & Kirby-a	41	82	123	256	428	600
2-S&K-a	23	46	69	136	223	310
3-6-S&K-a	20	40	60	120	195	270
V2#1-7,10-12 (#7-18)-S&K-a	20	40	60	114	182	250
8,9-No S&K-a	11	22	33	62	86	110
V3#1-3(#19-21)-Last precode (3-4/55)	10	20	30	58	79	100
4,6(#22,24), V4#1,3(#25,27)	10	20	30	54	72	90
V3#5(#23)-Meskin-c	10	20	30	56	76	95
V4#2(#26)-All S&K issue	19	38	57	109	172	235
V4#4(#28)-S&K-a	15	30	45	86	133	180
V4#5,6(#29,30)	10	20	30	58	79	100

YOUNG DR. MASTERS (See The Adventures of Young Dr. Masters)

YOUNG DOCTORS, THE
Charlton Comics: Jan, 1963 - No. 6, Nov, 1963

	GD	VG	FN	VF	VF/NM	NM-
V1#1	3	6	9	20	31	42
2-6	3	6	9	14	19	24

YOUNG EAGLE
Fawcett Publications/Charlton: 12/50 - No. 10, 6/52; No. 3, 7/56 - No. 5, 4/57 (Photo-c: 1-10)

	GD	VG	FN	VF	VF/NM	NM-
1-Intro Young Eagle	18	36	54	103	162	220
2-Complete picture novelette "The Mystery of Thunder Canyon"	10	20	30	58	79	100
3-9	9	18	27	50	65	80
10-Origin Thunder, Young Eagle's Horse	8	16	24	44	57	70
3-5(Charlton)-Formerly Sherlock Holmes?	7	14	21	35	43	50

YOUNG GUNS SKETCHBOOK
Marvel Comics: Feb, 2005 ($3.99, one-shot)

1-Sketch pages from 2005 Marvel projects by Coipel, Granov, McNiven, Land & others 4.00

YOUNG HEARTS
Marvel Comics (SPC): Nov, 1949 - No. 2, Feb, 1950

	GD	VG	FN	VF	VF/NM	NM-
1-Photo-c	18	36	54	105	165	225
2-Colleen Townsend photo-c from movie	13	26	39	74	105	135

YOUNG HEARTS IN LOVE
Super Comics: 1964

	GD	VG	FN	VF	VF/NM	NM-
17,18: 17-r/Young Love V5#6 (4-5/62)	2	4	6	9	13	16

YOUNG HEROES (Formerly Forbidden Worlds #34)
American Comics Group (Titan): No. 35, Feb-Mar, 1955 - No. 37, Jun-Jul, 1955

	GD	VG	FN	VF	VF/NM	NM-
35-37-Frontier Scout	10	20	30	54	72	90

YOUNG HEROES IN LOVE
DC Comics: June, 1997 - No. 17; #1,000,000, Nov, 1998 ($1.75/$1.95/$2.50)

1-1st app. Young Heroes; Madan-a 4.00
2-17: 3-Superman-c/app. 7-Begin $1.95-c 3.00
#1,000,000 (11/98, $2.50) 853 Century x-over 3.00

YOUNG INDIANA JONES CHRONICLES, THE
Dark Horse Comics: Feb, 1992 - No. 12, Feb, 1993 ($2.50)

1-12: Dan Barry scripts in all 3.00
NOTE: ***Dan Barry** a(p)-1, 2, 5, 6, 10; c-1-10. **Morrow** a-3, 4, 5p, 6p. **Springer** a-1i, 2i.*

YOUNG INDIANA JONES CHRONICLES, THE
Hollywood Comics (Disney): 1992 ($3.95, squarebound, 68 pgs.)

1-3: 1-r/YIJC #1,2 by D. Horse. 2-r/#3,4. 3-r/#5,6 4.00

YOUNG JUSTICE (Also see Teen Titans, Titans/Young Justice and DC Comics Presents: ...)
DC Comics: Sept, 1998 - No. 55, May, 2003 ($2.50/$2.75)

1-Robin, Superboy & Impulse team-up; David-s/Nauck-a 4.00
2,3: 3-Mxyzptlk app. 3.00
4-20: 4-Wonder Girl, Arrowette and the Secret join. 6-JLA app. 13-Supergirl x-over. 20-Sins of Youth aftermath 3.00
21-49: 25-Empress ID revealed. 28,29-Forever People app. 32-Empress origin. 35,36-Our Worlds at War x-over. 38-Joker: Last Laugh. 41-The Ray joins. 42-Spectre-c/app. 44,45-World Without YJ x-over pt. 1,5; Ramos-c. 48-Begin $2.75-c 3.00
50-($3.95) Wonder Twins, CM3 and other various DC teen heroes app. 4.00
51-55: 53,54-Darkseid app. 55-Last issue; leads into Titans/Young Justice mini-series 3.00
#1,000,000 (11/98) 853 Century x-over 3.00
...: A League of Their Own (2000, $14.95, TPB) r/#1-7, Secret Files #1 15.00
...: 80-Page Giant (5/99, $4.95) Ramos-c; stories and art by various 5.00
...: In No Man's Land (7/99, $3.95) McDaniel-c 4.00
...: Our Worlds at War (8/01, $2.95) Jae Lee-c; Linear Men app. 3.00
...: Secret Files (1/99, $4.95) Origin-s & pin-ups 5.00
...: The Secret (6/98, $1.95) Girlfrenzy; Nauck-a 3.00

YOUNG JUSTICE (Based on the 2011 Cartoon Network series)
DC Comics: No. 0, Mar, 2011 - No. 25, Apr, 2013 ($2.99)

0-19: 1-Miss Martian joins; Joker app. 2-Joker-c/app. 5-Kid Flash & Aqualad origins 3.00
20-25: 20-(11/12) Starts Invasion; 5 years later 3.00
FCBD 2011 Young Justice Batman BB Super Sampler (7/11) Flash app. 3.00

YOUNG JUSTICE: SINS OF YOUTH (Also see Sins of Youth x-over issues and Sins of Youth: Secret Files)
DC Comics: May, 2000 - No. 2, May, 2000 ($3.95, limited series)

1,2-Young Justice, JLA & JSA swap ages; David-s/Nauck-a 4.00
TPB (2000, $19.95) r/#1,2 & all x-over issues) 20.00

YOUNG KING COLE (...Detective Tales)(Becomes Criminals on the Run)
Premium Group/Novelty Press: Fall, 1945 - V3#12, July, 1948

	GD	VG	FN	VF	VF/NM	NM-
V1#1-Toni Gayle begins	34	68	102	199	325	450
2	16	32	48	94	147	200
3-4	15	30	45	86	133	180
V2#1-7(8-9/46-7/47): 6,7-Certa-c	13	26	39	72	101	130
V3#1,3-6,8,9,12: 3-Certa-c. 5-McWilliams-c/a. 8,9-Harmon-c	12	24	36	69	97	125
2-L.B. Cole-a; Certa-c	16	32	48	94	147	200
7-L.B. Cole-c/a	21	42	63	124	202	280
10,11-L.B. Cole-c	19	38	57	109	172	235

YOUNG LAWYERS, THE (TV)
Dell Publishing Co.: Jan, 1971 - No. 2, Apr, 1971 (photo-c)

	GD	VG	FN	VF	VF/NM	NM-
1	3	6	9	16	23	30
2	2	4	6	11	16	20

YOUNG LIARS (David Lapham's...)(See Vertigo Double Shot for reprint of #1)
DC Comics (Vertigo): May, 2008 - No. 18, Oct, 2009 ($2.99)

1-18: 1-Intro. Sadie Dawkins; David Lapham-s/a/c in all 3.00
...: Daydream Believer TPB (2008, $9.99) r/#1-6; Gerald Way intro. 10.00
...: Maestro TPB (2009, $14.99) r/#7-12; Peter Milligan intro. 15.00
...: Rock Life TPB (2010, $14.99) r/#13-18; Brian Azzarello intro. 15.00

YOUNG LIFE (Teen Life #3 on)
New Age Publ./Quality Comics Group: Summer, 1945 - No. 2, Fall, 1945

	GD	VG	FN	VF	VF/NM	NM-
1-Skip Homeier, Louis Prima stories	18	36	54	105	165	225
2-Frank Sinatra photo on-c plus story	20	40	60	117	189	260

YOUNG LOVE (Sister title to Young Romance)
Prize(Feature)Publ.(Crestwood): 2-3/49 - No. 73, 12-1/56-57; V3#5, 2-3/60 - V7#1, 6-7/63

	GD	VG	FN	VF	VF/NM	NM-
V1#1-S&K-c/a(2)	63	126	189	403	689	975
2-Photo-c begin; S&K-a	34	68	102	199	325	450
3-S&K-a	22	44	66	132	216	300
4-6-Minor S&K-a	16	32	48	94	147	200
V2#1(#7)-S&K-a(2)	21	42	63	126	206	285
2-5(#8-11)-Minor S&K-a	15	30	45	83	124	165
6,8(#12,14)-S&K-c only. 14-S&K 1 pg. art	17	34	51	98	154	210
7,9-12(#13,15-18)-S&K-c/a	21	42	63	126	206	285
V3#1-4(#19-22)-S&K-c/a	20	40	60	117	189	260
5-7,9-12(#23-25,27-30)-Photo-c resume; S&K-a	17	34	51	98	154	210
8(#26)-No S&K-a	10	20	30	58	79	100

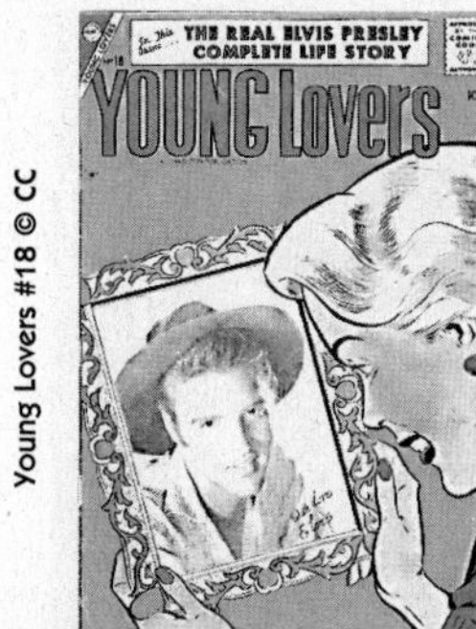

Young Lovers #18 © CC

Young X-Men #1 © MAR

Youthful Romances #5 © Pix-Parade

	GD 2.0	VG 4.0	FN 6.0	VF 8.0	VF/NM 9.0	NM- 9.2
V4#1,6(#31,36)-S&K-a	15	30	45	88	137	185
2-5,7-12(#32-35,37-42)-Minor S&K-a	14	28	42	78	112	145
V5#1-12(#43-54), V6#3,7,9(#57,61,63)-Last precode	9	18	27	54	72	90
V6#1,2,4-6,8(#55,56,58-60,62) S&K-a	11	22	33	62	86	110
V6#10-12(#64-66)	5	10	15	31	53	75
V7#1-7(#67-73)	4	8	12	28	47	65
V3#5(2-3/60),6(4-5/60)(Formerly All For Love)	4	8	12	25	40	55
V4#1(6-7/60)-6(4-5/61)	4	8	12	23	37	50
V5#1(6-7/61)-6(4-5/62)	4	8	12	23	37	50
V6#1(6-7/62)-6(4-5/63), V7#1	4	8	12	22	35	48

NOTE: ***Meskin** a-14(2), 27, 42. **Powell** a-V4#6. **Severin/Elder** a-V1#3. S&K art not in #53, 57, 61, 63-65. Photo-c most V3#5-V5#11.*

YOUNG LOVE
National Periodical Publ.(Arleigh Publ. Corp #49-61)/DC Comics: #39, 9-10/63 - #120, Wint./75-76; #121, 10/76 - #126, 7/77

	GD	VG	FN	VF	VF/NM	NM-
39	5	10	15	34	60	85
40-50	4	8	12	27	44	60
51-68,70	4	8	12	25	40	55
69-(68 pg. Giant)(8-9/68)	6	12	18	38	69	100
71,72,74-77,80	3	6	9	20	31	42
73,78,79-Toth-a	3	6	9	21	33	45
81-99: 88-96-(52 pg. Giants)	3	6	9	19	30	40
100	3	6	9	20	31	42
101-106,115-120	3	6	9	16	24	32
107 (100 pgs.)	7	14	21	49	92	135
108-114 (100 pgs.)	7	14	21	44	82	120
121-126 (52 pgs.)	4	8	12	26	41	55

NOTE: ***Bolle** a-117. **Colan** a-107r. **Nasser** a-123, 124. **Orlando** a-122. **Simonson** c-125. **Toth** a-73, 78, 79, 122-125r. **Wood** a-109r(4 pgs.).*

YOUNG LOVER ROMANCES (Formerly & becomes Great Lover...)
Toby Press: No. 4, June, 1952 - No. 5, Aug, 1952

	GD	VG	FN	VF	VF/NM	NM-
4,5-Photo-c	11	22	33	60	83	105

YOUNG LOVERS (My Secret Life #19 on)(Formerly Brenda Starr?)
Charlton Comics: No. 16, July, 1956 - No. 18, May, 1957

	GD	VG	FN	VF	VF/NM	NM-
16,17('56): 16-Marcus Swayze-a	11	22	33	64	90	115
18-Elvis Presley picture-c, text story (biography)(Scarce)	76	152	228	486	831	1175

YOUNG MARRIAGE
Fawcett Publications: June, 1950

	GD	VG	FN	VF	VF/NM	NM-
1-Powell-a; photo-c	14	28	42	81	118	155

YOUNG MEN (Formerly Cowboy Romances)(...on the Battlefield #12-20(4/53); ...In Action #21)
Marvel/Atlas Comics (IPC): No. 4, 6/50 - No. 11, 10/51; No. 12, 12/51 - No. 28, 6/54

	GD	VG	FN	VF	VF/NM	NM-
4-(52 pgs.)	22	44	66	132	216	300
5-11	15	30	45	85	130	175
12-23: 12-20-War format. 21-23-Hot Rod issues starring Flash Foster	15	30	45	83	124	165
24-(12/53)-Origin Captain America, Human Torch, & Sub-Mariner which are revived thru #28; Red Skull app.	326	652	978	2282	3991	5700
25-28: 25-Romita-c/a (see Men's Advs.). 27-Death of Golden Age Red Skull	148	296	444	947	1624	2300
25-2nd printing (1994)	2	4	6	8	10	12

NOTE: ***Berg** a-7, 14, 17, 18, 20; c-17? **Brodsky** c-4-9, 13, 14, 16, 17, 21-25. **Burgos** c-26-28. **Colan** a-14, 15, 20. **Everett** a-18-20. **Heath** a-13, 14. **Maneely** c-10-12, 15. **Pakula** a-14, 15. **Robinson** c-18. Captain America by **Romita**-#24?, 25, 26?, 27, 28. Human Torch by **Burgos**-#25, 27, 28. Sub-Mariner by **Everett**-#24-28.*

YOUNG REBELS, THE (TV)
Dell Publishing Co.: Jan, 1971

	GD	VG	FN	VF	VF/NM	NM-
1-Photo-c	3	6	9	14	19	24

YOUNG ROMANCE COMICS (The 1st romance comic)
Prize/Headline (Feature Publ.) (Crestwood): Sept-Oct, 1947 - V16#4, June-July, 1963 (#1-33: 52 pgs.)

	GD	VG	FN	VF	VF/NM	NM-
V1#1-S&K-c/a(2)	76	152	228	486	831	1175
2-S&K-c/a(2-3)	40	80	120	246	411	575
3-6-S&K-c/a(2-3) each	36	72	108	216	351	485
V2#1-6(#7-12)-S&K-c/a(2-3) each	32	64	96	188	307	425
V3#1-3(#13-15): V3#1-Photo-c begin; S&K-a	20	40	60	118	192	265
4-12(#16-24)-Photo-c; S&K-a	20	40	60	118	192	265
V4#1-11(#25-35)-S&K-a	20	40	60	114	182	250
12(#36)-S&K, Toth-a	20	40	60	118	192	265
V5#1-12(#37-48), V6#4-12(#52-60)-S&K-a	20	40	60	114	182	250
V6#1-3(#49-51)-No S&K-a	11	22	33	62	86	110
V7#1-11(#61-71)-S&K-a in most	15	30	45	88	137	185
V7#12(#72), V8#1-3(#73-75)-Last precode (12-1/54-55)-No S&K-a	10	20	30	56	76	95
V8#4(#76, 4-5/55), 5(#77)-No S&K-a	9	18	27	52	69	85
V8#6-8(#78-80, 12-1/55-56)-S&K-a	14	28	42	78	112	145
V9#3,5,6(#81, 2-3/56, 83,84)-S&K-a	14	28	42	78	112	145
4, V10#1(#82,85)-All S&K-a	14	28	42	82	121	160
V10#2-6(#86-90, 10-11/57)-S&K-a	8	16	24	52	99	145
V11#1,2,5,6(#91,92,95,96)-S&K-a	8	16	24	52	99	145
3,4(#93,94), V12#2,4,5(#98,100,101)-No S&K	5	10	15	31	53	75
V12#1,3,6(#97,99,102)-S&K-a	8	16	24	52	99	145
V13#1(#103)-Powell-a; S&K's last-a for Crestwood	8	16	24	52	99	145
2,4-6(#104-108)	4	8	12	28	47	65
V13#3(#105, 4-5/60)-Elvis Presley-c app. only	8	16	24	54	102	150
V14#1-6, V15#1-6, V16#1-4(#109-124)	4	8	12	27	44	60

NOTE: ***Meskin** a-16, 24(2), 33, 47, 50. **Robinson/Meskin** a-6. **Leonard Starr** a-11. Photo c-13-32, 34-65. Issues 1-3 say "Designed for the More **Adult** Readers of **Comics**" on cover.*

YOUNG ROMANCE COMICS (Continued from Prize series)
National Periodical Publ.(Arleigh Publ. Corp. No. 127): No. 125, Aug-Sept, 1963 - No. 208, Nov-Dec, 1975

	GD	VG	FN	VF	VF/NM	NM-
125	7	14	21	44	82	120
126-140	5	10	15	30	50	70
141-153,156-162,165-169	4	8	12	23	37	50
154-Neal Adams-c	5	10	15	31	53	75
155-1st publ. Aragonés-s (no art)	5	10	15	30	50	70
163,164-Toth-a	4	8	12	27	44	60
170-172 (68 pg. Giants): 170-Michell from Young Love ends; Lily Martin, the Swinger begins	5	10	15	30	50	70
173-183 (52 pgs.)	4	8	12	23	37	50
184-196	3	6	9	17	26	35
197-204-(100 pgs.)	7	14	21	44	82	120
205-208	3	6	9	16	24	32

YOUNG ROMANCE: THE NEW 52 VALENTINE'S DAY SPECIAL
DC Comics: Apr, 2013 ($7.99, one-shot)

1-Short stories by various; Superman/Wonder Woman-c by Rocafort; bonus valentines 8.00

YOUNG X-MEN
Marvel Comics: May, 2008 - No. 12, May, 2009 ($2.99)

1-12: 1-Cyclops forms new team; Guggenheim-s/Paquette-a/Dodson-c. 11,12-Acuña-a 3.00

YOUR DREAMS (See Strange World of...)

YOUR HIGHNESS
Dark Horse Comics: 2011 ($7.99, one-shot)

nn-Prequel to 2011 movie; Danny McBride & Jeff Fradley-s/Phillips-a/c 8.00

YOUR UNITED STATES
Lloyd Jacquet Studios: 1946

	GD	VG	FN	VF	VF/NM	NM-
nn-Used in **SOTI**, pg. 309,310; Sid Greene-a	25	50	75	150	245	340

YOUTHFUL HEARTS (Daring Confessions #4 on)
Youthful Magazines: May, 1952 - No. 3, Sept, 1952

	GD	VG	FN	VF	VF/NM	NM-
1- "Monkey on Her Back" swipes E.C. drug story/Shock SuspenStories #12; Frankie Laine photo on-c; Doug Wildey-a in al	36	72	108	211	343	475
2,3: 2-Vic Damone photo on-c. 3-Johnny Raye photo on-c	21	42	63	124	202	280

YOUTHFUL LOVE (Truthful Love #2)
Youthful Magazines: May, 1950

	GD	VG	FN	VF	VF/NM	NM-
1	16	32	48	94	147	200

YOUTHFUL ROMANCES
Pix-Parade #1-14/Ribage #15 on: 8-9/49 - No. 5, 4/50; No. 6, 2/51; No. 7, 5/51 - #14, 10/52; #15, 1/53 - #18, 7/53; No. 5, 9/53 - No. 9, 8/54

	GD	VG	FN	VF	VF/NM	NM-
1-(1st series)-Titled Youthful Love-Romances	30	60	90	177	289	400
2-Walter Johnson c-1-4	19	38	57	111	176	240
3-5	15	30	45	90	140	190
6,7,9-14(10/52, Pix-Parade; becomes Daring Love #15). 10(1/52)-Mel Torme photo-c/story. 12-Tony Bennett photo-c, 8pg. story & text bio.13-Richard Hayes (singer) photo-c/story; Bob & Ray photo/text story.	15	30	45	84	127	170
8-Frank Sinatra photo/text story; Wood-c/a	22	44	66	128	209	290
15-18 (Ribage)-All have photos on-c. 15-Spike Jones photo-c/story. 16-Tony Bavaar photo-c	14	28	42	82	121	160
5(9/53, Ribage)-Les Paul & Mary Ford photo-c/story; Charlton Heston photo/text story	14	28	42	80	115	150

6-9: 6-Bobby Wayne (singer) photo-c/story; Debbie Reynolds photo/text story. 7(2/54)-Tony Martin photo-c/story; Cyd Charise photo/text story. 8(5/54)-Gordon McCrae photo-c/story.

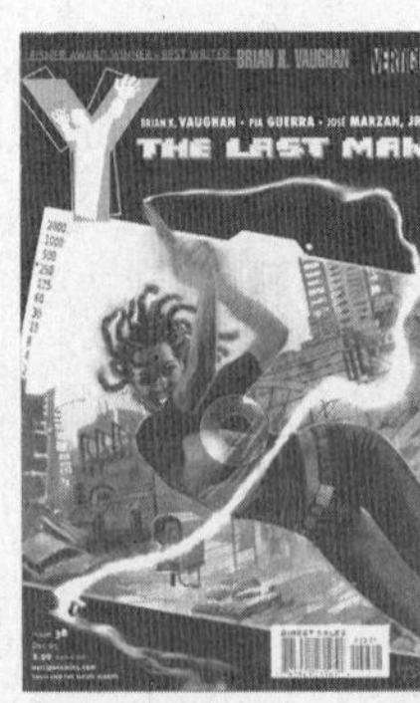

Y: The Last Man #38 © Vaughan & Guerra

Zago, Jungle Prince #4 © FOX

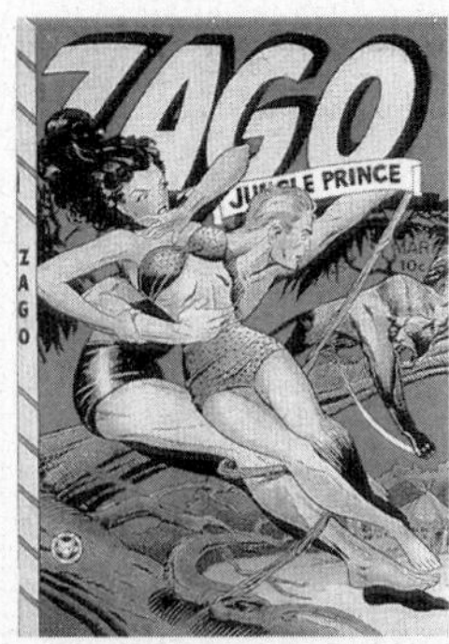

Zatanna (2010 series) #13 © DC

	GD 2.0	VG 4.0	FN 6.0	VF 8.0	VF/NM 9.0	NM- 9.2

(8/54)-Ralph Flanagan (band leader) photo-c/story; Audrey Hepburn photo/text story 14 28 42 76 108 140

YTHAQ: NO ESCAPE
Marvel Comics (Soleil): 2009 - No. 3, 2009 ($5.99, limited series)
1-3-English language version of French comic; Arleston-s/Floch-a 6.00

YTHAQ: THE FORSAKEN WORLD
Marvel Comics (Soleil): 2008 - No. 3, 2009 ($5.99, limited series)
1-3-English language version of French comic; Arleston-s/Floch-a 6.00

Y: THE LAST MAN
DC Comics (Vertigo): Sept, 2002 - No. 60, Mar, 2008 ($2.95/$2.99)
1-Intro. Yorick Brown; Brian K. Vaughan-s/Pia Guerra-a/J.G. Jones-c 7 14 21 46 86 125
2 3 6 9 15 22 28
3-5 1 2 3 5 6 8
6-10 5.00
11-59: 16,17-Chadwick-a. 21,22-Parlov-a. 32,39-41,48,53,54-Sudzuka-a. 3.00
60-($4.99) Final issue; sixty years in the future 6.00
... Double Feature Edition (2002, $5.95) r/#1,2 1 2 3 5 6 8
... Special Edition (2009, $1.00) r/#1, "After Watchmen" trade dress on cover 3.00
... - Cycles TPB (2003, $12.95) r/#6-10; sketch pages by Guerra 13.00
... - Girl on Girl TPB (2005, $12.99) r/#32-36 13.00
... - Kimono Dragons TPB (2006, $14.99) r/#43-48 15.00
... - Motherland TPB (2007, $14.99) r/#49-54 15.00
... - One Small Step TPB (2004, $12.95) r/#11-17 13.00
... - Paper Dolls TPB (2006, $14.99) r/#37-42 15.00
... - Ring of Truth TPB (2005, $14.99) r/#24-31 15.00
... - Safeword TPB (2004, $12.95) r/#18-23 13.00
... - Unmanned TPB (2002, $12.95) r/#1-5 15.00
... - Whys and Wherefores TPB (2008, $14.99) r/#55-60 15.00
... - The Deluxe Edition Book One HC (2008, $29.99, dustjacket) oversized r/#1-10; Guerra sketch pages 30.00
... - The Deluxe Edition Book Two HC (2009, $29.99, dustjacket) oversized r/#11-23; full script to #18 30.00
... - The Deluxe Edition Book Three HC (2010, $29.99, dustjacket) oversized r/#24-36; full script to #36 30.00
... - The Deluxe Edition Book Four HC (2010, $29.99, dustjacket) oversized r/#37-48; full script to #42 30.00
... - The Deluxe Edition Book Five HC (2011, $29.99, dustjacket) oversized r/#49-60; full script to #60 30.00

Y2K: THE COMIC
New England Comics Press: Oct, 1999 ($3.95, one-shot)
1-Y2K scenarios and survival tips 4.00

YUPPIES FROM HELL (Also see Son of...)
Marvel Comics: 1989 ($2.95, B&W, one-shot, direct sales, 52 pgs.)
1-Satire 4.00

ZAGO, JUNGLE PRINCE (My Story #5 on)
Fox Features Syndicate: Sept, 1948 - No. 4, Mar, 1949
1-Blue Beetle app.; partial-r/Atomic #4 (Toni Luck) 69 138 207 442 759 1075
2,3-Kamen-a 55 110 165 352 601 850
4-Baker-c 48 96 144 302 514 725

ZANE GREY'S STORIES OF THE WEST
Dell Publishing Co./Gold Key 11/64: No. 197, 9/48 - No. 996, 5-7/59; 11/64 (All painted-c)
Four Color 197(#1)(9/48) 10 20 30 66 138 210
Four Color 222,230,236('49) 6 12 18 41 76 110
Four Color 246,255,270,301,314,333,346 5 10 15 31 53 75
Four Color 357,372,395,412,433,449,467,484 4 8 12 28 47 65
Four Color 511-Kinstler-a; Kubert-a 5 10 15 31 53 75
Four Color 532,555,583,604,616,632(5/55) 4 8 12 28 47 65
27(9-11/55) - 39(9-11/58) 4 8 12 27 44 60
Four Color 996(5-7/59) 4 8 12 28 47 65
10131-411-(11/64-G.K.)-Nevada; r/4-Color #996 3 6 9 19 30 40

ZANY (Magazine)(Satire)(See Frantic & Ratfink)
Candor Publ. Co.: Sept, 1958 - No. 4, May, 1959
1-Bill Everett-c 14 28 42 80 115 150
2-4: 4-Everett-c 10 20 30 54 72 90

ZATANNA (See Adv. Comics #413, JLA #161, Supergirl #1, World's Finest Comics #274)
DC Comics: July, 1993 - No. 4, Oct, 1993 ($1.95, limited series)
1-4 3.00
...: Everyday Magic (2003, $5.95, one-shot) Dini-s/Mays-a/Bolland-c; Constantine app. 6.00
Special 1(1987, $2.00)-Gray Morrow-c/a 4.00

ZATANNA
DC Comics: Jul, 2010 - No. 16, Oct, 2011 ($2.99)
1-16: 1-Dini-s/Roux-a/c. 4,5,7-Hardin-a. 7-Beechen-s. 8-Chang-a. 11,13-16-Hughes-c 3.00
1-6-Variant-c by Bolland 6.00
...: The Mistress of Magic TPB (2011, $17.99) r/#1-6; variant cover gallery 18.00

ZAZA, THE MYSTIC (Formerly Charlie Chan; This Magazine Is Haunted V2#12 on)
Charlton Comics: No. 10, Apr, 1956 - No. 11, Sept, 1956
10,11 12 24 36 69 97 125

ZEALOT (Also see WildC.A.T.S: Covert Action Teams)
Image Comics: Aug, 1995 - No. 3, Nov, 1995 ($2.50, limited series)
1-3 3.00

ZEGRA JUNGLE EMPRESS (Formerly Tegra)(My Love Life #6 on)
Fox Features Syndicate: No. 2, Oct, 1948 - No. 5, April, 1949
2 69 138 207 442 759 1075
3-5 54 108 162 338 574 810

ZEN (Intergalactic Ninja)
Zen Comics Publishing: No. 0, Apr, 2003 - No. 4, Aug, 2003 ($2.95)
0-4-Bill Maus-a/Steve Stern-s. 0-Wraparound-c 3.00

ZEN INTERGALACTIC NINJA
No Publisher: 1987 -1993 ($1.75/$2.00, B&W)
1 2 4 6 10 14 18
2-6: Copyright-Stern & Cote 1 3 4 6 8 10
V2#1-4-($2.00) 3.00
V3#1-5-($2.95) 3.00
... :Christmas Special 1 (1992, $2.95) 3.00
... :Earth Day Special 1 (1993, $2.95) 3.00

ZEN, INTERGALACTIC NINJA (mini-series)
Zen Comics/Archie Comics: Sept, 1992 - No. 3, 1992 ($1.25)(Formerly a B&W comic by Zen Comics)
1-3: 1-Origin Zen; contains mini-poster 3.00

ZEN INTERGALACTIC NINJA
Entity Comics: No. 0, June-July, 1993 - No. 3, 1994 ($2.95, B&W, limited series)
0-Gold foil stamped-c; photo-c of Zen model 3.00
1-3: Gold foil stamped-c; Bill Maus-c/a 3.00
0-(1993, $3.50, color)-Chromium-c by Jae Lee 4.00
...Sourcebook 1-(1993, $3.50) 4.00
...Sourcebook '94-(1994, $3.50) 4.00

ZEN INTERGALACTIC NINJA: APRIL FOOL'S SPECIAL
Parody Press: 1994 ($2.50, B&W)
1-w/flip story of Renn Intergalactic Chihuahua 3.00

ZEN INTERGALACTIC NINJA COLOR
Entity Comics: 1994 - No. 7, 1995 ($2.25)
1-($3.95)-Chromium die cut-c 4.00
1, 0-($2.25)-Newsstand; Jae Lee-c; r/...All New Color Special #0 3.00
2-($2.50)-Flip book 3.00
2-($3.50)-Flip book, polybagged w/chromium trading card 4.00
3-7 3.00
Summer Special (1994, $2.95) 3.00
Yearbook: Hazardous Duty 1 (1995) 3.00
Zen-isms 1 (1995, 2.95) 3.00
Ashcan-Tour of the Universe-(no price) w/flip cover 3.00

ZEN INTERGALACTIC NINJA COMMEMORATIVE EDITION
Zen Comics Publishing: 1997 ($5.95, color)
1-Stern-s/Cote-a 6.00

ZEN INTERGALACTIC NINJA MILESTONE
Entity Comics: 1994 - No. 3, 1994 ($2.95, limited series)
1-3: Gold foil logo; r/Defend the Earth 3.00

ZEN INTERGALATIC NINJA SPRING SPECTACULAR
Entity Comics: 1994 ($2.95, B&W, one-shot)
1-Gold foil logo 3.00

ZEN INTERGALACTIC NINJA STARQUEST
Entity Comics: 1994 - No. 6, 1995 ($2.95, B&W)
1-6: Gold foil logo 3.00

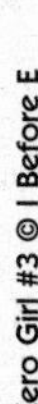
Zero Girl #3 © I Before E

Zip Comics #4 © MLJ

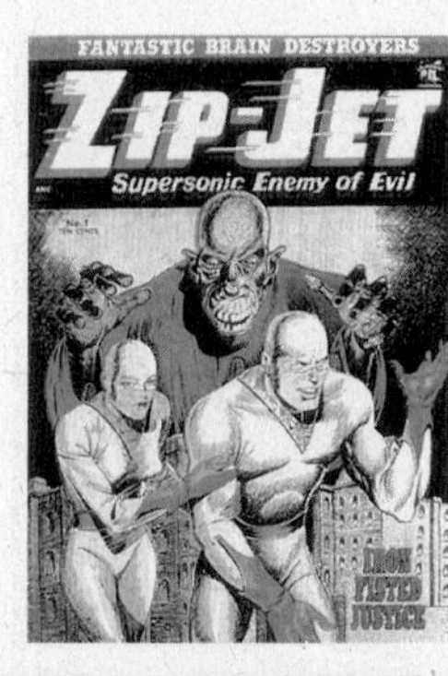
Zip-Jet #1 © STJ

ZEN, INTERGALACTIC NINJA: THE HUNTED
Entity Comics: 1993 - No. 3, 1994 ($2.95, B&W, limited series)

	GD 2.0	VG 4.0	FN 6.0	VF 8.0	VF/NM 9.0	NM- 9.2
1-3: Newsstand Edition; foil logo						3.00
1-($3.50)-Polybagged w/chromium card by Kieth; foil logo						4.00

ZERO GIRL
DC Comics (Homage): Feb, 2001 - No. 5, Jun, 2001 ($2.95, limited series)

	GD 2.0	VG 4.0	FN 6.0	VF 8.0	VF/NM 9.0	NM- 9.2
1-5-Sam Kieth-s/a						3.00
TPB (2001, $14.95) r/#1-5; intro. by Alan Moore						15.00

ZERO GIRL: FULL CIRCLE
DC Comics (Homage): Jan, 2003 - No. 5, May, 2003 ($2.95, limited series)

	GD 2.0	VG 4.0	FN 6.0	VF 8.0	VF/NM 9.0	NM- 9.2
1-5-Sam Kieth-s/a						3.00
TPB (2003, $17.95) r/#1-5						18.00

ZERO HOUR: CRISIS IN TIME (Also see Showcase '94 #8-10)
DC Comics: No. 4(#1), Sept, 1994 - No. 0(#5), Oct, 1994 ($1.50, limited series)

	GD 2.0	VG 4.0	FN 6.0	VF 8.0	VF/NM 9.0	NM- 9.2
4(#1)-0(#5)						4.00
"Ashcan"-(1994, free, B&W, 8 pgs.) several versions exist						3.00
TPB ('94, $9.95)						10.00

ZERO KILLER
Dark Horse Comics: Jul, 2007 - No.6, Oct, 2009 ($2.99)

	GD 2.0	VG 4.0	FN 6.0	VF 8.0	VF/NM 9.0	NM- 9.2
1-6-Arvid Nelson-s/Matt Camp-a						3.00

ZERO PATROL, THE
Continuity Comics: Nov, 1984 - No. 2 ($1.50); 1987 - No. 5, May, 1989 ($2.00)

	GD 2.0	VG 4.0	FN 6.0	VF 8.0	VF/NM 9.0	NM- 9.2
1,2: Neal Adams-c/a; Megalith begins						4.00
1-5 (#1,2-reprints above, 1987)						3.00

ZERO TOLERANCE
First Comics: Oct, 1990 - No. 4, Jan, 1991 ($2.25, limited series)

	GD 2.0	VG 4.0	FN 6.0	VF 8.0	VF/NM 9.0	NM- 9.2
1-4: Tim Vigil-c/a(p) (his 1st color limited series)						3.00

ZERO ZERO
Fantagraphics: Mar, 1995 - No. 27 ($3.95/$4.95, B&W, anthology, mature)

	GD 2.0	VG 4.0	FN 6.0	VF 8.0	VF/NM 9.0	NM- 9.2
1-7,9-15,17-25						5.00
8,16,26,27: 26-($4.95) Bagge-c						6.00

ZIGGY PIG-SILLY SEAL COMICS (See Animal Fun, Animated Movie-Tunes, Comic Capers, Krazy Komics, Silly Tunes & Super Rabbit)
Timely Comics (CmPL): Fall, 1944 - No. 4, Summer, 1945; No. 5, Summer, 1946; No. 6, Sept, 1946

	GD 2.0	VG 4.0	FN 6.0	VF 8.0	VF/NM 9.0	NM- 9.2
1-Vs. the Japanese	34	68	102	199	325	450
2-(Spring, 1945)	20	40	60	114	182	250
3-5	15	30	45	88	137	185
6-Infinity-c	17	34	51	98	154	210
I.W. Reprint #1(1958)-r/Krazy Komics	2	4	6	10	14	18
I.W. Reprint #2,7,8	2	4	6	10	14	18

ZIP COMICS
MLJ Magazines: Feb, 1940 - No. 47, Summer, 1944 (#1-7?: 68 pgs.)

	GD 2.0	VG 4.0	FN 6.0	VF 8.0	VF/NM 9.0	NM- 9.2
1-Origin Kalathar the Giant Man, The Scarlet Avenger, & Steel Sterling; Mr. Satan (by Edd Ashe), Nevada Jones (masked hero) & Zambini, the Miracle Man, War Eagle, Captain Valor begins	459	918	1377	3350	5925	8500
2-Nevada Jones adds mask & horse Blaze	271	542	813	1734	2967	4200
3-Biro robot-c	271	542	813	1734	2967	4200
4,5-Biro WWII-c	181	362	543	1158	1979	2800
6-8-Biro-c	168	336	504	1075	1838	2600
9-Last Kalathar & Mr. Satan; classic-c	194	388	582	1242	2121	3000
10-Inferno, the Flame Breather begins, ends #13	181	362	543	1158	1979	2800
11-Inferno without costume	129	258	387	826	1413	2000
12-Biro bondage/torture-c with dwarf ghouls	142	284	426	909	1555	2200
13-Electrocution-c	161	322	483	1030	1765	2500
14-Biro bondage/torture guillotine-c	132	264	396	845	1448	2050
15-Classic spider-c	161	322	483	1030	1765	2500
16-Female hanging execution-c by Biro (Rare)	155	310	465	992	1696	2400
17-Last Scarlet Avenger; women in bondage being cooked alive-c by Biro	174	348	522	1114	1907	2700
18-Wilbur begins (9/41, 1st app.); sci-fi-c	161	322	483	1030	1765	2500
19	123	246	369	787	1344	1900
20-Origin & 1st app. Black Jack (11/41); Hitler-c	232	464	696	1485	2543	3600
21,23-Nazi WWII-c	116	232	348	742	1271	1800
22-Classic Nazi Grim Reaper w/sickle, V for Victory-c	300	600	900	1950	3375	4800
24,25: 25-Last Nevada Jones	103	206	309	659	1130	1600
26-Classic Nazi/Japanese "Remember Pearl Harbor!" WWII cover; Black Witch begins; last Captain Valor	181	362	543	1158	1979	2800
27-Intro. Web (7/42) plus-c app.; Japanese WWII-c	226	452	678	1446	2473	3500
28-Origin Web; classic Baron Gastapo Nazi WWII-c	194	388	582	1242	2121	3000
29-The Hyena app. (scarce); Nazi WWII-c	155	310	465	992	1696	2400
30-WWII-c	97	194	291	621	1061	1500
31,33-35: All WWII-c. 34-1st Applejack app. 35-Last Zambini, Black Jack	81	162	243	518	884	1250
32-Classic skeleton Nazi WWII-c	129	258	387	826	1413	2000
36-38: 38-Last Web issue	57	114	171	362	619	875
39-Red Rube begins (origin, 8/43)	58	116	174	371	636	900
40-43	50	100	150	315	533	750
44-46: WWII covers. 45-Wilbur ends	55	110	165	352	601	850
47-Last issue; scarce	58	116	174	371	636	900

NOTE: *Biro a-5, 9, 17; c-3-17.* ***Meskin*** *a-1-3, 5-7, 9, 10, 12, 13, 15, 16 at least.* ***Montana*** *c-29, 30, 32-35.* ***Novick*** *c-18-28, 31.* ***Sahle*** *c-37, 38, 40-46. Bondage c-8, 9, 33, 34. Cover features: Steel Sterling-1-43, 47; (w/Blackjack-20-27 & Web-27-35), 28-39; (w/Red Rube-40-43); Red Rube-44-47.*

ZIP-JET (Hero)
St. John Publishing Co.: Feb, 1953 - No. 2, Apr-May, 1953

	GD 2.0	VG 4.0	FN 6.0	VF 8.0	VF/NM 9.0	NM- 9.2
1-Rocketman-r from Punch Comics; #1-c from splash in Punch #10	87	174	261	553	952	1350
2	52	104	156	328	552	775

ZIPPY THE CHIMP (CBS TV Presents...)
Pines (Literary Ent.): No. 50, March, 1957; No. 51, Aug, 1957

	GD 2.0	VG 4.0	FN 6.0	VF 8.0	VF/NM 9.0	NM- 9.2
50,51	8	16	24	40	50	60

ZODY, THE MOD ROB
Gold Key: July, 1970

	GD 2.0	VG 4.0	FN 6.0	VF 8.0	VF/NM 9.0	NM- 9.2
1	3	6	9	16	23	30

ZOMBIE
Marvel Comics: Nov, 2006 - No. 4, Feb, 2007 ($3.99, limited series)

	GD 2.0	VG 4.0	FN 6.0	VF 8.0	VF/NM 9.0	NM- 9.2
1-4-Kyle Hotz-a/c; Mike Raicht-s						4.00
TPB (2007, $13.99) r/#1-4						14.00
...: Simon Garth (1/08 - No. 4, 4/08) Hotz-s/a/c						4.00

ZOMBIE BOY
Timbuktu Graphics/Antarctic Press: Mar, 1988 - Nov, 1996 ($1.50/$2.50/$2.95, B&W)

	GD 2.0	VG 4.0	FN 6.0	VF 8.0	VF/NM 9.0	NM- 9.2
1-Mark Stokes-s/a						3.00
...'s Hoodoo Tales (11/89, $1.50)						3.00
... Rises Again (1/94, $2.50) r/#1 and Hoodoo Tales						3.00
1-(Antarctic Press, 11/96, $2.95) new story						3.00

ZOMBIE KING
Image Comics: No. 0, June, 2005 ($2.95, B&W, one-shot)

	GD 2.0	VG 4.0	FN 6.0	VF 8.0	VF/NM 9.0	NM- 9.2
0-Frank Cho-s/a						5.00

ZOMBIE PROOF
Moonstone: 2007 - Present ($3.50)

	GD 2.0	VG 4.0	FN 6.0	VF 8.0	VF/NM 9.0	NM- 9.2
1-3: 1-J.C. Vaughn-s/Vincent Spencer-a; two covers by Spencer and Neil Vokes						4.00
1-Baltimore Comic-Con 2007 variant-c by Vokes (ltd. ed. of 500)						6.00
2-Big Apple 2008 Convention Edition; Tucci-c (ltd. ed. of 250)						6.00
3-Convention Edition; Beck-c (ltd. ed. of 100)						6.00
...: Zombie Zoo #1 Virginia Comicon Exclusive Edition (2012, ed. of 150)						10.00
...: Zombie Zoo - WVPOP Exclusive Edition (2012)						10.00

ZOMBIES CHRISTMAS CAROL (See Marvel Zombies Christmas Carol)

ZOMBIES!: ECLIPSE OF THE UNDEAD
IDW Publ.: Nov, 2006 - No. 4, Feb, 2007 ($3.99, limited series)

	GD 2.0	VG 4.0	FN 6.0	VF 8.0	VF/NM 9.0	NM- 9.2
1-4-Torres-s/Herrera-a; two covers						4.00

ZOMBIES!: FEAST
IDW Publ.: May, 2006 - No. 5, Oct, 2006 ($3.99, limited series)

	GD 2.0	VG 4.0	FN 6.0	VF 8.0	VF/NM 9.0	NM- 9.2
1-5: 1-Chris Bolton-a/Shane McCarthy-s. 3-Lorenzana-a						4.00

ZOMBIES!: HUNTERS
IDW Publ.: May, 2008 ($3.99)

	GD 2.0	VG 4.0	FN 6.0	VF 8.0	VF/NM 9.0	NM- 9.2
1-Don Figueroa-a/c; Dara Naraghi-s						4.00

ZOMBIES VS. ROBOTS
IDW Publ.: Oct, 2006 - No. 2, Dec, 2006 ($3.99, limited series)

	GD 2.0	VG 4.0	FN 6.0	VF 8.0	VF/NM 9.0	NM- 9.2
1-Chris Ryall-s/Ashley Wood-a; two covers by Wood						15.00
2						10.00

ZOMBIES VS. ROBOTS AVENTURE
IDW Publ.: Feb, 2010 - No. 4, May, 2010 ($3.99, limited series)

	GD 2.0	VG 4.0	FN 6.0	VF 8.0	VF/NM 9.0	NM- 9.2
1-4-Short stories; Ryall-s; art by Matthews III, McCaffrey, & Hernandez; Wood-c						4.00

Zombie War #1 © Eastman & Skulan

Zoot #16 © FOX

Zorro (2008 series) #1 © Zorro Prods.

ZOMBIES VS. ROBOTS: UNDERCITY
IDW Publ.: Apr, 2011 - No. 3, Jun, 2011 ($3.99, limited series)

	GD 2.0	VG 4.0	FN 6.0	VF 8.0	VF/NM 9.0	NM- 9.2
1-3-Chris Ryall-s/Mark Torres; two covers on each by Torres and Garry Brown						4.00

ZOMBIES VS. ROBOTS VS. AMAZONS
IDW Publ.: Sept, 2007 - No. 3, Feb, 2008 ($3.99, limited series)

	GD 2.0	VG 4.0	FN 6.0	VF 8.0	VF/NM 9.0	NM- 9.2
1-3-Chris Ryall-s/Ashley Wood-a; two covers by Wood on each						5.00

ZOMBIE TALES THE SERIES
BOOM! Studios: Apr, 2008 - No. 12, Mar, 2009 ($3.99)

	GD 2.0	VG 4.0	FN 6.0	VF 8.0	VF/NM 9.0	NM- 9.2
1-Niles-s; Lansdale-s/Barreto-a; two covers on each						4.00

ZOMBIE WAR
IDW Publishing: Oct, 2013 - No. 2, Nov, 2013 ($3.99, limited series)

	GD 2.0	VG 4.0	FN 6.0	VF 8.0	VF/NM 9.0	NM- 9.2
1,2-Kevin Eastman & Tom Skulan-s/Eastman & Eric Talbot-a; 2 covers on each						4.00

ZOMBIE WORLD (one-shots)
Dark Horse Comics

	GD 2.0	VG 4.0	FN 6.0	VF 8.0	VF/NM 9.0	NM- 9.2
... :Eat Your Heart Out (4/98, $2.95) Kelley Jones-c/s/a						3.00
... :Home For The Holidays (12/97, $2.95)						3.00

ZOMBIE WORLD: CHAMPION OF THE WORMS
Dark Horse Comics: Sept, 1997 - No. 3, Nov, 1997 ($2.95, limited series)

	GD 2.0	VG 4.0	FN 6.0	VF 8.0	VF/NM 9.0	NM- 9.2
1-3-Mignola & McEown-c/s/a						3.00

ZOMBIE WORLD: DEAD END
Dark Horse Comics: Jan, 1998 - No. 2, Feb, 1998 ($2.95, limited series)

	GD 2.0	VG 4.0	FN 6.0	VF 8.0	VF/NM 9.0	NM- 9.2
1,2-Stephen Blue-c/s/a						3.00

ZOMBIE WORLD: TREE OF DEATH
Dark Horse Comics: Jun, 1999 - No. 4, Oct, 1999 ($2.95, limited series)

	GD 2.0	VG 4.0	FN 6.0	VF 8.0	VF/NM 9.0	NM- 9.2
1-4-Mills-s/Deadstock-a						3.00

ZOMBIE WORLD: WINTER'S DREGS
Dark Horse Comics: May, 1998 - No. 4, Aug, 1998 ($2.95, limited series)

	GD 2.0	VG 4.0	FN 6.0	VF 8.0	VF/NM 9.0	NM- 9.2
1-4-Fingerman-s/Edwards-a						3.00

ZOO ANIMALS
Star Publications: No. 8, 1954 (15¢, 36 pgs.)

	GD 2.0	VG 4.0	FN 6.0	VF 8.0	VF/NM 9.0	NM- 9.2
8-(B&W for coloring)	8	16	24	42	54	65

ZOO FUNNIES (Tim McCoy #16 on)
Charlton Comics/Children Comics Publ.: Nov, 1945 - No. 15, 1947

	GD 2.0	VG 4.0	FN 6.0	VF 8.0	VF/NM 9.0	NM- 9.2
101(#1)(11/45, 1st Charlton comic book)-Funny animal; Al Fago-c	21	42	63	122	199	275
2(12/45, 52 pgs.) Classic-c	15	30	45	83	124	165
3-5	11	22	33	62	86	110
6-15: 8-Diana the Huntress app.	9	18	27	52	69	85

ZOO FUNNIES (Becomes Nyoka, The Jungle Girl #14 on?)
Capitol Stories/Charlton Comics: July, 1953 - No. 13, Sept, 1955; Dec, 1984

	GD 2.0	VG 4.0	FN 6.0	VF 8.0	VF/NM 9.0	NM- 9.2
1-1st app.? Timothy The Ghost; Fago-c/a	11	22	33	64	90	115
2	8	16	24	42	54	65
3-7	7	14	21	37	46	55
8-13-Nyoka app.	9	18	27	52	69	85
1(1984) (Low print run)	1	2	3	4	5	7

ZOONIVERSE
Eclipse Comics: 8/86 - No. 6, 6/87 ($1.25/$1.75, limited series, Mando paper)

	GD 2.0	VG 4.0	FN 6.0	VF 8.0	VF/NM 9.0	NM- 9.2
1-6						3.00

ZOO PARADE (TV)
Dell Publishing Co.: #662, 1955 (Marlin Perkins)

	GD 2.0	VG 4.0	FN 6.0	VF 8.0	VF/NM 9.0	NM- 9.2
Four Color 662	5	10	15	30	50	70

ZOOM COMICS
Carlton Publishing Co.: Dec, 1945 (one-shot)

	GD 2.0	VG 4.0	FN 6.0	VF 8.0	VF/NM 9.0	NM- 9.2
nn-Dr. Mercy, Satannas, from Red Band Comics; Capt. Milksop origin retold	40	80	120	246	411	575

ZOOT (Rulah Jungle Goddess #17 on)
Fox Features Syndicate: nd (1946) - No. 16, July, 1948 (Two #13s & 14s)

	GD 2.0	VG 4.0	FN 6.0	VF 8.0	VF/NM 9.0	NM- 9.2
nn-Funny animal only	24	48	72	142	234	325
2-The Jaguar app.	20	40	60	117	189	260
3(Fall, 1946) - 6-Funny animals & teen-age	14	28	42	80	115	150
7-(6/47)-Rulah, Jungle Goddess (origin/1st app.)	123	246	369	787	1344	1900
8-10	74	148	222	470	810	1150
11-Kamen bondage-c	87	174	261	553	952	1350
12-Injury-to-eye panels, torture scene	60	120	180	381	653	925
13(2/48)	57	114	171	362	619	875
14(3/48)-Used in **SOTI**, pg. 104, "One picture showing a girl nailed by her wrists to trees with blood flowing from the wounds, might be taken straight from an ill. ed. of the Marquis deSade"	81	162	243	518	884	1250
13(4/48),14(5/48)-Western True Crime #15 on?	55	110	165	352	601	850
15,16	55	110	165	352	601	850

ZORRO (Walt Disney with #882)(TV)(See Eclipse Graphic Album)
Dell Publishing Co.: May, 1949 - No. 15, Sept-Nov, 1961 (Photo-c 882 on)
(Zorro first appeared in a pulp story Aug 19, 1919)

	GD 2.0	VG 4.0	FN 6.0	VF 8.0	VF/NM 9.0	NM- 9.2
Four Color 228 (#1)	18	36	54	122	271	420
Four Color 425,617,732	10	20	30	68	144	220
Four Color 497,538,574-Kinstler-a	11	22	33	72	154	235
Four Color 882-Photo-c begin;1st TV Disney; Toth-a	13	26	39	86	188	290
Four Color 920,933,960,976-Toth-a in all	10	20	30	66	138	210
Four Color 1003('59)-Toth-a	10	20	30	66	138	210
Four Color 1037-Annette Funicello photo-c	12	24	36	81	176	270
8(12-2/59-60)	7	14	21	48	89	130
9-Toth-a	8	16	24	51	96	140
10,11,13-15-Last photo-c	7	14	21	46	86	125
12-Toth-a; last 10¢ issue	8	16	24	51	96	140

NOTE: *Warren Tufts a-4-Color 1037, 8, 9, 10, 13.*

ZORRO (Walt Disney)(TV)
Gold Key: Jan, 1966 - No. 9, Mar, 1968 (All photo-c)

	GD 2.0	VG 4.0	FN 6.0	VF 8.0	VF/NM 9.0	NM- 9.2
1-Toth-a	7	14	21	44	82	120
2,4,5,7-9-Toth-a. 5-r/F.C. #1003 by Toth	4	8	12	28	47	65
3,6-Tufts-a	4	8	12	27	44	60

NOTE: *#1-9 are reprinted from Dell issues. **Tufts** a-3, 4. #1-r/F.C. #882. #2-r/F.C. #960. #3-r/#12-c & #8 inside. #4-r/#9-c & insides. #6-r/#11(all); #7-r/#14-c. #8-r/F.C. #933 inside & back-c & #976-c. #9-r/F.C. #920.*

ZORRO (TV)
Marvel Comics: Dec, 1990 - No. 12, Nov, 1991 ($1.00)

	GD 2.0	VG 4.0	FN 6.0	VF 8.0	VF/NM 9.0	NM- 9.2
1-12: Based on TV show. 12-Toth-c						3.00

ZORRO (Also see Mask of Zorro)
Topps Comics: Nov, 1993 - No. 11, Nov, 1994 ($2.50/$2.95)

	GD 2.0	VG 4.0	FN 6.0	VF 8.0	VF/NM 9.0	NM- 9.2
0-(11/93, $1.00, 20 pgs.)-Painted-c; collector's ed.						3.00
1,4,6-9,11: 1-Miller-c. 4-Mike Grell-c. 6-Mignola-c. 7-Lady Rawhide-c by Gulacy. 8-Perez-c. 10-Julie Bell-c. 11-Lady Rawhide-c						3.00
2-Lady Rawhide-app. (not in costume)						5.00
3-1st app. Lady Rawhide in costume, 3-Lady Rawhide-c by Adam Hughes	1	2	3	5	6	8
5-Lady Rawhide app.						4.00
10-($2.95)-Lady Rawhide-c/app.						4.00
The Lady Wears Red (12/98, $12.95, TPB) r/#1-3						13.00
Zorro's Renegades (2/99, $14.95, TPB) r/#4-8						15.00

ZORRO
Dynamite Entertainment: 2008 - No. 20, 2010 ($3.50)

	GD 2.0	VG 4.0	FN 6.0	VF 8.0	VF/NM 9.0	NM- 9.2
1-Origin retold; Wagner-s; three covers						3.50
2-20-Two covers on all						3.50

ZORRO MATANZAS
Dynamite Entertainment: 2010 - No. 4, 2010 ($3.99)

	GD 2.0	VG 4.0	FN 6.0	VF 8.0	VF/NM 9.0	NM- 9.2
1-4-Mayhew-a/McGregor-s						4.00

ZORRO RIDES AGAIN
Dynamite Entertainment: 2011 - No. 12, 2012 ($3.99)

	GD 2.0	VG 4.0	FN 6.0	VF 8.0	VF/NM 9.0	NM- 9.2
1-12: 1-6-Wagner-s/Polls-a. 7-12-Snyder III-a. 10-Lady Zorro on cover						4.00

ZOT!
Eclipse Comics: 4/84 - No. 10, 7/85; No. 11, 1/87 - No. 36 7/91 ($1.50, Baxter-p)

	GD 2.0	VG 4.0	FN 6.0	VF 8.0	VF/NM 9.0	NM- 9.2
1						5.00
2,3						4.00
4-10: 4-Origin. 10-Last color issue						3.00
101/2 (6/86, 25¢, Not Available Comics) Ashcan; art by Feazell & Scott McCloud						4.00
11-14,15-35-($2.00-c) B&W issues						3.00
141/2 (Adventures of Zot! in Dimension 101/2)(7/87) Antisocialman app.						3.00
36-($2.95-c) B&W						5.00
... The Complete Black and White Collection TPB (2008, $24.95) r/#11-36 with commentary, interviews and bonus artwork						25.00

Z-2 COMICS (Secret Agent...)(See Holyoke One-Shot #7)

ZULU (See Movie Classics)

Terry's Comics

WHO IS TERRY'S COMICS?

TERRY'S COMICS IS A COMIC BOOK DEALER WHO IS ALSO A COLLECTOR. TERRY'S COMICS IS ALWAYS LOOKING FOR QUALITY COMICS TO HELP REAL COLLECTORS FILL IN THEIR COLLECTIONS. I AM NOT ONLY LOOKING FOR NEAR MINT KEYS AS ARE MOST OTHER DEALERS. I SPECIALIZE IN TIMELY / ATLAS COMICS FROM THE 1940'S -1950'S

WHY SELL YOUR COMICS TO TERRY'S?

TRAVEL: I WILL COME TO VIEW YOUR COLLECTION, YOU DON'T HAVE TO MAIL IT TO ME.
CASH OFFERS: I CAN PAY FOR YOUR ENTIRE COLLECTION IN CASH IF YOU REQUEST IT.
HIGH PRICES PAID: I ALWAYS NEED NEW MATERIAL FOR MY CUSTOMERS. I WILL PAY MORE.
MONETARY RESOURCES: I HAVE A VERY LARGE LINE OF CREDIT THAT IS INSTANTLY AVAILABLE.
LOCATION: LOCATED IN THE SOUTHWEST AND AN ASSOCIATE IN THE NORTHEAST AND MIDWEST.
NO COST APPRAISALS: I DO NOT CHARGE YOU TO APPRAISE YOUR COLLECTION.
FINDERS FEE: I PAY A FINDERS FEE TO ANYONE THAT LEADS ME TO A COLLECTION PURCHASE.

TERRY'S COMICS

WHY WOULD YOU BUY FROM TERRY'S COMICS?

EXPERIENCE: WE HAVE BEEN BUYING AND SELLING VINTAGE COMICS SINCE 1976.
CUSTOMER SERVICE: WE HAVE THOUSANDS OF SATISFIED, REPEAT CUSTOMERS.
TIGHT GRADING : GRADING IS AS STRICT AS POSSIBLE TO KEEP ALL OUR CUSTOMERS HAPPY.
DISCOUNTS: MANY AVAILABLE, JUST ASK FOR THE BEST PRICE.
GUARANTEE: WE OFFER A FULL REFUND IF YOU ARE NOT SATISFIED.
SELECTION: WE HAVE ONE OF THE LARGEST SELECTIONS OF VINTAGE COMICS ANYWHERE.
CREDENTIALS: I AM A OPG ADVISER, CGC AUTHORIZED DEALER AND A NATIONAL CONVENTION EXHIBITOR.
FAST SHIPPING: MOST ORDERS ARE SHIPPED WITHIN TWO BUSINESS DAYS OF PAYMENT.

PERCENTAGE OF GUIDE I PAY YOU:
TIMELY : 80-200%
ATLAS : 55-200%
COVERLESS : 10-100% OF GOOD
DC GOLDEN AGE : 50 - 150%
HARVEY GOLDEN AGE 40-100%
MLJ: 60-120%
MARVEL SILVER AGE: 40-100%
DC SILVER AGE: 30-90%
WESTERNS: 25-55%

I WILL PAY YOU FOR POOR TO MINT GOLD & SILVER AGE COMICS, I WANT SUPERHERO, HORROR, CRIME , WAR, TEEN, ROMANCE, CLASSICS ETC.

EX. CAPTAIN AMERICA COMICS #1 G I PAY $12,000 OR FULL GUIDE. I CAN AND WILL BEAT ANY OFFER FOR TIMELY/ATLAS COLLECTIONS.

I WANT TO BUY YOUR JUNKY OLD COMICS.

FAX: (714) 288-8992
PHONE:(714) 288-8993
E-MAIL:INFO@TERRYSCOMICS.COM
WEBSITE: WWW.TERRYSCOMICS.COM
QUOTES: (800) 938-0325

PayPal VERIFIED

VISA MasterCard DISCOVER

TERRY'S COMICS
PO BOX 2065
ORANGE, CA. 92859

© Gilberton

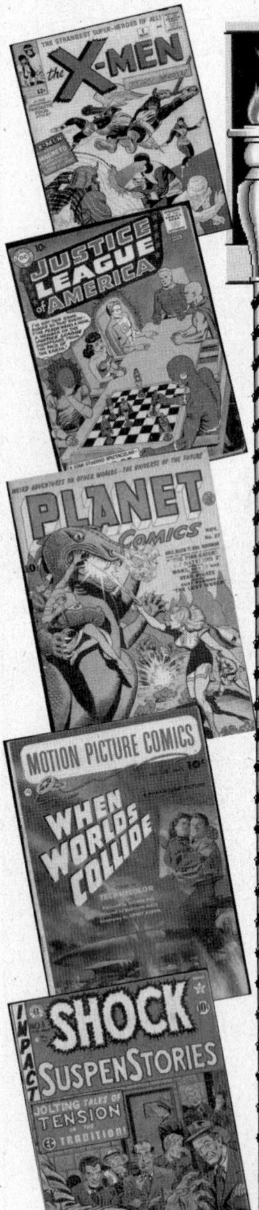

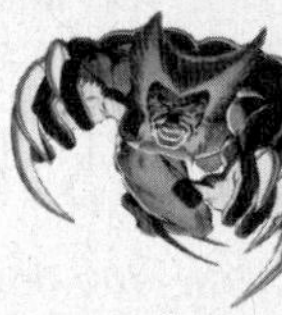

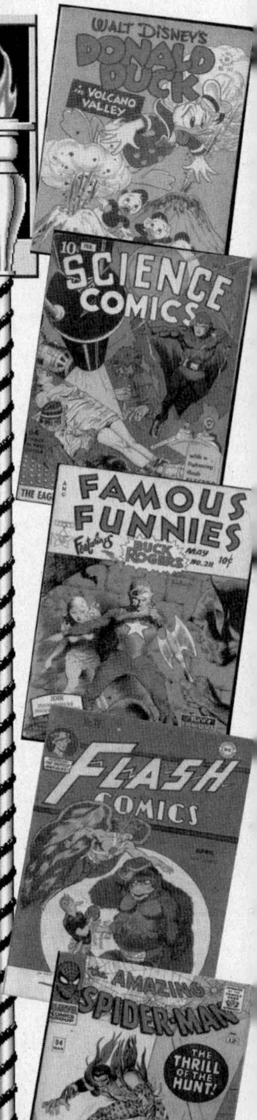

ALWAYS BUYING!!

No collection too large or small

Our tremendous inventory is updated daily

Immediate secure online shopping

Discounted daily specials

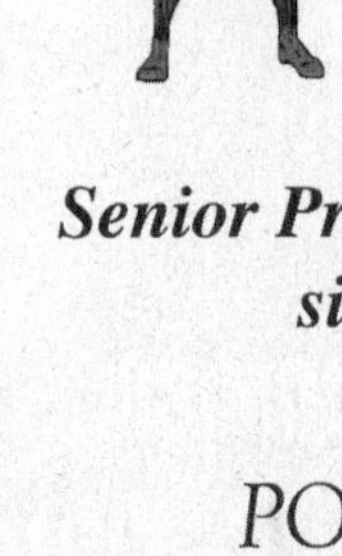

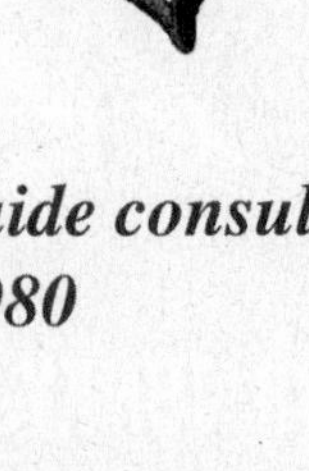

Senior Price Guide consultant since 1980

PO BOX 217
CRYSTAL BAY, NV 89402-0217
(775) 831-4848 FAX (775) 831-4483

Spider-Man, Wolverine © Marvel Comics; Superman © DC Comics

IF YOU ARE A SERIOUS COLLECTOR OF COMICS FROM THE 30'S, THROUGH THE 60'S, LOOKING TO FILL THE DIFFICULT HOLES IN YOUR COLLECTION...OR... TRYING TO UPGRADE YOUR FINES AND VERY FINES TO NEAR MINTS BUT CAN'T GO EVERYWHERE AND DON'T KNOW EVERYONE...?

SPECIALIZING IN WANT LISTS AND PURCHASING COLLECTIONS.

CALL US! WE'VE BEEN BUYING AND SELLING THE HIGHEST GRADE GOLD AND SILVER AGE BOOKS FOR OUR CLIENTS FOR THE LAST 33 YEARS!!!

856-845-4010

LET US SHOW YOU WHAT WE CAN DO FOR YOU...AND, IF YOU ARE SELLING YOUR COLLECTION, WE'LL FLY TO YOU ANYWHERE AND TREAT YOU RIGHT!

ASK AROUND (EVEN OUR COMPETITORS)...OUR REPUTATION CAN'T BE BEAT.

JHV ASSOCIATES

COMICS GUARANTY, LLC Charter Member Dealer

P.O. BOX 317, WOODBURY HEIGHTS, NEW JERSEY 08097

TEL: 856-845-4010 E MAIL: JHVASSOC@HOTMAIL.COM

www.JHVASSOCIATES.com

VISIT MY EBAY STORE JHV ASSOC

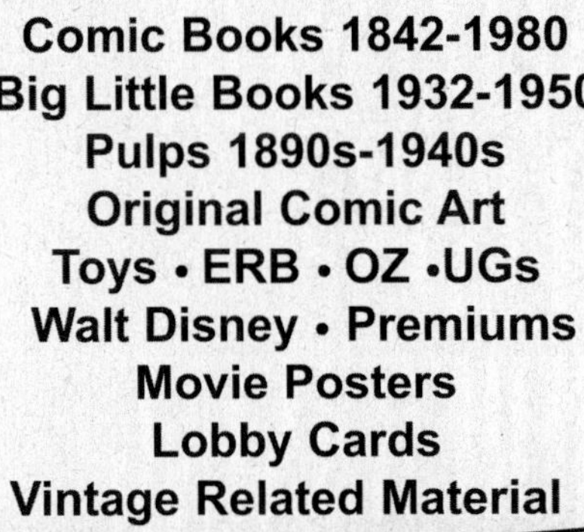

BUY • SELL • TRADE

www.BLBcomics.com

eBay STORE: **BLBcomics**

Remember to read Robert's long-running comics history articles in this guide introducing the Victorian & Platinum Era sections as well as the Origins of the Modern Comic Book 1929

• CHECK OUT THE MANY BARGAINS ON OUR WEBSITE •

WE BUY • FAIR PRICES • SECURELY PACKAGED • ACCURATE GRADING

Robert Beerbohm Comic Art **402.919.9393** BEERBOHMRL@gmail.com

PO Box 507 Fremont NE 68026

I BUY OLD COMICS 1930 to 1975

Any Title
Any Condition
Any Size Collection

Can Easily Travel to:
Atlanta
Chicago
Cincinnati
Dallas
Little Rock
Louisvillle
Memphis
St. Louis

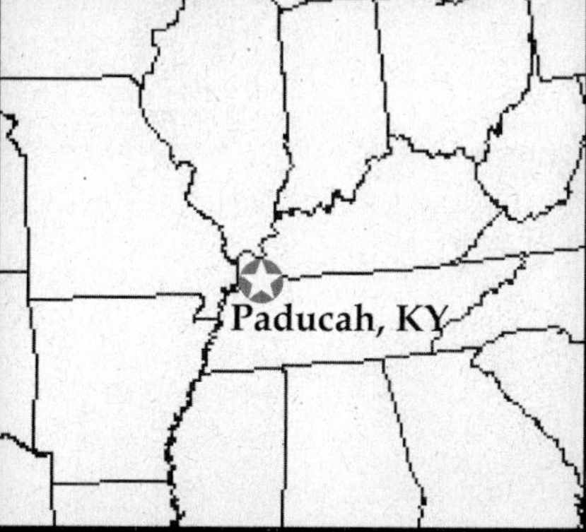

I want your comics:
Superhero
Western
Horror
Humor
Romance

Leroy Harper
PO BOX 212
WEST PADUCAH, KY 42086

PHONE 270-748-9364
EMAIL LHCOMICS@hotmail.com

Over 20 years of experience

All characters © 2014 respective holders. All rights reserved

Sparkle City Comics is the CGC Price Leader! Take a look at a few of our record sales...

Irrefutable facts instead of claims for a change.....

Tales of Suspense #39
CGC 9.2
$72,100 Sept/2011
(RECORD PRICE)
Sold For Less $56,763
May/2011
(Heritage)

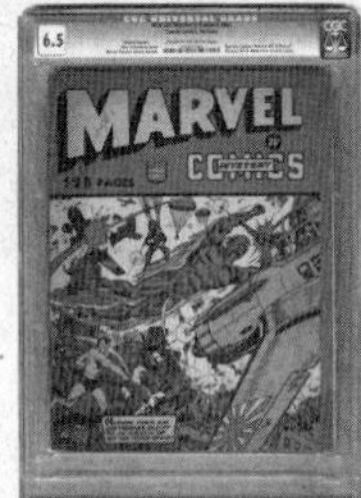

Marvel Mystery Annual
CGC 6.5
$31,100 Dec/2011
RECORD Price)
Sold For Less $26,290
Feb/2012
(Heritage) same exact book
2 months later

Fantastic Four #12
CGC 9.4
$48,201 Oct/2011
A 9.6 sold for $43,777
2 weeks later

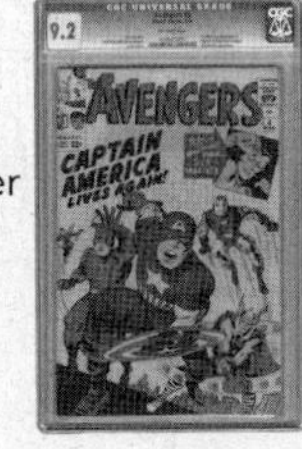

Avengers #4 CGC 9.2
$7,170 Nov/2011
A 9.2 sold a week earlier
for $5,750

Detective Comics #27 CGC 1.8
$116,100 Feb/2011 (RECORD PRICE)
A 2.0 Sold for $116,513 4 days earlier (Heritage)

Showcase #22 CGC 6.0
$6,200 RECORD PRICE
3 copies in 6.5 sold for less
during same period.

Tales of Suspense #59
CGC 9.6
$5,107 RECORD PRICE
sale 3 months later at $2,450

And Many More...
DETECTIVE COMICS #29 CGC 1.0 $9,600 RECORD PRICE
Tales to Astonish #44 CGC 9.6 $10,900 RECORD PRICE
Action Comics #13 CGC 1.5 $8,600 RECORD PRICE
Go to our website to view thousands of record sales at

www.sparklecitycomics.com

The secret?
eBay, the #1 place to sell comic books, and we are the # 1 seller, selling a million dollars a month!
We get more views, hits, and bids than every private auction website combined, not because we are great, but they cannot EVER afford to drive traffic like the billion dollar company eBay does, period.

eBay ID – sparklecitycomics
Positive Feedback – 44,000+
Platinum Top Rated Seller with
100% rating with 0 complaints

WE WANT TO BUY YOUR COMICS!!

CALL NOW 1.800.215.4006

buyingeverything@yahoo.com

GDC Gary Dolgoff Comics

800,000+ comics, art, etc. in stock! 1930s - 2000s

SUPPLYING

Dealers, Collectors, Investors Worldwide!

STRICT GRADING!
always 5,000+ Listings!
1930s - 2000s
Comics, Original Art,
Comic-Magazines,
CGC & More!
+ Thousands of SETS!

VISIT OUR: ebay store

eBay Top-rated seller

ebay id: 'gdcomics'

http://stores.ebay.com/Gary-Dolgoff-Comics

Don't use eBay? No Problem!

If you see something you like on there, then contact us!

STRICT GRADING!

FACT: Our strict grading really saves you 50%+ over 'industry-standard' grading... ASK ANYONE!

DEALERS & COLLECTORS

Buy from GD-COMICS & 'Line your pockets with a handsome-profit', every-time!

WE FILL WANT-LISTS! ASK FOR DETAILS!

Wouldn't it be nice to 'Never Over-Pay' Again?

TRY US OUT! WE CAN SUPPLY YOU FOR A LIFE-TIME...

COME VISIT OUR WAREHOUSE!

CALL OR WRITE US! OUR PLACE IS 'USER-FRIENDLY' & EASY TO-GET-TO...

Gary Dolgoff Comics

116 Pleasant St. Suite #213, Easthampton, MA 01027

PHONE: 413-529-0326 • EMAIL: gary@gdcomics.com

WEB: www.gdcomics.com • eBay ID: gdcomics

www.dougcomicworld.com

DOUG SULIPA'S

COMIC WORLD

Box 21986
Steinbach, Manitoba
CANADA R5G 1B5
Ph: 1-204-346-3674 (8am-11pm)
Web site: www.dougcomicworld.com
Email: dsulipa@gmail.com Ebay Auctions: "dwscw"
Mail order since 1971! Overstreet Advisor!
Specialist in EVERYTHING!

1,300,000 COMICS & RELATED ITEMS: Specializing in 1960-2010 = 95% of ALL comics by ALL companies in Stock. Likely THE World's BIGGEST selection with Approx. 200,000 DIFFERENT Comics & Related items in stock. PLUS a Great Selection of 1940s-1950s & older too. (We especially like to carry everything valued at under $100). ** (200,000 Alternatives; 40,000 Archie; 35,000 Charlton; 3000 Classics; 6000 Comic/Cartoon Paperbacks; 15,000 Comic Digests; 70,000 Comic Magazines; 3000 Dennis the Menace; Fanzines & related; 350,000 DC; 20,000 DELL; 20,000 Disney; 3000 French & Foreign Language comics; 30,000 Gold Key; 5000 Hanna-Barbera; 8000 Harvey; 450,000 Marvel; 12,000 Richie Rich; 2000 Treasure Chest; 1500 Undergrounds; 13,000 UK British Marvel; 6000 Warren). ** **PLUS a big selection of:** ACG, Adult Cartoon, Atlas/Seaboard, Atlas/Marvel, Bananas mags, BLBs, Capt. Canuck, CARtoons, CGC graded, Coloring Books, Calendars, CBG, Christian/Religious, Comic Reader/Journal, Cracked, Dynamite, Eerie Pub., Fanzines, Fawcett Westerns, Giveaways, Gladstone, Heavy Metal, Help, Horror, Humor/Parody, MAD, Misc. Golden Age, National Lampoon, Platinum Age, Portfolios, RBCC, Romance, Sick, Skywald, Spire, Stanley, 3-D, Treasuries, Trib Comic, War, Tower, UK - British Annuals & Comics, Westerns & MORE. We have most of the hard to find Cartoon, Humor, Love, Teen, War & Western Comics & most main-stream Superhero & other popular titles too. Please ***SEND your*** SERIOUS ***WANT LIST*** of 50 or less "Most Wanted" items.
eBAY: See our many current auctions on eBay, for all the types of material we sell as "**dwscw**" (Our Feedback is at over +2400 = 100% Positive, at time of writing). **ABE Books:** See the BOOKS, Paperbacks, Pulps & other items we have listed on the internet at ABE books = "www.abebooks.com" & search sellers = "Comic World". **POSTERS:** We have 10,000 Movie & Video store Posters (1960-up & some older), PLUS about another 10,000 Chain Store type posters; 3000 Comic & Comic Promo posters. Send your want lists! **100,000 Vinyl RECORDS:** Most Standard issue records 1960-90 in stock & selection of '50s(most $5-25); 8000 Cassette tapes. **600,000 NON-SPORT TRADING CARDS:** Decent selection of 1950s-1980 singles; Huge Selection of 1981-1995 Singles, Sets & inserts; MAGIC the GATHERING; VIDEO GAMES; Collectible Atari 2600, Coleco, Intellivision, Nintendo, Sega, Vic-20 & some newer games. **BOARD GAMES:** Approx 1500 Vintage 1950s to 1980s Board Games; Character, TV, Comic & Misc. **16,000 VHS MOVIES:** Most Popular Theatre Movies in Stock; 1000's of Out-of-Print; Most are $5-$15 range; 3000 DVDs; Selection of old NEWSPAPERS, Sunday Comic Pages (1960s-early 1980s); 1000 AVON collectibles; 1000 old SOFT DRINK bottles. **250,000 MAGAZINES:** One of the World's biggest selection of ALL types of mags 1940s-2000+, some older: [70,000 Comic related; 10,000 Fantasy/SF/Horror; 10,000 Sports Illustrated; 5000 Misc. Sports; 10,000 Music; 10,000 Car, Hot Rod, Motorcycle; 10,000 Playboy & Penthouse; 8000 Misc. ADULT 1950s-2000+ (No XXX); 20,000 NEWS MAGS: Life, Time, Newsweek, McLeans, Look, Saturday Evening Post, Colliers,etc.; 5000 TV/Movie/Personality; 15,000 Comic Digests; 5000 Misc DIGESTS; Readers, Coronet, Mystery, SF, Childrens, etc.; 10,000 TV GUIDES 1950s-2000+; 3000 PULPS]. ** PLUS: Adventure, Aircraft, Argosy, Beckett, Bettie Page, Boxing, Childrens, Cosmopolitan, Crafts, Dime Novels (1885-1925), Ebony, Golf, High Times, Hobbies, Martial Arts, Model Airplane Cars Trains, Muscle mags, National Geographic, Omni, People Mag, Popular Mechanics, New Yorker, Price Guide mags, Punch, Railroad, RPG/Gaming, Rolling Stone, Scandal & Tabloid, Stephen King, Teen, Tennis, Traci Lords, True Detective, True Romance, UFO, US mag, Video Games, War/Military, Western, Women's Fashion, Wrestling; *** Please ***SEND your*** SERIOUS ***WANT LIST*** of 50 or less "Most Wanted" items.
MANITOBA Collection: (20,000+ Comics from this mainly 1971-1988 HIGH GRADE Pedigree Quality Collection from all Publishers).
250,000 Mass Market PAPERBACKS: ALL TYPES 1940-2000 from VINTAGE Rarities to Common Reading copies (40,000 F/SF/Horror; 60,000 Mystery; 10,000 Vintage Adult; 6000 Comic/Cartoon, 2000 Rare Canadian Collins White Circle; 3000 scarce Harlequin, #1-2000; 12,000 War/Military, 6000 TV; 4000 Biography; 15,000 Western; 10,000 Historical Fiction; Occult/UFO=4000; 10,000 NON-Fiction; 10,000 Romance; 50,000 Misc. General Fiction. PLUS: Children/ Juvenile, Sports, Music, Movie, Juvenile Delinquent, Drug, Estoteric, Good Girl Art, JFK, Star Trek, Character/Personality, Ace Doubles, ERB, REH, History, Literature, Religion & MORE. **60,000 HARDCOVERS:** A huge selection, of ALL types 1900-1990s+ including many lower cost Book Club & cheaper Reading copies. Most in the $5-$35 range, some cheaper, some better.

** **We have 600,000 Pounds of Inventory:** Our Website lists the equivalent of 6000 Typed Pages, in over 160 Categories (& still growing) of what INVENTORY is IN STOCK & ready to sell. They are NOT catalogued by price & conditon. (1) REQUEST Condition, Price & confirmation of availability; (2) State preferred Condition; (3) List up to a MAXIMUM of 50 items that interest you; (4) We will respond ASAP.

** **NO COMPUTER ??** Send your want list, or phone it in. We can make printouts & send by Mail = Phone for Cost of Printing Out & shipping. We will sell BULK Store & Dealer stock. **BUY US OUT** = Buy all our entire Comics & Related items Inventory (Approx; $6-$10 Million Retail - Instantly become one of the World's Leading dealers) for US $900,000. >> SATISFACTION ALWAYS GUARANTEED: 99.9% Satisfaction Rate!! **Strict Grading!** FULL TIME Mail Order ONLY, from our WAREHOUSE (NO Retail store). MAIL ORDER since 1971, with OVER 25,000 DIFFERENT Satisfied Customers, with over 250,000 completed orders. VISA, MC, Amex, MO, PAYPAL.

WEBSITE: (www.dougcomicworld.com) If we don't have what you want, maybe no one does.

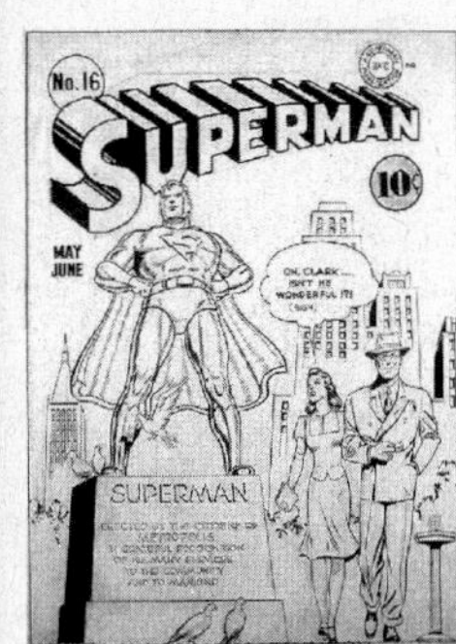

WANTED
COMIC BOOK ART
COMIC STRIP ART

BEFORE YOU SELL YOUR ART, CALL ME.

I CAN AND WILL PAY YOU MORE.

STEPHEN FISHLER
873 BROADWAY, SUITE 201, NEW YORK, NY 10003
TOLL-FREE 1.800.229.6387 OR CALL 212.260.4147 FAX 212.260.4304
STEPHENF@METROPOLISENT.COM

Maui Comics
& Collectibles
Maui, Hawaii

***Bruce Ellsworth (R.I.P.)** came to Maui and shared his love and knowledge of comics and the collecting business with me. He loved comics, and more so he loved underground comics. Bruce was not only a collector of comics, but of knives, paper ephemera, antique books, movie and rock posters, and just about anything else he could get his grubby little mitts on. He was a great mentor and a valued friend.*

In loving memory of
Bruce Ellsworth
Senior Advisor (since 1987)

Alika Seki. P.E.
Advisor (since 2012)
@ 1(808)298-5261 /
alikatime75@yahoo.com

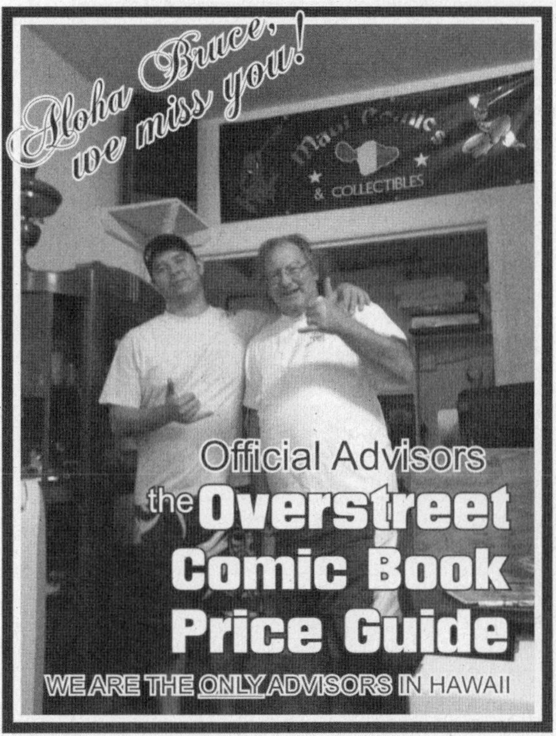

California Buyer Comics Magic the Gathering

You can visit us at:

Hi De Ho Comics
1431 Lincoln Blvd
Santa Monica, CA 90401

We want ALL comics (even Modern!)
We can travel to you and transport larger collections to our warehouse.

Internet or at Conventions:

Canvasstudios@gmail.com
Cardsgamescomics@gmail.com
text us at 714-225-8279
(Seek Out Cards Games Comics @ NY, San Diego, Chicago, & other fine Conventions.)

The lowest prices in Tennessee and Kentucky on New & Back Issue Comic Books, Graphic Novels, Trades & more!

We specialize in buying large collections!
(At our place or yours; we travel for large acquisitions.)

- 25% OFF *our already-low prices on ALL* BACK ISSUE COMICS, GRAPHIC NOVELS, TRADE PAPERBACKS & HARDBACKS!
- 10% OFF all NEW COMIC BOOKS (bought from our stands) & COLLECTOR'S SUPPLIES
- 25% OFF all NEW TRADE PAPERBACKS, HARDBACKS & GRAPHIC NOVELS (bought from our stands)
- 25% OFF all NEW COMIC BOOKS, GRAPHIC NOVELS, TRADE PAPERBACKS PAPERBACKS, HARDBACKS & GRAPHIC NOVELS when reserved with our subscription program. (15% at our Louisville store) Serving TN. & KY. since 1977

Also: **Toys, DVDs, Video Games, CCGs, Gaming,** more!

THE GREAT ESCAPE

NASHVILLE, TENNESSEE
West Nashville: 5400 Charlotte Avenue **(615) 385-2116**
(Note: our original Broadway location moved here on 11/1/10)
Madison, near **Opry Mills:** 111-B Gallatin Rd. N **(615) 865-8052**

BOWLING GREEN, KENTUCKY
Near Greenwood Mall 2945 Scottsville Rd. (270) **782-8092**

LOUISVILLE, KENTUCKY
In The Highlands: 2433 Bardstown Road **(502) 456-2216**
Email inquiries: contactus@thegreatescapeonline.com

OPEN NIGHTS & WEEKENDS: MON-SAT 10-9, SUN 11-7
www.TheGreatEscapeOnLine.com

SIGNATURE AUTHENTICATORS

The above fake Michael Turner signature is signed slowly and looks jagged. The marker used was lifted and repositioned several times throughout the signing and many areas are apparently very crude. **** NOT AUTHENTIC ****	An authentic Michael Turner signature is signed quickly, w/o hesitation, and is spontaneous. After comparing this to other Micheal Turner signatures, it is... *** AUTHENTIC ***

LET US AUTHENTICATE YOUR SIGNED COMICS SO WE CAN PROVIDE THE DOCUMENTATION AND CERTIFICATE OF AUTHENTICITY!

To learn more about our services please visit us at...

www.csacomics.com

Like Us On facebook

COMICS BY ANGELO

SOUTHERN CALIFORNIA BUYER OF VINTAGE COMICS AND TOYS

I buy graded comics, Golden Age, Silver Age, Timelys,
Underground comics, small collections, large collections

Call Angelo at 619-727-0414

Buy • Sell • Trade **ComicsByAngelo@gmail.com**

Batman and Wonder Woman Collectors

P.O. Box 604925
Flushing, NY
11360-4925

email: batt90@aol.com
wwali@aol.com

We buy pre-1975 Batman comics and memorabilia and Wonder Woman comics and memorabilia from all eras.
©DC Comics 2012

COSMIC COMICS!
LAS VEGAS, NV
4,000 SQFT. OF COMIC GOODNESS
LOCATED MINUTES FROM THE STRIP!
BUY
SELL
TRADE
Est. 1996
JIM SAYS:
OVER 50,000 BACK ISSUES
FROM THE 1950'S TO THE PRESENT!
10,000+ GRAPHICS NOVELS!
PLUS T-SHIRTS, TOYS AND DO-DADS!
Mention this ad for 10% off Back Issues
3830 E Flamingo Las Vegas, NV 89121
702-451-6611 • info@cosmiccomicslv.com
WWW.COSMICCOMICSLV.COM

BUSINESS CARD ADS

THE OVERSTREET COMIC BOOK PRICE GUIDE BUSINESS CARD ADS are a great way to advertise in the Guide! Simply send us your business card and we'll reduce it and run it as is. Have your ad seen by thousands of serious comic book collectors for an entire year! If you are a comic book or collectible dealer, retail establishment, mail-order house, etc., you can reach potential customers throughout the United States and around the world in our **BUSINESS CARDS ADS**!

For more information, contact our Advertising Dept.
Gemstone Publishing, Inc.
1940 Greenspring Dr., Suite I
Timonium, MD 21093
or e-mail **feedback@gemstonepub.com**.

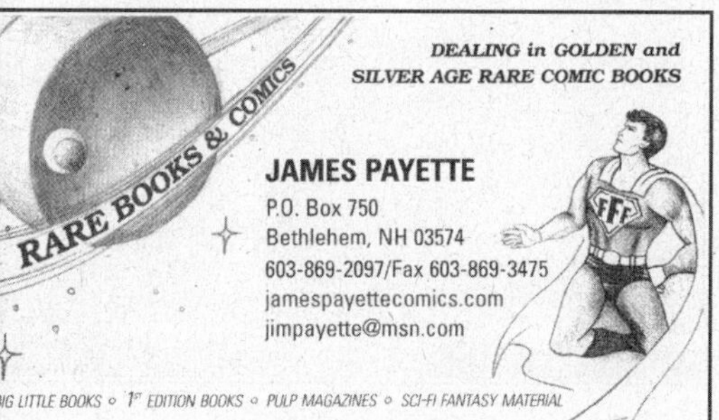

DEALING in GOLDEN and
SILVER AGE RARE COMIC BOOKS
RARE BOOKS & COMICS
JAMES PAYETTE
P.O. Box 750
Bethlehem, NH 03574
603-869-2097/Fax 603-869-3475
jamespayettecomics.com
jimpayette@msn.com
BIG LITTLE BOOKS ◦ 1ST EDITION BOOKS ◦ PULP MAGAZINES ◦ SCI-FI FANTASY MATERIAL

ALWAYS
BUYING
COMICS
.COM

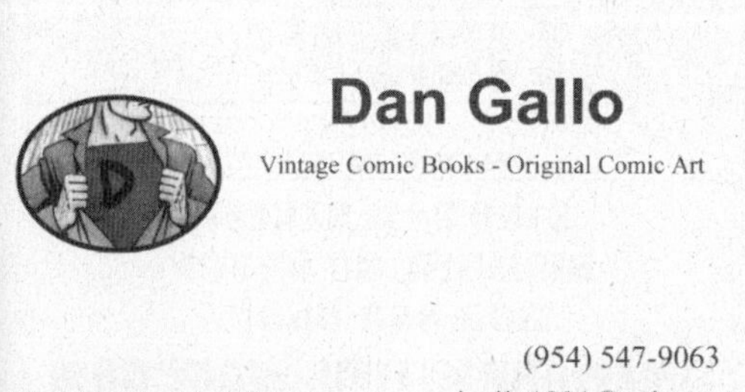

Dan Gallo
Vintage Comic Books - Original Comic Art
(954) 547-9063
e-Bay ID: dgallo1291
dgallo1291@aol.com

Top Five Selection on the Web!
Strict, consistent grading.
HC
NEW COLLECTIONS in the House!
EASY-TO-USE, secure WEBSITE!
FREE SHIPPING w/ $75 order!
info@houseofcomics.com
Call us at (510) 847-3376
www.HouseofComics.com

BUYING AND SELLING COMICS FOR 30 YEARS!
WORLDWIDE
COMICS
ALWAYS BUYING!
CALL US TODAY!
wwcomics.com
SENIOR OVERSTREET ADVISOR
STEPHEN RITTER • stephen@wwcomics.com
Tel: (830) 368-4103 • 29369 Raintree Ridge, Fair Oaks Ranch, TX 78015 (San Antonio Area)

Robert Yeremian
Owner

Hours:
Mon - Sat 11-7
Sun - 12-6

THE TIME CAPSULE
Buying and Selling

Comic Books, Toys
Records - LP's, 45's
CD's & Video Games,
Collectibles & More

537 Pontiac Ave.
Cranston, RI 02910
(401) 781-5017
ryeremian@aol.com

BUSINESS CARD ADS

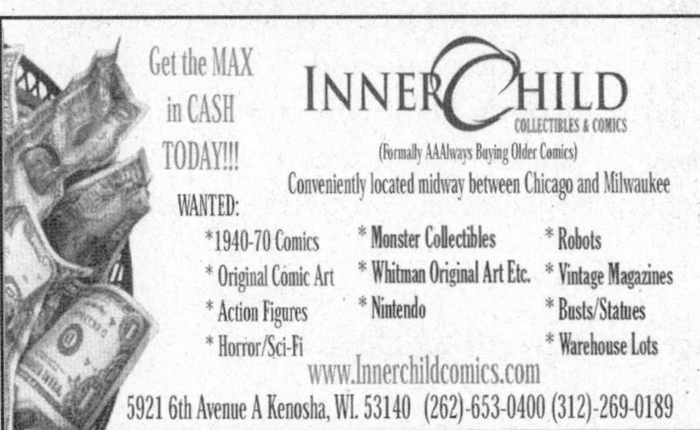

Get the MAX in CASH TODAY!!!
INNER CHILD
COLLECTIBLES & COMICS
(Formally AAAlways Buying Older Comics)
Conveniently located midway between Chicago and Milwaukee
WANTED:
*1940-70 Comics
* Original Comic Art
* Action Figures
* Horror/Sci-Fi
* Monster Collectibles
* Whitman Original Art Etc.
* Nintendo
* Robots
* Vintage Magazines
* Busts/Statues
* Warehouse Lots
www.Innerchildcomics.com
5921 6th Avenue A Kenosha, WI. 53140 (262)-653-0400 (312)-269-0189

Exclusive offering
ORIGINAL ARTWORK from
Golden Age Comic Book Artist
Vee Quintal Pearson
Hundreds of individual drawings,
figure studies & unpublished material
www.VeeQuintalComicArt.com

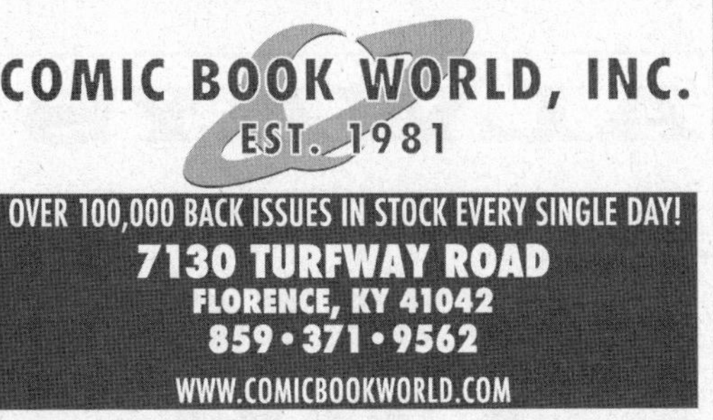

COMIC BOOK WORLD, INC.
EST. 1981
OVER 100,000 BACK ISSUES IN STOCK EVERY SINGLE DAY!
7130 TURFWAY ROAD
FLORENCE, KY 41042
859 • 371 • 9562
WWW.COMICBOOKWORLD.COM

Looking to buy, sell or trade

BATMAN
WONDER WOMAN
COLLECTORS

E-mail: batt90@aol.com
wwali@aol.com

COLLECTORS
P.O. Box 604925
Flushing, NY 11360-4925

TIME WARP
COMICS, GAMES, AND COLLECTIBLES
WWW.TIME-WARP.COM

3105 28TH STREET
BOULDER, CO 80301
303-443-4500
TIMEWARP1@TIME-WARP.COM

"Always buying Golden & Silver Age issues and collections."

Adam Black

Vintage Comic
Book Investor

Call today for a hassle-free phone consultation.

Cincinnati, OH **513-600-2719**

"King of Cards"
Mike Rea

"Rhymin"
Rich Rea

A TO Z CARDS, COMICS
& COINS

12-5 Sunday
10-7 Mon., Sat.
10-8 Tues., Wed., Thurs., Fri.

(734) 425-6780
32647 Ford Road
Garden City, MI 48135

www.YourAtoZ.com

BUSINESS CARD ADS

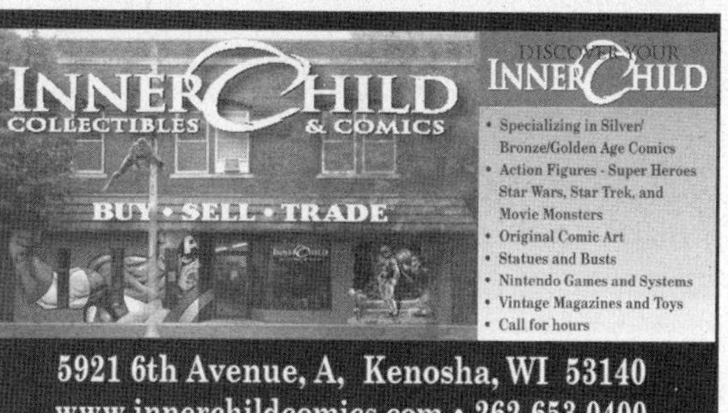

INNER CHILD
COLLECTIBLES & COMICS
BUY • SELL • TRADE
DISCOVER YOUR
INNER CHILD
• Specializing in Silver/ Bronze/Golden Age Comics
• Action Figures - Super Heroes Star Wars, Star Trek, and Movie Monsters
• Original Comic Art
• Statues and Busts
• Nintendo Games and Systems
• Vintage Magazines and Toys
• Call for hours
5921 6th Avenue, A, Kenosha, WI 53140
www.innerchildcomics.com • 262-653-0400

BUNKY BROTHERS
comics - pop culture
COMICS
Buy/Sell Vintage Comics
9155 Archibald Ave. Suite D
Rancho Cucamonga, CA
91730 USA
(Southeast Corner 7th & Archibald)
Open Mon - Fri 11:30am - 6:30pm
Sat 11:30am - 5:00pm
Sun - Call
Email: bunky@bunkybrothers.com
www.bunkybrothers.com
909.941.6402

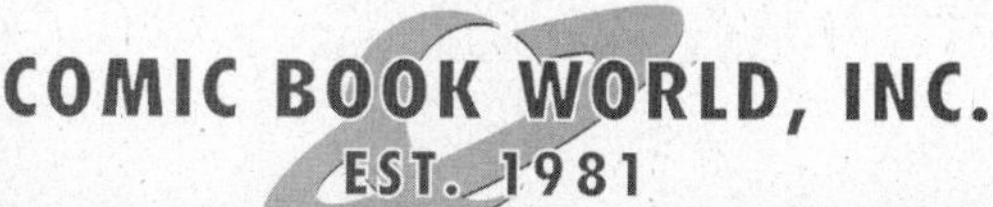

THE BEST COMIC BOOK STORE IN LOUISVILLE!

6905 SHEPHERDSVILLE ROAD

LOUISVILLE, KY 40219

502•964•5500

WWW.COMICBOOKWORLD.COM

COMICS LLC
Jesse James
President
*Comics *Gaming *Action Figures
www.jessejamescomics.com
Mon: 10am to 7pm
Wed: 9am to 9pm
Tues & Thurs: 10am tp 8pm
Fri-Sat: 10am to 9pm
Sunday: 11am to 7pm
10620 N. 43rd Ave #8
Glendale, AZ 85304
(602) 993-0392

30% OFF ALL COMIC BOOKS WITH MEMBERSHIP

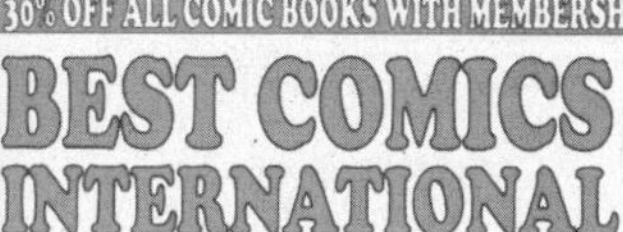

(Est.1991)

TOMMY MALETTA

•COMIC BOOKS•BACK ISSUES
•GRAPHIC NOVELS•TOYS•STATUES
•SPORTS MEMORABILIA

1300 JERICHO TURNPIKE NEW HYDE PARK, NY 11040
Phone: 516-328-1900 WWW.BESTCOMICS.COM

ComicStore.com
An E-Commerce Store
Serving Planet Earth

Always Buying!

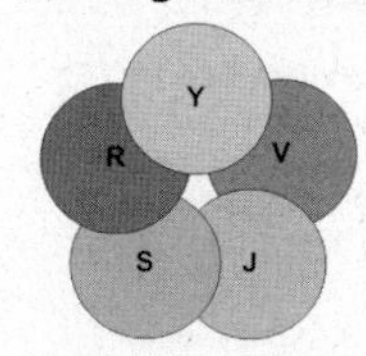

Txt (510) 470-1104
Info@ComicStore.com
Twitter: @ComicStoreCom
eBay ID: Shop_ComicStoreCom
eBay Store: ComicStoreCom

(407) 688-2768
P.O.Box 953972
Lake Mary, FL 32795

Email: pdyroff@cfl.rr.com
Ebay ID: pauldyroff
Ebay Store: Paul Dyroff Comics

www.paulscollectibles.com

Specializing in 1930s to 1970s Comics

Buying: Comics, Magazines, Big Little Books
Pulps, Paperbacks, Sunday Comics
WWII era, Non-Sports Cards, Newspapers
Certified eBay Trading Assistant - Consignments Wanted

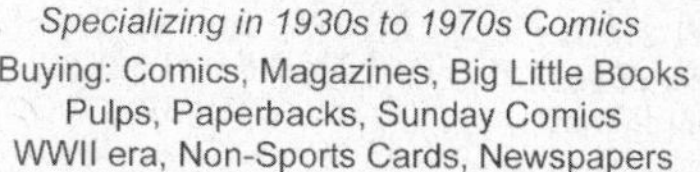

Outer Limits
Comic Books & Collectables

Buy • Sell • Trade

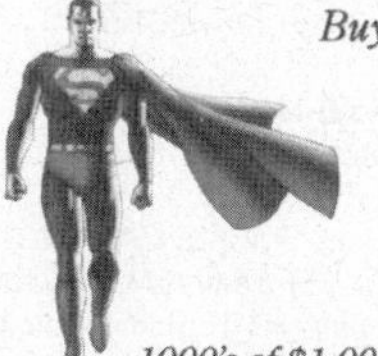

1000's of $1.00 Comics

Rod Matlack
427 S. Santa Fe Avenue
Pueblo, CO 81003
719.583.2750

DIRECTORY LISTINGS

(PAID ADVERTISING - STORE LISTINGS)

You can have your store listed here for very reasonable rates. Send for details for next year's Guide. The following list of stores have paid to be included in this list. We cannot assume any responsibility in your dealings with these shops. This list is provided for your information only. When planning trips, it would be advisable to make appointments in advance. Remember, to get your shop included in the next edition, contact us for rates.

Gemstone Publishing, Inc.
1940 Greenspring Dr., Suite I
Timonium, MD 21093
E-MAIL: feedback@gemstonepub.com

Items stocked by these shops are noted at the end of each listing and are coded as follows:

(a) Golden Age Comics
(b) Silver Age Comics
(c) Bronze Age Comics
(d) New Comics & Magazines
(e) Back Issue magazines
(f) Comic Supplies
(g) Collectible Card Games
(h) Role Playing Games
(i) Gaming Supplies
(j) Manga
(k) Anime
(l) Underground Comics
(m) Original Comic Art
(n) Pulps
(o) Big Little Books
(p) Books - Used
(q) Books - New
(r) Comic Related Posters
(s) Movie Posters
(t) Trading Cards
(u) Statues/Mini-busts, etc.
(v) Premiums (Rings, Decoders)
(w) Action Figures
(x) Other Toys
(y) Records/CDs
(z) DVDs/VHS
(1) Doctor Who Items
(2) Simpsons Items
(3) Star Trek Items
(4) Star Wars Items
(5) HeroClix

CALIFORNIA

The Comic Cellar
135 W. Main St.
Alhambra, CA 91801
PH: (626) 570-8743
comiccellar@comiccellar.com
www.comiccellar.com
(a-g,j,l-p,r,x,1-4)

Collectors Ink
2593 Hwy. 32
Chico, CA 95973
PH: (530) 345-0958
collectorsink@ymail.com
(a-k,r,t-x,z,1-5)

HighQualityComics.com
1106 2nd St., #110
Encinitas, CA 92024
PH: (800) 682-3936
FAX: (760) 723-0412
customerservice
@HighQualityComics.com
www.HighQualityComics.com
(a-f,j-m,p-x,1-4)

The Comic Cellar
628 S. Myrtle Ave.
Monrovia, CA 91780
PH: (626) 358-1808
comiccellar@comiccellar.com
www.comiccellar.com
(d,f,g,j,r,x,1-4)

Terry's Comics
Buying All 10¢ & 12¢
original priced comics
P.O. Box 2065
Orange, CA 92859
PH: (714) 288-8993 or
Hotline: (800) 938-0325
FAX: (714) 288-8992
info@TerrysComics.com
www.TerrysComics.com
(a,b,d-h,m,n,q)

ArchAngels
4629 Cass Street #9
Pacific Beach, CA 92109
PH: (310) 480-8105
rhughes@archangels.com
www.archangels.com

Bunky Brothers
9155 Archibald Ave.
Suite E
Rancho Cucamonga, CA
91730
PH: (909) 941-6402
FAX: (650) 347-2305
Bunky@BunkyBrothers.com
www.BunkyBrothers.com
(a-f,s-u,w,x,3,4)

A-1 Comics
818 Sunrise Ave.
Roseville, CA 95661
PH: (916) 783-8005
FAX: (916) 783-8040
Brian@A-1.com
www.A-1Comics.com
(a-j,m-o,q,r,t,u,w,x,1-5)

A-1 Comics
5361 Auburn Blvd.
Sacramento, CA 95841
PH: (916) 331-9203
FAX: (916) 331-2141
Brian@A-1.com
www.A-1Comics.com
(a-j,m-o,q,r,t,u,w,x,1-5)

Captain Nemo Games & Comics
565 Higuera St.
San Luis Obispo, CA 93401
PH: (805) 544-NEMO (6366)
CaptainNemo@CaptainNemo.biz
www.CaptainNemo.biz
(a-k,r,s,u,w-z,2-5)

Geoffrey's Comics
15900 Crenshaw Blvd.
Torrance, CA 90249
PH: (310) 538-3198
comicsonebay.com

COLORADO

RTS Unlimited, Inc.
P. O. Box 150412
Lakewood, CO 80215-0412
PH: (303) 403-1840
FAX: (303) 403-1837
RTSUnlimitedinc@gmail.com
www.RTSUnlimited.com
(a,b,c,e,f)

Outer Limits
427 S. Santa Fe Ave.
Pueblo, CO 81003
PH: (719) 583-2750
rodscomics@yahoo.com
(a-d,f,m,o,r,s,u,w-y,5)

CONNECTICUT

Matt's Sportscards & Comics
169 Elm St.
Enfield, CT 06082
PH: (860) 741-2522
E-Mail:
CardAndComicShop@cox.net
www.CardAndComicShop.com
(a-k,m,o,r,t,u,w,x,1,3,4)

FLORIDA

Emerald City Comics and Collectables, Inc.
4902 113th Ave. N
Clearwater, FL 33760
PH: (727) 398-2665
E-Mail: CowardlyLion
@emeraldcitycomics.com
www.emeraldcitycomics.com
(a-k,m,o,r-x,z,1-5)

Retail Slayer
Lake City, FL 32025
PH: (321) 377-2447
info@retailslayer.com
www.RetailSlayer.com
(d,g,h,j-m,q-u,w,x,z,1-5)

Paul Dyroff Comics
P.O. Box 953972
Lake Mary, FL 32795
PH: (407) 688-2768
pdyroff@cfl.rr.com
www.paulscollectibles.com
(a-c,e,l-p,r,s,t,v,x)

MightyMags.com
P.O. Box 22916
St. Petersburg, FL 33742-2916
PH: (727) 525-7111
MightyMagscom@aol.com
MightyMags.com
(a-c,e,p,1,3,4)

Classic Collectible Services
P.O. Box 4738
Sarasota, FL 34230
PH: (855) CCS-1711
CCSpaper.com

CGC
P.O. Box 4738
Sarasota, FL 34230
PH: (877) NM-COMIC
FAX: (941) 360-2558
www.CGCcomics.com

Emerald City Comics and Collectables, Inc.
9249 Seminole Boulevard
Seminole, FL 33772
PH: (727) 398-BOOK (2665)
E-Mail: CowardlyLion
@emeraldcitycomics.com
www.emeraldcitycomics.com
(a-k,m,o,r-x,z,1-5)

Culture and Thrills Collectibles Gallery
5205 N. Florida Ave.
Tampa, FL 33603
PH: (813) 237-5400
davidt@cultureandthrills.com
www.dtacollectibles.com
(a,b,c,e,f,l,m-x,3,4)

David T. Alexander Collectibles
P.O. Box 273086
Tampa, FL 33618
PH: (813) 968-1805
davidt@cultureandthrills.com
www.dtacollectibles.com
(a-c,e,l-o,r-t,v,x,3,4)

Pedigree Comics, Inc.
12541 Equine Lane
Wellington, FL 33414
PH/FAX: (561) 422-1120
CELL: (561) 596-9111
E-Mail: DougSchmell
@pedigreecomics.com
www.pedigreecomics.com

HAWAII

Maui Comics & Collectibles
10th Increment
Kahului, HI 96732
PH: (808) 298-5261
AlikaSeki@gmail.com
SekiEngineering.com
(a-c,e-g,j,l-n,p,s,t,w-z)

ILLINOIS

Yesterday
1143 W. Addison St.
Chicago, IL 60613
PH: (773) 248-8087
(a-c,e,f,l,n-p,r-t,v,x-z,1,3,4)

Dreamland Comics
105 W. Rockland Rd.
Libertyville, IL 60048
PH: (847) 680-0727
info@dreamland-comics.com
www.dreamland-comics.com
(a-j,r,t,u,w,x,1-5)

Revealed Treasures/ Comics4Less
165 N. Archer Ave.
Mundelein, IL 60060
PH: (847) 513-2666
oldcomics@yahoo.com
comics4less.com

Mellow Blue Planet
2212 5th Avenue
Rock Island, IL 61201
PH: (309) 788-1653
E-Mail: mellowblueplanet
@hotmail.com
www.mellowblueplanet.com
(a-f,h-l,o,q-x,z,1-5)

INDIANA

The Danger Room
833 East 53rd Street
Anderson, IN 46013
PH/FAX: (765) 646-6341
Raymond@Danger-Room.com
www.Danger-Room.com
(b-d,f-k,r,u-w,z,1,5)

Comics Ina Flash
P.O. Box 3611
Evansville, IN 47735-3611
PH/FAX: (812) 401-6127
comicflash@aol.com
www.comicsinaflash.com

Books Comics & Things
2212 Maplecrest Rd.
Fort Wayne, IN 46815
PH: (260) 493-6116
bct@bctcomics.com
www.bctcomics.com
(a-j,r,u,w,x,1-5)

Books Comics & Things
5808 W. Jefferson Blvd.
Suite C
Fort Wayne, IN 46804
PH: (260) 755-2425
jscott@bctcomics.com
www.bctcomics.com
(a-j,u,w,x,1-5)

IOWA

Mayhem Comics & Games
2532 Lincoln Way
Ames, IA 50014
PH/FAX: (515) 292-3510
shop@mayhemcomics.com
www.mayhemcomics.com
(a-k,r,u,w,x,z,1,3-5)

Mayhem Comics & Games
7500 University; Suite D
Des Moines, IA 50325
PH/FAX: (515) 271-8104
shop@mayhemcomics.com
www.mayhemcomics.com
(a-i,q,r,u,w,x-z,1-5)

KENTUCKY

The Great Escape
2945 Scottsville Road
Suites B17 & B18
Bowling Green, KY 42104
PH: (270) 782-8092
FAX: (270) 843-3090
thegreatescapebg@gmail.com
www.TheGreatEscapeOnLine.com

Comic Book World, Inc.
7130 Turfway Rd.
Florence, KY 41042
PH: (859) 371-9562
FAX: (859) 371-6925
cbwinfo@fuse.net
www.comicbookworld.com
(a-j,m,n,o,r,u,w,1-5)

Comic Book World, Inc.
6905 Shepherdsville Rd.
Louisville, KY 40219
PH: (502) 964-5500
FAX: (502) 964-5500
cbwdoug@bellsouth.net
www.comicbookworld.com
(a-j,n,o,r,u,w,1-5)

The Great Escape
2433 Bardstown Road
Louisville, KY 40205
PH: (502) 456-2216
FAX: (502) 458-2482
loutge@mw.twcbc.com
www.TheGreatEscapeOnLine.com

Leroy Harper
P.O. Box 212
West Paducah, KY 42086
PH: (270) 748-9364
LHCOMICS@hotmail.com

LOUISIANA

Excalibur Comics, Cards & Games
802 E. 70th St.
Shreveport, LA 71106
PH: (318) 868-4389
FAX: (318) 868-4369
excaliburccg@gmail.com
www.excaliburccg.com
(a-i,n,r,t,u,w,x,1,3-5)

MAINE

Top Shelf Coins & Comics
25 Central St.
Bangor, ME 04401
PH: (207) 947-4939
TopShelf@tcomics.com
www.tcomics.com
(a-f)

MARYLAND

E. Gerber
1720 Belmont Ave.; Suite C
Baltimore, MD 21244

Esquire Comics.com
Mark S. Zaid, ESQ.
P.O. Box 3422492
Bethesda, MD 20827
PH: (202) 498-0011
esquirecomics@aol.com
www.esquirecomics.com
(b-k,r,u,w,4,5)

Alternate Worlds
Yorktowne Plaza Shopping Center
72 Cranbrook Road
Cockeysville, MD 21030
PH: (410) 666-3290
AltWorldStore@comcast.net
www.Alternateworlds.biz
(b-j,q,r,u,w,x,1-5)

Comics To Astonish Inc.
9400 Snowden River Pkwy.
Suite 112
Columbia, MD 21045
PH: (410) 381-2732
comics2u@aol.com
www.ComicsToAstonish.com
(a-k,m,r,t,u,w,z,2,3,5)

Basement Comics
2113 Columbia Park Drive
Suite 2A
Edgewood, MD 21040
PH: (443) 831-2761
basmntcomx@aol.com
(a,b,c,e,l,m,n,o,r,s,4)

Greg Reece's Rare Comics
11028 Graymarsh Pl.
Ijamsville, MD 21754
PH: (240) 575-8600
greg@gregreececomics.com
www.gregreececomics.com
(a,b,c,e,f)

Cards Comics and Collectibles
100 A Chartley Drive
Reisterstown, MD 21136
PH: (410) 526-7410
FAX: (410) 526-4006
cardscomicscollectibles
@yahoo.com
www.cardscomicscollectibles.com
(a-d,f,g,j,t,w,5)

Diamond Comic Distributors
10150 York Road, Suite 300
Hunt Valley, MD 21030
PH: (443) 318-8001

Diamond International Galleries
1940 Greenspring Dr., Suite I
Timonium, MD 21093
GalleryQuestions@
DiamondGalleries.com
www.DiamondGalleries.com

MASSACHUSETTS

New England Comics
215B Harvard Ave.
Allston, MA 02134
PH/FAX: (617) 566-3509
support@newenglandcomics.com
www.newenglandcomics.com
(a-k,r,t,u,w,x,z,1-5)

New England Comics
716 Crescent St.
Brockton, MA 02302
PH/FAX: (508) 559-5068
support@newenglandcomics.com
www.newenglandcomics.com
(a-k,r,t,u,w,x,z,1-5)

New England Comics
316 Harvard St.
Coolidge Corner
Brookline, MA 02446
PH/FAX: (617) 566-0115
support@newenglandcomics.com
www.newenglandcomics.com
(a-k,r,t,u,w,x,z,1-5)

New England Comics
14A Eliot St.
Harvard Square
Cambridge, MA 02138
PH/FAX: (617) 354-5352
support@newenglandcomics.com
www.newenglandcomics.com
(a-k,r,t,u,w,x,z,1-5)

Gary Dolgoff Comics
116 Pleasant St.
Easthampton, MA 01027
PH: (413) 529-0326
FAX: (413) 529-9824
gary@gdcomics.com
www.gdcomics.com

That's Entertainment
56 John Fitch Highway
Fitchburg, MA 01420
PH: (978) 342-8607
www.ThatsE.com
(a-z,1-5)

SuperworldComics.com
456 Main St., Suite F
Holden, MA 01520
PH: (508) 829-2259
PH: (508) UB-WACKY
Ted@Superworldcomics.com
www.Superworldcomics.com
(a-c,m)

New England Comics
95 Pleasant St.
Malden, MA 02148
PH/FAX: (781) 322-2404
support@newenglandcomics.com
www.newenglandcomics.com
(a-k,r,t,u,w,x,z,1-5)

New England Comics
2184 Acushnet Ave.
New Bedford, MA 02745
PH/FAX: (508) 995-2693
support@newenglandcomics.com
www.newenglandcomics.com
(a-k,r,t,u,w,x,z,1-5)

New England Comics
732 Washington St.
Norwood, MA 02062
PH/FAX: (781) 769-4552
support@newenglandcomics.com
www.newenglandcomics.com
(a-k,r,t,u,w,x,z,1-5)

New England Comics
1511 Hancock St.
Quincy, MA 02169
PH/FAX: (617) 770-1848
support@newenglandcomics.com
www.newenglandcomics.com
(a-k,r,t,u,w,x,z,1-5)

New England Comics
We Buy Old Comics
Top Dollar Paid
Quincy, MA 02169
PH: (617) 770-1848
support@newenglandcomics.com
www.newenglandcomics.com
(a,b,c)

Bill Cole Enterprises Inc.
P.O. Box 60
Randolph, MA 02368-0060
PH: (781) 986-2653
FAX: (781) 986-2656
sales@bcemylar.com
www.bcemylar.com

Harrison's
252 Essex St.
Salem, MA 01970
PH: (978) 741-0786
FAX: (978) 741-0737
HarrisonsComics@hotmail.com
www.HarrisonsComics.net
(a-z,1-5)

The Outer Limits
437 Moody Street
Waltham, MA 02453
PH: (781) 891-0444
AskOuterLimits@aol.com
www.eOuterLimits.com
(a-p,r-z,1-5)

That's Entertainment
244 Park Avenue
(At the corner of Lois Lane)
Worcester, MA 01609
PH: (508) 755-4207
Ken@ThatsE.com
www.ThatsE.com
(a-z,1-5)

MICHIGAN

Motor City Comics
33228 W. 12 Mile Rd.
PMB 286
Farmington Hills, MI 48334
PH: (248) 426-8059
FAX: (248) 426-8064
michaelg@motorcitycomics.com
www.motorcitycomics.com
(a-c,l-o,r,v,w,x)

A To Z Cards and Comics
32647 Ford Rd.
Garden City, MI 48135
PH: (734) 425-6780
AtoZ@AtoZCardsandComics.com
www.YourAtoZ.com
(a-d,f,g,i,j,t,u,w,x,5)

Harley Yee Comics
P.O. Box 51758
Livonia, MI 48151-5758
PH: (800) 731-1029
FAX: (734) 421-7928
HarleyComx@aol.com
www.HarleyYeeComics.com

MINNESOTA

Nostalgia Zone
3535 East Lake Street
Minneapolis, MN 55406
PH: (612) 822-2806
order@nostalgiazone.com
www.nostalgiazone.com
(a,b,c,e,f,l-p,r,s,t,v,w,x)

NEBRASKA

Robert Beerbohm Comic Art
P.O. Box 507
Fremont, NE 68026
PH: (402) 919-9393
BeerbohmRL@gmail.com
www.BLBComics
(a,b,c,e,l-o,r)

NEVADA

Redbeard's Book Den
P.O. Box 217
Crystal Bay, NV 89402
PH: (775) 831-4848
FAX: (775) 831-4483
www.redbeardsbookden.com
(a,b,c,l,o,p)

Cosmic Comics!
3830 E. Flamingo Rd.
Suite F-2
Las Vegas, NV 89121
PH: (702) 451-6611
FAX: (702) 451-4609
info@CosmicComcsLV.com
www.CosmicComicsLV.com
(a-l,n,o,r,t-x,5)

NEW HAMPSHIRE

Rare Books & Comics
James F. Payette
P.O. Box 750
Bethlehem, NH 03574
PH: (603) 869-2097
FAX: (603) 869-3475
JimPayette@msn.com
www.JamesPayetteComics.com
(a,b,c,e,n,o,p)

NEW JERSEY

Nationwide Comics
Buying All 10¢ & 12¢
original priced comics
Derek Woywood
Clementon, NJ 08021
PH: (856) 217-5737 or
Hotline: (800) 938-0325
FAX: (714) 288-8992
dwoywood@yahoo.com
www.philadelphiacomic-con.com
(a,b,d-h,m,n,q)

Main Street Comics
74 N. Main St.
Milltown, NJ 08850
PH: (732) 828-7886
MSComics@aol.com
facebook.com/
MainStreetComicsNJ
(a-g,i,l,m,r,t,u,w-y,4)

Neat Stuff Collectibles
Brian Schutzer
704 76th Street
North Bergen, NJ 07047
PH: 1-800-903-7246
E-Mail: neatstuffcollectibles
@yahoo.com
www.NeatStuffCollectibles.com

All-Star Auctions
Nadia Mannarino
122 West End Avenue
Ridgewood, NJ 07450
PH: (201) 652-1305
FAX: (501) 325-6504
nadia@allstarauctions.net
www.allstarauctions.net

JHV Associates
(By Appointment Only)
P. O. Box 317
Woodbury Heights, NJ 08097
PH: (856) 845-4010
FAX: (856) 845-3977
JHVassoc@hotmail.com
(a,b,n,s)

NEW YORK

Silver Age Comics
22-55 31st Street
Astoria, NY 11105
PH: (718) 721-9691
PH: (800) 728-9691
FAX: (718) 728-9691
gus@silveragecomics.com
www.silveragecomics.com

Excellent Adventures Comics
110 Milton Ave. (Rt. #50)
Ballston Spa, NY 12020
PH: (518) 884-9498
jbelskis37@aol.com
www.excellentadventurescomics.com
(a-f,m-p,r-x,1-4)

Foxprowl Collectables
440 Ellicott St.
Batavia, NY 14020
PH: (585) 415-1173
foxprowl@yahoo.com
foxprowl.com or Facebook
(a-c,e-g,i-k,m,p-z,1-5)

Pinocchio Collectibles
1814 McDonald Ave.
(off Ave. P)
Brooklyn, NY 11223
PH: (718) 645-2573
a19gaba@aol.com
(b-d,f,i,w,x)

HighGradeComics.com
17 Bethany Drive
Commack, NY 11725
PH: (631) 543-1917
FAX: (631) 864-1921
BobStorms@
HighGradeComics.com
www.HighGradeComics.com
(a,b,c,e)

Best Comics
1300 Jericho Turnpike
New Hyde Park, NY 11040
PH: (516) 328-1900
FAX: (516) 328-1909
TommyBest@aol.com
www.bestcomics.com
(a,b,d,f,m,t,u,w,3,4)

ComicConnect.com
873 Broadway
Suite 201
New York, NY 10003
PH: (212) 895-3999
FAX: (212) 260-4304
support@comicconnect.com
www.comicconnect.com
(a,b,c,m,n,s,v)

Metropolis Collectibles
873 Broadway, Suite 201
New York, NY 10003
PH: (800) 229-6387
FAX: (212) 260-4304
E-Mail: buying@
metropoliscomics.com
www.metropoliscomics.com

Amazing Comics & Collectibles
P.O. Box 470
Sayville, NY 11782
PH: (631) 605-0143
info@amazingco.com
www.amazingco.com

Dan Gallo
Westchester County, NY
PH: (954) 547-9063
DGallo1291@aol.com
eBay ID: DGallo1291
(a,b,c,m)

NORTH CAROLINA

Heroes Aren't Hard To Find
1957 E 7th St.
Charlotte, NC 28204
PH: (704) 375-7462
FAX: (704) 375-7464
www.heroesonline.com

(a) Golden Age Comics
(b) Silver Age Comics
(c) Bronze Age Comics
(d) New Comics & Magazines
(e) Back Issue magazines
(f) Comic Supplies
(g) Collectible Card Games
(h) Role Playing Games
(i) Gaming Supplies
(j) Manga
(k) Anime
(l) Underground Comics
(m) Original Comic Art
(n) Pulps
(o) Big Little Books
(p) Books - Used
(q) Books - New
(r) Comic Related Posters
(s) Movie Posters
(t) Trading Cards
(u) Statues/Mini-busts, etc.
(v) Premiums (Rings, Decoders)
(w) Action Figures
(x) Other Toys
(y) Records/CDs
(z) DVDs/VHS
(1) Doctor Who Items
(2) Simpsons Items
(3) Star Trek Items
(4) Star Wars Items
(5) HeroClix

NORTH DAKOTA

Barry's Collectors Corner
1826 S. Washington St. #38
Grand Cities Mall
Grand Forks, ND 58201
PH: (701) 795-1386
UNDBKB@aol.com
(a-z,1-5)

OHIO

Up Up & Away!
4016 Harrison Avenue
Cincinnati, OH 45211
PH: (513) 661-6300
E-Mail: info
@upupandawaycomics.com
www.uuacomics.com
(a-g,i,m,u,w,2-5)

Bookery Fantasy
13, 15, 16 & 18 W. Main St.
Fairborn, OH 45324
PH: (937) 879-1408
BookeryFan@aol.com
www.BookeryFantasy.com
(a-j,l,n-p,s,u,w,x,z,1-5)

Colonel's Comics
7347 State Route 43
Kent, OH 44240
PH: (330) 931-8400
CBarrow007@aol.com
www.sellurcomics.com
(a,b,c)

Comics and Friends, LLC
7850 Mentor Ave.
Suite 1054
Mentor, OH 44096
PH: (440) 255-4242
comics.and.friends.store
@gmail.com
www.comicsandfriends.com
(a-g,i,j,l,m,n,r,t,u,w-z,1-5)

Parker's Records & Comics
1222 Suite C Rt. 28
Milford, OH 45150
PH/FAX: (513) 575-3665
dkparker39@fuse.net
www.parkersrc.com
(a-i,l,y)

OKLAHOMA

Legendary Comics
217 S. Perkins Rd.
Stillwater, OK 74074
PH: (405) 743-9100
Legendcmcs@aol.com
www.LegendaryComics.com
(a-f,r,w,5)

Want List Comics
(Appointment Only)
P.O. Box 701932
Tulsa, OK 74170
PH: (918) 299-0440
E-Mail: wlc777@cox.net
(a,b,c,m,n,o,s,t,x,3)

OREGON

Future Dreams
1847 East Burnside St.
Suite 116
Portland, OR 97214-1587
PH: (503) 231-8311
fdb@hevanet.com
www.futuredreamsbooks.com
(a-g,i,j,l-n,p-u,w,x,3,4)

PENNSYLVANIA

New Dimension Comics
Clearview Mall
101 Clearview Circle
Butler, PA 16001
PH: (724) 282-5283
butler@ndcomics.com
www.ndcomics.com
(a-l,n,o,r,t,u,w,x,1-5)

New Dimension Comics
Piazza Plaza
20550 Route 19 (Perry Hwy.)
Cranberry Township, PA
16066
PH: (724) 776-0433
cranberry@ndcomics.com
www.ndcomics.com
(a-l,n,o,r,t,u,w,x,1-5)

New Dimension Comics
Megastore
516 Lawrence Ave.
Ellwood City, PA 16117
PH: (724) 758-2324
ec@ndcomics.com
www.ndcomics.com
(a-l,n,o,r,t,u,w,x,1-5)

The Comic Store
28 McGovern Ave.
Lancaster, PA 17602
PH: (717) 397-8737
FAX: (717) 397-8903
comicstore@juno.com
www.comicstorepa.com

New Dimension Comics
Pittsburgh Mills
590 Pittsburgh Mill Circle
Tarentum, PA 15084
PH: (724) 758-1560
mills@ndcomics.com
www.ndcomics.com
(a-l,n,o,r,t,u,w,x,1-5)

New Dimension Comics
Pittsburgh Century III Mall
3075 Clairton Rd. #940
West Mifflin, PA 15213
PH: (412) 655-8661
century3@ndcomics.com
www.ndcomics.com
(a-l,n,o,r,t,u,w,x,1-5)

Comic Store West
2111 Industrial Hwy.
York, PA 17402
PH: (717) 845-9198
Bstoner@comicstorewest.com
www.comicstorewest.com
(d,f,h,t)

Hake's Americana & Collectibles
P.O. Box 12001
York, PA 17402
PH: (866) 404-9800
www.hakes.com

RHODE ISLAND

The Time Capsule
537 Pontiac Ave.
Cranston, RI 02910
PH: (401) 781-5017
thetimecapsule@mail.com
www.thetimecapsule.com
(a-h,l-o,s-z,2-4)

TENNESSEE

Cardsone.com
P.O. Box 3777
Cleveland, TN 37320
PH: (423) 472-3161
FAX: (423) 472-3148
Rsales@cardsone.com
www.cardsone.com

The Great Escape
111-B Gallatin Road North
Madison, TN 37115
PH: (615) 865-8052
FAX: (615) 865-8779
thegreatescapemadison
@gmail.com
www.TheGreatEscapeOnLine.com

The Great Escape
5400 Charlotte Avenue
Nashville, TN 37209
PH: (615) 385-2116
FAX: (615) 297-6588
Email: contactus
@thegreatescapeonline.com
www.TheGreatEscapeOnLine.com

TEXAS

Comic Heaven
P.O. Box 900
Big Sandy, TX 75755
PH: (903) 636-5555
www.comicheaven.net

Heritage Auction Galleries
3500 Maple Avenue
17th Floor
Dallas, TX 75219-3941
PH: (800) 872-6467
www.HA.com

Duncanville Bookstore
101 W. Camp Wisdom Rd.; Ste. J
Duncanville, TX 75116
PH: (972) 298-7546
AndyMac2570@aol.com
www.duncanvillebookstore.com

Worldwide Comics
29369 Raintree Ridge
Fair Oaks Ranch, TX 78015
PH: (830) 368-4103
stephen@wwcomics.com
wwcomics.com

William Hughes' Vintage Collectables
P.O. Box 270244
Flower Mound, TX 75027
PH: (972) 539-9190
FAX: (972) 691-8837
Whughes199@yahoo.com
www.VintageCollectables.net

The Pop Culture Company
11313 Katy Freeway
Houston, TX 77079
PH: (281) 798-0777
www.ThePopCultureCompany.com

Excalibur Comics, Cards & Games
2811 State Line Avenue
Texarkana, TX 75503
PH: (903) 792-5767
FAX: (903) 793-1158
excalicom1@aol.com
www.excaliburccg.com
(a-i,r,t,u,w,x,1,3-5)

VIRGINIA

Untamed Worlds
20722 Timberlake Rd.
Suite K
Lynchburg, VA 24502
PH: (434) 237-7115
info@untamedworlds.com
UntamedWorlds.com
(a-d,f-i,r,u,w,x,1,3-5)

WASHINGTON

Mill Geek Comics
17928 Bothell Everett Highway
Unit #C
Bothell/Mill Creek, WA 98023
PH: (425) 415-6666
millgeekcomics@gmail.com
(a-d,f-i,1-4)

Pristine Comics
2008 South 314th Street
Federal Way, WA 98003
PH: (253) 941-1986
www.PristineComics.com

WISCONSIN

Inner Child Collectibles and Comics
5921 Sixth Avenue "A"
Kenosha, WI 53140
PH: (262) 653-0400
StevenKahn@sbcglobal.net
innerchildcomics.com
(a-f,l-p,r,s,u-x,1-4)

Jef Hinds Comics
PO Box 44803
Madison, WI 53744-4803
PH: (608) 345-8750
jhcomics@jhcomics.com
www.jhcomics.com
(a-c,e,m-o,s,w)

CANADA

MANITOBA

Doug Sulipa's Comic World
Box 21986
Steinbach, MB., R5G 1B5
PH: (204) 346-3674
FAX: (204) 346-1632
dsulipa@gmail.com
www.dougcomicworld.com
(a-e,h,l,n-t,y,z,3,4)

PNJ Comics
"By Appointment Only"
Winnipeg, MB, R2W OM5
PH: (204) 416-8729
FAX: (204) 489-0589
info@pnjcomics.com
www.pnjcomics.com
(a,b,c)

ONTARIO

Big B Comics
1045 Upper James St.
Hamilton, ONT. L9C 3A6
PH: (905) 318-9636
FAX: (905) 318-9055
mailbox@bigbcomics.com
www.bigbcomics.com
(a-g,i,j,l,m,u-x,1-5)

Pendragon Comics & Books
3759 Lakeshore Boulevard West
Toronto, ONT M8W 1R1
PH: (416) 253-6974
pendragoncomics@rogers.com
www.pendragoncomics.com
(a-g,l,n-p,u)

QUEBEC

Heroes Comics
1166 Cure LaBelle
Laval, QC H7V 2V5
PH: (450) 686-9155
FAX: (450) 686-2097
heroescomics@videotron.ca
www.heroscomics.ca
(a-d,f-j,r,t-x,1-5)

INTERNET

Columbia Comics
(803) 361-6318
columbiacomics@gmail.com
columbiacomics.com

Comic Book Certification Service (CBCS)
PH: (844) 870-CBCS
www.CBCScomics.com

Comic Collectors Coop
PH: (507) 400-0661
info@Comicoop.com
www.Comicoop.com

ComicLink Auctions & Exchange
PH: (617) 517-0062
buysell@ComicLink.com
www.ComicLink.com

Cyberspace Comics
PH: (845) 649-7957
steve@cyberspacecomics.com
www.cyberspacecomics.com

GetCashForComics.com
PH: (866) 461-0640
buying@GetCashForComics.com

Hero Trader
PH: (239) 910-4089
info@herotrader.com
www.herotrader.com

HotFlips
PH: (800) 922-3547
www.HotFlips.com

MyComicShop.com
PH: (817) 860-7827
buytrade@mycomicshop.com
www.mycomicshop.com

Pacific Northwest Comics
PH: (206) 992-6424
TUNGLASHR@gmail.com
PH: (323) 620-3329
JB233@NYU.edu

Sharp Comics
PH: (410) 848-0275
Sales@SharpComics.com
www.SharpComics.com

Sparkle City Comics Auctions
PH: (800) 215-4006
buyingeverything@yahoo.com
www.sparklecitycomics.com

Torpedo Comics
PH: (866) 834-4115
TorpedoComics@gmail.com

Vault Grading
PH: (855) 222-5599
sales@vaultgrading.com
www.VaultGrading.com
www.VaultGradedComics.com

WE CAN HELP YOU RECLAIM YOUR CHILDHOOD WITHOUT COSTING YOU YOUR RETIREMENT!

Bringing you a diverse line of affordable collectibles in all of the categories we are traditionally known for, from political to pop culture! Die cast, action figures, wind-ups, slot cars, dolls, puzzles, Disneyana, banks, and much more!

New listings every week!
Items priced for immediate sale.
www.hakes.com

HAKE'S AMERICANA & COLLECTIBLES

P.O. Box 12001 • York, PA 17402 • Tel: (717) 434-1600 • Toll Free (866) 404-9800

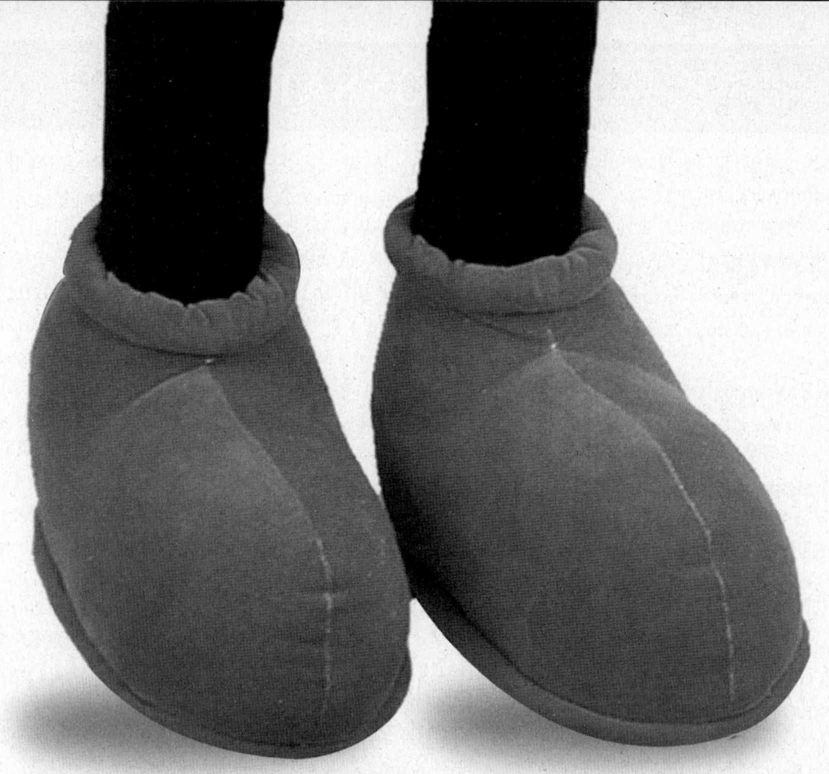

WALK IN THESE SHOES FOR A DAY!

THE ULTIMATE POP CULTURE EXPERIENCE!

WATCH YOUR FAVORITE POP CULTURE ICONS EVOLVE
FROM THE '20s TO THE PRESENT

GEPPI'S entertainment MUSEUM
301 W. CAMDEN STREET • BALTIMORE, MD 21201 • 410-625-7060
WWW.GEPPISMUSEUM.COM

GLOSSARY

a - Story art; **a(i)** - Story art inks; **a(p)** - Story art pencils; **a(r)** - Story art reprint.

ADULT MATERIAL - Contains story and/or art for "mature" readers. Re: sex, violence, strong language.

ADZINE - A magazine primarily devoted to the advertising of comic books and collectibles as its first publishing priority as opposed to written articles.

ALLENTOWN COLLECTION - A collection discovered in 1987-88 just outside Allentown, Pennsylvania. The Allentown collection consisted of 135 Golden Age comics, characterized by high grade and superior paper quality.

ANNUAL - (1) A book that is published yearly; (2) Can also refer to some square bound comics.

ARRIVAL DATE - The date written (often in pencil) or stamped on the cover of comics by either the local wholesaler, newsstand owner, or distributor. The date precedes the cover date by approximately 15 to 75 days, and may vary considerably from one locale to another or from one year to another.

ASHCAN - A publisher's in-house facsimile of a proposed new title. Most ashcans have black and white covers stapled to an existing coverless comic on the inside; other ashcans are totally black and white. In modern parlance, it can also refer to promotional or sold comics, often smaller than standard comic size and usually in black and white, released by publishers to advertise the forthcoming arrival of a new title or story.

ATOM AGE - Comics published from 1946-1956.

B&W - Black and white art.

BACK-UP FEATURE - A story or character that usually appears after the main feature in a comic book; often not featured on the cover.

BAD GIRL ART - A term popularized in the early '90s to describe an attitude as well as a style of art that portrays women in a sexual and often action-oriented way.

BAXTER PAPER - A high quality, heavy, white paper used in the printing of some comics.

BC - Abbreviation for Back Cover.

BI-MONTHLY - Published every two months.

BI-WEEKLY - Published every two weeks.

BONDAGE COVER - Usually denotes a female in bondage.

BOUND COPY - A comic that has been bound into a book. The process requires that the spine be trimmed and sometimes sewn into a book-like binding.

BRITISH ISSUE - A comic printed for distribution in Great Britain; these copies sometimes have the price listed in pence or pounds instead of cents or dollars.

BRITTLENESS - A severe condition of paper deterioration where paper loses its flexibility and thus chips and/or flakes easily.

BRONZE AGE - Comics published from 1970 to 1984.

BROWNING - (1) The aging of paper characterized by the ever-increasing level of oxidation characterized by darkening; (2) The level of paper deterioration one step more severe than tanning and one step before brittleness.

c - Cover art; **c(i)** - Cover inks; **c(p)** - Cover pencils; **c(r)** - Cover reprint.

CAMEO - The brief appearance of one character in the strip of another.

CANADIAN ISSUE - A comic printed for distribution in Canada; these copies sometimes have no advertising.

CCA - Abbreviation for **Comics Code Authority**.

CCA SEAL - An emblem that was placed on the cover of all CCA approved comics beginning in April-May, 1955.

CENTER CREASE - See **Subscription Copy**.

CENTERFOLD or CENTER SPREAD - The two folded pages in the center of a comic book at the terminal end of the staples.

CERTIFIED GRADING - A process provided by a professional grading service that certifies a given grade for a comic and seals the book in a protective **Slab.**

CF - Abbreviation for **Centerfold**.

CFO - Abbreviation for Centerfold Out.

CGC - Abbreviation for the certified comic book grading company, Comics Guaranty, LLC.

CIRCULATION COPY - See **Subscription Copy**.

CIRCULATION FOLD - See **Subscription Fold**.

CLASSIC COVER - A cover considered by collectors to be highly desirable because of its subject matter, artwork, historical importance, etc.

CLEANING - A process in which dirt and dust is removed.

COLOR TOUCH - A restoration process by which colored ink is used to hide color flecks, color flakes, and larger areas of missing color. Short for Color Touch-Up.

COLORIST - An artist who paints the color guides for comics. Many modern colorists use computer technology.

COMIC BOOK DEALER - (1) A seller of comic books; (2) One who makes a living buying and selling

comic books.
COMIC BOOK REPAIR - When a tear, loose staple or centerfold has been mended without changing or adding to the original finish of the book. Repair may involve tape, glue or nylon gossamer, and is easily detected; it is considered a defect.
COMICS CODE AUTHORITY - A voluntary organization comprised of comic book publishers formed in 1954 to review (and possibly censor) comic books before they were printed and distributed. The emblem of the CCA is a white stamp in the upper right hand corner of comics dated after February 1955. The term "post-Code" refers to the time after this practice started, or approximately 1955 to the present.
COMPLETE RUN - All issues of a given title.
CON - A convention or public gathering of fans.
CONDITION - The state of preservation of a comic book, often inaccurately used interchangeably with **Grade**.
CONSERVATION - The European Confederation of Conservator-Restorers' Organizations (ECCO) in its professional guidelines, defines conservation as follows: "Conservation consists mainly of direct action carried out on cultural heritage with the aim of stabilizing condition and retarding further deterioration."
COPPER AGE - Comics published from 1984 to 1992.
COSMIC AEROPLANE COLLECTION - A collection from Salt Lake City, Utah discovered by Cosmic Aeroplane Books, characterized by the moderate to high grade copies of 1930s-40s comics with pencil check marks in the margins of inside pages. It is thought that these comics were kept by a commercial illustration school and the check marks were placed beside panels that instructors wanted students to draw.
COSTUMED HERO - A costumed crime fighter with "developed" human powers instead of super powers.
COUPON CUT or COUPON MISSING - A coupon has been neatly removed with scissors or razor blade from the interior or exterior of the comic as opposed to having been ripped out.
COVER GLOSS - The reflective quality of the cover inks.
COVER TRIMMED - Cover has been reduced in size by neatly cutting away rough or damaged edges.
COVERLESS - A comic with no cover attached. There is a niche demand for coverless comics, particularly in the case of hard-to-find key books otherwise impossible to locate intact.
C/P - Abbreviation for **Cleaned and Pressed**. See **Cleaning**.
CREASE - A fold which causes ink removal, usually resulting in a white line. See **Reading Crease**.
CROSSOVER - A story where one character appears prominently in the story of another character. See **X-Over**.
CVR - Abbreviation for Cover.
DEALER - See **Comic Book Dealer**.
DEACIDIFICATION - Several different processes that reduce acidity in paper.
DEBUT - The first time that a character appears anywhere.
DEFECT - Any fault or flaw that detracts from perfection.
DENVER COLLECTION - A collection consisting primarily of early 1940s high grade number one issues bought at auction in Pennsylvania by a Denver, Colorado dealer.
DIE-CUT COVER - A comic book cover with areas or edges precut by a printer to a special shape or to create a desired effect.
DISTRIBUTOR STRIPES - Color brushed or sprayed on the edges of comic book stacks by the distributor/wholesaler to code them for expedient exchange at the sales racks. Typical colors are red, orange, yellow, green, blue, and purple. Distributor stripes are not a defect.
DOUBLE - A duplicate copy of the same comic book.
DOUBLE COVER - When two covers are stapled to the comic interior instead of the usual one; the exterior cover often protects the interior cover from wear and damage. This is considered a desirable situation by some collectors and may increase collector value; this is not considered a defect.
DRUG PROPAGANDA STORY - A comic that makes an editorial stand about drug use.
DRUG USE STORY - A comic that shows the actual use of drugs: needle use, tripping, harmful effects, etc.
DRY CLEANING - A process in which dirt and dust is removed.
DUOTONE - Printed with black and one other color of ink. This process was common in comics printed in the 1930s.
DUST SHADOW - Darker, usually linear area at the edge of some comics stored in stacks. Some portion of the cover was not covered by the comic immediately above it and it was exposed to settling dust particles. Also see **Oxidation Shadow** and **Sun Shadow**.
EDGAR CHURCH COLLECTION - See **Mile High Collection**.
EMBOSSED COVER - A comic book cover with a pattern, shape or image pressed into the cover from the inside, creating a raised area.
ENCAPSULATION - Refers to the process of sealing certified comics in a protective plastic enclosure. Also see **Slabbing.**
EYE APPEAL - A term which refers to the overall look of a comic

book when held at approximately arm's length. A comic may have nice eye appeal yet still possess defects which reduce grade.

FANZINE - An amateur fan publication.

FC - Abbreviation for Front Cover.

FILE COPY - A high grade comic originating from the publisher's file; contrary to what some might believe, not all file copies are in Gem Mint condition. An arrival date on the cover of a comic does not indicate that it is a file copy, though a copyright date may.

FIRST APPEARANCE - See **Debut**.

FLASHBACK - When a previous story is recalled.

FOIL COVER - A comic book cover that has had a thin metallic foil hot stamped on it. Many of these "gimmick" covers date from the early '90s, and might include chromium, prism and hologram covers as well.

FOUR COLOR - Series of comics produced by Dell, characterized by hundreds of different features; named after the four color process of printing. See **One Shot**.

FOUR COLOR PROCESS - The process of printing with the three primary colors (red, yellow, and blue) plus black.

FUMETTI - Illustration system in which individual frames of a film are colored and used for individual panels to make a comic book story. The most famous example is DC's *Movie Comics* #1-6 from 1939.

GATEFOLD COVER - A double-width fold-out cover.

GENRE - Categories of comic book subject matter; e.g. Science Fiction, Super-Hero, Romance, Funny Animal, Teenage Humor, Crime, War, Western, Mystery, Horror, etc.

GIVEAWAY - Type of comic book intended to be given away as a premium or promotional device instead of being sold.

GLASSES ATTACHED - In 3-D comics, the special blue and red cellophane and cardboard glasses are still attached to the comic.

GLASSES DETACHED - In 3-D comics, the special blue and red cellophane and cardboard glasses are not still attached to the comic; obviously less desirable than **Glasses Attached**.

GOLDEN AGE - Comics published from 1938 (*Action Comics* #1) to 1945.

GOOD GIRL ART - Refers to a style of art, usually from the 1930s-50s, that portrays women in a sexually implicit way.

GREY-TONE COVER - A cover art style in which pencil or charcoal underlies the normal line drawing, used to enhance the effects of light and shadow, thus producing a richer quality. These covers, prized by most collectors, are sometimes referred to as **Painted Covers** but are not actually painted.

HC - Abbreviation for Hardcover.

HEADLIGHTS - Forward illumation devices installed on all automobiles and many other vehicles... OK, OK, it's a euphemism for a comic book cover prominently featuring a woman's breasts in a provocative way. Also see **Bondage Cover** for another collecting euphemism that has long since outlived its appropriateness in these politically correct times.

HOT STAMPING - The process of pressing foil, prism paper and/or inks on cover stock.

HRN - Abbreviation for Highest Reorder Number. This refers to a method used by collectors of Gilberton's *Classic Comics* and *Classics Illustrated* series to distinguish first editions from later printings.

ILLO - Abbreviation for Illustration.

IMPAINT - Another term for **Color Touch**.

INDICIA - Publishing and title information usually located at the bottom of the first page or the bottom of the inside front cover. In some pre-1938 comics and many modern comics, it is located on internal pages.

INFINITY COVER - Shows a scene that repeats itself to infinity.

INKER - Artist that does the inking.

INTRO - Same as **Debut**.

INVESTMENT GRADE COPY - (1) Comic of sufficiently high grade and demand to be viewed by collectors as instantly liquid should the need arise to sell; (2) A comic in VF or better condition; (3) A comic purchased primarily to realize a profit.

ISSUE NUMBER - The actual edition number of a given title.

ISH - Short for Issue.

JLA - Abbreviation for Justice League of America.

JSA - Abbreviation for Justice Society of America.

KEY, KEY BOOK or KEY ISSUE - An issue that contains a first appearance, origin, or other historically or artistically important feature considered especially desirable by collectors.

LAMONT LARSON - Pedigreed collection of high grade 1940s comics with the initials or name of its original owner, Lamont Larson.

LENTICULAR COVERS or "FLICKER" COVERS - A comic book cover overlayed with a ridged plastic sheet such that the special artwork underneath appears to move when the cover is tilted at different angles perpendicular to the ridges.

LETTER COL or LETTER COLUMN - A feature in a comic book that prints and sometimes responds to letters written by its readers.

LINE DRAWN COVER - A cover published in the traditional way where pencil sketches are overdrawn with india ink and then colored. See also **Grey-Tone Cover**, **Photo Cover**, and **Painted Cover**.
LOGO - The title of a strip or comic book as it appears on the cover or title page.
LSH - Abbreviation for Legion of Super-Heroes.
MAGIC LIGHTNING COLLECTION - A collection of high grade 1950s comics from the San Francisco area.
MARVEL CHIPPING - A bindery (trimming/cutting) defect that results in a series of chips and tears at the top, bottom, and right edges of the cover, caused when the cutting blade of an industrial paper trimmer becomes dull. It was dubbed Marvel Chipping because it can be found quite often on Marvel comics from the late '50s and early '60s but can also occur with any company's comic books from the late 1940s through the middle 1960s.
MILE HIGH COLLECTION - High grade collection of over 22,000 comics discovered in Denver, Colorado in 1977, originally owned by Mr. Edgar Church. Comics from this collection are now famous for extremely white pages, fresh smell, and beautiful cover ink reflectivity.
MODERN AGE - A catch-all term applied to comics published since 1992.
MYLAR™ - An inert, very hard, space-age plastic used to make high quality protective bags and sleeves for comic book storage. "Mylar" is a trademark of the DuPont Co.
ND - Abbreviation for **No Date**.
NN - Abbreviation for **No Number**.
NO DATE - When there is no date given on the cover or indicia page.
NO NUMBER - No issue number is given on the cover or indicia page; these are usually first issues or one-shots.
N.Y. LEGIS. COMM. - New York Legislative Committee to Study the Publication of Comics (1951).
ONE-SHOT - When only one issue is published of a title, or when a series is published where each issue is a different title (e.g. Dell's *Four Color Comics*).
ORIGIN - When the story of a character's creation is given.
OVER GUIDE - When a comic book is priced at a value over *Guide* list.
OXIDATION SHADOW - Darker, usually linear area at the edge of some comics stored in stacks. Some portion of the cover was not covered by the comic immediately above it, and it was exposed to the air. Also see **Dust Shadow** and **Sun Shadow**.
p - Art pencils.
PAINTED COVER - (1) Cover taken from an actual painting instead of a line drawing; (2) Inaccurate name for a grey-toned cover.
PANELOLOGIST - One who researches comic books and/or comic strips.
PANNAPICTAGRAPHIST - One possible term for someone who collects comic books; can you figure out why it hasn't exactly taken off in common parlance?
PAPER COVER - Comic book cover made from the same newsprint as the interior pages. These books are extremely rare in high grade.
PARADE OF PLEASURE - A book about the censorship of comics.
PB - Abbreviation for Paperback.
PEDIGREE - A book from a famous and usually high grade collection - e.g. Allentown, Lamont Larson, Edgar Church/Mile High, Denver, San Francisco, Cosmic Aeroplane, etc. Beware of non-pedigree collections being promoted as pedigree books; only outstanding high grade collections similar to those listed qualify.
PENCILER - Artist that does the pencils...you're figuring out some of these definitions without us by now, aren't you?
PERFECT BINDING - Pages are glued to the cover as opposed to being stapled to the cover, resulting in a flat binded side. Also known as **Square Back or Square Bound**.
PG - Abbreviation for Page.
PHOTO COVER - Comic book cover featuring a photographic image instead of a line drawing or painting.
PIECE REPLACEMENT - A process by which pieces are added to replace areas of missing paper.
PIONEER AGE - Comics published from the 1500s to 1828.
PLATINUM AGE - Comics published from 1883 to 1938.
POLYPROPALENE - A type of plastic used in the manufacture of comic book bags; now considered harmful to paper and not recommended for long term storage of comics.
POP - Abbreviation for the anti-comic book volume, *Parade of Pleasure*.
POST-CODE - Describes comics published after February 1955 and usually displaying the CCA stamp in the upper right-hand corner.
POUGHKEEPSIE - Refers to a large collection of Dell Comics file copies believed to have originated from the warehouse of Western Publishing in Poughkeepsie, NY.
PP - Abbreviation for Pages.
PRE-CODE - Describes comics published before the **Comics Code Authority** seal began appearing on covers in 1955.

PRE-HERO DC - A term used to describe *More Fun* #1-51 (pre-Spectre), *Adventure* #1-39 (pre-Sandman), and *Detective* #1-26 (pre-Batman). The term is actually inaccurate because technically there were "heroes" in the above books.

PRE-HERO MARVEL - A term used to describe *Strange Tales* #1-100 (pre-Human Torch), *Journey Into Mystery* #1-82 (pre-Thor), *Tales To Astonish* #1-35 (pre-Ant Man), and *Tales Of Suspense* #1-38 (pre-Iron Man).

PRESERVATION - Another term for **Conservation**.

PRESSING - A term used to describe a variety of processes or procedures, professional and amateur, under which an issue is pressed to eliminate wrinkles, bends, dimples and/or other perceived defects and thus improve its appearance. Some types of pressing involve disassembling the book and performing other work on it prior to its pressing and reassembly. Some methods are generally easily discerned by professionals and amateurs. Other types of pressing, however, can pose difficulty for even experienced professionals to detect. In all cases, readers are cautioned that unintended damage can occur in some instances. Related defects will diminish an issue's grade correspondingly rather than improve it.

PROVENANCE - When the owner of a book is known and is stated for the purpose of authenticating and documenting the history of the book. Example: A book from the Stan Lee or Forrest Ackerman collection would be an example of a value-adding provenance.

PULP - Cheaply produced magazine made from low grade newsprint. The term comes from the wood pulp that was used in the paper manufacturing process.

QUARTERLY - Published every three months (four times a year).

R - Abbreviation for Reprint.

RARE - 10-20 copies estimated to exist.

RAT CHEW - Damage caused by the gnawing of rats and mice.

RBCC - Abbreviation for Rockets Blast Comic Collector, one of the first and most prominent adzines instrumental in developing the early comic book market.

READING COPY - A comic that is in FAIR to GOOD condition and is often used for research; the condition has been sufficiently reduced to the point where general handling will not degrade it further.

READING CREASE - Book-length, vertical front cover crease at staples, caused by bending the cover over the staples. Square-bounds receive these creases just by opening the cover too far to the left.

REILLY, TOM - A large high grade collection of 1939-1945 comics with 5000+ books.

REINFORCEMENT - A process by which a weak or split page or cover is reinforced with adhesive and reinforcement paper.

REPRINT COMICS - In earlier decades, comic books that contained newspaper strip reprints; modern reprint comics usually contain stories originally featured in older comic books.

RESTORATION - Any attempt, whether professional or amateur, to enhance the appearance of an aging or damaged comic book using additive procedures. These procedures may include any or all of the following techniques: recoloring, adding missing paper, trimming, reglossing, reinforcement, glue, etc. Amateur work can lower the value of a book, and even professional restoration has now gained a negative aura in the modern marketplace from some quarters. In all cases a restored book can never be worth the same as an unrestored book in the same condition. There is no consensus on the inclusion of pressing, non-aqueous cleaning, tape removal and in some cases staple replacement in this definition. Until such time as there is consensus, we encourage continued debate and interaction among all interested parties and reflection upon the standards in other hobbies and art forms.

REVIVAL - An issue that begins republishing a comic book character after a period of dormancy.

ROCKFORD - A high grade collection of 1940s comics with 2000+ books from Rockford, IL.

ROLLED SPINE - A condition where the left edge of a comic book curves toward the front or back; a defect caused by folding back each page as the comic was read.

ROUND BOUND - Standard saddle stitch binding typical of most comics.

RUN - A group of comics of one title where most or all of the issues are present. See **Complete Run**.

S&K - Abbreviation for the legendary creative team of Joe Simon and Jack Kirby, creators of Marvel Comics' Captain America.

SADDLE STITCH - The staple binding of magazines and comic books.

SAN FRANCISCO COLLECTION - (see **Reilly, Tom**)

SCARCE - 20-100 copies estimated to exist.

SEDUCTION OF THE INNOCENT - An inflammatory book written by Dr. Frederic Wertham and published in 1953; Wertham asserted that comics were responsible for rampant juvenile deliquency in American youth.

SET - (1) A complete run of a given title; (2) A grouping of comics for sale.

SEMI-MONTHLY - Published

twice a month, but not necessarily **Bi-Weekly**.

SEWN SPINE - A comic with many spine perforations where binders' thread held it into a bound volume. This is considered a defect.

SF - Abbreviation for Science Fiction (the other commonly used term, "sci-fi," is often considered derogatory or indicative of more "low-brow" rather than "literary" science fiction, i.e. "sci-fi television."

SILVER AGE - Comics published from 1956 to 1970.

SILVER PROOF - A black and white actual size print on thick glossy paper hand-painted by an artist to indicate colors to the engraver.

SLAB - Colloquial term for the plastic enclosure used by grading certification companies to seal in certified comics.

SLABBING - Colloquial term for the process of encapsulating certified comics in a plastic enclosure.

SOTI - Abbreviation for **Seduction of the Innocent**.

SPINE - The left-hand edge of the comic that has been folded and stapled.

SPINE ROLL - A condition where the left edge of the comic book curves toward the front or back, caused by folding back each page as the comic was read.

SPINE SPLIT SEALED - A process by which a spine split is sealed using an adhesive.

SPLASH PAGE - A **Splash Panel** that takes up the entire page.

SPLASH PANEL - (1) The first panel of a comic book story, usually larger than other panels and usually containing the title and credits of the story; (2) An oversized interior panel.

SQUARE BACK or SQUARE BOUND - See **Perfect Binding**.

STORE STAMP - Store name (and sometimes address and telephone number) stamped in ink via rubber stamp and stamp pad.

SUBSCRIPTION COPY - A comic sent through the mail directly from the publisher or publisher's agent. Most are folded in half, causing a subscription crease or fold running down the center of the comic from top to bottom; this is considered a defect.

SUBSCRIPTION CREASE - See **Subscription Copy**.

SUBSCRIPTION FOLD - See **Subscription Copy**. Differs from a **Subscription Crease** in that no ink is missing as a result of the fold.

SUN SHADOW - Darker, usually linear area at the edge of some comics stored in stacks. Some portion of the cover was not covered by the comic immediately above it, and it suffered prolonged exposure to light. A serious defect, unlike a **Dust Shadow**, which can sometimes be removed. Also see **Oxidation Shadow**.

SUPER-HERO - A costumed crime fighter with powers beyond those of mortal man.

SUPER-VILLAIN - A costumed criminal with powers beyond those of mortal man; the antithesis of **Super-Hero**.

SWIPE - A panel, sequence, or story obviously borrowed from previously published material.

TEAR SEALS - A process by which a tear is sealed using an adhesive.

TEXT ILLO. - A drawing or small panel in a text story that almost never has a dialogue balloon.

TEXT PAGE - A page with no panels or drawings.

TEXT STORY - A story with few if any illustrations commonly used as filler material during the first three decades of comics.

3-D COMIC - Comic art that is drawn and printed in two color layers, producing a 3-D effect when viewed through special glasses.

3-D EFFECT COMIC - Comic art that is drawn to appear as if in 3-D but isn't.

TITLE - The name of the comic book.

TITLE PAGE - First page of a story showing the title of the story and possibly the creative credits and indicia.

TRIMMED - (1) A bindery process which separates top, right, and bottom of pages and cuts comic books to the proper size; (2) A repair process in which defects along the edges of a comic book are removed with the use of scissors, razor blades, and/or paper cutters. Comic books which have been repaired in this fashion are considered defectives.

TTA - Abbreviation for *Tales to Astonish*.

UK - Abbreviation for British edition (United Kingdom).

UNDER GUIDE - When a comic book is priced at a value less than *Guide* list.

UPGRADE - To obtain another copy of the same comic book in a higher grade.

VARIANT COVER - A different cover image used on the same issue.

VERY RARE - 1 to 10 copies estimated to exist.

VICTORIAN AGE - Comics published from 1828 to 1883.

WANT LIST - A listing of comics needed by a collector, or a list of comics that a collector is interested in purchasing.

WAREHOUSE COPY - Originating from a publisher's warehouse; similar to file copy.

WHITE MOUNTAIN COLLECTION - A collection of high grade 1950s and 1960s comics which originated in New England.

X-OVER - Short for **Crossover**.

ZINE - Short for **Fanzine**.

CGC

How the Company Has Grown and How It Works

By the CGC Grading Team

The world of comic book collecting has grown and matured since the 2000 introduction of CGC (Certified Guaranty Company). Before the founding of CGC comic book transactions were mainly face to face deals with buyers and sellers reviewing the books and negotiating the sales price. The advent of the internet changed all that by opening up new opportunities in that comic books from across the country were as easy to buy as those across the street. But with this new market came risk. Risk of not knowing the seller and risk of buying a book virtually sight unseen except for an online image.

CGC was created to help bring order and stability to comic book sales, and to put an end to the risk and the chaos that accompanied online sales. CGC is the first independent, impartial, third-party comic book grading service. A proven and respected commitment to integrity, accuracy, consistency and impartiality has made CGC the leader in its field, becoming a tool to help people with their buying and selling decisions. The universally accepted grading scale ensures consistency and gives both dealers and collectors a sense of dependability when making purchasing decisions. With CGC certification, a collector knows what he or she is getting based on an accurate and comprehensive description that can be found on the CGC certification label.

If you've ever wondered about how it's done, here's a look at how CGC came together and how a book is certified.

The Formation of the Company

In January of 2000 CGC was launched under the umbrella of the Certified Collectibles Group, which includes Numismatic Guaranty Corporation (NGC), the largest third-party coin grading company in the world, Numismatic Conservation Services (NCS), the leading authority in numismatic conservation, Paper Money Guaranty (PMG), the world's leading currency certification company and Classic Collectible Services (CCS), the world's premier comic book restoration, restoration removal and pressing company.

The Collectibles Group sought out talented and ethical individuals to grade comic books. Experts needed a history of necessary skills to verify a comic book's authenticity and to detect restoration that can affect its value. To identify these individuals, many of the most respected individuals in the hobby were consulted, and, based on their recommendations a core grading team was selected.

The members of the CGC grading team come from diverse backgrounds, and many were comic book dealers at some time in their careers. Experience in the commercial sector can be an essential ingredient in becoming familiar with market standards. Upon joining CGC, all graders immediately cease all commercial trading. All CGC employees are prohibited from commercially buying and selling comic books to ensure they remain completely impartial, having no vested interest other than a dedication to serving clients through accurate and consistent grading.

When it was time to develop a uniform grading standard, the hobby's leaders were once again called upon. Everyone agreed that the *Overstreet Guide* was the foundation of this standard, but there were a number of subjective interpretations of its published definitions. It was critical to understand how these guidelines were being applied to the everyday buying and selling of comics. To accomplish this, approximately 50 of the hobby's top experts took part in an extensive grading test. Their grades were averaged and an accurate grading standard reflecting the collective experience of the hobby's most prominent individuals was thus developed. CGC now had the best standard and the best team to apply it.

With the graders in place and the grading scale established, the next step was to develop a tamper-evident holder for the long-term storage and display of certified comics. This proved to be a technical challenge. Exhaustive material tests were conducted to determine that the holders were archival safe. To create a true first line of defense, it was determined that the comic book should be sealed in a soft inner well, then sealed again inside a tamper evident hard plastic case with interlocking ridges to enable compact storage. The CGC certified grade appears on a label sealed inside the holder for an additional level of security.

Submitting Books

Comic books may be submitted for certification in two ways - they can be submitted by authorized dealers or by Collectors Society members. The Collectors Society is an online community with direct access to certification service from CGC, and submissions can be prepared using online submission forms or paper forms. Both dealers and Collectors Society members typically send their comics to CGC's offices by registered mail or through an insured express company. Submissions are also accepted at many of the Comic Cons that occur around the country throughout the year. CGC will grade on-site at selected shows.

Receiving the Books

Every day, CGC's Receiving Department opens newly arrived packages and immediately verifies that the number of books in each package matches the number shown on the submitted invoice. Once this is done, a more detailed comparison is made to ensure that their invoice descriptions correspond to the actual comics. This information is entered into a computer, and from this time forth, the comics will be traceable at all stages of the grading process by their invoice number and their line number within that invoice. Each book is checked to see that it is properly prepared for grading in an appropriately sized comic bag with backing board and then is labeled with a numbered barcode containing the pertinent data of invoice number and line item information for quick reading by the computer. Before any grading is performed, the book is examined by a CGC Restoration Detection Specialist. If any form of restoration work is detected, this information is entered into the computer, making it available to the grading team.

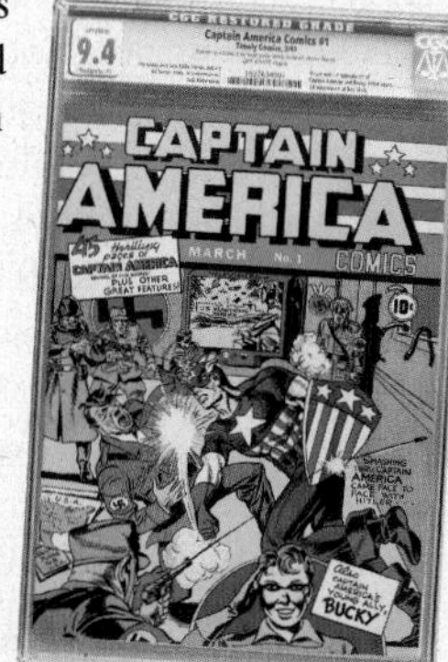

Each comic book receives a restoration check and the results appear on the label.

CGC RESTORED GRADE

Captain America Comics #1

Timely Comics, 3/41

Restoration includes: color touch, pieces added, reinforced, staples cleaned.

OFF-WHITE Pages

The Grading Begins

After being examined by a Restoration Detection Specialist, the book is then passed on to the graders. At this stage the comics have been properly sleeved and barcoded for grading and have been separated from their original invoice. This step is taken to ensure that graders do not know whose books they are grading, as a further guarantee of impartiality. The grading process begins by having the book's pages counted and entering into the computer any peculiarities or flaws that may affect a book's grade. Some examples of this would be "spine small stress lines," "staple rusted w/rust stained interior," "interior heavy tanning" and "bottom right front cover large crease." This information is entered into the "Graders Notes" field and a grade is assigned.

When other graders examine the comic, they are not able to see any previous assigned grades, so as to not influence their evaluation. Graders are only able to view previous Graders Notes after determining their own grade. The Grader may then add to the existing commentary if he believes more remarks are in order. The Grading Finalizer is the last person to examine the book. He makes a final restoration check before determining his own grade, at which time he reviews the grades and notes entered by the previous graders. If all grades are in agreement or are very close, he will assign the book's final grade. The book is then forwarded to the Encapsulation Department for sealing. If there is disagreement among the graders, a discussion will ensue until a final determination is made and the book forwarded.

Encapsulating the Comics

After each comic has been graded and the necessary numbers and text entered into their respective data fields, all the comics on a particular invoice are taken from the Grading Department into the Encapsulation Department. Here, appropriately color-coded labels are printed bearing the proper descriptive text, including each book's grade and identification number. This is critical, as it serves to make each certified comic unique and is also a significant deterrent to counterfeiting CGC's valued product. All of the above information is duplicated in a barcode, which also appears on the comic's label.

The newly-printed labels are stacked in the same sequence as the comics to be encapsulated with them, ensuring that each book and its label match one another. The comic is now ready to be fitted inside an archival-quality interior well, which is then sealed within a transparent capsule, along with the book's color-coded label. This is accomplished through a combination of compression and ultrasonic vibration.

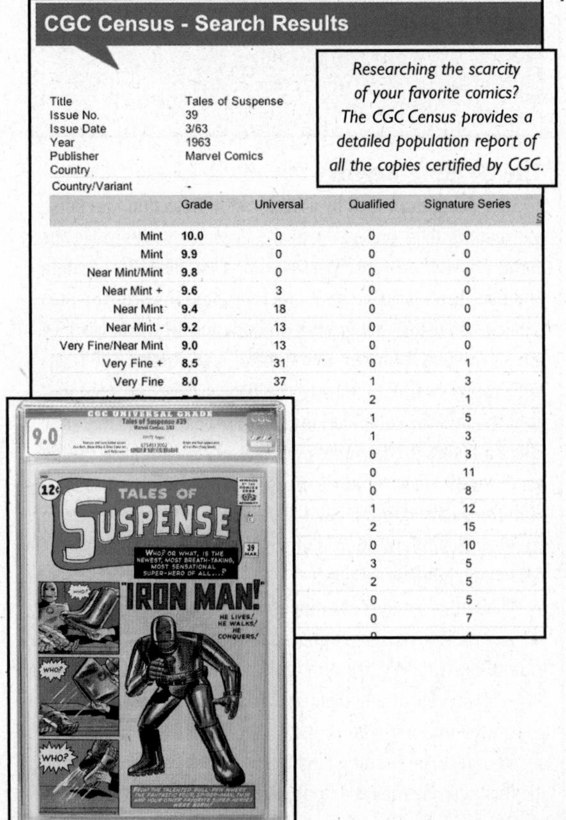

CGC Census - Search Results

Title	Tales of Suspense
Issue No.	39
Issue Date	3/63
Year	1963
Publisher	Marvel Comics
Country	
Country/Variant	-

	Grade	Universal	Qualified	Signature Series
Mint	10.0	0	0	0
Mint	9.9	0	0	0
Near Mint/Mint	9.8	0	0	0
Near Mint +	9.6	3	0	0
Near Mint	9.4	18	0	0
Near Mint -	9.2	13	0	0
Very Fine/Near Mint	9.0	13	0	0
Very Fine +	8.5	31	0	1
Very Fine	8.0	37	1	3
			2	1
			1	5
			1	3
			0	3
			0	11
			0	8
			1	12
			2	15
			0	10
			3	5
			2	5
			0	5
			0	7

Researching the scarcity of your favorite comics? The CGC Census provides a detailed population report of all the copies certified by CGC.

The Comics are Shipped

After encapsulation, all comics are returned briefly to the Grading Department for a quality control inspection. Here, they are examined to make certain that their labels are correct for both the grade and its accompanying descriptive information. Quality control also inspects each book for any flaws in its holder, such as scuffs or nicks. While these are quite rare, CGC is careful to make certain that the comics it certifies are not only accurately graded, but attractively presented as well. When all the comics have been inspected, they're delivered to our Shipping Department for packaging. The comics are counted and their labels checked against the original invoice to make certain that no mistakes have occurred. A Shipping Department employee then verifies the method of transport as selected by the submitter on the invoice and prepares the comics for delivery or they are held in CGC's vault for in-person pick-up by the submitter.

No matter whether the US Postal Service or some private carrier is used, the method of packaging is essentially the same. The encapsulated comics are placed vertically inside sturdy cardboard boxes. In 2005, CGC developed a custom shipping box to enable the highest level of stability during shipping. A copy of the submitter's invoice is included before the box is sealed and heavy tape is used to prevent accidental or unauthorized opening of the box while it's in transit.

The barcode of every comic book is scanned before it is placed into its shipping box. The status of the book is changed to "shipped" in our tracking system, and we retain a record of what books were shipped in which box. This is the final crucial step of our detailed internal tracking system.

The CGC Label

Comic books certified by CGC bear color-coded labels that have different meanings. Whenever purchasing a CGC-certified comic, be certain to note not only the book's grade but also its label category. A Universal label is denoted by the color blue and indicates that a book was not found to have any qualifying defects or signs of restoration. There is one exception to this policy: At CGC's discretion, comics having a very minor amount of glue and/or color touch-up may still qualify for a Universal label provided that they were produced approximately 1950 or earlier and that such restoration is noted underneath the assigned grade.

As its name implies, the Restored label, identified by its purple color, is used for books found to have restoration work performed on them. The grade assigned is based on the book's appearance, with the restoration noted. A distinction is made between Amateur and Professional restoration, this judgment being based on the materials used. Since the degree of work performed is also significant with restored books, there are a total of seven possible descriptions under the Restored label. Each description is prefaced with the word Apparent, followed by Slight, Moderate or Extensive in combination with the final descriptors Amateur or Professional. Examples of Restored labels might read Apparent Moderate Professional or Apparent Slight Amateur, both descriptions then being followed by the book's grade. Finally, comics which have had no restoration other than a trimming of their covers or edges are labeled as simply Apparent, followed by their grade.

The Qualified label is green, and this indicates that one qualifying defect is present on a book. An example of such a qualifying feature would be a missing Marvel Value Stamp that does not affect the story. While such a book technically may grade 1.5, it may appear to grade 9.6. In such instances, assigning a grade of just 1.5 does not fully represent the value of the comic to a collector. Through use of the green Qualified label, a comic buyer is able to make an informed decision as to what he is purchasing in terms of its overall desirability. Because of the complexity involved, green labels are assigned quite seldom and then only when considered absolutely necessary. In addition, comic books that have an unwitnessed signature, and therefore are not eligible for the Signature Series label (see below), get the Qualified label. This is the most common use for the Qualified label. This shows what the grade of the book would have been if the signature was not present.

CGC's Signature Series label is yellow, and this is used when a comic book has been signed or been sketched on by a creator in the presence of a CGC representative, assuring the signature's or sketch's authenticity. Only books that meet CGC's strict criteria for authenticity are eligible for the Signature Series label. In addition to the certified grade, the yellow label includes who signed it and when it was signed. If appropriate, a Signature Series label may state where a book was signed. In 2007, CGC introduced a Signature Series Restored label. Similar to the CGC Signature Series label in color, it is differentiated by a purple bar across the top. Restoration is noted in the same fashion as on the purple CGC Restored label, and, as with the regular Signature Series label, restored books must be signed in the presence of CGC representatives in order to be eligible for signature authentication.

CGC encapsulation is not limited to standard size comics. Magazines and small promotional comics are included as well.

The Evolution of CGC and CCG

In October of 2003, CGC began to certify comic book related magazines. The certification process and label system for magazines is exactly the same as for comic books. Some examples of comic book related magazines CGC certifies are *MAD Magazine, Vampirella, Creepy, Eerie* and *Famous Monsters of Filmland.*

More recently CGC introduced grading and encapsulation for *Sports Illustrated* and *Playboy* magazines, Movie Lobby Cards and Photographs making us the first independent, impartial, expert third-party grading service for all types of collectibles.

In a move intended to strengthen CGC's commitment to promoting the comic collecting hobby and enhance the collecting experience, CGC's parent company Certified Collectibles Group acquired Classics Incorporated, the world's premier comic book restoration, restoration removal and pressing company, in 2012. Previously located in Dallas, TX, Classics Incorporated relocated to Sarasota, FL to become an independent member of the Certified Collectibles Group under the new name Classic Collectible Services (CCS). Customers who wish to send books in for pressing, restoration or restoration removal are be able to send them to CCS and have them transfer directly to CGC for grading — creating a synergistic relationship that saves customers time, shipping and insurance expenses.

For more information on comic book certification and CGC's many services, please visit our website at www.CGCcomics.com

A Signature Series encapsulation provides an assurance of authenticity for the signature. In this case, it's the perpetually protected prodigious penmanship of the legendary Stan Lee.

All Golden & Silver Age fans need an Alter Ego™

Edited by Marvel Comics writer/editor **ROY THOMAS, ALTER EGO**—the greatest 'zine of the 1960s—is back, all-new, and focusing on Golden AND Silver Age comics and creators with articles, interviews, unseen art, P.C. Hamerlinck's **FCA** (**Fawcett Collectors of America,** featuring the archives of C.C. Beck), Michael T. Gilbert's **MR. MONSTER**, Bill Schelly, and more!

(84-page magazine with COLOR)
SINGLE ISSUES: $8.95 US
DIGITAL EDITIONS: $3.95 US

8-ISSUE SUBSCRIPTIONS:
$67 Standard US, $82 First Class US (Canada: $85, Elsewhere: $104 Surface Mail).

JUSTICE SOCIETY of AMERICA! $8.95 in the USA No.109 May 2012 80 PAGES FULL COLOR! PLUS: BERNARD BAILY

Characters TM & © their respective owners.

Call or write for a FREE CATALOG, or go online for an ULTIMATE BUNDLE, with all the issues at HALF-PRICE!

TwoMorrows. Celebrating The Art & History Of Comics.

TwoMorrows Publishing • 10407 Bedfordtown Drive • Raleigh, NC 27614 USA • 919-449-0344
E-mail: store@twomorrows.com • www.twomorrows.com

VISA MasterCard DISCOVER PayPal

If you love comics of the '70s & '80s, get a BACK ISSUE!

Characters TM & © their respective owners.

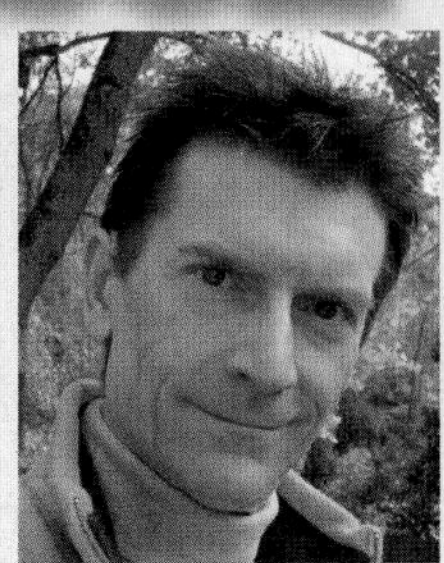

Edited by former DC and Dark Horse editor **MICHAEL EURY, BACK ISSUE** magazine celebrates comic books of the 1970s, 1980s, and today through recurring (and rotating) departments such as "Pro2Pro" (a dialogue between two professionals), "Greatest Stories Never Told" (spotlighting unrealized comics series or stories), and more!

(84-page FULL-COLOR magazine)
SINGLE ISSUES: $8.95 US
DIGITAL EDITIONS: $3.95 US

8-ISSUE SUBSCRIPTIONS:
$67 Standard US, $82 First Class US
(Canada: $85, Elsewhere: $104 Surface Mail).

Call or write for a FREE CATALOG, or go online for an ULTIMATE BUNDLE, with all the issues at HALF-PRICE!

TwoMorrows. Celebrating The Art & History Of Comics.

TwoMorrows Publishing • 10407 Bedfordtown Drive • Raleigh, NC 27614 USA • 919-449-0344
E-mail: store@twomorrows.com • www.twomorrows.com

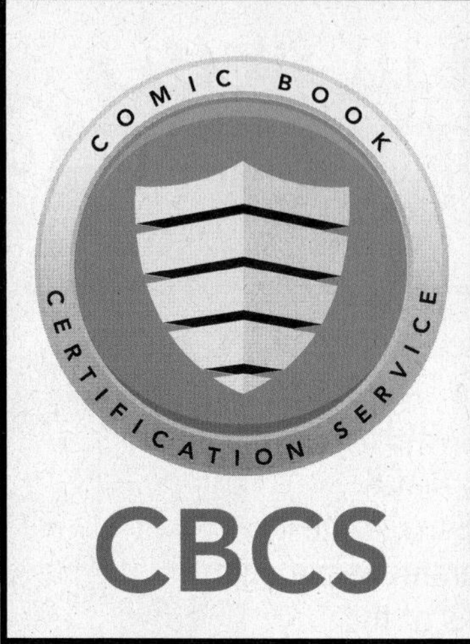

CBCS: An Introduction to the New Independent Grading Service

By J.C. Vaughn

His knowledge and enthusiasm for the world of comic books made Steve Borock an intriguing figure even before his tenures as President and Primary Grader for CGC and Senior Consignment Director for Heritage Auctions.

Over the years, in addition to his high profile professional occupations, he has capitalized on his connections to help others in need as a board member of The Hero Initiative and as auctioneer for the New York Comic Con and C2E2's fundraiser auctions for St. Jude Children's Hospital. He has also participated as an active Overstreet Advisor for years, as well as a Senior Advisor for The Overstreet Comic Book Grading Guide.

When we heard that he had joined the Comic Book Certification Service (CBCS) as President and Primary Grader, we wanted to know what brought him back to independent, third party grading, and how his new firm might distinguish themselves from their already established competition.

Overstreet: Independent third-party grading of comics is such a part of the industry or hobby now that it's difficult for many to remember how it was initially perceived when it was first introduced. What do you remember about the period in which it started?

Steve Borock (SB): The fact is that the majority of people who expressed an opinion thought it wouldn't work, and they weren't shy about saying so. There were some early proponents, of course, but they were vastly outnumbered. That said, the need for independent grading had become very apparent to a core group. The market was largely stagnant. Key dealers with keen eyes for grading and sterling reputations, enjoyed the trust of their peers, but there was no mechanism for others to build up to that level of consumer or peer confidence.

Internet sales, largely through eBay, opened a whole new frontier, but they also came with a significant number of disputes about the grades. The lack of independent, verifiable grades was an impediment to a larger, healthier market.

Overstreet: What sort of turning points do you remember in its evolution?

SB: After slow going at first, certification saw its first real victory in an auction staged by Greg Manning Auctions. Watchers were surprised by the prices realized. After that, through 2003-2004, the industry saw a dramatic increase in the number of certified comics available at conventions and from dealers.

Since then, we've seen the evolution of the business, an increase in high end liquidity, and a substantial increase in consumer confidence in the comics they're buying in person, online or from catalogs. It's no longer only confined by having to know the dealer in question very well. Instead, the consumer can focus on the critical factors: "Is this the comic I'm looking for, is it in the grade I want and is this the price I am willing to pay?" Between 1999, when I helped start CGC, and 2008, when I left, we saw the attitude of the marketplace entirely shift on the subject of certification.

Overstreet: That brings us to the present. Can the market support two grading companies?

SB: The answer to that is straight forward: Yes. If we didn't believe that, we wouldn't be here.

Overstreet: What will you do differently?

SB: We'll start with lower prices and faster turn times, which is self-explanatory. One of the things I'm happiest about is our holder. It is state-of-the-art and the interior sleeve will be made of a material called PETG, which is archival, crystal clear, incredibly smooth and free of any blemishes or imperfections. It is in the Mylar family, but can be molded and heat sealed. The label will contain more information, as we are splitting Restoration and Conservation into separate categories.

There is a big difference between a comic that has a spine split sealed to stop that spine split from getting worse and someone putting acrylic color touch on a cover just to make it look better. That color touch is not helping to conserve the comic as it's just there to make it look better, or worse, to fool an unsuspecting buyer into thinking it is in an untouched, higher grade.

Overstreet: You've done certification previously, and you've taken on other roles in the industry. What brought you back to grading?

SB: When I left grading to work at Heritage, I really thought that was it. In the end, though, there's something very compelling about this challenge. Even with our experience, we'll be the new kids on the block. We'll have to do something better just to get in the door. Again, I wouldn't be doing this if I didn't think we had something great to offer our hobby.

And speaking of experience, over the next few months people will come to know our staff, but I'm pleased to say that West Stephan is already on board. Between just the two of us, we start with about 70 years of grading, pedigree knowledge, and restoration detection experience from buying and selling as well as "professional" grading.

CBCS believes that our graders should have experience in the market place as that's how you truly learn to grade, learning and refining what hobbyists expect a grade should be when buying and selling. As many will tell you, grading is an art, not just a science. The overall look of an unrestored comic must really be factored into the grade

All of us at CBCS think that most things are better when there's competition. Consumers benefit from having selections to make. There is much competition in the card, paper money, and coin hobbies, why shouldn't our hobby have their choice of a certification company as well?

Overstreet: You've mentioned to us over the years that you believe transparency is a major component of consumer confidence. How will you address this at your new company?

SB: We feel that transparency is the key to helping the collecting community buy and sell comics. With that in mind, CBCS will have a published "grading guideline" on our website. We believe that this will also be a big help to collectors new to the hobby.

CBCS will have scheduled tours of our facility, so that our clients can see where their books are graded and how they are safely stored, as well as seeing the flow and professionalism of the certification process.

Further, once a comic is certified, we are going to give out grading notes for free on our website. Once someone has paid CBCS to certify his or her comic, it is only fair that a submitter should know how our grading team factored in the defects that resulted in the given grade.

Overstreet: Are there other things you'll be doing – or not doing – to bolster consumer confidence?

SB: In addition to our interactions with our customers, we believe it's also very important how we conduct ourselves when it comes to potential conflicts of interest. Neither CBCS employees – full or part time – nor any of their family members are allowed to buy and sell CBCS-certified comics or submit comic books for CBCS grading.

Now of course just about everyone at CBCS loves comics. They wouldn't be here otherwise, but if our grades are going to be perceived in a light that is beneficial to everyone, the trust factor has to be there. This is one way we will work to cultivate it. A CBCS employee who collects comics should not have any need to have a comic certified, as they should be able to purchase a comic for their personal collection using their knowledge of comics or having one of our graders to look that book over for them.

Another way is that CBCS employees, again, full or part time, are not allowed to sell ungraded comic books through auction houses or any anonymous sources.

Beyond that, CBCS pre-graders, senior graders and management are not allowed to accept gifts of any kind, including food, drink or entertainment, from any CBCS submitter or potential submitter. These CBCS employees must pay their own way, at all times, during conventions for items not reimbursed to them by CBCS.

Overstreet: In terms of practical, day-to-day operations, what do you see CBCS doing differently?

SB: We believe that dependability is a vital factor for those who submit their comics for certification. With that in mind, CBCS will have guaranteed turn times. It is unfair to our clients to offer a service and not deliver on a promise. In fact, we think we – and not the customer – should be penalized if we can't deliver on our promise, so if CBCS is more than a few days late shipping comics, our clients will be reimbursed with a certain amount of credit.

Overstreet: While maybe not as much as you, Steve, but like a lot of fans, collectors and dealers, we're very interested to see where all of this goes.

SB: This should be one hell of a ride! I hope our hobby accepts and loves what CBCS has to offer!

CBCS President and Primary Grader Steve Borock

CBM RETURNS IN A NEW FORMAT!

Overstreet's Comic Book Marketplace returns as a full-color, 192-page trade paperback with feature articles, interviews, commentary, comic book and original comic art market reports, great examples from comic art collectors, and much more!

COVER A

COVER B

COVER C

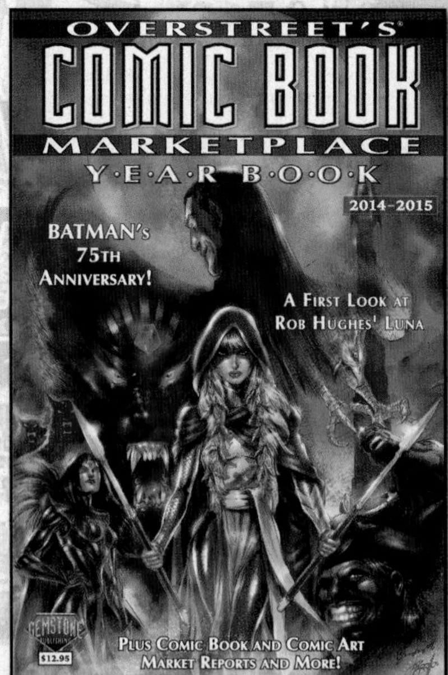

COVER D

All characters ©2014 their respective copyright holders. Overstreet® is a Registered Trademark of Gemstone Publishing, Inc. All Rights Reserved.

In *PREVIEWS* in July. On Sale in September.

GEPPI'S ENTERTAINMENT MUSEUM PRESENTS

The OVERSTREET HALL OF FAME

The Overstreet Hall of Fame was conceived to single out individuals who have made great contributions to the comic book arts.
This includes writers, artists, editors, publishers and others who have plied their craft in insightful and meaningful ways.

While such evaluations are inherently subjective, they also serve to aid in reflecting upon those who shaped the experience of reading comic books over the years. This year's class of inductees begins on this next page.

THE PREVIOUS INDUCTEES

Class of 2006
Murphy Anderson
Jim Aparo
Jim Lee
Mac Raboy

Class of 2007
Dave Cockrum
Steve Ditko
Bruce Hamilton
Martin Nodell
George Pérez
Jim Shooter
Dave Stevens
Alex Toth
Michael Turner

Class of 2008
Carl Barks
Will Eisner
Al Feldstein
Harvey Kurtzman
Stan Lee
Marshall Rogers
John Romita, Sr.
John Romita, Jr.
Julius Schwartz
Mike Wieringo

Class of 2009
Neal Adams
Matt Baker
Chris Claremont
Palmer Cox
Bill Everett
Frank Frazetta
Neil Gaiman
William M. Gaines
Carmine Infantino
Jack Kirby
Joe Kubert
Paul Levitz
Russ Manning
Todd McFarlane
Don Rosa
John Severin
Joe Simon
Al Williamson

Class of 2010
Sergio Aragonés
M.C. Gaines
Archie Goodwin
Winsor McCay
Mike Mignola
Frank Miller
Robert M. Overstreet
Mike Richardson
Jerry Robinson
Joe Shuster
Jerry Siegel
Jim Steranko
Wally Wood

Class of 2011
Jack Davis
Martin Goodman
Dean Mullaney
Marie Severin
Walt Simonson
Major Malcolm Wheeler-Nicholson

Class of 2012
John Buscema
Dan DeCarlo
Jean Giraud (Moebius)
Larry Hama
Kurt Schaffenberger
Bill Sienkiewicz
Curt Swan
Roy Thomas

Class of 2013
Mark Chiarello
Mike Deodato, Jr.
Bill Finger
Jack Kamen
Bob Kane
Andy Kubert

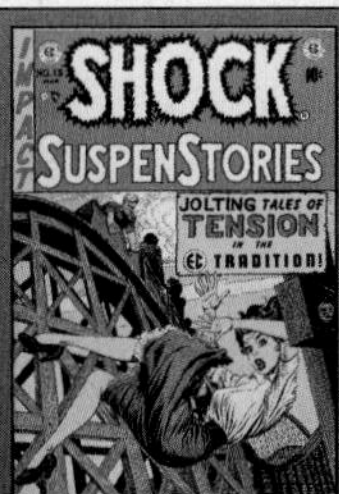

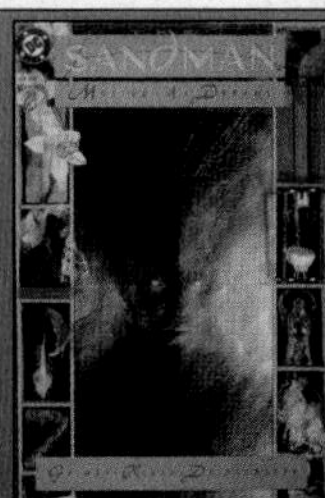

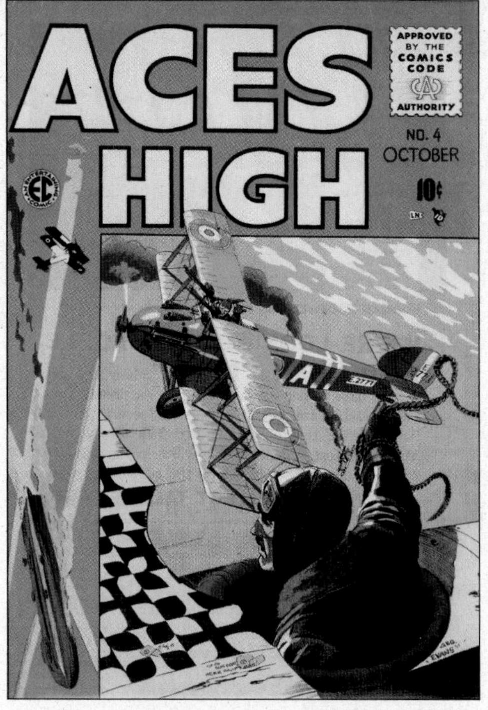

ACES HIGH #4
September-October 1955. © WMG

George Evans was a superb realistic illustrator in comic books and comic strips with a fascination for aviation art. He began in comics in the mid-1940s. Working first at Fiction House on *Planet Comics,* and *Wings Comics*, and aviation pulp illustrations, he next worked at Fawcett. After that, he moved to EC, and then did work for *Classics Illustrated*. He did the *Space Conquerors!* strip in *Boys Life* for several years in the '50s. During the early 60s, Evans contributed to Dell/Western/Gold Key, drawing *Tales of Terror*, *The Twilight Zone*, and *Frogmen*. He also ghosted pencils on the *Terry and the Pirates* comic strip from 1960 to 1973.

During the '60s Evans contributed stories to *Creepy* and *Blazing Combat*, and illustrated a children's book, *The Story of Flight*. In the '70s, he contributed to *National Lampoon*, and drew war and horror and *Blackhawk* for DC, did work for Marvel, and periodically ghosted *Secret Agent Corrigan* before taking over the art and writing in 1980. He also contributed to Dark Horse, Pacific, and Eclipse. Evans did *Corrigan* until retiring in 1996.

- *SCR*

CRIME SUSPENSTORIES #23
June-July 1954. © WMG

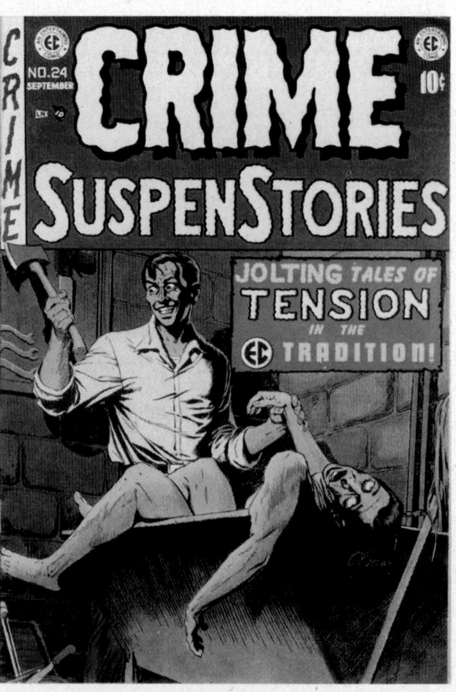

CRIME SUSPENSTORIES #24
September 1954 © WMG

PIRACY #7
October-November 1955. © WMG

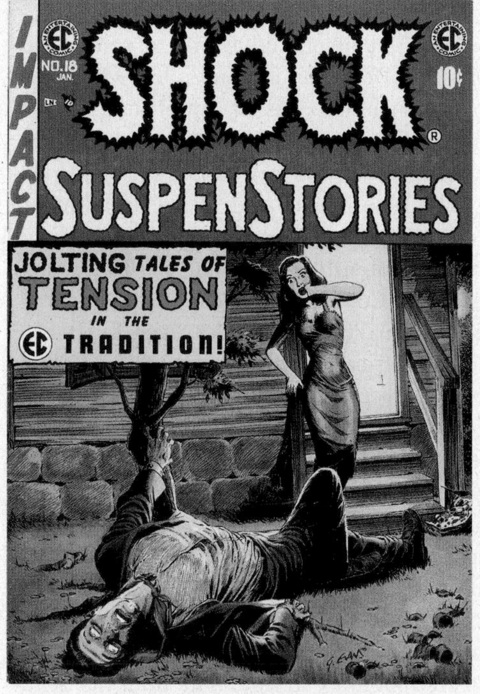

SHOCK SUSPENSTORIES #18
December 1954 - January 1955. © WMG

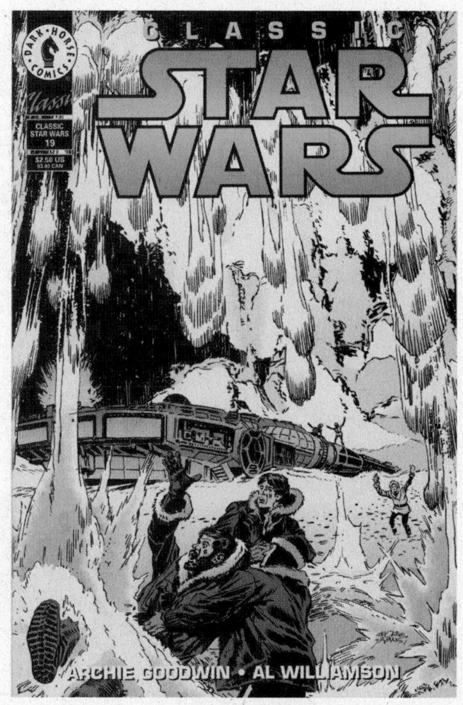

CLASSIC STAR WARS #19
May 1994. © Lucasfilms

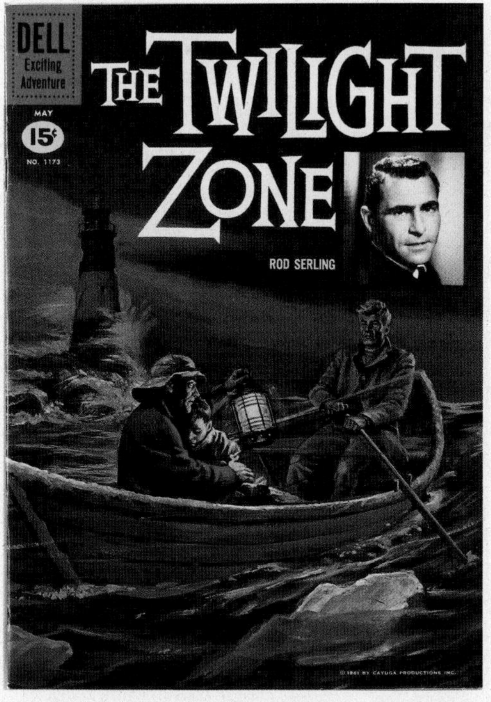

THE TWILIGHT ZONE FOUR COLOR #1173
March-May 1961. © Cayuga Productions

Despite the brevity of his comics career, Lou Fine is remembered as one of comics' best draftsmen. He began in comics in 1938 at the Iger & Eisner shop; his first published work was "Wilton of the West" in *Jumbo Comics* #4. He also supplied covers and stories for Fox, including "The Blue Beetle" and "The Flame," a series he co-created. At the same time, he established himself as an artistic superstar on "Dollman," "The Black Condor," "The Ray," and "Uncle Sam" for Quality Comics. However, by 1944, Fine had left comics to concentrate on newspaper and advertising strips. He ghosted the inking on Eisner's *Spirit* from 1942 until 1945. After this, Fine drew the syndicated strips *Taylor Woe* (1949) and *Adam Ames* (1959-1962). From 1965 until 1967, he drew the hard-boiled detective *Peter Scratch*. His sole '60s comic book work was the two-page, "The Man From Aeons" for *Wham-O Giant Comics* in 1967. His final strip was "Space Conquerors," which appeared monthly in *Boys' Life* until his death in 1971.
- *SCR*

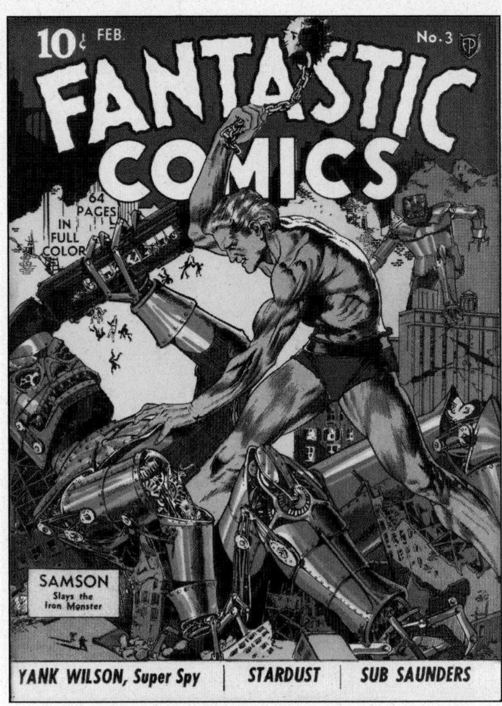

FANTASTIC COMICS #3
February 1940. © FOX

HIT COMICS #1
July 1940. © QUA

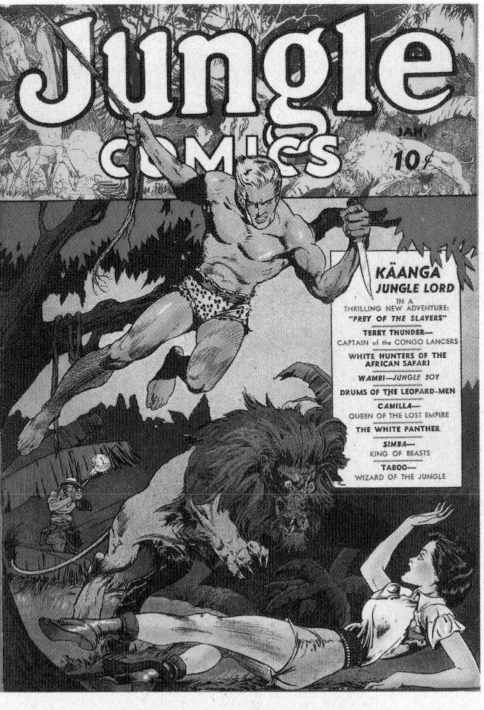

JUNGLE COMICS #1
January 1940. © Fiction House

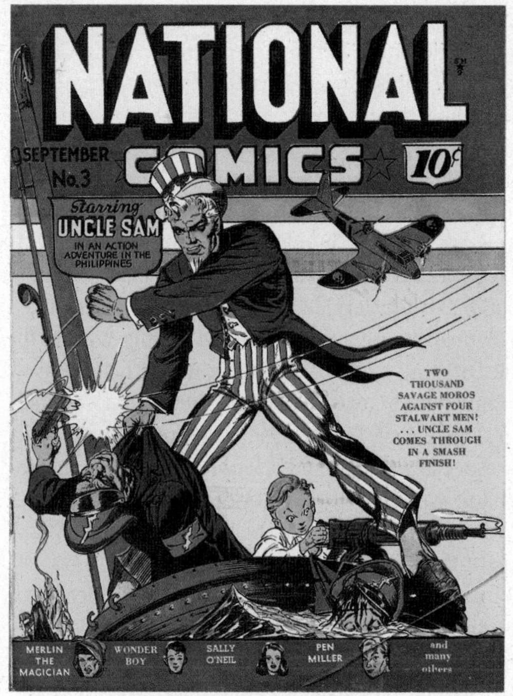

NATIONAL COMICS #3
September 1940. © QUA

PLANET COMICS #2
February 1940. © Fiction House

THE SPIRIT #7
Winter 1946. © Will Eisner Studios

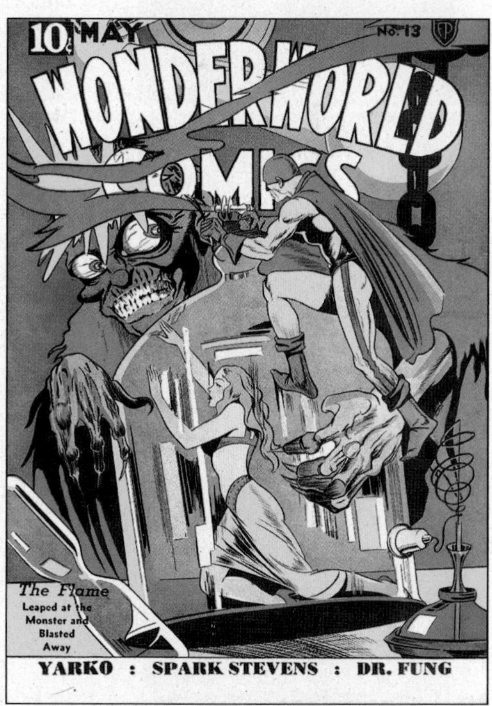

WONDERWORLD COMICS #13
May 1940. © FOX

FLASH COMICS #1
January 1940. © DC

The astonishingly imaginative and prolific Gardner Francis Cooper Fox was one of the Renaissance men of Comics. He wrote comic book scripts for several decades for a range of publishers including Timely, Avon, E.C., Marvel, and Warren, but was most closely associated with DC Comics. His career at DC lasted almost 30 years, and encompassed the creation of Zatanna, Hawkman and Hawkgirl, the Atom, The Justice Society of America, Johnny Thunder, the Flash, the Sandman, the Shining Knight, and Adam Strange. He also made significant contributions to the very earliest Batman stories, including creating Batman's parents, Thomas and Martha Wayne, the Bat-Gyro, the Batarang, and Batman's first use of his utility belt. At the same time he was the head writer for Max Gaines' All-American Comics line, he was also a productive writer of pulp fiction, especially horror and science fiction (though the versatile Fox also wrote adventure stories, westerns, sports stories, and romances). In the years between 1944 and 1982, he wrote one to three novels almost every year, publishing a staggering 12 novels just in 1974. In the '60s, Fox returned to Batman, creating the new Batgirl (Barbara Gordon), and reinventing the Justice League, the Atom, and Hawkman. His story "Flash of Two Worlds" in *Flash* #123 introduced the concept of Earth I and Earth II, thereby establishing the DC Comics multiverse, a concept that's been used ever since. His contributions to comics have been immeasurable, and he was DC's second-most prolific scripter (after Robert Kanigher), with 1,500 DC scripts to his credit.
- SCR

DETECTIVE COMICS #31
September 1939. © DC

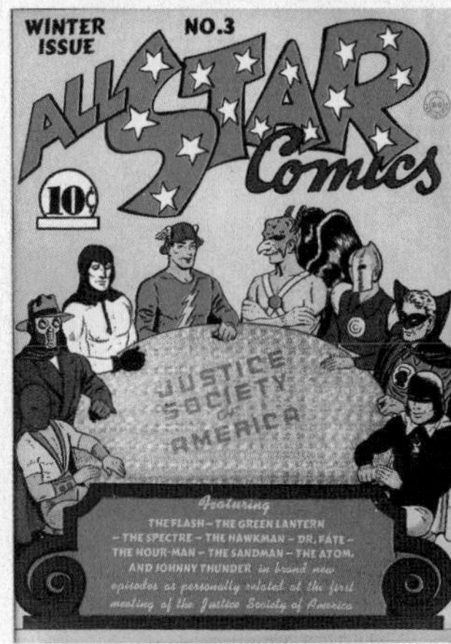

ALL STAR COMICS #3
Winter 1940. © DC

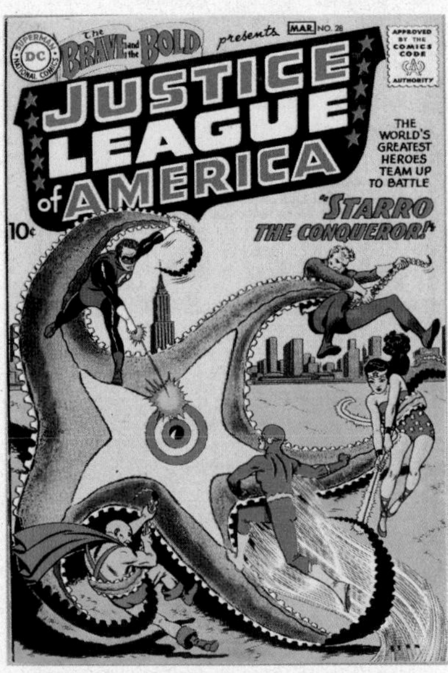

BRAVE AND THE BOLD #28
February-March 1960. © DC

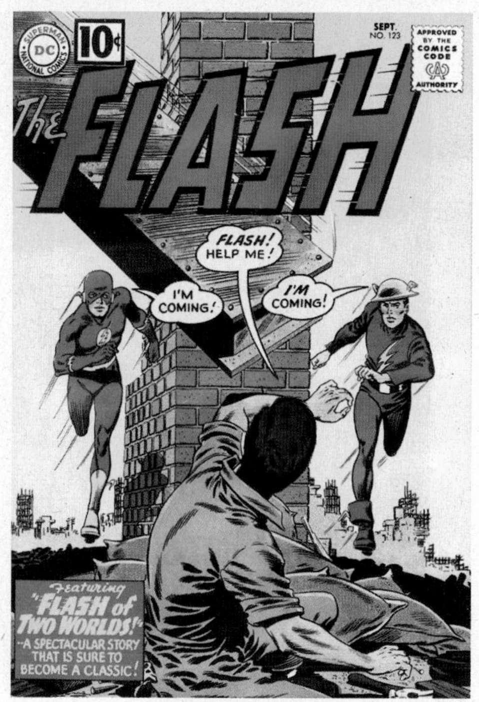

THE FLASH #123
September 1961. © DC

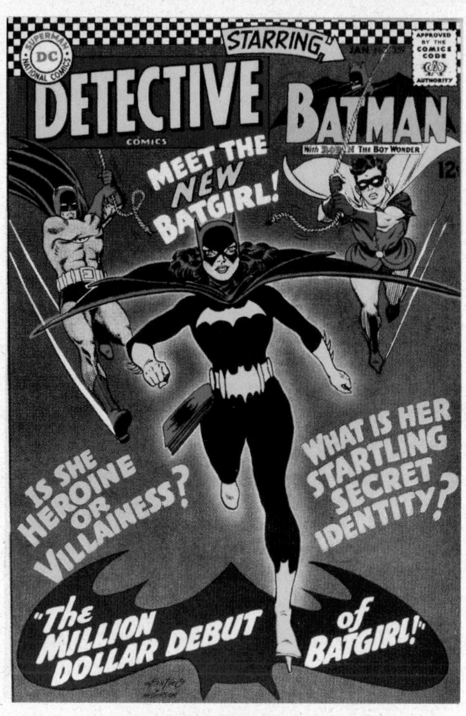

DETECTIVE COMICS #359
January 1967. © DC

JUSTICE LEAGUE OF AMERICA #51
February 1967. © DC

SHOWCASE #17
November-December 1958. © DC

Writer-artist Terry Moore's self-published *Strangers in Paradise* began as a three-issue miniseries at Antarctic Press, and then blossomed into two subsequent volumes from his own Abstract Studio imprint, the last of which ran 90 issues. The work earned him a very devoted fan following, which enabled the title to run more than 16 years. It spawned multiple reprints in soft cover, hardcover, and manga format editions, including a 20th anniversary omnibus in 2013. After the series concluded, Moore immediately launched *Echo*, an action-adventure science fiction series, which ran for 30 issues, and then *Rachel Rising*, a horror series. Like *Strangers in Paradise*, *Echo* and *Rachel Rising* feature strong female characters and realistic human interaction. Moore's success in self-publishing also lead to high-profile assignments in mainstream comics, including five issues of *Spider-Man Loves Mary Jane* and a nine-issue stint on *Runaways* for Marvel, and a variety of work for DC, Dark Horse, Bongo Comics, and Image Comics.
- JCV & SCR

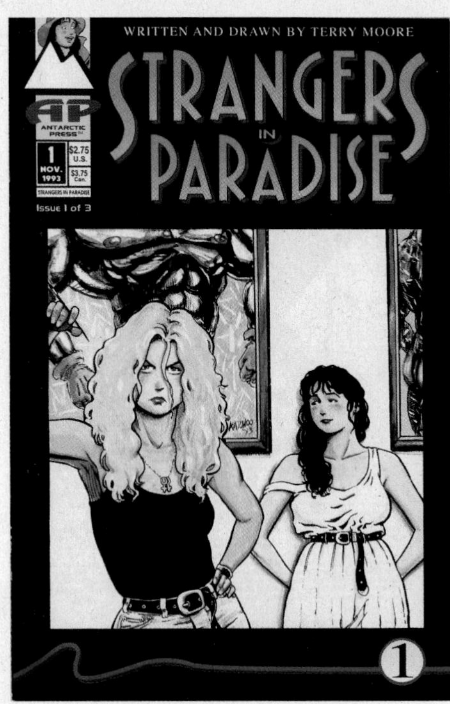

STRANGERS IN PARADISE #1
November 1993. © Terry Moore

STRANGERS IN PARADISE V2 #10
February 1996. © Terry Moore

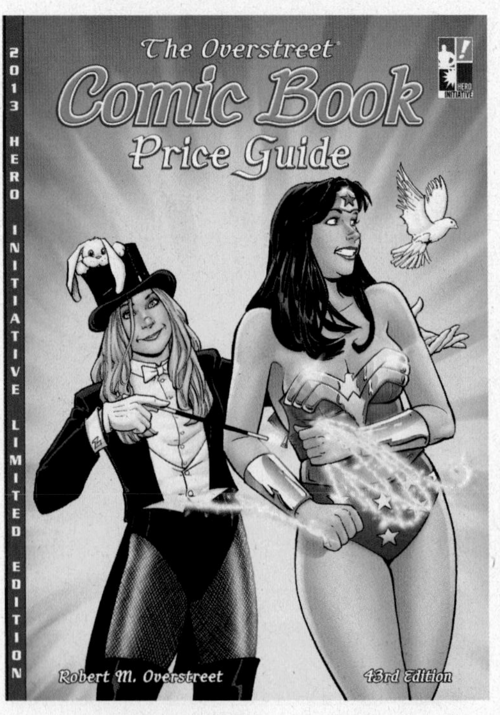

THE OVERSTREET COMIC BOOK PRICE GUIDE
43rd Edition, Hero Initiative variant. 2013.
© Terry Moore

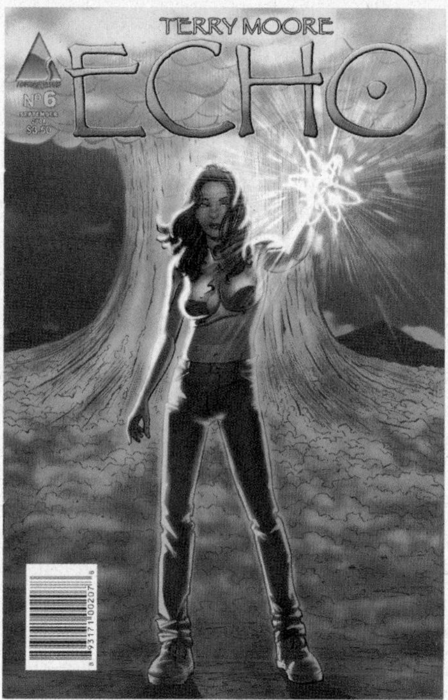

ECHO #6
September 2008. © Terry Moore

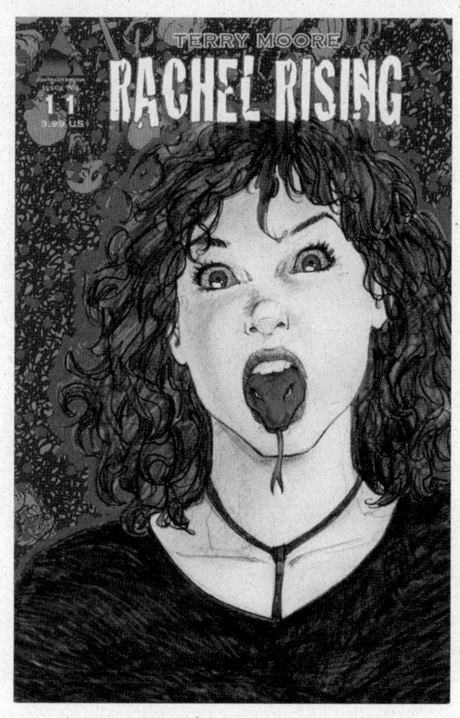

RACHEL RISING #11
2012. © Terry Moore

SPIDER-MAN LOVES MARY-JANE SEASON 2 #5
February 2009. © MAR

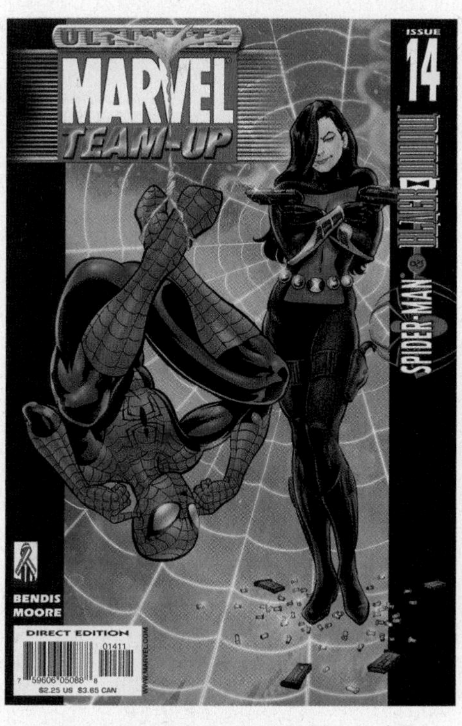

ULTIMATE MARVEL TEAM-UP #14
June 2002. © MAR

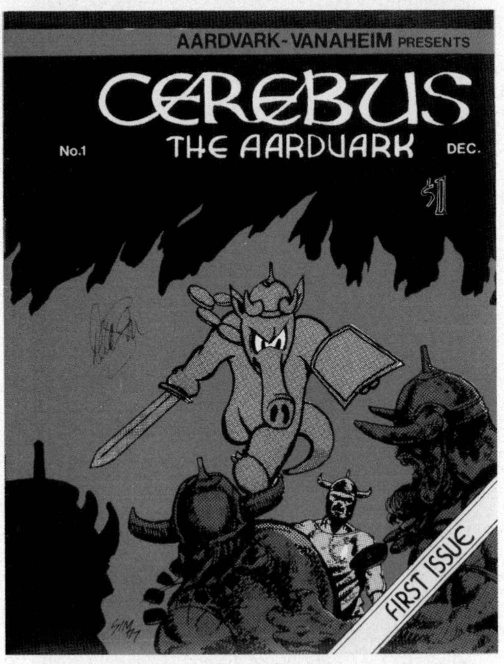

CEREBUS THE AARDVARK #1
December 1977 - January 1978. © Dave Sim

Dave Sim, the creator of *Cerebus the Aardvark*, is revered as one of the pioneers of the self-publishing and creators' rights movements. Although he has subsequently published interesting projects such as the online comic book biography of Canadian actress Siu Ta (entitled *Sui Ta, So Far*) and *Judenhass*, which Sim described as a "personal reflection on the Holocaust," and *Glamourpuss*, a comic book parody of fashion magazines, he is best known for his 300-issue, self-published comic, which he began in 1977. Initially a parody of *Conan the Barbarian* and *Howard the Duck*, *Cerebus* morphed into a vehicle for social satire that became increasingly sophisticated visually and explored weighty topics like politics, religion, metaphysics and gender roles. The 300 issues of *Cerebus* (constituting 6,000 pages) have been collected into 16 volumes. In 2009, Sim's web series, *Cerebus TV*, premiered, with new episodes appearing weekly. To date, more than 100 episodes have been produced.
- SCR

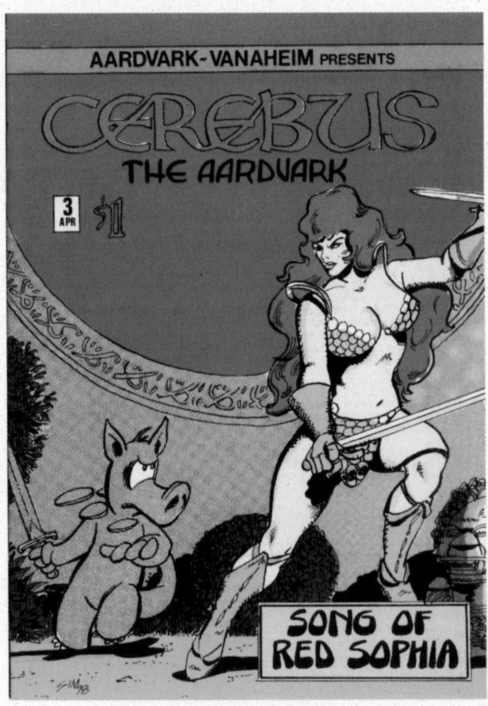

CEREBUS THE AARDVARK #3
April 1978. © Dave Sim

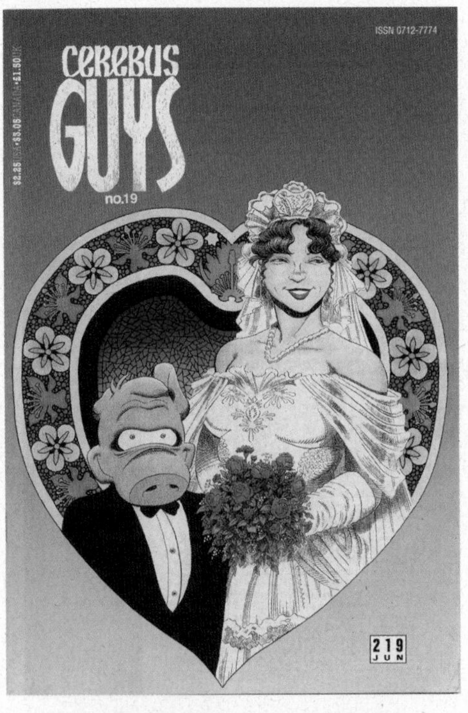

CEREBUS THE AARDVARK #219
June 1997. © Dave Sim & Gerhard

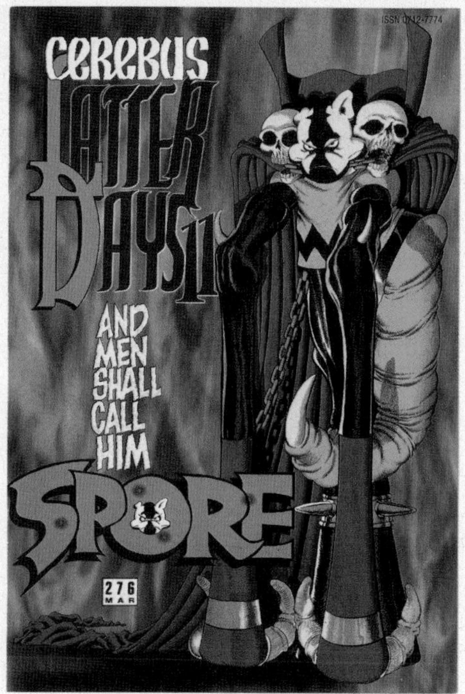

CEREBUS THE AARDVARK #276
March 2002. © Dave Sim & Gerhard

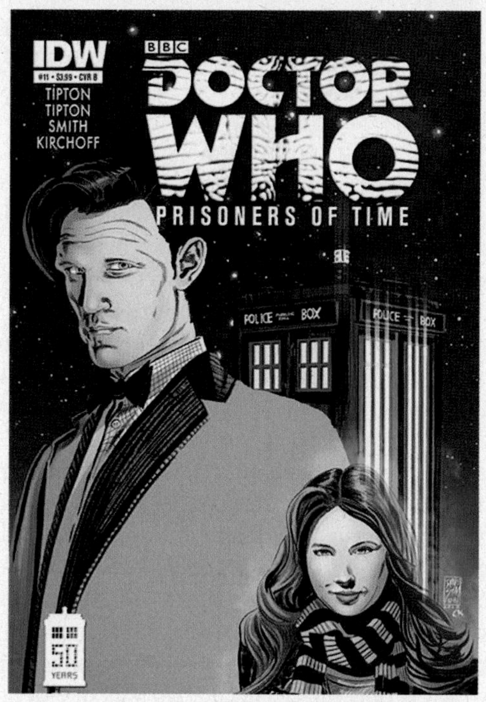

DOCTOR WHO: PRISONERS OF TIME #11
November 2013. © BBC

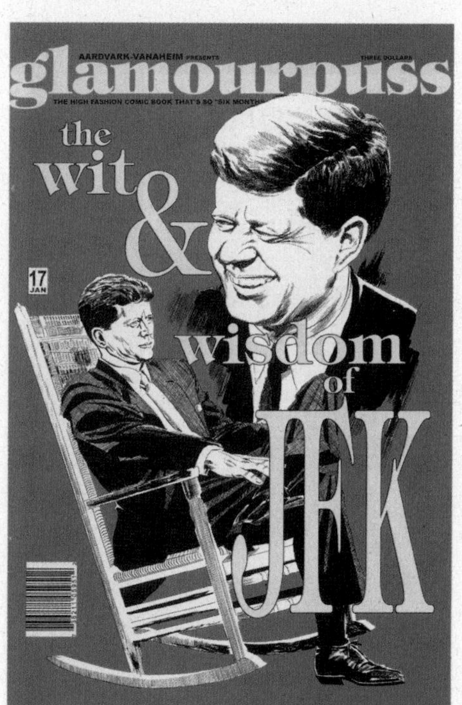

GLAMOURPUSS #17
January 2011. © Dave Sim

JUDENHASS Graphic Novel
2008. © Dave Sim

Jeff Smith, creator of the brashly funny and adventurous, all-ages *Bone*, is one of the most successful and honored of all self-published cartoonists, with 10 Eisner Awards, 11 Harvey Awards, one Inkpot Award, and two National Cartoonists Society Comic Book Awards, an astonishing legacy by any standards. While the 55 issues of *Bone* constitute the majority of his oeuvre, Smith has not rested on his many laurels. Since concluding the *Bone* saga in 2004, Smith's published works have included *Shazam!: The Monster Society of Evil* Prestige miniseries for DC, a retelling of the Golden Age Captain Marvel's epic struggle against the eponymous collection of villains, *RASL*, a science fiction series about a dimension-hopping art thief, the webcomic *Tüki*: *Save the Humans* (about the first humans to venture out of Africa), and the graphic novel, *Little Mouse Gets Ready*, a book intended for beginning readers. In 2007, Smith was named as the designer for Fantagraphics' complete collection of Walt Kelly's *Pogo* comic strips, which is only fitting, since *Pogo* was one of Smith's biggest influences as a cartoonist and writer.
- SCR

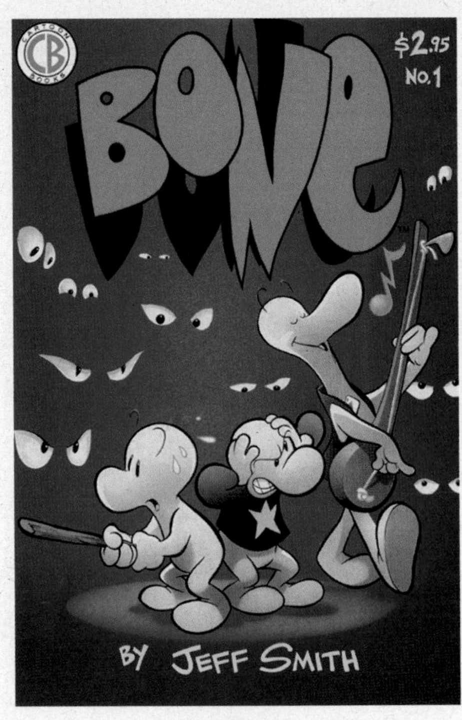

BONE #1
July 1991. © Jeff Smith

BONE #12
February 1994. © Jeff Smith

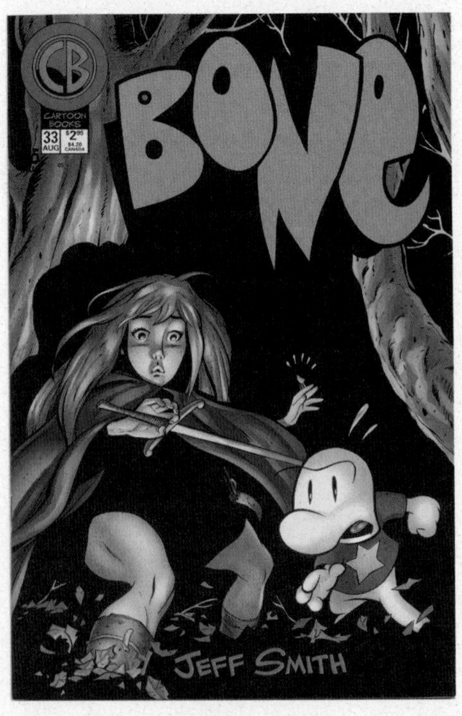

BONE #33
August 1998. © Jeff Smith

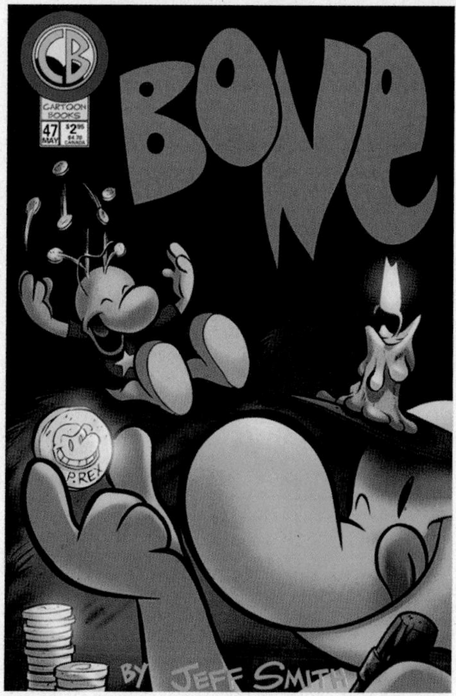

BONE #47
May 2002. © Jeff Smith

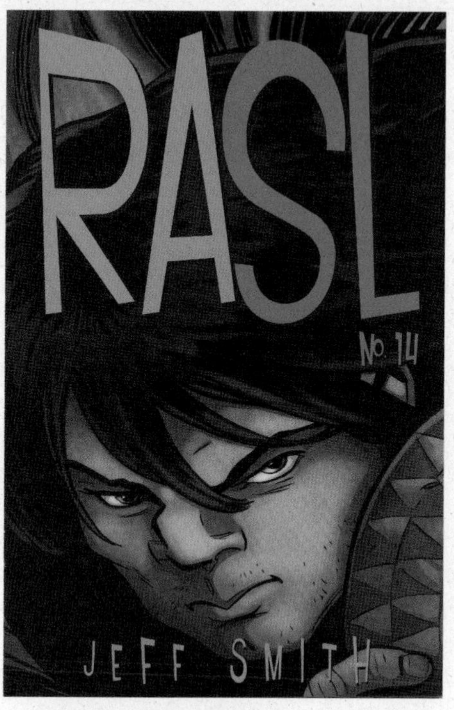

RASL #14
May 2012. © Jeff Smith

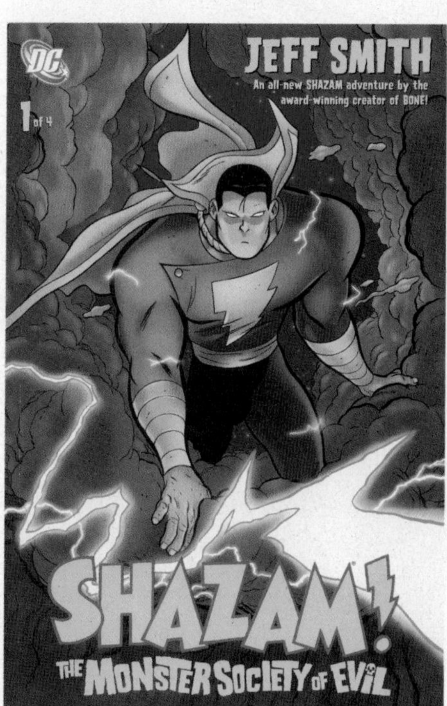

SHAZAM! THE MONSTER SOCIETY OF EVIL #1
2007 © DC Comics

STUPID, STUPID RAT TALES #1
December 1999 © Jeff Smith

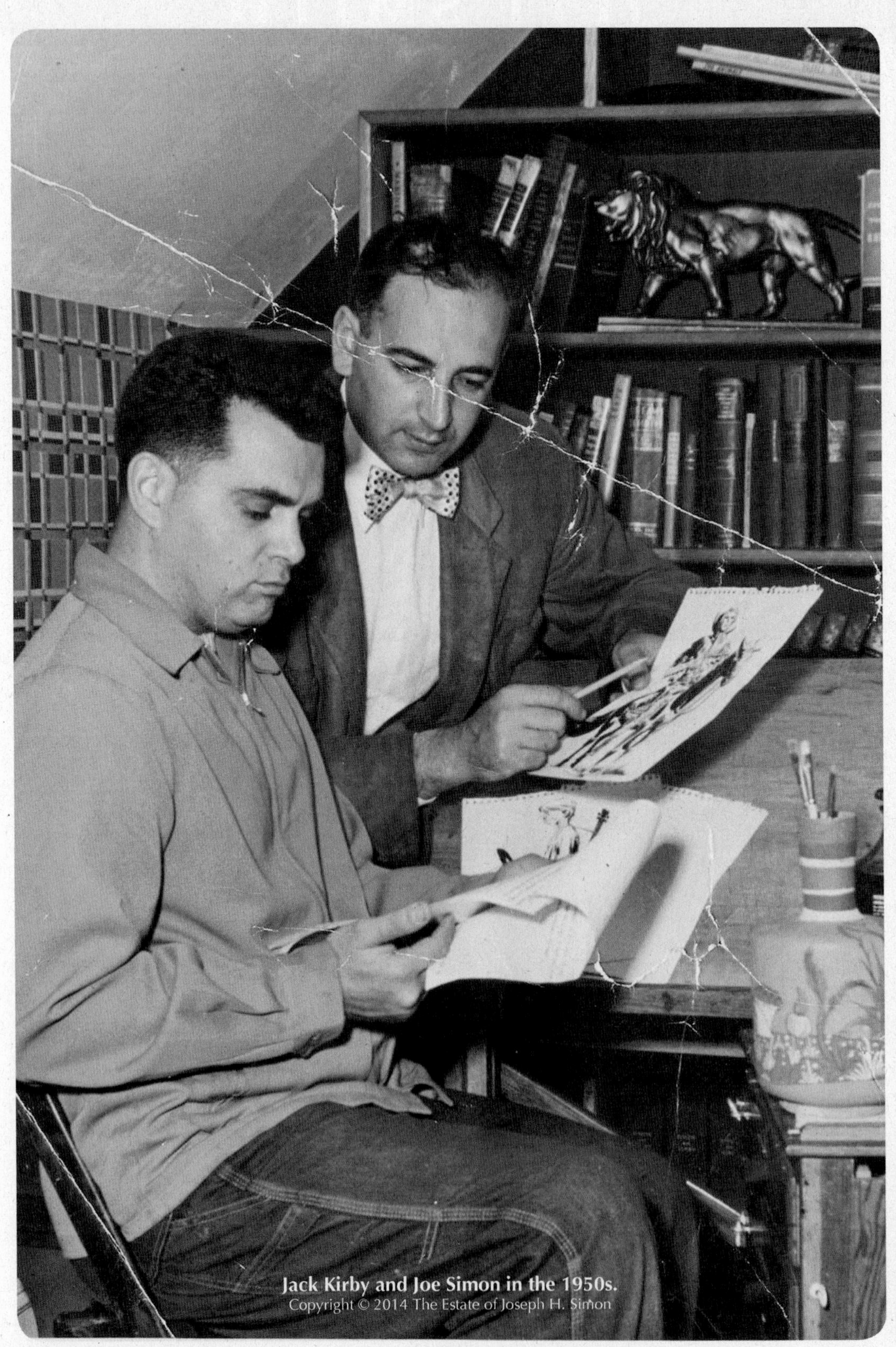
Jack Kirby and Joe Simon in the 1950s.
Copyright © 2014 The Estate of Joseph H. Simon

Joe Simon at 100

A Remembrance by **Steve Saffel**

Last October, Joe Simon would have celebrated his 100th birthday. Born Hymie Simon on October 11, 1913, he was renamed Joseph by his mother, Rose, who refused to accept what his father had put on the birth certificate. This set the stage for a man who would live life by his own rules, chart his own course, and succeed in ways most people only imagined.

I had the privilege of working with Joe for about a decade, on the six-book Simon and Kirby Library and the autobiographical *Joe Simon: My Life in Comics*. It was the experience of a lifetime. At every stage of his career, Joe was an innovator—something all writers and artists can learn from in today's era of comics self-publishing. If something was needed for Joe to get a particular job or assignment, he learned how to do what was needed. If one job folded, he found another, often taking his career in unexpected directions.

"I always knew another opportunity would come along, or that I'd be able to find something new and different," he wrote in his autobiography. Writer, artist, editor, designer, publisher—he taught himself to do it all at one time or another.

This urge to grow, to *evolve*, came very early in his life. The Great Depression hit when he was in his teens, so he had to adapt in order to survive. And adapt he did—becoming one of the industry's great pioneers and helping to create some of the most sought-after comics in history. His 90-year livelihood started when he was eight, as he explained in *Joe Simon: My Life in Comics.*

"I'd sit and make these elaborate pencil drawings of cowboys or horses or whatever the kids wanted, and sell them for a penny or two. Even as a young boy I was a working artist." He didn't take art classes, yet as a senior at Benjamin Franklin High School in Rochester, NY, his work appeared in the school newspaper and yearbook, exhibiting a distinctly art deco flair.

Joe Simon at the 2010 New York ComicCon

Copyright © 2014 Dana C. Hayward

Rochester was a center for the clothing industry and the location of a Bausch & Lomb optical plant. As a teenager he had to help support his family, and was one of the many newspaper vendors who would sell newspapers in front of the factories as the workers filed in and out in the mornings and evenings. Yes, young Joe Simon was a *bona fied* member of the Newsboy Legion.

***

After high school, while a lot of his friends went to college in Syracuse, Joe had to help support his parents. This was 1932 and the Depression was still going strong. So he immediately started looking for a job, and answered an ad for the "assistant art editor" at the *Rochester Evening Journal*, owned by the Hearst Corporation. He showed his drawings to art director Adolph Edler, and got the gig—earning $15 a week. Suddenly without any formal training, Joe had to produce.

Which he did, in spades.

Like his predecessor, Al Liederman, Joe drew political and sports cartoons, and illustrations for fiction that appeared in the newspaper. He got the *Journal* photographers to teach him how to use a camera and develop photos, while Adolph Edler taught him everything there was to know about preparing a newspaper to go to press, including the use of the airbrush to retouch photos.

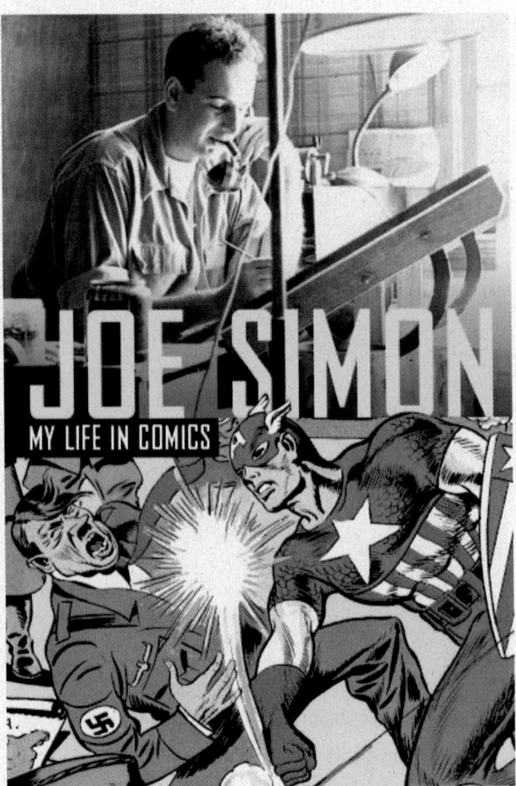

Almost overnight, Joe was a full-fledged newspaperman. While amassing this new array of skills, he always kept his eyes open, and grabbed each opportunity that came along.

One assignment took him to a semi-professional boxing match, for which he would produce sports cartoons. Joe went above and beyond, writing a complete article about the fight. The editors were thrilled with what he'd written, and started to send him to cover baseball, hockey, and more boxing matches. He found himself assigned to upstate New York boxing camps, where he rubbed elbows with greats like Primo Carnera, Joe Louis, and Max Baer.

That was where he met his idol, Damon Runyon, the writer whose work was adapted for the Broadway play *Guys and Dolls*. Over the years Runyon created characters like Nathan Detroit, Harry the Horse, and Good Time Charley. He had tremendous influence on Joe Simon's writing, evident in the Runyonesque comic book series "The Duke of Broadway," "Kid Adonis," and "The Vagabond Prince."

***

Joe loved his newspaper days. "The lessons I learned there were a chart for the future, like going through ten colleges, and coming out with all of the knowledge and experience to give me a lifetime of confidence." But the Hearst organization began to suffer financial declines, and started closing down some of their regional publications. Suddenly, Joe was out of a job. So in 1937 he decided to pack up his worldly possessions, and head for the one place he'd always wanted to be.

New York City.

In New York, some of his earliest work was advertising art for McFadden publications, where in 1939 the art director gave Joe a lead on a new type of publication—comic books. He sent Joe to Funnies Incorporated, a packaging company run by Lloyd Jacquet that sold material to publishers who didn't have in-house creative staff, including Centaur Comics and Timely Comics. Joe walked out of that meeting with an instant assignment—to write, pencil, ink, and letter an entire story.

There was only one hitch.

Joe had never before produced a comic book story. His work in the newspapers had consisted of single-panel cartoons and illustrations. Now he had to create an entire adventure out of thin air. So he went back to his rooming house and worked it out, producing a six-page western—most likely it was "Ranch

Telephone 2-3111 SYRACUSE AMERICAN—A Paper for People Who Think—SUNDAY, NOVEMBER 13, 1938 Telephone 2-3111 7

Introducing the 1939 AUTOMOBILES

In Syracuse and later in New York City, Simon produced advertising illustrations for newspapers and magazines.

A sample of Simon's fiction illustrations from the 1930s

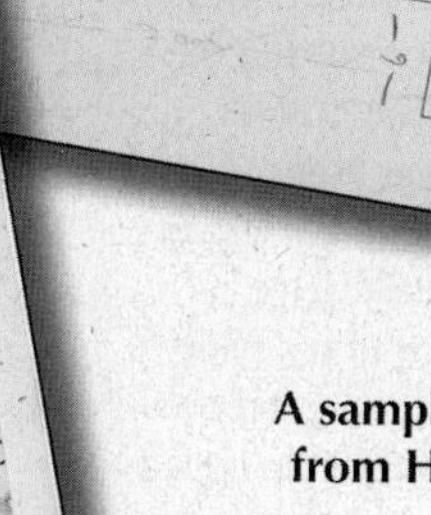

A sample of Simon's sports cartooning from Hearst newspapers of the 1930s

The cast of "The Duke of Broadway" by Joe Simon, from Stuntman #2.

Copyright © The Estate of Joseph H. Simon

OFF-TRAIL SUPER-SCIENCE NOVELETTE OF INTERPLANETARY ROMANCE!
THE GIRL FROM VENUS
by D. D. SHARP
Author of "Faster Than Light," etc.
Yes, atomic disintegration and argonite would give me the girl from Venus as my bride, and it would give us both health, wealth and complete happiness. . . . What it must also finally do, alas, was make Leatha indistinguishable from any other girl on the planet!
Giant passenger tubes went bellowing into space!

Simon and Kirby also produced illustrations for Martin Goodman's pulp titles.

Dude," which appeared in *Amazing-Man Comics* #10 (March 1940).

One assignment led to another, and before long he had thrown his fedora into the editorial arena, first at Fox Comics. There he met young Jacob Kurtzberg, and the team of Simon and Kirby was born. At about that time Martin Goodman tired of relying on Funnies, and decided to create his own editorial team. He poached Simon to be Timely's first in-house editor.

While at Timely, Joe and Jack continued their after-hours freelance work, producing the entire first issue of *Captain America Comics.* They took it to Goodman, who was so excited by it that he committed to launching the character in his own title. He also agreed to give Simon and Kirby a royalty 25% for every issue sold, after expenses. This seemed too good to be true—and it was. Goodman reportedly began using the Captain America profits to pay for all of the company expenses, so despite selling a million copies with issue #1, *Captain America Comics* paid almost nothing in royalties.

Thus, Simon and Kirby left Timely Comics.

***

Joe Simon's next major reinvention came about as a result of World War II.

While working at DC Comics, he joined the US Coast Guard and eventually was stationed in Washington, DC, as were Will Eisner and Al Harvey. In Washington he was assigned to the Combat Art Corps, whose task was public relations. There he produced the custom comic *Adventure is My Career*—editing, writing, penciling, and inking—and installments of the reality based comic strip *True Comics* which appeared in newspapers nationwide.

After the War he and Kirby reunited and began to produce material for Harvey Comics and Crestwood Publications (Prize Comics). For years superheroes had been their bread-and-butter, but in the post-war world the long-underwear crowd was floundering. *Stuntman* didn't catch on, and while Joe and Jack continued to sell stories in various genres—notably crime—it was clear that they needed something new.

That's when Joe made what may have been his greatest intuitive leap. It bothered him that comics ignored a huge portion of the audience. There were funny animal comics, Disney comics, and humor titles like *Archie*, but nothing specifically for young girls.

So once again he and Kirby produced an entire first issue—shouldering the full expense for *Young Romance* #1 (Sept.-Oct. 1947). They took it to Teddy Epstein and Mike Blier at Crestwood, who agreed to

A Joe Simon illustration for Sick magazine.

Copyright © The Estate of Joseph H. Simon

publish it. When Joe demanded that he and Jack receive 50% of the profits, Epstein and Blier balked, but eventually they gave in. The book was a huge success, lasting for 174 issues. Together he and Kirby had created a new comic book genre, one which would sell millions of comics and spawn legions of imitators.

At its height, the Simon and Kirby Studio turned out superhero, crime, romance, horror, military, and western titles, including the masterpiece *Boys' Ranch*. Encouraged by distributor Leader News, Joe and Jack created their own imprint, Mainline Publications, and launched four titles: *Bulls Eye*, *Police Trap*, *In Love*, and *Foxhole*. But Mainline was short-lived. Leader News also distributed the famous EC Comics, and when governmental hearings led to the cancellation of EC's entire comic book line, the distributor went out of business.

It was the beginning of an end. Joe Simon and Jack Kirby went their separate ways, and Joe began to gravitate away from comics... almost.

***

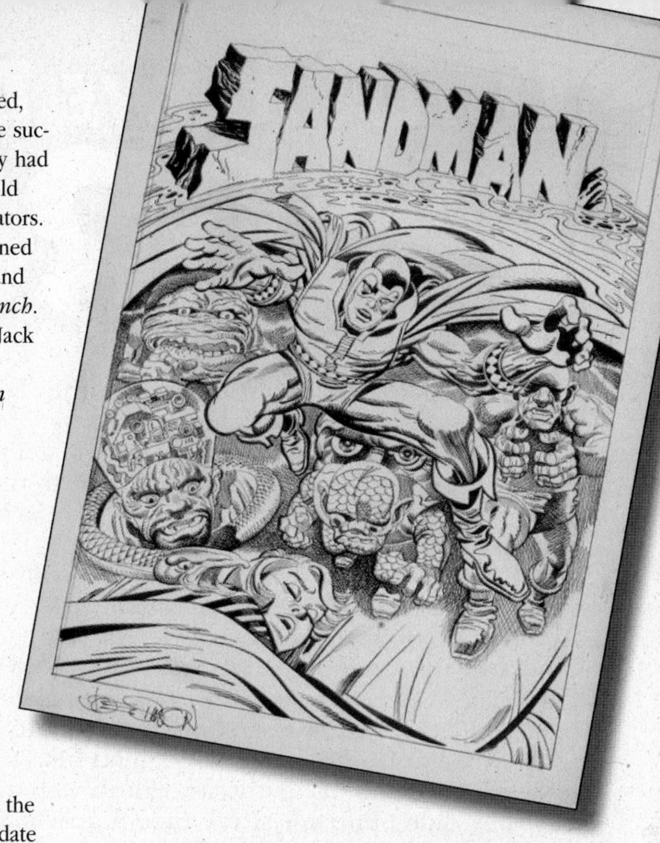

An unpublished version of the cover for *Sandman* #1, pencils by Jack Kirby, inks attributed to Joe Simon and Jerry Grandenetti.

Copyright © DC Comics

Martin Burstein was an old friend from Rochester. By the late 1950s he was prominent in the New York State Republican Party, and their candidate for governor was Nelson Rockefeller. Burstein enlisted Joe to help create a variety of promotional materials, including custom comic books spotlighting their candidates. This led Joe into doing commercial design for all sorts of clients, from direct-mail companies to the New York Electrical Contractors Association.

About the same time *MAD Magazine* was a massive hit, and Teddy Epstein wanted to get in on the action. He had Joe create *Sick Magazine*, employing illustrators like Bob Powell, Angelo Torres, and Jack Davis, as well as writers who went on to work for Jerry Lewis, Robin Williams, and the Smothers Brothers. *Sick* was a success, and Joe ended up owning 50% of the magazine.

So while he continued to dabble in comics, creating titles like *Thrill-O-Rama*, *Brother Power, The Geek*, *Prez*, and one more Simon and Kirby collaboration—a new *Sandman*—Joe never had all of his eggs in one basket. And he never lost that creative edge that took him down so many different paths.

He continued to pursue the copyright to his greatest creation, *Captain America*, and finally came to an agreement with Marvel Entertainment. That's why the Simon and Kirby byline appears on all of the Cap comics, and in the movies. Around the same time he suffered a stroke, yet in the decade that followed he signed a seven-book publishing deal with Titan, which led to the creation of the Simon and Kirby Library. In negotiating that contract, he made certain the Kirby Estate received a portion of the advances *and* the royalties.

Joe wrote two autobiographies: *The Comic Book Makers* (with his son Jim) and *Joe Simon: My Life in Comics*. I was fortunate enough to work with him as his editor on the latter, and it was a once-in-a-lifetime experience to watch him shape and polish that work. He retained his writing skills and editorial intuition until the day he died, shortly after his 98th birthday.

As we celebrate the 100th year since his birth, writers and artists can all learn from his experience, and chart their own courses. That was the example he set, and he lived by it for almost a century.

***

Steve Saffel is a Senior Acquisitions Editor and Dark Editorial Overlord at Titan Books, focusing on prose fiction. He's worked for Marvel Comics and Del Rey Books, and has reveled in the opportunity to work with many of the most creative folks in several fields.

LISTEN TO THE TALKING TREE: I AM GROOT!

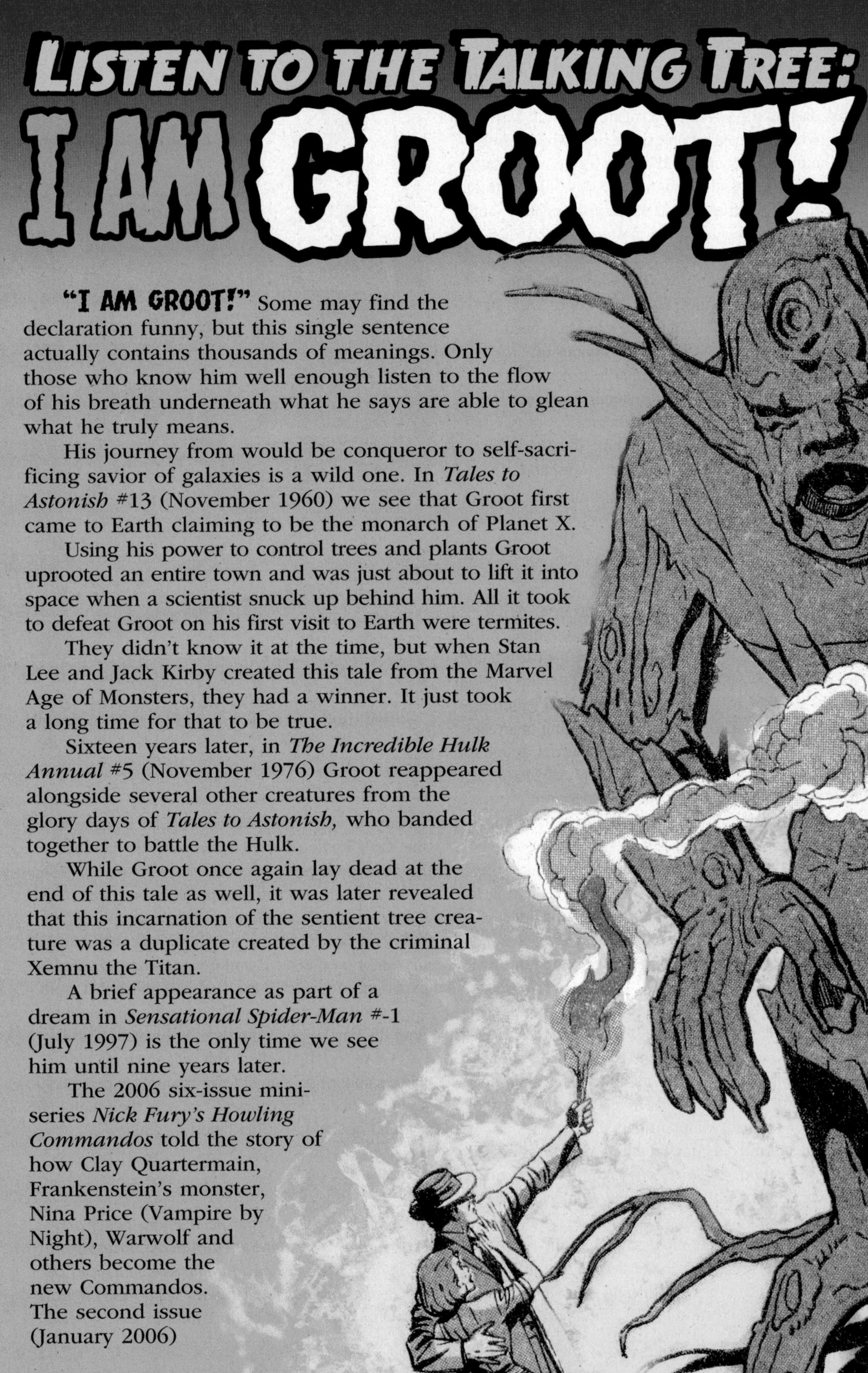

"I AM GROOT!" Some may find the declaration funny, but this single sentence actually contains thousands of meanings. Only those who know him well enough listen to the flow of his breath underneath what he says are able to glean what he truly means.

His journey from would be conqueror to self-sacrificing savior of galaxies is a wild one. In *Tales to Astonish* #13 (November 1960) we see that Groot first came to Earth claiming to be the monarch of Planet X.

Using his power to control trees and plants Groot uprooted an entire town and was just about to lift it into space when a scientist snuck up behind him. All it took to defeat Groot on his first visit to Earth were termites.

They didn't know it at the time, but when Stan Lee and Jack Kirby created this tale from the Marvel Age of Monsters, they had a winner. It just took a long time for that to be true.

Sixteen years later, in *The Incredible Hulk Annual* #5 (November 1976) Groot reappeared alongside several other creatures from the glory days of *Tales to Astonish,* who banded together to battle the Hulk.

While Groot once again lay dead at the end of this tale as well, it was later revealed that this incarnation of the sentient tree creature was a duplicate created by the criminal Xemnu the Titan.

A brief appearance as part of a dream in *Sensational Spider-Man* #-1 (July 1997) is the only time we see him until nine years later.

The 2006 six-issue mini-series *Nick Fury's Howling Commandos* told the story of how Clay Quartermain, Frankenstein's monster, Nina Price (Vampire by Night), Warwolf and others become the new Commandos. The second issue (January 2006)

by MARK SQUIREK

found Groot returning as a villain. When Gorilla-Man offers him the choice to join the Commandos or face imprisonment in #5 (April 2006), Groot switches sides.

After that mini-series ended, he was next found in a Kree prison in 2007's *Annihilation: Conquest*. In it, The Phalanx have invaded Kree space. The start of this battle finds Peter Quill (Star-Lord) at the center of the conflict. After taking refuge in the Kree prison, Quill assembled a team to fight the invasion. Included were Mantis, Bug, Rocket Raccoon, Groot, and others.

Their first battle shows Groot sacrificing himself while giving his team members time to escape. However a small sprig of his physical self remained. So he was revived, again. Once regrown, a second sacrifice led him to ignite his body in order to burn down the Babel Spire. This time it is Rocket Raccoon who saves a small bit of his friend.

Annihilation Conquest – Starlord #1 (September 2007) detailed the first time Groot and Rocket Raccoon teamed up. As guards monitor a prison conflict, they saw Rocket firing a repeating weapon larger than himself. The next panel revealed that Rocket was sitting in the palm of the giant tree, Groot. In that story, their friendship was cemented.

The team became the Guardians of the Galaxy.

Guardians of the Galaxy began in July 2008 and lasted 25 issues. It was followed by *The Thanos Imperative,* which in turn was followed by *Annihilators,* then *Annihilators: Earthfall,* and then the current *Guardians of the Galaxy* ongoing series.

In advance of the release of Marvel Studios' *Guardians of the Galaxy, Tales To Astonish* #13, particularly high grade copies, have started to command attention. Even *Where Monsters Dwell* #6, which reprints that story, has been the subject of new interest.

UNTOLD TALES: Curt Swan's STAR SEED

by Scott Braden

A recent conversation with freelance journalist and Overstreet Advisor Scott Braden led us to recall one of the more popular segments in our old magazine, Overstreet's FAN, Untold Tales, in which Braden explored – and told – those previous untold bits of behind-the-scenes comics history. We asked him to revisit the concept, and he delivered.

It's 1995, and the infamous comic book speculator boom of recent times past had nearly destroyed the industry. Enter Jim Shooter's Broadway Comics, a division of Lorne Michael's Broadway Video Entertainment, and a comic book publisher that valued quality – great characters, great storytelling — over quantity. And coming from a creative powerhouse like Shooter, who steered both Marvel Comics and Valiant to successful waters, Broadway Comics was also a publishing house where new ideas abounded.

One of the company's new ideas to make it to the four-color page was a young hero named Star Seed.

According to a Broadway Comics press release from June 1995, in Star Seed, "Dad was the alien Paul Gauguin. Mom is an exceptional Earth woman, who, 20 years ago, bore him a son. Xolus Cor is the Star Seed and his hybrid nature has given tremendous strength. He has also inherited some of his father's technology, which is good, because he's going to need all the help he can get to find his missing father. It's tough coming of age on a planet as savage as Earth – especially when you're truly one of a kind."

But Star Seed was more than just

Curt Swan's iconic image of Superman from the cover of *Superman Annual* #7 (1963) sold at Heritage Auctions in 2007 for $8,962.50.

When Swan opted out of doing Star Seed, pencil artist Andrew Wendel and inker Art Nichols got the assignment.

another comic book superman. Much more.

"I created Star Seed for a science fiction novel," Shooter revealed. "I planned out the whole story, but never got around to writing it. Broadway Comics were written by a team, like TV shows. JayJay Jackson, Pauline Weiss, Joe James, and I retooled my original concept and made it into a comic book series.

And for those who saw the outfit and the powers and thought of the character as a literal Superman, Shooter refutes this claim.

"Star Seed isn't anything like Superman," said Shooter. "If you mean was he sort of a centerpiece character, well maybe. But so was Fatale. They were our first, so in some ways, they were very special to us."

In any case, Star Seed was an important book for the burgeoning company — and needed an important artist. Enter comic book veteran Curt Swan.

"[Curt Swan was] a grandmaster," Shooter said. "A Hall-of-Fame, all-time-great superstar. The greatest Superman artist of all time. The definitive Superman artist."

To bring this all-star collaboration together — Broadway Comics and Swan — Shooter set the wheels in motion.

"I called him," said Shooter. "I worked with Curt for years at DC in the 1960s. He really wasn't doing much work

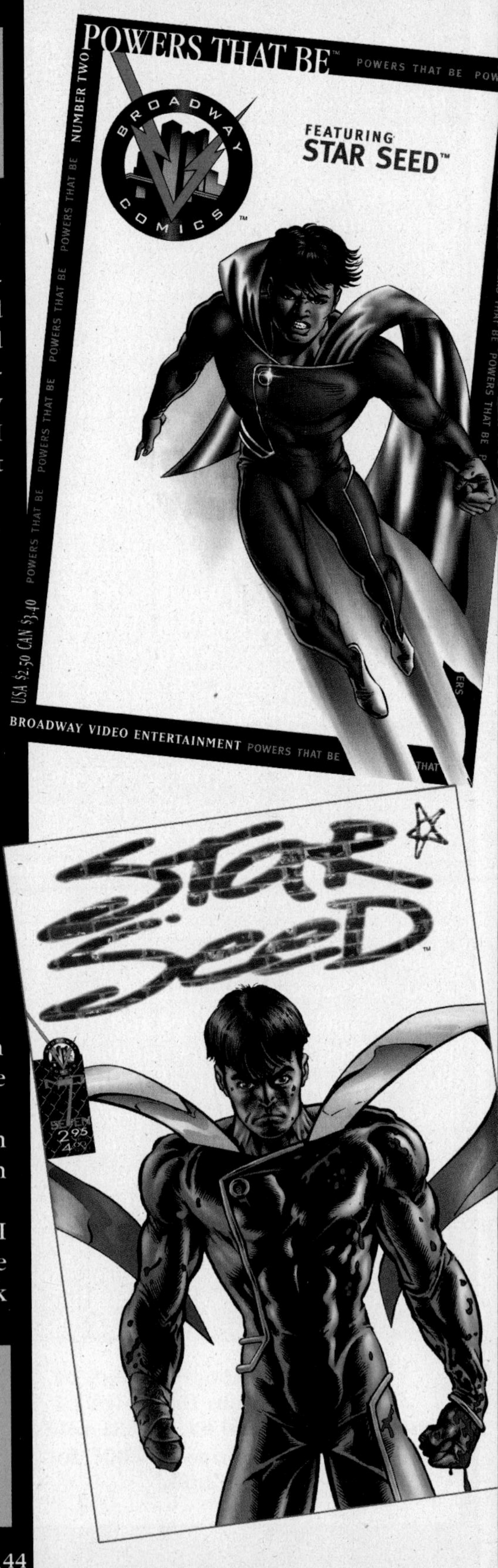

Broadway's *Powers That Be* #6 was followed by *Star Seed* #7, as the company changed many of their titles to the names of their featured characters.

around the time I asked him to draw Star Seed. Mostly retired. But as a favor to me, he agreed to draw Star Seed."

But having a great creator wasn't enough – especially if he wasn't familiar with how Shooter wanted to pursue storytelling.

"I wanted to use real locations, reference for everything," said Shooter. "Curt was used to the made-up world Superman flew around in back in the day. Made up buildings, cars, guns, etc. As I said, he was mostly retired, and he just didn't want to have to reference everything. Too much work, too much hassle. So in his gracious way, and with my complete understanding, he stepped down."

Not before creating some pages for Broadway, though. According to Shooter, the pages were given back to Swan. And with Swan's work going for big bucks in the collectors' market, they may just be worth something. Especially since Swan's *Action Comics* # 309 comic book cover brought in $112,015.75 in auction at Hake's Americana & Collectibles last fall.

Swan's original cover art for *Action Comics* #309, was sold by Hake's Americana & Collectibles for $112,015.75 on November 21, 2013.

But although Swan left the project, the book had to go on. Andrew Wendel filled Swan's shoes, and Star Seed made its debut *Powers That Be* #1 in late 1995. Although Broadway Comics was short-lived, those who read Star Seed's adventures remember them well.

But who knows what might have been with Swan at the artistic reins?

Where there's DANGER! MYSTERY! ADVENTURE! we find
The NEW CHAMP OF SPLIT-SECOND ACTION!
APR.-MAY., 1954
10¢
FIGHTING AMERICAN
PRIZE GROUP
with SPEEDBOY the wonder kid
WHO is the FIGHTING AMERICAN? Learn his secret in this issue!
Where there's DANGER! MYSTERY! ADVENTURE! we find
The NEW CHAMP OF SPLIT-SECOND ACTION!
JUNE, JULY, 1954
10¢
FIGHTING AMERICAN
PRIZE GROUP
with "SPEEDBOY," the wonder kid
THROW THEM DOWN THE SKY WELL! THAT'LL TAKE CARE OF THEM!
THEY WON'T LIVE TO TELL ABOUT THEIR VISIT TO GHOST CITY!

the FIGHTING AMERICAN AT 60

Captain America wasn't the only patriotic hero created by the legendary team of Joe Simon and Jack Kirby. In addition to the Guardian (blue outfit, carried a shield), the Silver Age Shield for Archie (who didn't carry a shield), the duo also developed the Fighting American, one of the first heroes to delve into satire.

Will Eisner's *The Spirit* had many satirical elements, as did Jack Cole's work on *Plastic Man*, and both are much heralded today, but in the Fighting American Simon and Kirby turned a rye eye toward what the politics of the day were when the series was launched in 1954.

Originally conceived as another riff on their established patriotic hero motif, the creators soured on the McCarthy-era definition of patriotism and ended up developing a character who parodied the climate and superheroes in general, but who still personified a more traditional patriotism including a love of free speech.

Radio announcer Johnny Flagg is murdered by foreign agents, but his younger, feeble brother, Nelson, allows his mind to be transferred to Johnny's rebuilt and enhanced body as the Fighting American. Joined by the requisite sidekick, Speedboy, he confronted menaces such as Hotsky Trotski, Poison Ivan, and Round Robin.

"It's impossible to know for sure, but the reason it failed to find public acceptance may also be why it is so highly regarded today - it didn't take itself or, apparently, the Cold War, seriously," wrote Don Makstein on his Toonopedia website.

Fighting American ran seven issues from Prize, its original publisher. An eighth issue was completed, but didn't appear until Harvey Comics released a one-shot in 1966 combined with the original #1.

The character returned when Marvel Comics collected all eight issues in a 1989 hardcover. A new incarnation debuted in a 1994 six-issue series from DC Comics, and Rob Liefeld brought the character back again under his Awesome Entertainment banner in 1997.

Another new version was announced more recently, but it did not happen. Titan Books has issued a new collection of the original Simon & Kirby material.

—J.C. Vaughn

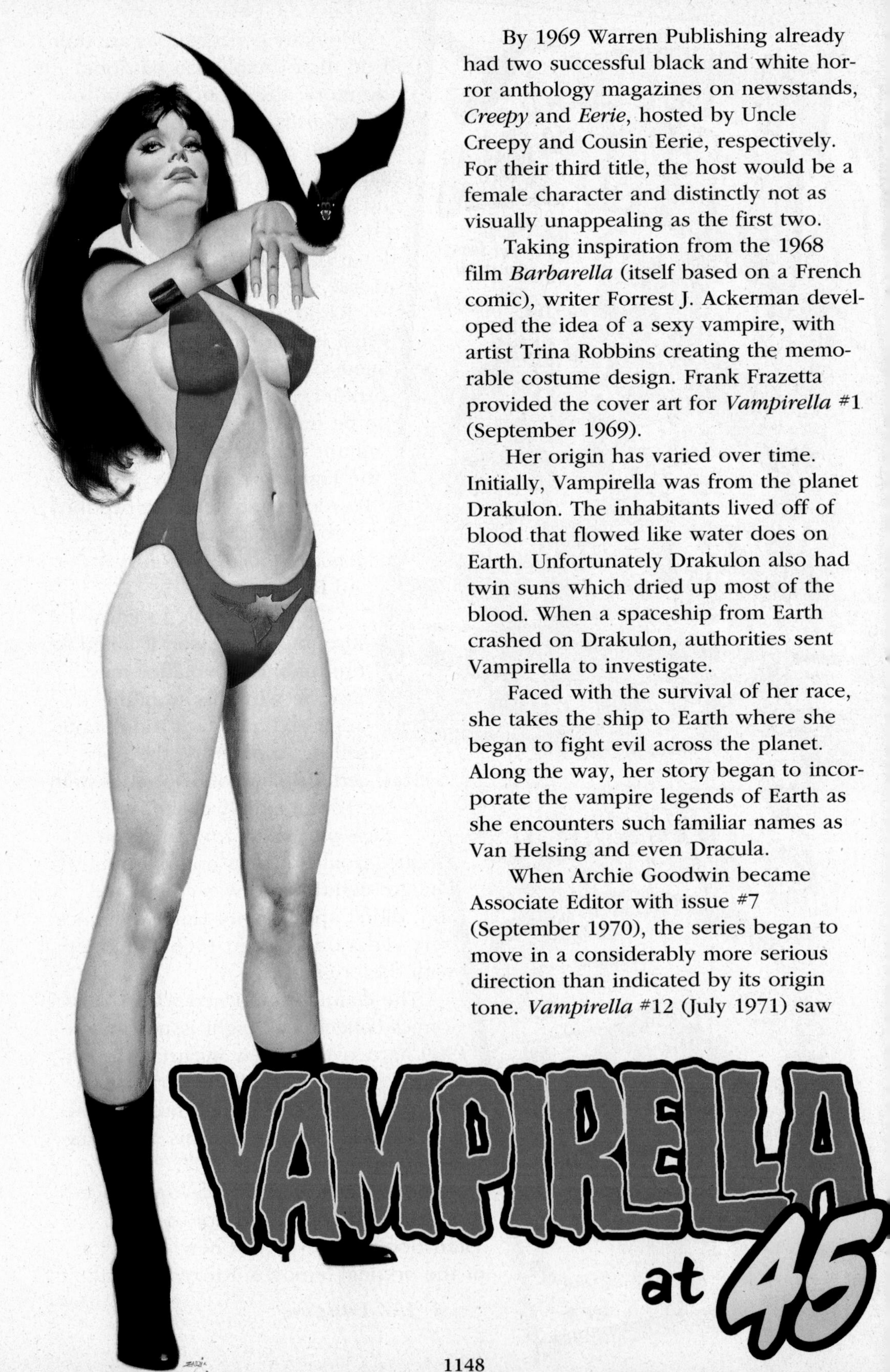

By 1969 Warren Publishing already had two successful black and white horror anthology magazines on newsstands, *Creepy* and *Eerie*, hosted by Uncle Creepy and Cousin Eerie, respectively. For their third title, the host would be a female character and distinctly not as visually unappealing as the first two.

Taking inspiration from the 1968 film *Barbarella* (itself based on a French comic), writer Forrest J. Ackerman developed the idea of a sexy vampire, with artist Trina Robbins creating the memorable costume design. Frank Frazetta provided the cover art for *Vampirella* #1 (September 1969).

Her origin has varied over time. Initially, Vampirella was from the planet Drakulon. The inhabitants lived off of blood that flowed like water does on Earth. Unfortunately Drakulon also had twin suns which dried up most of the blood. When a spaceship from Earth crashed on Drakulon, authorities sent Vampirella to investigate.

Faced with the survival of her race, she takes the ship to Earth where she began to fight evil across the planet. Along the way, her story began to incorporate the vampire legends of Earth as she encounters such familiar names as Van Helsing and even Dracula.

When Archie Goodwin became Associate Editor with issue #7 (September 1970), the series began to move in a considerably more serious direction than indicated by its origin tone. *Vampirella* #12 (July 1971) saw

artist Jose Gonzalez draw his first of many Vampirella stories. To this day, many fans consider him to be the character's definitive artist.

For over a decade the magazine brought solid horror to newsstands but by 1982 Warren was seeing serious problems that resulted in bankruptcy for the company. Their last issue was *Vampirella* #112 (March 1983).

Harris Publications acquired the rights to the character and published various one-shots, mini-series and series from beginning with *Vampirella* #113 in 1988 in its traditional magazine form. In 1991, Harris (through Dark Horse Comics) launched the mini-series *Vampirella: Morning in America* in a standard comic book format. Over the next 16 years, the company would publish the character with stories and art by a variety of top creators including Joe Jusko, Adam Hughes, Mike Mayhew, Michael Wm. Kaluta, Amanda Conner, Jimmy Palmiotti, Jeph Loeb and Tim Sale, among others.

In 2010 Dynamite Entertainment acquired the rights to the character and since then they have produced both archival collections of previous Vampirella stories and new original material by such creators as J. Scott Campbell, Alex Ross, Joseph Michael Linsner, Joe Madureira, Paul Renaud, Joe Jusko, Terry Dodson, and David Finch.

*– **Mark Squirek***

WOLVERINE™ at 40

Snikt! Snikt!

That is the sound of hell about to break loose.

It is also possibly the most famous sound effect ever created for a comic book since the medium began.

This year Wolverine turns 40. Today he ranks among the most popular characters to have ever originated in comic books, but four decades ago he had just made his brief first appearance in the last panel of *Incredible Hulk* #180 (October 1974).

In the follow-up, *Incredible Hulk* #181 (November 1974), he shared the cover with the Hulk and Wendigo. On it, artist and co-creator Herb Trimpe gave this new guy a teeth-gnashing desire to obliterate his opponent. He seemed vicious, fearless. He appeared to be energy incarnate. Chains burst around him and those claws just barely slipped by the Hulk's head. Compared to the Hulk, he looked small. It's Hulk, who wouldn't?

And that was just the cover.

As it turned out, Wolverine *was* small, at least in stature, but not in staying power. Writer and co-creator Len Wein and Trimpe tapped into something with the character's attitude and style in *Incredible Hulk* #181.

Wolverine was next featured in *Giant-Sized X-Men* #1 (July 1975). Since Wolverine's powers, his quick healing, his superior physical talents come from a

Herb Trimpe and Jack Abel's original art for Page 32 from *Incredible Hulk* #180, the first appearance of Wolverine, sold for $657,250 (including the buyer's premium) in Heritage's May 15-17, 2014 auction.

Summer 1975's *Giant-Size X-Men* #1 featured the first appearance of the new X-Men, a team that included – and would often be dominated by – Wolverine.

Frank Miller and Joe Rubinstein *Wolverine* (Limited series) #3 Cover Original Art Sold for $47,800 in November 2010.

natural mutation, it was only natural for him to join the X-Men.

It is that ability to heal so quickly that allowed him to live through having his skeleton laced with the metal alloy adamantium. The 68-page issue features a new restructure of the team by Len Wein and Dave Cockrum (Wein would soon bow out in favor of writer Chris Claremont, who would do much to shape Wolverine over the next two decades).

The story of the new team continued in *X-Men #94* (August 1975). Wolverine was cryptic and generally kept in the background until John Byrne took over as artist. He revised the character's costume and put more visual emphasis on Wolverine in the series. Fans began to respond to the character, partially inspired by his perceived willingness to use such force with almost blind fury.

He was and remained a bundle of contradictions. The ultimate loner, he was part of a team, and his friendship once given was given for life. His toughness is essential to his character, but he had moments of surprising subtlety. For years we were given hints as to his past, but nothing more.

In the original Wolverine mini-series in 1982, Claremont penned the defining line, "I am the best at what I do, but what I do best isn't very nice." Illustrated by Frank Miller, those four issues serve even more to highlight the multiple dichotomies of the character's nature, but there was still plenty they didn't reveal about his history.

Marvel Comics Presents, the long running, bi-weekly series in which he starred, filled in some of the blanks and added to Wolverine's riddles, but it wasn't until 2001's six-issue *Origins* that his background really got the spotlight. By that point, the character was already one of the most popular in the *X-Men* film franchise.

Since then his comic book incarnation has appeared in *Avengers, New Avengers, Wolverine and the X-Men, Savage Wolverine* and numerous other titles.

Even after all that time, though, there is still no more fear-inducing or thrilling sound effect than "SNIKT." When we see/hear it, we know someone's in trouble.

– Mark Squirek

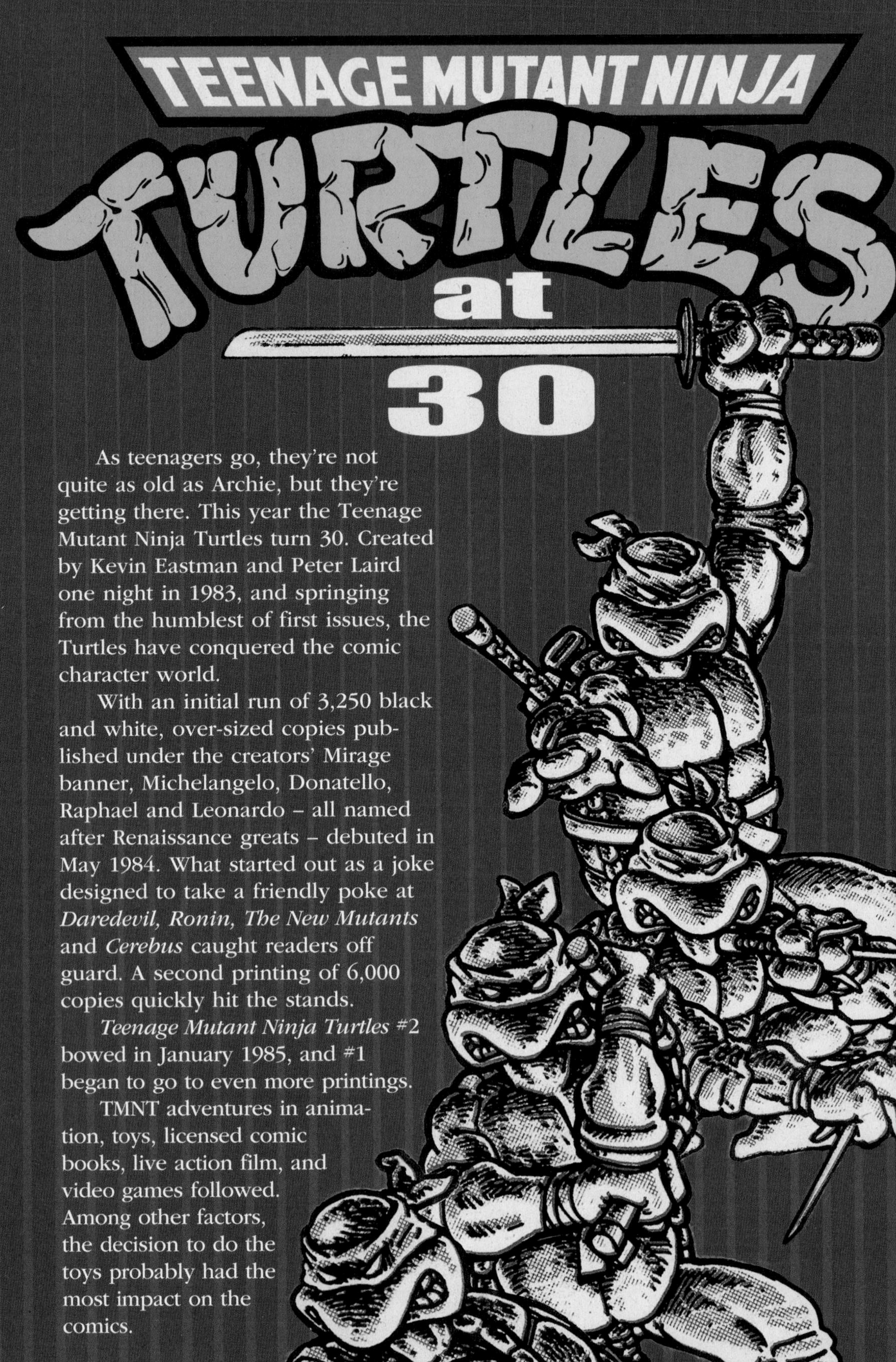

TEENAGE MUTANT NINJA TURTLES at 30

As teenagers go, they're not quite as old as Archie, but they're getting there. This year the Teenage Mutant Ninja Turtles turn 30. Created by Kevin Eastman and Peter Laird one night in 1983, and springing from the humblest of first issues, the Turtles have conquered the comic character world.

With an initial run of 3,250 black and white, over-sized copies published under the creators' Mirage banner, Michelangelo, Donatello, Raphael and Leonardo – all named after Renaissance greats – debuted in May 1984. What started out as a joke designed to take a friendly poke at *Daredevil, Ronin, The New Mutants* and *Cerebus* caught readers off guard. A second printing of 6,000 copies quickly hit the stands.

Teenage Mutant Ninja Turtles #2 bowed in January 1985, and #1 began to go to even more printings.

TMNT adventures in animation, toys, licensed comic books, live action film, and video games followed. Among other factors, the decision to do the toys probably had the most impact on the comics.

With the Playmates Toys line, changes were made to lighten the tone, which was initially funny but also decidedly more violent at first. Catch phrases such as "Cowabunga" were added and most significantly, their costumes became color coded. Michelangelo, Donatello, Raphael and Leonardo developed a love of pizza. The more kid-friendly animated version arrived in December, 1987. When it did, a brand new generation of young fans went wild. Ultimately that first series lasted an incredible 188 episodes until 1996.

During that time Playmates Toys ended up producing over 400 figures based on *TMNT*. Only *G.I. Joe* and *Star Wars* have ever sold more toys. These amazing numbers were helped by a 1990 film version which raked in over $200 million worldwide. There were sequels and reboots, of course.

Mirage initially produced 75 issues as well as multiple mini-series, one shots and spin-off titles closer in tone to the original than the cartoon. On the other hand, the series published by Archie, which ran from 1988 to 1995, reflected the cartoon's lighter tone. In 1996 TMNT moved to Image Comics for thirteen issues which ran from 1996-1999. Laird later disavowed the stories from this period. In 2001 the Turtles went home to Mirage where Laird produced 30 issues, ending in 20009.

In 2009, Nickelodeon purchased the Teenage Mutant Ninja Turtles from the Mirage Group and 4Kids Entertainment for $60 million. Presently IDW is producing comics based on the characters with Eastman's participation. As this edition of *The Overstreet Comic Book Price Guide* goes to press, a new *Teenage Mutant Ninja Turtles* film from producer Michael Bay is scheduled to be released in August 2014.

– Mark Squirek

#21 – "Silent Interlude" at 30

For those of us who were around when G.I. Joe: A Real American Hero #21 hit the stands in early 1984, it's hard to digest that three decades have passed since we first saw it. What's incomprehensible, though, considering its stature among artists and storytellers today, is the indifference that writer artist Larry Hama said greeted it upon its release. Hama answered a few questions about the project for us.

Overstreet: How did doing the silent issue of G.I. Joe come about in the first place?
Larry Hama (LH): There was some sort of scheduling glitch, and we had to produce a whole issue in something like three weeks. This was before internet and attached jpgs, so everything was on paper and had to travel via FedEx. It was seemingly impossible. I sat down with Denny O'Neil, and I said "if I write it and do pencil break-downs simultaneously, we can get a good finisher like Steve Leialoha and feed him pages as we go." Denny said George Roussos can color it in house as the pages come back. It then occurred to me that we could save a whole week if there was no lettering, and I proposed doing the whole issue "silent." Denny agreed immediately, but stressed that it couldn't just be a long fight, and there had to be characterization and drama. So I went home and started drawing. I wrote it and drew it in a little over three days. Oh, and the title page was lettered by Janice Chiang.

Overstreet: What sort of reactions did you get at Marvel before it was published?
LH: Not a lot of reaction at all. You have to remember that it was a "toy book" and that was the low rung on the totem pole back then. The main reaction was a bit of praise for getting the book out so fast. Although, I don't think we held the record for speed. I once did a double-length movie adaptation of a James Bond film "For Your Eyes Only," that we got out in one week from start to finish. I scripted it, Howard Chaykin penciled, and Vinnie Colletta inked.

Overstreet: What were the reactions like after it was published?
LH: It was totally ignored by the fan press. Nobody cared. We got a lot of letters from kids saying that without words it read too fast and they felt that they weren't getting their money's worth. A few kids sent the issue back, saying they got a defective copy because "all the words fell off."

Overstreet: Did you ever think you'd still be talking about it 30 years later or did you just think it was done, move on to the next one?
LH: None of us who worked on toy licensed properties thought that anybody would care about G.I. Joe or Transformers after the toys left the shelves and the commercials stopped running. There was no history to indicate otherwise. Maybe the difference was that a new generation of artists and writers were coming into the biz, who were taking the material seriously instead of viewing it as simply the ends to a pay check. I remember Neal Adams telling me back in the '70s that there was no such thing as a bad character, there was just bad interpretations of that character. That stuck with me.

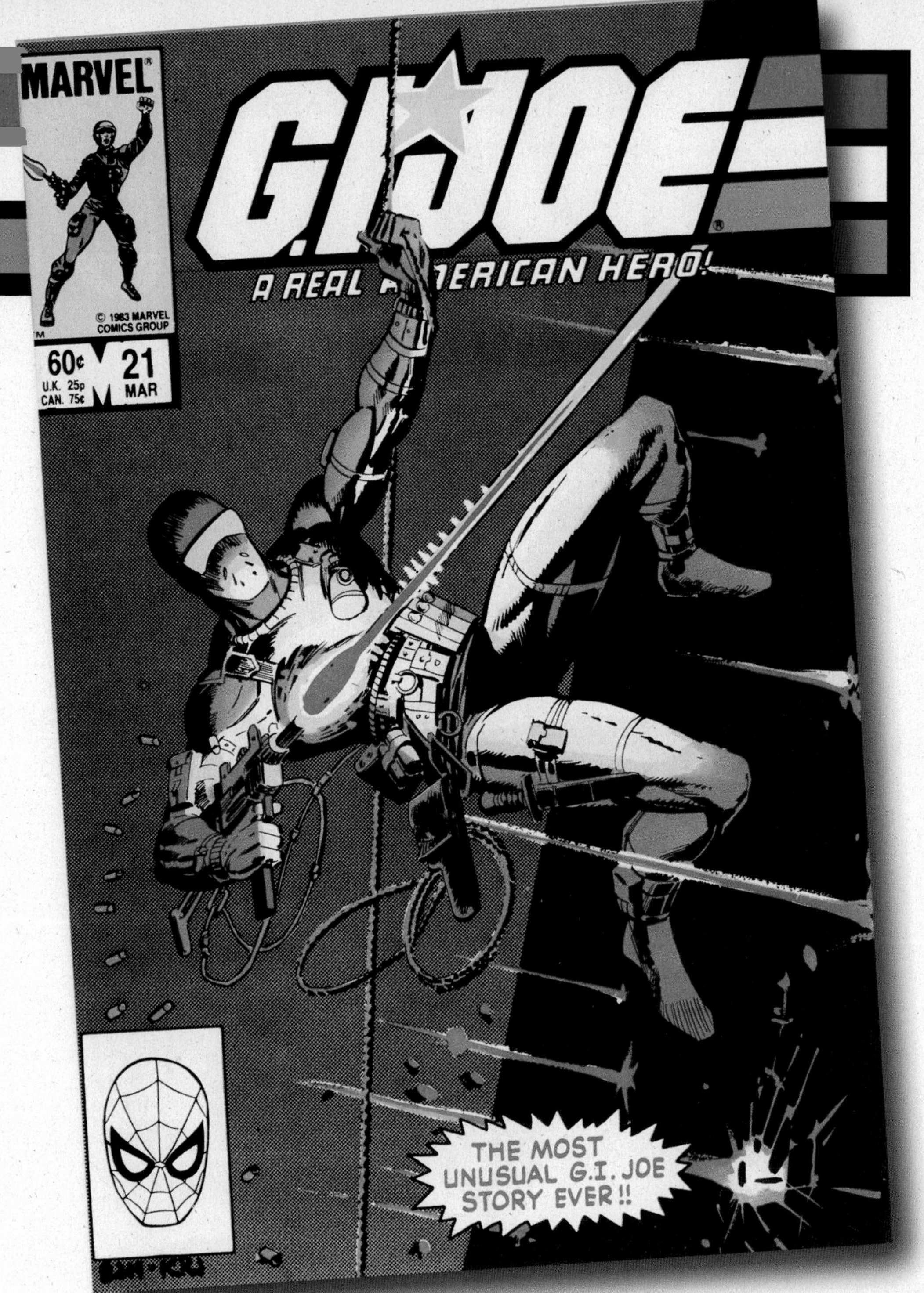

As we're going to press, publication is pending on a 30th anniversary edition of G.I. Joe: A Real American Hero #21 with additional material from IDW Publishing, where Hama continues to write the ongoing adventures of the characters.

A childhood love of samurai films and his introduction to Japanese woodblock prints while he was an illustration major at New York's Fashion Institute of Technology (FIT) were the fuel that sparked writer-artist Billy Tucci's creation of Ana Ishikawa, better known as the title character in *Shi*.

He had the initial idea as far back as high school.

"I conceived the idea of Shi and the lead character in my senior year at school.

The character of Ana Ishikawa was actually a male initially, thrust into a 'Montegue vs. Capulet' type of war that has been carried over from medieval Japan to the present," Tucci said.

But it was the art he discovered at FIT that was the catalyst to fully developing the story, he said.

"The beauty and dynamics of the woodblocks literally changed my life, and started the wheels turning in my head that wouldn't stop for over a decade," he said. "It wasn't until after college when I was doing freelance t-shirt art and working at Macy's as their children's wear designer that things started to change in both the characters, (the most important, being that our lead was now a female), the story and best medium to produce it. My childhood friend, illustrator and designer Barry Orkin, was the one who told me about the Sohei, the warrior monks of ancient Kyoto and Nara that really started things falling in place. It really unlocked an entire universe that was unique and original. It was also around that time that I became convinced that this story should be told not in novel form but rather in comics."

Always a student of history, he created a young woman caught between two ancient warring factions, between the old world and the modern age, between differing faiths and the yearning of her heart.

Shi: The Way of The Warrior #1 and the issues that followed sold like crazy in the heady days of the mid-1990s, propelling Tucci into the upper ranks of creator ownership. His imprint, Crusade, published numerous tales of Shi (which is Japanese for "death") and licensed comics for foreign publication as well.

After Tucci and co-writer Peter Gutierrez completed *Shi: The Way of the Warrior*, he teamed with writer Gary Cohn for *Shi: Senryaku,* which featured Ana's early life told through montages that mirrored the great events in history as portrayed by some of the best artists in the industry including Jim Lee, Joe Quesada, Jeff Smith, Jae Lee, Amanda Conner, Terry Moore, Stan Sakai, George Pérez, and Joe Jusko, among others.

Subsequently he produced a series of mini-series and one-shots chronicling the character's adventures, ending with 2005's *Shi: Ju-Nen*, published by Dark Horse before turning his attention to his acclaimed *Sgt. Rock: The Lost Battalion* and his passion project, *A Child Is Born.*

As he celebrates his character's 20th anniversary, Tucci said he's preparing a Shi graphic novel with a story that takes place 20 years after the original.

–J.C. Vaughn

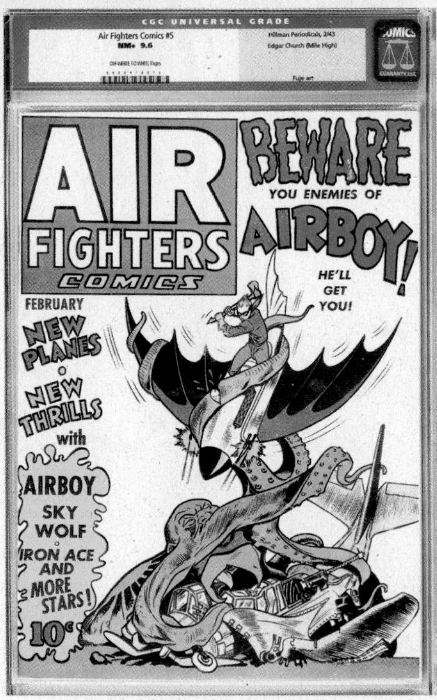

AIR FIGHTERS COMICS #5
February 1943. Mile High copy, and the only copy graded above a 9.0. © HILL

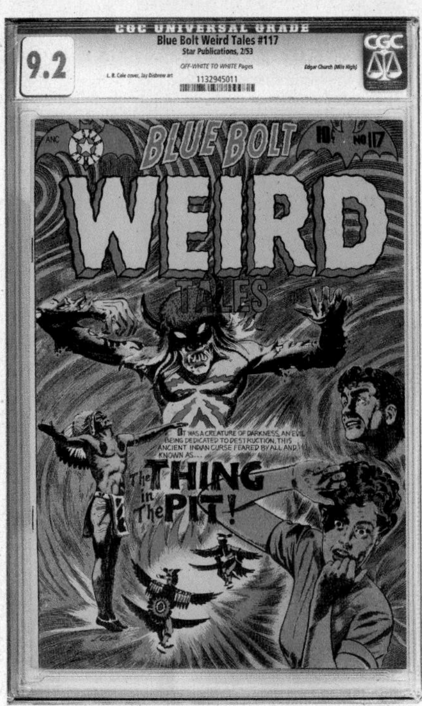

BLUE BOLT WEIRD TALES #117
February 1953. Mile High copy, highest graded.
© STAR

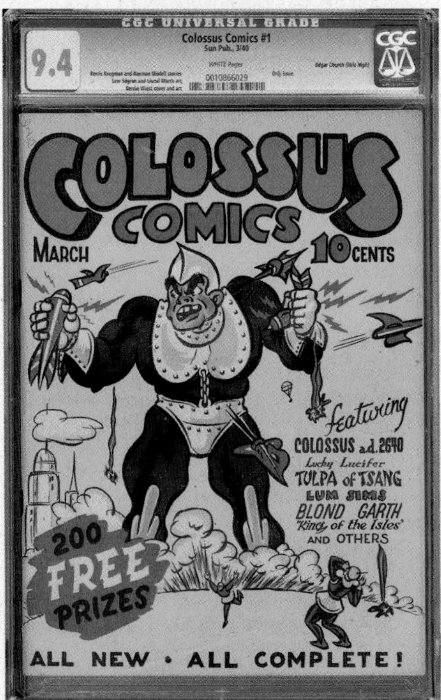

COLOSSUS COMICS #1
March 1940. Mile High copy, highest graded.
© Sun Publications

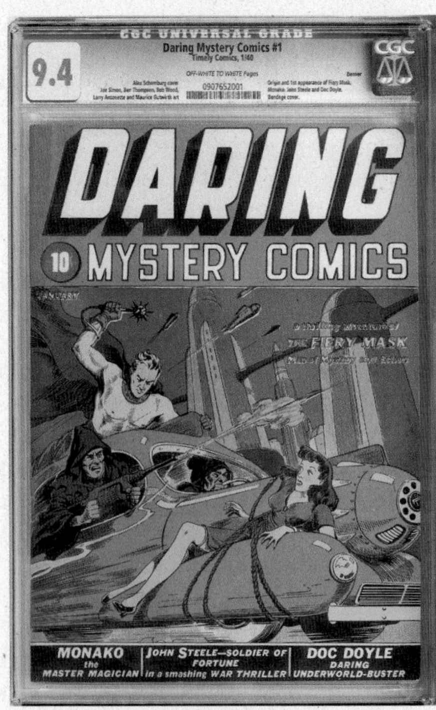

DARING MYSTERY COMICS #1
January 1940. Denver copy, highest graded.
© MAR

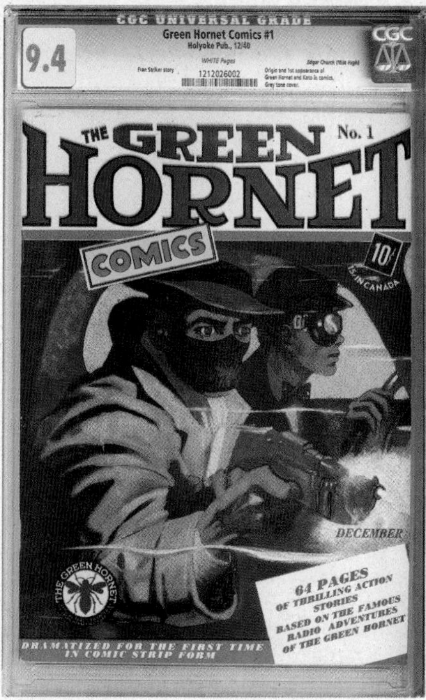

GREEN HORNET COMICS #1
December 1940. Mile High copy, highest graded.
© Holyoke

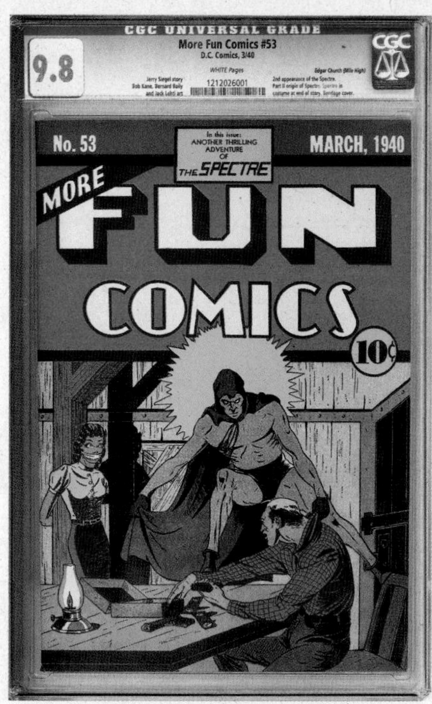

MORE FUN COMICS #53
March 1940. Mile High copy, highest graded.
The only 9.8 of the Top 30 Golden Age books. © DC

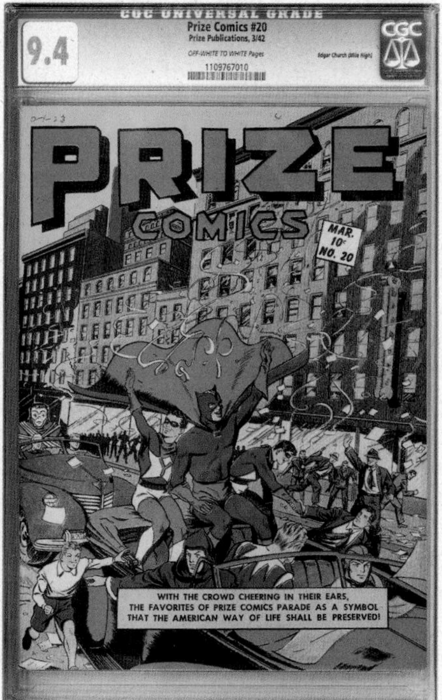

PRIZE COMICS #20
March 1942. Mile High copy, only copy ever graded.
© Prize Publications

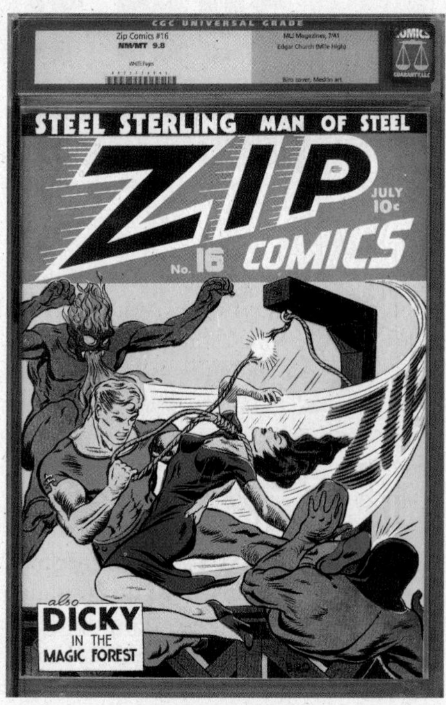

ZIP COMICS #16
July 1941. Mile High copy, one of only two known unrestored copies, highest graded. © MLJ

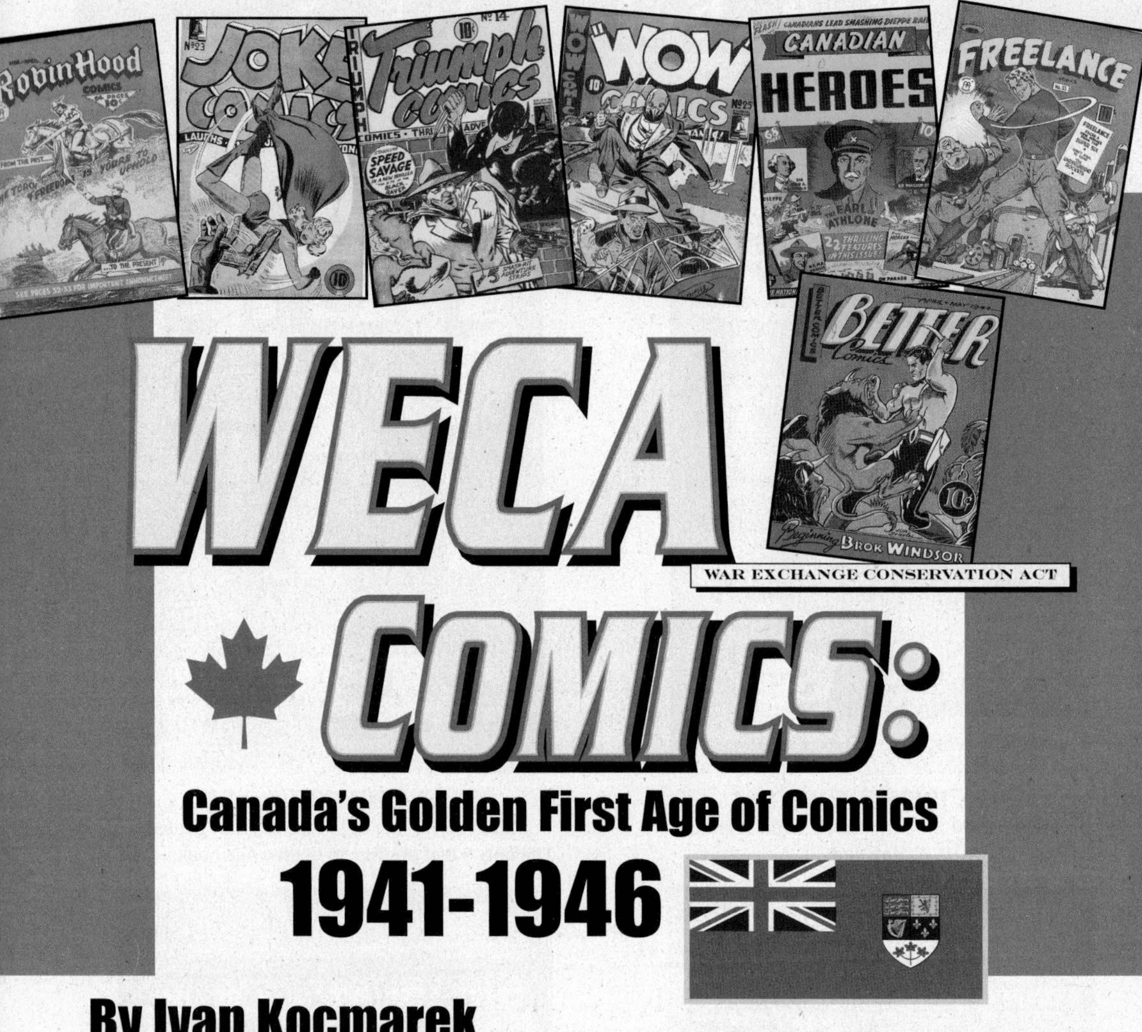

WECA Comics:

WAR EXCHANGE CONSERVATION ACT

Canada's Golden First Age of Comics 1941-1946

By Ivan Kocmarek

In his review of Jules Pfeiffer's *The Great Comic Book Heroes* (Bonanza Books, 1965), Canadian literary icon Mordecai Richler includes the following telling comment[i]:

> The last time we were asked to make do with Canadian comics was during the war years when in order to protect *our* balance of payments the government stopped the import of American comic books. The Canadian comic books hastily published to fill the gap were simply awful. We wouldn't have them. Banning American comics was a typically unimaginative measure, for whatever pittance the government made up in U.S. currency, it lost in home front morale.

This was 1967, Canada's Centennial year, five years before the 1972 Canada/Russia hockey series and a time when the country, as the bland Spam in the middle of a spicy British and American sandwich, thirsted for a sense of cultural identity. Richler's disdainful and jaundiced comments demonstrate that he must have been aware of only a regretful "sliver" of these war era comics or knew about them only from secondary sources. He couldn't have made the same comments had he known about Nelvana, Freelance, Active Jim and the Active Club, Johnny Canuck, Canada Jack and the Canada Jack Club, and the way that these creations informed and galvanized war era Canadian youth.

The first age of Canadian comics was a vibrant one whose sheen was just as "golden" (though not as lasting) as the one enjoyed by our neighbors to the south.

While in the States the birth of the superhero was innovative and seminal, filled with the Uncle Sam energy that spawned a star studded constellation of costumed defenders of justice and created an industry with an envious trajectory for the next decade, Canada's first superhero age was a struggle of opportunism in a window provided by our national government and the necessities of a war. It developed under the behemoth shadow of (and with the Anglo-American redraws, directly and heavily depended upon) the American comic conglomerates.[ii]

Canada entered the Second World War on September 10, 1939, nine days after Hitler invaded the Sudetenland and a week after England declared war on Germany. The U. S. jumped into the fray only the day after Pearl Harbor on December 8, 1941. A year before this, on December 6, 1940, the Canadian Parliament under Prime Minister William Lyon MacKenzie King, in an effort of protectionism, passed the War Exchange Conservation Act (WECA)[iii] to bolster the Canadian dollar and the war economy in general. Included in the list of banned imports were comic books.

All of a sudden the adolescent and pre-adolescent population of Canada (as small as it was compared to that of the U.S.) became an untapped and captive audience (read: customer base) for comic books that were no longer there. What must be noticed here is that WECA was passed in early December, 1940 and that the indicia date of the first Canadian comics to appear (*Robin Hood and Company* Vol. 1 #1[iv] and *Better Comics* Vol. 1, #1) was March, 1941. Given the fact that comics usually appear on the stands a month or even two months before their indicia dates[v], the turn-around time from nothing to finished product is amazing—capitalistic opportunism at its finest.

This window, opened at the start of 1941 was closed by the repeal of the War Exchange Conservation Act (WECA) by Canadian Parliament soon after the end of WWII (probably late 1945 or early 1946[vi]) and led to the quick return of the star-studded, glossy, full-

The typical interior black-and-white page of a Canadian White (from *Joker Comics* #4).

colored American comics to Canadian newsstands. Some Canadian comic titles that started up in 1941 and 1942 because of WECA continued to limp on through 1946, one by one dropping by the wayside, and by the end of 1946 became completely extinct.

Nostalgically and affectionately, these comics came to be known in fandom as the "Canadian Whites" because the interiors were printed only in black-and-white outline[vii]. My proposal, and many collectors of these books are now using this term, is that these books would better be referred to as "WECA" books because their existence was a direct product of the Act and their demise by the end of 1946 was an understandable result. These WECA books represent the first distinctively Canadian comics. They are the hardest to find and much rarer[viii] than almost all U.S. Golden Age comics.

To Canadians, the WECA comic books represent a precious and significant piece of our heritage. They were born directly out of our political past. They provided the pre-adolescents and adolescents of the day with a distinctly northern constellation of fantasy heroes and some who were singularly Canadian (Nelvana, Johnny Canuck, Canada Jack...). They provided those same kids, who didn't read newspapers and who had no TV to watch, with possibly (aside from weekly newsreels at the cinema and radio broadcasts) their only source of information on the war.[ix] Their value to Canadian culture is evidenced by the inclusion of John Bell's comprehensive collection of WECA Bell Features Publishing materials (including 380 copies of Bell WECA comics, original artwork, correspondence, contracts, copyright files, photographs, etc.) in the Collections of the National Archives of Canada in Ottawa.[x] On pg. 17 *of Better Comics* Vol. 1 #1, Vernon Miller[xi] makes it clear, for the kids of the day, what these comics were about when, in the third paragraph of a one page, blue text message with color borders entitled "Hello Boys, Hello Girls" he says: "This magazine, boys and girls, is drawn entirely by Canadian artists and published by a Canadian firm. Don't you think that is something to be proud of? We do." He signs off as "Uncle Verne."

The Canadian White era started with *Better Comics* #1, cover dated March 1941.

The WECA period *is* Canada's Golden Age[xii]. It was a six-year window of magic that stands on its own and needn't be framed by the parameters of the American Golden Age. It also needn't and shouldn't be restricted to archeological efforts of investigators and collectors scratching about in arcane ruins. Its present obscurity will not prevent it from enduring and endurance is what makes a piece or period of art classic[xiii].

WECA Books: The First Year

John Bell has already and exhaustively examined this WECA period from the publications standpoint. However, the comics themselves and their sequence deserve a closer look. The first year (1941) of WECA books started off with *Better* Vol. 1 #1 (Maple Leaf Publishing, Vancouver), *Robin Hood and Company* Vol. 1 #1 (Anglo-American Publisher's Limited, Toronto)—both with cover dates of March along with reprints of some Fox titles by Anglo-American[xiv] also with March cover dates. What should be noted as well is that even though *Better Comics* #1 has a cover and *indicia* date of March, 1941, if we look at the contests announced on the last folio page and the inside back cover, we find that entry deadlines are given as February 28. This means that the book had to be on the stands by no later than the beginning of February and, more likely, the middle of January, just about five weeks after the passing of the War Exchange Conservation Act (WECA). The publishers must have had some insider information about the Act going through or just anticipated it.

Better #1 must also be noted for having the first color WECA story in the inaugural "Iron Man"[xv] segment ("Iron Man and the City Under the Ocean"). *Robin Hood and Company* #1, on the other hand, collects together reprints from Ted McCall and artist Charles Snelgrove's *Toronto Evening Telegram* daily strips that appeared in the 1930s. Though after this issue, the comic takes on a regular size and format, it appears that the strips from the thirties continue to be reprinted for about the first year because panel size rarely varies and the early issues of this first year seem to have only one long, continuous story in each issue.[xvi]

Besides being Canada's first real comic book and first 15¢ comic, *Better* #1 starts off with a six-page semi-sci-fi story of "The Earth Torpedo" which looks like a Flash Gordon serial rocket that can tunnel through the earth. It carried its inventor Professor Miles and his nephew, Bobby, on adventures under the ground and this is the feature that gets front cover billing.. The irony (pun intended) is that *Better* #1, by analogy Canada's *Action* #1, would have been served better with Canada's first superhero (Iron Man) front and centre on the cover. The second six-page story features the incongruous Tiger Tex, a cowboy detective who has a talking parrot on his shoulder. "Iron Man and the City Under the Ocean," which begins on page 18, is the third, and only color, story in the issue, but it is the longest story at nine pages. Two other stories round out the book. A six-page period piece about 18th century press gang culture entitled "The Hidden Passage" and a four-page railroad adventure called "Roaring Rails." All were written and drawn by Vernon Miller except for "The Hidden Passage" which appears to have been written by F(rederick). P(ercival). Thursby (Marine Illustrator) and drawn by Vernon Miller. With its color covers (inside and out) *Better* #1 kicks off the WECA period and provides history's first answer to the question: "What is a Canadian comic book?"

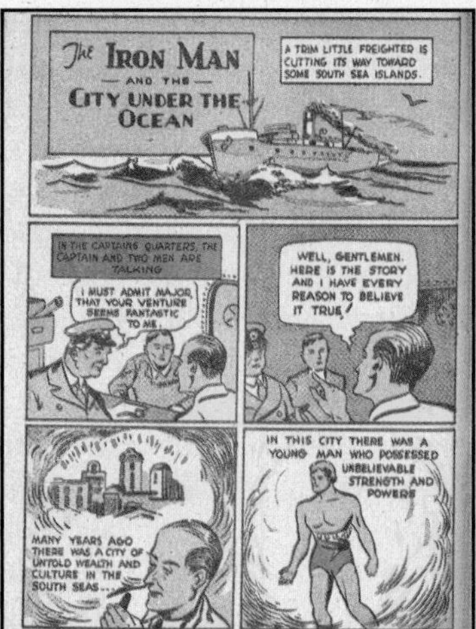

Canada's first superhero, Iron Man, debuted in the only color story within *Better Comics* #1.

A couple of months later, Maple Leaf put out *Lucky Comics* Vol. 1 #1 with a cover date of June, 1941. The first issue of *Lucky Comics* didn't bring us any superhero but features such as "Peter and Peggy and the Haunted Castle" by Ernie Walker and Vernon Miller, "Coast Patrol" by Ted Watson, "Ether Escapades" by Herb Frew and artist Verler, and "Wings over the Lions Gate" set in Vancouver harbor.[xvii] Though titled just *Lucky Comics* in the indicia, everywhere else throughout the issue (contest and editorial pages) as well as on the cover the full title was *Union Jack, Lucky Comics* and this continued for the first three issues. With *Lucky Comics*, Maple Leaf Publications (and it continued this later on in *Bing Bang* and *Rocket Comics*) demonstrated that its tradition would be to offer mainly down-to-earth adventure stories (in the fashion of British Boys and Girls Annuals which seem to have had a greater influence on Canadian comic tradition than they ever did on the American), along with funny animal and human caricature cartoon strips while downplaying superhero or science fiction/fantasy stories to usually one per issue. Yet *Lucky Comics* continued that high standard of production values that was more closely aligned with American output than Anglo-American displayed in *Robin Hood and Company* #1 and the other early books from that publisher.

In its second title, *Freelance* Vol. 1 #1 (July/August 1941)[xviii], Anglo-American brought out the first Canadian comic to offer "super-hero" adventure stories from cover to cover. The title character featured in this book was named after those medieval knights who had fulfilled their duties for one monarch or another and now could work on their own for any cause. Their lances were free (just as ironically we have "freelancers" in comic art and writing). They were "Have Gun, Will Travel" Paladins who solved other people's problems. He was the creation of Ted McCall and artist Ed Furness. The cover of *Freelance* Vol. 1 #1, which shows Freelance decking a Nazi soldier with the sub-text: "Smashing the Invader in Africa," seems to be the first Canadian war-themed cover and the first Canadian cover with a swastika on it. After Iron Man, Freelance represents the second superhero in Canadian Comics, even though he had no real super powers but was, a la Batman, an agile, acrobatic, resourceful

The first Canadian war-themed cover *Freelance* #1, (July/August 1941) was also its first with a swastika.

and skilled fighter. During the WECA period, Freelance was perhaps the best known and bestselling of all the heroes on offer.[xix]

The next book to appear, according to cover date, was from a new publisher and creator, Hillborough Studio in Toronto founded by Welsh-born Adrian Dingle[xx] and the Estonian Kulbach brothers Andre and Rene. *Triumph-Adventure Comics* Vol. 1 #1 (August, 1941)[xxi] gave us the second WECA war cover showing a WW2 dog fight with the main aircraft have the RAF/RCAF roundel prominent on the fuselage. This cover represents the lead story which features the account of squadron leader Spanner Preston, a young Canadian in the RAF, and his engagement of Luftwaffe Stukas during the evacuation of Dunkirk in 1940 when he was shot down behind enemy lines but managed to return heroically to allied safety and subsequent enlistment in British Intelligence back in London. That story occupies the first 16 pages of the book but, after a one-page filler, it's on page 18 that we get one of the singular zeniths of WECA and Canadian comic book culture in general.

Here is the first Nelvana of the Northern Lights story by her creator, Adrian Dingle[xxii]. In Nelvana we encounter the first featured female super hero in comics. She predates the first appearance of Wonder Woman (*All Star Comics#* 8, December 1941) by four cover date months. She is also the first superhero directly and identifiably tied to Canadian cultural identity.[xxiii] Nelvana is the semi-divine offspring of Koliak, King of the Northern Lights and a mortal mother who is not named. She can travel on the beams of the Aurora Borealis (which is really the spirit of her father placed in the sky as a result of an ancient curse) and call upon it for help. She also has a magical cloak that transforms her brother, Tanero, who can never be seen by a white man, into the shape of a Great Dane. Her first adventure takes place in the Great North of Canada above the Arctic Circle and involves her solving the crisis of a local tribe of Eskimos (a pejorative term now replaced by the term Inuit) who are no longer able to feed themselves from the natural resources around them because an evil foreign power called the Kablunets who are depleting those resources (conservation of natural resources itself a pure Canadian motif). [xxiv]

Nelvana of the Northern Lights - the first superhero tied to Canadian cultural identity.

A month after *Triumph Adventure Comics* #1 came another landmark book. Though technically not a Bell Features book because it was published by Commercial Signs of Canada (Cyril Vaughan Bell's name for the company before he decided to make it eponymous), *Wow Comics* #1 (September, 1941) was the inaugural issue of the one publishing company that began near the start of the WECA era and managed to last, in some form, through and past the end of that era. Alexander Ross in his interview based article from 1964 shares the following[xxv]:

> ...Bell happened to have a small color press in his sign-painting shop which was used occasionally for printing billboards and banners for used-car lots.
>
> When one of his sign-painters, Edmund Legault, revealed that his secret ambition was to become a newspaper cartoonist and that in his spare time he'd created a comic strip called *Dart Daring* and drawn several months of episodes. Bell decided to put his idle press to work and ran off fifty-two thousand copies of a Dart Daring comic book [*Wow Comics* #1]. ...the edition sold out within a week and Bell began to realize the vast extent of the market he'd discovered.

Wow Comics #1 was the first cover-to-cover full color[xxvi] Canadian comic.[xxvii] It was the showpiece for young artist Edmund Legault. What is characteristic of Legault's work is his panel arrangement. Rather than six or eight panel pages, Legault mostly prefered two or three panel designs and often made use of full page artwork. His multipanel pages sometimes place panels obliquely

Bell Features started its WECA run with *Wow Comics* #1, September 1941, featuring the art of Edmund Legault.

and can employ curved or circular panel borders. Because of his large panel arrangements, *Wow Comics* #1 contained only two stories, both featuring characters created, written, and illustrated by Legault in his idiosyncratic manner.

The lead-off and cover story was about a eighteenth century blond swashbuckler named Dartner "Dart" Daring and the cover is notable for its violence in depicting Dart's blood-tipped sword running through a pirate (yet it's less violent than the decapitation cover of the next issue – these two covers stand out in the tradition of WECA comic covers for their violence). In the story itself, Dart is shipwrecked off the coast of an island somewhere in the south seas and befriends a great ape there. In exploring the island's jungle he runs into a teenage "boy" (with a distinct cleavage that is obvious in many panels without Dart becoming aware of it) who is being tortured by a wild tribe. Dart, with the help of the great ape, rescues the boy but, after they escape, Dart sees that the ape is injured and demands the shirt from the "boy" to bind the ape's wounds. The "boy" is reluctant, so Dart rips it off "him" and, to his embarrassment, finally realizes he is dealing with a woman. This is how he meets the lead heroine of the series, Loraine Knight. The story ends in a literal cliff-hanger when Dart falls from a broken vine that he was using to climb down a cliff face over a whirlpool.

The other story in *Wow Comics* #1 is titled "Whiz Wallace and the Invisible Planet" and appears to be styled after Flash Gordon. Whiz is an airplane racer who is captured by a giant alien space creature and wakes up trapped in a paralysis beam inside the creature's rocket headed for space. While immobile he observes a large humanoid alien experimenting on a woman. The rocket enters a space firestorm and Whiz is freed and rescues the woman, who we learn is Elaine Kenyon[xxviii]. Their rocket reaches the Invisible Planet and after encountering some terrifying creatures (especially a giant spider-crab) they are rescued by a giant grasshopper and are welcomed by the civilization of the planet.

Within the next month, the third Anglo-American title appeared, *Grand Slam Comics* Vol. 1 #1, cover dated September/October 1941. It introduced three new Ed Furness series: "Clip Thomson," Royal Canadian Air Force officer, along with his pal Tub and "Don Shield and his famous Reverso Ray," and "The Crusaders," who are two adventurers named Bob and Paul with a rocket ship and other advanced technology whose "Bat-signal" sky sign is a rocket smoke trail cross. It must be noted that Ed Furness only illustrated "The Crusaders" and it was written by Les Gilpin. The last series introduced in *Grand Slam Comics* #1 was "Pat the Air Cadet," created and delivered by an individual signed simply, "Macduff."

A month or so after this came three issues with the cover date of November/December 1941. Two of them were Maple Leaf publications. *Bing Bang Comics* #1 featured a young "Bowery Boy" type tuff named Pinky while *Name-It Comics*, so "named" because Maple Leaf wanted to run a contest for its readers to come up with a name for the new title, continued the "Roaring Rails" series from *Better Comics* #1 and added detective "John Henry," the military themed "The White Knight," two adventure series "Mystery Mountain" and "Now You're Loggin'" and, most significantly, the sci-fi/fantasy Buck Rogers styled "Cosmo (And his White Magic)" which endured into the last year of the WECA books. The contest was won by a young man named Sheldon from Montreal and with the next issue *Rocket Comics* was born so that *Rocket Comics* Vol. 1 #2 is really the first issue of *Rocket Comics*.

The other book that came out with the cover date of November/December 1941 was an Anglo-American publication entitled *Aces 3 Comics*. A red-toned black-and-white cover introduced us to investigator Michael Lee and reprises three other military-themed features: "'Clip' Thomson." "'Pat' The Air Cadet," and "The Crusaders" from *Grand Slam Comics* #1. A few months later with issue four, its title would become *Three Aces Comics*.

One thing to notice is that while in the States at this time you've got swarms of DC, Timely, Fawcett, and MLJ superheroes buzzing and blazing all over its four-color planet and serving as the central comic book motif, in Canada, apart from Iron Man, Freelance, and Nelvana, we tended to concentrate on "more refined" Boys Annual type of content involving detectives, cowboys, swashbucklers, spacemen, and soldiers. Was it that Canadians, when they had the chance to produce their own comic book culture from scratch, couldn't – or chose not to – jump into the enterprise in a garish way? Perhaps again it was the influence of some sort of British Commonwealth Boys Annual legacy or was it that we just didn't have it in us? Why couldn't we come up with a Superman, Batman, Capt. Marvel or a Captain America[xxix]? But maybe that's not a negative point in the end because it shows us what made comics Canadian at that time.

In a strange way, Anglo-American circumvented this issue with its next releases. It decided to buy and license scripts from Fawcett Publishers in the U. S. which it then redrew using its own artists and published in its usual black-and-white form. This produced *Captain Marvel Comics* #1 and *Whiz Comics* #1 both with cover dates of January 1942. Whiz #1, for example, reproduces the scripts used for American *Whiz Comics* #22 (October 1941), though the covers of the two are very different. Ibis, Spy Smasher and all the usual Whiz characters were recreated for this Canadian anthology.

Around this time there also appeared a one-shot effort by mysterious Citren Publishers that reprinted MLJ's *Pep Comics* #22 (December 1941). The Canadian title was *Super Comics* and had no number. Its interior contents were the usual line drawn black-and-white. Most striking were the changes to the cover art which entailed the transformation of the Shield's breastplate Stars 'n Stripes into the Dominion of Canada's flag of the time, the Union Jack, and this followed through inside the book as well. The Japanese and Nazi standards on the heel of the spiked jack-boot (strange because the U.S. wouldn't enter the war for another year) were reduced to just one large Nazi symbol. The series would be resurrected in Canada two years later by F. E. Howard publications.

The next month, February 1942, brought three new titles onto the scene. The rarest and most unusual was a one-shot from Adrian Dingle's Hillborough Studio and was called *Top-Flight Comics*. Its inside front cover featured stamp size sketched portraits of the artists, Hugh Caulfield, Clayton Dexter, Dingle himself and Hunter Barker all probably done by Dingle. It had four solid features, all a dozen pages long each. Caulfield began the book with a finely drawn story about Happy Holden that was written by Jack Loudon. Happy is the pilot of a private plane on a geological expedition flying from Vancouver to Alaska that crashes into a lost prehistoric world beneath the arctic. The next is the swashbuckler cover story featuring The Rapier a seventeenth century Errol Flynn type good guy nemesis of pirates. Barker who, just like Dingle, seemed to have earned a reputation in the fine art field as an illustrator, offered two stories. "The Searunners" about a pair of teenage boys who have a run in with a U-Boat and Trigger Dunston, the mandatory tenacious Mountie, this time a corporal. Dingle finishes off the book with the "Arthurian" romance of a modern boy, Billy, who finds Excalibur and through it transforms periodically into an armored hero who battles evil in the world.

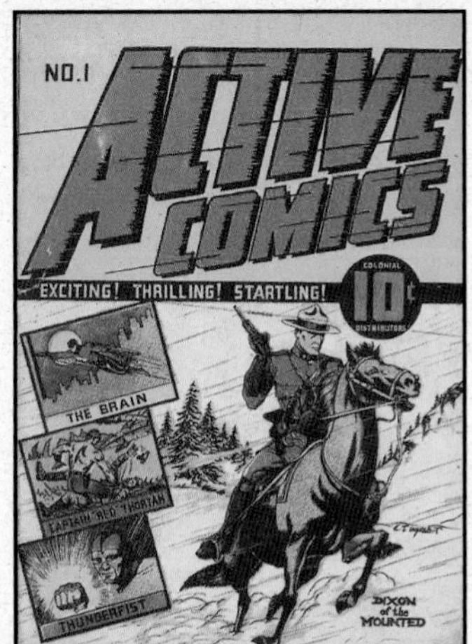

Active Comics #1 (Feb. 1942) introduced Thunderfist, Canada's first masked superhero.

The two other books with February 1942 indicia dates came from Cy Bell's stable of creators and provided a shot in the arm for the Canadian superhero genre. The first, *Active Comics* #1, had a lead-off story that introduced us to E. T. Legault's "Dixon of the Mounted" and this red-serge, stereotypical Mountie corporal blazed out at us from the front cover. The comic also featured a standard dashing adventurer in Al Cooper's "Capt. Red Thortan" who was a (as the text box on the splash page reads) "... soldier of fortune... [who] devotes himself to eliminate [*sic*] the enemies of democracy." But more significant to the WECA legacy were the other two stories in that issue.

The second story in *Active Comics* #1, written by E. T. Legault and drawn by Murray Karn, was the first Thunderfist story. Karn's somewhat static figures patently evoked Alex Raymond stylings. These early Cy Bell comics were all 64-pagers and stories were often a dozen pages or more and Thunderfist's "The Crime Crusher" gave us twelve pages of Canada's first masked (super) hero.[xxx] Randy Steele, an exceedingly strong and acrobatic individual, vengefully takes over the scientific research of his murdered inventor twin-brother Danny. He develops a bullet-proof, electrically charged costume with wrist devices that give him a super-powerful punch and ankle devices that allow him to travel along electrical lines with super speed. He also carries with him a tiny television screen that seems to be able to visualize any event in the world. With these costume powers he continues on in *Active Comics* until he signs off in a 4 part epic entitled Thunderfist and the Men from Mars in issues 23-26 written and drawn by Tedd Steele[xxxi].

Active #1's final story is a 15-pager from Leo Bachle featuring one of his creations, The Brain, in a story entitled "The Man with the Psychic Mind." The Brain is Gordon Bell who is born with psychic powers on the very day that his WW1 Canadian Victoria Cross-winner father dies. Gordon invents a flying suit made of secret mesh and covers the top half of his head with a black mask.[xxxii] The text box on that first splash panel describes The Brain: "With his power to visualize happenings far and near and his flying suit he devotes his life to ferreting out plots against the democratic world." The Brain ran until issue 27 of *Active Comics*.

The last of the three books to come out with the February 1942 indicia date was *Dime Comics* #1 and perhaps was the most significant. It contained only three long stories and sandwiched between 20 pages of Edmond Good's set up to a secret underground civilization adventure in "Rex Baxter and the Island of Doom" and 21 pages of Al Cooper's wonderful period war planes in "Kenneth 'Scotty' MacDonald" was Leo Bachle's 19 page introduction of the world to Johnny Canuck.

While Nelvana was Canadian by virtue of her origins in Canada's north and native mythology, Johnny had it stamped on his name and is therefore more closely aligned with the intent of American nationalistic superheroes such as Captain America, Fighting American, and Fighting Yank (in fact Yank and Canuck are analogous colloquial usages). Johnny's connection with the armed forces is not made clear in this first story and his uniform is not actually military issue. It consists only of jodhpurs and riding boots[xxxiii] as well as thin T-shirt that seems to disintegrate whenever he gets into action. Shot down over Libya, Johnny encounters a lost city with tremendous mineral wealth. He becomes their king and ends up defending them from a Nazi take over up to the point that, in the last few panels, he is praised by Churchill in London and reviled by Hitler in Berlin. *Dime Comics* #1, therefore, is best known for introducing Canada's first emphatically nationalistic comic book hero in the context of a global war.

The exploits of Johnny Canuck, Canada's first emphatically nationalistic comic book hero, started in *Dime Comics* #1 (Feb. 1942).

This brace of Bell issues marks the end of that first and perhaps most eventful year ever in Canadian comic book history. Political intervention and publishing opportunism gave Canadian kids dreams, adventures, and heroes they could call their own and this would prove out for the next five years to be the Canadian Golden Age of Comics.

Highlights of the WECA Years 1942-46

The next five years of the WECA period produced a number of significant occurrences in the story of Canadian comics.

1942

An unusual 52-page one-shot seems to have come out from the West Coast around April/May of 1942. It was a Maple Leaf book in all appearances, but the indicia attribute the publication to the governmental Community Standards Council of British Colombia.[xxxiv] This was *Your New World Comics* #1 with a cover that looked to be by Ernie Walker. It showed two fair-haired youngsters engrossed in observing, through a window, the bright Canadian future that lay ahead of them. The boy, chin in hand and pencil on his ear gazed through a window thoughtfully at a glistening, tall, almost Mormon-esque edifice. The girl, with compass points in one hand and a ruler in the other, measured out the building's blueprint—all a bit scary, really.

The date for the book comes from "Letter to Our Princess" dated April 10, 1942 on the inside front cover. The book contains mainly morally uplifting, historical, character building information and stories for kids. It has only three short comic panel stories. The first about explorer Alexander Mackenzie who traversed Canada from coast to coast ten years before the Lewis and Clark expedition in America. The others were a two color (red and blue) story of The Good Samaritan and a 5 pager "The Story of Our [Canadian] Flag." Just about all the other content is textual with accompanying illustrations.

Then in May of 1942 Cy Bell changed the name of his publishing company from Commercial Signs of Canada to Bell Features Publications and started placing that famous bell-shaped logo on all his comics starting with issues number 4 of *Active* and *Dime Comics*. *Joke Comics* #1 seems to have come out around March, 1942[xxxv]; no Bell logo appears on it or on #2. As its title and Lou Skuce's cover suggest, *Joke Comics* featured mainly cartoon laughs and humorous features and by issue four a standard line-up appeared on the cover including Ted Steele's "Private Stuff," Ross Saakel's "Spike and Mike," and most significantly a second Canadian female superhero called "The Wing" by John G. Hilkert[xxxvi].

The next significant event involved Bell Features as well. Adrian Dingle's Hillborough Studio folded after *Triumph Comics* #6 and

Top Flight Comics #1 both with cover dates of February 1942. When it resurfaced, probably about May 1942 with issue 7, *Triumph Comics* bore a Bell logo[xxxvii] and Adrian Dingle had become Art Director for Cy Bell's company. However, the real change to *Triumph Comics* with issue 7 was more than just a cosmetic one to its cover. Issue #7 jettisons the old Hillborough content apart from Nelvana and Tang and introduces two new costume hero stories. Ted A. Steele's new "Speed Savage" story was heavy on text and offered crime detective Speed who specialized in sports crimes and who became, as needs arose, avenging costumed sleuth the White Mask in long cape, broad fedora and white domino type mask. The other new masked marvel was Ross Saakel's Capt. Wonder who begins his comic existence as an anonymous young Canadian brought up, after his parents were killed by criminals, in a Himalayan temple. There three arcane gods from Valhalla, in a flash of Fawcett lighting, endow him with "...the strength of a hundered [*sic*] men, great wisdom and speed, the power to fly like a bird and swim like a fish...." *Triumph Comics* had become part of the Bell Features universe.

By June 1942 both Bell Features and Anglo-American had a new title each. Bell brought out *The Funny Comics* featuring Manny Easson's Dizzy Don a straw boater wearing Harry Langdon character who tripped successfully through adventure after adventure often encountering Nazis along the way. The first issue of *The Funny Comics* was much like *Joke Comics* #1 featuring a series of one page or multi-panel gag situations but this time centering on a single character in Dizzy Don. With issue #2 Dizzy became a full-blown Detective character usually solving a mystery in one lengthy story for half an issue and then reverting to regular gag pages for the second half of the book. Also, by June, Anglo-American had already acquired Fawcett scripts for Spy Smasher and started publishing that title as a re-drawn book.

The fall of this year saw Bell's final WECA base title appear. *Commando Comics* #1 (September – October 1942) [xxxviii] was a war themed comic which introduced characters such as Leo Bachle's Invisible Commando, Ace Bradley by E. B. C.(?), Adrian Dingle's Sign of Freedom and other characters such as Clift Steele, and Young Commandos (whose introductory story was handled by a young Mel Crawford). *Commando Comics* may very well be the fourth comic book of the war genre after Dell's *War Comics* #1 out in the spring of 1940, Fiction House's *Wings Comics* #1 which appeared in September 1940 and Quality's *Military Comics*, which first appeared in August 1941. American war comics didn't properly find their day until the time of the Korean War and after.

In October 1942, new publisher Educational Projects in Montreal initiated a title called *Canadian Heroes*, which featured true to life military, historical and athletic exploits related to Canada. Its most significant edition was Vol. 1 #5, dated March 1943. This issue introduced its only fictional, but most important character in relation to the history of Canadian comics.[xxxix] He was called Canada Jack, an expert gymnast and acrobat at the peak of human strength and ability. Just as Canada Jack was a stripped down, basic hero keeping in line with Educational Projects philosophy, so was his uniform. It consisted of a tank top undershirt with small crest in the centre of the chest and a set of stretch, gymnastics pants with a yellow stripe down the sides. He became popular enough to start the Canada Jack Club which was a network of readers who participated in war effort activities.[xl] Canada Jack ran until the end of the title with Vol. 5 #6 in October 1945.

Canadian Heroes #5 (March 1943) introduced Canada Jack, who became popular enough to start the Canada Jack Club.

Just after this, in the holiday period of 1942, Educational Projects also issued a new 68 page title called *Famous Adventure*

Stories which appeared to be a type of "classics" comics compendium of stories from literature, legend, and history. This issue has indicia that indicates it is #1 (though the cover doesn't have any indication of this) and that it was intended to be published monthly but it appears that only this issue came out. The apparent intention was to come up with a compilation analogous to America's *Classics Comics* which had begun a year earlier.[xli] The inside front cover makes it clear that the book wants to introduce young readers to these classic stories in the hope that they will go off eventually and find the originals. Stories include "The Three Musketeers" drawn by Joseph Hillenbrand, and "A Christmas Carol" and "Gulliver's Travels: The Voyage to Lilliput" by Sid Barron with other work by Leison, Herschel and L. Doff.

The end of 1942 and start of 1943 saw two Fawcett characters introduced and taking over leads in Anglo-American title. Captain Marvel, Jr. became lead and cover feature *Grand Slam Comics* Vol. 2 #1 dated December 1942 and Bulletman and Bulletgirl did the same in *Three Aces Comics* Vol. 1 #12, the January 1943 issue. Both of these lasted as leads and cover stars in their respective issues until the end of the summer in 1944, roughly a year-and-a-half (probably the terms of the original contract), when they disappeared and Canadian features again moved off the back pages onto the cover.

1943

By 1943 Canada had four functioning comic book publishing houses. Maple Leaf Books, out of Vancouver, produced four titles. Anglo-American Publications and Bell Features Publications, both based in Toronto, put out seven different titles each, and fledgling Educational Projects in Montreal issued its single title, *Canadian Heroes*. So, in the middle of the WECA period, there were at least 19 titles to look for on the stands.

Also in 1943, Anglo-American decided to reprint at least four of Samuel E. Lowe & Co.'s Mighty Midget Comics series. Known are *Bulletman*, *Captain Marvel Jr.. Golden Arrow*, and *Ibis the Invincible*. All the covers were the usual Double A two-tones, this time orange and black and were different (some slightly redrawn like the Ibis and Golden Arrow and others, like the Bulletman and Captain Marvel Jr., completely different). Contents also seem to be different and while all the back covers of the American issues have a small "Buy War Stamps" logo, the Canadian reprints have text ads for various Canadian non-comic companies.

In the spring of 1943, Bell Features issued a huge compendium one-shot called *Colossal Comics*. It contained six remaindered coverless Bell titles and ran over 300 pages and was priced at 39¢. Two different Adrian Dingle covers are known, one with a battleship overrunning a U-Boat and the other with a shot Japanese sniper falling from a palm tree. They have no numbers or indicia dates but are probably from this period because they were featured in ads and on back covers of books from this period such as *Active Comics* #15, *Wow Comics* #18 and *The Funny Comics* #11.[xlii]

Later in the year, Anglo-American also put out its first compendium of comics in annual form. This was the *Holiday Comics Gift Book* 35¢ giant, possibly meant to be the Canadian counterpart for Fawcett's 1942 American-issued, 196-page one-shot *Holiday Comics*. As indicated on the cover *Holiday Comics Gift Book* was mash-up of five Anglo-American comics.[xliii] It is not clear if the contents were consistent for every copy or if they varied with different remaindered "Double A" interiors. While the contents of the American giant were color reprints, the Canadian annual had the redrawn Canadian versions and a redraw of the *America's Greatest Comics* #2 cover that substituted Capt. Marvel, Jr., Kip Keene of the Mounted, and Sooper Dooper for Bulletman, Minute Man, and Mr. Scarlet. It was probably issued towards the end of the year and intended as a Christmas gift book.

Also in 1943, American publishers Timely somehow managed to get two 128-page, square-bound annuals published in Canada. These were the *Captain America 128-Page Annual* which featured the cover from U. S. *Captain America Comics* #22 (January 1943) with black and white interiors reprinted from U. S. *Marvel Mystery Comics* #33 and *Captain America Comics* #18. Back and inside covers were blank. The second

128-page Timely annual was the *Marvel Mystery 128-Page Annual* which had the cover of *Marvel Mystery* #33 and interiors that were black-and-white reprints of *Captain America* #22 and *Marvel Mystery* #41.[xliv] These two annuals have, up till now, realized the most expensive prices of any WECA books and the *Captain America Annual* is the only WECA book to make the Top 100 Golden Age Comic Books list in *The Overstreet Comic Book Price Guide*.

December 1943 saw the start-up of another Toronto publishing house, F. E. Howard Publications. Their MLJ reprints of American *Pep Comics* issues entitled *Super Comics* ran for six issues. All six were designated Vol. 2 probably in deference to Citren's earlier reprint of *Pep Comics* #22 (which was also entitled *Super Comics* but was not numbered and mainly contained reprints of American *Pep Comics* #44-48).[xlv] These comics are noted for having the costumes of MLJ characters The Shield and Captain Commando altered (re-drawn) to align them with Canadian iconology.

1944

Early in 1944 the Canadian Jewish War Congress published three small issues of *Jewish War Heroes*, which, if we can take the information on the last page of #3, came out of Montreal by H. J. Borrie Ltd. These were small (7-8 page) pamphlet type booklets in two-tone sepia and white printing. Today we might think of them as giveaway format and perhaps they were because they did not have prices on them. Writers and artists are not credited and the contents mostly consist of one page splash formats for each hero presented. Issue one was cover dated February 1944.

Early in 1944, Educational Projects advertised a Canadian reprint of E.C. Comics' giant *Picture Stories from the Bible: Complete Old Testament Edition* with a cover price of 60¢. From the ad appearing on p. 51 of *Canadian Heroes* Vol. 4 #1, the contents were supposed to be in full four color just like the American edition but it appears only to have been available through mail order and was "...enthusiastically endorsed by Editorial Advisory Council of Prominent Religeous [*sic*] Leaders." It is doubtful that this issue was ever actually published. Around the same time Educational Projects also put out a series of 30 or so paint books featuring classic themes such as *Aladdin and the Magic Lamp*, *The Three Musketeers*, *Alice in Wonderland*, etc. These were priced at 15¢ each and were available in book stores or by mail order. The same publishers put out a one-shot title called *Action Stories of the Mounties* which according to the cover was based on "true action stories from official records of the R.C.M.P." and reprinted Mountie stories from previous issues of *Canadian Heroes Comics*.

Copies of *Captain America 128-Page Annual* (1943) bring the most expensive prices of any WECA book on the market.

In the last half of 1944 two new publishing companies entered the fray, both based in Toronto.

The first, Feature Publications, put out just a single title called *Lightning Comics* that seems to have begun with issue #10 (cover dated Aug.-Sept. 1944) and run to #12 (dated Dec. 1944-Jan. 1945). Art was predominantly by Edward Schecter who exhibited a primitive but animated style, and the cover character was Captain Daring. Of note is Ross Mendes work on his Dr. Future and Pee Wee, Aram Alexanian's superhero Nemesis and Rover the Wonder Dog as well as Dartman by Hamilton in issue #12.

That same late summer, Al Rucker Publications opened its doors and its inverted triangle "A.R.P" logo began appearing on the stands beginning with its first comic book having the unwieldly title *Comic Section of Illustrated Weekender News Review* Vol. 1 #1 where "Comic" was the largest word in the banner. It turns out that the "Week Ender Illustrated News" was the sixteen page newspaper formatted middle section of the book and that the comic section announced on the front cover surrounded this. In Vol. 1 #1 there were 14 pages of black-and-white captioned newsprint photos (including a few of Frank Sinatra giving a concert in Boston and a couple of pages on the 1944 Miss Toronto pageant).[xlvi] The issue itself has the form of a regular comic book, albeit of slightly larger (11 x 8 inch) size as was common with earlier Rucker editions. It kept this title for the second issue but dropped the "Comic Section of..." portion so that the big banner word now was "Weekender" with its last three issues and it has become known as "[the] Weekender" to collectors.

Weekender Vol. 1 #1 used a slightly redrawn or traced cover from *Zip Comics* #45 (April 1944) and the contents are reprinted from that issue in black-and-white but replace the "Applejacks" story and a text story with a 12-page news/photo supplement. Though there is no indicia to confirm a date, the 10¢ price logo has the month "Sept." attached to it while later issue Vol. 1 #3 (which reprints parts of *Dynamic Comics* #12, November 1944) is dated September 1945.[xlvii] The date of September 1944 for *Weekender* Vol. 1 #1 is further supported by photos and stories in its news supplement section.

The fall of 1944 also saw Anglo-American introduce a number of new home-grown heroes. Cowboy hero The Purple Rider by Jack McKellar Calder began in *Three Aces Comics* Vol. 3 #8 (September 1944) and in the same issue month *Grand Slam Comics* Vol. 3 #10 introduced Commander Steele by Les Gilpin, as well as Red Rover and Dr. Destine both by Ed Furness. Fawcett heroes were pulled out of these titles but reactions in October letter columns were almost all positive with respect to these new characters.[xlviii]

1944 closed as positive year for Canadian comics. New publishers appeared and Anglo-American had introduced a successful new line of heroes. The next year, however, would prove to be one of the most significant and volatile ones for the WECA period of Canadian comics.

1945

The final few months of the war must have seemed like a left turn around an ominous corner for Canadian comic book publishers. The Reichstag was captured on the last day of April, 1945, compelling Hitler's suicide,[xlix] and the early May headlines began to acknowledge the defeat of Nazi Germany. Canadian publishers knew that this implied the imminent repeal of the War Exchange Conservation Act and a return of full-color, glossy, juiced-up American product to Canadian drug store stands. Up till this point, with the success of Canadian comics roaring at full throttle, Canadian comic book industry men like Ed Furness at one time "...thought this thing was going to go on forever."[l] But by this time all those involved in the industry must have seen the curtain beginning to fall.

In the best Canadian tradition, maple leaves flush themselves with color just before they are going to fall. So, too, Anglo-American obtained access to the newly acquired color printing press of Canada's leading national newspaper, *The Globe and Mail*, and started to issue comic books in color.[li] The last black-and-white issue of *Robin Hood Comics* was Vol. 2 #12 (Jan./Feb. 1945) and it introduced Kip Keene as the new starring figure in the Men of the Mounted series. The last black-and-white issue of the next oldest Anglo-American book, *Freelance Comics* was Vol. 3 #2 (and it featured one of the best WECA airplane covers). Into the crucible they went and emerged as a full-color, glossy cover, joint title called *Freelance – Robin Hood and Company* #27 dated July 1945, taking over the numbering from *Freelance Comics* since Vol. 3 #2 was its 26th issue. The same alchemy was used to produce a full color *Grand Slam – Three Aces Comics* Vol. 4 #44 dated July 1945 from *Grand Slam Comics* Vol. 4 #6 dated May 1945 and *Three Aces Comics* Vol. 4 #6 dated May 1945. The problem with this last blending is that the last black-and-white *Three Aces Comics* was its 42nd issue, leaving a mysterious gap and perhaps an unknown issue of *Three Aces*. In any event, Canadian comics could now compete with American books in the same spectrum should they need to.

After *Whiz Comics* Vol. 4 #6 (July 1945) and *Spy Smasher Comics* Vol. 3 #9 (April 1945 – the latest issue known), *Whiz-Spy Smasher*

Comics Vol. 4 #6 (though you would expect Vol. 4 #7) cover dated July 1945 emerged still in black-and-white. Anglo-American's *Captain Marvel Comics* continued on in black-and-white through 1945 unscathed. Both of these black-and-white titles fell off the radar with their December 1945 issues and Anglo-American was done with its Fawcett redraws.

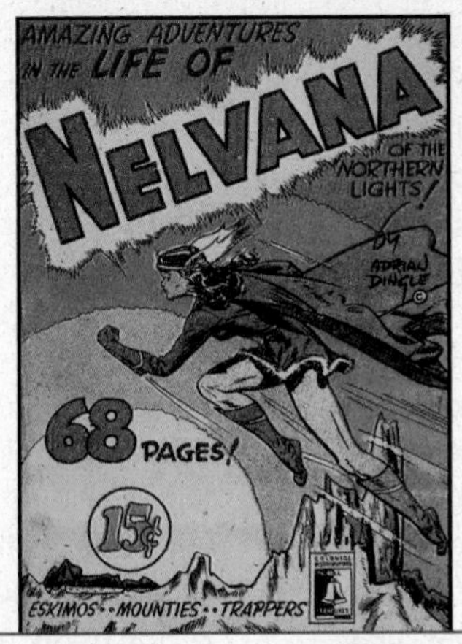

Of the six Bell Features compilation one-shots from 1945, *Nelvana* is the most sought after.

In 1945, Bell Features put out a series of six compilation issue one-shots with the following titles: *Nelvana, Phantom Rider, Speed Savage, Spike and Mike, Tang the Wonder Horse,* and *Thrilling Stories for Boys*. Each of these issues selected stories of the same feature from earlier Bell Comics issues and bound them together. Interiors were still in black and white but now you could get a collection of stories featuring your favorite character, all in one 68-page book for 15¢. Of these, the *Nelvana* issue is the one most sought after by collectors with *Speed Savage* perhaps next. The rarest of these appears to be the *Thrilling Stories for Boys* which brings together many of the three-to-four-page text stories that were accompanied by Murray Karn or Adrian Dingle illustrations.

Educational Projects put together a compilation issue of George Rae's Canada Jack entitled *Adventures of Canada Jack* as a one-shot at this time, as well as a 192-page compilation of other stories from *Canadian Heroes Comics* called *Picture Story Annual* that sold for 25¢.

Rucker Publications put out an unnumbered war book that had two cover variations but the same content. One was *(United Nations) Battle Heroes* with an uncredited "tank" cover and *(United Nations) War Heroes* with a soldier cover credited to Harold Bennett. At the same time, Rucker issued a reality-based one-shot crime comic called *Current Crimes*. After the end of the war the Rucker "inverted triangle" logo began to lose its text portion "If it's an Al Rucker Publication, it's true." Around this time (circa 1945) there is also an undated F. E. Howard one shot called *Lucky 7 Comics* that may have received American distribution.

By the start of September 1945 WWII had also ended on the Pacific front. Canadian parliament began to repeal the War Exchange Conservation Act in sections and American comics began to enter the country again and to dominate local newsstands.

Educational Projects didn't survive the year and stopped with the October 1945 issue of *Canadian Heroes* Vol. 5 #6. A few publishers like Anglo-American and Bell may still have thought their chances were more than fair for survival and even growth in the face of the American machine, the denouement had begun.

1946

The two Anglo-American double-titled full color books *Grand Slam –Three Aces* and *Freelance – Robin Hood* had run on in that form until the end of 1945, but by the spring of 1946 they split back into their individual titles. *Grand Slam – Three Aces Comics* Vol. 5 #50 (January 1946) reverted to *Grand Slam Comics* Vol. 5 #51 and *Three Aces Comics* Vol. 5 #51 both dated February 1946. *Freelance – Robin Hood* Vol. 3 #30 (January-February 1946) became *Freelance Comics* Vol. 3 #31 (April-May 1946) and *Robin Hood and Company* Vol 3 #1 (June-July 1946). With the Anglo-American change to full color in the previous year, the company also chose to start distributing these books in the UK. Similarly, some of the 1946 Anglo-American titles have indicia that show they were published in Cleveland, Ohio.[lii] Anglo-American's last issues, *Robin Hood and Company* Vol. 3 #34, *Grand Slam Comics* Vol. 5 #56, *Freelance Comics* Vol. 3 #35 were all cover dated December 1946 – January 1947, while *Three Aces Comics* Vol. 5 #55 was dated November-December 1946. Most importantly, Anglo-American had stuck to original content and with these last issues the WECA period had just managed to stick its nose into 1947.

It was in 1946 that publishers began printing comics specifically for distribution in the UK and the US and for many publishers content began to really shift from original Canadian material to American reprints and repackaged old Canadian content. Besides the 10¢ cover price, issues would now have a 9D (nine-pence) indicator and other books that we find from this period have a 9D or red one shilling sticker fixed to the cover. A full-page announcement on p. 8 of *Dime Comics* #27[liii] tells us that:

> On or about the 1st of the New Year [1946] all Bell Features Comic Books will be in full color and as usual [have] the greatest number of pages in America... back to the usual 68 page books. Boys and girls in the United States will be reading and enjoying the stories YOU know so well. Due to our books going into the States, there will be some changes in the present titles and stories... The black and white Canadian comic has only a few weeks to live and then your characters will live in full color.

Diversification and territorial expansion became a gasp for air to an industry drowning in a tidal surge of American four-color product.

The main Bell Features books began to reprint American stories) while retaining original Canadian covers that didn't relate to the contents (e.g., *Active Comics* #29) and then even inserted the word "New" into the titles (e.g., *New Active*, *New Triumph*, *New Dime*, *New Joke*, etc.) that started to appear in the Fall of 1946. At this time Bell also put out new titles that featured new and recycled content such as *Slam Bang Comics* #7 (which was the type of book promised in *Dime Comics* #27 and had new, full color Jeff Waring, Nitro, The Brain, Polka Dot Pirate stories and new story of the transformed Penguin as The Blue Raven) and #8, *Red Hot Comics* #1-3, *Unusual Comics* #1, and #1 and 2 of *FBI Comics*, *Johnny Canuck Comics*, and *Nitro Comics.*[liv] Other Bell titles from this time seem to be one-shot reprint titles such as *Capt. Wonder*, *The Brain*, *The Dreamer*, *Jet-Man*, *Terrific Comics*, and *Whittle Craft* (collecting together all the Bob Young Whittle Craft fillers that appeared in most of the Bell titles). After these, and with the end of 1946, Bell Features turned entirely to reprinting and repacking American content.

Al Rucker Publications continued with three issues of Volume 2 of their *Weekender* title throughout 1946 and through its Super Publications division began producing comics for additional distribution in the UK that still relied heavily on American Chesler Publications for comic content. One of these was a one-shot titled *Lucky Coyne Comics* that was actually a reprint of its own *Weekender* Vol. 1 #3 (Sept. 1945) with the cover from Chesler's *Dynamic Comics* #10. Its two issue Rocket Man Comics is probably another example of this. The one-shot *Scooter Comics* from April 1946 seems to have original teen-age hero and funny animal content with the specific aim of breaking the publisher in the US. By the end of 1946 Al Rucker Publications was gone.

One new Canadian publisher that decided to enter the fray while others were floundering was Superior Publishers which seems to have begun in 1946 with its Century Publications division, which focused on distribution of books in the UK. Some titles such as *Space Nomads Comics* and *Zor the Mighty Comics* (art by E. G. Letkeman), which ran for two issues each, seemed to contain original material. Others such as *Blazing Comics, Blue Circle Comics, Bombadier Comics, Circus Comics, Jeep Comics, Red Circle Comics, Skunky Comics, Star Studded Comics*[lv], *Three Ring Comics* (with the Prankster cover), *Tic Tac Toe Comics*, and *Twinkle Comics*, were one-shot or two issue runs of reprinted American material. Century Publications issued a second *Three Ring Comics* with the old Pep Comics 22 cover but with funny animal content specifically for distribution in the UK during 1946. Century Publications also sent a few of its titles such as *Zor the Mighty*, to the UK as coverless copies with the Century logo stamped in black on the first splash page.

In the spring of 1946, Maple Leaf books started carrying an alternate 6d (sixpence) indicator showing that their books too were intended for some British distribution and some final issues of each title lost the 10¢ indicator altogether leading to the conjecture that they may have only been issued in the UK. Maple Leaf also put out two issues in full color which were *Better Comics* Vol. 7 #3 (Dec. 1945-Jan. 1946) and 4 (Feb. –March 1946) and these were the only full color Maple Leaf editions . It then skipped the April-May 1946 issue and reverted back to black-and-white contents for separate June and July issues and its final two bi-monthly issues ending up with Vol. 3 #38 dated Oct.-Nov. 1946.

For the last couple of issues of each of the four Maple Leaf titles, the publishers chose a numbering system that reflected the actual number of issues of the title published. The last issue of *Lucky Comics* was Vol. 4 #34 (Oct.-Nov. 1946), of *Rocket Comics*, Vol. 4 #30 (Sept.-Oct. 1946), and of *Bing Bang Comics*, Vol. 3 #31 (Nov.-Dec. 1946).

Maple Leaf Publications is probably the least understood Canadian publisher and its issues are usually the hardest to come across. The final year of production is especially under-researched. It is clear that you need to pay attention to the actual dates of the comics from 1946 and not the volume numbering to get the right order.

By the start of 1947 the thrashing for survival had stopped and the First Great Age of Canadian Comics sailed off to the West. The last truly Canadian comic books from this era were those final four Anglo-American titles. After them only a few Canadian publishers decided to go on (Anglo-American, Bell Features, and Superior Publications) and those that did were reduced to reprinting or repacking some of their old materials or recently published American comics.

The Second Age of Canadian Comics would go on past the Comics Code and on into the middle 1950s, but that is grist for another article.

Author's note: *There is a small group of us in Canada who are working on a complete on-line database index of these WECA era comics in an effort to preserve their valuable part in our Canadian heritage and to further the knowledge of collectors in general about this broadly neglected area of comics fandom and collecting. Along with myself, Walter Durajlija, Jim Finlay, and most importantly, Stephen Lipson (who has the most comprehensive collection of WECA comics in the world) hope to have this done and up and running by the summer of this year. I am also greatly indebted to Walter, Jim, and Stephen for their assistance and feedback in the finalization of this, Jim Brigham's wonderful nuggets of information and the extensive work of John Bell that has gone before.*

ENDNOTES

[i] On p. 51 of Mordecai Richler, "The Great Comic Book Heroes," *Encounter*, May 1967 pp. 46-53. Compare this with Margaret Atwood's choice of Michael Hirsh and Patrick Loubert's *The Great Canadian Comic Books (Historical Perspective by Alan Walker and Afterword by Harold Town).* Toronto: Peter Martin Associates Limited, 1971 as one of her three favourite books of 1971 in "The books I enjoyed the most in 1971…" Financial Post (Fourth Section) Dec. 11, 1971 and Harlan Ellison's paean to Canadian forties Anglo-American comics in his forward: "Dreams of Joy Recaptured" to John Bell's *Canuck Comics* (1986).

[ii] There was a diluted "hiccup" of this initial situation later on in 1947 that started off a period of reprinting and repackaging of American comics that became the second era of Canadian comics that lasted into the mid-fifties—but that is the subject of another article.

[iii] You will find more detailed accounts of this period and the start of Canadian Comic Publishing Industry in the comprehensive output of John Bell's invaluable research, but especially in his most recent *Invaders from the north: how Canada conquered the comic book universe*, Dundurn Press, Toronto, 2006. Also "'Blood on the Snow' The Canadian Pulp Industry – The War Exchange Conservation Act, 1940" online from the National Archives of Canada (http://www.collectionscanada.gc.ca/pulp/027019-1100-e.html#tphp) which shows that the Canadian Pulp Industry seems to have started up in the same manner.

[iv] In my research I have yet to see a copy or scan of this issue which is reported to be tabloid (Sunday Comics) size without a proper cover and not as much accepted as being the first proper Canadian comic as Better Comics Vol. 1, #1. Note also the four Fox reprints (see footnote No. 15 below) that all have indicia dates of March 1941 as well but are bald colorless almost exact reproductions from cover to cover and therefore, least Canadian and not of the same order as the *Robin Hood* and *Better*.

[v] Contests were one of the main ways of engaging the young readers of these WECA books right from the start. There is a two page contests description on the last page and inside back cover of the first issue of *Better Comics*. In the sixth of seven rules provided, the deadline for entry submissions is February 28 which clearly implies that the book must have been on the stands at least by the beginning of February and probably in mid-January. The finished book follows so closely on the date of the enactment of WECA that I wonder if the publishers had an inkling of the political action and its impact before it was brought into being.

[vi] I can't find an exact date for the final repeal of the War Exchange Conservation Act, though it seems to have been dealt with gradually, selecting different provisions to repeal as the post war period went on.

[vii] The half-dozen or so major Canadian publishers of this period produce 40 plus individual titles that, in turn, had an output of over 700 separate issues (an accurate index is currently being worked on and should, for the first time, produce exacting statistics). Of these 95% of the interiors were in black-and-white outline and only 5% had color or some color interiors (most of the color books appeared just after the end of WWII in response to the threatening return of American books and they lasted about until the end of 1946).

[viii] Dealers who have been in the business for 20 or 30 years or more will tell you that they may have had tens of thousands of American Golden Age books come through their stores during that time while the WECA books probably numbered in the dozens. I would feel safe in placing a Gerber Scarcity Index of 8 and up for most of the WECA books with the exception of the full color versions that appeared after the war and those books from this same period that were exported to the U.K. as well as those distributed in the U.S. which would probably fall within the Gerber 6-7 category.

[ix] See Alexander Ross, "A Fond Portrait of those Wild War Comics," *Maclean's Magazine*, September 19, 1964, pp. 27-30. Kids were also able to

contribute to the war effort by joining the Canada Jack club.

[x] Descriptions of this collection are online at http://collectionscanada.gc.ca and listed under Bell Features Fonds [Textual Records] (1998-00563-1). Here is an excerpt from its description:

> ...including 380 copies of the original published comic books and 2,298 pieces of artwork for published comics. Works are by Harry Moyer, Adrian Dingle, Leo Bachle, F.G. Kelly, Gerald Lazare, John O'Henley, Lou Skuce, E.T. Legault, Murray Karn, Jack Kingsley, Ross Saakel, Edmond Good, Al Cooper, Allan Ross Mendes, Robert Patterson Young, Kenneth Edward Alton, Howard B. Cowan, Mickey Owens, Melville Crawford, T.A. Steele, Jack Trembley, Avrom Yanovsky, A.W. Nugent, and Manny Easson. Published comics include the following: Active, issues 1-28 (complete); Commando, issues 1-22 (complete); Dime, issues 1-15, 17-30; Dizzy Don, issues 4-20, 3 unnumbered issues; Joke, issues 1, 2, 4-10, 12-18, 20-26; Triumph, issues 1, 2, 5, 8-31, and 1 unnumbered; Wow, issues 1-10, 12-30; the Brain, issue 1; Doodlebugs, issues 1; FBI, issues 1-2; Jet-Man, issues 1, 10; Johnny Canuck, issues 2; Red Hot, issue 1; Slam-Bang, issue 7; Smasher, issue 7; Terrific, issues 2, 3; and Unusual, issue 1.

[xi] Vernon Miller was the one-man writer, artist and wrecking crew responsible for *Better Comics* #1 and the start of Maple Leaf Publications in general.

[xii] This also implies that the FECA period of hybrids, repacks, and reprints from 1947-1956 is its Silver Age—a step down in innovation, creativity and magic.

[xiii] The thirst for information among collectors about the WECA period is significant, and not just from Canadian collectors. Presently Stephen Lipson (who has the largest collection of these books, numbering over 450), Jim Finlay, Walter Durajlija, and I are working on a thorough and completely indexed database of WECA books and it should be available online by the time you read this.

[xiv] John Bell on p. 46 of his *Invaders from the north...* (2006) first brings attention to the fact that there may have been a number of reprints of other Fox books by Anglo-American early in 1941. *Fantastic Comics* 16, *Weird Comics* 12, Mystery *Men* 20, and *Big 3* #2 are known. These Fox reprints were without color and the covers were just line drawings and appear to be nothing more than reprints of the originals with the inside back covers of the originals becoming the back covers of the reprint (story order may have been different as well). They kept the March dates from the original covers and the indicia on the back covers do indeed indicate that they came out around March, 1941. It's strange that the reprints and the originals have the same release dates. Later Canadian reprints always appeared sometime after the American originals had been on the stands. It appears that Anglo-American may have tried to circumvent WECA with these black-and-white reprints and then was told that they could not do this after these first attempts came out.

[xv] Though the name of this character, would in most of us evoke the Marvel character that first appeared 22 years later in *Tales of Suspense* #39, he is more accurately a blonde-haired clone of another of that company's characters: Namor, the Sub-Mariner who first appeared in *Marvel Comics* #1, in October, 1939—a full year-and-a-half earlier.

[xvi] See (MacMillan 1986 p. 94)

[xvii] It must also be noted that this *Union Jack, Lucky Comics* also contains five full-page nautical illustrations by Marine Illustrator, F. P. Thursby.

[xviii] Maple Leaf books are noted for their vibrant, multi-color covers featuring well-proportioned figures and layouts. Anglo-American books, prior to the end of the war, are known for having two-color (white and a dominant choice from one of the primary colors, red, blue, or green and sometimes orange or occasional purple such as *Spy Smasher* Vol. 1 #7 and rarer yellow, *Robin Hood Comics* Vol. 1 #7) covers with cruder designs and, after signing agreements with Fawcett Publications, simply redrew many existing American covers.

[xix] See (MacMillan 1986, p. 96). In spite of this period popularity Freelance does not seem today to have the magic collectibility of a character like Nelvana whose appearances command higher prices.

[xx] Adrian Dingle is better known in Canada as a fine artist of landscapes and portraits (a career he pursued in earnest after the WECA period) than a comic book creator. His obituary in the *Globe and Mail* for December 23, 1974 was titled: Adrian Dingle: Well-known artist once drew comics."

[xxi] In 1946, the last WECA year, Bell Features for some perhaps legal reason, felt compelled to list the first issue dates for each of its titles on some of the back covers that appeared. Four of Bell's seven titles show no discrepancy with the cover dates that were printed, but three do and *Triumph Comics* was one of them. In this way, on the back cover of *Triumph Comics* #31 we find that June 1, 1941 is given as the actual date of the first issue of *Triumph Comics*. See notes 37 and 40 below.

[xxii] Dingle attributes the inspiration for *Triumph*'s Nelvana to the recounting of a legend brought back by Group of Seven artist Franz Johnson when he came back from an Arctic trip (See Sim, 2004 p. 30).

[xxiii] Michael Hirsh and Patrick Loubert, who along with Clive A. Smith, founded Canada's best known animation studio in 1971, paid tribute to the significance of Adrian Dingle's creation by naming their enterprise Nelvana Studios. If the first two names sound familiar, Hirsh and Loubert at this same time published an account of Bell Enterprises WECA books entitled *The Great Canadian Comic Books*, which, for many of us, was our first exposure to the world of WECA books and which has on its cover, Nelvana, front and centre. As of this writing there are plans to reprint the Nelvana stories from all 31 issues of *Triumph Comics* by, appropriately, two Canadian female comic aficionados, Hope Nicholson and Rachel Richey who managed to acquire her rights.

[xxiv] The rest of the book is notable for an exceptional sketch portrait of Winston Churchill on pg. 37; the first "Clue Catchers" mystery detective story; and the first "Tang" the colt story which is illustrated by Rene L. Kulbach. It is also important to note that, after the 6th issue Adrian Dingle took this title with him and joined Bell Features where the title lost the "Adventure" half of its banner and from issue 7 was known as plain *Triumph Comics*.

[xxv] Alexander Ross, "A Fond Portrait of those Wild War Comics," *Maclean's Magazine*, September 19, 1964 p. 29.

[xxvi] Rather than the brilliant full color seen in American books of this period, the color process used here can best be described as a "full color lite", where, though a range of colors is there, it is sapped of its energy and almost sun-faded or looking like water colors. Issues 2-8 in this series would regress to only two-color (e.g., orange and blue) interiors and after that just black-and-white line drawings..

[xxvii] Michael Hirsh and Patrick Loubert's *The Great Canadian Comic Books* (1971) is in a small way infamous for asserting that *Wow Comics* 1 was the first Canadian comic book but at that time the authors had no knowledge of earlier Maple Leaf or Anglo-American publications that preceded it. Ironically, they do reprint portions of stories from Hillborough Studio's *Triumph-Adventure Comics* but do not seem to have any idea that the first issue of this series preceded *Wow Comics* #1. *The Great Canadian Comic Books* is still a milestone in research, recognition and preservation of the tradition of the early years of Canadian comic books.

[xxviii] Both Loraine Knight and Elaine Kenyon, in later issues of *Wow Comics*, became the sources of inspiration for the cut-out fashion dolls carrying on the tradition that began five months earlier with the "Fun with Fashions" featuring Betty Shepherd in *Better Comics* Vol. 1 #2.

[xxix] In a way we did contribute to the creation of Superman with Joe Shuster, half of the creative team, being Canadian and Canadians have gotten better at being a little more garish by creating significant super heroes in recent years such as John Byrne's Alpha Flight, Dave Sim's Cerebus, Todd McFarlane's Spawn, Dean Motter's Mister X, and of course, Richard Comely's Captain Canuck.

[xxx] Actually beating out The Brain with his black skullcap mask by two stories

[xxxi] Karn took over the duties of writing the Thunderfist stories himself after the first 6 issues of *Active Comics* but left to join the Canadian armed forces after issue 12 when he turned 18 at which time Leo Bachle took over. Karn is also known for another strip he created from the start, Amazon adventurer Jeff Waring who first appeared in *Wow Comics* #7 and Tedd Steele is best known as the creator of "Speed" Savage in that same issue of *Wow Comics*. Karn did come back to do three more Jeff Waring stories for Bell Features after the war.

[xxxii] This mask is parodied in Ross Saakel's strip "The Noodle" and is worn by a hip toddler in a diaper. The Noodle began in *Active Comics* #4 with Saakel's first panel note stating "Any similarity to 'The Brain' is purely intentional." The Noodle ran from issues 4 to 27 of *Active Comics*.

[xxxiii] Jodhpurs and riding boots seem to be standard issue for many of the WECA heroes, not only understandably for the Mounties such as Dixon and Kip Keene, but also for characters such as Freelance, Capt. Red Thortan, Cosmo, and Terry Kane.

[xxxiv] This probably qualifies this as a public service comic and perhaps the first of its kind in Canada even though it was sold at a ten¢ price and not given away. It appears to have been commissioned out to Maple Leaf Publications by the provincial Standards Council.

[xxxv] See note 23 above. The back cover of *Joke Comics* #26 from the late spring of 1946 gives the date of the first issue of the title as March 13, 1942.

[xxxvi] Hilkert only drew the Wing for a couple of issues of *Joke Comics* (#4 and 6 and most likely #3 which would be her first appearance, though I

haven't come across a copy yet) and then she was revived by Jerry Lazare in issue 14 of the same title where she was featured for the first time on the cover (other cover appearances were *Joke Comics* #18 and 23). Hilkert also did a number of painted pulp covers from 1942-43, among them a half-a-dozen for the Ace Publications title *10 Story Detective*.

xxxvii In fact, it ran an ad on its inside front cover advising readers to look for this new "bell" trademark on issues of *Wow*, *Dime*, *Active* and *Joke* Comics and on its inside back cover displays the cover for *Wow Comics* #7 with the caption that the title "...is the largest selling comic magazine on the stands."

xxxviii The first ad for *Commando Comics* as "Coming Soon" seems to appear in *Dime Comics* #6 from July-August 1942 gives the probably availability date as around October 20th and an ad in *Dime* #7 (Sept. –Oct. 1942) shows that it is available. Also see note 23 above. The back cover of the last issue of *Commando Comics* (#22, Spring 1946) gives the date of the first issue of the title as October 17, 1942.

xxxix This issue also has a feature that deals with actor Raymond Massey's exploits in the Canadian Military.

xl This type of thing had already been initiated before at Bell Features with the introduction of Active Jim and the Active Club in issue 3 of Active Comics April, 1942.

xli It's important to note that it appears that American comic books with educational value such as *Classics Comics* did not seem to be included in the WECA ban and were able to be imported into Canada until in 1946 Gilberton began to issue versions printed in Toronto.

xlii This unnumbered compendium shouldn't be confused with the Elhil Publishing reprint book by the same title which came out about a half-dozen years later.

xliii The online Grand Comics Database www.comics.org gives the contents as Anglo-American issues *Captain Marvel Comics* Vol. 2 #1 and 2, *Grand Slam Comics* Vol. 2 #2, *Three Aces Comics* Vol. 2 #2, and *Freelance Comics* Vol. 2 #1, all from the early part of 1943.

xliv The contents of the *Captain America Annual* were published in the U.S. with the cover from *Marvel Mystery* #33.These two annuals are part of only a handful of Canadian Golden Age comics have been listed in *The Overstreet Comic Book Price Guide* up till now.

xlv F. E. Howard also put out an Archie Comics Special #1 in 1944 that reprinted *Pep Comics* #49. Later, in 1945 they put out an issue of *Captain Commando Comics* which reprinted stories from *Pep Comics* #45, 46, and 48 as well as containing some original E. G. Letkeman material (Dusty Rhodes, Zor the Mighty, Dr. Justice and The Space Nomads. In 1946, F. E. Howard put out a *Black Hood Comics* #1 which contains a mixture of reprints from *Pep Comics* # 46, 48, and 49 and recolored the Black Hood costume in red, rather than yellow, on the cover.

xlvi The other piece of evidence for the September 1944 date for this issue is a short captioned article that talks about the founding of the US Air Force on August 1, 1907 and that it was born "...thirty-seven years ago Tuesday." This means that Weekender Vol. 1 #1 (cover date September) was probably on the stands at the end of July in 1944.

xlvii This raises the question concerning the year-long gap between the first issue and the third.

xlviii For example, Virginia on the inside front cover of *Grand Slam Comics* Vol. 3 #11 from Toronto wrote:

> I cannot find words good enough or descriptive enough for the characters and stories you published in the September issue of GRAND SLAM COMICS. Commander Steele, Red Rover, Dr. Destine, and Pat the Air Cadet are perfectly thrilling, in fact, more than any other comic I've read in my life. I think this way of them because they carry off your thoughts to a mystic make believe world of your own, and to this I add they are interesting right to the very last world. I think many of your readers agree when I say GRAND SLAM COMICS are 'POSITIVELY TOPS'.

Another letter on the same page bemoans the loss of Captain Marvel Jr. as the cover and lead feature in *Grand Slam Comics* but the editor replies that he can still be found in *Spy Smasher Comics*.

xlix Mussolini had already been dead for two days.

l Quoted by Robert MacMillan in his "The War Years: Anglo-American Publishing Ltd." 1986, p. 99.

li MacMillan (1986) again quotes Ed Furness on p. 98: "The Globe and Mail, which printed our comics, had bought a four-color fountain for their daily press and Jimmy Harrison, who's the superintendent, said to Harold Sinnott, 'How'd you like to do your comics in color?' Well, of course, that was just fine."

lii Perhaps this was how Harlan Ellison became familiar with the Anglo-American books as evident in his "Dreams of Joy Recaptured" Forward to John Bell's *Canuck Comics* (1986).

liii On p. 30 of his "A McLean's Flashback: A Fond Portrait of those Wild Wartime Comics," McLean's Sept. 19, 1964, pp. 27-30 Alex Ross also informs us that:

> By the end of the war, Bell had bought a seventy-five-foot-long printing press with a seventy-five-thousand-dollar loan from the Industrial Development Bank and started reprinting old comic books with new covers for export to England. They were shipped a thousand at a time in old tea chests and the new covers were adapted to suit English tastes (*Wow Comics*, a title considered meaningless in the Midlands, became *Smasher Comics*).

liv *Nitro Comics* 2 sports the Adrian Dingle cover used originally on *Active Comics* 27 and then used again on an unnumbered issue of *New Dime Comics* which appeared in the late forties. Much like the latter many of these titles such as *Slam Bang*, *Unusual*, and *Red Hot* were used again in the late forties and early fifties, along with unnumbered versions of some of the "*New*..." titles to house reprinted American content. Note also that mastheads from old Bell titles such as *Dime Comics*, *Active Comics*, and *Triumph Comics* were used in the very late forties and early fifties with American cover reprints to house American content.

lv *Star Studded Comics* was a one-shot reprint of the American Cambridge House edition 25¢ book with a different blue background cover and with indica that showing Superior Publications.

Bibliography

Bell, John. ""The Golden Age of Canadian Comic Books and Its Aftermath (Super-Heroes & Others in English Canada, 1941-1966) ." Edited by Roy Thomas. *Alter Ego 36* (TwoMorrows Publishing), May 2004: 3-26.
Bell, John (Curator). "Guardians of the North: The National Superhero in Canadian Comic-Book Art, Exhibition Catalogue (Also issued in French under the title Protecteurs du Nord)." Ottawa: National Archives of Canada, 1992.
Bell, John (Editor). *Canuck Comics: A Guide to Comic Books Published in Canada.* Montreal: Matrix Books, 1986.
Bell, John. *Invaders from the north: how Canada conquered the comic book universe.* Toronto: Dundurn Press, 2006.
Carter, Derek. "Cultural Strip-Off A Review of The Great Canadian Comic Books by Michael Hirsh and Patrick Laubert, Patrick Martin Assoc., 1971." *Books in Canada* 1, #5 (December 1971): 1, 20.
Gilbert, Michael T. "Mr. Monster's Comic Crypt: Fred Kelly—An Appreciation." Edited by Roy Thomas. *Alter Ego*, #36 (2004): 45-51.
Harris, Peter. "Entries on Adrian Dingle, Freelance, James Llewellyn Frise, Nelvana, The Penquin, and Rex Baxter." In *The World Encyclopedia of Comics*, by Maurice Horn editor. New York: Chelsea House Publishers, 1976.
Lewis, David A. "One for the Ages: Barbara G+ordon and the (Il-)Logic of Comic Book Age-Dating." *International Journal of Comic Art* 5, #2 (2003): 296-311.
Loubert, Michael Hirsh and Patrick. *The Great Canadian Comic Books (Historical Perspective by Alan Walker and Afterword by Harold Town).* Toronto: Peter Martin Associates Limited, 1971.
MacMillan, Robert. "The War Years: Anglo-American Publishing Ltd." Edited by John Bell. *Canuck Comics: A Guide to Comic Books Published in Canada.* (Matrix Books), 1986: 92-101.
Offenberger, Rik. *A Brief History of Canadian Golden Age Archie Comics.* http://www.mightycrusaders.net/canada.htm.
Overstreet, Robert M.editor. *The Overstreet Comic Book Price Guide (42nd Edition).* Gemstone Publishing, 2012.
Pincombe, Robert. "Les Barker, a.k.a. Leo Bachle: The Astounding, True Life Adventures of Johnny Canuck." *Alter Ego*, 2004: 52.
Richler, Mordecai. "The Great Comic Book Heroes [Review]." *Encounter*, May 1967: 46-53.
Ross, Alexander. "A Fond Portrait of Those Wild Wartime Comics." *Maclean's Magazine*, September 1964: 27-30.
Sim, Dave. "Living In A World of Fantasy! (Cerebus Creator Dave Sim Talks with Canadian Comic Book Pioneers Adrian & Pat Dingle and Bill Thomas)." Edited by Roy Thomas. *Alter Ego*, #36 (May 2004): 27-35.
Sim, Dave. "My Teacher Was Just Alex Raymond Strips (A Conversation with Canadian Comic Artist/Writer Jerry Lazare." *Alter Ego*, #36 (May 2004): 37-43.
Theaker, Dan. "An Introduction to Canadian Comic Books ." #1. Arnprior, Ontario: Aurora Books, June 1986.
Thomas, Roy (Editor). "Reprint of Michael Hirsh and Patrick Loubert's The Great Canadian Comic Books (With Additional Illustrations)." Edited by Roy Thomas. *Alter Ego* (TwoMorrows Publishers) 3, #7 (August 2007).
Walker, Alan. "How Johnny Canuck Won the Second World War." Montreal Gazette, October 2, 1971: 24-6.
Woo, Benjamin. "An Age-Old Problem: Problematics of Comic Book History." *International Journal of Comic Art*, #10 (2008): 268-79.
—. "Red and White Tights: Representations of National Identity in Canadian Comic Books." *M. A. Thesis.* Burnaby: Simon Fraser University, 2006.

THE COUNTDOWN FOR THE SPECIAL 45TH ANNIVERSARY EDITION BEGINS NOW!

WOULD YOU LIKE TO ADVERTISE
IN THE BOOK KNOWN AS

THE BIBLE OF COMIC BOOK COLLECTORS?

SINCE 1970, THE OVERSTREET COMIC BOOK PRICE GUIDE
HAS BEEN THE GO TO DESTINATION
FOR SERIOUS COMIC BOOK ENTHUSIASTS,
DEALERS AND HISTORIANS!

- Full Page Color ads start at $2,500!
- Full Page B&W ads start at $900!
- Save 10% when you take three or more ads of the same size & type!
- Save 10% with our Early Bird rates!
- Save 20% with both discounts!

For additional rates, specs or technical information, contact

Michael Solof

Advertising Sales Coordinator

(410) 625-7062

somike@geppismuseum.com

Early Bird Deadline
December 2, 2014

Standard Rate Deadline
March 4, 2015

WWW.GEMSTONEPUB.COM

PAUL GULACY • CAPTAIN ACTION

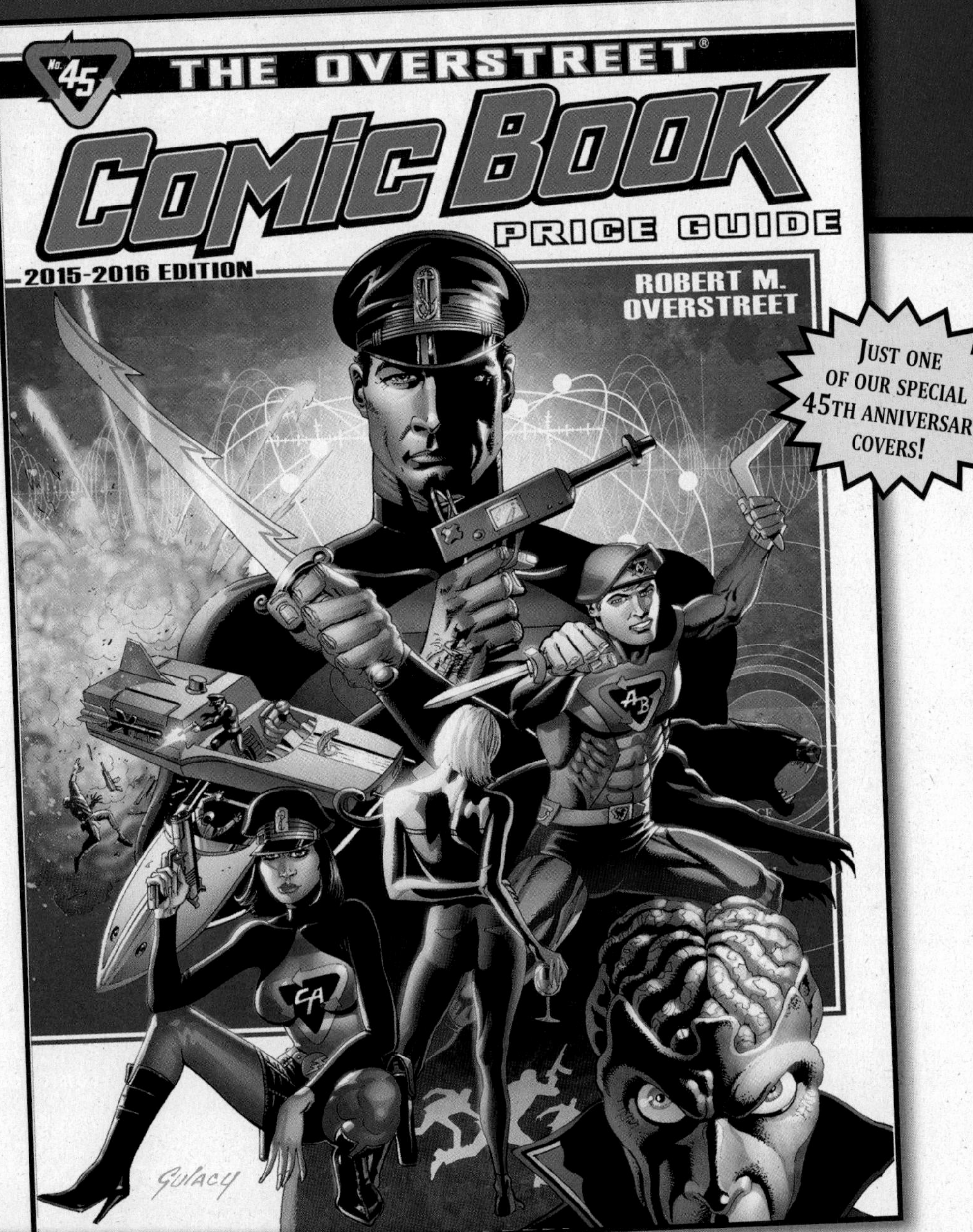

SEE PAUL GULACY'S ORIGINAL ART
AND SO MUCH MORE
AT GEPPI'S ENTERTAINMENT MUSEUM!

Captain Action and related characters
©2014 and TM Captain Action Enterprises, LLC.
Used by Permission.
Overstreet® is a Registered Trademark
of Gemstone Publishing, Inc.

WWW.GEMSTONEPUB.COM

EXPLORE THE BIGGER PICTURE OF THE WORLD OF COMICS!

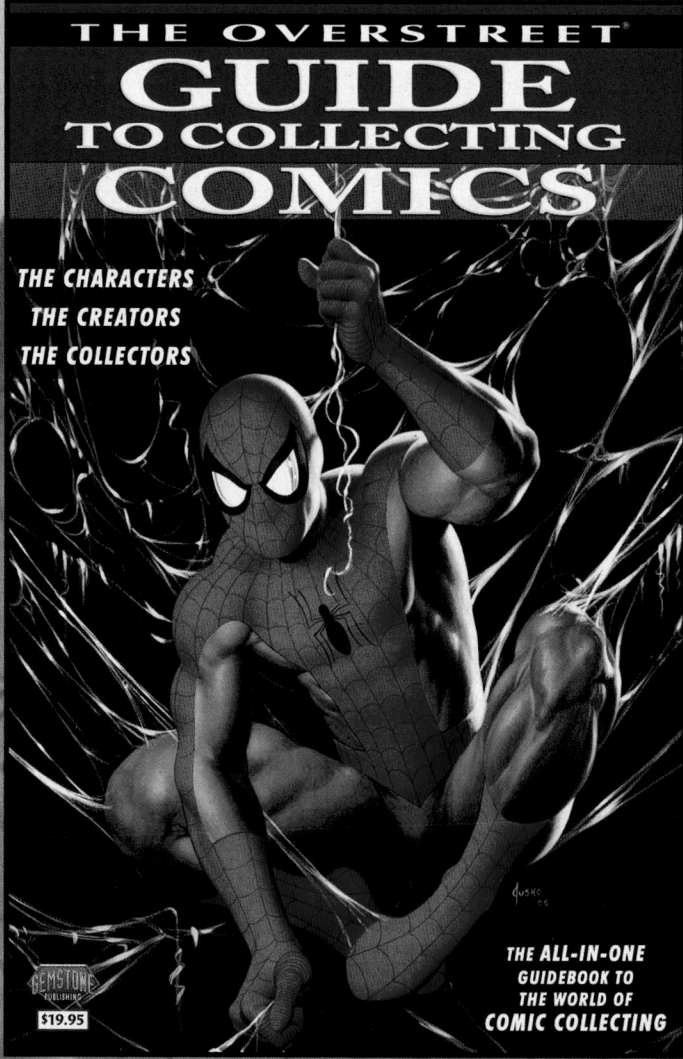

THE OVERSTREET® GUIDE TO COLLECTING COMICS

THE CHARACTERS
THE CREATORS
THE COLLECTORS

THE ALL-IN-ONE GUIDEBOOK TO THE WORLD OF COMIC COLLECTING

GEMSTONE PUBLISHING $19.95

"A wonderful info-packed gift idea for long-time fans and those new to the comics hobby!"
-- Joe Field, Flying Colors Comics

"The go-to name in comics values has created the go-to book for comics collecting."
-- Benn Ray, Atomic Books

"How To Collect Comics should be the title as it covers literally every aspect of learning the ins and outs of collecting comic books. I wish I had one of these when I first started out."
-- Vincent Zurzolo, Metropolis Collectibles & ComicConnect

"Wow! What a comprehensive look at the hobby in such a compact edition!"
-- Mike McKenzie, Alternate Worlds

"It's the perfect look at comics both for the beginner and, almost even more, for the experienced collector. It's a great gift for anyone who wants to introduce their friends and family to our crazy world."
-- Fred Pierce, Valiant Entertainment

It's like Comic Book Collecting 102 in a single book!

336 PAGES • FULL COLOR • SOFT COVER • $19.95

AT BETTER COMIC SHOPS NOW!

GEMSTONE PUBLISHING

WWW.GEMSTONEPUB.COM

COMIC AND ANIMATION ART COLLECTING REVEALED!

"Fantastic for a novice comic art or animation collector, but even better, even the most seasoned hobbyist will find some new information in many of the incredible articles. Overstreet has done it again! Another great book for our wonderful hobby!"
-- Steve Borock
President and Primary Grader
Comic Book Certification Service (CBCS)

"The perfect handbook to help understand the original comic book art market."
-- Dan Gallo
Comic Art Con

"There's no better one-volume introduction to collecting comics and animation art!"
-- Dean Mullaney
The Library of American Comics

"*The Overstreet Guide to Collecting Comic & Animation Art* is informative and incredibly exciting to read. It's full of pictures of incredible comic art, and a must-read for any comic art collector. The price is more than reasonable and the stories and art have a broad range of topics."
-- Nick Katradis
Collector

"Original narrative art is appreciated around the world. The basis of a cultural phenomenon, institutions routinely seek out and exhibit collections. It is amazing that a comprehensive guide that describes the factors and attributes that garner such attention has never been published until now."
-- Joe Mannarino
All Star Auctions

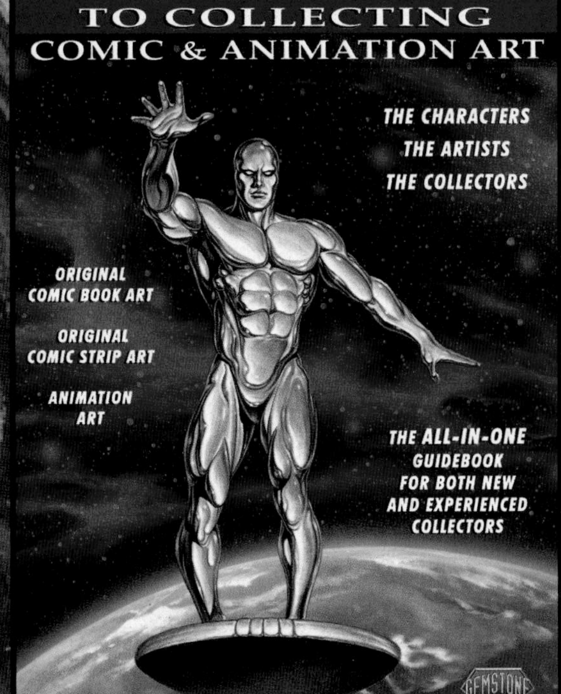

THE OVERSTREET®
GUIDE
TO COLLECTING
COMIC & ANIMATION ART
THE CHARACTERS
THE ARTISTS
THE COLLECTORS
ORIGINAL COMIC BOOK ART
ORIGINAL COMIC STRIP ART
ANIMATION ART
THE ALL-IN-ONE GUIDEBOOK FOR BOTH NEW AND EXPERIENCED COLLECTORS
GEMSTONE PUBLISHING
$12.95

Silver Surfer and Silver Surfer #1 image ©2014 Marvel Characters, Inc.
Overstreet® is Registered Trademark of Gemstone Publishing, Inc. All rights reserved.

Insights for Beginners and Experienced Collectors Alike!

160 PAGES • FULL COLOR • SOFT COVER • $12.95

AT BETTER COMIC SHOPS NOW!

WWW.GEMSTONEPUB.COM

DISCOVER
WHAT'S GONE BEFORE

www.gemstonepub.com

GEMSTONE PUBLISHING

BACK ISSUES NOW AVAILABLE

The Overstreet Comic Book Price Guide • Overstreet's FAN
Comic Book Marketplace • Overstreet's Comic Book Monthly
Overstreet's Golden Age & Silver Age Quarterly
Hake's Price Guide To Character Toys • The Overstreet Comic Book Grading Guide
Overstreet's FAN Edition Comics • And much more!

All characters ©2014 respective copyright holders.
Overstreet® is a Registered Trademark of Gemstone Publishing, Inc. All rights reserved.

OVERSTREET ADVISORS

DARREN ADAMS
Pristine Comics
Seattle, WA

WELDON ADAMS
Comics Historian
Fort Worth, TX

GRANT ADEY
Halo Certification
Brisbane, QLD, Australia

BILL ALEXANDER
Collector
Sacramento, CA

DAVID T. ALEXANDER
David Alexander Comics
Tampa, FL

TYLER ALEXANDER
David Alexander Comics
Tampa, FL

LON ALLEN
Heritage Comics Auctions
Dallas, TX

DAVE ANDERSON
Want List Comics
Tulsa, OK

STEPHEN BARRINGTON
Flea Market Comics
Chickasaw, AL

LAUREN BECKER
Warp 9 Comics
Clawson, MI

ROBERT BEERBOHM
Robert Beerbohm Comic Art
Fremont, NE

JON BERK
Collector
Hartford, CT

JIM BERRY
Collector
Portland, OR

JON BEVANS
Collector
Baltimore, MD

PETER BILELIS, ESQ.
Collector
South Windsor, CT

DR. ARNOLD T. BLUMBERG
Collector
Baltimore, MD

STEVE BOROCK
Comic Book Certification Service
St Petersburg, FL

KEVIN BOYD
Collector
Toronto, ONT Canada

SCOTT BRADEN
Comics Historian
Hanover, PA

RICHARD BROWN
Collector
Detroit, MI

MICHAEL BROWNING
Collector
Danville, WV

SHAWN CAFFREY
Finalizer/Modern Age Specialist
Certified Guaranty Co.

MICHAEL CARBONARO
Bestincomics.com
New York

BRETT CARRERAS
Brett's Comic Pile
Richmond, VA

GARY CARTER
Collector
Coronado, CA

CHARLES CERRITO
Hotflips
Farmingdale, NY

JEFF CERRITO
Hotflips
Farmingdale, NY

JOHN CHRUSCINSKI
Tropic Comics
Lyndora, PA

PAUL CLAIRMONT
PNJ Comics
Winnipeg, MB
Canada

ART CLOOS
Collector/Historian
Flushing, NY

GARY COLABUONO
Dealer/Collector
Arlington Heights, IL

BILL COLE
Bill Cole Enterprises, Inc.
Randolph, MA

OVERSTREET ADVISORS

TIM COLLINS
RTS Unlimited, Inc.
Lakewood, CO

ANDREW COOKE
Writer/Director
New York City, NY

JON B. COOKE
Editor - Comic Book Artist Magazine
West Kingston, RI

JACK COPLEY
Coliseum of Comics
Florida

JESSE JAMES CRISCIONE
Jesse James Comics
Glendale, AZ

FRANK CWIKLIK
Metropolis Comics
New York, NY

BROCK DICKINSON
Collector
St. Catharines, ONT Canada

PETER DIXON
Paradise Comics
Toronto, ONT Canada

GARY DOLGOFF
Gary Dolgoff Comics
Easthampton, MA

JOHN DOLMAYAN
Torpedo Comics
Las Vegas, NV

WALTER DURAJLIJA
Big B Comics
Hamilton, ONT Canada

KEN DYBER
Cloud 9 Comics
Portland, OR

TOMIS ERB
Comic Verification Authority
Brooklyn, NY

CONRAD ESCHENBERG
Collector/Dealer
Cold Spring, NY

MICHAEL EURY
Author
Concord, NC

RICHARD EVANS
Bedrock City Comics
Houston, TX

D'ARCY FARRELL
Pendragon Comics
Toronto, ONT Canada

BILL FIDYK
Collector
Annapolis, MD

PAUL FIGURA
Tenth Planet Comics and Games
Oak Lawn, IL

JOSEPH FIORE
ComicWiz.com
Toronto, ONT Canada

STEPHEN FISHLER
Metropolis Collectibles, Inc.
New York, NY

DAN FOGEL
Hippy Comix, Inc.
Cleveland, OH

BRAD FOSTER
SharpComics.com
Plainfield, IL

DAN GALLO
Dealer/Comic Art Con
Westchester Co., NY

STEPHEN H. GENTNER
Golden Age Specialist
Portland, OR

STEVE GEPPI
Diamond Int. Galleries
Timonium, MD

DOUG GILLOCK
ComicLink
Portland, ME

MICHAEL GOLDMAN
Motor City Comics
Farmington Hills, MI

TOM GORDON III
Collector/Dealer
Westminster, MD

JAMIE GRAHAM
Graham Crackers
Chicago, IL

DANIEL GREENHALGH
Showcase New England
Northford, CT

ERIC J. GROVES
Dealer/Collector
Oklahoma City, OK

OVERSTREET ADVISORS

GARY GUZZO
Atomic Studios
Boothbay Harbor, ME

JOHN HAINES
Dealer/Collector
Kirtland, OH

JIM HALPERIN
Heritage Comics
Auctions
Dallas, TX

JASON HAMLIN
Brett's Comic Pile
Richmond, VA

MARK HASPEL
Finalizer/
Pedigree Specialist
Certified Guaranty Co.,

JEF HINDS
Jef Hinds Comics
Madison, WI

GREG HOLLAND, Ph.D.
Collector
Alexander, AR

JOHN HONE
Collector
Silver Spring, MD

STEVEN HOUSTON
Torpedo Comics
Las Vegas, NV

BILL HUGHES
Dealer/Collector
Flower Mound, TX

ROB HUGHES
Arch Angels
Pacific Beach, CA

ED JASTER
Heritage Comics Auctions
Dallas, TX

NICK KATRADIS
Collector
Tenafly, NJ

BRIAN KETTERER
Collector
Baltimore, MD

DENNIS KEUM
Fantasy Comics
Goldens Bridge, NY

IVAN KOCMAREK
Comics Historian
Hamilton, ON

MICHAEL KRONENBERG
Historian/Designer
Chapel Hill, NC

BEN LICHTENSTEIN
Zapp Comics
Wayne, NJ

STEPHEN LIPSON
Comics Historian
Mississauga, ON

PAUL LITCH
Primary Grader
Certified Guaranty
Co., LLC

DOUG MABRY
The Great Escape
Madison, TN

TOMMY MALETTA
Best Comics
International
New Hyde Park, NY

JOE MANNARINO
All Star Auctions
Ridgewood, NJ

NADIA MANNARINO
All Star Auctions
Ridgewood, NJ

BRIAN MARCUS
Cavalier Comics
Wise, VA

WILL MASON
GetCashForComics.com
New York

HARRY MATETSKY
Collector
Middletown, NJ

DAVE MATTEINI
Collector
Mineola, NY

JON McCLURE
Comics Historian,
Writer
Portland, OR

TODD McDEVITT
New Dimension
Comics
Cranberry Township, PA

MIKE McKENZIE
Alternate Worlds
Cockeysville, MD

ANDY McMAHON
Duncanville Bookstore
Duncanville, TX

OVERSTREET ADVISORS

PETER MEROLO
Collector
Sedona, AZ

JOHN JACKSON MILLER
Comics Historian, Writer
Scandinavia, WI

STEVE MORTENSEN
Miracle Comics
Santa Clara, CA

MICHAEL NAIMAN
Silver Age Specialist
Chapel Hill, NC

MARC NATHAN
Cards, Comics & Collectibles
Reisterstown, MD

JOSHUA NATHANSON
ComicLink
Portland, ME

MATT NELSON
President, CCS
Sarasota, FL

TOM NELSON
Top Notch Comics
Yankton, SD

JAMIE NEWBOLD
Southern California Comics
San Diego, CA

CHARLIE NOVINSKIE
Silver Age Specialist
Lake Havasu City, AZ

VINCE OLIVA
Grader
CGC, LLC

RICHARD OLSON
Collector/Academician
Poplarville, MS

TERRY O'NEILL
Terry's Comics
Orange, CA

MICHAEL PAVLIC
Purple Gorilla Comics
Calgary, AB Canada

JIM PAYETTE
Golden Age Specialist
Bethlehem, NH

JOHN PETTY
Collector/Historian
Coram, NY

JIM PITTS
Avalon Collectibles
Mountain View, CA

BILL PONSETI
Collector
Newtown Sq., PA

RON PUSSELL
Redbeard's Book Den
Crystal Bay, NV

CATHY RADER
"Offbeat Archives"
Rare and Esoteric
Comics & Collectibles
Sioux Falls, SD

JEFF RADER
"Offbeat Archives"
Rare and Esoteric
Comics & Collectibles
Sioux Falls, SD

GREG REECE
Greg Reece's
Rare Comics
Ijamsville, MD

STEPHEN RITTER
Worldwide Comics
Fair Oaks Ranch, TX

ROBERT ROGOVIN
Four Color Comics
Scarsdale, NY

MARNIN ROSENBERG
Collectors Assemble
Great Neck, NY

CHUCK ROZANSKI
Mile High Comics
Denver, CO

BEN SAMUELS
Collector
St. Louis, MS

BARRY SANDOVAL
Heritage Comics Auctions
Dallas, TX

BUDDY SAUNDERS
Lone Star Comics
Arlington, TX

CONAN SAUNDERS
Lone Star Comics
Arlington, TX

MATT SCHIFFMAN
Bronze Age Specialist
Bend, OR

OVERSTREET ADVISORS

DOUG SCHMELL
Pedigree Comics, Inc.
Wellington, FL

BRIAN SCHUTZER
Sparkle City Comics
Neat Stuff Collectibles
North Bergen, NJ

ALIKA SEKI
Maui Comics and
Collectibles
Waiehu, HI

TODD SHEFFER
Hake's Americana
York, PA

FRANK SIMMONS
Coast to Coast Comics
Rocklin, CA

DOUG SIMPSON
Paradise Comics
Toronto, ONT Canada

ANTHONY SNYDER
Anthony's Comic
Book Art
Leonia, NJ

MARK SQUIREK
Collector
Timonium, MD

TONY STARKS
Silver Age Specialist
Evansville, IN

WEST STEPHAN
Comic Book
Certification Service
St Petersburg, FL

AL STOLTZ
Basement Comics
Havre de Grace, MD

DOUG SULIPA
"Everything 1960-1996"
Manitoba, Canada

CHRIS SWARTZ
Collector
San Diego, CA

BRIAN TATGE
Motor City Comics
Farmington Hills, MI

MAGGIE THOMPSON
Collector/Historian
Iola, WI

MICHAEL TIERNEY
The Comic Book Store
Little Rock, AR

TED VAN LIEW
Superworld Comics
Worcester, MA

JOE VERENEAULT
JHV Associates
Woodbury Heights, NJ

JOSEPH VETERI, ESQ.
Comic Verification Authority
Comic Con Art
Springfield, NJ

TODD WARREN
Collector
Fort Washington, PA

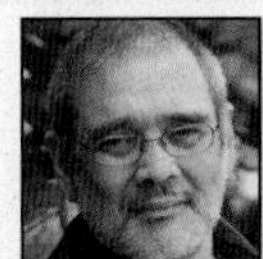

BOB WAYNE
DC Comics
New York City, NY

JEFF WEAVER
Victory Comics
Falls Church, VA

LON WEBB
Dark Adventure Comics
Norcross, GA

RICK WHITELOCK
New Force Comics
Lynn Haven, FL

MIKE WILBUR
Diamond Int. Galleries
Timonium, MD

MARK WILSON
PGC Mint
Castle Rock, WA

ALEX WINTER
Hake's Americana
York, PA

HARLEY YEE
Dealer/Collector
Detroit, MI

MARK ZAID
EsquireComics.com
Bethesda, MD

VINCENT ZURZOLO, JR.
Metropolis Collectibles, Inc.
New York, NY

OVERSTREET PRICE GUIDE BACK ISSUES

The Overstreet® Comic Book Price Guide has held the record for being the longest running annual comic book publication. We are now celebrating our 44th anniversary, and the demand for the Overstreet® price guides is very strong. Collectors have created a legitimate market for them, and they continue to bring record prices each year. Collectors also have a record of comic book prices going back further than any other source in comic fandom. The prices listed below are for NM condition only, with GD-25% and FN-50% of the NM value. Canadian editions exist for a couple of the early issues. Abbreviations: SC-softcover, HC-hardcover, L-leather bound.

1970

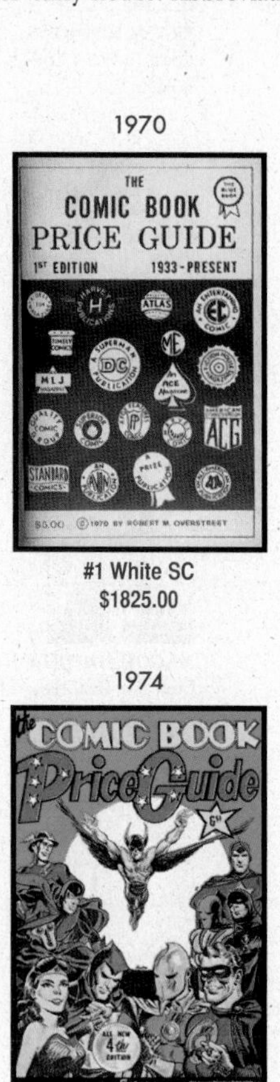

#1 White SC
$1825.00

1970

#1 Blue SC
(2nd Printing)
$1550.00

1972

#2 SC $650.00
#2 HC $1100.00

1973

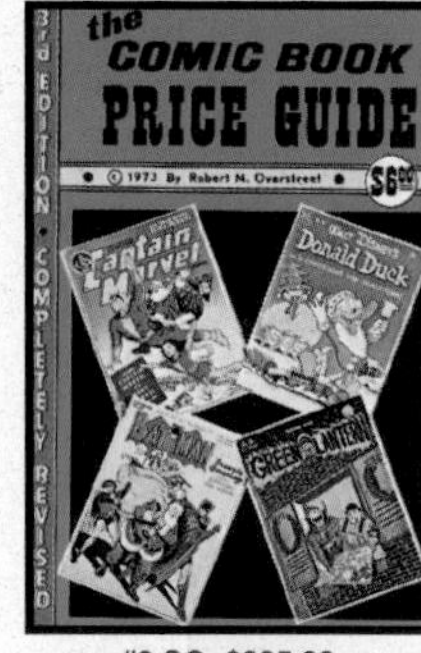

#3 SC $325.00
#3 HC $950.00

1974

#4 SC $165.00
#4 HC $475.00

1975

#5 SC $155.00
#5 HC $260.00

1976

#6 SC $105.00
#6 HC $155.00

1977

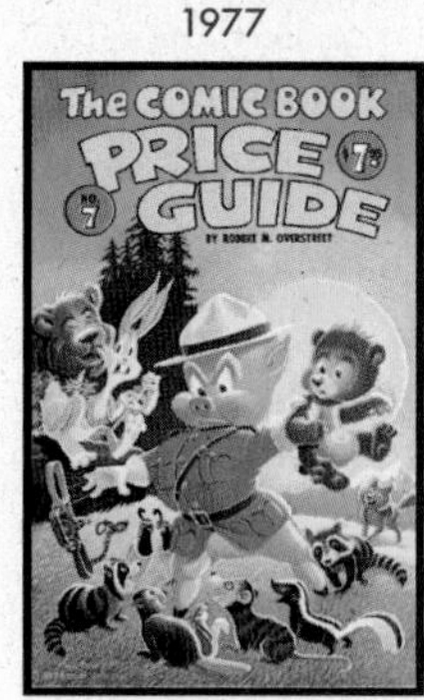

#7 SC $155.00
#7 HC $230.00

1978

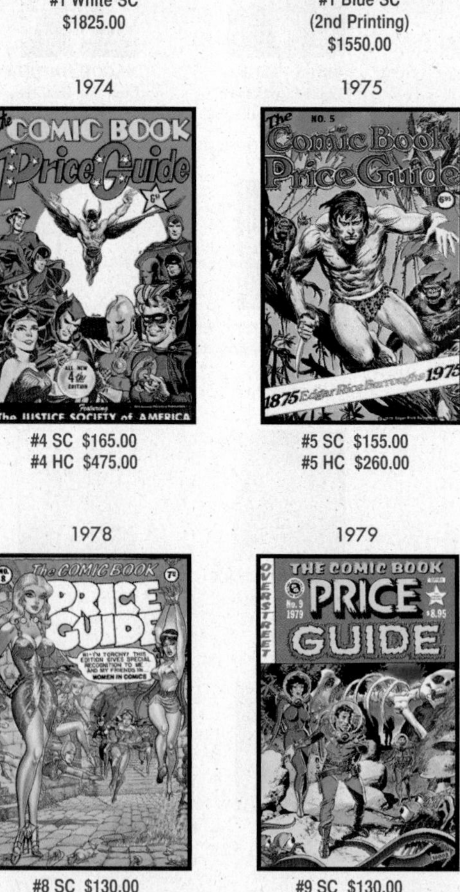

#8 SC $130.00
#8 HC $180.00

1979

#9 SC $130.00
#9 HC $180.00

1980

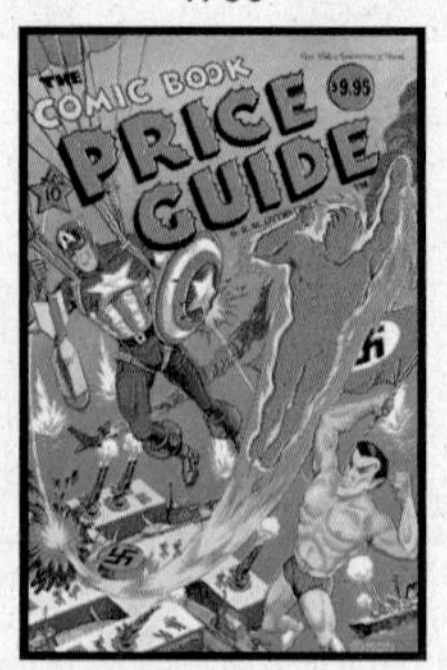

#10 SC $140.00
#10 HC $190.00

1981

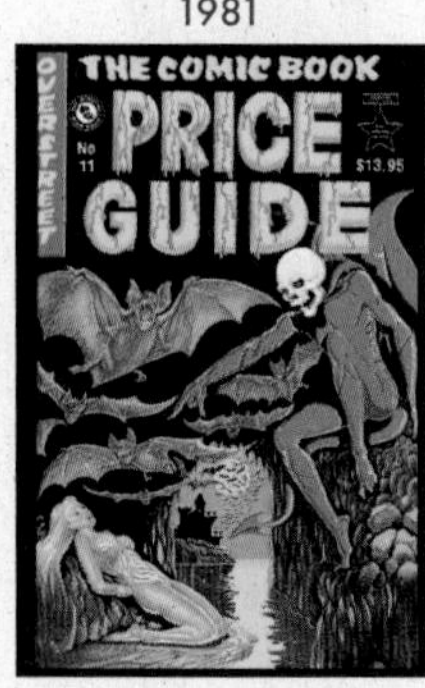

#11 SC $85.00
#11 HC $115.00

1982

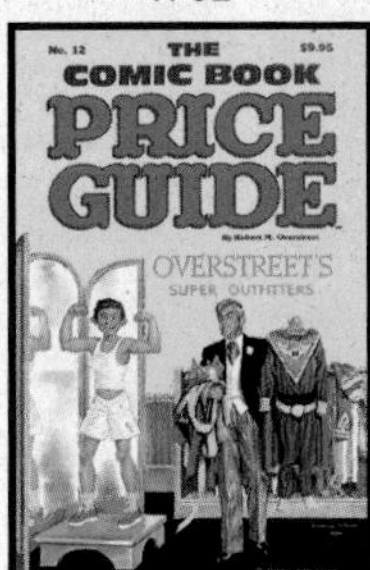

#12 SC $85.00
#12 HC $115.00

1983

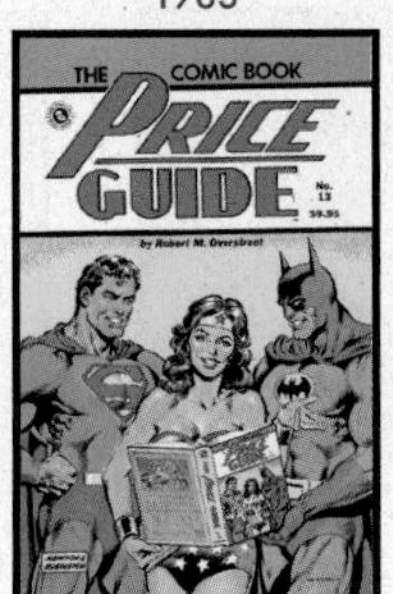

#13 SC $85.00
#13 HC $115.00

1984

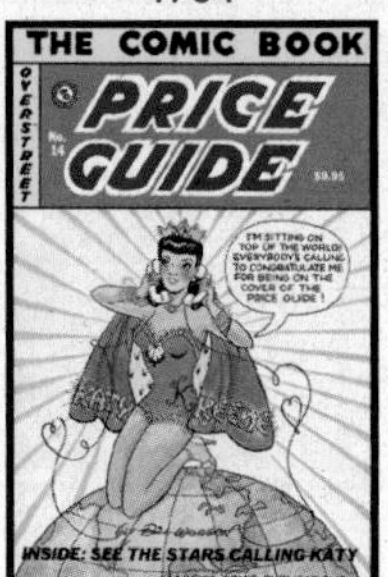

#14 SC $55.00
#14 HC $110.00
#14 L $170.00

1985

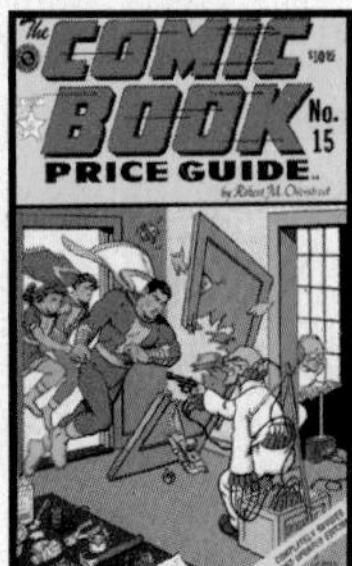

#15 SC $55.00
#15 HC $80.00
#15 L $160.00

1986

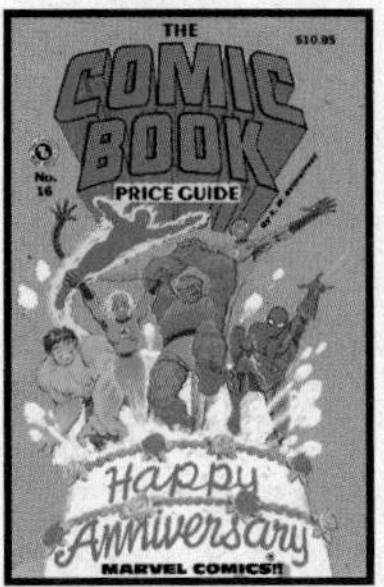

#16 SC $60.00
#16 HC $85.00
#16 L $170.00

1987

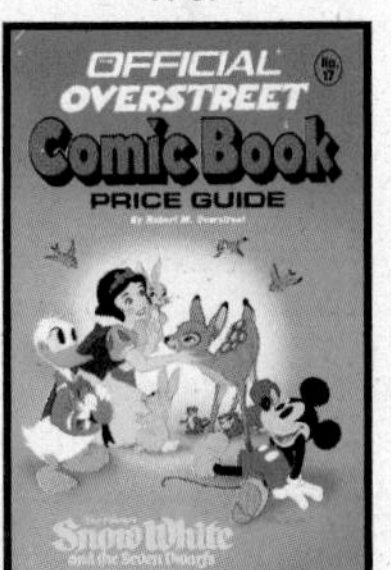

#17 SC $55.00
#17 HC $110.00
#17 L $160.00

1988

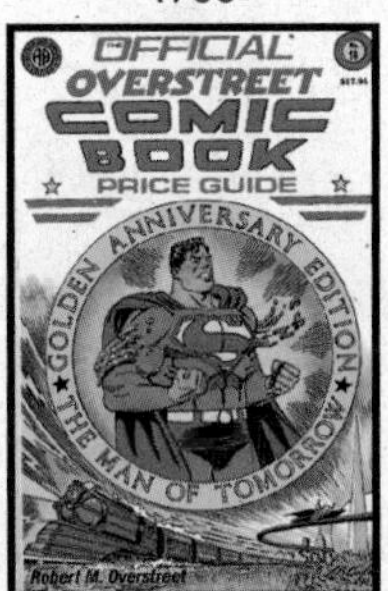

#18 SC $45.00
#18 HC $65.00
#18 L $160.00

1989

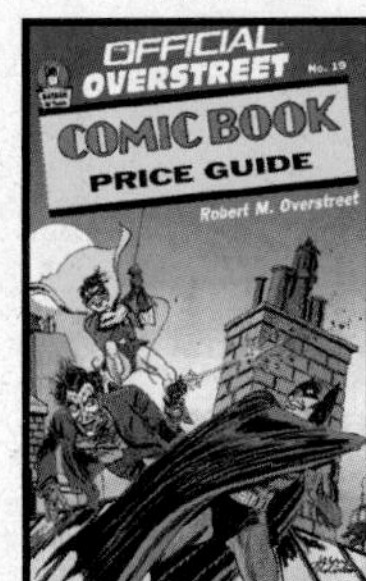

#19 SC $50.00
#19 HC $60.00
#19 L $170.00

1990

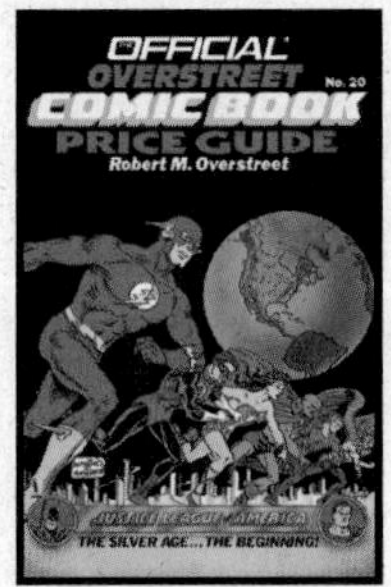

#20 SC $32.00
#20 HC $50.00
#20 L $135.00

1991

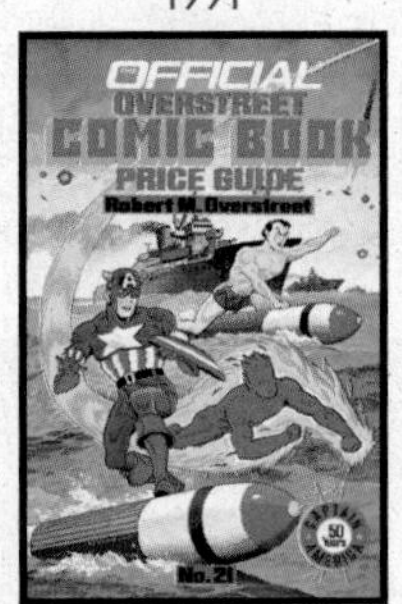

#21 SC $40.00
#21 HC $60.00
#21 L $145.00

1992

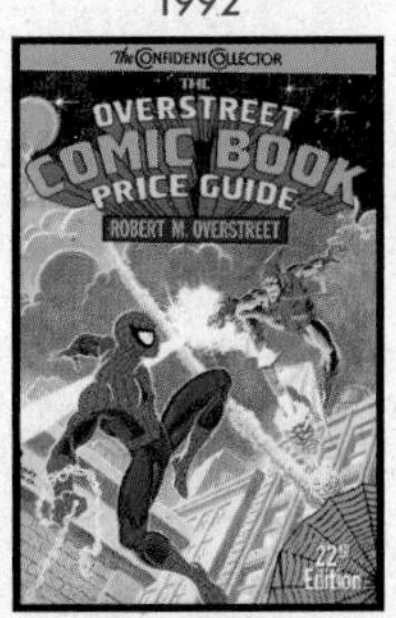

#22 SC $32.00
#22 HC $50.00

1993

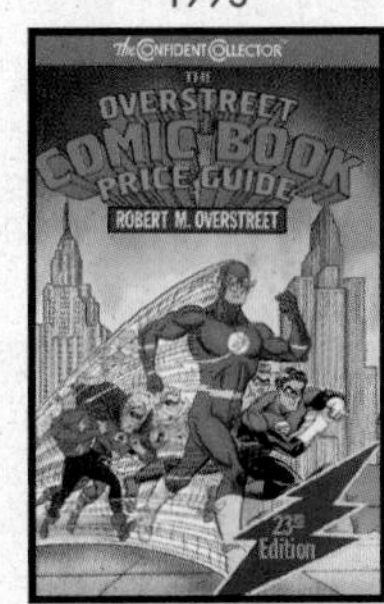

#23 SC $32.00
#23 HC $50.00

1994

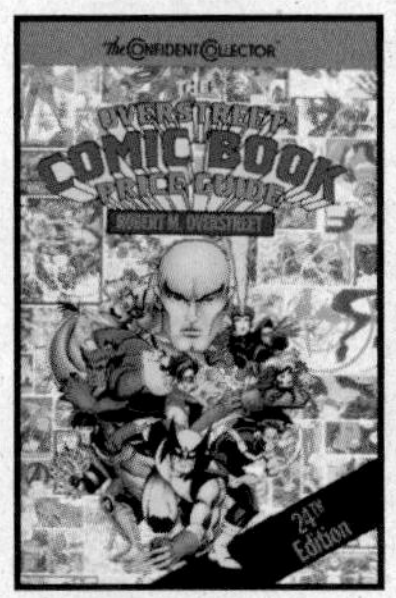

#24 SC $26.00
#24 HC $36.00

1995

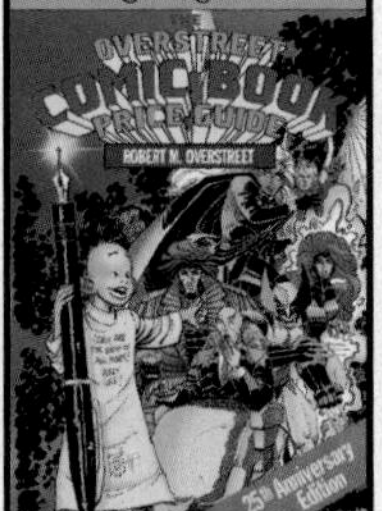

#25 SC $26.00
#25 HC $36.00
#25 L $110.00

1996

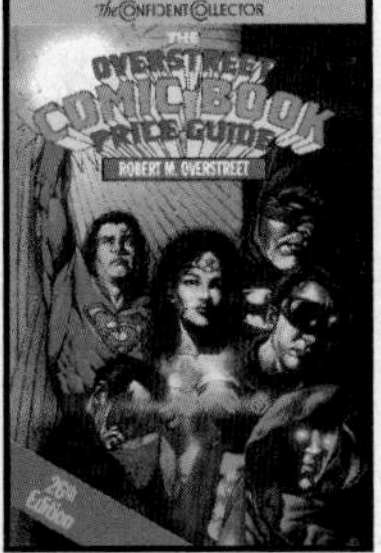

#26 SC $20.00
#26 HC $30.00
#26 L $100.00

1997

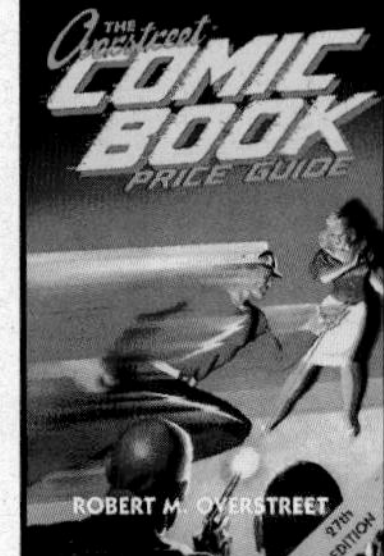

#27 SC $22.00
#27 HC $38.00
#27 L $125.00

1997

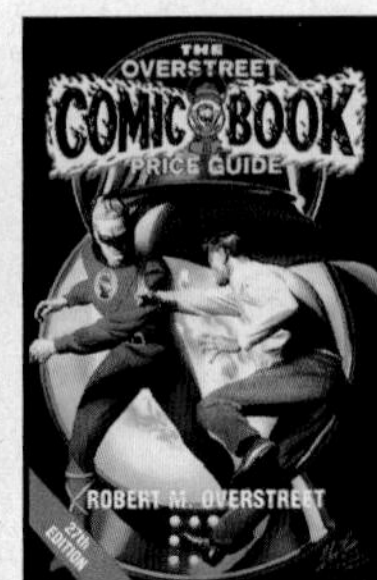

#27 SC $22.00
#27 HC $38.00
#27 L $125.00

1998	1998	1999	1999	2000	2000
#28 SC $20.00	#28 SC $20.00	#29 SC $25.00	#29 SC $20.00	#30 SC $22.00	#30 SC $22.00
#28 HC $35.00	#28 HC $35.00	#29 HC $40.00	#29 HC $37.00	#30 HC $32.00	#30 HC $32.00

2001	2001	2001	2002	2002	2002
#31 SC $22.00	#31 SC $22.00	#31 Bookstore Ed.	#32 SC $22.00	#32 SC $22.00	#32 Bookstore Ed.
#31 HC $32.00	#31 HC $32.00	SC only $22.00	#32 HC $32.00	#32 HC $32.00	SC only $22.00

2003	2003	2003	2004	2004	2004
#33 SC $25.00	#33 SC $25.00	#33 Bookstore Ed.	#34 SC $25.00	#34 SC $25.00	#34 Bookstore Ed.
#33 HC $32.00	#33 HC $32.00	SC only $25.00	#34 HC $32.00	#34 HC $32.00	SC only $25.00

2005	2005	2005	2006	2006	2006
#35 SC $25.00	#35 SC $25.00	#35 Bookstore Ed.	#36 SC $25.00	#36 SC $25.00	#36 Bookstore Ed.
#35 HC $32.00	#35 HC $55.00	SC only $25.00	#36 HC $32.00	#36 HC $32.00	SC only $25.00

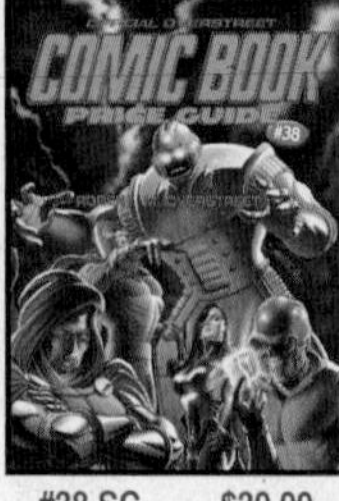

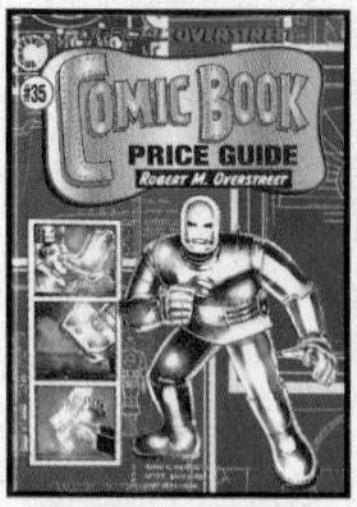

2007	2007	2007	2008	2008	2008
#37 SC $30.00	#37 SC $30.00	#37 Bookstore Ed.	#38 SC $30.00	#38 SC $30.00	#38 Bookstore Ed.
#37 HC $35.00	#37 HC $35.00	SC only $30.00	#38 HC $35.00	#38 HC $35.00	SC only $30.00

2009 — #39 SC $30.00 / #39 HC $35.00

2009 — #39 SC $30.00 / #39 HC $35.00

2009 — #39 Bookstore Ed. SC only $30.00

2010 — #40 SC $30.00 / #40 HC $35.00

2010 — #40 SC $30.00 / #40 HC $35.00

2010 — #40 HERO Initiative Ed. HC only $35.00

2011 — #41 SC $30.00 / #41 HC $35.00

2011 — #41 SC $30.00 / #41 HC $35.00

2011 — #41 HERO Initiative Ed. HC only $35.00

2012 — #42 SC $30.00 / #42 HC $35.00

2012 — #42 SC $30.00 / #42 HC $35.00

2012 — #42 HERO Initiative Ed. HC only $35.00

2013 — #43 SC $30.00 / #43 HC $35.00

2013 — #43 SC $30.00 / #43 HC $35.00

2013 — #43 HERO Initiative Ed. HC only $35.00

#31 Workbook - 2001 $35.00

#32 Workbook - 2002 $35.00

#33 Workbook - 2003 $37.00

#34 Workbook - 2004 $37.00

#35 Workbook - 2005 $37.00

#36 Workbook - 2006 $37.00

#37 Workbook - 2007 $37.00

#38 Workbook - 2008 $37.00

#42 Workbook - 2012 $45.00

#43 Workbook - 2013 $45.00

ADVERTISERS' INDEX

A

B

C

D

E

F

G

H

I

J

M

N

O

P

R

S

T

V

W

Y

Z

WWW.HAKES.COM

SOLD: $54,625

AMERICANA &
HAKE'S
SINCE 1967
COLLECTIBLES
A GEPPI'S ENTERTAINMENT AUCTIONS CO.

SOLD: $112,015

SOLD: $95,155

★CONSIGN NOW★

SOLD: $75,000

We Are America's First and Foremost Pop Culture Auction House

No One Has Done It Longer, No One Does It Better

Let Us Showcase Your Original Art -
We Will Present Your Items In The Best Way Possible

We Do Limit The Amount Of Art We Offer In Each
Auction So Every Piece Realizes Its Full Potential

World Record Prices Set In Every Auction

SOLD: $5,621

SOLD: $43,320

SOLD: $25,370

SOLD: $10,209

SOLD: $15,181

SOLD: $41,264

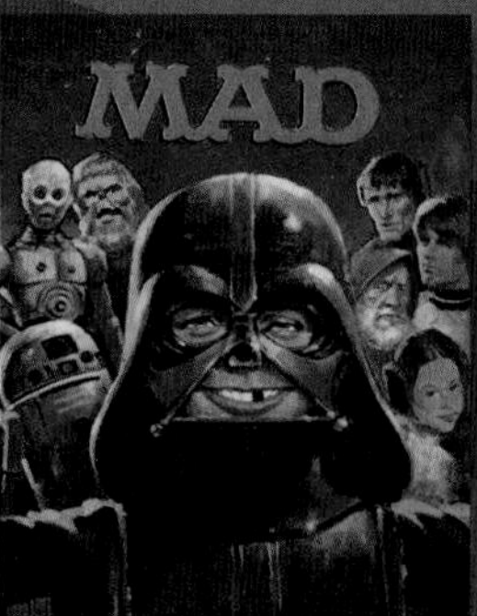

SOLD: $9,740

★CONSIGN NOW★
WWW.HAKES.COM

SOLD: $21,275

SOLD: $3,478

SOLD: $26,565

SOLD: $11,132

SOLD: $18,658

★ORIGINAL ART WANTED★PROVEN RESULTS★

SOLD: $11,500

SOLD: $3,452

SOLD: $10,120

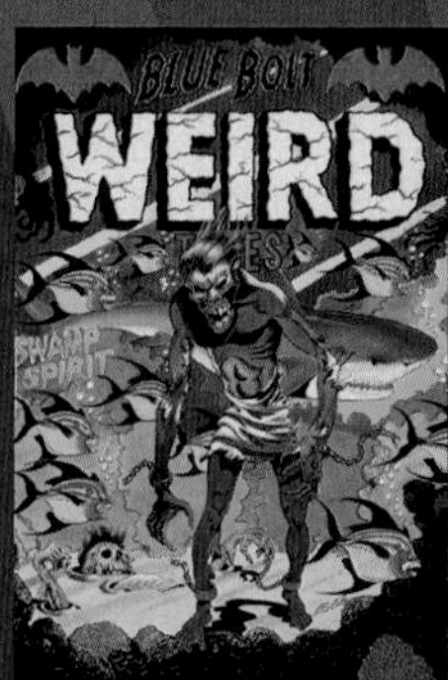

SOLD: $9,740

SOLD: $8,222

If interested in consigning contact:
Kelly McClain at mkelly@hakes.com or call 866.404.9800 ext: 1636
or Alex Winter at walex@hakes.com or call 866.404.9800 ext: 1632
Hake's Americana & Collectibles
PO Box 12001 - York, PA 17402
Toll Free: (866)404-9800

A DIVISION OF

THWARTING EVIL ON EVERY TURN!

ISSUE NO. 173 JULY

GTM GAME TRADE MAGAZINE

VILLAINY

DEVISE DASTARDLY DEEDS

IN THIS ISSUE:

- MAYFAIR GAMES AND *GTM* PARTNER TO BRING YOU EXCLUSIVE FREE GAME EXPANSIONS!
- THE TRUTH IS OUT THERE - IF YOU CAN FIND IT IN IDW GAMES' *THE X-FILES BOARD GAME!*

Each Month GTM Brings You Exclusive Information on the Industry's Most Popular Titles, Including:
SETTLERS OF CATAN • DC DECKBUILDING GAME • HEROCLIX
TICKET TO RIDE • CARCASSONNE • DORK TOWER

Exclusive Game Content in Every Issue!

We're on Facebook at  **.com/GameTradeMagazine**

• Read it • Buy it • Play It •

GAMETRADEMAGAZINE.COM

HERITAGE®

COMICS & COMIC ART AUCTIONS

WHEN IT'S TIME TO SELL, CONSIGN TO HERITAGE

THE WORLD'S LARGEST COLLECTIBLES AUCTIONEER

850,000+ Online Bidder-Members

More than $200 million worth of comics and comic art sold in the past 10 years, much more than all other auctioneers combined

500,000+ different people visit our website each month (source: compete.com, February 2013), no other comic dealer even comes close.

SOLD FOR $567,625! 2/13

SOLD FOR $274,850! 7/12

SOLD FOR $203,150! 8/13

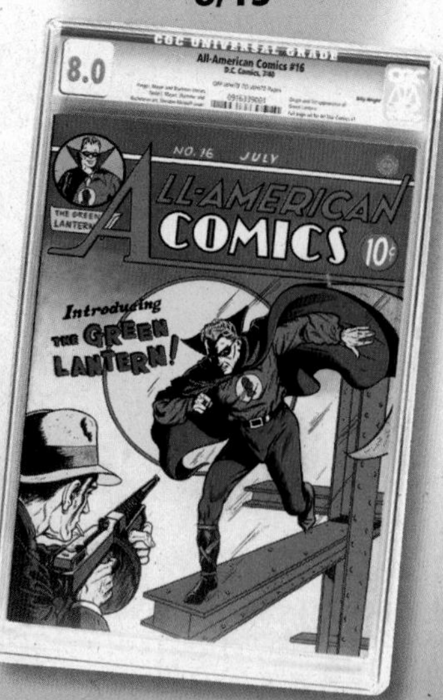

To discuss selling your comics or art at auction, call or email us today!

TO LEARN HOW HERITAGE GETS YOU MORE MONEY, SEE OUR ADS ON PAGES 6-7 AND 78–79!

3500 Maple Avenue | Dallas, Texas 75219 | 877.HERITAGE (437.4824) | Bid@HA.com

Annual Sales Exceed $900 Million | 850,000+ Online Bidder-Members

HERITAGE HA.com AUCTIONS

DALLAS | NEW YORK | BEVERLY HILLS | SAN FRANCISCO | HOUSTON | PARIS | GENEVA

TX Auctioneer licenses: Samuel Foose 11727; Robert Korver 13754; Andrea Voss 16406. • All comic auctions are subject to a 19.5% Buyer's Premium.
HERITAGE Reg. U.S. Pat and TM off.

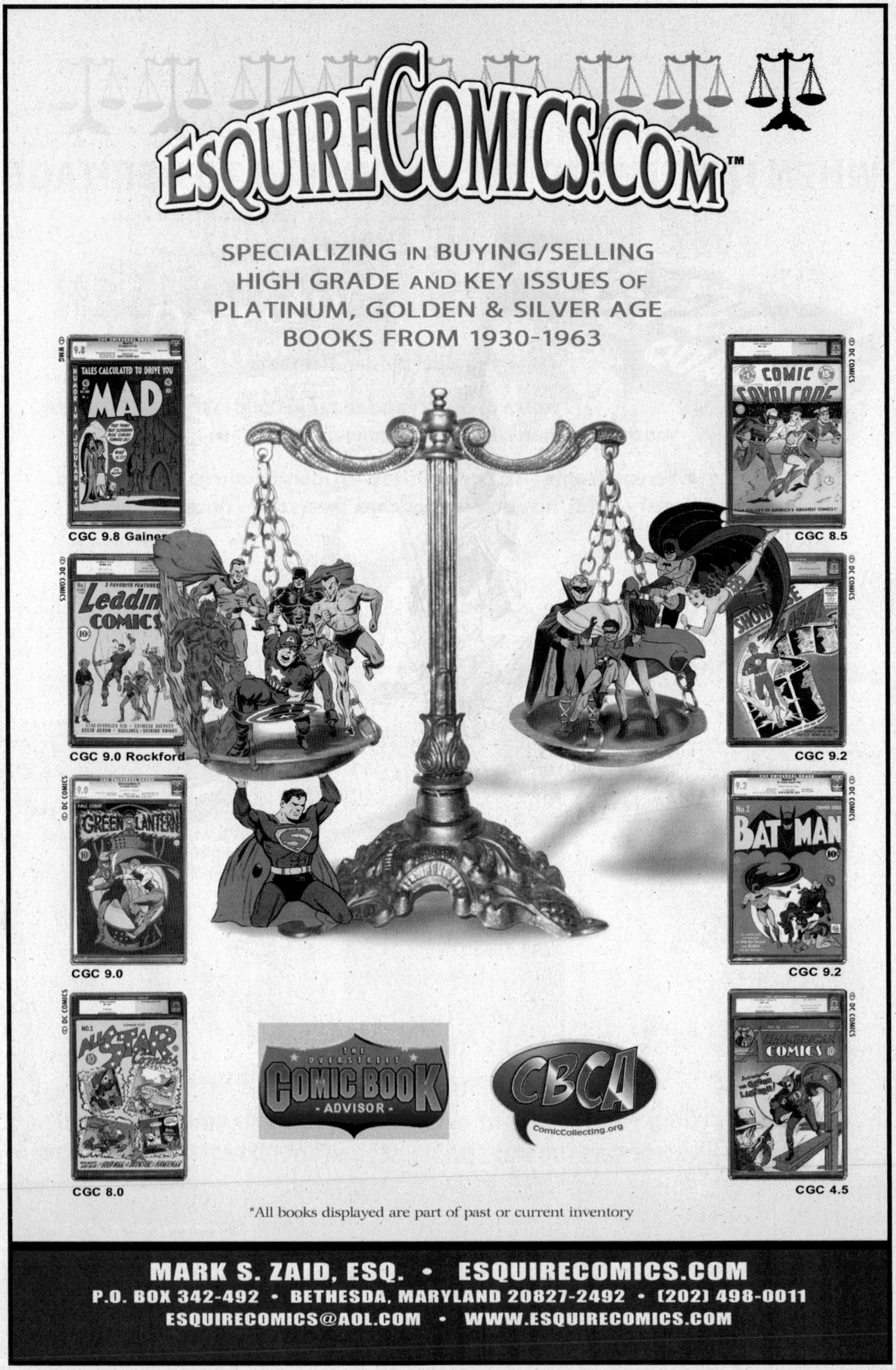

ESQUIRECOMICS.COM™

SPECIALIZING IN BUYING/SELLING HIGH GRADE AND KEY ISSUES OF PLATINUM, GOLDEN & SILVER AGE BOOKS FROM 1930-1963

CGC 9.8 Gaines

CGC 8.5

CGC 9.0 Rockford

CGC 9.2

CGC 9.0

CGC 9.2

CGC 8.0

CGC 4.5

*All books displayed are part of past or current inventory

MARK S. ZAID, ESQ. • ESQUIRECOMICS.COM
P.O. BOX 342-492 • BETHESDA, MARYLAND 20827-2492 • (202) 498-0011
ESQUIRECOMICS@AOL.COM • WWW.ESQUIRECOMICS.COM

COLLECTOR BUYING PRE-1965 COMIC BOOKS AND RELATED COLLECTIBLES

COMIC BOOKS

CLUB KITS • PREMIUMS

OTHER CHARACTER COLLECTIBLES

All characters ©2014 respective copyright holders.

I am the most serious collector you'll ever find... I LOVE THIS STUFF!

SEND YOUR SALE LIST!

Stephen A. Geppi

10150 York Road, Suite 300
Hunt Valley, MD 21030
443-318-8203
gsteve@diamondcomics.com

COLLECTOR BUYING MOST PRE-1967 COMIC BOOKS

PARTICULARLY INTERESTED IN:
Superhero comic books
Anything related to Batman
Anything related to Superman
Original comic book art
Pulp magazines

Why Sell to Me?

THIS IS A HOBBY, NOT A BUSINESS. THEREFORE, I CAN & WILL PAY MORE. I WILL BUY ENTIRE COLLECTIONS OR INDIVIDUAL PIECES. IMMEDIATE CASH IS ALWAYS AVAILABLE FOR PURCHASES.

DR. DAVID J. ANDERSON, D.D.S. • 5192 DAWES AVENUE
SEMINARY PROFESSIONAL VILLAGE • ALEXANDRIA, VA 22311
TEL (703) 578-1222 • FAX (703) 578-1222
DJA2@COX.NET